D1311996

A DICTIONARY OF AMERICAN ENGLISH

A DICTIONARY OF AMERICAN ENGLISH

ON HISTORICAL PRINCIPLES

Compiled at
THE UNIVERSITY OF CHICAGO

under the editorship of
SIR WILLIAM A. CRAIGIE
Co-editor of the Oxford English Dictionary

and

JAMES R. HULBERT
Professor Emeritus of English, the University of Chicago

VOLUME IV, RECORDER—ZU-ZU

THE UNIVERSITY OF CHICAGO PRESS

THE UNIVERSITY OF CHICAGO PRESS, CHICAGO 60637

Oxford University Press, London, England

PREFATORY NOTE TO VOLUME IV

THIS fourth and last volume of the Dictionary covers the later letters of the alphabet, including 88 pages of R (in addition to 31 in Volume III), 287 of S, 102 of T, 17 of U, 22 of V, 89 of W and X, and 15 of Y and Z. As in ordinary dictionaries, S occupies more space than any of the other letters.

The following summary of the main contents of the volume, on the same lines as in the previous Prefatory Notes, will serve to indicate a considerable number of the more important and interesting words included in its pages.

Among the terms descriptive of, or relating to, the country and its parts, the most numerous are those denoting natural features of land or water, as *red land, ridge, rim rock, rise* n. 1, *rising* n. 2, *rock* n. 1, *rolling prairie, sag* n. 1, *saline* n., *salt lick, salt marsh*, etc., *sand bank, sand hill, savanna, seaboard, sink* 1 and 2, *sink hole, slew* n.¹ and *slough, swale, swamp* n., *swash, swell* n., *table-land, upcountry* n., *upland* 1, *valley, wallow, wilderness, woodland; riffle* 1, *rift* 1, *rip* n., *ripple*¹, *river*¹ (with *river bottom*, etc.), *run* n. 1, *salt lake, schute* and *shoot* n. 1, *spring* n., *suck* n. 1, and *tidewater*. Proper names, some of which are frequent in attributive use, include *Red river, Rhode Island*, the *Rockies* or *Rocky Mountains, Santa Fe, Saratoga, Sea Island, Silver State, South* n., *South Carolina, Southland, Southwest, Tennessee, Texas, Trans-Alleg(h)anian* n. and a., *Trans-Mississippi, Trans-Missouri* a., *United Colonies, United States, Virginia, Wall Street, West* n. and adv., *Western Reserve, West Point, Wild West*, and *Yosemite*. Some other designations of localities or areas are *reservation, reserve* n. 2–6, *section* 1 and 2, *settlement* 2 and 3, *shire town, square* n.¹ 1 and 2, *state* n., *station* 1, *street* 1, *suburb, tier* n.¹, *town, township, uptown* n., and *village*.

Various means or methods of communication or transport are illustrated under *road* n., *roadway, ship canal, street railroad* and *street railway, subway, switchback, turnpike* n. 3, *wagon road, way* n. 1, and the more abstract *ride* n., *round trip, route* n. 1, *star route*, and *transportation*. The numerous names of vehicles include *rockaway, shay, sled* n., *sledge*², *sleigh* n. 1, *spider* 4, *stage* 2, *stagecoach* 1, *steam car, street car, sulky, surrey, toboggan* n., *travail, trolley*², *trolley car, truck* n.² 1, *wagon*, and *wheel* 6, together with the railroad *sleeper* 2, *sleeping car, smoker* 3, *smoking car*, and *stock car*. The more important or distinctive vessels are the *schooner* 1, *scout boat, scow* n., *skiff, sloop, steamboat* n., *steamer, steamship, stern-wheeler, team boat, towboat*, and *wharf boat*.

The terms denoting buildings or structures display considerable variety, ranging from the primitive *shack* n.³, *shanty* n., *tent*¹, *tepee*, and *wigwam* 1–4, to the *tenement house* and the *skyscraper* 4. They include *refectory, residence, restaurant, rotunda* 2, *saloon* 2, *sanitarium* 1, *schoolhouse, smokehouse, statehouse, state('s) prison, station house, still house, sugarhouse, tavern, theater, warehouse, washhouse*, and *watch-house*. Among the appendages, parts, etc., of buildings are *roof garden, stoop, underpinning* 1, *vault, veranda*, and *vestibule* n; also *shingle* n.¹, *slate* n. 2, *thatch, tile* 1, and *weather strip*.

Administrative and public services furnish a number of terms of historical interest, as *redemption, redistrict* v., *register* n.² 1 and v. 2, *registration, representation, resolution, resolve, resumption, return* n., *revenue* 2 and 3, *session, sovereign state, sovereignty, subtreasury, superior court, supreme court, tariff* n. and v., *tax* n., *taxable, taxpayer, territorial* a., *territory, treasury, unconstitutional* a., *veto* n. and v., *ward,* and *warrant* n. and v. There are numerous names of persons or bodies holding official positions or exercising special functions, as *recorder* 2 and 3, *register* n.[1], *registrar, representative, returning board, sealer*[1], *searcher* 1–3, *secretary* 1 and 2, *Secretary of State, secret service, selectman, senate, senator, sergeant, sheriff, solicitor-general, speaker, state board, State Department, surveyor, surveyor-general, tithingman, treasurer, trustee* n., *vice-president, viewer, vigilance committee, vigilante, watch* n. 1, *watchman, weigher,* and *yardmaster.*

Political terms are not remarkably numerous but cover some of the more important aspects or activities, as *re-eligibility, referendum, reform, republic, republicanism, spoils system, state sovereignty, state('s) rights, suffrage; slate* n. 4, *sticker* 1, *ticket* 2–5 (with *split, straight,* and *union ticket* 1 and 2). Among persons or bodies engaged in politics are *Red Republican, repeater* 4, *republican* n. 1 and 2, *ring* n. 3, *ringster* 1, *socialist, Tammany, third party, Whig, wide-awake* 2.

The historical terms, most of which either begin during the War of Independence or belong to the nineteenth century, include *redemptioner, regulator, signer, Son of liberty, Sons of America, sooner* 1, *submissionist, Tory*[2], *Unionist* n. 1 and a., *Union man* 1, *Washingtonian* n. (1 and 2) and a.; *regency, revolution, revolutionary* a., *Rump Congress, secede* v., *secesh* n., a., and v., *secession,* etc., *separation* 2, *Solid South, Stamp Act, Stars and Bars, Stars and Stripes, Star-spangled Banner, Thanksgiving* 1, *Thanksgiving day, Tippecanoe, training day, Union* n. 1 and a., *unpleasantness, unterrified* a. Indian habits or wars are represented by *scalp* n. 1 and v. 1, *scalping knife, scalp lock,* etc., *war belt, war dance* n. and v., *warpath,* etc., and *red stick.* With *slavery* and the *slave trade* is connected the *underground railroad.*

Military affairs figure to a considerable extent under the general terms *soldier* n. and *war,* and the special entries *recruiting* (*office, officer,* etc.), *redcoat, regiment, regimental* n. and a., *regular* n. and a., *Remington, revolver, rifle*[1], *rifleman, roster, Roughrider, saber, scout* n. and v., *sergeant, sergeant major, Springfield, squad, squadron, stockade* n. and v., *stockado, surgeon-general, sutler, train* n., *train-band, training, veteran, veteranize* v., *volunteer, War Department,* and *warrant officer.* The relatively fewer naval terms include *revenue cutter, sailing master, sailmaker, sailor* 1, *sea fencible, submarine* a., *submarine boat, torpedo* n. 2, *torpedo boat, vice-admiral* 1, and *wardroom* 1.

Religious bodies or movements, and persons connected with these, are represented by *rector* 2, *revivalist, revival man, ruling elder, saint* 1 and 3, *seeker, separatist, teacher* 1, *teaching elder, vestry* 1; *River Brethren, Roman Catholic* n. and a., *Sandemanian, Schwenkfelder* and *Schwenkfeldian* a., *Separate Baptist, Seventh-Day Baptist, Six-Principle Baptists, Shaker* 1, *Soft-Shell Baptist, Tunker, Unitarian* n. and a., *Universalist* n. and a., *Wesleyan* n. and a. Other terms connected with religion or the churches are *reformed* a., *reformed church, revival, rolling exercise, Sabbaday, Sabbath* n. and v., *Sabbath school, sacrament, Saybrook platform, society* 1 and 4, *synod, tabernacle, temple*[1], *theological school,* and *theological seminary.*

Under the heading of education come various designations of persons, as *rector* 1, *regent* 1 and 2, *schoolma'am, schoolmarm, schoolmaster, schoolmistress, school-teacher, tutor; scholar, sophister, sophomore;* also *senior, senior class* a., and *valedictorian.* Among educational institutions are *school* (with *school board, school district, school fund,* etc.), *reform school, singing school, spelling school, Sunday school; seminary* 1, *senior college,* and *university.* Of interest in that connection are also *spelling bee, spelling match, valedictory,* and *valedictory oration.*

Of the terms connected with games or sports the most noteworthy are *referee* 2, *regatta*, *rounce*, *tennis*, *tenpin(s)*, *ten-strike* 1, *tiger* 2, *trapball*, and *volley ball*.

A few designations of persons are formed on the names of states, viz., *Rhode Islander*, *South Carolinian*, *Tennesse(e)an* n., *Texan* n. 1 or *Texian* n., *Vermonter*, and *Virginian* n. National names are represented by *Scotch-Irish* n. and a., *Welsh* a., *Welshman* 1, and *Spaniard* 1. A few Indian tribes are distinguished as *River*, *Snake*, and *Upland Indians*, also the *Six Nations*, *root-diggers* or *-eaters*, and *wild Indians*, in addition to the special tribal names *Sac* or *Sauk*, *Seminole*, *Seneca*, *Shawnee*, *Shoshoni*, *Sioux*, *Siwash*, *Tuscarora* 1, *Uchee*, *Utah* or *Ute*, and *Wyandot(te)* 1. The Indian also figures under *red* n. 1 and a. 1, *red Indian* 1, *red people*, *redskin*, *savage* n. and a., and *warrior*.

Miscellaneous names of persons, some of which are characteristically American, include *refugee* n., *renegade* n., *reporter* 1 and 2, *residenter*, *rice-planter* 1, *river driver*, *riverman*, *road agent*, *roustabout*, *rowdy* n., *scab* n., *servant*, *settler* 1 and 2, *slave*, *slave-driver*, *solicitor*, *squatter* 1, *squire* n., *station agent*, *storekeeper*, *subagent*, *superintendent*, *supervisor*, *swamper*, *trapper*, *usher*, *voyageur*, *waiter* 1 and 2, *waiter girl*, and *wench*.

Business and commerce figure in the names of persons or groups of these, as *refiner* 2, *retailer*, *ring* n. 4, *speculator*, *syndicate* n., *trader* 1 and 2, *trust* n. 4, *undertaker*, or in terms indicating various aspects or products of industry or trade, as *refinery*, *refrigerator* 1, *sawmill*, *store* 1, and *variety store*, *trade* n. and v., *trading* 1, *truck* n.[1] 1, *vendue* n. and v.; mining supplies *riffle* 2, *riffle box*, and *rocker* 2, and logging *rollway*, *skid* n. and v., *skid road*, *skidway*, and *stumpage*. Among articles and apparatus are *rubber* 3, *telegraph*, and *telephone* n. There are many designations of currency, as *scrip* n. 1, *sharp shin*, *shilling*, *shinplaster* 1, *silver dollar*, *slug* n. 1, *Spanish dollar*, *specie*, *stiver*, *ten-cent* a., *tender*[1], *trade dollar*, *treasury note*, *two bits*, *two-cent*, *two-dollar*, and *V* 2 (= 5). Banking is represented by *reserve bank* (under *reserve* n. 7 b), *savings bank* 1, *state bank*, and *United States Bank*, and dealing in stocks by *short* a. 2 and adv., *stock board* 1, *stockbroker*, *stock exchange*, etc.

As in the earlier volumes, the names of trees and plants are numerous, both those which are common in British use and those which are distinctively American. Among the trees are the *red bay*, *red cedar*, etc., *rock maple*, *rock oak*, *saw palmetto*, *scrub oak*, *scrub pine*, *sequoia*, *shagbark* and *shellbark(ed)* hickory, *slippery elm*, *Spanish oak*, *spruce*, *sugar maple*, *sumac(h)*, *swamp oak*, *swamp pine*, *sweet gum*, *tamarack*, *tupelo* (*tree*), *turkey oak*, *walnut*, *white ash* 1, *white birch*, etc. Some of the more distinctive plant names are *redroot*, *redtop*, *ribbon cane*, *richweed*, *sagebrush*, *salt grass*, *sang* n., *scabish*, *shadbush*, *skunk cabbage*, *snakeroot*, *soap plant*, *sorghum* 1, *Spanish moss*, *spicebush*, *squash*[1], *sweet potato*, *tarweed*, *timothy* and *timothy grass*, and *Virginia creeper*. A number of special names are formed with the adjectives *red*, *white*, and *yellow*. The extended American use of *vine* may also be noticed.

The animal kingdom is represented by some of the larger and smaller quadrupeds, as the *red deer*, *Rocky Mountain sheep*, and *wapiti;* the *red fox*, *sable* n. 1, *seal* n.[1], *skunk* n. 1 and 2, *squirrel* 1, *wharf rat* 1, and *wildcat* n. 1; *snapper* 2, *snapping turtle* 1, *terrapin*, *turtle* 1, and *salamander* 1 and 2. Among the birds are the *redbreast* 1, *redhead*, *redpoll*[1], *reedbird*, *ricebird* 1, *ringneck* 2 and 3, *ring plover*, *robin*[1] 1 and 2, *ruffed grouse*, *sage hen* 1, *sand-hill crane*, *sapsucker*, *skunk blackbird*, *sora* and *sora rail*, *thrasher*[1], *turkey* 1, *turkey buzzard*, *veery*, *vireo*, and *vulture*. The noteworthy fishes are the *redfish*, *red horse* 1, *redmouth*, *roach* n.[1], *rock bass*, *salmon*, *salmon trout*, *scad*, *scuppaug*, *sea bass*, *sea robin* 1, *shad* 1 and 2, *sheepshead* n., *shiner* 2, *squeteague*, *squirrel fish*, *stone-toter*, *sucker* n. 1 and 2, *weakfish*, and *whitefish*. The only reptiles of importance are the *ribbon snake* and *ring snake*.

Articles of food or their accompaniments include *roasting ear, succotash, sweet corn, sugar* n. 1; *rusk* n., *slapjack, smearcase, taffy* 1, *tamale, waffle; saleratus biscuit, salt-rising bread*, and *sass* n. 1 or *sauce*. Names of drinks are *rum, sling* n., *switchel, tafia, whisky*, and the fanciful *redeye* 1, *rotgut* 1, *tanglefoot* 1, and *tangle-leg* 2. Undiluted liquor is *straight*.

The exuberant colloquial or slang element, which forms the most original feature of the purely American vocabulary, is no less conspicuous here than in the previous volumes, and by its variety precludes any attempt at classification. In many instances it arises by attaching a new sense to an ordinary word, such as the verbs *rip, rock, root, rustle, scoop, scoot, score, scratch, size, smile, straddle, streak*, etc., or the adjective *some*. In others a new phrase is created on the basis of common words, as in *a hard row to hoe* or *to hoe one's own row* (under *row* n. 5). In many, however, either the word itself, or the collocation is new and distinctive, as *red cent, right smart, rile* v., *riley* a., *ringtail, ring-tailed* a., *rip-roaring* a., *rooter, roughneck, rounder, rustler, saddy* n. and v., *salary grab, sash(a)y* v., *scads, scalawag, scrumptious* a., *seven-by-nine* a., *shad-bellied* a., *shavetail, shebang, shotgun, shuck* n. and v., *shyster, side show, sissy* n. and a., *six-shooter, skedaddle* n. and v., *skeesick(s), skyugle* n. and v., *slab-sided* a., *slangw(h)ang, slantindicular* a. and adv., *slick* n., a., v., and adv., *slumgullion, small potato, snoop* n. and v., *sockdolager, splurge* n. and v., *spread eagle, spread-eagleism, square meal, stampede* n. and v., *stemwinder, stogy, tacky* n. and a., *tarnal* a. and adv., *tarnation* n. and a., *teeter* n. and v., *tenderfoot* n. and v., *tote* n. and v., *trampoose* n. and v., *tuxedo, two-forty, Uncle Sam, vamo(o)se* v., *walking ticket, whangdoodle, whole hog, wildcat* n. 2–6, and *wildcat bank*, etc.

Those words in this volume which exhibit an interesting variety of senses, many of them new, are especially the nouns *rooster, rope, runner, salt, scrub, shake, shell, station, stock, striker, team, time, track*, the verbs *ride, set, skin, split, take, throw*, and both noun and verb in the cases of *roll, run, shoot, snake, spot, stake, stand, strike, stump*, and *turn*.

The nouns which enter into attributive collocations, some of which form a considerable number of separate entries, are *rice, river, road, rock, running, salt, sand, school, sea, sheep, side, silver, slave, spring, stage, state, steam, stock, stone, store, sugar, summer, swamp, timber, tobacco, town, tree, truck, turkey, Virginia, wagon, walnut, war, watch, water, wheat, wolf, wood*. The adjectives which furnish similar entries are especially *red, running, salt, scarlet, short, small, southern, Spanish, striped, Virginian, western, white, wild*, and *yellow*. It will readily be noticed that a large number of these collocations are marked as American, while others are predominantly so, being only rare or accidental in British use.

As in the third volume, the greater number of the words adopted from other languages are either of Spanish or Indian origin, the latter being the more numerous of the two. From Spanish have come *remuda, riata, rincon, rio*[1], *rodeo, roncador, ronco, ronquil, señor, señorita, serape* (also *sarape*), *sierra, sombrero, stampedo* n. and v., *tamale, tornillo, tulare, tule, vamo(o)se* v., *vaquero, vara*, and *vigilante*. The Indian words, of which only a limited number have come into general use, include *roanoke, rockahominy, sachem, sagakomi, sagamore, salal, samp, sannup, scup* n.[2], *scuppaug, scuppernong, seawan(t), sequoia, sewellel, siscoe, siscowet, skoke*[1,2], *skunk* n. and v., *sofky, squantum*[1,2], *squash*[1,2], *squaw, squeteague, succotash, sunck, supawn, tamarack, tautog, tepee, terrapin, toboggan* n. and v., *tomahawk* n. and v., *totem* n. and v., *tuckahoe, tupelo* (tree), *ulicon, unaker, wahoo*[1,2], *wampum, wampumpeag, wangun, wapiti, wappato, watap, wauregan* a., *weequashing, werowance, wicopy, woodchuck*, and *yaupon*. Next in order come the Dutch *rolliche, Santa Claus, sawbuck, schepel* and *skipple, schepen, schout, scow* n. and v., *slaw, sleigh* n. and v., *snoop* n. and v., *stadthouse*, *stiver, stoop, vendue* n. and v., *waffle*, and *wamus*. German has contributed *saibling, sauerkraut* or *sourcrout, smearcase, spiegel iron*, and *wienerwurst*. French is scantily represented by *vacher, vachery*, and *voyageur*. From other quarters have come the Slavonic *sherry-vallies* and *Suwarrow*[1] and the African *voodoo* n. and v.

A study of the above survey, together with those on similar lines given in the previous volumes, will go far to enable the reader to judge to what extent the compilers of the Dictionary have succeeded in achieving the aim stated in the Preface, viz., to record and illustrate 'not only words and phrases which are clearly or apparently of American origin, or have greater currency here than elsewhere, but also every word denoting something which has a real connection with the development of the country and the history of its people.' It may be affirmed with some confidence that a historical digest of all the material here collected would not only furnish a fuller account of the growth of the American language than any hitherto produced but would also exhibit the history of the colonies and the United States in many new and interesting aspects.

In the nature of things it is inevitable that even this extensive body of material should fall short of being complete and final. That end could only be attained if every page of every book, periodical, or newspaper of importance were carefully read and excerpted by competent collectors unlikely to miss anything of value—a task which is obviously beyond the limits of anything practical and feasible. It is the fate of dictionaries of this kind to leave something, possibly much, that still remains to be done, but part of their success lies in the fact that what they do contain serves as a solid nucleus for further research, indicates the lines on which such research will be most profitable, and enables the collector to ascertain readily whether he can contribute something new or significant. From this it follows that in time there may be such an accumulation of new material that a supplementary volume will become both desirable and necessary. When that time comes it will also be possible, if sufficient preparation has been made, to take account of the additions in new words, uses, or phrases which have been made to the vocabulary during the first half of the present century. Already a considerable amount of additional material has accumulated, chiefly quotations earlier than those that have been given. Any supplementary material, whether corrections of or additions to the present work or quotations for new words and meanings of the twentieth century, may be sent to the Department of English of the University of Chicago. Many earlier examples, as well as many addenda, have been contributed already by Major Sir St. Vincent Troubridge from his extensive reading in both British and American sources. To him also are due various improvements in the present volume.

The following list includes the names of many of those who have assisted the Dictionary project, chiefly by reading books and extracting quotations. The greater number of these rendered their assistance as part of the work done by them during attendance at courses in lexicography at the University of Chicago. Many others are not named, either because of fault in our records or because their contributions were of isolated quotations. Special acknowledgment is also due the many scholars and experts who helped with various problems.

Mildred D. Adams, Lois Allen, Doris L. Anderson, G. Anderson, Blanche B. Armfield, M. L. Aston, Marie Baldridge, Edna Barnes, C. L. Barnhart, Florence E. Barns, Louise Baugh, H. J. Bayliss, M. C. Beaman, N. S. Becker, Elizabeth C. Beers, H. M. Belden, A. T. Belknap, Gwendolyn Bell, Mary Bell, Edith Benjamin, Mrs. T. E. Bennett, E. Berg, Lois M. Bergstrom, Rae Blanchard, Grace Blankenship, H. F. Boettcher, D. F. Bond, Margaret Bowers, Aggie Boyet, Evelyn P.

Boynton, F. Bracker, G. W. Bradford, Flora Bradshaw, Mary E. Branch, Ruth Brannon, R. F. Brinton, Muriel I. Brothers, H. R. Brower, Minnie S. Buckingham, Mrs. W. E. R. Burk, Agnes Burns, Mary S. Button, S. M. Byrd, Ethel Byrns, H. F. Cameron, Mary Campbell, Ola M. Campbell, A. S. Cannon, Johnnie Lee Carlisle, Lillian E. Cashin, Grace A. Chapman, L. W. Chappell, Kathleen Clancy, Blanche Clark, W. O. Clough, Jennie A. Clymer, Mitchell Clymer, D. O. Coate, Manette Coffee, F. W. Collins, Lester Condit, Mary Cone, Frances Conlon, Helen D. Connell, Elsie Cornelison, Pearl J. Cosgrave, R. W. Coues, Mrs. John Cowan, Lucile Cox, Mary E. Craig, Julia F. Crane, Estella Cratty, R. N. Crawford, S. M. Crawford, E. H. Criswell, J. R. Crocker, Margaret Crockett, F. A. Croft, Mrs. Paul B. Cullen, A. R. Curry, Catherine Dalton, D. Dalton, L. L. Dantzler, Ellen C. Davidson, H. C. Davidson, E. R. Davis, E. B. Davis, Jean Davis, Zelia Denton, F. G. Dickason, L. T. Dickinson, J. Dickson, Mildred Dill, Lloyd Dodd, Caroline B. Donica, Jessie Douglas, T. W. Douglas, Helen Drew, C. J. Duffy, Ella Duke, E. H. Eby, Mary C. Ehrie, L. W. Elder, Frances Ell, Pocahontas Ellis, Ernestine Ernst, J. J. Eubanks, F. Evans, C. A. Exley, Mildred Farmer, W. Finke, Myrtle Finkelstein, Helen A. Fisher, J. F. Flanagen, Elizabeth Floyd, G. R. Floyd, A. V. Frankenstein, E. Froom, Wilbur Gaffney, Caroline Gardner, D. Garrett, Marye Garrett, P. D. Garrison, Jr., Floy P. Gates, Sister M. Josepha Geary, Eva O. Gholson, E. A. Gibson, Jewel W. Gibson, Bonnie Gilbert, Robert Goodman, Bessie A. Gorindar, Audrey Goza, P. S. Grant, C. P. Green, Dorothy Gregg, N. Grossblatt, Grace W. Gunning, E. E. Hale, Octavia Hale, R. W. Hale, R. F. Hamill, Geraldine Hammond, Lucy Harmon, Ruth Harrington, Edith Harris, Hubert Harris, L. M. Harris, Izola Harrison, B. Hartstein, M. Hathcock, E. F. Haugen, O. V. Hawkins, A. C. O. Haye, Grace Haynes, Rena Head, Ruth Heartsill, A. L. Hench, Telfair Hendon, Walter Hendricks, Adelaide C. Hibbard, F. C. Hilbish, Edgar Hirshel, Margaret Holderman, D. M. Holmquist, A. M. Holt, M. Hoogesteger, Ella M. Hooker, H. W. Horwill, Mary Howard, H. W. Howell, L. M. Hubbard, D. L. Hunt, K. W. Hunt, S. B. Hustvedt, B. B. Hutchen, Emma W. Jackman, Rose Jacobson, Kathleen A. Jarrell, Dora Johnson, F. M. Johnson, Goldie Johnson, Margaret Jones, Mrs. O. S. Jones, Mary P. Keeley, James Keeling, Keolla Kiersey, M. Kelly, Nelson Kilby, May A. Klipple, A. Koebele, Charlotte Kretsch, Elwood Kretsinger, L. Kryzanowski, Sherman Kuhn, G. L. Laffoon, R. M. Leader, H. D. Learned, Jane Leecraft, Frank Lewis, R. M. Limpus, L. Lincoln, Dorothy Long, Mary D. Long, P. W. Long, R. B. Long, R. L. Loos, Viola Loosbrock, A. Loucks, W. F. Luebke, C. F. Luther, Anna Lynch, T. O. Mabbott, E. S. McCabe, Lola B. McCallough, Lois McClellan, Ruth McEwen, Roy McKelvy, S. R. McLean, Earl McManus, Helen McMarries, J. B. McMillan, K. McMunn, Amelia Madera, Rosalind Maggid, M. W. Major, Alberta Malone, Alma B. Martin, Houstin Martin, J. V. Martin, Albert Mathews, J. C. Mathews, Mary Mayo, C. B. Meadins, Hazel Meadows, Jessie Mebane, Martha Meighan, Mamie Meredith, C. H. Merrill, Edna Middlebrooks, R. A. Mills, Pearl Minker, M. Molloy, Valentine Moon, G. Moore, Jessie E. Moore, Beth Moreland, Geraldine Moreland, Natalie Morrison, Grace E. Morse, Karen Mortensen, Agnes Moss, Nadine Neely, Ruby Nichols, C. S. Northup, D. Norton, Lena L. Notson, C. H. Osborne, Bernice Owens, F. L. Palmer, Elizabeth Pape, Julia Pardone, Anita Parker, W. S. Parker, T. M. Pearce, Elizabeth S. Peck, Mary H. Perkins, Mary R. Perkins, P. G. Perrin, Veda Perry, S. J. Petro, Andrew Phillips, Florence Phillips, Frances A. Pope, Alma Portman, F. A. Pottle, Louise Pound, J. C. Powell, Myrtle Pratt, Lenore P. Ramsey, R. L. Ramsey, G. L. Read, Grace Read, Elizabeth Reardon, Jesse Reed, Jr., Nell Reeser, Mrs. Frank

Reeves, Victor Reid, E. Reynolds, W. A. Rhoades, Permelia Rice, Virginia Rice, A. E. Richards, Mrs. Richeeker, Lou Ella Riffe, Docia Riley, Lois Roberts, E. E. Robins, G. A. Rollins, Hilda Ross, Irene Rothschild, Nellie Rushing, Waldo Sabine, Lela Sailors, I. S. Sanders, H. P. Sawyer, N. W. Sawyer, Irene Scales, Hazel Scandrett, Hortense Scheier, M. H. Schy, G. W. Scott, H. H. Scudder, E. D. Seeber, Anne R. Semple, M. Setterstrom, Emily Shafer, Robert Shannon, Leo Shapiro, G. H. Sharp, A. Shearer, Robert Shiley, Louise B. Sholl, Sarah T. Sisson, A. C. Smith, Dorothy Smith, Kate P. Smith, Nora O. Solum, Lucille Speakman, R. E. Spiller, G. W. Spohn, C. L. Start, E. C. Stauffer, Florence Stedman, J. M. Stein, Juanita Stickel, Hilda Stine, R. Stine, Mrs. O. A. Strange, Mabel Strong, Marjorie Stuff, F. Stumberg, Elizabeth Sturtevant, J. S. P. Tatlock, A. P. Taylor, Avera L. Taylor, Joseph Teplin, Thelma Terry, H. J. S. Thomas, D. C. Thompson, R. Thornley, G. Tozer, Bessie M. Trivitt, Margaret Trusler, Annie P. Turner, Edward Turner, Pearl Turner, Clarice E. Tyler, Ruth Upton, R. P. Utter, Helen Varkala, Edith Veatch, D. E. Voelker, Irene Wagner, Marda Walker, Mrs. A. B. Wallace, Marie A. Walls, F. Walton, Louis Wann, T. L. Ward, Jean Warinner, Georgia Watson, Everette M. Webber, Anna B. M. Wehman, Esther S. Weiss, Hanna Weiss, Georgia C. Weist, O. Wells, Elizabeth H. West, Peyton Wheeler, Forrest Whittemore, Lucy F. Wiatt, Emily M. Wilcox, O. E. Wilds, Flo Clark Williams, R. T. Williams, Eunice Wilson, Mrs. A. B. Winkler, Ola E. Winslow, Roberta Wood, E. Woodard, Emma Woods, Rozelle Work, A. T. Wright, J. M. Wyllie, Anna E. Yahn, Helen M. Yonan, M. D. Zabel, Eleanore Zorn.

Special mention should be made of the contributions of the following authors of doctoral dissertations on aspects of American English: E. H. Criswell, Frances G. Emberson, Woodford A. Heflin, Robert D. Highfill, Anna L. Keaton, who also gave editorial assistance one summer, and Lois M. MacLaurin.

The editorial staff on Volume IV has been practically the same as that for Volume II (and Volume III). Dr. Sarah M. Harris and Dr. Woodford A. Heflin resigned in the spring and summer of 1942, Dr. Heflin leaving for military service and Mr. Robert W. Wadsworth taking over his share of the editing. Dr. Frances G. Emberson joined the staff in 1940 to help with the verifying, proofreading, and editing.

The funds necessary to support the Dictionary during the eighteen years spent in collecting the material and editing and publishing it have come from various sources. The cost of gathering the material and the preparation of the first volume was defrayed largely by research funds from the General Education Board of New York. The American Council of Learned Societies underwrote the publication of the first two parts. The editing of the second volume and much of the third was generously supported by Mrs. R. S. Maguire. The preparation of the final volume, as well as of part of the third, was assisted by a grant from the Rockefeller Foundation. From its inception the Dictionary received the continuing and sustaining support of the University of Chicago.

EXPLANATION OF SPECIAL LETTERING AND SYMBOLS

The size of the (boldface) type used for the heading of each entry indicates the relative importance of words with respect to their history or present currency.

The date of the quotation is usually followed by the author's name in capitals, or in small letters when he is quoting a source or when the name is that of the editor of the work.

* indicates that the word or sense is found in English before 1600.

+ indicates that the word or sense clearly or to all appearance originated within the present limits of the United States.

‖ indicates that the term or sense is known only from the passage cited and may be an individualism.

{ } encloses the earliest, latest, or inclusive dates (so far as known) for the occurrence of the word or sense in England (or in other than American English), or a statement relative to this. When a definition is not preceded by a + mark but is followed by a date in braces later than that of the earliest quotation, it has been assumed that the sense is not (or is not with certainty) of American origin.

When none of these symbols is used, the inference is that the word or sense is to all appearance part of the common stock of English, although lexicographical evidence for deciding its precise origin is lacking.

† before a form in boldface type denotes that that spelling is obsolete.

[ ] frequently contains the etymology.

Editorial additions briefly elucidating some matter in a quotation are also given within brackets.

When enclosing quotations, brackets denote that such illustrations are inserted with a qualification, being sometimes anticipative of more definite American usage or illustrative of historical use and being sometimes the work of a non-American writer or of an American in a foreign environment.

' ' in the reference encloses the pseudonym under which the author produced the work quoted.

In references, large capitals indicate volumes, small capitals parts or sections, and lower-case letters chapters or prefatory pages, e.g. III., ii., xxi.

When a subordinate sense marked **b** follows a sense which is not marked **a,** this signifies that the subordinate sense is derived from (i.e. is not collateral with) this antecedent sense.

Numbered paragraphs, (1), (2), etc., are used to illustrate different contexts in which the word occurs.

Paragraphs preceded by (*a*), (*b*), etc., exhibit different forms or spellings of the word.

The printing of a word in small capitals signifies that further information will be found under that word.

LIST OF ABBREVIATIONS

(In addition to many others that are obvious)

a (before a date) . . = *ante*, before
a., *adj.*, adj. . . . . = adjective
abbrev. . . . . . . = abbreviation
absol., absol. . . . . = absolute, -ly
ad. (in etymologies) = adaptation of
adv., adv. . . . . . = adverb
app. . . . . = apparently
attrib. . . . . . . = attributive, -ly
B. '48 (etc.) . . . . = Bartlett, 1848
　　　　　　　　(1859, 1877)
B. and L. . . . . . = Barrère and Leland
　　　　　　　　(1889)
c (before a date) . . = *circa*, about
Cent. . . . . = Century Diction-
　　　　　　　　ary (1889–91)
Cf., cf. . . . . . . = compare
Cl. . . . . = Clapin (1902)
colloq. . . . . . . = colloquial, -ly
colloq.² . . . . . . = a lower grade of col-
　　　　　　　　loquialism
comb. . . . . = combination
dial., dial. . . . . = dialect
Dict. . . . . = Dictionary
E. . . . . = East
E. . . . . = English
ellipt., ellipt. . . . = elliptical, -ly
Eng. . . . . = England
esp. . . . . = especially

F. . . . . = Farmer (1889)
F., Fr. . . . . . . = French
f. (in etymologies) = formed on
F. and H. . . . . = Farmer and Henley
　　　　　　　　(1890–1904)
fem. . . . . = feminine
fig., fig. . . . . . = figurative, -ly
freq. . . . . = frequent, -ly
intr. . . . . = intransitive
It. . . . . = Italian
L. . . . . = Latin
masc. . . . . = masculine
mod. . . . . = modern
Mex. . . . . = Mexican
n., n. . . . . = noun
Obs., obs. . . . . = obsolete
occas. . . . . . . = occasional, -ly
O.E.D. . . . . . . = Oxford English Dic-
　　　　　　　　tionary
Pg. . . . . = Portuguese
Pick. . . . . = Pickering (1816)
p.p. . . . . = past participle
ppl. a., ppl. a. . . = participial adjective
pple. . . . . = participle
prep., prep. . . . = preposition
pron. . . . . = pronoun
pronunc. . . . . . = pronunciation
Prov. . . . . = Provençal

pr. pple. . . . . . = present participle
p.t. . . . . = past tense
q.v. . . . . = *quod vide*, which see
refl., refl. . . . . = reflexive
S. . . . . = South
Sc., Sc. . . . . . = Scotch
sc. . . . . = *scilicet*, namely
S.E. . . . . = South-East
Sp. . . . . = Spanish
spec., spec. . . . . = specifically
Stand. . . . . . . = Standard Diction-
　　　　　　　　ary (1893–95)
s.v. . . . . = *sub voce*, under the
　　　　　　　　word
S.W. . . . . = South-West
Th. . . . . = Thornton *Glossary*
Th. S. . . . . . . = Thornton *Supple-
　　　　　　　　ment*
tr. . . . . = transitive
transf., transf. . . = transferred sense
v., vb. . . . . . . = verb
var. . . . . = variant of
vbl. n. . . . . . . = verbal noun
W. . . . . = West
W. '06 (etc.) . . . = Webster, 1806
　　　　　　　　(1828, etc.)
Worc. . . . . . . = Worcester (1846,
　　　　　　　　1860)

3. A grooved cylinder or disk which, when played on a phonograph or dictaphone, reproduces sounds. {1906–} Also fig.

1896 *Critic* 21 Nov. 322/2 A man who uses a gramophone . . . talks into his machine and hands the records to his typewriter. **1902** LORIMER *Lett. Merchant* 214 The phonograph records of a fellow's character are lined in his face. **1915** *Victor Record Cat.* May, Dance Records. . . . Fox Trots.

4. Phrases. a. *To travel out of the record*, to deal with or consider matters not strictly contained in a record; to be irrelevant. {1770, 1772}

1816 *Ann. 14th Congress* 1 Sess. 583 But he believed he was traveling a little out of the record. **1832** DUNLAP *Hist. Amer. Theatre* 14 We shall take occasion to describe their boundaries . . . without abandoning that branch of history assigned to us, or as lawyers say 'travelling out of the record.' **1848** in Shields *S. S. Prentiss* 402 We are of opinion that Mr. Prentiss travelled out of the record in the use of the offensive expressions complained of. **1864** *Congress. Globe* App. 3 March 57/3 The committee even travel out of the record to find objects for assault.

+b. *To put* (one's self, a vote, etc.) *on record*, to make a definite declaration of one's attitude or opinion. {1919–}

1900 *Congress. Rec.* 11 Jan. 785/1, I would be perfectly contented if Senators would put their vote on record. **1905** *Springfield W. Repub.* 20 Oct. 1 The American association of bankers last week put itself on record as favoring government subsidies.

* Recorder.

* 1. A wind instrument of the flute kind.

1633 *N.H. Prov. Papers* I. 77 In the Garrett . . . 15 recorders and hoeboys.

* 2. One who records something in writing. **+a.** An official of an early town, court, etc.

1639 *Cambridge Rec.* 40 Wm Towne shall Regester eu[e]rie Birth Mariage Buriall . . . & give it in once eu[e]rie yeare to be delivered by the Deputies to the Recorder. **1641** *Mass. H. S. Coll.* 3 Ser. VIII. 227 Proceedings against delinquents in Criminall causes shall be briefly and destinctly entered on the Rolles of every Court by the Recorder thereof. **1643** *Rowley Rec.* 1 Mr. Thomas Nelson, Mr. Edward Carlton . . . are to Regester the severall lotts of all the Inhabitants . . . and to leave theirof a Coppy with the Recorder of the Shire. **1645** *Maine Hist. Soc. Coll.* 1 Ser. I. 368 William Waldern, Recorder of the province of Mayne, chosen and sworn for one year. **1651** *Southampton Rec.* I. 73 Richard Mills recorder of the lands of this town shall have two pence for every paper drawne. **1666** *Dorchester Rec.* 136 Ther should be a yeerly Choice of a Recorder to keepe the towne books. **1687** *Mass. H. S. Coll.* 4 Ser. V. 158 The Secretary . . . was also Recorder.

+b. An official of a modern county or court.

1816 U. BROWN *Journal* II. 228 Col[one]l Pindal now writes to the recorder of Deeds at Richmond. **1834** PECK *Gaz. Illinois* 101 All deeds, conveyances, mortgages, or title papers whatsoever, must be recorded in the 'recorder's office.' **1843** in Hines *Voyage* 428 A Recorder . . . shall keep a faithful record of the proceedings in the Legislative Committee, Supreme and Probate Courts. **1903** *Indian Laws & Tr.* III. 18 The owners of such locations shall relocate their respective claims and record the same in the office of the county recorder of Uintah County, Utah.

* 3. A judicial officer of certain municipalities, having variously designated duties in different places; a municipal judge with criminal jurisdiction of first instance.

1701 *Phila. Ordinances* (1812) 4 The present mayor, recorder and alderman . . . [shall] be the present justices of the peace and oyer and terminer. **1705** *Boston News-Letter* 26 Feb. 2/2 Capt. John Tudor is appointed Recorder of the City of New York. **1820** *Phila. Ordinances* (1834) 80 The recorder of the city of Philadelphia shall annually receive out of the state treasury the sum of nine hundred dollars. **1827** DRAKE & MANSFIELD *Cincinnati* 51 The Recorder is appointed by the Council, has charge of the laws and ordinances, and presides in the absence of the President of the Council. **1846** CORCORAN *Pickings* 34 'You are charged with disturbing the peace,' said the Recorder. **1870** M. H. SMITH *20 Years Wall St.* 470 The trial had produced a very marked effect on the recorder. **1883** SWEET & KNOX *Through Texas* 355 He is brought before the recorder to answer the following high crimes and misdemeanors.

+Recording telegraph. (See quot. 1876.) — **1860** PRESCOTT *Telegraph* 73 In 1837, Prof. S. F. B. Morse made known . . . his recording telegraph which justly retains his name. **1876** KNIGHT 1902/1 *Recording-telegraph*, a telegraph provided with an apparatus which leaves a record of the message transmitted.

* Recovery. Baseball. **+**The act of regaining possession of the ball after a fumble. — **1880** *Chicago Inter-Ocean* 28 June 8/3 Richmond . . . tried to get second on what looked like a passed ball, but which, by Flint's rapid recovery and beautiful throw to Quest, headed him off.

Recruiting, *n.* {1646–} *attrib.* Designating various places, etc., connected with recruiting soldiers. {1772–} — **1775** HANCOCK in *Essex Inst. Coll.* XXXVIII. 56 The resolutions of Congress . . . [desired] you to exert your utmost endeavours to promote the recruiting service in the army as well as in your particular Colony. **1794** *State P.* (1819) II. 55 There is a recruiting post at Temple. **1858** VIELÉ *Following Drum* 19 They were instructions . . . to establish a recruiting rendezvous to enlist soldiers for Uncle Sam. **1881–5** McCLELLAN *Own Story* 151 There was issued Gen-

eral Order No. 33, closing all the recruiting depots for the volunteers and stopping all recruiting. **1903** Fox *Little Shepherd* xxi, Dixie . . . trotted into the recruiting camp of the Fourth Ohio Cavalry.

Recruiting, *a.* Of persons: Who recruit soldiers. {1706–} See also RECRUITING OFFICER. — **1755** *Lett. to Washington* I. 101 My Son listed at first two pretty young Fellows his Neighbors as recruiting Serjeants. **1849** *Whig Almanac 1850* 26/2, 23 cents per day, hardships in war, and no hope at all, require the aid of a recruiting sergeant. **1859** J. B. JONES *Southern Scenes* 479 Our recruiting agents have ceased to send us more men from the North and the West. **1872** *Newton Kansan* 3 Oct. 3/4 The chair appointed an additional recruiting committee for each township.

Recruiting office. An office where recruits for military service are enlisted. Also attrib. — **1848** LOWELL *Biglow P.* 1 Ser. viii. 115 He looked through the dirty pane of the recruiting-office window. **1867** *Ore. State Jrnl.* 19 Jan. 2/2 A recruiting office is now open in Salem. **1894** ALDRICH *Two Bites* 55 The recruiting-office at Rivermouth was in a small, unpainted, weather-stained building.

Recruiting officer. An officer of the army or navy employed in getting recruits. {1706–} — **1776** [see DISCHARGE *n.*]. **1798** BENTLEY *Diary* II. 270 The recruiting Officer is still seen in our Streets, to provide men for the Frigate Constitution. **1866** 'F. KIRKLAND' *Bk. Anecdotes* 181/2 The recruiting officers were taking the names of those who desired to enlist. **1911** *Harper's Wkly.* 7 Jan. 20/3 The young man was accepted through the efforts of the recruiting officer.

Recruiting station. 1. A place where travelers can recruit their strength. **2.** A place where soldiers are recruited. — **(1) 1845** FRÉMONT *Exped.* 160 The bottoms of this river, (the Bear,) and of some of the creeks . . . form a natural resting and recruiting station for travellers. **(2) 1861** *Army Regulations* 29 A reward of thirty dollars will be paid for the apprehension and delivery of a deserter to an officer of the army at the most convenient post or recruiting station. **1883** *Century Mag.* Aug. 581/2 Every grog-shop in the ward was his recruiting station. **1898** PAGE *Red Rock* 42 Red Rock and Birdwood became recruiting-stations and depots of supply.

* Rectified, *a.* Of alcoholic liquors: Redistilled or purified. {1605–} — **1721** *New-Eng. Courant* 14–21 Aug. 2/2 Whether rectified Spirit of Wine may be drank, when there is no Rum or other Dram to be had. **1815** *Niles' Reg.* IX. 94/2 Rectified spirits . . . are to be found in our druggists' shops. **1832** [see COMMON *a.* 4 c].

Rectifier. {1611–} One who redistills or rectifies spirituous liquor. {1727–} — **1794** [see Low WINE]. **1840** *Niles' Nat. Reg.* 11 April 96/2 Among the sufferers [by the fire] were . . . Wm. Hefferman, and McMoran and McMechen, rectifiers. **1875** *Chicago Tribune* 13 Sept. 5/3 A rectifier is permitted to rectify spirits bought by him, and place the same upon the market under a rectifier's stamp. **1885** [see LICENSE 2].

* Rector.

* 1. The head of a college or school: (see esp. quots. 1851).

1686 in Peirce *Hist. Harvard* App. 67 There shall be allowed to the present Rector of the College . . . the remainder of the income not disposed underneath. **1719** *Mass. Col. Soc. Publ.* VI. 186 It Is thought Needful . . . to have a Resident Rector, who with one Tutor may be Sufficient to Instruct the Students. **1742** BRAINERD *Diary* (1902) 50, [I] spread before them the treatment I had met with from the rector and tutors of Yale College. **1838** *S. Lit. Messenger* IV. 576/2 To this the Ex-Rector of the College [Georgetown] responded. **1851** HALL *College Words* 255 The title of *Rector* was given to the chief officer of Yale College at the time of its foundation, and was continued until the year 1745. *Ib.* [In 1686] Mr. Joseph Dudley [of Harvard changed] . . . the title of *President of the College* to that of *Rector*. A few years after, the title of *President* was resumed.

+2. An Episcopalian clergyman in charge of a parish.

'In Eng. this term is reserved for the parson of a parish whose tithes are not impropriate' (Horwill).

1720 *Amer. Wkly. Mercury* 6 Oct. 1/2 The Humble Address of the Rector, Church Wardens and Vestry of Trinity Church in the City of New York in America. **1843** 'CARLTON' *New Purchase* I. 282 Now, in this 'fix,' will any man of broadcloth and French calf-skin, conjecture that our Rector's outer man exhibited signs of worldly pride? **1853** STOWE *Key* 247/1 The Rev. Alex. Glennie, rector of All Saints parish, Waccamaw, South Carolina, has for several years been in the habit of preaching with express reference to slaves. **1883** *Century Mag.* May 67/1 Mr. Strong put him in charge of Mr. Stanley, rector of the Episcopal Church in Waterport. **1908** LORIMER *J. Spurlock* 70, I've been rector of St. Aurea's now for ten years.

* Red, *n.*

+1. *pl.* Red men; Indians.

1804 C. B. BROWN tr. Volney *View* 351 A body might have been formed capable of defending itself both against whites and reds, the savage on the one hand, and the land jobber on the other. **1864** *Wkly. New Mexican* 29 July 2/2 A few shots were fired after the reds, but without effect. **1881** *Cimarron News & Press* 17 Feb. 2/2 It is high time that the Reds receive some punishment on account of their various misdeeds. **1923** [see HAPPY HUNTING GROUND].

+2. = RED CENT.

See also NARY *a.* b.

1853 *La Crosse Democrat* 7 June 4/2 He never intends to pay . . . a red of the sum of money. **1862** NORTON *Army Lett.* 80 [A Confederate bill] is a specimen of Confederate States art, beautiful to see, but 'not worth a red' to spend. **1898** ATHERTON *Californians* 39, I've given away my last red. **1914** — *Perch of Devil* 13 [He] hasn't a red to do the trick himself, but wants to go on a ranch as foreman.

3. In phrases.

To shoot the red, of turkeys, to develop the red coloring on the head and wattles {to sport the red 1897-}; +*in the red*, (see quotation).

1850 BROWNE *Poultry Yard* 163 A safer rule may be fixed at the season called 'shooting the red.' **1871** LEWIS *Poultry Book* 103 The following prescription . . . [is] an invaluable tonic for debilitated birds, especially in the mortality which is apt to prevail when 'shooting the red.' **1877** CATON *Antelope & Deer of Amer.* (1881) 149 Frontiersmen and hunters . . . say the deer is in the *red* or the *blue*, as it may be in the summer or the winter coat.

* Red, *a.*

I. +**1.** Used with reference to American Indians or their activities.

1775 ADAIR *Indians* 227 Three of them can make a successful campaign, even against their own watchful red-colour enemies. **1784** FILSON *Kentucke* 83, I am told the Shawanese, Delawares, Chicasaw, Cherokees, and all other the Red Flesh, have taken the Long Knife by the hand. **1822** *Ann. 17th Congress* 1 Sess. 320 The factories have been furnished with goods of a kind not suitable to Indians unless . . . fancy ribands . . . are indispensable to eke out the dress of our red sisters. **1836** IRVING *Astoria* I. 202 Red warriors entertained their white friends with dances and songs. **1843** 'CARLTON' *New Purchase* II. 45 Indianised-French-dances, and other odd things produced by this amalgamation of the red and white savages. **1864** *Wkly. New Mexican* 25 Nov. 3/3 You must not suppose that this is the first visit our red friends have made us. **1867** *Ib.* 11 May 2/3 A fight lately . . . resulted in the early demise of half a dozen of the red varment. **1872** EGGLESTON *End of World* 173 They did not smoke the pipe of peace, like red Americans. **1881** CHASE *Editor's Run in N. Mex.* 107 Maxwell opened the mouth of that cannon with a noise such as the New Mexico red faces had never heard before.

II. In specific names.

Only a selection of examples is included. Many others can be found in books on plants, birds, etc.

+**2.** Of various American plants and trees.

1742 HEMPSTEAD *Diary* 391 They are Sprouts taken up at the Root of our Red Sweeting. **1815** *Lit. & Phil. Soc. N.Y. Trans.* I. 172 The country abounded with . . . the white, yellow, and red marygold. **1819** E. DANA *Geog. Sk.* 245 Valuable forest trees growing not only on Bistrop's Grant, but in the adjacent region [include the] . . . mucilaginous elm and red elm. **1838** *Mass. Agric. Survey 1st Rep.* 18 Red grass or Fox grass. **1843** TORREY *Flora N.Y.* I. 43 Red Puccoon . . . is in considerable repute for its emetic, cathartic, and expectorant qualities. **1884** ROE *Nature's Story* 356 The earlier red grapes, including the Delaware, Brighton, and Agawam, not only furnished the table abundantly, but also a large surplus for market. **1899** CUSHMAN *Hist. Indians* 22 One branch of the Omahas asserted that their founder arose out of the water, bearing in his hand an ear of red maize.

b. Of varieties of wheat.

1792 *N.Y. State Soc. Arts* I. 73 The kind of wheat then most generally in use among farmers in that part of the country [Shelter Island] were the red-bald, and the spring or summer wheat. **1874** *Rep. Comm. Agric. 1873* 221 Red Mammoth.—Quantities of this wheat, grown in Illinois, were distributed for experimental purposes in the winter of 1871.

+**c.** Of varieties of apples.

1817 W. COXE *Fruit Trees* 169 Red Sweet. A very valuable cider apple, cultivated in East Jersey. **1849** THOMAS *Amer. Fruit Culturist* 164 Carthouse. . . . Red Romanite, of Ohio. . . . Much cultivated in Ohio valley and sold at New-Orleans. **1870** *Rep. Comm. Agric. 1869* 185 Red June. Origin, North Carolina; fruit, medium size.

+**3.** Of various American fishes and crustaceans.

1775 [see DRUM *n.* 3 b]. **1818** MITCHILL in *Amer. Monthly Mag.* II. 245 Red Scorpoena.—*Scorpoena rufa*, with a more ruddy colour of the skin. **1873** *Mich. Gen. Statutes* I. (1882) 581 Nothing in this act shall be construed as prohibiting . . . any person from catching mullet, suckers, redsides, wall-eyed pike, or sturgeon. **1881** McLEAN *Cape Cod Folks* 137 [He] related anecdotes redolent of 'red salmon.' **1883** *Nat. Museum Bul.* No. 27, A large 'Red Rock Crab' (*Echidnoceros setimanus*), living about the Farallone Islands, off San Francisco, is occasionally brought to the markets of that city as a curiosity. *Ib.* 493 *Acipenser rubicundus*. . . . Rock Sturgeon; Red Sturgeon. Mississippi Valley; Great Lakes, and northward. **1884** GOODE, etc. *Fisheries* I .244 A single species is known in California, the so-called Red Cusk, *Brosmophycis marginatus*. *Ib.* 265 Orange Rock-Fish (*Sebastichthys pinniger*) . . . is usually called simply 'Red Rock-Cod,' or 'Red Rock-fish.' **1896** JORDAN & EVERMANN *Check-List Fishes* 434 *Hexagrammos asper*. . . . Red Rock-trout. Alaska to Monterey. **1911** *Rep. Fisheries 1908* 314/2 The redfish (*Sebastodes melanops*) . . . is also known as 'red cod,' 'red rockfish,' etc.

+**4.** Of various American animals of a red or reddish color.

1781 PENNANT *Hist. Quadrupeds* II. 487 Red Mole. . . . *Talpa rubra Americana.* **1802** G. SHAW *Gen. Zool.* III. 11. 502 Red Bead Snake. *Coluber Guttatus.* . . . A native of Carolina. **1842** Red viper [see COPPERBELLY 2]. **1858** Red moose [see BLACK MOOSE]. **1867** *Amer. Naturalist* I. 394 Only the Red Sand-rat (T[*homomys*] *fulvus*) is at all common [in Ariz.]. **1879** GOODE in *Smithsonian Misc. Coll.* XXIII. IV. 19 *Lepus*

Americanus, var. *Washingtonii*.—Red Hare.—West of Rocky Mountains from Columbia River into British Columbia. **1883** *Century Mag.* Sept. 686/2 Presently I saw . . . three large, red weasels or ermines. **1893** *Nat. Duroc-Jersey Rec.* I. 17 The origin of the 'red hog' known today as the Duroc-Jerseys, cannot be positively traced. . . . In some of the counties of New York . . . they were called Red Rocks.

+**5.** Of various American birds having conspicuous red plumage or markings.

1688 CLAYTON *Va.* in *Phil. Trans.* XVII. 995 The Red Mocking . . . sings very well, but has not so soft a Note as the gray Mocking Bird. **1844** *Nat. Hist. N.Y., Zoology* II. 165 The Swamp Finch, *Ammodramus Palustris*, . . . is often called the Red Grass-bird in this State. **1883** *Century Mag.* Sept. 681/2 The nests were probably plundered at night, and doubtless by the little red screech-owl. **1917** *Birds of Amer.* II. 71 Red-tailed Hawk. *Buteo borealis borealis*. . . . Other Names.—Red Hawk; Hen Hawk [etc.].

+**6.** Of various insects.

1855 *Amer. Inst. N.Y. Trans. 1854* 282 The insect that has destroyed so much wheat in Western New-York and Pennsylvania and Northern Ohio this season, . . . is called the 'red weevil.' **1864** *Ohio Agric. Rep.* XVIII. 143 Late oats were injured by a red insect, called by farmers 'red lice.' **1894** *Vt. Agric. Rep.* XIV. 176 A little kerosene on the roosts will destroy the red mites that are so troublesome. **1895** *Dept. Agric. Yrbk. 1894* 290 An insect of some importance in the South is the square-necked or red grain beetle.

7. a. In combinations used attributively.

1788 WASHINGTON *Diaries* III. 350 In an equal No. of Rows . . . was sown the Red Horn Carrots. **1833** SILLIMAN *Manual of Sugar Cane* 13 The kind of Cane planted is Red Ribbon. **1866** LINDLEY & MOORE *Treas. Botany* 885/2 Its dark purplish berries . . . contain a purplish-red juice somewhat resembling red ink, and hence it is sometimes called the Red-ink Plant. **1883** *Nat. Museum Bul.* No. 27, 477 *Ictiobus bubalus.* . . . Red-mouth Buffalo-fish. Mississippi Valley. **1892** *Amer. Folk-Lore* V. 105 *Cladonia bellidiflora* (a common lichen), red-cup .noss. General in N.E. **1897** *N.Y. Forest, Fish, & Game Comm.* 2d Rep. 223 *Salmo mykiss.* . . . Black-Spotted Trout; Red-Throat Trout. **1897** SUDWORTH *Arborescent Flora* 76 *Cupressus guadalupensis.* . . . Arizona Cypress. . . . [Also called] Red-bark Cypress (Ariz.). Arizona Red-bark Cypress (*C. Arizonica*) (Cal. lit.). Guadalupe Cypress (Cal. lit.).

+**b.** In compounds with adjectives in -*ed*.

1825 NEAL *Bro. Jonathan* III. 420 The red-hearted, or upland beech. **1873** *Amer. Naturalist* VII. 328 Next comes the Red-vented, or Crissal Thrush (H[*arporhynchus*] *crissalis*); also inhabiting the Colorado and Gila valleys. **1883** *Nat. Museum Bul.* No. 27, 487 *Squalius elongatus.* . . . Red-sided Shiner; Red-sided Minnow. . . . Western Pennsylvania; Ohio Valley; Great Lakes; Upper Mississippi Valley. **1884** J. S. KINGSLEY, etc. *Stand. Nat. Hist.* II. 194 *Caloptenus femur-rubrum*, the Red-thighed Locust, is found throughout North America. **1917** *Birds of Amer.* II. 150 The Yellow-bellied Sapsucker and its western variant, the Red-naped Sapsucker (*Sphyrapicus varius nuchalis*), are the most migratory of all the Woodpeckers.

III. +**8.** In special combinations.

Red hill, a hill of red clay; *r. hot*, a long bun enclosing a frankfurter and, usually, a relish or condiment; *r. ibis*, a form of artificial fly used in fishing; *r. monkeys*, delirium tremens (slang); *r. nigger*, a contemptuous designation for an Indian; *r. pup*, =RED DOG 1; *r. rise*, (see quotation); *r. rover*, a children's game, or a particular participant in it.

1888 *Congress. Rec.* 12 Dec. 182/2 You may take the oldest red-hill in South Carolina, or Georgia, and fertilize it, . . . and you can make more cotton to the acre upon it than you could when it was virgin soil. **1903** ADE *People You Know* 111 [He had] a little something on the side for Red Hots. **1899** VAN DYKE *Fisherman's Luck* 27 H.E. G——, fishing with a small trout-rod . . . and an ancient red ibis of the common kind, rose and hooked a lordly salmon. **1850** LEWIS *La. Swamp Doctor* 118 In one of the upper apartments was a private patient, labouring under the disease indifferently known as the blue-devils, red-monkeys, seeing injuns, or man-with-the-poker. **1837** BIRD *Nick* I. 26, I killed two of the red niggurs. *c*1844 Red pup [see REDBACK 2]. **1888** *Encycl. Brit.* (ed. 9) XXIII. 203/1 These freshets, laden with the rich red loam of the plains, usually reach the lower inhabited portions of the State [of Texas] in periods of drought, and are termed 'red rises.' **1891** *Amer. Folk-Lore* IV. 224 Red Rover. The boy who is 'it' is called the 'Red Rover,' and stands in the middle of the street, while the others form a line on the pavement on one side.

+**Red adder.** =COPPERHEAD 1. — **1818** *Amer. Jrnl. Science* I. 84 *Scytalus Cupreus*, or Copper-head Snake, . . . [is known] in New-England, by the names of *rattlesnake's mate* and *red adder*. **1842** [see COPPER-BELLY 2]. **1859** BARTLETT 99 [The copperhead] has various other popular names, as Copper-belly, Red Viper, Red adder.

Red algae. *pl.* A class of algae characterized by red or violet pigment. — **1852** HARVEY in *Smithsonian Contrib. to Knowl.* V. v. 1 Rhodospermeæ, or Red Algæ. **1876** GOODE *Ib.* XIII. v. 60 On the coast of Maine, the bright-red variety of the Cod . . . is found only on bottoms covered with Red Algæ. **1901** MOHR *Plant Life Ala.* 148.

Red ant. Any of various ants of a red color, esp. a common house ant, *Monomorium pharaonis*. {1747-} — **1853** 'P. PAXTON' *Yankee in Texas* 161 A miserable dreary month . . . [was] enlivened only by the musquitoes, red ants, and a semi-occasional ray of moist, half-asleep sunshine. **1865** *Atlantic Mo.* June 734/1 Cockroaches and red ants never invade her premises. **1925** HERRICK *Man. Injurious Insects* 450 The tiny red ant, *Monomorium pharaonis*, is light-yellow and about one-sixteenth of an inch long. . . . It feeds on nearly everything it can find and is probably the most common house ant.

Red ash.[1] {1816-} +An American tree (*Fraxinus pennsylvanica*) having a strong, durable, brown wood. (Cf. GREEN ASH.) — **1784** CUTLER in *Mem. Academy* I. 492 *Fraxinus.* . . . The White Ash. The Red Ash. The Black Ash. The Prickley Ash. **1832** BROWNE *Sylva* 159 The red ash is a beautiful tree, rising perpendicularly to the height of 60 feet. **1860** CURTIS *Woody Plants N.C.* 54 Red Ash. . . . The young shoots . . . [are] clothed with a thick whitish down, which changes, in the Fall, to a reddish tint. **1892** APGAR *Trees Northern U.S.* 123 Red Ash . . . [is] a smaller and more slender tree than the White Ash.

+**Red ash.**[2] A variety of coal which when burned produces ashes of a reddish color. Also attrib. — **1857** GUNN *N.Y. Boarding-Houses* 60 Her coal merchant demurs about bringing a ton of Red Ash or Peach Orchard —until paid. **1874** RAYMOND *6th Rep. Mines* 507 Mr. Franklin B. Gowen . . . determined to make this large body of land available for the production of coal, the upper or red-ash veins having been worked out. **1882** *Century Mag.* July 345/2 Do you like the red-ash coal better than white ash, Deacon Emmett? **1907** *St. Nicholas* May 669/1 The coal is the red ash, burns very freely and gives plenty of heat.

+**Red Astrachan.** [See ASTRACHAN.] A red or reddish summer apple. {1853- (Rivers *Cat. Fruits* 11)} — **1847** IVES *New Eng. Fruit* 36 *Red Astracan.*—This beautiful apple is of medium size, of a round and rather flat form. **1856** *Rep. Comm. Patents 1855: Agric.* 290 Not much attention is given to summer apples, the 'Red Astrachan' being one of the best. **1863** *Horticulturist* XVIII. 262 Of Apples, we may mention American Summer Pearmain, Red Astrachan. **1875** BURROUGHS *Winter Sunshine* 163 The red astrachan [is] an August apple.

Redback.

+1. =DUNLIN.
Cf. RED-BACKED SANDPIPER.
1813 WILSON *Ornithology* VII. 25 Red-backed Sandpiper: *Tringa alpina;* . . . inhabits both the old and new continents, being known . . . in the United States, along the shores of New Jersey, by that [*i.e.*, the name] of the Red-back. **1917** *Birds of Amer.* I. 237.

+2. =RED DOG 1. *Obs.* Also attrib.
1841 *Jamestown* (N.Y.) *Jrnl.* 17 June 1/6 The following 'Red Back' Banks have resumed business and now redeem their notes in Albany. *c*1844 R. H. COLLYER *Amer. Life* 14, I have heard of a litter of dogs being sold and paid for by a litter of cats. This is no worse than some Banks in New York State known as 'red-back,' or 'red-dog' which were only redeemed by another known as 'red-pup,' one being about as valuable as the other.

+3. One of the treasury notes issued by the republic of Texas in 1838. Now hist.
1852 GOUGE *Fiscal Hist. Texas* 106 This deprived the holders of 'red backs' of even a promise to pay interest on their demands. **1872** MORRELL *Flowers & Fruits* 70 There was neither gold nor silver in circulation then. Texas did not have a supply of 'red-backs,' as was afterwards the case. **1889** H. H. BANCROFT *Works* XVI. 345 [The exchequer bills] soon suffered the same fate as the treasury notes, or red-backs as they were called from the color of the paper.

Red-backed, *a.* Having a red back. Used chiefly in the names of birds. {1768-} See also next. — **1709** LAWSON *Carolina* 126 The Red-back'd Snake [is found in Carolina]. **1839** STORER *Mass. Reptiles* 245 *S[alamandra] erythronota*. Green. The red-backed Salamander. . . . The motions of this species are very agile. **1839** AUDUBON *Ornith. Biog.* V. 335 Red-Backed Woodpecker. *Picus Pyrrhonotus.* . . . On the back between the shoulders was a large red space. **1858** BAIRD *Birds Pacific R.R.* 134 *Selasphorus Rufus*, Red-Backed Humming Bird. . . . This species is about the size of the common ruby-throated humming bird. **1917** *Birds of Amer.* III. 47/2 The Red-backed Junco (*Junco phæonotus dorsalis*) has a bright rufous back and a pink bill.

+**Red-backed sandpiper.** =DUNLIN. (Cf. RED-BREASTED SANDPIPER 2.) — **1813** [see REDBACK 1]. **1835** AUDUBON *Ornith. Biog.* III. 580 The Red-Backed Sandpiper, *Tringa Alpina*, . . . is abundant along the whole range of our coast. **1883** *Nat. Museum Bul.* No. 27, 150 *Pelidna alpina americana*, Red-Backed Sandpiper. North America and Northeastern Asia. **1911** FORBUSH *Hist. Game Birds Mass.* 284 The Red-backed Sandpiper feeds largely on worms, crustaceans, and insects.

Red bass. {1898-} +The red drum (*Sciaenops ocellata*), common along the Atlantic coast. (Cf. DRUM n. 3, DRUMFISH.) — **1842** *Nat. Hist. N.Y., Zoology* IV. 75 At Charleston, it [*i.e.*, the branded corvina] is called Bass, Sea Bass, and Red Bass. **1879** KILBOURNE & GOODE *Game Fishes U.S.* 37/1 In the Carolinas, Florida, and the Gulf, we meet the name 'Bass,' and its variations, 'Spotted Bass,' 'Red Bass,' [etc.].

+**Red bat.** A very common species of American bat (*Nycteris borealis*) of a red or reddish color. — **1812** WILSON *Ornithology* VI. pl. 150 Red Bat. **1884** J. S. KINGSLEY, etc. *Stand. Nat. Hist.* V. 167 The *Atalapha noveboracensis*, or Red Bat, is perhaps the most common of the Eastern American Bats.

+**Red bay.** A lauraceous tree (*Persea borbonia*) of the southern states. (Cf. ALLIGATOR PEAR, AVOCADO PEAR.)
*c*1730 CATESBY *Carolina* I. 63 The Red Bay. . . . The wood is fine grain'd, and of excellent use for Cabinets, &c. **1766** J. BARTRAM *Journal*

69 That which is called hammocky land is generally full of large evergreen and water-oaks, mixed with red-bay and magnolia. **1801** *Hist. Review & Directory* I. 147. **1833** SILLIMAN *Man. Sugar Cane* 19 [The hammocks are] characterized by the natural growth of . . . red bay, magnolia and cabbage-palmetto. **1869** *Amer. Naturalist* III. 401 A few of the prominent species worthy of mention are the Sweet Bay . . . ; the Southern Buckthorn . . . ; the Catalpa, or Indian-bean; also the *Persea Carolinensis*, or Alligator pear, sometimes called the Red Bay. **1901** MOHR *Plant Life Ala.* 96 The sweet illicium . . . and red bay (*Persea carolina*) are here met with.
attrib. **1734** Red bay timber [see HAND BOARD].

+**Red bay-tree.** =prec. — **1744** MOORE *Voy. Georgia* 116 To the South, is a little wood of red bay trees. **1802** DRAYTON *S. Carolina* 68 Red bay tree. . . . Grows in the lower country. **1846** BROWNE *Trees Amer.* 414 *Laurus carolinensis*, The Carolina Laurel-Tree. . . . [Also called] Red Bay-tree.

+**Red beds.** *W. Geol.* Reddish strata of sedimentary deposits. Also attrib. — **1888** *Encycl. Brit.* (ed. 9) XXIII. 202/2 West of this [in Texas] . . . is the gypsum country, consisting of the so-called 'red beds' of the western United States. **1890** *Cent.* 5016/2 *Red beds*, a conspicuous formation in the Rocky Mountains. . . . They are often eroded into fantastic and picturesque forms. **1905** *Forestry Bureau Bul.* No. 65, 7 The Red Beds Belt is named from the geological formation prevailing in western Oklahoma and the eastern part of the Texas 'Pan Handle.'

Red beech. {1889-} +A popular designation for the common American beech, *Fagus grandifolia.* — [**1637** see BEECH 1].] **1810** MICHAUX *Arbres* I. 27 *Red beech*, . . . dans les Etats du nord. **1814** PURSH *Flora Amer.* II. 624 *Fagus ferruginea* . . . is distinguished by the inhabitants by the name of Red Beech. **1851** SPRINGER *Forest Life* 30 Botanists are unable to find more than one kind of Beech, believing that the distinctions of 'white' and 'red' Beech in common use among the people describes but one species. **1894** *Amer. Folk-Lore* VII. 99 *Fagus sylvatica*, white beech, red beech, N.Y.

Red-bellied, *a.* In the names of American birds, fishes, etc.
See also RED-BELLIED NUTHATCH, SNAPPER, etc.
1709 LAWSON *Carolina* 126 Red-bellied Land-Snakes [are found in Carolina]. **1842** *Nat. Hist. N.Y., Zoology* III. 16 The Red-bellied Terrapin. *Emys rubriventris* . . . is one of the largest of the genus. *Ib.* IV. 236 [In] the Red-bellied Trout, *Salmo erythrogaster*, . . . not only the colors externally are extremely vivid, but the flesh is of a bright red approaching carmine. **1846** AUDUBON & BACHMAN *Viviparous Quads. N. Amer.* I. 292 *Sciurus Ferruginiventris* . . . Red-Bellied Squirrel. . . . Several specimens were received from California. **1917** *Birds of Amer.* II. 75/1 The entire under parts of the Red-bellied Hawk (*Buteo lineatus elegans*) are sometimes rich dark reddish. **1920** COPPER *Under Big Top* 44 That would be a red-bellied bream.

+**Red-bellied nuthatch.** The small Canada nuthatch (*Sitta canadensis*), the under parts of which are reddish brown in color. — [**1808** WILSON *Ornithology* I. 43 Red-bellied, black-capt nuthatch. *Sitta varia*.] **1839** PEABODY *Mass. Birds* 339 The Red-bellied Nuthatch . . . holds by its feet to the bark and sleeps, head downwards. **1870** *Amer. Naturalist* IV. 546 [The] Red-bellied Nuthatch . . . has as unmusical a note as ever fell upon one's ear. **1917** *Birds of Amer.* III. 203.

+**Red-bellied snapper.** =RED GROUPER. — **1879** *Smithsonian Inst. Coll.* XXIII. IV. 49 *Epinephelus morio*, . . . Red-bellied Snapper. . . . Southern Atlantic States. **1911** *Rep. Fisheries 1908* 316/2 The red grouper (*Ephinephelus morio*) is called . . . 'red-bellied snapper' in Florida.

+**Red-bellied snipe.** The long-billed dowitcher (*Limnodromus griseus scolopaceus*), in summer plumage. (Cf. DOWITCHER, GRAY SNIPE, RED-BREASTED SNIPE.) — **1883** [see GREATER *a.*]. **1917** *Birds of Amer.* I. 230/2 The Long-billed Dowitcher is known locally as . . . the Red-bellied Snipe.

+**Red-bellied woodpecker.** A red-headed woodpecker (*Centurus carolinus*) having under parts of a red or reddish color.
*c*1728 CATESBY *Carolina* I. 19 The Red-bellied Wood-pecker. . . . The belly near the vent . . . is stained with red. **1808** WILSON *Ornithology* I. 113 [The] Red-Bellied Woodpecker . . . prefers the largest, high-timbered woods, and tallest decayed trees of the forest. **1844** *Nat. Hist. N.Y., Zoology* II. 189 The Red Bellied Woodpecker . . . comes to us from the South in the spring, and advances as far north as Canada. **1874** COUES *Birds N.W.* 289 Red-bellied Woodpecker. . . . This is a rather southern species. **1917** *Birds of Amer.* II. 161/2 The Red-bellied Woodpecker . . . evinces a decided taste for fruit.

Redbelly. {1792-} +**1.** A fish, as the long-eared sunfish (*Xenotis megalotis*), having a salmon-colored belly. +**2.** The red-bellied terrapin, *Pseudemys rubriventris.* +**3.** *Red-belly squirrel*, a fox squirrel (*Sciurus niger rufiventer*) of the Mississippi Valley. +**4.** *Redbelly shiner*, the red-bellied dace, *Chrosomus erythrogaster.* — (1) **1791** W. BARTRAM *Travels* 14 We presently took some fish, one kind of which is very beautiful; they call it the red-belly. **1820** *Western Rev.* II. 49 A fine species, called Red-belly, Black-ears, Black-tail Sunfish, &c., . . . lives in the Kentucky, Licking, and Sandy rivers, &c. (2) **1877** BARTLETT 699 The most celebrated [terrapin] is the diamond-back; there are also the *yellow-bellies, red-bellies, loger-heads, snuff-boxes*, etc. (3) **1826** GODMAN *Nat. Hist.* II. 141 The Red-Belly Squirrel. . . . Its general colour is dark grayish brown above, with a bright yellowish red beneath. (4) **1820** *Western Rev.* II. 237 Redbelly

Shiner. *Luxilus erythrogaster*. . . . A very distinct and insulated species. . . . It is called Red belly Chub.

Red-berried elder. A variety of elder (*Sambucus racemosa*), bearing bright red fruit. {1731- (Miller *Gard. Dict.* s.v. *Sambucus* 4)} Also *redberry elder.* — **1789** [see FEVERBUSH]. **1795** WINTERBOTHAM *Hist. View* III. 388 Flowering Trees, Shrubs, &c. [include] . . . Red-berried elder. **1815** DRAKE *Cincinnati* 83 [The] red berried elder and witch hazle I have only found at the falls of the Little Miami. **1872** *Vermont Bd. Agric. Rep.* I. 279 S[ambucus] *Pubens*, Red Berried Elder, in dry, rocky soil, does not spread by running roots. **1887** *Harper's Mag.* July 303/2, I jumped out to secure . . . a branch of hobble-bush, or red-berried elder.

Redberry. +Any one of several American plants, esp. the red baneberry (*Actaea rubra*), producing bright red berries. — **1785** WASHINGTON *Diaries* II. 338, I discovered . . . the red berry of the Swamp. **1805** LEWIS in *L. & Clark Exped.* I. (1904) 299 The underbrush is willow, red wood, . . . the red burry and Choke cherry. **1806** CLARK *Ib.* V. (1905) 302 The [river] bottoms . . . [are] covered with timber . . . together with the red berry or Buffalow Grees bushes. **1819** WARDEN *Statistical Acct. U.S.* III. 136 The undergrowth [along the Missouri R.] consists of hazel, arrowwood, red-berry, crab-apple, wild pea vine, and rushes. **1916** BAILEY, etc. *Stand. Cycl. Horticulture* V. 2924/2 [*Rhamnus*] *crocea*. Red-berry. Evergreen shrub to 3 ft., with rigid often spinescent branches. . . . Calif.

+**Red birch.** The river birch (*Betula nigra*). (Cf. BROOM BIRCH.) — **1785** MARSHALL *Amer. Grove* 19 *Betula lenta*. Red Birch. This grows to a pretty large size. **1832** BROWNE *Sylva* 124 In Pennsylvania and New Jersey the name of Red Birch is given to the *Betula rubra*, to distinguish it from the white birch. **1850** S. F. COOPER *Rural Hours* 385 The *red birch*, also a tree of the largest size, is the kind used for brooms. **1894** COULTER *Bot. W. Texas* III. 413.

+**Redbird.** Any one of various small American birds of red or partially red plumage; esp. the cardinal or the summer tanager.

See also BLACK-WINGED *a.* and SUMMER REDBIRD.

1670 DENTON *Brief Desc. N.Y.* 6 There is also the red Bird, with divers sorts of singing birds. **1709** LAWSON *Carolina* 144 The Red-Birds (whose Cock is all over of a rich Scarlet Feather, with a tufted Crown on his Head, of the same Colour) are the Bigness of a Bunting-Lark. **1775** BURNABY *Travels* 17 In the woods there are . . . the red bird or nightingale, the blue-bird, the yellow-bird. **1810** WILSON *Ornithology* II. 38 The sprightly figure, and gaudy plumage of the Red-bird . . . will always make him a favorite. **1844** *Nat. Hist. N.Y., Zoology* II. 175 The Red-bird, or Summer Red-bird, comes to us from the South. **1894** TORREY *Fla. Sketch-Book* 114 Behind me a redbird was whistling. **1917** *Birds of Amer.* III. 63, 81.

Red-blooded, *a.* {1802-} *fig.* Masculine, virile; abounding in vitality and vigor. {1923-} — **1881** HAYES *New Colorado* 155 [Nothing] can be conceived more exasperating to a strong red-blooded man than to . . . have a villain take his watch and money. **1895** REMINGTON *Pony Tracks* 19 This time I found that I had a mount that was 'a horse from the ground up,' as they phrase it in the red-blooded West.

* **Redbreast.**

* **1.** Any one of various red-breasted birds, +esp. the migratory thrush or common American robin, *Turdus migratorius*.

1797 C. PRENTISS *Fugitive Ess.* 48 The readbreast mourns in solitary strains her absent mate. **1839** [see FIREBIRD]. **1858** *Atlantic Mo.* Oct. 598/2 The English Robin Redbreast has been immortalized in song. But the American Robin, (*Turdus migratorius,*) though surnamed Redbreast, is a bird of different species and different habits. **1917** *Birds of Amer.* I. 231 Knot. *Tringa canutus*. . . . [Also called] Beach Robin; Red-breast; Buff-breast.

+**2.** The red-breasted bream, *Lepomis auritus*.

1888 GOODE *Amer. Fishes* 66 In Pennsylvania it is called 'Sun Perch,' . . . elsewhere it is the 'Red Breast.'

Red-breasted, *a.* In the specific names of birds {1609, fig.; 1678-}: (see quotations).

1835 AUDUBON *Ornith. Biog.* III. 27 The great Red-Breasted Rail, or Fresh-Water Marsh-Hen, *Rallus Elegans*, . . . is abundant in South Carolina. **1852** BAIRD in Stansbury *Gt. Salt Lake* 322 *Pterocyanea raffelesii*. . . . The Red-breasted Teal appears to be a common bird in Utah. **1858** — *Birds Pacific R.R.* 222 *Sialia Sialis*, . . . Blue Bird; Red-breasted Blue Bird. . . . Eastern North America to a little west of Missouri river. *a*1862 THOREAU *Maine Woods* 321, I saw in Maine between July 24 and August 3, . . . *Turdus migratorius* (red-breasted robin). **1883** *Nat. Museum Bul.* No. 27, 163 *Mergus serrator*. Red-breasted Sheldrake. . . . Northern hemisphere, breeding in cold-temperate and subarctic regions. **1917** *Birds of Amer.* I. 126 Shoveler. . . . Other Names.—Spoonbill; . . . Red-breasted Shoveler.

Red-breasted merganser. A fishing duck, *Mergus serrator*. {1776-} — **1813** [see MERGANSER]. **1839** AUDUBON *Ornith. Biog.* V. 92 The Red-breasted Merganser is best known throughout the United States by the name of 'Shell-drake.' **1874** COUES *Birds N.W.* 584 Red-breasted Merganser; Fishing Duck. . . . Northern Hemisphere. **1917** *Birds of Amer.* I. 111/1 The Red-breasted Merganser is . . . an exceedingly expert diver.

+**Red-breasted sandpiper. 1.** The American knot, *Calidris canutus rufus*. (Cf. HORSEFOOT SNIPE 2.) **2.** =DUNLIN. (Cf. RED-BACKED SANDPIPER.) — **(1)** **1813** WILSON *Ornithology* VII. 43 Red-breasted Sandpiper

. . . [is a] prettily marked species. **1844** *Nat. Hist. N.Y., Zoology* II. 243 The Red-Breasted Sandpiper . . . [has] received several different names. **1888** [see HORSEFOOT SNIPE 2]. **1917** *Birds of Amer.* I. 231 Knot. *Tringa canutus*. . . . [Also called] Red Sandpiper; Red-breasted Sandpiper; Red-breasted Plover. **(2)** **1874** COUES *Birds N.W.* 489 *Tringa Alpina* var. *Americana*. American Dunlin; Black-bellied or Red-breasted Sandpiper.

Red-breasted snipe. {1802-} +The dowitcher, *Limnodromus griseus*. (Cf. GRAY SNIPE, RED-BELLIED SNIPE.) — **1813** WILSON *Ornithology* VII. 45 The Red-breasted Snipe arrives on the sea coast of New Jersey early in April. **1839** PEABODY *Mass. Birds* 371 The Red-breasted Snipe . . . arrives on our coast, from the south, in April. **1874** COUES *Birds N.W.* 479 The Red-breasted Snipe is a gentle and unsuspicious creature. **1917** *Birds of Amer.* I. 229 Dowitcher. *Macrorhamphus griseus griseus*. . . . [Also called] Red-breasted Snipe (summer).

Red-breasted thrush. The common American robin. *rare.* (Cf. MIGRATORY THRUSH.) — **1785** PENNANT *Arctic Zool.* II. 335 Red-breasted [Thrush]. **1808** WILSON *Ornithology* I. 39 The Red-breasted Thrush cannot brook the confinement of the cage. **1823** JAMES *Exped. Rocky Mts.* I. 263 *Turdus migratorius*—Red-breasted thrush.

Red-breasted woodpecker. {1729-} +The red-breasted sapsucker (*Sphyrapicus varius ruber*), of the California region. — **1839** AUDUBON *Ornith. Biog.* V. [79] [The] Red-breasted woodpecker, *Picus Ruber*, . . . has most of the habits of the common Red-headed Species. **1879** *Nat. Museum Proc.* I. 429 [The] Red-breasted Woodpecker . . . is a rather rare winter sojourner at Marysville and Murphy's.

Red brick. A brick of red color; an ordinary brick, as distinguished from a finishing brick or face brick. {1839-} Also collect. and attrib.

1845 *Lowell Offering* V. 190 The red-brick factories and boarding-houses . . . look as fresh as if just painted. **1874** ALDRICH *P. Palfrey* iv, Mr. Dent's glance . . . rested on the red-brick Almshouse. **1880** *Harper's Mag.* July 292/1 He had been living in an edifice of red brick, with granite copings, and an enormous fan-light over the door. **1902** ALDRICH *Sea Turn* 225 He began attendance at the little red-brick schoolhouse on the Hampton turnpike.

+**b.** A house built of red brick.

1905 'O. HENRY' *Four Million* 141 The restaurant was next door to the old red brick in which she hall-roomed.

+**Red brother.** An American Indian. Usually pl. — **1808** PIKE *Sources Miss.* 122, I was obliged to convince my red brethren that . . . I would not suffer them to plunder my men. **1820** in Morse *Rep. Indian Affairs* II. 13 Your red brethren, the Cherokees, Choctaws, Osages, the Six Nations, and other tribes, have had the same offers made to them. **1838** DRAKE *Tales Queen City* 102 The red brothers had assembled from the four winds. **1864** *Wkly. New Mexican* 9 Dec. 1/3 Horses and cattle [were] carried off by the *peaceable* red brethren.

+**Red buckeye.** A southern species of buckeye (*Aesculus pavia*) smaller than that found further north. — **1860** CURTIS *Woody Plants N.C.* 48 Red Buckeye . . . The root of this species is sometimes used as a substitute for soap in washing woollen cloths. **1901** MOHR *Plant Life Ala.* 133 Large live oaks, aged magnolias, and pignut hickories cover these heaps, along with dense copses of the red buckeye.

+**Redbud.** Any one of various American trees or species of trees of the genus *Cercis*, esp. *C. canadensis*, of the interior and southern United States; also, the buds of such a tree, used as a salad or garnish.

1705 BEVERLEY *Virginia* IV. 56 [The people of Va.] dish up [roots, herbs, etc.] various ways, and find them very delicious Sauce to their Meats; . . . such are the Red-buds, Sassafras-Flowers, Cymnels, Melons, and Potatoes. **1751** GIST *Journals* 59 We then went . . . thro rich level Land covered with small Walnut, Sugar Trees, Red-Buds. **1785** MARSHALL *Amer. Grove* 32 Red-bud, or Judas Tree. This grows naturally in several parts of North-America. **1821** NUTTALL *Travels Arkansa* 92 The Red-bud . . . was commonly in flower. **1871** *Ill. Agric. Soc. Trans.* VIII. 206 *Cercis Canadensis* (Red Bud) is quite common. **1897** SUDWORTH *Arborescent Flora* 253 *Cercis reniformis*. Texas Redbud. . . . [Also called] Redbud (Tex.). **1906** J. A. HARRISON *G. Washington* 61 Copses where the redbud and the Indian pink burned like flame in springtime.

attrib. **1709** LAWSON *Carolina* 100 The Red-Bud-Tree bears a purple Lark-Heel. **1770** *Md. Hist. Mag.* XIII. 72 Collect Locust & Red Bud seeds. **1872** *Harper's Mag.* Feb. 372/1 The redbud and dogwood blossoms had again appeared and vanished on the Kentucky hills.

+**Red bug.**

1. A reddish, six-legged, microscopic mite or chigger, *Trombicula irritans*.

Cf. CHIGOE 1, JIGGER.[1]

1827 WILLIAMS *West Florida* 29 Red bugs are numerous, especially in mossy woods. **1847** *Knickerb.* Nov. 394 A gross of red-bugs, of a size invisible to vulgar eyes, lay the foundation of as many ulcers. . . . The red-bug abounds only in decayed wood. **1872** [see CHIGOE 1 (b)]. **1903** *McClure's Mag.* Nov. 95/2 We'll have the tribe and the blue-bellies from the fort a scouring these hills till a red-bug couldn't hide.

2. The cotton-stainer, *Dysdercus suturellus*. Also *red cotton bug, cotton red bug*.

1837 WILLIAMS *Florida* 71 Red Cotton Bug, . . . an insect that pierces the capsule of the cotton, enters the seed and deposits its egg. **1856** *Rep.*

Comm. Patents 1855: Agric. 104 The 'red-bugs,' or . . . 'cotton-stainers,' generally make their appearance about August, or late in July. **1868** *Rep. Comm. Agric. 1867* 71 Another plant-bug (*Strachia histrionica*) . . . [hibernates] like the cotton red-bug.

+**Red cane. 1.** A variety of sugar cane the stalks of which are dark purplish red when mature. **2.** =PURPLE CANE 1. — (1) **1856** *Rep. Comm. Patents 1855: Agric.* 274 In general, the Red cane is said to yield less juice than the Red-striped. (2) **1862** *Ib. 1861: Agric.* 167 The Purple Cane, or American Red Cane, . . . is, however, no Black-cap.

Red cedar. {1843–, in Australia}

+**1. a.** Any one of various species of American trees of the genus *Juniperus*, esp. *J. virginiana*. **b.** The western red cedar, *Thuja plicata*. **c.** The incense cedar, *Libocedrus decurrens*.

[**1682** *Hist. Coll. S. Carolina* II. 28 This Country hath the Oak . . . and divers sorts of lasting Timber that England hath not; as Cedar white and red, Cypress, Locust, Bay. **1717** *Petiveriana* III. 11/2 Red Cedar. An Evergreen, its Wood sweet, very durable.] **1766** J. BARTRAM *Journal* 33 [This] rich hammock . . . [produced] red-cedar, celtis, a curious zanthoxylium, and several others. **1800** TATHAM *Agric. & Commerce* 113 The red cedar of Virginia is a native of the lower country. **1832** BROWNE *Sylva* 189 The Red Cedar, which belongs to the Junipers, is the most common species of its genus in the United States. **1884** SARGENT *Rep. Forests* 7 The red fir, the hemlock, and the red cedar (*Thuya*) are still important elements of the forests. **1897** SUDWORTH *Arborescent Flora* 64 *Libocedrus decurrens.* Incense Cedar. . . . [Also called] Red Cedar (Idaho). **1901** MOHR *Plant Life Ala.* 81 On these rugged grounds [in the Tenn. R. valley region] the red cedar . . . predominates. *Ib.* 133 On these shell banks [on the Gulf coast] the West Indian red cedar (*Juniperus barbadensis*) is frequently found in full perfection.

+**2.** A tree belonging to one of these varieties.
1817 *N. Amer. Rev.* V. 316 The stump of a red cedar stood near the shore. **1877** BURROUGHS *Birds & Poets* 86 The cedar-birds have known every red cedar on the place these many years. **1899** GOING *Flowers* 289 The very young 'berry' of a red cedar or a juniper is a close ring of carpels enclosing a few ovules.

+**3.** The wood of such a tree, esp. for use in construction.
1782 *Phila. Ordinances* (1812) 49 The said grate or grates shall be fixed in a frame of stone, or good red cedar. **1805** *Ann. 9th Congress* 2 Sess. 1082 The poles or sticks . . , are neatly made of red cedar. **1820** FLINT *Lett. from Amer.* 229 Red cedar is exceedingly durable as posts of rail-fences. **1871** BAGG *At Yale* 329 [The boat] was clincher-built, of red cedar, with box-wood ribs.

+**4.** Attrib. with *bucket, cigar box, post*, etc.
1742 *Harvard Rec.* II. 716 His Acco[unt] of Red Cedar Posts amounting to Thirty two pounds 10/ [shall] be allow'd. **1785** MARSHALL *Amer. Grove* 70 *Juniperus virginiana.* Red Cedar-Tree. . . . The berries are smaller than those of the Juniper. **1797** *Ann. 4th Congress* 2 Sess. 2113 It would be expedient . . . to secure some of the lands in South Carolina and Georgia, well clothed with live oak and red cedar timber, for the purpose of building ships of war. **1846** Red-cedar cigar-box [see CIGAR BOX]. **1851** *Knickerb.* XXXVII. 377 The country-bred traveller . . . inhales the odor of the red-cedar buckets. *a*1918 Red cedar shaft [see GIG *n.*[1]].

+**Red cent.** A cent. Usually in emphatic and negative expressions signifying an extremely small amount or a trifle. (Cf. RED *n.* 2.) — **1839** J. S. JONES *People's Lawyer* 1. i, It would not have cost you a red cent. **1845** *Knickerb.* XXVI. 191 What can they do with you then, if you . . . haven't got a red cent? **1875** HOLLAND *Sevenoaks* 39, I never charged him a red cent for nothin'. **1910** RAINE *B. O'Connor* 19 Not a red cent on the old man.

+**Red-chaff.** A variety of wheat. *Obs.* Chiefly in attributive use. — **1804** J. ROBERTS *Penn. Farmer* 103 Of the early yellow, and red chaff, from one to one and an half [bushels are sufficient]. **1849** *Cultivator* ns. VI. 125/2, [I] sowed six bushels of what is called red-chaff wheat, on the furrow. **1850** *Rep. Comm. Patents 1849: Agric.* 181 Cultivated more or less in this section . . . [are] the red-chaff bald, the crate, the club wheat. **1855** BROWNE in *Amer. Inst. N.Y. Trans. 1854* 590 Red-chaff white wheat, from England . . . is rather tender and probably would not succeed as a fall wheat, north of Virginia.

+**Red check.** (See CHECK *n.²* 7.)

Red cherry. {1731– (Miller *Gard. Dict.* s.v. *Cerasus*)}
+An American wild cherry, esp. *Prunus pennsylvanica.* Also attrib. and with defining terms. (Cf. PIN CHERRY.)
[**1717** *Petiveriana* III. 12/1 Red-Cherry. A large Tree in the Woods.] **1784** *Amer. Acad. Mem.* I. 449 The Large Red Cherry. A small tree. The Dwarf Red Cherry. A very low shrub. The Red Choke Cherry. A shrub. The Small Pale Red Cherry. A small tree, and the fruit hard and ill-tasted. **1832** BROWNE *Sylva* 135 The Red Cherry Tree is common only in the Northern States and in Canada, New Brunswick and Nova Scotia. **1900** Red cherry shrub [see FIRE CHERRY].

+**b.** The fruit of this tree or shrub.
1848 ROBINSON *Santa Fe Exped.* (1932) 8 On the banks of the creek we found an abundance of red cherries growing on small bushes. *a*1862 THOREAU *Maine Woods* 284 The Indian . . . sometime also ate the northern wild red cherries, . . . but they were scarcely edible.

+**Red children.** *pl. fig.* American Indians, thought of as occupying the relationship of children to the Great Father or president of the

United States. *Obs.* — **1801** [see HOUSE OF ENTERTAINMENT]. **1820** in Morse *Rep. Indian Affairs* II. 10 Your father the President, thinks that a great change in the situation of his Red Children has become necessary. **1849** *31st Congress 1 Sess.* Sen. Ex. Doc. No. 64, 187 It was the desire of their Great Father, the President of the United States, to be on terms of friendship and at peace with all his red children. **1866** *Rep. Indian Affairs* 298 Now, this is the principal desire of your red children.

Red clay. Clay of a characteristic red or reddish color; red ocher. {1756– (*Compl. Body Husb.* 7/1)}
1784 SMYTH *Tour* I. 81, I cut a most wretched figure being daubed from head to foot with red clay. **1823** JAMES *Exped.* I. 144 [Indian warriors] were painted with red clay. **1843** N. BOONE *Journal* (1917) 218 The caps were of a strata some ten feet thick, of friable over lying red clay. **1907** ANDREWS *Recoll.* 176 The soil was red clay and hard to dig.
attrib. **1862** *Ill. Agric. Soc. Trans.* V. 567 [Sugar cane] brought from the post-oak flats and red clay soil along the edge of the timber [etc.]. **1883** SMITH *Geol. Survey Ala.* 523 Above Elba there is a good deal of what are usually called 'red-clay hills.' **1888** 'CRADDOCK' *Despot* 34 The burly teams with their swinging gait to-and-fro preëmpted the narrow spaces of the red clay road.

∗**Red clover.** A Eurasian clover (*Trifolium pratense*), widely cultivated in the United States for fodder and as a soil-builder. Also attrib. (Cf. REDTOP CLOVER.) — **1723** [see CLOVER SEED]. **1806** LEWIS in *L. & Clark Exped.* V. (1904) 180 The other [species was] nearly as luxouriant as our red clover with a white flower. **1844** LEE & FROST *Oregon* 85 The [Clatsop] plain in its natural state is covered with a most luxuriant growth of the best quality of grasses, such as red clover, a species peculiar to that country. **1890** *Harper's Mag.* April 709/2 There are red and white clover, . . . gold-thread, and violets. **1901** MOHR *Plant Life Ala.* 828 The cultivation of red clover enters successfully into the system of farming.

∗**Redcoat.** +A British soldier serving in America, esp. during the Revolutionary War and the War of 1812. Now hist.
1674 JOSSELYN *Two Voyages* 153 Marching with Three hundred red-Coats, . . . [the British commissioners] took from the Dutch their chief town then called New-Amsterdam. **1702** SEWALL *Diary* II. 64 Capt Williams with his Red-Coats met us. **1775** *S.C. Hist. Soc. Coll.* II. 33 The people in New-England killed a great many of the red coats, and drove them to their ships. **1808** *Ann. 10th Congress* 1 Sess. II. 1479 No sooner did the red-coats, as they called the English, come within one hundred yards, than they threw down their arms. **1871** EGGLESTON *Hoosier Schoolm.* 96, I'd fit red-coats, in the war of eighteen-twelve. **1900** *Congress. Rec.* 29 Jan. 1262/2 [Marion and the other men were] making their little expeditions against the redcoats with 30, 40, or 100 men.
attrib. **1776** *Battle of Brooklyn* I. i, You have no doubt, my Lord, of splitting, and roasting, and pickling these red coat fellows. *c*1841 WHITMAN *Spec. Days* 351 The last occupant had left to join the red-coat soldiery.

+**Red-cob.** *attrib.* Designating a variety of Indian corn the ears of which have red cobs. — **1868** *Iowa State Agric. Soc. Rep. 1867* 166 The yellow dent and a reddish red-cob variety . . . are mostly esteemed. **1894** *Vt. Agric. Rep.* XIV. 36 Fodder grown from a later variety of western or southern red cob corn, [was] often cut before it was ripe.

+**Red-cockaded woodpecker.** A woodpecker (*Dryobates borealis*) of the pine woods of the southern states. — **1810** WILSON *Ornithology* II. 103 Red-cockaded Woodpecker. *Picus Querulus.* This new species I first discovered in . . . North Carolina. **1839** AUDUBON *Ornith. Biog.* V. 12 [The] Red-Cockaded Woodpecker . . . is found abundantly from Texas to New Jersey. **1858** BAIRD *Birds Pacific R.R.* 96 Red-cockaded Woodpecker. . . . This species is chiefly confined to the southern Atlantic States, being rarely seen as far north as Pennsylvania. **1917** *Birds of America* II. 144/2 Of the total food of the Red-cockaded Woodpecker over four-fifths is insects.

+**Red cotton grass.** (See quot. 1814.) — **1814** BIGELOW *Florula Bostoniensis* 16 *Eriophorum Cyperinum,* Red cotton grass. . . . A common and very tall meadow grass. . . . Spikelets . . . covered with dull reddish wool. **1833** EATON *Botany* (ed. 6) 329 *Scirpus eriophorum,* red cotton grass. **1840** DEWEY *Mass. Flowering Plants* 259 Red Cotton-Grass . . . [is] common in swamps and pools, and in rich muddy bottoms and banks.

+**Red crab.** {1674–} (See quot. 1884.) — **1883** *Nat. Museum Bul. No. 27,* 112 The Red and Rock Crabs are most abundant on the rocky shores of the northern side of the Golden Gate, where but little fishing is done. **1884** GOODE, etc. *Fisheries* I. 771 The Red Crab—*Cancer productus.* This is a very common species in the Bay of San Francisco.

Red-crested, *a.* Of birds: Having a red crest. {1785–} — *c*1728 CATESBY *Carolina* I. 17 The larger red-crested Wood-pecker weighs nine ounces. **1903** Fox *Little Shepherd* ii, A red-crested cock of the woods would beat his white-striped wings from spur to spur.

Red Cross. A well-known organization for alleviating pain and suffering caused by war or natural calamities. {1877–} Also attrib. — **1878** C. BARTON *Red Cross* (1881) 13 Organized in every state, the relief societies of the Red Cross would be ready with money, nurses and supplies. **1889** in *N.Y. Pub. Lib. Bul.* XLIV. 114 Red Cross ambulance sent on at once with him to Fort Robinson, with orders to return immediately to accompany column tomorrow. **1900** *Congress. Rec.* 2 Feb. 1429/1 It is impossible for the Red Cross Society . . . to go into a foreign country and receive a status there without the consent of the country to which it applies. **1920** *3d Nat. Country Life Conf. Proc.* 75 The Committee on health would include . . . the Red Cross.

+**Red crossbill.** The common crossbill, *Loxia curvirostra pusilla.* (Cf. AMERICAN CROSSBILL.) — **1867** *Amer. Naturalist* I. 44 The Common or Red Crossbill . . . is of desultory habits. **1879** *Nat. Museum Proc.* I. 412. **1917** *Birds of Amer.* III. 10/2 The White-winged Crossbill . . . seems to be somewhat less common than the Red Crossbill.

Red curlew. 1. =PINK CURLEW I. {1769, in Guiana} +**2.** The great marbled godwit, *Limosa fedoa.* (Cf. MARLIN.) — (1) **1731** CATESBY *Carolina* I. 84 *Numenius ruber.* The Red Curlew. . . . These Birds frequent the Coast of the Bahama Islands, and other parts of América between the Tropicks. (2) **1813** WILSON *Ornithology* VII. 30 Our gunners call it [*i.e.*, the godwit] the Straight-billed Curlew, and sometimes the Red Curlew. **1844** *Nat. Hist. N.Y.,* Zoology II. 253 [*Limosa fedoa*] is generally called the Marlin, and less frequently Red Curlew. **1917** *Birds of Amer.* I. 241.

Red currant. The fruit of *Ribes rubrum.* {1629–} Also attrib. with *jelly.* — [**1705** BEVERLEY *Virginia* II. 15 There grow naturally Two Sorts of Currants, one red, and the other black, far more pleasant than those of the same Colour in England.] **1805** LEWIS in *L. & Clark Exped.* II. (1904) 239 The fruit is a berry about the size and much the shape of the red currant of our gardins. **1847** PALMER *Rocky Mts.* 65 Today, as on yesterday, we found abundance of red, yellow and black currants, with some gooseberries, along the stream. **1887** I. R. *Lady's Ranche Life Mont.* 17 Buffaloberry jelly . . . is as good as red currant. **1903** FOX *Little Shepherd* xvii, The saddle of venison . . . [was] flanked by flakes of red-currant jelly.

+**Red cypress.** =BALD CYPRESS. Also attrib. — **1860** CURTIS *Woody Plants N.C.* 29 The *Red Cypress* has its heart of a reddish tint, is preferable to the others for timber, and cannot be split. **1883** SMITH *Geol. Survey Ala.* 292 *Taxodium distichum,* [is] the variety yielding the red cypress lumber. **1884** SARGENT *Rep. Forests* 184.

Red dace. {1880–4} +The shiner or redfin, *Luxilus cornutus.* — **1842** *Nat. Hist. N.Y.,* Zoology IV. 208 The Red-fin. *Leuciscus cornutus.* . . . Associated with the Brook Trout. It has the various popular names of Red-fin, Red Dace, and Rough-head. **1884** GOODE, etc. *Fisheries* I. 617 The 'Shiner,' 'Red-fin,' or 'Red Dace' abounds in all streams from New England to Kansas and Alabama. **1911** *Rep. Fisheries 1908* 309/2 *Dace,* a common name applied to different species of the *Cyprinidæ* family, generally modified by some descriptive prefix, as 'horned dace,' 'red dace,' etc.

* **Red deer.** +The common Virginia or white-tailed American deer (*Odocoileus virginianus*), so called from its appearance in its summer coat.

[?**1607** PERCY in Smith *Works* (1910) p. lxix, There is also great store of Deere both'Red and Fallow.] **1698** THOMAS *Pensilvania* 15 There are in the Woods abundance of Red Deer (vulgarly called Stags). **1709** LAWSON *Carolina* 123 Some take him [*sc.* the elk] for the red Deer of America; but he is not. **1781–2** JEFFERSON *Notes Va.* (1788) 55 There remains then the buffalo, red deer, . . . and water rat. **1852** MARCY *Explor. Red River* (1854) 67 The *Cervus Virginianus* (our red deer) has generally been considered the fleetest animal upon the continent. **1885** *Wkly. New Mexican Rev.* 18 June 4/6 [Near Santa Fe] wild turkeys are common; also the black-tailed and red deer.

Red devil. (See DEVIL *n.* 1.)

* **Redding.** +A mixture of water and red clay or ochre used to redden the hearth and sides of a fireplace. — **1866** A. D. WHITNEY *L. Goldthwaite* x, The brick hearth and jambs [were] aglow with fresh 'redding.'

+**Reddish egret.** A heron of the southern states and Central America, *Dichromanassa rufescens.* — [**1785** PENNANT *Arctic Zool.* II. 447 Reddish Egret. . . . Inhabits Louisiana.] **1835** AUDUBON *Ornith. Biog.* III. 411 The Reddish Egret is a constant resident on the Florida Keys. **1858** BAIRD *Birds Pacific R.R.* 662 *Demiegretta Rufa,* Baird. Reddish Egret. . . . Coast of South Florida and Gulf of Mexico to mouth of Rio Grande. **1887** RIDGWAY *Manual N.A. Birds* 131 Warmer portions of eastern United States, north to Florida and southern Illinois. . . . *A[rdea] rufa.* Reddish Egret.

Reddish-violet. (See quotation.) — **1856** *Rep. Comm. Patents 1855: Agric.* 273 The *Red-striped* [sugar] cane, which was originally brought from the Dutch colony of Java, and the *Violet* or *Reddish-violet,* which is only a variation from the former, . . . will generally prosper . . . [in] the Southern States.

Red dog.

+**1.** (See quot. 1886.) Now hist.

1838 *N.Y. Advertiser & Exp.* 21 April 1/4 Aptly enough are these banks called 'Wild Cat' and 'Red Dog.' *c*1844 [see REDBACK 2]. **1886** *Mag. Western Hist.* III. 202/2 The banks toppled to the earth. . . . They were known universally under the name of 'wild-cats.' The most worthless were styled 'red-dog.'

+**2.** A bill or note issued to serve as money by a wildcat or red-dog bank. Now hist. Also attrib.

1841 *Congress. Globe* App. 2 Sept. 343/1, I never heard it called 'Red Dog,' but, . . . that may be the proper name. **1860** *Harper's Mag.* March 568/1 [In] Marquette, Michigan, . . . wild-cat and red-dog money used to be current. **1885** *Santa Fé Wkly. New Mexican* 1 Oct. 3/1 Certificates of the red Warner proposes would be as unstable in value as the 'red dog' money of ante bellum days. **1912** *Lit. Digest* 5 Oct. 548 National banks [were created] . . . after the era of wildcat and red-dog private-banknote currency.

+**3.** (See quotation.)

1893 *Congress. Rec.* App. 4 Jan. 313/1 Some of the very lowest grades of flour, the flour which is called in common parlance 'red dog,' which is very little better than offal, sometimes goes abroad without any particular brand.

Red-ear kiss. A kiss bestowed upon a sweetheart by the finder of a red ear of corn at a husking bee. *Obs.* — **1828** *Yankee* Sept. 288/1 As for their delightful good old fashioned wheel-barrow kisses, I think, they are all of a piece with red-ear kisses, field-beds and bundling.

* **Redeem,** *v.* +*tr.* Of a government: **a.** To pay or satisfy the obligation created by (a bill of credit, note, warrant, etc.). **b.** (See quotation.) Cf. REDEMPTION I. — (*a*) **1748** *Mass. Province Laws* III. 456 The Principal End of your Meeting . . . is to take under Consideration what is further Necessary to be done by this Court for Redeeming our Bills of Credit. **1876** *Congress. Rec.* 25 July 4866/1 The first section of this bill requires coin-notes to be paid out, and consequently it involves the absolute necessity of redeeming those coin-notes. **1911** *Okla. Session Laws* 3 Legisl. 199 The State Treasurer is hereby directed tø immediately take up and redeem . . . all warrants heretofore issued. (b) **1895** *New Voice* 1 Aug. 3/4 Money is 'redeemed' by the Government issuing it for services when it receives it back again in taxes.

+**Red elder. 1.** =CRANBERRY TREE. (Cf. GUELDER-ROSE.) **2.** = RED-BERRIED ELDER. — (1) **1794** S. WILLIAMS *Nat. Hist. Vermont* 69 Vegetables . . . applied to medicinal purposes [include] . . . Red Elder. *Viburnum opulus.* **1819** WARDEN *Statistical Acct. U.S.* I. 429. (2) **1821** *Mass. H. S. Coll.* 2 Ser. IX. 155 Plants . . . indigenous in the township of Middlebury [Vt. include] . . . *Sambucus pubescens,* Red elder. [**1832** WILLIAMSON *Maine* I. 107 The Elder is of two species, the black and red.]

+**Red elm.** Any one of various American elms, esp. the slippery elm, *Ulmus fulva.* — **1805** CLARK in *Lewis & C. Exped.* I. (1904) 299 There is some timber in it's bottom lands, which consists of cottonwood red Elm, with a small proportion of small Ash. **1819** E. DANA *Geogr. Sk.* 245 The most valuable forest trees growing, not only on Bistrop's Grant, but in the adjacent region, [include] . . . mucilaginous elm and red elm. **1850** *New Eng. Farmer* II. 142 The Red or Slippery Elm is rare in this vicinity. **1897** SUDWORTH *Arborescent Flora* 180 *Ulmus crassifolia.* Cedar Elm. . . . [Also called] Red Elm (Tex.). *Ib.* 182 *Ulmus alata.* Wing Elm. . . . [Also called] Red Elm (Fla., Ark.).

* **Redemption.**

+**1.** The action on the part of a government of paying the value of its notes, warrants, etc.

Cf. REDEEM *v.*

1749 *Mass. Province Acts* III. 430 If the possessors aforesaid shall not offer such bills in exchange within one year from and after the said thirty-first day of March, . . . all right or claim to the redemption or exchange thereof shall determine and cease. **1780** J. JONES *Letters* 36 Would not the publication of extracts of the several acts of the States . . . , specifying the Funds established for support of redemption of the money, be of use? **1837** *U.S. Mag.* Oct. 19 We find such men as Mr. Macon . . . pledging the credit of the State for their redemption. **1884** BLAINE *20 Years of Congress* I. 470 It was quite practicable for them to keep a sufficient amount of legal-tender paper . . . to meet all the probable requirements of redemption. **1900** *Congress. Rec.* 13 Feb. 1751/1, I say to maintain the reserve for the redemption of greenbacks. *attrib.* **1868** *N.Y. Herald* 3 July 1/3 Stolen—From the Counter of the Redemption Department, at the United States Sub-Treasury, The following United States Coupon Bonds. **1894** LEAVITT *Our Money Wars* 113 The Law allowing the Interior Banks to keep Large Amounts of their Reserves in so-called Redemption Banks, or Banks in Money-Centers.

+**2.** The restoration of political control in the South to white people by the overthrow of the carpetbag regime. *Obs.*

1880 TOURGEE *Bricks* 380 All over the county, the process of 'redemption' was being carried on. **1884** *Century Mag.* April 862/1 Since the political 'redemption' of 1872–6, these methods have been wholly unnecessary.

Redemptioner. {1897–} +(See quot. 1815.) Now hist.

1771 *Md. Hist. Mag.* XIII. 174 Try, if & Redemptioner, to get Him on the terms agreed to by Robert, if an Indented servant get Him on the best terms you can. **1786** WASHINGTON *Diaries* III. 70 Received from on board the Brig Ann, from Ireland, two Servant Men . . . , redemptioners for 3 years service by Indenture. **1815** DWIGHT *Remarks on Rev. of Inchiquin's Lett.* 86 Your next topic of scandal is the state of those, whom you call Redemptioners; persons, who, wishing to come to America, and not having sufficient property to pay their passage, agree with the captain of the ship to become bound, as servants, for such a period of time as that their service will amount to the sum, which they have engaged to pay. **1871** *Congress. Globe* 9 Feb. 1094/3 A sea-captain . . . sold him into bondage as a 'redemptioner,' in which condition he was held for some years. **1893** EGGLESTON *Duffels* 57 Why did I leave my father's house to take you, a poor redemptioner just out of your time?

Redeye. {*a*1672–}

+**1.** Whisky, esp. of a poor quality. *slang.* Also attrib.

1819 QUITMAN in Claiborne *Life Quitman* I. 42 Whiting and I had to treat to 'red-eye,' or 'rot-gut,' as whiskey is here [Ky.] called. **1851** *Polly Peablossom* 50 That feller, Bonnel, sold me a pint of red-eye whiskey. **1867** *Picayune* 25 Dec., This man's whiskey ain't Red Eye. **1903** *N.Y. Sun* 15 Nov., Ben made for the nearest red-eye plant, and inside of an hour he was riotous and shooting up the town.

+**2.** Any one of various American fishes, esp. the rock bass. Also with specifying term. {the rudd, a1672}

Cf. GOGGLE-EYE I.

1820 RAFINESQUE *Ichthyologia Ohiensis* 31 Red-Eye. *Aplocentrus.*... Ohio Red-Eye. *Aplocentrus calliops*.... A beautiful fish from eight to twelve inches long. **1877** *Smithsonian Misc. Coll.* XIII. IX. 22 The name 'Red-Eye' in the region which this fish is supposed to inhabit is chiefly applied to the Rock-Bass (*Ambloplites rupestris*). **1883** *Nat. Museum Bul.* No. 27, 462 *Lepomis cyanellus.* Red-eye; Blue-spotted Sun-fish.... Great Lake Region; Mississippi Valley and southward to Mexico. **1900** *Everybody's Mag.* III. 523/1 [He] soon was engaged in drawing out sunfish and red-eyes. **1903** T. H. BEAN *Fishes N.Y.* 477 The blue-spotted sunfish, also known as the green sunfish and redeye, occurs from the Great Lakes region . . . south to Mexico.

‖**3.** A watchful eye. *slang.*

1833 J. HALL *Harpe's Head* 90 Keep a red eye out, boys,—that chap is not too good to steal.

+**4.** *Early China redeye*, a variety of bean.

1859 *Ill. Agric. Soc. Trans.* III. 503 The early China red-eye is very early and prolific.

+**5. a.** = RED-EYED VIREO.

a**1862** THOREAU *Maine Woods* 172 The birds sang quite as in our woods, —the red-eye, red-start, veery, wood-pewee, etc. **1892** TORREY *Foot-Path Way* 12 The Philadelphia's song is less varied than . . . the red-eye's. **1917** *Birds of Amer.* III. 103/2 Mr. Job . . . photographed several times a female Red-eye solicitously feeding two voracious young Cowbirds.

+**b.** (See quotation.)

1917 *Birds of Amer.* I. 261 Semipalmated Plover. *Ægialitis semipalmata.* . . . [Also called] Ring Plover; Red-eye; Beach-bird.

+**6.** (See quotation.) *Obs.*

a**1870** CHIPMAN *Notes on Bartlett, Red-eye,* . . . a copperhead.

+**Red-eyed vireo.** The little hangnest, *Vireo olivaceus.* (Cf. REDEYE 5 a.) — **1839** AUDUBON *Ornith. Biog.* V. 430, I found the nest of the Red-eyed Vireo nearly finished. **1858** *Atlantic Mo.* I. 207 The second [of the warbling flycatchers is known] as the Red-eyed Vireo. **1887** BURROUGHS in *Century Mag.* July 326 My hat fairly brushed the nest of the red-eyed vireo. **1917** *Birds of Amer.* II. 102.

Redfin. {1794-} +Any one of various widely distributed fishes of the families Cyprinidae and Catostomidae: (see also quot. 1890). Cf. RED HORSE. — **1818** [see DACE]. **1842** *Nat. Hist. N.Y., Zoology* IV. 207 The Red-fin, *Leuciscus cornutus,* . . . is usually found in clear limpid streams. **1890** *Cent.* 5020/2 *Redfin.* . . . The common yellow perch of the United States, *Perca flavescens.* . . . (Southern U.S.). . . . The red-cusk, *Dinematichthys* or *Brosmophycis marginatus.* **1899** VAN DYKE *Fisherman's Luck* 9 Magic . . . draws the little suburban boys . . . around the shallow pools where dace and redfins hide. **1911** *Rep. Fisheries 1908* 316/1 *Shiner,* a common name applied to the redfin (*Notropis cornutus*) from New England to Kansas and Alabama.

Red fir. {1848} +The Douglas fir; also, any one of various true firs of the western United States. — **1884** [see DOUGLAS FIR]. **1894** COULTER *Bot. W. Texas* III. 555 *Pseudotsuga Douglasii.* In the Guadalupe mountains and northwestward, 'Red fir.' **1897** SUDWORTH *Arborescent Flora* 57 *Abies nobilis.* Noble Fir. . . . [Also called] Red Fir (Cal., Oreg.). *Ib.* 58 *Abies magnifica,* Shasta Fir. . . . [Also called] Red Fir (Cal.), . . . California Red Fir (Cal. lit.).

*＊**Redfish.** +Any one of various American fishes of a red or reddish color or having red markings, as the channel bass (*Sciaenops ocellata*), the blueback salmon (*Oncorhynchus nerka*), etc.

1834 *S. Lit. Messenger* I. 121/2 The waters too, furnished their finny . . . treasures,—the red fish, buffalo [etc.]. **1842** *Nat. Hist. N.Y., Zoology* IV. 75 The Branded Corvina. *Corvina ocellata.* . . . It is called there [in New Orleans] *Poisson rouge* or *Red-fish.* **1881** *Amer. Naturalist* XV. 181 Only the quinnat and blue-back (then called red-fish) have been found in the fall at any great distance from the sea. **1882** *Nat. Museum Bul.* No. 16, 651 *Sebastes marinus,* Rose-fish; Red-fish. **1896** JORDAN & EVERMANN *Check-List Fishes* 412 *Pimelometopon pulcher.* . . . California Redfish; Fathead. **1911** *Rep. Fisheries 1908* 314/2 The redfish of California . . . is found from Point Conception to Cerros Island.

Red flannel shirt. A man's shirt of red flannel. — **1848** *Santa Fe Republican* 28 June 2/4 A proportionate lot of . . . Cinto laces, Red flannel shirts, . . . silk hose [etc.]. **1858** THOREAU *Maine Woods* 91 He wore a red-flannel shirt, woollen pants, and a black Kossuth hat. **1880** *Cimarron News & Press* 26 Feb. 3/1 A large assortment of . . . Red Flannel and Canton Flannel Shirts and Drawers at Porter's.

+**Red-flowering maple.** = RED MAPLE. — c**1730** CATESBY *Carolina* I. 64 The Red flowering Maple. These Trees grows to a considerable height; but their trunks are not often very large. **1775** BURNABY *Travels* 12 They are likewise adorned and beautified with red-flowering maples. **1819** E. DANA *Geogr. Sk.* 171 [The soil is] thickly covered with . . . honey locust, red flowering maple. **1832** BROWNE *Sylva* 107 The wood of the red-flowering maple is applicable to interesting uses.

Red fox. +The common fox (*Vulpes fulva*) of North America. Also attrib. (Cf. BLACK, CROSS-, SILVER FOX.)

[**1637** MORTON *New Canaan* 79 The Foxes are of two colours; the one redd, the other gray.] **1778** *Essex Inst. Coll.* XLIX. 109 Sold . . . 38 red fox skins, at 23s. **1789** MORSE *Amer. Geog.* 54 Beasts common to North America [include] . . . Red Fox, Gray Fox, Racoon. **1805** PARKINSON *Tour* 305 There are . . . the flying fox, black, red, great grey, and little grey fox. **1875** [see FUR-BEARER]. **1917** *Mammals of Amer.* 72/2 The Red Fox mates in February or early in March.

+**Red grouper.** A grouper (*Epinephelus morio*) common along the Gulf coast and the Atlantic coast south of Virginia. (Cf. RED-BELLIED SNAPPER.) — **1842** *Nat. Hist. N.Y., Zoology* IV. 21 This beautiful fish . . . is called by the fishermen, Groper and Red Groper. **1884** GOODE, etc. *Fisheries* I. 410 The Red Grouper . . . is found throughout the year on the 'grounds' at sea. **1911** [see RED-BELLIED SNAPPER].

+**Red haw.** The fruit of any one of various American trees of the genus *Crataegus,* esp. *C. coccinea.*

1717 *Petiveriana* III. 12/1 Red Haw. Of an agreeable Taste, and four times as big as ours in Europe. **1805** CLARK in *Lewis & C. Exped.* III. (1905) 33 Choke Cherries & red haws . . . act in different ways So as to make us Sick. **1824** DODDRIDGE *Notes* 86 Red haws grew on the white thorn bushes. **1849** [see BLACK HAW I].

b. A tree producing such fruit. In full *red haw tree.*

1787 *Amer. Acad. Mem.* II. I. 159 Black Haw, four inches diameter, and producing good fruit. Red Haw. **1823** JAMES *Exped.* I. 169 This band had . . . [subsisted] for some time upon the fruit of the red haws. **1871** EGGLESTON *Hoosier Schoolm.* 152 The roan . . . [went] past the familiar red-haw tree. **1881** *Amer. Naturalist* XV. 151 The larva of this Longicorn beetle infests what we call thorn apple or red haw. **1893** *Amer. Folk-Lore* VI. 141 *Cratægus coccinea,* var. *mollis,* red haw. Gen. in Central States.

Redhead. {1664-}

+**1.** An American duck or species of duck (*Nyroca americana*) allied to the canvasback.

1709 LAWSON *Carolina* 150 Red Heads . . . are very sweet food, and plentiful in our Rivers and Creeks. **1814** Wilson *Amer. Ornithology* VIII. 110 Red-Headed Duck. *Anas Ferina.* . . . The Red-head is twenty inches in length. **1891** [see COOT I]. **1917** *Birds of Amer.* I. 131/1 In the Redhead we have the counterpart of the Canvas-back.

+**2.** = RED-HEADED WOODPECKER. Also *redhead woodpecker.*

[**1764** REUTER *Wachau* 579 Red Heads . . . do much harm to the corn.] **1831** AUDUBON *Ornith. Biog.* I. 145 As soon as the Red-heads have begun to Visit a Cherry or Apple tree, a people along the trunk of the tree. **1832** WILLIAMSON *Maine* I. 150 The Woodpecker-family is so large with us, that we reckon seven species [including] . . . the red head, . . . [and] the speckled Woodpecker. **1869** *Amer. Naturalist* Jan. 599, I saw a Red-head Woodpecker high on the eastern slope of the Rocky Mountains. **1898** Fox *Kentuckians* 63 Stallards air as thick down thar as redheads in a deadenin'.

＊**Red-headed,** *a.* +In the names of various American birds: (see quotations and see also next).

1806 LEWIS in *L. & Clark Exped.* IV. (1904) 148 The read headed fishing duck is common to every part of the river. **1839** PEABODY *Mass. Birds* 392 The Red-headed Duck, *Fuligula ferina,* . . . often has the honor of being substituted [for the canvasback duck] in the market. **1843** MARRYAT *M. Violet* xliv, The most common birds of prey are . . . the black and red-headed vulture, the raven and the crow. **1845** W. T. THOMPSON *Chron. Pineville* 90 Out flew a large red-headed woodcock. **1917** *Birds of Amer.* I. 131 Redhead. *Marila americana.* . . . [Also called] Red-headed Raft Duck.

+**Red-headed woodpecker.** A very common American woodpecker (*Melanerpes erythrocephalus*), having a red head, and white and black plumage elsewhere.

c**1728** CATESBY *Carolina* I. 20 The Red-headed Wood-pecker . . . is the only one of the Wood-peckers that may be here domestick. **1805** LEWIS in *L. & Clark Exped.* III. (1905) 57 [A hunter] brought with him a red-headed woodpecker of the large kind common to the U States. **1834** in *Atlantic Mo.* XXVI. 339 Bee-martins, and red-headed woodpeckers gave me a vivid reminiscence of my poor, good old commonwealth. **1884** BURROUGHS in *Century Mag.* Dec. 222/2 A red-headed woodpecker . . . drums upon a lightning-rod on his neighbour's house. **1917** *Birds of Amer.* II. 156/1 The Red-headed Woodpecker is very fond of beech nuts and other mast.

Redheart. A red, heart-shaped variety of the cultivated cherry. {1707- (Mortimer *Art Husb.*)} Also attrib. (Cf. BLACK-HEART.) — **1833** *Md. Hist. Mag.* XIII. 377 Here were . . . numerous trees of ripe cherries, black hearts and red hearts. **1887** *Harper's Mag.* Dec. 31/1 Under the largest of two red-heart cherry-trees sat a girl shelling pease. **1904** GLASGOW *Deliverance* 238, I used to cut round old Fletcher's pasture . . . to keep from passin' by his red-heart cherry-tree that overhung the road.

Red-hearted, *a.* Having a red heart. Used in the names of various American trees, or to describe a tree beginning to decay. — **1784** *Amer. Acad. Mem.* I. 490 *Juglans.* . . . The White Walnut. The Red-hearted Walnut. The Oil-Nut, or Butter-Nut. **1825** NEAL *Bro. Jonathan* III. 420 [The church was] completely overshadowed by . . . the redhearted, or upland beech. **1901** *Dept. Agric. Yrbk. 1900* 206 The wood at first turns dark red-brown, and trees in this stage are known to the lumberman as 'red-hearted' timber.

+**Redheart hickory.** The shagbark. — **1897** SUDWORTH *Arborescent Flora* 113 *Hicoria ovata.* . . . Shagbark (Hickory). . . . [Also called] Redheart Hickory (Miss.).

+**Red hickory.** The mockernut hickory, or the pignut, *Carya glabra.* Also attrib. — **1709** LAWSON *Carolina* 99 There is another sort, which we call red Hiccory . . . ; of which Walking-Sticks, Mortars, Pestils, and several other fine Turnery-wares are made. **1775** *Amer. Husbandry* I. 313 The trees, which are the spontaneous product of the land, . . . abound with fine tall, red hiccories. **1813** MUHLENBERG *Cat. Plants* 88 Smooth hickory, red hickory, or pignut hickory. **1897** SUDWORTH *Arborescent Flora* 114 Mockernut (Hickory). . . . [Also called] Red Hickory (Fla.). *Ib.* 115 Pignut (Hickory). . . . [Also called] Red Hickory (Del.).

Red horse.

+**1.** Any one of various American suckers of the family Catostomidae; also, the red drum, *Sciaenops ocellata.*

1796 HAWKINS *Letters* 38 This is the most valuable creek known here for . . . trout, perch, rock, red horse. **1820** *Western Rev.* II. 303 Red-tail Sucker. *Catostomus erythrurus.* . . . Vulgar names Red-horse, Red-tail [etc.]. **1849** LANMAN *Lett. from Alleghany Mts.* 65 On inquiring of a homespun angler what fish the river did produce, he replied: 'Salmon, black trout, red horse, hog-fish, suckers and cat-fish.' **1881** TOURGEE *'Zouri's Christmas* v, 'It's a red-horse,' she cried; 'a baked red-horse!' **1911** *Rep. Fisheries 1908* 314/1 In Florida and the Gulf states, [the red drum is called] 'redfish' and 'red horse.'

+**2.** A Kentuckian. A nickname. *Obs.*

1835 HOFFMAN *Winter in West* I. 177 The spokesman was evidently a 'red-horse' from Kentucky. *c***1845** PAULDING *Amer. Comedies* (1847) 192 We've got some o' most all kinds: . . . Linsey-woolseys, Red-horses, Mudheads.

+**Red hunter.** An Indian huntsman. — **1806** *Ann. 9th Congress* 2 Sess. 1116 It continues the practice of both the white and red hunters to leave their skins . . . suspended to poles. **1872** *Amer. Naturalist* VI. 80 The early Jesuit missionaries and French *voyageurs* . . . found the buffalo . . . flying in countless numbers before the Red-hunter, or the prairie fire.

Red Indian. 1. An American Indian. {1831– (s.v. *Indian* sb. 2)} **2.** =PAINTED CUP. — **(1) 1835** AUDUBON *Ornith. Biog.* III. 202 The red Indian is making arrangements for his winter hunts. **1895** KING *New Orleans* 217 Is this your red Indian! **1914** STEELE *Storm* 124 The back country . . . had one day known a pirate and a desperado and a red Indian and a squire of dames. **(2) 1892** *Amer. Folk-Lore* V. 101 *Castilleia coccinea*, . . . Red Indians. Mass.

+**Redirect (examination).** *Law.* (See quotation 1889.) — **1889** *Cent.* 2048/2 The steps in the examination of a witness are the . . . direct examination by the party calling him, and the cross-examination by the opposite party; after which may follow a reëxamination or redirect examination by the former [etc.]. **1891** [see EXAMINATION 1]. **1909** E. L. BANKS *Mystery F. Farrington* 324 If the British attorney has finished his cross-examination, I will begin my re-direct.

+**Redistrict,** *v. tr.* To divide anew (a town or state) into districts, usually for the apportionment of representation. — **1850** in Parmenter *Hist. Pelham, Mass.* 198 Thomas Buffum, Monroe Eaton, Olney Cook [constitute] a committee to redistrict the town. **1867** *Ill. Agric. Soc. Trans.* VII. 510 Mr. Flag moved that the subject of redistricting the State be referred to a special committee of nine. **1905** *Springfield Wkly. Repub.* 22 Sept. 12 The results of the decennial census will form the basis for redistricting the state into senatorial and representative districts. **1911** *Boston Herald* 7 Aug. 4/1 A few legislators passed acts redistricting their states.

Red land.** Soil of a reddish hue {1712–}; in pl., sometimes a particular region. — *a1772** WOOLMAN *Journal* 70 We then crossed the river Susquehanna, and had several meetings in a new settlement, called the Red Lands. **1789** MORSE *Amer. Geog.* 49 It has intermixed with it reddish streaks and veins like a species of ochre, brought probably from the red lands, which lie up towards the mountains. **1857** OLMSTED *Journey through Texas* 67 This tract is known as the Red Lands of Eastern Texas. **1883** SMITH *Geol. Survey Ala.* 187 The red lands were the first to be cleared up by the original settlers.

+**Red larch.** The American larch or tamarack, *Larix laricina.* Also *red American larch.* Also attrib. — **1785** MARSHALL *Amer. Grove* 103 *Pinus-Larix rubra.* Red American Larch-Tree. **1803** LAMBERT *Descr. Genus Pinus* 58 The cones of both [trees] are sent from America annually to Mr. Loddige, one under the name of black & the other of the red Larch. **1838** INGRAHAM *Burton* I. 68 A gravelled walk [was] bordered by young evergreens, among which were the pine, hemlock, and hackamatack, or red larch. **1897** SUDWORTH *Arborescent Flora* 32 Tamarack. . . . [Also called] Red Larch (Mich.).

***Red lead.** A red oxide of lead, used chiefly in paints. — **1637** MORTON *New Canaan* 85 Red Leade is there likewise in great abundance. **1682** *Penna. Archives* 1 Ser. I. 47 Twenty ffower pounds of Red Lead. **1815** *Niles' Reg.* IX. 36/2 The Cincinnati Manufacturing Company have embraced in their plan, manufactories of white and red lead.

Red-legged, *a.* {1611–} +In the names of various American birds: (see quotations). — **1874** COUES *Birds N.W.* 646 *Larus (Rissa) Brevirostris,* (Brandt) Coues. Red-legged Kittiwake. . . . North Pacific, both Asiatic and American. **1917** *Birds of Amer.* I. 116 Black Duck. *Anas rubripes.* . . . [Also called] Red-legged Duck. *Ib.* 268 Ruddy Turnstone. *Arenaria interpres morinella.* . . . [Also called] Red-legs; Red-legged Plover; Chicken.

+**Red-legged grasshopper, locust.** A widely distributed locust, *Melanoplus femur-rubrum*; ?also, the Rocky Mountain locust (*M. spretus*), a migrating species extremely destructive to vegetation. — **1867** *Amer. Naturalist* July 271 The Red-legged Grasshopper . . . has been for several years immensely destructive in the far West, especially in Kansas. **1868** *Rep. Comm. Agric. 1867* 66 These insects destroy the red-legged locusts. **1925** HERRICK *Man. of Injurious Insects* 328 The red-legged grasshopper . . . injures corn, oats, rye, timothy, blue grass, and soy beans.

***Red lily.** +Any one of various American red-flowered lilies, as the wood lily, *Lilium philadelphicum.* — **1672** JOSSELYN *New Eng. Rarities* 42 Red Lillies grow all over the Country innumerably amongst the small Bushes. **1784** *Amer. Acad. Mem.* I. 434 Red Lily. Blossoms red, spotted with black. Common on borders of meadows. July. **1814** BIGELOW *Florula Bostoniensis* 82 *Lilium Philadelphicum,* Common red lily, . . . is a less showy, but equally beautiful species. **1872** TICE *Over Plains* 96, I here found a splendid red lily, as large as a cup, (*Lillium Philadelphicum*).

+**Red lion.** A children's game in which one of the players, called the red lion, attempts to catch the others. — **1853** B. F. TAYLOR *Jan. & June* 154 Here a game of goal is going on, and here, a game of 'red lion.' **1891** *Amer. Folk-Lore* IV. 225 Red Lion. The players 'count out' to see who shall be 'Red Lion,' who must retreat to his den.

+**Red locust.** The common American locust, *Robinia pseudoacacia.* — **1810** MICHAUX *Arbres* I. 38 Locust . . . *Red Locust* (Acacia rouge). **1832** BROWNE *Sylva* 298 From this variety in the color of the wood . . . are derived the names of Red, Green and White Locust.

+**Red lynx.** =BAY LYNX. — [**1875** *Smithsonian Misc. Coll.* XIII. I. 65 [Among] species of the Nearctic realm which occur in the Mexican region . . . the red lynx and raccoon are examples.] **1917** *Mammals of Amer.* 157.

Red man. {1610–}

+**1.** An American Indian. Also collect.

1744 *Present State Louisiana* 45 [The Choctaws] answered me . . . [that] knowing the Red Men and their Interests better than themselves, they [etc.]. **1772** in *Travels Amer. Col.* 519 He is a Red man and loves the Red People. **1826** BRADFORD *Kentucky Notes* 16 The Long Knives and the Redmen are at peace. **1894** *S. Dak. Hist. Coll.* I. 293 The government had extended its paternal hand over the red man. **1916** EASTMAN *From Deep Woods* 65, [I thought] of the time when red men lived here [in N.H.] in plenty and freedom.

+**2.** A company or gang of criminals that operated in West Virginia about 1870. *Obs.*

1893 CUSHING *Story of P.O.* 354 There was . . . an organization in West Virginia called 'Red Men' who were banded together for certain purposes known only to themselves.

+**Red maple.** Any one of various American maples, as *Acer rubrum,* having crimson flowers. (Cf. RED-FLOWERING MAPLE.) — **1770** FORSTER tr. Kalm *Travels* I. 167 The red Maple, or *Acer rubrum*, is plentiful in these places [near Chester, Penna.]. **1797** F. BAILY *Tour* 178 The colour of the blossom distinguishes it from the *Acer Rubrum*, or the red maple. **1814** PURSH *Flora Amer.* I. 266 *Acer rubrum.* . . . Commonly known under the name of Red-maple or Swamp-maple. **1883** ZEIGLER & GROSSCUP *Alleghanies* 307, My brother . . . was leaning partly out the front window there, where now glows the red maple. **1919** STURTEVANT *Notes on Edible Plants* 21 *A[cer] rubrum.* Red Maple. Swamp Maple. . . . In Maine, sugar is often made from the sap.

+**Red mavis.** The common thrasher or ground thrush, *Toxostoma rufum.* — **1854** [see BROWN THRASHER]. **1858** *Atlantic Mo.* Dec. 869/2 The Red Mavis (*Turdus rufus*) has many habits similar to those of the Cat-Bird. **1917** *Birds of Amer.* III. 179.

+**Red minnow.** Also *colloq.* **red minny.** Any one of various cyprinoid fishes, as *Lythrurus cyanocephalus* of the rivers of the central states. — **1820** *Western Rev.* II. 242 *Rutilus ruber* . . . is said to live in the small streams which fall into the Elkhorn and Kentucky. . . . It is commonly called Red-minny. **1890** *Cent.* 3778/2 Among these [cyprinoids] may be mentioned the red minnows of the genus *Chrosomus*, as *C. erythrogaster.*

+**Red money.** Paper money issued in 1780 by Maryland. *Obs.* — **1781** *Md. Hist. Mag.* II. 344 It is Projected to Give our Red Money a Value by making it a Tender in all Payments. **1782** [see BLACK MONEY].

Redmouth. {1729} +Any one of various red-mouthed fishes of the genus *Haemulon.* Also *redmouth grunt.* Also with specifying term. (Cf. FLANNELMOUTH.) — **1842** *Nat. Hist. N.Y., Zoology* IV. 89 The Speckled Red-Mouth, *Hemulon fulvo-maculatum*, . . . is a very savory food. **1879** GOODE in *Smithsonian Misc. Coll.* XXIII. IV. 47 *Hæmylum formosum*, . . . Squirrel Red-Mouth.—South Atlantic Coast of United States. **1884** GOODE, etc. *Fisheries* I. 398 [From] the brilliant red color of the inside of the mouth and throat, . . . they have sometimes been called Red Mouths, or Flannel Mouths. *Ib.*, The Red-mouth Grunt, *Diabasis aurolineatus*, is probably the Flannel-mouthed Porgy.

Red mulberry. {1717} +An American tree (*Morus rubra*), bearing reddish fruit. Also attrib. — **1743** CATESBY *Carolina* II. p. xxi, The Red Mulberry-Tree . . . is the only native mulberry of Carolina and Virginia. **1765** CROGHAN *Journal* 16 The whole country abounds with great plenty of the white and red mulberry tree. **1832** BROWNE *Sylva* 217 The red mulberry . . . attains the elevation of 60 or 70 feet. **1894** COULTER *Bot. W. Texas* III. 408 *Morus rubra.* (Red Mulberry.) Large tree, ripening its blackberry-like fruit in July.

Red neck. {1900} +**1.** (See quotation.) +**2.** The canvasback, or another duck. — **(1) 1830** ROYALL *Southern Tour* I. 148 This may be ascribed to the *Red Necks*, a name bestowed upon the Presbyterians in Fayetteville [N.C.]. **(2) 1872** *Wisconsin Laws* 186 No person shall catch, kill or otherwise destroy . . . any 'mallard or red neck' duck. **1888** TRUMBULL *Names of Birds* 47 In the neighborhood of Philadelphia hunters were in the habit of supplying the market with this duck [the canvasback], under the name of 'Red-head,' or 'Red-neck.'

Red-necked grebe. {1785-} +A large American grebe, *Colymbus grisegena holboelli.* — **1828** BONAPARTE *Synopsis* 417 [The] Red-necked grebe . . . inhabits the north of both continents. **1835** AUDUBON *Ornith. Biog.* III. 617 The Red-necked Grebe . . . is very common in the fur countries. **1844** *Nat. Hist. N.Y., Zoology* II. 276 The Red-necked Grebe is a northern species which occurs rarely on the coast of this State in winter. **1874** COUES *Birds N.W.* 730. **1917** *Birds of Amer.* I. 4 Holbœll's Grebe. *Colymbus holbœlli.* . . . [Also called] American Red-necked Grebe; Red-necked Grebe.

+Red oak.
1. An American oak (*Quercus borealis*), or any one of various related species.
1634 WOOD *New Eng. Prospect* 16 Of Oakes there be three kindes, the red Oake, white, and black. **1671** [see LIVE OAK 1]. *c*1729 CATESBY *Carolina* I. 23 The Red Oak. . . . The bark is dark colour'd, very thick and strong, and for tanning preferable to any other kind of Oak. **1784** SMYTH *Tour* I. 334 The woods consist of . . . oaks of many different kinds, such as red oak [etc.]. **1804–6** CLARK in *Lewis & C. Exped.* VI. (1905) 140 Hack berry and Hasel bushes are found as high up as the Council bluff also red oake and Sycamore. **1894** COULTER *Bot. W. Texas* III. 416.
2. Wood from such a tree.
1655 *Relation of Md.* 22 The timber of these parts is very good . . . ; the white Oake is good for Pipe-staves, the red Oake for wainescot. **1674** JOSSELYN *Two Voyages* 61, I shall add the ordering of Red-Oake for Wainscot.
3. A tree of such a species.
1638 *Mass. Bay Rec.* I. 227 [The line shall run] to a great red oake marked. **1685** *Manchester Rec.* 19 A county . . . Laid out . . . Land from A white oake on ye west side beinge ye corner bounds of sd Land with A heape of stones marked with 4 marks northerly to a red oake. **1710** *Plymouth Rec.* II. 33 The 40 Acrees of upland . . . laid out by us . . . is bounded as followeth begining at a Red oake [etc.]. **1799** *Wilmington* (N.C.) *Gazette* 5 Sept., 6207 acres on Bearskin swamp, beginning at a red-oak. **1835** *Survey of Property* Nov. (Pettigrew P.), To a littel red oak.
4. Attrib. with *bark, stake, stave,* etc.
1633 *Plymouth Rec.* I. 64 Lott lyeth on the easterly side of the fourth lott and att the south end bounded with a Rid oake stake. **1655** *Providence Rec.* II. 2 On the north East Corner [it is bounded] with a Red oake Tree. **1790** FRENEAU *Poems* (1795) 375 These rebels stood And wonder'd at the mischeifs they had done To such a pile, compos'd of red-oak wood. **1832** BROWNE *Sylva* 267 In the Middle States, a large part of the *red oak staves* are furnished by this species [the scarlet oak, *Quercus coccinea*]. **1901** H. ROBERTSON *Inlander* 310, I des gwine down to de branch to git me some red-oak bark.

Red osier. {1830-}
+1. The silky cornel, *Cornus amomum.*
1817–8 EATON *Botany* (1822) 252 *Cornus sericea,* red osier. . . . Properties similar to the *florida.* **1845** LINCOLN *Botany* App. 94/1.
+2. Another variety of dogwood, *C. stolonifera.* In full *red osier dogwood.*
*a*1862 THOREAU *Maine Woods* 174 There grew . . . *Cornus stolonifera,* or red osier, whose bark, the Indian said, was good to smoke. *Ib.* 314 *Cornus stolonifera* (red-osier dogwood), prevailing shrub on shore of West Branch.

Redowa. A waltz of Bohemian origin somewhat like the mazurka. {1862-} Also attrib. — **1859** *La Crosse Daily Union* 22 Oct. 2/2 The polka, redowa dances, waltzes . . . are to be utterly excluded from 'good society.' **1878** ROE *Army Lett.* 185 At the ball we danced *Les Variétés.* . . . It is thoroughly French, bringing in the waltz, polka, schottische, mazurka, and redowa. **1891** [see GALLOPADE].

Red owl. +An American screech owl (*Otus asio*), in its rufescent phase. — [**1785** PENNANT *Arctic Zool.* II. 231.] **1812** WILSON *Ornithology* V. 83 [The] Red Owl . . . [is] well known by its common name, the Little Screech Owl. **1839** PEABODY *Mass. Birds* 272 The Red Owl . . . rears its young in Massachusetts. **1884** BURROUGHS in *Century Mag.* Dec. 218 A winter neighbor of mine in whom I am interested . . . is a little red owl whose retreat is in the heart of an old apple-tree. **1917** *Birds of Amer.* II. 109.

+Red pea. A common field pea having red seeds. — **1805** PARKINSON *Tour* 352 He showed me some of the red peas so much famed in America. **1819** *Plough Boy* I. 130 Permit me to recommend to the notice of the farmers of your vicinity, the culture of the common red pea, (cow peas).

+Red people. The American Indians.
1765 CROGHAN *Journal* (1904) 161 We red people, are a very jealous and foolish people. **1778** *Va. State P.* I. 306 A small tract of Country . . . still belonged to the Red People. **1797** HAWKINS *Sk. Creek Country* 9 The purity of his actions has given him a standing among the red people. **1811** *Niles' Reg.* I. 318/1 Col. Hawkins . . . has secured the attachment of the red people. **1844** S. M. FULLER *Summer on Lakes* 216 He drank greedily, and too much of the physic. They said, it was his usual custom, when the red people bought the English physic. **1916** EASTMAN *From Deep Woods* 83 He had come again, this time as a Savior to the red people.

*Red pepper. Any one of various species of *Capsicum,* as *C. annuum,* or its fruit. — **1776** FITHIAN *Journal* II. 238 We got only some peaches — & a few red-peppers. **1834** A. PIKE *Sketches* 38 These New Mexicans

. . . have pushed out into every little valley which would raise half a bushel of red pepper. **1881** *Rep. Indian Affairs* 140 The Indians produce corn, wheat, pumpkins, melons, beans, red pepper. **1925** TILGHMAN *Dugout* 33 You get out them packages of red pepper and I'll fetch some more water.

+Red pepper pod. The fruit of a red-pepper plant. — **1850** GARRARD *Wah-To-Yah* xiii. 180 On Mr. St. Vrain's table was the national dish—*chile colorado*—a compound of redpepper pods and other spicy ingredients. **1866** W. REID *After the War* 499 [Whisky] was always watered down at least one-fourth, and the 'fine' was kept up by a liberal introduction of red pepper-pods. **1903** FOX *Little Shepherd* i, The kitchen utensils . . . had been piled on the hearth, along with strings of herbs and beans and red pepper-pods.

Red perch. {1898, in Tasmania} +**1.** The white perch, *Morone americana.* +**2.** The rosefish, *Sebastes marinus.* +**3.** = GARIBALDI 2. — (1) **1814** MITCHILL *Fishes N.Y.* 420 [The] Red Perch . . . is one of our most firm and savoury fish. **1819** WARDEN *Statistical Acct. U.S.* I. 431 The following fishes are found in the Lakes Champlain [etc.] . . . : red-perch, white-perch, pickerel [etc.]. **1903** T. H. BEAN *Fishes N.Y.* 529. (2) **1871** *Amer. Naturalist* V. 400 The common *Sebastes,* or 'Red Perch' at Eastport, feeds upon the same species. **1911** *Rep. Fisheries 1908* 313/1. (3) **1884** GOODE, etc. *Fisheries* I. 276 The names 'Gold-fish' and 'Red Perch' are also used, . . . referring to its brilliant orange colorations. **1885** [see GARIBALDI 2].

+Red pine. {1839-}
1. = NORWAY PINE.
1809 KENDALL *Travels* III. 145, I have referred the sapling of the lumberers to the yellow, red or Norway pine. **1851** SPRINGER *Forest Life* 38 The Norway, or Red Pine, as it is sometimes called. *a*1862 THOREAU *Maine Woods* 249 We landed on a rocky point . . . to look at some Red Pines. **1897** [see HARD PINE].
2. = GEORGIA PINE.
1832 BROWNE *Sylva* 229 This invaluable tree is known . . . in the Northern States, [as] Southern Pine and Red Pine. **1842** [see GEORGIA PITCH PINE].
3. Applied to various other American trees: (see quotations).
1845 FRÉMONT *Exped.* 233 The red pine . . . is here [in the Rocky Mts.] the principal tree. +**2.** W. MILLER *Dict. Names of Plants* 107/2 Pinetree, Red. *Pinus resinosa* and *Abies rubra.*] **1897** SUDWORTH *Arborescent Flora* 20 *Pinus ponderosa.* Bull Pine. . . . [Also called] Red Pine. *Ib.* 47 *Pseudotsuga taxifolia.* . . . Douglas Spruce. . . . [Also called] Red Pine (Utah, Idaho, Colo.).

Red plum. {1707- (Mortimer *Art Husb.* 546)} +Any one of various plums beariıg red or purplish red fruit, as *Prunus americana* and *P. nigra.* — **1845** D. McCLURE *Diary* (1899) 59 Red plums grow in great abundance in this country [near Pittsburgh]. **1819** SCHOOLCRAFT *Mo. Lead Mines* 28 Of these [wild fruits], the following is a catalogue: Grape, Red plumb, Percimmon [etc.]. **1843** TORREY *Flora N.Y.* I. 194 Red Plum. . . . Frequent in the valley of the Hudson. **1891** COULTER *Bot. W. Texas* I. 102 *Prunus americana.* . . . Wild yellow or Red Plum. Occurring sparsely on the San Antonio and its tributaries.

Redpoll.¹
1. A bird of the genus *Acanthis,* esp. the lesser redpoll, *A. linaria.* {1738-} Also *redpoll finch, greater redpoll.*
1814 WILSON *Amer. Ornithology* IX. 128 The *Red-polls* become very fat, and are then accounted delicious eating. *Ib.* (index), Red-poll Finch. **1877** BURROUGHS *Birds & Poets* 97 Other Northern visitors that tarried with me the same winter were the tree or Canada sparrow and the redpoll. **1884** — in *Century Mag.* Dec. 220/1 The Canada sparrow, . . . the red-poll, the cedar-bird, . . . sweep by me and around me in flocks. **1917** *Birds of Amer.* III. 12/2 The Greater Redpoll (*Acanthis linaria rostrata*) . . . looks like the Common Redpoll but is of greater size.

+2. *Redpoll warbler,* = PALM WARBLER.
See also YELLOW REDPOLL.
1844 *Nat. Hist. N.Y., Zoology* II. 89 The Red-Poll Warbler, . . . although very abundant in the Southern States from November to April, . . . has seldom been noticed in this State.

Redpoll.² One of a breed of hornless beef and dairy cattle of a red color. {1891- (Stephens *Bk. Farm* (ed. 4) III. 416)}
1893 G. W. CURTIS *Horses, Cattle* 166 Red-Polls are, in general appearance, hornless Devons. *Ib.,* If the Red-Polls are carefully bred, we may expect to see them grow rapidly in public favor.

+Red race. The race made up of or constituted by the American Indians. — **1841** A. W. BRADFORD (title), American Antiquities, and Researches into the Origin and History of the Red Race. **1883** ZEIGLER & GROSSCUP *Alleghanies* 19 The geographical genius of the red race can not be claimed as an argument in favor of the re-substitution of the Indian designation for . . . 'Mud Creek.' **1899** CUSHMAN *Hist. Indians* 81 Nature . . . is full of instruction, . . . yet we heeded not the symbolic whispers of her low, sweet plaintive voice pleading in behalf of the Red Race.

Red raspberry. A red or purplish red raspberry, +esp. the American *Rubus strigosus.* Also *red wild raspberry.* — **1818** *Amer. Jrnl. Science* I. 371 Red raspberry fully ripe. **1843** TORREY *Flora N.Y.* I. 214 *Rubus strigosus,* Red Wild Raspberry. . . . Rocky hill-sides. **1879** *Scribner's Mo.* May 14/2 But when the red raspberry blooms, the fountains of plenty are unsealed indeed.

+**Red Republican.** One who holds radically republican views and favors violent means for obtaining political reform. Freq. attrib. — **1852** STOWE *Uncle Tom* xxiii, That's one of your red republican humbugs, Augustine! **1853** LOWELL in *Putnam's Mo.* Nov. 463/2 Shun Red Republican hot waters. **1859** WILMER *Press Gang* 369 The Germans who meditated an attack on Bedini, were the members of an atheistical Red Republican association calling themselves Freemen. **1900** *Congress. Rec.* 7 Feb. 1616/1 The candidates and supporters of the Democratic party were held up before the people as a gang of socialists, red republicans, anarchists, and nihilists.

+**Red Republicanism.** The principles and policy of Red Republicans. *Obs.* — **1850** E. P. WHIPPLE *Oration 4 July* 29 We are proposing all those intricate problems which red republicanism so swiftly solves. **1855** in Hambleton *H. A. Wise* 255 Red Republicanism and licentious indulgence in the enjoyment of civil privileges, are as much to be feared . . . as any of the forms of monarchy and despotism.

+**Red river.** *attrib.* Designating objects found in or coming from the vicinity of the Red River in northeast Texas or the Red River of the North. — **1849** E. SMITH *Journey through Texas* 23 The cotton thus produced ranks in the New Orleans market as 'Red River' cotton, and is a fine and long staple. **1861** *Harper's Mag.* Feb. 306/1 Joe Rolette rode in a miniature Red River cart with his youngest boy . . . behind a diminutive mule. **1871** *Rep. Indian Affairs* (1872) 255 Nearly all these persons came into St. Cloud with one of the 'Red River trains,' a long procession of carts that comes annually laden with furs, from the Northwest and the British possessions. **1894** EGGLESTON in *Harper's Mag.* Feb. 467/1 The young man in the white blanket coat asked if we would like a Red River turtle.

Red rock. A rock that is red, esp. a sandstone of the Triassic period. Also attrib. — **1888** *Harper's Mag.* June 43/1 This is the 'red rock region,' the district of the Gypsum Hills. **1898** PAGE *Red Rock* 583 Hiram Still had one night seen the 'Indian Killer' standing by the red-rock.

+**Red rod.** The red osier (sense 1), or a similar plant. Also *red-rod cornus.* — **1785** MARSHALL *Amer. Grove* 36 *Cornus sanguinea.* American Red-rod cornus. . . . The bark of the young shoots is very smooth, and of a beautiful dark red colour. **1833** EATON *Botany* (ed. 6) 109 *Cornus sericea,* red osier, red-rod. . . . Berries bright blue. **1843** TORREY *Flora N.Y.* I. 290 *Cornus Sericea.* Swamp Dogwood, Red-rod. . . . Margin of swamps and banks of streams.

+**Red roncador.** The black croaker, *Rhinoscion saturnus.* — **1882** *Nat. Museum Bul.* No. 16, 572 *Sciæna saturna,* . . . Red Roncador. **1884** GOODE, etc. *Fisheries* I. 379 *Corvina Saturna.* This fish is known where found as the 'Red Roncador;' less commonly as the 'Black Roncador' or 'Croaker.' **1911** *Rep. Fisheries 1908* 314/2.

+**Redroot.** The American ceanothus, or any of various other American plants, as bloodroot, green amaranth, and climbing bittersweet.

1709 LAWSON *Carolina* 78 The Red-Root whose Leaf is like Spear-mint, is good for . . . sore Mouths. **1796** HAWKINS *Letters* 46 In the month of May on the small bushes, particularly the red root, there is to be seen . . . a white froth. **1810** WILSON *Ornith.* (1832) I. p. lxxxv, Here and there the white blossoms of the *Sanguinaria Canadensis,* or red root, were peeping through the withered leaves. **1833** EATON *Botany* (ed. 6) 85 *Celastrus scandens,* false bittersweet, staff tree, red root. . . . Retains its scarlet berries through the winter. **1872** *Vt. Bd. Agric. Rep.* I. 268 The green amaranth or red root . . . [will] fully perfect its seeds. **1899** *Mo. So. Dakotan* I. 176 The plow hung in an uncut red root. **1901** MOHR *Plant Life Ala.* 446 *Gyrotheca capitata.* . . . Red Root. . . . Carolinian and Louisianian areas. **1915** ARMSTRONG & THORNBER *Western Wild Flowers* 282 Redroot is another name. Mountain Lilac is the commonest name.

Redroot willow. =GLAUCOUS WILLOW. — **1817–8** EATON *Botany* (1822) 443 *Salix discolor,* red-root willow, basket willow.

+**Red russet.** Any of various reddish apples. In full *red russet apple.* — **1817** [see GOLDEN *a.* 1 (2)]. **1849** *New Eng. Farmer* I. 31/2 *Red Russet* apples . . . seem to be intermediate between the Baldwin and Roxbury Russet.

Red sandstone. A red sedimentary rock consisting chiefly of sand in a firmly compacted state. {1761–} — **1837** IRVING *Bonneville* I. 222 The 'Bluffs' . . . present to the eye a confusion of hills and cliffs of red sandstone. **1843** N. BOONE *Journal* 203 The same red sandstone and red clay . . . have colored the soil since we were one day off from the Arkansas. **1867** *Ore. State Jrnl.* 5 Jan. 1/1 Recently, in a lead mine near Memphis, Tennessee, some specimens of red sandstone were broken open. **1893** *Harper's Mag.* May 941/2 The notable buildings of Denver are built of Colorado red sandstone, granite, and other beautiful materials found in the mountains.

+**Red-shafted flicker.** =next. — **1858** BAIRD *Birds Pacific R.R.* 120 Red-shafted Flicker. . . . The prevailing color of the back, scapulars, and wings is brownish ash. **1869** *Amer. Naturalist* Jan. 599 [The] Red-shafted Flicker . . . is common throughout the Rocky Mountains.

+**Red-shafted woodpecker.** A western flicker (*Colaptes cafer collaris*) related to the golden-winged woodpecker. — **1831** WILSON, etc. *Ornithology* IV. 245 Red-Shafted Woodpecker. *Colaptes Mexicanus.* **1839** AUDUBON *Ornith. Biog.* V. 174 Red-shafted woodpecker. *Picus Mexicanus.* . . . The extent of its distribution is as yet imperfectly known. **1880** *Cimarron News & Press* 23 Dec. 1/4 The last member of this family is the red-shafted or Mexican woodpecker. **1917** *Birds of Amer.* II. 165/1 West of the Mississippi . . . [we find] the Red-shafted Woodpecker (*Colaptes cafer collaris*).

+**Red-shouldered blackbird.** The red-winged blackbird, or a related species. (Cf. MARSH BLACKBIRD.) — **1858** BAIRD *Birds Pacific R.R.* 529 *Agelaius Gubernator* . . . , Red-shouldered Blackbird. . . . Pacific Coast of the United States. Colorado River? **1917** *Birds of Amer.* II. 248 Red-winged Blackbird. *Agelaius phœniceus phœniceus.* . . . [Also called] Red-shouldered Starling; Red-shouldered Blackbird.

+**Red-shouldered buzzard.** =next. — **1844** *Nat. Hist. N.Y., Zoology* II. 10 The Red-Shouldered Buzzard, or Winter Hawk, . . . lays four or five bluish eggs. **1880** *Cimarron News & Press* 23 Dec. 1/5 Their representatives here are the red-tailed, red-shouldered, Swainson's, rough-legged and ferruginous buzzards. **1917** *Birds of Amer.* II. 74.

+**Red-shouldered hawk.** A common hawk (*Buteo lineatus*), of eastern North America. (Cf. HEN HAWK.) — **1812** WILSON *Ornithology* VI. 86 [The] Red-shouldered Hawk . . . preys on Larks, Sandpipers and the small Ringed Plover. **1871** *Amer. Naturalist* 173 This mode of migration is more characteristic, perhaps, of . . . the Red-tailed, Red-shouldered, and Broad-winged Hawks. **1895** *Dept. Agric. Yrbk. 1894* 220 Both it and the red-shouldered hawk, also known as 'hen hawk,' do occasionally eat poultry. **1917** *Birds of Amer.* II. 75/2 Red-shouldered Hawks are very valuable to the farmer.

+**Red-shouldered heron.** =GREAT BLUE HERON. — **1785** LATHAM *Gen. Synopsis Birds* III. 85 Red-Shouldered H[eron]. *Ardea Hudsonias* . . . By some supposed to be the *female* of the last [Great H.]. **1917** *Birds of Amer.* I. 184 Great Blue Heron. *Ardea herodias herodias.* . . . [Also called] Red-shouldered Heron.

+**Redskin.** An American Indian. {1851–}

1699 in H. E. Smith *Colonial Days* (1900) 49 Ye firste Meetinge House was solid mayde to withstande ye wicked onsaults of ye Red Skins. **1821** Schoolcraft *Narr. Travels* 346, I am a red skin. I do not know how to read and write. **1843** 'CARLTON' *New Purchase* I. 173, I felt like takin sides with the red skins myself. **1883** *Harper's Mag.* Oct. 807/1 A huge redskin . . . followed the General wherever he went. **1923** J. H. COOK *On Old Frontier* 49 The redskins would then have run to their own horses.

attrib. **1699** in H. E. Smith *Colonial Days* (1900) 49 My Honoured Father was as Active as ye Red Skin Men & sinewy. **1840** COOPER *Pathfinder* II. 124 Such the way red-skin woman do, when people in danger and want scalp. **1923** Redskin commerce [see COUREUR DE BOIS].

+**Red snake.** Any one of various snakes having red markings, esp. a harmless snake of the family Colubridae. — **1688** CLAYTON *Va.* in *Phil. Trans.* XVIII. 134 There is another sort of deadly Snake, called the Red Snake. **1744** MOORE *Voy. Georgia* I. 120 Besides the rattle-snake . . . there are also many others, as the black, the red, and the chicken snake. **1842** *Nat. Hist. N.Y., Zoology* III. 49 The Red Snake . . . is a beautiful little serpent, found under stones and logs.

+**Red snapper.** An important food fish (*Lutianus campechianus*) found on the Atlantic and Gulf coasts. — **1775, 1802** [see GRAY SNAPPER]. **1879** *Harper's Mag.* Dec. 26/1 The next dish was baked red snapper. **1894** *Scribner's Mag.* May 603/2 The epicure from the States would go wild with the display . . . of everything he might demand in the shape of . . . red snapper, green turtle [in the Rio Grande]. **1911** *Rep. Fisheries 1908* 316/2 The red snapper (*Lutianus aya*) is the most important of [the snappers].

Red spider. Any one of various spiderlike mites belonging to *Tetranychus* or a related genus. {1646–} — [**1856** *Rep. Comm. Patents 1845: Agric.* 79 Much injury is done to the cotton-leaf by a minute red spider.] **1873** *Amer. Naturalist* VII. 17 These six-legged forms are but the young of some eight-legged form such as Trombidium, to which belongs our common 'red spider.' **1892** KELLOGG *Kansas Insects* 106 The 'Red Spider' is not a spider, but a mite. **1925** HERRICK *Man. Injurious Insects* 395 The red spider . . . occurs all over the United States.

Red-spotted trout. {1883} **1.** The brook trout, *Salvelinus fontinalis.* **2.** =DOLLY VARDEN. — **(1) 1842** *Nat. Hist. N.Y., Zoology* IV. 235 Red Spotted Trout. . . . Those from running streams are better flavored than the pond trout. **(2) 1884** GOODE, etc. *Fisheries* I. 504 The Dolly Varden Trout—*Salvelinus Malma* . . . is known in the mountains as 'Lake Trout,' 'Bull Trout,' 'Speckled Trout,' and 'Red-spotted Trout.'

+**Red spruce.** A species of spruce (*Picea rubra*) found in the eastern states, usually in swamps. — **1810** MICHAUX *Arbres* I. 18 Abies nigra, . . . *Black* or *Double spruce,* nom . . . dans les Etats du nord. *Red spruce,* dans les mêmes contrées. **1832** BROWNE *Sylva* 99 From the influence of the soil upon the wood it [*Abies nigra*] is sometimes called Red Spruce. **1897** SUDWORTH *Arborescent Flora* 35 *Picea rubra.* . . . Red Spruce. **1905** *Forestry Bureau Bul.* No. 60, 16 The typical trees are red spruce, Fraser fir, and Carolina hemlock.

Red squirrel. +A small North American squirrel (*Sciurus hudsonicus*), many varieties of which are widely distributed throughout the United States. (Cf. CHICKAREE.)

[**1637** MORTON *New Canaan* 81 There are Squirils of three sorts, very different in shape and condition; one . . . is red, and hee haunts our houses and will rob us of our corne.] **1682** [see FOX SQUIRREL]. **1781–2** JEFFERSON *Notes Va.* (1788) 79 Aboriginals of . . . America. Lesser gray squirrel, Black squirrel, Red squirrel. **1805** PARKISON *Tour* 305 [There are] great grey, red, black, fox, and flying squirrel. **1879** *Smithsonian Misc. Coll.* XXIII. IV. 14 *Sciurus hudsonius,* . . . Red Squirrel; Chickaree.—Cismontane United States and Alaska. **1902** HULBERT *Forest Neighbors* 102 Other sounds there were . . . —the scream of the rabbit . . . ; the scolding of the red squirrel, disturbed and angry.

Redstart.** + =AMERICAN REDSTART. — *c1730** CATESBY *Carolina* I. 67 The Red-Start. . . . These Birds frequent the shady Woods of Virginia. **1812** WILSON *Ornithology* V. 119 The Redstart extends very generally over the United States. **1869** *Amer. Naturalist* III. 33 The Redstart was one of the commonest birds in the Missouri bottom-lands. **1917** *Birds of Amer.* III. 167/1 The Redstart . . . is perhaps the most restless and active of [the warblers].

Red stick.

+1. One of the sticks, painted red, used about 1812 by the Indian chief Tecumseh (?1768–1813) as the magic symbol of his war party. *Obs.* Also transf.

1819 *Niles' Reg.* XVI. *Suppl.* 102/2 [Tecumseh] carried with him a red stick, to which he attached certain mystical properties, and the acceptance of which was considered as the joining of his party; from hence the name red stick applied to all Indians hostile to the United States. **1845** SIMMS *Wigwam & Cabin* 1 Ser. 56 He had only consented to take up the red stick because it was reported by the black chief [etc.]. **1854** *S. Lit. Messenger* XX. 400 The red sticks were lifted by the Catawbas against the Shawnese.

+2. Originally, an Indian who accepted one of Tecumseh's red sticks and thus joined his war party; subsequently, any Indian warrior. *Obs.*

1817 *Niles' Reg.* XIII. 296/1 The number of hostile Indians, including the 'Red Sticks' and Seminoles, [is estimated] at more than two thousand. **1844** *Knickerb.* XXIV. 428 [He] declared that no foreign blood ran in his veins, but that he was a pure blooded 'Red Stick.' **1845** SIMMS *Wigwam & Cabin* 1 Ser. 121 [He] had proved his skill and courage in several expeditions against the Chowannee red sticks. **1846** MCKENNEY *Memoirs* I. 164 The sticks he [Tecumseh] distributed on that occasion being painted red, secured for those who agreed to co-operate with him, the title of 'Red-sticks.'

3. Attrib. with *class, dancing, party.*

1817 *Niles' Reg.* XII. 336/1 Never one of them has been known to join the red stick party. **1817** *State P.* (1819) XII. 339 From below where the Red Stick class reside. *Ib.*, I have heard . . . that the Red Stick party have commenced their Red Stick dancings again.

* Red stone.

* 1. Stone of a red color, +esp. that used by Indians for making pipe bowls. Also attrib.

1765 ROGERS *Acct. N. Amer.* 223 The bowl [of the calumet] . . . is made of a kind of soft red stone. **1778** CARVER *Travels* 101 The Indians get a sort of red stone, out of which they hew the bowls of their pipes. **1851** ROSS *In New York* 207 The stone on which the man was at work was a brown, or what is frequently called red stone. **1886** *Outing* Nov. 101/1 With the stem of the red-stone pipe held between his teeth, Paul said [etc.].

+2. (See quot. 1808.) *Obs.* Also attrib.

1808 CUMING *Western Tour* 473 The term 'Redstone' was also applied in New Jersey in 1790 to the above mentioned western counties of Pennsylvania. **1816** U. BROWN *Journal* I. 283 This day was heretofore appointed by the Masons . . . to walk in procession in the Town of Union which afforded an Opertunity to see many of the redstone farmers.

Redstreak. A kind of apple the skin of which is streaked with red and yellow. {1664-} — **1709** [see LONGSTALK 1]. **1760** WASHINGTON *Diaries* I. 147 Grafted 43 of the Maryland Red Strick. **1836** DUNLAP *Mem. Water Drinker* (1837) I. 48 The tale of grandfather's wars with the Indians . . . [is] interrupted by draughts of the precious juice of the crab, the spitzbergen, and the red-streak. **1875** BURROUGHS *Winter Sunshine* 140 Then comes the red streak, the yellow-sweet, and others.

+Red Strings. During the last stages of and immediately after the Civil War, a secret organization of the South, esp. in North Carolina, sympathetic to the Union. — **1871** [see HERO]. **1879** TOURGEE *Fool's Errand* 108 You mean the 'Red Strings' I suppose.

Red sumac(h). +Either of two sumacs (*Rhus glabra* and *R. copallina*) common in the eastern states: (see also quot. 1902). Cf. SMOOTH SUMAC(H). — **1813** MUHLENBERG *Cat. Plants* 32 *Rhus glabrum*, red, smooth Sumach. **1847** in *Readings in Ind. Hist.* 351 For Yellow Jaundice. Take a double handful of wild cherry tree bark . . . ; the same quantity . . . of the bark of the red sumach roots [etc.]. **1896** WILKINS *Madelon* 197 Every white alder-bush in the spring raised you up anew before me to madden me with vain longing, and every red sumach in the fall. **1902** CLAPIN 333 *Red sumac*, a tree, the leaves of which are largely used, by Indians and trappers, as a substitute for tobacco.

* Redtail.

+1. The red-tailed hawk. In full *redtail hawk.*

1812 WILSON *Ornithology* VI. 75 Early next morning the unfortunate Red-tail was found a prisoner. **1844** *Nat. Hist. N.Y., Zoology* II. 9 The Red-tail, Hen Hawk and Hen Harrier by which names it is designated, resides in our state during the whole year. **1894** *Outing* XXIII. 406/1 The red-tail hawk has his story of a cold wintry day. **1895** *Dept. Agric. Yrbk. 1894* 220 Fully 66 per cent of the red-tail's food consists of injurious mammals.

+2. a. The horny head, *Nocomis kentuckiensis.* **b.** The red horse, *Moxostoma aureolum.*

(a) **1820** *Western Rev.* I. 238 Kentuckian Shiner. . . . Vulgar names, Indian Chub, Red tail, Shiner, &c. (b) **1820** [see RED HORSE 1].

Red-tailed, *a.* Having a red tail. {1601-} — **1807** IRVING, etc. *Salmagundi* xviii. 476 Their lively prattle is as diverting as the chattering

of the red-tailed parrot. **1842** STORER in *Bost. Jrnl. Nat. Hist.* IV. 177 *Pomotis rubri-cauda.* Red-tailed Pomotis. Length of the fish five inches. **1845** Red-tailed roebuck [see BLACK-TAILED *a.* 1 b]. **1867** STORER *Hist. Fishes Mass.* 14 *Pomotis appendix.* . . . The Red-tailed Bream. **1874** *Vermont Bd. Agric. Rep.* II. 438 There is also the *Gastrophilus hemorrhoidalis*, or red-tailed bot fly.

+Red-tailed black hawk. A western variety (*Buteo borealis calurus*) of the red-tailed hawk, or a hawk of this variety. — **1858** BAIRD *Birds Pacific R.R.* 22 Red-tailed Black Hawk. . . . To a casual observer this bird would present somewhat the appearance of the black hawk of the United States. **1869** *Amer. Naturalist* III. 184 Two fine specimens of the Red-tailed Black Hawk . . . would not allow of a very near approach.

+Red-tailed buzzard. =next. — **1839** AUDUBON *Synopsis Birds* 6 *Buteo borealis.* Red-tailed Buzzard. **1858** BAIRD *Birds Pacific R.R.* 22 Red-tailed Black Hawk. . . . To a casual observer this bird would present somewhat the appearance of the black hawk . . . with the tail attached of the common red-tailed buzzard. **1874** COUES *Birds N.W.* 352 *Buteo borealis.* . . . Red-tailed Buzzard; Hen Hawk. **1887** [see BUZZARD]. **1917** *Birds of Amer.* II. 71.

+Red-tailed hawk. A common hen hawk of the United States, esp. *Buteo borealis* found in the East. — **1805** CLARK in *Lewis & C. Exped.* III. (1905) 257 Large red tailed Hawks, ravens & crows in abundance. **1831** AUDUBON *Ornith. Biog.* I. 265 The Red-tailed Hawk is a constant resident in the United States, in every part of which it is found. **1869** BURROUGHS in *Atlantic Mo.* May 582/2 [The turkey buzzards'] movements when in air are . . . identical with those of our common hen or red-tailed hawk. **1917** *Birds of Amer.* II. 71.

+Red-tap(e)y, *a.* Involved in or characterized by red tape or official formality or delay. *colloq.* — **1889** *Columbus Dispatch* 21 Jan., Whether the newspaper reports are extravagant, or the official reports are too red-tapy or timid, . . . it is hard to say. **1890** *Stock Grower & Farmer* 17 May 3/2 The money would be acceptable but the methods too red-tapey and slow.

Red-throated, *a.* Of birds: Having a red throat. {1743-} — [**1760** G. EDWARDS *Gleanings Nat. Hist.* III. 193 The Red-throated Fly-catchers.] **1844** *Nat. Hist. N.Y., Zoology* II. 286 The Red-throated Loon, *Colymbus septentrionalis*, . . . is comparatively a rare bird in this State. **1917** *Birds of Amer.* II. 150 Yellow-bellied Sapsucker. *Sphyrapicus varius varius.* . . . [Also called] Red-throated Sapsucker.

Red-throated diver. A variety of loon, *Gavia stellata.* {1768-} (Cf. CAPE-RACE.) — **1828** BONAPARTE *Synopsis* 421 The Red-throated Diver, *Colymbus septentrionalis.* . . . Inhabits the north of both continents. **1835** AUDUBON *Ornith. Biog.* III. 20 The Red-throated Diver is found . . . from Maryland to the extremities of Maine. **1874** COUES *Birds N.W.* 724 Red-throated Diver. . . . This species varies greatly in general size. **1917** *Birds of Amer.* I. 15.

Red thrush. {1885-} +=RED MAVIS. — **1789** MORSE *Amer. Geog.* 60 American Birds [which] have been enumerated [include the] Yellow Rump, Towhe Bird, Red Thrush. **1865** [see MAVIS]. **1917** *Birds of Amer.* III. 179 Brown Thrasher. *Toxostoma rufum.* . . . [Also called] Red Thrush.

Redtop. {attrib. 1800-}

+1. Any one of various pasture grasses, as bluejoint, *Calamagrostis canadensis.*

1792 MUHLENBERG in *Life & Corr. Cutler* II. 293 What is Bird-grass, Red-top, Wire-grass, Dog's-grass? **1829** EATON *Botany* (ed. 5) 447 *Windsoria seslerioides*, red-top. **1843** TORREY *Flora* N.Y. II. 458 *Poa serotina.* Red-top. . . . Wet meadows, valley of the Hudson and western parts of the State. **1850** *Rep. Comm. Patents 1849: Agric.* 135 They use herds-grass, and red-top, chiefly mixed with clover. **1891** WILKINS *Humble Romance* 92 The whole yard . . . [was] covered with a tall waving crop of red-top.

+2. Herd's grass, *Agrostis stolonifera major.*

1818 J. TAYLOR *Arator* 204 A large meadow in bottom land, of a grass called red top or herd's grass, was cut in dry weather. **1843** TORREY *Flora N.Y.* II. 441 *Agrostis vulgaris.* Red-top. Herd's grass. . . . Probably introduced from Europe. **1858** [see HERD'S GRASS]. **1901** MOHR *Plant Life Ala.* 370.

+Redtop clover. =RED CLOVER. — **1879** *Scribner's Mo.* Dec. 248/1 If the cultivator can wait for the . . . red-top clover he will find it far better. **1885** *South Fla. Sentinel* (Orlando) 29 July 4/2 Red top clover will grow and do well in our Sumter Co. soil. **1886** ROE in *Harper's Mag.* July 247/1 They began with red-top clover.

+Redtop grass. Any one of various pasture grasses naturalized in the United States, as herd's grass, *Agrostis stolonifera major.* — **1790** DEANE *New-Eng. Farmer* 115/1 The red top grass is so natural to every soil in this country, that all our old fields . . . are full of it. **1819** E. DANA *Geogr. Sk.* 108 Some of the prairas between fort Harrison and fort Meigs, are covered with red top and foul meadow grasses. **1870** *Rep. Comm. Agric. 1869* 88 *Agrostis vulgaris* (red-top grass) and *Agrostis alba* (white-top grass or white bent) are well known valuable meadow grasses.

+Redtop hay. Hay obtained from redtop grass. Also transf. — **1872** EGGLESTON *End of World* 65 When a man comes to Clark township . . . a cultivating a crap of red-top hay onto his upper lip, and a-lettin' on to be a singin'-master, I suspicions him. **1884** *Rep. Comm. Agric.* 233 The ergot of the red-top hay in Missouri and Illinois produced identical effects with that in the wild rye of Kansas.

+Red trout. The namaycush, or a similar trout. — **1766** ROWE *Diary* 94, [I] caught a fine Red Trout. **1884** GOODE, etc. *Fisheries* I. 48 The Lake Trout has other appellatives, such as . . . 'Tyrant of the Lake,'

'Laker,' 'Red Trout.' **1903** T. H. BEAN *Fishes N.Y.* 267 The lake trout has received many names, among which are . . . lunge, red trout, gray trout, and black salmon.

*****Reducer. 1.** One who reduces or smelts ore. **2.** (See quotations.) — **(1) 1876** RAYMOND *8th Rep. Mines* 286 Reducers cannot now buy directly of the miner. **(2) 1883** KNIGHT *Suppl.* 746/2 *Reducer,* a joint-piece for connecting pipes of varying diameter. The term is also applied to other pipe connections where one of the members has a smaller diameter. **1903** PRINGLE *Rice Planter* 56 An ever-flowing artesian well . . . throws water above the roof when a smaller pipe is put on,—a reducer, the man who bored the well called it.

+Reduction works. 1. A place where ores are reduced or smelted; a smeltery. **2.** (See quotation.) — **(1) 1865** *Harper's Mag.* Feb. 285/2 Down in a beautiful little valley . . . stand the reduction works . . . and peon quarters of the Mowry Silver Mines. **1872** TICE *Over Plains* 112 The reduction works . . . will not afford any relief to the Caribou mines. **1873** RAYMOND *Silver & Gold* 320 At the mouth of Little Cottonwood Cañon are Colonel Buell's reduction-works, comprising two Piltz furnaces. **1877** HODGE *Arizona* 85 Yet there is a scarcity of water at present for large reduction works. **1883** RITCH *Illust. N. Mex.* 35 A few reduction works, smelters and stamp mills have been erected and are in operation in nearly every county of the Territory. **(2) 1894** GOULD *Dict. Medicine* 1244/1 *Reduction-works,* a cremating establishment for disposing of the filth and refuse matter of a city.

Redweed. {1641-} **+1.** =POKEWEED. **+2.** =FIELD SORREL. — **(1)** [**1624** Smith *Gen. Hist. Va.* v. 170 [In the Bermudas] is also frequently growing a certaine tall Plant, whose stalke being als ouer couered with a red rinde, is thereupon termed the red weed.] **1667** *Phil. Trans.* II. 796 There grows a Berry (by report) both in the Bermudas and New England, call'd the Summer-Island-Redweed, which Berry is as red as the Prickle-Peare. **(2) 1894** *Amer. Folk-Lore* VII. 97 *Rumex acetosella,* red sorrel, red weed, West Va.

*****Red wheat.** A variety of wheat having red grains. — [**1840** *Niles' Nat. Reg.* 15 Aug. 384/3 Wheat. Good red commands $1.11 to $1.13.] **1868** *Mich. Agric. Rep.* VII. 349 Samuel Rappelye, Ridgeway, [exhibited] 1 bushel red wheat. **1870** *Rep. Comm. Agric. 1869* 251 In Suffolk County the product was about equal to that of the Bearded Red wheat.

***** **Red willow.** Any one of various trees and shrubs having reddish twigs, as the red osier.
Cf. KINNIKINNICK 2.
1784 *Amer. Acad. Mem.* I. 491 *Salix.* . . . The White Willow. The Red Willow. The Rose Willow. The Dogwood. The Osier. **1806** LEWIS in *L. & Clark Exped.* IV. (1905) 203 The red willow and 7 bark begin to put forth their leaves. **1824** DODDRIDGE *Notes* 26 Before the use of tobacco, the Indians smoked the inner bark of the red willow mixed with sumack leaves. **1895** *Outing* XXVII. 211/1 The lake . . . was covered with a growth of red willows and rushes. **1897** SUDWORTH *Arborescent Flora* 122 *Salix fluviatilis.* Longleaf Willow. . . . Red Willow (Mont.).
attrib. **1799** in Cuming *Western Tour* 426 He had nothing to smoke, but red-willow bark. **1883** *Harper's Mag.* Oct. 710/2 [We] cut a handful or two of red willow twigs.

b. The wood of a tree of this kind.
1814 BRACKENRIDGE *Views La.* 231 These skin canoes are stretched over the red willow.

+Red windflower. An anemone having red or reddish flowers. — **1861** WOOD *Botany* 203 A [*nemone*] *multifida.* Red wind-flower. . . . Rocks, northern Vt. and N.Y., W. to Lake Superior; rare. **1869** FULLER *Flower Gatherers* 28 Another species, the Red Wind Flower, has reddish purple blossoms.

Redwing. {1657-} **+1.** Any one of various birds of the genus *Agelaius,* esp. the red-winged blackbird. With defining term. **2.** (See quotation.) — **(1) 1778** CARVER *Travels* 474 The second sort [of blackbird] is the red wing, which is rather smaller than the first species. **1887** RIDGWAY *Manual N.A. Birds* 370 Bahaman Red-wing. **1917** *Birds of Amer.* II. 250 The Bi-colored Red-wing and the Tri-colored Red-wing might well be called California Red-wing and Western Red-wing. **(2)** *Ib.* I. 118 Gadwall. *Chaulelasmus streperus.* . . . [Also called] Red-wing.

Red-winged, *a.* {1712-} **+**In the names of American birds and fishes. — **1794** *Amer. Philos. Soc.* IV. 108 This ingenious gentleman was induced to suppose, from the peculiar melancholy cry of a red-winged-maize-thief, that a snake was at no great distance. **1839** AUDUBON *Ornith. Biog.* V. 3 Their habits are similar to those of the Red-winged Icterus. **1897** *N.Y. Forest, Fish, & Game Comm. 2d Rep.* 245 *Prionotus strigatus.* . . . Red-Winged Sea Robin.—Makes its appearance later than *P. carolinus.*

+Red-wing(ed) blackbird. The red-winged starling or marsh blackbird, *Agelaius phoeniceus.*
1803 in *Medical Repository* 2d Hexade II. 122 All the sorts [of birds] . . . are to be seen . . . at Plandome [N.Y.]. . . . Red-wing'd black-bird, Yellow-wing'd black-bird, Ground black-bird, or bob-lincoln. **1811** WILSON *Ornithology* IV. 37 Red-winged Starlings . . . are known by various names in the different states of the union; such as . . . Red-winged Blackbird, Corn or Maize Thief, Starling, &c. **1851** GLISAN *Jrnl. Army Life* 89 Of the birds and animals not usually eatable, there are the bird of paradise, red-winged and rusty-winged blackbird, blue-bird, buzzard, crow, [etc.]. **1883** *Century Mag.* Sept. 653/1 Among the most common birds are . . . the sharp-tailed finch, the red-wing blackbird, [and] the grassfinch. **1894** TORREY *Florida Sketch-Book* 97 Red-winged Blackbirds . . . piqued my curiosity by adding to the familiar *conkaree* a final syllable—the

Florida termination. **1904** STRATTON-PORTER *Freckles* 305 The red-winged blackbirds and bobolinks . . . came swarming by hundreds.

+Red-winged oriole. =prec. — **1785** PENNANT *Arctic Zool.* II. 256 The Red-winged Orioles build their nests in bushes. **1844** *Nat. Hist. N.Y., Zoology* II. 141 The Red-Winged Oriole . . . is regarded by the farmer with great aversion. **1917** *Birds of Amer.* II. 248.

+Red-winged starling. =RED-WINGED BLACKBIRD. — *c*1728 CATESBY *Carolina* I. 13 The red wing'd Starling. . . . They are the boldest and most destructive Birds in the Country. **1789** MORSE *Amer. Geog.* 60 American Birds [which] have been enumerated [include the] . . . Redstart, Red winged Starling, Swallow. **1811** WILSON *Ornithology* IV. 30 Red-winged Starling . . . [is a] notorious and celebrated corn-thief. **1881** *Amer. Naturalist* XV. 393 The Red-winged Starlings generally leave this region [in Iowa] before we have any severely cold weather. **1917** *Birds of Amer.* II. 248.

Redwood. {1634-}
+1. =RED WILLOW. *Obs.*
1778 CARVER *Travels* 31 About all the great lakes, is found a kind of willow, termed by the French, bois rouge, in English red wood. **1785** WASHINGTON *Diaries* II. 368 The Dogwood buttons were just beginning to open, as [were] the Redwood (or bud) blossom. **1805** LEWIS in *L. & Clark Exped.* I. (1904) 299 The under brush is willow, red wood, (sometimes called red or swamp willow). **1819** WARDEN *Statistical Acct. U.S.* III. 97 In the lower parts are found oak, elm, . . . red-wood, sumach.

+2. A species of unusually large and valuable California timber tree, *Sequoia sempervirens.*
1850 GLISAN *Jrnl. Army Life* 27 When in Oregon and California, the forests of the stately fir, and the majestic redwood perish by fire, they are succeeded by thickets of hazel, vine, maple and scrub oak. **1869** BRACE *New West* 93 The Sequoia belongs to the same family with the Red Wood. **1898** A. M. DAVIDSON *Calif. Plants* 161 There is another kind of redwood that grows in the magnificent forests along the northern coast of California. **1905** ATHERTON *Travelling Thirds* 162 The wonders of a Californian mountain-forest—of redwood and pine, madroño and oak.

+b. Building material obtained from this.
1854 BARTLETT *Personal Narr.* II. 19 He has now more than a hundred acres under cultivation, . . . protected by a post and rail fence of red wood. **1869** *Rep. Comm. Agric. 1868* 461 The red wood . . . is a valued commercial wood. **1891** WARNER in *Harper's Mag.* Jan. 172/1 A small flume eight or ten inches square of common redwood is laid along the upper side of a ten acre tract. **1895** GRAHAM *Stories of Foot-Hills* 143 The house itself was of unsurfaced redwood.

+c. =REDWOOD TREE.
1869 HARTE *Luck of Roaring Camp* 68 The redwoods . . . stood in Indian-file along the track. **1876** INGRAM *Centennial Exp.* 361 The big trees of California . . . were here represented by a piece of bark about eighteen inches thick taken from one of these monster red-woods. **1889** *Century Mag.* Feb. 601/2 There ain't much except ducks here—ducks an' redwoods. **1913** LONDON *Valley of Moon* 402 [The farm] must have redwoods on it.
transf. **1878** B. F. TAYLOR *Between Gates* 289 The young pioneers are the young redwoods of mankind.

+3. *Redwood sorrel,* (see quotation).
1915 ARMSTRONG & THORNBER *Western Wild Flowers* 272 Redwood Sorel. *Oxalis Oregana.* White, pink. Spring. Cal., Oreg., Wash.

+4. Attrib. in sense 2. **a.** Designating houses and other structures made of redwood lumber.
1863 *Harper's Mag.* June 25/1 [We settled] our score with the landlord of our red-wood hotel. **1879** HOWELLS *Lady of Aroostook* 66 'Now, if you were taking some nice girl with you!' . . . 'To those wilds? To a redwood shanty in California, or a turf hovel in Colorado?' **1882** *Century Mag.* June 226/2 Around the lofty redwood walls of these little bee-acres there is usually a fringe of chestnut-oak. **1883** *Ib.* Oct. 815/1 Living in a three-roomed, redwood log cabin, with a vine-covered booth in front, is an old man.

+b. Designating places and regions where redwood is the prevailing growth.
1882 *Nation* 19 Oct. 326/3 The Sierra forests [are] the only forests in California, outside of the redwood belt, of more than local importance. **1913** LONDON *Valley of Moon* 293 There's some fine redwood canyons, with good patches of farming ground that run right down to the ocean. *Ib.* 314 We'll collect . . . somewhere down in them redwood mountains south of Monterey.

+c. Designating pieces of redwood used in building houses, fences, etc.
1883 *Harper's Mag.* Aug. 337/2 [The hotel's] architecture and ornamentation belong to the new revival of good taste, the creed of redwood shingle and olive green. **1883** Redwood plank [see CITRUS FAIR]. **1893** HARTE *Susy* 62 The exposed *annexe* was filled with sharp resinous odors from the oozing sap of unseasoned 'redwood' boards. **1900** DRANNAN *Plains & Mts.* 577, [I had] had all my land fenced in with a picket fence made of red wood pickets. **1913** LONDON *Valley of Moon* 483 An ancient, rutted road . . . ran beside an equally ancient worm-fence of split redwood rails.

Redwood tree. {1745-} **+**A large coniferous tree of the genus *Sequoia* found in the coast ranges of California. — **1890** *Century Mag.* Dec.

180 Among other things which it would be of interest for him to see was mentioned a very large redwood tree. **1897** *Kissimmee* (Fla.) *Valley Gazette* 31 Dec. 4/7 The section of a California redwood tree . . . has been safely brought to Cliveden. **1900** HARTE *Treasure of Redwoods* 1 Mr. Jack Fleming stopped suddenly before a lifeless and decaying redwoodtree. **1913** LONDON *Valley of Moon* 412 There must be hills and valleys, and . . . lots and lots of redwood trees.

+**Ree corn.** (See quotation.) — **1881** *Rep. Indian Affairs* 36 Yield of crops raised by Indians from 580 acres, . . . estimated: Ree corn (a small early variety), 345 acres, 3,500 bushels.

* **Reed,** *n.*

* **1.** Any of several tall canelike grasses or their slender stems; spec., the ditch reed (*Phragmites communis*) or other species of *Phragmites* or of *Arundo.*

1607 in Smith *Works* (1910) p. xlii, We found here a *Wiroans* . . . who satt upon a matt of Reedes. **1626** *Plymouth Laws* 29 From hence forward no dwelling house was to be covered with any kind of thatche as straw reed &c. **1709** LAWSON *Carolina* 176 Their chiefest Game is a sort of Arithmetick, which is managed by a Parcel of small split Reeds. **1792** IMLAY *Western Territory* 41 The cane is a reed which grows to the height frequently of fifteen or sixteen feet. **1802** ELLICOTT *Journal* 184 The soil is . . . covered either with the large cane, (*arundo gigantea*) or the small cane or reed, (*arundo tecta*) **1870** KEIM *Sheridan's Troopers* 205 On these occasions at night, the party construct shelters made of reeds.

* **2.** *attrib.* Designating places where reeds grow.

*a*1656 BRADFORD *Hist.* I. 348 These but against the swampe and reedponde. **1683** *Jamaica* (L.I.) *Rec.* I. 250 What is given as above sayde is onely the boggy medow and reede grounde. **1819** E. DANA *Geogr. Sk.* 189 This portion of the land is interspersed with reed marshes, and the issue constant running water. **1862** *Harper's Mag.* June 31/1 At short intervals . . . there are lateral ridges running down into deep reed-brakes below. **1882** E. K. GODFREY *Nantucket* 266 A visit should be paid to Quaise or Masquetuck (the reed land).

* **Reed,** *v.* +*intr.* To shoot reedbirds. — **1853** *Knickerb.* XLII. 613 He's been 'reeding' too much for you, Sir.

Reedbird. {1648-} +The bobolink, esp. in its fall plumage; the flesh of this bird. Chiefly *S.*

1795 PRIEST *Travels* 90 [Among a] wonderful variety of small birds . . . , the *reed-bird,* or american ortolan, justly holds the first place. **1810** WILSON *Ornithology* II. 48 [The] Rice Bunting . . . [is] the Rice and Reedbird of Pennsylvania and the southern states. **1839** *Knickerb. Mag.* XIII. 437 He is the *reed-bird,* the much-sought-for tit-bit of the Pennsylvanian epicure. **1859** *Penna. Laws* 640 It shall be unlawful for any person or persons to shoot, kill, trap or destroy rail birds or reed birds. **1886** POORE *Reminisc.* I. 524 Quails, reed birds, chicken and lobster salads . . . were furnished in profusion. **1917** *Birds of Amer.* II. 242 Gunners . . . lie in wait for him on his southern migration, in order that banqueters may have their 'reed-birds on toast.'

+**Reed cane.** (See quot. 1818.) — **1817** S. BROWN *Western Gazetteer* 78 The Reed Cane . . . grows south of the ridge of hills. **1818** DARBY *Emigrant's Guide* 77 There are two very distinct species of the arundo, or large reed cane, growing in southern Louisiana; the *arundo gigantea,* and the *arundo aquatica.* **1833** FLINT *D. Boone* 151 Each is prepared with a bundle of long, dry, reed cane, or other poles, to which are attached splinters of burning pine.

* **Reed grass.** Any of various American grasses, esp. of the genera *Calamagrostis* and *Arundo.* Also with specifying terms. {1756 in Jamaica} — **1795** WINTERBOTHAM *Hist. View* III. 401 The States of New-England abound with . . . Reed grass, several species, Arundo, Brome grass [etc.]. **1869** *Amer. Naturalist* II. Feb. 653 The Reed-grass (*Phragmites communis*) grows in all wet places here [Pipestone Quarry, Minn.]. **1901** MOHR *Plant Life Ala.* 369 *Cinna arundinacea.* . . . Wood Reed Grass. *Ib.* 374 *Spartina polystachya.* . . . Salt Reed Grass.

Reed maker. A person who makes weavers' reeds. {1639-} — **1837** W. JENKINS *Ohio Gaz.* 421 There is [in Streetsborough] . . . 1 reed maker, and 1 post office. **1847** HOWE *Hist. Coll. Ohio* 244 In April, 1807, [Cadiz] . . . contained the following named persons, with their families: Jacob Arnold, innkeeper; . . . James Simpson, reed-maker [and others].

+**Reed organ.** (See second quot. 1909.) {1879} — **1851** CIST *Cincinnati* 221 The largest business in this line, is . . . that of making melodeons or melopeans and reed organs. **1909** *Sears, Roebuck & Co. Cat. No.* 118, 175 Beckwith Organs. The World Famous Line of Reed Organs. Unapproachable in Beauty, Workmanship, Finish and Tone. **1909** WEBSTER 1791/1 Two prevailing types of reed organ are the *harmonium,* in which the air is forced out through the reeds . . . , and the *American organ,* in which the air is drawn through them inward.

+**Reed shop.** A shop for the sale of weavers' reeds. — **1831** PECK *Guide* 285 [Union Co.] has . . . one reed and two slæ shops.

+**Reedy.** = REEDBIRD. — **1856** *Porter's Spirit of Times* 11 Oct. 90/3 Niggers ain't fit to shoot reedies. *Ib.,* The small boy . . . volunteers some information about a 'ree-ee-dy' that he just saw.

* **Reef.** *attrib.* and *comb.* Designating various fishes, insects, and other animals that live on or near reefs.

1879 KILBOURNE & GOODE *Game Fishes U.S.* 37/1 In the Carolinas, Florida, and the Gulf, we meet with the names 'Bass,' and its variations, 'Spotted Bass,' 'Red Bass,' 'Sea Bass,' 'Reef Bass,' and 'Channel Bass.' **1869** *Amer. Naturalist* III. 352n., We could find no evidence that the reef-builders at the present time . . . are working upon so high a northern

line. **1888** TRUMBULL *Names of Birds* 1 *Branta canadensis.* . . . Canada Goose: Common Wild Goose. . . . At Morehead, North Carolina, Reef Goose. **1890** *Cent.* 4219/1 *Reef-oyster,* an oyster growing naturally on reefs; a reefer. (Alabama to Texas.) **1884** GOODE, etc. *Fisheries* I. 846 The finer qualities of the marketable kinds [are found] in the deepest water in which the species occur, except perhaps in the case of the Reef Sponge. *Ib.* 488 About Grand Traverse Bay, Lake Michigan, two varieties [of lake trout] . . . are known as 'Reef Trout,' or when very large are called 'Racers.'

Reefer. {1890-} +(See quotation.) — **1881** INGERSOLL *Oyster-Industry* 247 *Reefer,* a natural reef-growing or untransplanted oyster. (Mobile to Texas.)

+**Reef fishing.** 'Fishing on or from coral reefs. (Florida, U.S.)' (*Cent.*)

* **Reel,** *n.*[1]

* **1.** One of various rotatory contrivances on which threads, yarns, or lines may be easily wound up or unwound.

1673 *Essex Inst. Coll.* L. 27 The inventory of the estate [includes] . . . a meale trough, . . . a hogskin, a Reele. **1771** HABERSHAM *Letters* 146, There should be more Basons and Reels. **1846** THORPE *Myst. Backwoods* 159 When we first looked into his collection of rods, reels, hooks and swivels, we told him [etc.]. **1889** [see JUMPER[1] 5].

b. *Off the reel,* without stopping; immediately. {1866-} *Right off the reel,* see RIGHT OFF *adv.* b.

1825 NEAL *Bro. Jonathan* I. 156 So then, says he to me, says he; sharp off the reel;—as 'cute a feller, that, as ever you seed.

+**2.** On a reaping machine, a rotatory contrivance with horizontal bars at the ends of the radial arms, by which the grain is pressed toward the cutters.

1876 KNIGHT 1890/2 The machine . . . had a reel with twelve vanes to press the grain toward the cutter. **1879** *Scribner's Mo.* Nov. 134/2 The plentiful reaping-machines with . . . their great overwhelming 'reels.' **1899** *Sat. Ev. Post* 10 June 795 The platform conceived by Cyrus H. McCormick for receiving the cut grain deposited thereon by the reel, . . . remains the same in principle today.

+**3.** A length of motion-picture film rolled up on a reel.

1916 DU PUY *Uncle Sam* 199 Among the reels shown was one which portrayed a visit of the President to New York.

4. *attrib.* and *comb.* Designating persons who operate or make reels.

1787 FRENEAU *Misc. Works* 410 Poor Richard, the reel-man, had nothing to say. **1887** *Courier-Journal* 28 Jan. 8/5 John Crowder, reel driver for No. 7 Engine Company, had two fingers of his right hand cut off yesterday afternoon. *Ib.* 19 Feb. 5/4 (*headline*), Capt. B. C. Milam, the Celebrated Reel Manufacturer, Completes a Beautiful Present for Mr. Cleveland. **1918** *Nation* 7 Feb. 130/1 [In the] flax mill he had worked as reel boy.

* **Reel,** *n.*[2] A lively country-dance, as the Virginia reel; the music played for such a dance. — **1774** FITHIAN *Journal* I. 184 [She moves] without any Flirts or vulgar Capers, when She dances a Reel or Country-Dance. **1835** [see DOUBLE-SHUFFLE]. **1840** in Buckingham *E. & W. States* II. 28 The match . . . will consist of a variety of Breakdowns, Jigs, Reels, &c. **1882** [see CONTRA-DANCE]. **1886** Z. F. SMITH *Kentucky* 256 [He] began to whistle a familiar reel he was accustomed to play on the violin.

* **Reel,** *v.* **1.** *intr.* To wind *up* a fishing line on a reel. {1873-} **2.** *tr.* To draw *in* (a fish) with a reel. {1881-} — (1) *a*1846 *Quarter Race Ky.* 30, I let him [a shark] run about fifty yards, and then reeled up. (2) **1857** HAMMOND *Northern Scenes* 43 Think of reeling in a twenty-pound pickerel. **1876** *Fur, Fin & Feather* Sept. 132/1 The moment he yields, the fisherman begins to reel him in.

* **Reeler. 1.** An instrument for reeling silk, yarn, etc. {-1629} ***2.** A person who operates a reel. +**3.** A motion-picture film of a designated number of reels. — (1) **1658** *Southold Rec.* I. 449 An Inventorie of the personall estate whereof Elizabeth Payne widdow dyed [includes]: . . . a wheele & reeler. **1853** FELT *Customs New Eng.* 54 Since the factories of our country have done the work which they used to do, reelers are scarcely ever seen in any of our households. (2) **1848** *Rep. Comm. Patents* 1847 450 This enables the reeler . . . to unite both threads into one. **1887** *Consular Rep.* Jan. p. lxxxiv. (*Cent.*), The syndicate were able to advance somewhat the price of cocoons, and to induce the reelers to provide themselves liberally for fear of a further rise. (3) **1916** 'BOWER' *Phantom Herd* 69 We've made quite a haul since you left. A bunch of one-reelers from Bently Brown.

+**Re-eligibility.** Eligibility for re-election to office. — **1785** MADISON *Writings* II. 174 For neither branch [of the Legislature] does it seem necessary or proper to prohibit an indefinite re-eligibility. **1788** JEFFERSON *Writings* VI. 426 There is another strong feature in the new Constitution, which I . . . strongly dislike. That is, the perpetual re-eligibility of the President. **1854** BENTON *30 Years' View* I. 207/1 Every contrivance is vicious, and also inconsistent with the re-eligibility permitted by the constitution, which prevents the people from continuing a member as long as they deem him useful to them. **1888** BRYCE *Amer. Commw.* II. II. xlix. 103 Some States limit his re-eligibility; but in those which do not there seems to exist no tradition forbidding a third term.

Reemer. A workman who opens the seams of the planking of a ship, so that they may be calked. — **1822** *Ann. 17th Congress* 1 Sess. 279 The

President [shall submit] . . . the amount paid for . . . armorers, reemers, caulkers, . . . and other laborers.

Re-emit, *v. tr.* To emit again, +esp. to reissue (bank bills and notes). — 1739 W. DOUGLASS *Discourse Currencies* 10 The Province of the Massachusetts-Bay . . . have since A. 1702 emitted and re-emitted Bills of publick Credit. 1759 FRANKLIN *Works* (1840) III. 203 The trustees of the loan office might reëmit the same sums. 1884 *American* VIII. 311 The notes are not held, when redeemed, but re-emitted.

*✱**Reeve.** (See quotation and cf. HOGREEVE.) — 1890 *Cent.* 5031/2 *Reeve,* a steward; a prefect; a bailiff. . . . The word enters into the composition of some titles . . . , and is itself in use in Canada and in some parts of the United States.

Re-export. {1792-} +A commodity exported after being imported; the amount of such a commodity. — 1761 GLEN *Descr. S. California* 48 The Exports of South Carolina Produce are inserted in one Account, and the Re-exports of imported Commodities and Manufactures in another. 1874 RAYMOND *6th Rep. Mines* 524 Tabular statement of imports, exports, and re-exports of gold and silver coin and bullion from 1867 to 1873, inclusive.

✱**Refectory.**

+**1. a.** A saloon. **b.** 'An eating-house, restaurant' (B. '59). 1834 in *Atlantic Mo.* XXVI. 742 Proceeded to Springfield, along a fine turnpike road, thickly planted with sorry-looking refectories, or grog shops. 1840 [see DRINKERY]. 1852 *Harper's Mag.* Sept. 488/2, I was at Lawson's Refectory last night.

✱**2.** In certain schools or religious communities, a room or building for eating in common. 1851 HALL *College Words* 256 *Refectory.* . . . At Princeton College, this name is given to the hall where the students eat together in common. Abbreviated REFEC. 1866 *Rep. Indian Affairs* 122, I have . . . arrived at the conclusion that to erect the buildings for dormitories, refectories [etc.] . . . will require . . . $11,500. a1870 CHIPMAN *Notes on Bartlett* 359 *Refectory,* . . . the place where the students of the Theo[logical] Sem[inary] take their food. 1920 HOWELLS *Vacation of Kelwyns* 11 A dining-room which had been the Family refectory . . . looked eastward.

Referee. {1621-}

1. A person to whom, either alone or with others, a dispute is referred for decision. {1670-} a1626 in Neill *Virginia Carolorum* 51 The Def't further alleadged that Sir George Yardley payde the Defts himselfe . . . and offered to make proof of it to us the Referrees. 1742 *Boston Rec.* 302 Such Award or Arbitrement . . . [shall be] delivered as the Act of the Referrees Mutually Chosen by the said Agents. 1920 [see FAMILY 2].

b. (See quot. 1850.) 1850 BURRILL *Law Dict.* (1860) 395/1 *Referee,* . . . a person to whom a cause pending in a court is referred by the court, to take testimony, hear the parties and report thereon to the court, and upon whose report, if confirmed, judgment is entered. 1882 McCABE *New York* 286 The proceedings are private, the courts turning the whole matter over to a referee.

2. In games or sports, an official who makes the contestants observe the rules; an umpire. {c1860-} In certain games a distinction is made between an *umpire* and a *referee.* In football, for instance, the latter is the final judge of all disputes and, in general, is judge of matters connected with the progress of the ball, but not generally of the players' acts. 1845 *Big Bear Ark.* 33 He was a general referee and umpire, whether it was a horse swap, a race, a rifle match, or a cock fight. 1856 *Porter's Spirit of Times* 6 Dec. 229/1 In [baseball] matches, an umpire is chosen on each side, and a referee to decide, when the umpires cannot agree. 1881 in P. H. Davis *Football* (1911) 469 The referee shall disqualify a player whom he has warned three times for intentional off-side playing. 1907 *St. Nicholas* Sept. 1013/1 The duties of the two umpires will be clearly defined so as to place responsibility upon the proper shoulders, and also to further assist the referee.

✱**Reference.** +*Surveying.* An observation of position in terms of longitude and latitude or some known point. — 1804 CLARK in *Lewis & C. Exped.* I. (1904) 139 After this I will put the Course Destance & references of each day first and remks. after. 1816 U. BROWN *Journal* II. 231 The reference he must take, was to go back to the Large Poplar at the beginning & start fair.

Referendum. The practice or principle of submitting a legislative act to a vote of the people or members of an organization. {1882-, of non-British practice} Also attrib. (Cf. INITIATIVE.) — 1870 *Mass. Statistics Labor Rep.* I. 358 We want the referendum. 1896 *Typographical Jrnl.* IX. 61 [Some] are attempting to procure the submission to a referendum vote of a proposition for representation from each union in an international convention. 1911 *Okla. Session Laws* 3 Legisl. 236 When a citizen, or citizens, desire to circulate a petition . . . invoking a referendum upon legislative enactments, such citizen or citizens shall [etc.].

✱**Refiner.**

1. An apparatus for refining ore. *Obs.* 1624 SMITH *Gen. Hist. Va.* III. 68 We spent some time in refyning, having . . . a refyner fitted for that purpose. 1713 *Wyllys Papers* 380 He . . . will Erect . . . a good and Sufficient house that will hold and contain . . . Two Substantial Reverbatory furnaces, Vizt. a Smelter and a Refyner.

✱**2.** One who refines metals, oil, etc.; one who owns or operates a refinery. See also SUGAR-REFINER. 1794 *Ann. 3d Congress* 1421 For the several expenses of the Mint, including the pay of a Refiner, . . . two thousand seven hundred dollars. 1802 *Steele P.* I. 291 There is one consideration of great weight in favor of the construction contended for by the Refiners. 1880 in Tarbell *Hist. Standard Oil Co.* I. 277 The oil refiners of Cleveland came to affiant as a representative of transportation. 1904 TARBELL *Ib.* I. 29 Iron works at Oil City and Titusville promised soon to supply the needs of both drillers and refiners.

Refinery. A place or establishment for the refining of metals, sugar, etc. {1727-41-} See also OIL REFINERY, SUGAR REFINERY. 1833 SILLIMAN *Man. Sugar Cane* 76 We are not at liberty to state the details of the excellent apparatus, in the refinery of Canby and Lovering. 1862 *Trial C. M. Jefferds* 8 He had a distillery, or refinery, or some kind of an establishment of that kind. 1865 *Atlantic Mo.* April 394/1 The oil drawn into barrels is . . . carried to the local refinery. 1894 *Harper's Mag.* Jan. 419/2 Before the invention of Henry Cort in 1774, the various kinds of refineries of pig iron could be classified as the low-hearth refinery and the bloomary. 1904 TARBELL *Hist. Standard Oil Co.* I. 19 Some of the great refineries of the country grew out of these rude beginnings. *attrib.* 1844 *Lexington Observer* 9 Oct. 4/1 10 Bbls. New Orleans Refinery Molasses . . . for sale low. 1888 *Amer. Almanac* 275 Occupations of the People of the United States. . . . Oil, mill and refinery operatives.

Refining. {1604-} *attrib.* +Designating places where oil is refined. — 1875 in Tarbell *Hist. Standard Oil Co.* I. 149 There are five refining points in the country, Pittsburg, Philadelphia, Cleveland, the Oil Regions and New York city. 1880 *Ib.* 277 Cleveland was to be wiped out as a refining centre. 1883 *Century Mag.* July 332/2 The United Pipe Lines [is] a corporation . . . having its termini at the seaboard and at the three principal refining cities of the interior.

Refix, *v.* {1611-} +*tr.* To repair or refit (a boat). *Obs.* Also absol. — 1666 *S.C. Hist. Soc. Coll.* V. 69 Therefore to worke wee goe againe and refix our boate. 1710 *Essex Inst. Coll.* XLII. 252 Ye said Brigantun is unloaden & refixt at Jamaica. 1780 *Va. State P.* I. 343 It is hoped that his vessel has been sufficiently damaged, as to oblige him to go to some harbour to refix.

Reflector. {1665-}

+**1.** =DUTCH OVEN 2. Also attrib. 1839 KIRKLAND *New Home* 262 Will he find fault with the clay-built oven, or even the tin 'reflector?' 1853 McCONNEL *Western Char.* 268 The housewife . . . would have thrown a 'Yankee reflector' over the fence. 1885 *Century Mag.* April 838 The biscuits were baked in the tin reflector oven.

2. A specially prepared surface of glass or metal for reflecting light in a certain direction. {1797-} 1832 WILLIAMSON *Maine* I. 23 The Lighthouse is 67 feet in height, . . . containing 15 patent lamps with reflectors, on a revolving triangle. 1844 *Knickerb.* XXIV. 287 A score or more of 'burning and shining lights' [are] flashed back by huge polished steel reflectors. 1880 E. JAMES *Negro Minstrel's Guide* 12 Lights should be placed in brackets, with reflectors. 1901 MERWIN & WEBSTER *Calumet 'K'* 19 A wall lamp, set in a dull reflector, threw shadows into the corners.

+**Reflunk,** *v. intr.* (See quotation.) *slang.* — 1829 *Va. Lit. Museum* 30 Dec. 460 To reflunk, 'to retreat, to back out.' Western States.

Reform. {1663-} *attrib.* Designating various parties, meetings, etc., connected with political and social reform. {1831-} 1851 COMMONS, etc. *Doc. Hist.* VIII. 317 A National Reform Convention is however to be held. 1857 *Atlantic Mo.* Nov. 74/2 Horatio and I one day looked in upon a reform meeting. 1874 Reform ticket [see GREELEY]. 1887 *Courier-Journal* 8 Feb. 1/2 The Reform Democrats Manage to Get Mr. Randall Into Very Deep Water. 1894 WISTER in *Harper's Mag.* Aug. 385/1 She was president of the Ladies' Reform and Literary Lyceum. 1901 DUNCAN & SCOTT *Allen & Woodson Co., Kansas* 599 In 1873 what was known as the Reform party was organized by Democrats and former Republicans. 1904 A. FRENCH *Barrier* 22 The reform politicians, those bees who buzzed continually and occasionally stung, had been after the young man.

Reformatory. An institution in which juvenile offenders are imprisoned and instructed; also, such a place for women. {1837-} — 1870 *N.Y. Laws* I. 320 The action of the commissioners . . . in locating said prison or industrial reformatory . . . at Elmira . . . is hereby approved. 1872 BRACE *Dangerous Classes N.Y.* 33 In the Reformatories of the country, . . . twenty-seven per cent. [of the inmates in 1868] were wholly illiterate. 1878 *Harper's Mag.* Dec. 109/1 Our reformatories . . . do not check the first steps in wrong-doing. 1887 *Courier-Journal* 16 Jan. 9/7 Sister Mary St. Ancelian, Mother Superior at the reformatory, . . . [asked the police] to take special pains to capture the runaway girls. 1912 NICHOLSON *Hoosier Chron.* 53 They were going to cut down the Reformatory's appropriation last winter.

Reform club. +A club organized to promote temperance. Also attrib. — 1877 *Mich. Gen. Statutes* I. (1882) 154 Reform club temperance societies may be incorporated in pursuance of the provisions of this act.

1882 RITTENHOUSE *Maud* 124 Then the Reform Club was organized, Mr Dietrich signed the pledge and now all is well with them.

* **Reformed,** *a.* Belonging to a church in some way changed or purified; having the views of a reformed church. Usually in specific names.

1648 *Platform Church-Discipline* (1772) 11 He joineth himself to another congregation more reformed. *c*1792 COXE *View U.S.* 373 There are and have been in the legislative, executive and judicial branches of the general government, persons of the following denominations—Episcopalian, . . . Reformed, Roman, and probably others. **1837** PECK *Gaz. Illinois* 73 A Seminary is about being established in a settlement of Reformed Presbyterians. **1844** Rupp *Relig. Denominations* 466 The Reformed Methodists took their origin from a feeble secession from the Methodist Episcopal Church, in . . . 1814. *Ib.* 502 Reformed Mennonite Society. **1847** DAVIDSON *Presbyterian Ch. in Ky.* 216 Campbellites . . . affected the title of Reformers, or Reformed Baptists, and spoke of 'The Reformation' as if there had never been any Reformation before. **1849** CHAMBERLAIN *Ind. Gazetteer* 189 The town contains . . . churches for the Episcopal and Reformed Methodists.

* **Reformed church.** A Protestant church brought to a better or purer state, esp. a Calvinistic body as distinguished from a Lutheran. Often in the official names of churches.

[**1617** BREWSTER in Bradford *Hist.* 44 Touching ye Ecclesiasticall ministrie, . . . we doe wholy . . . agree with ye French reformed churches.] **1670** I. MATHER *Life R. Mather* 51 [Many] Renowned Non-Conformists have scrupled Preaching Funerall Sermons; Also in some Reformed Churches that practice is wholly omitted. **1796** MORSE *Univ. Geog.* I. 545 The Germans [in Penna.] . . . consist of Lutherans, . . . Calvinists or reformed church, Moravians [and others]. **1807** *Ann. 10th Congress* 1 Sess. 1215 Mr. Findley . . . reported a bill for incorporating the Associate Reformed Church, in the City of Washington. **1850** HALE *M. Percival in Amer.* 264 Her first welcome was from one of the 'Reformed Church,' in New York. **1892** *York County Hist. Rev.* 76/2 Mr. Miller . . . [is] a devoted member and substantial aid to the Reformed Church.

* **Reformer.**

+**1. a.** (See quotation.)

1831 PECK *Guide* 258 The Reformers, or Methodist Protestant church, have several societies and preachers in the State [of Ill.].

+**b.** A Campbellite.

1834 PECK *Gaz. Illinois* 91 The Cambellites, or 'Reformers,' as they usually term themselves, have several large, and a number of smaller societies. **1837** *Ib.* (ed. 2) 215 A college . . . is contemplated to be brought into operation by the Baptist Reformers. **1850** GALLAHER *Western Sketch-Book* 222 Those of other denominations came,—the Methodists, the Campbellites, or Reformers, the Baptists, also. **1871** [see CAMPBELLITE 1].

* **2.** One who effects or advocates reform in politics, social matters, etc.

1848 GARRISON in W. P. & F. J. Garrison *W. L. Garrison* III. 231 Miss Thayer . . . [is] a 'Garrisonian' abolitionist, and a thoroughgoing reformer. **1857** *Atlantic Mo.* Nov. 74/2 The platform was crowded with male and female reformers. **1885** CRAWFORD *Amer. Politician* 59 John Harrington was a reformer. . . . He believed in an established Civil Service, in something which, if not exactly Free Trade, was much nearer to it than the existing tariff. **1902** MEYER *Nominating Systems* 70 The legalization of the caucus is often largely a semblance of reform, because many of the 'reformers' act under false pretenses.

+**Reform school.** (See quot. 1859.) — **1847** *Mass. Acts. & Resolves* 405 There shall be established, in the town of Westborough, . . . a school, for the . . . reformation of juvenile offenders, to be called the State Reform School. **1859** BARTLETT 359 *Reform School*, a school for the confinement, instruction, and reformation of juvenile offenders, and of young persons of idle, vicious, and vagrant habits. **1872** [see HOUSE OF REFUGE]. **1880** HOWELLS *Undiscovered Country* 133 You hain't any of them that's escaped from the reform school? **1913** LONDON *Valley of Moon* 3 An' her with seven, an' two of 'em in reform school.

* **Refreshing,** *a.* That refreshes the spirit or mind. {1823}

1697 SEWALL *Diary* I. 447 These thoughts were very refreshing to me. **1723** Sewall *Letter-Book* I. 14 It was exceedingly refreshing to me to hear from an ancient Acquaintance and so worthy a Friend as your Self. **1776** in Temple & Sheldon *Hist. Northfield, Mass.* 327 We had refreshing news that our men were returning to the camp. **1822** IRVING *Bracebridge Hall* I. 103 It was quite *refreshing* . . . when, in the course of the morning, a horn blew. **1858** SUMNER in S. Longfellow *H. W. Longfellow* II. 360 It is refreshing to be with persons whose knowledge and sympathies are so gratifying. **1893** *Nation* 31 Aug. 145/2 Mr. Johnson has a refreshing habit of frankness.

* **Refreshment.** *attrib.*

1. Designating various places where refreshments may be taken. {1849-}

1850 *Knickerb.* XXXVI. 288 Stepping to the refreshment-house, I heard [etc.]. **1855** M. THOMPSON *Doesticks* 136 Wherever a refreshment-table is spread, every man seems to regard it as his duty to fill himself to the very lips with all the 'delicacies of the season.' **1858** VIELÉ *Following Drum* 45 The principal public buildings at Whitehall seemed to be railroad depôts and refreshment saloons. **1863** A. D. WHITNEY *F. Gartney* xxxvi, Glory had already . . . given her a cake to eat from the refreshment

counter. **1907** *St. Nicholas* July 790 Here and there beneath the trees stood free refreshment stalls.

2. Designating persons or groups of persons who serve refreshments.

1866 MOORE *Women of War* 590 These ladies . . . and some others, formed the nucleus of the Cooper Shop Volunteer Refreshment Committee. **1880** 'MARK TWAIN' *Tramp Abroad* 335 The road was simply paved with refreshment-peddlers.

Refrigerant. {1676-} A freezing agent. — **1885** *Scientific Amer.* 9 May 291/3 Some experiments . . . appear to show that liquid oxygen is one of the best of refrigerants. **1887** *Courier-Journal* 22 Jan. 6/6 Carbonic Acid Gas to Replace Ice as a Refrigerant.

Refrigerating. {1684-} *attrib.* Designating containers fitted up as refrigerators. — **1869** *Rep. Comm. Patents 1868* I. 774/2 [The] Refrigerating Car . . . has a plurality of metallic chambers for the respective reception of 'way' and 'through' freight. **1875** *Chicago Tribune* 6 Oct. 4/1 The capitals of Europe are to be congratulated upon the successful transportation of American fruit to the English ports by the refrigerating-box plan.

Refrigerator. {1611-}

1. a. A box, room, or railroad car for keeping food or other articles cool. {1861-} **b.** An apparatus for rapidly cooling liquids, etc. {1824-}

1824 *Niles' Reg.* 19 June 253/1 He makes and sells . . . butter boxes, constructed on the principle, and somewhat on the plan of his excellent refrigerators. **1833** A. FERGUSSON *Notes Tour U.S.* 211 A *refrigerator*. This is a wooden chest. . . . There is a drawer or space at the bottom, to be filled with ice. **1838** *N.Y. Advertiser & Exp.* 7 Feb. 2/4 Since the introduction in this city of that most valuable utensil, the refrigerator, . . . the consumption of ice has greatly increased. **1871** W. G. CAMPBELL *New World* 193 Ice . . . is then kept in what is called a 'refrigerator.' **1874** KNIGHT 265/1 Fig. 632 shows a form of beer-cooler in which the kegs are kept in a refrigerator. **1879** BISHOP *4 Months in Sneak-Box* 256 They were packed in the refrigerator of a fleet-sailing boat. **1883** KNIGHT *Suppl.* 747/2 The storage, domestic, and railway car refrigerators are referred to. **1890** *Stock Grower & Farmer* 22 March 4/1 The refrigerators . . . are the cheapest and best and most economical means by which beef has ever been killed and cured. **1913** LONDON *Valley of Moon* 233 From the refrigerator he gave her all the ice she wished to carry.

+**2.** = COOLER 5. *slang.*

1883 HAY *Bread-Winners* 237 Have our prisoners taken down to the Refrigerator and turned over to the ordinary police.

3. *attrib.* **a.** Designating containers used for keeping things cool.

1871 *Vermont Bd. Agric. Rep.* IV. 50 In this shape the butter is packed in refrigerator cases. **1878** *Scientific Amer.* XXXIX. 290/2 New Refrigerator Basket. . . . [It] is designed as a receptacle for meat, butter, fish, and other perishable articles, for transporting and preserving them in hot weather. **1884** *Nat. Museum Bul.* No. 27, 1051 *Refrigerator oyster can.* Sheet-metal refrigerating can for oysters in bulk.

b. Designating persons or organizations whose business is connected with refrigeration.

1890 *Stock Grower & Farmer* 11 Jan. 5/2 Local slaughterers (the refrigerator men) have used a much larger number [of sheep] than ever before. **1893** AULD *Picturesque Burlington* 158 Many of these industries have established more than local fame, among the best known of which . . . [is] the Baldwin Refrigerator Co.

+**Refrigerator beef.** Beef stored or transported in refrigerators. — **1881** *Chicago Times* 4 June, American refrigerator beef sold at London and Liverpool to-day at 5½ d.

+**Refrigerator car.** A railroad car so constructed as to be kept artificially cool for the transportation of butter, meats, etc. — **1868** *Rep. Comm. Patents 1867* II. 1386/2 Refrigerator Car. . . . The air from the upper part of the inside of the car passes down through the ice chamber. **1872** *Vermont Bd. Agric. Rep.* I. 159 Previous to the time when refrigerator cars for conveying butter were put on the road, there was not even a 'butter day' here. **1881** *Chicago Times* 4 June, A Tiffany refrigerator-car will leave Chicago on Tuesday of each week. **1890** *Stock Grower & Farmer* 4 Jan. 4/3 The equivalent of nearly three car loads of cattle on the hoof can be packed in one of the new refrigerator cars. **1920** COOPER *Under Big Top* 237 Eighty miles away they found him, where he had ridden cramped, and half-frozen, in a refrigerator car.

Refugee, *n.* {1685-}

+**1.** An emigrant to America, as a French Huguenot, seeking refuge from religious or political persecution in Europe.

1704 *Va. State P.* I. 84 Diverse petitions [had been] heretofore presented by the ffrench Refugees, settled at Manicantown, praying for naturalizacon. **1882** *Nation* 20 July 44/3 Fifty-one families of Russian refugees, who came to this country a few months ago, returned to Europe on Friday, having failed to get work.

2. +**a.** A loyalist during the Revolutionary War who sought refuge under the protection of the British crown.

1778 T. HUTCHINSON *Diary & Lett.* II. 218 [Penobscot] is to be erected into a new Province, and to be given to the Refugees, upon the same quitrents as the N. Hampshire and other Grantees. **1783** *N.Y. City during*

Amer. Rev. (1861) 141 A very considerable embarkation of Refugees took place last week bound for Nova Scotia & Canada. **1797** *Encycl. Brit.* (ed. 3) XVI. 51/1 Since the revolt of the British Colonies in America, we have frequently heard of American refugees. **1888** LOWELL *Lit. & Polit. Addresses* 203 Most of the refugees who, during or after the Revolutionary War, went to England . . . found themselves out of place.

+b. A marauding Tory, esp. of New York State, fighting in guerrilla bands during the Revolutionary War.

Cf. COWBOY 1.

1780 J. ANDRÉ (*title*), The Cow-Chace, In Three Cantos, Published on Occasion of the Rebel General Wayne's Attack of the Refugees' Block-House On Hudson's River. **1781** *Md. Hist. Mag.* V. 129 The refugees in general were a set of gallows-marked rascals, fit for nothing but thieves. **1821** COOPER *Spy* xviii, The Cow-boys were sometimes called Refugees.

+3. A Canadian or Nova Scotian who came to help the United States during the Revolutionary War.

1783 *Jrnls. Cont. Congress* XXIV. 268 There are now serving in the Regiment . . . officers and men chiefly Refugees from Canada. **1785** *Ib.* XXVIII. 258 Whenever Congress can consistently make grants of land, they will reward . . . such refugees from Nova Scotia, as may be disposed to live in the Western country. **1796** *Ann. 4th Congress* 2 Sess. 1728 A tract of land . . . [shall] be immediately appropriated to compensate the refugees from the British provinces of Canada and Nova Scotia.

+4. During the Civil War, a person who left his home in order to seek refuge or to aid the other side.

1865 *Statutes at Large* XIII. 508 The Secretary of War may direct such issues of provisions, clothing, and fuel, as he may deem needful for the . . . supply of destitute and suffering refugees and freedmen and their wives and children. **1866** *Amer. Ann. Cycl. 1865* 393/1 A large number of refugees, who are returning to their homes on Government transportation, also receive their subsistence here [in Atlanta]. **1870** O. LOGAN *Before Footlights* 203 There were loyal refugees and rebel refugees. **1888** GRIGSBY *Smoked Yank* (1891) 236 The great fire [of Columbia, S.C.] . . . left thousands of people houseless and homeless. Many of these applied for permission to accompany our army when we continued our march. They were called refugees. **1896** [see HOME GUARD].

5. *attrib.* **+a.** In sense 2 with *horse, troop.*

1780 *Heath P.* III. 32 Colonel Delancy was with the refugee horse. **1823** THACHER *Military Jrnl.* 183 A captain of Colonel Delany's battalion of refugee troops, with about one hundred American royal regulars, was posted near a river.

+b. In sense 3 with *claim, land, tract.*

1812 *Niles' Reg.* II. 13/2 The speaker laid before the house . . . [a letter] on the subject of the refugee claims. **1812** MELISH *Travels* II. 222 A stripe of land about three miles broad, and 42 miles long . . . was appropriated to the relief of such as had to abandon their settlements in the time of the war, and take refuge in other places, and is thence called *refugee land.* **1837** W. JENKINS *Ohio Gaz.* 371 Refugee tract, . . . a narrow strip of country, 4½ miles broad from north to south, and extending eastwardly from the Scioto river, 48 miles.

+c. In sense 4 with *stirrup, style, train.*

The meaning of *r. stirrup* is uncertain.

1864 CUMMING *Hospital Life* (1866) 146/2 His two daughters were with him, and were keeping house in *two* rooms, refugee style. **1886** *Harper's Mag.* June 56/2 One was a side-saddle and another was an army saddle with refugee stirrups. **1888** GRIGSBY *Smoked Yank* (1891) 236 General Hazen asked me to take charge of the refugee train that was assigned to his division.

+Refugee, *v.*

A British example of 1750 in sense 2 is presumably a nonce use.

1. *tr.* To cause (a person) to become a refugee. Also *ppl. a.*

1806 HAWKINS *Letters* 429 It will be some time before the Creek young will get rid of the remains of that alloy which debased the agents and refugeed their associates. **1866** W. REID *After the War* 250 Many of his pupils were . . . negroes that had been 'refugeed' from the Red River country. **1874** COLLINS *Kentucky* I. 162 [There have been] about 1,200 deaths, within the year past, among the negroes refugeed at Camp Nelson.

2. *intr.* To seek or take refuge.

1864 CUMMING *Hospital Life* (1866) 157/2 Many of the citizens of Mobile . . . had *refugeed* from fear of an attack. **1877** *Harper's Mag.* Dec. 79/2 An old slave . . . told me she 'refugeed' from Virginia during the war. **1893** PAGE *Ib.* Dec. 18/1 After this thousands flocked to the city [Richmond], 'refugeeing' before the invading armies. **1904** R. E. LEE *Recoll. Gen. Lee* 270 In the early years of the struggle, my mother and sisters, when 'refugeeing,' had boarded . . . at his home.

+Refugee bean. A variety of snap bean, ? brought over by European refugees. — **1859** *Ill. Agric. Soc. Trans.* III. 503 The refugee bean (long, dark clouded,) has the same characteristics.

Refuse fish. (See quot. 1674.) — **1654** *Suffolk Deeds* II. 43 Twenty pownds in Currant mony beauer wheate butter or good refuse fish to be deliuered at Boston the first day of Nouember next at mony price. **1674** JOSSELYN *Two Voyages* 210 When they share their fish . . . they separate the best from the worst, . . . the second sort they call refuse fish, that is

such as is salt burnt, spotted, rotten, and carelessly ordered. **1710** *Essex Inst. Coll.* LVI. 283 Charles Pynn is . . . [credited with] 2 Qtls Refuse fish, 14 s. **1857** [see ROCK *n.* 13].

+Refuse (public) land. Pieces of comparatively undesirable public land either taken up last by settlers or left altogether unclaimed. *Obs.* — **1832** CLAY *Speeches* 225 This pretension may be . . . to graduate the public lands to reduce the price, and to cede the 'refuse' lands (a term which I believe originated with him [*i.e.*, Benton]) to the States within which they lie. **1838** *Indiana H. Rep. Jrnl.* 23 Sess. 506 A memorial and joint resolution on the subject of the refuse lands in the counties of Jackson, Scott, and Clark. **1845** *Indiana Senate Jrnl.* 29 Sess. 541 A joint resolution on the subject of the refuse public lands in Indiana.

Regalia. [Sp., 'royal privilege.'] A large cigar of a superior quality. {1874}

1839 BRIGGS *H. Franco* I. 28 He smoked none but the best regalias, which cost him three cents apiece. **1845** *S. Lit. Messenger* XI. 109/2 The meerschaum is not dearer to the German, than the regalia to the American student. **1856** *Porter's Spirit of Times* 15 Nov. 173/1 Monsieur Guerin . . . drew forth a regalia, lighting it from a coal raked out from the wood fire. **1870** TOMES *Decorum* 118 It is, moreover, a paltry ambition . . . to aspire to the distinction of being pointed out as . . . [the girl] who smoked one of Frank Tripup's fifty-cent regalias. **1909** WEBSTER 1795/2.

attrib. and *comb.* **1851** HALL *Manhattaner* 158 The fog . . . [was] as disagreeable to breathe as the smoke of a cabbage-leaf regalia cigar. **1869** *Boyd's Business Directory* 15 Tapping I. Pryor, regalia manufr.

+Regardless, *adv.* Ellipt. for *regardless of cost* (or *labor, consequences,* etc.); in spite of all. *colloq.* — **1872** 'MARK TWAIN' *Roughing It* 334 We are going to get the thing [*sc.* funeral] up regardless, you know. **1896** *Advance* 30 July 150 Miss Bond got herself up regardless, and came in resplendent in ruby velvet and white swansdown. **1904** W. H. SMITH *Promoters* 106 The stock certificates were gotten out regardless. **1911** QUICK *Yellowstone Nights* 289 We got . . . messages from him to rush S.F. 41144 to its passage, regardless.

Regatta. {1652–} A boat or yacht race, or a series of such races. {1775–} — **1835** *Harvardiana* II. 108 What a glorious regatta we might have. **1846** *Spirit of Times* 16 May 138/1 The Annual Regatta of the New York Yacht Club will come off on Thursday morning. **1856** *Porter's Spirit of Times* 4 Oct. 75/1.The third annual regatta of . . . [the San Francisco Yacht Club] came off in the harbor of San Francisco. **1883** *Century Mag.* Oct. 905/1 There is going to be a Ree-gatta on the river the day after tomorrow. **1905** *Ib.* Aug. 493/2 The English background lacks the gay and colorful beauty of our panoramic regattas.

∗Regency. **+ =** ALBANY REGENCY. Now hist. Also attrib. — **1830** Weed *Autobiog.* 367 Every day seems to drive it [the 'Old Elm Tree' establishment] farther from the Regency. **1830** WEED in Barnes *Mem. T. Weed* 40 Against the Regency, with its money, backed by 20,000 Masons, with their zeal, . . . how could there have been any other result? **1832** *Congress. Deb.* 13 March 2120 My honorable colleague, unwilling to submit to the drilling of the regency leaders, has taken the field 'upon his own hook.' *a*1882 WEED *Autobiog.* 121 Of the eight senators elected, six were Clintonians, and two Regency men.

Regenerator. {1740–} **+** (See quotation.) — **1871** *Harper's Mag.* Sept. 603 General Connor . . . and others who sided with him, in attempting to bring about a harmony between the people of Utah and the institutions of the republic, were stigmatized by the church party as 'The Regenerators.'

∗Regent.

+1. a. A member of a board governing a single state university or college, or supervising all the state schools, or other special educational institutions.

1813 *Niles' Reg.* V. 79/2 The regents of the university, expressly endeavored to effect this important object. **1838** (*title*), Annual Report of the Regents of the University of the State of New York. **1851** HALL *College Words* 256 Regent, . . . in the State of New York, the member of a corporate body which is invested with the superintendence of all the colleges, academies, and schools in the state. **1853** *Mich. Agric. Soc. Trans.* IV. 9 The legislature may . . . place the same [school] under the supervision of the Regents of the University. **1890** *Stock Grower & Farmer* 6 Sept. 3/1 The Board of Regents of the Agricultural College of New Mexico have issued invitations to the ceremonies of laying the corner stone of the college edifice. **1911** *Okla. Session Laws* 3 Legisl. 121 The Board of Regents of the State University . . . shall have the following . . . powers and duties [etc.].

+b. A member of the governing board of the Smithsonian Institute.

1846 POLK *Diary* (1929) 146, I rode out in my carriage to meet the regents of the Smithsonian Institute on the public grounds. **1906** *N.Y. Ev. Post* 1 Dec. 1 The regents of the Smithsonian Institution assemble for their annual meeting next Tuesday.

+2. In Harvard University, a disciplinary officer.

1814 *Harvard Laws* 7 The Regent and Proctors, shall reside in the College. **1851** HALL *College Words* 256 All weekly lists of absences, monitor's bills, petitions to the Faculty for excuse of absences [etc.] . . . are left with the Regent. **1902** CORBIN *Amer. at Oxford* 275 A Regent has among other duties a general charge of the rooms the fellows live in, and usually makes each room and its occupant a yearly visit.

+**3.** *pl.* The members of the Albany regency.

1838 *N.Y. Advertiser & Exp.* 6 Jan. 4/2 The Regents' skill, the Regents' power, Have vanished in a single hour.

+**Regidor.** *S.W.* [Sp.] A municipal officer: (see quotations). — **1834** A. PIKE *Sketches* 170 The Regidor, or Assistant Alcalde, Miguel Sena, has only perjured himself three times. **1838** C. NEWELL *Revol. Texas* 200 [Col. Bradburn] attempted to arrest George M. Patrick, the first Regidor, and acting Alcalde of Anahuac. **1848** BRYANT *California* xxii. 283 The first of these pueblos is governed by its corresponding body of magistrates, composed of an alcalde or judge, four regidores or municipal officers, a syndic and secretary. **1895** G. KING *New Orleans* 115 Instead of a superior council, there was a cabildo, with regidores, alcaldes, alguazils, alferez [etc.].

* **Regiment.** *Mil.* A body of soldiers commanded by a colonel; an army unit variously composed of battalions, a band, etc.

1654 JOHNSON *Wonder-w. Prov.* 191 The Government is divided into four Counties, . . . each containing a Regiment, over whom the chief Commander is only a Serjeant-Major. **1711** *Boston News-Letter* 11 June 2/2 In an Hours time the Troop of Guards and Regiment were under Arms. **1776** [see GRENADIER]. **1806** *Ann. 9th Congress* 1 Sess. 1250 The colonel or commanding officer of the regiment or garrison. **1861** *Army Regulations* 497 Vacancies occurring among the commissioned officers in volunteer regiments will be filled by the Governors of the respective States by which the regiments were furnished. **1890** [see CLOG-DANCER]. **1924** *Va. Adjt. General's Rep. 1922-23* 6 One regiment of light field artillery . . . [is] now being organized at Richmond.

Regimental, *n. pl.* The military uniform worn by soldiers of a particular regiment. {1742-} — **1754** WASHINGTON *Writings* I. 80 Regimentals . . . were not to be bought for less Virginia currency, than British officers could get for sterling money. **1771** *N.H. Prov. Papers* VII. 280, I order'd a compleat Suit of Regimentals to each Man as a Bounty for Enlistment. **1780** *Heath P.* III. 112 [Major André] was most elegantly dressed in his full regimentals. **1860** CLAIBORNE *Sam. Dale* 133 General Claiborne had presented him [*sc.* an Indian chief] with a splendid suit of regimentals. **1903** Fox *Little Shepherd* xviii, That fancy was that Chad should go in regimentals, as the stern old soldier on the wall.

Regimental, *a.* {1702-} Of persons: Belonging to a regiment. — **1778** Regimental commissioned officer [see CASTOR HAT]. **1781** *Va. State P.* I. 488 Several regimental pay-masters . . . are out of employ. **1816** *Ann. 14th Congress* 2 Sess. 273 Regimental quartermasters [shall be entitled] to the pay . . . of a lieutenant of infantry. **1866** 'F. KIRKLAND' *Bk. Anecdotes* 622/2 [She was] honored with the position of regimental bugler. **1917** J. A. MOSS *Officers' Manual* 485 *Regimental Monkey*, the drum major.

Regimental coat. A coat worn by members of a particular regiment. — **1781** *Va. State P.* I. 564 The tailors make '50 to 60 regimental coats a week' and are kept closely at work. **1787** TYLER *Contrast* II. i, This coat was my regimental coat in the late war.

* **Register,** *n.¹*

***1.** One of various public officers charged with making and keeping records of certain transactions, facts, or events: (see quotations). Usually an official title. {-1837}

See also COUNTY REGISTER.

1638 in J. Coffin *Hist. Newbury* 29 Edward Rawson shall . . . be the publick notary and register for the towne of Newbury. **1687** *Mass. H. S. Coll.* 4 Ser. V. 158 The late Secretary of our Colony [was required] to bring down all our books, records, and writings to the Secretary's or Register's office at Boston. **1709** *N.J. Archives* 1 Ser. III. 456 The said Barclay . . . moved the said court for a months time to answer the said bill, as this deponent is informed by the Register of the court. **1739** *Boston Gazette* 17 Dec. 3/1 John Boydell . . . came over from England into this Country in the Year 1716. . . . Register of the Court of Vice-Admiralty for this Province, New Hampshire, and Rhode-Island. **1784** FILSON *Kentucke* 38 A copy of the record must be . . . produced to the assistant register of the land-office. **1789** *Ann. 1st Congress* 78, I nominate, for the Department of the Treasury of the United States, . . . Joseph Nourse, (in office,) Register. **1831** PECK *Guide* 257 The officers in a land district are a Register and Receiver. **1852** *Whig Almanac* 1853 14/2 Holders or assignees of land warrants, on entering lands, are required to pay to the Register, the same compensation [etc.]. *a***1882** in McCabe *New York* 122 The Sheriff, County Clerk, District Attorney and Register, are the principal other officials. **1902** *Rep. Librarian of Congress* 44 The Register of Copyrights in his report . . . calls special attention to the need of indexing the earlier series of recorded books.

+**b.** *Register of deeds*, an official who registers deeds.

1735 *Boston Rec.* 129 The Town will proceed to the Choice of a . . . Register of Deeds for the County of Suffolk. **1777** *Essex Inst. Coll.* XLII. 315 Y[ou]r Brother is register of deeds. **1804** *Mass. Spy* 24 Oct. (Th.), Samuel Bartlett, Register of Deeds in Cambridge. **1857** *Lawrence* (Kan.) *Republican* 4 June 1 E. D. Ladd, Notary Public, Register of Deeds and Conveyancer. **1913** *Indian Laws & Tr.* III. 573 Copies [of a roll of the Chippewa Indians] may be made and filed for record with the registers of deeds of the various counties.

+**2.** (See quotation.)

1851 HALL *College Words* 257 *Register*, in Union College, an officer whose duties are similar to those enumerated under Registrar.

* **Register,** *n.²* (See also CASH REGISTER.)

***1.** A record of names, facts, transactions, or events; a book bearing this record.

1646 *Plymouth Laws* 85 A Clark . . . [shall be] appoynted and ordained to keep a Register of the day and yeare of the marriage byrth and buriall of every man weoman and child. **1722** FRANKLIN *Writings* II. 33 Two thousand Women . . . Enter their Names into a Register . . . with the Place of their abode. **1839** *S. Lit. Mess.* V. 100/1, I objected to his answering the question, if there was a register anywhere of the son's birth. **1870** [see FLAG *n.²* 4]. **1907** LONDON *Road* 85 [In] the office of the Erie County Penitentiary . . . we were to register, and on that register one or the other of my names will be found.

comb. **1646** *Plymouth Laws* 86 Every father, or mother . . . shall certify to the Towne clerk or register keeper, the name and day of the birth of every child.

b. An official document which describes a ship and records its owner or owners. {1825-}

1725 *Essex Inst. Coll.* XLV. 96 Ye said Colley kept ye sd Skooner in custody with ye Register. **1753** *Georgia Col. Rec.* VI. 396 Mr. Alexander Wylly of Savannah Merchant applyed to the Board for a New Register for a Schooner. **1818** *Niles' Reg.* XV. 104/1 Taylor swears, that he is . . . the sole owner of the schr. Romp, for which vessel he was then taking out a register.

+**c.** A book in which guests at a hotel, inn, etc., register their names.

1856 *Harper's Mag.* Dec. 66/2 He has nothing to do but to wander off to his hotel to look at the register and see if any body has come. **1871** HOWELLS *Wedding Journey* 98 The wayfarer . . . meekly wrote his name in the register. **1886** JAMES *Bostonians* 123 He had begun his career, at the age of fourteen, by going the rounds of the hotels, to cull flowers from the big, greasy registers which lie on the marble counters. **1902** HARBEN *A. Daniel* 151 Wilson is at the hotel. I saw his name on the register this morning.

2. A contrivance, as a metal plate, by which the draft can be regulated on a stove or furnace. {1610-}

1744 FRANKLIN *Works* I. (1887) 501 There are, moreover, two thin plates of wrought iron, viz., the shutter (vii.), and the register (viii.). **1815-16** *Niles' Reg.* IX. Suppl. 183/2 At about 6 o'clock in the morning the wood is nearly carbonated when the register is let down. **1897** F. C. MOORE *How to Build a Home* 56 The principal register of a furnace should always be so secured that it cannot be closed.

+**3.** A contrivance over an opening in the wall or floor of a room, by means of which the flow of heated air from a furnace can be regulated; also, the opening through which the air flows.

1847 *Rep. Comm. Patents 1846* 30 The openings from these furnaces, in the floors or walls of apartments, are usually covered with a kind of revolving valve, called the register. **1860** EMERSON *Conduct of Life* 133 People . . . who coddle themselves, who toast their feet on the register. **1883** *Century Mag.* May 158/1 The key of the book-case fell down the register last year. **1906** FREEMAN *By Light of Soul* 309 He found his mother warming herself by the sitting-room register.

* **Register,** *v.*

+**1.** *intr.* To record one's name, address, etc., in the register of a hotel.

1850 REID *Rifle Rangers* (1853) 41 Don't register till I come—I'll attend to that. **1879** BURDETTE *Hawkeyes* 62 Abou Tamerlik . . . , as he registered, spake cheerfully unto the clerk. **1893** 'MARK TWAIN' *£1,000,000 Banknote* 46, [I] registered at the Arlington Hotel, and went to my room. **1912** CROLY *M. A. Hanna* 459 Whenever prominent men registered at the hotel, Mr. Hanna managed to meet them.

2. a. *tr.* To put the name of (a voter) in a poll book. **b.** *intr.* To have one's name, address, etc., recorded in a poll book. {1832- (*Act 2 Will. IV* c. 65)}

(a) 1869 *Mich. Gen. Statutes* I. (1882) 129 The electors of each district shall vote in the respective districts . . . for which they are registered. **1889** *Century Mag.* Jan. 407/2, I ain't registered nuther. **1900** *Congress. Rec.* 4 Feb. 1800/2 Are your voters registered? **(b) 1900** *Ib.* 25 Jan. 1173/1 The exclusion of those who attempted to register was on account of the nonpayment of their taxes. **1903** HART *Actual Govt.* 205 Tramps and outcasts . . . are sometimes allowed to register from some place where they occasionally spend the night, and to vote.

+**3. a.** *tr.* To enroll (a student) in a school, or in various study and recitation classes. **b.** *intr.* To enroll in a school or class.

1894 *Univ. Chicago Register* 166/2 The student must register for each quarter. **1904** *N.Y. Tribune* 15 May, With less than 20 students to register, the founders of this beneficent work opened the school doors in November. **1905** *Univ. Chicago Official Publ.* IV. 7 To register for work.— After consultation with the Dean the student will enter on the registration card the courses which he desires to take. **1924** *Univ. Chicago Register* 103 Register, in the same office, for the courses of study desired for the ensuing quarter. **1925** F. B. O'REAR *Duties of Registrar* 154 Forms [are] presented for use in admitting students, in registering them for work, and providing course cards.

Registered, *a.* {1674–}

1. Of mail: Entered, for a special fee, in a special record in the post office, in order to insure greater security of delivery. {1874}

1872 *Pat. Off. Gazette* II. 653/2 Registered-Package Envelope.—William F. McCrary, Baker county, Oregon. 1886 *Statutes at Large* XXIV. 234 For transportation of silver coin, including fractional silver coin by registered mail or otherwise, seventy-five thousand dollars. 1893 CUSHING *Story of P.O.* 8 [The] Division of Registered Letters: prepares instructions for the guidance of postmasters relative to registered letters. 1925 *Postal Guide* July 103 Private insurance companies are willing to place additional insurance on registered mail if the sender desires to more fully protect his interests.

2. Of live stock: Having their pedigrees recorded.

1885 *Wkly. New Mexican Rev.* 12 Feb. 3/4 Mr. Leonard has now on sale at Albuquerque thirty thoroughbred imported and registered black polled Angus and Galloway bulls. 1890 *Stock Grower & Farmer* 24 May 4/2 177 head of registered Hereford cattle.

+Registered bond. A bond issued with the name of the holder written on the bond and recorded in a register. — 1861 [see COUPON BOND]. 1884 BLAINE *20 Years of Congress* I. 425 Its leading provisions were for the issue . . . of coupon or registered bonds not to exceed $500,000,000 in the aggregate. 1914 *Cycl. Amer. Govt.* I. 142/2 The holder of a registered bond cannot suffer loss if the security is stolen.

+Registered debt. A part of the national debt which, after the Assumption Act, was registered with the treasury but not funded by bonds. — 1794 *Ann. 3d Congress* 26 A statement of the Domestic Debt of the United States . . . 2d. The Registered Debt.

Registering punch. 'An instrument used by railroad conductors, with which they are required to cut from a card the amount of fares they receive' (B. '77).

Registrar. {1675–}

+1. A college or university official who keeps the records of students' enrollments and grades.

1813 *Niles' Reg.* V. 80/1 John W. Francis, M.D. Registrar. 1851 HALL *College Words* 257 At Harvard College, the Corporation appoints one of the Faculty to the office of *Registrar.* 1897 *Univ.* (Chicago) *Rec.* I. 274 The Registrar's Cash Statement. For the Spring Quarter ending June 24, 1896. 1921 *Educational Rev.* LXI. 148 The Registrar's Office as a Barometer of Educational Tendencies.

2. = REGISTER *n.*[1] 1. {1675–}

1882 McCABE *New York* 298 The *Hall of Records* . . . is occupied by the Registrar and his clerks. 1900 *Congress. Rec.* 31 Jan. 1367/1 When men of my age make an application to register, an ignorant, bitter partisan registrar could draw his head under his shell . . . and refuse . . . to adjudge. 1911 *Okla. Session Laws* 3 Legisl. 133 The clerk of the county court, the registrar of deeds, and the treasurer shall each have the power to appoint one or more deputies. 1924 [see BURIAL PERMIT].

* Registration.

1. The action or act of registering voters so that they may legally vote. Also attrib. {1832– (*Act 2 Will. IV* c. 65)}

1838 *N.Y. Advertiser & Exp.* 11 April 3/1 No wonder the loafers denounce a Registration Law! 1840 *Niles' Nat. Reg.* 13 June 229/1 The house of representatives . . . have passed a law for the registration of voters. 1864 *Mich. Gen. Statutes* I. (1882) 124 The city board of registration of the city of Detroit shall cause a session of the board of registration of each ward, or election district of said city, to be held on the first Monday in October. 1867 in Fleming *Hist. Reconstruction* I. 431 Interference by violence, or threats of violence, or other oppressive means to prevent the registration of any voter, is positively prohibited. 1903 HART *Actual Govt.* 73 The annual registration practically requires a man to appear twice, once to register and once to vote. 1911 *Okla. Session Laws* 3 Legisl. 231 Should the inspector of the elections have any doubt about the rights of the person offering for registration to vote, he may [etc.].

b. The extent or amount of such registration.

1892 *Boston Jrnl. & Nov.* 7/4 The registration this year is far ahead of any other, owing to several causes.

+2. Enrollment in a college or university. Also attrib.

1897 *Univ.* (Chicago) *Rec.* I. 199 June, Tuesday. . . . Matriculation and Registration of Incoming Students. 1905 [see REGISTER *v.* 3].

Registry fee. The fee paid for the registration of mail. — 1891 *Official Postal Guide* 732 The cost of registering mail matter is ten cents for registry fee, in addition to postage. 1912 *P.O. Dept. Ann. Rep.* 290 The registry fee was increased from 8 to 10 cents November 1, 1909.

Registry law. +A law concerned with the registration of voters. — 1840 *Boston Transcript* 30 March 2/2 The jacobins and sans-culottes of New York will lose an immense power by the Registry law. 1845 *Xenia Torch-Light* 4 Dec. 2/2 Dr. Olds introduced a bill to repeal the registry law which was read by title. 1865 *Ore. State Jrnl.* 23 Dec. 2/5 S. B. No. 1, the registry law, was indefinitely postponed.

Regrade, *v.* **+1.** To grade (a road) again. **+2.** To regroup the students of (a class). — (1) 1826 *Congress. Deb.* 18 Nov. 1572 (Ernst), The road . . . is to be re-graded. 1869 *Rep. Comm. Agric. 1868* 362 [Shells] may be readily . . . leveled in the construction of a new road, or regraded

when displaced by wear. 1884 *Century Mag.* March 649/2 The city was torn up from one end to the other, and regraded. (2) 1887 *Conv. Amer. Instructors of Deaf Proc.* 141 You may start out . . . with a class well graded, and before you have been at work three months you will find that you ought to regrade.

*Regret. (See quotations.) {1896} — 1859 BARTLETT 359 *Regret*, a note declining an invitation, and containing an expression of regret for the same. 1881 E. EDWARDS *Words, Facts & Phrases* 471 If a lady finds she cannot accept an invitation she says, 'I must send a regret.'

* Regular, *n.* Chiefly pl.

1. A soldier belonging to the standing army; a private professional soldier. {1756–7–}

1758 *Essex Inst. Coll.* XVIII. 105 The Regulars . . . were a most all swept off by Grape Shot. 1777 P. HENRY in Sparks *Corr. Revol.* I. 361 The deficiency in our regulars can no way be supplied so properly as by enlisting volunteers. 1811 *Ann. 12th Congress* 1 Sess. 2120 They supported the fame of American regulars. 1846 *Whig Almanac 1847* 9/1 The wretched pittance of seven dollars per month, now paid to our Regulars and Volunteers, is shamefully inadequate. 1866 'F. KIRKLAND' *Bk. Anecdotes* 327/1 The happiest thing of the day was the thrashing which General King's Brigade of Regulars administered to a Mississippi Brigade. 1895 *Chicago Strike of 1894* 364 They let the regulars and deputy marshals do it.

+2. During the Revolutionary War, a soldier of the British standing army.

1775 *Broadside Verse* (1930) 57 A bloody butchery by the British troops: or the runaway fight of the regulars. 1775 *Mass. H. S. Coll.* 4 Ser. I. 265 The George Tavern was burnt by the Regulars. 1776 *Battle of Brooklyn* I. iii, Spies from Flat Bush inform that the regulars are making a disposition to cross the hills. 1823 TUDOR *Life J. Otis* 39 In popular language, the common term for the British troops, during the revolutionary war, was the 'regulars.'

3. A regular customer, boarder, etc. {1898–}

1872 'MARK TWAIN' *Roughing It* 299 'Regulars' are permanent sources of news. 1898 *Kansas City Star* 20 Dec. 3/2 Only a small crowd turned out to witness the six events carded at Ingleside, but the regulars that were in attendance were well repaid. 1902 BANKS *Newspaper Girl* xvii, There are three kinds of workers on the New York press. . . . The 'regulars' are engaged on salary, and receive their weekly salaries every Saturday night. 1911 LINCOLN *Cap'n Warren's Wards* 183 Most of the male 'regulars' were in business about the city and therefore lunched elsewhere.

+4. A party member who faithfully stands by his party; a standpatter.

1904 *Indianapolis News* 27 July 6 The new chairman is a regular of the regulars. He is a Democrat, whether his party is for gold or for silver. 1914 [see HARD *n.* 2].

* Regular, *a.*

1. *Mil.* Belonging to the standing army; properly and permanently organized. {1706–}

1714 *Boston News-Letter* 18 Oct. 2/2 The Regular Forces Marching after His Excellency. 1756 in *Boston Transcript* 16 Sept. (1908) 17/5 Coll. Scott with a number of Regular officers had a Barbecue upon an Island. 1816 [see MILITARY LAND WARRANT]. 1854 BENTON *30 Years' View* I. 738/1 His appointment in the United States regular army was a conquest from the administration. 1900 *Congress. Rec.* 29 Jan. 1281/1 In the Regular Army . . . the soldier contributes monthly a small part of his pay.

2. *Politics.* **+a.** Of a candidate for office: Nominated or supported by the officially constituted organization of a party.

1827 *Hallowell* (Me.) *Gaz.* 20 June 3/1 If they vote for such a one solely because he is the 'regular candidate' as the cant phrase is, . . . let them take the consequences. 1872 [see GOVERNOR 3]. 1876 *N.Y. Ev. Mail* 21 Oct. (B.), When the average Democrat refuses to support the regular nominees, regardless of their personal characters, discipline is destroyed and disaster assured. 1887 *Boston Dem. City Com.* Bylaw 12 (Ernst), A regular Democratic nominee.

+b. Of a nomination or ticket: Made or chosen by the officially constituted party, esp. at a party convention.

1829 in Commons, etc. *Doc. Hist.* V. 156 Men who have long passed current as genuine and faithful . . . have aspired to break down the Regular nominations of the Democratic party. 1833 *Niles' Reg.* 16 Nov. 181/1 The highest on the 'regular' ticket . . . received 8,950 votes. 1866 *Ore. State Jrnl.* 3 Feb. 2/1 Their organ will be driven into the support of the 'regular Democratic ticket' by the politicians. 1902 MEYER *Nominating Systems* 17 [The people] were drilled into a blind acceptance of 'regular nominations.'

+c. Of a person or a vote: Supporting the established or official party organization; opposed to the insurgents.

1846 MACKENZIE *Van Buren* 182 He is a regular Democrat; was health officer in Philadelphia when he wrote the above letter. 1887 *Courier-Journal* 3 May 4/4 The 'regular' delegates (those whose credentials are indorsed by the chairman of the county or district committee) would be admitted without protest. 1892 *Congress. Rec.* 28 May 4802/1 The Ocala platform [was] repudiated by the regular rock-ribbed Democrats. 1900

Ib. 22 Jan. 1036/1 The white vote, the regular vote, in November substantially registers the action of the Democratic primaries in July. **1904** *Booklovers Mag.* Jan. 8 In the last two presidential contests he has been 'regular,' having voted for Bryan.

+d. Of a party: Recognized as the authorized party.
1864 *Ore. State Jrnl.* 16 April 2/5 He and O'Meara run [*sic*] on the same ticket, in opposition to the 'regular Democratic party.'

Regular, *adv.* {1710–} +(See quotations and cf. REGULAR WAY.) — **1865** *Harper's Mag.* April 616/2 People who have plenty of money buy for cash or 'regular'—which means that the stock will be delivered and paid for next day. **1870** MEDBERY *Men Wall St.* 50 Where the seller . . . hopes to get a better price, or cannot make a delivery of stock until next day, he sells *Regular.*

+Regular Baptist. (See quot. 1847.) — **1847** L. COLLINS *Kentucky* 110 This revival had the happy effect of bringing about a union between the *Regular* and *Separate* Baptists. These distinctive names were imported from Virginia, and mean the same as those of *Particular* and *General* Baptists in England—the former meaning those who hold to Calvinistic, and the latter those holding Arminian sentiments. **1849** CHAMBERLAIN *Ind. Gazetteer* 71 The Regular Baptists are numerous.

Regular session. +A session of Congress or of a state legislature that convenes at a time specified by law. — **1837** *Diplom. Corr. Texas* (1908) I. 264 There was no intention to bring up the subject of Texas and the question of its annexation, until the regular session which commences . . . on the first Monday in December. **1859** *Ind. H. Rep. Jrnl.* 4 Journal of the House of Representatives During the fortieth regular session of the General Assembly of the State of Indiana. **1912** NICHOLSON *Hoosier Chron.* 534 It was Morton Bassett's legislature . . . brought back to the capital to do those things which it had left undone at the regular session.

+Regular way. (See quot. 1900.) — **1857** *Merchants' Mag.* July 136 Very often in the report of stock sales, the letters r.w. are attached to certain operations. This 'regular way' means the delivery of the stock sold the next day. **1870** MEDBERY *Men Wall St.* 49. **1900** NELSON *A B C Wall St.* 157 *Regular, or regular way,* the term of sale employed when the delivery is to be made at or before 2-15 P.M. on the day succeeding that of the making of the contract.

Regulate, *v.* {c1630–}
+1. *tr.* To confine or control (hogs). *Obs.*
1642 *Dedham Rec.* III. 85 Whosoever . . . shall see an Swyne vnyoaked . . . shall put the same Swyne into the pownde to be Regulated vpon the penalty of 6d forfated for every Swyne. **1655** *Watertown Rec.* I. 1. 45 Thirteene Shillings . . . is for theire not regulating theire hogs.

+2. To punish (a person) by illegal or extralegal processes. Also *vbl. n.* Also *transf.* (Cf. REGULATOR 3.)
1824 BLANE *Excursion U.S.* 236 This practice of Regulating seems very strange to an European. **1835** PAULDING *J. Bull & Bro. Jon.* 86 He got taken up, and was very nigh being *regulated.* **1849** CHAMBERLAIN *Ind. Gazetteer* 112 If an individual or family disturbed the . . . community, . . . they were then *regulated,* as it was called. **1887** *Courier-Journal* 7 May 4/2 A small number of men . . . assume to 'regulate' the community in connection with this crime.

Regulating, *a.* {1710–} +Of persons or groups of persons: Belonging to an association of regulators (senses 2 and 3). *Obs.* — **1768** *Boston Chron.* 8 Aug. 315/1 The reforming or regulating people will not suffer process civil or criminal, to be executed, but where, and against whom they think proper. **1808** in Beadle *Undevel. West* 410 Should the accused person or persons raise up with arms in his or their hands, . . . in opposition to the regulating company [etc.]. **1828** J. HALL *Lett. from West* 291 The citizens formed themselves into a '*regulating company,*' a kind of holy brotherhood, whose duty was to purge the community of its unruly members.

Regulation. {1672–} +The mode or practice of policing or governing a society through regulators. Also *attrib.* — {**1768** *N.C. Col. Rec.* VII. 700 Regulators' Advertisement. . . . We are determined to have the Officers of this county under a better and honester regulation than they have been for some time past.} **1837** *S. Lit. Messenger* III. 648 The outrages of the borderers—the frontier law of 'regulation' or 'lynching' which is common to new countries all over the world, are ascribed to slavery. **1849** CHAMBERLAIN *Ind. Gazetteer* 112 There have been, no doubt, great abuses of attempted *regulation.* **1867** A. GREGG *Hist. Old Cheraws* 130 Such, however, was not the history of the Regulation Movement on the Pedee.

Regulator. {1655–}
+1. In Philadelphia, a surveyor who laid out the lines for house foundations, streets, etc. *Obs.*
1721 *Phila. Ordinances* (1812) 12 No person or persons . . . [shall] lay the foundation of any building, before they have applied themselves to the surveyors or regulators. **1782** *Ib.* 48 Regulators . . . [may] enter into or upon any lot or land . . . , and survey and measure the same.

+2. In the back country of the Carolinas, a member of various illegal or extralegal organizations: in South Carolina (1767–9) formed to purge the country of horse thieves and other criminals; in North Carolina (1768–71) formed to resist official extortion.
1767 in A. Gregg *Hist. Old Cheraws* 136 Those licentious spirits that have so lately appeared in the distant parts of the Province [of S.C.], . . . as-

suming the name of Regulators, have . . . illegally tried, condemned, and punished many persons. **1768** *Boston Chron.* 25 July 292/2 Charles-Town, (South-Carolina) June 23. . . . We daily hear of new irregularities committed by the people called regulators. **1768** *N.C. Col. Rec.* VII. 731 At a general meeting of the regulators on April 30th it was laid before us an Appointment of the Officers. **1769** [see MODERATOR 2]. **1771** *Mass. Spy* 27 June (Th.), The Regulators in the back settlements [at Cross Creek, N.C.] have given his Excellency and the troops under his command battle. *c*1774 J. ADAMS in Tudor *Life J. Otis* 506 Malcolm . . . had been active in battle against *the regulators* in North Carolina, who were thought in Boston, to be an injured people. **1784** SMYTH *Tour* I. 228 The Regulators of North Carolina were, and still are among the worthiest, steadiest, and most respectable friends to British government and real constitutional freedom. **1802** DRAYTON *S. Carolina* 196 Regulators . . . , rather than travel all the way to Charleston, for the purpose of carrying on prosecutions in the courts of law, inflicted summary punishment on all trespassers on their persons, or properties.

+3. A member of various other bands or volunteer committees, formed ostensibly to preserve order, prevent crime, etc., but actually, in many cases, to commit violence and crime.
1808 in Beadle *Undevel. West* 410 The blood of him or them shall not be required of any of the persons belonging to the regulators from the clan the person so killed belonged to. **1819** FAUX *Memorable Days* 318 These regulators [in Tenn.] are self-appointed ministers of justice. **1832** PAULDING *Westward Ho!* I. 96 Hence originated the institution called the *Regulators,* formerly common on the remote frontiers. **1839** HOFFMAN *Wild Scenes* 112 A disbanded regulator of the Georgia guard . . . had scented the contents of my master's saddle-bags. **1841** FOOTE *Texas* I. 233 Bands of *Regulators,* as they were called, pervaded the whole country, under the ostensible sanction of the Alcalde. **1842** *Amer. Pioneer* I. 229 To counteract which [*i.e.,* a gang of outlaws in Ky.] a company of regulators, as they were called, was raised. **1855** REYNOLDS *My Own Times* 180 In the counties of Massac and Pope [Ill.] in the year 1846, for several months the citizens were kept in constant alarm and excitement by two organized parties, known as 'Regulators,' and 'Moderators.' **1859** *Harper's Mag.* July 255/2 From *Arizona* we have intelligence of outrages by organized bands of ruffians, who, under the name of Regulators, attempted to expel the Mexican inhabitants from Sonorita Valley. **1861** Moore *Rebellion Rec.* I. III. 60 Mr. W. G. Ehrman of the Regulators' Committee of the State [of Md.] need not fear that he will be overlooked or forgotten. **1866** *Nation* I May 547/1 The freedmen . . . suffer chiefly from the terrorism of lawless bands of 'regulators' and 'nigger-killers.' **1877** *N. Amer. Rev.* July 8 Bands of 'regulators' traversed many parts of [La.]. **1879** *Cimarron News & Press* 20 Nov. 1/4 Law abiding citizens [of Ky.] are organizing and arming to protect themselves and the courts against assaults and threats of the so-called Regulators. **1918** CONNELLEY *Kansas* 432 A secret order of Free State men was formed at Lawrence which was variously called 'Defenders,' 'Regulators,' and 'Danites.'

+4. *Attrib.* in senses 2 and 3 with *camp, captain, struggle.*
1770 *N.C. Col. Rec.* VII. 848 John Wilcox fell in with us as we left ye Regelater Camp. **1845** *Amer. Whig Rev.* I. 124/1 Hinch, the Regulator Captain [in Shelby Co., Texas], had always been the unrivalled hero of such occasions. **1865** PIKE *Scout & Ranger* (1932) 128 He had taken a prominent part . . . in the Moderator and Regulator struggle in 1836-8.

＊Rein, *v.* +*tr.* To protect (a field) *from* stock. *Obs.* — **1799** WASHINGTON *Writings* XIV. 230 This field, after the rye has been eaten off by the sheep, is to be reined from stock of all kinds. *Ib.* 231 The other part . . . is to be equally well enclosed, and reined up from stock.

+Reina. [Sp., 'queen.'] A rockfish (*Hispaniscus elongatus*) of the California coast. — **1884** GOODE, etc. *Fisheries* I. 266 This species is known as 'Reina' (Queen) at Monterey. It is a small fish . . . and lives in deep water. **1911** *Rep. Fisheries* 1908 314/2.

＊Reindeer. An antlered northern deer of the genus *Rangifer,* +esp. the caribou (*R. caribou*), once inhabiting the northern part of the United States. Also *attrib.* — [**1744** A. DOBBS *Hudson's Bay* 19 They have . . . a kind of Deer they call *Cariboux,* (Rain-Deer).] **1796** *N.Y. State Soc. Arts* I. 345 The rein deer affords abundance of rich milk. **1831** in Cox *Adv. Columbia R.* II. 53 We have no buffalo or deer, except the *cariboux* (rein-deer); and not many even of those. **1917** *Mammals of Amer.* 34/2 By 1902 there had been introduced, [into Alaska] from Lapland and Siberia, 1720 Reindeer.

Reindeer moss. A many-branched lichen, *Cladonia rangiferina.* {1753–} — **1846** EMMONS *Agric. N.Y.* I. 5 We find an alpine region, where reindeer-moss and other lichens abound. **1907** *St. Nicholas* July 847/2 'Reindeer moss' supplies the reindeer with winter food.

+Reinsman. A person skilled in handling reins; a driver. Also *fig.* — **1855** in *Voice* 8 Feb. (1894), 30,000 . . . , deeming themselves as skilful reinsmen as those selected by the Boards of Excise, have assumed the driver's seat. **1870** M. H. SMITH *20 Years Wall St.* 263 His driver, an imported Englishman, is said to be the best reinsman in America. **1883** ZEIGLER & GROSSCUP *Alleghanies* 89 It will take a good reinsman to keep it from upsetting in the axle-deep ruts. **1904** *N.Y. Times* 13 Dec. 7 A number of well-known amateur reinsmen started from the Harlem River Speedway.

Relax. {1627–} +Diarrhea. *colloq. Obs.* {1733, in related sense} — **1805** *Lewis & Clark Exped.* VII. (1905) 164 Several of the men Sick with the relax. **1832** WYETH *Journal* 155 Our men troubled with the relax.

∗ Relay. *Telegraphy.* An instrument used in the process of strengthening a weak current in order to transmit long-distance messages. {1876-} Also attrib. — **1860** PRESCOTT *Telegraph* 81 The relay is a very essential apparatus in Morse's telegraphic system. **1876** KNIGHT 1915/2 *Relay magnet,* . . . a small electro-magnet requiring but a weak current to charge it, and having an armature [etc.].

+Relay station. A station where horses are changed on a stage or courier route. *Obs.* — **1870** KEIM *Sheridan's Troopers* 49 The nearest settlement was Pond City, quite an extravagant appellation for a relay station. **1895** REMINGTON *Pony Tracks* 7 It is over thirty miles to the first relay station or courier's camp. *a*1918 G. STUART *On Frontier* I. 150 There were relay stations along the route, where two minutes were allowed to change horses and mail.

∗ Reliable, *a.* That may be relied upon; trustworthy; dependable. {-1624, 1800-}
This word was once believed to be an Americanism. It is fully discussed by F. Hall in his work, *On English Adjectives in -able, with Special Reference to Reliable* (1877).
1792 in Cutler *Life & Corr.* II. 288, I have lately used the root, and find it a very reliable medicine. **1850** IRVING in P. M. Irving *Life W. Irving* IV. 70 You have built it [*i.e.*, your work] up with a care that renders it reliable in all its parts. **1883** HAWTHORNE *Dr. Grimshawe* (1889) 167 The visitor . . . glanced at his face, and then over his dress and figure, as if to gather from them some reliable data as to his station. **1883** HOUGH ed. Rogers *Journals* 4 The accounts of services here given, are in the main reliable.

Relief association. An association organized for giving relief to specified classes of persons. — **1863** KETTELL *Hist. Rebellion* II. 616 The majority of those persons went under the auspices of the 'National Freedmen's Relief Association.' **1882** GODFREY *Nantucket* 297 The Relief Association . . . was formed for the benefit of respectable elderly persons and invalids. **1883** [see CLEARING HOUSE 1].

+Relief committee. A committee organized to give relief. — **1842** *Picayune* 23 Jan. 2/5 The Relief Committee of the Firemen's Charitable Association will meet . . . at the Firemen's Insurance Office. **1864** CUMMING *Hospital Life* 128/1 There was a relief committee, from Lagrange, in the same car with us. **1892** HARRIS *On Plantation* 139 Where they lived remote from the relief committees, the families of the soldiers were not so well provided for as they had a right to expect.

+Relief note. A note issued by the state of Pennsylvania in 1841 to pay interest on the public debt, etc., bearing a promise to be received for all obligations due the state. — **1842** [see BLOWOUT 1]. **1853** *Fun & Earnest* 215 (Th.), Those ever-blessed Relief Notes, which our great sister State, the Keystone, so long paid her debts with. **1894** LEAVITT *Our Money Wars* 77 Pennsylvania, in this crisis, issued $3,100,000 of what was called 'Relief Notes.'

Relief party. *Hist.* + =NEW COURT PARTY. — **1847** L. COLLINS *Kentucky* 208 Chief Justice Boyle was head of the 'Old Court' of appeals, during the intensely exciting contest [*c*1825] . . . between the 'Relief' or 'New Court,' and the 'Anti-Relief' or 'Old Court' parties.

Relief society. A society organized for relief. — **1854** *Mass. Priv. & Sp. Statutes* X. 199 L. Cudkirk, M. Goodheim [and others] . . . are hereby made a corporation, by the name of the Hebrew Mutual Relief Society, in the city of Boston. **1863** CUMMING *Hospital Life* 99/2 He spoke very highly in praise of the Georgia Relief Society, and of the good which it had done. **1872** *Chicago Tribune* 5 Nov., People are too busily engaged in endeavoring to remain independent of Relief and Aid Societies. **1886** STAPLETON *Major's Christmas* 300 Nancy has a new dress, our minister my check for fifty dollars, and one hundred dollars to the Ladies' Relief Society of the parish.

Relief station. A place where aid is given to those requiring it. — **1860** GREELEY *Overland Journey* 199 Fort Bridger . . . [was] settled as an outpost and relief-station by the Mormons. **1904** *Chicago Tribune* 2 Aug. 2 The relief station . . . was besieged by large crowds all of yesterday.

∗ Religion.
+1. *To get religion,* to be converted; to become religious. *colloq.*
1772 in Fithian *Journal* I. 22 We have had a considerable stir of religion in college since you went away, Lewis Willson is thought to have got religion. **1805** Dow *Hist. Cosmopolite* (1848) 238 Next day I breakfasted . . . with a blacksmith, who once intended to flog me, but he now put a shoe on my horse, having since got religion. **1832** J. HALL *Legends of West* 46 Tom got religion at a camp-meeting, and for a while was quite a reformed man. **1876** 'MARK TWAIN' *Tom Sawyer* xxii. 179 There had been a 'revival,' and everybody had 'got religion,' not only adults, but even boys and girls. **1907** MULFORD *Bar-20* 105 But do you know what made him get religion all of a sudden? **1918** LINCOLN *Shavings* 117 If you ain't enough to drive the mate of a cattle boat into gettin' religion!

+2. *To experience religion,* (see EXPERIENCE *v.*).

∗ Religious, *a.* W. +Of a horse: Having no vicious traits. *colloq.* — **1869** *Overland Mo.* III. 127 It is amusing to hear one ask of another, when about to purchase a horse: 'Is he religious?'

+Religious boat. (See quotation.) — **1835** REED & MATHESON *Visit* I. 183 The steamer . . . is what is called a religious boat. There are Bibles strewed in the men's cabin, and a subscription-box for the Episcopal Tract Society.

Religious society. A society organized for religious purposes; a church organization. — **1779** *Mass. Constitution* iii, Religious societies . . . [should] make suitable provision at their own expense, for the instruction of the public worship of God. **1796** [see CHARITABLE *a.*]. **1831** PECK *Guide* 285 [The Germans] are subdivided into Lutherans and Dunkards, both of which have religious societies. **1909** *Indian Laws & Tr.* III. 387 The Secretary of the Interior is . . . directed to issue patents in fee to all religious societies and organizations . . . for the lands occupied by them.

∗ Relinquishment. +A tract of abandoned or relinquished land. — **1886** *Congress. Rec.* 28 June 6238/1 Nearly every land agent . . . advertises as a prominent feature of his business 'Relinquishments for sale.' **1897** *Outing* XXIX. 570/2 He had . . . bought a relinquishment up the river.

Reliquary case. A small box for keeping relics. — **1647** *Md. Archives* IV. 321 An Inventory of . . . goods, & Chattells. . . . An old brasse kettle, a gold Reliquary case [etc.].

∗ Relish. An article of food having a savory taste {1798-}; +esp. a pickled or preserved food eaten with other foods. — **1797** PRIEST *Travels* 32 About eight or nine in the morning [in Phila.] they breakfast on tea and coffee, attended always with what they call *relishes,* such as salt fish, beef-steaks, sausages, broiled fowls, ham, bacon, &c. **1832** TROLLOPE *Domestic Manners* II. 9 The herrings of the bountiful Potomac . . . are excellent 'relish,' as they call it, when salted. **1844** GODLEY *Lett. from Amer.* II. 43, I see one advertising for sale . . . 'relishes at all hours.' **1860** [see BAKED *ppl. a.* 2]. **1883** *Practical Housekeeping* 408 Cucumber Relish may be made of the large cucumbers.

+Reloan. An act involving the loan of the same money a second time. — **1790** *Ann. 1st Congress* 2021 The United States . . . [will provide for] all such part of the debts of the respective States, . . . [as shall] be subscribed towards a loan to the United States, upon the principle of either of the plans which shall have been adopted by them for the reloan of their present debt. **1802** *Ann. 7th Congress* 1 Sess. 1171 The bill before us authorizes a reloan of the whole Dutch debt. *Ib.* 1172, I will therefore move so to amend the bill as to make all the reloans reimbursable before 1809.

+Relocate, *v.*
1. *tr.* To locate a second time. (See LOCATE *v.* transitive senses).
1841 WEBSTER II. 457/2. **1866** *Rep. Indian Affairs* 76 If the Indians could be removed to some remote place equally fertile, and then relocated, it would no doubt be to their advantage. **1869** *Mich. Gen. Statutes* I. (1882) 229 Whenever a majority of the resident owners of any section . . . shall desire to have their corners and lines, or any of them established, re-located or perpetuated, such surveyor shall proceed to make the required surveys. **1874** RAYMOND *6th Rep. Mines* 517 They formed a code of laws, relocated the various outcrops, went to work in earnest and developed the mines. **1877** HODGE *Arizona* 129 In January, 1875, the mines were relocated under the superintendence of Col. William G. Boyle. **1885** *Harper's Mag.* May 835/2 Some individuals were able to relocate some of the old diggings. **1901** WHITE *Claim Jumpers* 232 Well, relocate them [*sc.* claims] ourselves, if that suits you better.

2. *intr.* To move and resettle.
1851 CIST *Cincinnati* 143 [This] determined the company to re-locate on higher ground. **1864** *Congress. Globe* 9 March 1018/2 In a larger number of cases these persons having taken homesteads, and again desiring to sell and relocate, . . . have paid for the lands. **1894** *Advance* 31 May, The congregation is preparing to re-locate in the north part of the city.

Relocation. {1746-7-} +The action or fact of relocating. — **1873** *Ill. Dept. Agric. Trans.* X. 371 The court shall appoint three viewers to examine and make the necessary re-location. **1876** RAYMOND *8th Rep. Mines* 221 Some relocations have been made under the act of 1872 and its amendments. **1901** [see DISCOVERY].

∗ Remember, *v. tr.* Used in the imperative in various war cries or slogans: (see quotations). — **1836** HOUSTON in Bolton & Barker *With Makers of Texas* (1904) 189 The whole line advancing in double-quick time, rung the war cry, 'Remember the Alamo!' **1888** A. E. BARR *Remember the Alamo* 378 It was from his [Sherman's] lips the battle-cry of 'Remember the Alamo!' sprang. **1898** *Forum* Nov. 283 The cry, 'To Hell with Spain! Remember the "Maine"!' presently grew faint, if it did not entirely die away.

+Remington. [Philo *Remington,* Amer. inventor (1816-89).] The name of a rifle. Usually attrib. — **1871** W. W. GREENE *Modern Breech-Loaders* 192 The Remington Rifle. This rifle was tried at Wimbledon, as long ago as 1866. . . . It has been extensively used in America, France, Denmark, and Austria, and also by the papal troops. **1873** *Rep. Chief of Ordnance* 87 The Board examined the alterations of the Remington gun. *Ib.* 88 The Board proceeded to test for rapidity of fire . . . Remington No. 86. **1890** *Cent.* 5175/2 *Remington rifle,* an arm extensively used in the armies of the United States, France, Denmark [etc.]. . . . The gun has been officially adopted by the United States Navy Department.

+Remonetization. The restoration of a metal, esp. silver, to its former use as legal tender. (Cf. DEMONETIZATION.) — **1876** *44th Congress 2 Sess.* Sen. Rep. No. 703, 99 It is not a particular silver coin, the remonetization of which is demanded, but it is the metal silver. **1878** *Rep. Secy. Treasury* 261 The expectation . . . that the remonetization of the silver dollar would be followed by an appreciation in the value of silver, has not yet been realized. **1900** *Congress. Rec.* 10 Feb. 1692/2 Now is the very time to renew . . . the movement toward the remonetization of silver to which we Republicans have so often pledged ourselves. **1925** BRYAN *Memoirs* 113 Many prominent Republicans were on record as in favor of remonetization.

+Remonetize, *v. tr.* To restore (silver) to its former use as legal tender. — **1877** *N.Y. Tribune* 16 Nov. (B.), You bankers had better accept my bill to remonetize silver. **1878** *N. Amer. Rev.* CXXVI. 315 If silver is remonetized, for instance, no number of states could nullify the law. **1882** ALDENHAM, etc. *Bimetallic Controversy* 225 If Germany to-morrow were to remonetise silver, with the same rapidity it would come up again.

+Remonta. *S.W.* [Sp.] (See quot. 1902.) — **1887** *Scribner's Mag.* II. 512/1 He is busy whipping up a *caballo* . . . or a *remontha.* **1902** CLAPIN 334 *Remonta,* . . . a Spanish word in use on the plains of the South-West, to signify a group of saddle-horses.

＊Remora. Any of several fishes of the genera *Echeneis, Remora,* etc., esp. *E. naucrates* and *R. remora.* Also with specifying terms. — **1818** MITCHILL in *Amer. Monthly Mag.* II. 244 White-tailed Remora. . . . Taken in the bay of New York, June 22, 1915. **1839** STORER *Mass. Fishes* 155 *The fourteen plated Remora.* . . . The only specimen I have met with . . . was kindly sent me by Dr. Yale. **1842** *Nat. Hist. N.Y., Zoology* IV. 309 The Common Remora. . . . Schoepff saw both this and the preceding species [Indian Remora] taken from the bottoms of vessels in the harbor of New York. **1884** GOODE, etc. *Fisheries* I. 446 The Remora was one of the first fishes observed by the early discoverers of North America. **1897** *N.Y. Forest, Fish, & Game Comm. 2d Rep.* 246 [The] Remora . . . is found in Gravesend Bay in summer only, attached to sharks, usually the sand shark.

Removability. Liability to be removed from office. {1836} — **1789** *Ann. 1st Congress* 404, I am not satisfied that removability shall be acquired only by impeachment. *Ib.* 679 The Senate . . . insisted on the amendment to the Treasury bill, respecting the removability of the Secretary by the President. **1828** WEBSTER, *Removability,* the capacity of being removable from an office or station.

Removal sale. A sale of goods at reduced prices before a store moves. — **1881** *Ore. State Jrnl.* 8 Jan. 5 Great Removal Sale! From now on until the first of March.

+Remuda. *S.W.* [Sp., 'exchange.'] A bunch of saddle horses kept to supply remounts. — **1892** *Dialect Notes* I. 251 *Remudo* or *remuda:* a 'bunch' of horses, about a score. Usually applied to geldings only. [Texas.] **1903** A. ADAMS *Log of Cowboy* 9 The *remuda,* under Bill Honeyman as horse wrangler, numbered a hundred and forty-two, ten horses to the man. **1910** RAINE *B. O'Connor* 212 He found . . . the whole *remuda* kicking up its heels. **1925** W. JAMES *Drifting Cowboy* 10, I sure had to do some tall scrambling when the remuda broke out of the corral.

＊Rendezvous, *n. attrib.* +Designating places where appointments or rendezvous are conveniently held. — **1719** *Lancaster Rec.* 190 [We were] Chosen and appointed a Commity . . . to Lay out the waies from the Randevou tree to the medows. **1738** *Lunenburg* (Mass.) *Proprietors' Rec.* 214 Lying and being in the northwesterly part of said Township Containing randizvous Lower meaddows. **1841** [see RENDEZVOUS *v.* 2].

Rendezvous, *v.* {c1645-}
1. *tr.* To bring together (troops) in a particular place. {1654-66; a1700, of ships}
'Now only U.S.' (O.E.D.).
1779 *N.H. Comm. Safety Rec.* 196 Wrote Letters to Colo Bellows, Colo Enoch Hale . . . about rendevousing their Continental Soldiers. **1780** JEFFERSON *Writings* IV. 83 He had proceeded so far as to rendezvous a considerable body of Indians. **1781** *Va. State P.* I. 601 A party of men belonging to Capt: Wood's Company happen'd to be rendezvoused in the neighborhood. **1895** *Outing* XXVII. 254/1 There the First New Hampshire Regiment was rendezvoused, twenty years before.
b. To bring together (people) in a designated place. {a1680, 1719}
1883 *N. Mex. Terr. Rep.* 77 A number of persons who had been indicted . . . for cattle stealing . . . were rendezvoused in the vicinity of Kingston. **1892** *Boston Jrnl.* 28 July 8/1 It was announced gravely . . . that the detectives had been 'rendez-voused' at a certain place.
+c. To bring together (cattle) from over a wide area. **1872** *Newton Kansan* 26 Sept. 2/4 Thirty thousand head of cattle are rendezvoused in Coffeyville.
+2. To meet (a person); to arrange (an appointment). **1841** COOPER *Deerslayer* v, I've come on this lake, Master Hutter, to rende'vous a fri'nd. *Ib.* viii, The Delaware and I rendezvous'd an app'intment, to meet this evening at sunset on the rendezvous-rock at the foot of this very lake.

Rendition. {1601-}
+1. The action of rendering a judgment or verdict.
1802 *Ann. 7th Congress* 1 Sess. 173 You might see one judge beginning a cause . . . and a different one entirely making the rendition of judgment. **1858** *Baltimore Sun* 17 Aug. (B.), On the rendition of the verdict, the large audience present manifested enthusiastic approbation. **1906** *Indian Laws & Tr.* III. 240 Upon the rendition of such judgment . . . the Secretary of the Interior is hereby directed [etc.].
2. The surrender *of* a person {1649, 1670}; +esp. a fugitive slave. *Obs.*
1854 F. CLARKE (*title*), The Rendition of Anthony Burns. **1860** in Victor *Hist. So. Rebellion* I. 86 The subject of the rendition of fugitive slaves can be adjusted. **1861** *Congress. Globe* 26 Feb. 1226/3 There has been difficulty about the rendition of fugitives from justice. **1864** Cox *8 Yrs. in Congress* 108 You are against the rendition of the black man in pursuance of the Constitution; and you give up a white man who has sought

an asylum on our shores. **1864** SALA in *Daily Telegraph* 13 Sept., Mr. Seward can scarcely place any obstacles in the way of the rendition of this man.
3. A translation, interpretation, or rendering *of* a text or its meaning. {1659, a1716}
'Now U.S.' (O.E.D.).
1858 *Nat. Intelligencer* 11 Nov. (B.), The closest possible rendition of the meaning of the original text of the Scriptures into English. **1870** *Congress. Globe* 23 Feb. 1511/2 What is the position of the gentlemen who advocate this rendition of this clause? **1875** STEDMAN *Victorian Poets* 275, I will not omit mention of Calverley's complete rendition of Theocritus.
+4. The acting or performance *of* a dramatic or musical piece. Also transf.
1877 FURNESS ed. *Hamlet* I. p. xiv, In their rendition of *Hamlet* by the Messrs Devrient, . . . the First Quarto has been proved by them to be more effective than the Second. **1881** *San Francisco Chron.* 4 April, The festivities of the occasion were enlivened by the rendition in a pleasing manner of a few instrumental selections. **1897** HOWELLS *Open-eyed Conspiracy* xi, Nothing could be more false than the motives and emotions of the drama as the author imagined them, but . . . their rendition by these sincere souls was yet more artificial.

Rendrock. A kind of dynamite used in blasting. {1881} — **1880** *Lib. Universal Knowl.* II. 628 The explosives were dynamite, rendrock, and vulcan powder. **1884** MATTHEWS & BUNNER *In Partnership* 51 An unattached goat . . . was fain to stay its stomach on a presumably empty rend-rock can. **1898** *McClure's Mag.* X. 521/1 A hand-car was loaded with rend-rock.

＊Renegade, *n.* +An Indian who continues his opposition to the whites after other Indians have made peace. — **1839** HOFFMAN *Wild Scenes* 104 Thy scalp-lock . . . will soon be twined in the fingers of the vengeful renegade! **1877** *Rep. Indian Affairs* 20 Raids by the renegades . . . became frequent. **1888** SHERIDAN *Memoirs* I. 89 The subjugation of the allied bands became a comparatively easy matter after the lesson taught the renegades who were captured at the Cascades.

Renegade, *a.* **a.** Traitorous; having deserted a cause or group. {1705} **+b.** Sometimes of an Indian: Unwilling to accept peace, otherwise accepted by his tribe, with the whites. — **1837** IRVING *Capt. Bonneville* I. 181 Kosato, the renegade Blackfoot, had recovered from the wound. **1887** *Rep. Indian Affairs* 53 A sudden and serious check to school operations was occasioned last September by the cold-blooded assassination of the Rev. R. A. B. Ffennell by a renegade Indian. **1890** [see BREECHCLOTH]. **1925** TILGHMAN *Dugout* 13 [It] was deserted save for three figures, the chief, a renegade white man . . . and Mak-teo.

＊Renegado. a. A white man who has deserted his people, +frequently to join the Indians. Also attrib. **+b.** An Indian at odds with his own people; =RENEGADE *n.* — **1677** HUBBARD *Narrative* I. 59 The Scouts brought in one Joshuah Tift, a Renegado English man of Providence. **1765** CROGHAN *Journal* 21 The French inhabitants hereabouts, are an idle, lazy people, a parcel of renegadoes from Canada. **1812** MARSHALL *Kentucky* 157 Some renegado white men, who . . . had fled from their own nation, and taken up with the Indians, incessantly instigated them to war, and to plunder. **1833** FLINT *D. Boone* 117 This vile renegado, consulted by the Indians as an oracle, lived in plenty. **1887** *Century Mag.* May 52/1 Those *renegados* so common in all Indian warfares and so numerous in every band . . . will join every revolt without regard to tribe or cause.

+Renewal system. A system of pruning vines by which the superfluous canes are cut away above the lowest buds of the cane. — **1862** *Rep. Comm. Patents 1861: Agric.* 474 This is what we call the 'renewal' system, and we consider it preferable to the 'spur' system. **1874** *Vermont Bd. Agric. Rep.* II. 279 That method called the *renewal* system is the best for this climate.

+Renig, *v.* [Var. of *renegue.] (Cf. NIG *v.*)
1. *intr.* To go back on what has been promised or said; to retract or make denial.
1784 ELLICOTT in Mathews *Life A. Ellicott* 27 The Hussey immediately Reniged and reclaimed the bid. **1853** *Morning Herald* (St. Louis) 28 June (Th.), All have bolted, renigged, and gone it helter-skelter, to a man. **1866** C. H. SMITH *Bill Arp* 153 When the Secretary read out my name all mixed up with the Republic I felt I was obleged to renig. **1897** LEWIS *Wolfville* 46 Two days later she raises the tariff to fifty cents on shirts. . . . But no one renigs. **1917** H. FRANCK *Vagabonding down Andes* 32 Hays renigged at the last moment, but I accepted the invitation issued to the 'general public.'
2. *Card-playing.* (See quotation.) {renegue, 1680-}
1864 DICK *Amer. Hoyle* (1866) 186 *Revoke,* or *Renig.*—Playing a different suit from the card led, though it is in the player's power to follow suit.

Rennet pudding. A junket pudding. — **1832** CHILD *Frugal Housewife* 62 Rennet pudding may be made at five minutes' notice.

+Reno. (See quotation.) — **1876** BOURKE *Journal* 8-22 Sept., Gambling Hells flourished: all games could be found. Three card monte, Reno, Poker, Roulette, and Faro.

Renominate, *v. tr.* To nominate (a person) another time for an office. — **1864** FRÉMONT in *Wkly. New Mexican* 24 June 2/1 If Lincoln be re-nominated, it would be fatal to the country to indulge and renew a power which has cost us some thousands of men needlessly. **1916** *N.Y. Times* 3 May 9/1 The 107 renominate Mitchel at dinner.

Renomination. {1885-} A nomination for a second, third, etc., term of office. {1891} — **1855** HAWTHORNE *Eng. Note-Books* (1870) I. 294 He thought the President had a fair chance of re-nomination. **1916** *N.Y. Times* 6 May 2/3 To friends he predicted the renomination of President Wilson.

+**Rensselaerite.** [Stephen Van *Rensselaer* (1765-1839), governor of New York.] A soft, fine, and compact variety of talc. — **1837** *N.Y. Nat. Hist. Survey 1st Rep. 2d Geol. District* 153, I propose to call it *Hemi-Prismatic Tabular* Spar. The trivial name I have conferred upon it, is *Rensselaerite*, in honor of the Hon. Stephen Van Rensselaer. **1843** *Nat. Hist. N.Y., Geology* III. 20 The *rensselaerite* of Dr. Emmons occurs in this district, near to Lewisburg furnace. **1862** DANA *Manual of Geol.* 81 *Rensselaerite* is a kind of soapstone of compact texture, and either gray, whitish, greenish, brownish, or even black, color.

***Rent,** *n.* For *rent*, +to be rented. — **1879** STOCKTON *Rudder Grange* i, There were none advertised for rent. **1884** *Boston Jrnl.* 6 Sept., Baltimore warehouses for Rent. **1889** *Century Mag.* Aug. 590/2 The last time I saw it, it was for rent. **1904** *Charlotte Observer* 27 May 4 For Rent . . . First class dwelling, No. 907 Elizabeth Avenue.

* **Rent,** *v.*

+**1.** *intr.* To secure the use of a place by paying rent.

1671 in Neill *Virginia Carolorum* 335 We suppose . . . that there is in Virginia above forty thousand persons . . . [of whom some] have come into settle and rent. **1911** OVINGTON *Half a Man* 44 [Negroes were] unable to rent in neighbourhoods suitable for respectable men and women.

+**2.** To let *for* a designated amount. {1815-28 with *at*}

1784 WASHINGTON *Diaries* II. 292 The Plantation on which Mr. Simpson lives rented well—viz. for 500 Bushels of Wheat. **1828** WEBSTER s.v., A tenement rents for five hundred dollars a year.

***3.** *tr.* To allow the use of (articles, persons, etc.) for a consideration; to hire *out.* {-1737, esp. of land and houses}

1801 *Phila. Ordinances* (1812) 174 The city commissioners are hereby authorised . . . to rent [hay scales] . . . as they now lease the public wharves. **1817** PAULDING *Lett. from South* II. 64 Our guide was a most ancient and venerable Hessian, who, to use his own expression, was *'rented'* out to the King of England, by the legitimate Prince of Hesse Castle. **1879** STOCKTON *Rudder Grange* i, It would not pay me to buy all these things and rent them out to you. **1895** *Outing* XXVII. 210/1 A few residents . . . eke out a meagre existence by renting boats to the occasional sportsman. **1903** *N.Y. Sun* 29 Nov. 26 We rent only new pianos of the most modern case design and of exquisite tone.

+**b.** *To rent,* to be rented out. {=Eng. to let} Also as an infinitive noun used attributively.

1861 *Chicago Tribune* 26 May 1/8 To Rent—Very Low—Two Floors. **1865** *Ib.* 15 April 1 House To Rent, And Furniture For Sale. **1904** *N.Y. Ev. Post* 18 June 2 The blossoming of 'To rent' signs on Broadway graphically shows the real situation.

4. To pay rent for the use of (things other than land, houses, or rooms). {1622, 1885}

'In Eng. one may pay *rent* for lands, houses, offices, and rooms, but most other commodities are *hired*' (Horwill). See HIRE *v.* 2.

1879 STOCKTON *Rudder Grange* xix, 'Mrs. Duffy,' said I, 'I want to rent a baby.' **1913** LONDON *Valley of Moon* 74 Couldn't rent animals like them. **1914** ATHERTON *Perch of Devil* ii, [She] rented the touring car she had used the night before.

+**Rent agent.** A real-estate agent who looks after the renting of properties. — **1891** *Harper's Mag.* June 60/2 David Berry became used to the surly calls of the rent agent. **1916** DU PUY *Uncle Sam* 212 It is a very small thing to send a man to a rent agent for a key to inspect lodgings.

***Rent corn.** +Indian corn taken in payment of rent. — **1863** in Rothert *Muhlenberg Co.* 276 My rent corn dispose of as soon as you can for the best price you can get.

* **Renter.** One who holds or occupies land or other property by paying rent {1766-}; a tenant farmer. {a1661-1792}

1655 *Boston Rec.* 125 A considerable part of the rent due . . . is nott brought in by the renters of the land according to the contract with the towne. **1659** *Ib.* 153 Lynde is reputed the rentor of the said land from the towne, according to a deed drawn at large. **1841** CIST *Cincinnati* 40 Houses still are . . . contracted for by renters, while in progress of building. **1882** SWEET & KNOX *Texas Siftings* 51 [He] tries to discourage us from our task of moulding public opinion by describing . . . the joyful glee of farming with negro renters 'on the shares.' **1891** O'BEIRNE *Leaders Ind. Territory* 44/1 Besides this he has two thousand acres of land under cultivation and forty-five renters. **1903** *N.Y. Ev. Post* 12 Sept., One of the largest firms of apartment renters up town. **1904** *Ib.* 8 Nov. 5 The cotton is all cultivated by renters, who pay $7 an acre. **1924** CROY *R.F.D.* No. 3 7 He cared nothing for casual conversation—especially with a 'renter.'

Rent money. Money with which to pay one's rent. — **1882** *Century Mag.* Oct. 832/2 A carpenter . . . proposed to pawn his edge-tools for rent-money. **1899** JEWETT *Queen's Twin* 202, I had to do every way to get my rent-money.

Rep.[1] An abbreviation for various words. *colloq.* {a1705-} +**1.** For REPUBLICAN. **2.** For *reputation.* {-1738} +**3.** For *representative.* — (1) **1817** *Niles' Reg.* XII. 16/2 The joint ballot of the legislature stood thus—for Wm. Findlay, 'rep.' 82. (2) **1873** BEADLE *Undevel. West* 367 A majority of citizens were negroes, with them a few whites of doubtful 'rep.' **1913** LONDON *Valley of Moon* 54 He's got a rep as a fighter. (3) **1905** *N.Y. Ev. Post* 28 Jan., We come face to face with six cowboys. They are the 'top hands' or 'reps' of a big cattle ranch.

Rep.[2] A textile of silk or wool, or both, having a transversely corded surface. {1860-} Also attrib. — **1864** STOWE *House & Home P.* 90 When I come to cover the lounges and our two old arm-chairs with marroon *rep,* it will make such a pretty effect. **1870** EGGLESTON *Queer Stories* 11 One of the green rep parlor chairs was speaking. **1897** 'THANET' *Missionary Sheriff* 142 Abbie did not see the hole in the green rep covering of the arm-chair.

Repacker. (See quot. 1828.) — **1671** *Cambridge Rec.* 197 [He] is Chosen to be the Repacker of meate. **1828** WEBSTER, *Repacker,* one that repacks.

Repair man. A man who makes a business of repairing things. — **1872** HUNTINGTON *Road-Master's Asst.* 27 It is a common practice for repair-men, when replacing mended iron, to squeeze it in perfectly tight. **1893** *Columbus Dispatch* 30 Sept., The defective tube was placed in its proper condition by Hallock, who is considered a fine repairman. **1918** OWEN *Typewriting Speed* 114 Another economy is to avoid the habit of needlessly calling for a repairman.

Repair shop. A shop where things are repaired or put back into good condition. {1899} — **1877** McCABE *Hist. Great Riots* 29 The two hundred employes of the repair-shops at Martinsburg were ordered by the leaders to join in the strike. **1882** — *New York* 318 In the yard . . . of the depot are numerous buildings for the shelter of cars and locomotives, coal sheds and repair shops. **1918** *Essex Inst. Coll.* LIV. 208 It was alleged . . . that the repair shops were run wastefully.

* **Repeal.** The act of repealing a law. **1.** (See quotations.) **2.** Used attrib. with reference to agitation by the Irish in the United States to abrogate the Union between Great Britain and Ireland. {1831-} — (1) **1766** ROWE *Diary* 90, I heard of an Express being Brought to town giving an acct. of the Repeal of the Stamp Act. **1848** *Santa Fe Republican* 23 Sept. 1/4 The cry of repeal [of the Mo. Compromise] will go forth and never cease until it has accomplished its purpose. **1925** *N.Y. Times* 15 Sept. 2/5 In December he will introduce an amendment to the Constitution providing for repeal of the Eighteenth Amendment. (2) **1842** *Niles' Nat. Reg.* 26 Feb. 416/2 National Repeal Convention. The delegates from the different states of the union to the National Irish Repeal convention assembled at Philadelphia on the 22d instant. **1843** in Sol. Smith *Theatr. Apprent.* 179 This is the language of those who have taken no part in the 'repeal meetings' in this country.

* **Repeat,** *n.* Horse racing. +The act of returning over a course just traversed. — **1856** *Porter's Spirit of Times* 25 Oct. 128/2 Nothing would have given the lovers of the trotting turf more pleasure than to witness a trot of three miles and repeat between such 'cracks' as these. **1903** A. ADAMS *Log of Cowboy* 131 A race horse can't beat an ox on a hundred miles and repeat to a freight wagon.

* **Repeat,** *v.* +*intr.* To vote more than once in a single election. (Cf. REPEATING.) — **1888** BRYCE *Amer. Commw.* II. III. lxiv. 469 Vagabonds . . . are ready to stuff ballot-boxes, to buy votes, to 'repeat,' etc.

* **Repeater.**

1. A watch or clock that, upon the pressing of a spring, will repeat the striking of the last hour and quarter hour struck. {1770-}

1838 *S. Lit. Messenger* IV. 59/1 A gemmed repeater . . . gave her the first intimation of the lateness of the hour. **1844** 'UNCLE SAM' *Peculiarities* II. 46 Mr. Smoulter . . . frequently consulted his gold repeater. **1875** HOLLAND *Sevenoaks* 6 A gold chain of fabulous weight . . . held his Jurgensen repeater.

+**2.** A firearm capable of firing a number of shots without being reloaded. {1886}

*c*1845 PAULDING *Amer. Comedies* (1847) 190 Some prefer Colt's repeaters, just for the sake, I calculate, of being singular. **1860** *Harper's Mag.* Feb. 426/1 Each of the company [was furnished] with one of the repeaters as a protection against the savage and thieving Camanche Indians. **1886** ROOSEVELT in *Outing* May 134, I fired three shots at her with the repeater. **1889** *Harper's Mag.* May 876/1 The elk . . . jump about, while the repeaters are mowing their fellows down.

+**3.** *Telegraphy.* (See quot. 1860.)

1860 PRESCOTT *Telegraph* 93 A repeater is an apparatus designed for the purpose of duplicating from one electric circuit to another the breaks and completions received from the transmitting station, for the purpose of renewing the power lost by the escape of the electric fluid into the earth through bad insulation **1869.** F. L. POPE *Electric Telegraph* 45 It was formerly customary to re-unite the messages at some intermediate station, but this duty is now usually performed by an apparatus called a *repeater.* **1876** KNIGHT 1917/2 The apparatus on the right-hand side of the repeater therefore remains quiet while the west is working.

+**4.** *Politics.* One who votes, or attempts to vote, more than once in an election.

1861 NEWELL *Orpheus C. Kerr* I. 244 This morning . . . I discovered six Repeaters among my men. Each of them voted six times last election day. **1868** [see COLONIST 2]. **1871** *Scribner's Mo.* I. 366 Repeaters changed their coats and hats after every vote. **1903** HART *Actual Govt.* 73 In some cities scores of thousands of illegal registrations stand from year to year, and are voted by repeaters who go from ward to ward. **1908** STEVENS *Liberators* 252 Repeaters went boldly from one polling place to another.

+5. A criminal repeatedly committed to prison.

*c*1882 in *Fortnightly Rev.* XLI. 389 A leader of a gang of repeaters before the ink on his fraudulent naturalization papers was dry. **1890** *Advance* 4 Dec. 909/4 The shortness of the term, the want of useful occupation, the freedom of association between prisoners, . . . breed a class of repeaters or rounders, as they are termed, some . . . recommitted more than a hundred times to the same prison. **1904** *N.Y. Ev. Post* 29 Jan. 4 A large percentage of the persons committed to the city institutions are 'repeaters,' who spend their lives in the jails and workhouses of different counties. **1924** G. C. HENDERSON *Keys to Crookdom* 5 These repeaters are observed to have certain very definite characteristics.

+6. One who repeats an athletic feat.

1895 *Outing* XXVI. 456/2 He is a 'repeater' of the first rank, such performances as winning two three-mile races in the same day . . . seeming easy for him.

*Repeating, *n.* +The action or practice of voting more than once in an election. Also attrib. — **1870** *Nation* 26 May 327/1 Mr. Sherman contrived to make it [the bill] also a means of preserving the purity of the ballot-box against white 'repeating,' false registering, false voting, and other approved Democratic machinery. **1875** *Chicago Tribune* 3 Nov. 1/3 This was done in the face of desperate and often successful attempts at repeating, notably in the Twentieth, Eighteenth, and Eighth Wards. **1903** STEFFENS in *McClure's Mag.* July 251 The repeating is done boldly, for the machine controls the election officers, often choosing them from among the fraudulent names. **1903** HAPGOOD *Autobiog. of Thief* 173 He was sent to Sing Sing for his repeating methods at election.

Repeating, *a.* {1688–} +Of firearms: Capable of firing several shots without reloading. {1858–}

1824 BLANE *Excursion U.S.* 47, I saw there several of the celebrated 'repeating swivels.' **1844** GREGG *Commerce of Prairies* I. 49 The 'repeating' arms have lately been brought into use upon the Prairies. **1854** *Penna. Agric. Rep.* 423 P. W. Porter, one Repeating Rifle. **1876** KNIGHT 1918/1 Colonel Colt is believed to be the first inventor of a really available repeating pistol. **1888** Repeating carbine [see CARBINE]. **1925** TILGHMAN *Dugout* 77 Her rifle was a new repeating Winchester.

+Repeating race. A race run to a certain point and back again over the same course. — **1868** WOODRUFF *Trotting Horse* 60 It is not the fast-trotting that will do the mischief, but the amount of work needful to put the youngster in fix for a repeating race.

Repeating watch. A watch that can be made to repeat the last hour and quarter-hour struck. {1688–} Cf. REPEATER 1. — **1712** *Boston News-Letter* 10 Nov. 2/2 Mr. Joseph Essex . . . performs all sorts of New Clocks and Watch works, viz. 30 hour Clocks, Week Clocks, . . . [and] new repeating Watches.

Repetitious, *a.* Employing or abounding in repetition; characterized by tedious repeating. {1675–} 'Common in recent American use' (*O.E.D.*). — **107** A succession, not much less repetitious or protracted, than that, in which school-boys of former times wrote. **1854** HAWTHORNE *Eng. Note-bks.* I. 136 An English legal document, . . . very long and repetitious. **1887** *Harper's Mag.* Sept. 515/2 The Governor . . . is entitled . . . to choke off an irrelevant or repetitious speaker.

Replant. A plant that is set out to replace another. — **1855** *Fla. Plantation Rec.* 133, I find that the replant is hard to live in consequence of the hot Son and rain. **1858** WARDER *Hedges & Evergreens* 66 It is extremely difficult to get replants to succeed well in a hedge-row that has grown even one season. **1868** *Ill. Agric. Trans.* VII. 172 The Gophers . . . will continue to take the re-plants year after year.

*Report, *v.*

1. *tr.* To present or return (a legislative bill) for formal consideration. {1667–}

1803 *Ann. 7th Congress* 2 Sess. 603 Mr Bayard . . . reported an amendatory bill; which was read twice. **1876** *Congress. Rec.* 14 Jan. 421/1 The civil-rights bill . . . was ordered to be reported regularly from a committee. **1883** *Rep. Indian Affairs* p. xxiv, The bill as read and referred was reported back by the Senate Committee. **1900** *Congress. Rec.* 20 Jan. 1015/2 The Secretary of War reported the bill back to us.

2. *intr.* To arrive at a place and present one's self. {1891}

1864 WEBSTER 1120/1 The officer reported to the general. **1885** GRANT *Personal Memoirs* I. 45 On the 30th of September I reported for duty at Jefferson Barracks. **1902** CORBIN *Amer. at Oxford* 296 At the tolling of a bell the student leaves all other affairs to report at a certain place.

*Reporter.

1. One employed to report speeches, meetings, or other facts and events, esp. for a newspaper or periodical; a newspaper reporter. {1813–}

1798 *Ann. 5th Congress* 1289 The House ought to render the reporters as independent and eligible as they could be. **1856** *Democratic Conv. Proc.* 21 These gentlemen should be admitted as reporters. **1870** O. LOGAN *Before Footlights* 245 The man who goes to a fire, and tells how many houses were burnt down, is a 'reporter.' **1882** McCABE *New York* 228 A reporter of one of the city dailies is on hand to 'write up' the wedding in the most glowing terms. **1902** LORIMER *Lett. Merchant* 105 Said he was a reporter and wanted to interview me on the December wheat deal. **1912** NICHOLSON *Hoosier Chron.* 138 The reporter and the caretaker were making no progress.

2. One officially appointed to report court proceedings, legislative debates, etc. {*a*1617–, of law cases}

1804 *Mass. Laws* 227 His Excellency the Governor . . . [shall] appoint some suitable person, learned in the law, to be a Reporter of the Decisions of the Supreme Judicial Court. **1812** *Ann. 12th Congress* 1 Sess. 1192 Mr. Key made some remarks which were not all distinctly heard by the Reporter. **1870** *Ill. Constitution* vi. § 9 The supreme court shall appoint one reporter of its decisions who shall hold his office for six years. **1894** Court reporter [see COURT 4].

+3. (See quotation.)

1895 *Westminster Gaz.* 12 Dec. 7/2 When a point was obtained, and the birds were fairly located, . . . the dog took his master right back to where the covey still lay crouched. . . . Such animals are called 'reporters.'

+Reporterize, *v. tr.* To subject to the influence of reporters. Also *ppl. a.* — **1888** *Harper's Mag.* July 314/2 Our reporterized press is often truculently reckless of privacy and decency. **1892** HOWELLS *Quality of Mercy* 152 The Events had been in the management of a journalist, . . . a certain Bartley Hubbard, who had risen from the ranks of the reporters, and who had thoroughly reporterized it in the worst sense.

+Reportorial, *a.* Characteristic of, pertaining to, or consisting of reporters. {1890} — **1858** *82d Anniv. of Amer. Indep.* (Boston) 6 As far as reportorial observation could extend, the best possible temper prevailed. **1860** *Independent* 20 Sept. (Chipman), Its editorial and reportorial departments. **1872** 'MARK TWAIN' *Roughing It* 422 From mere reportorial instinct, . . . [I] took out my watch and noted the time of day. **1899** T. HALL *Tales* 170 Hamilton had recently been dropped from the reportorial staff of the *Herald.* **1904** *Baltimore American* 13 June 6 Editorial and reportorial offices are now located in the second floor.

+Reportorially, *adv.* In the capacity or manner of a reporter. — **1862** *N.Y. Tribune* 22 April 1/4 At headquarters this morning—I mean those of Gen. Heintzelman, to which 1 am reportorially attached—I found things quiet enough. **1888** *Nation* 5 Jan. 3/3 The 'movements,' of troops near the frontier [are] a good thing to 'work up,' either editorially or 'reportorially.' **1901** *Pop. Science Mo.* Feb. 382 The newspaper must keep pegging away at it [*sc.* the weather], editorially and 'reportorially.'

‖Repose. (See quot. and cf. POSE.) — **1853** BOND *Minnesota* 240 The voyageur often finds 'a repose,' that is, something to place his burden upon while he rests, every three miles in crossing a portage.

*Representation.

1. The aggregate of the representatives of a given constituency; a delegation {1790–}; the representatives of a whole area, as of the entire country.

1787 *Constitution* i. § 2 When vacancies happen in the Representation from any State, the Executive Authority thereof shall issue Writs of Election. **1791** *Ann. 2d Congress* 177 The representation ought as nearly as possible to express not only the will, but to participate in the wishes and interests of the people. **1816** *Ann. 14th Congress* 1 Sess. 215 The small States should be districted for the election of their Representations.

2. The system or fact of being represented by delegates in a legislative or electoral body. {1769–}

1765 OTIS *Vindication of Brit. Colonies* (1769) 31 Were I convinced . . . that it is reasonable and best that the colonies should be taxed by parliament, without being allowed a representation [etc.]. **1836** *S. Lit. Messenger* II. 688 The proposed constitution . . . [allows the state govts.] direct representation in the Senate. **1868** [see ELECTORAL COLLEGE]. **1878** M. C. TYLER *Hist. Amer. Lit.* I. 154 Daniel Gookin . . . was the originator and the prophet of that immortal dogma of our national greatness—no taxation without representation. **1900** *Nat. Dem. Campaign Bk.* 4 The Porto Rico law . . . imposes upon the people of Porto Rico . . . taxation without representation. **1914** *Cycl. Amer. Govt.* III. 80/1 Proportional representation in legislative bodies is obtained in theoretical perfection when each political party or group is represented by a number of delegates in exact proportion to the number of votes cast for each group.

Representative. {1647–}

1. A member of a legislative body representing a particular constituency. {1671–}

Cf. DELEGATE 2 and 3, DEPUTY 1; see also HOUSE OF REPRESENTATIVES.

+a. A member of a colonial assembly, esp. of its lower house.

1635 *Essex Inst. Coll.* IV. 93/1 By the towne representative, 22nd of the 12th moneth. **1658** *Va. Statutes at Large* I. 502 Wee find . . . The present power of government to reside in such persons as shall be impowered by the Burgesses (the representatives of the people). **1693** *N.H. Prov. Papers* II. 89 Two men [are to be chosen] as Representatives to serve in General Assembly. **1721** *New-Eng. Courant* 7 Aug. 2/1 At a Town's Meeting [in Boston] . . . for electing four Gentlemen to serve them in the great and general Court or Assembly . . . John Clark, Elisha Cook, William Hutchinson Esqrs; and Mr. William Clark Merchant, were by a great Majority chosen their Representatives. **1775** *N.Y. Prov. Congress Jrnls.* I. 11/2 A committee from the House of Representatives of the Colony of Connecticut . . . [requested] a conference.

+b. A member of a state or territorial representative body, esp. the lower house.

1776 *N.Y. Prov. Congress. Jrnls.* I. 519/1 The style or title of this House . . . [shall be] 'the Convention of the Representatives of the State of New-

York.' **1777** *Ib.* II. 373/1 As chairman of a committee of the House of Representatives of this State [Mass.], I enclose you a copy of an act [etc.]. **1815** *Niles' Reg.* VIII. 63/1 A census has recently been taken in the state of New York . . . for the purpose of apportioning the senators and representatives in the state legislature. **1837** [see GENERAL COURT 1]. **1847** *Santa Fe Republican* 27 Nov. 3/1 The other being a member of the legislature, will soon have all his time occupied . . . as a representative. **1872** *Newton Kansan* 17 Oct. 2/1 He has served in . . . the Kansas Legislature, twice as Representative, from said county. **1915** G. CHANDLER *Iowa & Nation* 108 A representative must be a male citizen of the United States, at least twenty-one years of age.

+c. A person representing a congressional district or a state at large in the lower house of Congress.

1787 *Constitution* i. § 2 No person shall be a representative who shall not . . . be an inhabitant of that state in which he shall be chosen. **1798** MANNING *Key of Liberty* 60 The duty of a Representitive . . . is to act as all his constitutiants would if they ware all present. **1832** [see ELECT *v.* 2 c]. **1872** in *Statutes at Large* XVII. 28 The Tuesday next after the first Monday in November . . . is hereby fixed . . . for the election of Representatives and Delegates to the forty-fifth Congress. **1900** *Congress. Rec.* 3 Jan. 635/2 The people . . . have never accused the Representative from the Hermitage district of Tennessee of ever taking a cowardly or unpatriotic position.

+d. Used as a title.

1898 *Kansas City Star* 18 Dec. 4/1 Interest was added to the discussion . . . by an amendment offered by Representative Little. **1907** *St. Nicholas* July 800/1 On the step, looking bigger than ever, stood Representative Gilbert.

+2. *pl.* The collective members of the lower house of a legislature; a house of representatives.

1694 SEWALL *Diary* I. 389 Henry Ems the Baker has his name put into a Commission to be a Messenger to the Representatives when sitting. **1701** *Mass. Acts & Resolves* VII. 294 A Memorial of the Lt. Governour Council and Representatives, of your Majties Province of the Massachusetts Bay. **1714** *Boston News-Letter* 8 Nov. 2/1 The Governour, Gentlemen of the Council, and Representatives [in New Haven], in a full Body attended with the Officers of the Corporation, proceeded to the Centre. **1789** MACLAY *Deb. Senate* 15 The Clerk from the Representatives was at the door with a communication. **1862** *Harper's Mag.* Aug. 368/2 The bill . . . was finally passed by a small majority in each House, . . . in the Representatives, 107 to 102.

+3. *Hall of representatives,* = REPRESENTATIVE HALL.

1817 S. BROWN *Western Gazetteer* 98 The hall of representatives [is] on the second [floor of the state house].

+Representative district. A district which elects a representative to a state legislature. — **1846** *Mich. Gen. Statutes* I. (1882) 138 If such county shall be divided into two or more senatorial or representative districts, the inspectors of election [etc.]. **1851** *Ib.* 141 Said board shall also make a duplicate statement . . . when the county alone does not constitute a representative district.

Representative government. A government based upon a system through which the people govern through their chosen representatives. {1844-} — **1798** *Ann. 5th Congress* 1132 Ought we to conclude that . . . the representative government of the United States will be destroyed by the Representatives themselves? **1824** [see CULTIVATOR 1]. **1900** *Congress. Rec.* 5 Feb. 1502/1 We speak of self-government after the manner of our self-government—a representative government. **1913** LA FOLLETTE *Autobiog.* 129 Payne and his associates stood for the destruction of representative government.

+Representative hall. The chamber of the lower house of a legislative body. — **1865** RICHARDSON *Secret Service* 81 The Mississippi State House . . . is a faded, sober edifice of the style in vogue fifty years ago, with the representative hall at one end, the senate chamber at the other. **1873** *Newton Kansan* 27 Feb. 2/1 A resolution was passed excluding Dr. Rohrbacher of Sumner county from representative hall.

+Representatives' chamber. =prec. — **1789** *Ann. 1st Congress* 207 The oath should be administered to the President in the outer gallery adjoining the Senate Chamber, [rather] than in the Representatives' Chamber. **1823** TUDOR *Life J. Otis* 435 He found the door of the representatives chamber locked.

Reprize, *v. S.* **+***tr.* To prize (tobacco) another time. — **1758** *Lett. to Washington* II. 323, 3 hhd. . . . was to light & I Carried Tobco. from mudy hole and reprizd. & maid one heavier. **1898** *Treasury Decisions Customs* II. 799 Dealers in leaf tobacco are permitted to break original packages received by them, and rehandle, assort, and reprize the same.

Republic. {1603-}

1. A state having a government in which representatives are elected by, and responsible to, the people; a democratic state. {1604-}

1775 J. ADAMS *Familiar Letters* 66, I found . . . suspicions entertained of designs of independency; an American republic. **1862** Moore *Rebellion Rec.* V. II. 79 The confederates . . . were fresh, drilled troops, led on and cheered by their best Generals, and the President of their 'Republic.' **1886** ALTON *Among Law-Makers* 113 The President . . . [was cheered] as the Chief Magistrate of the greatest and mightiest Republic in the world!

+2. *spec.* **a.** The United States.

1789 *Hist. of Congress* (1834) 150 Concessions have been made from political motives, which, we conceive, may endanger the republic. **1848** *Commercial* (Wilmington, N.C.) 28 Nov. 2/2 (Th. S.), Mr. Jefferson styled those who contended for the veto power in the early days of the Republic, Monocrats. **1886** ALTON *Among Law-Makers* 9 Congress . . . is vested with the supreme power of the Republic. **1900** *Congress. Rec.* 20 Feb. 1996/1 The very scheme of government involved in itself . . . expansion of the protection of the Constitution over all parts of the domain of the Republic.

+b. One of the states of the Union.

1836 *S. Lit. Messenger* II. 282 Our own most beautiful system of Confederated Republics.

+c. = REPUBLIC OF TEXAS.

1836 *Diplom. Corr. Texas* I. (1908) 129 Many of the most important laws for the civil and military government of the Republic have been passed. **1840** *Texas Sentinel* (Austin) 22 Jan. 1/1 The land then became the property of the Republic. **1852** GOUGE *Fiscal Hist. Texas* 35 The first Congress under the Republic called for a report of the transactions of the treasury under the Provisional Government.

Republican, *n.* {1691-}

1. a. One who favors or supports a republican form of government. {1697-} **b.** One who believes in the principles of equality and liberty.

See also RED REPUBLICAN.

1775 BURNABY *Travels* 49 The Pennsylvanians . . . are great republicans, and have fallen into the same errors in their ideas of independency, as most of the other colonies have. **1778** HAMILTON *Works* VII. 537 These things wound my feelings as a Republican more than I can express. **1778** J. ADAMS *Familiar Lett.* 329 Stern and haughty republican as I am, I cannot help loving these people [the French] for their earnest desire and assiduity to please. **1787** MADISON *Federalist* x, And according to the degree of pleasure and pride we feel in being republicans, ought to be our zeal in cherishing the spirit and supporting the character of Federalists. **1837** *S. Lit. Messenger* III. 393 We were simple republicans from the United States of America. **1840** *Picayune* 16 Aug. 2/1 Any plain republican who wishes to have an idea of what a palace looks like, had better . . . just step on board magnificent steamer Gen. Pratte. **1863** NORTON *Army Lett.* 185 The marble columns . . . make up a scene of wonder and grandeur to a plain republican like me.

2. *spec.* **+a.** A member of a Pennsylvania political party opposed to the Constitutionalists (q.v., sense a). Now hist.

Cf. REPUBLICAN PARTY 1.

1782 J. ADAMS *Diary* Works III. 353 Vaughan has a brother in Philadelphia, who has written him a long letter about the Constitutionalists and the Republicans. *a*1821 BIDDLE *Autobiog.* 195, I found Council nearly divided between what were then called Republicans and Constitutionalists.

+b. A member of the early Republican party (sense 2); a Democratic Republican.

See also INDEPENDENT REPUBLICAN 1, JEFFERSONIAN REPUBLICAN, and cf. ANTI-FEDERALIST, DEMOCRAT 1, DEMOCRATIC PARTY.

1799 WASHINGTON *Writings* XIV. 181n., We are sure there will be none on the part of the *Republicans*, as they have very erroneously called themselves. **1804** C. B. BROWN tr. Volney *View* p. xii, I should have dwelt upon the grand source of their divisions, in their jarring political systems, which have split the nation into federalists and republicans. **1808** J. ADAMS *Works* IX. 602 The federal administration lasted twelve years. The republicans . . . have ruled eight years. **1809** KENDALL *Travels* III. 3 By the exclusive assumption of the name *republican*, the assuming party designs to throw, upon the other, the stigma, . . . of a fondness for regal government. **1814** [see FEDERALIST 1 b]. **1824** *Nat. Intelligencer* 10 Feb. 3/1 The Republicans of the United States are generally opposed to a Congressional Caucus. **1840** *Globe* (Washington) 11 April 3/6 The Republicans of Kinderhook have done their duty—they rallied en masse to the polls.

+c. A member of the modern Republican party organized in 1854-56.

See also BLACK REPUBLICAN, INDEPENDENT REPUBLICAN 2.

[**1854** A. E. BOVAY in Curtis *Republican Party* (1904) I. 177 Urge them [the opponents of the Kansas-Nebraska Bill] to forget previous political names and organizations, and to band together under the name I suggested to you at Lovejoy's Hotel in 1852. I mean the name 'Republican.'] **1858** *Harper's Mag.* May 832/2, 92 are Republicans, 22 Democrats, and 6 Americans. **1864** *Ore. State Jrnl.* 23 July 1/1 Did ever Whig or Republican preach secession, enforcing his doctrine with arms? **1872** [see FREE-SOILER]. **1887** *Courier-Journal* 21 Jan. 3/3 The dispatch to the Times . . . has created a stampede among the Republicans holding over there. **1913** LA FOLLETTE *Autobiog.* 374, I was then escorted to my desk in what was called the Cherokee Strip—a group of seats on the Democratic side of the house which was occupied by the Republicans in the Senate and only 31 Democrats.

+3. (See quotation.)

1832 FERRALL *Ramble* 88 The stumps . . . and 'republicans,' (projecting roots of trees, so called from the stubborn tenacity with which they adhere to the ground) . . . rendered the difficulties of traversing this forest [great].

+4. Commonly used in the names of newspapers. Also attrib.

1844 (*title*), Springfield Republican. **1852** 'MARK TWAIN' in *Hannibal Jrnl.* 23 May, The Burial of Sir Abner Gilstrap, Editor of the Bloomington 'Republican.' **1870** — *Galaxy* Nov. 732/1, I stood before the 'Republican' office and looked up at its tall unsympathetic front.

Republican, *a.* {1691–}

1. a. Favoring a republic; characteristic of one who believes in a republic. {1793–} **b.** Characteristic of, or belonging to, a republic. {1712–}

1778 in *S. Lit. Messenger* XXVII. 261/2 Pray inform our Republican friends of the true cause of that appointment, that they may not for a moment entertain a thought that we are lapsing into Aristocracy. **1787** *Constitution* iv. § 4 The United States shall guarantee to every State in this Union a republican form of government. **1807** IRVING, etc. *Salmagundi* 411 The multitude [complimented] his republican simplicity. **1841** [see FANDANGO 3]. **1850** *31st Congress 1 Sess.* Sen. Ex. Doc. No. 76, 3 New Mexico . . . asks to be admitted into the Union under a republican constitution. **1900** *Congress. Rec.* 31 Jan. 1363/1 The right of public discussion . . . [is] an absolutely essential force to the preservation and protection of this grand republican form of government of ours.

+2. Of or pertaining to the Democratic-Republican party.

[**1796** JEFFERSON *Writings* IX. 351, I had supposed the republican vote would have been considerably minor.] **1800** *Steele P.* I. 193 There is almost a certainty of there being a Republican ticket so far as to Mr. Jefferson. **1806** *Balance* V. 362/3 Much labor and expense have been taken . . . as appears from the account exhibited to the 'Republican Committee.' **1808** *Boston Courier* 3 Nov. 1/1 Republican convention . . . of republican delegates from every town in the county of Essex. **1813** *Niles' Reg.* V. 120/2 A majority of the votes in Alleghany county were in favor of the 'republican' candidates, the *judges* of the election. **1834** *Visit to Texas* xiii. 116 This 'Republican' meeting was held in a small log building. **1836** *S. Lit. Messenger* II. 284 Virginia was republican.

+3. Of or pertaining to the modern Republican party. **a.** Designating conventions or other meetings held by the members of the Republican party.

1856 *Porter's Spirit of Times* 4 Oct. 71/1 New Jersey . . . [was] discovered by the late Republican Convention, in their explorations for a candidate for Vice President. **1868** *N.Y. Herald* 10 July 6/3 Here is all the work of the Republican State Convention done. **1872** *Newton Kansan* 22 Aug. 3/1 A Republican County Convention will be held . . . to select delegates to attend . . . the Republican Congressional Convention. **1884** *Boston Jrnl.* 14 Aug., The Republican caucuses in Boston will be held on the evening of Wednesday, the 27th inst. **1893** *Harper's Mag.* Feb. 473 Mr. Curtis's reminiscences of the Republican National Convention of 1860 with a piece with his reminiscences of other similar events. **1905** *N.Y. Ev. Post* 6 Dec. 3 Vice-Chancellor Stevenson refused to make any injunctive order concerning the Republican primaries.

+b. Designating persons or groups of persons who belong to or represent the Republican party.

1860 B. ALCOTT *Journals* 330 Cast my vote for Lincoln and the Republican candidates generally. **1881** *Ore. State Jrnl.* 15 Jan. 2/1 The Tennessee legislature elected a republican greenbacker speaker of the house. **1888** *Nation* 12 Jan. 21/3 This outspoken declaration in favor of tariff reform . . . [comes from] the leading Republican Senator from the West. **1888** *Voice* 9 Aug., The Barney Rourke Association, a social organization named after that gin-miller and Republican 'boss.' **1900** *Congress. Rec.* 15 Jan. 813/2 Reported back by the Republican majority of that committee with the recommendation [etc.].

+c. Designating various newspapers that support the Republican party.

1861 E. COWELL *Diary* 318 The Republican journals continue their attacks on the policy of the President. **1873** *Newton Kansan* 15 May 2/2 Emporia having now two Republican papers is making rapid progress toward a division. **1881** *Ore. State Jrnl.* 8 Jan. 4/2 Their only daily in Milwaukee . . . has been sold to a company which will convert it into a Republican concern. **1913** LA FOLLETTE *Autobiog.* 251 The people were left with no large English-speaking Republican Daily to fight for their cause.

+d. Designating various committees of the party organization.

1870 *Republican Rev.* 20 Aug. 1/1 Will anybody inform us if there is a Republican County Committee in the county of Bernalillo? **1880** *Cimarron News & Press* 27 May 2/1 Whether a change in the Republican Central Committee would be beneficial to the party must be determined by the active politicians. **1884** *Boston Jrnl.* 24 Oct. 2/4 Among the contributions received by the Republican National Committee Wednesday was a $1 bill from an Irish girl in New Jersey. **1900** *Congress. Rec.* 10 Jan. 737/1 In 1884 he became a member of the national Republican committee.

+e. Designating various programs, lists, etc., endorsed by the Republican party.

1875 *Congress. Rec.* 27 Feb. 1888/2 Washington Jones, colored, . . . testified to voting the republican ticket, and being promised . . . a horse or mule, and forty acres of land. **1888** *Ib.* 19 Dec. 346/1 That poor, de-

luded victim of a bunco-steerer is not more certain to lose . . . than is the farmer as he struggles in the toils and meshes of Republican tariff legislation. **1904** *Omaha Bee* 16 Aug. 4 The republican campaign book stands upon . . . a record of promises made good.

+f. Used in the predicate.

1872 *Newton Kansan* 22 Aug. 2/1 [We] shall be known and found genuinely Republican. **1883** *Harper's Mag.* Dec. 162/1 Iowa went Republican . . . on the whole ticket by 30,000 plurality.

+4. Belonging to that part of the Pawnee tribe that once lived on the Republican River. (Cf. PAWNEE REPUBLICANS.)

1814 LEWIS & CLARK *Travels* (1817) I. opp. p. 1 (*map*), Great Pawnee & Republican Vill. 4000 Souls. **1907** HODGE, etc. *Amer. Indians* I. 707/1 *Kitkehahki*, . . . one of the tribes of the Pawnee confederacy . . . , sometimes called Republican Pawnee.

+Republican club. A political club supporting the Republican party. Also attrib. — **1867** in Fleming *Hist. Reconstruction* II. 18 You should organize Union Leagues and Republican Clubs. **1900** *Congress. Rec.* 23 Jan. 1097/1 Have you read Governor Voorhees's speech at the Republican club dinner in New York City?

+Republican dog. (See quotation.) — **1821** *Amer. Jrnl. Science* III. 27 There are also [on the north side of the Arkansas], it is said, prairie dogs, called by some republican dogs, on account of their living in large families.

Republican government. A government in which the sovereign power lies in the people or their elected representatives. — **1776** in F. Chase *Hist. Dartmouth Coll.* I. 659 Fear is the principle of a despotic, honour of a kingly, and virtue is the principle of a republican government. **1813** J. ADAMS *Works* X. 52 The nation would succeed in establishing a free republican government. **1855** in Hambleton *H. A. Wise* 312, I do not believe that a republican government can last long [without public discussion]. **1902** MEYER *Nominating Systems* 44 There should be sufficient interest . . . to struggle for the recovery of the place which a republican government promises to every citizen.

Republicanism.

1. The principles or theories of republican government; attachment to republican institutions. {1689–}

1771 BOUCHER *View of Causes Amer. Revol.* 104 A levelling republican spirit in the Church naturally leads to republicanism in the State. **1781** PETERS *Hist. Conn.* 93 Republicanism, schisms, and persecutions, have ever prevailed in this Colony. **1832** DUNLAP *Hist. Amer. Theatre* 41 Washington, . . . standing in the balcony in all the simplicity of republicanism, took the oath. **1848** *Santa Fe Republican* 24 May 2/3 Soon will we see Mexicans and Americans . . . pushing forward with that friendship and zeal, that Republicanism always brings about. **1872** R. G. McCLELLAN *Republicanism in Amer.* 22 Republican government . . . has in our country so completely leveled *caste*, sectionalism and intolerance . . . as to fully demonstrate the power of Republicanism.

2. +a. The principles or policies of the Democratic-Republican party. Now hist.

1801 CUTLER in *Life & Corr.* II. 44 Jefferson's speech though a mixed medley of Jacobinism, Republicanism, and Federalism . . . is extremely smooth. **1833** [see FEDERALISM b].

+b. The principles and policies of the modern Republican party.

1855 in Hambleton *H. A. Wise* 162 If Know-Nothingism is perpetuated, Republicanism is at an end. **1864** F. WOOD *Copperhead Catechism* 11 The chief aim of a Copperhead is . . . the annihilation of Republicanism. **1873** *Republic* I. 46 The leading lights of Democracy and Republicanism are alike frail and fallible. **1900** *Congress. Rec.* 22 Jan. 1035/1 The colored race casts a solid vote for the cause of Republicanism.

+3. A term or expression characteristic of the people of a republic, esp. of the U.S.

1868 HAWTHORNE *Our Old House* 47 He used to come and sit or stand by my fireside, . . . [with] kindly endurance of the many rough republicanisms wherewith I assailed him.

+Republican Methodist. *Hist.* One of a group of Methodists withdrawing from the Methodist Episcopal church in 1792 and after 1794 known as Christians. (Cf. CHRISTIAN *n.* 2, CHRISTIAN CONNECTION.) — **1844** Rupp *Relig. Denominations* 167 At first they took the name of 'Republican Methodists,' but at a subsequent conference resolved to be known as Christians only. **1919** *Census: Religious Bodies 1916* II. 448/2 James O'Kelley, of Virginia, with a considerable body of sympathizers, withdrew . . . and organized the 'Republican Methodists,' who later joined with others in . . . the 'Christian Church.'

Republican party. {1848–}

+1. In Pennsylvania, from about 1780 to 1800, a party advocating change in the state constitution.
Cf. REPUBLICAN *n.* 2 a.

1788 *Penna. Gazette* 9 Jan. 3/2 It is the duty of the antifoederalists, in a particular manner in Pennsylvania, to learn wisdom from the conduct of the republican party.

+2. The Democratic-Republican party.

1800 MONROE in Benton *30 Years' View* I. 354/1 The fair prospect of the republican party may be overcast. **1840** *Globe* (Washington) 16 April 3/5 The Republican party is sound to the core in this section of the State.

1847 POLK *Diary* (1929) 187 He had been in favour of Mr. Crawford as the nominee in the caucus of the Republican party.

+3. The modern national political party organized in 1854–56 to oppose the extension of slavery, later advocating a liberal interpretation of the constitution, protective tariffs, etc.

1857 BENTON *Exam. Dred Scott Case* 56 That jealous Republican party . . . had just come into power . . . upon the cry of saving the Constitution at the last gasp. **1867** H. LATHAM *Black & White* 72 On Saturday last a Caucus of the republican party was held. **1868** [see FREE-SOILER]. **1888** *Amer. Almanac* 268 In Missouri and West Virginia [in 1884], there was a 'fusion' of the Republican and the National Greenback parties, on one Electoral ticket. **1900** *Congress. Rec.* 20 Feb. 2009 Imperialism . . . is the new mission and the aspiration of the Republican party. **1924** *Forum* June 813 The Republican Party is a party dedicated to the maintenance inviolate of the rights of the States.

Republican society. +A society of Pennsylvania Republicans: (see REPUBLICAN *n.* 2 a). — **1779** *Penna. Gazette* 24 March 1/1 The members of the Republican Soc'y beg leave to address you.

+Republican state. A state that normally supports the Republican ticket. — **1857** BENTON *Exam. Dred Scott Case* 36 The only limitation upon its power was . . . in the obligation to dispose of the soil, to populate it, and to build up future Republican States upon it. **1925** BRYAN *Memoirs* 74 The state of Nebraska was a Republican state.

+Republican swallow. The cliff swallow (*Petrochelidon albifrons*), which lives in large flocks. — **1824** AUDUBON in *Lyceum of N.Y. Annals* I. 164 In the spring of 1815, I saw a few of these birds for the first time at Henderson. . . . I drew up at the time a description under the name of *H. republicana, Republican swallow*, in allusion to their mode of association for the purposes of building and rearing their young. **1917** *Birds of Amer.* III. 84 Cliff Swallow. . . . [Also called] Republican Swallow.

+Republic of Texas. The independent state of Texas between 1836 and 1845. — **1836** in Gouge *Fiscal Hist. Texas* 57 An act to establish a General Land-Office for the Republic of Texas. **1841** TYLER in *Pres. Mess. & P.* IV. 90 The resolution of the House of Representatives [requested] . . . information touching the relations between the United States and the Republic of Texas. **1845** [see ERECT *v.* 2].

* Repudiate, *v.*

1. *tr.* To refuse to pay (a public debt). {1863}

1841 *Week in Wall Street* 66 Villainy and irresponsibility . . . contributed . . . to induce a proposition, in some of the States, to disgrace themselves by repudiating their debts. **1852** GOUGE *Fiscal Hist. Texas* 247 Mississippi has repudiated the Union Bank bonds. **1855** *S. Lit. Messenger* XIX. 71/2 The spirited manner in which the State of Alabama had repudiated a public debt of some $500,000, gave him a favorable opinion of that people as a community of litigants. **1859** *Harper's Mag.* Sept. 570/2 When Rhode Island, by her legislation, from 1843 to 1850, repudiated her revolutionary debt, Dr. Richmond removed from that state to this borough.

2. In absol. use. {1843–, in reference to American state debts}

1853 *Knickerb.* XLII. 55 [He] was so disgusted when his state repudiated, that *he* repudiated *it*. **1858** *Harper's Mag.* March 448/2 The broker, finding he was from Illinois, . . . said, bluntly, 'Well, are you going to repudiate up there?' **1862** J. SPENCE *Amer. Union* 74 In each of the States that has repudiated there was a large majority of men thoroughly honourable in their private affairs.

‖**Repudiated state.** A state that has repudiated its debts. — **1847** SHELBURNE *Tourist's Guide* 257 A banker . . . asked me if I thought those repudiated States would ever be willing or able to meet the demands on them.

*Repudiation. The action of refusing to discharge a debt. {1843–, in regard to American state debts} — **1842** MANN *Oration 4 July* 69 The number of fraudulent bankruptcies, . . . the repudiation of State debts! **1844** *N. Amer. Rev.* Jan. 130 The word *repudiation*, in the sense in which it is now commonly used, was first adopted in the State of Mississippi. **1866** 'F. KIRKLAND' *Bk. Anecdotes* 126/1 Peabody, suffering from gout and Mississippi Repudiation, lost his temper. **1872** [see CARPETBAGGED *a.*]. **1886** *N.Y. Tribune* 14 July 2/1 The resolution was unpatriotic and an act of repudiation.

+Repudiationist. One who repudiates, or advocates repudiation of, some responsibility, esp. state debts. — **1862** *N.Y. Tribune* 21 Jan. (Chipman), Jeff. Davis was first known in public life as a Repudiationist. **1868** *Ore. State Jrnl.* 8 Aug. 2/1 Call us a Copperhead, . . . a repudiationist, and all the decent names you can think of. **1896** *Columbus Dispatch* 7 Oct. 4 Every day the repudiation of the repudiationists becomes more certain.

Repudiator. One who advocates repudiating a debt. {1843–, in regard to Amer. state debts} — **1879** *Nation* 13 Nov. 317/2 The people of the State appear now to be divided into two main parties by the McCulloch Bill, which the Repudiators desired repealed. **1886** ROOSEVELT *Life of Benton* 220 Before Jefferson Davis took his place among the arch-traitors in our annals, he had already been known as one of the chief repudiators.

+Request envelope. An envelope bearing a request that it be returned to the sender in a designated number of days if unclaimed. — **1865** *Rep. Postmaster-General* 8 To encourage the purchase of *request envelopes*, the law should be changed so as to allow the return of such letters to the writers free of postage. **1893** *Congress. Rec.* 18 Feb. 1802/1

You have allowed . . . the right of the Postmaster-General to have printed upon the request envelope, 'if not called for' within any number of days fixed, 'return to———.'

*Requisition. 1. Under the Articles of Confederation, an order made by Congress on the different states for money. **2.** 'A demand of the executive of one country or State upon another from a fugitive from justice' (B. '59). — **(1)** **1796** *Ann. 4th Congress* 2 Sess. 2699 The system of requisitions upon the States . . . utterly failed under the late Confederation. **(2)** **1842** *Niles' Nat. Reg.* 11 June 240/3 Requisition. A negro man against whom eight indictments were found in Arkansas, in July last, and who escaped into Canada. **1859** J. BROWN in Johnson *Anderson Co., Kansas* 107 The Governor of Missouri has made a requisition upon the Governor of Kansas for the delivery of all such as were concerned in the last named 'dreadful outrage.'

+Rescue grass. [Origin uncertain.] A brome grass (*Bromus unioloides*) cultivated in the southern states for forage and hay. — **1884** VASEY *Agric. Grasses* 106 *Bromus unioloides* . . . is said to have been introduced into Georgia by General Iverson, of Columbus, and by him called rescue grass. **1901** MOHR *Plant Life Ala.* 827.

Resentment. *New Eng.* A show of appreciation. {1651–1762} — **1743** *N.H. Prov. Papers* V. 669 We cannot but with grateful resentment acknowledge the great concern of the Lords Justices for our welfare & safety. **1849** *N. Amer. Rev.* July 104 A farmer in . . . New England, who had recently lost his wife, called upon a lawyer of the place for advice under his bereavement, remarking that he wished to make a proper resentment on the occasion.

* Reservation.

+1. A tract of land set aside by agreement between the government and an Indian tribe, reserved for the exclusive use and occupancy of the Indians; the Indians on such a tract of land.

Some states had set aside reservations before the national government was given power to make treaties with the Indians. See also INDIAN RESERVATION.

1789 *Ann. 1st Congress* I. 41 The reservation, in the treaty with the Six Nations, . . . is within the territory of the State of New York, and ought to be so explained as to render it conformable to the Constitution of the United States. **1792** *Mass. H. S. Coll.* 1 Ser. I. 285 The Indians are settled on all the reservations made by this state [N.Y.]. **1825** *Statutes at Large* VII. 245 From the lands above ceded to the United States, there shall be made the following reservations, of one mile square, for each of the half breeds of the Kanzas nation. **1866** *Wkly. New Mexican* 8 June 2/2 They told the sufferers not to lay it to the Mosque Navajos as they were not from the Reservation. **1871** *Rep. Indian Affairs* (1872) 283 The interests of the reservation were rapidly declining. **1873** COZZENS *Marvellous Country* 186 This reservation is about twenty-five miles long and seven miles wide. **1903** HART *Actual Govt.* 361 The Western people do not like to have reservations in their neighborhood, and constant pressure is put on the government to diminish or abolish them. **1923** J. H. COOK *On Old Frontier* 213 My friend Joseph Mousseau . . . still lives on Pine Ridge Reservation in South Dakota.

+b. With the specifying name of an Indian tribe.

1796 *Mass. H. S. Coll.* 1 Ser. V. 21 In the district comprehended between the Oneida reservation, and the Mohawk river, . . . there were, in 1785, but two families. **1835** JACKSON in *Pres. Mess. & P.* III. 135, I transmit herewith . . . four treaties for Potawatamie reservations. **1856** PIERCE *Ib.* V. 377 The sum of $16,024.80 . . . [remains] from the sales of Choctaw orphan reservations . . . of the treaty of 1830. **1876** RAYMOND *8th Rep. Mines* 324 The Uncompahgre district includes all lands drained by the Uncompahgre and its tributaries as far north as the Ute reservation. **1912** *Indian Laws & Tr.* III. 672 The purpose . . . is to restore the White Mountain Apache Indian Reservation . . . to the status existing prior to the said proclamation of March 2, 1909.

+c. *To leave* (or *be off*) *the reservation,* to go outside the limits of a reservation; to be away from one's appointed place; to go on a plundering expedition.

1871 *Republican Rev.* 25 Feb. 1/4 The Apaches of La Canada . . . have left the reservation. **1885** *Wkly. New Mexican Rev.* 5 Feb. 4/7 The Navajoes in New Mexico are reported to be off their reservation and depredating among the cattle. **1900** ADE *More Fables* 37 He bribed the Hired Girl to tell him Everything that happened while he was off the Reservation.

+2. A tract of land set apart for some other use; the action or fact of reserving such land.

See also FOREST RESERVATION, MILITARY RESERVATION.

1792 *Ann. 2d Congress* 1036 The claims covered by the first reservation are—1st. The bounties in land given by the said state of North Carolina in their Continental line. **1798** MORSE *Amer. Gaz.* 570 In these reservations [of Vt. land], liberal provision is made for the support of the gospel, and for the promotion of common and collegiate education. **1859** BARTLETT 361 Reservation, a tract of the public land reserved or set aside for some public use, as for schools. **1883** *Century Mag.* June 218/1 Between these two lines was a Government reservation.

+b. *Connecticut Reservation,* (see quot. 1901).

1812 MELISH *Travels* II. 257 We now entered into the *Connecticut Reservation,* at the 41st degree of latitude. **1901** JAMESON & BUEL *Encycl. Dict. Amer. Hist.* II. 50 The jurisdiction over this part [of w. Ohio] was ceded to the United States by Connecticut in 1786, but the ownership of the lands was retained by that State, which gave rise to the name, 'The Connecticut Reservation,' or 'Western Reserve.'

+3. An engagement of seats, rooms, etc., in advance of their use. *To make a reservation*, to reserve something for use at a designated time.

1906 LYNDE *Quickening* 118 That sleeping-car reservation for Thomas Gorden—have you secured it? 1907 *Springfield W. Repub.* 19 Dec. 16 A considerable number of New York and Boston people have made reservations at the Curtis hotel in Lenox for the holiday season. 1925 *Scribners' Mag.* July Advt. 32/1 Ward-Belmont [School] for girls. . . . Reservations for 1925–26 should be made as soon as possible to insure entrance.

+4. Attrib. in sense 1 with *farm, Navajo, plan*, etc.

1861 *Harper's Mag.* Aug. 308/1 In 1853 laws were passed for the establishment of a reservation system in California. 1866 *Weekly New Mexican* 8 June 2/1 Don Esteban Coruna . . . was killed by the reservation Navajos. 1877 *Rep. Indian Affairs* 40 The following are the productions of the reservation farm and garden. 1883 *Century Mag.* Aug. 518/2 About this time a bill . . . to provide homes for the Mission Indians on the reservation plan, was reported unfavorably upon by a Senate committee. 1887 *Pall Mall Gaz.* 31 Oct. 7/1 It is acknowledged on all sides (says an American contemporary) that the reservation policy is a failure. 1893 G. W. CURTIS *Horses, Cattle* 96 [We have made] careful, continued observation of the ponies belonging to the various 'Reservation' tribes.

+**Reservation Indian.** An Indian who resides on a reservation. — 1866 *Rep. Indian Affairs* 100 The reservation Indian is under the protection of the general government. 1891 *Harper's Mag.* Dec. 38/1 Possibly some took it with an admixture of tobacco and wild currant to make them drunk, or, in reality, very sick—which is much the same thing to a reservation Indian. 1916 EASTMAN *From Deep Woods* 125, I was much struck with the love of . . . independence in these, the first 'reservation Indians' I had ever known.

Reserve, *n.* {1644–}

+1. An alternate commissioner or deputy of a New England colony in the councils of the New England Confederation.

1652 *Mass. Bay Rec.* IV. 1. 77 Att a Gennerall Courte of Elecctjons, held at Boston, . . . Mr. Simon Bradstreete, Capt. Wm. Hawthorne, were chosen Commissioners. . . . Jno. Endecot, Esq. . . . Rich. Bellingham, Esq., Reserves. 1665 *Conn. Rec.* II. 18 Mr. Mathew Allyn [was chosen] a reserue.

+2. A place reserved for the future use or occupancy of an individual. In place names. *Obs.*

1700 *Md. Hist. Mag.* XX. 283 Olivers Reserve. *Ib.* 286 Richardsons Reserve.

+3. =WESTERN RESERVE. Also called *Connecticut reserve*. Cf. RESERVATION 2 b.

1798 in *Western Reserve Hist. Soc. Publ.* No. 96, 175 We the Subscribers are severally interested in the tract of Land called the Connecticut Reserve. 1805 *Statutes at Large* VII. 88 One hundred and seventy five dollars annuity as aforesaid, is the amount of the consideration paid by the agents of the Connecticut Reserve for the cession of their lands. 1808 JEFFERSON *Writings* III. 462, I have particularly contemplated . . . the acquisition of the eastern moiety of the peninsula between the lakes Huron, Michigan, and Erie, extending it to the Connecticut Reserve. 1817 S. BROWN *Western Gazetteer* 323 Mill-stones, grind-stones, and whetstones, are made in several parts of the Reserve. 1843 *Amer. Pioneer* II. 276 The missionary . . . laid his course for New England, on the Indian path from the Reserve along the lake shore to Buffalo. 1847 HOWE *Hist. Coll. Ohio* 188 The hardships and privations of the early settlers of the Reserve, are well described in the annexed article.

+4. A district or area reserved by the Indians for their own use; an individual Indian's reserved land.

1805 *Statutes at Large* VII. 98 The Mingoes . . . [reserve] also a tract of five thousand one hundred and twenty acres. . . . The latter reserve to be subject to the same laws [etc.]. 1818 F. HALL *Travels* 131 The river Credit is an Indian reserve, well stocked with salmon. 1845 HOOPER *Simon Suggs's Adv.* vi, He had brought with him to be 'certified' . . . an Indian woman whose 'reserve' was an excellent one.

+5. =RESERVATION 1: (see also quot. 1866).

1857 GIHON *Geary & Kansas* 20 The balance of this [Delaware Indian] reserve is now covered with squatters. 1864 *Wkly. New Mexican* 29 July 2/1 Gen. Carleton . . . has carried on a war against them [sc. Navajos] and inaugurated the policy of removing them from their country to a *reserve*, which has been set apart for their use, on the Pecos river. 1866 *Rep. Indian Affairs* 105 He reports several temporary reserves or farms, upon which small numbers of Indians have been collected. 1881 *Ib.* 7 The mesa known as Melno Park . . . is in the northeastern part of the reserve.

+6. Any other piece of land set aside for a special purpose. See also FOREST RESERVE.

1807 JEFFERSON *Writings* XVI. 422 We therefore met the chiefs . . . and agreed on a general boundary which was to divide their lands from those of the whites, making only some particular reserves, for the establishment of trade and intercourse with them. 1850 GLISAN *Jrnl. Army Life* 19 In view of more easily controlling the sale of contraband articles to . . . the

soldiers occupying military reserves in the Indian country, the government has found [etc.]. 1905 [see GRAZING 2].

b. (See quotation.)

1838 in Audubon *Ornith. Biog.* IV. 150 The pond is artificial, and such as in this country [S. Carolina] is called a 'Reserve.' It . . . is intended to preserve water sufficient, when needed, to irrigate and overflow the rice.

7. *attrib.* +**a.** In sense 4 with *Comanche, Indian, line.*

1865 PIKE *Scout & Ranger* (1932) 20 One faction . . . ascribed the murder to the Reserve Indians of Texas. *Ib.* 33 We saw no Indian signs until we got within three miles of the Reserve-line on the east. *Ib.* 47 A little further along was a pass, given . . . to a Reserve Comanche of an unpronounceable name.

+**b.** (*Federal*) *reserve bank*, one of the twelve banks created by the federal government for the deposit of reserves by member banks.

1913 *Statutes at Large* XXXVIII. 1. 251 The term 'member bank' shall be held to mean any national bank, state bank, or bank or trust company which has become a member of one of the reserve banks created by this Act. 1914 *Cycl. Amer. Govt.* III. 202/1 Twelve federal reserve banks were created. 1925 *New Republic* 18 March 90/2 There is, however, a much more powerful instrument in the hands of the reserve banks.

∗**Reserve,** *v.* +*tr.* To put (an Indian) on a reservation. *colloq.* (Cf. RESERVED *a.* 3.) — 1870 *Republican Rev.* 21 May 3/1 If they [the Utes] must be 'reserved' let their reservation be where they are most contented to stay.

+**Reserve city.** Any of certain cities in which national banks are required to keep certain minimum reserves against demand and time deposits. — 1900 *Congress. Rec.* 15 Feb. 1832/2 Ordinarily the country banks deposit their reserves and deposits in the reserve cities, which in turn deposit them in New York. 1913 *Statutes at Large* XXXVIII. 1. 262 The Federal Reserve Board shall be authorized: . . . To add to the number of cities classified as reserve and central reserve cities.

+**Reserve commissioner.** =RESERVE *n.* 1. — 1648 *Mass. Bay Rec.* III. 121 At a generall Court of Election, held at Boston, . . . there was chosen . . . Tho[mas] Dudley, . . . Reserue Commission[e]r.

∗**Reserved,** *a.*

+1. **a.** Of land: Kept free of settlements. **b.** Of public land: Retained unsold for some public use. See also RESERVED SECTION.

(a) 1764 *N.H. Hist. Soc. Coll.* IX. 145 Maj[o]r How . . . came to advise about settling upon ye Lds. reserved Land. (b) 1832 WILLIAMSON *Maine* II. 679 The '*reserved lands*' . . . were principally lots reserved for the future disposition of government, in the grants of townships; including probably parts of the nine Indian townships on the Penobscot river. 1844 *Indiana Senate Jrnl.* 29 Sess. 103 House Bill No. 11, entitled, an act in relation to patents to purchasers of lands in the reserved townships in Gibson and Monroe. 1890 [see FOREST LAND].

+2. *Constitutional law.* Not delegated to the federal government.

1835 *Nat. Intelligencer* 30 Oct. 3/1 The people of the District [of Columbia] . . . have reserved rights as well as others. 1890 *Cent.* 5101/2 *Reserved powers,* . . . specifically, those powers of the people which are not delegated to the United States by the Constitution of the country, but remain with the respective States.

+3. Of an Indian: Put on a reservation.

1864 *N. Mex. Press* 13 Sept. 1/3 Granting that actual depredators were unreserved Navajoes, it is evident the reserved ones became accessories after the fact.

+**Reserved section.** (See quot. 1817.) — 1804 PUTNAM in *Memoirs* 441 The printing . . . was Blanks for Leasing the reserved sections. 1817 BIRKBECK *Notes Journey in Amer.* (1818) 161 In the sale of public lands, there is a regulation, which I have before mentioned, that the sixteenth section, which is nearly the centre of every township, shall not be sold. It is called the reserved section; and is, accordingly, reserved for public uses in that township, for the support of the poor, and for purposes of education.

+**Reservee.** An Indian residing on a reservation. — 1835 *Indian Laws & Tr.* II. 445 And all such reservees as were obliged by the laws of the State in which their reservations were situated, to abandon the same . . . shall be deemed to have a just claim.

Reservoir. {1690–}

1. A tank, vat, or cistern, esp. for water. {1727–38}

1771 J. ADAMS *Diary* Works II. 268 They have built a shed over a little reservoir made of wood, . . . and into that have conveyed the water from the spring. 1787 CUTLER in *Life & Corr.* I. 206 A large reservoir of water is placed in the third loft of the house. 1792 BELKNAP *Hist. New-Hampshire* III. 114 Large troughs or vats, are placed in a central situation, to serve as reservoirs for the sap when collected. 1799 BROWN *A. Mervyn* viii, I proceeded to the bath, and, filling the reservoir with water, speedily dissipated the heat that incommoded me. 1809 A. HENRY *Travels* 69 The liquor was . . . conveyed into reservoirs or vats of moose-skin. 1827 [see CISTERN 1]. 1869 *Boyd's Business Directory* 73 Vats, Tanks and Reservoirs.

+**b.** A covered metal box attached to the side of a cooking range for keeping a supply of warm water.

1879 *Cimarron News & Press* 27 Nov. 3/1 We have a first class, New, No. 8 cooking stove with reservoir, extra warming oven [etc.].

2. A part of certain instruments or mechanisms in which a supply of fluid is kept. {1793–}

1784 CUTLER in *Life & Corr.* I. 106 Some particles of mercury [in a thermometer] had exuded through the leather of the reservoir. **1860** HAWTHORNE *Marble Faun* xliv, The lamp required to be replenished once . . . in three days, though its reservoir of oil was exceedingly capacious. **1909** WEBSTER 858/3 A pen with a reservoir in the holder.

3. A capacious receptacle made for the storage of water for irrigation, the water supply of a city, etc. {1705–}

1817 *Ann. 14th Congress* 2 Sess. 906 The lockage, aqueducts, culverts, feeders, and reservoirs of this navigation, are more expensive than all the canals required in the United States. **1832** DUNLAP *Hist. Amer. Theatre* 45 Nearly opposite . . . were the remains of aqueducts and reservoirs begun some time before 1775. **1840** *Niles' Nat. Reg.* 19 Dec. 256/1 The grand canal reservoir in Mercer County, Ohio, . . . is said to be the largest artificial lake in the world. **1885** *Wkly. New Mexican Rev.* 29 Jan. 4/2 Here large reservoirs and about two miles of substantial sluicing are to be constructed, and improved hydraulic machinery put in. **1890** *Stock Grower & Farmer* 1 March 7/1 Thirty five men are employed putting in a stone dam across the Pecos river, which is to form the reservoir that supplies the pipe line. **1907** *Indian Laws & Tr.* III. 275 The Secretary of the Interior . . . [is] authorized to acquire . . . all land . . . that he shall deem necessary in constructing a reservoir . . . on the Fort Hall Indian Reservation.

4. *attrib.* In senses 1 and 4 with *car, dam, site, system.*

1854 *Mass. Acts & Resolves* 238 On application made . . . in writing, by any person or persons owning . . . property liable to destruction or damage by the breaking of any mill or reservoir dam [etc.]. **1890** *Stock Grower & Farmer* 11 Jan. 4/4 The reservoir system [for irrigation] when adopted, has given general satisfaction. **1897** Reservoir car [see CONDUCTOR 2 b]. **1900** *Congress. Rec.* 3 Jan. 628/2 A petition . . . praying for the enactment of legislation . . . to promote the acquisition of reservoir sites.

✳ Residence.

1. A dwelling house; sometimes one of a superior or pretentious character. {1603–1844}

1835 INGRAHAM *South-West* II. 24 One or two private houses . . . [remind] one of the neat and beautiful residences on the 'coast.' **1852** EASTMAN *Aunt Phillis's Cabin* 25 The slight eminence . . . commanded a view of the residences of several gentlemen. **1853** *Harper's Mag.* Nov. 753/2 The protecting fence . . . shuts up 'the residence' from the plantation. **1881** *Rep. Indian Affairs* p. lxvi, Other buildings, including 'Odd Fellows Hall,' a large school-house, tenement-houses, and residences, are within the reservation. **1893** AULD *Picturesque Burlington* 116 Thus surrounded and enclosed by the college buildings and residences of the faculty, the old 'College Green' itself deserves more than passing mention.

2. *Attrib.* with *district, lot, plot, street.*

1861 *Chicago Tribune* 19 July 1/8 We have for sale several desirable Residence Lots on Wabash avenue. **1893** *Harper's Mag.* April 658/2 But I have strayed from the pretty residence districts of the city. **1895** *Outing* XXVII. 183/2 She led him . . . through the finest residence streets. **1906** LYNDE *Quickening* 93 The promoter had bought in the wooded hillsides facing the mountain, cut them into ten-acre residence plots, [and] run a graveled drive on the western side of the creek to front them.

+Resident. =RESIDENT GRADUATE. *Obs.* — **1851** [see RESIDENT GRADUATE].

✳ Residenter.

1. A resident or inhabitant: (see also quot. 1912). Now *local.* {1678–, in Scotland} Also *attrib.*

1797 in Hawkins *Letters* 464 By a residenter in the Cherokees, . . . I am informed [etc.]. **1816** U. BROWN *Journal* I. 269 E. Beeson introduces me to Phillip C. Pendleton Attorney at Law residenter in Martinsburgh. **1828** *Western Mo. Rev.* II. 252 But the eye traces, in new villages, neat houses, and establishments strongly contrasting with the old *outre* 'residenter' buildings, that New-England is gradually making its way. **1912** R. BINGHAM (Address 12 Dec. in Asheville, N.C.), 'Resident' . . . is never heard at all among the uneducated in Middle North Carolina, while 'residenter' is very common among them, and is never used in the sense of a mere resident. None but a citizen of long standing is ever called a 'residenter.'

+2. *Old residenter,* an early settler.

1827 *Western Mo. Rev.* I. 70 Hence arose a feud and a collision of authorities between the old and the new 'residenters.' **1838** FLAGG *Far West* II. 190 By the present degenerate race of villagers . . . the 'old residenters' [are referred to] as wonderful beings. **1873** 'MARK TWAIN' & WARNER *Gilded Age* 238 When I tell the old residenters that this thing went through [etc.]. **1898** WESTCOTT *D. Harum* 253, I ain't what ye might call an old residenter.

+Resident graduate. (See quotations.) *Obs.* — **1851** HALL *College Words* 258 In the United States, graduates who are desirous of pursuing their studies in the place where a college is situated . . . can do so in the capacity of *residents* or *resident graduates.* **1859** BARTLETT 361 *Resident Graduate,* graduates of colleges who are desirous of pursuing their studies at a college, without joining any of its departments. They may attend the public lectures . . . , and enjoy the use of its library.

✳ Resin. A solid or viscous organic secretion of plants and trees, esp. of the fir and pine trees.

1705 *Boston News-Letter* 30 July 2/2 For good and Merchantable Rezin or Turpentine *per* Ton. **1832** BROWNE *Sylva* 96 This resin [of the silver fir] is sold in Europe and the United States under the name of *Balm of Gilead.* **1899** CUSHMAN *Hist. Indians* 228 In case of sores, they applied a poultice of pounded ground ivy for a few days, then carefully washing the afflicted part with the resin of the copal-tree.

b. *Attrib.* with *plaster, soap, wood.*

1820 *U.S. Pharmacopœia* 123 Resin Plaster or Adhesive Plaster. **1855** COOKE *Ellie* 106 [He] drew from his overcoat pocket, a huge knot of resin-wood, crammed with combustible properties. **1877** BURDETTE *Rise of Mustache* 166 The 'strocky' appearance of your hair . . . instantly betrays the recent and extravagant use of resin soap.

Resk, *n.* [Dial. var. of *risk.*] Risk; danger; chance. — **1818** FESSENDEN *Ladies Monitor* 172 Provincial words [include]: . . . *resk* for risk. **1853** SIMMS *Sword & Distaff* (1854) 213, I've got nothing but the danger, and the cold, the resk and the exposure.

Resk, *v. tr.* To put (something) in danger; to run the hazard of; to venture. *dial.* — **1782** *Essex Inst. Coll.* XXXVIII. 54, I haue Resked my life for upward of Six years in the Publick Servis. **1853** SIMMS *Sword & Distaff* (1854) 86 We must resk nothing. **1921** GREER-PETRIE *Angeline at Seelbach* 3, I didn't nigh want to resk losing all them thar valuables. *Ib.* 6, I hadn't orter resked comin' to a big weaked city even with Lum.

✳ Resolute, *v.* ('Now *U.S.*' *O.E.D.*) +*intr.* To make or pass a resolution or resolutions. Also *tr.* and as *vbl. n.* — **1860** *Savannah Republican* 13 March (De Vere), When you have done resoluting, you will only have lost your time. **1887** *Courier-Journal* 25 Jan. 2/5 Therefore the revolutionary howlers 'resolute' that 'they still deem McDonald as their Senator, and will recognize no other.' **1888** BRYCE *Amer. Commw.* III. v. xc. 233 The discontented . . . flocked every Sunday afternoon to cheer denunciations of corporations and monopolists, and to 'resolute' against the rich generally. **1895** *Voice* 5 Sept. 4/5 The plutocratic organs . . . are talking of holding a national convention for the purpose of howling and resoluting. **1900** *Congress. Rec.* 17 Feb. 1901/2 They resolute, . . . and he bears the resolutions down and has read them to the House.

✳ Resolution. A decision or expression of opinion formally made by an assembly; a declaration proposed for adoption by an assembly. {1604–}

'Three kinds of resolutions are employed in Congress—simple resolutions, concurrent resolutions and joint resolutions' (1914 *Cycl. Amer. Govt.* III. 204/1). See also JOINT RESOLUTION, KENTUCKY 6, and cf. CONCURRENT *a.*

1671 *Doc. Col. Hist. N.Y.* XII. 487 The like Resolucon proposed as to Matinicock, It being a ffrontier Place, it is also allowed and approved of. **1776** *Jrnls. Cont. Congress.* IV. 15 The first resolution . . . [shall] be transmitted by express to Henry Middleton. **1787** *Constitution* i. § 7 Every Order, Resolution, or Vote to which the Concurrence of the Senate and House of Representatives may be necessary . . . shall be presented to the President of the United States. **1812** CUTLER in *Life & Corr.* II. 344 Town Meeting to consider Boston Resolutions, and to answer a letter from their Selectmen. **1842** [see EXECUTIVE *a.* 2 d]. **1877** *Harper's Mag.* March 596/1 As the debate on Foot's resolution advanced, Webster had not given it any attention. **1886** ALTON *Among Law-Makers* 45 A simple resolution extends only to the affairs of the body adopting it. **1924** E. W. HUGHES *Amer. Parliamentary Guide* 601 Resolutions as used in the practice of the Ohio General Assembly are of two kinds; House or Senate and Joint Resolutions.

attrib. **1925** BRYAN *Memoirs* 125 The resolutions committee harangued over the platform.

✳ Resolve. A declaration of purpose or opinion by a deliberative assembly; a resolution: (see quot. 1828). {1656–1713} 'Now *U.S.*' (*O.E.D.*).

1697 *Mass. Province Laws* VII. 151 Resolve for Approving, etc., the Division by the Inhabitants of Sandwich, of Scorton Neck and Shaume Neck. **1714** SEWALL *Diary* III. 6 At last the Deputies sent in this Resolve. **1778** HAMILTON *Works* VII. 540 A late resolve directs G. W. to fix the number of men [etc.]. **1828** WEBSTER s.v., Public acts of a legislature respect the state, and . . . the bills for such acts must pass through all the legislative forms. Resolves are usually private acts, and are often passed with less formality. **1866** LOWELL *Biglow P.* 2 Ser. 237 Who cares for the Resolves of '61, Thet tried to coax an airthquake with a bun?

✳ Resort. A place frequented by persons seeking health treatments, rest, or amusement. {1754–} Also *attrib.* and with defining term.

1862 Moore *Rebellion Rec.* V. 11. 147 Iuka . . . is a resort for invalids, on account of its splendid chalybeate springs. **1883** *Harper's Mag.* Sept. 521/1 The bustle of arrival and departure . . . [animates] the village in the way peculiar to American towns near a 'resort.' **1893** *Ib.* March 495 [They] now go to the so-called piny woods and mountain resorts of Georgia and the Carolinas. **1903** [see COMMUTATION]. **1919** HOUGH *Sagebrusher* 49 A few passengers from the resort hotel back in the town began to appear.

+b. A disorderly house or other place of questionable repute.

[1868 M. H. SMITH *Sunshine & Shadow* 432 One or two houses up town . . . became so notorious as resorts of the abandoned, that they were compelled to close.] 1888 *Nation* 9 Aug. 102/2 Tompkins . . . [enticed] a school-girl of thirteen . . . to 'a resort' outside the city.

Respectability. {1785-} Importance. — a1817 DWIGHT *Travels* II. 241 The District of Maine is fitted to derive its respectability especially from fishing, and commerce. 1824 MURRAY *Eng. Grammar* (ed. 5) I. 223 The respectability of the different opponents, will naturally induce the readers to pause and reflect.

*‑**Respectable,** a. Convenient; appropriate. *Obs.* — 1773 in F. CHASE *Hist. Dartmouth Coll.* I. 440, I directed the Printer to [announce a meeting] . . . at a place & spot most respectable to the College.

+**Respirometer.** 1. (See quotation.) 2. A measuring instrument used in studying respiration. — (1) 1883 KNIGHT *Suppl.* 753/1 *Respirometer*, the name adopted by Mr. Fleuss for his diver's apparatus for supplying air to a person beneath the surface of the water. (2) 1890 *Cent.* 5111/1.

*‑**Respond,** v. +1. *tr.* To answer, discharge, or satisfy, as by payment. +2. *intr.* (See quotation.) — (1) 1677 *Mass. Ct. of Assistants Rec.* I. 117 Wm. Long . . . was Attached and bound ouer in one hundred twenty & sixe pounds to respond the decree & Judgment of this Court. 1680 *Ib.* 171 The Secretary . . . shall require of the plaintiffe tenn pounds in money as Caution to respond the charges of sajd Court. (2) 1828 WEBSTER, *Respond*, . . . to be answerable; to be liable to make payment; as, the defendant is held to respond in damages.

Responsibility. {1787-} +(See quotation.) — 1890 *Cent.* 5112/1 *Responsibility*, . . . ability to answer in payment; means of paying contracts.

*‑**Responsible,** a. ‖Answerable to a charge. — 1650 in Hutchinson *Hist. Mass.* I. 452 You are required to attach the goods or lands of William Stevens to the value of one hundred pounds, so as to bind the same to be responsible at the next court at Boston.

*‑**Rest,** *n.*

*‑**1.** A support for steadying the barrel of a gun in aiming and firing.
1634 *Mass. Bay Rec.* I. 125 All the musketts, bandeleroes, & rests lately come ouer this yeare, shalbe equally devided. 1686 *Narragansett Hist. Reg.* III. 104, 2 guns, 1 rest. 1852 REYNOLDS *Hist. Illinois* 150 He saw Going . . . shoot a rifle, with a rest, ninety yards. 1897 LEWIS *Wolfville* 232 The big difference is that the East allers shoots from a rest; while the West shoots off hand.

2. An institution serving as a haven or shelter for persons of a designated class. {1892-}
1866 MOORE *Women of War* 434 In one of these trips of hospital visitation she found a collection of sick and convalescent soldiers at the 'Rest.'

+**3.** The action of resting a title. (See REST *v.* 1 c.)
1888 *Economist* 20 Oct. 2/1 This rest of the title is backed by a Policy of this Company.

*‑**Rest,** *v.*

1. *intr.* and *tr.* Of a field: to lie fallow; to allow (a field) to remain uncultivated. {1763}
1805 PARKINSON *Tour* 200 If the farm consists of four hundred acres, there are always two hundred lying to what they call resting (that is, without a crop) for two years. 1870 *Dept. Agric. Rep. 1869* 21 The term 'improved' includes . . . fallow and other temporarily uncultivated land —'resting' a field being the popular American substitute for rotation.

+**2.** *Law. intr.* To end voluntarily the introduction of evidence.
1876 HABBERTON *Jericho Road* 205 'Will the defense call any one?' 'No, your honor—we rest, . . . and trust to the good sense of the jury.' 1903 Fox *Little Shepherd* xiii, With this clear case against poor Jack, the Dillons rested. 1906 *Harper's Mo.* Nov. 837 On the 9th of April, the prosecution having rested, Judge Curtis opened for the defence.

+**b.** *tr.* To allow (a case) to stand as presented, without the adducing of further evidence; to cease presenting evidence in support of (a case).
1905 MITCHELL *Constance Trescot* 183 All the evidence for the plaintiffs was before the court, and Greyhurst sat down, stating that the plaintiff rested the case.

+**c.** To allow (a title to real estate) to stand without further or repeated searching of records.
1888 *Economist* 20 Oct. 2/1 Title Guarantee and Trust Co. . . . A title once examined and guaranteed is *rested* by this Company.

+**3.** To hang up (a hat or coat).
1897 LEWIS *Wolfville* 70 The old lady . . . asks me to rest my hat the second I'm in the door. 1911 HARRISON *Queed* 159 Won't you rest your coat, Mr. West? 1912 COBB *Back Home* 229 Judge Priest . . . made him rest his hat and overcoat . . . and sit down.

+**4.** *To rest up,* to regain strength by resting. Also *vbl. n.*
1909 WASON *Happy Hawkins* 351 One of 'em happened out here on a visit, to sort o' rest up. a1918 G. STUART *On Frontier* II. 192 There was never any such thing as 'resting up' or 'laying over'; the herd was kept moving forward all the time. 1922 Z. GREY *To Last Man* 284 Get rifle and ammunition, bake bread, and rest up before taking again the trail of the rustlers.

+**Restaurant.** A public dining room; an establishment in which meals are sold to the public. {1859-}
[1827 COOPER *Prairie* xix, Those delicious and unrivalled viands . . . are unequalled by any thing that is served . . . at the most renowned of the Parisian *restaurants*.] 1840 *Knickerb.* XV. 392 There are in the village numerous confectioners, charcutiers, and restorants. 1861 MCCLELLAN in *Own Story* 89 A colored gentleman . . . keeps a restaurant just around the corner in I Street. 1878 *Harper's Mag.* Feb. 336/1 The hotels, saloons, restaurants, and boarding cottages [of Atlantic City] . . . are innumerable. 1899 [see COMMUTATION TICKET]. 1914 'BOWER' *Flying U Ranch* 19 Parrots are so common, out on the Coast, that they use them in cheap restaurants for stew.

b. Attrib. with *apparatus, breakfast, business,* etc.
1867 *Atlantic Mo.* March 344/2 Some of them [*sc.* churches] are provided with a complete kitchen and restaurant apparatus. 1873 *Newton Kansan* 20 Feb. 3/2 Mr. Critchfield . . . has taken possession of Col. Irving's old restaurant stand. 1876 KNIGHT 1923/2 *Restaurant-car*, one adapted for affording meals to passengers on board while traveling. 1877 W. WRIGHT *Big Bonanza* 358 Out there they have no 'Hotel and Restaurant-keepers' Mutual Protection Association,' as they have in Virginia City. 1882 PECK *Sunshine* 127 The unsuspecting boarding-house keeper, or restaurant man, buys it and cooks it. 1904 A. DALE *Wanted, A Cook* 128 The restaurant breakfast can scarcely be said to be conducive to an overweening amiability. 1911 VANCE *Cynthia* 109 [He went] into the restaurant business.

+**Restauranter.** One who owns or operates a restaurant. — 1887 *Ohio State Jrnl.* 20 July, The headquarters of Mr. Kiesewetter are at Diebold's, an opulent restauranter and general purveyor to the wants of delegates. 1888 *Chicago Inter-Ocean* 7 March 4/5 A leading restauranter in New York has figured the average time of three thousand business men at their downtown luncheon is eight minutes.

+**Restaurat.** Variant of RESTAURANT. — 1833 *Niles' Reg.* XLIV. 178/1 A coffee room or *restaurat* will be established on the Third street front of the building. 1840 *Picayune* 7 Aug. 2/6 The subscriber . . . has reduced the price of Board to $5 per week at his Restaurat at the St. Charles Arcade Baths. 1841 *Ib.* 27 Aug. 2/3 A gentleman called for a bowl of gravy soup yesterday in a French restaurat. 1861 *N.Y. Tribune* 5 Aug. (Chipman), Restaurants, or 'restaurats,' as they are called [in New Orleans].

Restaurateur. 1. One who keeps a restaurant. {1796-} 2. A restaurant. {1804-, in France} — (1) 1827 COOPER *Prairie* I. 131 The viand might well have claimed a decided superiority over the meretricious cookery and laboured compounds of the most renowned restaurateur. 1856 *Harper's Mag.* Dec. 46/1 We repaired to a *restaurateur's*. (2) 1839 BRIGGS *H. Franco* II. 119, I got him to recommend me to a fashionable restaurateur. 1851 [see CAFÉ 1].

Rest cure. A method of restoring health by rest: (see quot. 1890); also, a place at which this method is applied. {1896} — 1890 *Cent.* 5114/1 *Rest-cure*, . . . the treatment, as of nervous exhaustion, by more or less prolonged and complete rest, as by isolation in bed. This is usually combined with over-feeding, massage, and electricity. 1892 S. HALE *Letters* 272 She is at a rest-cure. 1907 M. C. HARRIS *Tents of Wickedness* 448 They have been putting me through what they're pleased to call a 'rest cure.'

Restitutionist. A restorationist; one who believes in the 'restitution of all things' and the return of original purity. ('Chiefly *U.S.*' *O.E.D.*) +Often with reference to a specific sect in Massachusetts. — 1773 BOUCHER *View of Causes Amer. Revol.* 261n., Those who, during their connexion with Great Britain, were contented to be called Dissenters or Independents, are now pretty generally become, either Universal Restitutionists, Arians or Socinians. 1859 BARTLETT 362 *Restitutionists*, a religious sect which has recently sprung up in Worcester and some other places.

Restock, *v. tr.* To replenish; to furnish with a new supply. {a1680-}
1879 *Harper's Mag.* Oct. 715/2 Cattle in Western Texas are scarce, and . . . there are many advocates of stopping the drive entirely for a few years, in order to restock the country. 1891 O'BEIRNE *Leaders Ind. Territory* 46/2 They re-stocked this house and for several years did an extensive business over the entire Nation. 1905 *Forestry Bureau. Bul.* No. 61, 18 *Restock*, to renew a forest, either by natural or artificial means.

+**b.** *spec.* To replenish the supply of fish in (a stream or lake). Also *vbl. n.*
1869 *Rep. Comm. Agric. 1868* 319 Many curious facts have demonstrated the feasibility of restocking the salmon rivers. 1888 *Voice* 12 April, Lake George has greatly improved as a trout-fishing resort since the system of annual restocking began. 1892 *Vt. Agric. Rep.* XII. 159 There is nowhere a more practical illustration of restocking streams . . . than in Rutland County.

Restorationism. The belief that all men will at some time be restored to a state of happiness in the future life. {1896} Cf. UNIVERSALISM. — 1834 J. N. BROWN *Encycl. Relig. Knowl.* 1019/1 The Independent Messenger . . . is devoted to the cause of Restorationism. 1879 J. COOK *Marriage* 98 There is very little difference between Universalism and Restorationism. 1884 SCHAFF *Religious Encycl.* III. 1972/1 It is to be feared that belief in restorationism and annihilationism is increasing within orthodox communions.

Restorationist. One who believes in restorationism; spec., a member of a sect formed by a group seceding from the Universalist denomination in 1831 and affirming a doctrine of limited future punishment. (Cf. RESTITUTIONIST, UNIVERSALIST.) — **1834** J. N. Brown *Encycl. Relig. Knowl.* 1018/2 Though the Restorationists, as a separate sect, have arisen within a few years, their sentiments are by no means new. **1847** HOWE *Hist. Coll. Ohio* 218 There are 76 churches in Cincinnati, viz.: . . . 5 Disciples; 1 Universalist; 1 Restorationist; 1 Christian [etc.]. **1878** *N. Amer. Rev.* March 357 Now and then a purgatorial restorationist . . . is especially offensive for his use of these literal pictures of horror. **1892** *Critic* Oct. 177/2 He is a restorationist and this optimistic view . . . imparts a certain tinge to his handling of all themes.

+**Restorator.** [Fr. *restaurateur.*] A restaurant-keeper; a restaurant. — **1796** *Boston Directory* 261 Julien ———, restorator, Milk street. **1800** *Columbian Centinel* 31 Dec. 4/1 C. Delisle., Restorater, . . . continues to keep Boarders. **1815** in H. M. Brooks *Gleanings* IV. 129 The Subscriber . . . proposes opening a Restorator, for the accommodation of all who may honor him with their calls. **1848** *Boston Directory 1848–9* Advt. 23 The accommodation afforded to persons visiting Boston for partaking of meals . . . at Milliken's Temperance Restorator . . . is highly appreciated by those who are fond of good living. **1877** BARTLETT 793 *Restorator,* the keeper of a restaurant, or house of refreshment.

Restraint of trade. The prevention of free interchange of commodities. — **1890** *Statutes at Large* XXVI. 209 Every contract, combination in the form of trust or otherwise, or conspiracy, in restraint of trade or commerce among the several States . . . is hereby declared to be illegal. **1903** [see COMBINATION 2 b]. **1914** *Cycl. Amer. Govt.* III. 209/1 Any combination of competitors which aims at securing such a dominant position . . . that it will have the power . . . to fix prices, especially of the necessaries of life, will be regarded by the Supreme Court . . . as a combination in restraint of trade.

Restrictionist. +**1.** An opponent of the extension of slavery. Now hist. +**2.** One favoring the policy of protection of industry. {1849–} +**3.** One who favors legislation restricting sales of liquor. — **(1) 1820** *Niles' Reg.* XVIII. 258/2 We undertake to say that there is not a single *confessed* restrictionist elected throughout the whole territory. **1857** BENTON *Exam. Dred Scott Case* 87 Some of the most strenuous of the restrictionists had begun . . . to hold the language of conciliation. **(2) 1830** *Congress. Deb.* 5 May 893/2 We refer to England, that country which the restrictionists visit with such unmeasured abuse. **1832** *Ib.* 31 May 3226 Restrictionists, who call the people 'operatives,' ought to say subject instead of citizen. **(3) 1887** *Voice* 9 June 4 The restrictionists say, they wish to cut down the number of saloons by one-half.

+**Rest room.** A public room furnished and used as a place for relaxation and rest. {1929} — **1900** *Outlook* 6 Oct. 296 Rest-Rooms for Farmers' Wives. **1903** *Booklovers Mag.* Oct. 401 Every girl is given a half-hour intermission morning and afternoon to lounge in the rest-room and read or gossip. **1920** LEWIS *Main Street* 65 They've made the city plant ever so many trees, and they run the rest-room for farmers' wives. **1924** CROY *R.F.D. No. 3* 5 The 'rest-room' in the courthouse . . . was equipped with a mirror, a rocking-chair or two, and a scanty supply of old magazines.

+**Resubmissionist.** One who favors submitting to a second popular vote a prohibition amendment already in force. — **1889** *Voice* 7 March, The Resubmissionists [make the claim] that Prohibition has 'disarranged business.' **1890** *Public Opinion* 20 Sept. 547 The political alliance between the Resubmissionists and Democrats in Kansas places the 'straight-out' Prohibitionists in a peculiar position.

Result, *n.* {1626–} (See quot. 1828.) *Obs.* {1647–1701} — **1766** *Mass. H. S. Coll.* 3 Ser. V. 224 There will be some of us so faithful, as publicly to inform the world, that it was not the Result of this Council. **1828** WEBSTER, *Result,* . . . the decision or determination of a council or deliberative assembly; as the result of an ecclesiastical council. *New England.*

* **Result,** *v.* +*tr.* To make a decision *that,* etc. — **1812** N. WORCESTER *Bible News* (ed. 2) 176 (Pickering), According to Dr. Milner, the Council of Nice resulted, in opposition to the view of Arius, that the Son was peculiarly of the Father. **1816** PICKERING 164 Some of our writers on ecclesiastical affairs constantly use this verb, . . . thus: 'The Council resulted that the parties should do certain things.'

* **Resume,** *v. tr.* and *absol.* To begin again to make (specie payments). — **1838** *Congress. Globe* App. 23 April 307/2 Two Senators . . . intended by this means to enable the banks the sooner to resume species payments. **1840** *Niles' Nat. Reg.* 16 May 166/1 The law requires the banks in Pennsylvania to resume specie payments on the 15th January, 1841. **1841** *Ib.* 30 Jan. 352/3 Resumption in Pennsylvania. . . . The banks throughout this state have resumed.

* **Resumption.** The re-establishment of specie payments by a government or a financial institution; +often with specific reference to the resumption by the United States Treasury in 1879. In full *resumption of payment of specie,* etc. Also attrib.

1816 *Ann. 14th Congress* 1 Sess. 239 Unless the present Congress should take some efficient measure to compel the resumption of payment of specie, it was extremely doubtful whether it ever would be done. **1837** *Rep. Secy. Treasury* 17 The policy since pursued by most of them has been favorable to an early discharge of their engagements to the Treasury, and to a resumption of specie payments. **1875** [see CONTRACTION]. **1878** *N. Amer. Rev.* Jan. 156 Despite the stoppage of the resumption policy preparing by Secretary McCullough; . . . at last the inflationists calling themselves Republicans were foiled. **1884** *Century Mag.* Nov. 149 The commercial world on the passage of the Resumption Act began to adjust itself to the only true basis of financial security. **1894** LEAVITT *Our Money Wars* 185 The Resumption misery was fairly started. **1900** *Congress. Rec.* 10 Jan. 731/1 The refunding operations were being carried on in the seventies, but particularly in 1879, incident to the resumption of specie payments.

+**Resumptionist.** An advocate of the resumption of specie payments. — **1875** [see CONTRACTIONIST]. **1878** *Congress. Rec.* 26 Jan. 598/1 We are resumptionists. We deny . . . that there is [in the West] one particle of the spirit of repudiation.

Resurface, *v.* +*tr.* To supply with a new surface. {1929} Also *vbl. n.* — **1894** *Columbus Dispatch* 15 Sept., The resurfacing of the pavement about the Court House has progressed far enough to give the Judges some idea [etc.]. **1901** *Dept. Agric. Yrbk. 1900* 352 The road was resurfaced with limestone.

Resurrect, *v. tr.* To bring back or revive, as if from death; to bring to view. {1772–} Illustrated copiously in Th. and Th. S. — **1852** YOUNG in *Jrnl. of Discourses* I. 33 (Th.), I never want that to be resurrected. **1871** *N.Y. Tribune* 7 Feb. (De Vere), If Admiral Porter only lay still in his grave, if his friends did not resurrect him to offend the nostrils of the House [etc.]. **1876** 'MARK TWAIN' *Tom Sawyer* i. 18 She resurrected nothing but the cat. **1904** *Forum* July 132 The . . . offer made by General Reyes in behalf of the Bogota Government to resurrect and ratify the dead canal treaty.

Resurrectionizing. The exhuming of corpses for the purpose of selling them as anatomical specimens. {resurrectionize, *v.*, 1804–, in various senses; 1854} — **1819** F. J. DIDIER *Franklin's Lett.* I. 64, I had resolved never to meddle with *resurrectionizing* again, after the lesson I got in Baltimore! **1852** *Knickerb.* XL. 470 He had managed to pay his way through a couple of courses of lectures in a country college . . . by the not uncommon resource of poor devils in the study of medicine—*resurrectionizing.* **1871** *Cincinnati Commercial* 6 Feb. (De Vere), The leading gentleman of the resurrectionizing profession is one Cunningham, who, with two assistants, dug up the subjects and carried them to the medical schools in an express-wagon.

+**Resurrection note.** A bank note of the second Bank of the United States (1816–36) which was issued again by the successor of the bank, the Bank of the United States of Pennsylvania. *colloq.* — **1838** *Congress. Globe* App. 12 Feb. 80/1 (*caption*), Resurrection Notes. *Ib.* 23 April 305/3 A large proportion of these resurrection notes, as they have been aptly called, which have been issued and reissued by order of the new bank, are of the denomination of five dollars.

Resurrection plant. Any of various plants which, when dried up, can be made to re-expand by the application of moisture {1870–}, as the bird's-nest moss, *Selaginella lepidophylla.* — **1868** GRAY *Field Botany* 374 [The] 'Resurrection-Plant' . . . is a nest-like ball when dry, but when moist it unfolds. **1902** BAILEY, etc. *Cycl. Amer. Horticulture* IV. 1507/1 Resurrection plants are great curiosities. . . . The commonest ones . . . are members of the mustard family and the club moss family.

+**Resurrection robe.** A garment worn by a Millerite, in expectation of the second coming of Christ. — **1843** *Niles' Nat. Reg.* 4 March 16/3 Some of the devotees, attired in their resurrection robes, were actually nearly frozen to death waiting in a bleak, exposed situation out of doors, the awful consummation of all things.

Resurvey, *n.* A new survey {1768–}; the land surveyed anew. — **1662** *Va. Statutes at Large* II. 101 The fifty seaventh act prohibiting resurveighs not applying the expected remedies. **1702** *Reflections on Case of W. Penn* 9 The next thing to be consider'd is the Over-plus Land upon a Re-survey. **1765** HABERSHAM *Letters* 28 The vacant lands without the limits of these Grants cannot be . . . run out by our Surveyors, with any degree of certainty, which may make a resurvey of them absolutely necessary. **1785** *Md. Hist. Mag.* XX. 48 The whole space of the resurvey was at that time covered over with Ice. **1816** U. BROWN *Journal* I. 277 A resurvey had been made in the name of Thomas Brook.

* **Resurvey,** *v.* To make a fresh survey of land. {1784–} — **1746** *Md. Hist. Mag.* XVIII. 22 Beginning of Bedford Resurveyed. **1747** *Penna. Col. Rec.* V. 107 The said Road shall be Resurveyed and laid out according to the Courses it now runs.

* **Retail.** *attrib.* passing into *adj.*

1. Designating institutions, firms, etc., that sell goods in small quantities directly to the consumer.

1796 *Mass. H. S. Coll.* 1 Ser. V. 21 The number of retail houses is lessened. **1828** [see CHICKEN THIEF a]. **1854** 'O. OPTIC' *In Doors & Out* (1876) 122 The firm of Funk, Hunk, & Co. . . . had offered him three thousand dollars salary to superintend their retail department. **1882** McCABE *New York* 556 The principal retail firms possess large and magnificent buildings. **1916** J. W. FISK *Retail Selling* 31 This chain . . . makes a retail drug organization of enormous size and power.

2. Designating persons engaged in retail trade. {1716–}

1807 IRVING, etc. *Salmagundi* 268 Retail traders cannot go to the assembly. **1829** *Va. Lit. Museum* 30 Dec. 459 *Merchant.* . . . In many parts of the United States, it means a retail dealer. **1839** *Indiana H. Rep. Jrnl.* 23 Sess. 212 Mr. Matson presented the petition of sundry citizens . . . praying for a change in the law granting license to retail grocers. *a***1882** in McCabe *New York* 144 Retail venders of all kinds peddle their goods. **1898** *Kansas City Star* 18 Dec. 2/1 An effort will be made to form an alliance of the . . . hatters, garment workers, shoe workers, retail clerks and textile workers.

*Retailer. A dealer who sells goods in small quantities directly to the consumer.

1646 *Plymouth Laws* 86 Whosoever shall draw out and sell a lesser quantity or caske of wine than 10 gallons to any shall be accounted a retayler. **1696** *Mass. Province Laws* I. 238 The retailers, hucksters and traders of the town shall not . . . buy of any of the market people there, until the afternoon of every market-day. **1708** *Boston Rec.* 75 Damaris Perkins widdow her Petition for Lycence to Sell as a Retaylor Such Sperits as She distills in her Limbeck allowed. **1802** *Ann. 7th Congress* 1 Sess. 1325 Retailers of wines and spirits . . . shall pay for such licenses. **1902** LORIMER *Lett. Merchant* 133 The last car of lard was so strong that it came back of its own accord from every retailer they shipped it to.

+Retail store. A store in which commodities are sold in small quantities directly to the consumer. — **1785** MADISON *Writings* II. 162 Retail Stores are spreading all over the country. **1820** *Columbian Centinel* 29 Jan. 3/6 A valuable Stock of a Retail Store, consisting of Cloths, Cassimeres [etc.]. **1865** *Atlantic Mo.* Jan. 85/1 One of the largest retail stores in the New York dry-goods trade sells . . . ten million dollars' worth of fabrics per annum. **1882** MCCABE *New York* 267 Third avenue . . . is devoted to small retail stores.

*Retainer.¹ The act of a client in engaging an attorney, or a document attesting such an act. {1816-} 'Chiefly U.S.' (O.E.D.). — **1854** *N.H. Rep.* XXVIII. 302 A parol retainer of an attorney is sufficient to authorize him to commence a suit. **1868** *Calif. Rep.* XXXV. 534 The Court may require him [the attorney] to produce the evidence of his retainer.

*Retainer.² +(See quotations.) — **1811** *Tenn. Rep.* II. 167 A retainer to the camp must be a person who, from his situation and the nature of his employment, has a right to be at the camp, and within the line of sentinels. **1890** *Cent.* 5120/1 *Retainer*, . . . a sutler, camp-follower, or any person serving with an army who, though not enlisted, is subject to orders according to the rules and articles of war.

Reticule. {1727-38-} A small bag carried by women and used as a pocket or workbag. {1824-} — **1828** ROYALL *Black Book* II. 117 She followed me and put a bank note in my reticule. **1848** *Knickerb.* XXXI. 44 Aunt Patty was a great maker of . . . those old-fashioned articles, 'house-wifes' and 'reticules.' **1884** 'MARK TWAIN' *H. Finn* ix, We got . . . a reticule with needles and pins and beeswax and buttons and thread and all such truck in it. **1894** — *Those Twins* v, She toyed with her reticule a moment or two.

Retimber, *v. tr.* To supply (a mining shaft) with new supporting timbers. {1899-} — **1876** RAYMOND *8th Rep. Mines* 293 The 350-foot shaft has been straightened and retimbered and 350 feet of levels driven. **1882** *47th Congress* 1 Sess. H. R. Ex. Doc. No. 216, 297 The work of retimbering the old shaft has been completed.

‖Retiracied, *a.* Secluded. — **1856** *Knickerb.* March 267 There are no places in the world similarly *retiracied* which are less provincial or more agreeable [than certain New Eng. towns].

+Retiracy.

1. Retirement, seclusion.

1829 *Va. Lit. Museum* 30 Dec. 460 *Retiracy*, 'solitude' *Western States*. **1843** 'CARLTON' *New Purchase* I. 74, I'd a powerful sight sooner go into retiracy among the red, wild, Abor'rejines of our wooden country, nor consent to that bill. **1859** *La Crosse Daily Union* 11 Nov. 2/3 [The writing of a political history is] begun . . . amid the retiracy which is so favorable to its accomplishment. **1873** WALLACE *Fair God* 162 He left the house, and once more sought the retiracy of the gardens.

2. (See quot. 1848.) *Obs.*

1848 BARTLETT 274 *Retiracy*, sufficiency; competency. It is said, in New England, of a person who has retired from business with a fortune, that he has a retiracy; i.e. a sufficient fortune to retire with. **1860** *New Haven Palladium* (De Vere), When Mr. Watson found he had a sufficient retiracy, he gave up his lucrative business, and devoted himself to horticultural pursuits.

3. The act of retiring or being in retirement from a court room.

1864 *Harper's Mag.* April 711/2 After a few minutes retiracy the jury returned into court.

*Retire, *v.*

+1. *tr.* To put out (a player or side) in baseball; also *intr.*, to leave the home plate on being put out.

1874 *Chicago Inter-Ocean* 6 July 9/1 Schafer sent a fly to Treacy, at center, and was retired. *Ib.*, Cuthbert then sent a long fly to left field, and retired when it landed in Hall's hands, for it staid there. **1880** [see EARN *v.*]. **1896** KNOWLES & MORTON *Baseball* 101 The fielder who handles the ball in sufficient time to aid in retiring a base-runner is credited with an assist. **1917** MATHEWSON *Second Base Sloan* 180 The first batsman was retired on an easy toss from Chase to Jim.

+2. To withdraw or take (a thing) away from its usual place or the performance of its customary function.

1883 *Lisbon* (Dak.) *Star* 12 Oct., Eighteen packet boats have been retired by several of the packet lines . . ., owing to the low stage of water. **1888** *Amer. Humorist* (London) 2 June 5/2 Mr. Bonner retired him [a horse] from the track!

Retort, *v.* **1.** *tr.* To purify (gold amalgam) by heating in a retort. {1879-} +**2.** *intr.* To fall *off* or *away* when heated in a retort. — (1) **1850** KINGSLEY *Diary* 123 The boys retorted the last weeks work. **1909**

BANKS *Mystery F. Farrington* 33 He was now retorting gold in the most primeval fashion. (2) **1850** KINGSLEY *Diary* 151 [This amalgam] ought not to retort off more than ¼ as great pains has been taken to flirt it off dry from quicksilver. **1851** *Ib.* 166 We had 3654 dollars in amalgam and it retorted away to 2546 dollars.

+Retorter. One who retorts metals. — **1876** RAYMOND *8th Rep. Mines* 415, 2 amalgamators, 2 retorters and boiler-men.

Retoucher. One who touches up or improves things, esp. one who retouches photographs. — **1878** *Scribner's Mo.* March 687/2 The tools of the retoucher [of china in Germany] are . . . fine brushes and delicate instruments with which he removes the imperfections from each article or fills in what may be lacking. **1889** *Internat. Ann., Anthony's Photogr. Bul.* II. 372 The Retoucher who is compelled to approach within eight or nine inches of the negative, is damaging the sight. **1892** *Amer. Ann. of Photography* 102 The operator depends upon the retoucher to make a doubtful negative pass.

Retrocede, *v. tr.* To cede (territory) back to a state or country {1818-} — **1805** *Ann. 9th Congress* 2 Sess. 982 They then petitioned Congress . . . requesting that Congress would retrocede the territory to South Carolina. **1840** *Niles' Nat. Reg.* 25 July 326/1 Mr. Walker submitted a resolution instructing the committee for the District of Columbia to inquire into the expediency of retroceding all those portions of the District of Columbia not within the limits of the city of Washington to the respective states to which they formerly belonged. **1884** BLAINE *20 Years of Congress* I. 3 The entire territory [of La.] was retroceded to France.

Retrocession. {1681-} The return of territory to a country, state, or people. {1796-} — **1817** *State P.* (1819) XII. 19 In this treaty nothing is stipulated but the retro-cession of Louisiana. **1840** *Niles' Nat. Reg.* 17 Oct. 112/1 The vote on the question of the retrocession of the town and county of Alexandria to the state of Virginia was taken on Tuesday. **1894** ROBLEY *Bourbon Co., Kansas* 5 About 1825 the government began locating the various tribes of the more nearly civilized Indians from the East and South on reservations, by cessions, trades, treaties, removals, and retrocessions.

*Return, *n.*

*1. *pl.* =ELECTION RETURNS.

1689 *Penna. Col. Rec.* I. 268 For ye Reasons advertised in ye Returns thereof, given by ye Sheriff, [it] was not a good Election. **1787** *Constitution* i. § 5 Each House shall be Judge of the Elections, Returns, and Qualifications of its own Members. **1812** *Boston Gazette* 23 Nov. (Th.), Some returns from democratic towns are not made conformable to the Gerrymander law of last February. **1875** *Chicago Tribune* 4 Nov. 1/6 The returns . . . indicate that the so-called Republican candidate . . . has not an absolute majority of all the votes cast. **1911** *Okla. Session Laws* 3 Legisl. 79 Each special election commissioner, shall deliver to the county clerk, the ballot boxes containing the ballots, affidavits, and returns.

+b. *To go behind the returns,* (see quot. 1914).

1877 *Electoral Commission Proc.* 934 Much has been said here by those opposed to us about 'going behind the returns,' and the terrible consequences of such an act. **1914** *Cycl. Amer. Govt.* III. 211/1 *Returns, Can't Go Behind The,* a phrase indicating the demands of the Republican party, adopted by the electoral commission Feb. 7, 1877, in the Hayes-Tilden disputed election case, that the commission was not competent to investigate the eligibility of the list of electors submitted by the state authorities.

2. A report, usually formal, giving facts and statistics about a particular matter. {1787-}

1756 *Washington Writings* I. 398 A return of the stores at this place is enclosed. **1775** *Jrnls. Cont. Congress* III. 452 General Schuyler . . . has made a Return to Congress of the Cannon and other stores. **1827** DRAKE & MANSFIELD *Cincinnati* 66 From the following establishments and artizans no returns have been received. **1881** *Chicago Times* 14 May, The *Cincinnati Price Current* reviews the hog-packing returns as follows.

3. A list or enumeration of property subject to taxation.

1816 PICKERING 82 When a person neglects to make a return of his taxable property to the assessors of a town, those officers doom him. **1888** BRYCE *Amer. Commw.* II. II. xliii. 133n., In New York . . . if a person makes no return the assessors are instructed to 'doom' him according to the best of their knowledge and belief.

Return, *adv.* And return, and back again. — **1887** GEORGE *40 Yrs. on Rail* 88 The train . . . ran from Waukegan to Chicago and return every day.

+Returning board. In some states, a board composed of those appointed to determine officially the results of popular elections.

1874 *43d Congress.* 2 Sess. H. R. Rep. No. 101, 6 This conviction among them has been strengthened by the acts of the Kellogg legislature abolishing existing courts and judges, . . . by continuing the returning-board with absolute power over the returns of elections. **1877** BEARD *K. K. K. Sketches* 140 This society . . . succeeded to some extent in purifying the constitutions of the Returning Boards, those monster instrumentalities of fraud belonging to the Radical elective system here. **1880** *46th Congress 2d Sess.* Sen. Rep. No. 693, 344 We do not believe in the processes of Kellogg and the returning-board in Louisiana. **1893** *McClure's Mag.* I. 383/1 'The Potter Committee' [was] appointed to investigate the operations of the returning boards in the South.

attrib. **1878** Daly in J. F. Daly *A. Daly* 254 Excitement is at fever heat about the Returning Board trials. **1886** Z. F. Smith *Kentucky* 812 Even by the count of the celebrated *returning-board* expedient, Tilden's popular majority was 157,394.

Reunion. {1610-} +The return of the South to the Union. — **1863** *Rio Abajo Press* 4 Aug. 2/2 This is an important point for us 'Mudsills' to consider in view of 're-union' upon the basis of 'compromise.'

+**Revamp,** *v. tr.* To reconstruct, repair, patch up again. — **1850** Mitchell *Lorgnette* I. 141 Even the soberer subjects of History, he told me, must be re-vamped in some tasty way. **1865** *Atlantic Mo.* Feb. 186 The new-made lord Sent down his workmen to revamp the Hall. **1878** 'Mark Twain' *Ib.* May 617/2 He had to keep on procuring magazine acceptances and then revamping the manuscripts to make them presentable.

Revelator.

1. A revealer of things to come, esp. with reference to St. John, the author of the Book of Revelation. {1875-}

1801 *Mass. Spy* 20 May (Th.), They shall have their part (saith John the Revelator) in the lake which burneth. **1849** Whittier *Writings* V. 142 It should rather . . . call to mind what the Revelator hath said of the Holy City.

+**2.** Used of the president of the Mormon church.

1867 Dixon *New America* II. 12 The Mormon will put his trust in Joseph, as a natural seer and revelator. **1882** *Congress. Rec.* 13 March 1863/2 Brigham [Young] was a crafty old revelator and well knew how to impress his doctrines on people. **1895** *Denver Times* 5 March 8/2 Joseph Smith, the son of the martyr Joseph Smith, is now prophet, seer and revelator. **1900** *Congress. Rec.* 24 Jan. 1129/2 Although the president, prophet, seer, and revelator of the Church of Jesus Christ of Latter-Day Saints, Snow has five children.

+**Revengeless Christians.** (See quotation.) — **1796** Morse *Univ. Geog.* I. 283 [The Mennonists] call themselves the Harmless Christians, Revengeless Christians, and Weaponless Christians.

***Revenue.**

+**1.** =Revenuer. *dial.* or *illiterate.*

1883 Zeigler & Grosscup *Alleghanies* 357 My pards mout tak' ye a revenoo, an' let a hole thro' ye. **1901** *Munsey's Mag.* XXV. 422/2 If somebody sees the raiders, . . . word is passed along that 'the revenues are coming.' **1907** H. B. Wright *Shepherd of Hills* 69 He's just some revenue.

2. *attrib.* **a.** Designating boats and insignia of the Revenue-Cutter Service.

1795 *State P.* (1819) II. 398, I proceeded to Port Penn in the revenue barge. **1807** *Ib.* VI. 15, [I] went out and discovered the revenue colours in the boat. **1845** *Stat. at Large* V. 795 No revenue cutter or revenue steamer shall hereafter be built . . . , unless an appropriation be first made. **1881** *Naval Encycl.* 690/1 The revenue-steamer 'Reliance,' while pursuing blockade-runners . . . , was fired into by some land forces of the enemy.

b. Designating persons engaged in the revenue service.

1875 Wells *Practical Economics* 27 It was only necessary to say 'lead' to a United States district attorney, a collector, or revenue inspector, to seriously disturb his mental equanimity. **1882** *Congress. Rec.* 19 July 6194/1, I can see in my mind's eye . . . those one-gallows, straw-hatted fellows flying from the revenue officials to their mountain fastnesses. **1883** Zeigler & Grosscup *Alleghanies* 146 At fust we didn't know whether ye war gentlemen or a sheriff's posse, the road-boss or revenue galoots. **1884** Harris *Mingo* 132 Pap, do you reckon Mr. Woodward was a revenue spy after all? **1885** 'Craddock' *Prophet* 132 A party of revenue raiders had been heard of on the Big Smoky. **1893** *Harper's Mag.* March 602 'It was a revenue detective,' explained Mrs. Franklin; 'I mean the man who was shot.'

3. In special combinations.

Revenue act, a governmental act for raising revenue; *r. bond,* an obligation issued by a government or municipality to obtain funds for immediate use; *R. Department,* the department in the federal government charged with collecting revenue; *r. distillery,* a distillery paying the government a duty of so much per gallon upon the liquor made; *R. Marine,* =Revenue cutter b.

1791 Washington *Diaries* IV. 196 The discontents which it was supposed the last Revenue Act . . . would create subside as fast as the law is explained. **1856** MacLeod *F. Wood* 177 Last year the Comptroller borrowed upon revenue bonds, three millions six hundred and ninety-three thousand dollars. **1790** *Ann. 1st Congress* 1003, I likewise nominate the following persons to fill offices in the Revenue Department of the United States. **1868** Beecher *Sermons* (1869) I. 239, I am not now speaking of cellar distilleries, nor of the reformed revenue distilleries. **1868** *Stat. at Large* XV. 113 Hereafter no expenses of the revenue marine shall be paid out of any other fund.

+**Revenue agent.** (See quot. 1864.) — **1864** *Statutes at Large* XIII. 224 Revenue agents . . . [shall] aid in the prevention, detection, and punishment of frauds upon the internal revenue. **1901** *Munsey's Mag.* XXV. 419/1 In every district there is also an official known as a revenue-agent.

+**Revenue bill.** A congressional bill providing for the raising of revenue. — **1794** *Ann. 3d Congress* 697 Revenue Bill. . . . Laying additional duties on goods, wares, and merchandise, imported into the United States. **1833** *Niles' Reg.* XLIV. 1/1 Serious doubts began to be enter-

tained of the right of the senate to originate a revenue bill. **1842** in MacLeod *F. Wood* 95 The discussion of the revenue bill of last session, and motion of reference of the tariff portion of the President's message this session, have convinced me [etc.].

Revenue cutter. An armed government boat used to enforce revenue laws. {1801-} Also appositive.

1790 *Ann. 1st Congress* 2277 It shall be lawful for . . . the officers of the revenue cutters . . . to go on board of ships or vessels in any part of the United States. **1802** Ellicott *Journal* 298 [We] were accompanied over the bar by the Revenue Cutter, after which she fired a salute and left us. **1862** Kettell *Hist. Rebellion* I. 359 The Aiken . . . was a revenue cutter, surrendered by its commander to the Charleston authorities. **1866** Logan *Great Conspiracy* 125 The Texan Rebels seized the United States Revenue cutter 'Dodge' at Galveston. **1900** *Congress. Rec.* 4 Jan. 642/2 Mr. Mc-Millan . . . submitted a report, . . . recognizing the gallantry of Frank H. Newcomb, commanding the revenue cutter, *Hudson,* of his officers and men.

+**b.** *Revenue-Cutter Service,* (see quotation).

1890 *Cent.* 5134/3 Revenue marine, or *revenue-cutter service,* a corps organized in 1790 . . . for the purpose of guarding the coast and estuaries of the United States for the protection of the customs revenue.

Revenue law. A law providing for the raising of revenue. {1776-} **1789** *Ann. 1st Congress.* 162, I will not suppose the Government hazarded by making a revenue law that is right and justifiable on general principles. **1808** [see Cutter 2 b]. **1842** in MacLeod *F. Wood* 110 For high duties . . . encourage smuggling and other evasions of the revenue laws. **1873** *Newton Kansan* 17 April 2/1 The revenue law . . . provides for a tax of six mills.

Revenue man. =Revenue agent. {1841-} — **1884** Harris *Mingo* 102 Hog Mountain is to be raided by the revenue men by way of Teague Poteet's. **1901** Harben *Westerfelt* 112 She told me all about it the night the revenue men give you sech a close shave. **1917** Comstock *Man* 193 Blake . . . had a score to settle about the revenue men.

Revenue officer. =Revenue agent. {1776-} — **1791** *Ann. 1st Congress* 1844 A swarm of harpies, . . . under the denomination of revenue officers, will range through the country prying into every man's house and affairs. **1816** *Ann. 14th Congress* 2 Sess. 28 In some of the States . . . the public money is retained by a revenue officer. **1877** *N.Y. Ev. Post* 16 June (B.), The Moonshiner regards the revenue officer as a being to be extinguished. **1897** Brodhead *Bound in Shallows* 262 He said that last year they had a blind tiger there, and that the man who kept it shot a revenue officer dead.

+**Revenuer.** A term used by moonshiners for a revenue agent enforcing the laws against illicit distilling. *colloq.* — **1895** 'Craddock' *Mystery Witch-Face Mt.* 15 The 'revenuers' . . . never rode alone. **1923** *Dialect Notes* V. 210 Them revenuers made us hide out.

+**Revenue reformer.** One interested in reforming or changing the revenue laws. — **1870** *Nation* 19 May 311/1 The high protectionists are not sorry, while the revenue reformers are. **1882** *Ib.* 28 Dec. 544/3 The 'National Club of American Economists' . . . [will] fight the freetraders and revenue-reformers. **1887** *Courier-Journal* 2 Feb. 1/3 The Speaker will consult with the leading revenue reformers of the House tomorrow.

Revenue stamp. A government stamp to be affixed to certain goods and documents to represent the advance payment of taxes on them. — **1862** *Rep. Secy. Treasury* 9 Congress . . . authorized the use of postage and revenue stamps as a fractional currency. **1870** Medbery *Men Wall St.* 52 The acknowledgments are . . . covered with revenue stamps. **1887** *Postal Laws* 490 Any person employed in . . . the postal service who shall secrete, embezzle, or destroy any . . . [mail] which shall contain any note, bond, draft, check, warrant, revenue stamp [etc.], . . . shall be punishable by imprisonment at hard labor. **1893** Cushing *Story of P.O.* 1 He visits . . . the Bureau of Engraving and Printing, where the revenue stamps and greenbacks are manufactured.

+**Revenue tariff.** A tariff designed primarily to secure revenue as distinguished from a protective tariff (q.v.). — **1820** *Ann. 16th Congress* 1 Sess. 1966 They enacted . . . a revenue tariff, without the least regard to the situation of the country. **1845** *Xenia Torch-Light* 23 Oct. 2/1 The present Administration would not go strictly for a revenue Tariff. **1871** Grosvenor *Protection* 11 With a revenue tariff, . . . the controlling object is to secure duties with the least burden. **1887** *Courier-Journal* 19 Feb. 4/1 They are the identical arguments which the Courier-Journal has been pounding into the understanding of the people in its fight for a revenue tariff.

Reverberatory furnace. (See quot. 1881.) {1672-} — **1796** *Ann. 4th Congress* 2 Sess. 2571 The works consist of a fort, a citadel, an artillery store, and a reverberatory furnace. **1819** Schoolcraft *Mo. Lead Mines* 19 In A.D. 1797, Moses Austin . . . obtained a grant of land [in La.] from the Spanish authorities, in consideration of erecting a reverberatory furnace. **1881** Raymond *Mining Gloss., Reverberatory furnace,* a furnace in which ores are submitted to the action of flame, without contact with the fuel. The flame . . . strikes the roof (*arch*) of the furnace, and is *reverberated* downward upon the charge.

***Reverend,** *a.*

+**1.** Pure or undiluted. Usually of whisky. *colloq.*

1837 Wetmore *Gaz. Missouri* 336 'Muster courage to take . . . a tablespoonful, three times a day.'—'Jist reverend, without water, doctor?' **1853** Baldwin *Flush Times Ala.* 306 It aint as pleasant as sitting on a log by a camp fire, with a tickler of the reverend stuff. **1888** 'Craddock' *Despot* 467, I thunk the reverend stuff would fetch ye.

+2. *Reverend set*, (see quotations). *Obs.*

1826 FLINT *Recoll.* 15 A firm push of the iron-pointed pole on a fixed log, is termed a 'reverend' set. **1832** PAULDING *Westward Ho!* I. 83 They placed their shoulders against the long poles, one end of which was loaded with iron, and making what was called a 'reverend set,' walked steadily to the stern of the broad-horn, propelling her forward at the same time.

∗ Reverent, *a.* +Variant of REVEREND *a.* 1. — **1837** SHERWOOD *Gaz. Georgia* (ed. 3) 71 *Reverent*, for strong;—*reverent whisky, i.e.* not diluted. **1864** *Harper's Mag.* March 569/2 He put water in his liquor, instead of taking it 'reverent.'

+Reviewing stand. A temporary structure from which a parade or procession may be reviewed or seen to advantage. — **1897** *Boston Jrnl.* 15 Jan. 6/5 The local chapter . . . [suggested] a reform in . . . the erection of reviewing-stands for spectators on the occasion of processions on the next inauguration day. **1897** C. A. DANA *Recoll. Civil War* 288, I joined the company on the reviewing officers' stand, in front of the White House, in just the place which the reviewing stand now occupies on inauguration days.

Revival. {1651–}

1. *Revival of religion*, a period of renewed interest in and devotion to religion. {1757–}

1702 C. MATHER *Magnalia* I. 71/1 There was a notable Revival of Religion among them. *a*1817 DWIGHT *Travels* II. 277 Four considerable revivals of Religion have taken place in Somers during his Ministry. **1874** COLLINS *Kentucky* I. 25 The 'Great Revival' of religion begins in the Green river country.

2. A series of evangelistic meetings for awaking religious enthusiasm. {1849–}

1799 in Young *Jessamine Co., Ky.* 197, I have written several others to assist in holding the revival. **1807** MCNEMAR *Ky. Revival* 19 The first extraordinary appearances of the power of God, in the late revival, began about the close of the last century. **1864** *Wkly. New Mexican* 23 Dec. 2/4 In times of revivals as they are called, the organ is silent, and the singing gallery deserted, and every body gathers around the altar. **1925** BRYAN *Memoirs* 44, I attended a revival that was being conducted in a Presbyterian Church and was converted.

b. Attrib. with *agitation, extravagance, preaching, sermon.*

1889 *Pop. Science Mo.* June 148 Well-known examples of this [enthusiasm] in America are seen in the 'Jumpers,' 'Jerkers,' and various revival extravagances. **1891** *Atlantic Mo.* June 813/2 The old slaves are loath to give up the hysteric emotionalism of revival preaching. **1901** STILLMAN *Autobiog. Journalist* I. 37 Here there was nothing of the ghastly terrors of the great revival agitations. **1904** Revival sermon [see ENTHUSE *v.* 1].

Revivalist. A preacher who conducts or takes part in a religious revival. {1820–} Also attrib. — **1835** REED & MATHESON *Visit* I. 16 Mr. K., an active revivalist preacher, was to take the service. **1865** *Ore. State Jrnl.* 22 July 1/1 An anecdote is told of Finney, the 'revivalist,' . . . to the following effect. **1885** *Santa Fé Wkly. New Mexican* 20 Aug. 2/3 Sam. Jones, the revivalist, is a confirmed tobacco chewer. **1896** HARRIS *Sister Jane* 227 He was a revivalist, and although he was a methodist his preaching was acceptable to the members of all denominations.

+Revival man. In the Presbyterian church in Kentucky (*c*1803), a member of the faction led by Barton W. Stone, which was favorable to the enthusiasm of the contemporary revival movement; a New Light (sense 1 b). *Obs.* — **1847** DAVIDSON *Presbyterian Ch. in Ky.* 167 The clergy and people became divided into two distinct parties—the Orthodox and the New Lights—one assuming the honorable style of 'Revival Men,' and affecting superior sanctity and zeal, and stigmatizing the other unjustly as 'Anti-Revival Men.' *Ib.* 190 A division into two clearly defined parties was the inevitable result. To these parties were given by the former [*i.e.*, the enthusiastic party], the names of *Revival* and *Anti-Revival* men.

Revival meeting. A meeting or evangelistic service held during the course of a religious revival. {1843} — **1850** *Knickerb.* June 550 At a revival-meeting . . . one of the clergymen present read a passage from the Bible. **1875** *Chicago Tribune* 7 Dec. 8/1 The series of revival meetings to be held in the Green Street Tabernacle opened rather inauspiciously last evening. **1880** *Cimarron News & Press* 23 Dec. 2/5 The Jesuit Fathers are holding revival meetings at Las Vegas. **1909** WASON *Happy Hawkins* 187 I saw a photograph oncet of the bottomless pit at a revival meeting.

‖Revocal. Revocation. — **1862** *N.Y. Tribune* 9 June (Chipman), The President's revocal of General Hunter's proclamation was well received at Port Royal.

∗ Revolution. +The overthrow of British rule by the Revolutionary War; the Revolutionary War.

1789 *Ann. 1st Congress* 150 He recollected that, before the Revolution, very little was imported. **1811** J. ADAMS *Works* IX. 627 The last trial before a special court of Vice-Admiralty in Boston, before the revolution, was . . . for piracy and murder on the high seas. **1850** [see COWBOY 1]. **1894** *Harper's Mag.* Feb. 423/1 There was but little progress made in the iron industry till after the Revolution. **1915** TARKINGTON *Two Vanrevels* 8 After the Revolution, Carolinians and Virginians had come, by way of Tennessee and Kentucky.

b. Used with reference to the American Civil War.

1861 E. COWELL *Diary* 248 But to turn from all our insignificant affairs 'The Revolution' is stalking through this vast country with rapid strides.

Revolutionary, *a.* {1796–} +Of or pertaining to the Revolution or the Revolutionary War.

1798 *Ann. 5th Congress* 1337 He regretted to see so different a spirit animating our citizens now, from that which animated them in our Revolutionary struggle. **1813** *Ann. 12th Congress* 2 Sess. 69 The President communicated the memorial of Peter Charles L'Enfant, late a principal engineer and major in the Revolutionary Army of the United States. **1847** R. DODGE *Diary, Sk. & Reviews* 51 Some seven hundred of the men sat at dinner, in their odd uniform of immense coats, with gilt buttons, and cocked hats, in what we term, revolutionary style. **1893** PAGE in *Harper's Mag.* Dec. 14/1 The elements of character which the Virginian of the Revolutionary time inherited from his father he transmitted to his children. **1900** *Congress. Rec.* 10 Jan. 742/1 The sacred soil of his State . . . has gathered into its unreturning bosom for generations from colonial times, through Revolutionary times, . . . the bodies of so many noble men.

+b. *spec.* Of individuals who fought in the Revolutionary War.

1806 *Balance* V. 214/2 May the thundering sound of cannon, ever recall to our memory, the toils and dangers of our revolutionary heroes. **1818** *Niles' Reg.* XIV. 135/2 During the past week about 220 old revolutionary warriors appeared before judge Davis. **1819** *Ib.* XVII. 100/1 A great number of old revolutionary pensioners are now in town. **1825** *Catawba Jrnl.* 31 May, A band of revolutionary veterans, 60 or 70 in number. **1840** *Niles' Nat. Reg.* 1 Aug. 344/3 A revolutionary hero gone. **1900** *Congress. Rec.* 5 Feb. 1525/1 Daniel Webster once declared that our Revolutionary sires went to war about a preamble. **1907** *St. Nicholas* May 672/1 The four middle letters may be transposed so as to form the surname of a Revolutionary general.

+Revolutionary soldier. A soldier who took part in the Revolutionary War. — **1840** *Niles' Reg.* LIX. 157/2 At the extremity of the green, facing the college, a large platform was erected for the revolutionary soldiers. **1843** *Ib.* 23 Sept. 64/3 Revolutionary Soldiers. Henry Arnold, a soldier of the revolution, died in Washington, Pa. **1893** *Harper's Mag.* Jan. 238/2 This was the first allowance of pension of any sort to the widows of Revolutionary soldiers after the seven years' half-pay of 1780.

+Revolutionary War. The war for independence carried on by the American colonists against Great Britain (1775–1783). Also attrib. — **1800** HAWKINS *Sk. Creek Country* 26 These Indians were very friendly to the United States, during the revolutionary war. **1817** PAULDING *Lett. from South* I. 59, I have made an excursion to York; . . . celebrated as the place where the last blow of our revolutionary war was struck. **1844** RUPP *Relig. Denominations* 54 During the revolutionary war many of our churches were scattered by the male members being engaged with the army. **1891** EARLE *Sabbath* 104 In Lexington for many years after the Revolutionary War, the winter church-goers who came from any distance spent the nooning at the Dudley Tavern. **1907** *St. Nicholas* Sept. 1054/1 Jane McCrea . . . was killed by Indians during the Revolutionary War period.

Revolutioner. {1695–} +One who took part in the Revolutionary War. *Obs.* — **1835** CROCKETT *Tour* 52 General Morton is a revolutioner, and an officer in the society of old soldiers called the 'Cincinnati Society.' **1844** *Lexington Observer* 5 Oct. 3/4 There are no suitable husbands in either party for them, but the Old Revolutioners.

Revolutionist. {1710–} +One in sympathy with the South during the American Civil War. *Obs.* — **1861** in W. Lawrence *A. A. Lawrence* 171 Massachusetts troops fired on in Baltimore. Washington barely saved from the revolutionists. **1865** RICHARDSON *Secret Service* 17 Early in 1861, I felt a strong desire . . . [to learn] what the Revolutionists wanted, what they hoped and what they feared.

+Revolution war. =REVOLUTIONARY WAR. *Obs.* — **1795** *Mass. H. S. Coll.* 1 Ser. IV. 203 During the revolution-war, the publick opinion was . . . strongly in favour of the abolition of slavery. **1801** JEFFERSON *Writings* X. 226 All these petitions were depending . . . when the Revolution War broke out.

Revolver. A pistol in which a number of barrels, or, more usually, a cylinder suitable for separate charges or cartridges, revolves before the firing mechanism. {1848–}

[**1835** COLT in *Abridgm. Patent Specifications, Fire-arms* (1859) 84.] **1866** *Rep. Indian Affairs* 247 Whenever they become intoxicated . . . resort is had to the revolver and knife. **1899** in *Congress. Rec.* 15 Jan. (1900) 825/1 Wild, reckless cowboys gallop down the street, firing their revolvers right and left at everything in sight. **1920** HOWELLS *Vacation of Kelwyns* 35 He suddenly realized with a neuralgic poignancy that his revolver was meant to kill a man.

b. Attrib. with *barrel, belt, law, shot.*

*a*1861 WINTHROP *J. Brent* 208 They were close to us, within easy revolver shot. **1872** POWERS *Afoot & Alone* 129, I saw a youth . . . strap his spelling-book to his revolver belt. **1881** CHASE *Editor's Run in N. Mex.* 110 One good thing has resulted from the revolver law; people have learned to respect each other's rights. **1883** *Harper's Mag.* Oct. 710/2, The mouthpiece is . . . pierced with a bore about as large as a 0.45 revolver barrel.

Revolving, *a.* {1697–} Of mechanical apparatus or devices: Rotating, turning; making revolutions. {1814–}

1819 *Plough Boy* I. 123 Salmon's patent hay maker with revolving rakes. **1869** *Rep. Comm. Agric. 1868* 249 When a hedge becomes strong enough to turn stock, it is desirable to check its growth, . . . by cutting off the ends of the roots on the sides of the ridge . . . with a revolving colter. **1885** *Harper's Mag.* Jan. 284/1 Sliding knives or revolving cutters in 'trimming' machines pare off unnecessary parts. **1907** *St. Nicholas* Oct. 1104/2 It was his stated duty to attend one of the big revolving doors that opened upon the street. **1910** BOSTWICK *Amer. Pub. Library* 6 The 'revolving library' of Kittery and York, Me., [was] apparently so called because it was contained in a revolving case.

+b. Used of repeating firearms employing barrels or cylinders that rotate on an axis.

1850 *Rep. Comm. Patents 1849* 308 Having thus fully described my improved method of connecting the hammer with the cylinder of a revolving fire arm [etc.]. **1864** *Ib. 1862* I. 638 Improvement in Revolving Battery Guns. **1865** RICHARDSON *Secret Service* 200 Armed with revolvers and revolving carbines, members of the Guard had twelve shots apiece. **1886** *Harper's Mag.* Oct. 793/2 The types adopted by the United States navy are the Hotchkiss revolving cannon and rapid-firing single-shot guns, and the smaller calibre machine guns of Gatling.

+Revolving pistol. = REVOLVER. *Obs.* — **1844** *Lexington Observer* 24 July 3/4 The doctor, drawing a pair of Colt's revolving pistols, prepared to receive his excellency. **1847** PARKMAN in *Knickerb.* XXX. 24 The other jerked a little revolving pistol out of his pocket. [**1850** HINES *Voyage* 436 Edmonds armed himself with a revolving six barreled pistol that was sure fire.]

+Revolving rifle. A repeating rifle having a cylinder containing chambers for separate charges or cartridges that are brought in succession before the firing mechanism. *Obs.* — **1864** *Hist. North-Western Soldiers' Fair* 134 [Donations include] a revolving rifle, captured from a guerrilla. **1865** TROWBRIDGE *Three Scouts* 363 General Stanley . . . [was] giving them exercise and practice with their new revolving rifles.

+Re-wood, *v. tr.* To plant (land) again with trees; to repair (a bridge) with new wooden parts. — **1886** *N.Y. Tribune* (s.-w. ed.) 24 Dec. (*Cent.*), Rewooding the high lands where the streams take rise. **1908** *Indian Laws & Tr.* III. 333 For the purpose of rewooding and repiling the present old bridge, . . . the sum of twelve thousand dollars.

+Rheumatism root. 1. The twinleaf (*Jeffersonia diphylla*), which grows wild in the eastern states. (Cf. TWINLEAF.) **2.** The wild yam, *Dioscorea paniculata.* — (1) **1843** TORREY *Flora N.Y.* I. 34 *Jeffersonia diphylla.* Twin-leaf. Rheumatism-root. . . . [The root] is sometimes employed as a remedy in chronic rheumatism. **1847** WOOD *Botany* 153 This plant has in Ohio the reputation of a stimulant and antispasmodic, and is there significantly termed *rheumatism root.* **1898** CREEVEY *Flowers of Field* 308 Twin-leaf. Rheumatism-root. . . . A plant of low growth, not uncommon in the woods of western New York, southward and westward. (2) **1887** BENTLEY *Man. Botany* 706 The rhizome of *D*[*ioscorea*] *villosa*, the Wild Yam of the United States, is regarded as a valuable remedy in Virginia in rheumatism, and is hence commonly known as 'rheumatism root.'

+Rheumatism weed. 1. Any one of various evergreen herbs as the pipsissewa. {1798-} **2.** (See quotation and cf. DOGBANE, DOG'S-BANE.) — (1) **1784** *Amer. Acad. Mem.* I. 444 Rheumatism-Weed . . . abounds near White-Mountains. **1795** WINTERBOTHAM *Hist. View* III. 398 Among the native and uncultivated plants of New-England, the following have been employed for medical purposes: . . . Rheumatism weed, *Pirola minor* [and] Mouse ear, *Cerastium viscosum.* **1832** CHILD *Frugal Housewife* 28 Winter evergreen is considered good for all humors, particularly. Some call it rheumatism-weed. **1872** *Atlantic Mo.* June 748/2 The umbelled pyrola, or rheumatism-weed, . . . and the roots of the yellow dock, were favorite ingredients [for a 'diet drink' of herbs]. (2) **1894** *Amer. Folk-Lore* VII. 94 *Apocynum androsæmifolium*, rheumatism-weed, West Va.

‖Rheumatizzy, *a.* Conducive to rheumatism. *colloq.* — **1872** S. HALE *Letters* 79 These months . . . are rheumatizzy.

Rhexia. A genus of plants of the family Melastomaceae, or any plant belonging to this genus. (Cf. DEER GRASS, MEADOW BEAUTY.) — **1833** WHITTIER *Poetical Works* (1894) 262/1 The rhexias dark, and cassia tall. **1843** TORREY *Flora N.Y.* I. 227 Rhexia. . . . Perennial herbs. . . . Flowers showy, purple or yellow. **1863** *Rep. Comm. Agric. 1862* 159 The *Rhexias*, or, as our people call them, 'Meadow Beauties,' comprise the only native genus [of the tribe Melastoma]. **1887** BURROUGHS in *Century Mag.* July 327 Parts of New England have already a midsummer flower nearly as brilliant and probably far less aggressive and noxious, in meadow beauty, or rhexia.

Rhinoceros beetle. {1681-} **+(See quotations.)** — **1890** *Cent.* 5152/2 The common rhinoceros-beetle of the United States, *Dynastes tityus*, the largest of the North American beetles, has two large horns directed forward. **1908** KELLOGG *Amer. Insects* 12 The largest beetles in our country are the oddly shaped rhinoceros-beetles, Dynastes, found in the south and west.

+Rhode Island. *attrib.* [Name of a New England state.] Designating things found in or pertaining to Rhode Island. — **1872** *Atlantic Mo.* April 399 It required twenty-five hundred pounds in Rhode Island paper to buy one golden guinea. **1886** POORE *Reminisc.* I. 384 She could make a regal Cape Cod chowder, or roast a Rhode Island turkey. **1894** *Amer. Folk-Lore* VII. 91 *Chrysanthemum leucanthemum*, Kellup weed, Rhode Island clover, Montpelier, Vt.

+Rhode Island bent. A variety of lawn grass, *Agrostis capillaris.* — **1790** DEANE *New-Eng. Farmer* 123/1 The Rhode-Island bent, as it is called, or red top grass, will do with less drying than some other grasses. **1795** WINTERBOTHAM *Hist. View* III. 400. **1899** *Dept. Agric. Yrbk. 1898*

494 Creeping bent (*Agrostis stolonifera*) and Rhode Island bent (*A. canina*) are much prized for lawns.

+Rhode Islander. A native or inhabitant of Rhode Island. — **1679** *Conn. Rec.* III. 273 Our last Generall Court . . . resolued vigorously to pursue the outing of the Rohd Islanders from ye Narrogancett Country. **1752** [see NOVANGLIAN *a.* and *n.* 2]. *a*1817 DWIGHT *Travels* II. 37 Free born Rhode-Islanders ought never to submit to be priest-ridden. **1888** WHITMAN *Nov. Boughs* 384 One young sailor, a Rhode Islander, . . . told me, 'that must be the Holy Ghost we read of in the Testament.' **1905** *McClure's Mag.* Feb. 337/1 The political condition of Rhode Island . . . is shameful. But Rhode Islanders are ashamed of it.

+Rhode Island Greening. A variety of green or greenish apple; also, a tree producing this apple. — **1817** W. COXE *Fruit Trees* 129 Jersey, or Rhode-Island Greening. Sometimes called the Burlington Greening. **1850** *Rep. Comm. Patents 1849: Agric.* 271 The Rhode Island greening is the most celebrated and productive market variety. **1879** B. F. TAYLOR *Summer-Savory* 116 [He] gave me Rhode Island Greenings out of his Sunday-noon lunch. **1884** ROE *Nature's Story* 400 Those umbrella-shaped trees are Rhode Island greenings.

Rhodes scholar. (See SCHOLAR 3.)

Rhododendron. {1601-} A genus of shrubs or shrublike trees of the heath family that grows wild in mountainous regions; also, a plant of this genus. {1664-}

1814 BIGELOW *Florula Bostoniensis* 103 We have no shrub that surpasses the Rhododendron in elegance. **1839** *S. Lit. Messenger* V. 269/2 It is only in a few ravines that I saw the Rhododendron. **1875** R. H. DAVIS *Silhouettes* 255 Here and there a late rhododendron hung out its scarlet banner. **1924** RAINE *Land of Saddle-Bags* 133 A spring must be selected that flows under an impenetrable thicket of laurel (rhododendron).

b. Attrib. with *bell, bush, hybrid.*

1846 *Spirit of Times* (N.Y.) 9 May 131/3 [He] has now for sale fine large plants of his new Hardy Azalias, and Rhododendron Hybrids. **1901** HARBEN *Westerfelt* 316 He plunged into a tangle of laurel, rhododendron bushes, vines, and briers. **1903** Fox *Little Shepherd* ii, The laurel blooms and rhododendron bells hung in thicker clusters and of a deeper pink.

Rhodora. A flowering plant or shrub (*Rhodora canadensis*), found chiefly in New England. — **1839** EMERSON *Poems* (1867) 37, I found the fresh Rhodora in the woods. **1850** *New Eng. Farmer* III. 109 The Rhodora is a showy, early flowering shrub. **1869** FULLER *Flower Gatherers* 59 The Azaleas, or Swamp Honeysuckles, are beautiful cousins of the Rhodora. *a*1886 DICKINSON *Works* (1924) 82 The crocus stirs her lids, Rhodora's cheek is crimson.

+Rhody. = LITTLE RHODY. — *a*1859 in Bartlett 364 Old Newport, billow-cradled, see, On Rhody's verdant shore.

⁕ Rhubarb.

⁕1. Any one of various tall coarse plants of the genus *Rheum*, or a medicinal preparation made of the root of such a plant.

See also PIE RHUBARB and cf. PIEPLANT.

1693 Earle *Colonial Days N.Y.* 36 [A detailed school bill of the Lloyd boys] Wormwood & rubab for them. **1712** *Essex Inst. Coll.* X. 1. 94 [He] put in ginger, rum, sugar, and some powder of his, made of rhubarb, &c. **1776** *Jrnls. Cont. Congress* V. 712 A box of rhubarb [was] bought of Pelatiah Webster. **1820** *Columbian Centinel* 5 Jan. 4/3 Richard D. Tucker & Co. Have for sale . . . 34 cases Rhubarb. **1840** DEWEY *Mass. Flowering Plants* 104 *Rheum palmatum.* Rhubarb. Introduced from Asia, and rarely cultivated. **1898** A. M. DAVIDSON *Calif. Plants* 174 The beet and rhubarb . . . are nearly related to the dock and knot-weed. *a*1918 [see GOOSEBERRY 2].

2. Attrib. with *pie, seed, stalk,* etc.

1788 WASHINGTON *Diaries* III. 320, I sowed . . . one Row of Rhubarb seed. **1832** CHILD *Frugal Housewife* 69 Rhubarb stalks, or the Persian apple, is the earliest ingredient for pies, which the spring offers. **1834** in *Atlantic Mo.* XXVI. 492 We had apple-pie, and rhubarb-pie, or tart. **1868** *Mich. Agric. Rep.* VII. 351 C. F. Allen, Paw Paw, [exhibited a] specimen [of] rhubarb wine. **1902** *Harper's Mag.* May 944 Through the rhubarb thicket in the corner of the fence stalked a black bear.

⁕Rial. Any one of various coins of foreign origin formerly current in America with the value of about 12 1/2 cents; *rial of eight,* = PIECE OF EIGHT. (See also REAL.) — **1623** *Va. House of Burgesses* 24 His Riots and lascivious Filthiness with lewd Women, [was] purchased with Rials of Eight and Wedges of Gold. **1694** *Mass. H. S. Coll.* 4 Ser. I. 106 Rials pas for 9 pence. **1850** GARRARD *Wah-To-Yah* xvi. 199 Metcalf . . . [produced] a *rial's* worth of Mexican soft soap.

Rialto. {1901-} **+**A district in New York City frequented by stage players and theatergoers. — **1888** [see HAM FATTER]. **1903** *N.Y. Tribune* 13 Sept., If there be any to whom the Rialto is vain and the East Side intolerable. **1916** F. RIDER *New York City* 53 The theatre life of New York is comprised within the fairly narrow area of Broadway and the adjacent side streets, from 40th to 50th st.—a stretch popularly known as the 'Rialto.'

+Riata. [Sp. *reata.*] A rope or lariat. Cf. LARIAT *n.,* LARIAT(TE). **1848** BRYANT *California* xxiii. 291 A *riata* (rope) was then made fast to the broken bone, and the jaw dragged out. **1869** BREWER *Rocky Mt. Lett.* 26, [I] drew my lasso (riata) over them and hung up a blanket. **1880** [see LASSO *v.*]. **1890** HARTE *Waif of Plains* 173 With a cut of his riata over the animal's haunches, . . . they were both galloping furiously away. **1910** J. HART *Vigilante Girl* 196 But the riata, or lasso, at her pommel is probably purely for ornament.

b. *To coil up one's riata,* to die.
1871 *Overland Mo.* March 285/2, I'm a-coilin' up my *riata,* Jim.

∗ Ribbed, *a.*

1. Of knitted or woven fabrics: Having ribs or ridges on the surface. {1787-}
1756 *Essex Inst. Coll.* XLIII. 277 Smith wore when he went away . . . blue ribb'd Stockings. **1782** *Ib.* I. 13/1 You will be so kind as to Creadet me for . . . a patton of White Ribed Stuff for a Wescoat & Briches. **1825** [see MILLED *a.* 1]. **1890** *Harper's Mag.* Oct. 656/2 We each wore . . . ribbed bicycle stockings that came to our knees. **1904** WALLER *Wood-Carver* 38, I'm knitting 'ribbed' stockings.

+2. *Ribbed boiler, r. mussel, r. road,* (see quotations).
1833 FIDLER *Observations* 122 Such roads are denominated by the native, 'ribbed or corduroy roads,' an appellation not ill chosen. **1883** KNIGHT *Suppl.* 756/2 *Ribbed Boiler,* one with corrugations or projecting ribs to add to the surface exposed to the fire. Used for greenhouse boilers. **1883** *Nat. Museum Bul.* No. 27, 236 *Modiola plicatula,* . . . known as the Ribbed-mussel, is found from Georgia to Casco Bay, Maine.

∗ Ribbon. Also †ribband.

∗ 1. A fine fabric, often of silk or satin, woven in long, narrow strips; also, a piece or length of such a fabric.
1678 *New Castle Court Rec.* 322 There was taken out [of the chest] . . . 43 skaynes of thrid 40 skaynes of silke & one Remnant of old Ribband. **1711** *Springfield Rec.* II. 40 Eight yards & a Quarter of ribbin. **1825** NEAL *Bro. Jonathan* II. 46 His hair . . . [was] bound up with a piece of sky-blue 'worsted ribbon.' **1893** 'MARK TWAIN' *P. Wilson* iii, She added some odds and ends of rather lurid ribbon. **1912** NICHOLSON *Hoosier Chron.* 85 A dark young miss, with black hair tied with a red ribbon.

+2. The name of a variety of sugar cane.
Cf. RIBBON CANE.
1837 WILLIAMS *Florida* 106 Three kinds of cane are planted in the Territory, the creole, otaheita, and ribon.

+3. a. A long narrow strip of cloth especially prepared and inked for use on stamping devices and typewriters.
1876 KNIGHT 1936/2 Ribbons for hand-stamps are tapes saturated with an oily pigment. **1890** *Cent.* 5164/2 *Ribbon,* . . . a narrow web of silk for hand-stamps, saturated with free color, which is readily transferred by pressure to paper. **1918** OWEN *Typewriting Speed* 140 Work in a law office calls for the use of *black* ribbons on your machine.

+b. A narrow strip of paper used on a stock ticker; a ticker tape.
1882 MCCABE *New York* 338 The offers and bids . . . are noted on the long ribbons of the thousands of 'tickers.'

+4. A narrow band or streak of different color in slates.
1898 *19th Rep. Geol. Survey* VI. 257 The normal product of roofing slates is called No. 1 stock, and this is entirely free from ribbons.

+5. In miscellaneous uses.
To a ribbon, to a T, exactly; *ribbon arrangement, r. hog,* (see quotations).
1841 COOPER *Deerslayer* i, Now that's Judith's character to a ribbon! **1910** BOSTWICK *Amer. Pub. Library* 167 In some open-shelf libraries a so-called 'ribbon' arrangement of fiction has been adopted, in which the fiction is placed on one shelf around the room, with nonfiction classes above and below it. **1924** CROY *R. F. D. No. 3* 133 His ambition was to raise 'ribbon hogs'—hogs which would be awarded the prize at the local stock show.

+Ribbon cane. A variety of sugar cane the stalks of which when mature are marked with red or purplish longitudinal stripes. Also *ribbonplant cane.* (Cf. RIBBON 2.) — **1827** in Commons, etc. *Doc. Hist.* I. 215 Some ribbon plant cane have suckered on the 9th. **1833** SILLIMAN *Man. Sugar Cane* 10 The Ribbon Cane . . . appears to be a hybrid between the Violet and the Otaheitan varieties. **1837** WILLIAMS *Florida* 80 The Riband cane is said to keep it [nut grass] down. **1853** *Harper's Mag.* Nov. 749/1 The name of the Ribbon cane is suggestive of its appearance, for the purple is broken with golden stripes in every variety of penciling. **1901** MOHR *Plant Life Ala.* 825.

Ribbon grass. A variety of reed canary grass having white-striped leaves. {1786-} — **1817-8** EATON *Botany* (1822) 386 *Phalaris americana,* ribbon grass, wild canary grass. . . . Var. *picta,* leaves variously striped. This variety is the ribbon grass of the gardens. **1849** *New Eng. Farmer* I. 227 Ribbon Grass . . . is the beautiful striped grass occasionally used for garden borders. **1878** KILLIBREW *Tennessee Grasses* 204 *Ribbon Grass* . . . is exceedingly hardy and showy, but is of little value as a hay or pasture grass. **1884** VASEY *Agric. Grasses* 54 The well-known ribbon grass of the garden is a variety of [reed canary grass].

Ribbon snake. {1711-} +An American garter snake, *Thamnophis saurita.* — **1736** CATESBY *Carolina* II. 50 *Anguis gracilis fuscus.* The Ribbon-Snake. This is a slender Snake. **1791** W. BARTRAM *Travels* 273 The ribband snake is another very beautiful innocent serpent. **1827** WILLIAMS *W. Florida* 29 The garter, riband, green, chequered, and glass snakes, make up the account of this species, in West Florida. **1853** in Marcy *Explor. Red River* 205 This genus [*Eutænia*] is composed of numer-

ous species, some of them quite common, and known under the names of Riband, Striped, and Garter snakes. **1904** PRINGLE *Rice Planter* 105 There was a small ribbon snake, a foot long and one inch round!

+Rib pole. One of the poles or timbers on which the boards covering a log cabin were laid. *Obs.* — **1837** *S. Lit. Messenger* III. 82 The roofs of loose boards laid on long rib-poles betokened an abundance of timber. **1870** NOWLAND *Indianapolis* 50 Suspended by a rope (fastened to the rib-pole above), hung a thing that looked something in shape like the bow of a base viol.

Ribston(e) pippin. An excellent variety of winter apple. {Ribstone-Park pippin, 1769; 1796-} — **1817** W. COXE *Fruit Trees* 125 Ribstone Pippin. . . . It is an excellent table and baking apple. **1847** IVES *New Eng. Fruit* 39 Ribstone Pippin.—Fruit sometimes large, of a flat form; the skin is a mixture of russet and yellow. **1875** BURROUGHS *Winter Sunshine* 162 What a vigorous grower, for instance, is the Ribston pippin, an English apple.

Rib work. A basic or supporting structure having the appearance of ribs. {1894-} — **1848** BRYANT *California* xxi. 271 These *rancherias* consist of a number of huts constructed of a rib-work or frame of small poles. **1892** DANA *Syst. Min.* (ed. 6) 271 The crystals . . . affording a rectangular rib-work on the cross-section. **1895** *Outing* XXVII. 18/2 Over the rib-work thus formed, long strips of canvas are stretched.

∗Ribwort. A species of plantain (*Plantago lanceolata*) having long ribbed leaves, or a related species. — **1814** BIGELOW *Florula Bostoniensis* 34 *Plantago lanceolata,* Ribwort or field plantain. **1847** WOOD *Botany* 388 *P. major.* Common Plantain or Ribwort. . . . This species is a native of Japan, Europe and America, is very common, always at the door and by the wayside. **1894** *Amer. Folk-Lore* VII. 96.

∗ Rice.

I. ∗1. The edible seeds or grains of an annual grass (*Oryza sativa*), or the plant itself.
1637 *Conn. Rec.* I. 9 Windsor [is to provide] 50 peeces of Porke, 30 lb of Rice, 4 Cheeses. **1666** *S.C. Hist. Coll.* II. 13 The Meadows are very proper for Rice. **1715** *Boston News-Letter* 22 Aug. 2/2 The Indians . . . set their Horse loose into the Fields of Rice and Corn to Destroy it. **1789** MORSE *Amer. Geog.* 52 Rice . . . flourishes only in Georgia and the Carolinas. **1821** NUTTALL *Travels Arkansa* 73 Rice has been tried on a small scale, and found to answer every expectation. **1882** G. C. EGGLESTON *Wreck of Red Bird* 136, I thought the rice was wild—self-seeded. **1905** PRINGLE *Rice Planter* 252, I gave her four quarts of rice, some grist, a small piece of bacon, and some milk.

b. Preceded by defining terms.
1802 DRAYTON *S. Carolina* 127 Some of them, were called *fine rice,* as being more delicate, whiter, and more agreeably flavored. . . . Others were considered as *ordinary rice;* as being most nutritious, and serving for common food. And a third kind was called *clammy rice,* as adhering, when boiled, into one glutinous mass.

c. An aquatic North American grass (*Zizania aquatica*); wild rice.
1778 CARVER *Travels* 523 [The Indians place] their canoes close to the bunches of rice, in such position as to receive the grain when it falls. **1820** in *Wis. Hist. Coll.* VII. 199 The Indians around Sandy Lake, in the month of September, repair to Rice Lake to gather their rice. **1848** COOPER *Oak Openings* I. 78 There was a good deal of this rice at hand. **1876** *Wis. Hist. Coll.* VII. 266 Madam [an Indian woman] with the pole, forces the canoe slowly into the standing rice.

II. *attrib.* and *comb.* **2.** Designating places or regions where rice grows or is grown. {1625-}
See also RICE FARM, RICE FIELD, etc.
1765 J. BARTRAM *Journal* 13 These swamps are supposed to be the best rice-grounds. **1807** *Steele P.* II. 500 They had been trespassing on his rice land or bank. **1835** HOFFMAN *Winter in West* II. 256, I had seen the savage hills and plashy rice-pools of Wisconsan [*sic*]. **1874** LONG *Wild-Fowl* 49 When two persons are hunting in company in a rice-pond, it is well for one to take a stand on one of the large muskrat-houses. **1887** *Outing* June 259/2 To paddle through these rice-beds and shoot the ducks as they rise is considered the best sport.

b. Designating things associated with rice culture.
1836 SIMMS *Mellichampe* vi, The two got all their friends together, and *fout* . . . like so many tiger-cats, along the rice-dam, for two long hours by sun. *c*1852 in Stowe *Key* 154/2 The plantation hands . . . work all the time above their knees in water in the rice-ditches.

∗3. Designating foods prepared from rice.
See also RICE FLOUR, PUDDING, WAFFLE.
1802 CUTLER in *Life & Corr.* II. 71 Dined at the President's . . . [on] rice soup [etc.]. **1805** *Pocumtuc Housewife* (1906) 7 Get some rice Porridge or brewis and cold meat. **1832** CHILD *Frugal Housewife* 78 To make Rice Bread.—Boil a pint of rice soft [etc.]. **1833** *Md. Hist. Mag.* XIII. 364 Took breakfast with Mr. Grimke. . . . Salmon and rice-cake—cocoa and tea. **1846** *Knickerb.* XXVII. 552 A composition of butter, rice, and milk, dignified with the name of 'rice-custard.' **1850** *New Eng. Farmer* II. 162/1 Jellies for the Sick. . . . *Rice Jelly.*—Take of rice three spoonfuls [etc.]. *Ib.* 322/1 *Rice Balls.*—Pour upon half a pound of rice three pints of boiling milk [etc.]. **1870** W. BAKER *New Timothy* 40 There were rice batter-cakes for supper.

4. Designating machines or devices used in growing rice or preparing it for market.

See also RICE-PLANTER 2, RICE SIEVE.

1833 *Niles' Reg.* XLIV. 222/1 Rice threshing machines, are in operation at or near Savannah. **1850** *Rep. Comm. Patents 1849* 459 A patent has been granted . . . to cover the cylinder and the concave of cylindrical rice hullers. **1862** *Ib. 1861: Agric.* 646 Rice cleaning machines, Albert H. Wright, New York, N.Y., September 10. **1868** *Rep. Comm. Patents 1867* I. 896/1 *Rice Cultivator.* . . . The plow beams are adjustable laterally to the rear of the frame. **1876** KNIGHT 1938/2 *Rice-sower,* . . . a drill for planting rice. **1883** *Ib. Suppl.* 756/2 *Rice Drill*, a force-feed machine for drilling rice.

5. Designating persons having to do with rice.

See also RICEBIRD 2, RICE-PLANTER 1.

*c***1836** CATLIN *Indians* II. 159 The sugar planter, the rice, cotton, and tobacco growers . . . have only to turn their faces to the West. **1862** 'E. KIRKE' *Among Pines* 288 The rice-negro seldom lives to be over forty, and the cotton slave very rarely attains sixty. **1872** POWERS *Afoot & Alone* 44 These poor rice-eaters, and their grunting, gutteral, sea-island patois, might make you believe yourself on the deadly shores of the Senegal.

6. Designating insects injurious to rice.

See also RICE WEEVIL.

1882 *Amer. Naturalist* XVI. 1014 A New Rice Stalk-borer. . . . A new Lepidopterous insect which, in the larva state, bores the stalks of rice. **1883** *Science* I. 487/2 The rice-grub is the larva of a beetle (*Chalepus trachypygus*).

+Rice barrel. A barrel for rice. — *c***1729** CATESBY *Carolina* I. 38 Of the Saplings, or young Trees, are made the best Hoops for Tobacco, Rice, and Tar Barrels. **1742** *Georgia Col. Rec.* VI. 20 For all Pipes H[ogs]hds, Butts & Rice Barrils 2d. each. **1772** HABERSHAM *Letters* 220, I do not believe it wou'd be possible to buy rice barrels from the Coopers. **1853** SIMMS *Sword & Distaff* (1854) 277 He rolled over a pile of rice barrels.

Ricebird. {**1704**-}

1. Any one of various small birds that frequent rice fields, esp. the bobolink. {**1769**-}

*c***1728** CATESBY *Carolina* I. 14 The Rice-Bird . . . [is] esteemed in Carolina the greatest delicacy of all other Birds. **1796** [see CONQUEDLE]. **1808** SCHULTZ *Travels* II. 185 The rice bird is a small species of blackbird. **1887** *Courier-Journal* 6 May 4/7 Preparing to get across the Cape Fear river to shoot rice birds. **1917** *Birds of Amer.* II. 243/2 The havoc made on the ripening grain by the Rice-bird, as the Bobolink is commonly known . . . [in the rice fields of the South], is very great.

+2. A nickname for an inhabitant of a rice region, esp. a South Carolinian.

1777 *Md. Journal* 9 Dec. (Th.), Next comes in Sir H——y Cl——ton, . . . And swore he'd make the rice-birds think on. [**1809** WEEMS *Marion* (1833) 82 The British were a handful of hawks; the poor Carolinians [were but] a swarm of rice-birds.] **1861** *N.Y. Tribune* 15 Nov. 4/3 The surrounding country [near Beaufort, S.C.] embraces the best rice-fields of the South—so proverbially so, indeed, that the irreverent 'up-country' people are accustomed to call the aristocratic inhabitants of the region rice-birds; perhaps, also, in allusion to their worldly fatness. **1869** *Overland Mo.* III. 128 For a very obvious reason, the South Carolinians are called 'Rice-birds.'

+Rice bunting. =BOBOLINK. — **1783** LATHAM *Gen. Synopsis Birds* II. 188 Rice B[unting], *Emberiza oryzivora*. **1810** [see BOBOLINK 1 d]. **1839** PEABODY *Mass. Birds* 284 The Rice Bunting . . . is not nearly so much persecuted in New England as in other parts of the country. **1857** *Rep. Comm. Patents 1856: Agric.* 127 The 'Meadow Bird,' in Louisiana, the 'Reed Bird,' in Pennsylvania, the 'Rice-Bunting,' in the Carolinas, and the 'Bob-o-link,' in New York, and thence eastward, are all the same.

Rice corn. {**1681**-} A variety of Indian corn having grains somewhat resembling rice. — **1849** EMMONS *Agric. N.Y.* II. 265 Rice corn . . . is used principally for popping. **1850** S. F. COOPER *Rural Hours* 388 The varieties called rice-corn, and Egyptian corn, are used. **1851** J. F. W. JOHNSTON *Notes N. Amer.* I. 152 In some the horny part is large, as in the varieties known by the names of brown, Canada, rice, and pop corns.

Rice culture. The culture or cultivation of rice. — **1836** GILMAN *Recoll.* 222 Long tracts of land are devoted to rice-culture. **1854** *New Orleans Delta* 28 May, Mr. Britton has been traveling much through the Atlantic States . . . in quest of information upon the subject of rice culture and milling. **1856** OLMSTED *Slave States* 482, I should think, too, the horse-hoe . . . might be adapted to rice-culture.

+Rice cut-grass. A marsh grass (*Leersia oryzoides*), having grains resembling rice grains. Also *ricelike cut-grass*. — **1857** GRAY *Botany* 540 Rice Cut-grass. . . . Wet places; common. **1894** COULTER *Bot. W. Texas* III. 511 Rice cut-grass. . . . Margins of streams, often in shallow water, Texas to Minnesota and eastward. **1901** [see CUT-GRASS].

Rice farm. =RICE PLANTATION. — **1782** DENNY *Mil. Jrnl.* 46 Rice farms [are] around this neighborhood. **1887** R. H. DAVIS *Silhouettes* 21 A company was formed among the planters in the Gulf parishes to drain their marshes in order to establish large rice-farms.

Rice field. A field in which rice is grown. {**1704**-} Also attrib. — **1754** *S.C. Gazette* 8 Jan. 4 This reserve of back-water . . . supplies the rice field. **1765** HABERSHAM *Letters* 39, I find the Rice Field pernicious to my Health. **1836** [see DITCH *v.* 1]. **1885** *Rep. Indian Affairs* 117 The damage arising to the rice fields, fisheries [etc.] . . . leave [*sic*] these Indians [on the

White Earth reservation] in a pitiable condition. **1904** PRINGLE *Rice Planter* 67 The curing of hay is unknown to the rice-field darky.

Rice flour. Flour prepared from grains of rice. {**1769**-} — **1856** in Commons, etc. *Doc. Hist.* I. 125 Mr. Manigault wishes Mr. Clark to sell for him all the Rice flour made in his Mill. **1863** in *Century Mag.* XXXI. 769/2, I had nothing left but a sack of rice-flour. **1878** *Amer. Home Cook Book* 15 Mix the rice-flour smoothly with the water.

+Rice lake. A shallow lake or marsh, as those near the headwaters of the Mississippi, in which wild rice is found. *Obs.* — **1831** PECK *Guide* 14 A third [boat] may start from the rice lakes at the head of the Mississippi. **1834** — *Gaz. Illinois* 364 Here [around Green Bay] are large tracts of cranberry marshes, and rice lakes. **1849** *31st Congress 1 Sess.* H. R. Ex. Doc. No. 5, 11. 1031 [The Chippewas] compelled the Dakotah nation to abandon its ancient seat around the head-waters of the Mississippi, whose rice lakes and hunting-grounds the Chippewas at this day possess.

Rice land. Low wet land on which rice is or can be grown to advantage. {**1776**-} — **1743** CATESBY *Carolina* II. p. iii, *Rice Land* [in Carolina] is most valuable, though only productive of that grain, it being too wet for anything else. **1791** WASHINGTON *Diaries* IV. 194 The prices at which the Rice lands in the lower parts of the State are held is very great. **1807** [see RICE 2]. **1868** *Putnam's Mag.* May 502/2 [The] draining-canals in the rear of the rice-lands swarm with . . . fish.

Rice mill. A mill for removing the husk from rough rice. {**1842**-} — **1802** [see COG MILL]. **1829** B. HALL *Travels in N.A.* III. 163 Our first visit was to a Rice Mill. **1865** *Atlantic Mo.* May 627/1 It seems no extravagant ambition for a joint-stock company to aim at a rice-mill. **1888** BILLINGS *Hardtack* 406 The [signal] station was built on the top of a rice-mill.

Rice plantation. A plantation devoted to the cultivation of rice. {**1797**-} — **1787** in Commons etc. *Doc. Hist.* I. 323 Great Encouragement will be given to an Overseer of a sober industrious Character, to manage a Rice and Lumber Plantation, about Thirty Miles from Charles-Town. **1802** DRAYTON *S. Carolina* 8 The rivers which course along these lands, are bordered with the most fertile soils; and, upon them some of the best rice plantations are situated. **1843** *Knickerb.* XXI. 223 On the rice plantations however it is not so. **1903** PRINGLE *Rice Planter* 36 Flats are one of the heavy expenses on a rice plantation—large, flat-bottomed boats.

+Rice-planter.

1. The owner of a rice plantation.

1775 *Amer. Husbandry* I. 66 It concerns only those who have dealings with London, these are the tobacco and rice planters. **1791** WASHINGTON *Diaries* IV. 169 Captn. Alston is . . . one of the neatest Rice planters in the State of So. Carolina. **1847** *Knickerb.* XXIX. 198 [The agriculturists] are the rice-planters of Georgia and South Carolina, and the sugar-planters of Louisiana. **1856** OLMSTED *Slave States* 409, I left town yesterday . . . with a letter in my pocket to Mr. X., a rice-planter.

2. (See quotation.)

1876 KNIGHT 1938/1 *Rice-planter,* . . . an implement for sowing rice.

Rice-planting. The planting of rice. Also attrib. — **1853** SIMMS *Sword & Distaff* (1854) 188 It's lucky I do know something of rice planting. **1872** *Harper's Mag.* June 99/1 The visions that filled her sleeping hours were of new patterns and improved forms, with glimpses of money and rice-planting in the distance. **1903** PRINGLE *Rice Planter* 1 You have asked me to tell of my rice-planting experience.

∗Rice pudding. A pudding in which rice, sugar, and milk are the principal ingredients. — **1775** *Essex Inst. Coll.* XLVIII. 52 For diner I got a ris puden & bef & turneps. **1832** CHILD *Frugal Housewife* 63 If you want a common rice pudding to retain its flavor, do not soak it. **1850** S. F. COOPER *Rural Hours* 299 The rice-pudding, the plum tart, the apple-pie they are now eating, will no more compare with the puddings . . . at their good mother's table. **1899** *Boston Transcript* 15 Dec. 7/6 Their dinner is always the same 'bully beef,' which is very bad, and rice pudding. **1912** [see DESSERT].

+Ricer. A small press in which cooked potatoes, fruits, etc., are forced through perforations of the diameter, approximately, of a grain of rice. — **1896** *Columbus Dispatch* 21 Nov. 11 Cook one quart of blanched chestnuts in boiling stock till tender, press them through a ricer [etc.].

Rice sieve. A utensil used in separating rice from particles of husk, chaff, etc. — **1732** *S.C. Gazette* 16 Dec., Lately imported: . . . rice Seives, indian Cornmills. **1733** *Ib.* 20 Jan., Womens cloggs, rice sieves, reap hooks. **1739** *Georgia Col. Rec.* III. 429 For the present, we crave your Excellency's Goodness to allow, for the Use of the whole Congregation, some Rice Sieves.

+Rice swamp. A low swampy area, covered usually or periodically with shallow water, on which rice is or can be grown. — **1775** *Amer. Husbandry* II. 7 Rice-swamps . . . are shallow, sometimes fields of mud, at others thinly covered with water. **1821** WEEMS *Letters* III. 316 My friends . . . *all* shake their heads at mention of my traversing the low fenny Country & Rice Swamps on my solitary way home. **1864** NICHOLS *Amer. Life* I. 201 Even the malarias of the African coast or the rice-swamp may be met with proper precautions. **1884** F. Y. HEDLEY *Marching through Ga.* (1890) 325 The only route was a narrow causeway built up through the rice swamp.

+Rice waffle. A waffle made chiefly of rice. — **1845** SIMMS *Wigwam & Cabin* 2 Ser. 99 We had enjoyed all the warm comforts of hot rice-waffles, journey-cake, and glowing biscuit. **1887** *Century Mag.* Nov. 16/2 Little darkies . . . [were] supporting plates of hot batter-cakes, muffins, Sally Lunns, rice waffles.

Rice weevil. 1. An insect (*Sitophilus*, syn. *Calandra, oryzae*) highly destructive to rice. {1815-} Cf. BLACK WEEVIL. **+2.** *S.* The water weevil (*Lissorhoptrus simplex*), which feeds, in the larval stage, upon the roots and, as an adult, upon the leaves, of the rice plant. — **(1) 1838** *Mass. Zool. Survey Rep.* 83 *Calandra oryzæ*, the rice weevil, is very injurious to this useful grain, consuming its nutritious parts, and materially lessening its weight. **1858** *Mich. Agric. Soc. Trans.* IX. 224 The rice weevil . . . is very destructive in the Southern States to the growing crops of rice; it also attacks stored grain. **1895** *Dept. Agric. Yrbk.* 1894 280 The rice weevil derives both its popular and Latin name from rice (oryza), in which it was first found by its discoverer. **(2) 1900** WEBSTER *Suppl.* 178/1 *Rice weevil*, . . . the water weevil.

Richardson. [Sir John *Richardson*, Sc. naturalist (1787–1865).] Used in the possessive in the names of various birds and animals. — **1835** AUDUBON *Ornith. Biog.* III. 503 Richardson's Jager, *Lestris Richardsonii*, . . . visits the shores of Massachusetts and Maine. **1844** *Nat. Hist. N.Y., Zoology* II. 315 Richardson's Hawk Gull. *Lestris Richardsonii.* . . . They are Northern birds, breeding in the interior near the arctic circle. **1868** *Amer. Naturalist* II. 529 Richardson's Squirrel (*Sciurus Richardsonii*). I saw no true Squirrel in the eastern Rocky Mountains. **1874** COUES *Birds N.W.* 400 *Tetrao Obscurus* var. *Richardsoni.* . . . Richardson's, or Black-tailed Grouse. . . . In this slight variety of the common Dusky Grouse the general colors are darker. **1880** *Cimarron News & Press* 23 Dec. 1/5 Of the falcons we have the lanier, peregrine, pigeon, Richardson's and rusty-crowned falcon or sparrow hawk.

+Richweed. Any one of various American plants, as: **a.** The bugbane, *Cimicifuga racemosa.* **b.** = CLEARWEED. **c.** The horse balm, *Collinsonia canadensis.* **d.** The white snakeroot, *Eupatorium urticaefolium.*

1762 CLAYTON *Flora Virginica* 79 *Actæa racemis longissimis.* . . . *Nostratibus* Rich-weed *& aliquibus* Black-Snake-root. **1788** CUTLER in *Life & Corr.* II. 285, I likewise wish particularly to know what you find the Mayapple, Rich-weed, and Buffalo-clover to be. **1804** CLARK in *Lewis & C. Exped.* I. (1904) 79 In those small Praries or Glades I saw wild Timothy, lambs-quarter, Cuckle burs, & rich weed. **1814** BIGELOW *Florula Bostoniensis* 220 *Urtica pumila.* Richweed. . . . A weed about houses, distinguished by its stem, which is fleshy and almost transparent. **1817–8** EATON *Botany* (1822) 244 *Collinsonia canadensis*, horse-balm, rich-weed. . . . Strong scented, not unpleasant. **1859** BARTLETT 452 Stone-Root, (*Collinsonia Canadensis*,) a plant used in medicine. . . . It is also called Rich Weed. **1894** *Amer. Folk-Lore* VII. 92 *Eupatorium ageratoides*, richweed. Banner Elk, N.C.

+Rickrack.¹ [Reduplication of *rack*, 'to stretch.'] A kind of trimming made of serpentine braid. Also attrib. — **1884** RITTENHOUSE *Maud* 326 Splendid sempstress—clothes nearly all done—Rickrack and featheredge on the moon. **1910** C. HARRIS *Eve's Husband* 279 Poor Adam had lived for years with a wife who wore rick-rack braid on her petticoats because it was durable.

+Rickrack.² An echoic formation suggested by the rhythmic noise of oars in the oarlocks. — **1888** DORSEY *Midshipman Bob* 193 He had never heard such sweet music in his life as the 'rick-rack, rick-rack' of the oars in the thole-pins.

+Rico. *S.W.* [Sp. *rico* 'rich,' 'noble.'] A man of wealth, prominence, or influence. — **1844** GREGG *Commerce* I. 18 [He died leaving] sufficient property to entitle him to the fame of *rico* among his neighbors. **1857** DAVIS *El Gringo* 174 All classes indulge in it [the pastime of cock-fighting] more or less, from the peon in his blanket to the *rico* in his broadcloth. **1865** *Wkly. New Mexican* 3 Feb. 2/2 These Indians were Navajoes, and of the *ricos*.

*Riddle. +A sieve used by gold-miners in screening pay dirt. *Obs.* — **1849** WIERZBICKI *California* 41 On the upper edges of the boards, rests a box of boards, called a sieve or riddle. **1852** CLAPPE *Lett. from Calif.* 214 The 'riddle' . . . is made of sheet-iron perforated with holes about the size of a large marble.

Ride, *n.* A journey made in, on, or aboard any means of conveyance. {1779-}

The American practice of using 'ride' without regard to the method of conveyance is discussed by Horwill. (Cf. BOAT RIDE.)

1836 GILMAN *Recoll.* (1838) 42 Papa wished me to take a ride (*anglicè* drive) with him. **1843** *Lowell Offering* III. 49 Now we are wont to see . . . our delicate married ladies endeavoring to obtain the same benefit in morning rides in covered *air-tight* carriages. **1866** GREGG *Life in Army* 88 [The gamblers] were both honored with a ride upon a rail. **1899** MUIRHEAD *Baedeker's U.S.* p. xxx, Ride, applied to any mode of conveyance (horse, carriage, boat, etc.). **1909** *Springfield W. Repub.* 2 Sept. 16 There have been many picnics, drives and launch rides.

+b. *Out of ride,* (see quotation). *Obs.* **1859** BARTLETT 365 A stream is said to be 'out of ride' when it is past fording.

*Ride, *v.* **+1.** *tr.* To convey or haul in a cart or other vehicle. *Obs.* {1837} **1687** in Munsell *Annals of Albany* II. 97 It is very requisite that there be fyre-wood rid to ye indian houses. **1692** *Ib.* 121 Ye sheriffe . . . is required to see each trader ride a load of wood to the said house. **1778** *Mass. H. S. Proc.* 2 Ser. II. 443 Recd. two Waggoners to Ride wood. **1848** BARTLETT 276, I heard a witness in a court-room testify that he had 'rode some

hogs from the wharf to the store,' by which he meant that he carried a load of dead hogs on his cart.

+2. In polo, to edge an opponent *off*. **1897** *Outing* XXX. 487/1 Play into your comrades' hands, and watch out to edge or ride-off an adversary.

*3. *intr.* To go or travel in a wheeled vehicle. In British use 'now chiefly of travelling in public vehicles' (*O.E.D.*). Cf. RIDE *n.* 1, note. **1750** *Md. Hist. Mag.* XVII. 376 Capt. Meshack Botfield of Talbot County, riding out in a Chaise with his Wife, was accidentally flung out and much wounded. **1827** *Ib.* 261, I determined on taking a drive in the carriage, and at 11 rode over Cannon's bridge. **1873** ALDRICH *Marjorie Daw* 36 Yesterday afternoon my father and myself rode over to Rivermouth with the Daws. **1886** *Narragansett Hist. Reg.* V. 331 A party of six . . . rode through the swamp onto the island.

*4. To travel or journey *in* a boat or canoe. This use occurs sporadically in English from 1400 on. **1838** *S. Lit. Messenger* IV. 26/2 On the canal, they say 'riding' in the boats, instead of 'sailing.' **1850** WATSON *Camp-Fires Revol.* 63 Colonel Arnold rode in a birch canoe. **1899** ADE *Doc' Horne* 133, I used to go up there to rest and ride around in the boats for a few days at a time. **1905** *N.Y. Ev. Post* 14 Oct., Thousands . . . ride upon the excursion steamers up the Sound in the summer time.

+5. *College slang.* (See quotation.) **1851** HALL *College Words* 162 Hobbies are used by some students in translating Latin, Greek, and other languages, who from this reason are said to ride, in contradistinction to others who learn their lessons by study, who are said to dig or grub.

+6. (See quotation.) **1893** ROOSEVELT *Wilderness Hunter* 216 If the tree is too tall it [*sc.* the moose] 'rides' it, that is, straddles the slender trunk with its fore legs, pushing it over and walking up it until the desired branches are within reach.

7. In miscellaneous expressions. (See also LINE *n.* 13, RAIL *n.*¹ 3 c, d, and RANGE *n.* 1 f.)

To ride express, to ride as an express or messenger; *to ride* (something) *to the devil,* to be the ruin of (something); *to ride the fence,* to ride regularly along the fence around a cattle ranch to inspect and keep it in order; *to ride on trail,* (see quotation); *to ride a state,* to canvass or cover a state in the interest of a political candidate or campaign; *to ride the waves, to ride a log,* (see quotations); *to ride one's luck,* to depend upon one's luck; *to ride mail,* to carry the mail.

1775 *Jrnls. Cont. Congress* III. 265 John Powell's [account], for riding express, a ballance due to him amounting to forty-five dollars. **1865** *Wkly. New Mexican* 1 Sept. 2/3 Those are the men who have been riding the Territory to the devil for many years. **1881** CHASE *Editor's Run in N. Mex.* 49 Mr. Chase . . . has general supervision, with a boss on each ranch, to attend to all details, such as hiring the necessary help to 'ride the fences.' **1882** BAILLIE-GROHMAN *Camps in Rockies* 347 The process of driving cattle is called 'riding on trail,' one of the most laborious and dreary undertakings imaginable. **1882** *Narragansett Hist. Reg.* I. 292 He was a strong 'Governor Fenner man', and rode the State in his behalf. **1897** *Outing* XXX. 134/2 We had that most delightful experience which some ingenious wheelman has called 'riding the waves.' The fine dirt road . . . led over a succession of short hills, the down slopes of which were steep enough to carry one up the next ascent. **1905** *Forestry Bureau Bul.* No. 61, 44 *Ride a log, to,* to stand on a floating log. **1907** LONDON *Road* 218 He was riding his luck, and with each pass the total stake doubled. **1910** RAINE *B. O'Connor* 14 He was riding mail between Aravaipa and Mesa.

* Rider, *n.* **+1.** One who carries news, dispatches, letters, etc., over a given route. *Obs.* **1738** *Va. Gazette* 28 April, Riders are engag'd so conveniently, that no Post-Horse is to cross Potowmak or Susquehanna. **1756** *Md. Gazette* 12 Feb., A scheme is on Foot . . . for maintaining Riders from one Court-House to another. **1762** *Ib.* 4 Nov., The Calvert and Elk-Ridge Riders go every week in the year. **1776** in *S. Lit. Messenger* XXVII. 326/2 The distance I was from the Rider . . . have hitherto kept me from [writing]. **1788** FRANKLIN *Autobiog.* 352, I was satisfy'd without retaliating his refusal, while postmaster, to permit my papers being carried by riders.

+2. (See quotation.) *Obs.* **1767** *Doc. Col. Hist. N.Y.* VII. 937 Reservations were made of particular Lots under the names of some members of the Council and public officers. . . . These shares have been distinguished among the Inhabitants of that part of the Country by the name of Riders.

+3. In a rail fence, the top rail, placed in a crotch of crossed stakes or rails at the end of each panel. **1789** ANBUREY *Travels* II. 323 Above these stakes is placed a rail of double the size of the others, which is termed the rider, which, in a manner, locks up the whole, and keeps the fence firm and steady. **1800** TATHAM *Tobacco* 11 Into this cross one or more courses of heavy rails are laid (termed *riders*), which serve to lock and keep the whole partition secure. **1852** *Mich. Agric. Soc. Trans.* III. 185 My fences are . . . seven rails high, with stakes and riders. **1885** *Harper's Mag.* April 702/2 The 'riders' of his fences were always heavy and straight. **1903** Fox *Little Shepherd* xxx, The worm fences had lost their riders and were broken down here and there.

+4. = CIRCUIT RIDER.

1884 'CRADDOCK' *Tenn. Mts.* 15 The rider says thar's some help in prayer. *Ib.* 143 All them Peels . . . war gone down ter the Settlemint ter hear the rider preach.

+5. One experienced in the work done on horseback on a cattle ranch.

1888 *Century Mag.* Feb. 502/2, I had with my wagon a Pueblo Indian, an excellent rider and roper, but a drunken, worthless, lazy devil. **1894** *McClure's Mag.* July 101/1 The cowboys or 'riders' of each ranch cut out the cows of its brand.

+Rider, *v. tr.* To strengthen (a rail fence) with riders. Also *ppl. a.* — **1760** WASHINGTON *Diaries* I. 155 Good part of my New Fencing that was not Ridered was leveld. **1787** *Ib.* III. 208 Women [were] staking and ridering fence of the said field. **1858** WARDER *Hedges & Evergreens* 151 In Delaware . . . worm-fences, not ridered, were to be five feet high. **1891** *Harper's Mag.* March 544/2 Scarlet trumpet blossom . . . [was] flaring over the staked and ridered rail-fence. **1901** CABLE *Cavalier* xxv, We paused at a worm-fence. . . . It was staked and ridered.

∗ Ridge.

∗1. A long narrow stretch of elevated ground.

1624 in *Amer. Speech* XV. 383/1 Twelve acres of ground lying and being a narrow ridge of Land towards Goose hill betweene twoo Marshes. **1657** *Suffolk Deeds* III. 9 The other [creek] runns. towards the Narrow Ridge above sajd. **1703** *Providence Rec.* V. 61 An old fence . . . standeth on the midle of a Ridge of upland. **1784** FILSON *Kentucke* 20 We find . . . many knobs, ridges, and broken poor land. *a*1817 DWIGHT *Travels* II. 52 On the North-Eastern [side], shooting out from it as a spur, [is] a small ridge, called Newington Mountain. **1893** *Harper's Mag.* April 796/2 The land traversed by this gentleman is partly made up . . . of high rolling ridges, from which one can see the country for many miles around. **1914** STEELE *Storm* 9 The girl [was] scarcely discernible except when a ridge brought her against the sky.

attrib. **1868** *Iowa State Agric. Soc. Rep. 1867* 140 The ridge-land is the surest for wheat. **1903** Fox *Little Shepherd* ii, So he started out, brisk and shivering, along the ridge path with Jack bouncing before him.

b. In place names.

1700 *Md. Hist. Mag.* XX. 275 Gassaway Ridge. *Ib.* 288 Seneca Ridge. **1741** *N.H. Probate Rec.* III. 51 Catherine his sd. wife shall have as her full Part . . . that thirty Acres of Land Situate at a Place called Gravelly Ridge.

2. A range of hills or mountains. {1604–}

1720 *Va. House of Burgesses* 298 To the Westward of Virginia . . . there runs a Ridge or continued Chain of Exceeding high Mountains. **1781–2** JEFFERSON *Notes Va.* (1788) 16 Our mountains . . . are disposed in ridges one behind another, running nearly parallel with the sea-coast. **1835** MARTIN *Gaz. Virginia* 435 There are two ranges of highland, running nearly parallel with . . . the Clinch mountains,—one between Mocasin creek and Copper creek, denominated Mocasin ridge.

+Ridgeback. = RAZORBACK HOG. — **1872** *Harper's Mag.* April 663/2 She told me it was a 'ridge-back'—a 'jumping alligator,' a 'sub-soiler.'

Ridge board. {1833–} *transf.* +The highest part of a divide or watershed. — **1869** W. MURRAY *Adventures* 10 [The] ridge-board of the vast water-shed . . . slopes northward to the St. Lawrence.

Ridgepole. {1788–} ‖The crest of a mountain range. — **1788** MAY *Jrnl. & Lett.* 29 [We] began to ascend Alleghana. . . . At ten o'clock we were on the ridge-pole.

+Ridgepole pine. The lodgepole pine (q.v.), *Pinus murrayana.* — **1885** ROOSEVELT in *Century Mag.* June 225/2 The forest was composed mainly of what are called ridge-pole pines, which grow close together, and do not branch off until the stems are thirty or forty feet from the ground.

+Ridge prairie. (See quotation.) *Obs.* — **1882** *Econ. Geol. Illinois* II. 73 The prairies are therefore of two classes—those that are a little elevated and rather level near the lower course of the streams, and more elevated and rolling prairies on the higher ridges. The latter are the so-called 'ridge prairies.'

+Ridge road. A road along the crest of a ridge. { = Eng. ridgeway} — **1817** *N. Amer. Rev.* IV. 185, I have returned by the ridge road. **1839** *Knickerb.* XIII. 247 The ridge road . . . had placed us far in advance of the hound. **1871** *Harper's Mag.* Dec. 46/2 These 'ridge-roads' . . . form a system of ready-made highways. **1886** LOGAN *Great Conspiracy* 305 And what can that purpose be, but to throw his augmented right . . . along the ridge-road, upon Centreville?

∗Riding.¹ +An administrative division or district on Long Island. *Obs.* — **1665** *Smithtown Rec.* 6 There is a certain parcel or tract of land situate lying and being in the East Riding of York shire upon Long Island. **1675** in Easton *Indian War* 79 The Indyans of the north and west Ridings of Long Island shall . . . have their Guns restored to them. **1677** *Hempstead Rec.* I. 354 Plaintive is nonsuted because henery bomans home an being is not in this Riding.

∗Riding.²

I. +**1.** *Riding twice*, (see quotation). *Obs.*

1843 'CARLTON' *New Purchase* I. 137 Many horses indeed have two riders, a mode of horsemanship called in the Purchase 'riding twice.'

II. *attrib.* ∗**2.** Designating garments suitable for wear while riding.

1671 W. ADAMS in *Mass. H. S. Coll.* 4 Ser. I. 15, I received of Mr. Danforth 6 yards ½ Searge for a wescoat and riding breeches. **1685** *Conn. Rec.* I. 377, I give her . . . my saf gard and riding hood. **1711** *Springfield Rec.* II. 41, 14 silke rideing Girdles, 7 s. **1790** *Penna. Packet* 23 Sept. 4/4 Riding stays, turned stays, jumps, &c. **1826** COOPER *Last of Mohicans* xviii, He was seen tearing from a bush, and waving in triumph, a fragment of the green riding veil of Cora. **1894** FORD *P. Stirling* 202 His irreproachable riding-rig had been noticed. **1903** BRADY *Bishop* 33 Weighted with heavy boots, [and] canvas riding-trousers, . . . he yet ran as he had never run on Franklin Field. **1910** J. HART *Vigilante Girl* 194 Your maid Luisa . . . has your riding togs all laid out on the bed. **1916** WILSON *Somewhere* 176, I'm telling her to . . . get into these here riding pants of mine.

∗3. Designating an animal or a vehicle for riding on or in.

1756 *Lett. to Washington* I. 200 Your Riding mare [h]as had a Pretty Large Swelling under her Belly. **1759** ROWE *Letters* 337, I will speak to Mr. Trumbel this day for . . . the Riding Chaise.

+4. Designating agricultural machines upon which the operators ride.

1868 *Iowa State Agric. Soc. Rep. 1867* 151 Not many riding corn-planters are in use. *Ib.* 156 The corn . . . is cultivated according to the fancy of the farmers; some with shovel & some with barshear plows & others use the riding cultivator. **1924** CROY *R.F.D. No. 3* 24 The farmers tried to make up for it with increased machinery—riding plows, tractors, headers, trucks.

5. In miscellaneous combinations.

Riding bridle, a bridle suitable for use on a riding horse; *r. club*, a club the members of which are interested in and practice horseback riding as a recreation; *r. hall*, a hall or building where instruction is given in horseback riding; *r. outfit*, a saddle, cf. OUTFIT *n.* 4 note; *r. pistol*, a horseman's pistol; *r. road*, a road sufficient for travelers on horseback; *r. rock*, (see quotation); *r. stock*, horses suitable for riding; *r. way*, a ford.

1881 *Rep. Indian Affairs* p. xxxv, The Carlisle school has shipped to forty-two Indian agencies . . . 161 riding bridles, 10 halters [etc.]. **1916** WILSON *Somewhere* 197, I hear she has joined the riding club. **1884** ROE *Nature's Story* 60 There goes a squad to the riding hall. **1914** 'BOWER' *Flying U Ranch* 12 He bent over his sacked riding outfit, and undid it. **1769** *Md. Hist. Mag.* XII. 280 Macubbin has 2 or 3 Pair of riding Pistols under a foot long to sell. **1738** *Ib.* XV. 220 Your petitioner hath cleared a sufficient rideing road from George Oggs to Capt. John Risteaus. **1859** BARTLETT 365 *Riding rock*, a conspicuous rock at a ford, used to show the depth of the water and the safety of crossings. **1898** CANFIELD *Maid of Frontier* 113 Bring up only the riding stock; we will take no pack to-night. **1780** in Caulkins *Hist. Norwich, Conn.* (1866) 349 The upper riding-way in Doctor Perkins's intervale.

+Riding carriage. A vehicle in which persons ride. *Obs.* — **1792** BELKNAP *Hist. New-Hampshire* III. 117 White ash . . . serves for the frames of . . . riding carriages. **1796** *Ann. 4th Congress* 2 Sess. 2685 On every four-wheel riding carriage, except phaetons, and stage wagons, [is a tax of] six shillings per wheel.

Riding chair. = CHAIR 2. *Obs.* {1785–} — **1745** [see KITTEREEN]. **1779** *N.J. Archives* 2 Ser. III. 83 Any person . . . that has a riding chair to dispose of, may hear of a purchaser by applying to . . . this paper. **1788** in *Rep. Comm. Patents 1849* I. 543 A gentleman and his wife passed by us in a riding chair. **1808** *Ann. 10th Congress* 1 Sess. 2824 The said company shall be entitled to demand and receive . . . [tolls] for each chaise, sulky, or riding chair.

∗Riding coat. A coat worn, usually as a protection against rain, by one riding on horseback. — **1650** *Mayflower Descendant* X. 173 One cloake one Ryding coate and hood, [£] 1. **1707** SEWALL *Diary* 11. 187 [There] was so much Rain as to oblige me to put on my Riding Coat. **1775** FITHIAN *Journal* II. 111, I had cautiously put on my riding coat, to disguise the *clerical cloth.* **1905** N. DAVIS *Northerner* 153 Fatigue forgotten, she flung off her riding-coat . . . and went lightly about the preparations for supper.

Riding dress. A dress or habit worn by women when riding horseback. {1736–} — **1722** *Md. Hist. Mag.* XX. 65 Mrs. Mary Overard Dr. . . . To a Rideing Dress & Hatt. **1790** *Penna. Packet* 2 Jan. 4/2 A General and compleat Assortment of . . . Trimmings for Ladies Riding Dresses. **1833** J. HALL *Harpe's Head* 25 The light figure of Virginia was rendered more graceful by an elegant riding-dress. **1878** *Decorum* 275 The riding-dress should be made to fit the waist closely.

Riding habit. = prec. {1666–} — **1774** *Penna. Packet* 19 Sept. 1/3 Riding habits . . . done in the newest and most fashionable manner. **1823** COOPER *Pioneers* v, She stood dressed in a rich blue riding-habit. **1870** O. LOGAN *Before Footlights* 225 Your horse's legs go far down into ruts, bespattering your swellish riding-habit with a filthy, tenacious mire. **1905** VALENTINE *H. Sandwith* 103 She had never seemed more beautiful than to-day as she waited for him, dressed in her well-fitted riding-habit of Saxon cloth.

Riding horse. A horse suitable for riding. {1749–} — **1641** *Boston Rec.* 61 All dry cattle shall be driven of the necke, and not be suffered to abide there, except Riding horses. **1745** *N.H. Probate Rec.* III. 311, I give and Bequeath unto my Son John Nutter aforesaid my Riding horse. **1802** ELLICOTT *Journal* 221 Capt. Minor's riding horse, . . . [was] stolen from within two hundred yards of the camp. **1892** M. A. JACKSON *Gen. Jackson* 172 For a long time he was the riding-horse of the minister.

+Riding page. A page who rides in the discharge of his duties. — **1880** LAMPHERE *U.S. Govt.* 24/1 [There are employed] for the Senate Chamber; 3 riding pages, and 1 page for the office of the Secretary.

Riding place. {1665-} +A fording place on a stream. — **1679** *Conn. Rec.* 27 We went to the river . . . to the old rideing place. **1730** HEMPSTEAD *Diary* 219 Wee made a fence of Brush & poles & Thorn Trees to Stop the Riding place next Packer farm.

+**Riding postmaster.** A postmaster who carries mail on a horse. (Cf. POSTMASTER 1, note.) *Obs.* — **1737** *Penna. Gazette* 27 Oct., Henry Pratt is appointed Riding Postmaster for all the stages between Philadelphia and Newport in Virginia.

Riding saddle. A saddle used by one who rides horseback, as distinguished from a packsaddle or harness saddle. — **1846** SAGE *Scenes Rocky Mts.* xxxiii, Carefully hung in some fitting place, are seen his 'riding' and 'pack saddles.' *c*1857 *Kit Carson's Own Story* (1926) 87, I lost . . . one raft which had on it six rifles and a number (of) riding and pack saddles. **1910** J. HART *Vigilante Girl* 77 The head reposed on his riding saddle between the high pommel and cantle.

Riding school. A school in which horseback or other riding is taught. {1680-} — **1775** *Mass. H. S. Coll.* 4 Ser. I. 268 Our Meetinghouse . . . was destined for a Riding School for the Dragoons. **1810** BENTLEY *Diary* III. 507 We have a Circus which not only gives a riding School but a place for all the feats of rope dancers. **1882** *Wheelman* I. 70 Rinks and riding-schools sprang up in every city, town, and large village in the country. **1894** WARNER *Golden House* ii, I have to go up to the riding-school to see a horse.

Riffle. {1637-}
+**1.** A shoal, reef, or rocky obstruction in a river or a piece of shallow, rapid, or broken water caused by this.

1792 in *Amer. Speech* XV. 383 Thence . . . to a hickory by a Riffle in the river. **1796** F. BAILY *Tour* 149 These places . . . are called by the inhabitants 'Riffles;' I suppose a corruption from the word 'ruffle.' **1804** CLARK in *Lewis & C. Exped.* I. (1904) 205 [We] passed a very bad riffle of rocks in the evening. **1883** *Century Mag.* July 378/2 A line of loose rocks . . . cropped up nearly to the surface, producing a rapid, or riffle. **1919** ROOSEVELT in *Maine My State* 19, I had lost one of my heavy shoes in crossing a river at a riffle.

+**b.** *To make the* (or *a*) *riffle*, to cross a riffle or rapid; to overcome a difficulty, to succeed in an undertaking. *colloq.*

1859 A. S. DUNIWAY *Capt. Gray's Co.* 235 (Th.), I guess they'll make the riffle. **1875** *Atlantic Mo.* May 557 If I can make a riffle I want to git to Washington Territory once. **1887** M. ROBERTS *Western Avernus* 202 Fighting the stream at intervals, but 'making the riffle,' or crossing the rapid. **1899** HARTE *Jack Hamlin's Mediation* 24 'You'll make the riffle yet,' he said quietly. **1911** SAUNDERS *Col. Todhunter* 19, I'll try if I can make the riffle.

2. *Mining.* A bar, slat, or other obstruction placed across the bottom of a sluice box or other gold-washing apparatus to arrest particles of gold. {1865-}

1850 KINGSLEY *Diary* 120 Finished the riffles to the machine today. **1874** RAYMOND *6th Rep. Mines* 17 The *debris* . . . is brought, by means of undercurrents, riffles, and other appliances, in contact with the quicksilver. **1882** *47th Congress 1 Sess.* H. R. Ex. Doc. No. 216, 194 Cinnabar . . . is found in such quantities as to prove troublesome in washing for gold, filling the riffles where gold should lodge. **1910** J. HART *Vigilante Girl* 51 Sometimes the riffles would be clogged with coarse gold.

b. Attrib. with *bar, bed, block,* etc.
1876 RAYMOND *8th Rep. Mines* 349 About one-half of the ore going through the mill is saved by means of riffle-sluices. **1882** *47th Congress 1 Sess.* H. R. Ex. Doc. No. 216, 570 The dry earth, sand, or gravel . . . falls on the adjustable riffle-board . . . , the finer particles of dirt and dust being thrown away by the current behind before falling on the riffle-bed. **1883** KNIGHT *Suppl.* 824/2 *Sluices*, . . . boxes joined together, set with riffle blocks, through which is washed auriferous earth. **1889** MUNROE *Golden Days* 186 They were obliged to 'clean up' or remove what was lodged against the riffle-bars at least four times a day.

+**3.** (See quotation.)
1890 *Cent.* 5174/2 *Riffle*, . . . a piece of plank placed transversely in, and fastened to the bottom of, a fish-ladder.

+**Riffle box.** *Mining.* A cradle or boxlike contrivance having riffles or obstructions along the bottom for catching particles of gold. — **1850** A. T. JACKSON *Forty-Niner* (1920) 38 We caught an Indian cleaning up our riffle box Saturday night. **1871** RAYMOND *3d Rep. Mines* 70 The gold-saving method is the simplest—amalgamation in battery, copper-plate, riffle-boxes, and a tail sluice. **1889** MUNROE *Golden Days* 110 [A Long Tom] is simply a long trough ending in a 'riffle box.' *c*1900 R. L. HALE *Log of Forty-Niner* 99 In the basin bottom were all kinds of gear, from rifle boxes to tins for washing and cleansing gold.

||**Riffler.** =prec. *Obs.* In full *riffler box.* — **1850** KINGSLEY *Diary* 122 Made a panning trough to pour quicksilver from the riffler into and fix the pump. *Ib.* 137 It requires great care in making both these and the riffler boxes in order to have them hold quicksilver.

+**Riffling,** *a.* Forming a riffle or rapid. *Obs.* — **1754** *New Eng. Hist. & Gen. Reg.* XXII. 408 The navigation to Norridgewalk is considerably difficult by reason of the rapidity of the stream, and riffling falls.

Rifle.¹ {*a*1751-}
1. A firearm the barrel of which is grooved to insure greater accuracy and penetration for the bullet. {1810-}

1774 in Peyton *Adv. Grandfather* (1867) 132, [I provided] myself, Charles and Annetta with good rifles in exchange for our Spanish muskets. **1809** WEEMS *Marion* (1833) 75 O! that we had been there to aid with our rifles, then should many of those monsters have bit the ground. **1841** [see FISHING POLE]. **1882** BAILLIE-GROHMAN *Camps in Rockies* 5 The frontiersman when on horseback usually carries his rifle in front of him across the Mexican saddle. **1916** WILSON *Somewhere* 332 Old Pete, still not moving the rifle a hair's breadth, he calls out [etc.].

b. One who shoots with a rifle.
1846 *Spirit of Times* 6 June 174/3 The 'old man' was the best 'rifle' at a turkey 'shoot.' **1854** SIMMS *Southward Ho!* 468 Sir Henry Clinton marshalled his array . . . in order to make their valiant demonstration upon the little army of rifles, under Thompson, on the ever-famous 28th of June, 1776.

c. A rifled pistol.
*c*1852 in Stowe *Key* 175/1 A man told me . . . he would shoot me, and pulled a 'rifle' out of his pocket and showed it to me.

+**2.** A cannon the barrel of which is rifled.
1885 *Century Mag.* March 740 Her battery . . . consisted of two seven-inch rifles. **1898** *Scientific Amer. Suppl.* XLV. 16/1 A battery of six 6-inch rifles, two being carried in sponsons on the gun deck on each broadside.

3. Attrib. and comb. in sense 1. **a.** With *box, manufactory, powder.*

1837 *Niles' Nat. Reg.* 14 Jan. 320/2 *Rifle manufactory.* There is a manufactory of Cochran's many chambered rifle, for a company in New York. **1843** *Diplom. Corr. Texas* III. (1911) 1455, I issued special Order No. 5 . . . requiring Quarter Master General Wm. G. Cooke to procure for the use of the South western army, five kegs Rifle Pow[d]er. **1872** Rifle box [see BEECHER'S BIBLE].

b. In special combinations.

Rifle charge, an amount sufficient to charge a rifle; *r. coat, r. dress,* = RIFLE SHIRT; *r. frolic,* =RIFLE MATCH; *r. pan,* that part of a flintlock which holds the priming; *r.-picker,* a tool for keeping open the touchhole or tube of a gun; *r. pouch,* a bag for powder, shot, etc.; *r.-rammer,* a ramrod for a rifle; *r. team,* a team or group of marksmen; *r. trench,* =RIFLE PIT; *r. uniform,* a military uniform for a rifleman.

1850 LEWIS *La. Swamp Doctor* 171 Their big hearts had crumbled down to a rifle-charge of dust. **1877** *Rep. Indian Affairs* 5 The coat [ought] to be in shape like the old fringed rifle-coat or blouse. **1853** B. F. TAYLOR *Jan. & June* 207 You never wore a 'rifle-dress.' **1775** in A. Tomlinson *Military Jrnls.* 77 We had a rifle frolick. **1827** COOPER *Prairie* xxiii, It is not every savage that carries . . . as good a rifle-pan as this old friend of mine. **1846** McKENNEY *Memoirs* I. 74 He then pushed his rifle-picker through the hole. **1835** LONGSTREET *Ga. Scenes* 158 Ramrods, 10; rifle pouches, 3; bayonets, none. **1873** ROE *Army Lett.* 97 The sergeant carefully punches the sacks from one end to the other with a long steel very much like a rifle rammer. **1883** *American* VI. 245 Our American rifle-team has had its beating. **1885** *Century Mag.* June 300/2 The crest of the hill . . . was strengthened by rifle-trenches. **1813** *Niles' Reg.* III. 295/1 Trimmings for rifle uniforms, 59,350 yards.

∗**Rifle.²** A whetstone or a piece of wood covered with emery or some similar substance. 'Now *dial.* and *U.S.*' (*O.E.D.*). — **1842** KIRKLAND *Western Clearings* 58 But I have never learned to this day why a whet stone should be called a 'rifle.' **1871** DE VERE 532 *Rifle,* retains in some parts of the Union the meaning it has in Old English, viz., a whetstone for sharpening scythes, consisting either of the stone itself or of a strip of wood covered with emery. Its use is almost limited to the New England States and a few of the eastern counties of Virginia. **1884** ROE *Nature's Story* 246 All through the afternoon the musical sound of whetting the scythes with the rifle rang out from time to time. **1911** *Essex Inst. Coll.* XLVII. 13 'Whetting,' . . . is done by means of a sanded stick called a 'rifle.'

Rifle club. {1852-} *Hist.* +In the South after the Civil War, an organization ostensibly for rifle practice but really for the overthrow of the carpetbag regime. *Obs.* — **1878** in Fleming *Hist. Reconstruction* II. 410 White rifle clubs are ordered by the governor and President to disband and disperse. **1879** [see BULLDOZER 1].

Rifle company. A military company made up of riflemen. {1844-} — **1775** *Jrnls. Cont. Congress* III. 260 A captain of one of the rifle companies from Maryland. **1776** *Ib.* IV. 118 There is due, To Azariah Dunham on several certificates for provisions to several rifle companies, the sum of £7 15 0. **1847** HOWE *Hist. Coll. Ohio* 305 Vance's [blockhouse], built by ex-Gov. Vance, then captain of a rifle company, stood on a high bluff on the margin of a prairie.

Rifle corps. A military corps made up of riflemen. {1830-} — **1792** WAYNE in Putnam *Memoirs* 332 Within twenty days at farthest . . . will be as early as you could possibly obtain Volunteer Rifle Corps. **1811** *Ann. 12th Congress* 1 Sess. II. 2114 [The cavalry] were made to exchange positions with one of the mounted rifle corps. **1823** THACHER *Military Jrnl.* 121 The gallant Colonel Morgan, at the head of his famous rifle corps, . . . commenced the action. **1866** BANCROFT *Hist. U.S.* IX. 355 For a half-hour the rifle corps fought within the distance of forty yards.

+**Rifle frock.** A long, loose-fitting shirt or blouse worn by a rifleman. *Obs.* Also *transf.* — **1776** *Battle of Brooklyn* II. iii, Rifle guns and rifle frocks, will be as cheap in their camp tomorrow, as cods heads in New Foundland. **1782** TRUMBULL *M'Fingal* (1785) IV. 87 Rifle-frocks sent Generals cap'ring. **1811** *Niles' Reg.* I. 45/2 In this valuable class of cotton goods are included . . . rifle-frocks. **1823** COOPER *Pioneers* xxxiii, Having thrown a rifle frock over his shirt, . . . [a man] had issued from his retreat in the woods.

Rifle gun. A rifle. {1776-} — **1747** in Chalkley *Scotch-Irish Settlement Va.* I. 529 They were robbed of . . . a rifle gun (double tricked). **1775** *Warren-Adams Lett.* I. 58 They do Execution with their Rifle Gun at an Amazing Distance. **1811** SUTCLIFF *Travels* (1815) 119 Considerable business was done in locks, latches, and rifle guns. **1843** *Amer. Pioneer* II. 251 The man who carried the rifle gun and ammunition was so careless as to lose the bullet-pouch. **1903** Fox *Little Shepherd* i, Uncle Jim said once he aimed to give this rifle gun to me.

Rifleman. A soldier armed with a rifle rather than with a musket. {1792-}

1755 *Remembrancer* I. 132/1 The Congress have ordered one thousand more marksmen, or, as we call them, riflemen, to be raised. **1790** DENNY *Journal* 143 Half pound powder and one pound lead served out to each rifleman. **1812** *Niles' Reg.* II. 383/1, I left one company of riflemen, to conceal themselves near the bridge. **1866** 'F. KIRKLAND' *Bk. Anecdotes* 110/1 A third [sword was presented to Jackson] by the riflemen of New Orleans. **1919** HOUGH *Sagebrusher* 286 He received the fire of the entire squad of riflemen.

+**Rifle match.** A match or contest in rifle-shooting. — c**1845** [see COCKFIGHT *n.*]. **1880** 'MARK TWAIN' *Tramp Abroad* 626 [German newspapers] contain . . . no information about . . . yachting-contests, rifle-matches, or other sporting matters of any sort.

+**Rifle pistol.** A pistol having a rifled barrel. *Obs.* — **1849** PARKMAN *Oregon Trail* 428 The small bullet of the rifle pistol striking too far back, did not immediately take effect. **1883** 'MARK TWAIN' *Life on Miss.* xxix, I rose and drew an elegant rifle pistol on him.

Rifle pit. An excavation for the protection of riflemen firing upon an enemy. {1855-} — **1862** KETTELL *Hist. Rebellion* I. 310 On the northern slope of the bluff were two light batteries, and a rifle-pit one mile in length. **1867** Goss *Soldier's Story* 56 A line of rifle-pits connected Fort Williams, and Coneby and Compher redoubts, with Battery Worth. **1884** 'CRADDOCK' *Where Battle Was Fought* 127 The mists were crouching in the rifle-pits of the long picket-line. **1898** *McClure's Mag.* March 434/2 [The] spirit of the troops bore them . . . over the bristling rifle-pits on the crest.

+**Rifler.** =RIFLEMAN. *Obs.* — **1775** *Amer. Hist. Review* VI. 318 Dr. Appleton abroad p.m. saw 120 Riflers f'm Maryland on their March to the Camp. **1776** in Sparks *Corr. Revol.* I. 169 The two armed vessels . . . were attacked by parties of riflers ordered for that purpose. **1807** BARLOW *Columbiad* 195 Morgan in front of his bold riflers towers.

Rifle sand. Sand for use on a rifle for sharpening scythes. — **1882** *Narragansett Hist. Reg.* I. 312 The day for getting rifle sand (better known as 'Beach Pond Day') was the last Saturday of June. **1911** *Essex Inst. Coll.* XLVII. 13 Nearly all the grocery stores sold rifle sand.

+**Rifle shirt.** =HUNTING SHIRT. *Obs.* — **1778** *Essex Inst. Coll.* XLIII. 9 Brown or some other kind of your own fabrick in Stead [is ordered] to make Rifle Shirts or Frocks principally. **1784** SMYTH *Tour* I. 182 Their hunting, or rifle shirts, they have also died in variety of colours. **1793** *Gazette of U.S.* 24 Aug. (Th.), '1520 Rifle Shirts' were advertised for, *inter alia*, by the Treasury Department.

+**Rifle shoot.** =RIFLE MATCH. *Obs.* — **1888** *Boston Jrnl.* 22 Dec. 1/8 On Christmas morning there will be a rifle-shoot at Cider Mill Pond Range. **1892** *Boston Chron.* 26 Nov. 1/5 Rifle Shoot. Thanksgiving Practice by Company B, First Regiment.

+**Rifle whisky.** Cheap or inferior whisky. *Obs.* — **1856** *Harper's Mag.* Dec. 66/2 Already heavily laden with 'rifle whisky.' **1862** MOORE *Rebellion Rec.* V. II. 157 They consume almost unheard-of quantities of Bourbon and rifle-whisky. **1863** [see BUSTHEAD].

‖**Riflist.** =RIFLEMAN. — **1883** SWEET & KNOX *Through Texas* 580, I am going to have the figure on the monument represent an Alamo riflist in full uniform.

+**Rift.** [For *riff*, obs. var. of *reef*. Cf. *clift* for *cliff*.]

1. A barrier or obstruction in a stream or a fall or rapid caused by this.

1727 *Doc. Hist. N.Y. State* I. 459 The French . . . have no way but to come up from Montreal to the Lake against a Violent stream, all full of Rifts & Falls & Shallows. **1778** HUTCHINS *Va., Penna., Md., & N.C.* 21 The Muskingum is muddy, and not very swift, but no where obstructed with Falls or Rifts. **1784** WASHINGTON *Diaries* II. 313 The obstruction . . . [is] only a single rift of rocks across in one place. **1845** COOPER *Chainbearer* xxi, The most that can be done with it [the lumber] . . . will be to float it down to the next rift. **1879** *Scribner's Mo.* Nov. 21/1 In one hanging rift close by the bank . . . I took at five casts fifteen fish.

2. The wash of the surf on a beach or shore.

1866 STEDMAN *Poetical Works* (1873) 238 Light falls her foot where the rift follows after.

+**Rift timber.** (See quotation.) — **1875** TEMPLE & SHELDON *Hist. Northfield, Mass.* 14 Oak, or rift timber, as it was called, i.e., timber that could be easily split into clap-boards and shingles, was the only kind thought to be fit for use for buildings and fences.

Rig. {1822-}

+**1.** A plant, outfit, equipment, etc., for a particular purpose, esp. the engine, derrick, etc., for sinking and operating an oil well.

1845 *Niles' Reg.* 25 Oct. 128/3 The new rig works to a charm. **1860** GEO. T. CLARK *Diary* (MS.) 14 Saw Cole's rig which we bought after tea. **1868** *Iowa State Agric. Soc. Rep. 1867* 174, I consider the Victor mill & Cook's evaporator the best rig for making sirup profitably from cane, that I have examined. **1872** in Tarbell *Hist. Standard Oil Co.* I. 114 This forfeiture is not to apply to any wells where the erection of rigs is completed or under way. **1883** *Century Mag.* July 329/2 [The boiler] usually stands at some distance from the derrick, so that it will not be injured in case the rest of the 'rig' is destroyed by fire. **1885** *Santa Fé Wkly. New Mexican* 24 Sept. 2/4 He purchased for $1,800 the Dorifee ten-horse power artesian rig.

+**2.** *W.* The complete riding equipage of a cowboy.

1849 KINGSLEY *Diary* 41, I also saw a Spanish rig for horse riding which in part I think superior to ours. **1887** *Scribner's Mag.* II. 509/1 The common [cowboy] terms are . . . *rig, single-rig, double-rig.* **1904** STEEDMAN *Bucking Sagebrush* 54 They were saddled with the big California rigs. **1914** 'BOWER' *Flying U Ranch* 14, I've noticed that a hoss never has any respect or admiration for a swell rig.

+**3.** A horse-drawn vehicle, as a buggy, esp. one complete with its furnishings and the horse or horses that draw it.

1872 'MARK TWAIN' *Roughing It* 325, I mean to have the nobbiest rig that's going. **1883** RITTENHOUSE *Maud* 189 Mr Bates got a dashing rig with double team and we proceeded toward the Bay-road. **1903** A. ADAMS *Log of Cowboy* 207 There were two other occupants of the rig besides the driver. **1917** FREEMAN & KINGSLEY *Alabaster Box* 53 The wagon-shed behind the Brookville House sheltered an unusual number of 'rigs.'

+**b.** (See quotation.)

1893 CUSHING *Story of P.O.* 358 The only vehicle he could procure was an ox team with a certain indescribable paraphernalia, called a 'rig,' attached to a so-called wagon.

+**Rigdonite.** (See quotations.) *Obs.* — **1847** HOWE *Hist. Coll. Ohio* 284 The Mormons . . . [are] now divided into three factions, viz.: the Rigdonites, the Twelveites, and the Strangites. The Rigdonites are the followers of Sidney Rigdon, and are but a few in number. **1890** *Amer. Notes & Q.* V. 184/2 Sidney Rigdon's followers were or are called *Rigdonites.*

Rigger. One who rigs ships. {1611-}

1789 *Boston Directory* 180 Chase, James, rigger, Rand's-wharf, Ann-street. **1802** *Ann. 7th Congress* 221 The ropemakers, sailmakers, and riggers of the United states will feel the consequences. **1817** *Ann. 14th Congress* 2 Sess. 780 The riggers fit and put over head the rigging. **1881** EMERSON in *Scribner's Mag.* XXII. 90 If a scholar goes into a camp of lumbermen or a gang of riggers, these men will quickly detect any fault of character.

b. A fisherman who rigs lines, nets, etc.

1880 *Harper's Mag.* Aug. 340/1 There were, in the same way, trawlers, draggers, riggers, seiners.

∗ **Rigging.**

+**1.** The equipment, apparatus, or outfit needed for a particular kind of work, as skidding logs by steam power.

1849 THOREAU *Week on Concord* 68 They had teams with rigging such as is used to carry barrels. **1876** RAYMOND *8th Rep. Mines* 63 This claim has a splendid hydraulic rigging. **1895** JEWETT *Life of Nancy* 244, I don't want to move my riggin' nowhere for the sake o' two trees. **1905** *Forestry Bureau Bul.* No. 61, 44 Rigging, the cables, blocks, and hooks used in skidding logs by steam power.

+**2.** The exterior leather trappings of a saddle.

1847 HENRY *Campaign Sk.* 25 For the first time had the pleasure of riding a mustang with complete though rude Mexican rigging. **1891** *Century Mag.* March 774/1 [The mules] came into camp and ate the pads and rigging off the pack-saddles. **1923** J. H. COOK *On Old Frontier* 112 The California rider used a center-fire or broad single cinch, hung center from the rigging of his saddle.

Rigging loft.

1. A long room or workshop in which rigging for ships is fitted for use. {1821-}

1726 *New-Eng. Courant* 8 Jan. 2/2 A Fire broke out in a Rigging Loft on Mr. Clark's wharff. **1844** Rupp *Relig. Denominations* 430 They next hired a rigging-loft in William Street, and fitted it up for a place of worship. **1868** M. H. SMITH *Sunshine & Shadow* 465 He had heard of the meeting in the rigging-loft, and had come from Albany to worship with the little band. **1888** DORSEY *Midshipman Bob* 86 Then he arsks ef there's any more of 'em, and one man says yes, in the riggin'-loft.

+**2.** The place above the stage of a theater or the framework of beams from which the scenery is raised or lowered.

1870 O. LOGAN *Before Footlights* 95 Then there are men up in the rigging loft who attend to the flies and the curtain wheel. **1883** *Harper's Mag.* Nov. 879 Rigging Loft 90 ft. above stage. **1888** *Scribner's Mag.* Oct. 438 Looking upward from the floor of the stage, he would call them [the beams] the gridiron; standing on them, he would speak of them as the rigging-loft.

‖**Riggite.** (See quotation.) — **1771** FRANKLIN *Autobiog.* 282 This, and my being esteem'd a pretty good riggite, that is, a jocular verbal satirist, supported my consequence in the society.

* **Right,** *n.*

***1.** A legal claim or title to enjoy certain property, esp. commonage and land; a particular or defined share of land.

1635 *Watertown Rec.* I. 1. 2 No Foreainer . . . shall have any benefit either of Commonage, or Land undivided . . . except that they buy a man's right wholly in the Towne. **1694** *N.C. Col. Rec.* I. 396 Three of these rights are sold to Hannah Gosby. **1713** *Ib.* II. 3 Maj[o]r Christo Gale has allowed to prove upon oath the Importation of ffour rights for which he has not as yet taken up any Land. **1750** *N.H. Probate Rec.* III. 574 We Set off to Benjamin Smith . . . one whole Right in Canterbury it being sd. Deceased his origanal Right. **1794** S. WILLIAMS *Nat. Hist. Vt.* 337 In the grants of land that were made by him, there were three rights in each township reserved for religious purposes. **1876** *Ill. Dept. Agric. Trans.* XIII. 330 Both the 'rights' granted and the 'patents' acquired under the United States [to western territory] tended to isolate the incoming rural population. **1911** *Okla. Session Laws* 3 Legisl. 144 An order of confirmation . . . shall become effective only upon payment by the said county . . . to the owner or owners of said rights and properties.

***b.** A legal or moral title or claim to the use or enjoyment of certain privileges, activities, etc.

1733 HEMPSTEAD *Diary* 264, I wrote a Deed . . . for the Right of Comons belonging to Samll Raymond. **1776** JEFFERSON *Writings* II. (1893) 3 [I] hope respect will be expressed to the right of opinion in other colonies. **1803** *Ib.* (1905) X. 343 The agitation of the public mind on occasion of the late suspension of our right of deposit at New Orleans is extreme. **1842** *Niles' Nat. Reg.* 19 March 48 The object of Great Britain has been to interpolate the right of search into the law of nations. **1854** BENTON *30 Years' View* I. 22/2 Right of pursuit must attach. **1861** LOGAN *Great Conspiracy* 174 Sir, I have always denied, and do yet deny, the Right of Secession.

+**c.** *Right in the woods,* (see quot. 1784).

1784 SMYTH *Tour* I. 144 In some parts [of N.C.], each person, in possession of a plantation, has what is called a right in the woods; by which he is entitled to the property of a certain proportion of the live stock that runs wild. **1884** *Century Mag.* Jan. 444/2 In some parts of the Chesapeake region, and perhaps elsewhere, a customary 'right in the woods' pertained to every planter, and was matter of sale and purchase.

***2.** A moral, equitable, or legal claim to the privileges and immunities of a free person.

Often in phrase *Declaration of Rights,* a formal declaration frequently embodied in state constitutions. (See also EQUAL RIGHTS.)

1765 *Stamp Act Congress Jrnl.* 27 The congress . . . agreed to the following declaration of the rights and grievances of the colonists in America. . . . [Caption:] Declaration of Rights. **1776** *Amer. Archives* 4 Ser. VI. 461 Resolved unanimously [in Va.], that a committee be appointed to prepare a Declaration of Rights. **1776** FITHIAN *Journal* II. 182 The people here appear firm in support of the American Rights. **1790** *Mass. Constitution,* Preamble, We, . . . the people of Massachusetts, . . . do agree upon, ordain, and establish the following Declaration of Rights. **1852** GOUGE *Fiscal Hist. Texas* 167 If she [Texas] persists in her present course, she will also violate the important principle, contained in the 16th Article of the Declaration of Rights, which formed part of her constitution as an independent Republic. **1857** *Iowa Constitution* i. § 25 This enumeration of rights shall not be construed to impair or deny others. **1901** *Ala. Constitution* i. – 36 Everything in this Declaration of Rights is excepted out of the general powers of government. **1921** *La. Constitution* i. §15 This enumeration of rights shall not be construed to deny or impair other rights.

3. *Bill of rights.* +**a.** One of various formal declarations of the privileges and immunities of American citizens. +**b.** *spec.* The first ten amendments to the Constitution. Also fig. and in allusive context.

1798 MANNING *Key of Liberty* 11 In the Bill of Rights it declares all men to be free & equel. **1804** J. ADAMS *Works* II. 373 The first committee was instructed to prepare a bill of rights, as it was called, or a declaration of the rights of the Colonies. **1855** in Hambleton *H. A. Wise* 183 This principles of this organization are violative of the Constitution and of the Bill of Rights. *c***1862** BAGBY *Old Va. Gentleman* 72 A Virginian can say what he has got to say without regard to grammar—that vile infraction of the Bill of Rights and the liberties of the people. **1874** B. F. TAYLOR *World on Wheels* 49 Though the herder is quiet, civil, self-reliant, yet he is a peripatetic Bill of Rights.

***4.** *To rights,* immediately, at once. *Obs.* or *dial.* {1663–1731}

'Now *U.S.*' (*O.E.D.*).

1795 DEARBORN *Columbian Grammar* 139 Improprieties, commonly called Vulgarisms, . . . [include] T' writes for Immediately. **1815** HUMPHREYS *Yankey* 53, I'll be back, torights. **1834** C. A. DAVIS *Lett. J. Downing* 149 The Gineral got in a way he has of twitchin with his suspender buttons behind; and to rights he broke one off. **1848** *Knickerb.* XXXI. 178, I'm going to start a dairy to-rights.

+**5.** *Hunting.* The bird which when flushed flies up on the fowler's right.

1874 LONG *Wild-Fowl* 179 The experienced sportsman will usually kill his 'right' and 'left' easily.

***Right,** *a.* +In the names of positions on an American football team. (Cf. END, GUARD, HALFBACK, TACKLE.) — **1896** CAMP & DELAND *Football* 344 Instructions to Right End. . . . You should help the right tackle block his man. *Ib.* 345 Instructions to Right Half-Back. . . . You are responsible for the hole in this play. **1904** in P. H. Davis *Football* (1911) 446 Army vs. Yale. . . . Yale. . . . Right Guard, R. C. Tripp, '06.

***Right,** *v. tr. To right up,* to mend, repair, put in order. {1656} 'Now *dial.* and *U.S.*' (*O.E.D.*). — **1702** in Sheldon *Hist. Deerfield, Mass.* I. 283 Ye Town fort shall forthwith be Righted vp. **1787** WASHINGTON *Diaries* III. 173 The old fence round field No. 2 was righted up to keep creatures out of it. **1851** *Fla. Plantation Rec.* 363, 9 [slaves] Cleaning out stables and Righting up horse lot Fence.

***Right,** *adv.*

+**1.** Straightway; at once.

1849 LONGFELLOW *Kavanagh* xxix, If you don't go right about your business, I will come down. **1852** STOWE *Uncle Tom* xxi, I'll go right in the house, for paper and ink. **1901** *Munsey's Mag.* XXIV. 800/1 (*O.E.D.*), Yes, I'll go right down.

***2.** Precisely or exactly *here* or *there.* Often fig. 'Now chiefly *U.S.*' (*O.E.D.*).

1861 NORTON *Army Lett.* 25 Our camp is right there on the scene of the skirmish. *Ib.* 30 We are right here in the same camp. **1877** *Vermont Bd. Agric. Rep.* IV. 76 And right here is where we want the wisdom of this Board. **1893** FULLER *Literary Courtship* 98, I may as well say, right here, that I . . . had a rousing good time. **1905** *Springfield W. Repub.* 31 March 2 Right there is the main principle of the Japanese national policy. **1923** DUTTON *Shadow on Glass* 223 Right here came the conflict.

+**Right along,** *adv.* See ALONG *adv.* 2.

+**Right away,** *adv.* At once, immediately, without delay. — **1818** FEARON *Sketches* 5, I have been slick in going to the stand right away. **1842** DICKENS *Amer. Notes* 12, I saw now that 'Right away' and 'Directly' were one and the same thing. **1876** 'MARK TWAIN' *Tom Sawyer* iii. 36 But his face lit up, right away, for she tossed a pansy over the fence. **1919** *Maine My State* 47 It was right away after Poutrincourt's return to France that Champlain started out on an enterprise of his own.

+**Right bower.** (See BOWER.)

+**Right field.** *Baseball.* That part of the outfield to the right of the batter when in batting position; the position of a player covering this area. — **1868** [see FIELD 3 b]. **1878** *De Witt's Base-Ball Guide* 8 The above illustration shows the batsman standing so as to face for a hit to right-field. **1886** *Outing* March 697/2 Short-stop and right field are as yet unfilled.

+**Right fielder.** *Baseball.* A player stationed in the right field. — **1878** *De Witt's Base-Ball Guide* 21 The same may be said of the right fielder, as of the occupant of the left field. **1880** N. BROOKS *Fairport Nine* 7 'Hurrah for the Fourth of July!' shouted Bill Watson, a burly little chap, the right fielder. **1886** CHADWICK *Art of Pitching* 65 An apparently safe hit to right field is changed into an out . . . by the right-fielder. **1912** MATHEWSON *Pitching* 27 Kane, the little rightfielder on the Cincinnati club, was the first man up.

+**Right off,** *adv.* = RIGHT AWAY.

[**1758** S. THOMPSON *Diary* (1896) 12, I thought that they would have risen and marched right off.] **1787** TYLER *Contrast* II. ii, I was glad to take to my heels and split home, right off, tail on end. **1833** [see RIGHT UP *adv.* 1]. **1884** 'MARK TWAIN' *H. Finn* xxxiii, He wanted to know all about it right off. **1902** HARBEN *A. Daniel* 2, I want you to come to the house right off.

+**b.** *Right off the reel,* at once, directly. *colloq.* (Cf. REEL *n.*[1] 1.b.)

1848 BURTON *Waggeries* 11 [The captain] raised a pretty muss, I guess, right off the reel. **1899** ADE *Fables in Slang* 27 He could tell you quick—right off the Reel.

Right of way. {1768–}

+**1.** **a.** The right to construct a railroad. *Obs.* **b.** A narrow strip of land over which a railroad is built.

1838 *Indiana H. Rep. Jrnl.* 23 Sess. 101 Mr. Blair introduced bill No. 32, to grant the right of way to Illinois. **1883** *Rep. Indian Affairs* p. xxii, I had the honor to submit to the Department . . . the draft of a bill . . . to grant a right of way to the Carson and Colorado Railroad Company. **1902** WHITE *Blazed Trail* 407 On either side of the right-of-way lay mystery in the shape of thickets. **1918** *Essex Inst. Coll.* LIV. 205 This figure included all bridging, masonry, grading, rights of way, fences.

+**2.** **Right-of-way man,** one who surveys or opens up a right of way.

1891 *Harper's Mag.* Nov. 886/2 The first men to follow the engineers . . . are 'the right-of-way men.' **1906** LYNDE *Quickening* 77 We can't any more'n fire me, like he did the Southwestern right-o'-way man.

+**Right short.** *Baseball.* A position behind the base line running from first to second base, formerly occupied by a tenth player, but now played by the second baseman; also, the player occupying this position. *colloq.* In full *right shortstop.* — **1867** CHADWICK *Base Ball Reference* 84 [Let] the second baseman play at right short. **1868** — *Base Ball* 98 Parker . . . was playing right short. **1878** *De Witt's Base-Ball Guide* 21 The right-short will be the 'utility' man of the ten. **1886** CHADWICK *Art of Pitching* 86 [The second baseman] is required to cover second base and to play 'right short stop.'

+**Right smart.**

1. A considerable amount; a good deal. *local.*

1842 BUCKINGHAM *Slave States* II. 327, I asked here, whether the people made much maple-sugar in this neighbourhood; when the gentleman . . . answered, 'Yes, they do, I reckon, right smart.' **1862** NORTON *Army Lett.* 77 [The negro] could find 'right smart to do,' and felt very confident he could support his family. **1891** 'THANET' *Otto the Knight* 176 He chopped a right smart er wood fur me to-day. **1913** MORLEY *Carolina Mts.* 180 Neither are there 'hives' in the mountains, only 'bee-gums,' which the bees fill with 'right smart of honey.'

2. Attrib. with *heap, lot, way.*

This construction is an outgrowth of the use of *right smart* in expressions such as those in the first group below in which *smart* is sensibly an adjective. This use of *right* with an adjective is now archaic but survives in colloq. use, esp. in the South. For *right smart chance, sprinkling,* see CHANCE 1 (2), SPRINKLING 2.

[**1836** DUNLAP *Mem. Water Drinker* (1837) I. 80 His father is building a right smart house for him. **1866** C. H. SMITH *Bill Arp* 38 After right smart skirmishing the head of the raid fell back down the road to Alabama. **1917** FREEMAN & KINGSLEY *Alabaster Box* 56 Guess we'll have to set the Deacon down for a right smart real-estate boomer.]

1865 KELLOGG *Rebel Prisons* 395 There is a right smart heap of Sherman's men coming down through here. **1872** EGGLESTON *End of World* 34 You got a right smart lot of eggs, didn't you? **1917** COMSTOCK *Man* 25 It's a right smart way down.

* **Right up,** *adv.*

+**1.** = RIGHT AWAY. *Obs.*

1833 A. FERGUSSON *Notes Tour U.S.* 229 If a steward or a cabin-boy wishes to be very civil and smart, he assures you that he is going *right up* or *right off* to do your errand. **1844** *Knickerb.* XXIII. 100 His first thought doubtless would be for an omnibus 'right up.'

+**2.** *Right up and down,* honestly, plainly, without equivocation. *colloq.* Also as adj. (Cf. UP-AND-DOWN *a.* and *adv.*)

1828 *Yankee* I. 166/3, I love to deal right-up-and-down as you say here. **1837** BIRD *Nick* I. 66, I see'd the creatur' have . . . a right up-and-down touch of the falling-sickness. **1846** CORCORAN *Pickings* 73, I'm a butcher, right up and down. **1918** LINCOLN *Shavings* 246 Leander asked me right up and down if I wouldn't enlist if I was in his position.

Right whale. Any whalebone whale of the family Balaenidae. {1874–} Also attrib.

1725 DUDLEY in *Phil. Trans.* XXXIII. 256 The Right, or Whalebone Whale is a large Fish, measuring sixty or seventy Feet in Length. **1792** *N.Y. State Soc. Arts* I. 363 Profits . . . may arise from the gross matter or sediment contained in common right whale oil. **1834** *Congress. Deb.* 3 March 781 While the increase or decrease . . . of the sperm whale fishery ought to depend on somewhat certain calculations, the right whale fishery must fluctuate with circumstances. **1865** *Atlantic Mo.* Jan. 41/1 Captain Handy . . . [had] an eye for the beautiful as well as for right-whales. **1909** WEBSTER 816/3 The finbacks are more difficult to take and less valuable than the right whales.

Rigid. {1712} One of the strict followers of Robert Browne (d. 1633), the father of Congregationalism. — **1748** W. DOUGLASS *Summary* I. 444 The Rigids generally seceeded from the more moderate, and removed with their Teachers or Ministers without the Limits . . . of the Colony.

+**Rigolet.** *S.* [Fr.] A small stream, rivulet, or strait. — **1775** ROMANS *Nat. Hist. Florida* 227 On this river they are not in such plenty at the freshes as below, at the *rigolets,* on pearl river, and at the *Riviere aux Boeufs.* **1803** *Ann. 8th Congress* 2 Sess. 1504 By this creek the communication is kept up through the lake and the rigoleta to Mobile. **1879** BISHOP *4 Months in Sneak-Box* 219 We struck across the lake in a course which took us to a point below the 'Rigolets,' a name given to the passages in the marshes through which a large portion of the water of Lake Pontchartrain flows into the Gulf of Mexico.

Rile, *n.* [Var. of *roil.* Cf. BILE.] A turbid or disturbed condition of water or other liquid. Also *transf.* — **1848** LOWELL *Biglow P.* 1 Ser. viii. 108 'T'll take more fish-skin than folks think to take the rile clean out on 't. **1859** BEECHER *Notes from Plymouth Pulpit* 34 The muddy bottom sends its rile through all the waters.

Rile, *v.* {1838–} *tr.* To anger or vex exceedingly. Also with *up.* {1844–} 'Chiefly *U.S.* and *colloq.'* O.E.D.

1825 NEAL *Bro. Jonathan* I. 158 Bein' afeared he might ryle my blood. **1852** 'MARK TWAIN' in *Hannibal Jrnl.* 16 Sept., Renewed laughter . . . somewhat riled our hero. **1857** HOLLAND *Bay-Path* 32 It only raises the devil in me, and riles me all up. **1901** WILKINS *Portion of Labor* 87 If I've said anythin' that riled you, I'm sorry, I'm sure. **1914** S. H. ADAMS *Clarion* 12 'Oh, you can't rile me,' returned the quack.

+**Riley,** *a.*

1. Turbid, muddy. *colloq.*

1805 ORDWAY in *Jrnls. Lewis & O.* 240 [The water was] verry riley and bad tasted. **1850** KINGSLEY *Diary* 147 The river rose verry suddenly

again this morning & has been verry riley all day. **1880** N. BROOKS *Fairport Nine* 92 The coffee was 'riley,' as the boys said, not to say muddy. **1883** ZEIGLER & GROSSCUP *Alleghanies* 127, I'd use a snare. They're fust-rate tricks whar the water is still an' a little riley.

2. Angry or ill-tempered. *colloq.*

1847 ROBB *Squatter Life* 64 The boys and gals kept it up so strong, laffin at my scrape, and the pickle I wur in, that I gin to git riley. **1862** BROWNE *A. Ward: His Book* 100 'What's Old Revelashun got to do with my Show?' sez I, gittin putty rily. **1898** DUNBAR *Folks from Dixie* 85 Won't she be riley when she fin's out how mistaken she is?

* **Rill.** A small stream or rivulet. — **1738** BYRD *Dividing Line* (1901) 173 We encampt upon a small rill. *a*1817 DWIGHT *Travels* III. 304 We crossed . . . Wading River: an insignificant rill, from two to perhaps six feet in breadth. **1879** *Scribner's Mo.* Dec. 244/2 The rill ran a little way on my grounds. **1892** *Vt. Agric. Rep.* XII. 141 [With] the innumerable brooks and mountain rills, . . . it is well watered.

* **Rim.** The highest part of a hill; the edge or brink of a depression, coulee, etc. {1842–} — **1859** in F. Hall *Hist. Colorado* II. 520 Wind has blown snow off of the rim, but gravel is hard frozen. **1873** MILLER *Amongst Modocs* 174 We had reached the rim of a bench in the mountains. **1889** MUNROE *Golden Days* 160 They had no difficulty in following the rim of the depression. **1914** 'BOWER' *Flying U Ranch* 221 The herders jumped up and ran like scared cottontails toward the rim of Denson coulee.

+**Rim-fire.** *attrib.* Designating cartridges having the igniting substance disposed in the outer edge, rather than the center, of the base {1881–}; hence, *transf.,* designating saddles having two cinches. Also *absol.* (Cf. CENTER-FIRE.) — **1868** NORTON & VALENTINE *Rep. Munitions War* 27 It is impossible to explode the rim-fire cartridges, except by a concussion made by the hammer. **1894** *Harper's Mag.* Feb. 350/2 Tom Bailey called it [the saddle] 'a d—— rim-fire.' **1913** BARNES *Western Grazing Grounds* 381 Double Rig Saddle, a saddle with two cinches; a 'rim fire' saddle.

+**Rim rock.** *W. Geol.* Remaining portions of country rock, which once formed the sides or banks of rivers. — **1860** GREELEY *Overland Journey* 350 It is one of the arts of the miner to know just where to tunnel through the 'rim rock' so as to strike what was the bottom of the lake. **1876** RAYMOND *8th Rep. Mines* 122 The external character of this deposit is that of a broad channel . . . , with a well-defined rim-rock on the northern side. **1898** *Scribner's Mag.* XXIV. 571/1 It was a long, hard day's pull up the northern side of the mountain to the 'rim-rock' in deep snow. **1907** WHITE *Arizona Nights* 3 [We] followed it [a watercourse] into box canons between rim-rock carved fantastically.

+**Rincon.** *S.W.* [Sp. *rincón.*] A piece of land, esp. a small round valley or nook suitable for a house or village site. — **1888** E. M. JOHNSTONE *In Semi-tropic Seas* (Bentley), The territory . . . included all the arable lands from the 'Rincon' west to the sea. **1897** HOUGH *Story of Cowboy* 26 Many common descriptive words used in the ranch work . . . would be strange to the Northern rancher, such as *rincon* [etc.]. **1919** J. S. CHASE *Calif. Desert Trails* 243 In a *rincon* or elbow at the foot of the rise lay the hamlet of Banner.

* **Ring,** *n.*

* **1.** A small circular band or hoop, usually of gold or silver, worn on the finger as an ornament.

1622 'MOURT' *Relation* 33 We dismissed the Salvage, and gaue him a knife, a bracelet, and a ring. **1698** *Conn. Rec.* I. 545, I give him my gold ring. **1704** S. KNIGHT *Journal* 24 [She] run up stairs and putts on two or three Rings. **1788** *Columbian Mag.* May 271 Churches were places for people to shew once a week . . . their rings, snuff-boxes [etc.]. **1830** COOPER *Water Witch* III. v, His gaze had unconsciously become riveted on the rings of the hand he held. **1913** LONDON *Valley of Moon* 101 Her eye had glimpsed the topaz ring on the third finger of Saxon's left hand.

* **2.** A circle of metal for use in the nose of a swine to prevent it from rooting.

1636 *Plymouth Laws* 45 If any lose their rings or yoakes the first notice to be without fine. **1647** *Springfield Rec.* I. 192 In case any Swine . . . shall be found . . . w[i]thout yoke & ringe; It shall be lawfull . . . to drive them to the pound. **1679** *Conn. Rec.* III. 29 If any swine at Midleton be found on the common, without rings or yoakes, . . . they shall be liable to be pownded.

+**3.** A clique or faction of politicians or officeholders who act in concert for ends that are usually not in the public interest. {1882–}

1862 *Independent* 13 Feb. 4/4 [Parties] are more responsible in regard to the characters of those they nominate than are those . . . profligate rings that are so apt to take the control of a merely local election. **1870** *Nation* 6 Jan. 1/1 As to the virtuous country Democrats, the Ring now enjoys means of muzzling them. **1875** BURNHAM *Three Years* 23 Among the most efficient aids the U.S. government had in Louisiana, for the capture of the 'Thugs,' and the famous corrupt old 'ring,' at New Orleans. **1898** *Kissimmee* (Fla.). *Valley Gazette* 25 Feb. 1/1 He declares he is the candidate of no ring or clique. **1905** STEFFENS in *McClure's Mag.* Feb. 337/1 In the Senate there is a small ring (called the Steering Committee) which is coming more and more to be the head of the United States Senate.

attrib. **1875** *Chicago Tribune* 2 July 4/7 The Philadelphia *Inquirer* would object to enlarging Gov. Tilden's sphere of usefulness if any of Peter B.

Sweeney's Ring-spoils should be traced to his hands. **1883** *Century Mag.* July 419/2 Here the ring-politician mounts perpetual guard. **1903** *McClure's Mag.* Nov. 92/1 Philadelphia had a bad ring mayor.

+**4.** A combination of capitalists or stockbrokers who manipulate the market for selfish or corrupt purposes. {1880–}

1864 *Wkly. New Mexican* 24 June 1/3 Most of the parties who formed the 'ring' . . . sold their shares. **1879** *Harper's Mag.* Oct. 717 The inopportune arrival of several cargoes of Texan beef broke the ring and ruined the ringsters. **1896** SHINN *Story of Mine* 263 The trouble is with 'the ring'—the speculators who are trying to control something.

-**b.** *Finance.* (See quot. 1889.) Also attrib.

1889 *N.Y. Produce Exch. Rep.* 180 Where it appears that several parties have contracts between each other, corresponding in all respects (except as to price), and that a 'ring settlement' can be made, the party finding said 'ring' shall notify all parties thereto. **1902** NORRIS *Pit* 106 It was their duty to get the trades of the day into a 'ring'—to trace the course of wheat which had changed hands perhaps a score of times during the trading.

+**5.** In special combinations.

Ring fire, (see quotation); *r. heart,* a defect in lumber caused by a ring shake in the tree from which it comes; *r. hunt,* a hunt in which a large circular area is fired along its perimeter and the animals driven to the center; *r. oak,* (see quotation) *Obs.*; *r. relievo,* a children's game resembling prisoner's base; *r. road,* a circular course for a group of horsemen drawn up one behind the other; *r. rot,* (see quotation); *r. service,* a marriage service in which a ring is used; *r. shake,* (see quotation).

1852 REYNOLDS *Hist. Illinois* 194 Sometimes the hunters made what they called 'ring fires.' They set fire to the grass and leaves around a considerable tract of country, so as to enclose a number of deer, and other animals. **1874** KNIGHT 564/1 *Clear-stuff,* boards free from knots, wane, wind-shakes, ring-hearts [etc.]. **1799** J. SMITH *Acct. Captivity* 48 [We] agreed with them to take, what they call a ring hunt. **1709** LAWSON *Carolina* 92 White Iron, or Ring-Oak, is so call'd, from the Durability and lasting Quality of this Wood. **1891** *Amer. Folk-Lore* IV. 224 Ring Relievo. . . . The game continues until all players of the side that had the start are made captives. **1843** HALIBURTON *Attaché* 1 Ser. II. iv. 59 First and foremost, a ring-road is formed, like a small race-course. **1905** *Forestry Bureau Bul.* No. 61, 44 *Ring rot,* decay in a log, which follows the annual rings more or less closely. **1905** *Springfield W. Repub.* 23 June 14 The officiating clergyman was Rev. C. C. P. Hiller, and the ring service was used. **1905** *Scientific Amer. Suppl.* 25 March 24433/1 The defect known as cupshake, ringshake, . . . consists in a partial or entire separation of two consecutive annual rings, and appears on a cross section as one or more splits running concentrically around the log.

***Ring,** *v. tr.* To place a ring in the nose of (a pig) to prevent it from rooting. — **1636** *Mass. Bay Rec.* I. 187 The execution of the order against swine . . . agreed to bee suspended till the first of the first month, p[ro]vided they be rung. **1705** *Phila. Ordinances* (1812) 11 It shall not be lawful for any swine, hogs, shoats or pigs, to go at large . . . , whether yoked and ringed or not. **1859** T. D. PRICE *Diary* (MS.) 15 Aug., Helped Price Glynn to ring some pigs. **1924** CROY *R. F. D. No. 3* 134 She helped ring the old sows which had been rooting under the fences.

+**Ringbill.** =RING-NECKED DUCK. — **1856** AUDUBON *Birds of Amer.* VI. 320 In shape, the Tufted Duck, or Ring-bill, as it is called in Kentucky, resembles the Scaup or Flocking Fowl. **1888** TRUMBULL *Names of Birds* 60 Ring-Necked Duck: Ring-Necked Scaup. . . . At Chicago [it is known as the] Ring-Bill.

Ring-billed, *a.* (See quot. 1891 and see also RING-BILLED GULL.) — **1831** J. RICHARDSON, etc. *Fauna Bor.-Amer.* II. 421 *Larus zonorhynchus,* . . . Ring-billed Mew-Gull. **1883** *Nat. Museum Bul.* No. 27, 160 *Fulix collaris.* . . . Ring-billed Blackhead; Ring-neck. **1891** *Cent.* 5186/2 *Ring-billed,* . . . having the bill ringed with color. **1917** *Birds of Amer.* I. 137 Ring-necked Duck. *Marila collaris.* . . . [Also called] Ring-billed Duck.

+**Ring-billed gull.** The common or lake gull, *Larus delawarensis.* — **1844** *Nat. Hist. N.Y., Zoology* II. 309 The Common gull . . . , although called the Ring-billed Gull in the books, has received no other popular name than Brown Winter Gull. **1874** COUES *Birds N.W.* 638 The Ring-billed Gull is more generally distributed throughout the interior than the Herring Gull. **1917** *Birds of Amer.* I. 47/1 The California and Ring-billed Gulls generally nest together in big colonies on the inland lakes.

Ring bit. A severe bit having a ring for slipping over the lower jaw of the horse. — **1894** *Harper's Mag.* March 520/2 The Mexican 'punchers' all use the 'ring bit,' and it is a fearful contrivance. **1897** HOUGH *Story of Cowboy* 64 And still more cruel was the 'ring bit,' with its circle slipped over the lower jaw of the horse.

Ringed plover. (See RING PLOVER.)

Ringneck. {1895–} +**1.** =RING SNAKE 1. (Cf. RING-NECKED SERPENT.) +**2.** =RING PLOVER. +**3.** =RING-NECKED DUCK. — **(1) 1791** W. BARTRAM *Travels* 274 There are many other species of snakes in the regions of Florida and Carolina; as the . . . copper belly, ring neck, and two or three varieties of vipers. **(2) 1844** [see RING PLOVER]. **1872** COUES *Key to Birds* 244 Semipalmated Plover. Ring Plover. Ringneck. . . . North America, abundant. **1917** *Birds of Amer.* I. 264 Piping Plover. *Ægialitis meloda.* . . . [Also called] Ringneck. **(3)** *Ib.* 137 Ring-necked Duck. *Marila collaris.* . . . [Also called] Ring-neck.

Ring-necked, *a.* In the names of birds. {1834–} See also RING-NECKED DUCK. — **1887** BAIRD *Manual N. A. Birds* 206 *P[hasianus] torquatus.* Ring-necked Pheasant. **1888** TRUMBULL *Names of Birds* 60 Ring-necked Scaup: Ring-necked Black-Head. **1889** *Cent.* 3515/3 The great northern diver, ring-necked loon, or ember-goose . . . is from 30 to 36 inches long. **1917** *Birds of Amer.* I. 261 Semipalmated Plover. . . . [Also called] Ring-necked Plover.

+**Ring-necked duck.** The marsh bluebill (*Nyroca collaris*), widely distributed throughout North America. — **1831** J. RICHARDSON, etc. *Fauna Bor-Amer.* II. 454 *Fuligula rufitorques,* . . . Ring-necked Duck. **1856** [see BUNTY *a.* and *n.*]. **1874** LONG *Wild-Fowl* 278 The female of the ring-necked and scaup ducks . . . [differs] in the peculiar form of the bill. **1917** [see RINGNECK 3].

Ring-necked serpent, snake. {1840–} =RING SNAKE 1. — **1833** BROOKS *Zóphiël* (*note*), The ring necked serpent is still sometimes seen in North America. **1889** *Cent.* 1588/2 The best-known species [of *Diadophis*] is *D. punctatus,* the ring-necked snake, found in many parts of the United States.

Ring plover, Ringed plover. Any one of various widely distributed small plovers having a dark or dusky band encircling the neck and upper breast {1776– (Pennant *British Zool.* II. 666)}, +esp. the semipalmated plover or the piping plover. Also with specifying terms.

1785 PENNANT *Arctic Zool.* II. 485 Ringed and Black-crowned Plover. . . . [The ringed plover] inhabits America, down to Jamaica and the Brasils. **1812** WILSON *Ornithology* V. 30 The Ringed Plover is very abundant on the low sandy shores of our whole sea-coast, during summer. **1844** *Nat. Hist. N.Y., Zoology* II. 209 The Ring Plover, or Ring-neck as it is commonly called in this State, arrives here about the beginning of May. **1883** *Nat. Museum Bul.* No. 27, 147 *Ægialites curonicus.* Little Ringed Plover. Palæarctic region; accidental in California and Alaska (?). **1917** *Birds of Amer.* I. 261.

+**Ring rule.** Rule or government under the control of a political ring. — **1886** [see BOSS RULE]. **1895** *Outing* Dec. 184/2 That worthless bill . . . would relegate our city to the dark ages of ring rule. **1913** LA FOLLETTE *Autobiog.* 64 The only way to best boss and ring rule was to keep the people thoroughly informed.

Ringsail. (See quot. 1876.) — **1781** *Md. Hist. Mag.* VI. 312 Invoice of Schooner Nautilus's Materials. . . . 1 Ring Sail. . . . 1 Fish Hook. **1876** KNIGHT 1945/1 *Ring-sail,* . . . a small, light sail set on a mast on the *taffrail.*

Ring snake. {1901} +**1.** Any one of various American snakes of the genus *Diadophis,* as *D. punctatus.* ‖**2.** A snake fabled to roll along like a hoop: (see quotation and cf. HOOP SNAKE). — **(1) 1778** CARVER *Travels* 487 The Ring Snake is about twelve inches long. *a***1817** DWIGHT *Travels* I. 55 The Ring-Snake is long, slender, and black, with a white ring round its neck. **1836** EDWARD *Hist. Texas* 76 One will meet . . . at times with that beautiful, small, harmless creature, the ring-snake. **(2) 1899** *Animal & Plant Lore* 87 The 'ring snake' will, by taking its tail in its mouth, roll like a hoop.

+**Ringster. 1.** A member of a political ring. (Cf. RING *n.* 3.) **2.** A member of a price-fixing ring. (Cf. RING *n.* 4.) — **(1) 1875** *Chicago Tribune* 15 Dec. 4/1 The support secured for Mayor Cobb was sufficient . . . to defeat the unholy alliance of ringsters and politicians by which Boardman's nomination was first obtained. **1904** *Phila. Press* 9 Aug. 6 The infamous work in St. Louis and elsewhere by means of which Democratic ringsters fixed the elections to suit themselves. **(2) 1878** *Congress. Rec.* 20 March 1915/1 As the honest contractor will not go into a business where he has to evade the law, the ringster has it all his own way. **1879** [see RING *n.* 4]. **1904** TARBELL *Hist. Standard Oil Co.* I. 107 'Deserters,' 'ringsters,' 'monopolists' were the terms applied to [the refiners who had joined Rockefeller in creating a monopoly].

***Ringtail.** *slang. Obs.* +**1.** =ROARER 2. (Cf. RINGTAIL(ED) ROARER 2.) +**2.** *attrib.* Designating persons or things regarded as extraordinary. (Cf. next and see also RINGTAIL(ED) ROARER 1.) — **(1) 1840** *Boston Transcript* 15 April 2/1 When the Registry Law was first spoken of, the tail of the Democratic party, the roarers, buttenders, ringtails, O.K.'s, . . . and indomitables, talked strong about nullification and all that. **(2) 1859** *La Crosse Daily Union* 25 Oct. 2/4 Here lies James D. Potter, Who lived . . . as a Methodist Exhorter, With a regular ring-tail snorter. **1898** WESTCOTT *D. Harum* xxxvi, Ain't this a ring-tail squealer?

Ring-tailed, *a.* {1725–} +Extraordinary or unusual; monstrous. *slang.* (See also RINGTAIL(ED) ROARER 1.) — **1837** BIRD *Nick* I. 56 My name's Ralph Stackpole, and I'm a ring-tailed squealer! **1914** *Emporia Gazette* 13 Jan., He is a four-flusher, a ring-tailed, rip-snorting hell-raiser.

Ring-tail(ed) eagle. The golden eagle (q.v.) before it has attained full maturity. {1809–} — [**1809** G. SHAW *Gen. Zool.* VII. 71 Ring-tailed Eagle. . . . It is a native both of Europe and North America.] **1813** WILSON *Ornithology* VII. 15 The Ring-tail Eagle measures nearly three feet in length. **1869** BURROUGHS in *Atlantic Mo.* June 712/1, I saw the ring-tailed eagle, an immense, dusky bird. **1917** *Birds of Amer.* II. 82.

+**Ring-tailed marlin.** (See MARLIN.)

+**Ringtail(ed) roarer.**

1. (See quot. 1871.) *slang. Obs.*

1830 *Mass. Spy* 25 Aug. (Th.), I'm a ringtailed roarer from Big Sandy River. I can outrun, outjump, and outfight any man in Kentucky. **1836** *Crockett's Yaller Flower Almanac* 9, I am a raal ringtailed roarer. **1840** [see FOX *n.* 6 a]. **1871** DE VERE 224 A specially fine fellow of great size and strength is called a *ring-tailed roarer.*

2. = ROARER 2. *Obs.*

1862 LOWELL *Biglow P.* 2 Ser. iii. 100 A baldin hain't no more 'f a chance with them new apple-corers Than folks's oppersition views against the Ringtail Roarers.

+**Ringtoss.** A game in which rings are tossed, usually at an upright stick or peg. — **1879** HOWELLS *Lady of Aroostook* 88 A young person . . . played shuffle-board and ring-toss on the deck of the Aroostook. **1884** *Century Mag.* Jan. 359/1, [I] found the artist . . . demurely watching a game of ring-toss.

∗**Rink.** A sheet of ice or a smooth floor for ice or roller skating, respectively; also, a building having such a skating place. {1867–} Also attrib. — **1876** KNIGHT 1045/1 *Rink*, a skating-pond. **1886** *Harper's Mag.* July 174/1 The rink band opposite kept up a lively competition. **1893** *Ib.* Jan. 209/1 The rink was a large, bare structure of wood, with a circular arena for roller-skating. **1907** *St. Nicholas* June 696/2 On the rink . . . the hockey team was getting ready for the game with Cedar Grove School.

+**Rio.**[1] *S.W.* [Sp.] A river. Also attrib. Chiefly in proper names. — **1838** *Diplom. Corr. Texas* III. (1911) 849 The stock . . . had been dispersed during the campaign of 1836 across the Rio Grande into the Mexican territory. **1845** in Benton *Exam. Dred Scott Case* 104 He anticipated no time when the country would ever desire to stretch its limits beyond Rio del Norte. **1847** *Santa Fe Republican* 30 Oct. 2/4 A war party of the Apaches charged into the Rio. **1848** ROBINSON *Santa Fe Exped.* (1932) 31 The Rio bottom [near Sanden] . . . produces an abundance of grapes, apples and peaches. **1867** *Wkly. New Mexican* 22 June 2/3 Hon. J. Francisco Chaves arrived yesterday from the Rio Abajo. **1897** HOUGH *Story of Cowboy* 20 Each stream [is] called a rio, or river, no matter how small it may be.

Rio.[2] [See quot. 1922.] =next. — **1863** *Harper's Mag.* Oct. 627/2 A sharp skirmish . . . adds zest to your relish of a cup of Government Rio. **1922** W. H. UKERS *All about Coffee* 341/2 Brazil coffees are classified into four great groups, which bear the names of the ports through which they are exported; Santos, Rio, Victoria, and Bahia.

Rio coffee. [See prec.] A variety of Brazilian coffee. — **1859** *Ladies' Repository* Aug. 509/2 The learned lecturer over biscuits and Rio coffee had been rather severely handled. **1879** BAGBY *Old Va. Gentleman* 232, I smell the meat, the fish, the Rio coffee!

+**Rio Grande trout.** A trout (*Salmo virginalis*) found in the Rio Grande and other western streams. — **1883** *Nat. Museum Bul.* No. 27, 426 *Salmo spilurus*. Rio Grande Trout. Upper Rio Grande and Basin of Utah. **1896** JORDAN & EVERMANN *Check-List Fishes* 291.

Riot act. {1731–} *transf. To read the riot act*, to reprimand severely, to speak out with extreme plainness and vigor. *colloq.* {1920–} — **1866** C. H. SMITH *Bill Arp* 18 Your marshal here . . . don't read the riot-act, nor remonstrate, nor nothing. **1880** RANOUS *Diary of Daly Débutante* 157 Mr. Daly . . . read the riot act, as it were, and vanished into his den, leaving the naughty girls overwhelmed. **1898** *McClure's Mag.* March 400/2 Perhaps I didn't read the riot act to that conductor, to stop me right at the foot of the hill for a hot box. **1916** WILSON *Somewhere* 185 When Henrietta declared herself Alonzo read the riot act and declared marital law.

Rip, *n.*

1. A place in the sea where the water is violently disturbed, usually by the meeting of opposing tides. {tide rip, 1875–}

1775 ROMANS *Nat. Hist. Florida* App. p. lxxxviii, You will see a rip appear like breakers. **1807** *Mass. H. S. Coll.* 2 Ser. III. 73 Ships in storms get within the dangerous rips which lie off the island. **1882** GODFREY *Nantucket* 311 Standing here, one can see the 'rips' in the distance.

2. A stretch of broken water in a river; a rapid. {1888–}

1832 WILLIAMSON *Maine* I. 48 [The river] then passes the 'carrying place rips,' half a mile in length. **1850** JUDD *R. Edney* 199 The 'rips' [were] concealed from sight. *a*1861 WINTHROP *Open Air* 64 We must camp before we were hurried into the first 'rips' of the stream. **1885** C. A. STEPHENS *Adv. 6 Young Men* 79 The stream shoaled, and thenceforward we found 'rips' and 'bars' in plenty.

∗**Rip,** *v.*

+**1.** *To let rip*, to permit to run a course without hindrance, to let matters go. Freq. *to let her rip. slang.* {to let him rip, 1877}

1853 *Daily Morning Herald* (St. Louis) 19 Jan. (Th.), For we've got 'em on the hip Letter Rip! Letter Rip! **1866** GREGG *Life in Army* 225 The hands on board [the steamers] . . . are generally reckless of consequences, and disposed at all times to 'let her rip!' **1891** SWASEY *Early Days Calif.* 47, I try to banish the matter utterly from my mind, and say to myself, in the expressive language of modern slang, 'Let it rip.' **1894** *Outing* XXIV. 93 You have simply to sit still and 'let her rip,' as Mick puts it.

+**2.** *To rip and tear*, to rave, cavort, behave outrageously. *slang.* {to rip and swear, 1772}

1873 'MARK TWAIN' & WARNER *Gilded Age* 249 A man don't want to rip and tear around *all* the time. **1884** 'MARK TWAIN' *H. Finn* x, We just set there and watched him [*sc.* a catfish] rip and tear around till he drownded. **1916** *Dialect Notes* IV. 342 *Rip and tear*, to rave. N.Y., W. Res., Kan.

Ripple.[1] {1798–} + = RIFFLE 1.

1755 *N.H. Prov. Papers* VI. 431 The chief of ye way [there were] swift water falls and Ripples. **1784** WASHINGTON *Diaries* II. 315 The South Fork of Shannondoah [is] . . . impeded in its navigation by the rapid water and rocks . . . and a few other Ripples. **1807** in Pike *Sources Miss.* II. App. 20 We found [the Osage R.] a pellucid tranquil stream, with the exception of a few trifling ripples. **1812** MELISH *Travels* II. 87 We engaged a young man to take us over a bar, here called a *ripple*, a little way below. **1874** COLLINS *Kentucky* I. 547 Improvement to the descending navigation—by . . . the excavating of a channel through each of the principal shoals or ripples—was recommended. *a*1918 G. STUART *On Frontier* II. 113 The river . . . [is] fordable on all ripples.

+**b.** *To make the ripple*, = RIFFLE 1 b.

1874 in Fleming *Hist. Reconstruction* II. 42 He said he . . . would let me have it on my giving him the ripple. Told him I was not able to make the ripple.

Ripple.[2] {1660–} +'A toothed instrument for removing the seeds from broom-corn' (*Cent.*). — **1876** KNIGHT 1946/2 The ripple is used in the United States for stripping the seed from broom-corn.

Ripple grass. The ribwort, *Plantago lanceolata*. {1824–} — **1819** *Amer. Farmer* I. 149 My milch cows . . . were turned into a field well set with *Rib Plantain* or *Ripple Grass*, as it is generally called. **1833** EATON *Botany* (ed. 6) 266 *Plantago lanceolata*, rib-wort, snake-plaintain, ripple grass. **1899** GOING *Flowers* 359 The flower-spikes of the closely allied ripple-grass . . . were used as love-charms.

Rippling. {1669–} + = RIFFLE 1. *Obs.* — **1745** POTE *Jrnl. Captivity* 55 [It was] Likewise verey bad Paddling, on account of Ripplings and falls. **1755** L. EVANS *Anal. Map Colonies* 20 In Half a Mile [you] come to a little gentle Rippling, where the River may be forded on Horseback. **1832** WILLIAMSON *Maine* I. 57 Here are ripplings, to avoid which, a canal was cut twenty rods in length.

∗**Riprap,** *n.* +A foundation or sustaining wall made of loose stones; in pl., an artificial island in Chesapeake Bay.

1833 *Md. Hist. Mag.* XIII. 314 The ripraps directly opposite . . . will effectually secure the Bay. **1863** KETTELL *Hist. Rebellion* II. 481 President Lincoln . . . went across from Fortress Monroe to over a spot . . . about one mile below the Rip Raps. **1876** KNIGHT 1946/2 *Rip-rap*, . . . a foundation of loose stones. The artificial island in Chesapeake Bay, which is thus formed, is named the Rip-raps. **1880** *Cimarron News & Press* 9 Sept. 3/3 It is the intention of the company to raise the grade of the approaches on both sides, protecting the exposed surfaces by what is technically known as 'rip rap,' a kind of loose rock work. **1882** *Congress. Rec.* 7 Aug. 7006/1 The bridge . . . shall be built with the piers parallel to the current, leaving the water-way unobstructed by riprap or piling, or other obstructions.

transf. **1857** *Knickerb.* XLIX. 277, I once knew a druggist . . . who got along so well in dealing in all sorts of rip-raps . . . that he at last undertook to go heavily into the fancy segar-case business.

attrib. **1838** J. CHILDS *Western Railroad* (1839) 25 (Ernst), To guard the embankments by rip-rap walls.

+**Riprap,** *v. tr.* and *absol.* To make a riprap for; to protect (a river bank) with a riprap. Also *ppl. a.* and *vbl. n.* — **1848** *Soc. of N.Y. Aldermen* No. 9 (B.), If, in constructing a bulkhead, it should be determined to rip-rap to low-water mark. **1883** *American* VI. 297 The stream will be confined within permanent barriers by rip-rapped banks and levees. **1884** *Harper's Mag.* Sept. 504/1 Cliff ledges . . . [are] connected one terrace above the other, by . . . a natural riprapping of fallen fragments. **1903** *N.Y. Times* 15 Sept., Congress will be asked to riprap the entire river where there is danger of the current cutting through to the old course.

+**Rip-roaring,** *a.* First-rate, superior; full-blooded, full of vim and vigor. *slang.* — **1834** CARRUTHERS *Kentuckian* I. 62 There was a rip-roaring sight of slight o' hand and tumbling work there. **1845** HOOPER *Simon Suggs' Adv.* x, And I seed the biggest, longest, rip-roarenest blackest, scaliest . . . alligator! **1856** *San Francisco Call* 19 Dec. (Th.), That's a rip-roaring hat you've got. **1903** 'O. HENRY' *Roads of Destiny* 368, I'm feeling just like having one more rip-roaring razoo with you for the sake of old times.

+**Rip-roarious,** *a.* Uproarious, violent, tumultuous. *colloq.* — **1840** *Congress. Globe* 2 April 376/1 Here and there [was] a gentleman from both political parties, who had been drawn out by curiosity to witness their riproarious proceedings [at the Whig 'powwows']. **1855** *Knickerb.* XLV. 133 The multitude . . . Were yelling in one rip-roarious throng. **1890** *Harper's Mag.* April 796/2 Robert J. Burdette . . . divides his waning buzz of rip-roarious approbation between two mettlesome, cavorting, prankish steeds in the great American journalistic circus.

+**Rip-roariously,** *adv.* In a rip-roarious manner. *colloq.* — **1834** CROCKETT *Narr. Life* 78 The next day it rained rip-roriously.

Ripsack. = GRAY WHALE. — **1860** *Merc. Marine Mag.* VII. 213 It being difficult to capture them, they have a variety of names among whalemen, as 'Ripsack,' . . . 'Devil-fish.' **1884** GOODE, etc. *Fisheries* I. 31 The California Gray Whale . . . [is] called by whalemen 'Devil-fish,' 'Hard Head,' 'Gray Back,' 'Rip Sack,' and 'Mussel Digger.' **1911** *Rep. Fisheries 1908* 310.

Ripsaw, *v. tr.* To cut (lumber) with a ripsaw. — **1885** *Century Mag.* Nov. 33/1, [I] ripsawed the lumber up here.

+**Ripsnorter.** An exaggerated or bombastic designation for a person or thing regarded as markedly superior or striking. Also *transf. slang.* — **1840** *Crockett Almanac* 20/1 Of all the ripsnorters I ever tutched upon, thar never war one that could pull her boat alongside of Grace Peabody.

1885 *Santa Fé Wkly. New Mexican* 20 Aug. 2/6 Any galoot who wants the Ripsnorter for a year can have it left at his bar-room on payment of three red chips in advance. **1889** MUNROE *Dorymates* 84 Boys, we are in for a regular 'rip-snorter.' I never saw a nastier night. **1900** BACHELLER E. *Holden* 204 There he stood with the old bass viol. . . . ' 'S a *reel* firs'-class instrument,' he said. 'Been a rip snorter 'n its day.'

+Ripsnorting, a. =RIP-ROARING a. — **1846** *Yale Lit. Mag.* XI. 336 (Th.), What a rip-snorting red head you have got! **1904** *Topeka Capital* 2 June 4 Bryan will make a rip-snorting speech at the St. Louis convention. **1914** [see RING-TAILED a.].

+Ripstaver. =RIPSNORTER. *slang.* — **1833** *Sketches D. Crockett* 144 In ten minutes he yelled enough, and swore I was a ripstavur.

+Rip van Winkle. [The name of the principal character in Irving's well-known story.] *transf.* One who is unresponsive to change or behind the times; an animal that hibernates. Also attrib.

1856 HOFFMAN *Night Watch* 255 Why, Col. Murray, you are the veriest old 'Rip Van Winkle.' Have you also been asleep twenty years? **1857** *Harper's Mag.* Dec. 135/2 This announcement will . . . add another rivet, fastening upon us [in N.C.] the *sobriquet* of the Rip Van Winkle State. **1865** *Atlantic Mo.* April 392/1 Many . . . sold out at moderate prices to shrewd adventurers, who made themselves rich men before the dispossessed Rip Van Winkles awoke to a consciousness of what was going on about them. **1875** BURROUGHS *Winter Sunshine* 141 By mid-October, most of the Rip Van Winkles among our brute creatures have lain down for their winter nap.

+b. *Rip-van-Winkle-ish,* a., suggestive of the twenty-year sleep of Rip of van Winkle; *Rip-van-Winkle-ism,* an old-fashioned or out-of-date characteristic; ‖*Rip-van-Winkle-thump,* a religious exhorter.

1831 ROYALL *Southern Tour* II. 96 A low raised ignorant woman, into whom one of those Godly *Rip Van Winkle-thumps* from New York, had instilled holy, pious feelings. **1842** KIRKLAND *Forest Life* II. 228 [Reading an old-fashioned book] was counted among my Rip-Van-Winkle-isms. **1852** *Harper's Mag.* Aug. 420/2 A Pilgrim from the back woods . . . had just been awakened from a Rip-Van-Winkleish existence of a quarter of a century by the steam-whistle of the Erie Railroad.

* Rise, *n.*

1. A piece of rising ground; a small hill. {1639-}

1741 in *Amer. Speech* XV. 384/1 South Easterly . . . upon Reise of Land to a Stone. **1752** in *Travels Amer. Col.* 322 Here is the battery, on a rise of land which commands all the city. **1797** HAWKINS *Letters* 64 The Indians . . . sat down at a rise a little back. **1804** CLARK in *Lewis & C. Exped.* I. (1904) 121 The Countrey is leavel [near the Vermilion R.] . . . except Some few rises at a great Distance. **1871** *Harper's Mag.* Dec. 45/1 On a slight rise of ground at the opposite side of the creek stands a log-cabin. **1891** RYAN *Pagan of Alleghanies* 232 He tried to tell by distant muffled calls just what 'flat' or what 'rise' the hunters were on.

+2. *Rise ball,* in baseball, a pitched ball that curves upward. Now rare.

1886 *Outing* July 480/2 He is weak in catching a rise ball and in getting the ball started for second.

+3. (See quotation.)

1905 *Forestry Bureau Bul.* No. 61, 44 *Rise,* the difference in diameter, or taper, between two points in a log.

4. *To take its rise* {1630-}, of a stream, to have its source.

1773 FINLAY *Journal* 1 These two Rivers [the Chaudiere and the Kennebek] are supposed to take their rise on the height of land between those two Provinces. **1791** W. BARTRAM *Travels* 33 In these swamps several rivulets take their rise. **1834** PECK *Gaz. Illinois* 120 McLean county is watered by the Kickapoo, Sugar creek, and Salt creek, all which take their rise in the prairies of this county.

+5. *The rise of,* a little more than. *colloq.*

1834 in J. S. Bassett *Plantation Overseer* 66, I muste plante the rise of a hundred aceres in coten. **1845** HOOPER *Simon Suggs' Adv.* 141 Bill . . . has been ded the rise of twenty year. **1866** C. H. SMITH *Bill Arp* 41 It's now the rise of 42 years since I come into this cursed old world. **1903** FOX *Little Shepherd* xii, A leetle the rise o' six miles, I reckon. **1905** 'O. HENRY' *Roads of Destiny* 141, I've seen the rise of $50,000 at a time in that tin grub box.

+6. *To make a rise,* to make a raise. (See RAISE n. 4.)

1836 *Quarter Race Ky.* (1846) 24, I thought I'd make a rise on chuck-a-luck. **1851** HOOPER *Widow Rugby* 20 No matter how I make an honest rise, I'm sure to 'buck it off' at farrer.

+7. *S. And the rise,* and more.

1853 *S. Lit. Messenger* XIX. 220/2 He pretended to be thirty and the rise, but was, at the least, fifty. **1859** BARTLETT 367 The phrase 'and the rise,' is used in some parts of the South to mean 'and more'; as, 'I should think there were a thousand and the rise.'

* Rise, *v.*

+1. *tr.* To surmount or gain the top of (a hill, slope, etc.).

1796 HAWKINS *Letters* 29, I take to the left, . . . and rise up a steep hill. **1812** MARSHALL *Kentucky* 217 Indians . . . caught the horses as they rose the bank. **1846** in Claiborne *Life Quitman* I. 277 Soon we rose the swell

where the ricochet cannon ball cut down the seven Tennesseans. **1899** JEWETT *Queen's Twin* 199, I couldn't rise the hill if 'twas a windy day.

+2. To exceed (a number or amount).

Cf. RISE *n*. 5.

1838 in MATHEWS *Writings* (1843) 82/1 Brother George counted the strokes of his arm upon the cushion, and thinks he rose a hundred in the course of the sermon. **1877** JEWETT *Deephaven* 133, I like well enough to see a hog that'll weigh six hundred, . . . but for my eatin' give me one that'll just rise three.

+3. *How d'ye rise?* (see quot. 1848).

1846 CORCORAN *Pickings* 47 He commenced—'How are you, Squire—how d'ye rise?' **1848** *R.I. Words* (Bartlett MS.), *How d'ye rise,* a western salutation meaning how do you get along.

Risibility. {1620-} *pl.* +The risible faculties. — **1856** CARTWRIGHT *Autobiog.* 142, I had very hard work to keep down my risibilities. **1860** HAWTHORNE *Transformation* III. 161 An Italian comedy . . . [was] effective over everybody's risibilities except his own.

Risibles. *pl.* =prec. {1866-} 'Chiefly U.S.' (O.E.D.). — **1785** CUTLER in *Life & Corr.* II. 227 Your account . . . has distorted my risibles and given my sides a hearty shake. **1845** HOOPER *Simon Suggs' Adv.* 137 'Captain,' said Mr. Hadenskeldt, vainly endeavouring to control his risibles, 'let us attend to the trial now.' **1868** *N. Amer. Rev.* April 538 If the risibles of classical philologers are so easily provoked, . . . [we] regret that we do not form a member of so hilarious a body.

* Rising, *n.*

1. The adjournment of a legislative body. {1740-}

1700 *Penna. Hist. Soc. Mem.* IX. 21 After the rising of this assembly, he determines to send the laws for England. **1821** JEFFERSON *Writings* I. 15 On the rising of the House, . . . I happened to find myself near Governor W. Livingston. **1829** in Kennedy *Mem. W. Wirt* (1849) II. 263, I was so much pressed by the Supreme Court, about the time of the rising of Congress, that I could not find a moment for friendship.

* 2. A piece of rising ground; a small hill.

1671 in Summers *Ann. S.W. Va.* 3 At the foot [of a steep descent] . . . was a lovely descending valley about six miles over with curious small risings. **1702** *Providence Rec.* V. 129 The said seven acres of land is . . . bounded on the southwesterne Cornner with a stake & a heape of stones about it, on the south side of a small Riseing. **1757** *Lett. to Washington* II. 206 None of them would come into Town but Encamp'd on a Rising near it. **1784** FILSON *Kentucke* 16 The levels are not like a carpet, but interspersed with small risings, and declivities.

* 3. A leavening agent. Also attrib.

1817 *Niles' Reg.* XII. 165/2 The result was as above stated . . . being that kind of rising called here 'sotts,' a Dutch term, I presume. **1842** [see GRIDDLE 2]. **1876** M. F. HENDERSON *Cooking* 50 Rising-powder Proportions. To 1 quart of flour, use 2½ teaspoonfuls of baking-powder [etc.]. **1894** CLARK *On Cloud Mt.* 48 If ye was to put 's much risin' in 's what ye do back there in Illinoy, ye'd have every stone blowed out o' the oven when ye come to bake it.

Rising, *pr. pple.* {1610-}

+1. Fully as much as; rather more than.

1833 *Congress. Deb.* 30 Jan. 1482 We imported only, of the finer quality [of wool], a little rising four million pounds. **1883** JEWETT *Mate of 'Daylight'* 103 Forty years it must be, or rising forty. **1896** WILKINS *Madelon* 123 Old man in there, lived 'round these parts risin' eighty years.

+2. Upwards of, in excess of.

1817 PAULDING *Lett. from South* II. 121 'How much wheat did you raise this year?' 'A little rising of five thousand bushels.' **1842** KIRKLAND *Forest Life* II. 38 The last legislature . . . passed rising of two hundred laws. **1872** *Harper's Mag.* Sept. 507/1 The squire has . . . a daughter 'rising of sixteen,' who assists in the housekeeping. **1896** HARRIS *Sister Jane* 41 'How old is your baby?' inquired Mrs. Beshears. 'A risin' of five months,' replied the mother.

+Rising seat. (See quot. 1891.) — **1809** M. LEE *Quaker Girl of Nantucket* 28 (Th. S.), In the sing-song drawl once peculiar to the tuneful exhortations of the rising seat, he thus held forth. **1891** *Cent.* 5194/1 *Rising-seat,* . . . In a Friends' meeting-house, one of a series of three or four seats, each raised a little above the one before it, and all facing the body of the congregation. These seats are usually occupied by ministers and elders.

Rising sun. +**1.** The east. Used in Indian speech. +**2.** A quilt pattern suggestive of the sun when rising. Also attrib. — (1) **1841** COOPER *Deerslayer* xxvii, You are a man whose fathers came from beyond the rising sun; we are children of the setting sun. (2) **1895** 'CRADDOCK' *Mystery Witch-Face Mt.* 185 Some [quilts] were of the 'log cabin' and 'rising sun' variety. **1898** [see FOUR a. 2].

Rising vote. A standing vote. — **1896** *Internat. Typogr. Union Proc.* 2/1 Upon the previous question being ordered, [they] were unanimously adopted by a rising vote. **1912** Gaines *New Cushing's Manual* 153 In ordinary assemblies the usual mode of procedure is a rising vote. **1923** ROBERT *Parliamentary Law* 189 A single member can compel a rising vote to be taken.

Rived, *a.* Split or riven, rather than sawed. {*rive,* v.} — **1792** IMLAY *Western Territory* 134 [Log houses were] covered with rived ash shingles. **1838** *Yale Lit. Mag.* III. 7 The dwellings were almost entirely constructed of logs, and covered with rived boards. **1852** *Mich. Agric. Soc. Trans.* IV. 156 Either the rived or sawed bolt may be used. **1887** EGGLESTON in *Century Mag.* April 901/1 The earliest houses of worship in America belonged to the make-shift order of architecture,—four walls of . . . rived clapboards with earth filled in between.

∗ River.[1]

I. ∗**1.** A large stream of water flowing through the land into another stream, a lake, or the sea.

'An observing friend (who has been particularly engaged in geographical inquiries) first remarked to me, that in speaking of rivers, Americans commonly put the *name* before the word *River*, thus: Connecticut *river*, Charles *river*, Merrimack *river;* whereas the English would place the name after it, and say, the *river* Charles &c.' (Pickering).

1607 in Smith *Works* (1910) p. xliii, Certifying him of our intentyon vp the Ryver, he was willing to send guydes with us. **1681** *Derby Rec.* 77 The Bownds & quantities [of land] are as followeth . . . one lott lying from the River to the fence eastward [etc.]. **1705** *Boston News-Letter* 29 Oct. 2/1 There being 2 places over a little River lying near Sacho, . . . Capt. Browne very prudently divided his Company into 2 parts. **1783** HANCOCK in A. E. Brown *J. Hancock His Book* (1898) 234, I mean . . . one ship & one onely, provided you can meet with one to your mind in the River. **1805** CLARK in *Lewis & C. Exped.* VI. (1905) 20 The river makeing a Genl. Bend to the East 8 miles by land. **1892** M. A. JACKSON *Gen. Jackson* 175 The men gallantly waded the river.

b. A settlement along a river. *Obs.*

1644 *Conn. Rec.* I. 119 There shalbe noe Englishe grayne sould out of this Riuer to any other. *Ib.* 121 It is by this Court Ordered, that all the Inhabitants of this Riuer doe take spetiall notice of the said agreements.

2. In phrases.

To get on the river, to secure employment on a river, usu. on a river steamer; *to follow the river*, to gain one's livelihood by working on a river; *to go* (or *to sell*) *down the river*, to be sold (or to sell Negro slaves) into the severest kind of servitude, as that of the cane and cotton plantations on the lower Mississippi (*Obs.*); *to send up the river*, to send from New York up the Hudson to Sing Sing prison; to send to the penitentiary.

1875 'MARK TWAIN' *Old Times* i. 14 Boy after boy managed to get on the river. **1885** GRANT *Personal Mem.* I. 288 There were also many men . . . whose occupation had been following the river in various capacities from captain down to deck hand. **1893** 'MARK TWAIN' *P. Wilson* iii, Percy Driscoll slept well the night he saved his house-minions from going down the river. **1894** *Ib.* ix, Ole Marse Driscoll 'll sell you down de river. **1901** 'FLYNT' *World of Graft* 98 He was doin' fence work in York, an' I helped send 'im up the river for eight years.

II. *attrib.* and *comb.* **3.** Designating lands, usually for cultivation, situated on rivers.

See also RIVER BLUFF, RIVER FLAT 1, etc.

1704 *Conn. Rec.* IV. 493 A debt [is] due to Nathaniel Holt of Rhode Island for . . . part of a lot called the River lot. **1798** *Steele P.* I. 159 There is as fine an appearance of a Crop of Corn and Tobacco both at your River plantation as there ever was. **1817** S. BROWN *Western Gazetteer* 45 There are two kinds of these meadows—the *river* and *upland* prairies. **1819** E. DANA *Geogr. Sk.* 188 The river cane bottom land, we suppose to be equal in fertility to any on the continent. **1883** SMITH *Geol. Survey Ala.* 456 Nearly all of township 16 in this county is second-bottom or river-hummock land. **1892** *Vt. Agric. Rep.* XII. 132 Our hill farms . . . [are] not as productive . . . as our river farms.

4. Designating or pertaining to navigation, travel, or commerce on rivers.

1819 *N. Amer. Rev.* VIII. 9 A complete river navigation, on the best principles, in time, [may be] effected. **1851** CIST *Cincinnati* 318 It must tap the river travel at Cairo. **1871** GROSVENOR *Protection* 104 The lake and river tonnage built amounted to 14,475. **1892** *S. Dak. Hist. Coll.* I. 52 Fifteen of the hardest roughs employed in the river trade saw him passing the rude saloon. **1907** LONDON *Road* 183 The company formation was hopelessly broken up during the river-trip.

5. Designating persons or groups of persons who work or carry on operations adjacent to or upon a river.

See also RIVER DRIVER, RIVERMAN, etc.

1828 *Western Mo. Rev.* II. 14 River voyagers have run with pale faces to the 'Navigator,' when they have seen their boat approaching a dangerous place. **1841** CIST *Cincinnati* 43 Pedlars, river traders. **1864** NORTON *Army Lett.* 212 Company K is provost guard and river patrol. **1875** 'MARK TWAIN' *Old Times* ii. 34 We had a fine company of these river-inspectors along. **1883** GOODE *Amer. Fishes* 434 For the benefit of our river fishermen I quote two recipes. **1894** *Outing* XXIV. 57/1 One of the 'river-farmers,' as we style the owners of fat bottom-lands, had asked me to join him for a day's 'slopping round.' **1903** A. ADAMS *Log of Cowboy* 16 There was also present a river guard. **1908** WHITE *Riverman* 43 Only at the very last . . . did the river-jacks . . . zigzag calmly to shore.

6. Designating ways or thoroughfares on or by a river.

See also RIVER ROAD, RIVER STREET.

1832 *Louisville Directory* 102 The river route for emigrants was considered more dangerous than through the interior by land. **1835** SIMMS *Yemassee* II. 115 After a while came the tread of a horse rapidly driving up the river-trace. a**1862** THOREAU *Maine Woods* 251 The Allegash . . . here consists principally of a chain of large and stagnant lakes, whose thoroughfares, or river-links, have been made nearly equally stagnant by damming. **1902** WHITE *Blazed Trail* 211 The little procession . . . took its way up the river-trail.

7. Designating diseases prevalent in river regions.

1845 HOOPER *Taking Census* 157 The 'river ager' made Sol shake worse than that. **1853** STOWE *Key* 27/1 His young master was taken violently down with the river fever.

8. Designating mining operations, or places for mining, on or adjacent to rivers.

1850 A. T. JACKSON *Forty-Niner* (1920) 7 He is crazy on river mining. **1851** D. B. WOODS *At Gold Diggings* 13 The 'river diggings' include the bars and auriferous portions of the channels of the tributaries. **1871** RAYMOND *3d Rep. Mines* 128 *River sluicing.*—The future of the region under consideration will depend to a great degree on finding an outlet for its vast quantity of hydraulic dirt. **1897** *Consular Rep.* Oct. 146 Creek and river claims shall be 500 feet long.

9. In the names of fishes and other aquatic animals. (See also RIVER BASS, HERRING.)

River cat, any one of various catfish found in rivers; *r. chub*, (see quotation); *r. salmon*, the ordinary fresh-water salmon; *r. seal*, a seal which ascends rivers; *r. shrimp*, (see quotation).

1770 WASHINGTON *Diaries* I. 419 At this place . . . we found a Cat fish of the size of our largest River Cats. **1884** GOODE, etc. *Fisheries* I. 617 The 'Horny-head,' 'River Chub,' or 'Jerker' is one of the most widely-diffused of fresh-water fishes. **1888** GOODE *Amer. Fishes* 440 River-salmon, not anadromous. **1851** *Zoologist* IX. 3298 The fur-seal and river-seal are found. **1883** *Nat. Museum Bul.* No. 27, 117 The River Shrimp (*Palæmon Ohionis*) . . . occurs in the rivers of the Mississippi Valley.

10. In the names of plants. (See also RIVER BIRCH.)

River cottonwood, r. crowfoot, r. hawthorn, (see quotations); *r. maple,* red or swamp maple; *r. nymph,* the Virginia or scarlet strawberry; *r. pink,* a local name for the pink azalea, *Azalea nudiflora; r. swallow-wort,* a local name for a plant of the genus *Apocynum* found near streams.

1884 SARGENT *Rep. Forests* 172 *Populus heterophylla.* . . . River Cottonwood. Swamp Cottonwood. **1814** BIGELOW *Florula Bostoniensis* 139 *Ranunculus fluviatilis.* River crowfoot. . . . [Grows] in deep water. June. **1869** *Amer. Naturalist* III. 406 River Hawthorn (*Cratægus rivularis*). A hawthorn with black berries, . . . forming a shrubby tree fifteen to twenty feet high. **1851** SPRINGER *Forest Life* 25 It is said that the wood of this tree [Rock Maple] may be easily distinguished from the Red, or the River Maple. **1821** *Mass. H. S. Coll.* 2 Ser. IX. 150 Plants, which are indigenous in the township of Middlebury [Vermont include] . . . *Fluvialis fragilis?* Fescue grass, *Fragaria virginiana,* River nymph. **1892** *Amer. Folk-Lore* V. 100 *Rhododendron nudiflorum,* river pink. Cavendish, Vt. **1784** *Amer. Acad. Mem.* I. 423 *Apocynum.* . . . River Swallowwort. Blossoms yellowish white. At Winnipesoket-falls, in Providence-river. July.

11. In special combinations.

River and harbor bill, a congressional bill providing funds for improving the navigability and port facilities of rivers and harbors; *r. band,* (see quotation); *r. boot,* a boot of a type worn by lumberjacks; *r. connection,* a way or means of traveling by river; *r. divide,* a ridge separating the waters flowing into different rivers or river basins; *r. gambling,* gambling carried on aboard a river boat; *r. gold,* gold obtained from river diggings; *r. horn,* (see quotation); *r. island,* an island in a river; *r. landing,* a place on a river where goods and passengers are taken aboard or discharged; *r. life,* life or activity on or along a river; *r. log,* a log floating on a river; *r. report,* (see quotation); *r. shed,* a ridge or high ground between two rivers or river systems; *r. storm,* a storm in a river valley; *r. trunk,* the main stream or body of a river; *r. wash,* soil washed down and deposited by a stream; *r. yarn,* a story of river life.

1846 *Whig Almanac 1847* 38 The River and Harbor bill . . . was vetoed by the President. **1778** CARVER *Travels* 59 Near the River St. Croix reside three bands of the Nawdowessie Indians, called the River Bands. **1902** WHITE *Blazed Trail* 186 The long spikes of river-boots made an admirable weapon in the straight kick. **1851** CIST *Cincinnati* 320 Our river connections, canals, and turnpikes, are not embraced. **1876** Raymond *8th Rep. Mines* 68 The lateral ridges or present river-divides terminate to the east of them abruptly. **1866** MOORE *Women of War* 308 Before the war he had lived at Memphis and on the river, following the cognate and equally infamous branches of business, negro-trading and river gambling. **1890** HARTE *Heritage of Dedlow Marsh* 209 If we happen to strike river gold, thar's the stream for washing it. **1829** *Western Mo. Rev.* III. 16 A wooden trumpet, called a river horn [was] formerly used by keel and flat boat navigators on the western waters. **1913** LONDON *Valley of Moon* 479 I wouldn't trade a square mile of this kind of country for the whole Sacramento Valley, with the river islands thrown in and Middle River for good measure. **1851** CIST *Cincinnati* 198 The Phoenix Foundery, belonging to this firm, [is located] at the intersection of Smith street with the river landing. **1883** *Harper's Mag.* Oct. 799/2 [The Mississippi R.] was the arena on which all shades of Western and Southern river life and character were profusely displayed. **1850** JUDD *R. Edney* 357 The river-logs . . . are sometimes carried high up the bank. **1878** *Harper's Mag.* Dec. 95/2 At stations from which river reports are furnished, an observation of the depth and temperature of the water is made and reported . . . each day. **1682** *Southold Rec.* I. 385 Voated . . . that farmers to the westward [shall] repaire the highways to the Westward as far as the Rivershead. **1834** BRACKENRIDGE *Recollections* 20 We encountered a river storm, not many miles from the Mississippi. **1852** *Knickerb.* XL. 50 Rock-fish and trout at the mouths of the river-trunks are caught without trouble by the winders. **1910** RAINE *B. O'Connor* 224 Three men followed the riverwash beyond the limits of the town. **1901** CHURCHILL *Crisis* 334 Never had the Captain's river yarns been better told than at the table that evening.

***River.**[2] One who rives boards, shingles, etc. — **1640** *Mass. H. S. Coll.* 4 Ser. VI. 90 Wee are bold to intreat your . . . helpe for the suppressing pipe staff riuers and clabords in our towne. **1775** [see FROE].

River bar. A long, comparatively narrow formation of sand or gravel in or beside a river, esp. one containing gold-bearing soil. — **1874** RAYMOND *6th Rep. Mines* 20 A large percentage of the coarse gold contained in the gravel taken from the gulches and river-bars . . . was deposited along the beds of the streams farther down. **1882** *47th Congress 1 Sess.* H. R. Ex. Doc. No. 216, 108 The McGillivray mining property includes a number of low river bars. **1897** *Educational Rev.* Jan. 91 The spits and reefs along the South Atlantic coast of the United States are not river bars but wave formations.

+**River bass.** Any one of certain species of fresh-water fish, esp. black bass, found in the eastern United States. — **1877** *Smithsonian Misc. Coll.* XIII. IX. 20 River-Bass, *Lepomis.* **1883** *Century Mag.* July 376/2 The black bass . . . have received names somewhat descriptive of their habitat, as, lake, river, marsh, pond, . . . and Oswego bass. **1890** HOWELLS *Boy's Town* 30 There were men who were reputed to catch at will, as it were, silvercats and river-bass.

+**River birch.** **1.** The red birch, *Betula nigra.* **2.** (See quotation.) — **(1) 1884** SARGENT *Rep. Forests* 161 Red Birch. River Birch. . . . Used in the manufacture of furniture, woodenware, wooden shoes, ox-yokes, etc. **1892** APGAR *Trees Northern U.S.* 147 River or Red Birch. . . . Wild in Massachusetts, south and west; often cultivated. **1894** COULTER *Bot. W. Texas* III. 413 River or Red birch. . . . Banks of streams. **(2) 1897** SUDWORTH *Arborescent Flora* 142 *Betula lenta.* Sweet Birch. . . . River Birch (Minn.).

+**River bluff.** A high, steep bank of a river, or the top of such a bank. — **1817** S. BROWN *Western Gazetteer* 203 The garrison is situated on the river bluffs. **1869** FULLER *Flower Gatherers* 122 They love rocky hills and river-bluffs. **1902** WISTER *Virginian* xxv, Against the empty ridge of the river-bluff lay the moon.

***River boat.** A steamboat used in river traffic. — **1851** *Harper's Mag.* Aug. 424/2 Mind travels with us on . . . a high-pressure river-boat. **1877** HALE *G. T. T.* 73 River boats never came as early as they said they should. **1885** *Century Mag.* April 923/2 The only Confederate vessel then in commission was a small river-boat. **1891** C. ROBERTS *Adrift Amer.* 16 This was the first time that I ever saw a real Mississippi river boat.

+River bottom. Low level land along the margin of a river.

1752 GIST *Journals* 75 The River Bottoms . . . were a Mile wide and very rich. **1814** BRACKENRIDGE *Views La.* 29 The river bottoms being generally fine. **1850** *Western Journal* IV. 322 The apple orchards were all in the river bottoms. **1885** *Rep. Indian Affairs* 176 The farming lands are scattered along the river bottoms. **1916** EASTMAN *From Deep Woods* 5 Most of us hugged the wooded river bottoms.

attrib. **1809** CUMING *Western Tour* 323 The river bottom lands generally yield from eighteen hundred to two thousand pounds to the acre. **1862** *Rep. Comm. Patents 1861: Agric.* 282 This [corn] was a river-bottom crop.

+**River Brethren.** A Baptist denomination resembling the Mennonites, organized about 1770 among Swiss immigrants in Pennsylvania, and subsequently divided into distinct factions adopting other names. — **1865** BELCHER *Relig. Denominations U.S.* 913 Others were organized into a body called, *The River Brethren*, partly from the locality in which they were first found, near the Susquehanna and Conestoga, and chiefly from their baptisms being celebrated only in rivers. **1867** DIXON *New America* II. 309 No sect escaped this rage for separation, for independence, for individuality; neither Unitarian, nor Omish; nor River Brethren, nor Winebrennarians. **1919** *Census: Religious Bodies 1916* II. 177/2 The general term 'River Brethren' was given to the entire body.

River channel. **1.** The bed or course of a river. {1833-} +**2.** (See quot. 1880.) — **(1) 1704** *Providence Rec.* XI. 81 The Towne surveior only laid out . . . a Piece of land forty foote square, & there being Considerable land betweene it and the River Channill [etc.]. **(2) 1871** RAYMOND *3d Rep. Mines* 185 So far we have no more than cracked the shell of our mines, the core and heart still lying in the hills and old river-channels. **1880** INGHAM *Digging Gold* 46 The class of deposits known as the ancient river channels or the 'blue lead' of California . . . are gold-bearing gravels found deep beneath the surface.

+**River driver.** (See quot. 1848.) — **1848** BARTLETT 276 *River Driver*, a term used by lumbermen in Maine, for a man whose business it is to conduct logs down running streams, to prevent them from lodging upon shoals or remaining in eddies. **1861** C. L. FLINT *80 Years Progress* (1872) 93/2 [When] there is sufficient freshet to float the timber, another gang, called 'river drivers,' takes charge of it. **1895** WIGGIN *Village Watch-Tower* 6 With the parting of the boom . . . and the shouts of the river-drivers, the little Lucinda had come into the world. **1910** *Springfield W. Repub.* 7 July 14 Maine lumbermen enjoy telling the casual summer visitor how great is the skill of their cant men and river drivers.

River duck. Any one of various ducks that frequent fresh water, as distinguished from a sea duck. {1837-} — **1874** COUES *Birds N.W.* 559 River Ducks. . . . Wild throughout the whole of North America. **1883** *Nat. Museum Bul.* No. 27, 141 With the exception of the 'shore birds' . . . , 'marsh birds' . . . , and the herbivorous Anatidæ (swans, geese, and river ducks), all water birds may be said to be piscivorous to a greater or less degree. **1917** *Birds of Amer.* I. 114 The River Ducks . . . get most of their food by searching the bottom in water so shallow that diving is not necessary.

+**River elm.** (See quot. 1817-8.) — **1817-8** EATON *Botany* (1822) 496 *Ulmus nemoralis*, river-elm, grove-elm. **1845** LINCOLN *Botany* App. 180/1. **1852** MARCY *Explor. Red River* (1854) 76 It is fringed upon each side with . . . river-elm.

River flat. **1.** A level extent of land along a river. {1862} +**2.** A flatboat for use on a river. — **(1) 1800** HAWKINS *Sk. Creek Country* 47 On the right side, off from the river flats, the land is waving. **1835** HOFFMAN *Winter in West* II. 60 The prairies . . . resemble what at the North are called 'river-*flats*,' or natural meadows. **(2) 1829** *Free Press* (Tarboro, N.C.) 27 Nov., The Subscribers will proceed to sell at the Grove, . . . Two excellent River Flats.

River front. Land, esp. in a city, fronting on a river.

1855 *Chicago W. Times* 16 Jan. 1/1 To lease for a term of years. 200 feet river front, ready docked. **1862** MCCLELLAN in *Own Story* 634 Our cavalry has been engaged in picketing and scouting one hundred and fifty miles of river-front ever since the battle of Antietam. **1880** *Harper's Mag.* Dec. 53 The magic wand which . . . transforms the river-front of Pittsburgh . . . is the sudden advent of a 'coal-boat' stage of water. **1898** WESTCOTT *D. Harum* 151 Some fellers . . . are talkin' of startin' a plant here, an' it ain't out o' sight that they'd pay a good price fer the river front. **1901** CHURCHILL *Crisis* 3 The low houses . . . crowded on the broad river front.

+**River grape.** A species of wild grape (*Vitis vulpina*) found along rivers in the eastern and southern states. (Cf. CHICKEN GRAPE.) — **1859** [see CHICKEN GRAPE]. **1901** MOHR *Plant Life Ala.* 108 The river grape . . . [is] also found on the bare ledges of these bluffs.

+**River grass.** Grass growing in or near a river: (see also quot. 1889). — **1856** *Porter's Spirit of Times* 18 Oct. 113/2 The Carp must be angled for . . . in the vicinity of banks of weeds, water-lilies, or river-grass. **1889** VASEY *Agric. Grasses* 25 *Panicum Texanum* (Texas Millet). . . . In some localities it is known as river grass.

+**River herring.** **1.** The mooneye, *Hiodon tergisus.* **2.** =ALEWIFE 1. — **(1) 1842** *Nat. Hist. N.Y., Zoology* IV. 266 [The river mooneye] is known under the popular names of *Herring, River Herring,* and *Toothed Herring.* **(2) 1884** *Century Mag.* April 909 The different townships on Cape Cod protect the alewife, or 'river herring.' **1903** *N.Y. State Museum Bul.* No. 60, 199 The branch herring, river herring or alewife has a variety of additional names.

+**River hill.** A hill or stretch of elevated ground adjacent to a river. — **1818** FLINT *Lett. from Amer.* 103 The high grounds every where seen from the river, are called the river hills. **1834** in *Atlantic Mo.* XXVI. 491/2 Hemlock trees . . . [are found] on river hills. **1842** *Amer. Pioneer* I. 431, I was coming to the river hill.

+**River Indians.** (See quot. 1910.) — **a1704** *Mass. H. S. Coll.* 2 Ser. V. 33 Betwixt Kenebecke and Connecticut were . . . the River Indians, such who had seated themselves in several commodious plantations up higher upon Connecticut river. **1754** *Ib.* 3 Ser. V. 33 A considerable number of Indians from Stockbridge, being of the nation known by the name of the River Indians, were in town. **1774** *Doc. Hist. N.Y. State* I. 765 These Tribes have generally been denominated River Indians and consist of about Three hundred Fighting Men. **1910** HODGE, etc. *Amer. Indians* II. 392/2 *River Indians.* Used by Hubbard . . . as a collective term for the Indians formerly living on Connecticut r. above the coast tribes.

+**River land.** Land, esp. cultivable land, along a river. {1899} — **1781** PETERS *Hist. Conn.* 242 One acre commonly yields . . . from 40 to 60 bushels [of Indian corn] on river land. **1805** *Raleigh* (N.C.) *Register* 28 April, That valuable Plantation containing about one thousand Acres of River and Back Land. **1833** SILLIMAN *Man. Sugar Cane* 21 If, however, river lands . . . are selected, upon such I would unquestionably plant the Ribbon Cane. **1872** EGGLESTON *End of World* 283, I have only kept the river land.

Riverlet. =RIVULET. {1883-} — **1674** *New Eng. Hist. & Gen. Register* IV. 34, I give to my son . . . my house and home lot on the South side of the riverlet. **1704** *Conn. Hist. Soc. Coll.* VI. 272 Their Should be four houses fortyfied . . . , Two of which [are] to be on the north side of the Riverlett.

Riverman. One employed in traffic on a river {1722-}, +esp. a lumberjack. — **1830** COOPER *Water Witch* II. i, But we prate like gossiping river-men. **1845** SOL. SMITH *Theatr. Apprent.* 143 He stood in the front rank of that host of industrious and enterprising citizens known as River Men! **1875** 'MARK TWAIN' *Old Times* ii. 41 It was some little time, too, before his exploit ceased to be talked about by the river men. **1902** WHITE *Blazed Trail* 331 The riverman always mysteriously appeared at one side or the other. **1908** — *Riverman* 61 Each of these rivermen had two or three hundred dollars to 'blow' as soon as possible.

+**River meadow.** A stretch of level grassy land along a river. — **1854** [see FARMER BOY]. **1854** THOREAU *Walden* 256 In October I went a-graping to the river meadows. **1892** *Vt. Agric. Rep.* XII. 142 Fifty to seventy-five bushels of corn are raised on the river meadows.

+**River pilot.** One whose occupation is guiding or directing the course of a river boat. — **1883** *Harper's Mag.* Oct. 799/2 Mr. Clemens . . . in his character, first, as an apprentice to the occupation of a river pilot, . . . describes the characteristic features of the river. **1890** LANGFORD *Vigilante Days* (1912) 338 Captain Ankeny, an old river pilot, . . . knew every crook and rock in the channel.

+**River pirate.** One who engages in thievery and other piratical activities on or along a river. — **1860** [see COUNTERFEITER]. **1878** PINKERTON *Strikers* 229 River pirates of the lowest and most savage order came creeping up the Ohio. **1887** *Courier-Journal* 31 Jan. 8/1 The drift from above caused by the rise has about all passed, and the river-pirates were busy in their skiffs collecting it.

+**River rat.** A designation, usually of contempt or depreciation, for one who works or lives chiefly on a river. *colloq.* — **1884** *Harper's Mag.* March 513/1 Observe the river-rats clustering about the groggeries. **1897** BRODHEAD *Bound in Shallows* 31 She was a black-skinned little river-rat living yonder in the boom-house. **1905** *Forestry Bureau Bul.* No. 61, 44 *River rat*, a log driver whose work is chiefly on the river; contrasted with Laker. (N[orthern] F[orest].)

River road. A road along a river. — **1829** SHERWOOD *Gaz. Georgia* (ed. 2) 167/2 At Parker's . . . take a left hand, leaving the river road. **1862** Moore *Rebellion Rec.* V. II. 571 His infantry . . . passed through to that same river-road, and escaped. **1877** *Harper's Mag.* April 685/1, I followed the narrow river road along the banks. **1905** WIGGIN *Rose* 151 They saw Mr. Wiley driving down the river road.

***Riverside, River side.** The side or bank of a river; the side of a city bordering upon a river.

1624 in *Amer. Speech* XV. 385/1 The Land of William Prickett Conteyning by the river side ninetye and twoe pole. **1678** *Conn. Hist. Soc. Coll.* VI. 185 Thayr voate granted . . . a peice of land . . . beetwene goodman Cadwells ware house and the landing place . . . by the Riuer side. **a1817** DWIGHT *Travels* II. 77 He determined to make his way . . . to Hatfield by the river-side. **a1862** THOREAU *Maine Woods* 294, I should have so far to go to get to the river-side when he wanted me. **1897** C. A. DANA *Recoll. Civil War* 85 Admiral Porter . . . commanded the fleet which hemmed in the city on the river-side.

attrib. **1760** WASHINGTON *Diaries* I. 153 [No.] 3 Has 2 Pecks of sd. Earth and 1 of Riverside Land. **1881** *Amer. Naturalist* XV. 31 This belt of riverside timber is occupied by the Yuma Indians. **1891** COULTER *Bot. W. Texas* I. 63 Riverside grape. . . . Stream banks or near water.

River steamboat. A steamboat designed for service on rivers. {1851- (Mayhew *London Labour* III. 343)} — **1857** STACEY *Journal* 28 What an immense difference we find between the quiet Sundays at home and the bustling ones on board these river steamboats. **1865** *Atlantic Mo.* Jan. 81/1 The American river-steamboat . . . is another of the means by which Art has supplemented New York's gifts of Nature. **1913** LONDON *Valley of Moon* 432 Occasionally a river steamboat passed.

River steamer. =prec. {1851- (see prec.)} — **1833** COKE *Subaltern's Furlough* v, The American river steamers are noble vessels. **1851** *Knickerb.* XXXVIII. 469 So shall you see what our river-steamers are; what themes of just pride they are to every New-Yorker. **1866** GREGG *Life in Army* 247 The 'Commonwealth' was a first-class river-steamer. **1894** *S. Dak. Hist. Coll.* I. 288 An elevation gently sloping toward the river . . . affords good landing at the point where the river steamer Goddin lands her freight.

River street. A street along a river. — **1865** TAYLOR in *Atlantic Mo.* Jan. 17/1 The droshkies waited in the river-street a quarter of a mile below us. **1876** 'MARK TWAIN' *Tom Sawyer* 222 They moved up the river street three blocks. **1877** *Harper's Mag.* Jan. 301/2 It is not the pleasantest thing in the world to be obliged to pick your way through the river streets to the ferry.

+**River swamp.** A low region adjacent to a river, usually subject to overflow. — **1737** WESLEY *Journal* I. 402 Most river-swamps are overflown every tide by the river which runs through or near them. **1771** HABERSHAM *Letters* 145 The Rice in the River Swamps ripened uneven. **1826** FLINT *Recoll.* 262, I travelled forty miles along this river swamp. **1855** SIMMS *Forayers* 209 The river swamp is our hope just now.

+**River thief.** (See quot. 1859.) *Obs.* — **1859** BARTLETT 368 *River-Thief*, one of a class of thieves in New York city who in boats prowl about vessels at night and plunder them. **1882** McCABE *New York* 402 [They] look under the piers for the concealed boats of river thieves. *Ib.* 518 Another dangerous class of criminals are the river thieves, or 'River Pirates.'

+**River town.** A town on a river. — **1853** *Harper's Mag.* March 566/1 Scenes not in all respects unlike it have heretofore occurred . . . in certain of the chivalric river towns of the Southwest. **1864** NICHOLS *Amer. Life* I. 165 At the mouth of the Cumberland is a little straggling, wild, half-civilized river-town called Smithland. **1883** 'MARK TWAIN' *Life on Miss.* i, These cut-offs . . . have thrown several river towns out into the rural districts. **1907** *St. Nicholas* Aug. 948/1 Old river towns . . . have succumbed to the influence of the railroads.

Riverweed. {1671-} +Any one of various American aquatic plants of the genus *Podostemon*. Also attrib. — **1832** WILLIAMSON *Maine* I. 128 We have, also, . . . *Oar-weed, River-weed*, and *Succory*, as common herbs. **1867** *Atlantic Mo.* March 280/1 Sometimes a mere dark mass of river-weed would be floated by the tide past the successive stations. **1894** *Outing* XXIV. 366/2 They were quite ready to accept Horace Campbell's proposal to . . . try for pike at the hour when these fish are most eagerly prowling through their river-weed jungles.

+**River work.** Work done on a river. — **1865** *Atlantic Mo.* April 423/1 The John Adams . . . was an old East-Boston ferry-boat, . . . admirable for river-work. **1903** WHITE *Forest* 95, I instanced, too, some of the feats of river-work these men could perform.

***Rivet.** A short bolt the headless end of which is swaged to prevent retraction.

1810 *Austin P.* I. (1924) 168, 100 Rivets. **1869** *Boyd's Business Directory* 22 Buttons and Rivets. U.S. Patent Button and Rivet Company, 110 Leonard. **1907** *St. Nicholas* Oct. 1113/1 The rivets are heated. **1921** PAINE *Comr. Rolling Ocean* 175 She was staunch to the last rivet and angle-iron.

b. Attrib. and comb. with *clipper, company, cutter, machine.*

1868 *Mich. Agric. Rep.* VII. 362 T. Hogler, Grass Lake, [exhibited a] carriage bolt and rivet cutter. **1869** Rivet company [see prec.]. **1882** *47th Congress 1 Sess.* H. R. Ex. Doc. No. 216, 596 In this class belong rolling mills, bolt and rivet machines. **1883** KNIGHT *Suppl.* 759/2 *Rivet Clipper*, a tool like a bolt cutter for clipping the superfluous length of rivets before swaging the end.

Riveting machine. (See quot. 1876.) {1843-} — **1859** *Rep. Comm. Patents 1858* I. 562 Improved Riveting Machine. **1876** KNIGHT 1948/1 *Riveting-machine*, . . . a machine in which the operation of riveting boiler or other metallic plates is performed by steam-power. Its general principle is that of the punching-machine. **1883** *Ib.* 760/2 Small riveting machines are used for closing rivets on small articles of wear and convenience, such as brogans, boots, shawl-straps, valises, etc.

***Rivulet.** A small stream or river. — **1636** *Plymouth Laws* 51 A certaine Rivolett or Runlett there [was] comonly called Coahasset. **1702** *Conn. Rec.* IV. 390 [The] ferrymen . . . attend at Hartford rivulett. **1792** [see DRAIN *n.* 2 (b)]. **1815** DRAKE *Cincinnati* 69 In the rear of most bottom lands, there are brooks or rivulets. **1887** TOURGEE *Button's Inn* 2 Here ran one branch of an impetuous rivulet.

***Rix-dollar.** A silver coin having approximately the value of a dollar, issued by various European countries. — **1643** *Conn. Rec.* I. 86 Good Rialls of 8/8 and Reix Dollers shall passe betwixt man & man att fiue shillings a peece. **1715** *Boston News-Letter* 8 Aug. 1/2 There is about 80000 Rixdollars of the Coin struck [in Sweden]. **1741** *N.J. Archives* 1 Ser. VI. 118 Old Rix dollars of the Empire, eighteen penny weight and ten grains, four shillings and six pence.

***Roach,** *n.*[1] Also †**roch.** +**a.** Any of various cyprinoid or similar fresh-water fishes other than the carp. +**b.** Any of various sunfishes.

1637 MORTON *New Canaan* 91 There are in the rivers, and ponds, very excellent . . . Roches, Perches, Tenches, Eeles, and other fish. **1698** THOMAS *Pensilvania* 13 And for Fish, there are prodigious quantities of most sorts, . . . Roach, Eels [etc.]. **1709** LAWSON *Carolina* 160 We have . . . the same Roach; only scarce so large [as that in England]. **1799** WELD *Travels* 80 The Patowmac . . . abounds with . . . shad, roach, herrings, &c. **1832** WILLIAMSON *Maine* I. 159 The *Roach*, though rather scarce, is found in fresh ponds. **1848** THOREAU *Maine Woods* 59 Each [stood] with a sharpened stick . . . upon which he had spitted his trout, or roach, previously well gashed and salted. **1870** *Amer. Naturalist* IV. 100 A week later we found a few roach (*Stilbe Americana*). **1884** [see FALLFISH]. **1903** T. H. BEAN *Fishes N.Y.* 6 The roach is a common resident of lakes in New York and Brooklyn parks. *Ib.* 582 Other names for the species [*Leiostomus xanthurus*] are goody, oldwife, roach and chub. **1911** *Rep. Fisheries 1908* 314/2 Roach (*Semotilus corporalis*).—The largest chub found east of the Rocky Mountains.

+**Roach,** *n.*[2] Any of the various annoying or destructive insects called cockroaches, as *Blattella germanica* and *Periplaneta americana.* {1898} Also attrib. (Cf. CROTON BUG.) — **1837** B. D. WALSH tr. *Comedies Aristophanes* (1848) 89*n.*, 'Cock-roaches' in the United States . . . are always called 'roaches' by the fair sex, for the sake of euphony. **1853** 'P. PAXTON' *Yankee in Texas* 163 Texas, in fact, may be entomologically divided into . . . the ant country and the roach and flea country. **1892** [see COCKROACH]. **1925** HERRICK *Man. Injurious Insects* 454 Sodium fluoride has proved very effective for roaches in dwellings and store rooms.

Roach, *n.*[3] {1794-} +**1.** A roll of hair brushed upward. *colloq.* Also attrib. +**2.** An upward curve in the back of an animal. — **(1) 1884** HARRIS *Mingo* 43 Nor was his ideal of feminine beauty reached by the village belles, with their roach-combs. **1885** 'CRADDOCK' *Prophet* 17 His grizzled hair stood up in front after the manner denominated 'a roach.' **1898** DELAND *Old Chester Tales* 93 His yellow hair . . . every afternoon was curled up into a long, sleek roll called a 'roach,' and tied with a blue ribbon. **(2) 1889** *Century Mag.* Jan. 335/1 [The Texas pony has] a very long body, with a pronounced roach just forward of the coupling.

Roach, *v.* {1851-}

+**1.** *tr.* To trim the mane of (an animal); to clip (an animal's mane). Also *vbl. n.*

1818 *Missouri Gazette* 25 Dec. 4/5 His mane has been divided, and laid on both sides of his neck, and that part that laid on the left side, cut off as if to roach him. **1889** *Century Mag.* Jan. 335/2, I roached his mane and docked his tail. **1903** *N.Y. Ev. Post* 24 Oct., When brought to market he [the mule] undergoes the process of 'roaching,' which consists of removing all the hair of poor quality and scanty growth. **1919** WILSON *Ma Pettengill* 29, I had the boys . . . put each one of the cunning little mites [mules] into the chute and roach it so as to put a bow in its neck.

+**2.** To brush a person's (hair) upward.

1853 BALDWIN *Flush Times Ala.* 108 His hair was roached up, and stood as erect and upright as his body. **1894** 'MARK TWAIN' *Those Twins* v, The Judge . . . roached his gray hair up with his fingers. **1907** STEWART *Partners* 414 Clancy had took a shave and roached his hair.

+**Roachback.** Any animal with an upwardly curved back. — **1874** *Vermont Bd. Agric. Rep.* II. 402 Old Brown Dick was a roach-back, . . . while the buckskin McClellan was a regular hollow or sway back. **1893** ROOSEVELT *Wilderness Hunter* 266 Any bear with unusually long hair on the spine and shoulders . . . is forthwith dubbed a 'roach-back.' **1900**

SETON *Biog. of Grizzly* 135 The Roachbacks, as the Bitter-root Grizzlies are called, are a cunning and desperate race.

+Roach dace. (See quotation.) — **1842** *Nat. Hist. N.Y., Zoology* IV. 208 The Roach Dace. *Leuciscus pulchellus.* . . . According to Dr. Storer this species is found in the Eastern States.

+Roached, *a.*

1. Having an upward curve.

1776 *New Eng. Chron.* 25 Jan. (Th.), Strayed or stolen, a sorrel horse—roach'd back, 3 white feet. **1844** W. L. BROWN *Scribblings & Sk.* 176 (Th.), The two [horses] with roatched backs, and ears glued to their necks, were scrambling.

2. Of hair: Trimmed and brushed upward.

1790 *Augusta* (Ga.) *Chronicle* 13 March 3/1 (Th. S.), A Bay Horse, roached mane and a small switched tail. **1836** *S. Lit. Messenger* II. 303 [There were] rows of nags of all sorts and sizes, from the skeleton just unhitched from the plow, to the saucy, fat, impudent pony, with roached mane and bobtail. **1856** CARTWRIGHT *Autobiog.* 141 This young man had a mighty bushy roached head of hair.

+Roach mane. A horse's mane trimmed to within an inch or two of the skin. — **1781** *Royal Georgia Gaz.* 8 March (Th.), A Black Horse, about 13 and an half hands high, half roach main. **1835** J. T. IRVING *Indian Sk.* II. 4 She was mounted upon a little wall-eyed, cream-coloured pony, with a roach mane and a bobtail.

* Road, *n.*

I. *1. A sheltered stretch of water near shore. {–1720}

1622 'MOURT' *Relation* 46 [We] found there a fayre income or rode, of a Bay. **1654** *New Haven Col. Rec.* 70 He gaue his men order to goe out of ye harbour into the roade. **1697** SEWALL *Diary* I. 457 Johnson's ship was burnt in Charlestown Rode. **1720** [see CUT *v.* 20 a]. **1757** W. SMITH *Hist. N.Y.* 187 The Ships lie off in the Roads, on the East Side of the Town. **1778** *Essex Inst. Coll.* LII. 5 That night we anchored in the road. **1850** TAYLOR *Eldorado* iv, Those [vessels] which are obliged to lie in the open road are exposed to considerable danger.

*2. A way for communication and transportation, usually wide enough for vehicles.

See also COUNTRY ROAD, MACADAMIZED ROAD, etc.; GOOD-ROADS.

1639 *Conn. Hist. Soc. Coll.* VI. 5 All the fences to the great River to winser road shall be mended. **1675** *Providence Rec.* IV. 28 This towne . . . [has] in Consideration . . . A high way & a Comon Roade through that percell of Land. **1701** *Penna. Col. Rec.* II. 33 Ordered, That Nicholas Pyle, Saml. Lewis, Geo. Maires & Randal Vernon . . . view the Controverted parts of the said Road. **1752** W. TRENT *Journal* 79 They have opened up a road . . . with a land carriage only of eighty miles. **1803** *Ann. 8th Congress* 2 Sess. 1521 Instead of paying local taxes, each inhabitant is bound to make and repair roads, bridges, and embankments through his own land. **1854** BENTON *30 Years' View* I. 43/2 Formerly Indian traders followed 'traces:' now they must have roads. **1880** INGHAM *Digging Gold* 297 There is a good road from Spearfish City to the Blossburg coal bank. **1920** *3d Nat. Country Life Conf. Proc.* 93 Leading out from Springfield . . . are 50 miles of macadam roads.

+b. *Cumberland road,* = NATIONAL ROAD 2.

1816 *Ann. 14th Congress* 2 Sess. 21 Except the Cumberland road, the United States possesses neither canals nor canals, on which to legislate. **1854** BENTON *30 Years' View* I. 22/1 The Cumberland road, and the Chesapeake and Ohio canal, were the two prominent objects discussed. **1906** [see NATIONAL ROAD 2].

+3. = BUFFALO TRACE.

1765 CROGHAN *Journal* 13 We came into a large road which the buffaloes have beaten, spacious enough for two wagons to go abreast, and leading straight into the Lick. **1886** Z. F. SMITH *Kentucky* 22 The hardy explorers took one of these roads, or buffalo traces, as they are called and known even yet.

+4. a. The track over which railroad trains travel. **b.** A railroad company.

See also BRANCH ROAD.

1832 HONE *Diary* I. 59 The Mohawk and Hudson road is travelled by the power of a steam locomotive engine; the Saratoga, by a horse-power. **1849** CHAMBERLAIN *Ind. Gazetteer* 28 The business on this road has increased rapidly as it has been extended. **1872** TICE *Over Plains* 12 Waterville, the present terminus of the road, just one hundred miles west from here. **1880** *Harper's Mag.* Nov. 922/1 After a dusty stretch of road the train pulled up at a way-station. **1890** *Stock Grower & Farmer* 29 March 7/2 The Santa Fe road has promised to bring down a lot of buyers from Kansas. **1918** [see FREIGHT HOUSE].

5. *On the road.* {1642–} **a.** Of a circus, theatrical troupe, etc.: On tour. {1884–}

1870 O. LOGAN *Before Footlights* 367 The organ of the circus people . . . gives many curious details of circus-life Behind the Scenes, and 'on the road.' **1879** RANOUS *Diary of Daly Débutante* 62, I hear the older people tell such amusing stories of life 'on the road.' **1895** *N.Y. Dramatic News* 6 July 5/2 [He] will remain in the West until the season opens 'on the road.' **1920** *3d Nat. Country Life Proc.* 21 Several of them [*sc.* art exhibits] are already on the road.

+b. Traveling as a salesman.

1882 RITTENHOUSE *Maud* 125 Frank Metcalf . . . has to get a lot of checking done and be out on the road by ten tomorrow night. **1885** *Wkly.*

New Mexican Rev. 8 Jan. 3/6 He will start out on the road for Brittain, Richardson & Co. **1902** LORIMER *Lett. Merchant* 37, I raised his salary . . . , and put him out on the road to introduce a new product.

+c. Tramping; living as a tramp. *colloq.*

1897 'FLYNT' in *Forum* Feb. 735 It is the man who wilfully and knowingly makes a business of crime . . . that I have found in largest numbers 'on the road.' **1907** LONDON *Road* 194 As a sample of life on The Road, I make the following quotation from my diary.

II. *attrib.* and *comb.* **6.** Designating parts or appurtenances of a road.

See also ROADBED 1.

1662 *Plymouth Rec.* I. 46 The Towne have Refered the busines . . . concerning the Incroachment of Road Land upon some pte of the said land unto the deputies. **1819** *Mass. Spy* 3 Nov. (Th.), A salute was fired from a road bridge. **1853** THOMAS J. Randolph 113 It was his custom . . . [to] take his station by the road fence, leaning thereon, and stopping . . . passengers. **1865** NORTON *Army Lett.* 274 The water in the river . . . looks just like the road gutters after a heavy shower. **1897** MOORE *How to Build a Home* 5 The water ways should be intelligently studied . . . before planning the gutters, road-boxes, and sub-soil piping.

7. Designating legislative actions respecting roads.

1830 PAULDING *Chron. Gotham* 173 The great principle involved in this road bill. **1837** WETMORE *Gaz. Missouri* 17 Our representatives . . . employ their energies on unimportant subjects of discussion, such as road-laws, stray-laws, &c. **1850** *Knickerb.* XXXV. 22 His only books were a volume of almanacs, and a copy of road acts.

8. Designating persons or groups of persons who construct, maintain, or supervise roads.

See also ROAD COMMISSIONER, ROAD CUTTER, etc.

1835 HOFFMAN *Winter in West* I. 44, I hope the road-makers have not the conscience to call this Macadamizing. **1891** BUNNER *Zadoc Pine* 21 I'm a road-mender. You've got ter fill that hole up. **1898** *Kissimmee* (Fla.) *Valley Gazette* 11 Feb. 1/8 The county surveyor and road superintendent of Orange County have inspected and accepted the clayed road from Maitland to Atlamonte Springs Station. **1904** *Charlotte Observer* 17 Aug. 5 The small negro boy who attempted to set fire to the residence was sentenced to 18 months on the county road gang.

9. Designating machines used in constructing or maintaining roads.

1850 *Rep. Comm. Patents 1849* 302 Improvement in Road Scrapers. **1876** KNIGHT 1952/2 *Road-roller,* a heavy cylinder used for compacting the surfaces of a road. **1883** *Ib. Suppl.* 760/2 *Road Grader,* . . . *Road Leveler,* a scraper for leveling heaps of dumped earth thrown up to form a road. **1897** *Kissimmee* (Fla.) *Valley Gazette* 1 Dec. 4/5 Roadgrading machines are of great value in accomplishing the work. **1905** *Forestry Bureau. Bul.* No. 61, 44 *Road donkey,* a donkey engine mounted on a heavy sled, which drags logs along a skid road by winding a cable on a drum. It has a second drum for the haul-back. (P[acific] C[oast] F[orest].)

+10. Designating districts wherein the roads are kept up by local authority.

See also ROAD DISTRICT.

1858 *Texas Almanac 1859* 22 They shall also lay off these counties into road precincts, appointing an overseer for each, and designating all the hands liable to work on roads in each precinct. **1911** *Okla. Session Laws* 3 Legisl. 167 Any road improvement district . . . shall file in the office of the county clerk . . . a statement showing the total length of the line proposed.

+11. In special combinations.

Road beat, (see quotation); *r. belt,* a belt signifying an agreement with Indians for the maintenance of a road; *r. company,* a traveling theatrical company; *r. driver,* one who frequently drives a horse on the roads; *r. lottery,* a lottery to raise money for roads; *r. star,* an actor who is recognized as a star on the road outside of New York City; *r. walker,* one who walks along a railroad track to inspect it.

1895 *Dialect Notes* I. 399 Road-beat, part of the highway under the control of a single path-master. N.Y. e., s.e., Canada. **1765** CROGHAN *Journal* 156 [We] delivered them [*sc.* Indians] a Road Belt . . . to open a Road from the rising to the setting of the Sun. **1900** *Everybody's Mag.* II. 583/2 In the years of association which I have had . . . with 'road companies' I have become familiar with the types. **1897** *Boston Jrnl.* 4 Jan. 2/2 The half-mile track is convenient of access to road-drivers from the city. **1806** Road lottery [see LOTTERY OFFICE]. **1895** *N.Y. Dramatic News* 7 Dec. 11/4 Mr. Shea, already well established as a 'road' star, has quite captured New York also. **1897** *Voice* 4 March 8/1 The train was flagged by a road walker only a few feet away from the obstruction of stone and dirt on the track.

* Road, *v.* +*intr.* To travel on a road. Also *vbl. n.* — **1884** *Boston Herald* March, The horse . . . can trot better than 3 minutes and can road easy 40 miles per hour. **1890** *Atlantic Mo.* April 524/1 She accomplished forty-three miles in three hours and twenty-five minutes. This was great roading.

+Road agent. A highway robber. Also *attrib.*

1863 J. L. FISK *Exped. Rocky Mts.* 23 He had thrown away [his purse] in the grass, taking us for 'road agents.' **1874** ALDRICH *P. Palfrey* vii, That gang of marauders known as Henry Plummer's Road Agent Band . . . haunted the mountain-passes. **1876** W. M. FISHER *Californians* 74 These 'road-agents' are generally recruited among the distressed miners and farm-labourers of the mountain and country districts. **1893** ROOSEVELT *Wilderness Hunter* 412 Many of the desperadoes, the man-killers, and road-agents have good sides to their characters. **1917** McCUTCHEON *Green Fancy* 121 Book-agent by day, secret agent by night,—'gad, he may even be a road-agent.

b. *Road-agent spin,* a deft way of manipulating a revolver, supposedly used by road agents.

1908 BEACH *Barrier* 25 It was the old 'road-agent spin,' which Gale as a boy had practised hours at a time.

Roadbed. {bed of the road, *a*1825 (Loudon *Encycl. Agric.* 532)}

1. The graded surface or base of a road.

1850 *Western Journal* IV. 94 The importance of elevating a road bed above the level of the adjoining fields . . . is a fundamental requisite in making a good plank road. **1869** *Rep. Comm. Agric. 1868* 349 The road-bed is back-furrowed up. **1880** *Harper's Mag.* Nov. 925/1 A turn brings us upon scenes of wild, untutored nature, unspoiled by . . . Macadam's invention of road-bed.

2. The graded surface upon which the ties of a railroad are laid.

1840 TANNER *Canals & Railroads* 258 Road bed, that part of a rail-road upon which the superstructure reposes. **1858** W. P. SMITH *Railway Celebrations* 65 The Master of road has the general charge of all matters pertaining to the road-bed, the track [etc.]. **1885** *Wkly. New Mexican Rev.* 29 Jan. 2/6 The road bed has been laid nearly two years. **1903** E. JOHNSON *Railway Transportation* 36 The roadbed of the Columbia Railroad from Philadelphia to the Susquehanna River . . . illustrates [etc.]. **1918** *Essex Inst. Coll.* LIV. 217 The road-bed of the Boston and Maine was changed from Andover so as to pass through the south side of the new city.

+Road brand, *n.* A brand put on cattle being driven on the road: (see quotations). — **1883** SWEET & KNOX *Through Texas* 168 These are all branded with what is called the road-brand, usually a single letter, and only hair-deep. **1894** *McClure's Mag.* III. 111/2 When cattle are bought in one place to be driven to another and sold, a small, inconspicuous brand is put upon them, to protect them while on the trail; this is called a road brand. **1903** A. ADAMS *Log of Cowboy* 84 The road brand caught his eye.

+Road-brand, *v. tr.* To brand with a road brand. Also *vbl. n.* Sometimes in fig. use. — **1883** SWEET & KNOX *Through Texas* 175 He was rounded-up himself, and road-branded for the long trail. **1894** *McClure's Mag.* III. 101/1 Nothing is to be done but put a single brand on the animal, as in the case of . . . road-branding. **1903** A. ADAMS *Log of Cowboy* 12 Flood had spent the past two weeks across the river, receiving and road-branding the herd.

+Road commissioner. A county or local official who looks after or plans the construction of roads in his district. — **1829** in Commons, etc. *Doc. Hist.* I. 235 Spent the day in the board of Road Commissioners. **1842** KIRKLAND *Forest Life* I. 215 It will make him none the better road-commissioner, or supervisor. **1881** CARLETON *Farm Festivals* 146 Road Commissioner Reynolds . . . , as president, would state [etc.]. **1905** WIGGIN *Rose* 152 The road commissioner'll come along once a year.

+Road cutter. One employed to cut away brush and trees for the construction of a road. — **1755** *Lett. to Washington* I. 99 The Man is well known by Several in the Garrison, having hunted for them when they Covered the Road-Cutters. **1799** J. SMITH *Acct. Captivity* 5 My brother-in-law . . . was appointed commissioner, to have oversight of these road-cutters. **1880** *Lumberman's Gazette* 7 Jan. 28 After the log-makers come the 'road-cutters,' who clear away the brush and small logs.

+Road district. A district in which the maintenance and construction of roads are locally controlled. — **1838** *Indiana H. Rep. Jrnl.* 23 Sess. 87 The committee on roads [shall] be instructed to inquire into the expediency of increasing the size of road districts in this state. **1846** *Mich. Gen. Statutes* I. (1882) 241 There shall also be elected . . . one overseer of highways for each road district. **1869** *Rep. Comm. Agric. 1868* 352 The town trustees levy a road tax each year . . . [on] the taxable property in each road district. **1904** *Words & Phrases* 1 Ser. III. 2138 The term 'districts' means school districts, and has no reference to road districts.

+Roade, *n.* (See RODE.)

***Roader.** A horse for driving or riding on a road. {1825} — **1884** *Boston Jrnl.* 7 June, Any gentlemen wanting to purchase a strictly first-class roader or a trotter call on G. W. Gould. **1907** WIGGIN *New Chronicles of Rebecca* 153 Mr. Simpson had borrowed a 'good roader' and would himself drive the girl.

+Road hog. A person who drives down the middle of a road or in some other way prevents others from using it freely. (See HOG *n.* 1, note.) — **1898** J. PENNELL in *Harper's Mag.* April 680/2 Beware of Swiss drivers; they are the greatest 'road hogs' in Europe. **1913** LONDON *Valley of Moon* 84 You needn't be a road-hog because you're a Rube. **1922** *Commoner* Jan. 4 A pedestrian has the right of way . . . but what does it profit him if the speed-maniac and road-hog doesn't know it.

***Road horse.** A horse suitable for driving or riding on the road. {1743, 1790} — **1854** *Penna. Agric. Rep.* 130 The Committee on road horses report [etc.]. **1868** WOODRUFF *Trotting Horse* 38 Vast number of persons . . . keep good road-horses, if not fast trotters. **1894** *Vt. Agric. Rep.* XIV. 94 There has always been a demand for good road horses. **1899** [see FAMILY HORSE].

Road house. An inn or tavern alongside a road. {1857} — **1894** *Harper's Mag.* Oct. 804/2 Ye're a-keepin' a road-house, . . . one of them huckster taverns. **1909** 'O. HENRY' *Options* 104 We stopped at a road-house for dinner. **1923** WATTS *L. Nichols* 92 Mr. Nichols had had no opportunities for familiarizing himself with roadhouses.

Road map. A map showing the roads of a particular place. — **1883** *Wheelman* I. 315 The preparation of road maps and posting of guide-boards are to be important features in next season's work. **1924** *Lit. Digest* 9 Aug. 50 By using road signs and maps and inquiring your way along the road, make the jump from each village to the one that your map . . . indicates to be next.

+Roadmaster.

1. An employee of a railroad who has charge of road maintenance in a division.

1872 *Newton Kansan* 29 Aug. 3/3 Also the Walton claim . . . was sold to James Norton, road master A. T. & S. F. R.R. **1898** *Engineering Mag.* XVI. 66 The superintendent . . . is assisted by a trainmaster, a roadmaster or division engineer, a master mechanic, and a chief dispatcher. **1911** JENKS & LAUCK *Immigration Problem* 227 The road masters and section foremen prefer the Japanese as section hands.

2. An official in charge of maintaining or building a highway or country road.

1882 *Wheelman* I. 43 The road-master is elected for his popularity on account of his letting the farmers off easily. **1887** JACKSON *Between Whiles* 200 She saw . . . Sandy Bruce, . . . road-master, ship-owner, exciseman.

Road metal. Broken stones, cinders, etc., used in mending or building roads or ballasting a railroad bed. {1838} — **1818** FLINT *Lett. from Amer.* 60 The coal . . . may be quarried and carried out in wheel barrows, like road-metal. **1896** SHINN *Story of Mine* 81 The rule for breaking the quartz is to make it like good road metal.

+Road monkey. (See quot. 1905.) — **1895** *Stand.* 1542/2. **1905** *Forestry Bureau Bul.* No. 61, 45 Road monkey, one whose duty is to keep a logging road in proper condition. (N[orth] W[oods], L[ake] S[tates Forest].)

+Road overseer. A person charged with the upkeep of a stretch of road. — **1834** in *Atlantic Mo.* XXVI. 334 For mending roads, two instruments are used here, which many road-overseers in Virginia have long been vainly urged to employ. **1873** *Newton Kansan* 27 March 3/5 The two principal offices are those of Trustee and Road Overseer.

+Road runner. = CHAPARRAL COCK.

1858 BAIRD *Birds Pacific R.R.* 73 A single species [of *Geococcyx* is] known as the Paisano, . . . or sometimes Road Runner, on account of its frequenting public highways. **1877** HODGE *Arizona* 224 The chaparral cock, or California road runner, is found generally throughout the Territory. **1894** *Scribner's Mag.* May 597/2 Racing more rapidly than a horse can trot along the half-effaced trails in the mesquite brush is the 'road-runner,' or 'chapparal cock.' **1917** *Birds of Amer.* II. 127/1 The Road-runner is one of the most striking characters of the cactus belt of the Southwest.

transf. **1903** 'O. HENRY' *Roads of Destiny* 374 Hush up, you old locoed road runner.

Roadster. {1744–}

1. A horse for driving or riding on a road. {1818–}

1821 QUITMAN in Claiborne *Life Quitman* I. 64 He has given me some severe falls, but is now a fine roadster. **1856** *Rep. Comm. Patents 1855: Agric.* 39 We have many fine roadsters and saddle horses. **1864** *Ohio Agric. Rep.* XVIII. 3 Best pair matched roadsters. **1885** *Wkly. New Mexican Rev.* 2 July 2/4 Col. Grayson . . . paid the Duncan boys $365 for a span of roadsters. **1896** *Vt. Agric. Rep.* XV. 26 The class of horses that have made our state famous are the Morgan type of roadsters.

2. a. Anything that frequents roads. {1841–, of a person}

1850 S. F. COOPER *Rural Hours* 201 The yellow butterflies . . . are regular roadsters, constantly seen on the highway.

+b. A highwayman; a tramp; a wanderer: (see also quot. 1896).

1890 LANGFORD *Vigilante Days* (1912) 315 Henry Plummer was chief of the band; . . . Cyrus Skinner, fence, spy, and roadster. **1896** *Pop. Sci. Jrnl.* L. 255 The roadster proper is distinguished from the tramp by having a 'graft,' . . . a visible means of support. **1899** 'O. HENRY' *Roads of Destiny* 321 For the next ten minutes the gang of roadsters paid their undivided attention to the supper. **1901** *Scribner's Mag.* April 427/1 [He] was already a confirmed roadster, with an inordinate love for tobacco, and a well-developed taste for drink.

+3. a. A buggy or light carriage suited to travel on the road.

1892 *York County Hist. Rev.* 68 The former [repository and office] carries a fine line of . . . everything in light and heavy work from the most substantial farm truck to the lightest finished roadster.

+b. An automobile suited to travel on the road, esp. an open, single-seated car with a place for baggage or a rumble seat in the back.

1908 *Scientific Amer.* 8 Feb. 104 Cadillac. . . . Model G—Roadster, $2000. **1925** *Sat. Ev. Post* 4 July 51 Chevrolet for Economical Transportation. . . . Roadster, $525.

+**Road sulky.** A light, two-wheeled carriage suitable for use on the road. — 1853 *Knickerb.* XLII. 53 A well-built iron-gray was brushing up behind me in a road-sulky. 1868 WOODRUFF *Trotting Horse* 255 The little bay mare . . . in the battered road-sulky, kept making her long, low, sweeping stride directly in his wake.

+**Road supervisor.** A local official charged with looking after the roads. — 1869 *Rep. Comm. Agric. 1868* 348 The immediate supervision of construction and repairs is generally under the direction of local 'road supervisors.' 1881 *Ore. State Jrnl.* 8 Jan. 5/2 Quite a number of road supervisors have failed to make their reports. 1885 *Wkly. New Mexican Rev.* 5 Feb. 1/5 When any water pipe bursts . . . , it is made the duty of the police to at once notify the road supervisor.

Road tax. A poll tax for making and mending roads. {1801} — 1832 *East-Hampton Rec.* IV. 480 The commissioners of highways . . . [shall] exempt from the road tax all persons who will procure wagons [etc.]. 1844 *Indiana Senate Jrnl.* 29 Sess. 90 County auditors [shall have] longer time to make out a list of the road tax for the use of supervisors. 1873 BAILEY *Life in Danbury* 186 Once we passed a party of men engaged in national pastime of working out a road-tax. 1902 WHITE *Blazed Trail* 8 Those of us who have ever paused to watch a group of farmers working out their road taxes, must have gathered a formidable impression of road-clearing. 1914 *Cycl. Amer. Govt.* III. 230/2.

+**Road trotter.** 1. A horse that travels a road by trotting. 2. (See quotation.) 3. A road agent. — (1) 1868 WOODRUFF *Trotting Horse* 82 [Natural pacers] are often fine lasting road-horses, able . . . to make such fast brushes by pacing that no road-trotter can get by them. (2) 1917 *Birds of Amer.* II. 212 Horned Lark. *Otocoris alpestris alpestris.* . . . [Also called] Prairie Bird; Road Trotter; Wheat Bird. (3) 1921 *Okla. Chronicles* I. 83 The only way this 'road trotter,' as he was locally known, could be disposed of was to pay him a sum of money . . . and remain in possession of the claim or leave.

Road wagon. A vehicle for use on the highway, usually either a heavy wagon for transporting goods or a form of buggy. {a1787-} — 1833 *Congress. Deb.* 24 Jan. 1320 In 1829, the Kiskiminetas salt works, in Pennsylvania, employed two hundred road wagons. 1844 GREGG *Commerce of Prairies* I. 24 One or two were stout road-wagons, two were carts, and the rest Dearborn carriages. 1889 *Century Mag.* Feb. 602/1 The stout road-wagon was drawn by a good-looking pair of American horses. 1893 B. MATTHEWS in *Harper's Mag.* Dec. 29/1 The vehicles gathering at Madison Square . . . —coaches, private carriages, omnibuses, road-wagons of one kind or another. 1901 *Scribner's Mag.* April 422/1 He was drawing a light, bicycle-wheeled road-wagon. 1907 LILLIBRIDGE *Trail* 285 The wheels of the old road waggon had temporarily blazed a trail.

Roadway. a. A way used as a road. {1600-} **b.** The portion of a road on which the main traffic passes. {1807-}
1657 *Suffolk Deeds* III. 63 [There is] another Rode way betweene Weymouth Lyne & ye said lott, at ye weste ende. 1699 *Essex Inst. Coll.* XLII. 358 They layed out Six houes lots, . . . [and] a Conveniant Roadway. 1710 *Providence Rec.* XVII. 272 There must of nesesety be a Roade way layd out from ye Towne of Providence so Westward to Woodstock. 1862 *Rep. Comm. Patents 1861: Agric.* 345 The road-way will be a convenience in moving hay or manure. 1877 [see GAS COMPANY]. 1908 *Indian Laws & Tr.* III. 366 A roadway twenty feet wide shall be permitted across said lands from the Government school to the place of crossing the Mississippi River.

+**Roanoke.** [Algonquian *rawranoke.*] A kind of wampum used in the Virginia country. Now hist.
1624 SMITH *Gen. Hist. Va.* III. 58 *Rawranoke* or white beads . . . occasion as much dissention among the Salvages, as gold and siluer amongst Christians. 1634 *Relation of Beginnings of Md.* 15 [Indians] wear their hair generally very long, . . . and tye it about with a large string of Wampampegge, or Roanoke. 1656 *Va. Statutes at Large* I. 397 Peeces of eight that are good and of silver shall pass for five shillings, and Roanoke and Wompompeeke to keep their wonted value. 1705 BEVERLEY *Virginia* III. 4 Upon his Neck, and Wrists, hang Strings of Beads, Peak and Roenoke. 1804 BURK *Hist. Virginia* I. 174 But as to my daughter, I sold her, a few days since, to a great Werowance, for two bushels of Roanoke. 1900 *Harper's Mag.* March 511 Silver bangles, and ear-bobs, and strings of roanoke.

+**Roanoke chub.** (See quotation.) — 1883 *Century Mag.* July 376/2 In portions of Virginia they are called chub, southern chub, or Roanoke chub.

*****Roarer.**
+1. a. A person regarded by himself or others as a notable figure. {-1709, a roisterer} **b.** One who excels in some activity.
See also RINGTAIL(ED) ROARER.
1827 *Mass. Spy* 10 Jan. (Th.), The Albany beau drinks brandy and talks politics, and is in fact what he styles himself, 'a real roarer.' 1830 *Illinois Mo. Mag.* I. 71 He boasted . . . that his wife was as handsome as a pet fawn, and his children *real roarers.* 1836 HILDRETH *Campaigns Rocky Mts.* 237 Close to the wharf, upon the deck of a broadhorn, stood a fellow . . . styling himself the *'roarer,'* and declaring that he hadn't had a fight in a month, and was getting lazy. 1852 STOWE *Uncle Tom* viii, Tom's a roarer when there's any thumping or fighting to be done. 1869 — *Oldtown Folks* 117 She was spoken of with applause under such titles as 'a staver,' 'a pealer,' 'a roarer to work.' 1882 SWEET & KNOX *Texas*

Siftings 171 It was during the reign of Bob Augustine, 'the long-ranged Roarer of Calaveras Canyon,' as he familiarly called himself.

+**2.** *pl.* A name given a certain element of the New York Democratic party, esp. in the elections of 1840.
1840 *Boston Transcript* 15 April 2/1 The tail of the Democratic party, the roarers, buttenders, ringtails, . . . and indomitables, talked strong about nullification.

+**3.** An oil gusher.
1887 CREW *Treat. on Petroleum* 227 We have no right, perhaps, to expect a continuance of the 'roarers,' or 'gushers' as they are termed.

*****Roaring.** +(See quot. 1917.) — c1834 CATLIN *Indians* II. 13 It was in the midst of the 'running season,' and we had heard the 'roaring' . . . of the herd when we were several miles from them. 1917 *Mammals of Amer.* 41/2 The combined bellowing, or 'roaring' as it is called, of the [buffalo] bulls in the breeding time can be heard for miles.

*****Roast.** A part of an animal already roasted or cut to be roasted. 'More commonly used in Am. . . . In Eng. *joint* is preferred' (Horwill). — 1846 SAGE *Scenes Rocky Mts.* v, [Each campfire] was ornamented with delicious roasts, *en appolas,* on sticks planted aslope. 1877 *Harper's Mag.* Feb. 430/1 There is no dinner more satisfactory than one consisting first of a soup, . . . followed by a roast [etc.]. 1910 TOMPKINS *Mothers & Fathers* 70 Don't a roast of beef last nowadays!

Roast beef. Beef roasted for eating. {a1635-} Also transf. — 1694 [see MINCED PIE]. 1774 J. ANDREWS *Letters* 22 We were entertain'd with a very pretty collation, consisting of cold ham, cold roast beef, cake, cheese, etc. 1864 *Harper's Mag.* Feb. 341/2 They had contrived . . . to make what boys call 'roast beef' of his clothes—tying intricate knots in every portion of them that was tyable. 1907 *St. Nicholas* Aug. 934 Then the little pig that had roast beef . . . woke up.

+**Roast corn.** Corn roasted on the cob. Also attrib. — 1848 *Knickerb.* XVIII. 217 The roast-corn frolics . . . furnish sources of enjoyment. 1874 COLLINS *Kentucky* I. 112 [We went] through clouds of dust and over hot sands, with . . . only roast-corn for food.

*****Roaster.** A pan in which meat, etc., can be roasted. (See also APPLE-ROASTER.) {1799-} — 1658 *Southold Rec.* I. 449 An Inventorie of the personall estate whereof Elizabeth Payne widdow dyed possest [includes] . . . a brush, a roster [etc.]. 1841 *S. Lit. Messenger* VII. 662/1 There too lies a mutilated coffee-pot, a crownless hat and a lidless tin-roaster.

+**Roasting ear.** An ear of corn suitable for roasting.
1705 BEVERLEY *Virginia* III. 15 They delight much to feed on Roasting-ears; that is, the Indian Corn, gathered green and milky, . . . and roasted before the Fire, in the Ear. 1797 F. BAILY *Tour* 365 We longed very much for some of the old man's *roasting ears.* 1819 [see HOREHOUND 1]. 1871 *Rep. Indian Affairs* (1872) 473 [The Indians] have shown themselves, however poor they may be in raising corn, entirely successful in boiling roasting-ears.
attrib. 1812 MARSHALL *Kentucky* 128 [They] had exhausted all that kind of supply [*i.e.,* corn] long before the succeeding crop was fit for use, even in the roasting-ear state. 1895 *Outing* Sept. 436/2 [The raccoon] delights in . . . Indian corn, when the ears . . . are in the 'roastin' yere' stage.

+**Roasting-ear time.** The time of year when corn is in the roasting-ear stage; harvest time. — 1841 *S. Lit. Messenger* VII. 219/2 The Weyanokes . . . here celebrated . . . the green corn dance, (roasting-ear time). 1867 EDWARDS *Shelby* 338 Ever sence roastin-ear time. 1895 *Outing* Sept. 434/2 It is 'roastin' yere an' coon-time now.'

Roasting furnace. A furnace in which metallic ores, etc., are exposed to protracted heat to remove impurities. {1839} — 1869 J. R. BROWNE *Adv. Apache Country* 495 Mr. Vanderbosch . . . erected a roasting furnace in March, 1864. 1876 RAYMOND *8th Rep. Mines* 288 Devices half-way between the common grate and gas-generators . . . have been employed for some time . . . in roasting-furnaces used for slagging.

*****Roasting iron.** (See ROASTIRON.)

Roasting pan. A pan in which foods may be roasted. — 1815 *Niles' Reg.* IX. 94/2 Grid irons, griddles and roasting pans [were manufactured]. 1879 A. D. WHITNEY *Just How* 156 Put the roasting-pan with the gravy on the fire.

Roasting stick. {1688} A long stick for holding a piece of meat, etc., so as to roast it at an open fire. — 1812 MARSHALL *Kentucky* 161 The Indians . . . [left] some bits of meat on their roasting sticks. 1843 FRÉMONT *Explor. Rocky Mts.* 24 Having disposed our meat on roasting sticks, we proceeded to unpack our bales. 1882 in Z. F. SMITH *Kentucky* 206 Pieces of meat were upon the roasting-sticks.

*****Roastiron.** A gridiron. *Obs.* {-1519} Also *roasting iron.* {-1573} — 1650 *Conn. Rec.* I. 444 The goods and Cattle of John Brundish: . . . rostiron, spitt. 1650 *Mayflower Descendant* X. 173 One brandlet one rostiron one frying pan. 1654 *Essex Probate Rec.* I. 189 Axe, wedges, Rostiron, Trevett & other old iron. [1775 *Essex Inst. Coll.* XIII. 186, 1 pr. H[an]d Irons, 1 pr. roast[in]g do.]

*****Robber.** *attrib.* In the names of insects. {1831-} — 1871 *Amer. Naturalist* IV. 686 A robber-fly (*Proctacanthus Philadelphicus* . . .) burrows in the sand of the shores of Plum Island, Mass. 1876 *Vermont Bd. Agric. Rep.* III. 676 The spined soldier bug and the banded robber bug also prey upon the larvae of the potato beetle.

+**Robber's roost.** A place on the floor of the New York Stock Exchange: (see quotation). — 1885 *Harper's Mag.* Nov. 830/1 The guerrillas . . . have formerly fixed the unsavory appellations of 'Hell's Kitchen' and 'Robber's Roost' upon certain localities of the floor.

+Robber tariff. A tariff with high protective rates. Also attrib. — **1890** *Congress. Rec.* 12 Aug. 8452/2 [The burning of Indian corn as fuel] is heralded as an evidence of . . . the operation of this 'robber tariff.' **1892** *Ib.* 8 July 5908/1, I have sat here and have seen the advocates of the 'robber tariff' skulk behind a pretended protection to labor. **1894** *Ib.* 31 Jan. 1755/2 Under our robber-tariff system there was a license granted . . . to rob the farmers and laborers of the country.

*Robe. +A blanketlike garment or rug made, or resembling one made, of a dressed skin or skins.
See also BUFFALO ROBE.
1805 LEWIS in *L. & Clark Exped.* II. (1904) 376, I have also observed some robes among them of beaver, moonox, and small wolves. **1823** JAMES *Exped.* I. 145 Cut Nose now presented to the agent his crow and bison robe ornamented with hiero-glyphicks. **1876** *Wide Awake* 291/2 The bear's carcass was taken down, and the skin . . . was in time nicely tanned for a robe. **1900** GOODLANDER *Fort Scott* 25 [The Osage Indians] would buy what goods they wanted at one dollar's worth at a time until they had traded up all the bullion they had got for their ponies and robes. **1909** RICE *Mr. Opp* 178 Just take all that robe.
comb. **1850** GARRARD *Wah-To-Yah* iii. 55, I returned . . . with full complements of goods for robe trading.

+**b.** *To cast one's robe,* to go on the warpath.
1814 BRACKENRIDGE *Views La.* 254 Frequently when unsuccessful, they 'cast their robes,' as they express it, and vow to kill the first person they meet, provided he be not of their own nation.

+**Robert o' Lincoln.** A bobolink. — **1855** BRYANT *Poetical Works* (1903) 230 Robert of Lincoln bestirs him well. **1874** B. F. TAYLOR *World on Wheels* 253 There in the meadow . . . Robert o' Lincoln should ring his chime of bells.

*Robin.[1]
+**1.** A large, red-breasted thrush, *Turdus* (syn. *Merula*) *migratorius*.
Examples in the second group illustrate the former practice of hunting robins for sport or for food.
(1) **1703** SEWALL *Diary* II. 74 The Robbins cheerfully utter their Notes this morn. **1774** FITHIAN *Journal* I. 121 The finest morning we have yet had; the Robbins, & blue Birds singing all around us. **1808** WILSON *Ornithology* I. 35 Robin. . . . Scarce a winter passes but innumerable thousands of them are seen in the lower parts of the whole Atlantic states, from New Hampshire to Carolina. **1884** ROE *Nature's Story* 115 That handsome bird, the blue jay, so wild at the East, is as tame and domestic as the robin in many parts of the West. **1897** FLANDRAU *Harvard Episodes* 112 You lie and watch the industrious robins rip elastic angle-worms from the sod. **1917** *Birds of Amer.* III. 237/1 Practically all of the Robins who breed in the temperate zone migrate to warmer latitudes in the autumn.
(2) **1759** *Essex Inst. Coll.* XLIX. 6 Supped on Robens which my Chum and Wingate Killed. **1775** *Ib.* LIII. 86 Killed some robins. **1805** PARKINSON *Tour* 310 There is a bird they call a robin, something like our fieldfare, which they shoot. **1872** *Md. Laws* 664 The robin may be shot from and after the first day of September until the first day of May. **1917** *Birds of Amer.* III. 238/2 Incredible though it may seem, until within a few years ago, the Robin was classified, in several of the southern States, as a 'game bird,' and as such was killed in countless thousands for food or for 'sport.'
attrib. **1823** COOPER *Pioneer* 9 Did ye think to stop a full grown buck with . . . that robin pop-gun in your hand? **1867** *Common Sense Cook Book* 54 Robin pie. . . . Lay ten or twelve robins, previously rolled in flour, [in a pie dish].

+**b.** Specifically called *American robin.*
1798 *Monthly Mag.* May 331/2, I noticed several kinds of birds . . . peculiar to the North-American continent, viz. the Virginian nightingale; . . . the American robin, larger than ours; and the blue variegated jay. **1839**, **1844** [see MIGRATORY THRUSH]. **1867** LATHAM *Black & White* 31 The American robin is a red-breasted thrush.

‖**c.** *Robin snow,* a snow in the spring after the return of the robins.
1857 THOREAU *Journal* IX. 286 The slight robin snow of yesterday . . . is already mostly dissipated.

+**2.** In the names of various other birds. Freq. attrib.
See also ENGLISH ROBIN, GOLDEN ROBIN, etc.
1869 *Amer. Naturalist* III. 31 Oregon Robin (*T*[*urdus*] *nævius*). I found this beautiful thrush common near the summit of the Coeur d'Alene Mountains. **1884** COUES *N. Amer. Birds* 632 *Tringa.* . . . Robin Sandpiper. Bill about as long as, or rather longer than, the head. **1917** *Birds of Amer.* I. 231 Knot. *Tringa canutus.* . . . [Also called] Robin-breast; Beach Robin; Red-breast. *Ib.* 140 Buffle-Head. *Charitonetta albeola.* . . . [Also called] Dopper; Robin Dipper; Little Black and White Duck (male).

3. The name, or part of the name, of various fishes. {1618-} See also ROUND ROBIN, SEA ROBIN.
+**a.** The round robin, *Decapterus punctatus.* +**b.** The sailor's-choice, *Lagodon rhomboides.* +**c.** A sea robin. **d.** The flying gurnard, *Dactylopterus volitans.*
1884 GOODE, etc. *Fisheries* I. 393 The 'Sailor's Choice' . . . bears several other names, being known about Cape Hatteras as the 'Robin' and 'Pinfish.' **1894** *Outing* XXIV. 263/2 The robin grunted vigorously as I re-

lieved him of the hook. **1896** JORDAN & EVERMANN *Check-List Fishes* 489 *Cephalacanthus volitans.* . . . Flying-robin; Mucielago.

‖**Robin.**[2] (See quotation.) — **1877** BARTLETT 534 Robin, a flannel undershirt.

*Robin redbreast. + =ROBIN[1] 1.
1761 KALM *Resa* III. 46 Af Angelsmännerna och de Svenska kallades han *Robin-red-breast;* men är vida skild ifrån den med det namnet i Ängeland. **1774** FITHIAN *Journal* I. 232 Not a bird, except now & then Robin-Redbreast, is heard to sing in this Feverish Month. **1803** *Mass. H. S. Coll.* I Ser. IX. 202 Among the birds usually observed in this place [Compton, R.I.] are the robin red-breast, [and the] sparrow. **1865** BURROUGHS in *Atlantic Mo.* May 517/1 Shortly after Robin-Redbreast, with whom he associates, . . . [arrives] the Golden-Winged Woodpecker. **1917** *Birds of Amer.* III. 236.

+**Robin runaway.** The ground ivy, *Glecoma hederacea.* (Cf. GILL-GO-OVER-THE-GROUND.) — **1784** [see GILL-GO-OVER-THE-GROUND]. **1789** DUNLAP *Father* II. i, Old women's prescriptions—hoarhound, cabbage leaves, robin-run-away, dandy-grey-russet, and the like. **1892** *Amer. Folk-Lore* V. 102 *Nepeta Glechoma,* Robin runaway. N.H.

+**Robin's-egg.** Short for next. Used attrib. — **1873** PHELPS *Trotty's Wedding* xiv, In her upper drawer . . . she saw her robin's-egg sash and gloves.

+**Robin's-egg blue.** A bluish green color. Also attrib. or as adj. — **1887** WILKINS *Humble Romance* 15 [He purchased] a dress-pattern of robin's-egg blue silk. **1918** LINCOLN *Shavings* 256 The said mill arms were painted a robin's-egg blue.

+**Robin shot.** Shot of a size suitable for shooting robins. *Obs.* — **1792** PRENTICE *Fugitive Ess.* 145 We stand, nor dread the windy storm, Nor all the robin-shot, that rattle From those on t'other side the battle. **1844** *Knickerb.* XXIII. 440 [Get] half a dozen pounds of No. 4 shot. None of the fine mustard-seed or robin.

+**Robin snipe. 1.** =RED-BREASTED SANDPIPER 1. **2.** =DOWITCHER. — (1) **1844** *Nat. Hist. N.Y., Zoology* II. 243 The Robin Snipe, as it is called by our sportsmen, appears on the shores of this State in May. **1872** COUES *N. Amer. Birds* 256 Robin-snipe. . . . Bill equalling or rather exceeding the head. (2) **1917** *Birds of Amer.* I. 229 Dowitcher. . . . Other names [include] Robin Snipe; Sea Pigeon; Driver; [etc.].

+**Robin wheat.** ? A moss belonging to the genus *Bryum.* — **1886** BERGEN in *Pop. Science Mo.* XXIX. 368 The birds are not the only harvesters of the pretty moss known as robin-wheat. **1892** — in *Amer. Folk-Lore* V. 105 *Bryum* sp., robin-wheat. Mansfield, O.

Rob Roy. {1866-} *Rob Roy cloak,* a woman's cloak of a style now obsolete. — **1863** *Ladies' Repository* Nov. 645/2 A scanty but brilliantly-colored Rob Roy cloak . . . was drawn tightly around the primmest little figure you can imagine outside of 'fairie land.' **1863** A. D. WHITNEY *F. Gartney* xvi, Aunt Faith, in her pumpkin hood and Rob Roy cloak, . . . came over once in two or three days.

Rochelle powder. Seidlitz powder. — **1820** *Columbian Centinel* 2 Dec. 4/1 Maynard & Noyes . . . have prepared and now offer for sale, Rochelle Powders for making Rochelle Water. **1868** S. HALE *Letters* 54 The taste is fearful. Rochelle Powder, potash, salt, mustard, rotten eggs, anything else vile you can think of.

Rochelle salt. A colorless crystalline salt, mildly purgative. {1753-} — **1790** *Columbian Centinel* 15 Sept. 4/2 Purging Rochelle Salts, Spanish Liquorish Ball, and one bale of Morocco Leather . . . will be sold at the very lowest prices. **1820** *U.S. Pharmacopœia* 195 Tartrate of Potass and Soda Called Rochelle Salt.

*Rock, *n.*
I. 1. A large detached mass of stone; a boulder of some size. {1709-} **a.** Used as or in connection with a boundary.
1641 *New Haven Col. Rec.* 49 The small lotts shall begin att the great rock on the farre side of the mill river. **1668** *Derby Rec.* 10 The bounds of which tract of Land is . . . A small Rock south. **1698** *Boston Rec.* 233 [The line is to run] from thence to . . . a great Rock in Col: Shrimptons ground called the night pasture. **1722** *York Deeds* XI. 2 [The land is] bounded as followeth Vizt. Beginning at a great Rock.

b. Used as a building material.
1646 *New Haven Col. Rec.* 221 The rocks, soe farre as they reach serve for a fence. **1677** *Derby Rec.* 31 [The town] reserves the Stons of the rock and the rocks for the Use of the Town. **1701** *Essex Inst. Coll.* XXXVI. 82 For . . . tending the mason and drowing of Rockes and bringing of Clay of brick. **1712** SEWALL *Diary* II. 344, I lay'd a Rock in the North-east corner of the Foundation of the Meetinghouse. **1800** *Mass. H. S. Coll.* I Ser. VI. 219 The inhabitants are supplied abundantly with rocks for building of cellars from the hills.

c. Constituting an obstacle in farming or traveling.
1700 *Essex Inst. Coll.* VIII. 217, I had 4 men to dig rocks. **1777** in Jay *Correspondence* I. 166 They will be obliged to contend with Hills, Rocks, Gullies & Trees on *all* sides. **1803** CUTLER in *Life & Corr.* II. 125 When you cannot go over the ponds, could you not . . . haul the rocks, with the cart or drag, off the plow land in the farm. **1805** CLARK in *Lewis & C. Exped.* III. (1905) 16 The Indian horses pass over those Clifts hills beds & rocks as fast as a man. **1848** ROBINSON *Santa Fe Exped.* 43, 10 of Sandeval's miles . . . we found to be about 20, over a rough-and-tumble route, amongst rocks and gullies. **1880** ROLLINS *New Eng. Bygones* (1883) 41 He tilled the soil in summer and split rocks in winter.

2. A stone of small size, esp. one convenient for throwing. *local.*

'*U.S.* and *Austr.*' (*O.E.D.*).

1817 *Essex Inst. Coll.* VIII. 231 The people . . . kept up their carousal through the night, screeching like savages, beating drums, throwing of rocks against buildings. **1838** S. PARKER *Tour Rocky Mts.* 48 It is one of the peculiarities of the dialect of the people in the westernmost states, to call small stones rocks. And therefore they speak of throwing a rock at a bird, or at a man. **1882** BAILLIE-GROHMAN *Camps in Rockies* 190 The Western 'boy' never says 'throw a stone,' but 'throw,' or 'heave, a rock.'

+3. = PLYMOUTH ROCK 1.

1801 J. ALLYN *Sermon* (22 Dec.) 34 May the rock of the pilgrims . . . be associated with those christian virtues. **1807** *Columbian Centinel* 7 Jan. 2/3 The footsteps of our fathers, the revered rock, and their more sacred relics are proper objects to employ our contemplations. **1820** TICKNOR in *Life, Lett. & Jrnls.* I. 328 The first thing was of course the Rock, on which the first boatload . . . landed. **1823** THACHER *Military Jrnl.* 27 A visit of a few days to my friends at Plymouth, gave me an opportunity to pay my respects to the *rock.*

+4. *W.* Mineral ore, or a specimen of ore.

1885 *Santa Fé Wkly. New Mexican* 10 Sept. 4/3 The boys came home with their pockets full of 'rocks.' **1896** SHINN *Story of Mine* 78 The quartz prospector . . . only pans out a few ounces of powdered rock. **1902** WISTER *Virginian* xv, Are they taking much mineral out? Have yu' seen any of the rock?

+5. (See quot. 1881.)

1881 INGERSOLL *Oyster-Industry* 247 Rock.—A growth of native oysters massed into a rock-like bottom or ridge. (Chesapeake and southward.) **1883** *Nat. Museum Bul.* No. 27, 214 Whenever the solid beds or 'Rocks' were encountered, they were found to be long and narrow ridges.

+6. (See quotation.)

1905 *Forestry Bureau Bul.* No. 61, 18 In forest description rock refers to those characteristics of the underlying formation which affect the forest; as for example, its outcrop, composition, and the rapidity of its disintegration.

II. +7. A rockfish, esp. the striped bass.

1698 THOMAS *Pensilvania* 14 There are prodigious quantities of . . . large sort of Fish, as Whales . . . , Rock, Oysters. **1705** BEVERLEY *Virginia* II. 31 There come up likewise into the Freshes from the Sea, Multitudes of Shads, Rocks, Sturgeon, and some few Lampreys. **1796** HAWKINS *Letters* 38 This is the most valuable creek known here for fish in the spring and summer. Sturgeon, trout, perch, rock, red horse. **1857** *Harper's Mag.* March 439/1 At the dinner-table, . . . boiled rock, stewed cat-fish, white perch, and broiled shad disputed the claim on his taste and attention. **1894** *Scribner's Mag.* May 603/2 The epicure . . . would go wild with the display and the ridiculous cheapness of . . . June fish, rock [etc., at the mouth of the Rio Grande R.].

+8. A piece of money. *slang.* Usually pl.

1840 *Picayune* 31 July 2/2 He was just on the eve of leaving town with his 'pockets full of rocks.' **1846** CORCORAN *Pickings* 143 Here I am in town without a rock in my pocket. **1853** 'P. PAXTON' *Yankee in Texas* 124 [He] picked up a pocketful of rocks when cattle-huntin' wer in season. **1882** [see KING-PIN]. **1903** *N.Y. Sun* 8 Nov., It is known who are the men with a large accumulation of rocks behind them and who are the ones who are merely bluffing.

III. *attrib.* and *comb.* **9.** Designating tracts or areas where rocks are plentiful.

1638 *Essex Inst. Coll.* IV. 183/2 John Blackleech desireth 50 acres of Land . . . vpon exchange of 50 acres of his Rock grounde for yt. **1870** *Rep. Comm. Agric. 1869* 422 Chickens . . . have free range over a fifteen acre 'rock lot.' **1891** RYAN *Pagan* 96 The rest of that rock-land is going to break away sometime.

10. Designating geological or topographical features made up of or characterized by rocks.

See also ROCK STONE.

1797 HAWKINS *Letters* 171 The first rockfalls in the river . . . are 5 miles below the second falls. **1842** BUCKINGHAM *E. & W. States* III. 225 Not long after leaving Peru [Ill.], we passed on our right, a singular promontory, called by some Rock Fort, and by others Starved Rock. *a*1862 THOREAU *Maine Woods* 262 Being struck with the perfect parallelism of these singular rock-hills, . . . I took out my compass. **1881** Rock eddy [see BIN(N)ACLE]. **1886** WINCHELL *Walks & Talks* 53 We have seen . . . the rock-bluffs bounding . . . the basins of the great lakes. **1897** BRODHEAD *Bound in Shallows* 234 The falls of the Cumberland . . . [plunged] down the crescent break in the rock-bed.

11. Designating things made up or built of rocks.

See also ROCK ROAD.

1825 NEAL *Bro. Jonathan* III. 409 The black snake and copperhead have gone to the old rock heaps. **1896** *Dialect Notes* I. 423 *Rock fence,* a stone wall. N.Y.c.

12. In the names of plants and trees: (see quotations).

See also ROCK CHESTNUT OAK, ROCK CLUB MOSS, etc.

1819 *Western Rev.* I. 228 *Betula rupestris.* Rock Birch. . . . I have discovered this shrub in the cliffs and on the sandstone rocks of the Kentucky river in Estill County. **1817-8** EATON *Botany* (1822) 435 *Rubus saxatilis,* brier herb, rock blackberry. *Ib.* 414 *Pteris atropurpurea,* rock brake. . . . From three to ten inches high, bluish green, leaves stiff. **1819** *Western Rev.* I. 230 The *Cornus polygama* of the flora of Louisiana. . . . Its vulgar names are Rock-dogwood or White-berry. **1898** A. M. DAVIDSON *Calif. Plants* 72 The rock fern or Polypodium came above ground so quickly that it was hard to catch the leaves unrolling. **1862** *Rep. Comm. Patents 1861: Agric.* 485 'Rock grape,' *Vitis rupestris.* . . . Grapes small, black. **1778** CARVER *Travels* 517 Rock Liverwort is a sort of liverwort that grows on rocks, and is of the nature of kelp or moss. It is esteemed as an excellent remedy against declines. **1842** BUCKINGHAM *Slave States* II. 286 A new kind of wheat has been lately introduced into this part of Virginia, called the Rock Wheat, from the circumstance that a few years ago a single head of wheat, of peculiarly large size and product, was seen growing out of the crevice of a rock in a wheat field.

13. In the names of fishes: (see quotations).

See also ROCK BASS, ROCK COD, etc.

1884 GOODE, etc. *Fisheries* I. 410 There is a small species (*Serranus trifurcus*) . . . found only in the vicinity of Charleston, South Carolina, and Pensacola, Florida, where it is called the 'Rock Black-fish.' **1857** *Harper's Mag.* March 442/1 The refuse fish commonly taken [in N.C.] are sturgeon, rock-cats, trout [etc.]. [**1836** J. RICHARDSON, etc. *Fauna Bor.-Amer.* III. 246 The rock-codling . . . they take near Cape Isabella.] **1883** *Nat. Museum Bul.* No. 27, 129 *Panulirus interruptus.* . . . Rock-lobster. . . . Pacific coast, Point Conception, California, southward. Used as food. **1842** *Nat. Hist. N.Y., Zoology* IV. 147 The Rock Mullet, *Mugil petrosus,* . . . ranges from Brazil to the coast of New York. **1896** Rock salmon [see MEDREGAL 2]. **1883** *Nat. Museum Bul.* No. 27, 493 *Acipenser rubicundus.* . . . Stone Sturgeon; Rock Sturgeon; Red Sturgeon. Mississippi Valley; Great Lakes, and northward.

14. In the names of animals: (see quotations).

1878 BEADLE *Western Wilds* 457 The rock rabits (conies?) ran from covert to covert with a peculiar low moaning cry. **1893** ROOSEVELT *Wilderness Hunter* 124 We heard the shrill whistling of hoary rock-woodchucks.

15. In special combinations.

Rock coal, anthracite, stone coal; *r. codder,* (see quotation); *r. cut, r. cutting,* a way, as for a railroad, cut through rock, cf. CUT *n.* 1 c; *r. fight,* (see quotation); *r. gas,* natural gas obtained by boring through rock; *r. gypsum,* gypsum that occurs in massive form; *r. honey, r. ice cream, r. punch,* (see quotation).

1858 *S. Lit. Messenger* XXVI. 189/2 Ef thar had bin . . . a fier-plais instid uv a great to burn rock cole, the thing would uv bin kumpleat. **1896** *Boston Transcript* 21 Nov. 20/1 Rock codders . . . [are] small boats that go out for a day's fishing. **1873** BEADLE *Undevel. West* 139 From Wasatch we pass through a long rock-cut and tunnel. **1873** 'MARK TWAIN' & WARNER *Gilded Age* 419 By and by there is Newark, . . . then marshes, then long rock-cuttings, devoted to the advertisement of patent medicines. **1784** SMYTH *Tour* I. 89 The rock fight . . . is occasioned by such amazing number of those fishes, here called Bass-Rocks, coming up to the falls [near Halifax, N.C.] at the same time to spawn, that a dog thrown into the river then, would not be able to swim across, nor could live in it one quarter of an hour. **1888** *Harper's Mag.* June 47/2 To coal as a manufacturing energy has recently been added rock-gas. **1843** N. BOONE *Journal* 3 June 203 The water was sulphurous, and the rock gypsum and red stone dipping to the S.W. very slightly. **1815** KIRBY & SPENCE *Introd. Entomology* I. 323 What is called rock-honey in some parts of America . . . is the produce of wild bees, which suspend their clusters . . . to a rock. **1887** *N.Y. Tribune* 7 April 2/2 Granites . . . are a rough kind of sorbets. They are sometimes called rock punch and rock ice-cream, and are made of fruit juice, sugar and water.

Rock, *v.* {1600-} **+***tr.* To throw stones at; to stone. — *a*1848 in Bartlett 277 They commenced rocking the Clay Club House in June. **1853** 'P. PAXTON' *Yankee in Texas* 116 When man or boy, biped or quadruped, bird or beast is pelted, the unfortunate recipient of projectile favors is said to be rocked, unless indeed wood be put in requisition. **1872** HOLMES *Poet* 379 The boys would follow after him, crying, 'Rock him! Rock him! He's got a long-tailed coat on!' **1892** GUNTER *Miss Dividends* 194 [The rattlesnake] has bitten himself twice since I 'rocked' him. **1923** *Dialect Notes* V. 219, I rocked 'im off o' the place. [McDonald Co., Mo.]

+Rockahominy. [Algonquin Indian.] Indian corn parched and pounded into a fine powder; hominy. Also attrib. Now hist.

1674 in Jillson *Dark & Bl. Ground* 18 [They] gave him Rokahamony for his journey. **1705** BEVERLEY *Virginia* III. 18 Each Man takes with him a Pint or Quart of Rockahomonie, that is, the finest Indian Corn, parched, and beaten to Powder. **1709** LAWSON *Carolina* 178 Rockahomine Meal . . . is their Maiz, parch'd and pounded into Powder. **1738** BYRD *Dividing Line* (1901) 144 Rockahominy . . . is parcht Indian Corn reduc'd to powder. **1743** CATESBY *Carolina* p. x, [Carolina Indians] thicken their broths with Roccahomony, which is indeed, for that purpose much preferable to oatmeal or French barley. **1902** M. JOHNSON *Audrey* i, Platters of smoking venison and turkey, flanked by rockahominy and hoe-biscuit.

+Rock and brandy. Rock candy and brandy. — **1872** POWERS *Afoot & Alone* 109 You, Mr. Ox-driver, with your Baptist and Methodist, and Rock and Brandy, why don't you throw that sapling from the road?

+**Rock and rye.** Rock candy and rye whisky. Also fig. — **1880** *Congress. Rec.* 23 April 2692/1 [These heroes] were . . . the cream, or, . . . the very 'rock and rye' of the democracy. **1884** *Ib.* App. 21 April 145/2 The breechless sons of the Lothians were not averse to a wee drop of 'rock and rye.' **1886** Howe *Moonlight Boy* 31 Tibby Cole . . . visited a medical friend who had once prescribed rock and rye for his cough.

+**Rockaway.** [*Rockaway*, N.J., from Indian name.] A four-wheeled pleasure carriage, orig. having a standing canopy top and removable side curtains.

1846 Lowell *Letters* I. 121 Dr. Liddon Pennock has driven by me in his rockaway. **1857** *Lawrence* (Kan.) *Republican* 23 July 4 Fanny was soon in the rockaway and we drove off. **1884** Roe *Nature's Story* 192 With the aid of the family rockaway the entire party were at the boat-house before the sun had passed much beyond the meridian. **1912** Cobb *Back Home* 287 She drove her old rockaway down to the engine house.

attrib. **1845** Noah *Gleanings* 174, I keep a little Rockaway wagon. **1895** *Outing* XXVII. 5/2 The rockaway shaft had been broken only the day before.

+**Rockaway carriage.** =prec. — **1846** *Spirit of Times* 9 May 121/1 The price of a 'Rockaway' carriage which will carry eight persons depends very much on its finish. **1904** T. E. Watson *Bethany* 210 In the old-fashioned, rockaway carriage, the young preacher was driven, . . . to the Roberts home.

+**Rock bass.**

1. Any one of various fishes of the family Centrarchidae especially common in the streams of eastern and upper central North America.

[**1811** Lesueur *Hist. Poissons* III. 88 Le centrarchus . . . sous le nom anglais de 'rock basse.'] **1815** *Lit. & Phil. Soc. N.Y. Trans.* I. 496 White, black, and rock basse, are also seen in great numbers. **1842** *Nat. Hist. N.Y., Zoology* IV. 27 Fresh Water Bass. *Centrarchus aeneus.* . . . In Lake Champlain . . . it is called Rock Bass. **1884** Goode, etc. *Fisheries* I. 404 The Rock Bass . . . prefers clear waters, and is not often found in muddy bayous. **1891** O'Beirne *Leaders Ind. Territory* I. 210 There are two other species of this fish, the calico, or striped, and the rock bass. **1897** *Outing* 438/1 The boys called the rock-bass the 'black bass.'

2. A sea bass, as the black sea bass (*Centropristes striatus*) of the Atlantic coast, or the cabrilla (*Paralabrax clathratus*) of the Pacific coast.

1884 Goode, etc. *Fisheries* I. 407 The Sea Bass is called . . . at New Bedford also 'Rock Bass.' *Ib.* 413 The Cabrilla—*Serranus clathratus.* . . . Farther South [than Monterey] it is known to the 'Americans' usually as 'Rock Bass.' *Ib.*, The Johnny Verde—*Serranus nebulifer.* . . . This species receives the name 'Rock Bass' and 'Cabrilla' with the other species. **1911** *Rep. Fisheries 1908* 308/2 *Cabrilla*, a name applied indiscriminately to several serranoid fishes of the southern coast of California. They are also called 'rock bass,' 'kelp salmon,' 'Johnny Verde' [etc.].

+**Rock bird.** =Purple sandpiper. — **1796** Morse *Univ. Geog.* I. 212 Spotted Tring. Rock bird. *Tringa maculata.* **1917** *Birds of Amer.* I. 232 Purple Sandpiper. *Arquatella maritima maritima.* . . . Also called Rock Plover; Rock-bird; Rockweed Bird.

+**Rock-bottom.** (Cf. Bottom rock.)

1. a. (See quot. 1866.) **b.** The very bottom; a fundamental basis or issue.

1866 *Ore. State Jrnl.* 24 Nov. 2/2 A sound democrat, or 'rock bottom,' never shrinks from the requirements of his master. **1904** Harben *Georgians* 200 Now cool off, an' let's git down to rock bottom. **1911** Harrison *Queed* 45 In fact they had to retort by mortgaging their property to the hilt and cutting expenses to rock-bottom.

2. Attrib. in sense: Lowest possible; fundamental or basic.

1884 *Lisbon* (Dak.) *Star* 10 Oct., Boots, shoes and rubbers in great variety and at rock-bottom prices. **1904** W. H. Smith *Promoters* 182 These are the rock-bottom reasons for what we did and did not do. **1906** *Springfield W. Repub.* 30 Aug. 1 The specifications for bids let us down to the rock bottom fact that the U.S. has to turn to the despised coolies for aid.

+**Rock-breaker.** A machine for crushing stones. — **1874** Raymond *6th Rep. Mines* 409 It may be necessary to separate from the massive pieces the fine ore and clay . . . without sending them through the rock-breakers. **1876** — *8th Rep. Mines* 29 On this floor is placed one Wheeler's patent rock-breaker. **1882** *47th Congress 1 Sess.* H. R. Ex. Doc. No. 216, 71 The rock . . . [is] broken by a Blake rock-breaker. **1896** Shinn *Story of Mine* 218 All larger fragments roll into the jaws of a rock breaker.

+**Rock chestnut oak.** The chestnut oak (*Quercus prinus*) of the eastern states. — **1810** [see Rock oak]. **1832** Browne *Sylva* 285 The rock chesnut oak is sometimes 3 feet in diameter, and more than 60 feet high. **1897** Sudworth *Arborescent Flora* 156 *Quercus prinus.* Chestnut Oak. . . . [Also called] Rock Chestnut Oak (Mass., R.I., Pa., Del., Ala., Ill.).

+**Rock club moss.** =Festoon pine. — [**1771** J. R. Forster *Flora Amer. Septentr.* 48 *Lycopodium rupestre*, rock Club-moss.] **1843** Torrey *Flora N.Y.* II. 511 *Selaginella rupestris.* . . . Small Rock Clubmoss. . . . Dry rocky places: not rare.

Rock cod.

1. A variety of true cod found on rocky bottoms and ledges. {1705-}

1634 Wood *New Eng. Prospect* (1865) 45 Besides here is a great deale of Rock-cod and Macrill. **1807** *Mass. H. S. Coll.* 2 Ser. III. 56 The rock cod is taken in autumn. **1839** Storer *Mass. Fishes* 120 Several varieties . . . are known by the names of 'Rock Cod,' 'Shoal Cod,' &c. **1884** *Harper's Wkly.* 1 Nov. 721/2 The professionals and toughened amateurs . . . haul in sea-bass, black-fish, flukes, rock cod, . . . or whatever else comes to hand.

+**2.** Any one of various fishes of the Pacific coast distinguished, by this name, from the buffalo cod. Also *rock codfish.*

1838 S. Parker *Tour Rocky Mts.* 198 The rock codfish were not known to inhabit the waters about the mouth of the Columbia, until the present year. **1872** [see Flatfish]. **1884** Goode, etc. *Fisheries* I. 268 The name 'Rock Cod' applied to other Chiroids and to Sebastichthys, and thence even transferred to *Serranus*, comes from an appreciation of their affinity to *Ophiodon*, and not from any supposed resemblance to the true codfish. **1911** *Rep. Fisheries 1908* 310/2 The name 'grouper' is also applied to the rock cod of southern California.

+**Rock crab.** Any one of various crabs, as *Cancer irroratus*, found on rocky shores. — **1837** Williams *Florida* 105 The Rock Crab is common on the Atlantic coast. **1873** *Rep. Comm. Fisheries 1871–2* 312 The common 'rock-crab' . . . is widely diffused along our coast. **1883** *Nat. Museum Bul.* No. 27, [Among] the most valuable of these [crabs] are . . . the Common Crab, Rock Crab, and Red Crab . . . of the Pacific Coast. **1884** Goode, etc. *Fisheries* I. 772 The Pacific Rock Crab does not often occur on the shore between tides.

+**Rock-crusher.** =Rock-breaker. — **1897** *Outing* May 136/1 The men do their own work without the use of a rock crusher. **1897** *McClure's Mag.* Nov. 79/1 The surrounding hills echo with . . . the continual churning sound of rock-crushers.

+**Rock drill.** A drill or boring machine for penetrating rock. — **1876** Raymond *8th Rep. Mines* 37 Had it not been for the Burleigh rock-drill the work would have been abandoned long since. **1876** Knight 1958/2 McKean's rock-drill is operated by compressed air.

+**Rock elm.** The cork elm, or the wood of this; also, the slippery elm (*Ulmus fulva*), or the American elm. — [**1843** Holtzapffel *Turning* I. 85 Rock Elm . . . is extensively used for boat-building.] **1884** Sargent *Rep. Forests* 123 *Ulmus racemosa.* . . . Rock Elm. Cork Elm. . . . Hickory Elm. **1892** [see Cork elm]. **1897** Sudworth *Arborescent Flora* 180 *Ulmus pubescens.* . . . Slippery Elm. . . . [Also called] Rock Elm (Tenn.). *Ib.* 181 *Ulmus americana.* White Elm. . . . [Also called] Rock Elm.

* **Rocker.**

1. A piece of wood having a convex undersurface, used on a child's cradle, a chair, etc. {1793-}

1760 Eliakin Smith *Acct. Bk.* (MS., Forbes Lib., Northampton, Mass.), Pair of rockers on a cradle 5/. **1787** Cutler in *Life & Corr.* I. 269 He also showed us . . . his great arm chair, with rockers. **1848** in Bryant *California* 457 [The miner's cradle] is on rockers six or eight feet long. **1887** 'Craddock' *Keedon Bluffs* 29 The fire-light even revealed in a dusky nook a rude box on rockers.

attrib. and comb. **1850** Judd *R. Edney* 158 There are the Rocker-footed and the Square-footed; the vulgar, in stepping, go over from the heel to the toe, like the rocker of a cradle. **1893** Howells *Coast of Bohemia* 57 [She sat] up slim, graceful and picturesque, in the feather-cushioned rocker-lounge.

2. =Cradle *n.* 3.

1833 *Md. Hist. Mag.* XIII. 346 The gravel is washed, by being thrown into what is called a rocker, or cradle. [**1858** *Times* (London) 1 Dec. 10/1 The only mode of 'washing' here [in Br. Columbia] is with the 'rocker,' an inefficient, laborious, and slow, implement.] **1872** [see Hydraulic *n.*] **1885** *Wkly. New Mexican Rev.* 5 March 3/3 Our placer beds were . . . worked by the ignorant peons of wealthy Mexicans who got their first idea of even the 'rocker' from the early Spanish explorers. **1901** Grinnell *Gold Hunting in Alaska* 91 A rocker runs just like a baby's cradle, from side to side.

+**3.** =Rocking-chair.

1852 in Stowe *Key* 135/2 Will be sold, . . . Hair-seat Chairs, Sofas, and Rockers. **1883** 'Mark Twain' *Life on Miss.* xxxviii, Cane-seat chairs, splint-bottomed rocker. **1900** Dix *Deacon Bradbury* 92 Mart finally sank gasping into the big rocker. **1917** Comstock *The Man* 201 She trembled and drew near to the two in the old chintz-covered rocker.

+**4.** (See quot. 1876.)

1853 B. F. Taylor *Jan. & June* 155 Then who says, the boys sha'n't skate? Who grudges them the 'rockers'? **1873** Phelps *Trotty's Wedding* xvi, He had a pair o' new rockers, Christmas, that he hadn't tried. **1876** Knight 1958/2 *Rocker*, . . . a low-down skate with a rounding sole.

5. (See quot. 1876.)

1876 Knight 1958/1 *Rocker*, . . . the comb-like steel tool used in making the ground-work of the mezzotint process. **1885** *Harper's Mag.* Jan. 233/2 The instruments necessary . . . [are] a 'rocker' or 'cradle' with which to lay the ground [etc.].

6. A keel having a marked upward curve; a curve on a keel. {1876-}

'Chiefly *U.S.*' (O.E.D.).

1880 *Harper's Mag.* Aug. 401 False keels, or rockers, . . . have been tried upon deep-water cruises. **1895** *Outing* Aug. 382/1 Two thirds of the keel is almost flat, with a very slight rocker at the heel and a more pronounced curve under the fore-foot.

+Rocker sieve. A miner's cradle or rocker; a cradlelike device for washing out mud from the contents of a dredge. — **1869** *Overland Mo.* III. 301/2 The united crash of pebbles on hundreds of quickly agitated rocker sieves, sounded in his ear like the roar of a cotton factory. **1883** *Nat. Museum Bul.* No. 27, 575 Cradle or Rocker Sieve, for washing the contents of the dredges.

Rockery. An artificial mound of rough stones and soil in or upon which plants are cultivated for ornament. {1845-} — **1870** *Rep. Comm. Agric.* 1869 173 A rockery properly located and tastefully arranged is capable of affording much of interest and pleasure. **1871** *Scribner's Mo.* I. 233/1 In the older part of the cemetery . . . is a rockery, covered with creeping vines. **1923** WYATT *Invis. Gods* 27 He had regarded with approval the rockery and a red chair-swing in the garden.

Rocket.

1. A tube of pasteboard containing an inflammable mixture which when ignited propels the tube upward or forward. {1611-}

1701 *Boston Rec.* 12 Nor shall any person hereafter fire or throw any . . . Rocket or Serpent, or other fireworks in any of the streets. **1830** *Harper's Mag.* Dec. 73 The dawn of a new period was welcomed by musical strains . . . , by crackers, bombs, and 'flowers' (rockets, etc.). **1920** HOWELLS *Vacation of Kelwyns* 165 The rockets shot sideways and ascended in unexpected tangents.

+2. A form of school or college cheer.

1868 in *Westminster Gaz.* 26 Sept. (1901) 3/1 Three cheers . . . were given with a will, followed by the usual tiger and 'rocket.' **1879** *Princeton Book* 387 The twofold tradition in regard to the origin of the college cheer, or Nassau rocket.

Rockfish.

1. Any one of various fishes, as those of the family Scorpaenidae, found on rocky bottoms or among rocks. {1611-} Also with specifying terms.

1605 ROSIER *True Relation* 105 We got about thirty very good and great Lobsters, many Rockfish . . . and fishes called Lumpes. **1732** *Georgia Col. Rec.* III. 407 That River abounds . . . with Trout, Perch, Cat and Rock Fish. **1797** HAWKINS *Letters* 73 It is remarkable . . . for having great quantities of Rockfish at its mouth during the summer season. **1816** U. BROWN *Journal* I. 349 as large as Rock fish . . . has attacked men when in a bathing. **1886** *Outing* Dec. 242/2 It was now decided to try our luck with the rock-fish. **1911** *Rep. Fisheries* 1908 314/2 Rockfish (*Scorpænidæ*). . . . There are a large number of species, known to the fishermen as 'priest fish,' 'rock cod,' and 'rockfish,' with many qualifying prefixes, as . . . 'grass,' 'green,' 'orange,' 'red,' 'yellow' [etc.]

+2. a. Any one of various groupers found in the waters off Bermuda, Florida, etc.

1743 CATESBY *Carolina* I. p. xxxii, Common Names of the Fish of Carolina [include] . . . Sun-fish, Black-fish, Rock-fish. **1884** GOODE, etc. *Fisheries* I. 413 The Rock-fish of Key West . . . is said by Mr. Stearns to be very common. **1896** JORDAN & EVERMANN *Check-List Fishes* 374 *Mycteroperca bonaci*. Marbled Rockfish. West Indies, Pensacola to Brazil. **1911** *Rep. Fisheries* 1908 310/2 Grouper (*Epinephelus*). . . . The different species are known as 'red grouper,' . . . 'rock-fish,' etc.

+b. The striped bass, *Roccus saxatilis*.

1815 *Lit. & Phil. Soc. N.Y. Trans.* I. 503 The largest rock-fish . . . are called green heads. **1884** GOODE, etc. *Fisheries* I. 425 In the North it is called the 'Striped Bass,' in the South the 'Rock-fish' or the 'Rock.'

+c. The log perch, *Percina caprodes*.

1882 *Nat. Museum Bul.* No. 16, 499 *P. caprodes*. . . . Log Perch; Rockfish. **1884** GOODE, etc. *Fisheries* I. 417 This species is known as the 'Rockfish,' 'Hog-fish,' or 'Log Perch.' **1889** *Cent.* 2851/3 A darter, *Percina caprodes*, of the family *Percidæ* and subfamily *Etheostominæ*, inhabiting American fresh waters, [is] also called *hog-molly*, *log-perch*, and *rockfish*.

+d. The killifish, *Fundulus majalis*.

1883 *Nat. Museum Bul.* No. 27, 451 Bass-fry; Rock-fish. . . . This species is very abundant in shallow and brackish waters. It is the largest of the cyprinodents. **1896** JORDAN & EVERMANN *Check-List Fishes* 309.

+e. (See quotation.)

1891 *Cent.* 5207/2 Rockfish, . . . one of several species of serranids. (Local, U.S.)

+3. 'A codfish split, washed, and dried on the rocks' (*Cent.*).

+Rock house. 1. A house built of rocks. **2.** (See quot. 1883.) — (1) **1818** FORDHAM *Narr. Travels* 155 They had a strong rock house among the hills. **1889** *Harper's Mag.* Dec. 120/1 Thet thar rock house o' his'n, . . . I 'low it's the beatenes' house in creation. (2) **1883** SMITH *Geol. Survey Ala.* 438 Underneath the overhanging cliffs, or 'rock houses,' as they are termed, grow abundantly some of our rarest and most beautiful ferns. **1901** MOHR *Plant Life Ala.* 17 Thomas Minott Peters . . . first brought to light the delicate and extremely rare fern, *Trichomanes petersii*, . . . with others like it hidden in the dark recesses of rocky defiles and the so-called 'rock houses.'

+Rockies. *pl.* The Rocky Mountains.

*a*1861 WINTHROP *J. Brent* 60 The Wasatch range tones off into the great plains between it and the Rockys. **1881** *Rep. Indian Affairs* 46 The rain which should descend here, does not until . . . the foot-hills of

the Rockies are reached. **1890** *Stock Grower & Farmer* 26 April 5/3 The falling weather has been general on the eastern slope of the Rockies. **1900** *Congress. Rec.* 6 Feb. 1568/1 We already had a million square miles of territory this side of the Rockies. **1907** LONDON *Road* 143 At the summit of the Rockies, . . . the shack came forward for the last time.

∗Rocking. Mining. **+**The action of using a rocker (sense 2). Also attrib. — **1850** [see CRADLE *n.* 3]. **1882** *47th Congress 1 Sess.* H. R. Ex. Doc. No. 216, 568 This rocking and panning amalgamator for saving fine gold and floured mercury. **1896** SHINN *Story of Mine* 42 We started to rocking with my water.

+Rocking-chair. A chair mounted upon rockers. {1855-} — **1830** *Collegian* 93 Next sat Airy luxuriating in a cushioned rocking-chair. **1865** A. D. WHITNEY *Gayworthys* 203 Huldah . . . sank, utterly wearied, into her low wooden rocking-chair in the doorway. **1896** HARRIS *Sister Jane* 30, I rose from my rocking-chair and walked nervously about the room. **1920** HOWELLS *Vacation of Kelwyns* 45 She dropped into a rocking-chair and began to unfold her trouble to the Sisters, seated in rocking-chairs before her.

Rocking-horse. A wooden horse mounted upon rockers for children to ride. {1804-} — **1846** CHILD *Fact & Fiction* 244 He received an old tatterdemalion rocking-horse from the son of a gentleman. **1897** *Outing* XXX. 107/1 A large percentage of the best drivers have . . . ridden everything from a rocking-horse to a runaway thoroughbred. **1904** STRATTON-PORTER *Freckles* 64 They do move like a rocking-horse loping.

+Rock maple. A maple (*Acer saccharum*) abundant in the eastern half of the United States; the sugar maple: (see also quot. 1832).

1775 *R.I. Hist. Soc.Coll.* VI. 4 The timber [is] large and of various kinds, such as Pine, Oak, Hemlock and Rock Maple. **1800** in Bentley *Diary* II. 331 [Memphremagog] is circumscribed with a remarkably fine tract of Country, covered with a heavy growth of . . . Rock maple, black & yellow birch, & ash. **1832** BROWNE *Sylva* 104 In the extensive country of Genesee, both species [the sugar maple and the black sugar maple, *A. nigrum*] are indiscriminately called *Rock Maple* and *Sugar Maple*. **1850** JUDD *R. Edney* 308 Superb rock-maples overhang the roof of an iron foundery. **1880** TOURGEE *Bricks* 124 The elegant residences of the owners were . . . hidden among great groves of rock-maples. **1897** [see HARD MAPLE].

b. Attrib., often in sense: Made of the wood of rock maple.

1842 *Lowell Offering* II. 274 A huge rock-maple fire was burning brightly on the old kitchen hearth. **1848** D. P. THOMPSON *L. Amsden* 11 A body of three or four hundred straight, tall, and thrifty rock-maple trees . . . composed the sugar-place. **1858** THOREAU *Maine Woods* 97 We had two . . . rock-maple paddles, one of them of bird's-eye maple.

+Rock oak.

1. = ROCK CHESTNUT OAK. Also attrib.

1699 *Conn. Rec.* IV. 304 Running eastward three hundred rod to a rock-oak tree markt. **1773** *Ib.* XIV. 172 [Resolved] that the rock-oak aforesaid with stones about it is the southwest corner of Midletown. **1810** MICHAUX *Arbres* I. 23 *Rock Chesnut Oak*, . . . seul nom donné à cette espèce dans les Etats de New-York et de Vermont. *Rock et rocky oak*, . . . dans cette même partie. **1897** SUDWORTH *Arborescent Flora* 156.

2. The California blue oak, *Quercus douglasii*.

1860 GREELEY *Overland Journey* 349 Black and rock-oak are found in some of the mountain valleys. **1897** SUDWORTH *Arborescent Flora* 160 *Quercus douglasii*. . . . (California) Rock Oak.

Rock oil. Petroleum. {1668-} — **1855** in Tarbell *Hist. Standard Oil Co.* I. 265, I herewith offer you the results of my . . . researches upon the rock-oil, or petroleum, from Venango County, Pennsylvania. **1890** *Harper's Mag.* Oct. 723/1 It was generally supposed that the 'rock oil' which then began to be produced there in such quantity was a newly discovered material.

+Rock oyster. a. An oyster found growing upon a rock and not in a bed. **b.** An oysterlike bivalve, esp. *Hinnites giganteus* of the Pacific coast. — **1881** INGERSOLL *Oyster-Industry* 247. **1891** *Cent.* 5208/1. **1913** LONDON *Valley of Moon* 278 Some oysters first—I want to compare them with the rock oysters.

Rock pine. {1889-} **+1.** The jack pine, *Pinus banksiana*. **+2.** (See quot. 1905.) — (1) **1894** *Amer. Folk-Lore* VII. 100 *Pinus Banksiana*, shore-pine, rock-pine, Grand Lake section of Penobscot River. (2) **1897** SUDWORTH *Arborescent Flora* 100. **1905** *Forestry Bureau Bul.* No. 66, 33 The rock pine (*Pinus ponderosa scopulorum*), commonly called bull pine or yellow pine, is a variety of the western yellow pine of the Rocky Mountains, which it closely resembles.

Rock ptarmigan. (See quot. 1917.) — [**1819** SHAW *Gen. Zool.* XI. 290.] **1872** COUES *N. Amer. Birds* 235 Rock Ptarmigan. Tail black, . . . with a black transocular stripe. **1917** *Birds of Amer.* II. 22 Rock Ptarmigan. *Lagopus rupestris rupestris*. . . . The Rock Ptarmigan is common on the mainland of Alaska.

Rock-ribbed, *a.* {1776} *fig.* Firm; uncompromising; unyielding.

1887 *Courier-Journal* 3 May 414 Mr. Straus is a rock-ribbed Democrat. **1896** *Internat. Typogr. Union Proc.* 41/2 In the opinion of a vast majority of our members . . . as well as those of other rock-ribbed trade unionists [it] was regarded as a prolonged struggle. **1906** *Forum* July 3 Even Senator Tillman, a rockribbed, uncompromising Democrat, does not withhold the credit that is justly due. **1911** HARRISON *Queed* 292 Various feelings had gradually stiffened an early general approval into a rock-ribbed resolve.

+Rock road. A road paved with rocks. — **1850** *Western Journal* IV. 75 If rock and lumber were equally convenient, I would make rock roads. **1903** Fox *Little Shepherd* iii, There were towns . . . with rock roads running through them in every direction and narrow rock paths along these roads.

Rock-rooted, a. {1815–} *fig.* Firmly or unalterably fixed in opinion or policy. — **1890** *Congress. Rec.* 7 June 5802/1 Every rock-rooted advocate of the gold standard is in favor of [this provision]. **1902** CLAPIN 339 *Rock-rooted,* a qualification applied to the Democratic party, fondly by its members, and in derision by its foes.

Rock rose. {1629–}

1. Any plant of the family Cistaceae {1731–}, +as the frostweed. Also attrib.

1836 LINCOLN *Botany* App. 88 *Cistus . . . canadensis,* (rock-rose). **1840** DEWEY *Mass. Flowering Plants* 80 Cistineæ. The Rock Rose Tribe. **1843** TORREY *Flora N.Y.* I. 77 *Helianthemum. . . .* Rock-Rose. . . . The North American species of this genus produce two sorts of flowers. **1915** ARMSTRONG & THORNBER *Western Wild Flowers* 304 Rock-rose. *Helianthemum scoparium. . . .* A pretty plant, with many, slender stems and narrow, yellowish-green leaves.

+2. a. The shrubby St.-John's-wort, *Hypericum prolificum.* **b.** The resurrection plant, *Selaginella lepidophylla.*

1860 CURTIS *Woody Plants N.C.* 109 *Hypericum.* Of this we have five woody species, all with yellow flowers, one of which (*H. prolificum*) is occasionally cultivated under the name of *Rock Rose.* **1885** HAVARD *Flora W. & S. Texas* 527 *Selaginella lepidophylla,* Spring. (Siempre Vive; Rock Rose.) Very remarkable moss-like plant.

Rock salt. Salt occurring in nature in a solid form. {1707–} — **1752** *Boston Ev. Post* 4 Dec., Choice Rock Salt. **1779** *N.J. Archives* 2 Ser. IV. 37 A few casks of French, shore, and rock salt. **1819** SCHOOLCRAFT *Journal* 71 He represents the existence of rock-salt between the head of the south fork of White River and the Arkansaw. **1856** *Porter's Spirit of Times* 25 Oct. 130/3 The ground rock salt is most valued. **1886** WINCHELL *Walks Geol.Field* 131 The sediments . . . would be deposited upon the bed of rock-salt.

+Rock saxifrage. The early saxifrage (*Micranthes virginiensis*) of eastern North America. — **1817–8** EATON *Botany* (1822) 448 *Saxifraga virginiensis,* rock saxifrage. . . . On and near ledges of rocks. **1840** DEWEY *Mass. Flowering Plants* 45 S[axifraga] *Pennsylvanica,* Water Saxifrage, and *S. Virginiensis,* Rock Saxifrage, are named from their usual habitations.

+Rock slide. A mass of rock and earth precipitated as a landslide. — **1877** *Field & Forest* II. 186 Pointing to a rock-slide composed of masses of stone ranging in size from a pebble to the enormous boulder, he said, 'These are the graves.' **1910** RAINE *B. O'Connor* 240 Leroy had hardly passed beyond the rock-slide before the others.

+Rock snipe. =PURPLE SANDPIPER. — **1835** AUDUBON *Ornith. Biog.* III. 558 Their marked predilection for rocky shores has caused them to be named 'Rock Snipes' by the gunners of our eastern coast. **1888** TRUMBULL *Names of Birds* 182 [The purple sandpiper] is the Rock-bird, Rock Plover, and Rock Snipe at Rowley and Salem, Mass. **1917** *Birds of Amer.* I. 232 Purple Sandpiper. *Arquatella maritima maritima. . . .* Other Names.—Rock Sandpiper; Rock Snipe; Rock Plover.

*Rock stone. A stone; a stony formation. — **1685** *Plymouth Rec.* I. 184 The bounds of Nathanell Woods 2 Acres of land . . . [extend from] a Rock stone set into the ground [etc.]. **1725** *Bristol* (Va.) *Vestry Bk.* 23 Each Chapple are to be . . . fraim'd on good Sils under pin'd with good blocks or rock-stones. **1789** WASHINGTON *Diaries* IV. 49 From thence to Ashford . . . [the lands are] very hilly and much mixed with rock stone. **1836** EDWARD *Hist. Texas* 114 He would there see a . . . prairie . . . covered with small rock-stones.

+Rock swift. The white-throated swift (*Aëronautes saxatalis saxatalis*) of western North America. — **1869** *Amer. Naturalist* III. 186 [Of] the Rock Swift (*Panyptila melanoleuca*), a few . . . breed in some cliffs near [San Diego]. **1874** COUES *Birds N.W.* 265 White-throated or Rock Swift.

+Rock tripe. (See quot. 1866.) — **1866** LINDLEY & MOORE *Treas. Botany* 1172/2 *Tripe de Roche.* This name, or that of Rock Tripe, is given in North America, in consequence of the blistered thallus, to several species of lichens belonging to *Gyrophora* and *Umbilicaria,* but especially to the latter. **1901** MOHR *Plant Life Ala.* 63 On the summit of Chehawhaw Mountain rock-tripe, a large lichen (*Umbilicaria*), covers . . . the bare crags. **1907** *St. Nicholas* July 847/1 'Rock-tripe,' another lichen, has been eaten in the arctic regions in times of famine.

Rock trout. {1844–8} **1.** The boregat (*Hexagrammos decagrammus*), or any of various related fishes of the Pacific coast. **2.** (See quotation.) — **(1) 1876** *Smithsonian Misc. Coll.* XIII. VI. 65 Fishes, (western coast:) Rock trout, (*Chirus constellatus*). **1884** GOODE, etc.*Fisheries* I. 267 A family of fish of considerable importance on our Pacific coast is that of the *Chiridæ,* or Rock Trouts, no representatives of which are known in the Atlantic. **1911** *Rep. Fisheries 1908* 314/2 Rock trout (*Hexagrammos*), a group of fishes of considerable importance on the Pacific coast. They are the true greenlings. The different species are known as 'sea trout,' 'starling,' . . . 'red rock trout,' etc. **(2) 1891** *Cent.* 5208/3 *Rock-trout,* . . . the common American brook-trout, *Salvelinus fontinalis,* as occurring in Lake Superior.

Rockweed. Any one of various kinds of seaweed growing on rocks washed by the tides. {1626–1777} — **1698** *Providence Rec.* VI. 198 My son Elisha shall have free Egress and Regress . . . to fetch Rockweede for his vse at any time on the said Neck. **1722** [see KELP 1]. **1790** DEANE *New-Eng. Farmer* 148/2, I have sometimes defended the plants . . . by encircling them with rock-weed. **1839** *Mass. Agric. Survey* 2d *Rep.* 89 Result of ten experiments of seeding Potatoes, twenty hills each, manured with a small handful of Rock-weed. **1888** GOODE *Amer. Fishes* 171 He took the sprays of rock-weed in his hands and pulled them slowly to him.

Rock wren. {1882–} +Any one of several wrens of the genus *Salpinctes* found in the rim-rock region of the West. — **1858** BAIRD *Birds Pacific R.R.* 357 *Salpinctes Obsoletus.* Rock Wren. . . . High central plains through the Rocky mountains to the Coast and Cascade ranges. **1869** *Amer. Naturalist* III. 183 The Rock Wren . . . and Cactus Wren . . . chirrup loudly from the tiled roof or dense thickets. **1893** ROOSEVELT *Wilderness Hunter* 68 In the rough canyons [is] the rock wren, with its ringing melody. **1917** *Birds of Amer.* III. 188/2 The Rock Wren is not unlike its cousin in its household eccentricities.

*Rocky, a. **+1.** Disreputable, coarse. **+2.** Hard, difficult, tough. — **(1) 1851** A. T. JACKSON *Forty-Niner* (1920) 82 [The men] told stories, some of them pretty rocky. **1891** *Univ. of Mich. Daily* 18 March, Last year it [the filling of programs for the Junior Hop on the night before] was pronounced 'rocky' by all. **(2) 1873** MILLER *Amongst Modocs* 71 We may have a rocky time down there, my boy. **1889** L. C. D'OYLE in *Cornhill Mag.* Jan. 56 It'll be a little bit rocky on some of us. **1898** POST *10 Years Cowboy* 56, I don't believe I'm a coward, but there are things about this business that are a little bit too rocky for comfort.

+Rocky Ford. attrib. Designating a class of muskmelons originally grown around Rocky Ford, Colorado. — **1899** ADE *Fables in Slang* 2 There came into the room a tall, rangy Person with a Head in the shape of a Rocky Ford Cantaloupe. **1916** *Farmers' Bul.* No. 707, 22 The Rocky Ford melon is not a new variety of melon.

+Rocky Mountain.

1. *pl.* A great mountain range in the western part of North America.

Cf. CHIPPEWAN, CHIPPEWAYAN, a.

1804 CLARK in *Lewis & C. Exped.* I. (1904) 210 The Snake Indians . . . inhabit the Rockey Mountains. **1818** *Niles' Reg.* XIV. 208/1 Old col. Boone . . . may yet be driven to the Rocky Mountains, and even there be *disturbed* in 8 or 10 years. **1837** IRVING *Bonneville* I. 43 Up this stream he determined to prosecute his route to the Rocky Mountains. **1864** *Rio Abajo Press* 21 June 2/1 We have had no warm weather yet here on top of the Rocky mountains. **1876** CROFUTT *Trans-continental Tourist* 70 We are now near the summit of the great 'back-bone' of the continent—the Rocky Mountains. **1900** *Congress. Rec.* 31 Jan. 1354/1 The Rio Grande River . . . rises in the Rocky Mountains in Colorado.

2. *attrib.* in *sing.* **a.** Designating people, places, and things associated with the Rocky Mountains.

1832 *Congress. Deb.* 9 June 3397 If the Government wanted the services of those Rocky Mountain boys, they must pay for it. **1847** PARKMAN in *Knickerb.* XXX. 236 Several gaudy articles of Rocky Mountain finery . . . garnished the walls. **1850** GARRARD *Wah-To-Yah* x. 130 The hardy frequenters of the Rocky Mountain hunting grounds and beaver streams. **1865** *Wkly. New Mexican* 22 Sept. 1/3 After an experience of several years with the Rocky Mountain Indians, I am compelled to the conclusion that it is impossible to civilize the adult Indians. **1868** *N.Y. Herald* 30 July 4/3 The Western Indians and our Rocky Mountain Travellers. **1887** Rocky Mountain states [see FOREIGNISM]. **1900** *Congress. Rec.* 24 Jan. 1122/1 In our own . . . Rocky Mountain region you would find an optimistic enumerator who would go through a mining district. **1913** LONDON *Valley of Moon* 104 Del Hancock was . . . going I don't know where to raise a company of Rocky Mountain trappers to go after beaver.

b. In the names of birds frequenting the Rocky Mountain region.

Other examples can be found in ornithological works.

1825 BONAPARTE *Ornithology* I. 6 [The] Rocky Mountain Antcatcher, *Myiothera obsoleta,* . . . is one of those beings which seem created to puzzle the naturalist. **1858** BAIRD *Birds Pacific R.R.* 224 *Sialia Arctica. . . .* Rocky Mountain Blue Bird. . . . Rocky Mountain range and south to Mexico. **1872** *Harper's Mag.* Dec. 20/2 The eyes of the ornithologist are dazzled with the dark blue-green iridescent plumage of the bold and fearless Rocky Mountain blue jay. **1839** AUDUBON *Ornith. Biog.* V. 302 Rocky-Mountain Flycatcher. *Muscicapa Nigricans.* **1869** *Amer. Naturalist* III. 83 Rocky Mountain Golden-eye (*Bucephala Islandica?*). I saw some dark headed ducks, perhaps this species, . . . high up the Little Blackfoot River. **1887** RIDGWAY *Manual N.A. Birds* 262 Higher Rocky Mountains, from Colorado to eastern Montana (Fort Custer). . . . *M[egascops] asio maxwelliæ.* Rocky Mountain Screech Owl. **1878** *Nat. Museum Proc.* I. 417 *Melospiza fasciata,* [var.] δ. *fallax.*—Rocky Mountain Song Sparrow. **1917** *Birds of Amer.* III. 84 Cliff Swallow. *Petrochelidon lunifrons lunifrons. . . .* [Also called] Crescent Swallow; Rocky Mountain Swallow; Moon-fronted Swallow.

c. In the names of animals, insects, and fishes found in the Rocky Mountain region.

See also ROCKY MOUNTAIN GOAT, ROCKY MOUNTAIN LOCUST, etc.

1828 RICHARDSON in *Zoological Jrnl.* III. 517 Rocky Mountain Dormouse. *Ib.* 520 Rocky Mountain Flying Squirrel. **1909** WEBSTER 944/1

The allied migratory Rocky Mountain grasshopper (*M[elanoplus] spretus*) . . . sometimes travels in vast hordes in the region west of the Mississippi. **1826** GODMAN *Nat. Hist.* II. 144 The Rocky Mountain Ground-Squirrel. *Sciurus Lateralis*. . . . First seen by Lewis and Clark. **1884** GOODE *Fisheries* I. 542 Rocky Mountain White-fish—*Coregonus Williamsoni*. . . . It is found throughout the Rocky Mountain region, in cold, clear lakes.

 d. In the names of trees and plants growing in or associated with the Rocky Mountain region.

1871 *Amer. Naturalist* V. 66 We find the rocky slopes all yellow in some places with the flowers of the Rocky Mountain Barberry. . . . This is *Berberis aquifolium* of the author. **1849** EMMONS *Agric. N.Y.* II. 263 Rocky-mountain corn . . . is cultivated at present only as a curiosity. **1892** *Amer. Folk-Lore* V. 98 *Coreopsis tinctoria*, Rocky Mt. flower. Mansfield, O. **1882** *Century Mag.* Sept. 770/1 The narrow valley and the steep declivities . . . [were] heavily timbered with the red fir and the Rocky Mountain pine (*Pinus ponderosa*).

 +Rocky Mountain goat. =MOUNTAIN GOAT. Also with defining terms. (Cf. GOAT ANTELOPE.) — **1842** *Nat. Hist. N.Y., Zoology* I. 112 Rocky Mountain Goat . . . , larger than the common goat. **1868** *Amer. Naturalist* Dec. 537 The Rocky Mountain Goat is almost unknown to the traders at Fort Benton. **1885** *Century Mag.* Oct. 973/2 He killed a Rocky Mountain goat. **1917** *Mammals of Amer.* 56/2 Allen Rocky Mountain Goat.—*Oreamnos montanus missoulae*. . . . Found in Montana.

 +Rocky Mountain locust. A migratory grasshopper (*Melanoplus spretus*) formerly traveling in large hordes west of the Mississippi River. — **1878** *Rep. Comm. Agric. 1877* 264 The Rocky Mountain Locust, or Grasshopper of the West. **1892** KELLOGG *Kansas Insects* 24 The State was invaded by the Rocky Mountain Locust in 1866.

 +Rocky Mountain rat. The brushy-tailed wood rat, *Neotoma cinerea*. Also *Rocky Mountain wood rat*. — **1859** BAIRD *Mammals N. Amer.* 499 Rocky Mountain Rat. **1868** *Amer. Naturalist* II. 534 Rocky Mountain Wood-Rat (*Neotoma cinerea*). On the banks of the Missouri above Fort Union, were frequently seen large nests.

 +Rocky Mountain sheep. The bighorn (*Ovis canadensis*), or a related species. (Cf. MOUNTAIN SHEEP.)

[**1804** CLARK in *Lewis & C. Exped.* I. (1904) 239 We precured two horns of the animale the french Call the rock Mountain Sheep.] **1817** S. BROWN *Western Gazetteer* 202 Rocky Mountain Sheep are the most common animal. **1858** PETERS *Kit Carson* 405 The mountain districts . . . [abound] in the famous Rocky Mountain sheep. **1877** HODGE *Arizona* 222 The wild goat, or Rocky Mountain sheep, is quite plentiful in some of the mountainous districts. **1891** *Scribner's Mag.* Oct. 445/1 In pursuit of Rocky Mountain sheep, the hunter . . . must have a fondness for the mountains. **1917** *Mammals of Amer.* 50/2 Over these hills and ravines the Rocky Mountain Sheep bound up and down.

 +Rocky oak. =ROCK CHESTNUT OAK. (Cf. ROCK OAK 1.) — **1801** MICHAUX *Histoire des Chênes* 6 Chêne chataignier (des montagnes). *Mountain Chesnut Oak, Roky Oak.* **1810** — *Arbres* I. 23 *Rock chesnut oak*, . . . seul nom donné à cette espèce dans les Etats de New-York et de Vermont. *Rock* et *rocky oak*, . . . dans cette même partie.

 *Rod, *n.*

 *1. A linear measure equal to 16½ feet.

The sing. is sometimes used for the plural, esp. in colloq. speech. (Cf. POLE *n*.[1] 2 a.)

1635 *Watertown Rec.* I. 1. 1 There shall be foure Rods in breadth on each side of the River. **1666** *Warwick Rec.* 452, I Leiftenant Eliza Collins doe ingadge forth with to mend up twenty rodd of fence uppon . . . Mr John potters Lott. **1710** *Derby Rec.* 73 The South end is 24 rods. **1774** FITHIAN *Journal* I. 194 This [is] not more than three times as many Rod. **1822** FOWLER *Journal* 124 The Hot Watter Head kept the Ground Cleane for a few Rods Round the Spring. **1880** CABLE *Grandissimes* 424 Some rods within the edge of the swamp, . . . a dense growth of willows and vines and dwarf palmetto shut out the light of the open fields. **1902** HULBERT *Forest Neighbors* 23 A few rods up-stream was a grassy point which the rising waters had transformed into an island.

 +2. =LIGHTNING ROD.

[**1750** FRANKLIN *Writings* I. 102 Would not these pointed rods probably draw the electrical fire silently out of a cloud?] **1755** *S.C. Gazette* 24 July, The House of Mr. John Raven . . . was struck with Lightening, altho' it had an electrical Rod fixed to one of the Chimnies. **1851** CIST *Cincinnati* 216 The whole country, of which Cincinnati is the business centre, purchases these rods. **1900** STOCKTON *Afield & Afloat* 392 The rod was placed there that lightning might come down it, not that it might go up.

 +3. The drawrod of a freight train; *to ride the rods*, to steal a ride on the framework underneath a freight car.

1907 LONDON *The Road* 24 The tramp, snugly ensconced inside the truck, . . . has the 'cinch' on the crew—or so he thinks, until some day he rides the rods on a bad road. **1924** J. TULLY *Beggars of Life* 56, I beat it through De Kalb last night on the rods of a manerfest meat train.

 *Rod, *v.* **+tr.** To supply with lightning rods. — **1888** *Scientific Amer.* LVIII. 358 (*Cent.*), Several other houses in the town were rodded in the same way. **1897** F. C. MOORE *How to Build a Home* 64 A dwelling of his . . . was rodded in the best manner.

 ‖**Rodder.** One who erects lightning rods. — **1879** STOCKTON *Rudder Grange* xiii, I don't see how the rodder would 'a' got his ladder at all if the dog hadn't made an awful jump at him, and jerked the ladder down.

 +Rode. [Of obscure origin.] A rope for securing an anchor. — **1634** WOOD *New Eng. Prospect* (1865) 45 They are constrayned to . . . hale their Boats by the sealing, or roades. **1679** *Boston Rec.* 135 Allowed James Babson of Cape Ann towards a roade taken out of his Boate in the time of ye fire, . . . 20 s. **1726** PENHALLOW *Indian Wars* 58 [They] quit one of their boats by cutting their roads and lashings. **1891** *Cent.* 5210/1 Rode, . . . a rope attached to a boat-anchor or killock. *Perley.* (Bay of Fundy.)

 Rodent. {1835-} ‖ =RAT *n.* 6. — **1896** *Internat. Typogr. Union Proc.* 31/1 For two days after the beginning of the real struggle the paper (or half of it) was gotten out by rodents.

 Rodeo. [Sp., 'a going round, a cattle ring.']

 1. A round-up of cattle, usually held once a year on western ranches, for the purposes of branding, counting, inspecting, etc. {1834, in Chile}

1851 *Calif. Laws* 445 Every owner of a stock farm shall be obliged to give, yearly, one general rodeo. **1877** HARTE *Story of Mine* (1896) 423 It is only two years ago, before the rodeo, that I was here for strayed colts. **1890** *Stock Grower & Farmer* 5 April 6/1 The spring rodeo commenced March 20th at the mouth of Tonto. **1897** HOUGH *Story of Cowboy* 112 The rodeo was shiftless and imperfect, and many cattle got through year after year unbranded. **1919** WILSON *Ma Pettengill* 79 Finally we got the cows and calves home . . . and started a general rodeo for the dry stock.

attrib. **1892** ATHERTON *Doomswoman* xxiv, The platform on one side of the circular rodeo-ground. **1921** F. S. HASTINGS *Ranchman's Recoll.* 232 A certain outlaw speckled yearling . . . had thrown every boy with rodeo aspirations who had tried to ride him.

 +b. ?A herd of cattle.

1897 HOUGH *Story of Cowboy* 21 This is an old cattle country. Countless *rodeos* have crossed these hills.

 +2. A public exhibition of features of the round-up, such as lassoing, mustang-breaking, etc.

1914 'BOWER' *Flying U Ranch* 16 They have them rodeos on a Sunday, mostly, and they invite everybody to it, like it was a picnic. **1921** HASTINGS *Ranchman's Recoll.* 233 This is the chief type of rodeo—a show put on by all the ranch boys in a particular community. Professionals are barred. **1925** W. JAMES *Drifting Cowboy* 6 At them rodeos there's two men handling each horse, where with the round-up wagon on the range each man handles his horse alone.

 Rodman. {1888-} A surveyor's assistant who holds up the rod used in surveying. — **1856** WHIPPLE *Explor. Ry. Route* I. 5 The chainmen and rodmen being ignorant of their duties, little more than teaching them could this day be accomplished. **1899** *Success* 6 May 391 Mr. Martin got work as a rodman on the Brooklyn water works. **1903** *N.Y. Ev. Post* 31 Oct., He began in 1880 as a rodman, driving stakes for the surveyors.

 +Rodman gun. [Gen. T. J. *Rodman*, Amer. soldier (1815-71).] A smoothbore, muzzle-loading gun or cannon cast with a hollow core and cooled from the interior. — **1862** Moore *Rebellion Rec.* V. 11. 420, I could clearly distinguish the sharp, crashing thunder of our Rodman guns from that produced by the enemy's pieces. **1863** KETTELL *Hist. Rebellion* II. 429 The gun known as the Union or Rodman gun is a 15-inch columbiad.

 Rod of Aaron. [See AARON'S ROD.] ‖One of various plants often called *Aaron's rod*, characterized by tall flowering stems. — **1873** *Harper's Mag.* April 752/1 Sensitive plants and the rose of Sharon, Adam's-needle and rod of Aaron.

 *Roe.

 *1. The eggs of fish, freq. cooked and served as food

1682 ASH *Carolina* 26 [It produces] Sturgeon, of whose Sounds Iceing glass, of whose Roes Caviare are made. **1807** GASS *Journal* 128 The fish they take in this river are of excellent kinds, especially the salmon, the roes of which when dried and pounded make the best of soup. **1905** PRINGLE *Rice Planter* 165 A fresh trout with a roe . . . [was] a present from Casa Bianca.

 2. Attrib. with *mullet, sauce, shad*; also, *roe corn*, a single fish egg.

1869 *Rep. Comm. Agric.* 1868 321 These boxes contain each two thousand roe 'corns.' **1883** *Century Mag.* Aug. 549/2 Another cook will prepare the roe sauce to accompany the shad. **1884** GOODE, etc. *Fisheries* I. 451 The 'Roe Mullet' weigh about two and a half pounds, and are caught in November and until Christmas. **1884** ROE *Nature's Story* 195 There was a great roe-shad hanging by his gills.

 +Rogerene. [John Rogers, nonconformist of colonial Connecticut (1648-1721).] A member of a small religious sect of Baptist origin in Connecticut, whose doctrines and practice were opposed to some of the formal usages of churches, participation in military service, etc. Also *Rogerene Quaker.* Now hist. — **1754** HEMPSTEAD *Diary* 625 A Co[m]pany of the Rogerens . . . held their meeting after our meeting was over. **1820** *Niles' Reg.* XVIII. 366/1 A contagious disorder is now raging among the sect known by the name of Rogereen Quakers in Grotan. **1865** *Mass. H. S. Coll.* 4 Ser. VII. 584n., [John Rogers was] the founder of the sect of Rogerenes, of whom a small number still remain.

 *Rogue.

 +1. A pirate ship.

1689 SEWALL *Diary* I. 278 Two Rogues to windward of us, which the Man of War keeps off but can't come up with them. **1707** *Boston News-*

Letter 7 April 2/2 The Shallops give account of such a Ship seen this week . . . ; 'Tis feared to be a Rogue by his working.

+2. a. *Rogue's gallery,* a collection of photographs of criminals.

1864 NORTON *Army Lett.* 223 The process of transportation affords excellent opportunities for taking photographs of 'black-legs,' etc., for the Rogues' Gallery. **1882** McCABE *New York* 372 Here are the offices of . . . the Detective Squad, the Chief Surgeon, and the 'Rogue's Gallery.' **1901** RIIS *Making of American* 272 The 'gallery' at Headquarters is the rogues' gallery, not generally much desired.

+b. *Rogue's Island,* (see quotation).

1865 *Atlantic Mo.* Feb. 190/2 Rhode Island—then sometimes called Rogue's Island, from her paper-money operations—refused to give up the refugee rebels.

Roil, *n.* The stirring up of water. Also fig. — **1693** C. MATHER *Wonders Invis. World* (1862) 189 Some very great Saints of God, have sometimes had hideous Royls raised by the Devil in their minds. **1895** *Outing* XXVI. 62/1 The roil disturbed the spot where the fish was endeavoring to escape.

∗**Roil,** *v. tr.* To stir up or muddy (a stream); also, fig., to stir up or disturb (a person or his emotions). {-a1734; now *dial.*} Cf. RILE *v.* — **1771** J. ADAMS *Diary* Works II. 290 His imagination is disturbed, his passions all roiled. **1818** FEARON *Sketches* 97 We were mightily *roiled* (vexed) when they [*sc.* public roads] were first cut. **1854** THOREAU *Walden* 245 I could dip up a pailful without roiling it. **1870** LOWELL *Poetical Works* (1896) 409/2 A day at Chartres, with no soul beside To roil with pedant prate my joy serene. **1879** *Congress. Rec.* 3 June 1738/1 The Potomac River . . . is liable to be roiled. **1907** *Springfield W. Repub.* 17 Jan. 6 The publication of such a work naturally roiled the publishers of Webster's international dictionary.

+Roiler. [f. *roil* v., 'to salt fish.'] (See quotation.) — **1891** *Cent.* 5212/2 *Roiler,* a machine for salting small fish, as a revolving box turned by means of a crank. (North Carolina.)

Roily, *a.* [f. ROIL *n.* or *v.*] Muddy, turbid. {1866, *dial.*} — **1823** COOPER *Pioneers* xx, Nor catch a woodman's hasty snap, For fear . . . [the sap] should get roily. **1862** NORTON *Army Lett.* 98 Sometimes we have excellent water, and again we can get nothing but roily swamp water. **1895** *Outing* XXVI. 63/1 He abruptly departed, leaving behind him a trail of roily water. **1911** J. F. WILSON *Land Claimers* 22 Drenching showers filled the creek bottom with roily water.

+Rokeag(e). [See quot. 1910.] (See quot. 1848 and cf. PINOLE.) — **1848** BARTLETT 278 *Rokeage,* or *Yokeage,* Indian corn parched, pulverized, and mixed with sugar. **1910** HODGE, etc. *Amer. Indians* II. 394/1 *Rokeag,* . . . spelled also *roucheag* and *rokee.* The word is from Quiripi (Quinnipiac) *rok'hig,* abbreviated from *rokehigan,* and . . . means '(what is) softened.'

+Rokee. (See prec.)

∗**Roll,** *n.*[1]

∗**1.** An official list or register.

1641 *Mass. H. S. Coll.* 3 Ser. VIII. 223 Everie man shall have libertie to Record in the publique Rolles of any Court any Testimony given upon oath in the same Court. **1792** *Ann. 2d Congress* 464 The superintending officers at elections are empowered to appoint three clerks to attend, and to keep three rolls or checks, setting down the names of the voters therein with the names of the candidates. **1871** RAYMOND *3d Rep. Mines* 117 Nearly one-half the entries in the roll of the assessor make no mention of the mine which produced the ore. **1913** *Indian Laws & Tr.* III. 572 The roll herein provided for shall be made in triplicate and shall show the allotment number or numbers, together with the description of the property allotted.

∗**2.** A quantity of material rolled or twisted into cylindrical shape: **+a.** A mass *of* tobacco leaves; *in roll,* rolled up in cylindrical form.

1633 *Va. Statutes at Large* I. 205 Noe tobacco . . . shall be made upp in rolle except betweene the first day of August and the last day of October. **1648** *Boston Rec.* 187 Two hogshead . . . [were] in leafe & two in rowle. **1706** [see LEAF TOBACCO]. **1814** BRACKENRIDGE *Views La.* 91 [He] presented them a few rolls of tobacco.

attrib. **1633** *N.H. Prov. Papers* I. 73 He sent me from the Isle of Sholes 6 lb. of role tobaca.

∗**b.** A small portion of bread dough baked in any of various shapes.

1771 FRANKLIN *Autobiog.* 254 Having no room in my pockets, [I] walked off with a roll under each arm. **1835** LONGSTREET *Ga. Scenes* 36 Waffles were handed to Ned, and he tooke one; . . . and so on of muffins, rolls, and corn bread. **1907** ANDREWS *Recoll.* 234 After a cup of coffee and a roll, [he] rode horseback for an hour or so.

+3. A package of paper money; money in general.

a1854 W. NORTH *Slave of Lamp* 33, 'I guess the whole pile [of bills] are bogus,' muttered Confidence Bob, as he turned over his roll. **1900** DIX *Deacon Bradbury* 87 He bent over the uncleared breakfast-table and counted out a part of the roll. **1904** *N.Y. Times* 16 May 5 It was as easy to be separated from one's 'roll' at a shell game there a quarter of a century ago as it was ten years ago. **1916** WILSON *Somewhere* 401 He's got his roll out and wants to pay for the car right there.

+4. A specific cut of beef.

1884 *Harper's Mag.* July 299/1 The division is made into . . . loins, ribs, mess, plates, chucks, rolls, rumps.

+5. The rolled-up bedding and other personal belongings of a cowboy.

1907 WHITE *Arizona Nights* 157 'Rolls' were scattered everywhere. A roll includes a cowboy's bed, and all of his personal belongings. When the outfit includes a bed-wagon, the roll assumes bulky proportions.

6. In special combinations.

Roll lift (attrib.), of a drawbridge, operating on rollers; *roll pudding,* ?a pudding in the form of a roll.

1893 EGGLESTON *Duffels* 189, I broke into my stock of school-boy stories of the jokes about the 'cat,' or roll pudding we had twice a week. **1899** *Boston Transcript* 22 July 6/2 The outside section of the big, new, roll-lift draw over Fort Point Channel will be thrown open for use of all trains.

Roll, *n.*[2] {1688-} **1.** Undulation in the surface of land; a ridge. {1874-} **2.** A game of bowling. — **(1) 1850** KINGSLEY *Diary* 152 It is generally level without much roll. **1866** *Ill. Agric. Soc. Trans.* VI. 177 As the table land approaches the brook from either ridge, rough rolls or ridges occur. **(2) 1855** HOLBROOK *Among Mail Bags* 58, [I] agreed to meet him there early in the evening for a 'roll.'

∗**Roll,** *v.*

I. **+1.** *tr.* To shift (timber) for purposes of stacking, loading, transportation, and the like. {in general sense, 1375-}

1640 *Boston Rec.* 54 The timber he may rowle upon the marsh. **1739** HEMPSTEAD *Diary* 355, I was at home all Day setting up Crotches & roling Logs on the Wall. **1848** *Fla. Plantation Rec.* 57, I will finish roling logs today. **1902** WHITE *Blazed Trail* 195, I'll get you a gang of bully boys that will roll logs till there's skating in hell!

+2. *local.* To transport (tobacco or a cask of tobacco) by rolling the cask. Also *vbl. n.* Now hist.

Cf. ROLLING HOUSE, ROLLING ROAD 1.

1696 *Md. Laws* (1765) xxiv. § 8 [The] Governor of this Province, hath caused four Rolling Roads to be marked and cleared, for the rolling or transporting Tobacco or Goods by Land. **1724** JONES *Virginia* 55 The Tobacco is rolled, drawn by Horses, or carted to convenient Rolling Houses. **1856** OLMSTED *Slave States* 360 Until within a recent period, much tobacco has been brought to market, from the more remote districts of North Carolina and Virginia, by a very rude method, called 'rolling.' **1884** *Century Mag.* Jan. 446/2 The cask was strongly hooped, and then rolled by human strength along the hot and sandy roads often fifteen or twenty miles to the inspector's warehouse.

3. To press or flatten (iron) with a roller. {of copper, 1837-}

1795 *Essex Inst. Coll.* LIV. 103 A mill to roll and slit iron into sheets is required. **1870** EMERSON *Soc. & Solitude* 25, I admire . . . the skill which . . . engages the assistance of the moon . . . to grind, and wind, and pump, and saw, and split stone, and roll iron. **1881** [see FAGOT 1].

+4. To crush (sugar cane) by running it between rollers.

1862 *N.Y. Tribune* 4 March 17/3 All the cane grown is never rolled.

+5. *absol.* **a.** To bowl. {cf. *rolling* vbl. sb.[2] 1, quot. 1583} **b.** *Print.* To ink with a roller.

(a) 1852 HAWTHORNE *Notebooks* 262 There is a bowling-alley on the island, at which some of the young fishermen were rolling. **(b) 1880** 'MARK TWAIN' *Tramp Abroad* 586 In our country printing-offices the apprentice first learns how to sweep out and bring water; then learns to 'roll.'

II. With adverbs. **+6.** *To roll in.* **a.** To retire to bed. *colloq.*

1890 *Stock Grower & Farmer* 17 May 5/3 The older hands soon rolled in leaving him and the kids around the fire.

b. To arrive, as in a vehicle. *colloq.*

1904 'O. HENRY' *Heart of West* 270 The invited guests . . . rolled in from the Gila country, from Salt River, from the Pecos. **1916** Du PUY *Uncle Sam* 38 Meantime the genial examiner had rolled in upon the bank.

c. To bring *in* in large quantities. *colloq.*

1914 ATHERTON *Perch of Devil* 173 A moving picture show rolls in dimes.

+7. *To roll off,* to cover (a certain distance) on a bicycle.

1895 *Outing* XXVI. 361/1, I had rolled off seventy-seven miles.

+8. *To roll out.* **a.** To begin a journey; to depart.

1850 L. V. LOOMIS *Jrnl. Birmingham Emigrating Co.* 13 They hitched up and 13 men, 5 wagons and 23 Horses rolled out. **1923** J. H. COOK *On Old Frontier* 34 We will roll out tomorrow.

b. To get up, as by unrolling from blankets.

1884 W. SHEPHERD *Prairie Exper.* 237 The cook's voice shouts 'Roll out.'

+9. *To roll up,* to accumulate a large number of votes in an election.

1859 *La Crosse Union* 24 Oct. 2 He ought . . . to pitch in and help roll up a big majority for Randall. **1877** *Congress. Rec.* App. 24 Feb. 123/2 At the October election the democratic party of Georgia rolled up an astonishingly magnificent majority of 75,000 votes. **1900** *Ib.* 23 Jan. 1103/2 They answered them by rolling up a plurality of 5,665 votes for the member from Utah out of a total vote of 67,805.

+Rolled iron. Iron that has been formed into sheets or bars. {1884} — **1789** *Ann. 1st Congress* 167 The same [impost] . . . was laid upon . . . castings of iron, or slit or rolled iron. **1835** HOFFMAN *Winter in West* I. 77 Contracts are frequently made for $38 per ton to take the blooms at St. Louis and return them rolled iron. **1880** *Harper's Mag.* Dec. 57/1 There are in Pittsburgh thirty-five rolling-mills . . . whose product is here fashioned into one-quarter of all the rolled iron made in the broad republic.

+Rolled oats. *pl.* Oats prepared by crushing with heated rollers. Also attrib. Also *rolled oatmeal.* — **1888** *Puget Sound Gazetteer* July 12/1 The peculiar aroma of the old system is not imparted to the rolled oatmeal or the flour. **1888** HARGIS *Graded Cook Book* 514 Breakfast. Rolled Oats. **1901** GRINNELL *Gold Hunting in Alaska* 5 For breakfast, rolled oats mush, baking powder biscuit [etc.].

+Rolled steak. Steak rolled around some stuffing and baked. — **1883** RITTENHOUSE *Maud* 204, I got dinner—green peas, mashed potatoes, rolled steak with dressing and bread pudding and didn't spoil a thing.

Roller. **+1.** =ROLL *n.²* 1. **+2.** *Baseball.* An easily batted ground ball. **3.** (See quotation.) — (1) **1849** KINGSLEY *Diary* 88 The land on the left rises in rollers from 10 to 50 feet. **1850** COLTON *3 Years Calif.* 321 Our course . . . lay among mountain spurs, till we reached the rollers, which ridge the plain of the San Joaquin. (2) **1880** *Chicago Inter Ocean* 15 May 7/1 Flint sent a roller to Crane, and he touched the first batter on the way to second. **1912** MATHEWSON *Pitching* 101 The last batter hit an easy roller to Wagner. (3) **1891** *Cent.* 5214 *Roller,* . . . the rockfish or stripedbass, *Roccus lineatus.* [Maryland.]

+Roller boy. A boy who inks the rollers in a printing office. — **1849** *Knickerb.* XXXIV. 12 Our very roller-boy has got principles, or else he would be discarded indignantly down the stairs of this office. **1868** *Ore. State Jrnl.* 24 Oct. 1/6, [I am] a thorough printer myself, having served in all its gradations from printer's devil, roller-boy, and copy holder, to compositor and reporter and thence to the hard eminence of the chair editorial. **1896** HOWELLS *Impressions & Exper.* 27 He became a rollerboy, and served long behind the press.

+Roller cloth. =ROLLER TOWEL. — **1862** 'G. HAMILTON' *Country Living* 11, I become acquainted . . . with the *modus operandi* of 'rollercloths.' **1877** PHELPS *Story of Avis* 224 A roller-cloth would do, dear.

+Roller mill. (See quotations 1876, 1883.) {1882} — **1876** KNIGHT 1964/1 *Roller-mill,* a machine for bruising flaxseed, before grinding under edge-stones and pressing. **1883** *Ib. Suppl.* 763/1 *Roller Mill,* . . . a mill in which wheat is made into flour by a cracking process, by passing between rollers consecutively arranged in pairs. **1890** *Stock Grower & Farmer* 24 May 7/1 The Star roller mill of Las Vegas [N.M.] has proved a public benefaction. . . . San Miguel county will have flour to sell this year. **1892** *York County Hist. Rev.* 68 The roller mills at Glen are one of the imposing factors in this direction.

+Roller rink. A rink for roller skating. — [**1884** *Milnor* (Dak.) *Teller* 27 June, Only a few months ago and we read with dismay the approach of the roller rinktum.] **1885** *Wkly. New Mexican Rev.* 26 Feb. 3/5 In Santa Fe a roller rink can be kept open all summer, the nights being so delightfully cool. **1888** *Nation* 31 May 449/3 Children are protected from cruelty, from acting in theatres, from roller-rinks, and from toy-pistols.

+Roller skate. A skate mounted on small wheels. {1874-} — **1863** *Rep. Comm. Patents 1861* I. 280 A roller skate provided with two rows of tubular adjustable rollers, and the whole constructed and operating as shown and described. **1881** *Harper's Mag.* March 543/1 Children glide peacefully along the asphalt on roller-skates. **1895** *N.Y. Dramatic News* 9 Nov. 14/2 Major Newell . . . did some graceful clog dancing on roller skates. **1910** J. A. MITCHELL *Dr. Thorne's Idea* 53 Seizing a roller skate, . . . she hurled it with accurate aim.

Roller skating. The act or process of skating on roller skates. {1874-} Also attrib. — **1884** *Outing* III. 396/2 Roller-skating has received new impetus, and rinks are opened in all parts of the country. **1885** *South Fla. Sentinel* (Orlando) 1 April 1/8 Lawn tennis is said to have brought in, like roller skating, a new and peculiar disease. **1888** *Boston Jrnl.* 4 Oct. 2/4 The roller-skating craze . . . has died out in this section. **1894** GARLAND in *Harper's Mag.* June 144/1 [The hotel] had been a roller-skating rink in other days.

Roller towel. An endless towel running on a roller. {1862-} Also attrib. — **1845** *Knickerb.* XXV. 444 Beside the window was the linen roller-towel. **1882** 'M. HARLAND' *Eve's Daughters* 409 She had . . . a roller-towel rack screwed upon the wall at one side. **1902** *Harper's Mag.* May 977/2 [They] dried themselves on a common roller-towel.

+Roller worm. (See quotation.) — **1899** *Dept. Agric. Yrbk. 1898* 259 A caterpillar known as the bean leaf-roller or 'roller-worm' is injurious in the Gulf States to leguminous plants.

+Rolliche. Also **rollitje, rullitie.** [Du. *rolletje* 'little roll.'] (See quot. 1848.) — **1832** WATSON *Hist. Tales N.Y.* 127 The Dutch . . . cherish, by anniversary remembrances, . . . their tutelary protector, Saint Nicholas: . . . garnishing their tables with 'Malck and Suppawn,' with *rullities,* and their hands with long stemmed pipes. **1848** BARTLETT 280 *Rullichies,* . . . chopped meat stuffed into small bags of tripe, which are then cut into slices and fried. An old and favorite dish among the descendants of the

Dutch in New York. **1864** *Rio Abajo Press* 24 May 1/2 He would call for olykrocks, krollers, rollitjes, etc., with a cup of tea. **1890** E. L. BYNNER *Begum's Daughter* i. (*Cent.*), [The burghers of New Amsterdam] ate their supaen and *rolliches* of an evening. **1896** EARLE *Col. Days Old N.Y.* 118 On a swing-shelf were *rolliches* and head-cheese and festoons of sausages.

b. (See quotation.)
1844 SEDGWICK *Tales & Sk.* 79 He received a rooletjeer (doughnut) from the kind hand that had supplied this diurnal want of nature . . . for the last forty years.

✳ Rolling, *n.*
+1. =LOGROLLING 1. (Cf. ROLLING FROLIC.)
1847 in Howe *Hist. Coll. Ohio* 358 Many times were we called from six to eight miles to assist at a rolling or raising.

+2. In special combinations.
Other examples of technical uses can be found in Knight.
Rolling bank, (see quotation); *r. dam,* a dam constructed without sluiceways, in order to force the surplus water over the top; *r. place,* =ROLLING HOUSE; *r. season,* the time of the year when sugar cane is ground.
1902 *Forestry Bureau Bul.* No. 34, 25 Logs which were cut and skidded in the fall were hauled during the winter to the shore of some stream, where they were piled in huge tiers on the 'banking grounds,' as they were called on the Susquehanna, or 'landings' or 'rolling-banks,' in northern New York. **1815** *N.Y. Lit. & Phil. Soc. Trans.* I. 151 A rolling dam was made over the river, and a canal of one hundred rods was cut. **1708** *Md. Hist. Mag.* XVII. 218 But the Slovenly Planter will be ashamed to have his Tobacco brought to These Townes and Rolling places. **1833** SILLIMAN *Man. Sugar Cane* 14 Rains . . . occur during the rolling or grinding season.

✳ Rolling, *a.*
+1. Of land: Undulating; resembling the swell of the ocean. {1890-}
See also ROLLING PRAIRIE, ROLLING ROAD 2.
1804 CLARK in *Lewis & C. Exped.* I. (1904) 45 Found the prarie composed of good Land and plenty of water roleing & interspursed with points of timber land. **1815** DRAKE *Cincinnati* 92 The central or Mississippi district, may be characterized as a plain— . . . arid and rolling in the south-east. **1827** COOPER *Prairie* xxiv, They found the vast plain, the rolling swells, . . . and the scattered thickets, covered alike in one white, dazzling sheet of snow. **1837** MARTINEAU *Society* I. 321 We fairly entered the 'rolling country' to-day. **1854** *33d Congress 1 Sess.* H. R. Ex. Doc. No. 2 no II. 1. 24 The sand-hills . . . , like the rolling prairie hills to the north, increase in height. **1872** 'MARK TWAIN' *Roughing It* 25 Just here the land was rolling. **1925** TILGHMAN *Dugout* 1 Far scattered over the rolling Western plains, . . . the old dugouts tell their story of the past.

2. Turning over and over or making somersaults in a religious frenzy. (Cf. ROLLING EXERCISE.)
1807 MCNEMAR *Ky. Revival* 69 There were regular societies of these people in the state of Ohio. . . . Jerking, barking, or rolling, dreaming, prophesying, and looking . . . at the infinite glories of mount Zion.

3. In special uses.
Rolling John, (see quotation); *r. plant,* =ROLLING STOCK; *r. press,* (see quotation); *r. screen,* a screen used in the sifting of grain; *r. towel,* = ROLLER TOWEL.
1780 *N.J. Archives* 2 Ser. IV. 175 The merchant and country boults, hoisting works and rolling screen are all in good order. **1787** CUTLER in *Life & Corr.* I. 269 Another great curiosity was a rolling press, for taking the copies of letters or any other writing. A sheet of paper is completely copied in less than two minutes, the copy as fair as the original, and without effacing it in the smallest degree. **1864** WEBSTER 1146/3 *Rollingplant,* the locomotives and vehicles of a railway. **1869** STOWE *Oldtown Folks* 263 We performed our morning ablutions, refreshing our faces and hands by a brisk rub upon a coarse rolling-towel of brown homespun linen. **1881** INGERSOLL *Oyster-Industry* 247 *Rolling John,* a detached sponge drifting about the bottom. (Florida.)

+Rolling exercise. (See first quotation.) — **1807** MCNEMAR *Ky. Revival* 61 The rolling exercise . . . consisted in being cast down in a violent manner, doubled with the head and feet together, and rolled over and over like a wheel, or stretched in a prostrate manner, turned swiftly over and over like a log. **1847** HOWE *Hist. Coll. Ohio* 46 'Bodily exercises,' . . . have been classified by a clerical writer as 1st, the *Falling* exercise; 2d, the *Jerking* exercise; 3d, the *Rolling* exercise [etc.].

+Rolling frolic. =LOGROLLING 1. (Cf. ROLLING *n.* 1.) — **1822** WOODS *English Prairie* 213 Rolling frolics, are clearing wood-land, when many trees are cut down, and into lengths, to roll them up together, so as to burn them, and to pile up the brushwood and roots on the trees. **1835-7** HALIBURTON *Clockmaker* 1 Ser. xxvii. 262 Is it a vandew, or a weddin, or a rollin frolic, or a religious stir, or what is it?

+Rolling house. *local.* [f. ROLL *v.* 2.] A warehouse or place of deposit for tobacco. Now *hist.* — **1705** *Va. State P.* I. 97 The same storage shall be paid, as is directed by an Act appointing Rowling houses, &c. **1728** *Md. Hist. Mag.* XVIII. 12 John Ensor [is appointed] overseer of the roads . . . from Brittains Ridge Rolling house to the extent of that hundred. **1884** *Century Mag.* Jan. 436/1 By the beginning of the eighteenth century private 'rolling houses' . . . had become common.

Rolling mill. a. A machine which rolls out or flattens metals, grain, etc. {1799-} +b. An establishment where such machines are in use.

1787 CUTLER in *Life & Corr.* I. 249 On the Pennsylvania side of the Delaware is a famous forge, slitting-mill, and rolling-mill for grinding and bolting flour. **1815** *Mass. H. S. Coll.* 2 Ser. IV. 186 There is also a rolling mill under the same roof. **1849** *Knickerb.* XXXIV. 514 The rolling-mill . . . is a grand place for a mass-meeting. **1869** STOWE *Oldtown Folks* 235 He might as well have put the tips of his fingers into a rolling-mill. **1880** *Harper's Mag.* Dec. 57 There are in Pittsburgh thirty-five rolling mills wherein eight hundred boiling or puddling furnaces are seething. **1906** LYNDE *Quickening* 31 From the tall chimneys of a rolling-mill a dense column of smoke was ascending.

* **Rolling-pin.** A cylinder, commonly of wood, for rolling out dough for pastry, etc. — **1658** *Southold Rec.* I. 449 An Inventorie of the personall estate whereof Elizabeth Payne widdow dyed possest [includes]: . . . a rollinge pinn—a battledore [etc.]. **1711** *Essex Inst. Coll.* IV. 187/1, I give to Mercy & Sarah Oliver . . . My Waggon, Rowling pin, My Red Petticoat. **1828** LESLIE *Receipts* 12 Some think it makes common paste more crisp and light to beat it hard on both sides with the rolling-pin. **1898** PAGE *Red Rock* 182 She gave him a rolling-pin, and he set to work with it industriously.

+**Rolling prairie.** A tract of undulating prairie land; also, collect., the whole area of such land.

Cf. ROLLING *a.* 1.

1827 COOPER *Prairie* i, A train of wagons issued from the bed of a dry rivulet, to pursue its course across the undulating surface, of what, in the language of the country of which we write, is called a 'rolling prairie.' **1837** IRVING *Bonneville* I. 43 A march of nine miles took them over high rolling prairies to the north fork. **1857** CHANDLESS *Visit Salt Lake* 10 A short mile's walk brought one to camp on a slope of the glorious 'rolling prairie,' the finest descriptive name Americans have invented. **1872** TICE *Over Plains* 25 Tonganoxie, a small village, is situated on a fine rolling prairie. **1877** CAMPION *On Frontier* 8 Around us was a rolling prairie. **1893** *Harper's Mag.* April 697/2 Dense forests . . . gradually encroach upon the 'rolling prairies.'

b. Prairie land having an undulating or gently rolling surface.

1830 DEWEES *Lett. from Texas* 129 Above this region commences a surface which is peculiar to the greater part of our country, usually known by the name of 'rolling prairie.' **1846** in Emory *Military Reconn.* 386 The ground is what is called 'rolling prairie,' of gentle curves, one swell melting into another. **1857** BRAMAN *Texas* 169 The middle portions of the State are all of an undulating description, called here *rolling prairie*. **1885** *Rep. Indian Affairs* 129 The lands included in this reservation are . . . composed of river-bottom, high rolling prairie, and mountains. **1901** DUNCAN & SCOTT *Allen & Woodson Co., Kansas* 5 The uplands are gently rolling prairie.

+**Rolling road. 1.** *local.* A road over which casks of tobacco are rolled to a warehouse, market, etc. Now hist. (Cf. ROLL *v.* 2.) **2.** A road over rolling country. — **(1) 1696** [see ROLL *v.* 2]. **1714** *Md. Hist. Mag.* XVIII. 8 Petition of William Summers . . . [concerning] having cleared a Rolling Road. **1738** *Ib.* 18 The subscribers have altered their Rowling Road leading from Soldiers Delight to the Iron works. **1859** BARTLETT 370 *Rolling-Roads*, so called in Maryland and Virginia, from the old custom of rolling tobacco to market in hogsheads. . . . This mode of transportation was still in use twenty years ago. **(2) 1893** *Outing* XXII. 133/1 To Rosalia and Oakesdale was a fair rolling road.

Rolling stock. On a railroad, the locomotives, cars, and other equipment operating on rails. {1853-} — **1858** *Penna. R.R. Ann. Rep.* 14 The rolling stock upon the Pennsylvania Railroad . . . [included] 18 Baggage Cars. **1877** [see ENGINE 5]. **1890** *Stock Grower & Farmer* 11 Jan. 6/2 The railroad . . . found itself deficient in stock yards and in rolling stock. **1907** LONDON *Road* 177 The trains were composed of . . . the riff-raff of worn-out and abandoned rolling-stock that collects in the yards of great railways.

+**Rolling weed.** (See first quot. and cf. TUMBLEWEED.) — **1888** *Century Mag.* Jan. 453/2, I secured a 'tumble-weed' or 'rolling-weed,'—one of those globular perennials of the plains that when dead is pulled up by the wind and goes rolling around over the prairies at the mercy of the blast. **1891** *Cent.* 6527/2.

+**Roll stone.** A stone which has been rounded by attrition or friction. — **1845** FRÉMONT *Exped.* 124 We halted . . . on the most western fork of Laramie river—a handsome stream . . . with clear water and a swift current, over a bed composed entirely of boulders or roll stones. **1872** *Vermont Bd. Agric. Rep.* I. 688 A young man . . . brought me a fine specimen of gold from a rollstone he found, while digging a well.

Roll-top desk. A desk having a cover which rolls down. {1901} — **1887** *Trial H. K. Goodwin* 15 That shows the position of the roll-top desk which was in the front office. **1902** *Rev. of Reviews* (London) April 382/2 Every reporter has a roll-top desk. **1923** HERRICK *Lilla* 173 A young woman looked up from the roll-top desk where she was running over a typed list of names.

+**Rollway.** [f. ROLL *v.* 1.]

1. A stack of logs on a river bank, platform, etc., awaiting transportation by water or rail.

1855 *Michigan General Statutes* (1882) I. 995 It shall be lawful for such company to cause such rollways or jams to be broken. **1881** *Chicago Times* 16 April, I anticipate considerable trouble and expense breaking the rollways. **1902** WHITE *Blazed Trail* 92 The roll-ways are then broken, and the saw logs floated down the river to the mill.

2. A slope or chute on the bank of a river used for precipitating logs into the water; a banking ground or landing place for logs.

1855 *Michigan General Statutes* (1882) I. 994 Such corporations shall have authority to make and construct all . . . necessary rollways, booms, piers [etc.]. **1878** *Lumberman's Gazette* 9 March 216/2 The lumbermen have kept their rollways free from logs and therefore there will not be any to break out later in the season. **1879** *Scribner's Mo.* Nov. 19/2 The rivers abrading against these sand-hills occasionally cause precipitous bluffs . . . or such an elevation as is known in a lumberman's parlance as a 'roll-way.' **1903** WHITE *Blazed Trail Stories* 30 The rollways became choked with the logs dumped down on them from the sleighs.

Romal. (See RUMAL.)

* **Roman,** *a.*

* **1.** In the names of plants and fruits.

1784 *Amer. Acad. Mem.* I. 489 Ambrosia. . . . Conot-Weed. Roman Wormweed. . . . It is used in anticeptic fomentations. **1817** W. COXE *Fruit Trees* 132 Roman Stem. This apple was first propagated in the neighbourhood of Burlington New-Jersey. **1817-8** EATON *Botany* (1822) *Artemisia pontica*, Roman artemisia. *Ib.* 206 *Blechnum borealis*, Roman fern. **1856** *Rep. Comm. Patents 1855: Agric.* 295 Of apples we have . . . the 'Roman Beauty,' and the 'Pawpaw Sweeting,' for fall and early winter.

2. In special uses.

Roman fall, a type of headdress; *R. pearl*, a kind of imitation pearl; *R. stripe*, a pattern of variegated stripes of bright colors.

1876 W. M. FISHER *Californians* 10 A few women move about, tricked out fine as their surroundings permit—'Roman falls,' 'Grecian bends,' top-heavy *coiffures*. **1878** *Decorum* 281 Gold or Roman stripe are all very effective when worn with appropriate dresses. **1881** RITTENHOUSE *Maud* 36 My Roman-pearls were a slight consolation.

Roman Catholic, *n.* A member of the Roman Catholic church. {1605-}

1744 BRAINERD *Diary* (1902) 165 Several people seemed much concerned about their souls, especially one who had been educated a Roman Catholic. **1789** MORSE *Amer. Geog.* 354 The Roman Catholics, who were the first settlers in Maryland, are the most numerous religious sect. **1834** PECK *Gaz. Illinois* 92 The *Roman Catholics* are not numerous. **1864** in Arny *Items regarding N. Mex.* 34 The Pueblos are all nominally Roman Catholics. **1903** BRADY *Bishop* 128 He had been a Roman Catholic in the beginning.

Roman Catholic, *a.* Of or pertaining to Roman Catholicism. {1614-} — **1817** S. BROWN *Western Gazetteer* 27 There is a post-office and a chapel for the Roman Catholic worship. **1847** L. COLLINS *Kentucky* 139 Maryland . . . had been founded by Lord Baltimore, and a band of colonists professing the Roman Catholic religion. **1872** McCLELLAN *Golden State* 405 The Roman Catholic Church . . . works its affairs with the precision of machinery. **1894** LEAVITT *Our Money Wars* 263 This smart young man . . . decamped to Canada in company with a Roman Catholic priest.

+**Romanite.** =RAMBO. — **1817** [see RAMBO]. **1847** IVES *New Eng. Fruit* 46 Rambo, or Romanite.—This apple is much cultivated in Pennsylvania.

+**Roncador.** [Sp., 'snorer.'] Any one of various sciaenoid fishes of the Pacific coast. Often with specifying adjectives. (See also RED RONCADOR.) — **1882** *Nat. Museum Bul.* No. 16, 572 *Sciæna stearnsi*, . . . Roncador. **1884** GOODE, etc. *Fisheries* I. 379 *Corvina saturna* . . . is known where found as the 'Red Roncador,' less commonly as 'Black Roncador' or 'Croaker.' *Ib.*, *Umbrina roncador* . . . is generally known as the 'Yellow-tailed' or 'Yellow-finned Roncador.' **1890** Little roncador [see KINGFISH 3]. **1911** *Rep. Fisheries 1908* 314/2.

+**Roncher.** [Of obscure origin.] (See quot. 1877.) — **1877** BARTLETT 535 *Roncher*, a thing enormous of its kind; a blow of great force, synonymous with 'sockdolager.' **1897** ROBINSON *Uncle Lisha's Outing* 238, 'I got holt of a ol' roncher an' he yanked me in, so naow. I wish I'd got him. He was a ol' roncher.' And he began to cry piteously over the loss of the fish.

+**Ronchil.** (See RONQUIL.)

+**Ronco.** [See RONCADOR.] **1.** *Texas.* (See quot. 1883.) **2.** (See quotations.) — **(1) 1883** *Nat. Museum Bul.* No. 27, 442 *Micropogon undulatus*. . . . Croaker; Ronco; Verrugato (Cuba). . . . This is a food-fish of small size but good quality. . . . In the Southern States it is abundant. **1884** GOODE, etc. *Fisheries* I. 378. **(2) 1896** JORDAN & EVERMANN *Check-List Fishes* 384 *Hæmulon*. . . . Roncos or Grunts. . . . *Hæmulon plumieri*. . . , Ronco Ronco; Ronco Arará. *Ib.* 397 *Bairdiella ronchus*. . . , Ronco; Corvina. Atlantic coasts of tropical America, generally common in the West Indies.

Rondle, Rondelle. A circular piece, esp. the crust that forms upon the surface of molten metal as it cools. {1839, in France} — **1876** KNIGHT 1970/1 *Rondle*, . . . a round plate or disk. The term is applied to the crust or scale which forms upon the surface of molten metal in cooling. . . . Spelled also *rondelle*. **1878** PRESCOTT *Speaking Telephone* 288 A rondelle of firewood is fixed normally to the tube by its centre.

Rondo. {1797-} +A gambling game played with balls on a table. Also attrib. — 1852 A. T. JACKSON *Forty-Niner* (1920) 159 'Monte,' 'Red and Black,' 'Chuck-a-luck,' 'Twenty-one,' 'Rondo,' and 'Fortune Wheels' are the banking games. 1859 T. W. PALMER *New & Old* 229 With card and dice, roulette wheels and rondo balls, he fooled himself to the top of his bent. 1873 BEADLE *Undevel. West* 90 The 'Big Tent' . . . is filled with tables devoted to monte, faro, rondo coolo, fortune-wheels, and every other species of gambling known.

+**Ronquil.** [ad. Sp. *ronquillo* 'slightly hoarse.'] Any of various fishes of the northwest coast of North America, esp. *Bathymaster signatus*. — 1882 *Nat. Museum Bul.* No. 16, 619 *Icosteidæ* (The Ronquils). . . . This group, as at present constituted, is composed of three very diverse genera, each of a single species, inhabiting the deeper waters of the North Pacific. *Ib.* 623 B[*athymaster*] *signatus*, . . . Ronquil. 1884 GOODE, etc. *Fisheries* I. 361 An allied form is *Bathymaster signatus* Cope, the 'Ronchil,' found in deep water from Puget Sound northward.

* **Rood.**

* **1.** A square measure equivalent usually to one-fourth of an acre.

1635 *Cambridge Prop. Rec.* 4 Moore in old ffeild about one acker and a roode. 1679 *Waterbury Prop. Rec.* 11 Three roods of the best of this Land shall be accounted one acher. 1708 *Conn. Hist. Soc. Coll.* VI. 289 One Rood of Land out of the Highway or Common where his Barn now Standeth. 1850 CLAY in Abbot *South & North* 107, I will never, *never*, NEVER, by word or thought, by mind or will, aid in admitting one rood of free territory to the *everlasting curse* of human bondage!

* **2.** A linear measure of varying length, usually seven or eight yards.

1659 *Portsmouth Rec.* 379, [I] sell unto Ellexander Enos one Acre of land . . . ye one Side . . . being Tenn Roodes and one halfe broode. 1678 *Derby Rec.* 82, 52: Roods long on Each Side & 25 Roods wide att Each end . . . makes: 8 acres more or less. 1766 J. BARTRAM *Journal* 26 A large stream of water . . . may be smelt at some roods distant. 1799 J. SMITH *Acct. Captivity* 26 The town was about eighty rood above the mouth of the creek.

* **Roof.**

* **1.** The upper covering of a building; the ceiling of a room; the top; also transf., a house.

1653 *Boston Rec.* 114 Every howseholder shall provid a pole of above 12 foot long, with a good large swob at the end of it, to rech the rofe of his house to quench fire. 1698 in Burr *Witchcraft Cases* (1914) 63 It was a much greater [surprise], to be so near the danger of having my Head broke with a . . . great Hammer brushing along the top or roof of the Room from the other end. 1710 *Harvard Rec.* I. 391 Mr. Treasurer is therefore desired to take Effectual Care for the taking of the said Slate roof. 1825 NEAL *Bro. Jonathan* I. 367 When you are strong and hearty, it will be time enough, then, for you to leave my roof. 1848 BARTLETT 173 *Hay barrack*, . . . a straw-thatched roof supported by four posts. 1858 PETERS *Kit Carson* 243 [When a fandango is given] gambling is carried on under the same roof. 1907 *St. Nicholas* June 738/1 Now draw the shingles of the roof, the clapboards, the panels to the door.

b. Short for ROOF GARDEN.

1896 *N.Y. Dramatic News* 11 July 11/1 Eunice Vance comes to the Casino roof next month. *Ib.* 18 July 8/4 The roof is one of the coolest places in town.

2. Attrib. with *board, guard, line,* etc.

1853 FOWLER *Home for All* 187 Put on your four rafters, first beveling . . . the whole of their lower edges, to correspond with the pitch of your roof-boards. 1857 VAUX *Villas* 54 Some degree of picturesqueness can always be obtained by the treatment of the roof-lines. 1874 B. F. TAYLOR *World on Wheels* 218 There is singing everywhere: . . . from the second rail of the fence, a gust of melody; from the roof-ridge, a solo. 1876 KNIGHT 1973/2 *Roof-guard*, . . . a device for preventing snow from sliding from a roof. 1886 *Pall Mall Gaz.* 11 Sept. 3/2 The 'Roof-sleepers of New York' . . . describes, however, what is a grim reality. The hot weather has driven the poor of New York to the roofs for slumber. 1887 'CRADDOCK' *Keedon Bluffs* 29 A great fire flared on the hearth, illuminating . . . the ladder leading up to the shadowy regions of the roof-room. 1891 EARLE *Sabbath* 63 Sometimes a little pew or short gallery was built high up among the beams and joists over the staircase which led to the first gallery, and was called the 'swallows' nest,' or the 'roof pue,' or the 'second gallery.'

b. In special combinations.

Roof houseleek, the common houseleek (*Sempervivum tectorum*), often found on roofs; *r. slate, r. slating,* slate of the kind used in roofing {r. slate, 1803}; *r. water,* rainwater falling from the roof of a building. {1910}

1800 BENTLEY *Diary* II. 342, I brought away a specimen of the Roof House leek, which was a beautiful species. 1818 *Amer. Jrnl. Science* I. 342 A few miles north, this slate is distinctly marked, and in about 12 miles, forms hills of *roof slate* in Hosack, New-York. 1832 WILLIAMSON *Maine* I. 175 Argillite, . . . is used, when sufficiently soft, for writing-slates, and also for roof-slating when it splits well. 1879 *Harper's Mag.* June 134/1 During storms the roof water increases this action.

+**3.** In phrases.

To raise the roof, to protest emphatically or noisily, to blow up; *through the roof,* (*fig.*), (see quotation).

1860 M. J. HOLMES *Maude* 57 Ole master'll raise de ruff, case he put 'em away to sell. 1906 *Springfield W. Repub.* 25 Oct. 2 The question was raised whether a boss so placed in office 'through the roof,' rather than by working his way up, would be able to make good.

Roofer. **1.** (See quot. 1846.) {1855-} **2.** (See quotation.) — (1) 1846 WORCESTER 619/1 *Roofer,* one who roofs or makes roofs. *Pict. Ann.* 1897 *Columbus Dispatch* 27 Feb., On Court street, . . . a lot of roofers were at work yesterday putting on a new roof for a house. (2) 1859 MATSELL *Vocabulum* 74 *Roofer,* a hat.

+**Roof garden.** A garden or place for recreation and rest on the roof of a building, esp. one at which refreshments are served and dramatic or musical entertainment is presented.

1894 MATTHEWS in *Harper's Mag.* Jan. 223/2 There's a comic opera at the Garden Theatre, with a variety show up in the roof garden afterwards. 1898 *Daily News* (London) 15 Aug. 3/1 The New York theatres are rejoicing in the possession of . . . roof gardens. 1902 BELL *Hope Loring* 26 *He* owns a theatre in New York, my brother does. It has a roof-garden, and he makes loads of money. 1903 *Charities* 3 Oct. 287 The experiment of treating tuberculosis cases upon a roof garden is reported to be an unqualified success. 1910 BOSTWICK *Amer. Pub. Library* 285 In crowded city districts it is often a good plan to place an open-air reading room on the roof. . . . Boxes of flowers, etc., add gayety and serve to justify the name of 'roof garden,' popularly given to such reading rooms.

b. Attrib. with *idea, restaurant, vaudeville.*

1895 *N.Y. Dramatic News* 6 July 2/1 The growth of the roof garden idea has undoubtedly tended toward the obliteration of the regular forms of theatrical amusement during the heated term. 1909 'O. HENRY' *Options* 294 After dining we went to a roof-garden vaudeville that was being much praised. 1917 COMSTOCK *Man* 343 They were at a roof garden restaurant.

***Roofing.** attrib. Designating materials used in making roofs. {1815-} — 1865 *Chicago Tribune* 10 April 1 Roofing Paper, Fifty tons, superior quality, for sale cheap. 1874 *Vermont Bd. Agric. Rep.* II. 736 Several hundred squares of roofing slates were made that year. 1881 *Century Mag.* Dec. 319/2 Over these planks is to be a layer of roofing-felt or mortar.

Roof pole. A pole serving as a support for a wigwam or tent; a rafter in the roof of a house. — 1844 WHITTIER *Poetical Works* (1894) 26/2 And, adown the roof-pole hung, . . . In the smoke his scalp-locks swung. 1855 LONGFELLOW *Hiawatha* 164 The roof-poles of the wigwam Were as glittering rods of silver. 1885 EGGLESTON in *Century Mag.* April 873/2 The most honored guest might have to reach his chamber under the roof-poles by ascending steps on the outside. *a*1918 G. STUART *On Frontier* II. 135 Not a twig of wood on the road or at camp so had to take some of the roof poles to cook with.

***Rooftree.** The principal beam or ridgepole in a roof; hence, by extension, the roof itself, or the shelter provided by it. — 1838 FLAGG *Far West* I. 187, I reached the log-cabin of an old pioneer from Virginia, beneath whose lowly roof-tree I am seated at this present writing. 1852 MITCHELL *Dream Life* 39 Aye, your heart clings in boy hood to the roof-tree of the old family garret. 1878 JACKSON *Travel at Home* 279 A man sitting on his piazza may rest his feet on the roof-tree of his neighbor next below. 1888 PERRIN *Ky. Pioneer Press* 29 There is no account, however, of Samuel getting any of it [sc. property] upon leaving the family roof-tree. 1893 'THANET' *Stories* 44 The black roof-tree of the cottage sagged in the middle.

***Room,** *n.* In special combinations.

Room associate, a roommate; *r. bell,* a bell in a room, as in a hotel, for summoning a servant or attendant; *r. clerk,* in a hotel, lodging house, etc., a clerk who assigns rooms to patrons; *r.-hunter,* one in search of a room; *r. paper,* wall paper.

1845 *Lowell Offering* V. 18 'Now don't form plans at present, for curtailing expenses,' said her room-associate. 1860 GREELEY *Overland Journey* 78 Leavenworth.—Room-bells and baths make their final appearance. 1916 DU PUY *Uncle Sam* 49 The room clerk had suggested that it was the custom of the hotel that guests without baggage should pay in advance. 1883 CABLE *Dr. Sevier* 44 The room-hunters got away. 1873 'G. HAMILTON' *Twelve Miles* 45 The silence and stupidity of room-paper were wont to reign.

***Room,** *v.* +intr. To occupy a room or rooms; to lodge. — 1817 *Essex Inst. Coll.* VIII. 241 We are boarding with two of the college students, and room with them. 1866 J. H. WARD *Life & Lett. J. G. Percival* 32 In the last two years of his college life he roomed in the fourth story . . . of what is now Old South-Middle College. 1898 HARPER *S. B. Anthony* I. 12 That summer she boarded eleven factory hands, who roomed in her house. 1911 'O. HENRY' *Rolling Stones* 178 Stickney roomed at 45 West 'Teenth St.

+**Roomage.** Space or capacity. Obs. — 1843 WHITTIER *Poetical Works* (1894) 20/2 Pack [my ship] with coins of Spanish gold, From keel-piece up to deck-plank, The roomage of her hold. 1865 BURRITT *Walk to Land's End* 209 Mat and seat the rotunda of St. Paul's, and the nave of Westminster, to every foot of their magnificent roomage. *Ib.* 399 [Dunster Castle] entertained Charles II in its best guest and banquet-room, and William Prynne with coarser roomage and fare.

+**Roomer.** One who rents a room in a private home or lodging house, usually one who gets his meals elsewhere. — 1871 BAGG *At Yale* 46 *Roomer,* a word used by landladies to designate a lodger or occupant of a room who takes his meals elsewhere. 1893 *Chicago Tribune* 24 April 2/1

A room . . . which the householder would be willing to rent to a permanent roomer for $4 a week will cost $2.25 a day to transients after the Fair opens. **1906** 'O. HENRY' *Four Million* 50 She would sit on the steps of the high stoop with the other roomers. **1923** WATTS *L. Nichols* 68 Some rented out to roomers from cellar to attic.

+**Rooming house.** A house other than a hotel in which rooms or apartments, usually furnished, are rented. — **1893** *Spectator* 16 Sept. 366/1 We go to no hotel, but look for what Americans call a 'rooming house,' i.e., a house which lets furnished apartments. **1898** *Advance* 27 Jan. 118/2 Certainly he had never seen a rooming-house like it. **1909** *Washington Times* 2 March 1 Hundreds of persons who never slept in any but first-class hotels when away from home will tonight get their rest in rooming houses. **1924** RAINE *Troubled Waters* 54 Hotels were jammed, rooming houses doing a capacity business.

+**Room-keep,** *v. intr.* (See quot. 1871.) — **1871** DE VERE 491 The new word, *to roomkeep,* arising from the exigency which forces impoverished Southern families to content themselves with renting a few rooms and keeping house in them, has not yet obtained currency. **1911** HARRISON *Queed* 213, I don't find anything in the tenets of my religion that requires you to go off and room-keep with Professor Nicolovius.

+**Roommate.** One who shares the same room or rooms with another or with others. — **1789** DUNLAP *Father* IV. i, We were room-mates at Halifax. **1834** BRACKENRIDGE *Recollections* 106, I had three room mates. **1882** THAYER *From Log-Cabin* 283 'And that is why you sweep as well as you study?' interrupted the room-mate, in a complimentary tone. **1919** HOUGH *Sagebrusher* 19 Mary Warren and her room-mate, Annie Squires, met at a certain street corner.

Room rent. The rent paid for the use of a room. — **1818** *N. Amer. Rev.* March 427 The room rent and wood are estimated upon the condition that two students live in a College room. **1848** JUDSON *Mysteries N.Y.* II. 41 Shirley handed her a ten dollar bill. . . . 'Pretty good room-rent, for a half hour!' said the woman. **1884** CABLE *Dr. Sevier* 174 The good woman thought it but right somewhat to increase the figures of their room-rent.

+**Room trader.** (See quot. 1900.) — **1887** *Courier-Journal* 7 May 7/3 New England again became weak in company with Reading, both being especially heavy sufferers from the operation of the bearish room-traders. **1888** *Economist* 10 Nov. 7/3 The business was left chiefly to room traders and scalpers. **1900** NELSON *A B C Wall St.* 158 *Room trader,* a man who is a member of an exchange and speculates for his own profit and loss.

+**Roorback.** [The name given an imaginary traveler in the United States in whose alleged book of travels a statement damaging to the character of James K. Polk (1795–1849) was supposed to occur.] A falsehood circulated for political effect. Also attrib.
1844 *N.Y. Post* Sept. (Th.), The Roorback stories of the Whig partizans do not hang together. **1855** in Hambleton *H. A. Wise* 321 The present canvass has been prodigiously fruitful in all sorts of Roorbacks, humbugs . . . and even . . . falsehoods. *Ib.* 324 The third Roorback . . . of the Know Nothings, is 'that the influx of foreigners depreciates the price of labor.' **1896** *Boston Jrnl.* 31 Oct. 5/2 Do not allow roorbacks to scare you. **1922** McCORMAC *J. K. Polk* 273 For the purpose of injuring Polk in the North, the Whigs circulated widely the 'Roorback' canard the gist of which was that a gang of slaves branded with the initials 'J.K.P.' had been seen on their way to southern markets.

*****Roost.**
+**1.** A place in a forest or woods to which wild birds come regularly to roost and nest.
See also PIGEON ROOST.
1845 COOPER *Chainbearer* xiv, Multitudes of pigeons . . . were frequently found in their 'roosts,' as the encampments that they made in the woods were often termed in the parlance of the country. **1870** KEIM *Sheridan's Troopers* 154 We were in the midst of a favorite roost of immense numbers of wild turkeys. **1923** J. H. COOK *On Old Frontier* 4 Countless flocks . . . [would] congregate at what were called 'roosts.'

b. *fig.* A resting place.
1858 HOLMES *Autocrat* 164 The world has a million roosts for a man, but only one nest. **1864** LOWELL *Fireside Travels* 106 The only roost was in the garret, which . . . contained eleven double-beds, ranged along the walls. **1891** C. ROBERTS *Adrift Amer.* 23, I selected what appeared to me to be about the best spot for a roost, and . . . made a fairly comfortable bed.

+**2.** *To rule the roost,* to exercise authority, to be master. *colloq.*
Apparently a modification of the much older expression *to rule the roast,* in the same sense.
1828 ROYALL *Black Book* II. 315 These priests will rule the roost. **1893** *Boston Jrnl.* 20 April 5/3 England Rules the Roost. Her Ships at Hampton Roads Admittedly the finest.

Rooster. {rooster house, 1831, *dial.*}
1. The male of the domestic chicken; a cock. {1875–, *dial.*} Also attrib.
'Chiefly *U.S.* and *dial.*' (*O.E.D.*). The widespread use of this term in the United States has been ascribed to verbal modesty. Squeamishness about using the word *cock* is alluded to in the first group of examples.

(1) **1840** *Picayune* 25 Oct. 2/5 The Baltimore Clipper suggests that cocktails should henceforth be called rooster's shirts! **1841** H. PLAYFAIR *Papers* II. 111 The wives and daughters of the senators and representatives of the young states, occasionally, it is true, . . . gave different names to various animate and inanimate objects; such as 'little rocks' for stones, 'rooster' for game-cock. **1863** MASSETT *Drifting About* 256 [We had] a bottle of rooster-tail to sustain us on our return trip to Oregon city. **1871** DE VERE 380 [It is] absurd prudishness to shrink from the good old English word *Cock,* and translate it into the unmeaning *Rooster.* **1880** BENET *Americanisms* 13 When as a young 'nullifier' he was wearing his cockade, a 'nice' young lady told him how much she admired his pretty *roostercade.*
(2) **1772** A. G. WINSLOW *Diary* 45 Their other dish . . . contain'd a number of roast fowls—half a dozen, we suppose, & all roosters at this season no doubt. **1813** *Niles' Reg.* IV. Suppl. 192/1 A rooster mounted a parapet and crowed heartily. **1868** BRACKETT *Farm Talk* 26 Their fast horses, thousand-dollar sheep, and big roosters, are altogether too 'fast' for us common farmers. **1907** *St. Nicholas* Aug. 941/1, I have a rooster in the back yard that, I think, will interest you, as you are a naturalist.
attrib. **1809** WEEMS *Marion* (1833) 74 [The British officers] would look and grin on each other as sweetly as young foxes, who, prowling round a farm yard, had suddenly heard the cackling of the *rooster pullets.*

b. A representation of a cock used as a weather vane.
[**1857** HAMMOND *Northern Scenes* 107 Perched upon a staff, a few feet above the ridge pole, was a weather-cock, fashioned out of a piece of board in the shape of a rooster.] **1881** *Harper's Mag.* March 530/2 Every house [in Albany was] . . . surmounted by a rooster.

+**c.** A cock or representation of a cock used as a symbol of the Democratic party. Also attrib.
1870 NOWLAND *Indianapolis* 149 It was during this canvass [in 1840] that Tom gave to the Democratic party their emblem, which they have claimed ever since, the chicken cock, or rooster. **1888** *Boston Jrnl.* 12 Nov. 2/4 In New York . . . it is said literally acres of roosters have nodded and bobbed about. Some men pinned roosters and brooms on their hats and shoulders until the streets resembled a masquerade.

2. A man, a fellow: (see also quot. 1909). {1871–}
1840 *Knickerb.* XV. 293 There was 'ne'er a one left but the old rooster, as know'd how to take care of his self.' **1872** *Newton Kansan* 17 Oct. 1/7 As the deceased had consented that 'the Young Roosters' at the college could have his body, it was placed in a wagon. **1881** *Phila. Record* No. 3428, 2 It is not . . . in the nature of things that a rooster in the Legislature should quietly submit to be lectured by a rooster outside of the legislature. **1909** *Dialect Notes* III. 364 *Rooster,* a lascivious man. [e. Ala.] 'He's a regular old rooster.' **1921** PAINE *Comr. Rolling Ocean* 252 What was that rooster's name?

+**3.** The cock or hammer of a firearm.
1856 *Porter's Spirit of Times* 1 Nov. 140/2 Well now, daddy, says he, I lost the *rooster* off the lock of my gun.

+**4.** (See quotation.) *Obs.*
1871 De Vere 262 Rooster . . . indicates a bill, or proposed law, which will benefit the legislators—and no one else—for as the rasorial fowl scratches for his sustenance, so his figurative namesake is supposed to scratch the dunghill of modern legislation.

+**5.** (See quotation.)
1905 *Forestry Bureau Bul.* No. 61, 38 *Gooseneck,* . . . a wooden bar used to couple two logging trucks. (Gen[eral].) Syn.: rooster. (P[acific] C[oast] F[orest].)

+**6.** *pl.* A violet, as the common purple violet (*Viola cucullata*) of the eastern states, or the palm violet, *V. palmata.* Also *rooster fight, rooster hood. colloq.*
1884 ROE in *Harper's Mag.* June 94/1 [The] purple violets . . . were slaughtered by hundreds, for the projecting spur under the curved stem at the base of the flower enabled the boys to hook them together and 'fight roosters,' as they termed it. **1892** *Amer. Folk-Lore* V. 92 *Viola* (sp. unknown), rooster hoods. Buncombe Co., N.C. **1893** *Ib.* VI. 138 *Viola palmata,* roosters. Ferrisburgh, Vt. *Viola palmata,* var. *cucullata,* Johnny-jump-ups. Banner Elk, N.C. Roosters. N.Y. **1916** *Dialect Notes* IV. 345 *Rooster-fight,* a violet: so called [in Tenn.] from the practice of 'fighting' them together to see which would pull the other's head off.

+**7.** *Roosters' heads,* (see quotation).
1894 *Amer. Folk Lore* VII. 94 *Dodecatheon Meadia,* var., shooting stars, roosters' heads, Santa Barbara Co., Cal.

+**Rooster's egg.** (See quotations.) *colloq.* — **1899** GREEN *Va. Word-Book* 308 Rooster's egg, a small hen's egg. **1899** *Animal & Plant Lore* 12 A 'luck egg' is the egg of a rooster; also called a 'rooster's egg.' De Kalb Co., Ill. **1914** *Dialect Notes* IV. 152 *Rooster's egg,* a fertilized egg. [Me.] . . . In Mass. rooster's egg is used facetiously for a large egg.

Roosting. {1604–}
+**1.** =PIGEON ROOST. *Obs.*
1869 *Mich. Laws* I. 213 No person . . . shall use any gun . . . to maim, kill, or destroy any wild-pigeon or pigeons within their roostings.

+**2.** In special combinations.
Roosting ground, an area upon which wild fowls roost; *r. party,* a marauding party; *r. pond,* a pond upon which wild ducks stay at night.
1860 *Md. Laws.* cix. § 1 No person shall . . . shoot at or shoot any water fowl bedded in flocks, either upon the feeding or roosting-grounds of said water fowl. **1809** WEEMS *Marion* (1833) 183 Learning next morn-

ing, that a roosting party were out, Marion detached my brother Colonel Horry . . . to attack them. **1874** LONG *Wild Fowl* 161 The ducks will be seen coming from the roosting-ponds.

Roosting place. {1725-} +A place in the forest where wild fowl roost. (Cf. ROOST 1.) — **1812** WILSON *Ornithology* V. 103 [Wild pigeons] return . . . in the evening, to their place of general rendezvous, or as it is usually called, the roosting place. **1874** LONG *Wild Fowl* 159 When driven from one of these roosting-places . . . they congregate in another.

* Root, *n.*

* 1. The underground part of a plant, used as food.

1705 BEVERLEY *Virginia* IV. 56 Roots, Herbs, Vine-fruits, and Salate-Flowers. **1733** *Boston Rec.* 46 Whosoever shall . . . Expose to Sale, . . . any flesh Poultry Eggs, Butter, Meal, Chees, Frute, Hearbs, Rootes . . . Shall be fined. **1798** *Phila. Ordinances* (1812) 153 [There] shall be a row of stands . . . for exposing to sale all manner of roots, herbs and vegetable provisions. **1807** GASS *Journal* 212 We also got . . . sweet roots which they call Com-mas. **1866** *Rep. Indian Affairs* 74 The Indians have for several years raised enough grain and roots for their own subsistence. **1883** *Ib.* 155 Most of these . . . move about from one locality to another as their necessity for a supply of fish, game, roots, or berries may demand.

b. *Root of scarcity,* = MANGEL-WURZEL. {1787-}
1788 WASHINGTON *Diaries* III. 322, I sowed . . . the Seed of the Runkel Recbar, or Root of Scarcity.

2. *attrib.* and *comb.* **a.** Designating food or drink prepared from roots.

1670 *S.C. Hist. Soc. Coll.* V. 166 Here we had nutts and root cakes such as their women useily make as before. **1806** ORDWAY in *Jrnls. Lewis & O.* 352 We bought a little dark couloured root bread which is not good but will Support nature. **1856** SIMMS *Charlemont* 201 To purse up his mouth as if I was giving him root-drink, when I was telling him about Mother Frey's spoiling the fish!

b. Designating machines or implements for removing tree roots or cutting up vegetable roots. {1807-}

1850 *Rep. Comm. Patents 1849: Agric.* 412 A root-cutter and a grater are all that is necessary. **1856** *Mich. Agric. Soc. Trans.* VII. 54 D. O. & W. S. Penfield, Detroit, [exhibited] one iron root puller. **1876** KNIGHT 1975/2 The knives of the root-slicer *c* are attached to the arms of a fly-wheel. **1884** *Rep. Comm. Agric.* 178 A powerful root-extractor . . . gives a sufficient leverage.

3. In special combinations.

Root collar, (see quotation); *r. doctor,* =HERB DOCTOR; *r. potato,* the common potato; *r. spur,* a root extending laterally from the trunk of a tree.

1905 *Forestry Bureau Bul.* No. 61, 19 *Root collar,* that place at the base of a large tree where the swelling which is the direct result of the ramifications of the roots begins. **1890** *N.Y. Age* 19 April (Th. S.), Carmier was what people call down here a root doctor. **1828** *Western Mo. Rev.* II. 53 The third article is on *root potatoes.* **1851** SPRINGER *Forest Life* 23 The general outlines of the Yellow Birch often resemble the Elm, the root-spurs rise high up the trunk.

* Root, *v.*

+**1.** *intr.* To work hard, as for a livelihood; to plug or dig. *colloq.*

1856 HALL *College Words* (ed. 2) 395 *Root,* . . . to study hard. **1876** *Billings' Farmer's Alliminax* 18 Ever since Adam waz ordered to root, or perish, thare haz been an endless lot ov labor saving masheens, invented. **1902** LORIMER *Lett. Merchant* 110 Once he was turned loose to root for himself, he instinctively smelled out the business.

+**2.** *intr.* To shout, cheer, or work enthusiastically *for* the success of an athletic team or of an individual. *slang.*

1897 FLANDRAU *Harvard Episodes* 164 The fellows who had promised to vote for Wolcott . . . were beginning now to 'root' for him vigorously. **1903** *Boston Transcript* 3 Oct., Next him sat a lady who rooted industriously and vigorously for Pittsburg. **1923** WATTS *L. Nichols* 26 Everybody rootin' for the other fellow.

+**Root beer.** A beverage prepared with extracts obtained from various roots. Also attrib. — **1843** *Knickerb.* XXII. 85 [Let] the temperance halls and the root-beer *perambulatories* make answer. **1856** KANE *Arctic Explor.* I. 387, I will stay only long enough to complete my latest root-beer brewage. **1865** *Atlantic Mo.* Jan. 59/1, I have not heard his opinions concerning cider, or root-beer. **1882** FREDERIC *Lawton Girl* 165 Old Ikey Peters . . . started a sort of fish store, along with peanuts and toys and root beer. **1910** C. HARRIS *Eve's Husband* 127 They notice if he takes even a glass of root beer.

Root cellar. (See quot. 1923.) {1822-} — **1868** BEECHER *Norwood* 535 The grain-room, the root-cellars, the straw-sheds, the mill-room . . . seemed like parts of a city rather than of a barn. **1881** *Rep. Indian Affairs* 121 Agency Buildings at Poplar River are agent's house, . . . root cellar, 20 by 40, log, dirt roof. **1910** *Outlook* 25 June 367 No sooner are the foundations laid than the housewife sees that a root cellar must be added. **1923** *Dialect Notes* V. 219 *Root cellar,* an underground storage room for vegetables. [McDonald Co., Mo.]

Root crop. A crop, as potatoes, cultivated chiefly for the underground parts of the plants. {1834-} — **1858** C. FLINT *Milch Cows* 191 The potato is the first of the root crops to be mentioned. **1868** *Mich. Agric. Rep.* VII. 155 Indian corn, in many instances, did not recover from

the check it received, and root crops were much lessened in yield. **1888** *Vt. Agric. Rep.* X. 46 The potato is the most important root crop with us.

Root-digger. {1865-} +An Indian who subsists chiefly on roots; a root-eater. (Cf. DIGGER 2.) — **1837** IRVING *Bonneville* II. 84 Captain Bonneville unexpectedly found an owner for the horse which he had purchased from a Root Digger at the Big Wyer. **1845** FRÉMONT *Exped.* 148 Several families of Root Diggers . . . were encamped among the rushes on the shore. **1847** *29th Congress 2 Sess.* H. R. Doc. 76, 6 Yam pe-uc-coes, or 'Root Diggers,' . . . range generally on the headwaters of the Canadian and Red rivers. **1848** PARKMAN in *Knickerb.* XXXI. 123 The 'Root-Diggers,' a wretched tribe beyond the mountains, turn them to good account by making them into a sort of soup. **1873** BEADLE *Undeveloped West* 420 Here [in the Indian Territory] are sixty thousand red men who are neither hunters nor root diggers; they are agriculturists, herdsmen and mechanics.

Root-digging. The action of digging up roots, esp. with reference to the Indian root-diggers. {1877-, in Austral.} Also *ppl. a.* — **1845** FRÉMONT *Exped.* 202 With them were a few Snake Indians of the root-digging species. **1846** SAGE *Scenes Rocky Mts.* xiii, We were variously occupied in hunting, root-digging, and moccasin-making. *a*1861 WINTHROP *Canoe & Saddle* 196, I can find no object that can compare with this root-digging Klickatat. **1871** *Rep. Indian Affairs* (1872) 293 Most of them [*sc.* the Methows] cultivate small patches of potatoes and corn; . . . the remainder [of their subsistence comes] from hunting, fishing, and root-digging.

Root-eater. {*a*1735-} +An Indian belonging to any one of various tribes or groups noted for dependence upon roots for food. (Cf. ROOT-DIGGER.) — **1836** IRVING *Astoria* I. 276 Another class [of the Snake Indians], the most abject and forlorn, . . . are called Shuckers, or more commonly Diggers and Root eaters. **1850** SCHOOLCRAFT *Information resp. Indian Tribes* I. 522 Population of the Territory of Utah . . . [includes] Yumpatick-ara, Root-Eaters. **1886** *Amer. Philos. Soc. Proc.* XXIII. 299 Seven bands exist among the Comanche, as follows: I. Yamparika Yampa (root)-Eaters. **1907** HODGE, etc. *Amer. Indians* I. 390/2 The root-eaters were supposed to represent a low type of Indian.

Rooter. {1648-} +One who gives enthusiastic support, esp. to an athletic team. — **1895** *Stand.* 1550/1 *Rooter,* . . . one who gives encouragement, as by applauding. **1899** ADE *Fables in Slang* 27 He had been a Rooter from the days of Underhand Pitching. **1902** CORBIN *Amer. at Oxford* 153 Yale may outplay Harvard, but if Harvard sufficiently outcheers Yale she wins, and to the rooters belongs the praise. **1914** S. H. ADAMS *Clarion* 55 You're a good rooter for the business. **1924** P. MARKS *Plastic Age* 88 Shouts of 'Score! Score! Score!' went up from the Raleigh rooters.

+**Root fence.** (See quot. 1792.) *Obs.* — [**1792** BELKNAP *Hist. New-Hampshire* III. 108 When the roots [of the mast pine] have been loosened by the frost, they are . . . cut and dug out of the ground, and being turned up edge way, are set for fences to fields.] **1853** LOWELL in *Putnam's Mo.* II. Nov. 459/2 Sometimes a root-fence stretched up its bleaching antlers.

Root graft. A scion designed to be grafted on to the root of a stock. — **1859** *Rep. Comm. Patents 1858* I. 377 Improvement in Machines for Cutting Root grafts. **1872** *Ill. Dept. Agric. Trans.* IX. 68 The root-grafts grow and live as well as any.

+**Root hog or die.** An expression, usually of imperative force, indicating the necessity of either working hard or suffering undesirable consequences. *colloq.*

1834 CROCKETT *Narr. Life* 118 We therefore determined to go on the old saying, root hog or die. **1866** *Iowa Agric. Soc. Rep.* 1865 358 It has been a common practice with farmers . . . to raise them [*sc.* hogs] upon the principle of 'root hog or die.' That is to turn them out in to the woods or on to the prairies to get their own living. **1890** HARTE *Waif of Plains* 4 One of the wagons bore on its canvas hood the inscription, . . . 'Root Hog, or Die.' **1913** LONDON *Valley of Moon* 395 Root hog or die is on every wagon sheet.

b. Hence *root-hog-or-die law, policy, principle, variety.*

1853 PAIGE *Patent Sermons* III. 193 (Th.), Obliged to go upon the root-hog-or-die principle. **1875** *Chicago Tribune* 8 Dec. 8/3 A tax-eating official . . . could add to the wealth of the State with his little hoe on a good farm if the Root-hog-or-die-law was carefully read to him and enforced. **1879** TOURGEE *Fool's Errand* 150 The 'root-hog-or-die' policy of the great apostle of the instantaneous transformation era became generally prevalent. **1881** PIERSON *In the Brush* 16 The swine were of the original 'root-hog-or-die' variety.

Root house. {1765-} A house for storing potatoes, carrots, etc. {1805-} — **1790** *Penna. Packet* 30 March 4/2 On the premises are . . . two arched stone root houses. **1871** *Rep. Indian Affairs* (1872) 432, [I] have constructed two root-houses for stowing away vegetables.

Root louse. A form of plant louse of the family Aphididae which feeds on roots. — **1874** *Dept. Agric. Rep. 1873* 161 Neither on these vines nor on any others near them could a true *root*-louse . . . be found. **1891** *Cent.* 5225/3. [**1908** KELLOGG *Amer. Insects* 172 Of more economic importance are some of those plant-lice which infest crop-plants, . . . the apple-tree root-louse, . . . the corn-root louse, the hop-louse, [etc.].]

Root-washer. A machine for washing roots. — **1819** *Plough Boy* I. 123 Root washer, an improved one for washing potatoes, turnips, &c. **1876** KNIGHT III. 1976/2 *Root-washer,* a machine which usually consists of a slatted cylinder revolving in a tank of water.

Rootworm. Any one of various insect larvae that feed on the roots of plants, as the strawberry rootworm, *Paria canella*. (See also CORN-ROOT WORM.) — 1802 *Mass. H. S. Coll.* I Ser. VIII. 190 Five [worms] . . . are very destructive to Indian corn. . . . The fourth is the *root-worm*. 1883 *Science* II. 143/2 Insects affecting the strawberry . . . [include] the crown-borer, the root-worm, and the crown-miner.

* Rope, *n.*

*1. A length of large cord made of hemp, cotton, etc.

1640 *Conn. Rec.* I. 448 An Inventory of the goods and Cattell of James Olmestead: . . . fiue pyke forks, one rope, on fanne. 1707 *Boston Rec.* 56 Capt. Thoms Hutchenson is desired to provide a hammer, a Lanthorn & a rope. 1796 MORSE *Univ. Geog.* I. 557 A flat[boat], large enough to carry a team of six horses, runs on a strong rope, fixed and stretched across [the river]. 1837 IRVING *Bonneville* II. 52 The Shoshokees . . . manufacture good ropes, and even a tolerably fine thread, from a sort of weed found in their neighborhood. 1893 [see CRAB *n.*[1] 2]. 1907 *St. Nicholas* July 825/2 Untie that rope from around the stump there.

+2. = LASSO *n.*

1850 GARRARD *Wah-To-Yah* xix. 217 [Beavers are as] shy as a coyote as runs round camp to gnaw a rope. 1888 *Century Mag.* Feb. 506/1 The rope . . . is the one essential feature of every cowboy's equipment. 1907 WHITE *Arizona Nights* 317 Each had, of course, his saddle, spurs, and 'rope.' 1919 WILSON *Ma Pettengill* 54 Some way when he had got his rope over a job the hondoo wouldn't seem to render. He couldn't cinch anything. 1924 MULFORD *Rustlers' Valley* 156 The foreman . . . passed in, swinging his rope.

3. In phrases. a. *To know the ropes,* to know one's way about, to be acquainted with all the ins and outs of a situation. *colloq.* {1874-}

1840 DANA *Two Years* ix. 74 The captain . . . had been on the coast before and 'knew the ropes.' 1856 M. THOMPSON *Plu-ri-bus-tah* 186 The old man 'Knew the ropes,' and wouldn't go there. 1894 HOYT *Texas Steer* (1925) II. 21 The secretary knows the ropes and can show his employer the town. 1905 'O. HENRY' *Roads of Destiny* 134 You'll want somebody who knows the ropes to look out for you.

b. *To learn the ropes,* to find how the land lies, to become acquainted with all the tricks or dodges. *colloq.*

1850 MITCHELL *Lorgnette* II. 186 The belle of two weeks standing, who has 'learned the ropes,' is . . . anxious indeed to show her complacent daring. 1857 *Knickerb.* Jan. 38 [He was] just getting under way and learning the ropes in the store of Mr. Coolidge Claflin. 1905 PHILLIPS *Social Secretary* 24 You'll soon learn the ropes.

‖c. *To draw the rope,* (see quotation).

1891 F. CHASE *Hist. Dartmouth Coll.* I. 225 The worms . . . would climb the wheatstalks and eat them off close to the head, which would then fall to the ground and be at once devoured. Ineffectual attempts were made to prevent this by 'drawing the rope;' that is, by constantly sweeping the worms from the stalks by a rope stretched taut and drawn back and forth across the fields.

*4. *attrib.* and *comb.* **a.** Designating persons having to do with a rope or ropes.

1832 DUNLAP *Hist. Amer. Theatre* 128 As the good people of Boston were denied rational amusement, they accepted the efforts of the tumbler and rope dancer. 1855 WOOD *Recoll. Stage* 398 Herr Cline, one of the most agreeable and graceful of rope performers. 1917 SINCLAIR *King Coal* 19 There was a wire-haired and almond eyed Korean, . . . a 'rope-rider' in Hal's part of the mine.

b. Designating objects made of a rope or of ropes. {1704-}

1856 KANE *Arctic Explor.* I. 386 What remains to complete our camp-plot is the rope barrier. 1868 WOODRUFF *Trotting Horse* 249 A little, rough-coated bay mare . . . [was] tied at the tail of the wagon by a rope-halter some three or four feet long. 1874 LONG *Wild-Fowl* 109 An old powder-keg, . . . fitted with a rope-handle, makes [a pail]. 1884 W. SHEP-HERD *Prairie Exper.* 37 A man, armed with a rope-lasso, catches a calf by throwing it over his head. 1888 DELAND *J. Ward* 8 [He] caught her by the mane and a rope bridle. 1901 MERWIN & WEBSTER *Calumet 'K'* 5 'Slack away!' he called to the engineers, and he cast off the rope sling. 1902 WISTER *Virginian* xviii, After the rope corral we had to make this morning . . . the ropes was all strewed round camp.

c. In special combinations.

Rope apple, r.-broken, (see quotation); *r. drive,* a rope or ropes used to transmit power; *r. elevator,* (see quotation); *r. funeral,* a hanging or lynching; *r. pin,* a tent pin; *r. railway,* (see quotation and cf. CABLE RAILROAD); *r.-spinner,* a machine used in ropemaking; *ropewalking,* the gymnastic feat of walking a rope; *r. yellow,* (see quotation).

1709 LAWSON *Carolina* 109 Rope-Apples . . . are small apples, hanging like Ropes of Onions. 1882 BAILLIE-GROHMAN *Camps in Rockies* 99 She was not even 'rope-broken,' i.e. accustomed to the rope-halter. 1901 MER-WIN & WEBSTER *Calumet 'K'* 144 [Here would be] the rope-drive for the transmission of power from the working to the distributing floor. 1876 KNIGHT 1979/2 Rope Elevator, an elevator in which the platform or cage is raised and lowered by means of a rope and winding mechanism. 1895 *Congress. Rec.* 15 Jan. 1003/2 The judge feels that he has sent enough men to the penitentiary and attended enough rope funerals of the outlaws of that [Indian] country to make it a very paradise of peace. 1904 STRATTON-

PORTER *Freckles* 326 The men were driving the rope-pins. 1876 KNIGHT 1983/1 *Rope-railway,* a railway on which the cars are drawn by ropes wound upon drums rotated by stationary engines. 1848 *Rep. Comm. Patents 1847* 162 The crop is certainly short of an adequate supply for the bagging looms and rope spinners now in operation. 1881 *Mich. Gen. Statutes* I. (1882) 539 Any person . . . who shall apprentice, give away, let out or otherwise dispose of any such child to any person in or for the vocation, service or occupation of rope or wire walking . . . shall be deemed guilty of a misdemeanor. 1884 SARGENT *Rep. Forests* 517 Tar, produced by burning the dead wood and most resinous parts of the long-leaved pine in covered kilns, is graded as follows: 'Rope yellow,' or Ropemakers' tar —the highest grade, produced with a minimum of heat from the most resinous parts of the wood [etc.].

* Rope, *v.*

1. *tr.* To catch (a horse, calf, etc.) with a rope; to lasso. {1884-, in Austral.}

'*U.S. and Austr.*' (O.E.D.). Cf. ROPING 2.

1848 RUXTON *Life Far West* i, Maybe you'll get 'roped' (lasso'd) by a Rapaho. 1853 'P. PAXTON' *Yankee in Texas* 38 If he [the horse] has been once properly 'roped,' all that is necessary is to get one upon his neck. 1881 *Cimarron News & Press* 17 Feb. 3/1 He had 'roped' a calf, which by a sudden turn brought his horse backwards upon the rider. 1895 REMING-TON *Pony Tracks* 130 Having 'roped' a stray pony two days before, . . . the lightest *vaquero* was put on his back. 1923 'BOWER' *Parowan Bonanza* 65 She . . . can sling a pack or rope a critter better than lots of men that draw wages for doing it.

b. *transf.* To capture (a person).

Cf. ROPING 1.

1890 *Stock Grower & Farmer* 18 Jan. 3/2 It is hoped they [stockmen] will succeed in roping a few of the thieves. 1916 DU PUY *Uncle Sam* 120 Peterson should be 'roped.'

2. (See quotation.)

1883 'S. BONNER' *Dialect Tales* 23 This person was engaged in the curious operation of 'roping' her hair—that is, dividing it into small strands, each one of which was wrapped tightly to its end with a white cotton string.

+3. *To rope in* (or *into*), to ensnare, allure, deceive, take in. *slang.*

Cf. ROPING 1.

1840 *Picayune* 18 Sept. 2/2 The persons rightly concluded it was an effort to 'rope in,' and told Trainer so. 1859 *La Crosse Daily Union* 10 Nov. 1/2 The speculators did not expect to be roped in after the manner indicated. 1885 *Wkly. New Mexican Rev.* 2 July 4/3 Smokey Jones claims that he was roped into this snap by Chicago sharpers. 1890 *Buckskin Mose* 133 Young men who wished to grow wealthy without patient toil . . . [and] whose practice in . . . 'roping in a greeney,' had become too well known. 1911 BURGESS *Find the Woman* 76 It was a funny story how young Michael Carnarvon got married. . . . You see, young Carnarvon was really what you might call roped in.

+b. To draw into something. {1899-}

1868 'MARK TWAIN' in Marsh *Man. of Reformed Phonetic Shorthand* 91 She ropes us in at the church fairs.

Rope dancing. Dancing, balancing, or walking on a rope. {1704-} — 1734 *Boston Selectmen* 259 The Application. . . . Praying for Liberty to Entertain the Town with the Diversion of Rope Dancing . . . [was] disallow'd. 1789 *Holyoke Diaries* 121 At Donegan's Rope dancing. 1879 *Mich. Public Acts* 200 Any puppet-show, wire or rope dancing, or other idle show, acts or feats.

+Rope ferry. A ferry operated by a rope. — 1771 in *New Eng. Mag.* ns. XII. 350/1, I arrived at a place called the Rope Ferry. 1791 WASH-INGTON *Diaries* IV. 182 Passing through the village . . . just below the . . . falls in the Congaree (which was passed in a flat bottomed boat at a Rope ferry,) I lodged at Columbia. c1835 FOBES *Arnold's Exped.* 31 We came to a large stream . . . and to a crossing by means of a rope ferry. 1891 'THANET' *Otto the Knight* 217 A rope ferry spans the river below.

* Rope house. A building in which ropes are made. — 1752 HEMP-STEAD *Diary* 585, I ranged the S. Cornner of Natts Rope House &c. 1755 *Ib.* 652 Ephm. mowed this Side the Rope House & Rope walk. 1876 RAYMOND *8th Rep. Mines* 132 There is a blacksmith-shop, a rope-house, two large carpenter-shops, and one machine-shop.

* Ropemaker. One whose occupation is making ropes. — 1653 *Charlestown Land Rec.* 128, [I] the wife of John harrison, of boston, Rope-maker . . . [sell] my house and garden. 1701 *Boston Rec.* 10 Whoever Shall Kindle or make any fire open or abroad, within two rodds of any . . . combustable matter Subject to take fire (except in Ship Carpenters building yards, Sett work coopers, and Ropemakers works, . . .) Shall forfit . . . ten Shillings. 1774 *Washington Diaries* II. 138 A Rope Maker, one Paterson, Dined here. 1812 MELISH *Travels* II. 55 Professions exercised in Pittsburg: . . . Inkpowdermakers, rope-makers, tobacconists. 1888 *Amer. Almanac* 275.

Ropemaking. The occupation of making ropes. {1791-} Also attrib. — 1803 in *Cincinnati Misc.* I. 268 His companion is a young man who is master of the ropemaking business. 1847 *Rep. Comm. Patents 1846* 73 A machine for rope-making . . . has also been patented.

* Roper.

+1. One who uses a lasso.

1808 PIKE *Sources Miss.* 160 Taking the wild horses, in that manner, is scarcely ever attempted, even with the . . . most expert ropers. 1888

ROOSEVELT in *Century Mag.* Feb. 506/2 A really first-class roper . . . is usually fit for little but his own special work. **1893** — *Wilderness Hunter* 26 Then two of the best ropers rode into the corral and began to rope the calves. **1907** WHITE *Arizona Nights* 147 The three ropers sat their horses, idly swinging the loop of their ropes.

+2. A person who acts as a decoy, esp. one who works in the interest of a gambling house. Also *roper-in*.

1840 *Picayune* 31 Oct. 2/3 He had not well landed on the Levee, so famous for cotton bags, sugar, . . . 'ropers in,' and other 'dry goods.' **1868** M. H. SMITH *Sunshine & Shadow* 406 'What are you going to do with yourself to-night?' is carelessly asked by the roper-in. **1875** *Chicago Tribune* 30 Oct. 5/6 The gamblers and their ropers, steerers, and hangers-on maintained a sort of rear guard near the main entrance. **1889** *Columbus Dispatch* 6 Sept., One man was met by a 'roper' at the Court House, & thinks he was drugged.

Ropewalk. A place or establishment where ropes are made. {1692-}

1671 *Boston Rec.* 72, [I] haue layd out of my feild a highway of 12 foote wide from the fort lane to John Harrisons rope walke. **1723** *New-Eng. Courant* 29 April 2/1 A Man and Woman [were] scuffling together in a jesting manner, at a Rope Walk at the South End. **1789** MORSE *Amer. Geog.* 260 A covered rope-walk, and one of the best distilleries in America, were erected. **1810** *Agric. Museum* I. 46 In this town there are now at work 9 rope walks. **1860** MORDECAI *Virginia* 25 A grassy walk . . . extended for a considerable distance, down to where Foster's rope-walk afterward stood. **1893** *Harper's Mag.* May 826/2 The farm-house . . . is shown on Lyne's map, immediately to the south of the Broadway rope-walk.

Rope yard. A yard or open stretch of ground where ropes are made. {1664-} — **1676** *Boston Rec.* 103 Costs granted against Richard Woody in John Harrisons action about the towne high way where his rope yard is. *c*1792 COXE *View U.S.* 314 One rope yard carried on extensively. **1851** CIST *Cincinnati* 186 Nine rope-yards.—One hundred and thirty hands.

Rope yarn. A yarn forming part of a strand of rope, or material for making ropes. {1623-} Also *fig.* — **1684** I. MATHER *Providences* (1856) i. 15 [They would] tie fast with Rope-yarns. **1790** *Penna. Packet* 7 May 3/4 For Sale at New-York, . . . rope yarns, ratlin stuff, bolt ropes and marlines. **1813** *Niles' Reg.* V. 285/1 Some . . . anchored upon an enemy's lee shore, their fate hanging upon a rope yarn. **1879** L. FARRAGUT *Life D. G. Farragut* 33 If you touch a rope-yarn of this ship, I shall board instantly.

* Roping.

+1. Ensnaring, taking in, entrapping. Also *roping in*. Also *attrib.* (Cf. ROPE *v.* 1 b, 3.)

1840 *Picayune* 15 Sept. 2/4 Henry H. Taylor . . . went the 'big figure' in the 'roping in' business. **1848** BARTLETT 278 *Roping in*, cheating. A very common expression in the South-western States. **1891** HARTE *Sappho of Green Springs* 219 We want an end to this roping-in of white folks to suit your little game. **1912** *Chambers's Jrnl.* April 240/1 Counterfeiting is mostly done by printers, and often it is necessary [for a detective] to employ the method known as 'roping,' which means learning the facts of a man's manner of life and habits by getting a job, working with him, and forming a personal acquaintance with him. **1916** DU PUY *Uncle Sam* 121 A detective less experienced in roping might have considered an opportunity to go to this man's hotel with him as a piece of good fortune.

2. The action of lassoing stock with a rope. {1890-, in Austral.} Also *attrib.* (Cf. ROPE *v.* 1.)

1890 *Stock Grower & Farmer* 4 Jan. 5/2 Thursday afternoon the roping match took place. **1902** WISTER *Virginian* i, The passenger's dissertation upon roping I was obliged to lose, for Medicine Bow was my station. **1907** WHITE *Arizona Nights* 274 The roping and throwing and branding . . . filled our days with . . . the unusual.

+Roque. [f. CROQUET.] A form of croquet played on a court having a border or surrounding embankment. — **1899** [see CROQUET]. **1906** *Springfield W. Repub.* 30 Aug. 16 A 16-years-old lad who never before had played in a big tournament won the national championship at roque.

+Roram, Rorum. [Origin unknown.] A woolen material faced with fur, used for making hats; a hat made of this. Usually *attrib.* with *hat*. — **1796** *Aurora* (Phila.) 2 Jan. (Th.), Richard Robinson has on hand an assortment of Beaver, Castor, and Roram Hats. **1811** *Niles' Reg.* 21 Dec. 292/1 Philip J. Hahn . . . makes and sells . . . rorum, castor, or common fur hats. **1832** WATSON *Hist. Tales N.Y.* 153 What were called roram hats, being fur faced upon wool felts, came into use directly after the peace. **1833** A. GREENE *Life D. Duckworth* II. 219 He had . . . exchanged his old ram-beaver for a bran-new rorum. **1845** DRAKE *Pioneer Life Ky.* 231 Other arrangements were being made for the life before me, such as . . . purchasing a white roram hat.

Roscoe's yellowthroat. [Wm. *Roscoe*, Br. historian and philanthropist, (1753-1831).] =MARYLAND YELLOWTHROAT (Coues). *Obs.* — **1831** AUDUBON *Ornith. Biog.* I. 124 Roscoe's Yellow-Throat. *Sylvia Roscoe*. . . . In general appearance, this species so much resembles the preceding, that had not its habits differed so greatly from those of the Maryland Yellowthroat, I might have been induced to consider it as merely an accidental variety. **1839** PEABODY *Mass. Birds* 313.

* Rose.

I. *1. A plant or flower belonging to the genus *Rosa*.

1676 GLOVER *Va.* in *Phil. Trans.* XI. 629 They have likewise in their Gardens Roses, *Clove-Gilliflowers* and variety of other sorts of Flowers.

1792 IMLAY *Western Territory* 207 Every part of the country abounds in a variety of natural flowers . . . marshmallows, violets, roses of different sorts, &c. **1815** DRAKE *Cincinnati* 83 The most elegantly flowering trees and shrubs are the following, . . . black haw, the different species of roses [etc.]. **1843** TALBOT *Journals* 14 The prairie is covered with the greatest profusion of flowers. The rose, daisy, anemone, lupine. **1898** E. C. HALL *Aunt Jane* 266 Crumbling timbers were knit together by interlacing branches of honeysuckle and running roses.

2. With specifying terms.

See also BRIER ROSE, CHEROKEE 6 b, CLIMBING ROSE, etc.

1785 MARSHALL *Amer. Grove* 135 *Rosa carolinensis*. Wild Virginian Rose. . . . The flowers are single, of a red colour and late coming. **1814** BIGELOW *Florula Bostoniensis* 121 *Rosa Caroliniana*. Swamp rose. . . . This rose grows in swamps and wet grounds, sometimes forming thickets of itself. **1817-8** EATON *Botany* (1822) 433 *Rosa alba*, white rose. **1843** TORREY *Flora N.Y.* I. 218 *Rosa lucida*, Dwarf Wild Rose. . . . Borders of swamps; also in dry thickets, fields, and hill-sides. **1847** *Santa Fe Repub.* 23 Oct. 1/4 Longevity of the Damask Rose. There is a rose bush flourishing in a garden near Bristol, Pa., known to be more than one hundred years old.

II. *attrib.* **3.** Designating substances made, or supposedly made, from roses.

1864 *Ore. State Jrnl.* 12 March 3/5 Hembold's Improved Rose Wash cures secret diseases. **1866** A. D. WHITNEY *L. Goldthwaite* iii, I have some rose-glycerine here in my bag.

4. Designating occasions on which roses are used.

1895 *N.Y. Dramatic News* 23 Nov. 17/3 Friday evening will be known as 'rose evening,' every lady being presented with a rose as she enters the theatre. **1898** FORD *Tattle-Tales* 251, I didn't see you at Mrs. Grainger's rose-cotillion Tuesday, Mr. Stuart.

5. In the specific names of plants and trees.

See also ROSE ACACIA, ROSEBAY, etc. Other examples can be found in books on plants.

1784 *Amer. Acad. Mem.* I. 480 *Erigeron*. . . . Rosebetty. Blossoms in the circumference purple. **1887** BURROUGHS in *Century Mag.* July 328 The steeple-bush, or hard-hack, had more color, as had the rose-gerardia. **1877** PHELPS *Story of Avis* 92 He felt her presence in the room like he felt Aunt Chloe's rose-hyacinth in the atmosphere. **1907** *St. Nicholas* Aug. 939/1 The *Pogonia* group is represented by the rose-pogonia or snakemouth. **1850** S. F. COOPER *Rural Hours* 154 The midsummer flowers are beginning to open. Yellow evening primrose, purple rose-raspberry [etc.]. **1843** TORREY *Flora N.Y.* II. 375 *Carex Rosea*, Rose Sedge. . . . Moist woods and low grounds. **1815** DRAKE *Cincinnati* 83 [The] rose willow, leather wood and aspen, seem to be confined to the more northern portions of this tract.

6. In the specific names of birds and insects.

See also ROSE BUG, ROSE SLUG.

1875 *Rep. Comm. Agric. 1874* 125 Rose beetles, *Macrodactylus subspinus*, were quite injurious to cultivated grapes in Washington, Kansas. **1884** COUES *Key to Birds* (ed. 2) 314 *Cardellina*, . . . Rose Fly-Catching Warblers. **1868** *Amer. Naturalist* II. 163 Among the injurious hymenoptera . . . is the Rose Saw-fly (*Selandria rosæ*) and *S. cerasi*. **1832** WILLIAMSON *Maine* I. 172 Spiders: several species, such as black, gray, . . . jumping, rose Spiders. **1884** COUES *Key to Birds* (ed. 2) 318 *P[yranga] æstiva*, . . . Rose Tanager. Summer Red-Bird. **1889** *Cent.* 819/2 *C. rubra* is the rose warbler, entirely red with silvery auriculars; . . . found in Texas and southward. **1891** *Cent.* 5233/1 *Rose-worm* . . . , the larva of the common tortricid moth, *Cacæcia rosaceana*, which folds the leaves of the rose and skeletonizes them.

7. In special combinations.

+*Rose catarrh, r. cold*, a variety of hay fever attributed to the inhaling of rose pollen; *r. comb*, a flat comb characteristic of the Hamburg fowl and certain others {rosecombed, 1885}; *r. crown*, =prec.; **+***r. fever*, =*rose cold*; *r. gasburner*, (see quotation); *r. jar*, a container for dried rose leaves; *r. rust*, of certain rusts attacking roses.

1888 HUNTER *Encycl. Dict.* VI. 184/2 *Rose-catarrh, rose-fever*, . . . a catarrh or slight fever like hay-asthma, prevailing in parts of the United States. **1872** M. WYMAN *Autumnal Catarrh* 4 The popular name, 'Hay Fever,' . . . has been applied to the 'June Cold' or 'Rose Cold.' **1850** BROWNE *Poultry Yard* 52 The fleshy rose comb of the golden Hamburgh terminating in a sharp point behind . . . is seen in no other variety of fowl. *Ib.* 40 Most of our ordinary breeds have a rose crown. **1851** WORTLEY *Travels in U.S.* III. 22 [Hay asthma] is known in the U.S., and is called there, rose-fever. **1876** KNIGHT 1984/1 *Rose Gas-burner*, a burner giving a circle of small flames. **1894** *Harper's Mag.* Jan. 310/1 A rose-jar stood on one [table] in the corner. **1817-8** EATON *Botany* (1822) 498 *Uredo rosae-centifoliae*, rose rust. . . . On the leaves of the centfoil rose.

+Rose acacia. (See quot. 1898.) — **1833** EATON *Botany* (ed. 6) 306. **1852** MOTLEY *Correspondence* I. 129 The acacias (rose acacias) under my window . . . are not leafless. **1898** CREEVEY *Flowers of Field* 482 Rose Acacia. . . . *Robinia hispida*. . . . A shrub indigenous south of Virginia. . . . It grows from 3 to 8 feet high, and bears large, rose-colored blossoms.

Roseate spoonbill. A wading bird (*Ajaia ajaja*) with bare head and throat, and pink plumage. (Cf. PINK CURLEW 2.) — [**1785** LATHAM *Gen. Synopsis Birds* III. 16 Roseate Spoonbill, *Platalea Ajaja*. . . . The plumage is a fine rose-colour.] **1813** WILSON *Ornithology* VII. 123 Roseate Spoonbill: . . . inhabits the sea shores of America from Brasil to Georgia. **1887** RIDGWAY *Manual N.A. Birds* 123 Tropical America in general, north to southern Atlantic and Gulf States, and casually (formerly at least) to California and southern Illinois.... Roseate Spoonbill. **1917** *Birds of Amer.* I. 175/1 There is no large wading bird of North America that bears such brilliant plumage as the Roseate Spoonbill.

Roseate tern. A tern (*Sterna dougalli*) whose breast is roseate in the breeding season. {1813-} — **1835** AUDUBON *Ornith. Biog.* III. 297 The Roseate Tern spends the breeding season along the southern shores of the Floridas. **1869** *Amer. Naturalist* III. 234 The Least Tern, the Arctic Tern, Wilson's Tern, and the Roseate Tern, still breed on our [Mass.] coast. **1917** *Birds of Amer.* I. 64/1 The Roseate Tern is the embodiment of symmetry and grace.

* **Rosebay.** Any one of several species of *Rhododendron* or *Azalea.* {1760-} Freq. with specifying terms.
See also AMERICAN ROSE-BAY.
1781-2 JEFFERSON *Notes Va.* (1788) 38 Dwarf-rose bay. *Rhododendron maximum.* **1813** MUHLENBURG *Cat. Plants* 20 *Azalea viscosa*, Clammy, white-flowered rosebay. *Ib.* 43 *Rhododendron catabiense*, Catawba rosebay. **1843** *Amer. Pioneer* II. 120 'Laurel ridge' . . . [is] so named from the profusion of *Rhododendron*, or Rosebay, and *Kalmia latifolia*, or Laurel, which clusters along its rocky sides. **1898** *Atlantic Mo.* Oct. 498/2 The purple rhododendron or mountain rose-bay (*R. Catawbiense*) . . . was to be found here [in N.C.]. **1901** MOHR *Plant Life Ala.* 654 *Rhododendron catawbiense*.... Catawba Rhododendron. Rose Bay.

* **Rosebay tree.** =prec. — **1795** WINTERBOTHAM *Hist. View* III. 391. **1834** *S. Lit. Messenger* I. 97/2 The underwood is . . . diversified with immense tracts of the *Kalmia Latifolia* and the large rose-bay-tree, (*Rhododendron Maximum*).

Rose blanket. 'A blanket of fine quality, having a rose, or a conventional device resembling a rose, worked in one corner' (*Cent.*). — **1759** *Newport Mercury* 26 June 3/2 Just Imported by Simon Pease, jun.... best Rose Blankets. *a***1811** HENRY *Camp. Quebec* 102 Our attention was much more attracted by the costly feather beds, counterpanes, and charming rose-blankets, which the house afforded. **1820** *Columbian Centinel* 8 Jan. 3/4 A great variety of Dry Goods: . . . Rose Blankets.

Rose-breasted, *a.* {1801-} +In the names of American birds. (See also ROSE-BREASTED GROSBEAK.) — **1884** COUES *Key to Birds* (ed. 2) 348 *C[arpodacus] f[rontalis] rhodocolpus*, . . . Rose-Breasted Finch. *Ib.* 389 *Z[amelodia] ludoviciana*, . . . Rose-Breasted Song Grosbeak.

+**Rose-breasted grosbeak.** A grosbeak (*Hedymeles ludovicianus*), usually black and white, with a rose-colored breast. — **1810** WILSON *Ornithology* II. 135 [The] Rose-Breasted Grosbeak . . . [is found] in the state of New York, and those of New England. **1839** PEABODY *Mass. Birds* 329 The Rose-Breasted Grosbeak . . . may be seen standing with its wings lifted. *a***1866** *Conn. Gen. Statutes* 483 No person shall willfully shoot . . . [the] humming-bird, rose-breasted grosbeak, and phebe. **1917** *Birds of Amer.* III. 67/1 The Rose-breasted Grosbeak is held in high esteem because of his habit of preying upon the Colorado potato-bug.

Rosebud. {1611-} +**1.** A debutante. Used attrib. (Cf. BUD *n.*[2]) +**2.** *Rosebud Senator*, Senator Henry B. Anthony of Rhode Island (1815-84). A nickname. — **(1) 1885** *Harper's Mag.* March 544/2 The girls have gone to a 'rose-bud' dinner at the Mays', though I can't say I approved of it. **1890** *Century Mag.* Aug. 582 They flutter their brief hour in society.... Some of them hold on like grim death to rosebud privileges. **(2) 1885** *Congress. Rec.* 21 Jan. 908/1 [H. B. Anthony] was called 'the rosebud Senator,' . . . as a tribute to the healthful glow which mantled his cheek, or from the fact that . . . he constantly wore a bud or other flower.

+**Rose bug.** The rose beetle, *Macrodactylus subspinosus.* — **1800** *Mass. Spy* 1 Oct. (Th.), He suggests that the Rosebug is the pre-existing state of those worms. **1838** *Mass. Zool. Survey Rep.* 69 The rose-chaffer or rose-bug . . . attacks, without much discrimination, almost every tree, shrub, and plant. **1850** *New Eng. Farmer* II. 213 Rose-bugs have been so common in some of the Eastern States, that on the sea-shore they have floated in winrows on the sands. **1910** *Outlook* 25 June 436 Then came armies of creatures to swarm over the tender rose leaves and scoff at hellebore and ashes. What these left when satiated the rose-bugs appropriated.

* **Rosebush.** A shrub of the genus *Rosa.* — **1749** *N.J. Archives* 1 Ser. VII. 429 A rose bush standing on said road. **1785** MARSHALL *Amer. Grove* 135 The Rose-Bush.... The Seeds numerous, oblong, hairy, and joined within on all sides of the Seed-vessel. **1847** [see ROSE 2]. **1883** *Century Mag.* Nov. 137/2 It had a broad piazza, with rose-bushes, and the grounds around were full of flowers. **1914** 'BOWER' *Flying U Ranch* 173 Over there in them rosebushes you oughta find enough bresh.

+**Rosefish.** A rose-colored fish, esp. a marine food fish (*Sebastes marinus*). {1855} Cf. HEMDURGAN, NORWAY HADDOCK, RED PERCH 2. — **1731** *Essex Inst. Coll.* XLII. 223 We spy'd the Fin of a Whale . . . , & Supposing it to be a Rose fish, ran forward to see it. **1839** [see HEMDURGAN]. **1884** GOODE, etc. *Fisheries* I. 262 The Rose-fish is much esteemed as an article of food. **1911** *Rep. Fisheries 1908* 314/2.

+**Rose-flowering locust.** =HONEY LOCUST b. — **1810** MICHAUX *Arbres* I. 38 *R[obinia] viscosa.* Rose flowering locust. **1832** BROWNE *Sylva* 299 The rose-flowering locust is not so large as the preceding species. **1897** *Arborescent Flora* 263 *Robinia viscosa.* Clammy Locust.... Rose-Flowering Locust (Tenn.).

+**Rose-flowering raspberry.** The purple-flowering raspberry, *Rubus odoratus.* — **1847** WOOD *Botany* 249 Rose-flowering Raspberry. Mulberry.... Fruit broad and thin, bright red, sweet. **1847** DARLINGTON *Weeds & Plants* 125 Odorous Rubus. Rose-flowering raspberry.... The fruit of this is pleasantly flavored,—but is rarely perfected under cultivation.

Rose geranium. Any one of several cultivated plants of the genus *Pelargonium*, or the blossom of one of these. {1867-} — **1832** S. J. HALE *Flora* 59 Geranium, Rose. *P[elargonium] Capitatum.*... Flowers rose-scented and colored. **1854** M. J. HOLMES *Tempest & Sunshine* 333 [The bouquet] consisted of three large, full blown roses, round which were ranged in a perfect circle, some dark green leaves of rose geranium. **1869** FULLER *Flower Gatherers* 70 Bring me a blossom from that Rose-geranium in the window. **1899** GOING *Flowers* 126 Sometimes like the leaves of the rose-geranium, they are curiously slashed.

* **Rosemary.** A fragrant shrub, *Rosmarinus officinalis;* also, its leaves or foliage. — **1660** *Suffolk Deeds* III. 528 Receaved with som dredgare & Rosmary. **1709** LAWSON *Carolina* 78 Our Pot-herbs . . . are Angelica wild and tame, . . . sweet Bazil, Rosemary, Lavender. **1792** IMLAY *Western Territory* 207 Of herbs, &c. we have of the wild sort . . . thyme, Indian leaf, rosemary. **1818** BRYANT *Poetical Works* (1903) 34 Silent lovers . . . Came often . . . to strew Their offerings, rue, and rosemary and flowers. **1872** POWERS *Afoot & Alone* 299 You will find . . . sage, and mint, and rosemary, and purple tar-weed.

+**Rosemary pine.** Any of various species of pine found in the southeastern United States. — **1859** G. W. PERRY *Turpentine Farming* 26 Rosemary pine.—There is less of this kind of pine than any other that is used for turpentine. **1897** SUDWORTH *Arborescent Flora* 25 *Pinus tæda.* Loblolly Pine.... Rosemary Pine (Va., N.C.). *Ib.* 30 *Pinus palustris.* Longleaf Pine.... Rosemary Pine (N.C.).

Rose of Sharon. {1611-} +A common shrub, *Hibiscus syriacus.* — **1860** DARLINGTON *Weeds & Plants* 67 Syrian Hibiscus. Rose of Sharon. Shrubby Althæa. **1924** BAILEY *Man. Cultivated Plants* 496 Rose-of-Sharon . . . [is] much grown for its summer and autumn bloom of open-bell-shaped rose or purple [flowers].

Rose slug. a. The larva of a black sawfly (*Cladius isomerus*), which feeds upon the leaves of rosebushes. **b.** *Rose-slug sawfly*, the adult insect. {rose saw-fly, 1840} — **1877** *Vermont Bd. Agric. Rep.* IV. 98 One pound of tobacco soap to seven gallons of water is an efficient solution for . . . the rose slugs. **1892** KELLOGG *Kansas Insects* 4 No injury is done . . . by the four-winged hymenopterous insects, (the Raspberry- and Rose-slug Saw-flies.) **1922** *Farmers' Bul.* No. 1252, 4 The bristly rose slug . . . occurs in the States east of the Mississippi River.

* **Rose tree.** A rosebush, usu. one grown in natural form and not attached to a supporting wall or trellis. — **1737** BRICKELL *N. Carolina* 24 The Pleasure Gardens of North Carolina, are not yet . . . Adorned with many beautiful fragrant Flowers; there being only some few Rose-Trees, Bead-Trees, Orange-Trees. **1857** *Lawrence* (Kan.) *Republican* 11 June 3, I saw a rose-tree surrounded by a tuft of grass. **1891** WILKINS *New Eng. Nun* 24 A rose-tree outside the window waved; soft shadows floated through the room.

Rosette.

1. A decoration in the shape of a rose. {1802-}
1790 *Penna. Packet* 11 Dec. 3/2 Imported, . . . [Ladies'] elegant beaded rosettees, for shoes. **1844** *Knickerb.* XXIV. 89 His varieties of mouldings, consols, centre-flowers, rosettes and capitals . . . have long been the admiration of hundreds. **1863** [see FLAG-RAISING 1]. **1907** *St. Nicholas* Aug. 896/1 There were high-heeled pink slippers and a long pink feather with a gold rosette that was tarnished and dull.

+**2.** Any one of various diseases which attack specific plants, usu. causing rosetting of the leaves and stunted growth. Freq. with designating term.
1892 *Dept. Agric. Rep. 1891* 370 Dr. Smith has this year given considerable attention to peach rosette in Georgia. **1893** *Ib. 1892* 238 Inoculations have cast some doubt on the identity of the peach and plum rosette. **1894** *Farmers' Bul.* No. 17, 14 Rosette clearly belongs to the same type of disease as yellows.... In trees attacked in this manner all of the leaf buds grow into compact tufts or rosettes. **1920** *Ib.* No. 1129, 13 Rosette . . . has so far proved to be the most serious [disease] with which the pecan industry has to contend. **1924** *Ib.* No. 1414, 2 Symptoms of wheat rosette . . . first become evident in the spring after growth of the healthy plants is well started.
attrib. Ib. No. 1414 Pref., The rosette disease is recognized in the field in the spring by stunted and rosetted plants.

+**Rose vine.** A climbing rose. — **1856** *Harper's Mag.* Dec. 7/2 The cottage . . . [was] overrun with honey-suckle and eglantine, with the rose-vine and the clinging ivy. **1879** STOCKTON *Rudder Grange* vi, Euphemia tied up the rose-vines. **1883** RITTENHOUSE *Maud* 189 The Government Street residence [was] . . . soft in color, . . . with innumerable portions fancifully railed, and made glorious by great clambering rose-vines laden with blooms.

Rosewood. {1660-} *attrib.* Designating pieces of furniture, etc., made of rosewood. — **1847** BRIGGS *Tom Pepper* I. 145 Old Gil's parlor was well filled with rosewood chairs and sofas. **1854** M. J. HOLMES *Tempest & Sunshine* 134 The letter was placed in the rosewood box by the side of its companions. **1857** *Lawrence* (Kan.) *Republican* 23 July 4 The saucy young miss . . . has led her indulgent papa to the auction room to secure for her use that 'magnificent rosewood piano.' **1875** HARTE *Tales of Argonauts* 9 He looked . . . at the crimson satin and rosewood furniture. **1880** E. JAMES *Negro Minstrel's Guide* 4 Rosewood bones, 50 & 75 cts. per set. **1882** MCCABE *New York* 232 Rosewood caskets vary in price, according to the trimmings, from $90 to $150.

∗ Rosin. Also **rozin.**

∗ **1.** The resin or solid substance remaining when crude turpentine is distilled.

1634 WOOD *New Eng. Prospect* 17 The Firre and Pine bee trees that . . . afford good masts, good board, Rozin and Turpentine. **1693** *Springfield Rec.* II. 213 John Dorchester . . . should lay out the tract of Two miles Square to the Makers of Rosin. **1705** *Boston News-Letter* 30 July 2/2 For good and Merchantable Rezin or Turpentine per Ton, each ton containing 20 Gross Hundreds (net Rozin or Turpentine) to be brought in 8 Barrels, Three Pounds. **1789** MORSE *Amer. Geog.* 414 The exports [of North Carolina include] . . . turpentine, rosin, Indian corn. **1851** CIST *Cincinnati* 247 Purchasers [of varnish] . . . are not likely to experience imposition, which the introduction occasionally, of rosin, in an article where the maker's name is not apparent, . . . exposes them to, at times. **1882** G. C. EGGLESTON *Wreck of Red Bird* 165 This is the country where they waste nothing; they bark the trees to get resin; they distil the resin and make turpentine; what's left is rosin. **1904** *Scientific Amer.* XCI. 407/2 This whole mass [of turpentine, tar, etc.] is now placed in a copper retort, similar to that used in distilling the pure rosin.

2. *attrib.* **a.** With *box, canvas, dross,* etc.

1790 *Penna. Packet* 11 Dec. 3/2 Imported, . . . Rosin boxes. **1840** *Picayune* 28 July 4/5 400 Barrels Rosin Dross, an excellent article for steamboats. **1868** G. G. CHANNING *Recoll. Newport* 18, I was held over a rosin-pan to be smoked. **1913** LONDON *Valley of Moon* 81, He goes down sideways, strikin' his face first on the rosin-canvas.

+**b.** In the specific names of plants.

Rosin plant, the compass plant (see COMPASS 3 and cf. ROSINWEED); *rosinwood,* =CREOSOTE BUSH.

1839 in *Mich. Agric. Soc. Trans.* VII. 419 *Silphium gummiferum*. . . . Rosin-plant. **1854** BARTLETT *Personal Narr.* I. 94 Rosin wood, or creosote plant, a most disgusting, strong-smelling shrub.

+**Rosin heel.** A poor white. A nickname. (Cf. BOGUE *n.* 2.) — **1826** FLINT *Recoll.* 319 [The people of Western Florida] are a wild race, with but little order or morals among them; they are generally denominated 'Bogues,' and call themselves 'rosin heels.' **1866** W. REID *After the War* 416 'The rossum heels live in thar,' a newsboy on the train informed me.

Rosin oil. An oil obtained from rosin. {1866-} — **1850** *Rep. Comm. Patents 1849* 474 The oil here referred to, and called rosin oil, is obtained by the destructive distillation of common rosin. **1883** KNIGHT *Suppl.* 766/1 *Rosin oil,* a compound of melted rosin and linseed oil.

+**Rosinweed.** Any one of various American plants, esp. of the genus *Silphium,* which exude a resinous gum or odor. (Cf. COMPASS 3.) — **1831** *Jamestown Jrnl.* 13 July 1 Sunflowers and rosin-weed . . . abound [in Wis.]. **1848** BRYANT *California* ii. 28, [I have noticed] the rosin-weed, the stalk . . . of which, on being broken, exudes a gum of the consistence and odor of turpentine. **1893** *Farmers' Bul.* No. 10, 12 Rosinweed (*Grindelia squarrosa*) . . . grows in the native prairie, often so thick as to check the growth of grass. **1901** MOHR *Plant Life Ala.* 64 The borders of fields and woods, meadows and pastures, appear to be emphatically the home of golden-rods, rosinweeds, sunflowers, and Rudbeckias.

∗**Ross,** *n.* The rough scaly outer part of the bark of trees. {1840-} 'Chiefly U.S.' (O.E.D.). — **1778** CARVER *Travels* 497 The wood of this tree greatly resembles that of the common ash, but it might be distinguished from any other tree by its bark; the ross or outside bark being near eight inches thick. **1811** [see BLACK OAK 1 c (2)]. **1846** THORPE *Myst. Backwoods* 77 The 'ross,' or outside of the bark, is scraped off until it is smooth.

+**Ross,** *v. tr.* (See quot. 1864.) Also *ppl. a.* — **1864** WEBSTER 1140/3 *Ross,* to divest of the ross, or rough, scaly surface. **1874** *Vermont Bd. Agric. Rep.* II. 729 An ax should never be used to ross the bark. **1876** KNIGHT 1984/1 Rossing-machine. *Ib.* 1985/1 Rossing Attachment for Saw-Mill. **1878** *Vermont Bd. Agric. Rep.* V. 109 It injures a tree to ross it.

+**Rosser.** A rossing machine. — **1876** KNIGHT 1984/2 A common use of the rosser is in saw-mills, . . . to remove the bark from the log in advance of the path of the saw.

Roster. {1727-}

+**1.** A list of the officers of a regiment, brigade, etc.

1859 BARTLETT 371 *Roster.* 1. In Massachusetts, a list of the officers of a division, brigade, regiment, etc., containing, under several heads, their names, rank, corps, place of abode, etc. . . . . 2. The word is frequently used instead of Register, which comprehends a general list of all the officers of the State. **1889** CUSTER *Tenting on Plains* 358 The regiments looked well on the roster, but there were in reality but few men. **1893** *Nation* 20 April 301/1 The roster of German officers has been considerably enlarged.

+**2.** (See quotation.)

1891 *Calif. Statutes* 31 March 454 The Secretary of State is hereby authorized to compile, publish, and distribute one thousand copies of a State Blue Book or Roster.

∗**Rot,** *n.* +**1.** =BOLL ROT. +**2.** =ROTGUT WHISKY. — (1) **1819** *Niles' Reg.* XVI. 416/1 The *rot* is said to be making sad work among the cotton, in different parts of the southern states. **1828** *Western Mo. Rev.* II. 52 What prodigious loss has resulted from that disease in cotton, which of late years has been so fatal to crops, the *rot!* **1856** *Rep. Comm. Patents 1855: Agric.* 233 The 'rot' has been attributed to a variety of causes, such as changes in the atmosphere, . . . and to the growth of fungi. (2) **1860** GREELEY *Overland Journey* 201 A grocery devoid of some kind of

'rot,' as the fiery beverage was currently designated, was to them a novel and most distasteful experience.

∗**Rot,** *v. intr.* and *tr.* To soak or steep (hemp, flax, etc.) in water; to ret. {1836-} — **1765** WASHINGTON *Diaries* I. 213 Abt. 6 oclock put some Hemp in the Rivr. to Rot. **1786** WASHINGTON *Diaries* III. 121 Directed it [flax] to be critically examined and taken up this afternoon, if it should be sufficiently rotted. **1836** *Knickerb.* VIII. 47 [The moss] is rotted and dressed in much the same manner as flax, and is used in making 'pure hair mattresses!' **1862** *Rep. Comm. Patents 1861: Agric.* 23 'Rippling,' . . . 'rotting,' or steeping the [flax] straw [etc.] . . . have been considered as purely agricultural operations.

Rotary, *a.* **a.** Of machines: Rotatory; operated by rotation. {1799-} **b.** Of a stove. — **1843** [see KNITTING b]. **1850** *Rep. Comm. Patents 1849* 328 We claim . . . the above described rotary sewing machine. **1864** *Harper's Mag.* Sept. 503/2 She sent cousin Mary . . . a large, old-fashioned rotary cooking stove. **1887** *Courier-Journal* 17 Jan. 3/4 There is now in the shops of the Union Pacific a mammoth rotary snow-plow. **1892** *York County Hist. Rev.* 85/1 A thoroughly equipped printing house . . . [with] a Rotary press and sixty-odd fonts of type of new styles.

Rotary (steam) engine. A steam engine in which the piston revolves in the cylinder or the cylinder revolves about the piston. {1838-} — **1819** *Niles' Reg.* XVII. 129/2 We exhibit a view and give a description of the rotary steam engine. **1837** *Jamestown* (N.Y.) *Jrnl.* 29 March 1/6 The advantage of the rotary over the piston engine consists in its simplicity and economy. **1848** *Rep. Comm. Patents 1847* 69 Two other rotary steam engines have been patented. **1891** *Atlantic Mo.* June 808/1 Represented [among patents taken out by colored people] are . . . a rotary engine, a printing press, . . . and a telephone transmitter.

∗**Rotation.**

1. A regular alternation or succession of crops on a piece of land, for the maintenance of fertility. {1778-}

1794 JEFFERSON *Writings* IX. 287, I have therefore determined on a division of my farm into six fields, to be put under this rotation. **1846** *Spirit of Times* 18 April 89/3 Rotation of crops, is a subject of which little is known in American husbandry. **1895** *Univ. Nebraska Calendar 1895-6* 86 A treatment of each of the principal field crops . . . [will include] cultivation, harvesting, preservation, position in rotation. **1911** HARRISON *Queed* 228 Next morning's *Post* . . . discussed rotation of crops.

+**2.** Succession in political office by different persons representing, usually, different political parties. Also attrib.

1838 *N.Y. Advertiser & Exp.* 14 Feb. 1/2 Trouble in the democratic camp . . . is probably a practical result of the 'rotation' and 'spoils' principle of the party. **1870** *Nation* 13 Jan. 20/1 One has only to examine the opinions which now exist . . . touching the civil service of this country, and especially that feature of it known as 'rotation in office.' **1884** *Century Mag.* April 809/2 Indeed, there would be more excuse for rotation in office here than in any other branch of the Government.

Rote. (See quot. 1870.) {1610-1682} 'Now *U.S.*' (O.E.D.). — **1855** HALIBURTON *Nature & Hum. Nature* 210 [When] the rote is on the beach, it tells me it is the voice of the south wind giving notice of rain. **1870** LOWELL *Letters* II. 65 *Rote* is a familiar word all along our seaboard to express that dull and continuous burden of the sea heard inland before or after a great storm. **1900** JEWETT in *Atlantic Mo.* Aug. 153/1, I can hear the rote o' them old black ledges way down the thoroughfare.

Rotgut. {1633-}

+**1.** =ROTGUT WHISKY.

1819 QUITMAN in Claiborne *Life Quitman* I. 42 Whiting and I had to treat to 'red-eye' or 'rot-gut,' as whiskey is here called. *a***1846** *Quarter Race Ky.* 87, I rid up an axed the speaker 'how much Tarrif there was on rot-gut?' **1876** BOURKE *Journal* July 28–Sept. 8, A bottle of the Sutter's best whiskey . . . tasted very good because it had such a fine label. Without the label, I am quite assured, we'd have called it 'rot-gut' or 'hell-fire.' **1901** HARBEN *Westerfelt* 146 We'll have to leave these barrels o' rot-gut with you.

+**2.** *Rotgut minnow,* (see quotation).

1884 GOODE, etc. *Fisheries* I. 618 [The shiner] has no tangible importance as a food-fish. Its flesh spoils very quickly after the fish is taken from the water, hence the name 'Rot-gut Minnow,' applied to it in Alabama.

+**Rotgut whisky.** Whisky of an inferior quality, usually raw. *slang.* — **1850** A. T. JACKSON *Forty-Niner* (1920) 12 Half the men in sight were full of rot-gut whiskey. **1866** MOORE *Women of War* 173, I hope we shall meet again, where we shall have something better than corn bread baked in ashes, and rot-gut whiskey at fifteen dollars a quart. **1899** *Everybody's Mag.* I. 31/2, I guess you could argue on the quality and quantity of rot-gut whiskey a good engineer ought to drink. **1903** HAPGOOD *Autobiog. of Thief* 216 If one of them had five cents, he would go into a morgue (gin-mill where rot-gut whiskey could be obtained for that sum).

Rotherham plow. A form of plow now obsolete. {1762-} — *c***1797** LATROBE *Journal* 61 [Washington] gave the preference to the heavy Rotherham plow from a full experience of its merits. **1805** PARKINSON *Tour* 493 A few of the swing or Rotherham ploughs are used.

Rotten borough. {1812-} *transf.* +Used allusively, designating states or other republican political units, esp. those controlled by corrupt means, lacking sufficient population to justify their representation. Also attrib. — **1900** *Congress. Rec.* 17 Jan. 922/2 Silver bars . . . come from what the Republican party seeks to call the unpatriotic States, 'rotten boroughs' of the West. *Ib.* 5 Feb. 1520/1 [The Philippine Islands] will be admitted as States . . . [whenever] the party in power . . . thinks it needs a few more rotten-borough electoral votes. **1905** STEFFENS in *McClure's Mag.* Feb. 342/1 The worst of these rotten boroughs are the 'hill towns.'

Rotten-egg, *v. tr.* To pelt with rotten eggs. {1884–} — **1878** DALY in J. F. Daly *A. Daly* 253 The Shaughraun was played here last week & was a dire failure—the wake scene being rotten-egged three nights in succession. **1892** *Boston Jrnl.* 24 Oct. 1/4 Capt. R. F. Kolb, late candidate for Governor, . . . and S. S. Booth, fusion candidate for Elector . . . , were rotten-egged by a dozen or more persons. **1904** DARROW *Farmington* 250 If the men had any spirit they would go there some night and rotten-egg him out of town.

Rotten limestone. Limestone that is partially decayed. — **1843** *Knickerb.* XXI. 171 Entangled among the roots of the saw-palmetto, there is the greatest quantity of rotten limestone. **1846** LYELL *Second Visit* II. 42 The common name for the marlite, of which this treeless soil is composed, is 'rotten limestone.' **1868** *Rep. Comm. Agric.* 1867 428 The 'rotten limestone' formations of Alabama and Mississippi are unsurpassed for fertility. **1870** *Ib. 1869* 550 Prominent in this group is the 'rotten limestone,' celebrated among geologists for the great quantity of remarkable fossils which have been found in it.

Rotten marsh. A marsh having very soft, yielding soil. — **1649** in *Amer. Speech* XV. 386/1 Part of which is likewise Rotten Marsh amounting to three hundred and fifty acres. **1651** *Ib.,* Many rotten Marrishes and Swampps there was to passe over.

Rotunda. {a1700–} ‖1. ?A conical mound. 2. A large circular room. {1841–} — (1) **1791** W. BARTRAM *Travels* 520*n.*, *Chunk yard,* a term given by the white traders, to the oblong four square yards, adjoining the high mounts and rotundas of the modern Indians. (2) **1828** COOPER *Notions* II. 158 Four historical paintings . . . are destined to fill as many compartments in the rotunda, or the great hall of the capitol. **1867** *Ore. State Jrnl.* 9 Feb. 2/2 The great rotunda, a circular hall under the dome, is also on this floor. **1886** POORE *Reminisc.* I. 46 The then recently completed *rotunda* of the Capitol—Mr. Gales took pains to have it called *rotundo* in the *National Intelligencer*—was a hall of elegant proportions. **1907** ANDREWS *Recoll.* 183, I gave my orders lying on my back on the floor of the rotunda of the capitol.

+**Roucheag.** (See ROKEAGE.)

* **Rough,** *n.*

+**1.** A rough draft. *Obs.*

1699 SEWALL *Diary* I. 502 Agree for 15£ and draw a rough of it and take his hand to it. **1710** *Harvard Rec.* I. 395 A rough of sundry Articles was drawn up. **1796** *Steele Papers* I. 144 A rough of a letter which may at some future period compose part of a circular.

+**2.** A ruffian in the service of a political leader or group, esp. the Democratic party.

1868 *Ore. State Jrnl.* 28 Nov. 1/3 Suddenly a party of Democratic 'roughs' came surging by. **1872** BRACE *Dangerous Classes N.Y.* 27 These youthful ruffians . . . are the 'roughs' who sustain the ward politicians. **1875** *Chicago Tribune* 27 Sept. 7/3 A most unparalleled outrage was perpetrated to-night by the Democratic roughs of Cuyahoga Falls. **1876** *N.Y. Tribune* Oct. (B.), Three or four men . . . who are in reality detectives sent to look after the Democratic roughs.

* **Rough,** *a.*

* **1.** In the names of plants and trees.

Many more examples can be found in botanical works.

1785 MARSHALL *Amer. Grove* 139 *Salix nigra,* Rough American Willow, . . . rises often with a leaning or crooked trunk to the height of about twenty feet. **1814** BIGELOW *Florula Bostoniensis* 203 *Helianthus divaricatus.* Small, rough Sun flower. . . . A showy plant, not uncommon in woods and thickets. **1817–8** EATON *Botany* (1822) 170 *Amaranthus retroflexus,* rough amaranth. *Ib.* 341 *Lonicera hirsuta,* rough woodbine, . . . twines around trees from left to right to the height of twenty or thirty feet. *Ib.* 465 *Solidago aspera,* rough golden-rod. **1860** CURTIS *Woody Plants N.C.* 101 Rough syringa (*P[hiladelphus]*). . . . The leaves quite rough on the upper side and whitish. **1868** GRAY *Field Botany* 257 *S[ymphytum] asperrimum,* Rough C[omfrey]. Cult. in some gardens. **1878** KILLEBREW *Tenn. Grasses* 181 Rough Meadow Grass—(*Poa Trivialis*). . . . In the North it is a common meadow and pasture grass.

2. In the names of fishes and mollusks. {1648–}

1842 *Nat. Hist. N.Y., Zoology* IV. 5 The Rough Yellow Perch. *Perca serrato-granulata.* . . . With roughened radiated lines on the head. *Ib.* 5 The Rough-Headed Yellow Perch. *Perca granulata.* . . . Head roughened by granulations. *Ib.* 208 The Red-fin, *Leuciscus cornutus,* . . . has the various popular names of Red-fin, Red Dace, and Rough-head. **1883** *Nat. Museum Bul.* No. 27 193 Species of *Haliotis* that are of commercial importance: The White Sea Ear, . . . the 'Rough Sea-Ear,' or *Haliotis corrugata. Ib.* 245 Drill or Rough Whelk . . . [is found on the] Eastern coast of the United States to Massachusetts Bay. *Ib.* 406 *Limanda aspera.* . . . Rough Flounder. . . . Very abundant throughout the Gulf of Alaska. **1911** *Rep. Fisheries 1910* 310/1 The name [flounder] is variously applied to the flat fishes found on all our coasts, as 'American sole,' . . . 'rough limanda,' . . . 'rough dab,' 'Greenland turbot' [etc.].

+**3.** In special uses: (see quotations).

1865 *Ore. State Jrnl.* 28 Oct. 2/2 Two 'rough gamblers,' a new name for thieves, were found hanging from a hay frame, at Virginia City, Montana Territory. *Ib.* 30 June 312 'Rough Gambling.'—That's what they call robbing the stage over in Idaho.

Rough-and-tumble, *n.*

1. A form of fighting in which no rules are observed and no tactics barred. {1810–}

1792 BRACKENRIDGE *Adv. Capt. Farrago* 55, I will use no unfair method of biting, or gouging, or worse practice, common in what is called rough-and-tumble. **1824** DODDRIDGE *Notes* 184 This mode of fighting was what they called [in western Va. *c*1780] rough and tumble. **1825** NEAL *Bro. Jonathan* II. 43 Like to have a tussel, . . . or a good clever game o' rough an' tumble? **1839** C. A. MURRAY *Travels* I. 153 It might be supposed, that the coarse and brutal method of fighting, still frequently adopted in this state [Ky.] under the name of 'rough and tumble,' is sufficiently savage to satisfy the parties concerned. **1857** CHANDLESS *Visit Salt Lake* I. 118 The fingers of both were a good deal mauled; but rags and plaister set all right. Such is 'Rough-and-tumble.'

2. The haphazard give-and-take of rough, adventurous living, struggling, etc.

1840 DANA *Two Years* xxviii. 306, I had spent nearly a year [in the brig] and got the first rough and tumble of sea-life. **1852** *Boston Jrnl.* 13 Dec. 8/4 In the *rough and tumble* of political contest these [Irish] factions are not to be depended upon by either Liberals or Conservatives. **1884** LOWELL *Writings* VI. 31 There is more rough and tumble in the American democracy than is altogether agreeable to people of sensitive nerves and refined habits. **1897** *Century Mag.* May 104/2 You have gone through all the rough and tumble of army service and frontier life.

Rough-and-tumble, *a.* Characterized by disregard of all rules and formalities; irregular, disorderly. {1887–} — **1833** J. E. ALEXANDER *Transatlantic Sk.* II. 86 We went on at a 'rough and tumble' rate as he called it, and arrived with aching bones at the house of a lonely settler. **1848** IRVING *Knickerb.* (rev. ed.) IV. ix, They were represented as . . . expert at boxing, biting, gouging, and other branches of the rough-and-tumble mode of warfare. **1872** HOLMES *Poet* 323 Their appropriate sphere . . . is not literature, but that circle of rough-and-tumble political life where the fine-fibred men are at a discount. **1884** MATTHEWS & BUNNER *In Partnership* 53 Mr. Kilburn is a gentleman unaccustomed to rough-and-tumble encounters. **1905** *Forestry Bureau Bul.* No. 61, 41 A *rough and tumble landing* is one in which no attempt is made to pile the logs regularly.

+**Rough-and-tumble,** *adv.* In a rough or irregular manner. — **1818** PALMER *Travels U.S.* 131, I understand the question is generally asked, *Will you fight fair, or take it rough and tumble?* **1842** *Amer. Pioneer* I. 385 The two persons clenched each other 'rough and tumble' and both rolled into the brook. **1846** THORPE *Myst. Backwoods* 183, I can strike as hard as fourth proof lightning, and keep it up, rough and tumble, as long as a wild-cat.

Rough-billed pelican. (See quot. 1891.) — **1785** LATHAM *Gen. Synopsis Birds* VI. 586 Rough-billed Pelican. . . . This species . . . is found in some parts of America. **1823** JAMES *Exped.* I. 266 *Pelecanus erythrorhynchos*—Rough-billed pelican. **1871** *Amer. Naturalist* IV. 758 On the evening of the 15th of June, 1870, a most remarkable specimen of the rough-billed pelican (*Pelicanus erythrorhynchus*) was shot by Captain Oliver Maisonville. **1891** *Cent.* 5241/1 *Rough-billed,* . . . having a rough horny excrescence on the beak: specific in the phrase *rough-billed pelican, Pelecanus trachyrhynchus* (or *erythrorhynchus*). This remarkable formation is deciduous, and is found only on adult birds during the breeding season.

+**Rough-board,** *v. tr.* To cover with rough boards. — **1849** BROWNE *Poultry Yd.* 87 Rough-board it [a poultry house] from the apex downward by the sills to the ground.

Rough-bred, *a.* **1.** Of persons: Brought up in a rough, uncultivated environment. **2.** Of animals: Bred with no regard for pedigree. — **(1)** **1855** MITCHELL *Fudge Doings* I. 45 He is one of those genuine, rough-bred country Americans. **(2)** **1892** *Vt. Agric. Rep.* XII. 154 The successful sheep men of the State are, as a rule, breeding for mutton or for the rough-bred Merinos.

Rough dry, *a.* Of clothes: Dry but not smoothed or ironed. — **1856** STOWE *Dred* I. 181 Clothes look rough-dry, as if they had been pulled out of a bag. **1881** *Harper's Mag.* Sept. 578/2 My sister . . . said I couldn't have [my seersucker coat] . . . , because it was 'rough dry.' **1904** GLASGOW *Deliverance* 325 He seized the iron and ran it in a few hasty strokes over the rough-dry garment.

Rougher. One who tends a roughing-down set of rollers in a steel mill. {1893–} — **1890** *Columbus Dispatch* 27 May, The row between the roughers and catchers and the heaters and rollers. **1897** 'THANET' *Missionary Sheriff* 225 Sol Joscelyn was a rougher in the steel-works across the river. **1898** *Scribner's Mag.* XXIII. 311/1 The man with the scanty flaxen mustache was a rougher in a steel mill.

Rough-leaved, *a.* Of plants and trees: Having rough leaves. {1668–} — **1785** MARSHALL *Amer. Grove* 156 *Ulmus americana,* American rough leaved Elm-Tree, . . . rises to the height of about thirty feet. **1813** MUHLENBERG *Cat. Plants* 17 *Cornus asperifolia,* Rough-leaved dogwood. **1843** TORREY *Flora N.Y.* II. 439 *Vilfa aspera.* Rough-leaved Vilfa. . . . Sandy fields and hill-sides: not common. *Fl.* September. **1868** WHITTIER *Poetical Works* (1894) 84/2 Nightshade and rough-leaved burdock [grew] in the place Of the sweet doorway greeting of the rose.

Rough-legged buzzard. =ROUGH-LEGGED HAWK. — [**1840** BLYTH *Cuvier's Animal Kingdom* 171 The Rough-legged Buzzard. . . . One of the most widely diffused of Birds.] **1844** [see BLACK HAWK]. **1869** *Amer. Naturalist* III. 227 Less than twenty years ago our shores abounded, in spring and fall, with the Rough-legged Buzzard. **1880** *Cimarron News & Press*

23 Dec. 1/5 Their representatives here are the red-tailed, red-shouldered, Swainson's, rough-legged and ferruginous buzzards. **1917** *Birds of Amer.* II. 79 Rough-legged Hawk. *Archibuteo lagopus sancti-johannis.* . . . [Also called] Rough-leg; Rough-legged Buzzard; Black hawk.

Rough-legged falcon. {1763-} +=next. — **1811** WILSON *Ornithology* IV. 59 Rough-legged Falcon. *Falco Lagopus.* **1839** PEABODY *Mass. Birds* 267 The Rough-legged Falcon, *Falco lagopus,* and Falco Sancti Johannis are supposed to be two distinct species. **1864** *Amer. Naturalist* III. 518 The Rough-legged Falcon and Black Hawk are the same. **1874** COUES *Birds N.W.* 755/3 Falcon, rough-legged.

✶**Rough-legged hawk.** +A large hawk (*Buteo lagopus sancti-johannis* or a related species) having feathers extending to the toes. (Cf. BLACK HAWK.) — **1811** WILSON *Ornithology* IV. 60 The Rough-legged Hawk measures twenty-two inches in length. **1874** COUES *Birds N.W.* 365 The contrast between the physique of Rough-legged Hawks and their venatorial exploits, is striking. **1895** *Dept. Agric. Yrbk.* *1894* 219 The rough-legged hawk, and the ferruginous roughleg, or squirrel hawk, . . . are among our largest and at the same time the most beneficial hawks. **1917** *Birds of Amer.* II. 79/1 The Rough-legged Hawk breeds in Alaska and Canada and is but a winter migrant to the States.

+**Rough-lock,** *v. tr.* (See quot. 1884.) Also *vbl. n.* — **1859** MARCY *Prairie Traveler* iii, Rough-locking is a very safe method of passing heavy artillery down abrupt declivities. **1884** W. SHEPHERD *Prairie Exper.* 197 The hind-wheels were rough-locked, that is, a large linked chain was tied round the rim of the wheel in such a way that the wheel rides upon the chain, which drags along and cuts into the ground. **1888** CODY *Wild West* 548 We locked both wheels on each side, and then rough-locked them.

+**Roughneck.** A rough, uncouth, uncultivated fellow; a rowdy. *slang.* Also attrib. — **1836** CROCKETT *Exploits* 58 You may be called a drunken dog by some of the clean shirt and silk stocking gentry, but the real rough necks will style you a jovial fellow. **1903** *N.Y. Sun* 25 Nov. 2 The police were kept on the jump chasing away gangs of 'rough necks' (the pet name for the rowdies in Sam Parks's late union) who went from building to building trying to intimidate members of the new union. **1916** WILSON *Somewhere* 288 He really wanted . . . to study insect life and botany and geography and arithmetic, . . . instead of being killed off in a sudden manner by his rough-neck parent. **1923** 'BOWER' *Parowan Bonanza* 251 What's that rough neck doing here?

✶**Roughness.** +Hay, fodder, corn shucks, etc., as distinguished from grain. *colloq.* Also *transf.* — **1846** *Knickerb.* Oct. 313 There can't nobody stay here to save souls without some kind of *roughness* to keep up natur'. **1868** *Putnam's Mag.* June 711/1 The 'black 'un' had sought to burn her 'roughness,' . . . shucks, or corn-husks. **1888** WARNER *On Horseback* 142 'Roughness,' we found out at the other house, meant hay in this region. **1897** W. E. BARTON *Hero in Homespun* 184 [They] gave them [*sc.* horses] some 'roughness,' as John called the bundles of blade fodder.

+**Rough oak.** =IRON OAK. — **1847** DARLINGTON *Weeds & Plants* 308 *Q[uercus] obtusiloba.* . . . Obtuse-lobed Quercus. Barrens White Oak. Post Oak. Rough Oak. . . . The wood is very durable. **1892** APGAR *Trees Northern U.S.* 153 *Quercus stellata,* . . . Post-oak, Rough or Box White oak. . . . A medium-sized tree, 40 to 50 ft. high, with very hard, durable wood.

+**Rough on rats.** A proprietary form of rat poison. — **1885** *Wkly. New Mexican Rev.* 15 Jan. 3/1 At the bottom of the coffee pot was found a paper of 'Rough on Rats.' **1893** 'THANET' *Stories* 8 Onct he tooked Rough on Rats and I found it out and I put some apple butter in the place of it.

Rough rice. Unhusked rice. {1763-} Also attrib. — **1791** *Ann. 1st Congress* 1741 The petition of Col. Henry Laurens was . . . presented and read, praying compensation for ten thousand bushels of rough rice, supplied the late Continental army. **1845** POLK *Diary* I. 121 The Brittish Minister . . . held a long unofficial conversation with him . . . on the rough rice question and some others. **1859** *Ill. Agric. Soc. Trans.* III. 530 From fifty to eighty pounds of rough rice can safely be expected. **1893** *Harper's Mag.* Feb. 385/1 All the rough rice raised in Louisiana is milled in New Orleans in twelve or fifteen mills.

Roughrider. {1791-} +**1.** A cowboy of the western plains. +**2.** *pl.* (See quot. 1914.) — (1) **1888** ROOSEVELT in *Century Mag.* Feb. 505/2 The rough-rider of the plains, the hero of rope and revolver, is first cousin to the backwoodsman of the Southern Alleghanies. **1898** CANFIELD *Maid of Frontier* 30 They were . . . rising and falling in the gallop with the careless ease of the southwestern rough rider. (2) **1899** ROOSEVELT in *Scribner's Mag.* Jan. 7/1 When finally the Generals of Division and Brigade began to write in formal communications about our regiment as the 'Rough Riders,' we adopted the term ourselves. **1905** *N.Y. Times* 3 March 3 The Rough Riders are never so called in the formal literature of the inauguration. **1914** *Cycl. Amer. Govt.* III. 236/1 *Rough Riders,* a popular designation given the First United States Volunteer Cavalry organized by Leonard Wood and Theodore Roosevelt for service in the Spanish-American War, and recruited largely from the cowboys of the western plains.

+**Roughsc(r)uff.** A person of very low class; collect., the rag, tag, and bobtail. — **1843** STEPHENS *High Life N.Y.* II. 15 No ginuine gentleman ever gits mad with sich a ruff-scuff. **1859** BARTLETT 371 *Rough-Scuff,* the lowest people; the rabble. **1865** 'MARK TWAIN' *Sketches* (1926) 161 Of which wretched conglomeration of the ruff-scruff and rag-tag-and-bob-tail of noble old Calaveras he is the appropriate leader. **1904** *Atlantic Mo.* March 301 The only nationalities more hated by the trade-unionist are the political rough-scuff of Europe, . . . such as the Armeniᵃns, Greeks, and Syrians.

Roughskin. +=ROUGHNECK. — **1840** *Jamestown* (N.Y.) *Jrnl.* 28 Oct. 2/6 Some hardy roughskins from the pine knots up the Alleghany were sauntering up town. **1859** BARTLETT 371 *Roughskins,* a gang of Baltimore bullies.

+**Rough-winged (bank) swallow.** A swallow of the American genus *Stelgidopteryx,* as the bridge swallow, *S. serripennis.* — **1838** AUDUBON *Ornith. Biog.* IV. 595 In its general appearance . . . the Rough-winged Swallow is extremely similar to the Bank Swallow. **1872** COUES *Key to Birds* 114. **1878** *Nat. Museum Proc.* I. 409 *Stelgidopteryx serripennis.—* Rough-winged Bank Swallow. **1917** *Birds of Amer.* III. 93/1 The Rough-winged Swallow is a much duller looking bird than the Bank Swallow, with which it is apt to be confused.

+**Rounce.**

1. (See quotations.)

1864 DICK *Amer. Hoyle* (1866) 478 The game of Rounce, as played in the United States, is derived from the German game of *Ramsh,* and in its principal features resembles Division Loo. **1891** *Cent.* 5242/2 *Rounce,* . . . a game of cards, played with a full pack by not more than nine persons. Each player starts with fifteen points, and for every trick he takes subtracts one from the score; the player who first reaches zero wins.

2. *Marbles.* (See quot. 1922.)

This sense may be of different origin from sense 1.

1888 EGGLESTON in *Century Mag.* May 78/1 Their cries of 'rounses,' 'taw,' . . . and 'vent' might often be heard. **1922** *Dialect Notes* V. 187 *Rounce,* a call given when one's taw is so placed that he cannot shoot at the ring or at an opponent. If he calls 'Rounce' he may select a convenient place to shoot from, unless his opponent first calls, 'Vence ye rounce.' Also *rounin's,* n. Ky.

✶**Round,** *n.*

‖**1.** *pl.* Short for *rounds of applause.*

1845 SOL. SMITH *Theatr. Apprent.* 18, I was sure to receive a suitable number of 'rounds' at the end of each speech.

+**2.** *Baseball.* An inning. *Obs.*

1907 *St. Nicholas* July 819/1 That round began with the score a tie. Each side had made two runs.

3. *To go the rounds,* of news, reports, etc., to pass from one to another in an entire set or group. {to go the round, 1669-}

1837 *Jamestown* (N.Y.) *Jrnl.* 22 March 3/2 There is a story going the rounds in relation to the president-elect. **1857** *Lawrence* (Kan.) *Republican* 9 July 3 We notice a paragraph going the rounds of the papers. **1859** BARTLETT 371 To say that an article is 'going the rounds of the papers,' . . . is called an Americanism in England. **1862** NORTON *Army Lett.* 55 Everything of the kind has to go the rounds, you know.

✶**Round,** *a.* In the names of trees and plants. (See also ROUND RUSH.)

+*Round black Virginian walnut,* =BLACK WALNUT 1; +*r. corn,* (see quotation); +*r. potato,* an Irish potato.

1785 MARSHALL *Amer. Grove* 66 *Juglans nigra.* Round black Virginian Walnut. . . . Upon being bruised [the leaves] emit a strong aromatic flavour, as doth also the external covering of the fruit. **1889** *Cent.* 1268/3 *Round corn,* a trade-name for the grain of a class of yellow maize with small, round, very hard kernels. **1801** *Hist. Review & Directory* I. 150 Round potatoes. *Solanum Tuberosum.*

✶**Roundabout.**

+**1.** =ROUNDABOUT JACKET. *Obsolescent.*

1836 HILDRETH *Campaigns Rocky Mts.* I. 28 The fatigue uniform [was] a blue roundabout trimmed with yellow lace, white pantaloons, and forage caps. **1850** JUDD *R. Edney* 18 He wore a red shirt, and a roundabout, sometimes called a monkey-jacket. **1877** BURDETTE *Rise of Mustache* 25 [An] epoch in a boy's life . . . was marked by the transition from the old-fashioned cadet roundabout to the tail-coat. **1904** *N.Y. Ev. Post* 7 Jan. 7 Only yesterday this young man was playing about the streets of Washington, a schoolboy in roundabouts.

+**b.** A wrapper or dressing gown worn by women.

1841 *S. Lit. Messenger* VII. 525/1 The garment is a long, loose roundabout, connecting in front with strings, and is much worn, even at the present time. **1895** WIGGIN *Village Watch-Tower* 103 Mother had let her slip on her new green roundabout over her nightgown.

+**2.** An armchair having a rounded back and sides. In full, *r. chair.*

1840 *Knickerb.* XVI. 115, I sat in my roundabout chair the other evening. **1845** *Lowell Offering* IV. 175 [He sat] in a large flag-bottomed 'roundabout' on the opposite side of the fireplace.

+**Roundabout jacket.** A short, close-fitting jacket. (Cf. COATEE.) — **1800** *Lancaster* (Pa.) *Jrnl.* 20 Sept. (Th.), A Negro Man . . . had on . . . a callico roundabout jacket. a**1811** HENRY *Camp. Quebec* 35 [My wardrobe] consisted of a roundabout jacket, of wollen, a pair of half worn buckskin breeches. **1841** J. L. STEPHENS *Central Amer.* I. 17 My costume was not becoming so dignified a position . . . ; I took my seat, in a roundabout jacket.

Round ball. {1688-} +A game of ball resembling baseball. *Obs.* — **1841** *Picayune* 25 May 2/2 We would go to Cleveland ourselves just for one game of round ball, provided we could not enjoy it at less cost. **1856** *Porter's Spirit of Times* 27 Dec. 276/3, I have thought . . . a statement of my experience as to the Yankee method of playing 'Base,' or 'Round ball,' as we used to call it, may not prove uninteresting. **1871** CUTTING *Student Life Amherst* 112 'Wicket' and 'Round Ball,' were quite common once, though of late years, 'Base Ball' has entirely superceded them.

+**Round clam. 1.** =HARD CLAM. (Cf. QUAHOG 1.) **2.** (See quotation.) — (1) **1843** *Nat. Hist. N.Y., Zoology* VI. 217 This species is the common Round Clam, much prized as an article of food. **1883** *Nat. Museum Bul.* No. 27, 233 *Venus mercenaria* . . . is the 'quahaug,' or 'round clam.' (2) *Ib.* 241 *Saxidomus aratus* . . . is the 'Round Clam' of the Pacific coast.

+**Round-crested duck.** =HOODED MERGANSER. — **1731** CATESBY *Carolina* I. 94 The round-crested Duck. . . . The Head is crowned with a very large circular Crest. **1917** *Birds of Amer.* I. 112.

✱**Round dance.** A form of dance in which the participants form a ring, or dance or turn in a circle. — **1683** [see CANTICOY n. 1]. **1863** 'G. HAMILTON' *Gala-Days* 367, I was led away into some one or other of the several halls to see the 'round dances.' **1878** *Harper's Mag.* April 680/1 There were . . . girls that believed in round dances and theatres. **1899** CUSHMAN *Hist. Indians* 499 All these dances excelled in purity of sentiment to dances adopted by us, such as the 'round dance.'

Rounder. {1624–} +One accustomed to make the rounds of low resorts; a petty criminal; a man about town. *slang.*

1854 *Congress. Globe* App. 17 Jan. 1220/3, I have always found him [President Franklin Pierce] a very kind and agreeable man,—what the 'rounders' in New York would term a 'glover.' **1891** *Boston Jrnl.* 7 July 2/4 The regular rounders . . . are beginning to receive long sentences under the new drunkenness law. **1908** HORNBLOW *Profligate* 128 Bradley, who was an old rounder, smiled in pity at Billie's ignorance. **1920** SANDBURG *Smoke & Steel* 51 A rounder leered confidential.

transf. **1879** DALY in J. F. Daly *A. Daly* 330 [We] are old 'rounders' and familiar with the voice, gait and peculiarities of most of the actors and actresses on the American stage.

+**b.** (See quotation.)
1903 *Charities* 3 Oct. 283 The class of persons known as 'rounders,' people who go from one hospital to another seeking advice and treatment, a species of medical mendicants.

Roundhead. {1641–} **a.** (See quot. 1829.) +**b.** A Pennsylvanian. A nickname. *Obs.* Also attrib. — **1829** ROYALL *Pennsylvania* I. 152 [Professed Christians] have a number of names here, as in other States, 'Greybacks, Round-heads, &c.' **1862** KETTELL *Hist. Rebellion* I. 377 A reconnoissance in force, consisting of . . . three hundred of the 'Roundheads,' . . . drove the enemy completely from the island. **1863** Moore *Rebellion Rec.* V. 1. 24 Two companies of the Pennsylvania 'Roundhead' regiment . . . were cut off by the rebels.

+**Round herring.** One of certain sea fishes resembling herrings, as *Etrumeus sadina.* — **1842** *Nat. Hist. N.Y., Zoology* IV. 268 The Saury, *Elops saurus,* . . . appeared to be little known to the fishermen, who spoke of having seen it before, and called it the Round Herring. **1882** *Nat. Museum Bul.* No. 16, 263 *Etrumeus,* . . . Round Herrings. **1903** T. H. BEAN *Fishes N.Y.* 190 De Kay saw only a single specimen of the round herring from the harbor of New York.

+**Round-horned elk.** The American elk or wapiti. (Cf. AMERICAN ELK 2, ELK 2.) — **1781–2** JEFFERSON *Notes Va.* (1788) 57. **1842** *Nat. Hist. N.Y., Zoology* I. 119 The American Stag . . . is called in various parts of the country, . . . *Wapiti, Grey Elk,* and *Round-horned Elk.*

✱**Roundhouse.** +A circular building used for the housing and switching of railroad locomotives.

1870 *Rail-Road Gazette* (De Vere), Engineers and firemen often . . . have to spend considerable time about the round-house. **1881** CHASE *Editor's Run in N. Mex.* 164 The Atchison, Topeka and Santa Fe company . . . are building a large round house. **1898** HAMBLEN *Gen. Manager's Story* 62, I walked out, and strolled over to the round-house, to have a look at the engines. **1923** J. H. COOK *On Old Frontier* 94 When we reached Denison, I did not go to the roundhouse with the engine.

+**b.** Attrib. with *conclave, man, yarn-spinner.*
1895 *Chicago Strike of 1894* 214 A number of switch tenders, yard clerks, flagmen, tower men, and roundhouse men left their work. **1901** MERWIN & WEBSTER *Calumet 'K'* 290 Risks run . . . supplied round-house and tug-office yarn spinners with stories that were not yet worn off. **1904** LYNDE *Grafters* 286 [A] roundhouse conclave [was] held daily by the trainmen who were hung up or off duty.

Rounding up. {1769–} +The driving together or assembling of cattle into a compact herd. (Cf. ROUND UP *v.*, ROUND-UP *n.*) — **1876** WHILLDIN *Descr. W. Tex.* 16 It soon became evident that a place near us had been selected for 'rounding up.' **1879** *Harper's Mag.* Nov. 887/1 In June and July, and in September and October, 'rounding up,' or the grand collection and separation, takes place. **1880** *Cimarron News & Press* 15 July 2/4 Rounding up and branding in small parties is in progress throughout the country.

Round jacket. =ROUNDABOUT JACKET. {1872} — **1838** *N.Y. Advertiser & Exp.* 17 Feb. 1/5 A man with a round jacket on cannot walk along the wharves without being asked if he is willing to ship. **1840** *Knickerb.* XV. 139 In summer, it [the newsman's dress] consists of a round jacket and trowsers. **1869** BARNUM *Struggles* 145 [The Doctor] puts on a Yankee roundjacket and broadbrimmed hat.

+**Round-leafed violet.** (See ROUND-LEAVED VIOLET.)

Round-leaved, *a.* In the names of plants that have round or nearly round leaves. {1634–} See also ROUND-LEAVED MAPLE, ROUND-LEAVED VIOLET. — **1814** BIGELOW *Florula Bostoniensis* 39 *Cornus circinata.* Round leaved Cornel. . . . An erect slender shrub. . . . Fruit bluish. **1818** *Mass. H. S. Coll.* 2 Ser. VIII. 170 In July the lover of plants is gratified with . . . the round-leaved mallows. **1843** TORREY *Flora N.Y.* I. 289 *Cornus Circinata.* Round-leaved Dogwood. . . . Shady banks of rivers. *a*1862 THOREAU *Maine Woods* 207 Of smaller plants, there were the dwarf-cornel, great round-leaved orchis [etc.]. **1919** STURTEVANT *Notes on Edible Plants* 141 *C[ardamine] rotundifolia.* Round-leaved Cuckoo Flowers. Water-Cress.

Round-leaved maple. The vine maple (*Acer circinatum*), found in northwestern North America. — [**1846** BROWNE *Trees Amer.* 93 *Acer circinatum,* The Circinal-leaved Maple. . . . Round-leaved Maple, Britain.] **1869** W. MURRAY *Adventures* 128 A silver beech or round-leaved maple relieved the sombre color with lighter hues. **1892** APGAR *Trees Northern U.S.* 88 Round-leaved or Vine Maple. . . . A small tree or tall shrub . . . ; cultivated; from the Pacific coast.

+**Round-leaved, -leafed, violet.** (See quot. 1891.) — **1818** *Mass. H. S. Coll.* 2 Ser. VIII. 168 Among our herbaceous wild plants, the first that appear are the delicate claytonia, the graceful three-lobed hepatica, [and] the round-leaved violet, with its fine nodding blossoms. **1821** *Amer. Jrnl. Science* III. 274 Roundleaved violet in blossom. **1843** TORREY *Flora N.Y.* I. 71 Round-leaved Violet. . . . Remarkable among the stemless violets for its yellow flowers. **1891** *Cent.* 6761/3 *Round-leafed violet, Viola rotundifolia* of cold woods in eastern North America.

Round log. An unhewn log. Also attrib. — **1871** EGGLESTON *Hoosier Schoolm.* 95 He came upon a queer little cabin built of round logs. **1881** *Rep. Indian Affairs* 27 [Among the] houses on the reservation occupied by the Indians [are] . . . Round-log houses, 121. **1884** 'MARK TWAIN' *H. Finn* xxxii, Phelps's was one of these little one-horse cotton plantations . . . [having a] round-log kitchen, with a big broad, open but roofed passage joining it to the house.

Round-posted, *a.* +Of a chair: Having round upright posts or supports. — **1845** *Knickerb.* XXV. 444 The chairs around the room were the same strait-backed, withe-bottomed, round-posted, unpainted seats that they had been from my earliest recollection. **1857** HAMMOND *Northern Scenes* 170 The horns on his [a buck's] head were like an old-fashioned round-posted chair.

+**Round rimmer.** (See quot. 1848.) *Obs.* — **1842** C. MATHEWS in *Bro. Jonathan* Extra 26 Nov. 35/2 All over the region of East Bowery . . . the powerful class of Round-Rimmers; a fraternity of gentlemen, who, in round, crape-bound hats . . . carry dismay and terror wherever they move. **1848** BARTLETT 279 *Round-rimmers,* hats with a round rim; hence, those who wear them. In the city of New York, a name applied to a large class of dissipated young men by others called Bowery Boys and Soap-locks.

✱**Round robin.** +=CIGAR FISH. — **1709** LAWSON *Carolina* 159 We have another sort of Pearch, which . . . are distinguish'd from the other sorts, by the name of Round-Robins; being flat, and very round-shap'd. **1884** GOODE, etc. *Fisheries* I. 325 The Round Robin, or, as it is called at Pensacola, the 'Cigar-fish,' occurs . . . along the coast of the United States north as far as Wood's Holl. **1897** *N.Y. Forest, Fish, & Game Comm. 2d Rep.* 238 *Decapterus punctatus,* . . . Round Robin.—The spotted scad is not recognized in Gravesend Bay. **1911** *Rep. Fisheries 1908* 314/2 Round robin (*Decapterus punctatus*), a food fish found along the coast from the Gulf to Woods Hole. It is also called . . . 'scad.'

+**Round rush.** (See quotations.) — **1883** SMITH *Geol. Survey Ala.* 291 The following is a list . . . prepared by Dr. Charles Mohr, of Mobile: . . . Open river swamps—*Zizania aquatica* (wild rice), *Scirpus lacustris* (round rush), *Phragmites communis* [etc.]. **1901** MOHR *Plant Life Ala.* 50 The slender stems of these tall reeds and rushes sway to and fro above the . . . round rushes (*Juncus* spp.), galingales [etc.].

+**Round sauce.** (See quot. 1859 and cf. LONG SAUCE.) — **1857** *Knickerb.* XLIX. 273 They'd blamed all the long and round sauce in a kitchen-garden for not growing up into a hickory pole. **1859** ELWYN *Glossary* 95 Long *sarse,* and short *sarse,* and round *sarse,* are not unfrequently applied to different vegetables: carrots, beets, and potatoes are so called, according to their respective dimensions.

+**Round shave.** A tool used for cutting boxes in the pines of a turpentine orchard. — **1703** *N.C. Col. Rec.* I. 591 Henry Norman [shall] pay . . . one Drawing Knife one Round Shave. **1859** G. W. PERRY *Turpentine Farming* 54 Hands, when working with the roundshave, would cut off chips so large that, on reaching the ground, they could be heard for some distance.

Roundsman. {1795–} +(See quot. 1891.) — **1868** *N.Y. Herald* 31 July 6/5 Patrolman Jas. Mee . . . is hereby appointed roundsman on the force. **1891** *Cent.* 5246/1 *Roundsman,* . . . a police officer, of a rank above patrolmen and below sergeants, who goes the rounds within a prescribed district to see that the patrolmen or ordinary policemen attend to their duties properly, and to aid them in case of necessity. **1903** *N.Y. Ev. Post* 27 Nov. 2 Several hundred patrolmen reported to-day for examination for promotion to the rank of roundsman.

+**Roundstone.** (See quot. 1891.) — **1883** *Century Mag.* XXVI. 221/2 Gangs of street paviors were seen and heard here, there, and yonder, swinging the pick and ramming the roundstone. **1891** *Cent.* 5246/1 *Roundstone,* . . . small round or roundish stones collectively, used for paving; cobblestone. (Local, U.S.)

+**Round trip.** A complete trip to a destination and back again. {1892–} Also attrib.

1860 *Dinsmore's Amer. R.R. Guide* Sept. 142 Round trip tickets. **1873** MILLER *Amongst Modocs* 15 [He] proposed to take me into his employ for the round trip. **1887** *Courier-Journal* 9 May 3/3 What round-trip fares shall be placed in the race sheets? **1901** MERWIN & WEBSTER *Calumet 'K'* 202 One train . . . made the round trip from Bemis every day. **1911** J. F. WILSON *Land Claimers* 151 Spencer . . . making the round trip between dawn and dark. **1921** PAINE *Comr. Rolling Ocean* 223 We signed for the round trip in the Liberty Chimes, but we don't feel like taking her all the way home.

Round-up, *n.* {1769–} (Cf. ROUND UP *v.*, ROUNDING UP.)

+**1.** *W.* The driving together of cattle scattered over a wide area for counting, establishing ownership, etc.

1878 BEADLE *Western Wilds* 437 These cattle . . . are collected by a grand 'round-up.' **1887** *Scribner's Mag.* II. 508/1 The terms of the 'round-up' and the 'branding' and sheep-shearing are more or less piquant. **1902** WISTER *Virginian* xvii, During the many weeks since the spring round-up, some of these animals had as usual got very far off their range. **1914** 'BOWER' *Flying U Ranch* 88 This was a good three-quarters of an hour earlier than the Flying U outfit usually bestirred themselves on these days of preparation for roundup and waiting for good grass. **1924** DALE in D. & Rader *Okla. Hist.* (1930) 583 Each fall and spring were held the 'round ups.'

+**b.** Attrib. with *boss, captain, outfit,* etc.

1885 *Wkly. New Mexican Rev.* 26 March 1/6 Round-up parties have already been started for that section. **1890** *Stock Grower & Farmer* 14 June 5/3 The herder was found by the Long S roundup outfit, about six miles west of Sulphur draw. **1893** ROOSEVELT *Wilderness Hunter* 23 Close beyond the trees on the further bank stood the two round-up wagons. **1907** WHITE *Arizona Nights* 112 The round-up captain appointed two men to hold the cow-and-calf cut. **1920** HUNTER *Trail Drivers Texas* I. 313 The round-up boss would let no one ride through the herd and . . . unnecessarily disturb them.

+**2.** A meeting or reunion of old friends or associates.

1880 *Harper's Mag.* Feb. 380/2 Why, we old fellows have a round up 'most every year in Denver. **1887** HAYES *Jesuit's Ring* 270 We'll have a round-up of your old friends.

+**3.** A canvass or check up; a settlement.

1886 *Phila. Times* 3 May (*Cent.*), That exception . . . will probably be included in the general round-up tomorrow. **1892** *Boston Jrnl.* 29 Nov. 3/1 Round-Up of the Boston Aldermanic Districts. **1904** CRISSEY *Tattlings* 42 A hatchet-faced lawyer . . . made a quick round-up of the representatives of the corporate interests and vested rights of the state.

+**4.** A bringing together by the police of criminals and suspicious characters.

1899 *Chicago Record* 17 Jan. 12/1 A 'round-up' of all suspicious characters was begun. **1903** *N.Y. Times* 23 Sept., Thirty-three alleged members of East Side gangs were arrested by detectives in a round-up Monday night.

+**5.** The group or company of cowboys, horses, etc., engaged in a cattle round-up.

1903 'O. HENRY' *Rolling Stones* 86 The round-up had ridden on but a few moments before. *a*1918 G. STUART *On Frontier* II. 178 It was a novel sight to witness the big spring roundup pull out.

Round up, *v.* {1615–} (Cf. ROUNDING UP, ROUND-UP *n.*)

1. *tr.* To drive (live stock) together into a compact herd; to collect or bring in. {1847–, in Australia} Also transf. 'Orig. *U.S.* and *Austr.*' (*O.E.D.*).

1876 *Congress. Rec.* 30 June 4309/2 [The Mexican raiders] 'round up' a herd of cattle, and start with them at a full run for the Rio Grande. **1883** SWEET & KNOX *Through Texas* 160 All the cows and calves had been 'rounded up,' and the calves cut out and corralled. **1888** J. J. WEBB *Adventures* 237 We saw the Indians busily engaged in 'rounding up' and driving off a herd of mules. **1890** *Stock Grower & Farmer* 25 Jan. 4/4 Twenty stockmen have formed a pool for the purpose of rounding up their cattle and sheep. **1902** LORIMER *Lett. Merchant* 135 They started me out to round up trade in the river towns . . . near Cairo. **1909** WASON *Happy Hawkins* 201, I ain't a-layin' no plans to have the lala-ka-dinks from the civilized parts o' this country come out an' round up my langwidge. **1925** TILGHMAN *Dugout* 24 The men had little difficulty in rounding up some twenty head.

b. In absolute use. {1890–, in Australia}

1869 *Overland Mo.* III. 126 At night they 'round up' or 'corral.' **1879** *Harper's Mag.* Nov. 887/1 Each day they 'round-up;' the horsemen scour the country, and, with the skill coming from long practice, gather the cattle together. **1895** *Voice* 9 May 5/4 Who is it that are simply acting as cowboys, rounding up for the herd-groom of perdition? **1907** WHITE *Arizona Nights* 80 When we came to round up in the fall, we cut out maybe a dozen of those T.O. cattle.

+**2.** *tr.* To seek out and bring together; to capture or bring in (persons).

1885 *Wkly. New Mexican Rev.* 15 Jan. 2/5 Mr. Twitchell went down to 'round-up' the gang and was so far successful as to spot the leader. **1895**

Outing XXVII. 242/1 We might be fortunate enough to 'round up' some Indians and capture them. **1910** *N.Y. Ev. Post.* 24 Dec. Suppl. 1 At least four successful attempts to round up these fortune-tellers have been made.

+**3.** *absol.* To come to a stop, as for camping or spending the night.

1885 (newspaper), We have reached the point where we intend to round-up for the night. **1911** HARRISON *Queed* 6 Trucks were rounding up for stable and for bed.

+**Round whitefish.** =MENOMINEE WHITEFISH. — **1883** *Nat. Museum Bul.* No. 27, 417 *Coregonus quadrilateralis.* . . . Round Whitefish. . . . Lakes of New England; Upper Great Lakes [etc.]. **1911** [see MENOMINEE WHITEFISH].

+**Roundwood.** =MOUNTAIN ASH. — **1848** THOREAU *Maine Woods* 59 The wood was chiefly yellow birch, spruce, fir, mountain-ash, or round-wood, as the Maine people call it, and moose-wood. **1850** *New Eng. Farmer* II. 159 In the spring of 1847, one of my neighbors took from the forest some small mountain ash, or round-wood, as it is sometimes called.

*Rouse.** +A violent stir. Hence *rouse-out.* Also transf. — **1824** IRVING *Tales Trav.* I. 61 He revolutionized the whole establishment, and gave it such a rouse that the very house reeled with it. **1885** C. A. STEPHENS *Adv. Six Young Men* 122 The result was a most unwelcome rouse-out shortly after ten o'clock. **1916** SANDBURG *Chicago Poems* 125 The silk and flare of it [a red scarf] is a great soprano leading a chorus Carried along in a rouse of voices reaching for the heart of the world.

+**Rousement.** A religious stirring up or general excitement. Also transf. — **1883** *Congregationalist* 27 Sept. (*Cent.*), Deep strong feeling, but no excitement. They are not apt to indulge in any more rousements. **1886** *Advance* 9 Dec. 792/2 Dr. James Powell was also present to add to the 'rousements. **1904** *Springfield W. Repub.* 23 Sept. 2 Gen. Scott made his famous trip westward really to present his military figure to the people and arouse their enthusiasm. But the rousement failed to come.

Rouser. {1611–} A striking or unusual person, place, or event. *colloq.* {1808–, *dial.*} — **1828** WEBSTER, *Rouser,* one that rouses or excites. **1837** *Harvardiana* III. 238 The folks . . . are going to have a stark rouser of a ball. *c*1849 PAIGE *Dow's Sermons* I. 217 The third-named gentleman is a rhinoceros, and a rouser! **1879** *Harper's Mag.* Sept. 542 Ah! that's a rouser, is that hotel; it has more'n a hundred rooms all furnished beautiful from top to toe.

Roust, *v.* colloq.

1. *tr.* To rouse or stir (someone or something) *up;* to rout (someone or something) *out;* to raise (something). {1658–, now *dial.*}

1845 KIRKLAND *Western Clearings* 179 You ha'n't hid nothing, have ye? If you have, you'd better rowst it out at once't! **1850** COLTON *Deck & Port* 299 We rousted our anchors this afternoon from the bed in which they have slumbered for the last six weeks. **1871** HAY *Pike Co. Ballads* 14 We rousted up some torches, And sarched for 'em far and near. **1883** *Peterson's Mag.* June 469/2 Awhile ago you was all rousted-up about goin' to New York village to see Mrs. Larne. **1884** 'MARK TWAIN' *H. Finn* vii, Why didn't you roust me out? **1888** 'CRADDOCK' *Despot* 302 An' he kem ter the house, an' knocked an' knocked, an' never rousted up nobody. **1905** LINCOLN *Partners* 115 Roust out that bottle and heave it overboard.

+**2.** *intr.* To get *up* or turn *out;* to get busy.

1884 HARRIS *Mingo* 162 It twon't never do in the roun' worl' for to be a-makin faces at 'im from the groun'. Roust up, roust up. **1900** MUNN *Uncle Terry* 172, I genrally roust out by daylight. **1912** WASON *Friar Tuck* 67, I knew it was my duty to roust out an' keep Horace from gettin' more sleep'n my treatment for his nerves called for.

Roustabout. {1883–, in Austral.}

+**1.** A deck hand or water-front laborer.

1868 *Putnam's Mag.* Sept. 342/2 As the steamer was leaving the levée, about forty black deck-hands or 'roustabouts' gathered at the bows. **1884** 'CRADDOCK' *Where Battle Was Fought* 131 Soon the levee was swarming with the dusky figures of roustabouts. **1894** 'MARK TWAIN' *P. Wilson* xviii, Deck-han's en roustabouts 'uz sprawled aroun' asleep on de fo'cas'l'. **1909** RICE *Mr. Opp* 172 The roustabouts crowded along the rail, ready to make her fast.

2. An unskilled laborer, usually a transient who does odd jobs. {1883–, in Austral.}

1877 *Harper's Wkly.* 17 March 3/3 The vagabonds, the roustabouts, the criminals, and all the dregs of society seem to be Democrats. **1881** HAYES *New Colorado* 77 He was a kind of ro[u]stabout, or dish-washer, to a camping outfit. **1883** 'S. BONNER' *Dialect Tales* 121 After a time a negro passed near the cotton-shed—one of the kind called 'roustabouts' in that part of the country—people who live in a happy-go-lucky sort of way. **1911** HARRISON *Queed* 35 It takes a Whitney to invent the cotton gin, but the dullest negro roustabout can operate it. *a*1918 G. STUART *On Frontier* II. 179 Every man, whether owner of the largest herd or a humble roustabout, takes his orders from the captain.

‖**Rouster.** =ROUSTABOUT 1. — **1883** *American* VI. 40 Men . . . who used to be rousters, and are now broken down and played out.

*Rout,** *n.* A reception or large evening party. *Obs.* {1742–} Also attrib. (Cf. DRUM *n.* 4.) — **1772** A. G. WINSLOW *Diary* 18, I went directly from it [a funeral] to Miss Caty's Rout. **1796** WANSEY *Excursion U.S.* 125 [Mrs. George Washington] has routs or levees, whichever the people chuses to call them. **1867** *Common Sense Cook Book* 103 [Recipe for] rout biscuit. *Ib.* [Recipe for] rout cake. **1893** *Harper's Mag.* Feb. 371/2 Here [at the Pickwick Club, in New Orleans], after the opera or a country ride, or rout of any sort, the most brilliant beauties of the old and the new town may be seen.

＊**Rout**, *v.* +*tr.* To awaken (someone); to cause (someone) to get *out* of bed. — **1787** CUTLER in *Life & Corr.* I. 287 The people at the White House were gone to bed, but I soon routed them. **1852** WHITMORE *Diary* 1 July, Got routed out early this morning. **1887** HARTE *Crusade of Excelsior* 20 The skipper's been routed out at last, and is giving orders. **1892** *N.Y. Sun* 8 May 2/7 He ran to a neighbouring farmhouse, routed out the people.

＊**Route**, *n.* Also **rout.**

＊**1.** A regular course or road.

1778 HUTCHINS *Va., Penna., Md., & N.C.* 50 The rout from Lake St. Clair to Lake Huron, is up a straight or River, about 400 yards wide. **1807** GASS *Journal* 207 We continued our rout about ten miles. **1841** BUCKINGHAM *America* I. 237 Persons speak of the *rout* they intend to take in a journey, instead of *route*.

+**b.** With particular reference to mail.

1792 *Ann. 2d Congress* 58 The route by which the mails are at present conveyed shall in no case be altered. **1821** *Ann. 17th Congress* 1 Sess. 47 Praying that the route of the mail from Savannah to Augusta . . . may not be altered. **1871** DE VERE 356 A special car is, on all the more important routes, as the Post-Office Department calls the lines, provided for a mail-agent. **1874** *Rep. Postmaster-General* 209 Each railway post-office clerk, route agent, or post-office clerk . . . is required to attach to each package . . . a facing or label slip bearing the address of the package, the office or route upon which it was made up.

attrib. **1867** LOCKE *Swingin' Round* 141 We shel hev Post Offisis, and Collectorships, and Assessorships, and Furrin Mishns, and Route Agencies, and sich.

+**2.** A newsboy's territory.

1841 *Jamestown* (N.Y.) *Jrnl.* 5 May 2/4 He succeeded in obtaining possession of a route for a morning penny paper. **1850** MATHEWS *Moneypenny* 119 Go upstairs, and tell Wages to give you the St. John's Park route. **1890** H. O. WILLS *Twice Born* 26, I carried a 'route' for the Troy *Daily Press.*

Route, *v.* {1890}

+**1.** *tr.* To send or direct (someone or something) on a certain line of travel. Also *vbl. n.*

1832 McCLUNG *Sk. Western Adventure* 132 The Indians, astonished at seeing men route themselves in this manner, sallied out of their redoubts and pursued the stragglers. **1894** *Forum* Oct. 253 Outside agencies and travelling agents . . . secure the routing of passengers and freight by their respective [railroad] lines. **1897** *Boston Morn. Herald* 9 Sept. 8/4 (Ernst) The railroad committee . . . requested that same be hung in shipping offices and be used in routing freight. **1899** *N.Y. Ev. Post* 28 Jan., [Telegraphic] messages from the United States are generally routed as follows.

+**2.** To arrange (mail) in the order of delivery.

1893 CUSHING *Story of P.O.* 235 Here are the carriers themselves, engaged in 'routing' the mail.

+**Route agent. 1.** A postal employee assigned to duty on a railroad train who receives, assorts, and delivers mail along the route, and accompanies it in transit between post-office and railroad station or steamboat. *Obs.* **2.** A road agent. — **(1) 1855** HOLBROOK *Among Mail Bags* 415 No letters should be given to Route Agents upon the cars or steamboats, except such as cannot be written before the closing of the mail at the post-office. **1877** *Harper's Mag.* March 615/1 The mail-bag contained mutilated letters . . . , and the sachel the working tools of a route agent upon the Pennsylvania Railroad. **1880** TOURGEE *Invisible Empire* 416 They did not intend to allow any negro route agents, . . . or negro brakesmen, on the road. **(2) 1897** LEWIS *Wolfville* 197 It's shorely the need of money drives this Slim Jim to turnin' route-agent an' go holdin' up the stage.

+**Route step.** An order of march in which the men break step, and need not maintain silence. — **1867** *Atlantic Mo.* March 272/2 The 'route step' is an abandonment of all military strictness. **1872** ROE *Army Lett.* 51, I feel sorry for the men, but they always march 'rout' step and seem to have a good time. **1884** *Century Mag.* Dec. 281 Troops in crossing were given the order, 'Route step,' as the oscillation of the cadence step or trotting horse is dangerous to the stability of a bridge. **1911** *Infantry Drill Reg.* (War Dept.) 99 *Route step* and *at ease* are applicable to any marching formation.

+**Routing clerk.** (See quot. 1889.) — **1888** *N.Y. Tribune* (F.), As the messages drop they are taken out, slid through steam rollers that copy them, and drop them on a revolving, endless belt, that takes them off to the routing clerks and the messengers. **1889** FARMER 465/1 *Routing Clerks,* clerks in the U.S. Telegraph Service who despatch messages.

Rove beetle. {1781-} Any one of a large family of beetles (Staphylinidae), frequently found on decaying matter. — **1771** FORSTER *Cat. Animals N.A.* 27 Rove-beetle. **1862** *Rep. Comm. Patents 1861: Agric.* 596 Figure 19 represents a large family of insects which have received the common name of 'rove beetles,' technically *Staphylinidæ,* from the typical genus *Staphylinus.* **1869** *Rep. Comm. Agric. 1868* 307 Many of the rove beetles . . . are found in decaying animal and vegetable substances.

＊**Rover.** +**1.** A variety of plover. +**2.** A native or inhabitant of Colorado. A nickname. — **(1) 1780** *Narragansett Hist. Reg.* I. 100 Went to

the harbor's mouth a gunning and killed one rover. **(2) 1872** *Harper's Mag.* Jan. 317/2 Below will be found a careful compilation of the various nicknames given to the States and people of this republic. . . . Colorado, Rovers. **1902** CLAPIN 341.

+**Roving commission.** A commission appointed by Congress for a special investigation, usu. with vaguely defined authority; authorization or instruction given by Congress to an official, allowing him considerable freedom of operation. — **1867** *Congress. Globe* 22 March 273/2, I think it would be safer to leave this matter [of certain state claims] to the direct inspection of the War Department, than to send out a roving commission. We have had enough of these roving commissions. **1882** *Congress. Rec.* 9 March 1737/2 If that is to be the mission that Congress is to enter upon by these roving commissions, taking testimony and printing whatever any set of gentlemen may give as their own views, . . . I for one shall oppose it. **1894** *Ib.* 25 April 4098/1 Is it a legitimate expenditure of the public money to send out consuls with roving commissions to hunt up commerce for a certain class of our people?

Roving frame. {1825} A machine used in the process of converting wool or cotton into roves. — **1814** *Niles' Reg.* VI. 16/2 A roving frame or machine that will rove the same quantity for the same fineness, [will cost] 50 dollars. **1876** KNIGHT 1996/2 The roving-frame for worsted . . . takes in two slivers from the cans of the *drawing-frame* and elongates them four times. **1885** *Harper's Mag.* July 250/1 The 'speeder' or 'roving-frame,' is really the first machine of the spinning department.

Roving head. A kind of roving frame used in the manufacture of worsted. — **1815** DRAKE *Cincinnati* 143, 71 roving and drawing heads . . . have been made. **1876** KNIGHT 1996/2.

＊**Row,** *n.*

I. ＊**1.** A number of buildings or lots in a line; a particular street in a town.

1638 *Charlestown Land Rec.* 2 One roode of grounde . . . scituate in the middle row, butting northwest upon the markett place. **1663** *Providence Rec.* V. 205 The which percell of land is scituate . . . in the Rowe of the Towne. **1715** *Boston News-Letter* 14 Nov. 2/2 Good Cheshire Cheese . . . to be seen at his Ware-House in Merchants-Row Boston. **1872** *Chicago Tribune* 11 Oct. 1/6 The fire originated in Francis Larken's row, in Main Street. . . . Patterson's brick row was also destroyed.

2. A line of plants in a field, garden, or nursery. {1733-} Also attrib.

1786 WASHINGTON *Diaries* III. 52 Finished drilling the Barley at that place in 66 Rows. **1827** in Commons, etc. *Doc. Hist.* I. 214 Most of the plant cane, and also stubbles of Creole cane in new land mark the row. **1852** STOWE *Uncle Tom* xl, He set his basket down by the row. **1870** WARNER *Summer in Garden* xv, I planted . . . the rows a little less than three feet apart; but the [potato] vines came to an early close in the drought. **1905** *Forestry Bureau Bul.* No. 61, 19 *Row planting,* a method of planting in which the young trees are placed in rows, the distance between the rows being greater than the distance between the young trees in the rows.

+**3.** A story in a building.

1872 S. C. WOOLSEY *What Katy Did* iii, Which row are you going to have a room in?

+**4.** A wall.

1883 *Century Mag.* Sept. 686/2 A pair of brown-thrashers . . . were flitting from bush to bush along an old stone row in a remote field.

II. In phrases. **5.** With *hoe* v. in reference to sense 2 above. +**a.** *A hard* (or *long,* etc.) *row to hoe,* a difficult and tedious undertaking; a dreary prospect.

1835 CROCKETT *Tour* 69, I never opposed Andrew Jackson for the sake of popularity. I knew it was a hard row to hoe; but I stood up to the rack. **1839** S. SMITH *Down East* 127, I pity the man that has a helpless, shiftless wife; he has a hard row to hoe. **1866** LOWELL *Biglow* P. 2 Ser. xi. 244 We've gut an awful row to hoe In this 'ere job o' reconstructin'. **1873** M. HOLLEY *My Opinions* 21 Step-mothers have a pretty hard row to hoe. **1898** HAMBLEN *Tom Benton's Luck* 104, I've had a pretty tough row to hoe down there in New York. **1902** HARBEN *A. Daniel* 59, I have faith in your future, but you've got a long, rocky row to hoe. **1907** *Scribner's Mag.* July 124 If I am to maintain both my household and my self-respect, I have indeed a hard row to hoe.

+**b.** *To hoe one's* (*own*) *row,* to work independently or without assistance, to hold one's own in an encounter.

1841 *Knickerb.* XVII. 362 Our American pretender must, to adopt an agricultural phrase, 'hoe his own row,' . . . without the aid of protectors or dependents. **1845** *Cincinnati Misc.* I. 156/2 Mike did not greet our envoy in very pleasant style, but kept the fair weather side out, knowing that my friend was able to *hoe his own row.* **1860** HOLLAND *Miss Gilbert* 455 You are too much for me, Miss Gilbert; I can't hoe my row at all with you. **1862** NORTON *Army Lett.* 111, I can dispute and 'argufy' with a man and 'hoe my row,' but I never quarrelled with a woman yet but I got the worst of it. **1863** 'G. HAMILTON' *Gala-Days* 64, I could pick you up a dozen girls . . . who should be abundantly able to 'hoe their own row' with them anywhere. **1895** *Century Mag.* July 378/2, I wouldn't marry a man that couldn't work in open daylight for a livin'. I'd ruther hoe my own row.

+**c.** In other phrases with *hoe* v.

A new row to hoe, a new venture or undertaking; *to hoe another row,* to begin a new venture; *to hoe a big row,* to perform an important task.

1836 CROCKETT *Exploits* 28, I have a new row to hoe, a long and a rough one, but come what will I'll go ahead. *Ib.* 95 Our worthy was discharged from the company, and compelled to commence hoeing another row. **1900** *Congress. Rec.* 7 April 3899/1 Any man who can serve in Congress twenty-five years, hoe as big a row as Bland did, and grow all the time, is big enough for any position whatsoever.

6. In other phrases. +*a. Not to be worth* (or *amount to*) *a row of pins* (or *beans*), to be utterly trivial or worthless. Cf. BEAN 2 b.

1863 NORTON *Army Lett.* 169 He worries himself homesick and isn't worth a row of pins. **1903** *N.Y. Times* 17 Sept., The letter of Buchanan suspending us doesn't amount to a row of beans. **1903** *N.Y. Ev. Post* 18 Sept. 12 The work doing from Ann Street to Bowling Green does not amount to a row of pins.

+*b. To be at the end of* (one's) *row,* to have exhausted one's resources; to be played out.

1904 HARBEN *Georgians* 2 The old chap certainly is gettin' desperate. . . . It's my opinion he's at the end o' his row.

*Row, v. +*tr. To row up* (someone), to attack vigorously or punish severely (someone). *Obs.* Cf. SALT RIVER. — **1838** LOWELL in Hale *Lowell & Friends* 46 When I recite Locke, he [Mr. Frost] generally spends three quarters of the time in endeavoring to row up that delectable writer. **1845** *N.Y. Tribune* 10 Dec. (B.), We should really like, of all things, to row up the majority of Congress as it deserves in regard to the practice. **1850** LOWELL in Scudder *J. R. Lowell* I. 303, I am tired of controversy, and though I have cut out the oars with which to row up my friend Bowen, yet I have enough to do. **1871** DE VERE 346 To *row up* became soon identical with severe scolding or actual punishment.

Rowan berry. The fruit of the rowan tree {1814–}, or the tree itself. (Cf. next.) — [**1897** SUDWORTH *Arborescent Flora* 211 *Pyrus americana.* . . . Mountain Ash. . . . Rowan Berry (Ont.).] **1904** *McClure's Mag.* March 454/2 Again came autumn to the Quah-Davic, with . . . the wax-vermilion bunches of the rowan berries reflected in each brown pool.

*Rowan tree. A cultivated European species of mountain ash, *Sorbus aucuparia,* +or a related American species. (Cf. MOUNTAIN ASH.) — **1857** GRAY *Botany* 125 *P[yrus] aucuparia,* the cultivated European Mountain-Ash or Rowan-tree, is known by its paler, shorter, and blunt leaflets, and larger fruit. **1891** *Cent.* 5250/1 *Rowan-tree,* . . . the mountain-ash of the Old World, *Pyrus aucuparia;* also, less properly, either of the American species *P. Americana* and *P. sambucifolia.* **1892** R. H. DAVIS *Silhouettes* 4 Ef I was in the old place, . . . 'n could go set by father 'n mother every morning, whar they're lyin' among the rowan trees, I'd get young agin 'n lose this torment.

*Rowboat. A boat designed to be propelled by oars. — **1779** PUTNAM in *Memoirs* 140 The enimy have a roe-boat up as far as Sailsburys Island. **1847** LANMAN *Summer in Wilderness* 171 The Indian canoe is now giving way to the more costly but less beautiful row boat. **1882** MCCABE *New York* 402 The men live on the steamer, and patrol the water front of the city in row boats. **1909** 'O. HENRY' *Options* 299, I'll buy a catboat and a rowboat.

Row-de-dow. Noise; excitement: (see also quot. 1787). {row-de-dowing, 1832; 1887} *colloq.* — **1787** TYLER *Contrast* III. i, There was a soldier fellow, who talked about his row de dow, dow, and courted a young woman. **1832** *Congress. Deb.* 13 March 2128 [Political candidates] who have no military merit of their own, . . . in the rub-a-dub and row-de-dow excitement, . . . come in for their share of the 'spoils of the victor.' **1854** M. J. HOLMES *Tempest & Sunshine* 70, I can't eat with this 'ere shovel, and if I take my fingers, Tempest'll raise a row de dow. **1871** STOWE *Sam Lawson* 194 Since the gret fuss and row-de-dow about it, it's kind o' died out.

+**Rowdy, n.** [Of obscure origin.] A lawless backwoodsman; a rough, quarrelsome person. {in general use, 1865–}

1820 FLINT *Lett. from Amer.* 264 These I must call Americanisms, and will subjoin some examples: Rowdy—Blackguard. **1823** FAUX *Memorable Days* 318 The Rowdies of Kentucky . . . frequently decoy travelers, supposed to have money, out of the road, and then shoot them. **1844** *Lexington Observer* 5 Oct. 1/3 A gang of drunken rowdies attacked a Methodist Camp Meeting. **1860** OLMSTED *Back Country* 413 In the class furthest removed from this on the frontier . . . [are] border ruffians, of whom the 'rowdies' of our eastern towns are tame reflections. **1885** *South Fla. Sentinel* (Orlando) 8 July 2/2 Every portion of Orlando . . . [demands] protection from rowdies by our police. **1894** 'MARK TWAIN' *P. Wilson* x, He found the 'nigger' in him . . . giving the road . . . to the white rowdy and loafer. **1919** *Maine My State* 331 A tough looking rowdy . . . aimed a blow at him.

+**Rowdy, a.** {1872–}

1. Of a rough, disorderly, or uncouth nature.

1823 FAUX *Memorable Days* 324 A line of houses on the lonely road to Missouri is . . . kept up by these Rowdey robbers and murderers for the reception of travellers, and villains to rob them. **1843** 'CARLTON' *New Purchase* I. 76 A rowdy school-master of the Purchase . . . used this preventive. **1856** DERBY *Phoenixiana* 196 [You] accuse us of singing rowdy songs, nights. **1869** 'MARK TWAIN' *Innocents Abroad* 112 There was . . . no swaggering intrusion of services by rowdy hackmen. **1882** BAILLIE-GROHMAN *Camps in Rockies* 23 The West . . . is a very lusty, not to say rowdy country. **1898** HARPER *S. B. Anthony* I. 120, I explained the rowdy treatment of the other minister.

+**2. Difficult.**

1838 *S. Lit. Messenger* IV. 119/1 He's had rowdy work, poor soul, dodging through the swamps to keep out the way of the enemy.

+**Rowdy, v.** [Cf. ROWDY *n.*] *tr.* and *intr.* To bully (someone); to behave in the manner of a rowdy. Also *vbl. n.* — **1825** PAULDING *J. Bull in Amer.* 209 Notwithstanding . . . their being regulated and rowdied, . . . not one [emigrant] in a thousand ever goes home again. **1887** RILEY *Afterwhiles* (1894) 31 The dear little girl . . . [would] come rowdying up from her mother, And clamoring there at my knee. **1887** *Courier-Journal* 18 Feb. 1/3 There was a good deal of noise and 'rowdying.'

Rowdy-dowdy, a. Noisy; boisterous; rough. {1882–} — **1854** CUMMINS *Lamplighter* 260 To offer herself as a champion for that rowdy-dowdy child. **1855** *S. Lit. Messenger* XXI. 221/2 Noxatra is . . . a rowdy-dowdy village of three or four thousand inhabitants, including free negroes, pigs, and puddles.

+**Rowdyish, a.** [Cf. ROWDY *n.*] Inclined to be rowdy. {1874} — **1841** J. Q. ADAMS *Diary* 529 All this was as false and hollow as it was blustering and rowdyish. **1872** 'MARK TWAIN' *Roughing It* 168, I felt rowdyish and 'bully.' **1890** *Harper's Mag.* June 156/2 The fun [is] hoydenish and rowdyish.

+**Rowdyism.** [Cf. ROWDY *n.*] The behavior characteristic of rowdies. {1874} — **1842** *Chicago American* 30 Aug., Let the police be more energetic . . . or we shall soon gain a reputation for rowdyism. **1853** *La Crosse Democrat* 22 Nov. 3/2 The village has occasionally been disgraced by rowdyism and disorder. **1872** *Newton Kansan* 10 Oct. 2/3, I saw no rowdyism or drunkenness. **1891** O'BEIRNE *Leaders Ind. Territory* 41/2 Since he has become a guardian of the public welfare it is notable that the town has enjoyed absolute freedom from lawlessness and rowdyism. **1900** *Congress. Rec.* 31 Jan. 1365/2 Wherever there is a failure of the expression of the popular will through the ballot box, the result is disclosed in rowdyism and assassination and lynching.

*Rowen. The second growth of grass or hay in a season. 'Now chiefly *dial.* and *U.S.*' (*O.E.D.*).

1743 *Holyoke Diaries* 35 Began to mow Rowens. **1839** BUEL *Farmer's Companion* 229 The after-growth, or rowen, is very abundant. **1844** EMERSON *Nominalist & Realist* Ess. 2 Ser., The frugal farmer takes care that his cattle shall eat down the rowen. **1909** *Springfield W. Repub.* 7 Oct. 8 While yet the clover blooms in the rowen.

* b. Such grass or hay used as fodder.

1796 J. ADAMS *Diary* Works III. 417 A soft fine rain . . . [will] lay the foundation of fine rowen and after feed. **1874** *Vermont Bd. Agric. Rep.* II. 405 Lambs . . . will learn to be handled without fear; and by putting rowen in their racks, they will soon learn to eat. **1888** *Vt. Agric. Rep.* X. 36 Feed hay . . . till rowen is large enough, then rowen till fodder corn comes to maturity. **1894** *Ib.* XIV. 61, I feed cotton-seed meal, corn meal, rowen and hay.

+**Row flat.** A flatboat propelled by rowing. — **1777** *N.J. Archives* 2 Ser. I. 335 If it suits the purchaser, [he] may have the use of a row flat and landing. **1790** *Penna. Packet* 27 Sept. 3/4 Taken up a-drift in the river Delaware, on the 12th inst. a Row Flat.

*Row galley. A galley propelled by oars. Now hist. — **1740** W. STEPHENS *Proc. Georgia* I. 626 They might possibly send out Row-Gallies and Launches. **1776** *Jrnls. Cont. Congress* IV. 406 The General [shall] be authorized to direct the building of as many . . . row gallies . . . as may be necessary. **1886** Z. F. SMITH *Kentucky* 174 One of the more novel features . . . was the fitting up of an armed row-galley, with breastwork protections on the sides, for the patrol [in 1781] of the Ohio river.

Row grass. (Identity of plant not known.) — **1788** WASHINGTON *Diaries* III. 335 The ground . . . had been sown with Barley and Row grass.

*Rowing.

*1. The act of propelling a boat by the use of oars.

1869 *Nation* 3 June 432/2 We feel pretty sure that the manner of rowing of the American crew will be finer than that of their antagonists. **1887** *Outing* March 588/2 We are speaking of the exceptional successful exponents of bad rowing. **1897** FLANDRAU *Harvard Episodes* 113 The College . . . crowds your days and nights with the interests of rowing and base-ball, and the First Ten.

+**2. With *up*. A castigation.** *Obs.* (Cf. ROW v.)

1846 *N.Y. Tribune* 30 Jan. (B.), The most spicy part of the proceedings in the Senate was the rowing up which Mr. Hannegan gave Mr. Ritchie of the Union newspaper. **1856** *N.Y. Herald* 7 May (De Vere), We hope the President gave his Secretary a good rowing up; he certainly deserved it for his imbecility.

*3. Attrib. in sense 1 with *boat, man, match*, etc.

1830 COOPER *Water Witch* III. 105 [A] swift rowing-boat awaited his return. **1873** 'MARK TWAIN' & WARNER *Gilded Age* 200 Picnics, rowing matches . . . —Alice declared that it was a whirl of dissipation. **1887** J. HAWTHORNE in *Century Mag.* June 179/2 The parallel bars was another favorite exercise of the rowing-men. **1892** *Outing* Jan. 277/2 In 1887 the rowing tank was first put into practical use in the Yale gymnasium. **1894** *Ib.* April 68/1 They put on . . . long stockings and rowing tights. **1894** *Ib.* 71/2 Rowing topics are carefully avoided.

Rowing club. A club made up of persons interested in rowing as a sport. {1866} — **1884** BUNNER in *Harper's Mag.* Jan. 303/2 You may sit on the sliding seats of the . . . Rowing Club's shells. **1898** *Outing* April 10/1 This Union is composed of the Rowing Club, the Track Athletic Association [etc.].

+**Rowing machine.** An apparatus used for practice in rowing. — **1872** *Rep. Comm. Patents 1871* 495 William B. Curtis . . . [claims this] combination, in a rowing machine, . . . all constructed, arranged, and operating substantially as described. **1885** HOLMES *Mortal Antipathy* ii, Y' ought to see 'em . . . pull in them rowin'-machines. **1898** *Outing* April 11/1 The early work of the crew candidates consisted of . . . daily practice on the rowing machines. **1905** 'O. HENRY' *Four Million* 59 Let the mantel turn to a rowing machine. **1911** HARRISON *Queed* 89 He went around like a museum guide, introducing . . . to the visitor under its true names and uses . . . a rowing-machine, the horizontal and parallel bars [etc.].

+**Rowing weight.** =prec. — **1876** TRIPP *Student-Life* 346 Hawes had invented a machine called a rowing-weight. **1887** J. HAWTHORNE in *Century Mag.* June 179/2 Rowing-weights were not invented until two years later.

+**Roxbury Russet.** [*Roxbury*, Mass.] A variety of long-keeping apple originally grown in New England. Also *Roxbury Russeting*. — **1821** THACHER *Amer. Orchardist* 136 Roxbury russeting . . . is one of the best known, and most valuable fruits in Massachusetts. **1832** *Genesee Farmer* II. 320/1 Catalogue of Fruit Trees . . . for sale at the Horticultural Garden. . . . Roxbury Russet, Rhode Island Greening, [etc.]. **1847** IVES *New Eng. Fruit* 44 Roxbury Russet.—This apple is well known, and extensively cultivated in New England. **1861** *Ill. Agric. Soc. Trans.* IV. 468 Our farmers set in the early orchards of Wisconsin a large proportion of Roxbury Russets . . . and Spitzenbergs. **1880** *Harper's Mag.* March 573/2 She set right to a-parin' them Roxbury russets.

+**Roxbury waxwork.** [Cf. prec.] =BITTERSWEET 2. — **1870** *Amer. Naturalist* June 215 Bittersweet (*Celastrus scandens*), also called Roxbury Waxwork, . . . is a hardy climber. **1892** *Amer. Folk-Lore* V. 94 *Celastrus scandens*, Roxbury wax-work. E. Mass.

* **Royal,** *a.*

1. In names of foods.

1867 *Common Sense Cook Book* 96 Royal Iceing [*sic*] for Cakes. **1884** 'CRADDOCK' *Where Battle Was Fought* 114, 'I am going to make,' she remarked incidentally, as it were, '—Royal pudding for dinner on account of Somebody's sweet tooth.'

2. In specific names and other special combinations.

Royal catchfly, +*r.* (*red*) *fox*, (see quotations); *r. horned caterpillar*, (see quotation); *R. Pearmain*, a name applied to certain varieties of apples {1825- (Loudon *Encycl. Agric.* 599)}; *R. refugee*, +a loyalist seeking protection under the British crown; *R. Rider*, +a member of an order auxiliary to the second Ku-Klux Klan.

1901 MOHR *Plant Life Ala.* 497 *Silene regia.* . . . Royal Catchfly. . . . Flowers deep scarlet. Perennial. **1905** ELLIOT *Check List Mammals* 382 *Vulpes regalis.* . . . Royal Fox. **1917** *Mammals of Amer.* 73/1 Royal Red Fox.—*Vulpes regalis.* . . . Northern Plains from Dakota to Alberta, east to Manitoba and Minnesota. **1891** *Cent.* 5251/1 *Royal horned caterpillar*, the larva of *Citheronia regalis*, a large bombycid moth of beautiful olive and crimson colors. **1817** W. COXE *Fruit Trees* 122 Royal Pearmain.—Is a fine, large apple, rather flat in its form, of a rich russet colour, blended with red. **1778** *Mass. Spy* 15 Oct. 2/3 All the Royal Refugees in this city are desired to meet at a certain time and place, to deliberate on matters of the greatest importance. **1923** *N.Y. Times* 4 June 3/5 The congregation had had no warning that the Klansmen and Royal Riders were to attend the service.

+**Royal Americans.** (See AMERICAN *n.* 3 a.)

Royal Arch Mason. {1823} +One who has received the seventh degree in the York rite in American masonry. — **1867** *Mich. Gen. Statutes* I. (1882) 1147 Any ten or more residents of this state being members either of any commandery of knights templars, council, chapter of royal arch masons [etc.]. **1898** A. G. MACKEY *Hist. Free-Masonry* 1282 Several Royal Arch Masons in the upper part of South Carolina . . . had received their degrees in Master's lodges.

Royal fern. =BOG ONION b. {1860-} — **1890** [see BOG ONION]. **1901** MOHR *Plant Life Ala.* 123 Coarse beard grass . . . and royal fern . . . form conspicuous features in the aspect of the vegetation.

Royalist. {1643-} +In the American Revolution, a supporter of the king and the British government. Now hist. — **1809** FRENEAU *Poems* II. 186 To a Concealed Royalist. **1823** THACHER *Military Jrnl.* 93 An enterprize of little importance has lately been put in execution by a detachment of royalists from New York. **1832** DUNLAP *Hist. Amer. Theatre* 42 The Lutheran Church . . . had escaped the flames, to serve the royalists for a store-house. **1871** *Scribner's Mo.* II. 44 As the Army of the Revolution passed . . . Royalists and Republicans were out of doors to see the goodly show.

+**Royal palm.** An ornamental palm (*Roystonea regia*) of southern Florida and Cuba. — **1861** *Smithsonian Rep. 1860* 440 The Palm, . . . [found] in large groves, between Capes Sable and Romano, . . . was called 'Royal Palm,' and said to grow 120 feet high. **1884** SARGENT *Rep. Forests* 218 *Oreodoxa regia.* . . . Royal Palm. . . . Wood heavy, hard. **1897** SUDWORTH *Arborescent Flora* 105.

+**Royal tern.** A large tern (*Thalasseus maximus*), found in the southern states. — **1858** BAIRD *Birds Pacific R.R.* 859 *Sterna Regia.* . . . The Royal Tern. . . . Atlantic coast of the southern and middle States and California. **1874** COUES *Birds N.W.* 669 *Sterna* (*Thalasseus*) *Regia.* Royal Tern. . . . My personal observations on this species are confined to the coast of North Carolina. **1917** *Birds of Amer.* I. 59/2 The Royal Terns were largely exterminated in many sections of their range by the gunners of the millinery trade some years ago.

* **Royalty.**

1. A duty paid for the right to manufacture a patented article, for the use of land, etc. {1839-, a payment to the landowner by a mine lessee; 1879-}

1864 WEBSTER 1153/1. **1875** *Scribner's Mo.* Dec. 280/1 A creator and inventor has a natural right to the product of his brain, and wherever and by whomsoever that product is used, he is entitled to a royalty. **1900** *Congress. Rec.* 2 Feb. 1458/2 The Five Civilized Tribes, with their great trust fund, with their great income from occupation tax, and especially from their income by way of royalties.

2. An amount, constituting a proportion of the income from sales or a fee for performance, paid to the author or creator of a literary or artistic work. {1883-}

1880 *Scribner's Mo.* May 138/1 Houses which . . . paid no royalties to authors . . . availed themselves of the experience and outlay of American publishers. **1883** 'MARK TWAIN' *Life on Miss.* xxxii, I've edited books for that kind of people: and the moment they get their hands on the royalty —. **1888** *Nation* 26 Jan. 71/1 At 10 per cent. royalty [the book] would have given the author nearly $3,000. **1907** *St. Nicholas* June 680/1 It did not bring its author a considerable royalty. **1911** VANCE *Cynthia* 70 You had your eye on royalties—and a play to exploit yourself in.

Royal yard. *Naut.* The yard next above the topgallant yard. {1883} — **1839** *Knickerb.* XIII. 42 Send him some ratlin-stuff, so that he can set up brace-backstays abaft, and cross his royal yards, and call all hands up anchor. **1840** DANA *Two Years* xi. 89, I also connected with our arrival here . . . my first act of what the sailors will allow to be seamanship—sending down a royal yard. **1849** KINGSLEY *Diary* 26 Wind to-day quite varriable—sent down the royal yard. **1850** COLTON *Deck & Port* 183 We fidded our topgallant-masts; crossed our royal yards.

Royston crow. {1611-} ?+The common American crow, *Corvus brachyrhynchos*. Probably so called because confounded with the English hooded crow. — **1781-2** JEFFERSON *Notes Va.* (1788) 77 Besides these [birds], we have The Royston crow. *Corvus cornix.*

R. R. Abbrev. of RAILROAD. In attrib. use. — **1884** *Gringo & Greaser* 15 Feb. 4/1 Bernalillo County is having a R. R. bond boom and meetings are holding in Albuquerque. **1889** in *N.Y. Pub. Lib. Bul.* XLIV. 114 1st Halt at 7:05 by a bank of chalk earth thrown out of R. R. cutting. **1924** *Union Pacific Mag.* Jan. 6/1 He has been . . . Chairman, Executive Committee, . . . Oregon-Washington R.R. and Navigation Co.

* **Rub,** *v.*

1. *intr.* To chafe. *Obs.*

1784 WASHINGTON *Diaries* II. 281 My Horses, . . . from the extreme heat of the Weather began to Rub and gaul.

+**2.** *To rub out,* to kill or do for. *slang.* {1890, Austral.} 'Chiefly *U.S.*' (*O.E.D.*).

1848 RUXTON *Life Far West* i, Thar was old Sam Owins—him as got rubbed out by the Spaniards at Sacramenty, or Chihuahuy. **1856** BONNER *Life J. P. Beckwourth* (1931) 62 If you are fortunate you will discover the Black Feet before they see you. . . . If they discover you first, they will rub you all out. **1878** BEADLE *Western Wilds* 192 Can't you see I'm rubbed out?

3. *To rub it in,* to emphasize or impress unduly, as by reiterated jibes, references, etc. {1870-}

1851 *Polly Peablossom* 146 When it comes to rubbin' it in, I always in gen'rally kinder r'ars up. **1887** *Courier-Journal* 16 Jan. 8/4 'Der boss manager' . . . has decided to play them another series, and rub it in. **1900** *Everybody's Mag.* II. 431/2, I'm not fitted for anything better than Piccadilly, I know, but you needn't rub it into one. **1911** BURGESS *Find the Woman* 63 Wasn't that rubbing it in?

+**4.** *To rub snuff,* (see SNUFF 1 b.)

* **Rubber.**

+**1.** (See quotation.) *Obs.*

1825 PICKERING *Inquiries Emigrant* (1831) 71 One [practice is] in common use in the Eastern part of Maryland, of girls taking a '*rubber*' of snuff—that is, taking as much snuff as will lie on the end of the forefinger out of a box, and rubbing it round the inside of the mouth!

+**2.** One skilled in rubbing down race horses and athletes.

1840 *Picayune* 29 Oct. 2/1 A negro boy, belonging to Mr. John Campbell, a rubber in his stable, has confessed. **1893** Philips *Making of Newspaper* 211 The sporting writer . . . has a large and valuable acquaintance with owners, trainers, rubbers, jockeys, bettors, and bookmakers. **1895** WILLIAMS *Princeton Stories* 185 Another sub and William, the negro rubber, picked Wormsey up. **1902** McFAUL *Ike Glidden* 173 The gelding had been taken in charge by the professional rubber and the stable men.

+**3.** A rubber overshoe. Usually pl.

See also INDIA RUBBER 2.

1842 *S. Lit. Messenger* VIII. 516/2 The *younkers* who would go 'a Maying,' very prudently provided themselves with rubbers and tippets before encountering the rough southeaster. **1873** BAILEY *Life in Danbury* 76 You couldn't borrow an umbrella or a pair of rubbers from any one. **1883** RITTENHOUSE *Maud* 227, [I] got her rubbers and a new hat. **1902** MacGOWAN *Last Word* 297, I thought English ladies didn't wear rubbers. **1912** NICHOLSON *Hoosier Chron.* 455, I don't understand why you won't wear rubbers.

+4. A brake on a vehicle.

1850 in Glisan *Jrnl. Army Life* 32 The third vehicle, having no rubbers, or brakes, to the wheels, went so fast . . . that the driver was thrown from his seat.

5. *attrib.* **a.** Made of rubber.

See also RUBBER BLANKET, RUBBER BOOT, etc.

1849 KINGSLEY *Diary* 78 Some of the fellows went in swimming this afternoon by takeing rubber beds. **1866** 'F. KIRKLAND' *Bk. Anecdotes* 385/1 A full broadside from the Hartford was let go at her antagonist, but it was like throwing rubber balls against a brick wall. **1880** *Harper's Mag.* Aug. 399/2 A poncho and havelock cap comprise the rubber clothing outfit. **1883** KNIGHT *Suppl.* 771/2 *Rubber Center Spring*, a car or vehicle spring with a caoutchouc cylinder or block inclosed in a spiral spring, or otherwise associated. **1907** *St. Nicholas* June 736/1 So she bought . . . a big rubber balloon for 25 cents. **1911** VANCE *Cynthia* 298 She had no rubber cap. **1921** *Daily Telegraph* (London) 29 Aug. 9/3 Aviator J. F. Blake, flying low [over New Haven], dropped several inflated rubber inner tubes to three women who were struggling in the heaviest surf waves this summer.

b. In special combinations.

Rubber company, a group of associates in the rubber business; *r. currency*, (see quotation); *r. man*, a man financially interested in the rubber trade; *r. prince*, an outstandingly successful dealer in rubber (cf. PRINCE 1 a); *r. saw*, (see quotation).

1882 PECK *Sunshine* 128 The tripe is expensive, owing to the royalty that has to be paid to the rubber company. **1904** *N.Y. Ev. Post* 22 Nov. 8 Speaker Cannon talked disparagingly of 'rubber currency,' this being his interpretation of the word 'elastic.' **1889** *Boston Jrnl.* 22 Jan. 2/3 The rubber men and the lumber men are now having their innings. **1904** 'O. HENRY' *Cabbages & Kings* 4 Frank Goodwin, an American resident of the town, . . . [was] a banana king, a rubber prince. **1876** KNIGHT 1998/1 *Rubber-saw*, a tool used in cutting india-rubber. . . . It is a circular knife, driven at high speed, and kept constantly wet by a jet or spray of water.

Rubber blanket. A waterproof blanket made wholly or chiefly of rubber. — **1864** *Harper's Mag.* May 859/2 [The soldiers] were well provided with those almost indispensable comforts, rubber blankets. **1876** *Wide Awake* 170/1 He carried her down, and put her in the boat with a rubber-blanket around her. **1898** *Boston Herald* 11 Nov. 5/4 They lay their ponchos or rubber blankets on the beds. **1902** McFAUL *Ike Glidden* 158 On the end of the rope was fastened a bundle tied and wound up in a rubber blanket.

Rubber boot. A boot made of rubberized fabric. — **1863** 'G. HAMILTON' *Gala-Days* 271 The man who gave rubber-boots to women did more to elevate woman than all theorizers . . . that were ever born. **1873** PHELPS *Trotty's Wedding* xvi, I had my hat and rubber-boots on before Bob had finished his message. **1883** *Century Mag.* Oct. 925/2 Rubber boots reaching to the hip are of course necessary. **1920** HOWELLS *Vacation of Kelwyns* 43 By that time Kite . . . was hulking back to the barn full of hushed blasphemy from the crown of his flap-brimmed straw hat to the soles of his high-topped rubber boots.

Rubber coat. A coat made of rubberized fabric. — **1850** KINGSLEY *Diary* 157, I put on my Rubber Coat and built a chimney outside the tent. **1880** LAMPHERE *U.S.Govt.* 181/1 Cadets . . . will supply themselves with . . . 1 rubber coat [price] $4.54. **1887** *Courier-Journal* 1 May 3/3 Rubber Coats [for sale]. *a*1918 G. STUART *On Frontier* I. 69 Rubber coats and shoes were unknown at that time.

Rubber goods. *pl.* Articles made of rubber. — **1853** *Pathfinder Railway Guide* Sept. Advt., Goodyear's Patent Vulcanized Rubber Goods, In great variety, Wholesale and Retail. **1868** *Rep. Comm. Patents 1867* I. 888/2 Machine for Filling Cylindrical Molds for Rubber Goods. **1887** *Courier-Journal* 11 Jan. 3/4 Edward Landstreet, trading as Landstreet & Co., rubber goods, made an assignment to-day. **1911** PERSONS, etc. *Mass. Labor Laws* 140 A great many of Dr. Coggeshall's rubber factory patients have worked on light rubber goods.

Rubber shoe. =INDIA-RUBBER SHOE. — **1844** *Knickerb.* XXIV. 284 Old rubber-shoes! old rubber-shoes! Humble theme for heavenly Muse. **1870** EMERSON *Soc. & Solitude* 257 Newton was a great man, without telegraph, or gas, or steam-coach, or rubber shoes.

Rubber-soled, *a.* Of shoes: Having soles made of rubber. — **1884** *Harper's Mag.* Jan. 304/1 If you can buy . . . a pair of rubber-soled shoes, and a [tennis] racket, . . . you may readily gratify your whim. **1897** *Outing* July 377/1 A pair of rubber-soled lacrosse or tennis shoes, are first-rate for wear about camp.

Rubber tree. =INDIA-RUBBER TREE. {1880-} — [**1847** LOWELL *Biglow P.* I Ser. iv. 49 Rubber-trees fust began bearin' Wen p'liticle conshunces were comin' into wearin'.] **1871** DE VERE 420 Gum-trees are not unfrequently called *Rubber*-trees. **1897** SUDWORTH *Arborescent Flora* 191 *Ficus aurea*. Golden Fig. . . . Rubber Tree (Fla.). **1907** *St. Nicholas* May 636/1 When we were at supper we had music out of a rubber tree.

＊Rubstone. A form of whetstone. — **1687** SEWALL *Letter-Book* I. 75 Send me for my own proper accountt . . . six duz of rub stones. **1759** *Newport Mercury* 3 July 5/3 Just Imported . . . Sealing Wax, Snuff Boxes, Rubstones, Nails. **1843** *Nat. Hist. N.Y., Geology* I. 316 Rubstones or whetstones of various degrees of fineness, hardness, and sharpness of grit . . . have been obtained in Monticello. **1850** *Rep. Comm. Patents 1849* 358 The scythe . . . is more easily sharpened at the heel with the rub stone.

+**Ruby-crowned kinglet.** An American kinglet, *Regulus calendula*. — **1844** *Nat. Hist. N.Y., Zoology* II. 64 The Ruby-Crowned Kinglet . . . feeds on small seeds, on insects which infest trees, and their lurking larvae. **1867** *Amer. Naturalist* I. 109 Ornithological Calendar for April. 1st to 10th. . . . Ruby-crowned Kinglet. **1917** *Birds of Amer.* III. 222/2 Unlike the partly concealed marking which gives the Ruby-crowned Kinglet his name, the corresponding ornamentation of the Golden-crowned species is always plainly observable.

+**Ruby-crowned warbler.** =prec. — **1785** PENNANT *Arctic Zool.* II. 413 Pine, Yellow, and Ruby-Crowned Warbler. **1917** *Birds of Amer.* III. 221 Ruby-crowned Kinglet. *Regulus calendula calendula.* . . . Other Names.—Ruby-crowned Wren; Ruby-crown; Ruby-crowned Warbler.

+**Ruby-crowned wren.** =RUBY-CROWNED KINGLET. — [**1758** G. EDWARDS *Gleanings Nat. Hist.* I. 95 The Ruby-crowned Wren . . . hath [on top of the head] a spot of an exceeding fine red or ruby colour.] **1808** WILSON *Ornithology* I. 83 [The] Ruby-Crowned Wren . . . visits us early in the spring from the south. **1834** AUDUBON *Ornith. Biog.* II. 547 The Ruby-crowned Wren is found in Louisiana and other Southern States, from November until March. **1917** *Birds of Amer.* III. 221.

Ruby silver. A dark red or black sulphide of silver. {1815-} — **1880** *Cimarron News & Press* 26 Feb. 1/4 Experts have pronounced the specimens shown genuine ruby silver. **1882** *47th Congress 1 Sess.* H. R. Ex. Doc. No. 216, 177 The vein . . . contains black sulphurets and ruby silver. **1884** *Century Mag.* Nov. 57 It was . . . richer than the best of the ruby silver down in the Gunnison.

Rubythroat. {1783-} =next. — **1877** *Harper's Mag.* April 659/2 Looking up from a seat in the grove, I saw the ruby-throat drop down on its nest. **1892** TORREY *Foot-Path Way* 135 Could such truancy be habitual with the male ruby-throat?

Ruby-throated humming bird. The common humming bird (*Arhilochus colubris*) of eastern North America. {1782, of S. Amer.} — **1823** JAMES *Exped.* I. 265 *Trochilus colubris*—Ruby-throated humming-bird. **1831** AUDUBON *Ornith. Biog.* I. 248. **1874** COUES *Birds N.W.* 271. **1907** *St. Nicholas* May 655/2, I was very much interested one day last summer, in watching a ruby-throated humming-bird.

＊Ruck. ‖Nonsense; rubbish. *colloq.* *Obs.* — **1890** *Scribner's Mag.* Aug. 159 [He] wears gloves, and takes his meals private in his room and all that sort of ruck.

+**Ructious,** *a.* Extremely annoyed; difficult. *colloq.* — **1833** NEAL *Down-Easters* I. 14 Ryled—ructious—there ye go agin! . . . jest as eff you never heerd o' bein' ryled afore? **1897** *Kissimmee* (Fla.) *Valley* 3 March 1/6 T. P. Howard is having a ruxious old time splitting rails for T. H. Anier as the timber is so tough.

Rudbeckia. [mod. L. from *Rudbeck*, surname of two Swedish botanists at Uppsala before Linnaeus.] Any plant of the North American genus *Rudbeckia* of the family Carduaceae; a coneflower. — **1819** WARDEN *Statistical Acct. U.S.* II. 325 The natural meadows [in Ky.] are covered with . . . the purple-flowered rudbeechia [sic]. **1821** NUTTALL *Travels Arkansa* 148 These vast plains . . . were now enamelled with innumerable flowers, among the most splendid of which were the . . . Rudbeckias, fragrant Phloxes, and the purple Psilotria. **1886** *Boston Jrnl.* 21 July 2/3 In effective arrangement were yellow lilies, hardhack, rudbekia . . . and many smaller varieties of field flowers. **1901** MOHR *Plant Life Ala.* 48 Fleabanes, Rudbeckias, and other tall, coarse composites are characteristic of the prairie flora.

＊Rudder. A device or contrivance attached to the sternpost of a boat for steering it. — **1649** R. WILLIAMS *Letters* (1874) 165 His creditors in the Bay came to Portsmouth and unhung his rudder. **1711** *Boston News-Letter* 21 May 2/2 Capt. Ting had his Rudder struck off on the Shoales of Cape Florida. **1843** A. E. SILLIMAN *Gallop Amer. Scenery* (1881) 4 The broad Potomac, stretched tranquilly onwards, undisturbed save by the . . . lazy creak of the rudder of some craft. **1924** *Pat. Off. Gazette* 8 July 389/1 A composite rudder [is] adapted to be acted upon by the water currents forced thereagainst by said propeller.

Rudder fish. Any one of various fishes that follow vessels or are found about floating logs, casks, etc. {1792-} Also attrib. (Cf. BARREL-FISH, HARVEST FISH a, LOGFISH, PILOT FISH 2 a.)

*c*1733 CATESBY *Carolina* II. 8 *Perca Marina sectatrix*. The Rudder Fish. . . . Ships Rudders are seldom free from them. **1818** *Amer. Monthly Mag.* II. 244 Rudder-fish, or Perch Coryphaena. . . . Taken by a hook near a wharf of the city. **1839** STORER *Mass. Fishes* 55 *Trachinotus argenteus*. The Rudder Fish. **1882** *Nat. Museum Bul.* No. 16, 445 S[eriola] *zonata*, . . . Rudder Fish. **1884** GOODE, etc. *Fisheries* I. 332 The Rudder-Fish family, *Stromateidæ*. **1903** T. H. BEAN *Fishes N.Y.* 457 At Charleston the [harvest] fish is called rudderfish. **1911** *Rep. Fisheries 1908* 314/2 Rudder-fish (*Kyphosus sectatrix*), a small fish abundant about Key West.

＊Ruddy *a.* In the specific names of fishes and birds. {1785-} See also RUDDY DUCK, PLOVER. — **1842** *Nat. Hist. N.Y., Zoology* IV. 9 The Ruddy Bass. *Labrax rufus* . . . come into our markets from New Jersey and Long Island, where they are obtained in brackish streams. **1891** *Cent.* 5258/2 *Ruddy-rudder*, the long-eared sunfish, *Lepomis auritus*: so called from the red color of the tail. (New Jersey and Delaware.) **1917** *Birds of Amer.* I. 152 Ruddy Duck. . . . [Also called] Ruddy Diver. *Ib.* 270/1 The Black, or Black-headed, Turnstone . . . averages a trifle smaller than the Ruddy Turnstone. *Ib.* III. 219 The Wren-Tits are divided locally, because of slight variations, into four groups— . . . [one of which is the] Ruddy Wren-Tits.

+Ruddy duck. A small American duck (*Erismatura jamaicensis rubida*), the flesh of which resembles that of the canvas back. — **1813** WILSON *Ornithologist* VIII. 128 The Ruddy Duck is fifteen inches and a half in length. **1844** *Nat. Hist. N.Y., Zoology* II. 327 The Ruddy Duck. *Fuligula Rubida.* . . . Its food consists of marine and freshwater plants and seeds. **1917** *Birds of Amer.* I. 153/1 The sprightly, comical little Ruddy Duck is a distinctly North American species and is distributed widely over the continent.

Ruddy plover. The surf snipe or sanderling, *Crocethia alba.* — [**1785** PENNANT *Arctic Zool.* II. 486 Ruddy [Plover]. . . . Inhabits Hudson's Bay.] **1813** WILSON *Ornithology* VII. 129 The Ruddy Plover is eight inches long, and fifteen in extent. **1872** COUES *Key to Birds* 257 Ruddy Plover . . . ; head, neck and upper parts varied with black, ashy and bright reddish. **1917** *Birds of Amer.* I. 239.

*****Rue.** An herb (*Ruta graveolens*) used in medicine, or any one of various similar plants. (See also GOAT'S RUE, MEADOW RUE.) — **1698** THOMAS *Pensilvania* 21 [There are] most sorts of Saladings, . . . as Mustard, Rue, Sage, Mint. **1709** LAWSON *Carolina* 78 Wormseed, Feverfew, Rue, Ground-Ivy spontaneous, but very small and scarce. **1790** ASBURY *Journal* II. 88, I took a strong decoction of rue and wormwood. *a*1862 THOREAU *Maine Woods* 174 There grew the beaked hazel, . . . rue [etc.]. **1907** *St. Nicholas* Sept. 987/2 There were . . . Poison ivy and 'sour-grass,' thistle and rue and thorn.

+Rue anemone. A small American wild flower (*Anemonella thalictroides*) resembling both the meadow rue and the anemone. — **1817-8** EATON *Botany* (1822) 174 *Anemone thalictroides*, rue anemone. **1843** TORREY *Flora N.Y.* I. 24 Rue Anemone. . . . Although so strongly resembling *Anemone* in its flower, the fruit shows that its true place is in the genus *Thalictrum.* **1861** WOOD *Botany* 203 Rue Anemone. . . . A fine little plant of early spring. **1884** ROE *Nature's Story* 182 Burt now appeared with a handful of rue-anemones.

+Ruffed grouse. The mountain pheasant (*Bonasa umbellus*) of the eastern half of the United States. Also with defining terms. (Cf. PARTRIDGE 2, PHEASANT 1 *a*.) [**1752** G. EDWARDS *Gleanings Nat. Hist.* I. 79 The Ruffed Heath-cock, or Grous. **1772** *Phil. Trans.* LXII. 397 The Ruffed Grous, *T*[*etrao*] *Umbellus.*] **1812** WILSON *Ornithology* VI. 45 Ruffed Grous. This is the Partridge of the eastern states, and the Pheasant of Pennsylvania and the southern districts. **1842** BUCKINGHAM *Slave States* II. 301 Here also we saw several of the birds which the Americans call pheasants, but which is generally considered to be the 'ruffed grouse.' **1858** BAIRD *Birds Pacific R.R.* 641 Where this bird [the bobwhite] is called quail, the Ruffed Grouse is generally called partridge. **1881** *Mich. Gen. Statutes* I. (1882) 585 No person or corporation or company shall, at any time, kill . . . any deer, ruffed grouse, colin or quail. **1905** *Springfield W. Repub.* 15 Sept. 5 The hunter may bag woodcock or ruffed grouse, commonly called partridge, after October 1. **1917** *Birds of Amer.* II. 17/2.
   comb. **1856** *Porter's Spirit of Times* 22 Nov. 193/1 The only shooting which is to be had . . . is ruffed grouse shooting.

*****Ruffle.** **+1.** The calyx of a cotton bloom. **+2.** Something resembling a ruffle: (see quotations). — **(1)** **1856** *Rep. Comm. Patents 1855: Agric.* 109 Upon opening such a ruffle, this small spider was almost invariably found snugly ensconced in its web. **1874** *Rep. Comm. Agric. 1873*, 162 The egg of the boll-worm is usually placed in the so-called ruffle or envelope of the flower. **(2)** **1862** AGASSIZ *Contribs. Nat. Hist. U.S.* IV. 88 Four [of the bunches of organs on the jellyfish] are elegant sacks, adorned, as it were, with waving ruffles projecting in large clusters. **1872** COUES *Key to Birds* 18 The condor has a single ruffle all around the neck, of close, downy feathers.

+Ruffled grouse. =RUFFED GROUSE. — **1850** S. F. COOPER *Rural Hours* 13 Our Partridge or Pheasant, or Ruffled Grouse, as we should rather call it, are a more hardy bird. **1897** *N.Y. Forest, Fish, & Game Comm. 2d Rep.* 311 Popular synonyms [for the Ruffed Grouse]: . . . Ruffled Grouse; Drumming Grouse.

Ruffled shirt. A shirt adorned with ruffles. {1768-} **1754** *Va. State P.* I. 249, 2 fine Ruffled Shirts and 2 plain shirts for themselves and Wives . . . [were] sent by the Governor to them. **1799** J. SMITH *Acct. Captivity* 10 They gave me a new ruffled shirt, . . . also a tinsel laced cappo. **1843** HAWKS *D. Boone* 104 They all started for their boats —Simon Girty, with his ruffled shirt and soldier coat, marching at their head. **1882** [see HAIR TRIGGER 1]. **1905** RICE *Sandy* 271 A few feet farther away hung a portrait of her grandfather, brave in a high stock and ruffled shirt.
   transf. **1860** HOLMES *Professor* 19 Joe Warren, the first bloody ruffled-shirt of the Revolution, was as good as born here.

+Ruffle(d)-shirted, *a.* Clad in a ruffled shirt. *contemptuous.* — **1835** LONGSTREET *Ga. Scenes* 85 The *ruffled-shirted* little darlings of the present day [would be] under the discipline of paregoric. **1856** CARTWRIGHT *Autobiog.* 132, I got clear of my ruffle-shirted dandy.

+Ruffle shirt. =RUFFLED SHIRT. Also *transf.* and *attrib.* — **1838** DRAKE *Tales Queen City* 64 The colonists presented . . . a curiously grotesque appearance, loitering about the 'station' in ruffle shirts and coonskin caps. **1839** BRIGGS *H. Franco* II. 190 'Kill the 'ristocrat.' 'Off with his ruffle shirt,' . . . were sounds that rose up above the confused din. **1840** KENNEDY *Quodlibet* 158 If he [a merchant] . . . makes a little fortune, we can call him a . . . Ruffle Shirt. *c*1840 in Buckingham *E. & W. States* II. 117 Mr. Van Buren . . . has nothing in his palace but champagne, . . . and 'prime Havannas;' and these choice things are only dealt out to his

'silk-stocking and ruffle-shirt friends.' **1848** *Knickerb.* XVIII. 520 It was asserted . . . that he wore a ruffle-shirt and overshoes.

+Ruffle-shirter. (See quotation.) *Obs.* — **1842** *Knickerb.* XIX. 305 Many a taunt . . . was thrown at the ruffle-shirters [*i.e.*, upper-class, private-school boys], as the town boys called them.

+Ruffscruff. (See ROUGHSC(R)UFF.)

Rufous, *a.* In the names of birds of a reddish color. Usually in combination with adjectives or past participles. {1782-} — *c*1830 *Waldie's Select Library* II. 86/3 He disturbs a solitary rufous thrush engaged in washing its plumes. **1869** *Amer. Naturalist* III. 75 Rufous-backed Titmouse (*P. rufescens*). I met with this only in the dense forests of the higher Cœur d'Alene Mountains. **1872** COUES *Key to Birds* 140 Rufouscrowned Finch . . . ; crown uniform chestnut. **1884** *Ib.* (ed. 2) 434 *Myiarchus,* . . . Rufous-Tailed Flycatchers. *Ib.* 466 *A*[*mazilia*] *cerviniventris,* . . . Rufous-Bellied Humming-Bird.

***** **Rug.**
   *****1.** A coverlet for a bed. *Obs.*
   1633 *N.H. Prov. Papers* I. 77, In the Great House [are] 3 ruggs and 2 pentadoes. **1685** *Conn. Rec.* I. 377, I will and bequeath to my Cousen Martha Henderson . . . the rug that is on Cousen Steel's beed. **1711** *Essex Inst. Coll.* IV. 186/2 My bed & bolster, two pillows, green rugg, green curtains [etc.]. **1775** FITHIAN *Journal* II. 65 The weather these two days past is . . . so cold that I have slept under a sheet, blanket, coarse rugg, & my own cloaths! **1853** FELT *Customs New Eng.* 54 Rugs . . . as coarse nappy coverlets, for common beds, were used by our primitive families.
   2. A piece of carpeting or a skin used on the floor but not tacked down. {1810-}
   1828 WEBSTER, *Rug,* . . . a coarse nappy woolen cloth used for a bed cover, and in modern times particularly, for covering the carpet before a fire-place. **1882** LATHROP *Echo of Passion* i, She had risen as she spoke, and threw the novel down on the rug. **1884** MATTHEWS & BUNNER *In Partnership* 233, I was sitting just now before the hearth, with my feet in the bearskin rug you sent us two Christmases ago. **1896** JEWETT *Pointed Firs* 10 She stood in the centre of a braided rug.
   +3. (See quotation.) *Obs.*
   1792 BELKNAP *Hist. New-Hampshire* III. 129 There is a natural tough sward commonly called a *rug*, which must either rot or be burned before any cultivation can be made.

*****Rugged,** *a.* **+**Strong, hardy, robust. Also in comb. — **1816** PICKERING 167 Englishmen notice our use of *rugged*, in this sense, as a peculiarity; in expressions of this kind—a rugged, i.e., robust child; rugged health. **1838** *Knickerb.* XII. 199 They were hale, rugged urchins. **1872** HOLMES in *Atlantic Mo.* Dec. 729/2, I ain't quite so rugged as I used to be. **1890** *Harper's Mag.* April 747/2 She is not what you would call a rugged-looking baby.

+Ruinatious, *a.* (See quot. 1871.) *colloq.* — **1845** JUDD *Margaret* 210 The War was very ruinatious to our profession. **1871** DE VERE 629 *Ruinatious,* an enlarged and intensified form of *ruinous*, frequently used in the West and South.

*****Rulable,** *a.* **+**Permissible according to the rules. — **1889** *N.Y. Produce Exch. Rep.* 305 It shall be rulable to reject any . . . packages varying widely in color or quality from the bulk of the lot. **1890** L. C. D'OYLE *Notches* 170 He would take a cigar—not considered exactly fair, perhaps, but 'rulable' (occasionally) according to the standard of the country.

*****Rule.** A strip, usually of wood, marked in feet, inches, etc., and used for measuring. Also comb. — **1718** *Boston Selectmen* 35 One wooden Rule. **1787** *Ky. Gazette* 24 Nov. 2/3 Samuel Blair, Has for sale, . . . augers and two foot rules, very cheap for cash. **1805** *Austin P.* I. (1924) 96, 6 Rules. **1888** *Amer. Almanac* 275 Occupations of the People of the United States. . . . Sawyers, . . . Scale and rule makers. **1907** *St. Nicholas* Sept. 977/2 On the larger one were spread . . . a square, a rule, a pair of dividers and other tools of the draftsman.

*****Ruling elder.** In some religious bodies, as in the Presbyterian church, one chosen to act with the minister in managing church affairs in a parish or congregation. — **1642** LECHFORD *Plain Dealing* 15 Some Churches have no ruling Elders. **1670** ELIOT *Brief Narr.* [2] One of the Indians . . . should have been ordained Ruling-Elder. **1720** D. NEAL *Hist. New-Eng.* I. 21 A Settlement was not so much as thought of, till Mr. John Robinson, and Mr. William Brewster, the former an Independent Minister, the latter a Ruling Elder in the same Church, . . . bravely accomplish'd it. **1858** D. K. BENNETT *Chronology of N.C.* 27 He was during many years a ruling elder in the Presbyterian church. **1892** M. A. JACKSON *Gen. Jackson* 199 He prayed for the ruling elders.

+Rullichie, Rullitie. (See ROLLICHE.)

Rum.
   I. 1. An alcoholic liquor prepared chiefly from molasses or the juice of sugar cane. {1667-}
   The second group of examples illustrates the use of rum in trade with the Indians. (Cf. KILL-DEVIL 1, NEW ENGLAND RUM.)
   (1) **1654** *Conn. Rec.* I. 255 Whatsoeuer Berbados Liquors, commonly caled Rum, Kill Deuill, or the like, shall be landed in any place [etc.]. *c*1700 *Brookhaven Rec.* 5 If any one of ye Trustes after Worning given, Doth not appeare . . . , [he] shall forfit a pinte of Rum. **1734** *Harvard Rec.* I. 143 No Undergraduate shall keep by him Brandy, Rum, or any other distill'd Spirituous Liquors. **1787** [see JULEP]. **1812** *Ann. 12th Congress* 1 Sess. II. 1525 Rum is an article of great importation. **1830** WATSON *Philadelphia* 218 Rum distilled from molasses was once an article largely

manufactured and sold in Philadelphia. **1881** CHASE *Editor's Run in N.M.* 126 Character and rum have no connection. **1914** [see KEG *n.* 1].

(2) **1657** *Mass. Bay Rec.* III. 425 This Court doth . . . prohibite all persons . . . henceforth to sell . . . to any Indian . . . rum, strong waters, [etc.]. **1699** E. WARD *Trip to New-Eng.* 47 The Ground upon which Boston (the Metropolis of New-England) stands, was purchas'd . . . for a Bushel of Wampum-peag and a Bottle of Rum. **1701** WOLLEY *Journal N.Y.* (1902) 38 The Skins of all their Beasts . . . they barter . . . for Rum, Brandy and other strong Liquors. **1766** ROGERS *Ponteach* I. i, I've Rum and Blankets, Wampum, Powder, Bells. **a1772** WOOLMAN *Journal* 188, I perceived that many white people often sell rum to the Indians. **1788** FRANKLIN *Autobiog.* 375 We told them that if they would continue sober during the treaty, we would give them plenty of rum when business was over.

+**b.** Intoxicating liquors in general.

1858 HOLMES *Autocrat* 219 Rum I take to be the name which unwashed moralists apply alike to the product distilled from molasses and the noblest juices of the vineyard.

+**2.** *Rum, Romanism, and Rebellion,* (see quot. 1914).

1885 *Wkly. New Mexican Rev.* 19 March 1/4 Rev. Dr. Burchard, who so suddenly sprang into notoriety through the utterance of the famous alliteration, 'rum, romanism and rebellion,' has been asked by his church council to resign his ministry. **1914** *Cycl. Amer. Govt.* III. 241/1 *Rum, Romanism and Rebellion,* a phrase characterizing the Democratic party, used by Rev. Samuel D. Burchard, spokesman of a delegation of Protestant clergymen, October 30, 1884, in an address in New York City.

II. *attrib.* and *comb.* **3.** Designating places where rum is made, drunk, or sold.

See also RUM HOLE, MILL, SHOP.

1739 W. STEPHENS *Proc. Georgia* I. 291 Our vile Rum-Houses . . . had brought forth a Gang of mature Villains. **1815** *Mass. H. S. Coll.* 2 Ser. IV. 124 A rum distillery was established in 1738. **1843** *Yale Lit. Mag.* VIII. 117 The landlord of this same Wild Goose Hotel had become notoriously infamous as keeping one of the most unconscionable rum shanties in the land. **1880** *Harper's Mag.* Nov. 878/1 And Chesterfield was not exceptionally a rum place.

4. Designating containers for rum.

See also RUM BARREL, RUM JUG.

1771 *Md. Hist. Mag.* XIII. 266 Nimble Came up in a Terrible Condition from his Carrying the Rum Cags. **1779** *York Co., Va., Rec.: Wills* 28 April, 1 mahogany rum case with 2 doz. double flint bottles. **1833** *Niles' Reg.* XLIV. 408/2 Indian corn and meal, rum puncheons, staves and headpieces, hoops for rum and sugar casks, nails for sugar casks [are free of duty]. **1845** *Knickerb.* XXV. 299 [They] refreshed themselves with draughts from their rum-canteens. **1857** *Quinland* I. 281 The former keeper had been suddenly summoned . . . to leave his rum-tubs. **1863** *Boston Herald* 24 May 4/2 (Ernst), Rum-coolers are getting fashionable, if ice does sell at a penny a pound.

5. Designating persons who have to do with rum.

See also RUM-SELLER, RUM-SUCKER 1.

1775 ROMANS *Nat. Hist. Florida* 228 A wine-bibber or rum guzzler . . . can hardly avoid falling a prey to this bad air. **1809** KENDALL *Travels* II. 277 The *rum-carriers*, as they called the traders, found means to elude this. **1813** *Ann. 12th Congress* 2 Sess. 1096 The inspectors of dry goods would be as accommodating to the wants of the Government, as the rum tasters had been. **1855** M. THOMPSON *Doesticks* 272 [The street was] filled with big placards, posters, music, . . . rum-bullies, banners, bonfires, and lager-bier. **1860** GREELEY *Overland Journey* 289 [The Chinaman] is an inveterate gambler, an opium-smoker, a habitual rum-drinker, and a devotee of every sensual vice. **1860** *Harper's Mag.* April 607/1 Jew clothiers, rum-dealers, and gamblers followed the crowds of working-men.

6. In special combinations.

‖*Rum-and-gum*, a beverage made chiefly of rum; +*r. bud*, (see quotation); *r. cistern*, a large receptacle for rum; +*r. grog*, a grog made with rum; +*r. interest*, those interested in the rum traffic as manufacturers or dealers; *r.-pouring*, a ceremonial involving the pouring out of rum; *r. prize*, a captured vessel laden with rum; *r. sour*, a mixed drink consisting of rum, water, and lemon or lime juice; *r. tax*, a tax on rum; *r. trade*, traffic in rum.

1861 NEWELL *Orpheus C. Kerr* I. 212 [The South Carolina gentleman] clears a mighty track of everything that bears the shape of . . . peach-and-honey, irrepressible cocktail, rum-and-gum. **1848** BARTLETT 280 *Rum-Bud*, . . . a redness occasioned by the detestable practice of excessive drinking. Rum-buds usually appear first on the nose. **1889** BRAYLEY *Boston Fire Dept.* 211 Hugh McLaughlin . . . was instantly killed by the bursting of a rum cistern on July 30. **1806** *Balance* V. 142/3 A certain candidate has placed in his account of Loss and Gain. . . . : Loss. 720 rum grogs. **1883** *Century Mag.* Sept. 782/2 Such a righteous restoration of the law to its own place will be claimed . . . by the rum interest as a victory for them. **1880** CABLE *Grandissimes* 240 Once the blacks attempted by certain familiar rum-pourings and nocturnal charm-singing to lift the curse. **1777** in *S. Lit. Messenger* XXVII. 252/2 A small vessel in which Bannister is interested has carried a Rum Prize into N. Carolina. **1865** *Harper's Mag.* Oct. 562/1 Punch got on board . . . next morning in clothes drenched with 'rum-sours' and sea-water. **1830** *Jamestown* (N.Y.) *Jrnl.* 15 Dec. 1/2 The road is mostly macadamized in fine style as all our roads might be were it not for the oppressive operation of the rum taxes. **1859** WILMER *Press Gang* 172 A salutary dread of public opinion . . . may make the journalist a little cautious, in his mode of encouraging and promoting the rum trade.

Rumal. A cotton or silk material with a handkerchief pattern, or a square of this. Also *romal*. {1683–} Also attrib. — **1710** T. BUCKINGHAM *Naval Exped.* (1825) 79, I brought from Hartford . . . 5 handkerchiefs, (three white ones and two Rumals). **1732** *S.C. Gazette* 16 Dec., Coarse Chints, cotton Romalls. **1767** [see BANDANNA 2 b]. **1820** *Columbian Centinel* 1 Jan. 4/2 Apthorp and Parker . . . offer for sale . . . 50 ps. extra fine blue Moomy Choppa Romals. **1904** CHURCHILL *Crossing* 349 He mopped his brow with his blue rumal handkerchief.

Rum barrel. A barrel for rum; a barrel of rum. — **1764** *N.H. Hist. Soc. Coll.* IX. 151, [I] had a new rum barrel of Mr. Webster towards a barrel of cider he had of me. **1765** CROGHAN *Journal* 158 You stoped up the Rum Barrel when we [Indians] came here, 'till the Business of this Meeting was over. **1834** CARRUTHERS *Kentuckian* I. 97 There sat two or three starched lookin dogs on so many old rum bar'ls.

+**Rum cherry.** The wild black cherry (*Padus serotina*), used in making or flavoring rum. — **1836** LINCOLN *Botany* App. 129 *Prunus . . . virginiana*, (wild-cherry, rum-cherry, cabinet-cherry.) . . . In dense forests, it grows to a very great height. **1843** *Knickerb.* XXI. 585 They had been feeding him upon that inebriating article of food, rum-cherries. **1884** SARGENT *Rep. Forests* 68. **1897** SUDWORTH *Arborescent Flora* 245 *Prunus serotina*. Black Cherry. . . . Rum Cherry (N.H., Mass., R.I., Miss., Nebr.).

Rumford. *attrib.* [Sir Benjamin Thompson, Count *Rumford*, American-born physicist (1753–1814).] Designating various devices used in cooking or heating. Also ellipt. for *Rumford kitchen*. — **1811** *Agric. Museum* I. 42 The dinner was principally prepared hot on the ground, by means of a portable Rumford kitchen. . . . The utility of the portable Rumford had not probably been experienced in the field on any previous occasion in New England. **1831** R. COX *Adv. Columbia R.* 301 A bright brass footman . . . was suspended from the shining bars of a Rumford grate. **1845** THOREAU *Journal* I. 388 An annual rent . . . entitles him to the benefit of all the improvements of centuries,—Rumford fireplace, back plastering, Venetian blinds.

+**Rum hole.** A dram shop or groggery of a low type. *slang.* — **1836** *Dialogue betw. Strike & Steady* 5, I once suspected that the keepers of rum holes . . . were at the bottom of the whole. **1857** *Quinland* II. 187 They halted at the door of an old, low, decayed, dirty-looking building, beneath which was an oyster-cellar and 'rum-hole.' **1881** HOWELLS *Modern Instance* xxxvi, But if it was to search the States prisons and the jails, the rum-holes and the gambling-hells, . . . I should have some hopes of identifying him. **1887** ALDEN *Little Fishers* v, I'll hunt out towns where the fellows have just been left to stay in the streets, or else go to the rum-holes.

Rum jug. A jug for rum. — **1843** *Knickerb.* XXII. 34 The *Paroxysm* was in bad condition, full of mud, grass, clams, . . . broken rum-jugs. **1853** *Ib.* XLII. 318 He called an undoubted 'customer' to the stand, a man who would know a rum-jug 'at sight.' **1871** STOWE *Sam Lawson* 13 There, to be sure, sot ol Cack beside a great blazin' fire, with his rum-jug at his elbow.

+**Rummery.** =RUM HOLE. — **1851** *Alta Californian* 16 Aug., So putting off to the nearest rummery, he drowned all his recollections. **1857** *Lawrence* (Kan.) *Republican* 25 June 3 It has been . . . the prevailing sentiment in Quindaro that no rummeries should be allowed to exist here. **1866** 'F. KIRKLAND' *Bk. Anecdotes* 407/1 Two elaborate gentlemen from Philadelphia . . . invited Captain Baggs to take a drink in a neighboring rummery. **1898** *Advance* 12 Nov., His re-election does not prove that the people of the state are going to sell out to the rummeries.

+**Rum mill.** =RUM HOLE. *slang.* (Cf. GIN MILL.) — **c1849** PAIGE *Dow's Sermons* I. 144 Every rum-mill, groggery and tippling-shop . . . is a trap set by the devil to catch those who are guilty of not having over three cents. **1870** KEIM *Sheridan's Troopers* 16 The passengers retired to an adjacent 'rum mill.' **1881** HAYES *New Colorado* 152 The passage . . . from the express-office and the 'rum-mill' to the vice-regal palace and the ancient *pueblo*, is effected so speedily. **1889** BARRÈRE & LELAND I. 238/1 *Charter the bar, charter the grocery, to* (American), to buy all the liquor in a groggery or 'rum-mill' and give it away freely to all comers.

+**Rummy,** *n.* **a.** One who frequents rum shops; a low character; a sot. **b.** (See quot. 1890.) — **1860** EMERSON *Conduct of Life* 57 He led the 'rummies' and radicals in town-meeting with a speech. **1884** 'MARK TWAIN' *H. Finn* xix, I'd ben a-runnin' a little temperance revival thar 'bout a week. . . . I was makin' it mighty warm for the rummies. **1890** C. L. NORTON *Polit. Americanisms* 96 *Rummies*, a local name for the political opponents of the temperance party in Maine. **1894** 'MARK TWAIN' *P. Wilson* xi, Half of the company was composed of rummies and the other half of anti-rummies. **1913** LONDON *Valley of Moon* 59 You'd better tell the rummy to beat it.

+**Rummy,** *a.* Affected by or pertaining to rum. — **1834** *Jamestown* (N.Y.) *Jrnl.* 29 Jan. 1/5 The Massachusetts Masons, . . . like the rummy deacon, who fell from his horse—have merely 'got off to get on better.' **1843** *Amer. Pioneer* II. 372 He departed, muttering curses loud and deep, and in a voice peculiarly *rummy*. **1864** WEBSTER 1156/3 *Rummy*, of or pertaining to, rum; as, a rummy flavor.

Rum omelet(te). An omelet flavored with rum or served with a rum sauce. — **1851** HALL *Manhattaner* 161 It was orthodox to eat rum-omelette with 'pompano'-fish. **1903** [see DOUGH-BIRD].

***Rump.** +**1.** *pl.* (See quotation.) **2.** *attrib.* in *sing.* Designating legislative bodies composed of only a remnant of their membership and hence regarded as without authority. (See also RUMP CONGRESS, RUMP CON-

VENTION.) ‖3. *Rump President*, (see quotation). — (1) 1842 BYRDSALL *Hist. Loco-foco Party* 178 Hence the Equal Rights Party became divided within itself; the majority for union called the opposing minority Rumps, and the latter called the majority Buffaloes. (2) 1897 *Boston Jrnl.* 16 Jan. 7/3 The 'rump' house in Del. met today. *Ib.*, It was learned today that the 'rump' Senate has also been meeting regularly. *Ib.*, A full 'rump' Legislature is therefore in existence. (3) 1866 *Ore. State Jrnl.* 15 Sept. 3/2 A 'Rump President.'—It would seem, according to his theory, that [Johnson] . . . is not the President of the United States, but only of the States that voted for him.

+Rump Congress. {Rump Parliament, 1670–}

1. The Congress of the Reconstruction period, which excluded members elected by the states of the Southern Confederacy. Now hist.

1867 LOCKE *Swingin' Round* 136 Clear out the rump congress. 1868 *N.Y. Tribune* 8 July 3/1 [A Democratic government] will be a strong enough 'Government' then to take care of the carpet-bag gentry and the military machinery by which they may have swindled themselves into the Rump Congress. 1877 BEARD *K. K. K. Sketches* 17 There was no logical plan supporting that system of political manœuvres set in motion by the 'Rump Congress.'

‖**2.** The last Congress that met under the Articles of Confederation.

1889 *Century Mag.* April 803/2 It was indeed a Rump Congress.

+Rump convention. A nominating convention composed of a minority or remnant of a party. — 1872 *Newton Kansan* 31 Oct. 3/2 Delegates to the rump convention of W. B. Chamberlin openly charged him with packing the convention. 1903 *N.Y. Times* 28 Aug., The Bryan following will walk out after having made their protest. Then will come a rump convention.

Rum punch. An alcoholic beverage of which rum is the principal ingredient. {1737–} — 1701 WOLLEY *Journal N.Y.* (1902) 42 Their quaffing liquors are Rum-Punch and Brandy-punch. 1758 *Lett. to Washington* II. 398 To 40, Gallons of Rum Punch. 1847 *Santa Fe Republican* 13 Nov. 3/1 All kinds of Liquors, Hot Whiskey Punch, Tom & Jerry, Rum Punch, Refreshments, oyster suppers, Sardines [etc.]. 1891 *Cycl. Temperance* 288/2 The sickness among the people is owing to the excessive drinking of rum punch.

Rum-seller. One who sells rum. {1828–} — 1781 *Md. Hist. Mag.* V. 125 [We took in] seven passengers, who were sutlers or rum-sellers to Gen. Washington's army. 1853 *S. Lit. Messenger* XIX. 602/2 He didn't look to me like a rum-seller. 1872 TALMAGE *Abominations* 204 Let our citizens . . . take off their hats to the rum-seller. 1900 *Congress. Rec.* 25 Jan. 1200/2 A rumseller is as bad as a polygamist.

Rum-selling. The business of selling rum. — 1738 W. STEPHENS *Proc. Georgia* I. 91 The People here will not yet easily think Rum-selling a Crime. 1859 WILMER *Press Gang* 227 Being engaged in the lucrative business of rum-selling, this wretch could afford to disburse a little money. 1869 J. H. BROWNE *Great Metropolis* 474 Dirt and over-crowding, and rum-selling, and prostitution, and wretchedness in every form, are fit neighbors for pawnbrokers' shops.

+Rum shop. A shop where rum is sold; a saloon. Also transf. — 1738 W. STEPHENS *Proc. Georgia* I. 122 Those Rum-Shops were become as common among the People, in Proportion, as Gin-Shops formerly at London. 1863 *Boston Herald* 2 Aug. 2/5 They are just fit to stay in this city, vegetate in the back slums, read the News and Express, bum round rum-shops. 1898 WISTER *Lin McLean* 130 The act-drop fell, and male Denver, wrung to its religious deeps, went out to the rum-shop. 1921 PAINE *Comr. Rolling Ocean* 140 Bless my soul, what sort of a condemned rumshop have I stumbled into?

+Rum sling. Sling made with rum as the chief ingredient. (Cf. GIN SLING.) — 1827 *Mass. Spy* 25 July (Th.), It vas not a rum sling; no, nor a gin sling; no, nor a mint vater sling. 1845 *Big Bear Ark.* 43 Curse that rum sling—there was too much sugar in it.

+Rum-sucker. 1. A confirmed rum-drinker; a toper. *slang.* **2.** A variety of moss. — (1) 1858 *N.Y. Tribune* 9 July (B.), The stock . . . run after [salt] with an acquired appetite as strong as that of a rum-sucker. 1866 GREGG *Life in Army* 153 The surgeon that will advise you to this course, is likely to be a rum-sucker himself. 1888 *Voice* 10 May, If rum-suckers kill fool Prohibitionists we consent. (2) 1892 *Amer. Folk-Lore* V. 105 *Polytrichum commune*, rum-suckers. Stratham, N.H.

Rum toddy. A toddy made of rum. {1820–} — [1771 in *New Eng. Mag.* ns. XII. 348/2 We drank some New England rum-toddy.] a1841 HAWES *Sporting Scenes* II. 76 A hot rum-toddy might be swallowed with additional benefit. 1865 *Atlantic Mo.* April 511/1 Their master had the happy eccentricity of getting more amiable with every rum-toddy. 1878 COOKE in *Harper's Mag.* Sept. 575/1 He loved to . . . take a hot 'nip' of rum toddy.

*Run, *n.*

*1. A small stream; a branch, brook, or channel, or the low land through which it runs: (see also quot. 1908).

'Chiefly *U.S.* and *north. dial.*' (O.E.D.).

1605 ROSIER *True Relation* (1887) 134 Searching vp in the Iland, we saw it [a pond] fed with a strong run. 1649 *Warwick* (R.I.) *Rec.* 83 Jo Cook is granted yt pece of land . . . down to ye Rune by Jon Lipets. 1663 in *Amer. Speech* XV. 386/2 Thence over a small run or Bottom and a ridge. 1703 *Providence Rec.* V. 179 The said ffifty acres of land . . . is at

the head of a Run of Water which Runneth through Timothy Sheldon his land. 1770 WASHINGTON *Diaries* I. 442 There is no body's of Flat rich Land to be found—till one gets far enough from the River to head the little runs and drains. 1837 W. JENKINS *Ohio Gaz.* 122 Clarksburg, a post town . . . situated on the west bank of Hay run, a branch of Deer creek. 1908 G. H. PALMER *Life A. F. Palmer* 277 With us [in New England] that which runs swiftly a part of the year, and shows a dry bed for the remainder we fittingly call a run.

2. A measure of yarn: (see quot. 1875). {1878}

1734 *Conn. Rec.* VII. 512 There shall also be paid . . . for every yard that is . . . made of yarn that is eight runs to the pound, two shillings per yard. 1842 *Amer. Pioneer* I. 146 In 1790, twenty-nine families in Northfork, Connecticut, raised and spun twelve hundred runs of silk. 1875 TEMPLE & SHELDON *Hist. Northfield, Mass.* 161 Spinning was commonly done by the run. A run of yarn consisted of twenty knots, a knot was composed of forty threads, and a thread was seventy-four inches in length, or once round the reel. 1891 COOKE *Huckleberries* 144 The wool was carded, spun, washed, and put into the dye-tub, one 'run' of yarn that night.

+3. An upper and a lower millstone operating as a unit. Also collect.

1798 *Smithtown Rec.* 351 The grist mill house . . . [will] carry three run of stones with three Bolting mills. 1815 *Niles' Reg.* IX. 187/1 The whole expence in generating steam sufficient to drive two run of stones upon this principle will not exceed two hundred and twenty dollars. 1847 HOWE *Hist. Coll. Ohio* 157 The stream at present furnishes power for twenty two runs of stone. 1853 *Mich. Agric. Soc. Trans.* IV. 157 The power required to drive a machine is something less than the power required for one run of mill-stone. 1885 GRANT *Pers. Memoirs* I. 493 Every plantation . . . had a run of stones propelled by mule power, to grind corn for the owners and their slaves.

4. *Mining.* **a.** A continuous vein of metallic ore or coal. {1747–}

1807 *Steele P.* II. 505 We had not observed a very glowing description of certain gold runs, or mines, which have been discovered in North Carolina. 1857 *Harper's Mag.* Sept. 459/1 The leases of the operators usually covered a 'run' upon the out-crop, or strike of the vein, of from fifty to seventy yards. 1882 *47th Congress 1 Sess.* H. R. Ex. Doc. No. 216, 471 The common run is regarded as satisfactory in quality, but rich chimneys are reported as existing.

+b. = MILL RUN *n.*

1852 WHITMORE *Diary* 16 Oct., Tended stamps. Made a very good runn this week. 1871 *Republican Rev.* 17 June 2/3 They are now making a run of nine days. 1876 RAYMOND *8th Rep. Mines* 212 A run of this ore made in November yielded at the rate of $80 per ton. 1882 *47th Congress 1 Sess.* H. R. Ex. Doc. No. 216, 450 A small run was made by the McLaughlin & Cassell mill, at Central.

c. (See quotations.)

1864 WEBSTER 1157/3 *Run,* . . . the horizontal distance to which a drift may be carried. 1881 RAYMOND *Mining Gloss., Run,* certain accidents to the winding apparatus.

5. The migration of a shoal of fish ascending a river to spawn; a shoal of fish. {1820–}

1832 WILLIAMSON *Maine* I. 54 The run of salmon and shad, both in Androscoggin and Kennebec, is almost at an end. 1870 *Rep. Comm. Agric. 1869* 600 There is usually a fall run of salmon, but the fish are not so good as the spring run. 1881 *Amer. Naturalist* XV. 178 The great majority of the quinnet salmon and nearly all the blue-back salmon enter the rivers in the spring. The run of both begins generally the last of March. 1914 STEELE *Storm* 67 This little man . . . was worth ten in a run of fish or a gale of wind.

+6. *Baseball.* The completion by a player of a circuit of the bases under prescribed conditions of play; a score. {1746–, in cricket}

See also HOME RUN and cf. ACE.

1868 CHADWICK *Base Ball* 45 A run is scored the moment the player touches the home base without being put out, or without his being obliged to return to the base he left. 1885 *Santa Fé Wkly. New Mexican* 10 Sept. 4/3 The Browns made one run owing to Otero's fumble and wild throw to first base. 1910 *Spalding's Base Ball Guide* 131 Off Summers, 3 hits, 4 runs in 5 at bats in 1–3 inning.

+7. A platform or a similar place for the loading and unloading of wagons.

1870 *Huntington Rec.* III. 585 The said land . . . [is] sufficient . . . to build two runs, so called, or three runs . . . to load brick at. 1920 COOPER *Under Big Top* 226 Many a man [is saved] from injury at the unloading runs.

+8. The amount of sap that flows when sugar maples are tapped; the amount of maple sugar made at a particular time.

1890–3 TABER *Stowe Notes* 40 The early runs are not so sweet as the later. 1896 *Vt. Agric. Rep.* XV. 33 Car loads of the last run of the Vermont maple orchards are sent to these cities each year. 1898 N. E. JONES *Squirrel Hunters of Ohio* 21 A 'run' of sugar-water was not dependent upon a special act of Congress.

+9. *Football.* The action of running on the part of a player who is advancing the ball.

Cf. RUNNER 12.

1893 STAGG & WILLIAMS *Amer. Football* 43 In defending his territory against these runs the end stands at the most remote part of the field for assistance to help him.

+10. *W.* A stampede by a herd of cattle.

1903 A. ADAMS *Log of Cowboy* 38 We may never have a run the entire trip.

+11. (See quotation.)

1912 G. M. HYDE *Newspaper Reporting* 29 [The reporter] is ordinarily put on a *beat*, or *run*; this is simply a daily route or round of news sources which he follows as regularly as a policeman walks his beat.

12. In phrases. **+a.** *To get the run upon*, (see quotation).

1848 BARTLETT 280 'To get the run upon one,' is to make a butt of him; turn him into ridicule.

+b. *To keep* (or *lose*) *the run of*, to keep (or fail to keep) in touch with or informed about.

1862 MAURY in Corbin *Life M.F. Maury* 212, I shall . . . very much wish to keep the run of public sentiment. **1873** 'MARK TWAIN' & WARNER *Gilded Age* 32 That child has . . . kep' the run of the med'cin, and the times of giving it. **1876** 'MARK TWAIN' *Tom Sawyer* 21, I wish to geeminy she'd stick to one or t'other—I can't keep the run of 'em. **1893** — *£1,000,000 Bank-Note* 29 You couldn't afford to lose the run of business and be no end of time getting the hang of things again when you got back home. **1893** 'THANET' *Stories* 145, I've been in this block, Mrs. Carleton and me, ever since it was built; and, some way, between us we've managed to keep the run of all the folks in it. **1918** LINCOLN *Shavings* 320 I kind of lost run of the time.

* Run, *v.*

I. In transitive senses. **+1.** To survey, mark out, or establish (a line or bounds).

(1) **1641** *R.I. Col. Rec.* I. 114 Mr. Porter . . . and Mr. Jeoffreys shall run the line between the Touns. **1680** *Conn. Rec.* III. 50 [It is necessary that the divideing line between this colony and the colony of the Massachusetts . . . be run and marked out. **1707** M. MINOR *Diary* (1915) 103 I run a line with W Denison. **1745** HEMPSTEAD *Diary* 443, I was out to Mr. Tabers Sawmill farm to run Lines & measure 12 acres of Land. **1798** *Ann. 5th Congress* I. 677 They spoke on the subject of running the line between the United States and the Indians. **1802** ELLICOTT *Journal* 203 The chiefs gave a strong talk against running the line.

(2) **1660** *Essex Inst. Coll.* XXXVII. 229 Mr. John Gardener . . . [is] desired . . . to Run the bounds betwixt Bostone, Charlstown and Lynn . . . by a merridian Compass. [**1671** *Conn. Rec.* II. 152 This Court appoynts Lut Thomas Munson to runn the depth of the bownds of Brandford and Guilford to the northwards.] **1711** HEMPSTEAD *Diary* 2, I Ran ye Bounds. **1714** SEWALL *Diary* III. 22 Went to the Salt works and Run the Bounds.

+b. To lay off or plow out (rows or furrows).

1851 *Fla. Plantation Rec.* 348, 3 [slaves] Runing Roes for Cain. **1873** *Maine Bd. Agric. Rep.* XVIII. 126 The rows want to be run straight. **1885** 'CRADDOCK' *Prophet* 3 It might be marveled that so many furrows were already run.

2. To mold (bullets or shot). {1690–, in general sense}

1748 J. NORTON *Redeemed Captive* 5 The Serjeant ordered . . . another to run some Shot, having Shot-Moulds. **1780** *Narragansett Hist. Reg.* I. 99 Went to Godfrey's to run shot. **1807** *Ann. 10th Congress* 1 Sess. 420 Some of the men were engaged in running bullets. **1852** ELLET *Pioneer Women* 227 She was often occupied during the whole day or night in running bullets.

b. To obtain (tar) by the distillation of wood.

1856 SIMMS *Charlemont* 368 Don't you smell tar?—They're running it now!

c. To mold (candles).

1884 JEWETT *Country Doctor* 10 Be they the last you run?

+3. To bring forward or support as a candidate for office. {1862–}

1792 HAMILTON *Works* VIII. 286 To be run in this quarter as Vice-President. **1892** *Courier-Journal* 3 Oct. 4/4 The Democrats are running candidates in every district in the state.

+4. To navigate (a stream or difficult parts of a stream) in a canoe or other boat. {1892–}

1805 LEWIS in *L. & Clark Exped.* III. (1905) 23 There were five shoals neither of which could be passed with loaded canoes nor even run with empty ones. **1839** [see DALLE]. **1864** NICHOLS *Amer. Life* I. 172 Many of these bends may be avoided at high water, by taking the cross cuts, called 'running a *chute*,' when the whole country for twenty miles on each side is submerged. **1875** 'MARK TWAIN' *Old Times* ii. 37 Each of our pilots ran such portions of the river as he had run when coming up-stream. **1895** REMINGTON *Pony Tracks* 131 We were about to start on a cruise down a river which the lumbermen said could not be 'run,' as it was shallow and rocky.

+b. To go up or down (a stream) in fishing.

1879 *Scribner's Mo.* Nov. 20/2 In running a grayling stream, the feeling is one of peace and quietude.

+c. To pass up and down (a river) while employed on a steamboat.

1901 CHURCHILL *Crisis* 7, I thought I'd made a mistake to let him run the river. *Ib.* 296 He owns two slaves now who are running the river.

+5. To manage, carry on, boss (a business, enterprise, etc.). {1891–}

The first quotation may not belong under this sense.

1827 *Mass. Spy* 3 Oct. (Th.), Running a Bank. **1864** *Daily Telegraph* (London) 23 Dec. 5/5 'To run' is a . . . modern American locution. You may 'run' anything—a railroad, a bank, a school, a newspaper. **1885** HARTE *Maruja* 90 It is said that he offered to 'run' the distant estate of Joaquin Padilla from his little office amidst the grain of San Antonio. **1902** HARBEN *A. Daniel* 215 My cousin . . . was runnin' the restaurant under the car-shed. **1920** LEWIS *Main Street* 386 Sister Bogart about half runs his church.

+b. Used with reference to political domination or management.

1872 *Newton Kansan* 31 Oct. 3/2 This man aspires to run Harvey county by such trickery. **1882** *Nation* 28 Sept. 256/1 The decision . . . was in the hands of the politicians who 'fix' and 'run' primaries. **1886** ROOSEVELT in *Century Mag.* Nov. 74/1 The men who take part in and control, or, as they would themselves say, 'run' [political machines], . . . are familiarly known as machine politicians. **1905** STEFFENS in *McClure's Mag.* Feb. 339/2 The good people took the bribes and let the best people run the government.

+c. To control, direct, or guide (a person).

1888 BRYCE *American Commw.* I. i. ix. 115 It is often said of the President that he is ruled, or as the Americans express it, 'run,' by his secretary. **1890** S. HALE *Letters* 242 Cornelia is running me, and she is really just the right sort.

+d. *Agric.* To operate or have in operation (a plow); to cultivate (a crop).

1839 in Bassett *Plantation Overseer* 117, I have got my cotton land the half of it cleaned up and is running four plows. **1866** *Rep. Indian Affairs* 136 The Navajoes . . . were running forty-seven ploughs. **1879** TOURGEE *Fool's Errand* 84 No nigger shant be allowed to . . . run no crop on his own account herearter.

+e. *Stock exchange.* To carry on (a deal) or secure (a corner) involving some commodity.

1875 *Chicago Tribune* 2 July 7/3 Sturges was running a corner. **1887** *Courier-Journal* 3 May 4/7 There was considerable talk . . . that a deal in wheat is being run here and that a corner will soon develop. **1888** *Economist* 27 Oct. 7/3 He has worked upon the fear of the short interest that a corner might be run.

+f. To operate (a game of chance).

1885 *Santa Fé Wkly. New Mexican* 10 Sept. 4/4 They ran games at Houston until the town became unpleasant, and then came to Las Vegas. **1903** A. ADAMS *Log of Cowboy* 260 Every gambling house ran from two to three monte layouts.

+6. To chase and shoot (buffalo) on horseback.

1833 CATLIN *Indians* I. 219 On this journey we saw immense herds of buffaloes; and although we had no horses to *run* them, we successfully *approached* them on foot. **1848** PARKMAN in *Knickerb.* XXXII. 507 The chief difficulty in running buffalo . . . is that of loading the gun or pistol at full gallop. **1889** *Nat. Museum Rep. 1886–7* 470 Next to the still-hunt the method called 'running buffalo' was the most fatal to the race, and the one most universally practiced. **1900** DRANNAN *Plains & Mts.* 300, I met about thirty Kiowa Indians going out to run the buffalo near there.

+7. To tease or josh. *colloq.* {1888, in Austral.}

1835 HONE *Diary* I. 134 This is a club . . . where they sup, drink champagne and whiskey punch, talk as well as they know how, and run each other good-humouredly. **1860** HOLLAND *Miss Gilbert* 349 Now what's the use of running a feller?

+8. To entice (a Negro slave) *off* or away from his master; to steal.

1853 SIMMS *Sword & Distaff* (1854) 13 It strikes me that we might run the negroes without committing you. **1855** — *Forayers* 368 Your negroes might be run this very night. **1864** SALA in *Daily Telegraph* 23 Aug., The negroes his agents have bought in North Carolina, or 'run off,' i.e. stolen, in Kentucky. **1882** HARTE *Flip* 20 He's down on tramps ever since they run off his chickens.

+9. = DRIVE *v.* 6.

Cf. LOG-RUNNING.

1840 *Jamestown* (N.Y.) *Jrnl.* 26 Feb. 2/3 The streams are lined with lumber, ready at the proper season, to be run to market. **1864** *Mich. Laws* 23 Such corporation shall have a lien upon the logs, timber, or other floatables, driven, boomed, rafted, or run. **1896** *Monthly Weather Rev.* Nov. 407 The driving of piles in the Mississippi River . . . to hold a 'sheer boom' for the purpose of running the logs.

+10. To slip by without paying (something); to evade.

1867 'LACKLAND' *Homespun* 68 My conscience will never fully acquit me . . . of the guilt of having *run* that toll of a penny on many an occasion.

+11. To meet the needs of or be sufficient for, to support (a person or group).

1871 'Mark Twain' *Sk., New & Old* 95, I had . . . unsalable turnips enough to run the family for two years! **1904** Harben *Georgians* 207 Don't bother. I have enough cash to run me. **1909** Wason *Happy Hawkins* 280 She was in the habit of estimatin' just how little nourishment it would take to run her to the next feed.

+12. To examine (a net) for fish.

1880 *Harper's Mag.* May 855/2 The boatman . . . turns directly back and 'runs the net'—passing the cork line through the hands. *Ib.* 856/1 The net is 'run' twice or three times and is then taken up.

+13. To publish (an advertisement or story) in a newspaper.

1884 Nye *Baled Hay* 202 He wouldn't run any of his ads. **1912** G. M. Hyde *Newspaper Reporting* 30 [If] the editor decides not to print the story, he *kills* it; otherwise he *runs* it.

+14. (See quot. 1894.) Also transf.

1894 *McClure's Mag.* July 101/2 [The brand] is simply drawn, or 'run' upon the hide, using a long, sharp-pointed, hot iron rod for a pencil; and those so made are called 'running brands.' **1897** Lewis *Wolfville* 179 'That's straight,' says Dave Tutt, 'you-alls can't run no brand on melodies.'

II. In intransitive senses. **15.** Of fish: To pass to or from the sea; to migrate. {1887–, in n. Pacific}

1743 Catesby *Carolina* II. p. xxxiii, Herrings in March leave the salt waters, and run up the rivers. **1806** Lewis in *L. & Clark Exped.* IV. (1905) 95 These women informed us that the small fish began to run which we suppose to be herring from their discription. **1881** *Amer. Naturalist* XV. 178 Of these species, the quinnat and blue-back salmon habitually 'run' in the spring, the others in the fall. *a***1884** in Goode, etc. *Fisheries* I. 376 [Kingfish] occasionally run to a considerable distance up the rivers. **1888** *Forest & Stream* 3 May 291/3 Do the late running fish always run late? **1902** White *Conjuror's House* 81 At this season the game was poor, and the fish hardly yet running with regularity.

+16. To float down a stream. Used especially of ice.

1805 Clark in *Lewis & C. Exped.* II. (1904) 8 The drift wood beginning to run. **1807** Gass *Journal* 61 The weather became very cold, and the ice began to run in the river. **1865** *Atlantic Mo.* Jan. 42/2 Between these two periods the ice never ceased running. **1867** Richardson *Beyond Miss.* 145, I found the ice running so heavily, that it was impossible to cross. **1884** Roe *Nature's Story* (1902) 192 Don't go out again when the ice is running.

+17. To be a candidate for a political office.

1844 M. C. Houstoun *Texas* (1845) 216 At the present moment there are several persons who are about to 'run' as they call it, for the Presidency. **1851** Quitman in Claiborne *Life Quitman* II. 147 A majority of the people have declared against the course of policy . . . upon which alone I had consented to run as a candidate. **1873** *Newton Kansan* 15 May 1/6 Joseph Medill was asked if he would run again for Mayor of Chicago. **1891** O'Beirne *Leaders Ind. Territory* 118/1 Mr. Perry ran for Representative in the Push-ma-la-ta district. **1910** C. Harris *Eve's Husband* 148 There was less excuse for his running on the liquor ticket. **1912** Nicholson *Hoosier Chron.* 54, I'd go into their counties and spend every cent I've got fighting 'em if they ever ran for office again.

+18. To serve as a runner or tout *for* a boarding house. Cf. Runner 5 b.

1891 C. Roberts *Adrift Amer.* 228, I went with him to the house he was running for.

III. In phrases with nouns.

(See also Blockade *n.* 1 b, Face *n.* 1 b, Gauntlet.)

+19. *To run (the) bases*, to make the circuit of the bases in baseball. Cf. Base-runner, Base-running.

1845 in *Appletons' Ann. Cycl.* XXV. 77/2 A player, running the bases, shall be out if the ball is in the hands of an adversary or on the base, or the runner is touched by it before he makes his base. **1868** Chadwick *Base Ball* 43 The moment the striker has hit a fair ball he ceases to be 'the striker' and becomes 'a player running the bases.' **1907** *St. Nicholas* June 693/2 'Yes,' laughed Chub, 'we run bases.'

+20. *To run into the ground*, (see quot. 1859). *colloq.*

1836 *Quarter Race Ky.* (1846) 16 It's no use to run the thing into the ground. **1847** Field *Drama in Pokerville* 122 Mr. Wimple couldn't advise, really, the season was so completely 'run into the ground.' **1859** Bartlett 374 *To Run into the Ground*, to carry to excess, to overdo a thing, and thereby mar it. Probably a hunter's phrase, to express the earthing of a fox or other game. **1884** Gronlund *Coöp. Commonwealth* 74 After having run this Social 'Order' into the ground, it will be supplanted by a new principle.

+21. *To run a saw on* (someone or something), to make (someone or something) the object of jesting or ridicule. Also *to run it on*.

*a***1846** *Quarter Race Ky.* 68 'Running a Saw' on a French Gentleman. By 'Ginsangandson,' of Philadelphia. **1851** Hall *Manhattaner* 169 The

'Picayune' had always joked at classes, or run the saw on 'genera.' **1899** C. King *Trooper Galahad* 110 The members of the troop . . . thought to 'run it' on the 'doughboy' captain.

22. In less common phrases with nouns.

To run (one's) *board*, to leave without paying for one's board; *to r. the cards*, to tell one's fortune by means of cards; *to r. the guard*, to pass a guard or sentinel without leave; *to r. haunts*, to chase a ghost; *to r.* (one's) *luck*, to trust to luck; *to r. meat*, to pursue buffalo on horseback (*Obs.*); *to r. post*, to act as courier.

1897 Howells *Open-eyed Conspiracy* vii, It will be quite enough for the hotel-keeper if they run their board. I shall have to pay for it. **1884** Harris in *Century Mag.* Nov. 122, I'll run the cards and see what they say. **1848** *Santa Fe Republican* 2 April 1/2 Patrick Duffy . . . was shot recently while attempting to 'run the guard' with two other soldiers. **1900** *Congress. Rec.* 11 Jan. 784/2 When the dogs would rush in there was not a thing up there [in the tree], and the darkies would immediately say 'Let's go home; that dog was running haunts.' **1877** Campion *On Frontier* 7 We determined to 'run our luck' and 'play our own hand.' **1850** Garrard *Wah-To-Yah* i. 15 The next time you run meat, don't let the horse go in a trot and yourself in a gallop. **1848** Bryant *California* xxii. 281 Besides keeping the Indians in subjection, they [*sc.* pickets] run post with a monthly correspondence.

IV. 23. In phrases with prepositions.

To run around, +to plow by passing on both sides of the drill; *to r. for,* ‖to depend upon; +*to r. on,* (see quotation); *to r. over,* +to treat unfairly or slightingly; *to r. round,* +in surveying, to traverse the bounds of (a piece of land); *to r. through,* +to cultivate lightly and rapidly; *to r. upon,* 'to quizz, to make a butt of' (B.).

1851 *Fla. Plantation Rec.* 373 Ploughs Runing around cotton and splitting cotton middles. **1841** Longfellow in S. Longfellow *H. W. Longfellow* I. 391, I have to run for luck as to horses, which is not so agreeable. **1841** Webster 514/2 *To run on,* . . . to press with jokes or ridicule; to abuse with sarcasms; to bear hard on. **1836** *Quarter Race Ky.* 23, I would not advise any man to try to run over me. **1748** Washington *Diaries* I. 5 We set out early with Intent to Run round ye sd. Land. **1853** T. D. Price *Diary* (MS.) 6 July, Finished running through the corn. **1852** *Knickerb.* XXXIX. 403 It takes a long while for some men to learn to take it coolly when they are run upon.

V. In phrases with adverbs. **24.** *To run off* {1683–}, +to turn out on a typewriter.

1901 Merwin & Webster *Calumet 'K'* 106 Now, we'll write to Mr. Brown—no . . . ; I'll do that one myself. You might run off the other and I'll sign it.

***25.** *To run on to* {1847–}, +to run across.

1902 Wister *Virginian* ii, Meet a man once and you're sure to run on to him again.

***26.** *To run out.* +**a.** To survey or ascertain the bounds of tracts, areas, etc.

1671 *S.C. Hist. Soc. Coll.* V. 298 Another Surveyor . . . doth proffer to run out all parcells of land above 500 Akers at a Penny per Acre. **1742** *Georgia Col. Rec.* VI. 22 Thomas Ellis [appeared] in behalf of Mr. Tho: Salter in order to Obtain Directions from this Board touchg his Running out a Tract of 500 Acres of Land. **1798** [see Military *a.*]. **1842** *Amer. Pioneer* I. 379 A young man . . . made known his desire to have a district to run out. **1873** T. D. Price *Diary* (MS.) 5 Sept., Appraisers and viewers with surveyor run out piece of land. **1905** Cole *Early Oregon* 28 When school closed I assisted them in running out their land claims.

b. (1) Of land: To lose fertility; to become exhausted.

1838 Haliburton *Clockmaker* 2 Ser. iv. 60 The land gets run out in his hands, and is no good for ever after. **1857** *Lawrence* (Kan.) *Republican* 4 June 2 Any land which does not occasionally receive a deposit of organic-decayed vegetable-matter . . . [will] finally run out.

(2) Of plants: To degenerate, to lose vigor.

1838 *Mass. Agric. Survey 1st Rep.* 128 The herds-grass and red top, entirely run out by the second and third years after sowing. **1864** *Maine Agric. Soc. Returns 1863* 91 Some thought the potatoe had 'run out,' had lost its original vigor. **1878** Killebrew *Tenn. Grasses* 98 English Rye Grass . . . is said to impoverish land rapidly and will run out in a few years.

(3) Of a breed of persons or animals: To degenerate or decline in character or virtue.

1863 *Rep. Comm. Agric. 1862* 48 We often hear the complaint that the breed [of swine] has 'run out.' **1867** Lowell *My Study Windows* 97 The New England breed is running out, we are told!

+c. Baseball. tr. (See quot. 1867.)

1867 Chadwick *Base Ball Reference* 139 A player is 'run out,' when he is caught between two bases and is put out by one or other of the fielders. **1885** — *Art of Pitching* 140 The fielders run an opponent out when they touch him while he is half way, or nearly so, between the bases.

d. (1) To drive out (grass); to take the place of.

1872 *Vermont Bd. Agric. Rep.* I. 281 Some farmers have thought that it [*sc.* oxeye daisy] runs out [timothy]. **1873** *Ib.* II. 190 One objection often urged against cutting grass early and taking two crops a year . . . [is] 'It runs the grass out.' **1878** *Ill. Dept. Agric. Trans.* XIV. 295 Kentucky blue grass was best adapted for a good dairy farm; it would run out all other grasses.

(2) To vanquish (a competitor); to force (someone) to leave or run away.

1877 WANAMAKER in Appel *Biog. Wanamaker* (1930) 87 Dry Goods people . . . would spend fabulous sums 'to run John Wanamaker out.' **1885** *Wkly. New Mexican Rev.* 19 March 4/2 James Masterson . . . was run out of the county. **1890** *Lippincott's Mag.* March 312 Old Jim Blazer . . . ran two men out of the regiment. **1890** HARTE *Heritage of Dedlow Marsh* 191 It's only a question of my being *run out* of 'Frisco. **1924** CROY *R. F. D. No. 3* 189 He's got to be run out.

+e. To yield or produce.

1876 RAYMOND *8th Rep. Mines* 19 The Sunderland, with a furnace of 15 tons of daily capacity, ran out 1,500 flasks last year.

* 27. *To run over*, + (see quotations).

1857 *Hoyle's Games* (Amer. ed.) 288 Run Over.—Should you wish to bet more or 'bluff' off your adversary. **1864** DICK *Amer. Hoyle* (1866) 173 If bets are not limited, he [the player] can bet or 'run over' as much as he pleases.

* 28. *To run up*, + (see quotation).

1891 *Cent.* 5271/3 To run up, . . . to execute by hanging: as, they dragged the wretch to a tree and ran him up. (Western U.S.)

*Runabout. +A light, open-topped vehicle, as a buggy; a light automobile of a roadster type. {1902- } — **1891** *Cent.* 5272/3. **1899** ADE *Fables in Slang* 155 He took her riding in his new Runabout every Evening. **1903** [see BROUGHAM]. **1911** FERBER *Dawn O'Hara* 54 Dr. Briggs's patient runabout will be standing at his office doorway. **1922** PARRISH *Case & the Girl* 119 Where was it the three of you went on Sunday in the runabout, Captain West?

+Run-around. A felon or whitlow. *colloq.* (Cf. RUNROUND 2.) — **1872** TALMAGE *Sermons* 224 Some hypochondriac with a 'run-around' or a 'hang-nail.' **1913** LONDON *Valley of Moon* 352 His finger was hurting too much, he said. . . . 'It might be a run-around,' Saxon hazarded.

*Runaway.

* 1. One who runs away from servitude or deserts a master.

1637 R. WILLIAMS *Letters* (1874) 67 There are all the Runaways harbored. **1676** *Conn. Rec.* II. 276 Lnt. Joseph Orton is by this Court appoynted . . . to grant warrants in ciuill actions . . . [for] stopping of runn awayes. **1711** *Boston News-Letter* 17 Dec. 2/2 A Carolina Indian Woman . . . [was] taken up as a Runaway. **1803** *Lit. Mag.* (Phila.) Oct. 68 The negro fellow advertised in the late papers as a runaway. **1865** *Atlantic Mo.* April 505/2 Nobody in the town twitted him as a runaway.

attrib. **1643** *Va. Statutes at Large* I. 253 If any such runnaway servants or hired freemen shall produce a certificate [etc.]. **1682** *Plymouth Laws* 195 Such Indians whither such a runaway Indian is come shall forthwith give notice of the said Runaway to the Indian Constable. **1739** *Md. Hist. Mag.* XVIII. 18 It seems to be an account against James Gibbons for 2 years runaway time and charges of taking him.

+2. The action of a horse or team that bolts or dashes away out of control.

1850 GARRARD *Wah-To-Yah* xxi. 258 Three of the muleteams made handsome runaways. **1868** *Ore. State Jrnl.* 31 Oct. 3/1 Colonel Henderson had a runaway on Thursday. **1898** *Kansas City Star* 18 Dec. 1/5 Miss Agnes Peterson was hurt in a runaway caused by the driver of an express wagon.

‖3. = RUNWAY 1.

1891 *Fur, Fin, & Feather* March 182/1 To one who has sat all day on a Herkimer county (New York) runaway without seeing anything, the deer would seem to be 'pretty tolable plenty.'

Runaway Negro. A Negro slave escaped from bondage. *Obs.* Also attrib. — **1699** *N.C. Col. Rec.* I. 514 A particular law . . . injoyns all persons on a penalty to apprehend runaway Negroes. **1776** LEACOCK *Fall Brit. Tyranny* IV. iii, What? do you accuse his worship of turning kidnapper, and harbouring run-away negroes? **1784** SMYTH *Tour* II. 102 Run-away Negroes have resided in these places for twelve, twenty, or thirty years and upwards. **1884** HARRIS *Mingo* 197 What would be done with us if people found out we had been harbouring a runaway negro? **1894** 'MARK TWAIN' *P. Wilson* xviii, I 'uz pass'n' by one o' dem places in Fourth Street whah deh sticks up runaway-nigger bills.

Runaway slave. A slave escaped from bondage. *Obs.* — **1811** SUTCLIFF *Travels* (1815) 76 Whenever he saw a Negro, whom he judged to be a runaway slave, he would . . . jump from his work-board. **1833** *Niles' Reg.* XLIV. 183/1 An important trial was recently held . . . in which were involved some interesting questions touching runaway slaves. **1852** STOWE *Key* 67/1 She causes a reward to be offered for the recovery of a runaway slave, 'dead or alive.' **1880** CABLE *Grandissimes* 12 Runaway slaves were not so rare.

*Rundlet. = next. — **1636** WINTHROP in R. C. Winthrop *Life J. Winthrop* II. 151 There is in one of them a rundlet of honey, which she desires may be sent to her against she lie down. **1757** HEMPSTEAD *Diary* 687, I sent Adam over to Stonington to carry a Rundlet of Tarrwater for Joshua &c. **1841** *Lowell Offering* I. 225 Abigail, . . . taking out a large rundlet, which might contain two or three gallons, poured the contents into a couple of pails. **1895** M. A. Jackson *Gen. Jackson* 523 He commended to my own use a rundlet of cognac.

*Runlet. A small cask or keg. Also comb. (See also prec.) — **1633** *N.H. Prov. Papers* I. 77, 1 runlett with bone ashes and crucibles. **1708** *Essex Inst. Coll.* I. 172/2 The same sloop took . . . twelve three gallond

and twelve four gallond Runlits. **1845** HOOPER *Simon Suggs' Adv.* 72 They come from the runaway Seminole and the runlet-making Cherokee! **1866** *Harper's Mag.* March 544/2 One day an old farmer left in his store . . . an eight-gallon keg, called in those days a '*runlet*.'

*Runnel. A small stream of water; a brooklet or rill. — **1640** *Boston Rec.* 57 The lands of Mr. Rich . . . [are] limitted by fences and marsh towards the norewest, with a winter runnell and pouder horn Creeke. **1656** *Braintree Rec.* 7 This way was layed out into the common . . . straight from the runnill of water in the county highway. **1851** A. CARY *Clovernook* 272, I have seen them [*sc.* girls] sitting . . . on the slope of a hill, washed at the base by a runnel of silvery water. **1867** 'LACKLAND' *Homespun* 109 That stick . . . helped her across the moist places and glistening little runnels. **1910** J. HART *Vigilante Girl* 233 'Do you see anything to frighten her?' . . . 'Nothing unless it is that little runnel of dust-covered water there.'

*Runner.

I. ‖1. (See quotation.)

1709 LAWSON *Carolina* 162 Runners . . . have Holes in the Sand-Beaches and are a whitish sort of a Crab.

+2. An Indian courier or bearer of messages.

See also INDIAN RUNNER.

1753 WASHINGTON *Diaries* I. 46, [I] desired him to send for the Half-King; which he promised to do by a runner in the Morning. **1792** in Putnam *Memoirs* 266 It may be necessary for you to conciliate some chiefs by money and also to obtain runners. **1826** COOPER *Last of Mohicans* ii, Yon Indian is a 'runner' of the army. **1896** *Harper's Mag.* April 709/2 Thanks to the efforts . . . of the runners from the allied tribes of the lower lakes, the Chippewas and all the tribes of the upper lakes had taken the tomahawk.

+3. A black snake.

1795 in S. Williams *Nat. Hist. Vt.* (ed. 2) I. App. 485 In a field in Connecticut, . . . I approached with caution within twenty feet of a black snake, about seven feet long, having a white throat, and of the kind which the people there call runners or choking snakes. **1855** SIMMS *Forayers* 549 We got glimpse of a few runners (black-snakes), but they were quite too swift of foot for the hunters.

+4. In the names of fishes: **a.** The blackfish or tautog, *Tautoga onitis.* **b.** An amber fish, *Elagatis bipinnulatus.* **c.** = HARDTAIL.

(a) **1814** MITCHILL *Fishes N.Y.* 399 Tide black-fish or runners. The name of this fish is derived from the colour of its back and sides. (b) **1884** GOODE, etc. *Fisheries* I. 332 This West Indian fish, known at Key West as 'Skipjack' or 'Runner,' . . . usually moves in small schools of a dozen or two individuals. **1897** *N.Y. Forest, Fish, & Game Comm. 2d Rep.* 238 *Elagatis bipinnulatus.* . . . Runner. . . . This tropical species has once before been recorded from Long Island. (c) **1896** JORDAN & EVERMANN *Check-List Fishes* 346 *Caranx crysos.* . . . Hard-tail; Runner; Jurel; Yellow Mackerel. . . . Cape Cod to Brazil.

+5. One who solicits support or patronage. {1899}

1824 *Microscope* (Albany) 21 Feb. (Th.), Our wholesale property-speculators and their gentry in livery, called runners. **1847** ROBB *Squatter Life* 101 A steamboat runner came to their aid. . . . 'Passage up the Missouri, sir?' inquires the runner. **1855** *Chicago Times* 19 March 3/2 William Rodge, a runner for passengers, was fined $5 by His Honor yesterday for practising his profession without a license. **1872** *Chicago Tribune* 19 Oct. 6/1 For the purpose of inducing as many as possible to be transferred by his buses, Mr. Parmalee employs agents or runners. **1883** *Harper's Mag.* Nov. 814/1 The runners for several livery-stables offered to provide special transportation.

+b. *spec.* One who endeavors to procure patronage for a boarding house or hotel.

Cf. RUN *v.* 18.

1840 DANA *Two Years* xxxvi. 459 The decks were filled with . . . landlords and boarding-house runners. **1852** *Knickerb.* XL. 279 Albany caps the climax in respect of 'runners' for hotels, steamers, and luggage. **1879** B. F. TAYLOR *Summer Savory* 87 The House of Hanover . . . may designate a hemlock tavern in the West, where a tempestuous runner shouts 'All aboard for the Hanover House!' **1898** CAHAN *Imported Bridegroom* 164 a burly shaven-faced 'runner' of an immigrant hotel . . . sprang to their rescue.

+6. A prisoner allowed to act as messenger and to perform other offices about a prison.

1833 T. HAMILTON *Men & Manners* I. 176 [At the Boston prison] there is, however, a class of men, consisting of ten or twelve, called *runners* and *lumpers,* whose duty consists in moving about the yard. **1912** DREISER *Financier* 679 Some of the prisoners, after long service were used to 'trusties' or 'runners,' as they were locally called; but not many.

+7. One who pursues buffalo on horseback.

Cf. RUN *v.* 6.

1837 IRVING *Bonneville* II. 180 The 'runners,' mounted on the fleetest horses, were full tilt after the buffalo.

+8. = BASE-RUNNER.

1845 in *Appletons' Ann. Cycl.* XXV. 77/2 A player, running the bases, shall be out . . . if the runner is touched by it [the ball] before he makes his base. **1885** [see FORCE-OFF]. **1888** *Cosmopolitan* Oct. 450/2 He rushed down toward third base to coach one of his runners home. **1910** *Spalding's*

Base Ball Guide 346 If by accident . . . a thrown ball hits the umpire, on fair ground, the runner must return to his base. **1917** [see FAIR *a*. 2 b].

+9. One who accompanies a fire engine to a fire either as a fireman or as a hanger-on.

1881 *Harper's Mag.* Feb. 372/1 The boys . . . [were] not members of the companies but only 'runners' with the engines.

+10. (See quot. 1881.)

1881 INGERSOLL *Oyster-Industry* 247 *Runner.*—Vessels engaged in transporting oysters from the grounds to the market; they also buy the stock they carry. (Chesapeake.) **1891** *Cent.* 5274/1.

+11. The driver or engineer of a locomotive. {1889}

'Chiefly *U.S.*' (O.E.D.).

1874 FORNEY *Catechism of Locomotive* 547 Every locomotive runner should . . . have an exact knowledge of the engine intrusted to him. **1901** *Munsey's Mag.* XXV. 749/1 A new express locomotive . . . glided up to the platform under the hand of . . . one of the most experienced runners on the road.

+12. *Football.* A player who runs with the ball.

Cf. RUN *n*. 9.

1893 CAMP *College Sports* 121 A runner was placed behind the heavier mass, a pretending, or 'fake,' runner nearer the middle, and a man at the ball to put it in play. **1893** STAGG & WILLIAMS *Amer. Football* 43 The end-rusher has to meet the runner under most trying circumstances.

+13. One who directs or carries on a business.

Cf. RUN *v*. 5.

1893 M. HOLLEY *Samantha at World's Fair* 4 His parents . . . [were] good respectable . . . people . . . and runners of a cheese factory.

II. 14. One of the two long pieces of wood or metal upon which a sled or sleigh slides. {1837-}

1762 *Boston News-Letter* 7 Jan. 3/3 Wanted, a pair of good runners. **1802** *Mass. Spy* 24 March (Th.), A lad . . . was suddenly pitched off before one of the runners. *a*1862 THOREAU *Maine Woods* 196 Runners . . . are used only in the winter, when the snow is several feet deep. **1907** *St. Nicholas* Aug. 906/2 There, at Will's feet, stood the beautiful sled, so long, and low, and slender upon its shining runners.

+b. A heavy timber or structure serving as a temporary supporting track or way for a heavy object that is being moved. {1833}

1815 *Niles' Reg.* IX. 201/2 [We] moved the one-half of the arch off sideways, forty-six feet, on to the runners one hundred and eighty-five feet long. **1871** *Scribner's Mag.* Nov. 46 (O.E.D.), The barn or house was pried up, and great runners, cut in the woods, placed under it, and under the runners were placed skids. **1881** *Harper's Mag.* Jan. 195/2 We ran our engine on runners—simple runners made of planking.

+c. A skate, or a blade of a skate. {1893}

1860 WORCESTER 1348/1 *Skate,* . . . a sort of shoe . . . furnished with an iron runner, used to slide or travel on the ice. **1876** KNIGHT 2192/2 In an in-door sport suggested by skating, the sole has rollers instead of a runner. **1887** [see CLUB SKATES].

+Runner bird. = ROAD RUNNER. — **1885** *Santa Fé Wkly New Mexican* 17 Sept. 4/2 One of the greatest enemies of snakes in Arizona is the runner bird.

Runnet. = RUNNEL. {1601-} *Obs.* — **1644** *Providence Rec.* II. 3 Daniell Abbot hath sould . . . one other share of medow the north part next the riuer and runit. **1664** *Rowley Rec.* 152 [To] Robert Hesseltine . . . one acre . . . bounded by a small Runet of water on the west. **1704** *Providence Rec.* V. 184 The land . . . was bounded . . . farther Norwest by a small Walnut tree Neare a small Runnett Comeing downe the hill.

∗ Running, *n.*

+1. The surveying or marking out of a boundary line.

Cf. RUN *v*. 1.

1662 *Dedham Rec.* IV. 47 Ensigne Daniell Fisher and Edward Richards were mutually chosin . . . to setle and determine the runinge of the Devision line. **1706** *Providence Rec.* XI. 105 The reunning of the devideing line betweene the lands of Providence & ye lands of Pautuxett. **1715** *Mass. H. Rep. Jrnl.* I. 4 A Committee [is ordered] to prepare the Draught of a Vote, to bring forward, the Running of the Line between this Province and the Colony of Rhode-Island. **1797** *Ann. 5th Congress* I. 305 The running and marking of the boundary line, between the colonies of East and West Florida, and the territory of the United States, have been delayed by the officers of His Catholic Majesty.

2. The sap that has exuded from a pine. {1753}

1832 BROWNE *Sylva* 232 The scraping is a coating of sap . . . which is taken off in the fall and added to the last runnings.

+3. A scolding. *colloq.*

1832 S. SMITH *Life J. Downing* 158, I feel a little put out with Dr Burnham for an unhansome running he gave me 'tother day.

+4. (See quot. 1849.)

Cf. RUN *v*. 6.

1839 TOWNSEND *Narrative* 158 They have listened to the garrulous hunter's details of 'approaching,' and 'running,' and 'quartering.' **1849** PARKMAN *Oregon Trail* 91n., The method of hunting called 'running,' consists in attacking the buffalo on horseback and shooting him with bullets or arrows when at full speed.

+5. The act of standing as a candidate for office.

Cf. RUN *v*. 17.

1870 *Nation* XI. 1 He has never failed in getting such offices as he wanted, the record of his 'running' being about as good as that of any man in the country.

+6. = DRIVING *n*. 4.

Cf. RUN *v*. 9.

1880 *Michigan Rep.* XXXVIII. 603 Kelsey was to manage the logging in the woods and running of the logs to the mill.

7. Attrib. (passing into adj.) in special combinations.

Running account, a cursory, rapid account with few details; *r.-horse man,* one who raises and trains horses for running in races; *r. plate,* a light steel horseshoe used on race horses; *r. shot,* a shot at running game; *r. slough, r. story,* (see quotations); *r. switch,* on a railroad, a flying switch; *r. turf,* horse racing as a sport or business: (see quotation); *r. walk,* (see quotation).

1912 G. M. HYDE *Newspaper Reporting* 224 The second part, the running account, corresponds to the running account of the game as it will be taken up with the long football story. **1868** WOODRUFF *Trotting Horse* 65 It may be well enough for him to approach . . . the forcing method of the running-horsemen. **1877** CAMPION *On Frontier* 18 The shoes [were] taken off our horses and replaced by 'running plates.' **1886** ROOSEVELT in *Outing* May 134 He makes an unusually large percentage of misses on running shots. **1875** *Amer. Naturalist* IX. 387 Sometimes these ponds [in the river bottoms in Ill.] unite, retain a permanent connection with the stream and, at low water, flow towards it with a slow current, forming what are called 'running sloughs.' **1907** GIVEN *Making a Newspaper* 202 Any report which grows as the day advances is called a 'running story.' **1887** GEORGE *40 Yrs. on Rail* 34 When we took a car out we had to push it by hand and shove it on a side-track by a running switch. **1868** WOODRUFF *Trotting Horse* 134 There is not another instance in the annals of either the running or the trotting turf. **1893** G. W. CURTIS *Horses, Cattle* 60 The running walk—more commonly known as the 'single-foot'—is by odds the most elegant saddle gait.

∗ Running, *a.*

1. Of cash, money, etc.: In use or available for use. {running cash, 1679-}

1691 C. MATHER in *Mass. Bay Currency Tracts* 17 Is there not hereby 40,000 l Running Cash in the Country more than ever was. **1705** *Boston News-Letter* 12 March 1/2 The present running Coins within this Province are so debased & impaired by Rounding and Clipping [etc.]. **1768** *Baltimore Rec.* 39 Mr. Alexander Lawson . . . demanded the sum of 200 £ running Money. **1769** *Md. Hist. Mag.* X. 134 Ordered, That Mr Jacques pay to Nathaniel Watkins the sum of £3 running Cur[renc]y. **1862** *Rep. Comm. Patents 1861: Agric.* 112 A much less amount of *running capital* is required than for cotton factories.

∗ 2. Of plants: Creeping; climbing; sending out runners. Usually in specific names.

1840 DEWEY *Mass. Flowering Plants* 67 L[espedeza] *procumbens.* Running Bush Clover. . . . Blossoms in August. **1843** TORREY *Flora N.Y.* I. 111 *Malva rotundifolia.* Dwarf Mallow. Running Mallow. . . . Often a troublesome weed in gardens. **1847** DARLINGTON *Weeds & Plants* 127 R[ubus] *Canadensis.* . . . Canadian Rubus. Dewberry. Running Brier. **1865** *Maine Bd. Agric. Rep.* X. 60 The running juniper he had grubbed up root and branch, which was not a work of much labor if entered into with determination. **1887** *Harper's Mag.* Jan. 308/2, I usually raise my running squashes among the corn. **1889** VASEY *Agric. Grasses* 83 *Trifolium stoloniferum* (Running Buffalo Clover) . . . is found in rich open woodlands, and in prairies in Ohio, Illinois, Kentucky, and westward. **1894** *Amer. Folk-Lore* VII. 93 *Chiogenes serpyllifolia,* running birch, Vt. **1898** E. C. HALL *Aunt Jane* 266 In the middle of the garden stood a 'summerhouse,' or arbor, whose crumbling timbers were knit together by interlacing branches of honeysuckle and running roses.

+Running blackberry. The swamp blackberry (*Rubus hispidus*), or a related species. (Cf. DEWBERRY, LOW BLACKBERRY, LOW-BUSH BLACKBERRY.) — **1814** [see LOW BLACKBERRY]. **1832** WILLIAMSON *Maine* I. 114 Of the Bramble kind we have . . . the upright and running Blackberry, or Dewberry. **1919** STURTEVANT *Notes on Edible Plants* 507 R[ubus] *hispidus.* Running Blackberry. Swamp Blackberry.

Running block. (See quot. 1889 and cf. BLOCK *n*. 5.) — **1876** KNIGHT 2004/1. **1885** *Century Mag.* Aug. 506/2 The running-block, caught to the gunwale with a snap-spring, . . . keeps the sail flat and holds it well. **1889** *Cent.* 590/1 A running block is attached to the object to be raised or moved; a standing block is fixed to some permanent support. **1901** MERWIN & WEBSTER *Calumet 'K'* 99 Max, you get a light rope and a running block, and hang a hook on it.

+Running board.

1. (See quots. 1834, 1843). *Obs.*

1817 *Essex Inst. Coll.* VIII. 240 [We] were obliged to give it up after being at the expense of putting on running boards, and hiring two men to pole her up. **1834** BRACKENRIDGE *Recollections* 37 One night . . . [I lay] on the running board (a plank at the edge of the boat, on which the men walk in pushing with the pole). **1843** *Amer. Pioneer* II. 271 Keel-boats . . . were provided with running boards, extending from bow to stern, on each side of the boat. . . . The crew, divided equally on each side, set their poles near the head of the boat, and bringing the end of the pole to their shoulders, with their bodies bent, walked slowly down the running board to the stern.

2. A board or narrow platform along the side of a locomotive, street car, automobile, etc.

1864 WEBSTER 1158/1 *Running board*, a narrow platform extending along the side of a locomotive. **1874** FORNEY *Catechism of Locomotive* 337 The *running-boards* are planks . . . placed on each side of the boiler to enable the locomotive runner or fireman to go from the cab to the front end of the engine when it is running. **1903** *Elect. World & Engineer* 14 Nov. 795/2 The 'mule' has two large hooks for the towropes and has also a running board and guard hand rail. **1917** MATHEWSON *Second Base Sloan* 284 The cars that buzzed and clanged their way past Wayne were filled to the running-boards. **1923** WATTS *L. Nichols* 235 She sat down on the running-board of the car.

+**Running brand.** *W.* An iron rod, usually curved at the end, for running brands on cattle; a brand made with such an iron. (Cf. RUN *v.* 14.) — **1883** SWEET & KNOX *Through Texas* 160 The other, called a running brand, is a long piece of iron curved at the end. **1894** [see RUN *v.* 14].

+**Running business.** (See quot. 1849.) *Obs.* — **1809** KENDALL *Travels* III. 296 On the Province Point . . . I was taught to expect to find a store inhabited, and in the bustle of the *running* business. **1849** AUDUBON *Western Jrnl.* 53 Matamoras contains many Mexicans who do both a wholesale and retail 'running business,' that is, smuggling.

+**Running catch.** *Baseball.* (See quot. 1868.) — **1858** *Chadwick Scrapbook* (E. J. Nichols). **1868** CHADWICK *Base Ball* 45 A running catch is made when the ball is caught on the fly while the fielder is on the run. **1885** — *Art of Pitching* 140 Running Catch.—These catches are among the prettiest a fielder can make.

+**Running exercise.** An impelling desire to run, engendered by emotional excitement aroused at revivalistic religious services. *Obs.* (Cf. FALLING, JUMPING EXERCISE, etc.) — **1834** *Biblical Repertory* VI. 350 The running exercise was also one of the varieties, in which the person was impelled to run with amazing swiftness. *c*1843 B. W. STONE *Biography* (1847) 41 The running exercise was nothing more than, that persons feeling something of these bodily agitations, through fear, attempted to run away. **1847** HOWE *Hist. Coll. Ohio* 46 'Bodily exercises' . . . have been classified by a clerical writer as 1st, the *Falling* exercise; 2d, the *Jerking* exercise; 3d, the *Rolling* exercise; 4th, the *Running* exercise.

Running expenses. Ordinary daily expenses. — **1876** *Vermont Bd. Agric. Rep.* III. 307 Most of us farmers need the avails of all our surplus produce, to pay our running or current expenses. **1883** *Century Mag.* Oct. 808/1 Another $4000 does not more than meet its running expenses. **1889** MUNROE *Golden Days* 26 [Pay] all running expenses out of it.

+**Running gear.**

1. The moving or working parts, as wheels, pulleys, etc., of a mill, cotton gin, or the like.

1662 *East-Hampton Rec.* I. 201 Mr Backer shall have seven pounds for this yeare for tendinge the mill and maintayninge the running geares that is coggs and rounds. **1688** *Essex Inst. Coll.* XXXV. 214 John Hale & John Emery . . . [are] To make all the running Geers [of the mill] as water wheele Cog wheele & Trundle head. **1725** *New-Eng. Courant* 18–25 Jan. 2/2 The Wind . . . carry'd off the Top of the Mill, with the Shaft, Vanes, and running Geer, and brake them to Pieces. **1834** in Bassett *Plantation Overseer* 73 The cogs was all wayes a workinge out and the runinge geares that is hear I cant under take to pick a crop with them. **1901** MERWIN & WEBSTER *Calumet 'K'* 262 'Where is he now, Max?' 'Down in the cellar putting in the running gear for the 'cross-the-house conveyors.'

2. *Naut.* The ropes or chains used to work or set sails, yards, etc.

1838 COOPER *Homeward B.* xx, The standing rigging are the bones and gristle; the running gear the veins in which her life circulates. **1856** KANE *Arctic Explor.* II. 48 We can burn hemp and cast-off running-gear.

3. (See quot. 1876.)

1857 STROTHER *Virginia* 230 A shadowy group was dimly visible, a carriage mounted on the running-gear of a wagon, and drawn by four horses. **1876** KNIGHT 2004/1 *Running-gear*, . . . the entire portion of the vehicle below the bed or body. Specifically, the wheels, axles, perch (if any), hounds, bolsters, and tongue. **1888** J. J. WEBB *Adventures* 300 The wagons were a curiosity. The running gear and bodies (were) so dilapidated that repair seemed impossible. **1904** PRINGLE *Rice Planter* 132, [I] told him to take the body off of the little wagon, leaving only the running-gear.

Running horse. **1.** A race horse. {1608-} +**2.** *W.* A horse used for riding on hunts, scouting expeditions, etc., as distinguished from a pack animal. — **(1)** **1771** *Md. Hist. Mag.* XIV. 127 Half the shed [is] to Contain two stalls for Running Horses. **1800** *Steele P.* I. 185 Please to send me out his pedigree and the Certificate of his performances as a runing Horse. **1892** *Courier-Journal* 3 Oct. 8/3 Senator Fair's son Charles . . . has invested heavily in running horses with a view to a turf campaign next year. **(2)** **1837** IRVING *Bonneville* II. 183 Some of the men, throwing themselves upon the 'running horses' kept for hunting, galloped off to reconnoitre. **1846** WEBB *Altowan* I. 191 They had hoped to find the baggage-animals and the running-horses.

+**Running iron.** *W.* An iron rod used for making a running brand (q.v.). — **1894** *McClure's Mag.* July 101/2 The running-irons, or *guachos*, . . . are now considered bad form by progressive cattlemen. **1897** HOUGH *Story of Cowboy* 115 With the handy 'running iron,' or straight rod, . . . could not the cow thief erase a former brand and put over it one of his

own? **1907** WHITE *Arizona Nights* 317 That vehicle . . . transported such articles as . . . the running irons for branding.

+**Running mate. 1.** A horse that serves as a pacemaker for another or that works with another. **2.** *Politics.* A candidate running on the same ticket with another, but for a subordinate office. Often used of a candidate for vice president. — **(1)** **1868** WOODRUFF *Trotting Horse* 284 He has been . . . especially great for his knack at going with a running-mate. **1890** *Stock Grower & Farmer* 29 March 7/1 Dandy had a running mate that was just as different from him as could be. **(2)** **1902** WHITLOCK *13th District* 61 There were . . . pictures of the candidate himself, . . . and pictures, too, of his 'running mate,' the candidate for vice-president. **1905** F. A. MATHEWS *B. Duane* 157 You're a fit running mate fer the President of the United States. **1912** *N.Y. Ev. Post* 4 July 1/5 (Th. S.), Gov. Wilson said to-day: 'Gov. Marshall bears the highest reputation . . . , and I feel honored by having him as a running mate.'

+**Running oak.** A species of small shrubby oak found on the coast from North Carolina to Florida. — **1810** MICHAUX *Arbres* I. 24. **1832** BROWNE *Sylva* 287 Like the upland willow oak, it is confined to the maritime parts of the Carolinas, Georgia and the Floridas, where it is called Running Oak. **1897** SUDWORTH *Arborescent Flora* 164 The following shrubby species occurs on the coast from North Carolina to Florida: . . . *Quercus sericea.* Running Oak.

Running order. In a machine or something likened to a machine, a state, condition, or arrangement in which operation is feasible. — **1827** SHERWOOD *Gaz. Georgia* 152 Soon, say in summer of 1831, much will be in running order. **1850** KINGSLEY *Diary* 112 Got up steam again today and tried the larboard engine and have got both in running order. **1873** *Mich. Gen. Statutes* I. (1882) 829 Every corporation owning a road in use shall . . . draw over the same the merchandise and cars of any other corporation . . . : Provided, such cars are of the proper gauge, are in good running order, and properly loaded. **1897** BRODHEAD *Bound in Shallows* 13 When things were finally in running order and the Nashville steamers had a landing and a freight-house, . . . the hotel had ceased being fine and imposing.

Running race. A race in which horses run, as distinguished from one in which they trot or pace. — **1868** WOODRUFF *Trotting Horse* 66 The running-race for two-year-olds is commonly but a short dash. **1874** B. F. TAYLOR *World on Wheels* 75 The writer knew a young man—not so young as he was—who happened to be in New York when the great running-race between Fashion and Peytona occurred on the Union Course, Long Island.

+**Running season. 1.** The season at which buffalo travel from one grazing region to another. **2.** The rutting season for deer. — **(1)** **1833** CATLIN *Indians* I. 249 The 'running season,' which is in August and September, is the time when they congregate into such masses in some places, as literally to blacken the prairies for miles together. **1851** M. REID *Scalp Hunters* iv, 21 It was now the 'running season,' but none of the great droves had crossed us. **(2)** **1868** *Amer. Naturalist* II. 471 Then begins the running season, when bucks grow careless, or fearless, or both.

+**Running swamp blackberry.** (See quots. 1843, 1857.) — **1843** TORREY *Flora N.Y.* I. 217 *Rubus hispidus.* Running Swamp Blackberry. . . . Swamps and wet woods; sometimes in rather dry, but shady situations. **1857** GRAY *Botany* 121 *R[ubus] hispidus.* (Running Swamp-Blackberry.) . . . Fruit of a few large grains, red or purple, sour. **1889** *Cent.* 571/3.

+**Running time. 1.** =RUNNING SEASON 1. **2.** =RUNNING SEASON 2. **3.** The time usually devoted to a certain activity; schedule time. — **(1)** **1806** CLARK in *Lewis & C. Exped.* V. (1905) 294 It is now running time with those animals. **(2)** **1890** L. C. D'OYLE *Notches* 60 The loud, shrill, snorting whistle peculiar to the buck in 'running' time. **(3)** **1911** HARRISON *Queed* 143 Queed . . . pulled into supper only three minutes behind running-time.

Running track. A track on which contests in running are held. — **1883** *Harper's Mag.* Oct. 416/2 The running track, commonly used for trotting as well, has . . . seen some notable achievements. **1907** *St. Nicholas* June 694/1 'And a new running track,' added Dick.

Runny, *a.* Having a tendency toward excessive softness or fluidity. {*dial.*} — **1817** *Niles' Reg.* XII. 165/2 This flour would prove similar to a previous baking of new flour (which was *runny*). **1913** STRATTON-PORTER *Laddie* vii, He slid in a whole plateful of bread, another of cake. . . . Then we took some of every thing that wasn't too runny.

Run-off. {1894-}

+**1.** *Railroad.* An instance of running off or leaving the rails by a locomotive or car.

1855 *Chicago W. Times* 9 Aug. 1/8 The frequency of these run-offs demands the special attention of all railroad directors. **1872** HUNTINGTON *Road-Master's Asst.* 87 It is best always to keep spare [switch] rods on hand, to be used in case of a run-off.

+**2.** The amount of water that runs off a particular area during a rain or from a stream or spring. Also attrib.

1893 *Rep. Geol. Survey 1892–3* 149 The run-off, that is, the quantity of water flowing from the land. *Ib.* 150 For comparison with this run-off map a similar map showing the mean annual precipitation is introduced. **1895** J. W. POWELL *Physiographic Processes* 6 The mean run-off by streams is more than half the run-off. **1897** *N.Y. Forest, Fish, & Game Comm. 2d Rep.* 504 In the growing period . . . the run-off is only a very small per cent. of the total rainfall. **1911** QUICK *Yellowstone Nights* 244 The spring itself . . . dribbled out a mighty small amount of run-off.

Run-out. [from RUN *v.* 26 c.] *Baseball.* +An instance of running a player out. *Obs.* — **1868** CHADWICK *Base Ball* 66 We give the first letters of fly, tip, run out, and home run. **1877** *Nat. League Constitution & Rules* 41 An assist should be given to each player who handles the ball in a run-out or other play of this kind.

+**Runround. 1.** A side channel in a river which comes back into the stream. **2.** =RUN-AROUND. *colloq.* — **(1) 1848** THOREAU *Maine Woods* 51 The frequent 'run-rounds' which come into the river again, would embarrass an inexperienced voyager. **(2) 1857** *Knickerb.* XLIX. 97 There comes us [*sic*] a 'run-round' on the end of our pen-finger. **1879** WEBSTER *Suppl.* 1577/3 *Run-round,* . . . a felon or whitlow. (*Vulg. U.S.*)

Run side. The side or bank of a run. — **1655** in *Amer. Speech* XV. 387/1 Beginning at Mr. Knipes corner by the run side. **1709** LAWSON *Carolina* 31 This Night we lay by a Run-side, where I found a fine yellow Earth. **1736** FRANKLIN *Poor Richard's Almanac 1737* 3 It is most luxuriant near to Run Sides, if the Soil be rich, and not too moist. **1835** BIRD *Hawks* I. 264 Have you sat in his flower-garden? have you walked on his path by the Run-side?

+**Runtee.** [Of obscure origin; perhaps from Amer. Indian.] 'A circular piece of flat shell drilled edgeways and probably strung and originally used as an ornament' (Hodge). Now hist. — **1705** BEVERLEY *Virginia* III. 59 They also make Runtees of the same Shell, and grind them as smooth as Peak. **1883** *Bureau Amer. Ethnol. 2d Rep.* 229 There is quite a close resemblance between these objects [beads] and the 'runtees' of the early writers.

Runty, *a.* Small, undersized, ill-made. {1834–} '*U.S.* and *dial.*' (*O.E.D.*). — **1807** IRVING, etc. *Salmagundi* vi, Jeremy and his two sisters . . . are a trio of as odd, runty, mummy-looking originals as ever Hogarth fancied. **1846** *Knickerb.* XXVII. 42 What then is the Sack Degenerate? As its name implies, it is emphatically a 'runty' scion of the parent Sack Proper. **1886** PAGE in *Harper's Mag.* Oct. 696/1 A few hens . . . , a brood of half-grown chickens . . . , and a runty pig tied to a 'stob,' were the only signs of thrift. **1909** RICKERT *Beggar in Heart* 332 There is a resemblance . . . [to] the Earl. . . . That little, runty, half-baked, half-peeled codling!

+**Runway.**
'Chiefly *U.S.*' (*O.E.D.*).
1. A path, track, or way customarily followed by animals.
1839 HOFFMAN *Wild Scenes* 63 [The deer] kept swimming along the shore, close under the steep bank, looking up at it every now and then, as if in search of a 'runway.' **1875** BURROUGHS *Winter Sunshine* 73 Though a very lively creature at night, with regular courses and runways through the wood, [the hare] is entirely quiet by day. **1890** *Harper's Mag.* Oct. 651/2 The man stationed was a mile apart on what he said were the paths, or 'runways,' the deer would take. **1902** HULBERT *Forest Neighbors* 85 The Canada lynx came down the runway that follows the high bank. **1923** COOK *On Old Frontier* 70, I concealed myself . . . about one hundred yards from the mouth of the runway through which the horses would go to get a drink.
b. The underground passageway used by a mole; the way or course run by a fish.
1870 WARNER *Summer in Garden* vii, 60 The mole . . . had rooted up the ground like a pig. I found his run-ways. **1894** *Outing* XXIV. 453/1 After a minute's rest, to let him settle in his runway, I made a cast.
c. A place in which fowls may run.
1871 LEWIS *Poultry Book* 8 The hennery should be placed in a warm, dry location . . . with runways ample to allow of plenty of exercise. **1913** LONDON *Valley of Moon* 459 A goodly portion was devoted to whitewashed henhouses and wired runways wherein hundreds of chickens were to be seen.
2. An artificial track or open way serving as a gangway or road.
1883 HOWE *Country Town* (1926) 36 Pushing this into my wagon with the assistance of his wife, after we had first made a runway of boards, I hauled him to Fairview. **1888** *Scribner's Mag.* Oct. 444/2 If there is a 'runway,' which is an elevation like the rocky ascent in the second act of 'Die Walküre,' . . . it is 'built' by the stage-carpenters. **1901** MERWIN & WEBSTER *Calumet 'K'* 104 Gangs of laborers . . . [were] piling them [*sc.* planks] on 'dollies,' to be pushed along the plank runways to the hoist. **1902** LORIMER *Lett. Merchant* 25 Those steers just naturally follow along on up that runway and into the killing pens. **1904** *N.Y. Sun* 9 Aug. 1 The women became hysterical and stampeded for the wagon runway in the middle of the [ferry]boat.
b. (See quotation.)
1905 *Forestry Bureau Bul.* No. 61, 39 *Gutter road,* The path followed in skidding logs. . . . [Also called] runway.
3. The bed or channel of a stream.
1874 B. F. TAYLOR *World on Wheels* 250 Like the dusty 'run-ways' of thy brooks, soft pulses have grown dry and dumb. **1879** WEBSTER 1577/3.

+**Rural (free) delivery.** A branch of the government postal service operating in rural sections. Also attrib. — **1892** *Congress. Rec.* 28 May 4815/1 [Mr. Watson of Ga.] is perfectly consistent in advocating a rural free delivery system which would mount carriers on horseback and send them to every habitation in the land to deliver and collect the mails. **1893** CUSHING *Story of P.O.* 1006 A very important effect of the rural free delivery has been to increase the pay of postmasters where it has been tried. **1900** *Congress. Rec.* 16 Jan. 873/1 You talk about the Postmaster-General acting without authority by going further in expenditure in rural delivery than he ought to. *Ib.*, The rural free delivery service has come to stay. **1912** NICHOLSON *Hoosier Chron.* 605 Rural free delivery wagons [were] throwing off magazines and newspapers.

Rural school. =COUNTRY SCHOOL. Also attrib. — **1884** *Bureau of Educ. Bul.* No. 6, 11 The rural schools of our country provide elementary instruction for more than one-half of our school population. **1897** *Rep. Committee of 12* (N.E.A.) 61 Rural schools suffer from lack of trained teachers. In them, as a general thing, are young graduates from the village high school, or some favorite among neighborhood families. **1918** *Ala. Dept. Educ. Bul.* No. 56, 49 The teachers of rural schools in the United States drift from place to place more than do the members of any other profession. **1920** *3d Nat. Country Life Conf. Proc.* 134 In countless communities the rural-school grounds consist of but a stingy half-acre. **1925** *Rural School Leaflet* (Bureau of Educ.) No. 37, 2 Higher institutions of learning are now offering courses to administrators and supervisors of rural schools as well as to teachers.

* **Rush,** *n.*¹
* **1.** Any one of various plants of the genus *Juncus,* or of allied genera.
In many quotations, it is impossible to distinguish the genus or species referred to.
1634 WOOD *New Eng. Prospect* 96 In Summer they [*sc.* Indian women] gather . . . Hempe and Rushes, with dying stuffe of which they make curious baskets with intermixed colours and portractures of antique Imagerie. **1676** GLOVER *Va.* in *Phil. Trans.* XI. 627 Their Marshlands bear sedges and rushes after the manner of ours. **1737** BRICKELL *N. Carolina* 22 Stargrass . . . is used with good Success in most Fevers in this Country; Rushes of several sorts. **1766** [see BOTTOM *v.* 1]. **1807** GASS *Journal* 14 Here the soil is good . . . with some grape vines, and an abundance of rushes. **1899** GOING *Flowers* 177 The rushes are most abundant on roadsides and river-shores.
b. With specifying terms.
See also BOG RUSH and cf. sense 2.
1814 BIGELOW *Florula Bostoniensis* 84 *Juncus tenuis.* Slender rush. . . . A small, hardy species, common about foot paths and road sides. **1817–8** EATON *Botany* (1822) 449 *Scheuchzeria palustris,* less flowering rush. . . . In ponds and marshes. **1840** DEWEY *Mass. Flowering Plants* 205 *Luzula melanocarpa,* Blackfruited Rush, has a black capsule. **1843** TORREY *Flora N.Y.* II. 329 *Juncus bufonius.* Toad Rush. . . . Low grounds, and around ponds: common. **1894** *Amer. Folk-Lore* VII. 103 *Scirpus lacustris,* black rush, Minn.
+**2.** Any plant of the genus *Equisetum,* esp. *Equisetum hyemale,* sometimes used for fodder.
See also DUTCH RUSH, SCOURING RUSH, and cf. HORSETAIL, SCRUBGRASS.
1803 LEWIS in *Jrnls. of L. & Ordway* 55 The banks appear every where to abound with the *sand* or *scrubing Rush.* **1806** — in *L. & Clark Exped.* III. (1905) 333 This [blubber] they usually expose to the fire . . . and then eat it either alone or with the roots of the rush. **1817** BRADBURY *Travels* 15 On the islands which we passed there is abundance of *Equisetum hyemale,* called by the settlers *rushes.* **1819** D. THOMAS *Travels Western Country* 44 Scrub Grass is called in Scipio, 'Rushes.' **1821** NUTTALL *Travels Arkansa* 58 The scrub-grass or rushes, as they are called here (*Equisetum hiemale*), . . . appear along the banks in vast fields. **1834** PECK *Gaz. Illinois* 195 The rushes, which cover the prairies around, furnish winter food for cattle. **1854** *La Crosse Democrat* 28 March 1/5, I have known cattle to keep in good order all winter on rushes.
* **3.** *attrib.* and *comb.* **a.** Designating objects made of rushes.
1809 IRVING *Knickerb.* III. iii, The young ladies seated themselves demurely in their rush-bottomed chairs. **1894** ROBINSON *Danvis Folks* 270 [The] housewife . . . dropped the rush curtain under which she had watched him.
* **b.** Designating places where rushes grow.
1831 PECK *Guide* 105 In all the rush bottoms they [*sc.* cattle] fatten during the severe weather on rushes. **1835–7** HALIBURTON *Clockmaker* 1 Ser. 191 Her bare legs put me in mind of the long shanks of a bittern down in a rush swamp, a drivin away like mad full chizel arter a frog.
c. In the names of plants or birds.
1817–8 EATON *Botany* (1822) 338 *Limnetis juncea,* rush salt grass. *Ib.* 466 *Solidago juncea,* rush-stalk golden-rod. . . . Stem brownish. **1821** *Mass. H. S. Coll.* 2 Ser. IX. 151 Plants, which are indigenous in the township of Middlebury, [Vt.] . . . *Juncus effusus,* Rush grass. **1841** THOREAU *Journal* I. 265 The rush sparrow sings still unintelligible.

* **Rush,** *n.*²
+**1.** *College slang.* A good recitation.
1847 *Yale Banger* 22 Oct., In dreams his many *rushes* heard. **1851** HALL *College Words* 260 At Yale College, a perfect recitation is denominated a *rush.* **1871** BAGG *At Yale* 47.
+**2.** A general scrimmage or mass encounter between the students of two or more different classes.
Cf. RUSHING 1.
1860 *Yale Lit. Mag.* XXVI. 22 As a basis, a Rush tacitly assumes that it is promoting a rivalry that is proper and praiseworthy. **1871** BAGG *At Yale* 47. **1905** *Springfield W. Repub.* 6 Oct. 9 President Hyde delivered his opening address at the chapel, after which the annual rush between the

freshmen and sophomores took place. **1916** EASTMAN *From Deep Woods* 68 The two classes met in a first 'rush.'

3. A migration to new territory. {1850–}

See also GOLD RUSH.

1873 BEADLE *Undevel. West* 746 Five thousand Americans had . . . settled in California before the 'great rush' of 1849. **1890** *Stock Grower & Farmer* 8 March 6/4 The rush into the Cherokee lands will equal that into Oklahoma. **1898** [see KLONDIKE].

4. *To make a rush for* (something), to rush precipitately upon (something).

1837 BIRD *Nick of Woods* I. 229 The abbregynes ar' making a rush for the cabin. **1897** *Kissimmee* (Fla.) *Valley* 14 April 3/2 [One of the wolves] creeps as close as possible to the one [antelope] they have selected and then makes a rush for it.

+5. *With a* (*perfect*) *rush, in a rush, on the rush,* in a hurry.

1845 SOL. SMITH *Theatr. Apprent.* 152 Poker is decidedly a dangerous game to play at—particularly with strangers; but when you find yourself in possession of *four aces,* go it with a perfect rush! **1876** 'MARK TWAIN' *Tom Sawyer* xviii. 149 He is always in such a rush that he never thinks of anything. **1898** *McClure's Mag.* X. 352 The gray-backs came through with a rush. **1901** JAMES *Sacred Fount* 75 Last night she was on the rush.

+6. In special combinations.

Rush edition, an edition of a paper produced very rapidly; *r. job,* a piece of work requiring completion as soon as possible; *r. season,* a period when work is urgently demanded; *r. smoker,* a smoking party for prospective members of a student organization; *r. work,* work at a rapid rate.

1901 C. MOFFETT *Careers of Danger* 381 Already the mail clerks are swarming at the pouches, like printers on a rush edition. **1901** MERWIN & WEBSTER *Calumet 'K'* 126 But if you ever try to put me on a rush job, I'll quit and buy a small farm. **1906** SINCLAIR *Jungle* 124 Liable again to be kept overtime in rush seasons. **1899** QUINN *Penna. Stories* 60 It was not long before Theta Chi gave him a bid to a rush smoker. **1904** *N.Y. Herald* 17 Sept. 1 He stated that in six weeks rush work would be required to repair the boilers to make them serviceable.

∗ Rush, *v.*

To rush the growler, see GROWLER 2 b.

+1. *intr.* To make a good or a perfect classroom recitation; to pass an examination with success.

1848 *Yale Banger* 23 Oct., Then for the students mark flunks, even though the young men may be rushing. **1862** *Yale Lit. Mag.* XXVIII. 37 (Th.), If they rush as well in their lessons as they do in front of the Gymnasium, their marks will be very high. **1887** *Lippincott's Mag.* Aug. 291 The students gather in the recitation-rooms, where they 'rush' or 'flunk,' according as they have studied the night before or been 'out on a lark.'

+2. *tr.* With *it.* To do a thing energetically.

*a***1856** in Hall *College Words* (ed. 2) 365 Leg it, put it, rush it, streak it. **1859** BARTLETT 375 The old negro is rushing it with his fiddle.

+3. (See quotation.)

1889 *Electrical Rev.* 30 Nov. 10/4 Nearly all [telegraph operators] are ambitious to send faster than the operator at the receiving station can write it down, or in other words to 'rush' him.

+4. To cultivate (a person) assiduously; spec., to lavish attentions on (a student) in order to persuade him to join a particular fraternity. *colloq.*[2]

1899 F. NORRIS *McTeague* 226 Marcus had 'taken up with' Salina a little after Trina had married, and had been 'rushing' her ever since. **1899** QUINN *Penna. Stories* 60 That Fraternity began rushing him.

Rusher. {1654–}

+1. A person who rushes to new territory.

1871 DE VERE 629 *Rushers,* in California and all the gold-bearing districts of the West, is the comprehensive name of persons going to the mines. **1892** *Current Hist.* Nov. 433 As many of the 'rushers' are very poor, there is sure to be great suffering in the territory.

+2. *Football.* A player in the rush line.

1883 *Atlantic Mo.* May 682/1 A handsome check of an attempt to break through the line of rushers, in a scrimmage . . . is recognized. **1887** [see RUSH LINE]. **1893** POST *Harvard Stories* 25 The brown oval would go curving and spinning over the heads of the rushers.

+3. An energetic, aggressive person.

1889 *Century Mag.* Oct. 874/1 The pretty girl from the East is hardly enough of a 'rusher' to please the young Western masculine taste. **1902** MCFAUL *Ike Glidden* 121 She's such a rusher 'twon't take her no time if I kin only git her.

Rush hour. The period when traffic or business is heaviest. {1898–} — **1898** *Kansas City Star* 18 Dec. 4/4 A five cent fare is provided for the first twenty years and six tickets for twenty-five cents, good only for the 'rush hours.' **1899** *Chicago Record* 11 Jan. 1/7 The question of supplying proper facilities for travel [on street cars] during the 'rush' hours of the day . . . receives particular attention from railroad managers. **1904** A. FRENCH *Barrier* 183 More cars at the rush hours, and more attention to the suburbs. **1909** 'O. HENRY' *Options* 304 During rush hours a Mexican youth . . . aided him in waiting on the guests.

∗ Rushing.

+1. (See quot. 1888.)

1878 *N. Amer. Rev.* March 236 'Hazing,' 'rushing,' secret societies . . . are unknown at Oxford and Cambridge. **1879** *Princeton Book* 385 'Rushing' is not native to Princeton. **1888** BRYCE *Amer. Commw.* III. VI. cii. 454*n.*, Sophomores and freshmen have a whimsical habit of meeting one another in dense masses and trying which can push the other aside on the stairs or path. This is called 'rushing.'

2. *Football.* The action of advancing the ball by massing a number of players against a particular point of the opposing line.

1883 *Atlantic Mo.* May 681/2 Avoirdupois and strength are at a premium for rushing, blocking, and tackling. **1889** *Scientific Amer.* LIX. 304 In rushing . . . , when the 'backs' or 'half-backs' come together, the front lines get the most shocks.

+Rush lily. (See quotations.) — [**1884** W. MILLER *Dict. Names of Plants* 119/2 Rush-Lily, the genus *Sisyrinchium.* Purple, *Sisyrinchium grandiflorum.* White. *Sisyrinchium grandiflorum var. album.*] **1891** *Cent.* 5278/1 *Rush-lily,* . . . a plant of the more showy species of blue-eyed grass, *Sisyrinchium,* especially *S. grandiflorum,* a species with brightyellow flowers, native in northwestern America, occasionally cultivated.

+Rush line. *Football.* The line of players who carry or sustain the brunt of attack. Also *fig.* — **1887** *Century Mag.* Oct. 891/2 Across the field stretch the foot-ball infantry, the 'rush-line,' or 'rushers.' **1895** *Outing* Dec. 251/1 The Canadian game . . . [might be improved] by a reduction of the number of men on the rush line. **1906** *Life* 4 Oct. 366 We hear of a surprising prevalence among the young men of brains who come nowadays from the universities of the disposition to get into the political rush-line and have something to say about government. **1921** PAINE *Comr. Rolling Ocean* 3 He tore through a rush-line.

∗ Rusk, *n.* **a.** A hard, crisp bread, formerly used on board ship. *Obs.* **b.** A piece of light bread or cake, often baked to a state of crispness. {1759–} Also with defining term. **+c.** (See quot. 1891.)

1711 SEWALL *Diary* II 316 Finding the Tide not made, we Land at the Castle; eat Rusk and drank. **1830** WATSON *Philadelphia* 237 The supper consisted of tea, chocolate, and rusk—a simple cake, now never seen amidst the profusion of French confectionary. **1845** *Xenia Torch-Light* 31 July 4/3 Fresh Rusks and Bread, will be kept constantly on hand. **1852** EASTMAN *Aunt Phillis's Cabin* 72 We *always* have rusk. **1861** H. JACOBS *Life Slave Girl* 135 There were hot muffins, tea rusks, and delicious sweetmeats. **1880** CABLE *Grandissimes* 153 An inspiring smell of warm rusks . . . rushed through the archway. **1891** *Cent.* 5278/2 *Rusk,* . . . bread or cake dried and browned in the oven, and reduced to crumbs by pounding, the crumbs being usually eaten with milk. (New Eng.)

attrib. **1852** STOWE *Uncle Tom* xviii, Our friend, Tom, . . . had been in the kitchen during the conversation with the old rusk-woman.

+Rusk, *v.* [f. RUSK *n.*] (See quotation.) — **1891** *Cent.* 5278/2 *Rusk,* to make rusk of; convert, as bread or cake, into rusk. . . . (New Eng.)

+Russ. *local.* [See quot. 1851.] A kind of stone and concrete pavement. In full *Russ pavement.* — **1849** G. G. FOSTER *N.Y. in Slices* 9 The sight of the here-and-there patches of good, solid, smooth Russ pavement, puts us in a good humor. **1851** ROSS *In New York* 15, I must speak of a new form which is called the 'Russ Pavement,' named after Horace P. Russ, Esq., who first introduced it. **1856** S. F. BATEMAN *Self* i. i, The horses slipped on the Russ pavement. **1864** DALY in J. F. Daly *A. Daly* 62 My throat . . . is as full of rocks now as Broadway when Russ or Belgian is being laid.

Russelet. =RUSSEL(S). — **1790** *Columbian Centinel* 29 Sept. 20/4 [For sale,] a few Worsted Goods, such as Lastings, Satinets, Russelets, and Florentines.

Russel(l)'s willow. ?=CRACK WILLOW. (Cf. BRITTLE SALIX, WILLOW.) — **1813** MUHLENBERG *Cat. Plants* 91 *Salix Russeliana,* Russel's willow.

∗Russel(s). A kind of woolen material formerly used in making garments and shoes. *Obs.* {–1703} Also *attrib.* — **1710** T. BUCKINGHAM *Naval Exped.* 30 Five yards black Russels, at 9 s. 6 d. **1751** *Boston Ev. Post* 25 March, Women's callimanco & russel shoes. **1794** *Mass. Spy* 1 May 4/2 Ready for Sale . . . Russel, Calimanco, . . . Moreen, yellow Canvas. **1801** *Spirit Farmer's Mus.* 235 Sal, put on your russel skirt.

∗ Russet. An apple with mottled, brownish coloring. {1708–} Also *russet apple.* {1887} Freq. with specifying term.

1709 LAWSON *Carolina* 108 The Golden Russet thrives well. **1836** *Russet apple* [see LONG-NECKED SQUASH]. **1856** *Rep. Comm. Patents 1855: Agric.* 290 For fall and winter varieties, the 'Fall Pippin,' 'Seek-no-further,' 'Canfield,' 'Russet,' 'Lady,' and the 'Siberian crab,' are the most profitable. **1858** *Ill. Agric. Soc. Trans.* III. 347 Some cultivators rank the . . . American Golden Russet and Fallenwater or Fallenwalder, as perfectly hardy. **1868** Gale's Russet [see PIPPIN 2]. **1871** HOLLAND in *Scribner's Mo.* II. 321 The pyramids of russets that lately rose on every side . . . are beginning to grow small. **1921** FOLGER & THOMSON *Comr. Apple Industry* 408 The Roxbury and the Golden Russet are most commonly found on the market.

+Russet-backed thrush. A thrush (*Hylocichla ustulata*). Also *russet-back, russet thrush.* — **1876** WHITMAN *Spec. Days* 86 Down in the apple-trees . . . were three or four russet-backed thrushes. **1879** *Nat. Mu-*

seum Proc. I. 396 *Turdus ustulatus.*—Russet-backed Thrush.... Its delicious song is not likely to be forgotten by one who has heard it. **1881** WHITMAN *Diary* (1904) 58 The song of the catbird, wren, or russet thrush within hearing. **1917** *Birds of Amer.* III. 231 Russet-backed Thrush. *Hylocichla ustulata ustula....* Other Name.—Russet-back. *Ib.* 232/2 The Russet-backed Thrush must be considered as one of the positively beneficial birds.

*Russeting. A russet apple. {1607–} — **1676** GLOVER *Va.* in *Phil. Trans.* XI. 628 The Countrey... [affords] all sorts of English Apples, as Pear-mains, Pippins, Russetens, Costards. **1770** *Md. Hist. Mag.* XIII. 69, 4 Barrills of Apples, Russetins, Golden Pippins. **1827** *Harvard Reg.* Nov. 273, I pared, I trow, full many a russeteen.

Russia. Used attrib. {1656–}

1. Designating materials or objects originally made in Russia.

1650 ASPINWALL *Notarial Rec.* 416 For the Acco[unt] of Tho[mas] Lacock mer[chant]... 20 bed ticks. 12 russia lether chaires. **1741** *S.C. Gazette* 26 March, Just imported... Silesias, Buchrams, Russia Diaperete. **1758** *Newport Mercury* 19 Dec. 4/2 George Hazard... has to sell... Russia Linen, Cotton and Linen Checks. **1761** *Essex Inst. Coll.* XLVIII. 95 The Assortments are as follows,... Cheshire and Gloucester Cheese; best prime Russia Duck; gun powder; all sizes shot. **1775** *Jrnls. Cont. Congress* III. 258 An account... for sundry sail cloth, Russia Sheeting. **1790** *Penna. Packet* 1 Jan. 4/2 Just Arrived by the Mary Ann,... Lampblack, whiting, Russia matts, corks. **1842** *Nat. Hist. N.Y., Geology* II. 302 In fine, it [iron made from Cook ore] resembles very nearly the old *Russia sable,* so celebrated in this country. **1859** *Rep. Comm. Patents 1858* I. 530 The process of manufacturing sheet-iron, to possess most of the qualifications of 'polished Russia sheet-iron.'

b. Designating garments made of Russia duck.

1804 CLARK in *Lewis & C. Exped.* VI. (1905) 278, 11 pr Russia Overalls. **1841** *Knickerb.* XVII. 49 His duck trowsers and Russia shirt... bespoke him every inch a sailor.

2. In the names of plants, fowls, and animals.

1818 J. MOFFATT *Let. to E. Pettigrew* (Univ. N.C. MS.) 6 Aug., More than a thousand bushels of Russia Turnips may be raised. **1851** CIST *Cincinnati* 279 The hogs used for this market, are generally a cross of Irish Grazier, Byfield, Berkshire, Russia and China. **1854** *Penna. Agric. Rep.* 205 Wm. B. Slyder, for best pair Russia ducks.

Russia matting. (See quot. 1876.) — **1839** in Audubon *Ornith. Biog.* V. 504 The nest... with us has uniformly been built of Russia matting. **1876** KNIGHT 2005/2 *Russia-matting,* matting manufactured in Russia from the inner bark of the linden.... Much used for packing.

*Russian, *a.*

1. Native to, made in, or coming from Russia, or resembling something brought from Russia.

1827 *Hallowell* (Me.) *Gaz.* 20 June 4/4 (*advt.*), Received... Russian Diaper. **1856** *Porter's Spirit of Times* 29 Nov. 207/1 The Russian sable—the scarcest, and consequently the dearest fur we have—is, we understand, smuggled into this country. **1883** KNIGHT *Suppl.* 772/2 Russian Iron.... We have no doubt but that in time the American product, or 'imitation Russia,'... will eventually be made equal in all respects to the genuine Russian. **1883** *Wheelman* I. 305 The tea is... made, in fact, into what is called *tschai,* or Russian tea. **1884** *Nat. Museum Bul.* No. 27, 1044 Sturgeon roe is prepared and put up in cans under the trade names 'American caviare' and 'Russian caviare.'

2. Of persons or groups of persons: Of Russian birth or descent.

1872 MCCLELLAN *Golden State* 70 While in California, the count was so delighted with the country that he arranged for the founding of a Russian settlement. **1903, 1907** [see GERMAN JEW]. **1907** *St. Nicholas* May 669/1 Father and I went to see the Russian emigrant colony here lately.

3. In the names of plants and animals.

See also RUSSIAN THISTLE.

1819 *Plough Boy* I. 46 There were six competitors for the premium offered for the best acre of the *Ruta Baga* or *Russian Turnip.* **1845** LINCOLN *Botany* App. 104/2 *Galanthus... plicanthus,* (Russian snow-drop,) flowers smaller than the preceding. **1856** *Rep. Comm. Patents 1855: Agric.* 63 The 'China' breed [of hogs] is the most prevalent [in Beaver Co., Pa.], though some keep the 'Russian.' **1872** *Atlantic Mo.* May 551 Within a few years past, huge Russian wolf-hounds are frequently to be seen in the streets of New York. **1894** Russian cactus [see RUSSIAN THISTLE]. **1897** SUDWORTH *Arborescent Flora* 188 *Morus alba tatarica....* Russian Mulberry. **1917** COMSTOCK *Man* 43 A Russian hound... lay before the fire.

+Russian America. A name for Alaska prior to its purchase by the United States. *Obs.* Also *Russian American* a. — **1818** *Ann. 17th Congress* 1 Sess. 2139 Until 1816 the settlements of this Power did not reach to the southward of 55°, and were of no consideration, although dignified by them with the title of Russian America. [**1822** *Ib.* 2159 The Emperor Paul I... granted, in 1799, to the Russian American Company its first charter of incorporation.] **1840** DANA *Two Years* xxvi. 281 The only vessel was a brig under Russian colors, from Asitka, in Russian America. *a***1918** [see CHINOOK 4].

+Russian thistle. A prickly weed (*Salsola pestifer*); ?also, the saltwort, *S. kali.* — **1894** *Amer. Folk-Lore* VII. 97 *Salsola Kali,* var *Tragus,* Moguin, Russian thistle, Russian cactus, Dak. **1898** *Mo. So. Dakotan* I. 103 Only tiny triangular spots remained dry in the lee of broken corn-

stalks and scattered Russian thistles and the black clods of newly turned earth. **1913** BARNES *Western Grazing Grounds* 63 The Russian thistle (*Salsola tragus*) is also commonly called tumble weed.

*Rust, *n.*

*1. Any one of certain fungi causing a plant disease characterized by brownish spots; such a disease or one similar in appearance. Also with modifying terms.

1768 WASHINGTON *Diaries* I. 281 This [wheat] was also injured by Rust as well as by the frosts. **1790** DEANE *New-Eng. Farmer* 20/1 The pods are liable to be hurt by a black rust. **1814** J. TAYLOR *Arator* 153 There are two calamities only common to wheat, which may not be avoided with certainty; those of the Hessian fly and rust. **1847** PALMER *Rocky Mts.* 188 The rust and smut... are unknown in Oregon. **1883** [see FLEA BUG]. **1890** *Rep. Secy. Agric.1889* 416 The quince trees at Vineland, N.J., are annually affected with... orange rust (*Rœstelia aurantiaca*).

b. Attrib. with *blight, mite.*

1874 *Rep. Comm. Agric. 1873* 201 Thus far it would seem that the rust-blight is unknown to [cultivators in Texas]. **1884** *Rep. Comm. Agric.* 372 Emulsions... do not kill the eggs of the Rust-mite.

+2. (See quotation.)

1877 BARTLETT 543 *Rust,* discoloration in mackerel, sometimes caused by leakage of the brine in which they are packed.

*Rust, *v.* +*intr.* To become affected with rust. — **1869** *Rep. Comm. Agric. 1868* 415 The wheat rusted badly on the blade and slightly on the stalk. **1924** CROY *R. F. D. No. 3* 22 All men in this district... helped one another when the hay was falling down, when the wheat was rusting.

Rustication. {1623–} Dismissal from a college or university for a specified time, as a punishment. {1779–} — **1734** *Harvard Rec.* I. 152 [Refusal shall] be punished by Admonition, rustication, degradation or expulsion. **1850** THAXTER *Poem before Iadma* 14 The Student... thinks that he would rather die than suffer 'rustication.' **1866** LOWELL *Biglow P.* 2 Ser. viii. 189 The young man he speaks of was... put under his care during a sentence of rustication from—— College.

+Rusticoat potato. A variety of potato with reddish-brown skin. — **1775** in *Boston Transcript* 26 April III. 12/7, I have a fine prospect of a Crop of Rusty Coats Portators and winter Squashes this fall. **1782** J. ADAMS *Familiar Lett.* 404 But how much more luxurious it would be to me to dine... upon rusticoat potatoes with Portia!

Rustle, *n.* {1759–} +*To get a rustle on,* to get a move on. *colloq.*[2] (Cf. MOVE *n.*) — **1892** CRANE *Maggie* (1896) 101 Hi, you, git a russle on yehs! [**1899** C. W. GORDON *Sky Pilot* xxi, It's about time for me to get a rustle on.]

*Rustle, *v.*

+1. *intr.* To move energetically or hurriedly; to work actively *for* something; to look out *for* one's self. Also with *around. colloq.*[2]

1872 R. B. JOHNSON *Very Far West* 195, I've rustled upwards from a picayune printin' office down to New Orleens. **1884** 'MARK TWAIN' *H. Finn* xii, We'll rustle around and gather up whatever pickin's we've overlooked. **1885** JACKSON *Zeph* 1, Ther's men thet's rustled more'n he did; but 'tain't in some men *to* rustle. **1889** VASEY *Agric. Grasses* 57 No attempt is made by stockmen to feed cattle in the winter; they are expected to 'rustle around,' as the phrase is, and find their living. **1890** *Stock Grower & Farmer* 22 March 5/3 The reception committee at Fort Worth was evidently new at the business. Every visitor had to 'rustle' or get left. **1903** *N.Y. Tribune* 18 Oct., The hardy Western ponies, accustomed to 'rustling' for their own food. **1916** 'BOWER' *Phantom Herd* 243 He turns you out thinking he'll let you rustle for yourself awhile.

+2. *tr.* To acquire (something) by putting forth effort; to collect, get together, forage around for. Freq. with *up. colloq.*[2]

*a***1846** *Quarter Race Kentucky* 94 He nailed my thumb in his jaws, and rostled up a handful of dirt and throwed it in my eyes. **1880** *Cimarron News & Press* 8 April 3/1 Mr. John J. Vandemoor,... of the New York Mining Record, was in town this week, rustling business for that excellent journal. **1889** *Nat. Museum Rep. 1886–7* 451 His first care is to start out with his largest gunning-bag to 'rustle some buffalo chips' for a camp-fire. **1891** *Advance* 29 Jan., Some of the members have arranged... to go out on the hills and 'rustle up' wood. **1893** WISTER in *Harper's Mag.* Dec. 53/1, I'll be able to rustle up near five hundred dollars. **1897** LEWIS *Wolfville* 210 The cook's startin' in to rustle some chuck. **1902** WHITE *Blazed Trail* 176 The first thing we want to do is to rustle some money. **1905** *Springfield W. Repub.* 15 Dec. 15 The animals could 'rustle' enough off the range to get through the winter months. **1914** E. STEWART *Lett. of Woman Homesteader* 245 After I rustled some water I made myself and the kiddies a little more presentable. **1924** MULFORD *Rustlers' Valley* vi, I can rustle you a snack in a minute.

+b. To round up or herd together (live stock), esp. as a professional cowboy or ranchman. Also with *in, up. colloq.*[2]

1896 DICE *Counterfeiting Exposed* 30 [He] 'rustled' up a good big herd of cattle. **1900** GARLAND *Eagle's Heart* 156, I'm getting mighty near too old to enjoy rustlin' cattle together. **1903** A. ADAMS *Log of Cowboy* 53 Our foreman... sent Honeyman to rustle in the horses. *Ib.* 177 He was called to help rustle the horses. **1910** RAINE *B. O'Connor* 88 Thought you was rustling cows for a living somewheres in burnt Arizona.

+c. To acquire (live stock) by theft; to rob. *colloq.*[2]

1893 *Aberdeen* (S. Dak.) *Sun* 5 Jan. 7/4 Rustling cattle is an exciting trade and very profitable, but extremely hazardous. **1897** LEWIS *Wolfville* 161 If this yere party's rustlin' the mails, we-alls can't call his hand too quick. **1910** RAINE *B. O'Connor* 209 Slow elk . . . is veal that has been rustled.

Rustler. {1820-}

+1. A lively, industrious, ambitious person.

1872 'MARK TWAIN' *Roughing It* 333 But pard, he was a rustler! You ought to seen him get started once. **1889** MUNROE *Golden Days* 261 He's a rustler, he is! **1897** 'MARK TWAIN' *Following Equator* 365 What a rustler he was after the slumbrous way of Manuel, poor old slug! **1901** GRINNELL *Gold Hunting in Alaska* 47 His companion was a 'rustler.'

+b. A cook on a ranch.

1887 *Scribner's Mag.* II. 508/1 The cook on a ranch used to be called a 'rustler.' **1902** CLAPIN 343 *Rustler,* . . . formerly, a ranchman's term for a cook, on a ranch, from the fact that the work incumbent to it requires considerable activity and energy.

+c. An animal that forages about for its provender.

1890 *Harper's Mag.* April 689/2 The California sheep . . . are of unusual size, known as 'rustlers,' because they must rustle about for their food.

+2. A cattle thief.

1882 *N. Mex. Terr. Rep.* 98 The trail of the rustlers . . . was found. **1884** *Gringo & Greaser* 15 Feb. 4/2 The stockmen should be ready with a hemp necktie, to give the rustler a 'choker' reception. **1905** *N.Y. Ev. Post* 27 Jan. 4 A 'rustler,' as the term is used in the West, means a man who steals other people's cattle and puts his own brand on them. **1924** MULFORD *Rustlers' Valley* 219 Reckon they're watchin' for th' rustlers.

∥Rustlerdom. The region or territory frequented by rustlers.—

1897 HOUGH *Story of Cowboy* 291 It was legally impossible to do so in any of the courts sitting in rustlerdom!

✳Rustling, *n.* **+1.** Active, ambitious effort. **+2.** The stealing of cattle. — (1) **1872** R. B. JOHNSON *Very Far West* 191 'Rustling' is an Americanism, denoting the process of fighting against odds for a living. **1886** *Milnor* (Dak.) *Teller* 2 July 4/1 It may be expected that some tall rustling will be indulged in during the next few weeks. (2) **1903** A. ADAMS *Log of Cowboy* 93, I know a few of the simple principles of rustling myself. **1924** MULFORD *Rustlers' Valley* x, There had been no sign of rustling for months.

✳Rustling, *a.* **+1.** Brisk, active, up and coming. **+2.** Of range animals: Accustomed to foraging for themselves. — (1) **1882** *Century Mag.* Aug. 508/2 To do a rustling business is to carry on an active trade. **1884** *Milnor* (Dak.) *Teller* 17 Oct. 8/7 C. C. Groger, a rustling real estate dealer of Forman, Sargent county, was in the city most of the week. **1902** *Greenwood* (Ark.) *Democrat* 22 May 1/6 The rustling editor of the Greenwood Democrat was in town Saturday. (2) **1890** *Stock Grower & Farmer* 29 March 4/2 The condition of rustling animals is . . . deplorable.

Rusty, *n.* {1890, *dial.*} **+**Something exceptional; a prank, antic, caper, etc. Usu. *to cut* (*up*) *rusties. slang.*

1835 BIRD *Hawks* II. 245 Neversomever, I'll try for a spell ag'in, and the next'll be a right-down rusty! **1837** NEAL *Charcoal Sk.* (1838) 111 It won't do for us to be cutting rusties here at this time o' night. **1849** *Knickerb.* XXXIV. 90 Nobody has any 'inducement' to cut up such 'rusties' there. **1853** *S. Lit. Messenger* XIX. 602/2 We cut up our rusties at his hotel. **1871** DE VERE 537 *Rusties,* in Pennsylvania and Ohio, the name given to the restive movements of an unquiet horse. **1920** HUNTER *Trail Drivers Texas* I. 300 [In cowboy lingo] *'cutting a rusty'* . . . means doing your best.

✳Rusty, *a.* In the names of birds, fishes, and plants.

See also RUSTY-COAT POTATO, RUSTY-CROWNED FALCON, etc.

[**1785** PENNANT *Arctic Zool.* II. 452 Rusty-crowned [Heron]. . . . Crest and hind part of the neck of a deep ferruginous color. . . . Inhabits North America. **1787** LATHAM *Gen. Synopsis Birds* Suppl. I. 89 Rusty Oriole. . . . The edges of the feathers are rust-coloured.] **1811** WILSON *Ornithology* III. p. xiii, Rusty Flycatcher, wings and tail black; plumage above brown; inhabits the southern states. **1813** MUHLENBERG *Cat. Plants* 86 *Fagus ferruginea,* Rusty-leaved Beech. **1839** STORER *Mass. Fishes* 141 *P[latessa] ferruginea.* . . . The Rusty Dab. This species is occasionally brought to our market, in the winter season only. **1844** *Nat. Hist. N.Y., Zoology* II. 137 The Rusty Crow Blackbird. *Quiscolus Ferrugineus.* . . . Their geographical range extends from 24° to 68° north. **1884** GOODE, etc. *Fisheries* I. 197 The Sand Dab, or Rough Dab, *Hippoglossoides platessoides,* also sometimes known as the Rusty Flounder, is taken in winter by the line fishermen of New England. **1897** SUDWORTH *Arborescent Flora* 339 *Viburnum ferrugineum.* . . . Rusty Stagbush.

+Rusty-coat potato. (See RUSTICOAT POTATO.)

+Rusty-crowned falcon. The sparrow hawk, *Falco sparverius.* — **1872** COUES *Key to Birds* 214 Rusty-crowned Falcon. . . . Crown ashyblue, with a chestnut patch. **1880** *Cimarron News & Press* 23 Dec. 1/5 Of the falcons we have the . . . pigeon, Richardson's and rusty-crowned falcon or sparrow hawk. **1917** [see GRASSHOPPER *n.* 2 e].

+Rusty gold. Native gold with a coating which interferes with amalgamation. — **1872** TICE *Over Plains* 227 In the refining crucible this 'rusty gold' gives a regulus of 99 per cent. **1881** RAYMOND *Mining Gloss., Rusty gold,* Pac., free gold, which does not easily amalgamate, the particles being coated, as is supposed, with oxide of iron.

+Rusty grackle. =RUSTY(-WINGED) BLACKBIRD. — **1811** WILSON *Ornithology* III. 41 [The] Rusty Grakle . . . frequents corn fields. **1839**

AUDUBON *Ornith. Biog.* V. 483 [The] Rusty Grakle . . . is found on the shores of the Columbia River. **1867** *Amer. Naturalist* I. 54. **1917** *Birds of Amer.* II. 263 Rusty blackbird. . . . [Also called] Rusty Grackle.

+Rusty(-winged) blackbird. A blackbird (*Euphagus carolinus*) with blue-black feathers which turn rust-colored in the fall. (Cf. RUSTY GRACKLE.) — **1851** GLISAN *Jrnl. Army Life* 89 Of the birds and animals not usually eatable, there are the . . . rusty-winged blackbird, blue-bird, buzzard, crow. **1858** BAIRD *Birds Pacific R.R.* 551 Rusty Blackbird. . . . From Atlantic coast to the Missouri. **1870** *Amer. Naturalist* IV. 52 Since the first week in December there have been two, and part of the time three, Rusty Blackbirds constantly about one of my barns. **1917** *Birds of Amer.* II. 264/1 When the first sharp frosts come, . . . the Rusty Blackbird begins to appear.

Rutabaga. A variety of turnip (*Brassica napobrassica*) with a large root; the Russian or Swedish turnip. {1800-} Also *rutabaga turnip.* — **1806** MACMAHON *Amer. Gard. Cal.* 427 The Swedish turnep, or *Roota Baga,* as it is called, . . . requires to be sown in a different season. **1819** *Plough Boy* I. 46 There were six competitors for the premium offered for the best acre of the *Ruta Baga* or *Russian Turnip.* **1854** *Penna. Agric. Rep.* 43 Henry A. Carpenter, . . . one-fourth acre sugar beet and one-fourth acre ruta baga. **1880** INGHAM *Digging Gold* 325 An old prospector . . . lived in the San Juan country two months on 'ruta baga turnips.' **1896** *Internat. Typogr. Union Proc.* 58/2, 2 lbs. rutabagas, 70¢.

+Rutherfordite. [f. Rutherford Co., North Carolina.] (See quot. 1891.) — **1857** DANA *Mineralogy* 209. **1891** *Cent.* 5282/3 *Rutherfordite,* a rare and imperfectly known mineral found in the gold-mines of Rutherford county, North Carolina: it is supposed to contain titanic acid, cerium, etc.

+Rutland beauty. A species of bindweed (*Convolvulus sepium*) cultivated as a hedge. — **1847** WOOD *Botany* 444 Rutland Beauty . . . is cultivated as a shade for windows, arbors, &c. **1869** FULLER *Flower Gatherers* 228 One species, the *Calystegia sepium,* is much cultivated in gardens, and called 'Rutland-Beauty.' **1892** *Amer. Folk-Lore* V. 101.

+Rutland wriggle. [?Duke of *Rutland.*] (See quotation.) — **1817** PAULDING *Lett. from South* I. 235 [American bucks] walked with the genuine *Rutland wriggle;* that is to say, on tiptoe, and with a most portentous extension of the hinder parts.

✳Ryal(l). =RIAL. — **1682** *N.H. Hist. Soc. Coll.* VIII. 75 Fish, two ryals under price current. **1704** S. KNIGHT *Journal* 42 Mony [in Conn.] is pieces of eight, Ryalls, or Boston or Bay shillings.

✳Rye.

✳1. A cereal grass (*Secale cereale*); the seed or grain of this plant, used extensively for food.

1645 *Suffolk Deeds* I. 65 Two fourth parts of one hundred & fifty quarters of Rye. *c*1680 HULL *Diaries* 218 The blast this year took hold of Conecticot and New Haven; yet the Indian, barley, pease, and rye was spared. **1765** ROGERS *Acct. N. Amer.* 50 The produce of the soil [in N.H.] is chiefly Indian corn, rye, oats, pease. **1784** CUTLER in *Life & Corr.* I. 97 In Wakefield are fine fields of rye. **1803** *Lit. Mag.* (Phia.) Dec. 172 Good rye is likewise cultivated [in Penna.] to profit. **1857** E. STONE *Life J. Howland* 31 People generally bought indian corn or rye in the grain and sent it in wheel barrows to the old grist mill. **1906** T. F. HUNT *Cereals in Amer.* 352 The by-products of rye are rye bran and distillers' grains.

+2. =RYE WHISKY.

See also OLD RYE.

1890 *Buckskin Mose* 248 But for the quantity of rye we had all of us been swallowing, the others must have seen through this impudent operation. **1894** *Outing* XXIV. 127/1 The remnant of rye in the little flask was fairly divided. **1913** LONDON *Valley of Moon* 392 Some drink rain and some champagne . . . ; But I will try a little rye.

3. *attrib.* Designating foods and drinks made from rye grain or meal

See also RYE AND INDIAN (BREAD), RYE COFFEE, etc.

1805 *Pocumtuc Housewife* (1906) 34 Rye Doughnuts. **1830** SANDS *Writings* II. 240 All her aches and symptoms had disappeared, in consequence of having taken . . . a glass of rye-jack and bitters. **1858** *Harper's Mag.* May 854/2 Prior to the period of the general Temperance Reformation in New England, . . . every shopkeeper sold codfish and rye gin. **1867** *Common Sense Cook Book* 9 Rye Batter Cakes. **1871** DE VERE 41 In some parts of the West, another mush is frequently used, but as it is made of rye after the manner of a Hasty Pudding, it is called *Rye Mush.* **1891** JEWETT in *Atlantic Mo.* May 617 Rye drop-cakes, then, if they wouldn't give you too much trouble. **1892** *Nation* 3 March 168/2 The receipts which I selected were mush, Johnny cake, and Boston rye-and-cornmeal bread.

+Rye and Indian (bread). Bread made from a mixture of rye and corn meal. Now hist. (Cf. INDIAN BREAD 1.) — **1805** *Pocumtuc Housewife* 6 Johnny cake or hoe cakes are a good change from Rye and Indian bread. **1840** *Knickerb.* XVI. 18 There were eggs and fried ham, . . . rye-and-Indian bread. **1875** STOWE *Deacon Pitkin's Farm* 57 [There was] the equally inevitable smoking loaf of rye and Indian bread, to accompany the pot of baked pork and beans. **1887** TOURGEE *Button's Inn* 224 She passed around a hot plateful of toasted slices of 'rye and Indian.' **1898** [see RYE COFFEE].

Rye brome grass. {1812- (Withering *Brit. Plants*)} =CHEAT[1] *a.* — **1814** BIGELOW *Florula Bostoniensis* 26 *Bromus secalinus.* Rye Brome grass. . . . Stem erect, three feet high. **1840** DEWEY *Mass. Flowering*

Plants 240 Rye Broom-Grass . . . is the well-known chess of the wheat field.

+**Rye coffee.** A drink prepared from roasted grains of rye or from toasted rye bread. Now hist. — **1819** *Plough Boy* I. 35 The same correspondent . . . recommends the substitute of *rye coffee*, for that of exotic growth. **1836** *Knickerb.* VIII. 278 We had rye coffee and hominy for breakfast. **1890** *Amer. Notes & Q.* V. 259 We have still a tolerably vivid impression of the 'hard times' which followed the financial crisis of 1817, . . . and most especially the advent of rye-coffee. [**1898** HARPER *S. B. Anthony* I. 14 A drink of 'coffee' [was] made by browning crusts of rye and Indian bread, pouring hot water over them and sweetening with maple syrup.]

Rye field. {1762–} A field of rye. — **1658** *Lancaster Rec.* 60 [The way is] staked up to goodman Prescotts Ry feild. **1780** *N.J. Archives* 2 Ser. IV. 448 Yesterday 13 were found dead in a rye-field. **1849** CHAMBERLAIN *Ind. Gazetteer* 37 The course of feeding is sometimes . . . [in] a late rye field. **1866** 'F. KIRKLAND' *Bk. Anecdotes* 551/2 He came to a rye-field, where he encamped for the night.

Rye grass. Any one of several species of grass, as: **a.** Ray grass. {1753–} **b.** Lyme grass. Also attrib. and with defining terms. (See also ITALIAN RYE GRASS and cf. DARNEL, WILD RYE.)

1747 FRANKLIN *Writings* II. 384, I Sowed an Acre more with two bushells of Rye-Grass Seed. **1792** IMLAY *Western Territory* 41 The country is . . . covered with cane, rye grass, and the native clover. **1804** J. ROBERTS *Penna. Farmer* 47 Rye grass, when young in the spring, is proper for fattening horses or beasts. **1847** WOOD *Botany* 621 *E[lymus] villosus.* Rye Grass. . . . Dry grounds, Free States. **1863** RANDALL *Pract. Shepherd* 234 Many spontaneous clovers and grasses come in, such as . . . rye or ray grass . . . , and several of the fescue grasses. **1884** VASEY *Agric. Grasses* 107 *Lolium perenne.* (Rye grass and Italian Rye grass.) A perennial grass, introduced from Europe. **1895** *Dept. Agric. Yrbk. 1894* 436 A striking species of rye grass, called giant, or western rye grass, . . . grows in the Northwest and on the Pacific Slope. *a*1918 G. STUART *On Frontier* II. 47 The floor of the rest of the place is covered with rye grass or willow twigs.

✳**Rye meal.** Meal made from rye. — **1648** *Mass. H. S. Coll.* 4 Ser. VI. 68, Remember me about the German receipt for making strong water with rye meall without maulting of the Corne. **1783** PARKMAN *Diary* 300 Brot over . . . Cider Barrels, Meat Tubs, . . . Rye Meal & Indian Corn. **1856** *Rep. Comm. Patents 1855: Agric.* 163 The 'Boston Brown Bread,' contains two parts of corn to one of rye-meal. **1895** [see PANDOWDY].

+**Rye whisky.** Whisky made from the grain of rye. (Cf. RYE 2 and OLD RYE.) — **1785** in Ramsey *Tennessee* (1853) 297 Good distilled rye whiskey, at two shillings and six pence per gallon. **1853** *S. Lit. Messenger* XIX. 88/2 Ned Ellet . . . had taken in charge one Nash, a horse-thief, and also a tickler of rye whisky. **1878** KILLEBREW *Tenn. Grasses* 408 Rye whiskey is famous as a beverage the world over. **1897** FLANDRAU *Harvard Episodes* 328, I think I should like a little, a very little, rye whiskey and water.

S

Saase. (See SAUCE.)

+**Saba bean.** (See SAB(E)A BEAN.)

+**Sabatin.** (See quotation.) — **1895** KING *New Orleans* 67 There were . . . potatoes, sabatins (a kind of egg-plant), figs, bananas, pecans, pumpkins.

+**Sabbaday.** *New Eng.* [Contraction of SABBATH DAY.] The Sabbath *colloq.* or *dial.* Also attrib. — *c*1772 *Essex Inst. Coll.* LVI. 292 Thare was in the yeare 1738 a great athcak one sabbady. **1825** NEAL *Bro. Jonathan* I. 105 Ony lass Sabba'day,' at ever was, *me* and Bold Eagle—what a feller he is! **1858** *Harper's Mag.* Nov. 856/2 A thousand terrible thoughts rushed into her mind; . . . above all, the loss of her 'Sabber-day' dinner. **1868** BEECHER *Norwood* 47 Duties never conflict, you said, only Sabby-day morning last. *a*1870–91 [see SABBA(TH)-DAY HOUSE].

+**Sabbaday house.** (See SABBA(TH)-DAY HOUSE.)

Sabbatarian. {1613–} A member of a Christian sect which observes the seventh day of the week as the Sabbath; a Seventh-Day Baptist. {1645} Also attrib. — **1725** *Boston News-Letter* 14 Jan. 2/2 Eight of the Sect called Sabbatharians, that committed the Murder of Capt. Symmonds, . . . were there Executed. *a*1817 DWIGHT *Travels* III. 37 About one fourth of the people of Westerly are supposed to be Sabbatarians, or seventh-day Baptists. **1833** J. FINCH *Travels* 120 The sect of Sabbatarians were numerous in this part of the country. **1867** DIXON *New America* II. 308 This body was divided into Old School Baptists, . . . Sabbatarians, Campbellites [etc.].

* **Sabbath,** *n.*

* **1.** A day of rest and religious observance; usually, a synonym for Sunday, the first day of the week.

1630 in Bradford *Hist.* 330 Being at Salem ye 25. of July, being ye saboath, after ye evening exercise, Mr. Johnson received a letter from ye Gov[erno]r. *a*1656 BRADFORD *Ib.* 106 This being the last day of ye weeke, they [some of the Pilgrims] prepared ther to keepe ye Sabath. **1722** *New-Eng. Courant* 17 Dec. 1/1 The Prohibition extends to our very Beasts; yet not only they, but our Servants also, work on the Sabbath. **1734** *Harvard Rec.* I. 136 All disorders on said evening [*i.e.*, Saturday], Shall be punished as violations of the Sabath are. **1800** in Morse *Life O. W. Holmes* I. 11 She always commenced the Sabbath at sunset on Saturday. **1809** KENDALL *Travels* I. 115 One Sunday, or as it is here [in Conn.] uniformly denominated, one *sabbath,* I accompanied an entire family to church. **1825** NEAL *Bro. Jonathan* I. 34 In Connecticut . . . it is their doctrine that the 'Sabbath' begins from the going down of the sun on a Saturday afternoon. **1898** HAMBLEN *Gen. Manager's Story* 5 My father was a stern puritanical clergyman, who considered a smile on the Sabbath to be a sin.

* **2.** The seventh day of the week, Saturday, observed as a day of rest by some religious denominations.

1771 FRANKLIN *Autobiog.* 268 Keimer likewise kept the Seventh day, Sabbath. **1870** EMERSON *Soc. & Solitude* 151 The old Sabbath, or Seventh Day, [is] . . . a clean page which the wise may inscribe with truth.

+**3.** *To travel beyond the Sabbath,* to go into a region where the Sabbath and other civilized usages are not observed.

1826 FLINT *Recoll.* 178 It is a common proverb of the people, that when we cross the Mississippi, 'we travel beyond the Sabbath.'

4. Attrib. and comb. with *assembly, bell, breaker,* etc.

1654 JOHNSON *Wonder-w. Prov.* 46 Their Sabbath-Assemblies prove very thin if the season savour not. **1688** *East-Hampton Rec.* II. 222 We Resolve to take a list of ther Names and present them to the next sesions for sabath breakers. **1852** STOWE *Uncle Tom* xxxv, A fair-haired woman had led him, at the sound of Sabbath bell, to worship and to pray. **1853** M. BLAKE *Mendon Association* 56 Similar resolves were passed respecting the Sabbath, and the American and Foreign Sabbath Union. **1864** STOWE *House & Home P.* 319 Sabbath-keeping is the iron rod of bigots. **1866** MOORE *Women of War* 103 The Sabbath exercises in the Representatives' Hall, observed by no means discontinued. **1897** BRODHEAD *Bound in Shallows* 66 Two women advanced in the little garden-path before it, stiff in Sabbath prints.

‖**Sabbath,** *v. intr.* To spend the Sabbath. — **1730** B. LYNDE *Diary* (1880) 17 Sabbathed at Mr. Claps, and at Lord's Supper with him. **1732** *Ib.* 27 Sabbath'd at York.

Sabbath-breaking. The violating of the usual religious observance of the Sabbath. {1651–} — **1653** *Boston Rec.* X. 27 My selfe have often seene & heard offences . . . such as . . . quareling, mutines, sabboth breakings, thefts ffrorgeries & such like. **1693** C. MATHER *Wond. Invisible World* (1862)‖ Swearing, Sabbath-breaking, Whoring, Drunkenness, . . . do not make a Gentleman, but a Monster. **1815** Mills & Smith *Missionary Tour* 29 Sabbath-breaking, profanity and intemperance prevail [in New Orleans] to a fearful extent. **1837** *S. Lit. Messenger* III. 349 Sabbath breaking is . . . no obscure feature in this great system of bustle and business. **1900** WINCHESTER *W. Castle* 128 Slab City was famed, far and wide, for its profanity and Sabbath-breaking.

* **Sabbath day.** (Cf. SABBADAY.)

* **1.** Sunday.

1622 'MOURT' *Relation* 59 On the Sabboth day wee rested. **1699** *N.J. Archives* 1 Ser. II. 292 People . . . will upon no consideration suffer a waggon to travell on the Sabbath day. **1825** [see GO-TO-MEETING *a.* 2]. **1899** CUSHMAN *Hist. Indians* 46 The Sabbath day is regarded [by the Indian] with much more reverence.

2. Attrib. and comb. with *catechizing, clothes,* etc.

1760 *Boston Gazette* 12 May, The Committee of Tradesmen hereby advise their Constituents and others . . . to shift themselves and put on their Sabbath Day Clothes. **1867** HOLMES *Guardian Angel* 34 Its depressing influence . . . followed her to the Sabbath-day catechisings. **1876** *Scribner's Mo.* Jan. 322/2, I'd quite as lieve they'd go to the play as ask me to go to their Sabbath day play-house. **1891** EARLE *Sabbath* 90 Correspondingly thin cloth or kid or silk slippers, . . . were the holiday and Sabbath-day covering for the feet.

+**Sabba(th)-day house.** A small house which could be heated in winter, built near a church for the use of churchgoers during intervals between services. *Obs.*

Sabbath-day houses are usually thought to have been peculiar to New England, but are reported from Texas in *Dial. Notes* VI. 336.

*a*1870 CHIPMAN *Notes on Bartlett* 375 *Sabba'day-Houses.* Cottages near a church had for warmth, &c., at recess of public worship.—Old New England use. **1876** J. E. TODD *John Todd* 40 Near by were a number of rough, stone-built 'Sabba'-day houses,' where they flocked at noon, for warmth in winter (they had chimneys), and coolness in summer. **1887** EGGLESTON in *Century Mag.* April 906/2 This extreme scrupulosity about Sabbath-keeping was doubtless the moving cause of the building of the 'Sabbath-day houses.' **1891** EARLE *Sabbath* 102 The 'noon-house,' or 'Sabba-day house' or 'horse-hows' . . . was a place of refuge in the winter time, at the noon interval between the two services.

Sabbath-keeper. {1854} +One who observes Saturday, the seventh day of the week, as a day of rest and worship. — **1844** RUPP *Relig. Denominations* 73 There were many other severities practised upon the Sabbath-keepers in New England. **1901** STILLMAN *Autobiog. Journalist* I. 5 All who did not hold to the finest scruple of conscience . . . were excluded from the communion as a precaution against the Sunday keepers becoming a majority in the church and taking it away from the Sabbath keepers.

Sabbath school.

1. Sunday school. {1845}

1820 *Boston Selectmen* 131 The application for liberty to use the Boylston school house on Fort hill for a Sabbath school . . . was granted. **1832** WILLIAMSON *Maine* II. 688 Sabbath-schools . . . [were established] in Philadelphia, about 1811, and have since spread over the United States. **1863** J. C. POWER *Rise Sunday Schools* 22 A Sabbath School was organized at that time in connexion with the church. **1900** *Congress. Rec.* 23 Jan. 1104/2 A wonderful petition is rolled in . . . from Sabbath schools, sectarian churches, and societies.

2. Attrib. and comb. with *celebration, children,* etc.

1856 M. J. HOLMES *Homestead* I. ii, I dare say [she] thinks you a very nice woman, for how can her Sabbath-school teacher be otherwise. **1863** *Ladies' Repository* Jan. 5/1 A Sabbath school celebration of the Fourth of July . . . made the most definite impression upon my mind. **1866** MOORE *Women of War* 357 My Sabbath school lessons . . . are now remembered and prized. **1866** GREGG *Life in Army* 209 It was sung by the colored Sabbath School children.

+**Sabbath warden.** An officer who enforces laws governing Sabbath observance. — **1768** *Duxbury Rec.* 340 Jacob Peterson and Robert Samson were chosen Sabbath Wardens.

+**Sabe,** *n.* [See next.] Understanding; practical knowledge; knack. *colloq.*[2] (Cf. SAVEY *n.*) — **1875** HARTE in *Scribner's Mo.* Dec. 244 A little keer and a little sabe on my part, and there's that family in the gulch made comfortable. **1890** *Stock Grower & Farmer* 12 July 6/1 They ain't old enough to have no sabe—what Injuns call tum tum. **1913** LONDON *Valley of Moon* 311 We ain't got the *sabe,* or the knack, or something or other.

+**Sabe,** *v.* W. [Sp. *saber* 'to know.'] *intr.* To understand or comprehend. (See also SAVEY *v.*) — **1879** *Scribner's Mo.* Oct. 814/2 'I sabe.' The

Judge dropped into slang as Silas Wegg descended to poetry. **1885** *Wkly. New Mexican Rev.* 2 April 3/4 The bill permitting Mexicans who do not sabe English to act as jurymen. **1912** RAINE *Brand Blotters* 258, I sabe you'd better not try to sit in at this game.

+**Sab(e)a bean.** [*Saba*, an island in the W. Indies.] A variety of bean. — **1793** *Holyoke Diaries* 128 Planted Corn & Beans & Sabea Bean. **1815** *Ib.* 162 Planted beans, Giraud, Saba & Cranberry.

Saber, Sabre.

Saber is the 'obs. or U.S. form of *Sabre*' (*O.E.D.*).

1. A curved cavalry sword. {1680–}

1806 *Webster* 263/1 *Saber*, a cimetar, falchion, short broad sword. **1840** *Niles' Nat. Reg.* 8 Aug. 366/1 Each dragoon [is] to furnish himself with . . . a sabre and a cartouche box. **1863** C. A. DANA *Recoll.Civil War* 137 About seventy horsemen will go along with their sabers and carbines to keep off the guerillas. **1902** 'O. HENRY' *Roads of Destiny* 195 Opposite hung the major's old cavalry sabre that he had carried at Shiloh.

2. Attrib. with *bayonet, belt, club*, etc.

1861 *Army Regulations* 397 Sabre belt. **1866** 'F. KIRKLAND' *Bk. Anecdotes* 320/2 They heard the tramp of horses and the jingle of sabre scabbards. **1879** TOURGEE *Fool's Errand* xl. 295 The Klan, and its more subtle and complete successors, under various and sundry names, 'Rifle-Clubs,' 'Sabre-Clubs,' 'Bull-dozers,' and so forth, had fully established themselves throughout the country. **1885** *Century Mag.* Sept. 779 My saber . . . hung to my waist by the saber-knot. **1890** *Buckskin Mose* 42 Each of them was furnished with a Sharp's carbine with a sabre-bayonet, and a revolver.

Saber-fish. The cutlass fish, *Trichiurus lepturus*. {1863, in Cuba} — **1883** *Nat. Museum Bul.* No. 27, 437 Sabre-fish. . . . On the east coast of the United States north to Cape Cod. **1891** *Cent.* 5287/2 *Saber-fish*, . . . the hairtail or silver-eel.

‖**Sabertasched,** *a.* Wearing a sabretache. — **1862** *N.Y. Tribune* 25 March 6/1 You daily meet . . . long-haired city lawyers blown out into burly sabertasched dragoons.

∗**Sable,** *n.*

+**1.** The pine marten (*Martes americana*), or a related species.

1674 *Cal. State P., Amer. & W.I.* VII. 581 The natural inhabitants of the woods, hills, and swamps [in Maine include] . . . musquashes, sables, [and] squirrels. **1765** ROGERS *Acct. N. Amer.* 263 The *Martin*, or *Sable*, lives principally among the mountains. **1791** *Mass. Laws* (1801) I. 509 No person . . . shall hereafter, in either of the months of June, July, August or September, . . . [kill] Minks, Sable or Martin. **1839** [see ERMINE]. **1893** ROOSEVELT *Wilderness Hunter* 153 The marks . . . showed the loping progress of the sable. **1917** *Mammals of Amer.* 114/2 The Sable is principally trapped during the colder months, from October to April, when the fur is in good condition.

2. A type of iron, originally stamped with a sable. {1815} Also attrib.

1798 in H. M. Brooks *Gleanings* IV. 72 Cash given for . . . old Sable or Swedes Iron. **1820** *Columbian Centinel* 1 Jan. 3/1 Now landing from the brig Fame, . . . 25 tons new Sable Iron.

∗**Sable,** *a.* +Of Negroes: Black, dusky. Now freq. jocular.

1794 HUMPHREYS *Industry* 11 Bleed on, blest tree! and as thy sweet blood runs, Bestow fond hope on Afric's sable Sons. **1821** COOPER *Spy* xiii, It was only by odd moments he was enabled to impart to his sable brother . . . any portion of the wonderful incident. **1846** *Chicago Jrnl.* 6 Nov., Benefit of the Sable Melodists on which occasion will be performed a new Ethiopian Opera. **1857** *Lawrence* (Kan.) *Republican* 4 June 4 Is the sable African alone entitled to your sympathy and consideration? **1880** *Scribner's Mo.* Feb. 566/2 The sable and semi-sable pickers exchange their berry tickets and pennies as eagerly as we buy Vienna rolls. **1885** [see INSINUENDO].

absol. **1856** M. J. HOLMES *L. Rivers* 51 A group of sables . . . were discussing the furniture of the 'trump'ry room.'

+**Sable trap.** A trap for taking sables. — **1760** *New Eng. Hist. & Gen. Reg.* XXXVI. 30 Indians and Canadians . . . had been watching their sable traps. **1784** *Belknap P.* II. 188 We saw . . . abundance of sable-traps, and one bear-trap. **1851** SPRINGER *Forest Life* 118 Proprietors of a line of sable-traps would take the opportunity on the Sabbath to visit them.

+**Sac.** Also **Sack.** (See also SAUK.)

1. A tribe of Algonquian Indians living formerly in Michigan, later in Wisconsin and Illinois, and now in Oklahoma, Iowa, and Kansas. Often pl.

The Sacs and Foxes confederated in 1760.

[**1670** *Relations des Jésuites* (1858) 98/1 Leur langue . . . est la même que celle des Saki. **1722** COXE *Descr. Carolana* 48 The Nations who dwell on this River, are Outogamis, . . . Sacky, and the Poutouatamis.] **1820** [see Fox *n.* 2]. **1843** MARRYAT *M. Violet* xliii, The Sacs and Foxes . . . are on a good understanding with the Latter-day Saints. **1900** *Congress. Rec.* 26 Jan. 1221/1 What was the number of Indians . . . known as the Sac and Fox of the Mississippi, residing in the State of Iowa?

b. An Indian belonging to this tribe.

1810 *Ann. 12th Congress* 1 Sess. 1858 A considerable number of Sacs went . . . to see the British superintendent. **1848** BRYANT *California* iii. 41, I asked him if he was a Kansas? His reply was 'No—Sac.'

2. Attrib. with *chief, Indian, nation, tribe*.

1789 *Ann. 1st Congress* 41 [The treaties] with the sachems and warriors of the Wyandot, Delaware, . . . and Sac nations, . . . appear to have been negotiated [etc.]. **1840** *Niles' Nat. Reg.* 8 Aug. 356/2 The Sac and Fox Indians and Winnebagoes have had a talk. **1862** *Harper's Mag.* Sept. 463/2 The household traps and plunder of a Sac chief. **1877** JOHNSON *Anderson Co.*, (Kansas) 137 The Sac and Fox tribes of Indians were located on a reservation in Franklin and Osage counties.

+**Sacalait.** [Fr.; perhaps a perversion of some Indian word.] A name locally applied to certain fishes: (see quotations). — **1884** GOODE, etc. *Fisheries* I. 407 The Crappie—*Pomoxys annularis*. . . . Other names are . . . 'Sac-a-lait' and 'Chinquapin Perch' in the Lower Mississippi. *Ib.* 466 *Fundulus grandis*, is known at Pensacola by the name of 'Sac-à-lait.' **1891** *Cent.* 5288/3 Sacalai, same as *crappie*. **1903** T. H. BEAN *Fishes N.Y.* 463 Still other names of local application [for the calico bass] are barfish, bitter head, tinmouth, *sac-a-lait*, lamplighter [etc.]. **1911** *Rep. Fisheries 1908* 312 *Mummichog*. . . . On the Gulf [they are known] as 'sac-a-lait.'

+**Sacaton.** [Sp. *zacatón* fr. Nahuatl *çacatl, zacatl*, 'grass, reed.'] A coarse perennial grass of the Southwest, *Sporobolus wrightii*. Also *sacate*. — **1863** *37th Congress Sp. Sess.* Sen. Ex. Doc. No. 1, 16 'Sacaton' indicates water near surface. **1865** *Harper's Mag.* Jan. 147/1 The grass [of n. Sonora] consists of three principal varieties; the sacatone, a coarse, thick, and strong variety, growing in bunches; the mesquit [etc.]. **1873** ARMY *Items regarding N. Mex* 27 The 'sacaton' a grass growing 6 feet high also abounds [in the bottom lands of the Red R.]. **1894** *Dialect Notes* I. 325 *Zacáte*. . . . Also *sacáte*. **1913** BARNES *Western Grazing Grounds* 54 There are great areas along the rivers and in the alkali lands which grow a fine crop of sacaton . . . , sometimes, but erroneously called salt grass.

+**Sacatra.** [Fr., of obscure origin.] (See quotation.) — **1859** BARTLETT 375 *Sacatra*, the name given in Louisiana to the offspring of a griffe and a negress.

Saccharometer. An instrument for measuring the sugar content of a solution. {1784–} — **1833** SILLIMAN *Man. Sugar Cane* 36 An instrument called the Saccharometer, or Hydrometer of Baumé, is frequently used, in order to learn the saccharine richness of cane liquor. **1863** *Rep. Comm. Agric. 1862* 131 We have frequently been deceived in strong, rank looking cane, and found, upon applying the test of the saccharometer, that it would weigh only from five to six degrees Baumé. **1884** *Ib.* 37 The quality of the cane was tested . . . and the juice weighed with a very delicate saccharometer.

+**Sachamaker.** [App. from Algonquian *sachama* 'sachem.'] A sachem or sagamore; an Indian tribal chief. *Obs.* (Cf. SAGAMORE.) — **1675** *Doc. Hist. N.Y.* XII. 519 The 20th inst. three of the Nevisans Sachemakas, were here with me. **1682** *Indian Laws & Tr.* III. 696 The said Sachemakers doe hereby acknowledge themselves fully satisfyed. **1687** BLOME *Isles & Terr. in Amer.* 103 Another made a Speech to the Indians, in the Name of all the Sachamakers or Kings. **1701** WOLLEY *Journal N.Y.* (1902) 44 When we were at dinner . . . , a Sackamaker or King came in with several of his Attendants.

+**Sachem.** Also **sachim.** [Algonquian.]

1. A chief of an Indian tribe. Also attrib.

See SAGAMORE, note.

1622 'MOURT' *Relation* 120 The Company . . . [resolved] to retaine Nepeof, another Sachim or Gouvernour. **1631** Force *Tracts* II. iv. 6 This man least favoureth the English of any Sagamore (for soe are the kinges with vs called, as they are Sachims Southwards). **1670** ELIOT *Brief Narr.* 9 The Sachem of this Place is named Nomplion. **1723** *Amer. Wkly. Mercury* 5–12 Feb. 3/1 About a Fortnight ago dyed at Westerly, Ninnicraft the Great Sachem. **1777** ROBERTSON *Hist. America* I. iv. 343 In Florida, the authority of the sachems, . . . was not only permanent, but hereditary. **1781** PETERS *Hist. Conn.* (1829) 42 Gratitude, or pride, induced all those English-made sachems to assign deeds to their creators. **1839** *Mass. H. S. Coll.* 3 Ser. IX. 93 Before this country was visited by the Europeans, it is believed that the sagamore and sachem . . . came to their offices by hereditary right. **1882** E. K. GODFREY *Nantucket* 164 The Mayhews . . . may not have been able to purchase the Indian or 'sachem rights,' but it is certain there were no 'associates' until 1659.

transf. **1885** HOLMES *Mortal Antipathy* iv, The Mysterious Stranger is the name some give him, but we girls call him the *Sachem*, because 'he paddles about in an Indian canoe.'

2. *transf.* The head of any government; a political leader.

1684 *Doc. Hist. N.Y. State* I. 402 Wee have put ourselves under the Great Sachim Charles that lives over the Great Lake. **1776** J. ADAMS *Works* IX. 387 The patricians, the sachems, the nabobs, call them by what name you please, sigh, and groan, and fret. **1803** *Ga. Republican* 12 May 3/4 (Th. S.), Let our wine sparkle high while we gratefully give The health of our Sachem [Jefferson], and long may he live. **1817** *Mass. Spy* 2 April (Th.), There is a respect due to our sachems, which this vulgar state of things diminishes.

3. A governing officer of the Tammany Society in New York, or one of its early associated societies.

[**1786** in Kilroe *St. Tammany* 95 The example of these holy Sachems, has had a great effect.] **1787** *Ib.* 120 The members of St. Tammany's Society in the City of New York are requested to meet at their wigwam, . . . on Tuesday. . . . By order of the Sachem. **1819** *Mass. Spy* 10 March (Th.),

This toast astounded not only their Sachem, William Mooney, but put the whole wigwam into confusion. **1890** *Boston Jrnl.* 1 July 4/1 Richard Croker . . . is to be entertained this week by the Tammany sachems, who profess to see in him a much abused but now exonerated man.

b. *Grand Sachem*, the chief officer of a Tammany society. **1810** *Ohio Arch. & Hist. Q.* XXII. 354, I, Michael Leib, Grand Sachem of the Tammany Society, or Columbian Order, No. One, in the State of Pennsylvania, do . . . empower you . . . to build up and open a Wigwam at Chillicothe, in the State of Ohio. **1813** *Niles' Reg.* IV. 76/2 The Grand Sachem [shall] be requested to communicate, to the relatives of the deceased, a letter of condolence. **1882** [see GRAND *a.* 1]. **1905** *Springfield W. Repub.* 15 Dec. 1 Congressman W. Bourke Cockran was elected grand sachem of Tammany Hall in New York last week.

4. (See quotation.)
1871 DE VERE 379 The Scissor-tail (*Tyrannus carolinensis*) . . . does not shrink from attacking even hawks and eagles in defence of his young. The Narragansett Indians and other tribes called him, in appreciation of his bravery, the Sachem.

‖**5.** A water pipe or hose.
1889 S. HALE *Letters* 226 Peter Larkin came and coupled the sachem and turned on the ram.

+Sachemdom. The district governed by a sachem. *Obs.* — **1764** HUTCHINSON *Hist. Mass.* I. 459 There seems to have been two cantons or sachemdoms of the Cape Indians. **1794** STILES *Hist. Judges of Charles I.* 109 King Philip's war . . . was attended with exciting an[d] universal rising . . . of the Indians through New-England, except the Sachemdom of Uncas, at Mohegan. **1859** [see SACHEMSHIP].

+Sachemess. The wife of a sachem. *Obs.* — **1761** NILES *Indian Wars* II. 327 When the sachemess, or squaw sachem, . . . saw the fate of her husband, she was more flexible.

+Sachemic, *a.* Of or pertaining to a sachem. Also in comb. — **1847** EMORY *Military Reconn.* 37 We met ten or fifteen sachemic looking old Indians. **1885** J. S. KINGSLEY, etc. *Stand. Nat. Hist.* VI. 163 The sachemic office was hereditary [among the Five Nations], descending, not from father to son, but to the sister's children.

+Sachemore. =SAGAMORE. *Obs.* — **1751** GIST *Journals* 72 This Beaver is the Sachemore or Chief of the Delawares.

+Sachemship. The office or jurisdiction of a sachem. Now hist. — **1651** *Conn. Rec.* I. 228 Hee is not satisfied in Saquassens being exalted vnder our power to great Sachemship. **1859** BARTLETT 375 *Sachemdom,* or *Sachemship,* the government or jurisdiction of a sachem. **1880** *Lib. Universal Knowl.* X. 870 [The Oneidas were] divided into three clans . . . and nine sachemships. **1881** L. H. MORGAN *Houses Amer. Aborigines* 28 Fifty Sachemships were created and named in perpetuity.

+Sachem snake. A snake resembling the milk snake. — **1842** *Nat. Hist. N.Y., Zoology* III. 39 In Suffolk county, a large snake resembling this [milk snake] has been described to me under the name of Sachem Snake. **1910** HODGE, etc. *Amer. Indians* II. 402/1 A Long Island serpent, probably the milk-snake, has been called sachem-snake.

Sack, n.*¹ A kind of white wine. Now hist. Also attrib. — **1633 *N.H. Prov. Papers* I. 72 Pd. . . . Capt. Mason for 8 galls. of sack. **1647** *Md. Archives* IV. 320 A syluer sacke cup. **1653** *Boston Rec.* 41 There is also . . . a Sacke Bowle, a silver hot water cup [etc.]. **1686** *Conn. Rec.* III. 408 Every butt or pipe of Sherry, Sack, Malaga, . . . twenty shillings. **1729** SEWALL *Diary* III. 394, I made a good Fire, set Chairs, and gave Sack.

** Sack, n.*² A bag or container made of cloth; often a measure of some commodity.
1645 *Conn. Probate Rec.* I. 21 A sacke wth some biskitt in yt, another old Sacke used for a bedd. **1662** *Plymouth Laws* 136 In case any master Carrier . . . shall have cause to suspect any such goods may bee concealled in any cask or sacke amongst other goods [etc.]. **1820** *Amer. Antiq. Soc. Coll.* I. 66 He undertook this journey afoot . . . having no other provision but a little sack of roasted Indian corn. **1848** BRYANT *California* iv. 55 They were packing several large sacks of fur-skins. **1880** *Cimarron News & Press* 24 June 3/2 Messrs. B. & M. received last week some 400 sacks of wool. **1912** RAINE *Brand Blotters* 91 He loaded the sack on its back and drove off.

+b. *To be left to hold the sack*, to get the worst of a situation. (Cf. BAG *n.* 2.)
1904 W. H. SMITH *Promoters* 343 They are the ones that are always left to hold the sack.

** Sack, n.*³ **a.** A loose gown worn by women. (Cf. DRESSING SACK.) **b.** A loose-fitting coat. {1883-} (Cf. SACK COAT.)
1756 in Singleton *Social N.Y.* 246 Put her on a negligee, A short sack, or shepherdee. **1768** *Holyoke Diaries* 70 Altered my Blue Sack. **1773** TRUMBULL *Progress of Dulness* III. 54 A genius, that can . . . cast the nativity with ease Of gowns, and sacks and negligees. **1848** *Knickerb.* XXXI. 221 He had muffled up in his sack, neck-cloth and gloves. **1863** 'M. HARLAND' *Husks* 43 Sarah divested Jeannie of her sacque and dress. **1865** 'G. HAMILTON' *Skirmishes* 211 Old coats . . . and gowns, and sacks . . . [will not] be worn. **1873** PHELPS *Trotty's Wedding* ii, He wore a gray sack with a leather belt to it. **1881** *Harper's Mag.* April 736/1 A sacque opening nearly to her waist in a V shape showed a tattooed neck. **1883** HOWELLS *Woman's Reason* xxi, The two women laughed together, and began to pull up their sacks. **1894** B. MATTHEWS in *Harper's Mag.* Sept. 580/1 There were a few men in sacks and cut-aways; but the most of them had dressed for the occasion.

+Sack, *n.*⁴ (See SAC.)
+Sack, *v.* *Logging.* **a.** *tr.* To straighten out (a log slide or the upstream end of a log drive) by returning logs that have strayed or lodged. **b.** *intr.* To work at recovering strayed logs. Also *vbl. n.* and *ppl. a.* — **1860** *Harper's Mag.* XX. (*O.E.D.*), Another frequent and laborious part of the drive is sacking. **1902** WHITE *Blazed Trail* 334 Intense rivalry existed as to which crew 'sacked' the farthest down stream in the course of the day. **1905** *Forestry Bureau. Bul.* No. 61, 45 *Sack the rear, to,* to follow a drive and roll in logs which have lodged or grounded. *Ib., Sack the slide, to,* to return to a slide logs which have jumped out. **1908** WHITE *Riverman* 12 The moving of them [*sc.* stranded logs] was deferred for the 'sacking crew.'

Sack coat. A short, loose-fitting coat worn by men. — **1847** MAGOFFIN *Down Santa Fé Trail* 253 The general was dressed in his famed old gray sack coat. **1853** P. KENNEDY *Blackwater Chron.* 93 He wears an old brown sack-coat. **1887** J. HAWTHORNE in *Century Mag.* June 183/1 Here are crimson and blue hats, jerseys, and sack-coats. **1900** *Boston Transcript* 6 June 20/1 The men do not wear overcoats, but dress in heavy sack coats made of blankets. **1918** *Sears, Roebuck & Co. Cat.* No. 137, 441 Single breasted sack coat closing with three buttons.

*Sacking. A coarse, strong fabric of which sacks, bags, etc., are made. {1707-} — **1833** *Niles' Reg.* XLIV. 269/1 Linens to be admitted at an ad valorem duty of 15 per cent. . . . [include] twilled sacking: [and] warenderps. **1887** [see COT 1]. **1901** MERWIN & WEBSTER *Calumet 'K'* 323 With a hammer and nails, and a big piece of sacking he went down the leg again.

Sacking bottom. A coarse cloth bottom fastened beneath a framework, esp. a bedstead. {sacking bottom'd, c1710; 1881} — **1744** HEMPSTEAD *Diary* 425, [I was] fitting a new Bedstid that I Sent with Sacking Bottom. **1779** *York Co., Va., Rec.: Wills* XXII. 28 April, Mahogany bedstead with sacking bottom. **1833** CATLIN *Indians* I. 191, I am reclining on a sacking-bottom, made of the buffalo's hide. **1868** G. G. CHANNING *Recoll. Newport* 254 Sometimes it [*i.e.*, the bedstead] was furnished with a 'sacking bottom.'

+Sack pants. Loose-fitting trousers. — **1856** KANE *Arctic Explor.* II. 98 [My outfit] consists of— . . . an extra jumper and sack-pants for sleeping.

+Sack suit. A man's suit having a sack coat. — **1895** *N.Y. Dramatic News* 6 July 14/4 Four button sack suit, $25. **1908** 'O. HENRY' *Options* 194 One of them . . . 'roller-coasters' flew the track and killed a man in a brown sack-suit.

*Sacrament. **1.** *spec.* The ceremony of the Lord's Supper in various Christian churches. **2.** (See quotation.) — (1) **1665** *Plymouth Laws* 38 All men and women . . . may be admitted to the Sacrament of the Lord's supper. **1680** *Conn. Rec.* I. 355, I give to the South Church in Hartford £10 in plate for the use of the Sacrament. **1744** MACSPARRAN *Diary* 20 Anstis went . . . to be at a Husking instead of the Sacrament, wch she has not received since she lay in. **1850** in Rothert *Muhlenberg Co.* 200 Delivered an address and administered sacrament. (2) **1847** DAVIDSON *Presbyterian Ch. in Ky.* 134 From this time such crowds flocked to the sacraments, as these occasions [camp meetings] were called, that sufficient accommodations could not be procured for them.

Sacrament day. A Sunday on which the Lord's Supper is celebrated. — **1687** SEWALL *Diary* I. 176 May 15th was our Sacrament-day. **1725** [see EXERCISE *n.* 1]. **1759** *Essex Inst. Coll.* XLIX. 3 Mr. Barnard's Text, it being Sacrement Day, was that famous prophecy of Jacob's, Genesis, xxxix, 10.

+Sacramento perch. A fresh-water fish (*Archoplites interruptus*) something like the perch, found in the Sacramento and other rivers of the Pacific coast. — **1883** *Nat. Museum Bul.* No. 27, 461. **1896** JORDAN & EVERMANN *Check-List Fishes* 354 Sacramento Perch. Sacramento and San Joaquin rivers, California. **1911** *Rep. Fisheries 1908* 315/1 *Sacramento perch* . . . , sunfish of the Sacramento and an excellent food fish.

+Sacramento pike. The squawfish or yellowbelly (*Ptychocheilus oregonensis*), or a related species. — **1883** *Nat. Museum Bul.* No. 27, 487 Sacramento 'Pike'; 'Whitefish.' . . . In cold streams its flesh is excellent. **1896** JORDAN & EVERMANN *Check-List Fishes* 247 Sacramento Pike. . . . Rivers of Oregon and Washington . . . ; also in the Sacramento, San Joaquin, [etc.] . . . rivers of California. **1911** *Rep. Fisheries 1908* 315/1.

Sacred bean. +The American lotus or water chinquapin, *Nelumbo lutea.* (Cf. NELUMBO.) — **1817-8** EATON *Botany* (1822) 361 Sacred bean. . . . A most superb plant. **1850** S. F. COOPER *Rural Hours* 275 One of the noblest plants of our country . . . [is] the Nelumbo, or sacred bean. **1898** CREEVEY *Flowers of Field* 118 Sacred Bean. . . . The numerous pistils . . . produce bean-like, eatable seeds.

Sacred desk. +A pulpit. (Cf. DESK 2.) — **1772** *Boston Gazette* 28 Sept. (Th.), [That they] should select a Runagate to be their Monitor from the sacred desk. **1824** *Baptist Mag.* IV. 309 While sitting in the holy sanctuary and listening to the sweet accents of mercy from the sacred desk, her distress vanished at once. **1866** *Congress. Globe* 24 Jan. 401/3, I have seen in the sacred desk what were called eloquent clergymen, full Africans.

Sacred fire. {1693-} +A ceremonial fire burned as a rite by some Indian tribes, esp. the Pueblo tribes of New Mexico. — **1849** *31st Congress 1 Sess.* Sen. Ex. Doc. No. 64, 68 The old man and his daughter . . . were tending the sacred fire at Pecos. **1885** *Santa Fe Leader* 15 June, From that flight to this hour, his [Montezuma's] worshippers have kept . . . in their *estufas* the sacred fire. **1899** Cushman *Hist. Indians* 364 The women . . . [were] seated on skins close to the place of burial or sacred fire.

*Sacrifice.

*1. The act of offering something of value to a deity, +as practiced by various American Indian tribes; also, the thing so offered. Also attrib.

1705 BEVERLEY *Virginia* III. 42 The Indians offer Sacrifice . . . when they travel or begin a long Journey. **1791** LONG *Voyages* 35 The dances among the Indians [include]: . . . 9. The marriage dance. 10. The sacrifice dance. **1808** PIKE *Sources Miss.* 31 A small *red capot* hung upon a tree . . . was a sacrifice by some Indians to the *bon Dieu.* **1820** *Amer. Antiq. Soc. Trans.* I. 275 They perform the sacrifices and all the religious ceremonies of the nation.

+2. *Baseball.* = SACRIFICE HIT.

1880 *Chicago Inter-Ocean* 29 June 8/3 Force's winning run came off a wild throw by Ward, a sacrifice, and single. **1891** *Courier-Journal* 4 Oct. 5/1 Merritt's sacrifice and a single by Clausen scored two runs. **1917** MATHEWSON *Second Base Sloan* 246 The Billies caused consternation by . . . advancing a man to third on a sacrifice and an error.

+Sacrifice hit. *Baseball.* (See quot. 1889.) — **1880** *Chicago Inter-Ocean* 29 June 8/2 Anson's sacrifice hit and out advanced Williamson to third. **1889** CAMP *College Sports* 177 A 'sacrifice hit' is a ball so batted as to advance a base-runner while it gives an opportunity of putting out the man batting it. **1910** [see HIT *n.* 2].

Sacrifice rock. (See quotation.) — **1802** *Mass. H. S. Coll.* 2 Ser. III. 7 [The Indians] still however preserve a regard for sacrifice rocks, on which they cast a stick or stone, when they pass by them.

*Saddle, *n.*

*1. A seat for the rider of a horse; usually made of leather, with straps and stirrups at the sides.

See also CALIFORNIA SADDLE, MEXICAN SADDLE, PACKSADDLE and McCLELLAN 1.

1640 *Conn. Rec.* I. 448 An Inventory of the goods and Cattell of James Olmestead: . . . collers & harnes, saddell and pannell, halters & brydle. **1678** *New Castle Court Rec.* 349, 1 saddle and brydle girts and Croopers. **1707** *Boston News-Letter* 10 Feb. 2/2 He could not give a good account how he came by . . . a certain Horse, Bridle and Sadle found in his Possession. **1787** in V. W. Howard *Bryan Sta. Heroes* (1932) 42 Blair makes and sells all kinds of men's and women's saddles. **1835** HOFFMAN *Winter in West* I. 90 The effects of the Yankee were generally limited to a Dearborn wagon, a feather bed, a saddle and bridle. **1893** SANBORN *S. Calif.* 177 The saddle is studded over with silver ornaments. **1920** [see CUTTING *n.* and *a.* 3].

*2. Something resembling a saddle: (see quotations).

1833 SILLIMAN *Man. Sugar Cane* 35 These [scums] are pushed backwards by wooden oars, over the saddles separating the kettles. **1876** KNIGHT 2009/2 *Saddle. . . .* (*Railway.*) *a.* The bearing or brass resting on the journal of a car-axle in the axle-box. . . . *b.* A chair or seat for a railway-rail. **1876** INGRAM *Centennial Exp.* 343 The chains are carried over the top of the tower [of the bridge] on wrought-iron chairs or saddles. **1905** *Forestry Bureau. Bul.* No. 61, 45 *Saddle,* the depression cut in a transverse skid in a skid road to guide the logs which pass over it. (P[acific] C[oast] F[orest].)

+3. A pair of numbers in a policy game.

1882 McCABE *New York* 551 If a single number is chosen and drawn, he wins \$5; two numbers constitute a 'saddle.'

4. In phrases.

To pay saddle, (meaning uncertain); *to keep the saddle,* to remain on horseback.

1773 *Md. Hist. Mag.* XV. 57 The strongest reason ag[ains]t High fees to officers is the Saddles they Pay, & if by a Law they were obliged to swear they payed no saddles &c I would willingly give them Liberall Allowances, as it would secure the Residence of the Principall Officers among us. **1873** MILLER *Amongst Modocs* 15 Our work consisted in keeping the saddle eight or ten hours a day.

5. *attrib.* **a.** Designating parts of or articles used with saddles.

1676 SEWALL *Diary* I. 27 Saddle Cover [was] lost. **1678** *New Castle Court Rec.* 361, 2 saddle Ruggs & 3 old Blancketts. **1750** HEMPSTEAD *Diary* 546, I mended my old Sadle pad. **1759** *Newport Mercury* 26 June 4/3 Imported, . . . Saddle Heads, Tuff Nails [etc.]. **1790** *Penna. Packet* 2 Feb. 4/1 To be Sold by Jesse Sharpless, at his Saddle Manufactory, . . . A few setts of the best saddle nails. **1856** A. CARY *Married* 184 The bridle rein was twisted around the saddle horn. **1883** *Century Mag.* Aug. 523/1 Mats, called 'cocas,' . . . are much sought after by California ranchmen as saddle-mats. **1898** CANFIELD *Maid of Frontier* 185 His horse came up to his ranch . . . with the gun still in the saddle scabbard.

b. Designating places where saddles are made or kept.

1779 E. PARKMAN *Diary* 194 Snow-Banks very high one nigh my saddle-house 6 feet high. **1790** Saddle manufactory [see sense a]. **1837** W. JENKINS *Ohio Gaz.* 55 This town . . . [contains] two saddle and harness shops.

c. Designating animals broken to the saddle or made to carry packsaddles.

1853 'P. PAXTON' *Yankee in Texas* 132 It's a big pile to give for a saddle mule. **1890** *Stock Grower & Farmer* 21 June 6/3 H. W. Thaxton, of Roswell, has for disposal 200 head of saddle ponies. **1903** A. ADAMS *Log of Cowboy* 17 Then the entire saddle stock was driven in, so as to be at hand

in case a hasty change of mounts was required. **1907** WHITE *Arizona Nights* 316 Señor Johnson owned . . . two hundred broken saddle animals.

d. In special combinations.

Saddle gun, a gun carried in a holster on a saddle; +*s. man,* a traveler on horseback; *s. race,* a race run by saddle horses.

1886 *Outing* April 7/1, [I] had with me the little forty-sixty Winchester saddle gun. **1819** AMPHLETT *Emigrant's Directory* 71 *Saddle-men,* as they are termed here, command the best attentions of the host. **1868** WOODRUFF *Trotting Horse* 158 In the saddle-race, he beat me the first heat.

*Saddle, *v.* +**1.** *tr.* To fasten (a bird's nest) on a limb like a saddle. +**2.** *To saddle the market,* (see quotation). — **(1) 1831** AUDUBON *Ornith. Biog.* I. 303 The nests were fixed to a horizontal bough, but were not *saddled* upon it so deeply as those of the Wood Thrush are. **1857** *Rep. Comm. Patents 1856: Agric.* 134 The centre of the nest is saddled on the bough, being made thinner in the part resting thereon. **1881** *Amer. Naturalist* XV. 217 [The nest of the short-legged pewee] was saddled to a horizontal limb after the fashion of our wood pewee. **(2) 1870** MEDBERY *Men Wall St.* 137 Saddling the market, is to foist a certain stock on the street.

+Saddleback (caterpillar). (See quotations.) — **1891** *Cent.* 5297/2 *Saddleback,* . . . the larva of the bombycid moth *Empretia stimulea;* so called on account of the saddle-like markings on the back. **1908** KELLOGG *Amer. Insects* (ed. 2) 384 The saddle-back caterpillar, *Sibine* (Empretia) *stimulea,* has a striking squarish green blotch on the back.

Saddlebag, *n.* One of a pair of bags usually slung behind the saddle. {**1841**-} Also attrib. — **1773** FINLAY *Journal* 43 The rider had saddle bags quite full besides. **1790** *Penna. Packet* 2 Feb. 4/1 He also hath . . . Portmanteaus, Trunks, Saddle-bags [etc.]. **1816** *Austin P.* I. (1924) 262, Bot of Moses Austin . . . 2 Saddle Bags Locks. **1834** A. PIKE *Sketches* 16 Lewis was allowed to wait with . . . his saddle-bags full of clothes. **1901** DUNCAN & SCOTT *Allen & Woodson Co., Kansas* 619 The doctor of 1858, . . . with saddle-bags like paniers to a pack mule, would make a strange comparison with the well-dressed and well-barbered M. D. of the present era.

+Saddle-bag John. General John Pope (1822-92). A nickname. — **1884** *Century Mag.* Oct. 815 Pope was saddled with the title of 'Saddle-bag John,' in memory of his famous order about head-quarters being on horseback.

+Saddlebag(s), *v. intr.* To catch on an obstruction and be held up on it. Also *transf.* — **1884** 'MARK TWAIN' *H. Finn* xiii, [They] went a-floating down, stern first, about two mile, and saddle-baggsed on the wreck. **1905** *Forestry Bureau Bul.* No. 61, 45 *Saddlebag,* as applied to a boom, to catch on an obstruction and double around it.

+Saddle blanket. A blanket used under the saddle on a horse, mule, etc. — **1817** FORDHAM *Narr. Travels* 98 My cloak and saddle-blanket, spread on the floor, from my couch. **1848** *Ladies' Repository* VIII. 162 [They] slept on their saddle-blankets under the open canopy of heaven. *a***1918** G. STUART *On Frontier* I. 237 Spreading down our saddle blankets for a bed and our saddles for pillows we lay down.

Saddle horse. A horse suited for riding. {**1662**-} — **1755** FRANKLIN in *Autobiog.* 395 Every saddle or pack horse, is to be valued by indifferent persons chosen between me and the owner. **1810** WEEMS *Letters* III. 2 It was plannd that I shou'd . . . get a gigg, or even a saddle horse. **1818** FLINT *Lett. from Amer.* 114 Price of a fine saddle horse, 200 to 300 [dollars]. **1893** G. W. CURTIS *Horses, Cattle* 58 The American Saddle Horse is now recognized among the newly formed breeds. **1920** J. GREGORY *Man to Man* 103 A dozen saddle-horses were tied at the hitching-rail.

+Saddleleaf. The American tulip-tree, *Liriodendron tulipifera.* — **1820** in Mathews *Mem. Charles Mathews* (1839) III. 149 If you have not got any in the grounds, a saddle-leaf is beautiful. **1891** *Cent.* 6525/3 *Tulip-tree. . . .* An old name, *saddletree* or *saddle-leaf,* refers to the form of the leaf.

*Saddler.

*1. One who makes, repairs, or deals in saddles.

1663 *Boston Rec.* 19 Francis Smith hath imployed his sonne in the mannifacture of a sadler. **1777** *N.J. Archives* 2 Ser. I. 539 [The house] is well situated for a sadler, . . . or any tradesman. **1809** CUMING *Western Tour* 222 Pittsburgh [has] . . . six saddlers and harness-makers. **1849** CHAMBERLAIN *Ind. Gazetteer* 152 There are in Adams county . . . two saddlers. **1879** *Cimarron News & Press* 27 Nov. 3/2 J. F. Bond, the pioneer saddler of Trinidad, keeps the largest stock of goods. **1892** *York County Hist. Rev.* 48 J. N. Folckemmer, Harness-maker and Saddler, . . . occupies a shop and salesroom.

b. In possessive: Designating things used by a saddler.

1788 *Kentucky Gazette* 19 April 1/1 Now Selling by Tegarden and M'Cullough, . . . Sadlers Tacks Buckles and Bosses. **1816** *Austin P.* I. (1924) 263, 1 Saddler's Hammer. **1859** in F. Hall *Hist. Colorado* II. 523, [I have] got plenty buckskin needles and saddler's silk now.

+2. A saddle horse. *colloq.*

1888 *Boston Jrnl.* 16 June 1/1 Another auction sale of choice family horses (including matched pairs and saddlers). **1893** G. W. CURTIS *Horses, Cattle* 58 The origin of the Saddler is, of course, found in thoroughbred blood. **1904** *N.Y. Tribune* 17 July, Mrs. Roosevelt rode her favorite saddler Yganka.

+Saddle rock. [Said to be named for a rock in Little Neck Bay, Long Island.] (See quotations.) In full *saddle rock oyster.* — **1881** INGERSOLL *Oyster-Industry* 244 *Fancy Oysters.*— . . . In New York, these are 'Saddle Rocks,' 'Blue Points,' etc. *Ib.* 247 *Saddle Rock Oysters.*—A trade name in New York for the largest and finest oysters. **1891** *Cent.* 5298/1 *Saddle-*

rock, . . . a variety of the oyster, *Ostrea virginica*, of large size and thick, rounded form.

Saddler sergeant. {1865} +(See quotation.) — **1891** *Cent.* 5298/1 *Saddler-sergeant*, . . . in the United States a non-commissioned staff-officer of a cavalry regiment.

* Saddlery.

+1. Saddles and other articles made by a saddler. {1833–}
1711 *Boston News-Letter* 22 Oct. 2/2 To be Sold . . . Pipes, Sadlery, Bunting, Millenary Goods [etc.]. **1790** *Penna. Packet* 3 Feb. 2/4 A quantity of hinges, locks of all sorts, . . . sadlery, coffin furniture [etc., will be sold]. **1815** *Niles' Reg.* IX. 35/2 Plated saddlery and carriage mounting of all kinds . . . are manufactured. **1865** *Ore. State Jrnl.* 18 Nov. 4/5 Sam. Ashley, Manufacturer of all kinds of Harness and Saddlery. **1894** *Scribner's Mag.* May 603/2 The sewing-machine . . . has been followed [on ranches] by . . . revolvers, saddlery, and cotton goods.
attrib. **1787** *Md. Gazette* 1 June 3/3 Saddlery tools, in sets.

2. A place where saddles are made. {1841–}
1835 HOFFMAN *Winter in West* I. 40, I have examined the manufacture of these gorgeous trappings at the saddleries in some of the towns in passing. **1837** PECK *New Guide* 177 In Pittsburgh . . . there are twenty-six saddleries and forty-one tanneries.

+Saddle train. A procession of travelers on horseback; a train of animals carrying packsaddles. — **1861** *Harper's Mag.* Feb. 299/2 Fortunately, a saddle-train which had passed to Genoa . . . returned a little after daylight. **1878** JACKSON *Travel at Home* 104 Those who wish to see . . . , the setting-off of saddle-trains, . . . would better take rooms on the front. **1896** SHINN *Story of Mine* 51 Saddle trains were started for passengers before any vehicle could get over the passes.

*Saddletree. + =SADDLELEAF. — **1843** *Penny Cycl.* XXV. 34/2 *Tulip-tree.* . . . In America where it is native, it is also known by the names White wood, Canoe wood, Saddle-tree. **1866** LINDLEY & MOORE *Treas. Botany* 688/1 The leaves large, . . . four-lobed and somewhat like a saddle in shape; hence the tree is sometimes spoken of as the Saddle-tree.

+Saddy, *n. Pa.* [f. next.] A curtsy. — **1870** *Nation* 28 July 56/2 The child was directed to 'make a saddy.'

+Saddy, *v.* [Origin uncertain: (see quot. 1859).] *intr.* To curtsy; in vocative use, to express thanks. Also *vbl. n. colloq.* — **1835** CROCKETT *Tour* 34 It would do you good to see our boys and girls dancing. None of your stradling, mincing, sadying. **1835** BIRD *Hawks* I. 155 'Come now, my old boy, here's a dollar.' . . . 'Saddy, massa; God blessa massa!' **1859** BARTLETT 375 *To Saddy*, to bob up and down; to curtsy like a child. Probably a child's corruption of *Thank ye*, applied to the curtsy which accompanies the phrase. c**1873** DE VERE *MS. Notes* 549 *Saddy* is pure Philadelphian. 'I remember once ask[in]g my mo[ther] what it meant and her reply = "Save ye," but doubtful.' It was used in Va. 100 y[ear]s ago.

Sadiron. =FLATIRON. {1832–} — **1761** [see GRIDIRON *n.* 1]. **1787** *Md. Gazette* 1 June 1/2 Hardware, of all kinds, . . . Sad-Irons in casks of 2 cwt. **1815** *Niles' Reg.* VIII. 141/1 There are in Pittsburgh, three large and extensive air-founderies, cast all kinds of hollow-ware, . . . smiths' anvils, sad irons, steam-engine castings [etc.]. **1871** GROSVENOR *Protection* 202 The protective tariff of 1842 . . . imposed duties higher than ever before imposed on . . . sadirons. **1896** *Internat. Typogr. Union Proc.* 63/2, 4 sad irons, $2.16.

* Safe, *n.*

*1. A kind of cupboard or box in which provisions are kept safe from insects, etc.; a meat safe.
1649 *Conn. Rec.* I. 496 An Inventory of the Estate of Mr. William Whiting: . . . a clock, a safe, a bedstead. **1815** *View N.Y. State Prison* 35 Wheelbarrows, swifts, safes, tables, and indeed almost everything appertaining to the business [of carpentering] are manufactured. **1875** STOWE *We & Neighbors* 55 [In] the Kitchen and kitchen pantry . . . she looked into the flour barrel, the sugar barrel, the safe, the cake box. **1905** PRINGLE *Rice Planter* 197, I told her to broil a nice, 'cubator chicken and put it in the safe.

2. A strong metal box for valuables, intended to be secure against fires and burglary. {1838–}
Cf. SALAMANDER 3.
1820 *Boston Selectmen* 174 A fire proof safe in the Selectmens room for the security of the records. **1874** ALDRICH *P. Palfrey* xiii, The monotonous ticking of the chronometer, pinioned against the wall above the massive iron safe, was the only sound. **1898** WESTCOTT *D. Harum* 137 Everything had been put away, and the safe and vault closed. **1923** DUTTON *Shadow on Glass* 197 Bartley gave the box to the clerk to keep in the safe.
b. Attrib. and comb. with *blower, breaker, lock, wall.*
1853 *Rep. Comm. Patents 1852* I. 306 Improved Burglar-Proof Plates for Doors, Safe-Walls, Vaults, etc. **1859** *Ib. 1858* I. 543 Improved Safe Lock. **1870** M. H. SMITH *20 Years Wall St.* 320 A safe-breaker from Boston, a bank-robber from Philadelphia, a New York thief, have each their own way of doing things. **1887** *Courier-Journal* 6 Feb. 12/6 A band of burglars and safe-blowers . . . has in five years past stolen $20,000.

* Safe, *a.*

+1. *Politics.* **a.** Of men, esp. candidates for office: Not likely to disturb vested interests; dependable. **b.** Of a political district: Certain to vote for a given candidate.

1862 LOWELL *Biglow P.* 2 Ser. iii. 109 Long 'z ye sift out 'safe' candidates thet no one ain't afeared on. **1905** STEFFENS in *McClure's Mag.* XXIV. 352/2 The gubernatorial chair [in R.I.] never had amounted to much more than an empty honor for 'safe men.' **1914** [see COLONIZATION 4].

+2. *Baseball.* Of a hit: That enables the runner to reach a base.
1868 CHADWICK *Base Ball* 45 A 'safe hit' is made when the ball is either sent bounding out of reach of the in-fielders or sent similarly over their heads and yet not far enough out to be caught by the out-fielders. *Ib.* 89 Sumner secured his first base on a safe ball to left field.

3. In special combinations.
Safe chance, a good financial risk; *s. player*, a person who takes no chances.
1863 'M. HARLAND' *Husks* 117 To matrimonial speculators, as in financial circles, he was known as a 'safe chance.' **1901** ADE *40 Modern Fables* 155 He hoped that all of the Old Ladies and the Safe Players would dust the Cracked Ice out of their Laps and get busy.

+Safe deposit. A place for storing valuables. Usu. attrib. — [**1783** in Sparks *Corr. Revol.* IV. 27 West Point . . . may be made a safe deposit where every military article may be kept in good order and repair.] **1880** W. NEWTON *Serm. Boys & Girls* (1881) 338 (*O.E.D.*), I went down into the vaults of one of our great safe-deposit buildings. **1882** *Century Mag.* March 769/1 They did not ask for the key of the safe-deposit box, or for other evidence. **1896** *Typographical Jrnl.* 1 July p. iii (*advt.*), Safe Deposit Vault. . . . Finest and only vault of the kind in the State. **1904** 'O. HENRY' *Four Million* 153 Our romance has been a pallid thing of a marriage or two, a satin rosette kept in a safe-deposit drawer, and a life-long feud with a steam radiator. **1912** IRWIN *Red Button* 298 From there he went to a safe deposit bank.

* Safety.

+1. a. *Football.* The downing of the ball behind the goal line of the team in possession of the ball; also, the score made in such a play by the other team.
1881 in P. H. Davis *Football* (1911) 469 If the game still remains a tie the side which makes four or more safeties less than their opponents shall win the game. **1893** CAMP *College Sports* 92 A 'safety' is made when a side are so sorely pressed that they carry the ball behind their *own goal line*, and not when it is kicked there by the enemy.

+b. *Baseball.* A safe hit.
1917 MATHEWSON *Second Base Sloan* 105 Billy White led off with a safety to left.

2. A bicycle of the modern type having two wheels of equal size. {1877–}
1891 *Advance* 10 Sept., The brethren had been every where, in the mountains, in the woods, riding up and down the highways on safeties. **1896** *N.Y. Dramatic News* 11 July 11/3 They have recently been presented with three safeties by a well-known bicycle firm.

+3. *Committee of safety*, (see COMMITTEE 2 a).

4. *attrib.* Designating machines, contrivances, etc., constructed with a view to safety in operation, or to the safe use or keeping of things protected by them.
1840 *Niles' Nat. Reg.* 4 April 71/2 Lake, sound and sea going steamers [are] to have an equipment of . . . safety boats sufficient to carry all the passengers and crew. **1845** Safety chain [see FOB CHAIN]. **1846** McKENNEY *Memoirs* I. 26 One set [of vouchers was] for the Treasury Department, one for my office proper, and the third for a safety vault. **1847** *Rep. Comm. Patents 1846* 33 A patent has been granted for an improvement in the safety stirrup. **1869** *Boyd's Business Directory* 822/1 Root's Wrought Iron Sectional Safety Boiler Has no large sheet-iron shell to explode. **1872** HUNTINGTON *Road-Master's Asst.* 130 There is a kind of switch, known as Tyler's Safety Switch, much used on many New England roads. **1873** *Pat. Off. Gazette* 24 June 697/1 Safety-Platform for Elevators.—Robert Dunbar, Buffalo, N.Y. **1877** W. WRIGHT *Big Bonanza* 211 In all of the leading mines safety-cages are in use; also, safety incline-cars, or 'giraffes.' **1907** *St. Nicholas* Sept. 1004/1 Off it came and disclosed a beautiful double-barreled, breech-loading shot-gun, with pistol-grip and safety-guard.

+Safety barge. (See quot. 1859.) — **1827** McKENNEY *Tour to Lakes* 22, [I] have already selected the Safety barge, the Lady Clinton, for my conveyance. **1828** HONE *Diary* I. 2 After seeing three of my children, . . . under way in the safety barge, . . . we started. **1857** *Amer. Jrnl. Science* Nov. 359 Redfield was the first to devise and carry into execution the plan of a line of *safety barges* to ply on the Hudson between New York and Albany. **1859** BARTLETT 376 *Safety Barge*, a passenger boat towed by a steamboat at such a distance from it as to avoid all apprehension of danger to the passengers.

Safety fund. +A fund contributed to by different banks as a pledge for redemption of their banknotes, as under the New York banking law of 1829. Also attrib. — **1832** *Congress. Deb.* 7 March 2040 All the banks in this connexion are authorized by the law creating the safety fund . . . to take seven per cent. on all discounts for more than sixty days. **1834** C. A. DAVIS *Lett. J. Downing* 41 Major, Mr. Van Buren wants Amos Kendall to go and make report about the State Banks, and their Safety Funds. **1838** Safety Fund Country Bank Bill [see COUNTRY BANK]. **1855**

Knickerb. XLV. 471 Wouldn't he have skinned me if he could, with his discount, one and a quarter per cent for safety-fund money?

+**Safety-fund bank.** A bank that contributes to a safety fund. — **1832** *Congress. Deb.* 8 March 2074 Suppose one of these safety fund banks to be established in a country village. **1837** HONE *Diary* I. 254 But three banks at Buffalo, all safety-fund banks, are under injunction and their doors closed. **1857** *Harper's Mag.* Dec. 115/1 All the banks . . . should receive at par . . . the notes of certain specified Safety-Fund Banks.

Safety lamp. A lamp with a safety device on it. {1816-, a miner's lamp} — **1873** 'G. HAMILTON' *Twelve Miles* 105 As a safety-lamp it [the American student lamp] is unparalleled. **1881** RAYMOND *Mining Gloss.* 73 *Safety-lamp*, a lamp, the flame of which is so protected that it will not immediately ignite fire-damp. **1887** [see HEATER 3].

+**Safety touchdown.** =SAFETY 1 a. — **1887** *Century Mag.* Oct. 889/2 A 'safety' touch-down counts two points against the side which makes it.

Safety valve. A valve in a boiler for permitting excess steam to escape. {1815-} — **1813** *Niles' Reg.* III. Add. 1/2 When the steam lifts the safety-valve, it is then let into the cylinder. **1875** 'MARK TWAIN' *Old Times* vii. 131 The pent steam shrieking through safety-valves.

* **1. Saffron.**

* **1.** An orange-red product of the autumnal crocus, used for coloring, flavoring, and medical purposes.

1651 *Mayflower Descendant* X. 202 Cloves nuttmeggs Turmericke . . . Safforon a little of all; a box. **1695** SEWALL *Diary* I. 408, I went to Capt. Daviss and fetched some Trecle Water and Syrup of Saffron. **1713** *Mass. H. S. Coll.* 6 Ser. V. 276 If the measeles coms amongst you, its best to giue sage and baum tea, with a little safron, and keep warm. **1815** *Niles' Reg.* IX. 94/2 Saffron . . . [is] to be found in our druggists' shops. **1882** PECK *Sunshine* 171 The green-looking 'father' is . . . waiting for the clerk to open the door so he can get some saffron to make tea of.

* **2.** The autumnal crocus, *Crocus sativus.*

1791 MUHLENBERG *Index Florae* 159 *Crocus sativus*, Saffron. **1840** DEWEY *Mass. Flowering Plants* 195 Saffron . . . has much less reputation than formerly; found rarely in our gardens.

* **3.** In the names of other plants.

1737 BRICKELL *N. Carolina* 20 The Pot-Herbs [include] . . . Bastard Saffron; and several sorts of Mustard. **1817-8** EATON *Botany* (1822) 225 *Carthamus cærulius*, blue saffron.

Saffron tea. A drink for medicinal purposes, made from saffron or the leaves of the safflower. — **1839** *Chemung* (N.Y.) *Dem.* 25 Dec. (Th.), I have been taking julips, and a little saffern tea. **1875** HOWARD *One Summer* xi, That formidable woman . . . threatened the invalid with a heavy dose of castor-oil, which was to be followed at once, she volubly declared, by a large bowl of saffron tea.

+**Safrano (rose).** A variety of tea rose. — **1869** S. B. PARSONS *On the Rose* 48 Safrano. . . . Its half-opened bud is very beautiful, and of a rich, deep fawn color. **1876** WARNER *Gold of Chickaree* 234 'Have you?' said Hazel, intent upon placing a Safrano rose.

* **Sag,** *n.*

+**1.** A depression in a flat country; a low place in a line of hills; a bog or marshy place.

1727 in *Amer. Speech* XV. 387/1 Thence along the North Side of the Mountains . . . to a Corner Several Saplins by a Sagg. **1741** *Ib.* 387/2 To two Hiccory's on the side of a Sagg. **1850** *Rep. Comm. Patents 1849: Agric.* 443 Strawberries are met with . . . on the edges of 'sloughs' or 'saggs,' where the soil is deep and moist. **1869** BOWLES *Our New West* 107 We suddenly came out of the trees into . . . a gap or sag in the mountains. **1876** RAYMOND *8th Rep. Mines* 55 [There is] a depression or 'sag' in the main ridge between Clear and Sly Park Creeks. **1897** *Advance* 2 Sept. 304/2 The last place where threshing had been done, . . . was two miles across the sag of Sewanee. *a*1918 G. STUART *On Frontier* II. 118 There are plum bushes in every sag and ravine.

+**2.** A decline in price.

[**1891** *Daily News* (London) 4 March 2/2 In the American market there is a slight but general 'sag.'] **1897** HOUGH *Story of Cowboy* 334 Then in time came . . . the 'sag' in the cattle business.

* **Sag,** *v.* +(See quotation.) — **1879** WEBSTER *Suppl.* 198/1 *Sag*, . . . to loiter in walking; to idle along; to drag or droop heavily.

+**Sagaban.** [?Amer. Ind.] 'The root of the *Apios tuberoso*, used as food by the Indians of the North-west' (B. '59).

+**Sagaciate,** *v. colloq.* [From *sagacious.*] **1.** *intr.* To thrive or get along. **2.** *tr.* To endure. — (1) **1880** HARRIS *Uncle Remus* ii, 'How duz yo' sym'tums seem ter segashuate?' sez Brer Rabbit. (2) **1890** *Amer. Folk-Lore* III. Dec. 311 *Sagatiate*, . . . came into use here [in Phila.] between 1853 and 1859, being used only in the phrase, 'How does your corporosity sagatiate the inclemency of the weather?'

+**Sagakomi.** [Can. Fr., from Algonquian. Cf. Chippewa *sagâkomin* 'smoking-leaf berry.'] The bearberry (*Arctostaphylos uva-ursi*) or other shrub the leaves of which were mixed with or used as a substitute for tobacco; also, the leaves or the smoking mixture. Also attrib. — **1703** LAHONTAN *New Voyages* II. 53 They are forc'd to buy up Brasil Tobaco, which they mix with a certain Leaf of an agreeable Smell, call'd *Sagâkomi.* **1778** CARVER *Travels* 31 A weed that grows near the great lakes, in rocky places, . . . is called by the Indians Segockimac. **1805** CLARK in *Lewis & C. Exped.* I. (1904) 266 Two men of the N W Compy arrive with letters and Sackacomah. *Ib.* III. (1905) 273 A young Chief . . . produced for us to eate . . . cramberries & Sackacomey berries, in bowls made of horn.

Sagamite, Sagamity. [Can. Fr., from Algonquian.] A gruel or hominy made of corn. — [**1698** tr. Hennepin *New Discovery* (ed. 2) 116 A potful of Sagamite, or Pottage of Indian Corn, with some fat meat.] **1797** IMLAY *Western Territory* (ed. 3) 236 [Maize] is eaten different ways: the most common method is to make it into sagamity, which is a kind of gruel made with water, or strong broth. **1821** NUTTALL *Travels Arkansa* 81 A [Quapaw Indian] mother weeping over the grave of her son, poured upon it a great quantity of Sagamitty (or hominy). **1880** CABLE *Grandissimes* 26 They sat down to bear's meat, sagamite and beans.

+**Sagamore.** Also †**sagamo.** [Of Algonquian origin.] An Indian chief or leader.

Originally, among the Algonquian Indians, a lesser chief, the head of one of the tribes in a confederation presided over by a sachem. At times, however, *sagamore* has been considered synonymous with *sachem.* (Cf. SACHEM.)

[**1613** PURCHAS *Pilgrimage* 628 The said Sagamos lost the pipe.] *c*1618 STRACHEY *Virginia* 160 Many provinces . . . [are] governed in chief by a principall commaunder or prince . . . who hath under him divers petty kings, which they call Sagamoes. **1630** HIGGINSON *New-England* 18 The greatest Saggamores of the countrey do vs can not make aboue three hundred Men. **1690** *Mass. H. S. Coll.* 4 Ser. V. 251 The sagamores of the Five Nations were come to Albany. **1764** HUTCHINSON *Hist. Mass.* I. 463 They gave the title of Sachem to the chief, and sometimes that of Sagamore. **1839** *Mass. H. S. Coll.* 3 Ser. IX. 93 For the ancient appellations of Sagamore and Sachem, are substituted, in modern times, Governor and Lieutenant-governor. **1877** CAMPION *On Frontier* 82 A deputation of 'Sagamores' sent to the Pottowattomie chiefs asking for a contingent. **1919** *Maine My State* 104 At Mattawamkeag, the Sagamores of the Indian village welcomed them with hospitality.

b. Used as a title with the given name of a particular Indian.

1677 HUBBARD *Narrative* I. 76 Sagamore Sam, old Jethro, and the Sagamore of Quohaog, were taken by the English. **1758** J. WILLIAMS *Redeemed Captive* (1758) 25 An Indian came to the City (Sagamore George of Pennacook) from Cowass. **1834** WHITTIER *Poetical Works* (1894) 496/1 He who harms the Sagamore John Shall feel the knife of Mogg Megone.

+**Sagamoreship.** *Obs.* An Indian territory ruled over by a sagamore; the state or powers of a sagamore. — **1654** JOHNSON *Wonder-w. Prov.* 66 This Towne lies in the Saggamooreship, or Earldome of Aggawam. **1687** BLOME *Isles & Terr. in Amer.* 232 The three Kingdoms, or Sagamorships of the Mattachusets, . . . were now . . . reduced. **1760** NILES *Indian Wars* I. 178 Philip being now become the next heir to the crown, or sagamoreship, doubtless studied some method of revenge on the English for his brother's death.

+**Saganash, Sagenash.** [Algonquian *sagaunash.*] In Indian parlance, an Englishman; a white man. — **1825** W. BIGGS *Narr. Captivity* 13 He asked me if I was a Sagenash, (an Englishman). **1904** WHITE *Silent Places* 68, I know the language of the saganash.

Sagathy. A lightweight woolen material. *Obs.* {1707-} Also attrib. — **1705** *Boston News-Letter* 30 April 2/2 William Rogers . . . [has] a sagathy colour'd Jacket like a Searge. **1724** *New-Eng. Courant* 15 June 2/1 He carried away with him . . . a light colour'd Sagathee Jacket. **1751** MACSPARRAN *Diary* 62, I pd. . . . Capt. Harrison £45: 10 for a Piece of black Sagathee he sometime ago sent me. **1790** [see DUROY].

* **Sage.**

* **1.** A mint plant of the genus *Salvia*, esp. *S. officinalis*, with aromatic leaves used in flavoring; the dried leaves of this plant.

1698 M. THOMAS *Penna. & N.J.* 21 Besides what grows naturally Wild in the Country, and that in great plenty also, as Mustard, Rue, Sage, Mint. **1789** MORSE *Amer. Geog.* 53 Of the various aromatic and other kinds of herbs are balm, savory, thyme, sage. **1865** *Atlantic Mo.* Feb. 146/1 The good, prim dames . . . were proud . . . of their beds of thyme and sage. **1878** *Amer. Home Cook Book* 56 Fill it with sage and onion stuffing.

+**2.** Any of several species of *Artemisia*, esp. *A. tridentata*, growing wild on the western plains and plateaus; sagebrush; a plant of one of these species.

Cf. BLACK SAGE.

1805 LEWIS in *L. & Clark Exped.* II. (1904) 29 The wild hysop sage . . . and some other herbs also grow in the plains and hills. **1837** IRVING *Bonneville* II. 57 The valleys were . . . scantily clothed with a stunted species of wormwood, generally known among traders and trappers by the name of sage. **1845** FRÉMONT *Exped.* 124 The road . . . was made extremely rough by the stiff tough bushes of *artemisia tridentata*, in this country commonly called sage. **1853** Marcy *Explor. Red R.* 274 *Artemis[i]a filifolia* . . . is one of the numerous species called *sage* by the hunters. **1875** [see GREASEBUSH]. **1905** *N.Y. Ev. Post* 3 June, Perhaps he has many a break-down before he gets back to camp, since he has to go bouncing over the sages. **1913** BARNES *Western Grazing Grounds* 43 [There are] many varieties of sage.

3. *attrib.* +**a.** Designating areas covered by sagebrush.

1845 FRÉMONT *Exped.* 172 To our left, below, was the great sage plain. *Ib.* 227 [Some of the Indians] appeared to have been out on the sage hills to hunt rabbits. **1848** BRYANT *California* ix. 134 The plain . . . is covered with wild sage, with a few occasional blades of dead bunch-grass between the sage-hillocks. **1850** SAWYER *Way Sketches* 73 We now drove nine miles down the river over a sage country.

+b. In the names of plants.
1847 Wood *Botany* 415 P[*lectranthus*] *parviflorus*. . . . Sometimes seen in house cultivation and called *Sage Geranium!* It is a large, coarse plant. **1862** *Rep. Comm. Patents 1861: Agric.* 477, I request the *Sage grape.* **1862** *Harper's Mag.* May 745/2 Dried and cracking wastes of wild mustard, sage-weed, and bunch grass.

+c. Designating birds and animals of the sage country.
1869 *Amer. Naturalist* III. 82 [The] Sage Fowl (*Centrocercus urophasianus*) . . . is very rare [near Fort Benton]. **1868** *Ib.* II. 536 [The] Sage Hare (*Lepus artemisia*) . . . is more rare near Fort Benton. **1884** Coues *Key to Birds* 375 *Amphispiza*. . . . Sage Sparrows. **1917** *Birds of Amer.* III. 174 Sage Thrasher. *Oreoscoptes montanus*. . . . Also called Sage Thrush.

Sage-and-tansy ale. A beverage brewed from sage and tansy. — **1712** *Essex Inst. Coll.* X. 94 We were brewing sage and tansey ale.

+Sagebrush.
1. a. =Sage 2. **b.** An area covered by sagebrush.
1861 *N.Y. Tribune* 5 July (Chipman), The sorry shrubs known as 'grease-wood' and 'sage-brush' thinly cover the plain. **1866** *Ore. State Jrnl.* 10 Nov. 1/1 We traveled through an alkaline country which affords but little grass, and no wood, save sage brush. **1872** 'Mark Twain' *Roughing It* 33 If the reader can imagine a gnarled and venerable live-oak tree reduced to a little shrub two feet high, with its rough bark, its foliage, its twisted boughs, all complete, he can picture the 'sage-brush' exactly. **1890** Custer *Following Guidon* 71 The dull sage-brush, or grease-root, or the sparse buffalo-grass, were all that the sun spared from its scorching rays. **1907** White *Arizona Nights* 27 Onpeacable citizens Texas Pete used to plant out in the sage-brush.

2. *attrib.* **a.** Designating types of land on which sage-brush grows.
1870 *Rep. Comm. Agric. 1869* 612 The southern portion of Idaho . . . consists of fertile valleys traversing sage-brush plains and table-lands. **1888** *Amer. Humorist* (London) 2 June 3/3, I expect to see the sagebrush deserts of Nebraska and Nevada under cultivation. **1900** *Congress. Rec.* 3 Feb. 1474/2 The land is arid sagebrush land. **1902** 'Mark Twain' in *Harper's Mag.* Feb. 431 No poking around all over the sage-brush range an hour and a half in a mass-meeting crowd for *him.* **1907** White *Arizona Nights* 191 We began to toil in the ankle-deep sand of a little sage-brush flat.

b. Designating a mining process for the reduction of ore.
1877 W. Wright *Big Bonanza* 139 The wonders performed by the 'sage-brush process,' as it was called, were being heralded through the land. **1896** Shinn *Story of Mine* 84 A mill on the Comstock . . . advertised reduction of ores by the 'sage-brush method.'

c. *Sagebrush state*, a state where sagebrush grows in abundance, esp. Nevada.
1904 *N.Y. Ev. Post* 6 May 7 A senator from one of the 'sagebrush' States —Mr. Newlands of Nevada. **1917** *Boston Ev. Globe* 11 April 16/4 Nevada has been known for many years as the Sagebrush State.

+Sagebush. A bush of sage (sense 2). — **1807** Gass *Journal* 204 Sage bushes . . . grow in great abundance on some parts of these plains. **1866** *Rep. Indian Affairs* 125 Some twenty-five acres of land have been cleared from thick sage bushes. **1902** 'Mark Twain' in *Harper's Mag.* Jan. 269/2 He started on a run, racing in and out among the sage-bushes.

Sage cheese. Cheese flavored with sage leaves or sage extract. {1714-} — **1699** Sewall *Diary* I. 492 Eat sage Cheese, drunk Beer and Cider and came homeward. **1833** Neal *Down-Easters* I. 24 The end of one [chest] being stove . . . , the deck was instantly littered with all sorts of down-east travelling haberdashery—. . . a new bridle, part of a sage-cheese [etc.]. **1861** *Ill. Agric. Soc. Trans.* IV. 102 The Sage cheese on exhibition for your inspection was made July 22, 1859. **1909** Webster 1868/2.

+Sage chicken. =next. — **1873** in Custer *Boots & Saddles* 293 A pair of sage-chickens, a pair of curlew, and a jack-rabbit complete my present collection. **1902** Wister *Virginian* 53 At our noon meal we . . . shot some young sage chickens, which were good at supper. **1914** E. Stewart *Lett. Woman Homesteader* 18 Occasionally a bunch of sage chickens would fly up out of the sagebrush.

+Sage cock. The largest of the American grouse (*Centrocercus urophasianus*); spec., the male of this species. (Cf. Cock of the plains, Prairie cock, etc.) — **1852** Baird in Stansbury *Gt. Salt Lake* 319 Sage Cock . . . is found on the plains skirting the Rocky mountains. **1874** in Coues *Birds N.W.* 404, I have heard it said that the Sage Cock migrates, but this is not so. **1886** Roosevelt in *Outing* Aug. 525 This is the great Sage Cock, a bird of fine appearance. **1917** *Birds of Amer.* II. 30/1 The Sage Cock has a sharp cackle.

+Sage desert. W. A plateau or plains area covered with sagebrush. — **1845** Frémont *Exped.* 161 The dark and ugly appearance of this plain obtained for it the name of the Sage Desert. **1869** J. R. Browne *Adv. Apache Country* 513 In the alkali plains and sage-deserts and rugged mountain ranges of Nevada, you find him with his pick and shovel. **1870** Pine *Beyond the West* 215 There are [in Oregon] many . . . sage deserts.

+Sage grass. (See quot. 1903.) — **1886** *Consular Rep.* Jan. 40 Those hundreds of thousands of acres of once valuable Southern lands . . . [are] now lying to waste in worthless 'sage grass.' **1903** *Dialect Notes* II. 328 *Sage-grass*, sedge-grass. Also called 'broom-sage.' [s.c. Mo.]

+Sage grouse. =Sage cock. — **1889** Farmer 469/1 *Sage-Hen*, otherwise known as the Cock of the Plains, and for which the name of

Sage-Grouse has been suggested. **1917** *Birds of Amer.* II. 31/1 The Sage Grouse seldom is to be found far from the sagebrush.

+Sage hen.
1. The sage cock; spec., the female of this species.
1847 Palmer *Rocky Mts.* 143 The small game are hare, rabbit, grouse, sage hen, pheasant, quail, &c. **1848** E. Bryant *California* x. 148 The sage-hens, or the grouse of the sage-plains, . . . have been frequently flushed, and several shot. **1852** *S. Lit. Messenger* XVIII. 416/1 'Sage-hens' . . . are fine game and probably a species of grouse. **1870** Beadle *Utah* 222 We entered a region abounding in jack-rabbits and sage-hens. **1888** Roe *Army Lett.* 378 Faye and Captain Rives often bring in large bags of mountain grouse and young sage hens. **1917** *Birds of Amer.* II. 30/1 Thus far the systematists have not been able to find a subspecies of the Sage Hen.

2. A native or resident of Nevada. A nickname.
1872 *Harper's Mag.* Jan. 318/1 [People from] Nevada, [are called] Sage-Hens.

+Sage of Monticello. [From name of estate in Va.] Thomas Jefferson (1743-1826). — **1839** 'M. Pencil' *White Sulphur P.* 19 It was here in the shade of these elms, that the sage of Monticello was wont to spend so much of his time. **1912** Nicholson *Hoosier Chron.* 196 If you're going back to the Sage of Monticello, how do you think he would answer that?

+Sage rabbit. Any of several rabbits of the West, as *Sylvilagus nuttalli*. — **1846** Sage *Scenes Rocky Mts.* iv, [The] sage rabbit . . . is nearly three times the size of the common rabbit, and of a white color, slightly tinged with grey. **1867** *Amer. Naturalist* I. 534 The Sage Rabbit (*L. artemisia*) is as abundant in Arizona as the Jackass-rabbit. **1879** Goode, etc. *Cat. Animal Resources U.S.* 20 *Lepus sylvaticus*. . . . Sage Rabbit.

Sage tea. A tea made from sage leaves. {1705-} — **1704** Sewall *Diary* II. 116 Drunk a porringer of Sage Tea, upon which I sweat very kindly. **1775** Asbury *Journal* I. 142 The gargle . . . was sage tea. **1805** Clark in *Lewis & C. Exped.* I. (1904) 252 George Drewyer taken with the Pleurisy last evening. Bled & gave him Some Sage tea. **1887** Wilkins *Humble Romance* 407 Beside this bottle stood another of sage tea; that was for her head.

+Sage-willow. A gray willow *Salix tristis*. — **1846** Emerson *Rep. Trees & Shrubs Mass.* 256 The sage willow is a slender, hoary plant, or a spreading tufted bush. **1891** *Cent.* 5303/2.

∗Sago. A species of dry, granulated starch prepared from the trunks of certain palms, cycads, etc.
1775 Romans *Nat. Hist. Florida* 130 Sago might be here produced as well as in Georgia, for the tree from which the basis of this drug is taken abounds particularly in East Florida. **1810** *Columbian Centinel* 27 Jan. 4/3 Goodwin & Whiting . . . Have for sale . . . Sago, Cut Nails. **1862** Cumming *Hospital Life* (1866) 46/2 The stove . . . answers for what little I have to cook—beef-tea, toast, sago, and arrow-root.

b. Attrib. with *jelly, oatmeal, pudding.*
1790 *Penna. Packet* 2 Jan. 4/2 Sago oatmeal. . . . For Sale By John Dorsey. **1832** Child *Frugal Housewife* 32 Sago Jelly. The sago should be soaked in cold water. **1873** Phelps *Trotty's Wedding* xi, You look like sago-pudding—and—horsehair stuffing.

+Saguaro. [Mex. Sp.] =Giant cactus. — **1881** *Amer. Naturalist* XV. 982 By far the most conspicuous and remarkable form is the *Cereus giganteus*, locally known as the 'saguara' cactus. **1907** White *Arizona Nights* 220 [The] snake . . . looked just like a sahuaro stalk. **1916** Peixotto *Our Hispanic Southwest* 64 Tall saguaros reared their fluted columns like giant candelabra.

+Saguaro woodpecker. =Gila woodpecker. — **1884** Coues *Key N.A. Birds* (ed. 2) 488 Saguaro Woodpecker. **1917** *Birds of Amer.* II. 163.

Saibling. [Dial. Ger.] **1.** A char (*Salvelinus alpinus*) introduced into the United States from Europe. {1896} Also attrib. — **+2.** The Sunapee trout, *S. aureolus.* — (1) **1884** Goode, etc. *Fisheries* I. 501 The Saibling is, in its habits, perhaps more similar to the well-known Blue-backed Trout or Oquassa Trout of Rangely Lake, Maine, than to our Brook Trout. *Ib.* 504 In selecting a place in which to deposit the saibling eggs . . . , the Commissioner of Fisheries has endeavored to find a lake as similar as possible in depth and temperature to the larger Swiss lakes. (2) **1911** *Rep. Fisheries 1908* 315/1 Saibling (*Salvelinus aureolus*), the Sunapee trout of Maine and New Hampshire.

∗Sail, *n.*
∗1. A piece of canvas or other strong material used to catch the wind so as to propel a boat.
1624 Smith *Gen. Hist. Va.* III. 60 We seeing them [sc. Indians] prepare to assault vs, left our Oares and made way with our sayle to encounter them. **1714** *Boston News-Letter* 12 April 2/2 Canvas of Sundry Sorts for small Sails, and mending. **1894** *Outing* May 148/2 The sail is laced to a yard and boom. **1907** *St. Nicholas* July 812/2 It may seem odd that in these days of steam, steel, and dynamos, so much time should be spent in learning sails.

2. Attrib. with *canvas, duck, needle,* etc.
1654 *Essex Probate Rec.* I. 197, 20 yds. of Sayle Canvas. **1711** *Boston News-Letter* 17 Sept. 2/2 There will be exposed to Sale . . . Hats, Sail Twine, Earthen Ware, Guns. **1791** *Amer. Hist. Rev.* XII. 84 That [manufactory] for Sail Duck is counted a valuable acquisition to the state. **1828** Sherburne *Memoirs* 55 Their manner of curing them [sc. fish] is to salt them lightly, and with a sail needle and twine string them up by the head, and dry or smoke them. **1841** *Diplom. Corr. Texas* I. (1908) 495

The letter I sent by a Sail Packet just ready from New York. **1844** *Knickerb*. XXIII. 507 You'll see all their steam-ships and their sail-ships they splurge so much about, lying high and dry.

∗Sail, *v.* **+**To sail in(to), to attack boldly; to go into something without hesitation or restraint. *slang.* — **1856** M. THOMPSON *Plu-ri-bus-tah* 69 'Sailing in,' without regard to Any of the Laws of 'Fancy.' **1868** *Congress. Globe* 2 May 2353/2 How he would sail into them! **1883** 'MARK TWAIN' *Life on Miss.* xxvi, Old General Pillow . . . sailed in, too, leading his troops as lively as a boy. **1903** LEWIS *Boss* 52 Half an hour before six, blow your whistle an' sail in. **1911** LINCOLN *Cap'n Warren's Wards* 202 So sail in and show us what you're made of.

Sailboat. A boat provided with sails. Also attrib. {*a*1835} — **1798** C. WILLIAMSON *Descr. Genesee* iii, The number of sail-boats have greatly increased on the lake. **1831** HOLLEY *Texas* (1833) 47 From Brazoria to Bolivar, I came in a sail-boat. **1851** MELVILLE *Moby-Dick* 115 The stout sail-boat that had accompanied us began ranging alongside. **1900** STOCKTON *Afield & Afloat* 311 He bought a better sailboat than he had ever owned. **1911** LINCOLN *Cap'n Warren's Wards* 333 He had gone to see the sail boat man.

Sail carriage. ?Something to carry a sail which was wetted and placed over a roof to protect it from fire. — **1829** *Mass. Laws* 237 The said Firewards . . . are hereby authorized . . . [to appoint] twenty men to each Sail Carriage. *Ib.*, The said Firewards shall have the care . . . of the public Engines, Hose and Sail Carriages, Fire Hooks and Ladders.

∗Sailcloth. Canvas or other strong material used for sails. Also attrib. — **1714** *Boston News-Letter* 26 April 2/2 To be Sold by Publick Vendue or Outcry . . . several sorts of Sail Cloth, Kentings, Linings, Earthern Ware. **1776** [see DUCK *n.*² 1]. **1790** *Penna. Packet* 26 April 2/3 The Boston Sail Cloth Factory alone gives employment to upwards of 300 persons. **1848** BURTON *Waggeries* 19, I hadn't on nothin' . . . only a blue cotting shirt and sail-cloth pantys. **1914** STEELE *Storm* 3 He came into the shed and sat down on a pile of old sail-cloth.

∗Sailfish. One of various fishes having a saillike dorsal fin, **+**esp. *Istiophorus americanus*. — **1879** GOODE, etc. *Cat. Animal Resources U.S.* 39 *Histiophorus americanus*. . . . Sail-fish.—Atlantic Coast of America. **1882** TENISON-WOODS *Fish & Fisheries N.S. Wales* 190 Sail-fish. *Carpiodes*. N. America. **1884** GOODE, etc. *Fisheries* I. 357 The occurrence of the Sail-fish is . . . very unusual. *Ib.* 615 The Carp Sucker—*Carpiodes cyprinus*. The different species (*Ictiobus cyprinus, carpio*, etc.) known as 'Carp,' 'Carp Suckers,' 'Spear-fish,' 'Sail-fish,' 'Quill-back,' etc., abound in all the larger bodies of water south and west of New York. **1903** T. H. BEAN *Fishes N.Y.* 405 The sailfish lives in the warmer parts of the Atlantic, ranging northward to France and, occasionally, to Cape Cod.

∗Sailing. *attrib.* Designating various kinds of boats that are propelled by sails. {1707–} — **1721** *New-Eng. Courant* 14 Aug. 2/2 On the 4th Inst. at Night were drowned going to Thomsons Island in a small sailing Boat, Mr. Heskew, and a Young Man whose Name was Holland. **1785** *Md. Hist. Mag.* XX. 52 He hath at high tides frequently passed over the bank . . . in battaus canoes and sailing Yawles. **1880** *Harper's Mag.* Aug. 396 The crank *Rob Roy* was superseded, as a sailing canoe, by the *Nautilus*. **1907** *St. Nicholas* July 812/2 They used to put their knowledge into practice on an extended cruise on the sailing-ship *Monongahela*.

Sailing master. An officer in charge of navigating a vessel {1836–}; **+**formerly, in the United States Navy, a warrant officer next below a lieutenant.

'The grade was merged in that of *master* in 1862' (W. '09). **1779** *N.H. Comm. Safety Rec.* 194 Appointed—Curtice Sailing Master of the Armed Ship Hampden. **1794** *Ann. 3d Congress* 1426 There shall be employed, in each of the said ships, . . . one sailing-master, one purser . . . and eight midshipmen. **1813** *Ann. 12th Congress* 2 Sess. 49 A detachment of men arrived from New York, accompanied by Sailingmasters Watts and Chisson. **1853** COZZENS *Prismatics* 110 The jolly sailing-master . . . departed from the place as mad as a bear with a sore head. **1907** 'O. HENRY' *Roads of Destiny* 113, I gave orders to the sailing-master that the arms, ammunition, and provisions were to be landed at once.

Sailing orders. {1692–, of the sea} *fig.* **+**The orders or directions pertaining to land travel, esp. of a wagon train. — **1857** STACEY *Journal* 44 We received our sailing orders this morning. **1878** [see BEATEN *ppl. a.* 2].

Sailing party. A party at which the chief entertainment is sailing. — **1877** BAGBY *Old Va. Gentleman* 11 Of fish-fries, barbecues, sailing-parties, sora and duck shooting, . . . I need not speak at length.

Sailing vessel. Any ship propelled by sails. — **1748** FRANKLIN *Exper. on Electricity* 38 It appears at the stern and in the wake of every sailing vessel. **1775** *Jrnls. Cont. Congress* III. 203 A swift sailing vessel . . . [shall] be fitted . . . for a cruize of three months. **1866** W. REID *After the War* 59 We passed a little sailing vessel manned by blacks. **1908** HANDSAKER *Pioneer Life* 15 The other routes were by sailing vessels around Cape Horn or by the Isthmus of Panama.

Sail loft. A loft or place where sails are cut out and made. {1769} — **1759** *Newport Mercury* 5 June 4/1 To be Sold. A Warehouse and Cooper's Shop, With the Sail-Loft, and the Part of the Wharf whereon the same stands. **1832** DUNLAP *Hist. Amer. Theatre* 17 The place has since been occupied as a sail-loft. **1888** DORSEY *Midshipman Bob* 84 At Flushing . . . they was laid in a old sail-loft, and left.

∗Sailmaker.

∗1. One who makes and repairs sails.

1656 *Suffolk Deeds* III. 340 Six pounds & tenn shillings . . . [paid] by willjam Talbott of the same Boston Sailmaker. **1685** *Boston Rec.* 78 Wil-

liam Colman . . . became surety . . . for Samuel Baylie, Saylmaker. **1704** *Boston News-Letter* 22 May 2/1 He was lately an Apprentice to Mr. Bulfinch Sail-maker of Boston. **1733** *S.C. Gazette* 183/1 Goods lately Imported, and to be Sold . . . Sailmakers Thread and Spinnel. **1776** FITHIAN *Journal* II. 205, I paid off my last weeks board with a sail-maker in Crown-Street. **1865** *Chicago Tribune* 10 April 1 Ship Chandlers and Sail Makers, Twines and Cordage of Every Description. **1886** *Outing* May 169/2 A squall carried away our . . . flying jib—a good job for the sail maker.

+2. *U.S. Navy.* A warrant officer in charge of all articles made of canvas.

1794 *Ann. 3d Congress* 1426 There shall be employed, in each of the said ships, . . . one sail-maker, one carpenter. **1839** *Knickerb.* XIII. 43 The sail-maker . . . proceeded to sew him up in his hammock. **1881** *Naval Encycl.* 713/2 [A] sailmaker . . . [receives] from $700 to $1800 a year as pay.

+Sailmaker's mate. *U.S. Navy.* A petty officer who assists or acts for the sailmaker (sense 2). — **1794** *Ann. 3d Congress* 1426 The following petty officers . . . shall be appointed by the captains of the ships: . . . one cockswain, one sail-maker's mate, two gunner's mates. **1796** *Ann. 4th Congress* 2 Sess. 2786, 2 Sail-maker's Mates, [$]13 [per month]. **1881** *Naval Encycl.* 713/2 [A] sailmaker's mate [is] a petty officer of a man-of-war, working at sail-making under the directions of the sailmaker.

∗Sailor. Also †sayler, sailer.

∗1. One who sails vessels; a member of a ship's crew; a seaman below the rank of an officer.

1622 'MOURT' *Relation* 70 One of the Saylers found aliue vpon the shore an Hering. **1714** *Boston News-Letter* 7 June 2/2 Deserted also from the said Capt. Sherburn's Ships, the Sophia, the two following Sailors. **1776** A. ADAMS *Familiar Lett.* 187 Captain Burk, who accompanied the *Defence*, being a prime sailer, he came up first. **1842** *Knickerb.* XX. 496, I observed a dozen sailors pulling an anchor. **1907** *St. Nicholas* July 812/2 When the new sailor gets his uniform from the paymaster, he often finds that it doesn't fit.

+2. The female blackpoll warbler. *local.*

1785 PENNANT *Arctic Zool.* II. 401 Black-Poll [Warbler]. . . . Inhabits during summer, Newfoundland and New York; Called in the last, *Sailor*.

3. Short for SAILOR HAT.

1898 *Kansas City Star* 18 Dec. 11/3 Choice of our entire line of Walking Hats and Sailors worth up to 50¢ for 25¢.

4. In possessive combinations: (see quotations.)

1835 AUDUBON *Ornith. Biog.* III. 298 A kind of small molluscous animal . . . floats near the surface, and bears the name of 'sailor's button.' **1839** in Buckingham *Slave States* (1842) I. 577 [A meeting] to assist in promoting the benevolent object of forming a Sailors' Home for the port of New Orleans. **1895** *Stand.* 1572/2 Sailor's pocket, the egg-case of a skate or oviparous shark. *Ib.*, Sailor's-purse, an egg-pouch of oviparous rays and sharks, which is mostly found empty on the sea-shore. . . . (Humorous.)

5. Attrib. with *boarding house, jacket, preacher, trousers.*

1805 CLARK in *Lewis & C. Exped.* III. (1904) 197 They had scarlet & blue blankets Salor Jackets, overalls. **1840** GARRISON in W. P. & F. J. Garrison *Life W. L. Garrison* II. 427 Taylor, the 'sailor preacher,' behaved in a most outrageous manner. **1851** M. REID *Scalp Hunters* xx, These calzoneros are cut after the fashion of sailor-trousers, short waist, tight round the hips, and wide at the bottoms. **1895** G. KING *New Orleans* 239 Commodore Patterson constructed a battery . . . and manned it by an impressment of every nautical-looking character to be found in the sailor boarding-houses of New Orleans.

Sailor hat. A hat similar to those formerly worn by sailors. — **1869** TOURGEE *Toinette* (1881) 414 In an instant the little sailor-hat, floating away upon the foaming waters of the cascade, was all that could be seen of the brave young boy. **1893** [see KID' 3 a, first quot.]. **1907** 'O. HENRY' *Heart of West* 266 Panchita tripped demurely out her gate in a thin, trim white lawn and sailor hat.

Sailor knot. Any knot used by sailors. {sailors' knot, 1882} — **1872** 'MARK TWAIN' *Roughing It* 447 Forth he strode, a picture to look at, . . . [with] a liberal amount of black-silk neck-cloth tied with a sailor-knot. **1893** POST *Harvard Stories* 13 [We'll] stick our sailor-knots in our shirt fronts and be right in the top flight.

Sailorman. =SAILOR 1. {*a*1840– (Barham *Ingold. Leg.*)} — **1790** TYLER *Contrast* II. ii, A parcel of sailor men and boys got round me. **1888** STOCKTON *Dusantes* 119 'Aye, aye, sir!' said the black-bearded sailor men. **1906** *N.Y. Ev. Post* 16 June, Apart from the annual regatta, there are endless minor 'brushes' for 'fresh-water sailormen.'

+Sailor plant. (See quotation.) — **1891** *Cent.* 5306/3 Sailor-plant, . . . the beefsteak-plant or strawberry-geranium, *Saxifraga sarmentosa*.

+Sailor's-choice. One of various fishes, as a small porgy, *Lagodon rhomboides;* a pigfish, *Orthopristis chrysopterus;* and a grunt, *Haemulon parra.*

*c*1860 in Goode, etc. *Fisheries* I. 399 The 'Sailor's Choice' makes its appearance in our waters about the month of April and continues with us until November. **1879** GOODE, etc. *Cat. Animal Resources U.S.* 46 *Lagodon rhomboides*. . . . Sailor's Choice.—West Indian Fauna and north to Cape Cod. **1882** *Nat. Museum Bul.* No. 16, 551 *Pomadasys fulvomaculatus*. . . . Sailor's Choice; Hog-fish. **1888** GOODE *Amer. Fishes* 80 *Diabasis chromis* the 'Sailor's Choice.' **1911** *Rep. Fisheries* 1908 315/1 Sailor's choice (*Lagodon rhomboides*). . . . The name is also applied to the pigfish (*Orthopristis chrysopterus*) in South Carolina.

Sailor suit. A suit modeled after a sailor's garb. — **1880** *Harper's Mag.* Aug. 337/2 Excursionists in sailor suits were playing croquet. **1882** RITTENHOUSE *Maud* 77 Robin has on . . . a little blue sailor-suit. **1903** BURNHAM *Jewel* 77 Jewel hummed a tune as she took off her sailor suit.

Sail vessel. A boat or ship propelled by sails. — **1846** *S. Lit. Messenger* XII. 19/2 The absence of sail-vessels [at the levee of a Western city] at once suggests, to the mind of an Eastern man, the idea of a new world. **1855** [see CENTERBOARD]. **1869** *Causes Reduct. Tonnage* (1870) 210 The cost per ton for building the hulls of sail-vessels or steamers would be, probably, if any were building, from $40 to $45.

Sainfoin. Also †**sanfoin, saintfoin.**

1. A Eurasian perennial herb (*Onobrychis viciaefolia*) grown as a forage plant {1626–}; the seed or leaves of this plant.

1724 JONES *Virginia* 41 Many raise good Clover and Oats, and some have planted Sanfoin. **1781–2** JEFFERSON *Notes Va.* (1788) 40 Our grasses are lucerne, st. foin, burnet, timothy, ray and orchard grass. **1788** WASHINGTON *Diaries* III. 330, 4 bushels of Sainfoin . . . was in soak. **1794** *N.Y. State Soc. Arts* I. 156 Sainfoin, considered like hay, is one of the most friendly foods to neat cattle. **1848** *Rep. Comm. Patents 1847* 194 Mr. Cretté tried the experiment of mixing it with clover, sainfoin and burnet. **1895** *Dept. Agric. Yrbk. 1894* 393 A package marked '*Burnet,*' costing 16 cents a pound, contained 47 per cent of sainfoin, which costs 6 cents a pound.

+2. 'A western American fabaceous herb (*Psoralea onobrychis*)' W. '09.

* Saint.

I. +1. A member of the early New England Puritan church.

1649 ELIOT *Glorious Progress* 18 It is a day of small things, an Embrio which the Lord expecteth should be furthered by the prayers of the Saints and Churches. **1651** (*title*), The Psalms Hymns and Spiritual Songs of the Old and New Testament, . . . for the Use, Edification, and Comfort, of the Saints. **1736** in *Amer. Hist. Review* I. 88 With Respect to Rum, the Saints of New England I fear will find out some trick to evade your Act of Parliament.

+2. A member of a Tammany Society.

1812 PAULDING *Beauties of Brother Bull-us* 38 Brother Hector *Bull-us* is of all men living the best fitted to . . . play tricks for the entertainment of the *Saints* of Tammany.

+3. A Latter-Day Saint or Mormon.

1842 J. C. BENNETT (*title*), The History of the Saints; or, an Exposé of Joe Smith and Mormonism. **1852** STANSBURY *Gt. Salt Lake* 124 'The saints' were directed to build a magnificent temple. **1874** B. F. TAYLOR *World on Wheels* 38 The locomotive . . . brought the Gentiles and the 'Saints' shoulder to shoulder. **1885** *Wkly. New Mexican Rev.* 5 Feb. 1/6 He said the saints were being persecuted in Arizona. *a*1918 G. STUART *On Frontier* I. 120 The Lord was on the side of the Saints.

II. *attrib.* or *appositive.* **4.** In the specific names of plants.

See also ST. ANDREW'S CROSS, ST.-JOHN'S-WORT, etc.

1743 CLAYTON *Flora Virginica* 88 *Ascyrum foliis ovatis*, . . . St. Andrews-wort. **1791** *Amer. Philos. Soc.* III. 115 *Chrysanthemum*? (St. Anthony's cross). **1833** EATON *Botany* (ed. 6) 86 [*Centaurea*] *solstitialis*, (St. Barnaby's thistle). **1892** *Amer. Folk-Lore* V. 91 *Nigella Damascena*. . . St. Catherine's flower. **1874** *Rep. Comm. Agric. 1873* 434 Apples—Red and White Astrachan, Duchess of Oldenberg, Saint Lawrence [etc.]. **1847** WOOD *Botany* 256 *S*[*piræa*] *hypericifolia*. St. Peter's Wreath. . . . Cultivated in gardens and shrubberies.

5. In the names of birds and fishes.

1883 *Nat. Museum Bul.* No. 27, 177 *Tachybaptes dominicus.* Saint Domingo Grebe. . . . North to Rio Grande Valley, in Texas, and Lower California. **1889** *Cent.* 2235/2 *St. George's fish*, the common starfish, *Asterias vulgaris. Stimpson.* **1873** *Amer. Naturalist* VII. 327 The St. Lucas thrush (*H*[*arporhynchus*] *cinereus*) . . . agrees with the thrasher . . . in being thickly speckled with brownish-black.

St. Andrew's cross. {1615–} +A woody plant (*Ascyrum hypericoides*) having petals in the form of an X. (Cf. ANDREW'S CROSS.) — **1738** BYRD *Dividing Line* (1901) 111 Abundance of St. Andrew's cross in all the woods. **1869** FULLER *Flower Gatherers* 245 The *Crux Andreae* or St. Andrew's Cross, is interesting from the regularity of its parts.

*St.-John's-wort. Any plant of the genus *Hypericum*. (Cf. JOHN'S-WORT.) — **1753** ELIOT *Field-Husb.* 92 There is another Weed called St. John's Wort; it fills the Ground. **1831** R. COX *Adv. Columbia R.* 318 St. John's wort . . . has been successfully applied as a fomentation in topical inflammations. **1843** TORREY *Flora N.Y.* I. 86 *Hypericum perforatum.* Common St. John's Wort. . . . Fields, pastures and road-sides; too common in most parts of the State. **1915** ARMSTRONG & THORNBER *Western Wild Flowers* 292 St. John's-wort. *Hypericum concinnum.* . . . The flowers are an inch or more across, with bright golden petals.

St. Louis. *attrib.* +Designating a limestone near St. Louis, Missouri. — **1862** DANA *Manual Geol.* 307 The St. Louis limestone (250 feet thick), overlaid by ferruginous sandstone (200 feet). **1879** *Encycl. Brit.*

(ed. 9) X. 350/2 St. Louis group.—Limestones with shale, in places 250 feet.

+St. Michael('s) pear. A variety of pear. Also attrib. — **1837** HAWTHORNE *Twice-told Tales* (1879) I. 118 They strung him up to the branch of a St. Michael's pear tree. **1849** *New Eng. Farmer* I. 368 From Colonel F. R. Bigelow, Medford, very good St. Michael pears. **1871** *Harper's Mag.* Dec. 57/1 [She] helped herself as she liked to . . . the delicious greengages, and 'St. Michael' pears.

St. Nicholas. 1. The patron saint of virgins, children, etc.; Santa Claus. ‖**2.** Christmas time. — (1) **1773** in Singleton *Social N.Y.* 309 Last Monday the anniversary of St. Nicholas, otherwise called Santa Claus, was celebrated at Protestant Hall. **1846** *Knickerb.* XXVII. 83 The sable attendants [were] clad in the authentic costumes of a period held in loving remembrance by every true son of Saint Nicholas. (2) **1830** WATSON *Philadelphia* 242 The 'Belsh Nichel' and St. Nicholas has been a time of Christmas amusement from time immemorial among us.

St. Patrick's Day. A holiday, March 17, celebrated particularly by Irish Americans. — **1871** *Republican Rev.* 18 March 1/3 St. Patrick's Day . . . passed off in Albuquerque without any public or other demonstration. **1914** *N.Y. Times* 17 March 7/3 The observance of St. Patrick's Day will begin with a mass this morning at St. Patrick's Cathedral.

*St.-Peter's-wort. (Cf. PETER'S-WORT.) **a.** Any herb of the genus *Ascyrum.* {1733–} +**b.** The snowberry, *Symphoricarpos racemosus.* — **1785** MARSHALL *Amer. Grove* 14 *Ascyrum Hypericoides.* St. Peter's Wort. . . . The flowers are sparingly produced at the tops of the stalks. *Ib.* 82 *Lonicera Symphoricarpos*, Indian Currants, or St. Peter's Wort, . . . often sends off a few weak trailing branches lying upon the ground. **1843** TORREY *Flora N.Y.* I. 84 *Ascyrum.* . . . St. Peter's Wort. . . . *Ascyrum stans.* Upright St. Peter's Wort. **1894** TORREY *Fla. Sketch-Book* 28 St. Peter's-wort, a low shrub, thrives everywhere in the pine barrens.

+St. Tammany. (See TAMMANY.)

* Sake. *Sake's alive, my sakes* (*and sorrows*), exclamations of surprise or astonishment. {*dial.*}

Sakes alive is '*dial.* and *U.S.*' (*O.E.D.*).

1846 *Law sakes alive* [see LAW SAKES *interj.*]. **1859** STOWE *Minister's Wooing* xii, 'Sakes alive!' said little Miss Prissy after dinner. **1863** A. D. WHITNEY *F. Gartney* v, Oh, my sakes and sorrows! Ain't she just like a princess? **1889** JEWETT *Betty Leicester* 10 My sakes, how you talk! **1894** 'MARK TWAIN' *P. Wilson* viii, Sakes alive, it's 'mos' enough to buy a tol'-able good second-hand nigger wid. **1920** WILSON *Red Gap* 275 A going concern—my sakes, yes!

* Saker. An old form of cannon. *Obs.* — **1628** *Va. House of Burgesses* 50 Send us a Barque . . . [and] lade her hither wth. meale, 12 feild carriages for demi Culverin, 4 for saker, & 4 for minion. **1642** *Conn. Rec.* I. 72 [He] doth prmise to lend the Country two peeces of Ordnance, Sakers or Minions. **1654** JOHNSON *Wonder-w. Providence* 191 His great Artillery [is] well mounted, and cleanly kept, half Canon, Culverins and Sakers.

+Sala. *S.W.* [Sp., a new borrowing.] A large hall, sometimes used for dining. — **1834** A. PIKE *Sketches* 96 The sala, or long hall, . . . was garnished with vast quantities of buffalo meat. **1844** GREGG *Commerce of Prairies* I. 204 The winter rooms . . . are most frequently entered through the *sala* or hall. **1898** ATHERTON *Californians* 19 Mrs. Polk would sing these old love-songs of Spain to the accompaniment of the guitar which had entranced her caballeros in the *sala* of her girlhood. **1902** — *Splendid Idle Forties* 12 The floor was bare, the furniture of horsehair; . . . it was a typical Californian sala of that day.

* Salad. Also †**sallet.**

*1. a. Any one of various vegetables or herbs used, in a raw state, as an article of food. +**b.** *S.* Cooked greens.

1622 J. PORY *Descr. Plymouth Col.* 41 After their powdered sallets . . . they may refresh and quench their thirst. **1701** WOLLEY *Journal N.Y.* (1902) 41 They are obstinate and incessant Smoakers, both Indians and Dutch, especially the latter, whose Diet especially of the boorish sort, being Sallets and Bacon, . . . require the use of [tobacco]. **1769** Holyoke *Diaries* 71 Sallad up in the Garden. **1821** NUTTALL *Travels Arkansa* 107, I met with a new species of *Sysimbrium* . . . [which] might perhaps be better worth cultivating as an early sallad, than the *Barbarea americana*, or winter sallad. **1860** MORDECAI *Virginia* 211 A few vegetables also volunteered their verdure; such as dandelions—an excellent salad—butter-cups [etc.]. **1886** Z. F. SMITH *Kentucky* 157 The indigenous salads and early berries came next, and finally the feast of garden vegetables. *attrib.* **1634** in C. C. Hall *Narr. Early Md.* 40 The ground is heare, as in very many places, covered with . . . saxafras, vines, sallad-herbes, and such like. **1705** BEVERLEY *Virginia* IV. 56 They have several Roots, Herbs, Vine-fruits, and Sallad-flowers peculiar to themselves. **1777** *N.J. Archives* 2 Ser. I. 392 Some sallad seed, which my wife found, she sowed, and was to have half the sallad. **1912** COBB *Back Home* 75 The smoked hog jowls hung in rows, fairly begging people to carry them off and boil them with salad greens.

2. *spec.* Lettuce. {1877–}

'*Dial.* and *U.S.*' (*O.E.D.*).

1838 *Phila. Ledger* July (B.), Salad goes to head by the middle of May, on Vancouver's Island. **1851** MELVILLE *Moby-Dick* 124 A king's head is solemnly oiled at his coronation, even as a head of salad.

*3. A dish of herbs, vegetables, fruits, etc., usually served uncooked and seasoned with salt, oil, vinegar, or other dressing.

1731 *Essex Inst. Coll.* XLII. 233 At supper [we] were regaled with Bony-clabber, soop, Sallet, roast Shad, & Bread & Butter. **1788** [see CRANBERRY SAUCE]. **1860** [see GREEN PEAS]. **1885** CRAWFORD *Amer. Politician* 149 Mr. Biggelow had just brought Joe some salad.

transf. **1840** *S. Lit. Messenger* VI. 347/1 Fighting! said Ryburn, striving to turn the conversation; that's my sallad as the saying is.

attrib. **1871** *Scribner's Mo.* II. 103 Salad mayonnaise requires experience and a certain knack. **1882** Salad club [see COOKING *vbl. n.* c].

+Salad bird. =GOLDFINCH 1. — **1808** WILSON *Ornithology* I. 21 [Goldfinches] pass by various names expressive of their food, color, &c. such as Thistle-bird, Lettuce-bird, Sallad-bird [etc.]. **1917** *Birds of Amer.* III. 13.

Salad dressing. A dressing for use on salads. {1836–} — **1878** *Decorum* 156 We should not find . . . salad-dressing. **1887** RITTENHOUSE *Maud* 392, [I] spend frequent hours in the kitchen devising wonderful croquettes, salad-dressings and blanc-manges. **1893** *Harper's Mag.* Jan. 200/2, I must make the salad dressing, mustn't I?

∗Salad oil. An oil for use on salads. — **1622** 'MOURT' *Relation* 142 Butter or Sallet oyle, or both is very good. **1746** *S.C. Gazette* 22 Sept., Good Sallad Oyl of Cessamum or Benny Seed. **1776** *Essex Inst. Coll.* XLIX. 100 Sold by order Capt. Samuel Williams . . . : 264 boxes Lisbon lemons; . . . 20 cases salad oil. **1865** *Atlantic Mo.* May 605/2, I never eat anything with salad oil in it.

+Salad tree. The redbud, *Cercis canadensis.* — [**1756** KALM *Resa* II. 204 Sallad-trä . . . i god jord.] **1813** MUHLENBERG *Cat. Plants* 42. **1897** SUDWORTH *Arborescent Flora* 252 *Cercis canadensis.* Redbud. . . . Salad Tree (Del.).

+Salal. [See quot. 1896.] The fruit or berries of *Gaultheria shallon,* a small shrub found on the Pacific coast; also, the shrub itself or its wood. (Cf. SHALLON.)

[**1805** CLARK in *Lewis & C. Exped.* III. (1905) 274 An old woman presented . . . a kind of Surup made of Dried berries which is common to this Countrey which the natives Call Shele wele (*She-well*).] **1866** [see SHALLON]. **1896** *Garden & Forest* IX. 292 Salal, or Sallal.—A Chinook Jargon word, from the last two syllables of *klkwu-shala,* the Chinook name of the fruit of the plant. **1911** J. F. WILSON *Land Claimers* 127 They fed it [the fire] high with dry branches, putting a last touch to it by an armful of salal. **1915** ARMSTRONG & THORNBER *Western Wild Flowers* 342 It is called Salal by the Oregon Indians, who value the black, aromatic berries as an important article of food.

b. Attrib. with *berry.*
1838 S. PARKER *Tour Rocky Mts.* 202 The salalberry is a sweet and pleasant fruit, of a dark purple color, and about the bigness of a grape. **1855** GLISAN *Jrnl. Army Life* 249 Berries afford them a good substitute for bread; such as the blackberry, . . . salalle-berry, salmon-berry [etc.]. *a*1861 WINTHROP *Canoe & Saddle* 43 [The Indian] brought me sallal-berries, and arbutus-leaves to dry for smoking.

∗Salamander.
+1. A species of pocket gopher (q.v.).
1805 LEWIS in *L. & Clark Exped.* I. (1904) 289 Their work resembles that of the salamander common to the sand hills of the States of South Carolina and Georgia. **1841** LYELL *Trav. N.A.* (1845) I. 161 We also saw small hillocks . . . made by a very singular animal, which they call a salamander, because, I believe, it is often seen to appear when the woods are burnt. **1885** *South Fla. Sentinel* (Orlando) 8 April 1/6 The gophers (Florida salamanders) proved its [the garden's] destruction.

2. Any one of various small harmless amphibians, usually of the genus *Ambystoma,* resembling lizards. {1611–}
Cf. HELLBENDER 1.
*c*1830 *Waldie's Select Library* II. 84/3 The object first observed was the tail of a beautiful salamander. **1839** STORER *Mass. Reptiles* 249 *Salamandra dorsalis.* . . . The many spotted Salamander. **1842** *Nat. Hist. N.Y., Zoology* III. 81 The Blue-spotted Salamander, *Salamandra glutinosa,* . . . sometimes is found six inches long. **1868** *Amer. Naturalist* II. 493 It [is] extremely probable, that all Siredons are merely larval Salamanders.

+3. A fireproof iron safe. In full *salamander safe. Obs.*
1845 *Cincinnati Misc.* I. 194 Iron safes . . . of the kind termed *Salamanders,* [are] being made. **1846** *Xenia Torch-Light* 2 April 1/4 His skin would make a good salamander safe. **1857** *Harper's Mag.* Oct. 710/2 Mr. Wiseman . . . bought a splendid salamander safe to put in his state-room.

∗Salary. **+**In special combinations.
Salary day, the day on which salaries are paid; *s. judge,* a judge who receives a salary rather than fees; *s. list,* a list of those who regularly receive salaries; *s. loan shark,* one who loans money at an excessive rate, taking as security an assignment on the borrower's wages; *s. officer,* an officer who receives a salary; *s. system,* a system in which services are paid for by salaries.
1870 O. LOGAN *Before Footlights* 92 These envelopes are all prepared before 'salary-day' arrives. **1789** *Ann. 1st Congress* 784 We must have a double suit of salary judges, attorneys general, marshals, clerks, and constables. **1845** SOL. SMITH *Theatr. Apprent.* 21, I supposed (of course) that I should immediately be placed upon the salary list. **1914** KEATE *Destruction Mephisto's Web* 123 In the exposé of grafts, the Salary Loan Shark should be placed at the head of the list. **1816** *Ann. 14th Congress* 2 Sess. 240 The only difference between a salary officer and a per diem, is simply in the mode of payment, and not in the amount. **1880** 'MARK TWAIN' *Tramp Abroad* 585 When we borrowed the feeing fashion from

Europe a dozen years ago, the salary system ought to have been discontinued, of course.

+Salary grab. An act of Congress (March 3, 1873) by which the members made substantial retroactive increases in their own salaries. Also *salary grabber, salary grab session.* Now hist. — **1873** *Tribune Almanac* 25 The Salary Grab. . . . The back pay dates from March 4, 1871. **1875** *Chicago Tribune* 5 Oct. 2/3 Tipton, the Nebraska salary-grabber, and a young man named Weir, . . . have been advertised for weeks by monster posters, personal drumming, etc. **1886** ALTON *Among Law-Makers* 138 The people of the country were furious when they heard of this 'salary-grab.' **1887** *Nation* 8 Dec. 452/3 A notorious illustration of what may happen . . . was the once renowned 'salary-grab session,' when the retiring members voted to increase their salaries retroactively just before Congress expired. **1895** MYERS *Bosses & Boodle* 126 The 'Salary grab,' was passed by this Congress.

+Salary man. A man who receives a salary. — **1719** *Mass. Bay Currency Tracts* 193 Salary Men, Ministers, School-Masters [etc.]. . . . are pincht and hurt more than any. **1763** *Essex Inst. Coll.* XLIX. 139 Our provinces . . . have greatly wronged many hundreds of thousands of orphans, helpless persons, generous creditors, and salary men, by means of their awful breaches of their public faith. **1824** *Baptist Mag.* IV. 358 The situation of clergymen is quite different from other men, even other *salary* men.

∗Sale. **+**In special combinations.
Sale block, a block on which slaves were exposed for sale (*Obs.*); *s. brand,* (see quotation); *s. crop,* a crop grown to be sold; *s. garden,* a garden in which vegetables are raised for sale; *s. money,* money obtained from a sale; *s. note,* (see quotation).
1887 HARRIS in *Century Mag.* April 847/2 The prisoner was made to stand on the sale-block so that all might have a fair view of him. **1844** GREGG *Commerce of Prairies* I. 186 No matter how many proprietors a horse or mule may have had, every one marks him with a huge hieroglyphic brand, which is called the *fierro,* and again, upon selling him, with his *venta,* or sale-brand. **1850** *Rep. Comm. Patents 1849: Agric.* 131 Our forefathers . . . [were] at too great a distance from market to cultivate any other as a *sale* crop than tobacco. **1851** CIST *Cincinnati* 191 J. S. COOK, has recently commenced a sale garden and nursery. **1656** *Suffolk Deeds* II. 246 [He] hath hereby full power and Authority . . . out of the Sale money to satisfye himselfe the aforesaid sume of forty six pounds. **1862** BOUVIER *Law Dict.* II. 495/2 *Sale note,* a memorandum given by a broker to a seller or buyer of goods, stating the fact that certain goods have been sold by him on account of a person called the seller to another person called the buyer.

Salem grass. =FEATHER GRASS 2. — **1749** FRANKLIN *Writings* II. 386, I threw in . . . a bushell of Salem Grass or Feather-Grass.

+Salemite. A native or inhabitant of Salem, Mass. *Obs.* — **1702** C. MATHER *Magnalia* (1853) I. 72 Some of the passengers . . . came over with those of our first Salemites. **1708** *Essex Inst. Coll.* X. 77, [I] found at our house when we came back the Salemites.

+Saleratus. [f. mod. L. *sal aeratus* 'aerated salt.']
1. A name originally used for potassium bicarbonate, but later applied to sodium bicarbonate or baking soda.
1837 S. GRAHAM *Treatise on Bread* 46 (Ernst), Pearlash or saleratus is also used by them [*sc.* public bakers] in considerable quantities. **1848** BRYANT *California* viii. 123 We have passed several small lakes or ponds, incrusted with the carbonate of soda or common saleratus. **1857** *Lawrence* (Kan.) *Republican* 11 June 4 Saleratus is becoming almost as necessary with our people in the production of bread, as flour. **1882** BAILLIE-GROHMAN *Camps in Rockies* 56 The baking powder, or 'saleratus' (the grandest word in the trapper's very abridged dictionary), cannot be found.

transf. **1908** 'O. HENRY' *Options* 66 And here was a man whose saleratus you had et.

2. Attrib. with *bread, cake, factory, water.*
1846 *Knickerb.* XXVII. 510 The white sal-æratus cake and the 'water bewitched' are quickly devoured. **1849** CHAMBERLAIN *Ind. Gazetteer* 186 In the county . . . [is] an extensive saleratus factory. **1872** *Harper's Mag.* Jan. 221/2 The meal was a substantial one of fried bacon, saleratus bread, corn-dodgers, and coffee. **1877** JEWETT *Deephaven* 61 We tried clear alcohol, and saleratus-water.

+Saleratus biscuit. A biscuit leavened with saleratus. — **1872** [see SALT-RISING BREAD]. **1898** F. H. SMITH *C. West* 35 Set out before him were fried eggs . . . ; saleratus biscuit, full of dark spots; and coffee in tin cups. **1905** 'O. HENRY' *Trimmed Lamp* 50 There is one day when all we Americans who are not self-made go back to the old home to eat saleratus biscuits.

Sale(s) day. A day fixed for the public sale or exchange of property. — **1868** *Harper's Mag.* Aug. 372/1 The first Monday of the month . . . is always 'sale day' in South Carolina. **1877** *Vt. Dairymen's Ass. Rep.* VIII. 19 Attempts have been made . . . to falsify the truth of history, by representing that the first effort to establish 'sales days' or a country cheese market was made at Utica in 1870. **1884** HARRIS *Mingo* 246 Last sale-day he took me off behind the Court-house. **1887** — in *Century Mag.* April 841/2 Only last sale-day you mighty nigh jolted the life out of Bill-Tom Saunders.

+Sales girl. A girl or a woman employed to sell goods or merchandise. — **1837** *Courier-Journal* 2 Feb. 4/7 In order to cripple his old partner, he offered superior inducements to the sales girls to go with him. **1903** LOOMIS *Cheerful Americans* 255 The anxious-looking shoppers . . . [were]

making the evening the worst in the year for tired sales-girls. **1907** *St. Nicholas* June 683/2 'White suede gloves, please, elbow length,' she said to the salesgirl.

+Saleslady. =SALESWOMAN. { =E. 'shop-girl'} — **1870** *Phila. Ledger* 16 Dec. (De Vere), Wanted. Two competent sales-ladies. **1892** *Harper's Mag.* Feb. 439/1 Every girl behind a counter is a saleslady. **1906** *Atlantic Mo.* Jan. 32/1 Salesladies and female clerks and stenographers . . . disclose in their features [independence and shrewdness]. **1917** J. F. DALY *Life A. Daly* 511 It was in America, of course, that a young person described herself as a sales-lady.

∗**Salesman.** ∗**a.** One who sells goods in a store or shop; a clerk. +**b.** A commercial traveler (q.v.). — **1851** *Knickerb.* XXXVIII. 653 Our friend . . . is about to embody, in his sales, a series of practical lectures upon auctioneering in general, with imitations of the more prominent metropolitan functionaries who call themselves 'salesmen.' **1884** CABLE *Dr. Sevier* xlvii, Shop-keepers and salesmen at their doors [were] catching what they could of his words. **1902** LORIMER *Lett. Merchant* 131 A real salesman is one-part talk and nine-parts judgment; and he uses the nine-parts of judgment to tell when to use the one-part of talk.

+**Sale(s) molasses.** Molasses bought at a store, as distinguished from that made at home. — **1854** H. H. RILEY *Puddleford* 92 Longbow . . . used sales-molasses for common, every, most every day. **1863** RANDALL *Pract. Shepherd* 147 Cow's milk . . . is generally mixed with a little 'sale' molasses [for young lambs].

+**Sales people.** *pl.* Those employed to sell goods or merchandise. — **1876** *Scribner's Mo.* Feb. 599/2, I walked through the crowds of purchasers and salespeople. **1905** *Washington Star* 24 Nov. 20 Wanted—the services of experienced salespeople for every department.

+**Salesroom.** A room in which sales are made. { =sale-room} — **1840** *Knickerb.* XVI. 226 A crowded audience [was ejected] from his sales-room, because an unlucky wight had the temerity to bid six-pence for a tattered copy of Paradise Lost. **1851** ROSS *In New York* 24 Many congregate around the doors of these sales-rooms. **1880** *Harper's Mag.* Nov. 904/1 Try to sell one of your pretty 'services' . . . at any of the leading shops or sales-rooms. **1892** *York County Hist. Rev.* 85 The salesroom . . . carries a fine line of . . . dress goods in wool, merino and cotton goods.

+**Sale stable.** A large barn or other building where horses are kept for sale. — **1851** CIST *Cincinnati* 216 We have . . . forty-five livery and sale stables. **1875** *Cincinnati Times* 1 July 2/8 Metropolitan Livery, Boarding and Sale Stables. **1892** HOWELLS *Quality of Mercy* 206 The horses, good, bad, and indifferent, were sent to a sale-stable in Boston.

Saleswoman. A woman employed to sell goods in a shop or store. {1704-} — **1865** *Atlantic Mo.* March 319/2 The great establishment is still continued, with . . . its wealth of costly goods, and its long array of tortured saleswomen. **1880** *Harper's Mag.* June 36/2 Thousands of young women are occupied as saleswomen in the retail stores of Sixth Avenue. **1906** *N.Y. Ev. Post* 7 Feb. 4 There is a great deal of snobbery among women workers, the saleswoman feeling herself superior to the factory-worker. **1919** HOUGH *Sagebrusher* 20 Her frock was that of the sales-woman, her gloves were badly worn.

+**Salina.** [New borrowing from Sp.] =next. — **1844** GREGG *Commerce* I. 176 The *Salinas* are public property. **1850** *Western Journal* IV. 375 There are a number of *Salina's*, or mines of pure salt. **1890** PEARY in *Scientific Amer. Suppl.* LXII. 11710/3 Less than three miles of level swampy *salinas* reach to the surf of the Pacific.

∗**Saline,** *n.* A salt spring, lick, pond, or marsh; a salt mine or salt works.

1766 [see SALT *n.* 5]. **1804–5** LEWIS in *L. & Clark Exped.* VI. (1905) 55 The mountains, salines, trading establishments, and all the other remarkable places . . . are also laid down on this map. **1844** GREGG *Commerce of Prairies* II. 186 There have been several *Salines*, or mines (if we may so term them) of pure salt, discovered in different parts of the Prairies. **1888** *Harper's Mag.* April 739/2 The waters of the bay were already marbling over the salines and half across the island.

∗**Saline,** *a.* **1.** Of land: Containing valuable salines. +**2.** *Saline fund*, a fund accruing to a state treasury from the sale or lease of salt lands. — (1) **1821** NUTTALL *Travels Arkansa* 219 Such is the appearance of the saline plains of the Arkansa. **1837** PECK *New Guide* 312 Funds, in part, have been provided, from the sales of certain saline lands belonging to the state [of Ill.]. **1844** *Indiana Senate Jrnl.* 29 Sess. 113 The committee on education [shall] be instructed to enquire into the expediency of appropriating a part of the saline lands of Brown county for the support of a school for the poor and orphans. (2) *Ib.* 171 That class of children designated in the resolution . . . will participate in the benefits arising from the saline fund.

Saline spring. A spring the water of which is salty. {1872-} — **1808** *Ann. 10th Congress* 2 Sess. 905 In the Western country there were saline springs which produced better salt than that imported. **1836** J. HALL *Statistics of West* 21 Saline springs are distributed throughout the whole region. **1840** in *Mich. Agric. Soc. Trans.* VI. 289 Several saline springs and deer-licks were examined in the valley.

Sally port. An opening in a fortification for the passage of troops. {1649-} Also transf. — **1738** BYRD *Dividing Line* (1901) 230 In their houses they always contrive a sally-port, . . . so they may escape. **1756** [see BLIND *n.* 1]. **1807** *Ann. 10th Congress* 1 Sess. I. 457 Captain Bissel . . . took me through the sally port to the back of the garrison. **1872** ROE *Barriers Burned Away* xxxiv, At the sally-port of the distant barracks bayonets were gleaming.

∗**Salmon.**

∗**1.** A large, highly esteemed food fish (*Salmo salar*) found on the North Atlantic coast and in rivers, which it ascends for spawning.

1616 SMITH *New England* 10 Much Salmon some haue found vp the Riuers. **1675** JOSSELYN *Two Voyages* 141 Salmon and Lampres are catch'd at the falls of Rivers. **1712** SEWALL *Diary* II. 348 The Govr invites Col. Hutchinson by name to come and eat Salmon with him Election-day morn. **1792** [see DIPPING NET]. **1814** MITCHILL *Fishes N.Y.* 435 Common Salmon. . . . Their season is the middle of May, or beginning of June. **1840** *Niles' Nat. Reg.* 25 April 128/2 The 'first salmon' caught in the Kennebec this year was sold in Boston on Friday last for forty-two dollars. **1869** *Rep. Comm. Agric. 1868* 322 The sea-going salmon . . . [has] very nearly [become extinct] upon our eastern coast. **1903** T. H. BEAN *Fishes N.Y.* 246 To the Penobscot the salmon come most abundantly in June and July.

+**2.** Any one of various food fishes somewhat resembling the true salmon, as the pickerel and the pike perch, found in lakes and rivers in the interior of the United States.

1765 ROGERS *Acct. N. Amer.* 177 In the rivers round Lake Ontario are salmon in great plenty. **1843** *Niles' Nat. Reg.* 18 March 48/3 Fresh salmon, caught in the waters of Lake Ontario on Tuesday last, were eaten in New York on Saturday. **1849** LANMAN *Lett. Alleghany Mts.* 65 Their salmon is none other than the genuine pickerel of the North and South. **1856** [see GROWLER 1]. **1884** *Century Mag.* April 908/1 The pike-perch becomes a 'salmon' in the Susquehanna, Ohio, and Mississippi rivers.

+**3.** Any one of various fishes allied to the true salmon, esp. of the genus *Oncorhynchus*, found along the northern Pacific coast, and in streams flowing into the Pacific.

1806 LEWIS in *L. & Clark Exped.* IV. (1905) 163 The common Salmon and red Charr are the inhabitants of both the sea and rivers. **1837** [see FISH FEAST]. **1844** LEE & FROST *Oregon* 192 The Indians scattered to their various quarters to engage in removing to their fishing-grounds against the arrival of the salmon. **1871** RAYMOND *3d Rep. Mines* 196 At the Cascades of the Columbia, the Des Chutes, and other rivers, not too much obstructed, salmon are speared or hooked in great abundance by the Indians. **1891** [see HUMPBACK 2].

4. *attrib.* and *comb.* **a.** Designating ponds, streams, etc., frequented by salmon. {salmon river, 1753}

1687 SEWALL *Diary* I. 188 Hutchinson and Self rode to the Salmon-falls. **1761** NILES *Indian Wars* II. 402 At the head of this neck was a fine salmon-pond. **1833** *Knickerb.* I. 283 The salmon lakes, and the trout streams . . . [were] given by the master of life to his red men. **1845** FRÉMONT *Exped.* 201 One of the guides informed me that this was a 'salmon water.' **1886** H. P. WELLS *Salmon-Fisherman* 75 The Mic-mac type of birch-bark canoe . . . [is] used on many salmon-streams. **1886** *Critic* 16 Oct. 183 A map and an annotated list of salmon-rivers locate them chiefly north of the St. Lawrence.

b. Designating persons, articles, and contrivances connected with the catching and preserving of salmon.

1828 SHERBURNE *Memoirs* 55 Wilds and myself were invited by the Governor to assist rowing his barge up the river, where he had salmon nets. **1869** *Mass. Acts & Resolves* 681 Whoever takes or catches fishes . . . in any other manner than by . . . sweep-seine or salmon-pot, shall forfeit a sum not less than five dollars. **1881** *Amer. Naturalist* XV. 182 These distorted males are commonly . . . rejected by the canners and salmon-salters. **1886** H. P. WELLS *Salmon Fisherman* 42 An enamelled water-proofed salmon-line is an expensive thing. *Ib.* 49 Some salmon-reels are now to be had with a drag.

5. In special combinations.

Salmon bake, a social gathering at which salmon are baked and eaten; *s. cache*, a hiding place for a supply of salmon; *s. harvest*, the taking or catching of salmon; *s. house*, a temporary lodge or habitation used by Indians at a salmon fishery; *s. perch*, a fish resembling a salmon and a perch; *s. season*, the season when salmon are usually taken.

1919 *Dialect Notes* V. 58 A merry crowd . . . participated in a most enjoyable salmon-bake. **1844** LEE & FROST *Oregon* 177 Salmon caches . . . are cellars which they [*sc.* the Dalles Indians] dig in the sand, where they deposit . . . the fruits of their summer's toil, and their winter's hope. *Ib.* 242 The Indians were now all engaged in the salmon harvest, and we met with them in their salmon houses at the Dalls. **1819** *Western Rev.* I. 308 The most delicate fishes are the Salmon-perch, the Bubbler [etc.]. **1844** LEE & FROST *Oregon* 299 Apr. 24th.—The salmon season has now commenced.

+**Salmonberry.** Any one of various plants or their fruits of the genus *Rubus*: **a.** The cloudberry (q.v.) **b.** A white-flowered raspberry, *R. parviflorus*. **c.** A raspberry (*R. spectabilis*) of the Pacific coast region.

1855 GLISAN *Jrnl. Army Life* 249 Berries afford them a good substitute for bread; such as the . . . salmon-berry. *a*1861 WINTHROP *Canoe & Saddle* 142 His heart grew big and swollen with hope, as the black salmon-berry swells in a swamp in June. **1873** MILLER *Amongst Modocs* 149 There was a little lake belted by wild roses and salmon berries. **1901** GRINNELL *Gold Hunting in Alaska* 16 The other day we picked three quarts of salmon berries. **1915** ARMSTRONG & THORNBER *Western Wild*

Flowers 236 Salmon-berry. *Rubus spectabilis*. . . . It is rather confusing that this should be called Salmon-berry in the West, for in the East that is the common name of *Rubus parviflorus*.

Salmon cannery. A place where the business of canning salmon is carried on. — **1891** WELCKER *Tales 'Wild & Woolly West'* 10 Attached to the salmon cannery was a store. **1911** [see CANNERY].

Salmon-canning. The canning or preserving of salmon. Also attrib. — **1882** *Harper's Mag.* Dec. 13/1 The salmon-canning establishments are large unsightly structures. **1919** J. COBB *Canning Fishery Products* p. ix, Salmon canning is the most important fish canning industry of the Pacific coast.

Salmon fisher(man). One who fishes for salmon. {1678-} — **1837** IRVING *Bonneville* I. 75 Captain Wyeth, and his New-England band of beaver hunters and salmon fishers, now dwindled down to eleven. **1886** H. P. WELLS *Salmon-Fisherman* 6 But two formidable obstacles confront the American angler at the outset of his career as a salmon-fisherman. **1891** CHASE & CLOW *Industry* II. 119 Salmon fishers . . . fix weirs or sluices across the rivers.

Salmon fishery. A place where salmon are taken in large numbers. {1762-} — **1822** in Morse *Rep. Indian Affairs* I. 38 At the falls of the Columbia river . . . is an immense salmon fishery. **1844** LEE & FROST *Oregon* 198 Here is an excellent salmon fishery, and from two hundred to three hundred Indians spend one-third of the year at these Shoots. **1866** *Rep. Indian Affairs* 83, I granted permission to several of them . . . to visit the Dalles salmon fishery.

+Salmon-killer. N.W. (See quot. 1891.) — **1884** GOODE, etc. *Fisheries* I. 458 The name 'Salmon-killer' is applied to them about Seattle. **1891** *Cent.* 5315/2 *Salmon-killer*, a sort of stickleback, *Gasterosteus aculeatus*, var. *Cataphractus*, found from San Francisco to Alaska and Kamchatka, and destructive to salmon-fry and -spawn. **1896** JORDAN & EVERMANN *Check-List Fishes* 324.

Salmon pool. (See quot. 1890.) — **1886** H. P. WELLS *Salmon-Fisherman* 128 Nothing about salmon-fishing will probably astonish the experienced trout-fisherman . . . more than . . . a 'salmon-pool.' **1890** *Cent.* 4618/3 *Salmon-pools*, eddies where the salmon collect. Formerly, in some parts of New England, these pools or eddies were numbered, and the fishermen living near the streams had certain rights in them.

* **Salmon trout.** +Any one of various American fishes, as the namaycush and the Dolly Varden.

1705 *Boston News-Letter* 22 Oct. 2/1 Our men were refresh'd with variety of Fish, especially Salmon Trouts, some whereof 2 foot long. **1726** PENHALLOW *Indian Wars* 113 Our men were well entertained with moose, bear, and deer, together with salmon-trout. **1791** in Imlay *Western Territory* (1797) 460 [Among the] very fine fish . . . are to be found excellent salmon of two different kinds, salmon-trout of a very large size, [and] white and yellow perch. **1806** CLARK in *Lewis & C. Exped.* IV. (1905) 166 The Salmon Trout are seldom more than two feet in length. **1842** *Nat. Hist. N.Y.*, *Zoology* IV. 239 The Lake Trout, *Salmo confinis*, . . . is the well known Lake Salmon, Lake Trout, or Salmon Trout of the State of New York. **1883** [see DOLLY VARDEN]. **1884** GOODE, etc. *Fisheries* I. 474 The Steel-head—*Salmo Gairdneri*. . . . Large individuals are often called 'Salmon Trout.' **1911** *Rep. Fisheries 1908* 311/2 In different localities the individuals . . . are known by the local names 'salmon trout,' 'namaycush,' 'togue' [etc.].

attrib. **1844** FRÉMONT *Exped.* 219 Such a salmon-trout feast as is seldom seen was going on in our camp.

+Salometer. An instrument for measuring the salinity of water; a salinometer. — **1849** LANMAN *Lett. Alleghany Mts.* 158 When tested by a salometer, . . . it [the water] ranges from twenty to twenty-two degrees. **1860** MAURY *Phys. Geog. Sea* (Low) ii. § 102 (*O.E.D.*), The salometer confirms it.

Saloon.

1. A drawing-room or parlor. {1728-} Now hist.

'Now *U.S.*' (*O.E.D.*). Cf. BOWLING, CONCERT, ICE CREAM SALOON. **1799** WELD *Travels* 89 The hall, or saloon as it is called, is always a favourite apartment, during the hot weather, in a Virginian house. **1828** COOPER *Notions* I. 261 A young American . . . is just as happy in the saloon, as she was a few years before in the nursery. **1856** STOWE *Dred* II. 121 A large circle of family and plantation hands gathered together in the pleasant, open saloon. **1860** MARSH *Lectures Eng. Lang.* 440 The aim of a numerous class of popular writers is . . . to make books . . . speak the dialect of the saloon.

+2. A place where intoxicating liquors are sold and drunk. Cf. DRINKING, GAMBLING, etc., SALOON; also, BAR-ROOM, GROCERY 2. **1841** *S. Lit. Messenger* VII. 764/1 After going into the saloon (grog-shop) to 'freshen the nip'— . . . they led me into the upper tier of boxes. **1869** BREWER *Rocky Mt. Lett.* 10 'Saloons,' 'bar-rooms,' 'sample-rooms,' 'liquor stores,' 'lager beer,' etc., furnish most of the signs on the places of business. **1884** [see DISPENSATORY]. **1890** CUSTER *Following Guidon* 157 A cavalry horse, tied in front of one of the saloons in town, had been stolen. **1902** WHITE *Blazed Trail* 155 He arrived out of breath in a typical little mill town consisting of the usual unpainted houses, the saloons, mill, office, and general store. **1925** TILGHMAN *Dugout* 29 Lafe Ballard . . . came out of the Lalla Rook saloon.

+3. The main room or compartment of a railroad parlor car.

1891 *Harper's Mag.* March 581/1 Then came the more spacious saloon reserved for the smokers, and furnished with a *buffet*.

+4. Attrib. and comb. in sense 2 with *band*, *building*, etc. **1873** *Newton Kansan* 24 April 3/2 He will continue the saloon business. **1874** PINKERTON *Expressman & Detective* 160 He formed the acquaintance of several old saloon-loafers. **1889** *Voice* 20 June, [The brewer] holds a chattel mortgage on the saloon furniture and frequently on the household effects of the licensee. **1903** *N.Y. Ev. Post* 2 Oct. 2 A Park Row bar-tender . . . refused to reveal the combination of the saloon safe. **1905** Saloon band [see DANCE HALL]. **1917** SINCLAIR *King Coal* 42 The company lets the saloon-buildin'.

+Saloonatic. [Suggested by *lunatic*.] A saloon-keeper; one who favors the saloon system. *slang. Obs.* — **1878** BEADLE *Western Wilds* 386 The principal saloonatic had secured a rare attraction: a band of fifteen Chippeways were performing the 'war dance' before his door. **1891** *Voice* 19 Nov., The voice of 'The Pioneer-Press' is the voice of a saloonatic. **1909** RICE *Mr. Opp* 95 We will hurl grape and cannister into the camps of the saloonatics until they flee the wrath to come.

+Saloonist. =next. *Obs.* — **1882** *Ohio State Jrnl.* (Columbus) 9 Oct., Some pretty harsh comments were made . . . at the action of the saloonist. **1887** *Courier-Journal* 16 Feb. 4/6 The outfit was complete and the liquor sold by the saloonist was of the best.

+Saloon-keeper. One who keeps a saloon in which intoxicating liquors are sold and drunk. — **1873** *Newton Kansan* 2 Jan. 2/2 A saloon keeper named Sullivan was shot. **1884** *Century Mag.* May 147/2 The average saloon-keeper in Ohio is a law-breaker. **1899** [see EAST SIDE]. **1922** PARRISH *Case & Girl* 177 The other broke through the big saloon-keeper's guard.

+Saloon man. A man engaged or interested in the saloon business; a saloon-keeper. — **1886** STAPLETON *Major's Christmas* 89 Soon them evilomened birds, the saloon men, went off with their goods. **1894** WISTER in *Harper's Mag.* May 912/2 Toussaint walked between Cutler and the saloon-man to jail. **1902** WHITE *Blazed Trail* 45 Pat McGinnis, the saloon man, enticed him in. **1903** [see EMPIRE STATE 1].

* **Salt**, *n.*

I. ***1.** Sodium chloride, a well-known condiment and preservative.

1641 *Plymouth Rec.* I. 7 Mr. John Jenney is desirous to set up the making of salt. **1688** SEWALL *Diary* I. 206 Salem Gentlemen come wiliiy to Town early in the morn and buy up a great quantity of Salt. **1709** LAWSON *Carolina* 63 The New-England-Men and Bermudians visited Carolina . . . and carry'd out what they made, bringing them, in Exchange, Rum, Sugar, Salt, Molosses, and some wearing Apparel. **1777** *Warren-Adams Lett.* I. 313 They have Salt at half a Dollar a Bushell. **1812** MARSHALL *Kentucky* 43 Capt. Boone . . . with thirty men went to the Blue Licks, on Licking River, to make salt for the different garrisons in the country. **1897** [see KNAPSACK].

b. In various transf. and fig. uses: (see quotations).

1835 BIRD *Hawks* II. 78 The only murdering I ever knowed of among them, was that of Andy Parker; and that I uphold to be salt for gruel,— fair grist for cheating the miller. **1843** STEPHENS *High Life N.Y.* II. 261 Salt won't save you if that scamp of your'n don't shell out. **1868** BRACKETT *Farm Talk* 64 A feller couldn't make his salt to pay two hundred for 'em.

c. *pl.* Mineral salts taken as a purgative or cathartic. {1772-}

1804 CLARK in *Lewis & C. Exped.* I. (1904) 117 Capt. Lewis took a Dost of Salts to work off the effects of the arsenic. **1826** in Peck *Guide* (1831) 223 The practise of taking salts and other aperients . . . is injurious. **1877** [see BONESET 1 b]. **1888** *Vt. Agric. Rep.* X. 40 [He] would give a dose of salts two or three days previous to calving.

***2.** =SALTCELLAR.

1654 *Harvard Rec.* I. 209 Plate belonging to the Buttery . . . [includes] One Silver Salt. **1678** *New Castle Court Rec.* 362 The Inventory of Henry Salters Goods. . . . A silver porringer & Silver Salt. **1707** [see CUP I]. **1791** *Ky. Petitions* 184, I give and bequeath . . . four salts with their glasses and shovels.

3. =SALT MARSH 1. {1621-} Usu. pl.

1674 in Alvord & Bidgood *Trans-Allegheny Region* 223 They went down ye river and came to ye mouth of ye salts. **1709** [see BIRCH *n.* 1]. **1796** *Ann. 4th Congress* 2 Sess. 2694 All tide-swamps, not generally affected by the salts or freshes, of the first quality, are rated at six pounds per acre. **1802** DRAYTON *S. Carolina* 63 Yellow Jassmin . . . grows plentifully on the large sea islands, and parts of the lower country not far removed from salts. **1859** [see FRESH *n.* 2].

4. A sailor. Usually with *old*. {1877-}

1840 DANA *Two Years* i. 7 My complexion and hands were quite enough to distinguish me from the regular *salt*. **1851** *Harper's Mag.* Dec. 137/1 The veteran Nantucket salt comes off second best. **1873** *Newton Kansan* 30 Jan. 3/4 Prairie people may not all know that the 'old salts' do not measure distances on water as they do the goodly acres. **1895** G. KING *New Orleans* 81 De Kerlerec was an officer of the Marine, a gruff, bluff old salt. **1907** *St. Nicholas* June 677/1 There are in Portsmouth . . . 'old salts' who love to . . . spin long yarns of the 'good old days.'

II. *attrib. and comb.*

The attributive use of the noun cannot in all cases be rigidly distinguished from the adjective.

5. Designating topographical formations characterized by the presence of salt.

See also SALT CREEK, LAKE, RIVER, SPRING, etc.

1766 in *Travels Amer. Col.* 469 We halted near the Saline or Salt Run. **1803** *Ann. 8th Congress* 2 Sess. 1504 There exists about one thousand miles up the Missouri ... a salt mountain. **1816** *Niles' Reg.* X. 354/1 The Saline is a valuable salt flat. **1852** MARCY *Explor. Red River* (1854) 19, I shall ... push forward as far as possible into this most inhospitable and dreaded salt desert. **1856** WHIPPLE *Explor. Ry. Route* II. 53 The salineras or salt-pits upon the plains between Rio Pecos and the Del Norte will become another important source of mineral wealth to the settlers of New Mexico. **1859** BARTLETT 377 *Salt-Bottom*, a plain or flat piece of ground covered with saline efflorescences. **1865** PIKE *Scout & Ranger* (1932) 119 On its banks was a salt bluff, which rendered it brackish. **1880** CABLE *Grandissimes* 356 The day broke across ... crisp salt pools and passes.

6. Designating things relating to salt as an article of commerce.

1807 *Ann. 10th Congress* 1 Sess. I. 1209 The House were predetermined against the continuance of the salt duty. **1809** KENDALL *Travels* II. 133 The water is now drawn into the last range of vats or rooms, called *salt-rooms*. **1845** *Cincinnati Misc.* I. 271 It [was] necessary to cut the tree down to prevent further mischief or injury to a salt shed. **1871** GROSVENOR *Protection* 301 In one salt establishment wages had been decreased. **1883** 'MARK TWAIN' *Life on Miss.* xli, The old brick salt-warehouses clustered at the upper end of the city. **1891** O'BEIRNE *Leaders Ind. Territory* 83/1 In 1863 he engaged in the salt business at the old salt works at that place.

7. Designating containers in which salt is kept.

See also SALT BOX, SALTCELLAR, etc.

1840 DANA *Two Years* 203, I went up to the town on horseback, with a great salt-bag behind the saddle. **1847** FIELD *Drama in Pokerville* 174 Others ... protect their skins by ripping and forming cowls of empty salt sacks. **1853** RAMSEY *Tennessee* 714 The salt gourd, in every cabin, was considered as a treasure. **1876** Salt bottle [see MESS PAN]. **1908** GALE *Friendship Village* 222 [She] observed, vigorously using a salt-shaker, 'but then I always believe, myself, in havin' everything properly seasoned in the kitchen.'

8. In special combinations.

+*Salt block, -catcher, gauge,* (see quotations); +*s. log,* a log in which notches have been cut to hold salt for live stock; *s. question,* +the question or problem in the South during the Civil War of securing salt; +*s.-raker,* one who collects salt in a salt pond; +*s. reservation,* an area of salt lands reserved to itself by a state government for use in the public interest; +*s. sick,* (see quotation); *s. trough,* a trough at which stock is salted. {1832}

1876 KNIGHT 2023/1 *Salt-block,* an apparatus for evaporating the water from a saline solution. The technical name for a salt-factory. **1735** *Ga. Hist. Soc. Coll.* II. 51 About six at night I crossed the salt-catchers, being the head of the Cambake river, in a small canoe. **1864** WEBSTER 1166/3 *Salt-gauge,* an instrument used to test the strength of brine or salt-water. **1800** HAWKINS *Sk. Creek Country* 45 They select a place of good food, cut down a tree or two, and make salt logs. **1864** *Index* (London) 2 June 343/1 Soon after the blockade many thought that we [confederates] should 'go up' on the salt question—couldn't salt our meat, and should be starved into subjection. **1837** in Audubon *Ornith. Biog.* V. 257 Fishermen, and salt-rakers, ... frequent the keys to the windward of this place. **1837** W. JENKINS *Ohio Gaz.* p. x, Laws were passed for leasing the school lands, and salt reservations. **1868** *Rep. Comm. Agric. 1867* 97 In Duval county, Florida, a disease vulgarly named 'salt-sick,' supposed to result from eating plants growing near salt water, has been fatal [to cattle]. **1797** HAWKINS *Letters* 92 The Indians ... charge their neighbors with ... making pens for their cattle and hogs, and salt troughs for their stock.

* **Salt,** *a.*

1. Of plants: Growing near salt water or in other places where salt is present.

1743 MACSPARRAN *Diary* 12 My wife paid him ... for 7½ Days works, vizt 2 ab't Salt Sedge. **1837** IRVING *Bonneville* I. 167 There was abundance, too, of the salt weed. **1900** WEBSTER *Suppl.* 182/3 *Salt reed grass* ..., a tall reedlike grass (*Spartina polystachya*), common in salt meadows. **1913** BARNES *Western Grazing Ground* 57 Salt sage (*Atriplex*) is the one most generally called by the generic name sage by stockmen all over the West.

* **2.** Of foods: Treated, cured, or seasoned with salt.

See also SALT BEEF, SALT FISH, etc.

1835 INGRAHAM *South-West* I. 29 Them ar' chaps up thar, ha'nt lived on salt grub long. **1844** LEE & FROST *Oregon* 222 This gentleman furnished us with some excellent salt salmon. **1857** STACEY *Journal* 83 We have mutton every day instead of 'Old Ned,' in other words, salt bacon. **1896** *Vt. Agric. Rep.* XV. 22 When the public can ... [learn to] prefer fresh to salt butter, a very much larger amount will be consumed. **1902** BANKS *Newspaper Girl* 142 Salt Codfish. Ready for immediate use.... Ebenezer Emmett, packer.

* **Salt,** *v.*

* **1.** *tr.* To treat (meat) with salt for preserving or curing it. Freq. with *down, up.*

1634 WOOD *New Eng. Prospect* (1865) 38 [Fish] are left on the dry ground, sometimes two or three thousand at a set, which are salted up against winter. **1675** *Conn. Rec.* II. 381 The Councill ... aduised that the people of those plantations would kill and salt up what of their cattell were fitt to kill. **1750** T. WALKER *Journal* 52, I departed, Leaving the others to provide and salt some Bear. **1796** [see BARK *v.*¹ 1]. **1879** *Scribner's Mo.* Nov. 21/1 We killed and salted down—a hundred and twenty pounds of fish. **1895** *Dept. Agric. Yrbk. 1894* 68 Very much of the meat is canned or salted.

+**b.** To make away with or kill (a person); to deflate. *slang.* Also *vbl. n.*

1840 SIMMS *Border Beagles* (1855) 258 This agent of his excellency ... once fairly salted, ... we shall have no trouble for some time to come. **1913** LONDON *Valley of Moon* 61 You're too fresh to keep.... You need saltin' down.

+**c.** To cover or prepare (the carcass of a deer) with poison so that it may serve as a bait in poisoning wolves.

1891 *Fur, Fin, & Feather* 187/2 [The buffalo-hunter] brings down a deer, whose carcass is generously 'salted' with a white powder, which is odorless, but deadly.

+**2.** To provide (live stock) with salt.

1819 SCHOOLCRAFT *Mo. Lead Mines* 35 [Horses] subsist themselves in the woods, ... nothing more being required than to look after them, to see that no bells are lost, that they are duly salted, and that they do not go astray. **1838** ELLSWORTH *Valley of Wabash* 40 The hogs should be regularly salted while feeding. **1878** in Summers *Ann. S.W. Va.* (1929) 1586 Mr. Cornut, on going out to salt them, discovered that three of the most valuable [horses] were missing. **1903** FOX *Little Shepherd* xxi, Sheep ran bleating toward him, as though he were come to salt them.

+**b.** *To salt the cow to catch the calf,* to achieve one's ends by indirect means. *colloq.*

1823 CROCKETT *Autobiog.* (1923) 44, I went on the old saying, of salting the cow to catch the calf.

Salt beef. Beef cured in salt or brine. {1745-} — **1779** E. PARKMAN *Diary* 158 At eve she returns with a present of Salt Beef. *a*1800 TWINING *Visit* 348 The American captains ... [had] the reputation of keeping rather an indifferent table—living, it was said, principally on salt beef and sour-crout. **1861** NORTON *Army Lett.* 24 Our rations are of the best quality, except our salt beef, which is not sweet. **1910** [see COMMISSION MERCHANT].

Salt boat. A boat used in transporting salt. *Obs.* {1791-} Also *salt boatman.* — **1839** HOFFMAN *Wild Scenes* 118, [I] took my passage in a salt-boat to Cincinnati. **1842** *Amer. Pioneer* I. 283 James Sloan was first known as a salt boatman on Niagara river in 1807 or 8. **1884** [see COAL BOAT].

Salt-boiler. One who makes salt by boiling salt water. *Obs.* {1748-} Also as a nickname. — **1655** *Suffolk Deeds* II. 183, I John Morse of Boston in New England Salt boyler, doe Acknowledge myself to owe [etc.]. **1833** *Niles' Reg.* XLIV. 395/1 Several salt boilers at Harwich remarked that some clam shells on the sea shore contained minute chrystals of salt. **1885** *Mag. Amer. Hist.* April 394/2 *Salt Boiler, The,* a nickname of the Hon. Thomas Ewing, Senator, and a member of Harrison's and Taylor's Cabinets. When a boy he is said to have worked as a boiler at the salt springs of Ohio.

Salt box.

1. a. A box in which salt is kept for domestic use; a saltcellar. {1611-} +**b.** A large shallow box in which meat is cured.

1647 *Essex Probate Rec.* I. 71 One salt boxe, ... 2 Reaphookes, one pitchfork. **1775** *Essex Inst. Coll.* XIII. 186, 1 salt Box, 1 pr Snuffers. **1835** Hoffman *Winter in West* II. 117 ... he throws the meat into a 'salt-box,' from which the 'packer' receives it. **1885** HOWELLS *Silas Lapham* viii, 'Well, now,' said Walker, beating the bottom of his salt-box to make the salt come out.

+**2.** Attrib. with reference to a type of frame building suggestive of a salt box.

1876 INGRAM *Centennial Exp.* 717 [The cabin] was built of logs in the 'salt-box' style and entirely open in front. **1900** SHELTON (*title*), The Salt-Box House: Eighteenth Century Life in a New England Hill Town.

+**Salt cedar.** An ornamental shrub or small tree (*Tamarix gallica*) which grows in the warmer parts of the United States. — **1881** *Harper's Mag.* April 731/1 Salt cedars and stunted live-oaks ... were the only trees growing from the thin soil. **1895** *Dept. Agric. Yrbk. 1894* 425 Along the Gulf coast of Texas and the shores of southern California 'salt cedar' is doubtless a good sand binder.

* **Saltcellar.** A small container for salt used at the table. — **1640** *Essex Probate Rec.* I. 12, I give unto my sister above said three peuter platters and a double salt seller. **1720** SEWALL *Letter-Book* II. 106 To be Bought.... Four Duzen of small Glass Salt-cellars. **1845** *Knickerb.* XXVI. 513 A salt-cellar was produced upon the board just filled with coarse but very pure salt. **1907** 'O. HENRY' *Roads of Destiny* 343 Take away this empty salt-cellar.

+**Salt creek.** A creek the waters of which are salty.

1639 *Portsmouth Rec.* 8 It is Mutually agreed ... that these quanteties [be grown].... William Hutchinson flour Hundreth [on the] North side of ye salt Crick. **1694** *Jamaica* (L.I.) *Rec.* I. 431 John Pruden ... [has sold] a cartain lott parcel tract & meashur of salt meadow . . . [bounded] by a certain salt creek on ye west. **1748** ELIOT *Field-Husb.* i. 3 Last Fall I began upon it and drew a Ditch of four foot wide from a large Salt Creek. **1907** ANDREWS *Recoll.* 84, I walked down to Salt Creek, three miles and back.

+b. *To row up Salt Creek,* to row up Salt River (s.v. SALT RIVER 2).

1843 'CARLTON' *New Purchase* I. 261 If I don't row you up salt crick in less nor no time, my name's not Sam Townsend.

Salted pork. =SALT PORK. — **1763** E. Singleton *Social N.Y.* 358 No kind of provisions . . . are to be sold anywhere but in the common Market Houses of this city (except live fish, bread, flour, salted beef, salted pork). *a*1811 HENRY *Camp. Quebec* 23 We gave salted pork, and they returned two fresh beaver tails. **1845** COOPER *Chainbearer* vii, [The tavern] afforded nothing to drink but rum, and nothing to eat but salted pork and potatoes.

* Salter.

*1. a. One who makes salt. **b.** One who salts meat, fish, etc. {1611–}

1640 *Boston Rec.* 47 Also Beniamyn Negoose, a Salter, is Allowed to be an Inhabitant. **1755** [see CUTTER 1]. **1800** *Mass. H. S. Coll.* 1 Ser. VII. 248 The *splitter* . . . splits them [the fish] completely open, and hands them to the *salter* who salts and piles them in bulk. **1846** *Knickerb.* XXVII. 512 [The fish] are thrown into the hold where the 'salter' gives them the finishing stroke. **1881** *Scientific Amer.* XLIV. 408/2 In this state it [cowhide] is sold to the salters.

2. *New Eng.* (See quotation.)

1891 *Cent.* 5319/1 *Salter,* . . . a trout about leaving salt water to ascend a stream. (New Eng.)

+3. One who salts cattle. (Cf. SALT *v.* 2.)

1903 *N.Y. Ev. Post* 30 Sept. 7 The 'salters' . . . have reported a good grazing season.

+Salt factory. A place where salt is processed; a saltworks. — **1835** HOFFMAN *Winter in West* I. 76 At the mouth of the glen we paused to look at a salt factory. **1837** W. JENKINS *Ohio Gaz.* 85 It has . . . ten or twelve salt factories.

* Salt fish. Fish cured by salting, as distinguished from fresh fish.

1689 SEWALL *Diary* I. 276 Had a Dish of Fowls and Bacon with Livers: a Dish of Salt Fish [etc.]. **1777** in Quincy *Hist. Harvard* II. 541 The Steward shall not be obliged to provide salt fish, but shall procure fresh fish as often as he can. **1805** PARKINSON *Tour* 221 The greater number of people in America live on salt fish and smoked bacon. **1866** A. D. WHITNEY *L. Goldthwaite* vi, Let's go in, and get salt-fish and cream for our breakfast. **1899** JEWETT *Queen's Twin* 47 [He took] an armful of dried salt fish from a corded stack in the back of the wagon.

attrib. **1844** *Knickerb.* XXIV. 470, I was about to partake of a salt-fish dinner. **1884** *Nat. Museum Bul.* 1096 Salt-fish market. . . . Piles of fish and barrels on the wharf.

Salt furnace. A furnace operated in connection with a salt works. — **1822** FOWLER *Journal* 124 The Smoke appeered like that of a Salt furnis. **1837** W. JENKINS *Ohio Gaz.* 393. 2 salt furnaces . . . [make] from 400 to 500 barrels of salt per week. **1847** HOWE *Hist. Coll. Ohio* 263 His pack-saddle [was] stolen by the boilers, . . . thrown into the salt furnace, and destroyed.

Salt grass. Any one of various grasses, as *Distichlis spicata* or some species of *Spartina,* found (1) in salt flats, meadows or marshes, or (2) in arid alkaline plains in the west.

(1) **1704** *Providence Rec.* XIV. 279 A piece of Ground . . . beareth a sort of salt Grass which is Called Thatch. **1774** HUTCHINSON *Diary & Lett.* I. 240 The grass appears unlike our salt grass: more like what some call bastard grass. **1812** IRVING *Knickerb.* (1927) 461 A little rural retreat . . . [was] infested, in the summer time, with musquitoes; but otherwise very agreeable, producing abundant crops of salt-grass and bull-rushes. **1875** *Fur, Fin & Feather* (ed. 3) 118 Very soon after feeding on the succulent salt-grasses . . . [the ducks] acquire the delicious flavor for which they are so highly esteemed. **1891** *Scribner's Mag.* X. 470 The tangled growth of hedge, cat-tails, elder and salt-grass.

attrib. **1834** AUDUBON *Ornith. Biog.* II. 377 Their flight was precisely similar . . . when perched on . . . stalks of salt grass-hay.

(2) **1843** FRÉMONT *Explor. Rocky Mts.* 21 There was a bluish grass . . . called by the voyageurs '*herbe salée,*' (salt grass). **1852** STANSBURY *Gt. Salt Lake* 235 The only vegetation today has been a little dwarf artemisia, grease-bush, rabbit-bush, [and] salt-grass. **1877** CAMPION *On Frontier* 241 A long day's march . . . brings us . . . [to] a flat meadow of 'salt grass.' **1894** COULTER *Bot. W. Texas* III. 546 *D[istichlis] spicata.* . . . Salt Grass. . . . Common in saline soil, throughout Texas and Northward. **1913** BARNES *Western Grazing Grounds* 43 There is also sacaton (*Sporobolus airoides*), sometimes but erroneously called salt grass.

+Salt-grassy, *a.* Abounding in salt grass. *colloq.* — **1898** N. BROOKS *Boys of Fairport* 195 That flat, marshy, salt-grassy isthmus . . . connected the hilly peninsula of Fairport with the mainland.

Salt hay. Hay made from salt grass. {1763–}

1648 *Mass. H. S. Coll.* 4 Ser. I. 204 Salt hay and fresh there thousands are of acres I do deeme. **1732** HEMPSTEAD *Diary* 252 In the foren[oon] I went to Mamacock & fetcht a L[oa]d of Salt hay alias Rushes. **1794** *Mass. H. S. Coll.* 1 Ser. III. 198 Stout's creek, . . . where a number of tons of

salt hay were annually cut, now scarcely exists. **1802** [see FODDER *v.* 1]. **1885** JEWETT *Marsh Island* 41 The men folks would all be off about the salt hay.

attrib. **1733** HEMPSTEAD *Diary* 265 [We] fetched a L[oa]d of Salt Hay Rushes fro[m] Mamacock. **1843** *Knickerb.* XXII. 34 Range your eye along the summits of the salt hay-stacks.

+Salt-haying. The harvesting of salt-grass hay. — **1860** *Harper's Mag.* Aug. 336/1 He could get well helping the Deacon all one summer on the smack and the salt-haying.

+Salt hole. (See quot. 1894.) — **1691** *Jamaica* (L.I.) *Rec.* I. 391 What salt holles shall fall in ye sd. meadow ye sd. Mr. Whitte to make up with mowable meadow. **1894** *Dialect Notes* I. 333 *Salt holes,* pool holes of small size filled with salt water. Frequent in marshes. [N.J.]

Salt horse. Corned beef or salt beef. *slang.* {1840–} Also transf. — **1846** MELVILLE *Typee* 1 There is nothing left us but salt-horse and sea-biscuits. **1877** 'MARK TWAIN' *Punch, Brothers, Punch!* 37 We stepped into the Revere House, thinking maybe we would chance the salt-horse in that big dining-room for a flyer. **1888** *Century Mag.* July 467/1 He knew that 'salt-horse' and 'cow-feed' were nicknames for corned-beef and vegetables. **1905** LINCOLN *Partners* 96 If you're dyin' to eat salt-hoss and smell bilge, you can do it.

*Salt house. A house in which salt is made or stored. *Obs.* Also attrib. — **1638** *Essex Inst. Coll.* IX. 70 Ther is granted to Mr. John Winthrop Jun. liberty to set a Salt house vpon Ryalls side. **1667** Salthouse beach [see CARRY *v.* 2 b]. **1713** *Charlestown Land Rec.* 206 The way ishuing out of fish street . . . to the Salt house is agreeable to the former record. **1785** WASHINGTON *Diaries* II. 383 Sowed the following Nuts and Seeds . . . immediately back of the Salt House. **1846** SOL. SMITH *Theat. Apprent.* 34 The old salt-house . . . had been occupied by Mr. Ludlow as a theatre.

Salting trough. A trough in which meat is salted. *Obs.* {1842–} — **1648** *Conn. Rec.* I. 507 An Inventory of the Estate of Thomas Nowell: . . . one butter churne, 2 Runletts, . . . one salting trough. **1652** *Mayflower Descendant* XI. 94 One hogshead and a salting trough and a little Tubb. **1654** *Essex Probate Rec.* I. 189 In the Cellar [were]: . . . a salting trough & Cover.

Salt junk. Beef salted and dried. {1837–} Cf. SALT BEEF, HORSE. — **1792** CUTLER in *Life & Corr.* I. 486, I had infinitely rather sit down with you to a piece of salt junk at nine o'clock than be tormented with the parade and delay of Philadelphia entertainments. **1852** STANSBURY *Gt. Salt Lake* 171 A very few days' immersion . . . [changed] its character from corned beef to what the sailor called 'salt junk.' **1884** *Century Mag.* Nov. 110 A half loaf of 'soft tack' . . . was issued, together with a piece of 'salt junk,' about as big and tough as the heel of my government shoe. *c*1900 R. L. HALE *Log of Forty-Niner* 26 The usual fare is hard baked biscuit . . . and beef as salt as salt itself, to keep it from spoiling, named in sea-language 'salt-junk,' and 'salt-horse.'

Salt kettle. A large kettle in which salt is made by boiling down salt water. — **1834** A. PIKE *Sketches* 101 A country store, including everything saleable, from a salt-kettle to a yard of tape. **1886** Z. F. SMITH *Kentucky* 296 Many fires [were] burning under the salt kettles in the distance.

Salt lake. A lake the water of which is salty.

1799 *Amer. Acad. Mem.* II. 11. 77 The *mossy plant,* growing in abundance in the bottom of the salt lake, . . . in shallow places may be seen almost covering the whole of it. **1836** IRVING *Astoria* I. 196 The real object of the expedition . . . [was] to cross the mountains to the great salt lake in the west. **1873** COZZENS *Marvellous Country* 61 Across this vast sandy plain two or three blue specks were visible, which . . . were salt lakes. **1901** *Amer. Rev. of Reviews* XXIV. 309/1 Throughout the Staked Plains, numerous small and picturesque salt lakes lie nestled among cliffs of sandstone.

+b. *transf.* The Atlantic Ocean.

1826 COOPER *Mohicans* xvii, The enemies of the great king across the salt lake are his enemies.

+c. =PLAYA.

1859 BARTLETT 326 These *playas* . . . are also called 'salt lakes' from the nitrous efflorescence with which they are often covered when dry.

+Salt lick. A place where animals lick the earth for impregnated saline particles; a salt spring or shallow salt pond. Cf. LICK *n.* 1.

1751 GIST *Journal* 42 Upon the N Side of Licking Creek . . . are several Salt Licks, or Ponds, formed by little Streams or Dreins of Water. **1796** *Statutes at Large* I. 466 Every surveyor shall note in his field-book the true situations of all mines, salt licks, salt springs and mill seats. **1802** ELLICOTT *Journal* 15 The salt lick, or spring, is situated in the bed of a small creek. **1873** *Winfield* (Kan.) *Courier* 18 Jan. 3/2 We have salt licks on the west of town. **1907** J. L. HOWE *Inorganic Chemistry* 47 Salt springs, known as salt licks, are found in many parts of the country, and at these vast herds of wild animals used to congregate for the purpose of obtaining salt as food.

attrib. **1755** L. EVANS *Anal. Map Colonies* 29 Great Salt Lick Creek is remarkable for fine Land.

Salt mackerel. Mackerel cured or preserved with salt. — **1805** *Pocumtuc Housewife* (1906) 6 Salt Mackerel and Shad freshened over night and boiled are good. **1855** 'P. PAXTON' *Capt. Priest.* 54 She wants in exchange . . . a salt mackerel. **1877** JEWETT *Deephaven* 102 There were the . . . 'kits' of salt mackerel. **1891** *Century Mag.* April 931, I enjoyed that boiled salt mackerel.

*Salt-maker. One who makes salt. — 1806 LEWIS in *L. & Clark Exped.* IV. (1905) 11 Willard had continued his hunt from point Adams towards the salt makers. 1812 MARSHALL *Kentucky* 43 Capt. Boone was out hunting meat for the salt-makers. 1847 L. COLLINS *Kentucky* 217 These works were then occupied by the families of the salt makers. 1888 *Amer. Almanac* 275.

+Salt manufactory. A place where salt is made; a salt works. — 1777 *Ky. Petitions* 44 If the Claimants do not immediately errect Salt manufactories at the different springs [etc.]. 1823 JAMES *Exped.* I. 33 Near Shawneetown are extensive salt manufactories. 1869 *Mich. Gen. Statutes* I. (1882) 436 The inspector shall not . . . have any interest whatever, directly or indirectly, in any salt manufactury.

*Salt marsh.

*1. A coastal marsh overflowed periodically by the sea; an area of low flat land subject to overflow by salt water.
1624 SMITH *Gen. Hist. Va.* IV. 162 For salt marshes or Quagmires, in this tract of James Towne Riuer I know very few. 1700 *N.H. Probate Rec.* I. 457, I give to my Son John five acres of Salt Marsh. 1784 *Ib.* III. 709 The Salt Marsh . . . [is] bounded Northerly by English Grass Land. 1806 [see MAT]. 1858 PETERS *Kit Carson* 286 That gentleman lived in a salt marsh, which is to be found in the valley of San Louis. 1872 MCCLELLAN *Golden State* 210 Large tracts of alkali desert and salt marsh is found. 1885 *Harper's Mag.* Jan. 198/1 The road lay through the bleak country side of the salt-marshes which stretched themselves away toward the sea. 1901 [see GROUNDSEL 2].

+2. (See quot. 1882.)
1836 SIMMS *Mellichampe* iv, [The pony] smells . . . as if it had fed on cane-tops and salt-marsh all its life. 1882 G. C. EGGLESTON *Wreck of Red Bird* 28 The little marsh islands . . . are simply bars of mud on which a kind of rank grass, called salt marsh, grows.

3. In specific names of plants, animals, etc. {1855–}
1843 TORREY *Flora N.Y.* II. 136 *Blitum? maritimum.* Salt-marsh Blite. . . . Salt-marsh, Long Island [see CENTAURY]. 1854 EMMONS *Agric. N.Y.* V. 225 *Spilosma acræa.* Salt marsh Caterpillar. 1862 *Harper's Mag.* Nov. 737/2 The *Simulia œstuarium*—'Salt-marsh fly'—is a nuisance found every where . . . near salt marshes. 1894 COULTER *Bot. W. Texas* III. 527 *S*[*partina*] *stricta.* . . . Salt Marsh-Grass. . . . Salt marshes, mostly near the coast. 1911 *Rep. Fisheries 1908* 317/2 [Salt-water terrapins] are also called 'salt-marsh turtle' and 'diamond-back.'

+Salt-marsh hay. =SALT HAY. *Obs.* — 1655 *N.H. Probate Rec.* I. 31, I give unto my Sonne-inlaw . . . the farthermost stack of Salt Marsh hay. *c*1680 HULL *Diaries* 243 Being salt-marsh hay, it smothered, and did not hastily burn.

+Salt meadow. A meadow adjacent to, or occasionally overflowed by, the sea; a salt marsh.
1656 *New Haven Rec.* I. 288 It was don . . . by the cattell hurrying downe in to ye salt meddows. 1700 *N.H. Probate Rec.* I. 463, I do also give him . . . the half of all my salt meadows. 1709 *Providence Rec.* XVII. 252 One share of salt meadow . . . & Two pieces of salt marsh. 1789 MORSE *Amer. Geog.* 287 Along the sea coast the inhabitants subsist principally by feeding cattle on the salt meadows. 1808 PIKE *Sources Miss.* 160 The river bottoms full of salt ponds; grass similar to our salt meadows. 1891 WILKINS *New Eng. Nun* 375 It was quite a crowd that reached the marsh that the Foster people called the salt-meadow.
attrib. 1742 *Duxbury Rec.* 272 The town also voted that David Allen should improve the town's salt meadow marsh this present year. *a*1841 HAWES *Sporting Scenes* I. 193 Lie down in the bottom of the boat, in the dry salt-meadow grass. 1862 *Harper's Mag.* Nov. 737/2 Who does not know . . . 'the Salt-Meadow Gnat' North?

+b. (See quotation.)
1833 CATLIN *Indians* I. 219 We came in contact with an immense saline, or 'salt meadow,' as they are termed in this country, . . . some hundreds of acres of the prairie which were covered with an incrustation of salt.

Salt meat. Meat cured by salting. {1617–} — 1732 FRANKLIN *Poor Richard's Almanac 1733* 15 Salt meat should be sparingly eat. 1880 *Harper's Mag.* Feb. 358/2 Hence the Belhavenites often sat down to a dinner of salt meat and johnny-cake. 1895 G. KING *New Orleans* 65 Their food was trappers' fare, biscuit and salt meat.

*Salt pan.

*1. A large shallow vessel in which salt water is evaporated.
1648 *Mass. H. S. Coll.* 4 Ser. VI. 71, I am advised not to send your salt pan to Boston. *a*1656 BRADFORD *Hist.* 142 Neither was their salt-pan come. 1708 *N.J. Archives* III. 305 He proposes to himself (by ye product of Salt, and ye ashes made under ye Salt Pans) to support & carry on ye said Pot-ash Work. 1792 POPE *Tour S. & W.* 18 Mr. Beall's Boat . . . was a moveable Fortification; having about one Hundred and Fifty Salt Pans so arranged, as to render a few Men within, capable of repulsing ten Times their Number without. 1887 *Prince Society Publ.* XVII. 64 The patent recites . . . the making of salt-pans and salt.

*2. A shallow depression by the sea from which salt is obtained by the natural evaporation of the sea water allowed to flow into it. *Obs.*
1654 *Boston Rec.* 15 Sixteene accres of upland and salt marsh more or lesse, by the salt pan sold to Edward Pason. 1688 *Duxbury Rec.* 62 The

said meadow was disposed of . . . from said tree and stake along the beach to a place where the salt pan stood [etc.].

3. *Geol.* A lake or other natural undrained depression in which water collects and upon evaporation leaves a deposit of salt. {1785–, in Africa}
1849 EMMONS *Agric. N.Y.* II. 15 The *Salsola kali* is common about the salt-pans and fields moist with chloride of sodium.

*Saltpeter, Saltpetre.

*1. Potassium nitrate, used chiefly in the manufacture of gunpowder.
1631 WINTHROP *Hist.* (1853) I. 458 Bring . . . good store of saltpetre. 1680 *Conn. Rec.* III. 298 We have no Salt Peter raysd in our Colony. 1757 *Lett. to Washington* II. 74, I have sent from this place . . . .50 pounds Saltpeter. 1789 MORSE *Amer. Geog.* 289 Col. Ford . . . was enabled, by the ample supply of saltpetre furnished by the patriotic inhabitants to make [powder]. 1803 *Ann. 8th Congress* 2 Sess. 1504 Caves of saltpetre are found in upper Louisiana. 1883 ALLEN *New Farm Book* 58 Nitrate of Potash, (Saltpetre,) and Nitrate of Soda. These are both found in a crude state in native beds.

2. Attrib. and comb. with *bed, dust, house,* etc.
1642 *Boston Rec.* 70 The Constables are appointed . . . to take care for the building a salt peter howse. 1686 SEWALL *Diary* II. 10* To make a Salt-Petre Bed. . . . Let the Bank be made upon rising Ground. 1775 *Amer. Hist. Review* I. 304 A Specimen of the Saltpetre Rock in Virginia was sometime past produced in Congress. 1842 *Amer. Pioneer* I. 359 They were every day engaged in bringing saltpetre dust from a cave at some distance from the fort. 1881 'M. HARLAND' *Common Sense* (rev. ed.) 527 To Relieve Asthma. Soak blotting or tissue paper in *strong* saltpetre water [etc.].

Saltpeter cave. A cave in which saltpeter occurs in abundance. — 1781 in *Amer. Speech* XV. 388 At a Spanish oak and white oak in the edge of a great Savanah near a Saltpeter Cave. 1820 *Western Rev.* II. 35 The salt-petre caves of the Western Country, possess antiseptic qualities equal to the embalming spices and bitumens of Egypt. 1847 L. COLLINS *Kentucky* 500 There are numerous saltpetre caves. 1869 *Rep. Comm. Agric. 1868* 397 Saltpeter Caves in the South.

+Salt plain. A plain the soil of which is impregnated with salt; an alkali desert (q.v.). — 1791 W. BARTRAM *Travels* 68 Low salt plains . . . produce Barilla, Sedge, Rushes, &c. 1843 N. BOONE *Journal* 199 One of the Salt Plains was within 20 miles. 1852 STANSBURY *Gt. Salt Lake* 189 We have been constantly occupied for the last four days in endeavouring to reach our companions on the salt-plain of the western shore. 1873 *Winfield* (Kan.) *Courier* 19 June 3/2 Mr. McClurg also had the skins of several small animals and birds, common to the great salt plains.

+Salt pond. a. =SALT PAN 2. {1697–} b. A pond of salty water. — 1643 in *Amer. Speech* XV. 388/1 Unto the branches of the Salt pond. 1685 *Jamaica* (L.I.) *Rec.* I. 284 [The] said acor of midow and a halfe is to be without salt ponds. 1708 *Boston Rec.* 74 Mr. Stephen Minot is desired to imploy workmen to make a Sufficient foot way next beyond the Salt ponds. 1817 S. BROWN *Western Gazetteer* 19 [Near the Illinois R.] are many coal mines, salt ponds, and small lakes. 1874 *Scribner's Mo.* Nov. 29/1 The sportsman . . . [may] fish from the salt-ponds. 1902 *Harper's Mag.* April 815 The incomparable, limitless prospect of meadow and salt pond and bar and sea.

Salt pork. Pork cured with salt. {1745–} — 1723 [see PUDDING 5]. 1750 BIRKET *Cursory Remarks* 33 We dined upon Salt pork and Turneps. 1823 JAMES *Exped.* I. 171 We are now reduced again to salt pork of a very inferior quality. 1871 EGGLESTON *Hoosier Schoolm.* 81 Floating islands of salt pork [were] fished out of oceans of hot lard. 1902 HULBERT *Forest Neighbors* 40, I'd rather have salt pork.

+Salt prairie. (See quotations.) — 1836 *S. Lit. Messenger* II. 354 In the peninsula of Michigan . . . I saw for the first time a salt or wet prairie which is only a swampy meadow, grown up in a rank, coarse, sedgy grass. 1859 BARTLETT 377 *Salt Prairie,* in Texas and New Mexico, the tracts of salt efflorescence which often cover a wide space.

Salt region. A region where salt is abundant. — 1832 BAIRD *Valley Miss.* 123 The 'salt region' extends 15 miles along the [Kanawha] river. 1836 J. HALL *Statistics of West* 58 At a distance of about sixty miles from the mouth [of the Kanawha R.] . . . commences the richest *salt region* in the United States. 1843 N. BOONE *Journal* 221 Mounds of the same material show from afar projected against the horizon in the Salt region.

*Salt rheum. +Any one of various skin eruptions, as eczema.
1809 KENDALL *Travels* I. 325 [The disease] of which I heard the name in every one's mouth, is the *salt rheum.* 1841 *Knickerb.* XVII. 293, I should say it was salt rheum. 1872 MCCLELLAN *Golden State* 168 [The grindelia] has long been known to the Indians and native Spanish of California . . . as a cure . . . in many skin diseases, as salt-rheum, nettlerash, and many others. 1873 BAILEY *Life in Danbury* 290 He is too afraid of the new kinds of insects, small-pox, and salt-rheum.

+b. *Salt-rheum weed,* = BALMONY.
1847 WOOD *Botany* 400 *C*[*helone*] *glabra.* Snake-head. Salt-rheum Weed. . . . A plant of brooks and wet places.

+Salt rising. A leaven consisting of a salted batter of flour or meal used in bread-making.
[1833 TRAILL *Backwoods of Canada* (1846) 137 [The wife of a Canadian settler] must know how to manufacture *hop-rising* or *salt-rising* for leav-

ening her bread.] **1846** FARNHAM *Prairie Land* 333 They make a large loaf in their iron ovens which is fermented by what they call *salt-rising.* **1880** *Scribner's Mo.* Jan. 426/1 The whole feminine conclave launched out into a . . . discussion of the relative merits of salt-risin's, milk-emptin's, and potato yeast. **1898** HARPER *S. B. Anthony* I. 161 The process of yeast-making was . . . not well understood by the average housekeeper, so a substitute was found in 'salt-risings.'

attrib. **1846** FARNHAM *Prairie Land* 138 When tea-time approached, . . . the 'salt risin' loaf . . . [was] put to baking. **1907** *N.Y. Ev. Post* (s.-w. ed.) 20 June 4 The general suffrage seems to go to . . . Virginia ham, salt-rising biscuits, apple dumpling.

+**Salt-rising bread.** Bread leavened with salt rising. — **1865** *Atlantic Mo.* April 400/1 Maggie . . . described the process of making 'salt-rising' bread. **1872** EGGLESTON *End of World* 12 The Germans . . . were not yet civilized enough to like the yellow saleratus-biscuit and the 'salt-rising' breads of which their neighbors were so fond. **1898** E. C. HALL *Aunt Jane* 6, I took the premium on my salt-risin' bread and sponge cake. **1920** HOWELLS *Vacation of Kelwyns* 27 It seems like what they used to call salt-rising bread.

+**Salt river.**

1. A river up which the tide comes to, or almost to, its source. *Obs.*

1659 *Providence Rec.* I. 97 A percell of land . . . lieth upon the salt River at the furthermost side of the towne boundes. **1704** *Ib.* V. 224 Sd Cove . . . lieth adjoyneing to the North side of the salt River called Pautuckett. **1791** W. BARTRAM *Travels* 31 Numerous small rivers and their branches . . . they call salt rivers, because the tides flow near to their sources.

b. Used attrib. in sense: Rude, uncultivated, backwoodsy, esp. with ref. to speech. *Obs.*

1835 FLINT in *Athenæum* 511/2 There is, in fact, a well-known rivalry between the collectors of the Downing dialect of New England, and the Crocket or Salt River dialect of the South and West. **1835** *Knickerb.* VI. 177 She grew up the oddest compound of . . . prose-poetry, mock-sublime, Jersey-Yankeeism, and Salt-river slang and roaring, that it has ever been my fortune to meet. *Ib.* 178 This tender mourner of the album and the beech could out-face a Salt-river roarer in West country slang.

2. *To row* (someone) *up Salt River*, or variants: To get the better of, to treat severely. Often with reference to political defeats. *slang.*

1832 TROLLOPE *Domestic Manners* II. 117 This was one of those threats which in Georgia dialect would subject a man to 'a rowing up salt river.' **1839** HOFFMAN *Wild Scenes* 133 Tecumseh afterward rowed [him] up Salt River. **1852** *Chicago Democrat* 11 Nov., One Thomas Holt, lately a clerk in the Chicago Post Office, when last seen, . . . was on his way up 'Salt River' with Gen. Scott. **1860** G. W. Bungay *Bobolink Minstrel* 70 That's the way you feel, my dear, When sailing up Salt River. **1910** *N.Y. Ev. Post* 1 Oct., That imaginary stream called 'Salt River,' up which defeated candidates are supposed to be rowed, is one of the most felicitous of all our political Americanisms, although its authorship is unknown.

Salt rock. 1. Rock salt or rock impregnated with salt. {1693–} **2.** (See quotation.) — **(1) 1784** FILSON *Kentucke* 17 Near this water is found a pure salt rock. **1805** *Ann. 9th Congress* 2 Sess. 1102 On a branch of the Arkensas . . . the Indians find the salt rock. **1865** PIKE *Scout & Ranger* (1932) 115 Coming upon a bluff of saltrock . . . beneath which was a sort of cavern, filled with cold brine, I plunged into it. **(2) 1837** W. JENKINS *Ohio Gaz.* 322 The water is obtained by boring into a stratum of whitish sand stone, (called salt rock) at a depth of from about 350 to 700 feet.

Salt spoon. A small spoon, usually having a round bowl, for serving salt at table. {1858–} — **1840** [see BRITANNIA 3]. **1865** STOWE in *Atlantic Mo.* Feb. 231/1 Look at that black spot on the salt-spoon! **1869** ALCOTT *Little Women* II. 36 [Meg] promised her aid,—gladly offering anything . . . from her little house itself to her very best salt-spoons.

Salt spring. A spring the water of which is salty. {1647–} Also attrib. — **1651** *Conn. Rec.* I. 223 If the said John Wenthrop Esqr shall discouer . . . stone salt, salt springs, or any other the like, . . . the said John Wenthrop Esqr . . . shall injoye [them] foreuer. **1786** *Mag. Amer. Hist.* I. 242 About 30 miles from Louisville there is a salt spring called Bullets Lick. **1802** *Ann. 7th Congress* 1102 The grant of the Scioto salt springs, will at present be considered as the most valuable. **1853** *Mich. Agric. Soc. Trans.* IV. 9 The Legislature may appropriate the twenty-two sections of salt spring lands now unappropriated. **1888** [see LICK *n.* 1].

***Salt water.**

***1.** Water impregnated with salt; sea water.

1608 SMITH *Works* (1910) 17 Within 4 or 5 daies iourney of the falles, was a great turning of salt water. **1684** *Plymouth Rec.* I. 180 [The way is] bounded by the Clifts & Saltwater to the southerly end of Plymouth bounds. **1704** *Providence Rec.* V. 199, [I] have bargained & Sold . . . foure acres of land . . . on the Westerne side of the Cove or salt Water which lieth before the Towne of Providence. **1843** N. BOONE *Journal* 208 [They went through] a lake near a mile long, of salt water. **1904** TARBELL *Hist. Standard Oil Co.* I. 4 Persons [were] drilling for salt-water to be used in manufacturing salt.

2. *attrib.* +**a.** Designating newcomers recently arrived from overseas. *Obs.*

*c***1797** LATROBE *Journal* 63 The ferryman . . . is one of several who are children of a man and woman, negroes, brought from Africa—called here salt-water negroes. **1818** FEARON *Sketches* 93 If I had my will there should never be a salt-water man employed in the States.

b. In the specific names of various fishes and birds.

1814 MITCHILL *Fishes N.Y.* 433 Salt-water Catfish. *Silurus marinus.* A splendid fish. **1835** AUDUBON *Ornith. Biog.* III. 35 The Salt-Water Marsh Hen swims with considerable ease. **1844** *Nat. Hist. N.Y., Zoology* II. 259 The Saltwater Meadow-Hen, *Rallus crepitans*, . . . appears along the shores of this State about the latter end of April. *Ib.* 327 The Ruddy Duck, *Fuligula Rubida*, . . . is frequently called the Saltwater Teal. **1883** *Nat. Museum Bul.* No. 27, 452 *Fundulus grandis.* . . . Killifish; Mummichog; Salt-water minnow. Atlantic coast of Southern United States. **1884** GOODE, etc. *Fisheries* I. 269 At the mouth of the Chesapeake [the tautog is called] 'Salt-water Chub.' **1889** FARMER 141/2 In New York it [the chogset] is known . . . as the Salt Water Perch.

+**Salt-water marsh.** =SALT MARSH 1. — **1754** *Georgia Col. Rec.* VI. 427 [The land was] bounded on the back by a Salt Water Marsh. **1834** [see FIDDLER 2]. **1883** *Nat. Museum Bul.* No. 27, 155 Louisiana Clapper Rail. Salt-water marshes of Gulf coast.

+**Salt-water tailor.** =BLUEFISH 1. — **1859** BARTLETT 469 In the towns on the Potomac, the Blue fish is called a *Salt-water tailor.* **1883** *Nat. Museum Bul.* No. 27, 448 Skipjack; Salt-water Tailor; Horse-mackerel. . . . This is a food-fish of great importance. **1911** *Rep. Fisheries 1908* 317/2 The 'salt-water tailor' is the bluefish . . . of North Carolina, Virginia, and Maryland.

+**Salt-water terrapin.** Any one of various terrapins, as the diamond-back, found in salt or brackish water. — **1842** *Nat. Hist. N.Y., Zoology* III. 10 The Salt-water Terrapin . . . is the well known and justly prized Terrapin of epicures. **1911** *Rep. Fisheries 1908* 317/2 The salt-water terrapin (*Malaclemmys palustris*) is very highly prized for food.

+**Salt-water trout.** A weakfish. — **1737** BRICKELL *N. Carolina* 234 The Salt-Water Trouts . . . have blackish and not Red Spots. **1884** GOODE, etc. *Fisheries* I. 362 About Cape Cod they are called 'Drummers' . . . [and in] the Southern Atlantic States . . . 'Sea Trout' and 'Salt-water Trout.' **1911** *Rep. Fisheries 1908* 316/2 Squeteague (*Cynoscion regalis*). . . . It is known as . . . 'shad trout,' 'sea trout,' and 'salt-water trout' in the Middle and South Atlantic states.

Saltweed. {1847} +An annual plant of the genus *Atriplex*, found in the dry alkaline regions of the West. — **1836** IRVING *Astoria* II. 133 There was . . . a miserable growth . . . of a plant called saltweed, resembling pennyroyal. **1837** — *Bonneville* I. 167 There was abundance, too, of the salt weed; which grows most plentiful in clayey and gravelly barrens. **1881** *Macmillan's Mag.* July 237/1 Vegetation wholly fails [in the Bad Lands of Wyoming], save here and there a bunch of salt-weed.

***Salt well.** A bored well that supplies brine for salt-making. Also attrib. — **1815** *Niles' Reg.* IX. 186/2 The salt wells of this gentleman are sunk to the astonishing depth of 420 feet. **1841** CIST *Cincinnati* Advt. Hose and Salt Well Joints. **1888** *Scribner's Mag.* Jan. 29/2 In the salt-wells . . . the miners were annoyed by the increasing flow of the green, bad-smelling stuff. **1904** TARBELL *Hist. Standard Oil Co.* I. 5 Certain of these deserted salt wells were opened years after.

***Salt works.** A place where salt is made. — **1625** BRADFORD *Hist.* (1912) I. 428*n.*, The generality can daily afford [comfort], having built houses, . . . erected salt works [etc.]. **1798** C. WILLIAMSON *Descr. Genesee* iv, The salt works at Onondago are now under the direction of the State. **1812** *Ann. 12th Congress* 1 Sess. 2242 A tract of not less than six miles square shall be reserved . . . for the use and support of the public salt works on Saline creek. **1909** *Nat. Conservation Congress Proc.* 58 We have great salt works in Louisiana which we mine as you do coal or iron.

***Saltwort.** (See also BLACK SALTWORT.) **a.** =GLASSWORT a. **b.** A plant of the genus *Salsola.* — **1784** [see GLASSWORT]. **1814** BIGELOW *Florula Bostoniensis* 65 *Salsola Caroliniana.* American Saltwort. . . . Salt marshes. July, August. **1843** TORREY *Flora N.Y.* II. 140 *Salicornia herbacea.* Common Saltwort, or Samphire. . . . Salt-marshes, Long Island, Staten Island. **1886** MITCHELL *R. Blake* 339 Rigid salt grasses and the broadening rings of salt-wort . . . lent each their hues to make one vast mottled mistiness.

+**Saltzburgher.** A member of a group of colonists from Salzburg, Austria, who settled in Georgia. Now hist. — **1737** *Georgia Col. Rec.* III. 135 The use of the Missionaries and School-master for the Saltzburghers, [£]50. **1737** WESLEY *Journal* I. 370, I had occasion to make a very unusual trial of the temper of Mr. Boltzino, pastor of the Saltzburghers. **1739** in McCall *Hist. Georgia* I. 92 We the Saltzburghers, and inhabitants of Ebenezer, . . . [intreat] your excellency . . . [to send] another transport of Saltzburghers, to be settled at Ebenezer. **1741** *Georgia Col. Rec.* III. 385 [The] Saltzburghers, . . . with the Saltzburghers that went before, were settled in a Town called by them Ebenezer.

+**Salutatorian.** The member of a graduating class in high school or college, usually the second highest student in scholastic rank, who delivers the salutatory address on commencement day. — **1847** WEBSTER 978/2. **1871** BAGG *At Yale* 592 The 'Salutatorian' is in like manner the 'second best.' **1881** RITTENHOUSE *Maud* 13 Rosa Goldstine is to be valedictorian and Tillie Vincent salutatorian. **1904** *N.Y. Ev. Post* 4 March 7 By vote of the Yale faculty there will be no appointment of valedictorian and salutatorian after the present year.

Salutatory, *n.* {1641–}

+**1.** An address pronounced by a student at commencement, esp. the salutatory oration given by the salutatorian.

1779 *N.J. Archives* 2 Ser. III. 670 John Woodford [gave] the Salutatory in Latin. **1849** *Amherst Indicator* II. 96 We ask our friends 'out in the world,' whenever they meet an educated man of the class of '49 not to ask if he had the Valedictory or Salutatory, but if he takes the Indicator. **1881** RITTENHOUSE *Maud* 13 Mabel, ten times as smart as all the rest put together, . . . [was] not even given the salutatory. **1895** WILLIAMS *Princeton Stories* 283 Other honors . . . [included] the class oratorship on Class Day, and then the Latin salutatory to-day. **1905** *N.Y. Ev. Post* 12 June 12 The annual class day exercises of the University of Pennsylvania were held to-day. H. B. Taylor delivered the salutatory.

+2. A printed address of greeting to the readers of the first issue of a newspaper or magazine.

1880 *Scribner's Mo.* July 455 Its salutatory is worth quoting as a piece of brave crowing. **1887** *Lit. World* (Boston) 25 June 206/2 In his salutatory the editor declares his paper to be 'a very modest effort to assist in a practical way the "Literary Movement in Chicago."'

Salutatory, *a.* {1818-} +Pertaining to an address of greeting. Used esp. of the oration delivered by the salutatorian at the opening of commencement exercises. — **1670** *Mass. H. S. Coll.* 4 Ser. I. 13 Our class declaimed their last declamations . . . with an oration salutatory and valedictory. **1725** [see BACHELOR 1]. **1779** *N.J. Archives* 2 Ser. III. 670 The exercises . . . [included a] salutatory latin oration by George Merchant. **1856** *S. Lit. Messenger* XXII. 68/2 This gentleman . . . was graduated [at Princeton] in 1791, having the Salutatory Oration in Latin assigned him.

Salutatorily, *adv.* By way of greeting. *Obs.* — **1847** WEBSTER 978/2. **1863** A. D. WHITNEY *F. Gartney* vi, 'Well, Melindy,' said Mrs. Griggs, salutatorily.

*****Salvage.** (See SAVAGE.) *Obs.*

Salvation Army. A charitable and religious organization of a quasi-military form which works chiefly among the poorest and neediest classes in large cities. {1880-} Also attrib. — **1884** *Milnor* (Dak.) *Teller* 19 Sept., Fifty-two pretty American girls . . . enter a town singing 'The Star-Spangled Banner' and otherwise convincing people that they are not a Salvation Army detachment. **1894** *Harper's Mag.* Oct. 699/1 [A boy] imitated the rich girlish voice of a young Salvation Army lass. **1905** 'O. HENRY' *Strictly Business* 37 Do you know of any immediate system of buncoing the community out of a dollar or two except by applying to the Salvation Army?

Salver. A tray or dish used in serving food or other refreshments. {1661-} — **1707** *Boston News-Letter* 17 Feb. 2/2 Stolen on Tuesday night . . . One Salver with a Foot to it. **1790** *Columbian Centinel* 29 Sept. 19/3 Two very handsome Salvers, one pair Butter-Boats [are for sale]. **1856** STOWE *Dred* II. 336 Tiff busied himself in arranging cake and fruit on a silver salver. **1887** I. ALDEN *Little Fishers* xii, Miss Eva . . . [called him] to help arrange the salver.

+Sam.¹ [Abbrev. of Uncle *Sam.*] Uncle Sam or the United States government; the Know-Nothings. *Obs.*

1855 M. THOMPSON *Doesticks* 244 [The Know-Nothings made me] solemnly swear . . . death and destruction to all foreigners, and eternal fidelity to 'Sam.' **1856** J. L. CHAPMAN (*title*), Americanism versus Romanism, or, The Cis-Atlantic Battle between Sam and the Pope. *a*1870 CHIPMAN *Notes on Bartlett* 378 *Sam*, a nickname given, as referring to their cant about Uncle Sam, to the Know-Nothing or Native American party.

+b. *To see Sam,* to become impressed with the merits or popularity of the Know-Nothing party. *Obs.*

1855 *Olympia* (Wash.) *Pioneer* 6 July (Th.), It is a common thing to hear men boast that some fellow has 'seen Sam' or is 'Right on the Goose.' **1866** *Congress. Globe* 18 Jan. 308/1 Just at the close of the polls I looked back over my shoulder, and saw 'Sam' a short distance behind.

+Sam.² = next.

1867 DIXON *New America* II. 13 Sam—all negroes there are Sams—may be a Methodist. *Ib.* II. 15 Since the South has been made free for Sam to live in, he has turned his back to the cold and friendly North, in search of a brighter home.

Sambo. {1748-} A Negro. A nickname. Also in a generic sense. {1866-}

1806 FESSENDEN *Democracy Unveiled* II. 24 Our *daughters* and our *wives* . . . Will strengthen Jefferson's resources By Sambo's social intercourses. **1837** *S. Lit. Messenger* III. 86/1, I don't think you love him much yourself, Sambo. **1866** in Fleming *Hist. Reconstruction* I. 92 Sambo is a freeman by force of presidential proclamation. **1885** LOWELL *Letters* II. 301 Haven't they resuscitated Sambo in a shape as *descomunal* as ever after we had dismounted him once and for all?

+Sam Hill. A euphemism for *hell.* — **1839** *Havana* (N.Y.) *Republican* 21 Aug. (Th.), What in sam hill is that feller ballin' about? **1865** TROWBRIDGE *Three Scouts* 64 When you might a' married!—why in Sam Hill didn't ye, then? **1883** *Century Mag.* Oct. 895/2 [Girls] will lie like Sam Hill to make believe they aint [engaged]. **1897** ROBINSON *Uncle Lisha's Outing* 189 Sam Hill! Look aout! **1918** FREEMAN *Edgewater People* 314 What in Sam Hill made you treat her so durned mean fur?

+Samp. [Algonquian *nasamp.*] Coarse meal of Indian corn, or a kind of porridge made from this. Also attrib.

Cf. NASAUMP.

1643 WILLIAMS *Key* (1866) 41 From this the English call their Samp . . . eaten hot or cold with milke or butter. **1672** JOSSELYN *New-Eng. Rarities* 53 The English make a kind of loblolly of [corn] . . . , which they call sampe. **1761** *Huntington Rec.* II. 448 Jacob Brush should have Lyberty to Build a samp Mill in the Meeting house Brook. **1805** *Pocumtuc House-*

wife (1906) 8 Saturday night they will expect . . . Samp when corn is new. **1850** *Harper's Mag.* Nov. 729/2 Among the relics preserved . . . [is] a samp-pan that belonged to Metacomet, or King Philip. **1893** B. MATTHEWS in *Harper's Mag.* Dec. 33/1 Then a canvas-back apiece . . . with samp, of course, and a mayonnaise of celery.

+Sample ballot. (See quot. 1897.) — **1897** *Congress. Rec.* 18 Feb. 1970/1 [The law of Illinois] provided, also, that accompanying these ballots should be eight 'instructive ballots'—ballots prepared for the instruction of the voters, sample ballots. **1898** *Mo. So. Dakotan* I. 73 If a voter had to vote on the merits of every law passed by the legislature, he would probably throw away his sample ballot in disgust and go afishing.

*****Sampler.** A piece of needlework, usu. having the alphabet, mottoes, etc., worked in ornamental characters, as an exercise in embroidering. — **1694** *Conn. Rec.* I. 414 To his daughter Elizabeth I give my white worked Sampler. **1758** *Newport Mercury* 19 Dec. 4/2 Any Person desirous of sending Children, may . . . have them instructed in . . . Embroidering, Tent Stitch, Samplers, &c. **1837** *S. Lit. Messenger* III. 601, I should be called up like a froward girl that mindeth neither book nor sampler. **1893** *Harper's Mag.* March 512/1 A sampler . . . [was used] as a screen between the sofa and the fire. **1907** *St. Nicholas* July 779 This Sampler, faded now and worn, Her childish fingers made.

Sample room. {1895}

+1. = SALOON 2.

1869 BREWER *Rocky Mt. Lett.* 10 'Saloons,' 'bar-rooms,' 'sample-rooms,' 'liquor stores,' 'lager beer,' etc., furnish most of the signs on the places of business. **1885** *South Fla. Sentinel* (Orlando) 29 April 3/1 A gentleman from Georgia is about to start a sample and billiard room. **1890** WIGGIN *Timothy's Quest* 8 There were groceries, with commodious sample-rooms attached, at each corner. **1896** *Chicago Rec.* 13 Jan. 11/6 For Sale—Corner Sample-room . . . license paid.

2. A room in which various commodities are displayed as samples. {1895}

1892 *York County Hist. Rev.* 62/1 To the side is the reading and sample-rooms for the commercial traveler.

+Sample trunk. A specially fitted trunk in which a commercial traveler carries his samples. — **1887** [see COMMERCIAL TRAVEL(L)ER]. **1915** *Current Affairs* 25 Jan. 8/2 (Ernst) Salesmen's sample trunks.

+Sampling rod. (See quotation.) — **1886** *Harper's Mag.* July 208/1 On arrival at the city they [*sc.* cereals] are sampled by means of a hollow iron sampling-rod, whose valve opens to admit the grain as the rod is thrust into the hatches of a vessel, or the interior of a car, and closes so as to retain the sample when it is drawn out.

+Samp mortar. A mortar in which Indian corn is reduced to coarse meal. *Obs.* — **1713** HEMPSTEAD *Diary* 30, I was at home al day fixing Sampmorter & killing Sheep. **1825** WOODWORTH *Forest Rose* I. ii, Didn't you get up softly and put the big samp-mortar in your place? **1838** *Knickerb.* XII. 195 It was not uncommon in a calm time, to hear the samp mortars a-going quite across the Sound.

Sam(p)son-post. {1860; earlier, *Sam(p)son's post*} +Oil drilling. (See quot. 1881.) — **1865** *Harper's Mag.* April 573/2 The walking-beam is a heavy horizontal piece of timber, supported in the centre by a Samson-post. **1881** RAYMOND *Mining Gloss.* 74 *Sampson-post,* an upright post which supports the walking-beam, communicating motion from the engine to a deep-boring apparatus.

+Sancho. [Sp.] In the game of sancho pedro, the nine of trumps. — **1880** DICK *Amer. Hoyle* (ed. 13) 210 *Sancho* . . . may be taken with any trump higher than the Nine. **1899** CHAMPLIN & BOSTWICK *Cycl. Games & Sports* (ed. 2) 7/2 The nine of trumps (called Sancho) [counts] nine points.

+Sancho pedro. [Sp.] A gambling card game derived from auction pitch. So called from the trump cards *sancho* and *pedro* (qq.v.). Cf. PEDRO SANCHO. — **1890** *Cent.* 4356/2 *Pedro,* . . . in the game of sancho-pedro, the five of trumps. **1899** CHAMPLIN & BOSTWICK *Cycl. Games & Sports* (ed. 2) 7/2 Pedro Sancho, or Sancho Pedro. . . . Any number of persons may play.

*****Sand.**

*****1.** A well-known material in granular form resulting from the disintegration of rocks.

1622 'MOURT' *Relation* 19 We found a little path to certaine heapes of sand, one whereof was covered with old Matts. **1722** *Boston Rec.* 171 Voted That no person presume to digg & Carry away of the Sand, Gravel, Earth, Tirf, or Stones. **1838** FLAGG *Far West* I. 67 Pure white sand [is] . . . transported to Pittsburg for the manufacture of flint glass. **1883** *Harper's Mag.* Aug. 327/2 [In] silent moulding rooms . . . delicate, thoughtful manipulation of sand that is to shape the fluid metal goes on.

2. = GRIT *n.²* *colloq.*

'Chiefly U.S.' (O.E.D.).

1875 HARTE *Tales of Argonauts* 71 Blank me if I didn't think he was losing his sand. **1883** *Harper's Mag.* Jan. 202/2 Good, solid man he was, too, with heaps of sand in him. **1903** ADE *In Babel* 181 There don't seem to be anybody around here that's got the sand to take her away from Mr. Branford.

3. In phrases. +**a.** *To have sand in one's craw,* to have courage, grit, determination.

1872 *Newton Kansan* 5 Dec. 3/3 We hope to see Mr. Pettibone with sufficient 'sand in his craw' for this new position [of police judge]. **1881** *N.Y. Times* 18 Dec. 4/3 To have 'sand in one's craw.' To be determined and plucky. Equivalent to 'grit.' **1884** 'Mark Twain' *H. Finn* viii, When I got to camp . . . there warn't much sand in my craw.

+b. Miscellaneous phrases.

To knock the sand from under, to undermine or get the better of; *to throw sand in the wheels, to raise sand,* (see quotations).

1847 Robb *Squatter Life* 73 [He was] conning a most powerful speech, one that would knock the sand from under Hoss. **1877** Bartlett 793 To *throw sand in the wheels,* to cast obstructions in the way of an undertaking. **1892** *Dialect Notes* II. 231 'To raise sand' is slang [in Ky.] for to get furiously angry, the same as 'to raise Cain.'

4. *attrib.* and *comb.* **a.** Designating contrivances and persons having to do with sand.

See also Sand pump.

1785 Washington *Diaries* II. 438 *Tools and Implemts.* Open Iron Wire Sieve, 1; Sand Sieve, 1. **1789** *Boston Directory* 182 Dinsdel John, sand dealer. **1796** *Ib.* 225 Bates, Elisha, sandman, Fish street. **1871** *Franklin Inst. Jrnl.* March 196 This steam sand jet has already been introduced to clean cast iron hollow ware.

b. Designating topographical features composed of or covered with sand.

See also Sand bar, Sand bluff, etc.

1821 Fowler *Journal* 20 We Set out Early and maid ten miles up the River the Sand Knobs still on the Right. **1839** in W. Kennedy *Texas* I. 40 At that time the main channel was situated one-third of the distance from Decrow's house to the sand hammocks near the present end of the peninsula. **1840** *Knickerb.* XVI. 269 Here steep sand-cliffs were observed, rising from the water . . . about two hundred feet. **1864** *Harper's Mag.* Nov. 694/1 Desert mesas and sand-bottoms formed the characteristic features of our journey. **1869** Browne *Adv. Apache Country* 50 After coursing along the belt of the great sand-desert on the left, we struck into the Colorado bottom. **1880** Cable *Grandissimes* 34 A beautiful land of low, evergreen hills . . . [looked] out across the pine-covered sand-keys of Mississippi Sound. **1894** Wister in *Harper's Mag.* July 207/2 'Mong them sand humps. **1912** Raine *Brand Blotters* 147 You'll find that break mark every eight feet or so in the sand wash.

c. In the names of plants that grow in sandy soil.

See also Sand brier, Sand bur, etc.

1793 Cutler in *Life & Corr.* II. 279 The Hudsonia . . . is called Sand-bind, from the circumstance of its being found only on the sea-shore, in a loose sand . . . confined by the plant. **1915** Armstrong & Thornber *Western Wild Flowers* 88 Sand Dock. *Rumex venosus.* . . . The small inconspicuous flowers develop into clusters of showy valves or wings. **1884** Sand jack [see Bluejack 2]. **1898** A. M. Davidson *Calif. Plants* 201 Some of these native spring time weeds are, the poppy, . . . owl's clover, sand-lupines, [and] chilicothe. **1833** Eaton *Botany* (ed. 6) 46 [*Atriplex*] *arenaria,* sand orache. . . . Stem reddish, angular, very branching; about a foot high. **1915** Armstrong & Thornber *Western Wild Flowers* 104 Sand Puffs. *Abronia salsa.* . . . This plant is . . . delicately tinted and . . . decorative in form. **1819** *Western Rev.* I. 93 Peculiar to this [Ky.] region . . . [is] *Capraria multifida,* Sand Ragweed. **1879** *Scribner's Mo.* Sept. 651/1 After laboriously cleaning their fish, they laid them among the sand-reeds. **1803** Lewis in *Jrnls. of L. & Ordway* 55 The banks appear every where to abound with the sand or scrubing Rush. **1915** Armstrong & Thornber *Western Wild Flowers* 240 Sand Strawberry. *Fragaria Chiloensis.* . . . A charming plant. **1898** A. M. Davidson *Calif. Plants* 174 The wild four-o'clock and the sand verbena are classed in this group [of beautiful weeds].

d. In the specific names of fishes found along sandy shores or bottoms.

See also Sand dab, launce, smelt.

1817 in *Amer. Monthly Mag.* II. 204 The fishermen . . . call it [*Opsanus cerapalus*] by the name of *Yellow-Kusk, Sand Codling, Slimer,* etc. **1839** Bird *Robin Day* 4/1, [I showed] an extraordinary tact in roasting crabs and fiddlers, oysters, and sand-eels. **1911** *Rep. Fisheries 1908* 318/2 The sand-whiting (*M[enticirrhus] saxatilis*) . . . is abundant from Chesapeake Bay to Texas. **1884** Goode, etc. *Fisheries* I. 449 About Cape Hatteras the names 'Jumping Mullet' and 'Sand Mullet' occur. **1882** Sand pike [see Sauger]. **1884** Goode, etc. *Fisheries* I. 671 The Sand Shark—*Odontaspis littoralis.* This species . . . is found on our coast from New England southward to Charleston.

e. In the names of various birds found in sandy regions.

See also Sand bird, Sandpeep, etc.

1847 Emory *Military Reconn.* 40 Swarms of wild geese and sand cranes passed over camp. **1917** *Birds of Amer.* I. 249 Spotted Sandpiper. *Actitis macularia.* . . . [Also called] Tilt-up; Sand Lark; See-saw. **1838** Audubon *Ornith. Biog.* IV. 584 Bank Swallow or Sand Martin. *Ib.* 587 Although small, the Sand Swallow is a rather hardy bird.

f. In the names of various animals and insects usually found in sandy regions.

See also Sand crab, Sand dollar, etc.

1879 *Scribner's Mo.* Sept. 650/1 Truth compels us also to admit that sand-adders are quite partial to the Hook. **1884** J. S. Kingsley, etc. *Stand. Nat. Hist.* II. 185 Throughout the Rocky Mountain region . . . are found several species of large, fierce-looking insects . . . popularly known as sand-crickets. **1852** Wiley *Life in South* 30/1 *Sand-fiddler,* . . . the local name for a small animal of the shell-fish kind, which abounds on the

[N.C.] beach. **1881** *Harper's Mag.* Dec. 75/1 The fluttering butterfly . . . is pounced upon in mid-air by the great sand-hornet.

5. In special combinations.

Sand barge, a barge used in transporting sand; *s. blow, s. burst,* a large, deep, circular cavity in the ground caused by an earthquake; *s. club,* = Sandbag n. 2; *s. collar,* a mass of eggs deposited in the sand by a marine snail; *s. heat,* heat or warmth found in a sandy soil; *s. hog,* a laborer who works underground as in building a subway (*colloq.²*); *s. house,* a sand heap; *s. iron,* (see quotation); *s. ore,* = Bog ore; *s. spout,* (see quotation); *s. whirl,* = prec.

1840 Dana *Two Years* 203, I had got everything in order—patch upon patch, like a sand-barge's mainsail. **1846** Lyell *Second Visit* II. 176 Within a distance of a few hundred yards, were five more of these 'sand-bursts,' or 'sand-blows,' as they are sometimes termed here. **1873** *Winfield (Kan.) Courier* 11 Sept. 1/7 A weapon of a peculiarly dangerous and for a time mysterious nature . . . is a sand club, formed by filling an eel skin with sand. **1918** Lincoln *Shavings* 159 They walked along the beach, picked up shells, inspected 'horse-foot' crabs, jelly fish and 'sand collars.' **1815** *Mass. H. S. Coll.* 2 Ser. III. 166 The soil of Plymouth is favourable to the growth of Indian corn, which requires a sand heat, checked however by latitude. **1907** *N.Y. Ev. Post* (s.-w. ed.) 11 Feb. 6 The 'sand hogs,' or 'muckers,' are the common laborers of the tubes. **1781** Peters *Hist. Conn.* (1829) 210, I must go to my sand-houses. **1796** Morse *Univ. Geog.* I. 464 The Rev. Dr. Jared Eliot, of Killingworth, invented sand-iron, or the making of iron from black sand, in 1761. **1805** D. McClure *Diary* (1899) 131 The country abounds with Sand or bog oar. **1872** *Chicago Tribune* 24 Dec. 2/7 Half a dozen 'sand-spouts'—columns of sand drawn up by whirlwinds—were to be seen on the Twenty-two-Mile Desert yesterday afternoon. **1890** *Stock Grower & Farmer* 4 Jan. 7/2 You see objects like enormous giants moving across the waste swiftly. They are sand-whirls.

∗ Sandbag, *n.*

∗ 1. A strong cloth or canvas bag filled, or to be filled, with sand for use in fortifications.

1758 *Lett. to Washington* II. 320 The half of the Sand Bags . . . will serve to carry up to Fort Cumberland the Corn that may be got. **1781** *Va. State P.* I. 596 [The Engineer] asks for a supply of Sand-Bags. **1861** *Army Regulations* 116 Sand-bags, forming loop-holes, are placed at intervals on the parapet. **1897** *McClure's Mag.* X. 154 The ironclads and steamers [were] protected in vulnerable parts by bulwarks of hay, cotton, and sandbags.

+2. A tube of strong flexible material filled with sand and used by thugs as a weapon.

1887 *Courier-Journal* 17 Jan. 2/6 He was struck with a sand-bag. **1894** *Harper's Mag.* Oct. 808/2 Burglars are harmless beasts, provided the man who is being robbed has the sense . . . not [to] go groping about . . . trying to get shot or hit in the back of the neck with a sand-bag. **1903** Ely *Evolution Indust. Soc.* 127 If I knock you down with a sand-bag and rob you, is that to be called competition?

Sandbag, *v.* {1860–} *+tr.* To fell (a person) with a sandbag. Also fig. — **1887** *Courier-Journal* 2 Feb. 6/2 The next day Claytor turned up at Central Station with a fairy story that he had been sand-bagged on his way home. **1896** Ade *Artie* 110 Even if he does scrub-bag a few of them rich blokies what's the diff? **1901** *Congress. Rec.* 23 Jan. 1345/1 [This district] is lying in wait, as it were, from one year's end to the other, awaiting an opportunity to sandbag the public.

+Sandbagger. 1. A robber or ruffian who uses a sandbag. Also fig. **2.** A sailboat using sandbags as ballast. — **(1) 1882** Peck *Sunshine* 203 Suppose all the men that have been robbed in the past year by cowardly sandbaggers, could have 'put up their hands.' **1887** *Courier-Journal* 8 Feb. 2/4 An Improvement On the American Sandbagger. **1893** *Chicago Tribune* 26 April 6/4 One of the Chicago papers recently complained that Illinois had no first-class highwaymen. It must have overlooked the legislative 'sand-baggers.' **(2) 1894** *Outing* XXIV. 401/2 [He] enjoys the sea in every form, whether racing in a sandbagger, cruising in a schooner, or taking his ease beneath the shady awning of a big steam yacht.

∗ Sand bank. A large deposit of sand; a sand bar. — **1673** in *Amer. Speech* XV. 388/2 The sand banks on the Sea board Side. **1709** [see Cassine 1]. **1789** Morse *Amer. Geog.* 41 It is rapid in such parts of the river as have clusters of islands, shoals and sand-banks. **1833** Wyeth *Oregon* 22 Have not the people of that sand-bank, Nantucket, redeemed it from the ocean? **1836** Irving *Astoria* I. 145 The channel of the river frequently shifted from side to side, according to the bends and sandbanks. **1892** M. A. Jackson *Gen. Jackson* 55 After a night of toil they sought shelter under a sand-bank.

Sand bar. A deposit of sand in the form of a bar, ridge, shoal, etc., found in or along rivers or coasts.

1781-2 Jefferson *Notes Va.* (1788) 5 The Missisipi, below the mouth of the Missouri, is always muddy, and abounding with sand bars. **1796** *Ann. 4th Congress* 2 Sess. 2572 A large pier, as the foundation for a battery on a sand-bar opposite Mud Island, to make a cross fire, has been completed. **1806** *Ann. 9th Congress* 2 Sess. 1111 The sand bars . . . extended so far into the bend as to leave little more than the breadth of the boat. **1843** Talbot *Journals* 4 [We became] finally the prey of an insidious sand-bar. **1893** *Scribner's Mag.* June 715/1 Logs block up the river by . . . grounding on sand-bars. *a*1918 G. Stuart *On Frontier* II. 17 The river was low and full of sand bars.

+**b.** *Sand-bar willow*, (see quotations).

1884 SARGENT *Rep. Forests* 168 *Salix longifolia*. . . . Sand-Bar Willow. . . . Very common throughout the Mississippi River basin, and reaching its greatest development in the valleys of Oregon and northern California. **1897** SUDWORTH *Arborescent Flora* 122.

+**Sand barren.** A tract of poor, light, sandy land having scanty vegetation. — **1766** [see HUMMOCK 1]. **1865** *Atlantic Mo.* Jan. 77/1 The low sand barrens and wet alluvial flats . . . compelled Philadelphia and Baltimore to retire their population. **1870** EMERSON *Soc. & Solitude* 144 In Massachusetts, we fight . . . the blowing sand-barrens with pine plantations.

Sand beach. A beach consisting of, or covered with, sand. — **1709** [see SAND BIRD]. **1798** *Doc. Hist. N.Y. State* I. 674 The shore is a sand beach free from rocks. **1807** GASS *Journal* 31 We encamped on a sand beach on the north side. **1872** MCCLELLAN *Golden State* 455 The sand beach for miles at this point is hard, level, and clean. **1907** *St. Nicholas* July 791/1 They finally ran the boat on the little sand beach.

Sand bird. One of various birds, esp. a snipe or a sandpiper, found on the seashore; a shore bird. {1878} — **1709** LAWSON *Carolina* 151 The Sand-Birds are about the Bigness of a Lark, and frequent our Sand-Beaches. **1745** E. KIMBER *Itinerant Observer* 11 There is a very extraordinary Bird in this Country, which frequents the Sea Beaches, &c., call'd a Sand-Bird, which almost melts in the Mouth. **1832** WILLIAMSON *Maine* I. 149 Beach, or Sand-bird is about the size of a swallow. **1869** ALCOTT *Little Women* II. 197 [A] sand-bird came tripping over the beach. **1917** *Birds of Amer.* I. 234 White-rumped Sandpiper. . . . [Also called] Sand-bird; Bull Peep.

+**Sand blackberry.** An American species of blackberry (*Rubus cuneifolius*) found in the eastern states. — **1843** TORREY *Flora N.Y.* I. 217 *Rubus cuneifolius*. . . . Sand Blackberry. . . . Abundant in New-Jersey. **1901** MOHR *Plant Life Ala.* 541 Sand blackberry. . . . The 'Topsy' variety of blackberry originated from this species.

Sand blast. A stream of sand driven by air or steam upon a surface to be cleaned, cut, engraved, etc.; the apparatus for directing such a stream. {1888-} Also attrib. — **1871** *Franklin Inst. Jrnl.* March 193 The Resident Secretary . . . [cut] the surface of a plate of glass by a sand blast. **1876** *Vermont Bd. Agric. Rep.* III. 636 The sand blast proper is made up of an apparatus through which sand and steam pass and strike upon the stone. **1898** *Engineering Mag.* XVI. 145/2 The Sand-Blast Process as Applied to the Cleaning of the Walls of Pardee Hall, Lafayette College.

+**Sand bluff.** A bluff or headland composed of sand. — **1834** PECK *Gaz. Illinois* 352 [The] sand bluffs of the Mississippi, in Warren and Mercer counties . . . furnish convenient landings for steam boats. **1837** IRVING *Bonneville* I. 223 He found it at the foot of a sand-bluff, a little to the east of the Wind River mountains. **1853** *Harper's Mag.* March 433/2 The elevation of the sand bluff at this point is probably 400 feet. **1862** MOORE *Rebellion Rec.* V. II. 165 The yellow sand bluff rises to the height of a hundred and fifty feet.

Sand board. {1817-} +(See quot. 1876.) — **1846** *30th Congress 1 Sess.* H. R. Ex. Doc. No. 41, 441 We saw many axletrees, wagon tongues, sand-boards, and ox yokes, that had been broken and cast aside. **1876** KNIGHT 2025/1 *Sand-board*, . . . a bar over the hind axle and parallel therewith. It rests upon the hind hounds where they cross the axle.

✱**Sand box.** +(See quotation.) — **1859** BARTLETT 379 *Sand-Box*, a primitive sort of spittoon, consisting of a wooden box filled with sand.

+**Sand brier.** =HORSE NETTLE. — **1819** *Western Rev.* I. 93 [Among] the trees and plants peculiar to this [Ky.] region . . . [is] *Solanum Carolinianum*, Sand briar. **1894** [see BULL NETTLE].

Sand bug. {1854-} +**a.** A sand wasp: (see quotation). +**b.** A marine crustacean (*Emerita talpoida*) which digs in the sand. — **1855** OGILVIE *Suppl.* 346/2 *Sand-bug*, a hymenopterous insect, the *Ammophila arenaria*. (American.) **1884** GOODE, etc. *Fisheries* I. 779 The Sand Bug . . . is rather an odd species of Crab, related to the Hermit Crabs.

+**Sand bur.**

1. a. =BUR GRASS. **b.** Any one of various weeds bearing prickly burlike fruit, as *Solanum rostratum*, found usually in unfertile sandy soil. **c.** The prickly calyx of such a plant.

1834 A. PIKE *Sketches* 48 To add to our comforts, the ground here was covered with sand-burs. **1846** *30th Congress 1 Sess.* H. R. Ex. Doc. No. 41, 445 In the corn fields we find . . . the sand burr, and various species of the sunflower tribe. **1892** *Amer. Folk-Lore* V. 105 *Cenchrus tribuloides*, sand-burr. Ill. and westward. **1904** *Topeka Capital* 11 June 4 A sandbur will grapple on to a man's coat tail and stay there all day. **1920** [see HEDGEHOG GRASS].

2. *To stick to* (something) *like a sand bur*, to cling tenaciously.

1870 EGGLESTON *Queer Stories* 53 It sticks to you like a sandburr. **1914** 'BOWER' *Flying U Ranch* 76, I'm sticking to the truth like a sand burr to a dog's tail.

+**Sand cherry.** The fruit of the dwarf cherry (*Prunus pumila*) of the Great Lakes region, or a related species (*P. besseyi*) of the western United States; also, the plant bearing the fruit. — **1778** CARVER *Travels* 30 Near the borders of the Lake [Michigan] grow a great number of sand cherries. **1843** TORREY *Flora N.Y.* I. 195 Sand Cherry. . . . Sandy and rocky shore; Highlands of New York; rare. **1923** [see SAND HILL 2].

Sand crab. a. =LADY CRAB. **b.** Any one of various crabs of the family Ocypodidae. {1851-} Also transf. — **1843** *Nat. Hist. N.Y.*, Zo-

ology VI. 6 This [*Platycarcinus irroratus*] and the succeeding species [*Platycarcinus sayi*] are both designated by our fishermen as the *Spotted Crab* and *Sand Crab*. **1881** *Harper's Mag.* April 745/2 Dina bestowed as much attention as possible on the bereft sand-crab. **1883** SWEET & KNOX *Through Texas* 24 The calling of each other names, such as 'sand-crabs' and 'mud-turtles,' is one of the harmless ways in which they ventilate their spleen. **1907** *St. Nicholas* July 856/2 The fires light the sand-crab's lair.

+**Sand creek.** W. =DRY CREEK. — **1846** SAGE *Scenes Rocky Mts.* xiii, We soon came to a large sand creek. **1907** COOK *Border & Buffalo* 96 In the sand creek at the south end of the grove were several holes of fresh water.

Sand dab. A flatfish: **1.** The rough dab, *Hippoglossoides platessoides*. {1880-4-} +**2.** A flounder (*Limanda ferruginea*) found along the Atlantic coast of North America. — (1) **1839** STORER *Mass. Fishes* 143 *Platessa dentata*. . . . This species [is] known by the fishermen as the 'Sand-dab' in the Boston market. **1843** *Nat. Hist. N.Y.*, Zoology V. 178 [Certain mollusks] were found in the stomachs of the *P. dentata*, or Sand-dab. **1884** GOODE, etc. *Fisheries* I. 197 The Sand Dab, or Rough Dab, . . . is taken in winter by the line fishermen of New England. (2) **1903** T. H. BEAN *Fishes N.Y.* 726 *Limanda ferruginea*. . . . Sand Dab. . . . This is also known as the rusty dab.

+**Sand dollar.** Any one of various flat, round sea urchins, as *Echinarachnius parma*. — **1883** *Nat. Museum Bul.* No. 27, 123 The so-called 'Sand Dollar,' (*Echinarachnius parma*), inhabits the east coast. **1884** GOODE, etc. *Fisheries* I. 839 The Sand Dollar . . . is found all the way from New Jersey to Labrador. **1893** HALE *New Eng. Boyhood* 148 Here we had our first real knowledge of what sea-urchins are, and what people call 'sand dollars.'

Sand dune. A dune or hill of sand, usually on the coasts of large lakes or the sea. {1830-} Also in proper names. — **1840** in *Mich. Agric. Soc. Trans.* VI. 287 A narrow tract of land on the lake coast . . . [is] occupied by a series of recent sand dunes. **1878** HARTE *Drift from Two Shores* 10 Toiling from the settlement over the low sand dunes, a carriage at last halted. **1898** ATHERTON *Californians* 324 It was a summer of raging trades which seemed to lift the sand dunes from their foundations. **1917** S. MATHER in *Nat. Park Service Rep.* 16 The Interior Department . . . will control the destinies of the Sand Dunes National Park.

Sandemanian. A believer in the religious teachings of Robert Sandeman (1718-71), a disciple of John Glass. {1810-} Now hist. (Cf. GLASSITE.)

1787, 1801 [see GLASSITE]. **1856** GOODRICH *Recoll.* I. 398 It was, in fact, the sanctuary of the Sandimanians, or, according to the popular accent, Sandaminians; a small sect of forty members then [1809], and now dwindled to a still smaller number. **1884** SCHAFF *Religious Encycl.* III. 2109/1 The sect, . . . called 'Glassites' in Scotland, and 'Sandemanians' in England and America, never attained any high degree of prosperity.

b. Attrib. (passing into adj.) with *church, conference, meetinghouse.*

1766 STILES *Extracts & Miscellanies* 566 In the late Times of Oclocracy some small Damages have been done to the Sandimanian Meeting House. **1773** *Mass. Col. Soc. Publ.* VI. 115 The Fire likewise communicated with the Sandemanian Meeting House. **1856** GOODRICH *Recoll.* I. 400 The Sandimanian church at Danbury [Conn.] now numbers three male and fifteen female members. **1877** HALE G. T. T. 52 [If] they are delegates from the United Sandemanian Conference of Louisville to the United Sandemanian Conference of Cincinnati, we shall have psalmody.

Sandemanianism. The doctrines, organization, and worship peculiar to the Sandemanians. Now hist. — **1771** J. ADAMS *Diary Works* II. 270 When the Doctor took his hat to go . . . , [Colburn] kissed him before all the company in the room. This is sandemanianism. **1856** GOODRICH *Recoll.* I. 401 Sandimanianism, which originated in a hard, sarcastic mind, subsided into a sort of amiable and tranquil Quakerism.

Sanderling. A small sandpiper (*Crocethia alba*) found on beaches. {1602-} — **1637** MORTON *New Canaan* 69 Sanderlings are a dainty bird, more full boddied than a Snipe. **1844** *Nat. Hist. N.Y.*, Zoology II. 245 The Sanderling . . . changes its upper reddish summer plumage for the grey livery of winter. **1883** *Nat. Museum Bul.* No. 27, 150 Sanderling. . . . Nearly cosmopolitan during migrations, but breeding only far northward. **1917** *Birds of Amer.* I. 240/2 The Sanderling's common note is a sharp *chit*.

+**Sand field.** A field or extensive expanse of sandy ground. Also attrib. — **1836** *S. Lit. Messenger* II. 664 You half-starved old sand-field Jersey Kill-Deer! **1873** COZZENS *Marvellous Country* 236 The great plateau of the West, with its sand-fields sparkling in the sunshine, stretched out as far as the eye could reach.

Sand flat. a. A level plain of light sandy soil. {1839-} **b.** A level sand bar. — **1794** [see CREEK THATCH]. **1807** IRVING, etc. *Salmagundi* iii, I would prefer at any time to travel with an ox-team through a Carolina sand-flat. **1826** AUDUBON *Ornith. Biog.* II. 41 The dead fish that frequently are found about the sand-flats of rivers. **1839** *S. Lit. Messenger* V. 474/1 They would thus avoid the disagreeable route by stage, through the tame sandflats and miry swamps. **1886** WINCHELL *Walks & Talks* 137 The junction of two streams and the location of a sand-flat could sustain no relation to strata three or four hundred feet beneath. **1911** *Rep. Fisheries 1908* 314 [The razor shell] is a common inhabitant of sand bars and sand flats in New England.

Sand flea. {1796-} **a.** + =BEACH FLEA. +**b.** Any flea found in sandy regions. — **1807** *Mass. H. S. Coll.* 2 Ser. III. 54 The sand flea is abundant on the beach: carcases left there are soon devoured by them. **1843** [see BEACH FLEA]. **1889** MUNROE *Dorymates* 138 The sand-fleas have made a meal of [the fish]. **1920** LINCOLN *Mr. Pratt* 221 He was a regular sand-flea for bobbing up where you didn't expect him.

+**Sand flounder.** Any one of various flounders that frequent sandy bottoms. — **1842** *Nat. Hist. N.Y., Zoology* IV. 296 The pigmy flat-fish, *Platessa pusila*, . . . is known in the markets under the name of Sand Flounder. **1884** GOODE, etc. *Fisheries* I. 199 The Spotted Sand Flounder, *Sophopsetta maculata*, . . . [is] found from Bucksport, Maine, to Fort Macon, North Carolina. **1893** [see DAYLIGHT 2].

Sand fly. Any one of several small biting flies, as the no-see-'em or punkie. {1748-} — **1736** WESLEY *Journal* I. (1909) 191, I wrapped myself up . . . , in a large cloak, to keep off the sand-flies. **1789** [see HORNET 1]. **1832** WEEMS *Letters* III. 345 Those day & night tormentors of men & beast, the *sand flies & musquitoes*, drove me back. **1869** BEECHER *Sermons* I. 298 Be afraid of sand-flies, be afraid of mosquitoes. **1903** [see DEER FLY].

+**Sand grape.** An American wild grape, *Vitis rupestris* or *V. linsecomii*. — **1891** COULTER *Bot. W. Texas* I. 62 Abounding in the sandy post-oak woods of eastern Texas it is called 'post-oak grape' or 'sandgrape.' **1893** *Amer. Folk-Lore* VI. 139 *Vitis rupestris*, sand grape; sugar grape. West Va. **1915** HUSMANN *Testing Grape Varieties* 15 *V[itis] rupestris* (sand, sugar, or rock grape). . . . Open places in poor soils and along gravelly banks and ravines.

Sand grass. Any one of various grasses that grow along sandy shores or in sandy soils. {1857-} — **1857** GRAY *Botany* 556 *T[ricuspis] purpurea*. (Sand-Grass.) . . . In sand, Massachusetts to Virginia along the coast, and southward. **1882** MCCABE *New York* 110 The sand grass and brambles grow thickly over the lowly, lonely graves. **1894** COULTER *Bot. W. Texas* III. 539 *S[ieglingia] purpurea*. . . . Sand Grass. . . . Sandy shores, eastern Texas to Michigan and along the Gulf and Atlantic coasts. **1894** *Amer. Folk-Lore* VII. 104 *Calamagrostis longifolia*, sand-grass, Central Neb.

* Sand hill.

1. A hill, dune, or other natural elevation composed of or covered with sand. Usually pl.

1622 'MOURT' *Relation* 10 [They found] the ground or earth, sand hils much like the Downes in Holland. *c*1729 CATESBY *Carolina* I. 32 [Larks] frequent the Sand-Hills upon the Sea-shore of Carolina. **1817** E. PETTIGREW *Let.* 19 May (Univ. N.C. MS.), The sand hills are alive with inhabitants. **1846** SAGE *Scenes Rocky Mts.* iv, Ranges of broken sand-hills mark the transition to the high arid prairies in the rear. **1899** CHESNUTT *Conjure Woman* 10, I lives des ober yander behine de nex' san'-hill.

b. A designation for a particular locality where such hills abound.

1806 *Ann. 9th Congress* 2 Sess. 1134 The great chain or dividing ridge, [is] commonly known by the name of the sand hills. **1864** *Wkly. New Mexican* 16 Dec. 2/2 At the 'sand hills' they killed another. **1884** *Century Mag.* June 280/1 The young man would attend to all that was to be done at Sand Hills.

2. Attrib. with *boy, country, pony*, etc.

1813 *Raleigh* (N.C.) *Minerva* 19 Nov., Arrived, . . . the northern, eastern, southern, and western transport fleets of gigs, single and double chairs, and sand-hill ponies. **1858** *S. Lit. Messenger* XXVI. 230/1 We had . . . a class of sand hill boys and gopher trapping girls. **1913** BARNES *Western Grazing Grounds* 65 These latter species are . . . most common . . . in the sandhill region of western Nebraska. **1923** J. H. COOK *On Old Frontier* 95 We passed through the sandhill country at the season when the sand cherries were ripe.

+**Sand-hill crane.** The brown crane (*Grus canadensis tabida*); also, the little brown crane (*Grus canadensis*).

1805 CLARK in *Lewis & C. Exped.* III. (1905) 176 Jo [Fields] killed a Sand hill Crane. **1839** TOWNSEND *Narrative* 125 We observed great numbers of the brown, or sandhill cranes, . . . flying over us. **1857** *Rep. Comm. Patents 1856: Agric.* 87 A domesticated brown sand-hill crane . . . spent much time in hunting about the fields for the nests of meadow-mice. **1877** HODGE *Arizona* 223 [Among] the most common of the birds of Arizona are . . . pelicans, herons, [and] sand-hill cranes. **1891** *Cent.* 5330/3 *Grus canadensis* . . . properly applies only to the northern brown or sand-hill crane, somewhat smaller . . . [than] the southern brown or sand-hill crane, *Grus mexicanus* or *G. pratensis*. **1907** LILLIBRIDGE *Trail* 115 He can . . . stalk a sandhill crane where there isn't cover to hide your hat. **1917** *Birds of Amer.* I. 200/2 When the Sandhill Crane is crippled by a broken wing or otherwise, he may become an exceedingly ugly antagonist.

transf. **1872** EGGLESTON *End of World* 200 Jonas had been all his life, as he expressed it in his mixed rhetoric, 'a wanderin' sand-hill crane.'

+**Sand-hiller.** *S.* A poor white or cracker inhabiting a sand-hill region, particularly in South Carolina and Georgia. — **1856** OLMSTED *Slave States* 506 The sand-hillers . . . are small, gaunt, and cadaverous. **1865** CHESNUT *Diary from Dixie* 401 Why do they remain Sandhillers from generation to generation? **1881** DE FOREST *Bloody Chasm* 147 She has lived and slaved like a sand-hiller. **1886** *Amer. Philological Assoc.* XVII. 46 Common Southern expressions [include] . . . *sandhillers*, poor whites of sandy districts.

+**Sand-lapper.** An inhabitant of a sandy region: (see quot. 1903). *colloq.* — **1836** SIMMS *Mellichampe* viii, He is some miserable overseer—a sand-lapper from Goose Creek. **1841** — *Scout* xiv, He was a little, dried-up, withered atomy—a jaundiced 'sand-lapper,' or 'clay-

eater,' from the Wassamasaw country. *a*1846 [see COWCUMBER]. **1903** *Outlook* 7 Nov. 576 A South Carolinian mentioned that the people of his State were often nicknamed 'sandlappers.'

Sand launce. Any one of various small eellike marine fishes of *Ammodytes* or related genera. {1776-} — **1814** MITCHILL *Fishes N.Y.* 363 Sand launce, *Ammodytes tobianus*. **1842** *Nat. Hist. N.Y., Zoology* IV. 317 The American Sand-launce, *Ammodytes americanus*, . . . is not a rare species. **1897** *N.Y. Forest, Fish, & Game Comm. 2d Rep.* 235 [The] Sand Launce . . . appears in Gravesend Bay in July, but is more plentiful in winter.

+**Sand lot.** An unoccupied piece of sandy ground or vacant lot in or adjacent to a city, freq. serving as the scene of unorganized games and sports. Also attrib.

The term first came into use in San Francisco from the fact that the followers of Denis Kearney held meetings on a lot of this kind on the west side of the city. (Cf. KEARNEYISM, KEARNYITE.)

1885 *Mag. Amer. Hist.* Feb. 201/2 One Dennis Kearny . . . made his headquarters in what were known as the 'Sand Lots,' near San Francisco. **1893** *Congress. Rec.* 13 Oct. 2495/2 The 'sand-lot orators,' the Dennis Kearney type, . . . ought to be in the house of correction now. **1898** ATHERTON *Californians* 37 She drew Helena into a sand lot opposite. **1902** *Advocate of Peace* Feb. 35 Race prejudice and jealousy, instigated by sand-lot demagogues, enlisted the more ignorant laboring men against the quiet and industrious Asiatics. **1913** LONDON *Valley of Moon* 78, I've known [about his bad thumb] since he first got it as a kid fightin' in the sandlot at Watts Tract.

+**Sand-lotter.** A member of a radical political element; orig., = KEARNYITE. — **1887** *Advance* 17 Feb. 107 [The California Chinese Mission] raised the last year in California $3,756, hoodlums, sandlotters and politicians to the contrary notwithstanding. **1894** *Nation* 12 July 20/2 The decent people . . . outnumber the Sand-lotters and other anarchists by five to one.

+**Sand myrtle.** A low evergreen shrub (*Leiophyllum buxifolium*) found along the Atlantic coast. — **1814** PURSH *Flora Amer.* I. 301 *Ammyrsine buxifolia*. . . . Being known by the name of Sand-myrtle among the inhabitants of New Jersey. **1860** CURTIS *Woody Plants N.C.* 100. **1861** WOOD *Botany* 492 *Leiophyllum*, Sand Myrtle. . . . Small, smooth shrubs, with erect branches. **1882** *Harper's Mag.* June 71 Of the smaller shrubs now in bloom we find the sand-myrtle, with its terminal umbellike clusters of small pinkish flowers.

Sandpaper. Strong, coarse paper rendered abrasive by having sharp sand firmly glued to one side. {1825-} — **1842** *Nat. Hist. N.Y., Geology* II. 179 [Potsdam sandstone furnishes] a sharp-gritted sand for sawing marble, and for sand paper. *a*1862 THOREAU *Cape Cod* 101 We found on the shore . . . Cockles, or Cuckoos (*Natica heros*), and their remarkable *nidus*, called 'sand-circle,' looking like . . . a flaring dickey made of sandpaper. **1897** *Outing* XXX. 197/1 Rubbing with sandpaper completes this part of the operation.

Sandpapering machine. A machine for sandpapering flat surfaces, buffing the soles of shoes, etc. {1885-} — **1869** *Boyd's Business Directory* 52 Sand Papering Machines. Potter & Co. . . . Williamsport, Pa. **1885** *Harper's Mag.* Jan. 286/1 1855.—Buffing or sand-papering machine.

+**Sandpeep.** Any one of various small sandpipers. (Cf. PEEP 1 a.) Also transf. — **1872** COUES *Key to Birds* 254 This species [the least sandpiper] and the last [the semipalmated sandpiper] are usually confounded under the common name of 'sandpeeps.' **1898** N. BROOKS *Boys of Fairport* 194 Charles Fitts shot ten sand-peeps and a teal-duck yesterday. **1905** LINCOLN *Partners* 198 It sounds foolish to think a bow-legged sandpeep with a sprained brain like Peleg's can know about the Lord Almighty's gales.

+**Sand pine.** **1.** A smooth-barked pine, *Pinus clausa*, found in sandy regions, esp. in Florida. **2.** (See quotation.) — **(1)** **1884** SARGENT *Rep. Forests* 199 *Pinus clausa*. . . . Sand Pine. Scrub Pine. Spruce Pine. **1901** MOHR *Plant Life Ala.* 131 The dead tops and branches of the sand pine (*Pinus clausa*) . . . increase the impression of aridity on these desolate shores. **(2)** **1897** SUDWORTH *Arborescent Flora* 23 *Pinus contorta*. Twisted Pine. . . . Sand Pine (Oreg.).

* Sandpiper. Any one of various small wading birds that frequent sandy or muddy shores and utter piping notes. {1674-}

1827 *Western Mo. Rev.* I. 324 These muddy bayous and stagnant waters are often so covered with these leaves that the sandpiper walks abroad on the surface of them, without dipping its feet in the water. **1849** AUDUBON *Western Jrnl.* 51 For six or eight miles we went merrily on, watching the little sand-pipers and turn-stones. **1882** GODFREY *Nantucket* 242 The harrier, . . . sandpiper, field plover, black duck are . . . present at the proper season. **1907** *St. Nicholas* Aug. 897/2 The sandpipers flitted back and forth on their thin little legs.

b. With specifying terms.

1813 WILSON *Ornithology* VII. 36 The Ash-colored Sandpiper . . . inhabits both Europe and America. **1828** BONAPARTE *Synopsis* 317 The Schinz's Sandpiper, *Tringa Schinzii*, . . . [is] found from beyond the Mississippi to the Atlantic shores. **1835** AUDUBON *Ornith. Biog.* III. 451 The Buff-Breasted Sandpiper . . . is often seen near Boston. **1874** COUES *Birds N.W.* 484 Baird's Sandpiper . . . is generally distributed over the Missouri region. **1911** E. H. FORBUSH *Game Birds* 283 The Red-backed Sandpiper . . . is found often in the interior of North America.

Sand plain. A plain the surface of which is composed of light sandy soil. {1903-} — **1817-8** EATON *Botany* (1822) 325 On the sand plains, at the foot of Pine-rock, in New-Haven, a [juniper] root . . . often sends off shoots. **1836** J. HALL *Statistics of West* 13 [The valley of the Mississippi] extends . . . to the great sand plains of the west. **1842** *Nat. Hist. N.Y., Geology* II. 378 The great sand-plain . . . lies between Leraysville and Wilna or Carthage. **1873** *Newton Kansan* 27 Feb. 2/2 Surrounding sand plains will not hinder it.

+**Sand plum. 1.** =BEACH PLUM. **2.** A western variety (*Prunus angustifolia watsonii*) of the chickasaw plum. — **(1) 1843** TORREY *Flora N.Y.* I. 194 Beach Plum. Sand Plum. Low, with straggling branches, seldom thorny. *c*1870 CHIPMAN *Notes on Bartlett* 379. **(2) 1909** *Cent.* 1022/3 *Sand-plum, Prunus Watsoni*, a shrub of sandy lands from Nebraska to Arkansas.

+**Sand prairie.** =SAND PLAIN. — **1834** *Visit to Texas* 115 [The town] is situated on a sand Prairie, where are hardly any signs of vegetation. **1846** SAGE *Scenes Rocky Mts.* xviii, There was not a drop of water to allay our thirst short of the river, fifteen miles distant,—over an open sand-prairie. **1857** WILLIS *Convalescent* 243 Our journey of the next day, over the sand-prairies to Siasconset . . . must be the theme of still another letter.

Sand pump. A heavy metal cylinder provided with a suitable valve used for removing wet sand, pulverized rock, etc., from a drilled well. {1902-} — **1865** *Atlantic Mo.* April 393/1 The earth is then removed from the inside of this pipe by means of a sand-pump. **1883** *Century Mag.* 329/1 A rude shed . . . shelters . . . the machinery for working the drill and sand-pump.

Sand rat. {1781} +A pocket gopher or pouched rat. Also transf. — **1846** in Emory *Military Reconn.* 388 Piles of loose earth, like small ant hills . . . are formed by the sand rats or gophers. **1867** *Amer. Naturalist* I. 394 Only one, the Red Sand-rat (*T. fulvus*) is at all common [in Ariz.]. **1917** J. A. Moss *Officers' Manual* 485 Sand-rat, an officer or soldier on duty in the rifle pit at target practice.

Sand reef. =SAND BAR. — **1883** 'MARK TWAIN' *Life on Miss.* xxiv, You can tell a sand-reef—that's all easy. **1920** LEWIS *Main Street* 6 She heard again the startled bells and thick puffing of high-stacked river steamers wrecked on sand-reefs sixty years ago.

Sandrock. a. =SANDSTONE. {1798} +A rock composed of sandstone. — **1804** LEWIS & CLARK *Exped.* VI. (1905) 159 [Specimen] found exuding from a Strata of sand rock on [one] of the Bluffs. **1838** COLTON *Ind. Delineated* 60 The silicious strata, or sand rocks, . . . are generally soft and crumbling. **1864** *Harper's Mag.* Dec. 55/2 The sand-rocks there are about 20 feet thick. **1885** *Century Mag.* Jan. 466/1 There are a number of theories concerning the formation of natural gas, and the deposit of the sand-rock in which it is obtained.

+**Sand-shoal duck.** =PIED DUCK. — **1813** WILSON *Ornithology* VIII. 91 [The pied duck] is called by some gunners the Sand Shoal Duck, from its habit of frequenting sand bars. **1844** *Nat. Hist. N.Y., Zoology* II. 326 This Duck, well known on this coast under the name of Skunk-head, and Sand-shoal Duck on the coast of New-Jersey, is not, however, very abundant.

Sand smelt. Any one of various small fishes of the family Atherinidae. {1836-} — **1855** BAIRD in *Smithsonian Rep. 1854* 338 The Silverside Sand-Smelt. *Atherinopsis notatus.* . . . It is found quite abundantly everywhere throughout Egg Harbor bay. **1884** [see GREEN SMELT 2]. **1911** *Rep. Fisheries 1908* 316/1.

Sand snipe. Any one of various sandpipers. {1848-} — **1806** LEWIS in *L. & Clark Exped.* IV. (1905) 135 The common snipe of the marshes and the smal sand snipe are the same of those common to the Atlantic Coast. **1840** *Knickerb.* XVI. 27 We were all despatched . . . on different errands; some to shoot sand-snipe, and others to collect driftwood for fuel. **1849** *Ib.* XXXIV. 554 [There are] all the varieties of long-billed birds, including ox-eyes and sand-snipe. **1917** *Birds of Amer.* I. 249.

Sand spit. A point of low sandy land that projects out into a body of water. — **1886** *Outing* April 59/2 [Alligators] can be seen lying motionless on the banks and sand spits, sunning themselves. **1886** *Ib.* Dec. 247/1 It is provoking to be . . . landed on a little sand-spit, backed by a marsh full of mosquitoes. **1914** STEELE *Storm* 80 To the left I made out the low, gray line of a sand-spit.

Sand spurry. Any one of various plants of the genus *Spergularia*. {1866 (*Treas. Bot.* s.v. *Spurry*)} — **1868** GRAY *Field Botany* 68 *Spergularia*, Sand Spurry. . . . A sort of Sandworts with scaly-membranaceous stipules, and reddish flowers. **1891** COULTER *Bot. W. Texas* I. 30. **1901** MOHR *Plant Life Ala.* 501 Sand Spurry. . . . Fruit purplish.

Sandstone.

1. Rock formed chiefly of consolidated siliceous sand. {1668-}

1799 *Amer. Acad. Mem.* II. II. 79 A pure *sand stone* as white as milk, [is] found in great abundance in a place between Poughkeepsie and New York. **1819** FLINT *Lett. from Amer.* 158 Western Pennsylvania possesses . . . limestone, sandstone, and salt springs. **1857** STACEY *Journal* 107 On top of a mesa, near camp, . . . we found most beautiful sandstone. **1916** [see LIMESTONE 1].

b. A sandstone or a piece of a sandstone rock used as a marker at a grave.

1846 *Knickerb.* XXVII. 55 They would put up a small red sand-stone scratched upon with the baby's name. **1870** NOWLAND *Indianapolis* 35 A rude 'sand-stone' marks the head.

2. Attrib. with *bluff, butte, cliff,* etc.

1823 JAMES *Exped.* I. 33 Between them are some low sandstone hills. **1846** W. G. STEWART *Altowan* I. 114 On its right bank runs a low range of sandstone bluffs cut down perpendicularly to the green sward. **1865** *Atlantic Mo.* May 565/2 The sandstone cliff, . . . in alternating horizontal shades of red, fronts the sea. **1872** BOURKE *Journal* Nov. 25 Passed between two sandstone buttes. **1873** COZZENS *Marvellous Country* 52 We visited some remarkable sandstone formations near by. **1882** MCCABE *New York* 460 The Metropolitan Museum of Art . . . is constructed of red brick with sandstone trimmings.

Sand storm. *W.* and *S.W.* A wind storm that bears along clouds of sand. {1774-} Also transf. — **1872** MCCLELLAN *Golden State* 308 Sandstorms interrupt the traveller and fill the air with clouds of impenetrable dust. **1885** *Wkly. New Mexican Rev.* 21 May 4/1 The mosquitos are too numerous and sand storms too frequent. **1899** A. THOMAS *Arizona* 103 'There's only one sandstorm ahead of you.' . . . 'What's that sir?' . . . 'Mrs. Canby.' **1913** J. B. ELLIS *Lahoma* 251 They haven't lived in the West, neighboring with real things like alkali plains and sand-storms.

Sand sucker. {1862-} +**1.** (See quotation.) +**2.** The California whiting, *Menticirrhus undulatus.* — **(1) 1881** INGERSOLL *Oyster-Industry* 247 *Sand-Sucker*, Holothurians, Nereids, and other soft animals buried in the low-tide sands, and showing tentacles. (Florida, Gulf coast.) **(2) 1896** JORDAN & EVERMANN *Check-List Fishes* 401 *Menticirrhus undulatus.* . . . California Whiting; Sand Sucker. Southern California, north to Santa Barbara. **1911** *Rep. Fisheries 1908* 318/2.

+**Sand violet.** Any one of various violets that grow in sandy soil, esp. the bird's-foot violet. — **1880** COOKE in *Harper's Mag.* Dec. 87/1 When I was married to Ethan, . . . if he didn't fetch me a big bunch of sand-violets . . . for to match my eyes and my skirt. **1889** COOKE *Steadfast* 313 The crowds of mild blue sand-violets with golden eyes smiling upward to the kindred blue of the June heaven. **1893** *Amer. Folk-Lore* VI. 138 *Viola pedata*, sand violet. Conn.

Sand wasp. Any one of various solitary wasps that burrow in the sand. {1802-} — **1869** *Rep. Comm. Agric. 1868* 310 The several families of sand-wasps, mud-daubers, &c., build their nests in the earth. **1871** [see DAUBER]. **1907** *St. Nicholas* June 748 [Illustration reading:] The sand wasp using a rock. Pounding down the earth with a small pebble.

Sandwich tern. {1785-} +Cabot's tern (*Thalasseus sandvicensis acuflavidus*), found during the breeding season along the coast from North Carolina to Texas. — **1835** AUDUBON *Ornith. Biog.* III. 531, I never saw the Sandwich Tern on any other portion of our coasts than between the Florida Keys and Charleston. **1844** *Nat. Hist. N.Y., Zoology* II. 303 The Sandwich Tern has been little noticed on our coast. **1874** COUES *Birds N.W.* 673 *Sterna (Thalasseus) Cantiaca.* Sandwich Tern. . . . Atlantic coast of North America to Southern New England. **1917** *Birds of Amer.* I. 59.

*Sandwort. Any one of various plants of the genus *Arenaria* or *Moehringia*, found usually in dry, sandy soils. — **1784** *Amer. Acad. Mem.* I. 446 *Arenaria.* . . . Sandwort. Blossoms redish white. **1814** BIGELOW *Florula Bostoniensis* 108 *Arenaria rubra.* Common sandwort. . . . A spreading plant, with small, delicate, red flowers. **1892** TORREY *Foot-Path Way* 104 The splendid black-and-yellow butterfly . . . did not disdain to sip also from the sandwort's cup.

Sandy, a. +In special applications.
Sandy barrens, s. bottom land, a barren or piece of bottom land the soil of which is sandy; *s. mocking bird, s. toad*, (see quotations).

1849 CHAMBERLAIN *Ind. Gazetteer* 278 Intermixed with them [*sc.* the timbered lands] are sandy barrens, and swamps. **1845** *Cultivator* ns. II. 253 Upon some of the Wabash sandy bottom lands, the corn is fine. **1891** *Cent.* 5333/2 *Sandy mocking-bird*, the brown thrush, or thrasher. **1870** BEADLE *Utah* 471 The 'horned toad' or 'sandy toad,' scientifically ranked *Phrynosoma*, is found on all the high, dry plains . . . [and] is calloused on the belly like an alligator.

‖**Sandy-hill crane.** =SAND-HILL CRANE. — **1825** W. BIGGS *Narr. Captivity* 21, I had . . . sandy-hill cranes, boiled in leyed corn, which made a very good soup.

+**San Franciscan, n.** A resident or native of San Francisco, California. — **1875** *Scribner's Mo.* July 277/2 San Franciscans are remorseless critics. **1878** J. S. HITTELL *Hist. San Francisco* 448 Home is less and the street more for the San Franciscans than for the citizens of New York. **1903** C. KEELER *San Francisco* 24 The most spectacular of the fortunes . . . were amassed by two San Franciscans, J. C. Flood and W. S. O'Brien.

+**San Franciscan, a.** Of or pertaining to San Francisco, California. — **1885** BAYLOR *On Both Sides* 227 The glasses rattled as if in a San Franciscan earthquake.

+**Sang, n.** Short for GINSENG.

1843 'CARLTON' *New Purchase* I. 256 The storekeeper was obliged to book the nine and a quarter cents, to be paid in 'sang.' **1886** *Harper's Mag.* June 58/2 Formerly, digging 'sang,' as they call ginseng, was a general occupation. **1897** W. E. BARTON *Sim Galloway's D.* 20 The sang was short this year.

b. Attrib. with *hoe, run.* (See also SANG-DIGGER.)

1859 BARTLETT 379 In Alleghany Co., Maryland, is Sang Run near which is a well-known 'sanging ground.' *Ib.*, Sang-Hoe, the implement used in gathering ginseng.

+**Sang, v. intr.** To gather ginseng. Also *vbl. n.* — **1848** BARTLETT 282 *Sang* . . . is or was also used in Virginia as a verb; *to go a sanging*, is to be engaged in gathering ginseng. **1877** *Field & Forest* III. 40 Why, I have sanged all over [the mountain]. **1892** ALLEN *Blue-Grass Region* 249 In the wildest parts of the country . . . entire families may still be seen 'out sangin'.'

Sangaree, *n.* Wine diluted and spiced. {1736-} — **1744** *Mass. H. S. Coll.* 1 Ser. VII. 185 The Indians . . . were regaled with some bumbo and sangree. **1784** SMYTH *Tour* I. 42 [He] continues to drink toddy or sangaree, all the afternoon. **1833** COKE *Subaltern's Furlough* I. 27 He set about making a glass of port-wine sangaree. **1888** DELAND *J. Ward* 400, I'll have Betty bring you a sangaree. **1904** STUART *River's Children* 76 They sipped iced orange syrup or claret sangaree.

Sangaree, *v. tr.* To make into a sangaree. {1860} — **1835** INGRAHAM *South-West* I. 115 [Devotees of domino are] clustered around the tables, with a tonic, often renewed and properly sangareed, at their elbows.

+Sang-digger. One whose occupation is that of digging ginseng. — **1878** in Summers *Ann. S.W. Va.* 1567 These hill-sides are a godsend to 'sang-diggers.' **1885** M. THOMPSON *Byways & Bird Notes* 97 These ginseng-diggers—or 'sang-diggers,' as they are called—are queer folk.

*Sanglier. A wild hog. *Obs.* {-1725; *obs.*} — **1805** *Ann. 9th Congress* 2 Sess. 1104 There were innumerable quantities of . . . deer, foxes, sangliers, or wild hogs [etc.].

Sanguinaria. A genus of perennial herbs having only one species, the bloodroot (sense 1); a plant of this genus. {1875-} — **1839** BRYANT *Poetical Works* (1903) 185 The quick-footed wolf . . . crushed the flower Of sanguinaria, from whose brittle stem The red drops fell like blood. **1841** PARK *Pantology* 414 Lobelia . . . and sanguinaria, or blood root, have also emetic properties.

*Sanicle. 1. Any plant of the genus *Sanicula*. 2. (*Bastard*) *American sanicle, false sanicle,* (see quotations). — (1) **1778** CARVER *Travels* 516 Sanicle has a root which is thick towards the upper part. **1792** IMLAY *Western Territory* 207 Of herbs, &c. we have . . . burnet, nettle, sanicle. **1814** BIGELOW *Florula Bostoniensis* 67 *Sanicula Marilandica.* Sanicle. (2) **1731** MILLER *Gard. Dict., Mitella,* . . . Bastard American Sanicle. . . . American Mitella. **1840** DEWEY *Mass. Flowering Plants* 45 *M[itella] diphylla,* False Sanicle, . . . grows abundantly in moist woods, and blooms in June. **1889** *Cent.* 2818/2 *H[euchera] villosa* is sometimes called the *American Sanicle.*

Sanitarium.

1. A hospital or health establishment for the care of invalids, patients taking rest cures, etc. {1851-65}

The usual term in British use has been *sanatorium,* a word which has also been used, esp. in recent years, in America. See the quotation which follows:—**1901** *Chicago Tribune* 16 Feb., 'Sanatorium' is the proper title for an institution devoted to the curing of disease.

1877 PHELPS *Story of Avis* 426 They could return and start the sanitarium or the boarding-school. **1890** *Harper's Mag.* March 612/2 There were other members of the Sanitarium. **1898** *Kissimmee* (Fla.) *Valley Gazette* 4 March 3/1 W. C. Parsons . . . is now with his wife at the St. Helena Sanitarium in California. **1913** LONDON *Valley of Moon* 513 There's some talk of a big sanitarium back in the hills.

+2. A region or place used, or suitable for use, as a health resort.

1880 *Harper's Mag.* Sept. 543/2 This whole [Blue Ridge] mountain region [will be] the great sanitarium for the older States. **1885** *Wkly. New Mexican Rev.* 4 June 1/6 The historical interest which ever attaches to the old City of Holy Faith [Santa Fe], seems to make it one of the most desirable sanitariums.

Sanitary, *a.*

+1. Tending to promote health.

'App. found only in U.S. writers' (*O.E.D.*).

1853 KANE *Grinnell Exped.* 298 All hands went out for a sanitary game of romps in the cold light. **1865** LOWELL in *N. Amer. Rev.* Oct. 606 Solitary communion with Nature does not seem to have been sanitary or sweetening in its influence on Thoreau's character. **1872** FISKE *Myths & Myth-Makers* 61 In Sweden sanitary amulets are made of mistletoe-twigs, . . . [as] a specific against epilepsy and an antidote for poisons.

2. Of or pertaining to cleanliness as practiced for the prevention of disease, or to agencies promoting this. {1842-}

1862 *Harper's Mag.* Aug. 313/2 Here . . . we have . . . one of the wharves sacred to the Municipal Sanitary office. **1872** BRACE *Dangerous Classes N.Y.* 61 The recent Sanitary Acts of New York attempt to hold in check the mode of building tenement-houses. **1883** *Rep. Indian Affairs* 2 By the adoption of good sanitary measures . . . the Indians were kept . . . remote from the agency, . . . until the pestilence subsided. **1890** *Stock Grower & Farmer* 18 Jan. 3/2 Governor Prince, at the request of the New Mexico Sanitary board, has issued a quarantine proclamation.

+3. *absol.* **a.** The United States Sanitary Commission. **b.** A Sanitary fair.

1865 *Atlantic Mo.* Feb. 233/2, [I shall attempt] to answer for others the very questions which my fortnight with the Sanitary has answered for me. **1866** 'F. KIRKLAND' *Bk. Anecdotes* 587/2 You can give it back to the Sanitary. **1867** *Atlantic Mo.* April 422/1 To this hour, therefore, the 'Sanitary' looms up in the eye of people at home.

4. Belonging to or provided by the U.S. Sanitary Commission.

The adj. here partakes of the nature of an absolute used attributively. **1865** *Atlantic Mo.* Feb. 242/1 Two to three Sanitary wagons, loaded with hospital stores of all sorts, . . . move with each army corps. **1866** MOORE

Women of War 359 A lady was on the Sanitary boat with comforts for the sick. **1867** *Atlantic Mo.* April 422/1 The connection which the people had with the army was in a very large walk of experience, carried on through 'Sanitary' agencies.

+Sanitary commission. One of various commissions, set up by different agencies, to look after the health and sanitary conditions of certain people, esp. of the armies during the Civil War.

1861 *Rep. Sanitary Comm.* 5 By direction of the Sanitary Commission, I respectfully submit the following report. **1865** RICHARDSON *Secret Service* 235, I went up the Tennessee River by a boat crowded with representatives—chiefly women—of the Sanitary Commissions of Cincinnati, St. Louis, and Chicago. **1866** MOORE *Women of War* 115 She went, . . . with several other ladies, and some gentlemen of the Christian and Sanitary Commissions, to labor on the hospital transports. **1898** *Kansas City Star* 19 Dec. 2/5 The sanitary commission's work can all be done by a state veterinarian. **1923** WYATT *Invis. Gods* 176 The president of the so-called 'Sanitary commission' . . . railroaded the infamous anti-civil-service act through the State legislature.

attrib. **1865** KELLOGG *Rebel Prisons* 327 Another supply of Sanitary Commission stores reached us while in this condition. **1866** LOWELL *Bigelow P.* 2 Ser. p. lxix, Being asked to write it out as an autograph for the Baltimore Sanitary Commission Fair, I added other verses.

+Sanitary fair. During the Civil War, one of various fairs conducted to raise funds for the work of the U.S. Sanitary Commission. — **1865** *Nation* I. 379 The editor exhibited . . . his business capacity and his knowledge of 'Young America' at the time of the Northwestern Sanitary Fair. **1866** MOORE *Women of War* 348 [A] great number of persons . . . saw Mrs. Hoge . . . and [her] most successful labors at the great Sanitary Fair of Chicago. **1866** 'F. KIRKLAND' *Bk. Anecdotes* 587/2 The Boston Sanitary Fair called forth some pleasing illustrations of the sunny side of human nature. **1876** [see FAIR *n.*[1] 3].

+San Jose scale. [From *San Jose,* Calif., where it was first introduced.] A scale insect (*Aspidiotus perniciosus*) very injurious to fruit trees. — **1887** *Calif. State Bd. Agric. Biennial Rep. 1885-1886* 12 Reports come in rapidly from various sections of the State of the appearance of the San José scale, even so far north as Geyserville, in Sonoma County. **1912** *Yrbk. Dept. Agric. 1911* 462 Several colonies of beetles were liberated in various parts of the United States where the San Jose-scale was abundant.

‖Sanko. (See quotation.) — **1856** *Porter's Spirit of Times* 18 Oct. 109/1, I can show the handsomest pair of matched family *puppies* that there is in this State [Mass.]—perfect little sankoes, seven weeks old.

+Sannup. Also **sanop, sanapp,** etc. [Algonquian.] An Indian brave who is married. Now hist.

1628 *Mass. H. S. Coll.* 3 Ser. VIII. 177 Sanops must speak to sanops, and sagamores to sagamores. *a*1649 WINTHROP *Hist.* I. 89 Three of his sanapps . . . brake into a neighbor's house. **1682** R. RAWLINSON *Narr. Captivity* 25 A Squaw . . . spoke to me to make a shirt for her Sannup. **1792** Belknap *Hist. New-Hampshire* III. 378 Our family [included] . . . my late mother's daughter, whom I therefore called my sister, her sanhop, and a pappoose. **1832** WILLIAMSON *Maine* I. 491 All conversation between one [an Indian wife] and an Englishman, in the presence of her 'sanup,' or husband, is quickly chided by him. **1855** *Knickerb.* XLV. 430 The good minister . . . beheld the 'senap' laid out, drunk as a piper, by the road-side.

Sanpan. {sampan, 1620-} +(See quotation.) — **1897** *Outing* July 362/2 [Put in Bay] has a boat whose style is peculiar to the place. It is called a 'sanpan,' and is an eight-foot punt, made of a few pine boards, which in light winds simply skims along the surface of the water.

+Santa Claus. Also †**Santaclaus, St. Claes, Santa Klaus.** [Du. *sinterklaas,* corruption of *Sant Nikolaas.*]

1. =ST. NICHOLAS 1.

1823 COOPER *Pioneers* iv, Remember there will be a visit from Santaclaus to-night. **1850** S. WARNER *Wide, Wide World* xxviii, I used to think that Santa Claus came down the chimney. **1871** DE VERE 94 The one Dutchman whom all American children hold dear . . . is Santa Klaus. **1881** *Ore. State Jrnl.* 1 Jan. 7/3 Santa Claus' Headquarters! Wm. Beck & Son. **1897** *McClure's Mag.* X. 192 Yes, Virginia, there is a Santa Claus. *attrib.* **1886** STAPLETON *Major's Christmas* 201 Papas and mammas . . . planned the Santa Claus performance which was to come when the inquisitive eyes were closed in slumber.

‖2. Christmas time.

1830 WATSON *Philadelphia* 242 The 'Belsh Nichel' and St. Nicholas . . . is the same also observed in New York under the Dutch name of St. Claes.

Santa Cruz. [Island in W. Indies.] +Attrib. with *punch, rum.* — **1855** Santa Cruz rum [see BITTERS 1]. **1869** 'MARK TWAIN' *Innocents* 149 The uneducated foreigner could not even furnish a Santa Cruz Punch.

Santa Fe. *attrib.*

+1. Designating persons connected with the Santa Fe expedition.

1841 *Picayune* 12 Aug. 2/3 It is probable that the troops consisting of the Santa Fé soldiers and volunteers, have . . . had a meeting with hostile Indians. *Ib.* 7 Sept. 2/2 The volunteers, who went out to co-operate with the Santa Fé pioneers, have returned. *Ib.* 25 Sept. 2/3 The body of white men is supposed to be the Santa Fé troops.

2. Designating various routes, equipment, etc., connected with the early trade with Santa Fe, New Mexico.

1841 *Picayune* 27 April 2/4 The Texans think they will be able to divert much of Santa Fé trade to the new Republic. **1843** N. BOONE *Journal* 207 Most of one day's march was on the Santa Fe trace. **1844** GREGG *Commerce of Prairies* I. 33 Besides the Santa Fe caravans, most of the Rocky Mountain traders . . . take this town [Independence, Mo.] in their route. *Ib.* 85, I do not believe there have been a dozen deaths upon the Santa Fé route. **1848** PARKMAN in *Knickerb.* XXXII. 95 Here we saw his large Santa Fe wagons standing together.

Santa Fean. +A resident or citizen of Santa Fe, New Mexico. — **1840** *Boston Transcript* 8 Feb. 2/1 This fair Santa Féan must be more bewitchingly beautiful than even the 'blushing beauties' of . . . the City of Brotherly Love. **1850** GARRARD *Wah-To-Yah* x. 140 Doniphan's regiment . . . [had] no force to support it, and its certain defeat would give the Santa Feeans additional courage. **1885** *Wkly. New Mexican Rev.* 1 Jan. 4/2 A lady well known and beloved by many Santa Feans, died suddenly of heart disease.

+**Santa Fe expedition.** A quasi-military and commercial expedition sent out by the Republic of Texas to lay claim to eastern New Mexico in 1841. — **1841** *Picayune* 9 Nov. 2/1 The Courier seems to doubt the accuracy of the information respecting the safe arrival of the Santa Fé Expedition, at its place of destination. **1842** *Ib.* 18 Jan. 2/3 The prisoners taken in the Santa Fé expedition had arrived at Mexico.

+**Santa Fe road.** =SANTA FE TRAIL. — **1844** GREGG *Commerce of Prairies* II. 63 Our courts of justice have since dealt with those who killed Chavez, in 1843, on the Santa Fé road. **1860** GREELEY *Overland Journey* 22 The great California trail, like the Santa Fé and all other primitive roads through this prairie country, keeps along the highest 'divides.' **1867** *Wkly. New Mexican* 4 May 1/3 General Hancock's Indian expedition . . . [was] bound for Fort Larned, on the Santa Fe road.

+**Santa Fe tea.** (See quotation.) — **1859** BARTLETT 379 *Santa Fé Tea,* an infusion of leaves of the *Alstonia theæformis,* used in New Mexico.

+**Santa Fe town.** Any town in New Mexico east of the Rio Grande, an area once designated by Texas as a county in Texas. *Obs.* — **1841** *Picayune* 3 Sept. 1/6 The principal part of both the population and trade connected with the Santa Fe towns are supposed to lie on the east side of the river, and within the Texan boundary.

+**Santa Fe trader.** One who transported goods, esp. over the Santa Fe Trail, for trade in Santa Fe, New Mexico. — **1843** *Niles' Nat. Reg.* LXV. 128/3 Santa Fe Traders. Intelligence brought by the last arrival from Santa Fe, places beyond doubt the safety of the party. **1847** PARKMAN in *Knickerb.* XXIX. 163 A multitude of shops had sprung up to furnish the emigrants and Santa Fé traders with necessaries for their journey. **1848** ROBINSON *Santa Fe Exped.* (1932) 7 We met more Santa Fé traders.

+**Santa Fe trail.** A road or trail over which trade was conducted from about 1822 to about 1880 between Independence, Missouri, and Santa Fe, New Mexico. — **1850** GARRARD *Wah-To-Yah* x. 125 [We] followed the Santa Fe Trail, which kept the river bank. **1881** CHASE *Editor's Run in N. Mex.* 205 The old Santa Fe trail . . . has not been used for three years. **1885** *Wkly. New Mexican Rev.* 22 Jan. 4/7 Since the supplanting of the Prairie schooner and Santa Fe trail with palace cars for cattle . . . upon a steel trail, the old city has been receiving many enterprising additions of modern types. **1925** *Kansas City Star* (Bell), Some Kansans seem to think they can't get to heaven except by the Santa Fe trail.

+**Santee.**[1] (See quotation.) — **1819** SCHOOLCRAFT *Mo. Lead Mines* 98 The *santee,* consisting of two stones, 3 feet long, and 3 feet 6 inches wide, . . . [which] reach from the bottom of the ash-pit, to a foot above the basin-stone, . . . keeps the lead, slag, &c. from running into the fire arch, and is an important part of the [ash] furnace.

+**Santee.**[2] [From name of Indian tribe or river in S. Car.] A kind of cotton. — **1820** *Western Carolinian* 25 July, *Cotton*—Sea-Island, 35 *a* 37½ cts. lb.—Santee, 30 *a* 32. **1824** *Catawba Journal* 7 Dec., Santees [have been sold] at 19 *a* 21.

+**Santo.** *S.W.* [Sp.] A small statue or image of a saint. — **1834** A. PIKE *Sketches* 146 The santos and other images had been brought from Mexico.

* **Sap.**

* **1.** The juice circulating in trees. +With specific reference to the sugar maple.

1787 CUTLER in *Life & Corr.* II. 398 The sap is extracted in the months of February and March. *c*1790 COXE *View U.S.* 77 The easy and profitable practice of making sugar from the sap or juice of the maple tree, had prevailed for many years in the northern and eastern states. **1850** [see BUSH *n.* 2]. **1880** *Vt. Agric. Rep.* VI. 112 Wooden troughs were used for catching and storing the sap. **1915** E. ATKINSON *Johnny Appleseed* 47 Sap was running, and squaws were boiling sugar in the maple groves.

+**2.** Attrib. and comb. with *boiling, bush, cider,* etc.

1842 *Amer. Pioneer* I. 346 'Sap porridge,' . . . when made of sweet corn meal, and the fresh sacarine juice of the maple, afforded both a nourishing and a savory dish. **1843** *Knickerb.* XXII. 161 One felled the proper trees, taking care to leave the sap-trees, the sugar-maple, untouched. **1845** COOPER *Chainbearer* xx, I don't think anything of bringing you . . . a little water, . . . nor should I had we any beer or sap-cider. **1852** *Knickerb.* XXXIX. 477 Somebody . . . has been describing 'The Pleasures of

Maple-Sugar-Making in the Country,' . . . [including] the sudden 'sap-freshet.' **1861** *Boston Herald* 12 April 2/6 Owners of sap orchards can afford to work day and night. **1875** BURROUGHS *Winter Sunshine* 119 A 'sap-run' seldom lasts more than two or three days. **1877** BARTLETT 793 *Sap-Boiling,* the boiling of sap from maple-trees, for the purpose of making sugar. *a*1882 WEED *Autobiog.* 12, I now look with great pleasure upon the days and nights passed in the sap-bush.

+**b.** Designating containers for sap, or apparatus used in the making of maple sugar and syrup.

See also SAP BUCKET, SAP TROUGH.

1849 *Knickerb.* XXXIII. 279 'The Sugar Bush' has vividly recalled to memory . . . the pale-blue smoke curling up from the 'sap-works.' **1872** *Vermont Bd. Agric. Rep.* I. 215 When I was a boy I purchased one hundred sap-tubs, and commenced sugaring on my own hook. **1874** *Ib.* II. 719 The 'sap-gatherer' or 'draw-tub,' as it is called, is a hogshead containing from one hundred to one hundred and fifty gallons. *Ib.* II. 729 Russia iron is the best material for home made sap pans as the nitre can be removed from it more easily. **1876** KNIGHT 2028/1 *Sap-boiler,* a furnace with pans for evaporating the sap of the maple. **1878** *Vermont Bd. Agric. Rep.* V. 105 The sap was lugged with sap yoke and pails on their shoulders. *Ib.,* We now have the Eureka sap spout, the tin bucket [etc.]. **1904** WALLER *Wood-Carver* 51, [I] drew trees and sheep and loggers' camps on the flat stones beneath the crotch set for the sap-kettles.

+**Sapa(e)n.** Variant of SUPAWN. — **1754** in Fries *Moravians in N.C.* II. 530 Now [we] must eat Sapan (Indian Corn Porridge) alone, it is well that we have cows, which affords a little milk to it. **1850** S. F. COOPER *Rural Hours* 387 We have *sapaen,* or hasty-pudding.

+**Sap beetle.** 'A beetle which feeds on sap; specifically, any beetle of the family Nitidulidæ' (*Cent.*).

+**Sap bucket.** A receptacle for maple sap. — **1845** JUDD *Margaret* I. 12 [Here were] frows, sap-buckets, a leach-tub. **1853** *Harper's Mag.* March 562/1 The 'sap-buckets' [are] taken from the garret and got ready for the delicious juice of the sweet sugar-maple. **1902** HULBERT *Forest Neighbors* 154 He invaded the sugar-bush by night, gnawing deep notches in the edges of the sap buckets and barrels.

Saphead. A stupid or foolish person. {1828} — **1798** FESSENDEN *Orig. Poems* (1806) 44 The poet . . . squibs each jacobinick saphead. **1843** STEPHENS *High Life N.Y.* I. 51 A feller must be a sap-head if he can't . . . give a gal the mitten when he thinks she desarves it. **1884** 'MARK TWAIN' *H. Finn* iii, You don't seem to know anything somehow—perfect saphead. **1901** *Munsey's Mag.* Aug. 746/1 'That pitiful fool, that sap head!' he thought.

* **Sapling.**

* **1.** A young tree of slight diameter. Also attrib.

1622 'MOURT' *Relation* 35 The houses were made with long yong Sapling trees. **1663** *Plymouth Rec.* I. 69 Lott . . . extends north 14 degrees east to a younge Rid oak sapline. **1791** [see NOTCH *v.* 2 (second quot.)]. **1847** ROBB *Squatter Life* 74 You'll cum to the 'saplin acre.' *a*1918 G. STUART *On Frontier* I. 26 These slab seats . . . had slanting holes bored in them . . . into which short pieces of saplings were inserted for legs.

+**2.** =SAPLING PINE.

1809 KENDALL *Travels* III. 53 The yellow or red pine, (*pinus pinea,*) [is] called by the French colonists *sapin,* and by the English corruptly sapling. **1851** SPRINGER *Forest Life* 41 This difference is accounted for by the rapidity with which the sapling grows.

+**Sapling pine.** The apple pine or white pine, *Pinus strobus.* (Cf. PUMPKIN PINE.) — **1810** MICHAUX *Arbres* I. 17 Pinus strobus, *White pine.* . . . *Pumkin pine* . . . , *Sapling pine* . . . ; dénominations secondaire dans les Etats de Vermont, New-Hampshire et le District de Maine. **1832** BROWNE *Sylva* 242 The secondary denominations of Pumpkin Pine, Apple Pine and Sapling Pine . . . are derived from certain accidental peculiarities. **1851** SPRINGER *Forest Life* 41 That variety called sapling Pine, bull sapling, &c., usually grows on high, hard-wood land.

+**Sapo.** [Sp.] =SARPO. — **1891** *Cent.* 5339/1 *Sapo,* . . . the toad-fish, *Batrachus tau.* **1896** JORDAN & EVERMANN *Check-List Fishes* 466 *Porichthys notatus.* . . . Cabezon; Sapo. Pacific Coast from Puget Sound to Panama.

Sapodilla. A large tropical American tree, *Sapota achras* {1697-}; the fruit of this tree. {1750-} — **1751** WASHINGTON *Diaries* I. 24 After Dinner . . . there was Granadella, the Sappadilla [etc.]. **1866** W. REID *After the War* 182 Limes, and sapadillos, and 'sour sops,' were the common fruits of the season. **1891** *Cent.* 5339/1 *Sapodilla,* a large tree, *Achras Sapota,* native in tropical America, cultivated there and in other tropical regions for its fruit, the sapodilla or sapodilla-plum.

+**Sap pine. a.** The pitch pine, *Pinus rigida.* **b.** The loblolly pine, *P. taeda.* — **1808** PIKE *Sources Miss.* II. App. 54 The whole of this course lays through ridges of pines or swamps of pinenet, sap pine, hemlock, &c. **1832** BROWNE *Sylva* 238 In swamps, . . . [the wood] is light, soft, and composed almost wholly of sap; it is then called Sap Pine. **1897** SUDWORTH *Arborescent Flora* 26 *Pinus tæda.* Loblolly Pine. . . . Sap Pine (Va., N.C.). *Ib.* 27 *Pinus rigida.* Pitch Pine. . . . Sap Pine (lit.).

+**Sapsago.** [Corruption of G. *schabzieger.*] (See quot. 1846.) — **1846** WORCESTER 630/2 *Sapsago,* . . . a kind of Swiss cheese, of a dark olive-green color. . . . *Farm. Ency.* **1877** BARTLETT 551.

+**Sap sour.** (See quotation.) — **1888** *Boston Jrnl.* 15 Sept. 2/4 A new disease . . . among the grape vines of the Santa Ana and San Gabriel valleys of California . . . is termed the sap-sour.

+**Sapsuck.** =next. — **1889** RILEY *Pipes o' Pan* 41 The catbird in the bottom, and the sap-suck on the snag.

+Sapsucker. Any one of several varieties of small woodpeckers, esp. those of the genus *Sphyrapicus*.

1805 *Lewis & Clark Exped.* VI. (1905) 187, [I saw] the small woodpecker or sapsucker as they are sometimes called. **1839** [see DOWNY WOODPECKER]. **1846** *30th Congress 1 Sess.* H. R. Ex. Doc. No. 41, 502 This morning I got a little sapsucker, 'sitta Carolina.' **1850** S. F. COOPER *Rural Hours* 301 The downy woodpecker, and the hairy woodpecker . . . are called sap-suckers by the country people. **1862** [see BARK-EATER]. **1880** *Cimarron News & Press* 23 Dec. 1/4 Of the several small species commonly called 'sap suckers,' a variety of the yellow-bellied is perhaps the most striking. **1906** *N.Y. Ev. Post* 10 Nov. Suppl. 1 The sapsucker in its tippling operations wastes quantities of sap. **1917** *Birds of Amer.* II. 152/1 The [red-breasted] Sapsucker sometimes arouses the wrath of the farmer.

transf. **1866** *Wkly. New Mexican* 29 Dec. 2/3 This style of argument is peculiar to the Gazette and the coterie of government 'sap suckers' who control its columns.

+Sap-sucking woodpecker. A sapsucker, esp. the yellow-bellied woodpecker, *Sphyrapicus varius*. (Cf. BARK-EATER.) — **1862** *Ill. Agric. Soc. Trans.* V. 732 The wounds made by the Sap-Sucking . . . Woodpecker are carried down to the wood. **1884** COUES *Key to Birds* (ed. 2) 485.

+Sap sugar. Maple sugar. — **1800** D'ERES *Memoirs* 63 The squaws in particular, would make me many and valuable [presents] . . . , consisting of sap-sugar. *a*1871 in De Vere 418 The boys enlivened by . . . whiskey sweetened with sap-sugar, and small beer. **1895** JEWETT *Nancy* 105 [She] handed us sap sugar on one of her best plates.

+Sap trough. A container for maple sap. {1840, Can.} — **1804** FESSENDEN *Orig. Poems* (1806) 41 Your love I well repaid By . . . a sap-trough neatly made. **1823** COOPER *Pioneers* xiv, I wanted him to . . . take the cow and the sap troughs. **1847** Howe *Hist. Coll. Ohio* 484 Sixteen of Williamson's men crossed, two at a time, over in a large sap-trough. **1897** ROBINSON *Uncle Lisha's Outing* 84, These 'ere boots . . . [are] stiffer'n sap troughs.

+Saque. Corruption of ACEQUIA. — **1847** J. T. HUGHES *Doniphan's Exped.* (1907) 91 A large saque interrupted our progress.

+Sarape. Also **zarape.** [Sp.] Variant of SERAPE. — **1834** A. PIKE *Sketches* 138 Everything is new, strange, and quaint; . . . the zarape or blanket of striped red and white. **1844** GREGG *Commerce of Prairies* I. 209 An additional value is set upon the fine *sarape* on account of its being a fashionable substitute for a cloak. **1852** *Knickerb.* XXXIX. 224 Throwing a *sarape* across the saddle, . . . I mounted a fine-limbed, powerful gray. **1893** *Harper's Mag.* Feb. 386/1 The monte table was only a sarapé spread on the arid yellow dust of the sand waste.

+Saratoga. [f. *Saratoga* Springs, N.Y.]

1. A fashionable type of summer resort.

[**1852** MITCHELL *Dream Life* 156 All the lax gaiety of Saratoga palls on the appetite.] **1856** F. DE W. WARD *Summer Vacation Abroad* 78 Bath [England] is well known as the Saratoga of the British realm. **1869** TOUSEY *Papers from over the Water* 187 Leamington is one of England's Saratogas. **1915** A. KILMER in *Leaves of My Life* 101 Buxton is an English Saratoga.

2. = SARATOGA TRUNK.

1874 B. F. TAYLOR *World on Wheels* 72 It is not a carpet-bag, nor a valise, nor a Saratoga, but a leather portmanteau. **1877** W. WRIGHT *Big Bonanza* 417 A lady . . . had a 'Saratoga' of the three-decker style at Carson City. **1882** BAILLIE-GROHMAN *Camps in Rockies* 187 The other two . . . got at the 'Saratogas' containing our spare clothes. **1897** GUNTER *Don Balasco* xi, [A dandy's] three trunks . . . [gave] the captain of the *Flying Fish* more disgust than all the Saratogas of the ladies.

3. Attrib. with *bandbox, basket, corn cake, wave.*

1877 W. WRIGHT *Big Bonanza* 417 Monk . . . hates the sight of one of those ponderous specimens of architecture in the trunk-line known as the 'Saratoga bandbox.' **1884** RITTENHOUSE *Maud* 276 Then we bought five bolts of satin ribbon for the 'Saratoga baskets.' **1884** NYE *Baled Hay* 223 A raven-black Saratoga wave, hanging on the back of a chair, has been known to turn white in a single night. **1889** *Hood's Cook Book* 2 For Saratoga corn-cake the white kind [of corn meal is used].

+Saratoga chip. A very thin potato chip. — **1880** ROE *Army Lett.* 262 The Saratoga chips were delicate and crisp and looked nice. **1887** *Nation* 6 Oct. 278/3 (title), Saratoga Chips and Carlsbad Wafers. **1903** BURNHAM *Jewel* 207 In the midst of the discussion of lamb chops and Saratoga chips, . . . in walked Dr. Ballard.

+Saratoga potato. =prec. — **1880** 'MARK TWAIN' *Tramp Abroad* 574, I have made out a little bill of fare: . . . Porter-house steak. Saratoga potatoes. **1890** McALLISTER *Society* 100, I had . . . Spanish mackerel, Saratoga potatoes, soft shell crabs [etc.].

+Saratoga trunk. A very large traveling trunk. — **1861** NEWELL *Orpheus C. Kerr* I. 280 [One woman brought] six Saratoga trunks full of moral reading for our troops. **1872** *Harper's Mag.* Dec. 20/2 Already Saratoga trunks are seen where but a dozen years since the bear and deer only were met. **1898** N. E. JONES *Squirrel Hunters of Ohio* 301 At the rear each coach was provided with a capacious boot for the accommodation of Saratoga trunks and U.S. mail-bags. **1904** *Springfield W. Repub.* 24 June 7 The convention hall is . . . big and chilling . . . [like] the inside of a titanic Saratoga trunk, with its swelling cover represented by the enormous roof arches.

+Saratoga water. Water from Saratoga Springs, New York. — **1833** in Mackenzie *Van Buren* 245 He could do the friendship I want as easily as rise and drink a glass of Saratoga water at the Springs. **1893** *Harper's*

Mag. Jan. 323/1 In front of me was the sign: 'Saratoga water. All you wish for five cents.'

* Sarcenet, Sarsenet.

* 1. A very fine soft silk fabric used esp. for linings; a kind or piece of this; a dress made of this cloth.

1733 *S.C. Gazette* 4 Aug., Just Imported, . . . white sarsnetts. **1775** in Singleton *Social N.Y.* 247 Henry Wilmot, in Hanover Square, sells . . . modes, sarsinets, peelong. **1810** *Columbian Centinel* 6 Jan. 4/4 R. W. Gerry [sells] . . . Sinchaws; India Sarsnets. **1842** KIRKLAND *Forest Life* I. 18 With a veil of green sarcenet closely drawn to save my precious eyes . . . , I commenced my journey. **1873** 'G. HAMILTON' *Twelve Miles* 113 Sarcenet and muslin and straw matting have their victories no less renowned than plush.

2. Attrib. with *bow, dress, lining*, etc.

1710 SEWALL *Diary* II. 285 [The pallbearers wore] White Sarsnet Scarvs and Gloves. **1802** BOWNE *Life* 136 Mrs. Derby has insisted on my wearing the sarsnet dress today. **1833** NEAL *Down-Easters* I. 34, I saw . . . the sarsnet-lining of her little straw-bonnet. **1883** *Harper's Mag.* Dec. 90/1 She in time even let them fix a pair of goodly sarsenet bows to each end of it.

Sarcophagus. {1601-} +(See quotation.) — **1871** DE VERE 538 *Sarcophagus* almost universally serves in America to designate the metallic burying-cases, which are largely used to transport bodies from distant places to their last home, and presents a striking instance of the preference given here to the high-sounding terms, however unmeaning and inappropriate they may be.

* Sardine, *n.*

* 1. a. Any of various small or young fishes resembling or related to the true sardine of Europe, +as the young herring and menhaden, or, in North Carolina, an anchovy, *Anchoviella epsetus*. Also attrib. +**b.** *pl.* These fish, as well as the European sardine, preserved as food, usually put up in cans. Also attrib.

1842 *Civilian & Galveston City Gazette* 1 Oct. 1/3 Fancy Groceries as preserves, Jellies, . . . Sardines. **1847** *Santa Fe Republican* 13 Nov. 2/4 Sardines, 350 boxes Sardines for sale low. **1865** BOUDRYE *Fifth N.Y. Cavalry* 262 The prisoners lie close-packed like sardines in a can. **1877** BARTLETT 551 *Sardines*, . . . menhaden prepared in resemblance to the sardines prepared in Europe. **1881** *Ore. State Jrnl.* 1 Jan. 2/2 Sardines—Qr. boxes, $1.75. **1884** *Nat. Museum Bul.* No. 27, 1064 Sardine cannery. . . . Miniature models of the cans, soldering implements, &c., are shown in position. Camden, Me. **1900** STOCKTON *Afield & Afloat* 263 Isn't that a box of sardines? **1911** *Rep. Fisheries 1908* 307/1 The silver anchovy (*Anchovia browni*) . . . is also known as 'sardine' and 'spearing.' *Ib.* 316/1 Different species [of silversides] are known as . . . 'merit-fish,' 'sardine,' 'California smelt' [etc.].

+**2.** *transf.* (See quotations.)

1856 Sacramento item (Th.), The many lads . . . seemed to think the actor very green; But who, I ask, is most of a sardine? **1861** *New Haven Palladium* 27 Dec. (Chipman), We 'Old Whales' or, as we [*sc.* sailors] are sometimes termed, 'Sardines,' are not supposed by some 'land-crabs' to have much of a taste for [roast fowl]. **1870** LUDLOW *Heart of Continent* 118 The name for a spindling little fellow, whom the plainsman does not wish to compliment, is 'You Sardine.'

║Sardine, *v. tr.* To pack closely. — **1896** *Advance* 24 Dec. 916/2 [We have room for] 200, yet there are 350 people outside . . . , and in some way we are going to sardine them in.

Sarge. Short for SERGEANT. *colloq.* — **1867** Goss *Soldier's Story* 98 You look hungry too, Sarg. *Ib.* 258 Sarge, the Colonel has got his mad up, and you'll be sent into the stockade.

Sargo. {1880} +(See quotations.) — **1884** GOODE, etc. *Fisheries* I. 400 'Sargo,' *Pristipoma Davidsoni*, is found from San Pedro southward to Cerros Island. **1896** JORDAN & EVERMANN *Check-List Fishes* 390 *Diplodus argenteus*. . . . Sargo. West Indies: Florida and the Bermudas. **1911** *Rep. Fisheries 1908* 310/2 Different species [of grunt] are known as . . . 'sailor's choice,' 'sargo,' 'pork-fish,' etc.

+Sarpo. [Var. of SAPO.] A species of toadfish, as *Opsanus pardus*. — **1879** *Nat. Museum Proc.* II. 336 These fish were called in Pensacola by the names 'Sea Robin' and 'Sarpo;' the latter being doubtless a corruption of the Spanish 'Sapo,' meaning 'toad.' **1883** *Nat. Museum Bul.* No. 27, 433.

Sarracenia. [f. D. *Sarrazin* of Quebec.] A genus of American bog herbs; a pitcher plant. — **1786** ABERCROMBIE *Gardener's Asst.* 66/1 *Sarracenia*, or side-saddle flower. Purple, Yellow. **1796** C. MARSHALL *Gardening* (1813) 370 Sarracena is a native of the bogs of North America. **1802** ELLICOTT *Journal* 287 Several species of that beautiful plant, the saracinia, are frequently met with in the margins of swamps. **1818** *Mass. H. S. Coll.* 2 Ser. VIII. 171 Among the plants in the neighbouring towns . . . [is] the purple sarracenia. **1855** [see BLUE FLAG 1].

* Sarsaparilla. (See also SASSAPARILLA, SAXAFARILLA.)

1. * a. Any of various species of *Smilax* of Central and South America. **b.** Any of various other plants resembling, or used as a substitute for, sarsaparilla, +esp. a species of *Aralia*. Freq. with qualifying adjectives. {1840-}

1637 MORTON *New Canaan* 66 There is abundance of Sassafras and Sarsaperilla. **1672** JOSSELYN *New Eng. Rarities* 59 We have in New-England two Plants, that go under the name of Sarsaparilia. **1737** BRICKELL *N. Carolina* 22 Sarsaparilla, White Hellebor, [and] several sorts of Thistles [grow here]. **1778** CARVER *Travels* 512 *Sarsaparilla.* The root of this plant . . . is the most estimable part of it. **1784** *Amer. Acad. Mem.* I. 432 *Aralia.* . . . Sarsaparilla. The roots . . . make an ingredient in diet drinks. **1814** BIGELOW *Florula Bostoniensis* 74 *Aralia nudicaulis.* Wild Sarsaparilla. . . . A well known aromatic plant. . . . Woods and thickets. **1836** EDWARD *Hist. Texas* 43 Let us look at some of the roots and plants below, such as . . . the sarsaparilla. **1847** DARLINGTON *Weeds & Plants* 156 *A. nudicaulis.* . . . Naked-stem Aralia. Sarsaparilla. False Sarsaparilla. **1869** CURTIS *Woody Plants N.C.* 116 Sarsaparilla. (*S[milax] glauca.*) . . . It is not the Sarsaparilla of the druggists, but is said to be often mixed with it. **1878** [see MAY APPLE 1].

*2. a. The dried root of these plants or a medicinal preparation made from them. **+b.** A beverage flavored with sarsaparilla.

*c***1618** *Mass. H. S. Coll.* 4 Ser. I. 246 He found . . . good store of sarsaparilla gathered. **1846** *Spirit of Times* 9 May 131/3 Sands's Sarsaparilla for the Removal and Permanent Cure of all Diseases, arising from an Impure State of the Blood. **1865** *Atlantic Mo.* Jan. 59/1, I have not heard his opinions concerning . . . sarsaparilla, or ginger-pop. **1890** *Boston Jrnl.* 9 May 2/2 Cases like yours may possibly be cured by the use of Hood's Sarsaparilla.

+3. Attrib. in sense 2 with *baron, bottle*, etc.

1840 *Picayune* 28 July 3/4 Sarsaparilla Syrup and Vegetable Universal Pills, to cleanse the blood from all impurities. **1844** 'UNCLE SAM' *Peculiarities* I. 43 On the outside . . . is printed the following thirsty announcement: . . . Congress Water, Sarsaparilla Soda, Ginger Champaign [etc.]. **1849** WILLIS *Rural Letters* 329 It may sound something like a 'sarsaparilla testimonial.' **1856** *Porter's Spirit of Times* 11 Oct. 90/3 The smallest boy brings out from part of his jacket a sarsaparilla bottle. **1902** LORIMER *Lett. Merchant* 244 Some men go through life on the Sarsaparilla Theory—that they've got to give a hundred doses of talk about themselves for every dollar which they take in. **1904** 'O. HENRY' *Cabbages & Kings* 4 She found . . . in the form of Frank Goodwin, . . . a rubber prince, a sarsaparilla, indigo, and mahogany baron.

*Sarsenet. (See SARCENET.)

Sash.[1]

1. A frame, usually of wood, in which glass is fitted, forming a window; the sliding frame of a sash window. {1681-}

1698 in Burr *Witchcraft Cases* (1914) 73 My Window was all broke with a violent shock of Stones and Brick-bats: . . . one huge one made its way through the great square or shash of a Casement. **1714** SEWALL *Diary* II. 424 Mr. Banister open'd his sashes, to whom the Govr. made a deep bow as he rode along. **1771** *Copley-Pelham Lett.* 130, I should like to Direct how to make the Sashes somthing different from what is usual with you. **1838** *U.S. Mag.* I. 351 [He] threw up the sash as if to inhale the cool night air. **1883** *Harper's Mag.* Aug. 464/1 He pushed up the sash [of the pantry window]. **1920** HOWELLS *Vacation of Kelwyns* 76 They dashed the sashes down as a torrent of rain beat against the glass.

+2. (See quotations.)

1838 *Civil Engineer* I. 148/1 [Potomac Aqueduct.] Wales, or stringers, twelve by six inches, to guide sheet piling, called in America the lower and upper *sash.* **1875** KNIGHT 950/1 *Gate-saw,* a mill-saw which is strained in a *gate* or *sash* to prevent *buckling.*

3. *attrib.* and *comb.* **a.** Designating various parts of, or things used in, sash windows.

1733 *S.C. Gazette* 183/1 Lately Imported, and to be Sold, . . . Sash Glass. **1746** *Harvard Rec.* II. 757 [They] are about to . . . make sash Lights, of Glass of 8 & 10 Inches. **1761** Sash-weight [see CART BOX]. **1769** in Sheldon *Hist. Deerfield, Mass.* I. 475 Spreading, turning & haking sash timber five weeks. **1777** *Essex Inst. Coll.* XLIX. 106 Sold by order of Capt. William Pickman, viz: . . . sash pulleys, shutter bolts [etc.]. **1790** *Penna. Packet,* 1 March 1/1 Will commence the Sale of a Large and General Assortment of . . . hand vizes, bell cranks, sash fastners [etc.]. **1897** F. C. MOORE *How to Build a Home* 60 The owner will furnish all locks, knobs, hinges, sash-lifts, and sash-fasteners.

b. With *factory, maker.*

1827 DRAKE & MANSFIELD *Cincinnati* 66 No returns have been received . . . [from] 1 Sash Maker. **1837** W. JENKINS *Ohio Gaz.* 126 There are . . . 2 steam engine shops, 1 iron foundry, 1 sash factory [etc.].

*Sash.[2] A scarf or band worn around the waist or over one shoulder. {1681-} — **1757** *Lett. to Washington* II. 36, I expect the Like number of Shoulder Knotts, Sashes, & Gorgetts. **1774** [see GORGET 2]. **1805** *Ann. 9th Congress* 2 Sess. 1083 The dress of the women is a long loose robe . . . tied round with a fancy sash, or girdle. **1866** LOCKE *Struggles Nasby* 314 He wuz dressed with a sash over his shoulder. **1913** LONDON *Valley of Moon* 104 [He] had a silk sash around his waist he'd learned to wear in California from the Spanish.

Sashararer. Corruption of *certiorari,* a writ issued by a superior court calling up the records of an inferior court on a particular case. *colloq.* Also attrib. — **1855** *Knickerb.* XLV. 186 The only remedy at law for the respondent was the *sasherara.* **1857** *Ib.* XLIX. 642 Let the suit be instituted; and if resisted, let it be carried on by a sasherarar. **1867** HAR-

RIS *Sut Lovingood* 33, [I] fell asleep a-think'n bout bein a rale sashararer lawyer, hoss, saddil bags, an' books.

+Sash(a)y, *v.* [Corruption of *chassé.*] *intr.* To glide or move *around;* to go about; to go. *colloq.* — **1860** HOLMES *E. Venner* vii, The Doctor looked as if he should like to rigadoon and sashy across as well as the young one he was talkin' about. **1865** 'MARK TWAIN' *Sketches* (1926) 159 For all they're so handy about keeping her sasshaying around from shanty to shanty . . . none of 'em's ever got a good word for her. **1890** FREDERIC *Lawton Girl* 97 M'rye she took Melissa's part, and so I kind o' sashayed out. **1910** McCUTCHEON *Rose in Ring* 263 Then he up and sashayed to New York. **1917** — *Green Fancy* 165 Been sashaying in society?

‖Sashrary, *v. tr.* To have the records of (a case) reviewed by a superior court by virtue of a writ of certiorari. *colloq.[2]* — **1840** KENNEDY *Quodlibet* 229 So what does he do but sashrary the case!

Sash saw. a. A small saw used in making sashes. {1812} **+b.** A thin saw operated in a frame. Also attrib. — **1794** [see COMPASS 2]. **1866** *Ore. State Jrnl.* 23 June 4/5 We have on hand a full set of Mill Irons for a sash saw mill. **1877** *Scribner's Mo.* XV. 151/2 The old 'sash-saw' was so thin that it had to be kept strained within a frame or 'sash,' to prevent its 'buckling' or bending when crowded into the cut.

Sash window. A window with sliding sashes. {1686-} — **1711** *Mass. H. S. Coll.* 6 Ser. V. 240 Its best you obserue the manner of the sash windows, how thay are balanced with weights. **1761** NILES *Indian Wars* II. 502 There were several handsome buildings in the fort, especially the governor's house,—three stories high, with sash-windows. **1789** WASHINGTON *Diaries* IV. 30 There is a . . . great similitude in their buildings— . . . two flush stories with a very good show of sash and glass windows. **1857** VAUX *Villas* 142 The large bay projection in the parlor is proposed to be constructed . . . with three sash-windows fitted into it.

Sass, *n.* Also *sas.* {*dial.* in 19th c.} [Var. of *sauce.*]

1. a. Garden vegetables. {1875, *dial.*} **+b.** Stewed fruit or preserves served at a meal as dessert. *colloq.*

See also APPLE-SASS, GARDEN SAUCE.

1775 *Essex Inst. Coll.* XLVIII. 43 Steven Barker come down and brought us som sas. **1836** *Crockett's Yaller Flower Almanac* 31 All the sass was touched. **1852** M. L. DUNCAN *America* 389 Variety and ingenuity in cake-making, and 'sass' as the Dutch call sweetmeats.

2. Impertinent talk. *colloq.* {sauce, 1835-}

In this sense, *sass* is the normal American pronunciation rather than *sauce,* which is seldom heard.

1853 G. C. HILL *Dovecote* 88, I've a precious good mind to duck you for your sass! **1876** 'MARK TWAIN' *Tom Sawyer* i. 23 If you give me much more of your sass I'll take and bounce a rock off'n your head. **1897** 'THANET' *Missionary Sheriff* 21, I shall take more advantage of it if you give me any sass.

Sass, *v.*

1. *tr.* To talk disrespectfully or impertinently to (a person). {sauce, 1864-}

1856 DERBY *Phoenixiana* 125 The squire he goes round a walkin And sasses all respectable persons With his talk of pills he's invented. **1867** 'MARK TWAIN' *Sketches* (1879) 96 You ought never to 'sass' old people—unless they 'sass' you first. **1881** COOKE *Somebody's Neighbors* 242 First she pestered me, 'n' then she sassed me. **1896** *N.Y. Dramatic News* 18 July 2/3 When he was requested to desist he 'sassed' the officer. **1920** LEWIS *Main Street* 118 There had to be one man in town independent enough to sass the banker!

2. *To sass back,* to reply impertinently.

1884 'MARK TWAIN' *H. Finn* xxvii. 237 The king sassed back, as much as was safe for him. **1891** HOLMES *Over Teacups* 154, I suppose Me-Number-Two will 'sass back.'

*Sassafras. Also †*saxafras, sassifax.*

*1. A North American aromatic tree (*Sassafras variifolium*) of the laurel family; a tree or the wood of this species.

See also CALIFORNIAN *a.* 2, quot. 1897. The genus *Sassafras* includes an obscure Chinese species as well as the American.

[**1577** FRAMPTON tr. Monardes *Joyfull Newes* II. 46 Of the Tree that is brought from the Florida, whiche is called Sassafras.] **1602** BRERETON *Virginia* 12 The finder of our Sassafras in these parts, was one Master Robert Meriton. **1634** in C. C. Hall *Narr. Early Md.* 45 We cannot sett downe a foot, but tread on Strawberries, . . . acchorns, walnutts, saxafras etc. **1682** ASH *Carolina* 6 The Sassafras is a Medicinal Tree. **1728** *Boston Rec.* 12 No Popler, . . . Sassifax, Black ash, Basswood, or Ceder Shall be Corded up. **1774** in Peyton *Adv. Grandfather* (1867) 127 The forest of Kentucky consists of . . . cedar, sassafras, wild cherry and many other descriptions peculiar to the country. **1797** HAWKINS *Letters* 108 The sassafras [is] begining to bloom. **1815** DRAKE *Cincinnati* 120 The sassafras is found even on the banks of lake Champlain. **1826** COOPER *Mohicans* ix, They brushed the sassafras, causing the faded leaves to rustle. **1876** HALE *P. Nolan's Friends* ix, Could she have passed that flaming sassafras without so much as noticing it? **1897** SUDWORTH *Arborescent Flora* 202 Saxifrax (Fla.). . . . Sassafrac (W.Va.). Sassafrac (Del.). **1907** *St. Nicholas* Oct. 1137/1 We all know the sassafras in bloom.

*2. a. A part of the sassafras tree, esp. the bark, used medicinally.

1613 PURCHAS *Pilgrimage* 632 Jamestown [furnishes] . . . many commodities, as Furres, Dies, Mineralls, Sassafrasse, Sturgeon. **1619** *Va.*

House of Burgesses 10 All Tobacco & Sassafras [shall] be brought by the planters to the Cape Merchant. **1724** [see INDIAN DOCTOR]. **1815** *Niles' Reg.* IX. 94/2 Oils, of mint, sassafras, worm and penyroyal and castor; . . . are to be found in our druggists' shops. **1843** TALBOT *Journals* 29 The following are external applications: sassafras, American elm. **1884** NYE *Baled Hay* 208 An excellent liniment for toothache or neuralgia, is made of sassafras, oil of or[i]ganum [etc.].

b. = SASSAFRAS TEA.

1863 *Rio Abajo Press* 14 April 2/3 Sassafras.—Those who use this drink will find [etc.]. **1871** EGGLESTON *Hoosier Schoolm.* 88 He drank his glass of water, having declined even her sassafras. **1912** NICHOLSON *Hoosier Chron.* 44 Sassafras in the spring, and a few doses of quinine in the fall, . . were all the medicine that any good Hoosier needed.

3. Attrib. with *clump, leaf, root,* etc.

1650 *Portsmouth Rec.* 378 James Sands . . . haue sould . . . fortie fower acres of land . . . [bounded] South west with a Sassafrax tree. **1672** JOSSELYN *New Eng. Rarities* 46 We made our Beer of Molosses, Water, Bran, chips of Sassafras Root, and a little Wormwood. **1699** *Derby Rec.* 207 The north corner is a stone and a saxafax stak. **1776** *N.J. Archives* 2 Ser. I. 191 Said swamp has in it a large quantity of beach, white oak, and sassafras timber. **1792** POPE *Tours S. & W.* 55 [They] rekindle more [fire] by the Friction of a round Sassafras Stick, in an Augur Hole bored into a Piece of dry Poplar. **1824** DODDRIDGE *Notes* 284 A large poultice of chewed sassafras leaves . . . is the dressing which the Indians usually apply to recent gun shot wounds. *c*1866 BAGBY *Old Va. Gentleman* 52 This black-legged little spectre . . . crashes through the sassafras clump.

+**Sassafras bush.** A low-growing sassafras. — **1854** *Spirit of Times* 4 Nov. 447/3 Presently we cum to a sasafrac bush. **1880** *Harper's Mag.* July 174/1 Sassafras bushes thrust up their crimson tops through the broken flooring. **1903** Fox *Little Shepherd* ii, He came upon a cow browsing on sassafras-bushes right in the path.

+**Sassafras laurel. 1.** = MOUNTAIN LAUREL 2. **2.** = SASSAFRAS 1. — (1) **1866** LINDLEY & MOORE *Treas. Botany* 821/2 O[reodaphne] *californica* is a common tree in the mountainous parts of California, where it goes by a variety of names, such as Mountain Laurel, Spice-bush, Balm of Heaven, Sassafras Laurel. (2) **1878** HOBLYN *Dict. Medicine* s.v., *S. officinale,* or Sassafras Laurel, grows in North America.

+**Sassafras soap.** Soap scented with sassafras. — **1860** HOLLAND *Miss Gilbert* 108 Arthur took his accustomed seat at the head of the table, with Leonora at his right hand, . . . [in an] atmosphere of sassafras-soap. **1863** TAYLOR *H. Thurston* 137, I never washed my face with sassafras soap. **1898** WESTCOTT *D. Harum* xii, He performed his ablutions (not with the sassafras soap).

Sassafras tea. A tea made from sassafras bark. (Cf. SASSAFRAS 2 b.) {1783} — **1802** C. PETTIGREW *Let. to E. P.* (Univ. N.C. MS.), I have always found Sassafras tea from the bark of the roots good in a Cold. **1841** *S. Lit. Messenger* VII. 219/2 The Weyanokes . . . celebrated . . . the medicine dance, with savage incantation . . . and drinking libations of sassafras-tea. **1897** W. E. BARTON *Sim Galloway's D.* 24 [She] hastened her preparation of a hoe-cake and a cup of sassafras tea. **1912** NICHOLSON *Hoosier Chron.* 44 Sassafras tea and a circus every spring; I always take both.

Sassaparilla. Also **sassyperiller,** etc. Variants of SARSAPARILLA. Now *colloq.*

1624 Smith *Gen. Hist. Va.* IV. 149 Medicinals and Perfumes, Sassaparilla, and many other physicall drugs . . . are the meanes whereby they raise [their wealth]. **1790** *Penna. Packet* 1 Jan. 4/2 Just Arrived by the Mary Ann, . . . Spanish sassaparilla. **1862** BROWNE *A. Ward: His Book* 124 Old man Townsin's Fort was to maik Sassyperiller. **1885** *Harper's Mag.* Aug. 398/1 Sassprilla's good for the blood this time er year. **1894** *Amer. Folk-Lore* VII. 89 *Aralia nudicaulis,* sassafariller, Banner Elk, N.C.

+**Sass tea.** = SASSAFRAS TEA. — **1847** ROBB *Squatter Life* 72 The matron of the house boiled him some hot 'sass-tea,' which, the old man said, relieved him mightily.

+**Sassy,** *a. colloq.* [Dialect var. of *saucy.* Cf. SASS *n.* 2]

1. Of persons or of their manners and speech, etc.: Impertinent; presumptuous; cheeky. {saucy, 1530-}

1831 S. SMITH *Life J. Downing* 128 If I should give out now . . . , them are sassy chaps in Portland would laugh at me. **1843** 'CARLTON' *New Purchase* II. 154, I'll cut out your sassy tung. **1867** *Atlantic Mo.* Jan. 106/1 It's enough to have a sassy hired man round. **1883** EGGLESTON *Hoosier School-Boy* 44 He's too sassy. **1918** LINCOLN *Shavings* 22 Why, you little sawed-off, dried-up, sassy son of a sea cook!

transf. **1917** COMSTOCK *Man* 12, I kept the sassy little hen.

2. Of an article of dress: Smart; cute; stylish.

1862 BROWNE *A Ward: His Book* 200 A hansum yung gal, with . . . a sassy little black hat tipt over her forrerd, sot in the seat with me. **1885** JEWETT *Marsh Island* 80 Ain't she got a sassy bow?

*** Satchel.** A small bag for use in traveling or for carrying books.

1809 IRVING *Knickerb.* v. iv, Two lean sided hungry pettifoggers [were] mounted on Narraganset pacers, with . . . green satchels under their arms. **1869** J. R. BROWNE *Adv. Apache Country* 184 She pulled [a book] out of a satchel belonging to one of the party. **1898** *McClure's Mag.* X. 285 She was . . . directing the neighbor to push the satchel far enough under the seat. **1902** 'O. HENRY' *Roads of Destiny* 46 There was two quarts of the finest old silk-velvet Bourbon in that satchel.

attrib. and *comb.* **1855** *Knickerb.* XLV. 14, I bore away a volume of Cowper's poems . . . in a satchel-bag. **1887** *Courier-Journal* 20 Feb. 5/4 (*headline*), Alleged Satchel-Snatcher.

Sateen. A glossy, satinlike cotton or woolen fabric. {1878-} — **1881** *Art Interchange* 27 Oct. 93/1 Sateen, velvet and serge are also used [for mantel scarves]. **1883** *Peterson's Ladies' Nat. Mag.* June 500/1 The jacket of the checked sateen has a waistcoat of the plain sateen. **1887** *Courier-Journal* 6 Feb. 1/5 Monday we will show 150 styles of our own importations of French Satines. **1925** *Sears, Roebuck & Co. Cat.* No. 160, 75/3 Coat . . . is lined throughout with the best grade of woven shadow stripe sateen.

*** Satin.**

***1.** A silk fabric of a glossy surface; a garment made of this material.

1725 SEWALL *Letter-Book* II. 188 Madame Usher's Chest [contained] . . . one full Suit of Striped Satin lined with Cloth-coloured Lutestring. **1787** TYLER *Contrast* I. i, She is to be married in a delicate white sattin. **1878** *Harper's Mag.* Jan. 277/2 The only stuffs to be had [in Monterey, in 1849] were Chinese satins and the harshest English merinoes. *a*1882 in McCabe *New York* 204 What would . . . Madame Blanche [be] without her silks or satins? **1907** *St. Nicholas* Aug. 895/2 [The dress] was funny and wide-skirted, of pink satin, with a tight pointed bodice trimmed with yellowed lace.

2. *attrib.* and *comb.* passing into *adj.* **a.** Designating things made of, or covered with, satin.

1705 *Boston News-Letter* 9 July 2/1 They found on Board a flowered sattin pair of Stays. **1760** ROWE *Letters* 362, 1 p[ai]r Black Sattin Shoes. **1761** *Essex Inst. Coll.* XLVIII. 95 [In] the Assortments are . . . Ladies satten hats. **1810** *Columbian Centinel* 3 Jan. 3/2 Stolen from the waggon . . . 2 do brown and green Satin Slips. **1840** *Niles' Nat. Reg.* 2 May 144/1 We examined yesterday a box of figured satin ribands. **1875** STOWE *We & Neighbors* 412 An engagement ring . . . lay snugly ensconced in its satin case. **1891** WILKINS *New Eng. Nun* 94 He wore a beautiful coat an' a satin vest.

b. In the specific names of plants, birds, fishes.

See also SATIN BELL.

1907 *St. Nicholas* Aug. 943 [Illustration reading:] The satin bower bird. **1882** LATHROP *Echo of Passion* iv, Marigolds and satin-flowers . . . were growing in the midst of rank weeds. **1884** Vasey *Agric. Grasses* 121 *Muhlenbergia glomerata* (Satin Grass). . . . Glenwood, Pope County, Minn. **1897** SUDWORTH *Arborescent Flora* 317 *Chrysophyllum monopyrenum.* . . . Satinleaf. **1814** MITCHILL *Fishes N.Y.* 456 Satin-striped Herring, *Clupea vittala,* . . . inhabits the salt water. **1897** SUDWORTH *Arborescent Flora* 205 *Liquidambar styraciflua.* Sweet Gum. . . . Satin Walnut.

+**Satin bell.** (See quotations.) — **1898** A. M. DAVIDSON *Calif. Plants* 123 Mariposas are . . . sometimes called globe tulips, . . . the satin-bell or fairy's lantern. **1915** ARMSTRONG & THORNBER *Western Wild Flowers* 58 Satin-bell. White Globe Tulip. *Calochortus albus.*

Satinet. Also **satinette.**

1. a. An imitation or thin satin, made of silk, or of cotton and silk. {1703-} +**b.** A fabric made of a cotton warp and woolen filling; a garment made of this.

(a) **1714** *Boston News-Letter* 22 Feb. 2 To be Sold by Publick Vendue or Outcry . . . Sundry European Goods, as Silks, Satinets. (b) **1787** *Md. Gazette* 1 June 3/3 Fustians; Jeans; Satinet. **1816** [see COATEE 1]. **1845** *Knickerb.* XXV. 91 We became a boy again in brown sattinets. **1866** *Maine Agric. Soc. Returns 1865* 26 Ornamental articles . . . have given place to home made clothes for men's and women's wear, such as . . . satinets. **1881** *Rep. Indian Affairs* 370.

2. Attrib. with *coat, company, factory, mill.*

1837 *Mass. Priv. & Sp. Statutes* VII. 729 Elisha Curtis, Walter H. Bowdoin [and others] . . . are hereby made a manufacturing corporation, by the name of 'The Springfield Satinet Company.' **1837** MARTINEAU *Society* II. 227 At Lowell, in Massachusetts, there was in 1818, a small satinet mill, employing about twenty hands. **1841** *Niles' Nat. Reg.* 9 Oct. 96/1 The large sattinet factory . . . was destroyed by fire. **1868** *Ore. State Jrnl.* 3 Oct. 3/1 [They will have] Satinet Coats, Beaver Coats, Overcoats.

Satinwood. The hard, light-colored wood of certain trees, as *Zanthoxylum flavum* of Florida and the West Indies; a tree productive of this kind of wood. {1823-} Also *attrib.* — **1792** IMLAY *Western Territory* 214 Satin-wood tree. Not classed. **1832** WILLIAMSON *Maine* I. 108 The other [maple] . . . is almost as handsome in cabinet work as satin wood. **1884** SARGENT *Rep. Forests* 31 *Xanthoxylum Caribæum.* . . . Satin Wood. Semitropical Florida. **1897** SUDWORTH *Arborescent Flora* 265 *Xanthoxylum cribrosum.* Satinwood.

*** Sauce.** Also **sarse, saase.** (See also SASS *n.*)

1. Chiefly *New Eng.* Vegetables, either cooked or uncooked. *Obsolescent.* {1629; dial. 1813-}

This sense is retained chiefly in the combination *garden sass,* or *garden sauce* (q.v.). See also LONG, ROUND, SHORT SAUCE.

[**1705** BEVERLEY *Virginia* IV. 56 Roots, Herbs, Vine-fruits, and Salate-Flowers . . . [the people of Virginia] dish up . . . , and find them very delicious Sauce to their Meats.] **1709** *Harvard Rec.* I. 388 The Steward Proposes to allow . . . an half penny towards Sawce. **1743** *N.H. Probate Rec.* III. 187, I Bequeath her also . . . two hundred Pounds of Beef with all Sauce accordingly whether Cabbage Potatoes or whatever she . . . Shall think necessary. **1771** *Boston Ev. Post* 29 July 3/2 [The] old Negro . . . [was] well known in this Town, for bringing Sauce to Market. **1825** NEAL *Bro. Jonathan* I. 72 Still to be met with, all over the 'Western Country,' . . . [are] sweet corn, pumpkin pies, and *sarse* (vegetables). **1837** *Jamestown* (N.Y.) *Jrnl.* 12 April 1/6 Though a garden affords neither bread nor meat, yet it yields such a rich variety of sauce as renders less of either necessary.

+2. Stewed or preserved fruit.

See also APPLE SAUCE, CRANBERRY SAUCE.

1845 KIRKLAND *Western Clearings* 24 Among custards, cakes, and 'saase' or preserves, of different kinds, figured great dishes of lettuce [etc.]. **1848** *R.I. Words* (Bartlett MS.), *Sweet Sauce*, another name for [preserves]. **1868** *Ill. Agric. Soc. Trans.* VII. 554 [Apples of a winter variety] make a fine fresh sauce late in the winter. **1869** BARNUM *Struggles* 248 Those who have heard John E. Owens in 'Solon Shingle,' are aware that preserved fruits are in New England called 'sauce,' by the vulgar pronounced 'sass.' **1884** F. E. OWENS *Cook Book* 322 Earthern milk crocks unglazed are best adapted for stewing berries or any sauce.

3. *attrib.* and *comb.* **a.** In the sense of a soft or liquid substance used with other food. **+b.** In senses 1 and 2.

1774 FITHIAN *Journal* I. 251 Mrs. Carter imports . . . a pair of fashionable Goblets; Pair of beautiful Sauce-Cups. **1816** PICKERING 169 Those farmers, who supply the markets with vegetables, are sometimes called by their brethren, *sauce-marketers.* **1851** CIST *Cincinnati* 260 Pickles, preserves, sauce makers. **1858** HOLMES *Autocrat* 357 You know those odious little 'saäs-plates' that figure so largely at boarding-houses. **1861** NORTON *Army Lett.* 12 [At the glass factory] a boy would . . . turn out a beautiful salt-cellar . . . , a sauce-dish, or whatever the mold happened to be. **1878** *Amer. Home Cook Book* 125 Equal quantities of medium-sized onions, cucumbers and sauce-apples.

Sauce boat. A small vessel from which soft or liquid sauce is poured over meat, puddings, etc. {1747-} — **1790** *Penna. Packet* 7 Dec. 3/3 Joseph Anthony, Junior, . . . Has Imported . . . Sauce boats and mustard tankards. **1807** IRVING etc. *Salmagundi* xvi. 419 A mighty sweet disposed old dowager . . . had a sauce-boat launched upon the capacious lap of a silver-sprigged muslin gown. **1865** A. D. WHITNEY *Gayworthys* 282 Cousin Wealthy brought in . . . a tiny, shallow, silver sauceboat, filled with yellow cream. **1878** *Amer. Home Cook Book* 74 Serve the broth in a sauce boat.

Saucepan.

1. A pan with a handle, used for boiling and stewing. {1686-}

1678 *New Castle Court Rec.* 361 4 Tin Saws Pans. **1702** *Essex Inst. Coll.* XLII. 161 Inventory of ship Providence Galley. . . . A fish Hook, a Copper Sauce panne [etc.]. **1766** [see COOLER 1]. **1867** EDWARDS *Shelby* 255 The bear roamed at will among the regiments, thrusting his ugly face into sauce-pans and stew-kettles. **1889** [see FARINA 3].

+2. (See quotation.)

1844 *Nat. Hist. N.Y., Zoology* VI. 57 [The king crab] is also called the *Sauce-pan,* in allusion to the shape of its shield, which is frequently used as a bale for boats.

✳ Saucer. A small shallow dish used: **a.** To hold food and other things. **b.** To place under a cup. {1753-}

1640 *Conn. Rec.* I. 448 An Inventory of the goods and Cattell of James Olmestead: . . . 1 frudishe, 2 little sasers. **1784** *Mass. Centinel* 10 July 3/3 This Day, Will be sold, by Publick Vendue, . . . 4 doz. Cups and Saucers. **1806** *Austin P.* I. (1904) 104 Articles Wanted from Orleans [include] . . . Cups, Saucers, Tureens, Tea Potts. **1850** [see CUP 1]. **1904** GLASGOW *Deliverance* 252 His trouble with Maria all came of his reproving him for drinking out of his saucer. **1907** *St. Nicholas* June 736/1 She bought a paint-box with two little saucers in it for 10 cents.

attrib. **1902** L. RICHARDS *Mrs. Tree* 86, I'll make you a saucer-pie next time I'm baking.

Sauerkraut. Fine-cut cabbage fermented in a brine of its own juice. {1633-} Also *attrib.* (Cf. SOURCROUT.) — *a***1813** WILSON *Foresters* 9 Torrents of Dutch from every quarter came, Pigs, calves, and *saur-craut* the important brine. **1863** P. S. DAVIS *Young Parson* 48 [You] eat the best of roast beef, while I have to put up with sauerkraut and spec. **1888** *Century Mag.* March 807/1 The representative Americans of the present day . . . [are] the Micks and the Pats, the Hanses and the Wilhelms, redolent still of the dudeen and the sauerkraut barrel. **1923** WATTS *L. Nichols* 20 Nothing was so profitable as getting up a reputation for a specialty, be it sauerkraut, [or] schnittlach.

+Sauger. [Probably Amer. Ind.] A pike perch (*Cynoperca,* syn. *Stizostedion, canadensis*) smaller than a wall-eyed pike. — **1882** *Nat. Museum Bul.* No. 16, 526 *Stizostedium canadense.* . . . Sauger; Sand-pike; Gray-pike; Horn-fish. **1893** *Outing* XXII. 88/1 She fished on, adding now a bass, then a pike or a sauger to her trophies. **1911** *Rep. Fisheries 1908* 311/1 The name [horsefish] is also applied to the sauger.

+Sauk. Variant of SAC. Also *attrib.* — **1806** PIKE *Sources Miss.* I. App. 20 The Sauks and Reynards are planting corn. **1835** HOFFMAN *Winter in West* I. 257 The old fellow . . . had been breathing revenge . . . against the Sauks and Foxes. **1836** J. HALL *Statistics of West* 53 On this prairie is a small village of the Sauk and Fox Indians. **1852** REYNOLDS *Hist. Illinois* 8 They claimed relationship with the Pottowatamies, and perhaps the Sauks and Foxes also.

Sault. [Fr.] A waterfall. — [**1600** Hakluyt *Voyages* III. 234 The Captaine prepared two boats to goe vp the great River to discouer the

passage of the three Saults or falles.] **1809** A. HENRY *Travels* 16 The Sault de Saint-Louis . . . is the highest of the *saults,* falls, or *leaps,* in this part of the Saint-Lawrence. **1817** S. BROWN *Western Gazetteer* 250 Ships of great burthen can approach to the sault or rapides. **1848** BARTLETT 408 The rapids of the St. Lawrence, and those connecting the Upper Lakes, retain the French name; as *Sault* St. Mary, etc. Pronounced *soo.*

Saury. A name given to various long fishes, as the big-eyed herring (*Elops saurus*) and the billfish (*Scombresox saurus*). {1771-} — **1842** *Nat. Hist. N.Y., Zoology* IV. 268 The Saury is a southern species. **1882** *Nat. Museum Bul.* No. 16, 374 *Scomberesox,* Lacépède. Sauries.

✳ Sausage.

✳1. Ground or minced meat, esp. pork, commonly enclosed in the intestine of an animal, tied off into short lengths or links. (Cf. BOLOGNA 1.)

1796 F. BAILY *Tour* 103 Their breakfasts [in Norfolk] consist of beef-steaks, sausages, stewed veal, fried ham, eggs. **1812** *Austin P.* I. (1904) 209 [We] made Coffee and fryd Sausages &c for Breakfast. **1853** BALDWIN *Flush Times Ala.* 37 He would make as many links of sausage as any hog that ever squealed. **1881** *Harper's Mag.* May 828/2 A hastily improvised sausage had been made by stuffing some of the finely chopped liver, heart, etc. into the larger intestines. **1910** TOMPKINS *Mothers & Fathers* 245 A gray-bearded man . . . [was] frying sausages.

2. *attrib.* and *comb.* **a.** Designating the forms in which sausage is made or served.

1791 FRENEAU *Poems* (1795) 421 Pig's head, or sausage link, or bullock's tongue. **1867** *Common Sense Cook Book* 10 [Recipe for] Sausage Fritters. **1891** WILKINS *New Eng. Nun* 164 Mis' Gill she sent us in two sausage-cakes. **1894** FORD *P. Stirling* 375 Three Newport swells . . . drank half-bean coffee and ate hot sausage rolls.

b. Designating machines that cut up sausage meat or make it into links.

1845 *Knickerb.* XXV. 406 It is ten to one that there lurks beneath it [the Yankee countenance] the knowledge of . . . some 'self-acting back-action saussage-stuffer.' **1848** D. P. THOMPSON *L. Amsden* 104 Jim Walker . . . was to our house . . . to borrow a sassage-filler for his wife. **1850** *New Eng. Farmer* II. 379 Sausage or Mincing Machine. This is a small, compact machine, remarkably strong and durable. **1854** *Penna. Agric. Rep.* 127 A model of a Sausage cutter was exhibited. **1869** *Overland Mo.* III. 130 Swine's flesh, bread, sage, and other matters of nourishment and seasoning, chopped fine, . . . [are] squirted out into links from the end of a sausage-gun. **1876** KNIGHT 2031/2 *Sausage-grinder,* . . . a machine for mincing meat for sausages.

c. Designating persons who make or sell sausages.

1874 COLLINS *Kentucky* I. 145 He is the only one authorized to buy the hogs from Jefferson and Bullitt counties, except the small lots to sausage dealers. **1882** PECK *Sunshine* 56 May we never live to make a million dollars if it wasn't the red-faced sausage man.

✳ Savage, *n.* Also †salvage.

✳1. An uncivilized person; spec., the American Indian. Now hist. in spec. sense.

The Indians have been given many similar names: see ABORIGINES *n.,* BARBARIAN *n.,* HEATHEN, NATIVE 1, PAGAN, etc.

1605 ROSIER *True Relation* (1887) 109 The Salvages came first to us. **1677** *Plymouth Laws* 187 Captive salvages were taken . . . in our late warrs. **1709** LAWSON *Carolina* 223 The Indians . . . eat abundance of Broth, except the Savages whom we call the naked Indians, who never eat any Soupe. **1725** *New-Eng. Courant* 7 June 1/1 We have, through the favour of God, destroyed more of the Salvages. **1775** ADAIR *Indians* 382 The constancy of the savages in mortifying their bodies, to gain the divine favour, is astonishing. **1841** *Picayune* 11 Sept. 2/4 The savages, who, proverbially, never fight but at advantage, will not dare attack so formidable a party [as the Santa Fe expedition]. **1881** *Amer. Naturalist* XV. 26, I discovered a dozen naked savages. **1923** [see MOCCASIN 1].

+2. *S.W.* A wild Indian, as distinguished from a Pueblo. *Obs.*

1863 *Rio Abajo Press* 10 Feb. 3/1 Our population has suffered sufficient from the depredations of savages. **1871** *Republican Rev.* 22 April 2/1 A party of savages made an attack upon a ranch, within sight of Camp Crittenden. **1882** *Terr. Rep. N. Mex.* 92 A body of about forty savages had crossed the A. & P. R. R., east of Laguna.

✳ Savage, *a.*

✳1. Uncivilized; +belonging to the Indian race.

1630 *Plymouth Laws* 25 Authority [is given] to us . . . to take . . . all such persons . . . as shall attempt to inhabite or trade with the savage people. **1638** *Md. Council Proc.* I. 75 Situate among divers Salvage nations, the incursions . . . of the Salvages . . . may probably be feared. **1807** BARLOW *Columbiad* 240 Are these . . . the swords Thy hand unsheath'd and gave the savage hordes? **1843** TYLER in *Pres. Mess. & P.* IV. 271 A war of several years' continuance with the savage tribes of Florida still prevailed. **1870** KEIM *Sheridan's Troopers* 141 The extraordinary fertility, the abundance of timber and game, rendered the valley of the Washita an inviting spot for the savage warrior and his kindred.

+b. *S.W.* Belonging to a non-Pueblo Indian tribe. *Obs.*

1885 *Santa Fé Wkly. New Mexican* 24 Sept. 1/2 In November, 1849, New Mexico had 36,950 savage Indians, divided into ten tribes of 4,750 lodges.

+2. *Savage as a meat ax,* (see MEAT AX).

+Savagerous, a. [Coined from *savage* and *dangerous.*] Fierce; savage. Cf. SEVAGAROUS a., SERVIGROUS a. *slang. Obs.* — **1843** *Spirit of Times* (Phila.) 25 Aug. (Th.), The Editor calls his savagerous enemy a remarkably pious and moral young man. **1850** *Wilmington* (N.C.) *Commercial* 7 March 1/6 (Th. S.), Of all the untiring, unaccountable, and unspeakable 'Savagerous' rumpuses ever kicked up Cape Horn takes the banner. **1866** C. H. SMITH *Bill Arp* 54 It is, perhaps, . . . the most savagerous beast that ever got after tories and traitors.

+Savagerous, *adv.* Savagely. *slang. Obs.* — **1848** BURTON *Waggeries* 16 Lookin' at the strannger darned savagerous, says he, 'Who the hell are *you?*'

+Savanilla. The tarpon, *Tarpon atlanticus.* — **1884** GOODE, etc. *Fisheries* I. 611 [The tarpon is] the 'Savanilla' of Texas. **1911** *Rep. Fisheries 1908* 317/2.

*Savanna. Also †savanoe, savannah.

*1. A treeless, grass-covered plain, esp. in the South; a lowland meadow.

1671 *S.C. Hist. Soc. Coll.* V. 333 You will finde . . . great Creeks, mar[s]hes, or Savanoes on the other side [of certain pine lands]. **1709** *N.C. Col. Rec.* I. 715 [Bath] will be the centre of trade, . . . surrounded with most pleasant savannas, very useful for stocks of cattle. **1741** *Ga. Hist. Soc. Coll.* II. 249 The savannahs, (so they call the low watery meadows, which are usually intermixed with pine lands). **1817** BRADBURY *Travels* 307 The whole of the Illinois and western territories . . . is an assemblage of woodland and prairie and savannas. **1837** WILLIAMS *Florida* 11 This part of the country is curiously diversified with savannas, lakes, ridges of hammock, and plains of pine barren. **1851** *Knickerb.* XXXVIII. 465 For fifteen years he has roamed the wild savannas of the Missouri territory. **1900** *Congress. Rec.* 1 Feb. 1412/1 Battalions have come trooping from the savannas, the plains, and the mountains of the South. **1905** *Forestry Bureau Bul.* No. 64, 7 Loblolly is the first pine to take possession of the savannas, or marshy prairies.

+b. Flat grassland covered with scattered trees. (See also PINE SAVANNA.)

1865 *Reader* 23 Sept. 236/3 The army has been moving through magnificent pine-woods—the savannahs of the South, as they are termed.

2. Attrib. with *ground, land, marsh, pineland.* {1697}

1709 LAWSON *Carolina* 45 We travell'd . . . over pleasant Savanna Ground. **1741** *Ga. Hist. Soc. Coll.* I. 159 Savannah Land . . . is extremely proper for husbandry. **1791** W. BARTRAM *Travels* 197 This range or chain of morasses . . . appeared to me to be fed or occasioned by the great wet bay-gale or savanna Pine lands. **1827** *Western Mo. Rev.* I. 317 It is a wide savanna marsh, . . . covered with high cane grass.

+Savanna bunting. = SAVANNA SPARROW. — **1844** *Nat. Hist. N.Y., Zoology* II. 161 The Savannah Bunting is quite common in this State. **1917** *Birds of Amer.* III. 25.

+Savanna crane. ?The whooping crane, *Grus americana.* — **1791** W. BARTRAM *Travels* 220 Amongst other game, they brought with them a savanna crane which they shot in the adjoining meadows.

+Savanna cricket. (See quotations.) — **1791** W. BARTRAM *Travels* 276 There is yet an extreme diminutive species of frogs, which inhabits the grassy verges of ponds in savannas: these are called savanna crickets. **1842** *Nat.Hist. N.Y., Zoology* III. 70 *Hylodes gryllus.* . . . At the South, it is called Savannah Cricket. **1853** *Harper's Mag.* Nov. 771/1 The chirp of the savanna-cricket . . . fell upon my ear.

+Savanna finch. = SAVANNA SPARROW. — **1811** WILSON *Ornithology* IV. 72 Savannah Finch . . . is probably the most timid of all our Sparrows. **1828** BONAPARTE *Synopsis* 109 The Savannah Finch . . . inhabits near the Atlantic coast from Savannah to New York. **1839** AUDUBON *Ornith. Biog.* V. 516 The Savannah Finch was found . . . on the Rocky Mountains and about the Columbia River.

+Savanna frog. = SAVANNA CRICKET. — **1827** WILLIAMS *W. Florida* 29 Except the little savanna-frog, these embrace all the species with which we are acquainted.

+Savanna grass. Conjugated paspalum, *Paspalum conjugatum.* — **1859** G. W. PERRY *Turpentine Farming* 9 The land needs no cultivation, but every kind of turf should be turned over, such as . . . wire grass, savanna grass and broom-sage grass.

+Savanna partridge. = CANADA GROUSE. — **1808** PIKE *Sources Miss.* 73 My Indians killed fifteen partridges, some nearly black, with a red mark over their eyes, called the Savanna partridge.

+Savanna sparrow. A small white and brown sparrow (*Passerculus sandwichensis savanna*) or a related variety. — **1811** WILSON *Ornithology* III. 55 The female of the Savannah sparrow is five inches and a half long. **1869** *Amer. Naturalist* III. 230 The Savannah Sparrow . . . is evidently a sea-sider. **1882** *Century Mag.* Jan. 361/2 New England [birds include]: . . . Savannah sparrow, chickadee. **1901** GRINNELL *Gold Hunting in Alaska* 15 Other familiar birds now rearing their broods here are the barn swallow, Savannah sparrow and tree sparrow. **1917** *Birds of Amer.* III. 25/2 The better known member of this family . . . is the Savannah Sparrow.

*Save, v.

1. *tr.* To take advantage of (something) while the opportunity is present.

1808 PIKE *Sources Miss.* 118 Embarked early, and wishing to save the fresh, I pushed hard all day.

+2. *W.* To secure by killing, to kill. *colloq.*

1833 J. HALL *Harper's Head* 38, I knew I had *saved* him [the buck]. **1849** KINGSLEY *Diary* 34 One of our sailors struck a porpess this morning but did not save him. **1853** 'P. PAXTON' *Yankee in Texas* 118 The gentleman need not have wasted so much breath in excusing himself for having *saved* a notorious rascal. **1877** CAMPION *On Frontier* 344 The boys [were] anxious to lose no chance of 'saving' an Indian.

+3. *To save the Union,* to preserve the United States under the Constitution as one nation.

1857 BENTON *Exam. Dred Scott Case* 123 The abrogation of the Missouri Compromise (which saved the Union). **1862** LINCOLN in Logan *Great Conspiracy* 433, I would save the Union. **1888** GRIGSBY *Smoked Yank* (1891) 31 The government was at that time trying to save the Union and slavery too. **1904** PAGE in *McClure's Mag.* March 551/2 Horace Greeley's old paper, the *New York Tribune,* has recently . . . felt compelled to declare that the War was primarily undertaken to save the Union and not to emancipate slaves.

Savey, Savvy, *n.* Knowledge; understanding. *colloq.²* {1785–, W. Indies or Sc.} Cf. SABE *n.* — **1870** HARTE *Poems* 54 Hed n't no savey— hed Briggs. **1883** DE VERE in *Encycl. Brit.* (ed. 9) *Amer. Suppl.* I. 197/2 *Savey* is the one *Spanish* word which is used all over the southern part of the Union. **1902** MACGOWAN *Last Word* 149 You've got no sort of *savey.* **1924** CUMMINS *Sky-High Corral* 36, I don't get the savvy of this.

Savey, Savez, *v.tr.* and *intr.* To know; to understand. {1785–, chiefly W. Indies} — **1850** [see FOFARRAW *n.* and *a.* 1]. **1897** LEWIS *Wolfville* 45 You've got to quit; savey? **1912** [see MUTTONHEAD]. **1925** SCARBOROUGH *Wind* 47 Oh, I savez.

*Savin, Savine.

1. +a. The red cedar, *Juniperus virginiana.* +b. The creeping juniper, *J. horizontalis.* c. Any of several other related or similar shrubs and trees.

a**1649** WINTHROP *Hist.* II. 62 Within 12 miles of the top was neither tree nor grass, but low savins. **1709** LAWSON *Carolina* 90 Savine . . . grows every where wild. **1774** FITHIAN *Journal* I. The Land . . . is covered for most of the way with Large Pines, & shrubbery Savins. **1787** CUTLER in *Life & Corr.* I. 201 Brought home the savin and bear's-foot. **1817–8** EATON *Botany* (1822) 324 *Juniperus sabina,* savin. . . . A low shrub. **1837** WILLIAMS *Florida* 76 Some of the burnt barrens will not produce even pine or scrub oaks, but are usually partially covered with clumps of savin. **1861** STOWE *Pearl Orr's Isl.* I. 8 Only savins and mullens . . . diversified the sandy wayside. **1884** SARGENT *Rep. Forests* 186 *Torreya taxifolia.* . . . Stinking Cedar. Savin. Western Florida. **1894** COULTER *Bot. W. Texas* III. 556 *J[uniperus] Virginiana.* (Red cedar or Savin.) . . . Throughout northern, central, and western Texas.

2. Attrib. with *bush, juniper, tree.*

1672 JOSSELYN *New Eng. Rarities* 3 In these Gullies grow Saven Bushes which being taken hold of are a good help to the climbing Discoverer. **1709** *Braintree Rec.* 73 The Selectmen of Braintree . . . layd out a Private Drift way . . . from the Savin Tree to a forked Stump upon the plaine. **1813** MUHLENBERG *Cat. Plants* 93 *Juniperus sabina,* Savin juniper.

Savings bank.

1. A banking institution for the deposit and accumulation of small savings, usually at interest. {1817–}

See also POSTAL SAVINGS BANK.

1818 *Holyoke Diaries* 168 My Father gone to meeting of Savings bank. **1837** HONE *Diary* I. 256 The savings-bank also sustained a most grievous run. **1851** ROSS *In New York* 42 The present number of *Banks* in the city, exclusive of 'Savings' Banks,' is 38. **1866** *Ore. State Jrnl.* 3 March 3/2 A savings bank for colored people . . . now has $30,000 of deposits. **1900** *Congress. Rec.* 21 Feb. 2015/1 The establishment of a system of savings banks in connection with the postal service would be of incalculable benefit to the wage-earners.

+2. A container in which coins may be saved, esp. one with a coin slot and openable only after the insertion of a certain number of coins.

1869 ALCOTT *Little Women* II. 12 [He brought] every kind of tinware, from a toy savings-bank . . . to a wonderful boiler. **1882** [see CLOTHES CLOSET]. **1922** *Sears, Roebuck & Co. Cat.* No. 144, 474/1 The Home Five Coin Savings Bank. . . . They register accurately.

3. Attrib. in sense 1 with *book, clause, insurance system.*

1880 *Harper's Mag.* Dec. 92 [She] utterly refused to give up her savings-bank book to the deacon. **1887** *Courier-Journal* 30 Jan. 5/1 Mr. Cobb . . . opposed the bill with the savings-bank clause left out. **1909** BRANDEIS in *Amer. Statistical Assoc.Publ.* IX. 414 The Massachusetts savings-bank insurance and pension system was first put into operation on June 18, 1908.

Savings institution. a. = SAVINGS BANK 1. {saving institution, 1830} b. (See quot. 1834.) — **1832** *Encycl. Amer.* XI. 216/2 *Savings Institutions,* or, as they are often called *Savings Banks,* are an institution of recent origin, but have already accomplished much good. **1834** in *Atlantic Mo.* XXVI. 483/1 *Savings Banks* here . . . pay no interest on deposits. Savings *Institutions* pay interest on deposit, varying from 2 to 5 per cent. **1845** in W. Lawrence *A. A. Lawrence* 200 My wish has been . . .

[to make] it the interest of the Savings Institution to sell their building to the Athenæum.

*Savoy. A variety of cabbage. In full *savoy cabbage*. Also attrib. — 1709 LAWSON *Carolina* 77 [We have] Coleworts plain and curl'd, Savoys. 1790 [see LOW DUTCH *a*.]. 1805 PARKINSON *Tour* 338 Cabbages are very much used; and the Savoy sorts grow very well. 1886 *N.Y. Agric. Exper. Station* (Geneva) *Rep.* 200 The smooth or less blistered sorts [are] known as *cabbages*, and the more blistered ones as *Savoys* or *Savoy cabbages*.

*Saw, *n.*

*1. A tooth-edged metal plate, band, or tube, used for cutting wood, bone, etc. Often with defining term.

See also BUCKSAW, CIRCULAR SAW, CROSSCUT SAW.

1634 WOOD *New Eng. Prospect* 52 [Each settler should bring] all manner of Augers, piercing-bits, Whip-saws, Two-handed saws, Froes. 1715 *N.H. Probate Rec.* I. 759, I give to my dear wife the use of my Saw at the lower mill on Dover side. 1845 FRÉMONT *Exped.* 247 The other party, to whom he had committed his wagons, and mill-irons, and saws, took a course further to the south. 1875 KNIGHT 734/2 Dovetail-saw.... There are several varieties. 1907 *St. Nicholas* Aug. 919/1 All the tools he used were a brace and bit for boring the holes, a saw, a hammer, and a try-square.

+2. A cotton-gin saw.

1835 INGRAHAM *South-West* II. 289 The teeth of the saws catch and carry through the lint from the seed. 1847 [see MOTE *n*.]. 1882 *Century Mag.* Jan. 477/2 The brush ... feeds the cotton to the saws. 1902 *Twelfth Census* IX. 338/2 A modern ginnery containing 4 gins of 70 saws each ... requires an 80-horsepower engine.

3. *attrib.* and *comb.* a. Designating various machines for setting saws.

1847 *Rep. Comm. Patents 1846* 49 A patent has also been granted ... for a saw-dressing machine. 1853 *Mich. Agric. Soc. Trans.* IV. 84 Improved saw-set for setting cross cut, mill and circular saws. 1859 *Rep. Comm. Patents 1858* I. 565 Improved Saw-Filing Machine. *Ib.* 565 Improved Saw Gummer. 1866 *Ill. Agric. Soc. Trans.* VI. 52 Improved Saw Upset: N. F. Stone & Co.

+b. *Lumbering.* Designating groups of persons who use saws in felling and trimming trees.

1902 WHITE *Blazed Trail* 9 The 'saw-gangs,' three in number, prepared to fell the first trees. 1905 *Forestry Bureau Bul.* No. 61, 29 Bank, ... the logs cut or skidded in one day above the required amount and held over by the saw crew or skidders.

c. In the names of worms and beetles.

1885 *Library Mag.* April 292/2 [The ivory-bill's] principal food is a large flat-headed timber-worm, known in the South as *borer* or *saw-worm*. 1895 *Dept. Agric. Yrbk. 1894* 287 The saw-toothed grain beetle ... is of common occurrence in granaries, in groceries, ... and in barns.

*Saw, *v.*

‖1. *intr.* To move. (Cf. CUT *v.* 3.)

1801 *Spirit Farmers' Mus.* 235 Now saw as fast as e'er you can do.

+2. *tr.* To dupe; to play a trick on (someone). *slang. Obs.*

1846 CORCORAN *Pickings* 80 [He spoke] in a tone that acknowledged he had been *sawed*. 1847 FIELD *Drama in Pokerville* 68 The manager was 'sawed.'

3. In phrases. a. *To saw wood* (or ‖*gourds*), +to pass the time sleeping, snoring, or doing nothing about a particular matter. Often in political context.

1870 LUDLOW *Heart of Continent* 91 In five minutes ... we were all 'sawing gourds' together in the land of Nod. 1894 *Congress. Rec.* 24 Jan. 1347/2 Is it possible that the framers of the bill hold a grudge against the voters who 'sawed wood' last November? 1908 'O. HENRY' *Options* 75 During all these wintry apostrophes, Barbara, cold at heart, sawed wood —the only appropriate thing she could think of to do.

b. *To saw the air* {1602–}, +in batting, to swing at and miss a pitched ball.

1880 *Chicago Inter-Ocean* 19 May 2/5 Shaffer sawed the air three times without hitting anything, and retired.

+Sawbelly. 1. The summer herring, *Pomolobus aestivalis*. 2. The branch herring, *Pomolobus pseudoharengus*. — (1) 1884 GOODE, etc. *Fisheries* I. 582 Around the Gulf of Maine this species is also known by the names 'Kyack' or 'Kyauk,' 'Saw-belly,' and 'Cat-thrasher.' (2) 1903 T. H. BEAN *Fishes N.Y.* 200 The branch herring, river herring or alewife ... [is] the sawbelly of Maine.

Sawbill. A bird with a serrated bill, esp. a merganser {1843–} or +a motmot. Also attrib.

1827 McKENNEY *Tour to Lakes* 249 The ducks we have seen are all, or nearly all, of one species. They are the saw-bill. 1840 *Knickerb.* XVI. 216 We frequently drove up the saw-bill and the duck and mallard from their hitherto undisturbed nooks in the stream. 1844 [see DUN DIVER *a*.] 1872 COUES *Key to Birds* 178 In the ... *Momotidæ* (motmots or sawbills), the middle and outer toes are perfectly coherent for a great distance. 1917 *Birds of Amer.* I. 111 Red-breasted Merganser. *Mergus serrator*.... [Also called] Saw-bill; Common Saw-bill. *Ib.* 112 Hooded Merganser. *Lophodytes cucullatus*.... [Also called] Saw-bill Diver.

Sawbill duck. A merganser. {1849} — 1839 *Knickerb.* XIII. 432 The sportsmen of our party here brought us the partridge, pigeon, and saw-bill duck. 1917 *Birds of Amer.* I. 112 Hooded Merganser. *Lophodytes cucullatus*.... [Also called] Little Saw-bill Duck.

+Saw brier. Any of several species of brier, such as the bull brier. — 1806 *Ann. 9th Congress* 2 Sess. 1142 The saw briar, single rose briar, and china root briar [grow near the Washita R.]. 1821 NUTTALL *Travels Arkansa* 180 This route was ... often entangled with brambles, and particularly with the tenacious 'saw-brier' (*Schrankia horridula*).

+Sawbuck. [Du. *zaagbok*.]

1. A sawhorse, esp. one with the legs projecting above the cross; any piece of furniture of similar construction. Also fig.

1862 *Rep. Comm. Patents 1861: Agric.* 141 The sheep is then laid upon his back in a kind of saw-buck. 1869 'MARK TWAIN' *Innocents* 58 The saddles ... consisted of a sort of saw-buck, with a small mattress on it. 1877 BURDETTE *Rise of Mustache* 308 You might as well tell a joke to a sawbuck as to his wife. 1878 B. F. TAYLOR *Between Gates* 237 [The horse] made a saw-buck of her legs. 1906 CHURCHILL *Coniston* 390 He was standing with his foot upon the sawbuck and the saw across his knee. 1920 LEWIS *Main Street* 83 In back yards their sawbucks stood in depressions scattered with ... flakes of sawdust.

b. A horse. *slang. Obs.*

1882 BAILLIE-GROHMAN *Camps in Rockies* 366 Dismounting from my tired 'sawbuck,' I proceeded to examine the arrangement.

2. A ten-dollar bill.

So named in allusion to the X shape of the sawyer's sawbuck.

1850 *Knickerb.* XXXVI. 297 Send me the two double 'saw-bucks.' 1857 *Quinland* II. 166, I know fifty fellows ... that for one end of a saw-buck a-piece, would be on hand with a whole company of voters at their heels. 1870 NOWLAND *Indianapolis* 315 In former years he was ever ready to ... risk what he called a 'sawbuck' (a ten dollar note), on his success.

3. Attrib. in sense 1 with *attachment, attitude, saddle*.

1855 M. THOMPSON *Doesticks* 322 Macduff ... stands over the conquered Macbeth in a grand saw-buck attitude. 1900 *Scribner's Mag.* Sept. 270/2, I never tired of seeing the two Indians throw the hitches by which they fastened tents, boxes, heads, or anything at all, to the saw-buck attachments on the pack-saddles. 1907 WHITE *Arizona Nights* 17 We skirmished around and found ... a sawbuck saddle with kyacks.

+Saw-cut (grub). See quotations. — 1859 *Harper's Mag.* July 164/2 Our disciple of nature ... hears the busy chirp of the 'saw-cut' under the bark. *Ib.* 165/1 The flies are carefully put away, another foot-link is attached to the line—the saw-cut grubs are substituted. Down glide the larvæ ... and in a few minutes up comes the fish.

*Sawdust.

*1. Small particles of wood made in the process of sawing.

1804 J. ROBERTS *Penna. Farmer* 18 Sawdust, tanners bark, and rotten leaves, are best for the compost dunghil. 1863 RANDALL *Pract. Shepherd* 170 The bottom of the pen should be kept clean with straw, saw-dust, or corn-cobs. 1907 ANDREWS *Recoll.* 129, I had sawdust put between the plaster and clapboards.

+2. *attrib.* Designating various things and persons connected with a circus.

1883 *Century Mag.* March 746/1, I was not flattered at being taken for a sawdust artist. 1884 RITTENHOUSE *Maud* 319, I felt like the queen of the saw-dust arena. 1887 CUSTER *Tenting on Plains* 380, I hardly knew whether I was myself or the venturesome young woman who spends her life in taking airy flights through the paper-covered circles in a saw-dust ring. 1895 *N.Y. Dramatic News* 5 Oct. 16/3 Eddie Arlington ... has left the ranks of the sawdust field and embarked in the paths of financial journalism.

‖Sawdust country. A section of the country after most of the timber has been cut up. Also attrib. (Cf. *Cut-over land* s.v. CUT-OVER *a*.) — 1894 *Home Missionary* Oct. 327 It might seem wise to let the little churches organized in this 'sawdust country' drop into oblivion. *Ib.* 328 These small, rural, sawdust-country churches are to our city churches what mountain rills are to rivers.

+Sawdust pudding. (See quotations.) — 1840 SPARKS ed. Franklin *Works* I. 85*n*., The guests ... were surprised to see nothing before them but two puddings made of coarse meal, commonly called *sawdust puddings*. 1844 'UNCLE SAM' *Peculiarities* I. 166 A sawdust pudding ... [is] a capital fritter, made of the scrapings produced when meat is so frozen as to be separated into pieces by a saw.

*Sawed, *a.*

*1. Of timber, or boards: Cut or made by sawing.

1732 *S.C. Gazette* 48/2 Any Person who wants the Frame of a House, or any other sawed Timber, or Boards for Exportation, may ... hear more particular from Mr. Robert Austin in Charlestown. 1831 PECK *Guide* 181 Hundreds of cabins are made without ... a single piece of sawed plank. 1894 *Harper's Mag.* Feb. 480/1 A new tariff bill ... adds a large number of articles to the free list, including ... salt, sawed lumber, agricultural implements, and many chemicals.

+2. a. Intoxicated. *slang. Obs.* b. Fooled. *Obs.*

See also SAW *v.* 2.

1833 A. GREENE *Life D. Duckworth* II. 176 He was seldom downright drunk; but was often ... most infernally sawed. 1847 FIELD *Drama in Pokerville* 199 The thoroughly 'sawed' victim made way for him as if he had been the cholera incarnate! *a*1856 in Hall *Coll. Words* (ed. 2) 461.

Sawed-off, *a.*

1. Shortened by having an end cut off by a saw. {1895}
1869 BRACE *New West* 93 A little house . . . built on the sawed-off stem of one tree, gives one a most impressive idea of their size. **1897** 'MARK TWAIN' *Following Equator* 378 It was a vulture standing on the sawed-off top of a tall and slender and branchless palm. **1912** RAINE *Brand Blotters* 80 The 'shotgun messenger' was indolently rolling a cigarette, his sawed-off gun between his knees.

+2. Short, under average height. Also absol.
1887 GEORGE *40 Yrs. on Rail* 22, I remember . . . the little sawed-off cars jolting along the uneven track. **1901** WHITE *Westerners* 220 Most marvellous was a clean-limbed, deep-chested, slender running horse, accompanied by a sawed-off English groom. **1902** LORIMER *Lett. Merchant* 160, I didn't understand football, but understood that little sawed-off.

+Sawed-off shotgun. A shotgun with its barrel cut off short. — **1898** *Scribner's Mag.* Jan. 86/2 There was another roar from the messenger's sawed-off shotgun. **1910** J. HART *Vigilante Girl* 137 Alden looked with interest at the 'sawed-off shotgun.' **1916** DU PUY *Uncle Sam* 11 Who is there around here who has a sawed-off shotgun?

***Sawer. 1.** =SAWYER 1. **+2.** =SAWYER 3. — **(1) 1630** *Mass. Bay Rec.* I. 74 Carpenters, joyners, brickelayers, sawers, and thatchers shall not take aboue 2s. aday. **1633** *Ib.* 109 Sawers, masons, clapboard-ryvers, brickelayers, . . . &c., shall not take aboue 2s. a day. **(2) 1833** *Niles' Reg.* XLIV. 394/1 We notice in the engineer's report the improvements making in the navigation of the Ohio and Mississippi rivers in removing snags, sawers, &c.

Saw-filer. 1. A machine for filing saws. **2.** A person whose business is to file saws. {1881} — **(1) 1859** *Rep. Comm. Patents 1858* I. 564 Improved Saw Filer. **(2) 1882** *Harper's Mag.* July 233/1 The workmen . . . hired a saw-filer in the neighborhood to ring the bell four times daily.

Sawfish. Any of several sharklike fishes of the genus *Pristis* having along each edge of the snout a row of strong toothlike structures. {1664-} Also attrib. — **1815-6** *Niles' Reg.* IX. Suppl. 190/1 Two Saw Fish were caught on Saturday and Monday last. **1843** MARRYAT *M. Violet* xliv, The saw fish is peculiar to the Mississippi and its tributaries. **1902** NORRIS *Pit* 365 In the 'front library,' . . . [were] 'whatnots' crowded with shells, Chinese coins, lacquer boxes, and the inevitable sawfish bill.

Sawfly. Any of the Hymenoptera of the extensive superfamily Tenthredinoidea. {1773-} — **1792** BELKNAP *Hist. N.H.* III. 182 Insects. . . . Oak Apple Fly, *Cynips*.—Several species. Saw Fly, *Tenthredo betulæ*. **1837** WILLIAMS *Florida* 71 Saw Fly.—*Tenthredo*. Pine timber, cut in the summer, is pierced full of holes by this living auger. **1884** *Rep. Comm. Agric.* 387 Wheat and Grass Saw-Fly. . . . My acquaintance with this insect has so far been confined to the larvae only. **1925** HERRICK *Man. Injurious Insects* 333 The Western Wheat-Stem Sawfly. *Cephus cinctus*. . . . This native sawfly . . . is now a serious pest on spring wheat.

+Saw gin. A cotton gin in which the fibers of cotton are torn from the seed by toothed disks or circular saws. — **1801** MILLER & WHITNEY in *Amer. Jrnl. Science* XXI. 222 The machine for separating cotton from its seeds, [is] commonly called the Saw Gin. **1812** *Ann. 12th Congress* 1 Sess. 2190 If the saw gin of Whitney had not been brought to light, the green seed cotton could only be cultivated by those planters who have a superabundant number of laborers. **1854** *Fla. Plantation Rec.* 102 Thar was no saw gins in town. **1882** *Century Mag.* Jan. 477/2 Several minor modifications of the saw-gin . . . seem to have merits.

Saw grass. Any of certain grasslike herbs having sharp teeth along the edges of the leaves {1855-}, esp. any species of *Cladium*, as +*C. jamaicensis* of the southern states. — **1822** *Notices East Florida* 24 (Th. S.), They were obliged to defend their horses' feet with wrappings of cow-hide, in order to prevent their being injured by the sharp saw grass. **1829** EATON *Botany* (ed. 5) 383 *Schoenus effusus*, saw grass. **1848** *S. Lit. Messenger* XIV. 531/2 The saw grass was at least four feet above the heads of the men seated in the boats. **1883** [see BONNET 2]. **1908** CHAMBERS *Firing Line* 153 Westward no trail lay save those blind signs of the Seminoles ac oss the wastes of open timber and endless stretches of lagoon and saw-grass which is called the Everglades.

Sawhorse. 1. A rack or frame on which wood is sawed by hand. {1778} **+2.** A packsaddle. — **(1) 1848** [see BUCK *n.*[2]]. **1887** ALDEN *Little Fishers* iv, Astride a saw-horse in the yard . . . was a curly-headed boy. **1920** LEWIS *Main Street* 222 Juanita Haydock, Rita Simons, and Raymie Wutherspoon sat on a sawhorse. **(2) 1886** S. HALE *Letters* 164 The saddle for donkeys here is a simple saw-horse.

***Sawing.** +(See quotation.) — **1857** *Mich. Agric. Soc. Trans.* VIII. 166 'Sawing' . . . means working against each other, or *one* trying to dip the sheep on one side whilst the *other* is trying to do the reverse.

Sawing mill. =SAWMILL. {1722-} — **1619** *Va. Ho se of Burgesses* 17 He is utterlie ignorant in the busines of the Sawinge Mills. **1724** JONES *Virginia* 131, I shall say little of Sawing-Mills, since they are already in Use.

+Saw log. A log of a suitable size and length for sawing into boards. — **1831** BUTTRICK *Travels* 57 There were also many rafts of boards and shingles timber and saw logs. **1854** BROMWELL *Locomotive Sk.* 162 The ox-teams are busy tugging off the saw-logs. **1866** *Rep. Indian Affairs* 184 Agent Burleigh . . . purchased 90,000 feet of saw-logs. **1894** *Voice* 22 Nov. 4/3 That may be but a straw which shows the blowing of the wind, but it has the size of a saw-log. **1905** *Forestry Bureau Bul.* No. 64, 34 They have cut all the sawlogs on the tract.

***Sawmill.**

***1.** A factory or mill in which logs are sawed into boards by power-driven machinery; also, a machine for sawing lumber. (See also STEAM SAWMILL.)
1634 WOOD *New Eng. Prospect* (1865) 19 Here no doubt might be good done with saw mils. **1676** *Mass. H. S. Coll.* 4 Ser. V. 8 [They] fell to burning, beginning with Mr. Tilden's sawmill. **1708** *Boston News-Letter* 8 Nov. 4/2 There is a choice good Farm . . . [with] a good large New House, and a good Saw Mill. **1770** PITTMAN *Present State* 24 Many of the planters have saw-mills, which are worked by the waters of the Mississippi in the time of the floods. **1813** *Niles' Reg.* IV. 111/2, I apply the power by means of a connecting rod or rods (or pitman, as it is called when applied in saw-mills). **1847** *Santa Fe Republican* 1 Oct. 1/4 The point which we would recommend for the construction of the first dam, is about two miles above the saw mill. **1884** *Rep. Comm. Agric.* 138 There are 1,569 sawmills in operation in [Penna.]. **1912** *Indian Laws & Tr.* III. 537 The Secretary of the Interior is authorized to use this money, . . . in the purchase of a sawmill and logging equipment.

b. *Portable (circular) sawmill*, a portable machine by which logs can be sawed into boards.
1854 *Penna. Agric. Rep.* 98 The committee also notice a portable circular saw mill. **1892** *York County Hist. Rev.* 66 They operate a portable sawmill.

2. Attrib. with *boiler, dam, gate*, etc.
1675 *Essex Inst. Coll.* LVI. 301 Samil Dudley of Exeter, clerk, conveyed to Moses Gillman . . . 40 acres of a sawmill grant. **1716** *Duxbury Rec.* 113 We began at the waste gate belonging to the saw mill . . and run from said gate Easterly as the old saw mill dam stood. **1819** in Shields *S. S. Prentiss* 65 The lot of two acres on the bank of the river on which a saw-mill house is erected belongs to myself. **1843** *Yale Lit. Mag.* VIII. 406 There are multitudes of people in the land, . . . whose first idea when coming to the premises would be, what lots of saw-mill logs there are here. **1851** HOOPER *Widow Rugby* 89 You've set and watched a saw-mill gate jerk up and down. **1860** *Harper's Mag.* May 856/1 The prisoner's 'counsel' (called the saw-mill lawyer) thought he had a green one in the people's witness. **1871** *Republican Rev.* 29 April 2/2 Take what was the 'Sibley Trail,' now known as the Saw Mill road. **1883** *Harper's Mag.* Sept. 642/2 At Huntsville, Texas, five men [were] killed by the explosion of a saw-mill boiler. **1892** *Financial World* (Boston) Aug. 7/1 We can furnish him about every form of security . . . from a government down to a saw-mill industrial.

Sawmiller. The proprietor or operator of a sawmill. {1881} — **1845** THOREAU *Journal* I. 361, I lodged at the house of a saw-miller last summer. **1878** *No. Amer. Rev.* May 501 Printers, gunsmiths, sawmillers, . . . and others shall pay twenty-five cents on every hundred dollars' worth of gross receipts.

Sawmill work. A sawmill plant. — **1654** *Suffolk Deeds* II. 26, I Edward Colcott . . . doe hereby giue . . . vnto Thomas Rucke . . . one third parte of a saw mill worke. **1739** W. STEPHENS *Proc. Georgia* I. 402 One Tyrrel, appointed Director of the Saw-Mill Work at Old Ebenezer.

+Saw palmetto. a. A common dwarf palmetto (*Serenoa serrulata*) of the South. (Cf. PALMETTO SCRUB.) **b.** A similar palm (*Paurotis wrightii*) of southern Florida.
1797 HAWKINS *Letters* 85 The whole country was a pine barron, with wire grass and saw palmetto. **1844** *Knickerb.* XXIII. 46 My arms were only sufficient to . . . keep him clear of the saw-palmetto. **1861** *Amer. Cycl.* XII. 704/1 The saw palmetto . . . occurs on the southern islands of South Carolina, and in sandy soils southward to Florida. **1865** CUMMING *Hospital Life* 160/1 Gentlemen's and ladies' hats are made out of saw palmetto. **1894** TORREY *Fla. Sketch-Book* 3 The ground [was] covered thickly with saw palmetto. **1919** STURTEVANT *Notes on Edible Plants* 100 B[rahea] *serrulata* H. Wendl. Saw Palmetto. Southern United States.

***Saw pit.** An excavation over which a log is sawed with a two-man saw, one man standing in the pit. Also attrib. — **1636** *Boston Rec.* 12 The sawe pitte [is to be] gotten filled. **1681** *East-Hampton Rec.* II. 109 Diging ye Sawpit. **1732** HEMPSTEAD *Diary* 251, I was drawing up the Timber to make a cogg wheel & a Sawpitt. **1788** MAY *Jrnl. & Lett.* 73 Made a saw-pit for sawing boards. **1830** WATSON *Philadelphia* 280 The Hon. James A. Bayard . . . fought a duel with another member in a disused saw-pit shed. **1890** *Century Mag.* Dec. 179 Marshall discovered gold in 1848 . . . about forty miles to the north of the saw-pits.

+Sawteat blackberry. A variety of blackberry. — **1795** WINTERBOTHAM *Hist. View* III. 395 Sawteat blackberry or bumblekites, *Rubus fruticosus*.

Saw tooth. {1601-} +An ownership mark put on animals. — **1779** *N.J. Archives* 2 Ser. III. 231 A red heifer . . . with a half crop in the left ear . . . and a saw-tooth on the same.

+Saw-whet (owl). =LITTLE OWL 2. — **1834** AUDUBON *Ornith. Biog.* II. 567 The Little Owl is known in Massachusetts by the name of the 'Saw-whet,' the sound of its love-notes bearing a great resemblance to the noise produced by filing the teeth of a large saw. **1844** *Nat. Hist. N.Y., Zoology* II. 30 The *Little Owl* or *Saw-whet* as it is called in Massachusetts and this State, is found in every part of the Union. **1894** *Outing* XXIII. 406/1 The little 'saw whet' under his tiny glass globe. **1917** *Birds of Amer.* II. 107 Saw-Whet Owl.

Saw-whetter. {1840-, in Canada} **+1.** (See quot.) **+2.** A person whose business is sharpening saws. *Obs.* — **(1) 1784** BELKNAP *Jrnl. Tour to White Mts.* (1876) 10 The Dr. saw a blue bird, with a white head, which is said to be a *saw-whetter*. **(2) 1789** *Boston Directory* 196 Pike Timothy, saw whetter.

∗Sawyer.

∗1. A workman who saws timber into boards, or wood into proper lengths for fuel.

1626 *Plymouth Laws* 28 [No] smiths sawyers or whatsoever . . . shall use their science or trades . . . for any strangers or foreigners. **1641** *Conn. Rec.* I. 65 Sawyers shall not take aboue 4s. 2d. for slitt worke or three inch planke. **1724** JONES *Virginia* 38 Several of them [*sc.* slaves] are taught to be Sawyers, Carpenters, Smiths, Coopers, &c. **1765** TIMBER-LAKE *Memoirs* 59 A pair of sawyers would divide the same tree into eight or ten [boards] in much less time. **1820** *Amer. Antiq. Soc. Coll.* I. 75 Sawyers, [were] most necessary of our workmen for building our ship. **1885** *Rep. Indian Affairs* 196 The sawyer, who is a half-breed, runs the saw-mill.

+b. A lumberman who fells trees by sawing.

1880 *Lumberman's Gazette* 28 Jan. 1/3 A Wisconsin lumber-camp is divided into 'choppers,' 'sawyers' and 'swampers.' **1893** *Atlantic Mo.* Feb. 196/1 Each man . . . [is] hired for a definite purpose, as . . . barker, sawyer, bull-puncher, or skid-greaser. **1900** *Bureau Statistics* (Treas. Dept.) *Summary* Nov. 1116 The swampers . . . follow the sawyers. **1905** *Forestry Bureau Bul.* No. 61, 37.

+2. a. A beetle whose larvae burrow in wood. {1890-} **b.** The katydid.

1789 ANBUREY *Travels* II. 452 [In Va.] the log huts in which the soldiers reside . . . [have been] nearly destroyed by an insect that . . . preys upon the solid part of the timber; and these insects . . . have the appellation of sawyers. **1804** LEWIS in *L. & Clark Exped.* VI. (1905) 127 The green insect known in the U' States by the name of the sawyer or chittediddle was first heard to cry on the 27th. of July. **1908** KELLOGG *Amer. Insects* 285 The sawyers, various species of the genus *Monohammus*, are beautiful brown and grayish beetles.

+3. A log or tree caught in a river so that it or its branches 'saw' back and forth with the waves.

Cf. PLANTER 3.

1797 F. BAILY *Tour* 256 These sawyers are large trunks of trees. **1807** C. SCHULTZ *Travels* II. 30 Sawyers . . . receive a regular vibratory motion. . . . Some of these have a very quick motion; others again are slower, frequently disappearing from one to twenty minutes. **1833** J. HALL *Legends of West* 139 In the middle of the river was a large sawyer, . . . the entire trunk of a majestic oak. **1847** LANMAN *Summer in Wilderness* 21 Immediately in the foreground [are] a solitary sawyer and the hull of a sunken steamboat. **1883** 'MARK TWAIN' *Life on Miss.* xl, At this point begins the pilot's paradise: a wide river . . . [with] no bars, snags, sawyers, or wrecks. **1907** STEWART *Partners* 49 Down in the current I seen a sawyer.

+4. A sawing machine or sawmill.

1840 *Picayune* 6 Aug. 2/6 For sale . . . a first rate steam sawyer.

+5. = DOGFISH 2.

1884 GOODE, etc. *Fisheries* I. 659 The Bowfin or Johnny Grindle—*Amia calva*. . . . It occurs in the Great Lakes, where it is called 'Dogfish' and 'Sawyer.' **1911** *Rep. Fisheries 1908* 308/1.

Saxafarilla, Saxifarilla. Obs. var. of SARSAPARILLA. Also attrib. — **1634** WOOD *New Eng. Prospect* 13 In the woods, without eyther the art or the helpe of man, . . . [grow] mirtle, saxifarilla, bayes, &c. **1748** HEMP-STEAD *Diary* 498, I was about Town all day to get Saxafarilla Roots to make a Drink.

Saxhorn. One of various brass wind instruments with valves. {1852-} Also attrib. — **1856** *Daily Democratic Press* (Chicago) 19 Aug. 2/7 B. K. Mould & Co., Chicago, advertise for sale a number of Sax Horns of the best French manufacture. **1857** *Ill. Agric. Soc. Trans.* II. 291 The sax-horn band, of Warren, enlivened the occasion with some excellent music. **1867** *Chicago Times* 18 Sept. 5/3 The band . . . nightly have made the air (un)musical with their cracked trombones and ear-splitting saxhorns.

∗Saxifrage.

+1. Misused for SASSAFRAS. Also attrib.

1616 SMITH *New England* 16 [Trees here include] plumtree, hazell, saxefrage. **1670** DENTON *Brief Desc.* 4 The greatest part of the Island is very full of Timber, as . . . Maples, Cedars, Saxifrage, Beach. **1678** *Wyllys Papers* 271 We have ordred John barker to Remove his fence beg[inn]ing at the fence at his house to a saxifrage bowe.

∗2. a. Any plant of the genus *Saxifraga* or of the related genus *Micranthes*. **b.** Any of certain other plants, as the burnet saxifrage, etc. Freq. with defining terms.

1765 J. BARTRAM *Journal* 17 It is entangled with a large species of water-numularia, persicaria, water-grass, and saxifrage. **1817-8** EATON *Botany* (1822) *Sanguisorba canadensis*, burnet saxifrage. . . . The leaves resemble the burnet. **1843** TORREY *Flora N.Y.* I. 255 *Saxifraga Pennsylvanica*. Pennsylvanian Saxifrage. . . . In swamps and wet meadows; common. **1857** GRAY *Botany* 143 Lettuce Saxifrage. . . . Cold mountain brooks, Pennsylvania . . . and throughout the Alleghanies southward. **1867** ME-LINE *Santa Fé & Back* 14 Here we begin to see the aloe, prickly-pear, and saxifrage. **1885** *Outing* Nov. 177/1 At its top there is a cluster of small white flowers known as saxifrage. **1898** A. M. DAVIDSON *Calif. Plants* 178 Most of the California saxifrages are found in shaded canons or on high mountains. **1915** ARMSTRONG & THORNBER *Western Wild Flowers* 202

Saxifrage. *Micranthes rhomboidea* (*Saxifraga*). . . . A little alpine plant, growing in moist soil, or on mossy rocks.

‖Saxlingham. (See quotation.) — **1745** in Watson *Philadelphia* 179 [From one advertisement of the year 1745, I take the following now unintelligible articles of dress] naffermamy, saxlingham.

∗Saxon. +Short for SAXON MERINO. Also attrib. — **1852** [see GRADE *n.* 8 a]. **1856** *Rep. Comm. Patents 1855: Agric.* 53 A large proportion of our sheep, however, are a cross with the Spanish and Saxons. **1863** *Rep. Comm. Agric. 1862* 23 [Alpaca] fleeces are . . . used for many purposes to which our Saxon or merino wools . . . are inapplicable. **1883** ALLEN *New Farm Book* 419 The Saxon . . . is one of the varieties of the pure-bred Merino.

+Saxon merino. A breed of fine-wooled sheep; a Saxony merino. Also attrib. — **1854** *Penna. Agric. Rep.* 65 There is not a Merino or Saxon Merino Sheep on the ground. **1863** RANDALL *Pract. Shepherd* 25 The woolen tariff enacted in 1824, gave a new impulse to the production of fine-wool and . . . Saxon Merinos were imported . . . into the United States. **1893** G. W. CURTIS *Horses, Cattle* 250 It is believed that Mr. Berry was the first to apply the name 'Black-Tops,' and that he did so to distinguish them from the light colored, delicate Saxon Merinos.

Saxony. {1844-} attrib. Designating a breed of sheep developed in Saxony, Germany. — **1831** PECK *Guide* 173 Little is said or done to . . introduce the marino, or saxony breed. **1842** *Nat. Hist. N.Y., Zoology* I. 112 The quality of the fleece was still farther improved in 1824, by the introduction of what are termed *Saxony sheep*. **1862** *Rep. Comm. Patents 1861: Agric.* 120 The Saxony Merino. . . . They are a fine-boned, well-formed sheep. **1863** *Rep. Comm. Agric. 1862* 47 About the year 1824, and subsequently, occurred the 'Saxony speculation' which resulted in the importation of individuals of the Saxony breed by Judge Hayes.

∗Say, *n.*¹ A fine, thin kind of woolen cloth resembling serge. *Obs.* — *c*1645 *Harvard Rec.* I. 11 It[em] Greene say & Nailes . . . 2 [s.]. **1660** *Essex Probate Rec.* I. 322 A pece of grene say, 10s. **1711** [see GRAZET]. **1773** FRANKLIN *Writings* VI. 121 Nor shall any worsted, bay, or woollen yarn, cloth, says [etc.] . . . be water-borne even across the smallest river or creek.

+Say, *n.*² [Thomas Say, Amer. naturalist (1787-1834).] In various names of a species of flycatcher: (see quotations). — **1825** BONAPARTE *Ornithology* I. 20 [The] Say's Flycatcher, *Muscicapa Saya*, . . . now before us is a male. **1917** *Birds of Amer.* II. 200 Say's Phœbe. *Sayornis sayus*. . . . Other Name.—Say's Pewee.

∗Say, *n.*³

+1. *To have the say*, to have the authority.

1838 *Jamestown* (N.Y.) *Journal* 11 July 1/5 One thing I am determined on and that is, that the folks who succeed best in hauling the Two Pollies in the stream shall have the say in rigging on her up for the voyage. **1863** HOPLEY *Life in South* II. 332 The Yankees have the *say* all to themselves. **1902** WISTER *Virginian* xiii, Somebody has to have the say, I reckon.

+2. *Poker.* A player's turn to bet or pass. *Obs.*

1864 DICK *Amer. Hoyle* (1866) 123 When it comes to the dealer's 'say,' . . . he will also make the same bet if he pleases. **1884** 'CRADDOCK' *Where Battle Was Fought* 35 [He] calmly awaited Estwick's 'say.' **1887** KELLER *Draw Poker* 23 The next say belongs to the next player to the left.

∗Say, *v.*

+1. *quasi-interj.* Used to call attention to a statement or question. *colloq.* {I say, 1611-}

1854 M. J. HOLMES *Tempest & Sunshine* 12 Say, you scapegrace, come up here. **1869** 'MARK TWAIN' *Innocents* 35 Now, say—my friend—don't you know any better? **1888** *Amer. Humorist* (London) 5 May 72/1 Say, boys, let's climb the mountain. **1902** BANKS *Newspaper Girl* 40 Say, don't you worry about that scoop. **1912** NICHOLSON *Hoosier Chron.* 169 Say, the janitor service in this old ark is something I couldn't describe.

+2. *Poker.* To bet or pass at one's turn.

1887 KELLER *Draw Poker* 23 If no straddle has been made, the first player to the left of the age must 'say.'

+Saybrook platform. A platform of church discipline and polity adopted by a synod of the Connecticut Congregational church at Saybrook in 1708.

Much the same as the Cambridge platform (q.v.). Cf. PLATFORM *n.* 1.

1825 NEAL *Bro. Jonathan* I. 5 [He had been] defeated at his own game—Divinity—with his own weapons—the Saybrook platform, and Bible. **1838** COOPER *Homeward B.* xxvii, It is likely Mr. Monday is a Church-of-England man and we both belong to the Saybrook Platform! **1844** G. B. CHEEVER *Lect. Pilgrim's Progress* 201 Other men would have sprinkled their pages with conversations about . . . the Saybrook Platform. **1879** *Congress. Rec.* 21 Feb. 1715/2 The 'Saybrook platform' was the formula into which the really liberal . . . principles of their religion had been cramped and crowded.

Say-so. The mere word of a person; an assertion; the right of command. {1637-; now *dial.*} *colloq.*

1804 *Balance* 30 Oct. 347 (Th.), If the Democrats' say-so could make Mr. Jefferson a Christian, he would long ago have been one of the greatest in our country. **1844** KIDDER *Mormonism & Mormons* 53 How could they know? . . . Certainly on no other grounds than his [Joseph Smith's] 'say so,' which is good for nothing. **1853** BALDWIN *Flush Times Ala.* 118, I'm obleeged to you for your perlite say so, and so forth. **1855** *Harper's Mag.* Oct. 603/2 They would ha' disappeared . . . if I hain't put in my say so.

1890 *Congress. Rec.* 9 May 4432/1 We need not depend on anybody's say-so. **1902** WHITE *Blazed Trail* 195 In questions of policy mine is the say-so every trip.

* **Scab,** *n.*

+**1.** A workman who accepts lower wages than those prescribed by a trade union, or who refuses to join a union; one who works after a strike has been called, or in the place of a union man on strike. {1881-}

1806 Commons, etc. *Doc. Hist.* III. 74, I concluded at that time I would turn a scab. **1811** *Selected Cases N.Y.* I. 262 The offending member was then termed a *scab* and wherever he was employed no others of the society were allowed to work. **1887** *Harper's Mag.* April 822/2 Why is an honest, hard-working laborer derided as a 'scab'? **1889** SALMONS *Burlington Strike* 259 The man who takes the place of another when that other engages in a struggle with a corporation, is a 'scab.' **1917** SINCLAIR *King Coal* 136 Mike Sikoria . . . talked about 'scabs,' and the dreadful things that honest workingmen would do to them.

2. *attrib.* and *comb.* +**a.** Designating commodities produced or handled by nonunion organizations.

1881 *Chicago Times* 11 June 2/2 Three hundred saloon-keepers of New York have joined hands with the striking brewers by refusing to purchase scab beer. **1887** *Courier-Journal* 1 Feb. 2/5 They declare that they will not handle 'scab' freight. **1888** *Nation* 12 Jan. 22/1 There had been a similar difficulty . . . regarding 'scab coal' from the Lehigh region.

+**b.** Designating commercial organizations, business places, etc., employing nonunion workmen.

1888 *Nation* 5 April 269/3 The employees refused to move a carload of flour that came out of the 'scab' warehouse. **1895** *Chicago Strike of 1894* 123 When you travel take the Great American Scab Route, the Chicago, Burlington and Quincy Railroad. **1896** *Typographical Jrnl.* IX. 232 He gave the work to the Topeka scab outfit. **1898** *Mo. So. Dakotan* I. 106 Hats are made in union factories and in scab factories.

+**c.** Designating nonunion workmen engaged in various employments.

1889 SALMONS *Burlington Strike* 430 The strike was declared off, and scab switchmen were employed in their places. **1891** 'THANET' *Otto the Knight* 21, He was bossing a boycott on a poor widow woman who wouldn't turn a scab carpenter out of her boarding-house. **1898** *Mo. So. Dakotan* I. 107 Unions . . . [provide] a class of workmen superior in every way to the non-union or 'scab' employee. **1913** *Industrial Worker* (Spokane, Wash.) 3 July 1/3 The Utah Construction Co. . . . filled the town of Tucker . . . with a force of armed thugs, gunmen, scabherders and professional strike breakers.

Scab, *v.* {1632-}

+**1.** *tr.* and *intr.* To behave as a scab; to take (another workman's job). {1905} Also *to scab it*.

1806 in Commons, etc. *Doc. Hist.* III. 75 Their business was to watch the Jews that they did not scab it. **1889** SALMONS *Burlington Strike* 357 The men . . . declared they had never scabbed a day in their lives. **1895** *Chicago Strike of 1894* 308 If there is a strike ordered I will be damned if I am going to scab. **1898** *Scribner's Mag.* Oct. 445/2, I won't scab any man's job. **1917** SINCLAIR *King Coal* 298 Is there anybody here who'll scab on his fellows?

+**2.** *tr.* To ostracize (a worker) as a scab, or to declare (a shop) a nonunion organization and to boycott it.

1806 in Commons, etc. *Doc. Hist.* III. 73, I was liable to be scabb'd. . . . If I did not join the body, no man would set upon the seat where I worked; . . . they would neither board or work where I was unless I joined. *Ib.* 77 In a little time after this his shop was scabbed.

Scabbard fish. {1836-}

+**1.** The cutlass fish (*Trichiurus lepturus*), found on the coasts of the southern United States, or any of several related species.

1883 *Nat. Museum Bul.* No. 27, 437 *Trichiurus lepturus.* Silvery Hairtail; Scabbard-fish; Sabre-fish; Silver Eel. Warm seas. On the east coast of the United States north to Cape Cod. **1897** *N.Y. Forest, Fish & Game Comm. 2d Rep.* 236 [The] scabbard fish . . . is very rarely seen in [Gravesend Bay]. **1903** T. H. BEAN *Fishes N.Y.* 403 The scabbard fish frequents warm seas and ranges north to Cape Cod and Lower California.

2. Any long, slender fish of the genus *Lepidopus.* {1836-}

1884 GOODE, etc. *Fisheries* I. 336 The 'Scabbard-fish' of Europe . . . also occurs in the Gulf of California.

+**Scabbarding.** The spacing of lines of type. *Obs.* — **1786** CUTLER in *Life & Corr.* II. 270 Size of the paper, scabbording of the lines, . . . scabbording of the prefaces . . . were all particularly specified in the contract. **1818** *N. Amer. Rev.* May 118 If a printer, he is adroit at *scabbarding.*

+**Scabbish.** (See SCABISH.)

* **Scabious. a.** Any cultivated plant of the genus *Scabiosa,* esp. the sweet scabious, *S. atropurpurea.* +**b.** Any of various native plants, esp. certain plants of the genus *Erigeron.* (See also SWEET SCABIOUS.) — **1676** GLOVER *Va.* in *Phil. Trans.* XI. 629 There grow wild in the Woods, Plantane of all sorts, . . . Centory, Scabious, [and] Groundsel. **1778** CARVER *Travels* 515 Herbs [include] . . . Wake Robin, Betony, Scabious, Mullen

[etc.] **1830** LINDLEY *Introd. Nat. Syst. of Botany* 200 *Erigeron philadelphicum* and *heterophyllum* . . . are commonly sold under the name of Scabious. **1832** S. J. HALE *Flora* 163 Scabious. *Scabiosa atro-purpurea.* . . . The dark *purple* has been called 'Mourning Bride.' **1891** *Cent.* 5365/3.

+**Scabish.** Also **scabbish.** [Origin obscure.] **a.** The evening primrose (*Oenothera biennis*) or a related plant. Also with specifying term. **b.** = SCABIOUS b.

1817-8 EATON *Botany* (1822) 364 *Œnothera biennis,* scabish, tree-primrose. . . . Phosphorescent. **1821** *Mass. H. S. Coll.* 2 Ser. IX. 153 Plants, which are indigenous in the township of Middlebury [Vt. include] . . . *Oenothera biennis,* Scabish. [*Oenothera*] *chrysantha,* Dwarf scabish. **1828** RAFINESQUE *Medical Flora* I. 162 *Erigeron Philadelphicum.* English Name—Skevish Fleabane. . . . Vulgar Names—Skevish, Scabish, Sweet Scabious [etc.]. **1874** *Vermont Bd. Agric. Rep.* II. 779 *Heteraspis pubescens.* Very common on the scabish. **1891** *Amer. Folk-Lore* IV. 149 A very rough, coarse, rank-growing weed in the swamps, which I think now was some kind of Aster, grandmother called *Scabish.* **1892** *Ib.* V. 96 *Œnothera fruticosa,* scabbish. N.H.

Scad. a. A fish of the genus *Trachurus.* {1602-} +**b.** The cigar fish (*Decapterus punctatus*), or a related species. +**c.** = GOGGLER.

1671 *S.C. Hist. Soc.Coll.* V. 336 Fish there are in both riuers multitudes, As Bass, . . . scad, Thornbacks, drumes, &c. **1882** *Nat. Museum Bul.* No. 16, 432 *Decapterus punctatus.* . . . Scad; Round Robin. **1884** GOODE, etc. *Fisheries* I. 326 The Scads, known in England as the 'Horse-Mackerels,' appear to occur in all temperate and tropical waters. **1885** [see GOGGLER]. **1903** T. H. BEAN *Fishes N.Y.* 425 The scads [*Trachurus*] are described by European writers as occurring . . . in enormous schools. . . . Only a few specimens have been recorded on our Atlantic coast. *Ib.* 427 The big-eyed scad [*Trachurops crumenophthalmus*] is taken in the fall in Gravesend bay. **1911** *Rep. Fisheries 1908* 314 Round robin (*Decapterus punctatus*) . . . is also called 'cigar-fish' and 'scad.'

+**Scadoodles.** [Cf. SCADS and OODLES.] =next. *slang.* — **1869** *Overland Mo.* III. 131 A Texan never has a great quantity of any thing, but he has 'scads' of it, or 'oodles,' or 'dead oodles,' or 'scadoodles,' or 'swads.'

+**Scads.** *pl.* [Origin obscure.] **a.** ?Dollars. **b.** A large sum of money; a great quantity *of* anything. *slang.*

1809 *Amer. Mag.* Nov. 1 [This] land of our dads . . . is a dinger at nailing the scads. **1856** Sacramento item (Th.), So off he went with good three hundred 'scads.' **1869** [see SCADOODLES]. **1894** HARTE *Bell-Ringer of Angel's* 13 Arthur would yet be seen . . . 'dropping his scads' at draw poker. **1904** W. H. SMITH *Promoters* 52 England . . . found she could raise scads of opium in India, but had no market for it. **1923** WATTS *L. Nichols* 214 The old girl surely did have it—scads of it, he said to himself; and this certainly was his lucky day.

* **Scaffold,** *n.*

* **1.** A raised framework for drying hay, meat, fish, or tobacco.

1634 WOOD *New Eng. Prospect* (1865) 48 There was made here a ships loading of fish the last yeare, where still stands the stages, and drying scaffolds. **1741** *N.H. Probate Rec.* III. 71 [We] have Set off to Susanna . . . The South Part of the Barn . . . and the East Scaffold for hay. **1784** SMYTH *Tour* II. 134 The scaffolds . . . are generally erected all round the tobacco houses. **1806** CLARK in *Lewis & C. Exped.* IV. (1905) 235 Those who remained in camp were employd in . . . makeing a scaffold and cutting up the meat in order to dry it. **1874** *Vermont Bd. Agric. Rep.* II. 522 The single cow is . . . fed from the scaffold of choice hay, . . . and the pile of beets, turnips or potatoes.

+**2.** (See quotations.)

1814 BRACKENRIDGE *Views La.* 203 A kind of scaffolds . . . were erected . . . by the neighboring settlers for the purpose of shooting the deer by moon light. . . . The hunter ascends the scaffold, and remains until the deer approaches. *Ib.* 261, I saw a great number of small scaffolds . . . on which human bodies were exposed. . . . In this they [the Mandans] are different from the Arikaras, who bury their dead as we do.

* **Scaffold,** *v.*

+**1.** *tr.* Of American Indians: To expose (a corpse) on a scaffold.

1775 ADAIR *Indians* 323n., [They] scaffolded their dead kinsman. **1805** CLARK in *Lewis & C. Exped.* I. (1904) 325 An Indian woman was scaffeled in the Indian form of Deposing their Dead. **1814** BRACKENRIDGE *Views La.* 225 An Indian chief . . . was scaffolded here some years ago.

+**2.** To place on a scaffold for drying purposes or for safekeeping. Freq. with *up.*

1799 J. SMITH *Acct. Captivity* 39 Sometime in February, we scaffolded up our fur and skins. **1804** CLARK in *Lewis & C. Exped.* I. (1904) 197, I scaffeled up the Deer & returned. **1808** PIKE *Sources Miss.* 2 [The Sacs] were employed in spearing and scaffolding a fish, about 3 feet in length, with a long flat snout.

+**Scalage.** The amount by which anything is scaled down; the amount which timber measures. — **1853** *Congress. Globe* 1 March 961/1 Gentlemen . . . will come in, who have got their scalage at eighty-seven and a half cents on the dollar. **1878** *Michigan Rep.* XXXVI. 168 Allen agreed to deliver . . . merchantable lumber . . . [equivalent] to the total scalage of the logs delivered.

+**Scalawag, Scallawag.** Also **scallywag.** *colloq.* [Origin obscure.]

1. A scamp; a loafer; a rascal. {1891}

1848 BARTLETT 284 *Scalawag,* a favorite epithet in western New York for a mean fellow; a scape-grace. **1861** *Md. Hist. Mag.* V. 312 It would be hard to rake up a meaner looking set of scallawags than the regular privates. **1869** J. R. BROWNE *Adv. Apache Country* 183 [She] had been eight days at this infernal place among a set of scallywags who didn't understand her lingo. **1885** JEWETT *Marsh Island* 17, I asked that young scalawag who drove me over this noon. **1903** *McClure's Mag.* Sept. 462 The honest, conservative citizen remains at home, while the able scalawag runs his organization.

2. A poor or worthless animal.

1854 *N.Y. Tribune* 24 Oct. (*Cent.*), The number of miserable 'scallawags' is so great that . . . they tend to drag down all above themselves to their own level. **1872** *Vermont Bd. Agric. Rep.* I. 312 Valuable sheep have been messed with the skalawags of the flock. **1878** *Ill. Dept. Agric. Trans.* XIV. 286 The cows in the Northwest, as a whole, are 'scalawags.'

3. A Southerner who supported the Congressional plan of reconstruction after the Civil War; a white Republican in the South.

1868 *N.Y. Herald* 10 July 10/2 There was nothing left in his old State but scallawags and carpet baggers. **1871** *Congress. Globe* 4 April 253/3 Those who were born in the South and remained faithful to the Government, or have since joined the Republican party, are stigmatized as the 'scalawags,' or low persons of the baser sort. **1874** in Fleming *Hist. Reconstruction* II. 153 The people ought to . . . drive every carpet-bagger and scalawag out of the State. **1898** PAGE *Red Rock* 339 One's a carpet-bagger and t'other a scalawag. **1911** SIMONS *Social Forces in Amer. Hist.* 298 The army of men that were thus marshaling the negroes for the Republican party was made up in part of Northern adventurers ('carpet-baggers') and so-called Southern 'Union men' ('scalawags').

4. Attrib. in senses 1 and 2 with *appointee, beef, Indian,* etc.

1885 *South Fla. Sentinel* (Orlando) 8 April 1/7 Chicago beef, New York butter . . . will disappear [from Fla.] as well as the warlike racing Florida hog and scalawag beef. **1888** BRYCE *Amer. Commw.* II. II. xliv. 164 A group of such 'scallawag' members . . . increase their legislative income by levying this form of taxation [blackmail] upon the companies of the State. **1891** WELCH *Recoll. 1830–40* 123 It would be a very 'scalawag' Indian to whom he would answer tan-ta-gig-egac (no trust). **1902** Scalawag steer [see FAT *v.* 1]. **1906** *Nation* 12 July 27 Those scalawag appointees of McKinley's . . . have recently had to be removed from the consular service in China. **1907** *Cincinnati Enquirer* 10 July 6/1 In anticipation of statehood the territories seem to have been overrun by a lot of scalawag politicians.

* **Scald.**

1. a. A disease of animals, affecting the hoofs. {1886}

+**b.** A disease of plants resembling wilt.

1791 W. BARTRAM *Travels* 208 The traders and Indians call this disease the water-rot or scald. **1895** *Stand.* 1590/3 *Scald,* a destructive disease of cranberries, due to a sphaeriaceous fungus: applied also loosely by farmers and fruit-growers to any sudden wilting or decay, of unknown origin, of leaves and fruit. **1899** *Farmers' Bul.* No. 91, 10 Tip Burn, Leaf Burn, or Scald. This disease of the [potato] leaves . . . is often confused with early blight. **1916** *Ib.* No. 727, 28 Sun scald sometimes occurs during the winter on the south or southwest side of the trunks, especially in the case of high-headed trees.

+**2.** (See quotations.) {1795–, patch of sun-scorched land} Freq. pl. Also attrib.

1862 *Ill. Agric. Soc. Trans.* V. 170 A stratum of hard-pan, . . . when exposed, or the surface soil washed from it, is known as the 'scalds.' *Ib.* 175 The drains are put in below the band of 'scald' clay. **1871** *Ib.* VIII. 205 In the northeastern portions of the county, however, are occasional 'scalds,' caused by the removal of the surface soil from a finely comminuted arenaceous subsoil. **1882** *Econ. Geol. Illinois* II. 124 Where the soil becomes shallow, and the hard-pan reaches the surface, there we find the so-called 'scalds,' or barren spots, in the fields.

* **Scale,** *n.*[1]

* **1.** A weighing apparatus. Freq. pl.

1642 *Plymouth Laws* 73 All the Milners within this Govern[men]t shall provide and keepe weights and scales in their millnes. **1790** *Penna. Packet* 8 May 4/4 Thomas Seddon, . . . has for Sale . . . Gold scales and weights. **1816** *Austin P.* I. (1924) 264, I Sett Apothecaries Scales. **1861** *Army Regulations* 242 Cattle presented for acceptance must be weighed upon the scales. **1922** *Sears, Roebuck & Co. Cat.* No. 144, 835/1 This scale has no loose weights.

2. Attrib. and comb. with *box, maker, man,* etc.

See also SCALE BEAM, SCALE HOUSE.

1655 *Suffolk Deeds* III. 209, I John Saers of Casco bay scale maker . . . Haue bargained & Sold . . . one Island. **1708** SEWALL *Diary* II. 226 Mr. Tho. Banister junr. . . . [was fined] 10s. Breach of the peace for throwing the pots and Scale-box at the maid. **1783** in Chalkley *Scotch-Irish Settlement Va.* I. 232 It is certified that the scale man is Peter Hane. **1794** COXE *View U.S.* 450 [Among the manufactures, . . . [are] scale plates.

1864 *Hist. North-Western Soldiers' Fair* 79 [Donations include] Buffalo Scale Works, E. C. Butler, Agent, 1 platform scale.

+**3.** A spree; a drinking frolic. *Obs.*

1825 PICKERING *Inquiries Emigrant* (1831) 27 Though they are seldom seen drunk, when on a 'scale,' or drinking frolic, [the Americans] are often seen near half-and-half. **1835** TODD *Notes* 37 Bacchanalian orgies [in New York City] are called *scales.*

* **Scale,** *n.*[2] +A graduated table *of* prices, values, etc. {1865–} —

1780 *Mass. Province Laws* V. 1413 The following scale shall be the rule . . . for settling the rate of depreciation on all contracts. **1788** JEFFERSON *Writings* VI. 433 A scale of their value [that of U.S. bills of credit, etc.] for every month has been settled according to what they sold for at market, in silver or gold. **1792** *Va. Rep.* (Washington) I. 130 This account ought to be subject to the legal scale of depreciation for May 1780. **1832** *Jamestown* (N.Y.) *Jrnl.* 25 Jan. 1/3 It seems to be universally agreed that the present scale of rates [for newspapers, etc.] should be altered so as to lighten the burden of postage. **1896** *Internat. Typogr. Union Proc.* 27/1 He agreed to continue paying the scale.

Scale, *n.*[3] +A piece of money. — **1871** DE VERE 296 Among the less generally known terms [for money] are . . . *wherewith, shadscales,* or *scales,* 'for short.' **1874** B. F. TAYLOR *World on Wheels* 28 But promise him a 'scale'—scale, skilling, shilling.

* **Scale,** *n.*[4] +An estimate of the amount of lumber in a given collection of logs or standing timber. Also attrib. — **1877** *Michigan Rep.* XXXIV. 376 To conclude the parties in that respect by his scale. *Ib.* XXXV. 521 The scale bill showed four hundred and ninety three thousand five hundred and seventeen feet of white pine. **1903** WHITE *Blazed Trail Stories* 43 The firm agreed to pay six dollars a thousand, merchantable scale, for all saw-logs banked at a rollway.

* **Scale,** *v.*[1]

+**1.** *tr.* To reduce (something) in amount; to reduce (an amount) according to a fixed scale. Freq. with *down.* Also *vbl. n.*

1790 *Ann. 1st Congress* 1161 If the Government . . . finds that it will work an evil . . . , to discharge those notes . . . at their nominal value, they are not to be blamed for scaling them. **1852** GOUGE *Fiscal Hist. Texas* 184 Scaling debts is not paying them. **1882** *Nation* 21 Sept. 232/2 All the others must be equally conscious of their deserts in order to get a proper proportion when the 'scaling down' comes. **1890** *Congress. Rec.* 25 June 6499/2 When an employer feels that his margin is slipping away from him, the first thing done is to scale down the price of wages. **1911** HARRISON *Queed* 292 Public institutions . . . could consider themselves lucky if they did not find their appropriations scaled down by a fourth or so.

+**2.** To proportion (votes) according to a scale.

1856 HAMBLETON *H. A. Wise* 29 The vote was then taken, and was scaled on the principle of allowing each county represented a number equal to its Democratic vote in the presidential election of 1852.

+**3.** *Lumbering.* Of timber: To produce, measure, or work out at (a given amount of lumber).

1853 LOWELL in *Putnam's Mag.* Nov. 466/1 Their eye, accustomed to reckoning the number of feet a tree will *scale,* is rapid. **1858** THOREAU *Maine Woods* 148 The largest pine belonging to his firm . . . 'scaled' in the woods four thousand five hundred feet. **1878** *Lumberman's Gazette* 16 March, This firm have been hauling timber that will scale almost an average of 2500 feet per each piece. **1911** J. F. WILSON *Land Claimers* 78 I can figure out how much your trees will scale.

+**4.** *Lumbering.* To measure (logs) or estimate the yield of (timber). Also *ppl. a.*

1867 LOWELL in *Atlantic Mo.* Jan. 27, I expect I can Scale a fair load of wood with e'er a man. **1877** *Michigan Rep.* XXXV. 506 These logs . . . had been scaled, and . . . they actually conformed to the contract. **1903** WHITE *Blazed Trail Stories* 48 Not a log do I scale for ye, Jimmy Bourke. **1905** *Forestry Bureau Bul.* No. 61, 46 *Scale book,* a book especially designed for recording the contents of scaled logs.

+**5.** To grade or rank.

1890 *Stock Grower & Farmer* 29 March 5/1 Rams must weigh 110 pounds in carcass, clip 25 pounds of wool, and scale 75 points to be standard. Ewes . . . can be scaled or not.

+**6.** *intr.* To taper *off* or diminish.

1898 F. H. SMITH *C. West* 60, I guess she'll scale off. . . . The glass is a-risin', too.

* **Scale,** *v.*[2] +(See quot. 1870.) — a**1870** CHIPMAN *Notes on Bartlett* 382 *To scale.* 1. To go, or make go, sideling. 2. To skip, ricochet, or cause to do so.—New England. **1877** BARTLETT 644 Scaling stones (upon the water) was a common New England expression for what the English boys call 'making ducks and drakes.'

Scale-bark. {1884–} +=SCALY-BARK. — **1837** BIRD *Nick* I. 101 Thar may be something of the scale-bark and parsimmon about me.

Scalebeam. A weighing instrument with a sliding weight on a horizontal bar; the bar used in such a device. {1723–} **1678** *New Castle Court Rec.* 361 One Large Scales Beame. **1777** *N.J. Archives* 2 Ser. I. 530 To be sold, a very good scale beam, ropes and scale dishes all fit for immediate use. **1802** *Ann. 7th Congress* 2 Sess. 1242 Six scale beams, scales, and weights. **1869** *Overland Mo.* III. 129 A large number [of eastern Texans] made the scale-beam kick at two hundred.

+**Scale bug.** Any of numerous insects of the family Coccidae, which are destructive to plants. — **1883** *Century Mag.* Oct. 811/2 The orange's worst enemy is a curious insect, the scale-bug. **1888** *Nation* 10 May 383/3 Another speaker . . . expressed much pleasure at the happy comparison of a protective tariff to the 'scale-bug'—an ineradicable pest and blight wherever it appeared. **1895** M. GRAHAM *Stories of Foot-Hills* 90, I'd stick at home closer'n a scale-bug to an orange-tree.

+**Scale carp.** A variety of the common carp (*Cyprinus carpio*) in which the body is completely scaled: (see quot. 1903 and cf. MIRROR CARP). — **1878** *Rep. Comm. Fisheries* VI. p. xlii, About half of the scale carp . . . remained in Baltimore. **1903** T. H. BEAN *Fishes N.Y.* 167-8 Three varieties are recognized, the scale, the mirror and the leather carp, based chiefly on the scaling of the body.

+**Scale(d) dove.** (See quot. 1891.) — **1884** COUES *Key to Birds* (ed. 2) 570 *Scardafella inca*. . . . Inca Dove. Scaled Dove. **1891** *Cent.* 5370/1 *Scale-dove*, . . . an American dove of the genus *Scardafella*, as *S. inca*, or *S. squamata*, having the plumage marked as if with scales. **1917** *Birds of Amer.* II. 52.

+**Scaled partridge.** A partridge (*Callipepla squamata*) found in the Southwest. — **1858** BAIRD *Birds Pacific R.R.* 646 Scaled or Blue Partridge. . . . Valley of Rio Grande of Texas. . . . Most abundant on the high broken table lands and mezquite plains. **1872** COUES *Key to Birds* 238. **1880** *Cimarron News & Press* 30 Dec. 1/5 The scaled partridge or blue quail has a short, full, soft crest.

+**Scaled quail.** =prec. — **1874** [see BLUE QUAIL]. **1917** *Birds of Amer.* II. 8/1 The Scaled Quail is a desert species.

Scalefish. {1601-} +a. (See second quot. 1891.) {1857, in New Brunswick} +b. =SCABBARD FISH 2. — **1714** *Essex Inst. Coll.* XLII. 354 Account of merchantible Cod & Scale fish on board the Johanna. **1805** *Columbian Centinel* 31 July Extra 2/3 (Ernst), 200 qnts scale fish. **1832** [see HALIBUT]. **1891** *Cent.* 5365/2 *Scabbard-fish*. . . . Also called *scalefish* and *frost-fish*. Ib. 5370/1 *Scale-fish*, . . . a dry-cured fish, as the haddock, hake, pollack, cusk, or torsk, having much less commercial value than the cod, which is distinguished as *fish*. (A fishmongers' name.)

+**Scale house.** A place where large scales, as for weighing animals, are kept. Also attrib. — **1754** *S.C. Gazette* 5 Feb. 3/1 A Scale-House Beam, Scales and Weights, compleat. **1868** *Ill. Agric. Soc. Trans.* VII. 442 In this division of the stock yards there are three scale houses. **1885** *Rep. Indian Affairs* 80 To the southeast . . . is one large cattle corral, . . . with scales and scale-house.

+**Scaler.**[1] *Lumbering.* One who determines the volume of logs. — **1877** *Michigan Rep.* XXXIV. 376 The contract . . . is held not to impower the scaler to go into the percentage. **1893** *Scribner's Mag.* June 710/1 The logs [are] rolled off the sleighs, measured by the quick-witted scaler. **1900** BRUNCKEN *N. Amer. Forests* 82 He may . . . act as 'scaler,' that is, measure the amount of logs cut by some contractor. **1903** WHITE *Blazed Trail Stories* 33 Jimmy Hall, the scaler, laid his flexible rule on the face of each log.

+**Scaler.**[2] {1611-} +(See quotation.) — **1891** *Cent.* 5370/3 *Scaler*, . . . an instrument resembling a currycomb and usually made of tin, used for removing scales from fish.

+**Scallawag.** (See SCALAWAG.)

＊**Scallop.** A variety of shellfish (*Pecten irradians*), or a related species.
1637 MORTON *New Canaan* 91 There are, Cockles, and Scallopes; and divers other sorts of Shellfishe. **1709** LAWSON *Carolina* 162 The Skellops, if well dress'd, are a pretty shell-fish. **1859** *Huntington Rec.* III. 446 No person other than a resident of the Town of Huntington shall take or catch any . . . scallops or mussels within the bounds of said Town. **1883** *Nat. Museum Bul.* No. 27, 239 *Pecten tenuicostatus* . . . is the 'Great' or 'Giant' scallop. **1911** *Rep. Fisheries 1908* 315/1 Scallop. . . . An edible bivalve found off the coasts of Long Island, Rhode Island and southern Massachusetts in paying quantities.

b. Attrib. with *dredge, fishery, net.*
1881 INGERSOLL *Oyster-Industry* 247 *Scallop Net*, the small dredge used in catching scallops. (New Bedford.) **1883** *Nat. Museum Bul.* No. 27, 268 Implements [used in the shellfish fishery include] . . . Scallop-dredge. **1886** *Amer. Naturalist* XX. 1001 It is only between Cape Cod and New Jersey that any commercial scallop-fishery exists.

Scalloper. {1881-} +One who gathers scallops. — **1881** INGERSOLL *Oyster-Industry* 247 *Scalloper*, a scallop-fisher. **1887** GOODE, etc. *Fisheries* v. II. 570 The scallopers will tell you everywhere that the more they [scallops] are raked the more abundant they become.

+**Scallyhoot,** v. W. [Origin obscure.] intr. (See quot. 1889.) — **1869** *Overland Mo.* III. 128 A mustang . . . [will] 'get up and scallyhoot' a short distance. **1889** FARMER 473/1 *Scallyhoot, To*, to be off; to skedaddle. A Texas form. **1903** 'O. HENRY' *Roads of Destiny* 96 Same old Whipperwill Creek skallyhootin' in and out of them motts of timber.

+**Scallywag.** (See SCALAWAG.)

＊**Scalp,** n. (See also SCULP n.)
1. a. A patch of skin and hair taken from the head of an enemy and preserved as a trophy by a North American Indian. {1601, of the anthropophagi}
1674 GOOKIN in *Mass. H. S. Coll.* 1 Ser. I. 162 They always carefully preserve the scalps of the head, drying the inside with hot ashes. **1748** WASHINGTON *Writings* I. 3 We were agreeably surprized at ye sight of thirty odd Indians coming from war with only one scalp. **1805** LEWIS in *L. & Clark Exped.* III. (1905) 29 [If] others get the scalps or first lay

their hand on the dead person the honor is lost to him who killed them. **1859** MARCY *Prairie Traveler* vi, He who can count the greatest number of scalps is the most highly honored by his tribe. **1888** SHERIDAN *Memoirs* I. 24 The few friendly Indian scouts . . . held a grand pow-wow and dance over the scalps of the fallen braves. **1901** WHITE *Westerners* 86 [He] took down from the tent pole the string of scalps. *a*1918 G. STUART *On Frontier* II. 73 These same Indians with scalps of women and children . . . dangling from their belts, appeared at the council.

b. An Indian scalp taken by a white man.
1689 *Plymouth Laws* 212 Eight or ten pound per head . . . [shall be given] for every fighting man of the enimy whose scalp shall be brought in. **1724** in Sheldon *Hist. Deerfield, Mass.* I. 425 What you sent me shows wt wages or Premiums on scalps. **1791** H. M. Brooks *Gleanings* IV. 105 [We] do promise to pay One Hundred Dollars for every hostile Indian's scalp, with both ears to it. **1876** BOURKE *Journal* 15 June, We only got eleven scalps. **1907** WHITE *Arizona Nights* 162 The Mexican government was offering a bounty for Apache scalps.

+**2.** The skin from the head of an animal, esp. a predatory animal for which a bounty has been offered.
1703 *Narragansett Hist. Reg.* III. 162 All persons who shall kill any Sheep or Lambs . . . shall be obliged to carry in the Skalp with Ears of the same. **1847** ROBB *Squatter Life* 80 This creatur' of a faction wants to have every man's rifle stamped with the state arms, and then made pay a license to the state before he can git a bonus for wolf-scalps. **1865** PIKE *Scout & Ranger* (1932) 113 The Comanche people wore the buffalo scalp. **1872** *Fur, Fin & Feather* (ed. 2) 140 The scalps of the animals destroyed may be presented to any justice of the peace. **1873** Gopher scalp [see BOUNTY n. 3]. **1890** *Stock Grower & Farmer* 22 Feb. 3/1 The bounty law must be fixed up so that scalps will be paid for. **1901** DUNCAN & SCOTT *Allen & Woodson Co., Kansas* 15 [The county board] offered a bounty of twenty-five cents for wolf scalps.

+**3.** In fig. use, esp. of political victories or defeats.
[**1850** *Congress. Globe* App. 21 Feb. 190/3 The hon. member said . . . he would either have our votes or our *scalps*.] **1872** *Congress. Globe* 16 Feb. 1076/3 [This hall is not,] as the honorable Senator from Mass. of today would have it, an arena for the exhibition of political scalps. **1885** *Wkly. New Mexican Rev.* 9 April 2/4 Poor Judge Trimble! The metropolitan sheets of the Central city [Albuquerque] are often after his scalp. **1890** *Congress. Rec.* 17 March 2323/1 The force was run in season and out of season for the purpose of taking Democratic scalps. **1914** GERRY *Masks of Love* 171 The Middle Western Syndicate . . . has made up its mind to have my scalp.

4. *attrib.* and *comb.* **a.** In sense 1 a with *chant, feast*, etc.
See also SCALP DANCE, SCALP HALLOO, etc.
1829 COOPER *Wish-ton-Wish* xxv, 'Tis the scalp-whoop, and the warriors are very glad. **1834** *Knickerb.* IV. 372 Talking Potato was not destined to grow up under the ascendant star as a warrior, scalp-taker, and man-killer. **1835** WHITTIER *Poetical Works* (1894) 504/2 The Norridgewock . . . Shakes his scalp-trophies to and fro Exultingly. **1846** SAGE *Scenes Rocky Mts.* xx, The murderers had the impudence to ask a scalp-feast. **1847** ROBB *Squatter Life* 105 A red skin, ef he'd come on a scalp visit, would a bin diskivered by either. **1881** *Harper's Mag.* April 659/2 William and Mary's classical course for his young braves . . . would not improve them in deer-stalking or scalp-lifting. **1884** *Century Mag.* May 138/1 But mingling with these unpleasant sounds came the rapid movement of the scalp-chant, hum, hum, hum. **1898** *McClure's Mag.* Feb. 382/2 He moved in the direction of his desire, chanting the Apache scalp-music.

b. In other senses with *blade, bounty,* etc.
1712 SEWALL *Diary* II. 351 Council would have had Subsistence and £100 Scalp-money. **1819** E. EVANS *Pedestrious Tour* 239 Malden . . . is a wretched looking place. It appears, indeed, like a scalp shop. **1829** COOPER *Wish-ton-Wish* xxviii, The Sergeant hath a right to claim the scalp-bounty, for the man that is slain. **1835** BIRD *Hawks* I. 79 He acquired a singular reputation as a bold and successful scalp-hunter. **1850** GARRARD *Wah-To-Yah* xvii. 201 'When an Injun's a "gone beaver," we take a knife like this,' pulling out his long scalpblade. Ib. xx. 247 [Kit Carson's] prowess in scalp-taking and beaver-taking is the theme of many campfires.

+**Scalp,** v. {1806-} (See also SCULP v., SCALPING.)
+**1.** *tr.* To mutilate (an enemy) by taking his scalp in the manner of an American Indian.
1693 *Mass. Province Laws* VII. 395 [He] found his Brother killed & scalped. **1696** SEWALL *Diary* I. 432 One Peters and Hoyt scalp'd at Andover this week. **1747** FRANKLIN *Plain Truth* 8 The French and their Indians . . . ravage the Frontiers of New York, and scalp the Inhabitants. **1818** FORDHAM *Narr. Travels* 179 The Kentuckians have adopted the Indian custom of scalping the dead. **1869** 'MARK TWAIN' *Innocents* 205, I have camped with Indians, . . . I have roamed with them, scalped them, had them for breakfast. **1881** *Rep. Indian Affairs* 103,I succeeded in capturing the Indian . . . that murdered and scalped a poor, innocent, old white man. **1909** [see MANITO].
fig. **1849** HAWTHORNE in J. Hawthorne *N. Hawthorne & Wife* II. 384 I shall do my best to kill and scalp him in the public prints. **1871** BAGG *At Yale* 252 The Fresh of '72 were for a time in the habit of wearing caps made of paper, . . . so that if they chanced to be 'scalped' their loss would be trifling. **1891** *Cent.* 5372/1 *Scalp*, . . . in *Amer. polit. slang*, to destroy the political influence of, or punish for insubordination to party rule.

+**2.** To level *off.*

1825 LORAIN *Pract. Husbandry* 335 The Yankee farmer first chops the fallen timber, then scalps off the grubs level with the ground. **1895** *Stand.* 1591/3.

+**3.** *colloq.* **a.** *To scalp the market,* to buy and sell grain or stocks, taking small profits or losses quickly as the market fluctuates. **b.** *tr.* To make (a certain profit) in this way.

1886 *Harper's Mag.* July 213/2 [The scalper buys] any quantity of grain that may be offered, sells it at an advance of 1/8 cent per bushel, thus scalps the market. **1897** *Boston Globe* 29 Aug. (Ernst), The broker himself would be selling the stock at 104 in New York, thereby 'scalping' one-fourth and making a handsome profit at no risk. **1902** LORIMER *Lett. Merchant* 201 Then I saw what looked like a safe chance to scalp the market for a couple of cents a bushel.

+**4.** *intr.* (See quotation.)

1889 FARMER 473/1 *Scalp, To.* . . . To drive a hard bargain. . . . To speculate in unused railway tickets.

+**Scalp dance.** A dance participated in by Indians to celebrate a victory and display the scalps taken as trophies.

1791 J. LONG *Voyages* 35 The dances among the Indians are many and various, . . . [including] the scalp dance. **1836** IRVING *Astoria* I. 228 There were war-feasts, and scalp-dances, with warlike songs and savage music. **1841** BUCKINGHAM *America* I. 101 The 'scalp dance' of the Sioux is among the most revolting. **1865** PIKE *Scout & Ranger* (1932) 95 The grand scalp dance was commenced. **1894** WISTER in *Harper's Mag.* June 128/2 A scalp-dance went on, besides lesser commotions and gatherings. **1901** *Harper's Mag.* April 741/1 Everybody rejoiced, and there were many scalp-dances.

Scalper. {1795-}

+**1.** One who takes the scalp of an enemy, in the manner of an American Indian.

1760 NILES *Indian Wars* I. 174 This reminds me of an account we had of a notable old scalper among [the Indians]. **1841** COOPER *Deerslayer* v, My gifts are not scalpers' gifts, but such as belong to my religion and colour. **1900** DRANNAN *Plains & Mts.* 60 When the story of my killing the two Indians got out, I came to be generally called 'the boy scalper.'

+**2.** (See quotation.)

1874 J. C. MCCOY *Hist. Sk. Cattle Trade* 292 So soon as an incoming train is announced nearing the stock yards, the hurrying tramps of solicitors, called 'Scalpers,' may be heard hustling toward the unloading platform. If there is a shipper on the train whose stock is not consigned, they . . . [present] the business cards of the commission firms which have the Scalpers employed.

+**3.** (See quot. 1909 and also TICKET SCALPER.)

1875 *Chicago Tribune* 8 Dec. 12/3 The new town grew up to be . . . the great commercial centre of rail-road-ticket 'scalpers.' **1885** *Wkly. New Mexican Rev.* 8 Jan. 4/6 Chicago scalpers are selling tickets to New York via the Chicago & Atlantic at $11.50. **1897** *Chicago Tribune* 15 Sept. 10/3 (*caption*), Scalpers are aided. **1909** WEBSTER 1888/3 *Scalper,* . . . a person who buys and sells railroad or other tickets at reduced prices.

+**4.** (See quot. 1900.)

1886 *Harper's Mag.* July 213/2 The 'Pit' is the scalper's delight. **1900** NELSON *A B C Wall St.* 158 A scalper is a room trader who takes 1/8 and 1/4 profits and losses, trading for his own account, and confining his attention to the smallest fluctuations. **1903** *N.Y. Ev. Post* 26 Sept., The buying was only moderately brisk and mainly confined to small scalpers.

+**Scalp halloo.** A shout of victory, celebrating the taking of a scalp or scalps. (Cf. SCALP YELL.) — **1799** J. SMITH *Acct. Captivity* 6 The scalp halloo . . . is a long yell or halloo, for every scalp or prisoner they have in possession. **1823** DODDRIDGE *Logan* II. ii, The [Indian] scalp-halloo has not been heard. Our young men can hardly make it. **1847** L. COLLINS *Kentucky* 200 When within half a mile of the fort, they [*sc.* Indians] raised the scalp halloo, and fired their guns. **1886** Z. F. SMITH *Kentucky* 400 The dependent inmates of the houses were [never] entirely exempt from the echo of . . . the scalp halloo that sent tidings of another victim to savage atrocity.

Scalping. {1739-}

+**1.** The action of taking an enemy's scalp. {1747-}

Perhaps the first two quotations should be regarded as examples of the verbal form.

1757 *Lett. to Washington* II. 62 In the Mean Time order them out in Parties with some of Your Men a Scalping. **1835** WHITTIER *Mogg Megone* (1894) 500/2 The almost infant Norridgewock . . . plucks his father's knife away, To mimic, in his frightful play, The scalping of an English foe. **1837** IRVING *Bonneville* I. 141 [He] recounted tales of . . . sackings, burnings, plunderings, scalpings. **1883** SWEET & KNOX *Through Texas* 39 A silver-handled hunting-knife . . . would be handy in case any scalping would have to be done.

fig. **1850** GALLAHER *Western Sk.-Book* 389 He regarded the cutting to pieces, or, as he sometimes expressed it, the 'scalping and tomahawking' of a beautiful hymn, which the judgment and good taste of the church has sanctioned . . . as a grievous outrage.

2. a. The selling of railroad tickets at less than the usual rates or prices. **b.** (See quot. 1900.)

1882 *Nation* 5 Oct. 276/2 A corporation like the Pennsylvania Railroad must protect itself against loss through 'scalping.' **1887** *Courier-Journal* 19 Jan. 2/4 After reorganizing the firm confined its operations chiefly to 'scalping.' **1900** NELSON *A B C Wall St.* 158 *Scalping,* following the varying changes of the market, and taking small profits or losses with the rapidity with which the market fluctuates.

3. Attrib. and comb. with *act, business, ground,* etc.

See also SCALPING KNIFE, SCALPING PARTY.

1750 in Temple & Sheldon *Hist. Northfield, Mass.* 381 Our Men will not venture out after the Enemy on any Scalping Act whatsoever. **1755** *Lett. to Washington* I. 130 We have had no Scalping work hear this Week. **1758** *Va. State P.* I. 254 We are in fine scalping ground I assure you. **1826** COOPER *Mohicans* iii, His closely shaved head, on which no other hair than the . . . scalping tuft was preserved was . . . [adorned with] a solitary eagle's plume. **1888** *Economist* 20 Oct. 6/3 There is a fair amount of scalping trade, but the public show little interest in the list. **1897** *Boston Globe* 29 Aug. (Ernst), The whole history of the rise and fall of the arbitrage or scalping business is a story of the perfection of telegraphic communication.

Scalping knife. A knife used for the scalping of an enemy. {1759-} Now hist.

1756 WASHINGTON *Writings* I. 353 Ensign Smith & 12 men of the Regiment . . . took a number of . . . scalping knives. **1791** J. LONG *Voyages* 23 He draws the scalping knife from its sheath. **1811** *Niles' Reg.* I. 311/2 Every Indian was provided with a . . . scalping knife. **1837** IRVING *Bonneville* II. 24 [They] flourished over his head their tomahawks and scalping-knives. **1861** E. COWELL *Diary* 379, 300 Cherokee Indians . . . [are] in full war costume, with tomahawks, and scalping knives. **1899** *Mo. So. Dakotan* I. 177 Soon the whole Sioux nation was on the war path with tomahawk and scalping knife. *a*1918 G. STUART *On Frontier* II. 73 Treaties were forgotten; . . . tomahawk and scalping knife sharpened.

+**Scalping party.** An expedition for the purpose of scalping. — **1756** *Doc. Hist. N.Y. State* I. 481 We are yet much troubled by scalping parties. **1757** *Lett. to Washington* II. 60 As You will have a Number of Indians at Fort London, . . . send them out in scalping Parties. **1779** *Va. State P.* I. 323 Governor Hamilton . . . [gave] instructions to Officers going out with scalping parties of Indians & whites. **1779** BLEECKER *Hist. Maria Kittle* 45 Here the savages were joined by several scalping parties. **1867** PARKMAN *Jesuits in N. Amer.* 337 Small scalping-parties infested the Huron forests.

+**Scalp lock.** A long lock of hair left unshaved by American Indians as a challenge to their enemies.

1826 COOPER *Prairie* xviii, A large and gallant scalp-lock seemed to challenge the grasp of his enemies. **1835** IRVING *Tour on Prairies* 29 Their hair was cropped close, except a bristling ridge on the top, . . . with a long scalp-lock hanging behind. **1843** HAWKS *D. Boone* 81 His hair is shaved, leaving nothing but the scalp-lock. **1870** KEIM *Sheridan's Troopers* 195 The scalp-lock, or hair growing on a diameter of two inches on the vertex of the skull, is artistically plaited. **1884** *Century Mag.* May 142/1 His scalp-lock was tied with otter fur. **1916** EASTMAN *From Deep Woods* 53 It's more than likely he'll have your scalplock before morning.

+**Scalp pole.** A pole erected by Indians for the display of scalps taken as trophies. — **1800** HAWKINS *Sk. Creek Country* 82 The two last towns raised the scalp pole. **1833** CATLIN *Indians* I. 240 [Scalps are] hung out, over the wigwams, suspended from a pole, which is called the '*scalp-pole.*' **1865** PIKE *Scout & Ranger* (1932) 95 The entire tribe, save the women, were whirling in circles around the scalp pole. **1873** COZZENS *Marvellous Country* 124 The scalp-pole was handed round by the oldest of the squaws.

+**Scalp song.** (See quotations.) — **1823** JAMES *Exped.* III. 60 Two or three other little detached squads were now seen to approach, also singing the scalp song. **1832** *Jamestown* (N.Y.) *Jrnl.* 25 April 1/3 Every evening she was brought out and compelled to dance her death dance and sing her scalp song, amid the shouts of infuriated savages. **1835** SIMMS *Yemassee* II. 78 The warriors . . . [howled] out the sanguinary promise of the scalp-song.

+**Scalp yell.** The victorious yell an Indian gives at the moment he scalps a man. (Cf. SCALP HALLOO.) — **1792** BRACKENRIDGE *Mod. Chivalry* (1937) 58 A warrior . . . separates it [*sc.* a scalp] from the head, giving, in the mean time, what is called the scalp yell. **1846** MCKENNEY *Memoirs* I. 107 They were at no loss to know that the yells were 'scalp yells'; but had not heard with sufficient accuracy to decide whether they indicated scalps be *taken* or *given.* **1913** LONDON *Valley of Moon* 465 He drew his finny prize to the bank . . . with the scalp-yell of a Comanche.

***Scaly,** *a.* In specific names of plants, birds, etc.: (see quotations). Also in attrib. and adj. compounds.

See also SCALY-BARK HICKORY.

1709 LAWSON *Carolina* 91 White, Scaly-bark Oak . . . is used . . . in building Sloops and Ships. *c*1729 CATESBY *Carolina* I. 21 There is another kind of white Oak, which in Virginia is called the Scaly white Oak. **1791** *Amer. Philos. Soc.* III. 114 *Hydrophyllum canadense* (Scaly-root). **1833** EATON *Botany* (ed. 6) 329 *Scirpus cæspitosus,* scaly rush. **1851** BARRY *Fruit Garden* 367 The Scaly Aphis or Bark Louse . . . is a dark brown scale insect, that infests the bark of the apple tree. **1872** COUES *Key to Birds* 227 *Genus Scardafella* . . . *Scaly Dove.* General coloration much as in the ground dove. **1883** *Nat. Museum Bul.* No. 27, 131 *Lepidonotus squamatus.* . . . *Scaly Worm.* Atlantic coast, New Jersey to the Arctic Ocean. Used as bait.

Scaly-bark. +The nut of the scaly-bark hickory. — **1893** *Advance* 23 March, You all buy some 'scaly-barks.' **1909** CALHOUN *Miss Minerva* 66 You can get all the . . . scalybarks and fig leaves . . . you want to, but don't you tech a single apple.

+**Scaly-bark hickory.** The shagbark hickory, *Carya ovata.* — **1781-2** JEFFERSON *Notes Va.* (1788) 37 Scaly bark hiccory. *Juglans alba cortice squamoso.* **1814** PURSH *Flora Amer.* II. 637 This useful tree is known by the name of Shell-bark Hickory, Shag-bark and Scaly-bark Hickory, on account of its bark, which is torn in loose fragments. **1832** BROWNE *Sylva* 184 The singular disposition of the bark . . . has given rise to the descriptive names of Shellbark, Shagbark and Scalybark Hickory. **1882** *Econ. Geol. Illinois* II. 3 The timber . . . consists principally of the . . . laurel oak, scaly-bark hickory, ash [etc.]. **1897** SUDWORTH *Arborescent Flora* 113 *Hicoria ovata.* . . . Shagbark (Hickory). . . . Scalybark Hickory (W.Va., S.C.).

+**Scaly-bark hickory nut. a.** =prec. **b.** The nut of the scaly-bark hickory. — **1775** ADAIR *Indians* 360 Filberts . . . are as sweet and thin-shelled, as the scaly bark hiccory-nuts. **1786** WASHINGTON *Diaries* III. 30 Spaded up some of the ground in my botanical garden for the purpose of planting the scaly bark hickory nut of Gloucester in. **1906** 'O. HENRY' *Rolling Stones* 8, I saw . . . a little flaxen-haired man with a face like a scaly-bark hickory-nut.

*Scammony.** A purgative drug obtained from *Convolvulus scammonia* or a similar plant; also, the plant. (Cf. IPECACUANHA, JALAP, MECHOACAN.) — **1672** JOSSELYN *New Eng. Rarities* 58 Briony of Peru . . . or rather Scammony; some take it for Mechoacan. **1732** *S.C. Gazette* 132/2 Lately imported, and to be sold, . . . Scammony, Opium. **1737** BRICKELL *N. Carolina* 21 [Ipecacuana] and the Scamony grow in high Sandy Ground, in many Places in Carolina. **1855** I. C. PRAY *Mem. J. G. Bennett* 199 The manufacturers of aloes, scammony, and gamboge, [have been enabled] to erect massive structures of stone, brick, and iron.

Scamp. {1782-} +The bacalao (*Mycteroperca falcata*), a southern fish so called because of its ability to steal bait without being caught; also, the closely related species *M. phenax.* — **1882** *Nat. Museum Bul.* No. 16, 538. **1884** GOODE, etc. *Fisheries* I. 413 Another fish of this genus, *Mycteroperca falcata*, is called at Pensacola by the name 'Scamp.' **1896** JORDAN & EVERMANN *Check-List Fishes* 375 *Mycteroperca falcata phenax.* . . . Scamp; Bacalao.

+**Scamper-down.** A rollicking dance. — **1847** HOWE *Hist. Coll. Ohio* 121 It is doubtful if the anniversary of American independence was ever celebrated in Cleveland by a more joyful and harmonious company, than those who danced the scamper-down, . . . forty-six years ago in the log cabin of Major Carter.

*Scant,** *a.* and *adv.*

1. *adj.* Barely amounting to (a given measure).
'Chiefly *U.S.*' (O.E.D.).
1856 KANE *Arctic Explor.* II. 70 We have just a scant two day's allowance of meat for the sick. **1893** *Chicago Tribune* 25 April 7/1 It was a close call, Bob Lytle . . . running her to a scant head.

*2.** *adv.* Barely or scarcely. {-1808}
'Now *arch.* (?*U.S.*)' (O.E.D.).
1837 HAWTHORNE *Twice-told Tales* (1879) I. 163 Scant a mile above their heads, was that bleak verge, where the hills throw off their shaggy mantle of forest trees. **1867** HOWELLS *Ital. Journeys* 12 We were rushing (at the rate of five miles scant an hour). **1880** 'MARK TWAIN' *Tramp Abroad* 156 Two foot large, on the stabboard, two and a half scant on the labboard! **1885** 'CRADDOCK' *Prophet* 23, I war married when I war sixteen,—sixteen scant.

*Scantling.**
1. A small piece of wood. {1663-}
1638 *Dedham Rec.* III. 39 Crosse cutting every 2: foote over to be alowed six pence & soe euery scantling after yt. Rate. **1713** *Va. State P.* I. 175 The Scantlines at £4.10 p: Thousand. **1773** *Md. Hist. Mag.* XV. 281 They may goe to the Island to get the scantlings for the Corn House. **1889** 'MARK TWAIN' *Conn. Yankee* 289 About two hundred yards off . . . we built a pen of scantlings. **1920** *3d Nat. Country Life Conf. Proc.* 15, I experimented with some scantlings set upright upon a hayrick.

+**2.** *collect.* Lumber or timber, esp. yellow pine, of small dimensions.
1743 *Georgia Col. Rec.* VI. 68 The Reverend Mr. Bolzius [petitioned] this Board to allow him a Quantity of Boards, Planks, and Scantling. **1786** WASHINGTON *Diaries* III. 5, [I] directed them to get me . . . scantling for Plow stocks. **1802** C. PETTIGREW *Let. to E. P.* (Univ. N.C. MS.), Shingles & Scantling are coming greatly into demand to the southward. **1831** PECK *Guide* 188 Scantling is usually estimated the same as plank or boards, one inch thick. **1903** *Amer. Architect* 8 Aug. 43 Joist and scantling of various kinds . . . have been put together in what has sometimes been called basket-framing.
attrib. **1833** SILLIMAN *Man. Sugar Cane* 45 The molasses cisterns . . . [are] covered with five or six inch scantling beams.

Scapegallows. {1819-, *dial.*} An evildoer or criminal deserving to be hanged. — **1799** WASHINGTON *Writings* XIV. 154 None but the riff-raff of the Country, and the scape-gallowes of the large cities will be to be had. **1828** ROYALL *Black Book* II. 30 The cadets . . . went sneaking along like so many scapegallows. **1839** BIRD *Robin Day* 10 My own particular associates at school were . . . in fact, a set of such imps and scapegallows as would now be considered fit for a House of Refuge. **1854** S. SMITH *Down East* 132 You are a scoundrel and a scape-gallows.

Scapegrace. {1809-} *local.* +The red-throated diver or loon, *Gavia stellata.* — **1835** AUDUBON *Ornith. Biog.* III. 24 In the neighbourhood of Boston, and along the Bay of Fundy, they are best known by the names of 'Scape-grace' and 'Cape-racer.' **1891** *Cent.* 5375/3 Scapegrace. . . . (Local, New. Eng.) **1917** *Birds of Amer.* I. 15 Red-throated Loon. . . . [Also called] Cape Racer; Scape-grace.

+**Scape pipe.** The escape pipe of a steamboat. — **1838** FLAGG *Far West* I. 51 The stern roar of the scape-pipe, gave evidence of the fearful power summoned up to overcome the flood. **1842** *S. Lit. Messenger* VIII. 65/2 The old cotter's wood trees on its [the Ohio River's] sandy margin, had never then heard the noise of the 'scape-pipe. **1874** 'MARK TWAIN' *Old Times* vii. 132 Tall columns of steam burst from the 'scape-pipes' of both steamers.

+**Scap net.** [Cf. SCOOP NET.] A net used for catching bait or fish. — **1844** LEE & FROST *Oregon* 105 At the falls . . . [the Indians take salmon] with what is sometimes called a scap-net. **1892** *Harper's Mag.* Dec. 115/2 Sou'westers, fishing-tackle, scap-nets [etc.] . . . filled up the rest of the window.

Scarcity (plant or root). The mangel-wurzel. {root of scarcity, 1787-; scarcity plant, 1803} — **1788** WASHINGTON *Diaries* III. 335 None of the Scarcity plant . . . was discoverable. *Ib.* 350, I planted 3 Rows of the Seed of the Scarcity Root. **1817-8** EATON *Botany* (1822) 203 *Beta cicla*, white beet, scarcity. **1821** *Mass. Spy* 11 April (Th.), The Red Scarcity Root . . . is now dignified by the name of mangle wurtzel. **1847** DARLINGTON *Weeds & Plants* 274 A large rooted variety of B[eta] Cicla, . . . called Mangel Wurtzel, or Scarcity Root, is sometimes cultivated for stock. **1857** GRAY *Botany* 367 *Beta vulgaris*, the Beet, with its varieties, the Scarcity and Mangel Wurtzel.

*Scare,** *v.*

+**1.** To frighten (game) out of concealment. With *out* or *up*. Also transf.
1846 *Spirit of Times* 25 April 97/1 He is also to send us the rattles of the biggest snake ever scared up in 'Old Norf Caline.' **1852** WATSON *Nights in Block-House* 169 Ad was equal to two or three common men in scarin' up and shootin' red-skins. **1866** COOKE *Surry* 399 We will try and scare up some game beyond the river. **1874** LONG *Wild-Fowl* 142 We probably won't scare out any very large batches of ducks.

+**2.** *fig.* To scare *up*, to discover, produce, or arrange (something).
1841 Letter 12 July (MS.), We had 'the best music that has been scared up' for a long time. **1857** *Quinland* II. 166, I can scare up more votes in this city than any other big chicken without feathers that walks the pave and crows on the corner. *a*1861 WINTHROP *J. Brent* 137, I allowed 't would pay to scare up a dance. **1890** *Stock Grower & Farmer* 1 Feb. 4/2 A country the like of which can not be 'scared up' in many thousands of miles travel. **1907** FREEMAN *Lavinia* 298, I'll see if Almira can't scare you up a cup of coffee.

*Scare fly.** A device for scaring away flies. {1862} — **1846** *Xenia Torch-Light* 23 April 1/5 We have seen many a 'scare crow,' but never before a *scare-fly.*

Scare head, *n.* A newspaper headline of a sensational nature. {1888-} Also *scare headline.* — **1887** *Courier-Journal* 15 Feb. 6/4 The 'scare' head which follows . . . is an evidence that the country paper tries hard to keep pace with the times and its metropolitan contemporary. **1897** STEFFENS in *Scribner's Mag.* Oct. 461/1 One of the . . . most offensive of these tricks is the use of the 'scare head.' **1904** *N.Y. Ev. Post* 27 Aug. 4 No well-conducted daily would throw 'scare headlines' upon the account of a missionary convention. **1911** HARRISON *Queed* 228 The three-column scare-head over their bitterly partisan 'story' ran thus.

+**Scare-head,** *v. tr.* To place in a prominent headline. Also *ppl. a.* — **1889** HOWELLS *Hazard of Fortunes* II. 281 He read . . . the deeply scare-headed story of Conrad's death. **1902** NORRIS *Responsibilities of Novelist* 300 The name of the leading lady or leading man is 'scare-headed' [on theater bills] so that the swiftest runner cannot fail to see. **1911** HARRISON *Queed* 219 The *Chronicle* . . . scareheaded a jaundiced account of the affair.

Scare headline. (See SCARE HEAD *n.*)

+**Scaresome.** (See quot. 1859.) *colloq.* — **1845** JUDD *Margaret* 275 It's cruel skeersome about there. **1859** BARTLETT 383 Scaresome or *Skeersome*, frightful.

*Scarf,** *n.*[1] A strip of silk or other material, worn over the head or shoulders or around the neck. — **1676** *N.H. Probate Rec.* I. 175, I give Scarfs to all my Barers to the grave. **1708** SEWALL *Diary* II. 247 Gave Mr. Walter a Lutestring scarf. **1844** *Lexington Observer* 2 Oct. 1/4 In our stock may be found an excellent assortment of . . . shawls, mantillas, and scarfs. **1904** STRATTON-PORTER *Freckles* 37 She tucked [in] the coarse scarf she had knit for him.

+**Scarf,** *n.*[2] [Origin obscure.] A line or groove cut in the body of a whale. — **1851** MELVILLE *Moby-Dick* 331 The blubber in one strip uniformly peels off along the line called the 'scarf.' **1874** C. M. SCAMMON *Marine Mammals* 63 A scarf is cut along the body and through the blubber.

+**Scarf,** *n.*[3] [?Variant of *kerf.*] A V-shaped or diagonal cut through a limb or tree. — **1863** *Maine Agric. Rep.* VIII. 36 The bark of the stock opposite the scarf with a thin sliver of wood is cut down. **1887** BILLINGS *Hardtack* 180 When an army first went into camp trees were cut with the scarf two or three feet above the ground.

+**Scarf,** *v.* [f. SCARF *n.*[2]] *intr.* To cut off the blubber of a whale. — **1851** MELVILLE *Moby-Dick* 332 And thus the work proceeds; . . . the mates scarfing, . . . and all hands swearing occasionally. **1887** GOODE, etc. *Fisheries* v. II. 278/1 The second mate 'scarfs,' or cuts the body blubber.

+Scarily, *adv.* [f. SCARY *a.*] In a frightened manner. — **1845** SIMMS *Wigwam & Cabin* I Ser. 107 My heart . . . [was] jumping up and down as scarily as a rabbit's. **1880** HOWELLS *Undiscovered Country* 133 The light . . . was held scarily aloft above the head of an elderly woman who surveyed them with an excited face.

∗ Scarlet, *a.*

1. In the specific names of plants and trees.

There are other examples in books on botany.

a. As simple modifier.

See also SCARLET MAPLE, SCARLET OAK, etc.

1709 LAWSON *Carolina* 95 The Scarlet Trumpet-Vine bears a glorious red Flower. **1785** Scarlet honey suckle [see FRENCH HONEYSUCKLE]. **1817-8** EATON *Botany* (1822) 342 *Lychnis chalcedonica*, scarlet lichnis. **1846** THORPE *Myst. Backwoods* 50 The scarlet creeper and fragrant jasmine . . . shed upon . . . Rousseau a shower of fragrance. **1850** *New Eng. Farmer* II. 126 Scarlet Columbine is a well-known May flower. **1860** CURTIS *Woody Plants N.C.* 82 Scarlet haw (*Cratægus coccinea*). . . . The fruit is bright red. **1868** *Rep. Comm. Agric.* 1867 306 The common scarlet Azalea (*Azalea calendulacea*,) hybridized by the pollen of the yellow Azalea (*Azalea Pontica*,) produced flowers finely variegated with the colors of the parent plants. **1898** A. M. DAVIDSON *Calif. Plants* 142 The other flower . . . has several common names, painted cup, scarlet painter's brush, Indian plume, etc. **1901** MOHR *Plant Life Ala.* 115 *Clinopodium coccineum*, the scarlet basil, is a low undershrub with dazzling flame-colored flowers.

b. In combination with participial adjectives.

See also SCARLET-FLOWERING *a.*

1795 WINTERBOTHAM *Hist. View* III. 391 Scarlet-flowered horse chesnut. **1813** MUHLENBERG *Cat. Plants* 48 *Cratægus coccinea*, Scarlet-fruited hawthorn. **1892** APGAR *Trees Northern U.S.* 104 *Cratægus coccinea*, Scarlet-fruited thorn. . . . Fruit scarlet, round or pear-shaped.

2. In names of animals.

See also SCARLET IBIS, SPARROW, TANAGER.

1672 JOSSELYN *New Eng. Rarities* 37 The Scarlet Muscle . . . [is a] kind of Muscle which hath a purple Vein, which . . . yieldeth a perfect . . . scarlet juice. **1842** *Nat. Hist. N.Y., Zoology* III. 81 The Scarlet Salamander, *Salamandra coccinea*, . . . appears to dwell almost constantly on land. **1842** HOLBROOK *N. Amer. Herpetology* III. 127 *Rhenostoma coccinea*. . . . The Scarlet Snake. *Ib.*, The 'Couleuvre écarlate' (Scarlet Snake) of Bosc is quite another animal, doubtless the *Calamaria elapsoidea*. **1847** LANMAN *Summer in Wilderness* 60 Here an eagle and hawk, a partridge and scarlet-bird. **1917** *Birds of Amer.* I. 171/1 The great Scarlet Flamingo is a rare bird in the United States.

Scarlet-flowering, *a.* In the names of trees and shrubs. — [**1731** P. MILLER *Gardeners Dict.* s.v. *Pavia*, The Scarlet Flowering Horse-Chesnut . . . is a Native of America.] **1775** BURNABY *Travels* 12 [The woods] are likewise adorned and beautified with . . . scarlet-flowering chesnuts. **1785** MARSHALL *Amer. Grove* 3 The Scarlet flowering Maple . . . grows to a pretty large size in a rich soil. *Ib.* 129 *Rhus glabrum carolinense*. Carolinian Scarlet-flowering Sumach.

+Scarlet ibis. An ibis (*Guara rubra*) of tropical America. — [**1785** PENNANT *Arctic Zool.* II. 458.] **1813** WILSON *Ornithology* VIII. 41 Scarlet Ibis . . . is found in the most southern parts of Carolina. **1839** AUDUBON *Ornith. Biog.* V. 62, I have found the Scarlet Ibis less numerous than even the Glossy Ibis. **1883** *Nat. Museum Bul.* No. 27, 144 Scarlet Ibis. . . . Accidental (?) in Louisiana and Southern Texas.

+Scarlet maple. The red maple. {1833} — **1813** MUHLENBERG *Cat. Plants* 95 Scarlet, white, red, or soft maple. **1850** S. F. COOPER *Rural Hours* 64 The sugar, the scarlet, and the silver maples, are assuredly very fine trees. **1879** [see NORWAY MAPLE].

∗Scarlet oak. A N.A. oak (*Quercus coccinea*) with leaves which turn scarlet in the fall. — [**1731** P. MILLER *Gardeners Dict.* s.v. *Quercus*, The Virginian Scarlet Oak.] **1775** *Amer. Husbandry* I. 376 Scarlet oak . . . [is used] in ship building. **1832** BROWNE *Sylva* 266 The Scarlet Oak is first seen in the vicinity of Boston. **1850** *New Eng. Farmer* II. 142 The Scarlet Oak, cultivated upon a lawn, and permitted to stand alone, is a very ornamental tree. **1884** 'CRADDOCK' *Tenn. Mts.* 60 The scarlet-oak emblazoned the mountain side.

Scarlet runner (bean). A high-climbing bean (*Phaseolus coccineus*) with bright red flowers. {1824-} — **1806** B. McMAHON *Amer. Gard. Cal.* 580 Bean, The Dwarf Kidney. . . . Running Kinds. . . . Scarlet Runners. **1871** *Harper's Mag.* Aug. 385/1 He stopped by the window and peeped through the scarlet runners. **1894** *Ib.* July 296/2 Scarlet-runners . . . bloomed in sweet profusion. **1899** JEWETT *Queen's Twin* 107 Scarlet-runner beans made haste to twine themselves to a line of strings for shade.

Scarlet sparrow. The scarlet tanager. — [**1764** G. EDWARDS *Gleanings Nat. Hist.* III. 278/1 The Scarlet Sparrow . . . [came] from Mr. Brook, Surgeon, of Maryland in North America.] **1917** *Birds of Amer.* III. 79 Scarlet Tanager. *Piranga erythromelas*. . . . [Also called] Pocket-bird; Scarlet Sparrow.

+Scarlet tanager. The redbird, *Piranga erythromelas*. (Cf. SCARLET SPARROW.) — **1810** WILSON *Ornithology* II. 42 [The] Scarlet Tanager . . . is one of the gaudy foreigners . . . that regularly visit us from the torrid regions of the south. **1839** PEABODY *Mass. Birds* 319 The Scarlet Tanager . . . [is] retired in his habits. **1880** *Harper's Mag.* June 79 Scarlet

tanagers gleam like living bits of fire. **1912** N. WOODROW *Sally Salt* 11 There's a scarlet tanager flying through the blue.

∗Scary, *a.* Timorous, easily frightened. {1842-} — **1800** WEEMS *Letters* II. 160, I have always been very scary about our monies. **1816** U. BROWN *Journal* I. 358, [I] felt a little scary, when about half way the wind blew fresh down the River. **1884** JEWETT *Country Doctor* 6, I don't feel scary at being left sole alone. **1910** J. HART *Vigilante Girl* 30 Now that our scarey friends have gone, let's sit down and have a chat.

+Scat, *n.*¹ Short for *scattered vote.* — **1808** *Mass. Spy* 9 Nov. (Th.), Democratic 'Scats,' 26.

+Scat, *n.*² In phrases: *Quicker than* (or *like*) *scat*, in a great hurry. *colloq.* — **1833** J. S. JONES *Green Mt. Boy* I. iii, I'll have the square discharge him quicker than s'cat. **1889** 'MARK TWAIN' *Conn. Yankee* 480 But the scheme fell through like scat. **1897** ROBINSON *Uncle Lisha's Outing* 86 One o' the boys . . . hed his fork into 't . . . quicker 'n scat. **1909** STRATTON-PORTER *Girl of Limberlost* 325 Quicker 'an scat there was her ma a-whirling.

+Scat, *v.* [? A hiss plus *cat*.] **1.** *intr.* To go off hastily. Usually in imperative. **2.** *tr.* To drive off by saying *scat*. — (1) **1870** A. D. WHITNEY *We Girls* 218 'Scat!' cried Stephen. And Ruth scatted. **1908** 'O. HENRY' *Options* 199 Now, scat, both of you! (2) **1876** *Wide Awake* 307/2 Mamma jumped and scatted her.

+Scat my cats. An exclamation of surprise or impatience. *colloq.* — **1898** WESTCOTT *D. Harum* xlviii, 'Scat my Cats!' he cried.

∗Scattered, *a.* +Of votes: Tallied from scratched tickets or from tickets the count of which has been delayed until after most of the other votes have been counted. — **1808** *Mass. Spy* 4 May (Th.), The Federal Senators are certainly chosen, unless scattered votes are uncommonly numerous. **1841** G. COMBE *Notes U.S.* I. 97 If an individual voter is not satisfied with the 'ticket' of his party, he may erase any names from it he pleases, and add others. . . . These votes are regarded as thrown away, and technically are said to be 'scattered.'

+Scatter gun. A shotgun. *colloq.* — **1836** H. R. HOWARD *Hist. V. A. Stewart* 140, I have a choice scatter-gun. **1844** GREGG *Commerce of Prairies* I. 48 The frontier hunter sticks to his rifle, as nothing could induce him to carry what he terms in derision 'the scatter-gun.' **1895** *Outing* XXVI. 66/1, I reckon yer pretty handy with that scatter-gun. **1923** J. H. COOK *On Old Frontier* 4 Pidgeon shooting was good . . . for anyone who owned or could borrow a 'scatter-gun.'

∗Scattering, *a.*

1. a. Of houses or settlements: Lying spread out over a considerable area; sporadic or straggling. {c1710} **b.** Of settlers: Living far from other inhabitants; widely separated.

'Now chiefly *U.S.*' (*O.E.D.*).

1671 *Doc. Col. Hist. N.Y.* XII. 485 All ye ffrontier Scattering Plantacons [must] be ordered immediately to thrash out or remove all their Corne. **1775** *R.I. Hist. Soc. Coll.* VI. 4 Here are few scattering inhabitants. **1809** CUMING *Western Tour* 60 The country afforded no variety, being still, hill, dale, woods, and scattering farms. **1834** *Visit to Texas* 15 A few scattering settlers are found in that tract of country. **1848** BENNETT *Mike Fink* 11/1 Front street . . . could then boast but a few scattering houses. **1904** *McClure's Mag.* March 557/1 In them days . . . ranches were scatterin'.

2. Of trees, snow, etc.: Dispersed; found at infrequent intervals; sporadic. {1697-}

1666 *S.C. Hist. Soc. Coll.* V. 63, [I found] on the Outside of the woods some single scattring Pine trees. **1713** HEMPSTEAD *Diary* 19 Some Scatering Snow. It Snowed at night also a little. **1805** LEWIS in *L. & Clark Exped.* II. (1904) 94 [The course was] to the upper part of some scattering timber at the entrance of a small creek. *c*1835 CATLIN *Indians* II. 61 We could just discern amongst the scattering shrubbery . . . , the tops of the Camanchee wigwams. **1874** RAYMOND *6th Rep. Mines* 312 A few men collected some scattering fire-brick and built a reverberatory furnace. **1891** *Cent.* 5383/2 *Scattering*, . . . separated from the school, as fish: hence, sparse; scarce. (New Eng.) **1906** LYNDE *Quickening* 60 The forest . . . reached a long finger of scattering oaks down to the opposite side of the creek.

+3. Of votes: Cast for candidates receiving a very small poll, as for a write-in candidate on a scratched ticket.

1766 J. ADAMS *Diary* Works II. 185 There were six different hats with votes for as many different persons, besides a considerable number of scattering votes. **1789** *Mass. Centinel* 11 April 3/2 The whole number of votes last given in, is 3328, of which the Hon. Mr. Sedgwick has 1564. . . . Scattering votes, 64. **1832** S. SMITH *Life J. Downing* 165, I believe the votes [for me] are put in the papers along with the scattering votes. **1863** *Rio Abajo Press* 18 Aug. 4/3 All votes not given for our candidates will be 'scattering.' **1888** *Amer. Almanac* 225 The 2,143 'Scattering' votes for President in 1884 were cast for St. John, Prohibition.

Scaup duck. One of various sea ducks, esp. the broad-bill (*Nyroca marila*) {a1672-} +and the smaller American species, *N. affinis*.

[**1785** PENNANT *Arctic Zool.* II. 565 Scaup Duck. . . . Inhabits America, as high as Hudson's Bay.] **1813** WILSON *Ornithology* VIII. 84 Scaup Duck. . . . This Duck is better known among us by the name of the Blue Bill. **1835** AUDUBON *Ornith. Biog.* III. 226 The opinion, derived from Wilson's account of the Scaup Duck, that it is met with only along our sea coasts, in bays, or in the mouths of rivers, as far as the tide extends, is incorrect. **1874** LONG *Wild-Fowl* 277 The female of the ring-necked and scaup ducks . . . are alike in general color. **1889** [see FLOCKING FOWL]. **1917** *Birds of Amer.* I. 135 Scaup Duck. . . . [Also called] American Scaup Duck; Greater Scaup Duck; Troop-fowl.

*   **Scavenger.** One who collects refuse; a street-cleaner. — **1668** *Boston Rec.* 39 Att a publique mettinge . . . were chosen . . . Scauengers. **1797** *Phila. Ordinances* (1812) 145 House dirt . . . [is] to be raked out of the gutters, and water courses . . . that the scavengers may remove the same. **1883** *Century Mag.* July 428/2 The city scavengers . . . went knocking from house to house. **1924** MAXEY *Outline Municipal Govt.* 225 In a number of cities garbage is collected neither by the city nor by contractors, but by licensed scavengers.

   Scavenger beetle. Any beetle which feeds on decaying matter. {1854} — **1854** EMMONS *Agric. N.Y.* V. 263 (*index*), Scavenger beetles, 57. [*Ib.* 57 The *Necrophaga* perform the part of scavengers in destroying and burying carrion.] **1862** *Rep. Comm. Patents 1861: Agric.* 594 Several large families . . . are commonly called 'scavenger,' or 'carrion beetles,' . . . because they are chiefly found in decomposed animal matter.

*   **Scene.** *pl.* Slides, hangings, or other apparatus used on a stage to give the appearance of reality to the action of the play. — **1739** *N.Y. Wkly. Journal* Feb., No Body [is] to be admitted . . . behind the Scene's. **1751** *N.Y. Post-Boy* 22 April, Mr. Murray . . . [has] agreed to give him a night, clear of all Expences, for his Half of the cloaths, Scenes, &c. belonging to the Play-House. **1812** *Niles' Reg.* I. 340/2 Thirty-five scenes were at the moment hanging exclusive of the flies. **1851** NORTHALL *Curtain* 17 [He] found the stage, with the curtains, wings, scenes, and borders all in flames.

   Scene-painter. One who paints scenery for a theater stage. {1749-} — **1832** DUNLAP *Hist. Amer. Theatre* 54 Major Andre and Captain Delancy were the scene painters here also. **1833** *Century Mag.* Oct. 954/1 The scene-painters . . . are required to consider . . . the needs of the action. **1863** MASSETT *Drifting About* 46 This part, I may mention, was very effectively rendered by the celebrated scenepainter, Mr. Henry Isherwood.

   Scenery. {1748-} The slides, painted hangings, etc., of a theater stage. {1774-} — **1773** in Singleton *Social N.Y.* 285 The scenery, decorations [etc.] . . . are allowed by the most critical judges of theatrical splendour to be more magnificent than could be expected. **1839** *Chicago American* 19 Aug., Mr. Jefferson . . . is now in Chicago preparing *entire new scenery*, and improving the theater building. **1911** C. POLLOCK *Footlights* 246 There is no scenery, no furniture, no 'properties.'

   Sceneshifter. One who shifts scenery during the performance of a play, opera, etc. {1752-} — **1817** [see CANDLE SNUFFER 1]. **1851** NORTHALL *Curtain* 174 The scene-shifter seems also affected with the sulks. **1888** *Scribner's Mag.* Oct. 444/2 Meanwhile the 'grips,' as the scene-shifters are called, have hold of the side scenes ready to shove them on.

   Scenic artist. A scene-painter. — **1846** *Chicago Jrnl.* 23 Dec. 3/2. Scenic artist, L. G. Hager, Stage carpenter, Geo. Wetsell. **1856** *Porter's Spirit of Times* 20 Dec. 262/3 Laura Keene's Theatre. . . . Scenic artists, Messrs. Almy and Hawthorne. **1908** *J. Cohn's Off. Theatrical Guide* XIII. 58 Academy of Music. . . . Frank Platzer, scenic artist.

+   **Schap(p)s.** Variant of CHAPS. (See also SHAPS.) — **1844** W. SHEPHERD *Prairie Exper.* 41 The cow-boys, with their *schaps*, i.e. leather-leggings and flopping wide-brimmed hats, are trooping off. **1896** *Christian Educ.* Jan. 7/1 A cowboy with spurs, schapps, sombrero and lariat, was a new sight to Miss Selby.

*   **Schedule,** *n.*
'*Scene, Scepter, Schedule,* . . . you must read as if they were wrote, *Sene, Septer, Sedul*' (**1727** W. Mather *Young Man's Companion* 22). 'In England the universal pronunciation at present seems to be with (ʃ); in the U.S., the authority of Webster has secured general currency for (sk)' (*O.E.D.*).

+**1.** 'In the State of Rhode Island, the printed "Acts and Resolves" of the General Assembly' (B '59).
   1836 (*title on binding*), Schedules of the General Assembly [of R.I.].

+**2.** A plan of procedure for moving from one operation or action to another, with the time indicated when each operation is to be begun and completed; the running time, or the time of arrival and departure, of a train.
   1866 C. H. SMITH *Bill Arp* 21 We tried our durndest to comply with your schedule. **1873** HALE *In His Name* vi, Halting was not in John of Lugio's schedule for that afternoon. **1887** GEORGE *40 Yrs. on Rail* 86 [We] ran on a schedule of our own throughout the journey. **1904** *Newark Ev. News* 13 June 6 It is on the schedule for the new Equal Taxation Commission to organize to-morrow. **1911** PERSONS, etc. *Mass. Labor Laws* 109 Most important of these enforced concessions was the temporary reduction to a ten-hour [factory] schedule at Fall River.

+**b.** A program.
   1904 *N.Y. Ev.Post* 12 May 1 Never has there been such a large schedule of speakers at a meeting of the Rapid Transit Commission as this afternoon.

+**3.** A printed or written outline of a procedure planned according to time; a time-table.
   1864 NORTON *Army Lett.* 282 That is all that ever caused the name to be printed on anything but time-tables and schedules of a one-horse railroad. **1883** WARNER *Roundabout Journey* 2 We travel fast and we reach

places at the time named on the schedule. **1891** *Scribner's Mag.* Sept. 270/1 A steamer to-day leaves her wharf at the moment of time set forth in her schedule. **1904** LOUNSBURY *Stand. of Pronunciation in Eng.* 203 Their names appear in guide-books and train schedules.

attrib. **1903** WISTER *Philos.* 4 10 A delayed train makes the last few miles high above schedule speed.

+**4.** In phrases.
Ahead of schedule, ahead of the time called for in a schedule; *according to schedule*, according to the time planned; *on schedule*, on time as indicated in a schedule.
   1885 *Century Mag.* Jan. 397/2 The conductor of the Bleecker street car . . . must have got ahead of his schedule. **1906** 'O. HENRY' *Rolling Stones* 23 Tuesday, the day set for the revolution, came around according to schedule. **1909** *Springfield W. Repub.* 19 Aug. 10 The train was running exactly on schedule when the party left it.

   Schedule, *v.* {1862-} +**1.** *intr.* To file a list or schedule: (see quotation). +**2.** *tr.* To plan, arrange, or announce *for* a definite time. Also *ppl. a.* — (1) **1855** *Chicago W. Times* 20 Sept. 1/3 Sherman, late editor of the defunct Beardstown *Gazette*, last week scheduled—i.e., took the benefit of the insolvent law of this state, and turned out his property, under oath, to his creditors. The schedule of his assets was as follows. (2) **1898** PAGE *Red Rock* 478 The trial would come off as already scheduled. **1904** *N.Y. Ev.Post* 30 Sept. 1 The archbishop is scheduled to speak this afternoon at the Academy of Music. **1907** M. C. HARRIS *Tents of Wickedness* 188 Dinner . . . was not eaten till two hours after its scheduled time.

+**Schedule return.** *spec.* A report including, or consisting of, a list of students attending certain schools. — **1837** PECK *Gaz. Illinois* 68 In each county a school commissioner is appointed, to . . . receive schedule returns of the number of scholars that attend each school.

+**Schedule time.** The time called for in a schedule. — **1881** HAYES *New Colorado* 94 [The engineer] rounded the curves in about half of schedule time. **1897** 'MARK TWAIN' *Following Equator* 290 This train . . . goes twenty and one-half miles an hour, schedule time. **1908** 'O. HENRY' *Options* 204 The San Augustine Rifles got back home on schedule time.

*   **Scheme.** +(See quot. 1856.) — **1853** Root & Lombard *Songs Yale* 22 His bleared eyes gleam o'er that horrid scheme! **1856** HALL *College Words* (ed. 2) 400 The printed papers which are given to the students at Yale College at the Biennial Examination, and which contain the questions that are to be answered, are denominated *schemes*.

‖**Schemy,** *a.* Artful; scheming. *colloq.* — **1891** 'THANET' *Otto the Knight* 250 He was schemy, too.

+**Schenectady barge.** A barge built in Schenectady, New York: (see quot. 1836). *Obs.* — **1805** PIKE *Sources Miss.* I. App. 3, I have therefore hired two Schenectady barges. **1836** IRVING *Astoria* I. 144 Another [boat] was of a larger size, . . . and known by the generic name of the Schenectady barge.

+**Schepel.** Also **schipple.** [Du.] A measure of about three-fourths of a bushel. *Obs.* — **1658** *Hempstead Rec.* I. 43 Our tithe may be paid unto the Governor according to our agreement, being one hundred schepells of wheate. **1677** *New Castle Court Rec.* 149, 20 schipple of wheat to bee delivered att New Yorke. **1702** in Munsell *Ann. Albany* IV. 153 S. V. Cortland . . . [has] said summe in hand, L2: 18: 6, and 4 schepels somer Tarwe, or wheat.

   Schepen. [Du.] +In the Dutch settlements of New York, a municipal officer with duties similar to those of an alderman. Now hist. {c1481-1756, in the Netherlands} — **1664** in *N.Y. State Lib. Hist. Bul.* No. 2, 147 Jacob Kip, and Jaques Cousseau, are also Chosen to the Office of Schepens, in this City of New Yorke. **1673** *Doc.Col.Hist.N.Y.* XIII. 476 Ye Schepens or Magistrates of respective Townes . . . [shall] Governe as well their Inhabitants as Strangers. **1809** J. ADAMS in *Scribner's Mo.* XI. 576/2 There is not a Burgomaster, Pensionary, Counsellor, or Schepen—and there are near five thousand of them all—who does not understand this subject better than Hamilton did. **1896** EARLE *Colonial Days N.Y.* 240 A judgment was recorded from each burgomaster and *schepen* as to what punishment would be proper.

   Schiedam (schnapps). Gin of the type made in Schiedam, Holland. {1821-} (Cf. HOLLAND GIN.) — **1834** NOTT *Novellettes* I. 12 He made Cognac brandy, Jamaica rum, Scheidam, and eke Cologne gin. **1848** BRYANT *California* xxvii. 338 Our host brought out some scheidam and *aguardiénte*. **1865** *Atlantic Mo.* April 451/2 The Devil, with his . . . Scheidam schnapps, has kept a pretty even pace with [reform]. **1890** *Century Mag.* Nov. 51 There were . . . booths for gin, cider, and Schiedam schnapps.

*   **Schismatic.** *spec.* +A member of one of the seceding religious groups of about 1800, distinguished from the New Lights (sense 1 b), for instance, by a difference of conviction on the part to be played by faith and blind impulse. — **1807** McNEMAR *Ky. Revival* 42 On this occasion, as far as the way was opened for a separation the subjects of the revival, who were sincere in their profession, generally came forth, and united with the seceding body, which were distinguished by the name of *Schismatics*. **1834** *Biblical Repertory* VI. 339 There sprang up that fruitful crop of heresy and schism, that afterwards assumed the shape, as well as the name, of *New Lights, Schismatics, Marshallites, Unitarians,* and *Shakers*.

   Schist. *Geol.* Any metamorphic crystalline rock having component minerals divided into parallel planes. {1795-} — **1781-2** JEFFERSON *Notes Va.* (1788) 28 Near the eastern foot of the North mountain are immense bodies of *Schist*, containing impressions of shells in a variety of forms. a**1817** DWIGHT *Travels* II. 418 The rocks on the Eastern side of these mountains are chiefly a shining schist. **1895** *Geol. Soc. Amer. Bul.* VI. 21 March 254 Schists . . . invariably accompany the limestone.

Schnapps. A strong Holland gin or other spirituous liquor. (See also SCHIEDAM (SCHNAPPS).) {1818-} — **1838** COOPER *Homeward B.* xx, Mr. Monday has tried the virtue of the schnapps on them. **1849** G. G. FOSTER *N.Y. in Slices* 85 The other . . . [answered] with the most limpid assurance to the various demands for gin, Monongahela, or schnapps. **1891** BUNNER *Zadoc Pine* 149 Mr. Onderdonck took his portion of post-prandial Schnapps.

∗Scholar.

∗1. One who is taught in a school; a pupil.

Except in rural communities this usage seems to be obsolescent.

1643 *New Eng. First Fruits* (1896) 3 If any Schollar shall be found to transgresse any of the Lawes of God, or the Schoole, . . . he shall be lyable . . . to correction. **1674** SEWALL *Diary* I. 4 He should be . . . whipped before all the Scholars. **1743** FRANKLIN *Poor Richard's Almanac 1744* I I think such Language between old Men and Scholars unbecoming. **1831** SLOCOMB *Amer. Calculator* 3 The questions . . . are such as I have long been . . . asking my scholars. **1879** *Cimarron News & Press* 20 Nov. 3/1 The public school in Cimarron opened on Monday last with a large attendance of scholars. **1904** DARROW *Farmington* 56 If we scholars did not grow up to be exemplary men and women, it surely was not the fault of our teachers or our parents.

+2. *Scholar of the house*, at Harvard and Yale colleges, a student granted a scholarship and charged with the duty of taking account of the buildings and fences. *Obs.*

1667 *Harvard Rec.* I. 49 The schollars of the house shall take a strict account of all the Buildings, Chambers, studyes, & fences. **1774** *Yale Laws* 22 The Scholar of the House . . . shall be obliged to view any damage done in any Chamber. **1843** BELDEN *Sk. Yale College* 86 Scholars on this foundation are to be called 'scholars of the house.' **1876** *Scribner's Mo.* April 760/1 We cannot pause to describe those shadowy functionaries [at Yale], the Beadle and the Scholar of the House.

3. *Rhodes scholar*, a college or university male student who has received one of the scholarships established by Cecil Rhodes (1853-1902), and tenable at the University of Oxford, England.

1904 *Dial.* 16 Jan. 36/2 Within a few weeks the process of selecting Rhodes scholars . . . will be in active operation. **1908** *Nation* 5 Nov. 436/2 Students with adequate means have preferred to go to Germany at their own expense, rather than to go to Oxford as Rhodes scholars.

∗Scholarship. A grant of money or tuition given a student to enable him to pursue his studies. — **1654** *Harvard Rec.* I. 209 The Country allows the Colledge annually 15 lbs. for 4 Schollarships. **1823** J. M. DUNCAN *Travels U.S.* I. 175 These exhibitions, or scholarships as they are termed, have each a capital of about £560 sterling. **1844** *Lexington Observer* 2 Oct. 2/5 Two Scholarships to Let for the ensuing Session in Morrison College. **1886** H. D. BROWN *Two College Girls* 172 Lots of the fellows at Harvard have scholarships. **1902** *Living Age* 17 May 446 Where . . . are the great political advantages that it has been said will flow from the Rhodes scholarships?

+Schoodic. *attrib.* Designating the landlocked salmon or trout of the Schoodic Lakes of Maine. — **1872** *N.Y. Agric. Soc. Trans. 1871* 352 An eleven pound Schoodic salmon is the largest on record. **1884** GOODE, etc. *Fisheries* I. 470 The 'Land-locked' or 'Fresh-water' Salmon, known also . . . in different parts of Maine as 'Schoodic Trout,' 'Sebago Trout,' or 'Dwarf Salmon,' probably never visit salt water.

∗School.[1]

See also BOARDING, COMMON, DISTRICT, FREE, etc., SCHOOL.

∗1. A place or institution for instruction in any branch of knowledge; a schoolhouse; +a college or university.

Unless otherwise implied, *school* usually refers to a school of the pre-college rank.

1644 *Harvard Rec.* I. 4 The Chamber over ye Schoole. **1656** *Rowley Rec.* 95 If he keep the scolle seuen years this [loan of] fiue pound is to bee void. **1717** *Mass. Col. Soc. Publ.* VI. 183 The Lower house . . . [shall] declare ye place they desire ye sd School to be Setled in. **1767** FITHIAN *Journal* I. 1 A letter to my Father, begging him to put me to School. **1791** in Jillson *Dark & Bl. Ground* 107 A small single room cabin of one story . . . is built as a school. **1836** *Diplom. Corr. Texas* I. (1908) 134 Liberal allowances for Schools, colleges, internal improvements etc. ought to be made. **1865** *Wkly. New Mexican* 10 Feb. 1/3 There are no schools, no means of education, except what is put forth by Bishop Lamy by his private exertions. **1904** *Delineator* Oct. 657 College pillows are of blue denim, with 'Yale' embroidered in white; of crimson, with 'Harvard' in white letters; . . . and similarly with the names and colors of other schools.

b. *At school*, in attendance at a school. {1846}

1647 ELIOT *Day-Breaking* I His son . . . is now at school in Dedham. **1898** WESTCOTT *D. Harum* 388 She was summoned to Andover by the serious illness of her only son, who is at school there.

c. *To keep school*, =next. {1828-30-}

1658 *Dedham Rec.* IV. 2 Michall Metcalfe . . . shall keepe Schoole vntill this daye month. **1746** *Holyoke Diaries* 8 Son Edward . . . went to keep school.

∗d. *To teach school*, to teach in a school. {-1740}

'Now *dial.* and *U.S.*' (O.E.D.).

1655 *East-Hampton Rec.* I. 83 The house where the scoolmaster was a teachinge scoole. **1677** SEWALL *Diary* I. 35 His Son . . . might obtain Mr. Sanfords House and authority therein to teach School. **1848** *Knickerb.* XVIII. 68 He . . . taught Stokeville school. **1860** M. J. HOLMES *Cousin Maude* 145 James De Vere had once taught school. **1903** WIGGIN *Rebecca* 81 They suspicioned I was tryin' for a place to teach school.

2. A division of study or administration in a university. {1873-}

1835 J. MARTIN *Descr. Virginia* 82 The different branches of science and literature . . . taught [at the U. of Va.] are styled *schools*. **1851** HALL *College Words* 263 In some American colleges, the different departments for teaching law, medicine, divinity, &c. are denominated *schools*. **1871** BAGG *At Yale* 32 Connected with the college are four professional 'schools' or 'departments,' of which . . . the oldest is the Theological. **1891** *Univ. Chicago Official Bul.* No. 1, 8 The officers . . . who give instruction . . . shall constitute the Faculty of that Academy, College or School.

3. *attrib.* and *comb.* **a.** Designating persons connected with schools.

See also SCHOOL BOARD, SCHOOL COMMISSIONER, etc.

1775 *Essex Inst. Coll.* XIII. 185 My own School Runners perform'd the whole [of the house cleaning]. **1782** in S. E. Baldwin *Simeon Baldwin* 108 Mrs. Caldwell the Albany Schoolmadam was with us. **1842** KIRKLAND *Forest Life* I. 215 [Education] will make him none the better . . . school-inspector. **1845** W. T. THOMPSON *Chron. Pineville* 44 Mr. Boss Ankles . . . [based] his claim to consideration on the ground of his being a 'schoolkeeper' and a professor of music. **1846** FARNHAM *Prairie Land* 22 Either [the Banner or her peerless captain] were sufficient to have put to flight the sentimentality of a legion of school-misses. **1889** *Our Little Ones* Aug. 312, I think the school visitor may be here to-morrow. **1911** PERSONS, etc. *Mass. Labor Laws* 181 The child must also present a certificate from a school physician. **1923** HERRICK *Lilla* 117 The larger cities had begun to pay high salaries for their school superintendents.

b. Designating things owned by students for use in school.

See also SCHOOLBOOK.

1796 WEEMS *Letters* II. 35 Subjoind. is his list of such books as he thinks will sell well, . . . viz. Small school Bibles. **1856** GOODRICH *G. Go-ahead* 14 If the reader will consult any school map, he will get a clear idea of the various countries in Farther India. **1863** A. D. WHITNEY *F. Gartney* vi, You might mend up one of your old school dresses for her. **1874** *Rep. Vermont Bd. Agric.* II. 735 Mr. Allen conceived the project of making school slates from this quarry. **1890** HOWELLS *Boy's Town* 61 His poem . . . was probably a simple, unconscious imitation of something that had pleased him in his school-reader. **1902** LORIMER *Lett. Merchant* 239 Of course I told Hank that Boston wasn't all that it was cracked up to be in the school histories.

c. Designating equipment, departments, etc., of schools.

1835 *Knickerb.* V. 57 My school-bench commanded a view of a long and distant range of the Catskills. **1854** *Penna. Agric. Rep.* 276 Another great reform would be the introducing of a school library into every district school. *Ib.* 405 Best School Desks and Chairs. **1911** PERSONS, etc. *Mass. Labor Laws* 199 The boy's mother said . . . that he was thirteen . . . (just one year younger than she subsequently swore at the Somerville school office).

d. Designating activities found or conducted in schools.

See also SCHOOL-KEEPING, MEETING, -TEACHING.

1835 *Knickerb.* April 273 [The figures drawn on the slate] would be led on by what they call in school-sports, a go-devil, prancing about all in high horns, and a spear on the end of his tail. **1868** *N.Y. Herald* 10 July 9/5 School Commencement.—The annual commencement exercises . . . were held . . . yesterday morning. **1883** HOWELLS *Woman's Reason* xv, She used to act in the school exhibitions. **1920** — *Vacation of Kelwyns* 136 Parthenope found him at the school examination.

+e. In special combinations.

School agent, a book agent who sells books to schools; *s. bond*, a bond issued to borrow money for school purposes; *s. election*, an election in which the voters vote upon such matters as issuing school bonds; *s. land office*, a land office that handles the business of renting and selling school lands; *s. law*, a law that deals with control and maintenance of schools; *s. pin*, a pin of a design chosen to represent a school; *s. rate*, a tax rate levied to support schools; *s. reservation, reserve*, an area of land set aside for the support of schools; *s. town*, a town sufficiently large to have its own schools.

1879 *Harper's Mag.* July 215/2 The rival school agents . . . were very fortunate in their contracts with the professors. **1873** *Winfield* (Kan.) *Courier* 18 Sept. 2/3 School Bonds [are selling] at 90 cents. **1903** *Evanston* (Ill.) *Press* 11 April, The readers of The Press will note the call for the annual school election in another column of the paper. **1911** *Okla. Session Laws* 3 Legisl. 242 The Commissioners of the School Land Office shall cause the land to be appraised. **1873** *Harper's Mag.* March 631/1 The new school law of Maryland authorizes the establishment of . . . schools for colored children. **1903** WHITE *Blazed Trail Stories* 99 You wear your school-pin still, so you are not yet 'out.' **1660** *Dedham Rec.* IV. 18 Jonathan Fayerbanke Senior . . . made it apeere that his youth is aboue age to pay to the Schoole Rate and is therefore abated 4s, 9d. **1842** *Niles' Nat. Reg.* 11 June 233/3 A bill relating to the school reservations in the states of Alabama and Mississippi, was . . . passed. **1908** *Indian Laws & Tr.* III. 360 The Secretary of the Interior . . . [is] authorized to cause that part of the Cheyenne school reserve . . . to be appraised. **1898** DUNBAR *Folks from Dixie* 235 Miltonville had just risen to the dignity of being a school town.

*School.² *attrib.* **a.** In the specific names of fish or shellfish that appear in schools. **b.** *S. fish*, any fish that appears in schools. — **1814** MITCHILL *Fishes N.Y.* 368 The Shoal-cod, or School-cod, (*Gadus arenosus,*) . . . is taken on the level and sandy bottoms. **1876** GOODE *Cat. Fishes of Bermudas* 11 The smaller school-fishes. **1884** GOODE, etc. *Fisheries* I. 372 The smaller fish of the species [the red drum] are called simply 'Bass,' or 'School Bass.' *Ib.* 783 In and about Vineyard Sound, Massachusetts, two varieties of Lobsters . . . are distinguished as 'School Lobsters' and 'Rock Lobsters.'

School bell. A bell rung to summon children to school. {1862} — **1702** SEWALL *Diary* II. 61 Set out from Salem as the School-Bell rung. **1810** in Richardson C. *Miner* 56 The school bell rung.

School board. A body of persons, usually elected, charged with providing and maintaining the public schools of a school district or city; a board of education (q.v., under EDUCATION). {1870-} — **1857** *Harper's Mag.* Sept. 571/2 Can you inform me where the president of your school board resides? **1898** *Kansas City Star* 18 Dec. 2/2, I look confidently for the time when the men of the mill and the factory will be seen . . . on the school board. **1911** *Okla. Session Laws* 3 Legisl. 219 Their children shall be enumerated for that year by the school board for the district in which they shall attend school.

Schoolbook. A book of instruction used in schools. {1751-} — **1745** FRANKLIN *Writings* II. 296 At present I only send for a few school books. **1796** WEEMS *Letters* II. 45 His books shd. be little entertaining histories, school books, some Novels, &c. **1822** *Ann. 17th Congress* 1 Sess. 61 American school books are plenty and cheap. **1891** RYAN *Pagan* 133 The Bible is the only school-book he had, 'most. **1925** BRYAN *Memoirs* 314 Education [in the Philippines] has become widespread, . . . aided largely by American schoolbooks.

attrib. and *comb.* **1896** *Internat. Typogr. Union Proc.* 241 Ginn & Co., [are] school-book publishers. **1900** *Congress. Rec.* 25 Jan. 1167/1, I insist more upon brain capacity than I do upon a schoolbook education.

*Schoolbutter. {-a1700} *S.* +An insulting word used by school-boys. — **1835** LONGSTREET *Ga. Scenes* 84, I fell down . . . , running after that fellow that cried 'school-butter.' **1886** *Amer. Philol. Ass. Trans.* XVII. 46 *School-butter* (challenge to country school). **1901** H. ROBERTSON *Inlander* 20 He took off his coat . . . , [and] struck into the chorus with the mortal insult:—'*School-butter! school-butter!*' **1912** *Dialect Notes* III. 588 When he yelled *school butter* at us, we yanked him off the wagon and blacked his eyes.

+**School commissioner. a.** A public official elected or appointed to superintend the schools of a county or state. **b.** A member of a school board.

1838 *Indiana H. Rep. Jrnl.* 2 Sess. 126 It [shall be] the duty of school commissioners to appoint township trustees. **1845** *Ill. Rev. Statutes* 109 Transfers or assignments, shall be proven by certificate of the school or acting canal commissioner. **1857** *Quinland* I. 273 To-day I have been before the School Commissioners to be examined and get my certificate of qualification for teaching a common school. **1859** BARTLETT 384 *School-Commissioner*, the officer whose duty it is to have the administration and superintendence of public instruction in a State. **1873** *Harper's Mag.* March 629/2 New York has a school commissioner for each Assembly district. **1917** SINCLAIR *King Coal* 117 Observing a bulge on the right hip of the School-commissioner, Hal put out his hand towards it.

+**School committee.** A school board. So called esp. in New England, Delaware, and North Carolina.

1790 *Boston Rec.* 215 The Article in the Warrant relative to explaining the Commission given to the School Committee . . . [was] read. **1821** [see COURSE *n.* 2 b]. **1837** *S. Lit. Messenger* III. 590/1 One Mr. Lawrie Todd . . . [was] an active member of the school committee. **1859** BARTLETT 384 *School-Committee*. . . . These committees usually serve without compensation. **1883** *Century Mag.* Sept. 654/2 A few years ago, the school committee in one of the towns decided on a change of geographies. **1911** PERSONS, etc. *Mass. Labor Laws* 20 An investigation [was made] by the school committee.

Schooldame. A schoolmistress. {a1652, 'an old woman who keeps a small school for young children'} — **1709** *Essex Inst. Coll.* X. 84 Paid ye school dame. **1738** *Lunenburg* (Mass.) *Rec.* 102 Ye town will provide a School master for the first six months and School Dames for ye other six months. **1767** *Essex Inst. Coll.* XXI. 234 Thomas Dresser Joshua Tarr [were chosen] a Committee to Look out for a Scool Dame. [**1852** PARKER *Ten Sermons Religion* (1859) 19 He must study the anicular lines on the school-dame's slate.]

+**School director.** A local officer in charge of the district schools; a member of a school board. — **1890** *Stock Grower & Farmer* 4 Jan. 7/3 All justices of the peace, constables, school directors and mayordomos of acequias [in N. Mex.] shall be elected. **1892** *York County Hist. Rev.* 45 Mr. W. J. Young is school director, taking an active part in educational matters. **1914** *Cycl. Amer. Govt.* III. 254/2 School directors in general manage and control the schools, buildings and the school property.

+**School district.**

1. Any area established as the unit of organization for the local administration of schools.

1809 KENDALL *Travels* I. 128 There are thirteen school districts [in Berlin, Conn.]. **1831** *Jamestown* (N.Y.) *Jrnl.* 19 Jan. 2/1 There are nine thousand and sixty-two school districts in this state. **1850** *Mich. Gen. Statutes* I. (1882) 60 The legislature shall provide by law for the removal of any officer elected by a county, township, or school district. **1873** *Winfield* (Kan.) *Courier* 15 May 3/1 One of the farmer boys of school district No. 24 . . . came in Tuesday. **1911** *Okla. Session Laws* 3 Legisl. 218 The county superintendent . . . [may] permit children, living in any school district in this state at a distance of two miles or more from the school house at the home district, to attend school in another district.

2. *Attrib.* with *board, election, library, meeting.*

1830 S. SMITH *Life J. Downing* 92 Resolved, That it be recommended . . . [to call] school district meetings. **1893** *Harper's Mag.* April 708/1 The right of suffrage [for women] . . . is confined to municipal and school-district elections. **1898** *Kansas City Star* 21 Dec. 2/2 A case . . . involved the question whether, as to railroad legislation, the legislatures of theoretically sovereign states should be reduced to the level of city councils or school district boards. **1910** BOSTWICK *Amer. Pub. Library* 6 Similar to these [town libraries], . . . were school-district libraries.

+**School farm. a.** A farm, or farm land, the income from which goes toward the support of a school or schools. **b.** A farm connected with a school, on which students work or learn agriculture. Also transf.

1734 *Mass. H. Rep. Jrnl.* XII. 110 A Petition of the Town of Reading, praying for a Grant of Land for a School Farm of the quantity of two thousand acres. **1866** in Fleming *Hist. Reconstruction* I. 323 The 'school farms' . . . shall be sold, . . . and the proceeds . . . shall be invested in United States bonds, the interest of which shall be appropriated, . . . to the support of the schools. **1871** *Rep. Indian Affairs* (1872) 589 A school-farm of 50 acres of excellent land affords employment for the boys and a large part of the supply for the table. **1898** *Kansas City Star* 20 Dec. 2/5 Ex-President Grover Cleveland has decided to abandon the 'school farm' which he . . . undertook earlier in the summer.

+**School fund.** A fund set up and maintained, esp. by a state government, for the support of public schools.

1812 MELISH *Travels* II. 428 The *school fund* [in N.Y.] amounts to 483,326 dollars. **1818** *Conn. Constitution* viii. § 2 The School Fund, shall remain a perpetual fund, the interest of which shall be inviolably appropriated to the support and encouragement of the public or common schools throughout the State. **1837** W. JENKINS *Ohio Gaz.* 53 This township has a school fund of about $5000, arising from a sale of school section No. 16. **1858** *Texas Almanac 1859* 22 This supplementary Act makes it the duty of the Chief Justices to apportion the School Fund annually among the children of their respective counties. **1870** *Penna. Laws* 420 One-half [of the fines paid by fishermen] . . . to go to the informer and the other half to the school fund. **1900** *Congress. Rec.* 31 Jan. 1353/2 We have a magnificent permanent school fund from this lease money and from the sale of our land. **1914** *Cycl. Amer. Govt.* III. 256/1.

* **Schoolhouse.**

***1.** A building for the use of a school.

*c*1640 *Harvard Rec.* I. 19 The least study [is] a loft in that which was the schoolhouse. **1686** SEWALL *Diary* I. 157, I go to the meeting at the School-house. **1745** *N.H. Hist. Soc. Coll.* VII. 362 [The town voted] to build school housen. **1817** S. BROWN *Western Gazetteer* 61 The court house, jail, and school house are of brick. **1845** *Xenia Torch-Light* 31 July 1/2 No one would suspect, on looking at the well-managed farms, . . . and the occasional brick school-houses, that scarcely five years have elapsed since the first plough was driven into this prolific soil. **1900** [see LYCEUM 3]. **1925** BRYAN *Memoirs* 246 The schoolhouse is the dearest friend of a free people.

+**b.** (*Little*) *red schoolhouse*, a small country schoolhouse, usually of red brick. Often used as a symbol of the rural schoolhouse.

1862 BROWNE *A. Ward: His Book* 71 A C of upturned faces in the Red Skool House. **1899** in *Congress. Rec.* (1900) 15 Jan. 825/1 The little red schoolhouse appeared upon the hilltops and in the valleys of Kansas. **1904** *Nation* 28 Jan. 76/1 All classes of our educational institutions, from the little red schoolhouse to a Harvard or a Yale, may turn out citizens who are utterly careless of their duties . . . as members of our democracy.

2. *Attrib.* with *building, education, frame*, etc.

1688 SEWALL *Diary* I. 231 Little Hannah . . . , being enter'd a little within the Schoolhouse Lane, is rid over by David Lopez. **1717** *Braintree Rec.* 91 Their should be a Reconsideration of the late vote of ye Town, about the new school house frame set up. **1814** *Boston Selectmen* 113 Proposals were received from Mr. David Greenough respecting the terms of purchase of part of the school house lot. **1831** PECK *Guide* 298 Upper Alton [has] . . . a brick school-house building. **1852** REYNOLDS *Hist. Illinois* 180 McDonough never received any *schoolhouse* education, whatever. **1872** *Newton Kansan* 12 Sept. 3/2 The new school house site has been chosen on the west side of the square. **1907** *St. Nicholas* May 630/1 The schoolhouse yard and every open lot in the neighborhood were scenes of animated and noisy struggles between rival teams.

+**Schoolhouse preacher.** (See quotation.) — **1872** *Harper's Mag.* March 638/2 The State of Maine has an order of clergy called 'school-house preachers,' who farm it, or work at some trade during the week, and on Sunday 'exercise their gift.'

+**School-keeping.** The action of keeping school. {1857-} — **1651** *Dedham Rec.* III. 191 The time of Couent. in ye schoole keepeinge. being expired. wt. may be the resolution of ye Town. **1775** in Johnston *N. Hale* 139 School keeping is a business of which I was always fond. **1824** *Baptist Mag.* IV. 386 From his application to books after he commenced school-keeping, . . . he entered upon the ministry with enlightened views of the work. **1860** HOLMES *E. Venner* ii, It is customary to allow half-time to students engaged in school-keeping. **1882** THAYER *From Log-Cabin* 238 How would you like to try your hand at school-keeping, James?

+**School land.** Land set aside for the support of public schools.

1649 *Suffolk Deeds* I. 91 Humphrey Johnson of Roxbury granted unto William Chenie of Roxbury twenty Acres of land in Roxbury bounded wth . . . the schoole lands & Richard Peacocks northwest. **1668** *Braintree Rec.* 9 The Towne of Brantry did consent to lay the Schoole land; that is to say the Annuall Income of it; for a salliry for a Schoole master. **1775** *N.H. Hist. Soc. Coll.* IX. 89, I might . . . lay out for the Clearing the School Lands to the Amount of £500. **1836** W. O'BRYAN *Travels* 55 Lands called School lands are appropriated for their support. **1881** *Ore. State Jrnl.* 1 Jan. 4/3 Notice Is Hereby Given . . . for the Sale of School lands. **1901** *Amer. Rev. of Revs.* XXIV. 306/1 These so-called 'school lands' now comprise 4,444,144 acres. **1917** SINCLAIR *King Coal* 168 He was buying school-lands from the state.

+**School lot.** A town lot set aside for a school. — **1720** *Lunenburg* (Mass.) *Rec.* 18 Ye. School Lott [shall] be Laid out as Near ye Center of ye house lotts as May be. **1759** *Newport Mercury* 3 July 3/2 The Proprietors also propose to grant . . . one hundred Acres for a School-Lot, Burying-Ground, and Training-Field, in each Township. **1842** *Nat. Hist. N.Y., Geology* II. 61 Another very handsome variety occurs in Warrensburgh, on the school lot. **1859** [see GOSPEL].

+**Schoolma'am.** A schoolmistress. *colloq.* (See also COUNTRY SCHOOL b.) — **1844** *S. Lit. Messenger* X. 557/1 The children crowded around 'mamma,' drawing her as far as possible from the formidable 'school ma'am.' **1864** NICHOLS *Amer. Life* I. 59 [We] were taught by the same schoolmasters in winter, and the same 'schoolma'ams' in summer. **1900** MUNN *Uncle Terry* 84 You are not a bit like the schoolma'am of my boyhood. **1919** HOUGH *Sagebrusher* 46 Reckon she's a school ma'am?

‖**Schoolma'amish,** *a.* Like a schoolma'am. — **1887** FREDERIC *Seth's Brother's Wife* 24 She was held to be too serious and 'school-ma'am-ish' for pleasant company.

+**Schoolmarm.** Variant of SCHOOLMA'AM. *dial.* or *humorous.* {1888} Also *attrib.* — **1848** *S. Lit. Messenger* XIV. 385/1 The teacher, (or school-marm, as they called her), was on her feet. **1872** *Ill. Dept. Agric. Trans.* IX. 275 Their thoughtful, stiff, precise, school-marm mode of utterance always seems to say to you: 'I am a pedant.' **1887** *Courier-Journal* 29 Jan. 4/7 (*headline*), A Prominent Warren-county Farmer Asked to Pay for the Ruin of a Pretty young School-marm. **1902** WISTER *Virginian* vi, She'd be just the schoolmarm for Bear Creek.

∗**Schoolmaster.** A male teacher in a school.

1635 *Boston Rec.* 5 Our brother Philemon Pormont, shalbe intreated to become scholemaster. **1659** *Dedham Rec.* IV. 3 It shall be at the libertie of the school master to refuse such. **1702** SEWALL *Diary* III. 398 Two Schoolmasters chiefly for Winter. **1774** *Amer. Hist. Review* VI. 72, I being reduced to the last shilling was obliged to engage to go to Virginia for four years, as a schoolmaster for Bedd, Board, washing and five pounds during the whole time. **1806** *Balance* 9 Sept. 282/1, I have known a school-master frequently employed to draw wills. **1833** *Jamestown* (N.Y.) *Jrnl.* 3 July 1/3 Our Schoolmasters are . . . 'boarded around.' **1903** Fox *Little Shepherd* v, The schoolmaster laughed—Chad had asked him a question at last that he couldn't answer.

+**School meeting.** A meeting of citizens called to consider school matters. — **1834** *Jamestown* (N.Y.) *Jrnl.* 26 Nov. 1/6 This is about the fortieth time I have been to School Meeting on this spot. **1883** HOWE *Country Town* (1926) 34 At the school-meetings he was the second to speak.

∗**Schoolmistress.** A woman who teaches school. — **1715** SEWALL *Diary* III. 50 Mrs. Anne Kay . . . Was a good Woman, and a good School-Mistress. **1796** *Ann. 4th Congress* 2 Sess. 2694 A like tax has been imposed on . . . employments, faculties, and professions; clergymen, mechanics, schoolmasters, and schoolmistresses excepted. **1814** *Mass. H. S. Coll.* 2 Ser. III. 111 The salary . . . of a school mistress, [is] one dollar and a half per week, and board. **1870** 'F. FERN' *Ginger-Snaps* 171 The same system of dress is recommended for Sunday-school girls, schoolmistresses, church-singers, and the lower orders generally.

+**School money.** The money in a school fund. — **1757** *Duxbury Rec.* 323 [The town] voted that . . . a Committee . . . make up accounts with the Town's trustees, about the Town's stock of School money. **1832** WILLIAMSON *Maine* II. 677 Each town being required to raise a sum in school-money, equal to 40 cents a person. **1871** EGGLESTON *Hoosier Schoolm.* 221 Ralph found himself . . . glad to hear from Mr. Means that the school-money had 'gin aout.'

+**School rick.** *local.* [App. formed on the analogy of *bishopric*.] A school district. *Obs.* — **1789** in Parmenter *Hist. Pelham, Mass.* 227 Each School Rick Shall Build and Maintain their own School Houses. **1797** *Ib.* 228 The Assessors Shall Commit District Lists of the Assesment of every School Rick to their Trustees.

Schoolroom. A room in which a school is conducted; a room in a schoolhouse. {1775-}

1773 FITHIAN *Journal* I. 61, I have to myself in the Evening . . . my Liberty, either to continue in the School room, in my own Room, or to sit over at the great House. **1835** HOFFMAN *Winter in West* I. 239 The room . . . [is] fitted up with desks and benches as a school-room. **1872** *Newton Kansan* 26 Sept. 3/2 The Mite Society will hold a ten cent sociable in the school room. **1905** RICE *Sandy* 101 The change from the road to the school-room was not without many a struggle on Sandy's part.

+**School section.** A section of government land given to state governments for the support of public schools.

'The states admitted between 1802 and 1848, except Texas, received the 16th section in each surveyed township of the public domain; the states admitted since 1848, with a few exceptions, have received the 16th and 36th sections, in some cases two more, in each surveyed township' (1914 *Cycl. Amer. Govt.* III. 256/1).

1835 *Indiana Mag. Hist.* XXII. 438 This was an action brought by the Trustees of a school Section for money due on two years rent. **1846** *Xenia Torch-Light* 8 Jan. 2/4, I wish . . . to ask you a few questions about the law regulating our school sections. **1872** TICE *Over Plains* 134 We then visited other mines farther down on the plain; and among them the shaft on the 16th, the school section. **1899** *Mo. So. Dakotan* I. 175 The near colt shied at a monster tumble weed racing across the schoolsection. **1918** *Statutes at Large* XL. II. 2237/1 School section allowed Montana in lieu of lands in Huntley irrigation project.

+**School ship.** A ship on board which a nautical training school is conducted. Also appositive. — **1841** *S. Lit. Messenger* VII. 7/2 The means of creating officers [for the navy] . . . are to be derived from the school-ship. **1867** LONGFELLOW in S. Longfellow *H. W. Longfellow* III. 89 We stopped near the school-ship, which was crowded with boys, all singing an evening hymn. **1879** WHITMAN *Spec. Days* 136 From 7 to 9, [I was] aboard the United States school-ship Minnesota. **1903** *N.Y. Times* 7 Oct. 6 The annual graduation exercises of the schoolship St. Mary's were held last night on board the ship.

+**School society.** A private organization for the support of schools. — **1754** HEMPSTEAD *Diary* 623, I Rid out in the Neck to hear the Clerk of the School Society. **1812** *Ann. 12th Congress* 1 Sess. 2255 The Trustees of the Georgetown Lancaster School Society.

+**School system.** The plan and arrangement of the schools in a given community. (See also COMMON SCHOOL 3 b.) — [**1834** *Jamestown* (N.Y.) *Jrnl.* 26 Nov. 1/6 Without any school system, the children [in Iceland] learn to read around the family fire.] **1869** BRACE *New West* 79 The general school system of California . . . is more centralized. **1884** *Gringo & Greaser* 15 Feb. 3/1 Of all the humbug impositions that afflict our Territory, none is so glaring . . . as our miserable excuse for a school system. **1911** PERSONS, etc. *Mass. Labor Laws* 218 We should know how many children . . . the school system could no longer control, as well as those it still retains.

+**School tax.** A tax, usually levied by a school district, town, or county, for the support of public schools. — **1789** *Mass. Acts & Resolves* 12 Whenever the Rents and Incomes of the School Lands . . . shall be insufficient . . . , the said District may . . . grant such School Taxes as may be necessary. **1818** *Niles' Reg.* XIV. 174/2 To $6 20, the present state tax, the school tax, would add $2 24. **1841** *Niles' Nat. Reg.* 26 June 272/3 The school tax for the year is $61,803, equal to $22 for each district. **1876** *Harper's Mag.* Dec. 159/1 A voter came up and asked for a ticket against the school tax. **1918** *N.Y. Laws* II. 367 Suffolk county, school taxes, collection by town collectors.

School-teacher. A teacher in a school. (See also COMMON SCHOOL 3 d, quot. 1844.) — **1855** BARNUM *Life* 13 My first school-teacher was a Mr. Camp. **1864** *Wkly. New Mexican* 17 June 1/4 Eight young ladies have emigrated from Lowell, Mass., to Washington Territory, where they are to be employed as school teachers. **1898** PAGE *Red Rock* 513, I am the school-teacher at the Bend. **1912** NICHOLSON *Hoosier Chron.* 399, I'm a school-teacher, . . . a member of the gray sisterhood of American nuns.

+**School-teaching.** The business or occupation of teaching school. — **1846** *Indiana Mag. Hist.* XXIII. 459 After he came to the west his occupation was that of school-teaching. **1865** *Atlantic Mo.* March 379/2 The censurable point of the aspiration consists in being dissatisfied with the humbler vocation of school-teaching, and in pining after the loftier career of milliner. **1912** NICHOLSON *Hoosier Chron.* 421 This school-teaching ain't good for you.

+**School trustee.** One who acts as trustee for school properties; a member of a school board. — **1844** *Indiana Senate Jrnl.* 29 Sess. 292 A bill to authorize the school trustees of congressional townships to act as examiners of common school teachers. **1890** *Nation* 10 April 291/2 [Politicians'] daughters or sisters are imposed as teachers on the School Trustees. **1898** DUNBAR *Folks from Dixie* 240 The younger men thought that he was rather overplaying his rôle of school trustee.

+**Schooner.** Also **skooner, scooner.** [Origin uncertain: see note.]

The story that the word originated about 1713 in Gloucester, Mass., when the first schooner was supposedly launched, is commonly repeated. A bystander is reported to have exclaimed, 'Oh, how she scoons!' And the captain is said to have replied, 'A scooner let her be!' This story, as quoted in Babson's *Hist. Gloucester* (1860), p. 252, was first recorded in 1790. It is unsupported, however, by any New England evidence for the use of *scoon* or *scun*, a Sc. and northern Eng. dialect word, meaning 'to skim along the surface of the water.'

1. A fore-and-aft rigged vessel, orig. having but two masts, with the smaller sail on the foremast.

See also FISHING SCHOONER, FORE-AND-AFT SCHOONER, LUMBER SCHOONER.

1716 *Boston Rec.*XXIX. 231 James Manson ye Skooner Mayflower from North Carolina. **1720** *Essex Inst. Coll.* XX. 26 Two small vessels are mentioned upon the inventory of his property, viz.: 1 skooner valued at £200, one small skooner at £22. **1721** MOSES PRINCE *Let.* in J. Babson *Hist. Gloucester* 252 Capt. Robinsons . . . was the first contriver of schooners, and built the first of the sort about eight years ago. **1742** *Georgia Col. Rec.* VI. 22 John Penrose . . . was Building a Scooner. **1765** WASHINGTON *Diaries* I. 214 My Carpenters had in all worked 82 days on my Schooner. **1834** PECK *Gaz. Illinois* 18 [Lake Michigan] affords fine navigation for schooners and steam boats. **1862** in McClellan *Own Story* 500, I despatched eleven steamers . . . and six schooners, with five batteries of heavy horse-artillery. **1916** DU PUY *Uncle Sam* 126 You had a trim little schooner.

b. *Schooner-of-war.*

1836 AUDUBON *Ornith. Biog.* III. 391 During several weeks which I spent . . . on board the United States schooner-of-war the Spark.

2. A tall beer glass. {1895-}

1877 BARTLETT 557 A Bowery merchant affirms that the resemblance of the Brooklyn bridge to a German's nose lies in the fact that schooners move under it. **1885** *Santa Fé Wkly. New Mexican* 30 July 4/2 We fellows who deal in schooners don't get much of a margin. . . . It's the exclusive pony-glass dealers who harvest the nickles these warm days. **1904** MACKAYE *Panchronicon* 247 Bring me a schooner of light lager. **1923** 'BOWER' *Parowan Bonanza* 43 Jim brought his schooner of beer over, and sat down.

3. Short for PRAIRIE SCHOONER.

1890 C. W. HASKINS *Argonauts Calif.* 205 Heavily loaded 'schooners' . . . could often be seen . . . stringing along the road for miles. **1901** WHITE *Claim Jumpers* 170 Soon after they passed the canvas 'schooners' of some who had started the evening before.

4. Attrib. and comb. in sense 1 with *barge, load, man,* etc.

1804 *State P.* (1819) V. 35 Several vessels of the above description, which are mentioned to be schooner-rigged. **1819** E. DANA *Geog. Sk.* 199 Fort St. Stevens stands on the west bank of the Tombigbee, at the head of schooner navigation. **1819** *Western Rev.* I. 361 The River is navigated by steam boats, barges, keel boats, schooner barges [etc.]. **1866** *Outing* VIII. 23/2 In addition to her propelling power she has a schooner rig. **1884** CABLE *Dr. Sevier* 130 Richard saw him . . . superintending the unloading of a small schooner-load of bananas. **1884** *Nat. Museum Bul.* No. 27, 674 Schooner-smack 'Storm King.' **1897** *Outing* XXX. 335/2 The happy owner of a small yacht . . . is no worse off in this particular than he who owns a steamer or a schooner-yacht. **1914** STEELE *Storm* 270 Then he scrutinized the rank of schooner-men flanking me.

+Schooner wagon. =PRAIRIE WAGON. — **1882** *Century Mag.* July 345/1 Deacon Joel, passing her, alone in his schooner-wagon, should insist upon her riding.

Schottische. A dance resembling the polka {1859-}; the music for such a dance. Also attrib.

1852 *Knickerb.* XXXIX. 155 The 'Schottische,' [was] danced by one of our ladies and a blushing young man. **1862** NORTON *Army Lett.* 61 Our band entertained the *messieurs* with the 'Marseillaise,' and afterward with schottisches, polkas, cotillions, etc. **1895** L. G. FRAZER, etc. *Dancing* 424 It is difficult to see why the title ['barn dance'] is specially applied to this Scotch lilt and schottische hops. **1902** WISTER *Virginian* x, Miss Wood . . . was dancing the schottische.

+Schout, Scout(e). Also **skoute**. [Du.] In the Dutch settlements of New York, a local officer vested with judicial functions. Now hist. {c1481-1673; 1867, in the Netherlands}

1664 in *N.Y. State Lib. Hist. Bul.* No. 2, 159 Scout, Burgomastrs. & Schepens ordered to summon a court. **1673** *Jamaica* (L.I.) *Rec.* I. 91 Deputis . . . [were] to make choice . . . of one for a skoute and one for a secretary. **1695** *Doc. Hist. N.Y. State* I. 631 Wee doe give & graunt unto the said Pattentees . . . full power & authoritie to Elect & nominate a certaine officer amongst themselves to execute the place of a Scoute. **1809** IRVING *Knickerb.* III. ii, This potent body consisted of a schout or bailiff, with powers between those of the present mayor and sheriff. **1896** EARLE *Colonial Days N.Y.* 237 The *schout* judged this epithet to be a slander and an affront to the Secretary.

+Schute. Variant of CHUTE *n.* in various senses.

1812 MARSHALL *Kentucky* 74 [The falls are] rendered still more alarming and dangerous by the irregularity of the schutes. **1848** *S. Lit. Messenger* XIV. 685/2 As the water descends not more than about ten feet in running three hundred yards, the place might be more appropriately termed a schute than a fall. **1861** *N.Y. Tribune* 12 Sept. 6/1 He 'took the schute,' as our raftsmen would say, and slid down into Tennessee to confer with his allies. **1862** *Ib.* 9 June 8/5 It is generally supposed among boatmen that their business is done for this season, the canals, locks, schutes, &c., being completely wrecked and destroyed. **1872** *Penna. Laws* 966 Any person or persons . . . owning dams across said river or tributaries shall . . . erect the necessary schutes, . . . to enable fish to ascend said streams at all times. **1890** *Stock Grower & Farmer* 5 April 6/1 Frank Huntington

and Jim Leonard left for their ranch on Friday morning with lumber and other necessary material for building a branding schute.

+Schuylkill. A river and county in Pennsylvania: Used in specific names. — **1854** ELLIOTT *Fruit Book* 247 Schuylkill . . . [also called] Cape Grape. . . . Its value is only as a wine grape. **1883** *Nat. Museum Bul.* No. 27, 491 Schuylkill Cat . . . is one of the best known and most esteemed of our cat-fish.

+Schwenkfelder. Also **Swingfelter.** A member of a sect founded by Kaspar Schwenkfeld (1490-1561), of Silesia: (see quot. 1883). {Schwenkfeldian, 1562-1587, 1886} — **1789** MORSE *Amer. Geog.* 313 The Germans [in Pa.] . . . consist of Lutherans, . . . and Swingfelters. **1789** *Columbian Mag.* III. 28 The Swingfielders . . . hold the same principles as the Friends. **1844** Rupp *Relig. Denominations* 663 Schwenkfelders are a denomination of Christians. **1867** DIXON *New America* II. 309 No sect escaped this rage for separation, . . . [neither] Swedenborgians, nor Schwenkfelders. **1883** *American* VI. 372 The Schwenkfelders, who are now extinct in Europe, linger on in Pennsylvania.

Schwenkfeldian, *a.* Belonging to the sect of Schwenkfelders. — [**1876** R. BARCLAY *Inner Life* 243 In 1734, forty Schwenkfeldian families travelled to England, and finally emigrated to Pennsylvania.] **1888** SCHAFF *Hist. Christian Ch.* VI. 574 He founded a new sect . . . which is perpetuated among the Schwenkfeldian congregations in Eastern Pennsylvania.

+Scientific school. A school in which technological subjects are taught. — **1868** *Ore. State Jrnl.* 11 July 1/2 It was proposed to establish scientific schools in connection with Harvard and Yale. **1870** *Rep. Comm. Educ.* 52 The argument . . . is a plea for artisan, art, industrial, and scientific schools as a part of the common school system.

Scientist. {1840-} +Short for CHRISTIAN SCIENTIST. — **1895** *Amer. Art Jrnl.* 26 Jan., The solo singer, however, was a Scientist, Miss Elsie Lincoln. **1906** BELL *C. Lee* 100, I thought Scientists did not like doctors! **1914** E. STEWART *Lett. Woman Homesteader* 12, I certainly got as warm as the most 'sot' Scientist that ever read Mrs. Eddy could possibly wish.

* Scissors. Also **sizors, sizers.** *pl.* A well-known cutting instrument resembling shears but smaller. Often *pair of scissors.*

1646 *Mass. H. S. Coll.* 4 Ser. VI. 379 He stole also a pair of sizors. **1678** *New Castle Court Rec.* 362 Inventory . . . 5 Combe brushes & 5 payer of sizers 4 parcells of knitting needles. **1711** *Springfield Rec.* II. 41, 9 pair of sizers at six pence the Pair. **1806** *Austin P.* I. (1924) 102, 1 doz. Cast Steel Scissors. **1859** STOWE *Minister's Wooing* xxx, [She] was ready with thimble, scissors, or thread, whenever any one needed them. **1878** *Rep. Indian Affairs* 396 Scissors, 4 and 6-inch. **1907** *St. Nicholas* Sept. 1034/2 With sharp-pointed scissors we will open one of these egg-cases.

attrib. **1845** KIRKLAND *Western Clearings* 101 Their feet [had] never been coaxed into shoes of the size and shape of a scissors-sheath. **1870** E. B. FOOTE *Plain Talk* 421 We have knife-sharpeners, scissors-sharpeners, and pencil-sharpeners. **1879** STOCKTON *Rudder Grange* i, The bedstead was what is sometimes called a 'scissors-bed.' We could shut it up.

‖ b. *To give* (someone) *scissors,* to overcome or get the better of (someone).

1847 ROBB *Squatter Life* 31 Thar is a fellar of the inimy who's dead bitter agin us and our team, so you must gin him scissors!

Scissor(s)-grinder. {1893-} One who grinds or sharpens scissors. — **1841** HAWTHORNE *Notebooks* (1932) 88 The squirrel . . . frequently uttered a sharp, quick, angry noise, like that of a scissors-grinder's wheel. **1855** M. THOMPSON *Doesticks* 155, [I imitated] the loving accents of the scissor-grinder's wheel. **1861** H. N. BAKER *(title)*, Tim, the Scissor's Grinder. **1869** LOWELL *Under the Willows* 20 Here The Scissors-grinder, pausing, doffs his hat.

Scissortail. The swallow-tailed flycatcher (*Muscivora forficata*) of the southern states and Mexico, or a related species. {1839-, of S. Amer.} In full *scissortail flycatcher;* also, *scissor-tailed flycatcher.* — **1858** BAIRD *Birds Pacific R.R.* 169 *Milvulus forficatus,* Scissor-tail, Swallow-tailed Flycatcher, . . . [is the] 'Bird of Paradise' of the Texans. **1889** *Cent.* 2334/2 *Fork-tailed flycatcher,* an American tyrant-flycatcher. . . . Also called *scissortail.* **1917** *Birds of Amer.* II. 191/2 It needs but little study of the food of the Scissor-tailed Flycatcher to show that where the bird is abundant it is of much economic value.

Scoale beame. Variant of SCALEBEAM. — **1674** *Harvard Rec.* I. 61 Kitchins Utensils, . . . 1 Great Iron Scoale Beame.

+Scoke. (See SKOKE.[1])

+Scoldenore. [Of obscure origin.] =OLD SQUAW. — **1873** THAXTER *Isles of Shoals* 109 Boats go out after sea-fowl, . . . [among which are] old wives, called by the natives *scoldenores.* **1917** *Birds of Amer.* I. 141.

* Sconce. A candle-holder. — **1714** *Boston News-Letter* 29 March 2/2 To be Sold by Publick Vendue or Outcry. . . . Glass Sconces and Gilt. **1790** *Penna. Packet* 1 March 1/1 This Day . . . Will commence the Sale of . . . Brass pullies, sconces, chimney hooks [etc.]. **1846** POE *Works* (1902) V. 169, I took from their sconces two flambeaus. **1885** EGGLESTON in *Century Mag.* April 881/1 Spermaceti candles . . . suited better than any others the gilt and carved sconces.

+Sconk cabbage. =SKUNK CABBAGE. — **1836** AUDUBON *Ornith. Biog.* III. 478 There he lies, snugly squatted beneath the broad leaves of the 'sconk cabbage' or dock.

+Scooner. (See SCHOONER.)

* **Scoop,** *n.*

* **1.** Any one of various shovellike utensils used for bailing out liquids or dipping up loose materials.

1679 *Boston Rec.* 132 Every family shall be ordered by the Selectmen to have a proportion of Buckets swobbs and scoopes. **1870** KEIM *Sheridan's Troopers* 129 A delapidated sombrero . . ., taken from a side glance, gave Joe's head the appearance of a huge scoop. **1881** *Harper's Mag.* April 649/2 The sap . . . was conveyed to the kettles in barrels, from which it was transferred by scoops. **1887** STOCKTON *Dusantes* 44 [A tin pan] answered very well as a scoop.

+2. =SCOOP BONNET.

1846 *Knickerb.* XXVIII. 304 The head was honored with an ancient 'straw scoop.' **1846** FARNHAM *Prairie Land* 101 The whole was surmounted by a capacious sugar-loaf Navarino scoop.

‖3. An opening or vista.

1854 LOWELL *Letters* I. 216 You get a gleam of the sea through some scoop in the woods.

4. (See quot. 1879.) *rare.*

1879 WEBSTER *Suppl.* 1577/3 *Scoop,* . . . a sudden breaking down of prices for the purpose of buying stocks at cheaper rates, followed by a rise. (*Cent.*) **1913** *Stand.* 2196/3.

+5. =BEAT *n.* 4.

1886 *Phonetic Jrnl.* 6 Feb. 63/1 In American newspaper offices an item of news is valued largely according to the likelihood of its being an exclusive piece of information, or a 'scoop.' **1894** 'O. HENRY' *Rolling Stones* 167 We handed to a member of our reportorial staff, . . . instructions to go to Washington, interview President Cleveland, and get a scoop . . . on all other Texas papers. **1902** LORIMER *Lett. Merchant* 107 This is a bully scoop for you, boys. **1917** SINCLAIR *King Coal* 197 He might find one . . . who would yield to the temptation of a 'scoop.'

+6. (See quotations.)

1881 INGERSOLL *Oyster-Industry* 247 *Scoop,* a light kind of dredge. (Chesapeake.) **1911** *Essex Inst. Coll.* XLVII. 14 Today, a long plank or pole called a 'scoop' drawn by horses and having a plank for a man to stand on, drags all the hay at once to the stack.

* **Scoop,** *v.*

+1. *tr.* To obtain, take, or get, often surreptitiously, in a wholesale or thorough manner. Often with *in* and *up*. *slang.* {1901-} Also *fig.*

1850 COLTON *3 Years Calif.* 440 [The Roman Catholic church] could scoop up whole tribes of savages, dazzling them with the symbols of religion. **1876** *Congress. Rec.* 19 July 4718/2 [It may have been necessary] to pop down upon that identical reservation and, as they say out West, scoop it. **1882** McCABE *New York* 160 He runs seventy 'busses on this line and scoops in three 'r four hundred a day. **1894** 'O. HENRY' *Rolling Stones* 233 [A married woman] has some rights of her own, and everybody else's she can scoop in. **1900** BONNER *Hard Pan* 3 White Pine scooped the last dollar he had.

+2. To get the advantage of, use up, take in (a person). Also with *in. colloq.*

1867 RICHARDSON *Beyond Miss.* 134, 'I am badly scooped' meant [in Kansas]: 'I am used up' or 'defeated.' **1872** 'MARK TWAIN' *Roughing It* 333 They've scooped him. **1889** *Boston Jrnl.* 30 March 2/3 The Mexican Consul . . . [charged] from $3 to $4 for passports to cross the Mexican line, and scooped in many tenderfeet. **1916** THOBURN *Stand. Hist. Okla.* II. 750 They had just been 'scooped,' with no chance to present their side of the case, and they were dumbfounded.

+b. *Newspaper.* To get ahead of (a rival) in securing or publishing news.

1898 *Boston Jrnl.* 17 Oct. 3/6 You don't suppose I am going to let her get scooped on the news of this engagement, do you? **1902** BANKS *Newspaper Girl* 59, I was not scooped after all, but how in the world had that article got there? **1911** FERBER *Dawn O'Hara* 9 He left them in the ditch on the big story of the McManus indictment, and the whole town scooped him.

‖3. To propel one's self by rowing as with a scoop.

1886 STOCKTON *Mrs. Lecks* 50, I'll never leave this place if I have to scoop myself out to sea with an oar.

+4. *intr.* Of a whale: To feed; to take in large mouthfuls of brit.

1887 GOODE, etc. *Fisheries* v. II. 264 Again the whale may be 'scooping' or feeding.

5. *tr.* and *intr.* 'To take with a dredge, as oysters'; 'to use a scoop; dredge; as for oysters' (*Cent.*).

+Scoop bonnet. A woman's bonnet shaped somewhat like a scoop. — **1846** FARNHAM *Prairie Land* 102 Sometimes her scoop bonnet covered half my field of vision. **1892** *Lippincott's Mag.* June 645 On her head she wore an enormous white scoop bonnet. **1905** LINCOLN *Partners* 30 [Portraits] of ladies in flowered scoop bonnets . . . gazed down upon him with rigid disapproval.

Scooper. {1668-} +(See quotation.) *Obs.* — **1857** *Ill. Agric. Soc. Trans.* II. 313 The scooper, which was a large, clumsy machine, and very heavy, was used for breaking up prairies.

+Scoop hat. =SCOOP BONNET. *Obs.* — **1865** *Atlantic Mo.* Feb. 149/2 Dame Tourtelot, . . . her great scoop hat trimmed with green, . . . kept her keen eyes fastened intently upon the minister. *Ib.* May 597/1 He came to look upon . . . the yellow ribbons within the scoop-hat of Almira Tourtelot . . . as the types of goodness.

+Scooping net. =next. — **1806** LEWIS in *L. & Clark Exped.* III. (1905) 350 The Clatsops Chinnooks &c. in fishing employ . . . the scooping or dipping net with a long handle. **1835** AUDUBON *Ornith. Biog.* III. 565 Negroes were there amusing themselves by raising shrimps . . . with scooping nets.

+Scoop net. =DIP NET. {1895, fig.} — **1792** BELKNAP *Hist. New-Hampshire* III. 90 The Indian scoop-net is shaped like a pocket. **1817** S. BROWN *Western Gazetteer* 225 At the end of [the pole] . . . is affixed a scoop-net. **1883** *Nat. Museum Bul.* No. 27, 110 Soft Crabs . . . are secured almost entirely by means of scoop-nets from the beaches, or in the hands. **1896** *Boston Transcript* 21 Nov. 20/1 The fish are then dipped out with great scoop nets, and are sold to the cod fishermen.

+Scoop shovel. An implement consisting of a broad flat scoop fitted to a handle, used for scooping up loose earth, coal, etc. Also *attrib.*

1850 HINES *Voyage* 160 With the help of . . . a couple of scoop-shovel canoes, we succeeded in crossing without accident. **1855** THOMPSON *Doesticks* 218 [The picture] is either a female rag-picker with a scoop-shovel, or a Virginia wench with a hoe-cake in her hand. **1886** *Century Mag.* 28/1 The snow fell in heavy masses 'as if thrown from a scoop-shovel.' **1898** *McClure's Mag.* Jan. 216/1 The fireman [had not] interrupted for an instant the steady pendulum-like swing of the fire-door and the scoop-shovel.

b. *Scoop-shovel bonnet,* =SCOOP BONNET. *Obs.*

1884 'MARK TWAIN' *H. Finn* xvii, One was a woman in a slim black dress . . . and a large scoop-shovel bonnet.

Scoot, *n.* **1.** An act of scooting. *colloq.* {1864-} Also *attrib.* or as *adj.* +**2.** (See quotation.) — (1) *c*1870 CHIPMAN *Notes on Bartlett* 385 'He made a scoot,' went 'on a run.' 'Scoot train,' one that omits stopping at a particular station; an express train. New England. (2) **1905** *Forestry Bureau Bul.* No. 61, 36 Dray, a single sled used in dragging logs. One end of the log rests upon the sled. (N[orthern] F[orest].) . . . [Also called] go-devil, lizard, scoot [etc.].

Scoot, *v.* Also †skoot, skute.

1. *intr.* To slide suddenly or rapidly. {*dial.*}

1837 NEAL *Charcoal Sk.* (1838) 75 Notwithstanding his convulsive efforts to clutch the icy bricks, he *skuted* into the gutter. **1851** MELVILLE *Moby-Dick* 475 The enormous casks . . . scoot across the slippery decks, like so many land slides. **1866** *Harper's Mag.* Jan. 271/2 His feet 'skooted' forward, his legs followed, and the ponderous brother came down upon the floor. **1895** *Dialect Notes* I. 342.

+2. To go swiftly or hurriedly; to dart. Often with adverbs. {scout, 1758-1810} Cf. SKEET *v.* 1.

'The modern *scoot* was app. imported into general British use from the U.S.' (*O.E.D.*).

1841 *Jamestown* (N.Y.) *Jrnl.* 10 June 4 Didn't he . . . scoot through the briar bushes and the gals snikkered out. **1871** *Harper's Mag.* Sept. 640 The dog sprang between the legs of the bystanders and 'scooted' out of the door. **1890** H. M. FIELD *Bright Skies* 58 While the flocks of ducks go 'scooting' by, the herons stand with quiet dignity. **1909** WASON *Happy Hawkins* 301 Then he . . . scooted over to an eatin'-house, comin' back with a lot o' stuff an' some coffee.

+b. *tr.* To cause to go hastily or at once. Cf. SKEET *v.* 2.

1899 HARTE *Mr. J. Hamlin's Meditation* 140 [Bill] scooted him down to Spindler's and collected the money from Spindler himself afore he'd give him up.

Scooter. {1825-}

+1. *S.* A long narrow plow used for opening or breaking rather than for stirring the soil. In full *scooter plow.*

1820 in *Henderson's N.C. Almanack* (1823) 25 The ridges are opened with a small plough called a scooter, something like a shovel plough. **1870** *Rep. Comm. Agric.* 1869 290 Rows were laid off five apart with an ordinary scooter plow. **1897** *Plantation Missionary* Aug. 44/1 [We open] the rows with a scooter. **1920** *3d Nat. Country Life Conf. Proc.* 46 The same old hoe and the same old scooter plow are brought forth at the same time of the year.

+2. A sailboat for use on water or on ice.

1903 *N.Y. Times* 13 Dec., The 'scooter' . . . is built with a bottom and a deck which are duplicates of each other. **1904** *Scientific Amer.* 5 March 201/1 Incredible speed is attained by the larger and more completely equipped scooters. *Ib.* 201/2 There are . . . few more interesting sights seen than those afforded by a scooter plunging at full speed from the ice into the water. **1909** *Cent. Suppl.* 620-1 *Ice-scooter.* . . . These scooters may be run alternately through water and over ice.

+Scoot horn. (See SCOUT HORN.)

+Scophilite. (See SCOVILITE.)

Scorcher. {1874-} *fig.* Something that scorches; a searing attack. *slang.* {1888-} — **1842** in *Corr. R. W. Griswold* (1898) 120 The review in The Examiner . . . is a 'scorcher.' **1869** 'MARK TWAIN' *Innocents* 453 Every time they read me a scorcher of a lecture I mean to talk back in print.

∗ Score, *n.*

1. In a game, the record of points won by a player or players. {1742–}

Illustrated with reference to baseball and football.

1880 N. BROOKS *Fairport Nine* 185 The Fairports, with skilful playing and good running, succeeded in adding 2 more to their score. **1895** WILLIAMS *Princeton Stories* 251 Higher up were footballs hung in clusters with scores painted upon them. **1907** [see SCORE-KEEPER].

attrib. **1868** CHADWICK *Base Ball* 64 In the . . . score sheet . . . to the left the initials represent the words Runs, Outs, Times, Bases [etc.].

+2. *Baseball.* A batting list. *rare.*

1893 CAMP *College Sports* 292 The batsmen must take their positions . . . in the order in which they are named on *the score.*

∗ Score, *v.*

+1. *intr.* To slab or split off the outer parts of a tree trunk that is to be hewed. (Cf. SCORER 3.)

1752 in *Travels Amer. Col.* 320 Four hands schooring. *Ib.* 320, I finished hewing in the forenoon three at schooring.

+2. *tr.* To castigate (a person or thing); to rate or denounce severely.

1812 PAULDING *J. Bull & Bro. Jon.* 107 [She] fell upon Beau Napperty, and scored him at such a rate, that [etc.]. **1835** *Ib.* (new ed.) 126 The first fellow that . . . undertook to score Jonathan, was one Farmer Parkinson. **1892** LOUNSBERRY *Studies in Chaucer* III. 223 Even poor Lipscomb . . . was soundly scored for his grossness and vulgarity. **1903** *N.Y. Times* 5 Dec. 5 Bishop Burgess in a sermon which he delivered yesterday plainly scored 'Parsifal,' although he did not once mention the name of the opera.

+3. *Baseball. tr.* and *intr.* To make (a score or run) or to cause (a fellow player) to make one; to make a score. Also *fig.* {1782–, in cricket}

1868 CHADWICK *Base Ball* 46 A nine is said to be 'whitewashed' when they are put out in an inning without being able to score a single run. **1887** *Courier-Journal* 26 May 2/6 Neither side scored until the second inning. **1889** 'MARK TWAIN' *Conn. Yankee* 339 The Boss scores on his first innings. **1912** MATHEWSON *Pitching* 108–9 Schlei made a base hit . . . and scored both men.

Score book. **+1.** *Baseball.* A book in which scores and details of play are recorded. {1862–, of cricket} **+2.** A book in which the grades or marks of students are recorded. *Obs.* — **(1) 1868** CHADWICK *Base Ball* 41 Whenever a player is put out, . . . an 'out' is recorded in the score books. **1878** *De Witt's Base-Ball Guide* 30 In an ordinary score-book, each fielder is numbered from one to nine. **(2) 1871** BAGG *At Yale* 584 If by chance a student should get hold of the score-book of his division he would not be able to make out very closely the significance of the hieroglyphics contained therein.

Score-keeper. *Baseball.* +One whose duty it is to keep a record of scores or runs. — **1880** N. BROOKS *Fairport Nine* 40 The score-keepers had to allow them a home run for Jake Coombs. **1907** *St. Nicholas* June 721/1 The score was twelve to ten in favor of the Junior Giants, according to . . . Liberty Jim, official score-keeper for the occasion.

∗ Scorer.

+1. A sharp cut or slash, as with a switch or whip. *colloq.*

1845 HOOPER *Simon Suggs' Adv.* 24 He came down with a *scorer* across Simon's shoulders.

+2. = SCORE-KEEPER. {1773–, in cricket}

1867 CHADWICK *Base Ball Reference* 30 A regular scorer . . . should be competent to record the fielding as well as batting score of the game. **1891** N. CRANE *Baseball* 79 *Assist,* the credit given by the scorer to a fielder who handles the ball in assisting to put out a player.

+3. An axman who scores or slabs off the outer portions of a tree trunk in preparation for the work of the hewer.

1880 *Lumberman's Gazette* 7 Jan. 28 The scorers and liner fell the trees and roughly trim the two opposite sides.

∗ Scoria. Rough, cinderlike masses formed by lava as it cools. {1830–} Also *attrib.* — **1792** BELKNAP *Hist. New-Hampshire* III. 37 A company of persons . . . have found further evidences of internal fires; particularly a large quantity of *scoriæ*. **1852** MARCY *Explor. Red River* (1854) 9 In the course of the march to-day, we met with numerous detached pieces of copper ore, mixed with volcanic scoria. **1897** HOUGH *Story of Cowboy* 29 In the wild region of the Bad Lands, . . . the red scoria buttes and banks . . . are burned out of the earth.

Scoring. [SCORE *v.* 2.] +A rating, castigation. — **1863** *Harper's Mag.* March 569/1 We had not paid our circuit preacher . . . and we expected a scoring from the elder.

+Scorpene. [From Sp. *escorpina* or It. *scorpina.*] (See quotation.) — **1884** GOODE, etc. *Fisheries* II. 263 This species [*Scorpæna guttata*] is known by the names 'Scorpene,' 'Scorpion,' and 'Sculpin.' **1896** JORDAN & EVERMANN *Check-List Fishes* 433.

∗ Scorpion.

+1. *S.* Any one of various harmless lizards, esp. those of the genus *Sceloporus.*

1709 LAWSON *Carolina* 131 The Scorpion Lizard, is no more like a Scorpion, than a Hedge-Hog; but they very commonly call him a Scorpion. **1827** WILLIAMS *W. Florida* 28 The largest [lizard] is about seven inches long. . . . The old inhabitants call him the scorpion. **1839** *S. Lit. Messen-*

ger V. 113/1 'Scorpions' . . . [are] a genus greatly meliorated, and as I may say, mitigated from the fabulous *scorpio.*

∗2. Any one of various nocturnal arachnids found in warm regions.

1851 GLISAN *Jrnl. Army Life* 69 Sleeping on the ground . . . is not at all unpleasant in moderately fine weather, except when . . . scorpions or snakes, become too sociable. **1877** HODGE *Arizona* 227 The scorpion is found in limited quantities, and its sting is painful but not necessarily dangerous. **1923** J. H. COOK *On Old Frontier* 28 There were plenty of tarantulas, centipedes, and scorpions, with rattlesnakes too numerous to mention.

+3. a. = CABEZON. **b.** = SCORPENE.

(a) 1884 GOODE, etc. *Fisheries* I. 259 The names 'Cabezon,' 'Sculpin,' 'Scorpion,' [etc.] . . . are applied to this species [*Scorpænichthys marmoratus*]. **(b) 1884, 1896** [see SCORPENE].

+4. In special combinations.

Scorpion bile, inferior whisky (slang); *s. bug,* (see quotation); *s. lizard,* (see sense 1, quot. 1709); *s. mouse,* any of certain short-tailed mice of the genus *Onychomys* found in the western states.

1865 'MARK TWAIN' *Sketches* (1926) 163 Our reserve [voters were] . . . full of chain-lightning, sudden death and scorpion-bile. **1891** *Cent.* 5411/1 *Scorpion-bug,* a large predaceous water-beetle whose raptorial fore legs suggest a scorpion; a water-scorpion. **1890** *Stock Grower & Farmer* 4 Jan. 7/2 The most curious of all was a little beast that I shall name the 'scorpion mouse' because it appears to feed upon scorpions exclusively.

Scotch, *n.* **1.** = SCOTCH SNUFF. {1774– (Foote *Cozeners* Wks. III. 76)} **2.** Short for SCOTCH WHISKY; a drink of this. {1886–} Also *attrib.* (See also HOT SCOTCH.) — **(1) 1874** B. F. TAYLOR *World on Wheels* 95 There is a faint suspicion of 'Scotch' on her upper lip. **1891** WELCH *Recoll.* 1830–40 183 It was not uncommon to see a couple of portly old gentlemen meeting on the street offering their boxes of Maccaboy, Rappee or Scotch, each to the other. **(2) 1898** WESTCOTT *D. Harum* v. [He] was induced to go the length of 'Scotch and soda.' **1904** Mackaye *Panchronicon* 248 Give me a Scotch high-ball.

∗ Scotch, *a.*

1. Of persons: Native to Scotland, or of Scottish ancestry. {1606–}

Cf. SCOTCH-IRISH *n.*, SCOTCH-IRISH *a.*, SCOTCHMAN.

1729 *Amer. Wkly. Mercury* 22 May, There is just arrived from Scotland, a parcel of choice Scotch Servants; Taylors, Weavers, Shoemakers and ploughmen. **1798** I. ALLEN *Hist. Vermont* 41 A number of Scotch emigrants [were encouraged] to settle at New Haven falls. **1896** P. Ross *Scot in Amer.* 268 The establishment gave employment to 1,800 hands, mostly Scotch.

∗2. Of things: Obtained from Scotland, or made in the Scottish fashion.

See also SCOTCH CAP 1, SCOTCH CLOTH, etc.

1759 *Essex Inst. Coll.* XIX. 70 It Came out in order this Day that no officer in ye Rigement Should wear a Scotch bonet. **1779** *York Co., Va., Rec.: Wills* XXII. 28 April, 1 Scotch carpet £10. **1833** *Niles' Reg.* XLIV. 269/1 To be admitted at an ad valorem duty of 15 per cent. under the act of 14th July, 1832: . . . Irish, Scotch and English linen sheetings. **1875** *Chicago Tribune* 1 Oct. 1/1 French, English, and Scotch Suitings, Overcoatings, and Cloths of every description.

3. Of dances: Originating in, or characteristic of, Scotland.

1891 WELCH *Recoll.* 1830–40 376 [In] the 'Scotch Reel,' . . . each lad must needs have two lassies. **1895** L. G. FRAZER, etc. *Dancing* 424 It is difficult to see why the title ['barn dance'] is specially applied to this Scotch lilt.

4. In the specific names of plants.

See also SCOTCH BROOM, SCOTCH CABBAGE, etc.

1840 DEWEY *Mass. Flowering Plants* 109 *Campanula rotundifolia.* Hair Bell, or Scotch Bell. A beautiful and slender plant. **1849** EMMONS *Agric. N.Y.* II. 141 Scotch Wheat. Its origin is unknown. Berry large, and resembles the Indiana. **1891** *Cent.* 5412/1 *Scotch heath* or *heather,* . . . (U.S.), the common heather, *Calluna vulgaris.*

+Scotch broom. (See quot. 1891.) — **1817–8** EATON *Botany* (1822) 471. **1868** GRAY *Field Botany* 100 C[ytisus] (or *Sarothamnus*) *scoparius,* Scotch Broom. Shrub, from Europe. . . . Hardy in gardens N.; running wild in Virginia. **1891** *Cent.* 5412/1 *Scotch broom,* an American designation of the common broom, *Cytisus scoparius.*

Scotch cabbage. A variety of cabbage having a round or flattened head. *Obs.* {1825– (Loudon *Encycl. Agric.* 799)} — **1805** PARKINSON *Tour* 339 The Scotch, or drum-head cabbage, is in great request, . . . and is used for what they call sour-crout, for the winter. **1849** [see DRUMHEAD 2].

∗ Scotch cap.

∗1. A man's round, brimless, woolen cap ornamented with two streamers. Also *attrib.*

1840 DANA *Two Years* 150 Putting on . . . red shirts, and Scotch caps, we began taking out and landing our hides. **1865** *Atlantic Mo.* May 595/2 He bartered one day a new pocket-knife . . . for a knit Scotch cap, half-worn. **1890** FREDERIC *Lawton Girl* 75 Lucinda . . . toiled in the Scotch-cap factory in the village. **1893** *McClure's Mag.* Aug. 252/2 Scarlet knit Scotch caps . . . completed the camp uniform.

+2. (See quotations.)

1891 *Cent.* 5412/2 *Scotch-cap,* . . . the wild black raspberry. **1900** WEBSTER *Suppl.* 186/2 *Scotch cap,* the wild black raspberry . . . ; also, the salmon berry.

Scotch cloth. A cheap fabric somewhat resembling lawn. *Obs.* {1675-} Also attrib. — **1696** SEWALL *Letter-Book* I. 167 Several pieces of Serge, Stuff and Scotch-Cloth, to the value of about Thirty pounds. **1713** *Mass. H. S. Coll.* 6 Ser. V. 269, [I] send . . . two peices of lining Scotch cloth for the children. **1721** *Amer. Wkly. Mercury* 5 Oct. 4/2 [He has] a New Scotch-cloth Shirt, white Linnen Britches.

Scotch gray(s). {Scotch greys, 1805-} A variety of buckwheat or of potato. Also attrib. — **1849** EMMONS *Agric. N.Y.* II. 48 Scotch Grays Potato . . . [is] complained of as disposed to become watery and rather strong. **1856** *Rep. Comm. Patents 1855: Agric.* 204 The variety [of buckwheat] principally raised is known as the 'Scotch grey.'

+Scotch-Irish, *n. collect.* Persons of Scottish and Irish ancestry, esp. those from northern Ireland.

1744 *Mass. H. S. Coll.* 1 Ser. VII. 177 The inhabitants [of Lancaster, Pa.] are chiefly High-Dutch, Scotch-Irish, some few English families, and unbelieving Israelites. **1789** MORSE *Amer. Geog.* 313 [The Irish of Penna.] have sometimes been called Scotch-Irish, to denote their double descent. **1835** SHIRREFF *Tour* 236 He had never heard of Scotchmen before, and insisted I must be one of the Scotch-Irish which I afterwards learnt means, in this part of the world [Ill.], the inhabitants of the north of Ireland. **1853** *S. Lit. Messenger* XIX. 40/1 In Western Virginia . . . that shrewd and thrifty race called 'Scotch-Irish' are mostly settled. **1883** *Harper's Mag.* Feb. 421/2 The so-called Scotch-Irish are the descendants of the Englishmen and Lowland Scotch who began to move over to Ulster in 1611.

b. *Scotch-Irisher, Scotch-Irishman,* a person of Scotch-Irish blood.

1823 COOPER *Pioneers* xxxiii, I was out among the Scotch-Irishers. **1903** Fox *Little Shepherd* x, Broadcast, through the people, was the upright sturdiness of the Scotch-Irishman, without his narrowness and bigotry.

+Scotch-Irish, *a.* Of or pertaining to the descendants of those Scots who settled in northern Ireland early in the seventeenth century. — **1828** J. HALL *Lett. from West* 295 Scotch-Irish Pennsylvania claims the honour of his [Hugh Glass's] nativity. **1844** *Knickerb.* XXIII. 404 It is now no more than a hundred years since a small band of Scotch-Irish Presbyterians settled in [a valley in central N.Y.]. **1893** PAGE in *Harper's Mag.* Dec. 14/1 Stout Scotch-Irish settlers filled up the [Shenandoah] Valley. **1905** VALENTINE *H. Sandwith* 3 These hoary timbers had witnessed . . . the coming of the Scotch-Irish pioneers.

*Scotchman. A man of Scottish nationality; an immigrant from Scotland. — **1679** *Jamaica* (L.I.) *Rec.* I. 194 A tenn acre Lot of upland . . . [is] joyneing on Alexsander Smith a scotch man. **1682** *Mass. H. S. Coll.* 4 Ser. V. 83 One Jeffryes, a Scotchman, . . . contrived her [the ship's] escape two days before the trial. **1700** *N.J. Archives* 1 Ser. II. 328 They turned out an Englishman who was Sherif & put in a Scotchman who they thought would Obey them without Reserve. **1773** WASHINGTON *Diaries* II. 122 In the afternoon came . . . two Scotchmen empowered by a Number of Familys about Glasgow to look out Land for two hundred Familys. **1867** EDWARDS *Shelby* 66 This gunner was a debonair, gallant, sunbrowned Scotchman. **1905** *North Carolina Booklet* IV. x. 11 Governor Gabriel Johnson was himself a Scotchman.

Scotch plaid. {1785-} +A fabric having a pattern of colored bars or stripes crossing each other in imitation of a Scottish tartan. Also attrib. — **1868** *Ore. State Jrnl.* 5 Dec. 2/5 Scotch plaids, it is said, will be 'the thing' for ladies' walking suits this winter. **1873** PHELPS *Trotty's Wedding* v, She had on a Scotch-plaid dress. **1878** *Decorum* 282 A costume of Scotch plaid is in excellent taste.

Scotch snuff. Finely ground snuff of a characteristic strength and pungency prepared from well-dried tobacco. {1815-} Also fig. — **1733** *S.C. Gazette* 7 April, To be sold . . . cut Tobacco, Scotch Snuff, and Pigtail. **1779** *N.J. Archives* 2 Ser. III. 600 For sale . . . Scotch snuff of an excellent quality. **1853** BALDWIN *Flush Times Ala.* 310 You must mash Sam Boyd and Jo Holt into Scotch snuff.

Scotch terrier. A short-legged terrier of a breed originating in Scotland. {1863} — **1865** *Atlantic Mo.* April 493/1 Some [rooms are] so stately, so correct, that they would paralyze even the . . . most impudent Scotch terrier. **1883** THAXTER *Poems for Children* 13 Little Scotch terrier, little dog Rags, Looks in her face. **1912** *Outing* April 119/2 This Lowland dog . . . was in early days called the Scotch terrier.

Scotch whisky. Whisky made in Scotland, or of the type distilled there. {1855-} Also attrib. — **1848** JUDSON *Mysteries N.Y.* I. 115 'Mountain-dew.' Scotch whiskey. **1853** SIMMS *Sword & Distaff* (1854) 457 Old rum and fiery French brandy and genuine Scotch whiskey took the place . . . of more courtly spirits. **1872** *Atlantic Mo.* May 551 In summer and winter alike, hot Scotch whiskey-punch, served in large goblets, was the staple [in N.Y. City]. **1880** *Harper's Mag.* Aug. 354/1 A flask of Scotch whiskey . . . was his one catholic remedy . . . for cuts, fevers, colds, or rattlesnake bites.

Scoter. Any one of various ducks of the genera *Oidemia* or *Melanitta* {1674-}, as the American scoter. Also *scoter duck.* Also with specifying terms. (See also SURF SCOTER.) — **1813** WILSON *Ornithology* VIII. 135 Scoter Duck: *Anas nigra* . . . [is] more usually met with in the northern than southern districts. **1887** RIDGWAY *Manual N.A. Birds* 113 Northern North America; south, in winter, to Chesapeake Bay, the Great Lakes, and southern California. . . . *O[idemia] deglandi.* White-winged Scoter.

1902 WHITE *Blazed Trail* 87 Butterballs and scoters paddled up at his approach. **1917** *Birds of Amer.* I. 149/1 The American Scoter, Black Coot, or Little Gray Coot . . . is the least numerous of the three Scoters.

*Scour, *n. pl.* +A form of diarrhea in cattle and sheep. {sing. 1764-} — **1848** *Rep. Comm. Patents 1847* 507 They say the disease called the 'scours' is the principal one to which sheep are liable. **1863** MITCHELL *My Farm* 223 His calves will very likely take the 'scours.' **1882** *Maine Agric. Rep.* XXVI. 25 Over-loading the stomach after a long fast is almost sure to be followed by indigestion and scours, diseases which are very common among young calves.

*Scour, *v.* *To scour up* {1611-, fig.}, +to impart a polish to by scouring. — **1833** S. SMITH *Life J. Downing* 175 He put on his regimentals and scoured up the old piece of a scythe that he used to have for a sword. **1870** J. P. SMITH *Widow Goldsmith's Daughter* vii, Being called back to scour up the pot-hooks, polish the crane [etc.].

*Scourer.

*1. A contrivance for cleaning the bore of a gun.

1633 *N.H. Prov. Papers* I. 80, 3 spounges, 2 scowrers. **1651** *East-Hampton Rec.* I. 18 All that are fitt to beare armes shalbe sufficiently provided with . . . scourer shotbagg rest bolt and a fitt thing to carrie powder in. **1702** *Essex Inst. Coll.* XLII. 162 Inventory of ship. . . . Scourer for small arms.

‖2. (See quotation.)

1831 R. COX *Adv. Columbia R.* 186 The bride was . . . consigned to the care of one of the men's wives, called 'the scourer,' . . . who had her head and body thoroughly cleansed from all the Indian paint and grease with which she had been saturated.

3. An apparatus for cleaning grain or removing hair from hides by scouring or rubbing.

1859 *Rep. Comm. Patents 1858* I. 378 Scourer G, blast spouts E F, and fan C, [are] combined and arranged relatively with each other. **1883** KNIGHT *Suppl.* 784/1 Scourer, a form of grain cleaner in which the berry is subjected to a rubbing action to remove all extraneous matters. **1885** *Harper's Mag.* Jan. 276/2 Hides brought to the currying, after having been properly split, flattened, pin-wheeled, and tanned out, are put under a 'scourer,' a machine constructed of a number of diminutive wheels, which are made to move powerfully and swiftly over the yet damp hide.

+Scouring plow. A plow for shallow surface cultivation rather than for breaking purposes. — **1856** *Rep. Comm. Patents 1855: Agric.* 170 It was ploughed as near it as possible with a double-shovel scouring plough. **1861** *Ill. Agric. Soc. Trans.* IV. 204 [The corn is] plowed four times in its cultivation . . . , the two last times with scouring plows.

+Scouring rush. Any one of various species of plants of the genus *Equisetum,* esp. *E. hyemale,* suitable for use in scouring wood or metal: (see also quot. 1847). — **1817-8** EATON *Botany* (1822) 273 *Equisetum hyemale,* scouring rush. **1847** EMORY *Military Reconn.* 13 We find in the bottoms . . . scouring rush (*Equisetum hyemale,*) a powerful diuretic upon horses. **1899** GOING *Flowers* 251 The horsetails, or scouring-rushes, . . . shed spores.

Scours. (See SCOUR *n.*)

*Scout, *n.*

*1. One who keeps watch upon or reconnoiters an enemy's movements and positions.

See also INDIAN SCOUT 1 and 2.

1624 SMITH *Gen. Hist. Va.* III. 90 [Captain Smith,] vnderstanding by his Scouts the arrivall of such a Fleet, . . . supposed them *Spanyards.* **1676** I. MATHER *K. Philip's War* (1862) 101 Some that were sent forth as Scouts were killed or Captivated. **1704** *Boston News-Letter* 15 May 2/1 Some [Indians] were trackt about three miles . . . and 'tis believed they saw our Scouts. **1790** WASHINGTON *Diaries* IV. 114 The County Lieutenants of that District [were] to employ 4 scouts in each of the Frontier Counties for the purpose of discovering the movements of the Indians. **1826** COOPER *Mohicans* xiv, The scout now told the sisters to dismount. **1898** WISTER *Lin McLean* 57 Tommy Postmaster had paid high for a necklace of elk-tushes the government scout at McKinney sold him. **1923** J. H. COOK *On Old Frontier* 89 He had charge of the Pawnee Indian army scouts for some time.

*2. *On a scout,* or variants of this. **a.** Engaged in a scouting expedition; occupied with spying out or being on the watch for information. {1687-}

See also INDIAN SCOUT 3.

1675 *Lancaster Rec.* 107 Hugh Clarke . . . being the last weeke vpon the Scout with Capt. Gibbs, . . . they found seuerall houses deserted. **1716** CHURCH *Philip's War* 46 [He] was minded to send some of them out on a Scout. **1775** *Essex Inst. Coll.* LIII. 84 Went down to Charlestown upon scout. **1903** Fox *Little Shepherd* xxiv, Dan is out on a scout.

+b. Endeavoring to escape officers of the law; on the dodge.

1891 O'BEIRNE *Leaders Ind. Territory* 74/1 Paul was arrested and Ben Dillard fled from the locality, and spent some four years on the scout, after which he gave himself up.

*3. = SCOUTING PARTY. {-a1619}

1693 in Temple & Sheldon *Hist. Northfield, Mass.* 125 The scout of 4 men . . . lighted on new tracks which they followed. **1723** *Amer. Wkly. Mercury* 29 Aug. 2/1 A Scout of about 10 or 12 Indians (as he thought) came Sudenly upon them. **1779** *Mass. H. S. Coll.* 2 Ser. II. 453 A Small Scout went out this day. **1798** I. ALLEN *Hist. Vermont* 92 He sent a scout of about 300, mostly Indians, to hunt at the mouth of Otter Creek. **1867** EDWARDS *Shelby* 412 At Current river a scout of fifty were encountered.

4. (See quot. 1851.) *Obs.* {1708-}

1846 *Yale Lit. Mag.* XI. 282 In order to quiet him, we had to send for his factotum or scout, an old black fellow. **1851** HALL *College Words* 264 *Scout,* a cant term at Oxford for a college servant or waiter. . . . Sometimes used in American colleges.

+5. *Baseball.* A player stationed in the field; a fielder. *Obs.*

1856 *Porter's Spirit of Times* 27 Dec. 276/3 One of these swiftly-delivered balls . . . is sure to give the outmost scout employment. **1871** EMERSON *Works* X. 309 [To] the baseball players, . . . the bat, the catcher, and the scout are equally important.

6. Attrib. with *fashion, force, game,* etc.

See also SCOUT BOAT, SCOUT HORN, etc.

1758 *Essex Inst. Coll.* XVIII. 187 The Rangers exercise in Scout marches and Bush fighting. **1775** ADAIR *Indians* 336 Now and then I put up the whoop on different sides of the path, . . . [to] intimidate the opposite scout-party. **1836** SIMMS *Mellichampe* xviii, We must play a scout-game with the rascal. **1853** — *Sword & Distaff* (1854) 491 Having ascertained, scout-fashion, all the necessary particulars in the case, Frampton rejoined his party. **1900** DRANNAN *Plains & Mts.* 194 Almost the entire scout force were from New York.

∗ Scout, *v.* (See also SCOUTING.)

∗1. *intr.* To act as a scout or spy.

1675 *Conn. Rec.* II. 406 The Councell allso wrote a letter . . . to desire them to scoutt abroad and pick up such of the enemie as they shall find. **1689** *Mass. H. S. Coll.* 4 Ser. V. 203 Some parties of our friend[ly] Indians . . . [can serve] as a flying army to scout upon the heads of the out towns and plantations. **1705** *Boston News-Letter* 14 May 2/2 His Excellency has ordered Major Walton to detach a Company to Scout from Nitchewanock to Wells. **1840** COOPER *Pathfinder* I. 255 The Sarpent and I were out scouting about the garrison there. **1888** HARTE *Argonauts of N. Liberty* 198 It's one of their gang—scouting. **1902** WHITE *Blazed Trail* 211 Shearer and Andrews, the surveyor, were scouting up the river.

2. *tr.* To examine or search carefully (a place or region). {1704-}

1675 *Conn. Rec.* II. 411 The Councill ordered him . . . to march and scout the woods as far as Wongunck. **1782** *Essex Inst. Coll.* I. 13/2 My dutey will consist in scouten the woods. **1881-5** MCCLELLAN *Own Story* 190 After again scouting the woods, Col. Devens returned to his advanced position. **1895** REMINGTON *Pony Tracks* 147 We go ashore and 'scout the place.'

+Scout boat. A boat used in scouting operations. {1902-} — **1717** *S.C. Statutes at Large* III. 24 For the scout boat on Port Royal Island, [there shall be] a Captain and six private men. **1741** *S.C. Hist. Soc. Coll.* IV. 25 A Sum of £10,000 annual Expense . . . in maintaining Garrisons, Lookouts, Scout Boats [etc.], would be saved to the Publick. **1836** E. L. JOHNSTON *Recoll. Ga. Loyalist* 40 My father had an appointment under Government . . . ; this was the command of a scout boat. **1862** MOORE *Rebellion Rec.* V. II. 182 The scout-boats of Com. Montgomery notified him of the presence of the Federals.

Scouter. A scout. {1642-45} — *c*1776 in Irving *Life Washington* II. 606 [Governor Trumbull described him as] a famous scouter and wood-hunter. **1827** COOPER *Prairie* xviii, This is a scouter in his war-paint! There should be more of his tribe at no great distance. **1855** SIMMS *Forayers* 358 But suppose he should be surprised, Bertha, by some of these scouters? **1867** EDWARDS *Shelby* 232 Sears . . . [was] one of the truest scouters who ever fired pistol.

+Scout horn, Scoot horn. (See quot. 1884 and cf. BOAT HORN 2.) — **1855** 'P. PAXTON' *Capt. Priest* 183 He contented himself . . . keeping his hands busy with the scout-horn wetting the sails. **1884** *Nat. Museum Bul.* No. 27, 779 *Scout-horn,* a wooden pole having a piece of a leather boot-leg fastened to one end so as to form a scoop. . . . Used in former years to wet the sails of small vessels in order to make them set flat and hold the wind when sailing close-hauled.

Scouting.

1. Spying out; reconnoitering. {1644-}

1676 in A. S. Hudson *Hist. Sudbury, Mass.* 202 Said men are to be improved in scouting between town and town. **1704** *Boston News-Letter* 7 June 2/1 If it were possible for me by any means to bring the Queens good Subjects in the several parts, to do their duty in Watching & Scouting. **1840** COOPER *Pathfinder* I. 237, I fancy the open air, long hunts, scoutings, forest fare, and the sleep of a good conscience may always keep the doctors at a distance. **1865** BOUDRYE *Fifth N.Y. Cavalry* 42 Picketing and scouting were not very desirable.

2. Attrib. with *capacity, design, excursion,* etc.

1761 NILES *Indian Wars* II. 440 Lieutenant Dorman went out on a scouting design against the enemy. **1845** FRÉMONT *Exped.* 214 One of our best men . . . had gone out on a scouting excursion. **1854** SIMMS *Southward Ho!* 294 Coulter persuaded the old African . . . to set forth on a scouting expedition to the farmstead. **1855** — *Forayers* 251 He was . . . to exercise his best *scouting* capacities. **1866** *Rep. Indian Affairs* 162 Five Indians . . . came in one of my scouting stations. **1881** STODDARD *E. Hardery* 88, I can imagine it's a scouting raid, inside the enemy's lines.

Scouting party. A body of men on a scouting expedition. — **1756** ROGERS *Journals* 17 They discovered a scouting party of three or four hundred Indians. **1790** FANNING *Narrative* 12 We kept scouting parties, through the country. **1812** [see INDIAN SIGN]. **1895** M. A. JACKSON *Gen.*

Jackson 548 A Federal scouting party could have come up the Hazel Grove road and seized him as prisoner of war.

Scout man. A scout or spy. *Obs.* — **1739** W. STEPHENS *Proc. Georgia* I. 457 Three of the Scout-men, straggling unwarily into the Woods, were attacked. **1795** PUTNAM in *Memoirs* 407 A few Spyes or Scout men under proper direction will afford every reasonable Protection against the Small Sculking parties of Savages.

Scout path. A trail along which scouts or scouting parties usually passed. *Obs.* — **1750** in Temple & Sheldon *Hist. Northfield, Mass.* 378 About twelve or fifteen Indians Way-laid the Scout-Path from Fort Dummer to Colerain.

Scout shallop. A shallop suitable for use in reconnoitering. *Obs.* — **1693** *Essex Inst. Coll.* XLII. 111 [They] did set forth & mainetaine a Scout Shallop for about fiue months in the Sumer. **1704** SEWALL *Diary* II. 98 Read Brothers Letter . . . about a Scout-Shallop. **1832** WILLIAMSON *Maine* II. 46 Furnished with 14 transports, 36 whaleboats, and a scout-shallop, he sailed [in 1704] from Boston.

+Scovilite, Scophilite. One of the Scovil faction, commissioned by the governor of South Carolina in 1768 to suppress the Regulators (sense 2); also applied during the Revolution to certain active Tories. — **1855** SIMMS *Forayers* 217 All these rascals, Scophilites, Yahoos, foragers, tories, . . . are all in the king's commission. *Ib.* 218 The Scophilites and Yahoos, sir, were notorious long before the beginning of the war. **1899** E. MCCRADY *Hist. S.C. Royal Govt.* 595 He conferred a high commission to suppress these disorders on a man whose name was variously written, Scovil or Schovel or Schofield. . . . The Governor . . . sided with the Scovilites, his creatures.

+Scow, *n.* [Du. *schouw.* See note below.] A large, flat-bottomed boat, usually serving as a ferryboat or lighter.

Also in Scotland and Ulster (1841-) by independent adoption from Dutch.

1669 in Munsell *Ann. Albany* IV. 10 The Governor hath given me Orders . . . to provyde a scow to help ye souldiers in their provision of fire wood. **1714** HEMPSTEAD *Diary* 34, I workt at huttons al day about ye horse Boat or Scow. **1781** JEFFERSON *Writings* II. (1893) 485 Scows I am afraid cannot be used for the Transportation of your cannon. **1835** A. PARKER *Trip to Texas* (1836) 16 The Scows used exclusively for grain, flour, lumber, &c., . . . are employed by the farmers to carry their own produce to market. **1883** 'MARK TWAIN' *Life on Miss.* xxx, A dozen rude scows were scattered about. *transf.* **1901** MERWIN & WEBSTER *Calumet 'K'* 69 The Pages aren't sending out any six-mile-an-hour scow to do their quick work.

b. Attrib. with *boat, gang, load,* etc.

1714 HEMPSTEAD *Diary* 38, I fetched ye Scow load of Railes & Posts. **1828** FLINT *Geog. Miss. Valley* I. 230 The ferry flat is a scow-boat. **1891** *Scribner's Mag.* Oct. 483/1 The oyster next falls into the hands of the 'scow-gang,' men whose specialty it is to remove them from the floats. **1906** *N.Y. Ev. Post* 8 Oct. 12 Scowmen and bargemen along the North and East River fronts. **1913** LONDON *Valley of Moon* 269 At the foot of Castro street . . . the scow schooners, laden with sand and gravel, lay hauled to the shore in a long row.

+Scow, *v. intr.* and *tr.* To cross by means of a scow; to transport (something) in a scow. *Obs.* — **1749** W. DOUGLASS *Summary* I. 460 The ferry is about 80 rod, and . . . runs 2 or three knots, scowed over in about 9 minutes. **1751** MACSPARRAN *Diary* 58 He and a Boy. . . were Scowing wood. **1828** WEBSTER s.v.

Scrabble. {1842-}

+1. A scratching or scrambling; a scrimmage or tussle; a rough-and-tumble effort. {as vb. 1638-, 'to scramble'}

1794 *Gazette of U.S.* 21 Feb. (Th.), The Frenchman . . . in a scrabble swore he would have another hem to his shirt, and in the very scrabble lost his shirt. **1826** BRYANT *Let. to S. S. Bryant* 13 June (MS.), I am obliged to have a pavillion [because of the mosquitoes], or spend my sleeping hours in a perpetual scrabble. **1849** T. T. JOHNSON *Sights Gold Region* 66 We often got caught by the waves, and had a grand scrabble to reach dry land. **1894** ALDRICH *Two Bites* 145 The next sound I heard was the scrabble of the animal's four paws as he landed on the gravelled pathway. **1911** SAUNDERS *Col. Todhunter* 43 Whoever wins will win after the toughest scrabble you and me ever saw in Missouri politics.

+2. A scattered or scanty growth.

1896 ADE *Artie* 113 There was a scrabble of soft beard on his chin.

∗ Scrag. +Any one of various small whales having the skin near the tail covered with protuberances. In full *scrag whale.* Also *scrag right whale, scrag-tail whale.* {1850}

1701 WOLLEY *Journal N.Y.* (1902) 47 A Scrag-tail Whale is like another, only . . . his bone is not good. **1725** DUDLEY in *Phil. Trans.* XXXIII. 258 The Scrag Whale is near a-kin to the Fin-back. **1835** MACY *Hist. Nantucket* 28 A whale, of the kind called 'scragg,' came into the harbor. **1874** C. M. SCAMMON *Marine Mammals* 67 Our observations, however, make it certain that there is a 'scrag' Right Whale in the North Pacific. **1884** GOODE, etc. *Fisheries* I. 31 The Scrag is of special interest on account of its influence in first developing the whaling industries of Nantucket.

Scraggly, *a.* Irregular, loose-limbed, scraggy. {*dial.*} Also comb. — **1869** STOWE *Oldtown Folks* 534 That's all we scraggly old people are good for. **1884** NYE *Baled Hay* 198 A flippant nation of scoffers had utilized that volume to press autumn leaves and scraggly ferns in. **1887** WILKINS *Humble Romance* 220 The walls of the little room had a scraggly-patterned paper on them. **1901** WHITE *Claim Jumpers* 44 The stranger was a tall, scraggly individual, dressed in the usual flannel shirt and blue jeans.

***Scramble,** *v.* +*tr.* To beat or stir (eggs, etc.) in cooking them. Also transf. — **1864** WEBSTER 1183/3 *Scramble*, to mix and cook in a confused mass; as, to scramble eggs. **1865** *Atlantic Mo.* June 656/1, I might have scrambled you, or boiled you, or made a pasch-egg of you. **1875** M. LONGWORTH *Teresina in Amer.* I. 280 [If] the *chef de cuisine* has ordered the eggs that morning to be scrambled, as they call the mess, then you must . . . eat them scrambled or go without. **1891** RYAN *Told in Hills* 100 The girl . . . [did not look] up from the eggs she was scrambling in the bake-oven of a few minutes before. **1903** *Munsey's Mag.* May 247/1 She scrambled eggs and bacon, and ate them.

Scrambled egg. +An egg of which the white and the yolk are stirred or mixed together while cooking, often with the addition of a little milk. {1897-} Usually pl. — **1864** SALA in *Daily Telegraph* 9 Feb., Bring me . . . some scrambled eggs. *c*1866 [see GOOBA-PEA]. **1867** DIXON *New Amer.* II. 96 The eggs, hard eggs, boiled eggs, scrambled eggs, are delicious. **1884** F. E. OWENS *Cook Book* 65 Scrambled eggs . . . must not be hard.

Scrap basket. A basket for scraps or remnants, esp. of cloth; a wastebasket. — **1895** WILLIAMS *Princeton Stories* 270 Tucker tossed his cap and Symington's gracefully into the scrap-basket. **1903** WIGGIN *Rebecca* 240 The pillow-cases are from Mrs. Cobb, . . . the scrap-basket from Living and Dick. **1914** S. H. ADAMS *Clarion* 21, [I] hung the scrap-basket on the stenographer's ear when she tried to hold me up to sign some letters, jumped out of the fifth-story window, and here I am.

Scrapbook. {1825-} **a.** A notebook. **b.** A blank book in which newspaper clippings, pictures, etc., are pasted for preservation. {1854-} — **1830** *Collegian* 173 In noting down in a little scrap-book whatever had struck my eye . . . , I spent the noon hour. **1846** *Xenia Torch-Light* July 3/5 [The engravings] are a handsome addition to a Scrap Book. **1896** *Voice* 18 June 6/4, I have a scrap-book of newspaper clippings that is a symposium of Billingsgate mudballs, with Crane for the target. **1902** *Harper's Mag.* May 969/2 It jars me to reflect that . . . the school-girl with her scrap-book and the fiend with his awful album are all of a piece with *me!*

***Scrape,** *n.* +Crude turpentine scraped from the trunks of turpentined trees. In full *scrape turpentine.* — **1856** OLMSTED *Slave States* 343 It is occasionally . . . scraped off, and barreled by itself. It is, therefore, known in market as 'scrape.' **1863** 'E. KIRKE' *Southern Friends* 131 Your trees are old, and now yield little of anything but scrape. *Ib.* (note), 'Scrape' turpentine is only about half as valuable as 'dip.' **1884** SARGENT *Rep. Forests* 517 The following grades of turpentine are recognized in the trade: . . . 'Scrape' or 'Hard Turpentine'—the product of the scrapings of the boxes. **1896** *Pop. Science Mo.* Feb. 470 The product thus obtained is 'scrape,' or 'hard turpentine.'

***Scrape,** *v.*

+**1.** *tr.* To level (ground) or clear its surface of weeds, grass, etc., preparatory to planting a crop. *Obs.*

1647 WILLIAMS *Letters* (1874) 146 The Indian hills . . . [are] only scraped or levelled. **1772** *Md. Hist. Mag.* XIV. 150 We want a good Season much, most of our tob[acc]o ground being Scraped.

+**2.** To cultivate (cotton) to a shallow depth and thin it with hoes or special plows.

1827 *Western Mo. Rev.* I. 82 The cotton . . . is thinned carefully, and plows, in the form of scrapers, are used, as the technical phrase is, to scrape it out. **1829** in Commons, etc. *Doc. Hist.* I. 235 Hoes scrapeing cotton in Sheep pasture. **1835** INGRAHAM *South-West* II. 283 The cotton . . . is thinned out, or as it is called, 'scraped.' **1854** *Harper's Mag.* March 453/1 The dexterity displayed by the negroes in scraping cotton is most calculated to call forth the admiration of the novice spectator.

***Scraper.**

+**1. a.** A heavy, two-handled scoop drawn by oxen or horses and used chiefly for excavating, as in road-making. **b.** A tool for comparatively shallow cultivation of row crops.

1823 *New Eng. Farmer* II. 9 The most expeditious, effectual, and economical mode of making a drain would undoubtedly be to use oxen, and a scraper or ox-shovel, as it is sometimes called. **1857** in Commons, etc. *Doc. Hist.* I. 276 In this age of improvement, with scrapers and cultivators, and all the endless variety of labor-saving ploughs. **1874** *Vermont Bd. Agric. Rep.* II. 658 In this work the scraper may be used with profit. **1885** *Rep. Indian Affairs* 157 If I could get their Great Father to give them three large plows and scrapers I would let them know. **1906** [see DIRT ROAD].

+**2.** A dredge for taking oysters, scallops, etc.

1881 INGERSOLL *Oyster-Industry* 247 *Scraper*, a small dredge. Chiefly spoken of with reference to scallops. (New England.) **1887** GOODE, etc. *Fisheries* v. II. 571 For a rocky bottom a dredge is used which has the blade immovably fastened to the arms; otherwise it does not differ from the 'kettle-bail' and it is known as a 'scraper.'

***Scraping.** +**1.** =SCRAPE *n.* +**2.** Shallow cultivation of a crop, designed to thin it and to remove grass, weeds, etc. — (1) **1832** BROWNE *Sylva* 232 The scraping is a coating of sap which becomes solid before it reaches the boxes. (2) **1854** *Harper's Mag.* March 453/1 If the weather be favorable, the young plant is discovered making its way through in six or ten days, and 'the scraping' of the crop, as it is termed, now begins.

1863 *Rep. Comm. Agric. 1862* 109 As soon as the third leaf appears the process of 'scraping' commences.

+**Scrapple.** Scraps of meat, usu. pork, boiled with corn meal or flour, and allowed to set. Freq. sliced and fried: (see also quot. *c*1870). — *c*1870 CHIPMAN *Notes on Bartlett* 387 *Scrapple*, equal parts of buckwheat flour and wheat flour boiled in the liquor produced in making 'Head-Cheese,' and used as 'Hasty Pudding' is after cooling.—Pennsylvania. **1872** NAPHEYS *Prev. & Cure Disease* I. 59 The sausage and scrapple of New Jersey. **1881** *Harper's Mag.* Jan. 181 Milk, eggs, sausage, scrapple, vegetables, and poultry, all fresh from the farm. **1890** *Voice* 20 Mar., His palate is so rich in appetites for scrapple, baked beans, moose steak. **1904** *N.Y. Ev. Post* 15 Jan. 7 Those who are acquainted with scrapple, who love sausage [etc.]. **1920** BOK *Americanization* 213 Bok was telling Kipling one day about the scrapple so dear to the heart of the Philadelphian as a breakfast dish.

***Scratch.** *attrib.* passing into *adj.* In special applications.

Scratch awl, a form of awl used by carpenters for marking timber, plank, etc.; *s. block,* a block or pad of paper for scribbling; *s.-gravel,* rough-and-tumble, slam-bang; *s. hit* (*Baseball*), a hit that barely enables the batter to reach first base; *s. hitter,* a baseball player who secures a scratch hit or hits; *s. match,* a match ignited by being scratched on a rough surface; *s. paper, s. player,* (see quotations); *s. shot,* a shot which barely or by luck reaches its mark; *s. ticket,* (see quotation); *s. vote,* a vote or ballot that has been scratched (cf. SCRATCH *v.* 1).

1894 ROBINSON *Danvis Folks* 238 The carpenter . . . was bustling about with a square and scratch-awl. **1897** FLANDRAU *Harvard Episodes* 192 On the table . . . his note-books and scratch block were lying open. **1862** Moore *Rebellion Rec.* V. II. 306 It was a fair stand-up, knock-down and scratch-gravel fight between the two iron-clad nondescripts—the Union Essex and the rebel Arkansas. **1917** MATHEWSON *Sec. Base Sloan* 166 Four men faced Chase in the third, the first getting a scratch hit, the second sacrificing him to the next bag. **1886** *Outing* July 477/2 Many is the man who does much towards producing runs, and yet . . . at the end of the season stands below the 'scratch' hitter. **1891** WELCH *Recoll.* 1830-40 359*n.*, Locofoco or scratch matches first came into use about [1840]. **1905** *Dialect Notes* III. 93 *Scratch-paper*, paper used for memoranda. 'The commandant doesn't like for you to use the delinquency blanks as scratch-paper.' **1895** J. P. LEE *Golf* 181 *Scratch Player*, one who receives no allowance in a handicap. **1916** DU PUY *Uncle Sam* 154 If he could make a scratch shot and land on the coco of Mr. Goliath he would win. **1859** BARTLETT 386 *Scratch Ticket*, properly *scratched ticket*, an election ticket with one or more names of candidates erased. **1888** BRYCE *Amer. Commw.* I. I. xiv. 203 Surprises and scratch votes are not uncommon.

***Scratch,** *v.*

+**1.** *Polit. tr.* To cancel or scratch off (a name or names) from those appearing on the ticket of one's party; to repudiate (a candidate) or bolt (a ticket) in this manner. Also *vbl. n.*

1841 *Whig Almanac* 3 Messrs. Ritner and Shulze, the Harrison Senatorial Electors, were *scratched* by a number of voters. **1870** *Congress. Globe* 24 May 3761/1 It is the habit of the American voter as a rule to scratch his ticket, to take from it such names as do not please him. **1880** *Scribner's Mo.* Oct. 909/1 They sometimes take the liberty of scratching a name, but they prefer . . . to vote the regular ticket. **1912** NICHOLSON *Hoosier Chron.* 248, I've never scratched a ticket since I first voted. *absol.* **1888** BRYCE *Amer. Commw.* II. III. lxvi. 494 The number of candidates is often so great . . . that many who would be glad to 'scratch' or 'paste' have really no data for doing so. **1906** QUICK *Double Trouble* 284 When this 'advanced thought' platform of yours comes to be voted on, there won't be any one for it except thick-and-thin party men who 'never scratch.'

+**2.** *intr.* To make *for* with all speed; to turn or swing; to move or depart in haste. *colloq.*

1847 ROBB *Squatter Life* 109, I'm cussed if I hadn't to turn round, too, and scratch for the snag again! **1875** 'MARK TWAIN' *Old Times* iii. 49, I've got to scratch to starboard in a hurry. **1887** *Outing* May 120/1, I fired the gun and the horses scratched away from the mark. **1903** WHITE *Blazed Trail Stories* 5 This little town will scratch fer th' tall timber . . . when the boys goes in to take her apart.

+**3.** *To scratch for one's self,* to look out or care for one's self. *colloq.*

1850 WATSON *Camp-Fires Revol.* 30 Then each one had to scratch for himself. **1856** A. CARY *Married* 304 Shaking off the other child, [she] told him to scratch for hisself a time, while she began to prepare the supper.

+**4.** *To scratch gravel. colloq.* **a.** To go or depart in utmost haste. **b.** To work hard for a living.

1854 M. J. HOLMES *Tempest & Sunshine* 103 You'd better scratch gravel for home. **1864** *Rio Abajo Press* 10 May 1/1 Ike, as a matter of course, 'scratched gravel,' and left a blue streak behind. **1892** HARRIS *On the Plantation* 130, I'm a-gwine ter scratch gravel. **1898** WESTCOTT *D. Harum* xxv, Till I was consid'able older 'n you be I had to scratch grav'l like all possessed.

+**Scratch coat.** (See quot. 1891.) Also *scratch-coated* a. — **1823** COOPER *Pioneers* xi, Festoons and hieroglyphics met the eye in vast profusion along the brown sides of the scratch-coated walls. **1853** FOWLER *Home for All* 44 My own [finish] consists simply of a coat of common mortar, . . . [put on] just as you would put on the scratch-coat of an inside wall. **1884** *Century Mag.* April 870/1 The east wing [of the N.Y. City Hall was] put under scratch-coat. **1891** *Cent.* 5418/2 *Scratch coat*, in *plastering*, the rough coat of plaster first laid on. . . . It is named *scratch-coat* from the fact that it is usually roughened by scratching the surface with a pointed instrument before it is set hard, in order that the next coat may more strongly adhere to it.

+Scratched ticket. *Polit.* A ticket which has been scratched by the voter. — **1870** MAVERICK *Raymond & N.Y. Press* 340 A citizen wishing to vote a 'scratched' ticket, putting the name of Hans Breitmann, Republican German, in place of that of Timothy Finnegan, Democratic Irishman, finds [etc.]. **1887** *Courier-Journal* 18 Feb. 1/3 At the suggestion of one of the Democratic judges the scratched tickets were separated.

* Scratcher.

+1. (See quotations.) *slang.*

1859 MATSELL *Vocabulum* 77 *Scratcher*, a forger; a copyist. **1894** *N.Y. Amer. Rev.* April 454 The actual forger [in a professional forgery gang] . . . is known among his associates as the 'scratcher.'

+2. (See quot. 1888.)

1880 *Scribner's Mo.* Feb. 621/2 Mr. Evarts will be obliged to look among the 'scratchers,' . . . for the indorsement of . . . Civil Service reform. **1888** M. LANE in *America* 1 Nov. 16 *Scratchers*, voters who erase from the ticket the name of any candidate for whom they do not wish to vote.

+3. (See quotation.)

1891 *Cent.* 5418/2 *Scratcher*, . . . a day-book. (U.S.)

+4. (See quotation.)

1905 *Forestry Bureau Bul.* No. 61, 19 *Scratcher*, an instrument used for marking trees. It usually consists of a hooklike gouge fastened to a flat, elliptical iron hoop.

Scratch grass. {1886-} +A common species of tearthumb, *Tracaulon sagittatum.* — **1790** DEANE *New-Eng. Farmer* 114/2 There are several other grasses produced in this country, as quitch grass, dogs grass; and scratch grass, resembling arsmart, on the uplands. **1833** EATON *Botany* (ed. 6) 275 *Polygonum sagittatum*, prickly knotweed, scratch grass. **1891** *Amer. Folk-Lore* IV. 148 *P. Hydropiper* was *Smartweed* [in N.H.], and *P. sagittata, Scratch-grass.*

* Scratching.

+1. *pl.* A place to which wild turkeys resort for scratching and feeding. (Cf. SCRATCHING PLACE.)

1845 *Big Bear Ark.* 148 Bout the fust ov Octobur we ginerally takes to huntin rigler in the scratchins. **1846** THORPE *Myst. Backwoods* 63, I hunted the gobbler always in the same 'range,' and about the same 'scratchins.'

+2. (See quotation.) *Obs.*

1857 BORTHWICK *3 Years in Calif.* 144 The Americans called it 'scratching,' which was a very expressive term for their [Chinese miners'] style of digging.

+3. The failure to support a candidate, usu. by marking out or erasing his name from a ticket: (see also quot. 1902).

[**1860** MORDECAI *Virginia* 92 Each third year, one of the members should be *elected out.* . . . This ostracising process was termed *scratching.*] **1882** *Nation* 16 Nov. 422/1 The 'scratching' movement, one among the several small beginnings of the overwhelming Independent sentiment of to-day, was started in New York in 1879. **1888** BRYCE *Amer. Commw.* II. III. lxviii. 530 To abstain from voting for the names on your party ticket to whom you object is . . . scratching. **1892** *Courier-Journal* 3 Oct. 1/8 Party lines were not drawn much, and there was free scratching by members of both parties. **1902** CLAPIN 351 *Scratching*, an electioneering dodge, which consists in distributing narrow slips of paper gummed on the back, and bearing printed names of candidates, so that voters may readily rearrange the ballots to suit their own preferences.

‖Scratching place. A place to which pinnated grouse resort for scratching and feeding. (Cf. SCRATCHING 1.) — **1810** in Wilson *Ornithology* III. 110 To some select and central spot where there is very little underwood, they [sc. grouse] repair from the adjoining district. From the [mating] exercises performed there, this is called a *scratching place.*

Scrawl. {1693-} *local.* +(See quot. 1828.) — **1828** WEBSTER, *Scrawl*, . . . in *New England*, a ragged, broken branch of a tree, or other brush wood. **1845** JUDD *Margaret* I. 169 She crossed the Porta Salutaris and all the scrawls of the stump fence.

+Scrawny, *a.* [?Var. of *scranny*.] Scrawly; scrubby; mean; meager; thin. Also *scrawniness.* — **1833** STOWE in C. E. Stowe *Life* (1889) 70 This envelope was written in a scrawny, scrawly, gentleman's hand. **1843** 'CARLTON' *New Purchase* I. 122 But what are these *scrawney* little trees fenced in to prevent cattle from eating them down? **1863** HAWTHORNE *Our Old Home* 385, I often found, . . . [in] my dear countrymen . . . , a certain meagreness, (Heaven forbid that I should call it scrawniness!). **1880** INGHAM *Digging Gold* 327 Very few of the old-time, scrawny or shabby wooden structures remain to be seen. **1897** H. MONROE in *Columbus Dispatch* 4 Feb. 7/7, I saw . . . the scrawny, ragged men and women shuffling lackadaisically from door to door.

Screamer. A person of unusual size, strength, capabilities, etc. *slang.* {1850-} (Cf. ROARER 1.) — **1831** *Louisville Pub. Adv.* 17 Oct. 2/3 The principal character in this production, is, to use his own elegant language, a *screamer.* **1835** C. F. HOFFMAN *Winter in West* II. 186, I am as good a little fellow as ever mother brought forth: she said I was a screamer, the moment she saw me. **1845** KIRKLAND *Western Clearings* 44 She's a screamer of a girl. **1861** NEWELL *Orpheus C. Kerr* I. 16, I took to

a gal that stuck out all around like a hay-stack, an' was a screamer at choir-meetin' and such like. **1909** WASON *Happy Hawkins* 42, I'd allus heard 'at he was a rip-snortin' screamer, an' here he was talkin' low an' level like.

* Screech owl. +Any one of various small American owls of the genus *Otus*, esp. *O. asio* of the eastern states. Freq. with specifying terms. — **1812** WILSON *Ornithology* V. 83 Red Owl. . . . This is . . . well known by its common name, the Little Screech Owl. **1837** WILLIAMS *Florida* 73 There are many birds in Florida. . . . [Among these is the] Screech Owl, *S[trix] assio.* **1884** HARRIS in *Century Mag.* Nov. 121 The screech-owl would shake and shiver in the depths of the woods. **1917** *Birds of Amer.* II. 111 A species closely allied to the Screech Owls is the Spotted Screech Owl (*Otus trichopsis*).

Screen door. A light door consisting of a frame covered with screen wire or netting, which is used in addition to an outer door. {1840-} — **1883** RITTENHOUSE *Maud* 225 And after he'd gone I stood staring and staring out of the screen-door at nothing. **1900** DIX *Deacon Bradbury* 59 The light screen-door swung to behind him with a slight slam. **1919** HOUGH *Sagebrusher* 259 She heard it on the gallery floor inside the slamming screen door.

* Screw, *n.*

+1. *College slang.* (See quot. 1851.) *Obs.*

1810 *Harvard Lyceum* 8 Sept. 102 Haunted by day with fearful screw. **1828** *Harvard Reg.* Feb. 378 One must experience all the stammering and stuttering—the unending doubtings, and guessings to understand fully the power of a mathematical *screw.* **1851** HALL *College Words* 265 An excessive, unnecessarily minute, and annoying examination of a student by an instructor is called a screw. . . . The instructor is often designated by the same name. . . . At Bowdoin College an imperfect recitation is sometimes thus denominated. **1855** S. WILLARD *Memories of Youth* I. 256 Apprehension of the severity of the examination, or what in after times, by an academic figure of speech, was called screwing, or a screw, was what excited the chief dread.

+2. A press for baling ginned cotton. Also *screw press.*

1824 *Catawba Jrnl.* 23 Nov., I will sell . . . a prime fifty saw Gin, a Screw, &c. **1852** *Fla. Plantation Rec.* 72, I will Commence getting timbers for the Screw. **1874** KNIGHT 635/2 There are various forms of cotton-presses, known as the screw, toggle, beater [etc.] . . . presses.

3. *To put the screws on*, or variants: To put pressure upon or to force payment of a debt. {1860-}

1845 JUDD *Margaret* II. 313 We are too lenient, we didn't put on the screws half hard enough. **1853** THOMAS *J. Randolph* 286 If I had not caught him in Baltimore, and put the screws to him, . . . I never should have got the money. **1894** P. L. FORD *P. Stirling* 241 Then I can put the screws on him safely, you think? **1905** N. DAVIS *Northerner* 164 The devil! Who's turning the screw?

4. *attrib.* and *comb.* Designating persons, establishments, and things in some way associated with the mechanical device known as a screw.

See also SCREW-DRIVER, SCREW PLATE, etc.

1812 MELISH *Travels* II. 55 Professions exercised in Pittsburgh [include]: . . . lock-smiths, screw and hinge-makers, clock and watch-makers. **1827** DRAKE & MANSFIELD *Cincinnati* 65 Two Plane Stock, Bit and Screw Factories. **1838** FLAGG *Far West* I. 57 These screw-wheels float upon the surface parallel to the shore, . . . and are connected with the gearing in the Millhouse upon the bank by a long shaft. **1859** *Rep. Comm. Patents 1858* I. 584 Improved Screw Wrench. **1876** KNIGHT 2073/2 *Screw-rudder*, an application of the screw to purposes of steering, instead of a rudder. **1885** *Harper's Mag.* Jan. 286/1 The 'screw-nailing' machine, . . . with a whirl and a thump drives a screw-nail severed from a coil of brass wire through the thickest of tough leather. *Ib.* 286/2 Cable-nailing machine; succeeded by standard screw machine in 1876.

* Screw, *v.*

+1. *tr.* To press (hay or cotton) in bales or bundles with force exerted through a screw. Also *ppl. a.*

1713 HEMPSTEAD *Diary* 26, I spent most of ye day about fitting Mr Coits press & Screwing 1 bundle hay. c**1775** GAGE in Loring *Hundred Boston Orators* (1852) 675 He and I . . . stopped to watch some young men screwing hay for the troops in Boston. **1823** THACHER *Military Jrnl.* 46 Next in the martial procession are a train of carts, loaded with fascines and hay, screwed into large bundles of seven or eight hundred weight. **1827** in Commons, etc. *Doc. Hist.* I. 287 In a steam cotton-press house . . . they work, watch and watch by candle-light, screwing cotton. **1849** *Knickerb.* XXXIII. 359 At the base of a high cliff I looked up and saw . . . a mass of solid, shining gold, as large as a bunch of screwed hay!

2. *College slang.* (See quot. 1851.) *Obs.* {1626, 1639}

1819 A. PEIRCE *Rebelliad* 53 Who would let a Tutor knave Screw him like a Guinea slave! **1851** HALL *College Words* 265 *Screw*, To press with an excessive and unnecessarily minute examination. **1865** *Atlantic Mo.* June 738/2 He was every day 'screwed' by his tutor upon some technical point of the language.

+Screw auger. An auger having spiral channels. Also *attrib.* and *transf.* (Cf. POD AUGER.) — **1792** IMLAY *Western Territory* 114 The juice [of the maple] was found to ooze as effectually from an incision made with a screw auger of ⅛ of an inch diameter. **1812** *Ann. 12th Congress* 1 Sess. 1446 The inventor of that useful instrument the screw-auger, . . . was an inhabitant of New England. **1825** NEAL *Bro. Jonathan* III. 149 They were at work with . . . broad axes, and screw augers. **1833** — *Down-Easters* I. 15 Never hearn tell o' the rain water doctor? some calls him the screw-auger doctor, and some the steam-doctor. **1840** WEBSTER *Letters* (1902) 671, I have heard of Thompson's Medicine, some called 'screw auger,' some called 'wild-cat.'

+Screw bean. *S.W.* The curiously twisted spiral pod of the screw pod mesquite; also, the tree producing this. — **1866** LINDLEY & MOORE *Treas. Botany* 930/1 *Prosopis pubescens*, . . . is the Screw-bean or Screw Mezquit of the Americans. **1873** ARNY *Items regarding N. Mex.* 110 Mesquite, or *screw bean.*—This in the valleys of the Gila becomes a considerable tree. **1877** HODGE *Arizona* 246 The bean . . . which is called the screw bean, resembles a bunch of the alder tags and is screw shaped. **1897** SUDWORTH *Arborescent Flora* 251.

Screw-driver. A tool having a blunt blade used for turning screws into and out of their places. {1812-} — **1779** *York Co., Va., Rec.: Wills* XXII. 28 April, 1 doz. draw rings, screw driver, and gimlet. **1859** *Rep. Comm. Patents 1858* I. 569 Improved Ratchet Movement for Screw Drivers. **1883** [see CHISEL *n.* 1]. **1911** VANCE *Cynthia* 229 He fell to his knees before the door, struck a match, found the screw-driver, and attacked the lock.

Screw eye. **+1.** A slang term for a cross-eyed person: (see also quot. 1844). **2.** A screw the head of which is a loop or eye. {1873-} — **(1) 1836** *Quarter Race Ky.* 23 He and the claimant went to old screw-eye [the judge]; and he decided I had lost. **1844** 'UNCLE SAM' *Peculiarities* I. 135 Miss Angelina Spifflenberg . . . has one of the most powerful squinting or screw eyes in this or any other country. **(2) 1883** KNIGHT *Suppl.* 786/1 *Screw Eye*, a loop with threaded shank, to be screwed into an object. **1890** *Internat. Ann., Anthony's Photogr. Bul.* III. 241 The plate is placed level, resting on three screw-eyes. **1907** *St. Nicholas* June 731/1 Into the top of the strip of wood on the table drive a medium-sized screw-eye.

+Screw mesquite. *S.W.* =SCREW-POD MESQUITE. — **1866** [see SCREW BEAN]. **1867** *Amer. Naturalist* I. 400 The food of these [bush] rats . . . [includes] the curious spirally-twisted fruit of the 'screw-mezquite' (*Strombocarpa pubescens*). **1881** *Ib.* XV. 30 Another [species is] called the screw mezquit . . . , on account of its short pods being closely twisted into the shape of a screw.

Screw plate. **a.** A hardened steel plate having in it dies of various sizes for making small screws. **b.** A holder for dies used in cutting screw threads. {1677-} a**1656** BRADFORD *Hist.* 287 Some have seen them [*sc.* Indians] have their scruplats to make scrupins them selves. **1780** *N.H. Comm. Safety Rec.* 234 Ordered the Board of War to provide & send . . . one Screw Plate. **1794** *Mass. Spy* 1 May 4/2 Daniel Waldo, jun. Has just received . . . Vices, Plyers, Screw Plates [etc.]. **1850** *Fla. Plantation Rec.* 60 Roberson says he will want . . . an inch screw plate with stock and dies. *attrib.* **1851** CIST *Cincinnati* 260 Screw plate factories.

+Screw-pod mesquite. *S.W.* A tree (*Prosopis pubescens*) bearing pods of a characteristic spiral form. — **1884** SARGENT *Rep. Forests* 62 *Prosopis pubescens.* . . . Screw Bean. Screw-Pod Mesquit. Tornilla. . . . [Reaches] its greatest development within the United States in the valleys of the lower Colorado and Gila rivers. **1897** SUDWORTH *Arborescent Flora* 251.

Screw propeller. A ship's propeller somewhat in the form of a huge screw. {1839-} — **1848** *Rep. Comm. Patents 1847* 71 Another for an improvement in casings and screw propellers. **1907** *St. Nicholas* Aug. 928/1 The idea of a screw-propeller, however, was not lost.

Screw steamer. A steamship having a screw propeller. {1848-} — **1858** *S. Lit. Messenger* XXVI. 88/1 We have screw steamers of three classes. **1887** BILLINGS *Hardtack* 271 When the war broke out, the available vessels were mainly a few ships-of-the-line, frigates and screw steamers.

+Screwstem. Any plant of the genus *Bartonia*, the stems of which are sometimes spiral or twisted. — **1817-8** EATON *Botany* (1822) 202 *Bartonia paniculata*, screwstem. **1847** WOOD *Botany* 454 *C*[*entaurella*] *autumnalis.* . . . Screw-stem. . . . *C. Moseri.* . . . Moser's Centaurella or Screw-stem.

+Screw-wood. =SCREW-POD MESQUITE. — **1844** GREGG *Commerce of Prairies* II. 78 In the immediate vicinity of El Paso there is another small growth called *tornillo* (or screw-wood), so denominated from a spiral pericarp. **1847** RUXTON *Adv. Rocky Mts.* (1848) 174.

+Screw worm (fly). (See quotations.) — **1891** *Cent.* 5422/2 *Screw-worm*, the larva of a blow-fly, . . . which deposits its eggs or larvæ on sores on living animals. **1908** KELLOGG *Amer. Insects* 344 A flesh-fly of serious importance is the terrible screw-worm fly, . . . which lays its eggs on flesh . . . and often in the nasal passages of domestic animals and human beings. **1925** HERRICK *Man. Injurious Insects* 423 The Screw-Worm Fly, *Chrysomyia macellaria*, . . . is a native insect occurring all over the United States but most injurious in the South and Southwest.

Scribener. (See SCRIVENER.)

*Scrimmage.
*1. An irregular or petty encounter between small bodies of armed enemies; a skirmish. {-1643}
1776 R. LINCOLN *Papers* (1904) 3 Scrimages had happened between the lines. **1841** COOPER *Deerslayer* xxii, They feel their loss here, in the late skirmmage, to their heart's cores. **1853** 'P. PAXTON' *Yankee in Texas* 111 Col. Ting . . . was in nearly every scrimmage in '36.

+2. *Football.* The play which begins on the line of scrimmage when the center puts the ball in play and ends when the ball is dead. {of Rugby, 1857-}
1879 in P. H. Davis *Football* (1911) 468 A scrimmage takes place when the holder of the ball . . . puts it down on the ground in front of him and puts it in play while on side. **1887** *Century Mag.* Oct. 888/1 American players, working out the scrimmage into a new form, have changed the possibilities of the game very greatly. **1896** CAMP & DELAND *Football* 412 The man who puts the ball in play in a scrimmage, and the opponent opposite him cannot pick up the ball until it has touched some third man.

Scrimmaging. {1887-} +The carrying out of a scrimmage or skirmish by small bodies of enemies. *Obs.* — **1776** R. LINCOLN *Papers* (1904) 3 They have Scrimageing from there every Day. **1853** SIMMS *Sword & Distaff* (1854) 135 We've had a mighty sharp scrimmaging here for more than three hours.

Scrimshander, Scrimshandy. [Origin obscure.] *Naut.* The making or ornamenting of knicknacks and useful articles as the carving of whales' teeth, ivory, etc., as practiced by seamen; the articles so made. {scrimshaw, 1864-} Also *attrib.* (The bulk of the evidence for this word is American.) — **1851** MELVILLE *Moby Dick* 14, I found a number of young seamen . . . examining by a dim light divers specimens of *skrimshander*. *Ib.* 302 Other like skrimshander articles, as the whalemen call the numerous little ingenious contrivances they elaborately carve out of the rough material, in their hours of ocean leisure. **1883** *Internat. Fisheries Exhib. Cat.* (London) 198 Collection illustrating the games, amusements, literature, art-work of the fishermen; musical instruments, carvings ('scrimshandy'), &c.

Scrimshawing. Also **skrimshonting.** [Origin obscure.] (See quots. 1882, 1887.) Also *scrimshawed* p.p. — **1882** E. K. GODFREY *Nantucket* 65 The word 'skrimshonting' is often heard, and is applied to the doing of any small job requiring ingenuity, like the carving of a whale's tooth or the making of a small box. **1883** *Internat. Fisheries Exhib. Cat.* (London) 207 Walrus tusks scrim-shawed, and frame made of walrus ivory. **1887** GOODE, etc. *Fisheries* v. II. 231 Scrimshawing is . . . the art . . . of manufacturing useful and ornamental articles at sea.

Scrip, *n.* {1762-} Often collective.
+1. A certificate of indebtedness issued as currency, or in lieu of money.
Certain classes of these certificates were redeemable in land at the option of the holder: (see sense 2). See also CITY SCRIP, PRICE RAID SCRIP, TREASURY SCRIP.
1790 FRENEAU *Poems* (1795) 429 Vast loads [he] amass'd of scrip, and God knows what. **1831** *Congress. Deb.* 4 Jan. 405 The bill, in fact, proposed an exchange of scrip for land. **1840** *Niles' Nat. Reg.* 2 May 136/3 The board of public works, in Illinois, have issued a large amount of scrip, generally for sums of $100 and upwards. **1856** *Harper's Mag.* June 117/2 Scrip, to the amount of more than a million dollars, has been already issued to defray the cost of the Indian war in Oregon. **1875** *Ib.* Sept. 565/1 'Scrip' was issued for the domestic debt of the State, and was receivable for State dues. **1898** *Kissimmee* (Fla.) *Valley Gazette* 18 Feb. 3/5 It is suggested that scrip be issued for the amount. *attrib.* **1849** *31st Congress 1 Sess.* H. R. Ex. Doc. No. 5, II. 1178 Up to the 5th instant we issued . . . scrip certificates of $25. each, 460.

+b. =FRACTIONAL CURRENCY, SCRIP.
1873 'G. HAMILTON' *Twelve Miles* 216 The widow who bestowed her ten-cent scrip may have been really more benevolent. **1880** HOWELLS *Undiscovered Country* 142 'There,' she said, handing Egeria some bits of scrip, 'it's ten cents apiece to the Junction.' **1887** BILLINGS *Hardtack* 63 This was before scrip was issued by the government to take the place of silver.

+2. A certificate or warrant redeemable in land to an amount described on the warrant; land scrip.
Usually issued by the federal government, either to private claimants or to states under the Morril act of 1862, but also by state governments and land companies controlling large land grants. (See also COLLEGE SCRIP, HALF-BREED SCRIP, LAND SCRIP.)
1828 *Texas Laws* (B. '59, p. 192), So much of the vacant lands . . . shall be surveyed and sectionized . . . as will be sufficient to satisfy all claims for scrip sold, soldier's claims, and head-rights. **1838** C. NEWELL *Revol. Texas* 185 It may be well to make a few remarks upon Empresario Grants, Texas Land Companies, and their 'Scrip.' **1852** *Stat. at Large* X. 143 [This] scrip shall be receivable in payment for any lands owned by the United States subject to sale at private entry. **1870** *Rep. Comm. Agric. 1869* 471 Scrip to the amount of 100,000 acres still remains unsold. **1884** *Congress. Rec.* 10 June 4994/2 The [lumbermen] have long been in the habit of getting it [pineland] under different forms of scrip, under the soldiers' additional scrip, under the Sioux half-breed scrip, under the Cherokee scrip, and every other damnable kind of scrip that could be had.

‖Scrip, *v. tr.* To secure (land) in redemption of land scrip. *colloq.* — **1882** *Century Mag.* Sept. 769/1 They 'scrip' the adjoining sections of Government land, or take it up with desert land claims.

Serito(i)re. (See SCRUTO(I)RE.)

*Scrivener. A professional copyist; a secretary or notary. *Obs.* — **1661** *Suffolk Deeds* III. 514 John Sanford of Boston . . . in New England Scrivenor and Sarah his wife sends Greetings. **1677** *Mass. H. S. Coll.* 3 Ser. VII. 50 The Deputies . . . doe make choice of Mr. John Hayward, the scrivener, to be the man. **1703** *Boston Rec.* 33 Granted to Benja. Eliot the Shop . . . formerly Let to John Howard, Scribener. **1771** FRANKLIN

Autobiog. 269 The two first were clerks to an eminent scrivener or conveyancer in [Phila.]. **1810** [see COPYIST].

+**Scrod,** *n.* [Origin obscure.] (See quotations and cf. ESCROD.) — **1856** J. REYNOLDS *Peter Gott* 92 Peter Gott, in addition to the money he had saved, had a pile of nice scrods. **1859** BARTLETT 388 *Scrods,* (*Shreds?*) small pieces of fish, or small fish for boiling. New England. c**1870** CHIPMAN *Notes on Bartlett* 388 *Scrod.* . . . In Mass. pronounced *scrōde* and used to designate a small fish split and slightly salted. Comp. Ger. *schroeder.* **1884** GOODE, etc. *Fisheries* I. 201 In the vicinity of Cape Ann the young Cod, too small to swallow a bait, are sometimes known to the fishermen as 'Pickers,' and throughout all Eastern Massachusetts the name 'Scrod,' or 'Scrode,' is in common use. **1894** *Outing* XVIII. 404/1 Scrod are those [cod] weighing under the three pounds.

+**Scrod,** *v.* [f. prec.] (See first quotation.) — **1891** *Cent.* 5425/3 *Scrod,* . . . to shred; prepare for cooking by tearing in small pieces: as, *scrodded* fish. **1895** *Stand.* 1607/1.

+**Scrofulaweed.** The downy rattlesnake plantain, *Perarium pubescens.* — **1817-8** EATON *Botany* (1822) 294 *Goodyera pubescens,* rattlesnake leaf, scrophula-weed. **1836** LINCOLN *Botany* App. 101.

Scroll saw. (See quot. 1876.) Also attrib. {scroll sawing, 1874} — **1851** CIST *Cincinnati* 206 In the first story are located . . . the machinery for a scroll saw . . . , and the apparatus by which the veneering is done. **1868** *Mich. Agric. Rep.* VII. 361 G. S. Wormer & Son, Detroit, [exhibited] 1 scroll saw machine. **1876** KNIGHT 2077/1 *Scroll-saw,* a relatively thin and narrow-bladed reciprocating-saw, which passes through a hole in the work-table and saws a kerf in the work. **1882** 'M. HARLAND' *Eve's Daughters* 50 The bit of fancy-work is to Mamie what Willie's chest of tools . . . or scroll-saw is to him.

+**Scrouger.** A person or thing extraordinary or startling in size, capabilities, etc. *colloq.* — **1840** *Picayune* 31 Oct. 2/1 Get ready for a scrouger, boys. **1855** *Harper's Mag.* Dec. 40/2 The race was excitin,' a parfect scrouger—the steam yelled and the hands swore. **1861** NEWELL *Orpheus C. Kerr* I. 230 We had one of the she-critters aboard—and she was a scrouger, I tell ye!

* **Scrub,** *n.*

1. *collect.* Stunted trees or brushwood; a region overgrown by these. {1833-, of Australia}

1809 A. HENRY *Travels* 281 At four o'clock in the afternoon, we reached a little scrub, or bushy tract, on which we encamped. **1888** FERGUSON *Experiences of Forty-Niner* 128 We camped one night in the mountains . . . where there were patches of scrub. **1903** WHITE *Forest* 152 The forest slants down to your feet in dwindling scrub. **1910** [see CHAPARRAL 2].

2. *Stock-raising.* **a.** A horse of a poor or inferior breed. **1834** CARRUTHERS *Kentuckian* I. 12, I would bet my horse Talleyrand against an old field scrub that that fellow is a Yankee. **1861** *Ill. Agric. Soc. Trans.* IV. 255 It costs but little or no more to raise a valuable colt than a poor scrub. **1888** *Harper's Mag.* Jan. 325/1 The colonel's horse—an old 'scrub' he had borrowed—'bucked.'

* **b.** A poor or worthless bovine animal; a cow from mongrel stock. {–1581} Also in generic sense. **1868** *Iowa State Agric. Soc. Rep. 1867* 130 A few of our farmers have half and one-fourth blooded young bulls and heifers, a cross with the scrub and short-horns. **1890** *Stock Grower & Farmer* 22 Feb. 4/2 As to 'scrubs' we cannot vouch. **1905** *Springfield W. Repub.* 28 July 5 The term 'scrub' is applied, by agricultural writers, to cattle that have no particular breeding, no matter how good or bad they may be.

+**3.** Tobacco of an inferior quality. **1840** *Picayune* 20 Sept. 2/5 The stock on hand for sale is now reduced to less than 500 hhds., a great part of which consists of scrubs.

+**4.** (See quotations.) {in general sense, 1589-} **1866** CARPENTER *At White House* 96 'Well,' continued Mr. Lincoln, . . . 'I belonged . . . to what they call down South, the "scrubs"; people who do not own slaves are nobody there.' **1907** H. BINNS *A. Lincoln* 27 He was now increasingly conscious . . . of a destiny before him, incompatible with the circumstances either of a 'Southern Scrub' or of a poor farmer in the backwoods of Indiana.

+**5.** A ball player not belonging to the first or best team; the team made up of such players. Usually pl. **1893** CAMP *College Sports* 140 He'd rather play against any team in the association than against the 'scrubs.' **1895** WILLIAMS *Princeton Stories* 190 Once when the scrub had the ball they gave the signal for a trick which they had been saving up as a surprise for the 'varsity. **1910** *N.Y. Ev. Post* 15 Oct. Suppl. 1 These men, wrapped in gray blankets, who line the low fence surrounding the field on the day of the big game, are the 'scrubs,' or second team men.

+**b.** (See quot. 1910.) **1896** WHITE *Real Issue* 66 Just before school was called Piggy Pennington was playing 'scrub.' **1910** *Dialect Notes* III. 447 *Scrub,* a game of baseball played by a half dozen or more persons (when there are not enough to 'choose up' for two nines), in which the players move up as a batter is retired. **1917** MATHEWSON *Second Base Sloan* 126 At the end of a week or so they were playing 'scrub' every noon-hour.

+**6.** Attrib. in sense 5 with *game, match, nine.* Also in transf. use with *center, crew,* etc. **1868** CHADWICK *Base Ball* 45 Either of the nines in a match game, or of the contesting parties in a scrub match, constitutes the 'side' in a game. **1880** N. BROOKS *Fairport Nine* 173 During the summer, several 'scrub'

games had been played by the Fairports. **1884** NYE *Baled Hay* 69 When I get in sight the 'scrub nine' close up. **1892** J. L. FORD *Dr. Dodd's School* 5 The school eleven . . . were playing a practice game of foot-ball with a scrub eleven enrolled for the occasion. **1893** WILLIAMS *Princeton Stories* 180 The scrub halves had fallen on him from the other direction to keep him from being shoved back. **1901** FORD *House Party* 202, I rowed better than he, having been on the 'varsity scrub crew. **1920** CAMP *Football without Coach* 63 You will have your regular center playing against a scrub center.

Scrub, *a.* {1710-}

1. Of vegetation: Stunted, low-growing, dwarfed. {1749-} Also in fig. context.

1779 *Mass. H. S. Coll.* 2 Ser. II. 465 Their breastwork was made of pine Logs coverd with green skrub bushes. **1816** U. BROWN *Journal* I. 266 Thence 20 miles . . . over the poorest Ugly Hills I ever saw, Abounded with . . . Jack Oaks and other Scrub Wood. **1871** *Harper's Mag.* Sept. 493/1 Now and then we pass clumps of scrub-growth clad in russet and gold. **1875** CARLETON *Farm Legends* 2 His little scrub thicket of pupils sent upward a half-smothered hum. **1882** MCCABE *New York* 443 A low scrub underbrush grew rankly over it. **1894** *Harper's Mag.* Aug. 338/1 The trees . . . are not to be compared with those of the scrub forests of Long Island. **1901** DUNCAN & SCOTT *Allen & Woodson Co., Kansas* 581 The once scrub brush has grown into young forests in places.

b. Of different kinds of trees: Small, dwarfed. Also in specific names.

1817-8 EATON *Botany* (1822) 204 *Betula glandulosa,* scrub birch, . . . very abundant in the marshes about Stockbridge, Mass. **1849** *31st Congress 1 Sess.* Sen. Ex. Doc. No. 64, 78 [Along the Rio Chaco] scrub cedars, very thinly scattered, were to be seen on the heights. **1874** COUES *Birds N.W.* 148 The Clay-colored Sparrows nest abundantly . . . among the innumerable scrub-willow copses of the valley. **1883** SMITH *Geol. Survey Ala.* 226 *Barrens soil* from near Cluttsville, Madison county. . . . Vegetation [includes] . . . scrub hickory, wild gooseberry, blackberry. **1889** *Century Mag.* April 903/2 We suddenly left them [*sc.* pines] for the scrub mesquite which bars your passage. **1897** *Outing* XXIX. 427/1 He draws cautiously up towards a clump of scrub hemlock.

2. Of a domestic animal: Common or poor; of an inferior or mongrel breed or stock. {1870, Australia}

1823 COOPER *Pioneers* xvii, Billy Kirby would then be seen, sauntering around the taverns, the rider of scrub-horses, the bully of cock-fights. **1868** *Iowa State Agric. Soc. Rep. 1867* 99 Raise and fatten a scrub steer and put him into market at four years old. **1868** BRACKETT *Farm Talk* 43 The calf's sire was a 'scrub' bull. **1872** *Ill. Dept. Agric. Trans.* IX. 204 A common scrub hog can scarcely be found in the country. **1889** WARFIELD *Cattle-Breeding* 50 Indeed I have myself known prize animals in the showyard that were by Short-horn bulls out of native or 'scrub' cows. **1891** C. ROBERTS *Adrift Amer.* 37 An old man . . . owned about twenty scrub colts, which he used to let run wild. a**1918** G. STUART *On Frontier* II. 201 Among them [were] two fairly good 'scrub' race horses.

+**b.** With reference to breeds or types of such animals or to such stock in general.

1839 *Indiana H. Rep. Jrnl.* 23 Sess. 232 Those [calves] of our scrub breed will only bring . . . **1858** C. FLINT *Milch Cows* 50 The term 'native,' or 'scrub,' is applied to a vast majority of our American cattle, which, though born on the soil, and thus in one sense natives, do not constitute a breed, race, or family. **1868** *Iowa State Agric. Soc. Rep. 1867* 130 The general idea pervades . . . that a larger . . . animal of blooded stock can be produced by the same amount of feed than can be made with the same feed fed to scrub stock. **1897** *Kissimmee* (Fla.) *Valley Gazette* 22 Dec. 2/3 Unfortunately, these cattle are of the scrub type and run very light in weight.

+**3.** In special combinations.

Scrub aristocrat, (see quotation); *scrubland,* inferior land overgrown with scrubs or scrubby vegetation {1852, Australia}; *s. politician,* a mediocre or contemptible politician; *s. tavern,* a low tavern or groggery; *s. white,* a white person of a low class.

1840 KENNEDY *Quodlibet* 158 If he . . . makes a little fortune, we call him a . . . Scrub Aristocrat. **1779** *Mass. H. S. Proc.* 2 Ser. II. 472 [We] came over skrub land this day. **1848** IRVING *Knickerb.* (rev. ed.) VII. i, He enabled every scrub-politician to measure wits with him. **1853** *Harper's Mag.* April 583/1 These houses were 'groceries,' a sort of scrub-tavern quite common in the western world, where very cheap and very bad liquor is sold to the miners. **1901** RYAN *Montana* 125 There are always a lot of scrub whites ready to take advantage of war signals.

Scrubbing brush. A brush used for scrubbing. {1681-} — **1746** *Md. Hist. Mag.* XXI. 380 Invoice of Goods. . . . 6 Hair Brooms, 6 scrubbing Brushes. **1848** *Knickerb.* XXXI. 24 Scoured worms! how be they scoured, Sir? With sand and scrubbing-brush? **1872** EGGLESTON *End of World* 25 The scrubbing-brush dropped in the pail of soapsuds. **1907** *London Road* 88 There were bath-tubs, hot water, soap, and scrubbing-brushes.

+**Scrub day.** The day upon which household scrubbing is regularly done. — **1873** PHELPS *Trotty's Wedding* vi, They have their 'scrub-days' and their dress-days. **1883** RITTENHOUSE *Maud* 244 This morning we woke up to find no girl, beside the house to sweep, extra chamber-work to do, and its being scrub day, baking day, churning day, mending day and the cold remains of some house-cleaning to do. **1912** IRWIN *Red Button* 227, I won't be fit for a thing to-morrow an' it's scrub-day, too!

+Scrubgrass. =SCOURING RUSH. — **1814** BRACKENRIDGE *Views La.* 206 Through all these islands, and on the Missouri bottoms, there are great quantities of rushes, commonly called scrub grass. **1819** D. THOMAS *Travels Western Country* 44 Scrub Grass is called in Scipio, 'Rushes.' **1821** NUTTALL *Travels Arkansa* 58 The scrub-grass or rushes . . . appear along the banks in vast fields.

+Scrub hill. A hill covered with scrubby trees. *Obs.* — **1788** M. DEWEES *Journal* (MS.) 5ᵛ Left the foot of the mountain and cross scrub hill. **1816** U. BROWN *Journal* I. 275 [I journeyed] some times a long on the margin of the River Potomac, and some times a little in those scrub Hills.

+Scrub-mop. A mop. — **1865** *Harper's Mag.* April 665/1 You can make brooms and scrub-mops . . . to sell.

+Scrub oak. Any one of various American dwarf oaks. Also attrib. (Cf. SHRUB OAK.)
These include *Quercus ilicifolia* and *Q. prinoides* of New England and the middle states, *Q. catesbaei* and *Q. myrtifolia* in the South, and various western species.
1779 *Mass. H. S. Proc.* 2 Ser. II. 474 The land the Army came by this day is very poor, chiefly skrub oak plains. **1796** HAWKINS *Letters* 16 The lands in this vale not rich, the timber small and mostly scruboak. **1808** PIKE *Sources Miss.* 40 Found some scrub oak. **1848** BRYANT *California* xi. 155, I noticed in one of the ravines to-day, the scrub-oak, or what is commonly called *black-jack.* **1857** STROTHER *Virginia* 116, I was hanging to the limb of a scrub oak. **1884** 'CRADDOCK' *Tenn. Mts.* 118 The few necessities . . . were in readiness to be transported . . . to Melinda's old home on Scrub-Oak Ridge. **1894** *Amer. Folk-Lore* VII. 99 *Quercus agrifolia,* scrub oak, evergreen oak, Cal. **1923** J. H. COOK *On Old Frontier* 6 This timber was a sort of scrub oak or blackjack.

+Scrub pine. Any one of various American dwarf pines, esp. the Jersey pine and the coastal form of the lodgepole pine. {1898–, in Australia}
1810 MICHAUX *Arbres* I. 16 *Jersey pine,* . . . dans New-Jersey où elle abonde. *Scrub pine,* nom usité en Virginie. **1849** *31st Congress 1 Sess.* Sen. Ex. Doc. No. 64, 131 A large part of the inhabitants are . . . gathering *piñones,* an edible fruit of the piñon, the common scrub pine of the country. **1884** SARGENT *Rep. Forests* 9 A scrub pine (*Pinus Murryana*), occupies vast areas, almost to the exclusion of other species. **1901** MOHR *Plant Life Ala.* 70 The scrub pine (*Pinus virginiana*) is found on the most broken and poorest places. **1923** WYATT *Invis. Gods* 17 Wild columbine . . . trooped in summer over the fern-runs up to the front terrace, and the Japanesy shadows of the black scrub pine that crowned it.

+Scrub race. An impromptu or casual race or contest; a race between scrub horses. Also *scrub racer, scrub racing.*
1807 IRVING, etc. *Salmagundi* xv. 405 He set out with a determination . . . to start in the scrub-race for honor and renown. **1836** *Knickerb.* VIII. 693 A new owner was on his back, and tearing through the pine barrens like a scrub-racer. **1837** *Ib.* X. 379 Look at him at a scrub-race, mounted on one of his father's colts. **1841** *Ib.* XVII. 276 The gentler sex . . . [have] the aid of such beaux as they can inveigle from amusements better suited to the dignity of the sex, such as drinking, scrub-racing. **1865** BOUDRYE *Fifth N.Y. Cavalry* 104 It was a scrub race,—across fields, fences and stone walls, we pressed after them. **1894** *Outing* XXIV. 145/1 In a scrub race the helmsman cracks on until the lee gunwale is almost on a level with the water.

+b. (See quot. 1914.)
1868 *N.Y. Herald* 10 July 6/5 The lines of division between the old republican and federal parties having entirely disappeared with the dissolution of the federal party, there was in 1824 a beautiful scrub race for the Presidency. **1880** *Harper's Mag.* Aug. 470 There was a 'scrub race,' and the election fell to the House of Representatives. **1914** *Cycl. Amer. Govt.* III. 274/1 *Scrub Race for the Presidency,* a derisive phrase applied to the personal contest for the presidency in 1824–5, between John Quincy Adams, Henry Clay, Andrew Jackson, and William H. Crawford, in which regularly organized parties were lacking. The electors failing to make a choice, the House of Representatives chose Adams.

+Scrub team. An athletic team, as in football, made up of players inferior to those on the 'first' team. — **1887** *Century Mag.* Oct. 895/1 The 'University team' . . . is pitted daily against a second, or 'scrub,' team of somewhat larger numbers. **1902** BELL *Hope Loring* 21, I am halfback on the scrub team here.

+Scrubwoman. A woman who does scrubbing; a charwoman. — **1885** *Century Mag.* Jan. 463/1 The men who control the theaters . . . are omnipotent to decide the casting of a tragedy or the pay of a scrub-woman. **1892** *Harper's Wkly.* 9 Jan. 42/4 The scrub-women . . . need all the intervening time to clean up and make these quarters ready for the business of the morrow. **1903** [see JANITRESS]. **1923** WYATT *Invis. Gods* 21 The scrubwoman on her knees . . . was wringing . . . her washrag.

‖**Scrumptious,** *n.* The gallant or fitting thing. — **1857** UNDERHILL & THOMPSON *Elephant Club* 159 He said his brother would see tu me, and do the scrumptious while he was gone.

+Scrumptious, *a.*
1. Nice; stylish; first-class. *colloq.* {1865–}
1830 S. SMITH *Life J. Downing* 50 The General Court . . . all had their hats off, and [were] looking pretty scrumptious. **1843** STEPHENS *High Life N.Y.* I. 173, I don't think there's anything very scrumptious about

the outside of the Theatre anyhow. **1889** DALY *Great Unknown* 10 But Cousin Ned's real scrumptious. **1901** ADE *40 Modern Fables* 95 Each would have on her most scrumptious Toggery. **1920** LEWIS *Main Street* 17 Probably the lumber yard isn't as scrumptious as all these Greek temples.

2. Fastidious; hard to please. *colloq.*
1835 KENNEDY *Horse Shoe Robinson* I. 87, I'm not over-scrumptious which. **1845** JUDD *Margaret* II. 314, I don't mean to be scrumptious about it, Judge.

Scruto(i)re, Scrito(i)re. =ESCRITOIRE. *Obs.* {1665–} Also attrib. — **1686** SEWALL *Letter-Book* I. 37, [I] have mislaid the Key of my Scritore and can't come at the papers. **1711** *Mass. H. S. Coll.* 6 Ser. V. 253 Send the key of the drawers of the scrutore. **1728** *Boston News-Letter* 18 Jan. 2/2 Lost a small Scrutoir Key. **1838** KENNEDY *Rob of Bowl* I. 127 Tell Nicholas Verbrack to look in my scritoire. **1853** RAMSEY *Tennessee* 132 These issues of the North-Carolina Treasury . . . are still found in great abundance in the scrutoires and chests of the old families.

Scuffle. A gardener's hoe designed for thrusting. {1841–, *dial.*} In full *scuffle hoe.* — **1797** S. DEANE *Newengland Farmer* (ed. 2) 95/2 *Dutch Hoe,* sometimes called a *Scuffle;* an iron instrument, with a sharp steeled edge, nearly in the shape of the letter D. **1825** LORAIN *Pract. Husbandry* 191 The scuffle (or D hoe as it is sometimes called) will destroy weeds growing on a level surface. **1856** *Mich. Agric. Soc. Trans.* VII. 55 D. O. & W. S. Penfield . . . [exhibited] 6 scuffle hoes. **1875** KNIGHT 2078/2 *Scuffle-hoe,* . . . a thrust-hoe having the blade in line, or nearly so, with the handle.

✳**Scull.** +A large piece of bark removed from a tree for use in making a bark canoe. *Obs.* — **1846** THORPE *Myst. Backwoods* 77 The 'scull' (scroll of bark) is then opened, and braces inserted to give the proper width to the gunnels of the canoe.

Scull boat. A boat, freq. a racing boat, propelled by sculls or short oars. {skulling boat, 1856} — **1870** *N.Y. Herald* 7 June 7/5 At the single scull boat race this afternoon there were five competitors.

Scullcap. (See SKULLCAP.)

+Scullduggery. [Var. of *sculduddery.*] Tricky, rascally conduct. *colloq.* (See also SKUL(L)DUGGERY.) — **1867** RICHARDSON *Beyond Miss.* 134 Smith and Brown . . . are up to some scull-duggery. **1894** LEAVITT *Our Money Wars* 116 [An] epitome of the financial scull-duggery of this year [1875] is given in . . . John Sherman's report as chairman of the Senate Finance Committee.

Sculling float. A flat-bottomed sculling boat. — **1874** LONG *Wild-Fowl* 89 The sculling-float . . . is rarely used in the pursuit of ducks where they are to be found in any considerable numbers. *Ib.* 230 They may also be approached, by using ordinary caution, in a sculling-float.

+Sculp, *n.* =SCALP *n. colloq.* Now hist. — **1758** *Essex Inst. Coll.* XVIII. 180 They obtained fifty-two Sculps & two Prisoners. **1804** *Lewis & Clark Exped.* VII. (1905) 64 They took the 65 of the Mahars sculps and had them hung on Small poles. **1845** SIMMS *Wigwam & Cabin* 1 Ser. 53 A pretty fellow . . . at his time of life to be looking after sculps of women and children. **1904** CHURCHILL *Crossing* 61, I wish the devils had every one of your fat sculps.

+Sculp, *v. tr.* =SCALP *v. colloq.* — **1758** *Essex Inst. Coll.* XVIII. 109 Taring his Nails out by ye Roots, Sculping alive and such like torments, they wou'd shout and yell . . . like so many Fiends. **1759** *Ib.* XIX. 188 [He] Killed and Sculpt one of ye Indians. **1775** RAUCK *Boonesborough* 168 [We] went down and found two men killed and sculped. **1834** CARRUTHERS *Kentuckian* I. 24 But as to shootin and sculpin Injins, that's a thing there is no bones made about. **1845** SIMMS *Wigwam & Cabin* 1 Ser. 44 They'll be sculped, every human of them, in their beds. **1904** CHURCHILL *Crossing* 61 We've all been burned out and sculped up river.

✳**Sculpin, Sculpion.** Any one of various fishes, mostly worthless, of the family Cottidae or Scelidae; also, one of certain other fishes. — **1761** OTIS in Tudor *Life J. Otis* 69 If he had taken an eel, or a smelt, or a sculpion, it was his property. **1810** BENTLEY *Diary* III. 491 The Sculpion, flounder, & eels are to be seen swimming near our wharves. **1839** STORER *Mass. Fishes* 23 *Hemitripterus Americanus.* . . . The Sea Raven, or deep water sculpin, . . . is taken in deep water. **1846** *Porter's Spirit of Times* 4 July 223/1 His first fish was, I believe, of that curious sort, commonly called 'Sculpin,' the abhorrence of all Fishermen. **1875** HOWARD *One Summer* xx, Mr. Tom Otis, in detaching a sculpin—a fish to which he was exceedingly partial—from his hook, threw into the raging sea a ring of considerable . . . value. **1896** JORDAN & EVERMANN *Check-List Fishes* 433 *Scorpæna guttata.* . . . Sculpin. Coast of California. **1911** *Rep. Fisheries 1908* 315/1 Sculpin (*Cottidæ*).—Several species of sculpin are found on the Atlantic and Pacific coasts.
attrib. **1864** LOWELL *Fireside Travels* 121 Why must great souls exhaust so soon Life's thin and unsubstantial boon? Existence on such sculpin terms, . . . What is it all but dross to me?

✳**Scummer.** A shallow utensil, usually perforated, for removing scum from the surface of a liquid. — **1648** *Conn. Rec.* I. 486 Inventory of the goods . . . of Richard Rissly. . . . A scummer, a cleansing dish. **1674** *Harvard Rec.* I. 61 Kitchins Utensils, . . . 1 Lawne sieve. 1 scummer. **1841** *Lowell Offering* I. 226 Abigail furnished us each with a large brass scummer.

+Scup, *n.¹ and v.* [Du. *schop.*] *local.* **1.** *n.* A swing. **2.** *v.* (See quotation.) — (1) **1848** BARTLETT 288 *Scup,* . . . a swing. A New York word. **1850** S. WARNER *Wide, Wide World* xi, What'll you give me if I'll make you a scup one of these days? (2) **1848** BARTLETT 288 *To scup,* . . . to swing. Common in New York.

+Scup, *n.²* Short for SCUPPAUG.
1848 BARTLETT 288 *Scup,* . . . a small fish abounding in the waters of New York and New England. In Rhode Island they are called *scup;* in New York, paugies, or porgies. **1873** *Rep. Comm. Fisheries* I. 74 The scup are known to be schooling, wandering fish of the high seas, and come from the Gulf Stream and from the Florida Cape. **1903** *N.Y. Ev. Post* 21 Nov., The porgy, the 'scup' of the more eastern waters, is reckoned a vulgar fish. **1911** *Rep. Fisheries 1908* 313/2 ['Pogy' is applied to] the scup (*Stenotomus chrysops*) along the southern coast.
attrib. **1860** *Harper's Mag.* Nov. 753/1 We had choice of a cruise on the Sound for scup fishing, or a bird-egging frolic to Muskegeet.

+Scuppaug. [Narraganset Indian.] A marine fish (*Stenotomus versicolor*) of the Atlantic coast, or a related fish (*S. chrysops*). — **1807** *Mass. H. S. Coll.* 2 Ser. III. 57 The skapaug in shape somewhat resembles the roach. **1815** *Mass. H. S. Coll.* 2 Ser. IV. 255 Tataug, scauppaug, eels, are the most common fish near the shores. **1833** *Niles' Reg.* XLIV. 415/1 He had probably given chase to some straggling bluefish or scuppaug (paugy, as the New Yorkers call them). **1860** *Harper's Mag.* Nov. 755/1 We . . . spent two hours or more in pulling out scuppaug. This is a species of perch, plump and white, weighing from one to three pounds. **1911** *Rep. Fisheries 1908* 315/2 Scup (*Stenotomus chrysops*). . . . Common local names are 'scuppaug,' 'paugy,' . . . etc.

+Scuppernong. [Algonquian river and lake name in N.C.]
1. = SCUPPERNONG GRAPE 1.
1829 *Free Press* (Tarboro, N.C.) 27 Feb., Among them the Scuppernong, a native of North Carolina, growing in a swamp. **1849** *New Eng. Farmer* I. 362 The Black Scuppernong bears from one to four berries on a bunch. **1869** *Rep. Comm. Agric. 1868* 443 Louis Froelich . . . says the Scuppernong gives the surest crop of grapes he has ever found or heard of in any wine-growing country. **1870** D. MACRAE *Americans at Home* (1908) I. 271 Experiments are being largely made in the planting of a native vine called scuppernong, which is found to flourish in soil where nothing else could live. **1885** *South Fla. Sentinel* (Orlando) 7 Oct. 4/1 Mr. John Padgett, of Enterprise, sold from one grape vine, this season, 770 quarts of scuppernongs. **1899** CHESNUTT *Conjure Woman* 19 Nex' mawnin' he tole some er de niggers 'bout de fine bait er scuppernon' he et de night befo'.
2. = SCUPPERNONG WINE.
1846 *Spirit of Times* 25 April 97/1 A keg of 'Scuppernong' is on its way to us, having been shipped from Wilmington, N.C. **1862** 'E. KIRKE' *Among Pines* 280 Her husband opened a sideboard, and brought forth . . . a decanter of Scuppernong. **1877** in Fleming *Hist. Reconstruction* II. 61, 62 Supplies for South Carolina: . . . scuppernong, sparkling Moselle [etc.].
3. Attrib. with *family, hock, pie,* etc.
1848 *Rep. Comm. Patents 1847* 470 Profits of a Scuppernong Vineyard. *Ib.* 471 For Scuppernong Hock, I put in the juice three pounds of double refined sugar per gallon. **1868** *Rep. Comm. Agric. 1867* 425 The Scuppernong family of grapes never fails [in La.]. **1903** *Outlook* 7 Nov. 584 A scuppernong pie . . . was the first grape pie I had ever eaten.

+Scuppernong grape.
1. A cultivated variety of the southern muscadine (*Muscadinia rotundifolia*), or its large, sweet, plumlike fruit.
1859 BARTLETT 389 *Scuppernong Grape.* . . . It is indigenous on the Scuppernong river and lake in North Carolina, and yields a highly esteemed wine. **1868** *Rep. Comm. Agric. 1867* 72 The Scuppernong grape alone is said to be exempt from the attacks of the grapevine borer. **1877** ROE *Army Lett.* 168, I was very ill for several days on the way up, the result of malaria—perhaps too many scuppernong grapes. **1901** MOHR *Plant Life Ala.* 136 The scuppernong grape yields its crops year after year with regular abundance.
2. = SCUPPERNONG WINE.
1887 *Courier-Journal* 8 May 18/5 Here's some of that scuppernong grape.

+Scuppernong grapevine. A vine which produces scuppernongs. — **1857** *Harper's Mag.* May 746/1 The dwellings in the Piny Woods . . . almost always have . . . a trellis supporting an extensive scuppernong grape-vine. **1904** PRINGLE *Rice Planter* 98 In addition to these they have a most prolific pear tree and a very large scuppernong grapevine.

+Scuppernong wine. A sweet, straw-colored wine made from scuppernongs. — **1825** *Catawba Jrnl.* 2 Aug., The editor . . . having had a taste of the Scuppernong wine from North-Carolina, extols it in the highest terms. **1828** *Free Press* (Tarboro, N.C.) 29 Aug., Also, some superior Scuppernong Wine. **1887** *Century Mag.* July 335/2 [She] begged Mrs. Colonel Ledbetter to give her her recipe for making the scuppernong wine she had heard so much praised.

+Scurvy-leaves. ?Water plantain: (see quotation). — **1674** JOSSELYN *Two Voyages* 80 Water-plantane, called in *New-England* water Suck-leaves, and Scurvie-leaves, you must lay them whole to the leggs to draw out water between the skin and the flesh.

Scuttler. {1867-} +A striped lizard (*Cnemidophorus sexlineatus*) of the South. — **1886** *Amer. Philol. Ass. Trans.* XVII. 46 *Scuttler* or *streakfield* (striped lizard).

* Scythe. An agricultural implement used for mowing, consisting of a long curved blade fixed to a long handle.
1641 *Conn. Rec.* I. 444 Goods of Richard Lyman deceased: . . . 2 scythes wth their tacklin. **1713** HEMPSTEAD *Diary* 25, I was about home fixing up Syths to go to mowing. **1795** *Essex Inst. Coll.* LIV. 103 To the anchor works may be annexed . . . a suitable apparatus for making shovels, scythes [etc.]. **1844** *Lexington Observer* 25 Sept. 4/1 8 doz. Scythes . . . just received and for sale. **1872** *Atlantic Mo.* April 308 A Pennsylvanian might dig a piece of iron out of his native hills, . . . but he was obliged to send it to England to be made into steel and a scythe. **1923** J. H. COOK *On Old Frontier* 3 Sturdy sons of the forest, they could swing the scythe or the grain-cradle from sunup to sundown.
attrib. **1744** *Md. Hist. Mag.* XXI. 244, 6 Grass Scythe Blades. **1786** WASHINGTON *Diaries* III. 77 At Dogue run . . . the Scythmen began last to cut. *a*1817 DWIGHT *Travels* I. 361 There are in this township . . . a saw-mill, a scythe-manufactory [etc.].

Scythe snath. The handle to which the blade of a scythe is fastened. {1839-} — **1783** E. PARKMAN *Diary* 300 Old iron 5/ Scythe Snath /8. **1841** *Lowell Offering* I. 16 All the neighbors . . . were expected to bring with them some implements of husbandry, such as ploughs, . . . scythe-snaths, rakes, [and] goads. **1866** *Rep. Indian Affairs* 292, 120 wedges for scythe snaths. **1881** *Ib.* 400.

Scythestone. A whetstone for sharpening a scythe. {1688-} — **1678** *New Castle Court Rec.* 349 An Inventory of ye goods Belonging to Richard Hunter [includes] . . . 9 sith stones. **1762** *Essex Inst. Coll.* XLIX. 276 To Be Sold. . . . Sickles, Scyths, Scyth Stones. **1787** *Md. Gazette* 1 June 3/3 Scythe stones; . . . tobacco and snuff boxes. **1843** *Nat. Hist. N.Y., Geology* III. 70 The rock is of excellent quality for grindstones, but too hard for scythe stones. **1881** *Rep. Indian Affairs* 438.

+Scythe whet. *local.* The veery or Wilson's thrush. — **1871** LOWELL *My Study Windows* 22 My walk under the pines would lose half its summer charm, were I to miss that shy anchorite, the Wilson's thrush, nor hear in haying-time the metallic ring of his song, that justifies his rustic name of 'scythe-whet.'

* Sea. In attrib. uses.
1. Designating things used at sea.
See also SEA BED, SEA BISCUIT, etc.
1636 *Essex Probate Rec.* I. 4 A Sea chest. **1638** *Md. Archives* IV. 87 3. thimbles, a sea-capp, a pcell of old books. **1660** *Essex Probate Rec.* I. 317 One Bible wth. 3 small seabookes. **1711** *Boston News-Letter* 29 Oct. 2/2 Had on when he went away, a dark coloured Se[a] J[a]cket, blew Breeches. **1734** *N.J. Archives* 1 Ser. XI. 392 A Servant Man named Lawrence Stakepole . . . had on a Felt Hat, an old Sea-Pea-Jacket lined with red [etc.]. **1751** WASHINGTON *Diaries* I. 26 Provided my Sea Store and dined with Mr. Carter. **1801** *Essex Inst. Coll.* LIII. 202 Our Sea stock . . . was to be in the greatest Abundance. **1851** MELVILLE *Moby-Dick* 44 There was a low rumbling of heavy sea-boots among the benches. **1854** COOKE *Va. Comedians* I. 215/2 My best military dresses are still at Yorktown, in the sea trunks.

*2. In the specific names of plants and animals.
Only a selection is given.

*a. Birds that frequent or live on the sea.
See also SEA BRANT, SEA DRAKE, etc.
1709 LAWSON *Carolina* 147 The Sea-Cock is a Gull that crows at Break of Day. **1858** BAIRD *Birds Pacific R.R.* 806 *Pelionetta Perspicillata.* Surf Duck; Sea Coot. . . . On and near seacoast of North America. **1917** *Birds of Amer.* I. 214 Coot. *Fulica americana.* . . . [Also called] Crow-bill; Sea Crow; Pond Crow. **1844** *Nat. Hist. N.Y., Zoology* II. 280 The Sea Dove, *Mergulus alle,* . . . occurs on the northwest coast near the mouth of the Columbia river. **1814** Wilson *Ornithology* IX. 129 In Mr. Wilson's history of the Bald Eagle, he confidently asserts that it is the same species as the Sea Eagle, in a different stage of color. **1917** *Birds of Amer.* I. 33 Skua. *Megalestris skua.* . . . [Also called] Sea Hawk; Sea Hen. **Ib.** 142 Harlequin Duck. *Histrionicus histrionicus.* . . . [Also called] Squealer; Sea Mouse. **1835** AUDUBON *Ornith. Biog.* III. 105 The Sea Parrot, as this bird [the Puffin] is usually called on the eastern coasts of the United States, . . . sometimes proceeds as far south as the entrance of the River Savannah in Georgia. **1709** LAWSON *Carolina* 147 The Sea-Pie, or gray Curlue, is about the Bigness of a very large Pigeon. **1917** *Birds of Amer.* I. 33 Pomarine Jaeger. *Stercorarius pomarius.* . . . [Also called] Gull Hunter; Sea Robber; Gull Chaser. **Ib.** 218 Northern Phalarope. *Lobipes lobatus.* . . . [Also called] Sea Goose; . . . Sea Snipe; Whalebird. **1813** WILSON *Ornithology* VII. 76 From their long pointed wings they are generally known to seafaring people and others residing near the sea shore by the name of Sea Swallows. **1624** SMITH *Gen. Hist. Va.* v. 171 [There are] many sorts of Fowles, as . . . Red-shankes, Sea-wigions, Gray-bitterns.

* b. Mammals and reptiles that live in the sea.
See also SEA COW, SEA LION, SEA OTTER.
1884 *Nat. Museum Bul.* No. 27, 643 *Callorhinus ursinus.* . . . Northern Fur Seal; Sea Bear. Coast of California northward. **1847** *Knickerb.* XXIX. 494 The staid and lofty lawyer . . . was bargaining with an old African woman for a lot of sea-terrapins. **1874** B. F. TAYLOR *World on Wheels* 228 The thing was a sea-tiger, and resembled an exaggerated seal. **1766** STORK *Acct. E. Florida* 52 There are three sorts of sea-turtle common in East-Florida, the logger-head, hawk's-bill, and green-turtle.

* c. Fishes, mollusks, jellyfishes, etc.
See also SEA BASS, SEA CLAM, etc.
1791 CUTLER in *Life & Corr.* I. 467 We found the Sea-anemone, or animal plant, in great perfection and of a large size. **1884** GOODE, etc. *Fisheries* I. 173 The best known species [of the devilfishes] are the Marbled Angler, *Pterophryne histrio,* and the Sea Bat, *Malthe vespertilio.* **1672** JOSSELYN *New Eng. Rarities* 152 Sea Bream . . . are plentifully taken upon the sea coasts. *a*1884 in Goode, etc. *Fisheries* I. 701 These shells have been called by different names, . . . such as . . . 'Rattle-snake's Tail,' 'Lob-

ster's Tail,' 'Sea-bug,' and 'Sea-caterpillar.' **1672** JOSSELYN *New Eng. Rarities* 24 Sea Bleak or Bley, or Sea Camelion. **1842** *Nat. Hist. N.Y., Zoology* IV. 159 The Sea Wolf, *Anarrhicas lupus*, . . . is known under the various popular names of Cat, Wolf-fish, and Sea Cat. **1855** BAIRD in *Smithsonian Rep. 1854* 341 The Sea Cat-Fish, *Ailurichthys marinus*. . . . The flesh is very indifferent. **1672** JOSSELYN *New Eng. Rarities* 24 Sea Cod or Sea Whiting. **1884** GOODE, etc. *Fisheries* I. 783 On the coast of Rhode Island, Lobsters are sometimes called 'Sea-craws,' from their resemblance to the fresh-water Cray-fish. *Ib.* 841 Among the Gorgonians occur the Sea-fans (*Gorgonia flabellum*), and the Sea-feathers or Sea-plumes. **1842** *Nat. Hist. N.Y., Zoology* IV. 381 The Bluish Sea Lamprey, *Petromyzon nigricans*, . . . is found attached to mackerel, haddock, and cod fishes. **1884** GOODE, etc. *Fisheries* I. 453 The 'Sea Mullet' ranges from eight to eighteen inches. **1855** BAIRD in *Smithsonian Rep. 1854* 346 The Bill-Fish [and] Sea-Pike . . . have been seen at Columbia, Pennsylvania, in the Susquehanna. **1891** *Cent.* 5445/3 *Sea-potato*, . . . an ascidian of some kind, as *Boltenia reniformis* or *Ascidia mollis*. (Local, U.S.) **1733** *Georgia Col. Rec.* III. 62 [Received] several Parcels of Sea Rod. **1842** *Nat. Hist. N.Y., Zoology* IV. 59 The Spotted Sea Scorpion, *Scorpaena bufo*, . . . has been observed from the Caribbean sea to Newfoundland. **1883** *Nat. Museum Bul.* No. 27, 476 *Clupea mediocris*. . . . Mattowacca; Sea Shad; Shad. Atlantic coast of North America. **1814** MITCHILL *Fishes N.Y.* 483 Long-toothed Sea Shark. *Squalus Americanus*. . . . This fish is occasionally taken at the very city of New York. *c*1733 CATESBY *Carolina* II. 2 *Saurus ex cineres nigricans*. The Sea Sparrow-Hawk. . . . This Fish was caught on the coast of Carolina. **1843** *Nat. Hist. N.Y., Zoology* VI. 2 The Sea-spider, or Spider-Crab, is very common on the coast of this State. **1911** *Rep. Fisheries 1908* 317/1 *Starfish*, a star-shaped animal . . . found all along the coast and known as 'five-finger,' 'sea-star,' 'star,' etc. **1883** *Nat. Museum Bul.* No. 27, 123 Two species of edible Sea Urchin . . . live upon our coasts.

* **d.** Plants growing along the seashore.

See also SEA GRAPE 2, SEA OAT, SEA ROCKET.

1814 BIGELOW *Florula Bostoniensis* 85 *Triglochin maritimum*. Sea arrow grass. . . . The cultivation of this plant for cattle has been recommended. **1901** MOHR *Plant Life Ala.* 132 The low islets closer to the main shore . . . [are fringed with] *Chenopodium berlandieri* and *Lycium carolinianum* (sea cherry). **1843** TORREY *Flora N.Y.* I. 12 *Ranunculus Cymbalaria*. . . . Sea Crowfoot. . . . Salt marshes on the seacoast of Long Island; also about the salt works of Salina and Syracuse. **1883** *Nat. Museum Bul.* No. 27, 123 At least three species of edible Holothurians or Sea-cucumbers occur upon the Eastern coast of the United States. **1915** ARMSTRONG & THORNBER *Western Wild Flowers* 110 Sea Fig, Fig-marigold. *Mesembryanthemum aequilaterale*. Pink. Spring. California. **1840** DEWEY *Mass. Flowering Plants* 98 *Acnida cannabina*. Sea Hemp. Grows in marshes about salt water. **1843** TORREY *Flora N.Y.* I. 93 Common Sea Quickweed, . . . *Houckenya peploides*. **1841** WOOD *Botany* 349 *A[rtemisia] Canadensis*. Sea Wormwood. . . . Shores of the great lakes. Plum Island.

* **e.** Plants that grow in the sea.

See also SEA GRAPE 1, SEAWEED.

1899 GOING *Flowers* 385 We may notice a green film which is caused by the growth of some tiny and humble cousins of the rich green 'sea-lettuce' which floats at the edge of tidal pools on rocky coasts. **1868** *Amer. Naturalist* II. 230 The Sea-thong (*Himanthalia lorea*) . . . at first grows like a cup.

3. In special combinations.

Sea fort, a fort built next to the sea {1879–}; *s. paper*, (see quotation); *s. power* {1849–}, the power of a nation to conduct maritime warfare {1883–}; *s.-service*, (see quotation).

1634 *Mass. Bay Rec.* I. 120 Mr. Beecher, Mr. Peirce, & Robte Moulton are desired to treate & bargaine with Mr Stevens & Mr. Mayhewe . . . for the building of the seaffort. **1813** *Ann. 12th Congress* 2 Sess. 72 All American mariners and apprentices . . . shall be comprehended and described in an official document, or sea paper, authenticated for the use of the vessel during the voyage. **1807** *Ann. 10th Congress* 1 Sess. 1198 The sea-power as yet controls the land-power. **1891** *Cent.* 5447/2 *Sea service*, . . . in the United States navy, service at sea or on board of a sea-going ship, as distinguished from *shore-service*.

+**Sea bass.** [Cf. Du. *zeebaars*.] **a.** Any of the fishes of the family Serranidae, esp. the black sea bass (*Centropristes striatus*) found along the Atlantic coast. **b.** The white sea bass (*Atractoscion nobilis*) or the jewfish (*Stereolepis gigas*) of the California coast. **c.** (See quot. 1883.)

1765 ROGERS *Acct. N. Amer.* 68 In the sea adjacent to this island [Long Island] are sea-bass and black-fish in great plenty, which are very good when fresh. **1775** BURNABY *Travels* 109 These waters [in N.Y.] afford various kinds of fish, black-fish, sea-bass, sheeps-heads, rock fish, lobsters, and several others. **1807** *Mass. H.S. Coll.* 2 Ser. III. 56 The sea bass is caught in every season except winter. **1848** BURTON *Waggeries* 22 [You] keep your table well supplied with hallibut and sea-bass, and black-fish, eh? **1883** *Nat. Museum Bul.* No. 27, 442 *Sciæna ocellata*. . . . Poisson Rouge; . . . Sea Bass; Spotted Bass. . . . This is a rival of the drum in size and is vastly more important as a food-fish. **1900** NORRIS *Blix* 129 There were . . . sheaves of fishing-rods, from the four-ounce wisp of the brook-trout up to the rigid eighteen-ounce lance of the king-salmon and sea-bass.

Sea bed. {1838} A bed used on a boat. Also *sea bedding*. *Obs.* — **1637** *Md. Archives* IV. 76 The Inventary of the goods & chattells of mr John Baxter [includes] . . . 1. rugg & an old sea-bed. **1664** *Essex Probate Rec.* I. 445 In the hall, . . . [were] 2 baggs & old seabeds & bedding. **1720** *Essex Inst. Coll.* XX. 26, 1 skooner valued at £200, a small skooner at £22.—Sea beding £4.

Sea biscuit. Hard-tack or pilot bread. {1680–90–} — **1725** *New-Eng. Courant* 17 May 2/2 All Gentlemen, Merchants and others, may have Wheat and Flower bak'd into Sea Bisket for 3s. per Hundred. **1846** MELVILLE *Typee* 1 There is nothing left us but salt-horse and sea-biscuit. **1883** 'MARK TWAIN' *Life on Miss.* lii, I spent my last 10 cts for 2 moons (*large, round sea-biscuit*).

* **Seaboard.**

+**1.** The coast line; the area or land adjacent to the coast line, esp. along the Atlantic coast. {1840–}

1788 ASBURY *Journal* II. 37 The Gnats are almost as troublesome here, as the mosquitoes in the lowlands of the seaboard. **1793** JEFFERSON *Writings* III. 277 On their seaboard they [*sc.* the United States] are open to injury. **1803** *Ann. 7th Congress* 2 Sess. 192 The seaboard can send few if any troops beyond the mountains. **1833** SILLIMAN *Man. Sugar Cane* 19 It is believed that the cane can be cultivated, profitably, on the sea board of Georgia. **1865** *Atlantic Mo.* June 693/1 Internal trade before the war consisted [partly] of the trade of the Lakes and the canals leading from them to the seaboard. **1891** WILKINS in *Century Mag.* Feb. 506/2 In the heart of this simple, humble young woman of the seaboard, . . . was love of the kind . . . that is better than marriage.

+**b.** *Atlantic seaboard*, the country along the Atlantic Ocean.

1851 CIST *Cincinnati* 312 Here are four trunk roads, each terminating . . . on the Atlantic sea-board. **1865** BURROUGHS in *Atlantic Mo.* May 523/2 The Wood-Thrush . . . [has a] liberal distribution throughout our Atlantic seaboard. **1886** LOGAN *Great Conspiracy* 84 Douglas . . . was triumphantly received by the chief cities of the Mississippi and the Atlantic sea-board.

2. Attrib. with *city*, *climate*, *cotton*, etc.

1640 in *Amer. Speech* XV. 389 A parcell of land att the Seaboard side. **1812** MELISH *Travels* I. 27 Sea-island cotton . . . is planted, and comes to maturity, in all the . . . islands along the coast . . . and is thence called *seaboard cotton*. **1835** HOFFMAN *Winter in West* I. 37, I used to think our sea-board climate as capricious as it could well be. **1843** *Knickerb.* Nov. 431 The average length of human life is thirteen per cent. greater in the mountain districts of New-Hampshire than it is upon the sea-board country of Massachusetts. **1858** *Harper's Mag.* July 278/1 In one of the seaboard States resided a Mr. Smith, since a Senator. **1860** in Logan *Great Conspiracy* 127 Everybody can see, too, how the bringing in of $300,000,000 of imports into Southern ports would enliven business in our seaboard towns. **1881** *Century Mag.* Dec. 317/1 It is hard for us here, in the seaboard cities, to realize that the good gifts of broad statesmanship . . . may come from the Galilee beyond the mountains.

+**Sea brant.** **1.** The white-winged scoter, *Melanitta deglandi*. **2.** (See quotation.) — **(1)** **1888** TRUMBULL *Names of Birds* 99 To some at Portsmouth, N.H., [*Oidemia deglandi* is known as] Sea Brant. **1917** *Birds of Amer.* I. 150 White-winged Scoter. *Oidemia deglandi*. . . . [Also called] Brant Coot; Sea Brant; May Whitewing. **(2)** **1891** *Cent.* 548/3 *Sea-brant*, . . . the brant- or brent-goose.

Sea bread. =SEA BISCUIT. {1876} — **1837** S. GRAHAM *Treatise on Bread* 93 (Ernst), The machine which the bakers call the break, [is] used in making crackers and seabread. **1846** MELVILLE *Typee* 37 He first brought to light about a pound of tobacco, . . . the whole outside being covered with soft particles of sea-bread. **1852** MITCHELL *Dream Life* 42 You would . . . make a very nice breakfast off of smoked herring and sea-bread. **1869** J. R. BROWNE *Adv. Apache Country* 241 In the meantime [we] lived on our sea-bread, roast beef, and the honey and wild fruits of the island.

+**Sea clam.** One or other species of clam found along the Atlantic coast, esp. the surf clam. — **1802** *Mass. H. S. Coll.* 1 Ser. VIII. 192 The sea clam, which is at present called the *hen*, the quahaug having lost that appellation, is bivalve. *a*1862 THOREAU *Cape Cod* 100 Our host told us that the sea-clam, or hen, was not easily obtained. **1883** *Nat. Museum Bul.* No. 27, 260 Hen Clam, Surf Clam, or Sea Clam . . . [is found from] Florida and Gulf of Mexico to Labrador. *Ib.*, *Cyprina islandica*. . . . Sea Clam. Long Island to Arctic Ocean.

***Sea coal.** **a.** Mineral coal, as distinguished from charcoal. Now hist. **b.** (See quot. 1895.) — **1714** *Boston News-Letter* 18 Oct. 2/2 To be Sold also . . . Sheet and Bar Lead, Sea Coal and Chalk. **1732** HEMPSTEAD *Diary* 253, I fetched a Load of Sea Coale for John from the Town wharff. **1788** MAY *Jrnl. & Lett.* 19 This mountain . . . abounds in good sea-coal, which they call here stone coal. **1822** *Missionary Herald* XVIII. 31 In the [Missouri] river is abundance of sea-coal fit for use. **1893** HALE *New Eng. Boyhood* 95 We had to illuminate the room with gas—made sometimes from turpentine, sometimes from 'sea coal,' as, like Shakespeare, we called it. **1895** *Stand.* 1610/3 *Sea-coal*, . . . [Rare, U.S.] Soft coal as distinguished from anthracite.

***Seacoast.** The shore of the land along the sea. Also attrib. — **1640** *Conn. Rec.* I. 52 The Courte . . . [is] to prosecute the murtherers . . . vppon consultation with . . . our neighbor Plantations aboute the sea coste. **1776** *Essex Inst. Coll.* XLIII. 188 They petition for two or three cannon and a Sea Coast Company. **1818** *Niles' Reg.* XV. 45/1 That road . . . is a great turnpike extending from Maine to Georgia in the general direction of the sea coast and main post road. **1880** CABLE *Grandissimes*

358 Would anyone hereafter dispute with him on the subject of Louisiana sea-coast-navigation? **1907** *St. Nicholas* June 676/1 The quaint old town by the sea, called Portsmouth, is the only sea-coast town in New Hampshire.

+Sea corn. The mass of yellow egg capsules of such marine snails as the whelks. — **1885** J. S. KINGSLEY, etc. *Stand. Nat. Hist.* I. 333 [The eggs of the whelk] are laid in hemispherical capsules, yellow in color, piled up in a heap, and presenting an appearance well-described by the name 'sea-corn' applied to them by the New England fishermen.

Sea cow. Any sirenian, as the manatee. {1613–} — **1682** ASH *Carolina* 31 There is farther to the Southward of Carolina . . . a Fish . . . call'd the Manacy or Sea-Cow. **1827** WILLIAMS *W. Florida* 24 The Indians state that the maneto, or sea-cow, used to resort to [the river]. **1911** *Rep. Fisheries 1908* 312/1 Manatee (*Trichechus latirostris*), a sirenian found on the Florida coast in very small numbers; also called 'sea-cow.'

＊Sea devil. 1. One of various ugly fishes. {1634–} **2.** (See quotation.) {1902–} — **(1) 1814** MITCHILL *Fishes N.Y.* 465 Bellows-fish, or common Angler. *Lophius piscator*. . . . They have named him also the *sea-devil*, on account of his ugliness. **1842** *Nat. Hist. N.Y., Zoology* IV. 377 The Sea Devil, *Cephaloptera vampirus*, . . . is one of those huge monsters of the deep, which are occasionally captured along our shores. **1882** *Nat. Museum Bul.* No. 16, 52 *Manta birostris*. . . . Sea Devil; Devil Fish. **(2) 1878** *N. Amer. Rev.* 230 A naval officer might almost stand aghast at the prospect of his ship being struck unawares by one of these stealthy and effective sea-devils [torpedo boats].

＊Sea dog. An experienced and seasoned sailor. {1855–} — **1823** COOPER *Pilot* II. 137 Ahead, heave ahead, sea-dogs! **1840** DANA *Two Years* xxiii. 230 The carpenter . . . was an old sea-dog, a Swede by birth, and accounted the best helmsman in the ship. **1897** *Outing* XXX. 588/2 Dear gallant old sea-dogs, these Amagansetters!

Sea drake. {1632} +(See quotation.) — **1861** COUES in *Phila. Acad. Nat. Sciences Proc.* 240 [Eiderducks] are universally known as 'Sea-ducks,' the males being always distinguished as 'Sea-drakes.'

+Sea drift. Any flotsam, esp. vegetable and animal matter cast up on the seashore. — **1816** *East-Hampton Rec.* IV. 396 If any person or persons shall cart . . . more than two loads of seaweed or sea-drift from the beach . . . they so offending shall forfeit the sum of five dollars. **1891** *Harper's Mag.* Sept. 592/1 Many among them have gathered to themselves a respectable covering of soil from the various sorts of sea-drift.

Sea duck. a. Any duck of the subfamily Fuligulinae. {1753–} **+b.** *New Eng.* An eider duck. — **1794** *Mass. H. S. Coll.* 1 Ser. III. 199 Sea fowl are plenty on the shores and in the bay; particularly the . . . black duck, sea duck, [and] old wife. **1835** AUDUBON *Ornith. Biog.* III. 343 We saw a great number of 'sea Ducks,' as the gunners and fishermen on that coast, as well as on our own, call the Eiders and some other species. **1869** *Amer. Naturalist* III. 226 Their numbers were immensely reinforced by myriads of sea-ducks from more northern seas. **1917** *Birds of Amer.* I. 147/1 The Massachusetts gunners call them [*sc.* eiders] Sea Ducks for they seem to prefer the outer ledges jutting into the sea.

Sea-elephant oil. Oil taken from the elephant seal. {1828–} — **1807** *Mass. H. S. Coll.* 2 Ser. III. 29 Two of the brigs go to Patagonia after sea elephant oil. **1818** *Niles' Reg.* XIV. 168/1 A ship has arrived at Nantucket with 1400 casks sea-elephant oil.

Sea fencible. (See quot. c1870.) Now hist. {1803, 'old coast-guard'} — **1813** *Ann. 13th Congress* 1 Sess. 35 The bill to authorize the raising a corps of sea fencibles was read the second time. **1814** BENTLEY *Diary* IV. 290, I had attached myself to Captain Ropes' Sea fencibles with the cannon of the United States. **1817** *Ann. 14th Congress* 2 Sess. 871 A bill . . . [was taken up] for allowing five years' half pay to the widows or orphans of any officer or soldier of the militia, rangers, sea fencibles. c**1870** CHIPMAN *Notes on Bartlett* 389 *Sea-fencibles*, name adopted in 1812–15 by volunteer troops, coast-guards composed of men past the age legally required for military service. Massachusetts.

+Sea food. Food taken from the sea, fish, shellfish, etc. Also attrib. — **1836** *Knickerb.* VIII. 423 She said that she had come to Screamy Point to get 'sea-food.' **1865** *Atlantic Mo.* May 601/1 Queer-shaped flat-boats . . . [are] ferrying over . . . some fish-peddler bound to the 'P'int' for 'sea-food.' **1906** *N.Y. Ev. Post* 10 March 5 Up State residents are among the best customers of the sea food, fruit and produce dealers in the downtown open markets.

+Sea goose. 1. A phalarope. **2.** (See quotation.) — **(1) 1835** AUDUBON *Ornith. Biog.* III. 118 The gunners of Eastport, who knew them under the name of Sea Geese, spoke of them as very curious birds. **1844** *Nat. Hist. N.Y., Zoology* II. 269 The Hyperborean Lobefoot, *Lobipes hyperboreus*, . . . occurs abundantly in Maine (where they are termed Sea Geese) and farther north. **1861** COUES in *Phila. Acad. Nat. Sciences Proc.* 229 Both [*Phalaropus fulicarius* and *P. hyperboreus* are] known by the uncouth and inappropriate, though curious name of 'Sea-geese.' **1880** *Harper's Mag.* Sept. 504/2 A quaint apparent exception, and the only one, to the universal rule of rapine . . . was a little bird somewhat larger than a sand piper—the sea-goose, so-called. **1917** *Birds of Amer.* I. 217, 218. **(2) 1891** *Cent.* 5440/3 *Sea-goose*, . . . a dolphin: so called from the shape of the snout.

＊Sea grape. 1. =GULFWEED. {1850} **2.** Any tree of the genus *Coccolobis*. {1806, in W. Indies} — **(1) 1825** LONGFELLOW *Poetical Works* (1893) 650/1 They rested by the coral throne, . . . Where the pale sea-grape had o'ergrown The glorious dwellings made for them. **(2) 1834** AUDUBON *Ornith. Biog.* II. 385 When the sea-grape is ripe, they feed greedily upon it. **1837** WILLIAMS *Florida* 114 The Caccalobe or sea grape ornaments all our southern coast with its abundant clusters. **1884** SARGENT *Rep. Forests* 118 *Coccoloba uvifera*. . . . Sea Grape. Semi-tropical Florida. **1897** SUDWORTH *Arborescent Flora* 191.

＊Sea horse.

＊1. The walrus. Also attrib.

1643 *New Eng. First Fruits* (1896) 11 [We have] Fish, as Cod, Haddock, . . . Seales, Whales, Sea-horse. **1764** HUTCHINSON *Hist. Mass.* I. 464 The Mohawks secured their bodies against the arrows of other Indians by a covering of seahorse skins. **1798** in H. M. Brooks *Gleanings* IV. 109 Cash given for Ivory, Sea-horse, and Sea-cows Teeth. **1855** GLISAN *Jrnl. Army Life* 177 The [stuffed] sea-horse and sea-lion attracting the larger share of attention from visitors.

＊2. Any of numerous small fishes of the family Syngnathidae, esp. of the genus *Hippocampus*. Also attrib.

1839 STORER *Mass. Fishes* 167 *Hippocampus brevirostris*. The short-nosed Sea-horse. **1860** *Harper's Mag.* March 490/2 The sea-horse is small, about three inches long. **1867** *Amer. Naturalist* I. 227 The structure of the Sea-horse's tail should be borne in mind. **1884** GOODE, etc. *Fisheries* I. 172 There are one or more species of the Sea-horse family on the Atlantic coast, and also one on that of California.

+3. (See quotation.)

1917 *Birds of Amer.* I. 80 Fulmar. *Fulmarus glacialis glacialis*. . . . [Also called] Molly Hawk; John Down; Sea Horse.

+Sea Island.

1. One of a chain of islands off the South Carolina, Georgia, and Florida coasts; also, pl., the whole chain of islands. Also attrib.

1763 *Hist. Coll. S. Carolina* II. 468 Marshes . . . abound much on the sea Islands. **1797** *Ann. 4th Congress* 2 Sess. 2133 Almost the whole of their [Ga.] sea-islands were examined for [timber]. **1802** DRAYTON *S. Carolina* 63 Yellow Jassmin . . . grows plentifully on the large sea islands. **1880** HARRIS *Uncle Remus* p. xiii, The dialect of the cotton plantations . . . [differs from] the lingo in vogue on the rice plantations and Sea Islands of the South Atlantic States. **1895** *Dept. Agric. Yrbk. 1894* 123 The storm of August 26, 27, 28, 1893, [was] familiarly known as the 'sea islands storm.'

2. Ellipt. for next. Also attrib.

1803 J. DAVIS *Travels* 78 Of cotton there are two kinds; the sea-island and inland. The first is the most valuable. **1819** *Niles' Reg.* XVII. 9/2 [The duty] will be considerably enhanced upon sea islands. **1856** *Rep. Comm. Patents 1855: Agric.* 319 [It is believed] that the 'Georgian,' or 'Short-staple,' is the Sea Island, carried into the interior. **1916** *Farmer's Bul.* No. 787, 7 [Egyptian cotton] will continue to be used by many mills . . . until the Sea Island growers improve their product.

+Sea-island cotton. A long and silky-fibered cotton (*Gossypium barbadense*), formerly grown on the Sea Islands. Cf. ISLAND COTTON.

1805 MICHAUX *Travels* 345 Sea Island Cotton . . . has a deep black seed, and very long fine wool. **1812** *Ann. 12th Congress* 1 Sess. 2190 Sea Island cotton can only be raised in a very limited district of the Union. **1828** in Commons, etc. *Doc. Hist.* I. 268 The Sea Island Cotton was introduced directly from the Bahama Islands into Georgia. **1858** *Texas Almanac 1859* 84 We have omitted to mention the numerous experiments now being made to grow the Sea-Island or black-seed cotton on our coast lands. **1870** J. YEATS *Nat. Hist. Commerce* (1872) 199 The best American cotton . . . is the celebrated Sea-island cotton, which grows on a row of islands situated along the coast of Georgia. **1897** *Kissimmee* (Fla.) *Valley* 2 June 1/4 The exhibit of sea-island cotton from Ocala and Gainesville attracts much attention.

＊Seal, n.¹

＊1. Any aquatic carnivorous mammal of the families Phocidae and Otariidae (suborder Pinnipedia) having flipperlike limbs adapted to swimming. (See also HAIR SEAL.)

1622 MOURT *Relation* 71 They returned with three greate Seales, and an excellent good Cod. **1643** [see SEA HORSE 1]. **1674** *Cal. State P., Amer. & W.I.* VII. 581 On the sea coasts [of Maine are], whales, grampus, seals, sharks [etc.]. **1789** MORSE *Amer. Geog.* 55 Beasts which are the same on both continents . . . [include the] Mole, Morse, Seal. **1806** LEWIS in *L. & Clark Exped.* IV. (1905) 99 The seal are found here in great numbers, and as far up the Columbia river as the great falls. **1856** GLISAN *Jrnl. Army Life* 327 The officers sometimes amused themselves with shooting at gulls, seals, and ducks. **1889** MUNROE *Golden Days* 83 They saw hundreds of black seals. **1916** *Outlook* 26 Jan. 172/1 As a trapper Uncle Sam has to guard the seals and sea otter in the northwestern seas, in compliance with the international sealing agreement of 1911.

2. *attrib.* and *comb.* Designating things made from the bodies of seals; designating various persons, actions, etc., connected with sealing.

1789 *R.I. Commerce* II. 405 First Seal Oil . . . 2/3 to 2/6 per Gallon. **1834** AUDUBON *Ornith. Biog.* II. 200 The remains of a deserted camp of seal-catchers was easily traced from our deck. **1873** E. S. PHELPS *Trotty's Wedding* v, She took a second-class passage . . . for Alaska, and went into the seal fisheries shortly after. **1876** *Narr. Polaris Exped.* (Navy Dept.) 219 Hans set some seal-traps, without success. **1916** *Outlook* 26 Jan. 172/2 It is now possible to make the seal leathers here, as furriers are now willing and able to undertake the seal tanning and preparing.

∗ Seal, n.²

∗ **1.** An engraved, inscribed, or embossed stamp used for making an impression in wax, etc., on documents; often worn on a watch chain.

1633 *Plymouth Laws* 34 All other measures [are] to be brought in to the constable . . . , and so to be sealed by him with the seale appoynted for that end. **1689** *Conn. Probate Rec.* I. 506, I give to Nathaniel Dickinson's wife . . . my silver Thimble & Seale. **1759** *Newport Mercury* 26 June 4/3 Imported . . . and to be sold by Jacob Richardson, . . . Gun-hammers, Gun-Locks, Watch Chains and Seals. **1789** *Ann. 1st Congress* I. 73 He brought up . . . an engrossed bill to provide for the safe-keeping of the acts, records, and seal of the United States. **1852** STOWE *Uncle Tom* i, He wore a heavy gold watch-chain, with a bundle of seals of portentous size. **1872** E. EGGLESTON *End of World* 62 He's got more seals to his ministry a-hanging onto his watch-chain than I ever seed.

2. +**a.** In the early New England church, a sacrament.

1637 *Essex Inst. Coll.* I. 39/1 He refuseth to come to Assembly and to p[ar]take in ye seales. **1648** *Platform Church-Discipline* (1772) 10 Their elders in their own church shall receive none to the seals but visible saints.

b. *Seals of* (or *to*) *his ministry*, evidences of successful ministerial labors, as converts, church members, etc. Now rare.

Cf. sense 1, quot. 1872. *Seal of apostleship*, see 1 Cor. 9:2.
1759 *Plymouth Church Rec.* I. 313 He has had many Seals of his ministry. **1818** *M.E. Church Annual Conf. Minutes* 308/2 A goodly number of the seals of his [Wm. Patridge's] ministry are, we trust, now with him in heaven.

+**3.** A strip of easily torn metal put on a railroad box car to seal it.

1885 *Santa Fé Wkly. New Mexican* 10 Sept. 3/7 John Hubbard, breaking seal of railroad car; two years.

∗ **Seal,** *v.* +*tr.* In the Mormon church, to marry (a woman) to a man as a spiritual wife. (See also SEALED *a.* 2.) — **1852** STANSBURY *Gt. Salt Lake* 136 If a man once married, desires to take him a second helpmate, . . . the woman is then 'sealed' to him under the solemn sanction of the church, and stands, in all respects, in the same relation to the man as the wife that was first married. **1861** *New Amer. Cycl.* XI. 739/1 Polygamy is inculcated and wives are 'sealed' to saints here on earth to augment their power in the heavens. **1884** MILLER in *Lancaster* (Pa.) *New Era* 15 April, Sealed unto Him.

∗ **Sealed,** *a.*

∗ **1.** Of weights and measures: Stamped with a mark as a guarantee. {−1615}

1633 *Plymouth Laws* 34 Ye new bushell, being a sealed bushell brought out of England of Winchester measure should be alowed and no other. **1701** *Boston Rec.* 11 [Butchers shall] be provided with good and sufficient Scales and sealed weights. **1861** *Ill. Agric. Soc. Trans.* V. 153 The quantity of wheat . . . was one hundred and eighty-nine and one-half bushels, measured in a sealed half bushel.

2. Of a Mormon: Married by the Mormon Church: (see also quot. 1856).

1856 FERRIS *Mormons at Home* 114 The extra wives of the Mormons are called by some of them 'spirituals,' by others sealed ones, while our landlady calls them 'fixins.' **1857** *Harper's Mag.* Feb. 404/1 In Utah, Judge Drummond . . . instructed them to indict all 'sealed' persons who had not been legally married.

∗ **Sealer.**¹ An official charged with affixing a seal or mark to certain materials, measures, etc., as proof of weight, quality, etc. {−1592}

1645 *Plymouth Col. Rec.* XI. 199 The sealler shall haue . . . a peny for euery waight under a quarter of a pound. **1657** *Springfield Rec.* I. 256 Robert Ashly was chosen Sealer. **1712** *Southampton Rec.* II. 175 Manassah Kempton chosen sealer to seal wates and mesures. **1712** *Boston Rec.* 160 The Sel. men have Nominated & Chosen Capt. Timo Clark, to be . . . veiwer & Sealer of Moulds. **1728** *Ib.* 223 The Several Sealers of wood appointed within this Town are hereby Directed not to Seal any Range of wood not corded as aforesaid. **1905** *Municipal Code of Chicago* 902 (Index), City Sealer.

Sealer.² **1.** One who hunts seals. {1842−} **2.** A vessel used in hunting seals. {1820−} — (1) **1825** COOPER *L. Lincoln* xvii, The sealers of New England have been able to discover Terra Australis. **1865** *Atlantic Mo.* Jan. 42/2 Put that question to a sealer or fisherman. (2) **1856** OLMSTED *Slave States* 539 Has there ever been a Georgia whaler? or a Georgia sealer? **1873** BAILEY *Life in Danbury* 209 There is a sealer fitting out here that is a marvel to seamen. **1890** *Advance* 29 May, Sealskins captured by United States cruisers from illegal sealers.

Sealer of leather. =LEATHER-SEALER. *Obs.* — **1643** *Mass. Ct. of Assistants Rec.* II. 138 Hugh Mason, and Geo. Munnings, being presented for sealers, & searchers of leather. **1688** *Huntington Rec.* I. 520 Joseph whittman was chossen to bee a sealler of Leather that is Putt to saile. **1703** *Braintree Rec.* 54 Lt. Samuel Penniman should be a sealer of Leather for this Town this year. **1796** *Boston Directory* 298 Sealers of Leather: Thomas Bradlee, David Hollis [etc.].

Sealer of (or **for**) **weights and measures.** One who attaches a mark of guarantee to a weight or measure; an inspector of weights and measures. {1835}

1647 *Watertown Rec.* I. 1. 22 Isack mixter is Chosen Sealer for waightes & measures. **1650** *Boston Rec.* 100 Mr. Jerimy Houchin is chosen Sealer of the weights and measures this yeare. **1721** *Braintree Rec.* 103 Sealer of Weights and Measures was John Bass. **1858** *Wis. Rev. Statutes* 176 There shall be an election of . . . one sealer of weights and measures; and one overseer of highways. **1906** *Springfield W. Repub.* 1 March 16 P. J. Tetrault, sealer of weights and measures, . . . found that every one of them was selling butter that was one ounce short of a pound.

+**Seal-fat,** *a.* Very fat and sleek. — **1848** RUXTON *Life Far West* ii, 'Any buffalo come in?' 'Heap, and seal-fat at that.' **1850** GARRARD *Wah-To-Yah* v. 73 [Cottonwood bark] renders them [*sc.* animals] 'seal fat.' **1898** CANFIELD *Maid of Frontier* 112 The weather'll be warmer an' my horse seal fat.

Sealing.¹ The action or occupation of hunting seals. {1848−} Usu. attrib.

1807 *Mass. H. S. Coll.* 2 Ser. III. 29 The sealing voyages to Patagonia last about a year. **1835** COOPER *Monikins* vii, The sealing-business . . . is my ra'al occupation. **1839** *S. Lit. Messenger* V. 3/1 Fanning and his associates . . . in a few years made Stonington famed for sealing. **1880** *Harper's Mag.* Aug. 485, His whaling, sealing and other ships were to be found in the North Pacific. **1900** DRANNAN *Plains & Mts.* 579 There were six sealing boats with the schooner.

∗ **Sealing.**² +Among the Mormons, the ceremony or action of taking a spiritual wife. — **1856** B. J. FERRIS *Mormons at Home* 114 These lefthand marriages are called sealings. **1857** *Harper's Mag.* Feb. 404/1 In Utah, Judge Drummond charged the Grand Jury that the Mormon ceremony of 'sealing' does not constitute a legal marriage. **1882** WAITE *Adv. Far West* 137 These marriages are always performed in their sacred and secret Temple, in a singular manner, and are called 'Sealings.'

Sealing hammer. A hammer used for stamping a seal on something. — **1713** *Boston Rec.* 182 Ye other Sealing hammers & Staves [shall] be brought in to ye Treasu[re]r.

Sealing water. Water in the trap of a water drain, which serves to cut off the air of the sewer. — **1884** *Century Mag.* Dec. 260/2 The current thus produced is to carry the sealing-water with it. **1885** *Ib.* Jan. 259/1 The whole volume of sealing-water is rarely removed with a single motion.

∗ **Sealing wax.** A substance, plastic when heated, used to seal documents or letters. — **1657** *Mass. H. S. Coll.* 4 Ser. VII. 81 Sir, I pray you send me some sealing wax. **1722** *New-Eng. Courant* 8 Jan. 1/2 Whether so many L-tt-rs taken out of the Office open'd, ought always to be attributed to the Badness of the Sealing-Wax? **1790** *Penna. Packet* 8 May 4/4 Thomas Seddon . . . has for Sale . . . Sealing wax and wafers per lb. **1876** HALE *P. Nolan's Friends* iii, I have sealing-wax enough and parchment enough for a King's ransom.

Sea lion. {1601−}

1. Any of a number of large, eared seals of the Pacific Ocean, esp. *Eumetopias jubata* (syn. *E. stelleri*) of the North Pacific, and the California sea lion, *Zalophus californianus*. {1697−}

1836 IRVING *Astoria* II. 227 The flesh, . . . with the eggs of sea fowls, preserved in oil, an occasional sea lion, a few ducks in winter, and some wild roots, composes their food. **1872** McCLELLAN *Golden State* 239 Seals and sea-lions, are also found either in the rivers or bays. **1881** R. H. DAVIS *Silhouettes* 113 It was the very question she had asked about the sea-lion in the Park yesterday. **1911** *Rep. Fisheries 1908* 315/2 Sea-lion (*Eumetopias jubata*). . . . They are killed with guns and lances.

+**2.** *local.* An inferior Texas cow driven up from the Gulf coast. *colloq.*

1890 *Stock Grower & Farmer* 16 Feb. 3/3 The purchase, in 1886, of ten thousand head of scrubby south Texas cattle, 'dogies' or 'sea lions,' at very high prices, was the cause of the great losses by the Delano-Dwyer company. **1892** *Scribner's Mag.* June 738/1 'Dogies,' 'sea-lions,' and 'long-horns' were favorite nicknames for the cattle.

Seal ring. A finger ring engraved with a seal. {1608−} — **1638** *Md. Archives* IV. 89 One seale-ring. **1701** *N.H. Probate Rec.* I. 474, I will and bequeath . . . the picture of Captain Thomas Daniel my husband, deceased, and his Seal-Ring. **1888** CABLE *Bonaventure* 158, I like a handsome seal-ring. **1919** HOUGH *Sagebrusher* 190 Quickly he slipped off the seal ring from his own finger and passed it to Sim Gage.

∗ **Sealskin.**

∗ **1.** The skin of a seal; also, a garment made of sealskins.

1790 *Penna. Packet* 3 Sept. 1/4 For Sale, A Parcel of Seal and Elephant Skins. **1820** *Boston Advertiser* 3 July 2/5 Alligator and seal skins. **1878** *Rep. Indian Affairs* 131 The demand for their fish, oil, and seal skins . . . was] immediate and sure. **1887** *Courier-Journal* 11 Jan. 8/6 $160 Sealskins for $100.

2. *quasi-adj.* Made of sealskin. {1769−}

1834 C. A. DAVIS *Letters Jack Downing* 39, I out with my seal-skin wallet. **1845** *Big Bear Ark.* 81 His crop of hair was surmounted by the funniest little seal-skin cap imaginable. **1869** *Rep. Comm. Agric. 1868* 177 In winter the dry grasses . . . are shaped to correspond with the foot, and placed between the foot and the seal-skin sole of the winter boots worn in that country [the Yukon]. **1881** McLean *Cape Cod Folks* 17, I had a new sealskin coat that very winter. **1881** Howells *Modern Instance* i, [He] pulled the seal-skin gloves from his long hands. **1893** M. Howe *Honor* 104 She could at last afford a sealskin sacque.

+**Sealskin trunk.** A trunk covered by sealskin. — **1693** *Conn. Probate Rec.* I. 422, I also desire my son John Buttolph shall have my great Seal Skin Trunk. **1714** Sewall *Letter-Book* II. 37 Put all in a seal-skin trunk of a suitable bigness. **1840** *Picayune* 9 Oct. 3/1 Found, A common seal-skin Trunk.

* **Seaman.** A sailor below the rank of an officer; a mariner.
1643 *Suffolk Deeds* I. 7 The sd. shippe shall be compleately fitted with a master and fowerteene able seamen, and a boy. **1778** *Jrnls. Cont. Congress* X. 29 The bounties given to seamen by the resolve of Congress of the 29 March, 1777, is not to be stopped out of their wages. **1796** *Ann. 4th Congress* 2 Sess. 2787 Pay of the officers, seamen, and marines [per month]. **1840** Dana *Two Years* xxxvii. 477 The exertions of the general association, called the American Seamen's Friend Society, . . . have been a true blessing to the seaman. **1907** *St. Nicholas* July 812/1 Many of our seamen begin their career at seventeen aboard the frigate *Constellation.*

b. *Seamen's rights,* +spec., during the Napoleonic wars, the right of American seamen to be free from impressment on the high seas.
1813 Clay in *Ann. 12th Congress* 2 Sess. 676/2 If we fail, let us fail like men—lash ourselves to our gallant tars, and expire together in one common struggle, fighting for 'seamen's rights and free trade.'

Sea marsh. A marsh kept wet by the overflow of the sea. {*a*1746}
— **1827** *Western Mo. Rev.* I. 317 It is a wide savanna marsh, . . . covered with high cane grass, in appearance not unlike the sedge of the sea marshes at the north. **1880** Cable *Grandissimes* 354 Orleans Island . . . is a narrow, irregular, flat tract of forest, swamp, . . . and sea-marsh lying east and west. **1887** R. H. Davis *Silhouettes* 37 They separated in a few minutes, Knight taking his way to the sea-marshes.

+**Seam diggings.** Gold diggings in an earth seam or narrow stratum.
— **1873** Raymond *Silver & Gold* 25 Among what may justly be ranked as new discoveries is a description of gold-bearing deposits denominated 'Seam Diggings.'

Seaming lace. Lace used to cover or ornament a seam. {1616–} — **1644** *Essex Probate Rec.* I. 38, 1 holland sheet with a seaming lace. **1684** *Essex Inst. Coll.* XXV. 154 A sheet with a seeming Lace.

+**Sea mink.** (See quotations.) — **1888** Goode *Amer. Fishes* 123 The King-Fish . . . [is] known as . . . the 'Sea Mink' in North Carolina. **1911** *Rep. Fisheries 1908* 311/2 Kingfish (*Menticirrhus saxatilis*), a food fish found on the coasts of the Middle and South Atlantic states, and occasionally on the Gulf coast. It is called . . . 'sea mink' in North Carolina.

* **Seamster.** A seamstress; one who sews. {'Now only applied to one of the male sex'} — **1859** Bartlett 390 *Seamster,* a seamstress. **1892** A. E. Lee *Hist. Columbus, Ohio* I. 255 Gov. Worthington . . . favored the fair seamsters with some fine apples from his Ross County orchard. **1892** *Current Lit.* X. 41 The sailor who sews on the binding [of a flag] . . . is an excellent 'seamster.'

Seamstress, Sempstress. A woman whose occupation is sewing. {*a*1613–} — **1796** *Boston Directory* 228 Box Mary, sempstress, Cambridge street. **1811** Weems *Letters* III. 54 My clothes linnens &c. are in the hands of the Taylor & semstress. **1863** A. D. Whitney *F. Gartney* xxi, Half a dozen seamstresses, and as many sewing-machines, were busy . . . in making up the delicate draperies. **1905** [see Meeting seed].

+**Sea oat.** A grass (*Uniola paniculata*) found on the southern coast. — **1894** Coulter *Bot. W. Texas* III. 545 U[*niola*] *paniculata.* (Sea Oats.) . . . Drifting sand along the coast, southern Texas to New Jersey. **1901** Mohr *Plant Life Ala.* 130 On the crests and steep sides of the hillocks the so-called sea oat . . . forms open patches.

Sea otter. An otter (*Enhydra lutris*) of the North Pacific coast. {1664–} Also ellipt. for next. — **1805** [see Drum *n.* 3]. **1844** Lee & Frost *Oregon* 72 Beaver was valued at two dollars per skin, though worth five dollars; land otter at fifty cents, though worth five dollars; sea otter at twelve dollars, worth from forty-five to sixty dollars. **1894** *Outing* XXIII. 389/1 The pursuit of the sea-otter, the shyest and most valuable of all pelagic animals, is the chief means of their support. **1904** White *Silent Places* 3 The silver-fox, the sea-otter, the sable, . . . these [names] and others sang like arrows cleaving the atmosphere of commoner words.

Sea-otter skin. The skin or pelt of the sea otter. — **1822** *Ann. 17th Congress* 2 Sess. 402 There was that year [1805–6] sent [to Canton] 17,445 sea-otter skins. **1836** Irving *Astoria* I. 97 Some [Indians] brought a few land-otter and sea-otter skins to barter. **1849** A. Ross *Adv. Oregon River* 89 The chief's robe is made of sea-otter skin and other valuable furs. **1883** Goode *Fishery Industries U.S.* 42 Sea-otter skins . . . , valued at $3,750, were taken in California.

Sea perch. A spiny-finned fish resembling the true perch {1601, 1857–}, +as the black sea bass or the conner. — **1765** Rowe *Diary* 86 We caught above sixteen dozen. of pond and sea perch. **1807** *Mass. H. S. Coll.* 2 Ser. III. 57 The sea perch is very large and excellent: it is caught in the spring. **1843** Marryat *M. Violet* xliv, The sea-perch (*Lupus Maritimes*), the ecrivisse, and hundred families of the 'crevette species,' offer to the Indian a great variety of delicate food for the winter. **1911** *Rep. Fisheries 1908* 308/2 Chogset (*Tautogolabrus adspersus*) . . . is also called 'cunner,' 'sea perch,' 'perch,' [etc.].

Sea pigeon. {1620–} +**1.** (See quotations.) +**2.** =Dowitcher. — (1) **1871** *Harper's Mag.* July 190 Another mollusk, one of the shell-less

kind, is a great soft body, of the shape and size of a half-grown pigeon; the resemblance to the latter being so great, it has obtained the name seapigeon. **1885** Holder *Marvels of Animal Life* 169 One of the sea-slugs, a great green creature, commonly known on the [Florida] reef as the seapigeon. (2) **1909** Webster 1907 *Sea pigeon,* . . . the dowitcher. *New Jersey.*

+**Sea poose.** Also sepoose, sea puss, sea purse. [Origin uncertain. For sense 1, see *Southampton Rec.* I. 69*n.*]

1. *Southampton, L.I.* A channel from a bay to the sea providing water power for a mill. *Obs.*
1650 *Southampton Rec.* I. 69 [They] are to have for their paines 3s per day at the seapoose. **1653** *Ib.* 94 Mr Rayner & Iohn White are appointed & left to agree (if they can) with the miller concerneing the alteration of his mill to ease the towne of the burthen of opening the sepoose. **1654** *Ib.* 102 William Ludlam ingageth to grind, . . . the Towne being at theire liberty for opening the sepoose.

2. (See quot. 1891.)
*a*1841 Hawes *Sporting Scenes* I. 102, I kept watch of him—when I came to a sea poose—I went in and to the east of it. **1891** *Cent.* 5445/3 *Seapurse,* . . . a swirl of the undertow making a small whirlpool on the surface of the water; a local outward current, dangerous to bathers. Also called *sea-pouce* and *sea-puss.* (New. Eng. and New Jersey coasts.) **1904** *N.Y. Tribune* 29 May, McDonald was a good swimmer, but, getting caught in a sea puss, was shot out to the deep sea with great velocity.

* **Seaport.** A port on the seacoast; ||an inland river port. Also attrib. — **1691** Sewall *Diary* I. 354 General Court passes an order for prohibiting Frenchmen being in the Seaports or Frontier towns. **1773** in Fithian *Journal* I. 39 The town . . . is making vast strides towards being a sea port-town. **1816** U. Brown *Journal* II. 48 [Parkersburg, W. Va.] will become a City as well as a safe & Extensive Harbor & Sea-port. **1883** *Harper's Mag.* June 161/2 Near one of our Atlantic sea-ports there resides an old whaling captain.

+**Sea purse, Sea puss.** (See Sea poose.)

+**Sea quail. 1.** A turnstone. **2.** Cassin's anklet, *Ptychoramphus aleuticus.* — (1) **1888** Trumbull *Names of Birds* 186 In Connecticut at Saybrook and Lyme, [*Arenaria interpres* is called] Sea Quail. **1891** *Cent.* 5445/3 *Sea-quail,* . . . the turnstone, *Strepsilas interpres.* (Connecticut.) (2) **1917** *Birds of Amer.* I. 20 Because of its plump shape and size, it [Cassin's anklet] has been called a 'Sea Quail.'

Sea raven. {1601–} +A sculpin (*Hemitripterus americanus*) of the Atlantic coast. — [**1672** Josselyn *New Eng. Rarities* 29 Sea-Raven.] **1836** J. Richardson, etc. *Fauna Bor.-Amer.* III. 50 The Sea-raven . . . inhabits the cod-banks on the coast of New York, Nova Scotia, and the Gulf of St. Lawrence. **1842** *Nat. Hist. N.Y., Zoology* IV. 57 The Sea Raven is subject to great variations in its color. **1897** *N.Y. Forest, Fish, & Game Comm. 2d Rep.* 244 Sea Raven. . . . Spawns in November.

* **Search,** *n.*[1] A sieve. *Obs.* — **1647** *Essex Probate Rec.* I. 70 A search & a boxe, . . . a flaskett. **1837** Peck *New Guide* 127 Instead of bolting cloths, the frontier people use a sieve, or as it is called here, a 'search.'

Search, *n.*[2] *Right of search,* the right, in international law, to stop and search ships for contraband by a warship of a belligerent nation. {1817–} — **1798** *Ann. 5th Congress* 1907 Gentlemen appeared to confound the right of search with the right of capture. The right of search is universal. **1809** *Ann. 10th Congress* 2 Sess. 1255 We admit the right of search for contraband of war.

* **Search,** *v.* **1.** *tr.* To inspect (leather). *Obs.* **2.** *Search me,* +I have no idea; I know nothing about the matter. *colloq.*[2] — (1) **1642** *Watertown Rec.* I. 1. 8 [They] are appointed by the Towne to search and seal Leather according to the order of Court. (2) **1901** Merwin & Webster *Calumet 'K'* 37 'What's the matter with the G. & M. anyway?' . . . 'Search me,' said Dennis. 'They've tied us up for these two weeks.' **1904** 'O. Henry' *Cabbages & Kings* (1916) 47 'What's her tonnage?' 'Search me!' said Smith. 'I don't know what she weighs in at.' **1917** McCutcheon *Green Fancy* 56 'Wasn't it an automobile accident?' 'Search me.'

* **Searcher.**
* **1.** A customhouse officer who searched for dutiable or contraband goods. *Obs.*
*a*1649 Winthrop *Hist.* I. 320 Mr. Hibbins . . . was plaintiff, for £500, which the searchers lost from him in the ship. **1661** *Portsmouth Rec.* 107 Mr. Hinory Percey and frances Braiton are Chosen Serchers for prohibited wine and strong watars. **1761** Glen *Descr. S. Carolina* 48, I therefore think it would be of Service, if the Commissioners of the Customs were to appoint another Searcher for this Province. **1775** *Essex Inst. Coll.* XIII. 179 [Oatmeal is] ranged under the Head of Provision, which it seems lays at the Arbitrium of the Searcher.

+**2.** An inspector of leather. *Obs.*
1642 *Mass. Bay Rec.* II. 19 The said searchers . . . shall seale & marke such leather as they shall find sufficient. **1656** *Conn. Rec.* I. 287 Nor shall any searcher or sealor of Leather refuse with convenient speede to seale any Leather suffitiently tanned haveing timely notice. **1689** *Southampton Rec.* II. 305 Manassah Kempton [was] chosen sealer and searcher of leather.

+**3.** An inspector of meats or fish. *Obs.*
1654 *Boston Rec.* 118 Chosen for Searchers and packers of Flesh and Fish: William Dinsdayle and John Barrell.

+4. *New Eng.* 'An instrument resembling an auger, used in the inspection of butter, to ascertain the quality of that contained in firkins' (B. '59).

Searchlight. An apparatus for projecting a powerful beam of light; the light so projected. {1883-} — **1886** *Harper's Mag.* June 21/2 Space is still to be found . . . for electrical apparatus for lighting the ship, for search light, and other ordnance purposes. **1897** *Outing* XXX. 95/1 Steamers plying upon the river are equipped with search lights, by the aid of which the fowl are mercilessly slaughtered at night. **1923** WATTS *L. Nichols* 153 The search-lights on the tall buildings went jigging wildly up and down the sky.

Search warrant. A warrant legally issued authorizing the search of a house or other premises for stolen goods, etc. {1751- (Fielding *Amelia* III. xi)} — **1739** W. STEPHENS *Proc. Georgia* I. 306 It was thought proper to send out several Officers with a search Warrant. **1814** *Niles' Reg.* VI. 38/2 Mr. Adams asked him to serve a search-warrant on Jacob Bigelow. **1867** RICHARDSON *Beyond Miss.* 103 A search-warrant was placed in the hands of Sheriff Samuel Walker. **1905** VALENTINE *H. Sandwith* 197 The man, not having secured a search-warrant from the Dunkirk sheriff, finally went off.

+Sea rig. Clothes worn at sea. — **1840** DANA *Two Years* 6, I made my appearance on board at twelve o'clock, in full sea-rig. **1865** A. D. WHITNEY *Gayworthys* 127 Gershom was to . . . sign his shipping articles and go with his uncle to get his 'protection,' and his sea rig.

+Sea robin. {1899-, *dial.*}
1. a. Any of several gurnards of the genus *Prionotus*.
1814 MITCHILL *Fishes N.Y.* 430 Gurnard, or Sea Robin. *Trigla lineata.* **1839** STORER *Mass. Fishes* 12 *Prionotus strigatus*. Sea Robin. . . . This species . . . is frequently taken in the vicinity of Holmes Hole. **1884** in Goode, etc. *Fisheries* I. 256 Among the fish that may be classed as edible, . . . is the Sea-Robin, Grunter, or Gurnard. **1894** *Outing* XXIV. 263/2 Here's a sea-robin! A curious grunting fellow, 10 in. long, with a great fin, like a butterfly's wing, projecting from each side of his throat. **1911** *Rep. Fisheries* 1908 315/2 Sea robin (*Prionotus carolinus*). . . . They are also called 'gurnards,' 'wing-fish,' 'sea bat,' etc.

b. A toadfish.
1879 *Nat. Museum Proc.* II. 336 These fish were called in Pensacola by the names 'Sea Robin' and 'Sarpo.' **1911** *Rep. Fisheries* 1908 315/2 Sea robin . . . is also applied to the toadfish (*Apsanus tau*) in the Gulf.

2. The red-breasted merganser.
1891 *Cent.* 5447/1 *Sea-robin*, . . . the red-breasted merganser, *Mergus serrator*. (Rowley, Massachusetts.) **1917** *Birds of Amer.* I. 111.

Sea rocket. Any plant of the genus *Cakile*. {1611-} — **1814** BIGELOW *Florula Bostoniensis* 157 *Bunias edentula*. American sea rocket. . . . A fleshy, maritime plant. . . . Grows abundantly at Cape Ann. **1843** TORREY *Flora N.Y.* I. 66 *Cakile maritima*. Sea Rocket. . . . Sandy seashore of Long-Island, and shore of Lake Erie at Portland harbor. **1901** MOHR *Plant Life Ala.* 522.

Sea salmon. 1. A salmon that lives in the sea. **+2.** Either of two weakfishes, *Eriscion nebulosus* and *Cynoscion nobilis*. — (1) **1842** *Nat. Hist. N.Y.*, *Zoology* IV. 241 The Common Sea Salmon. *Salmo salar.* **1871** *Harper's Mag.* Aug. 466/1 Whether this fish be really a 'landlocked salmon'—that is to say, a true sea salmon that has changed its habits to such an extent as to dwell permanently in the fresh-waters—is the subject of inquiry. (2) **1909** WEBSTER 1907/3.

Sea serpent. {1646-} A large marine animal often reported seen, and said to resemble more or less a serpent. {1671-} — **1674** JOSSELYN *Two Voyages* 23 They told me . . . of a Sea-Serpent or Snake, that lay quoiled up like a Cable upon a Rock at Cape-Ann. **1832** WILLIAMSON *Maine* II. 671 The present [1818] is the third year, a monster of the deep called a *Sea-Serpent*, has been oftentimes seen along our eastern coasts. **1843** *Niles' Nat. Reg.* 22 July 336 The Sea Serpent, once more, 70 to 80 feet in length, its head elevated eight or nine feet above water, was gazed at for an hour by Capt. Cotton of the schr. Brilliant on the 12th May, Cape Ann bearing W. 15 miles. **1883** *Harper's Mag.* Oct. 714/2 Any ignoramus . . . can believe in the existence of the sea-serpent.

+Seashore cotton. =SEA-ISLAND COTTON. — **1802** DRAYTON *S. Carolina* 134 That raised on lands adjacent to the sea and salt water, called *island* or *sea shore cotton*, being black seed, is preferred to the *green seed* cotton.

∗ Seaside.
∗ 1. The land bordering the sea.
In early New England frequently used in the descriptions of lands.
1641 *New Haven Col. Rec.* 59 So many of those (who have the small lotts by the sea side) as will resign their land beyond the East River shall have 6 acres for every single person. **1679** *R.I. Col. Rec.* III. 58 Made two small purchases of two tracts of land by the sea side. **1698** *Providence Rec.* XI. 36 He may have a peece of land by ye sea side.

2. Attrib. in the names of plants and trees. {1696-}
1785 MARSHALL *Amer. Grove* 20 The Species are, I. *Betula-Alnus glauca.* Silver-Leaved Alder. . . . *Betula-Alnus maritima.* Sea-Side Alder. **1843** TORREY *Flora N.Y.* II. 261 *Triglochin maritimum*. Seaside Arrow-grass. . . . Salt marshes on the Island of New-York, and on Long Island. **1829** EATON *Botany* (ed. 5) 172 *Chloris petraea*, sea-side chloris. **1837** WILLIAMS *Florida* 37 The seaside grape, different kinds of plumbs, and custard apples are frequently found in the hammocks. *c*1729 CATESBY *Carolina* I. 32 The Sea-side Oat . . . I observed growing no where but on Sand-Hills;

so near the Sea, that at high Tides the water flows to it. **1784** *Amer. Acad. Mem.* I. 449 The Beach, or Sea-Side Plumb. There are several varieties of this species growing plentifully on Plumb-Island. **1901** MOHR *Plant Life Ala.* 473 *Quercus myrtifolia*. . . . Seaside Scrub Oak. . . . Coast from South Carolina to Florida, west to Alabama.

+Seaside finch. An Atlantic-coast salt-marsh sparrow, *Ammospiza maritima*. — **1811** WILSON *Ornithology* IV. 68 Sea-side Finch. . . . This species derives its whole subsistence from the sea. **1839** PEABODY *Mass. Birds* 326 The Seaside Finch . . . visits the interior only when driven by easterly storms. **1844** *Nat. Hist. N.Y.*, *Zoology* II. 163 The Seaside Finch, as its name imports, is common along our maritime borders. **1917** *Birds of Amer.* III. 30.

Seaside resort. A resort at the seaside. — **1879** *Harper's Mag.* July 163 Nowhere else in all sea-side resorts will he be likely to get so much . . . elbow-room. **1882** MCCABE *New York* 508 During the summer New York thieves are to be found at all the watering-places and seaside resorts. **1901** 'FLYNT' *World of Graft* 137 [They] went on a jaunt to a sea-side resort on their profits in the transaction.

∗ Sea snail. a. Any of various marine gastropods, as the species of *Littorina*. **b.** A fish of the family Liparididae. {*a*1672-} — **1871** *Harper's Mag.* July 189 One of the few forms of shell-fish that seem to be entirely oceanic, or independent of any dépôt, is the janthina, or sea-snail. **1883** *Nat. Museum Bul.* No. 27, 244 Pennywinkle, or Sea Snail . . . [is found] from Connecticut to Nova Scotia. **1884** GOODE, etc. *Fisheries* I. 253 The Lump-Suckers: Lump-Fish and Sea-Snails. The Sea-Snails—Liparididæ. **1911** *Rep. Fisheries* 1908 313/2 *Periwinkle*, a common name for the sea snail (*Littorina*) and whelk (*Fulga*), which are used for bait and sometimes for food on the north Atlantic coast.

∗ Season, n.
1. A rain or a spell of wet weather, esp. one regarded as favorable for the setting out of plants. {1707, in Jamaica}
1724 JONES *Virginia* 39 They transplant and replant [tobacco] upon Occasion after a Shower or Rain, which they call a Season. **1784** SMYTH *Tour* II. 130 In the first rains, which are here called seasons, after the vernal equinox, the tobacco plants are carefully drawn while the ground is soft. **1841** in Bassett *Plantation Overseer* 152 With seasons [he] would have made at least 130 bags of cotton. **1918** *Dialect Notes* V. 19 This cotton needs a good season.

2. The period of the year regularly devoted to some particular activity, as theater-going, hunting, etc. {1687-}
1750 in Singleton *Social N.Y.* 272 A company of comedians from Philadelphia . . . intend to perform [in a building on Nassau Street, N.Y.] as long as the season lasts. **1840** *Picayune* 3 Nov. 2/1 The house was better by five hundred dollars than any other of the present season. **1876** *Fur, Fin & Feather* Sept. 96/1 The season for chicken-shooting commences from the first to the twentieth of August. **1886** *Outing* April 94/2 In 1883, the nine was much strengthened, and consequently had a very successful season. **1907** *St. Nicholas* May 610 The grand entertainment and show . . . opened the season at 'Festival Park.'

∗ Season, v. tr. To fertilize (land). *Obs.* {-1589} — **1722** *New-Eng. Courant* 9 April 2/2 If the Ground fails, it must be seasoned with Beans, or the like.

+Season check. (See quot. 1905.) — **1887** KIRKLAND *Zury* 32 Ye see that thar season-check in the butt-end? **1905** *Forestry Bureau Bul.* No. 61, 33 *Check*, a longitudinal crack in timber caused by too rapid seasoning. . . . Syn.: season check.

∗ Seasoner. **+**'A seaman or fisherman who hires for the season; by extension, a loafer; a beach-comber' (*Cent.*).

∗ Seasoning.
+1. A fever or other illness often suffered during the first year of settling in a new country. {1774-}
The first quotation may belong under sense 2.
1670 DENTON *Brief Desc. N.Y.* 17 The Climate [of N.Y.] hath such an affinity with that of England, that . . . the name of seasoning, which is common to some other Countreys hath never there been known. **1705** BEVERLEY *Virginia* IV. 69 The first Sickness that any New-Comer happens to have there, he unfairly calls a Seasoning. **1724** JONES *Virginia* 50 Abundance of Damps and Mists . . . makes the People subject to Feavers and Agues, which is the Country Distemper, a severe Fit of which (called a *Seasoning*) most expect, some time after their Arrival in that Climate. **1826** FLINT *Recoll.* 132 Emigrants generally suffer some kind of sickness, which is called 'seasoning,' implying that it is the summit of the gradual process of acclimation.

2. The process or the period of illness by which a person is acclimatized to a new country. {*a*1859-}
1807 IRVING, etc. *Salmagundi* x, Strangers always . . . undergo a *seasoning* [in Penna.] as Europeans do in the West Indies. **1819** C. B. JOHNSON *Lett. from Penna.* 94 These [stagnant ponds and marshes] are so common in the western states, that a 'seasoning' is spoken of as . . . a matter of course. **1843** *Amer. Pioneer* Oct. 443 The mumps, and perhaps one or two other diseases, prevailed, and gave us a seasoning.

+Season passenger. A railway passenger who travels on a season ticket. — **1856** W. H. SWIFT *Mass. Railroads* 14 There is a return of the Commutation or Season Passengers, for the years 1852, 1853, and 1854.

Season ticket. A ticket entitling the holder to railway transportation, admission to a theater, etc., during a specified period. {1835-} Also fig. — **1820** *Columbian Centinel* 2 Dec. 1/1 For sale, a Boston Theatre

Season Ticket, at a fair price. **1854** THOREAU *Walden* 210 Those passengers who have a season ticket and see it often, are better men for the sight. **1887** GEORGE *40 Yrs. on Rail* 40, I want two season tickets between Boston and New York.

+**Sea spin.** =HORSEFOOT CRAB. — **1782** CRÈVECŒUR *Letters* 146 Each master of a family [in Nantucket] is obliged to allow him two hundred horse feet, (*sea spin,*) with which this primitive priest fertilizes the land of his glebe.

Sea sucker. (See SEERSUCKER.)

*** Seat,** *n.*

1. A place suitable for an estate; a country estate. {1607-}

1635 in *Amer. Speech* XV. 390/1 Extending into the woods from a seat or tract of land called Marchants Hope. **1677** *New Castle Court Rec.* 155 John Johnson . . . [desires] of this wor[shi]pp[fu]ll Court a grant to take up . . . a seate of Land. **1704** S. KNIGHT *Journal* 59 Here were good Buildings, Especially one, a very fine seat, w[hi]ch they told me was Col. Hethcoats. **1782** *Warren-Adams Lett.* II. 171 It gave me great pleasure to hear, that you and Mrs. Warren were settled . . . at so beautiful a Seat as that of the late Govr. Hutchinson. **1835** HOFFMAN *Winter in West* I. 53 The increasing number of farm houses, and occasionally a handsome seat tastefully planted among them, . . . indicated our approach to the City of Pittsburg. **1857** *Harper's Mag.* July 205/1 Country residences and farms were common enough every where, but up the river people had 'seats.'

2. One of the places provided in a legislative assembly or political convention for the seating of its members; a right to sit as a member of a legislative assembly; a legislative position or office. {1774-}

1787 JAY in Sparks *Corr. Revol.* IV. 153 Members who will find it convenient to make their seats subservient to partial and personal purposes. **1789** *Ann. 1st Congress* 15 The following members of the Senate appeared and took their seats. **1837** *U.S. Mag.* I. 75 He was formerly a journeyman printer of New York; but . . . won a seat in Congress. **1856** *Democratic Conv. Proc.* 13 According to the rules of the Convention, seats have been provided for the delegations from each State. **1887** *Boston Jrnl.*, 16 of the members who owe their seats to his money have formed what the New York Aldermen would call a 'combine,' and demand $10,000 apiece before they will vote for Hearst. **1900** *Congress. Rec.* 3 Jan. 635/2 My duty is to look after my own seat and let Roberts look after his.

‖**3.** A place of employment.

1806 in Commons, etc. *Doc. Hist.* III. 77, I was afraid if he dismissed me that I could not get another seat in the city, for the next employer would be under the necessity of discharging me likewise.

+**4.** A membership on a stock exchange.

1882 MCCABE *New York* 337 A seat in the Board costs about $6000, and is the absolute personal property of its owner. **1889** GIBSON *Stock Exchanges* 74 'Seats' now can only be obtained by purchase from retiring members. **1900** NELSON *A B C Wall St.* 15 Memberships . . . are called seats.

*** Seat,** *v.*

***1.** *tr.* To establish (a person or people) in an area as a settler or settlers. *Obs.* {-1776; 1910}

1612 SMITH, etc. *Virginia* II. 96 Master West hauing seated his men at the Falles, presently returned. **1697** *Md. Hist. Mag.* XV. 115 The Indians for these three months last past he has observed to be more Insolent than in all the ffour years time he had been Seated before. **1750** T. WALKER *Journal* 39 The Duncards . . . [have] not long been seated here. **1797** WASHINGTON *Writings* XIII. 406 If . . . they could have been first seated as tenants. **1817** S. BROWN *Western Gazetteer* 165 Where the French inhabitants are seated, the lots are narrow, houses thick.

+**2.** *tr.* To establish (a plantation or estate); to furnish (land) with settlers; to occupy as settlers. *Obs.*

1620 in Bradford *Hist.* 117, I would that the first plantation might hear be seated. **1650** *Md. Archives* I. 288 Others that have seated Plantations haue again deserted them suffering there said Land . . . to lye wast. **1677** *New Castle Court Rec.* 87 John Taylor . . . [desires] a warrant . . . to take upp 600 acres of land . . . promising to seate the same out of hand w[i]th a conciderable family. **1710** *Va. House of Burgesses* 293 If persons can be allowed to claim more land than they are able to occupy, they keep out others who might seat the same. **1738** BYRD *Dividing Line* (1901) 22 The terms both of taking up and seating land were much easier in Carolina. **1778** *Va. State P.* I. 308 The said Slaughter was to have the tract of Land aforesaid, provided he seated it with a certain number of families within a limited time. **1794** WASHINGTON *Writings* X. 366 It would give me pleasure to see these lands seated by particular societies.

3. To provide with seats. {1818-}

1691 *Huntington Rec.* II. 94 The towne [is to provide] . . . stuff to seat ye sd. house. **1856** CARTWRIGHT *Autobiog.* 45 [Presbyterians and Methodists would] seat the shed, and here they collect together from forty to fifty miles around.

+**4.** To assign seats to people in (a meetinghouse or other building). *Obs.*

See also SEATING 1, SEATER 2.

1693 *Braintree Rec.* 29 Thomas Ball and Samuel Tompson are chosen to Seat the Meeting hous by apointing persons to ther places. **1707** *Manchester Rec.* I. 118 A committie chosen to seate our meting hous. **1718**

SEWALL *Diary* III. 208 Visited Mrs. Bethiah Kitchen. . . . She treated Capt Osgood very roughly about Seating the Meetinghouse. **1733** *Suffield Doc. Hist.* 256 At a meeting . . . warn'd to try ye minde of ye Town Relating to seating the meeting House.

+**b.** (See quotation.)

1828 WEBSTER, In New England, where the pews in churches are not private property, it is customary to *seat* families for a year or longer time; that is, assign and appropriate *seats* to their use.

+**Seated land.** (See quot. 1877.) — **1680** *Doc. Col. Hist. N.Y.* XII. 653, [I] haue made severall Surveys both of seated & Unseated Lands. **1877** W. H. BURROUGHS *On Taxation* 208 In Pennsylvania, prior to 1844, seated lands, that is, lands occupied by residence, or cultivation, could not be sold for taxes.

+**Seater.**

1. *Va.* A settler established on land. *Obs.*

1653 *Va. House of Burgesses* 90 Provided that such seaters settle advantageously for security. **1822** *Amer. Beacon* (Norfolk) 19 Feb. 2/2 Mr. Clay quoted several laws of the colony of Virginia, passed near two centuries ago, providing that the true owner should compensate the seater of land.

2. *New Eng.* One who assigns the seats in a meeting-house. *Obs.* (Cf. SEAT *v.* 4.)

1693 *Braintree Rec.* 29 Seaters of the Meeting hous. **1702** *Suffield Doc. Hist.* 141 In this fourth vote, which is the rule given for the seaters to act by; estate is the first thing mentioned. **1713** SEWALL *Diary* II. 389 Mr. Pemberton . . . would not have me resign my Seaters place now.

*** Seating.**

1. The action of settling on land or of settling a country. {1603-}

1650 *Md. Archives* I. 288 Divers persons who haue heretofore taken vpp land within this Province haue neglected the seating thereof for a long time. **1672** *Doc. Col. Hist. N.Y.* XII. 498 If your Honore plese to grant vs . . . the land . . . wee shall take spedey care fore the seating of it. **1713** *N.C. Col. Rec.* II. 66 A tract of Land . . . is Lapsed for want of Seating. **1821** DOUGHERTY *Light to People of Ky.* 1 No such seating and improvements had been made thereon.

+**b.** The establishment *of* a town or colony. *Obs.*

*c*1669 *Doc. Hist. N.Y. State* I. 87 The seating of towns together is necessary in these parts of America, especially upon the Maine Land. **1699** *Phil. Trans.* XXI. 441 At the first Seating of Maryland there were several Nations of Indians in the Country. **1779** *Ky. Petitions* 53 From the first-seating of This Town both the inhabitants and travilers has found it very inconvenient to get across the Kentucky River.

+**2.** The action of assigning seats in a meetinghouse. Now hist. Also attrib.

1685 SEWALL *Diary* I. 119 Mrs. Harris and Baker present their mutual offences against each other as to their seating before Mr. Willard and the Overseers. **1891** EARLE *Sabbath* 49 Many men were unwilling to serve on these seating committees, . . . protesting against it on account of the odium that was incurred.

3. *concrete.* Material for covering the seats of chairs, etc. {1833-}

1790 *Penna. Packet* 11 Dec. 1/2 A very choice Parcel of Hair Seatings, of various widths and patterns. **1824** *Stat. at Large* IV. 26 [The duty] on hair cloth and hair seating, [shall be] thirty per centum ad valorem.

+**Seatmate.** One who shares a seat with another, esp. in a school. —
1859 *Ladies' Repository* Nov. 645/1 She will tickle the neck of her seatmate with a bit of grass. **1883** WILDER *Sister Ridnour* 47, I thought about . . . the footprints made by Johnny and his seat-mate. **1903** WIGGIN *Rebecca* 61 Her seat-mate, Emma Jane, had made up a little mound of paper balls.

*** Sea toad.** +**1.** A sculpin. **2.** A toadfish. — (1) **1842** *Nat. Hist. N.Y. Zoology* IV. 52 The Common Bull-Head, *Cottus virginianus*, . . . is known [as] Sea Robin, Bull Head, Sea Toad, and Pig Fish. **1884** GOODE, etc. *Fisheries* I. 258 On our Atlantic coast are found several species of this family [Cottidae], generally known by the name 'Sculpin,' and also by such titles as . . . 'Sea-toad,' and 'Pig-fish.' (2) **1891** *Cent.* 5449/3 *Sea-toad,* . . . the toadfish, *Batrachus tau.*

Seat of government. A capital city or a town where government is administered. — **1789** *Ann. 1st Congress* 84 The bill to establish the seat of Government of the United States [shall] have the first reading at this time. **1805** *Phila. Ordinances* (1812) 107 By the removal of the seat of government from the city of Philadelphia, it has become inconvenient to present the mayor elect to the governor to take oath. **1831** PECK *Guide* 293 The great National Road, now constructing . . . to the seat of government in Missouri. **1857** *Lawrence* (Kan.) *Republican* 28 May 1 An act was then passed for the removal of the seat of government to the Shawnee Mission. **1910** *Indian Laws & Tr.* III. 432 Traveling and incidental expenses of special agents, . . . in lieu of all other expenses, including expenses of going to and from the seat of government.

Seat of justice. +A town where a court sits; a county seat. — **1806** *Ann. 9th Congress* 2 Sess. 1005 Uniontown being the seat of justice for Fayette county, Pennsylvania. **1831** PECK *Guide* 287 Waterloo is the seat of justice. **1849** CHAMBERLAIN *Ind. Gazetteer* 288 Lawrenceburgh, the Seat of Justice of Dearborn county, is situated on the Ohio river.

+**Seat of the courts.** =SEAT OF JUSTICE. — **1789** *Penna. Mag.* VI. 117 The Name of the principal Town or Seat of the Courts is Louisbourg.

Sea trout. {1745–}

1. Any of several fishes, +esp. one of the weakfishes, as *Cynoscion regalis* and *Atractoscion nobilis*.

1766 STORK *Acct. E. Florida* 52 Those mostly made use of . . . [include the] cat-fish, sea-trout, and black-fish. **1864** NORTON *Army Lett.* 212 Sea trout—Thompson caught one the other day that weighed twenty-six pounds. **1884** GOODE, etc. *Fisheries* I. 362 With the other members of the genus [the squeteague] is spoken of under the name 'Sea Trout.' **1891** *Cent.* 5449/3 *Sea-trout.* . . . 1. Any catadromous trout or char, as the common brook-trout of the United States, *Salvelinus fontinalis*. **1897** *Outing* XXX. 217/2 So we went mud-larking about the river's mouth after sea-trout. **1911** *Rep. Fisheries* 1908 316/2 Squeteague (*Cynoscion regalis*) . . . is known as . . . 'gray trout,' 'sun trout,' 'shad trout,' 'sea trout,' and 'salt-water trout' in the Middle and South Atlantic states.

+2. A rock trout, *Hexagrammos decagrammus*.

1884 GOODE, etc. *Fisheries* I. 267 From San Francisco southward, the names 'Rock Trout' and 'Sea Trout' are common. **1911** *Rep. Fisheries* 1908 315/2 *Sea trout,* a name given to . . . the spotted rock trout or greenling . . . south of San Francisco.

Sea turn. A brief change in the direction of the wind bringing a cool breeze from the ocean. {1627}

1643 WILLIAMS *Key* (1866) 111 This Southwest wind is called by the New-English, the Sea turne, which comes from the Sunne in the morning, about nine or ten of the clock Southeast, and about South, and then strongest Southwest in the after-noone, and towards night, when it dies away. **1792** BELKNAP *Hist. New Hampshire* III. 23 Sometimes the extreme heat of several days, produces, in the maritime parts, a sea turn, and in the inland parts, a whirlwind. **1815** *Mass. H. S. Coll.* III. 216 The extreme heat of summer is mitigated by sea turns. **1880** ALDRICH *Stillwater Tragedy* iii, Presently his influence began to be felt like a sea-turn. **1896** JEWETT *Pointed Firs* 134 No surprises of sea-turns or southwest sultriness might be feared.

+**Seaver's Sweet.** A variety of apple. — **1847** IVES *New Eng. Fruit* 46 *Cann Apple.* . . . This apple is cultivated by some, under the name of Seaver's Sweet.

+**Seawan(t), Sewan(t).** [Algonquian. Cf. Narraganset *siwân* 'unstrung shell beads.'] Wampum. Now hist.

1627 *N.Y. Hist. Soc. Coll.* I. 346 As an employment in winter they make sewan, which is an oblong bead that they make from cockle shells. **1675** *Doc. Col. Hist. N.Y.* XII. 524 The belts of sewant were written upon, to be kept in token of a continuance of Peace. **1701** WOLLEY *Journal N.Y.* 29 Their Money is called Wampam and Sea-want, made of a kind of Cockle or Periwinkle-shell. **1843** *Nat. Hist. N.Y., Zoology* VI. 217 From the internal purple part of the shell, the colored beads of the aborigines were formerly manufactured, constituting the *seawan* or *wampum.* **1851** SCHOOLCRAFT *Information resp. Indian Tribes* I. 85 Four grains of sewan made a penny.

***Seaweed.** **a.** Any plant growing in the sea; spec., any marine alga, as kelp, rockweed, etc. **b.** *collect.* A mass of such plants. — **1674** JOSSELYN *Two Voyages* 40 We met with abundance of Sea-weeds called Gulf-weed coming out of the Bay of Mexico. **1743** HEMPSTEAD *Diary* 413, [I] carted Seaweed from the Shore. **1779** *N.J. Archives* 2 Ser. III. 9 The soil very good for corn and rye, and with a small expence (by bringing on the sea-weed) will be very good for raising wheat. **1837** [see MARSH MUD]. **1907** *St. Nicholas* May 621/1 A pebble, . . . a piece of seaweed, an oyster-shell . . . interested him deeply.

***Sea wolf.** Any of the marine blennies having strong teeth, esp. *Anarhichas lupus.* (Cf. WOLF FISH.) — **1701** WOLLEY *Journal N.Y.* (1902) 47 A Dubartus is a Fish of the shape of a Whale, which have teeth where the Whale has Bone, . . . they are call'd by some the Sea-Wolf. **1818** *Amer. Monthly Mag.* II. 242 Sea Wolf—*Anarrhicas lupus,* . . . was taken by the fishermen when angling for cod, and brought into Boston. **1838** *Mass. Zool. Survey Rep.* 41 Sea-wolf, is not only eaten by the inhabitants of several countries of the north of Europe, . . . but is even *here* esteemed by many, and thought inferior to but very few of our fishes. **1844** De Smet *Oregon Missions* 60 My Indians, having shot a sea-wolf, made a great feast.

+**Sebago salmon.** [f. *Sebago* Lake, Me.] A landlocked salmon, *Salmo sebago.* — **1883** *Nat. Museum Bul.* No. 27, 425 Sebago Salmon. . . . Saint Croix River and lakes of Maine. Extensively introduced into other lakes and into streams southward. **1911** *Rep. Fisheries* 1908 315/1 The landlocked salmon, or fresh-water salmon, or Sebago salmon . . . , is found in fresh waters, generally landlocked.

+**Sebago trout.** =prec. — **1884** GOODE, etc. *Fisheries* I. 470 The 'Land-locked' or 'Fresh-water' Salmon, known also . . . in different parts of Maine as 'Schoodic Trout,' 'Sebago Trout,' or 'Dwarf Salmon,' probably never visit salt water.

Secede, *v.* {1755–}

1. *intr.* Of a person: To withdraw from one's associates; to retire. *Obs.*

1702 MATHER *Magnalia* (1853) I. 240 The ministers and Christians by whom New-England was first planted, . . . [were inspired] to secede into a wilderness, they knew not where. a**1811** HENRY *Camp. Quebec* 24 Having now seceded many miles from the last white inhabitants . . . it became us therefore to proceed cautiously.

b. To withdraw from a political convention. {1755–, to withdraw from any association}

1831 HONE *Diary* I. 38 Such men as Gallatin, Griswold, Carow, and King . . . should have protested and seceded from the convention. **1860** W. T. SHERMAN in *Sherman Lett.* 84 If the seceders again secede to Richmond, and there make a Southern nomination, . . . Lincoln may run in.

+2. *To secede from the Union,* to withdraw from the Federal Union.

1825 JEFFERSON *Writings* I. 20 Possibly their colonies might secede from the Union. **1830** *Congress. Deb.* 10 May 947/1 The case of the southern States is utterly hopeless and incurable. They must secede from the Union. **1851** *Harper's Mag.* June 129/2 My counsel is, secede from the union of these United States. **1900** *Congress. Rec.* 23 Jan. 1104/1 The great States of the South were seceding from the Union.

+3. *ellipt.* = sense 2.

1833 *Jamestown* (N.Y.) *Jrnl.* 20 Feb. 1/6 If a State has a right to secede and thereby to dissolve the Union as far as she is concerned—she may exercise it at one time as well as another. **1861** BUCHANAN in *Pres. Mess. & P.* V. 657 In several of the States which have not yet seceded the forts, arsenals, and magazines of the United States have been seized. **1865** PIKE *Scout & Ranger* (1932) 127 The cry was 'secede, secede!' **1886** LOGAN *Great Conspiracy* 104 If you Secede, your representatives will go out of Congress.

+**Seceded state.** One of the Southern states that seceded from the Union just prior to the Civil War. — **1861** in Kettell *Hist. Rebellion* I. 293 [Kentucky] has determined that the proper course for her to pursue is to take no part in the controversy between the government and the seceded states but that of *mediator* and *intercessor.* **1865** LINCOLN in Fleming *Hist. Reconstruction* I. 115 We all agree that the seceded States, so called, are out of their proper practical relation with the Union. **1866** 'F. KIRKLAND' *Bk. Anecdotes* 35/1 The condition of the seceded States and the course to be pursued with the garrison at Fort Sumter, were discussed.

Seceder. {1755–}

1. One who secedes from a church body; esp., a member of the Secession church of Presbyterians, originating in Scotland in 1733. {1758–}

1784 WASHINGTON *Diaries* II. 297 After hearing . . . their Religious principles (which had brought them together as a society of Cederders) . . . ; I told them I would make them a last offer. **1789** [see COVENANTER]. **1815** *Niles' Reg.* VII. 339/2 The public buildings are . . . a Presbyterian meeting-house, a Methodist meeting, two for the Seceders and one Roman chapel. **1829** ROYALL *Pennsylvania* II. 234 He is a *Seceder,* and what that is the heaven knows. **1863** J. L. FISK *Exped. Rocky Mts.* 31 We passed 'Soda Springs,' a small town of 'Morrisites,' seceders from Mormonism. **1863** TAYLOR *H. Thurston* 43 He was first a Seceder . . . but differed with them on the doctrine of Grace.

+2. One who advocated secession from the Union; a Southerner belonging to a seceding state.

1833 MARSHALL in Logan *Great Conspiracy* 28 Numerous important historical facts . . . remove the foundation on which the Nullifiers and Seceders have erected that super-structure which overshadows our Union. **1860** *Boston Transcript* 19 Dec. 2/1 Some of the leading seceders, professedly those members of Congress, . . . are a little confused. a**1861** WINTHROP *Open Air* 296 To him and his guns, flanking the approaches and ready to pile the moat full of Seceders, the country owes the safety of Fortress Monroe. **1887** BILLINGS *Hardtack* 22 These events [at Fort Sumter] . . . opened the eyes of the 'Northern Doughfaces' . . . to the real intent of the Seceders.

3. *Attrib.* in sense 1 with *church, meetinghouse, minister.*

1817 S. BROWN *Western Gazetteer* 287 Piqua has . . . one Seceder meeting house in the town. **1847** HOWE *Hist. Coll. Ohio* 256 Millersburg contains . . . 1 Seceder church. **1856** CARTWRIGHT *Autobiog.* 60 There was [a school] . . . , taught by a well-educated teacher, a Seceder minister.

+**Seceding state.** A state that secedes, or has seceded, from the Union. — **1833** MADISON in Benton *30 Years' View* I. 357/2 A seceding State mutilates the domain, and disturbs the whole system from which it separates itself. **1865** PIKE *Scout & Ranger* (1932) 132 They would proclaim that the North was utterly demoralized and powerless to coerce the seceding States into obedience. **1885** LOGAN *Great Conspiracy* 138 The Seceding States of the South were strengthening their attitude by Confederation. **1888** LOWELL *Lit. & Polit. Addresses* 211 The Democratic party was quite as efficient in bringing that war upon us as the seceding States themselves.

+**Secesh,** *n.* [f. SECESSION.] *colloq.* or *slang.*
Used only by Northerners as a jocular or disparaging word.

1. *collect.* The army of the Southern Confederacy; secessionists. Often without article.

1861 NORTON *Army Lett.* 32 The guards soon found the *secesh* to be a great hog that was wandering round in the woods. **1867** LOCKE *Swingin' Round* 97 Washington had stunk with secesh ever since he vetoed the bill. **1898** FORD *Tattle-Tales* i, A brigade of 'secesh' were charging to a railroad embankment. **1901** STILLMAN *Autobiog. Journalist* I. 332 My backwoodsmen . . . meant to go to 'shoot secesh,' not to be regular infantry.

2. A secessionist during the Civil War. Also as *pl.*

1862 HOLMES *Pages Old Vol. Life* 36 'These are two wounded Secesh,' said my companion. **1866** C. H. SMITH *Bill Arp* 169 The old squire was a powerful secesh, and hated the Yankees amazin. **1870** O. LOGAN *Before*

Footlights 229 For three long minutes I was a blasted Secesh, totally devoid of principle; a fiendish slaveholder, without any slaves. **1887** BILLINGS *Hardtack* 244 But a large number of soldiers . . . recognized no white man south of Mason and Dixon's line as other than a 'secesh.'

+**Secesh,** *a. colloq.* or *slang.*

1. Of persons: **a.** Belonging to the Southern Confederacy; being a secessionist.

In this sense the word may be regarded as the noun used appositively. **1861** *Chicago Tribune* 26 May 1/4, I might have to shoot a 'Secesh' fellow right through the mazzard. **1862** HOLMES in Motley *Correspondence* II. 57 Mr. Conway, . . . Virginia born, with seventeen secesh cousins, . . . [told] of his late experiences at the seat of Government. **1865** KELLOGG *Rebel Prisons* 200 The following, [was] written by a 'secesh' young lady to her lover. **1866** 'F. KIRKLAND' *Bk. Anecdotes* 71/2 A secesh Colonel had sold his negro to the Confederate government. **1904** *Buffalo Commercial* 10 Sept. 6 The reporters eagerly interviewed those old-fashioned 'Secesh' editors from the 'late Confederate states.'

b. Supporting or sympathetic to the cause of the Southern Confederacy.

1867 *Congress. Globe* 21 Nov. 769/1 Mr. Butler voted . . . with the leading 'Secesh' members of [the legislature of Tenn.]. **1868** *Ore. State Jrnl.* 8 Aug. 1/3 Seymour is a good enough Secesh Democrat for that branch of the party.

2. Of things: Made or owned by persons of the Southern Confederacy.

1861 NORTON *Army Lett.* 35 We dug *secesh* potatoes to roast. **1862** *Ib.* 74, I picked up a *secesh* bullet there too. **1866** GREGG *Life in Army* 74 All along the route, secesh chickens, hogs, geese, ducks, turkeys, horses, mules, &c., were missing. **1867** Goss *Soldier's Story* 41, I was mixed up in some 'right smart tall grass' . . . on account of the stealing of a Secesh goose. **1876** J. E. TODD *John Todd* 428 Near it is a long, double-barreled gun—'my Secesh gun.'

3. Of or pertaining to the Southern Confederacy in its operation of the Civil War.

1862 NORTON *Army Lett.* 59 We pitched our picket tents which we carry with us on the ground lately occupied by a *secesh* regiment. **1863** *Rio Abajo Press* 29 Sept. 3/2 Eight gentlemen from Texas . . . are said to have left that State to escape the Secesh conscription. **1863** in 'F. Kirkland' *Bk. Anecdotes* 77/1 A plan . . . is now disclosed to some General in each military department in the Secesh States. **1864** *Congress. Globe* 27 May 2529/1 The secessionists got hold of the meeting, and . . . passed the most violent secesh resolutions. **1875** BURNHAM *Three Years* 21 It was found exceedingly difficult to pass . . . unchallenged, if a man even secretly entertained any but the most radical 'secesh' opinions.

4. Used in the predicate: Having the opinions of the Southerners during the Civil War; sympathetic toward the South.

1863 BOUDRYE *Fifth N.Y. Cavalry* (1868) 339 An oyster man . . . Was Union on the York, but Secesh on James river. **1865** PIKE *Scout & Ranger* (1932) 157, [I took] good care to be just secesh enough to give confidence. **1869** HALE *Ingham Papers* 200 The old gentleman was as secesh as Bertha was loyal. **1887** BILLINGS *Hardtack* 234 So many who really were 'secesh' claimed to be good Union men, it came latterly to be assumed that the victim was playing a false rôle.

+**Secesh,** *v. colloq.* and *jocular.* **1.** *intr.* To secede; to withdraw. ‖**2.** *tr.* To get *seceshed*, to get separated. — **(1) 1861** Moore *Rebellion Rec.* I. 111. 126 He has plenty of money, which I find is a good thing to secesh with. **1862** BROWNE *A. Ward: His Book* 185 If any State wants to secede, let 'em Sesesh! **1867** LOCKE *Swingin' Round* 23, I seceshed with 100 niggers to git 200. **(2) 1862** LOWELL *Biglow P.* 2 Ser. iv. 119 We've succeeded in gittin' seceshed an' dissolved.

+**Seceshdom.** =SECESSIA. *jocular.* — **1861** *N.Y. Tribune* 23 Nov. 8/1 Private advices from Seceshdom speak of the elation which succeeded the first excitement produced by the arrest of Mason and Slidell.

+**Secesher.** A Southern secessionist. *slang.* — **1861** NEWELL *Orpheus C. Kerr* I. 75, I happened to light on a very fat secesher, who was doing a little running for exercise. **1862** BROWNE *A. Ward: His Book* 190, I went amung the Seseshers with no feeling of annermosity. **1866** 'F. KIRKLAND' *Bk. Anecdotes* 105/1 'Long come two or free hundred ob dem seceshers.

+**Secesh flag.** =SECESSION flag. *jocular.* — **1861** NORTON *Army Lett.* 18 He made a little *secesh* flag. **1862** BROWNE *A. Ward: His Book* 200 She wore a little Sesesh flag pin'd onto her hat.

‖**Seceshly,** *adv.* In the manner of the secessionists. — **1862** *Congregationalist* 7 Feb. (Chipman), Some sour, seceshly inclined tavern-keeper.

+**Secessia.** The land of the secessionists or the Southern Confederacy. *jocular.* Also *transf.* — **1861** NORTON *Army Lett.* 26 We are in Secessia and the meanest part of it, too. **1862** MOORE *Rebellion Rec.* V. 11. 303 They anticipated a triumph for 'Secessia.' **1866** 'F. KIRKLAND' *Bk. Anecdotes* 461/1 'Yes, indeed,' broke in fair Secessia.

Secession. {1604-} The action of seceding from a political union {1660-}, with special reference to the withdrawing from the Union by the Southern states.

+**1.** In discussions before December 20, 1860.

1830 *Congress. Deb.* 10 May 948/2 Make good the charge, prove the injury, and they [the people of N.Y.] will consent to the secession [of S.C.] to-morrow. **1832** M. CAREY *Olive Branch No. III* (Ernst), The strong probability of a secession, at least of South Carolina. **1851** in A. C. Cole *Whig Party in So.* 196 Of all the vagaries that ever straggled into the brain of a politician, the one of peaceable secession of a State from the Union, is the most absurd. **1857** BENTON *Exam. Dred Scott Case* 181 All the nullification newspapers opened for secession for that new cause. **1860** LONGFELLOW in S. Longfellow *H. W. Longfellow* II. 409 Secession of the North from freedom would be tenfold worse than secession of the South from the North.

+**2.** In reference to actual secession after December 20, 1860.

1860 in Logan *Great Conspiracy* 115 The Secession of South Carolina is not an event of a day. **1861** E. COWELL *Diary* 241 Professor Anderson is 'loafing about' having been driven from the South by secession. **1865** in Fleming *Hist. Reconstruction* I. 141 The American people have now put their final and effectual veto upon this doctrine of 'Secession.' **1884** BLAINE *20 Years of Congress* I. 573 The purpose of the secession . . . [was] the establishment of an independent slave-empire.

+**b.** In fig. contexts.

1861 *Vanity Fair* 16 Feb. 77/2 Thank Goodness March the Fourth is near, To nip Secession's nose. **1871** WHITMAN *Democ. Vistas* 30, I have mark'd the brazen hell-faces of secession and slavery gazing defiantly from all the windows and doorways. **1872** *Newton Kansan* 5 Sept. 4/3 The only garment that fits him at all is the old, torn, bullet-riddled jacket of secession.

+**3.** *quasi-adj.* Sympathetic to secession.

1861 W. T. SHERMAN in *Sherman Lett.* 131 The young active element is all secession, the older stay-at-homes are for Union and Peace.

4. *attrib.* +**a.** Designating attitudes, feelings, etc., reflecting sentiment favorable to secession.

1860 *Boston Transcript* 20 Dec. 2/1 The Secession Feeling at the South is decreasing in intensity in some states. **1861** *Chicago Tribune* 15 April 1 In all that the Chicago *Times* has said of the secession movement. . . . not one word has yet been uttered in condemnation of the traitors and rebels. **1865** *Atlantic Mo.* April 441/2 This was an elderly, somewhat cold and forbidding personage, of Secession sympathies. **1866** 'F. KIRKLAND' *Bk. Anecdotes* 602/1 He met a young lady of secession proclivities. **1872** *Newton Kansan* 17 Oct. 1/2 Mr. Greeley has especial trouble to explain his secession sentiments uttered in 1861.

+**b.** Designating persons or groups of persons sympathetic to or participating in secession.

1861 *Chicago Tribune* 19 July 1/2 It was obtained by an officer of the Ohio Volunteers from a Secession family near Ravenswood. **1861** in E. McPherson *Polit. Hist. Great Rebellion* (1864) 391/2 A caucus was held in this city [Washington] by the Southern Secession Senators. **1862** in McClellan *Own Story* 347 There is in front of us to impede our advance the secession Army of the Rappahannock, so called. **1865** PIKE *Scout & Ranger* (1932) 131 One week the secession orators would herald to excited audiences that independence could be consummated without any war at all. **1866** 'F. KIRKLAND' *Bk. Anecdotes* 110/2 A secession minister comes into the store kept by a Quaker.

+**c.** Designating objects worn to show sympathy toward secession.

1862 *Mass. Hist. Soc. Proc.* V. 375 A pair of secession slippers, taken, by the police in Baltimore, from a person on his way to the shoemaker to have them made up. **1863** HOPLEY *Life in South* I. 137 At an annual State exhibition in Georgia, a lady presented a 'Secession bonnet,' of home manufacture. **1886** POORE *Reminisc.* II. 80 It was not uncommon to meet on Pennsylvania Avenue a defiant Southerner openly wearing a large Virginia or South Carolina secession badge.

+**d.** In special combinations.

Secession dinner, a dinner given to benefit the secessionists; *S. Ordinance,* the ordinance adopted by a South Carolina convention giving official sanction to that state's secession from the Union; *s. ticket,* a political ticket bearing the names of candidates advocating secession.

1865 *Wkly. New Mexican* 4 Aug. 2/2 It was fashionable for some folks, to rend their linen over the fancied wrongs of the South, and to preside 'with dignity,' at secession dinners. **1860** *Boston Transcript* 21 Dec. 2/5 The official despatch to the President, announcing the passage of the Secession Ordinance, was received last evening. **1861** *N.Y. Tribune* 8 Nov. 6/1 Thousands, Sir, voted the Secession ticket just to prove . . . that they abhorred free-nigger barbarianism!

Secessional, *a.* {1838-} Addicted to the doctrines of secession. — **1861** *Vanity Fair* 22 June 284/2 But if that secessional person only knew how many thousand New-York people live in Clover, . . . he would probably retire from seceding.

+**Secession convention.** Any of the state conventions convened in the South to consider or declare secession from the Union. — **1860** *Boston Transcript* 19 Dec. 4/2 The South Carolina Secession Convention. **1893** PAGE in *Harper's Mag.* Dec. 10/2 Here [in Richmond] sat and deliberated the Secession Convention during the period when Virginia stood as the peace-maker between the two sections.

+**Secessiondom.** =SECESSIA. — **1862** 'E. KIRKE' *Among Pines* 63 This, the reader will please remember, was the state of things . . . in the *very heart* of Secessiondom. **1868** *N.Y. Herald* 1 July 6/4 But New York has had enough experience of the dogmatic philosophers of secessiondom.

+**Secessioner.** =SECESHER. *slang.* — **1863** *Harper's Mag.* July 282/1 The pesky officers using up on them seceshioners roads all the stuff that was sent to make breeches. **1865** *Nation* I. 457 We ha'n't no use for secessioners, not for nothin'.

+**Secession flag. a.** The flag of the Southern Confederacy. **b.** Any particular flag of this kind. — **1861** *Chicago Tribune* 26 May 1/6 He carried . . . [a] secession flag. **1863** HOPLEY *Life in South* I. 283 Before the confirmed Secession of Virginia from the Northern States' Government, the 'Secession flag,' as an indication of the prevailing sentiment, was set floating from many public buildings and private dwellings. **1866** 'F. KIRKLAND' *Bk. Anecdotes* 582/2 Miss Lee wore upon her bonnet a min[i]ature silken secession flag.

+**Secessionism.** {1899–} +The principles or doctrines of those who advocated secession from the Union. Now hist. Also fig. — **1861** *N.Y. Herald* 16 Nov. (Chipman), Their faith in secessionism will give place to a keen appreciation of their own interests. **1865** *Nation* I. 38/1 So outspoken is its secessionism that it has lately been warned by the military that its course must change or its publication stop. **1898** *Voice* 5 May 6/5 Lincoln . . . found himself in possession of a bankrupt government, confronted by an arrogant secessionism.

+**Secessionist.** In the Southern and border states, one who advocated secession from the Union; one who supported the Confederacy. {1881–, in general sense}

1851 *Harper's Mag.* Dec. 120/1 The same division prevailed in the Congressional contest, the nominees being Unionists and Secessionists. **1851** *Whig Almanac 1852* 43/2 The Co-Operationists . . . carried six districts; and the Secessionists . . . carried one. **1861** *Chicago Tribune* 19 July 1/4 St. Louis. . . . Alexander Lewis, a well-known horse-dealer and secessionist, appeared on the street to-day, with his rifle in hand, defying anybody who didn't believe in Jeff. Davis. **1862** in Collins *Kentucky* I. 109 The secessionists, or known sympathizers with secession, . . . will be held strictly responsible. **1903** W. E. CURTIS *True A. Lincoln* 188 Mr. Blair . . . from the beginning was in favor of prompt and energetic measures against the secessionists.

b. *quasi-adj.* Sympathetic toward secession.
1869 BRACE *New West* 277 The region about Los Angeles . . . was somewhat secessionist, or at least opposed to the Government, during the war.

+**Secession sympathizer.** One who sympathized with the doctrines of secession. — **1861** in Linton *Life Whittier* 136, I do not like to find fault with the Administration, as in so doing I *seem* to take sides with the secession-sympathisers of the North. **1863** Cox *8 Yrs. in Congress* 309 It is for this that gentlemen on the other side hurl at us epithets of 'secession sympathizers,' 'disloyal men.' **1864** *Wkly. New Mexican* 10 June 2/2 Secession sympathizers were then in the employ of government.

+**Seckel.** Ellipt. for next. Also attrib. — **1852** *Horticulturist* VII. 48 Those [pears] of merit which were in season with the Seckel and Virgalieu . . . are as follows. **1858** *Ill. Agric. Soc. Trans.* III. 338 Some years since one of my Seckle trees began to blight badly in the bark. **1868** *Ib.* VII. 521 He will never forget to associate the exquisite flavor of the Seckel . . . with that name. **1890** *Cent.* 4343/3 The Seckel is an American variety—the fruit small, but unsurpassed in quality.

+**Seckel pear.** [See quot. 1817.] A sweet and juicy variety of pear, usually reddish brown in color. — **1817** W. COXE *Fruit Trees* 159 Seckle Pear.—So called from Mr. Seckle of Philadelphia, the proprietor of the original tree. **1847** BRIGGS *Tom Pepper* I. 145 One of them fished up a seckle pear, and the other a paper of figs. **1867** HOLMES *Guardian Angel* 25 Her cheek had a little of the russet tinge which a Seckel pear shows. **1882** *Harper's Mag.* May 892/2 A Marquette strawberry . . . [resembles] in size a Seckel pear.

‖**Seco.** Corruption of ACEQUIA. (See also SAQUE, SEQUIA.) — **1862** *Harper's Mag.* May 742/1 The vineyards were but partially cultivated, and the secos, or ditches for the irrigation of the land, were entirely dry.

∗**Second,** *n.*

1. *pl.* An inferior article or articles. {c1600, 1812–} +**a.** Tobacco leaves of an inferior quality or the plants that produce them: (see quot. 1724).
1658 *Va. House of Burgesses* 107 Proposed whether ground leaves or seconds are merchantable tobacco. **1666** *Md. Archives* II. 143 All Sound tobacco . . . free from ground leases [*sic*] and Seconds shall be held Merchantable. **1724** JONES *Virginia* 117 They have a Law against Seconds, . . . [intended] to prohibit all Persons from manufacturing a second Crop from the Leaves that sprout out from the Stalk after the first Leaves are cut off. **1775** *Amer. Husbandry* II. 80 These *seconds* . . . do not usually grow so high as the first plant, but notwithstanding they make very good tobacco.

b. *pl.* Inferior grain, or flour made from it. {sing., 1743 (Ellis *Mod. Husb.* IV. III. 63; *pl.* 1823–} Also attrib.
1742 *Md. Hist. Mag.* XX. 263 You are to bring down what seconds and Bran Mr. Brown has ready of the Produce. **1774** FITHIAN *Journal* I. 262 The steady Rate of flour weekly, for the great House is 100 Lb of which 50 is the finest, & 50 the Seconds. **1857** GUNN *N.Y. Boarding-Houses* 231 Take 'seconds' flour and saleratus, mix and form your biscuit. **1891** CHASE & CLOW *Industry* II. 94 The 'firsts' or best grains, and the 'seconds' or poorer grains, were put into separate sacks.

2. A second wife.
1667 SANFORD *Letter Book* 42 My Beest Respects premised unto yor Self & my good Cozen yor Second.

+**3.** *Parliamentary law.* **a.** An act or utterance in which a motion is seconded. **b.** One who seconds a motion.

1812 *Ann. 12th Congress 1 Sess.* 1462 The Speaker said he conceived that every motion must receive a second before it could be announced from the Chair. *Ib.* 1472 A reversal of the rule that the plurality of the members is to govern . . . [would] make the mover and his second superior to the whole body. **1894** T. B. REED *Manual Gen. Parl. Law* 77 No second is required in the House of Representatives to an ordinary motion. **1915** H. M. ROBERT *Rules of Order Rev.* 36 The chair should repeat the motion before calling for a second.

∗**Second,** *a.*

+**1.** Of a district, church, bank, etc.: Organized, incorporated, or named as the second of its kind in a given community. (Cf. FIRST *a.* 1.)
1684 *Providence Rec.* XIV. 92 Tenn acrs of low land & Swampye in ye lue of five acrs of Meaddow in ye second devision. **1827** R. KNIGHT *Six Principle Baptists* 290 The Gloucester Second Church . . . was organized about 1780. **1846** LYELL *Second Visit* II. 98 In the Second Municipality [of New Orleans] . . . the Anglo-Americans have . . . started ten newspapers. **1894** LEAVITT *Our Money Wars* 49 The Act of April 10, 1816, chartered the second Bank of the United States.

2. a. Of a person holding office or official position: Next to the highest in rank or responsibility. {1702–}
See also COMPTROLLER 3 b.
1721 *New-Eng. Courant* 4 Sept. 2/1 The following Persons were compelled to go with them, viz. Henry Piper chief Mate, Mathew Gilliat second Mate, James Fearon Carpenter. **1808** *Stat. at Large* II. 482 Each company of artillery [shall have] one captain, one first and one second lieutenant [etc.]. **1816** *Ib.* III. 281 For compensation to the second assistant postmaster general, one thousand six hundred dollars. **1871** *Rep. Indian Affairs* (1872) 573 Each had a principal and second chief, and a speaker of the council. **1883** 'MARK TWAIN' *Life on Miss.* xxxvii, Among the forty-seven wounded were the captain, chief mate, second mate, and second and third clerks.

+**b.** Of a hired person: Assistant to another.
See also SECOND GIRL, SECOND MAN 2.
1905 *Indian Laws & Tr.* III. 131 For pay of second blacksmith, and such iron and steel and other materials as may be required, . . . one thousand dollars. **1905** *Forestry Bureau Bul.* No. 61, 46 *Second faller*, the subordinate in a crew of fallers. (P[acific] C[oast] F[orest].)

+**3.** Appended to a personal name: Being the second person of that name; junior.
1803 *Mass. Spy* 2 Feb. (Th.), Daniel Heywood, 2d. *Ib.* (Th.), Wm. Caldwell, 2d. **1805** *Ib.* 11 Sept. (Th.), Jonas Sibley. Jonas Sibley, 2d. **1821** *Ib.* 18 April (Th.), All persons are cautioned not to harbour or trust David Rich, David Attwood, Ezekiel Davis, 2d., Margaret Moore, &c., Paupers of the town of Oxford.

+**4.** Of a theater balcony, gallery, etc.: Next above the first balcony, gallery, etc.
1871 *Chicago Ev. Jrnl.* 26 Aug., Above the first balcony is the second balcony. **1872** *Chicago Tribune* 13 Oct., Just at the left of this is the flight of stairs leading to the second circle. **1891** EARLE *Sabbath* 63 Sometimes a little pew or short gallery was built high up among the beams and joists over the staircase which led to the first gallery, and was called the 'swallows' nest,' or the 'roof pue,' or the 'second gallery.' **1896** BIRKMIRE *Planning Amer. Theatres* 46 Seats [are] arranged as follows: . . . first box-tier, 32 boxes, 160 people, second box-tier, 32 boxes.

+**5.** *absol.* = SECOND BASE.
1862 *Chadwick Scrapbook* (E. J. Nichols). **1886** CHADWICK *Art of Pitching* 72 A runner is on second. **1897** *Outing* June 299/2 Dean at second is fielding well. **1907** *St. Nicholas* June 719/2 The stains of grass and earth . . . he had succeeded in acquiring by many an exciting 'slide for second.'

+**6.** In special combinations.
Second branch of the legislature, the lower house of a legislature; *s. low ground*, second bottom; *s. office*, the office of vice president; *s. principal meridian*, *s.-quality white*, *s. soil*, (see quotations); *s. termer*, one serving a second term in the penitentiary; *s. work*, work done by a second girl.
1787 in T. Speed *Polit. Club*, *Danville, Ky.* 139 What ought to be the powers of the second branch of the legislature in a commonwealth? **1771** *Va. Gazette* 7 Feb. 3/2 It is all first and second low Grounds, very level, and will produce any Thing usually cultivated in this Colony. **1856** *Democratic Conv. Proc.* 68 [John C. Breckenridge's] elevation to the second office in the Government, is an auspicious augury of the return of Kentucky to the Democratic faith of her fathers. **1834** PECK *Gaz. Illinois* 93 The 'Second Principal Meridian' is a line due north from the mouth of Little Blue river in Indiana. **1829** B. HALL *Travels in N.A.* III. 220 The different kinds of cotton are, 'first quality white,' 'second quality white,' and 'yellow.' **1857** *Ill. Agric. Soc. Trans.* II. 347 In some sections of the state, in digging wells, a 'second soil,' so called, is found about eighteen or twenty feet below the surface, wherein wood, tree tops and bark of trees are imbedded in a black soil similar to the upper. **1889** *Columbus Dispatch* 25 Sept., The established belief [is] that second-termers are numerous. **1878** COOKE *Happy Dodd* 125 She would make a good child's nurse, or she could do second work.

Second Advent. {1736–} *attrib.* +**a.** Designating persons believing in the imminence of the second coming of Christ. +**b.** Designating the doctrines or organizations of such persons. (Cf. MILLERITE.) — **1844** RUPP *Relig. Denominations* 668 Second Advent Believers. [Account] by

N. Southard, Editor of the Midnight Cry. **1847** LOWELL *Biglow P.* I Ser. iv. 61 An excellent deacon of my congregation (being infected with the Second Advent delusion) assured me [etc.]. **1860** HOLMES *E. Venner* xxiv, Some of the Second-Advent preachers had been about, and circulated their predictions among the kitchen-population of Rockland. **1891** MCCLINTOCK & STRONG *Cycl. Biblical Lit.* XI. 53/1 On the 18th of May, 1842, the 'Second Advent Association of New York City and Vicinity' was formed.

+Second Adventist. =MILLERITE; ADVENTIST. — **1849** in Wellcome *Hist. Second Advent Message* 580 Wm. Miller, distinguished as the founder of the sect known as 'Second Adventists, or *Millerites*,' recently died at his residence in the State of New York. **1857** *Harper's Mag.* Oct. 712/1 Pete is a stubborn Millerite, or Second-Adventist, always setting 'the last day' some months ahead. **1873** PHELPS *Trotty's Wedding* xii, When I turn Second Adventist and get ready to fly, I'll wear them. **1891** HOLMES *Over Teacups* 313 No melodramatic display of warring elements, such as the white-robed Second Adventist imagines, can meet the need of the human heart.

∗**Secondary,** *a.* Of education: Next above the elementary rank. {1876-} — **1852** *Ind. Hist. Soc. Publ.* III. 615 Those engaged in studies of a more advanced character, constitute another class, termed secondary. **1889** *Cent.* 1845/2 Education is further divided into *primary education* . . . ; *secondary,* that received in grammar and high schools or in academies; *higher* . . . ; and *special* or *professional.*

Secondary school. A school intermediate between an elementary school and college; a high school. {1861, in France; 1902} Also attrib. — **1835** *S. Lit. Messenger* I. 275 Secondary schools . . . [teach] the rudiments of Arithmetic, Geography, English Grammar [etc.]. **1894** *Harper's Mag.* May 964/1 This principle . . . will make a great simplification in secondary-school programmes. **1908** [see ELEMENTARY EDUCATION].

+Second bank. The bluff or embankment that rises from river-bottom land. *Obs.* — **1797** F. BAILY *Tour* 212 This second bank subsides into a plain country. **1817** S. BROWN *Western Gazetteer* 52 *Rising-Sun*— Is delightfully situated on the second bank of the Ohio. **1823** JAMES *Exped.* I. 62 The second banks . . . are here raised about seventy feet.

+Second base. *Baseball.*
1. The base behind the pitcher's box.
1845 in *Appletons' Ann. Cycl.* XXV. 77/2 The bases shall be from 'home' to second base, forty paces [etc.]. **1880** N. BROOKS *Fairport Nine* 186 Joe Fitts attempted to run to second base. **1912** MATHEWSON *Pitching* 202 Sheckard flied out to Seymour, Kling being held on second base.

2. A second baseman, or the position played by him.
1868 CHADWICK *Base Ball* 43 The regular order of positions of a base ball nine is as follows: Catcher, Pitcher, First Base, Second Base, Third Base [etc.]. **1880** N. BROOKS *Fairport Nine* 24 George Bridge, their second base, was the decentest boy of the gang. **1886** *Outing* April 104/1 Terry, '85, of Yale, was offered the position of second base of the Metropolitan nine.

+Second baseman. A baseball player who plays at second base. **1867** CHADWICK *Base Ball* 84 [Let] the second baseman play at right short. **1887** *Courier-Journal* 25 Jan. 8/4 Burdock, once the king of second basemen, is searching for an engagement. **1924** C. D. WARDLAW *Fundamentals of Baseball* 7 The second-baseman . . snaps the ball to the short-stop.

∗**Second-best,** *a.* +In quasi-adverbial use: *To come off* (or *out) second best,* to be defeated. {1870} — **1774** J. ANDREWS *Letters* 68 In ev'ry affray as yet the officers have been the aggressors and came off *second* best. **1777** A. ADAMS *Familiar Lett.* 319, I am glad to hear of fighting, even though we come off second-best. **1863** 'M. HARLAND' *Husks* 24 A plate or cup . . . had come off second best . . . in an encounter with some other member of the crockery tribe. **1879** *Scribner's Mo.* Oct. 884/2 [He] was never known to come out 'second best' in a horse-trade.

+Second board. (See quot. 1909.) — **1855** *Chicago W. Times* 29 March 1/4 The market at the Second Board, which was a strong one at the opening, closed 1-2 per cent off. **1909** WEBSTER 1909/1 *Second board,* . . . the second call on exchanges . . . ; on the New York Stock Exchange, the second printed list of sales, for the period from 12 M. to 2 P.M.

+Second bottom. The second or higher level of bottom land. — **1691** in *Amer. Speech* XV. 390/1 On ye second bottom of ye upper back Creek. **1788-** [see BOTTOM *n.* 1 b].

Second class, *n.* +A class of mail comprising newspapers and other periodicals. — **1863** *Stat. at Large* XII. 705 The second class embraces all mailable matter exclusively in print, and regularly issued at stated periods. **1880** LAMPHERE *U.S. Govt.* 242/2 Mailable matter of the second class, deposited in a letter-carrier post-office for local delivery, shall be delivered through boxes. **1883** *Postal Guide* 733 'Nixes' is a term used . . . to denote matter of domestic origin, chiefly of the first and second class, which is unmailable.

Second-class, *a.*
1. a. Of a conveyance: For use of passengers paying a fare next below the highest fare. {1837-8-}
1850 *Phila., Wilmington, & Balt. R.R. 12th Rep.* 22 One large new night car and one second-class car are nearly finished. **1874** PINKERTON *Expressman & Detective* 51 He went immediately to the second-class car. **1883** *Harper's Mag.* Nov. 968/2 In this country first, second, and third class cars are not common on our railways.

b. Of persons: Entitled to ride in a second-class conveyance.
1878 B. F. TAYLOR *Between Gates* 257 A dilapidated stage . . . looked just fit to . . . carry second-class passengers and dead-heads. **1903** E. JOHNSON *Railway Transportation* 144 Second-class passenger traffic is not stimulated in the United States.

2. Inferior; not of the best kind.
1873 MILLER *Amongst Modocs* 133 Six-foot Sandy was . . . a sort of cross between a first-class miner and a second-class gambler. **1882** MCCABE *New York* 544 The second-class [gambling] houses, or 'hells,' lie principally along Broadway and prominent streets leading from it.

+3. a. Of mail matter: Consisting of newspapers and other periodicals. Of postal rates: Established as the charge for carrying newspapers and other periodicals.
See FIRST-CLASS *a.* 2 b, note.
1873 *Postal Laws* 176 (Ernst), Postage on second-class matter must be prepaid. **1877** *Rep. Postmaster-General* 246 Why . . . should *book manuscript* be excepted from the first-class rate and charged only the low second-class rate? **1893** CUSHING *Story of P.O.* 410 It has its fiends who want their publications admitted to the mails as second class matter when they are not second class matter at all. **1924** *Postal Guide* 10 Application for entry of a publication as second-class matter or registry as a news agent should be made through the postmaster to the Third Assistant Postmaster General, Division of Classification.

Second classman. +At Annapolis, a third-year man. — **1888** DORSEY *Midshipman Bob* 128 His class-mates backed him to a man, so did the second-classmen.

Second day. Monday. In attrib. use. (Cf. FIRST DAY.) — **1705** SEWALL *Diary* II. 147, I refer'd them to second-day Morning Decr. 10. to meet at the Secretary's office.

+Second-day dress. A dress worn by a bride on the day after her wedding. (Cf. next.) — **1898** HALL *Aunt Jane* 163, I had on my 'second-day' dress, the prettiest sort of a changeable silk.

+Second-day wedding. (See quotations.) — *a*1860 JUDD *Hist. Hadley* (1905) 238 There were occasionally, second-day weddings, or wedding festivities kept up the second day. **1877** BARTLETT 566 *Second-Day Wedding,* a reception or evening party given by the parents of the bridegroom, or by the new-married couple in their own house, soon after their marriage.

Second degree. +1. In the early history of Harvard, the M.A. degree. +2. A grade of crime only less serious than first degree. — (1) **1671** SEWALL *Letter-Book* I. 18 Sir Bayly intends to see the College in the spring; in order to the taking of his 2d Degree. **1704** *Boston News-Letter* 24 July 4/1 Mr. Thomas Weld . . . took his Second Degree at Cambridge on the 5th Instant. **1734** [see DEGREE 1]. (2) **1821-** [see DEGREE 2].

Second fiddle. *To play second fiddle,* to act or be in a subordinate capacity. {1862} Cf. THIRD *a.* 2. — **1831** *Jamestown Jrnl.* 21 Sept. 2 The Buffalo Journal . . . [has] long played second fiddle to the Craftsman. **1857** *Lawrence* (Kan.) *Republican* 9 July 3 His mission seems to consist in playing second fiddle to the other performers. **1884** *Boston Jrnl.* 13 Sept., There was a time when the Globe, as a Democratic paper, did not play second fiddle to the Herald. **1884** *American* VIII. 182 They seem willing to have us play second-fiddle to any European power.

Second floor. +The floor of a building above the ground floor. {1821-, 'next but one above the ground-floor'} Also attrib. — **1846** E. WAYLEN *Reminiscences* 230 Meals were taken in a capacious dining room on the first floor. *Ib.* (note), Called the 'second-floor' in America. **1866** A. D. WHITNEY *L. Goldthwaite* iv, The proprietor . . . showed them a commodious second-floor corner-room. **1871** ROE *Army Lett.* 8 It has . . . two rooms and a very large hall closet on the second floor. **1912** T. R. SULLIVAN *Heart of Us* 49 They climbed into a light, airy room occupying the entire second floor.

+Second girl. A housemaid of subordinate position. — **1871** HOWELLS *Wedding Journey* 25 The human wave is beginning to sprinkle the pavement with cooks and second-girls. **1889** *Century Mag.* March 787/1 One might suppose . . . that Milly Robinson had been born labeled 'Mrs. Dansken's Second Girl.' *c*1895 NORRIS *Vandover* 61 A respectable-looking second girl hurried past him carrying her prayer-book.

Second growth.
1. The growth that follows the destruction of the virgin forest: (see also quot. 1900). {1825 (Loudon *Encycl. Agric.* 805)}
1829 COOPER *Wish-ton-Wish* ii, Much of the surface of this opening, too, was now concealed by bushes, of what is termed second growth. **1896** *Vt. Agric. Rep.* XV. 85 What we need fear is that this second-growth shall be of an inferior class of trees. **1900** BRUNCKEN *N. Amer. Forests* 67 Where lumbermen, cutting construction material, speak of 'second growth,' they merely refer to timber which they left standing thirty or forty years ago. **1905** *Forestry Bureau Bul.* No. 61, 20.

2. Attrib. with *maple, mountain spruce,* etc. {1863, in Brazil}
1858 THOREAU *Maine Woods* 156, I saw no soft, spreading, second-growth white pines. **1869** *Rep. Comm. Agric.* 1868 414 An old second-growth pine-field, . . . seeded to wheat in 1866-'67, . . . was plowed thoroughly across the old furrows. **1880** *Vt. Agric. Rep.* VI. 116 Good second growth maples produce the sweetest sap. **1897** *Outing* XXX. 231/2 The paddle used is of second-growth mountain spruce.

Secondhand, *a.* {1654–}

1. Not new; previously used. {1673–} Often designating various vehicles.

1733 FRANKLIN *Poor Richard's Almanac 1734* 1, I have bought a second-hand coat. **1747** *Boston Gazette* 21 July 4/2 A very good second-hand chair and harness to be sold. **1779** *Ib.* 13 Dec. 3/3 A second-hand Chariot with harness compleat. **1790** *Columbian Centinel* 6 Oct. 28/1 To Be Sold, Two very good second hand Chaises. **1802** ELLICOTT *Journal* 5 The other [boat was] a second hand keel-boat. **1814** *Nat. Intelligencer* 28 July 4/4 For Sale, A strong, well-built second hand Coachee. **1880** 'MARK TWAIN' *Tramp Abroad* 267 He sold the old carriage and bought a cheap second-hand buggy. **1923** J. H. COOK *On Old Frontier* 5, I had purchased . . . a good second-hand Texas saddle for $5.

2. Of a shop or store: Dealing in secondhand goods.

1888 ROE *Army Lett.* 359 We did not desire to turn our houses into sec-ond-hand shops. **1901** CHURCHILL *Crisis* 48 We shall skip likewise a most affecting scene at Mr. Canter's second-hand furniture store.

+**Secondhand land.** (See quotation.) — **1893** *Scribner's Mag.* June 699/1 The days of 'looking' Government timber are wellnigh over. The landlooker is now engaged in estimating what is called 'second-hand land,' the land of private owners.

Second man. +**1.** An Indian sub-chief. +**2.** A man who assists a man servant or a hired man. (Cf. SECOND GIRL.) — (1) **1772** in *Travels Amer. Col.* 505 A young man who I had sent two Days ago with a Message to Emistisiguo and 2d Man of the Little Tallassies was Returned. (2) **1905** *Washington Star* 24 Nov. 20 Wanted—a thoroughly competent white second man.

Second-rate, *a.* {1669–} +Of land or soil: Of a quality poorer than that of first-rate lands, sometimes determined by an official appraisal. (Cf. FIRST-RATE *a.* 1.)

1784 FILSON *Kentucke* 16 The inhabitants distinguish its quality by first, second, and third rate lands. **1831** PECK *Guide* 47 The bottoms [in La.] are only second rate land. **1834** PECK *Gaz. Illinois* 99 Second rate lands are taxed two dollars and forty cents per quarter section. **1863** *Rep. Comm. Agric. 1862* 61 The 'second-rate pine lands' form the largest pro-portion of Florida.

Second reader. *Christian Science.* +The member of a Christian Sci-ence church elected to read from the Bible in the Sunday services. — **1896** *N.Y. Tribune* 27 Sept. 11. 2/4 Those who had heretofore been known as pastors were hereafter to be known as readers, their titles to be First Reader and Second Reader, and were to be officially appointed by the church. **1906, 1920** [see FIRST READER 2].

Second summer. (See quotation.) — **1808** ASHE *Travels* 194 The summer is not violently hot, being tempered by a perpetual breeze; and the autumn [in Ky.] is distinguished by the name of the Second Summer.

Second table. +A table for people not qualified by some standard to sit at the regular table with others. Also fig. — **1850** *Congress. Globe* 11 March 500/2 Upon steamboats they [*sc.* Negroes] are seated at the 'second table.' **1856** *Ib.* 9 Aug. 2015/1 If we vote for Mr. Buchanan we shall come in at the second table, and can never expect to sit at the first table.

***Secret,** *n.* ‖?A privy. — **1787** *Md. Gazette* 1 June 1/2 To be rented, a three story Brick House, . . . [with] a large Smoke House and Secret, a large yard [etc.].

***Secret,** *a.* In the name of: +**a.** A committee set up to obtain pow-der, guns, etc., for carrying on the Revolutionary War. +**b.** A Com-mittee of Correspondence set up by Congress. — [**1775** *Jrnls. Cont. Con-gress* II. 253 Resolved, that a secret Committee be appointed to contract and agree for the importation and delivery of . . . gunpowder.] **1776** *Ib.* IV. 345 Resolved, That the Committee of Secret Correspondence be di-rected to lay their proceedings before Congress. *Ib.* V. 856 The Secret Committee having informed Congress that a vessel was arrived with sundry articles by them imported [etc.]. **1777** *Ib.* VII. 216 Resolved, . . . That another warrant issue on the same loan officer, in favour of the Secret Committee, for ten thousand dollars. *Ib.* 274 Resolved, That the style of the Committee of Secret Correspondence be altered, and that, for the future, it be styled the Committee for Foreign Affairs.

Secret agent. One who secretly investigates or acquires information for a principal.

1837 *Diplom. Corr. Texas* III. (1911) 827 The Government of the United States . . . [sent] a secret agent to Texas to enquire into her situation and powers. **1855** HOLBROOK *Among Mail Bags* 25 The gentleman at this time at the head of the Post Office Department, had not been a very ar-dent believer in the necessity or usefulness of 'Secret Agents,' so called. **1866** COOKE *Surry* 255 You think, my dear, that Fenwick, the Yankee spy, blockade-runner, and secret agent, had better get off, eh? **1917** Mc-CUTCHEON *Green Fancy* 256 He is a secret agent from the embassy.

Secretare. [Fr. *secrétaire.*] =SECRETARY 3. {1838–} — **1771** *Md. Hist. Mag.* XIV. 136 If you have moved it thence it may be in the old secretare in the Chappell.

*** Secretary.**

*** 1.** One whose office is to conduct correspondence, keep records, and perform various other duties for a private per-son, corporation, or public body.

Colonial secretaries to legislative bodies performed, in some cases, ad-ministrative functions.

1645 *New Haven Col. Rec.* 224 The secretarie confessed his vnfitnesse for the place by reason of a low voyce, a dull eare & slow apprehensions. **1687** *Mass. H. S. Coll.* 4 Ser. V. 158 A warrant was issued out to require the late Secretary of our Colony to bring down all our books [etc.]. **1775** *Jrnls. Cont. Congress* II. 94 Resolved, . . . That there be a secretary to the Major general, acting in a separate department. **1789** *Ann. 1st Congress* 43 It [should] be the duty of the Secretary of the Senate . . . to give the necessary directions to the different printers, to furnish each member with such paper as he shall choose. **1848** *Ladies' Repository* VIII. 251 He is, evidently, a man of business, and is the secretary of the bench of bishops. **1868** (*title*), Seventh Annual Report of the Secretary of the State Board of Agriculture of the State of Michigan. **1904** *N.Y. Ev. Post* 17 March 7 It was while Mr. Thurber held the office of private secretary to President Cleveland that its title was changed from private secretary to secretary to the President. **1923** DUTTON *Shadow on Glass* 71 The secre-tary informed us she had closed [the safe].

*** 2.** An executive officer presiding over a department of state. +**a.** An officer responsible to Congress under the Ar-ticles of Confederation. Also in official titles.

1778 *Jrnls. Cont. Congress* X. 153 Resolved, That a proper person be ap-pointed to act as secretary of ordnance, and paymaster to the Board of War and Ordnance. **1778** J. ADAMS *Familiar Lett.* 353 The new secretary at war makes a vast parade of the number of men in their service by land and sea. **1781** *Jrnls. Cont. Congress* XIX. 43 Resolved, That an office be forthwith established for the Department of Foreign Affairs . . . ; That there shall be a secretary . . . to be stiled 'Secretary for foreign affairs.' **1789** *Ann. 1st Congress* 51 Resolved, That the Secretary of Foreign Affairs under the former Congress be requested to peruse the said convention.

+**b.** In the official names of certain cabinet members under the Constitution.

See also HOME SECRETARY, SECRETARY OF STATE 1.

1789 *Ann. 1st Congress* 71 Whenever the Secretary of the Treasury shall be removed from office by the President of the United States, . . . the assistant shall . . . have the charge and custody of the records. **1789** Sec-retary of War [see NORTHWESTERN *a.* 1]. **1798** *Ann. 5th Congress* 584 Resolved, That this bill . . . [be entitled] 'An act to extend the privilege of franking letters and packets to the Secretary of the Navy.' **1849** *Whig Almanac 1850* 22/1 The head . . . , the Secretary of the Interior, is ap-pointed in the same manner as other heads of departments. **1861** Secre-tary of the Treasury [see COUPON BOND]. **1864** *Wkly. New Mexican* 10 June 2/3 A whisper went through the church, 'That's the wife of the Secretary of War.' **1868** HAWTHORNE *Notebooks* I. 84 When I asked him whether it would be well to make a naval officer Secretary of the Navy, he said, 'God forbid.' **1886** ALTON *Among Law-Makers* 69 The Secretary of the Interior . . . is a sort of jack-of-all-trades. **1889** *Stat. at Large* XXV. 659 The Department of Agriculture, shall be an Executive Department, under the supervision and control of a Secretary of Agriculture. **1900** *Congress. Rec.* 20 Feb. 1992 Let that go to the Secretary of Agriculture. **1903** Secretary of Commerce [see COMMERCE]. **1913** *Statutes at Large* XXXVII. 1. 736 There is hereby created an executive department in the Government to be called the Department of Labor, with a Secretary of Labor.

+**c.** Ellipt. or as title in sense 2 b.

1795 HAMILTON *Works* VII. 108 In this respect the Comptroller is a check upon the Secretary. **1865** *Nation* I. 706 Secretary Seward has ad-vised the North Carolinians, . . . to ratify the Constitutional Amend-ment. **1869** in Leavitt *Our Money Wars* 109 The Secretary began issuing certificates simultaneously with the issue of Greenbacks. **1894** *Harper's Mag.* April 804/1 Secretary Carlisle issued a circular offering $50,000,000 ten-year five-per-cent. bonds for public subscription.

+**d.** A secretary for a territory of the United States.

1807 *Ann. 10th Congress* 1 Sess. 2813 Each of the Secretaries of the Mississippi, Indiana, Louisiana, and Michigan Territories, appointed under the authority of the United States [shall] be entitled to the annual sum of one thousand dollars. **1880** *Cimarron News & Press* 17 June 2/2 W. G. Ritch has been confirmed by the senate as secretary of the ter-ritory.

3. A writing desk or case with conveniences for arranging papers. {1833–}

1815 [see BUREAU 1]. **1836** GILMAN *Recoll.* (1838) 251 In one room was an oldfashioned secretary, towering to the ceiling, where a few worm-eaten books leaned against each other. **1877** *Harper's Mag.* April 682/1 The money was kept in a secretary. **1910** C. HARRIS *Eve's Husband* 138 He was seated at an old 'secretary' in the parlor, . . . his hands busy sorting letters.

+**Secretary bookcase.** (See quotation.) — **1855** *Chicago W. Times* 18 Oct. 1/7 A secretary book case, of very handsome black walnut, . . . has six large drawers, . . . writing desk, etc.

+**Secretary of Congress.** Under the Articles of Confederation, the officer who acted as secretary to the Continental Congress. — **1778** *Jrnls. Cont. Congress* XI. 611 Resolved, . . . that the Committee of Commerce, the Marine Committee, the Committee of Treasury, Board of War and Ordnance, and secretary of Congress, be authorized to increase the salary of their clerks. **1785** *Ib.* XXIX. 629 [It was moved that] the Secy. of Con-gress be directed to write the Executives of the several States informing them that [etc.]. **1789** *Ann. 1st Congress* 34 The committee appointed the 13th of April to confer with a committee of the House of Representatives, upon the future disposition of the papers in the office of the late Secretary of Congress, made a report.

Secretary of State. {1620–}

+**1.** A cabinet officer of the United States government in charge of all foreign affairs.

1789 *Ann. 1st Congress* 90, I likewise nominate Thomas Jefferson, for Secretary of State. **1795** *Ann. 3d Congress* 1299 The Secretary of State . . . has had an official communication of a Decree rendered by the National Assembly of France. **1846** POLK *Diary* (1929) 62 Forty or fifty persons . . . called; among them the Russian Minister, Secretary of State and the Secretary of the Navy and several members of Congress. **1925** BRYAN *Memoirs* 176, I next name him after I became Secretary of State.

+**2.** An officer of a state government whose chief duty is the making and keeping of records.

1803 *Mass. Register* 35 John Avery, Secretary of State.—Office, Floor of the New State-House. **1837** MARTINEAU *Society* III. 323 Pennsylvania. 1832 and 1833. Receipts. . . . Fees, Secretary of State's office, [$]728.33. **1845** in *Tall Tales of S.W.* (1930) 25 Judge Douglass, of Illinois, . . . soon made himself District Attorney, member of the Legislature, Register of the U.S. Land office, Secretary of State. **1911** *Okla. Session Laws* 3 Legisl. 236 It shall be the duty of the appellants to serve notice upon the Secretary of State, in writing, of such an appeal.

Secretary type. *Printing.* A black-letter type imitating handwriting. {1877} — **1845** *Xenia Torch-Light* 23 Oct. 3/5 Having lately procured a new font of Secretary Type, we are prepared to print all kinds of Blanks.

Secret service. Any service rendered the government that may not be divulged {1710– (Addison *Lett.* 212)}; +a branch of government employment formally organized in the Treasury Department in 1864–5. Also attrib.

1776 *Jrnls. Cont. Congress* VI. 985 That the Secret Committee take proper and effectual measures to procure a quantity of hard money . . . for the purpose of secret services. **1846** *Xenia Torch-Light* 30 April 2 The President refused to communicate the manner in which the secret service fund had been expended under the administration of John Tyler. **1868** L. C. BAKER *Hist. U.S. Secret Service* 45 General Walbridge then said to me, 'Baker, you are the man of all others to go into this secret service.' **1880** LAMPHERE *U.S. Govt.* 66/2 The Secret Service Division sprung from an annual appropriation made for the prevention and punishment of counterfeiting. **1904** *N.Y. Ev. Post* 8 Nov. 1 In the private car with the President was Secretary Loeb, several White House servants, and a number of secret service men.

Secret society. A society in which the members are sworn to keep secret certain specified features of the society. {1829–} Also attrib. (Cf. GREEK-LETTER SOCIETY.) — **1851** HALL *College Words* 129 At Dartmouth College, the electioneering for members of the secret societies was formerly called *fishing*. **1865** *Atlantic Mo.* March 380/2 If anything could have created secret societies, it would have been the Fugitive-Slave-Law excitement. **1876** HABBERTON *Jericho Road* 94 Some of the most determined horse-owners in each county formed secret societies. **1880** INGHAM *Digging Gold* 231 Cities in the Black Hills . . . erected churches, schools and secret society buildings of various sorts. **1907** *St. Nicholas* June 696/1 Don't you think, pet, that you are a little too young to belong to secret societies?

Sectarian school. A church school. {1903} — **1842** MANN *Oration 4 July* 65 [They] have separated their children from the mass, and gathered them into class, and clan, and sectarian schools. **1880** *Cimarron News & Press* 2 Sept. 2/2 Sectarian schools . . . should rely wholly on private and sectarian sources for their support. **1900** *Congress. Rec.* 3 Feb. 1471/2 All appreciate the good that sectarian schools have done in these reservations.

*Sectary. A religious sect. Obs. {1643, 1651; obs. rare} — **1750** GIST *Journals* 38, I have no Design or Intention to give Offence to any particular Sectary or Religion. **1764** HUTCHINSON *Hist. Mass.* I. 431 What they called a sectary sprang up in the Massachusetts Colony. **1783** *Maryland Jrnl.* 24 Oct. (Th.), Perhaps you may have in view the Whirlers, a sectary lately broke out to the Eastward, and to which one of your erring saints became a convert.

*Section.

+**1.** In the public-land survey, an area of land, almost always one mile square, constituting a division of a township; 640 acres.

See also FRACTIONAL, HALF, QUARTER, SCHOOL SECTION.

1785 *Jrnls. Cont. Congress* XXVIII. 209 The plats of the townships . . . shall be marked by subdivisions into sections of 1 mile square. **1796** *Stat. at Large* I. 466 One half of the said townships, . . . shall be subdivided into sections, containing, as nearly as may be, six hundred and forty acres each. **1809** CUMING *Western Tour* 197 This Crouse is a wealthy man, having . . . a farm of two sections, containing thirteen hundred acres. **1836** J. HALL *Statistics of West* 169 All the lands within each district, are . . . divided into *townships* of six miles square, and each of these [is] subdivided into thirty six *sections* of one mile square, containing six hundred and forty acres each. **1849** CHAMBERLAIN *Ind. Gazetteer* 420 North of Eel river are about 40 sections of barrens intermixed with small prairies. **1890** *Stock Grower & Farmer* 8 March 5/3 The intervening sections of the Atlantic and Pacific railroad land grant [in Ariz.] are owned by the cattle men and are not fenced. **1924** CROY *R.F.D. No. 3* 3 He had only one

hundred and twenty acres of land, while most of the farmers had a quarter, or a half section, even a section.

+**b.** Often followed by a number used to describe it in the land survey.

1837 W. JENKINS *Ohio Gaz.* 119 Its territory consists of sections 5, 6, 7 [etc.], in township 11, and range 21. **1865** *Ore. State Jrnl.* 18 Nov. 3/2 The undivided half of 38 acres situated in Township 18 and in Section 12, Lane County Oregon. **1903** *Indian Laws & Tr.* III. 8 Section sixteen shall become a part of the reservation heretofore set apart for the use and occupancy of the Torros band.

+**2. a.** A distinct part of the country; a territory set apart by geographical, economic, or cultural lines. **b.** In relatively small areas, as in a town or county: A quarter or district.

'Since the French Revolution this word has been much used here instead of *part, quarter, &c.*' (Pickering).

1814 M. CAREY *Olive Branch* 186 To sow discord, jealousy and hostility between the different sections of the union, was the first and grand step in their career. **1838** *U.S. Mag.* IV. 56/2 Mr. Thompson, of S.C., especially called attention to . . . [the fact] that that view of it originated with the section of country . . . represented by that gentleman [from Mass.]. **1842** M. CRAWFORD *Journal* 6 The country along the river particularly on the Ohio side is a beautiful and apparently level and rich section. **1865** COX *8 Yrs. in Congress* 21 Crittenden and himself [Douglas] were championing the interests of all sections, and striving to avert in time the calamities which were pressed by extremists, North and South. **1881** *Rep. Indian Affairs* 7 In this section . . . the coal beds were discovered. **1910** FRANCK *Vagabond Journey* 478 They dogged my footsteps through shrieking slum sections, down alleyways reeking with refuse.

+**3.** *Railroad.* **a.** A division of a sleeping car constituting an upper and lower berth, or, when these are not made up, two double seats facing each other.

1866 [see BERTH 2 b (2)]. **1878** JACKSON *Travel at Home* 28 Our first anxiety as to whether we should each get a 'section' was soon merged in our second. **1895** ROBINSON *Men Born Equal* 372 The porter finished our section. **1910** RAINE *B. O'Connor* 11 Down the aisle to the vacant section opposite her [went] a procession whose tail was composed of protesting trainmen.

+**b.** One of two or more trains running on the same schedule.

1872 *Newton Kansan* 3 Oct. 3/2 The caboose and the next three cars to it of the 1st section was badly smashed up.

+**c.** A part of the right of way under the care of a section gang (q.v.).

1883 SWEET & KNOX *Through Texas* 121 He superintended the hands working in that section. **1890** *Stock Grower & Farmer* 18 Jan. 5/2 Hines was a poor Irishman who . . . formerly worked on a section for the Southern Pacific company.

4. attrib. +**a.** In sense 3 c with *boss, foreman, man,* etc.

1872 HUNTINGTON *Road-Master's Asst.* p. iii, The enormous expense of track repairs . . . may be greatly reduced by a reform in the every-day practice of the track-layer and section-master. *Ib.* 116 Section-men are passing over the road with a hand-car, going to or from work. **1883** SWEET & KNOX *Through Texas* 121 Mr. O'Lafferty was section boss of No. ——. **1883** *Wheelman* I. 329 Having proved himself faithful and competent, he was assigned to the position of section foreman. **1891** C. ROBERTS *Adrift Amer.* 71 Section work is track repairing.

+**b.** In sense 1 with *boundary, map.*

1882 *Nation* 14 Sept. 220/2 The section map . . . indicates that a portion of this tract had in 1880 from 6 to 11 inhabitants to the square mile. **1902** WHITE *Blazed Trail* 114 Officials had run careless lines through the country along the section-boundaries.

Sectional, *a.* {1816–}

+**1.** Of feelings, actions, etc.: Belonging to, or springing from, the people of a certain section. {1886–}

1806 *Ann. 9th Congress* 1 Sess. 1042 Let a narrow, selfish, local, sectional policy prevail, and struggles will commence. **1830** *Congress. Deb.* 24 Feb. 194/2 Averse as the democracy of the East is to slavery, . . . [they] never will join, in the sectional tirade against the South, as 'black States.' **1842** *Whig Almanac 1843* 27/2 In the debate which ensued upon the revision of the Tariff, all these sectional jealousies were sedulously inflamed. **1852** STOWE *Uncle Tom* xviii, Let us for a while lay aside our sectional prejudices, and come out to dinner. **1873** *Republic* I. 48 Sectional sentiment evidently is not yet . . . dead. **1922** TARKINGTON *Gentle Julia* 256 A sectional rancour seemed all at once to affect the young man.

+**2.** Of an issue or question: That divides one section from another.

1856 *Democratic Conv. Proc.* 25 We reiterate . . . the well considered declarations of former Conventions upon the sectional issue of Domestic Slavery. **1881** BUEL *Border Outlaws* 96 In the early part of the great sectional conflict, her devoted husband was sacrificed. **1900** *Congress. Rec.* 25 Jan. 1172/1 We ought to be done with fighting these old and sectional questions.

3. Made up of sections that fit together.

1862 *Harper's Mag.* Aug. 321/2 We come to one of the most important adjuncts of a mercantile marine—the dry, or sectional dock. **1876** KNIGHT

2086/2 *Sectional Steam-boiler*, . . . one built up of portions secured together in such a way that the size may be increased by addition of sections. **1907** 'O. HENRY' *Roads of Destiny* 74 A word from me was more to them than a whole deckle-edged library from East Aurora in sectional bookcases was from anybody else.

+Sectional feeling. A feeling aroused among people of a certain section through a consciousness of differences between their own interests and the interests of people in other sections. — **1816** *Ann. 14th Congress* 2 Sess. 359 There is much cause to fear that in such a state of things, sectional feelings would prevail over principles of justice. **1836** J. HALL *Statistics of West* 206 In no portion of the Union is there more of a *national*, and less of a *sectional* feeling, than in the west. **1866** *Appletons' Ann. Cycl.* 451/1 He congratulated the people that . . . the country was restored to its former tranquillity, minus slavery and sectional feeling. **1904** *Chicago Ev. Post* 27 Oct. 1 Rivalry for horse show honors between the East and the West has become keen even to the edge bordering upon sectional feeling.

+Sectionalism. Disproportionate confinement of interest to a particular section; sectional feeling or interests. {1886} — **1855** Hambleton *H. A. Wise* 205 That platform [is] the only sure foundation of a national party, and the only bulwark against the uniting and dangerous agitation of sectionalism. **1860** LOWELL *Writings* V. 37 It is idle to talk of sectionalism, abolitionism, and hostility to the laws. **1872** *Harper's Mag.* Jan. 230/1 Her protectors . . . had only that weak sentiment of sectionalism which prevailed in the Northern Border States. **1898** *Kansas City Star* 20 Dec. 12/1 Judge Emory Spear introduced the President, who spoke of the [Civil] war and its results in wiping out sectionalism.

+Sectionalist. One who has sectional feeling. — **1858** W. P. SMITH *Bk. Railway Celebrations* 258 Whatever disunionists or sectionalists may do or say—the more they try to tear us apart, the more the iron road and lightning wire must bind us together. **1862** in Dicey 6 *Mos. Federal States* II. 86 There were abolition fanatics there [in the North], it was true—sectionalists, traitors, brothers of Southern secessionists.

Sectionalize, *v.* {1854-} +*tr.* To divide along sectional lines. Also *ppl. a.* — **1871** *Congress. Globe* 3 April 420/2 The South regarded the government as sectionalized in the election of President Lincoln. **1879** *Appletons' Ann. Cycl.* 111/1 We denounce and condemn the efforts of both the old political parties to create a solid North or a solid South, and thereby sectionalize the country. **1893** *Nation* 13 April 279/2 But so far is it from being true that there had been 'nothing active on the part of the South' in sectionalizing the Union, it would rather seem more correct to say that she had the larger share in the process.

Sectionally, *adv.* From a sectional standpoint. {1869, of the U.S.; 1891} — **1878** *N. Amer. Rev.* March 316 Less than one-third of the country is united almost solidly and sectionally to oppose the restoration of silver money to its former estate.

+Sectional party. A political faction or party devoted primarily to the interests of one section. — **1849** A. MACKAY *Western World* I. 225 Perhaps the most purely sectional party in this country is that of the Nullifiers. a**1850** CALHOUN *Works* I. 308 As a federal government, extending over vast territory, the tendency will be, in the first place, to the formation of sectional parties. **1858** DOUGLAS in Logan *Great Conspiracy* 67, I am opposed to organizing a sectional party, which appeals to . . . Northern passion and prejudice against Southern institutions. **1902** G. C. EGGLESTON *D. South* 314 A strong political party at the North . . . was a strictly sectional party in its composition, having no existence anywhere at the South.

+Section corner. The corner of a surveyed section of land. — **1817** *Niles' Reg.* XII. 97/2 At the distance of every mile, between the township corners, *section* corners are established. **1840** *Knickerb.* XVI. 206 Such ransacking of the woods for section corners, ranges, and base lines! **1873** *Winfield* (Kan.) *Courier* 3 July 3/2 You can even have your lines straightened between section corners when the stones have been knocked down and removed from their original position.

+Section gang. A gang of workmen who take care of a section of railroad track. Also attrib. — **1891** C. ROBERTS *Adrift Amer.* 172, I came to a section-gang at work. **1907** LONDON *Road* 178 That section-gang boss and assistant prepared to meet death. **1909** CALHOUN *Miss Minerva* 66 Did you-all hear 'bout that 'Talian Dago that works on the section gang eating a buzzard?

+Section hand. A workman on a section gang. — **1873** *Newton Kansan* 27 Feb. 3/2 A drunken section hand . . . laid down upon the railroad track to take a nap. **1876** CROFUTT *Trans-continental Tourist* 64 From this city west the railroad laborers—section hands—are all Chinamen. **1911** JENKS & LAUCK *Immigration Problem* 227 The road masters and section foremen prefer the Japanese as section hands. **1925** TILGHMAN *Dugout* 97 The Santa Fe railroad employed many Mexicans as section hands and as laborers about the shops.

Section house. {1856-} +A house or building serving as living quarters or headquarters of a section gang. — **1878** BEADLE *Western Wilds* 51 A section house by the roadside . . . mark[s] the site where sales to the amount of millions were made in two months. **1903** *N.Y. Ev. Post* 29 Aug., Crowbars and tools were identified as having been taken from the railroad section house.

+Sectionize, *v.* {1876-} *tr.* To divide land off into several portions or sections, to be sold or allocated separately to settlers or members of an Indian tribe. Also absol. and as *vbl. n.* — **1828** *Laws of Texas* Nov. (B.), So much of the vacant lands of the republic [of Mexico] shall be surveyed and sectionized, as will be sufficient to satisfy all claims. **1871** *Rep. Indian Affairs* (1872) 185 [Various tribes] were induced either to sectionize, or

in some way to admit white settlers. **1873** BEADLE *Undevel. West* 399 He is the only Choctaw in the district who is in favor of sectionizing and admitting white immigration.

Section line. A line running between two sections. {1828, in Australia} Also attrib. — **1872** *Newton Kansan* 12 Sept. 2/4 The farmers . . . are leaving space for a road along the section lines. **1873** *Winfield* (Kan.) *Courier* 11 Jan. 3/3 Section line roads of Lucius Hubbard and others was laid over under the rule. **1902** HULBERT *Forest Neighbors* 116 That same land-looker came pacing down a section line and halted squarely in front of him. **1906** *Indian Laws & Tr.* III. 178 In the Choctaw, Chickasaw, and Seminole Nations public highways or roads . . . may be established on all section lines.

Securityship. The condition of standing security for another person. — **1797** *Steele P.* I. 149 He has engaged in it purely to exculpate him from his Security Ship for his brothers. **1854** BENTON *30 Years' View* I. 117/2 [Nathaniel Macon] was opposed to securityships, and held that no man ought to be entangled in the affairs of another.

Sedan.

1. A covered chair for carrying one person, borne on two poles by two men. {1635-} Also *sedan chair*. {1750-}

a**1649** WINTHROP *Hist.* II. 264 [He] presented the governour with a sedan, which (as he said) was sent by the viceroy of Mexico to his sister. **1715** SEWALL *Diary* III. 47 The Gov[erno]r . . . was carried from Mr. Dudley's to the Town-House in Cous. Dummer's Sedan. **1790** MACLAY *Deb. Senate* 220 Johnson was brought in a sedan. a**1821** BIDDLE *Autobiog.* 213, I had Dr. Franklin's sedan chair brought. **1893** *Harper's Mag.* March 600, 'I had thought of asking the Senator to come along with us.' . . . 'In a sedan-chair?'

+2. An automobile having both the front and back seats enclosed in the same compartment.

1909 WEBSTER opp. p. 156 (*caption*). **1915** *Lit. Digest* 21 Aug. (*cover advt.*), A touring car when the windows are down. . . . With the windows raised, a luxurious sedan. **1922** *Short Stories* Feb. 98/1 The sedan had been equipped with an exhaust foot warmer or heater.

*****Sedge.**

*****1. a.** Any grasslike plant of the family Cyperaceae, esp. one of the genus *Carex*. **b.** The sweet flag, *Acorus calamus*. **c.** The yellow iris, *Iris pseudacorus*.

Sedge may possibly sometimes be short for BROOM SEDGE: (cf. SEDGE FIELD).

1613 PURCHAS *Pilgrimage* 635 There is [in Virginia] . . . flax surpassing ours in growth and goodnesse, exceeded by a new-found stuffe of a certain sedge or water-flagge. **1731** *Southampton Rec.* III. 2 Samuel Cooper and Samuel Bishop [are allowed] to fetch theire sedge off. **1791** W. BARTRAM *Travels* 68, Low salt plains . . . produce Barilla, Sedge, Rushes, &c. **1805** PARKINSON *Tour* 53 The whole of the different fields were covered with either the stalks of weeds, corn-stalks, or what is called sedge—something like spear-grass upon the poor limestone in England. **1805** LEWIS in *L. & Clark Exped.* II. (1904) 272 The high lands are thin meagre soil covered with dry low sedge. **1839** in *Mich. Agric. Soc. Trans.* VI. 264 Most of the swamps and marshes are covered with a luxuriant growth of sedge, tamarack, and cranberry vines. **1849** [see CUT-GRASS]. **1898** A. M. DAVIDSON *Calif. Plants* 170 What is commonly called the tule, in California, is really a sedge, so is the Papyrus of our gardens. **1907** *St. Nicholas* Aug. 939/1 The *Pogonia, Arethusa*, and *Limodorum* groups grow along grassy lake shores and among the shimmering sedges of our marshes in June.

*****2.** With defining words.

Only a selection is given. See also BROOM SEDGE, FOX SEDGE.

1814 BIGELOW *Florula Bostoniensis* 218 *Carex crinita*. Chaffy Sedge. . . . A tall, elegant grass, remarkable for its long, pendulous, bristly spikes. **1843** TORREY *Flora N.Y.* II. 379 *Carex trisperma*. Three-seeded Sedge. . . . Sphagnous swamps, and wet mountain woods. *Ib.* 410 *Carex eburnea*. Bristle-leaved White Sedge. . . . A delicate little species, nearly allied to *C. alba* of Europe but quite distinct.

3. Attrib. with *flat, island, meadow, pond*.

1711 *Duxbury Rec.* 211 All their salt and sedge Islands, and sedge flats . . . should next be laid out as followeth. **1747** in *Amer. Sp.* XV. 390/1 The Land . . . is near to the westermost end of sedge pond. **1809** *Huntington Rec.* III. 247, I Moses Scudder . . . have granted bargained and sold . . . a certain piece of salt or sedge meadow.

*****Sedge boat.** +A boat for transporting sedge. — **1839** *Knickerb.* XIII. 503 Sedge-boats could pass with their sails set. **1843** *Ib.* XXII. 33 Here two negro boatmen . . . had consented to . . . row us out in their new sedge-boat.

Sedge-field. *quasi-adj.* +Feeding on wornout ground. Also fig. (Cf. BROOM SEDGE 1, quots. 1819, 1860.) — **1867** HARRIS *Sut Lovingood* 30, I'se allers intu sum trap whut wudn't ketch a saidge-field sheep. **1905** N. DAVIS *Northerner* 42 That sort of talk is what Hugh calls 'sedge-field Democracy.'

Sedge grass. =SEDGE 1. {1865} Also attrib. — **1749** ELIOT *Field-Husb.* ii. 21 For sundry Vessels have been in these Towns from other parts, to load with sedge-grass. **1783** *Huntington Rec.* III. 109 No Person within the Township of Huntington . . . should go upon the Marshes . . . to cut any sedge grass before the first Day of September. **1858** *Texas Almanac 1859* 126 He found that the hog-wallow prairie and the rank, coarse sedge grass, common in that part of the State, did not suit sheep. **1891** *Century Mag.* Jan. 425, I found a sedge-grass field of about twenty acres. **1910** *Nation* June 345/2 Last year's thick sedge grass reaches to the knees.

+Sedge ground. Ground covered with sedge. — **1667** *Plymouth Rec.* I. 95 Graunted unto James Clarke a certaine . . . p[ar]te of the pond or sedge ground. **1740** *Mayflower Descendant* XI. 5 Richard Mayo & Rebecca Mayo . . . [sold] that lot of Medow or sedge ground lying in Eastham. **1910** C. HARRIS *Eve's Husband* 30 That look of relief and timid animation, like signs of early spring upon the poor brown sedge-ground of an old field.

+Sedge hen. The clapper rail, *Rallus longirostris crepitans.* — **1888** TRUMBULL *Names of Birds* 127 At Pocomoke City, Md., and at Eastville, Va., Sedge-Hen. **1890** *St. Nicholas* June 638/1 We got forty-two sedge-hens, on a high tide. **1917** *Birds of Amer.* I. 204.

Sedition act, law. *spec.* +A law of July 14, 1798, passed by the Federalist-controlled Congress to suppress opposition to the government. (See also ALIEN 2.) — **1800** *Aurora* (Phila.) 19 May (Th.), He replied that he was not at liberty to say—we had a sedition law—which will soon be done away. **1801** HAMILTON *Works* VII. 193 As to the sedition law, we refer you to the debates in Congress. **1802** *Ann. 7th Congress* 1 Sess. 803 We have had a Sedition act, calculated to secure the conduct of the Executive from free and full investigation. **1814** J. ADAMS *Works* VI. 518 If these things are so in Virginia, . . . where the sedition act, the gag law, was so unpopular; where can we look . . . [for] a candid freedom of the press?

∗ See, *v.*

+1. *tr.* In poker, to meet or accept (an amount wagered) by staking a similar amount. {1599–, of other games} Also transf.

1842 *Picayune* 11 Jan. 1/6, I see your five thousand, and bet you twenty thousand dollars more. **1859** *Harper's Mag.* Sept. 572/2, I'll make my blind good and see your *Simon*, and go ten better. **1887** KELLER *Draw Poker* 24 If any player has deposited any amount in the pool and does not wish to 'see' the raise of any subsequent player, he may retire from the game. **1910** *N.Y. Ev. Post* 28 Feb. (Th.), Argentina has to see the Brazilian navy and go it one or two better.

2. *To see about* {1869–}, (see quot. 1848).

1848 BARTLETT 289 *To See About*, to attend to; to consider. **1858** HAWTHORNE *Fr. & It. Note-Books* (1872) I. 40 J—— and I then went to the railway-station to see about our luggage.

3. *Not to see it*, to be unable to see the propriety, rightness, etc., in (a situation, policy, etc.). *colloq.*

1865 *Ill. Agric. Soc. Trans.* VI. 169 When I look at the collector of the port of New York's tables of the importation of foreign wool, I, in the slang of the day, 'don't see it.' **1866** LOWELL *Biglow P.* 2 Ser. p. xlvi, 'I don't see it' was the popular slang a year or two ago, and seemed to spring from the soil; but no, it is in Cibber's 'Careless Husband.' **1867** CRAWFORD *Mosby* 263 When handed his musket, he refused to take it, stating his reasons to the officer commanding the company, and to General Barton. They 'couldn't see it,' but marched him back to the Soldier's Home.

+4. To bribe (persons) with a certain amount.

1869 BARNUM *Struggles* 692 The New York Legislature . . . [had] refused us a charter unless I would 'see' the 'ring' a thousand dollars' worth, which I declined. **1873** 'MARK TWAIN' & WARNER *Gilded Age* 141 'It will take a good deal of money to start the enterprise,' remarked Mr. Bolton, who knew very well what 'seeing' a Pennsylvania legislature meant. **1888** BRYCE *Amer. Commonw.* I. i. xv. 213 Professional 'lobbyists' . . . make it their business to 'see' members and procure, by persuasion, importunity, or the use of inducements, the passing of bills . . . which involve gain to their promoters. **1906** *N.Y. Ev. Post* 8 Jan. 7 When a corporation desires legislation, that is, legislation that requires that legislators should be 'seen,' it sends its bill to Albany.

+5. To understand (a person). *colloq.*

1873 BEADLE *Undevel. West* 369 'Marshal's got a good thing, though.' 'I *see* you; best place to make money in the United States.'

Seeboy. (See STABOY.)

+Seecatch. [Russ. *sekach.*] An adult male fur seal. {1896} — **1881** H. W. ELLIOTT *Rep. Seal Isl. Alaska* 42 The 'see-catchie' which have held the harems from the beginning to the end of the season, leave for the water. **1884** GOODE, etc. *Fisheries* I. 77 One old 'See-catch' was pointed out to me . . . as an animal that was long known to the natives as a regular visitor.

∗ Seed.

+1. Gunpowder. *humorous. Obs.*

1825 NEAL *Bro. Jonathan* II. 73 Halloo; you! major!—where's the seed?

+2. (See quot. 1851.) *slang. Obs.*

1849 *Yale Tomahawk* 27 Nov., But we are 'seeds' whose rowdy deeds Make up the drunken tale. **1851** HALL *College Words* 266 Seed. In Yale College this word is used to designate what is understood by the common cant terms, 'a youth'; 'case'; 'bird.' **1852** *Yale Tomahawk* May (Hall), Each one a bold seed, well fit for the deed.

3. (See quot. 1881.) {1721–}

1881 INGERSOLL *Oyster-Industry* 248 *Seed*, infant or young oysters, suitable or intended for transplanted growth in artificial beds. **1887** GOODE, etc. *Fisheries* v. II. 524 The seed used is gathered . . . sometimes by tonging in deep water, where oysters lie on the bottom singly or nearly so. **1891** *Scribner's Mag.* Oct. 472/1 The oysterman . . . loads his vessel with 'seed.'

4. *In the seed*, +of cotton, not ginned.

1829 A. SHERWOOD *Gaz. Georgia* (ed. 2) 259 Suppose, again, that government should erect at every man's door a Tariff Cotton Gin, which should give every man as much ginned cotton as he delivered in the seed. **1833** in Bassett *Plantation Overseer* 54 You wanted to now how much coten you had in the seede.

5. *Old seed*, += HAYSEED 3. *jocular.*

1887 GEORGE *40 Yrs. on Rail* 157 'Here old seed, get into this hack,' said one driver. **1897** GARLAND *J. Edwards* 185 Why don't you old seeds quit quarrelin' an' go to fightin'?

∗ 6. *attrib.* and *comb.* **a.** Designating fine, specially selected wheat, maize, etc., preserved for raising a new crop.

See also SEED CANE, SEED CORN, etc.

1806 *Balance* V. 296/2 This difference arises solely from my cleaning my seed-wheat. **1809** A. HENRY *Travels* 233, I distributed seed-maize among the Indians here, which they planted accordingly. **1839** *Farmers' Mo. Visitor* I. 68/1 If farmers would *scald* their seed peas, before sowing them, they would not be troubled with the bug. **1852** STANSBURY *Gt. Salt Lake* 125 A pioneer company, consisting of one hundred and forty-three men, . . . agricultural implements and seed-grain, manfully set out in search of a home beyond the Rocky mountains. **1884** *Rep. Comm. Agric.* 309 [Cabbage-bugs] got into my garden and utterly destroyed my . . . mustard, seed-turnips, and every other cruciform plant. **1903** PRINGLE *Rice Planter* 12, I keep the key to the seed-rice loft, though Marcus has all the others.

∗ b. Designating agricultural implements used in sowing and cleaning seed.

See also SEED DRILL, -SOWER.

1819 *Plough Boy* I. 123 Bennet's seed machine for sowing grass seed. **1850** *Rep. Comm. Patents 1849: Agric.* 463 The seed is sown with a seed-barrow or drill. **1859** *Rep. Comm. Patents 1858* I. 373 The combination of the seed-distributor, and clearing-blades, and propelling axle. **1864** *Ohio Agric. Rep.* XVIII. 66 [The] Western Empire Separator and General Seed Cleaner . . . cleans and separates all kinds of grain and seed.

c. Designating the parts of plants that bear or contain the seeds. {1671–}

1839 BUEL *Farmer's Companion* 149 Burying the crown, causes grain to tiller better, that is, to send up more seed-stocks. **1841** HAWTHORNE *Notebooks* (1932) 82 She strings the seed-berries of roses together. **1855** LONGFELLOW *Hiawatha* 245 The only weapon That could wound him, . . . Was the seed-cone of the pine-tree. **1855** *Mich. Agric. Soc. Trans.* VI. 222 Our potato fields will blossom as freely as the rose and bear seed balls as in former years. **1869** *Rep. Comm. Agric. 1868* 204 The orange-colored capsules open, and show the scarlet seed-covers. **1890** HOWELLS *Boy's Town* 54 The boys gathered the little cheeses, as they called the seed-buttons which formed when the flowers dropped off.

7. In special combinations.

Seed Baptist, (see quotation and cf. TWO-SEED BAPTIST); *s. cigar*, a cigar made of or wrapped with seed-leaf tobacco; *s. cooky*, a cooky flavored with caraway seed; *s. dealer*, one who deals in seeds; *s.-eater*, a bird that eats seeds; *s. forest*, (see quotation); *seed-oil mill*, a mill in which oil is pressed from cotton seed; *s. ore*, ore found in the form of grains; *s. room*, a room for seed; *s. spot*, (see quotation).

1839 CASWELL *America* 314 A miserable sect of Seed Baptists, or Snake Baptists, is said to exist in the west, who carry the Calvinistic system to a tremendous length. They hold that all mankind are divided into two classes, the seed of the woman and the seed of the serpent. The seed of the woman are necessarily saved, and the seed of the serpent necessarily lost. **1892** *York County Hist. Rev.* 47 J. S. Overbaugh & Co., manufacturers of Fine Seed and Havana Cigars. **1861** STOWE *Pearl Orr's Isl.* I. 26 She gave it nuthin but these 'ere little seed cookies. **1895** *Dept. Agric. Yrbk. 1894* 420 Seed dealers should treat all cereals offered for sale. **1884** BURROUGHS in *Century Mag.* Dec. 220/1 Even the slate-colored snowbird, a seed-eater, comes and nibbles. **1905** *Forestry Bureau Bul.* No. 61, 20 Seed forest, a forest composed wholly or mainly of trees grown from seed. **1881** *Harper's Mag.* Dec. 726/2 There are now fifty-nine seed-oil mills in the South. **1796** MORSE *Univ. Geog.* I. 683 In the cavities between [large rocks of iron ore], lie an ochre and seed ore. **1868** *Mich. Agric. Rep.* VII. 21 The tool-room for the Horticultural Department has been enlarged, . . . an office and seed-room provided. **1901** *Forestry Bureau Bul.* No. 61, 20 Seed-spot, a small area, usually in a burn or in an opening in the forest, which is sown with tree seed.

Seed bag. 1. A bag in which seed is kept. **2.** (See quot. 1864.) — **(1)** **1867** HARRIS *Sut Lovingood* 92 Vinegar jugs, seed bags, yarb bunches, . . . all mix'd dam promiskusly. **1883** 'S. BONNER' *Dialect Tales* 86 'That ain't the pint at all,' says Sister Sweet, 'whether 'twas carpet-rags, or seed-bags, or satin robes for the rich.' **(2)** **1864** *Harper's Mag.* Dec. 55/2 The seed-bag is a simple leather bag containing dry flax-seed, which, . . . when in position rapidly swells so as to shut the whole orifice and leave the well of oil undisturbed by superincumbent water. **1883** *Century Mag.* July 330/1 Then the 'tubing,' two inches in diameter, is put in, and a 'seed-bag' is forced down between it and the casing. **1890** *Harper's Mag.* Oct. 727/2 He went to Tarentum, witnessed the methods of boring for salt, and the exclusion by 'seed bags' of fresh water and petroleum.

Seed bed. {1660–} *S.* A small, specially prepared plot or area in which sweet potatoes are placed to produce draws. — **1837** WILLIAMS *Florida* 111 The potato is planted in seed beds.

Seedbox. {1733–} +A North American plant (*Ludwigia alternifolia*) having a boxlike seed vessel. — **1817–8** EATON *Botany* (1822) 341 *Lud-*

wigia alternifolia, seed box. . . . Damp. **1843** TORREY *Flora N.Y.* I. 237. **1893** *Amer. Folk-Lore* VI. 142 Seed-box. West Va.

Seedcake.* **1. A sweetened cake flavored with caraway seed. +**2.** =COTTONSEED(-OIL) CAKE. — **(1) 1805** *Pocumtuc Housewife* (1906) 29 Gingerbread, seedcakes and doughnuts will suffice for daily needs. **1837** in Kittredge *Old Farmer* (1904) 93 Wheat loaves, gingerbread, hot buns and seed-cakes—these are all very clever. **1881** *Century Mag.* Nov. 138/1 Go to buy seed-cakes at the cart: baker wont give no tick. **1905** *N.Y. Ev. Post* 4 Aug. 7 Angel cake, sponge cake, and ice-cream cake have conspired to relegate the seed cake to practical oblivion. **(2) 1881** *Harper's Mag.* Oct. 726/2 The mass of kernels left is made into seed-cake, a most desirable food for stock.

+**Seed cane.** (See quot. 1892.) — **1829** SHERWOOD *Gaz. Georgia* (ed. 2) 255 The stacks or banks in which seed cane is preserved during winter, are called mattresses. **1833** SILLIMAN *Man. Sugar Cane* 11 This early attention is given to the saving of seed on account of the injury occasioned to Seed Cane by frost. **1853** *Harper's Mag.* Nov. 756/2 The 'seed-cane' once deposited in its place, it is covered with earth from three to four inches deep. **1892** *Mod. Lang. Notes* Nov. 393 *Seed cane*—the seed or plant cane . . . of the first year's growth.—Also the cane reserved for planting.

***Seed corn.** +Grains of Indian corn for planting. — [**1619** *Va. House of Burgesses* 17 Yet are wee at this tyme very much unprovided of any good seed-corn.] **1635** *Mass. Bay Rec.* I. 142 Noe Indean corne (except seede corne) shalbe sold for above vi *s* per bushell. **1759** in Commons, etc. *Doc. Hist.* I. 115 Nor should there be less care observed in selecting the Seed corn from the crib. **1831** HOLLEY *Texas* (1833) 103 They were compelled . . . to obtain their seed-corn over land. **1894** *Vt. Agric. Rep.* XIV. 47 Can common seed corn be raised at a profit?

Seed cotton. Unginned cotton. {1835–} — **1797** F. BAILY *Tour* 285 The seed-cotton loses three-fourths of its weight by jenning. **1833** in Bassett *Plantation Overseer* 54 Dear sir I cant give you the amount of your seede coten. **1854** *Harper's Mag.* March 455/2 Each hand picks from two hundred and fifty to three hundred pounds of 'seed cotton' each day. **1889** *Century Mag.* April 914/1 Tom offered to bet the seed cotton in his patch that Bill could fix up something.

Seed cucumber. ?The single-seed cucumber, *Sicyos angulatus*. — **1792** IMLAY *Western Territory* 211 Papaw. This fruit grows upon a tree from twelve to twenty-six feet high. It is in shape more like a seed cucumber than any thing else. It is ripe about midsummer. **1890** WIGGIN *Timothy's Quest* 199 We're goin' to pickle seed cowcumbers to-morrer.

Seed drill. =DRILL *n.*[2] 2. — **1792** *N.Y. State Soc. Arts* I. 86 But some years ago a farmer in Somerset county, in New-Jersey, first introduced a seed-drill of his invention. **1856** *Rep. Comm. Patents 1855: Agric.* 198 The seed-drill, however, has been somewhat extensively used of late [for sowing wheat]. **1884** *Rep. Comm. Agric.* 567 The seed is sown by hand or by seed-drill.

***Seeder.** An implement for sowing seed. {1899–} — **1868** *Iowa State Agric. Soc. Rep. 1867* 226 The seeder can be adjusted in five minutes. **1881** *Rep. Indian Affairs* 400. **1885** *Advance* 12 March, We shall soon be a-field with plow, harrow and seeder, making ready for the wheat and corn.

***Seed-grower.** One who grows plants for their seed. {1824–} — **1859** *Ill. Agric. Soc. Trans.* III. 501 Seed growers are very careful in their selections of roots for seed. **1885** *Amer. Naturalist* XIX. 1041 One head of cross-bred awnless barley was received from Mr. Horsford, a seed-grower in Vermont.

+**Seed hemp.** (See quot. 1862.) — **1765** WASHINGTON *Diaries* I. 213 Began to pull the Seed Hemp—but was not sufficiently ripe. **1862** *Rep. Comm. Patents 1861: Agric.* 114 The male [hemp] is called the blossom-hemp, and the female the seed-hemp.

Seeding machine. (See quot. 1876.) — **1831** *21st Congress 2 Sess.* H. R. Doc. No. 50, 3 Planting, seeding, mowing, and thrashing machines. **1859** *Rep. Comm. Patents 1858* I. 474 Improvement in Seeding Machines. **1862** *Rep. Comm. Patents 1861: Agric.* 646 Straw-cutters, . . . Seeding-machines, . . . Separators, Grain. **1876** KNIGHT 2088/1 *Seeding-machine* . . . an implement for sowing seed. The term, in its general sense, may include machines for planting in hills, drills, or broadcast, but it is confined more usually to machines for distributing seed in drills or broadcast.

Seeding plow. (See quot. 1876.) — **1862** *Rep. Comm. Patents 1861: Agric.* 643 Ploughs, Subsoil, . . . Plough, Seeding. **1876** KNIGHT 2088/2 *Seeding-plow*, a plow with a box, which drops or scatters seed in the furrow or on the fresh-turned earth.

Seed leaf. {1693–} +Broad-leaved tobacco used for cigar wrappers; a variety of tobacco having exceptionally broad leaves. Also attrib. In full *seed-leaf tobacco*. (Cf. BROADLEAF 2.) — **1868** *N.Y. Herald* 1 July 9/4 Considerable activity has prevailed in seedleaf. **1887** *Courier-Journal* 8 Jan. 4/3 The seed-leaf States are a unit for repeal. **1892** *York County Hist. Rev.* 22 Mr. Munchel . . . manufactures from the best and most carefully-selected Havana and American seed-leaf a number of favorite and deservedly popular brands of fine cigars. **1895** *Dept. Agric. Yrbk. 1894* 145 The seed-leaf, or Havana, tobacco is produced in such quantities and such excellence as to give a distinct character to localities in Massachusetts, Connecticut [etc.].

Seedling. A young plant or tree grown from a seed: (see also quot. 1905). {1660–} Also attrib. — **1828** J. Q. ADAMS *Diary* 377 In the southern seedling-bed a few black walnuts and shagbarks are still coming up. **1848** *Rep. Comm. Patents 1847* 196 Fifteen specimens of Vandermark seedling . . . measured over a foot in circumference! **1862** *Rep. Comm. Patents 1861: Agric.* 186 Hovey's Seedling [a strawberry] is very valuable. **1884** *Rep. Comm. Agric.* 371 A small seedling orange infested with Rust-mite was covered with a nail-keg and fumigated. **1905** *Forestry Bureau Bul.* No. 63, 9 In forest description a seedling is understood to mean a tree grown from seed which has not reached a height of 3 feet.

Seedling apple. An apple or apple tree raised from an apple seed; a variety of such apples. — **1843** *Indiana Mag. Hist.* III. 189 Forty-three new seedling apples competed for a premium. **1883** *Harper's Mag.* Dec. 56/1 Our seedling apple, the Highland Beauty. **1916** THOBURN *Stand. Hist. Okla.* I. 262 Seedling apples and peach trees were by no means uncommon.

Seed oats. *pl.* Oats suitable for sowing. {1801–} — **1772** *Md. Hist. Mag.* XIV. 139, I will send yr. seed Oates & some flour next week. **1773** *Ib.* XV. 58 How Came you to feed with seed Oates formerly sent you, be more Carefull. **1874** *Vermont Bd. Agric. Rep.* II. 224 [He] now furnishes seed oats to his neighbor.

Seed-planter. A device for planting seeds. — **1850** [see PLANTER 4]. **1852** *Mich. Agric. Soc. Trans.* III. 30 Best seed planter, for hand or horse power, for hills and drills. **1863** *Rep. Comm. Patents 1861* I. 313 The attachment to hand corn or seed planters of a tube [etc.].

Seed potato. An Irish or sweet potato selected for planting. {1744– (Ellis *Mod. Husb.* I. 104)} — **1742** *N.H. Probate Rec.* III. 115, I Give to my Dear and Loving Wife . . . Ground . . . for to plant one bushel of Seed pertators. **1787** WASHINGTON *Diaries* III. 192 Examined the Seed Potatoes . . . and found them all rotten. **1854** *Fla. Plantation Rec.* 554/2 2 banks of seed potatoes. **1874** *Vermont Bd. Agric. Rep.* II. 227 [Mr. Foster] selects seed potatoes as particularly as corn.

***Seedsman.** A dealer in seeds. {1691–} — **1789** *Boston Directory* 199 Spriggs Thomas, gardner and seedsman. **1895** *Dept. Agric. Yrbk. 1894* 392 One of the most common practices of a certain class of seedsmen is to give seed a high-sounding name.

Seed-sower. A mechanical implement for sowing seed. — **1850** *Rep. Comm. Patents 1849: Agric.* 113 Their seed-sowers and grain-crushers . . . do much to expedite the labors of the farm. **1874** *Vermont Bd. Agric. Rep.* II. 236 Sow seed with a seed sower at the rate of four pounds per acre. *Ib.* 239, I never could regulate a seed sower so as to distribute beet seed evenly.

+**Seed store.** A store or shop where seeds are sold. — **1833** A. FERGUSSON *Notes Tour U.S.* 21, I frequently visited the *seed-store* of Mr Thorburn. **1839** [see GENERAL *a.* 2]. **1861** *Ill. Agric. Soc. Trans.* V. 379 A third class political 'clerk' presides over a sort of 'National Seed Store.'

+**Seed tick.** Any one of various ticks, esp. the cattle tick, in its first or young stage.

1705 BEVERLEY *Virginia* IV. 66 Seed-Ticks are no where to be met with, but in the track of Cattle. **1789** ANBUREY *Travels* II. 395 There are two sorts of insects extremely troublesome, which are the woodtick, and the seed-tick. **1837** BIRD *Nick* I. 218 You'll say it war only the squabbling of seed-ticks and blue-bottle flies. **1889** CUSTER *Tenting on Plains* 139 What was most aggravating were two pests of that region, the seed-tick and the chigger.

b. *Seed-tick coffee*, any one of various coffee substitutes in use in the South during the Civil War. *Obs.*

1888 *Century Mag.* Sept. 266/1 With 'seed-tick' coffee and ordinary brown sugar costing fabulous sums and almost impossible to be obtained, it is small matter of wonder that the unsatisfied appetite of the rebel sharpshooter . . . often impelled him . . . to call a parley with the Yankee across the line.

+**Seed tree.** (See quot. 1905.) — **1896** *Vt. Agric. Rep.* XV. 87 They always leave a sufficient number of seed trees. **1905** *Forestry Bureau Bul.* No. 61, 20 *Seed tree*, any tree which bears seed; specifically a tree which provides the seed for natural reproduction.

Seed warehouse. A seed store; a warehouse in which seed is stored. — **1863** *Horticulturist* Jan., Advt. 6 Alfred Bridgeman, Seed Warehouse, Etc., 876 Broadway New York. **1874** *Rep. Comm. Agric. 1873* 213 The Department is not a seed-warehouse.

***Seedy,** *a.* +(See quot. 1851.) *slang. Obs.* — **1848** *Yale Gallinipper* Nov., And snowballs falling thick and fast As oaths from seedy senior crowd. **1850** *Yale Battery* Feb., A *seedy* Soph beneath a tree, practicing *Trigonometry.* **1851** HALL *College Words* 267 *Seedy*, rowdy, riotous, turbulent.

***Seeker.** **1.** *cap.* A member of a small religious sect which professed to be seeking further revelation. {1617–} +**2.** One seeking for religion. *colloq.* — **(1) 1654** JOHNSON *Wonder-w. Prov.* 231 Familists, Seekers, Antinomians and Anabaptists . . . are so ill armed, that they think it best sleeping in a whole skin. **1702** C. MATHER *Magnalia* (1853) I. 63 There have been also some unhappy sectaries, viz.: Quakers and Seekers. **(2) 1801–3** J. LYLE *Diary* (MS.) 39 When I spoke to seekers I cautioned them against depending on a Jesus yet unknown. **1836** GILMAN *Recoll.* (1838) 270*n.*, Persons of colour . . . become *seekers* in any church, and under any leader they prefer. **1880** *Scribner's Mo.* July 423/2 Saints and 'seekers' came hurrying in. **1888** [see ANXIOUS SEAT 1]. **1890** *Harper's Mag.* Jan. 285/2 Every negro in the county was there—. . . hardened sinners who had never even been seekers at the mourners' bench—they were all there.

Seek-No-Further, Seek-No-Farther. {1670–, a variety of apple} A variety of red-streaked winter apple; an apple of such a variety. — **1817** W. COXE *Fruit Trees* 131 Seek No Further. This apple is a native of one of the Eastern states; it is a large fruit, of a . . . yellowish green colour. **1862** [see NONESUCH 2]. **1895** *Dept. Agric. Yrbk. 1894* 211 In this zone we enter the true agricultural part of our country, where apples

(Oldberg, Baldwin, Greening, wealthy, seek-no-further, and others), . . . attain their highest perfection.

Seep. **1.** A small spring. {1824, *dial.*} +**2.** (See quot. 1909.) — **(1) 1881** BOYD *Resources South-west Va.* 251 Much salt has been made there by boiling the water caught at one of the brine seeps. **(2) 1909** WEBSTER 1912/3 *Seep*, . . . a spot where . . . petroleum oozes out slowly.

Seepage. Slow seeping or oozing; also, that which oozes. {1825-} '*Sc.* and *U.S.*' (*O.E.D.*). — **1874** RAYMOND *6th Rep. Mines* 324 A delivery of one thousand inches continuously . . . will require (to allow for evaporation and seepage) 1,400 inches to be taken from the Pecos. **1883** 'MARK TWAIN' *Life on Miss.* xxx, The flood (or possibly the seepage) had lately been ravaging it. **1900** *Engineering Mag.* XIX. 766/1 The authorities believed it would be impossible to deal with the seepage. **1911** VANCE *Cynthia* 313 There had been a slight seepage of moisture through one joint.

+**Seepy,** *a.* (See quotation.) — **1859** BARTLETT 393 Seepy land is land under cultivation that is not well drained. Maryland and Virginia.

Seersucker. Also †**sea sucker.** A light, striped fabric, formerly of linen, but now often of cotton, having an irregularly crinkled surface. {1757-}

1733 *S.C. Gazette* 20 Jan., Imported, . . . padusoys, seersuckers. **1817** *Niles' Reg.* XIII. 289/2 The prizes made by the privateers under the Mexican flag, are to a very large amount of merchandize, such as . . . muslins, seersuckers, calicoes, &c. **1866** A. D. WHITNEY *L. Goldthwaite* xiii, Leslie had made for her a small hoop, . . . and laced a little cover upon it, of striped seersucker, of which there was a petticoat also to wear above. **1881** *Argus* (Grundy Center, Iowa) 9 June 1/6 Buntings, Seersuckers, Ginghams, Lawns, etc.

b. Attrib. with *coat, cutaway, gown,* etc.

1722 *Md. Hist. Mag.* XX. 64 India Gown & petticoat . . . Burdett Ditto . . . Sea Sucker Do . . . Cloak & Scarf [etc.]. **1725** *Boston News-Letter* 24 June 2/2 A seersucker jacket & breeches. **1863** A. D. WHITNEY *F. Gartney* xxiii, He was there, . . . with his straw hat and seersucker coat on, inspecting and giving orders. **1897** STUART *Simpkinsville* 94 The pegs are usually covered with the linen dusters and seersucker cutaways of the younger men. **1904** *N.Y. Times* 25 July 1 They started out this morning in muslins and seersucker suits.

+**Seesaw pan.** (See quotation.) — **1833** SILLIMAN *Man. Sugar Cane* 100 The syrup flows, readily, into the evaporating vessels—which are the . . . bascule pans, called also, tilt or see-saw pans.

Segar. Variant of CIGAR. {1735-1833}

1785 *Notes & Q.* 9 Ser. VII. 437/1 Any person who shall be found smoaking any pipe or segar in the streets, . . . [shall] pay the sum of two shillings for every such offence. **1798** *Mass. Spy* 21 Feb. (Th.), A segar, and fifteen or sixteen glasses of Don Pedro. **1805** PARKINSON *Tour* 331 They have generally a husking-feast; . . . and, after they have done, they have a supper, smoke segars, and drink whiskey. **1816** *Ann. 14th Congress* 1 Sess. 1873 Duty . . . on segars, two dollars and fifty cents per thousand. **1875** *Chicago Tribune* 15 July 1/1 No Key West or other Domestic Segars in stock. **1911** HARRISON *Queed* 86 I'll bet segars you wake up . . . feelin' like a dish of stewed prunes.

b. Attrib. and comb. with *box, maker,* etc.

1805 *Columbian Centinel* 31 July, extra p. 1/3 (Ernst), Japaned segar boxes. *Ib.*, Silver segar tubes. **1809** WEEMS *Marion* (1833) 63 'Pooh!' replied the count, . . . puffing out his cheeks as when a segar sucker explodes a cataract of smoke from the crater of his throat. **1837** WILLIAMS *Florida* 121 The city contains . . . five segar makers. **1869** *Boyd's Business Directory* 13 Noll & Carr, segar manufacturers.

+**Sego (lily).** *W.* [Shoshonean Indian.] A showy-flowered perennial plant (*Calochortus nuttallii*), or its edible bulb: (see also quotation 1875). — **1852** STANSBURY *Gt. Salt Lake* 160 *Sego* . . . is much used by the Indian tribes as an article of food. **1870** BEADLE *Utah* 161 Wolves, raw hides, rabbits, thistle roots, *segos*, and everything that would support life was resorted to. **1875** *Amer. Naturalist* IX. 18 The general Indian name of 'Sego' is applied indiscriminately to all the edible bulbs of [s. Utah]. **1883** *Harper's Mag.* Oct. 709/2 That is the sego . . . and it is good to eat. **1915** ARMSTRONG & THORNBER *Western Wild Flowers* 64 [The mariposa] is called Sego Lily . . . in Utah and is the 'State flower.'

***Segregate,** *v.* +**1.** *tr.* (See quotation.) Also as *adj.* **2.** To force (Negroes) to live, go to school, etc., apart from the rest of the community. {*in general sense} — **(1) 1881** RAYMOND *Mining Gloss.*, *Segregate*, Pac. To separate the undivided joint ownership of a mining claim into smaller individual 'segregated' claims. **1919** A. H. FAY *Glossary of Mining* 601/1. **(2) 1908** R. S. BAKER *Following Color Line* 299 All through my former chapters I have been showing how the Negroes are being segregated. **1914** B. T. WASHINGTON *Selected Speeches* 247 Wherever the Negro is segregated, it usually means that he will have poor streets, poor lighting, . . . and poor sanitary conditions generally.

Segregation. **1.** (See quotation.) **2.** The separation of Negroes from whites with respect to places of residence, schools, etc. {1615-, in general sense} Also attrib. — **(1) 1866** *Ore. State Jrnl.* 6 Jan. 3/1 Divorces are now called 'Segregations.' **(2) 1903** B. T. WASHINGTON, etc. *Negro Problem* 215 The Afro-American people have been held together rather by the segregation decreed by law . . . than by ties of consanguinity. **1916** *Virginia Rep.* 692 The cities and towns of this State have the power . . . to pass segregation ordinances separating the places of residence of white and colored citizens, respectively.

Seidlitz powder. A compound effervescing powder consisting of sodium bicarbonate, Rochelle salt, and tartaric acid; a dose of this. {1815-} Also attrib. — **1845** *Knickerb.* XXV. 107 One blue pill every night for a week; seidlitz-powder in the morning. **1849** T. T. JOHNSON *Sights Gold Region* 5 Our polite and attentive stewardess . . . [was busy with] Seidlitz powders, for which there was a perpetual outcry. **1855** M. THOMPSON *Doesticks* 218 [The stage] reminded me forcibly of an empty seidlitz-powder box, turned up edgeways. **1866** *Ore. State Jrnl.* 13 Jan. 1/1, I will give you a Seidlitz powder.

***Seign(i)orage.** The difference between the market value of bullion and the face value of the coins minted from it; the bullion representing this difference. Also attrib. — **1894** *Harper's Mag.* June 154/1 Vetoed the Bland seigniorage bill, providing for the coinage of all the silver bullion in the Treasury. **1896** *Boston Jrnl.* 28 Jan. 10/6 Senator Gorman recommends a plan . . . of authorizing the coinage of all the silver bullion and coining the seigniorage. **1900** NELSON *A B C Wall St.* 158 *Seignorage*, the difference between the commercial value of bullion in coin and the face value of the coin. **1914** *Cycl. Amer. Govt.* III. 286/2 *Seigniorage* . . . constitutes a profit to the government.

* **Seine.** A net used in taking fish.

1634 WOOD *New Eng. Prospect* 52 Here likewise must not be forgotten all vtensils for the Sea, as . . . Sharke-hookes, Seanes, or Basse nets, large and strong. **1798** Hawkins *Letters* 490 All the men, women and children of Tuckabatchee turned out a-fishing; their seine was made of cane platted, 160 feet long, 30 feet at each end, tapering, and the middle about 4 feet broad. **1855** BAIRD in *Smithsonian Rep. 1854* 337 One specimen [of the hair-finned dory] was taken in August while hauling the seine in the surf. **1911** *Rep. Fisheries 1908* 317/2 [The tarpon] is caught on hooks and in seines.

b. Attrib. and comb. with *fishery, heaver, house, maker.*

1796 *Boston Directory* 248 Glyde, Samuel, seine maker, Sudbury street. **1876** *Wide Awake* 139/2 When the seine-house door had been fastened open, . . . Mr. Bushnell and his wife stood without looking in. **1884** GOODE, etc. *Fisheries* I. 604 In the Albemarle the important Shad seine-fisheries begin early in March. **1901** *Scribner's Mag.* April 504/1, I was seine-heaver on her for two seasons.

Seine boat. A boat suitable for carrying and operating a seine. {1602-} — **1856** OLMSTED *Slave States* 351 There are two large seine-boats, in each of which there is a captain, two seine-tenders, and eight or ten oarsmen. **1880** *Harper's Mag.* Sept. 496/2 He came upon a crew ready to set off in a long, sharp, white seine-boat. **1889** MUNROE *Dorymates* 37 The great thirty-foot, double-ended seine-boat, rowed by eight men, had left the schooner. **1901** *Scribner's Mag.* April 496/1 Every vessel in the fleet . . . looked to the painter of the seine-boat astern.

Seiner. **1.** One who uses a seine in fishing. {1602-} +**2.** =SEINE BOAT. — **(1) 1845** HOOPER *Daddy Biggs' Scrape* 189 The part above is resorted to by those who fish with the rod; and that below, by seiners. **1884** GOODE, etc. *Fisheries* I. 571 A gentle ripple indicates their position . . . and is of great assistance to the seiners in setting their nets. **1889** *Columbus Dispatch* 12 Oct., Seiner fined . . . for violating the fishing law by seining in the Scioto River. **(2) 1880** *Harper's Mag.* Aug. 340/1 There were . . . trawlers, draggers, riggers, [and] seiners. **1906** J. B. CONNOLLY *Out of Gloucester* 8 She's a seiner out of Gloucester.

Seine twine. Twine for making seines. {1875-} — **1770** *Boston Gazette* 2 April, The right sort of three-threaded Sein Twine. **1809** *Ann. 10th Congress* 2 Sess. 1537 [This bill prohibits the exportation of] seine, sail, or sewing twine. **1824** *Catawba Jrnl.* 30 Nov., Cotton Bagging, Bale Rope, bagging and sein Twine.

Seining. The taking of fish with a seine. {1836-}

1671 *Plymouth Laws* 283 No Stranger . . . shall make use of our Lands or Shoar, for Sayning or halling of Fish. **1793** *Mass. H. S. Coll.* 1 Ser. III. 167 So unfavorable is it [the river], . . . to seining or fishing, that the exclusive privilege of fishing is annually sold for less than twelve shillings. **1876** *Fur, Fin & Feather* Sept. 139/2 Considerable seining has been done.

attrib. **1887** GOODE, etc. *Fisheries* v. I. 267 The common method of dressing [mackerel] on a seining schooner is as follows: The men engaged in dressing are divided into gangs [etc.]. **1901** *Scribner's Mag.* April 496/1 The Gloucester seining fleet had been cruising off Georges Bank.

Select committee. (See quot. 1914.) {1643-} — **1789** *Ann. 1st Congress* 431, I will withdraw the motion, and move you, sir, that a select committee be appointed to consider and report such amendments. **1802** CUTLER in *Life & Corr.* II. 71 The Select Committee have this day reported a bill for . . . enacting a new naturalization bill. **1857** BENTON *Exam. Dred Scott Case* 118 The bill was the work of a Select Committee, eight in number. **1914** *Cycl. Amer. Govt.* I. 358/1 Select committees are appointed to make special investigations, to consider particular subjects not falling into the usual legislative categories, to take charge of celebrations or the like. Often these are joint committees.

Select council. +The upper of two legislative bodies which together form a city council. — **1796** *Phila. Ordinances* (1812) 90 The said freemen shall . . . also elect, by ballot, twelve persons . . . to be members of the select council. **1811** MEASE *Philadelphia* 93 There are two legislative branches, viz. Select and Common Councils. The first consist of twelve, the latter of twenty members. **1822** *Mass. Laws* VIII. 735 The administration [in Boston] . . . shall be vested in . . . one select Council, . . . to be denominated the Board of Aldermen; and one more numerous Council, . . . to be denominated the Common Council; which Boards in their joint capacity, shall be denominated the City Council.

+**Select councilman.** A member of a select council. — **1892** *York County Hist. Rev.* 14 Mr. Stauffer is a native of this city and is select councilman for eight years.

+**Select court.** *New Eng.* A court of selectmen. *Obs.* — **1677** *Plymouth Laws* 184 Complaint is made that the order of Court made June 1675 concerning Celect Courts that there should be but two in a towne annually [etc.]. **1681** *Ib.* 192 It is enacted by this Court That each Towne of this Gov[e]r[n]ment doe provide a booke wherin shall be entered all those orders of Court as are or shalbe made for direction of said Celect Courts by the Secretary.

+**Selectman.** *New Eng.* One of a board of town officers chosen annually to administer the affairs of the town.

1635 in Frothingham *Hist. Charlestown, Mass.* 51 An order [was] made by the inhabitants of Charlestowne at a full meeting for the government of the Town by Selectmen. **1691** *Boston Rec.* 206 James Taylor is chosen Treasurer . . . to imploy and disburse such publique stocke as shall come into his hands by direction of the Selectmen. **1703** *Cambridge Prop. Rec.* 219 Mr. Sam[ue]ll Sparhawke hath moved to ye Select Men yt he may have a high Way layd out to his Meadow. **1798** *Boston Rec.* 45 [That] the Aqueduct Corporation be allowed the privilege of securing by booming their logs on such part of the beach at the foot of the Common . . . as the Selectmen . . . may appoint. **1808** CUTLER in *Life & Corr.* II. 340 Town Meeting, in consequence of a Letter from the Selectmen of Boston. **1885** *Boston Jrnl.* 8 Jan. 1/6 The Selectmen [of Watertown] have voted to protest against the action of Cambridge in using the streets of the town to lay out their Stony Brook water main. **1920** HOWELLS *Vacation of Kelwyns* 193 She'd ought to be put somewheres, but as long as she's got enough to live on the selectmen can't touch her.

transf. **1858** HOLMES *Autocrat* 280 The selectmen of an African kraal-village would have had more respect for their ancestors.

+**Select school.** A private school, esp. one appealing to parents desiring exclusiveness. Also *select boarding school.* — **1831** PECK *Guide* 246 Belleville Academy . . . is a select boarding school for boys. **1847** HOWE *Hist. Coll. Ohio* 272 There are 5 public and 4 select schools. **1849** CHAMBERLAIN *Ind. Gazetteer* 281 Four select schools . . . [have] 317 scholars. **1868** *Ore. State Jrnl.* 5 Sept. 3/2 Miss Kate L. Andrew will open a Select School in the Public School House, on Monday, September 7th. **1903** *Congress. Directory* (57th Congress Sess.) 21 Attended common and select schools there.

+**Select townsman.** *New Eng.* =SELECTMAN. *Obs.* — **1648** *Suffolk Deeds* III. 454 Benjamine Ward doth hereby binde himself . . . to pay vnto . . . ye present Select Townesmen of Boston . . . three pounds per Annm. **1649** *Springfield Rec.* I. 215 The Select Townsmen shal have full power and authority to Lay out all common Highways. **1664** *Ib.* II. 55 No Inhabitant shall sell or in any manner pass away his house lott . . . before he hath made the Select Townsmen acquaynted who his Chapman is.

+**Select watch.** *New Eng.* A body of night watchmen selected to patrol the streets of a town and serve as policemen. *Obs.* — **1699** *Boston Rec.* 238 And it was then unanimusly agreed by all the above sd. Justices & Selectmen that a Select watch was most sutable for this town. **1707** *Ib.* 43 Voted the continuance and Support of the Select watch for the year ensueing.

***Selenite.** A form of gypsum occurring in thin plates resembling mica or as crystals. {1668–} — **1821** NUTTALL *Travels Arkansa* 168 The Canadian [R.] . . . is often impotably saline; 100 miles from its mouth, its banks are said to abound with selenite. **1852** MARCY *Explor. Red River* 24 Sulphate of lime . . . occurs in various degrees of purity, from the common plaster of Paris to the most beautifully transparent selenite I have ever seen. **1870** KEIM *Sheridan's Troopers* 135 A delicate selenite, composed of transparent crystals or crystalline masses, . . . was found in great abundance.

***Self-.**

1. Used with participial adjectives to denote machines, contrivances, etc., that work automatically. {1824–}

1830 PAULDING *Chron. Gotham* 12 She was . . . marking with a gold self-sharpening pencil a list of books. **1835** *23d Congress 1 Sess.* H. R. Rep. No. 55, 24 Cigars, self-igniting, John Marck, New York, April 16, 1834. **1847** *Rep. Comm. Patents 1846* 38 [In] a self-feeding pencil . . . the leads are placed in a receptacle, in such a manner that . . . they are forced in a continuous supply to the point. **1850** *Ib. 1849* 209 Improvement in Self-lighting Lamps. **1878** G. PRESCOTT *Speaking Telephone* 253 The apparatus employed . . . [was] an electro-magnet with a self-interrupting break-piece attached to its armature. **1882** *Century Mag.* Jan. 478/1 The machine is a self-packing press . . . the cotton being fed at the top from a hopper, and shot out below in the form of a small, neat package, safely inclosed in a strong canvas bag. **1883** *Scientific Amer.* 3 March 138/3 An improved bundle separating attachment for self-binding harvesters has been patented. **1883** KNIGHT *Suppl.* 795/2 *Self Dumping Coal Tub,* tubs arranged to dump automatically at a desired point.

+**2.** In special combinations.

Self-electioneering, electioneering for one's self; *s.-elevated,* elevated in rank or fortune through one's own efforts; *s.-heater,* a stove that has an automatic feed; *s.-milker,* a cow that sucks herself; *s.-propeller,* a steam engine that travels under its own power; *s.-rake,* an attachment to a harvesting machine for raking and depositing the cut grain in convenient piles (cf. SELF-RAKER); *Self-Savers,* (see quotation); *s.-stealer,* one who runs away from servitude; *s.-taxation,* taxation that is self-imposed.

1838 FLAGG *Far West* II. 58 The charge of self-electioneering is, indeed, a powerful engine often employed by political partisans. **1838** *U.S. Mag.* I. 412 Few men have *lived down* . . . [more] unresting attacks of calumny and abuse, than the self-educated and self-elevated farmer's boy of New England,—Amos Kendall. **1903** *N.Y. Sun* 22 Nov., A social reunion around the 'self-heater' where they played as children. **1863** MITCHELL *My Farm* 106 Self-milkers are not profitable. **1881** *Harper's Mag.* Jan. 205/2 The steam engines were self-propellers. **1868** *Iowa State Agric. Soc. Rep. 1867* 233 Price [of harvester] $155 as a hand-raker alone; $195 with self-rake attached. **1882** *Advance* 16 March, The 'Church of the Self-Savers,' a new Socialistic organization, held service Sunday in this city. **1856** OLMSTED *Slave States* 159 What a life it must be; born outlaws; educated self-stealers. **1810** A. TOWNSEND *Oration 4 July* 9 [The founders of Mass.] assumed the right of self-taxation.

+**Self-binder.** A harvesting machine which binds into bundles the grain which it cuts. — **1879** *Scribner's Mo.* Nov. 134/2 Finally [there is] the self-binder, that perfection of farm machinery. **1883** *Rep. Indian Affairs* 24 These ten . . . wanted to buy a 'self-binder,' and inquired the cost. **1885** *Ib.* 26, I have again organized clubs amongst the Indians for the purpose of purchasing self-binders, reapers, and mowing machines.

+**Self-boarder.** One who provides and prepares his own food. Also *vbl. n.* — **1849** CHAMBERLAIN *Ind. Gazetteer* 60 The expense for board is materially lessened by associations for the purpose, also by individual self-boarding. **1885** (letterhead of N.Y. State Normal & Training School), Board, fuel, washing, lights, $3 to $4 per wk. Self-boarders can live much cheaper.

+**Self-cocker.** A self-cocking firearm, esp. a revolver. — [**1863** *Battle-Fields of the South* I. 125 An Adam's self-cocker (unloaded).] **1875** *Chicago Tribune* 26 Nov. 5/2 The weapon . . . is a seven-shooter, self-cocker, and is a 32 calibre. **1881** HAYES *New Colorado* 177, I'll lend you a self-cocker like mine. **1893** ROOSEVELT *Wilderness Hunter* 421 My guns was Colt's self-cockers. **1902** WHITE *Blazed Trail Stories* 150 It was wonderful work, rattling fire, quicker than a self-cocker even.

+**Self-cocking,** *a.* Denoting a revolver the hammer of which can be raised and released by pulling the trigger. {1892–, as noun} — **1880** *Cimarron News & Press* 23 Dec. 3/1 Mr. T. O. Boggs of Tramperos, while in the act of drawing a self-cocking pistol from his pocket, accidentally discharged it. **1888** *Battle Creek Wkly. Jrnl.* 8 Feb., McCarty drew his revolver, a self cocking, 38 calibre, Smith & Wesson affair. **1902** HULBERT *Forest Neighbors* 161 Four shots, as fast as the self-cocking revolver could pour the lead into his body.

+**Self-culture.** The cultivation or development of one's abilities through self-imposed effort. — **1837** CHANNING *Works* (1886) 14/1 In this country the mass of the people are distinguished by possessing means of improvement, of self-culture, possessed nowhere else. **1859** *New Amer. Cycl.* VI. 254/1 From being the slave of his imaginative faculty, he [Dante] rose by self-culture and force of will to that mastery of it which is art. **1860** ABBOTT *South & North* 230 [We] wield all the powers of our government . . . to check every effort these defrauded children of God may make for self-culture.

+**Self-feeder.** *Mining.* A device which automatically supplies ore to the stamp mortars of a stamp mill. — **1876** RAYMOND *8th Rep. Mines* 48 The adoption of self-feeders reduces the expenses of treatment of ores to about $1 per ton. **1882** *47th Congress 1 Sess.* H. R. Ex. Doc. No. 216, 587 The mechanism . . . is driven by the cam shaft similarly to the self-feeders, over which so much ingenuity has been expended to regulate the delivery of ore to the mortars.

Self-government. {1734–} The administration by the people of a community, state, etc., of their own public affairs. {1870–} — **1790** JEFFERSON *Writings* III. 60 Every man, and every body of men on earth, possesses the right of self-government. **1822** *Ann. 17th Congress* 1 Sess. I. 79 Such control, vested in an independent magistracy, would be entirely hostile to every principle of self-government. **1901** WHITE in *McClure's Mag.* Dec. 148 He is merely a magnified type of hundreds of earthworms boring beneath the roots of self-government by cities and States. **1925** BRYAN *Memoirs* 246 Education is necessary to self-government.

***Self-heal.** Any one of various plants reputed to possess extraordinary healing properties, esp. *Prunella vulgaris.* — **1791** MUHLENBERG *Index Florae* 173. **1814** BIGELOW *Florula Bostoniensis* 149 *Prunella Pennsylvanica.* Self heal. . . . A handsome plant, native of meadows and moist pastures. **1843** TORREY *Flora N.Y.* II. 69 *Prunella vulgaris.* Common self-heal. . . . Healall. . . . Woods, road-sides, etc.; very common. **1915** ARMSTRONG & THORNBER *Western Wild Flowers* 444 Self-heal. . . . The name, often spelled Brunella, is said to be derived from an old German word for an affection of the throat, which this plant was supposed to cure.

+**Self-hunt,** *v.* Of a dog: To begin hunting without the direction of trainers or owners. Also *vbl. n. Obs.* — **1768** WASHINGTON *Diaries* I. 284 The hounds havg. started a Fox in self huntg., we followed. **1770** *Ib.* 369 Found some dogs that were self hunting.

+**Self-made man.** A man who has risen from poverty or obscurity by his own efforts. — **1832** *Congress. Deb.* 2 Feb. 277 In Kentucky, almost every manufactory known to me is in the hands of enterprising self-made men. **1877** *Harper's Mag.* Feb. 463/2 He was what is called a self-made man. **1892** HOWELLS *Quality of Mercy* 368 The self-made man can never be the society equal of the society-made man. **1914** ANTIN *They Who Knock* 76 [We regard] our self-made men as the noblest product of our democratic institutions.

+**Self-poise.** Poise attained through self-command. — **1854** LIPPINCOTT *Haps & Mishaps* 2 There is a maturity of thought . . . , a self-poise about him, which impress you. **1860** EMERSON *Conduct of Life* 177 A self-poise belongs to every particle. **1884** *Century Mag.* Jan. 453/2 He displayed excellent qualifications for either soldier or civilian—self-poise, a quick intelligence, close application.

+**Self-raker.** An attachment to a harvesting machine for raking and depositing the cut grain in convenient piles; a harvester having such an attachment. — 1857 *Ill. Agric. Soc. Trans.* II. 120 A self raker . . . may be just as simple in its structure as some *hand raker.* 1867 *Rep. Comm. Agric.* p. vi, The reaper . . . is supplemented with a self-raker. 1868 *Mich. Agric. Rep.* VII. 285 Thirty reaping machines were entered for trial, eight of which were self-rakers. 1879 *Scribner's Mo.* Nov. 134/2 The self-raker . . . drops it [*sc.* wheat] in convenient little bunches.

+**Self-rising** (flour). Flour to which has been added baking powder and salt in the proper proportions for biscuits, griddlecakes, etc. — 1865 *Chicago Tribune* 10 April 1 Rogers' Self Rising Flour. . . . You require no Baking Powder, Yeast or Cream Tartar and Soda. 1877 W. WRIGHT *Big Bonanza* 114 Many of the miners used a kind of flour, called 'self-rising.'

+**Self-rocker.** A chair provided with springs that assist in keeping it in motion when set to rocking. — 1893 *Harper's Mag.* April 800/1 The chair he sat in was a self-rocker—a little invention of his own. 1909 RICE *Mr. Opp* 97 She's going to select a plush self-rocker for the congregation to give the new preacher.

Selfward, *adv.* and *a.* ('Chiefly *U.S.*' *O.E.D.*) **1.** *adv.* Toward one's self. **2.** *adj.* Tending toward one's self. {1888-} — (1) 1887 *Springfield Repub.* 8 Oct., Contrary to the beneficent law of his being, he [*sc.* man] exercised this choice selfward. (2) 1888 *Advance* 15 Nov., I wonder if other ministers are prone to fall into this habit of selfward praying.

Selfwardness. The quality of being selfward. — 1889 *Advance* 28 March, The selfwardness of piety which Lent emphasizes.

+**Selkirk's violet.** A violet (*Viola selkirkii*) found in the northern states. — 1843 TORREY *Flora N.Y.* I. 70 Selkirk's Violet. . . . Woody hill-sides in the western part of the state. . . . A well-marked, but rare species. 1869 FULLER *Flower Gatherers* 110 One is called *Selkirk's* violet.

* **Seller.**

1. A book which sells well, or to a specified extent. Now freq. *best seller.*

1895 *Chicago Strike of 1894* 449 It is a good book, what we in the phrase of the business call 'a seller.' 1900 *Century Mag.* Feb. 646/2 Tragic novels are poor sellers, and one poor seller might cause the canceling of orders for his future novels. 1903 *Munsey's Mag.* Aug. 764/1 Many of its [the *Bookman's*] pages are devoted to correspondence with the salaried boomers of publishing houses relative to what are known as 'sellers'—meaning books that enjoy a wide sale. 1921 *Bookman* Dec. 298/1 The novel, 'Main Street,' which included among its targets people who buy best sellers, is itself a best seller.

+**2.** *Seller three* (*ten*, etc.), a stock exchange term indicating that a seller is expected to deliver property sold on the third (tenth, etc.) day but may do so earlier.

1869 'MARK TWAIN' *Innocents* 368 One forty-niner—damaged—at £23, seller ten, no deposit. 1882 MCCABE *New York* 341, I'll give an 1/8, seller three for the lot. 1888 *Economist* 20 Oct. 18/3 Sales were made on the Chicago Stock Exchange yesterday of . . . $5,000 Gas 5s at 83 3/8; $10,000 at 83 3/8, seller 3.

Seller's option. Finance. (See quot. 1891.) — 1857 *Merchants' Mag.* July 134 Sales at seller's option are generally a fraction below the current cash price. 1865 *Harper's Mag.* April 616/2 Stocks may be sold for cash, or regular, or on seller's option. 1891 *Cent.* 5481/1 *Seller's option,* in Exchange transactions, the option which a seller has, or has reserved to himself, of delivering the thing sold at any time within a certain number of days specified: usually abbreviated to *s.o.*

Selling out. +A political betrayal for a price. *colloq.* — 1857 *Lawrence* (Kan.) *Republican* 4 June 3 No humiliating compromise is proposed, and no selling out. 1888 BRYCE *Amer. Commw.* III. iv. lxxxiii. 110 When this transfer of the solid vote of a body of agitators is the result of a bargain with the old party which gets the vote, it is called 'selling out.'

+**Sell-out,** *n.* An agreement arrived at by collusion to the detriment of legitimate private or public interests. — 1883 HAY *Bread-Winners* 151 How much did the Captain give you for this sell-out? 1890 *Advance* 1 Feb. 3 The proposed sell-out of the State of North Dakota to the infamous Louisiana Lottery Company. 1906 *Watson's Mag.* Jan. 262 (*Cent. Suppl.*), The Tariff Act . . . was an ungodly and unblushing sell-out to the Sugar Trust.

Sell out, *v.* {1648-}

+**1.** **a.** *tr.* To transfer the support of (a newspaper) or to betray (someone) for some return. **b.** *intr.* To change one's position or to yield to a rival for gain.

(a) 1857 *Lawrence* (Kan.) *Republican* 2 July 1 If the *Times* has not been 'sold out' to the Border Ruffian party, it looks very much as if it had been 'chartered.' 1867 *Ore. State Jrnl.* 19 Jan. 3/1 The writer thinks the officers were 'badly sold out.' 1901 NORRIS *Octopus* 446 You've sold us out, you. (b) 1870 *Nation* 6 Jan. 1/1 The opposition candidate for the Speakership, . . . in the opinion of the bystanders, 'sold out' to his competitors. 1906 'O. HENRY' *Trimmed Lamp* 13 When I sell out it's not going to be on any bargain day.

+**2.** (See quot. 1870.) Also as adj.

1870 MEDBERY *Men Wall St.* 137 To 'sell out' a man, is to sell down a stock, which another is carrying, so low that he is compelled to quit his hold, and perhaps to fail. 1898 *Kansas City Star* 18 Dec. 5/1 Unless the receipts should be materially larger this week the sold out bulls will be

likely to scramble back into the market again. 1902 NORRIS *Pit* 323 He's going to try to sell us out, is he? All right. We'll sell, too.

Seltzer. An effervescent mineral water obtained from Nieder Selters in Germany, or water artificially made to resemble this. Also attrib. in full *Seltzer water.* {1741-} — 1810 *Columbian Centinel* 3 Jan. 4/1 The Seltzers and Soda Waters are not only resorted to in many disorders, but as grateful morning beverage to those who are curious in their fluids. 1877 MCCABE *Hist. Great Riots* 39 The only articles furnished that I know of were a jug of seltzer and a bottle of claret. 1882 PECK *Sunshine* 110 He walked off to a bottle of seltzer water. 1883 *Century Mag.* Nov. 43/2 Still positively recognizable are the arched structures at Nos. 270 and 272 Royal street, occupied now, alas! by a prosaic seltzer factory. 1898 FORD *Tattle-Tales* 60 Mr. Potter was seated in a library, smoking, with a glass of seltzer—and something else—at his elbow.

Semester. One of the two periods of instruction into which the school year of approximately thirty-six weeks is usually divided. {1827-, of Germany} Also attrib. — 1881 *Missouri Univ. Cat.* 40 The Juniors and Seniors . . . spent the balance of the semester in studying simple methods of teaching physics. 1890 WEBSTER 1308/1 *Semester,* . . . a period of six months; especially, a term in a college or university which divides the year into two terms. 1895 *Univ. Nebraska Calendar 1895-6* 33 The year is divided upon the semester plan. Each semester has eighteen weeks. 1914 ATHERTON *Perch of Devil* 1 For two years and a semester Gregory had been the most brilliant figure in the School of Mines.

Semiarid, *a.* Of an area: Having very little rain. Usually with *region.* — 1898 *Pop. Science Mo.* LII. 466 In the semiarid region the struggle for existence is so great. 1900 *Congress. Rec.* 31 Jan. 1353/1 We urge the adoption of a harmonious system of irrigation laws in all of the arid and semiarid States and Territories.

+**Semicolon butterfly.** An American butterfly (*Polygonia interrogationis*) having markings suggestive of semicolons. — 1841 T. W. HARRIS *Rep. Insects Mass.* 219 Semicolon Butterfly. . . . Under-side of the wings in some rust-red, . . . with a pale gold-colored semicolon on the middle of the hinder pair. 1854 EMMONS *Agric. N.Y.* V. 207 Semicolon Butterfly. . . . There seems to be some variety in the markings of this butterfly, though the general pattern is much the same.

+**Semimonthly,** *n.* A publication that comes out twice a month. — 1851 CIST *Cincinnati* 75 These are semi-monthlies.

+**Semimonthly,** *a.* and *adv.* **1.** *adj.* Taking place or appearing twice a month. **2.** *adv.* Twice a month. — (1) 1860 *36th Congress 2 Sess.* Sen. Ex. Doc. No. 1, I. 435 The present contract . . . provides for an additional monthly trip between New York and San Francisco, making the service tri-monthly instead of semi-monthly as heretofore. 1865 *Atlantic Mo.* Jan. 86/2 New York . . . [issues] seventy-four monthly, semi-monthly, or weekly magazines. (2) 1895 *Univ. Nebraska Calendar 1895-6* 250 The Hesperian is the pioneer paper of the University, published semi-monthly.

Seminar. 1. An informal meeting of students with a leader. **2.** A course of study or a meeting of advanced students who are doing original research under the guidance of a professor. {1892-} — (1) 1889 *Harper's Mag.* Jan. 273/2 In New York and Washington, if I am not misinformed, 'seminors' are held at regular intervals, at which a clever woman coaches other clever women in the political, literary, and ethical topics of the day. 1897 FLANDRAU *Harvard Episodes* 237 You're going to give us a seminar, you know—the exam comes tomorrow. (2) 1893 POST *Harvard Stories* 233, I am going to a seminar over in College House. 1893 *Advance* 27 April, The Seminar . . . is a society for the prosecution of independent work in some chosen field. There are to be eight of these Seminars [in the Chicago Theological Seminary] next year.

* **Seminary.**

***1.** A place of education, as an academy, high school, or college.

1708 *Boston News-Letter* 19 Jan. 2/2 The Reverend Mr. John Leveret was this Day declared President of Harvard Colledge . . . and the care of that Seminary put into his hands. 1790 *State P.* (1819) I. 15 Whether . . . [knowledge] will be best promoted by affording aids to seminaries of learning already established . . . will be well worthy of a place in the deliberations of the legislature. 1815 DWIGHT *Remarks on Review of Inchiquin's Lett.* 56 What is true of the Seminary at Andover, is believed to be true, substantially, of all the other Institutions. 1878 *Harper's Mag.* March 501/1 The teacher in our public schools who graduated from college or seminary twenty or thirty years ago finds himself [etc.]. 1898 PAGE *Red Rock* 399 Scholars . . . from other schools much farther off began to flock to Mrs. Welch's seminary.

b. A building in which such a school is conducted.

1831 PECK *Guide* 247 The buildings . . . [include] a *Seminary* which consists of a main building . . . with wings on each side. 1859 *Ladies' Repository* Jan. 43/1 The bell on the seminary had rung.

+**2.** =SEMINAR 2.

1879 *Ann. Rep. Johns Hopkins Univ.* 56 Seminary of American History. 1889 *Academy* 17 Aug. 103/2 The 'seminary' system seems to be making way [at Johns Hopkins], especially in the department of philology. The seminary is an association of the teachers, fellows, and scholars . . . for the prosecution of original studies by means of discussion and criticism. 1891 *Cent.* 5485/1-2 *Seminary,* . . . a seminary course: imitated from German use. Also *seminar.*

3. Attrib. in sense 1 with *chapel, dude, girl,* etc.

1838 *Indiana H. Rep. Jrnl.* 23 Sess. 126 A majority of the voters in the counties should vote for Seminary Trustees. 1845 *Indiana Senate Jrnl.*

29 Sess. 481 A joint resolution in relation to the titles of purchasers of seminary lands in Gibson county. **1848** *Indiana Gen. Ass. Doc. 1848-9* II. 285 The amount of principal and interest remaining due and unpaid, for seminary lots on reserve sections around the University buildings is . . . $3,669.00. **1877** *Harper's Mag.* March 563/1 He was . . . being repossessed for the time by an old-time effort to design a stained window for the seminary chapel. **1883** PECK *Bad Boy* 16 He chewed like a seminary girl chewing gum. **1891** GARLAND *Main-travelled Roads* (1922) 22 W'y, you damned seminary dude, I can break you in two!

+Seminole. [Creek *Simanôle* 'runaway, separatist.']

1. A Muskhogean Indian of a tribe found in Florida and Oklahoma and composed originally of Creek refugees; also, pl., the tribe of such an Indian. Also collective.

1789 *Amer. State P.: Ind. Affairs* I. 15 Some of the most southern towns of the Lower Creeks, or Seminoles, are within the territory of Spain. **1817** *Niles' Reg.* XIII. 296/1 The number of hostile Indians, including the 'Red Sticks' and Seminoles, [is estimated] at more than two thousand. **1866** 'F. KIRKLAND' *Bk. Anecdotes* 318/2 He fainted at the spectacle, and was soon after butchered by a Seminole. **1885** *Century Mag.* Aug. 602/2 The Creeks and Seminoles have not improved as much as the three other tribes, and are not considered so bright and energetic. **1910** HODGE, etc. *Amer. Indians* II. 500/2 While still under Spanish rule the Seminole became involved in hostility with the United States. **1917** *Cambr. Hist. Amer. Lit.* I. 195 His son William, [was] called by the Seminoles 'Puc-Puggy' (Flower-Hunter).

2. The language of the Seminole Indians.

1848 *S. Lit. Messenger* XIV. 482/2, I concluded at the time [that the opera] was written in Seminole, as the only word which I distinctly heard was en ca. **1857** *Knickerb.* XLIX. 634 The title given the place is *Atseena Otee*, which the largest landed proprietor says is Seminole for Cedar Key.

3. Attrib. with *father, nation, squaw, tribe.*

1835 SEALSFIELD *Morton* (1844) II. 24 Eine schmutzige, einer *Seminola squaw* vergleichbare Schöne zog ihre Kappe vom Kopfe. **1837** MARTINEAU *Society* II. 71 The Seminole fathers would not deliver them up. **1881** *Rep. Indian Affairs* p. lv, [They] were willing to incorporate the whole Seminole tribe into their nation. **1900** *Congress. Rec.* 2 Feb. 1455/2 In the Seminole Nation the survey and appraisement is already finished.

+Seminole Indian. An Indian of the Seminole tribe; also, pl., the tribe of Seminoles. — **1797** MORSE *Amer. Gazetteer* s.v. *Calos*, Not far from this is a considerable town of Seminole Indians. **1839** VAN BUREN in *Pres. Mess. & P.* III. 510 The Commissioner of Indian Affairs . . . [suggests] the propriety of setting apart a tract of country west of the Mississippi for the Seminole Indians. **1846** *Xenia Torch-Light* 30 April 1/7 The Seminole Indians . . . are well pleased with the country they have lately removed to. **1850** TAYLOR in *Pres. Mess. & P.* V. 45 The Senate . . . [called] for information in relation to the hostilities and outrages committed during the past year by the Seminole Indians in Florida. **1852** FILLMORE in *Pres. Mess. & P.* V. 171 The removal of the remnant of the tribe of Seminole Indians from Florida has long been a cherished object of the Government.

+Seminole war. The war of 1817–18 or the war of 1835–42, carried on by the United States against the Seminole Indians. — **1831** in Benton *30 Years' View* I. 167/2 The deliberations of the cabinet of Mr. Monroe on the occurrences of the Seminole war. **1842** *Whig Almanac 1843* 23/1 The Seminole war, which has cost the Nation so many millions of money, . . . had its origin as early as 1814. **1848** *Ib. 1849* 47/2 Such was the cause of Seminole and other wars with Indians, prior to 1843. **1854** BENTON *30 Years' View* I. 129/2 His invasion of Spanish territory during the Seminole War, had just come to his knowledge. **1869** *Ore. State Jrnl.* 2 Jan. 2/2 The Seminole war in Florida lasted about 7 years and cost $100,000 and 15,000 lives.

+Seminolian, *n.* and *a.* **a.** *n.* A Seminole Indian. **b.** *adj.* Of or pertaining to a Seminole Indian. *Obs.* — **1817** *Niles' Reg.* XIII. 191/1 Those negroes . . . , together with the barbarous Seminolians, have been robbing and murdering the frontier inhabitants. **1818** *Ib.* XV. 200/2 Little doubt is entertained but there will soon be a final termination of the Seminolian war.

+Semioccasional, *a.* Occurring or operating every now and then. *colloq.* — **1850** in *Yankee Humour* (1853) 113 Semi-occasional intoxication. **1878** *Congress. Rec.* 14 June 4612/1 A semi-occasional ship carries the mails.

+Semioccasionally, *adv.* Every now and then. *colloq.* — **1854** *Knickerb.* XLIII. 323 He preached semi-occasionally, at a private house. **1864** *Congress. Globe* 11 April 1557/3 He has had such [moments] at long intervals and semi-occasionally. **1903** *N.Y. Herald* 21 Oct. 10 The publishers continue to send the book semi-occasionally.

Semiofficial, *a.* Official to some extent. {1859-} — **1806** *Ann. 9th Congress* 1 Sess. 597 Must we have semi-official authority, even for a title-page? **1834** *Congress. Deb.* 8 Jan. 189 At length semi-official authority declared that the purpose was fixed. **1872** *Atlantic Mo.* March 38 Official and 'semi-official' organs begin to make their appearance in all quarters.

+Semipalmated plover. A plover (*Charadrius semipalmatus*) that breeds in the arctic region and appears as a visitor in various parts of the United States. — **1828** BONAPARTE *Synopsis* 296 The Semi-palmated Plover . . . [is] common all along the sea coast of the union. **1883** *Nat. Museum Bul.* No. 27, 147 *Ægialites semipalmatus*. Semipalmated Plover. . . . Nearly the whole of America, but breeding only far northward. **1917** *Birds of Amer.* I. 262/1 The Semipalmated Plover is the common Plover of the Atlantic seaboard.

+Semipalmated sandpiper. An American peep, *Ereunetes pusillus*. — **1813** WILSON *Ornithology* VII. 131 *Tringa semipalmata*. Semipalmated Sandpiper. **1823** JAMES *Exped.* I. 31 The semipalmated sandpipers were in large flocks. **1883** *Nat. Museum Bul.* No. 27, 150 Semipalmated Sandpiper. . . . Northern and Eastern North America, and, in winter, nearly the whole of tropical America. **1917** *Birds of Amer.* I. 239/1 The Semipalmated Sandpiper is a sociable little bird.

+Semipalmated snipe. The willet, *Catoptrophorus semipalmatus*. — **1813** WILSON *Ornithology* VII. 27 Semi-palmated Snipe . . . is one of the most noisy and noted birds that inhabit our salt marshes in summer. **1839** PEABODY *Mass. Birds* 369 The Semipalmated Snipe . . . [is] known by the name of Willet. **1844** *Nat. Hist. N.Y., Zoology* II. 251 The Willet, Semipalmated Snipe, or Stone Curlew, reaches this State about the beginning of May. **1917** *Birds of Amer.* I. 246.

+Semi-weekly, *n.* A paper that comes out twice a week. — **1840** *Niles' Nat. Reg.* 18 April 112/3 We see some errors in the list of our papers . . . , including semi-weeklies. **1873** F. HUDSON *Journalism* 277 With the daily there was a weekly and a semi-weekly. **1884** *Tenth Census* VIII. 111 Three months only the *Spy* ran as a tri-weekly, and but three months longer as a semi-weekly.

Semi-weekly, *a.* Appearing, arriving, etc., twice a week. — **1843** *Penny Cycl.* XXVI. 14/2 [In the U.S. there are] 1141 weekly, and 125 semi- or tri-weekly newspapers. **1865** *Atlantic Mo.* Jan. 86/2 The metropolis [New York City] . . . issues . . . one hundred and thirty-three weekly or semi-weekly journals. **1873** BEADLE *Undevel. West* 339 The semi-weekly mail arrived from the city. **1900** *Scribner's Mag.* Sept. 259/2, I climbed up on the semi-weekly stage.

***Senate.**

+1. The upper and smaller branch of a state assembly or legislature.

In the first two quotations the word is used in a general or anticipatory sense.

1775 A. ADAMS *Familiar Lett.* 74 We want him in the Senate; we want him in his profession; we want him in the field. **1777** HAMILTON *Works* VII. 498 In your time your [N.Y.] Senate . . . will be liable to degenerate into a body purely aristocratical. **1786** J. ADAMS *Works* IX. 548, I cannot conceive why the [Mass.] Senate did not concur with the House. **1814** *Portsmouth Oracle* 29 Oct. 2/5 A bill [is] before the Senate of this State, for raising two regiments of People of Colour. **1840** *Niles' Nat. Reg.* 7 March 4 The bill to abolish imprisonment for debt in Louisiana . . . was sent to the senate. **1887** *New Princeton Rev.* Sept. 178 The name 'Senate' was used for the Upper House in Maryland, Massachusetts, . . . and Virginia. **1918** *Va. Acts of Assembly* 788 Resolved, by the senate, the house of delegates concurring [etc.].

+2. The upper house of the United States Congress, composed of two senators from each state.

1787 *Constitution* ii. § 2 The President . . . shall have Power, by and with the Advice and Consent of the Senate, to make Treaties. **1789** *Annals 1st Congress* 18 The Senate appointed Charles Thomson, Esq. to notify George Washington, Esq. of his election to the office of President of the United States. *c***1808** J. ADAMS *Works* VI. 531 We have in fact, an aristocratical branch to our government, and that is, the senate. **1850** HONE *Diary* II. 369 The Senate of the United States is decidedly in the opposition. **1900** *Congress. Rec.* 1 Feb. 1375/2 There is no rule . . . of the Senate relating to the matter. **1917** *N.Y. Times* 3 April 1/6 President Wilson appeared before a joint session of the Senate and House.

+3. In special combinations.

Senate amendment, an amendment made by the Senate to a bill; *S. calendar*, the list of the bills before the Senate, showing the order in which they are to be considered; *S. clerk*, the secretary of the Senate, or one performing secretarial duties for a Senate committee; *S. document*, (see quotation); *S. investigating committee*, a committee appointed by the Senate to investigate a particular matter; *S. lobby*, a lobby which seeks to influence the actions of the Senate; *S. printer*, the printer to whom is intrusted the printing of the official documents, proceedings, etc., of the Senate. *Obs.*

1868 *N.Y. Herald* 4 July 3/2 The Senate Amendments to the Special Tax Bill. **1880** *Harper's Mag.* Aug. 484 800 [bills] remained unfinished on the Senate calendar. **1873** *Ib.* May 853/2 She won't . . . ask which of the Senate clerks is the Secretary of State. **1895** *Statutes at Large* XXVIII. 621 The executive and miscellaneous documents and the reports of each House of Congress shall be designated as 'House Documents,' 'Senate Documents,' 'House Reports,' 'Senate Reports,' thus making two classes for each house. **1890** *Stock Grower & Farmer* 25 Jan. 4/1 Some of the witnesses before the senate investigating committee have testified that the profit on each head of cattle they buy is only four dollars and ninety-five cents. **1868** *N.Y. Herald* 27 July 8/1 The Senate lobby was present in full force to-night. **1860** *36th Congress 1 Sess.* H. R. Rep. No. 249, 13 When he was elected Senate printer he repudiated all our agreements.

Senate chamber. {1737-} +The chamber or hall in which a senate meets. — **1785** WASHINGTON *Diaries* II. 372 We proceeded to business in the Senate Chamber. **1793** *Steele P.* I. 108 Take a peep into the Senate Chamber. **1837** JACKSON in *Pres. Mess. & P.* III. 289, I hereby convene the Senate of the United States to meet in the Senate Chamber on the 4th day of March next. **1884** *Century Mag.* May 63/2 The Senate Chamber and court rooms [of the capitol in Albany, N.Y.] are almost finished. **1912** NICHOLSON *Hoosier Chron.* 603 It was almost too much for my composure to behold her there, beyond question the best-dressed woman in the senate chamber.

+Senate committee. A committee chosen by a senate to perform some specific function, such as the gathering of information relevant to proposed legislation. — **1881** *Ore. State Jrnl.* 15 Jan. 4/2 One of the annual illustrations of the Democratic sense of humor . . . is the appointment of Mr. Vest to the chairmanship of the Senate Committee on Civil Service Reform. **1912** NICHOLSON *Hoosier Chron.* 463, I learned a good deal those winters I spent at the State House, when I was stenog to certain senate committees. **1925** BRYAN *Memoirs* 386 It was submitted to the Senate Committee on Foreign Relations.

+Senate district. =SENATORIAL DISTRICT. — **1850** *Mich. Gen. Statutes* I. (1882) 76 The legislature shall . . . divide the state into senate districts. **1881** *Ib.* 107 This state shall be and is hereby divided into thirty-two senate districts.

* Senator.

+1. One of the two representatives sent by each state to the United States Senate.

1787 *Constitution* Art. 1. Sect. iii, The Senate of the United States, shall be composed of two Senators from each State. **1808** *Ann. 10th Congress* 1 Sess. 184 The senate resumed the consideration of . . . the conduct of John Smith, a senator from the State of Ohio. **1846** POLK *Diary* (1929) 127 If a proposition such as they suggested was made, it must come from the Pennsylvania Senators. **1895** J. W. MOORE *Amer. Congress* 506 The President had expressed himself to several Senators as being satisfied with [the Wilson tariff bill]. **1912** NICHOLSON *Hoosier Chron.* 337 We, the delegates here assembled, do hereby pledge the party's support for the office of Senator in Congress to the Honorable Edward G. Thatcher.

+2. A member of the upper branch of a territorial or state assembly or legislature.

See also STATE SENATOR.

1792 IMLAY *Western Territory* 171 It has been the crude practice [in Ky.] hitherto, that each county should have two delegates and one senator to represent them. **1866** *Wkly. New Mexican* 22 Dec. 2/2 Hon. Manuel Barela, one of the senators from San Miguel county having resigned, a special election was held. **1873** *Harper's Mag.* March 573/1 The terms of Senators range from one to six years.

3. Prefixed as a title to the surname of a senator.

1852 STOWE *Uncle Tom* ix, Senator Bird was drawing off his boots. **1872** *Newton Kansan* 12 Dec. 2/1 Senator Pomeroy has introduced a bill . . . to create a new judicial district. **1882** *Nation* 26 Oct. 344/1 Senator Mahone, the chief of the progressive Repudiationists in Virginia, 'wants a place for a friend.' **1884** ROE *Army Lett.* 320 The 'Indian Commission' . . . consists of senator Dawes and fourteen congressmen. **1887** *Courier Journal* 29 Jan. 5/5 The chances [are] in favor of Senator Morgan, on the grounds that he is from the Gulf States. **1904** *Springfield W. Repub.* 9 Sept. 6 Senator Depew salts down William Allen White, who has stated that the senator tried to bully the president.

Senatorial, *a.* {1740-} +Of or pertaining to a state or federal senate or senator. — **1778** *Essex Co. Convention Result* 52 The senatorial convention may be composed of delegates from the several towns. **1790** MACLAY *Deb. Senate* 199 But as the matter, strictly speaking, was not *senatorial*, or such as belonged to us in our capacity as a public body, . . . it was withdrawn. **1873** *Newton Kansan* 13 Feb. 4/2 [He] has been bitter in hostility to what he called the senatorial ring. **1889** *N.Y. Times* 8 Sept., The investigation by the Senatorial commission into the dressed-beef combine was resumed here to-day. **1913** Senatorial contest [see CROWD *n.*].

+Senatorial courtesy. The deference due a senator, esp. in the matter of appointments to offices in his state. — **1884** THAYER *From Log-Cabin* 279 A custom of the United States Senate called 'Senatorial courtesy' . . . [is] the custom of allowing senators to designate who should be appointed to fill certain offices in their respective states. **1913** LA FOLLETTE *Autobiog.* 462, I was rudely thrusting this troublesome proposition upon them in violation of all the regulations governing 'senatorial courtesy.'

+Senatorial district. A division of a state or territory entitled to elect a senator to the state or territorial assembly or legislature. Also attrib. — **1834** *Congress. Deb.* 17 Feb. 567 The friends of the State and national administrations have recently had meetings in nearly every town, to elect delegates for their council and senatorial district conventions for the present year. **1851** *Mich. Gen. Statutes* I. (1882) 141 A duplicate statement of the votes given for senator . . . [is] to be delivered by him to the senatorial district canvassers. **1870** *Republican Rev.* 26 March 2/4 Where two counties compose one Senatorial district the delegates for Senator will be divided between such counties. **1891** O'BEIRNE *Leaders Ind. Territory* 51/2 Some years previously Mr. Hampton was employed . . . to take the census of the senatorial district.

Senatorship. {1602-} +The office or position of a state or federal senator. — **1851** LONGFELLOW in S. Longfellow *H. W. Longfellow* II. 208 Sumner came to dinner in very good spirits, feeling better about his senatorship. **1873** *Newton Kansan* 1 May 2/1 He has no intention of entering Kansas politics again and will not be a candidate for the Senatorship. **1898** *Kissimmee* (Fla.) *Valley Gazette* 14 Jan. 1/1 The inauguration address . . . was short and contained no reference to the contest for the senatorship. **1910** J. HART *Vigilante Girl* 204 He has an itch for office, although he has no chance for the senatorship.

* Send, *v.*

*1. *To send down,* +to send to prison.

1840 *Picayune* 2 Aug. 2/5 She scorned to find surety in $500 to keep the peace, so she was sent down. **1882** SALA *Amer. Revisited* (1883) 73 They were 'sent down' for ten days.

*2. *To send up.* **a.** To send to prison. {1897-} +**b.** (See quotations.) Also *vbl. n.*

(a) 1867 DALY *Under Gaslight* 11. 16 Here's me as was a-weeping every night, thinking as you was sent up for six months. **1880** 'MARK TWAIN' in *Atlantic Mo.* Aug. 228/2 He was 'sent up' for only two years. **1890** *Scribner's Mag.* Nov. 619/1 Some of them [*sc.* women sentenced to the workhouse] seem rather proud of the number of times they have been 'sent up.' **(b) 1902** WHITE *Blazed Trail* 82 He was engaged in 'sending up'; that is he was one of the two men who stand at either side of the skids to help the ascending log keep straight and true to its bed on the pile. **1905** *Forestry Bureau Bul.* No. 61, 46 *Send up, to*, in loading, to raise logs up skids with cant hooks, or by steam or horse power.

+3. *Baseball.* To send (*a ball*) *in*, to deliver a swiftly pitched ball to a batter.

1871 *N.Y. Herald* 22 Sept. 4/6 Wolters . . . never sent the balls in better than on this occasion.

Send-off. {1889-}

+1. A sending off or starting of contestants in a race.

1856 *Porter's Spirit of Times* 25 Oct. 131/2 Shockoe got the send-off with the word. **1875** *Chicago Tribune* 15 July 1/3 There was considerable jockeying, and . . . an even send-off [in the boat race] was not obtained.

+2. A good-will demonstration given a person or persons setting off on a journey, etc.; also, transf., a start. *colloq.* {1889}

1872 'MARK TWAIN' *Roughing It* 332 One of the boys has passed in his checks, and we want to give him a good send-off. **1887** HARTE *& Devil's Ford* 72 No opportunity was offered for a 'send off' suitable to the conditions of the parties. **1903** ADE *People You Know* 44 Proposing to every Girl the first time he met her . . . seemed to him such a cordial Send-Off for a budding Friendship.

+Sene. Abbrev. of SENIOR. *slang. Obs.* — **1846** *Yale Banger* 10 Nov., The Freshman Class . . . from time immemorial the target for all the venomed darts of rowdy Sophs., magnificent Juns., and lazy Senes. **1850** *Ib.* 2 Dec., A rare young blade is the gallant Sene.

+Seneca. Also †Senecke, Sinneque, Siniker. [Du. *Sennecaas*, a term used collectively for the Indians in the Lake Oneida region of western New York.]

1. *pl.* = SENECA INDIAN b.

[*c*1614 in *Doc. Col. Hist. N.Y.* I. opp. p. 11 (*map*), Sennecas.] **1664** *Mass. H. S. Coll.* 4 Ser. VI. 531, 3000 of the Seneckes, a people in league with the Mohawkes beyond them, are gathered together. **1694** *N.J. Archives* 1 Ser. II. 104 The Mennissinck Sachems . . . are afraid that the Sinneques have killed them. **1709** SEWALL *Diary* 11. 262, 300 Eastern Indians . . . were gon to the 5 Nations to pray leave to dwell with them, and . . . others refusing them, they were gon to the Senecas. **1789** *Indian Laws & Tr.* III. 698 The Ondawagas, or Senacas, Cayugas, Tuscaroras, Onondagas, and Oneidas, . . . did make, and conclude upon the following articles. **1823** J. M. DUNCAN *Travels U.S.* II. 77 The Five Nations were the Mohawks, Oneydas, Onondagoes, Cayugas, and Senecas. **1894** ROBLEY *Bourbon Co., Kansas* 7 These various tribes of New York Indians, consisting of the remnants of the Senecas, Onondagas, Cayugas, Tuscaroras, Oneidas, St. Regis, Stockbridges, Munsees and Brother-towns, were called the 'Six Nations.'

2. An Indian belonging to the Seneca tribe.

1699 *Va. State P.* I. 67 At last one of the great men & one Siniker (Seneca) came over to us. **1784** W. WALTON *Narr. Captivity B. Gilbert* 7 The other five were Senecas. **1793** *Mass. H. S. Coll.* 3 Ser. V. 155 This Seneca said that excepting the four nations before mentioned, the Indians were for peace. **1874** B. F. TAYLOR *World on Wheels* 31 The painted Senecas and the smoky Onondagas went gliding about like vanishing shadows.

3. Attrib. with *chief, tribe.*

1840 VAN BUREN in *Pres. Mess. & P.* III. 566 That improper means have been employed to obtain the assent of the Seneca chiefs there is every reason to believe. **1846** *Xenia Torch-Light* 11 June 1/1 An aged chief of the Seneca tribe . . . had not yet been to see him.

+Seneca grass. The odoriferous holy grass (*Hierochloë borealis*) of the northern states. — **1814** BIGELOW *Florula Bostoniensis* 245 *Holcus odoratus.* Seneca grass. . . . **1815** *Lit. & Phil. Soc. N.Y. Trans.* I. 72 There is a highly aromatic plant collected by the Indians in small quantities, called the Seneca grass. **1840** DEWEY *Mass. Flowering Plants* 243 Seneca Grass. . . . Sweet-scented American plant, spread widely over the country, but not of much utility. **1857** GRAY *Botany* 574 *H*[ierochloa] *borealis.* . . . Vanilla or Seneca Grass. . . . Moist meadows, Mass. to Wisconsin, and northward.

+Seneca Indian. a. An Indian belonging to the largest and most warlike of the tribes making up the Five Nations. **b.** *pl.* The tribe. — **1684** *N.H. Hist. Soc. Coll.* II. 199 The sd Mohauck, Senacar, or other Indians, [shall] be paid out of such monies as shall be raised in the sd

Province. **1724** JONES *Virginia* 5 The Senecaa Indians in their War Dress may appear as terrible as any of the Sons of Anak. **1775** ADAIR *Indians* 393 A party of the Senekah Indians came to war against the Katahba. **1840** *Niles' Nat. Reg.* 4 April 80/2 The treaty made with the Seneca Indians has been ratified by the senate. **1900** *Congress. Rec.* 26 Jan. 1232/2 Among the Seneca Indians a singularly beautiful belief prevailed.

+Seneca nation. The (or an) Indian nation of the Senecas. Also pl. — **1779** *N.H. Hist. Soc. Coll.* VI. 326 Near the end of this lake is the famous town of Kanadagago, the metropolis of the Seneca Nations. **1787** *Mag. Amer. Hist.* I. 383 The Indian who was killed was a principal man in the Seneca Nation. **1846** POLK in *Pres. Mess. & P.* IV. 428, I herewith transmit . . . a memorial addressed to the President and the Senate in relation to the treaty . . . of May 20, 1842, with the 'Seneca Nation of Indians.'

+Seneca oil. Crude petroleum found in the region formerly occupied by the Seneca Indians. Now hist. — **1795** J. SCOTT *U.S. Gazetteer* s.v. *Allegany*, In this county is Oil creek: It flows from a spring much celebrated for a bitumen resembling Barbadoes tar, and is known by the name of Seneca Oil. **1804** *Doc. Hist. N.Y. State* II. 1176 A sort of oil called by the Indians Seneca Oil . . . is excellent for wounds and other medicinal uses. **1883** *Century Mag.* July 325/1 Seneca Oil [was sold] as a remedy for rheumatism. **1904** TARBELL *Hist. Standard Oil Co.* I. 5 'Seneca Oil' seems to have been the earliest name under which petroleum appeared in the East.

+Seneca rattlesnake-root. =next. — **1738** TENNENT *Epistle to Mead* 5 A Root discovered by the Seneca Indians . . . was a certain Remedy against the Bite of the Rattle-snake, . . . and was distinguished by the Name of Seneca Rattle-snake Root. **1801** *Hist. Review & Directory* I. 145 Seneca rattlesnake-root. *Polygala Senega.* **1830** WATSON *Philadelphia* 616 About the year 1739, I saw much said in the Gazettes of the newly discovered virtues of the Seneka rattlesnake root.

+Seneca snakeroot. An American milkwort (*Polygala senega*), or the root of this, formerly valued as a remedy for snake bites. — [**1764** REUTER *Wachau* 571.] **1789** MORSE *Amer. Geog.* 415 Among others are the ginseng, Virginia snake root, Seneca snake root, an herb of the emetic kind. **1806** LEWIS in *L. & Clark Exped.* V. (1905) 61 Sheilds . . . had previously seen the tea of Sinneca snake root used in stead of the mint. **1869** FULLER *Flower Gatherers* 136 The *Polygala Senega* furnishes the Seneca Snake-root so highly valued as a medicine. **1878** *Rep. Indian Affairs* 82 The Seneca snake-root has been a source of profit and the means of great help to the destitute who raised no crop last year.

∗ Senior. [Short for SENIOR SOPHISTER.]

+1. A student in the last year of the regular four-year course in a college or high school.

1741 in Hall *College Words* 318 No Freshman shall be saucy to his Senior. **1798** A. HOLMES *E. Stiles* 251 About a week after he undertook the tuition of the Seniors. **1813** PAULDING *Sc. Fiddle* (1814) 64 No Latin now, or Heathen Greek, The *senior's* double tongue can speak. **1882** RITTENHOUSE *Maud* 50 The Seniors wore French-twists yesterday morning. **1893** POST *Harvard Stories* 70 Randolph presented him with . . . the advice to learn as soon as possible to tell a Senior from a Freshman. **1915** CAMPBELL *Proving Virginia* 10, I supposed a Senior had to study.

+b. Attrib. with *dormitory, oration, rhetorical, society.*

1851 in Hall *College Words* 270 The custom of delivering Senior Orations . . . is, I think, confined to Washington and Jefferson Colleges in Pennsylvania. **1871** BAGG *At Yale* 169 Senior-society men never mention their own society in the presence of others. **1881** *Ore. State Jrnl.* 8 Jan. 5/3 Prof.'s Johnson and Spiller will take charge of the senior and junior rheticals. **1907** *St. Nicholas* May 604/2 [His] belongings were already stowed away in his locker in the Senior Dormitory on the floor above.

+2. (See quot. 1847.)

1847 WEBSTER 1006/3 *Senior,* . . . one in the third year of his course at a theological seminary. **1912** *Chicago Theol. Sem. Register* May 48 Seniors begin to worry over their Theses.

+Senior bachelor. (See quotation.) — **1851** HALL *College Words* 270 *Senior bachelor,* one who is in his third year after taking the degree of Bachelor of Arts.

Senior class. +a. A class in college or high school made up of those in the fourth year of the regular academic course. Also attrib.

1770 FITHIAN *Journal* I. 10 The present Senior Class consists of ten. **1830** *Collegian* 118, I was thinking you were in the Senior Class. **1871** [see ORATOR]. **1900** WINCHESTER *W. Castle* 25 Wesley and Chester went to the city of Dorchester on some business for the Senior class. **1908** *Albion* (Mich.) *High School Cat.* 9 The plan of 'Senior Class Day' was also inaugurated.

+b. (See quotation.) *Obs.*

1816 *Ann. 14th Congress* 2 Sess. 270 Those [in the militia] over thirty-one, and under forty-five years of age, shall be called the senior class of militia.

+Senior college. A college offering the last two years' work required for the bachelor's degree. — **1899** *Univ. of Chicago Reg.* 37/1 The Faculties of the Schools of Arts, Literature, and Science have been organized as follows: (1) The Faculty of the Junior Colleges; (2) The Faculty of the Senior Colleges [etc.]. **1920** S. P. DUGGAN in Klapper *College Teaching* 28 Some other degree . . . [may be granted] at the end of the Senior College.

‖**Senioric,** *a.* Of or pertaining to a college senior. (Cf. FRESHMANIC.) — **1871** BAGG *At Yale* 167 Fifteen senioric shirt-bosoms were adorned by as many new badges.

+Senior preacher. In the Methodist church, a preacher superior in rank to another with whom he is associated in a common service. (Cf. JUNIOR PREACHER.) — **1845** *Indiana Mag. Hist.* XXIII. 212 The senior preacher in his second sermon commenced the controversy on the subject of Arianism.

+Senior senator. A senator who has served longer in the Senate than the other senator from his state. (Cf. JUNIOR SENATOR.) — **1885** CRAWFORD *Amer. Politician* 137 The next vacancy . . . would have occurred in about a year's time, at the expiration of the senior senator's term of office. **1900** *Congress. Rec.* 16 Jan. 854/1, I did not know that the senior Senator from Alabama (Mr. Morgan) was paired with the junior Senator from Iowa.

Senior sophister. {1685–} +A student in the fourth and last year of a college course. *Obs.* Also fig. — **1690** SEWALL *Diary* I. 314, I would not have you send any to me in whoes Book-Debts are old enough to be senior Sophisters, being of more than three years standing. **1720** [see BACHELOR 1 (2)]. **1757** in Hutchinson *Diary & Lett.* I. 68, I was examined at Harvard College, . . . my elder brother Daniel being there a Senior Sophister. **1766** in Peirce *Hist. Harvard* 246 The Senior Sophisters shall attend the Tutor *A* on Mondays.

+Senior year. The fourth and last year of a high school or college course. — **1796** MORSE *Univ. Geog.* I. 420 The undergraduates are not permitted to attend them [*sc.* medical lectures] till their senior year. **1853** *Songs of Yale* 4 The 'Biennial' is an Examination occurring twice during the course, . . . at the close of the Sophomore and of the Senior years. **1871** *Harper's Mag.* Nov. 950/1 During their Senior year, . . . he selected a subject in mental philosophy. **1893** POST *Harvard Stories* 233 There is a grinding bee in entrance Greek, in Jim de Laye's room—lot of foolish virgins like myself, who have put off the job until Senior year. **1924** S. S. COLVIN *Intro. to H. S. Teaching* 12 A number of high schools offer in their senior year a vocational course.

∗ Senna. a. Any one of various tropical herbs of the genus *Cassia*, +esp. American senna. Also attrib. **b.** The dried leaves of such a plant used in medicine. — **1732** *S.C. Gazette* 132/2 Lately imported, . . . sundry sorts of Druggs, viz. . . . Senna, Manna [etc.]. **1776** STORK *Acct. E. Florida* 48 The vines, the senna shrub, sarsaparilla, China-root, . . . are indigenous plants of East-Florida. **1801** *Hist. Review & Directory* I. 144 Senna. *Cassia ligustrina.* **1832** WILLIAMSON *Maine* I. 128 The *Senna,* a mild cathartic, is said to grow in the forest of Union.

+Señor. *S.W.* [Sp. A new borrowing.]

1. A Spanish gentleman or one of Spanish descent.

1847 *Santa Fe Republican* 4 Dec. 2/3 The Santa Fe House also expects to figure some day *seminaria proximo,* all of which the Senors and Senoras shall have timely notice of. **1850** GARRARD *Wah-To-Yah* xvii. 198 A señora in her nightdress . . . was the admiration of the mustached *señors* and half-wild *voluntarios.* **1880** CABLE *Grandissimes* 223 He ventured to reveal the foregoing incidents to the señor.

2. A title of respect used before a man's name, equivalent to *Mr.*

[**1848** *Santa Fe Republican* 1/4 [Indians] drove off all the stock belonging to Senor el Padre.] **1866** *Weekly New Mexican* 22 Dec. 1/3 Married. . . . Mr. James Edgar Griggs, formerly of New Jersey, to Miss Eugenia E., daughter of Señor Don Cristoval Ascarate. **1925** BURNS *Saga of Billy the Kid* 24 Señor McSween was a young lawyer looking for a good town in which to settle.

b. Used as a form of address.

1890 *Century Mag.* Dec. 178 Señor, I have made an important discovery. **1907** WHITE *Arizona Nights* 285 'Señor,' said he, 'you're off your feed.'

+Señora. *S.W.* [Sp. A new borrowing.] A lady of Spanish nationality or descent. Also a title of respect. — **1841** *Picayune* 10 April 2/4 The Señoras of Santa Fé and Taos invariably wear veils over their heads. **1854** *Harper's Mag.* April 588/2 [There is no lady] of more fashionable reputation than this same Tules, now known as *Señora* Doña Gertrudes Barceló. **1863** *Rio Abajo Press* 28 April 1/2 Senora Tules . . . screamed and ran back to the kitchen. **1893** [see DON 1].

+Señorita. *S.W.* [Sp. A new borrowing.]

1. A young Spanish lady or one of Spanish descent. Also a term of respectful address.

[**1823** QUITMAN in Claiborne *Life Quitman* I. 85 The belles . . . 'tote' their fans with the air of Spanish señoritas.] **1844** GREGG *Commerce of Prairies* II. 90 Two or three well-dressed señoritas sat discussing some of the fruitful topics of the day. **1863** *Rio Abajo Press* 5 May 1/3 Excuse me, senorita; I could make no use of your person if I should win; so we will play no more. **1887** *Scribner's Mag.* Oct. 510/1 The true cow-boy delights in the lingering waltz which the *señoritas* accord him. **1912** HOUGH *Story of Cowboy* 127 Some wandering teamster . . . met and wooed and married the señorita.

2. Any one of several small, beautifully marked kelpfish of the California coast. Also *señorita fish.*

1882 *Nat. Museum Bul.* No. 16, 604 *Pseudojulis.* . . . Señoritas. *Ib.,* P. *modestus.* . . . Señorita; Pesce Rey. **1884** GOODE, etc. *Fisheries* I. 275 The Señorita-fish, of California. At Monterey, California, this species, *Pseudojulis modestus,* is known as, 'Pescerey'; southward it is called 'Señorita.' **1896** JORDAN & EVERMANN *Check-List Fishes* 413 *Iridio semicinctus.* . . .

Kelpfish; Señorita. . . . Santa Barbara Islands to Cerros Island. *Ib.*, *Oxyjulis modestus*. . . . Señorita. . . . Monterey to Guadalupe Island. *Ib.* 467 *Gibbonsia evides*. . . . Kelpfish; Senorita. . . . South to Point Conception.

*Sense, *v. tr.* To comprehend, grasp, understand. {1891-} *colloq.* ('Chiefly *U.S.* and *dial.*' *O.E.D.*) — **1840** A. M. MAXWELL *Run through U.S.* I. 102 The noun *sense* they convert into a most comical verb—'I sense,' or 'She sensed him to do it.' *c*1851 WHITCHER *Bedott P.* xxviii. 345 But in the first place you must know what sort o' man Deacon Whipple was, or else you won't sense the joke. **1857** *Knickerb.* XLIX. 68 He's smart, now—do you sense that? **1897** BRODHEAD *Bound in Shallows* 257 You sense right well that I ain't looking for no word.

+Sensitive brier, briar. Any one of various plants, esp. prostrate herbs of the genus *Schrankia*, as *S. uncinata*, that are sensitive to the touch. (Cf. SENSITIVE ROSE.) — **1802** ELLICOTT *Journal* 287 The sensitive briar, (*mimosa instia*.) this beautiful and singular plant, is common to the poor, sandy land. **1869** *Amer. Naturalist* III. 163 Along the steep banks of the creeks and ravines, the sensitive Brier (*Schrankia*) is to be found. **1872** TICE *Over Plains* 15 Amongst the grass the beautiful rose colored flowers of the Sensitive Briar (*Schrankia uncinata*). **1891** COULTER *Bot. W. Texas* I. 98 *Schrankia*. Sensitive briar.

Sensitive fern. A North American fern (*Onoclea sensibilis*) the leaves of which show a tendency to fold together when plucked or when wilting. {1823-} — **1814** BIGELOW *Florula Bostoniensis* 257 Sensitive fern. . . . Low grounds. Perennial. **1843** TORREY *Flora N.Y.* II. 499 Sensitive Fern. . . . Moist woods and thickets: common. **1858** THOREAU *Maine Woods* 108 Horehound, horsemint, and the sensitive fern grew close to the edge, under the willows and alders. **1899** GOING *Flowers* 262 The Hartford climbing-fern and the common sensitive-fern and a few others have instituted a division of labor.

+Sensitive pea. Any one of various North American plants of the genus *Chamaecrista*, as *C. fasciculata* and *C. nictitans*, that droop or wilt upon being touched. (Cf. PARTRIDGE PEA.) — **1843** TORREY *Flora N.Y.* I. 190 *Cassia Chamæcrista*. Partridge Pea. Sensitive Pea. . . . Sandy fields: Staten Island; Long Island; . . . rare in the interior of the State. **1847** DARLINGTON *Weeds & Plants* 110 *C*[*assia*] *Chamæcrista*. . . . Partridge Pea. Sensitive Pea. Magothy-bay Bean. **1884** W. MILLER *Dict. Names of Plants* 175/2 [*Cassia*] *nictitans*. Sensitive Pea, or Wild Sensitive Plant, of N. America. **1907** BAILEY, etc. *Cycl. Amer. Agric.* II. 309/2 Partridge pea, Sensitive pea, Magothy Bay bean (*Cassia Chamæcrista*).

Sensitive plant. Any one of various plants, especially those of the genus *Mimosa*, that show motion in some of their parts when touched or irritated. {1659-} — **1789** MORSE *Amer. Geog.* 415 A species of the sensitive plant is also found here. **1852** MARCY *Explor. Red River* (1854) 79 We also found . . . a beautiful variety of the sensitive plant. **1873** *Harper's Mag.* April 752/1 Verbenas and pansies, mignonette; Sensitive plants and the rose of Sharon, . . . Growing together, the wild and the tame. **1908** [see MALTESE *a.* 1].

+Sensitive rose. The sensitive brier, *Schrankia uncinata*. — **1892** *Amer. Folk-Lore* V. 95 *Schrankia uncinata*, sensitive rose. West and South.

* Sentinel. Also †**centenall**. A sentry, guard, or watchman.

1622 'MOURT' *Relation* 24 [We] kept good watch with three Sentinells all night. **1709** *Boston Rec.* 99 Ordered. That Wm. Phelps be continued as a Centenall at ye South Battree. **1823** JAMES *Exped.* I. 145 Sentinels walked to and fro behind the benches. **1876** BOURKE *Journal* 13 March, Sentinels and videttes are inspected. **1898** PAGE *Red Rock* 119 Their names had been taken in by the sentinel before they were admitted to the Chief Provost's presence.

Sentry. An armed soldier posted at a particular place as a guard or observer. {1632-} Also attrib. — **1635** *Mass. Bay Rec.* I. 137 There shalbe forthwith a beacon sett on the sentry hill att Boston. **1755** *Lett. to Washington* I. 95 Two Indians took a fuzee from a Boy within Musket Shot of the Sentry. **1863** NORTON *Army Lett.* 144 As 'Corporal of the Guard' it is his duty to post and relieve the guards and keep an open ear for the call of the sentry. **1907** LONDON *Road* 94 There were machine-guns in the sentry-towers.

Sentry box. A small wooden structure or booth for sheltering a sentry in bad weather. {1716-} — **1702** *Boston Rec.* 29 Ordered that Mr. John Barnerd do forthwith build a Watch House of Eight foot Square, with a Centry box on the Top. **1776** *S.C. Hist. Soc. Coll.* III. 184 [To] Zach. Flurry, for centry-boxes at Dorchester,—£13. **1845** *Lowell Offering* V. 255 A small building, looking, for all the world, like a sentry-box, . . . is, in fact, one of those railroad depots. **1861** *Army Regulations* 62 If there be no sentry-box, they will secure arms.

Separate, *n*. {1612-}

+1. In New England, one of those who seceded from the orthodox churches as a result of the Great Awakening *c*1740; a New Light (q.v., sense 1). Now hist. Also attrib. Cf. SEPARATIST 1.

1842 TRACY *Gt. Awakening* 317 About a year afterwards, (October 9, 1745,) a Separate church was organized at Mansfield. **1884** Schaff *Religious Encycl.* III. 2160/1 *Separates*, an American Calvinistic Methodist sect, composed of Whitefield's followers, which sprang up in 1750 under the name of 'New Lights.' They were, however, subsequently organized into separate societies by Rev. Shubal Stearne, and then they took the name 'Separates.'

+2. An article or document issued separately; an offprint.

1886 *Rep. Secy. Treasury* I. 405 To the questions of 16, 17, and 18, in the 'separate' of January 18, 1886, no reply is given by the superintendent of the mint. **1892** *Athenæum* 12 Nov. 666/3 From time to time we received odd 'separates' of papers published in the *Proceedings* of the United States National Museum. **1894** *Harvard Teachers' Ass. Leaflet* No. 11, 4 The geographical report . . . might be reprinted in the annual report of the superintendent of public instruction, from which 'separates' could be struck off.

*Separate, *v.* +*tr.* (See quotation.) — **1888** *Civil Service Comm. 4th Rep.* 51 A statement of the number of persons who have been 'separated' from the classified service by removal, resignation, and death cannot be made.

+Separate Baptist. A member of a Baptist sect which originated in the revival movement of the Great Awakening (cf. SEPARATE *n.* 1) and was later widely extended in the South and West. Also attrib. — *a*1817 DWIGHT *Travels* III. 64 Of the number, who finally filled up its extent, were Calvinistic, Arminian, Sabbatarian, and Separate Baptists. **1847** L. COLLINS *Kentucky* 109 In 1793, an [unsuccessful] attempt was made to bring about a union between the Regular and Separate Baptists. **1882** Schaff *Religious Encycl.* I. 836/1 A sect . . . had been organized in 1751, in North Carolina, under the preaching of Shubael Stearns, and were called 'The Separate Baptists.' **1919** *Census: Religious Bodies 1916* II. 126/2 The strict Calvinistic doctrines of election, reprobation, and fatality have never been accepted by the Separate Baptist churches.

Separating machine. A machine for separating threshed grain from chaff or refuse; a machine for sorting leather strips according to their thickness. — **1862** *Rep. Comm. Patents 1861: Agric.* 648 Threshing and separating machines, Grain. **1885** *Harper's Mag.* Jan. 286/1 The date given . . . is as near as possible to the time when the machines . . . became accepted successes: . . . 1840.—Sole-leather 'separating' machine.

* Separation.

+1. The formal dismissal of an employee, student, etc., by his superiors.

1779 JEFFERSON *Writings* II. 179 The separation of these troops would be a breach of public faith. **1888** *Civil Service Comm. 4th Rep.* 51 The number of such 'separations' from the classified departmental service [follows]. **1897** FLANDRAU *Harvard Episodes* 229 He would feel [sorrow] at what the official college gracefully terms the 'separation' of Billy from the University.

+2. The withdrawing or seceding of a portion of a state from the whole unit, or of a state from the Union. Also attrib. *Obs.*

1785 J. SEVIER in Ramsey *Annals of Tenn.* (1853) 317 At the time of our declaration, we . . . thought your Legislature had fully tolerated the separation. **1795** J. SULLIVAN *Hist. of District of Maine* 396 Whenever the people can agree upon and procure a separation, it will give an energy to their public conduct . . . which can never be produced by any other means. **1832** WILLIAMSON *Maine* II. 532 The General Court employed measures calculated to cool and abate the high Separation-fever. **1861** in Lewis *How West Virginia Was Made* 83 It shall be in part the business of this Convention, to make the requisite preparatory arrangements for the separation from Virginia. **1862** KETTELL *Hist. Rebellion* I. 133 Troops were stationed at the polls to over-awe Union voters, and thus the vote for 'separation' was raised to 104,913 against 47,238 for 'no separation.'

Separationist. {1882-} **+1.** An advocate of the right of a state to withdraw from the Federal Union. **+2.** A believer in the rigid separation of white people and Negroes. — (1) **1833** CAREY *Olive Branch Once More* 11 Dec. 17 There is not in this part of the country one separationist in one hundred of our citizens. (2) **1888** CABLE in *Contemporary Rev.* March 452 No excellence . . . can buy for a 'man of colour,' from these separationists, any distinction between the restrictions of his civil liberty and those of the stupidest and squalidest of his race.

Separatist.

+1. A seceder from an American denomination; spec., a member of one of the congregations of Separates (q.v., sense 1) formed as a result of the New England revival of the middle of the eighteenth century.

1781 PETERS *Hist. Conn.* 199 The Bowlists, Separatists, and Davisonians, are peculiar to the Colony. . . . The second permit only the elect to pray. **1796** MORSE *Univ. Geog.* I. 426 Southeast from Salem . . . lies Marblehead, containing one Episcopal and two Congregational churches, besides a small society of Separatists. **1809** KENDALL *Travels* I. 291 It is divided into three societies, exclusive of a society of anabaptists, and another of *separatists*, or of the *new light*, which it either does, or lately did, contain. **1875** NORDHOFF *Communistic Societies U.S.* 69 Rapp [founder of 'Harmony Society'] and his adherents . . . were denounced as Separatists [*c*1787].

+2. A member of a communistic society of German origin established at Zoar, Ohio, in 1817. *Obs.*

1875 NORDHOFF *Communistic Societies U.S.* 99 Zoar [Ohio] is the home of a communistic society who call themselves 'Separatists,' and who founded the village in 1817.

Separator. 1. =GRAIN SEPARATOR. {1830-} 2. =CREAM SEPARATOR. {1884-} Also attrib. — (1) **1856** OLMSTED *Slave States* 475 Where steam-engines are employed, there are often connected with the thresh-ing-mill, very complete separators and fanners. **1864** *Ohio Agric. Rep.* XVIII. 61 Oviatt's Improved Thresher and Separator . . . made its first public appearance in the fall of 1863. **1898** *Mo. So. Dakotan* I. 130 The straw-burning traction engine at the head of the train with the big sepa-rator. (2) **1888** *Vt. Agric. Rep.* X. 19 The separator system is more ex-pensive for the creamery man at the start. **1892** *Ib.* XII. 127 Separators are located at the most eligible points. **1896** *Ib.* XV. 66 In the last Report of the Vermont Station are grouped the results of tests on 49 separators of 20 makes.

+**Sepawn.** (See SUPAWN.)

+**September butter.** Butter made during September. — **1839** *Mass. Agric. Survey 2d Rep.* 71 June butter . . . and September butter . . . are generally of a superior quality to that made at other seasons.

+**Sequia.** Also **Zequia.** Short for ACEQUIA. — **1846** in Bryant *California* xxxiv. 396 The Pimos Indians . . . irrigate the land by water from the Gila, as did the Aztecs, . . . the remains of whose sequias, or little canals, were seen by us. **1857** M. REID *War Trial* (B.), As the mustang sprang over the zequia, the flowing skirt of the manga was puffed forward. **1870** LUDLOW *Heart of Continent* 183, I found a number of 'sequis,' or distributing ditches, already run.

Sequoia. [*Sikwâyĭ*, a Cherokee Indian, inventor of the Cherokee syllabary.] A genus of trees which includes the big tree (q.v.) and the giant redwood of California; a tree of this genus. {1866–}

1870 EMERSON *Soc. & Solitude* 132 The mammoth Sequoias rose to their enormous proportions. **1872** McCLELLAN *Golden State* 163 In the State are the wild nutmeg, . . . vine-maple, and sequoia. **1890** *Century Mag.* Dec. 180/2 The Sequoias are found nowhere except in California. **1900** BRUNCKEN *N. Amer. Forests* 12 Of all the forests of the world these have the most gigantic trees, barring only the Sequoias of California. *attrib.* **1878** *Harper's Mag.* Jan. 244/1 Now shall we explain the rise of the sap in the great sequoia-trees of California?

+**Serape.** *S.W.* [Sp., app. from Amer. Indian.] A shawl or blanket worn as an outer covering especially by Spanish Americans. (See also SARAPE.) — **1844** GREGG *Commerce of Prairies* I. 286 They now, also, manufacture a singular species of blanket, known as the Serape Navajo, which is of so close and dense a texture that it will frequently hold water almost equal to gum-elastic cloth. **1853** BREWERTON *With Kit Carson* (1930) 150 The sides of their rooms are provided with huge rolls of serapes (a kind of coarse blanket, which forms one of their articles of trade with the adjoining provinces, being largely manufactured by the women of the country). **1886** HARTE *Snow-bound* 153 Falkner had exchanged his . . . *serape* for a beaver overcoat. **1894** *Harper's Mag.* March 515/2 With their gay *serapes* tied behind their saddles, they were as impressive a cavalcade of desert-scamperers as it has been my fortune to see. **1916** 'BOWER' *Phantom Herd* 68 He had finished [his work] with an old Mexican serape draped around his person for warmth.

***Serge.** Also †**searge, sarge, surg(e).**

*1. A comparatively heavy twilled fabric made of wool and used for suits, dresses, etc.; a similarly twilled but lighter fabric made usually of silk and used chiefly for linings.

1661 *Suffolk Deeds* III. 448, 18 yrds of searge at 6s. 6d per yrd. **1686** *Conn. Rec.* III. 196 Mr. Francis Thrasher . . . [had] layd out considerable to fit himself to promoate the trade of makeing cloath and searge. **1705** [see DRUGGET 1]. **1792** *Ann. 2d Congress* 1000 Great quantities of . . . serges . . . are made in the household way. **1844** *Lexington Observer* 25 Sept. 2/6 In our stock may be found . . . a great variety of Surges, Vel-vets [etc.]. **1883** in Wells *Practical Economics* 105 The average duty on the serges or lastings used in the manufacture of shoes is 85 per cent.

***b.** A suit made of serge.

1910 TOMPKINS *Mothers & Fathers* 351 Our blue serges had previously cost fifteen dollars a head.

2. Attrib. with *britches, coat, gown,* etc.

1640 *Essex Inst. Coll.* L. 228, I give unto Elizabeth Kellem a surg was-cot. **1678** *New Castle Court Rec.* 349, 1 searge suite. **1686** *Narragansett Hist. Reg.* III. 104 A camlet cote and sarge britches. **1710** T. BUCKING-HAM *Naval Exped.* (1825) 79, I brought from Hartford . . . a new black broad-cloth coat, a serge coat, a drugget jacket. **1888** ROE *Army Lett.* 374 Mrs. Ord pulled up and pinned up her serge skirt in a way that would have brought in a small fortune to a cartoonist. **1903** WALTZ *Pa Gladden* 268 Melonie Hathaway chose to wear the white serge gown and dove-gray Dunkard bonnet.

***Sergeant.** Also †**serjeant, sargent, sargint.**

*1. A town officer charged with attendance upon courts and the execution of local ordinances: (see quot. 1891).

Cf. TOWN SERGEANT.

1638 *R.I. Col. Rec.* I. 65 The Sergeant . . . is to serve all warrants di-rected unto him. **1652** *Providence Rec.* II. 67 The Serjeant shall serve the Writ. **1837** BANCROFT *Hist. U.S.* I. 429 A nominal mayor and aldermen, a chancery court and a court-leet, sergeants and white rods, can make [a city]. **1891** *Cent.* 5507/2 Sergeant, . . . in Virginia, an officer in towns hav-ing powers corresponding to those of constable; in cities, an officer having powers connected with the city court corresponding to those of sheriff, and also charged with collecting city revenues. **1906** J. S. GARLAND *New England Town Law* R.I. 119 In case of failure by the town to elect a ser-geant, the town council chooses that officer.

***2.** *Mil.* A noncommissioned officer next in rank above a corporal.

1642 *Plymouth Laws* 71 The Courts doth give power to the Townes to propound two or three persons to the Court to be in any cheefe place above the degree of Serjeants. **1704** *Boston News-Letter* 7 Aug. 2/1 The Sloop hail'd in to the Shoar, found the Boat sunk, and one Sargent dead, whom they brought off. **1754** *Lett. to Washington* I. 7 His duty . . . is only to give to Each Company their provisions & the Sargints to devide, & not he, for no one I can Employ will Undertake the whole. **1797** HAW-KINS *Letters* 94, [I] request you to furnish an escort of one Serjeant, one Corporal and 12 dragoons. **1807** GASS *Journal* 219 One of our sergeants shot a deer at a lick close to our camp. **1898** CANFIELD *Maid of Frontier* 104 The Sergeant stood straight and tall by the leaping camp-fire. **1925** TILGHMAN *Dugout* 36 The sergeant did not believe this, but he could not disprove it.

+**b.** *Sergeant clerk,* (see quotation).

1895 *Outing* XXVII. 252/1 [The new military code] changes the title of the brigade sergeant-major to that of sergeant-clerk.

3. A police officer next below a captain or a lieutenant in rank. {1839–}

1882 McCABE *New York* 374 Each precinct is commanded by a captain of Police, under whom are several Sergeants. **1898** CANFIELD *Maid of Frontier* 93, I'm an officer of the law now, Sergeant.

***Sergeant at arms.** (See quot. 1856.) — **1789** *Ann. 1st Congress* 122 It shall be the office and duty of a Sergeant-at-Arms to attend the House during its sitting. **1821** *Ann. 17th Congress* 1 Sess. 22 The resolution au-thorizing the Doorkeeper and Sergeant-at-Arms to employ an assistant and horses was . . . passed. **1856** BOUVIER *Law Dict.* (ed. 6), *Sergeant at arms*, an officer appointed by a legislative body, whose duties are to en-force the orders given by such bodies, generally under the warrant of its presiding officer. **1872** *Harper's Mag.* Dec. 95/2 Governor Stokes, of North Carolina, and Mountjoy Bailey, sergeant-at-arms of the Senate, were two of the players. **1925** BRYAN *Memoirs* 180 One of the assistants of the sergeant at arms . . . supplied me with water.

+**Sergeant attendant.** =SERGEANT 1. *Obs.* — **1640** *R.I. Col. Rec.* I. 101 Henry Bull is chosen Sargeant attendant for this yeare. **1641** *Ib.* 112 Thomas Gorton and Henry Bull are chosen Sergeant Attendants.

+**Sergeant fish.** 1. A fish of the family Rachycentridae; a fish (*Rachycentron canadus*) marked with stripes resembling those of the sleeve of a sergeant's uniform. 2. (See quotation.) — (1) **1883** [see LING]. **1889** *Cent.* 1073/1 The sergeant-fish . . . [is] of an olive-brown color with a broad blackish lateral band. **1903** T. H. BEAN *Fishes N.Y.* 448 Family Rachycentridae. Sergeant Fishes. Genus Rachycentron. . . . Probably only one species; a large, strong, voracious shore fish, found in all warm seas. (2) **1896** JORDAN & EVERMANN *Check-List Fishes* 369 *Centropomus undecimalis.* . . . Robalo; Sergeant-fish; Snook; Brochet de Mer. Coasts of Florida and Texas southward among the West Indies to Surinam or beyond.

***Sergeant major.**

1. *Mil.* A sergeant of advanced rating, as a master ser-geant or technical sergeant, attached to a regiment, usually at a headquarters, as an assistant to an adjutant. {1802–}

1840 COOPER *Pathfinder* II. 74, I have the honour to hold the colonel's appointment as Serjeant-Major of the 55th. **1861** *Army Regulations* 58 The Sergeant-Major will dress the ranks, count the files, verify the de-tails. **1870** KEIM *Sheridan's Troopers* 116 Elliott, with the sergeant-major of the regiment, and a handful of men started down the river after several fugitives. **1895** *Outing* Dec. 255/2 The non-commissioned staff com-prises a sergeant-major, a quartermaster-sergeant, a commissary-ser-geant [etc.].

2. The cow-pilot or demoiselle (*Abudefduf marginatus*).

1876 GOODE *Cat. Fishes of Bermudas* 38 The fish is sometimes called the 'Sergeant-major,' in allusion to the chevron-like bands of yellow on the sides. . . . Its accidental occurrence at Newport, R.I., has been re-corded. **1884** GOODE, etc. *Fisheries* I. 275 Among the reefs of Florida two or three species of the family *Pomacentridæ* are abundant . . . [including] the 'Sergeant Major,' *Glyphidodon saxatilis* . . . , called in Bermuda the 'Cow-pilot.'

***Sergeantship.** The office of a town sergeant. *Obs.* — **1638** *R.I. Col. Rec.* I. 65 Henry Bull is . . . invested with the authority aforesayd, and what else shall be found meet to concurr with that office of Sergeantship.

+**Sergiverous,** *a.* (See SERVIGROUS *a.*)

Seringa. {1740–} =SYRINGA. Also *attrib.* — **1845** *Knickerb.* XXV. 448 The well-pole came to the ground just over and behind a large seringa-bush. **1850** HALE *M. Percival in Amer.* 94 Let us play this rose-bush is Gertrude, and that seringa-tree Aunt Clara. **1868** A. D. WHITNEY *P. Strong* 35 Wide turf spaces . . . under lilacs, snowballs, and seringas, and horse-chestnuts and maples.

***Sermon.**

*1. A public discourse usually delivered by a minister from a pulpit and designed for religious instruction or exhor-tation.

1676 SEWALL *Diary* I. 27, I was thereby . . . put in mind likewise of Mr. Thachers Sermon. **1729** in Sheldon *Hist. Deerfield, Mass.* I. 459 His Custom was to Preach a Lecture once a month, and a Sermon the Friday before the Sacrament. **1780** *Essex Inst. Coll.* XV. 69 A Sermond being preched in S[ai]d Chu[rc]h by ye Rev[eren]d Mr. parker from boston. **1803** CUTLER in *Life & Corr.* II. 117 Mr. Willard, . . . an Episcopalian, preached in the Hall. Pretty good sermon. **1881** *Ore. State Jrnl.* 1 Jan. 6/1 Wearing his eyes and health out writing sermons that nobody will take the trouble to listen to. **1923** P. G. MODE *Frontier Spirit in Amer. Christianity* 157 With a preference for the topical style of sermon, . . . he stands out as the conspicuous product of the frontier.

+**2.** A discourse of this kind delivered on a special occasion or in commemoration of an important historical event. (See also ARTILLERY, ELECTION SERMON.)
1776 S. CONANT *Anniversary Sermon* (1777) 6 The most noted historical facts, relative to the coming over of our fore-fathers, have been named in the first public Sermon on this occasion. **1814** CUTLER in *Life & Corr.* II. 349 Proposed to the people a meeting on Thursday afternoon at 2 o'clock, with a view of delivering a century sermon, being 100 years since the foundation of this church and society.

Sermon book. A book containing sermons. {1772} *Obs.* — **1653** *Boston Rec.* X. 5 My son . . . [shall have] first made choyce out of my study of such Bookes as he shall desier whether Divinitie, Hystory or Milletary or any of my written Sermon bookes. **1694** *Conn. Probate Rec.* I. 414, I give to my daughter Mary Hinman a desk, and a sermon Booke.

* **Sermon time.** The time during which a sermon is being preached.
1677 SEWALL *Diary* I. 43 In Sermon time there came in a female Quaker. **1687** *Ib.* 175 On Sabbath-day Old Meeting and ours much disturbed in Sermon-Time the afternoon by a distracted Fr. Man. **1707** *Ib.* II. 201 Mr. Pemberton preaches more fully and vehemently against being cover'd in Sermon Time. **1761** in Tudor *Life J. Otis* 91 You must stand up in sermon time, you must look devout and deeply attentive. **1871** STOWE *Sam Lawson* 130 They'd be a writin' all sermon-time. **1881** HOWELLS *Modern Instance* iv, It was in the very heart of sermon-time, and he had the whole street to himself.

* **Serpent.**
1. A form of firework which burns with a zigzag or serpentine motion. {1634–}
1701 *Boston Rec.* 12 Nor shall any person hereafter fire or throw any . . . Rocket or Serpent, or other fireworks in any of the streets. **1751** WASHINGTON *Diaries* I. 23 An invitation from Mrs. Clarke and Miss Robts. to come and see the serpts fir'd being gunpd. **1783** CUTLER in *Life & Corr.* I. 94 In the evening very handsome fire-works were played off—a large number of sky-rockets, serpents, crackers, wheelworks, etc. **1869** ALDRICH in *Our Young Folks* April 214 Here . . . could be purchased the smaller sort of fireworks, such as pin-wheels, serpents, double-headers, and punk.

+**2.** *pl.* The Shoshoni, a tribe of Shoshonean Indians.
1843 DE SMET *Lett. & Sk.* 62, I visited . . . many other tribes, such as the . . . Cheyennes, Serpents, Crows, [etc.].

* **Serpentine.** (See quot. 1910.) Also attrib. — **1814** BRACKENRIDGE *Views La.* 68 A beautiful *serpentine* of a red color, is found about three hundred miles west of the Mississippi. **1838** S. PARKER *Tour Rocky Mts.* 71, I saw to-day . . . a considerable quantity of the most beautiful serpentine I ever beheld. **1882** *47th Congress 1 Sess.* H. R. Ex. Doc. No. 216, 639 Black powder is found most effective in soft serpentines and similar rocks. **1899** *Amer. Architect* 3 June 74/1 'Asbestic,' [consists] . . . of pulverized soapstone or serpentine rock, containing, as serpentine often does, a large proportion of asbestos. **1910** HODGE, etc. *Amer. Indians* II. 511/2 *Serpentine*, a magnesium silicate, of greatly varying texture and color, much used by the native tribes in the manufacture of ornaments, tobacco pipes, and ceremonial objects.

* **Servant.**
* **1.** One who performs domestic service in or about a house for hire.
The second group of examples illustrates American resentment against being called a *servant*. (See HIRED *a.* note.)
(1) **1632** *Plymouth Laws* 31 In case any shall faile their appointed time by themselves or assigns for themselves or serv[an]ts they forfeit ten shillings a day. **1651** *Mass. Bay Rec.* III. 242 If theire [youths'] beinge in any such place [tavern, etc.] be knowne to them, or any servant or other helpe in the family, or supplying the place of a servant, . . . such person shall forfeit the summe of fortie shillings. **1745** MACSPARRAN *Diary* 24 My first, best and most principal Servant was drowned. **1779** G. R. CLARK *Sk. Campaign Illinois* 56 He was obliged to Encamp three days in the most obscure part of the island with only a Servant to attend him. **1835** INGRAHAM *South-West* II. 252 Northern people . . . often bring free coloured, or white servants (helps) with them. **1903** Fox *Little Shepherd* ix, General Dean was walking swiftly down the hill, with Snowball's mammy . . . rushing after him, and the kitchen servants following.
(2) **1784** SMYTH *Tour* I. 356 Those ignorant backwoodsmen [in Kentucky] . . . would conceive it an indelible disgrace and infamy to be styled servants, even to his Majesty. **1818** [see HIRED HAND]. **1838** FELTON *Life in Amer.* 69 Servants they will not submit to be called; this term is especially resisted by the free-born sisterhood; they are, therefore, denominated *helps, helpers,* or *hands.* **1860** HOLMES *E. Venner* ix, Abel had Revolutionary blood in his veins, and though he saw fit to 'hire out,' he could never stand the word 'servant.' **1885** — *Mortal Antipathy* Postscript, Families used to import young men and young women from the country towns, who called themselves 'helps,' not servants.

+**2.** A slave. Used euphemistically. *Obs.*
1704 *Boston News-Letter* 17 July 2/2 He said he was a free Negro, . . . but upon being sent to Prison, he owned he was a Servant and made his Escape from his Master. **1809** KENDALL *Travels* II. 272 *Servant,* in the statute book of Connecticut, and therefore probably in common language, is put for *slave;* a violation of terms for which it would not perhaps be difficult to assign the motive. **1848** in Stowe *Key* 164 We expect to start our servants to the South in a few days. **1851** in Bassett *Plantation Overseer* 190, I nough write you a few lins concerning your plantation and servants.

+**3.** An immigrant intending or destined to become a servant or indentured servant in America. *Obs.*
1721 *New-Eng. Courant* 6 Nov. 4/1 A Ship lately bound from Dublin to Virginia with Servants, were oblig'd by the Servants (who rose upon the Ship's Crew and kill'd two of them) to put back into another Port. **1769** *Boston Chronicle* 25 Sept., Arrived from Ireland, The Ship King of Prussia, Arthur Darley, master, has on board 30 Servants. **1771** FRANKLIN *Writings* I. 290 It was an odd thing to find an Oxford scholar in the situation of a bought servant. **1856** OLMSTED *Slave States* 228 The term *servant* was, I believe, always applied, in the provincial days of Virginia, to white men and women, who were bound to service for a limited time, and the term slaves, to those held for life.

Servant girl. A girl employed as a servant. {1834–} — **1754** *Penna. Gazette* 8 Aug. 3/1 Run away. . . . A native Irish servant girl, . . . chunky and well-set, short legs, and pretty thick. **1770** *Penna. Chronicle* 17 Sept. 138/2 Absconded from her master's service . . . an English servant girl. **1883** WILDER *Sister Ridnour* 32 Whose servant-girl has walked disorderly this time?

Servant maid. A young girl or slave serving as a maid. {1661}– — **1654** JOHNSON *Wonder-w. Prov.* 191 One of Roxbury [was] sending to Boston his servant maid for a Barber-Chirurgion, to draw his tooth. **1704** *Boston News-Letter* 8 May 2/1 Four Indians Seized a Servant Maid of Richard Waldron's, Esq. **1714** *Ib.* 14 June 2/2 A Strong Lusty white Servant Maid's Time for about three Years and an half . . . to be disposed of. **1799** C. B. BROWN *A. Mervyn* i, Our servant-maid . . . had been conveyed to the hospital. **1853** SIMMS *Sword & Distaff* (1854) 88 [She] had consented to go forward on her route . . . under the guidance of Jenny, the servant-maid.

* **Servant man.** A free man or a slave employed as a servant. — **1711** *Boston News-Letter* 22 Oct. 2/2 Ran-away from his Master . . . a Servant Man named James Crage, a North Britain. **1720** *Amer. Wkly.* Mercury 31 March 2/2 Run away from Jacob Rice of Urbanna . . . two Servant Men. **1732** *S.C. Gazette* 88/1 A white Servant Man . . . wilfully drown'd himself in Black River. **1891** *Century Mag.* March 775 He started off with . . . Sanders, the colonel's servant-man.

* **Serve,** *v.* To serve up, +(see quotation). — **1848** BARTLETT 291 To serve up, to expose to ridicule; to expose.

* **Service berry.** Also **sarvice berry.**
+**1.** The fruit of the service-berry bush. {1861, in Canada (*Shad sb.* 4 b)}
Cf. JUNE BERRY, SHADBERRY.
[**1784** ASBURY *Journal* I. 477 The child he fed with . . . sawice berries.] **1805** ORDWAY in *Jrnls. Lewis & O.* 266 Our Intrepters wife found and gethered a fine persel of Servis berrys. **1843** TALBOT *Journals* 49 Had an abundance of haws and sarvice berries. **1891** RYAN *Pagan* 130 Even Becky Ann was over to see him, carrying . . . some scarlet service-berries, the gift of Bud. *a*1918 G. STUART *On Frontier* I. 184 She is going to stop at Hell Gate Cañon . . . and gather service berries.

+**2.** =next.
1805 LEWIS in *L. & Clark Exped.* II. (1904) 239 The suruice berry differs somewhat from that of the U. States. **1841** FARNHAM *Travels* (1843) II. 120 The service berry—choke-cherry—the elder—the shrub maple . . . clothed the ground. **1852** STANSBURY *Gt. Salt Lake* 79 The timber . . . consists of oak, . . . service-berry, and box-elder of large size. **1892** APGAR *Trees Northern U.S.* 107 *Amelanchier Canadensis.* . . . Shad-bush. Service-berry. . . . It varies from a low shrub to a middle-sized tree. **1915** ARMSTRONG & THORNBER *Western Wild Flowers* 216 Service-berry. June-berry. *Amelanchier alnifolia.* . . . When thickets of this shrub are in bloom on mountainsides the effect is very pretty.

+**Service-berry bush.** Any one of various American trees or shrubs of the genus *Amelanchier.* — **1807** *Gass Journal* 136, I saw service-berry bushes hanging full of fruit. **1839** TOWNSEND *Narrative* 210 The opposite side of the river is thickly covered with large timber . . . , intermixed with service-berry and currant bushes. **1845** FRÉMONT *Exped.* 122 The stream was wooded . . . with currant and serviceberry bushes. **1882** *Century Mag.* Oct. 867/1 The service-berry bushes bear blossoms like the English hawthorn. **1894** *Outing* July 306/1 The undergrowth was poplar, sarvice-berry bushes and other shrubs.

* **Service book.** A book containing a form or forms of divine service; a prayer book. — **1633** *N.H. Prov. Papers* I. 80, 2 service bookes. **1686** SEWALL *Diary* I. 139 Married by Mr. Randolph's Chaplain, at Mr. Shrimpton's, according to the Service-Book. **1864** STOWE *House & Home* P. 327 Whether it be printed in a church service-book or on secular sheets.

Service bush. +=SERVICE-BERRY BUSH. — **1839** AUDUBON *Ornith. Biog.* V. 464 The nest was in the branch of a small service bush. **1848** BRYANT *Calif.* xii. 167 A few poplar and pine trees, service-bushes, willows, and a variety of small shrubbery . . . ornament this narrow and romantic gorge. **1901** WHITE *Claim Jumpers* 126 The mountain laurel, the elders, the sarvis bushes . . . had disappeared. **1914** E. STEWART *Lett. Woman Homesteader* 19 There were . . . service-bushes and birches that shut off the ugly hills on the other side.

+**Service pension.** A stipend paid at regular intervals by the government to one who has served a prescribed time in the United States Army or Navy. Also attrib. — **1887** *Nation* 24 Feb. 160/1 A little band of greedy schemers . . . have been diligently pushing the 'service pension' project, which would place on the roll every man who ever served three months in the Union Army. **1893** EGGLESTON *Duffels* 185 In these late years I have been cured of my regrets; not by service-pension slogans and pension agent's circulars. **1900** *Congress. Rec.* 8 Jan. 680/1, I think Congress was generous when it passed the service-pension act applying to the Mexican war soldiers. **1914** *Cycl. Amer. Govt.* II. 668/2 A service-pension is granted to one who has been in military service for a prescribed length of time, usually without regard to the existence of any injury or disability of service origin.

* **Service tree.** +a. The American mountain ash, *Sorbus americana.* +b. = SERVICE-BERRY BUSH.
1737 BRICKELL *N.Carolina* 71 The Service Tree groweth to be very large, and beareth long Leaves like those of the Ash Tree. **1785** MARSHALL *Amer. Grove* 145 *Sorbus americana.* American Service Tree. . . . This grows naturally upon the mountains towards Canada. **1824** DODDRIDGE *Notes* 84 The service trees were the first in bloom in the spring. **1883** ZEIGLER & GROSSCUP *Alleghanies* 69 Up through the laurel tangles, out from under the service-trees, hawthornes, and balsams, came the pack. **1897** SUDWORTH *Arborescent Flora* 211 *Amelanchier canadensis.* . . . Service-tree.

+**Servigrous,** a. Also **sergiverous,** etc. = SEVAGAROUS a. *colloq.* —
1835 LONGSTREET *Georgia Scenes* 227 Pretty *sevigrous,* but nothing killing yet. **1886** *Amer. Philol. Ass. Trans.* 35 A gentleman from Ohio . . . mentions as recently imported [from Virginia] . . . *savigrous* (savage). **1887** 'CRADDOCK' *Keedon Bluffs* 215 His gran-dad Grisham . . . war knowed ter be the mos' servigrous singer they hed ennywhar. **1910** *Dialect Notes* III. 458 *Sergiverous,* a term of opprobrium, as 'He is a low-down *sergiverous* cuss.'

Serving maid. A servant girl, especially one who serves at table. {1693-} — **1869** TOURGEE *Toinette* (1881) 13 As the meal progressed the old man grew cheerier and . . . at its close, he called boisterously for the serving-maid to remove the remnants. **1871** HOWELLS *Wedding Journey* 25 They were frowsy serving-maids and silent.

* **Serving man.** A man employed as a servant or attendant. — **1846** MELVILLE *Typee* 280, I was at perfect liberty to have my face spanned by three horizontal bars [of tattooing], after the fashion of my serving-man's. **1887** PERRY *Flock of Girls* 99 The old serving-man . . . had been around the world with Mr. Peyton. **1920** HOWELLS *Vacation of Kelwyns* 55 Her aunt's serving-man had stood in line all night to get tickets for them.

+**Sesame grass.** = GAMA GRASS. — **1791** MUHLENBERG *Index Florae* 179 *Tripsacum dactyloides,* Sesame-grass. **1829** EATON *Botany* (ed. 5) 426. **1857** GRAY *Botany* 582 *Tripsacum.* Gama-Grass. Sesame-Grass. . . . *T. dactyloides.* . . . It is sometimes used for fodder at the South, where better is not to be had.

+**Sesquicentennial,** n. and a. The celebration of a one hundred and fiftieth anniversary. (Cf. CENTENNIAL n., CENTENNIAL a.) — **1880** *London & Prov. Mus. Trades Rev.* 15 Nov. 3/1 The Sesqui-centennial of Baltimore was celebrated during the second week of October. **1888** *Advance* 9 Aug., The sesquicentennial celebration of the church. **1896** *Handbook of Princeton* (t.-p.), Published by the Sesquicentennial Celebration Committee. **1925** *N.Y. Times* 15 Oct. 16/4 The 150th anniversary of the adoption of the Declaration of Independence will be officially observed . . . at the grounds of the Sesquicentennial Exposition.

* **Session.** A single sitting or a regular and continuous series of sittings: +a. Of a legislative body in a colony, state, or territory.
1715 *Mass. H. Rep. Jrnl.* I. 3 The usual Orders of the House were Read: And Ordered, To be the Orders, of the House during the Sessions thereof. **1749** *Conn. Rec.* IX. 418 The listers of the town of Bolton [shall] be ordered to bring in to this Assembly at their sessions in October next the sum total of the list of the polls. **1790** *Steele P.* I. 76 During the late session of the general assembly . . . the executive of the state received more communications from Mr. Steele, than from all our other members of Congress. **1832** DUNLAP *Hist. Amer. Theatre* 56 The Legislature of Pennsylvania was in session at this time. **1877** JOHNSON *Anderson Co., Kansas* 172 Then the citizens applied to the Territorial Legislature, at its session in 1861, for a charter of incorporation. **1903** *Evanston* (Ill.) *Press* 11 April, The session for that year was marked by the contest for the office of United States senator.
attrib. **1845** *Xenia Torch-Light* 4 Dec. 3/7 We hope to secure a wide circulation for the Session Journal in every section of the State. **1862** *Mich. Gen. Statutes* I. (1882) 288 Such [a] member has performed service . . . since the passage of act number one hundred and sixty-nine of the Session Laws of eighteen hundred and fifty-nine.

+b. Of the Congress of the United States.
1789 *Ann. 1st Congress* 19 That two Chaplains, of different denominations, be appointed to Congress for the present session. **1801** HAMILTON *Works* VII. 200 Instead of delivering a *speech* . . . at the opening of the present session, the President has thought fit to transmit a *Message.* **1843** [see CONCURRENT a.]. **1895** (*title*), The Executive Documents of the House of Representatives for the Third session of the Fifty-third Congress. **1906** *Forum* April 444 An early adjournment of the session is deemed essential.

* **c.** Of a court for the trial of cases.
1811 MEASE *Philadelphia* 95 The District Court . . . may hold its session in any part of the district. **1855** HOLBROOK *Among Mail Bags* 148 Several weeks were to elapse before the session of the Court. **1896** *Internat. Typogr. Union Proc.* 11/2 This transcript . . . will be filed in court when the sessions are renewed. **1911** *Okla. Session Laws* 3 Legisl. 137 It shall hereafter be the duty of the county judge of Delaware County, Oklahoma, to hold alternate sessions of the county court of said county.

* **Set,** *n.*
+**1.** The concerted action taken by a crew in poling a boat: (see quotations).
1826 FLINT *Recoll.* 25 They raise their pole, walk forward in Indian file, and renew their 'set,' as the phrase is, again. **1843** *Amer. Pioneer* II. 271 The crew . . . walked slowly down the running board to the stern—returning at a quick pace to the bow for a new sett.

+**2.** A suitable place to set a trap for an animal.
1834 A. PIKE *Sketches* 33 He took it on foot, with his six traps on his back, obtained a set for all of them, and went back to camp.

+**3.** A young oyster or the crop of young oysters *in* a given locality.
1881 INGERSOLL *Oyster-Industry* 248 'The Set is good in Somerset this year'; *i.e.,* there is an abundance of infant oysters. **1887** *Goode,* etc. *Fisheries* v. II. 540n., There is no word in the Northern States for infant oysters, except the terms 'set,' 'spat' [etc.]. **1906** *N.Y. Ev. Post* 23 Aug. 7 The oyster 'set' in Connecticut waters this year is a success.

* **Set,** *p.p.* and *a.*
1. Of a person: Obstinate; unchanging. {*dial.*}
1828 WEBSTER s.v., A man set in his opinions or way. **1863** A. D. WHITNEY *F. Gartney* xix, I always thought she was setter'n an old hen. **1897** FLANDRAU *Harvard Episodes* 204 John was too contemplative—too 'set'; he refused to accept freshman standards. **1907** FREEMAN *Winning Lady* 117 They're awful set, both of them.

+**2.** Ready, prepared. In phrases, as *Get set, All set.*
1844 GREGG *Commerce of Prairies* I. 51 Each teamster vies with his fellow . . . and it is a matter of boastful pride to be the first to cry out—'All's set!' **1882** BAILLIE-GROHMAN *Camps in Rockies* 3 'All set!' echoes from each of the horsemen in front. **1893** *Outing* XXII. 154/1 At the words 'Get set!' the arms are raised, the knees slightly bent, and . . . the starter braces his legs apart.

3. In special combinations.
Set bowl, a fixed lavatory bowl with running water and drainpipe; *s. gun,* a gun fixed at some point and left to be discharged by an animal's touching a spring or other device; *s. hoop,* a hoop for a barrel with a bulge; *s. pole,* a fishing pole left anchored for a period of time; *s. ring,* a finger ring set with a stone; *s. tub,* a built-in tub.
1899 HOWELLS *Ragged Lady* 185 He sympathized with her in her wish that there was a set-bowl in her room. **1882** *Century Mag.* March 723/2 Various kinds of traps, set-guns, and dead-falls are also employed against [the black bear]. **1850** *Rep. Comm. Patents 1849* 382 Revolving cylinders [are] to be used for the bending of . . . coopers' sett hoops. **1859** *S. Lit. Messenger* XXVIII. 143/2 Bill . . . 'lowed he'd watch the set pole. **1887** *Courier-Journal* 20 Feb. 4/6 Children's Solid Gold Band and Set Rings, 25¢, 50¢, 75¢ and $1. **1884** HOWELLS *Silas Lapham* 50, I presume you'll let me have set tubs.

* **Set,** *v.*
The use of *set* for *sit* is not uncommon in colloquial or uneducated American speech, but this use is of such long standing in English {*c*1205-} that it is not specially illustrated here. In dial. or colloq. use the p.t. is sometimes *sot.*

+**1.** *tr.* To plant (corn) in a hole fertilized usually with fish. *Obs.* {1612-, of beans, peas, etc.} Also *vbl. n.*
[**1631** in Hutchinson *Coll. Papers Mass. Bay* 52 Mens labour are precious heere in corne setting tyme.] **1633** *Plymouth Laws* 32 The said herrings alewives or shadds comonly used in the setting of corne [shall] be appropriated to such as doe or shall inhabite the towne of Plymouth. **1643** WILLIAMS *Key* (1866) 114 Against the Birds the Indians are very carefull . . . to set their corne deep enough that it may have a strong root. *a*1656 BRADFORD *Hist.* 116 He directed them how to set their corne.

* **2.** *To set much* (and variants) *by* (a person, thing, etc.), to think much of (a person, thing, etc.). {-1741}
1785 in Sparks *Corr. Revol.* IV. 118 A visit, which I shall set more by than the interest I possess in Massachusetts. **1831** S. SMITH *Life J. Downing* 137 The President sets a great deal by me, and . . . I have a good deal of influence with him. **1883** JEWETT *Mate of 'Daylight'* 2 Young fellers, they do set an awful sight by their own opinions. **1914** FREEMAN in *Harper's Mag.* Aug. 362/1, I set a lot by that bowl of goldfish.

* **b.** *ellipt.* With omission of the adverb or adverbial phrase. *colloq.* {-1664}
1848 BARTLETT 291 *To Set by,* . . . to regard; to esteem. **1865** A. D. WHITNEY *Gayworthys* 205 She sets by you as she does by her life. **1877** JEWETT *Deephaven* 35 She sets by her looks, though. **1899** A. BROWN *Tiverton Tales* 262 He always set by blue, didn't he, puss? **1922** — *Old Crow* 490 Folks set by me a spell. Then they stop.

+3. *To set a fire*, to start a fire.

'In Eng. one may say of an incendiary that he *sets fire to* a building or that he *sets* a building *on fire*, but not that he *sets a fire*' (Horwill).

1906 *N.Y. Ev. Post* 15 Nov. 3 Two fires in tenement house letter boxes were set to-day at an early hour.

*4. *To set away.* To go off; to set out. *Obs.* {1818, *n. dial.*}

1725 in *Travels Amer. Col.* 97, I sett away from my Camp abt Eight of the Clock. **1755** *Essex Hist. Coll.* LII. 78 Dined & set away in Compa[ny] with an Oyster bay man. **1774** FITHIAN *Journal* I. 148 Mr. Carter proposes to set away soon after Dinner.

*5. *To set one's self down*, +to take up a permanent position; to settle.

1818 FEARON *Sketches* 224 The squatter . . . 'sets himself down,' upon land which is not his own.

*6. *To set in.* Of a current or flood: To flow in toward the shore. {1719-}

1624 WINSLOW *Good News* 16 Here they perceived that the tide set in and out, with more violence.

*7. *To set off.* **a.** To deduct by way of compensation. {1735-}

1654 *Watertown Rec.* I. 1. 45 What fencing or repayre to the howse is necessary he is to doe it, & to sett off in his rent.

b. To mark off or reserve (a tract of land).

1714 *Duxbury Rec.* 98 Which reserve was to be set off unto him. **1717** *Mass. H. Rep. Jrnl.* I. 240 The Petitioners [shall] be set off a Precinct according to the Bounds mentioned. **1817** S. BROWN *Western Gazetteer* 64 [Jackson] was set off in 1815.

*8. *To set on*, +to begin working.

1637 *Dedham Rec.* III. 33 Yf they doe not within 6. dayes set on to build & improve the sayd lotts [etc.]. *Ib.*, They to haue Lotts layd out for them whensoeuer they will set on to improve ye same. **1816** U. BROWN *Journal* II. 351 He then set on & pulled all the old stufing out, which Consisted of some hair, some fur, some Raccoon Skins.

*9. *To set out.* **a.** To mark off (a piece of land).

1636 *Dedham Rec.* III. 20 Set out & measured . . . Lotts for seuerall men. *Ib.*, Set out and measured for Abraham Shawe 12: Acres.

+b. To start out *to* do something. {1888}

1812 *Niles' Reg.* 25 Jan. 391/1 The gang . . . lately set out to liquidate the middle states with counterfeit notes. **1832** S. SMITH *Life J. Downing* 164, I never see fellows so mad before in my life, unless it was Major Eaton . . . when he sot out to flog Mr Inghram. **1893** *Harper's Mag.* Jan. 313/2 Did he . . . deliberately set out to be a tyrant? **1908** FREEMAN *Shoulders of Atlas* 189 If I set out to have her, I'll miss my guess.

+c. To start (a fire) in prairie grass or in the woods.

1877 *Rep. Indian Affairs* 46 The fires . . . in the grass and sage-brush . . . [are] as likely to be 'set out' by white persons as by Indians. **1887** 'CRADDOCK' *Keedon Bluffs* 101 It might seem some outburst of fire which had been slyly 'set out' in the woods. **1895** 'CRADDOCK' *Mystery Witch-Face Mt.* 2 The fire . . . was 'set out' in the woods with the mission to burn only the leaves and undergrowth.

*10. *To set up.* +**a.** To start the bidding on (an article).

1848 BARTLETT 372 At public auctions an article is sometimes 'set up,' or 'started,' by the auctioneer at the lowest price at which it can be sold.

+b. To put (drinks, cigars, etc.) before a person; to treat. Often *to set 'em up. colloq.*

1851 A. T. JACKSON *Forty-Niner* (1920) 92 You can't do anything in this country without setting 'em up first. **1873** MILLER *Amongst Modocs* 132 The Howlin' Wilderness called out, 'Oh, what a hat! Set 'em up!' **1881** HAYES *New Colorado* 76 You bet he lived high; always set up the drinks. **1895** *Boston Jrnl.* 26 Dec. 4/5 The clerk set up the soda water. **1914** 'BOWER' *Flying U Ranch* 67 [They] found Denson himself pompously 'settin 'em up to the house.'

+c. With *to:* To court a girl. *colloq.*

1874 ALDRICH *P. Palfrey* vi, I'd wager a cookey, now, young Dent has ben settin' up to that Palfrey gal, an' there's ben trouble. **1886** *Harper's Mag.* Dec. 42/1 Why don't he set up to Sally Brent?

d. Occasional uses.

(1) To get ready *to* do something. (2) To train (a soldier) to stand or walk erect. {1865-}

(1) **1760** *Essex Inst. Coll.* XX. 290 About noon there Came a letter . . . to Come to Crown point for to set up to go to Sd Johns. (2) **1835** HOFFMAN *Winter in West* II. 91 The same pains should be taken with each individual horse, as in 'setting up' an ordinary recruit before subjecting him to company drill.

Setback.

1. A reverse; a check in one's plans or progress. {1674, 1895-}

1862 *N.Y. Tribune* 16 May 12/2 We'd had so cursed many set-backs lately. **1888** SHERIDAN *Memoirs* I. 454 The temporary set-back there to one division was soon redeemed by victory. **1896** *Internat. Typogr. Union Proc.* 10/2, I am not discouraged at the set-back received in the Superior Court of Marion County. **1903** *N.Y. Ev. Post* 29 Sept. 1 The cause of honest municipal government would receive a setback from which it would not soon recover.

+2. a. =BACK SET *n.* 2. **b.** A place set back from a stream; a bayou.

1877 BARTLETT 572 *Set-back*, the reflux of water made by a counter-current, by the tide from the sea meeting the flow of a river, by a dam, &c. **1895** REMINGTON *Pony Tracks* 139 The crane takes off from his grassy 'set back' in a deliberate manner.

+Setback euchre. A kind of euchre: (see quot. 1899). — **1845** *Big Bear Ark.* 176 It may be crack-loo, poker, brag, or set-back-euchre. **1899** CHAMPLIN & BOSTWICK *Cycl. Games & Sports* (ed. 2) 299/2 *Set-back Euchre.* . . . At the opening of the game each player's score is credited with five points. When he makes a point it is subtracted from the score, and when he is euchred he is set back two points, which are added to his score. He whose score is first reduced to nothing, wins.

+Set-out dance. (See quotation.) — **1791** J. LONG *Voyages* 35 The dances among the Indians . . . [include] the set out dance.

||Settable. Of land: Capable of being planted with corn. (See SET *v.* 1). — *a*1656 BRADFORD *Hist.* 260 They should only lay out settable or tillable land.

*Settee. A seat with a back, made to accommodate two or more persons; spec., a medium-sized sofa with arms, and + sometimes with rockers. {1716-}

1773 in Singleton *Social N.Y.* 83 [Joseph Cox from London makes] settees, couches, . . . and corner chairs. **1779** BLEECKER *Hist. Maria Kittle* 65 [He] laid his precious burden on a settee. **1815** *Niles' Reg.* IX. 36/1 Fancy chairs and settees, elegantly gilt and varnished [are manufactured]. **1839** *Jamestown Jrnl.* 6 Nov. 1/5 There he sat in state among a crowd of people, on an old-fashioned horse-hair settee. **1843** 'CARLTON' *New Purchase* I. 21 The gentlemen [were] to snooze gratuitously on the settees in the bar room. **1872** EGGLESTON *End of World* 90 She sat down upon an old-fashioned settee with rockers, and began to rock. **1876** [see CAR SEAT]. **1913** LA FOLLETTE *Autobiog.* 72 We sat on the settee and talked of general matters for some time.

+b. (See quotation.)

1891 *Cent.* 5527/3 *Settee*, . . . a small part taken off from a long and large sofa by a kind of arm: thus, a long sofa may have a settee at each end partly cut off from the body of the piece.

*Setter.

*1. A breed of dog or a dog of this breed.

1827 *Hallowell* (Me.) *Gaz.* 20 June 3/4 They report to have seen . . . 2 coach dogs, 8 spaniels and setters. **1835** HOFFMAN *Winter in West* I. I saw several fine setters which I had reason to suspect came into the country in this way. **1856** *Porter's Spirit of Times* 11 Oct. 97/1 The setter is, by far, the best dog to use in woodcock shooting. **1895** G. KING *New Orleans* 224 It was the voice of his dog, his favourite setter.

attrib. **1846** *Spirit of Times* (N.Y.) 4 July 226/1 Also a setter bitch and brace of pups, from the above dog. **1902** LORIMER *Lett. Merchant* 45 Your letter . . . twists around the point a good deal like a setter pup chasing his tail.

+2. A device in a typesetting machine.

1876 *Centennial Exp.* 208 All the preceding letters . . . were shoved along to the left upon the stick by a small piece of metal called the 'setter.'

*Setting. [Confused with *sitting*.] +**1.** A Quaker family meeting. +**2.** *Keep your setting*, keep your seat. — (1) **1825** NEAL *Bro. Jonathan* II. 163 It was a 'setting'—a sort of religious exercise, after a 'visitation.' (2) **1864** TROWBRIDGE *Cudjo's Cave* 93 Keep yer settin', keep yer settin', Mr. Villars. **1901** WILKINS *Portion of Labor* 97 Keep your settin', keep your settin'.

Setting hen. A brooding hen. {1829, *dial.*} — **1856** M. J. HOLMES *L. Rivers* 233 Wimmin may jest as well be putterin' about that as anything else, for their time ain't nothin' more'n an old settin' hen's. **1896** HARRIS *Sister Jane* 63 A settin' hen flew in my face. **1903** WIGGIN *Rebecca* 8, I felt like our setting hen when we shut her up in a coop.

+Setting out. The gifts made to a bride or a newly married couple, or equipment provided to start them off in married life. — **1839** KIRKLAND *New Home* 38 And Mr. Spangler gave me a nice settin-out besides. **1848** *Ladies' Repository* VIII. 337, I think you can afford to give that to Hen and Kate as a part of their 'setting out.' **1856** M. J. HOLMES *L. Rivers* 66 Among the rest was the 'blue set,' a part of her 'setting out.' **1885** *Harper's Mag.* Feb. 369/2 'They had a poor setting out,' my aunt Debby said, 'for the Professor wa'n't noways forehanded.' **1893** HOLLEY *Samantha at World's Fair* 632 A silver bedstead the Sultan is a-goin' to give to his daughter as a part of her settin' out when she marries.

+Setting pole. A pole used to propel a boat; a punting pole. {1824-}

1645 *Conn. Rec.* I. 473, 2 owers, 2 setting poles, an halespeare. **1698** in Burr *Witchcraft Cases* (1914) 68 Then the setting-Pole was divers times cast into the River. **1753** WASHINGTON *Diaries* I. 65, I put-out my setting Pole to try to stop the Raft. **1791** *Ib.* IV. 163 Vessels by the Aid of Oars and Setting poles are brought for the produce. **1828** FLINT *Geog. Miss. Valley* I. 151 The propelling power of the keel-boat is by oars, sails, setting-poles, the cordelle [etc.]. **1882** THAYER *From Log-Cabin* 193 James was standing on deck, with the setting-pole against his shoulders.

+Setting room. Variant of SITTING ROOM. Now *dial.* — **1741** *N.H. Probate Rec.* III. 30, I give to my beloved Wife . . . ye furniture of ye Chamber over our Setting room. **1832** WILLIAMS *Maine* II. 703 Our indigenous cherry, black-birch, and curl maple, . . . were shoved from the parlour and setting-room, to admit articles of foreign mahogany. **1875**

HARTE in *Scribner's Mo.* Dec. 253/2 Ye'll jest quit work, and make yerself comfortable in the settin'-room. **1904** GLASGOW *Deliverance* 312 'Where is he now?' 'Complaining over some bills in his setting-room.'

Setting up.

+1. Among certain Negroes, an action of sitting up late at night, as before a funeral or on Christmas Eve.

1836 GILMAN *Recoll.* (1838) 81 This solemnity is usually styled by the negroes 'a setting up.' **1905** PRINGLE *Rice Planter* 272 All the grown servants have gone to the 'setting up.'

+2. A person's size and build. *colloq.*

*a***1861** WINTHROP *J. Brent* 236, I've got a daughter myself, . . . jest about your settin' up.

+3. A useful article given to a bride or to a newly married couple.

1877 COOKE *Huckleberries* (1896) 33, I guess I'll let her hev that 'ere brown 'nd white heifer for a settin' up.

* Settle, *n.* A long wooden bench with a high back, sometimes having a box under the seat: (see also quots. 1830 and 1865).

1654 *Essex Probate Rec.* I. 200 Inventory of the estate of widow Elizabeth Hardie: . . . 2 litle tables, 1 form and a setle. **1744** FRANKLIN *Acct. Fire-Places* 6 They have no Comfort, 'till either Screens or Settles are provided. **1830** WATSON *Philadelphia* 183 Plain people used settees and settles,—the latter had a bed concealed in the seat, and by folding the top of it outwards to the front, it exposed the bed and widened the place for the bed to be spread upon it. **1854** CUMMINS *Lamplighter* iii, Drawing an old wooden settle up to the fire, he threw his shaggy great-coat over it. **1865** *Atlantic Mo.* April 455/2 The sill under the no'theast corner o' the meetin'-house has a little settle to it. **1896** WILKINS *Madelon* 78 Eugene lounged gracefully over to the hearth and sat down on the settle, and began reading his Shakespeare book. **1914** E. STEWART *Lett. Woman Homesteader* 111 Mrs. O'Shaughnessy and I sat on the old blue 'settle' at one side.

* Settle, *v.*

1. *tr.* To establish (a plantation, colony, or town) at a certain place. {1797–}

1635 *Mass. Bay Rec.* I. 156 There shalbe a plantacon setled. **1670** DENTON *Brief Desc. N.Y.* 2 Only a part of the Main Land belonging to New-York Colony, where several Towns and Villages are setled, . . . doth intercept the Manahatans Island. **1717** *Mass. H. Rep. Jrnl.* I. 202 A Petition of John Higginson, and Thirty-four others, . . . praying leave to go & Settle a Town there. **1796** MORSE *Univ. Geog.* I. 124 In order to preserve the chronological order in which the several colonies . . . were first settled, it will be necessary that I should just mention [the following].

2. a. *intr.* To take up one's residence in a certain place {1627–}; +spec., to locate on new land.

1679 *Conn. Rec.* III. 37 He may have a suitable proportion of land allotted to him for one of his sons to setle on. **1718** *Mass. H. Rep. Jrnl.* II. 46 He has not settled on the same. **1831** DEWEES *Lett. from Texas* 139 Families who emigrate . . . shall immediately present themselves to the Ayuntamiento of the place where they wish to settle. **1854** *La Crosse Democrat* 25 April 2/1 Sales are daily made to those who are settling permanently in our village. **1873** *Newton Kansan* 10 April 2/1 [The Germans] were to settle on the Santa Fe lands. **1920** LEWIS *Main Street* 8 We'd have bully times in Yankton, where I'm going to settle.

+b. *quasi-passive.* Of a place: To be settled or occupied.

1806 CLARK in *Lewis & C. Exped.* VII. (1905) 398 The Lands on the lower portion of that river is settling fast. **1834** PECK *Gaz. Illinois* 142 A large portion of this [Macoupin] county is excellent soil, and well proportioned into timber and prairie, and rapidly settling. **1853** BALDWIN *Flush Times Ala.* 82 The country was just settling up. **1907** LILLIBRIDGE *Trail* 271 We were on the other side of the river, before the country settled up.

3. a. *tr.* To appoint (a minister) to a charge. {1726–, 'chiefly *Sc.*'} **+b.** *intr.* To be ordained or installed *in* a ministry.

1788 *Presb. Church Constitution* 413 When any minister is to be settled in a congregation, the installment . . . may be performed either by the presbytery, or by a committee appointed for that purpose. **1828** WEBSTER, N D settled in the ministry when very young. **1832** WILLIAMSON *Maine* II. 465 The baptist society settled Elder Simon Lock. **1887** WILKINS *Humble Romance* 389 If Mr. Morton was settled over that church, he'd never go inside the door as long as he lived.

4. a. *tr.* To cause the grounds of (coffee) to sink.

1846 FARNHAM *Prairie Land* 332 The coffee is drawn back and settled with an egg. **1860** HOLLAND *Miss Gilbert* 98 We never settle our coffee with eggs after they get to be over a shilling a dozen. **1883** *Harper's Mag.* March 578/1 Should the coffee be settled with an egg or with fish-skin?

+b. To cause (a thing) to sink.

1847 LANMAN *Summer in Wilderness* 34 We ran into a downward-bound steamer, and settled her to the bottom.

+c. To melt (snow).

1888 *Forest & Stream* 15 March 147/2 The frequent chinooks have settled the snow faster than it fell.

5. a. *To settle* (one's) *hash,* (see HASH *n.* 2). **b.** *To settle* (a person's) *business,* to make an end of (a person).

1847 ROBB *Squatter Life* 127 The party proposed to settle his business at once.

* Settled, *a.*

1. Of a colonial court: Regular.

1675 *Plymouth Laws* 173 A case, which without much damage can not well be defered to one of the Cettled Courts.

2. a. Of a minister: Established over a charge. {1785} **b.** Of a ministry: Occupied by a resident minister.

1735 *Boston Rec.* 125 One [House Lot is] to be for the first Settled Minister. **1759** *Essex Inst. Coll.* XLIX. 2 Mr. Serls was a Settled Minister at Sharon. **1797** *Mass. H. S. Coll.* 1 Ser. V. 48 The teacher or minister, who was exempted from taxes, was such a settled minister. *a***1817** DWIGHT *Travels* IV. 397 Thirty-three were without any charge; or in the language of New-England, were not settled ministers. **1859** *Ladies' Repository* 511/1 They form an invincible argument in favor of an 'itinerant' in preference to that which, as if in mockery, is termed a 'settled' ministry.

+3. Of a country: Peopled with settlers.

1792 IMLAY *Western Territory* 149, I take notice only of the settled country. [**1831**] J. SINCLAIR *Correspondence* II. 12 In the settled part of it [Penna.], the land is divided into smaller farms.] **1835** JACKSON *Message to Congress* 7 Dec., The plan of removing the Aboriginal people who yet remain within the settled portions of the United States, to the country west of the Mississippi river, approaches its consummation. **1840** IRVING *Wolfert's Roost* 259, I had relatives in Lexington, and other settled parts.

+4. Of soap: Refined by fusing in weak lye or water.

1898 G. H. HURST *Soaps* 228 Three chief varieties of hard soap . . . known as 'curd,' 'fitted,' or, in America, 'settled,' and 'run' soaps. **1906** LAMBORN *Modern Soaps* 329 White settled soap made from tallow does not fulfil these requirements.

Settlement. {1626–}

I. +1. The action of settling in a new country. {1827–}

1675 *Conn. Rec.* II. 249 More to the number of eleven [are] preparing for setlement. **1776** *Decl. Independence*, We have reminded them of the circumstances of our emigration and settlement here. **1815** *Niles' Reg.* VIII. 135/1 At the first settlement of this place [in Kanawha Co., W. Va.] there was a great *Buffalo Lick.* **1872** TICE *Over Plains* 43 The concentration of the cattle trade here retards the growth, settlement, and improvement of the rich agricultural country. **1898** *Kissimmee* (Fla.) *Valley Gazette* 18 Feb. 2/1 The grant opened up for public settlement and claim, certain lands upon which the Seminoles had squatted. **1900** [see HOMESTEAD 3 b]. **1911** *Indian Laws & Tr.* III. 671 Executive order of June 14, 1879, . . . is hereby amended so as to permanently withdraw from settlement . . . all those tracts lying south of Salt River.

2. a. A place where a settler or settlers have established themselves; a village or town. {1697–} **+b.** *pl.* A collection or series of frontier places, including the houses, barns, clearings, etc., connected with them.

In sense b often used in contrast to the wild country beyond the frontier.

1711 *Boston Rec.* 84 The Town will purchace Land of the Proprietors of the New Settlements on the Neck. **1733** BYRD *Journey to Eden* (1901) 284 We went out of our way, to ly at a Settlement of his upon Cock's Creek. **1737** BRICKELL *N. Carolina* 116 The Mountain-cat . . . seldom appeareth or approacheth near the Settlements. **1788** FRANKLIN *Autobiog.* 403 He might have more horses to assist his flight towards the settlements. **1817** S. BROWN *Western Gazetteer* 131 The settlements extend from the mouth of the river . . . as far as the great jam of driftwood. **1823** [see INDIAN COUNTRY]. **1843** 'CARLTON' *New Purchase* I. 100 A settlement usually takes its name from the person that first 'enters upon the land.' **1847** ROBB *Squatter Life* 136 The fellars in the settlement seemed to be allfired pleased at my gittin' back. **1848** BRYANT *California* iv. 54 We met four trappers from the Rocky Mountains, returning to the 'settlements.' **1849** *31st Congress 1 Sess.* Sen. Ex. Doc. No. 64, 173 Horses, cattle, corn, and many articles of merchandise, can be had at Edward's settlement, on the north side of the Canadian. **1877** JOHNSON *Anderson Co., Kansas* 58 That was the first settlement on the South Pottowatomie above the Schutte farm. **1913** J. B. ELLIS *Lahoma* 81 Them moccasins will do famous until I can get you shoes from the settlements.

+3. With defining words indicating the nationality or race of the settlement.

See also EUROPEAN SETTLEMENT, WHITE SETTLEMENT.

1707 *Mass. Province Acts* VIII. 211 Committees of both Houses [shall] be appointed to Consider . . . Whither it be practicable to Insult the French Settlements in Nova-Scotia? **1741** *Georgia Col. Rec.* III. 398 The Choctaws . . . are upon the Frontiers between the English and French Settlements. **1775** ADAIR *Indians* 261 They were in the horse-pen, preparing that day to have set off with their returns to the English settlements. **1809** CUMING *Western Tour* 245 This was formerly an Indian settlement. **1826** FLINT *Recoll.* 10 Our journey from the beautiful Moravian settlements in Pennsylvania had been rendered sometimes tedious. **1872** McCLELLAN *Golden State* 75 On his way, at the Mohave settlements on the Colorado, all the party except Smith and two others were killed by the Indians. **1919** *Maine My State* 315 Our Swedish settlement today has three saw mills.

4. A part of a southern plantation reserved for the use of Negroes, either as living quarters or for farming. {1827, in Central Amer.}

1839 KEMBLE *Residence in Ga.* 18 There are four settlements or villages (or, as the negroes call them, camps) on the island. **1856** OLMSTED *Slave States* 417 At another plantation . . . I found the 'settlement' arranged in the same way, the cabins only being of a slightly different form. **1865** in Fleming *Hist. Reconstruction* I. 351 The inspector of settlements and plantations will . . . give them [*sc.* Negroes] a license to settle such island or district. **1884** *Century Mag.* April 859/2 The owner of broad acres finds it profitable to divide them into 'settlements' and rent them to the 'hands.'

II. +**5.** A sum of money or other property given a pastor in addition to his salary. Now hist.

1755 *Essex Inst. Coll.* XXI. 156 Voted . . . forty Pounds in the year 1756 for his Settlement. **1781** PETERS *Hist. Conn.* (1829) 232 Finding the Doctor's design was to become a churchman, the people demanded the settlement given him twelve years before. *a*1840 N. EMMONS *Works* I. p. xxvii, Before the war began, my people punctually paid my salary, and advanced one hundred pounds of my settlement a year before it was due by contract.

+**b.** 'A pastor's homestead as furnished by a parish, by a gift either of land, with or without buildings, or of money to be applied for its purchase' (*Cent.*).

*a*1840 N. EMMONS *Works* I. p. xxvii, I had just purchased a settlement, and involved myself in debt.

III. 6. *attrib.* In sense 2 with *company, master, road, store.*

1843 'CARLTON' *New Purchase* I. 89, I have travelled all day long upon a neighbourhood or settlement road. *Ib.* I. 142 They contrive to barter some produce at the settlement store for sugar, tea, coffee and paper. **1857** in Dana *Great West* 226 We, the undersigned, do hereby agree to form an Octagon Settlement Company. **1867** *Atlantic Mo.* Nov. 611/2 Backwoods melodies . . . had been invented for native ballads by 'settlement' masters.

+**Settlement Indian.** An Indian who lives in a village or at a settlement. — **1740** *S.C. Hist. Soc. Coll.* IV. 94 A free Negro . . . used to Scout with some Negroes and Settlement Indians as their Captain. **1775** ADAIR *Indians* 344 Our Settlement-Indians were at this time closely hunted, many were killed, and others carried off.

+**Settlement right.** A right to acquire a certain amount of land for a settlement. Also *transf.* — **1784** FILSON *Kentucke* 37 The Settlement and pre-emption rights arise from occupation. **1792** IMLAY *Western Territory* 10 This encouragement consisted in offering 400 acres of land to every person, who engaged to build a cabin, clear a piece of land, and produce a crop of Indian corn. This was called a settlement right. **1826** FLINT *Recoll.* 207 Every married man with a family went to the commandant of the district, and for a very trifling *douceur* obtained a settlement-right, amounting to an American section. **1838** *S. Lit. Messenger* IV. 294/2 All settlement rights were saved, . . . and we set about making new settlements.

* **Settler.**

+**1.** One who settles in new country. {1788-}

See also BACK SETTLER.

1739 W. STEPHENS *Proc. Georgia* I. 469 One Bunyon, a Builder of Boats and a Settler there, had . . . built a large Ferry-Boat. **1795** *Ann. 3d Congress* 1266 The farm of a settler might come close to the Indian line. **1836** [see HEADRIGHT 2]. **1857** *Lawrence* (Kan.) *Republican* 28 May 1 C. Stearns . . . supplies Emigrants and Settlers with everything they want to eat at the lowest prices. **1871** *Republican Rev.* 18 Feb. 1/4 He denied that the settlers in the Territories wished to protract the Indian wars for selfish ends. **1925** TILGHMAN *Dugout* 74 They burned houses and murdered what settlers they could.

collect. **1890** *Rep. Secy. Agric. 1889* 265 The settler . . . is growing a better crop of maize in all the eastern counties of the Centennial State than is the farmer of Michigan. **1925** BRYAN *Memoirs* 219 The settler . . . had invited in a relentless and apparently unmanageable power.

+**b.** *Actual settler*, one who actually lives in a newly settled region, as distinguished from a land speculator.

1779 *Ky. Petitions* 51 [We] pray that every Actual settler . . . may be entituled to Draw a free lott. **1790** A. HAMILTON *Works* VII. 50 Convenient tracts shall from time to time be set apart for the purpose of locations by actual settlers. **1838** C. NEWELL *Revol. Texas* 187 None but *actual settlers* could hold land in Texas, except perhaps by purchase from a *native* Mexican. **1862** [see HOMESTEAD *n.* 2]. **1899** in *Congress. Rec.* (1900) 17 Jan. 891/1 A large number of citizens . . . are actual settlers and home builders upon certain odd-numbered sections of public land.

+**c.** With adjectives indicating the time of settlement.

See also FIRST SETTLER, OLD SETTLER.

1798 *Doc. Hist. N.Y. State* I. 675 Those who were received by the Original Settlers as 'accepted Inhabitants,' might have been born in America. **1840** HALIBURTON *Clockmaker* 3 Ser. xiv, The meeting was held on the betterments of a new settler, near a bridge, to which several roads led. **1841** *Lowell Offering* I. 122 We emerged from the forest to a spot termed by the early settlers 'a clearing.'

+**2.** A founder of a town.

1701 *Phila. Ordinances* (1812) 1 At the humble request of the inhabitants and settlers of this town of Philadelphia. *c*1870 CHIPMAN *Notes on Bartlett* 395 *Settler*, 1. . . . the founder of a town, one who makes or gains a settlement.—New England.

3. A vessel or tub in which something is allowed to settle. {1674-}

1873 RAYMOND *Silver & Gold* 193 The settlers are cleansed of the deposited sand every forty-eight hours. **1882** *47th Congress 1 Sess.* H. R. Ex. Doc. No. 216, 568 Amalgamating pans and settlers have on their outside surface a series of three, four, or five spouts.

+**Settler's ax.** Any ax used by a settler, symbolizing the complete destruction of the forests. — **1863** TAYLOR *H. Thurston* 277 No settler's axe had cut away a single feather from the ragged plumage of the hills. **1881** *Harper's Mag.* April 650/2 With the . . . disappearance of the game before the settler's axe . . . the conditions of the Indian himself have radically altered.

** **Settling.** The action of making or causing to be made a settlement in a place. *Obs.* {1609-} Also *attrib.* — **1622** 'MOURT' *Relations* 38 It was controversial amongst vs, what to doe touching our aboad and setling there. **1643** in Bradford *Hist.* 496 In our setling . . . we are further dispersed upon ye sea coasts and rivers then was at first intended. **1664** *Brookhaven Rec.* 13 The Committy of Connecticut, appointed for Settleing business on Long Island. **1715** *Mass. H. Rep. Jrnl.* I. 5 A Report of the Committee for Setling of the Eastern Parts of this Province.

+**Settling clerk.** *N.Y. City.* A clerk who represents a bank in the bank clearing house. — **1896** WHITE *Money & Banking* 240 Each bank sends to the clearing house—a delivery clerk and a settling clerk. **1902** LORIMER *Lett. Merchant* 52 Bill Harris had found out that he was no good as a settling clerk.

Set-up. {1841-} +**1.** The call or order to sit down to a meal. +**2.** A personal bearing or carriage. +**3.** An arrangement or situation. — (1) **1843** 'CARLTON' *New Purchase* I. 180 When the 'set up' is ordered, the gentlemen instantly seat themselves alongside, and partly under the table. (2) **1890** T. C. CRAWFORD *Eng. Life* 147 [English soldiers] have a set-up not to be found in any of the soldiers of the Continental armies. (3) **1895** *Outing* XXVI. 66/1, I found an easy set-up and pocketed fifteen straight.

** **Setwork.** *Coopering.* +A method of making strong barrels or other vessels by bending and setting the staves; a vessel made by this method. *Obs.* Also *attrib.* — **1720** SEWALL *Diary* III. 276, [I] bid him leave off working at his Trade of Set-Work Coopering. **1824** DODDRIDGE *Notes* 146 I have seen him make a small neat kind of wooden ware called set work. **1843** *Amer. Pioneer* II. 110 In a few months . . . a sufficient amount of nice set-work pails were made.

+**Setwork cooper.** A cooper who makes barrels by setwork. *Obs.* — **1691** SEWALL *Letter-Book* I. 119, I received of Edward Spalding and Joseph Tompson, Executors of Will. Needham of Boston, N. E., Setwork Cooper, Fifty pounds. **1701** *Boston Rec.* 10 [No one] Shall Kindle or make any fire . . . within two rodds of any wooden house, warehouse, wood pile or any other combustable matter . . . except in Ship Carpenters building yards, Sett work coopers, and Ropemakers works.

+**Sevagarous,** *a.* Fierce, violent, mighty. *dial.* (Cf. SAVAGEROUS *a.*, SERVIGROUS *a.*) — **1837** BIRD *Nick* I. 96 The strongest man in Kentucky, and the most sevagarous at a tussle. **1845** SIMMS *Wigwam & Cabin* 2 Ser. 82 'A madman, eh?' 'Yes, and a mighty sevagerous one at that. . . . He's kill'd two men already.'

+**Sevenbark. a.** =NINEBARK. **b.** Any one of certain species of hydrangea, or the bark of such a plant. — **1762** CLAYTON *Flora Virginica* 77 *Spiræa floribus albis, foliis opuli.* Sevenbark. **1806** LEWIS in *L. & Clark Exped.* IV. (1905) 49 The seven bark or nine bark as it is called in the U' States is also common [near Ft. Clatsop]. **1901** MOHR *Plant Life Ala.* 535 *Hydrangea arborescens.* . . . Wild Hydrangea. Sevenbark. . . . Western Ohio Valley to Missouri, south to Florida, Mississippi, and Arkansas. *Ib.* 536 *Hydrangea quercifolia.* . . . Oak-leaf Hydrangea. Sevenbark. . . . The bark, 'sevenbark,' is used in domestic medicine.

Seven-by-nine, *a.* [In allusion to windowpanes measuring seven by nine inches.] +Inferior, insignificant, trivial. *colloq.*

1846 *Congress. Globe* 24 Dec. 86/2 He found the old threadbare charge . . . reechoed by every little paltry seven-by-nine Locofoco print. **1855** M. THOMPSON *Doesticks* 102 Wanted to see the world; so started for the seven-by-nine State of Rhode Island. **1884** HOWELLS *Silas Lapham* iv A. T. Stewart gave one of those French fellows sixty thousand dollars for a little seven-by-nine picture. **1894** *Ib.* 11 Jan. 743/2 Those little two penny, seven-by-nine protection furnaces were replaced by the magnificent Democratic furnaces.

Seven Cities. *spec.* +Several ancient towns of New Mexico, now thought to be the pueblos of Zuñi, whose reputed wealth first induced the Spaniards to come to the Southwest. Now hist. (Cf. CIBOLA.) — **1857** DAVIS *El Gringo* 58 The first knowledge the Spaniards of Southern Mexico had of this country was about the year 1530, when it was known as the country of the seven cities. **1872** TICE *Over Plains* 212 The architectural remains of Aztec, Tescucan and other semi-civilized Indians of Mexico, Central and South America, . . . has no semblance whatever to that of these Seven Cities. **1889** BANCROFT *Works* XVII. 30 At Vacapa Niza met natives from the east, known as 'pintados,' who had something to say of the 'seven cities.' **1895** *Amer. Hist. Ass. Rep. 1894* 92 In the spring of 1540 Francisco Vasquez Coronado . . . found the Seven Cities of Cibola.

Seven-day, *a.* Favoring or practicing observance of the Sabbath on Saturday; Sabbatarian. {seventh-day, 1684–} Cf. SEVENTH-DAY ADVENTIST, BAPTIST, GERMAN BAPTIST. — **1680** *Conn. Rec.* III. 299 There are 4 or 5 Seven-day men, in our Colony. **1898** WESTCOTT *D. Harum* xxxiv, If it wa'n't fer me she'd git in time as narrer as they seven-day Babtists over to Peeble.

Seven men. +A group of men, seven in number, elected annually in some New England towns to have charge of various public matters of local concern. *Obs.* — **1636** *Ipswich Rec.* 20 Feb., The seven men shall have no power to grant any Land in . . . the Cow pasture. **1644** *Dedham Rec.* III. 105 Michael Powell is Chosen . . . to be one of the 7 men for the year next ensuing. **1647** *Watertown Rec.* I. 1. 10 The seaven men chosen for ye assayers of the towne . . . [shall] giue Eury man satisfaction. **1656** *East Hampton Rec.* I. 103 It is ordered by the 7 men that for the payment of the towne rate wheate shalbe paid [etc.].

+**Seven-shooter.** A rifle or revolver that accommodates seven charges or cartridges in its magazine or chambers. — **1866** 'F. KIRKLAND' *Bk Anecdotes* 659/2 [The infantry] consisted entirely of West Virginia Union troops, armed with the Spencer seven-shooter. **1867** J. M. CRAWFORD *Mosby* 227 The enemy were armed with Spencer's seven-shooters, pistols and sabres. **1872** 'MARK TWAIN' *Roughing It* 23, I was armed to the teeth with a pitiful little Smith & Wesson's seven-shooter . . . , and it took the whole seven to make a dose for an adult. **1884** F. Y. HEDLEY *Marching through Ga.* (1890) 131 Trenches were occupied by dismounted cavalry, armed with seven-shooters.

*Seven-sleepers.** +An American jumping mouse: (see quotation). *Obs.* {1873– *dial.*, of a dormouse} — **1795** *Amer. Philos. Soc.* IV. 122 In the vicinity of Philadelphia, the *Dipus Americanus* is called, by some persons, the *Seven-Sleepers.*

+**Seventeen-year(s'-) locust.** The periodical cicada (*Cicada septendecim*), which remains under ground seventeen years (in the South, thirteen) before maturity. — **1844** *Yale Lit. Mag.* IX. 335 The articles on 'The Nebular Theory,' and 'The American Seventeen Year Locust,' speak well of the scientific interest which characterizes the 'rural institution.' **1868** *Rep. Comm. Agric.* 1867 68 Nothing more is seen or heard of the '17-years' locust,' in the same locality, for a certain period of years. **1879** *Scribner's Mo.* Aug. 502/1 The seventeen-year locust . . . requires seventeen years to perfect itself. **1907** *St. Nicholas* June 746/2 Seventeen-year locusts in emerging from their long life in the ground build similar chimneys or turrets.

+**Seventh-Day Adventist.** A member of a millenarian sect of Adventists who observe the seventh day as the true Sabbath. (Cf. MILLERITE.) — **1875** *Amer. Cycl.* XIV. 745/2 Seventh Day Adventists . . . originated as early as 1844. **1882** Schaff *Religious Encycl.* I. 32/1 The Seventh-Day Adventists, as they are now called, do not pretend to foretell the exact day of Christ's coming. **1904** [see ADVENTIST].

+**Seventh-Day Baptist.** One of a group of Sabbatarian Baptists organized in Rhode Island in 1671; also a Seventh-Day German Baptist.

1703 *Penna. Hist. Soc. Mem.* IX. 185 One William Davis, a Seventh-Day Baptist, had a dispute with him [George Keith] in the Keithian meeting-house. **1789** MORSE *Amer. Geog.* 206 Others [who] observe the Jewish or Saturday Sabbath . . . are called sabbatarian, or seventh-day baptists. **1835** REED & MATHESON *Visit* II. 72 [The Baptist denomination] reckons to have 3,397 clergy, . . . exclusive of the Freewill Baptists, the Seventh-day Baptists, and the Six Principle Baptists. **1863** TAYLOR *H. Thurston* 131 He accompanied the Misses Smith (Seventh-day Baptists) on a sleighing party. **1905** VALENTINE *H. Sandwith* 340 Hallett picked up a volume dealing with . . . the rise of the German Seventh Day Baptists.

b. Attrib. with *church, minister, society.*

1844 RUPP *Relig. Denominations* 100 The principles of the Seventh Day Baptist Society of Ephrata . . . may be summed up in a few words. **1895** WIGGIN *Village Watch-Tower* 71 The Seventh Day Baptist minister went so fur as to preach at him. **1901** STILLMAN *Autobiog. Journalist* I. 5 The relations of the historic First Seventh Day Baptist Church at Newport with the churches observing the 'Lord's-Day Sabbath' were always most kindly.

+**Seventh-Day German Baptist.** A member of a small Sabbatarian sect with monastic tendencies, composed of seceders from the Dunkers in Pennsylvania. — **1867** DIXON *New America* II. 308 In a very short time this [Baptist] body was divided into Old School Baptists, . . . Seventh-day German Baptists, Tunkers [etc.]. **1903** *Encycl. Amer.* VIII. s.v., A small body of seventh-day German Baptists, with five churches and some 200 members, is usually included among the Brethren.

+**Seven-thirty.** A U.S. bond: (see quot. 1879). Now hist. — **1879** WEBSTER *Suppl.* 1578/2 *Seven-thirty,* a United States Government bond, bearing seven and three tenths (thirty hundredths) per cent interest annually. **1890** *Harper's Mag.* Oct. 700/2 They were known by the name of 'seven-thirties' from their rate of interest.

*Seventy.** +**1.** *Mormon Ch.* (See quotations.) +**2.** *Committee of Seventy,* a citizens' committee formed in 1871 in New York City for the purpose of breaking the political power of the Tweed Ring. Now hist. Also attrib. — **(1) 1862** *N. Amer. Rev.* July 222 An apostle organizes, a patriarch blesses, a seventy travels and preaches (the word 'seventy' means a single person). *Ib.* 223 The 'Seventies' are separated into quorums of seventy members in each, of which there were, in 1855, thirty-

nine. **(2) 1871** *Nation* 7 Sept. 153/1 The committee of seventy . . . have already begun operations. **1872** *N.Y. Herald* 2 Nov. 2/3 The Committee of Seventy Boxes. The Committee of Seventy will provide at its boxes for voters, on the day of election, the following tickets, in bunches. **1914** *Cycl. Amer. Govt.* III. 468/3 A Committee of Seventy was formed in September, 1871, which brought about the destruction of the Ring.

Seventy-four-gun ship. A warship mounting seventy-four guns. {seventy-four, 1797–} — **1778** *Jrnls. Cont. Congress* XI. 555 The seventy-four gun ship now on the stocks . . . may be more profitably for the public, constructed a two-decker. **1797** *Ann. 4th Congress* 2 Sess. 2142 These frigates . . . might easily be converted into 74-gun ships. **1812** *Ann. 12th Congress* 2 Sess. 32 Mr. Taylor moved to strike out all the provisions of the bill for the building and equipment of 74-gun ships. **1870** 'MARK TWAIN' *Sk., New & Old* 122 That woman rose up till she appeared to be as tall and grand as a seventy-four-gun ship.

Seventy-six. +Used allusively with reference to 1776, the year of the Declaration of Independence.

1802 *Ann. 7th Congress* 1 Sess. 752 The veterans of '76 . . . wasted their youth and their substance in fighting our Revolutionary battles. **1806** FESSENDEN *Democracy Unveiled* II. 161 How many a Tory renegadoe, You've raised, . . . Above the Whigs of seventy-six. **1846** LOWELL *Biglow P.* 1 Ser. i. 10 They'd ha' done't ez quick ez winkin' In the days o' seventy-six. **1880** B. S. HEATH *Labor & Finance Revol.* (1891) 32 Our patriotic fathers of '76 fought seven long years.

attrib. **1806** *Balance* V. 2/2 False philosophy and seventy-six fever still predominate. *a*1817 DWIGHT *Travels* III. 192*n.*, These . . . in our newspapers were commonly called '76-men; men who . . . have disturbed the peace of society. *a*1848 in Northall *Yankee Hill* 121 He used to wear an old genuine '76 coat.

+**Seventy-sixer.** (See quotations.) — **1806** FESSENDEN *Democracy Unveiled* II. 162 Seventy-sixer, a cant word adopted by some of our mushroom patriots, to designate the men who first asserted American Independence in the year 1776. **1812** PAULDING *J. Bull & Bro. Jon.* (1814) 109 He bought one of those cocked hats usually called seventy-sixers, from having been in fashion about that time. **1837** *S. Lit. Messenger* III. 8 Here is a Gotham . . . weekly. . . . I say its a perfect seventy-sixer.

+**Seven-up.** =ALL-FOURS.

1836 SIMMS *Mellichampe* xviii, 'Old sledge' (or 'seven up'), . . . in that unsophisticated period, had not given place to brag and poker. **1844** J. COWELL *Thirty Years* 93 Two ardent devotees at seven-up . . . squatted on either side of him, and made his shoulders their table. **1872** 'MARK TWAIN' *Roughing It* 175 We played euchre and seven-up to strengthen the mind. **1925** TILGHMAN *Dugout* 42 [They] played seven-up for drinks.

attrib. **1846** *Spirit of Times* (N.Y.) 11 July 229/1 Said to be one of the best 'seven up' players in all Texas.

+**Seven-year apple.** A tropical shrub (*Casasia clusiaefolia*) or its applelike fruit. — [**1730** *Phil. Trans.* XXXVI. 434 The Seven Years Apple . . . ripens in seven or eight Months Time.] **1884** SARGENT *Rep. Forests* 95 *Genipa clusiæfolia.* . . . Seven-Year Apple. . . . The large insipid fruit . . . [is] popularly but incorrectly supposed to require seven years in which to ripen.

+**Seven-year itch.** The long lasting itch. *colloq.* — **1899** CHESNUTT *Conjure Woman* 154 Lawsuits wuz slow ez de seben-yeah eetch. **1909** CALHOUN *Miss Minerva* 10 She got the seven-year itch. **1911** SAUNDERS *Col. Todhunter* 17 That old woman's worse'n the sevenyear itch.

*Severe,** *a.* +Vicious, powerful, headstrong. *colloq.* — **1829** *Western Mo. Rev.* III. 120 They were in the habit of managing a wild, or, as the phrase was, a 'severe' colt. **1845** HOOPER *Taking Census* 151 Them's the severest dogs in this country. **1889** *Harper's Mag.* Jan. 270/1 He never killed a man who did not deserve killing. . . . He is called in the language of the country [Ky.], a 'severe' man.

Sewan(t). (See SEAWAN(T).)

+**Seward Whig.** [Wm. H. Seward, Amer. statesman (1801–72).] (See quot. 1914.) Now hist. — **1855** Hambleton *H. A. Wise* 233 The very few Democrats in the Legislature voted generally against the resolutions, and the Seward Whigs . . . seem to have gone in a body for them. **1914** *Cycl. Amer. Govt.* III. 300/2 *Seward Whigs,* a name given in New York politics, to distinguish those approving Seward's course in the U.S. Senate in 1850 regarding the compromise measures.

+**Sewee.** A member of a small (probably Siouan) tribe of Indians formerly living in what is now eastern South Carolina; also., *pl.,* the tribe of such an Indian. Also attrib. — **1677** *S.C. Hist. & Gen. Mag.* XI. 85 [At] Sewee . . . the Sewee Indians are seated. **1737** WESLEY *Journal* I. (1909) 402 Sewee-beans, [are] about the size of our scarlet, but to be shelled and eaten like Windsor beans. **1835** SIMMS *Yemassee* II. 56 He approached sufficiently nigh to distinguish a band of Sewees. **1856** W. J. RIVERS *Sk. Hist. South Carolina* 38 The Santees, Seewas, and Etiwans . . . lived between Charleston and Savannah.

+**Sewellel.** [?A corruption of *shewallal,* the Chinook name for a robe made of the skins of these animals. See Hodge, etc. *Amer. Indians* II. 516/1.] The mountain beaver (*Aplodontia rufa*), found in a limited area in the Pacific Northwest. — **1806** LEWIS in *L. & Clark Exped.* IV. (1905) 109 *Sewelel* is the Chinook and Clatsop name for a small animal found in the timbered country on this coast. **1884** J. S. KINGSLEY, etc. *Stand. Nat. Hist.* V. 121 The 'Showt'l' or 'Sewellel' of the aborigines . . . [is] known to more prosaic hunters and trappers as the 'Boomer' or 'mountain Beaver.' **1917** *Mammals of Amer.* 206 The Sewellel is a rodent about the size and general build of a Prairie Dog.

* Sewer.

1. An artificial channel, usually underground, for carrying off waste water and refuse from houses, towns, etc. {1606–}

1769 *Phila. Ordinances* (1812) 21 The best method and manner of . . . repairing the common sewers. **1782** *Ib.* 48 All regulations . . . of descents, water courses, common sewers. **1865** *Atlantic Mo.* Jan. 82/2 New York has constructed . . . one hundred and seventy-six miles of sewer. **1896** *Congress. Rec.* 26 Feb. 2180/1 The men that were employed on that sewer were a class of men who moved around wherever they could get a job.

2. Attrib. with *commissioner, department, drop*, etc.

1856 MacLeod *F. Wood* 202 Mr. Commissioner of Paving got raps on the knuckles for the gullies and displaced curb-stones and unclosed sewer-holes that he neglected to attend to. **1873** *Mich. Gen. Statutes* I. (1882) 672 The council . . . may establish a board of sewer commissioners for the city. **1878** Pinkerton *Strikers* 381 The excitement opened by a strike on the part of two hundred negro sewer-hands. **1883** *Harper's Mag.* Nov. 904/1 The stalwart laborer, with his nose right down in the foul-smelling earth, saturated with sewer gas and coal gas, never sickened at all. **1890** *Stock Grower & Farmer* 22 March 5/4 Fort Worth will be a different looking place in three years, when it gets its sewer system in and the sidewalks and pavements down. **1896** *Boston Transcript* 4 Aug. 3/5 Another great use of water is made by the sewer department for flushing sewers and puddling trenches. **1903** *N.Y. Ev. Post* 9 Oct. 8 They broke in the gratings over the sewer drops.

* Sewing. *attrib.* and *comb.* **a.** Designating articles used in connection with sewing.

1858 *S. Lit. Messenger* XXVI. 65/2 How many has it taken from the disease-inviting sewing-stool? **1867** Dixon *New America* II. 248 The Yankee mechanic, so prolific in the matter of cork-screws, sewing-frames, and nut-crackers has left the manufacture of traps to Solingen and Elberfelt. **1868** *Mich. Agric. Rep.* VII. 354 A. Dondero, Detroit, . . . [exhibited] 1 willow ladies' sewing chair. **1876** Knight 1705/2 Pins of peculiar forms and sizes are made for specific purposes, . . . such as the breast-pin, hair-pin, sewing-pin, etc. **1896** Harris *Sister Jane* 344 She put on her 'sewing-specs,' as she called them. **1901** White *Westerners* 312 Her hands passed fumblingly over the table, just missing the long sewing scissors. **1911** Ferber *Dawn O'Hara* 207 The simple women told the story of . . . [the] sewing stand, and carved bed.

b. In special combinations.

Sewing day, a day in which sewing is taught; *s. frolic*, (see quotation); *s. hall*, an early form of factory where women sewed; *s. party*, a social gathering at which sewing is done; *s. union*, =Sewing society.

1849 *31st Congress. 1 Sess.* H. R. Ex. Doc. No. 5 II. 1145 On sewing days the attendence was considerably greater. **1822** Woods *English Prairie* 213 Picking cotton, sewing, and quilting frolics, are meetings to pick cotton from the seeds, make clothes, or quilt quilts. **1864** *Harper's Mag.* Oct. 578/2 Later still [in Providence, R.I.] 'sewing halls' were established. **1845** *Lowell Offering* V. 268 We used to have sewing parties, tea parties, . . . and spinning frolics. **1863** Taylor *H. Thurston* 434 The Great Sewing-Union was not reorganized.

+Sewing bee. A social gathering of women who meet to sew, usually for benevolent purposes. — **1880** *Harper's Mag.* Aug. 354/2 There is church twice a month, sewing bees, and apple-butter stirrings. **1885** Custer *Boots & Saddles* 125 The ladies quietly arranged, as a surprise, a sewing-bee. **1914** E. Stewart *Lett. Woman Homesteader* 90 It was to be a sewing-bee, a few good neighbors invited, and all to sew for Grandma.

+Sewing bird. A clamp, part of which is shaped like a bird or a bird's beak, used for holding material that is being sewed by hand. — **1864** *Hist. North-Western Soldiers' Fair* 147 [Donations include] 1 pair brackets, 1 sewing bird, 2 bibs. **1868** in Hale *Ingham Papers* 224 Emily has a very good sewing-bird that was made there. **1876** Warner *Gold of Chickaree* 318 If you want . . . a thimble or a sewing-bird, or any little trifle like notepaper or a clotheshamper, help yourself!

+Sewing circle. A group of women who meet regularly to sew for charitable purposes; a meeting of such a group. Also attrib. — **1846** *Knickerb.* XXVII. 373 As if I too belonged to a sewing-circle, and read charity sermons. **1854** 'O. Optic' *In Doors & Out* (1876) 55 The missionary society . . . was composed of ladies, who met once a month at the sewing circle. **1883** Wilder *Sister Ridnour* 14, I tried to be faithful; I seldom missed a sewing-circle. **1900** Munn *Uncle Terry* 74 They were the subject of much after-church and sewing-circle talk. **1911** Burgess *Find the Woman* 7 Mrs. Hopbottom was at her sewing-circle.

Sewing cotton. Firmly twisted cotton thread used in sewing. {1826–} — **1811** *Niles' Reg.* 45/2 In this valuable class of cotton goods are included . . . sewing cotton. **1879** Stockton *Rudder Grange* iv, She had to purchase some sewing-cotton, and some other little things.

Sewing girl. A girl employed to sew. — **1856** M. J. Holmes *Homestead* iv. iv, She unfortunately asked, in a very sneering tone, 'how long since he had seen the sewing girl?' **1870** 'F. Fern' *Ginger-Snaps* 117, I don't like those sewing-girls. . . . Why don't they go into some respectable family as chambermaids, or nurses, or cooks? **1887** *Courier-Journal* 6 Feb. 7/2 A sewing-girl brought Mrs. Brown a dress.

Sewing machine.

1. A machine for sewing or stitching cloth, leather, etc. {1847–}

1847 *Rep. Comm. Patents 1846* 101 A very beautiful and perfect sewing machine has been patented this year. **1864** Nichols *Amer. Life* I. 380 The reaping and sewing machines of American invention are known everywhere. **1885** *Harper's Mag.* Jan. 284/1 The little shoemakers' shops disappeared before the march of the sewing-machine. **1897** *McClure's Mag.* Nov. 64/2 We ain't got . . . so much's a sewin'-machine. **1907** *St. Nicholas* May 627/1 She hurried up the steps and into the living-room, where Miss Smifkins was already at the sewing-machine.

2. Attrib. and comb. with *needle, operator*, etc.

1863 Moore *Rebellion Rec.* V. 1. 70 Elias Howe, Jr., the inventor of the sewing-machine needle, was a private in this regiment. **1865** 'Mark Twain' *Sketches* (1926) 163, I would go back there and argue the sewing-machine question around Coon's bar-room stove again. **1872** Brace *Dangerous Classes N.Y.* 313 One of the best features of this most practical 'institution' for poor girls is a Sewing-machine School. **1880** *Harper's Mag.* June 28/1 It is usually the agents not the companies that are concerned in the sewing-machine swindle. **1888** *Amer. Almanac* 275 Occupations of the People of the United States. . . . Sewing-machine operators, . . . Shingle and lath makers.

Sewing-machine agent. One who sells sewing machines by house-to-house canvassing. — **1873** Bailey *Life in Danbury* 58 [He] knocked down two sewing-machine agents with the other end. **1912** N. Woodrow *Sally Salt* 123 The sewing-machine agent awaited them.

Sewing needle. A needle for sewing. {1613–} — **1678** *New Castle Court Rec.* 362 The Inventory of Henry Salters Goods . . . [includes] 600 sowing needles. **1711** *Springfield Rec.* II. 41, 4 Hundred sowing needles at 3 shillings the hundred. **1759** *Newport Mercury* 26 June 4/3 Imported . . . and to be sold by Jacob Richardson, . . . London sewing and knitting Needles. **1864** *Rep. Comm. Patents 1862* I. 404 Improvement in Envelopes for Sewing Needles.

Sewing room. A room in a home or elsewhere used for sewing. — **1852** Hale *If, Yes, & Perhaps* 56, I always offered my services in the Sunday Schools and sewing-rooms. **1875** Stowe *We & Neighbors* 258 Maggie turned, and sullenly followed Eva into a little sewing room adjoining the parlor. **1902** L. Richards *Mrs. Tree* 178 She hurried across the shop, and entered the sewing-room. **1910** Tompkins *Mothers & Fathers* 78 We don't really need that sewing room at the back.

Sewing school. A school in which sewing is taught. {1809–} — **1771** A. G. Winslow *Diary* 12, I return'd to my sewing school after a weeks absence. **1865** *Atlantic Mo.* April 464/1, I quitted the sewing-school on a Friday evening. **1875** Stowe *We & Neighbors* 46 The girls help every week in a sewing-school.

* Sewing silk. Firmly twisted silk thread used in sewing.

1667 Sanford *Letter Book* 46 Sume good Silke Buttons for Brest and Coate with Sume Stitching & Soeing Silke. **1711** *Springfield Rec.* II. 41, 8 ounces of sowing silke. **1761** *Essex Inst. Coll.* XLVIII. 95 The Assortments . . . [include] garterings and ferrets; sewing silks. **1811** Sutcliff *Travels* (1815) 139, I also saw a quantity of sewing silk made in this country. **1892** *York County Hist. Rev.* 73 The goods carried embrace . . . embroidery and sewing silks.

attrib. **1840** *Niles' Nat. Reg.* 16 May 176/2 The sewing silk manufacture at Nantucket, continues in the same prosperous career. **1846** Farnham *Prairie Land* 119 Their most profound wonder was called forth by an embroidered sewing-silk shawl. **1869** *Rep. Comm. Agric. 1868* 289 The American sewing-silk machine is a great improvement over the old-fashioned one.

+Sewing society. A society or group of women, usually in a particular church, organized to sew for charitable purposes; a meeting of such a society.

Cf. Sewing circle.

[**1842** Dickens *Amer. Notes* I. 109 They have among themselves [at the State Hospital in Boston] a sewing society to make clothes for the poor.] **1845** Kirkland *Western Clearings* 120 Emma and her Mother did not join the sewing society. **1878** Cooke *Happy Dodd* 94 The ladies . . . announced at the Wednesday sewing-society that the congregation were invited to be at the parsonage. **1886** H. D. Brown *Two College Girls* 6 Mrs. Howe entertained the sewing society. **1920** *3d Nat. Country Life Conf. Proc.* 96 The 'steered' committee . . . gathers up the neighborhood discussion from the . . . sewing society.

attrib. **1883** *Wheelman* I. 351 The sewing-society circle are coming here to surprise us.

Sewing table. 1. A table or lapboard used in sewing. **2.** (See quotation.) — (1) **1863** A. D. Whitney *F. Gartney* xxi, In her low chair by her sewing-table, sat the young sister. **1883** Knight *Suppl.* 527/1 *Lap Table*, a sewing or cutting-out table, supported in or over the lap; a lap-board. **1900** Dix *Deacon Bradbury* 5 Mrs. Bradbury . . . placed a pile of pie-plates on the sewing-table. (2) **1876** Knight 2124/1 *Sewing-table*, a table or bench at which signatures of books are sewed to the cords or bands by which they are fastened together, and also secured in the cover.

Sewing twine. Firmly twisted twine used in sewing. — **1809** *Ann. 10th Congress 2 Sess.* 1537 [This bill prohibits the exportation of] seine, sail, or sewing twine. *a*1817 Dwight *Travels* III. 73 Sewing twine only is spun at present.

Sewing woman. A woman whose trade or occupation is sewing. {1847–} — **1853** Stowe *Key* 34/1 She will get spoiled, and go to raising her price,—these sewing-women are so selfish. **1865** *Atlantic Mo.* XV. 91 In a large city there are always hundreds of sewing-women begging from these hard employers the privilege of toiling all day. **1882** McCabe *New York* 275 Ballet girls, sewing women, all sorts of people who live by their wits, find homes here. **1902** Aldrich *Sea Turn* 180 Among her own acquaintances Mrs. Shaw would solicit work for the sewing-women.

∗ Sexton.

∗1. A subordinate official or janitor of a church, whose duties include the ringing of the church bell and, formerly, the digging of graves.

1717 *Boston Selectmen* 22 The T. Clerk . . . [shall] Supply ye Several Sextons or Bell Ringers . . . with the Penall Order . . . Relating to Regulating of Buryalls. 1790 in H. M. Brooks *Gleanings* II. 96 The sextons [of Salem] are desired to toll the Bells only four strokes in a minute. 1843 *Knickerb.* XXII. 83 The sexton of the church made his appearance. 1882 McCabe *New York* 208 The hostess summons to her aid the sexton of the fashionable church she attends. 1907 *St. Nicholas* Sept. 1014/1 By the favor of Uncle Seth Howe, the sexton, he had watched every step in the erection of the new organ.

2. Any of various carrion beetles which bury small dead animals by digging away the earth under them; a burying beetle. In full *sexton beetle.* {1840-}

1854 Emmons *Agric. N.Y.* V. 56 The latter [*Silpha*] are sometimes called sexton beetles, from their habit of burying all the small dead animals they meet with. 1869 *Rep. Comm. Agric. 1868* 307 The *Silphidæ* (burying or sexton beetles, scavengers, etc.) are found with dead animals, and sometimes on flowers. 1884 J. S. Kingsley, etc. *Stand. Nat. Hist.* II. 385 On account of their habit of burying small dead vertebrate animals, in which they lay their eggs, these beetles [*Necrophorus*] are often called sextons or grave-diggers.

Shack, *n.*[1]

1. A worthless fellow; a vagabond or lout. *colloq.*[2] {1682-} Now rare.

'*Dial.* and *U.S.*' (*O.E.D.*).

1843 Stephens *High Life N.Y.* I. 135 It aint common that you'll find a lazy shack of a feller very tight about money. 1846 Whitcher *Bedott P.* iii. 34 Her father was a poor drunken shack . . . , and her mother took in washin'. 1898 Westcott *D. Harum* 221 That ole shack! Who in creation could he git to take him?

2. A slow trot. Also *shack gait.*

1881 *Harper's Mag.* Feb. 375/2 [He] walked with a peculiar shack gait. 1900 Garland *Eagle's Heart* 144 He continued his steady onward 'shack' toward the West.

∗ Shack, *n.*[2]

1. Fallen mast, as beechnuts, acorns, etc. {1825-} Also *shack-fed.*

1849 W. Brown *America* 33 The pork which has been fed in the woods is called shack-fed, and is not so good as the corn-fed. 1858 in J. F. Morgan *Eng. under Norman Occup.* 57n., Wild hogs . . . grew fat upon the shack which every where abounded [near Sandusky, O.].

+2. (See quotation.)

1891 *Cent.* 5539/1 *Shack,* . . . in the fisheries, bait picked up at sea by any means, as the flesh of porpoises or of sea-birds, refuse fish, etc., as distinguished from the regular stock of bait carried by the vessel or otherwise depended upon. Also *shack-bait.* (New Eng.)

+3. A miscellaneous catch of fish at sea made up largely of cheap varieties, esp. of cod. Also attrib.

1904 *Mass. Com. Fisheries Rep.* 78 At first a shack trip referred particularly to a voyage on which cheap species of fishes constituted the bulk of the catch. *Ib.,* Such fish, tumbled in together, without effort at classification, are known as shack.

+Shack, *n.*[3] [Of obscure origin.] A shabby house, log cabin, hut, or shanty.

1878 *Rep. Indian Affairs* 42 Too much praise cannot be given to these homesteaders for . . . the erection of this building, while they, themselves, were living in shacks. 1891 Ryan *Told in Hills* 350 They laid him on the floor of the shack. 1901 White *Westerners* 222 Then yere's the cookee's shack. 1924 Mulford *Rustler's Valley* iv, The street was a busy one in front of a line of lighted buildings, frame, one-story shacks all.

b. Attrib. and comb. with *life, like, mate.*

1885 *Home Missionary* March 426 The rude shacklike store, has changed to an imposing structure of stone or brick. 1891 Ryan *Told in Hills* 191 From their tones one would gather the impression that all the splendors of a metropolis were as nothing when compared with the luxuries of 'shack' life in the 'bush.' 1909 *N.Y. Ev. Post* 4 Feb. (Th.), An Italian was murdered in his bunk by his shack-mate.

+Shack, *v.* [Possibly different words.] **1.** *intr.* (See quot. 1896.) **2.** *tr.* To go after, hunt up, or retrieve. — (1) 1833 *Trial E. K. Avery* 61, I *shacked* down some of the hills, (partly run). 1896 *Dialect Notes* I. 424 *Shack,* . . . to go at a slow trot. 'The old horse shacked along.' (2) 1891 *Cent.* 5539/1 *Shack,* . . . to go after, as a ball batted to a distance. (Local, U.S.) 1900 *Dialect Notes* II. 58 *Shack.* 1. To gather tennis balls. . . . 2. To go in search of, hunt up a person or thing.

∗Shackling, *a.* {1788-} +=next. — 1790 in Morison *Oxford Hist. U.S.* I. 127 His whole figure has a loose, shackling air. 1846 Polk *Diary* (1929) 114 Mr. Bancroft reminded Mr. Buchanan of a remark which he had made in the Cabinet some months ago, that the title of the United States north of 49° was a shackling one. 1883 Shields *S. S. Prentiss* 62 The boat itself was a rude, shackling craft, with rickety flooring and an abundance of bilge-water beneath.

Shackly, *a.* Rickety, dilapidated, ramshackle, loose-jointed. '*U.S.* and *dial.*' (*O.E.D.*). — 1843 *Indiana Mag. Hist.* III. 181 Shackly houses, huts and hovels . . . gave no great expectation of refinements. 1876 'Mark Twain' *Tom Sawyer* xxx. 228, I got to the old shackly brick store by Temperance Tavern. 1891 Wilkins *New Eng. Nun* 273 If folks want to wear them manufactured shoes, they can, . . . old shackly things! 1897 'Mark Twain' *Following Equator* 694 A gaunt, shackly, country lout six feet high . . . had on a hideous brand-new woolen coat.

∗ Shad.

1. An American clupeoid fish (*Alosa sapidissima*) of the Atlantic coast region. Usually collective.

See also CHICKEN SHAD.

1612 Smith, etc. *Virginia* I. 15 Of fish we were best acquainted with . . . Catfish, Shades, Pearch of 3 sorts. 1698 Thomas *Pensilvania* 13 And for Fish, there are prodigious quantities of most sorts, viz. Shadds . . . Sheeps-Heads [etc.]. 1709 Lawson *Carolina* 157 Shads are a sweet Fish, but very bony. 1771 Washington *Diaries* II. 16 Many Shad had been catchd on the Maryland shore. 1789 Morse *Amer. Geog.* 205 In the rivers and bays are plenty of . . . shad, lobsters, oysters and clams. 1803 *Mass. H. S. Coll.* 1 Ser. IX. 124 In the [Tioga] river, shad are caught in the spring. 1842 *Nat. Hist. N.Y., Zoology* IV. 255 American Shad . . . are sold at from six to ten dollars per hundred. 1884 *Century Mag.* April 827/1, I have . . . let my black man go fishing for the shad which are now running. 1911 *Rep. Fisheries 1908* 315/2 Shad (*Alosa sapidissima*), a very important food fish found on all the coasts and in some inland waters.

b. In figurative expressions.

1825 Neal *Bro. Jonathan* I. 272 If Bob had not broken his hold, he'd 'a been flat enough; 'like a shad in a platter.' 1835-7 Haliburton *Clockmaker* 1 Ser. xxvii. 258, I reckon you are as deff as a shad. 1875 Burroughs *Winter Sunshine* 233 They were like Number Three mackerel or the last run of shad. 1897 Brodhead *Bound in Shallows* 155 It's no use for me to worry myself thin as a June shad, though.

2. Used in the names of other fishes. **+a.** Without qualifying terms. (1) A mojarra, *Gerres cinereus.* (2) The crappie.

(1) c1733 Catesby *Carolina* II. 11 *Turdus cinereus peltatus.* The Shad. . . . This is esteemed a good Fish. (2) 1903 T. H. Bean *Fishes N.Y.* 460 Among the many names which have been applied to the crappie are: . . . John demon, shad, white croppie.

+b. With qualifying terms: (see quotations).

See also BUGSHAD and GIZZARD, HICKORY, MUD, OHIO SHAD.

1884 Goode, etc. *Fisheries* I. 569 In North Carolina . . . the names 'Yellow-tail' and 'Yellow-tailed Shad' are occasionally heard [for the menhaden]. *Ib.* 608 In the Potomac . . . [the hickory shad] is called the 'Tail- or Shad.' *Ib.* 610 In the Chesapeake region . . . [the mud shad is known as the] 'Winter Shad,' or 'Stink Shad'; . . . in the Saint John's River as the 'Stink Shad,' or 'White-eyed Shad.' 1896 Jordan & Evermann *Check-List Fishes* 282 *Alosa alabamæ.* . . . Alabama Shad. Gulf Coast of United States. 1897 Lake shad [see LAKE 3 d].

+3. =SHAD-BELLY COAT.

1856 Cozzens *Sparrowgrass P.* 137 If it were not for the broad-brimmed hat, and the straight coat, which the world's people call 'shad,' I would be a Quaker.

+4. =SHADBUSH.

1886 *Harper's Mag.* June 149/1 Kites, tops, hoops . . . all appear in due season as regularly as . . . the blossoms of the 'shad.'

5. *attrib.* **a.** Designating various contrivances for taking shad fish.

1780 *N.J. Archives* 2 Ser. IV. 320 To be sold or let for the season, a Shad Net. 1848 Bartlett 152 The large bow-nets in New York harbor, used for catching shad, are called *shad-fykes.* 1876 Goode *Classif. Animal Resources U.S.* 37 Shad-slides, used in the rivers of North Carolina.

b. Designating various fishes that resemble shad.

1790 *Penna. Packet* 1 March 3/3 William Robinson, Junr. . . . Hath for Sale, . . . Shad bass (or rock) and Halibut in barrels. 1832 Williamson *Maine* I. 158 There are two or three varieties [of shiner], one is like the minnow, another 'the shad-shiner.' 1888 — *Amer. Fishes* 100 C[alamus] *arctifrons*, the 'Shad Porgy' or 'Grass Porgy' of Key West. 1911 *Rep. Fisheries 1908* 316/2 Squeteague (*Cynoscion regalis*). . . . It is known as . . . 'shad trout,' 'sea trout,' and 'salt-water trout' in the Middle and South Atlantic states.

c. Designating persons who catch or sell shad.

1834 *Knickerb.* III. 355 'What'll you *guv* me for this 'ere lot?' said a tall shad-woman. c1840 in Northall *Curtain* 65 Abduction of Signora Low Rinde by shad-fishers. 1895 *Outing* XXVI. 445/1 On the end of the little point is a wharf, . . . littered with . . . the nets and apparatus of shad-fishermen.

d. In special combinations: (see quotations).

1871 De Vere 631 Shad-eaters, is the slang term very generally applied to members of the Legislature of the State of Connecticut—from an imaginary fondness for the excellent shad caught in those rivers. 1883 in Trumbull *Names of Birds* 157 [In Del.] snipe are called shad-birds by many of the fishermen. 1884 Goode, etc. *Fisheries* I. 606 The favorite spawning grounds of the Shad, or 'Shad Wallows,' as they are termed by the fishermen, are on the sandy flats.

+Shad-bellied, *a.*

1. Of a coat: Cut so that it slopes away in front. Cf. SHAD-BELLY COAT.

1832 KENNEDY *Swallow Barn* II. 5 A shad-bellied blue bobtail coat . . . was well adapted to show the breadth of his brawny chest. **1847** HOWE *Hist. Coll. Ohio* 257 The men [among the Dunkers] wear long beards and shad-bellied coats, and use hooks and eyes instead of buttons. **1874** EGGLESTON *Circuit Rider* 184 His coat is straight-breasted—shad-bellied as the profane call it. **1891** — in *Century Mag.* Feb. 540 Put him into a shad-bellied drab and he would still have retained traces of dudishness.

2. Of persons: Thin- or flat-bellied; lank.

a1846 *Quarter Race Ky.* 163 Do I know it, you no-souled, shad-bellied, squash-headed, old night-owl you! **1857** *S. Lit. Messenger* XXV. 305/1 He is a keen-made man, of the shad-bellied, weazel pattern. **1871** STOWE *Sam Lawson* 8 He was kind o' mournful and thin and shad-bellied.

+Shad-belly. 1. A term of contempt for a preacher. **2.** = SHAD-BELLY COAT. **3.** A Quaker. — (1) **1851** *Polly Peablossom* 80 Stop, there, you eternal shad-belly. (2) **1852** *S. Lit. Messenger* XVIII. 680/1 He had . . . doffed the cassock, or, rather, the shad-belly, for the gown. (3) **1859** [see SHAD-BELLY COAT].

+Shad-belly coat. (See quot. 1859.) — **1842** *Spirit of Times* (Phila.) 18 March (Th.), 'What do you ask for this?' said a gentleman in a shad-belly coat. **1859** BARTLETT 396 *Shad-Belly Coat*, one which slopes gradually from the front to the tails, and has no angle. Drab coats of this shape are worn by Quakers, who are hence sometimes called *shad-bellies*. **1891** WELCH *Recoll. 1830-40* 181 For an office, or careless coat, the frock was sometimes exchanged for a bottle green 'shad-belly' coat.

Shadberry. The shadbush. {1861, in Canada} — **1847** WOOD *Botany* 245 A[melanchier] *Canadensis*. . . . Shad Berry. June Berry. Wild Service Berry. . . . Fruit pleasant to the taste, ripening in June. **1897** SUDWORTH *Arborescent Flora* 212 *Amelanchier canadensis*. . . . Service-tree. . . . Shad Berry (Fla.).

+Shad blossom. = SHADBUSH. — **a1817** DWIGHT *Travels* I. 42 *Shad-blossom*. This tree grows about fifteen feet in height. **1875** HOLLAND *Sevenoaks* 288 The shad-blossoms were reaching their flat sprays out over the river.

+Shad-blow. = SHADBUSH. — **1846** BROWNE *Trees Amer.* 282 *Amelanchier canadensis*. The Canadian Amelanchier. . . . [Also called] Wild Pear-tree, Sugar Plum, June Berry, Shad-blow, Shad-flower. **1878** STOWE *Poganuc People* 182 The white blossoms of the shad-blow . . . shook themselves gaily out in the woods. **1892** *Amer. Folk-Lore* V. 95 *Amelanchier Canadensis*, . . . sugar plum; shad-blow. N.H.

+Shad box. A floating box used by fish culturists for hatching shad. Also *shad-hatching box.* — **1884** GOODE, etc. *Fisheries* I. 409 These eggs were placed in shad boxes. **1884** *Century Mag.* April 901/1 Green's Shad-Box. These, and the invention of Mr. Seth Green's floating shad-hatching box, were really all the important improvements or experiments made.

+Shadbush. Any one of various American shrubs or small trees of the genus *Amelanchier;* also, improperly, the flowering dogwood, *Cynoxylon floridum.* (Cf. JUNE BERRY.) — **1817-8** EATON *Botany* (1822) 181 *Aronia botryapium*, shad-bush, june-berry. **1844** *Lowell Offering* IV. 217 The 'shadbush, white with many blossoms,' . . . let fall its leaves . . . into the river. **a1862** THOREAU *Cape Cod* 152 The Shadbush (*Amelanchier*), Beach Plums, and Blueberries, . . . were very dwarfish. **1891** *Cent.* 5539/3 *Shad-bush.* . . . The name is sometimes given (erroneously) to the flowering dogwood, *Cornus florida.* **1905** *N.Y. Ev. Post* 29 July 5 The only tree which has buds at all like that of the beech, is the shadbush or June berry, *Amelanchier Canadensis.*

Shaddock. Also **shattuck.** A citrus fruit (*Citrus maxima*) resembling the grapefruit, but usually much larger and of poorer quality. {1696–, in W. Indies} Also attrib.

1720 SEWALL *Diary* III. 238 Mr. Cooper sends my wife a Present of Oranges and a Shattuck. **1812** STODDARD *Sk. Louisiana* 168 The Delta produces various kinds of excellent fruit; such as . . . citrons, and shaddock. **1873** *Harper's Mag.* April 751/1 Under the shattuck and lemon trees Grandpa dozes away at ease. **1895** *Dept. Agric. Yrbk. 1894* 211 This is the zone . . . of the citrus fruits—the orange, lemon, lime, and shaddock.

∗Shade, *n.*

+1. A slight structure, usually open at the sides, affording shelter from the sun or the weather.

1645 *New Haven Col. Rec.* 165 If he may have a little house or shade made att the water side to worke in . . . he will keep a ferry boate to carry people. **1677** *R.I. Col. Rec.* II. 560 No person shall suffer any Indian wigwam to be built upon his land, or shade made of mats or in other ways made for the entertaininge of Indians. **1773** in Fithian *Journal* I. 39 He has converted [a small tower] into a shade for horses. **1867** *Amer. Naturalist* I. 145 This year I made a shade open on all sides, protected by a roof to keep out the hot rays of the sun, and boards were arranged so that they could be raised up from the roof to give more light when the sun was behind the clouds. **1889** CUSTER *Tenting on Plains* 185 The staff-officers had caused a long shade to be built, instead of shorter ones.

∗2. A desolate place or one sheltered from the sun. +Used in place names. *Obs.* Also attrib.

1689 *Conn. Probate Rec.* I. 514, I give to my son Samuel . . . half that pece caled shade Land. **1693** *Norwalk Hist. Rec.* 86 To thirty acres and half at White Oak Shade. **1784** WASHINGTON *Diaries* II. 288 The Road

being exceedingly bad, especially through what is called the Shades of death. **1816** U. BROWN *Journal* I. 282, I have rode through . . . their Shades of Death (here is the tall pines) their savage Mountains & many other desprate Mountains.

3. A scarflike headdress or veil. *Obs.* {1706–}

1738 *Boston News-Letter* I June 2/2 Just Imported, . . . worsted Shades, Masks. **1751** *Boston Ev. Post* 13 May, Plain white & sprigged Gause, . . . Gause for shades. **1768** FRENEAU *Poems* (1795) 9 One must have her shawl, and one her shade. **1825** NEAL *Bro. Jonathan* III. 6 Her 'shade' . . . fell down to her feet. **1839** *S. Lit. Messenger* V. 795/1 But you could never have seen how she became her decent white lace cap, her flowing black lace *shade* . . . and her stiff brocades.

+4. = SUNSHADE.

1846 *St. Louis Reveille* I Jan., A full assortment of Umbrellas, Parasols, Parasolettes and Shades . . . at the lowest market prices. **1888** DALY *Lottery of Love* 21 Put up your shade, it's raining.

+5. A device, consisting usually of a length of stiff cloth mounted on a roller, for use at a window to regulate light, etc. (Cf. SHADE ROLLER.)

1867 A. J. EVANS *Vashti* xviii, Though a rose-coloured shade was lowered, the sash had been raised. **1875** *Scribner's Mo.* Dec. 288/1 Shades, made of fine wooden slats, are very suitable for kitchen windows. **1900** BONNER *Hard-Pan* 87 She saw the split and ragged shades in the windows. **1910** TOMPKINS *Mothers & Fathers* 335 The room is absurdly dark; suppose you pull up that shade.

6. In special combinations.

Shade card, a color chart; +*s. cord,* a pull-cord on a window shade; *s.-grown,* (see quotation).

1886 *Delineator* Nov. 403 These Shade Cards show 290 shades of Briggs' Imported Silk and Floss. **1904** RIIS *Roosevelt* 298 When he passed each window [he] would seize the shade-cord and give a little abstracted pull. **1906** *Springfield W. Repub.* 10 May The growing of wrapper tobacco in tents, or, in other words, shade-grown wrappers.

∗Shade, *v.* +*tr.* To reduce or lower (prices or rates) slightly. — **1875** *Chicago Tribune* 27 Oct. 6/4 Prices are not strong, the quotations being shaded on fair orders. **1898** WESTCOTT *D. Harum* 17 Mebbe we c'd shade the price a little. **1903** *Boston Transcript* 24 Oct. 22 To spur his freight traffic manager to get business without shading rates. **1913** STRATTON-PORTER *Laddie* ix, He said Mr. Pryor had shaded his price.

+Shade hat. A woman's or girl's hat having an unusually broad brim to protect the wearer's complexion from the sun. — **1871** *Harper's Mag.* Dec. 57/2 Shade hats, nubias, and fancy rigmaroles were not then invented. **1887** *Courier-Journal* 8 May 8/1 Mrs. J. Muirhead . . . has fine selections of shade hats. **1893** HOWELLS *Coast of Bohemia* 57 Fanning her comely face with her shade-hat, it occurred to her to say [etc.]. **1907** HARRIS *Tents of Wickedness* 112 'Worse than ever!' cried the girl, throwing herself down in one of the big wicker chairs and taking off her shade hat.

Shader. {1728–} +(See quot. 1839.) — **1839** *S. Lit. Messenger* V. 314/1 The people . . . have a mortal aversion to fine spreading trees; which under the *horrible* name of 'shaders' they extirpate in the most cruel manner. **1895** *Dept. Agric. Yrbk. 1894* 466 Thus the box elder, an excellent shader in certain portions of the West, is a failure as soil cover in others.

+Shade roller. (See quot. 1909.) — **1851** CIST *Cincinnati* 245 Shade and map-rollers, turning in ivory, done in a superior style. **1869** *Boyd's Business Directory* 601 Stewart Hartshorn, Sole Manufacturer of Hartshorn's Patent Self-Acting Shade Rollers. **1909** *Cent. Suppl.* 1205/3 *Shade-roller,* . . . a roller resting upon supports in a window or other place, upon which a window-shade, curtain, awning, screen, or map may be rolled.

+Shade tree. A tree, usually planted or set out, valued for its shade. {1885, in Bermuda} — **1806** *Balance* 22 July 228 (Th.), It is to be regretted that a shade tree, useful and ornamental as the poplar, should be in danger. **1832** BAIRD *Valley Miss.* 31 The china tree is a beautiful shade tree. **1868** BEECHER *Norwood* 524 As they proceeded, Pete pointed them to a field with scattering shade trees in it. **1895** *Outing* 444/1 Shade-trees had been allowed to grow for many years along the fences. **1922** TARKINGTON *Gentle Julia* 101 Incredibly elastic, the shade-trees were practising calisthenics.

Shad fish. {1679–} +=SHAD 1. — **1677** *Springfield Rec.* II. 131 And shad fish they may not sel for more than halfe pence apeice there. **1709** LAWSON *Carolina* 60 We met an Indian that had got a parcel of Shad-Fish ready barbaku'd. **1760** *Essex Inst. Coll.* XLVI. 256 There were 2500 and odd Shad Fish taken out of Merrimack-River, by one single Draft of a Net.

+Shad fishery. A place where shad are taken in quantity; the business or process of catching shad. — **1780** *N.J. Archives* 2 Ser. IV. 185 To be sold, the plantation . . . near several shad fisheries. **1811** SUTCLIFF *Travels* (1815) 49 On the former river there is a Shad Fishery. **1865** *Atlantic Mo.* April 464/1 These [seines] were very great affairs, being used in the shad-fishery on the Delaware.

+Shad-flower. 1. = SHADBUSH. **2.** = WHITLOW GRASS. — (1) **1836** LINCOLN *Botany* App. 185/1 Shad-flower. *Aronia.* **1843** TORREY *Flora N.Y.* I. 225. **1861** WOOD *Botany* 329 *Amelanchier.* Shad-Flower. Small trees or shrubs. West Va. (2) **1893** *Amer. Folk-Lore* VI. 137 *Draba verna,* shad flower. West Va.

+Shad fly. 1. Any one of several flies that appear about the time shad enter the rivers. **2.** An artificial fishing fly for catching shad. — (1)

*a*1862 THOREAU *Maine Woods* 237 We met with ephemeræ (shad-fly) midway, about a mile from the shore. (2) **1884** *Nat. Museum Bul.* No. 27, 944 Fly-Books. Containing salmon, black bass, shad, grayling, and trout flies.

+Shad frog. A leopard frog. — **1791** W. BARTRAM *Travels* 276 The shad frog, so called in Pensylvania from their appearing and croaking . . . at the time people fish for shad, is a beautiful spotted frog. **1827** [see GREEN FROG]. **1872** *Newton Kansan* 31 Oct. 1/7 The species called bull-frogs, or shad-frogs, are about the only kinds that are used for culinary purposes. **1897** *Chambers's Encycl.* V. 13/1 Widely distributed in the United States are two forms—the Shad- or Leopard-frog . . . and the Wood-frog.

+Shad herring. 1. =FALL HERRING. **2.** The thread herring, *Opisthonema oglinum*. — **(1) 1814** MITCHILL *Fishes N.Y.* 452 Long-Island Herring. *Clupea mattowacca*. . . . Some call this fish the *shad herring*, and some the *fall shad*. **1903** T. H. BEAN *Fishes N.Y.* 197. **(2) 1842** *Nat. Hist. N.Y., Zoology* IV. 265 The Spotted Thread Herring . . . appears in our waters about the beginning of September, where it is often called the Shad Herring.

+Shadine. 1. The round herring, *Etrumeus sadina*. **2.** (See quotation.) — **(1) 1782** CRÈVECŒUR *Letters* 132 Near Pochick Rip . . . they catch their best fish, such as, . . . cod, smelt, perch, shadine, pike, &c. **1796** MORSE *Univ. Geog.* I. 222 Sheeps Head Drum, Mossbanker, Shadine. **1842** *Nat. Hist. N.Y., Zoology* IV. 263 The Spotted Shadine. . . . Our species does not appear to be common. **(2) 1884** *Nat. Museum Bul.* No. 27, 1041 An effort was made a few years ago to introduce menhaden canned in oil, under the names of 'American sardines,' 'American boneless sardines,' and 'shadines.'

✶Shadow. A detective. {1890-} — **1859** MATSELL *Vocabulum* 78 *Shadow*, a first-class police officer, one who possesses naturally the power . . . to follow his quarry. **1860** *Harper's Mag.* July 233/2 A brace of Metropolitan 'shadows' . . . took the astonished Jim and his companion into their charge.

+Shad pole. A pole used in setting a shad net. — **1852** *Knickerb.* XXXIX. 572 We remarked that the shad-poles had almost entirely disappeared from the Hudson. **1856** COZZENS *Sparrowgrass P.* 86 Off the river there is a long perspective of shad-poles, apparently stretching from shore to shore. **1884** ROE *Nature's Story* 197 A moment later a shad-pole gyrated past me.

Shadrach. [Name of one of the three Hebrews preserved unharmed in the fiery furnace (Dan. 3).] +(See quot. 1841.) — **1841** WEBSTER II. 581/2 *Shadrach*, in the smelting of iron, a mass of iron in which the operation of smelting has failed of its intended effect. (*Local.*) **1891** *Century Mag.* Dec. 178 This mineral is a piece of what the iron-workers call shad-rach.

+Shad salmon. A fish of the family Coregonidae, such as the Otsego bass. — **1842** *Nat. Hist. N.Y., Zoology* IV. 248 The Common Shad Salmon . . . occurs in Lakes Erie and Ontario, and in the smaller lakes in the interior of the State. **1850** S. F. COOPER *Rural Hours* 376 It is a shad-salmon, but is commonly called the 'Otsego Bass,' and is considered one of the finest fresh-water fish in the world.

+Shad season. The season when shad are usually taken. — **1808** *Phila. Ordinances* (1812) 219 The said south side . . . [is] to be used during the shad and herring season only. **1843** *Knickerb.* XXI. 383 The fishermen during the shad-season freighted every one [ferryboat] that plied between the island and the city.

+Shad seine. A net, usually large, for taking shad. Also *shad seine boat, shad seine fisheries.* — **1785** WASHINGTON *Diaries* II. 357 Sent my Shad Sein and Hands to the Ferry to commence Fishing. **1884** *Nat. Museum Bul.* No. 27, 694 Potomac river shad seine-boat. . . . Used in the shad-fisheries of the Potomac River. **1884** GOODE, etc. *Fisheries* I. 604 In the Albemarle the important Shad seine-fisheries begin early in March. **1891** *Cent.* 5469/3 Seines vary in size from one small enough to take a few minnows to the shad-seine of a mile or more in length, hauled by a windlass worked by horses or oxen or by a steam-engine.

+Shad spirit. =MARSH SNIPE. — **1844** *Nat. Hist. N.Y., Zoology* II. 35, [I] was told that it was the Shad Spirit, announcing to the scholes of shad, about to ascend the river, their impending fate. **1883** *Century Mag.* Oct. 923/1 The fishermen . . . have dubbed its author the 'shad spirit.' **1917** *Birds of Amer.* I. 227 Wilson's Snipe. *Gallinago delicata*. . . . [Also called] Shadbird; Alewife-bird; Shad Spirit.

+Shad tree. =SHADBUSH. — **1818** *Mass. H. S. Coll.* 2 Ser. VIII. 169 The latter part of May appear . . . among the trees, the elm, ash, beech, aronia or shad tree, yellow and white birch, and red and sugar maples. **1821** *Amer. Jrnl. Science* III. 275 The wild red cherry tree, aronia or shad tree . . . blossom. **1832** WILLIAMSON *Maine* I. 114 [The boxwood] flowers in May, about the time the shad and their fellow travellers ascend the rivers in the spring, and is therefore called 'shad tree.' **1880** *Harper's Mag.* June 70 Yonder on the wooded slope the feathery shad-tree blooms like a suspended cloud of drifting snow.

+Shadwaiter. =MENOMINEE WHITEFISH. — **1879** GOODE *Cat. Animal Resources U.S.* 57 *Prosopium quadrilaterale.* . . . Shad-waiter. **1891** *Cent.* 5542/1. **1903, 1911** [see PILOT FISH 2 b].

✶Shady, *a.*
+1. (See quot. 1859.)
1859 MATSELL *Vocabulum* 78 *Shady*, quiet; out of sight; not easily found. **1872** EGGLESTON *End of World* 174 He disappeared, and he's been shady ever since.

+2. *To keep shady*, to keep quiet so as to escape notice or detection; *to keep* (someone) *shady*, to keep (someone) in hiding. *colloq.*
1847 FIELD *Drama in Pokerville* 81, I kep' shady, Miss Fanny, bress de Lord, I did. **1871** EGGLESTON *Hoosier Schoolm.* 135 Then you . . . go over to Jackson county and keep shady till we want you. **1887** STOCKTON *Hundredth Man* xii, I've promised to keep him shady. **1894** *Harper's Mag.* Oct. 700/2 'Keep him shady,' said the district leader. **1897** CLOVER *Paul Travers' Adv.* 51, I guess I can fix you out if you hang around here, but keep shady.

✶Shaft.¹ +A memorial obelisk or column.
1837 EMERSON *Poems* (1904) 159 Bid Time and Nature gently spare The shaft we raise to them and thee. **1873** HARTE *Stories & Poems* (1914) 217 The gray shaft that commemorated the Morristown dead of the last civil war obliterated the past. **1873** MILLER *Songs of Italy* (1878) 49 The town Raised that shaft on the spot. **1910** *N.Y. Ev. Post* 29 Sept., The gravestone is 'the marble shaft' or 'the simple stone which marks the spot where his mouldering dust is deposited.'

✶Shaft.² An excavation, either vertical or inclined, made in mining.
1721 *Conn. Rec.* VI. 253 Clearing and cleaning the said levels or shafts. **1789** MORSE *Amer. Geog.* 290 Besides a company opened a very large shaft on the side of the hill. **1814** BRACKENRIDGE *Views La.* 149 There is but one shaft, . . . sunk by Moses Austin. **1896** SHINN *Story of Mine* 218 Let us follow the course of an ore car from the mouth of the shaft. **1917** SINCLAIR *King Coal* 182 They could draw out the smoke and gases and clear the shaft.

b. Attrib. with *claim, coal, ladder, mine.*
1873 RAYMOND *Silver & Gold* 72 Shaft claims at San Andreas, Calaveras County. **1873** *Newton Kansan* 3 April 3/3, I am selling No. 1 shaft coal. **1888** *Harper's Mag.* June 47/2 In Linn County there are shaft mines at less depth. **1914** ATHERTON *Perch of Devil* 355 Miners hate the shaft ladder.

+Shaft furnace. (See quot. 1876.) — **1871** RAYMOND *Mines* 378 Smelting in Shaft Furnaces. **1874** — *6th Rep. Mines* 302 It is proposed to erect a shaft-furnace. **1876** KNIGHT 2128/2 *Shaft-furnace*, . . . one in which the ore, in a state of division, is dropped down a chimney through the flame.

+Shaft house. A structure at the entrance to a mine shaft for housing the hoisting machinery. Also attrib. — **1871** RAYMOND *3d Rep. Mines* 344 The quartz is brought from the mine, unless the mill is in or near the shaft-house, in wagons. **1880** *Cimarron News & Press* 19 Aug. 3/3 A large shaft house is being constructed upon the Smith copper lead. **1914** ATHERTON *Perch of Devil* 355 Not daring to summon the shaft house man, he was sneaking down the ladder. **1917** SINCLAIR *King Coal* 176 They came to the shaft-house of Number Two.

Shafting.¹ {1825-} +'A darkening of the shaft, or quill of a feather, as in some breeds of poultry' (*Cent. Suppl.*). — **1897** *Dept. Agric. Yrbk.* 1896 462 Shafting on the back will also help the black stripe in the saddles.

+Shafting.² The sinking of a shaft; also, collect., the shafts of a mine. — **1871** RAYMOND *3d Rep. Mines* 297 Aggregate of shafting over 5,000 feet. **1874** ALDRICH *P. Palfrey* vii, After four weeks of drifting, and shafting, and all manner of prospecting, they failed to find it again, and gave up. **1876** RAYMOND *8th Rep. Mines* 273 About 1,000 feet of shafting and drifting will represent the amount of work done.

Shaft mule. A mule that works in shafts or beside the shaft or tongue of a vehicle. {shaft-horse, 1769-} — **1847** PARKMAN in *Knickerb.* XXIX. 165 No sooner were our animals put in harness, than the shaft-mule reared and plunged. *Ib.* 393 He sat still in his seat on one of the shaft-mules.

✶Shag.¹ A woolen or silk cloth having a velvet nap. *Obs.* Also attrib.
1632 *N.H. Prov. Papers* I. 66, 90½ yards of shagge at 18d per yd. **1654** *Essex Probate Rec.* I. 178 Inventory: . . . one shagg wescoat & 3 cloath wescoats, 10s. **1710** T. BUCKINGHAM *Naval Exped.* (1825) 81 To six yrds. shagg, 12.0. **1762** in H. M. Brooks *Gleanings* IV. 37 Beaver Coating, Half-Thick, red Shagg, Bayes. **1850** *Rep. Comm. Patents 1849* 494 They had made with worsted a kind of cloth called shag.

✶Shag.² A niggergoose or cormorant.
1737 BRICKELL *N. Carolina* 212 The Shag is somewhat like the Cormorant. **1796** MORSE *Univ. Geog.* I. 214 Shag. *Pelicanus graculus*. Cutter. **1832** WILLIAMSON *Maine* I. 147 The Shag . . . is larger than a black duck. **1883** THAXTER *Poems for Children* 60 Tis the cormorant, dear little brother; The fishermen call it the shag. **1917** *Birds of Amer.* I. 97/2 The Cormorants have many local names, such as 'Shag,' 'Lawyer,' and 'Nigger Goose.'

+Shaganappi, *n.* N.W. [From Cree dial. of Algonquian.] 'Thongs of rawhide used for rope or cord' (Hodge).
[**1873** G. M. GRANT *Ocean to Ocean* 122 Shaganappi . . . does all that leather, cloth, rope, nails [etc.] . . . are used for elsewhere. **1880** *Scribner's Mo.* July 442/2 Should any part break in the course of a thousand-mile journey, shaganappi, or buffalo raw-hide thong, is in requisition. **1892** in C. W. Gordon *Life J. Robertson* 329 In the old days . . . every one had his pocket full of shaganappi.] **1891** *Cent.* 5543/2.

+Shaganappi, *a.* N.W. [See prec.] 'Tough; rough' (*Cent.*).

Shagbark. {1691–6, in the West Indies}

+1. The nut of the shagbark hickory tree.

1777 *Mass. Hist. Soc. Proc.* 2 Ser. II. 236 [Buy me] a bushel or two of shagbarks. **1820** *Columbian Centinel* 12 Jan. 3/5 [Auction] This day at 11 o'clock . . . 4 hhds. Shagbarks, 46 small casks superior Smyrna Raisins. **1892** TORREY *Foot-Path Way* 225 Our annual wild crop [consisted of] . . . shagbarks, acorns, and so forth. **1901** [see ENGLISH WALNUT].

+2. = SHAGBARK HICKORY. Also attrib.

1790 DEANE *New-Eng. Farmer* 190/7 But two sorts [of nut trees] . . . grow spontaneously in this country; the white walnut, and the shagbark. **1814** BIGELOW *Florula Bostoniensis* 229 *Juglans squamosa.* Shellbark. Shagbark. . . . The wood . . . is principally used for purposes where strength is required. **1834** C. A. DAVIS *Lett. J. Downing* 20, I got a white hat on, and a shag-bark stick. **1880** *Harper's Mag.* Nov. 865 There was a splendid tall shagbark close by.

transf. **1798** FESSENDEN *Orig. Poems* (1806) 45 Now jogs the bard, with *shag-bark* elbow.

+b. The wood of this tree.

1869 STOWE *Oldtown Folks* 483 Ef the deacon hain't come down with his shagbark! **1888** KIRKLAND *McVeys* 334, 'I'm going to cut up that wood!' 'You! Tackle that thar dry shag-bark?' **1894** *Advance* 20 Sept. 606/2 The teacher could be seen . . . carrying his blazing torch of shagbark.

+c. The bark of a shagbark hickory tree.

1920 HOWELLS *Vacation of Kelwyns* 16 [He looked] as if he were hewn out of hickory, with the shag-bark left on in places.

+Shagbark hickory. Any one of several closely related species of hickory, esp. *Carya ovata*, having bark of a shaggy or scaly character; a tree of such a species.

1751 J. BARTRAM *Observations* 67 A great hill, cloathed with large Magnolia, . . . shagbark-hickory, chestnut and chestnut-oak. **1814** PURSH *Flora Amer.* II. 637 *Juglans alba* . . . is known by the name of Shell-bark Hickory, Shag-bark and Scaly-bark Hickory, on account of its bark, which is torn in loose fragments. **1904** CRISSEY *Tattlings* 225 Old Benage was as rough as a shag bark hickory.

b. The nut of a shagbark hickory tree. Also *shagbark hickory nut.*

1796 MORSE *Univ. Geog.* I. 188 Nut fruit [in New Eng.]. . . . Shagbark Hiccory (*Juglans cineria?*)—Chesnut [etc.]. **1884** ROE *Nature's Story* 305 [He] fed it with an apple and shag-bark hickory-nuts.

c. The wood of a shagbark hickory tree.

1869 STOWE *Oldtown Folks* 479 Good straight shagbark-hickory was voted none too good for the minister.

+Shagbark walnut.

1. = SHAGBARK HICKORY. Also *shagbark walnut tree.*

1802 *Mass. Spy* 10 March (Th.), The growth of shagbark walnuts has been remarkably slow. **1813** MUHLENBERG *Cat. Plants* 88 *Juglans compressa* [or] *squamosa macrocarpa,* large-fruited shell-bark [or] shag-bark walnut. **1827** J. Q. ADAMS *Memoirs* VII. 323 In my summer-house nursery two more of my shagbark walnut-trees have come up. **1884** COOKE in *Harper's Mag.* Sept. 615/2 A cluster of shag-bark walnut-trees.

2. The nut of a shagbark walnut tree.

1843 STEPHENS *High Life N.Y.* II. 27 The head of the pin was as big as a shag-bark walnut. **1850** *Knickerb.* XXXV. 557 We knew a Wall-street bank-messenger formerly, whose feet looked like two parcels of shagbark walnuts. **1878** STOWE *Poganuc People* 220 The frost ripened the shag-bark walnuts.

Shagreen. a. A kind of untanned leather prepared from the skins of horses, camels, etc., and usually dyed green. {1677–} Also attrib. **b.** The prepared skin of a ray, shark, etc., having a hard rough surface. {1870–} — **1754** *S.C. Gazette* 1 Jan. 2/2 John Paul Grimke Jeweller, has just imported . . . tweeser cases, shagreen boxes. **1784** CUTLER in *Life & Corr.* I. 106 The thermometer was in a glass tube, which was placed in a shagreen case. **1790** *Penna. Packet* 6 Jan. 1/4 Shagreen and fish skin cases with lancets. **1871** *Scribner's Mo.* Feb. 458/1 Now a square sheet [of stationery], now an oblong, rules the day; of satin smoothness one month, rough as shagreen the next. **1911** *Rep. Fisheries 1908* 314/1 The skin [of rays] is sometimes manufactured into leather called 'shagreen.'

‖**Shagreened cutworm.** (See quotation.) — **1884** *Rep. Comm. Agric.* 292 The Shagreened Cut-Worm . . . , which has also been noticed to feed upon the cabbage-plant, appears to be confined to the Southern Atlantic States.

✳Shake, *n.*

To be great shakes, see GREAT SHAKES.

1. An earthquake, or the tremulous movement or shock of this. {1622–1793}

'Now only *U.S.' (O.E.D.).*

1705 *Boston News-Letter* 2 July 2/2 There was felt in this Town a small shake of an Earthquake. **1727** *Mass. H. S. Coll.* 4 Ser. II. 174 About an hour after this was another rumble with a small shake. **1887** *Courier-Journal* 7 May 2/1 *The Arizona Shake.* **1907** *Westminster Gaz.* 13 April 3/2 That earthquake at San Francisco—the 'shake,' as the local papers lightheartedly called it within a fortnight.

+b. *pl.* A section of country marked by large fissures or cracks in the earth caused by earthquakes.

1833 *Sketches D. Crockett* 108 [They] asked me if I didn't want to go down to the Shakes, and take a bear hunt.

+2. A long, split, unplaned shingle or clapboard.

(See also OAK SHAKE.)

1772 *R.I. Commerce* I. 420 We herewith send you all the Shakes we can yet get in. **1845** *Cincinnati Misc.* I. 164/2 It was a small one story-house, shingled with what they call 'shakes,' all over the West and Southwest. **1881** PIERSON *In the Brush* 51 The roof was made of 'shakes.' *a*1918 G. STUART *On Frontier* I. 75 We busied ourselves making clapboards or shakes out of sugar pines.

attrib. **1856** ROPES *6 Months in Kan.* 56 At a little 'shake' shop, we see tubs and pails. *Ib.* 172 Living in a 'shake' cabin, . . . is the fair little lady who helped me into my present 'quarters.' **1857** *Lawrence* (Kan.) *Republican* 9 July 3 You are always welcome to his [a squatter's] log or shake house.

+b. *pl.* (See quotations.)

1820 SCORESBY *Account Arctic Regions* I. 207*n.*, The staves [of casks taken apart are] closely packed up in a cylindrical form, constituting what are called *shakes* or *packs.* **1841** DANA *Seaman's Man.* 122 *Shakes,* the staves of hogsheads taken apart.

+3. = FEVER AND AGUE. *colloq.* Usually pl.

1825 PAULDING *J. Bull in Amer.* 9 Even if the poor man should happen . . . to be free from the ague; or 'shake,' as they call it. **1839** BIRD *Robin Day* 64 Fever-and-ague . . . fell to fumbling, as well as the 'shakes' would permit, in his pocket. **1872** NAPHEYS *Prevention of Disease* 251 The 'shakes' are . . . universal in some parts of the Mississippi valley. **1904** MACKAYE *Panchronicon* 138, I think my sister's got the shakes or suthin'. **1923** *Dialect Notes* V. 220.

+b. An attack of this.

1850 LEWIS *La. Swamp Doctor* 73, I thought of the last shake I had in far distant Massassip. **1856** OLMSTED *Slave States* 355 Even in the midst of a severe 'shake,' they would generally insist that they were 'well enough to dive.' **1888** J. J. WEBB *Adventures* 62 He had a good 'shake,' and being without a doctor or medicine, the prospect of a rapid journey was rather discouraging.

+4. (See quotation.) *colloq.*

1909 WEBSTER 1934/2 *Shake,* . . . short for *milk shake* or *egg shake,* etc., beverages of milk, or milk and egg, flavored and shaken thoroughly.

+5. *Fair shake,* a good bargain; a square or honest deal. *colloq.*

1830 *Central Watchtower* (Harrodsburg, Ky.) 22 May, Says I . . . any way that will be a fair shake. **1846** *Spirit of Times* 18 April 91/1 He was never allowed to have 'a fair shake.' Over a heavy course, at four miles, whose horse could have beaten him? **1902** WHITE *Blazed Trail* 218 That ain't a fair shake.

+6. *To give* (something or someone) *the shake,* or variants: To get rid of (something or someone); to give the slip to; to turn one's back on. *slang.*

1875 in J. F. Daly *Life A. Daly* 215, I desire to give the 'Two Orphans' a shake. **1883** 'MARK TWAIN' *Life on Miss.* iii, 27 But none of them herded with Dick Allbright. They all give him the cold shake. **1896** ADE *Artie* 127, I'm afraid the old folks'll think we're givin 'em the shake. **1909** WARE *Passing English* 84/2 Do you give me the cold shake?

✳Shake, *v.*

To shake a stick at, see the noun.

+1. *tr.* To cast off or turn one's back on (someone). *colloq.*

1872 'MARK TWAIN' *Roughing It* 336 He never shook his mother. . . . He give her a house to live in, and town lots, and plenty of money. **1876** *Scribner's Mo.* Jan. 443/2 To 'go back on' a friend or 'shake' a partner was one of the gravest of crimes. **1883** 'MARK TWAIN' *Life on Miss.* xliv, When at last he . . . became a paltry alderman, the public 'shook' him. **1895** HARTE *Clarence* 64 Tell me, Clarence, . . . you shook her, too!

+b. To leave (a place) or get rid of (something). *colloq.*

1876 'MARK TWAIN' *Tom Sawyer* xxxv. 271 Now these clothes suits me, and this bar'l suits me, and I ain't ever going to shake 'em any more. **1877** HARTE *Story of Mine* (1896) 226 It's high time you and me packed up our traps and 'shook' this yar shanty. **1910** [see DEADFALL 2 (a)].

2. *absol.* To shake hands. {1601}

'Now only *U.S. slang.' (O.E.D.).*

1873 CARLETON *Farm Ballads* (1882) 44 My neighbor Ager come this way, invitin' me to 'shake.' **1882** SWEET & KNOX *Texas Siftings* 137 Shake, ole fel! **1902** NORRIS *Deal in Wheat* 19 Shake on it, and hats off to my distinguished friend. **1914** [see GO *n.* 4].

Shakedown. {c1730–} += BREAKDOWN. — **1845** *Xenia Torch-Light* 31 July 1/7 The organ struck up, from which he concluded that some sort of 'shake down,' was about to commence. **1908** SINCLAIR *Metropolis* 226 When he felt like dancing a shakedown, he could take a run out to God's country.

+Shake-hands. A handshake. — **1874** EGGLESTON *Circuit Rider* 91 She made haste to wash and dry her hands, that she might have a 'good, old-fashioned Methodist shake-hands.' **1883** *Century Mag.* Oct. 895/1 Arthur assented, . . . congratulating himself that the shake-hands was disposed of. **1897** *McClure's Mag.* Dec. 162/1 He was a man without any pretensions, and always had a pleasant shake-hands for you.

✻ **Shaker.**

+**1.** A member of a celibate and communistic religious sect, introduced in America in 1774, whose devotions include a characteristic shaking or dance. {1648–, a Quaker or other sectarian}

1784 BELKNAP *Jrnl. Tour to White Mts.* (1876) 20 [His] wife had run away with the Shakers and carried off 25 of his dollars. **1814** *N.Y. State Soc. Arts* III. 82, I understand the Shakers have also planted it. **1867** DIXON *New America* II. 81 No one in either New York or Massachusetts can match the Shakers in producing seeds and plants. **1896** *Peterson Mag.* March 253/1 The years of watch-care which she had given to the child left in her charge, had created in her heart a love which the Manifesto taught to be earthly and unworthy a devout Shaker. **1920** HOWELLS *Vacation of Kelwyns* 156 The Shakers had brought the spring down from the upland above.

+**2.** (See quotation.) *Obs.*

1845 LYELL *Second Visit* I. 60 Large grasshoppers, with red wings, [are] called here [in New Eng.] shakers.

+**3.** Short for SHAKER BONNET.

1881 *Harper's Mag.* May 854/2, The bonnet . . . is far too fine. I will buy you a shaker at the store. **1897** LEWIS *Wolfville* 29 So the girl . . . puts on her shaker an' goes stampedin' off. **1905** WIGGIN *Rose* 9 Rose had tried on . . . children's gingham 'Shakers,' mourning bonnets for aged dames [etc.].

+**4.** A container in which drinks are mixed by shaking.

1889 J. G. WOOLLEY *Seed No. 1 Hard* (1893) 96 The bartender . . . makes the bits of ice, the spoon, the shaker, the strainer, the glasses, fairly play a tune.

+**5.** A container for salt, pepper, etc., having a perforated top.

See also *pepper-shaker* (1900) under PEPPER 4.
1910 TOMPKINS *Mothers & Fathers* 29 Miss Elsie would be terribly shocked at this shaker.

+**6.** Attrib. and comb. in sense 1. **a.** Designating plants grown or developed by the Shakers.

Cf. SHAKER('S) SEED.
1842 KIRKLAND *Forest Life* II. 113 Here's . . . patent pills—cure anything you like—ague bitters—Shaker yarbs. **1856** COZZENS *Sparrowgrass P.* 31 Our Shaker corn . . . gives himself a rousing shake, and flings big drops [of rain] around him. **1861** *Ill. Agric. Soc. Trans.* IV. 104 The product of the said half acre . . . [is] ninety-five and a half bushels of fine sized tubers, . . . the variety being the 'Shaker Potato,' flesh white.

b. Designating persons belonging to the Shaker sect.

1850 GALLAHER *Western Sketch-Book* 58 Three Shaker missionaries, from Lebanon, in New York, . . . succeeded in forming two small societies in Kentucky, and one in Ohio. **1856** CARTWRIGHT *Autobiog.* 32 Soon the Shaker priests came along. **1862** BROWNE *A. Ward: His Book* 33 My Shaker frends, I now bid you a welcome adoo. **1883** Shaker sister [see CRIMP *n.*² 2]. **1920** HOWELLS *Vacation of Kelwyns* 85, I heard of gem-pans fast enough from the Shaker ladies.

c. Designating things made or built by Shakers. Also in possessive.

See also SHAKER ROCKER, SHAKER ROCKING-CHAIR.
1848 *Knickerb.* XXXII. 76 We should like some of our country friends . . . to go into a Shaker barn. **1849** AUDUBON *Western Jrnl.* 152 Some of the mules drank five buckets of water . . . (the common shaker buckets). **1866** A. D. WHITNEY *L. Goldthwaite* x, She rocked herself back and forth in the Shaker chair. **1879** BISHOP *4 Months in Sneak-Box* 34 Bread and butter, with Shakers' peach-sauce, . . . contributed to furnish a most satisfactory meal.

d. Designating articles of clothing characteristic of Shakers' dress.

See also SHAKER BONNET.
1883 *Century Mag.* Feb. 525/1 A bonnet, hey? . . . It looks like a Shaker cap. **1905** WIGGIN *Rose* 154 She slipped on her gray Shaker cloak.

+**Shaker bonnet.** =QUAKER BONNET. — **1859** *Harper's Mag.* Sept. 504/1 Shaker bonnets for the girls and Canada straw hats for Ben and Peter. **1881** *Ib.* May 854/2 Here she bought a Shaker bonnet for her pupil. **1893** *Ib.* Feb. 446/2 The corners of the canvas hoods [were] erected, like Shaker bonnets, over their high-piled loads.

+**Shaker community.** =SHAKER VILLAGE. — **1817** *Niles' Reg.* XII. 371/1 At Enfield, Vermont, he visited the '*Habitation of the Shaken* [sic] *community*,' to use their own phraseology, or in more familiar language the Shaking Quakers. **1837** MARTINEAU *Society* II. 55, I visited two Shaker communities in Massachusetts. **1870** D. MACRAE *Americans at Home* II. 368 There are only some eighteen Shaker communities in the States. **1920** HOWELLS *Vacation of Kelwyns* 171, I thought of having the scene partly in a Shaker community.

+**Shakerdom.** The region occupied by Shakers; the Shakers collectively. — **1861** HOLLAND *Lessons in Life* 87, I object to their Style of life and piety, and to everything outside of Shakerdom. **1876** GLADDEN *Working People & Employers* 203 Shakerdom has but one prophet, and his name is Frederick Evans. **1891** HOLMES *Over Teacups* 66 Your imaginary wholesale Shakerdom is all very fine, said I.

Shakeress. A female Shaker. — [**1860** *Reynolds's Misc.* 15 Sept. 180/2 Two comely Shakeresses wait upon you.] **1870** D. MACRAE *Ameri-*

cans at Home II. 358 We follow the Shakeress . . . within doors.] **1880** HOWELLS *Undiscovered Country* 203 A score of the young Shakeresses . . . sorted and cleaned these simples.

+**Shaker family.** One of the units into which a Shaker society is divided: (see also quot. 1837). Also attrib. (Cf. FAMILY 2.) — **1837** MARTINEAU *Society* II. 55 There are fifteen Shaker establishments or 'families' in the United States. **1920** HOWELLS *Vacation of Kelwyns* 24 The caravan of the Kelwyns drew up under the elms at the gable of the old Shaker Family house.

+**Shakerism.** The beliefs and practices of the Shakers. {1868–} — **1807** R. MCNEMAR *Kentucky Revival* 95 If *Shakerism* were properly understood, there is no man in his senses could persecute it. **1822** MARY M. DYER (*title*), A Portraiture of Shakerism. **1838** *Knickerb.* XI. 535, [I] have none of this skill in Shakerism. **1856** CARTWRIGHT *Autobiog.* 53 The Shaker priests . . . swept members of different Churches away from their steadfastness into the muddy pool of Shakerism. **1867** DIXON *New America* II. 102 Shakerism as an actual fact in the domestic life of America . . . is far from being a mere folly. **1920** HOWELLS *Vacation of Kelwyns* 8 He was curious enough to ask some questions . . . about the general conditions of Shakerism.

+**Shake roof.** A roof made of shakes. Also *shakes roof.* — **1850** *Knickerb.* XXXVI. 73 They live in their cabin with its 'shakes roof' and mud-chimney. **1863** *Ladies' Repository* XXIII. 398/2 They are covered with what is called a 'shake' roof, that is, clapboards laid from one pole to another in rows overlapping each other. **1902** WILSON *Spenders* 19 There was a round hole in the 'shake' roof, fastidiously cut to fit a stovepipe.

+**Shaker rocker.** =next. *Obs.* — **1882** *Century Mag.* March 761/2 [I] sat down in the Shaker rocker. **1898** E. C. HALL *Aunt Jane* 4 The chairs were ancient Shaker rockers, some with homely 'shuck' bottoms.

+**Shaker rocking-chair.** A rocking-chair made, or of a type made, by the Shakers. *Obs.* — **1866** A. D. WHITNEY *L. Goldthwaite*, Miss Craydocke . . . came and placed her Shaker rocking-chair beside her. **1881** *Harper's Mag.* Sept. 579/1 Adams . . . perched on the arm of a scarlet Shaker rocking-chair. **1893** *Ib.* 476/2 He wrote, not at his desk, but sitting in a Shaker rocking-chair, with a pad upon his knee.

+**Shaker(s') seed.** Seed grown and sold by the Shakers. *Obs.* — **1835** TODD *Notes* 12 Tradesmen exhibit . . . such sort of placards as . . . 'Shakers' seed sold here,' meaning the society of Shakers forming a religious community near Troy, whose garden seeds are much approved. **1842** DICKENS *Amer. Notes* 80 'Shaker seeds,' 'Shaker herbs,' and 'Shaker distilled waters,' are commonly announced for sale in the shops of towns and cities. **1846** *Knickerb.* XXVIII. 340 Having a choice supply of 'Shaker's seeds,' procured in the States, I arranged some small beds.

+**Shaker village.** A community or settlement composed of, and managed by, Shakers. — **1824** in H. M. Brooks *Gleanings* IV. 125 An assortment of Steel & Silver Pens, from the Shaker Village. **1857** *Harper's Mag.* July 165/1 Stretching along upon a noble mountain terrace . . . lay the Shaker village. **1867** DIXON *New America* II. 80 This village is Mount Lebanon, . . . known to scoffers as a comic institution unattached, under the name of the Shaker Village. **1887** *Courier-Journal* 12 Feb. 5/1 He gave Dines $675 on coming to the Shaker village last fall.

Shake-up. {1857–}

+**1.** A hastily constructed building. Also attrib. in the sense of makeshift.

1873 BEADLE *Undevel. West* 728 Moorehead is a rather rough looking frontier town, consisting of . . . 'shake-ups' of pine lumber. *Ib.* 823 A man with ten thousand cattle upon the range, is content to . . . sit on a hickory 'shakeup' chair, sleep on shucks, live in a board or log 'shantie.'

+**2.** A change of personnel or reorganization in an office or other organization.

1887 *Courier-Journal* 6 Feb. 2/2 No Shake-up Probable. **1900** B. MATTHEWS *Confident To-Morrow* 145, I hear there's been another shake-up in the office. **1903** *N.Y. Ev. Post* 16 Sept., Big Police Shake-up. Eight Captains Transferred by Greene. **1914** S. H. ADAMS *Clarion* 100 There may be a shake-up coming under the new owner.

✻ **Shaking.** In special combinations.
Shaking fork, a kind of pitchfork used by threshers in removing the straw from threshed grain; *s. meadow, prairie*, meadow or prairie which shakes or trembles when walked upon; *s. shoe*, a shoelike trough that drops grain from the hopper of a mill into the eye of the millstone.

1854 *Penna. Agric. Rep.* 81 Joseph Bruederly exhibited two shaking forks. **1748** ELIOT *Field-Husb.* i. 4 Smooth, even, shaking Meadow . . . is called Cranberry Marsh. **1888** CABLE *Bonaventure* 143 Far out over the vast marshy breadths of the 'shaking prairie,' two still clouds . . . sparkled. **1850** *Rep. Comm. Patents: 1849* I. 351, I claim . . . as new . . . the arrangement of the horizontally sliding screen and shaking shoe.

+**Shaking ague.** Fever and ague, or an attack of this. *Obs.* — **1835** LONGSTREET *Ga. Scenes* 210 Nancy was cured sound and well by it, of a hard shakin' ager. **1855** SIMMS *Forayers* 164 Dick could easily simulate the sufferings of one seized with 'the shaking agy.'

+**Shaking Quaker.** A Shaker; also, pl., the sect of Shakers. A nickname. *Obs.* — **1782** *N.H. Hist. Soc. Coll.* I. 239 The people called Shaking Quakers, came to Mr. (Joseph) Flint's. **1806** FESSENDEN *Democracy Unveiled* I. 88 Did'st ever see a shaking quaker? **1823** THACHER *Military Jrnl.* 169 Shaking Quakers, or dancing quakers, . . . have no affinity either in principle or character to the established order of Quakers. **1864** NICHOLS *Amer. Life* II. 30, I have never seen a more remarkable people than the American Shakers, or, as they are sometimes called, Shaking Quakers.

+**Shalam colonist.** A member of the Faithist colony near Las Cruces, New Mexico. Now hist. — **1885** *Wkly. New Mexican Rev.* 23 April 3/4 The new bible used by the Shalam colonists . . . is purported to have been written by Dr. Newbrough, under inspiration.

Shale. A slatelike, argillaceous rock, often occurring above coal formations. {1747–}
1821 *Amer. Jrnl. Science* III. 245 Immediately above the shale, I have found [alum stone]. **1870** KEIM *Sheridan's Troopers* 136 The veins [of gypsum] . . . were universally found in extensive fields of red earth and shale. **1903** WHITE *Forest* 164, I knew well enough what he was standing on—a little ledge of shale. **1916** THOBURN *Stand. Hist. Okla.* I. 4 The rock formations . . . include those commonly known as limestone, sandstone, granite, gypsum, and shale.

+**Shallon.** =SALAL. — **1806** LEWIS in *L. & Clark Exped.* IV. (1905) 52 The *Shallon* is the production of a shrub which I have heretofore taken to be a speceis of loral. **1814** PURSH *Flora Amer.* I. 284 This elegant evergreen shrub is in high esteem among the natives, on account of its berries, which they call Shallon. **1866** LINDLEY & MOORE *Treas. Botany* 522/2 The Shallon or Salal of the north-west coast of America.

∗**Shalloon.** A light, closely woven, woolen material used chiefly for linings. — **1710** SEWALL *Letter-Book* I. 384 Send . . . a good Shaloon for Lining. **1784** *Mass. Centinel* 8 May 3/3 A servant's blue broadcloth coat quite new . . . lined with blue shalloon. **1811** *Niles' Reg.* 21 Sept. 46/1 Shalloons . . . can only be made of wool long enough to be combed.

∗**Shallop.** A light open boat propelled by oars or sails. — **1611** in A. Brown *Genesis U.S.* I. 507 A Spanish Carvall came into our River fitted with a shallop necessarie and propper to discover freshetts, Rivers and Creekes. **1707** *Boston News-Letter* 7 April 2/2 The Shallops give account of such a Ship seen this week. **1789** MORSE *Amer. Geog.* 346 The trade of this state [Del.] . . . is carried . . . in boats and shallops. **1835** HOFFMAN *Winter in West* I. 16, [I] pulled for the berth of my little shallop **1882** [see LANDING 3].

Shallopman. One who operates a shallop. {a1660–} — **1787** FRENEAU *Misc. Works* 416, I was always afraid Of sailors, and ships, and the shallopman's trade. **1810** *Phila. Ordinances* (1812) 230 [Any] shallop-man who shall violate this provision . . . shall forfeit . . . ten dollars. **1811** MEASE *Philadelphia* 59 In case flour has been injured by shallop-men, carters, or miller, the owner is entitled to damages to the extent of the injury.

Shallot. a. A plant of the onion kind (*Allium ascalonicum*), used for flavoring. {1664–} **b.** A small onion. — **1709** LAWSON *Carolina* 97 The Honey-Tree bears as great a Resemblance to the Locust, as a Shallot does to an Onion. **1798** HAWKINS *Letters* 322 Planted shallots and canteloup melons. **1822** WOODS *English Prairie* (1904) 305 Shalots . . . are planted by the Americans in preference to onions. **1886** EBBUTT *Emigrant Life* 72 Wild onions, or shallots, were very plentiful.

∗**Sham.** +A member of a secret organization in South Carolina that sought to continue the work of the Ku-Klux Klan after the disbanding of that organization. — [**1877** BEARD *K.K.K. Sketches* 155 The 'sham,' or counterfeit edition of the K.K.K., had no organized existence in either of the remaining Southern States.] *Ib.* 158 A resolution of *sine die* adjournment was actually passed, and the members having exchanged sad farewells and wept on each other's necks in view of the gloomy prospect before them, the 'Shams,' as they were derisively called, became masters of the situation.

‖**Shambler.** A horse that shambles. — **1861** WINTHROP *Canoe & Saddle* 219 Shabbiest led off on his shambler in quite another direction from mine.

∗**Shambles.** *pl.* +A slave market. *Obs.* — **1852** STOWE *Uncle Tom* xlv, An older sister went to the shambles to plead with the wretch . . . to spare his victims. **1860** ABBOTT *South & North* 177 There is no longer occasion to buy and sell your fellow-men in the shambles.

Shanghai, n. Also †Shanghae.
1. A long-legged chicken with feathered shanks, of a breed reputedly introduced from Shanghai, China; also, pl., the breed. {1853–}
1853 B. F. TAYLOR *Jan. & June* 85 Those heavenly hens, the Shanghais and Cochin Chinas. **1857** *Harper's Mag.* May 743/2 An obstreperous shanghai in a tree hard by was crowing for day. **1871** [see COCHIN CHINA]. **1888** 'CRADDOCK' *Despot* 45 She could have made soup out'n me, . . . ez onconsarned ez ef I'd been a Shanghai.
transf. **1859** *Gt. Republic Mo.* Jan. 70 (B.), I degenerated into a fop, and became a shanghai of the most exotic breed. **1902** HARBEN *A. Daniel* 156, I'm a mountain shanghai, I reckon it's fifteen mile on a bee-line to my shack.

‖**b.** *pl.* Long, slender legs.
1863 NORTON *Army Lett.* 187 He asked me if I could march twenty-five miles and not be sick. That was a thrust at my 'shanghais.'

+**2.** A long frock coat. In full *Shanghai* (*over*)*coat.*
1855 M. THOMPSON *Doesticks* 297, I could forgive thy Shanghae coats. **1856** *Porter's Spirit of Times* 22 Nov. 190/3, I have doffed the shanghai and donned the shooting-jacket. **1873** BAILEY *Life in Danbury* 11 He wore a Shanghai overcoat. **1901** HARRIGAN *Mulligans* 137 He wore a long black coat, termed 'shanghai.'

+**3.** In various other senses: (see quotations).
1857 UNDERHILL & THOMPSON *Elephant Club* 86 His hat was an antiquated shanghae—black on the crown and light underneath the brim. **1880** *Scribner's Mo.* Jan. 365/1 The 'shanghai' is the glaring daub required by

some frame-makers for cheap auctions. **1880** *Cimarron News & Press* 30 Sept. 2/4 Of late years . . . there are but few rough, bony shanghais, in the shape of oxen and steers, brought from Texas and from the West. **1881** INGERSOLL *Oyster-Industry* 248 Shanghai, a long, slender oyster.

4. *attrib.* **a.** In sense 1 with *chicken, fowl, rooster.*
1849 *New Eng. Farmer* I. 386 Shanghae fowls, by S. and G. Hyde. **1855** M. THOMPSON *Doesticks* 248, [I] have here publicly to acknowledge the receipt of . . . a Shanghae Rooster, with double teeth. **1860** HOLMES *E. Venner* xix, From those windows . . . , we could see . . . a Shanghai chicken.

+**b.** *Mil.* Designating a rapid manner of marching or drilling formerly in use at West Point. *Obs.*
1858 *S. Lit. Messenger* XXVI. 17/2 It is called in the familiar language of the camp, by the name of the 'Shanghai Drill.' *Ib.*, 18/1 They think the 'double quick' or 'Shanghai trot' too undignified for their years and ponderosity. **1867** HARRIS *Sut Lovingood* 196 A long necked passenger . . . cum rushin out in a shanghi trot.

+**c.** Shanghai fence, (see quotation).
1862 *Ill. Agric. Soc. Trans.* V. 692 Many men . . . are compelled to make . . . 'Shanghai' or 'Bloomer' fences (two-boarded fences).

+**Shanghai, v.** [*Shanghai*, China.] *tr.* To overpower (someone) by drugs or other means and ship him as a sailor, in order, usually, to secure premium money. — **1871** *N.Y. Tribune* 1 March (De Vere), Before that time they would have been drugged, shanghaied, and taken away from all means of making complaint. **1887** S. SAMUELS *Forecastle to Cabin* 46 To be carried or forced on board of a ship in this manner is what is termed in sailor parlance being 'Shanghaied.' **1898** *McClure's Mag.* April 535/1 Ye've been shanghaied 'long with three or four more of us.

+**Shanghaism.** *Polit.* The action, on the part of a candidate, of running for office on more than one ticket. — **1859** *La Crosse Daily Union* 22 Oct. 2/2 There will not be a remnant of Shanghaism left in Wisconsin.

+**Shanpips.** *pl.* A secret society reputed to have existed formerly among the Mormons. *Obs.* (Cf. DANITE, DESTROYING ANGEL.) — **1857** *Congress. Globe* App. 24 Feb. 280/3 They suppose that there is a secret society existing there, called *Danites, Shanpips,* or *Destroying Angels.*

Shanty, n. [Canadian Fr. *chantier.*]
1. A cheap, flimsy, hastily erected cabin, hut, or shack. {1832–, in Canada}
'Chiefly *U.S.* and *Canada*' (O.E.D.). See also CLAIM SHANTY, LUMBER *n.* 4 f.
1822 Z. HAWLEY *Tour* 31 [These people] lived in what is here [Ohio] called a *Shanty*. **1847** RUXTON *Adv. Rocky Mts.* (1848) 177 Scattered about were tents and shanties of logs and branches of every conceivable form. **1886** POORE *Reminiscences* II. 342 He gave him seed to sow, a shanty to live in, and some land to till. **1901** MERWIN & WEBSTER *Calumet 'K'* 266 He arose and tramped uneasily about the little shanty. **1920** HOWELLS *Vacation of Kelwyns* 193 She'll die in that shanty of her'n some night if she don't get killed first.

+**b.** Used, in depreciation or contempt, of more pretentious structures.
1848 COOPER *Oak Openings* I. 26 This term 'shanty,' . . . by a license of speech, . . . is often applied to more permanent residences. **1862** CUMMING *Hospital Life* 32/2 [The] house called a hotel . . . is a perfect shanty. **1862** *Ev. Standard* (London) 1 Dec., There is a two-story wooden shantee in Trenton that they call an hotel.

c. With defining terms indicating the materials used.
See also BARK, FRAME, LOG SHANTY.
1836 *Quarter Race Ky.* (1846) 14, I noticed many a . . . fellow force his skeary nag up to the opening in the little clapboard shanty. **1857** WILLIS *Convalescent* 256, I am thinking now of building a pine shanty in the glen. **1860** GREELEY *Overland Journey* 180 We stopped beside a stone and mud shanty of very rude construction.

d. Used by a lumberman or lumbermen.
1846 FARNHAM *Prairie Land* 208 The solitary wood-chopper, whose 'shantee,' [is] hidden among the trees. **1859** *Harper's Mag.* Aug. 319/2 [We saw] the shanties and desolate clearings of the lumber-men.

2. Attrib. with *boss, cake, family,* etc.
1846 *Knickerb.* XXVIII. 340, [I] became a proficient in making that unleavened bread known, *inter sylvas,* as 'shanty cake.' **1858** HALE *If, Yes, & Perhaps* 126 But his extempore train chose to stop at a forsaken shanty-village on the Potomac. **1872** BRACE *Dangerous Classes N.Y.* 152 The shanty family are never quite so poor as the tenement-house family. **1878** *Lumberman's Gazette* 6 April, The last of the shanty-teams of the season have about gone through here. **1894** *Outing* XXIV. 94/2 A shanty gang had turned a drive of square timber out of the branch. **1905** *Forestry Bureau Bul.* No. 61, 33 Chore boy, one who cleans up the sleeping quarters and stable in a logging camp, cuts firewood, builds fires, and carries water. . . . [Also called] shanty boss.

+**Shanty, v.** *intr.* To live (*out*) in a shanty. Also *vbl. n.* used attrib. — **1840** HOFFMAN *Greyslaer* I. 60, I never shanty out without a large fire. **1857** HAMMOND *Wild Northern Scenes* 197 They shantied on the outlet, just at the foot of the lake. *Ib.* 212 When we got back to our shantyin' ground, we were tuckered out you may believe. **1897** ROBINSON *Uncle Lisha's Outing* 38 Me an' this man shantied on your land here one spring.

+**Shanty boat.** A river boat provided with living quarters similar to those of a shanty. Also *shanty boatman.* — **1879** BISHOP *4 Months in Sneak-Box* 59 The shanty-boatman looks to the river . . . for his life.

Ib., The sweeps, or oars, . . . govern the motions of the shanty-boat. **1887** *Courier-Journal* 25 Jan. 2/3 A murder occurred . . . on a shanty-boat near Vidalia. **1897** *Outing* XXIX. 368/1 Later in the day we were joined by a very small boy from a shanty-boat. **1907** *Springfield W. Repub.* 28 March 13 At almost every landing place of any importance one will observe several house, or shanty-boats as they are called, anchored.

+**Shanty boy.** =SHANTYMAN. — **1893** *Scribner's Mag.* June 706/1 My Shanty Boy so bold and free will save me from all harm. **1902** WHITE *Blazed Trail* 184 His stake 'blown-in,' . . . the shanty boy would again start for the woods.

Shantyman. A lumberman or woodcutter. — [**1829** J. MACTAGGART *Three Years* I. 241 The *Shantymen* live in hordes of from thirty to forty together; throughout the day they cut down the pine trees.] **1893** *Scribner's Mag.* June 702/2 The typical shantyman works only fitfully in summer. [**1899** C. W. GORDON *Sky Pilot* iii, Latour . . . had been a shantyman himself.]

+**Shantytown.** A poor section of a city or town full of ramshackle or makeshift cabins or shacks; the inhabitants of such a section. — **1898** DELAND *Old Chester Tales* 178 The Judge's orchard [was] a place where Morrison's Shantytown took its outings and its apples. **1917** SINCLAIR *King Coal* 36 There's lots of people have boarders in shanty-town.

***Shape,** *n.* +Condition; mode or state of being. *colloq.* — **1865** NORTON *Army Lett.* 249, I got through it all in good shape. **1887** *Courier-Journal* 4 May 5/3 Things are getting in better shape. **1902** MACGOWAN *Last Word* 340 He's in bad shape now. **1905** *N.Y. Ev. Post* 24 Feb. 11 Repairs will be required to put it in shape to safely carry 120-ton locomotives.

* **Shape,** *v.*

‖**1.** *intr.* To shape one's course *for.*
1848 COOPER *Oak Openings* I. 49 Perhaps it would be best for me to shape at once for Ohio.

+**2.** To tend in a certain direction; to assume a particular aspect. *colloq.*
1865 NORTON *Army Lett.* 278 As things are shaping I do not much think I shall try. **1903** *N.Y. Times* 10 Sept., Matters are shaping for an effort on the part of the organized teamsters.

3. *To shape up.* +**a.** To put (something) into proper shape.
1885 *Harper's Mag.* Jan. 277/1 An experienced workman finishes the work of setting out by 'shaping up' the hides. **1890** *Stock Grower & Farmer* 8 March 3/1 All the replies received have been 'shaped up,' compiled and condensed.

+**b.** =sense 2.
1907 *Springfield W. Repub.* 2 May 3 It is not at all certain that matters will shape up so as to permit them to do this. **1919** HOUGH *Sagebrusher* 90 We're waiting . . . until things kind of shapes up. **1921** PAINE *Comr. Rolling Ocean* 293 Here is how it shapes up to me.

+**Shaps.** *pl.* =CHAPS. (Cf. SCHAP(P)S.) — **1882** BAILLIE-GROHMAN *Camps in Rockies* 394 His legs encased in the long leather *shaps* of the cowboy, reaching up to the hips. **1893** ROOSEVELT *Wilderness Hunter* 58 The men rode to the wagons . . . , some wearing leather shaps or leggings, others having their trousers tucked into their high-heeled top-boots. **1904** LYNDE *Grafters* 246 The cross-street was deserted save for a drunken cowboy in shaps and sombrero.

***Share.**¹ Also †sheare, *dial.* sheer.
***1.** One of the parts into which land is divided for occupancy or ownership by individual holders. *Obs.*
1628 *Plymouth Laws* 30 Every man of the surveighers [shall] have a peck of corne for every share of land layed out by them. **1662** *Oyster Bay Rec.* I. 9 John Risbile is to have ye first meadow sheer at matinicuk next to ye beach. **1687** *Providence Rec.* XVII. 82 His Estate . . . [includes] a 3rd part of a share of meaddow. **1700** *Ib.* V. 76, I Nicolas Power . . . [am] the true heir to the said six acre sheare of land. **1789** MORSE *Amer. Geog.* 260 They purchased a tract of about a mile square . . . and divided it into thirty parcels or shares.

2. One of the parts into which the capital stock of a company or corporation is divided. {1601-}
1778 in K. P. Bailey *Ohio Company of Va.* 325 The said Ohio Company . . . doth at present consist of twenty Shares. **1790** HAMILTON in *Ann. 1st Congress* 2012 The Secretary would propose a loan upon the principles of a tontine. . . . Each share to be two hundred dollars. **1839** *S. Lit. Messenger* V. 3/1 Let each member subscribe for not less than ten shares . . . in the South Atlantic Steam Navigation Company. **1859** J. B. JONES *Southern Scenes* 497 Have you any Pennsylvania Railroad shares? **1870** MEDBERY *Men Wall St.* 134 *Block*, a number of shares, . . . massed together, and sold or bought in a lump. **1904** C. A. CONANT *Wall St. & Country* 17 Bonds and ordinary shares prove unattractive to a certain type of investor.

+**b.** Used of bank stock.
1799 *Steele P.* I. 174 Mr. Miller . . . may have from me in the morning, any number of shares, not exceeding 90 at 37. **1814** *Niles' Reg.* VI. 152/2 The right of the state to subscribe certain shares in the Utica Bank. **1859** BARTLETT 91 How many shares in the —— Bank have been subscribed to-day?

+**3.** *On* (or *upon*) *(the) shares,* in accordance with an agreement by which the collaborators in an undertaking are to receive specified portions of the gain. (Cf. HALF *n.*)

*a*1656 BRADFORD *Hist.* 185 [The vessel] was rudly manned, and all her men were upon shars, and none was to have any wages but ye m[aste]r. **1792** BELKNAP *Hist. New-Hampshire* III. 216 Men can always be had to go on shares, which is by far the most profitable method, both to the employers and the fishermen. **1817** *Mass. Spy* 29 Jan. (Th.), To be let, upon Shares or Hire, a Farm. **1844** GREGG *Commerce of Prairies* II. 215, I requested a chief to take my horse and kill one [buffalo] 'upon the shares.' **1898** NICHOLAS *Idyl of Wabash* 36 He was a-workin' old Carter's farm on the sheers. **1924** CROY *R.F.D. No. 3* 9 Most of them were either working their father's land 'on shares,' or themselves were hired men.

4. In special combinations.
Share capital, the entire capital represented by shares; *s.-crop system,* the share system (q.v. below); *s. hand,* one who assists in producing a crop for a share of its proceeds; *shareman,* one who shares with others the gains of a fishing voyage; *s. system,* a system of farming in which a landlord and a tenant share in the risks and proceeds of a crop.
1885 WELLS *Practical Economics* 251n., The share capital and funded and floating debts of the railroads of the United States, for the year 1883, have been estimated at $6,765,000,000. **1907** *Springfield W. Repub.* 25 April 1 It is claimed that the difficulties of the South with the immigration laws can be met by reviving the old-time 'share-crop' system. **1911** JENKS & LAUCK *Immigration Problem* 83 Italian cotton tenants are showing the cotton growers of how much value careful cultivation, kitchen gardens and small store accounts may be to the cotton 'share hand' and tenant. **1687** *Conn. Rec.* III. 425 Fishermen . . . shall not presume to break off their voyage, . . . without the consent of the owner, master and share-men. **1831** FOWLER *Tour New York* 76 The *share*, or *halving system,* as it is called, is not very extensively practiced.

***Share.**² =PLOWSHARE. — **1644** [see COULTER]. **1662** *Essex Probate Rec.* I. 374 A shar & colter with expins. **1857** *Lawrence* (Kan.) *Republican* 11 June 3 After plowing eight or ten acres the share gets thick. **1867** 'LACKLAND' *Homespun* 285 The man of the hard hands . . . is turning up the sod with the gleaming share.

Shareholder. One who holds a share or shares in a corporation, a piece of property, etc. {1841-} — **1795** in Imlay *Western Territory* (1797) 575 The board of managers shall consist of a president and four members, to be chosen from among the share-holders. **1806** *Ann. 9th Congress* 465, I am a shareholder in a vineyard in Kentucky. **1881** *Ore. State Jrnl.* 1 Jan. 2/1 An individual shareholder of an insolvent national bank cannot be compelled to pay more than his full proportionate share of the bank's liabilities. **1911** *Okla. Session Laws* 3 Legisl. 86 The shareholders of trust companies . . . shall be additionally liable for an amount equal to the stock owned.

* **Shark.**
1. Any one of various large selachian fishes found chiefly in warm seas.
Freq. with defining terms. See also BONE SHARK, DOG SHARK, etc.
1616 SMITH *New England* 29 Cod, Hake, Haddock, Cole, Cusk or small Ling, Shark [etc.] . . . do heere, for want of vse, still increase. **1715** *Boston News-Letter* 11 July 2/2 A great Shark about 20 Foot long jumps out of the Water. **1764** in Singleton *Social N.Y.* 352 A shark ten feet long was taken at the New Dock. **1806** *Balance* 3 June 171/3 A former professor of chemistry in Columbia College . . . once dissected a shark and a sow. **1855** BAIRD in *Smithsonian Rep. 1854* 352 The blue shark was quite abundant in the bay during the summer. **1911** *Rep. Fisheries 1908* 316/1 Numerous species of sharks are found on the Atlantic and the Pacific coasts.

+**2.** =LAND SHARK 1. {1713-, in general sense}
1841 *Cultivator* VIII. 53 When you arrive in a new settlement, *beware of sharks.* **1870** BEADLE *Utah* 52 The Military Tract became the happy hunting ground of sharks and sharpers of every description. **1873** EGGLESTON *Myst. Metrop.* 52 He knows how to deal with these sharks.

+**3. a.** (See quot. 1856.) **b.** (See quot. 1914.)
1853 Root & Lombard *Songs of Yale* 45 No more look out for sharks. **1856** HALL *College Words* (ed. 2) 421 In student language, an absence from a recitation, a lecture, or from prayers, prompted by recklessness rather than by necessity, is called a *shark*. He who is absent under these circumstances is also known as a shark. **1909** *Springfield W. Repub.* 8 July 12 There is a distinction between the 'shark' and the 'grind.' . . . 'Sharks' play games. **1914** *N.Y. Ev. Post* 5 Jan.6 [The] 'shark' known to the American college world . . . [is] primarily, the student who devours and digests learning with ease . . . and, secondarily, one who excels in any line of activity.

+**4.** (See quotation and cf. LAND SHARK 2.)
1859 BARTLETT 397 *Shark,* a lean, hungry hog. Western.

+**Sharking.** [f. SHARK 1.] (See quot. 1859.) Also attrib. — **1859** BARTLETT 397 *Sharking,* fishing for sharks. **1881** in Godfrey *Nantucket* 146 No summer expedition is complete without one 'sharking expedition.' **1882** GODFREY *Ib.* 329 A visit can be made to the 'sharking grounds.'

***Sharp,** *a.* In combination with adjs. in *-ed,* in the specific names of trees, plants, fishes, and birds. {1611-} — **1785** MARSHALL *Amer. Grove* 68 *Juglans alba acuminata.* Long, sharp-fruited Hickery Tree. **1827** WILLIAMS *W. Florida* 30 Of Eagles, *Falco,* we have . . . Sharp Winged blue, *F. subceruleus*—rare. **1840** DEWEY *Mass. Flowering Plants* 133 *A[ster] acuminatus.* Sharp-leaved Aster. . . . [Grows] on mountains; August to October. **1843** TORREY *Flora N.Y.* II. 20 *Utricularia cornuta.* Sharp-horned Bladderwort. . . . Highlands of New-York; near Troy; about the Falls of Niagara. **1884** Sharp-headed Finner [see FINNER].

+**Sharper.** [f. *sharp* a.] (See quotations.) — **1881** INGERSOLL *Oyster-Industry* 248 *Sharpers*, elongated, protruding, sharp-ended oysters, dangerous to the feet in moving about the reefs. (Gulf coast.) **1887** GOODE, etc. *Fisheries* v. II. 548 Some [oysters] however, growing separately, ... [are] distinguished as 'sharpers,' from the fact that the ends of their shells are unusually sharp.

+**Sharpie.** (See quot. 1864.) Also attrib.
1864 WEBSTER 1215/2 *Sharpie*, ... a long, sharp, flat-bottomed sailboat. (*Local U.S.*) **1883** *Nat. Museum Bul.* No. 27, 267 A Connecticut sharpie ... used in the oyster and scallop fisheries. **1895** *Outing* XXX. 488/1 A balance-lug sail ... was subsequently replaced by a sharpie sail and jib. **1903** *Forest & Stream* 21 Feb. p. ix/4 Duck shooters' complete outfit ... consists of the cabin sharpie Fox, 37 ft. [etc.].

Sharp knife. +(See quotation.) — **1888** M. LANE in *America* 25 Oct. 15 Sharp Knife, Andrew Jackson.

*****Sharp-nosed,** *a.* In the specific names of fishes. {1769-} — **1814** MITCHILL *Fishes N.Y.* 462 The dissimilarity of the *blunt-nosed* and *sharp-nosed* sturgeon, is very obvious. **1836** J. RICHARDSON, etc. *Fauna Bor.-Amer.* III. 4 *Perca acuta*. Sharp-nosed Perch. This species was found in Lake Ontario. **1879** *Nat. Museum Proc.* I. 388 *Scoliodon terræ-novæ*. ... Sharp-nosed Shark. Very abundant in the harbor. [Beaufort Harbor, North Carolina.] **1884** GOODE, etc. *Fisheries* I. 666 The 'Eagle Ray,' or 'Sharp-nosed Ray,' *Mylobatis Fremenvillei*, ... is comparatively unusual in occurrence.

+**Sharps' (rifle).** [Christian *Sharps*, Amer. inventor (1811-74).] A breech-loading, single-shot rifle. — **1854** BARTLETT *Personal Narrative* I. 78 My Sharp's rifle ... loaded at the breech and primed itself. **1867** RICHARDSON *Beyond Miss.* 122 The old hero and his seven sons ... handled their Sharpe's rifles with fearlessness and accuracy. **1886** ROOSEVELT in *Outing* June 261 We opened fire on them [*sc.* deer], I with a Winchester, my companion with a 40-90 Sharp's rifle. **1897** LEWIS *Wolfville* 89 Dave's shootin' a Sharp's. **1908** MULFORD *Orphan* 169 My breach-loading sharps, .50 calibre.

+**Sharp shin.** [Named in allusion to the wedge shape of the segment.] One of five or ten segments of a cut coin, intended to pass current for one of four or eight segments of the coin. *slang.*
Cf. CUT MONEY.
1804 *Lancaster* (Pa.) *Jrnl.* 14 July (Th.), Three Sharpshins Reward. **1832** KENNEDY *Swallow Barn* I. 103 It is not of the value of a sharpshin. **1844** *Cincinnati Misc.* I. 6 A new [coinage of cut money] ... formed an additional quarter, or two additional eighths *to pay the expense of coinage*. This last description of change ... was nicknamed *sharp shins*.

+**Sharp-shinned hawk.** A North American hawk (*Accipiter velox*), widely distributed throughout the country. — **1823** JAMES *Exped.* I. 262 *Falco velox*. ... Sharp-shinned hawk. **1841** THOREAU *Journal* I. 306 What journal do the persimmon and buckeye keep, or the sharp-shinned hawk? **1887** RIDGWAY *Manual N.A. Birds* 227. **1917** *Birds of Amer.* II. 66/1 The Sharp-shinned Hawk has a body but little larger than a Robin's.

Sharpshooter. One who shoots a firearm accurately, esp. a soldier skilled in marksmanship; a sniper: (see also quot. 1918). {1802-} **1806** F. AMES *Works* I. 356 Are you sharp-shooters of Hampshire ready to get the bounty for Englishmen's scalps? **1821** in H. M. Brooks *Gleanings* IV. 141 The Subscriber, intending to give a grand treat to Sportsmen and Sharp Shooters, proposes to set up a number of fine Turkeys to be fired at. **1862** NORTON *Army Lett.* 73 Their sharpshooters were within thirty rods of us. **1918** FARROW *Dict. Mil. Terms* 551 *Sharpshooter*, ... in small-arms firing, a grade of rifleman just below that of expert rifleman.

+**Sharps rifle.** (See SHARPS.)

Sharp stick. (See quot. 1848.) — *a*1846 *Quarter Race Ky.* 120 The boys were all after him with 'sharp sticks' and 'hot bricks.' **1848** BARTLETT 295 'He's after him with a sharp stick;' i.e. he's determined to have satisfaction, or revenge. Western. **1871** *Trenton State Sentinel* 26 May (De Vere 631), The New York Tribune is still after Senators Carpenter, Conkling, and others, with a very sharp stick.

Sharptail. {1867} +(See quotations.) — **1891** *Cent.* 5554/2 *Sharptail*, ... the sharp-tailed grouse. **1917** *Birds of Amer.* II. 128 Pintail. *Dafila acuta*. ... [Also called] Peak-tail; Sharp-tail; Sprit-tail.

Sharp-tailed, *a.* {1678-} +In the specific names of birds. — **1811** WILSON *Ornithology* IV. 70 The Sharp-tailed Finch is five inches and a quarter long. **1831** WILSON, etc. *Ornithology* II. 260 *Fringilla Caudacuta*, Wilson. Sharp-tailed sparrow. **1858** BAIRD *Birds Pacific R.R.* 526 *Ammodromus Caudacutus*. ... Sharp-tailed Finch. ... Atlantic coast of the United States. **1883** *Nat. Museum Bul.* No. 27, 149 *Actodromas acuminata*. Sharp-tailed Sand-piper. Eastern Asia and Western Alaska. **1909** WEBSTER 1937/1 *Sharp-tailed duck*, ... the pintail duck. *Local, U.S.*

+**Sharp-tailed grouse.** A western grouse, *Pedioecetes phasianellus*. — [**1785** PENNANT *Arctic Zool.* II. 306 Sharp-tailed Grouse.] **1804-6** CLARK in *Lewis & C. Exped.* VI. (1904) 12 The Prarie Fowl common to the Illinois are found as high up as the River Jacque above which the Sharpe tailed Grows (grouse) commence. **1839** TOWNSEND *Narrative* 347, I returned to the fort in the afternoon with twenty-two sharp-tailed grouse. **1889** *Harper's Mag.* May 879/2 The sharp-tailed grouse had its eastern limit in Michigan. **1917** *Birds of Amer.* II. 29/2 The food of the Sharptailed Grouse is similar to that of the Prairie Grouse.

+**Shassay,** *v.* Variant of SASH(A)Y *v.* — **1871** *Harper's Mag.* XLIII. 640/2 Jake's instincts prompted him to 'shassay' around the fire.

+**Shasta.** [Amer. Indian.] A mountain peak in California: Used in the specific names of plants and trees. — **1893** *Stand.* 2248/1 *Shasta daisy*, a large, showy, cultivated variety of the ox-eye daisy. **1897** SUDWORTH *Arborescent Flora* 58 *Abies magnifica*. Shasta Fir. ... [Also called] Shasta Red Fir (var. *Shastensis*). *Ib.* 76 *Cupressus macnabiana*. Macnab Cypress. ... [Also called] Shasta Cypress (Cal.). **1915** ARMSTRONG & THORNBER *Western Wild Flowers* 34 Shasta Lily is a variety with a small bulb.

Shattuck. (See SHADDOCK.)

*****Shave,** *n.*[1] One of various tools used for scraping or removing thin slices from a surface. — **1645** *Essex Probate Rec.* I. 48, 2 chissells, one shave, one sickle. **1678** *Conn. Probate Rec.* I. 350, I give to John Ventrus my Tenant sawe, a shave & froe. **1718** *Boston Selectmen* 35 One brand, ... 2 punches, one Shave. **1859** *Mich. Agric. Soc. Trans.* X. 625 Wagon makers' shave, ... 25 [cents].

Shave, *n.*[2] {1604-}
1. An act of swindling; a swindle. {1863}
1834 C. A. DAVIS *Lett. J. Downing* 39, I've got some real shaves myself in that way. **1838** *Knickerb.* XII. 317 They speak of the above transaction but seldom, and invariably as 'the dead shave!' **1848** *Ib.* XXXII. 81 Ten dollars! ... What a shave! **1880** 'MARK TWAIN' *Tramp Abroad* 387 He went swinging along ..., as if he did not know he had just swindled a coroner by the closest kind of a shave.

+**2. a.** An exorbitant discount on a note. **b.** A premium charged for allowing a contract to be changed.
1855 *Chicago Times* 27 Jan. 2/2 When it [currency issued by certain banks] was offered at the very bank that had loaned it, ... the sucker offering it was compelled to stand a shave of from *ten to twenty per cent.* **1864** *Chicago Tribune* 9 April 4/2 [Bankers] have to pay the shave on a depreciated currency. **1898** WESTCOTT *D. Harum* 157 You've bled her fer shaves to the tune of sixty odd dollars in three years, an' then got your int'rist in full.

*****Shave,** *v.*
+**1.** *tr.* To discount (a note) at an exorbitant rate of interest. *slang.*
1807 IRVING, etc. *Salmagundi* 309 Those who *shave notes of hand* ... are the most respectable, because, in the course of a year, they make more money. **1818** *Niles' Reg.* XIV. 2/2 Very important men ... deal in and shave bank notes, as a regular business. **1848** W. ARMSTRONG *Stocks* 37 Ketchum, Rogers, and Bement ... do an immense business in shaving notes. **1896** FREDERIC *Damnation of T. Ware* 40 People tacitly inferred that he 'shaved notes.'

+**2.** To charge (a person) an exorbitant discount rate on a promissory note; to cheat (a person). *slang.* *Obs.*
1819 [see SHAVEE]. **1834** C. A. DAVIS *Lett. J. Downing* 39 We have been shav'd, ... most infarnally, with some of them 'ere State Banks. **1845** *Xenia Torch-Light* 31 July 1/7 The skinflint '*Individual*' Brokers, who have shaved the poor man from 20 to 50 per cent. for money loaned on mortgaged security.

Shaved head. *transf.* +An Indian. — **1846** SAGE *Scenes Rocky Mts.* iv, A thousand 'shaved heads' are upon us, half frozen for hair!

+**Shaved meat.** Jerked meat. — **1808** PIKE *Sources Miss.* App. III. 44 The travelling food of the dragoons ... consists of ... wheat biscuit and shaved meat, well dried, with a vast quantity of red pepper.

Shavee. {1826-} +A person whose note is discounted exorbitantly. — **1819** *Niles' Reg.* 20 Nov. 185/2 Every man who has 100 dollars is *shaving*, and everyone that wants $100 is trying to get *shaved*. ... *Shavers* and *shavees* are the bulk of the male population.

*****Shaver.** +One who discounts notes at exorbitant rates; a note-shaver. — **1807** IRVING, etc. *Salmagundi* 309 Your higher order of *shavers*, your true bloodsuckers of the community, ... grow rich on the ruin of thousands. **1812** PAULDING *J. Bull & Bro. Jon.* 111 He had put it [the cash] in the hands of a shaver, as they called him, ... who had placed it out at two per cent a month. **1859** *Harper's Mag.* June 137/1 Feels Arnul was a great shaver of small notes.

+**Shave rush.** Shave grass: (see quotations). — **1821** NUTTALL *Travels Arkansa* 53 A friable bed of dark-coloured argillaceous and sandy earth ... [contains] blackened impressions of leaves of an oak, ... with *Equisetum hiemale* or Shave-rush, and other vegetable remains. *Ib.* 78 It is from the prevalence of the cane, and the shave-rush (*Equisetum hiemale*), that the cattle are kept in tolerable condition.

+**Shavetail.** *slang.*
1. An unbroken mule.
1870 KEIM *Sheridan's Troopers* 89 [He] gave vent to a soliloquy in denunciation of 'shave-tails,' declaring that they were only sulky. **1897** LEWIS *Wolfville* 168 My off-wheel mule—a reg'lar shave-tail—is bad med'cine.

2. *transf.* A tenderfoot; a person not yet acquainted with certain things: (see also quot. 1917). Also attrib.
1899 T. HALL *Tales* 8-9 Not once ... has the boy asked his advice even about a camping place, which is quite customary and proper with 'shave-tail' officers. **1902** WHITLOCK *13th District* 426 He was a shavetail then, and didn't know a Piegan Indian from a Sioux. **1908** BEACH *Barrier* 283 The first shave-tail desperado that meets him will spit in his eye. **1917** J. A. MOSS *Officers' Manual* 485 *Shave-tail*, a new second lieutenant. So called after the young, unbroken mules in the Quartermaster Corps.

*Shaving.

+1. The discounting of notes at exorbitant rates; the business of buying and selling notes at profitable rates.

1816 *Niles' Reg.* X. 334/2 It ought to come, to relieve the people from the harpies that prey upon their labor in the '*shaving*' of notes. **1818** FEARON *Sketches* 13 The only business which was good for anything . . . was shaving, i.e. buying and selling bank-notes. **1838** *N.Y. Advertiser & Exp.* 21 March 3/1 The Star says *shaving* is at present quite a monopoly.

2. *attrib.* **a.** Designating the trade of, or things associated with, shaving the face.

1743 FRANKLIN *Writings* II. 232 Alexander Miller, Peruke-maker, . . . intends to leave off the Shaving Business after the 22nd of August next. **1836** *S. Lit. Messenger* II. 734 An old shaving-can . . . sat disconsolately on the chimney. **1851** CIST *Cincinnati* 226 A. E. Wetherill, manufacturer of perfumery, . . . soaps and shaving creams. **1865** *Atlantic Mo.* April 397/1 Tommy . . . took from the shelf first a tin pot strongly resembling a shaving-mug. **1871** 'MARK TWAIN' *Sk., New & Old* 258, [I] noted the numbers on the private shaving-cups in the pigeonholes. **1892** Shaving parlors [see HAIR-DRESSING PARLOR, ROOM].

b. Designating various tools and implements used in planing or shaving down wood or metal.

1841 *S. Lit. Messenger* VII. 527/2 A spacious garret . . . seemed to be used as a receptacle for . . . pitchforks, shaving horses, and sundry other implements of domestic industry. **1843** *Knickerbocker Mag.* XXII. 386 The rub-a-dub of the cooper's mallet, the creak of his shaving knife were still. **1888** *Century Mag.* May 84/1 He was surprised to find Barbara sitting on the 'draw-horse' or shaving-bench.

+Shaving bank. A bank that shaves notes. — **1848** BARTLETT 295 Banks, when they resort to any means to obtain a large discount, are also called shavers, or shaving banks.

Shaving box. A box for holding shaving soap. *Obs.* {1841} — **1775** *Penna. Ev. Post* 27 July 325/2 Brushes, shaving-boxes and black-ball of the best quality. **1790** *Penna. Packet* 19 April 4/2 He has likewise for Sale, . . . Razor strops, Shaving boxes, Shaving soap. **1840** *Picayune* 28 July 4/1 The following compose a part [of the merchandise]: . . . superior friction matches; . . . shaving boxes.

+Shaving mill. A small privateer. *Obs.* — **1781** *Indep. Chronicle* (Boston) 19 July 3/3 A small boat, one of the noted Shaving-Mills, which continually infest our bay, was captured. **1813** *Salem Gazette* 12 Oct. 4/1 The Fairhaven shaving mill . . . has sailed from Boston on a cruise. **1876** *Wide Awake* 243/2 A new 'shaving mill' . . . did double work of destruction.

+Shaving saloon. =BARBER SHOP. *Obs.* — **1846** CORCORAN *Pickings* 171 This shaving saloon is like himself—queer, very queer. **1855** MARRYAT *Mts. & Molehills* 306 In the 'shaving-saloons' the accommodation these establishments afford is indispensable to the California public. **1867** *Ore. State Jrnl.* 17 Jan. 3/3 New Shaving Saloon, Willamette Street.

Shaving shop. {1844} +A bank or a broker's office where notes or certificates are discounted at exorbitant rates. *Obs.* — **1836** CROCKETT *Exploits* 29 Placing one million of the public funds in some little country shaving shop with no more than one thousand dollars capital. **1840** *Picayune* 19 Sept. 2/3 There was a general run upon all the individual shaving shops, or self-instituted shinplaster manufactories. **1862** *N.Y. Tribune* 24 June 2/1 The only question was whether it [currency inflation] should be done by the banks and shaving-shops, or by the Government.

Shaving soap. Soap used to make a lather for shaving. {1844} — **1790** [see SHAVING box]. **1846** *Spirit of Times* (N.Y.) 9 May 131/1 The celebrity of 'Ring's Verbena Cream' throughout the United States has never been approached by any other Shaving Soap. **1898** *N.Y. Journal* 16 Sept. 11/6 Each contained toilet and shaving soap.

+Shaving ticket. A ticket entitling the holder to a shave or shaves in a barber shop. — **1864** *Hist. North-Western Soldiers' Fair* 82 W. A. Hetteck, Sherman House, [gave] 6 shaving tickets with 10 shaves each.

+Shawanee. (See SHAWNEE.)

+Shawanese salad. The Virginia waterleaf, *Hydrophyllum virginicum.* (See also *Shawanee salad* under SHAWNEE 2 b.). — **1784** FILSON *Kentucke* 24 The Shawanese sallad, wild lettuce, and pepper-grass, and many more . . . have excellent virtues. **1829** LOUDON *Encycl. Plants* 133 Hydrophyllum virginicum is used as a salad, under the name of Shawanese salad in North America.

Shawl. {1662–} An article of women's clothing worn about the head and shoulders. {1767–}

See also BLANKET SHAWL, CAMEL'S-HAIR b, CASHMERE 4, PAISLEY a.

1788 in H. M. Brooks *Gleanings* IV. 59 Few doz. purple & white Shawls. **1841** BACHE *Fire-Screen* 181 She sat . . . wrapped in that rich-looking dark shawl she was so fond of. **1857** *Lawrence* (Kan.) *Republican* 9 July 3 The Shawl was large, with white ground work, and a red border. **1879** HOWELLS *Lady of Aroostook* 73 Lydia was . . . wrapped against the freshening breeze in a red knit shawl. **1922** A. BROWN *Old Crow* 207 Charlotte appeared, done up in an old-fashioned shawl.

+Shawl society. (See quotation.) — **1871** BAGG *At Yale* 141 Psi U used to be called the 'shawl society,' in the old days when the wearing of that garment was deemed to smack somewhat of aristocracy and exclusiveness.

+Shawl strap. One of a pair of straps joined by a handle for carrying a shawl, etc. — **1873** PHELPS *Trotty's Wedding* xviii, The baby's swal-

lowed the shawl-straps! **1880** 'MARK TWAIN' *Tramp Abroad* 352 They must stand . . . laden with wraps and satchels and shawl straps.

+Shawmut. A variety of apple. — **1849** *New Eng. Farmer* I. 226 Shawmut.—This is a good apple till the latter part of May.

+Shawnee. Also **Shawanee, Shonee.** [Shawnee *Shawunogi* 'southerners.']

1. A member of an important Algonquian tribe of Indians, originally resident on the Savannah River; in pl., sometimes, the tribe. Also collective. In full *Shawnee Indian.*

1728 in Hildeburn *Century of Printing* 94 Two Indian Treaties . . . between the Honourable . . . Lieut. Governour of the Province of Pennsylvania, . . . And The Chiefs of the Conestogoe, Delaware, Shawanese and Canawese Indians. **1755** *Lett. to Washington* I. 149 The Cherokees have taken up the Hatchet against the French & Shawnesse. **1786** *Mag. Amer. Hist.* I. 177/2 Some few Shawness . . . come in frequently. **1812** *Niles' Reg.* II. 7/1 The Americans burned . . . all the corn of the Shawanees. **1817** *State P.* (1819) XII. 450 The balance of our men (except five Shonee Indians who had left us several days before). **1831** [see KICKAPOO]. **1837** BIRD *Nick* I. 15 The Shawanee and the Wyandot still hunted the bear and buffalo in the cane-brake. **1854** *S. Lit. Messenger* XX. 401 The Shawnese still deserved their chastisement. **1891** O'BEIRNE *Leaders Ind. Territory* p. viii/1 The Shawnees awaited their opportunity until the Tonkaway braves had departed on a big hunt.

quasi-adj. **1873** BEADLE *Undevel. West* 355 His first wife . . . was half Shawnee, from Canada.

2. *attrib.* **a.** With *camp, eardrops, tribe.*

1800 D'ERES *Memoirs* 15 About sixty Indians of the Shawanee tribe, came in birch canoes. **1821** NUTTALL *Travels Arkansa* 54 We stopped awhile at a Shawnee camp. **1855** WHIPPLE, etc. *Explor. Ry. Route* III. 51 [Figure D illustrates] one of a pair of Shawnee ear-drops, . . . made by a native artist.

b. In the specific names of plants.

1822 *London Hort. Soc. Trans.* 1 Ser. IV. 445 The Hydrophyllum Virginicum is called by the Americans of the Western States, *Indian Sallad,* or *Shawanee Sallad,* because these Indians eat it as such, when tender. Some of the first settlers do the same. **1909** *Cent. Suppl.* 1208/3 *Shawnee-haw,* . . . the larger withe-rod, *Viburnum nudum. Shawnee-wood,* . . . the western catalpa or catawba-tree, *Catalpa speciosa.*

+Shawnese, *a.* Also **Shawonese, Shawness, Shawanese.** Of or pertaining to a Shawnee or the Shawnees.

Probably from the *-ese* plural of SHAWNEE, on the analogy of such words as CHINESE.

1748 WEISER *Journal* 32, I made a Present to the old Shawonese Chief. **1786** *Mag. Amer. Hist.* I. 178 This evening a Mr. Soveraign came in from the Shawness towns. **1826** FLINT *Recoll.* 231 A rich commandant . . . married a Shawnese wife. **1846** *Xenia Torch-Light* 11 June 3/2 A letter [has been] lately received by him from an Indian named John Wolf, of the Shawanese tribe.

Shay. [f. CHAISE, mistaken for a pl.]

1. = CHAISE. {1806–7–} Also attrib.

1717 SEWALL *Diary* III. 139 The Governour went through Charlestown . . . , carrying Madam Paul Dudley in his Shay. **1779** *Essex Inst. Coll.* LVI. 24, I bought a shay . . . [for] £460 Massa. currency. **1836** GILMAN *Recoll.* (1838) 41 You may go to the barn and tackle the horse and shay. **1857** HOLMES *Poetical Works* 158/2 Have you heard of the wonderful one-hoss shay? **1887** WILLIAMS *Humble Romance* 139 We got in under the shay top as far as we could.

+2. (See quotation.)

1905 *Churchman* 18 Nov. 804 A 'shay' . . . is a kind of fishing boat.

+Shayite. =SHAYSITE. — **1787** *Maryland Jrnl.* 21 Dec. (Th.), Hail Congress, Conventions, Mobs, Shayites, and Kings. **1788** *Ib.* 29 Feb. (Th.), Rouse, ye Shayites, Dayites, and Shattuckites! Rouse, and kick up a dust before it is too late.

+Shays. [f. Capt. Daniel *Shays* (1747–1825), the leader of an insurrection in 1786–7 against the government of Massachusetts.] Used attrib. and in possessive. Now hist. — **1798** MANNING *Key of Liberty* 54 This Shais afair neaver would have hapned if the peopel had bin posesed of a true knowledge of their Rights. **1833** *Jamestown* (N.Y.) *Jrnl.* 13 Feb. 1/3 The Shay's insurrection in Massachusetts has been frequently alluded to of late as affording a parallel to the course expected from South Carolina.

+Shaysite. A follower of Daniel Shays in the insurrection of 1786–7: (see SHAYS). — **1792** *Mass. Spy* 13 Dec. (Th.), [He] acts like one of those who were called warm Shaysites, in whom there was much guile. **1798** MANNING *Key of Liberty* 46 They would call them Jacobines, Shasites, Disorganisers & Enemyes to all government. **1836** R. C. TORREY *Hist. Fitchburg, Mass.* 87 Capt. Shattuck was a distinguished Shaysite of Pepperell.

Sheaf oats. Oat plants bundled into sheaves. — **1765** CROGHAN *Journal* 19 The young reeds being preferable to sheaf oats. **1862** *Rep. Comm. Patents 1861: Agric.* 296 The seed heads . . . are far better as food for every kind of stock than sheaf oats. **1872** *Harper's Mag.* Jan. 227/2 His master . . . [was] set to work at chopping sheaf oats in a hay-cutter. **1894** *Outing* XXIV. 337/1 Ten minutes later the horses were quietly eating their corn and sheaf oats.

*Shear, n.

*1. pl. A cutting instrument with two blades that act simultaneously on opposite sides of the material being cut; large scissors.

1607 in Smith *Works* (1910) p. xliii, [We] presented . . . gyftes of dyvers sortes, as penny knyves, sheeres, belles. **1651** *Mayflower Descendant* X. 161, 4 moulds for bullets & shott and a paire of great sheers. **1761** in H. M. Brooks *Gleanings* IV. 26 Fine Lancashire Watch Plyers, Shears and Nippers. **1891** CHASE & CLOW *Industry* II. 143 A pair of great shears . . . clicked as though they enjoyed the feast. **1907** *St. Nicholas* Aug. 914/1 The other man was trimming the horse's mane with a pair of shears.

2. Attrib. and comb. with *blade, grinding, metal.*

1812 *Niles' Reg.* 25 Jan. 390/1 The subscriber . . . can furnish clothier's shear blades. **1876** KNIGHT 2134/2 *Shear-grinding Machine*, . . . a machine for grinding the blades of cotton and woolen shearing-machines. **1894** *Harper's Mag.* March 588/1 'Shear-metal,' [was] so called because it was first used for sheep-shears.

*Shear, v. 1. tr. Of sheep: To yield (a fleece). {1587, 1854} 2. To yield wool to (a certain amount). — (1) **1852** *Mich. Agric. Soc. Trans.* III. 139 An article upon Sheep, describing bucks that shear the big fleeces. **1876** *Vermont Bd. Agric. Rep.* III. 213 These sheep sheared a fleece of fine, downy wool, of from one and one-half to three pounds. (2) **1852** *Mich. Agric. Soc. Trans.* III. 146 Some of my best sheared but a little short of fifteen lbs. **1864** *Maine Agric. Rep.* IX. 9 It is not uncommon to have ewes shear eight pounds each in our section. **1904** 'O. HENRY' *Heart of West* 233 The sheep sheared six pounds all round this fall.

*Shearer. +An animal that yields a fleece through shearing. — **1864** *Ohio Agric. Rep.* XVIII. 236, I now have the best shearers I have ever kept. **1898** *Mo. So. Dakotan* I. 46 This class of lambs are found to be a little better shearers.

*Shearing.

*1. An occasion at which sheep are shorn.

1848 LOWELL *Poetical Works* (1896) 136/2 Your goddess of freedom, a tight, buxom girl . . . Who can sing at a husking or romp at a shearing. **1883** *Century Mag.* Oct. 817/1 A shearing at a large sheep ranch is a grand sight. **1890** *Stock Grower & Farmer* 8 Feb. 6/1 The Texas Wool-Growers' association has decided to hold a public shearing at the Topeka fair grounds on the first Tuesday in April.

2. Attrib. with *band, camp, contest,* etc., in sense: Pertaining to the shearing of sheep.

1866 *Iowa State Agric. Soc. Rep. 1865* 218 The shearing contest was lively. **1872** POWERS *Afoot & Alone* 300 A party . . . squatted around a fire by the shearing-camp. **1883** *Century Mag.* Oct. 817/1 In all . . . large [Indian] villages are organized shearing bands, with captains, that go from ranch to ranch in the shearing season. *Ib.*, There were a half dozen Indians lying on the ground outside this shearing shed. **1884** W. SHEPHERD *Prairie Exper.* 151 A few tumble-down open sheds guided you to the shearing corral.

*Shearing time. The time or season when sheep are sheared. {1742 (Ellis *Mod. Husb.* II. 138)} — **1654** *Essex Inst. Coll.* VI. 258/1 One yew [is] to be delivered for his use at the next shearing time. **1760** NILES *Indian Wars* I. 221 [They] were wont to come once a year at their shearing-time on the island. **1862** *Rep. Comm. Patents 1861: Agric.* 137 Shearing time . . . is the month of June. **1914** E. STEWART *Lett. Woman Homesteader* 87 When shearing-time came she went to a sheep-man.

Shearwater. a. Any of several seagoing birds, chiefly of the genus *Puffinus,* which usually skim close to the water in flight. {c1671-} +b. A skimmer of the genus *Rhynchops,* esp. the black skimmer.

1709 LAWSON *Carolina* 150 Shear-Waters are a longer Fowl than a Duck; some of them lie on the Coast, while others range the Seas all over. **1756** KALM *Resa* II. 153 Styrmannen, som var hemma i Philadelphia, kallade dem Shearwaters. **1791** [see RAZORBILL]. **1813** WILSON *Ornithology* VII. 85 Black Skimmer, or Sheerwater. *Rhincops nigra. Ib.* 87 The Sheerwater is most frequently seen skimming close along shore about the first of the flood. **1835** AUDUBON *Ornith. Biog.* III. 555 The Wandering Shearwater. *Puffinus cinereus.* I have found this species ranging from the Gulf of St. Lawrence to that of Mexico. **1883** *Century Mag.* Sept. 652/2 [Among them] birds on Cape Cod is . . . the black skimmer, or shearwater. **1917** *Birds of Amer.* I. 82/2 The best places to find Shearwaters, as well as the other 'ocean wanderers,' apparently are the fishing 'banks.'

Sheathing nail. A nail used to fasten sheathing to the bottom of a ship. {1611-} — **1656** *Suffolk Deeds* II. 241 Joshua Hewes . . . doth freely fully & absolutely Giue Graunt Bargaine sell enfeoffe & confirme vnto the said Henry Shrimpton all those sheathing nailes being eight thousand and fower hundred. **1715** *Boston News-Letter* 25 April 2/2 To be Sold . . . Sheathing Nails of sundry Sizes. **1742** *Md. Hist. Mag.* XX. 260, 4 Hundred weight of Eight penny sheething Nails.

+Sheathing paper. A building paper for sheathing. — c**1790** COXE *View U.S.* 62 The produce, manufactures, and exports of Pennsylvania . . . [include] sheathing and hanging paper. **1801** *Ann. 7th Congress* 2 Sess. 1225 Articles paying fifteen per cent. ad valorem . . . [include] cartridge and sheathing paper. **1854** EMMONS *Agric. N.Y.* 223 To protect a tree, Dr. Harris long ago recommended the use of sheathing paper. **1876** *Vermont Bd. Agric. Rep.* III. 239 The other three sides are boarded tightly, and lined with sheathing paper.

Sheath knife. A knife carried in a sheath. {1837-} — **1836** *Knickerb.* VIII. 693 [He] begged to borrow the Minorcan's sheath-knife. a**1862** THOREAU *Maine Woods* 231 His belt . . . contained a large sheath-knife. **1923** J. H. COOK *On Old Frontier* 110 A revolver and a sheath-knife were very necessary parts of a cowboy's equipment.

+She-balsam. The Fraser fir (*Abies fraseri*) of the southern Alleghenies. Also *she-balsam fir.* — **1884** SARGENT *Rep. Forests* 210 *Abies Fraseri.* . . . Balsam. She Balsam. High mountains of North Carolina and Tennessee. **1897** SUDWORTH *Arborescent Flora* 50 Fraser Fir. . . . [Also called] She Balsam (N.C.). She Balsam Fir (N.C.).

+Shebang. slang. [Of obscure origin.]

1. Civil War. A place where a soldier slept; a tent or hut; a headquarters. Also attrib.

1862 WHITMAN *Spec. Days* 27 [I am] among the groups around the fires, in their shebang enclosures of bushes. **1865** SABRE *Prisoner of War* 87 Get to hell off my Shebang. **1867** GOSS *Soldier's Story* 120 One of my company had his 'shebang' near the well. **1888** GRIGSBY *Smoked Yank* (1891) 193, I sat in my shebang, as we called it, at work on this stamp.

2. In various extended senses: A building; a carriage; a theater; an outfit; etc.

c**1870** CHIPMAN *Notes on Bartlett* 398 Shebang, . . . an engine-house. **1871** BAGG *At Yale* 47 Shebang, rooms, place of abode. Also a theatrical or other entertainment in a public hall. **1872** 'MARK TWAIN' *Roughing It* 327 You're welcome to ride here as long as you please, but this shebang's chartered. **1877** HARTE *Story of Mine* 85 That . . . don't fetch me even ef he'd chartered the whole shebang. **1885** BAYLOR *On Both Sides* 278 My shebang is around here just a step. **1890** HARTE *Heritage of Dedlow Marsh* 45 That old pirate . . . had a stock of the real thing from Robertson County laid in his shebang on the Marsh. **1901** HARBEN *Westerfelt* 198, I like to have my dealin's with the head of a shebang. **1910** MCCUTCHEON *Rose in Ring* 150 She's put the rest in to save the shebang. **1917** FREEMAN & KINGSLEY *Alabaster Box* 29 If we didn't want to sell this old shebang we'd be damn idiots.

*She-bear. A female bear. — **1847** HOWE *Hist. Coll. Ohio* 565 He once shot a she bear and 2 cubs in less than three minutes. **1872** TICE *Over Plains* 206 The squaws took up the fight with the fierceness of grizzly she-bears when fighting for their cubs. **1914** 'BOWER' *Flying U Ranch* 257, I'd rather nurse a she bear with the mumps!

+She-cattle. Cows. — **1885** *Santa Fé Wkly. New Mexican* 20 Aug. 4/1 There are now on the ranges of New Mexico sufficient she-cattle to fully stock the territory in five years. **1890** *Stock Grower & Farmer* 26 April 4/2 A decreased supply [may result from] . . . the wholesale marketing during the past three seasons of 'she-cattle.' **1903** A. ADAMS *Log of Cowboy* 12 The contract called for a thousand she cattle.

‖Shecoonery. A humorous corruption of *chicanery.* — **1845** THOMPSON *Chron. Pineville* 47 This town's got a monstrous bad name for meanery and shecoonery of all sorts. *Ib.* 48 He dwelt upon the verdancy of his neighbors, and the shecoonery which had been practised upon them.

+She-corn. (See quotation.) — **1705** BEVERLEY *Virginia* II. 29 The other has a larger Grain, and looks shrivell'd with a Dent on the Back of the Grain, as if it had never come to Perfection; and this they call *She-Corn.*

*Shed. Also †shead.

*1. A relatively small structure for storage or shelter, sometimes attached to a larger building as a lean-to, either open at the sides or closed in; a roof supported by pillars.

1637 *Dedham Rec.* III. 28 Lambert Genere hath undertaken . . . to build a sufficient shead to lodge the Swyne. **1653** *Boston Rec.* 6, I give . . . five pounds more towards the erecting of a platforme . . . with a shead of boards raysed over it. **1707** *Braintree Rec.* 66 The Selectmen . . . have allowed unto John Wilson Esqr. . . . Leave and Liberty to set up a shed containing Twelve foot front. **1725** in *Travels Amer. Col.* 166 Two Sheds to be repaired . . . are over two of the fflankers. **1771** [see COACH HOUSE 1]. **1833** SILLIMAN *Man. Sugar Cane* 30 The Canes . . . [are] delivered under a shed whose roof is a continuation of that of the Sugar house. **1868** *Rep. Comm. Agric. 1867* 240 It is generally the best economy to have all the farm store-room and stables under the same roof . . . rather than to build sheds for the purpose. **1880** *Harper's Mag.* Sept. 535/1 Near the Tennessee line their huts are often merely sheds. **1907** *St. Nicholas* June 692/2 The snow was sliding with sudden excited rustlings from the roofs of the barn and sheds.

b. A similar structure of large size used to shelter large objects such as machinery or railway cars. {1855-}

1840 *Picayune* 9 Sept. 2/1 A large warehouse or shed . . . was discovered on fire. **1878** JACKSON *Travel at Home* 6 An enormous shed is filled with [luggage].

+2. An open porch of a house.

1778 CARVER *Travels* 46 Before the doors are placed comfortable sheds, in which the inhabitants sit, when the weather will permit. **1856** OLMSTED *Slave States* 630, I observed remarkably comfortable, though cheap and rude, quarters for the negroes—each cabin being of good size, with brick chimney, and a broad shed or gallery before the door.

3. A refreshment stand of rough boards.

1879 *Harper's Mag.* June 70/1 The cook . . . instigated the artist to make a likeness of Aunt Sally, sitting in the shade of the shed.

+Shed chamber. N. Eng. A room under a shed roof. — **1889** COOKE *Steadfast* 74 Hiram Perkins, the hired man, . . . slept in the 'shed charm-ber.' **1895** A. BROWN *Meadow-Grass* 13 Mis' Jeremiah took her to the shed-chamber and trounced her soundly. **1922** — *Old Crow* 483 The bed . . . was the old four-poster he had packed away in the shed chamber.

✶**Shedder.** +A crab or other shellfish during one of its stages: (see quotations). — **1843** *Nat. Hist. N.Y., Zoology* VI. 11 During this interval, they are known under the name of Soft-shell Crabs, or Shedders. **1879** *St. Nicholas Mag.* Nov. 84/2 [The young crab] keeps on eating till he is bigger still; then he is called a 'Shedder.' . . . He still grows till he is called a 'Buster,' and then sheds. **1883** *Century Mag.* July 378/2 A dozen large craw-fish, . . . about to shed their outer cases, or shells, . . . are called 'shedders,' or 'peelers.' **1911** *Rep. Fisheries 1908* 309/1 While shedding . . . [crabs] are known as 'hard-shell,' . . . 'peeler,' and 'shedder.'

+**Shedder crab.** A crab in the shedder stage. (Cf. prec.) — **1848** *S. Lit. Messenger* XIV. 684/1 We will purchase a few shedder-crabs in the market. **1856** *Porter's Spirit of Times* 27 Sept. 57/2 Perhaps at this season the most killing bait, is the shedder crab. **1884** ROE *Nature's Story* 128, [I] fastened on my hook a peeled shedder crab.

+**Shed kitchen.** A shed room used as a kitchen. — **1872** EGGLESTON *End of World* 62 Got a mustache onto the top story of his mouth, somethin' like a tuft of grass on the roof of a ole shed kitchen. **1886** STAPLETON *Major's Christmas* 267 They followed her . . . to a shed kitchen, where there was a cook stove and a sink.

+**Shed porch.** =SHED 2. — *c*1850 BAGBY *Old Va. Gentleman* 250 Under a hastily-made shed-porch in front of the house will be found a number of rocking-chairs.

Shed roof. A roof on a shed; a roof of a type used on a shed. {1805-} — **1736** *Md. Hist. Mag.* III. 45 This Deponant Looking on the Shead-Ruff of Capt. Cressap's house he see [etc.]. **1817** *Essex Inst. Coll.* VIII. 235 These [arks] are . . . built like our mud-scows, with a shed roof over your head. **1847** HOWE *Hist. Coll. Ohio* 240 Seventy or eighty feet of the enclosure was composed of a row of log corn cribs, covered with a shed roof. **1857** VAUX *Villas* 97 The simplest form [of bay window] is a plain semi-octagon, with simple shed-roof, shown at L [*i.e.*, a three-way hip roof]. **1904** T. E. WATSON *Bethany* 8 Springing off from the main roof, other rafters reached downward to rest upon outer plates—forming a shed-roof; the half of this, being closed in with planks, made a shed room.

+**Shed room.** S. A ground-floor room jutting out from a house or cabin, and usually having a separate roof; a lean-to room. — **1835** LONGSTREET *Ga. Scenes* 205 She pointed to an open shed-room adjoining the room in which we were sitting. **1845** *Big Bear Ark.* 157 The girls took the bride into the shed room. **1879** *Scribner's Mo.* June 260/1 They had . . . a neat one-and-a-half story house, with piazza and two back shed-rooms. **1888** *Century Mag.* Oct. 897/1 She went quietly to her little shed-room at the end of the porch. **1904** [see prec.].

Shed-shaped tent. A tent with a pent roof. — *a*1862 THOREAU *Maine Woods* 246 A shed-shaped tent will catch and reflect the heat like a Yankee-baker.

✶**Sheep.**

I. ✶**1.** Any ruminant animal of the genus *Ovis*, esp. the domesticated species, *O. aries.*

See also COTSWOLD, LEICESTER, MERINO SHEEP.

1633 *Plymouth Laws* 31 No sheep [shall] be sold out of the colony. **1682** ASH *Carolina* 21 Their Sheep bears good Wooll. **1760** NILES *Indian Wars* I. 221 Each . . . [left] a farm at Block Island, which they stocked with sheep. **1849** *31st Congress 1 Sess.* Sen. Ex. Doc. No. 64, 106 [The Navajos'] stock . . . consisted mainly of sheep and horses. **1871** *Republican Rev.* 26 Aug. 1/2 When California was being first settled by Americans, hundreds of thousands of sheep were driven from New Mexico to California. **1912** WING *Sheep Farming in Amer.* 106 The sheep . . . will remain wet for 24 hours at least after emerging from the dip.

b. A wild sheep.

See also MOUNTAIN SHEEP, ROCKY MOUNTAIN SHEEP.

1804 CLARK in *Lewis & C. Exped.* I. 240 The Mandans Indians Call this Sheep *Ar-Sar-ta.*

II. *attrib.* and *comb.* **2. a.** Designating various actions connected with caring for or raising sheep. {1607-}

See also SHEEP-HERDING, SHEEP-RAISING, SHEEPSHEARING.

1672 *East-Hampton Rec.* I. 243 William Edwards of Easthampton have entered and Action of the case against Roger Earle for Unfaithfullnes in his shepekeping the Sumer last past. **1856** *Porter's Spirit of Times* 11 Oct. 99/3 Several farmers in Washington county [Pa.] have tried raising millet for sheep feeding. **1879** *Cimarron News & Press* 20 Nov. 3/6 E. S. Post, dealer in . . . Buckeye Mowers, Sulky Rakes, Sheep Dipping Tanks [etc.]. **1884** W. SHEPHERD *Prairie Exper.* 2 Cattle, cow-boys, round-ups, sheep-driving, herders, and life on the prairie, these are my text. **1890** *Cincinnati Christian Advocate* 5 Feb. 10/2 Culture is not a new suit of clothing, to be donned after one has finished his sheep-washing or his board-of-trade deal.

✶**b.** Designating persons who care for or deal with sheep.

See also SHEEP-FEEDER, SHEEP-GROWER, etc.

1693 *Huntington Rec.* II. 118 It was voted . . . that Rogger Quinte [be] sheepe keeper for this present yeare. **1868** *Mich. Agric. Rep.* VII. 400 The Sheep Breeders' and Wool Growers' Association of this county express . . . our views on this important interest. **1872** 'MARK TWAIN' *Roughing It* 240 They were expecting some sheep-drovers and their flocks. **1874** *Vermont Bd. Agric. Rep.* II. 431 Every sheep-owner knows what a commotion the appearance of these flies causes among his flock. **1883** Sheep-shearer [see HARVESTER 2].

✶**c.** Designating various pens or pasture lands in or upon which sheep are kept.

See also SHEEP COMMON, SHEEP PEN.

1718 HEMPSTEAD *Diary* 79, I was at home making the sheep fold. **1782** CRÈVECŒUR *Letters* 127 Several hundred of sheep-pasture titles have since been divided on those different tracks. **1792** *Mass. H. S. Coll.* 1 Ser. III. 156 Clerks of the sheep yard are appointed. **1810** *Steele P.* II. 631 We are converting the City into a Sheep walk on a great scale. **1865** *Harper's Mag.* June 12/1 He undertook to find accommodations in a vacant sheep-corral. **1868** *Mich. Agric. Rep.* VII. 47 Twelve half-blood Cotswold sheep . . . were put in the pens, at the south end of the sheep barn.

✶**d.** Designating parasites that infest sheep.

1789 MORSE *Amer. Geog.* 62 Of Insects found in America, we will mention, . . . Flea, Gnat, Sheep Tick [etc.]. **1874** *Vermont Bd. Agric. Rep.* II. 430 The sheep bot fly, *Œstrus ovis* . . . is found all over the Northern States. **1892** *Amer. Folk-Lore* V. 101 *Cynoglossum officinale*, sheep-lice. No. Ohio.

✶**e.** In the names of plants. Also in possessive.

See also SHEEPBERRY, SHEEP LAUREL, etc.

1806 *Ann. 9th Congress* 2 Sess. 1142 Common names of some of the . . . plants, growing in the vicinity of the Washita . . . [include] sheeps' clover, life everlasting, wild liquorice. **1854** *Mich. Agric. Soc. Trans.* V. 524, I planted one half with yellow sheep tooth dent. **1855** Sheep Fescue [see FESCUE]. **1858** *Harper's Mag.* May 841/2 A shrewd boy knows . . . in what pastures the purple smaller laurel—sheepsbane—grows. **1892** *Amer. Folk-Lore* V. 93 *Abutilon Avicennæ* sheep-weed; Mormon-weed; velvet-weed. Quincy, Ill. **1915** ARMSTRONG & THORNBER *Western Wild Flowers* 258 Pink Lady-fingers, Sheep-pod, *Astragalus Utahensis.* Pink. Spring, summer, autumn. Utah, Nev.

+**f.** In special combinations.

Sheep mountains, mountains inhabited by mountain sheep; *s. rock*, (see quot. 1859); *s. wagon*, a wagon used in a sheep camp.

1900 *Scribner's Mag.* Sept. 271/1 It seemed like a fairy-tale to be there, with the sheep mountains all around. **1859** COOPER & SUCKLEY *Nat. Hist. Washington Terr.* III. 137 Several rocky prominences in northern California . . . have the name of 'Sheep rocks,' where the bighorn exists. **1914** E. STEWART *Lett. Woman Homesteader* 8 About noon the first day out we came near a sheep-wagon.

Sheepback. A mass of rock made smooth and round like a sheep's back by the action of glacier ice. {1877} — **1875** *Amer. Naturalist* IX. 174 Many of the 'sheep backs' are still covered with a crust-like enamel. **1880** DANA *Man. Geology* 699 The rounded knolls of rock along the track of a glacier have been called *sheep-backs (roches moutonnees)* in allusion to their forms. **1906** *N.Y. Ev. Post* 10 Nov. Sat. Suppl. 1 The gray lumps of glacial boulders, the terraces, rock faults, ravine gashes, 'sheepbacks,' and even lines of strata are visible at a distance.

+**Sheepberry. 1.** The black haw, *Viburnum prunifolium.* **2.** The nannyberry (*Viburnum lentago*), or its black edible drupe. — **(1)** **1814** PURSH *Flora Amer.* II. 709 Sheep-berry. *Viburnum prunifolium*). **1897** SUDWORTH *Arborescent Flora* 338 Stagbush. . . . [Also called] Sheepberry (N.J.). — **(2)** **1817-8** EATON *Botany* (1822) 510 *Viburnum lentago*, sheepberry. . . . Berries black, oval, and pleasant-tasted: somewhat mucilaginous. **1884** SARGENT *Rep. Forests* 94 Sheepberry. Nannyberry. . . . Wood heavy, hard, close-grained, compact.

+**Sheep camp.** W. A camp serving as headquarters for sheep-herders. — **1883** SWEET & KNOX *Through Texas* 585 It is wonderful how many educated men, and men of rare talents and attainments, are to be met in sheep-camps and cattle-ranches. **1912** RAINE *Brand Blotters* 177, I played hell with one of his sheep camps.

Sheep common. {1707} +A share or right in common land used for pasturing sheep. — **1677** in Sheldon *Hist. Deerfield, Mass.* I. 180 Let out to Philip Matt on my 18 cow commons and 4 sheep commons at Pocumtuck, all the intervale land. **1792** *Mass. H. S. Coll.* 1 Ser. III. 156 The property is very unequally divided, varying from one sheep commons right to fourteen hundred sheep commons right. **1882** Godfrey *Nantucket* 89 The owner of 2⁄₀ part of an original share of land . . . would own . . . thirty-six sheep commons (meaning thirty-six undivided 1/20th parts) of a certain share in each of the old divisions.

Sheep country. Country used, or suitable to be used, for running sheep. {1872} — **1883** *Century Mag.* Oct. 807/1 For a few years the wide belt of good pasturage land along the coast was chiefly a sheep country. **1890** *Stock Grower & Farmer* 12 July 5/1 The country north of Prescott [Ariz.], is the best sheep country in the United States. **1898** *Mo. So. Dakotan* I. 45 Through her wide awake sheep men . . . she is widely known as a sheep country.

Sheep dip. A liquid preparation in which sheep are dipped to kill parasites. {1865-} — **1880** *Cimarron News & Press* 26 Feb. 2/5 Carbolic Sheep Dip . . . kills Ticks, Lice, and all parasites. **1897** HOUGH *Story of Cowboy* 281 Ex-cowboys . . . would have scorned to carry a 'bucket of sheep dip.'

Sheep dog. (See quot. 1879.) {a1774-} — **1872** POWERS *Afoot & Alone* 164 Here, too, are the calico flocks of goats, and the famous New Mexican sheep-dogs. **1879** WEBSTER *Suppl.* 1578/2 *Sheep-dog*, a dog for tending sheep;—in America, a common name for the colly. **1905** VALENTINE *H. Sandwith* 59 Two children in blue sunbonnets ran in advance of the horses chased by a barking sheep-dog.

Sheep-eater. +An Indian of certain Shoshonean tribes: (see quotations). Also attrib. — **1865** *Rep. Indian Affairs 1864* 175 These [Tukuarika] bands are generally known as 'the Sheep-Eaters,' and their number is estimated at one thousand. **1882** BAILLIE-GROHMAN *Camps in Rockies* 176 In the Wind River chain there existed up to quite recent times, a very interesting and very little-known community of Indians, known as the 'Sheepeaters.' **1890** LANGFORD *Vigilante Days* (1912) 135 That notorious scoundrel . . . bought a squaw from the Sheep Eater tribe of Bannack.

+**Sheep-feeder.** (See quot. 1906.) — **1862** *Rep. Comm. Patents 1861: Agric.* 128 Cheyney was at that time a noted sheep-feeder. **1906** *N.Y. Ev. Post* 27 Oct. Sat. Suppl. 1 A 'sheep feeder' is a man who receives the animals from the ranges into the feed lots, where they are fattened for market, and he is distinguished from a 'breeder,' who grows his sheep on the range.

Sheep fever. +An intense desire to go into the sheep business. — **1868** *Iowa State Agric. Soc. Rep. 1867* 408 The 'sheep fever' has proved the 'nub,' and wool-growers are rather disgusted. **1868** BRACKETT *Farm Talk* 27 A sheep-fever, or mania, rages throughout a portion of the country.

+**Sheep-grower.** One who breeds and raises sheep. — **1868** *Rep. Comm. Agric. 1867* 233 It is a matter well worthy the attention of sheep-growers. **1870** *Ill. Agric. Soc. Trans.* VII. 455 The general practice of crossing the coarse wool buck with fine wool ewes, is now thought by many first-class sheep growers, to be bad.

***Sheephead.** + =SHEEPSHEAD. — **1743** CATESBY *Carolina* II. p. xxxii, Common Names of . . . Sea Fish [include]: . . . Sea-Tench, Sheephead, Eel. **1812** STODDARD *Sk. Louisiana* 163 It produces a kind of fresh water sheep-head. **1864** NORTON *Army Lett.* 212 Sheephead, shaped like a pumpkin seed with teeth exactly like a sheep's, . . . [are abundant]. **1894** TORREY *Fla. Sketch-Book* 51, I never saw so much as a sheep-head or a drum lying at his feet.

***Sheep herd.** +A herd of sheep. — **1867** *Wkly. New Mexican* 2 Feb. 1/4 A band of Mescalero Apaches . . . made a descent upon a sheep herd a few miles below Las Cruces. **1880** *Cimarron News & Press* 19 Aug. 1/7 The Apaches made a raid upon the sheep herds of Valencia county.

+**Sheep-herder.** *W.* One who herds sheep, esp. in unfenced country. — **1871** *Republican Rev.* 13 May 1/2, 150 Krowas, killed two sheep herders. **1885** *Outing* Oct. 52/1, I would be sure to 'grubstake' every wandering Mexican sheep-herder that chanced along. **1890** *Stock Grower & Farmer* 24 May 7/2 The Mennonite colony of farmers . . . have been having some considerable trouble with the sheep herders. **1916** WILSON *Somewhere* 221 [Here's] this room still looking like the inside of a sheep-herder's wagon!

+**Sheep-herder's delight.** Hard liquor. *slang.* — **1873** *Harper's Mag.* Feb. 479/1 A peddler, . . . after taking several drinks of my sheep-herders' delight, . . . went off and stole his own pack. **1877** W. WRIGHT *Big Bonanza* 375 But let me come home full of tangle-leg, sheep-herder's delight, and tarant'ler juice. **1878** B. F. TAYLOR *Between Gates* 281 The man . . . has just tipped a tumbler of what he calls in his random recklessness, . . . 'the sheep-herder's delight.'

+**Sheep-herding.** The action or occupation of herding sheep. — **1891** C. ROBERTS *Adrift Amer.* 245 Sheep-herding will almost disappear when the wild beasts of Texas are extinct. **1908** 'O. HENRY' *Options* 48 I've never exactly done any sheep-herding.

Sheep house. A building in which to shelter sheep. — **1738** *N.H. Probate Rec.* II. 280 Samuel & Abigail White . . . shall Have . . . Division No Two in ye sd Barn . . . & No five of ye Sheep house. **1773** *Penna. Gazette* 27 Oct. Suppl. 2/2 To be sold, A valuable plantation . . . , with a calf and sheep-house. **1806** *Balance* V. 288/2 The sheep house may be situate at the end of the barn. **1838** *S. Lit. Messenger* IV. 232/1 Besides the dwelling-house, there are negro-quarters, . . . sheep-house, . . . and kitchen.

Sheep-killing dog. A dog that makes a practice of killing sheep. — **1864** *Ohio Agric. Rep.* XVIII. 388 And the millions of money that are thus annually lost by the farmars [*sic*] of Ohio, are just as causlessly [*sic*] lost as in the case of loss by sheep killing dogs. **1872** *Newton Kansan* 29 Aug. 4/2 Sheep-killing dogs are generally great cowards. **1898** E. C. HALL *Aunt Jane* 18 Job set there, lookin' like a sheep-killin' dog.

+**Sheep laurel.** A dwarf shrub (*Kalmia angustifolia*), resembling mountain laurel and poisonous to stock; also, the mountain laurel (q.v. sense 1 b). Cf. LAMBKILL. — **1810** MICHAUX *Arbres* I. 35 *Mountain laurel*, . . . dénomination la plus générale. *Sheep laurel*, . . . nom secondaire. **1869** FULLER *Flowers Gatherer* 138 And here is a third species, the *Angustifolia*, commonly termed, 'Sheep-Laurel.' **1897** SUDWORTH *Arborescent Flora* 315 *Kalmia latifolia.* Mountain Laurel. . . . [Also called] Sheep Laurel (Pa., Ohio).

***Sheepman.** +A sheep-breeder; one who owns sheep. — **1872** POWERS *Afoot & Alone* 297 These people in Southern California, . . . except these big sheep-men and stock-ranchers, is the meanest and mangiest people I know. **1885** *Wkly. New Mexican Rev.* 19 Feb. 4/1 Advices from Pajarito state that a lot of cowboys are creating trouble with the sheep men. **1892** *Vt. Agric. Rep.* XII. 154 The successful sheep men of the State are . . . breeding for mutton or for roughbred Merinos. **1905** *Forestry Bureau Bul.* No. 62, 8 The sheepmen and cattlemen are in frequent collision. **1919** HOUGH *Sagebrusher* 72 They might take me fer a sheep man.

+**Sheep meat.** Mutton. (Cf. SHEEP'S MEAT.) — **1859** BARTLETT 398 *Sheep-Meat.* Mutton is often so called in the West. **1884** *Gringo & Greaser* 1 Jan. 2/3 [We] munch our tortiers and sheepmeat on the wing.

+**Sheepnose.** Any of several varieties of apple. Also attrib. — **1817** W. COXE *Fruit Trees* 125 Bullocks Pippin . . . is more generally distinguished by the vulgar name of Sheep-nose, from a supposed resemblance between the form of the apple and that part of a sheep. **1859** ELLIOTT *Western Fruit Book* 188 Sheep nose. Medium, oblong, pale yellow, faint blush; flesh, firm, watery. November, December. **1888** 'CRADDOCK' *Despot* 82 He be right yander in that thar sheep-nose apple-tree.

Sheep pen. A pen in which sheep are kept. {1649–} Also †*sheeps pen.* — **1646** *New Haven Col. Rec.* 266, I have made a sheeps penne. **1767** WASHINGTON *Diaries* I. 239 Sowed Turnep Seed . . . in sheep pens at the House. **1879** *Scribner's Mo.* June 338/1 The other [sleeve] had been sacrificed in a scuffle in the sheep-pen. **1904** WALLER *Wood-Carver* 86 They came down to the sheep-pen for a wisp of hay.

+**Sheep poison. 1.** =LAMBKILL. **2.** (See quotation.) — **(1) 1814** [see LAMBKILL]. **1892** *Amer. Folk-Lore* V. 100 *Kalmia angustifolia*, sheep-poison. N.E. **(2) 1884** W. MILLER *Dict. Names of Plants* 124/2 'Sheep-poison,' Californian. *Lupinus densiflorus.*

+**Sheep-raiser.** One who breeds and raises sheep. — **1864** *Ohio Agric. Rep.* XVIII. 258 They had the best of attention from an old Berkshire sheep-raiser. **1874** *Rep. Comm. Agric. 1873* 280 Mr. Solomon Jewett, . . . one of the oldest and largest sheep-raisers in that State, . . . has now 450 acres sown in alfalfa. **1887** *Courier-Journal* 7 May 2/1 Cubert Gonzales, a larger sheep-raiser, rode over the range. **1922** Z. GREY *To Last Man* i, I reckoned you belonged to the sheep raisers who're on the outs with my father.

Sheep-raising. The action or occupation of breeding and raising sheep. {1880–} — **1832** *Encycl. Amer.* XI. 352/2 (*caption*), Sheep-Raising. **1857** *Rep. Comm. Patents 1856: Agric.* 50 This part of the State [of Ill.] is well adapted to sheep-raising. **1880** *Cimarron News & Press* 22 Jan. 1/4 In Colorado, Utah, New Mexico, Arizona and Texas sheep-raising has been enormously profitable. **1899** *Atlantic Mo.* June 754/2 Sheep-raising is one of the industries in which the white man [in N. Mex.] . . . has invested largely.

+**Sheep ranch,** *n.* A ranch devoted to the breeding and raising of sheep. Also attrib. — **1875** *Congress. Rec.* 20 Feb. 1537/1 This is not the sheep-ranch proposition. **1881** CHASE *Editor's Run in N. Mex.* 49 Mr. Chase and his partner Dawson own a sheep ranche 180 miles south-east of Cimarron. **1904** 'O. HENRY' *Heart of West* 230 You don't often hear as agreeable a noise as that on a sheep-ranch.

+**Sheep-ranch,** *v. intr.* To operate a sheep ranch. — **1879** HOWELLS *Lady of Aroostook* 65 They may sheep-ranch, too, for all I know.

Sheep range. A range over which sheep are herded. {1845} — **1863** *Rep. Comm. Agric. 1862* 41 These islands . . . are likely to become the best lands for sheep ranges. **1880** *Cimarron News & Press* 24 June 3/2 This week they expect the large clip of Don J. A. Baca, of Las Vegas, whose sheep range [is] in the eastern part of the county. **1908** 'O. HENRY' *Options* 53, I approve of Black Bill's retreat to the sheep-ranges.

+**Sheep saffron.** *S.* Sheep sorrel or a medicinal preparation made from it. — **1835** LONGSTREET *Ga. Scenes* 210, I reckon sheep-saffron the onliest thing in nater for the ager. **1850** LEWIS *La. Swamp Doctor* 151 How we . . . were perfectly unanimous in the conclusion that 'sheep safern' were wonderful 'truck!' **1856** CARTWRIGHT *Autobiog.* 135 The next time those monkey-catchers come they bring sheep-saffron.

Sheep's fescue (grass). A European grass (*Festuca ovina*), frequently cultivated for sheep pasturage. {1759–} — **1840** DEWEY *Mass. Flowering Plants* 241 Sheep's Fescue. Is recently introduced as a valuable grass. **1878** KILLIBREW *Tenn. Grasses* 184. **1884** VASEY *Agric. Grasses* 103 *Festuca ovina* (Sheep's Fescue grass).

+**Sheep's gray.** A mixture of white and black wool. Also attrib. and comb. — **1713** *Boston News-Letter* 2 Feb. 2/2 A Servant Man Named James Holms . . . [has] dark Sheeps gray coloured Stockings. **1852** *Mich. Agric. Soc. Trans.* III. 489 One piece of sheeps-gray cloth. **1862** 'K. KIRKE' *Among Pines* 235 He wore . . . a suit of the ordinary 'sheep's-grey.' **1889** *Century Mag.* Jan. 462/1 Then we had resort to coarse sheep's-gray jacket and trousers.

* **Sheepshead,** *n.* +One of several fishes having some resemblance to the head of a sheep: (see note). Sometimes with specifying terms.

These fishes include: **a.** A large food fish (*Archosargus probatocephalus*), abundant on the Atlantic and Gulf coasts. **b.** An allied fish of Florida, *Salema rhomboidalis* (syn. *Archosargus unimaculatus*). **c.** The fresh-water drumfish (*Aplodinatus grunniens*) of the Great Lakes and the Mississippi Valley. **d.** The dollarfish, *Poronotus triacanthus.*

1643 WILLIAMS *Key* (1866) 138 *Taut-aūog*, Sheeps-heads. **1687** BLOME *Isles & Terr. in Amer.* 119 The Sheepshead, so called, from the resemblance of its Mouth and Nose to a Sheep, is a Fish much preferred by some. **1701** WOLLEY *Journal N.Y.* 40 Bass and Sheepshead . . . are delicate Fish. **1724** JONES *Virginia* 41 There is Variety of excellent Fish, . . . especially Oysters, Sheepsheads, Rocks, . . . Drums. **1768** WASHINGTON *Diaries* I. 285, [I hauled] the Sein upon the Bar of Cedar Point for Sheeps heads. **1789** MORSE *Amer. Geog.* 205 In the rivers and bays are plenty of sheeps-head, black-fish, herring. **1815** *Lit. & Phil. Soc. N.Y. Trans.* I. 494 A very ill-tasted fish in Erie, is called the *sheep's head* on account of a supposed resemblance to its salt water namesake. **1842** *Nat. Hist. N.Y., Zoology* IV. 76 The Malasheganay, *Corvina richardsonii*, . . . in Lake Huron . . . is called Sheepshead. **1849** COOPER *Sea Lions* iv, He has a sheeps-head at the end of his line that will weigh eight or ten pounds. **1868** G. G. CHANNING *Recoll. Newport* 66 Hereabouts [in R.I.] were caught . . . the bass and tautog, and now and then a 'sheep's head.' **1884** GOODE, etc. *Fisheries* I. 275 The Red-fish, of California, . . . is very rarely called 'Sheepshead.' *Ib.* 333 The 'Butter-fish' of Massachusetts and New York, [is] sometimes known . . . about Cape Cod as the 'Sheepshead' and 'Skipjack.' **1896** JORDAN & EVERMANN *Check-List Fishes* 390 *Archosargus....* Sheepsheads. **1897** *Outing* XXX. 435/2 Most abundant . . . was the 'sheepshead' (freshwater drum), a good-looking, silvery fish. **1909** WEBSTER 1939/1 *Sheepshead,* . . . the salema.

+**b.** Used attrib. with *killifish, lebias, minnow,* to designate a killifish (*Cyprinodon variegatus*) of the Atlantic and Gulf coasts.

1814 MITCHILL *Fishes N.Y.* 441 Sheep's-Head Killifish. . . . Lives in the salt water. **1842** *Nat. Hist. N.Y., Zoology* IV. 215 The Sheepshead Lebias . . . [is] used as bait. **1896** JORDAN & EVERMANN *Check-List Fishes* 314 *Cyprinodon variegatus....* Sheepshead Minnow. Cape Cod to the Rio Grande.

+**Sheepshead,** *v. intr.* 'To fish for or catch sheepshead' (*Cent.*).

+**Sheepshead gull.** (See quotations.) — **1813** WILSON *Ornithology* VII. 76 By many it [the common tern, *Sterna hirundo*] is called the Sheep's-head Gull, from arriving about the same time with the fish of that name. **1844** *Nat. Hist. N.Y., Zoology* II. 305 The Silvery Tern, *Sterna argentea,* . . . is sometimes called the *Little Sheepshead* Gull.

+**Sheepsheading party.** A party organized to fish for sheepshead. — **1814** MITCHILL *Fishes N.Y.* 394 The outfit of a sheep's heading party is always an occasion of considerable parade and high expectation.

+**Sheepshead porgy.** A small sparoid fish (*Calamus penna*) of the Florida reefs. — **1884** GOODE, etc. *Fisheries* I. 394 A fish known as the 'Sheepshead Porgy' is said by Stearns to be common about the Florida Reefs.

+**Sheep-shearer machine.** A machine for shearing sheep. — **1868** *Mich. Agric. Rep.* VII. 361 G. S. Wormer & Son, Detroit, [exhibited] 1 American sheep shearer machine.

Sheepshearing. The act of shearing sheep {1607–}; the occasion when sheep are shorn.

1712 *Essex Inst. Coll.* X. 1. 95 Finished sheep shearing. **1775** *Holyoke Diaries* 88 Great meeting will be here this month, & Sheep shearing, high Frolicks, both. **1812** *Niles' Reg.* II. 192/1 On Thursday last, being the 8th anniversary of the Arlington Sheep Shearing, a number of gentlemen . . . assembled with their sheep as competitors for the various prizes. **1851** MELVILLE *Moby-Dick* 179 His spout is . . . white as a side of our Nantucket wool after the great annual sheep-shearing. **1883** [see GRAPE 4 b].

attrib. **1868** *Mich. Agric. Rep.* VII. 404 The usual preparations were made for a Sheep-Shearing Festival. **1890** *Stock Grower & Farmer* 26 July 3/1 Wm. Cook Scott . . . is introducing the Wolseley sheep shearing machine in America.

Sheep shears. *pl.* A pair of shears specially designed for shearing sheep. {1688–} — **1712** HEMPSTEAD *Diary* 10, I was att home & a mending my sheep shears. **1890** *Stock Grower & Farmer* 15 Feb. 6/3 Knives were used in shearing [in N. Mex.] and the first sheep-shears were brought into the territory and used in 1854.

*Sheepskin.

*1. The woolly skin of a sheep, esp. one used as a robe or garment; leather or parchment prepared from this skin.

1631 WINTHROP in R. C. Winthrop *Life J. Winthrop* II. 60 Bring two or three hundred sheep-skins. **1757** *Lett. to Washington* II. 158 Some trifling things may be had, vizt. Sheepskins, Hair Cloths. **1861** [see GUMBO BOX]. **1898** CAHAN *Imported Bridegroom* 156 The dim outline of Rouvke in top-boots and sheepskin [rose] . . . in the background. **1924** *Publisher's Weekly* CVI. 443/1 *Niger* morocco is a trade name for sheepskin with a coarse grain finish.

*2. A document made of parchment; +spec., a college diploma.

1804 D. WEBSTER *Private Corr.* I. 173 Feeling some anxiety about your 'sheep-skin,' I wrote to Merrill. **1827** COOPER *Prairie* vii, Why do not the surveyors of our States . . . cover their shining sheepskins with big words? **1900** MUNN *Uncle Terry* 29 Did you bring your sheepskin with you?

transf. **1843** 'CARLTON' *New Purchase* I. 141 [We] arn't no hirelins like them high-flow'd college-larned sheepskins.

3. Attrib. in sense 1 with *apron, bellows, boots,* etc.

1714 *Boston News-Letter* 18 Oct. 2/2 To be Sold . . . Grindstones, Calve and Sheep Skin Bellows, Hammers. **1751** *Va. Gazette* 28 Feb. 4/2 An Apprentice . . . had when he went away . . . a Pair of new tann'd Sheep Skin Breeches. **1809** WEEMS *Marion* (1833) 47 [You could see] the fences all strung along with starved tackies, in grape-vine bridles and sheepskin saddles. **1879** *Scribner's Mo.* Aug. 614/1 He wore . . . a sheep-skin apron tied about his waist. **1890–3** TABER *Stowe Notes* 4, I wear sheepskin boots with thick leather soles. **1919** HOUGH *Sagebrusher* 8 In the winter time he cast a sheepskin coat over all.

+**Sheep's meat.** Mutton. (Cf. SHEEP MEAT.) — **1833** J. STUART *Three Years N.A.* II. 126 The people, and especially the less rich classes, dislike mutton, which they call sheep's-meat. **1837** MARTINEAU *Society* II. 46 The inhabitants may be put in the way of obtaining tender 'sheep's meat.'

Sheep sorrel. a. A dwarf herb, *Rumex acetosella.* {1872; *sheep's sorrel} **b.** One of various wood sorrels. — **1807** GASS *Journal* 188, I also saw a great quantity of sheep-sorrel growing in the woods. **1832** KENNEDY *Swallow Barn* I. 284 His constitution resembles that waterish, gravelly soil that you see sometimes around a spring where nothing grows but sheep-sorrel. **1839** in *Mich. Agric. Soc. Trans.* VII. 413 *Oxalis stricta.*

Yellow wood sorrel. Sheep sorrel. **1893** *Amer. Folk-Lore* VI. 139 *Oxalis acetosella,* sheep sorrel. Jones and Del. Co., Ia. **1894** [see FIELD SORREL].

Sheepswool. 1. Wool from sheep. {1721} +**2.** A high grade of sponge. Also attrib. — (1) **1656** *Watertown Rec.* I. 1. 50 She [must] sett her selfe to the Carding of two Skaines of Cotton or sheeps wooll. **1735** *N.H. Probate Rec.* II. 535, I Give unto my beloved wife . . . five pound of Sheeps wool. **1866** A. D. WHITNEY *L. Goldthwaite* viii, Sticks and roots and bark, straw and grass and locks of dirty sheepswool, made up its bulk and its untidiness. (2) **1883** *Nat. Museum Bul.* No. 27, 126 Fully 75 per cent. in value of all the Florida Sponges marketed are of the Sheepswool variety. **1911** *Rep. Fisheries 1908* 316/1 *Sheepswool,* the highest grade of Florida commercial sponges.

*Sheer, *a.* Of fabrics: Thin, diaphanous. {–1727} 'Now *U.S.*' (*O.E.D.*). — **1836** GILMAN *Recoll.* (1838) 191 The sheerest muslin lay on that pale forehead. **1862** S. HALE *Letters* 13 Sheer white muslin, most elaborately trimmed with brilliant rose and Chine ribbon. **1898** CHOPIN in Rankin *K. Chopin* (1932) 267 She fastened a sheer white 'kerchief . . . about the old lady's neck.

+**Sheer boom. a.** (See quot. 1876.) **b.** Such a structure designed to shunt logs away from a bridge or the bank of a stream. — **1876** KNIGHT 2141/1 *Sheer-boom,* . . . a boom in a stream to catch logs and direct them toward a log-pond. One end is moored to the shore, and it has rudders . . . to catch the force of the current obliquely, and thus maintain its position at a certain angle across the direction of the stream. **1879** *Lumberman's Gazette* 1 Oct., The company have put in a row of piers to which they have attached a sheer-boom. **1882** *Congress. Rec.* 8 July 5817/1 [The clause] for the protection of Rock Island bridge by sheer-booms. **1896** *Monthly Weather Rev.* Nov. 407/1 The formation of the gorge is supposed to have been caused by the driving of piles in the Mississippi River . . . to hold a 'sheer boom' for the purpose of running the logs . . . into the Zumbra River for safe harbor. **1908** H. DAY *King Spruce* 334 Sheer-booms . . . were to be the silent herders that would edge the log-flocks away from the banks.

* Sheet.

1. A large piece of cotton or linen cloth used on a bed; a bed sheet.

1638 *Md. Archives* IV. 30 The Inventory of John Bryants goods [includes] . . . 1. cap, 3. sheets, 2. hatts. **1684** *Hempstead Rec.* I. 431 The Estate of John Smith: . . . Two chaff beds and two boulsters, five fether pillows, Six sheetes, three Coverlids [etc.]. **1721** *N.H. Probate Rec.* I. 684 My son Benjamin shall allso give her his sd mother two good sheets. **1794** in Buckingham *Newspaper Lit.* II. 229 Two sheets, a feather bed and hay-tick, I order sledded up to Natick. **1803** *Lit. Mag.* (Phila.) Dec. 172, I slept little on my musty dusty bed of chaff with one scanty sheet. **1875** STOWE *We & Neighbors* 406 Aunt Maria has her hands so full, . . . buying her sheets and towels and table-cloths, . . . that her nervous energies are all used up. **1923** HERRICK *Lilla* 107 His mother and sister . . . sewed all the sheets and household linen.

2. A piece of paper on which a number of bills or notes are so printed that they may be readily cut or torn apart. {1852–, of stamps}

1776 *Penna. Ev. Post* 2 March 110/2 A Sheet of Continental Money, . . . containing sixteen bills, being numbered 38019, and 38032. **1819** in Mackenzie *Van Buren* 155 If, however, you should receive . . . a supply of our notes, in sheets, or otherwise, you will not interfere.

+**3.** A large piece *of* gingerbread baked on a flat tin or in a shallow pan.

1825 NEAL *Bro. Jonathan* I. 108 Walk into you, any time, for half a sheet o' gingerbread. **1846** FARNHAM *Prairie Land* 31 It was . . . a pair of luscious brown sheets of gingerbread, which he had purchased at a Dutch farm-house. **1865** *Atlantic Mo.* June 665/2 Not a young farmer came into Hanerford . . . , who did not . . . buy a sheet of gingerbread . . . [for] the drive homeward.

*4. Used attrib. to designate various metals in the form of broad flat sheets.

See also SHEET COPPER, SHEET IRON.

1692 SEWALL *Letter-Book* I. 129 Holes are punched in sheet-Lead. **1778** *Essex Inst. Coll.* XLIII. 9 Boxes of Sheet Tin a third X. *c*1790 COXE *View U.S.* 39 By wind and water machines we can make . . . sheet-iron, sheet-copper, sheet-brass. **1847** *Rep. Comm. Patents 1846* 60 Letters patent have been granted for an improved mode of manufacturing spoons from sheet silver. **1851** CIST *Cincinnati* 237 Sheet-steel for sale. **1874** LONG *Wild-Fowl* 86 Strips of sheet-zinc should be . . . tacked smoothly around the edges of the bottom.

Sheet copper. Copper in sheets or thin pieces. {1720– (Steuart *Letter-bk.* 121)} – *c*1790 [see SHEET 4]. **1797** *N.Y. State Soc. Arts* I. 374 The dome [of the fireplace may be] either of marble or of sheet copper, japaned or guilded. **1887** *Amer. Naturalist* June 600 A horizontal disk of sheet-copper . . . would afford room for a number of paraffine imbedding-troughs.

Sheeting. Cotton or linen cloth woven sufficiently wide for bed sheets. Also with qualifying terms indicating the source of the commodity. {1711–}

1714 *Boston News-Letter* 9 Aug. 2/2 Several Sorts of Irish Linens for Shirting, Sheeting and Tableing. **1767** in H. M. Brooks *Gleanings* IV. 13, 22 yards of Hamburgh Sheeting. **1803** *Lewis & Clark Exped.* VII. (1904)

245, 45 1/2 Yds of 9/8 Flanders Sheeting . . . 14.49. **1803** *Austin P.* 1. (1924) 89, 1 ps Lancaster Sheeting. **1811** *Niles' Reg.* 21 Sept. 45/2 In this valuable class of cotton goods are included strong neat shirting and sheeting. **1893** *Harper's Mag.* Feb. 384/2 New Orleans has two large cotton-mills, making brown goods, sheetings, shirtings, unbleached and colored goods.

b. Attrib. with *cloth, cotton, linen.*
1730 *Md. Hist. Mag.* XIX. 185 One peece Irish Sheeting linen. a**1825** *Memorandum for E. Pettigrew* (Univ. N.C. MS.), 4 pieces sheeting cotton. **1876** *Vermont Bd. Agric. Rep.* III. 89 For a strainer, good sheeting cloth is not too thick, if the milking is properly done.

Sheet iron.
1. Iron in the form of broad thin sheets. {1816–} Also fig.
1776 *Jrnls. Cont. Congress* V. 443 Thomas Bates, blacksmith, [was] proposing to supply the continental troops with a quantity of camp kettles, of sheet iron. **1789** *Morse Amer. Geog.* 288 These works produce . . . sheet iron, and nail rods. **1841** *Knickerb.* XVII. 38 The black-board . . . consisted of a plate of sheet-iron well rusted. **1902** *Lorimer Lett. Merchant* 148 His creed was built of sheet iron and bolted together with inch rivets.

2. attrib. a. Designating articles made of sheet iron.
1833 *Md. Hist. Mag.* XIII. 346 About halfway down is a sheet iron riddle. **1850** *Sawyer Way Sketches* 107 A sheet-iron camp kettle, and a common bake kettle. **1862** *Rep. Comm. Patents 1861: Agric.* 162 The juice of the cane was immediately boiled in a sheet-iron boiler fastened in a furnace. **1871** Sheet-iron kettle [see Kettle 1 b]. **1880** *Harper's Mag.* Dec. 65 Tremendous sheet-iron oil-tanks . . . are to store away 2,000,000 barrels of 'dollar-crude.' **1924** *Mumford Sticks & Stones* 89 What Owen's generation actually did see, apart from sheet-iron façades, . . . was the Crystal Palace.

+b. In special combinations.
Sheet-iron band, a callithumpian band (*facetious*); *s. hat,* (see quotation). **1846** *Spirit of Times* (N.Y.) 18 April 88/1 His hat was what is commonly termed a 'sheet-iron' hat, being destitute of nap, and resembling a battered chimney pot. **1851** *Hall Manhattaner* 146 The happy couple . . . would have seen . . . a modest card of anonymous authority, calling on the Sheet-Iron-Band to appear that night for duty.

Sheet-iron stove. A small wood-burning stove made of sheet iron. — **1820** *Columbian Centinel* 1 Jan. 4/4 For Sale, . . . All kinds of Sheet Iron Stoves and Funnels. **1863** *Taylor H. Thurston* 131 The sheet-iron stove gave out a comfortable warmth. **1884** *Century Mag.* Nov. 109, I have seen a new regiment start out with all the indescribable material carried by raw troops, sometimes including sheet-iron stoves. **1918** *Essex Inst. Coll.* LIV. 212 Air tight sheet iron stoves . . . heated the portion near them.

Sheet-iron ware. Articles of merchandise made of sheet iron. — **1851** *Cist Cincinnati* 186 Value of . . . tin-ware and sheet-iron-ware, 30 per cent. **1878** *Rep. Indian Affairs* 47 Here are manufactured flour, tin, and sheet-iron ware. **1892** *York County Hist. Rev.* 47 D. H. Leppo, Tin and Sheet-Iron Ware, Stoves, &c.

Sheet music. Music published in the form of large, usually unbound, sheets. {1881} — **1857** *Lawrence* (Kan.) *Republican* 11 June 3 City Drug Store . . . Periodicals, Lithographs, Sheet Music, Etc. **1863** *Ill. Agric. Soc. Trans.* V. 256 Lay aside . . . all the sheet music that is laying around loose. **1880** 'Mark Twain' *Tramp Abroad* 229 By him lay . . . a well-gnawed slab of gingerbread as big and as thick as a volume of sheet music. **1915** *Chicago D. News Almanac 1916* 615/2 The Coe music collection . . . contains . . . 400 pieces of sheet music.

*Shekel. A coin; also, pl., money. *colloq.* {paper shekel, 1825–} **1871** *Bagg At Yale* 47 Shekels, money. **1889** *Munroe Golden Days* 181 There'll be monte lay-outs where . . . nobody'll lose a shekel. **1894** *Ford P. Stirling* 165 This money was all that he received for the time spent, but he was not working for shekels.

*Sheldrake. *local.* +Any one of various American ducks, esp. the canvasback.
See also **Hooded sheldrake.**
1616 *Smith New England* 29 Sheldrakes, Teale, Meawes, Guls, . . . and many other sorts, whose names I knowe not. **1781–2** *Jefferson Notes on Va.* 77/2 We have . . . Sheldrach, or Canvas back. **1793** *Mass. H. S. Coll.* I Ser. III. 86 There is a great number of wild fowl on this river and its waters, viz. swans, geese, shelldrakes, a variety of ducks and teal. **1813** *Wilson Ornithology* VIII. 104 At the Susquehannah they are called *Canvas-backs,* on the Potowmac *White-backs,* and on James' river *Sheldrakes.* **1882** *Godfrey Nantucket* 157 In the early spring, at Coatue and in the upper harbor, brant, sheldrakes, coots, and whistlers are to be found in considerable numbers.

*Shelf.
1. = Bench *n.* 2. {1818–}
1846 *Knickerb.* XXVII. 405 A village . . . was placed high up on a cool shelf of the mountain. **1847** *Henry Campaign Sk.* 283 There were two shelves, . . . the second covered with a vigorous growth of hackberry, oak, ebony, and peccan.

+2. A berth on a canal boat.
1847 *Robb Squatter Life* 90 Possessing a 'top shelf,' and conscious that we could sink but a few feet, I held my peace.

+3. A shelf fungus.

1907 *St. Nicholas* July 846/1 'Shelves,' often called 'devil's bread,' . . . grow on woodland stumps and trees and logs.

4. In special combinations.
Shelf goods, merchandise usually displayed for sale upon shelves; *s. list,* a list of books and other materials in a library in the order of arrangement on the shelves; *s. number,* a number placed on a book to indicate its position on a library shelf (cf. Call number); *s. paper,* paper placed on a shelf as a cover or ornament; *s.-worn,* showing marks of wear from having been kept on a shelf (*fig.*); *s. wrinkle,* a wrinkle in a garment resulting from its having been kept on a shelf.
1899 *Caddo Herald* 3 March 1 They have opened up a first-class stock of Hardware, consisting of a general line of Shelf Goods. **1910** *Bostwick Amer. Pub. Library* 171 The name 'shelf list' is sometimes improperly given to a class list. *Ib.* 166 The old 'fixed location,' in which every book always stood on the same shelf and bore a 'shelf number,' is now generally abandoned. **1901** *Merwin & Webster Calumet 'K'* 326 The three set to work, . . . covering the tables with pink and blue and white scalloped shelf-paper. **1887** *Tourgee Button's Inn* 188 [The invention's] out of season, . . . creased and shelf-worn. **1898** *C. A. Bates Clothing Bk.* No. 1107 There are no shelf wrinkles.

+Shelf hardware. ?Comparatively light hardware displayed for sale upon shelves. — **1865** *Ore. State Jrnl.* 18 Nov. 3/2 Goldsmith and Friendly . . . [are] displaying to the Public an Immense Stock of . . . Shelf Hardware. **1892** *York County Hist. Rev.* 57 The stock embraces . . . a large line of heavy and shelf hardware.

*Shell, n.
I. *1. The hard calcareous covering of a crustacean, mollusk, etc., +used as wampum or as ornaments by Indians.
1648 *East-Hampton Rec.* I. 3 Allsoe, they reserve libertie to fish in all convenient places for Shells to make wampum. **1724** *Jones Virginia* 11 They often wear Shells hanging upon their Breasts. **1831** *R. Cox Adv. Columbia R.* 158 These shells . . . are found in the neighbourhood of Nootka, and form an important article of local traffic.

+2. A person's head, mouth, or body. *colloq.*
1678 *B. Tompson Poetical Works* 125 Too big for my poor shell to Comprehend. **1845** *Knickerb.* XXV. 212 'Shut your shells!' answered Tom, in high dudgeon. **1906** *F. Little Lady of Decoration* 95 My old shell is too exhausted to move.

+3. A bare, rough, or unpretentious building with little or no furniture.
1852 *Stowe Uncle Tom* xxxii, They were mere rude shells, destitute of any species of furniture. **1880** *Harper's Mag.* Dec. 43 Which one of the old shells have you taken? **1920** *Howells Vacation of Kelwyns* 5 Even the summer shell was little known in the early eighteen-seventies.

+4. A long, light, narrow racing boat; a skiff or canoe.
[**1858** *Holmes Autocrat* 196, I run along ripping it up with my knife-edged shell of a boat.] **1875** *Fur, Fin & Feather* (ed. 3) 114/2 For weeks I have paddled my cedar shell in all directions. **1882** *Nation* 6 July 9/2 The Yale shell . . . is built some eight or ten feet longer than that of Harvard. **1887** *Century Mag.* June 179/1 A new boat—a 'shell'—was bought for the University crew.

5. A cartridge for a pistol or other firearm. Also attrib.
1908 *Chambers Firing Line* 165 The agile herd bounded past far out of shell-range. **1914** 'Bower' *Flying U Ranch* 73, I'd haze 'em into a coulee and turn loose with a good rifle and plenty uh shells. **1924** *Cummins Sky-High Corral* 47 She stole all my 30-30 shells.

II. attrib. and comb. 6. Designating materials, trimmings, etc., having a shell pattern.
1774 *Fithian Journal* I. 186 She is drest in a neat shell Callico Gown. **1867** *Harris Sut Lovingood* 137 Irish chain, . . . saw teeth, checker board, an' shell quilts . . . reigned triumphan' 'bout her hous'. **1870** A. D. Whitney *We Girls* v, She could make shell-trimmings and flutings. **1893** *Holley Samantha at World's Fair* 152 To suppose that anybody would be a-lookin' out for shell-work stockin's, a-carin' whether they wuz clam-shell pattern, or oyster shell.

7. Designating land or areas where marine shells are abundant in the soil.
1837 *Williams Florida* 56 The soil is rich shell land. **1883** *Smith Geol. Survey Ala.* 500 The belt of what is called in this county 'shell prairie' is about five miles wide. **1887** *South Fla. Sentinel* (Orlando) 16 Feb. 1/9 This [land] is what they call a shell hammock.

8. Designating articles made of tortoise shell.
1844 *Lexington Observer* 25 Sept. 1/4 Have just received . . . Shell, Twist and Side Combs. **1883** *Knight Suppl.* 805/1 *Shell Piece,* . . . one of the shields of tortoise-shell or horn, used with spring eye-glasses which clasp the nose. **1896** *Harper's Mag.* April 808/1 She replaced the dagger with a shell pin from her own hair. **1898** *Westcott D. Harum* 208 Mrs. Bixbee was grand in black silk and lace collar fastened with a shell-cameo pin not quite as large as a saucer.

+9. Designating light racing boats, or a race between such boats.
1858 *Holmes Autocrat* 189 My present fleet on the River Charles . . . [includes] a 'skeleton' or 'shell' raceboat. **1871** *Harper's Mag.* July 186 The shell-boats . . . made such good time that in 1869 a general challenge

was given. **1891** *Harper's Wkly.* 19 Sept. 715/2 The aquatic event of the day was the eight-oared shell race for the S.I.A.C. challenge cup.

10. Designating ways, walks, etc., surfaced with sea shells.
See also SHELL ROAD.

1884 CABLE *Dr. Sevier* 454 [Mary was] breaking the silence . . . by the soft grinding of her footsteps on the shell walk. **1887** CUSTER *Tenting on Plains* 273 The best part of all our detention was the shell drive along the ocean. **1908** CHAMBERS *Firing Line* 146 The little cavalcade made a startling clatter on the shell highway.

11. In special combinations.

Shell bank, (see quotation); *s. beans*, beans shelled before cooking, as distinguished from those cooked in the pod; *s. bluff*, a bluff consisting largely of sea shells; *s. button*, a hollow button made of a front and a back piece; *s.-cracker*, *shellhead*, *shellman*, *s. pot*, *s. pump*, *s. quail*, (see quotations); *s. vase*, a vase ornamented with shells.

1891 *Cent.* 5565/3 *Shell-bank*, a shelly bank or bar, usually covered at high tide, forming favorite feeding-grounds for various fishes. **1868** HAWTHORNE *Notebooks* II. 88 [We had] shell-beans, green corn, and cucumbers from our garden. **1765** J. BARTRAM *Journal* 7 This shell-bluff is 300 yards more or less along the river's bank. **1789** *Ann. 1st Congress* 796 Abraham Westervelt . . . [asks that] an exclusive patent may be given him for manufacturing shell buttons of different dimensions. **1891** *Cent.* 5565/3 *Shell-cracker*, a kind of sunfish, *Eupomotis speciosus*. [Florida.] *Ib.* 5566/1 *Shellhead*, the dobson or hellgrammite. [Georgia.] **1900** WEBSTER *Suppl.* 1902 *Shell man*, a swindler who plays the shell game. **1790** *Mass. Spy* 24 June (Th.), A negro man, saw, and caught, a small turtle, or what is more generally known [in Va.] by the name of shellpot. **1876** KNIGHT 2149/2 *Shell-pump*, (*Well-boring*), a tube with a clack-valve at its foot, used for removing the detritus from a bored shaft. **1884** COUES *Key to Birds* (ed. 2) 593 *Callipepla.* . . . Shell Quail. . . . One U.S. species. . . . *C. squamata.* . . . Scaled Partridge. Blue Quail. **1893** *Harper's Mag.* April 792/1 A little dingy brown place with paper blinds on the windows and shell vases on the mantel-shelf.

* Shell, *v.*

+1. *tr.* To remove (the grains) of Indian corn from the cob; to free (ears of corn) of the grains.

1639 *Md. Archives* I. 79 All contracts made for paym[en]t in Corne shall be understood of Corne shelled & a barrell of new Corne tendred in payment. **1767** [see COB *n.*¹ 1]. **1813** *Steele P.* II. 708, I Sold Sixty Bushels Corn . . . to be delivered at your plantation at the river on Monday next, please to have it Shelled and delivered that day. **1886** Z. F. SMITH *Kentucky* 127 Thirty men were sent . . . for the purpose of shelling corn for the supply of the fort.

+b. With *down, off, out.* Also absol.

1803 CUTLER in *Life & Corr.* II. 125 In bad weather, shell out your corn. **1825** NEAL *Bro. Jonathan* I. 53 The farmer . . . gives them [*sc.* his neighbors] notice, that he is ready to 'shell out'; or in other words, to undergo a husking. **1830** S. SMITH *Life J. Downing* 38 Uncle Joshua will have to shell out his bushel of corn. **1845** HOOPER *Taking Census* 163 Taking an ear of corn . . . and shelling off a handful, she commenced scattering the grain.

+2. To cover (an area) with shells to catch oyster spawn.

1871 in Ingersoll *Oyster-Industry* 76 We shall . . . shell the ditch again this summer, and keep up the cultivation. **1885** *Encycl. Brit.* XVIII. 110 Spawning oysters are frequently put down in the spring, two months before the ground is shelled.

+3. *To shell out* or *over*, to hand out or pay up. *colloq.*

1833 S. SMITH *Life J. Downing* 244 They were . . . shellin out the munny like corn. **1846** *Jamestown* (N.Y.) *Jrnl.* 26 Feb. 3/2 The County has two treasurers, . . . each calling on the Collectors of taxes to shell over. **1857** *Knickerb.* XLIX. 34, I reckoned I could make him shell over.

Shellac, *n. a.* Lac melted and made into thin plates. {1713-} **b.** Lac dissolved in alcohol and used chiefly as a varnish. Also attrib. — **1820** *Columbian Centinel* 1 Jan. 3/5 At Auction . . . 2700 Cow Hides, 19 cases of Shellac. **1881** *Ore. State Jrnl.* 8 Jan. 2/5 Brush over the back of the paper . . . a weak solution of white shellac in alcohol. **1898** *Kansas City Star* 18 Dec. 1/3 Freling wrapped the finger in a shellac dressing. **1907** *St. Nicholas* Oct. 1134/1 The web is to be preserved is sprayed with artist's shellac from an atomizer.

Shellac, *v. tr.* To coat or varnish (a surface, room, etc.) with shellac. {1884-} — **1876** *Scribner's Mo.* Feb. 488/1 It is made of plain white pine, brought to a good surface and shellacked. **1882** *Harper's Mag.* Oct. 688 The bedrooms are shellacked and some are stained of a deep tint. **1917** MATHEWSON *Second Base Sloan* 90 Wayne threatened to varnish or shellac the paper so that it would turn the rain.

+Shellbark.

1. = SHELLBARK HICKORY. Also attrib.

1805 PARKINSON *Tour* 374 There is a tree, the shell-bark, that bears a nut called hiccory. **1824** DODDRIDGE *Notes* 87 Some of the larger shell bark nuts . . . were little inferior to the English walnut. **1855** *S. Lit. Messenger* XXI. 125 And now the object of my search,—the shell-bark,—is reached. **1907** M. H. NORRIS *Veil* 26 The dreamer . . . seemed to see some lofty and slender shellbark lifting up its thousand golden buds in praise of spring.

2. A nut of the shellbark hickory.

1832 WATSON *Hist. Tales N.Y.* 54 Among the latter [items of Indian diet] were chesnuts, shellbarks, walnuts. **1869** FULLER *Flower Gatherers*

306 Mr. and Mistress Bunny were living . . . on shell-barks and acorns. **1885** *Harper's Mag.* Dec. 78/2 The chipmunk . . . [has] his hoard of hazel-nuts and shell-barks.

‖3. (*Shell bark.*) Bark that is scaly or flaky.

1845 DRAKE *Pioneer* 230, [I] found the old hickory . . . quietly as ever casting off now and then his 'shell bark.'

+Shellbark(ed) hickory.

1. a. The scaly-bark hickory, or a tree of this species. **b.** The thick shellbark hickory or king nut.

1785 MARSHALL *Amer. Grove* 69 *Juglans alba ovata.* Shell-barked Hickery. . . . There are several varieties of this in America. **1814** PURSH *Flora Amer.* II. 637 This useful tree is known by the name of Shell-bark Hickory, Shag-bark and Scaly-bark Hickory, on account of its bark, which is torn in loose fragments. **1847** DRAKE *Pioneer Life Ky.* 42 The usual number of ragged children . . . [played] under the shade of some shell-bark hickory. **1860** CURTIS *Woody Plants N.C.* 43 Shell-Bark Hickory. . . . The nuts are nearly pointless. **1901** MOHR *Plant Life Ala.* 84 The tulip tree . . . [is associated] with white ash and shell-bark hickory.

attrib. **1881** PIERSON *In the Brush* 23 [He] gave orders . . . to get the shell-bark-hickory torches that they had provided to light us home.

2. The nut of this tree.

1820 *Amer. Farmer* I. 335 In 1817, I planted 5 pecks of Shell-bark Hickory.

+Shelled corn. Indian corn removed from the cob. — **1676** *Md. Archives* II. 560 No ordinary keeper shall demand above . . . 4 lib. Tob[acco], ffor a Peck of Indian shell'd Corn. **1699** *N.C. Col. Rec.* I. 521 Ye Marshal [was ordered to] deliver ye two Hoggs and See Much Sheld Corn. **1714** *Essex Inst. Coll.* X. 1. 104, I agreed to give Mr. Ganson five bushels of shelled corn. **1809** CUMING *Western Tour* 175 The usual produce of an acre of this . . . soil, is from forty to fifty bushels of shelled corn. **1904** PRINGLE *Rice Planter* 108 These two acres made seventy-two bushels of shelled corn.

Sheller. {1694-}

1. A device for shelling corn, peas, etc.

1859 *Rep. Comm. Patents 1858* I. 361 The nature of this invention relates . . . to the form and arrangements of the shellers. **1868** *Iowa State Agric. Soc. Rep.* 1867 221, $60 for mill without sheller. **1877** [see FEEDER 6]. **1880** *Lib. Universal Knowl.* I. 164 For harvesting, we have mowing, reaping and binding machines, shellers, fruit-pickers, etc.

+2. (See quot. 1881.)

1881 INGERSOLL *Oyster-Industry* 248 *Shellers*, persons who open clams for market. (New Jersey.) **1887** GOODE, etc. *Fisheries* V. II. 593 As many as two dozen shellers are at work at one time. **1894** *Dialect Notes* I. 333.

+3. ?A hard-shelled crab.

1886 MITCHELL *R. Blake* 261 Don't know shellers. Why ther's them, and ther's paper shells, and ther's soft shells, . . . and them's all crabs.

* Shellfish.

*1. Various small aquatic animals, as oysters, crabs, etc., provided with a shell.

1622 'MOURT' *Relation* 109 [We] bought about a handfull of Meale, . . . and a small string of dryed shell-fish, as big as Oysters. **1702** C. MATHER *Magnalia* (1853) I. 558 This wampam . . . is made of the shell-fish which lies upon the sea-coast. **1792** POPE *Tour S. & W.* 92 The River abounds in Scale and Shell-Fish. **1855** [see MUSCLE]. **1899** 'O. HENRY' *Roads of Destiny* 312 The Italian beggars were creeping nearer their landing, laden with early vegetables and shellfish.

+2. A trunkfish. Also with specifying term.

1896 JORDAN & EVERMANN *Check-List Fishes* 424 *Lactophrys triqueter.* . . . Trunk-fish; Rock Shellfish. . . . West Indies, north to the Bermudas; Key West and Pensacola. *Ib.* 424 *Lactophrys trigonus.* . . . Common trunk-fish; Chapin; Shell-fish. West Indies, north to Bermuda and Key West.

+Shell game. A sleight-of-hand gambling game; thimblerig. Also attrib. — **1893** *Chicago Tribune* 19 April 2/6 He was working the shell game yesterday afternoon. **1899** *Congress. Rec.* 24 Jan. 1009/2 For one time in my life I ran up against a shell game. **1903** *N.Y. Times* 26 Sept. 9 The shell-game man had ceased from troubling.

Shell heap. An accumulation of domestic remains of aborigines who subsisted chiefly on shellfish. — **1882** *Amer. Antiquarian* IV. 201 Mr. Tooker . . . has found perfect clay pipes on shell heaps. **1892** *Boston Soc. Nat. Hist. Proc.* 30 (*Encycl. Dict. Suppl.*), The bones of such animals as are commonly found in the shell-heaps of Maine. **1896** JEWETT *Pointed Firs* (1910) 119 He remarked that he'd like to walk over an' see the shellheap. **1910** HODGE, etc. *Amer. Indians* II. 542/2 The inland fresh-water shell-heaps of Florida are composed of distinct genera of shells.

Shell lime. Lime obtained by burning sea shells. {1793-} — **1774** J. HARROWER *Diary* 87 This morning two Carpenters was put to new weather board my house . . . , and to new plaster it on the Inside with shell lime. *a*1817 DWIGHT *Travels* III. 56 The cement of this work, formed of shell lime and beach gravel, has all the firmness of Roman mortar. **1884** *Rep. Comm. Agric.* 321 Those [remedies] which gave the best results were, dusting the roots of the cabbages with fine bone dust, and the application of one teaspoonful of caustic shell-lime to each plant.

Shellmarble. (See quot. 1891.) — **1842** *Lowell Offering* II. 302 Brother has a piece of shell marble, which is extremely beautiful. **1891** *Cent.* 5566/2 *Shell-marble*, . . . an ornamental marble containing fossil shells.

Shell marl. Marl consisting in part of marine shells. {1759-} — **1839** BUEL *Farmer's Companion* 89 *Shell-marl* is a deposit of marine, and sometimes of land-shells. **1843** *Nat. Hist. N.Y., Geology* I. 11 Shell marl . . . is much used by the farmers. **1869** *Rep. Comm. Agric.* 1868 370 In the tertiary are found large and numerous beds of shell-marl and limestone. **1883** SMITH *Geol. Survey Ala.* 504 The marl bed . . . is a shell marl, which in places contains very little else than shells.

+**Shell money.** Wampum or peag. (Cf. SEAWAN(T).) — **1851** J. F. W. JOHNSTON *Notes N. Amer.* II. 465 From the purple interior of this shell the *wampum* or shell-money of the Indians was prepared. **1869** *Amer. Naturalist* i. III. 3 The use of shell-money has, in great measure, ceased at the points he mentions. **1872** McCLELLAN *Golden State* 44 The red man alone was supreme in his animal life, . . . [making] his shell money and flint-pointed arrow. **1907** [see HIAQUA].

+**Shell road.** *S.* A road the upper surface of which is made of sea shells. — **1840** *Picayune* 28 July 2/1 The shell road will be abandoned by the citizens, unless more security can be felt in traveling upon it. **1860** E. COWELL *Diary* 74 The 'shell road' . . . is formed of broken clam shells. **1883** RITTENHOUSE *Maud* 189 Flying over a white shell road, behind a pair of dapple grays, can you imagine anything more entrancing? **1911** *Rep. Fisheries* 1908 309/2 The famous shell roads of the South are constructed of [shells of the cuneata clam].

Shell rock. A hard rocklike formation consisting largely of sea shells. — **1837** WILLIAMS *Florida* 56 The bank is formed of concrete shell rock. **1891** *Scribner's Mag.* Oct. 475/1 The 'natural beds' . . . are known as . . . 'Shell Rock,' 'Cohansey beds' [etc.]. **1895** *Dept. Agric. Yrbk.* 1894 520 The shell rock was laid down in thickness only 3 to 4 inches.

+**Shelter belt.** (See quot. 1905.) — **1869** *Rep. Comm. Agric.* 1868 197 For a shelter belt, . . . this [maple] will be found suitable. **1886** *Leslie's Mo.* June 751/2 For shelter-belts on the prairies, evergreens are the more valuable. **1905** *Forestry Bureau Bul.* No. 16, 21 Shelterbelt, natural or artificial forest maintained as a protection from wind or snow.

+**Shelter hedge.** A close hedge for sheltering a garden or other ground. — **1858** WARDER *Hedges & Evergreens* 43 [The hemlock spruce] soon forms a . . . close shelter-hedge. *Ib.* 240 The common cedar is very efficacious and much used for producing a shelter-hedge.

Shelter tent. =DOG TENT. {1888-} — **1862** Moore *Rebellion Rec.* V. II. 84 Some of the shelter-tents, knapsacks, and blankets, fell into the hands of the enemy. **1881-5** McCLELLAN *Own Story* 331 All the troops slept on the muddy field, in the rain, with what protection their shelter-tents gave them.

+**Shenanigan.** [Of obscure origin.] Treacherous conduct; trickery; nonsense; foolery. *colloq.* — **1871** *Republican Rev.* 11 March 1/3 Let there be no 'shenanigan' amongst the wealthy, they have more to lose than the poor. **1897** *Outing* XXIX. 483/1 He is with a man who is firmly kind, but who will stand no shinanigan.

+**Shenkbeer.** (See quotation.) *Obs.* — **1871** DE VERE 142 The other extreme, an exceedingly weak and insipid beverage, *Shenkbeer*, the *Schenkbier* of Germany, is so called because it has to be put on draught (*schenken*) as soon as it is made, for fear of turning sour if not immediately consumed.

✱**Shepherd.**
+**1.** A person selected by a colonial town to have charge of the sheep of the inhabitants. *Obs.*
1645 *New Haven Col. Rec.* 167 Some have taken offence att the shepheards keeping his sheep and marking a penne for them towards the Oyster river. **1674** *Cambridge Rec.* 218 For A sheaperd John Jackson [was appointed]. **1716** *Huntington Rec.* II. 330 It was voated . . . they should have a shepherd in the town.

✱**2.** *W.* One who tends and has charge of a herd of sheep grazing at large.
1847 RUXTON *Adv. Rocky Mt.* (1848) 184 San Antonio . . . [is] inhabited by pastores and vaqueros—shepherds and cattle-herders. **1881** *Ind. Affairs* 139 Navajo children of school age are employed as shepherds. **1890** *Harper's Mag.* Oct. 806/2 The insane asylums of California contain many shepherds.

b. Attrib. with *girl, hut.*
1834 A. PIKE *Sketches* 40 There are some deserted ranchos, as they are called—that is, sheep-pens and shepherd huts. **1878** BEADLE *Western Wilds* 254 Every-where along the grass-plats were shepherd girls with considerable flocks.

Shepherdee. ?A garment of some kind worn by women. — **1756** in Singleton *Social N.Y.* 246 Put her on a negligee, A short sack, or shepherdee.

Shepherd('s)-holland. A variety of holland cloth. *Obs.* — **1644** *Wyllys Papers* 73 A good shephard holland strong & white. **1693** SEWALL *Letter-Book* I. 137 One p[iec]e Shepard's Holland or course Bag-Holland.

+**Shepherd spider.** (See quotation.) — **1864** WEBSTER 499/3 *Father-long-legs*, . . . a species of spider . . . called also *harvest-man, shepherd-spider*, and *daddy-long-legs*. (U.S.)

✱**Shepherd's-purse.** A weed (*Capsella bursa-pastoris*) bearing pods suggestive of a purse or pouch. — **1784** *Amer. Acad. Mem.* I. 466 *Thlaspi.* . . . Shepherd's Purse. Shepherd's Pouch. Blossoms white. **1795** WINTERBOTHAM *Hist. View* III. 398 Among the native and uncultivated plants of New-England . . . [is] Shepherd's purse, or pouch. **1814** BIGELOW *Florula Bostoniensis* 156 *Thlaspi Bursa pastoris*, Common Shepherd's purse, . . . [grows] in pastures and road sides. **1878** [see MAYWEED]. **1899** GOING *Flowers* 376 There is no month in the year in which one may not see the flowers of chickweed, sow thistle, and shepherd's-purse.

Sherbet. **a.** A cooling drink, usually consisting chiefly of fruit juices. {1603-} +**b.** (See quot. 1891.) — **1729** FRANKLIN *Writings* II. 115 He makes a Sign to have Things serv'd . . . generally, a little Sweetmeat, a Dish of Sherbet. **1841** *Knickerb.* XVII. 279 Though sugar was reasonably abundant, we searched in vain for any thing which would answer to hold our sherbet. **1863** TAYLOR *H. Thurston* 242 Such men may drink their sherbet. **1887** *South Fla. Sentinel* (Orlando) 23 Feb. 1/7 The bill of fare included ice cream . . . and sherbet. **1891** *Cent.* 5568/2 *Sherbet*, . . . a water-ice, variously flavored.

✱**Sheriff.**
1. The chief executive officer in a county, charged with preserving the peace and serving as the executive agent of the courts.
1646 *Va. House of Burgesses* 73 Then the said sherriffes shall have power to distrayne. **1689** *Plymouth Laws* 210 Ordered that the sheriffs or County Treasurers of the severall Counties . . . give in an accompt of all moneys. **1721** *Mass. H. Rep. Jrnl.* III. 142 The Goal in Cambridge . . . [is] Represented by the Sheriff as insufficient to secure the Indian Hostages. **1796** in Imlay *Western Territory* (1797) 553 There shall be appointed in each county . . . one sheriff, one coroner, one trustee, and a sufficient number of constables. **1841** *Diplom. Corr. Texas* III. (1911) 1333 The Sheriff, coroner, or other Ministerial officer of the County of Travis [etc.]. **1890** *Stock Grower & Farmer* 10 May 4/2 The sheriff of Lincoln county will officiate at a double hanging. **1925** TILGHMAN *Dugout* 31 You ain't quick enough to go up against our sheriff.

+**b.** A peace officer among reservation Indians.
1866 *Rep. Indian Affairs* 250 The chiefs and councillors shall appoint three sheriffs.

2. Used in possessive in phrases.
Sheriff's box, ?an inclosure in a court room for the use of a sheriff and his prisoners; *s. hammer* (often fig.), a hammer or gavel used by a sheriff at a sheriff's sale; *s. office,* the position or office held by a sheriff; *s. prison,* (see quotation).
1799 Rothert *Muhlenberg Co.* 45 The court house . . . [will have] a judge's bench . . . , a sheriff's box, a clerk's table and seat. **1865** *Atlantic Mo.* April 510/1 In process of time, 'debts of honor' and the sheriff's hammer had dissipated his entire clientage of blacks. **1909** PARKER G. *Cleveland* 36 The Sheriff's office . . . would give him the required leisure for the needed study. **1882** McCABE *New York* 418 Ludlow Street Jail . . . is sometimes called 'The Sheriff's Prison.' All persons arrested under process issued by the Sheriff of the county of New York are imprisoned here.

‖**Sheriffcy.** The office of sheriff. — **1841** in Jillson *Dark & Bloody Ground* 91 He remained in service for six months, . . . returning to the duties of his Sherriffcy [etc.].

+**Sheriff's sale.** A public sale of property conducted by a sheriff in compliance with a writ of execution. — **1817** *Ann. 14th Congress* 2 Sess. 850 A duty of 10 percent. [shall] be laid on all foreign goods sold at auction, with the exception of . . . sheriffs and marshals' sales. **1867** *Wkly. New Mexican* 2 Feb. 2/3 Sheriff's Sale. On the first Monday [etc.]. **1882** *Century Mag.* Jan. 379/1 The property was bought of a bankrupted owner, at sheriff's sale.

Sherman. [John *Sherman* (1823-1900), U.S. senator from Ohio.] Used attrib. with *Anti-trust act* and *Anti-trust law* to designate a law passed in 1890 prohibiting combinations in restraint of interstate or foreign trade. — **1899** GUNTON *Trusts & Public* 42 The Sherman anti-trust law . . . foreshadow[s] what is likely to come. **1908** *Independent* 16 July 137/1 In 1890 Congress enacted the Sherman Anti-Trust act.

+**Sherman Act.** [See prec.] A congressional act in force from 1890 to 1893 for artificially maintaining the price of silver through compulsory government purchase of silver bullion. Also *Sherman law.* — **1892** *Dem. Platform* in K. Porter *Nat. Party Platforms* 162 We denounce the Republican legislation known as the Sherman Act of 1890. **1894** *Harper's Mag.* Jan. 318/1 Mr. Voorhees's substitute repealing the Sherman law was passed by a vote of 43 to 32. **1909** PARKER G. *Cleveland* 211 In 1893 . . . [an] extra session [was] called to repeal the silver-purchase clause of the Sherman Act.

+**Sherman note.** [See SHERMAN.] One of the legal-tender treasury notes, redeemable in coin, issued in 1890 under the provisions of the Sherman Act. — **1894** MUHLEMAN in Nelson *A B C Wall St.* 104 The Secretary of the Treasury is to redeem the 'greenbacks' and 'Sherman notes' in gold. [**1897** *Daily News* (London) 10 Dec. 5/1 The second feature of the Secretary's plan . . . is the retirement of all the outstanding greenbacks and Sherman notes.] **1900** *Congress. Rec.* 11 Jan. 776/1 Sherman notes . . . are all to be disposed of under this bill.

+**Sherrivarrie,** *n.* =CHARIVARI *n.* (Cf. SHIVAREE.) — **1805** in *Amer. Pioneer* II. 229 When a *sherri-varrie* is announced, it is done by a running cry through the streets. **1837** WILLIAMS *Florida* 116 Sherivarees are parties of idle people, who dress themselves in grotesque masquerade, whenever a widow or widower are married.

+**Sherrivarrie,** *v. tr.* =CHARIVARI *v.* — **1843** *Amer. Pioneer* II. 229 At a later period, Edward Livingston, esq., was *sherri-varried* here [at New Orleans].

Sherry. A wine made in Jerez, Spain, or one or more or less resembling this wine. {1608-} Also attrib. — **1686** *Conn. Rec.* III. 408 There shall be paid to the treasurer . . . [for] every butt or pipe of Sherry, . . . twenty shillings. **1790** *Ann. 1st Congress* 1547 There shall be paid the following rates: . . . Upon every gallon of Sherry wine, twenty-five cents. **1847** BRIGGS *Tom Pepper* I. 270 We don't . . . drink a glass or two of sherry.

1872 [see CORNER GROCERY]. **1908** LORIMER *J. Spurlock* 190 We'll begin with some grapefruit, and fill up its crevices with a little old sherry.

+Sherry cobbler. A cobbler in which sherry wine is used. {1882} — **1841** *Knickerb.* XVII. 157 He was ignorant of the abstruser mysteries of a sherry cobbler! **1848** IRVING *Knickerb.* (rev. ed.) VII. iii, [The inhabitants of Md.] lay claim to be the first inventors of those recondite beverages, cock-tail, stone-fence, and sherry-cobbler. **1872** POWERS *Afoot & Alone* 167 In Franklin we found pretty stuccoed houses, . . . sherry cobblers (without ice), streets wide and shaded. **1910** DOUGLAS ed. Parkman *Oregon Trail* 361 *Sherry cobblers, brandy toddy,* beverages composed of spirits and water, sweetened.

+Sherry-vallies. *pl.* [Cf. Polish *szarawary.*] (See quot. 1848.) *Obs.* — **1778** C. LEE *Memoirs* (1792) 430 If you find them to be green breeches patched with leather, and not actually legitimate sherry vallies, such as his Majesty of Poland wears, . . . I will submit. **1825** *Amer. Folk-Lore* IV. 354 Shorrevals and overalls And Pantaloons he'll make. **1835** HOFFMAN *Winter in West* I. 91 That short man yonder . . . is just raising his blue cotton frock to thrust his hand into the fob of his sherrivalleys. **1848** BARTLETT 296 *Sherryvallies,* . . . pantaloons made of thick velvet or leather, buttoned on the outside of each leg, and generally worn over other pantaloons. They are now chiefly worn by teamsters. . . . When journeys were made on horseback, sherryvallies were indispensable to the traveller.

Shetland. *attrib.* Designating products of the Shetland Islands or things made of wool obtained there. {1790-} — **1863** 'M. HARLAND' *Husks* 12 Each . . . had upon her lap a basket of many-hued balls of double or single zephyr worsted, or Shetland or Saxony wool. **1885** *Century Mag.* June 269/2 That little shetland shawl, soft as spun silk and cobwebby as lace . . . —what could better fit her need? **1891** 'THANET' *Otto the Knight* 285 The groom in livery . . . [led] a wee Shetland pony. **1923** Shetland-wool fascinator [see FASCINATOR].

+Shian, Shienne. Variants of CHEYENNE. — **1830** *Western Mo. Rev.* III. 566 In a valley of this sort . . . dwelt the Shoshonee, and their subdued allies, the Shienne. **1850** GARRARD *Wah-To-Yah* xx. 245 B'ar's out playin' like shian *ki kun* (children).

*Shield.

*1. A piece of defensive armor carried in the hand or on the arm by an Indian.
1808 PIKE *Sources Miss.* III. App. 11 The Appaches . . . all carry a shield. **1827** COOPER *Prairie* xxvi, Spears, shields, lances, and arrows . . . had in their time done good service. **1876** *Chicago Tribune* 11 July 2/5 The shield of Sitting Bull . . . is embossed with an eagle. **1901** WHITE *Westerners* 64 Above the lodges . . . were suspended the spears and shields of the warriors.

+2. A policeman's badge.
1903 *N.Y. Ev. Post* 29 Oct. 3 The ex-policeman . . . turned in his shield in September. **1904** 'O. HENRY' *Trimmed Lamp* 84 They'll take away my shield and break me.

+3. *Shield of liberty,* a patriotic emblem of the U.S.
1864 *Wkly. New Mexican* 27 May 1/4 On the other side [of the two-cent piece] there is the shield of liberty, bearing the words, 'God our Trust.'

*Shift. A garment worn as underclothing; a woman's chemise. *Obs.* — **1636** *Essex Probate Rec.* I. 7 One stuffe petticoat & waskote, 4 shifts w[i]th shewes . . . [are] for Sara Dillingham. **1707** *Boston News-Letter* 15 Sept. 2/2 Had on . . . a white Shirt, as also a blue one with her. **1778** CARVER *Travels* 236 The [Indian] girls are covered from the neck to the knees with a shift and a short petticoat. **1822** Morse *Rep. Indian Affairs* II. 240 The wives and daughters of distinguished Indians . . . [wear] a shift of calico, fringed round the neck and bosom.

+Shift boss. A boss in charge of a shift of miners. — **1876** RAYMOND *8th Rep. Mines* 166 Rates of wages: . . . Foremen, per day, $8.00. Shift-bosses, per day, $6.00. **1896** SHINN *Story of Mine* 226 Each level of the mine has therefore three shift bosses.

*Shifting. +Underclothing. *Obs.* Also attrib. — **1678** *New Castle Court Rec.* 322, 3 3/8 yd. of Indifferent fyne Shifting Linnen. **1689** *Mass. H. S. Coll.* 4 Ser. V. 220 They want . . . linen cloth for shifting. **1724** *Narragansett Hist. Reg.* I. 181 Nathaniel Bundy . . . took ye widow Mary Palmister . . . in ye highway, with no other clothing but shifting, or smock . . . ; and was joined together in that honorable estate of matrimony.

+Shifting engine. *Railroad.* A switch engine. — **1878** PINKERTON *Strikers* 219 D. M. Watt . . . ordered an employee to descend from a shifting engine and change the switch. **1887** *Courier-Journal* 4 May 4/5 Two men . . . were struck by a shifting engine last night and instantly killed.

+Shifting-top buggy. A buggy with a top that folds back. *Obs.* — **1856** *Mich. Agric. Soc. Trans.* VII. 61 John Patton . . . [exhibited] shifting top buggy. **1865** *Wkly. New Mexican* 17 Feb. 2/3 For Sale. A Shifting Top Buggy.

+Shillagalee. *N.Y.* 'A low fellow; a scalawag' (B. '77).

*Shilling.

*1. A unit of money value reckoned at twelve pence or one-twentieth of a pound, either in English or +in colonial and early state money.
The value of a shilling differed from one colony or state to another: (see POUND[1] 2, note).
1623 *Va. House of Burgesses* 24 We agree with that Prime-one, who wished, that Corn might never be under eight Shillings a Bushel. **1683** [see PILLAR]. **1705** *Boston News-Letter* 11 June 2/2 There are to be Sold long Tobacco Pipes by the Cask, to be taken by the Contents, whole and

broken, at Three Shillings and Six Pence per Groce. **1789** *Ann. 1st Congress* 227 The price of molasses is about twenty-ninetieths of a dollar, the duty is about five, and the expense of the distillation may be six more, in all thirty-one-ninetieths, or two shillings and seven pence. **1791** *Mass. Spy* 28 April (Th.), A dollar consists only of the small number of six shillings. **1831** PECK *Guide* 151 One shilling per bushel, New England currency, is a common price [for wheat]. **1849** G. G. FOSTER *N.Y. in Slices* 82 The grocery keeper, for instance, buys butter of an inferior quality at twelve and a half or fourteen cents per pound, and retails it at two shillings. **1882** TUCKER in *Albany Institute Trans.* X. 336 The 'shilling' of our own State [N.Y.] is the 'levy' of Pennsylvania. **1891** *Cent.* 5572/2 Reckoning by the shilling is still not uncommon in some parts of the United States, especially in rural New England. **1906** J. A. HARRISON *G. Washington* 405 To this day the mountain people of Virginia rudely reckon in shillings (16 2/3 cents).

2. One of various silver coins current in the colonies, and in the states for some time after the Revolution.
These coins included the English shilling, the Spanish real (worth about 12½ cents) and the shilling pieces of the different colonial currencies. See also NEW YORK SHILLING, PINE-TREE SHILLING, YORK SHILLING.
1692 SEWALL *Letter-Book* I. 5 N. E. Shillings &c received of Mr. Nathl. Foot, £80 00. **1719** *Mass. Bay Currency Tracts* 183 Some Money was Coined here, as Shillings, Six-Pences, &c. **1846** FARNHAM *Prairie Land* 299, 'I reckon you may get three,' said the prudent husband, depositing a shilling in his palm. **1848** BARTLETT 135 The Spanish real of ⅛ of a dollar or 12½ cents is called . . . in New York, one shilling. **1850** *Knickerb.* XXXV. 166 He only gave Mr. Prettyman a shilling! **1891** WELCH *Recoll.* 1830-40 169 It was common, particularly in New England, to call . . . a shilling a *bit.*

+Shilling pavement. The sidewalk or pavement on the shilling side of Broadway in New York City. — **1849** G. G. FOSTER *N.Y. in Slices* 4 Nothing could more effectually stamp you as vulgar than to be seen stumbling over the crockery-crates and second-hand furniture of the shilling pavement.

+Shilling side. The west side of Broadway in New York City, esp. about Vesey Street, where a cheaper trade was conducted than on the other side of the street. *Obs.* — **1850** *Knickerb.* XXXV. 91 An animal of the 'porcine genus' . . . was reposing on the shilling-side of the great thoroughfare. **1870** M. H. SMITH *20 Years Wall St.* 197 On the dollar side or on the shilling side of the street he intended to create a business. **1922** WANAMAKER in *Appel Biog. Wanamaker* (1930) 132 He found himself on the wrong side of Broadway, the shilling side, next to the old Astor House.

Shimming. {1792-} +The action of filling up a space with a shim. — **1872** HUNTINGTON *Road-Master's Asst.* 78 When ballast is frozen so that track can not be surfaced by tamping, it is done by *shimming.* **1880** FORNEY *Car-Builder's Dict.* (Cent.), Shimming has been used in fitting on car-wheels when the wheel-seat of the axle was a little too small.

Shin, *v.* {1829-}

1. *tr.* To hit or kick (a person) on the shins. {a1845-}
1819 E. EVANS *Pedestrious Tour* 214 He was often heard to say to his troops in battle:—'Shin them, my brave boys!' **1846** *Yale Banger* 10 Nov., We have been shinned, smoked, ducked, and accelerated by the encouraging shouts of our generous friends.

2. To climb up. {1907}
1880 N. BROOKS *Fairport Nine* 9 Which of you fellows is best on shinning a lightning-rod?

+3. *intr.* To go *up* to; to move *around* actively; to walk. Also quasi-tr.
1837 NEAL *Charcoal Sk.* (1838) 106 Shin it, good man . . . ; shin it as well as you know how! **1843** STEPHENS *High Life N.Y.* I. 178 Darn me if I don't shin up to that gal for a partner. **1845** *N.Y. Com. Adv.* 13 Dec. (B.), The Senator was shinning around, to get gold for the rascally bankrags, which he was obliged to take. **1869** 'MARK TWAIN' *Innocents* 492, I would have made him shin out of Galilee quicker than any turtle ever did yet. **1879** *Harper's Mag.* Aug. 386 'Tain't much of a kerridge . . . , but I cal'late it's a little better'n shinnin' it. **1890** *Congress. Rec.* 18 Sept. 10188/2 They find a difficulty in shinning around to borrow money. **1904** *N.Y. Sun* 31 Aug. 2 He might find it difficult to shin around the corners of political dilemmas.

+b. To make an effort to borrow money.
See also SHINNING.
1834 A. GREENE *Perils Pearl St.* 125 Shinners may be divided into two classes: those who shin from necessity, and those who shin from profit.

+Shinanigan. (See SHENANIGAN.)

+Shindig. *slang.* 1. (See quot. 1859.) 2. A more or less noisy party or gathering of any kind; =SHINDY 1. — (1) **1859** BARTLETT 400 *Shin-Dig,* a blow on the shins. Southern. (2) **1873** HARTE *Mrs. Skagg's Husbands* 139 'Is this a dashed Puritan meeting?' . . . 'It's no Pike County shindig.' **1911** HARRISON *Queed* 229 He found a group of men . . . eagerly discussing the shindig.

Shindy. {1821-} 1. A commotion or row. *slang.* {a1845-} +2. *To cut a shindy,* to raise a commotion. — (1) **1829** B. HALL *Travels in N.A.* III. 325, I never saw a more complete row, or as a fellow near me called it, 'a more regular shindy.' **1867** LOCKE *Swingin' Round* 244 This occasioned another shindy. **1905** FREEMAN *Debtor* 294 'You must not say scrap.' 'A shindy, then.' (2) c**1849** PAIGE *Dow's Sermons* (B.), You . . . ought to be careful how you cut shindies under the broadsword of justice.

✳ Shine, *n.*

+1. A caper or trick. *colloq.*

1835–7 HALIBURTON *Clockmaker* I Ser. xvii. 143, I met . . . a real conceited lookin critter as you een amost ever seed, all shines and didos. *a*1861 WINTHROP *J. Brent* 31, I don't feel so sharp set on lettin' you hev that black after that shine. **1869** STOWE *Oldtown Folks* 235 She needn't think she's goin' to come round me with any o' her shines.

+b. *To cut a shine,* or variant: To cut a dido.

To cut up shines, see CUT *v.* 24 c; *to cut high shines,* see CUT *v.* 25 m.

1819 A. PEIRCE *Rebelliad* 72 Peele Dabney gaz'd, Sikes cut a shine. **1835** LONGSTREET *Ga. Scenes* 7 Come cutt'n your shines 'bout me agin.

+c. *To come a shine over* (a person), to impose on (one).

1847 ROBB *Squatter Life* 151 They couldn't come any of them thar shines over him.

+2. (See quotation.) *slang.*

1851 HALL *College Words* 278 *Shine.* At Harvard College this word was formerly used to designate a good recitation.

+3. A polish given a pair of shoes; a job at shining shoes.

1871 *Galveston News* 4 May (De Vere), As I left the cars, an imp with smutty face, Said: Shine? **1880** *Harper's Mag.* Feb. 397/2 107 Here does the hirsute mountain-dweller don the garb of civilization, and procure a 'shave' and a 'shine.' **1894** *Advance* 27 Dec. 458/1 A little boot-black . . . shivered in the March wind and waited for shines. **1902** LORIMER *Lett. Merchant* 178, I've seen a ten-cent shave and a five-cent shine get a thousand-dollar job.

+4. *To take the shine off* (a person), to lower (a person) in the eyes of others; to humble. *colloq.* {to take the shine from, out of, 1819–}

1834 C. A. DAVIS *Lett. J. Downing* 23 The review of Captain Finny's company did take the shine off them are Boston and Salem sogers. **1843** STEPHENS *High Life N.Y.* I. 74 If Cousin Beebe don't take the shine off these New Yorkers, . . . I lose my guess. **1868** BRACKETT *Farm Talk* 42 He is raising a bull calf, which, he says, he 'is bound shall take the shine off' anything in our county.

+5. *To take a shine to,* to take a liking or fancy to. *colloq.*

1840 *Crockett Almanac* 14, I wonst had an old flame I took sumthin of a shine to. **1847** LOWELL *Biglow P.* I Ser. ii. 23 It's a scorpion thet's took a shine to play with 't. **1881** M. J. HOLMES *Madeline* 221 Joseph . . . [is] the one who's taken such a shine to Jessie. **1901** CHURCHILL *Crisis* 143 I've taken a shine to this Bostonian, Joe. **1918** LINCOLN *Shavings* 134 I think he's taken a shine to me.

+6. *To make a shine with* (a person), to make a hit with (someone).

1847 ROBB *Squatter Life* 137 To make a shine with Sally, I sent over word that I would . . . bring with me my fust *pledge of affection,* meanin' the parasol.

✳ Shine, *v.*

+1. *tr.* In hunting at night, to throw a light in (the eyes of an animal); to fire-hunt (an animal).

1833 FLINT *D. Boone* 25 He had *shined the eyes* of a deer. **1843** HAWKS *D. Boone* 21 While the other *shines* him, . . . [the hunter] has a fair shot. **1885** *South Fla. Sentinel* (Orlando) 10 June 2/2 They took the small boat and pulled to the nearest key to shine deer. **1910** ROOSEVELT *African Game Trails* 226 The way to get this . . . nocturnal animal was by 'shining' it with a lantern at night.

fig. **1843** HAWKS *D. Boone* 23 Rebecca Bryan completely *shined his eyes;* and after a time, . . . [they] were married.

+2. *absol.* To engage in shining shoes.

1872 *Harper's Mag.* March 637/1 Charles Lewis . . . still lives and 'shines' on the shores of the majestic Susquehanna. **1887** *Ib.* June 161/1 While he was 'shining' I asked his price, which he said was ten cents.

+b. *tr.* To polish the shoes of (a person).

1885 BAYLOR *On Both Sides* 417 A ragged gamin . . . offered to 'shine' me for a 'dime.' **1888** *Century Mag.* July 462/2, I shined a young feller this mornin'.

+3. *intr.* To make a play for the attention or good will of another.

1841 *Jamestown* (N.Y.) *Jrnl.* 10 June 4/1, I had a great mind tu go off and shine round some other gal, jest for spite. **1853** *La Crosse Democrat* 27 Sept. 1/3 Still I think to talk sense to one and shine for the other. **1882** *Century Mag.* Oct. 827 It was then that David first set out to shine up to her. **1901** WILKINS *Portion of Labor* 454 You needn't come shinin' round Ellen and me.

+4. To succeed. *slang.*

1848 RUXTON *Life Far West* iv, One from the Land of Cakes . . . sought to 'get round' (in trade) a right 'smart' Yankee, but couldn't 'shine.' **1859** BARTLETT 401 *To Shine,* . . . to get along, succeed. Western.

✳ Shiner.

1. A silver or gold coin. *slang.* {1760–}

1788 *Mass. Centinel* 8 Oct. 25/1 The widow . . . paid down the shiners. **1810** *Repertory* (Boston) 16 Oct. (Th.), One hundred Eagles was the price; I paid the shiners in a trice. **1853** *La Crosse Democrat* 26 July 3/5 If you will give sixty-five dollars in California shiners. *a*1861 WINTHROP *J. Brent*

231 Most likely these shiners they won last night is some of the very sufferins Sizzum got from him.

+2. Any of a number of small, silvery, cyprinoid fishes found in American fresh waters, as the redfin (*Luxilus cornutus*), the chub (*Notemigonus crysoleucas*), etc.; loosely, any of several other silvery fishes, as the dollarfish, menhaden, etc. {1836, of young mackerel}

1792 *Mass. H. S. Coll.* I Ser. I. 113 [The lake] is supplied with pickerel, large perch, eels, shiners. **1820** RAFINESQUE in *Western Rev.* II. 240 Silverside Fallfish. . . . Vulgar names, Silverside, Shiner, White Chub, &c. Common in the streams of Kentucky. **1832** *N.H. Hist. Soc. Coll.* III. 87 The Shiner . . . is not as large as the Perch. **1845** THOREAU *Journal* I. 384, I catch shiners with fishworms, and bait the perch with them. **1854** HAMMOND *Hills, Lakes* 46 No sunfish, chub, shiner, perch, or any of the other kinds, so common in the fresh waters of the country. **1864** *Maine Agric. Soc. Returns 1863* 101 Where he takes shiners in quantity he may fail to secure a solitary trout. **1870** *Amer. Naturalist* IV. 100 During the last summer a few red-fins . . . and shiner (*Hypsilepis Kentuckiensis*), made their appearance. **1890** HOWELLS *Boy's Town* 30 My boy's experience was full of the ignominy of catching shiners and suckers. **1913** RILEY *Eccentric Mr. Clark* 109 The stream [is] noted more for its plenitude of 'chubs' and 'shiners' than the gamier two- and four-pound bass.

+b. With specifying terms.

1814 MITCHILL *Fishes N.Y.* 364 Cryptous broad shiner. *Stromateus cryptosus.* . . . A curious and beautiful fish. **1820** RAFINESQUE in *Western Rev.* II. 238 Goldhead Shiner. *Luxilus chrysocephalus.* . . . It is found in the Kentucky, Ohio, Cumberland, Green river, &c. **1842** *Nat. Hist. N.Y., Zoology* IV. 127 The Blunt-nosed Shiner, *Vomer brownii,* . . . appears in our waters in July and August. **1884** GOODE, etc. *Fisheries* I. 322 'Blunt-nosed Shiner,' . . . sometimes varied to 'Pug-nosed Shiner,' is in common use in the New York market and in Narragansett Bay. *Ib.* 616 The Golden Shiner—*Notemigonus chrysoleucus* . . . is a sluggish fish, frequenting ponds, bayous, and cut-offs.

✳ Shingle, *n.*[1]

I. ✳1. A small board sawed or split thin, with one end thinner than the other, used in making a roof, or in facing the side of a wall. Often collect.

See also CEDAR, CYPRESS, PINE SHINGLE.

1651 *Dedham Rec.* III. 191 The Meetinghouse shall be couered wth shingle. **1676** in Hutchinson *Coll. Papers Mass.-Bay* 487 The town contains about 2000 houses, most built with tymber and covered with shingles of cedar. **1710** *Harvard Rec.* I. 391 The said Slate roof . . . [shall be covered] wth board and Shingle. **1765** ROGERS *Acct. N. Amer.* 50 The chief commodities exported from this province [N.H.], are, . . . staves, boards, shingles, furs, &c. **1849** WILLIS *Rural Letters* 127 The cutting of shingles . . . [is] preferred by the young men to the . . . work of the farm-yard. **1882** COYNER *Hand-Book of Mormonism* 6 Large sums were raised in the Old World to pay for the glass and shingles of the Salt Lake Temple. **1904** PRINGLE *Rice Planter* 136 He could cut shingles in my swamp, where there was plenty of cypress.

+2. A shingle, any other board, or even a brass plate, bearing a name and used as a sign, esp. for a doctor's or a lawyer's office.

1842 *Spirit of Times* (Phila.) 18 May (Th.), One William Dermott hoisted his shingle yesterday. **1852** WEED *Lett. from Europe* 508 We only find plain Hiram Powers, whose 'shingle,' as we express it, hangs out to indicate his Studio. **1880** INGHAM *Digging Gold* 321 We saw a shingle out, 'Rooms to Let.' **1889** *Century Mag.* Jan. 406/2 [The] newly painted 'shingle' pronounced him 'Attorney at Law.'

+b. *fig.* A sign or indication that a person is beginning his professional career or is offering his services to the public.

This fig. sense often has a strange mixture of the literal sense.

*c*1844 R. H. COLLYER *Amer. Life* 34 The veriest jackass . . . is allowed by the famous bar-rules of Massachusetts . . . to set his 'shingle' amidst twenty thousand other 'lawyers.' **1894** FORD *P. Stirling* 14 Peter . . . had striven to get Watts to do the same [*i.e.,* to study law], with the ultimate intention of their hanging out a joint shingle in New York. **1903** *Cosmopolitan* Sept. 497 When a man once assumes the full title of architect and hangs out his shingle.

II. *attrib.* and *comb.* **3.** Designating wood or pieces of wood out of which shingles are made.

1647 *Springfield Rec.* I. 190 No man shall hence forth transport out of the town to other places, any . . . shingle tymber or pipe staves. **1838** ELLSWORTH *Valley of Wabash* 55 The shingle blocks are steamed. **1852** D. S. CURTISS *Western Portraiture* 46 Lumber received by Lakes for that year [1850]: Shingles, . . . Pickets, . . . Shingle Bolts.

+4. Designating machines, instruments, and factories employed in making shingles.

1802 *Mass. Spy* 17 Nov. (Th.), Dr. French of Conn. has invented a Shingle Dressing Machine. **1847** *Rep. Comm. Patents 1846* 90 One patent has been granted this year for an improved shingle-cutting machine. **1850** *Ib. 1849* 431 Some half dozen shingle machines have been patented within the year. **1876** KNIGHT 2151/2 *Shingle-planing Machine,* a machine in which roughly rived or sawn shingles are faced by planing in the direction of the grain of the wood. **1879** *Mich. Gen. Statutes* I. (1882) 552 Any person being in the possession or having the control of any saw-mill, shingle-mill [etc.].

+**5.** Designating buildings, or parts of buildings, covered with shingles.

1810 IRVING in P. M. Irving *Life W. Irving* I. 245 [Helping young artists] would, I am satisfied, be more pleasing in the sight of Heaven . . . than building a dozen shingle church steeples. **1839** BRIGGS *H. Franco* II. 206 The house was a little shingle cottage, with a projecting roof. **1869** *Rep. Comm. Agric. 1868* 56 Board and shingle sugar-houses.

6. Designating persons who make or handle shingles. {1792}

1817 PAULDING *Lett. from South* II. 177 The brickmaker made bricks, and the shingle-splitter, split his shingles. **1835-7** HALIBURTON *Clockmaker* I Ser. iii. 16 We shall be in time to get under cover in a shingle-maker's shed. **1856** *Harper's Mag.* Sept. 447/2 Joe Skeeters holds the office of shingle-counter for the Dismal Swamp Land Company. **1857** CHANDLESS *Visit Salt Lake* 214 Those connected with house-building: the dobie-maker, the mason, the shingle-layer [can thrive in Salt Lake City]. **1859** BARTLETT 401 *Shingle-weaver,* a workman who dresses shingles. **1895** *Outing* Oct. 71/1 We got into the home of the shingle getters.

+**7.** Designating boats and vehicles usually employed in carrying shingles, or a child's make-believe boat consisting of a shingle.

1833 COKE *Subaltern's Furlough* i, [We] overtook our black friend and his shingle sloop. **1895** *Stand.* 1653/2 *Shingle-rack,* a wagon or sleigh made for hauling shingles. **1897** STUART *Simpkinsville* 156 He's with my Tom, sailin' shingle boats in my goose-pond.

+**8.** In special combinations.

Shingle cake, a flat cake; *s.-caped overcoat,* an overcoat with two or more overlapping capes; *s.-whittling,* the pastime of whittling a shingle; *s. yard,* (see quotation).

1872 *Harper's Mag.* June 97/1 She had eaten nothing since morning save a reminiscence of her youth in shape of a molasses 'shingle-cake,' purchased of an old 'mauma' on the Aug. **1889** *Ib.* Aug. 386/1 [In] a shingle-caped overcoat, . . . he sat gravely and sturdily down amid his peers. **1851** HALL *Manhattaner* 50 He would . . . betake himself to shingle-whittling, or any other Yankee recreation which is as soothing to troubled nerves. **1895** *Stand.* 1653/2 *Shingle-yard,* a place where shingles of all kinds are stored for sale.

*✳**Shingle,** n.²* *attrib.* Designating places characterized by collections of small roundish stones. {1834-} — **1661** *Plymouth Rec.* I. 43 All the land lying . . . at the Eelriver swamp betwixt the Eelriver and the shingle brooke shalbee Reserved for comon. **1701** *Manchester Rec.* 96 On the norwest of the highway that goes to the Shingle place it is bounded with John Leyes on the north side. **1850** HINES *Voyage* 341 The prairies are all composed of shingle land. **1879** *Harper's Mag.* July 203 A guide who knew the shingle region was also hired.

*✳**Shingle,** v.*

*✳**1.** tr.* To put shingles on (a roof, house, etc.). {-1638}

1651 *Dedham Rec.* III. 197 He shall . . . shingle the penthouse ouer the Bell [of the meetinghouse]. **1712** HEMPSTEAD *Diary* 9, I went to Shingle-ling Sister mary's house. **1764** *N.H. Hist. Soc. Coll.* IX. 159 Reuben Kier came to shingle my barn. **1886** *Harper's Mag.* June 108/1 The houses . . . were shingled on the sides.
fig. **1834** C. A. DAVIS *Lett. J. Downing* 49 We are now . . . fitting and joining the beams and rafters of the message; and if Mr. Van Buren don't get back before we begin to shingle it, I guess his 'Safety Fund' will stand but a poor chance. **1847** *Santa Fe Republican* 2/4 The whole Territory of New Mexico is now shingled over with troops.

+**2.** To file overlapping claims on (a piece of land); to put several liens on (a property).

[**1832** CLAY *Speeches* (1842) 221 The same tract was not unfrequently entered various times by different purchasers, so as to be literally shingled over with conflicting claims.] **1869** *Congress. Globe* 7 Jan. 239/1 Where else are great cities built upon a soil shingled with mortgages drawing enormous rates of interest? **1886** Z. F. SMITH *Kentucky* 187 Thus were the means and the inducements furnished to *shingle* over one claim with another. **1892** *Ky. Centenary Celebr. by Filson Club* 137 There were few 'locations' that were not 'shingled' by opposing claims.

+**3.** To cut (the hair); usu., to cut (the hair) very short. Also absol. and *ppl. a.*

1857 HOLLAND *Bay-Path* 232, I don't s'pose . . . there's anybody in the settlement can shingle like me. **1883** HOWE *Country Town* (1926) 25 He shingled hair in a superb manner. **1890** *Buckskin Mose* 29 His beard . . . was shingled off short. **1907** *St. Nicholas* June 712/1 [With] Rob's merry tousel of the shingled head, . . . Fritzi felt her keenest grief and shame appeared.

+**4.** To cover like a shingled roof.

1858 HOLMES *Autocrat* 33 [A] middle-aged female, with a parchment forehead and a dry little 'frisette' shingling it.

+**5.** (See quotation.)

1859 BARTLETT 401 *To Shingle,* to chastise. A shingle applied *a posteriori* is a favorite New England mode of correcting a child.

Shingle ballast. [f. SHINGLE *n.²*] Small roundish stones used as ballast. {1801} — **1733** *Boston Rec.* 65 We now think of an Addition to the House . . . and of laying Shingle Ballast before the same. **1845** *S. Lit. Messenger* XI. 588/2 She must therefore be at the expense of taking in a large quantity of stones, called shingle ballast, to steady the ship.

*✳**Shingle nail.** A nail used in putting shingles on a roof. — **1755** *Holyoke Diaries* 15 The Newby. shingle Nails at 22/M. **1815** *Mass. H. S. Coll.* 2 Ser. IV. 186 One machine will . . . make 150 shingle nails in one minute. **1884** 'MARK TWAIN' *H. Finn* xxxvii, [We] found a couple of shingle-nails.

+**Shingle oak.** An American oak (*Quercus imbricaria*) used to make shingles. — **1814** PURSH *Flora* II. 627 The Shingle Oak rises to about forty or fifty feet. **1860** CURTIS *Woody Plants N.C.* 36 Shingle Oak. . . . In Illinois, it has been used for shingles, probably for want of a better material. **1897** SUDWORTH *Arborescent Flora* 176.

+**Shingle roof.** A roof made of shingles. {a1850} — [**1749** HEMPSTEAD *Diary* 528 Mostly Wooden houses covered with Long Ceder Shingle Roof & Sides.] **1831** *N.H. Hist. Soc. Coll.* V. 52 The shingle roof had been chiefly removed for a covering of zinc. **1904** *N.Y. Ev. Post* 2 April 5 The shingle roof of his house leaked.

+**Shingle-roofed,** *a.* Having a roof covered with shingles. — **1792** [see NEW YORKER]. **1847** HOWE *Hist. Coll. Ohio* 273 A hewed log and shingle-roofed building . . . was the first tavern. **1874** COLLINS *Kentucky* I. 23 They burn several towns, one with 120 houses (of which 80 were shingle-roofed).

+**Shingle sunbonnet.** A sunbonnet so made that pieces of shingle can be inserted in the sides to stiffen them. (Cf. SLAT SUNBONNET.) — **1856** S. ROBINSON *Kansas* 306 A woman dressed in bright-red calico, . . . and shingle sun-bonnet, sat there sewing on a muslin of gay colors.

+**Shingle titles,** *pl.* Land titles that overlap each other. — **1833** FLINT *D. Boone* 244 Almost every tract was covered with different and conflicting titles—forming what have been aptly called 'shingle titles.' **1843** HAWKS *D. Boone* 129 Almost all the titles conferred in this way became known as 'the lapping, or shingle titles.'

+**Shingle willow oak.** =SHINGLE OAK. — **1801** MICHAUX *Histoire des Chênes* 7 Quercus Imbricaria. Chêne A Lattes. *Shingles Willow Oak.* **1817** S. BROWN *Western Gazetteer* 24 [There are] three [species] of willow oak, upland, swamp, and *shingle,* so called from its being an excellent material for shingles.

Shingling. **a.** The cutting of shingles. **b.** The action of shingling a house, etc. {1703, 1910} Also transf. — **1670** *Essex Inst. Coll.* XLII. 45 Rich Sibly [was] granted liberty to fall 6 trees for his use for shingling. **1785** WASHINGTON *Diaries* II. 429 Finished the Shingling on the West front of the House. **1807** *Ann. 10th Congress* 1 Sess. I. 582 [These tomahawks] were such as were generally used for shingling. **1830** PICKERING *Inquiries Emigrant* 115 Their barns are thatched, but in a rough manner; the Americans call it shingling with straw!

+**Shingly,** *a.* **a.** Shaped like a shingle. **b.** Covered with shingles. Also *fig.* — **1856** GOODRICH *G. Go-ahead* 195 Mr. Fuz was a man of middle height, but of great breadth, his body being rather flat and shingly. **1857** WHITTIER *Poetical Works* (1894) 152/1 The painted shingly town-house, where The freeman's vote for Freedom falls. **1863** 'G. HAMILTON' *Gala-Days* 107 The rustic stone city . . . looks so attractive, so different from our hasty, brittle, shingly American, half-minute houses.

Shining, *a.* In the specific names of plants and animals. {1626-} — **1810** MICHAUX *Arbres* I. 41 Salix lucida. . . . *Shining willow,* (Saule luisant), nom donné par moi. **1814** PURSH *Flora* I. 9 [*Fraxinus*] caroliniana. . . . *Shining-ash.* In rocky situations, from Pensylvania to Carolina, scarce. **1842** *Nat. Hist. N.Y., Zoology* IV. 209 The Shining Dace, *Leuciscus nitidus,* . . . was taken in July, in Lake Champlain. **1869** *Amer. Naturalist* III. 472, I soon noticed . . . the Shining Flycatcher and Gila Woodpecker (*Centurus uropygidlis*), both of which were abundant [in California].

Shining Mountains. +The Rocky Mountains. *Obs.* — **1847** COYNER *Lost Trappers* 158 They [Rocky Mountains] were called by some of the first discoverers, the Shining Mountains, from the fact that the higher parts are covered with perpetual snows, which give them a luminous and brilliant appearance.

+**Shinleaf.** Any herb of the genus *Pyrola.* — **1817-8** EATON *Botany* (1822) 416. **1821** *Mass. H. S. Coll.* 2 Ser. IX. 154 Plants, which are indigenous in the township of Middlebury, [Vt., include] . . . *Pyrola rotundifolia,* Shin leaf. *Pyrola secunda,* One-sided shin leaf. a**1862** THOREAU *Maine Woods* 319.

*✳**Shinner.** colloq.* +**1.** One who begs for money. +**2.** One who moves about quickly. +**3.** (See quotation.) — (1) **1834** A. GREENE *Perils Pearl St.* 125 Shinners may be divided into two classes: those who shin from necessity, and those who shin from profit. a**1859** *N.Y. Ev. Post* (B.), No 'short shinner' feared rebuff, Who sued for pelf. (2) **1837** NEAL *Charcoal Sk.* (1838) 107 Berry . . . [was not] well calculated for a 'shinner' of the first class. (3) **1844** *Spirit of Times* (Phila.) 11 Feb. (Th.), Certain cunning men, . . . not farmers . . . , have purchased shabby looking carts, backed them up among the wagons, and every market day made them regular stands for the sale of beef, mutton, veal, &c. These men are called 'shinners.'

Shinning. {1873-} +The action of borrowing, or trying to borrow, money. *colloq.* (Cf. SHIN *v.* 3 b.) — **1839** *Jamestown Jrnl.* 20 Nov. 1/5 A shinning . . . is borrowing money to take up his own notes with. **1843** STEPHENS *High Life N.Y.* I. 5 Mr. Beebe's out a shinning now. **1853** *La Crosse Democrat* 6 Dec. 2/6 Shinning [is] on the decline. . . . Stocks are rising. **1871** DE VERE 306 This process of *shinning* is resorted to whenever the merchant or banker is *short.*

Shinny, *n.* A boys' game similar to hockey. {1672-} Also attrib.
— **1785** DENNY *Journal* 60 [The Indians were] exceedingly active at the game our boys call shinny or common. **1847** *Knickerb.* XXIX. 453 The fathers of the city . . . mean that everybody should enjoy them [the green enclosures], even boys with their shinny-sticks. **1889** *Amer. Notes & Q.* IV. 58 School-boys desired to make up a match for . . . 'shinny.' **1902** WILSON *Spenders* 177 He was a crackin' good shinny player.

Shinny, *v.*[1] [f. *shin* 'the fore part of the leg.'] To climb, esp. by using the arms and the shins of the legs without steps; etc. Also *vbl. n.* — **1888** DALY *Lottery of Love* 18 The way you shinnied up the side of the ship . . . converted me on the spot to the Blooming costume. **1906** *Washington Post* 22 May 2 As its girth precluded 'shinnying,' Gladden procured a ladder. **1922** A. BROWN *Old Crow* 126 He always escaped and 'shinnied' up the cliff opposite, by fissures the boys of every generation knew.

+Shinny, *v.*[2] [f. SHINNY *n.*] *fig. intr.* To blow hot and cold; freq., *to shinny on one's own side,* to keep to one's own side of the fence. — **1839** KIRKLAND *New Home* (1840) 305 My dear friends . . . stuck to me like wax, . . . never shinnyin' off and on, but up to the scratch. **1866** C. H. SMITH *Bill Arp* 144 Let 'em shinny on their own side, and git over among the folks who don't want us reconstructed. **1887** *Courier-Journal* 11 Jan. 1/1 If his Royal Highness does not like United States justice, he can 'shinny on his own side' of the water hereafter.

+Shin oak. Any of several species of dwarf oak. — **1844** GREGG *Commerce of Prairies* II. 200 Black-jacks . . . [are] intermixed with a very diminutive dwarf oak, called by the hunters 'shin-oak.' **1889** *Harper's Mag.* Dec. 121/2 The dwarf shinn-oaks . . . were overlaid here and there with a fine filmy network of love-vine. **1897** SUDWORTH *Arborescent Flora* 152 *Quercus breweri.* Shin Oak. *Ib.* 153 *Quercus gambelii.* Gambel Oak. . . . Shin Oak.

+Shinplaster. [*Shin* 'fore part of leg' and PLASTER 1.]
1. A piece of paper money or scrip issued upon inadequate security; a depreciated bank note. *colloq.*
The name was applied especially to: **a.** The numerous notes of small denomination issued by private bankers, municipalities, etc., during the depression of 1837-40. **b.** The fractional currency (q.v.).
1824 *Microscope* (Albany, N.Y.) 15 May (Th.), We advise our friends to exchange their 'shin plasters' for 'solid charms' as soon as may be. **1837** *Jamestown* (N.Y.) *Jrnl.* 19 July 2/2 The Van Buren party . . . have introduced 10,000 kinds of Shin Plasters nominally of any value from 100 to 5 cents. **1839** *S. Lit. Messenger* V. 272/2, I had seen nothing in circulation but Tennessee banknotes . . . and shin-plasters of all sorts and sizes from a dollar downwards. **1846** *Whig Almanac 1847* 11/1 The money of the Government is . . . to be exclusively Specie (its own Shinplasters excepted). **1869** 'J. BILLINGS' in *Ore. State Jrnl.* 2 Jan. 1/3, I gave one ov them a 50 cent shinplaster. **1870** MEDBERY *Men Wall St.* 286 The Revolutionary 'shin-plasters,' as the irreverent already styled them. **1900** *Congress. Rec.* 7 Feb. 1610/2 A reproduction of 'shin-plasters' [was] not expected at the opening of the twentieth century.

b. Attrib. with *bank, currency, inflation,* etc.
1838 *U.S. Mag.* Jan. 30 Mr. Strange . . . [was] no greater friend to the miserable 'shin-plaster' currency of the District. **1838** *N.Y. Advertiser & Exp.* 3 Feb. 1/2 The manner in which the bank and shin-plaster whigs bamboozle poor General Harrison . . . is very affecting. **1853** *La Crosse Democrat* 12 July 1/6 A Shinplaster Bank of St. Paul. **1874** *Chicago Times* 11 June 4/2 Willful Wallowing in the Slough of Shinplaster Inflation. **1888** *Century Mag.* Sept. 763/2 'Wild-cat' bank-notes of all sorts, shapes, and sizes vied with the 'shin-plaster' utterances of municipalities.

+2. 'A small square patch of brown paper, usually saturated with vinegar, tar, tobacco-juice, or the like, applied by poor people to sores on the leg' (*Cent.*).

+Shin wood. The ground hemlock. — **1778** CARVER *Travels* 505 Shin Wood . . . proves very troublesome to the hasty traveller, by striking against his shins. **1813** MUHLENBERG *Cat. Plants* 93. **1836** EDWARDS *Hist. Texas* 66 The names of the trees . . . [and] shrubs . . . [include] the Prickly Ash, the Shin-wood [etc.].

∗Ship, *n.*
∗1. Any large vessel for navigation, esp. a seagoing vessel.
1622 'MOURT' *Relation* 29 We found . . . [the river] not Navigable for Ships. **1643** *New Eng. First Fruits* (1896) 10 [We have] English Wheat . . . and all other provisions for Victualling of Shippes. **1771** FRANKLIN *Autobiog.* 267 The annual ship . . . [was] the only one at that time usually passing between London and Philadelphia. **1851** MELVILLE *Moby-Dick* 76 There were three ships up for three-years' voyages. **1917** *Lit. Digest* LIV. 1231 The ship *Aztec* which a German submarine sank . . . had been insured for $1,000,000.

2. An airship. {1928-, an airplane}
1873 *Winfield* (Kan.) *Courier* 12 June 1/7 His ship will have the buoyancy of one hundred and thirty thousand feet of hydrogen gas.

3. *attrib.* and *comb.* **∗a.** Designating things used or consumed on ships.
See also SHIP STUFF.
1636 WINTHROP in R. C. Winthrop *Life J. Winthrop* II. 158, I would have sent you some ship beer. **1648** *Conn. Rec.* I. 490 An Inventory of the Goods of Timothy Standly: . . . 1 shipp chest. **1740** W. STEPHENS *Proc. Georgia* I. 524, I had . . . given Directions, to remount as many [pieces of artillery] as needed it on Ship-Carriages (or Trucks). **1754** *S.C. Gazette* 1 Jan. 2/2 Exceeding good Flour, ship Bread, bar Iron, . . . just import-

ed. **1840** OLMSTED *Lett. Astronomy* 276 [Galileo's best telescope, magnified] only thirty times, which is no better than a common ship-glass. **1851** MELVILLE *Moby-Dick* 25 Laying a bit of ship biscuit on top . . . , he kindled the shavings into a sacrificial blaze. **1854** *Penna. Agric. Rep.* 394 Best Ship Axes.

∗b. Designating persons associated in some way with ships.
See also SHIP CARPENTER, SHIP JOINER, etc.
1643 *Suffolk Deeds* I. 51 The Ship men made answere yei would not deliver it. **1653** *Ib.* 326 This Indenture [was] made betweene John Cutting of Charlstowne in new England Shipp m[aste]r . . . & John ffrary. **1717** SEWALL *Letter-Book* II. 75 Jonathan now . . . joyns with him in his Ship-Chandlers Business. **1790** BENTLEY *Diary* I. 223 Becket, James, . . . Ship Builder. **1839** LEONARD *Adventures* (1904) 230 [They] make appointments with ship-traders to meet at some designated time and place. **1860** MORDECAI *Virginia* 141 He was the first to engage in the occupation of ship-broker in Richmond. **1869** *Causes Reduct. Tonnage* (1870) 112 American ship-captains are men of a higher grade than English ship-captains. **1904** *N.Y. Sun* 11 Aug. 3 The men who are called ship luggers . . . load meat aboard the steamships.

c. In special combinations.
Ship subsidy, a government subsidy for the operation of ships, used attrib.; *s. vessel,* a relatively small ship not propelled by steam.
1851 CIST *Cincinnati* 322 The construction and equipment of ship vessels . . . seems likely to become a permanent . . . business. **1900** *Congress. Rec.* 21 Feb. 2015/1 Sentiment is hereby declared to be opposed to the enactment of the Hanna-Payne ship subsidy bill.

∗Ship, *v.*
+1. *tr.* To transport (goods) by rail or other land transportation.
1857 *Harper's Mag.* Sept. 459/2 A few of the more enterprising operators . . . thought nothing of shipping two or three thousand tons per annum. **1877** JOHNSON *Anderson Co., Kansas* 195 Cattle are shipped over them. **1885** *Harper's Mag.* April 921/2 [We] shipped our . . . collection of luggage to the hotel. **1906** *Springfield W. Repub.* 15 Nov. 16 Over 2000 barrels of apples have been shipped out of Conway over the street railway. **1916** WILSON *Somewhere* 133 You can't expect us to be shipping steers every month.
absol. **1859** *Harper's Mag.* 425/2 Sug . . . knows that it is to his interest to ship by our line. **1890** *Stock Grower & Farmer* 4 Jan. 4/3 The railroads find their interests lie with the men who ship on the hoof.

+2. *intr.* Of perishable goods: To stand shipment.
1867 *Ill. Agric. Soc. Trans.* VII. 510 It ships well, and is a very good peach.

Shipbuilding. The business or action of building ships. {1717-} — **1729** FRANKLIN *Writings* II. 136 The Increase of our Currency . . . has encouraged . . . Ship-Building. **1784** [see HORSEJOCKEY]. **1814** BIGELOW *Florula Bostoniensis* 225 The wood of the white oak . . . is much used in ship building. **1878** INGRAM *Centennial Exp.* 631 Notable among [the resources and industries of Delaware] . . . are the agricultural, mechanical, and those of iron ship-building, morocco manufacturing and car-building. **1907** *London Road* 182 On the banks of the Des Moines was inaugurated a tremendous era of shipbuilding.

+Ship canal. A canal through which ships may be taken.
Cf. BOAT CANAL.
1798 I. ALLEN *Hist. Vermont* 268 A ship canal would be the means of importing salt. **1831** JACKSON in *Pres. Mess. & P.* II. 552 The magnificent project of a ship canal . . . from the Atlantic to the Pacific Ocean, now in serious contemplation, shall be executed. **1837** *Knickerb.* IX. 294 Who, ten years since, would have thought of a *ship canal* from the lakes to the ocean! **1849** TAYLOR in *Pres. Mess. & P.* V. 15 A contract . . . [has] been concluded with the State of Nicaragua . . . for the purpose of constructing a ship canal through the territory of that State to connect the Atlantic and Pacific oceans. **1867** *Atlantic Mo.* June 666/2 Those ship canals which Chicago is so set upon speedily creating, will give St. Louis also access to the Great Lakes. **1914** STEELE *Storm* 57 We approached the mouth of the ship-canal.

∗Ship carpenter. A carpenter who repairs or helps build a ship. — **1638** *Md. Archives* I. 6 Then came Edward Bateman of St. maries hundred, ship carpenter & claymed a voyce as freeman. **1714** *Boston News-Letter* 22 March 2/2 Ran-away from . . . his Ship, . . . William Netherton Ship Carpenter. **1871** GROSVENOR *Protection* 67 The ship-carpenters do not share in the benefits of the tariff. **1911** PERSONS, etc. *Mass. Labor Laws* 114 The Rev. William B. Tilden, minister of the New South Congregational Society, . . . had begun life as a ship carpenter.

+Ship channel. A channel used by ships. — **1775** in Sparks *Corr. Revol.* I. 73 The ship-channel . . . runs between the east head of Long Island and the south point of Deer Island. **1830** COOPER *Water Witch* III. 101 The Narrows . . . is the ordinary ship-channel of the port. **1875** 'MARK TWAIN' *Old Times* iv. 61 Ship channels are buoyed and lighted.

+Ship house. A structure built over a dock. — **1825** N. ADAMS *Annals Portsmouth* 388 Two ship houses [are] sufficiently extensive to cover the largest ships employed in the Navy. **1841** *S. Lit. Messenger* VII. 17/2 The dock was filled up, and a ship-house built over it. **1880** 'MARK TWAIN' *Tramp Abroad* 274 Sometimes one of these monster precipices had the slight inclination of the huge ship-houses in dockyards.

Ship joiner. A joiner or carpenter who does cabinet work, etc., for a ship. {1858-} — **1739** *Boston Rec.* 219 Mr. Benjamin Brown, (Shipjoyner) was Chosen. **1818** [see FRAME DWELLING]. **1840** MATHEWS *Politicians* I. i, Joe carries a whole block with him, besides his river influence among the . . . ship-joiners.

✱**Ship-keeper.** A person employed to take care of a ship in the absence of the crew. — **1796** BENTLEY *Diary* II. 170 A Negro . . . was Ship keeper in the harbour. **1866** 'MARK TWAIN' *Lett. Sandwich Islands* 68 'Ship-keeper,' a man who stands guard on a whaler and takes care of the ship when the boats and the crew are off after whales.

Shipment.

1. The act of shipping goods by sea {1802-} +or by land.
1798 I. ALLEN *Hist. Vermont* 268 Spring and fall shipments are seasonably made to New York. **1871** RAYMOND *3d Rep. Mines* 141 The shipment of ores to California during the two years was as follows. **1872** *Ill. Dept. Agric. Trans.* IX. 65 It is desirable . . . to have not only a profitable market, accessible by rail, or market for distant shipments, but a local market. **1904** [see EXPORTER].

2. A consignment of goods shipped by sea {1861-} +or by land.
1840 *Niles' Nat. Reg.* 4 July 278/1 The shipments [of coal] for the week . . . were 11,898 tons. **1925** FOSTER *Trop. Tramp Tourists* 144 The big mining camps at the top of the hill were calling for a large shipment of lumber.

Ship of state. The nation figuratively regarded as a vessel. {1675, ship of the state} — [**1835-7** HALIBURTON *Clockmaker* I Ser. 160 Where's that Ship of State, fitted up all the way from the forecastle clean up to the starn post?] **1847** *Santa Fe Republican* 4 Dec. 2/1 Nor can it be expected that men . . . in civil life should be able at once to . . . guide the ship of State. **1870** LONGFELLOW *Poetical Works* (1893) 103/2 Sail on, O Ship of State! Sail on, O Union, strong and great! **1900** *Congress. Rec.* 16 Feb. 1883/1, 20 per cent of the employees in all Departments in the city of Washington . . . are really barnacles upon the ship of state.

✱**Ship of war.** A warship. — **1690** SEWALL *Diary* I. 327, [I] visited the Ships of War and other Vessels. **1778** *Mass. Spy* 15 Oct. 1/2 Sailed from Boston harbour, on a cruize, in the Continental ship of war Raleigh. **1840** BANCROFT *Hist. U.S.* III. 202 A large ship-of-war from that station joined the expedition. **1845** POLK in *Pres. Mess. & P.* IV. 412 It has been a wise policy to afford to these important interests protection with our ships of war distributed in the great highways of trade throughout the world.

+**Shippen's Russet(ing).** (See quot. 1817.) — **1817** W. COXE *Fruit Trees* 124 Shippens Russeting . . . is a large flat apple, of an irregular form. **1833** *Genesee Farmer* 15 June 190/1 Roxbury Russet. Shippen's Russet.

✱**Shipper.**

1. One who ships goods by water. {1755, 1880}
1723 *New-Eng. Courant* 1 July 1/2 The Shipper, as well as the Workman and his Goods, meet with a Return of Five Hundred *per Cent.* in Oaths and Curses. **1789** JEFFERSON *Writings* VII. 274, I would advise our shippers of oil always to get the certificate of the French consul. **1895** E. CARROLL *Principles Finance* 298 The owners of the cargo or property used or destroyed, abandoned, or cast overboard, have a right to recover its value *pro rata* from the shippers whose property was saved.

+**2.** One who ships goods by land.
1840 *Niles' Nat. Reg.* 4 April 80/2 Principal transportation lines have resolved to give the shipper or owner the full advantage of the reduction of twenty cents per barrel [of flour]. **1869** *Ill. Agric. Soc. Trans.* VII. 420 Contract cattle were delivered this month, nearly all of which lost money to Western shippers. **1899** *Boston Herald* 8 Aug. 9/2 Chicago advices report that shippers in that city are not taking kindly to the new rate conditions. **1907** M. H. NORRIS *Veil* 38 Mr. George Edward Jones . . . [found], as a shipper's notice had informed him he should, the car-horse and cow.

+**3.** A commodity that is shipped or suitable to be shipped.
1881 *Tenth Census* III. III. 19 English shippers consist of leaf and strips. **1884** *Harper's Mag.* July 297/2 [In the cattle pen] may be gathered one hundred head of choice 'shippers.' **1887** *Courier-Journal* 19 Jan. 8/1 For the best quality Clarksville or Harkinsville district shipper, $50, [was] awarded to Mr. Hana.

✱**Shipping.** *attrib.*

1. Designating places, either on the water or inland, from which commodities are shipped. {1843}
See also SHIPPING POINT.
1766 STORK *Acct. E. Florida* 63 It is often necessary, in the West-Indies, to carry it [sugar] at a great expence by land, a considerable distance to the shipping-places. **1862** NORTON *Army Lett.* 66 It is twenty-four miles to Fortress Monroe, our nearest shipping station. **1877** HODGE *Arizona* 143 Yuma is the principal shipping and commercial town of the Territory. **1887** *Courier-Journal* 9 May 4/1 The business of shippers and shipping centers [has] been becoming better adjusted gradually to the new order of things. **1894** EGGLESTON in *Harper's Mag.* Feb. 473/2 They made their way to the shipping-post called Georgetown.

+**2.** Designating commodities suitable or intended for shipping.
1812 STODDARD *Sk. Louisiana* 126 Various articles, usually denominated naval stores, are produced here; such as hemp, pitch, tar, turpentine, and shipping timber. **1820** *Columbian Centinel* 1 Nov. 4/3 For sale . . . 3000 pair Shipping Shoes. **1863** *Ill. Agric. Soc. Trans.* V. 669 These remarks are

particularly applicable to those heavy descriptions of tobacco known in Virginia as heavy shipping leaf. **1869** *Ib.* VII. 420 Choice to extra, and second class shipping steers, remained throughout the month moderately steady. **1876** RAYMOND *8th Rep. Mines* 242 The ore-vein . . . yields a large portion of 'shipping' or first-class ore. **1894** *Tenth Census* III. III. 194 Dark Shipping tobacco is generally raised on rich lots. **1882** *47th Congress 1 Sess.* H. R. Ex. Doc. No. 216, 201 A shaft is down 75 feet, exposing a 3-foot vein, 15 inches of which is high-grade or shipping ore.

3. Designating persons or firms connected with the business of shipping. {1844-}
1857 *Harper's Mag.* Sept. 459/2 The coal . . . passed through the hands of the shipping merchants to those of the consumer. **1863** *Ib.* Aug. 338/2 I was . . . a third partner in a New York shipping-house. **1886** *Outing* May 164/2 The shipping commissioners came on board. **1889** MUNROE *Dorymates* 108, I see that you are cut out for a regular shipping agent. **1894** ALDRICH *Two Bites* 193 Mr. Nelson . . . mentioned to me casually that he was looking for a shipping-clerk.

Shipping plank. A plank suitable for use in building a ship. — **1640** *Mass. H. S. Coll.* 4 Ser. VI. 143 The towne agreed not to cutt any great tymber which is fitt for shipping planckes or knees.

+**Shipping point. a.** An inland town from which goods are shipped. **1863** *Ib.* Aug. 338/2 This is quite a shipping point, over the Chicago and Alton Railroad. **1890** *Stock Grower & Farmer* 19 April 6/1 The shipping point will be Lordsburg or Deming. **1904** TARBELL *Hist. Standard Oil Co.* I. 94 The same rate was put on refined oil from Cleveland, Pittsburg and the creek, to Eastern shipping points. **b.** A seaport for shipping goods. — **1872** *Ill. Dept. Agric. Trans.* IX. 173

Ship railway. A railway for carrying ships across land. {1891-} Also attrib. — **1881** *Chicago Times* 12 March 14/2 Captain Eads . . . will spend a month in making an inspection of his ship-railway route [across the Isthmus of Tehuantepec]. **1888** *Harper's Mag.* Feb. 379/2 A ship-railway has also been surveyed across the Florida peninsula to save the 600 miles of distance around and through the straits.

+**Ship's lawyer.** A poor lawyer. — **1894** *Congress. Rec.* 31 May 5547/2 [Judge Turner] decided that I might pass as 'ship's lawyer' to practice in this court.

+**Ship stuff.** **1.** A coarse or low-grade wheat flour. **2.** Material for use in making or repairing a ship. — **(1) 1771** WASHINGTON *Diaries* II. 23 Sold all the Flour I have left: . . . ship stuff at 8/4 pr. Cwt. *c*1790 COXE *View U.S.* 62 Produce, manufactures, and exports of Pennsylvania [include:] . . . midlings, ship-stuff, bran, shorts. **1818** *Niles' Reg.* XIV. 359/2 Petersburg, Va. inspections, for April, May, and June, 1818—7541 bbls superfine; . . . 18 do. ship stuff. **(2) 1884** SARGENT *Rep. Forests* 511 A few small mills saw oak from the immediate neighborhood into ship-stuff and car lumber.

Ship's writer. (See quotations.) — **1881** *Naval Encycl.* 745/2 Ship's Writer, a petty officer who, under the directions of the executive-officer, does the writing and keeps the watch-, muster-, conduct-, and other books of the ship. **1914** *Dialect Notes* IV. 151 Ship's writer, executive officer's yeoman.

✱**Ship timber.** Timber for building ships. — **1640** *Mass. H. S. Coll.* 4 Ser. VI. 90 They may as well cut it further of, it being so portable, and ship-timber being so heavy. **1774** J. ANDREWS *Letters* 43 The inhabitants . . . provided a number of teams, such as carry ship timbers. **1822** *Ann. 17th Congress* 1 Sess. 213 Persons are now engaged in cutting down and sending off the valuable ship timber on the public lands of Florida. **1919** HOUGH *Sagebrusher* 250 Down this stream ship timbers once had come.

Shipworm. Any of certain small mollusks that burrow in submerged wood: (see quotations). {1778-} — **1843** *Nat. Hist. N.Y., Zoology* VI. 249 The well known Ship-worm . . . scarcely extends north of the waters of this State. **1883** *Nat. Museum Bul.* No. 27, 241 Four species of the genus *Teredo* [are] found on the coast of the United States, and . . . these creatures are usually known as ship-worms. **1907** *St. Nicholas* Sept. 1039/2 This remarkable wood-cutting is done by a little sea animal, a marine mollusk, known to scientists as the *Teredo navalis* or ship-worm

✱**Shipwright.** A workman employed in the construction of ships. — **1631** *Va. House of Burgesses* 125 Tradesmen are wantinge, especially Shipwrites. **1715** *Boston News-Letter* 28 March 2/2 A Negro Man . . . to be Sold and seen at the House of Mr. William Peirce Shipwright in Lyn-Street near Charlstown Ferry. **1789** *Ann. 1st Congress* 123 A petition of the shipwrights of the city of Charleston, . . . was presented to the House and read. **1884** *Harper's Mag.* May 877/1 The demand for repairs to machinery] . . . gives a living to . . . shipwrights, boiler-makers, machinists, and laborers.

Shipyard. A yard or enclosure where ships are built or repaired. {a1700-} — **1713** *Boston News Letter* 14 Dec. 2/2 A Convenient Ship Yard with a Crane Dock and Work-House . . . to be Let. **1832** DUNLAP *Hist. Amer. Theatre* 40 The town was partially built on low swampy ground, intermingled with water to the ship-yards. **1889** BRAYLEY *Boston Fire Dept.* 59 It swept everything as far as the lower end of Water and Milk streets to Hallowell's ship-yard. **1913** [see NAIL *n.* 3].

✱**Shire.** New Eng. **1.** A county. *Obs.* **2.** Attrib. with *hall, meeting, treasure.* — **(1) 1641** *Mass. H. S. Coll.* 3 Ser. VIII. 226 Any Shire or Towne shall have libertie to choose their Deputies. **1764** HUTCHINSON *Hist. Mass.* I. 117 The colony . . . was divided this year [1643] into four counties or shires. **(2) 1641** *Mass. H. S. Coll.* 3 Ser. VIII. 229 The Generall or publique Treasure . . . shall never be expended but by the appointment of a Generall Court, nor any Shire Treasure, but by the appointment of the freemen thereof. **1658** *Boston Rec.* 144 Capt. James Olliver is chosen Commissioner to receive the proxyes for magistrates and County

Treasurer, and to carry them to the shire meeting. **1819** FAUX *Memorable Days* 215, I rambled round the town to the court-house, or shire-hall.

✶ Shire town. A county seat.
This word appears to have been used only by New Englanders.
1648 *N.H. Prov. Papers* I. 189 The Court doth think fitt that the shire town of Norfolke be referred to further consideration. **1669** *Watertown Rec.* I. i. 96 The invoyse . . . was Deliverd vnto Tho Flegg Commissioner: to cary to the sheire-towne of the County; as the law Requireth. **1717** SEWALL *Diary* III. 132 Cambridge is the Shire-Town for Middlesex. **1792** *Mass. H. S. Coll.* 1 Ser. I. 112 Worcester, the shire town of the county of Worcester, is situated 47 miles W. from Boston. **1809** BRECK in *Recoll.* (1877) 264 Chester . . . is the shire-town of the county of Deleware, in Pennsylvania. **1881** HOWELLS *Modern Instance* iii, It was the central town in the county, and yet not the shire-town. **1904** MABIE *Backgrounds of Lit.* 84 [Concord] was a shire-town, and it had business relations with lumbermen and farmers who came to it for supplies.

Shirk, *v.* {1633–}
+1. *New Eng. tr.* To shift (responsibility) *off upon* (or *on to*) someone.
1838 HAWTHORNE *Notebooks* (1932) 69 The horse he pronounced 'a dreadful nice horse to go; but if he could shirk off the work upon the others, he would.' **1845** LOWELL *Letters* I. 111, I would almost give half the rest of my life if I might shirk off upon somebody else all that is generally considered the pleasant result of a literary reputation. **1861** PHILLIPS *Speeches* (1863) 368 Burden it [cotton] by taxes with the full cost of a slaveholding government, . . . a tax it has never yet felt, having shirked it on to the North.

+2. *intr.* To shift *for* one's self. *Obs.*
1843 MATHEWS *Writings* 71/1 As for Harvest, let him shirk for himself. **1849** KINGSLEY *Diary* 76, I can shirk for myself pretty well. **1853** *Harper's Mag.* Oct. 708/2 He determined, as he expressed it, to 'leave the old homestead, and shirk for himself.' **1874** *Vermont Bd. Agric. Rep.* II. 422 They are then turned into the pasture to shirk for themselves.

+Shir(r), *n.* [Origin unknown.] **1.** (See quotations.) **2.** (See quot. 1891); also, a band of fabric gathered on both sides. Also *attrib.* — **(1)** **1858** SIMMONDS *Dict. Trade Products* 341/2 Shirr, an insertion of elastic cord between two pieces of cloth. **1876** KNIGHT 2157/1 *Shirr,* . . . an elastic cord inserted in cloth or between two pieces. **(2)** **1891** *Cent.* 5578/2 *Shirr, shir,* . . . a puckering or fulling produced in a fabric by means of parallel gathering-threads. **1894** S. GARDNER *Quaker Idyls* i, The stiff bonnets were relieved by silk shirrs of brown or gray. **1902** *Delineator* Dec. 623 A shirr-string, run through an underfacing, provides the means of closing.

+Shir(r), *v.¹* To make shirrs or gathers in (a garment or fabric). — **1891** *Cent.* 5578/2 *Shirr.* **1896** *Godey's Lady's Bk.* Feb. 223/2 Pretty shades may be made by simply taking a piece of crêpe paper . . . and shirring it several times, leaving sufficient at the top to form a full ruffle.

+Shir(r), *v.²* *tr.* (See quot. 1909.) — **1891** *Cent.* 5578/2. **1909** WEBSTER 1944/1 *Shirr,* . . . to break (eggs) into a dish with cream or crumbs and bake in the oven or cook in hot water on the fire.

+Shirred, *a.*
1. (See quotations.) {1882}
1847 WEBSTER 1023 *Shirred,* . . . a term applied to articles having lines or cords inserted between two pieces of cloth, as the lines of India rubber in shirred suspenders. **1876** KNIGHT 2157/1 *Shirred Goods,* . . . goods with elastic cords (*shirrs*) interwoven in suspenders, garters, etc.

2. Gathered; ornamented with gathered trimmings.
1860 S. WARNER *Say & Seal* lxxii, A simple plain shirred spring bonnet of blue and white silk. **1891** EARLE *Sabbath* 91 The good wives' heads bore . . . 'shirred lustring hoods.' **1900** *19th Cent.* XLVIII. 791 A perfectly-fitting gown . . . [with] ruffles and finely-shirred lace. **1907** WIGGIN *Old Peabody Pew* 114 Dark-haired Nancy under the shadow of her shirred hat.

+Shirred eggs. Eggs poached or baked in cream, crumbs, etc. {1892} Cf. SHIR(R) *v.²* — **1883** SALA *Amer. Revisited* I. 302 That woman's shirred eggs and sugar-cured ham should immortalise her.

✶ Shirt, *n.*
✶1. A garment of cotton, linen, or other material, for the upper part of the body, worn either with or without a coat; +a hunting shirt (q.v.).
See also BILED *a.* 2, BOILED *ppl. a.* 3, RUFFLED SHIRT.
1640 *Conn. Rec.* I. 449 An Inventory of the goods . . . of James Olmestead [includes] . . . 3 shirts. **1687** SEWALL *Diary* I. 191 A Boy of about 5 years old is burnt to death by his Shirt catching fire. **1721** *Ib.* III. 288 You are directed to take up a Blanket and Shirt for him. **1805** LEWIS in *L. & Clark Exped.* II. (1904) 378 The shirt of the men is really a commodious and decent garment. **1854** *S. Lit. Messenger* XX. 122/1 [He] was habited in his red flannel shirt. *a*1861 WINTHROP *J. Brent* 38 One chapter might be written on his fringed buckskin shirt. **1894** *Harper's Mag.* Jan. 267/1 He wore a coat of nankeen open over his collarless shirt. **1907** FREEMAN *By Light of Soul* 425 When a man had to have all his shirts and dickeys made he was helpless.

2. In phrases.
See also BLOODY *a.* 3 c.
+a. *To keep one's shirt on,* to keep calm or unexcited. *colloq.*

1854 HARRIS in *Spirit of Times* (N.Y.) 447/3, I say, you durned ash cats, just keep yer shirts on, will ye? **1861** *Chicago Tribune* 26 May 1/4 'Keep your shirt on, Mr. Wilkins,' was his elegant remark. **1920** SANDBURG *Smoke & Steel* 62, I can keep my shirt on.

+b. *To wave the shirt,* to wave the bloody shirt (q.v.).
1888 *San Francisco News Letter* 4 Feb., The machine had nominated Blaine and connubiated with Tammany and waved the shirt.

3. *Attrib.* and *comb.* with *factory, maker,* etc.
1855 M. THOMPSON *Doesticks* 40, [I] sold my trunk to buy a set of gold shirt-studs. **1863** *Horticulturist* Jan., Advt. 14 James Parrish, Shirt Manufacturer. **1880** *Harper's Mag.* June 29/2 The shirt-makers can do their work at home. **1886** J. A. PORTER *New Stand. Guide of Washington* 160 Branch Baltimore Shirt Factory. . . . Shirts Made to Order.

Shirt, *v.* {1601–} **1.** *intr.* To put a shirt on. ‖**2.** *tr.* To tear a shirt off (a person). — **(1)** **1754** in *N.H. Hist. Soc. Coll.* I. 279 The deponent sold the said Indians two shirts, and happened to see them when they shirted. **1755** *Essex Inst. Coll.* LII. 81 Dined alone on asparagus, shaved, shirted, &c. **1854** *Harper's Mag.* May 851/2 Then you could shirt and shave In old Kentucky. **(2)** **1834** CARRUTHERS *Kentuckian* I. 61, I call [it] a pretty tolerable neat job, to shirt a stranger the first night he comes to town.

+Shirt bosom. The front of a shirt. { =E. 'shirt front'} — **1852** *Harper's Mag.* Sept. 537/1 John placed it in the button-hole of the shirt-bosom. **1890** HOWELLS *Boy's Town* 141 The rest . . . would let you smooth them, or put them inside your shirt-bosom, or anything. **1911** *N.Y. Ev. Post* 2 Feb. 6 Annoying, is it not, to sit in your chair and have your shirt bosom rise up out of your waistcoat?

Shirt button. **+a.** A shirt stud. **b.** A button to be sewed on a shirt. {1851–} — **1678** *New Castle Court Rec.* 352, 3 Payer of shirt Buttons. **1715** *Mass. H. S. Coll.* 6 Ser. V. 312, I send you . . . some sets of shirt buttons. **1742** *Md. Hist. Mag.* XX. 178 Three or four Papers good shirt Buttons but not made on Wire. **1857** *Quinland* I. 120 Here is everything you want, . . . jack-knives, shirt-buttons, thread [etc.]. **1861** *Vanity Fair* 23 Feb. 85/1 He was seated with his face on his shirt buttons, and his feet on the fender.

+Shirtee. A false shirt front. — **1806** *Mass. Spy* 30 July (Th.). **1818** *Lancaster* (Pa.) *Jrnl.* 5 Aug. (Th.), A shirt, if you can afford it. But if you can't, then a shirtee, with pretty broad ruffles.

Shirting. A cotton or linen cloth suitable for shirts. {1604–} Also *attrib.* — **1675** *Conn. Rec.* II. 397 Procure, if possible, some shoes, shirting and other goods necessary for the soldiery. **1711** *Boston News-Letter* 22 Oct. 2/2 To be Sold by Mr. William Payne, Merchant, . . . Sundry sorts of Shirting Holland. **1729** *Md. Hist. Mag.* XVIII. 335, 40 Ells of Good Shirting Linnen. **1812** *Niles' Reg.* II. 408/2 Thirty dollars for the best piece of hempen or flaxen shirting [given to] Mrs. Margaret Knode. **1922** *Sears, Roebuck & Co. Cat.* No. 145, 414/2 An economical Shirting made of stout yarns . . . will wear a long time.

+Shirtman. A rifleman in the Revolutionary armies: (see quot. 1788). *colloq.* — **1775** *Penna. Gazette* 16 Aug. 2/3 The damn'd shirtmen, as they are emphatically called by some of his [the loyal governor's] minions. **1776** *Penna. Ev. Post* 30 July 376/1 The enemy's lookouts . . . cried out 'The shirtmen are coming.' **1788** W. GORDON *Hist. Independence U.S.A.* II. 112 Colonel Woodford had not more than 300 shirtmen (as they call the riflemen, on account of their being dressed in their hunting shirts).

✶ Shirt-sleeve. *attrib.* **+a.** Designating actions or occurrences in which men appear in their shirt sleeves. Also fig. **+b.** Designating persons who work in their shirt sleeves. Also fig. — **1855** M. THOMPSON *Doesticks* 320 The prompter would . . . suddenly disappear, until some fresh delinquency called for another shirt-sleeve advent. **1857** WILLIS *Convalescent* 296 Pray bring home with you . . . that New Orleans fashion of *shirt-sleeve promenade!* **1864** SALA in *Daily Telegraph* 27 Sept., The people are going to elect shirt-sleeve aldermen that work all day. **1908** *Pall Mall Gaz.* 20 April 2/2 The Congressmen have a preference for what they picturesquely describe as 'Shirt-sleeve Ambassadors'—men who they think will labour for their country's interests and scorn social fascinations.

+Shirt-sleeved, *a.* Appearing in shirt sleeves without a coat. {1889} — **1869** LOWELL *Poetical Works* (1896) 415/1 In this brown-fisted rough, this shirt-sleeved Cid, . . . My lungs draw braver air. **1883** 'MARK TWAIN' *Life on Miss.* xxxviii, The shirt-sleeved passengers cleansed themselves at a long row of stationary bowls in the barber shop.

Shirt tail. The end of a man's shirt; +a nightshirt; *to make a shirt tail,* to run in one's nightshirt. Also *attrib.* — **1845** HOOPER *Simon Suggs' Adv.* 13 From the time he was a 'shirt-tail boy,' [his wits] were always too sharp for his father's. **1846** W. G. STEWART *Altowan* I. 174 [He] made a shirt-tail across the prairie on the other side. **1855** WILLIS *Convalescent* 35 The event of the past month, to my children, has been a shirt-tail chase and capture of a 'possum. **1856** DERBY *Phoenixiana* 128 The San Diego Light Infantry in full uniform, consisting of Brown's little boy in his shirt-tail, fired a National salute with a large bunch of fire crackers. **1905** *Dialect Notes* III. 94 *Shirt-tail parade,* a nocturnal parade of students wearing night-shirts over their clothes to celebrate an athletic victory.

+Shirt waist. A woman's or boy's waist somewhat resembling a man's shirt. Also *attrib.* — **1887** PERRY *Flock of Girls* 30 The child was a small slender creature for a long time, . . . [with] simple unfurbeloved shirt-waist frocks. **1892** *Courier-Journal* 2 Oct. 1/3 Ladies' Fall Style. Shirt Waist at 75¢. **1902** [see FLOWER GARDEN]. **1904** *N.Y. Times* 11 May

5 Boys' shirt waists and blouses. **1911** BURGESS *Find the Woman* 108 Bessie was dancing with President Roosevelt at a shirtwaist ball!

+**Shitepoke**, *n.*⁴ [Origin unknown.] The green heron. (Cf. POKE *n.*⁴) — **1832** WILLIAMSON *Hist. Maine* I. 145 The Skouk . . . is vulgarly called a 'shite-poke.' **1844** [see POKE *n.*⁴ 1]. **1859** BARTLETT 402 *Shitepoke*, (*Butorides virescens*,) a widely distributed bird of the heron species, also called Green Heron and Fly-up-a-Creek.

Shittim wood. {1611–} +**1.** A southern sapotaceous tree, *Bumelia lanuginosa*. +**2.** =BEAR-BERRY 2. +**3.** The silver-bell tree, *Halesia carolina*. — (1) **1884** SARGENT *Rep. Forests* 102 *Bumelia lanuginosa*. . . . Gum Elastic. Shittim Wood. . . . Wood heavy, soft, weak. **1905** *Forestry Bureau Bul.* No. 66, 33 The mesquite, wild china, and shittimwood . . . reach up into the State [Kan.] from the south. (2) **1884** SARGENT *Rep. Forests* 41 *Rhamnus Purshiana*. . . . Bearberry. Bear Wood. Shittim Wood. . . . The bark . . . possesses powerful cathartic properties. (3) **1894** *Amer. Folk-Lore* VII. 94 *Halesia tetraptera*, shittimwood, West Va.

+**Shivaree**, *n.* [Corruption of CHARIVARI *n.*] A noisy demonstration, esp. as a serenade for a newly wedded couple; a racket, a confused noise. Also attrib. (Cf. SHERRIVARRIE *n.*) — **1843** 'CARLTON' *New Purchase* II. 231 The musicians . . . [let] off at each repetition of the demand peals of shiver-ree. **1850** A. T. JACKSON *Forty-Niner* (1920) 23 The boys . . . gathered and gave the couple a shivaree. **1875** 'MARK TWAIN' *Old Times* iii. 55, I started such a rattling 'shivaree' down below as never had astounded an engineer in this world before. **1911** QUICK *Yellowstone Nights* 211 The boys outside with their shivaree instruments ready . . . sang in unison.

+**Shivaree**, *v. tr.* To annoy or serenade (a person) with a shivaree. — **1872** EGGLESTON *End of World* 294 And among the manly recreations which they have proposed to themselves is that of shivereeing 'that Dutchman, Gus Wehle.' **1879** CABLE *Old Creole Days* 132 Why don't you shivaree him? **1910** *Guide* July 139/1 A crowd . . . started out to 'shivaree' (mob and din to madness) the dreaded old man.

***Shoal**, *n.*¹ A place, often in a river, where the water is shallow; a sand bar. Often in proper names.

1612 SMITH, etc. *Virginia* I. 50 The shoules [of the river] force the Channell . . . neere the land. **1688** SEWALL *Diary* I. 237 We go away East-South-East and the like, hoping to shape clear of Nantucket Shoals. **1719** *Amer. Wkly. Mercury* 29 Dec. 2/1 The Exchange Brigantine of this place . . . [was] drove on the Sholes between Cape Look Out and Cape Hatteras. **1778** HUTCHINS *Va., Penna., Md., & N.C.* 24 Navigation [of Kentucky Creek] is interrupted by shoals. **1802** ELLICOTT *Journal* 8 Our people were much fatigued by dragging our boats over the shoals. **1817** S. BROWN *Western Gazetteer* 239 The Muscle Shoals are about 100 miles south of Nashville. **1874** COLLINS *Kentucky* I. 17 [He] pitches camp above the mouth of Bear Grass creek, retiring of a night to a shoal above Corn Island. **1900** MUNN *Uncle Terry* 295 Both her husband an' son went down in a coaster one winter's night, on Monhegan Shoals.

+**b.** *Shoal mark*, a marker that indicates shoal water.

1875 'MARK TWAIN' *Old Times* iv. 77 [He] then began to work her warily into the next system of shoal marks.

***Shoal**, *n.*² A large number of fish. — **1648** *Mass. H. S. Coll.* 4 Ser. I. 202 Allewifes with their crowding sholes, in every creek do swim. **1771** WASHINGTON *Diaries* II. 16 The Herring began to run in large Shoals. **1814** [see BLACK DRUM]. **1871** *Scribner's Mo.* I. 283 An unprecedentedly large shoal of mackerel were running in.

Shoal, *v.* {1610–} *intr.* 'To lounge about lazily' (B.). — **1842** MATHEWS *Puffer Hopkins* 111 You shuffled up to the counter as if you were shoaling through the market, according to your well-known habits, stealing pigs' feet . . . to make broth of.

+**Shoal duck.** (See quot. 1891.) — **1807** *Mass. H. S. Coll.* 2 Ser. III. 54 The birds, which frequent this and the adjacent islands, are . . . the wild goose; the brant; the shoal duck [etc.]. **1844** *Nat. Hist. N.Y., Zoology* II. 333 The Eider Duck . . . is known on Long Island under the names of *Black* and *White Coot*, *Big Sea Duck*, and *Shoal Duck*. **1891** *Cent.* 5580/1 *Shoal-duck*, . . . the American eider-duck, more fully called *Isles of Shoals duck*, from a locality off Portsmouth in New Hampshire.

***Shoal-water.** *attrib.* +Designating aquatic birds and fish found frequently in shallow water. — **1874** LONG *Wild-Fowl* 136 The seeds . . . are the favorite food of mallard and other shoal-water ducks. **1884** GOODE, etc. *Fisheries* I. 201 [Cod] which live near the shores, but which are less closely limited to the reefs, . . . are called 'Shoal-water Cod,' 'Shore Cod,' 'Inshore Cod' [etc.]. *Ib.* 488 At Grand Haven there are two forms of Mackinaw Trout, known as the 'Shoal-water Trout' and the 'Deep-water Trout.'

+**Shoal(-water) cod.** (See quot. 1884.) — **1839** STORER *Mass. Fishes* 120 Several varieties . . . are known by the names of 'Rock Cod,' 'Shoal Cod,' &c. **1884** GOODE, etc. *Fisheries* I. 201 Another class of names appears to apply to those fish which live near the shores. . . . These are called 'Shoal-water Cod.'

***Shoat.** (See SHOTE.)

***Shock**, *n.* +A number of matured stalks of Indian corn cut and brought together in an upright position. — **1863** NORTON *Army Lett.* 174 He came out . . . like a mouse from a shock of corn. **1879** *Scribner's Mo.* Oct. 827/1 It did not take long to select a convenient 'shock' for a 'blind,' or ambush. **1920** *3d Nat. Country Life Conf. Proc.* 156 You will notice the cornfield and shocks of corn standing sentry.

***Shock**, *v.* +*tr.* To place (corn, corn tops, etc.) in compact shocks. — **1755** HEMPSTEAD *Diary* 657, I rid down to the Cornfield & helpt to shock up some Corn Topps that was cut yesterday. **1779** *Narragansett Hist.*

Reg. I. 94 Shocked corn storks. Caught a woodchuck. **1868** *Iowa State Agric. Soc. Rep. 1867* 210, I protect my vines in Winter by shocking corn-fodder around them. **1907** [see FODDER *n.* 1 b 2].

+**Shock corn.** Indian corn stored in shocks. — **1865** *Ill. Agric. Soc. Trans.* V. 27 So long as the present system of . . . placing shock-corn on the ground . . . shall prevail. **1868** *Iowa State Agric. Soc. Rep. 1867* 124 In fattening steers, I feed shock-corn twice a day. *Ib.* 126 Generally feed shock-corn . . . as long as to be had.

Shocker. One who places grain in shocks as it is cut or reaped. {1827–} — **1786** WASHINGTON *Diaries* III. 91 For every two Cradlers to allow 4 rakes, 1 shocker, and two Carriers. **1880** *Harper's Mag.* March 534/1 An army of 'shockers' follow the reapers, setting up the bundles to ripen before threshing. **1895** *Voice* 28 Nov. 7/4 [He] rapidly tumbles his wheat sheaves . . . into convenient bunches for the one lone shocker to set up and cap.

Shoddy, *n.* A fabric made, at least in part, of reclaimed wool {1847–}; woolen yarn obtained from refuse woolen rags {1832–}; inferior cloth. Also comb. — **1861** *Chicago Tribune* 26 May 1/3 Blouses made of shoddy, with pants, [cost] $10. **1869** *Boyd's Business Directory* 13 Mitchell & Bailey, shoddy manufrs. **1880** *Harper's Mag.* Feb. 356/1 The 'coats of sleazy cloth, and waistcoats of indifferent flannel,' of which Washington complained, may well stand as an early definition of modern 'shoddy.' **1892** *Courier-Journal* 1 Oct. 3/1 American woolen goods contained only forty-five parts of pure wool to fifty-five parts of cotton, shoddy and other adulterants.

Shoddy, *a.* {1882–} +Of a person: Pretentious by virtue of ill-gotten wealth, etc., but inferior in moral worth, character, breeding, etc. Also *shoddydom, shoddyite*.

'In the U.S. the word seems to have been first used with reference to those who made fortunes by army contracts at the time of the Civil War, it being alleged that the clothing supplied by the contractors consisted largely of shoddy.' (*O.E.D.*)

1862 *Congress. Globe* 7 July 3164/1 The anxiety of the 'shoddy' politicians to assail that address. **1863** *Boston Sun. Herald* 15 Feb. 2/3 There are shoddy lawyers, shoddy doctors, shoddy preachers, and shoddy teachers, . . . and, worse than all, there are shoddy newspapers whose especial business it is to puff up all the shoddy in the world and endeavor to make the people believe that it is the genuine article. **1870** M. H. SMITH *20 Years Wall St.* 199 A marble palace was to be erected on that site that would make all Shoddydom red with envy. **1873** BAILEY *Life in Danbury* 289 A New York shoddy lady is proud to boast that her daughter is at 'a fashionable boarding school.' **1882** McCABE *New York* 226 The acquaintance of some wealthy shoddy family is formed. **1883** *Harper's Mag.* Nov. 820/2 Unfortunately no part of the world . . . is absolutely free from the shoddyite, the cockney, and the snob.

Shoddy aristocracy. =SHODDYOCRACY. *Obs.* — **1865** *Daily Telegraph* (London) 4 Dec. 5/6 A few of the codfish, shoddy, and petroleum aristocracy. **1870** W. F. RAE *Westward by Rail* 57 [I have] seen notorious members of the 'Petroleum' and 'Shoddy' aristocracy of the United States excite the amazement of Frenchmen and Germans by their lavish expenditure.

+**Shoddyize**, *v.* (See quotation.) — **1871** DE VERE 299 A verb, even —to *shoddyize*—has been made to supply an apparent demand.

+**Shoddy(o)cracy.** (See quot. 1902.) — **1863** NORTON *Army Lett.* 169 Shoddycracy is pretty large in New York, . . . the hideous offspring of the monster war. **1865** *Newton Kansan* 9 Jan. 4/3 You have only mixed among the shoddy-ocracy of Fifth Avenue, but you have seen nothing of the genuine Knickerbocker society. **1902** CLAPIN 359 *Shoddyocracy*, people who have become rich by making contracts for shoddy goods, or in any other disreputable way.

***Shoe.**

1. The customary outer covering, usually of leather, worn on the human foot. {Usu.=E. 'boot'}

See also BOOT-AND-SHOE, FRENCH FALL SHOES, etc., and cf. BOOT¹ 1, BROGAN 1, etc.

1629 *Mass. Bay Rec.* I. 35, 8 dussen pair neats leathr shewes. **1692** in Burr *Witchcraft Cases* (1914) 156 [She] first threw her Muff at her; but that flying not home, she got off her Shoe, and hit Goodwife C. **1704** S. KNIGHT *Journal* 43 A tall country fellow . . . gave a scrape with his shovel like shoo, leaving a small shovel full of dirt on the floor. **1895** M. A. Jackson *Gen. Jackson* 571 Many . . . were without shoes and the entire command without provisions. **1909** RICE *Mr. Opp* 14 He was . . . mentally engaged in drilling oil-wells, composing poetry, and selling shoes.

+**b.** *Blast my old shoes*, an expression used for emphasis. *colloq.*

1835 LONGSTREET *Ga. Scenes* 6, I'll see you a fair fight, blast my old shoes if I don't!

2. *attrib.* and *comb.* **a.** Designating tools and materials used by shoemakers.

See also SHOE FINDINGS.

1742 *Md. Hist. Mag.* XX. 267 Send me one Dozen of Mens shoe Lasts Large and different sizes. c**1766** *York Co., Va., Rec.: Wills* XXI, [In a back room:] 1 Shoe Jack, 1 grain bin [etc.]. **1768** Shoe tack [see SHOE KNIFE]. **1820** *Columbian Centinel* 29 Jan. 3/6 Valuable Sale of . . . warranted Shoe Pincers. **1827** DRAKE & MANSFIELD *Cincinnati* 60 In the third story the manufacture of *shoe trees* is carried on. **1851** CIST *Cincinnati* 179 E. G. Webster & Co. . . . [use] English kids, drillings, and shoe-duck. **1876** KNIGHT 2164/1 *Shoe-shave,* . . . an implement on the principle of the spoke-shave, for trimming the soles of boots and shoes.

b. Designating places where shoes are made or finished. See also SHOE FACTORY, STORE.

1781 *Va. State P.* I. 449 Anderson's time as conductor of the shoe-manufactory had expired but he is willing to engage again. **1848** in Commons, etc. *Doc. Hist.* VIII. 200 Young women working in a book-bindery, shoe-bindery, milliner's shop, or any such.

c. Designating persons who bind, make, or sell shoes. See also SHOEMAKER, SHOE MAN.

1809 *Longworth's N.Y. Directory* 227 Shoebinder. **1844** *Lowell Offering* IV. 146 [Some] shoe-peddlers . . . came in, and made very strenuous exertions to attract our attention. **1897** BRODHEAD *Bound in Shallows* 246 Dillon talked with a shoe drummer in the hotel office. **1902** HARBEN *A. Daniel* 53 Percy Lee, Hamilton's shoe-clerk, hit back at that Savannah girl.

+**d.** In special combinations.

Shoe department, in a store, the department in which shoes are sold; *s. finder,* a person dealing in the tools and appliances used by shoemakers; *s. line,* a commercial supply or stock of shoes; *s. parlor,* =SHOE-SHINING PARLOR; *s. pocket,* (see quotation); *s. stand,* a location for a shoe store.

1887 *Courier-Journal* 2 Feb. 6/7 He will be assigned to the shoe department. **1909** *Boston Transcript* 19 July 14/5 The National Leather and Shoe Finders' Association. **1837** *S. Lit. Messenger* III. 618 Nothing in the 'shoe line' was mentioned. **1906** *Washington Post* 29 April 9 The improvised shoe parlor was in All Souls' Unitarian Church. **1876** KNIGHT 2162/2 *Shoe-pocket,* . . . a small leather pocket attached to a saddle for the purpose of carrying one or more extra horseshoes. **1887** *Courier-Journal* 6 Feb. 3/6 For Sale—A Good Shoe Stand—Stock and fixtures. . . . Schlesinger's Shoe Store.

+**Shoe bench.** A shoemaker's bench. — **1841** *Knickerb.* XVII. 362 A few weeks' rumination on the shoe-bench, or cogitation on the tailor's board, is sufficient to perfect either. **1891** *Harper's Mag.* June 57/1 An express wagon was . . . loaded with the old shoe bench.

Shoe binding. {1835–} Strips or strings of leather, ribbon, etc., used to strengthen or ornament the edges or seams of shoes. — **1759** *Newport Mercury* 5 June 4/1 To be Sold, . . . Womens and Mens Hose, Quality Binding, Shoe Ditto, black Silk Ferret [etc.]. **1761** *Essex Inst. Coll.* XLVIII. 95 The Assortments [include] . . . shoe bindings, qualities. **1777** *Warren-Adams Lett.* I. 359 The Mussel I should be very glad of, . . . and shoe binding, if it is to be had.

Shoeblack. One whose occupation is cleaning and polishing shoes and boots. {1778–} — **1772** J. ADAMS *Diary* Works II. 306 A porter, a shoeblack, or chimney sweeper, would be ashamed of the coarse, low, vulgar dialect of this sea officer. **1816** WEEMS *Letters* III. 156 What can I ever make to defray carriages, . . . shoe blacks, Barbers &c. &c. **1842** *Amer. Pioneer* I. 75 Our host . . . [had] to officiate in all the various departments appertaining to a hotel, from the landlord down to the shoe-black. **1877** *Harper's Mag.* Dec. 46/2 During the day their patronage comes from newsboys and shoe-blacks.

Shoe blacking. Blacking used on boots and shoes. {1902–} — **1837** *Yale Lit. Mag.* II. 81 So we pass on. Match-boxes, shoe-blacking, sugar-whistles, brass jews-harps. **1844** *Lexington Observer* 25 Sept. 2/5 A part of the stock is embraced in . . . Preserve and Pickling jars of all sizes, Superior Shoe Blacking, etc. etc. **1881** *Rep. Indian Affairs* 395.

Shoe boot. ?A boot of superior elegance; a dress boot. Also attrib. — **1789** *State Gazette of N.C.* (New Bern) 19 March, He carried off with him . . . a pair of shoe-boots. **1818** ROYALL *Lett. from Ala.* 106 [He] swore vengeance against every shoe-boot gentleman in the Bluff. **1845** HOOPER *Simon Suggs' Adv.* 23 If he was only to see one o' them fine gentlemen in Augusty, with his . . . shoe-boots a-shinin' like Silver.

Shoe box. 1. A box in which shoes are kept. **2.** A large, strong box in which shoes are shipped. **3.** A box of pasteboard in which a pair of shoes is usually sold. {1897–} — **(1) 1869** ALCOTT *Little Women* II. 355 Demi's shoe-box was a miracle of mechanical skill, though the cover wouldn't shut. **(2) 1866** *Harper's Mag.* Oct. 680/1 The General . . . sent to the Quarter-Master for an empty shoe-box. **1891** *Harper's Mag.* June 56/1 The great Lynn teams, piled high with clean wooden shoe boxes, came and went along the highways. **1902** MCFAUL *Ike Glidden* 236 Ansel stood on a shoe box and called the caucus to order. **(3) 1901** ADE *40 Modern Fables* 224 Farmers . . . come out of the Union Station carrying . . . Shoe Boxes full of Lunch. **1906** PRINGLE *Rice Planter* 305, I found him . . . still grasping the coverless shoe box with which he had appeared at the station.

***Shoe buckle.** A buckle used on the front of a shoe, as a fastening or ornament. — **1697** *Conn. Rec.* I. 563, I give unto my Brother Thomas his Eldest son Stephen my Shoo buckells. **1711** *Springfield Rec.* II. 42 Eleven pair of Shoe Buckles. **1791** *Ann. 1st Congress* 2130 [A duty] shall be laid on . . . shoe and knee buckles. **1850** *Rep. Comm. Patents 1849* 545 Shoe-buckles were another article in great vogue. **1889** *Century Mag.* April 826/2 [They] were dressed . . . with waistcoats and breeches and white gaiters, or spatterdashes, . . . covering the shoe-buckle.

+**Shoe-buttoner.** A small metal contrivance having a semicircular bend or hook at one end used for fastening button shoes. — **1881** RITTENHOUSE *Maud* 34, I'll bet my prettiest shoe-buttoner that Alice and Fred are engaged. **1905** 'O. HENRY' *Roads of Destiny* 138 Old Urique keeps anywhere from $50,000 to $100,000 . . . in a little safe that you could open with a shoe buttoner.

+**Shoe-deep,** *a.* Of snow: Deep enough to cover the shoes of one walking through it. Also *half shoe deep* a. — **1773** FITHIAN *Journal* I. 75 Last night there fell a Snow, which is about half Shoe-deep. **1783** *Huntington Rec.* III. 102 Saturday Night about 11 O Clock, . . . snow about shoe deep. **1891** WILKINS *New Eng. Nun* 174 There had been a light fall of snow the day before, but it was not shoe-deep.

Shoe factory. A factory in which shoes are made. — [**1835** J. MARTIN *Descr. Virginia* 143 There are 29 dwelling houses, 3 mercantile stores, . . . and 2 boot and shoe factories.] **1855** HOLBROOK *Among Mail Bags* 276, How many persons are employed in that shoe factory? **1887** *Courier-Journal* 3 May 1/4 A very extensive and disastrous lock-out has been inaugurated in the shoe-factories to-day. **1889** BRAYLEY *Boston Fire Dept.* 333 A fire on the 23d, in the buildings . . . occupied as a shoe-factory, caused . . . damage. **1915** CAMPBELL *Proving Virginia* 221 Still more [money] was in a large shoe factory.

+**Shoe findings.** *pl.* Supplies, materials (except leather), and tools for shoemakers. (Cf. FINDINGS.) — **1836** in Commons, etc. *Doc. Hist.* VI. 37, 20 dollars . . . it must cost him [the journeyman cordwainer] for shoe-findings, tools and implements. **1892** *York County Hist. Rev.* 26 H. B. Beard, Wholesale and Retail Dealer in Harness and Saddlery, Shoe Findings, &c.

Shoe knife. A knife having a sharp fixed blade, used by a shoemaker. {1859–} — **1768** in H. M. Brooks *Gleanings* IV. 38 Pen-knives, scissars, shears, shoe-knives, shoe tacks [etc.]. **1815** *Niles' Reg.* IX. 94/2 Shoe knives, stirrups and bridle bitts. **1887** *Courier-Journal* 8 May 5/1 A shoemaker . . . committed suicide . . . by cutting his throat from ear to ear with a small shoe-knife.

***Shoe leather.** *That ever trod* (or *wore*) *shoe leather,* that ever lived. *colloq.* — **1835** LONGSTREET *Ga. Scenes* 21, [I'm] jist a *leetle* of the best man, at a horse swap, that ever trod shoe-leather. **1851** *Polly Peablossom* 83 You are the most presumptuous people, you Methodists, that ever trod shoe leather. **1902** NORRIS *Pit* 341, I don't take that kind of talk from the best man that ever wore shoe-leather.

***Shoemake.** [From SUMAC(H).] An American tree or species of tree of the genus *Rhus,* esp. *R. glabra;* also, the bark or the root of such a tree.

1588 HARRIOT *Briefe Rep. Va.* B4 There is Shoemake well knowen. **1629** *Mass. Bay Rec.* I. 384, [I] wishe alsoe yt there be some sassaffras . . . sent vs, as a(lsoe good st)ore of shoomacke. **1634** WOOD *New Eng. Prospect* (1865) 18 The Diars Shumach, with more trees there be. **1799** *Herald of Freedom* (Edenton, N.C.) 27 March, 1408 acres . . . beginning at a pine stump in the center of a persimmon, sweet gum and shoemake. **1804–6** CLARK in *Lewis & C. Exped.* VI. (1905) 141 Shoemate commences. **1857** *N. Amer. Rev.* July 181 The gudewife no longer points to her 'shoe-make' (as the sumach-tree was formerly called). **1892** *Amer. Folk-Lore* V. 94 *Rhus glabra,* shoe-make. Ohio and Ill.

attrib. **1733** *S.C. Gazette* 24 March, Two Ounces of Shoemack Root.

***Shoemaker.** One whose occupation is making shoes.

1623 *Plymouth Laws* 28 [No] taylors shoemakers carpenters [etc.] . . . shall use their science or trades . . . for any strangers or foreigners till such time as the nescessity of the colony be served. **1698** *Mass. Province Acts* II. 313 No person . . . [using] the mystery or faculty of a shoemaker or cordwainer, shall [etc.]. **1793** *Mass. H. S. Coll.* 1 Ser. II. 7 There is a proportionable number of cabinet-makers, carpenters, smiths, and shoe-makers. **1840** *Knickerb.* XVI. 209 Near the only window was placed the work-bench and entire paraphernalia of the shoe-maker. **1904** [see HAT 2 d].

b. In appositive use.

1679 *Boston Rec.* 126 Warrant [shall] be given to a Constable to leauie by distresse vpon ye estate of Alexandr Calman shoomaker . . . for openinge of a shop in ye towne. **1684** *Ib.* 60 Andrew Marriner, shoomaker, . . . [entertained] at Geo. Cables. **1707** *Boston News-Letter* 6 Jan. 4/2 Samuel Neale of this Town Shoe-maker . . . departed this Life.

c. In or as the name of fishes.

1884 GOODE, etc. *Fisheries* I. 326 The Thread-fish—*Blepharis crinitus.* This fish, also known as the 'Shoemaker-fish,' is found along our coast from Cape Cod to the Caribbean Sea, as also on the Pacific coast of tropical America. *Ib.* 332 *Elagatis pinnulatus* . . . , known at Key West as 'Skipjack' or 'Runner,' and at Pensacola as 'Yellow-tail' or 'Shoemaker,' is, according to Stearns, 'abundant on the western and southern coasts of Florida.' **1903** T. H. BEAN *Fishes N.Y.* 104 *Catostomus nigricans.* . . . Hog Sucker; Stone Roller. . . . The name, shoemaker, was formerly applied to this species in Lake Erie, perhaps on account of the resemblance of its color to that of shoemaker's pitch.

+**Shoemaker loo.** (See quot. 1904.) — **1813** in Kittredge *Old Farmer* (1904) 95 Tom Teazer, well known at the grog shops for a dabster at shoemaker loo, . . . and all the village moon-cursers came in for their portion of the wreck. **1833** NEAL *Down-Easters* I. 71 Do you play checkers? . . . or shoe-make-loo [*sic*]? **1872** [see LOO 1]. **1904** KITTREDGE *Old Farmer* 96 'Shoemaker loo' was a round game at cards.

Shoemaker's shop. A shop in which shoes are made and repaired. — **1794** BENTLEY *Diary* II. 93 Mr. Collins . . . kept always in his Shoemaker's shop, articles for sale to Seamen. **1831** PECK *Guide* 289 St. Clair county has . . . two hatter's shops, three shoemaker's shops, five cabinet maker's shops. **1861** *Vanity Fair* 11 May 225/1 On the door-post of a shoe maker's shop in the Bowery, the following announcement is to be seen.

Shoemaking. The making of shoes. {1611–} Also attrib. — **1781** *Va. State P.* I. 449 W. Armstead giving to the Executive a statement of the shoe-making business under Mr. Mathew Anderson. **1864** [see BLACK-

SMITHING]. **1892** *York County Hist. Rev.* 62 This gentleman . . . has spent some years at shoemaking.

Shoe man. {1841-} One who makes or sells shoes. — **1862** *Independent* 27 March 4/4 The shoe-man says: 'Such a tax will simply break up the business.' **1887** *Courier Journal* 8 May 9 The Clothiers calumniate us for certain specified reasons; the Shoe Men villify [*sic*] us for others. **1899** HOWELLS *Ragged Lady* 59 The shoeman . . . [turned] with a pair of high-heeled bronze slippers in his hand.

+Shoepack. [SHOE and Lenape *paku*, a kind of shoe.] A shoe resembling a moccasin. (Cf. PAC, PACK.) — **1755** *Lett. to Washington* I. 99 It would be a good thing to have Shoe-packs or Moccosons for the Scouts. **1824** DODDRIDGE *Notes* 129 The gentlemen dressed in shoepacks, mocassons, leather breeches, . . . all home-made. **1897** ALLEN *Choir Invisible* 26 The small, sensitive feet, . . . covered with coarse shoe-packs tied with leather thongs. **1920** LEWIS *Main Street* 82 All over town small boys were squealing . . . 'Look at my shoe-packs!'

+Shoe peg.

1. A small wooden peg used to fasten shoe soles to the uppers or to each other.

1854 LIPPINCOTT *Haps & Mishaps* 13 The Yankee having whittled a large lot of unsaleable shoe-pegs into melon seeds. **1860** HOLMES *E. Venner* iii, Manufactures [of Pigwacket Centre], shoe-pegs, clothes-pins, and tin-ware. **1883** *Century Mag.* Sept. 789/2 One of the girls places a handful of large shoe-pegs on the desk of each of the youngest children.

2. A variety of Indian corn, or the grains of such corn, somewhat resembling the pegs used in shoemaking. Also attrib.

1873 *Kan. State Bd. Agric. Rep. 1872* 275 The Shoepeg variety . . . yields well and matures in midsummer. **1878** HARTE *Drift from Two Shores* 141 The honest Connecticut farmer was quietly gathering from his threshing-floor the shoe-pegs.

+Shoe-pegging machine. A machine which pegs shoes. — **1883** [see NAIL MACHINE]. **1883** KNIGHT 806/1 *Shoe Pegging Machine*, a machine which takes the pegs in the strip, feeds and cuts them, and pegs on the sole. **1894** HOWELLS in *Harper's Mag.* June 44/1 Somehow that shoe-pegging machine must come in.

+Shoe-shining parlor. A place where shoes are shined or blacked. Also *shoe-shine parlor.* — **1898** *Kansas City Star* 21 Dec. 1/4 Mrs. Edna Maxwell . . . ran a shoe shining parlor on West Ninth street. **1911** FAIRCHILD *Greek Immigration to U.S.* 127 In 1904 there were but three shoe-shine parlors in the hands of Greeks in the city. *Ib.* 173 These shoe-shining parlors are small store rooms.

Shoe shop. A shop where shoes are made or repaired. {1824-} — **1837** MARTINEAU *Society* II. 249 These are the 'shoe shops,' where the father of the family and his boys work. **1851** *Knickerb.* XXXVIII. 185 [He] was at the time working in his shoe-shop. **1883** FULTON *Sam Hobart* 41 The man . . . of the spindle, of the shoe-shop, and of the carpenter's bench, comes into association with the noblest, the most enterprising of the land. **1903** 'O. HENRY' *Roads of Destiny* 161 A guard came to the prison shoe-shop, where Jimmy Valentine was assiduously stitching uppers.

+Shoe store. A place where shoes, boots, and related merchandise are sold. — **1789** *Boston Directory* 175 Bond and Bryant, shoe-store. **1813** *Boston Selectmen* 84 He should occupy the room in the old Town house adjoining his shoe store. **1860** MORDECAI *Virginia* 221 His house . . . was bought and demolished by Mr. Hubbard, to make room for his extensive shoe-store. **1903** 'O. HENRY' *Roads of Destiny* 166 There wasn't an exclusive shoe-store in the place.

Shoestring. {1616-1755}

+1. A variety of tobacco. *Obs.*

1784 SMYTH *Tour* II. 129 There are seven different kinds of tobacco, . . . named Hudson, Frederick, Thick-joint, Shoe-string [etc.].

+2. A small amount of money; a small margin of capital. *colloq.[2]* Also *transf.*

1882 *Century Mag.* April 884/2 [He] could draw to a shoe-string, as the saying went, and obtain a tan-yard! **1904** *Cosmopolitan* May 89 He speculated 'on a shoe-string.'

+3. In phrases.

To tie one's shoestrings, to be prepared and on the alert; *to walk on one's shoestrings*, to be quite destitute.

1854 THOREAU *Walden* 85 Rescue the drowning and tie your shoe-strings. **1888** *St. Louis Globe Dem.* 16 Feb. (F.), I was literally walking on my shoe strings.

+4. *attrib.* Designating narrow, stringlike objects.

1897 *Pop. Science Mo.* L. 309 Bad roads and shoestring paths . . . fringe them. **1902** NORRIS *Pit* 337 His shoestring tie straggled over his frayed shirt front.

+Shoestring District. The Sixth Congressional District in Mississippi, as laid out in 1874, in a long, narrow shape, in order to exclude a large Negro population. (Cf. DUMB-BELL DISTRICT, GERRYMANDER *n.* 1 b.) — **1878** *Congress. Rec.* App. 13 June 478/2, I will promise to meet him on the northern border of 'the shoe-string district.' **1882** *Ib.* 13 Feb. 1105/1 The Shoe-string district in Mississippi . . . is child's play to the skillful carving of our Pennsylvania artists in fraud. *Ib.* 29 April 3442/1 What is known as the 'Shoestring district' . . . is about four or five hundred miles long, as I am informed, and about forty to fifty miles wide on an average.

+Shoe town. A town in which shoemaking is the principal industry. — **1883** in Wells *Practical Economics* 106 The best educated factory population in New England is that found in your 'shoe-towns.' **1896** *Internat. Typogr. Union Proc.* 25/1 Brockton, Mass., is another well organized shoetown.

+Shoe track. A track made by shoes, as distinguished from one left by moccasins or bare feet. — **1725** *Lancaster Rec.* 239 This day Capt Blancher saw some shoe tracks. **1758** *Va. State P.* I. 255 He saw a Shew track among them, which caused them to believe it to be had been white men. **1808** PIKE *Sources Miss.* 47 Finding some to be shoe-tracks, he conceived it to be the establishment of some traders. **1848** BRYANT *California* xvii. 223, I saw a plain and fresh shoe-track.

+Shook, *n.* [f. SHOOK *a.*]

1. A set of staves, boards, headings, etc., sufficient for a hogshead, barrel, or box, packed in a compact bundle for transport. {1860-}

1819 *Mass. Stat.* 19 June, For shooks and empty barrels, four cents. **1842** *Amer. Pioneer* I. 138 [He] threw overboard all the puncheon shooks and about fifty barrels of flour. **1886** PHELPS *Burglars* 10 What are shooks, Miss Corona? **1897** *Congress. Rec.* App. 31 March 12/2 Any ordinary person of fair ability can look into a car loaded with box shooks and easily determine about how many thousand feet of lumber it contains.

+2. (See quotation.) *Obs.*

1860 GREELEY *Overland Journey* 162 'Shooks,' or split saplings of cotton-wood, . . . incline gently to the transverse or longer sides.

3. *Attrib.* and *comb.* with *covered, machinery,* etc.

1860 GREELEY *Overland Journey* 162 The unchinked, barely shook-covered houses . . . are decidedly the cooler and airier. **1869** *Boyd's Business Directory* 19 Barrel, Shook and Stave Machinery. Holmes E. & B. **1888** *Amer. Almanac* 275 Occupations of the People of the United States. . . . Stave, shook and heading makers.

Shook, *a.* {1695-} +Reduced to shooks (sense 1). — **1768** *Mass. Gazette* 9 June (Th.), A few large shook hogsheads. **1794** MORSE *Amer. Geog.* (ed. 2) 206 Exported from the United States . . . Wood Staves and Heading, Shingles, Shook Casks.

Shook, *v. tr.* To reduce (a cask) to shooks: (see also quot. 1841). *Obs.* — c**1800** Gravestone epitaph in *Harper's Mag.* XXII. 283/2 Now food for worms, Like an old rum-puncheon, marked, numbered, and shooked. **1841** WEBSTER II. 593/2 *Shook*, to pack staves in casks. **1849** COOPER *Sea Lions* xxiii, [By] shooking the casks, room might be made aboard . . . for all my [seal]skins.

＊Shoot, *n.*

1. =CHUTE *n.* 1. {1613-}

For figurative phrases in this sense, see 7a and 7b.

1805 ORDWAY in *Jrnls. of Lewis & O.* 232 The falls continue all that distance in 5 different Shoots. **1843** *Amer. Pioneer* II. 271 A boatman who could not boast that he had never swung nor backed in a shoot, was regarded with contempt. **1900** WAYLAND *Hist. of Rockingham Co.* 419 My grandmother took me to the High Rock to see the boats come through the shoot.

b. (See quotation.)

1891 *Cent.* 5584 *Shoot*, . . . an artificial contraction of the channel of a stream in order to increase the depth of water.

+2. A smooth, precipitous way down which logs or cotton bales are allowed to slide. (Cf. CHUTE *n.* 2, 3.)

1848 BARTLETT 300 *Shoot*, or *Shute*, a passage-way on the side of a steep hill or mountain down which wood and timber are thrown or slid. **1858** *Harper's Mag.* Dec. 12/1 The other [compartment contains] a smooth-floored slide, or 'shoot,' by which the cotton is delivered. **1863** HOPLEY *Life in South* II. 333 On many of the Southern rivers there are wooden landings, with . . . 'shoots,' or long wooden slides for the cotton to be passed down the banks to the boat. **1876** CROFUTT *Trans-continental Tourist* 122 The logs are slid down the mountain sides in 'shoots.'

+3. A narrow passageway through which cattle or sheep are driven. (Cf. CHUTE *n.* 5.)

1868 *Ill. Agric. Soc. Trans.* VI. 319 Each railroad has one thousand feet of platform . . . provided with 'shoots,' leading directly into the yards and pens. **1880** *Harper's Mag.* Jan. 203/1 There were . . . three corrals connected by 'shoots,' or narrow passages. *Ib.* 205/1 Then they saw the sheep run through the shoot to be counted.

+4. *Baseball.* A pitched ball that curves or shoots away from a direct line. (Cf. OUTSHOOT 1.)

1885 CHADWICK *Art of Pitching* 14 Pitchers frequently have full command of one kind of a 'curve' or 'shoot' of a ball. **1886** — *Art of Batting* 34 What batsmen require . . . is to practice against . . . the various 'shoots.'

5. A shooting match. {1892-}

1897 *Boston Jrnl.* 6 Sept. 4/4 (Ernst), The annual state shoot of our militia . . . takes place today. **1908** *Outlook* 29 Aug. 280/1 Plenty of my friends . . . shoot on a big scale, moving from 'shoot' to 'shoot.'

+6. (See quotation.)

1905 *Forestry Bureau Bul.* No. 61, 22 A shoot is a sprout which has not reached a height of 3 feet.

+7. In various colloq. phrases. **a.** *To take the shoot*, to set forth boldly; to enter upon an indicated course of action.

1837 BIRD *Nick* II. 15 Then for rifle-butt, knife, and hatchet! . . . Take the shoot with full pieces, and let the skirmudgeons have it handsome! **1843** 'CARLTON' *New Purchase* II. 105 Pushed by the two on land [the horse] took the 'shoote;'—in this case a plunge . . . into water a little over nine feet deep! **1878** BEADLE *Western Wilds* 183 The new meetin' folks . . . took the abolition shoot. **1883** HAY *Bread-Winners* 252, I had to take the other shoot—he hadn't the sand to help.

‖**b.** *To take a shoot after*, to take a liking to.
1847 ROBB *Squatter Life* 143 That gal . . . wur about the pootyest creatur . . . I ever took a *shute* arter.

+**c.** *To be on the shoot*, to be ready to shoot, to be on the warpath. Also *to be on the cut and shoot*.
1873 MILLER *Amongst Modocs* 308 No one cared, so long as he fought with men who 'came from the shoulder,' or were on the 'cut and shoot.' **1880** *Harper's Mag.* July 193/1 Them tramps . . . knew we was on the shoot. **1890** *Century Mag.* Feb. 524/1 Some folks called him the 'Taos Terror' . . . , for he was on the shoot every time.

+**d.** *To come on a straight shoot*, to proceed in a direct, forthright manner.
1904 W. H. SMITH *Promoters* 72 You can't come at things on a straight shoot any more.

✳ **Shoot,** *v.*
I. +**1.** *intr.* Of Indian corn: To put out young ears.
1775 in Rauck *Boonesborough* 179 Corn planted 26 or 27 of April was tasseled or shot. **1851** *Polly Peablossom* 20 It was as vivifying as a shower of rain on corn that is about to shoot and tassel.

+**2.** *tr.* To blast (an oil or gas well) with dynamite or nitroglycerin in an effort to start or increase its flow.
1888 *Scribner's Mag.* May 576/1 [Explosives] are used in the petroleum industry to 'shoot' the wells, so as to remove the paraffine which prevents the flow of oil. **1897** *Kissimmee* (Fla.) *Valley Gazette* 1 Dec. 1/8 Sixty quarts of nitroglycerine had been hauled here for the purpose of shooting a gas well.

+**3.** To give up or quit. *slang.*
1883 HAY *Bread-Winners* 249 If I had all the cash he takes in to-night, I'd buy an island and shoot the machine business.

+**4.** *Baseball.* To throw (a ball) swiftly.
1912 E. V. COOKE *Baseballogy* 17 Shoot the ball to second. **1912** MATHEWSON *Pitching* 273 Flaherty would shoot the ball over to first as before.

II. In phrases.
To shoot craps, see the noun.
+**5.** *To shoot one's grandmother*, (see quot. 1859.)
1855 HALIBURTON *Nature & Hum. Nature* II. 297 You showed her she had shot her grandmother. *Ib.* (note), Shooting one's granny, or grandmother, means fancying you have discovered what was well known before. **1859** BARTLETT 402 *To Shoot one's Grandmother*, is a common though vulgar phrase in New England, and means, to be mistaken, or to be disappointed; to imagine oneself the discoverer of something in which he is deceived. The common phrase is, 'You've shot your granny.'

+**6.** *Shoot that hat!* or variant: (see quots. 1877, 1903.) *slang.* (Cf. sense 3.)
1876 *Ed. Burton's Songs* (B.), The slang the gang is using now, You'll hear from every lip; It's shoot the hat! and get it boiled; And don't you lose your grip. a**1877** *Danbury News* (B.), Oh, shoot the school. **1877** BARTLETT 585 To say, 'Shoot that dress,' is meant to convey the idea that the dress is inferior. **1903** FARMER & HENLEY VI. 188/1 *Shoot that (hat, man*—anything)! . . . a mild imprecation, 'Bother!'

+**7.** *To shoot off one's mouth*, to talk freely, with little regard for propriety, facts, or effects. *slang.*
1880 *Cimarron News & Press* 8 April 1/5 Nobby, you've . . . never yit shot off yer mouth on the marryin' biz. **1890** LANGFORD *Vigilante Days* I. 295 There you go, shooting off your mouth to me the first thing.

+**8.** *W.* To shoot (a person) *up*, to shoot or to shoot at (a person) in a lawless, reckless manner. *slang.*
1890 *Stock Grower & Farmer* 21 June 3/1 Three cowboys shot each other up. **1901** WHITE *Westerners* 31 If you try to shoot us up any, we'll kill every hoof you have. **1912** WASON *Friar Tuck* 198 A cattle man is never satisfied unless he has grabbed what he wanted away from someone else, an' then shot him up a little for kickin' about it.

b. *To shoot up* (a place), to rush or ride through (a place) shooting wildly or recklessly in all directions.
1890 *Stock Grower & Farmer* 18 Jan. 5/2 This so enraged the boys that they began shooting up the town. **1903** 'O. HENRY' *Roads of Destiny* 102 Liquor must be partaken of, the suburbs shot up. **1913** BARNES *Western Grazing Grounds* 27 Herders were killed, camps raided or 'shot up.'

+**9.** *To shoot the chutes*, to slide or go down a precipitous incline in a specially made type of toboggan or boat.
1895 *N.Y. Dramatic News* 30 Nov. 17/4 Shooting the Chutes, the latest craze that has struck the town, is . . . drawing large crowds. **1896** *Ib.* 11 July 10/2 Last week the delightful occupation known as shooting the chutes was shown in full swing.

+**10.** *To shoot a jam*, (see quotation).

1905 *Forestry Bureau Bul.* No. 61, 46 *Shoot a jam, to*, to loosen a log jam with dynamite.

+**11.** *To shoot it out*, to fight with firearms to a decision. *colloq.*
1912 RAINE *Brand Blotters* 327 Had he shown any sign of indecision, they would have taken a chance and shot it out.

✳ **Shooting.**
+**1.** *As sure as shooting*, certain or certainly. *colloq.*
1853 'P. PAXTON' *Yankee in Texas* 116 [To a southerner] drawing his comparison from his idolized rifle, a thing is '*as sure as shooting*.' **1876** HABLERTON *Jericho Road* 60 It'll be Lem's gain, sure as shootin'. **1907** *St. Nicholas* May 604/1 'If you did want to leave Hammond you could?' . . . 'Sure as shooting!' **1924** CROY *R.F.D. No. 3* 149 You're going to have trouble as sure as shootin'.

2. In special combinations.
Shooting affair, s. affray, a fight between individuals using firearms, esp. pistols; *s. bee*, =SHOOTING MATCH; *s. club*, an organization composed of those interested in shooting; *s. distance*, the distance at which shooting can be effective; *s. gun*, a gun that shoots, as distinguished from a toy; *s. place*, a place where shooting to improve marksmanship is done; *s. pouch*, a receptacle in which a hunter carries his powder, shot, etc.; *s. stand*, a place where those engaged in a shooting match stand; *s. tackle*, the equipment used by those who shoot; *s. team*, a number of marksmen who compete with others in shooting; *s. traps*, shooting tackle.
1871 *Republican Rev.* 13 May 1/2 Two shooting affairs took place at Elizabethtown on Wednesday last. **1879** *Cimarron News & Press* 27 Nov. 3/2 A shooting affray occurred in Otero in which Harry Bassett, the livery stable keeper, was killed. **1890** *Harper's Mag.* Dec. 160/1 Progressive shooting bees . . . had been held. **1893** *Post Harvard Stories* 16 The shooting-club team . . . was to shoot a clay-pigeon match against Yale before the game. **1845** *Big Bear Ark.* 27 A green-horn friend of mine . . . reached shooting distance before me. **1871** *Harper's Mag.* Oct. 691/2, I do want to see a real shooting-gun. **1651** *New Haven Rec.* 91, 7 acres of land . . . left for a shooting place for ye Trayne band. **1835** HOFFMAN *Winter in West* II. 72 The highly ornamented shooting-pouch [of the Indians] . . . must make no contemptible appearance. **1823** COOPER *Pioneers* xvii, The distance between the stump and shooting-stand was one hundred measured yards. **1871** *Knickerb.* XXIX. 429 A variety of shooting-tackle arranged in no very great order. **1893** *Post Harvard Stories* 13 Hudson was on the shooting-team. **1845** *Big Bear Ark.* 43 The fellows got together their shooting traps.

+**Shooting cracker.** A firecracker. *Obs.* — **1867** *Amer. Philos. Soc. Proc.* X. 344 There was also a loud report, described as resembling the noise of a large shooting-cracker. **1890** HOWELLS *Boy's Town* 110 The boys began to celebrate [Christmas] . . . with shooting-crackers and torpedoes.

Shooting ground. A place where shooting is done, either in hunting or at target practice. {1859-} — a**1835** in Audubon *Ornith. Biog.* IV. 5 Carroll's Island . . . has long been known as a great shooting ground. **1874** LONG *Wild-Fowl* 129 The place [was] a hotel near the shooting-grounds. **1897** *Outing* March 536/2 A shooting friend . . . and myself were staying at a farmhouse, near the shooting-grounds.

+**Shooting iron.** A firearm. {1891-} — **1787** TYLER *Contrast* III. i, He was afraid of some of them 'ere shooting irons. **1832** J. HALL *Legends of West* 260 This is a poor shooting-iron. **1881** HAYES *New Colorado* 117 What kind of shooting-iron have you? . . . Navy Colt? **1923** J. H. COOK *On Old Frontier* 26 Nobody in Texas had a better shooting iron than I.

Shooting match. A contest in marksmanship. — **1750** *Penna. Assembly Acts* (1762) II. 33 Horse-races, Shooting-matches, or other idle Sports. **1791** *Wheeleys Baptist Ch. Min.* Aug. (Univ. N.C. MS.), A Quary whether is it lawful for members to put in at Shuting matches and Shute for whatever is Set up answer'd No. **1813** *Niles' Reg.* IV. 35/1 Frequently [I] gained their applause for my activity at our shooting matches. **1881** *Ore. State Jrnl.* 1 Jan. 5/1 The seventh match . . . will take place at Albany next Monday. a**1918** G. STUART *On Frontier* I. 187 Jacobs and Gwin had a shooting match for one and two dollars a shot.

+**Shooting scrape.** An outbreak in which shooting occurs. *colloq.* — **1875** *Chicago Tribune* 22 July 8/1 A Legal Shooting Scrape. A Deputy Sheriff Who Couldn't Aim Straight. **1881** *Cimarron News & Press* 17 Feb. 3/2 Sheriff Wallace . . . does not propose that his term of office shall be so productive of shooting scrapes as were some of his predecessors.

✳ **Shooting star.** +Any of various plants of the genus *Dodecatheon*, esp. the American cowslip, *D. meadia.* — **1857** GRAY *Botany* 272 D[odecatheon] *Meadia.* . . . Very handsome in cultivation. In the West called Shooting-Star. **1871** *Amer. Naturalist* V. 215 A nearer view shows these flowers to be those of the shooting-star. **1882** *Century Mag.* Sept. 772/1 In early June there blooms a unique flower called the shooting star, shaped like a shuttle-cock. **1915** ARMSTRONG & THORNBER *Western Wild Flowers* 364.

Shooting stick. {1683-} +A gun. *Obs.* — **1858** *S. Lit. Messenger* XXVI. 468/2 No man in his senses would voluntarily go out with 'shooting-sticks to fire at his own money.' **1866** 'F. KIRKLAND' *Bk. Anecdotes* 237/2 Sambo . . . fell back in confusion when the 'shooting stick' was brandished toward his own breast.

+**Shootist.** One who shoots {1899}, +esp. a desperado or 'bad man.' — **1871** DE VERE 657 The man whose rifle brought down the largest amount of game became known as a famous shootist. **1873** BEADLE *Un-*

devel. West 371 He is reputed 'so quick on trigger,' that all other 'shootists' in the country have an awe of him. **1876** MILLER *First Fam'lies* 105 Experienced shootists, old hands at mortal combat with their kind, glanced from man to man. **1898** CANFIELD *Maid of Frontier* 177 He was knowed to be a shootist and there weren't nobody hankerin' for the job of bringin' him in.

*** Shop.**

***1.** A building in which various articles are made or repaired and, in some instances, sold.

'Gradually *store* supplanted *shop*, until now in ordinary American use *store* means any place of some size where things are sold, and *shop* commonly means a smaller place where things are done or made. Thus one would speak of a *shoe store*, where shoes are sold, but of a *shoe shop*, where shoes are mended. . . . The distinctions are not always clearly maintained, however' (1925 Krapp *Eng. Lang. in Amer.* I. 131–2). Quot. 1635 may belong to sense 2.

1635 *Essex Inst. Coll.* IV. 90/1 Divers speaches about convenient places for shops. **1647** *Watertown Rec.* I. I. 22 Setting vp a shop for a Smithes forge. **1701** [see CASK *n.* 1]. **1749** *N.H. Probate Rec.* III. 684, I give and bequeth to my beloved son . . . my Barn and shop with all my black smiths tools. **1800** [see HABIT-MAKER]. **1849** *Penn. R. R. Ann. Rep.* 49 For Warehouses, Shops, Locomotives, [etc.] . . . $1,990,000. **1892** *Congress. Rec.* 1 April 2843/1 The American producer, whether on the farm or in the shop, can knock the hind sights off the producer anywhere else. **1908** 'O. HENRY' *Strictly Business* 250 James left the hat-cleaning shop.

***2.** A building or room in which goods are sold.

1647 *Suffolk Deeds* I. 88 Such Commodities as the sd Tho: or his Executor shall choose at any shopp in Boston at money prices. **1724** [see JALAP 2]. **1787** TYLER *Contrast* v. ii, Why, I have been about to twenty shops, turning over pretty things. **1865** *Atlantic Mo.* Feb. 192/1 Thirty editions were sold in shops or hawked about by peddlars. **1892** *Vt. Agric. Rep.* XII. 130 Each town has a small village . . . where the churches, post-office, store, and various shops are located. **1907** ANDREWS *Recoll.* 194 [There was] not a single shop doing business.

+3. *To give the best one has in the shop*, to put forth one's best or maximum effort. *colloq.*

1873 *Newton Kansan* 20 Feb. 3/4 If they [Indians] opposed them they would give them the 'best they had in the shop.'

4. In special combinations.

Shop bell, a bell that rings in a shop when the door is opened; *s. building*, a building in which shop work is carried on; *s. chairman*, a union workman in a shop, selected to represent the union in adjusting differences with the employers; *s. clerk*, one employed as a clerk in a shop; *s. lady*, a woman or girl who works in a shop; *s. lot*, a lot upon which a shop is located; *s. room*, a room or a particular portion of space available for a shop or for shop work; *s. talk*, talk pertaining to a profession or occupation; *s.-tender*, one who tends a shop; *s. weight*, a weight used in weighing in a shop; *s. work*, work done in a shop; *shopworn*, worn or soiled by having been kept in a shop; *s. yard*, a yard adjoining a shop.

1851 HAWTHORNE *House of Seven Gables* 93 We will tie up the shop-bell for good and all! **1906** *Indian Laws & Tr.* III. 247 Shop building, four thousand dollars. [**1923** BLANCHARD *Outline of Brit. Labor Movement* 75 In America the shop chairmen of such industries as the men's clothing industry have more power and recognition than was ever accorded to the shop stewards of England.] **1911** HARRISON *Queed* 151 There is your public, . . . shop-clerks, stenographers [etc.]. **1908** 'O. HENRY' *Options* 43 The shop-lady did not retreat a hair's-breadth. **1816** PICKERING 127 *Lot.* . . . Hence, a house-lot, shop-lot, &c. **1898** *Kansas City Star* 18 Dec. 4/1 The bill contains . . . [items] for the erection of additional shop room, $2,000. **1881** *Scribner's Mo.* XXII. 864/2 Annoyed by the continual shop-talk of three passengers opposite, I . . . left my seat. **1845** *Lowell Offering* V. 282 There are hundreds of young men in Lowell, as shop-tenders, etc. **1780** *Va. State P.* I. 372 The Leads of our Windows & Shop Weights are already gone. **1883** *Rep. Indian Affairs* 162 We have carried forward our shop-work much on the same plan as last year. **1869** BARNUM *Struggles* 40 A large quantity of tin ware which had been in the shop for years . . . was considerably 'shop-worn.' **1656** *Suffolk Deeds* II. 239 To hold ye said dwelling house & Lean too therevnto adjoyning with ye shop yard, orchard & garden therevnto belonging.

Shopgirl. A girl employed in a shop where goods are sold. — **1768** FRENEAU *Poems* (1795) 12 No more the shop-girl could his talk endure. **1824** IRVING *Tales Traveller* I. 331 A hint to all haberdashers who have pretty daughters for shop-girls, and young students for customers. **1870** *Scribner's Mo.* I. 128 Old women . . . and shop-girls stop their chattering . . . to fill their reticules. **1890** CUSTER *Following Guidon* 257 The shop-girl is often a superior order of being even with experienced shoppers. **1912** NICHOLSON *Hoosier Chron.* 475 Mrs. Owen . . . was inveigling shop-girls to her farm and then putting them to work in her kitchen.

***Shopkeeper.** One who keeps a shop. — **1655** *Suffolk Deeds* II. 169 A difference on Accompts was dependeing betwixt Mr. Michell Rayner of London vintner . . . & Edward Burt of Charles towne shop keeper. **1740** *Ga. Hist. Soc. Coll.* II. 79 Shopkeepers, tradesmen, and artificers, . . . live very well on their business here, and many more might. **1807** *Mass. H. S. Coll.* 2 Ser. III. 28 The shop-keepers procure their goods from Boston and New York. **1876** GARFIELD in *Congress. Rec.* 4 Aug. 5184/1 [The Democrats] made you believe . . . that we were a community of shopkeepers, or sordid money-getters. **1925** *Scribner's Mag.* Oct. 408/2 A New York shopkeeper . . . courageously came to the aid of a neighbor who was being robbed.

***Shopman.** One who serves in a shop. {1758–} — **1844** EMERSON *Experience* Ess. 2 Ser., The chagrins which the bad heart gives off as bubbles, at once take form as ladies and gentlemen in the street, shopmen or barkeepers in hotels [etc.]. **1850** S. WARNER *Wide, Wide World* iii, Mrs. Montgomery was desiring the shopman to show her various kinds and sizes [of Bibles]. **1907** *St. Nicholas* June 736/2 The shopman said they were a dollar a pair! **1918** SANDBURG *Cornhuskers* 141 Cowpunchers, cornhuskers, shopmen, ready in khaki.

+Shopnote. A note or bill of credit exchangeable for goods in a shop. *Obs.* — **1739** W. DOUGLASS *Discourse Currencies* 23 Many factors . . . send Home a high Account of Sales, by the Shopkeepers giving a great Advance in Consideration of a very long Credit, and to be drawn out in Shop Notes. **1770** *Md. Hist. Mag.* III. 245 We have . . . stated an Account to shew at one View, what Part of each Shop-Note is for the Articles prohibited. *Ib.* XII. 368 The following will Answer the Shop note you wrote for—July 4: 1770 Bought for Cha: Carroll Esqr. By Mr. Harding of Dennis Dougherty.

Shopping. {1764–} *attrib.*

1. Designating localities frequented by shoppers.

1882 MCCABE *New York* 135 In 1830 . . . the portion between Chambers and Canal streets was the fashionable shopping quarter. **1893** *Harper's Mag.* April 652/2 [In Brooklyn] are several tenement districts and three considerable shopping centres. **1905** 'O. HENRY' *Four Million* 180 He hung about the shopping districts.

2. *Shopping bag*, a bag used by shoppers for carrying purchases; *s. store*, a store having a variety of goods that appeal to shoppers.

1893 *Harper's Mag.* April 659/2 [In Brooklyn] is a long double row of shopping stores, many of which . . . compare favorably with the best and largest of the department stores of New York. **1907** 'O. HENRY' *Strictly Business* 215 The girl laid on the table a worn red morocco shopping bag.

Shop sugar. ? Sugar procured in shops, as distinguished from that made at home. *Obs.* — **1687** SEWALL *Letter-Book* I. 74 If the mony hold outt send a barrel or two of shopp sugar and 3 or 4 sugar loves. **1714** *Boston News-Letter* 18 Jan. 2/2 To be Sold by Mr. Thomas Cushing at his Shop; . . . Shop Sugar by the Barrel or quarter of a Hundred.

*** Shore.** *attrib.* In special combinations.

Shore country, country bordering on the seashore; *s. dory*, a dory for use near shore; *s. duty*, duty on shore, as distinguished from duty at sea; *s. folks*, those who live ashore, as distinguished from seafarers; *s. hold*, (see quotation); *s. leave*, leave of absence given a sailor to spend time on shore; *s. pine*, (see quotation); *s. privilege*, privilege or permission to do something on a shore; *s. salt*, salt obtained on a shore; *s. seine*, a seine used near shore; *s. state*, a state bordering on the seashore; *s. suit*, a suit worn by a sailor when on shore; *s. town*, a town on the seashore; *s. trawl*, (see quotation); *s. use*, use on shore.

1843 *Knickerb.* XXI. 38 One of those arms with which the sea interlocks all the shore-country of Carolina. **1884** *Nat. Museum Bul.* No. 27, 698 *Shore Dory.* . . . The boats . . . are used by the shore fishermen of New England. **1880** *Lib. Universal Knowl.* XI. 408 Pay-masters . . . on shore-duty are employed in the naval purchasing agencies. **1889** JEWETT *Betty Leicester* 8 You wouldn't know us now from shorefolks. **1905** *Forestry Bureau. Bul.* No. 61, 46 *Shore hold*, the attachment of the hawser of a raft of logs to an object on the shore. (N[orth] W[oods], L[ake] S[tates Forest].) **1888** DORSEY *Midshipman Bob* 205 They set about making the most of their shore-leave. **1894** *Amer. Folk-Lore* VII. 100 *Pinus Banksiana*, . . . shore-pine, rock-pine, Grand Lake section of Penobscot River. **1856** *Huntington Rec.* III. 431 The President of Trustees . . . [is] empowered to commence suit against Samuell P. Hartt for back lease rent of shore privilege at Northport. **1779** *N.J. Archives* 2 Ser. IV. 22 For Sale, . . . a few bushels of good shore salts. **1884** GOODE, etc. *Fisheries* I. 289 It seems . . . absurd that the Massachusetts people should have supposed that the use of shore-seines was exterminating the Mackerel on the coast of Massachusetts. **1871** *Harper's Mag.* July 188 It is a shameful omission on the part of the people of the shore States, as well as those of the interior, that [etc.]. **1885** HOWELLS *Silas Lapham* 415 A young fellow in the shabby shore-suit of a sailor . . . got up from where he had been sitting. **1816** *Mass. H. S. Coll.* 2 Ser. VII. 115 Professed butchers . . . are constant in their attendance at the markets of Boston, Plymouth, Duxbury, and intermediate shore towns. **1884** *Nat. Museum Bul.* No. 27, 916 *Shore trawl.* . . . Used in near-shore fishing for cod, hake, and haddock. **1835** INGRAHAM *South-West* II. 11 Their religion was laid by for shore use.

Shore bird. Any one of various shore-inhabiting birds, chiefly of the suborder Charadrii. {1672–} — **1874** COUES *Birds N.W.* 448 The *Limicolæ*, or Shore Birds . . . , comprehend all kinds of Plover, Snipe, Woodcock, and birds collectively known as 'Bay Snipe,' as well as Phalaropes, Avocets, Stilts, Turnstones, and Oyster-catchers. **1882** *Century Mag.* Oct. 830/1 They all . . . dined on shore-birds shot on Saturday afternoon. **1883** *Ib.* Sept. 653/1 Among the most common birds [on Cape Cod] are . . . the shore birds. **1917** *Birds of Amer.* I. 255 The Plovers comprise the family *Charadriidæ* of the order of Shore Birds.

+Shore bug. Any insect of the family Saldidae. — **1895** COMSTOCK *Man. Study Insects* 134 Some of the Shore-bugs dig burrows, and live for a part of the time beneath the ground. **1904** KELLOGG *Amer. Insects* 202 By the edge of pond or stream may be found . . . the smaller, soft, long-oval, long-legged, running shore-bugs.

+**Shore dinner.** A dinner featuring various sea foods. — **1895** *Outing* XXVI. 408/2 Happy-Go-Lucky Beach is proud of their achievements . . . in the ordering of and presiding at a good shore-dinner. **1903** *Boston Transcript* 3 Oct. 4 The repast was a typical Rhode Island shore dinner.

Shore lark. =HORNED LARK. {1893} — [**1771** J. R. FORSTER *Flora Amer. Septent.* 12 Shore Lark. *Alauda alpestris.*] **1808** WILSON *Ornithology* I. 85 [The] Shore Lark . . . is one of our winter birds of passage. **1869** BURROUGHS in *Atlantic Mo.* May 583/2 A flock of birds . . . proved to be shore-larks, the first I had ever seen. **1893** *Scribner's Mag.* June 760/2 The artificial destruction of forest, and extension of the open country toward the Atlantic, have resulted in the eastward spread of many prairie birds, such as the shorelark and the bobolink.

Shore line. {1852–} attrib. +Designating a road or railroad along a shore. — **1862** *Rep. Comm. Patents 1861: Agric.* 344 The shore-line road from Boston to New York crosses a large number of these marshes in the State of Connecticut. **1872** *Travelers' Official Ry. Guide* Jan. Table 69, New Haven, New London and Stonington Railroad. Operated by New York and New Haven Railroad, as Shore Line Division.

Shoreman. {1643–} One who remains on shore but is engaged in, or connected with, the fishery business. {1761–} — **1670** *Essex Inst. Coll.* XLII. 45 The shoremen of this Towne that make or dry fish vpon our fish Iland haue liberty to Cutt flake stuffe vpon our Comons. **1710** *Ib.* 250 What fish was not utterly spoiled . . . was Carryed ashore & dryed by shoremen. **1800** *Mass. H. S. Coll.* 1 Ser. VII. 248 The shoremen and the women then wash and spread them [the fish] on the flakes.

+**Shoresman.** =prec. — **1872** TALMAGE *Sermons* 56 Some plain shoresman in rough fishing smack . . . brings them ashore in safety. **1883** GOODE *Fisheries Industries U.S.* 22 To the class of 'shoresmen' belong (1) the capitalists who furnish supplies and apparatus for the use of the active fishermen; (2) the shopkeepers from whom they purchase provisions and clothing; and (3) the skilled labourers who manufacture for them articles of apparel [etc.]. **1884** *Nat. Museum Bul.* No. 27, 839 *Halibut flitching knife.* . . . Used by shores-men to cut off flitches or strips of halibut for smoking and fins for pickling.

* **Short,** *n.*

1. *pl.* The bran and coarser parts of meal. {1765–}
1742 *Md. Hist. Mag.* XX. 166, I desire you will send the Bran Shorts & Middleings. *c*1790 COXE *View U.S.* 62 The produce, manufactures, and exports of Pennsylvania . . . [include] bran, shorts, ship-bread. **1850** *Rep. Comm. Patents 1849: Agric.* 102 These cows are fed with shorts or chip-stuff. **1924** CROY *R.F.D. No. 3* 2 [An automobile] carried out to the farm . . . harness, shorts, bran, stock feed.

2. *pl.* (See quotation.) {*c*1790–}
1795 WINTERBOTHAM *Hist. View* III. 440 Hemp . . . which breaks in the operation is called *shorts,* and is about half the value of long hemp.

+**3. a.** A broker who sells for future delivery securities or commodities which he does not have at the time of the sale. {1913–}
1849 G. G. FOSTER *N.Y. in Slices* 19 Some wild-looking 'short' . . . rushes down and hysterically inquires of his obliging neighbor, Mr. Smith, whether he hasn't a few hundred over. **1870** MEDBERY *Men Wall St.* 134 When the market is over sold, the shorts, if compelled to deliver, find themselves in a 'corner.' **1896** SHINN *Story of Mine* 190 Naturally the 'shorts' had their innings. **1904** 'O. HENRY' *Four Million* 213 He dashed into the inner office with the haste of a short trying to cover.

+**b.** *pl.* Short sales; the supply needed to meet short-sale contracts.
Freq. in phrase to cover shorts.
1870 [see SHORT *a.* 2]. **1881** *Harper's Mag.* April 734/2 'Spots,' 'futures,' 'longs,' and 'shorts' were unknown terms. **1902** NORRIS *Pit* 345, I'm going to buy in my July shorts.

+**4.** =SHORTSTOP 2.
1858 *Brooklyn Daily Times* 18 June (E. J. Nichols). **1870** *N.Y. Herald* 7 June 7/4 A change was made in placing their available men also, James Snyder going to short. **1887** *Courier-Journal* 26 May 2/6 Mc-Kean's work at short cost Cleveland the first game with the Baltimores to-day. **1897** *Outing* May 203/1 Chandler at short is being very hard pushed.

5. 'Whatever is deficient in number, quantity, or the like' (*Cent.*). {1886}
1886 *Rep. Secy. Treasury* I. 100 In counting the remittances of banknotes received for redemption during the year, there was found . . . $8,246 in 'shorts,' being amounts less than the amounts claimed. **1887** *Scientific Amer.* LVII. 194/3 [This coin package is] practically a self-counter, in which there can be no dangers of 'shorts' or 'overs.'

* **Short,** *a.*

1. *Short off* (or *out*) *for,* having an insufficient quantity of. *colloq.*
1779 PARKMAN *Diary* 110, I am so short out for good Hay that I send one horse to Mr Eben[eze]r Maynard . . . to be kept. **1822** DEWEES *Lett. from Texas* 25 We are rather short off for the milk just now.

+**2.** Having an insufficient amount of securities or commodities to meet obligations; pertaining to a transaction in 'shorts.'

1865 *Harper's Mag.* April 616/2 If he has sold 500 Hudson for future delivery, expecting it to fall, he is pronounced 'short of Hudson.' **1870** M. H. SMITH *20 Years Wall St.* 66 Men who are short—that is, men who sell what they have not got,—watch the selling to find the time when they can cover their shorts. **1875** A. DALY *Big Bonanza* (1884) 20 The market opened lively with a demand for speculative shares by those who have been 'short' of the leading stocks. **1885** *Harper's Mag.* Nov. 842/1 He 'buys in' by purchasing stock to meet a 'short' contract.

* **3.** In combination with adjectives in -*ed.*
See also SHORT-BILLED CURLEW, SHORT-BILLED (MARSH)WREN, etc.
a. In the names of plants.
See also SHORT-LEAVED PINE.
[**1802** DRAYTON *S. Carolina* 125 They are called *Guinea rice, bearded rice,* a *short grained rice,* somewhat like barley, and a species of *high land rice.*] **1813** MUHLENBERG *Cat. Plants* 96 *Acacia brachyloba,* Short-lobed acacia. **1821** NUTTALL *Travels Arkansa* 63 For the first time [I] recognised the short-podded honey-locust (*Gladitscia brachycarpa*). **1878** Killebrew *Tenn. Grasses* 232 *Gymnopogon Brevifolius,* Short Leaved Beard Grass.
b. Denoting various fishes or shellfishes.
See also SHORT-NOSED GAR.
1842 *Nat. Hist. N.Y., Zoology* IV. 345 The Short-nosed Sturgeon. *Acipenser brevirostris.* . . . I have seen it . . . in the markets at Norfolk. **1843** *Ib.* VI. 47 Numerous specimens of this species . . . [adhere] to the gills and inside of the mouth of the *Rhombus triacanthus,* or Short-finned Harvest-fish. **1855** Short-billed Pike [see PIKE *n.*[1] 2]. **1883** *Nat. Museum Bul.* No. 27, 189 *Ommastrephes illecebrosa* . . . is known as the 'short-finned squid.'

4. In special combinations.
Short ballot, (see quotation); *s. ear,* (see quotation), *Obs.*; *s. fielder,* a baseball player who plays the short-field position; *s. keeping,* keeping on short commons; *s. lay,* a large share in the profits of a voyage (cf. LAY *n.* 2); +*s. market,* (see quotation); *s. road,* (see quotation); *s. shoulder,* 'an undisputed proposition.' *Rare'* (Th.); +*s. trading,* short selling on an exchange.
1914 *Cycl. Amer. Govt.* I. 104/2 A short ballot is any voting paper which requires the selection of only a few important candidates. **1851** HALL *College Words* 188 At Jefferson College, Pennsylvania, a student of a sober or religious character is denominated a *long ear.* The opposite is *short ear.* **1874** CHADWICK *Base Ball Man.* 27 The Short Fielders. In the present position of the game there is but one. **1858** *Ill. Agric. Soc. Trans.* III. 458 The Longwools . . . will not bear to be herded in as large flocks as the Southdowns, and . . . will not stand as much short keeping. **1866** 'MARK TWAIN' *Lett. Sandwich Islands* 64 The Captain generally gets a tenth, twelfth or fourteenth [part], which is a 'short lay,' and the other officers in proportion. **1900** NELSON *A B C Wall St.* 159 *Short market,* an oversold market, with the aggregate contracts for the delivery of stocks exceeding the supply at a certain range of prices. **1905** *Forestry Bureau Bul.* No. 61, 38 *Go-back road,* a road upon which unloaded logging sleds can return to the skidways for reloading, without meeting the loaded sleds en route to the landing. (N[orthern] F[orest]). Syn.: short road. **1849** *Knickerb.* XXXIII. 543, I believe it's reduced to a positive 'short shoulder' that the Jersey Quakers eat more pickled sturgeon than any other class of people. **1900** NELSON *A B C Wall St.* 19 In this case (short trading) the rule of trading says that the interest belongs to your broker.

b. In names of plants and trees.
Short bean, a variety of beans bearing short pods; *s. corn,* a variety of corn producing short ears; *s. cotton,* short-staple cotton; *s.-leaf milkwort,* a species of milkwort characterized by short leaves; *s.-shucks,* a term used in Maryland and Virginia for the scrub pine; *short-wing fringe ash,* (see quotation).
1790 DEANE *New-Eng. Farmer* 20/2 The short bean is so called from its shape. **1786** WASHINGTON *Diaries* III. 143 Measured . . . 19 Barrls. of long Corn and 6 of Short. **1854** SIMMS *Southward Ho!* 249 Their cry is 'war,' even in the midst of prosperity, and when short-cotton is thirteen cents a pound! **1901** MOHR *Plant Life Ala.* 589 *Polygala brevifolia.* . . . Shortleaf Milkwort. . . . From New Jersey along the coast to Florida, west to Mississippi. **1897** SUDWORTH *Arborescent Flora* 27 *Pinus virginiana.* Scrub Pine. . . . [Also called] Short Shucks (Md., Va.). *Ib.* 324 *Fraxinus dipetala brachyptera.* Short-wing Fringe Ash.

* **Short,** *adv.*

+**1.** *To sell short,* to sell stock or goods on a stock exchange which the seller does not have at the time of the sale.
1861 Moore *Rebellion Rec.* I. III. 27 When one of the members of the Board offered to sell Government Stock 'short' on time, he was instantly hissed down. **1872** TALMAGE *Abominations* 116 He hears that a brother broker has sold 'short.' **1886** *Harper's Mag.* July 206/1 Parties in interest not unfrequently attempt to guard against loss from fluctuation of prices by selling short in the Chicago market. **1902** LORIMER *Lett. Merchant* 191 [Horshey] told me you had ordered him to sell a hundred thousand ribs short last week.

+**2.** *To go short,* =prec.
1870 MEDBERY *Men Wall St.* 192 [He] not seldom gives his broker the order to go short 500 shares on every stock called. **1902** NORRIS *Pit* 325 Crookes and his clique had sold five million bushels, 'going short,' promising to deliver wheat that they did not own.

+**Shortage.** A deficit or deficiency. {1898–} Also attrib. — **1868** (Newspaper, April), The 'shortage war' between the shippers of grain and the skippers who carry it, is practically over. **1880** *Harper's Mag.* Oct.

726/1 In an aggregate of six carloads there was only a shortage of *thirty pounds*. **1902** LORIMER *Lett. Merchant* 69 It didn't seem to have any real bearing on his claim for shortage on the last carload of sweet pickled hams he had bought from us.

+**Short-billed curlew.** The Hudsonian curlew. (Cf. CURLEW 2 a, JACK CURLEW.) — **1813** WILSON *Ornithology* VII. 22 The Esquimaux Curlew, or as it is called by our gunners on the sea-coast, the Short-billed Curlew, is peculiar to the new continent. **1858** [see HUDSONIAN a.]. **1917** *Birds of Amer.* I. 252.

+**Short-billed (marsh) wren.** A small wren (*Cistothorus stellaris*) that frequents marshes. — **1844** *Nat. Hist. N.Y.*, *Zoology* II. 58 The Short-Billed Wren . . . does not appear to be a numerous species in this State. **1874** COUES *Birds N.W.* 37 The Short-billed Marsh Wren . . . occurs along the whole Atlantic coast. **1917** *Birds of Amer.* III. 195.

Short boy. +(See quot. 1851.) *Obs.* — **1851** *Harper's Mag.* July 276/1 A large number of Germans . . . were attacked by a gang of desperadoes from New York, known as 'Short Boys.' **1857** in Brace *Dangerous Classes N.Y.* 22 Is not this crop . . . of shoulder-hitters and shortboys . . . the very fruit to be expected from this seed? **1880** [see DEAD RABBIT].

***Shortcake.** A cake made with plenty of shortening; a cake made of biscuit dough. — **1820** IRVING *Sketch Book* No. 6, 92 [There were] sweet cakes and short cakes. **1856** M. J. HOLMES *Homestead* VI. v, The venison steaks and Dillah's short-cake, smoking hot, were placed upon the old square table. **1893** *Harper's Mag.* March 505/1 They give you good eating—strawberries and short-cake—oh, my!

+**Short card(s).** =POKER² 1. Also attrib. — **1845** HOOPER *Simon Suggs' Adv.* 134 Thar never were a *peaceabler* or more *gentlemanlier* game o' short cards played. **1856** *Harper's Mag.* Dec. 68/2 He is not much of a hand at 'short cards.' **1876** HARTE in *Scribner's Mo.* May 45 It is worthy of a short-card sharp and a keno flopper. **1902** WILSON *Spenders* 293 This gambler he was the slickest short-card player ever struck hereabouts.

Shortclothes. *pl.* Smallclothes, knee breeches. — **1845** *Knickerb.* XXV. 1 Giant Woglog reäppeared to me here, . . . short-clothes and all. **1852** ELLET *Pioneer Women* 340 The French soldiers, with their blue coats turned up with white facings, and short-clothes, . . . formed a strong contrast. **1893** EGGLESTON *Duffels* 27 A planter . . . [was] clad in buckskin shortclothes.

Short-eared owl. The marsh owl, *Asio flammeus*. {1766- (Pennant *Brit. Zool.* (1768) I. 156)} — **1811** WILSON *Ornithology* IV. 64 Short-eared Owl: *Strix brachyotos* . . . is reputed to be an excellent mouser. **1839** PEABODY *Mass. Birds* 274 The Short-eared Owl . . . is another of those wanderers which occasionally leave their northern home to visit us. **1880** *Cimarron News & Press* 23 Dec. 1/4. **1917** *Birds of Amer.* II. 102/1 Marshes and bogs are the preferred habitat of this small and rather stupid Owl, the Short-eared.

+**Short field.** *Baseball.* That part of the playing field in which the shortstop plays. Also attrib. — **1868** CHADWICK *Base Ball* 73 The Irvingtons . . . took an out-fielder from his regular position, and placed him at short field. **1885** — *Art of Pitching* 101 Throwing fast when the fielder has time for a moderate and more accurate throw, is not 'good form' in short field work. **1898** *Kansas City Star* 18 Dec. 3/2 He will be found at short field on the senatorial team next season.

+**Short fielder.** =SHORTSTOP 1. *Obs.* — **1874** CHADWICK *Base Ball Man.* 27 The Short Fielders. In the present position of the game there is but one 'short-stop,' and he stands to the left of the in-field between the second and third base positions.

+**Short fielding.** *Baseball.* Playing as a fielder in the short field. — **1868** CHADWICK *Base Ball* 99 The play was the perfection of short fielding.

Short-grass. {1826-} *attrib.* +Designating a region where low prairie grass grows naturally. — **1844** GREGG *Commerce of Prairies* II. 139 We succeeded in reaching a spot of shortgrass prairie. **1900** *Congress. Rec.* 26 Jan. 1222/2 It is a part of the public domain, away out in what is called the short-grass country. **1923** *Kansas City Star* 23 April 22/2 That part of the state known as the short grass country needs a sod-soaker.

Short gun. A firearm that is relatively short; a carbine. *Obs.* — **1661** *Plymouth Rec.* I. 44 For the use of Abraham Jackson one short gun and a sword. **1689** *Conn. Probate Rec.* I. 594 My three side arms, one short gun or Carbine.

Short hair.

+**1.** *pl.* (See quot. 1914.) *slang. Obs.*

1875 *Nation* 1 April 218 A very real division of the Democratic party in this city into two sets of politicians known familiarly as 'Short Hairs' and 'Swallow Tails'—the former comprising the rank and file of voters, and the latter 'the property owners and substantial men.' **1894** STEAD *If Christ Came to Chicago* 36 Mayor Hopkins was elected by the silkstockings on the one hand and the shorthairs on the other. **1914** *Cycl. Amer. Govt.* III. 308/1 *Short Hairs*, a term . . . denoting the common man and 'toughs' in politics in contradistinction to the fashionable 'swallow tails.'

+**2.** *Short-hair grass*, (see quotation).

1913 BARNES *Western Grazing Grounds* 70 A short wiry but nutritious grass known locally as short-hair grass (*Calamagrostis breweriii*), . . . will stand an immense amount of grazing without being completely killed out.

Short haul. (See HAUL n.)

Shorthorn. An animal of the ox kind belonging to a breed developed in the north of England and highly valued for beef and milk; the breed to which such an animal belongs. {1826-}

1854 *Penna. Agric. Rep.* 237 That the large and seemingly over-grown Short-Horn or Durham should be a great milker, may seem paradoxical. **1862** *Rep. Comm. Patents 1861: Agric.* 431 Suppose we take two young short-horns as nearly alike as possible. **1884** *Rep. Comm. Agric.* 442 Many reports are made of the introduction of short-horns. **1903** [see RANGER 5]. **1913** BARNES *Western Grazing Grounds* 93 The Short-horn was found deficient in . . . rustling qualities.

b. Attrib. with *breed, breeder, cattle, cow*.

1848 *Rep. Comm. Patents 1847* 364 The introduction of short horn, Devon, Hereford and Ayrshire cattle . . . has proved of great advantage. **1858** C. FLINT *Milch Cows* 32 It is the pride of short-horn breeders to trace back to him. **1867** *Rep. Comm. Agric. 1866* 291 The original dam of the 'Cream Pot' breed of stock was a large, light roan short-horn cow. *a***1918** G. STUART *On Frontier* II. 178 We had now increased our herd . . . and were buying thoroughbred bulls of short horn breed to grade them up.

+**Short interest.** (See quot. 1900.) — **1888** *Economist* 20 Oct. 7/1 They point to the large short interest in St. Paul as an element of strength in that stock. **1900** NELSON *A B C Wall St.* 159 *Short interest*, that interest in the market which is represented by the aggregate sales of men who have sold at a price with the expectation of buying in at a cheaper price.

+**Shortleaf pine.** A species of pine having relatively short leaves or needles, esp. *Pinus echinata*. — **1796** HAWKINS *Letters* 24, [I] came . . . to oak and short leaf pine. **1800** — *Sk. Creek Country* 20 The growth of timber is oak, hickory, and the short leaf pine. **1883** Hale *Woods & Timbers N.C.* 210 All the oaks grow here [in Mecklenburg Co.]; also . . . shortleaf pine and some walnut. **1905** *Forestry Bureau Bul.* No. 64, 8 Loblolly successfully competes with shortleaf pine for occupancy [in e. Tex.].

+**Short-leaved pine.** =prec. Also *short-leaved yellow pine*. — **1743** CATESBY *Carolina* App. p. xxii, The Short-leav'd Pine is usually a small tree. **1802** DRAYTON *S. Carolina* 10 The high lands are covered with different kinds of oak . . . and short leaved pine. **1832** BROWNE *Sylva* 235 In the Middle States, . . . it is called Yellow Pine, in the Carolinas and Georgia, . . . Short-Leaved Pine. **1897** SUDWORTH *Arborescent Flora* 27 *Pinus virginiana*. Scrub Pine. . . . [Also called] Shortleaf Pine (N.C.). *Ib.* 29 *Pinus echinata*. Shortleaf Pine. . . . [Also called] Shortleaved Pine. . . . Shortleaved Yellow Pine.

+**Short-legged pewee (flycatcher).** A species of wood pewee (*Myiochanes richardsoni*), found in western North America. — **1839** AUDUBON *Ornith. Biog.* V. 299 Short-Legged Pewee Flycatcher. *Muscicapa Richardsonii*. **1858** BAIRD *Birds Pacific R.R.* 189 Short-legged Pewee. . . . High central dry plains to the Pacific; Rio Grande valley, southward to Mexico; Labrador. **1881** *Amer. Naturalist* XV. 217 The short-legged pewee . . . does not seem to be rare throughout this southern country.

Short meter. {1718-}

+**1.** (See quot. c1870.) *Obs.* Also attrib.

1836 L. BEECHER *Plea for Colleges* 71 Half-made, selfmade men . . . are united only in their contempt of a regular education, and their eulogies of modern mental supremacy, and a short metre course. *c***1870** CHIPMAN *Notes on Bartlett* 403 Short Metre, . . . a short course, as of study, &c.

+**2.** (See quot. 1877.) *Obs.* Also as adv.

1847 LOWELL *Biglow P.* 1 Ser. ii. 26 Ef it won't fer wakin' snakes, I'd home agin short meter. **1853** HALIBURTON *Sam Slick's Wise Saws* (1859) 41, I might just as well make short meter of it, and sell him at once. **1858** *Harper's Mag.* Sept. 567/1, I will hurry through the crowd and into the pulpit in short metre. **1877** BARTLETT 587 *Short Metre*, . . . in a short period; soon. To make short metre of a thing or piece of work is to do it quickly.

Short-neck. {1707-} +=PECTORAL SANDPIPER. — **1844** *Nat. Hist. N.Y.*, *Zoology* II. 242 The Pectoral Sandpiper, *Fringa Pectoralis*, . . . passes under the various names of Meadow Snipe, Jack Snipe, and Shortneck. **1917** *Birds of Amer.* I. 233.

+**Short-nosed gar.** A ganoid fish (*Cylindrosteus platystomus*) of the eastern and central United States. — **1883** *Nat. Museum Bul.* No. 27, 492 *Lepisosteus platystomus*. . . . Short-nosed Gar. Great lakes; rivers of the Ohio and Mississippi Valleys, southward to the Rio Grande; Florida. **1911** *Nat. Fisheries 1908* 310/2 The short-nosed gar . . . is smaller than the preceding and has the same geographic distribution.

+**Short-quartered shoe.** =LOW-QUARTER SHOE. *Obs.* — **1807** IRVING *Salmagundi* xi. 285 She wore a pair of short-quartered high-heeled shoes. **1832** DUNLAP *Hist. Amer. Theatre* 27 We see the beaux of 1761, with . . . their silk stockings, short-quartered shoes, and silver or paste buckles.

+**Short sale.** A contract made for the sale of securities or goods which the seller does not yet possess but which he expects to buy at a future time for less than his sale price. — **1885** *Harper's Mag.* Nov. 842/1 [Buying stock to fulfill a contract] is a self-protective measure, and is called 'covering short sales.' **1888** *Economist* 27 Oct. 7/3 They turned in to hammer them down with short sales, which has been a successful practice for some years past. **1911** *Amer. Year Book 1910* 385/2 All of these bills were directed against the use of 'options,' 'short sales,' and transactions in 'futures.'

+**Short sauce.** (See quot. 1859.) *Obs.* — **1815** [see LONG SAUCE]. **1859** BARTLETT 255 Beets, carrots, and parsnips are *long sauce*. Potatoes, turnips, onions, pumpkins, etc. are *short sauce*.

+**Short selling.** (See quot. 1900.) — **1888** *Economist* 10 Nov. 7/2 The situation, instead of being an encouragement to short selling, suddenly turned distinctly bullish. **1900** NELSON *A B C Wall St.* 159 *Short selling,* selling stocks and borrowing them for immediate delivery. When finally bought in the borrowed stock is returned.

Short session. +Before the Twentieth Amendment went into effect Oct. 15, 1933, the session of Congress beginning in December of even-numbered years and ending on March 3 following. — **1828** COOPER *Notions* II. 262 But the usual practice is to let the bodies separate, at the end of what is called the 'short session.' **1906** *Kansas City Star* 3 Dec. 2/2 Both houses of Congress were to meet today for the short session.

+**Short six. 1.** A variety of cigar. (Cf. LONG NINE.) **2.** A small candle, six of which weigh a pound. **3.** *To come to short sixes,* to fight it out. — (1) **1865** BROWNE *A. Ward; His Travels* 57 Tom Slink . . . used to smoke short-sixes. (2) **1890** J. JEFFERSON *Autobiog.* 146 The very cornerstone of Juliet's balcony contained twenty pounds of the best 'short sixes.' (3) **1834** SIMMS *Guy Rivers* I. 187 If you be not satisfied, why the sooner we come to short sixes the better.

+**Short-staple cotton.** Any one of several varieties of cotton the staple or fiber of which is relatively short. — **1802** *Steele P.* I. 341 Short Staple, or Green seed Cotton if the best Quality, 16 Cents. **1828** in Commons, etc. *Doc. Hist.* I. 267 This was the green seed or short staple cotton. **1891** CHASE & CLOW *Industry* II. 7 If they [*sc.* fibers] are long, the cotton is called long-staple cotton; if short, short-staple cotton.

Shortstop. *Baseball.*
+**1.** An infielder who covers the territory between second and third base.
1868 CHADWICK *Base Ball* 16 Though he hit the ball hard, it went directly to the short stop. **1897** *Outing* May 204/1 Stagg has the problem of finding a . . . short stop. **1917** MATHEWSON *Second Base Sloan* 129 He was the shiftiest shortstop I ever saw outside professional teams.
+**2.** The position played by such a fielder or the station at which he plays.
1878 *Harper's Mag.* Jan. 240/2 He could play short-stop better than any boy. **1887** *Courier-Journal* 26 Jan. 6/2 White . . . has lately signified his entire willingness to occupy his old position at short stop.

Short-story. *attrib.* and *comb.* Of or pertaining to a prose narrative complete in literary form and treatment but much shorter than a novel. {1898-} — **1887** *Harper's Mag.* Feb. 482/1 We are tempted to claim a national primacy in short-story writing. *Ib.* 483/2 A little question will usually enable him to decide whether he has hold of a short-story motive or a long-story motive. **1906** 'O. HENRY' *Trimmed Lamp* 219 That day he had 'lunched' . . . a short-story writer, and the famous conductor of a slaughter-house exposé.

+**Short-straw pine.** =SHORTLEAF PINE. — **1859** G. W. PERRY *Turpentine Farming* 22 We proceed now to the notice of the common short-straw pine.

+**Short sweetening.** Sugar. (Cf. LONG SWEETENING.) *colloq.* — **1885** *Harper's Mag.* Aug. 399/1 He set out the glass with its little quota of 'short sweetening' and a cut-glass decanter. **1886** *Ib.* June 62/2 These decoctions they mollify with home-made sorghum molasses, which they call 'long sweetening,' or with sugar, which by contrast is known as 'short sweetening.' **1914** B.T. WASHINGTON *Selected Speeches* 218 This good lady asked whether we wanted long or short sweetening in our coffee.

Short-tailed, *a.* In the names of various birds and animals having relatively short tails. {1684-} — **1813** WILSON *Ornithology* VII. 84 The short-tailed tern measures eight inches and a half from the point of the bill to the tip of the tail. **1857** *Rep. Comm. Patents 1856: Agric.* 84 Several species [of meadow-mice] . . . are commonly considered by farmers as one animal, known under various names, as 'Short-tailed Field Rats or Mice,' 'Bear Mice,' [etc.]. **1917** *Birds of Amer.* III. 192 House Wren. *Troglodytes aëdon aëdon*. . . . [Also called] Stump Wren; Short-tailed House Wren; Jenny Wren.

Short term. +A term of office shorter than a full term, usually the remainder of a full term of office vacated by death or resignation. — **1868** *N.Y. Herald* 15 July 5/2 The General Assembly to-day elected . . . General J. C. Abbott [U.S. senator] . . . for the short term. **1883** *Harper's Mag.* Sept. 642/1 Supreme Judge (short term) Martin D. Follet.

+**Shoshoni, Shoshone(e).** [Of obscure origin.]
1. An Indian of a northern tribe of the Shoshonean branch of the Uto-Aztecan family; also, pl., the tribe. Applied loosely to any Shoshonean Indian.
1805 LEWIS in *L. & Clark Exped.* II. (1904) 370 The Shoshoenes may be estimated at about 100 warriors. **1836** IRVING *Astoria* II. 40 They came to two lodges of Shoshonies. **1848** BRYANT *California* xi. 152 One of the men called himself a Utah, the other a Shoshonee or Snake. **1878** BEADLE *Western Wilds* 345 Soon the whole country was swarming with Bannocks and Shoshones. **1884** W. SHEPHERD *Prairie Exper.* 59 The Crows . . . came down to visit the Rapahoes, Shoshones, and other tribes.
b. The language of these Indians.
1843 MARRYAT *M. Violet* xiv, I addressed him in Shoshone, which beautiful dialect is common to the Comanches, Apaches, and Arrapahoes.
2. Attrib. with *agency, beauty, Indian,* etc.
1806 LEWIS in *L. & Clark Exped.* V. (1905) 4 The Shoshone man was displeased because we did not give him as much venison as he could eat. **1837** IRVING *Bonneville* I. 204 The Shoshonie beauties also flaunted about in all the colours of the rainbow. **1845** FRÉMONT *Exped.* 129 By the Shoshone and Utah Indians . . . it was called the Bitter-root river. **1886** *Outing* Dec. 198/2 Dick had a big tepé, with a Shoshone woman for his wife.

1900 *Congress. Rec.* 9 Feb. 1664/2 An amendment . . . for making necessary repairs of the Big Wind River Bridge on the Shoshone Agency, Wyo.

* **Shot.**
* **1. a.** A ball or bullet to be discharged from a gun or cannon. Usually collect. **b.** A quantity of small lead pellets, used as a single charge of a gun; a single pellet. {1770-}
See also BIRD-SHOT, BUCK-SHOT, DUCK SHOT, etc.
1619 *Va. House of Burgesses* 13 That no man do sell or give any Indians any piece shott or poulder. **1643** *Portsmouth Rec.* 21 It is . . . ordered that euery man [have] 4l. of shote lying by them. **1687** SEWALL *Letter-Book* I. 64 We desire her produce with the fraight be invested in six tone of shott, of which three ton Goose, two tone Duck, one tone pigeon. **1748** FRANKLIN *Exper. on Electricity* 10 Place an iron shot, of three or four inches in diameter, on the mouth of a clean, dry glass bottle. **1774** J. ANDREWS *Letters* 57 A quantity of the train came down to Scott's for the remainder of the shot, hand Granades, Cohorns. **1818** SCHOOLCRAFT *Journal* 27 Our dried meat and our shot are also nearly expended. **1855** in A. Lawrence *Diary & Corr.* 27 Sixty-three shot were picked out of the floor after the accident. **1892** M. A. JACKSON *Gen. Jackson* 351 The Confederates poured shot and shell upon the enemy.

2. A charge of powder. {1708-}
1671 in Alvord & Bidgood *Trans-Allegheny Region* 193 [We] presented him with three or four shots of powder.

3. In games and sports: An act of directing a ball; a stroke. {1868-}
1864 DICK *Amer. Hoyle* (1866) 422 If the striker . . . has not at least one foot on the floor while striking, the shot is foul. **1899** ADE *Fables in Slang* 16 They began to Tremble and fell down on their Shots.

+**4.** 'One piece or section of an extended seine or drift-net' (*Stand.*).
1880 BURROUGHS in *Scribner's Mo.* Aug. 492/2 The net is divided into 'shots.'

5. In phrases. +**a.** *Shot, lock, and barrel,* the entire thing, the whole caboodle. *colloq.* {stock, lock, and barrel, 1830-}
1834 CROCKETT *Narr. Life* 21 Away went their mill, shot, lock and barrel.
+**b.** *Shot in the neck,* a drink of liquor. *slang.* Cf. SHOT *a.*
1851 *Polly Peablossom* 180 The two then exchanged a 'shot in the neck.'
c. *A long shot* {1791-}, +a great deal; a long way; +*not by a long shot,* emphatically not.
1848 BARTLETT 215 Mr. Divver offered a resolution summarily removing the superintendent, and was quickly told . . . that he was going too fast by a long shot. . . . *Proceedings in the Case of Dr. Reese.* **1857** *Knickerb.* XLIX. 38 It was, by a long shot, the most Christian look I had ever seen him raise. **1884** in Tarbell *Hist. Standard Oil Co.* II. 114 They are not the Democracy of Ohio by a long shot. **1890** HARRIS in *Century Mag.* Dec. 290/1, I hain't dead yit. . . . Not by a long shot! **1903** LEWIS *Boss* 375 That Blackberry duck . . . is quite a flossy form of stock student and a long shot from a slouch. **1917** MCCUTCHEON *Green Fancy* 258 He fooled men a long shot keener than you are.

6. Attrib. in sense 1 with *belt, box, cartridge,* etc.
1633 *N.H. Prov. Papers* I. 79 Shott moulds pr. 1. **1707** *Boston News-Letter* 16 June 2/1 Capt Davies . . . bruis'd himself much upon the edge of a Shot Case. **1819** SCHOOLCRAFT *Mo. Lead Mines* 60 Jefferson county has . . . 3 shot manufactories. **1830** COOPER *Water Witch* III. 258 The smaller booms with the mess-chest and shot-boxes were all that lay between the group in the centre and the depths of the ocean. **1837** IRVING *Bonneville* II. 123 The experienced trapper sleeps . . . with his rifle beside him, the shotbelt and powderflask on the stock. **1876** KNIGHT 2166/1 *Shot-cartridge,* a round of ammunition for a shot-gun.

* **Shot,** *a.* +Intoxicated. *slang.* Freq. in phrase *shot in the neck.* (Cf. SHOT *n.* 5 b.) — **1835** TODD *Notes* 22 In Pennsylvania section originated . . . 'Well shot in the neck,' for intoxication. **1855** *Brooklyn Jrnl.* 18 April (B.), Mr. Schumacher [observed] . . . that some of the prisoners' attorneys got as often 'shot in the neck,' as the Under-Sheriff did in the head. **1864** *Harper's Mag.* May 856/2 He again sat down by the fire, . . . by which time he was pretty well 'shot.'

+**Shot bag.** A bag for carrying shot.
1638 *Md. Archives* IV. 32 Goods [include] . . . one fowling piece & shott bagge. **1716** CHURCH *Philip's War* 2 The Mount-hope Men . . . made a formidable appearance, . . . with their Powder-horns, and Shotbags at their backs. **1784** SMYTH *Tour* I. 180 Shot bag and powder-horn . . . hang from their necks over one shoulder. **1843** HAWKS *D. Boone* 33 By comparing that ball with those in his shot-bag, he found they were of the same size. **1872** 'MARK TWAIN' *Roughing It* 24 We also took with us a little shot-bag of silver coin. **1911** WHITE *Bobby Orde* xi, In the bunks . . . lay powder canisters, shotbags, wad-boxes.

+**Shotbush. 1.** The Hercules'-club, *Aralia spinosa.* **2.** (See quotation.) — (1) **1784** *'Amer. Acad. Mem.* I. 431 *Aralia*. . . . Berry-Bearing Angelica. Shot Bush. . . . Common in new plantations. **1902** CLAPIN 360 *Shot-bush,* . . . a prickly tree shrub, also humorously called *tear-coat.* A Southern term. (2) **1891** *Cent.* 5590/3 *Shot-bush,* . . . the wild sarsaparilla, *Aralia nudicaulis:* from its shot-like fruit.

*Shote, Shoat.

*1. A young hog.

1640 *R.I. Col. Rec.* I. 75 Mr. Potter, hee will lend one yearling, . . . John Briggs, one shote. 1737 W. STEPHENS *Proc. Georgia* I. 49 A young Shote, barbacue'd ouer a Fire in the Wood, was set on the Table. 1835 LONG-STREET *Ga. Scenes* 115 On leaving the dining-room, [he] was met at the door by Flora, with . . . a dish large enough to contain a goodly sized shote. 1914 E. STEWART *Lett. Woman Homesteader* 204 She and I talked of ash-hoppers, smoke-houses, . . . poke-greens, and shoats, until she fell asleep.

+2. An idle or contemptible person; a fellow. *slang.*

1800 WEEMS *Washington* (1840) 40 The poorest shoat, if wearing the proud epaulette of a Briton, might command a Wolfe, if so unlucky as to be an American! 1836 *S. Lit. Messenger* II. 664 You poor wretched shote! 1869 STOWE *Oldtown Folks* 134 Where a plague is that lazy shote of a boy?

+Shot gold. Placer gold found in pellets like shot. — 1873 ARNY *Items regarding N. Mex.* 76 The gold found in the gulches is shot-gold mostly. 1874 RAYMOND *6th Rep. Mines* 303 The gold is 'shot' gold, found on a sandstone bed-rock.

+Shotgun.

1. a. *generic.* Any smooth-bore gun for firing a single bullet or a charge of shot: (see quot. 1835). b. A gun of this type for shooting a charge of shot at short range. {1892}

1776 in Rauck *Boonesborough* 250 They were prevented from carrying anything away except one shot gun without any ammunition. 1807 *Ann. 10th Congress* 1 Sess. I. 430 A man next to me . . . had a shot gun. 1828 J. HALL *Lett. from West* 86 Luck's like a shot-gun, mighty uncertain. 1835 LONGSTREET *Ga. Scenes* 222 In olden time the contest was carried on chiefly with *shot-guns,* a generic term which in those days, embraced three descriptions of fire-arms—*Indian-traders,* . . . *the large musket,* and the *Shot-gun,* properly so called. 1853 GLISAN *Jrnl. Army Life* 118 My first success in deer hunting was with a shot-gun. 1868 *Ore. State Jrnl.* 28 Nov. 2/3 A shot gun, heavily charged with buck shot, lay on the bottom of the wagon. 1897 *Scribner's Mag.* Nov. 575/1 In his hand Pete held a shot-gun of the kind used by express messengers, with sawed-off barrels and heavy charges of buckshot in them. 1910 *Springfield W. Repub.* 24 Nov. 2 But the shotgun loaded with slugs or buckshot is a dangerous affair.

2. With defining terms.

1848 COOPER *Oak Openings* I. 47 He and Gershom . . . [took] four pieces of fire-arms; one of which was, to use the language of the west, a double-barrelled 'shot-gun.' 1881 *Ore. State Jrnl.* 1 Jan. 7 We keep a full line of Breech and Muzzle-Loading Shotguns. 1886 *Milnor* (Dak.) *Teller* June Guess I'll go for the galoot with a two-scatter shotgun.

3. *attrib.* passing into *adj.*: Enforced with a shotgun.

1880 *Congress. Rec.* 10 March 1450/1 The shot-gun policy, which worked so well in 1876, . . . has been continued up to the present time. 1883 *Century Mag.* July 431/1 To the merchant, 'shot-gun quarantines' throughout the southern Mississippi valley explained themselves. 1893 *Congress. Rec.* 5 Oct. 2171/2 You were not able to produce a single instance of intimidation or violence . . . in the period in which you say the elections were conducted under the 'old shotgun system.'

+Shotgun messenger. An express messenger armed with a shotgun. — 1893 *Chicago Tribune* 24 April 3/1 He also has pictures of 'Mike' Tovey, a 'shot gun' messenger. 1894 *Harper's Mag.* Oct. 673/2 The humorous Gazelle had . . . asked him to carry the package to Folsom for her, and deliver it there to a certain shot-gun messenger of the express company.

+Shot-(hole) borer. A bark beetle (*Scolytus rugulosus*) or one of several other related species of the family Scolytidae. Also attrib. — 1890 E. A. ORMEROD *Injur. Insects* (ed. 2) 331, I found that the cause of the injury was the 'Shot-borer' Beetle (as it is called in America). 1891 *Cent.* 5590/3. 1916 *Farmers' Bul.* No. 763, 2 The shot-hole borers or barkbeetles burrow into the bark.

+Shot ore. A kind of iron ore: (see quots. 1843, 1860). — 1804 *Mass. H. S. Coll.* 1 Ser. IX. 255 Ledge or shot ore, yields nearly 25 per cent. of good iron. 1843 *Nat. Hist N.Y. Geology* IV. 438 Bog iron is found in grains both loose and forming small masses in the soil. . . . It has the local name of *shot ore.* 1860 *Harper's Mag.* April 597/1 The ore . . . is composed of a very pulverulent although closely compacted mixture of small angular grains of magnetic iron ore, or magnetite, with small round granules of phosphate of lime or *apatite.* Such ore is called 'shot ore' by the miners, from its crumbling easily into small fragments.

Shot pouch. 1. A pouch, usually of leather, for carrying shot. {1732-, used by sportsmen} +2. =RUDDY DUCK. — (1) 1775 *S. C. Hist. Soc. Coll.* II. 32 You are come . . . to know the cause of our warriors cleaning their guns and putting on their shot-pouches. 1836 [see PARCHED CORN]. 1888 PERRIN *Ky. Pioneer Press* 28 A rifle and shot pouch comprised part of the editor's office furniture. 1916 EASTMAN *From Deep Woods* 31, I took . . . my shot-pouch and a well filled powder-horn. (2) 1888 TRUMBULL *Names of Birds* 111 Others at Detroit, and the 'punters' of St. Clair Flats, refer to the species [the ruddy duck] still as Fool-Duck, Deaf-Duck, and Shot-Pouch. 1917 *Birds of Amer.* I. 152.

Shot put. An athletic event consisting of throwing or casting with an overhand motion a spherical weight. — 1898 *Cap & Gown* (Univ. of Chicago) III. 121 June 6, Western Intercollegiate Track Meet. . . . Field Events. . . . Shot Put. . . . 38 ft. 9½ in. 1924 *Kansas City Times* 19 April 17/3 Wilson of Arkansas City . . . scored . . . second in the shotput, and third in the discus and javelin.

Shot tower. A high tower in which melted metal is dropped in slender streams to make shot. {1835} — 1817 PAULDING *Lett. from South* I. 90 One [city] has its steeples—the other its shot-towers; one has its Hudson & East rivers—the other its Delaware and Schuylkill. 1889 'MARK TWAIN' *Conn. Yankee* 438, I was the only person in the kingdom who knew how to manage a shot-tower.

*Shoulder.

1. In phrases.

+*To overleap one's shoulders,* to overextend oneself; +*to come from the shoulder,* to be open and straightforward.

1834 SIMMS *Guy Rivers* II. 102 The pedler had somewhat 'overleaped his shoulders,' as they phrase it. 1873 MILLER *Amongst Modocs* 308 No one cared, so long as he fought with men who 'came from the shoulder,' or were on the 'cut and shoot.'

2. *attrib.* a. Designating ornaments, insignia, etc., attached to the shoulders of coats or dresses.

1639 *Mass. Bay Rec.* I. 274 Some other superfluities . . . may easily bee redressed without . . . the spoile of garments, as immoderate great breches, knots of ryban, broad shoulder bands. 1678 *New Castle Court Rec.* 322, 2 pr. of sleeves and one shoulder knott [were stolen from Adam Wallis's chest]. 1907 ANDREWS *Recoll.* 152 The enlisted men should wear shoulder scales when in full dress.

b. Designating garments worn about the shoulders.

1790 FANNING *Narrative* 50, I had ordered . . . twenty-five men to have a certain dress made . . . , and red shoulder cape also. 1877 PHELPS *Story of Avis* 307 He found Avis . . . half wrapped in the shoulder-robe from the hammock. 1890 *Century Mag.* Dec. 300 [She] stood with her hand wrapped in . . . her shoulder shawl. 1900 DIX *Deacon Bradbury* 130 Mart and Emmeline submissively took their light worsted shoulder-wraps.

+Shoulder-hitter. One who hits from the shoulder; a ruffian or bully. *colloq.* — 1855 M. THOMPSON *Doesticks* 228 [At] the Bowery Theatre . . . adolescent 'shoulder hitters' and politicians in future take their first lessons in rowdyism. 1857 [see CHIP *n.* 7 a]. 1876 TRIPP *Student-Life* 275 Rumor gave him the reputation of being a first-rate 'shoulder-hitter.' 1903 LEWIS *Boss* 60 There were a round twenty of my Tin Whistles, each a shoulder-hitter and warm to shine in the graces of Big Kennedy.

Shoulder stone. A stone used as a shot in the shot put. — 1791 *Wheeleys Baptist Ch. Min.* July (Univ. N.C. MS.), Brother Richard Burch Came before the Church and acknowledged himself guilty of joining with the wicked in . . . throwing the Shoulder Stone.

Shoulder strap. {1688-} +A soldier, esp. an officer. — [1863 WHITMAN *Diary* 50 There is a rather notable absence of military uniforms on the floor of the house; . . . I do not see a single shoulder-strap.] 1895 REMINGTON *Pony Tracks* 241 One by one the 'shoulder-straps' crawl in through the hole in the tepee.

Shoulder-striker. =SHOULDER-HITTER. *colloq. Obs.* — 1860 HOLMES *Professor* 264 No 'shoulder-striker' hits out straighter than a child with its logic. 1866 LOWELL *Biglow P.* 2 Ser. p. lvii, *Shoulder-hitters:* I find that *shoulder-striker* is old, though I have lost the reference to my authority.

*Shout, *n.* +A cry expressive of religious feeling; a meeting at which worship is carried on by shouting. — 1862 E. W. Pearson *Lett. Port Royal* 27 We asked Cuffy if they considered the 'shout' as part of their religious worship. *Ib.* 34 They had had a 'Shout,' which I had heard distinctly at three o'clock in the morning. 1867 *Nation* 30 May 432/2 The true 'shout' takes place on Sundays or on 'praise' nights.

*Shout, *v.* +1. *intr.* To say something significant or to the purpose. *slang.* +2. Of a thing: To be obvious or conspicuous. *colloq.* — (1) 1875 *Scribner's Mo.* Nov. 142/1 Said he, perversely, 'Now yer shoutin'!' 1911 SAUNDERS *Col. Todhunter* 99 'You're shoutin' now, Colonel,' agreed Sim. (2) 1892 *Pall Mall Gaz.* 25 July 3/1 Figures which, to use an Americanism, fairly 'shout.'

Shouter. {1692-} +One who loudly supports a political candidate. *colloq.* — 1875 *Wkly. New Mexican* 13 Oct. 2/1 The Carleton and Perea 'shouters,' got up a procession with banners, transparencies and noise. 1904 *Rochester Post Express* 26 May 4 The canvass of the state was very thorough, Hearst shouters being busily engaged in every city and village.

*Shouting, *n.* +1. The action of uttering cries of exultation during religious excitement. +2. Attrib. with *bee, exercise, meeting.* — (1) [1807 McNEMAR *Ky. Revival* 69 There were regular societies of these people in the state of Ohio. . . . Praying, shouting, jerking, barking, or rolling.] 1871 *Ku Klux Klan Rep.* VI. 306, I have attended what they call their religious meetings; and they have what they call 'shouting.' 1904 DERVILLE *Other Side of Story* 19 Yet these same ministers encouraged 'shouting,' which might be considered as undignified in a church as dancing could be at home. (2) 1839 *Knickerb.* Sept. 213 He was sternly opposed to what are called 'shouting meetings.' 1877 *Harper's Mag.* April 707/1 At the shouting exercises on Sunday nights . . . his feet begin to move before the end of the first verse. 1902 HARBEN *A. Daniel* 116 He's come nigher . . . to turn me into the right way than all the shoutin'-bees I ever attended.

Shouting, *a.* {1600-} +Uttering cries of religious exultation. — 1874 EGGLESTON *Circuit Rider* 216 He'll marry some shouting girl, I suppose. 1888 *Times Democrat* 5 Feb. (F.), Sister Mary . . . was a shoutin' member of the church, as her name indicates.

+Shouting Methodist. A Methodist who shouts during religious excitement. — 1851 *Polly Peablossom* 87 Forgeron was from that time 'a shouting Methodist.' 1875 BURROUGHS *Winter Sunshine* 23 About the only genuine shouting Methodists that remain are to be found in the coloured churches.

*Shove, v.

*1. intr. To set out for a place; to push along. colloq. {-1581, 1721}

1856 'MARK TWAIN' Adv. Snodgrass 31, I shoved out for the Massasawit House. 1867 — Sk., New & Old 274, I then took what small change he had, and 'shoved.' 1904 'O. HENRY' in McClure's Mag. April 612/1 When dark came we fagged 'em a batch of bullets and shoved out the back door for the rocks.

2. tr. To get rid of or pass (a note, counterfeit money, etc.). slang.

1859 MATSELL Vocabulum 79 Shove, pass money. 'Shove the blunt,' spend the money. 'Shove queer,' pass counterfeit money. 1864 [see POSTAGE CURRENCY]. 1875 Chicago Tribune 11 Nov. 2/1 Discovery of a Scheme in New York for Shoving 'Queer' Railroad Tickets. 1885 LELAND Brandnew Ballads 35 The one [note] I shoved was never worth a continental dam.

||3. Baseball. To hit (a ball) to a particular place.

1912 C. MATHEWSON Pitching 109 Mowrey shoved a long fly to right field.

*Shovel.

*1. A more or less hollow scoop with a handle.

In quotation 1791 apparently a shovel-shaped saltspoon.

1634 WINTHROP in R. C. Winthrop Life J. Winthrop II. 126 [We have need of] spades and shovels. 1706 Boston News-Letter 7 Jan. 2/2 To be Sold, . . . 5 Iron Doors, Two great Shovels [etc.]. 1791 Ky. Petitions 184, I give and bequeath . . . four salts with their glasses and shovels. 1812 Niles' Reg. II. 131/1 The purveyor of public supplies advertises for . . . 2500 shovels. 1850 TYSON Diary in Calif. 9 You will soon become accustomed to the mode of proceeding, either with a shovel, pickax, pan, or washer. 1907 St. Nicholas June 719/2 Others brought shovels to smooth off the uneven places and to fill up any small holes.

2. Attrib. with bonnet, cultivator, factory, etc.

1780 Narragansett Hist. Reg. I. 105 Made a shovel pan for George. 1815 Mass. H. S. Coll. 2 Ser. III. 171 On the Town Brook [are] . . . one Cotton Factory, (brick); Shovel Factory; Anchor works. 1840 Niles' Nat. Reg. 17 Oct. 112/2 Shovel Manufacture. Oliver Ames . . . now owns three extensive factories. 1869 Rep. Comm. Agric. 1868 236 They are sometimes very expeditiously covered . . . with the mold-board or the shovel cultivator. 1873 Newton Kansan 9 Jan. 3/4 Shovelmen and a snow plow as advance guard, left this place for the west. 1901 CHURCHILL Crisis 324 It was a shovel bonnet, with long red ribbons that tied under her chin.

+Shovel and tongs, adv. With energy; relentlessly. — 1843 STEPHENS High Life N.Y. I. 40 Arter rolling up his shirt sleeves and spitting on his hands . . . , he went at it shovel and tongs. 1857 Lawrence Republican 13 Aug. 3 Of course it pitches into the Free-State men pellmell, shovel and tongs, head over heels.

*Shovelboard. (See SHUFFLEBOARD.)

*Shoveler, Shoveller. A river duck, Spatula clypeata. Often with specifying terms. {1674-}

1709 LAWSON Carolina 149 Shovellers (a sort of Duck) are gray, with a black Head. 1731 CATESBY Carolina I. 96 Anas Americanus luto rostro, the Blue-wing Shoveler. . . . The upper part of the wing is covered with pale blue feathers. 1789, 1813 Blue winged shoveller [see BLUE-WINGED a.]. 1813 WILSON Ornithology VIII. 65 The Shoveller visits us only in the winter. 1835 AUDUBON Ornith. Biog. III. 227 [Scaup Ducks] furrow the mud, in the manner of the Shoveller. 1917 Birds of Amer. I. 126 Shoveller. . . . [Also called] Red-breasted Shoveller.

Shoveler duck. =prec. — 1838 AUDUBON Ornith. Biog. IV. 241. 1886 ROOSEVELT in Outing Aug. 522/2 The mallard duck, shoveler duck, and broad bill are also common [along the Little Missouri R.].

+Shovelfish. 1. The paddlefish, Polyodon spathula. 2. =SHOVELHEAD. — (1) 1847 Knickerb. XXIX. 332 The shovel or spoon-bill fish is only found in the Alabama and its tributaries. 1911 Rep. Fisheries 1908 313/1 Local names are 'spoonbill,' 'duckbill cat,' and 'shovelfish.' (2) [1863 J. G. WOOD Illus. Nat. Hist. III. 200 The two smaller figures represent the Shovel-fish, so called from the curious form of its head.]

+Shovelhead. The shovel-nosed sturgeon, Scaphirhynchus platorhynchus. — [1881 Cassell's Nat. Hist. V. 45 The second genus, called the Shovel-head (Scaphirhynchus), is represented by a single species, . . . found in the Mississippi.]

Shovel-head(ed) shark. (See quotation.) — 1879 Nat. Museum Proc. I. 387 Reniceps Tiburo,—Shovel-headed Shark; Bonnet-head. Abundant [near Beaufort Harbor, N.C.]. 1882 Nat. Museum Bul. No. 16, 25 Reniceps tiburo.—Shovel-head Shark; Bonnet Head. . . . Atlantic Ocean; abundant southward.

+Shovelnose. A shovel-nosed fish. — 1709 LAWSON Carolina 155 Of these [sharks] there are two sorts; one call'd Paracooda-Noses; the other Shovel-Noses. 1842 [see HAMMER-HEAD(ED) SHARK]. 1894 Outing XXIV. 60/2 The big 'pike' was slow in its movements, and Jack had plenty of warning before the shovel-nose showed in the rapid right at his feet. 1911 Rep. Fisheries 1908 317/1 The various species [of sturgeon] are known as 'lake sturgeon,' 'white sturgeon,' 'shovelnose,' etc.

Shovel-nosed, a. Of a fish: Having a broad, flat nose or head. {1707-} — 1844 E. C. WATMOUGH Scribblings (ed. 2) 110 (Th.), One who cared as little about the picturesque as a shovel-nosed shark for an ice cream. 1849 31st Congress 1 Sess. H. R. Ex. Doc. No. 5, II. 1025 Hotan-ke . . . is applied . . . by the Sioux to the shovel-nosed sturgeon of the

Mississippi. 1894 Outing XXIV. 55/1 Our favorite game was the pike—the mottled, shovel-nosed rascal, called 'pickerel' in Jersey and in many other places.

Shovel plow. A plow having a simple triangular share. {1801-} — 1805 PARKINSON Tour 492 [What Americans] call a shovel-plough, [is] something like a paring-spade. 1847 DRAKE Pioneer Life Ky. 45 After a first 'breaking up' with the coultered plow, the shovel plow was in general use. 1862 Rep. Comm. Patents 1861: Agric. 285 Thus the one-acre crop of 263 bushels was ploughed with a shovel-plough three times. 1876 Ill. Dept. Agric. Trans. XIII. 328 The barshare and shovel plow have been succeeded by . . . the Pekin, the Peoria, [and] the Moline.

+Shovel weed. The shepherd's-purse. — 1893 Amer. Folk-Lore VI. 137 Capsella bursa-pastoris, shovel weed. Penobscot Co., Me.

*Shover. +One who passes counterfeit money. — 1889 Harper's Wkly. 21 Sept. 768/1 Eight persons, mostly 'shovers' or passers, were arrested in Russo's gang. 1896 Cincinnati Enquirer 21 Aug. 6/7 This is about the fourth time . . . that McCullough has been made the victim of shovers of the queer.

*Show, n.

1. A sign or indication of mineral, oil, etc. {1600}

1733 BYRD Journey to Eden (1901) 318 Within 2 Miles of the Mouth are good shews of Copper Mines. 1756 Lett. to Washington I. 231 Colo. Lomax . . . flatters himself with the Prospect of great Wealth from his Share of a Copper Mine . . . which has a Show of much rich Ore. 1870 CONE & JOHNS Petrolia 145 Few operators continue to test beyond a month, unless the 'show' of oil is very fine. 1890 Harper's Mag. Oct. 726/2 'The Pennsylvania Rock Oil Company' . . . purchased . . . all the land on Oil Creek upon which there was any 'show of oil.'

*2. a. A display or exhibition for the entertainment of spectators. b. A dramatic performance {1863-}; a circus.

1764 ROWE Diary 67 Went after dinner to see a Show at the White Horse wh[ich] was a very faint Representation of the City of Jerusalem. 1787 TYLER Contrast III. i, He would not go to a play for the world; he thinks it was a show, as he calls it. 1845 KIRKLAND Western Clearings 15 The winter . . . is generally the chosen period for . . . dancing, seeing 'shows,' and going to school. 1873 Winfield (Kan.) Courier 27 May 1/6 They kept as quiet as death, fearing that they would . . . be subjects of the displeasure of a circus man, if he should discover them 'dead-heading' it to his show. 1882 McCABE New York 640 The street is the paradise of beer saloons, . . . cheap theatres, and low-class shows. 1896 N.Y. Dramatic News 4 July 12/1 [The circus] well merited its title of the 'greatest show on earth.' 1920 COOPER Under Big Top 3 The traveling population of the show was greater than that of the village itself!

+3. An affair; a business or social matter; a concern. {1898-} To be the whole show, to be the most important person(s) in a matter. colloq.

These are fig. uses of sense 2.

1797 H. W. FOSTER Coquette 138 The show is over, as we yankees say; and the girl is my own. 1851 KINGSLEY Diary 171 He got 500 dollars for his share which takeing the show as we now have it I think was a plenty. 1867 LOCKE Swingin' Round 243 The delegashens bein all in, it wuz decided to go on with the show. 1889 Daily News (London) 9 Feb. 6/1 The U.B. endeavoured . . . to control the funds and operations of the League —to 'boss the whole show,' . . . making use of a familiar American expression. 1901 McCUTCHEON Graustark 123 We seem to be the whole show here. 1922 A. BROWN Old Crow 31, I hate the whole blamed show.

+4. An opportunity for doing something; a chance.

The 1579 quotation of the O.E.D. seems to have been a nonce use.

a1861 WINTHROP J. Brent 297 So we guv 'em a fair show, with a big stick of cotton-wood and a shingle apiece. 1873 BEADLE Undevel. West 581 The sand surrounding the mesa presents the poorest show for farming I ever saw. 1884 'MARK TWAIN' H. Finn xvii, I'm always kept down; I don't get no show. 1914 'BOWER' Flying U Ranch 188 Our only show is to stop with our toes on the right side of the dead line.

+5. =SHOW-DOWN 1 a.

1887 KELLER Draw Poker 29 The previous bettor may . . . call for a show for that amount.

6. attrib. a. Designating animals, places, etc., exhibited to the public or not for ordinary use. {1614-}

See also SHOW BOX, CASE, WINDOW.

1825 COOPER L. Lincoln iv, When she is grave, she walks with the stateliness of a show-beef. 1850 MATHEWS Moneypenny 66 [The boarding house] had a show parlor, with a sofa, and two ottomans. 1864 Ohio Agric. Rep. XVIII. 401 Every intelligent breeder knows how often we find first class 'show bulls' that turn out inferior breeders. 1890 Stock Grower & Farmer 21 June 5/3 He does not maintain a 'show ranch' for visitors.

b. Designating persons, places, etc., employed in, or connected with, the business of shows.

See also SHOW BOAT, SHOWMAN.

1845 SOL. SMITH Theatr. Apprent. 20, I posted off to Troy, to 'join the show-folks.' 1869 'MARK TWAIN' Innocents 199 These latter were not show-people. 1873 HIGGINSON Oldport Days 196 [She] grew up into a well-behaved mediocrity, unregretful of the show-tent. 1911 BURGESS Find Woman 169 But I had no idea showgirls got such good salaries! 1920 COOPER Under Big Top 180, I lived near the 'show lot' where all the big circuses gave their exhibits.

c. In special combinations.

Show dress, a dress worn by a slave while being shown for sale; *s. town,* a town where a show draws a good (or bad) house.

1853 STOWE *Key* 164/1 Gay calico was bought for them to make up into 'show dresses,' in which they were to be exhibited on sale. **1893** AULD *Picturesque Burlington* 52 Burlington is what is known in theatrical parlance as a good 'show town.'

* **Show,** *v.*

+1. a. *To show foot,* to put the foot forward preparatory to action. **b.** *To show leg,* to run away.

(a) 1825 NEAL *Bro. Jonathan* I. 269 Carter . . . began to 'show foot' for another, and more active demonstration. *Ib.* 271 [The wrestlers] drew up—made play—showed foot—half locked—sprang at each other. **(b) 1837** BIRD *Nick* I. 120, I'll fight for you, or run for you, . . . shake fist or show leg.

2. *To show one's hand,* to display one's cards; fig., to reveal one's position or intentions. {1879–}

1845 SOL. SMITH *Theatr. Apprent.* 149 Let us show our hands for the money already down. **1893** *Harper's Mag.* May 893/1, I must therefore tell you the whole scheme—show all my hand.

+3. *To show down,* in poker to display one's cards. In fig. use.

1893 *Congress. Rec.* 13 Oct. 2493/1 The Republican Senate saw their bluff, called them, and made them show down. **1902** LORIMER *Lett. Merchant* 234 They just had to . . . pass you the pot when you showed down. **1904** W. H. SMITH *Promoters* 129 Don't show down till you're called.

4. *To show out.* {1846–} **a.** To reveal or exhibit one's true character or views. ‖**b.** To make an ostentatious display; to show off.

(a) 1846 WHITCHER *Bedott P.* iv. 43 A body can't tell what sort of a woman a gal *will* make afore she's married—they don't always show out, you know. **1883** *Century Mag.* Aug. 598/1 [I] never show out in any way that I know there are young ladies or literature in the world. **(b) 1887** WILKINS *Humble Romance* 170 He's doin' it to show out.

5. *To show up.* {*tr.,* 1826–; *intr.,* 1883–} **a.** To make good one's pretensions. **b.** To turn up at a particular place; to make an appearance. {1890}

(a) 1883 'MARK TWAIN' *Life on Miss.* iii, 'Oh, come now, Eddy,' says Jimmy, 'show up.' **(b) 1888** *Lisbon* (Dak.) *Star* 3 Feb. 4/1 Will Worden is expected to show up next week. **1896** *Typographical Jrnl.* IX. 257 The following Monday he did not 'show up' at the shop. **1914** ATHERTON *Perch of Devil* 55 Mr. Compton . . . don't show up till nearly six.

+Show boat. A river boat carrying a troupe of actors and having a place where plays are performed. — **1869** *Atlantic Mo.* July 82/2 Jealousy may be as rife on a Mississippi show-boat as in the antechamber of any court in Europe. **1907** STEWART *Partners* 229, 'I'm with the show-boat,' he said, pointing farther up the river. **1909** RICE *Mr. Opp* 98 A new and handsome Show Boat will tie up at the Cove.

Show box. A box in which some object or curiosity is displayed as a show. {1748–} Also fig. — **1833** HAWTHORNE *Twice-told Tales* (1879) II. 134 [We rescued] the show-box of such a couple from a mob of great double-fisted countrymen. **1848** BUSHNELL *Work & Play* (1864) 35 It is merely to classify facts on a basis of comparison or abstraction; that is, to arrange a show-box and call it philosophy.

Show case. A glass case for displaying and protecting various articles. {1879} — **1839** BRIGGS *H. Franco* II. 2 Spruce looking gentlemen, . . . with glass show cases on the side walk, displaying . . . jewelry, and soaps, and penknives. *a*1861 WINTHROP *Open Air* 314 Nothing could be gayer or brighter or more party-colored than the confectioners' show-cases. **1923** VANCE *Baroque* 32 Aniello Barocco . . . was leaning on one of the show cases that fenced apart the makeshift office and the body of the shop.

+Show-down.

1. *Poker.* A play in which a bet is called, and the hand or hands are revealed.

1884 *Gringo & Greaser* 15 Feb. 2/2 In the show down Estevan held only a bobtail flush. **1898** W. C. MORROW *Ape, Idiot* 159 Never disclose your hand except on a showdown.

2. *fig.* In a business or other deal, an action bringing matters to an issue; an open disclosure of plans, means, etc. {1909}

1895 *Chicago Strike of 1894* 32 Where I had to deal with the devil and wanted a show-down, . . . I had enough sense to know that my only hope was to go into partnership with him. **1902** BELL *Hope Loring* 122 Remember to let him try it if it comes to a show-down. **1904** *N.Y. Globe* 28 March 2 A 'show-down' disclosed the fact that all the district leaders were with him. **1912** RAINE *Brand Blotters* 58 There will be a showdown some day.

* **Shower.**

***1.** A short fall of rain; a short-lasting, heavy rainstorm.

1732 FRANKLIN *Poor Richard's Almanac 1733* 11 Pleasant Showers. **1800** BOUCHER *Glossary* p. xlix, The soil is . . . washed away by the sudden and impetuous showers common in those countries [Va. and Md.], during the summer season. **1863** HOPLEY *Life in South* I. 94 'Shower' seemed but

a mild term for what we should call a hurricane, or violent tempest. **1907** *St. Nicholas* May 655/2 There had been a shower a short time before.

+2. = SHOWER BATH 1.

1851 *Knickerb.* XXXVIII. 178, [I] must go and take a 'shower' in the adjoining bath-room. **1873** 'MARK TWAIN' & WARNER *Gilded Age* 308 He has fell back on hot foot-baths at night and cold showers in the morning.

+3. A party at which presents are given a person or institution.

See also *kitchen shower* (under KITCHEN 4 d).

1904 *N.Y. Tribune* 27 Oct. 7 The managers of the Home for the Friendless invite the public to a linen shower and reception. **1905** *Dialect Notes* III. 94 *Shower,* a party given a prospective bride, at which she receives presents of some one kind.

Shower bath.

1. A bath taken under an overhead spray. {1803–}

1785 CUTLER in *Life & Corr.* II. 230 He still feels the good effects of the shower-bath. **1845** SOL. SMITH *Theatr. Apprent.* 216 A feeling of all-overish-ness, like that experienced by a timid child while enjoying (?) the luxury of a cold shower-bath. **1893** POST *Harvard Stories* 57 His hair was all damp and on end after his shower-bath at the boat-house.

b. A form of punishment.

1866 LOSSING *Hudson* 303 The terrible Shower Bath . . . is now seldom used [at Sing Sing Prison].

2. The place or apparatus for a bath under a spray. {1815–}

1797 MORSE *Amer. Gazetteer* s.v. *Bath,* A commodious bathing-house has been erected, . . . containing hot, cold, and shower baths. **1869** 'MARK TWAIN' *Innocents* 80 The general size of a store in Tangier is about that of an ordinary shower-bath in a civilized land. **1899** in *Congress. Rec.* 31 Jan. (1900) 1355/2 The great hospitals . . . have been provided with bath tubs, closets, shower baths [etc.].

* **Showing.** +A display or performance of an indicated kind. {1902} — **1869** *Rep. Comm. Agric. 1868* 51 This is a very meager showing, but an export of ten times the amount would be worse. **1876** RAYMOND *8th Rep. Mines* 453 We have been unable to obtain any data that justifies a showing so favorable. **1894** *Vt. Agric. Rep.* XIV. 97 When one sizes up the points of this horse he is not surprised at the good showing made by the animal. **1902** LORIMER *Lett. Merchant* 141, I would feel a good deal happier over your showing if you would make a downright failure or a clean-cut success once in a while.

Showman. One who exhibits a show; a proprietor of a show {*a*1734–}; one skilled in presenting things dramatically. — **1787** CUTLER in *Life & Corr.* I. 309 There are constant exhibitions from rope-dancers, mountebanks, jugglers, and show-men. **1851** NORTHALL *Curtain* 167 Barnum however displayed a little of the show-man. **1920** COOPER *Under Big Top* 46 Buffalo Bill was a showman.

+Showt'l. [Amer. Indian.] A marmotlike rodent (*Aplodontia rufa*) of the west coast region. Also with defining terms. — **1859** BAIRD *Mammals N. Amer.* 354 This animal . . . is now called Showt'l. **1884** [see MOUNTAIN 9 a]. **1917** *Mammals of Amer.* 206 On account of certain well-defined peculiarities, the Sewellel, or Showt'l has been placed in a family by itself, Rafinesque's Showt'l. . . . Pacific Showt'l. . . . California Showt'l. . . . Olympic Showt'l.

+Show window. A display window in a store. — **1855** M. THOMPSON *Doesticks* 118 [Ladies] used to perform their perpetual gyrations in the show-windows. **1890** *Stock Grower & Farmer* 25 Jan. 6/3 A most fitting emblem of that city has recently been placed in a New York show-window —a sponge eight feet in circumference. **1914** 'BOWER' *Flying U Ranch* 33 Where do you keep him when he ain't in the show window?

+Showy lady's-slipper. A pink-and-white-flowered American orchid, *Cypripedium reginae.* — **1857** GRAY *Botany* 454 Showy Lady's Slipper. . . . The most beautiful of the genus. **1898** CREEVEY *Flowers of Field* 81 Showy Lady's Slipper. . . . In peat-swamps . . . it may be seen to grow in numbers.

+Showy orchis. A North American orchid, *Galeorchis spectabilis.* — **1857** GRAY *Botany* 443 Showy Orchis. . . . On hills in rich woods, New England to Kentucky. **1890** *Cent.* 4141/3 The common American species of *Orchis* is *O. spectabilis,* the showy orchis.

* **Shredder.** +1. A machine for cutting up stalks of corn or cane for fodder. +2. A machine for shredding wheat. — **(1) 1887** *Century Mag.* Nov. 113/2 The canes . . . [go] first to a 'shredder.' **(2) 1909** *Cent. Suppl.* 1214/1 *Shredder.* . . . Prepared whole wheat is fed between each pair of rolls and is torn into long threads.

* **Shrew.** Any of several small molelike animals of the family Soricidae, +esp. *Sorex personatus* and *Blarina brevicauda.* Often with defining terms. (See also MOLE SHREW 1.) — **1826** GODMAN *Amer. Nat. Hist.* I. 77 Cats . . . will hunt and destroy shrews. **1868** *Amer. Naturalist* Dec. 528, I saw two shrews . . . running swiftly over some of the gigantic prostrate logs of arborvitae. **1885** *Ib.* Sept. 922 The little shrew, *Blarina parvula,* from Western Kansas. **1917** *Mammals of Amer.* 312 Rocky Mountain Water Shrew.—*Neosorex navigator navigator. Ib.,* The Marsh Shrew ranges from central Minnesota to the east base of the Rocky Mountains.

+Shrew mole. a. Any mole of the genera *Scalopus* and *Scapanus.* **b.** = MOLE SHREW. Also with defining terms. — **1826** GODMAN *Amer. Nat. Hist.* I. 84 The shrew-mole is found abundantly in North America, from Canada to Virginia. **1842** *Nat. Hist. N.Y., Zoology* I. 17 The Shrew-mole has a wide geographical range. **1905** ELLIOT *Check List Mammals*

466 *Neurotrichus gibbsi....* Gibbs' Shrew Mole. *Ib.* 467 *Neurotrichus gibbsi major....* Large Shrew Mole. *Ib., Neurotrichus gibbsi hyacinthinus....* Hyacinthine Shrew Mole.

+**Shrewsbury.** An oyster taken from the Shrewsbury River, New Jersey. — **1844** *Knickerb.* XXIII. 500 Here we are with ... our Shrewsburys, and Blue pointers, a shilling's worth of either worth all the shellfish that ever grew on the French coast.

Shrewsbury cake. A crisp, waferlike cake. {1728-} — **1805** *Pocumtuc Housewife* (1906) 31 Shrewsbury Cakes. **1867** *Common Sense Cook Book* 103 Shrewsbury Cakes.... Cut it [the dough] into small round cakes.

+**Shrewsbury fever.** (See quotation.) — **1849** *Knickerb.* XXXIV. 423 Although in these mountain districts we feel comparatively free from apprehension of the cholera, we have had an impressive reminder of the pestilence in the ravages which a disease, called the Shrewsbury fever, has made in a family living a few hundred feet behind us.

***Shrike.** Any of several birds of the family Laniidae, esp. of the genus *Lanius*. Also with specifying terms. (See also GREAT AMERICAN, LOGGERHEAD, NORTHERN SHRIKE.) — **1808** WILSON *Ornithology* I. 75 This habit of the Shrike of seizing and impaling grasshoppers and other insects on thorns, has given rise [etc.]. **1883** THAXTER *Poems for Children* 23 The wicked shrike Harshly creaks like some half-open door. **1917** California, Gambel's, Migrant shrike [see GAMBEL].

* **Shrimp.** Any of numerous crustaceans of the genus *Crago* or allied genera: (see also quot. 1871).

See also MANTIS SHRIMP.

1612 SMITH, etc. *Virginia* I. 15 Of fish we were best acquainted with ... Shrimps, Creuises, Oysters, Cocles, and Muscles. **1709** LAWSON *Carolina* 162 Shrimps are here very plentiful and good. **1770** PITTMAN *Present State* 5 Shrimps are found in the Mississippi as far as Natches. **1871** *Amer. Naturalist* V. 400, I have observed them [feed] ... upon several species of *Mysis* and *Thysanopoda*, called 'shrimp' by the fishermen. **1911** *Rep. Fisheries 1908* 316/1 Prawns are generally larger than shrimps, often attaining a length of 7 inches.

b. Attrib. and comb. with *boat, catcher, chaff,* etc.

1883 *Harper's Mag.* May 827/1 The Chinese shrimp-catchers are found in the cove at Potrero [Calif.] **1883** *Nat. Museum Bul.* No. 27, 117 On the coast of the Southern States, the shrimp fishery has attained considerable development in some sections. *Ib.* 701 Chinese *shrimp-boat....* Used in shrimp-fishing in San Francisco Bay, and generally in California. **1891** *Cent.* 5599/3 *Shrimp-chaff*, refuse winnowed from dried shrimps by Chinese in California, and exported to China as a fertilizer for tea-plants.

Shrinkage. A reduction in the size, amount, or numbers of a thing, assets, etc. {1800-} — **1770** WASHINGTON *Diaries* I. 390 The loss in the shrinkage if Green Wheat is not equal to that of its shattering ... when it is over-ripe. a**1848** *N.Y. Tribune* (B.), A new carriage-wheel has been invented, the spokes of which, should they become loose through wear or shrinkage, are made tight by a few turns with a wrench. **1870** M. H. SMITH *20 Years Wall St.* 49 Shrinkages in dry goods stores produce ruin. **1888** *Economist* 27 Oct. 3/2 The shrinkage that these [railroad] concerns have suffered is due mainly to growing competition and consequent reduction in rates.

Shropshire. Short for SHROPSHIRE-DOWN. {1886} Also attrib. — **1890** *Stock Grower & Farmer* 29 March 5/1 The breed are known as coarse wool Shropshires, an animal noted for weight and hardiness. **1892** *Vt. Agric. Rep.* XII. 146 The prize Southdown and Shropshire sheep of the State are here.

Shropshire-Down. A breed of sheep. — **1883** ALLEN *New Farm Book* 423 *Shropshire-Downs.*—Under this name a larger variety of the Down sheep has of late been introduced among us.

* **Shrub.**[1] In the specific names of plants and trees: (see quotations).

1789 MORSE *Amer. Geog.* 247 [The] shrub cranberry ... grows on low ground. **1836** GILMAN *Recoll.* 227 The shrub honeysuckle threw out its perfume beneath. **1813** MUHLENBERG *Cat. Plants* 85 *Morus scabra*, rough, shrub mulberry. **1771** J. R. FORSTER *Flora Amer. Septentr.* 6 *Ptelea trifoliata.* Shrub trefoil. Virginia. **1817-8** EATON *Botany* (1822) 441 *Salix recurvata*, shrub willow. **1785** MARSHALL *Amer. Grove* 168 *Xanthorhiza simplicissima.* Shrub Yellow Root.... This shrub ... might be employed to good purpose in dying cloaths.

Shrub.[2] {1747-} +(See quot. 1891 and cf. RASPBERRY SHRUB.) — **1787** *R.I. Commerce* II. 310 When our People begin to drink Punch, we will try what can be done with the Arrack and Schrub. **1860** HOLMES *Elsie Venner* vii, There would be lemonade and srub for those that preferred such drinks. **1891** *Cent.* 5602/2 *Shrub*, ... a cordial or syrup consisting of the acid juice of some fruit, as the raspberry, cooked with sugar and vinegar, and diluted with water when used.

* **Shrubby,** *a.* In the specific names of plants: (see quotations). — **1860** DARLINGTON *Weeds & Plants* 67 *H[ibiscus] Syriacus....* Syrian Hibiscus. Rose of Sharon. Shrubby Althæa. **1785** MARSHALL *Amer. Grove* 5 *Shrubby Bastard Indigo.* This grows naturally in Carolina ... to the height of ten or twelve feet. **1814** BIGELOW *Florula Bostoniensis* 169 *Hedysarum frutescens.* Shrubby Hedysarum.... A slender, whitish, woody plant, found in dry woods. **1785** MARSHALL *Amer. Grove* 55 *Glycine frutescens.* Carolinian Shrubby Kidney Bean.... The flowers ... are succeeded by long cylindrical pods of two cells. **1901** MOHR *Plant Life Ala.* 85 Coral-berry and shrubby St. John's wort (*Hypericum prolificum*) [form] the bushy covering of the ground.

Shrub oak. {1753} +=SCRUB OAK. — **1778** CARVER *Travels* 508 The Shrub Oak is exactly similar to the oak tree. **1790** DEANE *New-Eng. Farmer* 127/1 The use of the narrow hoe is ... to take up strong roots, such as those of the shrub-oak. **1832** WILLIAMSON *Maine* I. 109 The Shrub Oak grows 8 or 10 feet in height. **1907** *St. Nicholas* May 620/2 He wore ... stout shoes, [and] strong gray trousers to brave shrub-oaks and smilax.

Shruffy, *a.* Of land: Covered with scrubby growth suitable for fuel. *Obs.* — **1647** *Dedham Rec.* III. 123 Granted to Richard Ellice & his heirs for euer one parcell of shruffie meadow. **1659** *Ib.* IV. 8 Granted to Nathaneall Coaleburne and to his heyers for euer two smale parcells of shruffey vpland. **1662** *Ib.* 51 John Haward moue for a parcell of shrufie land adjoyneng to his meadowe.

Shuck, *n.* {1674-}

'Chiefly *dial.* and *U.S.*' (*O.E.D.*). See also CORN SHUCK.

+**1.** The husk of an ear of corn. Also collect.

a**1805** *Steele P.* II. 864 Anderson ... cribbed 40 waggon Loads of corn in shucks. **1854** *Fla. Plantation Rec.* 91 Evens ... sent me 26 barels in the Shuck. **1891** *Century Mag.* Feb. 489 Of these identical shucks the family bed is made. **1904** T. E. WATSON *Bethany* 11 Peas, potatoes, fodder, shucks—he always had more than enough.

+**b.** =CORN SHUCK 2.

1850 GARRARD *Wah-To-Yah* xiv. 175 The shucks are dried and cut in slips, one and a half inches broad by three in length.... When the shuck lights, the burning roll is drawn in the tube.

+**2.** The shell or husk of a hickory nut. {1674-1847, of other nuts}

1853 *Knickerb.* XLII. 369 He sat bolt upright in a hickory, eating nuts, and throwing the shucks on the ground. **1880** *Harper's Mag.* Nov. 865 There was a splendid tall shagbark close by, with branches fairly loaded with the white nuts in their open shucks. **1894** EGGLESTON in *Century Mag.* April 850 About Lake George, I find 'shuck' used ... for the outer covering of the hickory-nut.

+**b.** *S.* The shell of an oyster.

1859 BARTLETT 404 *Shucks....* At the South, where the word is most in use, it is also applied to the shells of oysters. **1881** INGERSOLL *Oyster-Industry* 248.

+**3.** Something worthless. Usu. pl. Often in phrases.

1843 W. T. THOMPSON *Major Jones's Courtship* 48 Tom Stallins had ... one grate big yaller cur, what wasn't worth shucks to trail. **1857** *Knickerb.* XLIX. 37 Nobody ever made shucks out of *you*. **1861** *Ill. Agric. Soc. Trans.* IV. 478, I would not give 'shucks' for it in our locality. **1876** 'MARK TWAIN' *Tom Sawyer* vii. 75 Church ain't shucks to a circus. **1886** HARRIS in *Century Mag.* Jan. 427/2 This yer one ... don't amount to shucks. **1894** 'MARK TWAIN' *P. Wilson* xi, Here they don't give shucks for his scientifics. **1906** *Washington Post* 11 May 6 It has not been very long since no political platform was worth shucks that did not contain a plank denunciatory of England. **1911** SAUNDERS *Col. Todhunter* 33 Fetchin' and carryin' for the girls, ... don't count for shucks.

+**b.** (See quotation.)

1871 DE VERE 47 During the Civil War ... the original Blue Backs of the Confederacy (so-called in opposition to the Green Backs of the Union) soon became known as Shucks, a name sufficiently significant of their evil repute as a circulating medium.

4. *attrib.* +**a.** Designating things stuffed or padded with corn husks.

See also SHUCK BOTTOM, SHUCK COLLAR.

1844 KENDALL *Narr. Santa Fé Exped.* II. 97 He gave us ... a shuck bed to sleep upon. **1851** *Knickerb.* XXXVII. 393 There was but an apology for a bed-stead, with a 'shuck' mattress on it. **1885** 'MARK TWAIN' in *Century Mag.* Feb. 547/2 There's always cobs around about in a shuck tick. **1896** READ *Jucklins* 128, [I saw] ... a red-looking negro, with a string of shuck horse collars.

b. In sense 1 b with *cigarette, cigarillo*.

Cf. SHUCK CIGAR.

1850 GARRARD *Wah-To-Yah* xii. 165 After rolling up and smoking a shuck *cigarillo*, [he] coiled himself before the fire in his one blanket to sleep. **1905** 'O. HENRY' *Roads of Destiny* 141 He rolled a shuck cigarette.

c. In special combinations.

Shuck basket, a basket for carrying corn shucks; *s. house*, a structure where corn is shucked; *s. tea*, tea made by steeping corn shucks in boiling water.

1866 C. H. SMITH *Bill Arp* 123 My worldly possessions ... [included] a shuck basket full of some second-class vittels. **1856** *Fla. Plantation Rec.* 487 I, Renty, gitten sills to go under shucke house. **1888** *Whitewater* (Wis.) *Reg.* 23 Feb., Oftentimes the simplest remedies, such as pine-water or shuck-tea, were made to serve a timely and efficient turn.

+**Shuck,** *v.*

1. *tr.* To remove the husks from an ear of (corn); to remove the husk from (a nut). Also absol.

The process of husking corn often includes the jerking of the ear from the cornstalk: (see CORN-HUSKING 1, CORN-SHUCKING 1).

1834 NOTT *Novellettes* II. 144 The farmers occasionally employed the mountaineers to ... shuck corn. **1883** *Century Mag.* Oct. 812/2 The nuts must be ... first picked, then shucked, then dried. **1901** CHURCHILL *Crisis* 491, I shuck an ear of corn before I buy it. **1922** CATHER *One of Ours* 79 Claude sent Dan to shuck on the north quarter.

b. To take the shells off (oysters).

1879 *Harper's Mag.* June 64/1 The oysters are generally shucked early in the morning. **1881** INGERSOLL *Oyster-Industry* 248 *Shuck*, to open oysters. (Baltimore and southward.) **1891** W. K. BROOKS *Oyster* 17 He said that . . . he could 'shuck' thirty-six oysters a minute.

2. To take *out* from a conveyance; to take *off*, to cast (a coat or other garment). Also *fig.*

1848 W. T. THOMPSON *Major Jones's Sk. Travel* 178 After shuckin out the passengers and baggage, . . . they tuck us down a steep hill to the steamboate. *a*1859 *Southern Sketches* 31 (B.), He'd shuck off his coat to fight. **1887** *Century Mag.* April 846/2 Now, will you shuck them duds? **1891** *Ib.* Nov. 62 They have never shucked their boyhood. **1906** *Ridgway's Wkly.* 20 Oct. 53 He emptied the papers on the floor, and fell listlessly to shucking off the wrappers. **1908** 'O. HENRY' *Options* 76 Please shuck the hide off that letter and read it.

3. *refl.* To undress (one's self); to strip (one's self) *of* something.

1845 *Big Bear Ark.* 93 He got behin' the door and shuck'd himself. **1877** W. WRIGHT *Big Bonanza* 378 Carter began to wriggle from side to side in the effort to 'shuck' himself of the long-tailed black coat. **1897** R. M. JOHNSTON *Old Times Middle Ga.* 37 Sam . . . shucked hisself out his workin'-clothes.

4. *intr.* **a.** To get *out* of one's clothes.

1848 W. T. THOMPSON *Major Jones's Sk. Travel* 117, I shucked out of my old clothes.

b. Of corn: To yield an amount of grain in shucking.

1871 *Ill. Agric. Soc. Trans.* VIII. 240 The hills of corn in a field planted five feet apart each way, and with four stalks to a hill, will not shuck any more corn per hill than those [etc.]. **1874** EGGLESTON *Circuit Rider* 12 The first comers . . . spent the time looking at the heap [of corn], and speculating as to how many bushels it would 'shuck out.'

+Shuck bottom. A chair seat padded with corn shucks. Also *attrib.* — **1872** EGGLESTON *End of World* 282 Jonas . . . was sitting on a 'shuck-bottom' chair. **1898** E. C. HALL *Aunt Jane* 4 The chairs were ancient Shaker rockers, some with homely 'shuck' bottoms.

+Shuck-bottomed chair. A chair with a shuck bottom. — **1841** *S. Lit. Messenger* VII. 775/1 The more provident part of the slaves . . . [manufacture] shuck-bottomed chairs, mats, shuck collars, brooms, and the like. **1888** EGGLESTON *Graysons* xxxi, He drew up another shuck-bottomed chair.

+Shuck cigar. A roll of tobacco enclosed in a corn shuck for smoking. — **1841** KENDALL in *Picayune* 26 June 2/2 Of the Mexican population [at San Antonio, Tex., the men are] . . . extremely fond of smoking *shuck cigars*. **1850** GARRARD *Wah-To-Yah* xviii. 211 In my dreams, *rebozas*, black eyes, and shuck cigars were mixed in admirable confusion.

+Shuck collar. A horse collar padded with corn shucks. — **1781** *Va. State P.* I. 589 Many of these [horses] are sent with 'shuck-collars.' **1841** [see SHUCK-BOTTOMED CHAIR].

+Shucker. **1.** A digger Indian. *Obs.* **2.** =CORN-SHUCKER. **3.** One who shucks oysters. — (1) **1836** IRVING *Astoria* I. 276 Another class [of the Snake Indians], the most abject and forlorn, . . . are called Shuckers, or more commonly Diggers and Root eaters. (2) **1874** EGGLESTON *Circuit Rider* 17 He started the whiskey bottle on its encouraging travels along the line of shuckers. **1882** *Century Mag.* Oct. 874/1 Two 'gin'r'ls' . . . proceed to divide the shuckers into two parties. (3) **1879** *Harper's Mag.* June 64/1 In the shining pans in front of the shuckers are quarts of clean . . . oysters. **1887** GOODE, etc. *Fisheries* v. II. 553 The average amount made by the shuckers . . . [is] $6 a week.

+Shucking.

1. a. A corn-husking bee. **b.** The action of removing the shells of nuts or oysters.

1817 ROYALL *Lett. from Ala.* 31, I only got a little lively at brother I's shucking. **1845** KIRKLAND *Western Clearings* 101 We were soon well pelted with nuts, and busily engaged in freeing them from their aromatic wrappers—an operation which we of the West call 'shucking.' **1871** EGGLESTON *Hoosier Schoolm.* 25 Spelling and 'shucking' are the only public competitions. **1879** *Harper's Mag.* June 64/1 Here the chief interest centres—the 'shucking' or opening of oysters.

2. *attrib.* Designating actions, instruments, etc., used in shucking corn or oysters.

1852 *Knickerb.* XL. 45 At a 'shucking-bee,' as they have to work, the feasting is gratis, for those who would feast. **1855** *Putnam's Mo.* Jan. 77/2 The following shucking song has nothing to recommend it to public attention, save the questionable rhyme to 'supper.' **1879** *Harper's Mag.* June 64/1 At the first glance into a shucking-house it looks terribly dirty. **1881** INGERSOLL *Oyster-Industry* 248 *Shucking stand*, a rude table, with boxed sides, etc., at which oysters are opened. (South.) **1884** *Nat. Museum Bul.* No. 27, 220 On each side of each alley are numerous stalls, each fitted with a 'shucking trough,' or box-like receptacle for the oysters. **1886** EBBUTT *Emigrant Life* 180 The hand is armed with a 'shucking-peg,' either of wood or iron fastened on with a thong,—which tears open the shucks on the ears of corn.

+Shuck pen. A pen in which corn shucks are put. — **1844** *S. Lit. Messenger* X. 486/1 The neighbor aforesaid had the comforts of a shuck-pen, in which to console himself for the night. **1895** HARRIS in *Scribner's Mag.* Dec. 726/2 Jeff, the little beagle, could have whipped a shuck-pen full of them without ever showing his teeth.

+Shucks, *interj.* An exclamation of disgust or regret. *colloq.* — **1847** FIELD *Drama in Pokerville* 68 And Mr. Bagly was there . . . [to shoot] any gentleman who might say 'shucks!' **1857** 'MARK TWAIN' *Adv. Snodgrass* 45 Shucks, a shiveree wasn't nothing longside it. **1879** BISHOP *4 Months in Sneak-Box* 179 His favorite expression seemed to be, 'Oh, shucks!' **1916** PORTER *David* 107 Shucks! It'll take more'n you ter make me think a crow can sing.

Shuffle, v. intr. To dance a double shuffle or the like. {tr., 1818–} — **1809** IRVING *Knickerb.* VII. i, He would occasionally give a nod of approbation to those of the young men who shuffled and kicked most vigorously.

Shuffleboard, Shovelboard. **a.** A game in which a disk or coin is driven by the fingers or the hand along a board or floor marked off with transverse lines; the board on which this game is played. **b.** A game similarly played with cues ('shovels') and large disks on the deck of a ship.

'The modern game as played in the U.S. is always called *shuffleboard*' (O.E.D).

1647 *Mass. Bay Rec.* III. 114 Vppon complaynt made of great disorder . . . by the vse of the game called shouelboard, it is therefore ordred . . . that no person shall henceforth vse the sd game of shoffle board. **1650** *Conn. Rec.* I. 527 No person shall henceforth vse the said Game of Shuffle Board. **1860** MORDECAI *Virginia* 219 Shovel-board and other innocent games were played at the cool and shaded spring. **1879** HOWELLS *Lady of Aroostook* 88 A young person . . . played shuffle-board and ring-toss on the deck of the Aroostook. **1910** J. HART *Vigilante Girl* 12 The [ship] passengers . . . play no games; the shuffleboard is unused.

Shuffler. {1611–} **+1.** A scaup duck. Also *attrib.* **+2.** The coot, *Fulica americana.* — (1) **1845** HOOPER *Taking Census* (1928) 111 Sol . . . went under the water in the 'Buck Hole,' 'like a shuffler duck with his wing broke.' **1852** BAIRD in Stansbury *Gt. Salt Lake* 324 Little Blackhead; Shuffler. Found across the continent. **1874** COUES *Birds N.W.* 573. (2) **1889** *Cent.* 1252/1 The common or bald coot of Europe is *F. atra*; that of America is *F. americana*, sometimes called *shuffler*. **1917** *Birds of Amer.* I. 214.

Shumach. (See SHOEMAKE.)
Shuman. (See SHAMAN.)

+Shun-pike. A way, esp. a side road, for avoiding a tollgate on a turnpike road. — **1853** W. McMURRAY *Speech* 28 March 17/1 (Th.S.), The Oswego Canal . . . has been called a 'shun pike.' **1881** PIERSON *In the Brush* 27, I saw tracks leading off into the woods, and was told that they were known as 'shunpikes.' **1903** STOCKTON *Captain's Toll-Gate* 6 A road . . . branched off from the turnpike . . . [and] entered the pike again beyond the toll-gate, and . . . it had seen a good deal of travel, which, in time, gave it the name of the shunpike.

Shut, a. Of a door, railroad switch, shutters: Closed. +With verbs *draw, push,* etc. — **1884** *Century Mag.* Nov. 13 [He] pushed the ground-glass door shut. **1902** WISTER *Virginian* xiv, Car wheels clicked over the main-line switch. A train-hand threw it shut after. **1911** HARRISON *Queed* 23 The last boarder rising drew shut the folding-doors into the parlor. **1924** MULFORD *Rustlers' Valley* xii, No one cared to light another lamp until . . . the shutters [had been] slammed shut.

Shut, v.

To shut (one's) face, head, pan, (see FACE *n.* 1 c, HEAD *n.* 5 a, PAN *n.* 7).

1. *To shut down.* {1794–} **a.** Of mountains, fog, and darkness: To come close down; to lower or fall. {1891–}

1779 *N.H. Hist. Soc. Coll.* VI. 320 Here the mountains shut down close on the river for 7 or 8 miles. **1869** *Onward* June 509 What's yonder? Is it a fogbank shutting down? **1962** CORBIN *Amer. at Oxford* 145 Long after the quick American twilight has shut down.

b. To close up (a mill or other establishment); to stop (work). {1880–} Also *absol.*

1850 JUDD *R. Edney* 377 Richard . . . was 'shutting down' the Mill, one day, in his lively way. **1876** RAYMOND *8th Rep. Mines* 226 The hands . . . forced the superintendent to shut down. **1891** C. ROBERTS *Adrift Amer.* 64 The contractor decided to 'shut down' the work. **1906** BELL C. *Lee* 243 Half the time this cheap negro labour . . . is drunk or striking, which often shuts down the plant for days at a time.

+c. Of a mill or other establishment: To close down.

1878 *Lumberman's Gazette* 8 Dec. 361 Eight of the steam saw mills at Muskegon were . . . expected to shut down this week for want of logs. **1903** *N.Y. Times* 16 Aug., The Hamilton Cotton Mills shut down to-day because of the state of the cotton market.

+d. To clamp down *on*, as by suppression or dismissal.

1886 JAMES *Bostonians* 149 She thought it prudent not to attempt to cut short the phrase . . . an imputation she should incur if, without more delay, she were to 'shut down,' as Verena said, on the young connoisseur. **1889** *Century* April 885/2 He shut down upon his wrath. **1891** WILKINS *New Eng. Nun* 106 She's been sewin' boots for Allen over at Wayne, but I heard the other day he was goin' to shut down on her.

⁂2. To shut out, +in baseball, to prevent (an opposing team) from scoring or from winning a single game.

1881 *N.Y. Herald* 17 July 10/3 The Domestics were shut out in every inning up to the eighth, when by bunching their hits they scored two earned runs on a single by Mahny. **1894** *Spalding's Base Ball Guide* 40 Nichols . . . shut out the St. Louis team without a game to their credit out of four games played. **1922** *Lit. Digest* 27 May 57/1 Another Robertson, of Yale, shut out Princeton without a hit.

+**Shutdown. 1.** An action of closing off something. **2.** *spec.* The discontinuance of work at a factory, oil well, etc. {1888, of America} — (1) **1857** *Knickerb.* XLIX. 35, 'I'll be just exactly shot if you *don't!*' he added with a patent diabolical shut-down. (2) **1884** *Boston Jrnl.* 16 Oct. 7 The Acushnet paper-mill at New Bedford has started up after a shut-down of two months. **1896** *Typographical Jrnl.* IX. 308 When a large concern feels a slight pressure on the strings of the exchequer there is a 'shut-down.' **1904** TARBELL *Hist. Standard Oil Co.* I. 121 In spite of the thirty days' shut-down, production was increasing.

Shute. {1790-} +Variant of CHUTE *n.* in various American senses. (See also SCHUTE, SHOOT.) — **1812** MELISH *Travels* II. 151 The water was low, and I observed three different passages, of which that on the Indiana side, called *Indian Shute*, is said to be the best. **1853** 'P. PAXTON' *Yankee in Texas* 46 Mr. Lefe Thompson . . . had cut the Gordian knot, and—as Judge Guffey would have said—'taken the shute.' **1857** *Harper's Mag.* Sept. 462/1 Miners . . . first make a small incision through the gangway pillar, which serves . . . as a shute for the excavated coal. **1865** [see FISH LADDER]. **1880** *Harper's Mag.* Oct. 726/1 Into a car goes a great *shute*, or nozzle; somebody pulls a lever, and, presto! away has gone that grain up into a weighing bin.

+**Shut-eye.** *Shut-eye flavor*, (see quotation). — **1848** LOWELL *Biglow* P. I Ser. p. x, I was not backward to recognize in them [*sc.* verses] a certain wild, puckery, acidulous (sometimes even verging toward that point which, in our rustic phrase, is termed *shut-eye*) flavor, not wholly unpleasing, nor unwholesome, to palates cloyed with the sugariness of tamed and cultivated fruit.

+**Shut-pan,** *n.* and *a.* [Cf. PAN *n.* 7.] *colloq.* **1.** *n.* The act of being secretive. **2.** *adj.* Close-mouthed. — (1) **1881–5** MCCLELLAN *Own Story* 161 The President [Lincoln] . . . said: 'Well, Mr. Blair, I was obliged to play shut-pan with you last night.' (2) **1889** *Century Mag.* Sept. 704/1, I shall be very 'shut pan' about this matter.

* **Shutter.**

1. A movable iron or wooden screen for a window or, less often, a door, to secure protection, privacy, etc. {1814-, but cf. WINDOW SHUTTER.}
See also FOLDING SHUTTER.
1695 SEWALL *Diary* I. 413 Was much pleas'd with our painted shutters. **1706** *Boston News-Letter* 7 Jan. 2/2 To be Sold . . . Two pair of Tongs, one Fork, and five Iron Shutters. **1799** in Rothert *Muhlenberg Co.* 45 A window in each room and shutters to each window. **1857** VAUX *Villas* 101 [Windows] may be fitted with . . . inside shutters, partly solid and partly filled in with slats. **1880** CABLE *Grandissimes* 117 The daughter presently threw open the batten shutters of its single street door. **1902** LORIMER *Lett. Merchant* 101 When it comes closing time for me it will make it a heap easier to know that some one who bears the name will take down the shutters in the morning.

+**b.** A screen to shut up a fire in a stove or fire box.
1744 FRANKLIN *Acct. Fire-Places* 15 The Shutter is . . . of such a Length and Breadth as to close well the Opening of the Fire-Place.

2. Attrib. and comb. with *bolt, fastener.*
1777 *Essex Inst. Coll.* XLIX. 106 Sold . . . shutter bolts. **1844** *Lexington Observer* 2 Oct. 4/1, 20 doz Shutter Fastners . . . just received and for sale by Edwin Stephens.

+**Shuttle train.** (See quot. 1891.) — **1891** *Cent.* 5607/1 *Shuttle train*, . . . a train running back and forth for a short distance like a shuttle, as over a track connecting a main line with a station at a short distance from it. **1923** *World Almanac* 503/2 A shuttle train runs between 50th Street and 59th Street, on Sixth Avenue.

Shy, *v.* {1650-} ‖'To hang about'(B.). — **1845** S. SMITH *J. Downing's Lett.* p. iii, [I] was kind of shying round, and looking at the everlastin' sight of books they've got.

* **Shy,** *a.*

+**1.** *Poker.* Short: (see quot. 1895).
1887 KELLER *Draw Poker* 28 The worst of all poker habits, owing the pool, or 'going shy,' as it is called, results from the non-observance of this very important rule. **1895** *Stand.* 1662/3 *Shy*, . . . having a less amount of money at stake than is called for by the rules of the game; short; as, to be shy a dollar in the pool.

+**2.** Short *of* or *on;* lacking; entirely without.
1895 *Denver Times* 5 March 1/3 (headline), J. W. Shannon, Burglar, . . . Was Shy Several Fingers. **1897** *Outing* XXX. 175/1 The guide's statement . . . was shy of the truth. **1904** *Chicago Ev. Post* 28 Sept. 4 The village justice . . . may have been a little shy in the matter of international law. **1916** 'BOWER' *Phantom Herd* 80 If they're shy on the number [of costumes], they better set down and make enough. **1921** PAINE *Comr. Rolling Ocean* 258 [By] the poor working-man, . . . they mean any greasy tramp that goes shy of a shave or a wash.

+**Shyster.** Also †**shuyster.** [Origin uncertain.] **a.** = SHYSTER LAWYER. **b.** Any unscrupulous or tricky person.
1849 FOSTER *N.Y. in Slices* 20 No Shyster disturbs his drunken meditations and no Keeper alleviates the agonies of returning sobriety. **1856** *Knickerb.* April 434 If these two 'shuysters' on the other side could get one more drink down your throat, you couldn't travel *at all.* **1859** *La Crosse Daily Union* 25 Oct. 2/3 The State Convention . . . [fell] into the hands of a set of political shysters. **1888** *Milnor* (Dak.) *Teller* 29 June

6/1 You might as well denounce the legal profession because of the shysters, . . . as to slam-bang newspapers because there are recreant editors and unfair reporters. **1923** CATHER *Lost Lady* 104, I suppose it takes longer to make an architect than it does to make a shyster.
attrib. **1870** MEDBERY *Men Wall St.* 123 Not a few individuals of the 'shyster' class . . . are ready to break their word. **1872** 'MARK TWAIN' *Roughing It* 487 Next we come to his Excellency the Prime Minister, . . . a lawyer of 'shyster' caliber. **1875** *Chicago Tribune* 2 Nov. 4/6 There are also some miscellaneous provisions directed against shyster corporations.

+**Shystering,** *n.* The activities of a shyster; living as a shyster. — **1882** HOWELLS *Modern Instance* xvii, I shouldn't like shystering. **1895** *Wkly. Examiner* (San Francisco) 19 Sept. 2/6 Those sharp practices generally passing under the name of shystering.

+**Shystering,** *a.* Tricky, unscrupulous. — **1860** *Knickerb.* LVI. 458 Outside of a kind of twopenny shystering smartness and snap-judgment genius, Dovey was . . . rather a cross between a Dutch dumpling and a one-horse blower. **1872** in R. G. White *Amer. View Copyright* 40 At Monday's session an unprepossessing person . . . made a 'shystering,' pettifogging speech.

+**Shyster lawyer.** A lawyer who preys upon his clients, esp. in the lower criminal courts, and conducts his business in an unprofessional and tricky way. — **1849** G. G. FOSTER *N.Y. in Slices* 20 He must . . . wait next day for the visits of the 'shyster' lawyers—a set of turkey-buzzards whose touch is pollution and whose breath is pestilence. **1904** *Brooklyn Eagle* 5 June, The courts swarm with fake accident cases, brought by shyster lawyers. **1923** VANCE *Baroque* 176 His shyster lawyer . . . called on me one day to protest against what he was pleased to term my persecution of his client.

Siberian, *a.* Of or characteristic of Siberia. {1719-} In the names of plants, animals, etc. {1763-}
1780 *N.H. Comm. Safety Rec.* 215 Gave a permit to Benja. Colby . . . to clear out for Pownalborough . . . [with] two Bushels of Siberian wheat. **1817** W. COXE *Fruit Trees* 106 The Siberian crab is a very beautiful apple. **1843** FRÉMONT *Explor. Rocky Mts.* 67 What was supposed to be the bleat of a hungry goat, . . . [we] found to proceed from a small animal of gray color, with short ears and no tail—probably the Siberian squirrel. **1852** *Horticulturist* VII. 176 German Greens, or Siberian Kale. . . . It is in reality, a sort of kale or cabbage, growing with spreading leaves like a turnip. **1872** COUES *Key to Birds* 130 Siberian Finch. Dusky purplish; neck above pale yellowish. **1884** *Ib.* (ed. 2) 284 *Motacilla ocularis*, Siberian Wagtail. **1892** *Apgar Trees Northern U.S.* 111 *Cornus alba*. (Siberian Red-stemmed Cornel.) . . . A shrub rather than a tree, cultivated from Siberia; hardy throughout. *Ib.* 185 *Abies Pichta*. (Siberian Silver Fir.) . . . A small to medium-sized cultivated tree.

Sibley. *attrib.* +Designating a tent or a stove of a type devised by General Henry Hastings Sibley (1811–94) and formerly used in the United States Army. Now hist. — **1861** in M. A. Jackson *Gen. Jackson* 185, I am writing under a Sibley tent, which is of a conical form. **1867** in Custer *Tenting on Plains* 516 We are in our tent, and enjoying a pleasant fire from our Sibley stove. **1907** ANDREWS *Recoll.* 149 The enlisted men occupied large, circular Sibley tents in each of which about a dozen slept.

* **Sick,** *a.*

* **1.** Suffering from illness; unwell; ailing.
'Now chiefly literary and *U.S.*'(O.E.D.). The examples in the first group show that this word has been regarded as an Americanism.
(1) **1789** WEBSTER *Dissertations Engl. Lang.* 389 [New Englanders] say, if a person is not in health, he is *sick*. The modern English laugh at them, because the English say a man is *ill*; and confine sick to express the idea of a nausea in the stomach. **1818** FEARON *Sketches* 221 A man's being *sick*, (the term applied to every species of illness,) is as common in this country, as being in distress in England. **1879** HOWELLS *Lady of Aroostook* 296 You must say ill. Sick is an Americanism.
(2) **1684** I. MATHER *Providences* (1856) viii. 192 Within a few dayes the sick party recovered. **1759** *Essex Inst. Coll.* XLIX. 1 My sister Betty had been quite Sick. **1836** *Diplom. Corr. Texas* I. (1908) 84, I was very sick yesterday and last night and am only able to sit up to day. **1920** ALSAKER *Eating for Health* 281 The parents have it in their power to keep the children well, sick half the time, or half sick all the time.

b. *Sick at* (or *to*) *the stomach,* having a desire to vomit; nauseated. {'s. at (or in) the s.,' 1653–1831}
1653 *Mass. H. S. Coll.* 4 Ser. VII. 466 She at times is sicke at her stomache. **1830** S. SMITH *Life J. Downing* 36 Rum, if they take tu much of it, makes folks *sick to the stomach*. **1872** *Vermont Bd. Agric. Rep.* I. 631 The men began to fall sick at the stomach, and some boys vomited and fell down. **1918** LINCOLN *Shavings* 51, I was sick at my stomach yesterday.

2. Used by, or suitable for, the sick. {1632-}
The adj. here partakes of the nature of an absolute used attributively.
1780 J. DODGE *Narrative* 23, I removed him to sick quarters. **1843** N. BOONE *Journal* 235 A Sick Camp was established there and many soldiers were buried. **1847** *Fla. Plantation Rec.* 302 Dye and Tempy in sick Barracks. **1848** PARKMAN in *Knickerb.* XXXII. 312 The commissary at the fort had given him an order for sick-rations. **1865** *Atlantic Mo.* Feb. 237/2 The sick home is a large three-story building. **1872** NAPHEYS *Prevention of Disease* 489 Sick-cookery does more than half do the work of the poor patient's weak digestion. **1873** PHELPS *Trotty's Wedding* viii, [He] sat back in his sick-chair and read the stories aloud.

3. *Sick and tired*, thoroughly tired or weary *of* something.
1884 NYE *Baled Hay* 124 We are sick and tired of pointing out different avenues of wealth only to be laughed at and ridiculed. **1890** CUSTER *Following Guidon* 57, I think we have rendered them sick and tired of war.

4. In special combinations.
Sick certificate, a certification of sickness; *s. excuse*, a certificate of sickness serving as an excuse; *s. lamp*, a lamp used in a sick room; *s. report*, *s. return*, a report or return of those in a military unit who are sick; *s. stomach*, a disease characterized by a sick or upset stomach.
1892 *Courier-Journal* 4 Oct. 1/4 The three cases were to have come up . . . this morning, but on the production of a sick certificate from Dann's attorneys, they were adjourned for one week. **1871** BAGG *At Yale* 582 The reason for rejecting a 'sick excuse' from a man who was not confined to his room is [etc.]. **1851** MITCHELL *Dream Life* 53 It is dreadful, when you . . . see nothing but the spectral shadows that the sick-lamp upon the hearth throws aslant the walls. **1809** *Ann. 11th Congress* 2491 The sick reports of four companies, which I attend, have enlarged considerably. **1862** STRONG *Cadet Life W. Point* 240 They all knew . . . what report the sick-return gave me. **1815** DRAKE *Cincinnati* 182 A disease called by the people the *Sick-stomach*, has prevailed . . . for several years.

Sick, *v.* Also **sic.**
1. In the imperative, addressed to a dog: To attack, fly at (an animal or person). {1908}
1845 HOOPER *Taking Census* (1928) 110 'Here, Bull!' shouted the widow, 'sick him, Pomp!' **1890** *Golden Days* 6 Sept. (*Cent.*), 'Sic 'em, Andy!' screamed Granny.

2. To urge or incite (a dog) to chase or attack. Sometimes with *at* or *on*.
1883 SWEET & KNOX *Through Texas* 660 If you were to sic him at a rabbit, . . . he wouldn't move a muscle of his eye. **1908** 'YESLAH' *Tenderfoot S. Calif.* 144 None of us cared, by gum, if they'd sicked a dog on us.

b. To encourage or incite (a person) to action of some kind. Usually with *on*.
1885 'CRADDOCK' *Prophet* 204 He sick-ed him on all the time. **1902** MACGOWAN *Last Word* 233 Sick 'em! It'll be interesting. **1923** VANCE *Baroque* 177 You ought to be able to locate that gang he sic'd on me last night.

Sick call. {1883-} *Mil.* **1.** A call or signal, usually sounded on a bugle, directing those who are sick to report for medical care; the occasion of such a call. {1918-} ‖**2.** (See quotation.) — (1) **1836** HILDRETH *Campaigns Rocky Mts.* 114 Every morning . . . 'sick call' blows. **1862** NORTON *Army Lett.* 81 There are calls 'To Strike Tents,' . . . 'Sick Call,' 'Officers Call,' 'Church Call,' etc. **1924** *Scribner's Mag.* Dec. 645/2 We got so many flat-footed recruits now that our morning sick calls look like a company drill. (2) **1865** KELLOGG *Rebel Prisons* 231, I went up to the sick-call, and was prescribed for by the Surgeon. *Ib.* 258 Outside was built a board fence the whole length of the stockade, and about three rods wide, where the doctors had the Sick Call.

＊**Sicken,** *v.* ‖*tr.* To stupefy (fish), so they may readily be taken. — **1872** *Fur, Fin & Feather* (ed. 2) 71 [No] person shall . . . sicken fish . . . in any stream, . . . [by any preparation] of a sickening, intoxicating, or destructive quality.

＊**Sickish,** *a.* Nauseating, sickening. — *a*1817 DWIGHT *Travels* II. 450 In passing these receptacles, we were saluted by a sweet, sickish effluvium, oppressive to the lungs. **1857** HAWTHORNE *Eng. Note-Books* II. 367 The atmosphere was a little faint and sickish.

Sickishly, *adv.* (See quot. 1841.) — **1841** WEBSTER II. 600/2 *Sickishly*, in a sickish manner. **1880** *Lit. World* (Boston) 24 April 139/1 Most writers upon him are either unpleasantly bitter or sickishly sweet.

＊**Sickle.**
＊**1.** A tool consisting of a long semicircular blade fastened to a short handle.
1622 'MOURT' *Relation* 75 [They] had no weapons but each one his Cicle. **1654** *Essex Probate Rec.* I. 165, 2 sickles, hand saw & a half bushell. **1824** DODDRIDGE *Notes* 77 The reaper . . . [struck] the point of the sickle through its [the rattlesnake's] head. **1875** in Wells *Practical Economics* 237 A few years ago men on the great fields of the West cut grain with sickles and with cradles.

2. In special combinations.
Sickle bar, the cutting mechanism of a mowing machine; +*s.-billed thrush*, =SICKLEBILL 2; +*s. grass*, a species of sedge (*Carex crinita*), or the tearthumb (*Tracaulon arifolium*); *s.weed*, (see quotation).
1862 *Ill. Agric. Soc. Trans.* V. 224 No 'tricks of the trade' such as . . . elevating the sickle bar above the proper cutting point were permitted to prevent a fair test. **1872** COUES *Key to Birds* 75 Sickle-billed Thrush. California Mockingbird. . . . Coast Region of California. **1854** *Mich. Agric. Soc. Trans.* VI. 149 In the low grounds are . . . marsh grass, sickel grass, three kinds of red top [etc.]. **1784** *Amer. Acad. Mem.* I. 440 *Polygonum foliis sagittatis, caule aculeato*. . . . Sickleweed. . . . Blossoms white, tinged with red.

Sicklebill. {1880-} +**1.** The long-billed curlew. In full *sicklebill curlew*. (Cf. CURLEW 3.) +**2.** The California thrasher, *Toxostoma redivivum*. — (1) **1872** COUES *Key to Birds* 262 *Numenius*, Long-billed Curlew. Sickle-bill. **1893** ROOSEVELT *Wilderness Hunter* 93 The sicklebill curlews . . . had for the most part gone southward. (2) **1881** *Amer. Naturalist* XV. 210 The California sickle-bill . . . is a resident . . . in Southern California.

+**Sicklepod.** An American species of rock cress, *Arabis canadensis*. — **1833** EATON *Botany* (ed. 6) 24. **1843** TORREY *Flora N.Y.* I. 55 Sickle-pod. Turkey-pod. . . . Rocky woods and hill sides. **1898** CREEVEY *Flowers of Field* 279 Sickle-pod . . . has sessile stem-leaves, acute at apex and base.

Sick nurse. {1821-} *spec.* +A Negro woman in charge of the sick slaves on a plantation. *Obs.* — **1842** BUCKINGHAM *Slave States* I. 133 Medicines were administered by a negro woman called the sick-nurse.

＊**Side,** *n.*
＊**1.** One of the halves of the body of a hog cured as bacon.
1650 *Essex Probate Rec.* I. 119 Two sides of pork, four sides and five roles of tob. **1818** in Commons, etc. *Doc. Hist.* I. 204 Took out of the store-room over the Kitchen 8 hams, 4 shoulders and 8 sides. **1900** BACHELLER E. *Holden* 172 A side of pork paid for many a long journey.

2. One half of a cowhide or oxhide.
1732 *S.C. Gazette* 128/1 To be sold, . . . about 600 sides of Leather in the Fatts, the greatest part of them tann'd. **1779** *Narragansett Hist. Reg.* I. 37 Returned home with a side of sole leather of Godfrey Hazard's. **1885** *Harper's Mag.* Jan. 274/2 The hides are . . . cut through the middle of the back to separate them into 'sides.'

+**3.** In either house of Congress, the part occupied by members of a given political party, or the members occupying the part. Usually with defining terms.
1873 *Republic* I. March App. p. xii, He 'would take care of the democratic side of the House.' **1886** ALTON *Among Law-Makers* 19 Seven [pages are appointed] for the Democratic side, and seven for the Republican side. **1900** *Congress. Rec.* 11 Jan. 777/1, I do not think there has been any such delay on this side of the Chamber.

4. *attrib.* and *comb.* **a.** Designating posts, planks, etc., at the sides of, and serving as supports for, various structures.
1637 *Mass. H. S. Coll.* 4 Ser. VII. 119 The side bearers for the second story . . . must not be pinned on. **1711** HEMPSTEAD *Diary* 2, I worked about ye corn & making a Side peice for Peter Manwarings Bedstid. **1832** BROWNE *Sylva* 297 [Locust] is also used for . . . the pins destined to attach the side planks to the frame. **1854** LOWELL *Writings* I. 186 What frame in what gallery ever enclosed such a picture as is squared within the groundsel, side-posts, and lintel of a barn-door? **1876** KNIGHT 1857/1 *Rail*, . . . one of the pieces connecting the posts of a bedstead. Known as head-rail, foot-rail, side-rail, according to position. **1898** *Engineering Mag.* XVI. 69 [The Pennsylvania R.R.] used the type [of car] known as gondolas, the side stakes being carried high enough to support the sides and roof.

b. Designating weapons carried at the side.
1755 *Lett. to Washington* I. 89, 4p. Side Pistols. **1886** *Century Mag.* Nov. 26/1 All wore moccasins, and were belted around the waist, and carried side-knives used by the hunters.

c. Designating actions or occupations engaged in on the side or incidentally.
See also SIDE LINE 3.
1870 MEDBERY *Men Wall St.* 129 All these neat side-transactions are known to the employees. **1903** HAPGOOD *Autobiog. of Thief* 37 We worked this as a 'side-graft,' for some time.

6. In special combinations.
Side bag, a bag carried by a woman at her side; *s.-bar whiskers*, whiskers on the side of the face or cheeks, (cf. SIDEBURNS); *s. bed*, ? a small bed placed beside another; *s. boom*, a boom along the side of a stream or other body of water; *s. bracket*, a gas- or electric-light fixture for the wall; *s. chain*, (see quotation); *s. cut*, a cut or piece of meat from the side of a hog; *s. draft*, a draft exerted on the side; *s. dumper*, (see quotation); *s. field*, a field on the side of a farm or holding; *s. flap*, (see quotation); *s. grade*, a slightly sloping ground surface; *s. hatchet*, a hatchet having the cutting edge beveled on one side only; *s. hunt*, (see quotation); *s. lamp*, a lamp used on or at the side of something; *s. latch*, a leather strap on the side of a bridle; *s. liner*, (see quotation); *s. log*, one of the logs forming the sides of a log house; *s.-looking*, looking sidewards; *s. order*, a small quantity of food, usu. served as a side dish; *s. partner*, one who works alongside another or alternates with another in the same job; *sidepiece*, a piece of leather at the side of an ambulance; *s. pond*, (see quotation); *s. stand*, a stand or location on or at the side; *s. stay*, (see quotation); *s. strap*, a strap on the side of a carriage; *s. tackle*, the right or left tackle on a football team; *s. tie*, one of the crossties next to a joint tie on which two lengths of railroad track are joined.
1903 BURNHAM *Jewel* 74 Jewel . . . opened her leather side-bag. **1882** PECK *Sunshine* 55 He was a red-faced man, with these side-bar whiskers. **1648** *Essex Probate Rec.* I. 98 One side bed for a child, 2 s. **1879** *Lumberman's Gazette* 1 Oct., Side-booms have been stretched along wherever there is any danger of logs escaping. **1897** F. C. MOORE *How To Build a Home* 57 Expense can be saved by dispensing with center outlets . . . , using side-brackets only. **1876** KNIGHT 2173/1 *Side-chain*, . . . one of the chains uniting the sides of the tender and engine, as a safety arrangement in the event of the drag-bar giving way. **1867** *Ill. Agric. Soc. Trans.* VI. 641 Prime Pork—Shall be packed with a header of side cuts. **1868** *Iowa State Agric. Soc. Rep.* 1867 223 There is no side-draft on the team. **1895** *Stand.* 2269/2 *Side-dumper*, in mining, a tram-car that can be tilted sidewise and thus emptied. **1651** *Portsmouth Rec.* 47 John brigs survayer for his side feild. **1876** KNIGHT 2173/1 *Side-flap*, . . . a piece of leather which hangs between the stirrup-strap and the skirting. **1860** *Ill. Agric. Soc. Trans.* IV. 37 [The Lancaster steam plow] could not maintain its position,

on even an easy side grade. **1895** *Stand.* 2269/3 *Side-hatchet*, a hatchet made on the principles of a side-ax. **1891** *Cent.* 5615/1 *Side-hunt*, a competitive hunt, in which the participants are divided into sides. **1899** *Mo. So. Dakotan* I. 156 He got a match from a drawer in his desk and lighted the one side lamp. **1846** THORPE *Myst. Backwoods* 13 The bridle envelopes the head . . . , crossing and recrossing, filled with side latches and throat latches. **1891** *Cent.* 5615/2 *Sideliner*, . . . a sidewinder, sidewiper, or massasauga. **1822** WOODS *English Prairie* (1904) 275 Two more of the side-logs [are placed] on the cross-logs. **1829** COOPER *Wish-ton-Wish* iii, A demure, side-looking young woman kept her great wheel in motion. **1900** ADE *More Fables* 205 His Brain felt as if some one had played a Mean Trick on him and substituted a Side-Order of Cauliflower. **1890** *N.Y. Post* 23 May (*Cent.*), The arrest was made by the witness's side partner, it being his night off. **1873** ALDRICH *Marjorie Daw* 109 'Tell Johnny Reb,' says Hunter, lifting up the leather side-piece of the ambulance, 'that' [etc.]. **1876** KNIGHT 2174/1 *Side-pond*, . . . a reservoir at the side of a canal-lock to economize the water in locking. **1870** MEDBERY *Men Wall St.* 34 We notice a boy at a side-stand with the morning share-list for sale. **1852** ELLET *Pioneer Women* 201 All men . . . were required to pull at the side stays, or short ropes attached to the upper side of the wagons, to prevent their upsetting. **1850** JUDD *R. Edney* 248 She sat on the black seat, with the curtain lifted, leaning on the side-strap. **1891** *N.Y. Tribune* 20 Oct. 5/4 He was of fine presence, standing six feet high, and was side-tackle on his college football team. **1872** HUNTINGTON *Road-Master's Asst.* 14 Side-ties (ties next the joint) should be of equal width and laid the same distances from the joint.

* **Side,** *v.*

+**1.** *tr.* To provide (a structure) with a side or sides. Also with *up*. Also fig.

1827 COOPER *Red Rover* I. 35 [It's] cloth that would do to side a house with. **1874** TAYLOR *World on Wheels* 119 [In the afternoon] the morning's frame was . . . raised, roofed and sided, and a doctrine or so put into it to keep house. **1877** *Rep. Indian Affairs* 40 Two dwelling-houses and one school-house have been sided up with weather-boards.

+**2.** *S.* To plow (a row crop) close to the drill.

1847 *Fla. Plantation Rec.* 244, 9 plows sieding cotton in brickyard cut. **1886** PAGE in *Century Mag.* June 200/2, I tell Hannah I ain' done sidin' meh corn.

Side arms. *pl.* Arms carried at one's side, as a sword, revolver, etc. {1760-} — **1689** *Conn. Probate Rec.* I. 594 The whole of my aforesaid House and Lands to be for my son. . . . Also my three side arms. **1774** J. ANDREWS *Letters* 72 One consequence . . . is, that none of the Soldiers, save those on duty, appear in the streets with side arms. **1865** *Nation* I. 207 [Few] were in the habit of carrying side-arms. **1898** *McClure's Mag.* X. 265 The officers . . . [could take] with them their side-arms and clothing.

+**Side bacon.** Bacon made from the side of a hog. (Cf. SIDE MEAT.) — **1850** SAWYER *Way Sketches* 108 [For] each man . . . [should be provided] fifty pounds of smoked side bacon. **1905** 'O. HENRY' *Roads of Destiny* 140 Frijoles and side-bacon would do me about as well.

+**Side-bar buggy.** A buggy having longitudinal sidepieces supporting the body. — **1899** TARKINGTON *Gentleman from Indiana* vii, Here and there the trim side-bar buggy of some prosperous farmer's son . . . flashed along the road. **1905** *N.Y. Herald* 19 Aug. 4/3 From the back country also come . . . old fashioned carriages, carryalls, sidebar buggies, Portland buggies. **1912** NICHOLSON *Hoosier Chron.* 388 You whistled, Morton, after you had pitched him and his side-bar buggy into the ditch and killed his horse.

* **Sideboard.** A piece of furniture for holding or displaying dishes, glasses, etc., in a dining room. {1671-} Also attrib. — **1771** *Copley-Pelham Lett.* 141, I noticed two such spaces with side boards in them. **1830** WATSON *Philadelphia* 183 Side-boards . . . were first introduced after the Revolution. **1865** *Atlantic Mo.* April 511/1 You have the sideboard-keys. **1881** [see CLAW-FOOT *a.*]. **1914** JAMES *Ivory Tower* 84 Doctor Hatch's own freedom . . . shared in . . . the appeal of the very form of the great sideboard.

Sidebone. {1819-} +A disease of horses causing the cartilages in the side of the hoof to turn to bone; also, the bony structure resulting from this disease. — **1886** *Amer. Agriculturist* (*Cent.*), Heaves, curb, spavin, sidebone, and ringbone are the most ordinary ailments in horses. **1891** *Cent.* 5614/3 Side-bones occur chiefly in the fore feet of draft-horses, and are an occasional cause of lameness.

+**Sideburns.** *pl.* [f. BURNSIDE, by confusion.] Short side whiskers. — **1887** *Chicago Jrnl.* 1 Aug., McGarigle has his mustache and small side-burns still on. **1912** WASON *Friar Tuck* 208 The one thing of his old life he refused to discard was his side-burns. **1923** *Dialect Notes* V. 220 *Sideburns*, burnsides. [McDonald Co., Mo.]

+**Side card.** In a poker hand having a pair, any card not paired; in other games, a nontrump card. — **1857** *Hoyle's Games* (Amer. ed.) 288 Should two or more hands come together of equal value in pairs, the better hand is decided by the highest side cards. **1864** DICK *Amer. Hoyle* (1866) 63 *Side-Cards*, lay cards.

+**Side check.** (See quot. 1895.) — **1895** *Stand.* 2269/2 *Side-check*, a check-rein that passes at the side of a horse's head instead of between the ears. **1904** *Cincinnati Enquirer* 30 Nov. 6 An Englishman, lately arrived in this country, protests against the side-check.

Side comb. A comb worn by women and girls at the side of the head. {1897-} Also transf. — **1824** *Mo. Intelligencer* 8 May 3/3 Tortoise Shell, Tuck and Side Combs. **1853** B. F. TAYLOR *Jan. & June* 85 [There

are] hens with very delicate side-combs, like our sweethearts. **1870** 'F. FERN' *Ginger-Snaps* 146 She don't shuffle round . . . with horn side-combs fastening six hairs to her temple. **1899** A. THOMAS *Arizona* 35 It's like any other side comb. **1908** 'O. HENRY' *Roads of Destiny* 60 When I'm hard at work I can see things through my side-combs.

Side drift. In a mine, a passage that leads off from a main cutting or tunnel. — **1872** 'MARK TWAIN' *Roughing It* 279 He disappeared in the gloom of a 'side drift.' **1876** HARTE in *Scribner's Mo.* XII. 312/1 He came upon Jack Hamlin, sitting upright in a side-drift.

Side entry. An entry at the side of a house. — **1885** JEWETT *Marsh Island* 195 The old farmer and his crony moved their chairs into the square side-entry. **1901** CHURCHILL *Crisis* 13 He did not discuss his ambitions at dinner with the other clerks in the side entry.

Side fence. A fence along the side of a lot, yard, etc. — **1644** *Essex Inst. Coll.* IX. 129 Such as shalbe defectiue in making vp their side fences . . . shall also be fined. **1660** *Portsmouth Rec.* 97 The said petar Taulmond is to maintaine . . . halfe Lott Strainge his side fence against the highway. **1879** STOCKTON *Rudder Grange* xiii, Then we climbed our side-fence.

Sidehill.

1. A hillside or acclivity. {1708-1807} 'Now *U.S.*' (*O.E.D.*).

1674 *Groton Rec.* 178 His houselot . . . [is] bounded on the north with the sidhill. **1711** *Mass. H. S. Coll.* 6 Ser. V. 242 You must all get out at the Barbers Bason, being a bad side hill. **1835** HOFFMAN *Winter in West* I. 232 The passage . . . was a mere fissure in the side hill. **1907** G. M. WHITE *Boniface to Burglar* 127 There I sat on the side-hill on Ohio soil.

2. Attrib. with *critter, field, lot, street*.

1849 WILLIS *Rural Letters* 93 It's a side-hill critter! Two off legs so lame, she can't stand even. **1862** *Rep. Comm. Patents 1861: Agric.* 415 During one season a side-hill lot on his farm . . . yielded no less than twelve tons of hay. **1891** HOWELLS *Imperative Duty* i, In the humbler side-hill streets, . . . [Negroes] have their homes. **1895** *Outing* XXVI. 331/1 A little side-hill field, with bold mountains showing in the background.

+**Sidehill plow.** (See quot. 1876.) — **1838** *Mass. Agric. Survey 1st Rep.* 68 In some parts of the county, the side hill plough with a changeable mould-board is used for all ploughing. **1854** *Penna. Agric. Rep.* 78 To Savery & Co., . . . for their side hill plow. **1876** KNIGHT 2173/1 *Side-hill Plow*, a plow whose cutting apparatus is reversible, so as to throw its furrow-slice to the right or left. . . . This enables the lead horse . . . to return in the furrow just made, the plow throwing the soil down hill while traveling in either direction.

Side hit. An adverse criticism or insinuation. — **1838** COOPER *Homeward B.* xvii, The latter was disposed to believe himself a subject of interest with this person, against whose exclusiveness and haughty reserve . . . he had been making side-hits ever since the ship had sailed. **1866** *Ore. State Jrnl.* 10 Nov. 4/1 A great many side hits are being made at the Plantation Bitters by a score or two of disinterested friends.

+**Side-hobbled,** *a.* Of a horse: Hobbled by having a forefoot and the hind foot on the same side fastened together. — **1806** LEWIS in *L. & Clark Exped.* IV. (1905) 317 We had all our horses side hubbled and turned out to graize. **1884** *Gringo & Greaser* 15 Feb. 2/2 Estevan Lopez thought he was a kicking mule and not being side hobbled let fly the business end against the doors.

+**Side judge.** (See quots. 1889 and 1914.) — **1846** *Knickerb.* Oct. 360 The attorneys . . . in company of the supreme court judge, the 'side-judge,' take the opportunity of having a bit of fun. **1859** *Harper's Mag.* March 568/2 Judge B——, of E—— County, in this State, was one of the *side* Judges of the old Court of Common Pleas. **1889** *Cent.* 3247/1 *Side judge*, a designation sometimes given to a magistrate, or each of two magistrates, of inferior rank, associated with a magistrate of higher grade for the purpose of constituting a court. **1914** *Cycl. Amer. Govt.* III. 308/2 In Pennsylvania there has been from early times a system of judges not learned in the law, who sit beside the regular judge. . . . The side judges have little influence on the decision of cases, for they cannot lay down any principles of law before the jury.

Side line, *n.* {1768-}

+**1.** A line along one side of the land allotted to a colonist. *Obs.*

1694 *N.C. Col. Rec.* I. 410 The dividing line . . . shall run paralel wth Cornelius Lerrys side line.

2. (See quot. 1844.) {1831}

1844 GREGG *Commerce of Prairies* I. 63 [With] the 'side line' (a hopple connecting a fore and hind leg) . . . an animal can hardly increase his pace beyond a hobbling walk; whereas, with a fore-hopple, a frightened horse will scamper off. **1887** *Outing* X. 11/1 'Side-lines' is the army substitute for hobbles.

+**3.** An auxiliary line of goods; a subordinate or secondary occupation or business.

1890 *N.Y. Tribune* 9 March (*Cent.*), Wanted—Salesman to carry as a side-line a new line of advertisement specialty. **1902** LORIMER *Lett. Merchant* 131 A good many salesmen have an idea that buyers are only interested in baseball, . . . and that business is a side line with them. **1914** S. H. ADAMS *Clarion* 304 There ain't hardly money enough in a side-line like the Pills to pay for the trouble of running it separate.

4. *Football.* One of the lines bounding the two sides of the playing field; also, the area just outside these lines.

1899 QUINN *Penna. Stories* 24 But the coaches on the side lines were not so jubilant. *a*1924 G. S. LOWMAN *Practical Football* 256 Some writers have designated that strip of territory five yards inside the sidelines . . . as the 'Bad Lands.'

+**Side-line,** *v. tr.* (See quot. 1837.) — **1837** IRVING *Bonneville* I. 36 The horses were 'side lined,' as it is termed: that is to say, the fore and hind foot on the same side of the animal were tied together. **1887** *Outing* X. 11/1 Making camp after dark, I had the horses *side-lined.* **1923** J. H. COOK *On Old Frontier* 69 The exhausted animals [are] lassoed, hobbled, or 'sidelined.'

Sid(e)ling. +(See quot. 1859.) *Obs.* Also attrib. — **1825** W. STRICKLAND in *Reports on Canals* 25 The passing or sideling places are formed by solid cast iron branches. **1859** BARTLETT 406 *Sidling,* a place at which to turn off on a railroad to wait for a passing engine.

Side mark. {1818-} +**1.** A mark or object on the side of a river enabling a steamboat pilot to know his bearings. **2.** (See quotation.) — **(1) 1875** 'MARK TWAIN' *Old Times* v. 90 That pilot can . . . give you such a lot of head-marks, stern-marks, and side-marks to guide you. **(2) 1905** *Forestry Bureau. Bul.* No. 61, 30 *Bark mark,* a symbol chopped into the side of a log to indicate its ownership. . . . Syn.: side mark. (N[orthern] F[orest].)

+**Side meat.** Bacon or pork from the side of a hog. (Cf. SIDE BACON.) — **1873** BEADLE *Undevel. West* 482 Two bright-eyed, graceful, copper-colored *señoritas* bring me a supper of coffee, side meat, eggs, and *tortillas de mais.* **1891** *Harper's Mag.* Aug. 486/2 The Mayor . . . set a piece of side meat to sizzling in a skillet. **1912** WASON *Friar Tuck* 394 Those who weren't hurt dangerous were given some side-meat and corn bread.

+**Side oat. a.** A species of oat in which the drooping panicle has branches on one side; spec., the Tartarian oat (*Avena orientalis*). **b.** *pl.* A grama grass used for forage (*Bouteloua curtipendula*) in which the racemes tend to be arranged on one side. — **1856** *Ill. Agric. Soc. Trans.* II. 105 My Tartarian oat . . . is a side oat, but has a thick, stiff straw. **1862** *Ib.* V. 196 He sows four bushels of seed to the acre, of black Tartarian or, as sometimes called, horse mane or side oats. **1909** *Cent. Suppl.* 1216/1 *Side-oats,* . . . a grama-grass . . . ranging from New Jersey to the Rocky Mountains and southward into Mexico.

+**Side porch.** A porch at the side of a house. — **1879** STOCKTON *Rudder Grange* xiii, We sat on the side porch, where it was shady. **1902** BELL *Hope Loring* 29 A tall persimmon-tree . . . overhung the roof of the side porch. **1922** TARKINGTON *Gentle Julia* 104 Florence sneezed frequently as she sat upon the 'side porch.'

Sider. {1841-} +A cowboy who rides by the side of the herd on a cattle drive. — **1869** *Overland Mo.* III. 126 The mighty herd . . . [has] 'siders,' who keep the stragglers out of the chaparral.

Side road. A branch road; a secondary road parallel to a main road. — **1861** in Logan *Great Conspiracy* 295, I sent down Col. Morell . . . to open a road down to Opequan Creek, within five miles of the camp at Winchester, on the side-roads it was upon. **1863** TAYLOR *H. Thurston* 193 The spot was reached by . . . taking a side road.

Side room. {1842-} +A small room at the end of a hall; a hall bedroom. — **1884** HOWELLS *S. Lapham* iii, The chambers were to be on the three floors above, front and rear, with side-rooms over the front door. **1893** — *Coast of Bohemia* 61 It's over the door, four flights up; it's what they call a side room. **1898** RANDELL *Amer. Politician in Eng.* 278 The girl . . . shared my little 'side-room;' they call hall-rooms that way in Boston.

* **Sidesaddle.**

* **1.** A woman's saddle so made that both feet of the rider are on the same side of the horse.

1648 *Conn. Rec.* I. 508, 1 cloakbag, 1 pillion, 1 sidesaddle and pillion cloath. **1810** M. DWIGHT *Journey to Ohio* 10 There is no chair or side saddle to be got. **1896** WILKINS *Madelon* 59 [She] put the side-saddle on the roan mare.

+**2.** = next a.

1817-8 EATON *Botany* (1822) 447 *Sarracenia purpurea,* side-saddle. . . . In marshes. **1839** in *Mich. Agric. Soc. Trans.* VII. 418.

+**Sidesaddle flower. a.** The common pitcher plant (*Sarracenia purpurea*), or its flower. **b.** *Californian sidesaddle flower,* the related species *Chrysamphora californica.* — **(a) 1738** CATESBY *Carolina* II. 69 *Sarracena.* . . . The under Part of the Flower . . . [resembles] somewhat the Seat of a Side-Saddle, from which in Virginia it has received its Name of Side-Saddle Flower. **1836** LINCOLN *Botany* 169 Side-saddle flower . . . is sometimes called Adam's cup, in reference also to the shape of the leaf. **1850** *New Eng. Farmer* II. 12/2 By taking up, in the autumn, the *Saracenia,* or Side-Saddle Flower, with the wet moss attached to its roots, . . . it will flourish. **1886** S. HALE *Letters* 169 Margy's glass pail [was] full of . . . side-saddle flower. **(b) 1891** *Cent.* 5616/3 *Darlingtonia Californica* has been called *Californian sidesaddle-flower.*

+**Side show.** At a circus, fair, etc., an attraction or exhibit of minor extent or importance. {1884-} Also transf.

1855 BARNUM *Life* 344 In attending to what might be termed my 'side shows,' or temporary enterprises, I have never neglected the American Museum. **1872** *Ill. Dept. Agric. Trans.* IX. 21 President Brown called attention to the . . . control of 'side shows' outside the Grounds. **1896** HARRIS *Sister Jane* 122 If we had that chap in the side-show, . . . he'd draw the crowds. **1900** *Congress. Rec.* 12 Feb. 1722/2 We are a side show. The headquarters will be in Wall street. **1924** CROY *R.F.D. No. 3* 212 They saw the sideshows, the Streets of Cairo.

b. Attrib. with *barker, man, riffraff,* etc.

1886 HOWE *Moonlight Boy* 73 One of his songs related to a side-show-man at a circus. **1894** 'MARK TWAIN' *P. Wilson* xvii, He scoffed at them as adventurers, mountebanks, side-show riff-raff, dime-museum freaks. **1909** *Guide to Chicago* (Chi. Assn. of Commerce) 141 Midway Plaisance . . . is the site of the side show section of the World's Fair. **1910** FRANCK *Vagabond Journey* 276 The secretary was a man . . . with the voice of a side-show barker. **1920** COOPER *Under Big Top* 65 Aside from the side-show tent was a smaller 'black top,' or tent made of black canvas.

Side-splitter. A side-splitting story or joke. — **1864** *Harper's Mag.* Feb. 422/1, I send you three samples [of letters] . . . , hoping thereby to reciprocate some of your side-splitters.

+**Sidetrack,** *n.* A railroad siding; a branch line. Also attrib. — **1840** *Albany & W. Stockbridge R. R. Engineers' Rep. 1840-1* 7 The relative . . . cost of these lines . . . [includes] all necessary buildings, dock and ferry landings, and side tracks. **1861** *Chicago Tribune* 26 May 1/8 For Sale. . . . Docking Lot, near Hough's Packing House, with a side track from the Alton & St. Louis R.R. **1876** CROFUTT *Trans-continental Tourist* 41 Waterloo is a small side-track station. **1880** *Cimarron News & Press* 25 March 3/2 Mr. Pat Colbert . . . is plying his old trade, having the contract for building the side track at Springer. **1917** MATHEWSON *Second Base Sloan* 63, An empty box car on a sidetrack invited them with a half-opened door.

+**Sidetrack,** *v.*

1. *tr.* To run (a train, car, etc.) on to a sidetrack. **1881** *Chicago Times* 14 May, [The corn] has been side-tracked and kept in the sun and rain somewhere along the road. **1886** *Leslie's Mo.* June 722/1 The next freight-train was to be side-tracked. **1890** *Stock Grower & Farmer* 22 March 5/3 The sleeping car of the New Mexico delegation was sidetracked in a hard part of the town. **1903** *N.Y. Ev. Post* 26 Sept., If a car is sidetracked as a result of congested traffic.

transf. **1880** *Cimarron News & Press* 19 Feb. 4/3 Short skirts are now worn for dancing dresses, and the gentlemen are no longer obliged to wait for the ladies to side-track their trains before they can pass.

b. *fig.* To put (something) aside; to divert (a person) from a main course or goal. Also reflex. and as *ppl. a.*

1889 *Christian Union* 21 March 356 He side-tracked himself and his platform. **1892** *Amer. Miss. Assn. 46th Ann. Rep.* 140 We are but bringing back to their lost inheritance these side-tracked brothers and sisters of our own Protestant lineage. **1897** MOODY in *Boston Jrnl.* 8 Jan. 5/4 [Sunday-school teachers] must go to work in dead earnest and not be side-tracked by anything under the heavens. **1900** *Congress. Rec.* 11 Jan. 784/1 Even my friend from South Carolina . . . seems to want to side track this amendment. **1911** HARRISON *Queed* 134, I must side-track My Book for two months or even longer!

2. *intr.* Of a train, to move on to a sidetrack; also, of a person, to shunt a train on to a sidetrack.

1888 *Harper's Mag.* March 650/1 One train had side-tracked to await the train from the opposite direction. **1898** HAMBLEN *Gen. Manager's Story* 185 The conductor came up and asked if I was going to sidetrack there.

b. *fig.* **To sidetrack on,** to leave the main subject for (something else).

1893 *Advance* 8 June, The business of the minister is to preach the gospel, not . . . to sidetrack on great moral issues.

+**Sidetracking.** Sidetracks, collectively. — **1892** A. E. LEE *Hist. Columbus, Ohio* II. 209 Sidetracking amply sufficient for the great mass of sojourning special trains was provided.

Sidewalk, *n.* {1667}

1. A walk or way, now usually paved, for pedestrians, beside a road or street. {1739} 'Now *U.S.*' (*O.E.D.*).

1807 *Boston Selectmen* 3 June 338 The Abuttors on the Easterly side of Hancocks Street . . . [have] regulated the side walk & paved the same. **1876** 'MARK TWAIN' *Tom Sawyer* ii. 26 Tom appeared on the sidewalk with a bucket of whitewash and a long-handled brush. **1892** M. A. JACKSON *Gen. Jackson* 211 A small group of soldiers was standing on the sidewalk. **1923** HERRICK *Lilla* 7 Lilla could just remember . . . a place of long white streets, with . . . broad cement walks—she had called it 'sidewalks.'

2. Attrib. and comb. with *farmer, flirtation,* etc.

1856 STOWE *Dred* I. 24 She has [developed] . . . a taste for side-walk flirtation. **1870** *Rep. Comm. Agric. 1869* 427 Mr. A. T. Stewart, had lately become 'a sidewalk farmer,' having gone out to Long Island and bought a little patch which he purposes to improve. **1875** *Chicago Tribune* 15 Aug. 16/4 The bridge-tenders, sidewalk-inspectors, and street employees . . . were paid off. **1882** McCABE *New York* 276 The sidewalk hucksters' stands give to it the effect of a partial illumination. **1883** *Century Mag.* Oct. 929/2 [Longfellow] often is judged by his least poetic work, . . . little sermons in rhyme that . . . become hackneyed as a sidewalk song. **1899** *Scribner's Mag.* Jan. 58/2, I followed the shadows of the sidewalk-trees down to the next corner. **1925** *Sears, Roebuck & Co. Cat.* No. 150, 751 Improved extension sidewalk skates.

+**Sidewalk,** *v. tr.* To provide (a street) with a sidewalk. Often *ppl. a.* — **1871** HOWELLS *Wedding Journey* 229 Up the odd side-walked street stretched an aisle of carriages. **1884** *Harper's Mag.* March 516/2 There is no store, no post-office, no sidewalked street—no nothing. **1893** *Home*

Missionary March 543 Miles of streets have been opened, graded, planked, and sidewalked.

+Sidewalk dealer. A trafficker in small wares on, or immediately adjacent to, a sidewalk. — **1870** *Scribner's Mo.* I 114 The sidewalk dealers . . . find extortion a losing game. **1872** *Atlantic Mo.* May 552/1 [The dog dealer] delivers himself of no 'patter,' like that of the sidewalk dealer in sundry small wares. **1882** McCABE *New York* 268 The sidewalk dealers appear to drive a thriving trade.

+Sidewalker. 1. One who idles about or loafs on sidewalks. **2.** (See quotation.) — **(1) 1849** G. G. FOSTER *N.Y. in Slices* 96 A filthy, ragged, idiotic vagabond, herding with negroes and low sidewalkers in the holes and corners of the City. **(2) 1891** *Cent.* 5617/2 *Side-walker*, . . . a laterigrade spider; a spider which walks or moves sidewise or otherwise with apparently equal ease, as *Salticus scenicus.*

+Side wheel. One of the large paddle wheels used on a side-wheel steamer.
1845 TYLER in *Pres. Mess. & P.* IV. 367 Side wheels have been ordered, as being best tested and least liable to failure. **1860** HOLMES *Professor* 365 She had neither side-wheel nor stern-wheel. **1886** *Outing* VIII. 15/2 Mr. Aspinwall altered this boat by putting on her side-wheels with feathering buckets.
b. Attrib. with *boat, gunboat, steamboat.*
1857 CHANDLESS *Visit Salt Lake* 2 Except during the 'June rise' side-wheel boats rarely go up [the Missouri R.]. **1862** Moore *Rebellion Rec.* V. II. 136 The small iron-clad and the side-wheel gunboats were badly crippled. **1891** WELCH *Recoll. 1830–40* 140 They seemed to have reached the ultimatum of perfection for side wheel 'steamboats.'

+Side-wheeler. =next. Also attrib. — **1866** W. REID *After War* 204 At last a light side-wheeler came steaming down the river for us. **1888** FERGUSON *Experiences Forty-Niner* 18 Struggling out by the aft gangway near the wheel, it being a side-wheeler, I . . . loosed myself. **1904** *N.Y. Times* 16 May 5 It was there that the two side-wheelers landed their passengers. **1909** *N.Y. Observer* 2 Sept. 315/1 The old-time side-wheeler ferry-boats were crowded from end to end.

+Side-wheel steamer. A steamboat propelled by paddle wheels at the sides. — **1857** MAURY in Corbin *Life M. F. Maury* 135 She was a side-wheel steamer. **1881** HAYES *New Colorado* 19 Into it [the Golden Gate] could freely . . . steam . . . the new side-wheel steamer from New York. **1899** CHESNUTT *Conjure Woman* 3 The last hundred miles . . . were up a river on a sidewheel steamer.

Sidewinder.[1] A heavy swinging blow with the fist. Also fig. (*'U.S. and dial.' O.E.D.*). — **1840** *Daily Pennant* (St. Louis) 14 May (Th.), Tim gives him a sockdologer and two side-winders, and leaves him for dead. **1860** HOLMES *Professor* 39 The boys of my time used to call a hit [*i.e.*, a retort] like this a 'side-winder.' **1871** *Harper's Mag.* Oct. 650 If he could give the erudite Charles King . . . what the 'boys' termed a 'side-winder,' it would set the post-office congregation in a roar.

+Sidewinder.[2] **1.** *S.W.* Any one of several small rattlesnakes, as the horned rattlesnake, *Crotalus cerastes.* Also transf. (Cf. MASSASAUGA.) **2.** (See quotation.) — **(1) 1885** J. S. KINGSLEY, etc. *Stand. Nat. Hist.* III. 402 The New Mexicans have named this animal the 'side-winder,' because of the slightly lateral motion which they have in passing forwards. **1907** WHITE *Arizona Nights* 27 He was a side-winder and a diamond-back and a little black rattlesnake all rolled into one. **(2) 1905** *Forestry Bureau Bull.* No. 61, 46 *Side winder*, a tree knocked down unexpectedly by the falling of another.

Sidewiper. {1893–} **+** =SIDEWINDER[2] 1. — **1877** HODGE *Arizona* 226 Another kind [of rattlesnake], called the side wiper, from its peculiar habit of locomotion sideways, instead of ahead, is found through most of the valleys and plains.

+Side yard. A yard at the side of a dwelling. — **1879** WHITMAN *Diary* (1904) 59 The window where I sit . . . opens on a spacious side-yard. **1922** TARKINGTON *Gentle Julia* 8 A boy of her own age emerged from the 'side-yard.'

Siding. {1603–}
+1. The boarding forming the side or sides of a frame building; a piece of lumber suitable for such a boarding. Often collective. {1866} Also attrib.
1829 COOPER *Wish-ton-Wish* xvii, [The dwellings were] constructed of a firm frame-work, neatly covered with sidings of boards. **1858** SIMMONDS *Dict. Trade Products* 343/2 *Sidings*, a name in America for long wedge-shaped boards, used for the sides or roofs of houses. **1874** LONG *Wild-Fowl* 89 Strips of weather-boarding, or 'siding,' as it is called out West, may be made to take their place. **1892** *York County Hist. Rev.* 69/2 Upwards of 40,000,000 feet of dressed lumber [are] annually turned out into . . . flooring, siding [etc.]. **1918** *Amer. Builder* April 83 Our Southern Pine products include . . . siding and flooring material.
+2. The reduction of timber to desired dimensions.
1875 KNIGHT 908/2 *Forming.* (*Shipbuilding.*) . . . This consists in:— *Siding;* . . . *Molding;* . . . *Beveling.* **1879** *Lumberman's Gazette* 15 Oct., But mulays were used in siding down for the gang.
‖3. A steep slope.
1895 REMINGTON *Pony Tracks* 188 On a sandy 'siding' he spread his feet and slid with an avalanche of detached hill-side.
+4. *attrib.* **a.** In sense 1 with *board, tile.* **b.** In sense 2 with *machine, mill.*

(a) 1876 KNIGHT 2568/2 Siding-tiles are used as a substitute for weather boarding. *Ib.* 2749/2 *Weather-board*, lapping siding-boards for houses. **(b)** *Ib.* 2175/1 *Siding-machine*, a machine for sawing timbers, or re-sawing boards into thin stuff for weather-boarding. **1879** *Lumberman's Gazette* 5 Nov., The machinery first put in included a mulay and a siding mill.

∗Sidling. +(See SID(E)LING.)

∗Siege.

∗1. The investment by an attacking force of a military stronghold. Also transf.
[**1746** (*title*), A Letter from William Shirley, Esq, Governor of Massachusets Bay, to His Grace the Duke of Newcastle: With a Journal of the Siege of Louisbourg.] **1826** FLINT *Recoll.* 163 After four days of unavailable siege, the Indians . . . went away. **1865** *Atlantic Mo.* May 636/1 Seventeen one-hundred pounders were burst during the siege of Charleston. **1870** KEIM *Sheridan's Troopers* 45 Sheridan was in a state of siege. **1897** *Outing* XXX. 248/1 Toward sundown the peccaries tired of their siege, and . . . trotted slowly into the depths of the forest.
+2. a. A long period devoted to a single purpose or spent in a single occupation. **b.** A period of prolonged illness, strain, or difficulty.
(a) 1833 CATLIN *Indians* I. 71 [Bogard was] just retiring from a ten years' siege of hunting and trapping in the Rocky Mountains. **1840** DANA *Two Years* 287 From this we escaped, having had a pretty good siege with the wooding. **(b) 1862** *Atlantic Mo.* May 558/1 We have had a siege of it. **1898** E. C. HALL *Aunt Jane* 9 She was as pale and peaked as if she had been through a siege of typhoid. **1902** HARBEN *A. Daniel* 58 For a while they have a siege of discontent.
3. Attrib. in sense 1 with *artillery, battery, gun*, etc.
1847 *Whig Almanac 1848* 24/2 Our own siege-train of 24-pounders . . . performed wonders. **1861** *Army Regulations* 399, 24 pdr. siege gun carriages. **1861** *Chicago Tribune* 26 May 1/6 The two siege pieces from St. Louis, arrived this evening. **1862** McCLELLAN in *Own Story* 267 It will be necessary to resort to the use of heavy guns and some siege operations before we assault. **1863** Moore *Rebellion Rec.* V. I. 2 Yesterday the Union siege-batteries opened their fire against the rebel works at Yorktown, Va. **1881–5** McCLELLAN *Own Story* 265 All that could be done was to . . . determine what could be effected with the aid of siege-artillery to cover the attack. **1888** *Century Mag.* Sept. 660/1 Pope . . . surrounded the place by siege-works in which he could protect his men.

Sierra. *W.* and *S. W.*
1. A ridge or range of hills or mountains rising in peaks suggestive of the teeth of a saw. {1613–, of Sp. Amer. and Spain} Also as proper name.
1844 GREGG *Commerce of Prairies* II. 77 The sierra which separates the waters of this river and those of the Rio Pecos was always visible on our left. **1848** BRYANT *California* xiv. 191 We pursued our wearisome journey over the next sierra. **1876** RAYMOND *8th Rep. Mines* 45 Water is taken from a series of lakes in the high sierra. **1907** LONDON *Road* 3, I could hear the sunny valleys of California calling to me over the cold crests of the Sierras.
+2. *attrib.* **a.** With *region, spur.* **b.** In specific names. See also SIERRA (NEVADA) JAY.
(a) 1873 BEADLE *Undevel. West* 255 From noon till 5 p.m. we endure the thumping of a Concord coach over the Sierra spurs. **1903** NORTH *Mother of Calif.* 104 The large sections of the Peninsula which are not sierra regions are usually either wide deserts or hot barren llanos, or plains. **(b) 1917** *Birds of Amer.* III. 236/1 The Sierra Hermit Thrush (*Hylocichla guttata sequoiensis*) is slightly darker and decidedly larger than the Monterey. **1917** *Mammals of Amer.* 73/1 Sierra Red Fox.—*Vulpes necator.* . . . High Sierra above 6000 feet altitude in California.

+Sierran, *a.* Of or pertaining to the Sierra Nevada Mts. — **1873** HARTE *Stories & Poems* (1914) 216 It was in a Sierran solitude, where I had encamped. **1886** — *Snow-bound* 3 Darkness had accompanied a Sierran stage-coach towards the summit.

+Sierra (Nevada) jay. (See quot. 1917.) — **1884** COUES *Key to Birds* 422 *Cyanocitta stelleri frontalis*, . . . Sierra Jay. **1917** *Birds of Amer.* II. 220/2 In the Rocky Mountain section of the United States . . . [is found] the Blue-fronted Jay or Sierra Nevada Jay.

Siesta. An afternoon rest or nap. {1655–} — **1804** C. B. BROWN tr. Volney *View* 108n., [In Philadelphia] the afternoon nap, or *siesta*, is taken only by the old, infirm, or indolent. **1851** HALL *Manhattaner* 183 Lunch is an agreeable interlude. So is . . . the siesta in the hot cabin. **1873** *Winfield* (Kan.) *Courier* 12 June 1/6 A series of prolonged yells and cheers aroused the camp from a pleasant siesta. **1890** HARTE *Waif of Plains* 23 Susy . . . seemed to have fallen quite naturally into her usual afternoon siesta. **1922** TARKINGTON *Gentle Julia* 111 Two [of her friends] had been ascertained, by telephonic inquiries, to be taking commanded siestas.

∗Sieve. Also †sive, seefe.

∗1. A domestic utensil having a bottom of mesh wire, perforated sheet metal, etc., used for screening out the coarser particles from flour, meal, etc.
1643 *Conn. Rec.* I. 455 The goods of Tho: Scott [include] . . . 1 spade, 1 hobing iron, 5 siues. **1678** *New Castle Court Rec.* 362 Inventory of Henry Salters Goods. . . . Ye bottom of a fine hair Sive: 5 Combe brushes [etc.]. **1779** *Broadside Verse* (1930) 190/1 It's hard and cruel times to live,

Takes thirty dollars to buy a sieve. **1884** F. E. OWENS *Cook Book* 126 Take large green cucumbers, peel them, put in cold water for an hour or two, then grate on a coarse grater into a sieve. **1892** *York County Hist. Rev.* 67 Another feature of the business is the manufacture of coal screens and sieves.

attrib. and *comb.* **1640** *Conn. Rec.* I. 453 Inuentory of Tho. Johnson. . . . 3 peeces of leather, halfe a pownd of pepper, a seefe bottom, o. 12. 1. **1646** *Charlestown Land Rec.* 102, [I] give unto William Kilcop, sive maker . . . , a generall Aquitance.

+2. = RIDDLE. Also *sieve box. Obs.*

1849 WIERZBICKI *California* 41 On the upper edges of the boards, rests a box of boards, called a sieve or riddle. **1874** *Vermont Bd. Agric. Rep.* II. 756 The heavy black sand in passing out of the sieve box carries a portion of fine gold with it,

* Sifter. A utensil for separating the coarser from the finer particles in flour, ashes, etc.; a sieve. {1611-}

1757 *Lett. to Washington* II. 158 Indeed some trifling things may be had, vizt. Sheepskins, Hair Cloths, Old Junk, Sifters. **1796** HAWKINS *Letters* 20 They exhibited to me a sample of their ingenuity in the manufacture of baskets and sifters, out of cane. **1844** *Knickerb.* XXIII. 72 The remaining list of commodities was made up of hats, caps, . . . slate-pencils and sifters. **1876** KNIGHT 2175/2 Sifters are used for sifting ashes from cinders; flour from lumps, etc.

b. A device for dusting plants with insect poison.

1879 *Rep. upon Cotton Insects* (Dept. Agric.) 246 Young's sifter. A device . . . for dusting Paris green upon potato-vines.

* Sight, *n.*

+1. (See quotations.)

1848 BARTLETT 303 In North Carolina the distance that can be seen on a road is called a sight. **1891** *Cent.* 5620/2 Sight, . . . a straight stretch of road, as one along which a sight may be taken in surveying; a line uninterrupted by a bend or an elevation: as, go on three sights, and stop at the first house. Also called *look.* (Western U.S.)

+2. (See quot. 1891.)

1849 KINGSLEY *Diary* 74, I began on some wheels for wheelbarrows but had a hard sight to get the lumber suitable for them, **1851** *Ib.* 173 Our sight for getting much more here is rather poor. **1891** *Cent.* 5620 Sight, . . . an opportunity for doing something; an opening; a chance; a 'show': as, he has no sight against his opponent. (Colloq.)

+3. *Poker.* A show of hands.

1857 *Hoyle's Games* (Amer. ed.) 288 A '*sight*' may be demanded. **1864** DICK *Amer. Hoyle* (1866) 177 Sight.—Every player is entitled to a 'sight for his pile.' **1887** *Courier-Journal* 23 Jan. 15/7 Then a rule sprang up that a man should be allowed a sight for his money.

4. One of the nails in the ends of a billiard table.

1864 DICK *Amer. Hoyle* (1866) 419 A line is drawn down the centre of the table, from the centre nails or sights in the head and lower cushions. **1899** CHAMPLIN & BOSTWICK *Cycl. Games & Sports* (ed. 2) 81 The first [spot], opposite the second 'sight,' is sometimes called the light red spot, the second, opposite the sixth 'sight,' the dark red spot.

5. In phrases. **+a.** *By a darned sight,* or variants: By a good deal. Usually in negative expressions. *slang* or *colloq.*

1834 C. A. DAVIS *Lett. J. Downing* 41 'Gineral, do you want another report?' 'Not by a darn'd sight.' **1840** *Niles Reg.* 9 May 149/2 He asked him if he was not going for Harrison and the whigs. 'No,' said he, 'not by a d——d sight.' **1884** 'MARK TWAIN' *H. Finn* i, I asked her if she reckoned Tom Sawyer would go there, and she said not by a considerable sight. **1896** HARRIS *Sister Jane* 63 That ain't all by a long sight.

+b. *To draw a sight upon,* to take aim at. Also fig.

1834 *Congress. Deb.* 25 Feb. 691, I supposed for once in my life I saw gentlemen in the open field, and might be able to draw a fine sight upon them. **1848** DRAKE *Pioneer Life Ky.* 218 You must . . . watch till the dawn of day when the animal comes to drink, and then 'draw a sight' upon his head.

c. *Sight unseen,* without examination. {1890, *dial.*}

1892 *Dialect Notes* I. 231 To trade knives sight unseen is to swap without seeing each other's knife. [Ky.] **1898** *Dept. Agric. Yrbk. 1897* 427 The intelligent farmer of to-day has got beyond trading 'sight unseen' or 'buying a cat in a bag.'

+d. *In sight,* (see quotation).

1900 NELSON *A B C Wall St.* 148 *In sight.* Merchandise available for immediate use, and a term applied to grain, cotton and coffee.

6. In special combinations.

Sight bill, a bill payable upon presentation (cf. SIGHT DRAFT); *s. chase,* a chase in which the dogs are in sight of their quarry; *s. check,* a check payable upon presentation; *s. reading,* reading or translating a foreign language at sight {1864, of music}; *s. rest,* a rest or support used in sighting a weapon, as a revolver; *s. writer,* a typist who has to look at the keys while typing.

1853 *S. Lit. Messenger* XIX. 89/2 Mr. Thompson agreed to accommodate him with a sight bill on his correspondent in Raleigh. **1897** *Outing* XXX. 127/1 [We are] just in time to witness a short but pretty 'sight chase.' The dogs have seen the fox. **1863** 'E. KIRKE' *Southern Friends* 232 I enclose you sight check of Branch Bank of Cape Fear on Bank of Republic, for $10,820. **1899** QUINN *Penna. Stories* 170 He never called us up on the regular lesson, . . . but kept us for the sight-reading. **1883** R. G.

WHITE *W. Adams* 121 He threw up his left arm, and took a sight rest on it [with his revolver]. **1918** OWEN *Typewriting Speed* 143 Many sight writers use all the fingers.

* Sight, *v.*

1. *intr.* To take aim; to take a sight or sights in surveying or running a line. {1896}

1787 *Md. Hist. Mag.* XIX. 265 Mr. Gay surveyor of the County . . . sighted with a compass from the tree. **1841** COOPER *Deerslayer* vii, A man sights suddenly, and fires quick, when his own life's in danger. **1847** DRAKE *Pioneer Life Ky.* 67, I 'sighted' by the stakes, as I laid the ground rails down. **1872** HUNTINGTON *Road-Master's Asst.* 18 A sprightly lad ten or twelve years old can . . . sight with great accuracy and rapidity.

+b. To look *around.*

1891 RYAN *Pagan* 40 Naw, I ain't hunting, . . . but as I was sightin' around the mountain, big Bill Riker, he come up to me.

2. *tr.* **a.** To take aim at. **+b.** (See quot. 1881.)

1871 *Harper's Mag.* Dec. 48/2 No sooner, however, did he 'sight,' or try to sight, the horseman in question, . . . than the thumping against the ribs again began. **1881** INGERSOLL *Oyster-Industry* 248 Sight, to be able to see oysters at the bottom and direct tongs to them. (Virginia.)

+3. *To sight in* (railroad ties), to align (railroad ties) by means of a sighting device.

1872 HUNTINGTON *Road-Master's Asst.* 16 A more ready method of laying the 'leading ties' is to 'sight them in' by the use of 'target boards.'

+Sight draft. A draft payable on presentation. — **1850** *Fla. Plantation Rec.* 60 Your favor of the 22d. ult. enclosing sight draft on Messrs. Habersham for $200 has been duly received. **1863** 'E. KIRKE' *Southern Friends* 214 He never draws against shipments, but holds on, and sells sight drafts, thus making the exchange. **1903** 'O. HENRY' *Cabbages & Kings* 209 It's a sight-draft on your president man for twenty thousand dollars.

*Sightly, *a.* **+**(See quot. 1828.) — **1828** WEBSTER, *Sightly,* . . . open to the view; that may be seen from a distance. We say, a house stands in a sightly place. **1873** 'MARK TWAIN' & WARNER *Gilded Age* 165 The University up there, on rising ground, sightly place, see the river for miles. **1912** *Buffalo Commercial* 2 June 12 The hotel occupies a sightly location.

+Sight piece. A gun sight, or the piece of metal upon which this is mounted. — **1835** HOFFMAN *Winter in West* II. 171*n.*, The long western rifle has three sight-pieces on the barrel. **1874** LONG *Wild-Fowl* 24 [The] sight-piece [should be] small and close to the muzzle.

* Sign, *n.*

To cut a sign, (see CUT *v.* 25 m).

+1. Evidence in the form of tracks, scratchings, broken twigs, etc., indicating the recent presence: **a.** Of men, usually Indians.

See also INDIAN SIGN.

1692 *Va. State P.* I. 44 We Ranged about to see if we could find ye tract of any Indians, but we could not see any fresh signe. **1746** *N.H. Hist. Soc. Coll.* IV. 208 By the sign of this ambush, and by the sign of their going off, in a single file, it was supposed there could not be less than 50 or 60 Indians. **1822** FOWLER *Journal* 97 The men are all feerfull of meeting With the Indeans as We . . . Have maid So much Sign in the Snow that the[y] will track us up. **1851** *Knickerb.* XXXVII. 396 Signs is tracks, Sir; Indian tracks. **1883** RITCH *Illust. N.Mex.* 103 Probably the Apache has been seen in the neighborhood for the last time, but the pioneers have not lost the habit of watching for his 'sign.'

+b. Of animals, esp. those hunted as game. Also with defining terms.

See also BEAR-SIGN 1, BEAVER SIGN, BUFFALO SIGN.

1804 CLARK in *Lewis & C. Exped.* I. (1904) 29 Great Deel of Deer Sign on the Bank. *Ib.* 68 Great Deel of Elk Sign. **1835** CROCKETT *Tour* 212 As we hunters used to say, where there is so much sign there must be game. **1853** 'P. PAXTON' *Yankee in Texas* 117 Nothing leaves a *mark* to him [*sc.* a Texan], he only sees *sign,* whether of bird or beast, friend or enemy. You hear of *turkey sign, bear sign, hog sign, cow sign, Indian sign,* etc. *a*1861 WINTHROP *J. Brent* 220 Here was the sign of horses, passed but now. **1870** *Amer. Naturalist* IV. 70 [They] paddle along shore, ever on the watch for 'otter sign.' **1895** *Outing* XXVII. 48/1, I scouted about in quest of sign.

2. A board suitably lettered for designating a shop or business, or the office of a doctor, lawyer, etc. Also *comb.* {1816-}

1842 *Knickerb.* XIX. 441 The [blacksmith's] sign-raising was celebrated by a neat supper. **1853** COZZENS *Prismatics* 31 [We] put up our two narrow, black tin signs, with gold letters, on a very white window shutter. **1865** 'G. HAMILTON' *Skirmishes* 158 The lawyer and the doctor put up their 'sign' and await briefs and patients. **1898** WESTCOTT *D. Harum* 361 The fact o' the matter is that I'm goin' to take down my sign. **1916** EASTMAN *From Deep Woods* 137, I opened my office, hung out my sign, and waited for patients.

+3. Short for SIGN LANGUAGE; also, a person's name in that language.

1857 *Lawrence* (Kan.) *Republican* 11 June 4 It is not easy to forget your *sign,* you are Col. Buchanan, and I am right glad to see you. **1870** KEIM *Sheridan's Troopers* 221 Each tribe, to begin with, has its name in sign.

+4. *Baseball.* A gesture, motion, etc., used to convey instructions or information secretly to a player.

1899 PATTEN *Frank Merriwell's Double Shot* 62 (E. J. Nichols). **1912** MATHEWSON *Pitching* 160 Ball-players are always looking to steal some sign so that they may 'cross' the enemy. In the language of the Big Leagues it is 'signs,' never 'signals.'

+5. In special combinations.

Sign jack, ?one who works on high advertising signs; *s. rider,* a cowboy riding the range in search of cattle or cattle thieves.

1890 *Stock Grower & Farmer* 11 Jan. 6/2 The sign riders cut the trail. **1906** *N.Y. Ev. Post* 17 Aug. 2 The 'sign-jacks' find regular employment from the bill-poster and street advertising companies.

∗Sign, *v.* 1. *intr.* (See quotation.) 2. *To sign off.* +a. To withdraw formally from membership in a religious body. With *to:* To change one's church membership *to* another denomination. Also *vbl. n.* +b. (See quot. 1859.) — (1) **1888** *Amer. Folk-Lore* I. 161 Sign, constantly used in Washington as a term for marking off the land for corn or potatoes. (2) **1838** EMERSON *Works* I. (1903) 143 In the country, neighborhoods, half parishes are *signing off,* to use the local term. **1859** BARTLETT 407 *To Sign off,* to release a debtor by agreeing to accept whatever he offers to pay; to give a receipt in full of all demands. An expression common among merchants. **1878** STOWE *Poganuc People* 12, 'I'm glad father signed off to the 'Piscopalians. . . .' 'My papa won't ever sign off.' *Ib.* 27 After the close of the [Revolutionary] war . . . the revolution came which broke up the State Church and gave to every man the liberty of 'signing off,' . . . to any denomination that pleased him.

∗Signal.

+1. =SIGN *n.* 4.

1878 *De Witt's Base-Ball Guide* 20 The left field . . . should watch the play of the pitcher, and attend to his signals. **1886** CHADWICK *Art of Pitching* 39 The most effective way of throwing to bases is to stand up straight and ready to throw to first base while looking at the catcher and awaiting the latter's signal.

2. In special combinations.

Signal-bearer, one who carries the flags, etc., used by surveyors; *s. camp,* a camp or place from which signals are sent; *s. code,* a code used in signaling; *s. kit,* a kit of articles used by signalmen; *s. lantern,* a lantern used as a signal; *s. master,* one in charge of a railroad signal system; *S. Office,* a government bureau in charge of signaling: (see SIGNAL SERVICE 2, quot. 1891); *s. party,* in an army, a detachment of signalmen; *s. point,* a place on a railroad at which there is a signal; *s. pole,* a pole or staff from which signals are displayed aboard ship.

1854 WHIPPLE, etc. *Explor. Ry. Route* I. 5 The parties at present are divided as follows: Mr. Albert Campbell, surveyor; . . . Messrs. Jones and Gaines, signal bearers [etc.]. **1884** *Century Mag.* April 827/1 Charles Caywood . . . kept the signal camp in the swampy woods back of Grimes's house. **1876** HABBERTON *Jericho Road* 94 Between the societies of neighboring counties there often existed signal-codes and unwritten extradition and reciprocity treaties. **1887** BILLINGS *Hardtack* 396 Details of men were made from the various regiments . . . to learn the use of the 'Signal Kit,' so called. The chief article in this kit was a series of seven flags. **1828** in Brayley *Boston Fire Dept.* 169 A signal lantern [shall] be procured and deposited in Engine-house No. 7. **1866** in Fulton *Sam Hobart* 103 The signal-master telegraphed all right to the Dayton office. **1872** *Harper's Mag.* Dec. 151 The appropriation by Congress to the Signal-office, with a view to the interests of agriculture as well as of commerce, was one of the results. **1862** MCCLELLAN in *Own Story* 302 If necessary, . . . communicate on return with signal party at Queen's creek. **1900** *Everybody's Mag.* II. 438/2 If a breakdown occurred between the signal points, there was no way to warn oncoming trains. **1838** COOPER *Homeward B.* vii, The master was busy . . . in getting down the signal-pole, . . . and otherwise superintending duty.

Signal bell. A bell used as a signal. {1897} — **1865** TROWBRIDGE *Three Scouts* 189 The signal-bell was ringing. . . . 'All aboard!' cried the conductor **1877** W. WRIGHT *Big Bonanza* 186 They answered every tap of the signal-bells as promptly . . . as though nothing were wrong below.

+Signal corps. An arm of the U.S. Army in charge of signal communications and information. — **1865** *Atlantic Mo.* June 753/1 Lieutenant Clemens of the Signal Corps, put off from the tug in a launch. **1880** LAMPHERE *U.S. Govt.* 147/2 In the Signal Corps proper officers and enlisted men skilled in all the uses of the appliances for signal duty are in the army. **1897** *Outing* XXX. 184/2 The active militia . . . consists of . . . two troops of cavalry, an ambulance corps and a signal corps. **1914** *Cycl. Amer. Govt.* III. 309 The Signal Corps of the United States Army exercises general supervision over the signal service, is charged with the construction, operation and maintenance of military lines of information, and performs all other services required by the field service regulations.

Signal fire. A fire lighted by Indians as a signal. {1849, in general sense} — **1849** *31st Congress 1 Sess.* Sen. Ex. Doc. No. 64, 212 They have been telegraphing with their signal-fires in several different directions. **1879** B. F. TAYLOR *Summer-Savory* 26 The night after his death the Indians kindled signal fires along the mountain peaks and thus telegraphed the event eighty miles down the river. *a*1918 G. STUART *On Frontier* I. 94 The Indians were burning signal fires on the mountains which boded no good to travelers.

Signalist. {1836} A signaler; one who sends signals. — **1881** *Appletons' Ann. Cycl. 1880* 548/1 He was enabled to furnish each army corps . . . with a competent force of skilled signalists.

Signalman. {1737–}

1. On a railroad, one who operates a signal. {1840–}

1867 DALY *Under Gaslight* IV. 40 The switch, with a red lantern and Signal man's coat hanging on it. **1892** *N.Y. Rev. Statutes* (1901) III. 3006 Any person who, being employed upon any railway as . . . bridge-tender, flagman, signal man [etc.], . . . is intoxicated, . . . is guilty of a misdemeanor.

2. One who makes or reads marine signals. {1737–}

1875 *Scribner's Mo.* Nov. 139/2 The Phonometer . . . is designed to assist the signal-man on steamships in marking the intervals of time at which the fog-horn or whistle is to be blown. **1878** *Harper's Mag.* Feb. 321/1 The signal man's face lengthened with amusement.

+3. (See quotation.)

1905 *Forestry Bureau Bul.* No. 61, 46 *Signal man,* one who transmits orders from the foreman of a yarding crew to the engineer of the yarding donkey. (P[acific] C[oast] F[orest].)

Signal officer. An officer in the signal service of the army. {1829, on a ship} — **1862** MOORE *Rebellion Rec.* V. 11. 213/1 My Signal-Officers, Lieuts. Taffts and Howard, are worthy of honorable mention. **1884** *Century Mag.* Oct. 814/1 The signal-officer . . . discovered that some of his men . . . were reporting the presence of . . . Confederate troops. **1920** *Lit. Digest* 12 June 80/3 While the war was still in progress the signal officers, using treetops as antennae, read messages from ships at sea, [and] from aviators in the sky.

+Signal service.

1. A system of communication by signals, or an organization operating such a system: (see sense 2, quot. 1891). Also fig.

1871 *Harper's Mag.* Aug. 406/1 The *military system* is one of the most . . . valuable features . . . of this Signal Service for the benefit of commerce. **1880** LAMPHERE *U.S. Govt.* 147/2 The Signal Service is divided into four branches. **1898** CANFIELD *Maid of Frontier* 105 The signal service inside of my shirt has never failed to telegraph me when to look out for the blue wind.

2. Attrib. with *bulletin, bureau, department,* etc.

1887 *Courier-Journal* 30 Jan. 7/7 The Signal-service department here received instructions to hoist the cold-wave flag, and a decided fall in temperature is promised. **1887** *Nation* 12 May 404/3 The information [in a guidebook] includes . . . the signal-service flags, postal rates [etc.]. **1888** *St. Paul Globe* 22 Jan., The signal service mercury sank to 41 deg. below zero this morning. **1891** *Cent.* 5624/2 *Signal-service Bureau,* from 1871 to the end of 1890, a bureau of the United States War Department, . . . having charge of military signaling and military telegraph-lines, and of the collection and comparison of meteorological observations, and the publication of predictions of the weather based upon them. **1892** *S. Dak. Hist. Coll.* I. 73 The next July, a signal service station was opened for business by the federal government. **1893** *Harper's Mag.* March 489/1 On our way to the cars we read a Signal Service bulletin announcing the temperature in New York to be 24°.

+Signal smoke. A smoke serving as a signal or sign to those at a distance. — **1834** A. PIKE *Sketches* 58 This day we had seen a large signal-smoke rise to the right behind a mountain. **1850** *Western Journal* IV. 236 Alarm smokes and signal smokes had now began to appear in every direction. **1854** WHIPPLE, etc. *Explor. Ry. Route* I. 92 Lieutenant Ives . . . had left Picacho on Thursday, having seen our signal-smoke upon the evening previous. **1875** *Scribner's Mo.* Dec. 198/2 High up on the mountain to the east was a signal smoke.

Signal station. 1. A place used by military forces for sending and receiving messages by signaling. {1816–} +**2.** A place on a railroad at which signaling is done, as a flag station. — (1) **1861** in McClellan *Own Story* 181 The signal station at Sugar Loaf telegraphs that the enemy have moved away from Leesburg. **1862** MOORE *Rebellion Rec.* V. 11. 475 Their signal-stations on the Blue Ridge commanded a view of our every movement. **1885** *Wkly. New Mexican Rev.* 5 Feb. 4/1 Lieutenant W. A. Glassford, of the United States signal service . . . has been instructed to find a favorable site this side of the Spanish range for a new signal station. (2) **1876** CROFUTT *Trans-continental Tourist* 50 Barton, a signal station of very little importance. **1887** *Courier-Journal* 2 Feb. 3/2 The train stopped about a mile from Jeffersonville, at a signal station.

Signal tower. {1766–} *Railroad.* +A small tower or structure where signals, often semaphores, are set or controlled. — **1900** *Everybody's Mag.* II. 445/1 There has been erected a special signal tower at the great Horseshoe Curve on the Pennsylvania. **1917** MATHEWSON *Second Base Sloan* 15 Eight burnished rails . . . crossed their path, under a big signal tower.

Signature book. A book in which are kept for reference the signatures of customers. — **1890** *Harper's Mag.* Feb. 468/2 The paying teller . . . [uses the] 'Signature Book' . . . for comparison.

Signboard. {1632–} +A board, usually on a post beside a road, containing directions or information for travelers. — **1833** *Knickerb.* I. 88, I had been long enough in the west to feel independent of roads and sign-boards. **1835** *S. Lit. Messenger* I. 580 The post of a sign-board where several roads meet. **1852** *Ib.* XVIII. 702/1 The witness asserted the distance to be nine miles, 'because the sign-board said so.' **1883** *Wheelman* I. 298 They found a sign-board pointing to Swampscott and Lynn.

+Sign camp. A camp of one or more cowboys on the watch for cattle thieves. — **1897** LEWIS *Wolfville* 2 We'll show Red Dog an' sim'lar villages they ain't sign-camps compared with Wolfville. **1902** MACGOWAN

Last Word 15 He stayed with me when I was sole alone for three months, keepin' sign camp for the L Q on the Staked Plain.

Signer. {1611-} +One of those who signed the American Declaration of Independence in 1776. More fully *signer of the Declaration (of Independence)*. Also with defining terms.

1820 *Niles' Reg.* XVII. 441/1 There now remain but four signers of the declaration of independence. **1827** *Md. Hist. Mag.* XVII. 250 Having received from old Mr. C. Carroll (the last survivor of the signers of the declaration of Independence) a recommendation to the President [etc.]. **1881** *Harper's Mag.* March 530/2 Tradition whispers that in 1736 Philip Livingstone, one of the signers of the Declaration, saved the life of this historical elm. **1885** BAYLOR *On Both Sides* 18 Jenny [was] descended from a Virginia signer of the Declaration. **1892** *Nation* 21 April 295/1 What shall we say to the descendants of the Pilgrims, and the Signers, and the Knickerbockers? **1902** Declaration Signer [see DECLARATION 1 (*b*)].

+b. *Great Signer*, Thomas Jefferson (1743-1826), author and thirty-second signer of the Declaration of Independence.

1883 *Harper's Mag.* July 319/2 When the great Signer stopped talking the countryman rushed for his hat.

Signist. +*Pure signist*, one who favors the use exclusively of the manual or sign method in teaching the deaf, and regards oral instruction with disfavor. — **1894** *Educator* Oct. 161 The ranks of the 'pure signists' have been terribly broken into.

Sign language. A mode of communication by means of manual signs; used among the Indians. {1865, in general sense} — **1847** PARKMAN in *Knickerb.* XXX. 234 Knowing nothing at that time of the sign-language of the Indians, I could only guess at his meaning. **1865** PIKE *Scout & Ranger* (1932) 24 The chiefs of the different tribes . . . , in their eloquent sign language, and in broken English, expressed their friendship. **1878** BEADLE *Western Wilds* 544 Their communication at first is entirely by the 'sign language.' **1891** *Harper's Mag.* Dec. 31/1 [In] sign language [Chief Old Sun] . . . told us that his teeth were gone. **1925** TILGHMAN *Dugout* 20 Joe addressed her with a few words of Cheyenne and the universal sign language.

*∗**Sign manual.** +A sign made by the hand or hands; the system of signs made in this way. — **1833** CATLIN *Indians* I. 116 [The chief's] orders and commands . . . were uniformly given by signs manual. **1871** *Rep. Indian Affairs* (1872) 472 We labored under many great disadvantages in . . . having to depend on the 'sign-manual' altogether.

Sign-painter. One whose occupation is painting signs. {1776-} — **1725** *New-Eng. Courant* 15 Feb. 1/2, I would oblige every Sign-Painter to serve seven Years at College, before he presum'd to handle Pencil or Paint-Box. **1789** DUNLAP *Father* II. i, I employ'd an artist, commonly called a sign painter, to delineate my name upon a painted board. **1847** L. COLLINS *Kentucky* 232 [In] Christian County . . . [there are] three house and sign painters. **1896** *N.Y. Dramatic News* 11 July 4/3 The sign painters will go to work today on the new name. **1902** ALDRICH *Sea Turn* 185 The rest of the lodgers, with the exception of the sign-painter, met their indebtedness.

Signpost. A post on which a sign is displayed. {1620-} **1652** *Suffolk Deeds* I. 137 The signes of the Kings armes & signe posts. **1712** HEMPSTEAD *Diary* 17 Daniel Gard . . . Was Whipt 39 Lashes with a Single Codline at ye Sign-post. **1857** *Quinland* I. 107 Dr. Vampire was climbing the tavern sign-post in order to escape his old antagonist. **1907** *St. Nicholas* May 661/1 The sign post is posting its posters.

b. A guidepost. {1863-} In fig. use. **1857** WILLIS *Convalescent* 310, I was a sort of neighborly sign-post, saving him many a trudge. **1914** STEELE *Storm* 216 The man whose affairs carry him continually over them [*sc.* the paths of the ocean] is able, even on a thick night, to read the shadowy sign-posts of these thoroughfares.

‖**Siki.** (See quotation.) — **1807** *Mass. H. S. Coll.* 2 Ser. III. 58 The siki, or common clam, is found on the borders of the lagunes and in several other parts of the island.

+**Silent partner.** A partner who is not active in the management of a firm and whose name may not be included in the firm's title. — **1828** WEBSTER, *Silent*, . . . not acting; not transacting business in person; as a silent partner in a commercial house. **1894** LEAVITT *Our Money Wars* 221 His Wall St. concern . . . came to grief in 1890: also a concern in Buffalo in which he was a silent partner. **1898** *McClure's Mag.* X. 499/1 In this firm J. D. Fish, president of the Marine Bank, was to be a silent partner.

Silent system. (See quot. 1891 and cf. AUBURN SYSTEM.) {1836-7} — **1842** BUCKINGHAM *E. & W. States* II. 306 The system of discipline pursued here, is that which is called the Auburn, or Silent System, in contradistinction to the Philadelphia, or Solitary, System. **1891** *Cent.* 5628/1 *Silent system*, a system of prison discipline which imposes entire silence among the prisoners, even when assembled together.

Silesia. **a.** A linen fabric originally made in Silesia. {1727-} +**b.** A thin cotton fabric, commonly twilled, used for linings. — **1741** *S.C. Gazette* 26 March, Just imported . . . Silesias, Buckrams. **1869** ALCOTT *Little Women* II. 328, I want some twilled silesia. **1894** *Outing* XXIV. 323/2 My companion thrust a half-yard of silesia . . . into his own pocket.

*∗**Silk, *n.***

*∗**1.** **a.** Raw silk or thread made from raw silk.

1647 *Essex Probate Rec.* I. 70 A swath, a p[ar]cell of cruell, thread & Silke, 8s. **1668** Neill *Virginia Carolorum* 322 The Governor, Councell and Burgesses of his Majesties Collony of Virginia . . . pray that your Majestie will . . . accept their present of three hundred pounds of silke. *c*1790 COXE *View U.S.* 75 In the settled parts of the states, . . . [we have] rice,

indigo, cotton, silk [etc.]. **1836** *Niles' Nat. Reg.* 8 Oct. 96/3 *American silk.* Twenty skeins of beautiful sewing silk have been made by Mrs. Lewis, of Berkley county, Virginia, the product of worms raised on her own farm. **1903** *Dept. Agric. Yrbk.* 1902 89 The Entomologist, Dr. Howard, . . . [studied] especially the methods of reeling silk.

*∗**b.** Cloth made of the threads or fibers produced by silkworms; a garment made of such cloth.

1710 T. BUCKINGHAM *Naval Exped.* (1825) 80 To the Taylor for mowhair, silk and making my jacket, 12.5. **1797** *Ann. 4th Congress* 2 Sess. 1870 [The lot] is composed of . . . satin, silks, corduroys, velveretts, &c. **1822** *Ann. 17th Congress* 1 Sess. 319, 147 yards of silk for $116.61. **1904** A. DALE *Wanted: a Cook* 27, I found her in mauve silk—really magnificently made.

+**c.** *Fine as silk*, very fine indeed. *colloq.*

1836 CROCKETT *Exploits* 64 'That's fine,' say I. 'Fine as silk, colonel, and leetle finer,' says the other. **1905** BELASCO *Girl of Golden West* (1925) I. 61, 'I trust the Girl who runs the Polka is well?' . . . 'Fine as silk, Mr. Ashby.'

+**2.** *collect.* The fine soft styles of an ear of Indian corn. See also CORN SILK.

1770 WASHINGTON *Diaries* I. 395 Many Stalks were putting out entire new Shoots with young and tender Silk. **1839** LONGFELLOW *Hyperion* I. 120 He was, . . . 'a devilish handsome fellow;' . . . 'with a cream-colored mustache, as soft as the silk of Indian corn. **1894** EGGLESTON in *Century Mag.* April 850 The pistillate flower of the maize . . . was appropriately called the 'silk.'

+**b.** *In silk(s)*, of Indian corn, at the stage of development when the silk is most conspicuous.

1774 FITHIAN *Journal* I. 212 The Corn is beginning pretty generally to tassel, & I saw one hill in Silk. **1784** SMYTH *Tour* I. 295 This state of it is denominated *the Corn being in Silks*. **1847** DRAKE *Pioneer Life Ky.* 52 By the month of August the corn is in silk.

+**3.** The lash of a whip.

1845 *Knickerb.* XXV. 91 Behave thyself, or thou may'st 'feel the silk.' **1873** MILLER *Amongst Modocs* 368 The driver . . . snapped the silk under the heels of his leaders.

+**4.** *attrib.* (passing into *adj.*) and *comb.* **a.** Designating things, especially articles of clothing, made wholly or chiefly of silk.

See also SILK BRAID, SILK HAT, etc.

1659 *Watertown Rec.* I. 1. 62 From heance forth, none of our inhabitants, except such as the law doth allow, doe either weare silke goods, or silke skarfes. **1667** SANFORD *Letter Book* 46 Sume good Silke Buttons for Brest and Coate. **1707** *Boston News-Letter* 15 Sept. 2/2 [She] had on . . . a black and white silk Crape Petticoat. **1737** *N.J. Archives* XI. 517 The other lin'd with light colour'd Silk Poplin. **1767** HABERSHAM *Letters* 61, I want a dress, plain and grave Coloured Silk Coat,—a black silk waistcoat without sleeves [etc.]. **1788** in H. H. Brooks *Gleanings* IV. 108 Old Silk Caps for bathing. **1840** *Picayune* 22 Oct. 2/4 He sported a figured silk stock. **1844** *Lexington Observer* 2 Oct. 3/7 The Ladies Will there find . . . Silk Shirts, Silk Hose, and Half Hose. **1906** FREEMAN *By Light of Soul* 437 She did not get into bed, but took a silk comfortable off, and wrapped it around her. **1920** COOPER *Under Big Top* 127 With his cane in one hand and the silk topper slanted over one eye.

b. Designating persons, groups, activities, etc., having to do with the production of silk in the United States.

See also SILK COMPANY, SILK-GROWER, etc.

1772 HABERSHAM *Letters* 162 The aid from Parliament for the Encouragement of the Silk Culture here [in Savannah] is withdrawn. **1797** IMLAY *Western Territory* (ed. 3) 263 It would be highly advisable for the silk-planter to be very cautious. **1840** *Niles' Nat. Reg.* 23 May 192/3 An experiment in silk raising has been made in the vicinity of New Orleans. **1841** *Picayune* 9 May 2/3 Silk cocoons. Mr. Frederick A. Ross . . . offers to purchase two thousand bushels of good cocoons of the next crop raised in Eastern Tennessee and South Western Virginia. **1843** *Niles' Nat. Reg.* 17 June 256/2 The Tribune speaks of the report of the New England silk convention held at Northampton as most cheering document to all the friends of this new branch of American industry. **1848** *Rep. Comm. Patents 1847* 101 Five states [raise] about five-eighths of the silk crop. **1868** *Rep. Comm. Agric. 1867* 7 Silk husbandry was introduced at an early day into Louisiana. **1876** *Wide Awake* 323/1 The 'silk-farm' contains a number of sections of the most fertile land in the state. *Ib.*, The Marquis de Bossiere . . . established a silk colony in the little town of Williamsburg, Franklin Co., Kansas. **1887** *Advance* 14 July 447/1 Mrs. L. F. Baldy of California, is about to establish a colony of silk culturists in Maryland.

c. Designating places, activities, etc., connected with the manufacturing or processing of silk.

See also SILK COMPANY, SILK FACTORY, etc.

1759 ELIOT *Field-Husb.* vi. 133 This . . . is the more pleasing, as it has a favourable Aspect upon the Silk Manufactory. **1836** *Niles' Nat. Reg.* 1 Oct. 80/3 *Silk print works.* . . . A new brick building . . . [has] been erected for the printing of silks and ginghams. **1856** *Porter's Spirit of Times* 13 Dec. 245/2 Burglars . . . had made an . . . entry into several silk warehouses. **1872** *Harper's Mag.* Nov. 836/2 Now the silk-mill on the old farm draws its supplies of the raw material from China and Japan. **1923** *Lit. Digest* 13 Jan. 14/2 'Unrest and discontent' are apparent among the workers [in Paterson, N.J.] to an extent which threatens the destruction of the city's prestige as a silk market.

Silk, *v.* +**1.** *tr.* To free (an ear of corn) from silk. +**2.** *intr.* Of Indian corn: To produce silk. (Cf. SILKED *a.*) — (1) **1847** DRAKE *Pioneer Life Ky.* 52 My first business in the morning was to pull, and husk and silk enough [corn] for breakfast. **1892** *York County Hist. Rev.* 59 [They] make a specialty of . . . 'silkers' for silking corn. (2) **1878** BEADLE *Western Wilds* 132 Corn [might] be made to tassle and silk in greenbacks. *Ib.* 245 Corn will not silk. **1902** *Monthly Weather Rev.* July 346/1 The month closed with the . . . oat harvest far advanced . . . ; corn mostly silking or earing.

+**Silkaline, Silkolene.** A soft cotton fabric resembling silk. Also attrib. — **1896** *Internat. Typogr. Union Proc.* 64/1, 12 yds. silkaline, $1.80. **1911** 'O. HENRY' *Rolling Stones* 197 The last wrinkle and darn of their blue silkolene cotton tights had vanished from the stage.

+**Silk ball.** (See quot. 1884.) — **1741** W. STEPHENS *Proc. Georgia* II. 135 Silk Balls . . . were to be taken at a good and certain Price. **1884** *Science* 9 May 562 The term 'silk-balls' was doubtless employed at times to designate cocoons; but that is quite different from 'raw-silk' and 'raw-silk balls,' which . . . might more appropriately apply to the twisted hanks of raw silk.

Silk braid. (See quot. 1891.) Also attrib. — **1761** in H. M. Brooks *Gleanings* IV. 28 Mohair Lupings, Silk Braid ditto, flatt and round Silk Lace and Frogs for Button Lupes. **1877** *Harper's Mag.* March 603/1 There is a lady who wants to match a confounded bit of silk braid, drab bordering on the lilac. **1891** *Cent.* 5630/1 *Silk braid*, a fine and closely worked braid of silk, made for the decoration of garments, and sometimes of furniture.

+**Silk bunting.** (See quot. 1891.) — **1884** COUES *Key to Birds* 387 *Spiza*, Silk Bunting. **1891** *Cent.* 5630/1 *Silk-bunting*, . . . an American bunting of the genus *Spiza* (formerly *Euspiza*), as the black-throated *S. americana*, whose plumage is peculiarly close and smooth.

Silk company. A company organized to produce silk. — **1836** *Niles' Nat. Reg.* 15 Oct. 112/2 The Massachusetts Silk company have at present 78,000 mulberry trees in flourishing condition. **1840** *Ib.* 16 May 176/2 The silk company at Northampton have completely resuscitated their establishment.

Silk-dyer. One who dyes silks. — **1708** *Boston News-Letter* 6 Dec. 4/2 Ran-away from his Master Ambrose Vincent, Silk Dyer of Boston, . . . an Irish Lad call'd Darby Ragan. **1789** *Boston Directory* 199 Smink Peter, musician and silk-dyer.

Silked, *a.* {1844–} +Of Indian corn: In the stage when the silk is first prominent. — **1879** *Scribner's Mo.* Nov. 134/1 Leagues of Kansas corn, seen in . . . their glory of silked and tasseled and sunlit strength.

+**Silker.** [f. SILK *v.* 1.] A device for removing the silk from ears of corn. — **1892** [see SILK *v.*].

Silk factory. A silk mill. {1835–} Also transf. — **1833** COKE *Subaltern's Furlough* xii, [In] Mansfield . . . a silk factory has been lately established. **1869** *Rep. Comm. Agric. 1868* 300 A company was formed to erect a silk factory at San José, California. **1876** *Wide Awake* 269/1 It was woven in his silk factory [in Kansas]. **1883** *Century Mag.* Sept. 694/2 Paterson is one of the greatest silk factories of the world.

Silk-grass. The silklike fiber or fibrous part of any one of a number of plants; also, the plant producing this. {1620–}

Among the plants (not all grasses) in connection with which the term has been used are various tropical American species belonging to the amaryllis and pineapple families (Amaryllidaceae and Bromeliaceae), several species of the American genus *Yucca*, esp. *Y. filamentosa* (beargrass), and two western American grasses, the needle grass (*Stipa comata*) and the bunch grass (*Oryzopsis cuspidata*).

1610 *Estate of Va.* 55 A kinde of hempe or flax, and silke grasse doe grow there naturally. **1664** *Essex Probate Rec.* I. 457, 2 beds mad of silkgras with bolster and blankits. **1743** CLAYTON *Flora Virginica* 152 Yucca flore albo, foliorum marginibus filamentosis. Silkgrass. **1775** ROMANS *Nat. Hist. Florida* 156 Silk Grass grows on the most barren sand hills of Florida. **1805** LEWIS in *L. & Clark Exped.* III. (1905) 12 A couple of bags wove with the fingers of the bark of the silk-grass. **1832** WILLIAMSON *Maine* I. 127 Milkweed, sometimes called *Silk-grass*, . . . bears pods four inches in length enfolding a downy substance, soft like silk and good for bedding. **1859** BARTLETT 26 *Bear-Grass*, . . . sometimes called Silk Grass, from the fibres which appear on the edges of the leaves, . . . is not a grass. **1884** W. MILLER *Dict. Names of Plants* 57/2. **1891** *Cent.* 5630/2 *Silk-grass*, . . . a grass, *Oryzopsis cuspidata*, of the western United States, whose flowering glumes are densely covered with long silky hairs; also, the similar *Stipa comata* of the same region.

Silk-grower. One who grows or cultivates silkworms for their use in producing silk. — **1845** *Knickerb.* XXV. 407 The silk-growers entered upon their business in earnest. **1869** *Rep. Comm. Agric. 1868* 292 It is probable, . . . from opinions expressed by silk-growers, that the number of cocoons will double annually. **1884** EGGLESTON in *Century Mag.* Jan. 433/2 The Queen of George III. wore a full court-dress of this silk—the last of all the garbs produced by loyal American silk-growers for English royalty.

***Silk hat.** A high cylindrical hat covered with a kind of silk plush. {1834–} — **1840** *Picayune* 3 Oct. 3/2 Just received . . . from New York and Philadelphia, a complete assortment of . . . Silk Hats. **1857** *Rep. Comm. Patents 1856: Agric.* 107 The general introduction of silk hats . . . [has] resulted happily for the persecuted muskrats. **1890** H. PALMER *Stories of Base Ball Field* 11 The discovery by the 'bleachers' of a silk hat in the grand stand was the signal for a whole afternoon of sport at the wearer's expense. **1920** COOPER *Under Big Top* 127 An elderly man who affected a silk hat, Prince Albert and cane, investigated a noise in the hallway to find a six-foot chimpanzee.

+**Silk plant.** A species of plantain, *Plantago rugelii*. — **1806** *Ann. 9th Congress* 2 Sess. 1142 The silk plant, wild endive, wild olive [etc., grow] . . . along the river side. **1852** STANSBURY *Gt. Salt Lake* 175 Among the springs was found . . . a plant I had not before seen—called by some of the men silk-plant. **1894** *Amer. Folk-Lore* VII. 96 *Plantago Rugelii*, . . . silk-plant, Fla.

Silk-reeling. The unwinding of raw silk from cocoons into skeins. Also attrib. — **1842** *Amer. Pioneer* I. 146 We lately visited Mr. Harrison's silk reeling establishment in Cincinnati. **1888** *Harper's Mag.* June 47 Silk reeling is one of the industries [of Kansas].

Silk shoe. A shoe partly made of silk. *Obs.* — **1772** A. G. WINSLOW *Diary* 17 My silk shoes compleated my dress. **1789** MORSE *Amer. Geog.* 182 The town of Lynn is particularly famous for the manufacture of womens silk and stuff shoes. **1813** *Niles' Reg.* V. 190/1 Women's stuff and silk shoes [are manufactured in the U.S.].

***Silk stocking.**

***1.** A stocking made of silk.

1677 SEWALL *Diary* I. 34 Ordered to buy 2 pair of Silk Stockings. **1770** *Penna. Chron.* 17 Sept. 138/1 They also scour, stove, foot, mend and graft all sorts of silk stockings in the neatest and best manner. **1854** BENTON *30 Years' View* I. 57/2 He always appeared in the Senate in full dress; short small-clothes, silk stockings, and shoes. **1907** *St. Nicholas* May 626/1 Rosamond wore blue silk stockings and bronze slippers with high heels.

+**2.** A member of the silk-stocking gentry. Chiefly in political usage.

1891 *Cent.* 5630/1 *A silk-stocking*, a person of this [luxurious or wealthy] class. **1894** STEAD *If Christ Came to Chicago* 36 Hopkins was elected by the silk stockings on the one hand and the shorthairs on the other. **1903** *Independent* 12 Nov. 2663/1 The mass of voters look upon him as a 'silk stocking'—as one who neither understands nor sympathizes with their life. **1914** *Cycl. Amer. Govt.* III. 309/1 *Silk Stockings*, a derisive appellation bestowed by the 'practical politicians' upon those citizens of wealth and high social position who occasionally interfere in politics in support of some reform measure or candidate.

3. Attrib. and comb. in sense 2 with *academy, company*, etc.

1798 *Ann. 5th Congress* 1948 If they wished to place them in a ridiculous point of view, or to procure for them the name of the *Silk Stocking Company*, or any other term of derision, they could not take a more effectual course to obtain it. *c***1840** in Buckingham *E. & W. States* II. 117 'Prime Havannas' . . . are only dealt out to his [Van Buren's] 'silk-stocking and ruffle-shirt friends.' **1869** TOURGEE *Toinette* (1881) 154 She had managed to pick up . . . 'a tolerable English education,' . . . [possibly] through the charity of some teacher at the 'Silk-Stocking Academy,' on 'Gentleman Ridge.' **1903** *N.Y. Ev. Post* 30 Oct. 2 Political conditions change even in the 'silk stocking' quarter—the middle reaches of Manhattan, between 14th Street and 96th Street. **1903** *N.Y. Sun* 28 Nov. 4 He is the representative of the wealthy intellectual, the cultured, the 'silk stocking' element, for which the people in general have no abiding affection.

+**Silk-stocking gentry.** (See quot. 1891.) — **1812** JEFFERSON *Writings* XIII. 163, I trust . . . the Gores and Pickerings will find their levees crowded with silk stocking gentry, but no yeomanry. **1836** CROCKETT *Exploits* 58 You may be called a drunken dog by some of the clean shirt and silk stocking gentry. **1843** MATHEWS *Writings* 43/1 The one [party] was known as the Silk-stocking Gentry: the other by the comprehensive appellation of the Loafers. **1891** *Cent.* 5630/1 Silk-stockings . . . were formerly regarded as extravagant and reprehensible, and as worn by men were regarded as an indication of luxurious habits; hence, the *silk-stocking gentry* or *element*, the luxurious or wealthy class.

Silk stuff. Material made of silk. {1730–} — **1663** *Md. Archives* I. 472 They had found the Silke stuffe which made only 3 Poke Baggs and noe more. **1711** *Springfield Rec.* II. 40 Six Yds & a halfe of silke stuff. **1711** *Boston News-Letter* 19 Feb. 2/2 Stolen or carried privately away . . . a double gown, one side silk-stuff the other russel; a second double Gown of silk-stuff and a Petticoat of the same.

+**Silk-top palmetto.** (See quot. 1890.) — **1884** SARGENT *Rep. Forests* 217 Silk-top Palmetto. Semi-tropical Florida. **1890** *Cent.* 4249/1 *Silk-top palmetto*, the name in Florida of *Thrinax parviflora*, found there and in the West Indies: a tree some 30 feet high, turned to minor uses. **1897** SUDWORTH *Arborescent Flora* 103.

Silkweed. {1857–} +Any one of various American plants of the genus *Asclepias*. Also attrib.

1784 *Amer. Acad. Mem.* I. 424 The seeds are contained in large pods, and are crowned with white down, . . . resembling silk, which has occasioned the name of Silkweed. **1828** *Western Mo. Rev.* II. 194 Among the varieties of flowers on the margin of the river, the most common is the *asclepias*, or silk weed. **1854** EMMONS *Agric. N.Y.* V. 263 Silkweed insect, 124. *Ib.* 124. This insect is common on the silkweed . . . in June and July. **1870** *Rep. Comm. Agric. 1869* 61 The *asclepias*, or silk-weed fiber, may be mentioned here as the principal plant, aside from flax and hemp, on which attempts at cottonizing were made. **1891** *Amer. Folk-Lore* IV. 148 Mrs. Hayward, who came from Middleborough, Mass., when I spoke of *Milkweed*, always understood Asclepias, which I was taught to call *Silkweed*.

* **Silkworm.** The larva of any one of various moths which produce silken cocoons of commercial value.

1676 GLOVER *Va.* in *Phil. Trans.* XI. 628 Mulberry-Trees . . . were planted at first to feed Silk-worms. **1724** JONES *Virginia* 60 Mulberry Trees and Silkworms thrive there to Admiration. **1796** WANSEY *Excursion U.S.* 193 Near Princetown are large plantations of the Italian mulberry tree, for the culture of the silk worm. **1848** *Rep.Comm. Patents 1847* 441 Various plans have been proposed and adopted for cocooneries or feeding-sheds for the silk-worm. **1898** HARPER *S. B. Anthony* I. 42 While at New Rochelle Susan becomes greatly interested in the culture of silk-worms.

b. Attrib. with *egg, mulberry, season.*

1739 W. STEPHENS *Proc. Georgia* I. 310 The Silk-Worm Season now demanding good Store [of mulberry leaves], Camuche persuaded Mr. Jones to purchase [young trees]. **1741** *Ib.* II. 98 Mr. Hird . . . [had] Orders from the General to call on me, to furnish him with some Silk-Worm Eggs. **1743** CATESBY *Carolina* II. p. xxi, The Italian or Silk-Worm Mulberry . . . [was] introduced into Virginia by Sir William Berkley.

Silky, *a.* {1611–} In the names of various trees and plants. — **1843** TORREY *Flora N.Y.* I. 6 *Clematis ochroleuca.* . . . Silky Virgin's Bower. . . . It flowers in May, and ripens its fruit early in July. **1884** SARGENT *Rep. Forests* 171 *Salix Sitchensis.* . . . Silky Willow. . . . A low, much-branched tree, . . . or more often a straggling shrub. **1891** COULTER *Bot. W. Texas* I. 150 C[ornus] *sericea.* Silky cornel. . . . Common in the Atlantic States and extending into eastern and northern Texas. **1894** *Ib.* III. 502 P[anicum] *lachnanthum.* (Silky Panic-grass.) . . . Dry plains, western Texas.

Silky fowl. A breed of domestic fowl having soft, white, fluffy plumage. — **1850** BROWNE *Poultry Yard* 81 Among the monstrosities of the domestic fowl . . . may be mentioned . . . the 'silky' and 'negro' fowls, with white silky plumage, and with skin, combs, and bones which are black. **1871** LEWIS *Poultry Book* 70 The sole value of the Silky fowl is as a mother to Bantams, or other small and delicate chickens.

Silo. **a.** A pit for the storage of food. *Obs.* {1835–} **b.** An air-tight chamber, either below or above ground, for the storage and fermenting of fodder. {1881–}

1860 DOMENECH *7 Yrs. in Deserts N. Amer.* II. 278 Winter family provisions are also placed in silos like those of the Arabs. **1876** KNIGHT 2182/2 *Silo,* a large shallow ditch protected by thatch or boards from rain, sun, and air, and used as a store-pit for potatoes or beets. **1884** *Vt. Agric. Rep.* VIII. 32 L. C. Fisher's silo [was] built in bay of barn, cemented at bottom and side. **1906** *Indian Laws & Tr.* III. 238 New silo, and equipment thereof, two thousand dollars. **1917** *Univ. Ariz. Agric. Exper. Sta. Ann. Rep. 1916–8* 394 Silos [are] indispensable . . . in the hot, dry climate of Arizona.

attrib. **1894** *Vt. Agric. Rep.* XIV. 45 The adoption of the silo system for storing, preserving and feeding the corn crop . . . will save seven-eighths or nine-tenths of the usual loss.

* **Silver.**

I. * **1.** A whitish metallic element, used as a medium of exchange; coin made of this metal.

1639 *Plymouth Laws* 65 No man shall give, trade, truck . . . with the Natives or Indians . . . to give or pay him any money gould or silver. **1691** C. MATHER in *Mass. Bay Currency Tracts* 15 Do not Bills Transmit to Remote Parts, vast summs without the intervention of Silver? **1716** *Mass. Bay Currency Tracts* 168 The Fishery was then the *N.E. Silver Mine,* and if Peace continue, may prove the principal Means to draw in Silver again. **1787** CUTLER in *Life & Corr.* I. 376, [I] have delivered him one hundred and ten dollars more in silver. **1838** HAWTHORNE *Notebooks* (1932) 47 There was a pedler there from New-York state, who sold his wares by auction, . . . making change with silver or bills. **1887** *Courier-Journal* 16 Jan. 4/5 A sample box of this wonderful Chewing Gum [will be] sent prepaid to any address on receipt of ten cents in silver.

+**b.** Freq. in contexts related to the demonetization of silver in 1873 and to the free-coinage movement.

See also FREE SILVER and cf. FREE COINAGE.

1876 *44th Congress 2 Sess.* H. R. Ex. Doc. No. 3 p. liv, From 1793 . . . to 1834, the silver and the gold dollar were alike authorized to be received as legal tender in payment of debt, but silver alone circulated. **1885** *Wkly. New Mexican Rev.* 8 Jan. 4/2 The single standard advocates are making [an effort] in congress to suspend the coinage of silver. **1893** *McClure's Mag.* I. 386/2 Everybody has an opinion about silver. **1900** *Congress. Rec.* 7 Feb. 1620/2 The Republican party has stealthily stricken down silver, and that party alone is responsible for the condition of silver to-day.

* **2.** The metal as found in mines, or as used in the arts.

1654 *Harvard Rec.* I. 209 One stone pott tipt with Silver. **1761** in H. M. Brooks *Gleanings* IV. 26 Stone Buttons in Silver, by the Card, black ditto in Silver. **1819** E. DANA *Geogr. Sk.* 160 Some silver . . . [is] found in divers places within [Tenn.]. **1865** *Wkly. New Mexican* 29 June 1/3 Silver is the prominent and most abundant mineral of the Territory. **1900** *Congress. Rec.* 17 Jan. 902/2 There was a greater production of silver in the State of Colorado than of gold.

* **3.** Articles made of silver.

1732 FRANKLIN *Writings* II. 184 We got a Tea-Table with all its appurtenances of China and Silver. **1792** *Fayetteville* (N.C.) *Gaz.* 7 Aug., He will give one hard Dollar an ounce for old or cut Silver. **1869** STOWE *Oldtown Folks* 567 There was a splendid lunch laid out in the parlor, with all

the old silver in muster. **1905** RICE *Sandy* 180 It's nothing short of criminal to keep all this old mahogany buried here in the country, and the cut-glass and silver.

II. *attrib.* and *comb.* **4.** * **a.** Designating various minerals and mineral compounds in which silver is present.

1631 *Suffolk Deeds* III. 54 Robert Aldworth and Gyles Elbridge . . . [shall pay] vnto our Soueraigne Lord the Kinge . . . One fifth part of all the yeald & Silver Oare. **1837** DANA *System Mineralogy* 417 Brittle Silver Ore, *Lunites rhombicus.* . . . Brittle Silver Glance. **1870** *Republican Rev.* 26 March 2/3 We acknowledge the receipt from Mr. James Pitts of Algodones of several rich specimens of silver quartz. **1876** RAYMOND *8th Rep. Mines* 275 The mines of Bingham Cañon produced last year a total of about 30,000 tons of ore, carrying silver-lead. **1896** SHINN *Story of Mine* 82 A very able and intelligent mill man of Nevada City, began to study the silver sulphurets of the Comstock.

* **b.** Designating various deposits productive of silver ore.

1868 *N.Y. Herald* 6 July 7/3 Such a report, designating the localities of gold bearing rocks and placers and silver lodes, . . . would many times repay the expense of the commission. **1874** RAYMOND *6th Rep. Mines* 329 At the southern extremity of the San Pedro Mountain a party of prospectors recently made the discovery of a silver-ledge.

c. Designating persons who prospect for, mine, or otherwise handle silver ore.

1877 W. WRIGHT *Big Bonanza* 486 Two mining superintendents were one day discussing the bonanza, when one of them said to his brother silver-hunter [etc.]. **1883** 'MARK TWAIN' *Life on Miss.* xxi, So I became a silver miner in Nevada. **1896** SHINN *Story of Mine* 1 An old Nevadan silver freighter . . . walked all day long for many . . . years beside his high ore wagon.

* **5.** Designating things made of silver.

See also SILVER PLATE 1, SILVERWARE.

1653 *Boston Rec.* 41 A Silver Porringer, a Sacke Bowle, a silver hot water cup, 3 silver spoones . . . were kept for our owne use. **1678** *New Castle Court Rec.* 267 One sword with a silver whyer handell. **1704** *N.H. Probate Rec.* I. 528 My Will is that . . . one Silver tankard, six silver spoons [etc.] . . . Remain undevided. **1748** *Mayflower Descendant* X. 109, I do order that the Silver Snuffers and Stand and a Spoon that my mother Farnum useth may be left with my Dear Wife. **1783** E. Parkman *Diary* 300 Inventory of the Goods . . . of Ebenezer Parkman. . . . One Silver Watch [etc.]. **1806** *Ann. 9th Congress* 2 Sess. 1120 He received a silver pin from a hunter. **1869** *N.Y. Times* 12 May 1/2 In presenting the silver spike to Dr. Durant yesterday, in performance of his part in the exercises attending the laying of the last rail of the great Pacific Road. **1873** ALDRICH *Marjorie Daw* 15 A green mould is settling on the names of the deceased, carved on the silver door-plates. **1893** *Harper's Mag.* Feb. 456/2 The clink of the high goblets against the silver waiter [was] reminiscent of a by-gone and more prosperous period.

b. Designating coins made of silver. {1764–}

See also SILVER DOLLAR, MONEY, PAY.

1704 S. KNIGHT *Journal* 42 Mony is pieces of eight . . . or Good hard money as sometimes silver coin is termed by [the people of Conn.]. **1741** *N.J. Archives* 1 Ser. VI. 118 Ecu's of France, or silver lewis, seventeen penny weight twelve grains, four shillings and six pence. **1778** CARVER *Travels* 509 The flowers of it [wintergreen] are . . . in the form of a rose, but not larger than a silver penny. **1843** 'CARLTON' *New Purchase* I. 257 He emptied all the contents on the counter, viz: two silver fips, three 'chaw'd bullits.' **1873** *Statutes at Large* XVII. 427 On the reverse of the silver trade-dollar, the weight and fineness of the coin shall be inscribed. **1874** EGGLESTON *Circuit Rider* 253 Postage cost a silver quarter on every letter.

6. +**a.** Designating various actions, meetings, etc., connected with the effort to remonetize silver.

See also SILVER STANDARD 2.

1877 *Harper's Mag.* March 627/2 The joint resolution providing for the appointment of commissioners to attend an international conference on the silver question was defeated in the House. **1885** *Wkly. New Mexican Rev.* 12 Feb. 2/4 The silver convention recently held in Denver passed some very sensible resolutions. **1889** *Cent.* 553/2 [The] Bland Silver Bill . . . reëstablished the silver dollar . . . as a legal tender. **1900** *Congress. Rec.* 14 Feb. 1807/1 Such counties as Jasper and Greene, counties which were heretofore Republican, went hellbent for the silver heresy.

+**b.** Designating persons or groups of persons seeking the remonetization of silver.

See also SILVER STATE 2.

1885 *Century Mag.* Sept. 804 Is it the 'silver barons' or the 'gold bugs' [who are responsible for the depression]? **1887** *Courier-Journal* 5 Feb. 1/6 A number of Representatives . . . are regarded as 'silver men,' or as leaning toward a soft-money policy. **1893** *Nation* 29 June 467/1 The very little game which our silver-bugs . . . are trying to play on us. **1896** *Westminster Gaz.* 10 July 2/1 The 'Silver Senators'—that is, the representatives of silver-producing States. **1896** BRYAN in *Rev. of Reviews* Aug. 174 Our silver Democrats went forth from victory unto victory. **1897** R. L. METCALF *Great Fight for Silver* 316 'The Silver Knight of the West,' William Jennings Bryan, of Nebraska, set the convention on fire. **1900** *Congress. Rec.* 7 April 3808/2 The benignant philanthropy of 'Silver Dick' Bland will be discussed and applauded by the historian. **1901** *N. Amer. Rev.* Feb. 271 The silver cabal won at every point. **1903** *Congress. Direc-*

tory (57th Congress 2 Sess.) 10 [Teller] was reelected in January, 1897, as an Independent Silver Republican.

∗7. In the specific names of plants, birds, fish, etc.

See also SILVER BELL, SILVER EEL, etc.

1884 GOODE, etc. *Fisheries* I. 612 'Silver Bass,' *Hyodon selenops*, . . . is confined to the rivers of the Southern States. **1884** VASEY *Agric. Grasses* 121 *Andropogon argenteus*, Silver Beard Grass. From W. S. Robertson, Muscogee Ind. **1848** THOREAU *Maine Woods* 81 It is a country full of evergreen trees, of mossy silver birches and watery maples. **1890** HOWELLS *Boy's Town* 30 There were men who were reputed to catch at will, as it were, silvercats and river-bass. **1786** WASHINGTON *Diaries* III. 141 Received . . . a Cock and Hen of the Silver Pheas[an]t. **1870** *Amer. Naturalist* IV. 109 The frost-fish are occasionally seen with a few herring in the small ditches, and are known then by juvenile anglers as the 'silver pike.' **1917** *Birds of Amer.* I. 231 Knot. *Tringa canutus*. . . . [Also called] Blue Plover; Silver Plover. **1881** *Amer. Naturalist* XV. 178 The silver salmon [predominates] in Puget sound . . . [and] in most of the small streams along the coast. **1892** APGAR *Trees Northern U.S.* 181 *Picea pungens*. (Silver Spruce.) . . . From the Rocky Mountains. **1911** *Rep. Fisheries 1908* 318/2 The surf-whiting (M[enticirrhus] *littoralis*), also called the 'silver-whiting,' is common from the Carolinas to Texas. **1871** *Amer. Naturalist* V. 92 By some they [Lepismas] are called 'silver witches.'

8. In special combinations.

Silver debt, a debt to be paid in silver money; *s. medium*, a medium of exchange consisting primarily of silver; *s. palace*, a deluxe palace car; *s. plater*, one who plates articles with silver; *s. scheme*, (see quotation and cf. MANUFACTURE BANK); *s. soap*, a soap for cleaning silverware.

1778 *N.H. Hist. Soc. Coll.* IX. 108, I have been for some time receiving old Silver Debts paid numerically in paper Dollars. **1720** *Mass. Bay Currency Tracts* 353, I can see no likelihood of our having a Silver Medium. **1867** TROBRIAND *Vie Militaire Dakota* 10 Les 'sleeping cars' sur le chemin de fer de Chicago ne sont pas aussi luxueux que ceux qui sont pompeusement appelés 'silver palaces' (palais d'argent) sur la route de New York à Chicago. **1815** *Niles' Reg.* VIII. 141/2 There are . . . 2 silver platers; 3 trunk makers [etc.]. *a*1780 HUTCHINSON *Diary & Lett.* I. 51 The merchants set up what they called a Silver Scheme, issuing notes to be redeemed in ten years with silver. **1873** PHELPS *Trotty's Wedding* xiv, Silvers it right over, and so much easier than silver-soap!

+Silver bell, Silver-bell tree. A southeastern tree (*Halesia carolina*) having bell-shaped white flowers; less often, a related tree, *H. diptera*. — **1785** MARSHALL *Amer. Grove* 57 Silver-Bell Tree. . . . The Corolla is of one petal, bell'd and bellied. **1847** DARLINGTON *Weeds & Plants* 218 The *Halesia*, or Silver Bell, two species of which . . . are common in cultivation. **1869** *Rep. Comm. Agric. 1868* 203 Trees with conspicuous or fragrant flowers. The dogwood . . . ; silver bell (*Halesia diptera*). **1919** STURTEVANT *Notes on Edible Plants* 297 Silver-Bell Tree. Wild Olive. . . . The ripe fruit is eaten by some people and when green is sometimes made into a pickle.

+Silver certificate. A certificate or piece of paper currency issued by the United States treasury against a deposit of silver coin. — **1882** *Statutes at Large* XX. 165 Silver certificates, when held by any national-banking association, shall be counted as part of its lawful reserve. **1890** *Stock Grower & Farmer* 1 Feb. 4/4 We would abolish the national banks, and replace their circulation with greenbacks, or silver certificates. **1896** [see GOLD CERTIFICATE]. **1900** *Statutes at Large* XXXI. 47 Hereafter silver certificates shall be issued only of denominations of ten dollars and under. **1905** *N.Y. Ev. Post* 1 Sept. 7 The cart-wheel dollar and its paper equivalent, the silver certificate.

+Silver dollar. A silver coin of the United States, worth 100 cents.

The silver dollar was authorized by Congress in 1792 and first issued in 1794. Its weight was changed in 1837 from 416 grains to 412.5 grains of standard silver. (Cf. BLAND, STANDARD SILVER, TRADE DOLLAR.)

1804 FESSENDEN *Orig. Poems* (1806) 159 Pewter platter, Which cookmaid Dolly scours so white, It shines like silver dollar bright. **1818** *Niles' Reg.* XIV. 108/1 Ten or twelve years since, golden half eagles were as current in Baltimore as silver dollars were at Boston. **1872** POWERS *Afoot & Alone* 273 When I arrived in Los Angeles, I had just one silver dollar left. **1885** *Wkly. New Mexican Rev.* 15 Jan. 2/2 Make the silver dollar worth a dollar in commerce and let the mints turn out all they can. **1917** *Nation* 27 Sept. 354/1 If the price should now by chance go much above $1.29 per ounce, the silver dollar would again disappear from circulation.

Silver eel. a. A common eel, so called after it has reached sexual maturity. {1838} **b.** A cutlass fish. — **1807** *Mass. H. S. Coll.* 2 Ser. III. 56 There are two species of eels; one of which is called the silver eel. **1842** *Nat. Hist. N.Y., Zoology* iv. 311 We have examined the Silver Eel of the fishermen. **1882** *Nat. Museum Bul.* No. 16, 910*n*. [*Trichiurus lepturus*] is known as 'Sabre-fish' and 'Silver Eel,' on the coast of Texas.

Silveret. A kind of fabric. *Obs.* — **1754** *S.C. Gazette* 28 May 3 Mathewes & Lloyd Have just imported . . . mantuas and other silks, grandurells, montagues, and silverets, white lead ground in oil [etc.]. **1759** *Newport Mercury* 3 July 5/2 Just Imported from London . . . , Crapes, large Brass Kettles, Shalloons, figur'd Stuffs, Thicksets, Silverets [etc.].

+Silverfin. A fresh-water minnow of the eastern and central states, as *Erogala whipplii*. — **1883** *Nat. Mus. Bul.* No. 16, 179 Silver-fin. . . . Pennsylvania and Central New York to Mississippi Valley. **1903** T. H. BEAN *Fishes N.Y.* 145 The silverfin ranges from western New York to Virginia and west to Minnesota and Arkansas.

Silver fir. Any of several true firs having leaves silver white underneath {1707–}, +as the balsam fir (q.v.) and the white fir, *Abies concolor*. Also with specific terms.

1791 *Jefferson Writings* VIII. 205 Either unknown or rare in Virginia, were . . . the silver fir, white pine, pitch pine [etc.]. *a*1817 DWIGHT *Travels* II. 210 This, I presume, is the silver fir. **1832** WILLIAMSON *Maine* I. 111 The Fir, which yields a fine balsam, is often called 'silver fir.' **1879** *Scribner's Mo.* May 55/2 Then there is the noble silver fir (*Picea nobilis*) singly and very effectively illustrated. **1880** BESSEY *Botany* 412 The genus *Abies* contains . . . the Giant Silver Fir, *A. grandis*, of Oregon and California. **1892** APGAR *Trees Northern U.S.* 187 *Abies pectinata* (European or Common Silver Fir.) . . . Good specimens can be found as far north as Massachusetts.

Silverfish.

1. Any of several silver-colored fishes. {1703–, in non-British waters}

1775 ROMANS *Nat. Hist. Florida* App. 52 The fish caught here are . . . silver-fish, jew-fish, rock-fish [etc.]. **1804** CLARK in *Lewis & C. Exped.* I. (1904) 110 Cought . . . a kind of perch Called Silver fish, on the Ohio. **1842** *Knickerb.* XIX. 113 Farewell to thy lakes and silver-fish. **1884** GOODE, etc. *Fisheries* I. 611, I saw large numbers of Silver-fish eight or ten miles up the Apalachicola River. **1889** *Scribner's Mag.* Aug. 156/2 [The tarpon] is the 'Silver-fish' of Pensacola, the 'Grande Écaille' . . . , and the 'Savanilla' of Texas. **1893** M. HOWE *Honor* 231 On either side of them were walls of tremulous water-weeds, through which shone silver-fish. **1911** *Rep. Fisheries 1908* 317/2.

2. (See quotation.) {1855–}

1890 *Cent.* 3413/2 In the United States these insects [of the genus *Lepisma*] are commonly called *fishtail*, *silvertail*, and *silverfish*.

+Silver fox. A color variety of the red fox; a neckpiece made of the fur of this animal. (Cf. BLACK, CROSS-, RED, SILVER-GRAY FOX.) — **1806** CLARK in *Lewis & C. Exped.* IV. (1904) 88 The Silver Fox . . . is very rare even in the countrey where it exists. **1826** GODMAN *Amer. Nat. Hist.* I. 274 The Black or Silver Fox . . . resembles the kindred species in the unpleasant odour it diffuses. **1902** WISTER *Virginian* iv, Skins of bear and silver fox lay upon the floor. **1918** LINCOLN *Shavings* 225 If you knew what a silver fox costs . . . you would be more careful in your language.

+Silver gar(fish). A needlefish. — **1859** BARTLETT 32 *Bill-fish*, . . . a small sea-fish fond of running up into fresh water during the summer. . . . Also called Sea-pike, Silver Gar-fish, etc. **1883** *Nat. Museum Bul.* No. 27, 450 Needle-fish; Silver Gar-fish. . . . This species ascends far up the streams. **1897** *N.Y. Forest, Fish, & Game Comm. 2d Rep.* 233 The silver gar is to be found in Gravesend Bay from June to September. **1903** BEAN *Fishes N.Y.* 318 The silver gar . . . is found along our coast from Maine to Texas. **1911** *Rep. Fisheries 1908* 310.

Silver-gray. {1712–}

+1. A conservative member of the Whig party supporting the Compromise of 1850. *Obs.* Also attrib.

1853 *Knickerb.* XLII. 653 'Woolly-Heads' were 'about,' and 'far-off the coming shone' of dignified 'Silver-Grays.' **1859** BARTLETT 408 *Silver Grays*. This term originated in the State of New York, and was applied to the conservative portion of the Whig party. . . . It was observed that many were men whose locks were silvered by age, which drew forth the remark from some one present, 'There go the silver grays!' **1884** BLAINE *20 Years of Congress* I. 524 Among the representatives of New York . . . [was] Ex-Governor Washington Hunt, whose Silver-Gray conservatism had carried him into the Democratic party.

2. A variety of the Dorking breed of chickens. {1889}

1871 LEWIS *Poultry Book* 54 The pure Duck-wing Game fowls are the Silver Grays.

+Silver-gray fox. =SILVER FOX. Also attrib. — **1778** *Essex Inst. Coll.* XLIX. 109 Sold . . . 3 silver gray fox skins. **1847** Emory *Military Reconn.* 405 Amongst the animals, we have . . . the silver-grey fox, (*canis cinerea argentus*). **1917** *Mammals of Amer.* 75/1 The Cross Fox and the Black, or Silver Gray, Fox are merely color phases of the Red Fox.

+Silver-gray squirrel. (See quotation.) — **1857** *Rep. Comm. Patents 1856: Agric.* 66 [The southern grey or Carolina squirrel, *Sciurus carolinensis*] is known among hunters as the 'Silver-grey Squirrel.'

+Silver hake. A food fish (*Merluccius bilinearis*) common on the New England coast. — **1884** GOODE, etc. *Fisheries* I. 240 The Silver Hake commonly inhabits the middle depths of ocean. **1903** T. H. BEAN *Fishes N.Y.* 692 The whiting is known by the additional names of hake and silver hake.

+Silverism. The doctrines of the silverites. — **1895** *Forum* Feb. 674 The panic of '93 was . . . due to two socialistic crazes: silverism and protectionism. **1896** *St. Louis Globe-Dem.* 22 June 4/2 Silverism in the shape which it had then was comparatively harmless. **1906** *Springfield W. Repub.* 20 Sept. 2 They are helping him [Mr. Bryan] to bury the silverism of his earlier period.

+Silverite.

1. A citizen of Silver City, Nevada.

1877 W. WRIGHT *Big Bonanza* 122 Here the Silverites determined to make the Indians smell 'villainous saltpeter.'

2. One advocating the use of silver as a monetary standard; a bimetallist advocating a silver, as well as a gold, standard.

1886 *Science* VII. 267 The attempt is made to cast a slur upon the 'silverites' by calling them inflationists. **1896** *Typographical Jrnl.* IX. 120 This sheet is supported by local silverites who have greenbacks to burn. **1900** *Congress. Rec.* 14 Feb. 1775/1 The battle of the standards was fought and lost by the Silverites in 1896.

+Silver king. 1. A man of importance in the silver industry. **2.** The tarpon, *Tarpon atlanticus.* — (1) **1889** EGGLESTON in *Century Mag.* March 791/2 We should possibly have more eminent men in the Senate and fewer 'lumber barons,' 'silver kings,' and creatures of railroad corporations. (2) **1889** *Scribner's Mag.* Aug. 164/1 No one could boast of having even hooked a 'Silver King.'

Silver-leaf. {1728-} *attrib.* Designating various trees with silver-colored leaves.

1847 WOOD *Botany* 507 Abele or Silver-leaf Poplar. **1861** *Ill. Agric. Soc. Trans.* IV. 449 Some one moved to recommend the Silver Leaf Maple for general cultivation. **1901** MOHR *Plant Life Ala.* 84 Silver-leaf linden (*Tilia heterophylla*). **1918** LINCOLN *Shavings* 95 She had taken [a table] out under the shadow of the silver-leaf tree.

Silver-leaved, *a.* In the specific names of plants. {1731-} — **1785** MARSHALL *Amer. Grove* 2 *Acer glaucum.* The Silver-leaved Maple. This tree grows frequently to the height of fifty or sixty feet. *Ib.* 20 *Betula-Alnus glauca.* Silver-leaved Alder. This grows naturally in low marshy ground. **1813** MUHLENBERG *Cat. Plants* 53 *Magnolia discolor,* Silver-leaved magnolia. **1843** TORREY *Flora N.Y.* I. 209 *Potentilla argentea.* Silver-leaved Cinquefoil. . . . Possibly only an introduced plant in this country.

Silver maple. {1800 (*London Med. & Phys. Jrnl.* IV. 246)} +An American maple (*Acer saccharinum*) with leaves silvery white underneath. — **1861** *Ill. Agric. Soc. Trans.* IV. 207 They are almost entirely silver maples, embracing 25,000 trees. **1905** in Dale & Rader *Okla. Hist.* (1930) 673 The trees 'wid glitterin' leaves' are silver maples.

*Silver mine. A mine productive of silver. Also fig. — **1624** *Va. House of Burgesses* 30 Certain forces [were] to march towardes the mountaines for the discovery of gold or silver mines. **1716** *Mass. Bay Currency Tracts* 168 The Fishery was then the N.E. Silver Mine. **1805** *Ann. 9th Congress* 2 Sess. 1100 [The Mine R., a tributary of the Red. R.,] is boatable about sixty miles to the silver mine, which is on the bank of the river. **1849** WIERZBICKI *California* 10 Silver-mines have been found in the vicinity of Pueblo. **1884** 'CRADDOCK' *Where Battle Was Fought* 48 The two had become exclusive owners of a certain silver mine in Colorado.

Silver money. *collect.* Coins made of silver. — **1678** *New Castle Court Rec.* 322 There was taken out [of a chest] . . . some silver monny & 2 pr of sleeves. **1711** *N.J. Archives* 1 Ser. IV. 112 [Some of us] cannot produce Silver Money to pay our Taxes. **1744** *N.H. Probate Rec.* III. 207, I giue and bequath unto my other four Children, . . . Twelve Pounds Ten Shillings Each, in silver money.

+Silver pay. Silver money. *Obs.* (Cf. PAY *n.* 1.) — **1654** *Portsmouth Rec.* 63 Tenn pounds . . . to bee payde at the Rate of silver pay. **1672** *East-Hampton Rec.* I. 347 A case tried . . . in a matter of Debt to the vally of foure shillings in Sillver pay. **1688** *N.J. Archives* 1 Ser. II. 29 There will be perhaps 20 percent loss between [country pay] & silver pay.

Silver perch. +a. Any of various fishes, as the crappie (*Pomoxis annularis*), having silvery coloring. +b. The mademoiselle. — (a) **1820** *Western Rev.* II. 53 *Pomoxis annularis.* . . . Vulgar names Gold-ring and Silver-perch. Found in August at the falls [of the Ohio R.], probably permanent. (b) **1855** BAIRD in *Smithsonian Rep. 1854* 331 The Silver Perch, *Corvina argyroleuca,* . . . is not unfrequently brought to market in New York. **1897** *N.Y. Forest, Fish, & Game Comm. 2d Rep.* 242 The young of the silver perch are found every summer in Gravesend Bay. **1911** *Rep. Fisheries 1908* 313/1 'Silver perch' [is applied] to the yellowtail (*Bairdiella chrysura*) in New Jersey.

* Silver plate.

1. Utensils made of silver {1610-}, often used in the colonies as a medium of exchange. (Cf. PLATE 3.)

1642 *Suffolk Deeds* III. 62 Received . . . of Edward Jackson Nayler in wt. chappell forty seven ounces 1/2 1/8 of Silver plate troy weight amounting in value with the fashion at five shillings fower pence per ounce to the summe of twelve pounds. **1718** *Smithtown Rec.* 39, I Richard Smith . . . leave to my wife Hannah one third of all moveables except silver plate. **1796** *Ann. 4th Congress* 2 Sess. 2681 Silver plate is valued by law at eight shillings and four pence per ounce. **1865** *Atlantic Mo.* Feb. 169/2 Costly silver plate is hired in large quantities from the manufacturer. **1870** MEDBERY *Men Wall St.* 290 Old Nat Prime moved that two services of silver-plate should be voted him, with a hundred fresh-minted dollars in them.

2. A photographic plate sensitized with a silver compound. {1845}

1841 EMERSON *Works* I. (1903) 264 The Daguerreotypist, with camera-obscura and silver plate, begins now to traverse the land.

Silver-plated, *a.* Covered or trimmed with a thin coat of silver. {1869-} — **1846** *Stat. at Large* IX. 46 [A duty shall be levied on] silver-plated metal, in sheets or other form. **1876** INGRAM *Centennial Exp.* 317 The Middletown Plate Company had . . . a fine display of silver-plated ware. **1905** *Sears, Roebuck & Co. Cat.* No. 115, 97 This set . . . consists of six silver plated crucible steel knives.

+Silver poplar. The white poplar, *Populus alba.* — **1847** DARLINGTON *Weeds & Plants* 332 Silver Poplar. . . . Some of the grass-plats in the public squares of New York have been quite overrun by the wide-

spreading suckers of this tree. **1861** *Ill. Agric. Soc. Trans.* IV. 448 The Silver Poplar is an abominable pest in loose soil, casting up suckers. **1897** SUDWORTH *Arborescent Flora* 137 *Populus alba canescens.* . . . Silver Poplar.

Silverside(s). a. Any of several small fishes of the family Atherinidae having silvery sides. {1881} **b.** Any of several fresh-water minnows. **c.** The silver salmon, *Oncorhynchus milktschitsch.* Also attrib.

1820 RAFINESQUE *Western Rev.* II. 240 Silverside Fallfish. *Rutilus plargyrus.* . . . Vulgar names, Silverside, Shiner [etc.]. **1839** STORER *Mass. Fishes* 62 *Atherina Boscii.* The small Silver Side. **1851** GLISAN *Jrnl. Army Life* 88 The purer streams from the hills abound in . . . sunfish, perch, and silver-sides. **1855** BAIRD in *Smithsonian Rep. 1854* 338 No use is made of these 'silver sides' on our coast, except as bait. **1883** *Nat. Museum Bul.* No. 27, 449 *Menidia dentex.* . . . Friar; Silversides. Atlantic coast of the Southern United States, entering streams. **1892** *Courier-Journal* 2 Oct. 17/8 Capt. Olsen . . . , while still fishing for groupers four miles off shore, hooked and landed a silverside salmon. **1911** *Rep. Fisheries 1908* 316/2 Some of the silversides (*Atherinidæ*) are wrongly called 'smelts.'

*Silversmith. One who works with silver. — **1744** FRANKLIN *Acct. Fire-Places* 36 Broken Bits of Black-Lead Crucibles from the Silversmiths, pounded fine, will do. **1815** *Niles' Reg.* VIII. 141/2 [There are] 8 silversmiths and watch makers. **1898** *Congress. Rec.* 1 July 6574/2 If you want to have a watch doctored, you take it to a silversmith.

+Silver standard. 1. The legal weight and fineness of silver in silver coins. {1860} **2.** A monetary standard in terms of silver. — (1) **1831** *Congress. Deb.* 22 Feb. p. cxl/2 An error . . . committed in establishing the money unit 'of the value of a Spanish dollar' . . . may be corrected by adhering to the established and existing silver standard. (2) **1900** *Congress. Rec.* 17 Jan. 905/1 The great majority of mankind was standing on the silver standard.

+Silver state. 1. *cap.* The state of Nevada. A nickname. **2.** A state producing silver or advocating free coinage of silver. — (1) **1871** *Harper's Mag.* Oct. 799/1 In our early days in the Silver State females were rarely to be seen in the frontier mining camps. **1907** *Boston Transcript* 9 Nov. 11. 9 Popular names of the States [include] . . . Silver—Nevada. Sucker—Illinois. (2) **1885** *Wkly. New Mexican Rev.* 8 Jan. 4/2 All the silver states and territories [should] organize to resist the effort which the single standard advocates are making in congress to suspend the coinage of silver. **1900** *Congress. Rec.* 14 Feb. 1803/2 The State of Missouri, outside of the city of St. Louis, was a silver State.

+Silvertip. A grizzly bear with hairs silvery-colored at the tips. Also *silvertip grizzly.* — **1891** *Scribner's Mag.* X. 449 They class the cinnamon, silver-tip, and grizzly, as grizzly bear. **1907** WHITE *Arizona Nights* 47 [He] intended to go after silver-tips somewhere in these very mountains. **1923** J. H. COOK *On Old Frontier* 138, I caught sight of a very large silver-tip grizzly lying down.

+Silvertop. 1. ?A mug of beer. *colloq.* **2.** A condition of grass in which the upper part whitens. **3.** *Silvertop palmetto,* the silver thatch (*Coccothrinax argentea*), with leaves white on the under side. — (1) **1840** *Picayune* 14 Aug. 2/2 It is hot . . . hot enough for an ice cream or a Silver Top. (2) **1890** *Amer. Naturalist* XXIV. 970 It is probable that these leaf-hoppers are responsible for much of the 'silver-top.' (3) **1884** SARGENT *Rep. Forests* 218 Silver-top Palmetto. Brickley Thatch. Brittle Thatch. Semi-tropical Florida.

Silverware. Utensils, esp. table ware, made of silver. {1860} — **1789** *Ann. 1st Congress* 167 The same [impost] . . . was laid . . . on gold, silver, and plated ware. **1860** GREELEY *Overland Journey* 33 The only iron safe . . . [was] plundered of some silver-ware. **1907** *St. Nicholas* June 700/1 A thief . . . stole papa's winter overcoat and a lot of silverware.

Silvery, *a.* {1600-} In the specific names of plants, fishes, etc. {1785-}

[**1781** PENNANT *Hist. Quadrupeds* I. 241 Silvery [Fox] . . . abound in the wooded eminences of *Louisiana,* which are every where pierced with their holes.] **1814** BIGELOW *Florula Bostoniensis* 255 *Asplenium thelypteroides.* Silvery Spleenwort. . . . This most beautiful fern grows to a pretty large size. **1814** MITCHILL *Fishes N.Y.* 364 Silvery hair-tail. *Trichiurus argenteus. Ib.* 417 Silvery Perch. *Bodianus argyro-leucos.* **1828** BONAPARTE *Synopsis* 360 The Silvery gull, *Larus fuscus,* . . . very common during winter near Philadelphia and New-York. **1839** PEABODY *Mass. Birds* 379 The Silvery Tern, *Sterna minuta,* . . . is seen . . . chasing insects over the pools and marshes. **1840** DEWEY *Mass. Flowering Plants* 57 *P[otentilla] argentea.* Silvery Cinquefoil. . . . Flowers yellow; June, in fields. **1842** *Nat. Hist. N.Y., Zoology* IV. 116 The Silvery Trachinote. *Trachinotus argenteus.*

+Simball. *New Eng.* =CYMBAL. — **1865** A. D. WHITNEY *Gayworthys* 36 After they had popped corn, and roasted apples, and eaten simballs, . . . they had all gone to bed. **1899** WILKINS *In Colonial Times* 19 Here's a piece of sweet cake and a couple of simballs.

+Simlin. Also **simblin, simmin.** =CYMBLING. Also attrib., comb., and fig. — **1804** CLARK in *Lewis & C. Exped.* I. (1904) 188 [The Arikara] raise great quantities of Corn Beens Simmins &c. **1814** BRACKENRIDGE *Views La.* 63 The common sun-flower, the bean, and the simblin . . . grow there [along the Arkansas R.] in their natural state. **1884** HARRIS *Mingo* 70 The line runs right across my simblin' patch. **1911** SAUNDERS *Col. Todhunter* 96 You impudent little simlin'-headed runt, you!

+'Simmon. A shortening of PERSIMMON. *colloq.* Also attrib.

1775 BOUCHER *Glossary* p.1, Brown linen shirts, and cotton jackets wear, Or only *wring-jaw* drink, and *'simmon beer.* **1834** *Knickerb.* III. 36 They seemed to me to fall just as fast as if I was shakin down 'simmons. **1839** *S. Lit. Messenger* V. 378/2 The longest pole, you know, takes the simmon. **1850** LEWIS *La. Swamp Doctor* 50 We all cum down like 'simmons arter frost. **1881** *Harper's Mag.* April 729/2 An' pleased they wuz ter see it—pleased as boys in 'simmon-time. **1904** 'O. HENRY' *Roads of Destiny* 350 That's why you see me cake-walking with the ex-rebs to the illegitimate tune about 'simmon-seeds and cotton.

∗Simnel. +=CYMBLING. — **1648** PLANTAGENET *Descr. New Albion* 28 Strawberries, Mulberries, Symnels, Maycocks and Horns like Cucumbers. **1705** BEVERLEY *Virginia* IV. 56 [The people of Va.] find them very delicious Sauce to their Meats; ... such are the Red-buds, Sassafras-Flowers, Cymnels, Melons, and Potatoes. **1709** LAWSON *Carolina* 77 [There are] Squashes, Simnals, Horns, and Gourds.

Simon. 1. A kind of game. **+2.** A dollar. *slang.* **3.** Short for *Simon-pure,* the real thing. — (1) **1853** 'P. PAXTON' *Yankee in Texas* 205 After playing 'Simon,' 'What is my Thought Like?' and a dozen similar games, one of the company arose. (2) **1859** *Harper's Mag.* Sept. 572/2, I was first in say, and bet a *Simon.* (3) **1875** BURROUGHS *Winter Sunshine* 21 The fish-crow, whose helpless feminine call contrasts strongly with the hearty masculine caw of the original Simon.

Simon Pure, *n.* {1815-} +A member of a New York City Locooco club. *Obs.* — **1840** *New Era* (N.Y.) 7 April 3/1 The Simon Pures, Kinderhook Club, and all others friendly to the good cause, are expected to attend.

+Simon-pure, *a.* Genuine; real; authentic. *colloq.* — **1840** *Maysville* (Ky.) *Eagle* 22 April 3/1 The Globe ... or indeed any other paper of the *Simon Pure* democracy. **1844** *Lowell Offering* IV. 172, I have not seen one of the old 'Simon Pure' Methodist bonnets since I have been here. **1887** *Courier-Journal* 20 Feb. 2/1 The real, simon-pure Congressman remains at the capitol engaged in the statesman business. **1898** NORRIS *Moran of Lady Letty* ii, The Chinamen sell it all over San Francisco as simon-pure cod-liver oil. **1902** LORIMER *Lett. Merchant* 74 Bill Budlong ... took a heap of pride in being the simon pure cuss.

Simpleton. {1650-} +(See quot. 1891.) — **1891** *Cent.* 5639/3 *Simpleton,* ... the American dunlin, purre, or ox-bird. **1917** *Birds of Amer.* I. 237.

+Sinch, *n.* (See CINCH *n.¹*)

+Sinch, *v.* Variant of CINCH *v.¹* — **1873** MILLER *Amongst Modocs* 187 A fractious mule ... for a time concluded not to be sinched again. **1878** E. B. TUTTLE *Border Tales* 36 All [mules] soon learn to swell themselves out when being sinched. **1889** MUNROE *Golden Days* 162 One hoss ... was the ... meanest ... old wall-eye that ever was sinched.

Sing, *n.* {1871-} A singing in company; a gathering or occasion for singing. *colloq.* {1884} — **1850** KINGSLEY *Diary* 140 We had a fine sing in the Evening which put me in mind of home. **1877** BARTLETT 594 *Sing,* a meeting for practice in singing. **1880** *Harper's Mag.* Aug. 346 The limit of social indulgence was the 'Sing'—a rendering of Moody and Sankey's hymns by the women around a cabinet organ. **1924** *Daily Maroon* (Univ. of Chic.) 6 June 1/5 Attendance records for the Sing seem about to be shattered by the influx of grads.

∗Sing, *v.* *To sing low,* to keep quiet. *colloq.* — **1866** C. H. SMITH *Bill Arp* 47 Now let me advise you to sing low about this fighting business. **1903** LEWIS *Boss* 70 Your Tin Whistles can join, man by man, but if they do they must sing low.

+Singers' seat. A seat or bench in a meetinghouse for the choir. — **1777** *Plymouth Church Rec.* I. 353 Deacon Crombie, our former Chorister, had left ye usual Singer's Seat. **1861** STOWE *Pearl Orr's Isl.* I. 72 Aunt Ruey ... had in her youth been one of the foremost leaders in the 'singers' seat.' **1878** — *Poganuc People* 102 The singers' seat ... was *our* singers' seat.

∗Singing.

+1. =SINGING SCHOOL.

1872 EGGLESTON *End of World* 118 She had walked to and from meeting and 'singing' with Humphreys. **1877** BARTLETT 595 *Singing,* in Pennsylvania, a singing-school.

2. Attrib. with *book, campaign, club,* etc.

1763 *Holyoke Diaries* 60 Spent evening at Singing Club. **1793** *Essex Inst. Coll.* XXII. 148 Voted to obtain ... 6 Singing Books for the use of the Parish. **1795** *Holyoke Diaries* 134, I was at Singing Concert. **1833** *Jamestown* (N.Y.) *Jrnl.* 6 March 2/5 The 'Singing Society' of this village meets this evening at the Presbyterian Church. **1845** CAULKINS *Hist. Norwich, Conn.* 149 In July 1726, six of the followers of Rogers were taken up at Norwich, for travelling on the Sabbath. ... One of them was a woman, ... called by them a *singing sister.* **1886** HOWE *Moonlight Boy* 7 Tibby Cole ... was a leader of brass bands, orchestras, and singing conventions. **1892** *Nation* 23 June 457/1 We shall, therefore, have the rare privilege of a canvass between men who are to be tried ... by the policies they stand for and by their respective administrations. This will not give us a 'singing campaign.'

+Singing fish. The midshipman (*Porichthys notatus*) or an allied fish. — **1884** GOODE, etc. *Fisheries* I. 253 The *Batrachidæ* are represented on the Pacific coast by the 'Singing-fish,' or 'Toad-fish,' *Porichthys porosissimus.* **1896** JORDAN & EVERMANN *Check-List Fishes* 466.

+Singing gallery. A choir loft. — **1818** BENTLEY *Diary* IV. 513 The amphitheatrical form of Singing galleries placed ... in front of pulpits

has had great favour. **1849** *Knickerb.* XXXIV. 276 A member of his choir ... most unadvisedly introduced his big fiddle into the 'singing gallery.' **1883** C. C. PERKINS *Hist. Handbook of Ital. Sculpt.* 139 [Della Robbia began] a series of ten alto-reliefs ... in 1433 for the balustrade of a singing-gallery (cantoria) in the Cathedral.

+Singing lecture. A church service consisting of both preaching and specially rehearsed singing. *Obs.* — **1723** *New-Eng. Courant* 3 June 2/1 On Thursday last a Singing Lecture was held at the Brick Church in Cornhill, and the Rev. Dr. Cotton Mather preach'd. **1779** E. PARKMAN *Diary* 96 A Singing Lecture at ye Request of ye Singing School.

Singing master. a. One who teaches singing {1711}; the master of a singing school. **+b.** A director of a choir or other singing group.

1754 in Singleton *Social N.Y.* 296 William Tuckey, singing master, desires to inform all lovers of psalmody that ... all persons may be taught by him on very reasonable terms. **1789** *Boston Directory* 190 Kimball John, singing-master. **1807** *Ann. 10th Congress* 1 Sess. 589 He has supplied us with schoolmasters, singingmasters, dancingmasters, and doctors in abundance. **1854** H. H. RILEY *Puddleford* 36 The singing-master boarded at our house. **1891** *Harper's Mag.* Oct. 813/1 The precentor, or singing-master, as he was called, was a tall young man in a black suit with white ruffles.

+Singing meeting. A church or community meeting for singing. — **1766** CUTLER in *Life & Corr.* I. 14 In the evening a singing meeting in the school-house; sang well. **1802** COWLES *Diary* 66 Cousin T. called after singing meeting. **1841** *Jamestown* (N.Y.) *Jrnl.* 24 June 1/3 He wouldn't so much as go down to the singing meetings that Gould kept a getting up. **1860** ABBOTT *South & North* 120 There is no church here, no village school, no singing-meeting, no social winter-evening gatherings.

+Singing Quaker. A Quaker given to singing under religious excitement. — **1684** I. MATHER *Providences* (1856) xi. 241 Observe the blasting rebukes of Providence upon the late singing and dancing Quakers. **1704** S. KNIGHT *Journal* 78 Says the woman are you singing quakers?

Singing school. A school for teaching singing; a meeting of people for practising singing. {1736}

1723 *New-Eng. Courant* 1 April 2/2 The Singing-School in that Place [a part of Boston] is broken up by Order of the Select Men. **1740** *N.Y. Wkly. Journal* 7 Jan. 4/1 Mr. Winter keeps a Singing School of Psalmody, near the lower End of the Broad Way. **1825** WOODWORTH *Forest Rose* I. ii, I don't calculate ... that you can say any thing to convince me that I didn't see Tom Clover kiss you last night, in the singing-school. **1856** M. J. HOLMES *L. Rivers* 234, I've kep' singin' school one term, besides leadin' the Methodis' choir in Slocumville. **1898** HARPER *S. B. Anthony* I. 23 She loved music, and wished to attend the village singing school. **1917** McCUTCHEON *Green Fancy* 61, I was comin' home from singin' school up at Number Ten.

+Singing seat. =SINGERS' SEAT. — **1774** *Essex Inst. Coll.* XXI. 271 Voted Liberty to build a singing Seat in the front of the Gallurry Pues. **1847** *Knickerb.* XXX. 527, [I] have obtained some notoriety in our parish choir for ... leading the singers in the First Congregational singing-seats. **1887** WILKINS *Humble Romance* 60 David Ayres, in his place in the second row of the singing seats, watched them soberly. **1891** WILKINS *New Eng. Nun* 25, I've sung in those singin'-seats forty year.

∗Single, *n.* Baseball. +A one-base hit. — **1858** *Chadwick Scrapbook* (E. J. Nichols). **1880** *Chicago Inter-Ocean* 29 June 8/3 Force's winning run came off a wild throw by Ward, a sacrifice, and single. **1912** E. V. COOKE *Baseballogy* 57 Grant us but a bingle E'en tho' it be a scratchy single.

∗Single, *a.*

+1. *Baseball.* Of a hit: Allowing the runner to gain first base.

1880 N. BROOKS *Fairport Nine* 181 Sam Perkins followed with a single baser, which advanced Pat Adams to the third base. *Ib.* 183 Dan Morey followed with a single base hit which put Eph to third base. *Ib.* 186 Eph Mullett ... made a two-base hit, Dan Morey following him with a single hit, which sent Mullett to third base.

∗2. In the specific names of plants and fishes: (see quotations). Also in attrib. and adj. compounds.

See also SINGLE SPRUCE.

1814 MITCHILL *Fishes N.Y.* 448 Single-bearded Flying Fish. *Exocaetus comatus.* **1817-8** EATON *Botany* (1822) 264 *Dianthus plumarius,* single pink. E[xotic]. *Ib.* 458 *Sicyos angulata,* single-seed cucumber. ... Cultivated every where; also indigenous. **1840** DEWEY *Mass. Flowering Plants* 114 *S[icyos] angulatus.* Single-seeded Cucumber. Grows also on the banks of streams. **1892** *Amer. Folk-Lore* V. 103 *Narcissus poeticus,* single daffy. Stratham, N.H. **1897** SUDWORTH *Arborescent Flora* 18 *Pinus monophylla,* ... Single-leaf Pinon. ... Fremont's Nut Pine.

3. In special combinations.

Single bed, bedstead, a bed for one person; *s.-decked car,* a stock car having only one deck; *s. jack,* a small hammer; *s. rifle,* a rifle having one barrel.

1849 WILLIS *Rural Letters* 137, I should have said that mine was a 'single bed.' **1867** A. J. EVANS *Vashti* xxxiii, A strip of faded carpet stretched in front of a small single bedstead. **1868** *Ill. Agric. Soc. Trans.* VII. 460 Sheep arrive here from the west in single decked cars. **1923** 'BOWER' *Parowan Bonanza* 12 Knock it [gold ore] off in chunks with a single-jack and gadget. **1897** *Outing* XXIX. 567/1, I had changed my single rifle to a double-barreled ball-gun.

✱**Single,** *v.* +**1.** *intr.* Of a horse: To single-foot. **2.** *To single out,* +(see quotation). — (1) **1864** WEBSTER 1233/3 Many very fleet horses, when overdriven, adopt a disagreeable gait, which seems to be a cross between a pace and a trot, in which the two legs of one side are raised almost, but not quite, simultaneously. Such horses are said to *single,* or to be *single*-footed. *W. S. Clarke.* (2) **1905** *Forestry Bureau Bul.* No. 61, 46 *Single out, to,* to float logs, usually cypress, one at a time, from the woods to the float road. (S[outhern] F[orest].)

+**Single bob.** An earmark put on an animal: (see quotation). — **1887** *Scribner's Mag.* II. 508/2 Words used in connection with . . . life on the plains: . . . singlebob, a slit ear dropping down.

+**Single-foot,** *n.* A gait of a horse in which each foot strikes the ground singly. Also attrib. — **1867** HARRIS *Sut Lovingood* 191 [He] started fur the back door, still on his all fours, in a single foot rack. **1877** ROE *Army Lett.* 179, I have been so pleased with . . . her delightful gaits—a little single foot and easy canter. **1882** STILLMAN *Horse in Motion* 117 Single-foot is an irregular pace, . . . distinguished by the posterior extremities, moving in the order of a fast walk and the anterior ones in that of a slow trot. **1897** HOWELLS *Landlord at Lion's Head* 154 This mare can walk like a Kentucky horse. . . . I believe I could teach her single-foot.

+**Single-foot,** *v. intr.* Of a horse: To go with a single-foot gait. Also *ppl. a.* and transf. — **1890** *Harper's Mag.* Jan. 246 The horse often single-foots faster than he trots. *Ib.* It is often said that a single-footing horse never trots well. **1891** *Ib.* Aug. 366/1 A noble little thorough-bred Kentucky saddle-horse . . . [can] single-foot up to twelve, and trot a 'forty gait as square as any track horse ever shod. **1903** 'O. HENRY' *Heart of West* 64, I singlefoots up beside him on my bronc.

+**Single-footed,** *a.* Of a horse: Having a single-foot gait. — **1864** [see SINGLE *v.*].

+**Single-footer.** A horse that single-foots. Also transf. — **1887** *Harper's Mag.* Sept. 490 He rode single-footers. **1891** *Ib.* Aug. 365/2 A single curb [is] lightly reining his quickly moving single-footer. **1897** LEWIS *Wolfville* 41 If they's single-footers like me an' ain't wedded none; . . . they wishes they has a wife a whole lot.

+**Single gold standard.** A monetary standard of gold only. Also attrib. — **1896** *St. Louis Globe-Dem.* 22 June 4/5 Silver was demonetized in 1873, and ever since that we have been on a single gold standard basis. **1900** *Congress. Rec.* 15 Jan. 813/2 The commissioners were abroad, commending the 'Indianapolis' scheme, based upon the permanent establishment of the single gold standard.

Single-hander. A boat operated by one person. — **1890** *Harper's Mag.* Sept. 594/1 If their pleasure be taken in a single-hander they are unhappy. **1893** *Outing* XXII. 145/2 The cost of a single-hander depends on the size of the boat.

Single-shot, *a.* Of firearms: Capable of firing only one shot without reloading. (Cf. REPEATING *a.*) — **1886** *Harper's Mag.* Oct. 793/2 The types adopted by the United States navy are the Hotchkiss revolving cannon and rapid-firing single-shot guns. **1897** *Outing* XXIX. 566/1, I gave my rifle—a single-shot express by Henry, with the falling-block system—to one of my men to hold.

+**Single spruce. a.** The white spruce, *Picea glauca.* **b.** The balsam fir, *Abies balsamea.* — (**a**) **1810** MICHAUX *Arbres* I. 18 *White* or *Single spruce* . . . , dénomination également en usage dans les Etats du Nord, le District de Maine et la Nouvelle-Écosse. *a*1817 DWIGHT *Travels* I. 38 The single spruce . . . is the link between the Hemlock and the white spruce, and is also used for Beer. **1832** BROWNE *Sylva* 93 *Abies alba* . . . in New Brunswick and the state of Maine [is called] *Single Spruce.* (**b**) **1909** *Webster* 1961/3 *Single spruce,* . . . the balsam fir.

Single standard. +A monetary standard based on one metal only; esp. the gold standard. Also attrib. — **1885** *Wkly. New Mexican Rev.* 8 Jan. 4/2 All the silver states and territories [should] organize to resist the effort which the single standard advocates are making in congress to suspend the coinage of silver. **1898** *Rep. Monetary Comm.* (Indianapolis Conv.) 97 Any attempt to [use both silver and gold] . . . will result in a single standard of the cheaper of the two metals.

+**Single-sticker.** A sailboat with only one mast. — **1893** *Boston Jrnl.* 13 April, The boat . . . will be in all the special races arranged for the big single stickers by the New York and other clubs. **1894** *Outing* XXIV. 193/1 The English way of rigging a single-sticker is being adopted in all our new racing craft.

+**Single stick vessel.** =prec. — **1886** *Outing* IX. 123/1 He asserted he could build a sloop which could beat any of the American single stick vessels.

+**Single tax.** A proposed tax by which the unearned increment, or the economic rent, of land would be taken as the sole source of public revenue. Also attrib. — **1879** GEORGE *Progress & Poverty* 383 A single tax on the value of land would hardly lessen the number of conscious taxpayers. **1889** [see next]. **1894** WARNER *Golden House* vi, She had heard him speak on the single tax at a labor meeting. **1924** *Jrnl. Polit. Econ.* Feb. 181 The single tax is unsound because it is based on a doctrine of 'natural rights.'

+**Single taxer.** One who advocates the single tax. — **1889** *20th Cent.* 6 April, He says that is a fair question which no Single-taxer ever answers, but that if it is evaded the whole single-tax theory vanishes. **1899** *Mo. So. Dakotan* I. 198 No single-taxer wants to interfere with your rights and possessions. **1905** *McClure's Mag.* Feb. 352/2 A single-taxer, a socialist, an advocate of the 'popular initiative for constitutional amendments' . . . , [marched] straight into the confidence of a majority of the voters of this conservative New England community.

+**Single track,** *n.* A railway track having only one set of rails. Also attrib. — **1838** *Civil Eng. & Arch. Jrnl.* I. 116 The estimated cost of the road, graded for a double track, and a single track laid, is 1,101,376.72 dollars. **1846** *Xenia Torch-Light* 2 April 2/7 The Legislature . . . authorized such persons as should become stockholders in said Company, to construct and maintain a Railroad, with single or double tract [*sic*]. **1849** *Whig Almanac 1850* 19/1 A single-track railway costs $40,000 per mile, where labor is cheap. **1898** *McClure's Mag.* March 390/1 When running a first-class train on a single-track branch, I had orders to meet and pass another first-class train at the junction. **1918** *Essex Inst. Coll.* LIV. 196 To lessen the expense, only a single track was at first laid.

+**Single-track,** *v. tr.* To construct (a railway line) with a single track. — **1874** *Boston & Chic. Ry. Trust Co. Bill* (Bay State Transp. League) 8 It will cost to single track the Massachusetts Central to Shelburne Falls $3,000,000.

+**Singletree.** (Cf. SWINGLETREE.)

1. The swinging bar to which the traces of a horse in harness are attached. {1890, in Australia}

1841 WEBSTER II. 609/1 A single-tree is fixed upon each end of the double-tree when two horses draw abreast. **1870** T. D. PRICE *Diary* (MS.) 26 Feb., Took double and singletrees to have ironed and neckyoke to have turned. **1890** LANGFORD *Vigilante Days* (1912) 283 Marshland climbed to the single-tree. **1913** LONDON *Valley of Moon* 351 The leaders slacked back an' darn near sat down on their singletrees when I . . . slammed on the brake.

2. 'A heavy horizontal bar sometimes used to spread the loop of a hoisting chain to prevent crushing the load.' (W. '09).

+**Singling.** Variant of *swingling.* In attrib. use with *board, knife.* — *a*1842 *Indiana Mag. Hist.* XV. 230 In early times flax was raised, pulled up, spread on the ground and rotted, the fibre broke on a break made for that purpose, then the shives were beat out by being held on a round top perpendicular board called a singling board. *Ib.*, A wooden knife was used to beat [the flax] with, which was made of oak or hickory, and called a singling knife.

+**Sing Sing.** A state prison at Ossining, New York. Also transf. — **1861** *Vanity Fair* 5 Jan. 5/1 Knives is at panic prices ever since Mulligan went up to Sing-Sing. **1870** EMERSON *Soc. & Solitude* 13 'Tis an extempore Sing-Sing built in a parlor. **1922** SANDBURG *Slabs Sunburnt West* 37 Let him eat out of the tin dishes at Sing Sing.

✱**Sink.**

✱**1.** A low-lying tract, area, or basin where water collects, forming ponds or marshes, or where it disappears by sinking or evaporation. {−1801} 'Now *U.S.*' (*O.E.D.*).

1690 *Va. Mag. Hist. & Biog.* XVIII. 101 The whole tract being a bout Seven hundred acres one halfe part being mine, cal'd halfe Sinke. **1780** in *Travels Amer. Col.* 652 Two springs and a sink on both sides of the branches. **1848** BRYANT *California* xvi. 214 We passed from the pools or 'Sink' over the low ridge of sand-hills, in a south course. **1878** BEADLE *Western Wilds* 106 What little [of the stream] is left has turned southward, and is lost in the 'sink.'

transf. **1861** *Harper's Mag.* March 465/2 The Whale Deep is a well-known sink in the otherwise regular bottom of the [Newfoundland fishing] banks, thirty miles in length by about twenty-five broad. . . . It appears to be a great depression or basin scooped out of the solid rock-bottom.

+**2.** =SINK HOLE.

See also LIME SINK.

1791 W. BARTRAM *Travels* 246 The ground . . . presented to view those funnels, sinks and wells in groups of rocks, amidst the groves. **1816** *Mass. Spy* 17 July (Th.), The only entrance into the [Mammoth] Cave is from the bottom of what the inhabitants call a 'sink,' which is a deep cavity in the earth, at the bottom of which there is generally a current of water. **1885** *Boston Jrnl.* 6 April 2/3 When the [water-filled sand] vein . . . comprises an acre or two it is called a 'sink.'

+**3.** =SINKBOX.

1856 LEWIS *Amer. Sportsman* 284 It is better . . . to have two or more double-barrelled guns in the sink. **1859** BARTLETT 24 *Battery,* a sort of boat used for duck-shooting in the Chesapeake, in which the shooter lies below the surface of the water. It is also called . . . a Surface-boat, Coffin-boat, Sink, or Box. **1874** LONG *Wild-Fowl* 252 The brush may be thrown off, and the labor of towing about the 'sink' avoided.

+**Sink boat.** =SINKBOX. — **1853** *Md. Laws* 220 If any person or persons shall use any sink boats . . . while engaged in shooting at . . . wild fowl, he or they shall be subject to a fine. **1877** BARTLETT 33 A friend in Maryland informs me that the usual term there is *Sink-boat,*—so called, because the whole body of the boat is below the surface.

+**Sinkbox.** (See quot. 1903.) — **1872** *Md. Laws* 76 Every applicant . . . shall pay to the Clerk of the Circuit Court . . . for a sink box, twenty dollars, . . . for each and every gunning season. **1900** *Outing* Nov. 147/1 On the Chesapeake . . . the 'sink-box' or 'battery' is much used. . . . It consists of a box big enough for a man to lie at full length, with flaps of wood and canvas extending on all sides, forming a platform about nine by thirteen feet. **1903** *N.Y. Sun* 8 Nov., A sinkbox . . . is a coffin-shaped boat with extending platforms, that sinks into the water until the platforms rest on the surface.

∗ Sinker.

+1. A muffin, biscuit, or dumpling; now esp. a doughnut. *slang.*

1870 BEADLE *Utah* 223 Our favorite dinner, when we could get the meat, was of fried ham and 'sinkers.' **1902** LORIMER *Lett. Merchant* 229 Any one who lets sinkers take the place of bread and meat gets bilious pretty young. **1906** *N.Y. Ev. Post* 10 Dec. 14 'Sinkers,' corn cakes, cream puffs, 'cookies,' and other standard foodstuffs. **1917** J. A. Moss *Officers' Manual* 485 *Sinkers*, dumplings.

attrib. **1898** *N.Y. Tribune* 13 May 5/3 Any beef-and-beans boy in a sinker shop in Park Row could have handled the two-year-old fillies almost as well.

+2. A small, pear-shaped object of stone or metal, used by Indians apparently as a weight.

1872 *Amer. Naturalist* VI. 640n., These 'plummets,' or 'sinkers,' as they are more commonly called in New England, are of quite common occurrence in the vicinity of Salem.

+3. (See quotation.)

1905 *Forestry Bureau Bul.* No. 61, 34 *Deadhead*, a sunken or partly sunken log. . . . [Also called] sinker.

∗ Sink hole. +A hole in the surface of the earth, freq. shaped somewhat like an inverted cone, formed by the action of water on the soil or underlying rock.

1749 in *Amer. Speech* XV. 392/1 Thence . . . to a small Hiccory Bush and a Hiccory Stake near a Sink Hole. **1806** LEWIS in *L. & Clark Exped.* V. (1905) 191 The road passing through an extensive high prarie rendered very uneven by a vast number of little hillucks and sink-holes. **1838** FLAGG *Far West* II. 212 My route for some miles wound . . . over a region which seemed completely excavated into sink-holes. **1871** *Rep. Indian Affairs* (1872) 560 The land is very difficult to irrigate, . . . [being] full of sink-holes. **1894** ALLEN *Ky. Cardinal* ix, I struck out across the country toward a big sink-hole in a field two miles away.

+b. (See quotation.)

1895 *Stand.* 1674/2 *Sink-hole*, . . . a place in a marsh where it is too soft to make a road, and which the winter's cold does not freeze over.

‖c. A large depression or enclosed valley.

1896 WHITE *Real Issue* 81 The Taylor Bottom . . . is a deep sink-hole, perhaps fifty feet deep, containing about ten square acres.

∗ Sinking, *a.* +Of streams or springs: Disappearing from sight; running into a sink hole. — **1780** in Summers *Ann. S.W. Va.* 733 Parker Atkinson [is to be overseer of the road] from the hollow of Doe Creek to the Steep Bank of Sinking Creek. **1781** in *Amer. Speech* XV. 392/2 Thence . . . to a Walnut and two hoopwoods in Chaplains line near a small Sinking Spring. **1784** *Ib.* 392/1 Thence . . . to three white oaks by the head of a Sinking run. **1792** *Ib.*, The buffaloe Road leads to Drennins lick and East side of a large Sinking branch.

+Sinkroom. *New Eng.* A room having a sink, esp. a room near a kitchen in which utensils are kept and the coarser operations involved in cooking are performed. Also attrib. — **1833** *Trial E. K. Avery* 55, [I] found him in the sink room. **1869** STOWE *Oldtown Folks* 66 The conversation was interrupted by a commotion in the back sink-room. **1887** WILKINS *Humble Romance* 331, I hadn't any more'n shut the sink-room door.

+Siouan, *a.* Pertaining to the Sioux Indians. — **1889** *Amer. Naturalist* XXIII. 75 The Siouan group had its habitat on the prairies between the Mississippi and Missouri. **1898** *Mo. So. Dakotan* I. 89 The term Dakota . . . was in use . . . among various Siouan tribes when first studied by white men.

+Sioux. [Fr., shortening of *Nadowessioux*, from Chippewa *Nâdowessi* 'little snake, enemy.']

1. *pl.* The largest and best-known of the Indian tribal groups of the Siouan stock; also, sing., an Indian belonging to a tribe of this group.

1805 LEWIS in *L. & Clark Exped.* I. (1904) 258 The Indians in our neighbourhood are frequently pilfered of their horses by the Recares, Souixs and Assinniboins. **1827** COOPER *Prairie* xxx, The keen weapon . . . meeting the naked breast of the impetuous Sioux, the blade was buried to the buck-horn haft. **1888** ROOSEVELT in *Century Mag.* May 39/1 [The country through which the Little Missouri R. flows] was the last great Indian hunting-ground across which . . . Sioux and Cheyennes . . . wandered in chase of game. **1894** WISTER in *Harper's Mag.* June 119/1 Forty Sioux were reported up the river coming to visit the Crows. **1916** [see HOSTILE *a.*].

transf. **1892** *Harper's Mag.* March 493/2 The 'bull-dog' . . . is the Sioux of the insect world, as pretty as a warrior in buckskin and beads.

2. Attrib. with *agent, band, brave,* etc.

1808 PIKE *Sources Miss.* 14 His design was to winter with some of the Sioux bands. *c*1834 CATLIN *Indians* II. 2 In his hand he held a beautiful Sioux pipe. **1836** IRVING *Astoria* I. 149 His [a French Creole's] regular, or habitual wife, was a Sioux squaw. **1869** *Ore. State Jrnl.* 2 Jan. 2/2 The Sioux war on the Plains . . . commenced in 1852. **1872** *Chicago Tribune* 25 June, The characters are a mixed set having among them guerrillas, trappers, Sioux braves [etc.]. **1912** NICHOLSON *Hoosier Chron.* 56 She had seen somewhere a photograph of a Sioux chief whose austere countenance was very like the minister's. **1923** J. H. COOK *On Old Frontier* 95 [He had] been employed in handling many Sioux ponies at the expense of their rightful owners.

∗ Sir.

∗ 1. A title or designation (rendering L. *dominus*) given to a bachelor of arts. *Obs.*

1688 SEWALL *Letter-Book* I. 88 Received Sir Shove's Letter. **1763** in Peirce *Hist. Harvard* 234 Voted, . . . That Sir Sewall, B.A., be the Instructor in the Hebrew and other learned languages for three years. [**1854** ed. J. Seccombe *Father Abbey's Will* 7 Some of the 'Sirs' as well as undergraduates were arraigned before the college government.]

+2. (See quot. *c*1870.) *Obs.*

1789 *Essex Inst. Coll.* XXV. 311 One of them fired and killed my honoured Sir. *c*1870 CHIPMAN *Notes on Bartlett* 408 *Sir*, not infrequent for father; said of parents by children; and of a father by his wife. Salem, Mass., until near 1840. . . . E.g. 'Your sir,' the mother would say to her child respecting his father, her husband.

∗ 3. A respectful term of address used in speaking to or with anyone.

1805 PARKINSON *Tour* 19 Among the white men in America, they are all *Mr.* and *Sir.* **1850** CARLISLE *Travels* 11 'Sir,' as an American always begins, 'on the prairies of Illinois this day Lord Mansfield administers the law of commerce.' **1852** BRISTED *5 Years in Eng. Univ.* II. 35, I have known southern and western gentlemen whose conversation seemed to consist of successive enunciations of 'Sir!' with a few words between to connect them.

+b. Added to *yes* or *no* as an intensive. (Cf. No SIR-EE.)

1799 *Aurora* (Phila.) 8 Aug. (Th.), Yes Sir! and [France] has been successful beyond any former experience. **1876** 'MARK TWAIN' *Tom Sawyer* vii, No, sir, it ain't fair. **1888** 'CRADDOCK' *Despot* 40 Yes, sir. . . . None like 'em now. **1906** FREEMAN *By Light of Soul* 398 'You don't mean to say they did all that?' said the other woman. 'Yes, sir, they did.'

∗ Siren. 1. An eel-shaped American amphibian of the family Sirenidae. {1791-} **+2.** (See quotation.) — (1) {1765 J. ELLIS tr. Linnaeus in *Phil. Trans.* LVI. 192, Dr. Garden's very rare two-footed animal . . . must be a new and very distinct genus, and should most properly have the name of *Siren.*] **1796** MORSE *Univ. Geog.* I. 224 The Siren or Mud-iguana, a fish of the order, *Branchiostegi*, . . . was first observed by Dr. Garden of Charleston (S.C.). (2) **1891** *Cent.* 5655/3 *Siren*, . . . one of the *Sirenia*, as the manatee, dugong, halicore, or sea-cow; any sirenian.

Sirenian. (See quot. 1911.) {1804-} — **1883** *Science* I. 346/1 The discovery of a new fossil sirenian in South Carolina brings the number of known existing and extinct forms in North America to eight. **1884** GOODE, etc. *Fisheries* I. 114 We have, then, upon our coasts two representatives of the Sirenians. **1911** *Rep. Fisheries 1908* 316/1 *Sirenians*, large marine mammals, more or less fishlike in form, such as manatees, sea-cows, etc.; found in warm seas.

Sirocco. {1617-} *W.* A dry, hot wind, usually from the south. Also attrib. — [**1836** EDWARD *Hist. Texas* 242 [They] threw themselves into the midst of our tranquil community, . . . overthrowing confidence and hope—like the scorching blasts of the sirocco winds.] **1848** ROBINSON *Santa Fe Exped.* (1932) 20 The dreaded Sirocco . . . burns us even through our clothes. **1872** TICE *Over Plains* 258 We here entered into a sirocco that blew a perfect gale from the south. **1893** *Harper's Mag.* April 712/2 Successive droughts and siroccos destroyed the crops in the western half of [Kan.].

∗ Sirop. *S.* +(See quotation.) — **1887** *Century Mag.* Nov. 116/1 The cane-juice runs into the largest kettle, called 'the grand,' . . . and in the course of the boiling is ladled successively into the others, called, in order, the 'prop' or 'proxy,' the 'flambeau,' the 'sirop,' and the 'battery.' . . . 'Sirop' is French for syrup.

∗ Sirup. (See SYRUP *n.*)

+Sis. Short for *sister. colloq.* — **1835** *Knickerb.* VI. 293 All the friends called her sister,—which, as the half was easier to be bandied about than the whole,—soon dwindled into 'sis.' **1880** TOURGEE *Bricks* 129 Sit closer, Sis, where I can see you better. **1891** RYAN *Pagan* 133 Folks call boys 'bud' sometimes, jist like they call girls 'sis.' **1902** *Harper's Mag.* March 620/2 'You'd better file, sis,' he said.

Sisal hemp. A tropical plant (*Agave sisalina*) or a plant related to this; the strong, durable fiber obtained from the leaves of such a plant. {1843-} — **1847** *Rep. Comm. Patents 1846* 73 The other [fabric] is a material for skirts, having slivers of untwisted sisal hemp woven in at intervals with the filling. **1856** *Ib. 1855: Agric.* 242 Dr. Henry Perine, who was for a time Consul at Yucatan, . . . introduced into the southern part of this State [Fla.], the Sisal hemp. **1863** *Rep. Comm. Agric. 1862* 62 High, rolling sandy districts . . . are, owing to their calcareous quality, well adapted for the growth of Sisal hemp.

+Siscoe. Variant of CISCO. — **1875** *Amer. Naturalist* IX. 135, I received . . . a collection of deep-water 'Siscoes' taken in Lake Tippecanoe, Kosciusko Co., Indiana. **1880** *Lib. Universal Knowl.* VI. 11 Herring are found all along the coast; and in the lakes there is a similar fish known as the siscoe. **1893** HOLLEY *Samantha at World's Fair* 457 We had fish for breakfast too—siscoes.

+Siscowet. (See quot. 1902.) — **1849** H. W. HERBERT *Fish & Fishing* 145 The Siskawitz is rather shorter and stouter than the Mackinaw fish. **1853** *Harper's Mag.* March 442/1 The *siskowit*, a fish peculiar to Lake Superior, . . . in delicacy of flavor, is thought by epicures to surpass all others. **1884** GOODE, etc. *Fisheries* I. 496 The Siscowet, or 'Siskawitz,' is a form of Lake Trout, which, according to many authorities, is a distinct species, and which has been observed only in Lake Superior. **1902** *Amer. Folk-Lore* XV. 258 *Siscowit.* This name, which has also the forms *siscowet, ciscoette,* . . . etc., is applied both to a variety of the great lake trout 'Mackinaw trout' (*Salmo namaycush*), and to a lake herring (*sisco*), [and] is by some writers referred to 'an Ojibwa *siskawit.*' **1911** *Rep. Fisheries* 1908 311/2 The 'siscowet' is another variety of [lake trout].

+Siscowet salmon. [See prec.] A large variety of the namaycush. — **1882** *Nat. Museum Bul.* No. 16, 318 Siscowet Salmon . . . is probably a local variety rather than a distinct species.

+Sissy, *n.*

1. = SIS. *colloq.*

1855 SIMMS *Forayers* 189 Keep close, and don't get up till sissy tells you. **1892** GUNTER *Miss Dividends* 80 Mr. Kruger is on hand to . . . say with paternal voice, 'Sissy, Dad's happy now.'

2. An effeminate man or boy. *colloq.*

1899 T. HALL *Tales* 131 Well, you are a sissy. **1911** FERBER *Dawn O'Hara* 42 The hero is a milk-and-water sissy, without a vital spark in him. **1918** in *Liberty* 11 Aug. (1928) 8/1 Captain Johnson announced . . . that he wanted no nissies in his outfit.

+Sissy, *a.* Effeminate, girlish. *colloq.* — **1891** *Harper's Mag.* Aug. 485/2 [He] sat near me, deep in conversation with a young gentleman with sissy whiskers. **1893** *N.Y. Mercury* May (Ware), Sissy men in Society.—Powdered, painted and laced. **1899** T. HALL *Tales* 121 Scotty was, in the newspaper vernacular, 'a sissy boy,' or, in other words, a bit effeminate. **1902** WILSON *Spenders* 291 The men . . . are a-getting to be a sissy lot these days. **1917** MATHEWSON *Second Base Sloan* 261 A lot of his sissy friends waves little pink flags.

+Sissyish, *a.* =prec. — **1889** HOWELLS *Hazard of Fortunes* II. 64 The New York fellows carried canes . . . ; and they were both sissyish and fast.

Sister city. A city thought of as having a status similar to that of another. — **1845** HONE *Diary* II. 266 Our sister city [Boston] of the Bay State has been without a chief magistrate for some time past. **1872** TICE *Over Plains* 84 Cheyenne, unlike its sister city, Denver, will, therefore, never [etc.]. **1873** *Harper's Mag.* Jan. 296/1 Energetic and skillful as its [*i.e.*, New York's] Fire Department may be, it . . . was no more so than the forces of its sister cities.

+Sisterhood of States. The states, thought of as a group, making up the American Federal Union. — **1832** *Congress. Deb.* 16 June 3627 Can you forget . . . the constitution you have sworn to support, the sisterhood of States which has cherished you? **1900** *Congress. Rec.* 25 Jan. 1207/2 A condition precedent to her admission into the sisterhood of States, was . . . an express prohibition against polygamy.

+Sister state. A state associated with the others in the American Federal Union. — **1777** *Boston Rec.* 285 We are sure, that very large, & much wanted Supplies, the Property of this State & expected here, are now ordered into some of the Sister States. **1798** I. ALLEN *Hist. Vermont* 225 The right of the people of Vermont to be admitted a sister State into the union was acknowledged by a great majority of the citizens. **1807** *Steele P.* II. 522 [The grants] ought from considerations of respect to a Sister State to be confirmed. **1900** *Congress. Rec.* 25 Jan. 1184/1 The new State . . . is invested with equality of privilege and function with all her sister States.

+Sister union. A union thought of as having aims and a status similar to those of another. — **1874** *Internat. Typogr. Union Proc.* 14 A member of a union going to work in the jurisdiction of a sister Union upon permit is amenable to the law of the latter Union. **1896** *Ib.* 49/2 We also suggested to the International officers the idea of printing and mailing blank resolutions to sister unions to be filled out.

✱Sit, *v.* In phrases with adverbs and prepositions.

A few of the quotations here given show the confusion between *sit* and *set* which is common in both England and America.

1. To sit by {1824-}, +to be near or present; to sit up to a table for a meal. *colloq.*

1845 KIRKLAND *Western Clearings* 109 Mr. and Mrs. Lightbody sat by, but Mr. Poppleton was again the spokesman. **1854** M. J. HOLMES *Tempest & Sunshine* 118 Come, boys, set by and have some fodder! **1888** KIRKLAND *McVeys* 273 He 'set by,' and resting his forehead on his arm was sound asleep when she came back in five minutes with bread, and milk, and cold meat.

✱2. To sit down, to settle, to take up one's abode. {-1579}

1634 *Mass. Bay Rec.* I. 129 The Scottishe & Irishe gentlemen . . . shall haue liberty to sitt downe in any place vpp Merimacke Ryver. **1637** *Conn. Rec.* I. 10 Mr. Haine & Mr. Ludlowe shall goe . . . to parle with the bay aboute our settinge downe in the Pequoitt Countrey. **1702** C. MATHER *Magnalia* (1853) I. 50 Their design was to have sat down some where about Hudson's River. **1817** BRADBURY *Travels* 332 The rapidity with which one of these colonies acquires wealth or property will appear by a comparison of their present state with their situation when they first sat down. **1842** *Amer. Pioneer* I. 226 One man sat down six miles east of him.

✱3. To sit in, +to join a group in playing cards, etc. *colloq.*

1868 S. HALE *Letters* 44 Before we got to lunch two Englishmen *sot in.* **1903** A. ADAMS *Log of Cowboy* 179 When one was frozen out another sat in and took his place. **1922** McNEAL *When Kansas Was Young* 187 A Texan . . . suggested to Major Drumm that he would like to 'sit in' but that he was somewhat hampered in the way of cash.

✱4. To sit up. +**a.** (See quot. 1856.) *colloq.*

1846 McKENNEY *Memoirs* I. 138 'Sit up, sit up, stranger, and join us,' said the hardy settler. **1856** S. WARNER *Hills of Shatemuc* xvi, 'Will you

sit up, cousin?' . . . : the meaning of the request being that he should move his chair up to the table. **1894** WILLIAMS *Pembroke* 38 If you don't set right up an' eat it, it will be gettin' cold.

+b. To sit up and take notice, to show marked interest. *colloq.*

1909 *N.Y. Ev. Post* (s.-w. ed.) 8 March 2 The crowd that fell upon Washington was of such a size that the District authorities sat up and took serious notice. **1914** ATHERTON *Perch of Devil* 175 When he does sit up and take notice he doesn't so much as wink. **1921** PAINE *Comr. Rolling Ocean* 104 What really made Judson sit up and take notice was the unexpected sight of 'Kid' Briscoe.

+c. To sit up (of) nights (fig.), to work hard; to be anxious; to spare no pains. *colloq.*

1855 B. YOUNG in *Jrnl. of Discourses* II. 320/2 If you persecute us, we will sit up nights to preach the Gospel. **1890** *Congress. Rec.* 26 April 3873/1, I sit up of nights trying to work out how I can obtain his approval. **1910** *N.Y. Ev. Post* 4 Aug. (Th.), The President is reported as . . . sitting up nights waiting for Mr. Ballinger to come round and hand in his resignation.

Sit-down. An occasion, esp. a meal, at which people are seated. — **1851** *Harper's Mag.* Nov. 849/2 No supper cards for a 'sit-down' to fried oysters and Burgundy. **1878** STOWE *Poganuc People* 139 But after tea there came the genial hour of the social sit-down in front of the andirons. **1907** LONDON *Road* 74 Even a 'set-down' could not have lured me away.

+Sitio. *S.W.* [Sp.] (See quot. 1859.) — **1825** *Austin P.* II. (1924) 1202 The twelfth article of the law says the Empresarios shall receive (5) five Sitios (Leagues) of pasture land. **1834** *Jamestown* (N.Y.) *Jrnl.* 19 Nov. 2/2 The law allows a married man [in Texas] to have not exceeding a Sitio. **1859** BARTLETT 409 The sitio is a league of land of 5,000 varas, and is equal to 4,428 English acres.

+Sitka. *attrib.* In the names of trees and birds found in the region of Sitka, Alaska. — **1884** SARGENT *Rep. Forests* 580 The most valuable tree of this region [Alaska] is the Sitka cedar (*Chamæcyparis Nutkaensis*). *Ib.* 178 *Chamæcyparis Nutkaensis.* . . . Yellow Cypress. Sitka Cypress. **1917** *Birds of Amer.* III. 222/2 The Sitka, or Grinnell's Ruby-crowned, Kinglet (*Regulus calendula grinnelli*) is similar to the more widely distributed Ruby-crown. **1897** SUDWORTH *Arborescent Flora* 41 *Picea sitchensis.* . . . Sitka Spruce.

✱Sitter. +(See quotations.) — **1868** *Ore. State Jrnl.* 19 Dec. 2/5 'Sitters,' as they are called, . . . sit about on chairs [in saloons] to sleep off the effects of drink. **1905** J. M. RICHARDS *With John Bull & Jonathan* 139 The greater privacy of the hotels in England greatly impressed me, as no 'loungers,' or 'sitters' as they are called in America, are allowed to frequent them.

Sitting room.

1. A room for sitting in, as distinguished from a bedroom, kitchen, etc. {1806-} Cf. SETTING ROOM.

1771 *Copley-Pelham Lett.* 147 The Arches at the sides of the Chimnie in the Sitting Room, I like. **1833** *Knickerb.* I. 204 His friend entered the common sitting-room of Squire Buckmere's family. **1898** E. C. HALL *Aunt Jane* 11, I went down into the sittin'-room to get Jacob's cyarpet-bag. **1925** BRYAN *Memoirs* 40 Grandma's room—the back sitting room—was my first schoolhouse.

b. Attrib. with *furniture, table, window.*

1852 STOWE *Uncle Tom* xxxix, Looking from the sitting-room windows, Cassy and Emmeline could see the troop. **1892** *Harper's Mag.* Dec. 78/1 Mrs. Wayne . . . [was] whacking dust from the sitting-room furniture with a turkey wing. **1921** PAINE *Comr. Rolling Ocean* 13 He dumped his wages upon the sitting-room table.

2. The part of a poultry house where hens sit.

1850 BROWNE *Poultry Yard* 89 In the sitting room . . . [the hen] may remain in perfect quietude till she hatches her brood.

Sitting shot. A shot made from a sitting position. — **1874** LONG *Wild-fowl* 151 If it was later in the day, it might be to our advantage to try a sitting-shot. **1894** ROBINSON *Danvis Folks* 24, I never missed a settin' shot in my life.

+Sitting-up visit. A visit to a woman soon after the birth of a child when she is again able to sit up. — **1761** *Holyoke Diaries* 49 Made Mrs. Ropes a Sitting up visit. **1772** A. G. WINSLOW *Diary* 15, I made a setting up visit to Aunt Suky.

+Siwash. *N.W.* [Chinook jargon, from Fr. *sauvage.*] An Indian of the northern Pacific coast. Also *attrib.* and *transf.*

1852 *Olympia* (Wash.) *Courier* 30 Oct. (Th.), The Siwash chiefs were maddened now to frenzy. **1865** *Ore. State Jrnl.* 1 April 2/3 The whites having misused the generousness of the 'Siwashes' sent a runner up the river. **1902** WHITE *Blazed Trail Stories* 138 Billy! . . . come down here, you siwash. **1904** E. ROBINS *Magn. North* 293 You soon learn it is the Siwash custom.

b. The trade language or jargon used by the Siwashes and those having dealings with them.

1902 *Skagway Daily Alaskan* 23 Aug. 3/1 The governor was forced back upon his ability to talk siwash, hoping thereby to control the Indian vote. **1908** BEACH *Barrier* 56 Address me in Siwash or in English unless we are alone.

∗Six, *a.* +In special combinations.

Six-and-a-quarter-cents coin, (see quotation); *S. Companies*, six benevolent and commercial associations for Chinese emigrants, originating about 1850, to supply cheap coolie labor in the United States; *s.-mouthed barker*, =Six-shooter; *s.-reel*, a reel danced by three couples; *s.-spotted mite*, a mite injurious to oranges; *s. ways for Sunday*, disordered; *s.-wheeler*, a railroad car having six pairs of wheels.

1880 N. Brooks *Fairport Nine* 125 The fourpence ha'penny, or six-and-a-quarter-cents coin, . . . circulated then. **1876** W. M. Fisher *Californians* 58 All these are commonly spoken of as 'The Six Companies.' **1890** *Buckskin Mose* 167, I've one of my own, an a Colt's six-mouthed barker, too. **1833** Longstreet *Ga. Scenes* 12 Off went the party to a good old republican six reel. **1890** *Rep. Secy. Agric. 1889* 341 Since the appearance of the Six-spotted Mite of the Orange in 1886, the Florida press has made frequent reference to it. **1840** *Jamestown (N.Y.) Jrnl.* 9 Dec. 2/1 Thro' the aperture [in his hat], red hair in abundance stood six ways for Sunday. **1907** London *Road* 39 When you go underneath on the rods, be sure to avoid the 'six-wheelers,'—they lead to disasters.

Six bits. *pl.* Seventy-five cents. (Cf. Four bits.) — **1840** *Jamestown (N.Y.) Jrnl.* 12 Aug. 3/4 If he grumbles we'll give him six bits. **1869** J. R. Browne *Adv. Apache Country* 368 They talk of charging six bits. **1916** Sandburg *Chicago Poems* 16 A dago working for a dollar six bits a day.

Six-horse. *attrib.* Designating conveyances drawn by, or a team consisting of, six horses. Also fig. — **1782** Crèvecœur *Letters* 96 We met several large Lancaster six-horse waggons. **1833** J. S. Jones *Green Mt. Boy* I. iii, For the rale genuine grammar larnin' I am a six-horse team and a big dog under the wagon. **1844** *Lexington Observer* 25 Sept. 2/7 At the same time and place will be sold . . . an Ox-cart, and a Six Horse Wagon. **1872** *Harper's Mag.* Dec. 22/1 On this line also lies Guy Hill, . . . down which the six-horse coach is driven at full speed. **1913** London *Valley of Moon* 441 At the end of the railroad, they saw the six-horse stages leaving for Middletown and Lower Lake.

+**Six-mule.** *attrib.* Designating conveyances drawn by six mules, or a team of six mules. — **1873** Harte *Tales of Argonauts* 202 Mr. Titherick . . . was then driving a six-mule freight wagon. **1878** Beadle *Western Wilds* 53, I took a position as engineer of a six-mule team. **1888** *Century Mag.* Nov. 159/1 The army wagon, the big blue wagon, the six-mule wagon, the U.S. wagon, Was blessed or was cursed. **1895** Remington *Pony Tracks* 5 Now the general steps out of the car and hands the commission into a six-mule ambulance.

+**Six Nations.** The confederation of Iroquois Indians as enlarged in the early eighteenth century by the addition of the Tuscarora to the Five Nations. Also *Six Allied Nations*.

1726 Penhallow *Indian Wars* 101 The delegates of the six nations of Iroquois, . . . being disposed to come to Boston, were kindly entertained there. **1754** *Mass. H. S. Coll.* 3 Ser. V. 16 In regard to . . . the treaty to be entered into at Albany with the said Six Allied Nations, you shall refer yourselves [etc.]. **1787** Franklin *Writings* X. 98 If the Six Nations would send down half a dozen of their young Lads to that College, the Government would take care that they should be well provided for. **1813** *Niles' Reg.* IV. 400/1 The *Six Nations* are the Mohawks, Oneidas, Onondagoes, Senecas, Cayugas, and Tuscaroras. **1891** Welch *Recoll. 1830–40* 111 The Seneca tribe of Indians, traditionally the most savage of the 'Six Nations' of the historic Iroquois. **1907** *St. Nicholas* July 832/1 [The Indians were] under the command of Brandt, the famous Chief of the Six Nations.

attrib. **1751** Croghan *Journal* (1904) 58 One of the Six Nation Kings from the Head of Ohio came to the Logstown to the Council.

∗Sixpence.

∗1. A sum of money having the value of six pennies; a coin of this value. *Obs.*

1635 *Watertown Rec.* I. 1. 1 The towne Clarke shall have six pense for every Lott of land that he shall Inroll in the towne Booke. **1707** *Springfield Rec.* II. 75 Every one that shal Speake in a Tumultuous manner shal pay six pence to ye Town Treasury. **1789** *Ann. 1st Congress* 227 Other rum usually costs about three shillings, or three shillings and six pence.

b. *transf.* A designation for a person. {1600} Used in the phrase *the same old sixpence*.

1833 S. Smith *Life J. Downing* 185 He is the same old sixpence he used to be. **1896** Jewett *Pointed Firs* 89, I declare if you ain't the same old sixpence! **1898** Westcott *D. Harum* 60 Ann and Jeff are just the same old sixpences as ever.

+**2.** (See quot. 1848.) *Obs.*

1818 Fearon *Sketches* 13 A beggar . . . was relieved with a Spanish silver piece called a sixpence: it was the sixteenth of a dollar. **1848** Bartlett 135 The half real of $\frac{1}{16}$ of a dollar is called in New York a *sixpence*. **1891** Welch *Recoll. 1830–40* 169 It was common, particularly in New England, to call a sixpence or a half dime, a *fip*.

+**Six-Principle Baptists.** A sect of Baptists professing six doctrines enumerated in Heb. 6:1-2. Also attrib. in sing. — **1835** Reed & Matheson *Visit* II. 72 [The Baptist denomination] reckons to have 3,397 clergy . . . and this, exclusive of the . . . Six Principle Baptists. **1884** Schaff *Religious Encycl.* III. 2191/1 *Six-Principle Baptists*. . . . In 1880 they had not more than a dozen (very weak) churches in New England, all but two in Rhode Island. **1919** *Census: Religious Bodies 1916* II. 102/1 A number of members withdrew and in 1653 organized the General Six Principle Baptist Church, the six principles being . . . : Repentance,

faith, baptism, laying on of hands, resurrection of the dead, and eternal judgment.

+**Six-rail fence.** A rail fence having six rails. — **1835** Paulding *J. Bull & Bro. Jon.* (new ed.) 171 He could jump over a six-rail fence without touching. **1853** B. F. Taylor *Jan. & June* 61 One meets six-rail fences every day.

Six-rowed barley. A type of barley with six rows of grains to the spike: (see quots.) {1762} — **1847** Darlington *Weeds & Plants* 393 *H[ordeum] vulgare.* . . . Common Hordeum. Barley. Four-rowed Barley. . . . In Western New-York . . . it is usually called Six-rowed Barley,—though that name would seem more properly to belong to another nearly allied species (*H. hexastichum*)—if, indeed, it be really distinct. **1857** Gray *Botany* 570. **1907** Bailey, etc. *Cycl. Amer. Agric.* II. 202/1 The four-rowed barley does not seem to be a distinct variety, but a variation of the six-rowed, as often the six-rowed barley drops two rows midway up the spike, the upper part being nearly four-rowed.

+**Six-shooter.** A revolver capable of firing six shots without reloading. *colloq.*

See also Navy six(-shooter) and cf. Five-shooter.

1853 Brewerton *With Kit Carson* (1930) 188 'Six shooters' . . . lay prepared for instant use. **1876** Miller *First Fam'lies* 105 The ugly black muzzle of a six-shooter was in the Parson's face. **1890** *Harper's Mag.* Dec. 160/2 That six-shooter you gave Pete was . . . a pretty gun. **1923** J. H. Cook *On Old Frontier* 59 [A man] wearing a Mexican sash about his waist and packing a pair of . . . six-shooters, would have no trouble getting something to eat.

b. Attrib. with *gun, sermon, war dance.*

1873 Miller *Amongst Modocs* 144 Sometimes they have a six-shooter war dance in the streets. **1890** *Stock Grower & Farmer* 21 June 3/1 A terrible six-shooter sermon came to us from Socorro county last week. Three cowboys shot each other up. **1920** Hunter *Trail Drivers Texas* I. 232 A 'hog-leg,' . . . better known as a six-shooter gun.

+**Six-shooting,** *a.* Of firearms: Capable of firing six shots without reloading. — **1855** Holbrook *Among Mail Bags* 194 Plenty of Sharp's rifles and Colt's six-shooting cavalry pistols . . . [enabled the] men and passengers . . . to fire three or four hundred shots without any delay in loading. **1858** Vielé *Following Drum* 224 A belt full of pistols, a sword buckled to the side, and a six-shooting rifle, composed his supply of firearms.

+**Sixteen-shooter.** A magazine rifle capable of firing sixteen shots without reloading. In full *sixteen-shooter rifle.* — **1865** Richardson *Secret Service* 480 He and his companions were now armed with sixteen-shooter rifles, revolvers, and bowie-knives. **1875** *Chicago Tribune* 2 Dec. 3/2 He was armed with a sixteen-shooter. **1894** Eggleston in *Harper's Mag.* Feb. 475/1 George had a sixteen-shooter.

+**Sixteenth section.** In a surveyed township, the section numbered sixteen, granted to the state by the federal government for school purposes. (Cf. School section.) — **1837** Wetmore *Gaz. Missouri* 72 This mine is on a tract of school-lands, commonly called sixteenth section. **1880** *Cimarron News & Press* 9 Sept. 2/1 Under our organic law each 16th and 32d section of public land is reserved for school purposes. **1914** *Cycl. Amer. Govt.* III. 256/1 The states admitted between 1802 and 1848, except Texas, received the 16th section in each surveyed township of public domain.

Sixteen to one. +The ratio, exactly or approximately, between the market values of gold and silver respectively, used especially as a popular phrase during the silver-coinage controversy, 1875-1900. — **1854** Benton *30 Years' View* I. 443/2 The value of gold is 16 to 1 over silver. **1896** *Typographical Jrnl.* IX. 368 'Bimetallism' and '16 to 1' adorn each end of the first page heading. **1903** *Forum* July 4 Mr. Bryan seems determined to drag into the next campaign the obnoxious ghost of sixteen to one. **1914** *Cycl. Amer. Govt.* III. 313/2 *Sixteen to One.* . . . It was quite generally believed that this was the ratio adopted under the mint act of 1793.

+**Six United Nations.** =Six Nations. *Obs.* — **1752** W. Trent *Journal* 96 We join with the Six United Nations of Indians. **1776** *Va. State P.* I. 273 The said Six United Nations . . . did grant to the said Traders . . . all that Tract of Land.

Six-week(s). *attrib.* +In the names of various quick-growing plants. Also absol. — **1763** Holyoke *Diaries* 58 Sowed 6 w(ee)ks beans. **1775** Adair *Indians* 406 The smaller sort of Indian corn . . . ripens in two months from the time it is planted; though it is called by the English, the six weeks corn. **1859** *Ill. Agric. Soc. Trans.* III. 503 Early yellow six-weeks [beans] and early Valentine (long red mottled,) are excellent for snaps. **1877** H. C. Hodge *Arizona* 54 The wild grasses of the country are very nutritious, embracing varieties of . . . six week grass, many varieties of bunch grass, etc. **1894** Coulter *Bot. W. Texas* III. 533 *B[outeloua] aristidoides.* . . . Six-weeks mesquit. . . . Western Texas to California.

∗Size, *v.*

+**1.** *tr.* To sum up or take the measure of (something); to estimate, to form an opinion about (a person, thing, etc.). Usually with *up.*

1877 'Mark Twain' *Punch, Brother, Punch!* 73 Somehow, it [a lawsuit about a cat] seemed to 'size' the country [Bermuda]. **1885** *Santa Fé Wkly. New Mexican* 24 Dec. 2/5 They know everybody can 'size up' a man at a glance. **1894** *Vt. Agric. Rep.* XIV. 97 When one sizes up the points of this horse he is not surprised at the good showing. **1917** B. Matthews *These Many Years* 205, I was always greeted . . . with the transfixing glance which seemed to 'size me up,' to use our expressive Americanism.

+b. *intr.* To turn out, amount to, or compare with; to prove to be upon investigation.

1884 NYE *Baled Hay* 126 Time, at last, makes all things size up in proper shape. **1902** WISTER *Virginian* v, Give me your opinion how it sizes up with the letters they write back East. **1914** JAMES *Ivory Tower* 91 The question of what Gray's 'interest' . . . might size up to.

2. *tr.* (See quotation.)

1889 C. T. DAVIS *Bricks & Tiles* (ed. 2) 147 It is necessary to grind the same clay . . . several times, . . . before it comes to the proper degree of plasticity for moulding; this operation is called 'sizing the clay.'

+3. *To size* (someone's) *pile*, or variant: To match or equal an opponent; to bet with; to estimate correctly (someone's) resources. Also in allusive context. *colloq.*

1840 HALIBURTON *Clockmaker* 3 Ser. xi. Come, I'll size your pile. . . . Plank down a pile of dollars . . . of any size you like, and I'll put down another of the same size. **1853** BALDWIN *Flush Times Ala.* 113 The jury shortly after returned into court with a verdict which 'sized their pile.' **1864** NICHOLS *Amer. Life* I. 387 To make a bet with a man is to size his pile. **1873** BEADLE *Undevel. West* 198 They are satisfied to 'size your pile' and take quarter of it. **1889** 'MARK TWAIN' *Conn. Yankee* 300, I was resolved he should have at least one [bath] . . . , if it sized up my whole influence and bankrupted the pile.

Sizz, *v.* {a1700} *intr.* To sizzle or hiss. {1788–} 'Chiefly *dial.* or *U.S.*' (O.E.D.). Also *fig.* — **1858** *S. Lit. Messenger* XXVI. 123/1 My eyes wus a akin and my hed a sizzing. **1862** *N.Y. Tribune* 21 June 3/1 [My notes] had cost many miles of travel . . . under a sun whose rays fairly made the flesh to sizz. **1887** *Voice* 1 Sept., Touch any one of the 900 delegates . . . and he (or she) will sizz. **1903** BRADY *Bishop* 158 He kin watch the thing [a fuse] sizzin' along the floor better in the dark.

‖**Sizzer.** Something that sizzles, as a firecracker. — **1897** *Chicago Tribune* 5 July 6/4 The last cracker will have cracked, the last torpedo will have popped, the last 'sizzer' will have hissed.

+Skallyhoot, *v.* (See SCALLYHOOT *v.*)

*Skate, *n.*[1] Any fish of the genus *Raja* or of allied genera, **+**as *R. laevis* of the Atlantic coast.

1616 SMITH *New England* 17 And scarce any place, but Cod, Cuske, Holybut, Mackerell, Scate, or such like, a man may take with a hook or line. **1778** J. ADAMS *Diary* Works III. 116 This forenoon a fisherman came alongside, with hakes, skates, and gurnards. **1806** CLARK in *Lewis & C. Exped.* III. (1905) 320 One of the men Call this fish a Skaite, it is properly a Thornback. **1867** LONGFELLOW in S. Longfellow *H. W. Longfellow* III. 96 Called on Agassiz, and found him busy dissecting a huge skate. **1891** [see DRUMFISH]. **1911** *Rep. Fisheries 1908* 314/1 [Rays] are also called 'skates,' 'torpedoes,' 'devil-fishes,' etc.

Skate, *n.*[2]

1. A metallic runner that may be clamped or fitted to a shoe, used to glide over ice. {1662–}

1701 WOLLEY *Journal N.Y.* 71 Upon the Ice its admirable to see Men and Women as it were flying upon their Skates. **1756** ROGERS *Journals* 11 We proceeded down the lake, on the ice, upon skaits. **1790** *Penna. Packet* 1 Jan. 1/3 Frederick W. Starman . . . has just received . . . from Amsterdam . . . Skates. **1855** GLISAN *Jrnl. Army Life* 163 It was difficult to realize that it was the same old dam . . . which I used to . . . glide over on skates. **1911** *Sears, Roebuck & Co. Cat.* No. 123, 1051/1 The runner of this skate is made of the very best cold rolled cast steel.

b. An ice-boat runner.

1781 S. PETERS *Hist. Conn.* 320 In the winter, the sleigh is used; a vehicle . . . carrying six persons in its box, which hangs on four posts, standing on two steel sliders or large scates. **1907** *St. Nicholas* July 781/1 You make a frame-work of timbers, kind of three-cornered like, and stick a skate or a runner at each corner.

c. = ROLLER SKATE.

1907 *St. Nicholas* June 736/2 So Doris said she would . . . wait until she had enough for the skates. **1925** *Sears, Roebuck & Co. Cat.* No. 150, 751 Children's Extension Skates With Steel Self Contained Ball Bearing Rolls.

2. A spell or exercise at skating.

1853 KANE *Grinnell Exped.* 214 Took a skate this morning over some lakelets recently frozen over. **1873** C. GORDON *Boarding-School Days* 68 The first call was turned into a skate together on the Hudson. **1889** *Advance* 11 April 294 Bound for the smooth sheet of ice . . . for a skate.

3. Attrib. and comb. in sense 1 with *blade, grinder,* etc.

1838 INGRAHAM *Burton* I. 143 It [a sleigh] was placed on *runners* sixteen inches high, shaped like skate-irons. **1871** GROSVENOR *Protection* 191 Sanford had pushed his skate-manufacture to success. **1876** KNIGHT 2192/2 *Skate-grinder,* a machine for grinding skates, straight-edged or rockers. **1895** *Outing* XXVII. 202/1 Skate blades *deeply* grooved, or 'guttered,' as it is termed, are a nuisance.

+Skate, *n.*[3] **1.** (See quot. 1890.) **2.** A contemptible person. *colloq.*[2] Often *cheap skate.* — **(1) 1890** *Dial. Notes* I. 75 Skate, . . . a worn-out horse. Plymouth, Mass. . . . Cape Cod and New Hampshire. **1916** WILSON *Somewhere* 24 As soon as they set foot to the ground have them skates of yours run away. **(2) 1896** *Typographical Jrnl.* IX. 6 The voracious and rapacious 'skate' . . . roars himself hoarse in advocacy of reform, gaining position and prominence, only to sell himself in the end to the best advantage. **1896** Cheap skate [see HORSE 6 b]. **1913** LONDON *Valley of*

Moon 84 Them cheap skates . . . with a couple of gallons of gasoline an' the price of a machine a-thinkin' they own the roads your folks an' my folks made.

Skate, *v. intr.* To glide over ice with skates. {1730–} — **1696** SEWALL *Diary* I. 439 Many Scholars go in the Afternoon to Scate on Freshpond. **1774** FITHIAN *Journal* I. 94 The Parson . . . & others are to come to Captain Turburvilles Mill-Pond to Skate before they go to the Ball. **1842** HAWTHORNE in S. Longfellow, *H. W. Longfellow* I. 450, I get up at sunrise to skate! **1889** DALY *Great Unknown* 12 You ought to see me skate.

Skating. {1723–} Attrib. with *cap, club,* etc. {1763–}

1856 *Porter's Spirit of Times* 27 Dec. 272/3 One, if not more, skating clubs could employ their time pleasantly, in the shallow waters up town. **1861** *Vanity Fair* 26 Jan. 41/2 How nice Mrs. Mendip looked to-day in her . . . chinchilla skating cap! **1864** *Hist. North-Western Soldiers' Fair* 81 [Donations include] Washington Skating Park Company, a lot of Skating Tickets. **1884** *Century Mag.* July 376/2 When are we of you most fond, Race-course, merry skating-pond? **1885** CRAWFORD *Amer. Politician* 87 The skating party . . . will be very select, you know. **1900** MUNN *Uncle Terry* 94 They all met at the old mill pond and had a skating frolic.

Skating rink. A rink for skating {1867–}, or for roller skating. — **1871** *Mich. Gen. Statutes* I. (1882) 1231 Any number of persons . . . desiring to form a corporation for the purpose of constructing, owning, and maintaining any skating park or rink . . . [may] associate for that purpose. **1885** [see OPERA HOUSE]. **1904** 'O. HENRY' *Roads of Destiny* 294 He was manager at different times of a skating-rink, a livery-stable [etc.].

+Skedaddle, *n.* A hurried flight or retreat; a scurry. {1870–} *colloq.* — **1861** *N.Y. Tribune* 26 Oct. 6/1 We may expect to witness such a grand *Skedaddle* of Secesh and its colored property as was never seen before. **1872** *Newton Kansan* 7 Nov. 4/1 A carousal, an epistle, a cowhide, a pistol, and a skedaddle.

Skedaddle, *v.* **+**intr. To retire hastily; to decamp; to absquatulate. *colloq.* {1867–}

It is not clear that the English dialectal use of this verb in the transitive, *i.e.*, 'to spill (milk, etc.)' {1862}, was the source of American usage during the Civil War.

1861 *N.Y. Tribune* 10 Aug. 5/5 No sooner did the traitors discover their approach than they 'skiddaddled,' (a phrase the Union boys up here apply to the good use the seceshers make of their legs in time of danger). **1862** *Rocky Mt. News* (Denver) 10 May (Th.), A gay bachelor, who has figured in Chicago for nearly a year, has skedaddled, absquatulated, vamosed, and cleared out. **1863** *Rio Abajo Press* 27 Jan. 2 The rebels skedaddled so speedily, that they left a great many dead on the field. **1884** HARTE *On Frontier* 239 The claim's played out, the partnership's played out, and the sooner we skedaddle out of this the better. **1904** GLASGOW *Deliverance* 45, I've upset the boy's cage of white mice and they're skedaddling about my legs. **1917** FREEMAN & KINGSLEY *Alabaster Box* 88 Now watch me skedaddle for that cream!

+Skedaddler, *n.* One who skedaddles. *colloq.* {1869} — **1862** *N.Y. Herald* 7 July 1/6 The skedaddlers, who brought the first news, exaggerated every thing they saw. **1863** *Boston Sun. Herald* 22 Feb. 3/2 Skedaddlers from the United States who become frightened at the prospect of a draft. **1872** *Vermont Bd. Agric. Rep.* I. 259 [In bee colonies] there are no skedaddlers, no jealousies.

+Skeesick(s). Also **skeezicks.** A good-for-nothing; a rascal. Often used playfully. *colloq.* — **1850** *Frontier Guardian* 2 Oct. (Th.), Though Kister, that skeezecks, with Hall at his back Should come again thieving. **1858** *Harper's Mag.* Dec. 138/2 He's the same little skeesick that told me to call for *Jones!* **1869** HARTE *Luck of Roaring Camp* 43 That 'ar d——d old skeesicks knows it. **1892** *Amer. Folk-Lore* V. Sept. 236 Skeezicks. . . . In my boyhood, in western New York, the word was applied to persons, usually children, who had been in mischief, and where the prank had caused sorrow to person or damage to property. **1917** McCUTCHEON *Green Fancy* 65 The old skeezicks that's been drivin' his car lately come down half-dressed.

Skeet, *v.* [Possibly a survival of *skeit, skete,* obsolete variant of SKATE *v.*] *[dial.]* **1.** *intr.* = SCOOT *v.* 2. **2.** *tr.* = SCOOT *v.* 2 b. — **(1) 1837** NEAL *Charcoal Sk.* (1838) 97 You must skeete, even if you have to cut high-dutchers with your irons loose. *a*1855 J. F. KELLY *Humors* 251, I skeeted down them steps into the Common to let off my corked up risibilities. **1921** GREER-PETRIE *Angeline at Seelbach* 3 Jest then, here come a . . . darky a skeetin' to-ward us. **(2) 1871** 'MARK TWAIN' *Sk., New & Old* 248 If you'll just give me a lift we'll skeet him into the hearse and meander along.

+Skeeter. Colloquial shortening of MOSQUITO. {1893, in Australia} Also *transf.* — **1852** STOWE *Uncle Tom* xx, Law, Miss Feely whip!—wouldn't kill a skeeter, her whippins. **1904** 'O. HENRY' *Heart of West* 112 Got up, the little skeeter, and licked Ross. **1914** FREEMAN *Copy-Cat* 92 Skeeters were biting me.

*Skein, *n.*[1] A quantity of thread, yarn, or match.

1653 *Boston Rec.* 31 Other things [were] drawne in to make this the more probable . . . as some farthing skeanes of thread. **1675** ANDROS in Easton *Indian War* 58, I have . . . despatcht this Sloope with . . . fifteen Musketts, and foure Skeynes of Match. **1768** *Boston Gazette* 9 May, The young Women of the Presbyterian Congregation . . . generously gave Mrs. Parsons the spinning of two Hundred and seventy Skeins of good Yarn. **1851** *Polly Peablossom* 37 He would mutter to himself . . . : 'Leghorn bonnet for Sal—12 skeins of flax thread.' **1912** *Sears, Roebuck & Co. Cat.* No. 124, 97 Golden Crown German Knitting Yarn. . . . Four skeins to the pound.

Skein.² {1837-} +A metal thimble protecting the spindle of a wooden axle. — **1847** *30th Congress 1 Sess.* H. R. Ex. Doc. No. 41, 517 The lower 'skeen' of the spindle was broken. **1881** *Rep. Indian Affairs* 402 Skeins, wagon, 2½ × 6½ inch.

****Skeleton.** attrib. +Designating land or water conveyances stripped down light. — **1846** *Spirit of Times* 18 April 90/2 This match was made to go in 'skeleton wagons.' **1858** HOLMES *Autocrat* 189 My own particular water-sulky, a 'skeleton' or 'shell' raceboat. **1867** 'LACKLAND' *Homespun* 181 A fly, a sulky, or a skeleton gig could be seen somewhere about the yard.

Sketch. {1668-} A short, light play or musical performance. {1861-} Also attrib. — **1789** W. DUNLAP *Darby's Return* (t.-p.), A comic sketch. As performed . . . for the benefit of Mr. Wignell. **1847** C. WHITE *Policy Players* (1874) t.-p., The Policy Players. An Ethiopian Sketch, in One Scene. **1887** *Courier-Journal* 25 Jan. 3/3 Everybody knows that Andy and Annie Hughes are among the cleverest of Irish sketch artists. **1915** [see ETHIOPIAN DRAMA].

Skewer. A long metal or wooden pin, used esp. to hold meat together while cooking. {1679-} — **1709** LAWSON *Carolina* 125 Roast a Bat on a Skewer, then pull the Skin off. *a***1846** *Quarter Race Ky.* 144 He took a long wooden skewer, and . . . thrust its point through a small piece of bear fat. **1914** E. STEWART *Lett. Woman Homesteader* 11 How much better that I were down in Denver, even at Mrs. Coney's, digging with a skewer into the corners seeking dirt which *might* be there.

+**Skew-gee,** *a.* Of a person: All mixed up; uncertain. *colloq.* — **1897** BRODHEAD *Bound in Shallows* 165 When folks gets all skew-gee brooding on things, why, it seems only right to straighten 'em out.

Ski, Skee. One of a pair of long strips of wood attached to the feet for gliding over snow. {1885-} — **1888** *St. Paul Globe* 22 Jan., County Superintendent Engstrom is visiting the country schools on skis. **1903** *N.Y. Tribune* 20 Dec., Lumbermen are buying skees for their convenience in crossing pathless tracts of snow.

Skid, *n.* {1609-10-}

1. A plank or piece of timber on which a heavy object is pushed or rolled. {1846-}

1800 TATHAM *Tobacco* 11 *Skids* are two or more strong saplings or other pieces of long timber, upon which timber, hogsheads, &c. are rolled. **1884** [see DRAG *n.* 1 b]. **1899** *N.Y. Journal* 16 June 4/2 Skids . . . are wide planks stretched between the curb and the buildings.

+**2.** *Lumbering.* One of several logs or timbers so laid that other logs can be slid over them, or piled upon them; esp., one of the transverse timbers forming a skid road.

1848 BARTLETT 304 *Skid*, a piece of light timber from ten to twenty feet in length, upon which heavier timber is rolled or slid from place to place. **1851** *Harper's Mag.* Sept. 518/1 New 'skids' are nicely peeled, by hewing off the bark smoothly, and plentifully as well as calculatingly laid along the road. **1880** *Lumberman's Gazette* 14 Jan., Some of the lumbermen have from 8,000,000 to 10,000,000 [logs] on the skids. **1893** *Atlantic Mo.* Feb. 194/2 Then the load itself, three logs tandem, coupled with chains, slid over the greased skids. **1905** *Forestry Bureau Bul.* No. 61, 46 *Skid*, a log or pole, commonly used in pairs, upon which logs are handled or piled (Gen.); or the log or pole laid transversely in a skid road (P[acific] C[oast] F[orest]).

comb. **1893** *Atlantic Mo.* Feb. 194/2 The 'skid-greaser,' . . . halting at every two steps to grease the worn skid over which the logs were about to pass.

Skid, *v.* {1674-}

+**1.** *tr.* To move (logs) on skids; to pile (logs) on skids. Also absol.

1878 *Lumberman's Gazette* 18 Dec. 426 Operators have been cutting and skidding for the past thirty or forty days. **1888** *Scribner's Mag.* Dec. 655/2 The logs are then 'skidded' by horses or oxen into skidways. **1897** *Ib.* Dec. 731/2 The trees themselves were trimmed, and then sawed into logs of desired lengths, and these were 'skidded' into piles. **1905** *Forestry Bureau Bul.* No. 61, 44 *Rigging*, the cables, blocks, and hooks used in skidding logs by steam power.

+**2.** (See quotation.)

1905 *Forestry Bureau. Bul.* No. 61, 46 *Skid*, . . . as applied to a road, to reenforce by placing logs or poles across it.

+**3.** *intr.* Of timber: To amount to a given quantity or number when piled up on the skids.

1902 WHITE *Blazed Trail* 49 That 'seventeen' white pine . . . won't skid over three hundred thousand.

+**Skidder.** (See quot. 1905.) — **1883** *Evangelist* (N.Y.) 8 March (Cent.), The skidders haul the logs to the pile. **1902** WHITE *Blazed Trail* 45 The sawyers, the swampers, the skidders, and the team men turned and put on their heavy blanket coats. **1905** *Forestry Bureau Bul.* No. 61, 47 *Skidder.* 1. One who skids logs. (Gen[eral].) 2. A steam engine, usually operating from a railroad track, which skids logs by means of a cable. (Gen.) Syn.: steam skidder. 3. The foreman of a crew which constructs skid roads. (P[acific] C[oast] F[orest]). *Ib.* 32 [4.] *Bummer,* a small truck with two low wheels and a long pole, used in skidding logs. . . . Syn.: drag cart, skidder.

+**Skiddy.** A type of carriage. — **1868** *N.Y. Herald* 22 July 1/2 Carriages, Second Hand Skiddy, Coupe and light Rockaways, eight leather top Buggies, all in good order.

+**Skid road.** *Lumbering.* A trail along which logs are dragged to the skidway; a road made with transverse skids. — **1880** *N.Y. Adirondack Survey 7th Rep.* 176 Advised that lumbermen had cut 'skid-roads' on which logs were drawn . . . , I changed the route. **1893** *Atlantic Mo.* Feb. 194/1 The procession [was] . . . advancing toward us down the skid road. **1900** *Bureau Statistics* (Treas. Dept.) *Summary* Nov. 1116 The Swampers . . . clear away the brush and other obstruction from around the tree, so that the logs can be gotten to the nearest skid road. **1905** *Forestry Bureau Bul.* No. 61, 45 *Saddle,* the depression cut in a transverse skid in a skid road to guide the logs which pass over it. (P[acific] C[oast] F[orest].)

+**Skidway.** *Lumbering.* (See quot. 1893.) — **1878** *Lumberman's Gazette* 6 April, These pole roads can be laid in the 'branch roads' direct to the skidways. **1893** *Scribner's Mag.* June 707/1 The skidway consists of two logs or timbers about ten feet apart, laid perpendicular to the log-road and well blocked up, upon which a tier of logs is placed ready to be loaded. **1902** WHITE *Blazed Trail* 80 The logs are piled in a gigantic skidway to await the spring freshets. **1906** *Churchman* 7 April 544 Other logs were piled up on a platform, called a 'skidway.'

****Skiff.** A small, light boat, as a light sailboat or rowboat.

1638 *Md. Council Proc.* I. 86, 2 Pinnaces & 1 Skiff . . . shall be pressed and fitted for the transporting and landing of the said Compa[ny]. *a***1649** WINTHROP *Hist.* I. 54 Three of the governor's servants were from this day to the 1 of December abroad in his skiff among the islands. **1773** FINLAY *Journal* 4 The Indians, one at the head and the other at the stern of these crank skifs, stood upright and set them up the stream with poles. **1821** NUTTALL *Travels Arkansa* 20 To-day I left Pittsburgh in a skiff, . . . in order to proceed down the Ohio. **1867** RICHARDSON *Beyond Miss.* 29 Crossing in a skiff I stood upon the soil of Kansas. **1881** INGERSOLL *Oyster-Industry* 248 *Skiff,* the peculiar, special oyster-boat used at Keyport, New Jersey. It is shaped like a small, shallow yawl. **1913** LONDON *Valley of Moon* 269 That night, long after dark, the little, half-decked skiff sailed up the Oakland Estuary.

comb. **1819** SCHOOLCRAFT *Mo. Lead Mines* 41 His boat . . . was built skiff-fashion, with a flat bottom.

Skift. Variant of SKIFF. {1783} — **1656** *Suffolk Deeds* I. 2 [We are] desired by Jno. Blackman to App[rize] a smale skifte taken vp adrift. **1816** U. BROWN *Journal* II. 222 Wm. Wells . . . prevails with me to go with him down the River 1¼ Miles to what he called a skift. **1885** *Century Mag.* Aug. 505/2 Visitors call it a skiff, natives a skift.

****Skillet.** Also †**skillite, skellet(t).**

****1.** A cooking utensil having a long handle. **a.** A small saucepan having three or four legs. *Obs.* **b.** A frying pan.

1630 in R. C. Winthrop *Life J. Winthrop* II. 38 Be sure to have ready at sea 2 or 3 skillets. **1644** *Essex Inst. Coll.* L. 333 One little skellett & one fryinge pann, 2s. 1d. **1692** *Conn. Probate Rec.* I. 463, I giue to Elizabeth Thomson . . . a coper skillite. **1740** *N.H. Probate Rec.* II. 809, I Give & Bequeath to my . . . wife . . . my Brass Skellet. **1810** *Inventory of Articles at Mount Vernon* 43 In the Kitchen . . . 3 Dutch Ovens . . . 2 Skillets [etc.]. **1853** 'P. PAXTON' *Yankee in Texas* 90 [His] small stock of furniture [included] . . . a skillet to bake his bread in. **1883** ZEIGLER & GROSSCUP *Alleghanies* 151 The small, round skillet with cover (Dutch oven they call it) was set over a bed of coals. **1917** MATHEWSON *Second Base Sloan* 73 [Nearby lay] an iron skillet with the handle broken off.

2. (See quot. 1891.)

1688 SEWALL *Letter-Book* I. 85, I have sent you . . . one Skillet of fine silver, . . . proper for a Goldsmith. **1891** *Cent.* 5671/1 Skillet, . . . in metal-working, a form into which the precious metals are run for sale and use as bullion, flatter than an ingot.

+**Skilly-pot, Skilliport, Skilpot.** [Du. *schildpad.*] (See quot. 1909.) — **1807** IRVING, etc. *Salmagundi* iv, Harsimus— . . . famous place for *skilly-pots;* Philadelphians call 'em tarrapins. **1853** COZZENS *Prismatics* 110 Here he was . . . royally feasted upon skilliports and snappers, . . . and other delicacies. **1909** WEBSTER 1968/5 *Skilpot,* . . . the red-bellied terrapin.

+**Skilts.** (See quot. 1845.) — **1845** JUDD *Margaret* I. 9 Her father and elder brother wore . . . a sort of brown tow trousers known . . . as skilts . . . reaching just below the knee, and very large, being a full half yard broad at the bottom. **1885** EGGLESTON in *Century Mag.* April 802/2 'Skilts' . . . came in time to take the form of the modern trousers.

****Skim.** +**1.** A thin sheet *of* ice. {1897, in Canada} **2.** (See quotation.) — **(1)** **1869** 'MARK TWAIN' *Innocents* 206 [Lake Tahoe] never has even a skim of ice upon its surface. **(2)** **1894** REMINGTON in *Harper's Mag.* Feb. 355 [They] can tell when and where he is going to strike as quickly as a boxer who knows by the 'skim on the eye' of his opponent.

+**Skimback.** **1.** The creek chub, *Semotilus atromaculatus.* **2.** = QUILLBACK. — **(1)** **1820** RAFINESQUE in *Western Rev.* II. 239 [The] Bigback Chubby, *Semotilus dorsalis,* . . . is found in the Kentucky, and several other rivers. Vulgar names, Big back Minny or Chub, Skimback, &c. **(2)** *Ib.* 301 Sailing Sucker. *Catostomus velifer.* . . . It has received the vulgar names of Sailor fish, Flying fish, and Skimback, because, when it swims, its large dorsal fin appears like a sail, and it often jumps or flies over the water for a short distance. **1888** GOODE *Amer. Fishes* 437 The 'Spear-fish,' 'Sail-fish,' 'Quill-back' or 'Skim-back' of the Ohio River is a fish often seen in the markets.

****Skimmer.**

****1.** A utensil for skimming liquids. Also *fig.*

1640 *Conn. Rec.* I. 448 An Inventory of the goods and Cattell of James Olmestead: . . . one skimer, on ladle [etc.]. **1717** *Mass. H. S. Coll.* 6 Ser.

V. 365 One apple roaster, 2 brass skimmers. **1814** J. TAYLOR *Arator* 205 Impurities rising to the top are taken off by a skimmer with holes in it, to let the cyder through. **1858** FLINT *Milch Cows* 223 A large white clamshell is very commonly used instead of a skimmer [for milk]. **1881** CHASE *Editor's Run in N. Mex.* 178 [One can] get knocked down or converted into a skimmer, with holes of 45 calibre, anywhere in [Leadville].

+**b.** (See quot. 1881.)

1881 INGERSOLL *Oyster-Industry* 248 Skimmer, flat, shallow pans of tin or zinc, with perforated bottom, in which the openers empty their measures of oysters, and where the liquor is allowed to drain away. **1884** *Nat. Museum Bul. No. 27*, 221 The oysters are thus run into a sheet-iron or zinc receptacle called the 'skimmer' . . . and are there cleaned of shell fragments.

+**2.** A form of the skim-colter plow.

1814 J. TAYLOR *Arator* 139 Thenceforth the tillage consists of a streak or furrow of a mere weeding plough called a skimmer, cutting with two wings twenty-four inches—drawn by one horse. **1854** in Commons, etc. *Doc. Hist.* I. 210 Three skimers ploughing Tobacco.

+**3.** = BLACK SKIMMER. {1826, in generic sense}

1838 AUDUBON *Ornith. Biog.* IV. 204 The hoarse cries of the Skimmers never ceased more than an hour.

+**4.** (See quot. 1891.)

1881 INGERSOLL *Oyster-Industry* 248 Skimmer, the *Cyprina islandica*, or big beach clam. (South shore of Long Island.) **1891** *Cent.* 5671/3 *Skimmer*, . . . one of several bivalves whose shells may be used to skim milk, etc.

+**Skimmer hat.** (See quot. 1830.) — **1830** WATSON *Philadelphia* 176 Other articles of female wear . . . [include] a 'skimmer hat,' . . . of a very small flat crown and big brim, not unlike the present Leghorn flats. **1840** A. M. MAXWELL *Run through U.S.* II. 18 Fellows called Tunkers . . . wear little white *skimmer* hats.

Skim-milk. *attrib.* +Weak; washed-out; second rate. — **1835–7** HALIBURTON *Clockmaker* 1 Ser. xxviii. 274 It was none o' your skim-milk parties, but superfine uppercrust real jam. *a***1845** T. KIRKMAN *Jones's Fight* 30 (Th.), Bimeby a sort of skim-milk looking feller cum and tuck a seat rite close by her. **1891** RYAN *Pagan* 82 He ain't one o' yer skim-milk, dauncy ones. He's as stout as a young bull.

Skimming dish. {1688–} +A boat or yacht of light draft. *colloq.* — **1884** in *Outing* VIII. 58/1 These [light-draught boats] are the 'skimming-dish,' the 'pumpkin-seed' and the 'flat-iron' models. **1897** *Ib.* XXX. 337/1 The boats entering this year's races will probably be all of one general type as to hull-saucers and skimming-dishes.

* **Skin,** *n.*

* **1.** An animal's hide or pelt, often used as a garment, rug, etc.

1621 'MOURT' *Relation* 114 We would not offer them any such iniury, though it would gaine vs all the skins in the Countrey. **1675** in Easton *Indian War* 85 Now is the vsual Tyme of our Hunting, and to gett a litle Provision and some Skins for Cloathing. **1708** *N.C. Col. Rec.* I. 691 Another branch of the Trade of the Country is the Indian Trade for skins & furrs. **1772** in *Travels Amer. Col.* 508 A Blanket which is commonly sold for six pound of drest skins they would sell for a buck skin in the Hair. **1833** WYETH *Oregon* 84 The white trader barters a tawdry bauble of a few cents' value, for a skin worth fifty of it. **1866** *Rep. Indian Affairs* 83 The Indians upon this reservation . . . dwell in tents built of skins and mats. **1911** *Rep. Fisheries 1908* 315/2 The walrus, eared seals, and earless seals . . . are captured for their oil, skins, and flesh.

+**2.** In miscellaneous senses.

a. A whip. **b.** A medicine bag. **c.** *College slang.* Cribbing. (Cf. SKIN *v.* 1.) **d.** = SHEEPSKIN 2. **e.** Short for SKIN GAME.

(a) **1845** SIMMS *Wigwam & Cabin* 2 Ser. 91 Only you be quiet; or we'll have to give you the skin. (b) **1847** LANMAN *Summer in Wilderness* 106 By breathing into the nostrils of the skin, he imparts to it a particular charm. (c) **1855** in E. C. Porter *Songs of Yale* (1860) 40 'Twas plenty of skin with a good deal of Bohn. (d) **1860** *Ib.* 69 Oh, worthless sheep, thy fleece all golden Might catch a foolish Jason's eyes, But never one who had beholden, Though from afar, the 'skin' we prize. (e) **1899** TARKINGTON *Gentleman from Ind.* vii, We been running no skin. . . . You gotter prove it was a skin.

3. *attrib.* and *comb.* **a.** Designating persons or groups of persons who hunt for or handle hides.

See also SKIN-HUNTER.

1774 in Chalkley *Scotch-Irish Settlement Va.* I. 180 Charles Beard to be bound . . . to learn trade of breechers makers and skin dressers. **1801** HAWKINS *Letters* 379 Your traders . . . are skin catchers and have more regard for their own interests than to yours. **1837** IRVING *Bonneville* I. 92 These, though generally included in the generic name of free trappers, have the more specific title of skin trappers. **1841** COOPER *Deerslayer* i, Am I a man like to let any sneaking, crawling, skin-trader get the better of me?

b. Designating things made wholly or partially of skins.

See also SKIN CANOE, SKIN LODGE.

1804 CLARK in *Lewis & C. Exped.* I. (1904) 87 The Indians pass this [the Platte] river in Skin Boats which is flat and will not turn over. **1837** BIRD *Nick* II. 115 Show me a bit of skin-rope for halters. **1870** 'O. OPTIC' *Field & Forest* 287, I had dressed myself in my best clothes, discarding forever my hunting frock and skin cap. **1881** *Rep. Indian Affairs* 40

Their descendants live, not in bark huts, or skin 'tipi,' but in comfortable log-houses.

+**c.** In special combinations.

Skin balloon, (see quotation); *s. faro*, a skin game at faro; *s. government*, (see quotation); *s. trade*, the trade in animals' skins.

1895 *Outing* XXVI. 399/1 The balloon is a 'skin balloon' made of silk. **1882** MCCABE *New York* 545 'Skin faro,' the only game played here, offers no chance whatever to the player. **1900** *Congress. Rec.* 25 Jan. 1165/2 It is not what some people have called 'skin' government—government according to the color of the skin. **1772** ROMANS in P. L. Phillips *Notes on B. Romans* 120 Mobile will . . . become the only Mart, for the Skin Trade from the Chactaw, Chickesaw, and Upper Creek Nations.

* **Skin,** *v.*

+**1.** *tr.* To crib or receive help in reciting (a lesson) or taking (an examination); to plagiarize. Also absol. and as *vbl. n.* *slang.*

1835 TODD *Student's Manual* 115 Should you allow yourself to think of going into the recitation-room, and there trust to 'skinning,' as it is called in some colleges. **1837** *Yale Lit. Mag.* II. 138 A student is said to *skin* a problem, when he places the most implicit faith in the correctness of his neighbor's solution of it. **1854** in E. C. Porter *Songs of Yale* (1860) 63 But now that last Biennial's past, I 'skinned' and 'fizzled' through. **1871** BAGG *At Yale* 632 Whether the Williams men were too honest or too stupid, or too closely watched, to skin successfully, does not appear.

+**b.** To help (another) *through* a recitation or examination.

1871 BAGG *At Yale* 641 A high-stand man who was well up on mathematics, . . . in consideration of $10, was to attempt to 'skin him through' his 'Puckle' Annual.

2. To fleece (a person) of his money; to swindle {1851–}; +to get the better of (another).

1839 BRIGGS *H. Franco* II. 76, I wish I may be blown into a gin shop if I warnt skinned clean. **1848** E. BRYANT *California* xxv. 325 Between the government of Mexico and the traders on the coast, California has been literally *skinned*. **1873** *Winfield* (Kan.) *Courier* 15 Feb. 1/5 Schenck used to skin Ulysses alive, and rather weaned him from the game. **1885** *South Fla. Sentinel* (Orlando) 29 April 3/5 [On] pay day . . . he immediately starts a gambling shop and keeps it open till he has skinned every possible victim. **1905** 'O. HENRY' *Trimmed Lamp* 62 Don't try to skin me, because I know all about the number of gallons of H_2O in the Croton reservoir. **1923** 'BOWER' *Parowan Bonanza* 246 There's nothing . . . like the friendship game to skin a man with.

+**b.** To obtain (money or goods) by a swindle.

1843 STEPHENS *High Life N.Y.* I. 241 Miss Josephine Burgess was a setting in her back shop a thinking over . . . the dollars and cents she'd skinned out of the gal's wages. **1889** 'MARK TWAIN' *Conn. Yankee* 335 [The] appropriation was . . . the River and Harbor Bill of that government for . . . the chance it afforded for skinning the surplus.

+**3.** To open or keep open (one's) eyes. *colloq.* {1887–}

1846 W. G. STEWART *Altowan* I. 167, I thought Parfin had kept his eyes skinned to wear his scalp so long in the Indian country. **1865** *N.Y. Herald* (F. and H.), Keep a padlock on yer mouth and skin yer weather eye. **1898** FREDERIC *Deserter* 69 That German fellow . . . kept them big eyes of his skinned for me all day long.

+**4.** To exhaust the strength of (land) or the ore of (a mine). Also *vbl. n.* {1867, 'to exhaust (a stream) by excessive fishing'}

1850 *Cultivator* ns. VII. 369 Many of the original settlers . . . moved west . . . to run another round of 'skinning' and starving. **1872** *Vermont Bd. Agric. Rep.* I. 371 The condition is all that can be taken out by what is called 'skinning' the land. **1895** *Forum* Sept. 8 [The poor whites] are rapidly learning to renovate the soil which had been 'skinned' in the days of slavery. **1907** WHITE *Arizona Nights* 164 For a while they tried gold washing, but I had the only pocket—and that was about skinned.

5. +**a.** To plow merely the surface of (the ground).

1861 *Ill. Agric. Soc. Trans.* IV. 373 If he has not a good team he will find himself skinning the ground or resting his animals.

+**b.** To strip (land) of its vegetation. Also *ppl. a.*

1907 *N.Y. Ev. Post* (s.-w. ed.) 18 July 6 Lands in the watershed of the Mohawk range cost a dollar an acre for 'skinned' wood-lots. **1912** MATHEWSON *Pitching* 218 The diamond at Marlin is skinned—that is, made of dirt, although it is billed as a grass infield.

+**6.** **a.** With *out:* To display or spread (a card hand).

1873 MILLER *Amongst Modocs* 44 Four aces! and what else? Skin 'em out, skin 'em out! **1884** CARLETON *Thompson St. Poker Club* (1889) 42 Mr. Williams proudly skinned out three jacks and a pair of kings.

+**b.** To look at one's own (cards) by opening them slightly.

1884 CARLETON in Wilder *Wit & Humor* VI. 1141 Mr. Williams . . . skinned his cards, . . . and said he would 'Jess—jess call.' **1895** *Cornhill Mag.* Aug. 174 Each man skinned his cards and tried his hardest to look disappointed. **1896** ADE *Artie* 11 He had to . . . skin his cards three or four times.

+**c.** To peel off (a note) from a roll of money.

1903 'O. HENRY' *Cabbages & Kings* 84 Henry skinned a twenty off his roll. **1908** LORIMER *J. Spurlock* 294 The Major skinned a hundred-dollar bill from his roll.

+7. To beat (a person or thing) all hollow; to eclipse; to outdo. *colloq.*

1901 'O. HENRY' *Cabbages & Kings* 47, I guess you've got us skinned on the animal and vegetation question. **1911** QUICK *Yellowstone Nights* 110 Purty good little places, . . . but the home place skins 'em all. **1913** LONDON *Valley of Moon* 309 The Porchugeeze has got us skinned a mile.

8. +**a.** *intr.* To shin or climb *up* something.

1871 'MARK TWAIN' in *Galaxy* Jan. 156/1 The beaver skun up a tree. **1916** WILSON *Somewhere* 312, I guess you can see plain enough now he ain't no rabbit, the way he skinned up that tree.

+**b.** To abscond; to make off. Often with *out.*

1873 *Winfield* (Kan.) *Courier* 27 May 3/1 We are under special obligations to a certain red-headed gentleman (?) of our acquaintance for pompously sauntering into our office, . . . and then skinning out for the post office without even telling us he would come again. **1891** *Fur, Fin, & Feather* 168/1 You skin away from this humstid. **1907** 'O. HENRY' *Roads of Destiny* 84, I threw him a dollar and skinned for the steamer. **1913** LONDON *Valley of Moon* 324 When it heard me comin' it skinned out most likely.

+**c.** To slip *through;* to get by without much to spare.

1902 LORIMER *Lett. Merchant* 141, I would feel a good deal happier . . . if you would make a downright failure or a clean-cut success once in a while, instead of always just skinning through this way. **1920** CAMP *Football without a Coach* 57 The best a runner can hope for is a chance to skin through that opening before it ceases to exist.

9. In phrases. +**a.** *To ʼskin the cat*, to raise the feet and legs between the hands while hanging on a bar, thence putting them over the bar and drawing the body up over the bar: (see also quot. 1893). Also fig.

1845 JUDD *Margaret* II. 199 The boys . . . [were] snapping-the-whip, skinning-the-cat, racing round the Meeting-house, or what not. **1873** [see HOGCHAIN]. **1893** *Amer. Folk-Lore* VI. 143 A boy hangs by the hands from a trapeze, and passes his legs through the circle formed by the wooden rod and the upper part of his body. Boys commonly 'skin the cat' both forwards and backwards. **1905** *N.Y. Ev. Post* 14 Oct., We have learned how to hide behind the back log of 'environment' or to 'skin the cat' in morality on the score of 'heredity.'

+**b.** *To skin mules*, to drive a team of mules. Cf. MULE-SKINNER 1.

1923 *Dialect Notes* V. 221 John's a-skinnin' mules now. [McDonald Co., Mo.]. **1924** *Scribner's Mag.* Dec. 645/1, I've skun mules in this man's army goin' on eleven years.

Skin beetle. (See quotation.) — **1862** *Rep. Comm. Patents 1861: Agric.* 594 Intermediate between the carnivorous *coleoptera*, that feed upon other insects, and the wood-boring or vegetable-eating tribes, are several large families . . . [called] 'burying beetles,' 'skin beetles,' 'bone beetles,' &c., because they are chiefly found in decomposed animal matter.

+**Skin canoe.** A canoe made of skins stretched over a frame. — **1808** PIKE *Sources Miss.* 155 [We] nearly compleated the frame of a skin Canoe. **1814** BRACKENRIDGE *Views La.* 231 These skin canoes are stretched over the red willow. **1870** *Amer. Naturalist* IV. 597 Let us take a small skin canoe and spend a day on the river.

+**Skin game.** A gambling game in which the players have little or no chance of winning against the bank or table; a fraudulent game. Also attrib. and transf. — **1868** M. H. SMITH *Sunshine & Shadow* 405 The square game . . . is played only by gentlemen, and in first-class houses; . . . the skin game . . . is played in all the dens and chambers, and in the thousand low hells of New York. **1895** CHAMBLISS *Diary* 169 Mr. Garrett made up his mind that he would rid San Francisco of one 'skin game' at least. **1900** GARLAND *Eagle's Heart* 239 We've been overrun with 'rollers' and 'skin-game' men. **1904** W. H. SMITH *Promoters* 98 We built the bridges finally, of course we did, for we weren't really working a skin game.

+**Skin-hunter.** One who hunts wild animals for their hides. — **1886** ROOSEVELT in *Outing* March 611 The brutal skin-hunters and meat-butchers of the woods and prairies have done their work. **1897** HOUGH *Story of Cowboy* 331 Hunter and trapper, skin hunter, gambler . . . —all mingled in an eddy and boil of tumultuous, vigorous life.

*Skink. (See BLUE-TAILED a.)

+**Skin lodge.** An Indian lodge made by stretching skins over a framework. — **1823** JAMES *Exped.* I. 187 The travelling huts, or as they are usually denominated, skin lodges, are neatly folded up, and suspended to the pack-saddle of the horse. **1832** CATLIN *Indians* I. 43 They then sometimes erect their skin lodges amongst the timber, and dwell in them during the winter months. **1885** *Rep. Indian Affairs* 35 In 1879 not a family lived . . . in anything, but a canvas or skin lodge.

*Skinner.

+**1.** During the Revolutionary War, a member of a marauding gang usually roaming in territory between the British and American lines in Westchester County, New York, and professing allegiance to the American cause. Now hist.

1821 COOPER *Spy* xviii, The skinner . . . had been left alone by . . . his gang. **1857** [see COWBOY 1].

+**2.** In miscellaneous senses.

a. One who skins a lesson. (Cf. SKIN *v.* 1.) **b.** A type of knife suitable for skinning an animal. **c.** ? A plow that breaks only the surface of land. **d.** Short for MULE-SKINNER (sense 1).

(a) **1871** BAGG *At Yale* 632 A desperate skinner, going up to recite an examination of which he knew nothing, has laid upon a lower edge of his instructor's desk a page or more of mathematical formulæ. (b) **1872** *Amer. Naturalist* VI. 223 The specimen could have been used as a knife, or 'skinner,' although now its edge is too irregular and dull for skinning. (c) **1873** *Newton Kansan* 24 April 3/3 [As] the breaking season is near at hand . . . farmers . . . should . . . buy a Skinner. (d) **1924** *Scribner's Mag.* Dec. 645/1 The skinner with the longest words travels the fastest.

Skinning knife. A knife designed for skinning an animal. {1884} — **1859** in F. Hall *Hist. Colorado* II. 521 Dug and panned to-day until my belt knife was worn out; so will have to quit or use my skinning knife. **1925** TILGHMAN *Dugout* 56 Sharpening his big skinning knife, . . . [he] cut his finger.

*Skip, *n.* +**1.** *Railroad.* A section of the track or grading left temporarily unfinished. +**2.** An animal of an inferior grade. — (1) **1868** *Ore. State Jrnl.* 21 Nov. 2/5 The grading has been completed from East Portland to Lake Labish with the exception of two or three short 'skips.' *Ib.* 5 Dec. 2/5 A section of about seventy miles [has been] made ready for the ties, excepting some short skips of trussel and rock work. (2) **1892** *Courier-Journal* 2 Oct. 21/6 Pigs and skips $4.25 @ 5.05. **1911** [see CANNER 2].

*Skip, *v.*

*1. *intr.* To leave hurriedly; to make an escape. *colloq.* 'Now U.S.' (O.E.D.).

1715 M. MINOR *Diary* (1915) 127 Desember . . . 27 Thomas Brumlees time was out, . . . 29 Brumly skipt. **1887** STOCKTON *Hundredth Man* xii, If either of 'em had skipped from under, all I had to do was to wash my hands of the whole business. **1892** HOWELLS *Quality of Mercy* 13 All of them had used others' money in speculation . . . and then had skipped, as the newspapers said. **1912** NICHOLSON *Hoosier Chron.* 143 We've had a bully day or two, but dad has skipped.

+**b.** Often *to skip out* (or *off*).

1865 GRIGSBY *Smoked Yank* (1891) 188 Thirteen [paroled men] . . . skipped out to-day. **1877** BEARD *K.K.K. Sketches* 78 Ghostly placards . . . were posted on their doors, commanding them to 'skip out' . . . , or expect the utmost vengeance of the Order. **1897** 'THANET' *Missionary Sheriff* 207 Parole of honor you won't skip off? **1922** PARRISH *Case & Girl* 123 He skipped out mighty sudden.

+**2.** *tr.* To leave (a place) hurriedly.

1882 BAILLIE-GROHMAN *Camps in Rockies* 18 'Skipping' three years ago his Iowa home, . . . he came West. **1885** *Santa Fé Wkly. New Mexican* 10 Sept. 4/7 George Handley, a laundryman at Albuquerque, has skipped the town. **1901** HARRIGAN *Mulligans* 25, I'm skipping the town.

+**3.** *To skip* (one's) *bail*, to run away while free on bail. Cf. JUMP *v.* 2 b.

1900 *Congress. Rec.* 5 Feb. 1521/2, I should like the gentleman to know that one lot of those ballot-box stuffers are in jail and every one of the others has skipped his bail.

*Skipjack.

1. Any of various fishes that skip or jump above the surface of the water. {1703-}

1791 W. BARTRAM *Travels* 67 The coasts, sounds, and inlets environing these islands, abound with . . . Skate, Skipjack [etc.]. **1839** STORER *Mass. Fishes* 49 *Pelamys sarda.* . . . The Skip Jack. This species is by fishermen incorrectly called 'Bonito.' **1842** *Nat. Hist. N.Y., Zoology* IV. 131 The Blue-fish, or, as it is sometimes called, the Horse Mackerel, Green-fish in Virginia, and Skip-jack in Carolina, is common . . . from May to Oct. **1849** KINGSLEY *Diary* 75 Some of the fellows caught a fish called skipjack to day which weighed some 6 lbs. **1882** [see JACK *n.*¹ 8 b]. **1882** *Nat. Museum Bul.* No. 16, 266 *Clupea chrysochloris*, Ohio Shad; Skipjack. **1884** GOODE, etc. *Fisheries* I. 324 The Jurel *Caranx pisquetus*. This fish [is known] . . . along the Florida coast as 'Jack-fish' and 'Skipjack.' *Ib.* 594 The Inland Alewife or Skipjack . . . is abundant throughout the Mississippi Valley in all the larger streams. **1911** *Rep. Fisheries 1908* 316/1 *Skipjack*, a local name applied to the skipper (*Scombresox saurus*) along the Atlantic and Gulf coasts; . . . to the runner (*Elagatis bipinnulatus*) about Key West; to the butterfly (*Poronotus triacanthus*) about Cape Cod; to the cutlass-fish (*Trichiurus lepturus*); . . . and to the leather jacket (*Oligoplites saurus*) on the Atlantic coast.

+**2.** A kind of boat.

1882 *Century Mag.* July 359/2 The skip-jack is another curious and by no means ungainly craft, evolved out of the sharpie by adding to the latter a rising floor. **1885** *Ib.* Aug. 510/1 Were the boats a little larger, like . . . the cat-boat that men call 'skip-jack,' . . . this fine effect would be lost. **1886** *Outing* April 58/1 There is the skip-jack, a much superior model for sailing.

+**Skip mackerel.** (See quotations.) — **1884** GOODE, etc. *Fisheries* I. 433 The Bluefish.—*Pomatomus saltatrix.* . . . About New York they are called 'Skip Mackerel.' **1911** *Rep. Fisheries 1908* 316/1 *Skipmackerel*, a name applied to the bluefish about New York.

+**Skippaug.** [Cf. SCUPPAUG.] (See quotations.) — **1842** *Nat. Hist. N.Y., Zoology* IV. 260 The Mossbonker. *Alosa menhaden.* . . . At the east end of the island, they are called *Skippaugs* or *Bunkers.* **1848** BARTLETT 222 *Menhaden*, . . . a fish of the herring kind. . . . In New York, [they are called] Mossbonkers and Skippaugs. **1849** D. WEBSTER *Private Corr.*

II. 337, [I] caught some fish, namely, tautog and skippog, the same, I suppose, as are called 'Porgee' in New York.

∗ **Skipper.**[1] The master or captain of a ship. — **1650** WILLIAMS *Letters* (1874) 197 A Dutchman skipper, Lorence, now following fishing here about us. **1762** *Md. Hist. Mag.* XVIII. 167 Mr. Mathew Travers, . . . Skipper of a Bay Schooner. . . was drowned. **1861** *Harper's Mag.* March 457/1 The crew of a [Newfoundland] 'banker' is generally composed of twelve men, including the 'skipper' or captain. **1914** STEELE *Storm* 209, I knew him for Charlie Dyer, skipper of that *Mary Sedgwick* that had gone to pieces on the Plymouth shore.

∗ **Skipper.**[2] One of various insects.

+**1.** A snapping beetle. Also with defining term.
1792 BELKNAP *Hist. New-Hampshire* III. 181 Skipper, *Elater oculatus.* **1813** BINGLEY *Animal Biog.* (ed. 4) III. 143 The Night-Shining Skipper. In the savannas of most of the warmer parts of America, these insects are to be seen in great abundance.

2. Any maggot infesting meat or cheese, as the worm of the cheese fly, *Piophila casei.* {1882-, *dial.*} Also attrib.
1805 PARKINSON *Tour* 221 The reason why [Americans] . . . smoke their bacon and fish, is, that there are many sorts of reptiles that would absolutely destroy it, were it not for the smoke, particularly what is called the skippers, or salt-worm. **1819** *Amer. Farmer* I. 126/3 We lost at least one third of our ham meat, by the skippers. **1859** *Ill. Agric. Soc. Trans.* IV. 100 The skipper fly . . . has been a pest to all cheese makers of Illinois. **1890** *Harper's Mag.* Feb. 444/2 It is like dislodging skippers from cheese with artillery.

3. Any of numerous small, butterflylike, lepidopterous insects of the family Hesperiidae. {1817-}
1850 *New Eng. Farmer* II. 12 That class of uneasy butterflies called *Skippers*, [are] so named from a singular habit they have acquired of jerking their wings, and thereby producing an undulating flight. **1867** *Amer. Naturalist* I. 221 The dun-colored Skippers (*Hesperia*) abound towards the middle of [June]. **1884** *Boston Jrnl.* 11 Oct. 2/4 [Insects] killed by the electric lights in the Capitol at Washington . . . [include] whirligigs, skippers, horned midgets.

4. A water skipper.
1854 EMMONS *Agric. N.Y.* V. 167 *Hydrometridae.* . . . Individuals of this family, . . . from their mode of progression over the surface of the water, have been called skippers.

+**Skipple.** [Du. *schepel.*] =SCHEPEL. *Obs.* Also attrib. (In quot. 1775 the word seems to be misused.) — **1678** *New Castle Court Rec.* 208 Captn. Cantwell has Received one Cowe and twenty skipple of wheat. **1701** WOLLEY *Journal N.Y.* 33 The Price of Provisions: Long-Island wheat three shillings a Skipple (a Skipple being three parts of a bushel). **1775** ADAIR *Indians* 362 A gentleman who had purchased a large quantity of it [hickory nuts], told me that a skippel, or three bushels, cost him only nine shillings of New York currency. **1784** W. WALTON *Narr. Captivity B. Gilbert* 62 This Family raised this Summer about one Hundred Skipple of Indian Corn. **1901** *Notes & Q.* 9 Ser. VIII. 283/2 The Skipple-measure or Short Bushel of New England.

+**Skipple stone.** A stone carried as a counterbalance to a load of grain measuring a skipple. *Obs.* — **1796** *Aurora* (Phila.) 13 Sept., Not far from Albany, among the Dutch A skipple-stone is used to balance weight On horse-back borne.

+**Skip straight.** (See quotation.) — **1887** KELLER *Draw Poker* 17 Efforts have been made to introduce into the game of Draw Poker what is known as the 'skip' straight—a sequence of alternate cards.

Skip-to-my-Lou. (See quotation.) — **1887** *Courier-Journal* 6 Feb. 14/5 The young people were to be engaged in playing 'Skiptummerlou,' which being interpreted means 'Skip-to-My-Lou,' a game strangely like a quadrille.

∗ **Skirmish,** *v.* +*intr.* To scurry or scout (*around*). — **1864** [see MOURNERS' BENCH]. **1893** HOLLEY *Samantha at World's Fair* 608 The males, from creation down, have been left free to skirmish round and get a livin' for themselves. **1907** WHITE *Arizona Nights* 17 We skirmished around and found a condemned army pack saddle with aparejos.

∗ **Skirret.** A species of water parsnip, *Sium sisarum.* — **1737** BRICKELL *N. Carolina* 18 The Garden Roots that thrive here are Parsnips, Carrots, Skirrets, [etc.]. **1775** ROMANS *Nat. Hist. Florida* 115 In the gardens we find . . . skirrets, leaks, scallions and other roots.

∗ **Skirt.**

∗**1. a.** An underskirt. **b.** The lower part of a woman's dress; an outer garment for women or girls covering the body from the waist down.
1644 *Essex Probate Rec.* I. 45 Too Diaper Napkins & one linnen skirt for a shift. **1857** M. J. HOLMES *Meadow-Brook* xxix, She had just time to adjust her skirts gracefully when there stood before her . . . the servant. **1913** LONDON *Valley of Moon* 72 Saxon completed her dressing, . . . stepping upon a chair so as to glimpse critically in the small wall-mirror the hang of her ready-made linen skirt.

+**2.** *To clear one's* (or *another's*) *skirts,* to avoid any blame; to absolve (someone) from taint of suspicion; to wash one's hands.
1854 S. SMITH *Down East* 27 Whether this man is to be convicted or not, I clear my skirts. **1898** WESTCOTT *D. Harum* 168 [He] cal'lated to clear his own skirts anyway. *a***1902** *N.Y. Tribune* (Clapin), You [do not] clear

the skirts of Gen. Grant and of your party, for the basest treachery to the people.

3. Attrib. and comb. with *clasp, elevator, supporter, wire.*
1864 *Hist. North-Western Soldiers' Fair* 130 [Donations include] 1 Goddess of Liberty skirt supporter, corset and shoulder brace. **1867** *Rep. Comm. Patents 1866* II. 805 Instrument for Puncturing Fabrics and Introducing Flat Skirt Wire Therein. **1876** KNIGHT 2196/2 Ingenuity is exerted in—Skirt-clasps. Skirt-elevators.

Skitter, *v.*

1. *intr.* To move or run lightly; to skim *along* a surface. {1875-}
1845 JUDD *Margaret* I. 175 On they went [on their sleds], skittering, bowling, sluice-like, wave-like. **1858** COOKE *Somebody's Neighbors* 15, I was . . . lyin' in my berth, hearin' the rats and mice . . . skitter over the floor. **1885** ROOSEVELT *Hunting Trips* 56 Some kinds of ducks . . . strike the water with their tails first, and skitter along the surface for a few feet before settling down. **1901** WHITE *Claim Jumpers* 117 The wind . . . skittered across cold-looking little pools of water.

+**2.** *tr.* To cause (an object) to skim or skip along a surface. Also *ppl. a.* and *vbl. n.*
1883 *Century Mag.* July 383/2 The angler, standing in the bow, 'skitters' or skips the spoon or bait over the surface. *a***1888** in Goode *Amer. Fishes* 37 When taken with a skittered minnow or bright fly on a light rod, we do not hesitate to class as a game fish the White Perch. **1903** WHITE *Forest* 246 Does yon trout to-day fancy the skittering of his food, or the withdrawal in three jerks?

+**b.** To make (an object) skim or sail through the air.
1907 *Harper's Mag.* Feb. 460 The younger boy skittered rocks at a chicken-hawk.

Skiver, *n.* **1.** (See quot. 1875.) {1800-} **2.** A tool or machine for skiving or cutting leather. — (1) **1820** *Columbian Centinel* 1 Jan. 4/2 For sale . . . 12 doz. red Skivers, 16 dozen red Roans. **1875** KNIGHT 1274/2 *Skiver,* a thin split of leather used for hat-linings, etc. **1885** *Harper's Mag.* Jan. 278/2 Their famous Southdown sheep furnish us with our 'skivers.' (2) **1850** *Rep. Comm. Patents 1849* 313, I claim . . . the application of a gauge or gauges to a skiver. **1902** *Boston Sun. Globe* 30 Nov. 26/5 The modern machinery comprises the molder, the skiver, of which there are three or four different kinds, the roller [etc.].

+**Skiver,** *v. intr.* (See quotation.) — *a***1891** *Shore Birds* 33 (Cent.), At the report of a gun the frightened flock will dart about in terror, *skiver,* as it is technically called.

+**Skoke,**[1] **Scoke.** [Massachuset *m'skok* 'that which is red.'] =POKEWEED or POKE *n.*[3] 1. Also attrib. — **1778** CARVER *Travels* 517 Gargit or Skoke is a large kind of weed, the leaves of which are about six inches long. **1796** MORSE *Univ. Geog.* I. 189 The following have been employed for medicinal purposes [in New Eng.]. , . . Mouse ear, . . . Gargit, or Skoke [etc.]. **1846** WHITCHER *Bedott P.* v. 50 She said he must take skoke berries and rum right off. **1850** *Knickerb.* XXXVI. 335 Those careless lines of mine were . . . indited in the red juice of the scoke, or poke-berry. **1896** *Garden & Forest* IX. 292/2 Skoke, . . . (*Phytolacca decandra*).

+**Skoke.**[2] Also **skoka.** [Probably short for Delaware *s'kakawunsh.*] =SKUNKWEED 1 a. — **1896** *Garden & Forest* IX. 292/2 Skoke, . . . *Symplocarcus fœtidus.* . . . Skoka is a variant of the name. **1910** HODGE, etc. *Amer. Indians* II. 595/1 *Skoka,* a name among herbalists for the skunkcabbage.

+**Skookum,** *n.* and *a.* [Chinook jargon 'powerful.'] **1.** *n.* Evil spirits; strong drink. **2.** *adj.* Strong. — (1) **1844** LEE & FROST *Oregon* 236 The doctors affirmed that they had been filled with skokoms. (2) *Ib.* 790/2 Quarts to the horses and quarts to the Siwashes and a skookum peck of trouble all round.

+**Skookum house.** *N.W.* A jail; a place of detention. — **1885** *Century Mag.* April 842 [An Indian] had recently been arrested by the agent, put in the 'skookum-house' (jail), and fined sixty dollars for having two wives. **1894** WISTER in *Harper's Mag.* Sept. 514/1 Maybe he catch E-gante, maybe put him in skookum-house (prison)? **1904** 'O. HENRY' *Whirligigs* 232 The skookum house for yours!

+**Skooner.** (See SCHOONER.)

+**Skouk.** [Origin uncertain; possibly the same word as SKOKE[1] or SKOKE[2]: note the parallel relationship between POKE *n.*[4] and POKE *n.*[3]] =POKE *n.*[4] 1. — **1794** MORSE *Amer. Geog.* 165 Green Bittern. Poke. Skouk. *Ardea virescens.* **1832** WILLIAMSON *Maine* I. 145 The Skouk is as large bodied as a partridge . . . and is vulgarly called a 'shite-poke.'

Skulking, *a.* Of an Indian or a group of Indians: Lurking about or hiding. {1619-, in general sense} — **1704** *Boston News-Letter* 22 May 1/2 Letters . . . acquaint us of some more damaging done by the Sculking Adversary. **1708** *Ib.* 14 June 2/2 On Monday last two men . . . were kill'd by the Sculking Indians. **1757** *Lett. to Washington* II. 122 The Skulking Party that has infested the Neighbourhood . . . may be thought . . . to be but a few. **1792** *Affecting Hist. F. Manheim* 13 The Indians . . . generally appeared in small skulking parties, committing great devastations.

Skullcap. {1682-} **a.** Any plant of the genus *Scutellaria,* in which the calyx resembles a helmet. {1760-} Also attrib. (See also MAD-DOG SKULLCAP.) +**b.** The marsh speedwell, *Veronica scutellata.* Also attrib.
1791 MUHLENBERG *Index Florae* 173 *Scutellaria,* Skull-cap. **1817-8** EATON *Botany* (1822) 508 *Veronica scutellata,* scull-cap speedwell. **1819**

Plough Boy I. 62 The scull-cap plant . . . is said to be an effectual remedy in cases of hydrophobia. **1821** *Mass. H. S. Coll.* 2 Ser. IX. 157 Indigenous in the township of Middlebury [Vt. is] . . . *Veronica scutellata*, Scull-cap, speedwell. **1869** FULLER *Flower Gatherers* 232 Grandmama calls it 'Skull-cap,' and says it is excellent for colds and fevers. **1915** ARMSTRONG & THORNBER *Western Wild Flowers* 446 Skullcap. *Scutellaria angustifolia.* . . . The calyx is curiously shaped and after the flower drops off resembles a tiny green bonnet.

+Skul(l)duggery. =SCULLDUGGERY. — *a*1877 in Bartlett 397 The Missourians . . . have two words to express the idea of underhand plotting; to wit, 'skullduggery' and 'chenanigan.' **1877** BARTLETT 796 *Skullduggery*, nonsense, foolery. **1892** *Boston Jrnl.* 7 Nov. 7/4 Unfounded Charges of Skulduggery in Ward 11. **1910** MCCUTCHEON *Rose in Ring* 188 There had been some skullduggery goin' on.

+Skulljoe. (See quotation.) — **1884** GOODE, etc. *Fisheries* I. 228 At Provincetown a Haddock salted and dried after being split is called by the name of 'Skulljoe,' or 'Scoodled Skulljoe.'

+Skunk, *n.* Also **squuncke, scunk,** etc. [Algonquian. Cf. Abnaki *segonku*.]

1. a. Any of several weasellike mammals of the genus *Mephitis*, well known for their power of ejecting an offensive-smelling secretion. **b.** Any of several other closely related American animals of the genera *Spilogale* and *Conepatus*.

The common skunk of the Northeast is of the species *Mephitis nigra;* of the North, *M. mephitis;* and of the West and South, *M. mesomelas.* (Cf. POLECAT.)

1634 WOOD *New Eng. Prospect* 22 The beasts of offence be Squunckes, Ferrets, Foxes. **1674** JOSSELYN *Two Voyages* 85 The *Squnck* is almost as big as a *Racoon.* **1781** PETERS *Hist. Conn.* (1829) 191 The Skunk is also peculiar to America. . . . He is black striped with white. **1806** LEWIS in *L. & Clark Exped.* IV. (1905) 73 The native wild animals, consisting of the Brown white or grizly bear . . . and polecat or skunk. **1823** JAMES *Exped.* I. 162 The flesh of the *skunk* we . . . [found] a remarkably rich and delicate food. **1842** *Nat. Hist. N.Y., Zoology* I. 29 The Skunk, *Mephitis Americana,* . . . is regarded as a fit subject for extermination. **1871** LEWIS *Poultry Book* 174, I then take Mr. Skunk by the tail. **1882** *Vt. Agric. Rep.* VII. 69 He believes the raccoon and the skunk are beneficial to the farmers in the destruction of vermin. **1902** WISTER *Virginian* xvi, There is a brown skunk down in Arkansaw. . . . Littler than our variety. **1925** TILGHMAN *Dugout* 4 Wolves and skunks abounded; otter and raccoons were found along the creeks.

2. With specifying terms.

1917 *Mammals of Amer.* 132/2 Western Striped Skunk, or California Skunk.—*Mephitis occidentalis occidentalis. Ib.,* Mearns Hooded Skunk, or Northern Hooded Skunk.—*Mephitis macroura milleri.* . . . It reaches the United States only in Southern Arizona. *Ib.* 135 The Spotted Skunk and its relatives of the genus *Spilogale* are the smallest of the North American skunks.

3. The fur of the skunk. {1884}

1862 TAYLOR in *Life & Lett.* 404 Sables are so expensive as to be vulgar and skunk . . . is infinitely handsomer.

4. A contemptible person.

1840 SIMMS *Border Beagles* I. 89 You can tell the people what a darned skunk of a fellow that Watson is. **1852** WATSON *Nights in Block-House* 30 He's a skunk—a flunky. **1885** BAYLOR *On Both Sides* 389 If, owing to that skunk Brown, you are disappointed out there, . . . write or telegraph me. **1925** TILGHMAN *Dugout* 54 Are you crying for that skunk that took you from home?

5. In miscellaneous applications: (see quotations).

1853 'P. PAXTON' *Yankee in Texas* 349 A severe defeat at the game of draughts was formerly, and, probably, is now, termed 'a skunk.' The man was 'skunked.' **1860** *Ill. Agric. Soc. Trans.* IV. 346 These skunks of the insect world [chinch bugs] are . . . many-sided, like the common house fly. **1877** *Vt. Dairymen's Ass. Rep.* VIII. 67 [Cheese that has deteriorated] in the vernacular is called skunks.

6. In phrases. **a.** *To skin one's own skunks,* to do one's own dirty work.

*c*1835 in Bartlett (1859) 122, Let every man skin his own skunks. **1892** *Amer. Folk-Lore* V. 60 Let them skin their own skunks. Said of any one who wishes to make a cat's paw of a person for his own disagreeable ends.

b. *To kill another skunk,* to create another stench or scandal.

1863 KETTELL *Hist. Rebellion* II. 582 The President hesitated in making another change in the war department, or, as he himself expressed [it] . . . , 'to kill another skunk.'

7. *attrib.* and *comb.* **a.** With *business, skin, trap.*

1862 TAYLOR in *Life & Lett.* 404 With my pelisse of raccoon and my cap of skunk-skin, I take my daily walk. **1894** WISTER in *Harper's Mag.* 908/1 Did you ever see a skunk-trap? **1898** WESTCOTT *D. Harum* 247 It was comin' to be a ch'ice between the chickin bus'nis an' the skunk bus'nis.

b. In the names of plants and fruits.

See also SKUNK CABBAGE, SKUNKWEED.

1817 W. COXE *Fruit Trees* 169 The Skunk Apple. . . . The name is derived from a nest of that animal found at the root of the original tree, in Middlesex county New-Jersey. *a*1817 DWIGHT *Travels* II. 312 Three sorts of currants are found in the forest: the red, the black, and a peculiar

kind, called Skunk currants. **1909** WEBSTER 1970 *Skunk grape,* the fox grape. **1894** *Amer. Folk-Lore* VII. 99 *Picea alba,* . . . skunk-spruce, Mt. Desert, [Me.], Washington Co., Me., Islands of Penobscot Bay, Me.

c. In the names of animals and birds.

See also SKUNK BLACKBIRD, SKUNKHEAD, SKUNK PORPOISE.

1876 LUDLOW, etc. *Rep. on Yellowstone* 65 *Gulo Luscus.* . . . In this region, they were spoken of as the 'Skunk-bear;' farther south they were called 'Carcajou.' **1836** *Penny Cycl.* V. 30/1 [The male bobolink's] variegated dress, . . . from a resemblance in its colours to that of the quadruped, obtained for it the name of 'skunk-bird' among the Cree Indians. **1917** *Birds of Amer.* I. 143 Labrador Duck. *Camptorhynchus labradorius.* . . . [Also called] Pied Duck; Skunk Duck. *Ib.* 151 Surf Scoter. *Oidemia perspicillata.* . . . [Also called] Skunk-head; Skunk-head Coot; Skunk-top.

+Skunk, *v.*

1. *tr.* **a.** In card games: To keep (a player) from getting a single point. Also *fig.* **b.** To defeat (an opponent) utterly.

1847 *Knickerb.* XXX. 15 While the righteous get High, Low, Jack, and the Game, the sinner gets skunked. **1848** BARTLETT 409 A presidential candidate who fails to secure one electoral vote is also *skunked.* **1853** [see SKUNK *n.* 5]. **1880** N. BROOKS *Fairport Nine* 37 Their only hope now was to 'skunk' the White Bears, who were coming to bat. **1904** CRISSEY *Tattlings* 365 A certain trio of choice scamps from the city hall gang would make a strong committee that could skunk the enemy.

2. College slang. To fail to pay a debt to (a person); to evade (a debt).

1851 HALL *College Words* 284 *Skunk,* at Princeton College, to fail to pay a debt; used actively; e.g. to skunk a tailor, i.e. not to pay him. **1859** BARTLETT 410 A student who leaves college without settling up, is said to skunk his bills.

3. *passive.* To be beaten (*out*) of something.

1877 W. WRIGHT *Big Bonanza* 541 'Skunked, by the holy spoons,' cried he. **1890** HASKINS *Argonauts Calif.* 250, I got skunked once out of a good claim.

4. (See quotation.)

1891 *Cent.* 5679/2 *Skunk,* . . . to cause disease in or of; sicken; scale, or deprive of scales: said of fish in the live-well of a fishing-smack. (New Eng.)

5. *intr.* To slink *away.*

1894 HARTE *Bell-Ringer of Angel's* 147 You heard how the new Sheriff . . . skunked away with his whole *posse* before one-eighth of my men.

+Skunk blackbird. a. The bobolink. **b.** *local.* The marsh blackbird.

There is some doubt about sense b; in quot. 1859 *marsh blackbird* may be used as another name for the bobolink.

1844 *Nat. Hist. N.Y., Zoology* II. 144 The Boblink, or Bob-o'link . . . as it is called in this state, is known in others by the various names of . . . American Ortolan, Butter-bird and Skunk Blackbird. **1855** BEECHER *Star Papers* 192 We followed that old Polyglott, the skunk-blackbird. **1859** BARTLETT 410 *Skunk blackbird,* the common marsh blackbird, so called in the rural districts of New England, New York, and Canada West. **1869** STOWE *Oldtown Folks* 409 That child can sing so like a skunk blackbird that you can't tell which is which. **1893** *Scribner's Mag.* 771/1 The bobolink's chief name was suggested by . . . his song; but another, skunk-blackbird, alludes to the skunk-like color and pattern of his dress. **1917** *Birds of Amer.* II. 241 Bobolink. *Dolichonyx oryzivorus.* . . . Other Names.—Skunk Blackbird; Skunk-head Blackbird [etc.].

+Skunk cabbage. One of various plants emitting a strong odor, esp. when bruised.

In the East and Northeast this name is applied commonly to the perennial herb, *Symplocarpus foetidus,* less commonly to the pitcher plant, *Sarracenia purpurea,* and, in early times, to the American hellebore (q.v.) and possibly to the pokeweed (see POKE *n.*3 2, note); on the Pacific coast it is applied to the plant *Lysichiton camstschatcense.* (See also SKUNK'S CABBAGE.)

1751 ELIOT *Field-Husb.* iii. 66 Take the Roots of Swamp Hellebore, sometimes called Skunk Cabbage, Tickle Weed. **1778** [see POKE *n.*3 2]. **1784** *Amer. Acad. Mem.* I. 407 *Arum Americanum.* . . . Scunk Cabbage. Skunkweed. The roots dried and powdered are an excellent medicine in asthmatic cases. **1789** [see POKE *n.*3 2]. **1832** WILLIAMSON *Maine* I. 128 Skunk-cabbage or Skunk-weed possesses an odour too distinctive ever to be mistaken. **1841** *Jamestown* (N.Y.) *Jrnl.* 7 April 1/3 Red dock, blue mullin and skunk cabbage we all know and have seen and suffered by. **1885** *Outing* Nov. 177/1 Do not overlook the purple spathes of the skunk cabbage. **1906** *Atlantic Mo.* Oct. 495 The first flower to bloom in this latitude when the winter frost loosens its grip upon the sod is the gross, uncouth, and noisome skunk cabbage. **1915** ARMSTRONG & THURBER *Western Wild Flowers* 138 [Wild peony] has a disagreeable smell, something like Skunk-cabbage, when crushed.

+Skunkery. A place where skunks are bred for their furs. — **1890** *Stock Grower & Farmer* 21 June 6/2 The skunkery is paying 200 per cent on the capital invested. **1897** *Boston Transcript* 11 Sept. 24/3 Minks have been bred for their skins in so-called minkeries, just as is being done with the skunks in what might be termed skunkeries.

+Skunkhead. 1. The extinct pied duck. **2.** The surf scoter, *Melanitta perspicillata.* Also attrib. — (1) **1844** *Nat. Hist. N.Y., Zoology* II. 326 This Duck [the Pied Duck, *Fuligula labradora*], well known on this coast under the name of *Skunk-head*, and *Sand-shoal Duck* on the coast of New-Jersey, is not, however, very abundant. **1875** *Fur, Fin & Feather* (ed. 3) 119 Of the various fowl called vulgarly coot, are the pied-duck (the skunk head), the velvet-duck [etc.]. (2) **1917** *Birds of Amer.* I. 151 Surf Scoter. . . . [Also called] Baldpate; Skunk-head; Skunk-head Coot [etc.].

+**Skunk horse.** (See quotation.) — **1805** *Balance* 22 Oct. 339 (Th.), A couple of impostors are exhibiting a piedbald or skunk horse, which they call a zebra, at the price of two shillings for grown persons.

+**Skunk porpoise.** (See quotations.) — **1884** GOODE, etc. *Fisheries* I. 16 The best known species on the Atlantic coast are the 'Skunk Porpoise,' or 'Bay Porpoise,' *Lagenorhynchus perspicillatus.* **1884** *Nat. Museum Bul.* No. 27, 632 The Skunk Porpoise . . . is very common off New England.

+**Skunk's-cabbage.** =SKUNK CABBAGE. — **1849** KINGSLEY *Diary* 15 The fruit grows on the extreme top with a blow or flower resembling our Skunks Cabbage. **1868** BEECHER *Norwood* 91 The great, succulent leaves of the skunk's cabbage were fully expanded.

+**Skunkweed.** **1. a.** The skunk cabbage, *Symplocarpus foetidus.* **b.** The American hellebore. **2.** (See quotation.) — (1) **1738** CATESBY *Carolina* II. 71 *Arum Americanum, Betæ folio.* The Scunk Weed. **1762** CLAYTON *Flora Virginica* 141 Polyandria. . . . Dracontium foliis subrotundis vulgo Skunck-weed. **1784** *Amer. Acad. Mem.* I. 407 Scunk Cabbage. Scunkweed. *Ib.* 409 In collecting the roots particular care ought to be taken that the *white hellebore*, or *poke root*, which some people call scunk weed, be not mistaken for this plant. (2) **1909** WEBSTER 1970 *Skunkweed*, . . . the polemoniaceous plant *Navarretia squarrosa* of California.

‖**Skyfalute,** *v. intr.* To cut high didoes. *slang.* — **1856** *Knickerb.* XLVII. 616 Well—we got ter skyfaluting about, and there was licker around, and pooty good rum.

+**Skygodlin,** *adv.* Obliquely. *slang. S.W.* — **1869** *Overland Mo.* Aug. 128 A mustang . . . will run 'skygodlin.'

Skylark. {1686–} +**a.** The horned lark or a related species. +**b.** =MISSOURI SKYLARK. — **1781–2** JEFFERSON *Notes Va.* (1788) 74. **1858** BAIRD *Birds Pacific R.R.* 403 *Eremophila Cornuta.* . . . Sky Lark; Shore Lark. **1874** COUES *Birds N.W.* 44, I saw no Skylarks after about the middle of September. **1907** *St. Nicholas* Oct. 1147/1 Down in the meadow a skylark is singing.

+**Sky pipit.** =MISSOURI SKYLARK. — **1884** COUES *Key to Birds* (ed. 2) 286 *Neocorys*, Sky Pipits.

Skyrocket. A rocket that ascends and explodes high in the air. {1688–} Also transf. — **1766** ROWE *Diary* 97 [They] had a large Bonfire & many sky Rockets. **1867** CRAWFORD *Mosby* 322 Sky-rockets were thrown into their camp. **1907** *St. Nicholas* July 787 J-ust you keep watch while my sky-rockets soar.

Skyrockety, *a.* High-flown; inclined to go up high. — **1890** *Voice* 23 Jan., I began to ask myself questions about this sky-rockety assemblage of words. **1896** *Godey's Lady's Bk.* April 348/2 That the sudden and sky-rockety increase last year was unnatural is generally admitted.

Skyscraper. {1794–}

+**1.** A bird that flies high.

1840 MATHEWS *Politicians* v. vi, I wish I had a brace of the sky-scrapers broiled for a luncheon. **1843** *Knickerb.* XXI. 10 Scare him [an eagle] away! Ha! old sky-scraper! Where's my gun? **1855** SIMMS *Forayers* 52 Open to the sky-scrapers, and the bouncing wild cats.

+**2.** A high hat or bonnet. Also attrib.

1847 J. A. EAMES *Budget of Letters* 397 She gave me a black silk bonnet . . . which stuck right up in the air after the fashion of the old 'sky scrapers.' **1884** HARRIS *Mingo* 89 Was it one of these sky-scrapers? *a*1885 in *Century Mag.* XXXV. 930/1 Milliner's wire . . . was used to give outline to the sky-scraper bonnets of the day.

+**3.** *Baseball.* A ball hit or thrown high into the air. Also attrib.

1866 *N.Y. Herald* 27 June 5/5 Goodspeed made three handsome fly catches; Mehl, Sweet and Dupignac each paying their share of attention to the 'skyscrapers.' **1907** *St. Nicholas* Sept. 996 A 'skyscraper' throw to first.

+**4.** A tall building.

1883 *Century Mag.* Sept. 724/1 The Georgia man . . . writes to the 'American Architect' to say that the American mind requires 'sky-scrapers.' **1891** *Boston Jrnl.* Nov., How the Sky Scrapers Are Built. **1903** KILDARE *My Mamie Rose* 288 We reach our stoop in the yawning dark cañon of the skyscrapers. **1913** LONDON *Valley of Moon* 82 The way led uptown, past . . . the Fourteenth Street skyscrapers.

Sky-scraping, *a.* {1840–} +**1.** Of buildings: Rising very high. +**2.** Of prices: High. — (1) **1891** *Boston Jrnl.* Nov., When entire streets are built with sky-scraping buildings, what disadvantages there will be. **1895** *Congreg. Chs. 9th Nat. Council Min.* 160 The poor man's cottage . . . is taxed two or three times as much, in proportion, . . . as the sky-scraping block of the millionaire. (2) **1904** *N.Y. Ev. Post* 12 March 10 Sky-scraping Prices at Last Brandus Picture Sale.

‖**Sky tavern.** A tavern in an upper story of a building. — **1827** MELLEN *Chronicle of '26* 25 What with . . . Sky-taverns, Wall-street, springs and watering halls, New York will loom. . . . The grandest, gayest, sharpest, sickliest of our clime.

+**Skyugle,** *n.* An instance of skyugling or an occasion when something is skyugled. *slang. Obs.* — **1864** *Army & Navy Jrnl.* 11 July (B.), A corps staff officer . . . informed me that he had been out on a general scyugle.

+**Skyugle,** *v. intr.* and *tr.* (See quots. 1864, 1877.) *slang. Obs.* — **1864** *Army & Navy Jrnl.* 11 July (B.), He had scyugled along the front, when the Rebels scyugled a bullet through his clothes; . . . he should scyugle his servant, who . . . had scyugled three fat chickens, for a supply of ice; . . . after he had scyugled his dinner, he proposed to scyugle a nap. **1877** BARTLETT 600 *Skyugle, Scyugle*, a queer word that originated with the Union soldiers during the late war. . . . 'It has not only a variety, but a contrariety of meanings.' **1877** W. WRIGHT *Big Bonanza* 375 It would do your hearts good to see that dog show off what a sense of appreciation he's got of me. Fellers, his gorgeous tail then stands aloft, he skyugles about. **1883** HARTE *Poetical Works* 145 And all of Smith's pigs were skyugled to boot.

* **Slab,** *n.*

* **1.** A rough, puncheonlike plank removed from the outside of a log in hewing it or in sawing it into planks.

1666 *East-Hampton Rec.* I. 248 A Pine slab by the well with my lath bench. **1780** E. PARKMAN *Diary* 226 Mr. Eleazar Rider, . . . having given me Slabbs &c, Stephen Maynard . . . brings a Load. **1817** *N. Amer. Rev.* IV. 180 Before they were covered with saw-mills and slabs, [the falls] must have formed a very picturesque spot. **1856** GOODRICH *Recoll.* I. 35 The school being organized, we were all seated upon benches, made of what were called *slabs*—that is, boards having the exterior or rounded part of the log on one side. **1900** BRUNCKEN *N. Amer. Forests* 66 He sees the immense accumulation of waste material, 'slabs,' and other debris encumbering the ground.

2. *attrib.* and *comb.* **a.** Designating things made of slabs.

1823 JAMES *Exped.* I. 154 'The figure four' . . . elevated the front of the trap upwards of three feet above its slab flooring. **1826** LONGFELLOW in S. Longfellow *H. W. Longfellow* I. 86 No green trees and orchards by the roadside; no slab-fences; no well-poles. **1845** *Knickerb.* XXVI. 411 There are houses of all grades provided, from the slab shanty to the comfortable frame-dwelling. **1867** RICHARDSON *Beyond Miss.* 141, I stopped at a little slab cabin. **1869** J. R. BROWNE *Adv. Apache Country* 402 Push open the rough board or slab door, and you have before you the . . . domestic life of the honest miner. **1878** STOWE *Poganuc People* 302 Nothing could be rougher . . . than the old school-house, . . . its rude slab benches and desks hacked by many a schoolboy's knife. **1883** HOWE *Country Town* (1926) 189 The man will die some of these days with . . . his slab house . . . and his handful of land paid for.

b. In special combinations.

Slab bonnet, =SLAT BONNET; *s.-bridged*, (see quotation); *s. car*, a car or truck used in or about a sawmill for conveying slabs; *s. company*, ? a company made up of slab-sided recruits; *s. pit*, a place where the slabs from a sawmill are burned; *s. saw*, a saw for cutting up slabs; *s. wood*, slabs used as firewood.

1891 RYAN *Pagan* 46 The face could scarcely be seen in the great shadows of a slab bonnet. **1866** LOWELL *Biglow P.* 2 Ser. p. lxii, Whoever has driven over a stream by a bridge made of *slabs* will feel the picturesque force of the epithet *slab-bridged* applied to a fellow of shaky character. **1879** *Lumberman's Gazette* 19 Dec., [The refuse] will fall into the slab car. **1833** in Kittredge *Old Farmer* (1904) 212 A captain of militia . . . had, like many other officers who commanded 'slab' companies, a troublesome set of fellows to deal with. **1879** *Lumberman's Gazette* 19 Dec., An elevator . . . is intended to be used in getting the slabs and clippings into the slab-pit. *Ib.*, The refuse will be run to the slab-saw and cut up. **1871** STOWE *Sam Lawson* 13 Cack allers had slab-wood a plenty from his mill.

Slab, *v.* {1703–} +**1.** *tr.* To convert into thick flat pieces. +**2.** *To slab off*, (see quot. 1859). — (1) **1866** LOSSING *Hudson* 70 There are also several mills for slabbing the fine black marble of that locality. **1893** *Advance* 11 May, A section of one thirty feet in diameter is to be slabbed. (2) **1835** CROCKETT *Tour* 212 You must take notice that I am slabb'd off from the election. **1859** BARTLETT 411 *To Slab off*, to throw aside as useless, like the outside piece of a log.

Slabber. {1718–} ‖**1.** Slobbering, slovenly talk. +**2.** *pl.* An ailment in horses and cows characterized by excessive dribbling at the mouth. — (1) **1840** DANA *Two Years* 44 The language of these people . . . [is] most brutish and inhuman. . . . It is a complete *slabber*. (2) **1843** TORREY *Flora N.Y.* I. 87 [St.-John's-wort] is generally believed, in this country, to be the most common cause of 'slabbers' in horses and horned cattle.

+**Slab-sided,** *a.* Flat-sided, long-legged; gawky, gangling. *colloq.* Also fig. — **1817** PAULDING *Lett. from South* II. 122 He was what is usually called a tall slab-sided Virginian. **1844** *Cincinnati Misc.* I. 20 Among our customers . . . was a long, slabsided, gangling fellow from the Western Reserve. **1881** *Amer. Naturalist* XV. 182 The male is slabsided, hook-billed and distorted, and is rejected by the canners. **1892** E. F. SHEPHARD *Speech* (Dec.), They said that we wanted every body to be good according to our pattern; that we were slab-sided, and that we were solemncholy. **1910** J. HART *Vigilante Girl* 143 The first pack-train . . . was headed by a tall, slab-sided mule.

+**Slab-sides.** Chap, fellow. *humorous.* — **1851** *Polly Peablossom* 83 How are you, old slab-sides?

Slack water, *n.* {1769–} A part of a river in which there is little or no current. {1867–77–} Also attrib. — **1836** J. HALL *Statistics of West* 38 At low stages the [Ohio] river becomes resolved into a succession of ripples, with extensive slack water basins between them. **1875** 'MARK TWAIN' *Old Times* ii. 25 The slack water ends here. **1908** WHITE *Riverman* 6 This stretch of slack water was always a terror.

+**Slack-water,** *v. tr.* To dam or impede (a stream) so as to produce stretches of slack or still water. Also as adj. — **1862** *Congress. Globe* 30 June 3033/1 If you slackwater the Susquehanna a few hundred miles up into New York, and then build a canal to Lake Erie, you will have navigation for your gunboats. **1863** KETTELL *Hist. Rebellion* II. 458 The Warwick river . . . had been slack-watered so as to swell the stream, and increase its depth and width. **1874** COLLINS *Kentucky* I. 54 Flat boats and water craft descending the slack-watered rivers, from a point above slack water, [are] not to pay tolls.

+**Slack-water navigation.** River navigation by means of locks and dams. — **1837** *Amer. Almanac* (Boston) 255 The works on the lower portion of the [Ky.] river . . . will form a slack-water navigation of 100 miles. **1850** *Western Journal* IV. 388 The Des Moines river slack-water navigation will form another arm. **1873** BEADLE *Undevel. West* 403 The Arkansas could have slack-water navigation a hundred miles or more above this. **1877** W. H. BURROUGHS *On Taxation* 28 It is difficult to see how the advantages of slackwater navigation . . . can be brought within the range of local objects.

Slack wire. A wire, loosely stretched between two supports, upon which an acrobat performs. {1825-} Also attrib. — **1753** *Amer. Wkly. Mercury* 20 Aug., The Surprizing Performances of the celebrated Anthony Joseph Dugee, . . . On a Slack Wire scarcely perceptible, with and without a Balance. **1845** SOL. SMITH *Theatr. Apprent.* 20 The season was eked out by the performance of harlequinades and pantomimes, intermixed with slack-wire arrangements. **1895** *N.Y. Dramatic News* 7 Dec. 13/4 Lottie Watson, the well-known slack-wire artist, . . . has since the close of the circus season been visiting friends and relatives.

Slag pot. A pot in which slag from a furnace is carried away. Also attrib. — **1876** KNIGHT 2198/1 The slag-pots are of cast-iron, tapering to a flat bottom, . . . or are made conical with three legs to stand on. **1876** RAYMOND *8th Rep. Mines* 29 The slag-pots are quadrilateral in form. **1906** LYNDE *Quickening* 384 The puffing locomotive had pushed the slag-pot car half way to the track end before Farley sat up.

+**Slam Bang,** *n.* A member of one of the political factions that opposed the Whigs. *Obs.* Also attrib. — **1837** *Jamestown* (N.Y.) *Jrnl.* 29 Nov. 2/2 Tory Executive power in its most tyrannical form combined in this country with the Fanny Wrights, the Loco Focos, and the Slam Bangs in order to break down the Whig party and Whig principles. **1838** MAYO *Polit. Sk. Washington* 19 n., See the infatuated proceeding . . . of the Slam-Bang-loco focos.

Slam-bang, *a.* Violent, noisy. *colloq.* — **1889** *Advance* 14 March, The friends of the Sabbath are not what some . . . slam-bang reformer would have the world believe. **1894** 'MARK TWAIN' *Those Twins* ii, 'Bob Ridley' is a common rackety slam-bang secular song.

Slam-bang, *v.* {1837-} +*tr.* To attack or denounce. *colloq.* — **1888** *Voice* (N.Y.) 12 July, You might as well denounce the legal profession because of the shysters . . . as to slam-bang newspapers because there are recreant editors.

+**Slam-Banger.** =SLAM BANG *n. Obs.* — **1840** *Maysville* (Ky.) *Eagle* 25 April 3/2 It is a subject of congratulations with all the Whigs, that the 'Slam-bangers,' 'Butt-enders,' *id est omne genus,* did not get a much heavier majority.

Slam-banging. Noise-making; tumult; clattering. *colloq.* Also fig. — **1843** *Knickerb.* XXII. 41 It was dismal to hear . . . the creaking on its rusty hinges and slam-banging of the sign of the Devil-Tavern. **1889** *Voice* 1 Aug., When you take up a Prohibition organ, you will find it full of political slang and slambanging. **1894** 'MARK TWAIN' *P. Wilson* vi, A prodigious slam-banging broke out below.

Slang.[1] A long narrow strip of land. *Obs.* {1610-} — **1658** *Providence Rec.* II. 18 This meddow haueing a narrow slang goeth from it to the aforsaide Riuer. **1690** *Ib.* XIV. 201 The westerne part of ye slangs of it [*sc.* the meadow] running up into ye land . . . to be unto said John Sayles. **1708** *Ib.* VII. 3 The slang of Meaddow he vseth to mow being within fence on ye East side the little Riuer.

Slang.[2] {1756-} The cant or jargon of a particular calling or profession {1802-12-}; colloquial language of a popular but ephemeral nature. {1818-} Also attrib. — **1832** KENNEDY *Swallow Barn* I. 52 He has slang for the stable boys, musty proverbs for the old folks. **1857** *Harper's Mag.* May 845/2 Not a few of our inferior newspapers abound in paragraphs, crammed with slang phrases. **1865** *Atlantic Mo.* April 417/2 A strange compound of the slang of the camp and the mystic phrases of the inspired prophets. a**1883** HOLMES in W. S. Kennedy *O. W. Holmes* 322 The use of slang . . . is at once a sign and a cause of mental atrophy. **1921** MENCKEN *Amer. Lang.* (ed. 2) 367 A very large part of our current slang is propagated by the newspapers, and much of it is invented by newspaper writers.

+**Slangw(h)ang.** Abusive or ranting utterance; balderdash, nonsense. *slang.* — **1834** BRACKENRIDGE *Recollections* 183 The dullest practised speaker is at home, compared to the young lawyer of genius, . . . who has acquired nothing of the ordinary *slang-whang.* **1859** *Harper's Mag.* July 164/1 Don't allow their vulgar slang-wang to have the slightest effect upon you.

+**Slang-whanger.** A low, noisy, ranting talker or writer. *slang.* — **1807** IRVING, etc. *Salmagundi* vii, These knights, denominated editors, or *slang-whangers,* . . . may be said to keep up a constant firing 'in words.' **1825** PAULDING *J. Bull in Amer.* 153 Princeton is the capital of old Kentuck, as these republican slang-whangers call it. **1857** *Harper's Mag.* Dec. 136/2 Parson Brownlow is one of the slang-whangers of the Southwest. **1892** T. & A. FITCH *Better Days* 304 The Tucson Star . . . used to be the chief of slangwhangers.

+**Slang-whanging.** The making, writing, or publishing of noisy, ranting, abusive harangues or addresses. *slang.* Also attrib. or as adj. — **1809** *Essex Register* 20 May (Th.), Federal Slangwhanging. **1836** CROCKETT *Exploits* 84 By his slang-whanging [he] drew a considerable crowd

around us. **1853** BALDWIN *Flush Times Ala.* 153 [Cave adapted] his talents to the slang-whanging departments of the [legal] profession. **1870** *Nation* 27 Jan. 58/1 The world would be in a dreadful state if a slang-whanging magazine or newspaper writer had only to call persons whom we all honor and admire Borgias. **1904** *Buffalo Commercial* 13 July 4 A clean campaign—one free from gross personal abuse and slang-whanging.

***Slant,** *v.* +**1.** *intr.* To have a bent or inclination *toward* something. +**2.** To go or move off. — **(1) 1850** LOWELL *Poetical Works* (1896) 325/2, I've always heard Our poor friend somewhat slanted Tow'rd taking liquor overmuch. **1869** STOWE *Oldtown Folks* 483 Your minister sartin doos slant a leetle towards th' Arminians. **(2) 1897** HOWELLS *Landlord at Lion's Head* 9 His father and brother . . . slanted after her.

+**Slantindicular,** *a.* and *adv.* Also **slantindickelar, slantingdicular,** etc. [From *slanting* and *perpendicular.*] **1.** *adj.* Slanting, sloping; also fig., indirect. *slang.* {1840-} **1832** T. COOPER *Memoirs of Nullifier* 37 (Th.), This is sorter a slantindickelar road, stranger. c**1840** NEAL *Beedle's Sleigh Ride* 7, [I] finally laid a plot to lug in the awful question in a sort of slantindickelar fashion. **1846** LEVINGE *Echoes from Backwoods* II. 93 Many of the passengers were afraid to leave their berths for days, taking what rest they could get by placing their feet in a 'slantingdicular' position against the top of their berths. **1887** WILKINS *Humble Romance* 245, I've felt as if I was slantendicular from heaven ever since I've been here.

fig. a**1864** in J. Bright *Sp. on Questions Pub. Policy* II. 339 When he was *not* before the world his walk was slantindicular.

2. *adv.* =next. *slang.*

1843 'UNCLE SAM' *Peculiarities* I. 161 Any man as don't predicate a whipping, had best not look slantendicular at *me,* that's all. **1847** *Chunkey's Fight* 138 (Th.), I'd shot him right through the breast, but sorter slantindickler. **1866** BUCKLAND *Curiosities Nat. Hist.* 3 Ser. I. 73 [The ducks] come down, as the Yankees say, 'slantindicular.'

+**Slantindicularly,** *adv.* In a slanting or sloping direction; obliquely. *slang.* {1869-} Also fig. — **1834** DE QUINCEY in *Tait's Mag.* I. 86 A sunrise and a sunset, ought to be seen from the valley or horizontally,— not, as the man of Kentuck expressed it, slantindicularly. a**1846** *Quarter Race Ky.* 137, [I] sort a cut him [the bear] slantindicularly through his hams. **1857** *Knickerb.* XLIX. 35 He had slantendicularly diverged from the path of moral correctitude.

+**Slapjack.** Variant of FLAPJACK 1. — **1809** IRVING *Knickerb.* VI. iv., To these [the Van Nests of Kinderhook] . . . we are indebted for the invention of slap jacks. **1845** J. W. NORRIS *Chicago Directory* 98 Exchange Coffee House. . . . Slapjacks and Maple Molasses, Mock Turtle Soup. **1885** *Outing* Oct. 76/1 Then comes supper, consisting of trout, fried potatoes, tea, and 'slapjacks.' **1890** GUNTER *Miss Nobody* ix, The old miner is one of those whole-souled Western anomalies who would divide his last *slap-jack* with you.

Slapper. {1781-} ‖A window shutter. — **1843** 'CARLTON' *New Purchase* I. 45 [The] window was a cubit square and had a flapper or slapper hung with leathern hinges.

+**Slap-stick.** A double lath used in low comedy or farce in dealing blows. Also attrib. with reference to rough comedy. {1925-} — **1896** *N.Y. Dramatic News* 4 July 9/3 What a relief, truly, from the slap-sticks, rough-and-tumble comedy couples abounding in the variety ranks. [**1907** *Wkly. Budget* 19 Oct. 1/2 A 'slap-stick,' the customary weapon in American theatre galleries.] **1919** HOLMES *Man fr. Tall Timber* 94 It was . . . one of those girl and slap-stick affairs.

+**Slash,** *n.*[1] [Of obscure origin.] A low, wet, swampy, or marshy area, often overgrown with bushes, canes, etc. Freq. pl.

1652 in *Amer. Speech* XV. 392/2 Beginning neer a wett slash. **1674** [see CANE 1]. **1797** HAWKINS *Letters* 89 This slash looks beautiful covered with reed to a considerable extent. **1832** J. HALL *Legends of West* 190 'Nothing but a slash.' 'What's that?' 'Why, sir, jist a sort o' swamp.' **1885** *N.H. Forestry Comm. Rep.* June 98 Forbid . . . the setting of fires between the first of May and the first of October, in any slashes, old pasture, field, or other place. **1904** T. E. WATSON *Bethany* 6 The grocery . . . stood on the flat, called the 'slashes.'

attrib. **1690** in *Amer. Speech* XV. 393/2 One thousand one hundred twenty nine acres . . . begining at a great pine by a piny Branch or Slash side.

***Slash,** *n.*[2]

+**1.** (See quot. 1905.)

1881 *Harper's Mag.* Oct. 688/2 Crawling through the densest slash of burned and fallen timber. **1904** *N.Y. Ev. Post* 18 June, A new trail leads through the timber 'slash' to the foot of a set of ladders. **1905** *Forestry Bureau Bul.* No. 61, 47 Slash. 1. The débris left after logging, wind, or fire. 2. Forest land which has been logged off and upon which the limbs and tops remain, or which is deep in débris as the result of fire or wind.

+**2.** The tops, branches, etc., of trees so felled as to impede, or give protection from, an enemy: (see also quot. 1887). *Obs.*

1886 MITCHELL *R. Blake* 16 Both sides were 'falling' trees to construct breastworks, abatis, and slashes. **1887** BILLINGS *Hardtack* 380 The territory covered by these fallen trees was called *the Slashes,* hence *Slashing.*

***Slash,** *v.*

+**1.** *tr.* To beat or tread down.

c**1834** CATLIN *Indians* II. 18 We will take that buffalo trail, where the travelling herds have slashed down the high grass.

+2. To clear (land) by cutting the growth upon it in a rapid, wasteful manner.

1857 *Quinland* I. 33 During the summer we 'slashed' about forty acres. **1885** *Century Mag.* April 836 He would have plenty to do 'slashing,' i.e., cutting down the trees preparatory to burning them.

+3. To cut down (timber or other forest growth) in an unplanned, destructive manner. (Cf. SLASHED *a.*)

1884 *Harper's Mag.* Sept. 502/2 The streams . . . were bordered by broad thickets of willows and cottonwoods convenient to 'slash.'

+4. To reduce or cut down (salaries, etc.) severely.

1906 *Washington Post* 29 April 6 A disposition was manifested in the Senate Committee to slash the salaries of members of the commission. **1910** *Springfield W. Repub.* 8 Dec. 8 It is not a pleasant thing to slash a presidential message to this extent.

Slashed, *a.* {1633-} +Of timber: Felled or cut down in a destructive manner. — **1843** *Yale Lit. Mag.* VIII. 332 His eye wandered far away over acres of slashed timber.

＊**Slasher.** +One who cuts down timber in a destructive or wasteful manner. — **1886** *Leslie's Mo.* June 450/2 [We] can say to the Eastern slashers, 'Go ahead and chop down your forests.'

Slashergaff, *a.* Violent, slam-bang. *slang.* — **1847** ROBB *Squatter Life* 31 We 'spect you . . . to pour it inter the inimy in slashergaff style.

‖**Slashett.** ? A small slash. — **1678** in *Amer. Speech* XV. 393/2 Thence . . . to a marked white oake in a slashett.

+**Slash ground.** (See quotation.) — **1877** BARTLETT 602 *Slash-Ground*, land on which the brush has been cut and left lying. New York.

＊**Slashing.**

+1. An area where timber has been cut or blown down.

1840 *Jamestown* (N.Y.) *Jrnl.* 1 July 2/5 On Monday, the body of Mr. Brown was found in a slashing. **1864** NORTON *Army Lett.* 211 Imagine a slashing of five hundred acres with an impassable swamp on each side. **1894** *Outing* XXIV. 186/2 We got into a spruce thicket of an old 'slashing'—the track of a hurricane. **1923** HERRICK *Lilla* 91 They set out on a trail that led through the slashings and past abandoned lumber camps.

+2. The felling of timber in such a way that the trees fall in heaps suitable for burning; the mass or debris of felled trees resulting from this.

1857 *Quinland* I. 34 When it came dry in the spring, we burned the 'slashing' we had made the previous summer. *a***1882** WEED *Autobiog.* I. 14 Slashing . . . brings the tops of fallen trees together so that they may be burned without the labor of cutting and piling the brush. **1887** BILLINGS *Hardtack* 380 When a line of works was laid out through woods, much *slashing*, or felling of trees, was necessary in its front.

+3. *pl.* = SLASH *n.*[1] 1.

*a***1864** T. WEED in Nichols *Amer. Life* II. 215 Cattle . . . were turned out to 'browse' in the 'slashings.'

+4. The cutting down of timber in a wasteful manner.

1874 *Vermont Bd. Agric. Rep.* II. 451 Mr. Hill, of Elmore, spoke of the waste . . . shown by farmers in cutting and slashing in the woods.

+**Slash pine.** Any one of various pines that grow in slashes or low coastal regions, as *Pinus caribaea*, and the loblolly and shortleaf pines. — **1882** HOUGH *Elem. Forestry* 328 Varieties [of *Pinus taeda*] are known in North Carolina as 'Swamp Pine,' 'Slash Pine.' **1884** SARGENT *Rep. Forests* 516 The naval stores . . . in the United States are principally produced from . . . the loblolly pine (*Pinus Tæda*), and the slash pine (*Pinus Cubensis*). **1897** SUDWORTH *Arborescent Flora* 29 *Pinus echinata*. Shortleaf Pine. . . . Slash Pine (N.C., Va., in part). **1901** MOHR *Plant Life Ala.* 323.

＊**Slat,** *n.*

1. One of the long, narrow pieces of wood on which rest the mattress, springs, etc., of a bed.

1857 GUNN *N.Y. Boarding-Houses* 96 Our bed did not possess its full complement of *slats* or cross-pieces. **1862** Higginson *Harvard Mem. Biog.* I. 242 The bulk of those now in bed must have lain on the slats of the bedstead. **1919** WILSON *Ma Pettengill* 292, I had kicked the slats out of my trundle-bed.

+2. Short for SLAT BONNET; one of the pasteboard strips used in such a bonnet.

1880 *Harper's Mag.* March 578/2 [She] goes to prayer-meetin' in her calico slat. **1891** *Century Mag.* Feb. 489 From the end of the tunnel formed by the uncompromising pasteboard slats a shrewd, hard, yellow, cadaverous face peers out.

3. *attrib.* Designating things made of long narrow planks or strips of wood.

1790 BENTLEY *Diary* I. 180 The Principal Garden is in three parts divided by an open slat fence painted white. **1853** FOWLER *Home for All* 115 A plank house can be lathed, and plastered, and finished for less than it costs to finish the slat-work wall, as it takes a greater quantity of mortar to level up and fill the crevices in the slat-work. **1884** Slat cattle-car [see CATTLE CAR]. **1893** AULD *Picturesque Burlington* 163 Wooden slat blinds for the inside of windows have retained their popularity for many years. **1901** CHURCHILL *Crisis* 488, I went straight to General Grant's headquarters,—just a plain, rough slat house.

＊**Slat,** *v.*[1] +*intr.* To place or fit slats. — **1874** *Vermont Bd. Agric. Rep.* II. 511 After they are all laid in their proper place, continue to slat between them, and so on above until completed.

＊**Slat,** *v.*[2]

1. *tr.* To cut or knock *off*.

1828 SHERBURNE *Memoirs* 55 The women and girls . . . rip them [the fish] open, . . . slat off their heads and split them. **1871** DE VERE 545 Fishermen on the Eastern coast . . . disengaged mackerel and other delicate-gilled fish by slatting them off the hook.

2. *Naut. intr.* Of sails: To flap or slap. {1881}

1840 DANA *Two Years* 38 The great jib flying off to leeward and *slatting* so as almost to throw us off of the boom. **1865** A. D. WHITNEY *Gayworthys* 254 The canvas [was] slatting out and in, in great bights.

b. In other contexts: To slap or bang.

1889 'MARK TWAIN' *Conn. Yankee* 144, I couldn't seem to stand that shield slatting and banging . . . about my breast. **1898** — in *Harper's Mag.* March 539/2 Nothing [had been] left for disorderly members to slat with.

+**Slat bonnet.** A cloth bonnet the sides of which are stiffened with narrow strips of pasteboard or wood. — **1880** *Harper's Mag.* March 577/1, I can go to prayer-meetin' in my slat bunnit well enough. **1899** CHESNUTT *Wife of His Youth* 132 Old Dinah saw . . . a tall, brown girl, in a homespun frock, swinging a slat-bonnet in one hand.

＊**Slate,** *n.*

＊**1.** = SLATE ROCK.

1630 HIGGINSON *New-England* 7 For Stone, here is plentie of Slates at the Ile of Slate in Masathulets Bay. **1705** [see CLAY 1]. **1802** DRAYTON *S. Carolina* 47 Good slate is found near the head waters of Lynch's creek. **1876** RAYMOND *8th Rep. Mines* 80 The Idaho Mine of Grass Valley . . . is situated . . . in a contact-formation of slate and greenstone. **1907** *St. Nicholas* May 669/1 The boys . . . pick the pieces of slate out of the coal.

＊**2.** A thin, rectangular piece of slate used for roofing. Usually *pl.*

1684 I. MATHER *Providences* (1856) x. 225 This unusual artillery of Heaven broke all the slates wherewith the houses were covered. **1743** *Holyoke Diaries* 33 The Slates for the chapel were begun to be cut in order to be put on it. **1860** MORDECAI *Virginia* 273 The roof was of boards, or slates or slabs.

＊**b.** Roofing slates collectively.

1674 *Md. Archives* II. 405 [The] state house and Prison . . . to be Covered with Slate or tile and in Mortar. **1789** MORSE *Amer. Geog.* 207 The roof is covered with slate. **1876** INGRAM *Centennial Exp.* 605 The roof was covered with Pennsylvania black slate.

＊**3.** A piece of slate, usually rectangular and framed, used, esp. by school children, for writing on.

1768 in Chalkley *Scotch-Irish Settlement Va.* I. 462, 3 yards coarse linen @ 2/6 and a slate. **1836** GILMAN *Recoll.* (1838) 50 We availed ourselves [of the opportunity] to draw figures on our slates. **1890** HOWELLS *Boy's Town* 64 The boys . . . held up their slates with things written on them to make the girls laugh. **1902** G. M. MARTIN *Emmy Lou* 8 [He] drove his pencil into his slate with a fervor that made Miss Clara rap sharply on her desk.

b. Such a slate used to keep a record, list, or score upon. Also *transf.* {1868-}

1782 HAMILTON *Works* VIII. 70 [The expense of the interior administration] amounts to about £15,000 as you will perceive by the inclosed slate. **1812** *Niles' Reg.* II. 378/2 A slate with the names of all the defenders of the house will be placed in the front room. **1883** SWEET & KNOX *Through Texas* 17 [He would say] to the bar-keeper, 'Them's mine: put 'em on the slate.' **1887** *Trial H. K. Goodwin* 39, [I] put his name and description on the slate.

+4. *Polit.* A list of candidates prepared beforehand for appointment, nomination, or election.

1865 *Harper's Mag.* July 228/2 Sometimes he [Lincoln] would 'break the slate,' as he called it, of those who were making a list of appointments. **1868** M. H. SMITH *Sunshine & Shadow* 317 In that little room . . . the 'slates' of ambitious and scheming politicians [have been] destroyed. **1902** MEYER *Nominating Systems* 42 The 'slate' for nomination [is] referred to a committee appointed by a chairman put up by the 'ring.' *transf.* **1913** LA FOLLETTE *Autobiog.* 12 Well, the fraternities made their slate and put it through.

+**b.** *To make up the slate,* (see quotation).

1892 WALSH *Lit. Curiosities* 1014 *Slate, to make up the.* In American political slang this signifies the secret understanding by which the leaders of a political party determine among themselves before the meeting of a nominating convention the names of the candidates for office which they desire and which they will endeavor by all their influence, open or covert, to have put in nomination by the convention.

5. *attrib.* and *comb.* **a.** Designating things made of or consisting of slate.

1710 *Harvard Rec.* I. 391 Mr. Treasurer is therefore desired to take Effectual Care for the taking of the said Slate roof. **1868** HAWTHORNE *Note-Books* I. 110 In the old burial-ground, Charter Street, [there was] a slate gravestone, carved round the borders. **1874** *Vermont Bd. Agric. Rep.* II. 740 [Upon] a large farm lying near that village, . . . was an extensive slate vein. **1876** Raymond *8th Rep. Mines* 65 It is foreign to my purpose to discuss at length the character and features of this slate-stratum. **1892** *Vt. Agric. Rep.* XII. 117 There is also a slate ledge in Waterford.

b. In special combinations.

Slate belt, a region or zone where slate is found; *s. dealer*, one who buys and sells slate; *s. mill*, a place where slate is mined or worked up into slates; *s. peg*, (see quotation); *s.-picker*, a boy who picks the pieces of slate from mined coal (cf. Cracker boy); *s. rag*, a rag or cloth used for cleaning a slate; *S. river pea*, a variety of pea; *s. roofer*, one whose occupation is roofing with slate; *s. run*, a run or stream that flows through a slate region; *s.-smasher*, one who breaks up a political slate; *s. work*, work done by school children on their slates; *s. writing*, writing on a slate done allegedly by a spirit or medium.

1882 *47th Congress 1 Sess.* H.R. Ex. Doc. No. 216, 458 On the eastern or slate belt great activity is manifested. **1874** *Vermont Bd. Agric. Rep.* II. 739 Mr. Reed . . . formed a stock company, Mr. Davidson, a heavy slate dealer of New Orleans, having a large interest therein. **1874** *Vermont Bd. Agric. Rep.* II. 739 A slate mill was built on the lake shore. **1876** Knight 2201/1 *Slate-peg*, a kind of nail used in securing slates on a roof. **1862** *Independent* 13 March 6/3 These slate-pickers and their sisters went through with poems, dialogues, and speeches. **1902** G. M. Martin *Emmy Lou* 20 She proffered him the hospitality of a grimy little slate rag. **1800** Tatham *Agric. & Commerce* 61 Plant black-eyed peas, Slate river peas, or cuckold's increase, in the interstices. **1874** *Vermont Bd. Agric. Rep.* II. 736 Allen entered into partnership with Thomas Christie, a slate roofer in Troy. **1807** Gass *Journal* 51 We passed a run on the south side called a slate run. **1869** *Cincinnati Enquirer* March (Clapin), Gen. Grant . . . is a great slate-smasher. **1871** *Rep. Indian Affairs* (1872) 459 In spelling, writing, map and slate-work these [Indian] children show much aptness and do well. **1885** *Century Mag.* July 382/2 She can do the trance business, and knocks, and slate-writing, and all that sort of thing.

***Slate,** *v.* +**1.** *tr.* To place (a person's name) on a political slate. +**2.** To free (coal) from pieces of slate. — (1) **1804** *Steele P.* I. 441 The Federalists have not nor do they intend slating a candidate. **1903** *San Francisco Argonaut* 31 Aug. 130 Henry Ash is now slated for the chairmanship of the Republican convention. (2) **1859** *Rep.Comm.Patents 1858* I. 705 Improvement in Machines for Slating Coal.

Slate-colored, *a.* In the names of birds: Of the color of slate; dark gray. {1811–} — **1874** Coues *Birds N.W.* 162 *Passerella Townsendii*, Slate-colored Sparrow. **1917** *Birds of Amer.* III. 47/1 East of the Rockies . . . the Slate-colored or Eastern Junco . . . occupies an area greater than any dozen varieties of the West. *Ib.* 177 Catbird. *Dumetella carolinensis*. . . . [Also called] Slate-colored Mockingbird; Black-capped Thrush.

+**Slate-colored hawk.** The sharp-shinned hawk, *Accipiter velox*. — **1812** Wilson *Ornithology* VI. 13 [The] Slate-colored Hawk . . . is a native of Pennsylvania, and of the Atlantic states generally. **1823** James *Exped.* I. 262 *Falco Pennsylvanicus*, Wilson—Slate-coloured hawk. **1844** *Nat. Hist. N.Y., Zoology* II. 17 The Slate-Colored Hawk . . . is noted for its attacks on the poultry yard.

Slate land. {1733–} +(See quot. *a*1817.) — *a***1817** Dwight *Travels* III. 217 The soil is generally what is called slate land; being either clay, or clay with a thin covering of sand. **1851** Cist *Cincinnati* 267 The Catawba and Isabella grape are said to succeed well on the slate lands.

Slate-maker. {1780–} +One who makes or assists in making a political slate. — **1868** *N.Y. Herald* 9 July 7/3 The slate makers were nigh frantic about the presentation of Mr. Greeley's name. **1883** *Century Mag.* May 67/2 There were no knots of slate-makers or wire-pullers; no one had a pet measure that he wanted to put through the convention. **1904** Crissey *Tattlings* 92 The druggist . . . walked into the room where the 'Big Three' slate makers were figuring out things.

Slate quarry. A quarry from which slate is obtained. {1611–} — **1806** *Ann. 9th Congress* 2 Sess. 1122 A little above the slate quarry, is a considerable plain. **1874** *Vermont Bd. Agric. Rep.* II. 739 About 1852 or 1853 Mr. Reed, a slater from New York, . . . opened a slate quarry on the west shore of the same lake.

Slate rock. A dense, fine-grained argillaceous rock that splits into thin plates; a piece of this. {1793–} — **1800** *Mass. H. S. Coll.* 1 Ser. VI. 222 The southern end [of the island] is a slate rock. **1838** *Mass. Agric. Survey 1st Rep.* 121 It takes a little more time to lay these slate rocks, than to lay bricks. **1874** *Vermont Bd. Agric. Rep.* II. 737 He bought what is called the Capin farm, covering a very extensive and valuable tract of slate rock.

+**Slather.** [Origin unknown.] A large quantity, a good deal, much. *colloq.* Usually pl. — **1876** 'Mark Twain' *Tom Sawyer* vii. 75 They got slathers of money—most a dollar a day. **1891** *Fur, Fin, & Feather* 169/2 [We found] slathers of black-tailed deer on our way up to the mountains. **1907** White *Arizona Nights* 10 A slather of rocks and stones come out of the mouth [of the mine]. **1911** Ferber *Dawn O'Hara* 142 It's going to be slathers of fun.

+**Slat sunbonnet.** =Slat bonnet. — **1878** *St. Nicholas* Oct. 797/1 As soon as they had thrown off their slat sunbonnets . . . , Nimpo was seized with a bright idea. **1891** *Century Mag.* Feb. 489 The whole array [is] made more incongruous by that homeliest head-gear, the slat sunbonnet. **1912** N. Woodrow *Sally Salt* 53 'Has he begun to bark yet?' a woman in calico wrapper and a slat sunbonnet asked.

Slattery, *a.* {1829–} ||Banging, clanging, rattling. — **1887** S. Hale *Letters* 172 Such a racket . . . there was that night, bang, bang, bang, slattery, rattly, everything on the loose.

***Slaughter,** *v.* +**1.** *tr.* To destroy (forests and timber) by wasteful and excessive cutting. +**2.** *Polit.* To defeat or overwhelm. *colloq.* — (1) **1896** *Vt. Agric. Rep.* XV. 85 Our lumber forests are being slaughtered. **1903** White *Blazed Trail Stories* 47 Fitzpatrick would not have the pine 'slaughtered.' (2) **1903** *N.Y. Ev. Post* 5 Oct. 3 McLaughlin's lieutenants are openly declaring that they will 'slaughter' the McClellan-Grout-Fornes ticket.

***Slaughterer.** One whose occupation is killing animals for food; a butcher. {1648–} — **1851** Cist *Cincinnati* 280 The slaughterers formerly got the gut fat for the whole of the labor thus described. **1890** *Stock Grower & Farmer* 11 Jan. 5/2 Local slaughterers (the refrigerator men) have used a much larger number [of sheep] than ever before.

* **Slaughterhouse.** A house where animals are killed for food. Also attrib.

1653 *Suffolk Deeds* I. 265 George Burden of Boston . . . [has sold] the slaughter house made by William Cotton. **1713** *Boston News-Letter* 3 Aug. 2/2 A Convenient dwelling House and Land, with a Slaughter-House thereon. **1802** *Charlestown Land Rec.* 254 Mr Timothy Keith encroached on the Town's land, at his Slaughter house, 5 feet. **1907** Andrews *Recoll.* 168 The natural or slaughter-house taste and odor was strong in both meat and soup.

+**b.** (See quotation.) *Obs.*

1789 in Cist *Cincinnati* (1841) 197 Guards . . . are allowed me at present, for the protection and defense of this *slaughter-house*, as some in this country, (Kentucky,) are pleased to term the Miami purchase.

Slaughter pen. A pen in which animals are killed for food. Also transf. — **1796** *Ann. 4th Congress* 2 Sess. 1720 Georgia was a slaughter-pen during the war. **1856** Simms *Charlemont* 27 These lads . . . raise hogs for the slaughter-pen. **1863** Norton *Army Lett.* 188, I will count up [my battles]. . . . Bull Run, Antietam, . . . Fredericksburg, the slaughter pen, skirmish at Richards' Ford [etc.]. **1878** *Rep. Indian Affairs* 151 For the first time in the history of this agency Indians have been induced . . . to perform the labor of the slaughter-pen.

* **Slave.**

+**1.** A Negro slave in what is now the U.S. Now hist.

1704 *Boston News-Letter* 6 Nov. 2/2 A Negro Woman Slave about 22 Years of Age, to be Sold by Mr. Nicholas Boone. **1797** Washington *Writings* XIII. 431*n.*, I had resolved never to become the Master of another slave by purchase. **1857** *Harper's Mag.* Oct. 688/1 Margaret Rine, the last slave in the State of New York, died recently on Long Island. **1894** Robley *Bourbon Co., Kansas* 66 Slaves were bought and sold in this county as late as August, 1857. **1907** *St. Nicholas* May 619/2 Others have said that he went there . . . in order to receive under his protection slaves who had succeeded in escaping from their Southern masters.

+**2.** (See quotation.) *Obs.*

*c***1838** Catlin *Indians* II. 213 This tribe [Sacs and Foxes] has a society which they call the 'slaves,' composed of a number of the young men of the best families in the tribe, who volunteer to be slaves for the term of two years.

3. *attrib.* and *comb.* **a.** With participial adjectives, as *slave-consuming*, *-cultivated*, *-cursed*, etc.

See also Slave-breeding, Slave-driving *a.*

1798 *Ann. 5th Congress* 2 Sess. 2058 At present the slaveholding parts of the State [Va.] are burdened with the heaviest part of the State taxes. **1828** Cooper *Notions* II. 296 The confederation is nearly equally divided into slave-owning, and what are called free states. **1837** in Mackenzie *Van Buren* 295 Our laws had . . . quite another [aspect] on the borders of slave-freeing Mexico. **1840** Garrison in W. P. & F. J. Garrison *Life W. L. Garrison* II. 393 If England would supply herself with free cotton from some other part of the world, to the exclusion of all slave-grown cotton, it is quite certain that, within seven years, American slavery would be peaceably abolished. **1853** Stowe *Key* 143/2 The immense acquisition of slave territory . . . now opens so boundless a market to tempt the avarice and cupidity of the Northern slave-raising States. **1860** Abbott *South & North* 291 The average value of land in slave-cursed South-Carolina. **1863** J. H. Simpson (*title*), Horrors of the Virginia Slave Trade and of the Slave-rearing Plantations. **1875** Slave-consuming [see Slave-breeding]. **1908** 'O. Henry' *Options* 89 Blandford Carteret . . . [became distinguished] for his pride, juleps, marksmanship, and vast slave-cultivated plantations.

b. Designating those who own or have to do with slaves.

See also Slave-breeder, Slave-catcher, etc.

*c***1835** in Stowe *Key* 198/2 To question whether slave-holders or slave-buyers are of the devil, seems to me like calling in question whether God is or is not a true witness. **1862** *N.Y. Tribune* 9 May 6/4 The Richmond aristocracy of Slave-chapmen would not forever have things their own way. **1832** Dunlap *Hist. Amer. Theatre* 23 The slave dealers of Newport . . probably thought a stage player a greater abomination than the kidnapper . . . of the miserable negro. **1856** Olmsted *Slave States* 196 The slave employer, if he finds he has been so unfortunate as to hire a sulky servant [etc.]. **1806** *Balance* V. 53/3 The wealthy slave holder is exempted from paying a cent. **1860** Abbott *South & North* 325 A compact . . . renders it necessary for us to join the slave-hunters. **1847** *Whig Almanac 1848* 6/1 Not even the most unscrupulous instruments of the Texas land speculators and slave-jobbers dared [etc.]. **1861** *N.Y. Times* 16 Dec. 4/5 The poor whites, hating profoundly the proud slave-lords, . . . are thoroughly discontented and ripe for profit. **1853** Stowe *Key* 36/1 Such men are to be found at the South in the relation of slave-masters. **1880** Tour-

GEE *Bricks* 162 A weak old woman, . . . though once a slave-mistress, was most sincerely rejoiced at the downfall of a system she had always regarded with regret. **1904** GLASGOW *Deliverance* 84 Where did he get the money to buy the place—he a slave-overseer? **1861** *N.Y. Tribune* 27 Dec. 7/2 Would-be savans establish a kind of difference of race between the slave-drivers, slave-breeders, and slave-traffickers of the South and the free men of the Union.

c. Designating laws and legislation relating to slaves and slavery.

See also SLAVE CODE.

1835 CHANNING *Works* (1886) 693/1 The very codes of slave legislation, . . . while they strip a man of liberty, affirm his right to life. **1841** EMERSON *Miscellanies* 271 He [a slaveholder] is the State of Georgia, or Alabama, with their sanguinary slave-laws, walking here on our northeastern shores. **1853** STOWE *Key* 103/2 The fact of so killing a slave is not of itself held presumption of murder, in slave jurisprudence.

d. Designating places where slaves are confined, usually while awaiting sale.

See also SLAVE PEN, SLAVE YARD.

1835 CHANNING *Works* (1886) 714/2 Slave-markets and slave-dungeons turn to mockery the language of freedom in the halls of Congress. **1852** STOWE *Uncle Tom* xxx, A slave-warehouse in New Orleans is a house externally not much unlike many others. **1860** ABBOTT *South & North* 200 There is no longer buying and selling—heart-crushing separations—slave-shambles! **1865** *Atlantic Mo.* April 432/2 [He] asked if I would wish to see the slave-jail. **1865** RICHARDSON *Secret Service* 64 Along the streets, you saw the sign, 'Slave Depot—Negroes bought and sold.' **1883** CABLE in *Century Mag.* June 219/1 Midway between Poydras and Girod streets [in New Orleans], . . . lay a *campo de negroes*, a slave camp, probably of cargoes of Guinea slaves.

e. Designating slaves serving in indicated capacities.

1856 OLMSTED *Slave States* 153 Slave-Lumbermen . . . are mostly hired by their employers at a rent . . . paid to their owners. **1871** GROSVENOR *Protection* 271 Allowing for . . . the omission of slave-laborers, it may be presumed that [etc.]. **1874** PINKERTON *Expressman & Detective* 43 Porter had become quite intimate with the slave-servants in the Exchange.

f. Designating societies in which slavery exists as an institution.

See also SLAVE STATE, SLAVE TERRITORY.

1856 E. G. PARKER *Oration 4 July* 23 (Ernst), Slave commonwealth. **1884** BLAINE *20 Years of Congress* I. 570 The haughty oligarchy of the South would have founded a slave republic which . . . would have changed the future of this continent. *Ib.* 573 The purpose of the secession . . . [was] the establishment of an independent slave-empire. **1886** LOGAN *Great Conspiracy* 20 [Jefferson] added to our domain the great French Slave Colony of Louisiana.

4. In special combinations.

Slave cabin, on a plantation, a cabin or hut occupied by one or more slaves; *s.-catching*, (see quotation); *s. coffle*, a group or caravan of slaves fastened together; *s. deck*, (see quotation); *s. despotism*, slavery as an institution; *s. government*, a government, as that of a state, in which slavery is legal; *s. hunt*, (see quotation); *s. institution*, an institution based upon slavery; *s. interest*, the interest of those owning slaves or favoring slavery; *s. line*, a line separating slaveholding states or territories from those that prohibit slavery; *s. melody*, a melody originated by or popular among slaves; *s. oligarch*, a member of the ruling class in a slaveholding society; *s. oligarchy*, a system of government, or a society governed, by a small number of slave-owners; *s. power*, the power and influence exercised by slave-owners and those favoring slavery; *s. quarter*, a place on a plantation where slaves live (cf. NEGRO QUARTER); *s. representation*, representation in Congress from a slaveholding state; *s. sale*, a sale of one or more slaves; *s. soil*, soil where slavery prevails; *s. song*, a song sung by slaves; *s. voyage*, a voyage for procuring slaves.

1858 WILLIS *Convalescent* 396 It was originally, probably, one of the slave-cabins of the estate. **1864** WEBSTER 1241/2 *Slave-catching*, the business of searching out and arresting fugitive slaves, to return them to their masters. **1842** CHANNING *Works* (1886) 880/1 It is even reported, that the slave-coffle is sometimes headed by the flag of the United States. **1840** *Niles' Nat. Reg.* 6 June 212/1 The slave decks on board of slave vessels . . . are formed of rough boards resting on water casks and stone ballast, and raised to within five feet of the deck. **1854** A. L. STONE *Oration 4 July* 13 (Ernst), The triumphant encroachment of the Slave Despotism on our soil. **1853** STOWE *Key* 123/1 Is there not the same dread through all the despotic slave governments of America? **1864** WEBSTER 1241/2 *Slave-hunt*, . . . a search after fugitive slaves. **1838** *Jeffersonian* (Albany) 2 June 125/1 Those who advocate the surpassing excellence of the slave institutions of the South have taken a bolder and more daring stand. **1833** *Congress. Deb.* 5 Feb. 1623/2 The South receives an equivalent for these exactions in some peculiar protection which is afforded by the constitution and the Union to our slave interest. **1854** BENTON *30 Years' View* I. 10/1 [The Missouri issue] divided Congress geographically, and upon the slave line. **1891** *Atlantic Mo.* June 813/2 The younger and progressive Negroes . . . are giving up, too, the old slave melodies. **1864** *Ore. State Jrnl.* 5 Nov. 1/5 We, the 'slave oligarchs,' [have] governed the Yankees till within a twelve month. **1885** *Mag. Amer. Hist.* April 395/1 Slave oligarchy.—The Slaveholders' Oligarchy is the more proper form. **1842** CHANNING *Works* (1886) 898/2 To unite with Texas . . . would be to ensure the predominance of the slave power. **1837** MARTINEAU *Society* II. 49 The slave-quarter is large. **1831** J. G. PALFREY *Oration 4 July* 13 (Ernst), Slave representation. **1835–7** HALIBURTON *Clockmaker* 1 Ser. xxvii. 267, I guess you needn't twitt me with our slave-sales for we deal only in blacks. **1854** BENTON *30 Years' View* I. 18/1 These treaties (Indian and Spanish) . . . extinguished slave soil in all the United States territory west of the Mississippi. **1881** *Harper's Mag.* May 818/2 The plaintive slave songs . . . have won popularity wherever the English language is spoken. **1804** *Ann. 8th Congress* 1 Sess. 1000 In various parts of the nation, outfits were made for slave-voyages, without secrecy, shame, or apprehension.

+**Slave auction.** An auction at which slaves are sold. Now hist. — **1839** CHANNING *Works* (1886) 787/1 Men whose reports of us determine our rank in the civilized world, associate with us the enormities of the slave-trade and of slave auctions. **1865** RICHARDSON *Secret Service* 30, I wish some of my old northern friends . . . could witness the scenes in the slave auctions. **1901** CHURCHILL *Crisis* 40 Was it possible that these people were coming to a slave auction?

+**Slave-breeder.** A slave-owner primarily interested in selling slaves and their offspring. *Obs.* — **1846** MACKENZIE *Van Buren* 276 [Canada] would now have been ruled by . . . the South Carolina and Virginia slave breeders and slave owners. **1860** ABBOTT *South & North* 54 The slave-breeders on the border States would sell off their stock. **1867** DIXON *New America* I. 16 Missouri . . . was then a slave state, with a sparse but fiery population of slave-breeders and slave-dealers.

+**Slave-breeding.** The breeding or rearing of slaves for the market. Usually contemptuous. *Obs.* Also attrib. — **1840** CHANNING *Works* (1886) 783/2 The northern slave States . . . have acquired a new interest . . . by humbling themselves to the condition of slave-breeding and slave-trading communities. **1857** W. R. ALGER *Genius Amer.* 7 [Virginia is] particularly celebrated now for four things, ruins, bankruptcy, arrogance, and slave-breeding. **1861** *N.Y. Tribune* 27 Dec. 7/2 Perhaps your next publication will altogether defend . . . slavery, slave-breeding and slave-trading. **1875** *Scribner's Mo.* Dec. 275/1 We leave the slave-breeding, and turn to the slave-consuming States.

+**Slave case.** A legal case involving or relating to a slave. *Obs.* — **1836** *Niles' Nat. Reg.* 26 Nov. 208/3 Another slave case. **1843** *Ib.* 19 Aug. 385 The Slave Case in Cincinnati.

+**Slave-catcher.** One whose occupation was searching out and returning fugitive slaves to their owners. *Obs.* — [**1765** TIMBERLAKE *Memoirs* 28 The old [Indian] warrior, commonly called the Slave Catcher of Tennessee, invited us to his camp.] **1852** STOWE *Uncle Tom* ix, Are you the man that will shelter a poor woman and child from slave-catchers? **1857** *Lawrence* (Kan.) *Republican* 11 June 2 The people . . . do not like to see their neighbors seized . . . for the offense of not helping a pack of slave-catchers do their dirty work. **1872** *Atlantic Mo.* April 426 A lasso might possibly be applied to a slave-catcher for once with good effect. **1882** WHITMAN *Spec. Days* 259 The members [of the Democratic nominating conventions were] . . . slave-catchers, pushers of slavery.

+**Slave code.** A system of state laws relating to slavery and the control of slaves. *Obs.* Also attrib. (Cf. BLACK CODE.) — **1835** CHANNING *Works* (1886) 703/1 'The slave can acquire nothing,' says one of the slave codes, 'but what must belong to his master.' **1858** DOUGLAS in Logan *Great Conspiracy* 70 If the People of a Territory want Slavery, they will encourage it by passing affirmatory laws, and the necessary police regulations, patrol laws and Slave Code. **1860** G. W. Bungay *Bobolink Minstrel* 24 [We'll] wipe out the slave-code teachers. **1865** in Fleming *Hist. Reconstruction* I. 176 There are no slaves now in Alabama. The slave code is a dead letter. **1893** *Harper's Mag.* April 701/1 The Legislature which assembled at Pawnee in July adopted the slave code of Missouri *en bloc*, . . . compelling every official, candidate, and voter to take an oath to support the fugitive-slave law.

+**Slave-driver.**

1. One employed or appointed to have charge of slaves or superintend them while at work. {1830–}

Cf. NEGRO-DRIVER.

1807 IRVING, etc. *Salmagundi* iii, Beautiful, O most puissant slave-driver, as are my wives, they are exceeded by the women of this country. **1857** GUNN *N.Y. Boarding-Houses* 127 The boarders said he'd been an overseer—or, as they termed it, *slave-driver*. **1885** BAYLOR *On Both Sides* 212 There was a dreadful slave-driver . . . carrying a wand with an iron tip heated red-hot.

2. *transf.* One in charge of others at work; a difficult or cruel taskmaster {1889}

1840 DANA *Two Years* 128 You've got a driver over you! Yes, a *slave-driver*—a *negro-driver!* **1854** THOREAU *Walden* 10 It is . . . worst of all when you are the slave-driver of yourself. **1892** *Courier-Journal* 1 Oct. 6/2 Since the abolition of slavery in the South the protected manufacturers of New England have been the slave-drivers of this country. **1901** MERWIN & WEBSTER *Calumet 'K'* 189 Do you think it would be worth something to the men who hire you for a dirty slave-driver to be protected from a strike?

+**Slave-driving,** *a.* Of or pertaining to the driving or superintending of Negro slaves. {1889 transf.} — **1830** *Congress. Deb.* 10 May 939/1 Here they may live and flourish, until some slave-driving politician and planter of South Carolina . . . again chains them to a miserable dependence on South Carolina cotton and British looms. **1859** J. B. JONES *Southern Scenes* 46 The reason alleged [for the ravage of one of his estates] was his alliance with the 'slave-driving' Blounts of the South. **1862** *N.Y. Tribune* 29 Jan. 5/2 The reciprocity swindle was fastened upon us by the slave-driving Democrats of the South. **1872** *Newton Kansan* 5 Sept. 4/3 The clothes he is in . . . belong to the . . . slave-driving Democracy.

+Slaveholders' rebellion. =REBELLION b; the Civil War. *Obs.* — **1861** *Chicago Tribune* 19 July 1/2 Senator Pomeroy's bill for the suppression of the slaveholders' rebellion, enacts that slavery be immediately abolished by proclamation. **1863** *Rep. Comm. Agric. 1862* 65 Surpassing all the enormities . . . of her past history is the great slaveholders' rebellion. **1865** RICHARDSON *Secret Service* 328 From the outbreak of the Slaveholders' Rebellion his name was one of the brightest in that noble but unfortunate army.

+Slaveholding state. =SLAVE STATE. *Obs.* — **1815** *Niles' Reg.* VIII. 66/1 Among the slave-holding states themselves, the progress of the black and white population has been steady and equal. **1840** *Picayune* 19 Sept. 2/5 When any man is found in a slaveholding state to express opinions so repugnant . . . , the most debasing punishment should be summarily inflicted on him. **1861** in Logan *Great Conspiracy* 149 The Slaveholding States are entitled to the faithful observance and execution of those laws. **1873** HOWELLS *Chance Acquaintance* i, Dr. Ellison . . . was too much an abolitionist to live in a slaveholding State with safety.

Slave labor. Labor performed by slaves; also, collect., slave laborers. {1871-} — **1820** *Ann. 16th Congress* 1 Sess. 1213 Free labor and slave labor cannot be employed together. **1853** STOWE *Key* 184/2 The filling up of all branches of mechanics and agriculture with slave labor necessarily depresses free labor. **1883** *Century Mag.* June 227/1 One pen brought out the underlying fact of slave labor. **1900** HALE *New Eng. Boyhood & Other Bits* 229 Place free and slave labor together, on fair ground.

+Slaveocracy, Slaveocrat, Slaveocratic. (See SLAVOCRACY, SLAVOCRAT, SLAVOCRATIC a.)

+Slaveownia. The slave-owning states. *Obs.* — **1862** *N.Y. Tribune* 21 March 6/4 [The Confederate] officers besought them . . . to recall . . . the reputation of Slaveownia for valor and chivalry. **1885** *Mag. Amer. Hist.* April 395/1 Slaveownia.—The word . . . did not come into general use.

Slave pen. A pen or enclosure for slaves awaiting sale. *Obs.* {1845} — **1846** WHITTIER *Writings* VII. 134 His rhetoric has a flavor of the slave-pen. **1874** COLLINS *Kentucky* I. 205 Trial for Killing . . . at the slave-pen in Memphis. **1901** CHURCHILL *Crisis* 35 Mr. Lynch's slave pen had been disgorged that morning.

+Slave property. Property consisting of slaves. *Obs.* — **1810** *Steele P.* II. 632 Being daily more & more disgusted with Tide Swamp and Slave property I should be glad to receive Terms or proposals for from 50 to 80 Negroes. **1839** CLAY *Speeches* (1860) II. 410 The total value . . . of the slave property in the United States, is twelve hundred millions of dollars. **1862** *N.Y. Tribune* 9 May 6/4 Is slave-property safer now than it was two years ago?

+Slave question. =SLAVERY QUESTION. *Obs.* — **1830** *Congress. Deb.* 25 Jan. 46/2 The weakness of the South, as connected with the slave question, exposes us to . . . constant attacks. **1848** *Santa Fe Republican* 29 Jan. 2/4 To the citizens of New Mexico, . . . the slave question and its final determination is of incalculable importance. **1866** 'F. KIRKLAND' *Bk. Anecdotes* 123/1 Mr. Calhoun . . . did not think the slave question . . . would produce a dissolution of the Union.

Slaver.

1. A vessel engaged in the slave trade. {1830-}
1827 COOPER *Red Rover* I. 71 It is the boatswain of the slaver in the outer harbour. **1840** VAN BUREN in *Pres. Mess. & P.* III. 619 After cruising off those parts of the coast most usually resorted to by slavers . . . , these vessels returned to the United States. **1890** *Harper's Mag.* Sept. 594/2 Living in quarters as crowded and bilgy as a slaver's hold.

+2. One who traffics in slaves. {1889-}
1833 COKE *Subaltern's Furlough* I. 175 No one uttered a word, but all looked hard at the slaver. **1850** COLTON *Deck & Port* 108 His moral firmness has made him the terror of every slaver. **1891** HOWELLS *Imperative Duty* vii, Was he some old slaver, like those in Mr. Cable's book?

***Slavery.** The social system or institution of holding human beings in bondage. {1728-} Now hist.
1773 FRANKLIN *Writings* VI. 39 A Disposition to abolish Slavery prevails in North America. **1819** E. DANA *Geogr. Sk.* 85 The tobacco plant, . . . as in all western states, where slavery is not permitted, is but little cultivated. **1864** ANDREWS *Recoll.* 187 The more rebels see that they cannot retain slavery, the more readily will they quit. **1893** *Harper's Mag.* April 700/1 The question of freedom or slavery in the Territory, and in the State to be, . . . was merely an incident in the tragedy.

b. Attrib. with *agitation, amendment,* etc.
1846 POLK *Diary* II. 76 There is but little doubt the Senate would have struck out the slavery proviso. **1854** BENTON *30 Years' View* I. 5/1 Slavery agitation took its rise . . . in the form of attempted restriction on the State of Missouri. **1865** COX *8 Yrs. in Congress* 406 Mr. Buchanan . . . proposed to save us from war by slavery amendments. **1886** LOGAN *Great Conspiracy* 490 An immediate decision by the Border-States to adopt . . . a policy of gradual Emancipation, would simultaneously solve the two intimately-blended problems of Slavery-destruction and Union-preservation.

+Slavery extension. The extension or spreading of slavery to new regions. Hence *slavery extensionist. Obs.* — **1848** McKee *National Conventions* (1901) 67 The political conventions recently assembled at Baltimore

and Philadelphia . . . [have nominated] candidates neither of whom can be supported by the opponents of slavery extension. **1850** *Whig Almanac 1851* 10/1 [A] number of 'Free-Soil Democrats' . . . could not vote for a speaker so thoroughly adverse as Mr. Cobb to their views of Slavery Extension. **1860** LOWELL *Writings* V. 40 Concede the demand of the slavery-extensionists. **1886** LOGAN *Great Conspiracy* 35 Threats and counter-threats of Disunion were made on either hand by the opponents and advocates of Slavery-extension through annexation.

Slavery question. The question or problem created by the existence of slavery as an institution. *Obs.* {1851-} — **1838** CLAY in *Corr. R. W. Griswold* (1898) 22 Should it be deemed necessary at a Convention to be holden in the fall, to ask my sentiments on the Slavery question. **1856** *Democratic Conv. Proc.* 25 The Democratic party will resist all attempts at renewing . . . the agitation of the slavery question. **1881** *Ore. State Jrnl.* 1 Jan. 1/3 All those in New York who were carefully watching the shifting phases of the slavery question were thinking seriously and sadly of John Brown. **1882** *Nation* 21 Dec. 531/2 To say that not one of these understood the slavery question . . . is only to repeat an acknowledged truism.

+Slave state. A state of the American Federal Union in which slavery was legal. Now hist. Also attrib. — **1809** *Ann. 10th Congress* 2 Sess. 428 In the slave States the allowance for the subsistence of a negro, is one peck of corn per week. **1848** *Californian* (San Francisco) 15 March 2/1 We left the slave States because we did not like to bring up a family in a miserable, can't-help-one's-self condition. **1857** BENTON *Exam. Dred Scott Case* 20 The owner cannot carry his slave State law with him into the Territory.

+Slave system. A system or social order in which slavery prevails as a legalized institution. — **1845** F. DOUGLASS *Narrative* 125, [I hope] that this little book may do something towards throwing light on the American slave system. **1853** STOWE *Key* 70/1 The author . . . was anxious . . . to have some understanding of the laws of the slave system. **1862** *N.Y. Tribune* 9 May 6/4 Is the slave system stronger politically [because of the efforts of Southern congressmen]?

+Slave territory. A territory or region where slavery is legalized. *Obs.* — **1847** LOWELL *Biglow P.* 1 Ser. iv. 50 We wunt hev an inch o' slave territory. **1851** *Harper's Mag.* July 274/1 [Mr. Webster] would never consent that there should be one foot of slave-territory beyond what the old Thirteen States had at the time of the formation of the Union. **1854** BENTON *30 Years' View* I. 18/1 There was not a ripple of discontent . . . at this mighty transformation of slave into free territory.

Slave trade. Traffic in slaves, esp. the bringing of Negro slaves to America. {1734-} Now hist.
1766 A. BENEZET *Caution to Gt. Britain* (1767) 3 The intent of publishing the following sheets, is more fully to make known the aggravated iniquity attending the practice of the Slave-Trade. **1806** *Balance* V. 47/1 Every state had agreed with congress, in their abhorrence of the slave trade. **1893** PAGE in *Harper's Mag.* Dec. 14/2 Virginia was the first State to declare the slave trade piracy. **1901** *Munsey's Mag.* Aug. 648/1 Purchased by a Baltimore firm for use in the slave trade, she was sent to Santiago, Cuba.

attrib. **1840** *Niles' Nat. Reg.* 15 Aug. 384/2 Slave trade decision. The schooner Catharine sent in by a British cruiser as being intended for the slave trade, is discharged by the decision of judge Betts. **1861** COX *8 Yrs. in Congress* 24 Governor McRae . . . [was] an original slave-trade secessionist, though educated in Ohio.

Slave trader. A ship employed in the slave trade {1875}; a person who trades or traffics in slaves. *Obs.* {1813} Also attrib. — **1821** J. Q. ADAMS *Diary* 270 There had not been found for these two years a single slave-trader wearing the American flag. **1842** CHILD *Lett. New York* (1846) 156 In New England, men look upon a slave-trader with as much horror as they do upon a pirate. **1861** *N.Y. Tribune* 18 Oct. 4/4 Wherever the slave traders resort, the name of our New-York Marshal is heartily cursed.

+Slave yard. A yard or enclosure where slaves are kept while awaiting sale. *Obs.* — **1866** MOORE *Women of War* 308 War had charms for him far beyond the milder horrors of the slave-yard and the smaller risks of the gaming-table. **1880** CABLE *Grandissimes* 121 Faintly audible to the apothecary . . . came from a neighboring slave-yard the monotonous chant and machine-like tune-beat of an African dance.

Slavist. One who favors or upholds slavery. {anti-slavist, 1832} *Obs.* — **1862** *Independent* 29 May (Chipman), Mr. Brown's figures are unanswerable, though doubtless some slavist will babble against them. **1889** H. O'REILLY *50 Yrs. on Trail* 15 The border warfare between the slavists and free-soilers.

‖Slavite. =prec. *Obs.* — **1831** *Liberator* 8 Jan. 1/2 (Th. S.), To say that a clerical slavite is bound to follow his own precepts, is preposterous. *Ib.* I. 115 (*Cent.*), The most abominable . . . spectacle which the wickedness of war presents in the sight of Heaven is a reverend slavite.

+Slavocracy. A dominant or powerful class made up of slave-owners and those favoring slavery. *Obs.* — **1848** *Whig Almanac 1849* 47/2 Borrowing . . . is very easy, in the estimation of this corrupt instrument of the slavocracy. **1865** *Nation* I. 202 The slaveocracy exists to-day in almost as much force as it existed before a shot had been exchanged. **1913** A. C. COLE *Whig Party in So.* 69 The economic and political interests of the southern Whigs were the 'special interests' of the slavocracy.

+Slavocrat. A member of the slavocracy. *Obs.* — **1859** BARTLETT 413 *Slavocrat,* a slaveholder. **1865** *Atlantic Mo.* Feb. 159/2 The slavocrats' revolution . . . will be the theme of the world. **1868** *Putnam's Mag.* May 596/1 There meet . . . the freedman and the once slavocrat.

+**Slavocratic**, *a.* Of or pertaining to a slavocrat. *Obs.* — **1857** *Lawrence* (Kan.) *Republican* 18 June 2 He excoriated this miserable slavocratic sham, which rejoices to call itself 'National democracy.'

+**Slaw.** [Du. *sla*.] =COLESLAW. Also *comb.* — **1861** WINTHROP *C. Dreeme* 157 Pad of butter. Plate of slaw, ready vinegared. **1883** RITTENHOUSE *Maud* 254 Mama had a lovely dinner, nicely served—turkeys, oysters, cran-berry sauce, celery, vegetables, slaw [etc.]. **1883** KNIGHT *Suppl.* 359/1 *Fruit Slicer*, an open-bottomed box with a follower, to contain fruit, and slipped back and forth in grooves over a knife fixed like that of a slaw-cutter beneath.—*Wharry.* **1891** *Cent.* 5688/2 *Slaw*, ... sliced cabbage, served cooked or uncooked as a salad. **1905** *N.Y. Ev. Post* 23 Sept. 2 Mince pie, hokey-pokey ice cream, over-ripe watermelon, frankfurters with hot slaw—all the less expensive and less desirable articles of diet go to stunt the gamin's growth.

***Slay.**[1] An instrument used in weaving; a reed. — **1648** *Essex Probate Rec.* I. 253 Three slayes ... ; three wheels. **1707** *Boston News-Letter* 7 April 2/2 All persons may be furnished at his Shop with all sorts of Sleas ready made on reasonable termes. **1831** PECK *Guide* 285 [Union county] has ... one reed and two slæ shops. **1892** HARRIS *On Plantation* 104 Aunt Crissy used to ... [keep] time with the ... dancing slays.

Slay.[2] (See SLEIGH.)

***Slead**, *n.* =SLED *n.* 1. *Obs.* — **1642** *Essex Inst. Coll.* L. 238 Cart, Slead & 3 Yoaks, 1 li. 6 s. **1712** HEMPSTEAD *Diary* 6 The Sleads are fetching wood fro Groaton on ye Ice. **1742** *N.H. Probate Rec.* III. 120, I also Give To my Three Sons ... all my farming Tackling, as Carts, Plows, Sleads.

Slead, *v.* {1689} +*tr.* =SLED *v.* 1. *Obs.* — **1712** HEMPSTEAD *Diary* 6 They Slead wood over into town from Groaton. **1718** *Ib.* 73, I workt at home al day. ... Sleading Stones with my Steers.

***Sled**, *n.*
'Now chiefly *dial.* and *U.S.* (O.E.D.). See also BOBSLED *n.*, DOG SLED.

***1.** A vehicle on runners for the conveyance of passengers or heavy loads over snow or ice.

1686 SEWALL *Diary* I. 165 Governour and Mr. Dudley ride in a Sled. **1701** *Boston Rec.* 12 No cart, Dray, Trucks or Sled drawn by either horse or horses, or horse and Oxen, shall be suffered to pass through any of the streets ... but with a sufficient driver. **1775** *Essex Inst. Coll.* XIII. 167 I have this day sent ... 6 casks by Young's Sleds. **1806** *Balance* V. 28/1 The machines may be easily conveyed on a waggon or sled. *a*1862 THOREAU *Maine Woods* 242 In the Aroostook country the sleds are required by law to be of one width. **1896** WILKINS *Madelon* 119 An ox-team drawing a sled laden with cedar logs. **1922** A. BROWN *Old Crow* 344 He sat looking out at the road, smooth with the grinding of sleds and slipping of sleighs.

+**b.** (See quotation.)
1832 COOPER *Pioneers* (rev. ed.) 3*n.*, Americans ... draw a distinction between a sled, or sledge, and a sleigh; the sleigh being shod with metal.

2. =HAND SLED.
Quot. 1680 may belong under sense 1.
1680 *N.H. Hist. Soc. Coll.* VIII. 43 The young man pulled both sled and father towards the house. **1869** STOWE *Oldtown Folks* 267 We had our sleds with us,—dear winter companions of boys. **1883** WILDER *Sister Ridnour* 200 We'd got Sammy a new sled. **1907** *St. Nicholas* Aug. 906/1 The expressman has just brought a perfect dream of a sled.

+**3.** A type of river boat: (see quot. 1832).
1832 FLINT *Hist. Miss. Valley* I. 151 The ferry flat is a scow-boat, and when used as a boat of descent for families, has a roof, or covering. These are sometimes, in the vernacular phrase, called 'sleds.' **1884** *Harper's Mag.* June 124/2 Of smaller vessels there were 'covered sleds,' 'ferry flats,' and 'Alleghany skiffs.'

4. Attrib. with *load, path, ride,* etc.
1726 *New-Eng. Courant* 26 Feb. 2/2 Allowing 3 Sled Load to one Cord, it comes out at 3 Shillings per Cord. **1804** FESSENDEN *Orig. Poems* (1806) 40 Oh, my Sophy! smile propitious, ... Nor, by conduct so capricious, Drive a sled-stake through my heart. **1854** M. J. HOLMES *Tempest & Sunshine* 176 His wife ... had not yet ceased laughing at Fanny's ludicrous description of her sled-ride. **1861** B. ALCOTT *Journals* 335, I get glimpses of Hawthorne as I walk up the sledpaths. **1873** BEADLE *Undevel. West* 727 The sled routes take a straight track from point to point.

+**Sled,** *v.*

1. a. *tr.* To convey (goods) by sled.
1706 *Essex Inst. Coll.* X. 73 Some wood sledded to ye water's side. **1743** MACSPARRAN *Diary* 11 Harry sledded stones this Forenoon. **1794** in Buckingham *Newspaper Lit.* II. 229 Two sheets, a feather bed and hay-tick, I order sledded up to Natick. **1831** WITHERS *Chron. Border Warfare* 232 Henry Fink and his son John, were engaged in sledding rails. **1882** T. D. PRICE *Diary* (MS.) 3 Feb., Mark sledded some wood to top of hill.

b. To move (something) about in the manner of a sled.
1855 *Knickerb.* XLV. 419 Ranting round the floor they run, Sledding a chair.

2. *intr.* To travel or ride on a sled. {1910}
1714 SEWALL *Diary* II. 430 Major Thaxter ... says he saw a man Sledding. **1780** A. ADAMS *Familiar Lett.* 377 The Bay has been frozen so hard that people have walked, rode, and sledded over it to Boston. **1832** WATSON *Hist. Tales N.Y.* 119 The western end of Garden street was ... a celebrated place for the boys in winter to sled down hill.

3. Of a load: To admit of being sledded.
1869 STOWE *Oldtown* 482 Now, p'r'aps, ef you'd jest tighten up the ropes ... , the hull load would sled easier.

+**Sledding.**

1. The action of conveying things on sleds or of riding on a sled; weather conditions affecting this.
1682 *Jamaica Rec.* I. 232 A way through the saide Lucasses Medow for sleding of hay. **1726** *New-Eng. Courant* 26 Feb. 2/2 The Sledding being now over, Country Loads of Oak Wood are sold. **1780** *Holyoke Diaries* 102 Rain. Sledding Spoild. **1804** *Essex Inst. Coll.* XXXIX. 325 We believe you have fine sledding. **1833** WATSON *Hist. Tales of Phila.* 157 There was also much sledding down the streets and hills descending to Pegg's run. **1890** JEWETT *Strangers* 36, I heard say yesterday that there was good sleddin'.

b. *Six weeks sledding in March,* ? a late spring.
1818 BENTLEY *Diary* IV. 505 We have an old saying, 6 weeks sledding in March.

2. *fig.* The action of getting on with a job, of earning a living, etc. Usually modified by an adj., as *hard, smooth.*
1839 GREELEY in *Corr. R. W. Griswold* (1898) 26 Payments are slack still, and we have rather hard sledding. **1855** *Knickerb.* XLV. 419 About that time it gets to be 'Hard sledding,' quite too hard for me. **1888** *Congress Rec.* 1 May 3589/1 For the farmer, in those days, there was mighty bad sledding on the road to Hard Scrabble. **1898** *N.Y. Ev. Post* 21 Oct. 1 Professional labor agitators do not always have smooth sledding in the field of politics. **1924** CROY *R.F.D. No. 3* 47 It was the duty of the 'contest manager' on the newspaper to originate some new feature each day, and often it was hard sledding.

***Sledge.**[1] A large, heavy hammer usually wielded with both hands. — **1647** *Suffolk Deeds* I. 70 Edward Gibones granted unto Richard Russell & Martha Coitmore ... one Crow of Iron one sledge one busking chesill [etc.]. **1798** I. ALLEN *Hist. Vermont* 41 [He] caused the miller to break the stones into small pieces with a sledge. **1877** MCCABE *Hist. Great Riots* 102 Men armed with heavy sledges would break open the cars. **1901** MERWIN-WEBSTER *Calumet 'K'* 5 There's Peterson now; up there with the sledge.

Sledge.[2]
1. A sled {1617–}, usually one with low runners for transporting heavy loads. {1684–}
See also DOG SLEDGE.
1745 SHIRLEY *Letter* (1746) 8 By the Help of Sledges [they] transported the Cannon and Mortars over these Ways. **1775** A. BURNABY *Travels* 50 In the winter, when there is snow upon the ground, it is usual to make what they call sleighing parties, or to go upon it in sledges. **1809** A. HENRY *Travels* 9, I discerned a *cariole*, or sledge, moving our way. **1842** HAWTHORNE *Twice-told Tales* (1851) II. 124 Next comes a sledge, laden with wood for some unthrifty housekeeper. **1869** STOWE *Oldtown Folks* 267 We had our sleds with us,— ... not the gayly painted, genteel little sledges with which Boston boys in these days enliven the Common, but rude, coarse fabrics. **1870** KEIM *Sheridan's Troopers* 183 Their affects [sic] were carried on dogs, or sledges drawn by that animal.

b. (See quot. 1884.)
1884 EGGLESTON in *Century Mag.* Jan. 446/2 Two skids fastened together made a 'drag' or 'sledge.' **1902** WHITE *Blazed Trail* 10 The logs would be dragged and hauled ... by means of ... a short sledge on which one end of the timber would be chained.

2. Attrib. with *bell, dog, journey,* etc.
1856 KANE *Arctic Explor.* I. 377 The instinct of a sledge-dog makes him perfectly aware of unsafe ice. **1864** *Harper's Mag.* Nov. 740 Our road was ... a sledge-track cut by lumbermen. **1881** *Harper's Mag.* Jan. 234/2 The sound of his sledge bells came through their closed doors. **1886** HARTE *Snowbound* 77 A man up at Strawberry fell under a sledge-load of wood in the snow. **1898** *McClure's Mag.* X. 297 During ... my sledge journey I got the impression that there was more motion in the ice the further we went north.

***Sledge hammer.** =SLEDGE.[1] — **1669** *York Deeds* II. 69 The Smyths shopp with bellows, anvell, beckorne, vice, sledge hammer & some ould irons. **1738** *N.H. Hist. Soc. Coll.* II. 80 [A committee are appointed] to procure ... sledge-hammer and tongs, fit for the work of a blacksmith. **1851** *Polly Peablossom* 79 He saw Forgeron, with a huge sledge-hammer in his hand. **1911** VANCE *Cynthia* 187 Rhode was stricken and carried off his feet, as by a blow of a sledge-hammer.

+**Sled-tender.** (See quot. 1905.) — **1860** *Harper's Mag.* March 444/2 The sled-tender is ready with team, tackle and fall, to raise the huge bodies of the fallen [trees] upon his sled, and transport them to the landing-places at the river. **1905** *Forestry Bureau. Bul.* No. 61, 47 *Sled tender*, a member of the hauling crew who accompanies the turn of logs to the landing, unhooks the grabs, and sees that they are returned to the yarding engine. (P[acific] C[oast] F[orest].)

Sleek, *adv.* {1602–} +Easily; smoothly. *slang.* (Cf. SLICK *adv.*) — **1806** *Spirit of Public Jrnls.* 114 Thus happy I hop'd I should pass, Sleek as grease down the current of time. **1814** *Niles' Reg.* VI. 39/1 If it had not been for the d——d guard ... , they would have had them away sleek. **1836** CROCKETT *Exploits* 16 The Hero ... had chalked out his course so sleek.

* Sleep, n.

+1. Among the Indians: A day, the measure of time between one sleeping period and the next.

1670 *S.C. Hist. Soc. Coll.* V. 166 The Caseeka . . . was within one sleep of us. **1761** NILES *Indian Wars* II. 582 He proposed . . . to return in 10 nights, or sleeps. **1844** GREGG *Commerce of Prairies* II. 298 Distances are represented by days' journey, which are oftener designated by camps or 'sleeps.' **1885** *Milnor* (Dak.) *Teller* 3 July 2/6 Cholera, chief of the Utes, . . . said he would give me two sleeps to get away in. **1919** CODY & COOPER *Buffalo Bill* 312 It was many sleeps away.

2. The state of a top spinning with such velocity that its motion is imperceptible.

1868 J. W. HOWE *From Oak to Olive* 25 Another, a top-spinning savage, continually whirls his top into that state which the boys call 'sleep.'

* Sleep, v.

1. *tr.* To provide (a person) with sleeping accommodations. {1884-}

1848 BARTLETT 306 She could eat fifty people in her house, but could not sleep half the number. **1883** *Gringo & Greaser* 1 Sept. 2/1 If we can find some other philanthropist who will kindly hash, beer and sleep us, we'll be there. **1912** RAINE *Brand Blotters* 47 He figured we couldn't eat and sleep him without extra trouble.

2. With adverbs. **+a.** *To sleep over*, to sleep beyond the time of usual awakening; (see quot. 1851). As *vbl. n.* {=E. 'to oversleep'}

1827 *Harvard Reg.* Sept. 202 They have indulged in the luxury of 'sleeping over.' **1851** HALL *College Words* 284 *Sleeping over*, a phrase equivalent to being absent from prayers. **1854** M. J. HOLMES *Tempest & Sunshine* 164 Claib, her husband, had adhered to his resolution of 'sleeping over.' **1871** BAGG *At Yale* 570 On Sunday mornings, too, there is an unusual amount of 'sleeping over,'—breakfast being often cut as well as chapel by the votaries of Morpheus.

+b. *To sleep up*, to catch up on one's sleep.

1884 'MARK TWAIN' *H. Finn* vii, We laid off after breakfast to sleep up, both of us being about wore out.

* Sleeper.

1. One of various strong timbers used to support a wall, floor, etc., esp. one of the joists laid directly upon the ground to receive the flooring of a ground story. {1607-}

1665 *Cambridge Rec.* 159 Granted liberty to seurall persons to fell timb[er] on the common . . . for sleepers & orchard fences. **1682** *Huntington Rec.* I. 343 Lewes shall [get] . . . six sleepers of good and sound timber. **1704** *Boston Rec.* 39 Lay the lower flowr with Sleepers & double boards. **1794** *Steele P.* II. 764 Archibald Casey is to hew loggs, sleepers, Joices [etc.]. **1833** *Niles' Reg.* XLIV. 395/1 The flooring was white pine plank, laid on oaken sleepers, the latter running crosswise. **1860** MORDECAI *Virginia* 305 The floor of the bridge had been taken up for repair, and the large sleepers remained.

+2. A railroad car arranged with compartments and berths for sleeping. Cf. PULLMAN, SLEEPING CAR.

1875 *Chicago Tribune* 11 Sept. 3/2 Every item of wood, iron, or upholstery which enters into the make-up . . . of a Pullman sleeper is Selected with Skilled Care. **1883** RITTENHOUSE *Maud* 188 He took us to the dressing-room in the sleeper. **1906** *Harper's Mag.* April 746 [He stood] in the aisle of the swaying sleeper. **1917** SINCLAIR *King Coal* 348, I came down on that sleeper last night.

attrib. **1914** 'BOWER' *Flying U Ranch* 52, I had the agent wire for sleeper berths on the 11:20.

+3. (See quot. 1907.) Also comb.

1894 *McClure's Mag.* III. 113/1 It is these ear-marks, . . . which makes the practice of 'sleeper branding' possible. **1907** WHITE *Arizona Nights* 78 A sleeper is a calf that has been ear-marked, but not branded. **1918** MULFORD *Man from Bar-20* 117 It's a sleeper. Somebody's took the trouble to cut th' notch [in its ear].

4. In miscellaneous senses.

a. ?A dormitory. **+b.** (See quot. 1864.) Also fig. **+c.** In athletic contests, a competitor who makes himself unnoticed in order to put opponents off guard. **d.** (See quotation.)

(a) **1754** *S.C. Gazette* 1 Jan. 4/1 The sleeper 15 feet square, and was built this year. **(b)** **1864** DICK *Amer. Hoyle* (1866) 208 A bet [in faro] is said to be a sleeper, when the owner has forgotten it, when it becomes public property, any one having a right to take it. **1896** G. W. DICE *Counterfeiting Exposed* 25 [He] was on a 'dead card' and liable to be 'swiped for a sleeper.' **(c)** **1892** *Outing* March 454/2 [Harmar was] beaten by Wells, a 'sleeper' from Amherst. **(d)** **1909** *N.Y. Ev. Post* (s.-w. ed.) 26 April 1 Attempts to smuggle gowns and women's wearing apparel by means of so-called 'sleepers,' or trunks which are brought over on the steamships without being accompanied by the owner.

* Sleeping. *attrib.* Designating various rooms or places for sleeping.

1841 COOPER *Deerslayer* xii, They entered the sleeping apartment of Hutter. **1870** *Pathfinder Railway Guide* Oct. 1 Palatial *Drawing Room* and Sleeping Coaches. **1874** KNIGHT 481/2 Car-seats . . . made reclining,

for night travel, . . . are termed 'sleeping-chairs.' **1890** *Stock Grower & Farmer* 11 Jan. 7/1 Here and there and everywhere are sleeping tents. *a*1904 WHITE *Blazed Trail Stories* 44 The camp consisted . . . [of] a cook-camp, a sleeping-camp, and a stable. **1923** WYATT *Invis.* Gods 111 The house was provided with an upstairs porch, one of the first sleeping porches in Chicago.

+Sleeping attorney. An attorney secretly retained to sleep in the same lodging that jurors sleep in, so as to be near to influence their decision in a case. — **1809** KENDALL *Travels* I. 184 It has been found that a *sleeping attorney* may be rendered very profitable.

+Sleeping bag. A large bag of warm material in which one may sleep. — **1856** KANE *Arctic Explor.* I. 196 We crawled into our reindeer sleeping-bags. **1898** *McClure's Mag.* X. 413 A sleeping-bag (a hair-mattress encased in reindeer skin) occupied the middle of the car. **1923** J. H. COOK *On Old Frontier* 6 We had no tents or bed tarpaulins or sleeping bags.

+Sleeping car. = SLEEPER 2.

1839 *Mechanics' Mag.* 5 Jan. 240 The introduction of the newly-invented sleeping cars on our railroads. **1860** GREELEY *Overland Journey* 8, I tried a 'sleeping car' for the third time and not very successfully. **1866** In Lossing *Civil War* (1868) II. 149 Mr. Lincoln merely took the sleeping-car in the night train. **1882** HOWELLS *Modern Instance* xiv, Our railroad tickets were nineteen [dollars], the sleeping-car was three. **1923** J. H. COOK *On Old Frontier* 30 A snoring man was an abomination in a cow-camp, as much so as he is today in a sleeping car.

b. Attrib. with *berth, company, porter.*

1882 PECK *Sunshine* 183 The sleeping car companies are discussing the idea . . . of placing safes in the cars. **1884** *Century Mag.* Oct. 945/1 The considerations here suggested are applicable . . . to sleeping-car porters and hotel waiters. **1901** CHURCHILL *Crisis* 324 In Shreve's time the cabins were curtained off, just like these new-fangled sleeping-car berths.

Sleeping room. A room for sleeping. {1727-} 'Now *U.S.*' (*O.E.D.*). — **1789** MAY *Jrnl. & Lett.* 125, I often find . . . the air of the sleeping-rooms thick and ropy. **1835** REED & MATHEWSON *Visit* I. 165 The sleeping-rooms, as they were called, were in the angles of the roof. **1872** *Chicago Tribune* 10 Nov. 9/4 There are in all 125 sleeping-rooms. **1902** WISTER *Virginian* 21 In this public sleeping room they had done what one does to secure a seat in a railroad train.

+Sleeping sawyer. A sawyer beneath the surface of the water. — **1807** SCHULTZ *Travels* II. 30 *Sleeping Sawyers* are the same as those just mentioned, except that their motion is entirely under water. **1819** SCHOOLCRAFT *Mo. Lead Mines* 224 When the tree does not reach within two or three feet of the surface of the water, they [the sawyers] are called *sleeping sawyers.*

* Sleepy, a. **+**In the specific names of plants and birds. — **1817-8** EATON *Botany* (1822) 459 *Silene antirrhina*, sleepy catchfly . . . Flowers small. **1891** *Cent.* 5691/2 *Sleepy duck*, the ruddy duck, *Erismatura rubida*; also called *sleepyhead, sleepy coot, sleepy brother.* (Atlantic coast, U.S.). *Ib.* 5951/1 *S[ipa] viridula*, var. *robusta*, of Mexico, New Mexico, etc., is reported to have a narcotic effect upon horses, and is called *sleepy-grass.*

Sleepy Hollow (chair). A type of easy-chair. {1834 (M. Edgeworth *Helen* I. 321)} — **1841** SEALSFIELD *Das Cajütenbuch* (1846) 330 Während sie sich in den *Sleepy Hollow* niederlies. **1880** *Harper's Mag.* Oct. 744/2 She seated herself in a Sleepy Hollow chair. **1885** BAYLOR *On Both Sides* 8 Two small red-plush tea-tables and sleepy-hollow chairs had been drawn near a glowing coal fire.

* Sleeve, n. Attrib. with *link* {1886}, *stud.* — **1820** *Columbian Centinel* 26 Jan. 3/5 [To be sold at auction:] Sleeve Links. **1860** E. COWELL *Diary* 150 A Mr. Christian . . . also gave him a pair of gold sleeve studs.

* Sleeve, v. tr. To put the arm about the waist of (a person) {1898, *dial.*}; to take (a person) by the sleeve. — **1834** CARRUTHERS *Kentuckian* I. 68 If there was a little knockin down and draggin out . . . among them dandy chaps, they would take better care how they sleeved decent men's daughters. **1885** JEWETT *Marsh Island* 95 He was squiring his mother at the head of the procession, sleevin' of her handsome, as if he liked it. **1896** — *Pointed Firs* 44, I see you sleevin' the old gentleman down the hill.

Sleeve button. 1. A cuff link. {1686-} 2. (See quotation.) — **(1)** **1773** in *Harper's Mag.* LXIV. 484/2 [Please return] lost sleeve-buttons to Mr. Todd, next door to the Coffee-House. **1828** SHERBURNE *Memoirs* 43 His shirt lay on the top of his clothes and his silver sleeve buttons lay upon his sheet. **1881** *Century Mag.* Nov. 50/2 A Cape Ann soldier shot a crow with his silver sleeve-buttons. **(2)** **1888** WHITMAN *Nov. Boughs* 71 In the slang of the New York common restaurant waiters . . . codfish balls [are known] as 'sleeve-buttons.'

+Sleigh, n. Also **†sley, slay, slae.** {1797-} [Du. *slee*, contraction of *slede.*] 'Chiefly *U.S.* and *Canada*' (*O.E.D.*).

1. = SLED *n.* 1; usu. a lighter vehicle for people.

1703 SEWALL *Diary* II. 91 Corps is brought to Town in the Governours Slay. **1708** *Boston News-Letter* 9 Feb. 2/2 Deleware River so froze that Loaden Slaes goes from hence upon it to Philadelphia. **1721** *New-Eng. Courant* 25 Dec., They went to church in a sley. **1759** in Rogers *Journals* 134, [I] send you twenty-two sleys to transport your sick. **1799** *Ann. 7th Congress* 2 Sess. 1429, I got into the sleigh, and went off. **1834** IRVING, etc. *Salmagundi* (1897), i. 12 n., Amongst the amusements . . . was that of making excursions in the winter evenings, on sleighs, to some neighboring village. **1892** *S. Dak. Hist. Coll.* I. 60 Over this mail route, in

February, 1871, came H. R. Vaughn, 'in an open one horse sleigh.' **1922** [see SLED *n.* 1].

b. = HAND SLED.
1869 *Boyd's Business Directory* 58 Wheelbarrows and Childrens' Sleighs. Newell & Sperry, Jordan.

+2. The bone of the upper jaw of a sperm whale.
1874 SCAMMON *Marine Mammals* 75 Next to and above the bone of the upper jaw (which is termed the 'coach' or 'sleigh').

3. Attrib. and comb. in sense 1 with *drive, frolicker,* etc.
1758 *Mayflower Descendant* X. 187 We Have Constantly Kept a Good Slay Path out in One Plais. **1772** *Boston Gazette* 3 Feb. 3/2 The ingenuity of some of those nocturnal Sley-frolickers, had added the Drum and Conkshell, or Pope-horn, to their own natural, noisy, abilities. **1802** *Mass. Spy* 24 March (Th.), A lad, seated on the fore part of a sleigh load of goods, was suddenly pitched off before one of the runners. **1855** *Knickerb.* XLV. 354 Already the sleigh-marks on the old snow were hidden. **1868** WHITTIER *Poetical Works* (1894) I. 273 Sleigh-drives on the mountain ways Defy the winter weather.

+Sleigh, *v. intr.* and *tr.* (See quot. 1806.) — **1728** SEWALL *Letter-Book* II. 264 They waited there for convenient snow to slay it to Salem. **1767** ROWE *Diary* 122, I went Sleighing in Bracketts sleigh. **1806** WEBSTER 281/1 *Sley,* to ride or convey in a sley. **1900** STOCKTON *Afield & Afloat* 249 She sometimes went sleighing.

+Sleigh bell. One of the small bells, usually of globular shape, attached to sleigh harness or to the sleigh itself. — *c*1790 in E. H. Smith *Amer. Poems* 208 Mind and have the sleigh-bells sent. **1823** COOPER *Pioneers* iii, The cheerful sound of sleigh-bells, however, attracted the attention of the whole party. **1885** CRAWFORD *Amer. Politician* 10 The sleigh bells tinkled unceasingly as the sleighs slipped by the window. **1908** [see DASH 1].

+Sleigh box. The box or body of a sleigh. — **1855** HOLBROOK *Among Mail Bags* 142 He drew from the sleigh-box . . . a revolver. **1867** 'LACK-LAND' *Homespun* 61 There in the sleigh-box, how snug and cosily they are squeezed together under the shaggy robes! *c*1873 DE VERE *MS. Notes* 186 *Bobs,* short, stout sleds, 2 of which are gen[erally] placed under 1 sleighbox or wagon box.

+Sleigher. One who rides in a sleigh. — **1861** *Harper's Mag.* Jan. 236/1 Away the merry sleighers bound, With jingling sound of bells.

+Sleighing. Riding in a sleigh for pleasure; the condition of the snow or ice that permits this.
1780 HAMILTON *Works* VIII. 33 When the sleighing arrives, it will be an affair of two days up and two days down. **1794** T. COOPER *America* 102 The snow had not yet fallen so thick, or so permanently, as to admit of the amusement of *sleighing.* **1832** WILLIAMSON *Maine* I. 100 During the whole of it [January], in many years, the sleighing is poor. **1885** HOWELLS *Silas Lapham* 403 The sleighing was incomparable. **1907** *St. Nicholas* Oct. 1098/1 There is snow-shoeing, skating, and sleighing.

b. Attrib. with *frolic, match, season,* etc.
1816 *Mass. Spy* 10 April (Th.), Either at a ball, party, sleighing match, or in a hack, the Spanish minister had signified something about the Floridas. **1837** NEAL *Charcoal Sk.* (1838) 177 We whole-souled people always plant sich articles in sleighing-time. **1842** 'UNCLE SAM' *Peculiarities* I. 44 Those who have sweet-hearts take them out on 'sleighing frolics.' **1860** E. COWELL *Diary* 20 This being the first 'sleighing weather' this winter, . . . the Concert was constantly being interrupted by the sleigh bells. **1882** MCCABE *New York* 401 During the sleighing season runaways are of daily occurrence.

+Sleighing party. A number of people taking a sleigh ride together; the occasion of such an amusement. — **1775** BURNABY *Travels* 88 In the winter, when there is snow upon the ground, it is usual to make what they call sleighing parties. **1798** *Holyoke Diaries* 175 On a sleighing party. **1807** IRVING, etc. *Salmagundi* ix, He remembers once to have been on a sleighing party with her. **1895** COFFIN *Daughters of Revolution* 87 [On] sleighing parties, . . . we pile into a double pung, ride in the moonlight.

+Sleigh ride, *n.* A ride in a sleigh, esp. as a social diversion or frolic. — **1828** H. FINN, etc. *Whimwhams* 22 Such worthy gentlemen happen to remember . . . a winter's breakfast at a country inn, after a sleigh-ride of ten miles for an appetite. **1872** HOLMES *Poet* 119 Your friends ought not to find fault with you if you do not care to join a party that is going on a sleigh-ride. **1887** GEORGE *40 Yrs. on Rail* 18 We had, in the autumn and winter, husking-bees, dancing parties, and sleigh rides to our heart's content. **1902** HULBERT *Forest Neighbors* 181 Not even a sleigh-ride on a winter's night can set the live blood dancing as it will dance and tingle up there above the clouds.

+Sleigh-ride, *v. intr.* To ride in a sleigh. — **1807** IRVING, etc. *Salmagundi* i, He recollects perfectly the time when young ladies used to go sleigh-riding . . . without their mammas. **1845** JUDD *Margaret* III. 407 In winter, we sleigh-ride, coast, skate, snow-ball. **1869** 'MARK TWAIN' *Innocents* 156 She would like well to sleigh-ride.

+Sleigh-rider. One riding in a sleigh. — **1833** *Knickerb.* I. 207 Arrived at the Plains, the sleigh riders stopped at a tavern. **1860** HOLLAND *Miss Gilbert* 415 The same muffled sleigh-riders—their heads bent to break the blast—the same gray sky, . . . had wearied and chafed Fanny Gilbert. **1883** *Wheelman* I. 434, I was making my first trial of it [*i.e.,* a bicycle] in the snow, among the sleigh-riders.

+Sleigh shoe. A protective covering of metal for a sleigh runner. — **1799** *Essex Inst. Coll.* LIV. 108, 3 [Tons] . . . Sleigh Shoes . . . 24 [dollars]. **1825** *Columbian Centinel* 5 Jan. 3/1 For sale by James Fullerton . . .

Steel Sleigh Shoes. **1845** J. W. NORRIS *Chicago Directory* 112 Stove Plates, Paint Mills, Sleigh Shoes of every description.

∗Slender, *a.*
1. In the names of plants: (see quotations). {1800– (Smith *Flora Brit.* I. 192)}
1814 BIGELOW *Florula Bostoniensis* 54 *Campanula erinoides.* Slender Bell flower. . . . Found in meadows among the high-grass, supporting itself . . . on surrounding plants. **1821** *Mass. H. S. Coll.* 2 Ser. IX. 156 Plants, which are indigenous in the township of Middlebury, [Vt., include] . . . *Sparganium natans?* Slender bur-reed. **1833** EATON *Botany* (ed. 6) 392 *Viola muhlenbergiana,* slender violet. **1840** DEWEY *Mass. Flowering Plants* 65 *V[icia] pusilla.* Slender Vetch. . . . South Boston, along fences. **1860** CURTIS *Woody Plants N.C.* 85 Slender gooseberry (*R. gracile*). . . . Delicate, and quite rare. **1901** MOHR *Plant Life Ala.* 386 *Festuca octoflora.* . . . Slender Fescue Grass.

2. In the names of fishes: (see quotations). {1836–}
1814 MITCHILL *Fishes N.Y.* 371 Slender Cod, *Gadus tenuis,* . . . is about fifteen inches long. **1842** *Nat. Hist. N.Y., Zoology* IV. 6 The Slender Yellow Perch. *Perca gracilis.* . . . Body elongated with a small black spot on its first dorsal. *Ib.* 262 The Slender Herring, *Alosa teres,* . . . is a rare species.

∗Sleuth. +A detective. — [**1872** H. P. HALSEY in *Fireside Companion* (title), Old Sleuth the Detective (Pearson *Dime Novels* 192).] **1901** 'O. HENRY' *Cabbages & Kings* (1916) 59 Goodwin followed at increased speed, but without any of the artful tactics that are so dear to the heart of the sleuth. **1916** DU PUY *Uncle Sam* 29 The sleuth would have sworn he had led the bookkeeper into a confession.

+Slew, *n.¹* Variant of SLOUGH. — **1805** CLARK in *Lewis & C. Exped.* VI. (1906) 116 Cath-lah-com-mah-tup's a Tribe of Multnom's South Side of the Wappato Island on a slew of the [Multnomah R.]. **1832** WYETH *Journal* 210 It is difficult to tell a returning slew from a river. **1882** *Century Mag.* Aug. 505/1 There is no waste land [in northern Minn.] save in little depressions which collect surface drainage and are called 'slews' (sloughs) in the local parlance. **1920** LEWIS *Main Street* 57 They ate their sandwiches by a prairie slew.

+Slew, *n.²* A great many; a lot. *colloq.* — **1840** THOMPSON *Green Mt. Boys* II. 268 He has cut out a road, and drawn up a whole slew of cannon clean to the top of Mount Defiance. **1858** *Harper's Mag.* May 767/2 By gracious! three thousand dollars is a 'tarnal slue of money! **1865** TROWBRIDGE *Three Scouts* 140 It'll take the hull ham to feed sich a slew of men! **1897** ROBINSON *Uncle Lisha's Outing* 2, I've seen slews on 'em [ducks] on the ma'shes. **1916** FREEMAN in *Woman's Home Comp.* Nov. 68 Phebe's nieces and nephews—she's got a slew of them—had sent her that fifteen-pound turkey.

Slew, *v. tr.* In passive: To get mired in a slough or swamp. {1904–} — **1846** FARNHAM *Prairie Land* 49 It was right good luck . . . that we didn't get *slued* afore we got to town. **1862** STANLEY in Baillie & Bolitho *Victorian Dean* 105 'Slewed,' in the extreme west [of the U.S.] is sloughed,' 'lost in a swamp.' **1867** *Atlantic Mo.* March 329/1 Many a farmer in those times has seen his load hopelessly 'slewed' within what is now Chicago.

+Slewer. *local.* **a.** A low or common person. **b.** (See quot. 1889.) *slang. Obs.* — **1848** W. T. THOMPSON *Major Jones's Sk. Travel* 107 They say here [in Phila.] that they [the servant girls] aint nothing but slewers—but I seed sum that I would tuck for respectable white galls if I had seed 'em in Georgia. **1889** BARRÈRE & LELAND 220/1 About fifty years ago in Philadelphia it was usual to speak of balls frequented by factory girls as 'slewers.'

‖Slew-eyed, *a.* Squint-eyed. — **1807** IRVING, etc. *Salmagundi* iv, Vernon *slew-eyed*—people of Brunswick, of course, all squint.

∗Slice. *local.* A fire shovel. (See also FIRE SLICE.) — **1641** *Essex Inst. Coll.* L. 230 One spitt and slice, 3 s. **1665** *Portsmouth Rec.* 401 A trew Inuentary of ye Estate of Joseph wayte. . . . Tramills and Slyce. **1848** BARTLETT 307 *Slice,* a common name in parts of New York and Canada for a large fire-shovel formed of a bar of iron flattened at one end. **1876** HAWTHORNE *Works* (1883) XII. 118 It was a sort of iron shovel (by housewives termed a 'slice') such as is used in clearing the oven.

Slick, *n.* {1626–}
+1. A member of a certain regulating band in Alabama. Now *hist.*
1833 *Niles' Reg.* XLIV. 202/2 It was insisted further, that the slicks had done much good.

+2. (See quotation.)
1836 WESTON *Visit* 59*n.,* ['Slick'] sometimes means 'insolence,' for they often say 'Give me no slick.'

+3. An oily surface on the sea.
1849 D. WEBSTER *Private Corr.* III. 333 You have seen on the surface of the sea, those smooth places, which fishermen and sailors call 'slicks.' **1876** *Fur, Fin & Feather* Sept. 132/1 This spread of oil is called a 'slick.' **1885** *Boston Jrnl.* 9 May 2/4 Fishermen are in the habit of watching for these 'slicks,' . . . as indicating the presence of schools of large fish feeding upon smaller ones. **1906** *Scribner's Mag.* Sept. 314 So out they went, chasing slicks and occasionally striking a school of big fish.

+4. A wild, unbranded horse.
1890 *Stock Grower & Farmer* 12 July 6/3 Seven of them were branded, the remainder were 'slicks,' or horses which had run wild from birth.

*Slick, *a.*

*1. Of animals: Plump; in good condition. {–1740; now *rare*}

1771 *Md. Hist. Mag.* XIV. 133 Great care is taken of Nimble & the Spavin'd Horse, the 1st is fat, as slick as a Race Horse. *c*1837 CATLIN *Indians* II. 181 The fleece (Hump) of a fat cow, was the luxury of luxuries; and for it we would . . . level our rifles upon the 'slickest' of the herds.

2. Of persons: **a.** Smart; clever. {1830–} *colloq.* or *slang.*

1818 FEARON *Sketches* 5, I have been slick in going to the stand right away.

*b. Smooth; plausible; ingratiating. *colloq.* {–1640}

1842 KIRKLAND *Forest Life* II. 4 [He] thought Seymour 'a leetle too slick' for his liking. **1875** HOLLAND *Sevenoaks* 282, I hate a slick man. **1904** CRISSEY *Tattlings* 432 One of the slickest lobbyists that ever attended a session was hanging around the legislature.

+c. Attractive; good-looking; well-groomed. *slang.*

1843 STEPHENS *High Life N.Y.* I. 178 By the hokey, she was a slick leetle critter. **1848** *Congress. Globe* 25 April 668/1 [The teachers] look 'so almighty slick,' that they will soon be released from school-teaching, by being called to preside over the houses of young Hoosiers. **1862** BROWNE *A. Ward: His Book* 27, As putty and slick lookin gals as I ever met.

+3. Of actions or words: **a.** Cleverly done or said; tricky; plausible. *colloq.*

1833 *Jamestown* (N.Y.) *Jrnl.* 25 Sept. 2/1, Of all the inventions I've hearn of Mr. Van Buren's, this is about the slickest. **1838** DRAKE *Tales Queen City* 30 Well, now, that's right down slick, anyhow. **1897** *Scribner's Mag.* XXII. 300/2 If that Darcy tries any of his slick, fake talk on Harry, . . . d—— if I don't knock his flannel mouth off him. **1898** WESTCOTT *D. Harum* 264 The way she . . . wheeled that hoss an' went out o' the yard a-kitin', was as slick a piece o' hoss bus'nis as ever I see. **1904** W. H. SMITH *Promoters* 19, I've seen the thing done a hundred times, with a slick word every time.

b. Easy; agreeable; promising; excellent. *colloq.* {1866, *dial.*}

1835 SIMMS *Partisan* 320 'Twas as slick going as down hill, with the wheels greased up to the hub! **1847** ROBB *Squatter Life* 142 Courtin' is all slick enough when every body's agreed. **1891** COOKE *Huckleberries* 227 There wa'n't nothin' too good for me them times, nothin' too slick for him to say. **1893** ROOSEVELT *Wilderness Hunter* 416 There was a boom on the town and it looked pretty slick. **1905** *McClure's Mag.* June 121/1 They certainly gave us a slick time. . . . Why our dinner cost nine dollars!

+4. Neatly arranged; excellently made. *colloq.*

1834 C. A. DAVIS *Lett. J. Downing* 2 It was so slick a kounterfit the Captain couldn't tell himself. **1843** STEPHENS *High Life N.Y.* I. 244 [The shopkeeper] went to a big drawer, where she kept her slickest dry goods, and cut off a lot of shiney red velvet. **1860** HOLLAND *Miss Gilbert* 131, I love to see a young man that keeps things slick around him. **1898** WESTCOTT *D. Harum* 269 A pair of satin-coated trotters drew him in the latest and 'slickest' model of top-buggies. **1900** MUNN *Uncle Terry* 176 A purty slick craft, boys.

+5. In phrases of comparison, such as *slick as grease, slick as molasses.*

1833 NEAL *Down-Easters* I. 62 He's royal Yankee I tell ye!—clear grit—smooth as ile; slick as grease, we say. **1836** [see GOOSE GREASE]. **1847** LOWELL *Biglow P.* 1 Ser. iv. 52 To the people they're ollers ez slick ez molasses. **1906** *Springfield W. Repub.* 16 Aug. 1 Two years ago everything was made as slick as molasses for Lieut.-Gov. Roberts.

*Slick, *v.*

+1. *tr.* To outsmart (a person); to put one over on. *slang.*

1836 H. R. HOWARD *Hist. V. A. Stewart* 20 On the day they published that they would be there to slick him, he had eighteen friends who came to his assistance.

2. *To slick down,* +to make (the hair) lie smooth. Also *transf.*

1834 C. A. DAVIS *Lett. J. Downing* 25 Every hair on it [was] slicked down with a dipped candle. **1841** *Knickerb.* XVII. 38 Mr. Cram . . . began to 'slick down' his hair. **1878** STOWE *Poganuc People* 153 The minit that Dr. Cushing . . . got folks kind o' slicked down and peaceable, Zeph would git up and stroke 'em all back'ards.

3. *To slick off,* +to polish off, to make elegant.

1846 LOWELL *Biglow P.* 1 Ser. i. 2 The parson kind o' slicked off sum o' the last varses.

+4. *To slick up.* **a.** To tidy up (a place); to make clean and neat.

1828 *Richmond Enquirer* 22 Aug. 4/1 (Th.), She calls it 'slicking up the room.' **1845** S. SMITH *J. Downing's Lett.* 43 Everything in the house was all slicked up a day or two beforehand. **1867** *Atlantic Mo.* Jan. 109/2 [The farm] looks more slicked up than ever it used to. **1918** LINCOLN *Shavings* 79 Mother was always a great one for keeping things slicked up.

+b. *passive.* Of a person: To be cleaned up and made attractive or presentable. Sometimes *to get slicked up.*

1831 S. SMITH *Life J. Downing* 134 My clothes had got so shabby, I thought I better hire out a few days and get slicked up a little. **1839**

KIRKLAND *New Home* (1840) 243 Mrs. Flyter was 'slicked up' for the occasion, in the snuff-colored silk she was married in. **1876** 'MARK TWAIN' *Tom Sawyer* xxxiii. 263 Come down when you are slicked up enough.

+c. *intr.* To make one's self clean, presentable, or attractive.

1841 *Knickerb.* XVII. 41 In a little while he recovered his self-possession, or, to make use of one of his own expressions, 'he slicked up.' **1867** *Atlantic Mo.* May 571/2 'Where's Kate?' 'Up stairs, a-slickin' up.' **1907** *Putnam's Mag.* July 486/2 Can't you wait till a gintleman polishes his finger nails? I'm slickin' up.

+Slick, *adv. colloq.* or *slang.* {1832–}

1. Quickly; well; easily; smartly. {1882}

1818 FEARON *Sketches* 59 If I did not he would send me off slick. *Ib.* 124 He is now progressing slick. **1825** LONGFELLOW in *S. Longfellow H. W. Longfellow* I. 59 They manage things there so *slick* that the college saves annually three thousand dollars! **1840** HOFFMAN *Greyslaer* I. 54, I've seen a good hunter . . . bring down a buck as slick with a bow and arrow as if it had been his own rifle. **1881** COOKE *Somebody's Neighbors* 90 He's got . . . a dry yard where the water all dreens off as slick as can be. **1902** WILSON *Spenders* 422 When they get in one hole, they say, 'Oh, if I was only in that other one, now, how slick I could climb out!'

2. Used as an intensive. {1832–}

1818 FEARON *Sketches* 123 Did she die slick right away? **1885** *Harper's Mag.* Aug. 485/2 The bullet . . . cut the rope, and let him slick down kerswosh into the sea.

3. In phrases of comparison, such as *slick as grease, slick as a whistle.* (See also SLEEK *adv.* quot. 1806.)

1811 *Mass. Spy* 20 March 4/1, I hop'd I should pass Slick as greese down the current of time. **1830** S. SMITH *Life J. Downing* 36 He's lost it, slick as a whistle. **1837** BIRD *Nick of Woods* I. 222 If I didn't fetch old dug-out through slicker than snakes. **1904** STRATTON-PORTER *Freckles* 256 She took us to be from McLean's gang, slick as grease.

+Slick and clean, *adv.* Completely. — **1857** *Quinland* II. 119 You'll be slick and clean out of the muss. **1900** DRANNAN *Plains & Mts.* 583 That fire wiped me out slick and clean.

+Slickens. [Cf. *slick* 'slime.'] (See quotations.) — **1882** *Century Mag.* XXV. 337 It is the lighter soils of the hydraulic mines and the pulverized matter from the quartz-mills of the mining region which constitute 'slickens.' **1894** *N.Y. Tribune* 1 Feb. 1/3 Above 500 acres . . . will be covered with 'slickens,' washings from the mines in the mountains, and thus be rendered valueless.

Slicker. {1851–3–}

+1. A long, loose, oilskin coat, esp. a yellow one.

1884 *Harper's Mag.* July 300/1 Carry . . . a rubber pillow, and a 'slicker.' **1888** *Ib.* July 244/2 The buffalo-grass sod . . . has become as impervious to water as a cow-boy's slicker. **1898** *Kansas City Star* 18 Dec. 7/5 A 'slicker' is a long yellow or black garment. **1914** E. STEWART *Lett. Woman Homesteader* 173 The rain ran off their slickers in little rivulets. **1925** *Scribner's Mag.* Oct. 9/2 What have you seen in the way of slickers? I want one for college wear.

+b. *Slicker roll,* a cowboy's roll wrapped in, or consisting of, his slicker.

1924 MULFORD *Rustlers' Valley* vi, Matt slipped the glass jar into his slicker roll.

+2. A smooth and clever trickster or cheat. *colloq.*

1900 'FLYNT' *Notes Itinerant Policeman* 62 Pickpockets! . . . You just bring the slickers in.

Slickings. + ? =FIXING 1 d. *colloq.* — **1847** FIELD *Drama in Pokerville* 53 'A little of the roast. if you please.' . . . 'None of the stuffin'!' 'Some of the slickin's!'

+Slicking up. The action of cleaning up and making presentable. *colloq.* — **1843** 'CARLTON' *New Purchase* I. 72 The caps . . . were worn expressly as the wives themselves said—'to save slicking up every day, and to hide dirt!' **1855** *Mich. Agric. Soc. Trans.* VI. 495 The farm needs a good deal of slicking up to make the general appearance equal to what nature has done for the land. **1907** *Springfield W. Repub.* 9 May 1 Denver has been having her period of spring slicking up.

*Slide, *n.*

1. =LANDSLIDE 1 {1664, 1829}; a snowslide.

1832 *N.H. Hist. Soc. Coll.* III. 227 Long *slides* were noticed, . . . extending through the dense forest from near the summits to the base of the mountains. **1843** *Nat. Hist. N.Y., Geology* I. 32 On some clay beds where slides have occurred, the angle of inclination is almost inappreciable to the eye. **1876** RAYMOND *8th Rep. Mines* 206 A fortunate 'slide' occurred, leaving a fine body of ore exposed on the hanging-wall. **1903** *N.Y. Ev. Post* 23 Sept., Another immense slide has occurred at Turtle Mountain.

+b. The mass of rock and earth dislodged by a slide.

1841 WHITTIER *Poetical Works* (1894) 173/2 Loose rock and frozen slide, Hung on the mountain-side. **1874** RAYMOND *6th Rep. Mines* 296 The shaft passes 45 feet through 'slide,' and then 155 feet on the vein.

+2. An otter or beaver slide. {1894}

See also BEAVER SLIDE, *otter slide* under OTTER 4.

1842 *Nat. Hist. N.Y., Zoology* I. 40 The steel trap is placed . . . at the bottom of one of their *slides*. **1868** *Amer. Naturalist* II. 157 In Missouri, where the river banks are steep the beaver constructs no canal, but 'slides.'

3. A vehicle or drag moved either on runners or on a smooth bottom. {1685–90–}

1858 D. K. BENNETT *Chronology N.C.* 102 'Slides' or 'sleds' . . . [had been] the useful and ornamental vehicles in that rolling region. **1884** 'CRADDOCK' *Tenn. Mts.* 156 Instead of a wagon, he had only a rude 'slide.' **1896** *Pilgrim Missionary* Sept. 10, [I] borrowed a mule and a slide, and hauled to the house some planks and pickets.

4. An inclined runway or plane on which heavy goods are dragged or slid by gravity. {1832, of Mexico}

1878 *Lumberman's Gazette* 16 March, The logs are then placed in the trough of the slide and very easily drawn by horses to their destination. **1886** HARTE *Snow-bound* 107 A slide was a rude incline for the transit of heavy goods that could not be carried down a trail. **1893** *Harper's Mag.* Jan. 174 The unavoidable flour-barrels came head foremost along a wooden slide. **1905** *Forestry Bureau Bul.* No. 61, 47 Slide, a trough built of logs or timber, used to transport logs down a slope.

b. = CHUTE 2. {1884, of Canada}

1858 SIMMONDS *Dict. Trade Products* 349/1 Slide, a place in a river for timber-logs or rafts to go down. **1880** *Lumberman's Gazette* 7 Jan. 28 The government constructs 'slides' for the passage of timber around shoals or rapids where there are no canals.

+5. (See quotation.)

1879 *Harper's Mag.* Nov. 889/1 Some [corrals] have what are called 'slides,' or passages gradually narrowing until but one animal can pass, and he, as he cannot turn around, can be easily branded.

+6. *Baseball.* The action of sliding into a base.

1886 CHADWICK *Art of Batting* 68 A slide in time saves an out. **1924** C. A. WARDLOW *Fundamentals of Baseball* 48 The 'feet-first' slide was introduced with the adoption of spikes.

* Slide, v.

+1. *intr.* To make off.

a1846 *Quarter Race Ky.* 62 Some fainted, others prayed, and not a few dropped their robes and 'slid.' **a1859** BARTLETT 415 We must cut our sticks and slide.—*R. S. Willis, Student's Song.* **1873** HARTE *Poetical Works* (1883) 149 She led William where he was covered by seventeen Modocs, and—slid!

+2. *Baseball.* To throw oneself toward a base with a slipping or gliding movement.

1868 CHADWICK *Base Ball* 26 Some base runners have a habit of sliding in on a base when they steal one. **1896** *N.Y. Dramatic News* 4 July 13/2 He has written many popular songs, including . . . 'Slide, Kelly, Slide.' **1924** C. A. WARDLOW *Fundamentals of Baseball* 48 A few players slide head first.

* 3. *To let slide,* to let (something) take its own course {–1611, 1885–}; to disregard; to let go to the devil.

1845 *Xenia Torch-Light* 4 Dec. 3/3 If there were anything in it worth the room we would copy it, but as we are certain our readers would not thank us for so doing, we let it 'slide.' **1858** J. S. HOLMES *Oration 5 July* 26 Already men have talked of 'letting the Union slide.' **1861** CHESNUT *Diary from Dixie* 119 [The Northerners] mean to let freedom slide a while until they subjugate us. **1863** *Congress. Globe* 29 Jan. 603/1 If the Union is to be saved or the negroes freed, are you in favor of emancipating the slaves and letting the Union slide?

* 4. *To slide out, fig.,* to escape difficulties, responsibility, etc.

[**1845** J. J. HOOPER *Taking Census* 150 We escaped . . . by a very peculiar knack we have of 'sliding out.'] **1877** BARTLETT 608 *To slide out,* . . . to avoid by artifice one's share of labor or responsibility.

* Slider.

1. A runner on a sled or other conveyance; also, a sled.

1781 S. PETERS *Hist. Conn.* 320 The sleigh . . . [carries] six persons in its box, which hangs on four posts standing on two steel sliders, or large skates. **1811** SUTCLIFF *Travels* (1815) 84 [When the Delaware R. is partly frozen,] they make use of a boat that has two sliders, one on each side the keel, shod with iron. **1887** *Courier-Journal* 11 Jan. 6/2 The sons of Main-street merchants [raced] on their handsome, bright-colored 'store' sliders.

+2. = REDBELLY 2. Also attrib.

1883 *Science* I. 149/2 The heart of the 'slider' terrapin. **1884** GOODE, etc. *Fisheries* I. 155 The 'Red-bellied Terrapin' . . . is also known under the names 'Potter,' 'Red-fender,' and 'Slider.' **1910** HART *Vigilante Girl* 88 They have some mud-turtles there called 'sliders.'

* Sliding, a. Of machinery, furniture, etc.: Capable of being slid or adjusted by sliding. {1680–} — **1724** *Md. Hist. Mag.* VI. 1 Two sliding windows . . . with good frame shutters. **1730** *Ib.* 12 Gunter's scale of boxwood, a sliding Gunter two feet long when shut, commonly called 'Seth partridges sliding rule.' **1826** FLINT *Recoll.* 108 [At the] sliding-tables . . . eighty passengers can sit down with comfort. **1856** *Mich. Agric. Soc. Trans.* VII. 61 John Patton . . . [exhibited] 2 sliding seat [buggies]. **1885** *Wkly. New Mexican Rev.* 2 April 4/5 The Springer stock yards are to be supplied with a 'sliding chute' for unloading fine cattle.

Sliding rule. A ruler provided with a ruled medial slide for making certain calculations; a slide rule. {1663–} — **1730** [see SLIDING a.]. **1767** in Commons, etc. *Doc. Hist.* I. 354 He carried with him . . . a sliding rule. **1794** *Mass. Spy* 1 May 4/2 Ready for sale . . . Gunter's sliding Rules.

Slim, *a.* {1657–}

+1. *local.* Of a person or his health: Poor.

1815 HUMPHREYS *Yankey* 40, I guess I be [homesick]; . . . I feel pritty slim. **1848** DURIWAGE & BURNHAM *Stray Subjects* 195, I never felt so slim in all my life. **1877** JEWETT *Deephaven* 169 She's had slim health of late years. **1902** L. RICHARDS *Mrs. Tree* 167 Mother's slim, I tell ye.

2. Of a crowd or attendance: Poor; scanty. {1852}

1836 *Quarter Race Ky.* 13 The muster at the stand [at a horse race] was slim. **1850** KINGSLEY *Diary* 138 The Co[mpany] did not work in the afternoon as some refused on account of haveing too 'slim a team.' **1880** 'MARK TWAIN' *Tramp Abroad* 45 Lecture courses upon specialties of an unusual nature are delivered to very slim audiences.

+3. Of a chance or opportunity: Small; poor; meager.

1851 KINGSLEY *Diary* 173, I think our prospect is rather more 'slim' this time than at any time before. **1855** *Chicago W. Times* 18 Oct. 1/1 Judge Trumbull might or might not have obtained the place of Senator . . . ; we think, however, his chances were slim. **1887** *Harper's Mag.* Feb. 490/1 My chances of seeing him draw his last breath were very slim. **1906** *McClure's Mag.* Feb. 344 When he started, the chances were slim.

+Slimer. [f. *slime* n. 'a viscous substance.'] A toadfish, *Opsanus tau.* — **1817** in *Amer. Monthly Mag.* II. 204 The fishermen . . . call it by the name of *Yellow-Kusk, Sand Codling, Slimer,* etc.

Slime table. An apparatus as a platform or inclined table for the treatment of slime. — **1883** RITCH *Illus. N. Mex.* 91 A slime table or 'buddle' . . . is for treating the dust or powdered ore. **1919** FAY *Glossary of Mining* 624/1.

+Slimpsy, *a.* Variant of SLIMSY. *colloq.* — **1888** *Century Mag.* Sept. 772/2, I feel ez slimpsy ez a dish-rag. **1895** *Missionary Herald* Dec. 493 These ladies have to stay in that slimpsy shed day and night. **1904** *N.Y. Ev. Post* 4 June, At first glance the material seems rather slimpsy. **1920** SANDBURG *Smoke & Steel* 105 Slimpsy, loose and ready to fall at a touch.

Slimsy, *a.* {1887–, *dial.*} +Flimsy; weak. *colloq.* Also *fig.* (Cf. SLIMPSY.) — **1845** JUDD *Margaret* II. 329 The building is old and slimsy, you know. **1848** BARTLETT 309 Slimsey, flimsey; frail. Most frequently applied to cotton or other cloth. **1863** *Harper's Mag.* March 537/2 You have slimsy muslins, I dare say? **1899** *Milwaukee Sentinel* 14 May 4/2 Of the same slimsy material the . . . claim is constructed.

+Sling, *n.* [Cf. G. *schlingen* 'to swallow.'] **a.** A drink consisting of spirit, usually gin, and sweetened water. **b.** A draft of liquor. *slang.*

See also BRANDY SLING, GIN SLING, RUM SLING.

1768 FRENEAU *Poems* (1809) I. 35 Rum ne'er shall meet my lips . . . In shape of toddy, punch, grog, sling, or dram. **1788** MAY *Jrnl. & Lett.* 26 He brought a case-bottle . . . filled with Hollands, of which each of us took a sling. **1812** PAULDING *J. Bull & Bro. Jon.* 122 It was a rare sight to see these fellows with a sling or a glass of grog before them. **1852** ELLET *Pioneer Women* 271 [They] refreshed themselves with a glass of sling, made of maple sugar and whiskey. **1877** COOKE *Huckleberries* 9 Fetch him up a good stiff sling. **1903** A. ADAMS *Log of Cowboy* 133 Just think of those long slings with red cherries floating around in them that we'll be drinking.

attrib. **1807** J. HARRIOTT *Struggles* II. 110 Mr. Miles . . . served his customers with sling-drams, grog, or cider, himself. **1848** BARTLETT 208 [Among] many and very singular names . . . given to the various compounds or mixtures of spirituous liquors and wines, . . . [is] Slingflip.

+Sling, *v.*[1] [f. SLING *n.*] *intr.* To take a sling; to drink alcoholic liquor. Also *vbl. n.* — **1833** J. E. ALEXANDER *Transatlantic Sk.* II. 7 He used to sling considerable heavy. **1840** HALIBURTON *Clockmaker* 3 Ser. xi, I ordered a pint o' the best [toddy], and so we slinged. **1867** SMYTH *Sailor's Word-Book* 632 On the American coast . . . the custom of *slinging* prevails . . . extensively, even where intoxication is despised.

* Sling, *v.*[2] +*tr.* In miscellaneous colloq. or slang uses.

a. To fling or toss (the foot) in dancing. **b.** *To sling ink,* to write. **c.** To handle (dishes or drinks); to mix. **d.** In a card game, to play one's (cards). **e.** Often with *on:* To put on (style). **f.** To shoot (lead) from a firearm. **g.** To tell (a story). {1904}

(a) 1834 *Knicker.* III. 34 When she dances she slings a nasty foot. **1879** *Cimarron News & Press* 20 Nov. 3/2 A tenderfoot can sling his heels higher at a baile than the average old timer. **(b) a1867** BROWNE *Works* (1876) 322 You axe me, sir, to sling sum ink for your paper. **1873** BEADLE *Undevel. West* 142 All who could sling ink became correspondents. **(c) 1872** *Newton Kansan* 28 Nov. 3/3 The way he'll sling the flowing bowl. **1889** H. O'REILLY *50 Yrs. on Trail* 7 As junior waiter . . . I could sling dishes around with the best of them. **1902** LORIMER *Lett. Merchant* 236 Hired a fancy mixer to sling together mild snorts . . . for the ladies. **(d) 1873** *Winfield* (Kan.) *Courier* 15 Feb. 1/5 [Jo] slings his cards with an enviable dexterity. **(e) 1875** *Scribner's Mo.* Nov. 142/1 You sling on too much style! **1878** BEADLE *Western Wilds* 184 [She] slung more style than a speckled show-horse. **(f) 1879** TOURGEE *Fool's Errand* 259 It's enough for you to have her sling a lump of cold lead through your carcass. **(g) 1896** HARTE *Poetical Works* 183, I kin not sling a fairy tale of Jinnys fierce and wild. **1899** — *Mr. J. Hamlin's Med.* 173 He jest slung yarns about his doin' thar.

+Sling-drinking, *a.* Of persons: In the habit of drinking slings. — **1835** PAULDING *J. Bull & Bro. Jon.* (new ed.) 146 She denounced them for a tobacco-chewing, . . . sling-drinking set. **1838** 'UNCLE SAM' in *Bentley's Misc.* IV. 586 A 'sling' drinking, bullying braggadocia from the 'old dominion'—(Virginia or Kentucky).

+**Slinger.** One who drinks slings habitually. — **1807** JANSON *Stranger in Amer.* 299 There is a numerous set of people in the Southern States, called *slingers*, and another, styled *eleveners*.

+**Sling shot. a.** =BLACK JACK 7. **b.** A boy's sling or catapult. **1849** KINGSLEY *Diary* 77 Many are getting up sling-shots, . . . but I hope we shall never have occasion to use them. **1891** H. HERMAN *His Angel* 149 He made a ghastly horrible sling-shot by filling a heavy tumbler with the iron tops screwed off from the fire-irons, and tying the lot in a handkerchief. **1904** *N.Y. Ev. Post* 24 June 2 The guards are authorized to carry slingshots . . . heavily loaded with lead. *Ib.* 3 Nov. 1 A keeper in Central Park charged the boy with shooting birds and squirrels in the park with a powerful slingshot. **1909** CALHOUN *Miss Minerva* 197 You can't even take your sling-shot, nor your air-gun [to school].

Slink. {1638–} +(See quotation.) — **1883** ZEIGLER & GROSSCUP *Alleghanies* 157 What's a slink? A year-old deer. When past a year old, the male deer is called a spike-buck.

* **Slip,** *n.*[1]

* **1.** A sloping pier or ramp extending out into the water as a landing place for vessels.
1669 *Boston Rec.* 50 Libertie is granted to Joseph Cocke to set vp a warehouse ouer the slip. **1734** *Boston Selectmen* 252 Granting Liberty for Laying down Ways at the slip in North Street for a Ferry. **1798** *Ann. 7th Congress* 2 Sess. 1310 The commissioners were enabled . . . to prohibit docks, slips, building on wharves, and other nuisances. **1850** JUDD *R. Edney* 42 Richard . . . descended the slip, some thirty feet, to the basin. **1906** PRINGLE *Rice Planter* 419 They got the flat to touch the slip at one end.

+**b.** 'An opening between wharves or in a dock' (*W.* '28); a ship's berth.
1796 *Gazette of U.S.* 6 Aug. (Th.), The abominable custom of filling up slips and docks with similar materials. **1821** W. DALTON *Travels U.S.* 3 Vessels, . . . being run into the little docks called 'slips,' can lay close alongside [the wharves]. **1868** *N.Y. Herald* 1 July 5/6 The Williamsburg ferry was attempting to enter the slip. **1891** *Scribner's Mag.* Oct. 514/1 The great ship backed majestically out of the slip. **1907** G. M. WHITE *Boniface to Burglar* 293 The ferry-boat that left the New York slip . . . bearing the party, also had me aboard.

+**2.** A mountain pass. {1739–, 'a passage'}
1788 CUTLER in *Life & Corr.* I. 427 Came through Dunning's Slip, where the river divides Dunning Mountains, and in a short distance passed through another Slip. **1858** in *Amer. Speech* XV. 393/2 Beginning on 2 beeches, dogwood and maple in a slip in the mountain above the forks of sd branch.

3. a. An article of women's dress, formerly an outer garment, now an undergarment. {1761–}
1797 BOWNE *Life* 11, I wish you to send me enough of all my slips to make long sleeves that you can. **1810** *Columbian Centinel* 3 Jan. 3/2 Stolen from the waggon . . . 2 do brown and green Satin Slips. **1868** G. G. CHANNING *Recoll. Newport* 46, I have spoken, casually, of my wearing frocks or 'slips.' **1907** *St. Nicholas* May 626/1 She wore a dainty gown of white muslin over a blue silk slip.

+**b.** A bedroom slipper.
1893 HOLLEY *Samantha at World's Fair* 155, I took my old slips, that had been my faithful companions for over two years. **1898** WESTCOTT *D. Harum* xviii, There's a pair of bedroom slips lined with lambs' wool.

+**4.** *spec.* A shoot or cutting from a sweet-potato plant.
1798 HAWKINS *Letters* 323 Planted potato slips. Planted sweet pepper. **1847** in Commons, etc. *Doc. Hist.* I. 196 July: . . . 3, planting slips. **1862** E. W. Pearson *Lett. Port Royal* 105 Sweet potatoes, planted with slips in July.

+**b.** A sweet potato developed from such a slip: (see quot. 1850).
1848 in Commons, etc. *Doc. Hist.* I. 199 November: . . . 15, 16, 17, 20, 21, digging slips. **1850** BURKE *Reminisc. Georgia* 126 The sweet potato . . . is of two kinds, called yams and slips. The yams are raised by planting the root in the spring as our farmers do the Irish potato, then when the tops of these are about six inches high, slips are cut from them and planted on another piece of ground. . . . The potato obtained in this way is called the slip, and is long and slender in form while the yam is short and thick.

+**5.** 'A long seat or narrow pew in churches' (*W.* '28). Chiefly *New Eng.*
'When there is a door, they are called pews; when without doors and free to all, slips. This, I believe, is the difference between them' (B. '48). **1823** *East-Hampton Rec.* IV. 426 That four slips be hired out . . . and the money for which they are hired be, applied towards painting the meeting house. **1838** FLAGG *Far West* I. 218 In lieu of pews, slips, or any such thing, a few coarse slabs of all forms and fashions. **1853** STOWE *Key* 22/1 A beautiful quadroon girl . . . sat in one of the slips of the church. **1906** CHURCHILL *Coniston* 15 Jethro Bass . . . sat in the rear slip.

+**6.** *Bookbinding.* (See quotations.)
1876 KNIGHT 2211/2 *Slip*, . . . the end of the twine to which the sheets are sewed, serving to attach the book to the boards. **1894** *Amer. Dict. Printing* 511 *Slip*, a cord used in fastening the back of a book.

7. *attrib.* +**a.** In sense 4 with *field*.

1848 in Commons, etc. *Doc. Hist.* I. 197 Feb. . . . 12, making slip field fence.

+**b.** In special combinations.
Slip cleat, (see quotation); *s. gap*, (see quotation); *s. runner*, in policy-playing, a person who carries slips with the winning numbers to the stations where the bets were made; *s. ticket*, (see quotation).
1873 BEADLE *Undevel. West* 41 Many plant trees for posts, using 'slip cleats,' that the wires may be moved every year or two on the growing tree. **1859** BARTLETT 167 A *Slip gap* is a place provided in a fence, where the bars may be slipped aside and let down. **1901** HARRIGAN *Mulligans* 65 The waiting policy players added to the hub-bub by their mutterings of discontent at the tardiness of the slip-runner. **1888** BRYCE *Amer. Commw.* II. III. lxvi. 493 A slip ticket is a list, printed on a long strip of paper, of the persons . . . recommended by the same party or political group for the posts to be filled up at any election.

* **Slip,** *n.*[2] (See quotation.) {c1425} 'Now *U.S.*' (*O.E.D.*). — **1859** BARTLETT 416 *Slip*, milk turned with rennet, etc., before the whey separates from the curd.

* **Slip,** *v.*
1. *intr.* Of bark: To peel off. {1878}
1788 DEANE in Cutler *Life & Corr.* I. 388, I have had chairs bottomed with the rind [of basswood], which will slip finely in June.

+**2.** *tr.* To provide (a church) with slips.
1837 in Chipman *Hist. Harwinton* 82 Voted to Slip the meeting house.

+**3.** In the post office, to provide (a bundle of letters, etc.) with a direction slip.
1887 *Postal Laws* 361 Letter and circular mail must always be properly 'faced up,' slipped, and tied in packages.

4. *To let slip*, to let fly.
1835–7 HALIBURTON *Clockmaker* 1 Ser. xxi. 199 The first flock of plover I see'd I let slip at them and missed them. **1848** BARTLETT 310.

5. *To slip up.* +**a.** To make a mistake; to fail. +**b.** To abscond.
(a) **1854** *Jrnl. of Discourses* II. 67/2 Some men think the way they are going to be saviors is to get as many wives as they can, and save them; now, they may slip up on that. **1866** *Wkly. New Mexican* 14 July 2/1 The knowledge that he has 'slipped up' and been exposed is more than sufficient punishment for the offense. **1888** *Century Mag.* June 279/1 Slip up in my vernacular! How could I? **1923** DUTTON *Shadow on Glass* 247 All of us slipped up. (b) *a*1855 J. F. KELLY *Humors* 263 Dr. P. St. C. Smith 'slipped up' one day, leaving the well done community of Boston and the environs, for fields more congenial to his peculiar talents.

Slip bar. =DRAWBAR 1. {1805} — **1681** *Southampton Rec.* II. 88 The said Iohn Woodruff is to keep a pair of slip bars for a highway. **1719** *Southold Rec.* II. 485 Gates or convenient slip bares may be set up upon the before mentioned open ways.

Slipe. 'A distance' (B. '48). *dial.* — **1835** CROCKETT *Tour* 145 Well, I've got a long slipe off from my steamboat. **1843** *Missouri Reporter* 19 May (Th.), They do not begin to be the party, 'by a long slipe.'

* **Slipper.**

* **1.** A light, low shoe, usually one of a type easy to put on and freq. one suitable for indoor wear only.
1686 SEWALL *Letter-Book* I. 38, I thank you . . . [for] the East-India slippers. **1800** *Mass. Laws* II. 903 Each manufacturer of . . . Sandals, Slippers or Goloshoes, shall have the exclusive right of stamping said articles. **1840** HONE *Diary* II. 4 In night-gown and slippers [I] was prepared for an hour's reading and an early bedding. **1853** *S. Lit. Messenger* XIX. 367/1 Above the slippers fell in artistically swelling folds, the tubes of a pair of yellow pantaloons. **1883** RITTENHOUSE *Maud* 154 Elmer looked somewhat amazed when he saw my new dress, white slippers and gloves. **1907** *St. Nicholas* Aug. 896/1 There were high-heeled pink slippers and a long pink feather. **1922** TARKINGTON *Gentle Julia* 186 Noble Dill went hopping upon a waxed floor and upon Julia's little slippers.

2. In miscellaneous senses.
a. A place that causes one to slip. **b.** A child's apron. **c.** *To give a person the slipper*, to leave a person holding the sack.
(a) **1828** *Yankee* I. 84/1 Sloughs, man-traps, slides, slippers and leg-breakers . . . abound here. (b) **1828** WEBSTER, *Slipper*, . . . a kind of apron for children, to be slipped over their other clothes to keep them clean. **1891** *Cent.* 5699/2. (c) **1835** in Bassett *Plantation Overseer* 51 He thinks he made six thousand Dollars . . . , if the expenses does not give him the *slipper* at the start.

+**Slipper-down.** 'A vulgar name in some parts of Connecticut for hasty pudding' (B. '48).

Slipper noose. A noose with a slipknot. — **1857** *Quinland* II. 43 The students had fastened up a number of small cords, by means of a 'slipper-neuse,' in which they suspended their books. **1860** [see CROWNER[2]]. **1875** BURROUGHS *Winter Sunshine* 162 [The rabbit] will put his head through the boy's slipper-noose.

+**Slippery elm.**
1. One of the red elms (*Ulmus fulva*) having a slippery inner bark; the wood of this tree.
1748 DRAKE *Pioneer Life Ky.* 73 Of the whole forest the red or slippery elm was the best. **1836** *Knickerb.* VIII. 73 Beware of a person . . . [vending] barks of prickly ash and slippery-elm. **1843** N. BOONE *Journal* 229

White oak, walnut and slippery elm on the creeks. **1860** CURTIS *Woody Plants N.C.* 55 Slippery elm. . . . As the trunk splits well, it is convenient for making of rails. **1905** *Forestry Bureau Bul.* No. 66, 37 The slippery elm . . . is a smaller tree than the white elm.

2. = SLIPPERY-ELM BARK.

1820 *U.S. Pharmacopœia* 155 Infusion of Slippery Elm. **1832** CHILD *Frugal Housewife* 28 Tea made of slippery elm is good for the piles. **1882** C. B. LEWIS *Lime-Kiln Club* 112 He was . . . handed a piece of slippery elm to keep his throat moist during his oratory. **1899** A. BROWN *Tiverton Tales* 69 'Slippery elm left by my dear father from his last illness,' she read.

attrib. **1882** PECK *Sunshine* 293 Canned peaches, that swim around in a pint of slippery elm juice in a tin can. **1889** COOKE *Steadfast* 118 [You] keep a wettin' his lips with that slipp'ry ellum tea in the mug.

3. The flannelbush (*Fremontodendron californicum*) of the west coast.

1884 SARGENT *Rep. Forests* 26 Slippery Elm. . . . The mucilaginous inner bark used locally in poultices. **1897** SUDWORTH *Arborescent Flora* 272.

+**Slippery-elm bark.** The mucilaginous inner bark of the slippery elm. — **1780** in *Travels Amer. Col.* 640 Bear fat is preserved sweet and pure by putting in a bunch of the Slippery Elem bark into it when rendering. **1846** THORPE *Myst. Backwoods* 76 A little pounded slippery-elm bark is used to caulk the seams [of the canoe]. **1894** *Outing* XXIV. 270/1 Fifteen or twenty of these pieces—looking very much like slippery-elm bark, . . . are placed in a bundle in layers.

Slipping. *New Eng.* +(See quot. 1895.) — **1895** *Dialect Notes* I. 394 *Slippin'*, sleighing. 'The slippin's pretty good.' Gardner, Mass. **1896** HOWELLS *Impressions & Exp.* 9 The 'slippin',' as the sleighing was called, . . . lasted from December to April.

+**Slipping bar.** = DRAWBAR 1. — **1667** *Southold Rec.* I. 229 Master Wells [was] to leav a convenient cart way . . . with a gatte or slipeing bares to go in and out at.

+**Slip potato.** = SLIP *n.*[1] 4 and 4 b. Also attrib. — **1862** E. W. Pearson *Lett. Port Royal* 72 They will probably be set to planting slip-potatoes. *Ib.* 111 The slip-potato crop is the only crop by which to judge of the negroes' capacity to take care of themselves. **1865** *Nation* I. 747/1 It was just time then to dig the slip potatoes.

+**Slippy-noose.** (See quotation.) — *c***1870** CHIPMAN *Notes on Bartlett* 416 *Slippy-noose*, a running knot.—New England.

+**Slip rail.** = DRAWBAR 1. {1828–, in Austral.} Cf. SLIP BAR. — **1725** *Huntington Rec.* II. 356 Benjamine Scudder shall have Liberty to Run his fence into the water or harbour . . . on condition the sd. Benjamin scuddar his heirs and assigns shall and do keep a good pair of slip Rails Convenient for the passing and Repassing of teams and carts.

+**Slip-shuck,** *v. tr.* To jerk an ear of (corn) from its plant so as to leave the husks, or at least the inner husks, on the ear. Also *ppl. a.* — **1850** *Rep. Comm. Patents 1849: Agric.* 155 A barrel of corn must be closely slip-shucked to average . . . a bushel of shelled corn. **1905** PRINGLE *Rice Planter* 228 The corn . . . has done very well—814 bushels of slip-shuck corn on seven acres. **1924** RAINE *Land of Saddle-Bags* 29 At 'gathering time' he hangs sacks of slip-shucked corn [from pulleys] and lets them slide down by gravitation.

* **Slit.** A straight cut, +used as an earmark on animals.

1636 *Plymouth Rec.* I. 1 [The cattle mark of] Steephen Tracy [is] a slitt under each eare. **1693** *N.C. Col. Rec.* I. 388 Diana ffoster records her marke . . . a cropp and 3 slitts on the left ear. **1736** *East-Hampton Rec.* IV. 13 Nathan Conklin . . . entereth for his ear mark an ell on the under side of the left ear . . . and a slit in the right ear. **1773** [see CROP *n.* 3]. **1846** *Portsmouth Rec.* 394 The Ear mark of the Creatures of Isaac S. Cory is a Slit in the Right Ear. **1885** *Wkly. New Mexican Rev.* 15 Jan. 2/6 Slit in right ear, tin tag in left.

Slitting mill. A mill for slitting iron bars into nail rods. {1667–} — **1716** [see NAIL *n.* 1]. **1781** *Va. State P.* I. 545 Proposals [have been made] to me for water, to Erect a Saw mill, Slitting mill, Boring Mill &c. **1809** KENDALL *Travels* I. 228 There is a slitting-mill in the north society. **1850** *Rep. Comm. Patents 1849: Agric.* 93 Within its present limits [those of Bristol Co., Mass.] are . . . seven rolling, slitting, and nail mills.

+**Slit work.** *collect.* Thin boards cut from larger boards or from logs. — **1636** *Springfield Rec.* I. 160 For ye sawinge of all ye boards & slit worke [etc.]. **1641** *Conn. Rec.* I. 65 Sawyers shall not take aboue 4s. 2d. for slitt worke or three inch planke. **1713** *Topsfield Rec.* I. 180 Carry Logs to Saw-Mills to make . . . Slit work. **1757** HEMPSTEAD *Diary* 682 Carted 1 Ld. slitt work from the sawmill. **1815** *Mass. H. S. Coll.* 2 Ser. IV. 55, 70,000 feet of boards, plank and slitwork were cut at the saw mill in the same year.

* **Sliver,** *n.* +**1.** A slice taken from the side of a small fish for use as bait. +**2.** (See quotation.) Also attrib. — **(1) 1869** *Maine Acts & Resolves* 24 Any person who shall cast or deposit . . . any pumice, scraps or other offal arising from the making of oil or slivers for bait . . . shall pay a fine. **1880** GOODE *Amer. Fisheries: Menhaden* 142 Fresh 'slivers' are preferred to those which have been salted. *Ib.* 147 The slivers (pronounced *slyvers*) are salted and packed in barrels. **(2) 1883** *Nat. Museum Bul.* No. 27, 336 *Sliver spade*, . . . a kind of spade used when cutting off the head of a whale for severing the connecting pieces of flesh, which are technically termed 'slivers.'

Sliver, *v.* {1605–} +*To let sliver*, to let slip or fly. — **1847** ROBB *Squatter Life* 111 As soon as I clapped peeper on him I let sliver.

Slivering. The action of cutting a sliver from a fish. Also attrib. — **1877** JEWETT *Deephaven* 104 We soon found what 'slivering' meant. **1880** GOODE *Amer. Fisheries: Menhaden* 147 The knife used is of a peculiar shape and is called a 'slivering knife.'

Slobberhannes. 'A game of cards for four persons, played with a euchre-pack' (*Cent.*); also, a point scored in this game: (see second quotation). — **1880** DICK *Amer. Hoyle* (ed. 13) 258 Slobberhannes . . . is an amusing game. *Ib.* 259 If a player scores *all* of the three foregoing points, he receives one point extra, which is called 'Slobberhannes.'

Slobgollion. (See quotation.) — **1851** MELVILLE *Moby-Dick* 465 It is called slobgollion; an appellation original with the whalemen. . . . It is an ineffably oozy, stringy affair, most frequently found in the tubs of sperm, after a prolonged squeezing, and subsequent decanting.

* **Sloe.** +**a.** = BLACK HAW. **b.** Any one of various American wild plums, as *Prunus americana*, *P. umbellata*, or the fruit of these. Also attrib.

1718 *Braintree Rec.* 155 We find ye way to straight at Mr. Crosbey's sloe bushes. **1737** [see BLACK THORN 1]. **1775** FITHIAN *Journal* II. 85 The *Sloe* . . . grows on a small bush . . . [and] looks like a heart-cherry. **1829** EATON *Botany* (ed. 5) 439 *Viburnum prunifolium*, black haw, sloe. **1835** IRVING *Tour on Prairies* 255 Among the thickets in the valleys, we met with sloes and persimmons. **1884** SARGENT *Rep. Forests* 67 *Prunus umbellata*. . . . Sloe. Black Sloe. . . . The black or red pleasantly acid fruit used as a preserve. **1897** SUDWORTH *Arborescent Flora* 237 *Prunus americana*. Wild Plum. . . . Sloe (Fla.). *Ib.* 339 *Viburnum prunifolium*. Stagbush. . . . Sloe (Tenn.).

* **Slogan.** A frequently repeated word or phrase, usually one associated with a particular party or group. {1704–} — **1854** *Harper's Mag.* IX. 564/1 As party bitterness has died away, . . . let us take up the old slogan: 'Hurrah for Jackson!' **1880** TOURGEE *Invisible Empire* xii, Wild-eyed lunacy . . . bursts forth among the Southern people at the utterance of the magic slogan of to-day, 'a war of races.' **1904** *Baltimore American* 30 Aug. 6 The Democratic campaign managers think they have discovered an entirely new and original campaign slogan in the demand for the independence of the Filipinos.

* **Sloo.** Variant of SLOUGH. — **1845** *Knickerb.* XXV. 194 Between these swells are sloughs, or 'sloos,' which are generally marshy. **1862** MOORE *Rebellion Rec.* V. II. 168 A bridge of cypress logs had been thrown over a 'sloo' between Flower Island and the Tennessee shore. **1902** WISTER *Virginian* 188 See them marshy sloos full of weeds.

+**Sloony.** A foolish, gawky fellow; a loony. *slang. Obs.* — **1828** ROYALL *Black Book* II. 95 P. W. is a great long sloony, with a gloomy countenance. **1850** NORTHALL *Yankee Hill* 44 The great folks . . . would snicker well to see such a sloony of a Yankee among them.

Sloop. A small one-masted vessel having a fixed bowsprit and a fore-and-aft rig. {1629–}

1692 *Maine Doc. Hist.* V. 366 [We] have had an Inuentory of the Tackell and Apparill & Stores belonging to s[ai]d Slope. **1704** *Boston News-Letter* 4 Dec. 2/2 Last Week arrived Captain Rhodes in a Sloop from Rhode-Island. **1771** FRANKLIN *Autobiog.* 258, I had a brother-in-law, Robert Holmes, master of a sloop that traded between Boston and Delaware. **1832** SANDS *Writings* II. 317 Jacobus Jacobson . . . owns a quarter in a sloop that Sails from our landing. **1900** STOCKTON *Afield & Afloat* 400 It had been proposed to him that he should go out in one of the numerous cat-boats or sloops which were idly lying at anchor.

b. Attrib. with *hire*, *load*, *navigation*, etc.

1671 *S.C. Hist. Soc. Coll.* V. 298, I suppose they have peticon'd your Honn[ou]rs to take off Mr. Colletons sloope hire from this place to Bermuda. **1687** SEWALL *Diary* I. 187 This day we receive a Sloop Load of Boards from the Salmon-Falls Saw-mill. **1818** *Niles' Reg.* XIV. 42/1 Champlain has a good sloop navigation. **1855** WILLIS *Convalescent* 26 With his early savings (as a sloop-skipper and steamboat pilot), he bought the river farm. **1885** *Outing* VII. 208/2 The only vessel in sight was the iron sloop-yacht Vindex.

+**Slooper.** ?The whistling swan, *Cygnus columbianus*. — **1835** J. MARTIN *Descr. Virginia* 484 There are two kinds [of swans], so called from their respective notes—the one the trumpeter, and the other the slooper.

+**Slooping.** The transporting or forwarding of goods in sloops. *Obs.* — **1854** *Budget* (Troy, N.Y.) 2 Aug. (Ernst), He prosecuted the mercantile business in connection with slooping.

Sloop man. A man in charge of a sloop. {1862–} — **1676** GLOVER *Va.* in *Phil. Trans.* XI. 625 The sloop man dropped his grap-line. **1715** *Essex Inst. Coll.* XLIV. 146 Doctor Henry Sweitzer's order . . . to deliver two hogsheads of Fish to Joshua Wetherell Sloopman or coaster. **1737** *Va. State P.* I. 229 Paid a Sloop man for 2 gal. of rum.

Sloop of war. A small warship carrying guns on the upper deck only. {1769–} — **1704** *Boston News-Letter* 19 June 2/2 Capt. Ebenezer Coffin in our Convoy Sloop of War, is arrived here this day. **1757** *Lett. to Washington* II. 82 A Sloop of War accompanys [a convoy of troopships]. **1813** BENTLEY *Diary* IV. 200 Lately a sloop of war has been launched at Charlestown Navy Yard. **1862** KETTELL *Hist. Rebellion* I. 361 She had been captured . . . by the United States sloop-of-war Saratoga. **1896** *Peterson Mag.* ns. VI. 294/2 He joined the sloop-of-war Saratoga.

* **Slop,** *n.* Kitchen refuse or swill, given as food to cows and pigs. Also attrib. and comb.

1805 PARKINSON *Tour* 39 [In winter people of Norfolk fed] their horses on blades, and their cows on slops. **1831** PECK *Guide* 172 With . . . a dairy and slop barrel . . . pork may be raised from the sow. **1851** *Polly Peablossom* 67 As for . . . what they calls Satartia, if this world was er kitchen, it would be the slop hole. **1867** 'MARK TWAIN' *Sk., New & Old*

251 You will . . . sit down in that slop-tub. **1872** NAPHEYS *Prevention of Disease* 56 Slop-fed unhealthy cows. **1912** DREISER *Financier* 127 A slopman, . . . who could come with a great wagon filled with barrels and haul away the slops from your back door, was absolutely essential.

* Slop, *v.*

+1. *tr.* To feed (a cow or pig) with slop or swill.

1848 DRAKE *Pioneer Life Ky.* 92 To slop the cows . . . was another [labor]. **1891** 'THANET' *Otto the Knight* 330 An' feedin' a chile ain't like sloppin' a pig, neither. **1923** WATTS *L. Nichols* 23 You got time t' slop them pigs I guess.

+2. *To slop over,* fig., to do or say more than is wise, through an excess of sentiment, zeal, emotion, etc. *slang.* {1896}

1861 BROWNE *Works* (1876) 117 The prevailin weakness of most public men is to slop over! **1872** *Congress. Globe* 23 Jan. 524/2 Amnesty . . . is magnanimity slopping over. **1902** PHILLIPS *Woman Ventures* 103 She felt that she had told the facts, and that she had avoided 'slopping over.'

Slop-basin. =next. {1778-} — **1731** in Singleton *Social N.Y.* 381 A set of China . . . or Earthen ware, such as Cups, Saucers, Slop-Bason, etc., proper for a modish Tea-Table.

Slop bowl. A bowl or basin for slops, esp. a receptacle for the dregs from teacups or coffee cups at the table. — **1810** *Columbian Centinel* 25 Aug. 4/2 For sale at Davis & Brown's Silver Ware and Jewellry Store . . . Sugar Basons, . . . Slop-Bowls. **1850** MITCHEL *Lorgnette* I. 195 [She wears] a hat, shaped like an inverted slop-bowl, with proper quantity of ribbon and flowers. **1884** *Harper's Mag.* Jan. 233/2 They presented him with a service of silver-ware richly chased and engraved . . . tea-pot, sugar-bowl, cream-cup, and slop-bowl.

Slope, *n.*[1] {1611-}

+1. A sloping or slanting cut made in the ear of a domestic animal to denote ownership.

1662 *East-Hampton Rec.* I. 193 Joseph ffoster marked a horse coult of his owne haveinge . . . a crop on the nere eare and a slope on the hinderpart of the same. **1751** *Portsmouth Rec.* 328 The Ear mark is two Slopes one on each Ear taken out behind the hinder part. **1859** in *Harper's Mag.* XX. 569/1 One stear a stag . . . [with] a slop on the under side of each yeare and the end of the rite yeare.

+2. An artificial descent in a stream to facilitate navigation. *Obs.*

1790 *Ky. Petitions* 145 Mills was suffered to be built . . . with ither good locks or slopes sufficient for boats to pass by the dams with safety. **1815-6** *Niles' Reg.* IX. Suppl. 165/2 Throw away all your notions of ford-ways, slopes and notches.

+Slope, *n.*[2] [SLOPE *v.*[2]] A moderate gait; a running away. *slang. Obs.* {1897-, *dial.*} — **1853** BALDWIN *Flush Times Ala.* 110, I augmented my speed into what might be denominated a gentle slope. **1859** BARTLETT 416 *Slope,* a running away, elopement, escape.

*Slope, *v.*[1] +*tr.* To mark (an animal) with a sloping cut in the ear. *Obs.* — **1666** *East-Hampton Rec.* I. 250 One sorrell horse coult . . . slopte on both sides of the right eare. **1705** *Portsmouth Rec.* 273 [A piece] Slopt of from the hinder part of the Said Crop. **1809** *Ib.* 371 The Ear mark of the Creatures of Elizabeth Brightman . . . is a Crop on the right ear, and a piece Slopt of from the hinder part of the said Crop.

+Slope, *v.*[2] [Origin unknown.] *intr.* To depart, decamp, make off. *slang.* Also *vbl. n.*

1839 MARRYAT *Diary in Amer.* II. 37 Here are two real American words; —'Sloping'—for slinking away; 'Splunging,' like a porpoise. **1845** *Xenia Torch-Light* 23 Oct. 4/1 The Col. was surprised to find his visitors had sloped. **1882** BAILLIE-GROHMAN *Camps in Rockies* 184 Instead of charging, as we had expected they would, they 'sloped.' **1901** JAMES *Sacred Fount* 70, I saw them a few minutes ago most distinctly 'slope.'

b. With adverbs and adverbial phrases.

1837 WETMORE *Gaz. Missouri* 325 We *sloped* over the mountains a few hundred miles to Lake Tinpanogos. **1843** STEPHENS *High Life N.Y.* II. 62 Then she sort of let her foot down by degrees, . . . and sloped off easy. **1864** *Chicago Tribune* 30 Aug. 2/2 The New Yorker . . . sloped for comfort to other quarters. **1866** C. H. SMITH *Bill Arp* 19, I'm afraid I'll get in a tight place among these bloods and have to slope out of it.

Slopshop. (See quots. 1878, 1891.) {1723-}

1775 *Jrnls. Cont. Congress.* III. 471 The Quarter-Master-General has no right to keep a slop-shop. **1807** J. R. SHAW *Life* (1930) 136 [At] a slop-shop . . . I equipped myself with a suit of clothes, from head to foot. **1878** PINKERTON *Strikers* 391 Upon the West Side [of Chicago] . . . there are innumerable . . . 'slop-shops,' or houses for the manufacture of ready-made clothing. **1891** NICHOLS *Business Guide* (ed. 28) 243 *Slop-shop,* a store where cheap ready-made clothing is sold.

b. Attrib. with *cut, robe, tailor.*

1853 KANE *Grinnell Exped.* 365 My latest rig [includes] . . . sailor pants of pilot cloth, slop-shop cut. **1891** *Century Mag.* April 932/2 The floor above . . . [was] the dwelling . . . of a slop-shop tailor. **1896** BRET HARTE *Barker's Luck* 102 He don't carry around no slop-shop robes and clap 'em on you whether they fit or not.

Slosh, *v.* {1844-}

+1. *intr.* To travel about; to walk around or loaf about. *colloq.*

1865 *Harper's Mag.* Jan. 146/2 In fact, she rather enjoyed sloshing around. **1876** 'MARK TWAIN' *Tom Sawyer* vi. 67 Devils don't slosh around much of a Sunday. **1908** McGAFFEY *Show-Girl* 58, I sloshed around town for a couple of years.

+b. To talk irrelevantly.

1880 *Harper's Mag.* Sept. 648/1 The Court . . . let him slosh around for a minute.

+2. *fig. tr.* To throw or toss (something) about in a careless or slipshod manner; to pour or dash (liquid). *colloq.*

1875 *Chicago Tribune* 3 Sept. 2/5 The Ring-paid scribblers and papers will slosh on the usual amount of whitewash. **1885** *Century Mag.* Nov. 63/2 If mining records was ever kep' as they'd ought to be, and not sloshed round so public like. **1902** *Emporia Gazette* 29 July, It pours over it the same oleaginous language that it once sloshed on Governor Roosevelt of New York.

Slot machine. A machine operated by inserting a coin in a slot {1892-}, +esp. such a machine serving as a gambling device. Also fig. — **1896** *Columbus Dispatch* 20 April 3/8 The new Republican mayor . . . has ordered all the slot machines out of town. **1897** *Chicago Tribune* 15 July 5/5 The bucket shops, clock games, and slot machines must go. **1911** 'O. HENRY' *Rolling Stones* 196 Mac McGowan was to . . . drop his silver talent into the slit of the slot-machine of fame and fortune that gives up reputation and dough.

* Slouch. +An inefficient or poor person, place, or thing. Usually in the phrase *no slouch of a (fellow, woodsman,* etc.). *colloq.*

1796 A. BARTON *Disappointment* III. i, He's no slouch of a fellow! **1840** HOFFMAN *Greyslaer* II. 23 You are no slouch of a woodsman to carry a yearling of such a heft as that. **1869** 'MARK TWAIN' *Innocents* 41 It shortly became a most lamentable 'slouch' of a journal. **1900** B. MATTHEWS *Confident To-Morrow* 52 Praxiteles was no slouch. **1910** McCUTCHEON *Rose in Ring* 273, I'm no slouch as a provider.

+b. With *at.*

1874 LONG *Wild-Fowl* 139 Well I guess you a'n't much of a 'slouch' at shooting. **1882** A. PERCY *Twice Outlawed* 79 You used to be no slouch yourself at it.

* Slough. Also †slow. (See also SLEW *n.*[1], SLOO, SLUE *n.*[1])

+1. A comparatively narrow stretch of backwater; a sluggish channel or inlet; a pond.

1665 *Springfield Rec.* II. 216 There is grannted to Inhabitants of Skeepmuck a highway from ye Slow beyond the Swan pond. **1714** *Charlestown Land Rec.* 217 The said Hunewell hath incroached & inclosed of the high way against his Orchard: between his old house & the Slough or Small Bridge. **1738** BYRD *Dividing Line* (1901) 27 [They] found all the Grounds bordering upon it very full of Sloughs. **1834** PECK *Gaz. Illinois* 237 A slough from the Mississippi approached and undermined the wall on one side in 1772. **1857** *Rep. Comm. Patents 1856: Agric.* 108 In these prairie water-courses and ponds, or sloughs, as they are called, the muskrats were very abundant. **1879** *Scribner's Mo.* Oct. 832/1 These sloughs or ponds occur very frequently upon the St. Paul and Pacific and Sioux City and St. Paul railroads. **1907** C. C. ANDREWS *Recoll.* (1928) 137 On our return trip, . . . one of our horses, an Indian pony, sank up to his neck in a slough.

+2. Attrib. in sense 1 and in general sense with *bass, hay, land,* etc.

1871 *Ill. Agric. Soc. Trans.* VIII. 172 The entire bed should be covered with coarse prairie or slough hay. **1874** LONG *Wild-Fowl* 150 Lager-beer . . . is much better to drink than slough-water. **1883** SMITH *Geol. Survey Ala.* 269 Black prairie slough soil, eight miles south of Montgomery. *Ib.* 272 The bottom soils . . . [vary] from the stiff black prairie slough lands . . . to light and rather sandy loams. **1884** *Harper's Mag.* March 601/1 Swamp and 'bay' (the word applied in Florida to slough and water-grass meadows) amplify the area. **1888** GOODE *Amer. Fishes* 56 'Marsh Bass,' . . . 'Slough Bass,' . . . are other names applied to one or both species [of black bass]. **1894** *Harper's Mag.* Aug. 457/1 If slough-shooting has a drawback, it is its lack of action. **1905** *Forestry Bureau. Bul.* No. 61, 48 *Slough pig,* usually a second-rate river driver who is assigned to picking logs out of sloughs in advance of the rear. (N[orthern] F[orest].)

+Slough grass. Any one of various grasses used chiefly for forage or hay found in or near sloughs. — **1860** *Ill. Agric. Soc. Trans.* IV. 488 Then [I] make a band of whatever material I have at hand, (slough grass is preferable. **1880** BESSEY *Botany* 455 *Muhlenbergia glomerata* and *M. Mexicana* constitute the 'Fine Slough Grass' of the Mississippi valley prairies. **1894** *Amer. Folk-Lore* VII. 103 *Agropyrum glaucum,* . . . slough-grass, pond-grass, Colorado.

*Slow, *n.*[1] +(See SLOUGH.)

*Slow, *n.*[2] *pl.* (See quotation.) *Obs.* — **1851** DUNGLISON *Med. Lexicon* (ed. 11) 564/1 *Milk Sickness,* Sick stomach, swamp sickness, Tires, Slows. . . . A disease occasionally observed in . . . Alabama, Indiana, and Kentucky, which affects both man and cattle, but chiefly the latter.

*Slow, *v.* *intr.* To slow *up,* to decrease speed. — **1881** *Century Mag.* Dec. 184/1 Slowing up, the great Cunarder gradually drew toward us. **1884** *N.Y. Sun* Aug.], If you'll slow up a trifle, . . . I'll get off here. **1886** ALTON *Among Law-Makers* 253 The train 'slowed-up.'

+Slow garter. (See quotation.) — **1842** *Nat. Hist. N.Y., Zoology* III. 45 The Striped Snake, *Tropidonotus tænia,* . . . is known under various popular names, such as Green Garter-snake, Slow Garter [etc.].

+**Slow lizard.** (See quotation.) — **1778** CARVER *Travels* 489 The *Slow Lizard* is of the same shape as the Swift, but its colour is brown.

+**Slue,** *n.*[1] Variant of SLOUGH. {1870-} — **1822** WOODS *English Prairie* 235 [We passed] a slue, or bayou . . . , on a drift-wood bridge. **1847** PALMER *Rocky Mts.* 186 There are some low ravines, (in the country called *slues,*) which are filled with water during freshets. **1873** 'MARK TWAIN' & WARNER *Gilded Age* 161 The indomitable engineer had carried his moving caravan over slues and branches.

+**Slue,** *n.*[2] (See SLEW *n.*[2])

+**Slue,** *v.* (See SLEW *v.*)

Slug, *n.* {1622-}

+**1.** Any one of various large gold coins of irregular shape privately issued in California about 1850. Now hist.

1854 *Daily Calif. Chron.* 6 Oct., We are too accustomed to see and handle the 'slugs' to be fobbed off instead, with a piece of thin, greasy paper. **1872** POWERS *Afoot & Alone* 303 A shining 'slug,' fresh from the San Francisco mint, [was] laid scrupulously in the place. **1907** *N.Y. Ev. Post* (s.-w. ed.) 5 Sept. 6 A rare relic in the form of an oblong 'slug,' such as passed current in the very early days of California for $50. *a*1918 G. STUART *On Frontier* I. 67 It was no unusual sight to see a man place a fifty dollar slug on a monte card.

2. A heavy piece or lump of crude metal; a gold nugget. {1894-}

*a*1861 WINTHROP *J. Brent* 33 It does look as bad off fur slugs as the cellar of an Indian's bank. **1872** 'MARK TWAIN' *Roughing It* 19 He would . . . pick up two or three pailfuls of shining slugs and nuggets of gold and silver. **1890** *Electrical Rev.* 19 April 2/4 'That is platinum, and it is worth about $150.' It was an insignificant looking slug.

+**b.** A thick lump *of* bacon.

1868 *Ill. Agric. Soc. Trans.* VII. 222 Our remedy is to drench them with lard or slugs of fat bacon.

+**3.** *Printing.* **a.** A lettered or numbered bar of metal to indicate a compositor; a compositor. **b.** A metal bar used for spacing. **c.** A line of type as cast by a linotype.

1871 RINGWALT, etc. *Amer. Encycl. Printing* 416/2 In daily-newspaper offices another species of slug, cast with the various letters of the alphabet on the top, are used to distinguish the matter set up by the different compositors, and the latter are frequently designated . . . as slug A, slug B, etc. **1893** Philips *Making of Newspaper* 103 'Slug 14' received his 'take' of copy at 2:35 A.M. **1924** *Publisher's Weekly* CVI. 190/2 *Slugs,* pieces of lead, about 3/4 inch high, and usually 6 or 12 points thick, used as spacing material between lines of type. The bar of metal with the type cast on it by the Linotype or Intertype is also called a slug.

attrib. **1894** SHUMAN *Steps into Journalism* 27 Most papers use 'big heads' or 'slug heads' over news articles exceeding one-half or two thirds of a column in length.

Slug, *v.* {1831-} +**1.** *tr.* and *intr.* Of a bullet: (see quotation).

+**2.** *To slug up,* to take a slug or drink of liquor. *slang. Obs.* — (1) **1876** KNIGHT 2217/2 The bullet, when forced to assume the sectional shape of the bore [of a breech-loading firearm] in the act of firing, is said to slug or to be slugged. (2) **1856** *Porter's Spirit of Times* 6 Sept. 7/1 Let's slug-up and prepare for business.

+**Slug caterpillar.** (See quot. 1891.) — **1841** GOULD *Invertebrata Mass.* 303 The most common of these slug-caterpillars, in Massachusetts, live on walnut-trees. **1891** *Cent.* 5706/3 *Slug-caterpillar,* one of the footless slug-like larvæ of the bombycid moths of the family *Limacodidæ.*

*Sluice, n.

*1. A channel, drain, or small stream for carrying off surplus or overflow water.

1644 *Essex Probate Rec.* I. 37, I giue Thomas my Son my Loomes & Sluices with there appurtenances. **1675** *Doc. Col. Hist. N.Y.* XII. 532 They were willing . . . to make & secure the Dick for a foott passage over by the river side with a sufficient sluyce to draine the water outt of the flye. **1713** *Charlestown Land Rec.* 179 Nathaniel Dows . . . Hath demised . . . unto the said John Underwood, all that peice [of meadow] . . . running upon a strait line from the sluce to [etc.]. **1793** in *Amer. Speech* XV. 394/2 Crossing the South Sluice 34 poles to his corner at the bank of Chain Island. **1831** PECK *Guide* 55 It requires only the cutting of a sluice through the levée at any place. **1874** KNIGHT 727/1 *Double-lock,* a canal-lock having two parallel chambers connecting by a sluice.

+**2.** In gold mining, a trough, flume, or series of riffle boxes through which water bearing auriferous gravel and sand is made to flow and deposit particles of gold.

1860 GREELEY *Overland Journey* 120 There are already sluices in operation at intervals for at least two miles up the runnel. **1872** McCLELLAN *Golden State* 266 Miners erect their sluices. **1883** *Century Mag.* Jan. 327/1 To use [the canyon] as a 'dump' or depository for the 'tailings' or débris of his sluices. *a*1918 [see DITCH *n.* 3].

+**3.** (See quot. 1905.)

1905 *Forestry Bureau Bul.* No. 61, 37 *Flume,* an inclined trough in which water runs, used in transporting logs or timbers. . . . [Also called] sluice, water slide, wet slide. **1908** WHITE *Riverman* 9 The sluice . . . had been built a good six feet above the level.

+**4.** Attrib. and comb. in sense 2 with *blanket, process, robber,* etc. Sometimes fig.

1869 HARTE *Luck of Roaring Camp* 21 The expatriated party [included] . . . 'Uncle Billy,' a suspected sluice-robber and confirmed drunkard. **1871** RAYMOND *3d Rep. Mines* 259 The sluice-tailings assay $5 per ton. **1873** BRET HARTE *Mrs. Skagg's Husbands* 121 A young man . . . was hung at Red Dog for sluice-robbing. **1876** RAYMOND *8th Rep. Mines* 74 Paid for sluice-blankets, [$]265.50. **1891** *Century Mag.* Feb. 533/2 This auriferous region . . . comprises the places . . . where the sluice and hydraulic processes were invented. **1905** 'O. HENRY' *Strictly Business* 81 Some of 'em [*sc.* women] are natural sluice troughs and can carry out $1,000 to the ton.

*Sluice, v.

+**1.** *tr.* To wash (auriferous sand or gravel) in a sluice. Also absol.

1850 A. T. JACKSON *Forty-Niner* (1920) 21 [We] washed up two days and sluiced top dirt the rest of the week. **1859** in F. Hall *Hist. Colorado* II. 521 Marsh Cook is sluicing a little with two boxes on bar of Vasquez Fork. **1869** BRACE *New West* 161 In many of these streams, whole hills have been 'sluiced' away. **1890** LANGFORD *Vigilante Days* (1912) 112 He quit sluicing and went to prospecting all over the country.

+**2.** (See quot. 1905.)

1877 *Lumberman's Gazette* 17 Nov. 309 The Chippewa will sluice down on the river mills at least 400,000,000 feet of logs. **1905** *Forestry Bureau Bul.* No. 61, 48 *Sluice,* . . . to float logs through the sluiceway of a splash dam. (N[orthern] F[orest].) **1908** WHITE *Riverman* 53 Three dams had to be sluiced through.

+**Sluice box.** =RIFFLE BOX. {1879, in S. Africa} — **1864** *Ore. State Jrnl.* 10 Dec. 3/1 Sluice boxes . . . were taken up by the wind. **1876** HARTE in *Scribner's Mo.* March 677/2 A walk of a few moments brought him to . . . the wooden sluice-box. **1896** SHINN *Story of Mine* 36 Sometimes a miner . . . would go home with his back aching from the labour of cleaning his sluice box every few minutes. *a*1918 G. STUART *On Frontier* I. 207 They also made some of the horses to set the sluice boxes on.

+**Sluiceway.**

1. An artificial channel or waterway; a sluice.

1779 *Mass. H. S. Proc.* 2 Ser. II. 461 The sluceway was broke up. **1878** JACKSON *Travel at Home* 252 A wooden sluice-way [is used] for mining purposes. **1902** WHITE *Blazed Trail* 326 Through the wide sluiceways a torrent foamed and tumbled. **1908** — *Riverman* 33 The six-foot lowering of the sluice-way had produced a fine current.

fig. **1858** *Beecher's Life Thoughts* 185 Some people . . . always make a drain or sluiceway by which the heavenly stream of God's favors escapes from them.

2. (See quotations.)

1851 *Harper's Mag.* Sept. 517/2 For taking logs down mountain sides, . . . we construct what are termed dry sluice-ways, which reach from the upper edge of a precipice down to the base of the hill. **1905** *Forestry Bureau Bul.* No. 61, 48 *Sluiceway,* the opening in a splash dam through which logs pass.

Sluicing. {1840-}

+**1.** The mining of gold by means of a sluice.

1860 *Harper's Mag.* April 614/1 The very general mode of mining known as 'sluicing' . . . employs not far from one half of the entire mining population of California. **1877** HODGE *Arizona* 63 Placers would pay well now, could water for sluicing or hydraulic washing be obtained. **1882** *47th Congress 1 Sess.* H. R. Ex. Doc. No. 216, 107 But little sluicing is now done except by Chinamen. *attrib. Ib.* 105 The Fox Creek and Boulder Creek sluicing claims have uniformly done well.

+**2.** A sluice or sluiceway used in gold-mining.

1869 HARTE *Luck of Roaring Camp* 67 It contained a rough, oblong box, —apparently made from a section of sluicing. **1885** *Wkly. New Mexican Rev.* 29 Jan. 4/2 Here large reservoirs and about two miles of substantial sluicing are to be constructed, and improved hydraulic machinery put in.

+**Slum.**[1] [Origin obscure.] A stew or other mixture of meat and vegetables, esp. potatoes and onions. Also transf. — **1847** J. MITCHELL *Reminisc. College* 117 Though the son of Vulcan found the pork and cabbage harmless, I am sure that slum would have been a match for him. **1871** BAGG *At Yale* 246 An olla podrida, hashed up from the remnants of yesterday's dinner, and fried into a consistency which baffled digestion, . . . was known as 'slum,' and was served both dry and wet. **1909** WASON *Happy Hawkins* 246 [He] started to peel spuds for the evenin' slum. **1924** *Scribner's Mag.* Dec. 648/2 The men took his slum and coffee to him.

+**Slum.**[2] Short for SLUMGULLION 1. Also fig. — **1874** RAYMOND *6th Rep. Mines* 350 The discharge near the top carries off light particles and slums. **1876** — *8th Rep. Mines* 27 This material . . . is like the slum or tailings from a mill. **1888** FERGUSON *Experiences of Forty-Niner* 53 It was a fine and attractive costume when . . . the weather was dry, but when the [buckskin] pants got wet in the slums, the legs elongated. **1890** *Scientific Amer.* 31 May 341/1 The alternate rise and fall of the hopper [in an ore concentrator is] caused by the vertically sliding beam, the slums, light gravel, etc., passing off through the waste flume at every upward motion.

+**Slumgullion.**

1. A muddy deposit in a mining sluice. Also transf. and fig.

1850 A. T. JACKSON *Forty-Niner* (1920) 30 The mud we were sending down the stream buried them under slumgullion. **1887** HARTE *Millionaire*

& Devil's Ford 146 We preach at them for playing in the slumgullion, and getting themselves splashed. **1896** — *Barker's Luck* 48 His fondness for paddling in the ditches and 'slumgullion' at one time suggested a water spaniel.

2. An insipid, unpalatable drink, as inferior tea. *slang.*

1872 'MARK TWAIN' *Roughing It* 44 Then he poured for us a beverage which he called 'Slumgullion.'

3. (See quotation and cf. SLOBGOLLION.)

1891 *Cent.* 5708/2 Slumgullion, . . . offal or refuse of fish of any kind; also, the watery refuse, mixed with blood and oil, which drains from blubber.

Slumming party. [f. *slumming* n. {1884-}] A party or group that visits the slums or low resorts for charitable purposes or out of curiosity. — **1884** *Boston Jrnl.* 1 Oct. 2/3 Slumming party engaged in conversation audibly. **1894** FORD *P. Stirling* 229 It's a society fad now to have what are called 'slumming parties.' . . . They get detectives to protect them, and then go through the tenements . . . and pry into their privacy and poverty, just out of curiosity. **1909** 'O. HENRY' *Options* 258 Along comes a slumming-party . . . , all in swallowtails.

Slump. {1895-}

+1. A slumping movement or fall.

1850 JUDD *R. Edney* 12 Move carefully! It is a slip, or a slump, all the way through. **1867** 'LACKLAND' *Homespun* 99 [A] black snake . . . slid down with a slump . . . into the water. **1900** S. HALE *Letters* 361, I let my huge bulk down with a slump.

2. A sudden or marked decline in prices. {1895-}

1887 *Courier-Journal* 17 Jan. 7/4 The crowd which had placed itself in a most comfortable attitude for a slump, had to bestir itself, [and] get in its short wheat. **1900** *Congress. Rec.* 7 Feb. 1613/1 The settlement of accounts on the 31st of December, 1899, was overshadowed by the 'slump' in the prices of all investments. **1919** SALTUS *Paliser Case* 35 The uncertain market; the slump, momentarily undiscernible; . . . these things were forgotten.

+3. *transf.* A period of temporary ineffectiveness; a sudden falling off in popularity, excitement, etc.; a decline. {1896-}

1889 HOWELLS *Annie Kilburn* xxv, What a slump!—what a slump! That blessed short-legged little seraph has spoilt the best sport that ever was. **1892** *Columbus Dispatch* 12 April, The last two weeks have seemed [?seen] a decided 'slump' in Hill stock in Washington. **1898** *N.Y. Tribune* 28 May 5/2 That alleged order for Rusie to pitch whether he had a sore arm or not may have had something to do with the slump in the work of the team within the last three days. **1912** MATHEWSON *Pitching* 179 Sometimes an umpire who has been good will go into a long slump when he cannot call things right and knows it.

+Slung shot. A weapon used chiefly by criminals consisting of a shot or other weight attached to a flexible handle or strap. Also attrib. (Cf. SLING SHOT a.) — **1842** *Spirit of Times* (Phila.) 29 Aug., Davis's companion struck him three violent blows with a slung-shot over the head. **1851** *Alta Californian* 19 July, We have . . . many thieves, burglars, and slung-shot murderers. **1881** BUEL *Border Outlaws* 117 A large slung-shot was found on his wrist. **1917** McCUTCHEON *Green Fancy* 302 He was put to sleep again by a crack over the head with a slung-shot.

Slur, *v.* {1602-} +*tr.* To coat or cover (a wall) with plaster or roughcast. — **1885** *Harper's Mag.* March 531/1 The rear wall is slurred.

+Slush fund. Orig., a contingent fund appropriated annually by Congress to be administered at the discretion of the disbursing officer, usually the Secretary of the Treasury; in later use, a fund for bribery, corruption, etc. — **1864** *Rio Abajo Press* 5 July 2/2 The polite Commissary informed us that they received twelve dollars a barrel for the [coffee] grounds, and thus added materially to the 'slush fund.' **1874** *Congress. Rec.* 17 April 3166/1 We have had this 'slush-fund' since 1866. **1908** STEVENS *Liberators* 300 Every insurance company that was operated for its promoters . . . contributed to the 'slush fund' at Albany.

Smack, *n.* {1611-} +A fishing vessel having a well in which fish may be kept alive. — *a*1891 *Fisherman's Memorial Bk.* 70 (Cent.), Many of them were made into smacks, so-called, . . . by building a water-tight compartment amidships, and boring holes in the bottom to admit salt-water.

+Smack, *v. tr.* To convey in a smack. — **1880** *Harper's Mag.* Aug. 350/2 The jigger . . . taking a haul of fish, 'smacking' a load of lobsters, wood, or ice. *Ib.* Sept. 499/1 The schooner Marthy . . . 'smacked' fish regularly to Portland.

Smacked, *a.* +(See quotation.) — **1886** *Amer. Philol. Ass. Trans.* XVII. 46 List of common Southern expressions: . . . *smacked* (ground—as smacked corn).

+Smack smooth, *a.* (See quotation.) *Obs.* — **1848** BARTLETT 409 *Smack smooth,* at the West, a term applied to land which is thoroughly cleared: i.e. smoothly cleared; level.

*Small, *a.*

1. In the names of plants.

See also SMALL BUCKEYE, CHERRY, MAGNOLIA.

1709 LAWSON *Carolina* 101 The small Bamboo is . . . a certain Vine, . . . growing in low Land. **1814** BIGELOW *Florula Bostoniensis* 50 *Convolvulus arvensis.* Small bindweed. . . . Flowers nearly white. *a*1817 DWIGHT *Travels* I. 46 The Small Laurel has little beauty. **1840** DEWEY *Mass. Flowering Plants* 144 G[alium] *trifidum.* Small Bedstraw. A small, sca-

brous plant. **1849** EMMONS *Agric. N.Y.* II. 317 Small Red cherry. Seasoned. **1860** CURTIS *Woody Plants N.C.* 44 Small-nut hickory (*C[arya] microcarpa*). The nut is roundish. *Ib.* 115 Small woodbine (*L[onicera] parviflora*). . . . [Flowers] greenish-yellow tinged with purple. **1883** SMITH *Geol. Survey Ala.* 233 Vegetation . . . [includes] hickory, post-oak, and small sourwood. **1889** VASEY *Agric. Grasses* 78 *Arundinaria tecta* (Switch Cane; Small Cane).

2. In the specific names of birds and animals.

See also SMALL PEWEE.

*c*1730 CATESBY *Carolina* I. 80 *Ardea stellaris minima.* The small Bittern. . . . I believe they retire from Virginia and Carolina more South. **1814** MITCHILL *Fishes N.Y.* 446 Small Silverside. *Atherina notata.* . . . Upper jaw somewhat jutting. **1842** *Nat. Hist. N.Y., Zoology* I. 34 The Small Weasel, *Mustella pusilla,* . . . is usually known under the name of the *Little Weasel.* **1917** *Birds of Amer.* I. 205 Virginia Rail. *Rallus virginianus.* . . . [Also called] Small Mud Hen; Fresh-water Marsh Hen.

3. In special combinations.

Small bolled cotton, a variety of cotton having small bolls; *s. business,* activity characteristic of business operated on a small scale; petty obstructionism; *s. game,* squirrels, woodchucks, etc., as distinguished from bear, deer, elk, etc.; *s. linen,* (see quotation); *s. news,* trivial or unimportant news; *s. part,* a minor role in a play; *s. planter,* a planter who farms on a small scale; *s. work,* work on small objects, tinkering.

1835 in Commons, etc. *Doc. Hist.* I. 184 Small bold cotton was backward in this country owing to the dry spring. **1855** *Chicago W. Times* 31 May 2/6 In any case, it seems 'small business' for the city . . . to carp and find fault about the bill. **1817** S. BROWN *Western Gazetteer* 147 Small game abound in all the upland forests. **1662** *N.H. Probate Rec.* I. 54 My wife shall have . . . Her small linin yt is to say Hancherchers neckclothes & Head linen. **1803** JEFFERSON in *Lewis & Clark Exped.* VII. (1905) 282, I recollect no other small news worth communicating. **1902** C. MORRIS *Stage Confidences* 200 A certain actress of 'small parts,' . . . suddenly broke out with [etc.]. **1863** *Rep. Comm. Agric. 1862* 60 Cuba tobacco is, next to sugar, most in favor with small planters. **1787** *Md. Gazette* 1 June 4/3 By trade a Coppersmith, and a good workman at small work.

b. With reference to Indians: (see quotations).

1832 CATLIN *Indians* I. 52 The Blackfeet proper are divided into four bands or families, as follow: . . . the 'Blood' band, of 450 lodges; and the 'Small Robes.' **1851** in Cushman *Hist. Indians* 89 In 1771, the eastern district of the Choctaw Nation was known as Oy-pat-oo-coo-la, signifying the 'Small Nation.'

Small arms. Firearms, as muskets, rifles, pistols, etc., that may be carried in the hand. {1710-} — **1689** *Maine Doc. Hist.* V. 10, I have delivered to Mr. Alden 31 Small arms. **1705** *Boston News-Letter* 3 Dec. 2/2 Capt. Foster's Mate desired him to go and help to bring down the small Arms. **1823** COOPER *Pioneers* xxii, On receiving this united discharge of small-arms, the front of the flock darted upward. **1892** M. A. JACKSON *Gen. Jackson* 340 Twenty thousand small-arms . . . fell into the hands of the Confederates.

*Small beer. Beer of a weak or inferior quality. Also attrib. and transf. — **1705** BEVERLEY *Virginia* IV. 57 Their richer sort generally brew their small-beer with malt. **1789** *Ann. 1st Congress* 224 Shall it be said that the General Government descends to small beer for its revenue, while strong beer remains duty free? **1844** KENDALL *Narr. Santa Fé Exped.* II. 125 To me it had the flavour of stale small-beer mixed with sour milk. **1873** *Newton Kansan* 24 April 4/2 Let us have done with these small-beer grumblings.

+Small boy. A young boy. The term is usually applied to boys of about five to ten years of age regardless of their size. — **1786** WASHINGTON *Diaries* III. 86 That Cowper Jack and Day, with some small boys and girls, . . . were assisting the farmer. **1821** COOPER *Spy* i, A small boy was directed to guide him to his room. **1889** *Atlantic Mo.* April 465/1 A small boy who first sees a military parade wishes to be a soldier. **1913** JAMES (*title*), A Small Boy and Others.

+Small buckeye. =RED BUCKEYE. — **1832** BROWNE *Sylva* 226 The Yellow *Pavia* . . . is here called *Big Buckeye,* to distinguish it from the *Pavia rubra,* . . . which is called *Small Buckeye.* **1846** — *Trees* 115 The Small Buckeye is a slender-growing tree or shrub.

Small change. Money in the form of small coins. {1875-} Also fig., and attrib. in sense: Petty, mean. — **1819** in Mackenzie *Van Buren* 156, I wish you to say to the bank that you want *Small Change;* and for that you will give them current bills. **1834** SIMMS *Guy Rivers* I. 17 It relieves young travellers, like yourself, of their small change. **1861** Moore *Rebellion Rec.* I. III. 40 White-slaves, peddling wretches, small-change knaves . . . are the levied 'forces' whom Lincoln suddenly arrays as candidates for the honor of being slaughtered by gentlemen. **1863** *Rio Abajo Press* 24 March 1/2 In regard to our minor currency, usually called 'small change,' it is difficult to realize [etc.]. **1864** LOWELL *Fireside Trav.* 192 A poor Anglo-Saxon must . . . look twice at his small change of quarters and minutes. **1905** A. H. RICE *Sandy* 290 He handed her some small change.

+Small cherry. =RED CHERRY. — **1832** BROWNE *Sylva* 135 Red Cherry Tree. *Cerasus borealis.* . . . [In] Maine and Vermont, it is called *Small Cherry* and *Red Cherry.*

Smaller. +'An ordinary-sized drink of liquor' (Th.). *slang. Obs.* — **1829** *N.Y. Mirror* 7 Nov. 138/2 'Sixteen smallers,' cried R——ds, 'it is deerskin.' **1835** BIRD *Hawks* II. 147 A smaller on that, Lingo,—come what will you lay? **1839** *S. Lit. Messenger* V. 66/1 Bill . . . had just commenced, after taking a 'smaller' himself, to serve out the liquor to them.

+**Small farmer.** One who farms on a small scale, almost or entirely without hired help. Also attrib. — **1835** HOFFMAN *Winter in West* I. 79 They were chiefly plain people, small farmers and graziers. **1849** WILLIS *Rural Letters* 175 Landscape gardening, as within the reach of small farmer people, is quite another thing. **1879** *Harper's Mag.* June 73/1 [The] small farmers hover around the outskirts of the crowd of fishermen. **1900** *Congress. Rec.* 19 Feb. 1938/2 Every promissory note which the small farmer or the large farmer . . . gives in order to carry on his farming . . . is taxed. **1913** LONDON *Valley of Moon* 327 The district . . . was 'small-farmer' country in which labor was rarely hired.

+**Small farming.** Farming performed on a small scale. — **1880** *Scribner's Mo.* Oct. 843/1 Small farming means, in short, meat and bread for which there are no notes in the bank. **1898** WESTCOTT *D. Harum* 171 Small farmin' ain't cal'lated to fetch out the best traits of human nature.

Small-flowered, *a.* {1789–} +In the names of American plants and trees having small flowers. — **1813** MUHLENBERG *Cat. Plants* 53 *Illicium*, Small-flowered, yellow, aniseed tree. **1817–8** EATON *Botany* (1822) 362 *Nicotiana paniculata*, small-flowered tobacco. **1843** TORREY *Flora N.Y.* II. 415 *Leersia Virginica*, Small-flowered White-grass. . . . Swamps and wet shady woods. **1901** MOHR *Plant Life Ala.* 507 *Asimina parviflora.* . . . Small-flowered Papaw. . . . Carolinian and Louisianian areas.

+**Small fruit.** (See quotations.) — **1879** WEBSTER *Suppl.* 1579/1 *Small fruits*, fruits raised in market-gardens. **1892** CROZIER *Dict. Bot. Terms* 164/2 *Small fruits*, a horticultural term for certain low-growing perennial, fruit-bearing plants and their product, including the strawberry, raspberry, blackberry, gooseberry, currant, huckleberry, and cranberry. The term includes grapes, but excludes cherries.

+**Small-fruited hickory.** A variety of hickory bearing fruit of comparatively small size. — **1847** DARLINGTON *Weeds & Plants* 306 The small fruited Hickory, C[arya] *microcarpa*, . . . is distinguished by its very small fruit. **1919** STURTEVANT *Notes on Edible Plants* 149 Small-fruited Hickory. Eastern North America. The nuts are edible but not prized.

+**Small grain.** Any one of various cereals, as wheat, oats, barley, etc., having grains smaller than those of Indian corn. Also attrib. — **1802** *Steele P.* I. 250 Cheapsides is sewed in Small Grain wheat ry and barly. **1816** *Niles' Reg.* X. 365/2 The small grains—wheat and rye, 'promise a heavy harvest.' **1839** BUEL *Farmer's Companion* 197 The small-grain crops are the greatest exhausters of the fertility of the soil. **1876** *Ill. Dept. Agric. Trans.* XIII. 301 The small grains are more mentioned [by early Fr. settlers] than Indian corn. **1892** *Courier-Journal* 1 Oct. 12/6 Churchill Hand-made Sour-mash Whisky. 40 per cent small grain.

+**Small-headed flycatcher, warbler.** (See quot. 1902.) *Obs.* — **1812** WILSON *Ornithology* VI. 62 [The] Small-headed Flycatcher . . . [is a] very rare species. **1839** PEABODY *Mass. Birds* 297 The Small-headed Flycatcher . . . has been found in Ipswich. **1870** *Amer. Naturalist* III. 577 Small-headed Flycatcher. . . . This rather apocryphal species is given by Peabody as having been met with at Ipswich by Dr. Brewer. **1902** RIDGWAY *Birds of N. & Middle Amer.* II. 709 *Wilsonia microcephala* Ridgway. Small-headed Warbler. . . . I am unable to satisfactorily dispose of this hypothetical species to any other.

Small-leaf. *attrib.* In the specific names of various plants and trees having small leaves. — **1897** SUDWORTH *Arborescent Flora* 234 *Cratægus uniflora*. Small-leaf Haw. *Ib.* 255 *Parkinsonia microphylla*. Small-leaf Horse Bean. . . . Palo Verde (Cal.). **1817–8** EATON *Botany* (1822) 432 *Rosa parvifolia*, small-leaf rose. **1901** MOHR *Plant Life Ala.* 89 Of smaller trees and shrubs, . . . small-leaf sugar maple, redbud, dogwood, and hazelnut prevail.

Small-leaved, *a.* In the specific names of various plants and trees having small leaves. {1812– (Withering *Brit. Plants*)} — **1813** MUHLENBERG *Cat. Plants* 48 *Cratægus parvifolia*, Small-leaved hawthorn. **1843** TORREY *Flora N.Y.* I. 180 *Desmodium ciliare*, Hairy Small-leaved Desmodium. . . . Sandy fields, hill-sides and copses. **1860** CURTIS *Woody Plants N.C.* 55 Small-leaved elm. (U[lmus] *alata*.) . . . The wood . . . is used for the naves of wheels. **1885** HAVARD *Flora W. & S. Texas* 508 *Acer grandidentatum*. (Small-leaved Maple). . . . The only maple of Western Texas. **1901** MOHR *Plant Life Ala.* 71 The following shade the rocky borders of the water courses: *Vaccinium tenellum* (small-leaved huckleberry).

+**Small magnolia.** The sweet bay, *Magnolia virginiana.* — **1785** MARSHALL *Amer. Grove* 83 Small Magnolia, or Swamp Sassafras, . . . grows naturally in low, moist, or swampy ground. **1868** GRAY *Field Botany* 43 Small M[agnolia] or Sweet Bay, [grows] wild in swamps N. to New Jersey and Mass.

*Small money.** Money of small size and low denomination; small change. — **1705** *Boston News-Letter* 8 Oct. 2/2 There is now Published an Almanack . . . : With a Table of the Weight of small Money. **1819** in Mackenzie *Van Buren* 156 Direct Mr. Wing to . . . request them to furnish him with small money for change. **1886** Z. F. SMITH *Kentucky* 562 When the want of small money became great, . . . about the beginning of the century, the need was met by cutting the Spanish dollar into four or eight parts.

+**Smallmouth (black bass).** =next. — **1884** GOODE, etc. *Fisheries* I. 401 The Small-mouth shares with the Large-mouth in the Southern States the names 'Jumper,' 'Perch,' and 'Trout.' *Ib.* 402 The Small-mouths found their way into the Hudson in 1825 or soon after. **1897** *Outing* Aug. 437/2 Most prized of the lot were the black bass, especially the small-mouth. *Ib.* 438/1 A small-mouth black bass was the prize first tried for.

+**Small-mouthed (black) bass.** A valuable fresh-water game fish, *Micropterus dolomieu.* — **1882** *Nat. Museum Bul.* No. 16, 485 Small-mouthed Black Bass. . . . Southern specimens usually have the scales of the lower part of the sides with faint dark streaks. **1883** *Century Mag.* July 376/2 There are but two well-defined species, the large-mouthed bass and the small-mouthed bass.

+**Small pewee.** =GREEN-CRESTED FLYCATCHER. — **1839** PEABODY *Mass. Birds* 295 The Small Pewee . . . is a very common summer bird. **1844** *Nat. Hist. N.Y., Zoology* II. 112 The Small Green-crested Flycatcher, or Small Pewee . . . , winters in Mexico. **1917** *Birds of Amer.* II. 207 Acadian Flycatcher. . . . [Also called] Small Green-crested Flycatcher; Green Flycatcher; Small Pewee.

Small potato. *fig.* +*pl.* A person or thing regarded as trivial, insignificant, paltry, etc. Also *small potatoes and few of* (or *in*) *a hill.* Usually pl.

1836 CROCKETT *Exploits* 25 This is what I call small potatoes and few of a hill. c**1849** PAIGE *Dow's Sermons* I. 199 Political foes are such very small potatoes, that they will hardly pay for skinning. **1889** *N.Y. Herald* 6 Oct. 11/1 Mr. Daly is small potatoes compared to the author of 'Divorçons!' **1922** A. BROWN *Old Crow* 465, 'I am,' thought Raven, returning to the . . . vernacular, 'very small potatoes and few in a hill.'

+**b.** Attrib. in sing. with *enemy, man, politician, reader.*

1840 *Picayune* 19 Aug. 2/1 Creole readers, Yankee readers, small potato readers, . . . hope you are well this morning. **1849** G. G. FOSTER *N.Y. in Slices* 102 Like monkeys and small-potato politicians, they have their appointed end. **1863** *Rio Abajo Press* 14 April 2/2 Their acts have shown them to be the smallest kind of 'small potatoe' enemies. **1880** *Harper's Mag.* Oct. 708 Yer small-p'tater men Will kin' o' work t' th' bottom uv the ben.

* **Smallpox.** A contagious disease characterized by fever, vomiting, and a pustular eruption. Esp. as prevailing among the Indians.

1635 R. MATHER *Journal* 30 Fevers, calentures, small pockes, & such diseases as have afflicted other passangers ye Lord kept from among us. **1643** *New Eng. First Fruits* (1896) 9 Sweeping away great multitudes of the Natives by the small Pox. **1690** [see MAQUA]. **1775** ADAIR *Indians* 251 Their own bad situation by the ravaging small-pox . . . induced the lower towns to lie dormant. **1822** MORSE *Rep. Indian Affairs* I. 92 The small pox, particularly, has frequently and in many tribes, made awful havoc. **1877** HODGE *Arizona* 169 The word moqui means death, and was applied to them by other tribes at a time long since, when the small-pox killed off large numbers of the tribe.

attrib. **1815–16** *Niles' Reg.* IX. Suppl. 182/1 The lady . . . voluntarily offered to go with her four children into the small pox hospital at Brooklyn.

b. In connection with inoculation as a preventive measure.

1721 *New-Eng. Courant* 6 Nov. 4/2 Whosoever shall come into this Town of Boston . . . presumptuously to bring the Small Pox on him or herself, or be inoculated, shall be forthwith sent to the Hospital or Pesthouse. **1776** *Mass. Spy* 17 July 3/3 The General Court have passed an act allowing of Hospitals for Innoculating for the small pox, in each county in this Colony. **1824** *New Eng. Farmer* II. 205 Small Pox. . . . A few years since, vaccination was very general; but of late it has been neglected.

attrib. **1868** G. G. CHANNING *Recoll. Newport* 17, I was but three and a half years old when . . . conveyed to the island . . . to be inoculated with small-pox virus.

c. As occurring in a *natural* or *common* way, as contrasted with occurrence from inoculation.

1776 J. ADAMS *Familiar Lett.* 148 We have this week lost a very valuable friend . . . by the smallpox in the natural way. **1788** FRANKLIN *Autobiog.* 349 In 1736 I lost one of my sons . . . by the small-pox, taken in the common way.

Small rice. (See quot. 1868.) — **1868** *Rep. Comm. Agric. 1867* 179 Other fans . . . divide it into three qualities, known as 'whole,' 'middling,' and 'small rice.' **1890** MCALLISTER *Society* 98 [We] had a dinner of small rice, pea pie, and roast turkey.

Small stores. Small articles, as soap, tobacco, etc., carried in a ship's store and sold to the crew. Also transf. Also attrib. — **1839** BRIGGS *H. Franco* I. 168, 'I suppose, Bob,' said one [sailor], 'we shall have small stores [in the way of food] all the voyage?' **1886** *Congress. Rec.* 17 June 5836/1 In the small stores account we find that Paymaster Smith . . . purchased over five thousand ditty boxes.

Small sword. A light sword suitable for thrusting, esp. used in fencing. {1687–} Also attrib. — **1756** in Singleton *Social N.Y.* 331 These are to give notice to all gentlemen who desire to learn the right Method and true Art of Defence and pursuit of the small sword in its greatest Perfection. **1809** in H. M. Brooks *Gleanings* IV. 144 Several amateurs . . . will play the Small-Sword, Cut-and-Thrust, Broad-Sword, and Cudgel or Cane Fighting. **1855** WOOD *Recoll. Stage* 274 A party of French artists also gave an exhibition of small sword exercise. **1865** *Atlantic Mo.* May 553/1 We had a fencing-master, and took regular lessons in the use of the small sword.

Small town. {1611–} *attrib.* passing into *adj.* Of or pertaining to a small city. — **1881** *Harper's Mag.* Jan. 223/2 Cosmopolitans, they do not sink into the ruts of small-town life. **1923** HERRICK *Lilla* 181 Gordon made various short tours in the state giving addresses before small town audiences.

∗Smart, *a.* (Cf. RIGHT SMART.)
Smart chance, sprinkle, sprinkling, (see the nouns).

+**1.** In good health, well. *N. Eng.*

1788 MAY *Jrnl. & Lett.* 116 Didn't feel smart enough to go to meeting. **1831** S. SMITH *Life J. Downing* 117, I didn't feel hardly smart enough to write. **1848** MITCHELL *Nantucketisms* 41, *I'm very smart,* I am very well. **1895** JEWETT *Nancy* 184 'How's William's folks?' 'They're smart.'

2. *Smart as a steel trap* (or *whip*), extremely alert, brisk, clever, etc. *colloq.*

1833 S. SMITH *Life J. Downing* 224 He'd come up again as smart as a steeltrap. **1874** B. F. TAYLOR *World on Wheels* 27 The 'drive' . . . was as smart as a whip, and profane. **1918** RIDEOUT *Key of Fields* 259 Times I think he's deeper'n a well and smarter'n a whip.

3. *Smart to work,* energetic, not lazy. *N. Eng.*

1890 JEWETT *Strangers* 137, I've be'n a smart woman to work in my day. **1902** FREEMAN *Six Trees* 91 The old woman always was smart to work.

4. *Smart hooping,* (see quotation).

1800 TATHAM *Tobacco* 54 [One method] of forming the hoop of tobacco hogsheads . . . resembles the method used in the construction of pales and tubs, called flat hooping; and the other is of the kind used for hooping casks for ordinary occasions, called smart hooping.

+**Smart,** *v.* [f. SMART *a.*] **1.** *tr.* and *intr.* To make or become spruce, well, or neat. Also with *up. colloq.* **2.** *To smart up,* to make smart or acquainted with new things. *colloq.* — (1) **1782** DALRYMPLE *Journal* 13, I shall have but little time to smart myself. **1839** KIRKLAND *New Home* (1840) 178, I see you've smarted up a good deal. **1860** *Ladies' Repository* May 279/1 Seems to me you are wonderfully smarted-up tonight! **1891** COOKE *Huckleberries* 251, I'm a goin' to stop till she's outdoors again and pootty well smarted up. (2) **1867** HOLMES *Guardian Angel* 359 He had got 'smarted up,' as his mother called it, a good deal.

+**Smart aleck.** A would-be clever person; a bumptious know-all. *colloq.* Also attrib. — **1873** BEADLE *Undevel. West* 140, I had the pleasure(?) of seeing at least a score of 'smart Alecks' relieved of their surplus cash. **1884** *Gringo & Greaser* 15 Feb. 2/1 Can't some smart Aleck, or some glib exposer, . . . tell us all about it? **1904** *Nat. Advertiser* 30 April 21 Smart-aleck efforts to get something for nothing. **1920** SANDBURG *Smoke & Steel* 224 Smart-alecks discussing 'educated jackasses.'

+**Smart grass.** =SMARTWEED. — **1845** JUDD *Margaret* II. 212 The geese . . . left only may-weed, smart-grass, and Indian tobacco.

Smart set. 'The extremely fashionable portion of society (sometimes with implication of being a little 'fast')' (*O.E.D.*). — **1890** McALLISTER *Society* 158 Behind what I call the 'smart set' in society, there always stood the old, solid, substantial, and respected people. **1898** HARRIS *Tales of Home Folks* 399 The 'smart set' had no kind of organization. **1900** ADE *More Fables* 106 All the Smart Set got ready to pike away for the Heated Term.

Smartweed. Any one of several species of *Persicaria,* as *P. hydropiper.* {1787–} — **1819** SCHOOLCRAFT *Mo. Lead Mines* 29 Plants from which colours have been extracted for dyeing . . . [are] shumac, upland dock, and smartweed. **1845** JUDD *Margaret* I. 105 Her little white and yellow chickens were peeping and dodging under . . . the star-tipped hedge-mustard, and pink-tufted smart-weed. **1867** HARRIS *Sut Lovingood* 75 A hollyhawk in a patch ove smartweed. **1884** *Century Mag.* Feb. 518/2 The old gray barns . . . were not too fine to have . . . a fringe of hemp, mayweed, and smartweed about their jagged underpinning. **1891** *Amer. Folk-Lore* IV. 148 *P. Hydropiper* was *Smartweed* [in N.H.].

+**Smarty.** A would-be witty person; a smart aleck. *slang.* — **1874** *Congress. Rec.* 4 June 4592/2, I said the colored people of my district were content with their condition. . . . A few exceptions . . . [are] 'smarties' or 'would-be' leaders. **1880** *Boston Transcript* 6 March (*Cent.*), 'Did you make the train?' asked the anxious questioner. 'No,' said smarty, 'it was made in the car-shop.' **1924** R. CUMMINS *Sky-High Corral* 16, I won't have no sneakin' smarty like you tellin' me what's what.

Smash, *n.* A spirituous drink with crushed ice, sugar, and a flavoring agent, as mint. {1859–, in Austral.} See also BRANDY SMASH, MINT SMASH. — **1872** *Harper's Mag.* Sept. 637/1 He engaged his old employer to compound . . . the soothing smash. **1873** MILLER *Amongst Modocs* 61 Come, take a smash! It will strengthen you up.

Smash, *v.* {1700–} +**1.** *tr.* To handle (baggage), esp. in a rough, careless manner. (Cf. BAGGAGE-SMASHER.) ‖**2.** To cultivate (land) with heavy implements that smash or crush the clods, vegetation, etc. — (1) **1865** *Atlantic Mo.* April 386/1 New trunks [were] more recklessly smashed, than would be possible at a later hour. **1872** BRACE *Dangerous Classes N.Y.* 317 They were mere children, and kept life together by . . . 'smashing baggages' (as they called it), and the like. (2) **1870** *Rep. Comm. Agric. 1869* 303 The thorough and deep cultivation of the soil by 'smashing' and cultivating with the ponderous implements employed in heavy lands facilitates drainage.

Smasher. {1794–} +=SMASH *n.* — **1849** G. G. FOSTER *N.Y. in Slices* 96 A good-looking female barkeeper . . . dispenses smiles and smashers.

‖**Smashfulness.** Propensity for breaking or smashing. — **1887** *Courier-Journal* 15 Feb. 4/3 The general smashfulness of the average baggageman . . . [has] long created suspicion in the public mind.

Smash-up. {1890–} +A collision or wreck, esp. on a railroad. *colloq.* — **1856** M. J. HOLMES *L. Rivers* 35 The old lady, sure of a *smash-up* this time, had attempted to rise. **1875** *Billings' Farmer's Allminax* 13 Got the orfull smash up on the rale rode. **1887** DALY *Railroad of Love* 47 There's been a collision on the road—a regular smash-up. **1923** WATTS

L. Nichols 354 There had been . . . a smash up; a delivery-wagon . . . had run head-on into that there stone.

∗**Smear.** +**1.** (See quotation.) +**2.** Something to spread on bread. — (1) **1877** BARTLETT 614 *Smear,* food; hash; grub, especially a society spread or supper. (2) **1891** 'THANET' *Otto the Knight* 330 You an' Bulah Norman wud . . . be projickin roun' my kitchin for light bread an' smear.

+**Smearcase.** [G. *schmierkäse.*] Cottage cheese. — **1829** ROYALL *Pennsylvania* I. 171 A dish, common amongst the Germans, . . . is curds and cream. It is very palatable, and called by the Germans *smearcase.* **1846** MAGOFFIN *Down Santa Fé Trail* 90 Their cheese is . . . made on the same principle as the Dutch smerecase. **1879** *Scribner's Mo.* Aug. 566/1 Loaf bread, . . . flanked by appetizing apple-butter, snowy smear-kase, and dulcet honey. **1894** *Harper's Mag.* Jan. 218/2 The 'cookey' (koekje), noodles, hodgepodge, smearcase, rullichies, cold-slaw, and other dishes that survive in New England.

Smeared dagger. (See quotations.) — **1871** C. V. RILEY *3d Mo. Ent. Rep.* 70 The Smeared Dagger . . . is another insect which is occasionally found upon the Grape-vine. [**1883** W. SAUNDERS *Insects Inj. Fruits* 325 The Smeared Dagger, *Apatella oblinita.*] **1891** *Cent.* 5713/3.

Smee(s). {1668–} +=PINTAIL 1. *local.* — **1888** TRUMBULL *Names of Birds* 38 In New Jersey, at Manasquan . . . [the pintail duck is known as] *Smee. Ib.* 39 Most of us . . . call it Sprig-tail, but I suppose its real name is Smees. **1917** *Birds of Amer.* I. 128.

∗**Smell,** *v. intr.* With *of:* To make use of the sense of smell in respect to a specified object. {1624, 1815} 'Now *U.S.*' (*O.E.D.*). — **1851** JUDD *Margaret* (ed. 2) 128 The big bear . . . smelt of her hand. **1852** CURTIS *Lotus-eating* 3, I have not yet done . . . smelling of all the flowers. **1912** HASKIN *Amer. Govt.* 276 He took out the cork, smelled of it, and then replaced it.

+**Smellage.** [Alteration of *smallage.*] Lovage, *Levisticum officinale.* — **1836** LINCOLN *Botany* App. 110 [*Ligusticum*] *levisticum,* (smellage,) leaves many. . . . Medicinal. **1855** *Mich. Agric. Soc. Trans.* VI. 149 The plants on the uplands are Columbo, . . . smellage, skoke or garget root.

Smelling bottle. A small bottle containing smelling salts for ready use. {1771–} — **1789** DUNLAP *Father* I. i, Have you a smelling-bottle, sir? **1854** COOKE *Va. Comedians* I. 281 Leaning over [he] took a smelling-bottle from the hand of the old dowager.

+**Smelling committee.** (See quotations.) — **1877** BARTLETT 614 *Smelling-Committee,* persons appointed to conduct an unpopular investigation. The phrase originated in the examination of a convent in Massachusetts by legislative order. **1888** WALLACE *Carpetbag Rule* 104 The colored members . . . elected a permanent chairman of the caucus, and that chairman appointed a committee of three to ferret out all the schemes which looked anything like money schemes. This committee was styled 'the smelling committee.'

Smelling salts. *pl.* An aromatic preparation used for preventing or relieving faintness, headache, or the like. {1840–} — **1841** BACHE *Fire-Screen* 96 Have either of you any hartshorn or smelling-salts? **1907** 'O. HENRY' *Roads of Destiny* 72 He first opened his eyes, pushed aside the smelling-salts, and asked: 'Where am I?'

+**Smell lemon.** A variety of gourd. — **1871** DE VERE 415 The little Smell-Lemon (*Cucurbita ovifera*), the fruit of which is about the size of a small orange, bright glossy red, with stripes of yellow.

∗**Smelt.**

∗**1. a.** Any of certain small fishes of the family Osmeridae, +as the American smelt (*Osmerus mordax*) of the east coast and the Pacific smelt (*Spirinchus thaleichthys*) of the northern west coast. **b.** Any of various fishes resembling the smelt.

1637 MORTON *New Canaan* 89 Of Smelts there is such abundance that the Salvages doe take them up the rivers with baskets, like sives. **1734** *Boston Rec.* 71 All Fish caught in Rivers, Ponds, and Brooks, shall be brought into and sold in the Market; Frost-fish and Smelts, excepted. **1782** CRÈVECŒUR *Letters* 132 Near Pochick Rip . . . they catch their best fish, such as . . . cod, smelt, perch [etc.]. **1818** *Amer. Monthly Mag.* II. 248 The length of the largest Smelts I have seen in New-York is about seven inches. **1857** UNDERHILL & THOMPSON *Elephant Club* 175, I could never afford more than a string of smelts. **1866** *Rep. Indian Affairs* 98 In this particular locality [Smith R., Calif.] there seems an inexhaustible supply of small fish called smelts. **1872** McCLELLAN *Golden State* 247 Rock-cod, a very bony fish, is plentiful; also tomcods, smelts, and soles or flatfish. **1900** *Boston Globe* 21 Oct. 2/3 They soon caught 13 smelts. **1911** *Rep. Fisheries 1908* 310 Eulachon (*Thaleichthys pacificus*). . . . On the Columbia River the name 'smelt' is used.

2. Attrib. with *brook, fishery, net.*

1668 *Boston Rec.* 41 The first tree we found in ye said Smelt Brooke is marked with B. **1884** *Nat. Museum Bul.* No. 27, 851 *Smelt-net.* Made of whalebone, with stone sinker. . . . Plover Bay, Alaska. **1884** GOODE, etc. *Fisheries* I. 543 The smelt fishery is increasing yearly in importance.

∗**Smelter.**

∗**1.** One who melts or reduces ore in order to extract metal; an owner of a smelter or smelting works.

1814 BRACKENRIDGE *Views La.* 149 The miners . . . dispose of their ore to the smelters. **1869** *Boyd's Business Directory* 14 Solomon Edward, smelter. **1876** RAYMOND *8th Rep. Mines* 271 It has been noticed by smelters in the valley that the percentage of lead in the ore is not as large as formerly.

+**2.** A smelting works. {1890} Also attrib.

1876 RAYMOND *8th Rep. Mines* 275 The Winnamuck Company shut down its smelter. **1883** RITCH *Illust. N. Mex.* 35 A few reduction works, smelters and stamp mills have been erected. **1896** *Columbus Dispatch* 4 Sept., The millionaire smelterman. **1907** *St. Nicholas* Oct. 1145/1 Small electric ore cars run to and from the smelter. **1914** ATHERTON *Perch of Devil* 9 [The] horizons . . . had always been obscured by the poisonous haze of smelters.

Smeltery. =SMELTER 2. *Obsolescent.* {1814-} — **1888** *Harper's Mag.* Sept. 592 The product of the smeltery, in 1886 had a money value of $1,105,190.76. **1895** *Cyclopedic Rev. Cur. Hist.* V. 225 The paralysis of mining [in Colo.] . . . has given way to an activity which has put almost every smeltery in operation.

Smelt house. =SMELTER 2. {1684-} — **1734** *Doc. Hist. N.Y. State* I. 724 The proprietor will rather send it [*sc.* lead] home in Oar than be at the charge to erect smelt houses here.

* **Smelting.** Attrib. with *company, furnace, house,* etc. {1610-} — **1835** HOFFMAN *Winter in West* I. 260 Smelting-furnaces of lead-ore . . . are scattered over the whole country between Rock River and the Ouisconsin. **1847** *Santa Fe Republican* 10 Sept. 2/3 The wealth of New Mexico can begin to show itself, Furnaces, Smelting houses, corn fields. **1867** *Atlantic Mo.* Feb. 216/1 To the east of the hotel there is a knoll, on which stand the smelting-works. **1876** RAYMOND *8th Rep. Mines* 229 The Galaxy, . . . and Disappointment . . . [have] each from 20 to 100 tons of excellent smelting-ore on the dumps. **1883** RITCH *Illust. N. Mex.* 81 A smelting and refining company is now erecting furnaces and reduction works.

+ **Smelt minnow.** The silvery minnow, *Hybognathus nuchalis.* — **1884** *Nat. Museum Bul.* No. 27, 481 *Hybognathus regius*. . . . Smelt Minnow. . . . Sometimes sold in early spring as 'smelt,' to which it bears almost no resemblance except in size and color.

Smethe. One of several varieties of ducks {smeath, 1622-}, +as the pintail duck. — **1674** JOSSELYN *Two Voyages* 101 Of ducks there be many more sorts, as . . . Plovers, Smethes, Wilmotes. **1888** TRUMBULL *Names of Birds* 38 Others at Tuckerton refer to it [the pintail duck] as *Smethe.*

Smew. 1. A European merganser (*Mergus albellus*): see quotations. {1674-} +**2.** =HOODED MERGANSER. — (1) **1813** WILSON *Ornithology* VIII. 126 The Smew, or White Nun . . . is another of those Mergansers commonly known in this country by the appellation of Fishermen, Fisher Ducks, or Divers. **1838** AUDUBON *Ornithology* IV. 350 The Smew is a bird of extremely rare occurrence in the United States. **1872** COUES *Key to Birds* 296 The smew, or white nun, *Mergellus albellus,* of Europe, has been attributed to N. Am. upon insufficient evidence, though very possibly occurring. (2) **1909** WEBSTER 1980/2 *Smew.* . . . The name is sometimes extended to the hooded merganser.

+ **Smidgen, Smidgeon.** Also **smitchin.** [Cf. SMITCH.] A small bit or part. *colloq.* — **1845** KIRKLAND *Western Clearings* 71 They wouldn't have left a smitchin o' honey. **1883** BEADLE *Western Wilds* 615 Not a smidgeon left—just bodaciously chawed up and spit out. **1886** *Amer. Philol. Ass. Trans.* XVII. 43 *Smidgen,* 'a small bit, a grain,' as 'a *smidgen* of meal,' is common in East Tennessee. **1897** ROBINSON *Uncle Lisha's Outing* 6 [We] want tu kerry . . . jest some pork an' taters an' a leetle smidgin o' bread tu start on. **1913** STRATTON-PORTER *Laddie* xvii, Robert wasn't a smidgin behind.

Smilax. Any of various greenbriers, as *Smilax rotundifolia* and *S. glauca.* Also with specifying terms. {1601-} — *c*1728 CATESBY *Carolina* I. 15 The Bay-leaved Smilax . . . is usually found in moist places. **1807** in *S. Lit. Messenger* XXIV. 308/1 The church steeple [was] garlanded to its summit with irregular festoons of smilax and ivy. **1839** AUDUBON *Ornith. Biog.* I. 302 The Green Briar, or Round-leaved Smilax, . . . is common along fences. **1880** *Harper's Mag.* July 184/2 The woods at either side were edged with natural hedges of mammoth fern, laurel, and serviceberries, . . . webbed together with the waxed dark green vine of the smilax. **1907** *St. Nicholas* Oct. 1120/1 Long festoons of smilax were hung in graceful curves all around the top.

Smilax china. The chinaroot, or, generically, plants resembling it. — **1772** ROMANS in P. L. Phillips *Notes on B. Romans* 124 [The Indians have] several Species of Smilax China, the Root of Which they pound into a flower, or more properly in an Impalpable Powder, and of this they make a kind of Bread. **1837** WILLIAMS *Florida* 79 Briar, China, Smilax China. . . . Best in damp soils, near streams.

* **Smile,** *n.* +A drink of liquor. {1889} — **1850** THAXTER *Poem before Iadma* 7 Hast ta'en a 'smile' at Brigham's. **1865** *Harper's Mag.* Feb. 288/2 After enjoying a luxurious dinner at head-quarters, and various hospitable 'smiles,' we rode back by the valley road. **1903** BURNHAM *Jewel* 222 Just a smile or two with the boys.

* **Smile,** *v.*

+ **1.** *intr.* To drink; to take a smile. *slang.*

1855 *Harper's Mag.* Dec. 36/2 Bob . . . requested them all to 'smile' at his expense. **1870** RAE *Westward by Rail* 337, I 'smiled' all the more readily because the morning was intensely cold. **1892** WALSH *Lit. Curiosities* 1016 'If asked to drink, what would you say?' He answered, 'I should smile.'

+ **b.** *tr.* To take (a drink).

1857 *Knickerb.* XLIX. 42 And having smiled about three fingers all round . . . I inquired [etc.].

2. *I should smile.* Used sarcastically to show disagreement or unwillingness. *colloq.*

1889 'MARK TWAIN' *Conn. Yankee* 112 They actually wanted *me* to put in! Well, I should smile. **1891** *Youth's Companion* LXIV. 138 Sing for nothing? Well, I should smile!

Smirky, *a.* Smiling affectedly. {17 . . , 1835} 'Sc. and U.S.' (O.E.D.). — **1835** LONGSTREET *Ga. Scenes* 215, I overtook a swarthy, bright-eyed, smerky little fellow, riding a small poney. **1880** 'MARK TWAIN' *Tramp Abroad* 440 He introduced himself, smiling a smirky smile.

Smitch. =SMIDGEN. *colloq.* {*c*1840} 'Sc. and U.S.' (O.E.D.). — **1876** *Wide Awake* 265/2, I ain't got a smitch o' work to do for myself. **1899** JEWETT *Queen's Twin* 73 Nobody's seen the l'aste smitch of her since.

* **Smite.** A very little bit; a smidgen. *local.* {1640} — **1843** 'CARLTON' *New Purchase* I. 175 Not a smite of noise. **1846** WHITCHER *Bedott P.* v. 50, I done all I could for him, but it dident do a smite o' good.

* **Smith.**

* **1.** One who works in metals, esp. a blacksmith.

See also BLACKSMITH, COPPERSMITH, etc.

1626 *Plymouth Laws* 28 [No] joyners smiths sawyers . . . shall use their science or trades . . . for any strangers or foreigners. **1649** WILLIAMS *Letters* (1874) 184, I hear a smith of your town hath left you, and saith I sent for him. **1755** *Lett. to Washington* I. 138 Let me know also the Allowance for Carpenters & Smiths when they are employed at their Trades. **1796** *Boston Directory* 281 Simmons, Simon, smith and farrier, Bishop's alley. **1857** *Lawrence (Kan.) Republican* 18 June 4 Many smiths never saw a breaker before they came here. **1881** STODDARD *E. Hardery* 60 'There's your bolts and hinges, Job,' exclaimed the red-headed smith.

b. As a possessive with *anvil, bellows, forge, work.*

1644 *Harvard Rec.* I. 7 For the Smithes worke, 6[s.]-11[d.]. **1647** *Watertown Rec.* I. 1. 22 Setting up a shop for a Smithes forge. **1781** *Va. State P.* I. 431 These [stores] consist of chests of tools, Smiths' bellows, axes [etc.]. **1815** *Niles' Reg.* VIII. 141/1 In Pittsburgh . . . are cast all kinds of hollow-ware, castings, cannons, cannon balls, smiths' anvils, sad irons [etc.].

2. Attrib. with *trade, work.*

1670 *East-Hampton Rec.* I. 332 [He] doe Ingage himself . . . to doe . . . all sorts of Smith worke . . . upon reasonable termes. **1781** in Summers *Ann. S.W. Va.* 1074 Ezekel Abel is appointed Guardian to John O Neil who is to give him one years schooling and learn him the Smith Trade.

+ **Smith and Weston.** A make of pistol. — **1867** DIXON *New America* I. 34 The new arm of the west, called a Smith-and-Weston, is a pretty tool. **1919** WINANS *Modern Pistol* 84 The smaller Civilian and Police Colt have not quite as good a stock . . . ; the same applies to . . . the Smith & Weston.

Smithery. {1625-} A smith shop. {1755, 1861-} — **1833** BOARDMAN *America* 16 Over one blacksmith's shop, I saw the word 'smithery.' **1843** 'CARLSON' *New Purchase* I. 100 A settlement . . . frequently [takes its name] from the person that establishes a ferry, a smithery, a mill.

+ **Smith shop.** A workshop in which a smith follows his trade. {1899} — **1710** *Boston Rec.* 105 Ordered That Compl[ain]t be made . . . Ag[ains]t Enoch Greenliefe for makeing a Smith Shop in his buildings. **1749** in Chalkley *Scotch-Irish Settlement Va.* I. 433 A road beginning at John Man's Smithshop on the south side of Peaked Mountain. **1857** *Ill. Agric. Soc. Trans.* II. 360 As smithshops were almost unknown in the country, horses were seldom shod. **1892** *York County Hist. Rev.* 68 The wheelwright and smithshop [is] 26x68 feet in area.

+ **Smithsonian,** *a.* Of or pertaining to J. L. M. Smithson (1765-1829) or the Smithsonian Institution. — **1840** *Niles' Nat. Reg.* 7 March 11/3 Mr. Adams rose . . . to make a report from the select committee on the Smithsonian bequest. **1851** *Santa Fe Gazette* 26 April, The Smithsonian Library contains near five thousand volumes. **1874** *Rep. Comm. Agric.* 1873 358 Among the important apparatus . . . recently procured may be mentioned a Smithsonian barometer.

Smithsonian Institution. An institution at Washington, D.C., endowed by an Englishman, J. L. M. Smithson: (see quot. 1835). — **1835** JACKSON in *Pres. Mess. & P.* III. 187 A bequest [has been made] to the United States by Mr. James Smithson, of London, for the purpose of founding 'at Washington an establishment under the name of the Smithsonian Institution, for the increase and diffusion of knowledge among men.' **1896** *Congress. Rec.* App. 6 Feb. 489/1 The Egyptian mummies across yonder in the Smithsonian Institution are not more dead than these plans. **1900** *Ib.* 1 Feb. 1400 It also had an estimate of $4,000 for observation of the total eclipse of the sun in May next, to be made by the Smithsonian Institution.

Smithsonite. [f. J. L. M. *Smithson.*] {*c*1835-} +Carbonate of zinc. — **1856** DANA *Rudim. Treat. Min.* 86 Carbonate of Zinc (Calamine, Smithsonite) is abundant in many of the localities of lead ores. **1896** CHESTER *Dict. Minerals* 251 *Smithsonite,* . . . found in drusy incantations or in botryoidal or stalactitic forms. **1922** *Mineral Resources 1919* (Bur. Mines) I. 245 The ores [in n. Ill.] are galena, smithsonite, sphalerite.

+ **Smith's shop.** =SMITH SHOP. *Obs.* — **1651** *Dedham Rec.* III. 179 Whensoeuer the said shopp shall be no longer vsed for a smithes shopp . . , then it shall be remoued. **1705** *Boston News-Letter* 22 Oct. 2/1 A fire broke out in a Smith's Shop. **1786** WASHINGTON *Diaries* III. 38 My drill or Barrel plow . . . requiring some alteration in the harrow, obliged me to bring it to the Smith's Shop. **1800** HAWKINS *Sk. Creek Country* 30 At the public establishment there is a smith's shop.

* **Smithy. 1.** A blacksmith's shop. Also attrib. +**2.** A blacksmith. This sense apparently has arisen through a misunderstanding of the word in Longfellow's 'The Village Blacksmith': (see *Amer. Speech* XVI. 151-2). — (1) **1744** FRANKLIN *Acct. Fire-Places* 29 Even the Smithy

Water in which hot Irons are quench'd, is found advantageous to the human Constitution. **1839** LONGFELLOW *Poetical Works* (1893) 14/2 Under the spreading chestnut tree The village smithy stands. **1884** *Century Mag.* Jan. 446/2 The plow in the colonies . . . was sometimes built by the farmer, and ironed at the nearest smithy. (2) **1847** *Graham's Mag.* April 262/1 Was he some Smithy, grim and old, Whose anvil iron changed to gold?

*Smock. +A variety of peach. — **1866** *Rep. Comm. Agric. 1865* 193 *Smock.*—A well known late variety, very productive, and valuable as a market peach. **1868** *Mich. Agric. Rep.* VII. 429 The most extensive for market are: Early Crawford, next, Early Barnard, Hale's Early, Late Crawford, and Smock (free).

Smock frock. A loose-fitting linen or cotton garment worn as a coat. {a1800-} — **1837** *Boston Advertiser* 17 Jan. 2/2 William Chambers . . . [is] charged with stealing at Gainsboro', two smock frocks.

***Smoke**, *n.*

***1.** In *pl.* or with *a:* A column or cloud of the visible volatile substance given off by a fire, +serving as a sign of an encampment, or used as a signal.

1689 *Maine Doc. Hist.* IX. 49 We discovered smokes att Spurwinke. **1726** PENHALLOW *Indian Wars* 37 [We] soon perceived a smoke, at about half a mile's distance. **1760** ROGERS *Journals* 182 The signal that I will make . . . will be a smoak and three guns, at a minute's interval each from the other. **1845** DE SMET *Oregon Missions* 147 [We] saw two smokes at the extremity of the plain. **1923** J. H. COOK *On Old Frontier* 15 Each man carried a flint and steel, together with a piece of punk or prepared cotton tape with which to build fires or 'make a smoke.'

2. a. A smudge used as protection against insects.
1765 ROGERS *Acct. N. Amer.* 140 It is difficult to sleep without a smoak in your bed-chamber, to expell [mosquitoes]. **1784** BELKNAP *Jrnl. Tour to White Mts.* (1876) 17 The people made little smokes in their cow-yards to defend their cows against the flies and mosquitoes.

b. A volume of smoke used to cure meat.
1805 CLARK in *Lewis & C. Exped.* III. (1905) 284 We fleece all the meat and hang it up over a small smoke.

3. ?A quantity of tobacco.
1792 *Hebron* (Conn.) *Rec.* (MS.), Pepoon, Silas, . . . 1 clock, 1 smoke 7/16. **1801** *Ib.*, Pepoon, Joseph, . . . 1 silver watch, 3 smokes 3rd rate.

4. A spell at smoking a pipe, cigar, etc.
1835 LONGSTREET *Ga. Scenes* 213 *Mrs. B.* [*to Mrs. S.*]. Well, let's light our pipes, and take a short smoke, and go to bed. **1837** IRVING *Bonneville* II. 89 Several warriors . . . came to have a talk and a smoke with the white men. **1847** EMORY *Military Reconn.* 24 It was in commemoration of a talk and friendly smoke between some two or three tribes of Indians. **1884** *Century Mag.* Oct. 874/1 That gentleman . . . was politely invited by the boys to stop and 'take a smoke.'

+**5.** Whisky. {Cape smoke, 'a brandy,' 1849-}
1904 'O. HENRY' *Cabbages & Kings* (1916) 49 On the bottles of . . . Scotch 'smoke' . . . behind the little counter the dust lay thick.

+**6.** *Watch my smoke,* watch me go; watch my speed. *colloq.*
1910 RAINE *B. O'Connor* 70 Watch my smoke. **1921** PAINE *Comr. Rolling Ocean* 10 Suspend judgment and watch my smoke.

7. In special combinations.
Smoke arch, (see quotation); *s. ball* {1753-}, a ball emitting smoke when ignited {1899}; *s.-belcher),* a steamboat that emits great volumes of smoke; *s. inspector,* an official whose duty is to prevent factories from emitting unreasonable amounts of smoke; *s.-washer,* (see quotation).
1864 WEBSTER 1248/1 *Smoke-arch,* the smoke-box of a locomotive. **1887** *Courier-Journal* 14 Jan. 8/6 Carbolic Smoke-Ball . . . will destroy the germ. **1843** 'CARLTON' *New Purchase* I. 43 A steamboat was a very *rara avis* on the Ohio river; at least such a smoke-belcher and spit-fire could not be found at any hour of the day and night. **1922** PARRISH *Case & Girl,* 133, I'm a smoke inspector. **1891** *Cent.* 5710/2 *Smoke-washer,* . . . a device for purifying smoke by washing as it passes through a chimney-flue.

***Smoke**, *v.*

I. 1. *tr.* To cure (fish or meat) by exposure to smoke. Also *ppl. a.* {as ppl. a., 1603-; 1767-}
1643 WILLIAMS *Key* (1866) 138 Breame. . . . Of this fish there is an abundance which the Natives drie in the Sunne and smoake. **1711** *N.J. Archives* 1 Ser. IV. 136, About 400 lb of Smokt Beef . . . hele take with him for his Company. **1788** MAY *Jrnl. & Lett.* 104 Breakfasted . . . in a really elegant manner, on fine coffee, loaf-sugar, venison, shad, and smoked shad. **1843** 'CARLTON' *New Purchase* I. 43 We had also *smoked* hams. **1880** *Harper's Mag.* Sept. 496/1 He came upon an important establishment where herring were smoked. **1905** PRINGLE *Rice Planter* 147 I was . . . brushing off the hams preparatory to smoking them.

+**b.** To thicken and harden (a skin shield) by exposure to smoke.
1833 CATLIN *Indians* I. 241 [By] the process of '*smoking the shield*' . . . . the skin is kept tight whilst it contracts to one-half of its size.

+**c.** *College.* To haze (a person) by exposing him to smoke.
1850 in Hall *College Words* (1856) 435 I would not have you sacrifice all these advantages for the sake of smoking future Freshmen. **1880** *Harper's Mag.* Nov. 950/1 They hazed and smoked Freshmen.

2. To inhale and expel the smoke of (burning tobacco, a pipe, etc.). {1687-}
1669 *Plymouth Laws* 158 Any p[er]son or p[er]sons that shalbe found smoaking of Tobacco on the Lords day . . . shall pay twelve pence. **1671** *S.C. Hist. Soc. Coll.* V. 334 Tobacco does very well; I have now in Cure as good as ever was Smoakt. **1766** ROGERS *Ponteach* I. iv, The Calumet I do not chuse to smoak. **1799** WELD *Travels* 14 A shocking custom obtains here [in Phila.], of smoking tobacco in the [theater]. **1869** J. R. BROWNE *Adv. Apache Country* 475 The other [man persists] in smoking bad cigars. **1900** BARBOUR *Mainwaring Affair* 8 Leisurely smoking a fine Havana, was Ralph Mainwaring.

3. To fill (a place) with smoke as protection against insects.
1766 J. BARTRAM *Journal* 41 This night was very warm, and the muskitoes troublesome, so that we smoaked our tent twice.

***4.** *fig.* To cause (a person) trouble or discomfort {-1680}; to make (a person) pay.
1834 SIMMS *Guy Rivers* II. 105 We shall smoke you before you get into Alabama. **1835** LONGSTREET *Ga. Scenes* 77 Maybe John Brown didn't smoke him for it. **1840** SIMMS *Border Beagles* I. 105 Watson thought to smoke him to the tune of two or three thousand dollars.

+**5.** Among the Sacs and Foxes, to obtain (a horse) by observing a special custom involving the act of smoking.
*c*1838 CATLIN *N. Amer. Indians* II. 213 Smoking horses is another of the peculiar and very curious customs of this tribe.

+**6.** To deceive or hoax (a person).
1847 ROBB *Squatter Life* 73 The Judge had no idea that Tom was smoking him.

+**7.** To furnish with tobacco.
1897 'MARK TWAIN' *Following Equator* 129 He will . . . feed you and slake you and smoke you with the best that money can buy.

II. 8. *intr.* To inhale and expel the smoke of a pipe, cigar, etc. {1617-}
1832 *New Eng. Mag.* III. 221, I snuffed and smoked and chewed. **1894** CHOPIN *Bayou Folk* 91 They sat at the pine table smoking and playing cards all the morning.

+**b.** Among the Indians, to exchange friendly greetings or to hold council by smoking: (see quotations).
1725 [see PIPE *n.¹* 2 a]. **1754** *Mass. H. S. Coll.* 3 Ser. V. 42 They have never invited us to smoke with them, (by which they mean the Commissioners had never invited them to any conference). **1827** COOPER *Prairie* xxv, He was not privileged then to smoke at the great council-fire of his nation. **1870** KEIM *Sheridan's Troopers* 189 If the band accepts the pipe and smokes, the request is granted, and the warriors of the band extend their cooperation.

***9.** To smart; to suffer. {-1773}
1818 ROYALL *Lett. from Ala.* 104 It's as fair cheatin says I, as I ever seed in my life; and you can make him smoke for it. **1878** BEADLE *Western Wilds* 442 The residents will make him 'smoke' with high taxes on his land.

10. Of a pipe or cigar: To serve (in a certain way) for smoking.
1883 *Harper's Mag.* July 174/2 These 'church-wardens' smoke freely and softly.

+**Smoked Yankee.** (See quotation.) — **1864** *Wkly. New Mexican* 10 June 2/3 In Baltimore they call the negro soldiers, who are abundant there, 'smoked Yankees.' The smoked ones like the title.

Smokehouse. {1672-}

+**1.** A building in which meat or fish is cured by means of dense smoke.
1759 *Newport Mercury* 10 April 4/2 To be Sold, . . . a choice Farm, . . . with a large dwelling House, a large Barn, good Stable, small Out-house and Smoke-house. **1776** CRESSWELL *Journal* 199 Nothing but hickory wood is burnt in these smoke-houses. **1835** in Bassett *Plantation Overseer* 49, [I] put up a . . . Smokehouse and a kitchen. **1868** *Iowa State Agric. Soc. Rep.* 1867 169 For corn, . . . hang it [*sc.* seed] up in the smokehouse or barn. **1893** 'MARK TWAIN' *P. Wilson* ii, A farm smokehouse had to be kept heavily padlocked. **1924** RAINE *Land of Saddle-Bags* 10 A smoke-house stands near by in the rear.

+**b.** A prison.
[**1857** GRIFFITH *Autobiog. Female Slave* 138 The 'lock-up' . . . had once been used as a smoke-house, but since the erection of a new one, was employed for . . . confining negroes.] **1889** *N.Y. Herald* 10 Jan. 8/4 [In Wilmington, Del., in 1740] the prison or 'cage,' sometimes called 'smoke house,' was a small one story brick building.

+**c.** *fig.* Anything having the appearance of a smokehouse or full of smoke.
1855 M. THOMPSON *Doesticks* 35, [I] rode to the railroad for the last time in the four-wheeled smoke-house.

+**2. a.** A building in which persons are exposed or subjected to smoke in order to disinfect them. *Obs.*
1792 BENTLEY *Diary* I. 394 At the Smoak house below the college, no representations that I had come from Salem would save me from a

Smoking. 1828 SHERBURNE *Memoirs* 29 There were little smoke-houses [for victims of smallpox] erected on a remote part of the island.

+b. A building for the disinfection of anything by the use of smoke.

1924 CROY *R.F.D. No. 3* The supers for the beehives must be cleaned and taken to the smokehouse.

Smokejack. {1675–} +(See quotations.) — **1891** *Cent.* 5719/1 *Smoke-jack,* ... on railways, a hood or covering for the end of a stove-pipe, on the outside of a car. **1909** WEBSTER 1981/1 *Smokejack,* ... a movable stack over the smokestack of a locomotive engine in a round-house stall.

Smoke pipe. A smokestack, esp. on a boat or locomotive. {1853} — **1815** *Niles' Reg.* IX. 108/1 At the upper end shall communicate with the external air a few inches above the smoke pipe. **1852** *Harper's Mag.* June 61/2 Taking a stand in the shelter of the enormous smoke-pipe, ... we watched the receding shores. **1882** *Century Mag.* Feb. 637/2 The pipes ... are heated by contact with the smoke-pipes. **1901** CHURCHILL *Crisis* 417 All the night the smoke-pipes were batting against the boughs of oak.

* Smoker.

1. One who smokes tobacco. {1617–}

[**1699** E. WARD *Trip to New-Eng.* 10 The Women (like the Men) are excessive *Smokers.*] **1835** INGRAHAM *South-West* I. 137 Relishing, with that peculiar zest which none but a smoker knows, a real Habana. **1851** *Knickerb.* XXXVIII. 184 They have built a kind of calf-pen for smokers, at the foot of Boston Common. **1881** *Ore. State Jrnl.* 1 Jan. 3/5 A lady wants to know why the railroad companies do not provide special cars for tobacco-chewers, as well as for smokers.

+2. *pl.* A grade of tobacco.

1881 *Tenth Census: Tobacco Culture* 15 Types of tobacco produced in different sections.... Domestic Cigar Tobacco and Smokers. **1895** *Dept. Agric. Yrbk. 1894* 145 Mahogany and yellow wrappers and smokers give a distinct character to localities in Virginia, North and South Carolina, and eastern Tennessee.

+3. A railway car or apartment designated for use by travelers who wish to smoke.

1882 SALA *Amer. Revisited* II. 140 The car known as the 'smoker' is usually relegated to the least eligible part of the train. **1887** *Courier-Journal* 17 Jan. 1/7 The passenger coach was twisted sideways off the track, but the smoker clung to the rails. **1922** J. A. DUNN *Man Trap* 154 The third coach ... was the smoker.

+4. A social occasion or party at which the guests smoke and chat. {1891, 'a concert at which smoking is permitted'}

1899 *N.Y. Journal* 7 Sept. 1/3 Smoker at the Waldorf-Astoria for the sailors of the Olympic. **1911** HARRISON *Queed* 196 After the bouts or the 'exhibition' of a Saturday, there was always a smoker.

+5. A smoking jacket.

1904 WALLER *Wood-Carver* 230 He sat before the library fire in his leather smoker.

+6. *local.* = CURLEW 3.

1888 TRUMBULL *Names of Birds* 198 Sickle-Bill Curlew.... Known also at Pleasantville [N.J.] to some of the gunners as *Smoker* or *Old Smoker* (the bill curving downward like the stem of a pipe). **1909** WEBSTER 1081/1. **1917** *Birds of Amer.* I. 251 Long-billed Curlew.... [Also called] Sabre-bill; Smoker.

Smokery. {1657–} =SMOKEHOUSE 1. — **1794** T. COOPER *America* 132 His *smokery* for bacon, hams, &c. is a room about twelve feet square.

+Smoke signal. A column or puff of smoke used as a signal. — **1873** COZZENS *Marvellous Country* 65 After leaving the Organos Mountains we had noticed Indian smoke-signals. **1885** *Outing* VII. 19/1 The Apache scouts sent up a second smoke-signal.

Smokestack. {1871–}

1. The funnel of a steamboat.

1859 *Harper's Mag.* April 606/1 [It was exciting] to listen to ... the hoarse breath of the smoke stacks as it came from the rosin-fed furnaces. **1861** NEWELL *Orpheus C. Kerr* I. 32 A fellow once took him [Lincoln] for a smoke-stack on a steamboat. **1880** 'MARK TWAIN' *Tramp Abroad* 249, I wished the sea had washed the rudder and the smokestack and the captain away. **1920** SANDBURG *Smoke & Steel* 248 A heave of hawsers and smokestacks, the swish of multiplied swoops and war dogs.

2. The chimney of a locomotive. {1890}

1871 *Congress. Globe* App. 27 Jan. 67/3 In the region around Lake Superior it was cold enough ... to freeze the smoke-stack of a locomotive. **1880** *Harper's Mag.* March 557/1 A freight train ... [was] thrown into lurid illumination by the sparks from the smoke-stack.

3. The tall chimney of a factory or other building. {1903}

1865 *Harper's Mag.* June 4/1 Smoke-stacks are blackening the air with their thick volumes of smoke. **1883** RITCH *Illust. N. Mex.* 97 For the smelter, ... the smoke-stack is ninety feet high. **1914** ATHERTON *Perch of Devil* 56 Anaconda Hill ... , with its tangled mass of smokestacks, ... looks like a gigantic shipwreck.

+Smoke talk. A meeting of two or more people at which informality and friendliness are fostered by smoking; an informal talk made while smoking. — **1893** *Boston Jrnl.* 25 March 2/2 The Association of Railroad

and Steamboat Agents of Boston held a smoke-talk at the Tremont House last evening. **1900** MUNN *Uncle Terry* 34, Can't you come around to my room to-night and have a smoke-talk? **1907** *Springfield W. Repub.* 24 Jan. 16 The Amherst club enjoyed the first of a series of informal banquets and smoke-talks to be held this winter.

Smoke tree. a. The Venetian sumac, *Cotinus coggygria.* {1887–}
+b. =CHITTAMWOOD. — **1846** G. B. EMERSON *Trees & Shrubs Mass.* 500 The Venetian Sumach, ... commonly called *Smoke-tree,* is much cultivated as a curious ... tree. **1850** JUDD *R. Edney* 85 [Her hair] hung on her like the fringe of the smoke-tree. **1868** GRAY *Field Botany* 84. **1892** APGAR *Trees Northern U.S.* 91 Smoke-tree.... A shrub or small tree, 6 to 10 ft. high, often planted for ornament. **1901** MOHR *Plant Life Ala.* 16 Passing over the detached spurs of the Cumberland Mountains ... he discovered the interesting American smoke tree ... , before known only from a single locality in the Indian territory.

+Smoke wagon. A railway train. *humorous.* — **1853** *La Crosse Democrat* 13 Dec. 3/2 You get into one of these smoke wagons.

* Smoking.

1. The action of fumigating a person.

1773 FINLAY *Journal* 25 He wou'd be oblig'd to undergo the ceremony of smoaking. **1792** [see SMOKEHOUSE 2 a].

2. *attrib.* Designating places, things, and activities connected with the smoking of tobacco. {1771–}

1809 CUMING *Western Tour* 223 Pittsburgh [has] ... one factury for clay smoking-pipes. **1809** A. HENRY *Travels* 299 Their practices of devotion consist in ... smoking-feasts, or feasts of the pipe, or calumet, held in honour of the spirits. **1816** *Ann. 14th Congress* 1 Sess. 590 [We] should be soon dismissed to a good hotel and smoking table. **1827** W. BULLOCK *Journey* p. xii, There are, also, a circulating library, and a smoking and drinking room for the gentlemen. **1831** R. COX *Adv. Columbia R.* 307 They all wear belts of variegated worsted, from which their knives, smoking-bags, &c. are suspended. **1854** CUMMINS *Lamplighter* 173 The same gentleman ... some years before wore a velvet smoking cap. **1884** NYE *Baled Hay* 125 This will furnish sufficient excuse for a man like us ... staying at home, ... [with] a loose smoking jacket on him. **1888** *Amer. Humorist* (London) 5 May 7/1 Came over from New York ... in the smoking compartment of a parlor car. **1892** *Harper's Mag.* Dec. 162 His father [was] made the recipient of a handsome solid silver smoking-set.

+Smoking bean. =INDIAN BEAN 2. — **1897** SUDWORTH *Arborescent Flora* 335. **1909** *Cent. Suppl.* 1233/2 Smoking-bean, ... so called from the custom of boys of smoking the pods.

+Smoking car. On a railway train, a car provided for the use of passengers who smoke. — **1857** *Harper's Mag.* Sept. 436/1 Jim Bug ... sat in the smoking-car. **1873** BAILEY *Life in Danbury* 243 Any conductor of a train that includes a smoking car can tell you all about it. **1887** GEORGE *40 Yrs. on Rail* 233 The smoking-car is the favorite resort for the jolliest men on the train. **1916** WILSON *Somewhere* 178 Certainly, go on, if it's anything that would be told outside of a smoking-car.

Smoking out. *College.* +The action of hazing a person by exposing him to excessive tobacco smoke. — **1871** BAGG *At Yale* 252 'Smoking out' is generally practised upon Freshmen before they become known as individuals.

+Smoking tobacco. Tobacco cut up and prepared for smoking. — **1796** MORSE *Univ. Geog.* I. 259 Snuff, chewing and smoking tobacco [are produced in the U.S.]. **1834** HAWTHORNE *Twice-told Tales* (1879) I. 116 Especially was he beloved by the pretty girls along the Connecticut, whose favor he used to court by presents of the best smoking tobacco in his stock. **1898** *N.Y. Journal* 17 Sept. 11/6 (Ernst), Each contained ... smoking and chewing tobacco.

*Smoky, *a.* +**1.** Of a mountain: Covered with mist. Also in proper name. +**2.** Of a horse: Vicious. — (1) **1825** NEAL *Bro. Jonathan* I. 105 See'd him jess now, comin' over the smoky mountain there. **1885** 'CRADDOCK' *Prophet* 1 Always touching the evasive clouds, the peaks of the Great Smoky Mountains are like some barren ideal. (2) **1899** *Scribner's Mag.* XXV. 13/2 Cow-boys often call vicious horses 'smoky' horses.

+Smoky City. Pittsburgh, Pennsylvania. A nickname. — **1859** *Ladies' Repository* Jan. 51/1 Pittsburg, Pennsylvania, is ... emphatically the 'Smoky City,' since bituminous coal is almost the only fuel consumed. **1902** CLAPIN 371.

+Smoky pie. (See quotation.) — **1884** COUES *Key to Birds* 419 *Psilorhinus,* Brown Jays. Smoky Pies.

+Smooch, *n.* [Var. of *smutch.*] A smear. — **1825** NEAL *Bro. Jonathan* II. 46 Cowhide shoes—newly greased, ... left a 'smooch' upon whatever they came near. **1870** A. D. WHITNEY *We Girls* iii, A smooch of stove-polish across her arm. **1901** *Harper's Mag.* April 669/1 A dark smooch appeared on his nose and cheeks.

Smooch, *v. tr.* To smear or dirty. {1631} Also *ppl. a.* ('Latterly U.S.' *O.E.D.*). — **1828** WEBSTER s.v. *Smutch.* In New England ... *smooch* ... signifies to foul or blacken with something produced by combustion or other like substance. **1835** WILLIS *Pencillings* I. 237 (*O.E.D.*), The attention and courtesies of every smooched petticoat far and near. **1845** *Knickerb.* XXV. 178 The *black snow-storm* ... from the chimney of our camphine reading-lamp [was] falling upon every thing around us; smooching fair works of art.

*Smooth, *n. local.* +'A meadow, or grass field' (B. '48). — **1845** JUDD *Margaret* I. 105 On the smooth in front of the house, her little white and yellow chickens were peeping and dodging under the low mallows ... and pink-tufted smart-weed.

✴**Smooth**, *a.*

1. In the specific names of plants, animals, birds, and fishes. {1603–}

See also SMOOTH-LEAVED *a.*, SMOOTH SUMAC.

1785 MARSHALL *Amer. Grove* 10 *Annona glabra*, Carolinian Smooth barked Annona, . . . grows naturally in Carolina. **1814** MITCHILL *Fishes N.Y.* 374 Smooth Blenny. *Blennius pholis.* . . . The skin was soft and uniform, without scales. **1817–8** EATON *Botany* (1822) 429 *Ribes uvacrispa*, smooth gooseberry. **1842** *Nat. Hist. N.Y., Zoology* III. 11 The Smooth Terrapin . . . occurs as far east as Rhode-Island. **1884** SARGENT *Rep. Forests* 164 *Alnus serrulata.* . . . Black Alder. Smooth Alder. **1884** GOODE, etc. *Fisheries* I. 269 The Tautog . . . is called 'Black fish;' in New Jersey also 'Black-fish' and 'Smooth Black-fish.' **1917** *Birds of Amer.* III. 81 Summer Tanager. *Piranga rubra rubra.* . . . [Also called] Smooth-headed Redbird; Bee Bird.

2. In special combinations.

Smooth iron, =FLATIRON; *s. plane*, (see quotation).

1671 *Portsmouth Rec.* 423, I give the Saw to Mary and the Smooth Iron. **1876** KNIGHT 2227/2 *Smooth-plane*, a smoothing or finishing-plane; the last used of the series of *bench-planes*.

+**Smoothbore**, *n.* A gun having an unrifled bore. {1859–}

1812 *Niles' Reg.* II. 398/1 It was the best smooth bore he ever shot with in his life. **1834** CARRUTHERS *Kentuckian* I. 21 Your smooth bores waste a deal of powder and lead upon the outlandish creters. **1886** *Harper's Mag.* June 6/1 Her battery consists of . . . 12 IX-inch smooth-bores. **1887** HARTE *Crusade of Excelsior* 58 The Señor was only showing us how they managed to shut up a smooth bore in this country. **1907** LILLIBRIDGE *Trail* 27 His finger was on the trigger of the old smoothbore. *fig.* **1875** 'MARK TWAIN' *Old Times* iii. 43 [He] was sure to subside into a very placable and even remorseful old smooth-bore as soon as they were all gone.

Smoothbore, *a.* {1859–} Of guns: Having an unrifled bore. {1860–} — **1799** *Ann. 7th Congress* 2 Sess. 1402 One had a rifle, and the other a smooth-bore piece. **1867** CRAWFORD *Mosby* 37 The Confederates were armed with old flint-lock muskets . . . and some old smooth-bore pieces of artillery. **1886** LOGAN *Great Conspiracy* 322 A smooth-bore battery of the Enemy . . . is driven back. **1902** WHITE *Blazed Trail* 129 He was armed with an old-fashioned smooth-bore muzzle-loader.

+**Smooth-bored gun.** A smoothbore. {1859–} — **1775** ADAIR *Indians* 275 He could not discharge it, as it was double-tricker'd, contrary to the model of their smooth-bored guns.

Smoothbore musket. A musket with an unrifled bore. {1879–} **1881** WILHELM *Military Dict.* 457/2 When smooth-bore muskets alone were used the bullets were chiefly spherical in form. **1894** ROBLEY *Bourbon Co., Kansas* 135 A quantity of smooth-bore muskets were sent to the end of the Pacific railroad.

✴**Smoothing.** Attrib. with *harrow, plane* {1678–}, *stone.* — **1660** *Mass. H. S. Coll.* 3 Ser. III. 136 You know I could never endure nor abide the smoothing plane. **1876** KNIGHT 2227/2 *Smoothing-stone*, a substitute for a smoothing-iron, made of steatite, attached to a plate and handle of metal. **1888** *Vt. Agric. Rep.* X. 48 Harrow with a smoothing harrow until corn is six inches high.

Smoothing iron. =FLATIRON. {1627–} — **1638** *Md. Archives* IV. 48, 1. smoothing iron. **1684** *Essex Inst. Coll.* XXV. 153 In the New house in the hall . . . a box smothing iron with 2 heaters. **1897** W. E. BARTON *Hero in Homespun* 36 It comes in like a smoothin' iron.

Smooth-leaved, *a.* In the specific names of plants. {1731–} — **1770** FORSTER tr. Kalm *Travels* I. 66 *Rhus glabra*, the smooth leaved Sumach, in the woods, on high glades, and old corn-fields. **1898** A. M. DAVIDSON *Calif. Plants* 176 All kinds of turnips are supposed to be cultivated forms of a common weed known as the smooth-leaved mustard.

+**Smooth sumac(h).** **1.** The red sumac, *Rhus glabra.* **2.** (See quotation.) — (1) **1814** BIGELOW *Florula Bostoniensis* 71 Smooth Sumach. . . . A common species of Sumach found about fences and borders of fields. **1901** MOHR *Plant Life Ala.* 600 Smooth Sumach. . . . The leaves are used for tanning and dyeing. (2) **1897** SUDWORTH *Arborescent Flora* 275 *Rhus copallina.* Dwarf Sumach. . . . Smooth Sumach.

✴**Smother.** +?=SMOTHERATION. — **1852** *32d Congress* 2 *Sess.* H. R. *Ex. Doc.* No. 23, 260 [The boat-fisherman of the Bay of Fundy] is kind and hospitable in his way; and the visitor . . . is treated to *fresh smother, duff*, and *jo-floggers*. [Note:] Potpie of sea-birds, pudding, and pancakes.

+**Smotheration.** {1826–} *New Eng.* 'A sailor's dish of beef and pork smothered with potatoes' (*Cent.*).

Smouch, *v.* 'Now *U.S.*' (*O.E.D.*). +**1.** *intr.* (See quotation.) **2.** *tr.* To pilfer or steal. {1826–} — (1) **1848** BARTLETT 314 *To Smoutch*, to gouge; to take unfair advantage. Colloquial in New York. (2) **1850** MATSELL *Vocabulum* 82. **1869** 'MARK TWAIN' *Innocents* 511, I have the books they will 'smouch' their ideas from. **1888** *New Princeton Rev.* V. 49 (*Cent.*), The rest of it was smouched from House's Atlantic paper.

Smouge, *v.* *tr.* and *absol.* =SMOUCH *v.* 2. — **1851** HALL *College Words* 286 *Smouge*, at Hamilton College, to obtain without leave. **1859** G. K. WILDER *Diary* (MS.) 5 May, No ticket [was] to be had so [I] smouged [my way] to Coldwater.

Smudge, *n.* {1767–}

+**1.** A smouldering fire emitting dense smoke for repelling mosquitoes, etc. {1880, in Canada}

1840 HOFFMAN *Greyslaer* I. 60 The thick fumes of his 'smudge' soon caused the insects to disappear. **1853** *Harper's Mag.* March 441/2 They have already lighted 'smudges' to drive away the gnats and mosquitoes. **1873** BEADLE *Undevel. West* 76 'Smudges' were lighted about the yard. **1901** GRINNELL *Gold Hunting in Alaska* 14, I keep a smudge burning in the tents so the boys may eat in peace.

+**2.** Attrib. with *box, fire, kettle, etc.*

1846 *Knickerb.* XXVIII. 341 You make a large 'smudge' fire outside that the smoke may drive these [insects] away. **1860** *Harper's Mag.* Oct. 584/1 Through the smudge-smoke . . . we could catch glimpses of dark eyes. **1882** G. C. EGGLESTON *Wreck of Red Bird* 55 'What is a "smudge box," Ned?' 'Simply a shallow box of earth set upon a post, to build a smudge upon.' **1902** WHITE *Blazed Trail* 148 Thorpe's old tin pail was pressed into service as a smudge-kettle. **1903** WHITE *Forest* 112 Your smudge-pan may drive away the mosquitoes.

✴**Smudge**, *v.* +*tr.* To make a smudge in (a place) to repel mosquitoes, etc.; to make (a fire) emit dense clouds of smoke. Also *vbl. n.* — **1846** FARNHAM *Prairie Land* 314 This process is more briefly designated by its technical name of '*smudging*'. **1860** *Harper's Mag.* Aug. 296/2 The blankets were spread in the tents, the tents smudged, or mosquito nets hung. **1866** *Ib.* Jan. 265/2 The others sat by the fire and 'smudged' it. **1891** *Cent.* 5722/1 *Smudge*, . . . to make a smudge in; fumigate with a smudge: as, to smudge a tent so as to drive away insects.

Smuggler. One who conveys goods clandestinely, to evade revenue, embargo, or importation laws. {1661–} — **1791** *Ann. 1st Congress* 2016 Either the smuggler undersells the fair trader, or he sells at the increased price occasioned by the duty. **1830** COOPER *Water Witch* III. 13 See that no boat quits the river to apprize the smugglers of their loss. **1843** [see NEGRO 3 d]. **1843** *Niles' Nat. Reg.* 20 May 192/3 Smug[g]lers caught. Seizures of dry goods . . . have been made by collector Brooks, of Detroit. **1916** DU PUY *Uncle Sam* 119 Thus was gained the first peep into the methods of the smugglers.

Smut. {1664–} A fungus disease of plants, esp. grain. {1665–} — **1652** *Mass. H. S. Coll.* 4 Ser. VII. 63 Send me 2 or 3 bushils of sumar wheat that is clean, without smut, for seed. **1772** *Md. Hist. Mag.* XIV. 148, I hope what was in or is still to shoot may be freer from the smut. **1847** PALMER *Rocky Mts.* (1904) 188 Rust and smut . . . are unknown in Oregon. **1899** *Dept. Agric. Yrbk. 1898* 652 The loss from smuts of grain is annually being reduced.

Smut face. +(See quotation.) — **1893** ROOSEVELT *Wilderness Hunter* 265 They insist on many species; not merely the black and the grisly, but . . . others with names known only in certain localities, such as the range bear, the roach-back, and the smut-face.

+**Smut grass.** A West Indian grass (*Sporobolus elongatus*) common in the southern states. — **1884** VASEY *Agric. Grasses* 63 *Sporobolus Indicus.* . . . is called smut grass, from the fact that after flowering the heads become affected with a black smut. **1894** COULTER *Bot. W. Texas* III. 518 Smut-Grass. . . . Introduced in rather moist land throughout the southern United States.

Smut machine. A machine for cleaning grain of smut. {1825– (Loudon *Encycl. Agric.* 406)} — **1803** *Mass. H. S. Coll.* 1 Ser. IX. 114 From these bins the wheat . . . is conducted through screws, fanning mills, smut machines, into the hoppers over the stoves for grinding. **1869** *Boyd's Business Directory* 54/2 Howes, Babcock & Co., . . . Manufacturers of 'Eureka' Smut and Separating Machine. **1883** KNIGHT *Suppl.* 825/2.

+**Smut mill.** =prec. — **1818** *Niles' Reg.* XV. 80/2 A *smut mill*, for cleaning wheat of smut, is in operation at Plattsburg. **1846** *Spirit of Times* 16 May 141/1 When [buckwheat is] carried to be ground, it is passed through a smut mill. **1871** DE VERE 547 *Smut-mill* or *smut-machine*, designates in the farmer's language a part of the flouring-mill which breaks and separates grains of wheat affected with smut.

✴**Smutty**, *a.* +In the specific names of birds. — **1884** COUES *Key to Birds* 425 *Perisoreus canadensis fumifrons*, . . . Smutty-nosed Jay. *Ib.* 783 *Priofinus melanurus*, Smutty-nosed Shearwater. **1917** *Birds of Amer.* I. 148 Scoter. *Oidemia americana.* . . . [Also called] Gray Coot; Smutty Coot.

✴**Snaffle bit.** A bridle bit having no curb, usually jointed in the middle. — **1667** SANFORD *Letter Book* 47 There was not any furniture to it more th[a]n a meane Snafle Bitt. **1759** *Newport Mercury* 26 June 4/2 Imported, . . . Snaffle and Curb Bitts. **1840** [see PELHAM BIT]. **1890** CUSTER *Following Guidon* 85, I was riding with a snaffle-bit to get a smoother gait. **1902** LORIMER *Lett. Merchant* 116 Money makes the mare . . . cut up, too, unless she's used to it and you drive her with a snaffle-bit.

✴**Snag**, *n.*

+**1.** A tree trunk or large branch embedded in the bottom of a river, bayou, etc., in such a way as to be dangerous to boats.

1804 CLARK in *Lewis & C. Exped.* I. (1904) 44 We got fast on a Snag Soon after we Set out. **1843** 'CARLTON' *New Purchase* I. 50 A snag is a miniature or youthful planter, or sometimes it is made by an upright branch of a large tree. **1875** 'MARK TWAIN' *Old Times* iii. 45 You can go up inside the old sycamore snag. **1897** DANA *Recoll. Civil War* 26 It was reported . . . that Bayou Macon was full of snags. **1912** COBB *Back Home* 312 Floating snags were going down.

2. *transf.* An impediment or difficulty. {1830–}

1829 KIRKHAM *Eng. Grammar* 207 He has run against a snag. **1851** HALL *Manhattaner* 76 [They] will run upon some snag in the under-currents of Louisiana law. **1870** MEDBERY *Men Wall St.* 101 The Rock Island corner of '63–'64 partly split upon this snag. **1923** J. H. COOK *On Old Frontier* 93 These were snags I had not been looking for in my attempt to become a train conductor.

+3. In special combinations.

Snag chamber, *s. room*, the front part of the hull of a river steamer, made into a water-tight compartment as a safeguard against the boat's sinking if snagged; *s. scow*, *s. vessel*, a scow or vessel for removing snags from waterways.

1829 B. HALL *Travels in N.A.* III. 364 All the boats on the Mississippi are now fitted with what is called a snag-chamber. **1820** *Niles' Reg.* XVIII. 112/2 The *steam boat* Columbus from New Orleans to Shipping-port, was . . . saved from sinking by having a snag room. **1907** STEWART *Partners of Providence* 176 The white snag-scow . . . did keep the snags pulled out of the mouth of the Missouri. **1847** LANMAN *Summer in Wilderness* 21 The snag-vessels can extricate them from their dangerous positions.

Snag, *v.* {1811–}

+1. *tr.* In passive: To be pierced by a snag. Said esp. of river steamers. Also in allusive context.

1807 GASS *Journal* 229 One of our best horses got snagged today, and was left here. **1836** J. HALL *Statistics of West* 239 Twenty-four [boats were] snagged, and *five* destroyed by being struck by other boats. **1847** PARKMAN in *Knickerb.* XXIX. 160 The 'Radnor,' since snagged and lost, . . . was loaded until the water broke alternately over her guards. **1849** *Knickerb.* XXXIII. 430/1 The situation of our streets during [March] . . . has been past description. . . . Our last omnibus was snagged, and sunk. **1880** BURNETT *Old Pioneer* 8 A single steamer . . . was snagged and sunk. **1898** POST *10 Years Cowboy* 62 The folks used to talk of that flatboat getting snagged. *fig.* **1834** CARRUTHERS *Kentuckian* I. 218, I'm snagged . . . if I wouldn't be apt to let the wind through his whistle.

+b. *intr. and passive:* To be caught on a snag. Also transf.

1866 *Harper's Mag.* Nov. 810/1 A Mississippi steamer, that snagged and went down on 'Yazoo Bend.' **1891** C. ROBERTS *Adrift Amer.* 211, I started to haul my line in, but found I was snagged. **1893** *Outing* XXII. 123/1 When the hook is snagged or fast in a tree it is often handy to be able to reel in.

+2. To break down, defeat, or trip. *slang.* Also *fig.*

1842 *Ainsworth's Mag.* II. 556 Feller citizens, jine me in snagging 'em. **1848** E. BENNETT *Mike Fink* 11/2 Open, Deb, . . . or by all the fishes of the Dead Sea, I'll snag this old door. **1898** *N.Y. Journal* 17 Aug. 6/6 The travellers thought to snag him.

+3. *fig.* To occupy or block as with a snag.

1852 PHILLIPS *Speeches* (1863) 38 A great mind, anchored in error, might snag the slow-moving current of society.

4. To clear (a river, etc.) of snags. {1882}

1889 *N.Y. Times* 21 July (Th. S.), [These men] are engaged in snagging the waterways.

+Snag boat. A boat designed to remove snags and other obstructions from waterways. — **1852** *Congress. Deb.* 3 May 2722 The snag boat had been employed in improving the navigation of the Mississippi. **1838** *Niles' Nat. Reg.* 13 Oct. 112/2 The United States snag boats are removing a number of coal boats sunken in the river. **1887** *Courier-Journal* 11 Jan. 3/5 Mr. O. Matthews . . . has been appointed Clerk of the Government snag-boat Wagner. **1893** *Harper's Mag.* Jan. 180 The crews of the snag-boats had been at work.

Snagged, *a.* {1658–} +Pierced or caught by a snag. — **1851** WORTLEY *Travels in U.S.* 112 In the papers you will often see whole columns, headed, 'Snagged,' containing a melancholy list of boats. **1867** RICHARDSON *Beyond Miss.* 21 A snagged steamer. . . . Our steamer . . . [would] shudder with horror at every snag grating against her hull. **1872** C. KING *Mountaineering in Sierra Nev.* 174, I made a dash for the snagged mule.

‖Snaggers. [Cf. SNIGGERS.] *I snaggers!* a mild imprecation. — **1833** A. GREENE *Life D. Duckworth* I. 92 Say nothing worse than—Darn it! I snaggers!

+Snagging. An instance of a steamboat's being pierced by a snag. *Obs.* — **1851** HALL *Manhattaner* 179 There may sometimes occur a snagging, . . . with perhaps a collision. **1880** 'MARK TWAIN' *Tramp Abroad* 95 [He] had gone to bed with his head filled with impending snaggings, and explosions, and conflagrations.

+Snaggled, *a.* **1.** Of teeth: Uneven; projecting. **2.** Intricate, difficult. — (1) **1884** BOURKE *Snake-Dance of Moquis* 360 His snaggled teeth, projecting tusk-like from an unnecessarily large mouth. **1888** 'CRADDOCK' *Despot* 389 The gleeful Bob, with distended ruddy cheeks, and two rows of snaggled white teeth, . . . continued his blithe circuit. (2) **1896** *Advance* 26 March 457/1 Snaggled problems grew plain as light.

∗Snaggy, *a.* +Of a waterway: Abounding in, or full of, snags. {1891–} — **1806** CLARK in *Lewis & C. Exped.* V. (1905) 380 The Sand bars . . . confined the [river] to a narrow Snagey Chanel. **1864** HOSMER *Color-Guard* xii, We passed into snaggy lakes at last. **1887** *Harper's Mag.* July 270/2 [The] snaggy, rafted, convoluted course was by universal avoidance relegated to an isolation almost insulting.

∗Snail.

∗1. Any one of various small gastropods.

1737 BRICKELL *N. Carolina* 169 The Snails are . . . not so plenty as with us in Europe. **1806** LEWIS in *L. & Clark Exped.* IV. (1905) 155 The

snail is numerous in the woody country on this coast. **1875** *Amer. Naturalist* IX. 387 The ponds are bordered by a belt of mud or sand, over which crawl hosts of Paludinas, Lymnæas, Physas, and other 'snails.' **1883** *Century Mag.* Sept. 719/1 The whole place is . . . seamed with iridescent tracks of snails.

+2. An oyster drill, as *Urosalpinx cinerea.* Also *snail bore.*

1881 INGERSOLL *Oyster-Industry* 248 *Snail-Bore.*—Mollusks of the genus *Urosalpinx*, etc. (New Jersey.) **1884** GOODE, etc. *Fisheries* I. 696 These small 'Snails,' 'Drills,' 'Borers,' and 'Snail-bores,' as they are variously called, belong to several species.

+3. *Snail hawk*, the everglade kite (*Rostrhamus sociabilis plumbeus*), which feeds on snails.

1917 *Birds of Amer.* II. 63 Everglade Kite. . . . Snail Hawk. . . . Tropical Florida.

∗Snake, *n.*

I. **∗1.** Any one of various long, limbless reptiles; a serpent.

See also BLACK SNAKE, BROWN SNAKE, etc.

1637 MORTON *New Canaan* 82 There are of Snakes divers and of severall kindes. **1750** T. WALKER *Journal* 71 My riding Horse was bit by a Snake this day. **1835** A. PARKER *Trip to Texas* 152 There are other snakes, not venomous, such as the coach-whip snake. **1904** STRATTON-PORTER *Freckles* 174 You're mortal afraid of snakes.

‖b. *pl.* An interjection.

1894 WISTER in *Harper's Mag.* Sept. 509/1 Snakes! but it feels good.

+2. An Indian belonging to any one of various Shoshonean tribes; also, *pl.*, any one of these tribes.

1821 J. FOWLER *Journal* 55 Last night on Counting them over find now four Hunderd of the following nations—Iltans—Arrapohoes—Kiawa Padduce—Cheans—Snakes. **1836** IRVING *Astoria* II. 16 The Snakes were to return to Fort Henry. **1848** BRYANT *California* xi. 152 One of the men called himself . . . a Soshonee or Snake. **1856** BONNER *Life J. P. Beckwourth* (1931) 88 One of the Snakes . . . strolled down to the Pun-nak lodges one evening. **1890** LANGFORD *Vigilante Days* (1912) 77 [With] a band of Snakes . . ., we can run off two thousand of the best of those animals. **1910** HODGE, etc. *Amer. Indians* II. 606/1 Snakes, a name applied to many different bodies of Shoshonean Indians, but most persistently to those of E. Oregon.

+3. = BLACK SNAKE 3.

1863 *Ladies' Repository* Aug. 488/1 [The teamster] made his snake ring again as he cracked it around his head.

+4. (See quotation.)

1891 *Cent.* 5725/1 *Snake-box*, . . . a faro-box fraudulently made so that a slight projection called a snake warns the dealer of the approach of a particular card.

II. In phrases. **+5.** In assertive expressions and in emphatic comparisons.

1789 *Columbian Mag.* III. 182 As sure as snakes it must be *tarnation* clever law. **1835** CROCKETT *Life* (1865) 242, I should lose my election as sure as there are snakes in Virginny. **1845** *Big Bear Ark.* 38 At it we went, like killing snakes, so good a man, so good a boy. **1854** S. SMITH *Down East* 331, I'm a-going to have some bread and flour cake . . . or else there's no snakes in Oquago. **1855** SIMMS *Forayers* 246 Inglehardt . . . is about as cold, as cunning, and as venomous as a snake in August.

+6. *To wake snakes*, (see quots. 1848, 1872). Also, in the imperative. *slang. Obs.*

1835 LONGSTREET *Ga. Scenes* 6 Oh, wake snakes, and walk your chalks! **1848** LOWELL *Biglow P.* 1 Ser. 147 *Wake snakes*, to get into trouble. **1872** DE VERE 212 The other meaning . . . makes waking snakes equivalent to 'running away quickly.'

7. *Above snakes*, from or above the ground; in height.

1851 WORTLEY *Travels in U.S.* 154 Look at those two tall Kentuckians, with their tufted chins, somewhere about seven feet 'above snakes.'

+8. In miscellaneous phrases.

To make snake, (see quotation); (to have) *snakes in one's boots*, (to have) delirium tremens; *why in snakes?* why in the mischief? *slang.*

1843 TALBOT *Journals* 42 A party of skirmishers . . . zig-zagging or as it is called 'making snake.' **1877** HABBERTON *Barton Exper.* ix, He's been plenty high on whisky for two or three days, . . . and they say he's got snakes in his boots now. **1891** *Scribner's Mag.* Sept. 293/1 Why in snakes should anybody want to be a sculptor?

III. *attrib. and comb.* **9.** In sense 1 in the specific names of, or with reference to, plants.

See also SNAKE CUCUMBER, SNAKEHEAD 1, etc.

1847 WOOD *Botany* 275 *C[ereus] flagelliformis.* . . . Snake Cactus. . . . From S. America. . . . Flowers of a lively pink color. **1832** KENNEDY *Swallow Barn* 232 The heirs of Swallow Barn . . . are hereafter to be pestered with this fine garden of wankopins and snake-collards. **1833** EATON *Botany* (ed. 6) 189 *Iris versicolor*, snake lily, blue flag. *Ib.* 266 *Plantago lanceolata*, rib-wort, snake-plaintain, ripple grass. **1844** *Lexington Observer* 3 July 1/3 The velvet Geraniums were . . . familiarly known as Snaketongue! **1893** *Amer. Folk-Lore* VI. 138 *Viola pedata*, . . . snake violet; horse-shoe violet. Swansea, Mass.; Boston, Mass.

+**10.** In sense 2 with *country, horse, nation.*
See also SNAKE TRIBE.
1814 BRACKENRIDGE *Views La.* 202 We had on board a Frenchman named Charbonet, with his wife, an Indian of the Snake nation. **1843** TALBOT *Journals* 45 The trappers prefer Snake Indians and Snake horses before any race of men or horses in the world. **1844** LEE & FOREST *Oregon* 211 He found a stone that he had picked up . . . in the Snake country.

11. In special combinations.
Snake-charmer, (see quotation); *s. curve,* a form of curve in a pitched baseball; *s. fat,* fat obtained from a snake; *s. hunt,* a hunt for snakes; *s. poison,* whisky (*slang*); *s.-poled,* badly beaten up (*slang*); *s. rail,* a strap rail (*Obs.*); *s.-room,* (see quotation) *colloq.*; *s. sign,* indication that a snake has been at a particular place; *s. staff,* a staff provided with a leather loop at one end for handling snakes; *snakeworm,* (see quotation).
1863 HOPLEY *Life in South* I. 93 Another sweet songster is the cat-bird, or 'snake-charmer,' thus named from its cry of alarm, as the popular belief is, when a snake is near. **1907** *St. Nicholas* June 720/1 The umpire . . . could throw an 'up shoot' and a 'snake curve' and never half try. **1897** HOUGH *Story of Cowboy* 211 Snake fat is good for softening leather. **1860** HOLMES *E. Venner* iv, After this there was a great snake-hunt, in which very many of these venomous beasts were killed. **1889** L. C. D'OYLE in *Cornhill Mag.* Jan. 51 It was variously called for as tangle-foot, snake-poison, . . . chain-lightning, or other fancy name, but it was *never* called for as *whisky.* **1838** DRAKE *Tales Queen City* 92 Many were trampled under foot, some *gouged,* others horribly *snake-poled.* **1862** *N.Y. Tribune* 26 June 1/4 The loose end of a snake rail threw the first car from the track. **1909** *Harper's Mag.* July 166/1 Higgins was then in the snake-room of the place—a foul compartment into which the stupefied and delirious are thrown when they are penniless. *a*1846 *Quarter Race Ky.* 93, I couldn't see no snake sign. **1889** *Century Mag.* Aug. 507 At present the snake-staff is used to handle snakes. **1891** *Cent.* 5726/1 *Snakeworm,* one of the masses of larvæ of certain midges of the genus *Sciara* . . . [which] often migrate in armies forming a snake-like body a foot or more long.

Snake, v. {1653-}
+**1.** *tr.* To drag or draw (a log or tree) along the ground.
1829 FLINT *G. Mason* 21 (Th.), Logs, sixteen feet in length, could be drawn, or as it is technically phrased, snaked into church. **1868** SOL. SMITH *Autobiog.* 11, I could . . . cut down and cut up trees, and 'snake' them to the farm. **1880** *Congress. Rec.* 22 Jan. 490/2, I could not fail to recall the wild sublimity of that early day when I snaked saw-logs. **1903** A. ADAMS *Log of Cowboy* 219 Old Joe and I had snaked them as fast as the axemen could get them ready.

+**b.** In transferred use.
1856 M. THOMPSON *Plu-ri-bus-tah* 135 Then he snaked the stars and stripes off. **1884** 'MARK TWAIN' *H. Finn* xxix, The lawyer . . . snaked a lot of old letters out of his pocket.

+**c.** In figurative use.
1883 *Phila. Times* No. 2810, 4 Some legal loophole . . . through which an evasion or extension can be successfully snaked. **1884** 'MARK TWAIN' *H. Finn* xix, You ain't the only person that's ben snaked down wrongfully out'n a high place. **1894** *Outing* XXIV. 448/2 After a full-back yo-heave-ho, old Joe was snaked into this glad, free life once more. **1902** LORIMER *Lett. Merchant* 74 Doc Hoover would . . . have to hold extra meetings for a couple of days to snake in that miserable Bill; but, in the end, he always got religion.

+**2.** To drag or snatch (a person or thing) *out* of a place. Also *fig.*
1834 C. A. DAVIS *Lett. J. Downing* 14 We snaked him out of that scrape as slick as a whistle. *a*1855 J. F. KELLY *Humors* 299 He forthwith made a preparation to 'snake out' a clever-sized fish. **1866** 'MARK TWAIN' *Lett. Sandwich Islands* 79 This chieftain . . . was able to snake an enemy out of the ranks with this spear at a distance of . . . even a hundred feet. **1881** PIERSON *In the Brush* 167 Together they 'snaked' him out of the house. **1905** LINCOLN *Partners* 200 If you've got a loose tooth a string and a door'll snake it out as quick as the dentist will.

+**b.** (See quots. 1841, 1848.) *Obs.*
1837 MARTINEAU *Society* I. 170 A hand-bill . . . declared that Thompson, the abolitionist, was to address them; and invited the citizens . . . to 'snake Thompson out, and bring him to the tar-kettle before dark.' **1841** H. PLAYFAIR *Papers* I. 129 Them State of Maine fellors . . . may be will *snake out* that genuyne British territory. [*Ib.* (note), A Yankeeism for *worming slily* into possession, or into a discovery.] **1848** LOWELL *Biglow P.* I Ser. 146 *To snake any one out* is to track him to his hiding-place.

+**3.** (See quot. 1859.) *Obs.*
1852 O. P. BALDWIN *Southern Sk.* 120 (B.), Any gal like me . . . ought to be able to snake any man of her heft. **1859** BARTLETT 421 *To Snake,* . . . to beat; to thrash. Southern.

+**b.** To cheat or swindle: (see quot. 1864).
*a*1861 WINTHROP *J. Brent* 183 They snaked me to the figure of a slug at their cheatin' game. **1864** DICK *Amer. Hoyle* (1866) 208 A game is said to be snaked, when the dealer's cards have been stolen and privately returned marked, or prepared in such a manner, as that, when they are dealt, the snaker knows what cards will win or lose.

+**4.** *intr.* To creep, crawl, or move in a snakelike manner. Also *to snake it.*
1844 *Public Ledger* (Phila. Pa.) 30 July 1/7 Is it right for fellows to snake it in the grass? **1852** STOWE *Uncle Tom* 54, I could get along and snake

through, even if justices were more particular than they is. **1855** SIMMS *Forayers* 104 Snake through the settlement! **1877** *Harper's Mag.* Jan. 293/1 That darned Potter feller's a-snakin' 'nd a-sneakin' round arter Phoebe. **1912** WASON *Friar Tuck* xxxviii, He had snaked up to him, and had got him by the throat.

Snakebird. {1831-} +The water turkey (*Anhinga anhinga*) of the southern states. — **1791** W. BARTRAM *Travels* 132 Here is . . . in the waters all over Florida, a very curious and handsome species of birds; the people call them Snake Birds. **1813** WILSON *Ornithology* IX. 80 The Snake-bird . . . seems to have derived its name from the singular form of its head and neck. **1853** *Harper's Mag.* Nov. 769/1 Here [in La.] you may see . . . the snake-bird, the pelican, and the ibis. **1889** *Cent.* 217/1 The American snake-bird, [or] darter, . . . inhabits swamps of the warmer parts of America. **1917** *Birds of Amer.* I. 93.

Snake box. 1. A box for snakes. {1886} +**2.** (See quot. 1891.) — (1) **1850** LEWIS *La. Swamp Doctor* 66 The snake-box was placed with the other baggage on the cabin deck. (2) **1891** *Cent.* 5725/1 *Snake-box,* . . . a faro-box fraudulently made so that a slight projection called a snake warns the dealer of the approach of a particular card. **1903** LEWIS *Boss* 374 They [are] handin' him out every sort of brace from an 'end-squeeze' . . . to a 'snake-box.'

Snake cucumber. 1. The snake melon (*Cucumis melo flexuosus*) or its long snakelike fruit. {1830- (Loudon *Hortus Brit.* 389)} **2.** The snake gourd, *Trichosanthes anguina.* — (1) **1817-8** EATON *Botany* (1822) *Cucumis anguinis,* snake cucumber. E[xotic]. (2) **1868** GRAY *Field Botany* 158 Snake-Cucumber or Vegetable Serpent, a tall climber, . . . the fruit very like a snake.

+**Snake dance.**

1. A religious dance among Indians, esp. one among the Hopi, in which live snakes are handled.
1772 in *Travels Amer. Col.* 517 The women danced the Snake dance, the leader haveing her legs Covered with Turpin shells which is filled with small stones on purpose to make a noise. **1877** JOHNSON *Anderson Co., Kansas* 139 [The Sac and Fox Indians] also danced the 'green corn' dance, and the 'snake' dance. **1884** BOURKE *Snake-Dance of Moquis* 199 The medicine of the snake-dance is known to only a few Moquis. **1891** *Bureau Amer. Ethnol. Rep.* VIII. 136 Among the Hopi, particularly at Walpi, the snake-dance is renowned.

2. a. A stage dance in some way suggestive of snakes or of an Indian snake dance. **b.** A parade of students celebrating an athletic victory by moving in a zigzag manner in Indian file.
1895 *N.Y. Dramatic News* 23 Nov. 4 Ida Siddons in her snake dance, two Italian pantomimists and the breathing paintings stood out in the olio like warts on a fat man's face. **1911** BURGESS *Find the Woman* 244 So he . . . went, reminding them of the [football] score and the snake-dance every time he opened a bottle.

Snake doctor. {1800-} +**1.** =SNAKE-FEEDER a. +**2.** The hellgrammite fly. — (1) *c*1862 BAGBY *Old Va. Gentleman* 92 [The water is] full of all manner of nasty and confounded 'mud-kittens,' 'snap'n turtles,' and snake doctors. **1885** 'CRADDOCK' *Prophet* 36 His listless gaze was riveted upon the quivering diaphanous wings of a snake doctor. **1899** *Animal & Plant Lore* 91 The dragon-fly is known as 'snake doctor' from his supposed professional services to snakes. (2) **1891** [see next]. **1901** L. O. HOWARD *Insect Book* 212 Names in use in Rhode Island . . . are: Dobsons, crawlers, . . . Ho Jack, snake-doctor, dragon, and hell-diver.

+**Snake-feeder. a.** A dragon fly. **b.** (See quot. 1891.) — **1861** *Ill. Agric. Soc. Trans.* IV. 341 [Suppose] we wished to multiply, artificially, the number of a particular species of *dragon-fly,* or *snake-feeder.* **1883** RILEY *Old Swimmin'-Hole* 11 The snake-feeder's four gauzy wings fluttered by. **1891** *Cent.* 5725/2 *Snake-doctor,* . . . the dobson or hellgrammite. . . . Also [in Ohio] *snake-feeder.* **1904** STRATTON-PORTER *Freckles* 219 The snake-feeders are too full to feed anything—even more sap to themselves.

+**Snake fence.** A zigzag or worm rail fence. — **1805** PARKINSON *Tour* 48 Snake-fences . . . are rails laid with the ends of one upon the other, from eight to sixteen in number in one length. **1837** MARTINEAU *Society* II. 35 Instead of the ugly, hasty snake-fence, there is a neatly built wall. **1880** *Scribner's Mo.* Feb. 505/2 The rail fence . . . is known in New England . . . [as] the snake fence, . . . from the slight resemblance of its zigzag line to the course of a serpent. **1917** COMSTOCK *Man* 116 The gate and snake-fence were carried away.

+**Snake hawk.** The swallow-tailed kite, *Elanoides forficatus.* — *c*1728 CATESBY *Carolina* I. 4 These are said to prey upon Lizards and other Serpents; which has given them by some the name of Snake-Hawk. **1873** *Amer. Naturalist* VII. 202 Numbers of exquisitely graceful swallow-tailed kites or 'snake hawks' . . . were seen sailing about. **1917** *Birds of Amer.* II. 60 Swallow-tailed Kite. . . . Other Names.—Swallow-tailed Hawk; . . . Fork-tailed Kite; Snake Hawk.

Snakehead. {1865-} Cf. SNAKE'S-HEAD.
+**1.** =BALMONY.
1784 *Amer. Acad. Mem.* I. 464 Snake-head. . . . Common by fences and amongst bushes in moist land. **1814** BIGELOW *Florula Bostoniensis* 153 Snakehead. . . . Found in brooks and wet ground. **1869** FULLER *Flower Gatherers* 271 We had still another flower . . . that Jimmy Carroll called *Snake-head.* **1904** BAILEY, etc. *Cycl. Amer. Horticulture* IV. 1673.

+2. *Railroad.* The loosened end of a strap rail driven upward through the floor of a car, to the danger or injury of the passengers. Now hist.

1848 BARTLETT 315 *Snake-Head,* an object of dread to travellers on railways.... Serious accidents have been caused by them. **1891** WELCH *Recoll. 1830–40* 31 One of the ever present fears of travelers riding on those strap rails were the so-called 'snake heads.'

+**Snake hunter.** During the Civil War, one of a body of Federal partisans organized to combat the Moccasin rangers. *Obs.* — **1862** *N.Y. Tribune* 3 June 5/1 Fremont has 'Snake-hunters,' gathered from the same class. **1866** 'F. KIRKLAND' *Bk. Anecdotes* 406/1 Captain Baggs got up ... a company of 'Snake-Hunters.'

+**Snake Indian.** =SNAKE 2.

1791 *Mass. H. S. Coll.* I Ser. III. 24 The tribes of Indians [were called] ... the Blackfeet tribe, the Snake Indians [etc.]. **1805** CLARK in *Lewis & C. Exped.* III. (1905) 47, [I] proceeded on up to join Capt Lewis at the upper Village of Snake Indians. **1836** IRVING *Astoria* II. 123 A solitary Snake Indian visited their camp. **1851** *Harper's Mag.* Dec. 122/2 The Snake Indians are becoming hostile and troublesome. **1868** *N.Y. Herald* 20 July 4/1 General Crook in Idaho has held a peace council with the Snake Indians.

attrib. **1855** GLISAN *Jrnl. Army Life* 209 He fitted out an expedition for the Snake Indian country.

+**Snake-killer.** The chaparral cock or road runner. — **1872** COUES *Key to Birds* 189 *Geococcyx,* ... Road Runner. Snake Killer. **1917** *Birds of Amer.* II. 126 Road-Runner.... [Also called] Snake Killer; Lizard Bird.

+**Snake medicine.** Whisky. *slang.* Also *attrib.* — **1865** *Harper's Mag.* Aug. 276/2 A fine spring of water, aided by a little snake-medicine, set us all right. **1901** CRANE *Monster* 199 [You] got up agin some snake-medicine licker.

+**Snakemouth. 1.** An orchid (*Pogonia ophioglossoides*) found in the eastern states. Also *snakemouth arethusa.* **2.** *pl.* (See quotation.) — (1) **1817–8** EATON *Botany* (1822) 397 Snake-mouth arethusa.... About 8 inches high, in damp places. **1821** *Mass. H. S. Coll.* 2 Ser. IX. 152. **1907** *St. Nicholas* Aug. 939/1 The *Pogonia* group is represented by the rosepogonia or snake-mouth. (2) **1894** *Amer. Folk-Lore* VII. 96 *Chelone,* sp., snake-mouths, Banner Elk, N.C.

+**Snake rail.** A strap or flat iron train rail, the ends of which frequently became loose, forming snakeheads. *Obs.* — **a1877** *N.Y. Tribune* (B.), The Winchester Railroad was built many years ago with the snake-rail, the ends of a large number of which, having become unfastened, spring up and down whenever a train passes.

+**Snakeroot.** The root or rhizome of any one of various American plants regarded as useful in cases of snake bite; the medicinal preparation made from this. {1703–} Also with specifying term.

See also BLACK SNAKE-ROOT, BUTTON (RATTLE)SNAKEROOT, etc.

1635 *Relation of Md.* 21 They have a roote which is an excellent preseruative against Poyson, called by the English, the Snake roote. **1713** *Mass. H. S. Coll.* 6 Ser. V. 276 If the measeles coms amongst you, its best to giue sage and baum tea, ... not too much snake roote. **1784** SMYTH *Tour* I. 290 The inhabitants, and negroes, likewise find and dig great quantities of snake-root. **1835** SIMMS *Partisan* (1854) 186 A bunch of the smaller snake-roots ... lay in the corner. **1862** STOWE *Pearl Orr's Island* II. 157 She's took camomile and orange peel and snake-root. **1901** MOHR *Plant Life Ala.* 672 The roots of this [*Gentiana villosa*] and *G. elliottii,* under the name of 'Sampson's snake-root,' are used in domestic medicine.

attrib. **1882** *Harper's Mag.* Nov. 855/1 He is no New-Englander, ... who has never heard of 'snakeroot tea.'

b. A plant supplying such a root or preparation. {1712–}

1709 LAWSON *Carolina* 78 The more Physical [herbs include] ... Monks Rhubarb, Burdock, Asarum wild in the woods, reckon'd one of the Snake-roots. **1743** CLAYTON *Flora Virginica* 112 *Aristolochia,* ... The Snake-root of Virginia. **1806** *Ann. 9th Congress* 2 Sess. 1142 The silk plant, wild endive, wild olive, pink root, snake root, ... growing along the river side. **1891** [see COLTSFOOT 2]. **1904** BAILEY, etc. *Cycl. Amer. Horticulture* IV. 1673 Snakeroot. Black S. *Cimicifuga racemosa* and *Sanicula Marilandica.* Button S. *Liatris.* Canadian S. is *Asarum.* Seneca S. *Polygala Seneca.* White S. *Eupatorium ageratoroides.*

Snake's-head. {1739–}

+**1. a.** =SNAKEHEAD 1.

1834 AUDUBON *Ornithol. Biog.* II. 150 The Snake's Head grows on the banks of rivers and swamps, in the Middle and Southern States. **1866** LINDLEY & MOORE *Treas. Botany* 1067. **1885** *Outing* VII. 180/1 Another stout herb with a spike of curiously formed white flowers is snakes-head.

+**b.** (See quotation.)

1915 ARMSTRONG & THORNBER *Western Wild Flowers* 572 Snake's Head. *Malacothrix Coulteri.* White. Spring. California.

+**2.** =SNAKEHEAD 2. Now hist.

1847 HONE *Diary* II. 328 The detail of loss of life by boiler-bursting, collisions, and snakesheads is as regular a concomitant of the breakfast-table as black tea. **1918** *Essex Inst. Coll.* LIV. 197 An unpleasant feature of primitive railroad travel was the 'snake's head' or end of a loosened rail punching through the floor of the car.

+**Snake's master.** (See quotations.) — **1841** W. KENNEDY *Texas* I. 133 A root called snakes'-master, which grows abundantly in the pine-

woods, is said to be an efficient remedy for the reptile's venom. **1844** M. C. HOUSTON *Texas* (1845) 244 In order, I suppose, to make one's mind easy [about rattlesnakes], you are told that 'the Indians' know an herb, which they call the 'snake's master.'

+**Snake tribe.** One of the tribes of Snake Indians; the Snake Indians collectively. — **1819** E. DANA *Geogr. Sk.* 54 Of these natives, ... the Snake tribe is the largest. **1837** IRVING *Bonneville* II. 48 These are of that branch of the great Snake tribe called Shoshokoes, or Root Diggers. **1910** HODGE, etc. *Amer. Indians* II. 606/1 The principal Snake tribes were the Walpapi and the Yahuskin.

*✻**Snakeweed.** +Any one of various American plants reputed to be valuable in treating snake bites: (see also quot. 1899). — **1642** LECHFORD *Plain Dealing* 47 He that is stung with any of them [*sc.* rattlesnakes] ... dyes, unlesse he timely get some Snake-weed. **1784** *Amer. Acad. Mem.* I. 475 *Prenanthes....* Snake-weed, Blossoms white. **1814** BIGELOW *Florula Bostoniensis* 70 *Cicuta maculata.* Water Hemlock. Snakeweed.... In wet meadows. **1899** *Animal & Plant Lore* 118 Ferns are popularly known as 'snake-weeds,' because snakes are supposed to harbor among them. Tennessee. **1913** [see FIREWEED].

Snaking. {1815–} +**1.** Creeping or crawling in a snakelike manner. +**2.** The killing of snakes. +**3.** The action of dragging (a saw log) out of a place. — (1) **1853** SIMMS *Sword & Distaff* (1854) 94 Keep you quiet now, while I do a little *snaking.* (2) **1862** *Harper's Mag.* June 33/2 The Colonel ... cried out 'Let the logs alone, and all of you go to snaking.' They piled up fifty-three [rattlesnakes] in the course of the evening. (3) **1883** *Harper's Mag.* Jan. 206/1 The snaking out of these logs is another source of casualty to the lumberman.

*✻**Snap,** n.*

+**1.** A sudden, brief spell *of* weather of an indicated kind. See also COLD SNAP.

1740 T. SMITH *Journal* (1849) 268 We had ... two or three snaps of cold weather, else constantly warm. **1875** STOWE *Deacon Pitkin's Farm* 33 The inclement New England skies ... forget to give their usual snap of September frost. **1884** H. C. McCOOK *Tenants Old Farm* 114 If there comes a snap of cold, ... [the larvae] creep for shelter into the bosom of the bud.

+**2.** A snap or string bean; a bean to be eaten unshelled. Usually *pl.* (Cf. SNAP BEAN.)

1842 KIRKLAND *Forest Life* II. 165, 'Snaps' are young green beans. **1859** *Ill. Agric. Soc. Trans.* III. 503 Early yellow six-weeks and early Valentine (long red mottled,) are excellent for snaps. **1881** TOURGEE *'Zouri's Christmas* ii, Sweet potatoes, snaps, and cabbages ... grew in the little truck patch. **1906** PITTMAN *Belle of Blue Grass C.* 241 The succulent 'snaps' or beans ... make the famous Kentucky dish.

+**3.** A trap, deception, or trick. *slang.*

1844 *Lexington Observer* 18 Sept. 3/1 Mr. Van Buren ... with his characteristic politeness *declined to be caught in any such snap.* **1885** *Wkly. New Mexican Rev.* 2 July 4/3 He was roped into this snap by Chicago sharpers. **1900** *Congress. Rec.* 15 Feb. 1850/2 Ex-Senator Vilas gave the snap away when he said [etc.]. **1919** HOUGH *Sagebrusher* 501 If that girl's not blind she'll get out and give this snap away.

+**4.** (See quotations.)

1864 DICK *Amer. Hoyle* (1866) 207 Snap, a temporary bank, not a regular and established game. [Faro.] **1909** *Cent. Suppl.* 1234/1 Snap, ... a temporary banking game; as, to deal a snap at faro.

+**5.** Vim, dash, zip, go. *colloq.*

1865 *Harper's Mag.* 145/2 [They] had no snap about them. **1892** *Congress. Rec.* 16 May 4292/2 What the people want in Kansas is snap, backbone, industry, and economy. **1920** LEWIS *Main Street* 415 Snap and speed are his middle name!

+**6.** (See quotation.)

1881 INGERSOLL *Oyster-Industry* 248 Snaps.—The most inferior oysters sent to market. (Maryland.)

+**7.** A person or thing that is extremely pleasant, easy-going, or easy; a sinecure. *colloq.*

See also SOFT SNAP.

1892 *Harper's Mag.* Feb. 439/1, I think travelling's a snap. **1897** FLANDRAU *Harvard Episodes* 120 [The college student would] ask his opinion of certain instructors and their courses,—whether this one was a 'snap,' and that one a 'stinker.' **1901** GRINNELL *Gold Hunting in Alaska* 95 The office is no 'snap.' **1925** BENEFIELD *Chicken-Wagon Family* 33 Arithmetic ... was a snap for the child.

8. *Photography.* A snapshot or quick exposure. *colloq.*

1893 *Amer. Annual Photography* VIII. 251 The exposures were mostly 'snaps.'

Snap, a.

+**1.** Quick, off-hand; held on short notice.

c1870 CHIPMAN *Notes on Bartlett* 422 Snap, rapid, quick, off-hand. 'A snap judgment,' 'snap bargain,' &c. **1879** *Congress. Rec.* App. 17 April 82/1 The decisions of all courts favor proceedings to admit aliens against technical and snap objections. **1896** *Ib.* 27 Feb. 2214/2 When the snap tally was taken, he ... went to the clerk. **1906** *N.Y. Ev. Post* 27 June 1 Many Tammany men expressed indignation over last night's 'snap' meeting.... Notices of the meeting were not sent out until yesterday morning. **1911** LINCOLN *Cap'n Warren's Wards* 136 This judgment was not of the snap variety.

+2. Of gloves: That fasten with a snap.

1893 M. Howe *Honor* 220 His wife wore . . . short white gloves of the species called 'snap' from the mode of fastening.

Snap, v.

+1. *Snap the whip*, (see quot. 1896).

1874 B. F. Taylor *World on Wheels* 152 You were the last boy on the string in the game of 'snap the whip.' **1890** Howells *Boy's Town* 70 You had been beguiled, as a little boy, into being the last in the game of snap-the-whip. **1896** *Dialect Notes* I. 424 *Snap the whip*, a boys' game in which a line of boys with hands joined run sharply and one end of the line suddenly stops, the other going round it in a circle.

2. *tr.* To turn *on* an electric light.

1911 Harrison *Queed* 68 Queed cleverly bethought him to snap on an electric light.

+3. To throw (a ball) with a quick, snappy jerk.

1912 Mathewson *Pitching* 262 He snapped it to third.

+4. *Football.* Of the center: To put (the ball) in play by passing it back to the player designated to receive it.

1920 Camp *Football without Coach* 48 The center would snap him the ball.

+5. Used in combination with nouns.

Snap law, (see quotation); *s. turtle*, a snapping turtle.

1863 *Congress. Globe* 7 Jan. 226/1 We had in operation [in Mass. until 1840] a terrible system, sometimes designated a snap law, by which a creditor could go, even in the night, and strip the debtor of everything he had in the world. **1841** H. Playfair *Papers* I. 32 'Half-horse, half-alligator,' with a 'streak of the snap-turtle,' is the usual appellation of those amphibious men who spend their lives on the banks, and as boatmen on the waters of the Mississippi.

+**Snap-back.** =Snapper-back. *Obs.* Also attrib. — **1893** Camp *College Sports* 96 Usually the 'snap-back' [puts the ball in play]. *Ib.* 99 This name [center rusher] has since given place almost entirely to 'snap-back.'

+**Snap bean.** Any one of several varieties of beans the young pods of which are prepared for cooking by 'snapping' or breaking them; a dish of such beans. Usually plural. — **1775** in Rauck *Boonesborough* 179 Had a mess of snap beans. **1831** Holley *Texas* (1833) 72 It bears a pod about the size and shape of the common snap bean. **1885** 'Craddock' *Prophet* 21 He applied himself with great relish to the bacon and snap-beans. **1910** C. Harris *Eve's Husband* 234 A man was ashamed if his snapbeans did not have the Government back of them.

Snap bug. =Click beetle. — **1834** McMurtrie *tr. Cuvier's Anim. Kingd.* 350 North America is extremely rich in this genus. The insect is usually called a *Snap-bug.* **1854** Emmons *Agric. N.Y.* V. 86. **1879** *Scribner's Mo.* Aug. 497/2 This springing power . . . has given it the improper name of 'Snap Bug.'

+**Snap company.** A theatrical company playing short engagements. — **1885** *Santa Fé Wkly. New Mexican* 24 Sept. 4/6 It is the custom, during the summer months, for 'snap' companies to travel through the country and gather shekels.

+**Snap convention.** A convention held on short notice. — **1892** *Courier-Journal* 3 Oct. 4/3 His hopes . . . were blasted by the nomination of Dr. J. F. Kinbley by a snap convention or 'conference' of Republican office-holders. **1914** [see Snapper 6].

*Snapdragon.** Any one of various plants, esp. of the genus *Antirrhinum*, having personate flowers suggestive of a dragon's mouth. Also attrib. — **1784** *Amer. Acad. Mem.* I. 464 *Antirrhinum.* . . . Blossoms yellow, with a mixture of scarlet. **1814** Bigelow *Florula Bostoniensis* 151 Toad flax. . . . The mouth . . . gapes open upon lateral pressure, a character which has given the genus the name of *Snap dragon.* **1892** *Amer. Folk-Lore* V. 93 *Impatiens fulva*, snap-dragon. N.H. **1915** Armstrong & Thornber *Western Wild Flowers* 466 Snap-dragon Vine . . . may be found growing in the bottom of the Grand Canyon.

Snape. A shaping tool used by carpenters. *Obs.* {1794-} — **1651** *Mayflower Descendant* X. 160 One Drawing knife 6 snape.

*Snaphance, Snaphaunce.** An early type of flintlock musket. *Obs.* Also attrib. — **1629** *Mass. Bay Rec.* I. 392 Wee haue . . . sent most of our guns snaphance, bastard muskett bore. **1658** *R.I. Col. Rec.* I. 403 Now it is declared, that both it and fyrelockes and snaphaunces with powder hornes bee alowed. **1677** *Plymouth Laws* 184 All p[er]sons required by the lawes of this Collonie to keep and maintaine armes . . . [shall] be att all times provided with sufficient fix feir lockes or snaphance muskets.

Snap hook. {1688-} (See quot. 1876.) {1889-} — **1850** *Rep. Comm. Patents* 1849 200 Having thus described . . . my improved barbs and spring snap hook, I do not claim [etc.]. **1876** Knight 2229/1 *Snap-hook*, a hook with a spring mousing by which it is prevented from accidental disengagement with the object to which it is attached.

+**Snap judgment.** A hasty, offhand judgment. Also attrib. — **1841** *Congress. Globe* App. 14 June 42/3 This extra session of Congress, called in time of peace to take snap judgments on the American people. **1860** *Knickerb.* LVI. 458 A kind of twopenny shystering smartness and snap-judgment genius. **1903** Brady *Bishop* 173 It was [his habit] not to deliver snap-judgments about anything. **1923** 'Bower' *Parowan Bonanza* 123, I ain't going to give snap judgment on a thing the size of this.

Snapped, a. {1900-} +1. *S.* Drunk. *slang. Obs.* +2. Of corn: That has been broken from the stalk without the removal of the inner husk from the ear. — (1) **1840** *S. Lit. Messenger* VI. 514/1 'Quit, Daniel, you'r *snapped*,' she said. **1844** [see Blue *a.* 5]. **1851** *Polly Peablossom* 46

Bennett and Smith were both at the grocery, the latter about two-thirds snapped. (2) **1868** *Iowa State Agric. Soc. Rep. 1867* 126 Feed in open lots from seventy-five to one hundred bushels of corn in the ear, snapped or pulled.

* **Snapper.**

1. a. Any one of various carnivorous marine fishes of the family Lutianidae. {1697-, in S. Seas} +b. *local.* Any one of various other fishes, as the rosefish and the red grouper. Also attrib.

See also Black, Brown, Gray, Red snapper.

1775 Romans *Nat. Hist. Florida* App. p. xix, A small reef . . . where vast quantities of groopers, snappers, amber-fish, . . . Jew-fish, &c. may be taken. **1839** Storer *Mass. Fishes* 26 The Norway Haddock. . . . By our fishermen it is known by the names of 'Rosefish,' 'Hemdurgan,' and 'Snapper.' **1884** Goode, etc. *Fisheries* I. 395 The Snapper Family—*Pristipomalidæ*. *Ib.* 396 Red Snappers are exceedingly abundant in these places, which are the so-called 'snapper banks.' **1888** Goode *Amer. Fishes* 76 Snapper-fishing is usually carried on with a bottom bait of skip-jack, blue-fish, or young shark. **1911** *Rep. Fisheries 1908* 314/2 Rosefish, . . . [also called] 'snapper,' 'hemdurgan' [etc.] . . . is caught on trawl lines.

+2. =Snapping turtle.

1796 *Aurora* (Phila.) 17 May (Th.), The crocodile throats of the gentle snappers or mud tortles in the Jersey market. **1807** Janson *Stranger in Amer.* 312 The natives call [land turtles] . . . snappers, and haw[k]sbills. **1872** De Vere 388 The Snapping Turtle . . . , also called simply Snapper, is a ferocious kind. **1886** *Scientific Amer.* 11 Dec. 370 The snapper has a voracious appetite.

+3. A cracker at the end of a whip. Also fig.

1835 Hoffman *Winter in West* I. 179 Jim cracked his snapper. **1878** B. F. Taylor *Between Gates* 156 Then that whip throws out fifteen feet of lash with an electric explosion at the end of it done up in a silk snapper. **1891** Holmes *Over Teacups* 306 If I had not put that snapper on the end of my whip-lash, I might have got off without the ill temper which my antithesis provoked. **1903** G. Bradford in *N.Y. Ev. Post* 29 Sept. 8 Senator Carmack . . . is simply adding a snapper to the lash of his vigorous denunciation of the whole Philippine policy.

+b. *transf.* A word or verse giving a smart or pointed finish to something.

1857 Holland *Bay-Path* xiv, You'd 'a said twenty lashes . . . and Mr. Moxon would 'a said twenty Amens on the end on 'em for a snapper. **1892** Child *Pop. Ballads* IV. 393/1 A copy . . . with the addition of one stanza for a 'snapper.'

+4. As the specific names of plants: (see quotations).

1840 Dewey *Mass. Flowering Plants* 75 Touch-me-not, or Jewel Weed . . [is] often called *Snapper*. **1892** *Amer. Folk-Lore* V. 93 *Silene cucubalus*, snappers. Salem, Mass.

+5. As the names of animals and birds: (see quotations).

1842 Buckingham *E. & W. States* III. 101 Rattlesnakes, copperheads, ground-vipers, and snappers—all of the venomous class of serpents—are occasionally found. **1891** *Cent.* 5727/2 *Snapper*, . . . one of various American flycatchers (not *Muscicapidæ*) which snap at flies, often with an audible click of the beak; a flysnapper.

+6. *Polit.* (See quotation.)

1914 *Cycl. Amer. Govt.* III. 324/2 *Snappers*, a nickname applied to the machine Democrats in New York in 1892, who, under the leadership of David B. Hill, held a very early state convention on short notice, called a 'snap' convention (Feb. 22, 1892).

+**Snapper-back.** In American football, the player who snaps the ball back; the center. — **1887** in P. H. Davis *Football* 475 Rule 12 altered so as to prohibit interference with the snapper-back until the ball is in motion. **1893** *Ib.* 483 The snapper-back [is] to have full and undisturbed possession of the ball. **1920** Camp *Football without Coach* 30 That involves a great deal harder work from the center rush or snapper back in getting the ball back to him.

Snapping, a. {1642-}

+1. Sharp, severe, or intense.

1845 *Knickerb.* XXV. 87, I've got a snapping head-ache.

+2. That makes a sharp, cracking noise.

1891 *Outlook* Dec. 238/1 In the tender light of the rising sun he creeps downstairs, avoiding that squeaking board and that snapping step.

+3. In the names of various animals and insects.

1837 Williams *Florida* 64 The Snapping Tortoise . . . grows to a huge size. **1838** *Mass. Zool. Survey Rep.* 62 The Elaters or snapping beetles . . . are well known by the faculty they have of throwing themselves upward with a jerk, when laid on their backs. **1842** *Nat. Hist. N.Y., Zool.* IV. 131 From the avidity with which they seize even an unbaited hook, they [sc. young bluefish] have received . . . the name of *Snapping Mackerel.* **1861** *Ill. Agric. Soc. Trans.* V. 416 There is scarcely an individual . . . unacquainted with the 'Spring-beetles,' or as they are often termed, 'Jumping-Jacks,' 'Snapping-Jacks.' **1869** *Rep. Comm. Agric. 1868* 93 Insects [of the family Elateridae] are known . . . in America as 'snapping beetles,' and erroneously 'snapping bugs.'

+**Snapping, adv.** Intensely. — **1857** in A. Allen *P. Brooks* (1900) I. 201 It is snapping cold here today. **1876** *Wide Awake* 19/1 The night was snapping cold. **1905** Wiggin *Rose* 93 The snapping cold weather and the depth to which the water was frozen were aiding it.

+**Snapping turtle.**

1. a. Any one of various American turtles of the family Chelydridae, as *Chelydra serpentina*. **b.** Any one of various soft-shelled turtles.

1784 SMYTH *Tour* I. 338 One kind of them bites very fiercely when incensed . . . ; these are called *Snapping Turtles*. **1846** LYELL *Second Visit* II. 156 On the shore of the lake we caught a tortoise, called here the snapping-turtle. **1884** GOODE, etc. *Fisheries* I. 153 The 'Snapping Turtle,' is very widely distributed. **1904** STRATTON-PORTER *Freckles* 332 [The men] sprawl on the table, scoop with their knives, . . . and duck their heads like snapping-turtles.

attrib. c**1866** BAGBY *Old Va. Gentleman* 48 A true Virginian . . . [must have] snappin'-turtle eggs. **1872** EGGLESTON *End of World* 24 This was spoken in a staccato, snapping-turtle way.

transf. **1830** *Amer. Beacon* (Norfolk, Va.) 28 Aug. 4/3 (Th. S.), On the subject of the tariff we [in S.C.] are not a little of the snapping turtle. **1856** CARTWRIGHT *Autobiog.* 306 She was one half alligator, and the other half snapping-turtle.

2. A person having the strength, ferocity, tenacity, etc. of a snapping turtle. *slang*.

1819 [see HALF HORSE (AND) HALF ALLIGATOR 1]. **1827** *Mass. Spy* 24 Oct. (Th.), The steamboats, snapping turtles, etc., looked upon him as being destined to establish permanently the inviolable rights of his native state. **1870** STEPHENS *Married in Haste* 207 There never was such a wicked, ungrateful, . . . little snapping-turtle as I am. **1900** HARRIS *On the Wing* 212 Jest tell him I'm a plain old snappin'-turtle from Georgia.

3. (See quotation.)

1920 HUNTER *Trail Drivers Texas* I. 297 An arrangement for holding the cattle while they are being branded is called a 'squeezer' or 'snappin' turtle.'

Snapsack. A knapsack. *Obs.* {1633–} — **1643** WILLIAMS *Key* (1866) 44 *Nemauanínnuit*, a snapsacke. **1689** *Plymouth Laws* 215 Each man to be provided with . . . suitable amunition & a snapsack. **1716** CHURCH *Philip's War* 33 They examined their Snapsacks. **1745** POTE *Jrnl. Captivity* 4 [They cut] our Small Sails in Peices with their knives to make Snapsacks.

Snap-shooting. (See quot. 1883.) {1872–} — **1874** LONG *Wild Fowl* 145 In this cross and overhead shooting, . . . snap-shooting won't do. **1883** *Century Mag.* Aug. 493/2 Snap-shooting is generally understood to consist in putting the gun to the shoulder and firing the instant it is in position. **1903** WHITE *Forest* 83 Don't attempt the real thing until your handling in a heavy sea has become as instinctive as snap-shooting or the steps of dancing.

Snapshot. {1808–} An instantaneous photograph, usually made with a small camera. {1890–} Also attrib. — **1890** *Boston Jrnl.* 1 March 12/5 They had permission to carry their Kodaks and take snap-shots as they passed through the streets. **1893** *Chicago Tribune* 22 April 7/7 'The Tribune' staff correspondent . . . caught a 'snap shot.' **1901** MERWIN & WEBSTER *Calumet 'K'* 288 Young men with snap-shot cameras waylaid Bannon. **1904** 'O. HENRY' *Cabbages & Kings* (1916) 200 You see a man doing nothing but loafing around making snap-shots.

✳**Snare.** A trap or device for taking wild animals. — **1778** CARVER *Travels* 290 Those [methods of beaver-hunting] generally practised, are . . . taking them in snares, cutting through the ice [etc.]. **1806** CLARK in *Lewis & C. Exped.* IV. (1905) 103 The nativs take a fiew of them [sc. raccoons] in snars, and deadfalls. **1859** *Ladies' Repository* Aug. 476/1 Snares, steel-traps, and dead-falls have proved very inefficient in the catching of bears.

Snare drum. A small drum having snares or strings of catgut stretched across the lower head. {1875–} Also transf. — **1873** ALDRICH *Marjorie Daw* 130 Morning and evening we heard the spiteful roll of their snare-drums. **1884** *Harper's Mag.* Sept. 513/2 The little snare-drum trotted bravely along. **1893** *Congress. Rec.* 21 Feb. 1914/1, I rose up from my seat in my office in Hartford, hearing a little snare drum. **1920** LEWIS *Main Street* 304 See that fellow there that's playing the snare-drum?

✳**Snarl.** + A large number; a swarm. *colloq.* — **1775** *Broadside Verse* (1930) 141/2, I see another snarl of men. **1825** NEAL *Bro. Jonathan* I. 76 There being 'a pootty consid'r'ble snarl o' gals, I guess' the supper was bravely furnished. **1860** HOLLAND *Miss Gilbert* 386 A snarl of people that didn't care anything about me. **1904** *N.Y. Tribune* 10 April, A veritable snarl of street urchins took possession of several benches in Lincoln Park.

✳**Snatch, v.** +**1.** *tr.* To arrest. *slang*. +**2.** To bring (a steamboat) quickly into a desired course. **3.** *To be snatched*, +(see quotation). — (1) **1860** *Harper's Mag.* Jan. 284/1 Colonel M'G—— . . . was 'snatched' for a violation of the same law. (2) **1875** 'MARK TWAIN' *Life on Miss.* ii. 40 Mr. Bixby . . . shouted through the tube . . . , 'Put her hard down! snatch her! snatch her!' **1877** BARTLETT 619 'Don't be snatched,' i.e., do not be in too great a hurry. South-western.

Snatch thief. A thief who snatches small objects as purses. {1903–} — **1887** *Courier-Journal* 1 May 13/2 Where the bonnet-buyer is there is the pickpocket and snatch-thief also. **1892** *Boston Jrnl.* 3 Nov. 3/7 A Snatch Thief Arrested.

✳**Snath.** Also **sneath, snathe.** The handle of a scythe. 'Chiefly *dial.* and *U.S.*' (O.E.D.) — **1644** *Essex Probate Rec.* I. 45 A sieth & a sneath. **1698** *Providence Rec.* VI. 211 A stubb sithe wth sneaths, nebbs & Rings. **1817** WEBSTER *Let. to Pickering* 15 [They] never have had occasion to mention . . . the *snathe* of a scythe. **1864** WHITTIER *Poetical Works* (1894) 246/1 O mower, lean on thy bended snath.

✳**Sneak, n.**
‖**1.** A scout.
1845 SIMMS *Wigwam & Cabin* 1 Ser. 45, I was a leetle too anxious to be altogether so careful as a good sneak ought to be.

+**2.** *To lead from a sneak*, in card-playing, to lead from a weak suit.
1891 'THANET' *Otto the Knight* 269 These primitive players led from 'sneaks.'

✳**Sneak, v.** +*intr.* To make off quietly. *colloq.* — **1896** ADE *Artie* 7, I'd 'a' sneaked early in the game. **1901** *Scribner's Mag.* April 409/1 Yell fire till the crowd comes, then sneak.

+**Sneak boat.** A shallow boat of light draught used chiefly by hunters in duck-shooting. (Cf. SINK BOAT.) — **1853** *Md. Laws* 220 Any person or persons [who] shall use any sink boats, sneak boats or floats, . . . shall be subject to a fine. **1889** *Scientific Amer.* 6 April 219/1 The usual length of a Barnegat sneakboat is 12 feet. **1898** *Kissimmee* (Fla.) *Valley Gazette* 28 Jan. 3/5, I found Carr in his new sneak boat duck shooting.

+**Sneak box.** =prec. Also attrib. — **1875** *Fur, Fin & Feather* (ed. 3) 120 Each gunner hiding his little sneak-box boat in the point of meadows . . . awaits the coming of the broad-bill flocks. **1883** KNIGHT *Suppl.* 826/2 The New Jersey sneak box is from 12' to 14' in length. **1906** *Atlantic Mo.* Aug. 240 The very moment one is captain of only a sneak-box one becomes arrogant.

+**Sneaking notion.** A secret or concealed idea: (see also quot. 1848). — **1815** HUMPHREYS *Yankey* 102, I've a sneaking notion . . . I'll git some grand promotion. **1843** W. T. THOMPSON *Major Jones's Courtship* 11, I always used to have a sort of sneakin notion of Mary Stallins. **1845** *Knickerb.* XXV. 182, I've experienced a kind of puppy-love, or what the Yankees call a 'sneaking notion,' but nothing more. **1848** BARTLETT 317 To have a sneaking notion for a lady, is to have a timid or concealed affection for her.

+**Sneak thief.** (See quot. 1859.) — **1859** MATSELL *Vocabulum* 82 *Sneak-thief*, a fellow who sneaks into areas, basement-doors or windows, or through front-doors by means of latch-keys, and entering the various apartments, steals any thing he can carry off. **1875** *Chicago Tribune* 7 Sept. 8/4 A sneak thief entered the carpenter shop. **1923** VANCE *Baroque* 189 The young man . . . reckoned him a respectable person by the cut of his sodden clothing, at least no sneak-thief.

+**Sneak-thieving.** Stealing without using force or violence, as by sneaking into places left unlocked or unguarded. — **1884** *Century Mag.* March 653/2 The offences are nearly all trivial, most of them being petty larceny and sneak-thieving. **1892** *Advance* 31 March, The designed effect of it [a gerrymander] may be termed a kind of political sneak-thieving.

Sneath. (See SNATH.)

Sneezewort. {1877–, Austral.} +Any one of several American perennial plants of the genus *Helenium*. — **1850** AUDUBON *Western Jrnl.* 237 The road . . . runs through a sandy soil, covered at present with what we call 'sneeze-weed.' **1880** CABLE *Grandissimes* 244 A frenzied mob of weeds and thorns wrestled . . . for standing-room—rag-weed, smart-weed, sneeze-weed. **1915** ARMSTRONG & THORNBER *Western Wild Flowers* 538 Sneeze-weed. *Helenium Bigelowii*. . . . The flowers are from an inch and a half to two inches across.

✳**Sneezewort.** + =prec. — **1840** DEWEY *Mass. Flowering Plants* 132 *H[elenium] autumnale*. Sneezewort. False Sun Flower. . . . bitter; fields; August. **1891** *Cent.* 5730/2 Sneezeweed. . . . Less properly called *sneezewort*.

+**Snell, n.** [Origin unknown.] A short piece of gut, horsehair, etc., used in fastening a fishhook to a longer line. — **1846** *Spirit of Times* 9 May 126/2 [The bass] was taken with a jointed rod, with a single gut snell, after half an hour's play. **1883** *Century Mag.* July 381/2 Reeling up his line to the snell of the hook, . . . he turned his left side to the riffle below. **1897** *Outing* XXIV. 331/2 Hooks mounted on strong gut snells.

+**Snell, v.** [From SNELL n.] *tr.* To tie (a fishhook) to a line. Also *ppl. a.* — **1891** *Cent.* 5730/2. **1893** *Outing* XXII. 123/2 Double-snelled Aberdeen, sizes 1 and 2, are very satisfactory hooks.

Snicker. A partly suppressed laugh. {1881–} — **1835** *Knickerb.* VI. 562, I was partially 'ware of a general *snicker*, through the room. **1848** *Ib.* XVIII. 65 There was a subdued 'snicker' from one end of the school-room to the other. **1865** *Ore. State Jrnl.* 12 Aug. 2/5 Just before services commenced a few young persons came in . . . and started up a series of jokes, giggles and 'snickers.'

Sniff. {1767–} +**1.** An insignificant person. *colloq.*[2] +**2.** (See quot. a1922.) — (1) **1890** GUNTER *Miss Nobody* xii, Going to marry that little sniff? (2) **1917** HERGESHEIMER *3 Black Pennys* xxiv, After dinner, when they were playing sniff. a**1922** in Appel *Biog. Wanamaker* 336 His own favorite game was 'sniff,' played with dominoes.

Snifter. {1780–} +A dram or small drink of liquor. *colloq.* — **1848** DURIVAGE & BURNHAM *Stray Subjects* 110 'Cobblers for the party,'— 'snifters for the crowd,'—or 'slugs for the entire company.' **1852** *Knickerb.* XL. 371 Uncle Jack . . . took a 'snifter' of Old Rye. **1876** 'MARK TWAIN' *Tom Sawyer* xvi. 138 Just one little snifter would fetch him. **1910** McCUTCHEON *Rose in Ring* 90 You need a snifter of brandy.

Sniggers. *I sniggers*, an expletive. *colloq. Obs.* {sniggers, 1633; odd 'sniggers, 1749} — **1835** *Knickerb.* V. 403 Judge my astonishment to see a brawny rustic rise, rub his hands, and begin with, 'I sniggers!' **1843** STEPHENS *High Life N.Y.* I. 115, I sniggers! if I didn't raly pity the poor gal.

*Snipe.

*1. a. Any of certain shore birds constituting the genus *Capella* (syn. *Gallinago*), +as the American snipe, *C. delicata*. b. Any of various other slender-billed shore birds, as certain sandpipers, dowitchers, etc.

1698 THOMAS *Pensilvania* 13 There are an Infinite Number of Sea and Land Fowl, of most sorts, *viz*. . . . Snipe, Curlew; as also Eagles. **1709** LAWSON *Carolina* 140 The Snipes here frequent the same Places, as they do in England. **1745** E. KIMBER *Itinerant Observer* 11 Snipes are also vastly plenty and good. **1811** MEASE *Philadelphia* 345 State Island is the great resort of snipes and woodcocks. **1880** *Harper's Mag.* July 218/1 The judge was out one morning in pursuit of snipe. **1925** BRYAN *Memoirs* 36 We got out at a pond near the road to shoot some snipe.

attrib. **1865** *Harper's Mag.* Sept. 415/2 Some adroit sportsmen, who amused themselves peppering me with snipe shot.

2. With specifying terms, chiefly in sense 1 b. {1785-}

See also DRUMMOND'S SNIPE, ENGLISH SNIPE, etc., Many species not illustrated here may be found in *Birds of Amer.* (1917) I. 225 ff.

1781-2 JEFFERSON *Notes Va.* (1788) 77 Yellow-legged snipe. **1813** WILSON *Ornithology* VII. 55 Yellow-shanks Snipe: *Scolopax flavipes* . . . is a plentiful species. **1835** AUDUBON *Ornith. Biog.* III. 322 The American Snipe is easily caught. **1917** *Birds of Amer.* I. 222 Avocet. *Recurvirostra americana.* . . . [Also called] Irish Snipe. *Ib.* 229 Dowitcher. *Macrorhamphus griseus griseus.* . . . [Also called] Brown Snipe (summer).

3. In miscellaneous colloq. and slang uses.

+a. (See quot. 1900.) +b. A cigar butt.

(a) **1870** MEDBERY *Men Wall St.* 131 In street *argot*, they are 'snipes' and 'lame ducks.' **1900** NELSON *A B C Wall St.* 159 Snipe, an obsolete term for a curbstone broker. (b) **1899** FLYNT *Tramping* 397 Snipe, cigar-butts.

Snipebill. {1678-} *local.* +'The bolt which connects the body of a cart with the axle' (WORC. '60).

Snippy, *a.* {1727-} Supercilious. *colloq.* — **1896** *Harper's Mag.* June 23/2 She's too snippy for me.

+**Sniptious,** *a.* (See quots. 1830, 1893.) — **1827** *Mass. Spy* 24 Oct. (Th.), We mought paddle our canoes together pretty snipshush like. **1830** *Va. Lit. Museum* 6 Jan. 479 *Sniptious and Ripsniptious,* 'smart, spruce.' *South and West.* **1893** M. A. OWEN *Voodoo Tales* 123 She hatter 'splain w'y she feel so snipshus (pert).

+**Snits.** *pl.* [Penn.-Ger. *schnitz* 'sections of apple.'] Slices of dried fruit. *local.* — **1848** *Knickerb.* XXXI. 222 A Dutchman smiles when he sees snits and scralls. **1871** DE VERE 144 The *Schnitzel,* slices of dried fruit, are almost universally called *snits.* **1903** *McClure's Mag.* Dec. 217/1 Don't eat them snits.

+**Snollygoster.** *S.* [Origin obscure.] (See quot. 1895.) *colloq.* — **1862** EMMETT *Black Brigade* (*Cent. Suppl.*), We am de snollygosters An' lubs Jim Ribber oysters. **1895** *Columbus Dispatch* 28 Oct. 4/3 A Georgia editor kindly explains that 'a snollygoster is a fellow who wants office, regardless of party, platform or principles, and who, whenever he wins, gets there by the sheer force of monumental talknophical assumnacy.'

+**Snook.**[1] [?f. *snook v.* 'to smell; to sneak about.'] **1.** *S.* A morsel of food; a bite. *colloq.* **2.** An informer. *colloq.* — (1) **1869** *Overland Mo.* III. 129 Many a Rebel cavalry-man . . . had sometimes gone forty-eight hours without a 'snook' of any thing. **1872** POWERS *Afoot & Alone* 92 Come, set up, stranger, and take a snook. (2) **1891** EARLE *Sabbath* 76 The ancient tithingman was pre-eminently a general *snook,* to use an old and expressive word,—an informer, both in and out of meeting.

Snook.[2] *pl.* **1.** A sergeant fish, *Rachycentron canadus.* {1697-, in W. Indies} **2.** = SERGEANT FISH 2. {1725-, in W. Indies} — (1) **1883** *Nat. Museum Bul.* No. 27, 448 Snooks. . . . Atlantic coast of the United States from Cape Cod to Florida; Gulf of Mexico. **1884** GOODE, etc. *Fisheries* I. 444 The 'Ling' or 'Snooks,' is considered one of the most important food-fishes of Maryland and Virginia. **1911** *Rep. Fisheries 1908* 309/1 Cobia . . . [is called] 'ling' and 'snooks' in western Florida. (2) **1896** JORDAN & EVERMANN *Check-List Fishes* 369 *Centropomus undecimalis.* Robalo; Sergeant-fish; Snook. . . . Coasts of Florida and Texas southward.

+**Snoop,** *n.* = SNOOPER. — **1891** *Cent.* 5733/2. **1891** *Amer. Folk-Lore* IV. 160 *Snoop.*—This word I have frequently heard in New England, used both as a verb and as a noun. It implies sneaking, spying, prying around.

+**Snoop,** *v.* [Du. *snoepen.*]

1. *intr.* To pry into; to loiter stealthily; to sneak *about* or *around.*

1832 SANDS *Writings* II. 291 The world has realms wherein to *snoop.* **1840** HOFFMAN *Greyslaer* II. 105 Both he and Bradshawe are snooping about the country. **1855** *Knickerb.* XLVI. 317 The level which the . . . engineers 'snooped' round and found out, hasn't 'a *parallel*' in all the adjacent region. **1875** HOLLAND *Sevenoaks* 237, I don't 'low no hired cusses to come snoopin' round my camp. **1891** *Amer. Folk-Lore* IV. 160 In Worcester, [Mass.,] where there are no resident families of Dutch descent . . . , it would be said: 'They caught him snooping at the door,' that is, peeping and listening. **1907** G. M. WHITE *Boniface to Burglar* 153 A bareheaded man wuz snoopin' about a barn . . . here yesterday. **1922** PARRISH *Case & Girl* 122 What're yer snoopin' round there for?

2. *N.Y.* (See quotation.)

1848 BARTLETT 318 *To Snoop.* . . . Applied to children, servants, and others, who clandestinely eat dainties or other victuals which have been put aside, not for their use.

3. *tr.* To pick or take *up.*

1880 *Harper's Mag.* Dec. 91/2, I should be snooped up in the fust gale.

+**Snooper.** One who pries or sneaks about. {1896} — **1891** *Cent.* 5733/2.

+**Snoopy,** *a.* 'Prying, sneaking' (*Stand.*).

Snoot. [Sc. and Amer. var. of *snout.] A person's nose. *humorous. colloq.* — **1879** *Chieftain* (Pueblo, Colo.) 25 March 2 The Colorado Springs *Gazette* . . . spends most of its efforts in the somewhat childish and unprofitable occupation of 'pulling snoots' at the majority of the stockholders. **1884** NYE *Baled Hay* 209 Read our . . . 'Ode to the Busted Snoot of a Shattered Venus De Milo.' **1920** LEWIS *Main Street* 320, I'm likely to . . . let loose with a punch in the snoot.

Snoozer. {1878-} +1. (See quotation.) +2. A city urchin who sleeps about in boxes, stairways, etc. — (1) **1848** BARTLETT 318 *Snoozer,* a thief who follows the business of robbing the boarders at hotels. He takes board and lodgings, and endeavors to share a room and become familiar with some country merchant; after which, by various tricks, he succeeds in robbing him. (2) c**1860** in Brace *Dangerous Classes N.Y.* 112 If you want to be snoozers, . . . you'll hang up your caps and stay.

+**Snore,** *n.* [Du. *snoer* 'a cord.'] (See quotation.) — **1848** BARTLETT 318 *Snore,* . . . a string with a button on one end to spin a top with. This term is retained by the boys of New York.

*Snore, *v.* +*I snore,* a mild oath. Chiefly New Eng. — **1790** *Mass. Spy* 30 Dec., In one village you will hear the phrase 'I snore,'—in another, 'I swowgar.' c**1815** PAULDING *Amer. Comedies* (1847) 34, I snore, I think the young fellows must have lost their gumption. **1845** JUDD *Margaret* I. 50, I han't lived in the woods to be skeered at owls, I snore. **1897** ROBINSON *Uncle Lisha's Outing* 124 Wal, I snore, if it don't look like one.

*Snort, *v. intr.* To laugh loudly. {1825} 'Dial. and *U.S.*' (*O.E.D.*). — **1834** C. A. DAVIS *Lett. J. Downing* 15 And then we all snorted and snicker'd. **1835-7** HALIBURTON *Clockmaker* 1 Ser. xix. 169, I thought I should have snorted right out two or three times.

Snorter.[1] {1601-} +A thing or person that is exceptional, big, noisy, or the like; a humdinger. *slang.* **1824** *Mo. Intelligencer* 29 May 1/3 Their sink, too you'd guess was a snorter With cross legs some like. **1831** H. FINN *Amer. Comic Ann.* 218 That jump wus a snorter. **1854** S. SMITH *Down East* 192 If it comes on to blow a real snorter, you furl all sails. **1872** *Harper's Mag.* Aug. 348/1 He hooked a . . . 'snorter.' **1909** WEBSTER 1985/1.

Snorter.[2] (See quotation.) — **1859** BARTLETT 424 *Snorter,* . . . the edge pieces of tortoise-shell.

Snot rag. A handkerchief. *coarse.* — **1895** *Dialect Notes* I. 400 *Snot-rag,* a handkerchief; common among schoolboys. **1917** SINCLAIR *King Coal* 9 You can keep your snot-rags.

+**Snout beetle.** Any beetle of the group Rhynchophora. Also with defining term. — **1862** *Rep. Comm. Patents 1861: Agric.* 603 The family *Curculionidæ* of authors includes . . . the 'snout-beetles' or 'weevils.' **1868** *Ill. Agric. Soc. Trans.* VII. 547 [Fruit] may be . . . seamed and blotched and disfigured by the industrious family of Snout Beetles. **1909** *Cent. Suppl.* 1235/1 *Scarred snout-beetle,* any member of the family *Otiorhynchidæ,* so called on account of a scar at the tip of the rostrum characteristic of this family of beetles.

+**Snouted weevil.** A snout beetle. — **1832** WILLIAMSON *Maine* I. 171 *Curculio quircus,* Snouted Weevil.

*Snow, *n.*[1]

*1. White crystals of congealed vapor that fall to the earth after being formed in the atmosphere; a fall of these crystals.

1630 HIGGINSON *New-England* 17 For two months space the Earth is commonly covered with Snow. **1717** C. MATHER *Diary* II. 439 As mighty a Snow, as perhaps has been known in the Memory of Man, is at this Time lying on the Ground. **1885** *Wkly. New Mexican Rev.* 8 Jan. 4/5 The San Juan valley is covered with three feet of snow.

+**2.** With reference to Indian speech: Winter.

1778 CARVER *Travels* 250 [Indians] in the interior parts . . . count their years by winters; or, as they express themselves, by snows. **1823** [see EAR *n.*[2] 3]. **1843** MARRYAT *M. Violet* xv, They would come every snow to the lodge of our Manitou. **1873** MILLER *Amongst Modocs* 242 One late and severe spring-time many thousand snows ago.

3. *attrib.* and *comb.* **a.** In the specific names of plants and fruits. {1775-}

1855 *Amer. Inst. N.Y. Trans. 1854* 362 Judge Livingston presented . . . his peculiar Snow apple, so called because it hangs on the trees until snow falls. **1784** *Amer. Acad. Mem.* I. 425 *Chenopodium.* . . . Snowbane. Fruit green or reddish. **1915** ARMSTRONG & THORNBER *Western Wild Flowers* 282 Snow Brush, Mountain Lilac. *Ceanothus velutinus.* **1814** PURSH *Flora Amer.* II. 709 Snow flock-tree. *Chionanthus.* **1891** *Cent.* 5342/2 The only species, *S[arcodes] sanguinea,* is a native of the Sierra Nevada in California, and is known as *snow-plant* from the place of its growth.

b. In the specific names of birds. {1648-}

1917 *Birds of Amer.* III. 40 Tree Sparrow. *Spizella monticola monticola.* . . . Other Names.—Snow Chippy; Winter Chip-bird [etc.]. **1837** *Oregon Snow-finch* [see OREGON 2]. **1884** COUES *Key to Birds* (ed. 2) 585 *Lagopus,* Ptarmigan. Snow Grouse. **1847** *30th Congress 1 Sess.* H. R. Ex. Doc. No. 41, 544 Flocks of the pretty snow lark were continually taking wing as we advanced. **1811** WILSON *Ornithology* IV. 53 Snow Owl: *Strix nyctea.* . . . Inhabits the coldest and most dreary regions of the northern hemisphere. **1884** COUES *Key to Birds* 377 *Junco,* Snow Sparrows.

+c. In special combinations.

Snow banner, (see quotation); *s. blockade,* a blockade resulting from the fall of snow; *s.-eater,* (see quotation); *s. fort,* a fort made of snow by children; *s. shoveler,* one who shovels snow.

1900 DRANNAN *Plains & Mts.* 234 Often long streams of glittering white stretch from its peaks, far out into space, and these are called 'snow-banners.' **1872** MCCLELLAN *Golden State* 367 The protracted snow block-ade on the overland road . . . demonstrated that but little interruption need be anticipated. **1886** *Science* 12 March 242/2 Warm west winds . . . are here [in e. Colo.] often called Pacific winds, also 'snow-eaters' and 'zephyrs.' **1853** G. C. HILL *Dovecote* 200 Some of us took to building snow forts near the school house. **1891** C. ROBERTS *Adrift Amer.* 114 We had in all three locomotives, two snow ploughs, and a gang of 75 snow-shov-ellers.

Snow, *n.²* A small, square-rigged vessel having a trysail mast close behind the mainmast. {snaw, 1676–1710; 1763–} — **1704** *Boston News Letter* 6 Nov. 2/2 Next morning was in sight of a Snow, Captain Lambard Commander. **1759** *Essex Inst. Coll.* XLIX. 19 A Snow . . . layd just a Head off us. *a*1821 BIDDLE *Autobiog.* 186 The snow was a two-masted vessel rigged very nearly like a brig.

* Snow, *v.*

+1. *To be snowed in,* to be forced to remain in a particular place by heavy snows. Also *ppl. a.*

1867 *Harper's Mag.* June 12/2 A party . . . from the town had been 'snowed in.' **1869** 'MARK TWAIN' *Innocents* 286 Appalled at the imminent danger of being 'snowed in,' we harnessed up and pushed on. **1882** [see BLOCKADE *n.* 3]. **1904** *N.Y. Ev. Post* 5 Feb. 3 The Wabash is devoting all its energies to clearing the line of delayed and snowed-in trains.

+2. *To snow under.* **a.** To bury under snow. **b.** *fig.* To overwhelm or overpower.

1880 'E. KIRKE' *Garfield* 32 Democrats vied with Republicans . . . in snowing him under with congratulations. **1897** 'MARK TWAIN' *Following Equator* 77 The storm rose and spread in a surprising way, and I was snowed under in a very few minutes. **1903** *N.Y. Times* 15 Sept., Snowed under by Republican votes. **1911** SAUNDERS *Col. Todhunter* 70 Stephen K. Yancey will snow Bill Strickland under so deep that [etc.].

* Snowball.

1. a. Any of certain white-flowered plants of the genus *Viburnum,* esp. the guelder-rose; a blossom of these plants. {1799–} **+b.** Any of certain other white-flowered plants, as the Jersey tea. Often with specifying terms and also attrib.

1817–8 EATON *Botany* (1822) 478 *Spiraea opulifolia,* nine-bark, snow-ball hardback. **1832** S. J. HALE *Flora* 165 Snow Ball, *Viburnum, opulus.* . . . A genus found in Europe, America, and Japan. **1834** AUDUBON *Or-nith. Biog.* II. 121 The Swamp Snowball, *Hydrangea quercifolia,* . . . found on the broken sandy banks bordering small water-courses. **1842** *Lowell Offering* II. 290 Unless, indeed, you could find a daisy, snow-ball, petunia, or rose hiding itself in the shrubbery. **1867** 'LACKLAND' *Home-spun* 239 Snow-balls, too, were growing in immense clusters in that yard. **1900** WEBSTER *Suppl.* 194/3 *Wild snowball,* . . . the New Jersey tea (*Ce-anothus Americanus*), so called from its clusters of small white flowers. **1909** *Cent.* 1235/1 *Little snowball,* the button-bush. *Cephalanthus occiden-talis.* **1923** WYATT *Invis. Gods* 84 Lilac and snowball heaped his grave.

+2. (See quotation.)

1848 BARTLETT 318 *Snowball,* a jeering appellation for a negro.

Snow bank. A bank or drift of snow. Also *fig.* {1803–} — **1779** E. PARKMAN *Diary* 194 Snow-Banks very high one nigh my saddle-house 6 feet high. **1838** *Knickerb.* XII. 341 The wind is playing a wintry dirge around my ears, and the snow-banks are rising. **1853** B. F. TAYLOR *Jan. & June* 249 A huge snow-bank of a cloud lay along the west at sun-set. **1887** GEORGE *40 Yrs. on Rail* 137 We ran into a snow-bank near Rosehill and stuck fast. **1907** *St. Nicholas* Aug. 872/1 But Chub was out-side up to his knees in a snowbank.

Snowberry. Any of various plants bearing white berries {1760–}, +as a North American shrub (*Symphoricarpos racemosus*), the blolly (*Chiococca alba*), and the creeping snowberry (*Chiogenes hispidula*). Also attrib. — **1803** JEFFERSON in *Lewis & Clark Exped.* VII. (1905) 393 We call it the snow-berry bush, no botanical name being yet given to it. **1847** EMORY *Military Reconn.* 19 Among the flowers and shrubbery was . . . the snowberry. **1858** THOREAU *Maine Woods* 155 The plants which cover the forest floor there are such as are commonly confined to swamps with us,—the *Clintonia borealis,* orchises, creeping snowberry, and others. **1898** E. C. HALL *Aunt Jane* 258 At the end of the long Dutch 'stoop' I found the wands of the snowberry. **1915** ARMSTRONG & THORNBER *Western Wild Flowers* 516 We often find Snowberries cultivated in old-fashioned gardens.

Snowbird.

1. Either the snow bunting or a finch of the genus *Junco.* {1750, in Canada; 1771–}

1674 JOSSELYN *Two Voyages* 100 The *Snow*-Bird is like a *Chaf-Finch,* go in flocks and are good meat. **1709** LAWSON *Carolina* 146 The Snow-Birds are most numerous in the North Parts of America, where there are great Snows. **1794** *Amer. Philos. Soc.* IV. 92 A small bird, our snow-bird, had been put into a cage containing a large rattle-snake. **1835** HOFFMAN *Win-ter in West* I. 168 Large flocks of snow-birds . . . made our route . . . more like a ride in the spring-time than a winter excursion. **1870** STE-

PHENS *Married in Haste* 188 Her hands flew up and down . . . like little snow-birds picking up seed. **1917** *Birds of Amer.* III. 45 The scientists . . . are disputing over the various races of Snowbirds, not sure just how many different species and varieties to list.

b. With specifying terms.

Only a selection is given. (See also OREGON SNOWBIRD.)

1850 S. F. COOPER *Rural Hours* 517 The arctic or Lapland snow-bird is not unfrequent in this State as a winter visitor. **1868** *Amer. Naturalist* II. 161 Western Snow-bird (*Junco Oregonus*). A specimen [was] shot at Fort Whipple, Arizona. **1873** *Ib.* VII. 634 The Black Snowbird breeds on the Graylock Range. **1917** *Birds of Amer.* III. 45 Slate-colored Junco, *Junco hyemalis hyemalis.* . . . [Also called] Blue Snowbird.

+2. =LESSER REDPOLL.

1811 WILSON *Ornithology* IV. 42 Lesser Red-poll. . . . They appear . . . with the first deep snow, and on that account are usually called by the title of Snow-birds.

+3. *fig.* (See quotation.)

1905 *N.Y. Ev. Post* 20 Nov. 6, 28 per cent. deserted after three months, and were presumably 'snow-birds,' that is, men who enlist to get food and clothing during the winter months.

Snow blind. Snowblindness. {as adj., 1748–} — **1870** *Amer. Nat-uralist* IV. 595 The painful inflammation of the eyes . . . is only too familiar to the northern voyageur under the name of 'snow blind.' **1880** INGHAM *Digging Gold* 345 The sun shining brightly upon the snow, troubled us somewhat with snow-blind.

Snow bunting. A finch (*Plectrophenax nivalis*) common in snowy re-gions. {1783–} — [**1771** J. R. FORSTER *Cat. Animals N. Amer.* 11.] **1839** PEABODY *Mass. Birds* 318 The Snow Bunting . . . come[s] riding on the snow-storms. **1877** BURROUGHS *Birds & Poets* 98 There is but one gen-uine snow-bird, . . . and that is the snow-bunting. **1917** *Birds of Amer.* III. 21/2 The Snow Bunting feeds almost exclusively from the ground.

Snowdrop. **a.** Any species of *Galanthus.* {1664–} **b.** The common anemone, *Anemone quinquefolia.* **+c.** The fringe tree. **+d.** The snow-berry, *Symphoricarpos racemosus.* — **1737** BRICKELL *N. Carolina* 22 Nar-cissus, Daffodil, Snow-Drops [are found here]. **1789** *Amer. Philos. Soc.* III. p. xxii, The Chionanthus (*Snow drop, Fringe tree,*) . . . grow[s] well near Philadelphia. **1817–8** EATON *Botany* (1822) 285 *Galanthus nivalis,* snow drop. **1863** E. W. Pearson *Lett. Port Royal* 159 There are a few snow-drops, very pretty. **1892** *Amer. Folk-Lore* V. 97 *Symphoricar-pus racemosus,* snow-drop. Mansfield, O.

Snowdrop tree. {1731–}

+1. =FRINGE TREE.

1785 MARSHALL *Amer. Grove* 33 *Chionanthus virginica.* Virginian Snow-drop Tree. The bark . . . is accounted by the natives a specific. [**1866** LINDLEY & MOORE *Treas. Botany* 270/2 *Chionanthus,* the Snowdrop tree of North America.]

+2. =SILVER-BELL TREE. Also with specifying term.

1813 MUHLENBERG *Cat. Plants* 46 Silverbell tree, or Four-winged Snow-drop tree. **1846** BROWNE *Trees Amer.* 366 *Halesia tetraptera,* The Com-mon Snowdrop-Tree. **1883** SMITH *Geol. Survey Ala.* 293 *Halesia diptera* (Snow-drop tree). **1897** SUDWORTH *Arborescent Flora* 323 *Mohrodendron dipterum.* . . . Snowdrop-tree. *Ib., Mohrodendron parviflorum.* . . . Small-flower Snowdrop-tree.

Snowflake. {1734–} =SNOW BUNTING. {1770–1845} — **1872** COUES *Key to Birds* 133 *Snowflake.* In breeding plumage, pure white, the back, wings and tail variegated with black. **1906** *Springfield W. Repub.* 5 April 5 Snowflakes are seen flocking with robins and song-sparrows. **1917** *Birds of Amer.* III. 20/1 Many a person . . . has seen the Snowflakes feeding . . . in the bitter biting zero weather of wind-swept fields.

+Snow flea. A small leaping insect, esp. of the genus *Leucojum,* com-mon in the East in early spring. — **1868** *Amer. Naturalist* II. 53 The little insects called snow-fleas . . . are found in winter at the foot of trees. **1888** COMSTOCK *Introd. Entomology* 61 Our common snow-flea . . . is sometimes a pest where maple sugar is made, the insects collecting . . . in the sap. **1908** KELLOGG *Amer. Insects* 64 The snow-flea . . . gathers in large numbers on the surface of snow in the late spring.

Snow fly. One or other species of small insects which appear on snow. {1668–} — **1879** E. P. WRIGHT *Animal Life* 491 In America we find that these little creatures [spring-tails] are at this day called snow-flies. **1891** *Cent.* 5735/2.

Snow goose. Any of several geese of the North Ameri-can genus *Chen.*

[**1771** J. R. FORSTER *Cat. Animals N. Amer.* 16 Snow Goose, *Anas nivalis.*] **1823** JAMES *Exped.* I. 266 *Anas (Anser,* Briss.) *hyperborea*—Snow goose. **1884** ROE *Nature's Story* 168 Have you ever obtained any snow-geese in our waters? **1917** *Birds of Amer.* I. 156/1 The Snow Goose is a western bird, closely resembling the Greater Snow Goose, which is confined main-ly to eastern North America.

+b. With specifying terms.

1883 *Nat. Museum Bul.* No. 27, 157 *Chen hyperboreus albatus* (Cass.). Lesser Snow Goose. *Ib., Chen rossi* (Baird). Ross's Snow Goose. **1889** *Cent.* 2576/1 *Blue snow-goose, Anser* or *Chen cærulescens,* a North Ameri-can goose closely related to the snow-goose. **1909** WEBSTER 1085/2 The greater snow goose (*C[hyperborea] nivalis*) occurs chiefly on the Atlantic coast; the lesser snow goose (*C. hyperborea*) on the Pacific coast and in the Mississippi Valley.

Snow-on-the-mountain. +A spurge (*Lepadena marginata*) hav-ing white bracts. (Cf. MOUNTAIN SNOW.) — **1880** T. MEEHAN *Native*

Flowers 2 Ser. I. 77 Snow on the Mountain.... Particularly attractive to the traveller over ... western railroads. **1891** *Amer.Folk-Lore* IV. 149 *Euphorbia marginata*, cultivated in flower-gardens is called *Snow on the Mountain*,—not a local name, I think. **1898** CREEVEY *Flowers of Field* 270 Snow-on-the-Mountain ... is cultivated in New York and New Jersey. **1913** CATHER *O Pioneers!* 36 In the bottom of the draws and gullies grew ... shoestring, and ironweed, and snow-on-the-mountain.

Snowplow. Any of several contrivances for moving snow off a road or railroad. {1829-} — **1792** BELKNAP *Hist. New-Hampshire* III. 79 When a deep snow has obstructed the roads, they are in some places opened by an instrument called a snow plough. It is made of planks, in a triangular form, with two side boards to turn the snow out on either hand. **1872** HUNTINGTON *Road-Master's Asst.* 102 There is hardly any first-class railroad in snowy parts of the country but is provided with some kind of 'big snow-plow.' **1887** *Courier-Journal* 11 Jan. 3/2 A west bound snow-plow ... ran into an east bound passenger train. **1905** *Springfield W. Repub.* 29 Dec. 3 Many of the street railways are buying larger snowplows.

+Snow shed. A shed built over a railroad track to protect it from snow. — **1869** *Congress. Globe* 5 April 502/2 The company coming from the Pacific side have stout snow-sheds over their roads. **1880** INGHAM *Digging Gold* 318 [We] passed through one of the longest snowsheds on the Union Pacific railway. **1898** HARPER *S. B. Anthony* I. 407 The train had ... drawn into a long snow-shed.

+Snowshoe.
1. A racketlike footgear enabling the wearer to walk on the surface of soft snow. {1681-, in Greenland and Canada} Cf. RACKET 1.

1666 *Doc. Hist. N.Y. State* I. 72 Ye french ... made use of Indian snow shoes which hath the very form of a Rackett tyed to each foote. **1704** *Boston News-Letter* 17 July 2/1 An Act directing that the Militia of the Frontiers be provided with Snow Shoes, &c. **1799** J. SMITH *Acct. Captivity* 38 The snow-shoes are made like a hoop net. **1808** PIKE *Sources Miss.* 69 [The dogs] went so fast as to render it difficult, for the men with snow shoes, to keep up with them. **1872** MCCLELLAN *Golden State* 145 The last raw-hide string from their snow-shoes was eaten. **1914** E. STEWART *Lett. of Woman Homesteader* 143 Gavotte came skimming along on the first pair of snowshoes I ever saw.

2. Attrib. with *dance, disease, evil,* etc.

1725 KIDDER *Exped. Lovewell* (1865) 78, I sent ... to Robert Richardson for fifteen of his Snow Shoe men. **1772** in Morse *Univ. Geog.* I. 100 As the Indians were hunting, some of them saw a strange snow-shoe track. **1809** A. HENRY *Travels* 68 The *snow-shoe evil* ... [proceeds] from an unusual strain on the tendons of the leg, occasioned by the weight of the snow-shoe, and brings on inflammation. *c*1836 CATLIN *Indians* II. 139 The *snow-shoe dance* ... [is] danced with the snow-shoes under the feet, at the falling of the first snow. **1891** *Cent.* 5736/2 *Snow-shoe disease*, a painful affection of the feet occurring in arctic and subarctic America after long journeys on snow-shoes. **1903** WHITE *Forest* 127 In the center ... lay an open box from which tumbled dozens of pairs of moose-hide snow-shoe moccasins.

Snowshoeing. The action of traveling on snowshoes or (quot. 1882) skis. — **1882** *Harper's Mag.* April 697/2 This sort of snow-shoeing [using Norwegian skis] is said to excel coasting, or even tobogganing. **1907** *St. Nicholas* Aug. 885/2 As the winter wore on, snow-shoeing, skating, skeeing kept them together for hours.

+Snowshoe rabbit. (See quot. 1890.) — **1890** *Cent.* 4924/2 *Snow shoe rabbit*, that variety of the American varying hare which is found in the Rocky Mountains.... It has been described as a distinct species, *Lepus bairdi.* **1917** *Mammals of Amer.* 274 Our Jack Rabbits and Snowshoe Rabbits are not Rabbits, but Hares.

+Snowslide. 1. A sudden sliding of a mass of snow; the snow piled up by this action. **2.** (See quot. 1905.) — (1) **1841** WHITTIER *Poetical Works* (1894) 11/1 Dazzling and white! save where the bleak, Wild winds have bared some splintering peak, Or snow-slide left its dusky streak. **1870** RAE *Westward by Rail* 223 Strong wooden sheds of about a thousand feet long, erected to guard the line against destruction from ... 'snow slides.' **1906** *N.Y. Ev. Post* 19 March 9 A snowslide which came down yesterday at the Liberty Bell mine damaged the tramway and considerable trestle work. **1914** E. STEWART *Lett. Woman Homesteader* 147 We could not pass the snow-slide. (2) **1905** *Forestry Bureau Bul.* No. 61, 48 *Snow slide*, a temporary slide on a steep slope, made by dragging a large log through deep snow which is soft or thawing.... [N[orth] W[oods].)

+Snow snake. A long, slender shaft of wood, variously decorated, thrown over the snow or ice in an Indian game. — **1850** *Regents Univ. of State N.Y. 3d Rep.* 78 Among the amusements of the winter season, in Indian life, is the game with Snow Snakes. **1888** *Science* XI. 37/1, I was recently surprised at not finding the snow-snake in the collection of Iroquois implements at the Museum of Natural History.

Snow squall. A flurry of snow. {1888} — **1775** *Mass. H. S. Proc.* 2 Ser. II. 287 The weather is attended with Snow Squalls. **1849** KINGSLEY *Diary* 55 We have had one or two quite heavy snow squalls this morning. **1907** *St. Nicholas* Oct. 1080/2 The snow-squall had passed.

Snowstorm. A storm consisting of a heavy fall of snow. {a1800-} — **1771** A. G. WINSLOW *Diary* 8, I was prevented dining at unkle Joshua's by a snow storm. **1784** HUTCHINSON *Diary & Lett.* II. 400 While you enjoy your vernal sun, I have here enjoyed an American snow-storm. **1861** MCCLELLAN in *Own Story* 177, I came back after dark in a driving snow-storm. **1925** BRYAN *Memoirs* 340 Then came a return to Denver in a blinding snowstorm.

∗Snowy, *a.* In the specific names of birds, plants, etc. {1777-}

1813 MUHLENBERG *Cat. Plants* 49 *Pyrus botryapium*, June berries, wild service, snowy pear. **1839** PEABODY *Mass. Birds* 271 The Snowy Owl, *Strix nyctea*, ... [is] often found in the most northern states. **1845** LINCOLN *Botany* App. 156/1 [*Ribes*] *niveum*, (snowy-flowered gooseberry,) has pendulous white flowers, and dark purple fruit. **1860** CURTIS *Woody Plants N.C.* 101 Snowy hydrangea (*H. radiata*).... The barren flowers ... are of pure white. **1869** *Amer. Naturalist* III. 231 The Snowy Egret, and the larger White Egret ... are occasionally tempted to visit our coast. **1880** CABLE *Grandissimes* 237 What surroundings! Endless colonnades of cypresses; ... the blue heron, the snowy crane [etc.]. **1884** *Rep. Comm. Agric.* 399 The Snowy Tree-Cricket ... will evidently be congregating in raspberry and blackberry patches. **1893** *Amer. Folk-Lore* VI. 141 *Amelanchier Canadensis*, snowy medlar. N.Y. **1917** Snowy Ring Plover [see SNOWY PLOVER].

Snowy heron. A small white egret, *Egretta thula.* — [**1785** LATHAM *Gen. Synopsis Birds* III. 1. 92.] **1828** BONAPARTE *Synopsis* 155 The Snowy Heron ... inhabits both Americas. **1855** *Knickerb.* XLVI. 222 Nightherons, snowy-herons, green-herons and little-herons construct their nests ... closely together. **1917** *Birds of Amer.* I. 188 Snowy Egret.... [Also called] Common Egret; Snowy Heron; Little Snowy.

+Snowy plover. A ring plover (*Charadrius nivosus*) of the West. — **1872** COUES *Key to Birds* 245 Snowy Plover ... several lateral tail feathers entirely white. **1917** *Birds of Amer.* I. 265 Snowy Plover. *Ægialitis nivosa.* ... Other Name.—Snowy Ring Plover.

∗Snub, *n.* +(See quotation.) — **1891** *Cent.* 5737/1 *Snub*, ... a stake, set in the bank of a river or canal, around which a rope may be cast to check the motion of a boat or raft. (U.S. and Canada.)

∗Snub, *v.*
1. *tr.* To check or stop (a boat) by taking a turn with a bowline about a post; to draw (a boat) *up* by shortening a line.

1840 COOPER *Pathfinder* II. 25 It was not a difficult task to snub so light a craft with ground-tackle of a quality better than common. **1872** 'MARK TWAIN' *Roughing It* 370 Snub up your boat. **1887** *Century Mag.* Aug. 483/2 A plain white-painted, three-hatched, and poop-cabined canal-host with ... a deck-hand forward to 'snub' her in the locks.

+2. To check (an animal or fish) with a line turned around a post or reel; to draw *up* close.

1888 *Century Mag.* March 660/1 The newly caught animal ... is taught this by being violently snubbed up. **1889** MUNROE *Dorymates* 78 Let him [*sc.* the fish] run a bit! ... Don't try to snub him yet. **1895** *Outing* XXVII. 224/1, I kept him [*sc.* a fish] snubbed up too closely for him to get a start. **1907** WHITE *Arizona Nights* 152 In such case he [*sc.* a calf] was snubbed up short enough at the end of the rope. **1913** BARNES *Western Grazing Grounds* 180 This is easily done by either throwing or snubbing them [*sc.* cattle] up to a strong post or fence and taking the points off.

Snubber. {1861-} +(See quotation.) — **1853** *Wkly. Oregonian* 12 March (Th.), A snubber, may it please the court, snubs the boat when she heaves to on the heel-path shore, and unships the whiffletrees in passing a lock.

Snubbing. {1600-} The action of checking a boat, animal, etc., by a line turned around a post. {1846} Also attrib. 'Naut. and U.S.' (O.E.D.). — **1850** *Knickerb.* XXXV. 21 One greases his pantaloons and slides down planes, with no snubbing posts save the bottom of a hill. **1862** *Rep. Comm. Patents* 1861: *Agric.* 107 This kyanized cordage ... was found ... less liable [than Manila rope] to *fray in snubbing.* **1897** *Outing* XXX. 356/2 Three men ashore carried snubbing-lines with which to check the boats in the locks. **1909** *Cent. Suppl.* 1235/3 *Snubbing-pitch*, ... in lumbering, the slope at which it is necessary to use a snub-line to control the downward movement of a load of logs. (Maine.)

Snucks. +*To go snucks*, 'to share equally' (B. '77). — **1872** EGGLESTON *End of World* 183 You'll get the 'old man' down on you, if you let a bird out of the trap in which he goes snucks.

Snuff.
1. Powdered tobacco prepared to be sniffed up into the nostrils. {1683-}

1723 *Amer. Wkly. Mercury* 8 Aug. 2/2 There is to be Sold, Choice Good Snuff (lately Imported from London). **1767** *Holyoke Diaries* 29 Began a bottle of Snuff. **1794** *Ann 3d Congress* 722 The House then took up the bill for laying a duty on snuff and refined sugar. **1855** BARNUM *Life* 89 A 'bean' in his box ... imparted a much improved flavor to the snuff. **1891** RYAN *Pagan* 130 People from the 'wooden' country ... [left] behind them a fine aroma of snuff and tobacco.

+b. *To rub snuff*, to dip and put snuff on the teeth, gums, etc. Also *to chew snuff*.
See also DIG *v.* 4, DIP *v.* 3.
1849 *Knickerb.* XXXIV. 117 The 'gude woman' sat in the corner 'rubbing snuff,' or 'dipping.' **1877** [see DIG *v.* 4]. **1891** RYAN *Pagan* 105 [Does] your deity of the lower world ... chew snuff?

+2. *In great snuff*, showily, gaily; *in high snuff*, in high feather.

1829 ROYALL *Pennsylvania* I. 26 One of the females . . . was dressed in great *snuff*, (as we say in the west). **1840** DANA *Two Years* 149 The Sandwich-Islanders rode down, and were in 'high snuff.'

3. Attrib. and comb. with *bean, bob, bottle*, etc.

1732 *S.C. Gazette* 24/1 Lost on Saturday last, between Charlestown and the Quarter-House, a Snuff-Mill. **1796** *Boston Directory* 243 Elliot, Simon, snuff manufacturer, No. 51, State street. **1827** DRAKE & MANSFIELD *Cincinnati* 65 Three Tobacco and Snuff Factories. **1845** GREEN *Texian Exped.* 138 He found in me no apologist for the 'snuff-dippers' and snuff-eaters of my own country. **1846** CORCORAN *Pickings* 54 [He pulled] out his horn snuff-bob. **1851** HOOPER *Widow Rugby* 94 Did you see . . . that old snuff-bottle? **1857** OLMSTED *Journey through Texas* 382 The Virginia habit of 'dipping' or snuff-chewing. **1869** TOURGEE *Toinette* (1881) 74 The well-laden snuff-brush, with its burden of 'Carolina Belle,' found its way into her mouth. **1871** DE VERE 63 The *dipping-stick* is also called *snuff-swab*. **1880** R. H. DAVIS *Silhouettes* 47 There it is, with German houses and German customs, dropped down right into the midst of Carolina snuff-rubbers, and Georgian clay-eaters. **1894** ROBINSON *Danvis Folks* 105, I'll git . . . a snuff bean, she lost hern a comin' hum. **1898** CANFIELD *Maid of Frontier* 34 [She] had discarded her snuff-twig and bustled about eager to serve her guests.

Snuffbox.

1. A box for holding snuff. {1687-}

1731 Singleton *Social N.Y.* 380 They must not use it when another is speaking, who ought to be heard with too much Respect, to admit of offering at that time from Hand to Hand the Snuff-Box. **1770** *Md. Hist. Mag.* XIII. 73 By the wagon, I send . . . the Tortois shell snuf Box which Motley left Here. **1819** *Columbian Centinel* 21 Aug., E. Copeland, Jr. has for sale a most elegant gold Snuff Box set with Pearls, &c. **1855** COOKE *Ellie* 135 [He] carried in his hand . . . an ebony snuff-box. **1913** MORLEY *Carolina Mts.* 169 In the pocket of many a mountain woman and pretty young girl to-day hides the snuff-box.

+**2. A species of tortoise.**

1877 BARTLETT 699 The most celebrated [terrapin] is the *diamond-back*; there are also the *yellow-bellies, red-bellies, loger-heads, snuff-boxes*, &c.

+**Snuff-dipper.** One who has the habit of dipping snuff. (Cf. DIPPER 6.) — **1845** GREEN *Texian Exped.* 137 We believe the most filthy of all practices is that of your 'snuff-dippers.' **1860** [see MOP 1]. **1896** *Amer. Missionary* Oct. 324 One sister who had been a snuff-dipper for more than twenty years was enabled by God's grace to give up the habit.

✲**Snuffer.**[1] *pl.* An instrument for snuffing out candles. (See also CANDLE SNUFFER 2.) — **1638** *Md. Archives* IV. 48, 1. old p. of brasse snuffers. **1759** *Newport Mercury* 26 June 4/3 Imported . . . Brass and Steel Snuffers. **1806** *Austin P.* I. (1924) 102, 1/2 doz. Steel Spring Snuffers. **1879** *Harper's Mag.* Dec. 34/2 You may buy . . . everything . . . from a pair of snuffers to a horse and wagon.

Snuffer.[2] {a1610-} A porpoise. — **1884** GOODE, etc. *Fisheries* I. 14 The little Harbor Porpoise, *Phocaena brachycion* Cope, [is] known to the fishermen as 'Puffer,' 'Snuffer,' 'Snuffing Pig.' **1911** *Rep. Fisheries 1908* 314/1.

+**Snuff stick.** A soft stick chewed at one end for dipping snuff. — **1870** W. BAKER *New Timothy* 103 Love her, and that snuff-stick 'tween her lips? **1891** RYAN *Pagan* 14 A stripling with a snuff-stick in his cheek. **1913** MORLEY *Carolina Mts.* 170 When a mountain woman refers to her 'toothbrush' the snuff-stick is what she means.

+**Snug fist.** One who spends money grudgingly; a tightwad. Used attrib. — **1837** *Jamestown* (N.Y.) *Jrnl.* 26 July 1/1 'That won't make the pot boil,' said an old snugfist farmer.

+**Snuggers.** [Cf. SNIGGERS.] *I snuggers*, a mild oath. *slang.* — **1843** STEPHENS *High Life N.Y.* II. 202, I snuggers, it made me feel streaked all over.

+**Snum**, *n.* *By snum*, by gosh! — **1825** NEAL *Bro. Jonathan* II. 315 By snum; but you're a foolish fellow!

+**Snum**, *v.* *intr.* *I snum*, I swear. *colloq.* — **1839** *Yale Lit. Mag.* IV. 357 (Th.), I snum, 'taint the thing for me. **1841** *Jamestown* (N.Y.) *Jrnl.* 10 June 4/1, I snum if I could scarcely believe my own natteral senses. **1890** M. J. HOLMES *Marguerite* (1896) 200, I snum if I can do it. **1916** WILSON *Somewhere* 333 Now, I snum! Here she's two-thirty!

✲**Soak**, *v.* +To pawn (something). *colloq.*[2] — **1882** SALA *Amer. Revisited* (1885) 382, [I would be] compelled to . . . 'soak my gem,' and 'Walker my diamonds'—to use the American euphemisms for the act of pawning their jewellery. **1913** LONDON *Valley of Moon* 409, I've had my hard times, an' fought a losin' strike, an' soaked my watch.

+**Soak-about.** (See quot. 1890.) *Obs.* — **1888** *Century Mag.* Jan. 369/2 The young master saw the boys playing at the boisterous and promiscuous 'soak-about.' **1890** HOWELLS *Boy's Town* 83 Soak-about . . . simply consisted of hitting any other boy you could with the ball when you could get it.

Soaked, *a.* {1600-} Of persons: Drunk, or full of liquor. *slang.* — **1737** *Penna. Gazette* 13 Jan. 2. **1852** A. T. JACKSON *Forty-Niner* (1920) 157 He bought his rum by the gallon and kept soaked all the time. **1914** GERRY *Masks of Love* 113 These Dutchmen are so soaked with beer they think they've bought their tickets for a Bayreuth songfest.

✲**Soap.**

✲**1.** Any one of various well-known chemical compounds consisting essentially of a fatty acid and an alkali, used for washing and cleansing.

1645 *Conn. Rec.* I. 473 From Seargeant Bryan more in sope, [£]3. **1726** PENHALLOW *Indian Wars* 28 The housewife . . . having boiling soap on the fire, scalded one of them to death. **1786** FRANKLIN *Writings* IX. 502, I have sent you also 2 Cakes of our fine Soap made of Myrtle Wax. **1802** *Ann. 7th Congress* 2 Sess. 1229 It is expedient to impose a duty . . . on soap. **1858** *Santa Fe Gazette* 22 May 1/1 We have succeeded in saving them [merchants] the trouble of going to St. Louis to buy their Soap and Candles. **1903** *Smart Set* IX. 96 Suppose you lost the soap in the tub.

+**2. Money, esp. that used for corrupt purposes.** *slang.*

1836 *Quarter Race Ky.* 24 When you offered to bet on the sorrel, I was out of soap. **1885** *Mag. Amer. Hist.* April 394/2 Soap.—Originally used by the Republican managers during the campaign of 1880, as the cipher for 'money' in their telegraphic dispatches. In 1884 it was revived as a derisive war cry aimed at the Republicans by their opponents. **1890** *Stock Grower & Farmer* 18 Jan. 4/4 The promoters of one or two wild cat irrigation schemes in this territory have secured laudatory notices . . . by the use of liberal quantities of 'soap.' **1894** *Congress. Rec.* 18 May 4920/1 A distinguished ex-President, now dead, said that soap was needed in a great campaign.

3. In special combinations.

Soap barrel, a barrel in which soft soap is kept; *s. boom*, a sudden rise in the commercial importance of soap; *s. chandler*, a dealer in soap; *s. cup*, a soap dish; *s. day*, a day on which homemade soap is prepared; *s. establishment*, =SOAP FACTORY; *s. house*, a house in which soap is made or stored; *s. oil*, (see quotation); *s. rock*, =SOAPSTONE 1; *s. stick*, transf., a gun; *s. tub*, a tub for waste to be used in making soap.

1873 BAILEY *Life in Danbury* 84 The victuals . . . tasted as though they had been fished out of the soap barrel. **1879** in Walsh *Lit. Curiosities* 114, I am looking for a soap boom every day. **1831** PECK *Guide* 296 A soap and tallow chandler. **1882** 'M. HARLAND' *Eve's Daughters* 69 [If you wish] to know whether your hostess superintended in person the preparation of your bed-chamber, consult the soap-cup. **1805** *Pocumtuc Housewife* (1906) 47 On soap day morning get breakfast out of the way early. **1861** *Vanity Fair* 6 April 157/2 Mr. Riggs had a large soap establishment. **1698** *Essex Inst. Coll.* III. 157/1, I give unto my beloved wife my . . . garding and yard . . . and the sope house. **1909** *Cent. Suppl.* 891/1 *Soap-oil*, the trade-name of the lowest of four grades of summer yellow cotton-seed oil. It is . . . used in soap-making. **1792** BELKNAP *Hist. New-Hampshire* III. 192 At Orford on Connecticut river, is found the Soap-rock. **1835** LONGSTREET *Ga. Scenes* 219 Wait till you see him lift the old Soap-stick, and draw a bead upon the bull's-eye. **1763** in Singleton *Social N.Y.* 360 The inside [of the rolls was] so bad that it was fit for no other use than the soap tub.

Soap apple. {1760} +(See quot. 1891.) — **1864** WEBSTER 1252/2. **1891** *Cent.* 5741/3 *Soap-plant*, . . . one of several plants whose bulbs serve the purpose of soap; particularly, the Californian *Chlorogalum pomeridianum*, of the lily family. . . . Also called *soap-apple* and *soap-bulb*, and . . . *amole*.

Soapberry. Any one of various trees of the genus *Sapindus*, especially *S. saponaria*. {1693-, of the fruit; 1716-} In full *soapberry tree*. {1725-} — **1818** NUTTALL *N. Amer. Plants* 257 Soap-berry. . . . Seacoast of Georgia. **1868** *Amer. Naturalist* II. 474n., The seeds of *Sapindus saponaria* (soap berry) would, probably, [serve to dress deer-skins]. **1897** SUDWORTH *Arborescent Flora* 295. **1919** *Smithsonian Rep.* 1917, 384 In addition to these are the paradise tree or bitterwood; soapberry tree [etc.].

✲**Soap-boiler.** A soap-maker. — **1637** *Boston Rec.* 18 George Woodward, sopeboylar, was found a delinquent. **1698** SEWALL *Letter-Book* I. 199 Mary Dafforne . . . [is] one of the surviving Daughters and Coheirs of Mr. Richard Woodey, . . . Soape Boyler. **1769** *Phila. Ordinances* (1812) 29 Distillers, soap-boilers and others . . . [discharge] stinking liquors. **1863** 'M. HARLAND' *Husks* 213 Mrs. Greyling's paternal progenitor was an opulent soap-boiler.

+**Soap bulb.** =SOAP APPLE. — [**1876** LINDLEY & MOORE *Treas. Botany* (rev. ed) 1279/2 *Chlorogalum pomeridianum*. . . . The bulbous root, when nipped in water, makes a lather . . . : hence it is known as the Soap-bulb.] **1891** [see SOAP APPLE].

Soap factory. A factory in which soap is made. {1861-} — **1840** *Niles' Nat. Reg.* 18 April 112/2 A frame soap factory was entirely destroyed. **1882** SWEET & KNOX *Texas Siftings* 66 Menger . . . ran a soap factory. **1923** WATTS *L. Nichols* 8 At Deercreek Valley station on the Big Four . . . [were] the soap- and glue-factories and the desiccating-plants.

Soap fat. 'The refuse of kitchens, used in making soap' (W. '79). In attrib. use. — **1837** NEAL *Charcoal Sk.* (1838) 95 Ever since these black stones was brought to town . . . them soap-fat and hickory-ashes men, has been going down. **1864** 'MARK TWAIN' *Sketches* (1926) 122 Those who may have kitchen refuse to sell, can leave orders and our soap-fat carts will visit the corner designated. **1877** *Harper's Mag.* Feb. 424/2 All the bits and ends . . . find their way to the soap-fat man and the swill tub.

Soapfish. 1. (See quot. 1891.) +2. (See quot. 1896.) — (1) [**1876** GOODE *Cat. Fishes of Bermudas* 60 A 'Soap-fish' also occurs, probably either *Rhypticus saponaceus* . . . or *Promicropterus maculatus*.] **1891** *Cent.* 5741/3 *Soap-fish*, a serranoid fish of the genus *Rhypticus* . . . : so called from the soapy skin. **1903** T. H. BEAN *Fishes N.Y.* 541. (2) **1896** JORDAN & EVERMANN *Check-List Fishes* 297 *Synodus foetens*. Lizard-fish; Lagarto; Soap-fish. Cape Cod to Brazil.

+**Soap gentian.** A common gentian (*Dasystephana saponaria*) of eastern North America. — **1817-8** EATON *Botany* (1822) 288. **1840**

DEWEY *Mass. Flowering Plants* 147 Soap Gentian. The leaves resemble some kinds of Saponaria, or Soapwort. **1869** FULLER *Flower Gatherers* 308 By some botanists this species has been confounded with the . . . *Soap-Gentian.*

+**Soap gourd.** *S.* A gourd used as a container for soft soap. — **1835** CROCKETT *Tour* 192, I'd give my head for a soap-gourd that Andrew Jackson never made the proposition. *c***1870** BAGBY *Old Va. Gentleman* 269 Benjamin dipped his paint-brush into the soap-gourd, . . . and kept on shaving. **1884** 'CRADDOCK' *Tenn. Mts.* 11 Ye ain't wantin' ter gin Vander the soap-gourd to drink outn'.

Soap grease. Grease for use in making soap. Also attrib. — **1805** *Pocumtuc Housewife* (1906) 47 Put it in the soap-grease barrel down cellar. **1867** HARRIS *Sut Lovingood* 251 Cum out yere, . . . yer wife's dam barril ove soap-grease, soften'd wif unbought whisky. **1880** DEMING *Adirondack Stories* 165 Large sections of the [bear] flesh were furtively used by the housewives for soap-grease.

Soap kettle. A kettle in which soap is made. — **1867** HARRIS *Sut Lovingood* 72 The ol'est gal wer sturn fus' in a soap-kittil. **1884** 'MARK TWAIN' *H. Finn* xxxiv, Tom he went to the soap-kettle . . . and fetched back the iron thing they lift the lid with. **1906** LYNDE *Quickening* 2 The iron . . . [is] just as good for plow-points and the like as it is for soap-kittles.

+**Soap lock.** A lock of hair, esp. a long earlock, soaped to make it lie smooth; one who wears such a lock; a rowdy or rough. *slang. Obs.* Also attrib. — **1840** *Picayune* 30 Aug. 2/2 Howard . . . is described as . . . wearing moustaches and soaplocks. **1848** BARTLETT 279 *Round-rimmers,* . . . in the city of New York, a name applied to a large class of dissipated young men by others called Bowery Boys and Soap-locks. **1852** *Knickerb.* XXXIX. 153 Some wore it [the hair] plastered down smoothly and straightly, in the most approved 'soap-lock' styles. **1887** *Harper's Mag.* March 643/2 There was also the Chatham Theatre, . . . beloved of newsboys and 'soaplocks.' **1891** WELCH *Recoll. 1830–40* 30 [Dickens wore] long hair and earlocks which were then denominated as 'soap-locks,' but deemed vulgar, except for the dudes and 'Bowery boys' of those days.

*∗**Soap-maker.** One who makes soap. — **1637** *Essex Inst. Coll.* IX. 58 Browne a sopemaker desireth admittance to the towne and is accepted. **1711** *N.C. Col. Rec.* I. 764 Women [are] Soap makers Starch makers [etc.]. **1838** HAWTHORNE *Note-books* (1932) 37 The soap-maker dropped his head, with a little snort, as it were, of wounded feeling. **1872** MCCLELLAN *Golden State* 53 They were good . . . soap-makers, herders of flocks, and tillers of the soil.

+**Soap plant.** Any one of various plants some part of which may be used as soap.

Among the more common of these plants are those of the genera *Agave, Yucca,* etc., of the southwestern states and Mexico, and the California plant, *Chlorogalum pomeridianum.* (Cf. AMOLE, SOAP APPLE, etc.)

1844 GREGG *Commerce of Prairies* I. 160 Among the wild productions of New Mexico is the *palmilla*—a species of palmetto, which might be termed the soap-plant. **1859** BARTLETT 425 *Soap-Plant,* (*Chlorogalum pomeridianum,*) a plant common in California and New Mexico, . . . which, when pounded and broken, answers the purposes of soap. **1873** COZZENS *Marvellous Country* 115 The soap-plant grew all around them in profusion. **1915** ARMSTRONG & THORNBER *Western Wild Flowers* 12 Amole Soap Plant. . . . The bulbs form a lather in water.

Soaproot. {1846–} +(See quots. 1891, 1909.) — **1891** *Cent.* 5742/1 *Soaproot,* . . . a Californian bulbous plant, *Leucocrinum montanum,* of the lily family. . . . Soaproot is used by the Digger Indians to take trout. **1898** A. M. DAVIDSON *Calif. Plants* 164 The bulbs of our soap-root are also used as soap. **1907** HODGE, etc. *Amer. Indians* I. 462/2 In parts of California extensive use was made of soap root and other plants for [drugging fish]. **1909** *Cent. Suppl.* 1236/2 *Soaproot,* . . . the soapwort, *Saponaria officinalis.* . . . The soap-plant, *Chlorogalum pomeridianum.*

Soapstone.
1. A massive variety of talc having a smooth, soapy feel. {1681–}

1774 *Md. Hist. Mag.* XVI. 30 The whole face of the Hill . . . Consists of vast irregular Broken Rocks of Soap Stone. **1850** *Western Journal* IV. 359 The whole soil is largely interspersed with a formation of marl and earthy limestone, so tenacious in some places as to . . . give the appearance of the yellow soap stone of our streams. **1892** *Vt. Agric. Rep.* XII. 133 In Waterville there is an inexhaustible quarry of soapstone. **1902** [see CHUCK-FULL *a.*].

+**2.** A piece of such stone used, when heated, as a griddle, foot-warmer, etc.

1887 *Courier-Journal* 29 Jan. 6/2 The Flower Mission . . . has already received and distributed more than two dozen of these soap-stones. **1890** *Century Mag.* XL. 531 [He] fished up a disused soapstone from somewhere, put it on the stove . . . , and stood erect and patient . . . till the soapstone was warm. **1905** LINCOLN *Partners* 28 Tempy, you do up that soapstone for his feet.

3. Attrib. and comb. with *back log, bag, cutter,* etc.

1810 *Columbian Centinel* 27 Jan. 4/2 Just received, a few soap-stone Back Logs, of large size. **1811** MEASE *Philadelphia* 352 Having crossed the Schuylkill at the ferry, [you may] proceed along its shore, visiting . . . a soap stone quarry. **1849** *New Eng. Farmer* I. 252 Cakes on a soapstone griddle required no fat to keep them from sticking. **1851** HOOPER *Widow Rugby* 45 Bill drew out his large soap-stone pipe. **1876** KNIGHT 2201/1 The softer, neater, and greatly superior article, known as soapstone pen-

cils, [is] made from a peculiar stone found near Castleton, Vt. **1878** COOKE *Happy Dodd* 93 Mrs. Ives gave it to me for a soapstone bag. **1882** MC-CABE *New York* 617 He was apprenticed to learn the trade of a grate-setter and soapstone-cutter. **1883** *Century Mag.* Aug. 596/2 He was sitting . . . with his feet on the hearth of the open soap-stone stove.

Soap weed. {1607–} +Any one of various soap plants found in the western and southwestern states. — **1848** ROBINSON *Santa Fe Exped.* 50 Here the soap-weed becomes almost a tree. **1897** LEWIS *Wolfville* 298 A leetle to the left of that soap-weed. **1906** *Springfield W. Repub.* 27 Sept. 3 The greatest, as well as most common, of all cacti is the 'soap weed.' **1923** J. H. COOK *On Old Frontier* 95 The sand cherries were ripe and at their best, as also were the blossoms on the soapweeds.

Soapwood. {1732–, W. Indies} *local.* +=DEER GRASS. *Obs.* — [**1743** CLAYTON *Flora Virginica* 41 *Rhexia calycibus glabris.* . . . Soopwood. **1771** J. R. FORSTER *Flora Amer. Septentr.* 17 *Rhexia virginica,* Soapwood.] **1791** MUHLENBERG *Index Florae* 168 *Rhexia,* Soap-wood.

*∗**Soapwort.** **1. a.** A plant of the genus *Saponaria.* +**b.** =COW-HERB. Used with specifying terms. +**2.** =SOAP WEED. — (1) **1791** MUHLENBERG *Index Florae* 169 *Saponaria,* Soapwort. **1817–8** Field soapwort [see FIELD 5 b]. **1843** TORREY *Flora N.Y.* I. 103 *Saponaria Vaccaria.* . . . Perfoliate Soap-wort. (2) **1890** CUSTER *Following Guidon* 202 The soapwort with its scentless blossom . . . was really used as a substitute for soap.

*∗**Soapwort gentian.** +=SOAP GENTIAN. — **1814** BIGELOW *Florula Bostoniensis* 64 Soapwort Gentian. . . . A very fine plant, distinguished by its large purple flowers. **1847** WOOD *Botany* 453 Soapwort Gentian. . . . Leaves . . . resembling those of the common soapwort.

Soary, *a.* Of or pertaining to soaring. — **1861** *N.Y. Tribune* 10 Oct. 6/2 The newspaper correspondents from Western Virginia are a very soary or a very hoaxy set of fellows. **1899** TARKINGTON *Gentleman from Ind.* ii, The orator winged away to soary heights.

Sociable. {1613–}
1. An open, four-wheeled, pleasure carriage having seats facing each other. *Obs.* {1794–}

1780 *N.J. Archives* 2 Ser. IV. 223 Wanted to exchange, a neat sulkey, almost new, for a sociable or handy one horse chair, equally good. **1825** *Catawba Jrnl.* 17 May, The subscriber . . . is now finishing . . . Sociables, Sulkeys, and a Mail Stage.

+**2.** An informal social gathering, often under the auspices of a church.

See also CHURCH SOCIABLE.

1826 LONGFELLOW in S. Longfellow *H. W. Longfellow* I. 74 [I] went with them to a little 'sociable' in the evening, where we had dancing. **1867** 'LACKLAND' *Homespun* 215 [The minister] is expected to lend his presence at all the bees, sociables, and society meetings. **1893** Philips *Making of Newspaper* 173, I was . . . supplying the managers of rural Sunday-school sociables with charcoal drawings of the donkey with the adjustable tail. **1920** LEWIS *Main Street* 59 We had the dandiest professional reciter at the Pythian Sisters sociable last winter.

+**3.** (See quot. 1876.) *Obs.*

1851 CIST *Cincinnati* 202 Dressing bureaus, sociables, and *vis-à-vis* are sure to catch the visitor's eye, and to open the visitor's purse. **1872** *Atlantic Mo.* May 544 She was lying on a little sociable or sofa, as he entered. **1876** KNIGHT 2234/1 *Sociable,* . . . a kind of couch with a curved S-shaped back, for two persons who sit partially facing each other.

Social, *n.* {1632–} +=SOCIABLE 2. {1893–} — **1872** *Newton Kansan* 22 Aug. 5/5 Parties, balls and socials . . . will be supplied with Fresh Oysters at all times at the old oyster depot. **1886** EBBUTT *Emigrant Life* 58 Sometimes, too, a 'social' is turned into a dance after the Methodists have gone home. **1922** A. BROWN *Old Crow* 225 There was always a line of cleavage at prayer-meeting, as at teas and 'socials,' between old and young.

*∗ **Social,** *a.*
1. Composed of those associating in a common service or attending an event for pleasure and relaxation.

1840 *S. Lit. Messenger* VI. 505/1 Mr. Hopper, notwithstanding the many privileges he had possessed in attending . . . social-prayer-associations, still remained a man of sin. **1842** BUCKINGHAM *Slave States* I. 546 The family give what is called 'a social party.' **1860** HOLMES *E. Venner* vii, Tickets to this 'Social Ball' were soon circulated. **1865** *Atlantic Mo.* March 366/1 In the larger cities of the East, . . . the club-house, the social-assembly, and a variety of public gatherings . . . take from the lecture-audiences the class that furnishes the best material in the smaller cities. **1871** BAGG *At Yale* 219 In the evening came a 'social reception' at the Art Building. **1880** *Cimarron News & Press* 19 Aug. 3/1 A social hop will be held in the court house to-morrow night. **1900** DIX *Deacon Bradbury* 24 She found resolute time for leading the little social functions of the town life. **1925** BRYAN *Memoirs* 28 In memory of these religious social gatherings my good wife has been led to set aside certain days for the bringing together of the representatives of the various denominations in a social way.

2. In special combinations.

Social capital, advantage in society; *s. coterie,* =social set; *s. equality,* equality in the social order, especially as between white people and Negroes; *s. gospel,* the gospel as it relates to one's place and conduct in society; *s. leader,* a leader in society or of a group in society; *s. letter,* a letter prompted by friendliness, geniality, etc., as distinguished from a business letter; *s. set*, a set, circle, or coterie in society; *s. standing*, standing or repute in society; *s.-status colonizer*, a person not legally resident in the ward in which he attempts to vote but having status in the community; *s. success*, success in society; *s. swim*, the social life, activities, etc., of those prominent in society; *s. work*, work in behalf of an underprivileged class or group in society; *s. worker*, one engaged in social work.

1877 HOWELLS *Out of Question* 26 As long as he could make social capital out of his obtrusive services to us he was very profuse with them. **1888** CLEWS *28 Yrs. Wall St.* 119 It was a kind of mutual admiration society, Drew being the king-pin of the social coterie. **1904** PAGE in *McClure's Mag.* April 621/2 The new missionaries went counter to the deepest prejudice of the Southern people...., and were believed to teach social equality. **1920** *3d Nat. Country Life Conf. Proc.* 61 It is the country church that needs to preach the social gospel. **1893** *Harper's Mag.* April 681/1 He could only gain his peep into the charmed circle if his political influence should become of importance to a social leader. **1921** T. A. CLARK *When You Write* 58 The friendly or social letter should have a considerably different form from the business letter. **1895** *Four Amer. Universities* 145 There are no Greek-letter fraternities to gather in and crystallize social sets. **1870** 'MARK TWAIN' *Sk., New & Old* 190 If a person of good family and high social standing steals anything, they call it *kleptomania.* **1870** *Congress. Globe* 13 April 2655/1 [G. S. Repplier] was a social status colonizer. **1870** *Scribner's Mo.* I. 65 She was the cap and crown of his social success. **1906** QUICK *Double Trouble* 234 Miss Scarlett ... was generally esteemed for ... her contributions to the sensations of a not overturbulent social swim. **1920** *3d Nat. Country Life Conf. Proc.* 192 The social-work agencies ... have not realized ... that the training of people to do social work as such in the country [etc.]. **1923** WATTS *L. Nichols* 39 Social workers, juvenile-court officials, humanitarians of every brand, would long since have reported the case.

+Social Band. A secret organization formed in Missouri in 1854 to carry Kansas for slavery. Now hist. — **1883** ANDREAS *Hist. Kansas* 90 Secret lodges were organized under various names—'Social Band' [etc.]. **1887** *Century Mag.* April 868/1 Secret societies under various names, such as 'Blue Lodges,' 'Friends Society,' 'Social Band,' 'Sons of the South,' were organized and affiliated.

Social club. A club organized to promote pleasant and profitable association among its members. — **1792** WEBSTER in E. Ford *Notes on N. Webster* I. 363 A number of Gentlemen meet at my house for the purpose of forming a social Club. **1881** *Ore. State Jrnl.* 15 Jan. 5/1 The social club had a most pleasant meeting.

+Social hall.

1. A drawing-room or salon on a river steamer for the use of the passengers.

1847 ROBB *Squatter Life* 154 Tom was picked up and carried into the Social Hall. **1858** *Harper's Mag.* Sept. 564/1 [Others] were seated in the 'social hall,' engaged in the fascinating game of 'poker.' **1872** EGGLESTON *End of World* 172 The throng of passengers ... drank with each other at the bar, smoked in the 'social hall.'

2. A large hall for assembly purposes; a building having such a hall.

1862 *N. Amer. Rev.* July 209 These dwellings, with the adjoining Council-House, History Office, Social Hall, and Hotel, give honor to the centre of the Mormon city. **1888** *Amer. Humorist* (London) 5 Aug. 8/1 In the Social hall are checkers, chess [etc.].

Socialist. One who believes in or advocates socialism. {1833–} [**1846** WORCESTER 674/2 *Socialist*, an advocate for socialism. *Ch. Ob.*] **1867** W. H. DIXON *New America* II. 225 The Perfectionist went far beyond the Socialist, the Shaker, and the Mormon, in his renunciation. **1887** F. A. WALKER in *Forum* May 231 That which characterizes the proper Socialist is a ... dislike of competition. **1895** *Chicago Tribune* 6 April 1 What the Populists and Socialists call the capitalistic class ... lives on its income from rents and bonds. **1920** [see DIVVY *v.* (1)].

b. Attrib. with *doctrine, meeting, paper.*

1896 *Internat. Typogr. Union Proc.* 47/1 This scheme ... found ready support ... from those who were opposed to the socialist doctrines. **1911** Socialist meeting [see COVER *v.* 3]. **1917** SINCLAIR *King Coal* 55 Minetti ... took an Italian Socialist paper.

+Social library. A library maintained, either by ownership of shares or by payment of subscription fees, by the particular group of persons entitled to use it. — **1814** *Mass. H. S. Coll.* 2 Ser. III. 102 There is a social library, which consists of about one hundred volumes. **1819** E. DANA *Geogr. Sk.* 80 There are two market houses, a bank, a printing office, and a good social library. **1835** *S. Lit. Messenger* I. 273 *Lectures and social Libraries* ... are among the chief glories of New England. **1910** BOSTWICK *Amer. Pub. Library* 7 The joint-stock form of library is in its simplest form a book club, as in the so-called 'social libraries' of Massachusetts.

Social science. Any one of various sciences, as economics, sociology, etc., that deal with various aspects of human society. {1846–} Also attrib. — [**1785** J. ADAMS *Works* IX. 540 The social science will never be much improved until the people unanimously know and consider themselves as the fountain of power.] **1849** *S. Lit. Messenger* XV. 77/2 On the Importance of the Social Sciences in the present day. **1897** HOWELLS *Open-eyed Conspiracy* vii, There's nothing for it but the Social Science Congress.

+Social sparrow. The chipping sparrow, *Spizella passerina.* — **1869** BURROUGHS in *Galaxy Mag.* Aug. 139/2 The social-sparrow, ... *alias* 'red-headed chipping-bird,' is the smallest of the sparrows. **1917** *Birds of Amer.* III. 41 Its confidence in the friendliness of man seems to be no less than that of the Robin and Bluebird, whence one of its names, the Social Sparrow.

∗ Society.

+1. a. *New Eng.* A parish or part of a town or settlement having its own place of worship. **b.** A Protestant church group whose members attend the same place of worship.

1739 *Suffield Doc. Hist.* 275 The Inhabitants of the West part of said Town ... [ask] to be Set off into a Distinct and Seperate Society. **1775** Baptist society [see BAPTIST 2]. **1809** KENDALL *Travels* I. 106 A society [in Conn.] is a community or corporation, established, for the most part, for the twofold object of religious worship and common schooling; but, in some instances, for religious worship only. It is also, at least in a *school* view, either the whole, or part of a town, defined by geographical limits. **1828** WEBSTER, In Connecticut, a number of families united and incorporated for the purpose of supporting public worship, is called an ecclesiastical society. **1831** PECK *Guide* 260 The *Christ-ians*, as they are termed, have some societies in Illinois. **1889** FREEMAN *Far-away Melody* (1891) 257 More people went into the Baptist Church, whose Society was much the larger of the two.

2. A number of persons united *for* a specified purpose. {1763–}

1797 *Ann. 4th Congress* 2 Sess. 1835 A society for the promotion of Agriculture ought to be established at the Seat of Government. **1822** MORSE *Rep. Indian Affairs* I. 75 Society for promoting the general welfare of the Indian tribes within the United States. **1867** DIXON *New America* II. 175 Are you a member of the Society for Promoting Equal Rights, as between the two sexes? **1906** *Forum* Sept. 571 The Society for the Suppression of Unnecessary Noise requests this Association [of automobile manufacturers] to assist in its movement.

+3. Among the Indians, a secret organization having some special religious or other significance.

1804 CLARK in *Lewis & C. Exped.* I. (1904) 130 Those who become Members of this Society must be brave active young men who take a Vow never to give back let the danger be what it may. **1886** *Rep. Bureau Amer. Ethnol.* 1885–86 151 The persons admitted into the society are firmly believed to possess the power of communing with various supernatural beings. **1906** [see DAKOTA].

+4. Short for SOCIETY OF FRIENDS.

1849 CHAMBERLAIN *Ind. Gazetteer* 73 The Society have about 5,000 children in this State.

+5. A secret club or organization among students, esp. a fraternity.

See also GREEK-LETTER SOCIETY, SECRET SOCIETY.

1871 BAGG *At Yale* 51 The sub-Freshman is pledged to his society months before he approaches the college walls. **1889** *Century Mag.* March 799/2 He was a member of neither of these societies, but of Delta Upsilon, a non-secret fraternity. **1915** F. W. SHEPARDSON *Phi Beta Kappa* 14 On Saturday, Jan. 6, 1781 five members [decided that] ... the society should disband.

+6. *attrib.* and *comb.* **a.** In sense 5 with *badge, pin, tax.*

1871 BAGG *At Yale* 65 No one without society badge or admission ticket could pass the entrance. *Ib.* 205 No undergraduate can shirk paying his 'society tax.' **1876** *Wide Awake* III. 99/1 His brother Tom ... wore a 'society pin.'

b. Designating persons or things belonging to, or having to do with, fashionable society.

1875 HUTTON *Plays & Players* 133 The unhealthful tendencies of many of the 'society,' 'upholstery,' 'emotional,' and 'Traviata' plays of the present. **1882** McCABE *New York* 228 An engagement ... is promptly announced in one of the 'Society journals.' **1897** HOWELLS *Open-eyed Conspiracy* iv, There isn't any society life at Saratoga that I can see. **1902** MACGOWAN *Last Word* 158 You are not happy ... doing those society letters which we know you loathe. **1902** BANKS *Newspaper Girl* 301 Miss Elizabeth Banks is society editor of this paper. **1923** 'BOWER' *Parowan Bonanza* 151, I don't aspire to be ... any society bird.

Society girl. A girl who is active in society, esp. one busy with social functions, entertainments, etc. — **1875** STOWE *We & Neighbors* 205 My sisters ... are society girls in the best sense. **1882** 'M. HARLAND' *Eve's Daughters* 256 The most useless, and frequently the most pitiable product of modern civilization is the Society Girl, bound to a wheel that whirls through a stated round of calls, receptions [etc.]. **1923** WATTS *L. Nichols* 209 Those society girls—— There were plenty more of them on the North Hill.

+Society hall. A hall in which members of a college society meet. — **1860** *Ladies' Repository* Jan. 60/2 [We] settled the affairs of the whole world in the society halls. **1871** BAGG *At Yale* 274 The hall, of more than twice the capacity of the society-halls, was crowded. **1887** *Lippincott's Mag.* Aug. 291 Others spend their evenings at the theatre, at their society hall, or in calling on their young lady acquaintances.

Society house. {1888–} +A house in which members of a college society or of a religious group live or meet. — **1887** *Lippincott's Mag.* Oct. 574 The candidate is invited to visit the society-house. **1891** EARLE

Sabbath 105 The New Canaan Church built on the green beside their meeting-house a fine 'Society House.'

+Society library. 1. =SOCIAL LIBRARY. **2.** The library maintained in a society (q.v., sense 1). — **(1) 1754** in Singleton *Social N.Y.* 339 Notice is hereby given to the proprietors of the New York Society Library that the books . . . are placed for the present . . . in their library room in the City Hall. **1823** J. & R. C. MORSE *Traveller's Guide* (1826) 14/1 The library [of Amherst Coll.] . . . contains 900 volumes, and the Society libraries have about 400 more. **1837** A. GREENE *Glance at N.Y.* 222 The New York Society Library . . . began [1754] with about 700 volumes. The price of a share was $12.50. **(2) 1809** KENDALL *Travels* I. 136 The number of books, in the respective town or society . . . libraries, is very small.

Society news. News of events or happenings in fashionable society. — **1875** C. F. Wingate *Views & Interviews* 93 How about society news? **1907** GIVEN *Making a Newspaper* 63 What is known as 'Society News' is collected by reporters, usually women, who depend upon acquaintances for some information.

Society of Friends. A religious body founded in England under the leadership of George Fox (1624–91) and commonly called Quakers. {1665- (J. Wiggan *Antichrist's Strongest Hold Overturned*)} — **1782** CRÈVECŒUR *Letters* 123 There are two places of worship, one for the society of Friends, the other for that of Presbyterians. **1817** *Ann. 14th Congress* 2 Sess. 442 Mr. Hopkins presented a petition of the religious society of Friends in Pennsylvania. **1869** *Atlantic Mo.* Oct. 474/1 The Mennists in many outward circumstances very much resemble the Society of Friends. **1900** *Congress. Rec.* 4 Jan. 646/2 Some of the writers of these letters are Quakers, members of the Society of Friends.

+Society reporter. One who reports society news for a paper. — **1888** [BRAINY *a.*]. **1895** CHAMBLISS *Diary* 250 Some complain of . . . society reporters and other public pests. **1916** SEITZ *Training for Newsp. Trade* 37 The society reporter . . . is well employed.

*Sock. 1. A knitted or woven short stocking worn esp. by men and children. **2.** *To knock the socks from*, to excel in some way. — **(1) 1747** FRANKLIN *Poor Richard Improved 1748* 3 A Man makes use of three Pair of Socks, of coarse Blanketing, or Duffeld for the Feet. **1830** PICKERING *Inquiries Emigrant* 72 In winter the latter [*i.e.*, women] wear stockings, and the former [*i.e.*, men] socks. **1862** JACKSON in M. A. Jackson *Gen. Jackson* 363 Don't send me any more socks. **1924** *Sears, Roebuck & Co. Cat.* No. 148, 233 Match their many little dresses and suits with any . . . of these prettily colored socks. **(2) 1864** *Harper's Mag.* Feb. 427/1 The good-natured people . . . predicted that when he took his seat in the House he would 'knock the socks' from some who had more reputation than he.

+Sockdolager. Also sogdollager, socdoliger. [Corruption of *doxology*.]

1. A tremendous blow; a finisher. *slang.* Also *fig.*

1830 *Va. Lit. Museum* 6 Jan. 479 *Sockdologer*, 'a decisive blow'—one, in the slang language 'Capable of setting a man a thinking.' **1859** *Harper's Mag.* Dec. 138/2 Page struck the unsuspecting and astonished individual a 'sockdollager.' **1865** *Jamestown* (N.Y.) *Jrnl.* 28 July 1/6 [The elephant] visited Typoo [another elephant] with a sock-dolager that fairly sent him on his beam ends. **1892** GUNTER *Miss Dividends* 36 'Won't it be a surprise?' . . . 'Yes,—I—reckon it will be a—sockdolager.' **1903** HAPGOOD *Autobiog. of Thief* 322 You're disfigured enough without my giving you another sockdolager.

2. An unusually large or exceptional person or thing.

1838 COOPER *Home as Found* II. 72 There is but one 'sogdollager' in the universe, and that is in Lake Oswego. **1842** *Knickerb.* XIX. 223 This [remark] seemed to be a 'socdoliger;' (which translated into Latin, means a *ne plus ultra*). **1891** COOKE *Huckleberries* 41 That's the sockdolager, old feller. **1910** *Dialect Notes* III. 458 *Sockdologer*, a very tremendous person or thing. 'Wasn't that a sockdologer of a man?'

3. (See quotation.)

1848 BARTLETT 319 *Socdolager*, a patent fish-hook, having two hooks which close upon each other by means of a spring as soon as the fish bites.

*Sod. *attrib.* and *comb.*

1. Designating structures built entirely or partially of sods or turf.

1838 ELLSWORTH *Valley of Wabash* 35 Sod fences, with a hedge of locust or the hawthorn, are found to be better and far neater than the ordinary ones. **1886** WILDER *Annals of Kan.* 849 F. H. Barnhart . . . [sends] a photo of a sod school house. **1892** in *S. Dak. Hist. Coll.* I. 46 They built three dwelling houses, a store, a sawmill and a sod fort. **1896** HOWELLS *Impressions & Exp.* 144 Their domiciles can be best likened for . . . discomfort to the dugouts or sod-huts of the settlers on the great plains. **1904** Sod-lodge [see HOGAN]. **1913** CATHER *O Pioneers!* 20 To the east, the sod stables, the cattle corral.

2. In special combinations.

Sod knife, a knife for cutting sod; *s.-planted*, of corn, planted on poorly prepared sod land; *s. plot*, a plot on which sod is allowed to form; *s. production*, a crop produced on sod land; *s. wheat*, (see quotation).

1856 *Mich. Agric. Soc. Trans.* VII. 54 D. O. & W. S. Penfield . . . [exhibited a] sod knife. **1879** *Scribner's Mo.* Nov. 134/1 Where it [*sc.* corn] has been sod-planted it is left untouched. **1860** B. ALCOTT *Journals* 329 Work all day on the slope and in the orchard for my sod-plot and strawberry bed. **1872** *Newton Kansan* 22 Aug. 5/2 Its 'sod' productions have

not been excelled in the State. **1841** *Cultivator* VIII. 147 'Sod wheat' is the term given to the first crop on the prairie.

*Soda.

1. Sodium bicarbonate or baking soda. {1851-}

1805 *Pocumtuc Housewife* (1906) 29 A manufactured article called soda is used in conjunction with cream tartar and sweet milk to make light delicious cakes. **1875** [see BISCUIT 2]. **1891** CHASE & CLOW *Industry* II 162 A little soda is added.

+2. In faro, the card which shows face up in the deal box before dealing begins. In full *soda card.*

1864 DICK *Amer. Hoyle* (1866) 208 *The Soda Card* is the top card of the deck when put into the dealing-box, preparatory to a deal. **1902** WILSON *Spenders* 122 That system of mine holds good all through the deal—you can play it from soda to hock and not lose out.

3. In special combinations.

Soda butte, a butte the soil of which contains a large proportion of sodium; *s. grass*, =SALTWEED; *s. mound*, a mound the soil of which is strongly impregnated with sodium; *s. prairie*, (see quotation).

1886 *Congress. Rec.* 14 Dec. 153/2 There are [in Yellowstone Park] hot springs and soda buttes. **1846** *30th Congress 1 Sess.* H. R. Ex. Doc. No. 41, 596 We encamp in soda grass. **1878** BEADLE *Western Wilds* 372 The plain is dotted by soda mounds from five to thirty feet in height. **1859** BARTLETT 426 *Soda-Prairie*, a plain covered with an efflorescence of soda, elsewhere called natron.

+Soda biscuit. A biscuit raised with soda. — **1858** *Harper's Mag.* Aug. 289/1 The green soda-biscuit and patent yeast-rolls of the present are compared with the crisp Johnny-cake of forty years ago. **1883** *Century Mag.* Aug. 527/1 Soda-biscuits delicately made. **1905** WIGGIN *Rose* 37 Who else could [bake] . . . such soda-biscuits, big, feathery, tasting of cream, and hardly needing butter?

+Soda cocktail. (See quot. 1889.) — **1868** *N.Y. Herald* 2 July 4/1 We have the Fourth of July thrown in with . . . its exhilarating associations so conducive of headaches and soda cocktails. **1879** *Newburgh* (N.Y.) *Daily Jrnl.* 22 Aug. 1/5 Well, give me a soda cocktail. **1889** *Cent.* 1081/1 *Soda cocktail*, a glass of soda-water with a little bitters.

+Soda cracker. A thin, crisp, flour cracker made from yeast dough to which soda has been added. — **1863** *Harper's Mag.* Feb. 313/1 Half a pound of soda crackers . . . and one red apple. **1873** BAILEY *Life in Danbury* 88, I ate some cold cabbage and a couple of soda crackers. **1896** *Internat. Typogr. Union Proc.* 54/1, 48 lbs. soda crackers, $2.88.

+Soda fount. =next 1. Also *attrib.* — **1848** [see GIN PALACE]. **1873** *Newton Kansan* 12 June 3/2 Munger & Ross have got their soda fount in full blast. **1904** DERVILLE *Other Side of Story* 110 The soda fount man does a flourishing business.

+Soda fountain. 1. A container for storing and dispensing soda water; also, a place or establishment at which soda water is dispensed from such an apparatus. **2.** A spring of mineral water containing soda. — **(1) 1828** [see MORGAN²]. **1855** *Chicago W. Times* 5 July 3/5 The kind-hearted knight of the soda fountain . . . handed her $5. **1922** TARKINGTON *Gentle Julia* 183 Is the soda fountain still running this late? **(2) 1878** BEADLE *Western Wilds* 372 The soda-fountains . . . boil furiously with a loud, bubbling noise.

+Soda powder. (See quot. 1890.) — **1820** *Columbian Centinel* 1 July 3/6 Maynard & Noyes continue to prepare Soda Powders, of superior quality. **1836** [see DRUG SHOP]. **1890** *Cent.* 4661/2 *Soda powder*, sodium bicarbonate 30 grains, tartaric acid 25 grains.

+Soda shop. A shop at which soda water is sold. — **1820** *Boston Selectmen* 161 All licensed victuallers, retailers, confectioners, and soda shops, must be closed in future on Sundays. **1843** *Knickerb.* XXII. 437 Men rush at the soda-shops. **1862** STRONG *Cadet Life W. Point* 128 The records of the soda shop may be found in the archives of the institution.

+Soda spring. A spring the water of which is impregnated with soda. Also as a proper name. — **1837** IRVING *Bonneville* II. 32 We have heard this also called the Soda spring. **1850** KINGSLEY *Diary* 134 He speaks of many interesting natural curiosities . . . among which are . . . the soda springs. **1890** LANGFORD *Vigilante Days* (1912) 79 At last they reached Soda Springs on Bear River. *a*1918 [see SODA WATER 2].

Soda water.

1. An effervescing beverage, orig. one containing some sodium bicarbonate, but latterly a drink consisting of flavored water highly charged with carbon dioxide. {1802-}

1820 *Columbian Centinel* 1 July 3/6 The reputation of the Powders, as the most convenient and best method of making Soda Water, is becoming well established. **1893** *Harper's Mag.* March 494 There were the same . . . peanuts and soda-water [in Jacksonville as in Asbury Park]. **1922** TARKINGTON *Gentle Julia* 183 You have more calls for soda water than you do for . . . real liquor?

2. Alkaline or saline water occurring in nature.

1872 *Harper's Mag.* Dec. 28/2 This is genuine soda-water—cooking soda with nearly an equal amount of sulphate of soda [etc.]. **1883** *Ib.* Oct. 712/1 In the extreme north [of Utah] is a magnificent subterranean reservoir of first-class soda-water. *a*1918 G. STUART *On Frontier* I. 147 At Soda springs on Bear river we drank our fill of soda water from a spring on the bank.

3. Attrib. and comb. in sense 1 with *apparatus, shop, vender, wagon.*

1825 WOODWORTH *Forest Rose* II. i, Set her up in a soda-water shop, or something of that kind. **1831** *21st Cong. 2 Sess.* H. R. Ex. Doc. No. 49, 52 Chemical Compositions. . . . Soda water apparatus, George Ott, Norfolk, Va. **1861** *Vanity Fair* 9 Feb. 63/1 He thought it was a yaller soda-water or cigar wagon. **1876** INGRAM *Centennial Exp.* 758 Concession contracts: . . . soda water venders, $20,000.

+**Soda-water fountain.** =SODA FOUNTAIN 1. — **1858** VIELÉ *Following Drum* 149 A bakery and even a 'pharmacie,' with a most pretentious soda water fountain, are found here. **1877** MINTURN *Travels West* 24 We made our way towards . . . a Gothic soda-water fountain. **1892** *Harper's Mag.* Dec. 142 [He] increased the apothecary's business by persuading him to send East for a soda-water fountain. **1902** LORIMER *Lett. Merchant* 217 [He] ran a soda-water fountain in the front of his store.

+**Sod corn. 1.** The first crop of corn on heavy prairie land. **2.** Whisky made from such corn. — (1) **1846** FARNHAM *Prairie Land* 214 A very respectable crop of corn, called by the farmers 'sod corn,' may be raised on the broken turf. **1873** *Winfield* (Kansas) *Courier* 22 May 2/3 [They] have been engaged in the manufacture of sod corn whiskey. **1898** [see DENT CORN]. (2) **1878** BEADLE *Western Wilds* 183 Chew's store . . . was the only place that sold bourbon—tothers only 'sod-corn.'

+**Sod crop.** The first crop on heavily sodded prairie land. — **1848** *Rep. Comm. Patents 1847* 539 This gave a sod crop without tending of thirty to forty bushels per acre. **1879** *Scribner's Mo.* Nov. 133/2 The sod crop . . . [is] often the settler's main or only reliance for the first year. **1888** *Congress. Rec.* 9 June 5078/2 Flaxseed or flax in this country [Minn.] is very largely . . . what we call a sod crop.

Sodded, *a.* {1652–} Of soil: Having a sod or turf. - **1874** *Vermont Bd. Agric. Rep.* II. 468 When rain falls upon naked or sodded soils, a portion is evaporated.

+**Soddy.** *W.* Short for SOD HOUSE. — **1893** *Pilgrim Missionary* June 8/1 Brother T—— has a large circuit of three churches, and lives in a 'soddy.' **1916** THOBURN *Stand. Hist. Okla.* II. 718 (*caption*), An Oklahoma Soddy.

+**Sod ground.** Prairie ground having a thick, heavy sod. — **1871** *Ill. Agric. Soc. Trans.* VIII. 238 Next in adaptation is the *sod ground* of our prairie State. **1883** *Rep. Indian Affairs* 98 We thought it useless to break up sod-ground for use one season only.

Sod house. *W.* A house having walls of sods or turf. {1832–} — **1872** *Kansas Mag.* Sept. 225/2 The sod-house of far Western Kansas, the cabin of Texas, and the adobe of Colorado, are not all so fortunate as to have a female occupant. **1889** *N.Y. Pub. Lib. Bul.* XLIV. 114 At one mile pass sod house on right of R. R. where main road joins trail. **1916** EASTMAN *From Deep Woods* 37 Curiosity led me back to the sod house.

+**Sod land.** Prairie land having a heavy sod during the first year of cultivation. — **1856** *Rep. Comm. Patents 1855: Agric.* 262 They were mostly sown upon sod-land. **1881** *Harper's Mag.* June 126/2 His average on sod land or after hemp is thirty-five bushels [of wheat]. **1886** EBBUTT *Emigrant Life in Kan.* 74 Indian corn does not grow so well as these on sod land.

Sodom apple. {1615–} +(See quotation.) — **1891** *Cent.* 5747/3 *Sodom-apple,* . . . sometimes, in the United States, the horse-nettle, *S. Carolinense,* and some similar species.

+**Sod plow.** (See quot. 1876.) — **1854** *Mich. Agric. Soc. Trans.* V. 53 1 sod plow for stiff soil. **1873** BEADLE *Undevel. West* 69 My host was going to Fremont 'to git his sod plow sot and sharped.' **1876** KNIGHT 2238/1 *Sod-plow,* a plow long in the share and mold-board, adapted to cut and overturn sod.

+**Sod (web) worm.** (See quotations.) — **1891** *Cent.* 5747/3 *Sodworm,* the larva of certain pyralid moths, as *Crambus exsiccatus,* which destroys the roots of grass and corn. **1925** HERRICK *Man. Injurious Insects* 308 The Sod Webworms. . . . There are at least six species of moths of the sub-family *Crambinæ* . . . whose larvæ feed on various grasses, weeds, and cereals.

Sofa. A long upholstered couch or lounge suitable for sitting or reclining. {1717–} — **1773** in Singleton *Social N.Y.* 83 [Joseph Cox from London] makes . . . sopha, settees, couches [etc.]. **1830** WATSON *Philadelphia* 183 Formerly they had couches of worsted damask . . . in lieu of what we now call sophas or lounges. **1880** *Harper's Mag.* July 264/1 She took her place upon the sofa. **1910** TOMPKINS *Mothers & Fathers* 43 To have something going on in the room is a relief when you are tied to a sofa.

+**Sofky, Sofkey.** [Creek Indian.] Hominy or thin corn gruel used by the Creeks and other southern Indians. Also attrib. — **1796** HAWKINS *Letters* 28 [She] gave me a basket of corn for my horses, a fowl, some sofkey (hommony) and ground peas. **1845** HOOPER *Simon Suggs' Adv.* 75 She had scarcely time to cook the sophky for her children. **1916** THOBURN *Stand. Hist. Okla.* I. 262 The fermented hominy which was known as 'tah-fula' . . . was the national dish of the Choctaws. The Creeks had a similar dish known as sof-ky.

*****Soft,** *n.* +**1.** A member of a political party advocating paper currency. *Obs.* +**2.** =SOFT-SHELL 3. Now hist. — (1) **1844** *Lexington Observer* 14 Aug. 3/2 The locofocos . . . are divided in that State [Mo.], and are known by the distinctive appellations of the '*Hards*' and '*Softs,*' in consequence of their views upon the currency question. (2) **1853** *N. Y. Tribune* 2 April 3/6 The Softs are composed of the remnants of the Van Buren and Adams party of 1848, and such Hunkers as Secretary Marcy and Gov. Seymour. **1888** BRYCE *Amer. Commw.* II. II. xlvi. 203 The Hunkers and Barnburners . . . subsequently passed into the 'Hards' and the 'Softs.' **1914** [see SOFT-SHELL 3].

*****Soft,** *a.*

*****1.** Of bakery products and cheese: Not firm; yielding readily to pressure.
1721 *Phila. Ordinances* (1812) 16 A biscuit or soft-bread baker. **1805** *Pocumtuc Housewife* (1906) 33 Soft Gingerbread. **1863** in Moore *Women of War* 133 [There were] boxes of tea, coffee, soft crackers, tamarinds, cherry brandy, &c. **1896** *Vt. Agric. Rep.* XV. 23 Fresh or soft cheese, like Neufchatel, is made from sweet milk.

+**2.** Of or pertaining to Soft-shelled Democrats. *Obs.*
1853 *Whig Almanac 1854* 41 Average Soft vote, 96,698. **1856** MACLEOD *F. Wood* 299 He could not really be called 'Hard' or 'Soft,' though a member of the latter organization and in full communion with it. **1859** *Harper's Mag.* Nov. 832/2 The 'Soft' chairman was thrown from the platform.

3. In the names of, or with reference to, aquatic creatures. {1601–}
1792 IMLAY *Western Territory* 154 The soft turtle . . . amply compensates for our having no other testaceous fish. **1871** DE VERE 388 Another tortoise of greater size and equal ferocity is the Softback (*Trionyx ferox*). **1875** *Mich. Gen. Statutes* I. (1882) 580 Nothing in this act contained shall prohibit the catching of soft fish. **1881** INGERSOLL *Oyster-Industry* 248 *Soft Oyster.*—The 'Virginia plant,' or southern oyster (Staten Island sound), as distinguished from the 'hard' native oyster. **1883** *Century Mag.* July 378/2 He then baited his hook with a 'soft craw.' **1883** *Nat. Museum Bul.* No. 27, 469 *Tylosurus marinus.* . . . Silver Gar-fish; Soft Gar; Billfish; Needle-fish. Atlantic coast.

4. In the names of plants and trees. {1785–}
1813 MUHLENBERG *Cat. Plants* 88 *Betula lenta,* Soft birch. **1814** Soft Monarda [see MONARDA]. **1843** TORREY *Flora N.Y.* II. 452 *Trisetum molle.* . . . Soft Trisetum. . . . Rocky banks of rivers. **1878** Killebrew *Tenn. Grasses* 327 *Bromus Mollis,* Soft Chess. . . . Troublesome weeds . . . in wheat fields. **1897** SUDWORTH *Arborescent Flora* 13 *Pinus strobus.* White Pine. . . . Soft Pine (Pa.). *Ib.* 15 *Pinus monticola.* Mountain White Pine. . . . Soft Pine (Cal.).

5. In special combinations.
Soft dollar, =PAPER DOLLAR; *s. shirt,* an unstarched shirt; *s. weather,* (see quotation).
1776 *Battle of Brooklyn* I. iv. There is not one of those horses but what is worth more than a hundred and fifty soft dollars—consider, Sir! **1900** NORRIS *Blix* 191 With a sensation of positive luxury . . . he put on a 'soft' shirt of blue cheviot. **1891** *Cent.* 5748/3 *Soft weather,* a thaw. [New Eng.]

+**Soft clam.** The long clam (*Mya arenaria*), of the Atlantic coast. Also attrib. — **1855** *Knickerb.* XLVI. 222 Along the strand, . . . those great delicacies, 'soft clams' and sand-crabs may be found. **1867** Soft clam fritter [see HARD CLAM]. **1883** *Nat. Museum Bul.* No. 27, 229 *Mya arenaria* is the . . . 'long,' or 'soft clam,' of Long Island Sound and the Middle States. **1903** *N.Y. State Museum Bul.* No. 71, 22 The soft or long-neck clam . . . is capable of locomotion only when very small. **1911** *Rep. Fisheries 1908* 309/1.

Soft coal. Bituminous coal, as distinguished from anthracite. {1789–} Also attrib. — **1865** *Atlantic Mo.* April 395/2 'Soft coal,' ventured Missele remembering her experience at the glass-works. **1885** HOWELLS *S. Lapham* xvi, The soft-coal fire in the grate purred and flickered. **1890** *Stock Grower & Farmer* 22 March 6/2, 75,000 gallons of water raised 20 feet at an expense of 100 lbs. of soft coal seems wonderful. **1914** STEELE *Storm* 220 The lookout first raised the Cape that afternoon, with the pall of soft coal standing up above its distant reach.

+**Soft corn.**
1. Indian corn of which the grains or kernels are relatively soft, either a special variety, e.g. *Zea mays amylacea,* or corn that has been affected by unfavorable weather conditions.
1751 J. BARTRAM *Observations* 60 Last of all was served a great bowl, full of Indian dumplings, of new soft corn, cut or scraped off the ear. **1770** *Md. Hist. Mag.* XIII. 72, I Have a great deal of soft Corn at all the Plantations. **1868** *Mich. Agric. Rep.* VII. 160 Early frosts made considerable 'soft corn.'

2. (See quot. 1859.) *slang.*
1834 CARRUTHERS *Kentuckian* I. 98 He's feedin me on soft corn, thought I. **1859** BARTLETT 426 *Soft Corn,* flattery. The more common terms are 'soft sawder' and 'soft soap.'

+**Soft crab.** =SOFT-SHELL CRAB. — **1805** PARKINSON *Tour* 315 Soft crabs . . . are reckoned great dainties. **1852** *Harper's Mag.* Sept. 533/2 He was eating one of the luxurious soft-crabs of that region [Richmond]. **1884** GOODE, etc. *Fisheries* I. 776 The terms 'Soft Crab,' 'Paper-shell,' and 'Buckler' denote the different stages of consistency of the shell [of the blue crab].

Soft drink. A drink or beverage containing no spirits or alcohol. {1880–} — **1892** *York Count. Hist. Rev.* 18 The general scope of the business includes the bottling of . . . soft drinks. **1894** *Outing* XXIV. 236/2 Each regiment had a 'canteen' of its own, where the men could buy . . . soft drinks. **1904** *Charlotte Observer* 9 June 4 Not a drop of liquor—not even a soft drink unless it be filtered water—will be on sale.

Soft grass. (See quot. 1889.) {1785–} — **1791** MUHLENBERG *Index Florae* 182 *Holcus,* Soft-grass. **1832** [see HAIR GRASS]. **1889** *Cent.*

2854/1 *Holcus.... H. lanatus*, the velvet-grass or meadow soft-grass, is extensively naturalized in the United States.... The species are known as *soft-grass* or *velvet-grass*.

Soft hat. A hat which is not hard like the bowler or derby; a crush hat. — 1873 [see CUTAWAY *a.*]. 1893 *Harper's Mag.* May 897/1 A gay, reckless gleam under the wide rim of his soft hat.

Softhorn. A greenhorn. *slang.* {1865–} — 1835–7 HALIBURTON *Clockmaker* 1 Ser. xxxi. 297 The blue-noses are the most gullible folks on the face of the airth,—'rigular soft horns. 1877 BARTLETT 796 *Soft-Horn*, a weak, credulous person. 1905 RICE *Sandy* 37 'Lor'! but you're a soft-horn,' said Ricks, contemptuously.

+**Soft maple.** The red, the silver, or the dwarf maple. Also attrib. — [1778 CARVER *Travels* 496 The Maple. Of this tree there are two sorts, the hard and the soft.] 1807 GASS *Journal* 195 The timber is mostly of the fir kind, with some cherry, ... soft maple and ash. 1884 *Rep. Comm. Agric.* 352 The ordinary food-plant of this species of bark-louse is the soft or silver maple 1896 *Vt. Agric. Rep.* XV. 38 Would you advise tapping soft maple trees? 1897 SUDWORTH *Arborescent Flora* 284, 287, 290.

Soft marsh. (See quotations.) — 1737 WESLEY *Journal* I. 402 Soft marsh ... is all a quagmire, and absolutely good for nothing. 1775 ROMANS *Nat. Hist. Florida* 30 The soft marshes are those, whose spungy nature allows the water easily to penetrate them.

+**Soft money.** (See quot. 1892.) Also attrib. — 1866 C. H. SMITH *Bill Arp* 119, I am not as much in favor of soft money as I was. 1875 *Chicago Tribune* 14 Oct. 1/7 You're a soft-money man, are you not? 1892 WALSH *Lit. Curiosities* 450 During the second half of the decade 1870–1880, ... 'soft money' ... was understood [to mean] an irredeemable paper currency such as was advocated by the Greenbackers.

+**Soft-shell.**

1. Any one of various aquatic animals, esp. crabs and clams, having a shell that is soft; these animals prepared as food.

1830 SANDS *Writings* II. 230 The soft-shell of the Red River [is a dish unrivalled in other parts of the world]. 1846 THORPE *Myst. Backwoods* 156 It is Turtle Lake from its abundance of 'green, amphibious soft-shells.' 1886 MITCHELL *R. Blake* 261 Soft shells ... ain't got no shells really. 1894 *Harper's Mag.* Oct. 804/1 Shuv them soft-shells this way. 1911 [see PAPERSHELL].

transf. 1847 FIELD *Drama in Pokerville* 84 Mr. Case ... did not require much urging, either, to join in the laugh against such a 'soft shell' as his phiz-battered principal was.

2. = SOFT-SHELL BAPTIST.

1845 *Knickerb.* XXVI. 285 A 'Hard-Shell' recently turned a 'Soft Shell' out of church. 1893 FARMER & HENLEY III. 270/2 The Soft-shells are of more liberal mind [than the Hard-Shells].

3. = BARN-BURNER. Now hist.

1853 *N.Y. Tribune* 2 April 3/6 A Soft Shell ... is a loud stickler for Union and Harmony. 1858 in Bartlett 426 The terms Hunker, Barnburner, Soft-shell, and Hardshell, have become obsolete, and hereafter we will be known only by the term Democrat. 1914 *Cycl. Amer. Govt.* III. 350/1 The 'Softs,' or 'Soft Shells,' were New York Democrats, in opposition to the regulars.

4. attrib. **a.** In the names of animals having soft shells. **b.** Designating a stage of development of a crab.

1818 *Amer. Monthly Mag.* II. 296 Soft shell Clam. These animals ... are excellent eating. 1846 THORPE *Myst. Backwoods* 17 In the depths of these ponds ... [is the] soft-shell terrapin. 1847 *Knickerb.* XXIX. 494 The congress-man sat ... [enjoying] a battle between a soft-shell turtle ... and a terrier puppy. 1883 GOODE *Fishery Industries U.S.* 51 This Crab is eaten in both the hard and soft shell condition. 1884 GOODE, etc. *Fisheries* I. 792 Soft-shell Lobsters are sometimes called 'Cullings.'

+**Soft-Shell Baptist.** A Baptist holding views more liberal than those of the Primitive or Hard-Shell Baptists. — 1845 [see HARD-SHELL BAPTIST]. 1871 DE VERE 241 The Soft Shell Baptists ... [allow themselves] to be indulgent to certain worldly usages, and to educate their ministers carefully for the pulpit.

+**Soft-Shell convention.** A convention of Soft-Shell Democrats. — 1856 *N.Y. Herald* 7 July (B.), The call of the Soft-shell Convention was signed by twelve men of the Free-Soil Buffalo stripe.

+**Soft-shell crab.** A crab that has recently shed its shell, the new one not yet being hard. — 1843 *Nat. Hist. N.Y., Zoology* VI. 11 During this interval, they are known under the name of Soft-shell Crabs, or Shedders. 1883 GOODE *Fishery Industries U.S.* 49 Soft-shell Crabs are ... seldom taken in marketable quantities excepting on the New Jersey coast. 1886 MITCHELL *R. Blake* 306 She sat in the kitchen by the fire, watching him roast soft-shell crabs.

+**Soft-Shell Democrat.** = SOFT-SHELL 3. — 1859 BARTLETT 426.

Soft-shelled, *a.* Having a soft shell. {1611–} Esp. in the names of animals.

1771 *Phil. Trans.* LXI. 267 We call it the *soft shelled* Turtle. 1796 Soft shelled clams [see CLAM *n.* 1]. 1804 *Md. Hist. Mag.* IV. 16 The Wabash affords an abundance of large turtles, called soft-shelled turtles, the outer coat being a hard skin rather than a shell. 1856 *Rep. Comm. Patents 1855: Agric.* p. xviii, The 'soft-shelled' almond ... is the variety recently introduced and distributed by this Office. 1857 *Ib. 1856: Agric.* 112 Soft-shelled tortoises ... can escape by diving. 1891 *Cent.* 5749/2 *Soft-shelled crab*, the common edible crab of the United States, *Callinectes hastatus*, when it has molted its hard shell and not yet grown another.

+**Soft-sheller.** A soft-shelled crab. *colloq.* — 1886 MITCHELL *R. Blake* 261 Women is often like soft shellers.

+**Soft snap.** A 'good thing'; a place or job requiring little or no work. *colloq.* — 1845 HOOPER *Simon Suggs' Adv.* 19 Simon Gets a 'Soft Snap' out of His Daddy. 1883 PECK *Bad Boy* 119 At first he thought he had a soft snap with me in the drug store. 1904 *N.Y. Times* 2 July 6 The average politician seemed to regard that office as a soft snap, for the performance of whose duties no training was required.

Soft soap, *n.*

1. Soap of a heavy, semiliquid consistency, often home-made. {1634–}

1744 FRANKLIN *Acct. Fire-Places* 28 A Brush will scour them perfectly; as will also a little strong Soft-Soap and Water. 1850 *Rep. Comm. Patents 1849: Agric.* 439 [We] wash the trees with soft-soap and water. c1870 BAGBY *Old Va. Gentleman* 268 That negro came forward with ... a gourd full of soft soap—this home-made, greasy, villainous stuff. 1912 NICHOLSON *Hoosier Chron.* 43 [I] know how to ... stir soft soap in an iron kettle. attrib. 1855 *Harvard Mag.* I. 19, [I] fell forward into an unemptied soft-soap keg.

+**2.** Flattery, soft sawder, blarney. *slang.* {1861–} Also attrib.

1830 *Ann. 21st Congress* 1 Sess. VI. 11. 774, I will not use the vulgar phrase and say he has been pouring soft soap down the backs of the New York delegation. 1832 *Jamestown (N.Y.) Jrnl.* 8 Feb. 3/1 Mr. Croswell and the soft soap editors are determined upon that. 1855 BARNUM *Life* 286 The first qualification necessary was a thorough knowledge of human nature, which of course included the faculty of judiciously applying *soft soap*. 1901 MERWIN & WEBSTER *Calumet 'K'* 345 We aren't handing out any soft soap at this dinner.

Soft-soap, *v. tr.* To flatter or soft-sawder (a person). *slang.* {as vbl. n., 1841–} — c1840 NEAL *Beedle's Sleigh Ride* 23 To see them flattering and soft soaping me all over. a1855 J. F. KELLY *Humors* 213 Get the fellow ashore if you can, talk to him, soft soap him. 1917 FREEMAN & KINGSLEY *Alabaster Box* 164 Anybody that's a mind to soft-soap them ... can lead them right around by the nose.

Soft spot. +**1.** *fig.* A lack of sound practical sense; a trace of tenderness or sentimentality. *colloq.* +**2.** (See quotation.) — (1) 1858 HOLLAND *Titcomb's Lett.* 46 You will be very apt, if you have a soft spot in your head, to think yourself above him. 1885 *Century Mag.* July 380/2 [He] had rather a soft spot in his heart for Violet. 1901 *McClure's Mag.* Dec. 152 [Platt's] delight in music still remains the soft spot which he turns to humanity. (2) 1900 NELSON *A B C Wall St.* 159 *Soft spot*, a weak point in the market.

Soft thing. *fig.* +Something extremely easy or pleasant; a snap. *colloq.* — 1867 CRAWFORD *Mosby* 103 Thinking they had a *soft thing* [they] were inside the house playing cards and drinking. 1880 *Harper's Mag.* 202/2 He told us that they [*sc.* the surveyors] 'had a soft thing.' 1898 FORD *Tattle-Tales* 153 Now, if you want a soft thing pay heed to what I write.

Sog. A large whale. — 1839 *Knickerb.* XIII. 379 He was a most extraordinary fish; or, in the vernacular of Nantucket, 'a genuine old sog,' of the first water. 1850 CHEEVER *Whale & Captors* 185 She's a beauty! a regular old sog!

Soger. {1640–1–} Among sailors, a seaman who shirks his duties. — 1840 DANA *Two Years* 154 *n.*, Soger (soldier) is the worst term of reproach that can be applied to a sailor. *Ib.* 276 The second mate swore at them for a parcel of 'sogers.' 1849 MELVILLE *Redburn* 58 Jackson was a notorious old *soger*.

Soggy, *a.* {a1722–} 'Chiefly *dial.* and *U.S.*' (*O.E.D.*).

1. Of things: Soaked with water or moisture; heavy.

1819 *Niles' Reg.* XVI. *Suppl.* 190/1 The boat's all soggy. 1863 TAYLOR *H. Thurston* 155 He looked out on ... fields of soggy, soaked snow. 1887 CUSTER *Tenting on Plains* 652 Everything we have is soggy with moisture.

b. Of sugar and pastry: Sodden; heavy. {1868–}

c1851 WHITCHER *Bedott P.* xxix. 375 It needs sugar, the best o' sugar, too, not this wet soggy-brown sugar. a1861 WINTHROP *Open Air* 118 We were ... compelled to struggle with real and not ideal pioneers for fried beefsteak and soggy doughboys. 1890 *Harper's Mag.* March 605/2 He would go in to eat a small slice of cold, soggy pie.

2. Of land: Boggy; soft with moisture. {a1722, 1805}

1867 *N.Y. Tribune* in *Blackwood's Mag.* Oct. 404/2 We marched ten miles over a soggy wilderness. 1880 ROLLINS *New Eng. Bygones* (1883) 68 The heart of an old wood ... hugs to its soggy sides such plants as love shade and moisture. 1896 *Godey's Lady's Bk.* April 351/2 These country roads are ... soft and soggy.

3. Of an appearance or a noise: Suggestive of wetness.

1877 DUHRING *Pract. Tr. Diseases Skin* 126 The skin ... is observed ... to have a soggy appearance. 1881 *Harper's Mag.* Oct. 650 Every footstep giving out a soggy wheeze from his old wet boots.

4. Of a person or an animal: Dull; without energy. {1911}

1867 HARRIS *Sut Lovingood* 105 All the old quilts ove wimen, an' the old soggy men ... visits 'im. 1873 ALDRICH *Marjorie Daw* 150 A menagerie with a soggy elephant, halts under the swinging sign. 1896 *Advance* 16 July 88/1 The Slavs are a passive, gregarious, soggy race.

*Soil. The ground with respect to its composition and as a source of vegetation. Also attrib. — **1634** Wood *New Eng. Prospect* (1865) 11 The Soyle is for the generall a warme kinde of earth. **1686** *Huntington Rec.* I. 472 Judge Palmer should bee taken in a pattenttee with us only in Refarance to soill Right of that land eastward of Cowharbor. **1794** [see Mill right]. **1872** *Newton Kansan* 22 Aug. 6/7 Fertile Soil, for Grain-growing and Stock-raising unsurpassed by any in the United States. **1898** *Dept. Agric. Yrbk.* 43 One of the first necessities in the development of a new district or in the improvement of an established district is an accurate soil map of the locality.

+**Soiling corn.** Corn planted to be fed as green fodder. — **1884** *Vt. Agric. Rep.* VIII. 355 [He] would plant soiling corn and not sow. **1888** *Ib.* X. 17 [He] raised no soiling corn.

Sojer, *v.* (See Soldier *v.*)

Sola bill. A bill of exchange drawn singly, as distinguished from bills drawn in sets. {1866} — **1737** W. Stephens *Proc. Georgia* I. 9 He brought a small Box with Sola Bills for a large sum. **1741** *Georgia Col. Rec.* III. 392 All Expences . . . should be defrayed and paid for in Georgia, in Sola Bills of Exchange only. **1750** *Ib.* VI. 323 The last Issue of Sola Bills was not sufficient to defray the Estimate to Michaelmas.

*__Solan goose.__ The common gannet, *Moris bassana.* — **1776** *Mass. H. S. Proc.* 2 Ser. II. 301 Gannets or Solen Geese . . . are almost as large as our Common Geese. **1917** *Birds of Amer.* I. 91 Gannet. *Sula bassana.* . . . [Also called] Soland Goose; Solan Goose; Solon Goose.

*__Solar,__ *a. absol.* +A salt made by solar evaporation. — **1859** *Ill. Agric. Soc. Trans.* IV. 103 Fourteen ounces of salt (solar being the best I ever used) is added. **1869** *Mich. Gen. Statutes* I. (1882) 439 All ground salt manufactured and put up for market, shall be legibly marked . . ; 'ground solar,' or 'ground boiled,' or 'ground steam,' or 'ground Chapin,' as the fact may be.

Solar (lard) lamp. A lamp giving a bright light, esp. an Argand lamp. {1841–} — **1844** *Lexington Observer* 25 Sept. 1/6 Patent solar lard lamps . . . $8.00. **1854** Cummins *Lamplighter* 111 She had trimmed the solar-lamp. **1887** Wilkins *Humble Romance* 405 If you ain't got the solar lamp a-settin' in a little bag!

Soldering iron. A tool used in melting and applying solder. {1688–} — **1859** *Rep. Comm. Patents 1858* I. 573 Improved Soldering-Iron. **1883** *Rep. Indian Affairs* 402 Soldering-irons, 36 ounces each.

Solder iron. =prec. — **1861** *Vanity Fair* 5 Jan. 3/1, I should have . . . thrust a hammer and a solder-iron into your hand.

*Soldier, *n.* (See also Soger.)

*__1. a.__ A member of an army. **b.** An ordinary enlisted man, as distinguished from an officer.

See also Citizen soldier, Old soldier 1.

1624 Smith *Gen. Hist. Va.* III. 44 Most of the souldiers recovered with the skilfull diligence of . . . our Chirurgian generall. **1639** *Springfield Rec.* I. 165 All above 15 yeares of age shall be counted for soldiers. **1675** Easton *Indian War* 16 Plimouth Soldiers were cum to have their Head Quarters within 10 Miles of Philip. **1717** *Mass. H. Rep. Jrnl.* I. 241 Praying a further Continuance of ten Souldiers in the Publick pay. **1758** [see Copper *n.*[1] 3 d]. **1790** *Ann. 1st Congress* 1272 At what period, sir, said he, did Congress contract with their soldiers? **1808** Pike *Sources Miss.* 1 One of my soldiers swam a channel . . . to inform me that the boat had stopt during the storm. **1888** Whitman *Nov. Boughs* 80, I find this incident in my notes (I suppose from 'chinning' in hospital with some sick or wounded soldier). **1913** London *Valley of Moon* 67 He was a soldier then, before the war.

2. =Hermit crab. {1666–}

1737 Brickell *N. Carolina* 247 The Soldier, is a kind of Shell-fish. **1834** Audubon *Ornith. Biog.* II. 445 The number of that strange species of crabs called *soldiers* was so great, that [etc.].

+3. An Indian brave with special duties: (see quotations).

See also Dog soldier.

1832 Catlin *Indians* I. 42 The chiefs have had to place 'soldiers' at my door . . . to protect me from the throng. **1848** Parkman in *Knickerb.* XXXI. 190 There were but few 'soldiers,' a sort of Indian police, who among their other functions usually assume the direction of a buffalo hunt.

+4. In miscellaneous senses: (see quotations).

1892 *Amer. Folk-Lore* V. 101 *Echinospermum Virginicum*, soldiers. E. Mass. **1902** Jordan & Evermann *Amer. Food Fishes* p. xlviii, The most useful [artificial flies for bass] may be named as follows: Coachman, professor, soldier [etc.]. **1904** P. Fountain *Great North-West* 224 A bird known locally [in Ohio] as 'the marshal,' and sometimes 'the soldier,' . . . is a very gaudy woodpecker.

5. In possessive combinations.

See also Soldiers' home, Soldier's-plume.

1884 *Congress. Rec.* 10 June 4994/2 [The lumbermen] have long been in the habit of getting it [pine land] . . . under the soldiers' additional scrip. **1865** *Atlantic Mo.* Feb. 247/2 Can we overestimate the influence of . . . these Soldiers'-Aid Societies, rising up in every city and village? **1837** *Jamestown* (N.Y.) *Jrnl.* 29 March 3/2 Soldiers' bounty lands can . . . be bought at still less. **1852** Gouge *Fiscal Hist. Texas* 66 It would be difficult for those who had bought up soldiers' certificates . . . to find purchasers. **1864** (*title*), History of the North-Western Soldiers' Fair Held in Chicago . . . , 1863. **1770** Washington *Diaries* I. 428, I marked two Maples, an Elm, and Hoopwood Tree as a Cornr. of the Soldiers L[an]d. **1866** Moore *Women of War* 127 And now [came] . . . representatives of Ladies' Aid Societies and Soldiers' Relief Societies. **1822** *Ann. 17th Congress* 1 Sess. 162 The holders of those soldier's Warrants Commenced locating them on the tract of land. **1923** *World's Work* 466/1 Soldiers' Widows and Their Pensions.

6. Attrib. and appositive with *boy, clothes*, etc.

1814 *Columbian Centinel* 3 Dec. U. Sam pays his soldier-servants in *Paper Money.* **1861** Moore *Rebellion Rec.* I. III. 91 My hungry soger-boys shall soon have meat and drink. **1861** *Vanity Fair* 15 June 281/1, I'd like to . . . have a marquee tent away off on a hill, where I could sit with soldier-clothes on, and watch the fight. **1920** *3d Nat. Country Life Conf. Proc.* 15, I had an opportunity to make a soldier monument.

b. In the specific names of plants and fish.

1882 *Nat. Museum Bul.* No. 16, 517 *P[œcilichthys] cœruleus.* . . . Soldier-fish. **1897** Sudworth *Arborescent Flora* 300 *Colubrina reclinata.* . . . Naked-wood. . . . Soldierwood.

Soldier, *v.* {1647–} +*intr.* To feign illness; to make only a pretense at working; to shirk. {1890} Also *vbl. n.* — **1825** Neal *Bro. Jonathan* II. 39 Is he sick or is he gwyin' a sojerin'? **1850** Kingsley *Diary* 108 There seems to be less sojering than usual. **1880** 'Mark Twain' *Tramp Abroad* 535 A fraud who pretended to be cutting steps . . . was 'soldiering' when we came upon him. **1903** *Boston Sun. Herald* 17 May 4/1 These physicians were appointed . . . for the ostensible purpose of preventing 'soldiering' among employes. **1917** J. A. Moss *Officers' Manual* 485.

Soldier beetle. A predatory lampyrid insect. {1855–} Also with specifying term. — [**1883** W. Saunders *Insects Inj. Fruits* 185 The larva of the soldier-beetle *Chauliognathus Americanus* . . . , is also a useful agent in destroying the curculio.] **1891** *Cent.* 5754/1 The Pennsylvania soldier-beetle, *Chauliognathus pennsylvanicus*, is common in the United States. **1904** Kellogg *Amer. Insects* 269 The nocturnal fireflies and their diurnal first cousins, the soldier-beetles, compose a coleopterous family, Lampyridae, of considerable size.

+**Soldier bug.** Any predatory pentatomid bug that sucks the blood of other insects. — **1868** *Mich. Agric. Rep.* VII. 175, [I] found [them] to be soldier-bugs, with their long harpoon bills thrust into a fine fat slug, and sometimes also into perfect beetles. **1876** *Vermont Bd. Agric. Rep.* III. 676 The spined soldier bug and the banded robber bug also prey upon the larvae of the potato beetle. **1884** *Rep. Comm. Agric.* 391 The Soldier-Bug. An undetermined species of *Podisus* affected wheat in the same manner.

Soldier crab. Either the hermit or the fiddler crab. {1668–} — **1814** [see Fiddler 2]. **1844** *Nat. Hist. N.Y., Zoology* v. 14 This bold demeanor has doubtless given rise to the name of *Soldier Crab.*

+**Soldiers' home.** An establishment where old or disabled soldiers are taken care of. — **1861** *Army Regulations* 343 The paymaster will deduct from the pay of all enlisted men twelve and a half cents per month for the support of the 'Soldiers' Home.' **1866** Moore *Women of War* 220 One of the most interesting places they found in the city [Vicksburg] was the Soldiers' Home. **1881** *Harper's Mag.* April 715/2 To the westward, are the handsome grounds of the Soldier's Home. **1900** *Congress. Rec.* 19 Jan. 1001/1 Part of his [the veteran's] meager pension [is] confiscated at Soldiers' Homes.

+**Soldiers' lodge.** (See quotation and cf. Dog soldier.) — **1878** *Rep. Indian Affairs* 159 The only party which could bolster him [Chief Spotted Tail] up is made up of the untamed and thoughtless young fellows of his tribe, who have established what is termed a 'soldiers' lodge,' and who have put the whole tribe under martial law.

+**Soldier's plume.** (See quotations.) — **1850** S. F. Cooper *Rural Hours* 168 The handsome, large purple-fringed orchis is also found here. . . . The country people call it soldier's plume. **1894** *Amer. Folk-Lore* VII. 100 *Habenaria psycodes*, . . . soldier's plume, N.Y.

+**Soldier vote.** *collect.* The political vote of returned soldiers. — **1887** *Nation* 10 March 197/3 The demagogues . . . are always bidding for the 'soldier vote.' **1900** *Congress. Rec.* 15 Feb. 1851/1 The pension attorneys are the organizers and managers of the so-called 'soldier vote.'

Sold land. +(See quotation.) — **1824** Doddridge *Notes* 104 We have no districts of 'sold land,' as it is called, that is large tracts of land in the hands of individuals, or companies who neither sell nor improve them.

*Sole. Any of certain flatfishes; also, the pole flounder of the east coast. Often with specifying terms.

The American species of sole, mostly of the genera *Achirus* and *Symphurus*, are of little food value. In popular usage, *sole* is applied to certain other flatfishes of excellent food value, as *Eopsetta jordani* and *Psettichthys melanostictus* of the west coast.

1674 *Cal. State P., Amer. & W.I.* VII. 581 There are infinite quantities of fish, such as . . . polluck, mackarel, soles, skate, lamperns [etc.]. **1709** Lawson *Carolina* 157 Soles . . . are as good, as in any other Part. **1748** Catesby *Carolina* II. p. xxxii. **1842** New-York Sole [see Coverclip]. **1884** Goode, etc. *Fisheries* I. 175 The American Sole, is found along our coast from Boston and Nahant to the mouth of the Mississippi River. *Ib.* 182 South of San Francisco . . . the young [of the bastard halibut are] . . . rarely distinguished from other 'Soles.' *Ib.* 186 *Parophrys isolepis* . . . is a Sole to the fisherman. *Ib.* 187 *Hippoglossoides Jordani* . . . is known universally as the 'Sole.' *Ib.* 188 The Slippery Sole—*Glytocephalus pacificus.* **1893** Post *Harvard Stories* 43 Mock turtle soup, and then filets of sole. **1903** Goode & Gill *Amer. Fishes* p. lxviii, *Psettichthys melanostictus:* 'Sole' of San Francisco. **1911** *Rep. Fisheries 1908* 310/1 The family of flounders is composed of the turbots (*Bothinæ*), the halibuts (*Hippoglossinæ*), the plaices (*Pleuronectinæ*), and probably the soles (*Soleidæ*).

∗Sole leather. Leather used, or suitable for use, on the soles of shoes. — 1638 *Md. Archives* IV. 74, 3. peices of sole-leather. 1715 *Boston News-Letter* 16 May 2/2 To be Sold . . . Jamaica Sole Leather very Good, cheaper than New-England Leather. c1790 COXE *View U.S.* 62 The produce, manufactures, and exports of Pennsylvania [include] . . . soal-leather, upper leather. 1857 *Lawrence* (Kan.) *Republican* 28 May 3 Just Received—1000 lbs. oak and hemlock Sole Leather. 1903 [see HEAD *n.* 8 a].

+**Solemncholy,** *a.* Excessively solemn. *rare.* {1863–} — 1772 Fithian *Journal* I. 27 Being very Solemncholly and somewhat tired, I concluded to stay there all night. 1835 KENNEDY *Horse Shoe Robinson* I. 62 Take [troubles] . . . as things that's not to be mended by a solemncolly longfacedness. 1893 *Harper's Mag.* Feb. 461/1 We sat round so solemncholy, . . . I vow if the thing didn't seem to me like some sort o' corpse.

∗**Solicitor.**

+**1.** An attorney representing a city, district, department, or the like. Often with *of,* followed by a designation of the department or agency employing him.

1830 *Stat. at Large* IV. 414 There [shall] be appointed, by the President of the United States, . . . some suitable person, learned in the law, to be solicitor of the treasury. 1840 *Niles' Nat. Reg.* 21 March 45/1 The bill . . . to abolish the office of solicitor of the general land office. 1858 D. K. BENNETT *Chronology N.C.* 45 He has been . . . solicitor of the Edenton District. 1907 *N.Y. Ev. Post* (s.-w. ed.) 5 Aug. 6 His term as solicitor, an officer who corresponds [in N.C.] to district attorney in New York, was in 1886.

∗**2.** A lawyer who conducts cases in a court of chancery; an attorney-at-law. In full *solicitor in chancery.*

'In the great majority of the states of the Union, where law and equity are both administered by the same court, it has naturally come about that the two offices of attorney at law and solicitor in chancery have practically been consolidated, although in the federal equity practice the term 'solicitor' is in general use. But in some states the office of solicitor in chancery is a distinct and separate office from that of attorney at law' (*Corpus Juris* [1916] VI. 568).

1842 *Diplom. Corr. Texas* III. (1911) 999 [In] my correspondence . . . you will find the opinions of Mr. Pringle, a distinguished solicitor. 1846 Solicitor-in-chancery [see ATTORNEY-AT-LAW]. 1852 *Knickerb.* XXXIX. 473 'Deputy-Sheriff P—— . . . was recently called upon to arrest a dulyregistered 'Attorney and Counsellor at Law, and Solicitor.' 1895 *Md. Supreme Ct. Rep.* LXXXI. 17 On March 9, 1893, all the creditors who had sued out attachments . . . were dismissed from the suit by the order of the plaintiff's solicitors.

+**3.** One who canvasses and solicits trade, donations, or the like.

1902 CLAPIN 376 *Solicitor,* a canvasser; one who solicits orders. 1903 SHUMAN *Pract. Journalism* 200 Have as many good solicitors out as necessary. 1918 *Nation* 7 Feb. 161/2 Life insurance salesmen as a class are . . . about the least ambitious . . . salesmen in the entire round of commercial solicitors.

∗**Solicitor-general.**

1. A law officer of the British crown in colonial America.

1692 *Conn. Hist. Soc. Coll.* III. 180 It is not fair play . . . to misinform the king's attorney general and solicitor general. 1823 TUDOR *Life J. Otis* 111 The office of Solicitor General was erected [c1761] expressly for [Jonathan Sewall].

+**2.** A law officer who assists the attorney-general of the United States.

1870 *Stat. at Large* XVI. 162 There shall be in said Department [of Justice] an officer learned in the law, . . . to be called the solicitor-general. 1900 *Congress. Rec.* 17 Feb. 1900/1 The oral argument was presented by the gentleman from Ohio, John K. Richards, the Solicitor-General, a most able lawyer and ex-attorney-general of Ohio.

+**3.** The chief law officer of certain states.

1879 ABBOTT *Dict. Terms Jurisprudence* II. 485/2 *Solicitor-general,* . . . in some of the states, the title of the chief law-officer, or one corresponding with the attorney-general in other states.

∗**Solid,** *n.* +A single color. — 1883 *Ev. Star* (Washington) 31 Oct. 3/6 Solids are all the go this season. 1908 GALE *Friendship Village* 4 Daisy and wild-rose patterns in 'solid,' and art curtains.

∗**Solid,** *a.*

1. Of persons: Financially able or established; well-to-do. {a1904, *dial.*}

1788 JEFFERSON *Writings* VII. 92, I wish to see the beef-trade with America taken up by solid hands. 1799 *Aurora* (Phila.) 8 Jan. (Th.), The solid men of Boston town. 1819 *Ann. 15th Congress* 2 Sess. 561 Solid capitalists . . . would have held only what they could pay for. 1860 *Century Mag.* Dec. (1881) 294/1, I have not had time to read the proceedings or address of the solid men of Boston. 1902 LORIMER *Lett. Merchant* 103 There isn't a solider man in the Boston leather trade than Jeremiah, nor a bigger scamp that the law can't touch than his son Ezra.

+**2. a.** Of a number of people, votes, etc.: United in support of, or opposition to, a person or cause.

1872 *Chicago Tribune* 14 Oct. 1/3 The Democrats are solid for Greeley in this county. 1884 *Harper's Mag.* Aug. 472/1 This perception may be due to the withdrawal of a candidate, and the transfer of his solid vote

to another. 1892 *Boston Jrnl.* 8 Nov. 4/4 A solid New England vote for protection and honest money will be glorious. 1905 *McClure's Mag.* XXIV. 342 Republicans do the same in their solid towns when we go in to outbid them.

+**b.** Of a person or newspaper, esp. in regard to politics: Regular; blindly partisan; steady.

1880 *46th Congress 2d Sess. Sen. Rep.* No. 693, 326 Q. These gentlemen . . . are both good Democrats? A. Yes, sir; they are solid Democrats. 1882 McCABE *New York* 601 The *Post* is regarded as the 'solidest' evening paper in the Metropolis. 1884 *American* IX. 180 He is, therefore, presumed to be solid as a Southern man. 1889 HOWELLS *Annie Kilburn* xviii, I'm solid for Mr. Peck every time.

+**c.** Closely associated *with;* having a dependable friendship *with.*

1882 PECK *Sunshine* 161, I was pretty solid with him. 1896 FREDERIC *Damnation of T. Ware* 366 That'll make you solid with the boys. 1912 NICHOLSON *Hoosier Chron.* 183, I advise you to make yourself solid with her.

+**3.** Of liquor: Straight.

1894 *Outing* XXIV. 49/1 He always took his liquor solid . . . ; he swallowed down two-thirds of a tumbler of raw Appleton rum.

Solid coin. Hard money. — 1789 *Ann. 1st Congress* 169 These articles are paid for principally, if not altogether, in solid coin.

Solidly, *adv.* {1611–} +Unanimously; as a unit. {1886} — 1865 in *Morning Star* (London) 14 March, I was told by a citizen of New York . . . [that] 100,000 Irish votes were given, as he expressed, solidly . . . for General M'Clellan. 1878 *Congress. Rec.* 8 April 2350/1 When I find republicans . . . voting solidly for an Irish Catholic democrat then I know there is a 'cat in the meal-tub.'

+**Solid South.** The southern states, so called chiefly for the practically invariable Democratic vote of the area since the Civil War.

1878 BEADLE *Western Wilds* 418 Now Texas is the most solid outpost of the 'Solid South.' 1878 *Congress. Rec.* 17 Dec. 242/1, I regret, that the necessity has ever existed in this country for what is termed 'a solid South.' 1884 BLAINE *20 Years of Congress* I. 489 While confronting the power of a solid South he [Lincoln] must continue to wield the power of a solid North. 1900 *Congress. Rec.* 15 Feb. 1842/2 As long as this condition remains do you expect to see anything but the solid South? 1903 *Sun* (N.Y.) 5 Nov. 6 The defeat of the Republicans in Maryland practically restores the 'Solid South' as completely Democratic. 1912 *Commoner* 15 Nov. 5 There was no break in the 'solid south.'

b. (See quotation.)

1885 *Mag. Amer. Hist.* April 395/1 *Solid South,* . . . latterly the united white vote (Democratic) as opposed to the solid Republican vote of the negroes.

Solitaire. {1716–}

1. A piece of jewelry having a diamond or other precious stone set by itself. {a1727–} Also attrib.

1750 [see EARRING]. 1762 in H. M. Brooks *Gleanings* IV. 37 Soletare Necklaces and Earings. 1867 'MARK TWAIN' *Sk., New & Old* 256 Miss R. P. . . . was attired in a simple white lace collar, fastened with a neat pearl-button solitaire. 1898 ATHERTON *Californians* 225 There were a few necklaces, stars, and ear-rings—of the vulgar variety known as 'solitaires.' 1912 IRWIN *Red Button* 350 You'll get a diamond solitaire as soon as I can beat it up-town!

2. One of various card games played by one person. {1746–; = Eng. 'patience'}

1868 A. D. WHITNEY *P. Strong* 109 It would be like a game of 'solitaire,' —'patience,' as they call it in the English novels. 1884 HARTE *On Frontier* 234 Taking a pack of well-worn cards from his pocket, [he] began to make a 'solitaire' upon the [barrel] lid. 1916 WILSON *Somewhere* 149, I'll bet he couldn't play an honest game of solitaire.

∗**Solitary,** *a.* +In the specific names of American birds. {1600–, of non-Amer. birds} Also absol.

1810 WILSON *Ornithology* II. 143 [The] Solitary Flycatcher, *muscicapa Solitaria,* . . . [is] occasionally found in the state of Georgia. 1813 *Ib.* 54 The Solitary Sandpiper is eight inches and a half long. 1839 PEABODY *Mass. Birds* 370 The Solitary Tattler, *Totanus chloropygius,* . . . is very unsuspicious. 1839 AUDUBON *Ornith. Biog.* V. 432 Solitary Vireo, *Vireo solitarius.* 1844 *Nat. Hist. N.Y., Zoology* II. 121 The Solitary Greenlet, *Vireo solitarius,* . . . is the rarest of the genus found in this State. 1865 BURROUGHS in *Atlantic Mo.* May 521/2, I have met here many of the rarer species, such as . . . the Solitary Warbler. 1892 TORREY *Foot-Path Way* 13 [The Philadelphia vireo's] song is practically certain to be confused with the red-eye's rather than with the solitary's. 1917 *Birds of Amer.* III. 234 Hermit Thrush. *Hylocichla guttata pallasi.* . . . [Also called] Solitary Thrush.

Solitary system. A system of solitary confinement for prisoners. — 1842 BUCKINGHAM *E. & W. States* II. 306 The system of discipline pursued here, is that which is called the Auburn, or Silent System, in contradistinction to the Philadelphia, or Solitary System.

Solo. {1695–} A carriage with room for one person only. {1787} Also attrib. — 1774 FINLAY *Journal* 52, I was in a Solo chair. 1789 *Ann. 1st Congress* 106 The articles enumerated for duty were . . . chaise, solo, or other two wheel carriages. **1793** COXE *View U.S.* 141 New-Jersey, in 1789, had . . . 1,549 one-horse chairs and solas.

+**Solograph.** (See quot. 1858.) Also attrib. — **1851** CIST *Cincinnati* 187 Hawkins, in addition to his daguerreotypes, produces what he terms a *solograph* picture. **1858** SIMMONDS *Dict. Trade Products* 352/1 *Solograph*, a name which has been given to some pictures on paper taken by the talbotype or calotype process.

* **Solomon's-seal. a.** Any plant of the genus *Polygonatum.* Also attrib. +**b.** One of various other plants. Usually with specifying terms. {1898, Tasmania}

1672 JOSSELYN *New Eng. Rarities* 45 Salomons-Seal, of which there is three kinds; . . . the second, Virginia Salomons-Seal. [**1760** J. LEE *Introd. to Botany* App. 327 Solomon's Seal, Pennsylvanian, *Uvularia*.] **1778** CARVER *Travels* 514 Solomon's Seal . . . grows on the sides of rivers, and in rich meadow land. **1805** CLARK in *Lewis & C. Exped.* III. (1905) 220, I Saw in my ramble to day a red berry resembling Solomons Seal berry. **1814** BIGELOW *Florula Bostoniensis* 80 *Convallaria racemosa.* Clustered Solomon's seal. **1857** GRAY *Botany* 467 *Smilacina.* False Solomon's Seal. . . . White, often fragrant flowers. **1868** A. D. WHITNEY *P. Strong* 36 Up in the pasture [is] the lesser Solomon's seal. **1869** FULLER *Flower Gatherers* 84, [I] continue to call it 'Dwarf Solomon's Seal.' **1892** *Amer. Folk-Lore* V. 103 *Habenaria orbiculata*, Solomon's seal. Barre, Vt. **1905** *Forestry Bureau Bul.* No. 60, 12 The ground cover is made up of . . . a scattering of goldenrod, asters, Solomon's seal, grasses, and other herbaceous plants.

So long, *n.* and *interj.* Goodbye. *colloq.* {1865-}

1860 WHITMAN *Leaves of Grass* 451, I whisper *So long!* And take the young woman's hand, . . . for the last time. **1897** CRANE *Third Violet* 130 'Well, so-long, boys,' said Hawker, 'I'll see you later.' **1916** SANDBURG *Chicago Poems* 117 And it's no use to beckon or say, So long.

* **Solve,** *v.* Baseball. +*tr.* To hit (a pitcher's delivery) effectively. — **1898** *N.Y. Tribune* 22 April 11. 1/3 Only in the second inning were the home players able to solve his [the opposing pitcher's] curves.

+**Sombrero.** *S.W.* [Independent borrowing from Sp.] A hat, esp. any of various kinds of broad-brimmed hats worn in the Southwest. {1770-, of Spain and Spanish America}

1836 LATROBE *Rambler in Mexico* 33 My accoutrement consisted of . . . a bag for seeds, and a broad-leaved palmetto *sombrero.* **1840** *Picayune* 18 Sept. 2/4 His *sombrero* was an enormous, heavy, broad-brimmed beaver. **1857** DAVIS *El Gringo* 190 The head is covered with a *sombrero* with a very wide brim. **1872** POWERS *Afoot & Alone* 170 A Mexican in a red gala shirt and a straw sombrero has just thrown the lazo over a steer. **1876** HARTE in *Scribner's Mo.* Feb. 560/1 They . . . doffed their glazed, stiff-brimmed, black *sombreros.* **1907** 'O. HENRY' *Heart of West* 266 He wore . . . his white felt sombrero on the back of his head.

+**Sombrero hat.** A broad-brimmed hat. — **1857** GUNN *N.Y. Boarding-Houses* 177 He wore . . . a broad *sombrero* hat. **1905** *Boston Transcript* 2 Sept. 22/7 Lumber jacks are . . . dressed in the style of a regular woodman, [with] shoe packs, heavy flannel shirts, sombrero hats.

* **Some,** *n.* +**1.** A great deal. *colloq.* +**2.** *And then some,* and more than that; and something more. *colloq.* — (1) **1850** KINGSLEY *Diary* 159, 30 ounces of amalgam, . . . I think is some for this bar. *Ib.* 163, 80 ounces in amalgam . . . is some & no mistake. (2) **1908** 'YESLAH' *Tenderfoot S. Calif.* ii. 22 It rains in sheets, in blankets, and in comforters, and then some. **1914** D. O. BARNETT *Letters* (1915) 19, I picked them out with those glasses, and let them have it, and then some!

* **Some,** *a.*

+**1.** In predicate position: Remarkable; deserving of special notice. *colloq.* or *slang.*

1845 *Knickerb.* XXV. 273 The way *he* put in the licks was some. **1849** *N.Y. Tribune* 15 May (B.), That [winter] . . . was admitted by the oldest inhabitant to be 'some' in the way of cold winters. **1863** *Rio Abajo Press* 24 Feb. 2 Our legislature is 'some' in the memorial line. **1888** EGGLESTON *Graysons* xiii, I used to think you wuz some at a hoe-down.

+**2.** In attrib. position: Worth talking about; unusual, extraordinary. *colloq.* or *slang.*

See also PUMPKIN 3.

1855 *Chicago W. Times* 31 May 1/7 In 1850 there was *some* excitement about the Presidential election time. **1914** ATHERTON *Perch of Devil* 80 'They're some geologists,' he added with unwilling admiration. **1921** PAINE *Comr. Rolling Ocean* 83 It takes some acrobat to keep his feet on the slippery gratings.

* **Some,** *adv.*

1. With adjectives: Somewhat. *colloq.* {1851-}

'*Dial.* and *U.S.*' (*O.E.D.*).

1804 *Lewis & Clark Exped.* VII. (1905) 31 Some rainy. **1834** *Georgian* (Savannah) 29 Dec. 3/2 [The woman is] large, and well set, and likely some marked with the whip. **1890** JEWETT *Strangers* 6 It must ha' been some inconvenient for ye. **1913** [see GUN PLAY].

b. With *different from, like, as, similar:* Somewhat, much.

1849 KINGSLEY *Diary* 70 Our Generous Captain put up a board to day on which the Latitude & Longitude is marked that we may all see, which I think is some different from Cap'n Bottums selfishness. **1862** NORTON *Army Lett.* 127 Things begin to look some like winter quarters. **1877**

JEWETT *Deephaven* 60 You look some as she used to. **1895** 'CRADDOCK' *Mystery Witch-Face Mt.* 230 Waal, Wat is some similar ter a balky horse.

+**2.** With verbs: Somewhat, to some extent.

1843 WHITTIER in Pickard *Life Whittier* I. 281, I think some of attending the great antislavery convention. **1889** *Internat. Ann., Anthony's Photogr. Bul.* II. 206 Having been troubled some of late to get clear results, . . . I have substituted distilled water for ordinary water.

+**b.** In emphatic use: Very well indeed. *colloq.*

1848 RUXTON *Life Far West* i, That one did shoot some. **1866** LOWELL *Biglow P.* 2 Ser. p. lxxix, Thet night, I tell ye, she looked *some!* **1907** *London Road* 181 That's going some.

* **Son.** A man regarded as a product of a certain institution, place, or action. (Cf. FAVORITE, NATIVE SON.) — **1726** *Harvard Rec.* II. 535 Voted, that the Humble thanks of the Corporation be returned by Mr. President to Mr. Hollis, . . . for his fixing his eye on the worthy Mr. Greenwood, a Son of this College, for that Service. **1807** GASS *Journal* 235 After taking our farewell of these good hearted, hospitable and obliging sons of the west, we proceeded. **1864** EDWARDS *Shelby* 474 Missouri's stalwart sons will again rush to uphold the Confederate banner. **1900** *Congress. Rec.* 27 Jan. 1245/1 Louisiana herself lost a well-beloved son, who was destined to play no unimportant part in carving her destiny.

* **Song.** *attrib.* +In the specific names of birds. — **1839** AUDUBON *Synopsis Birds* 132 *Coccoborus*, Song-Grosbeak. . . . *Coccoborus cœruleus.* Blue Song-Grosbeak. **1917** *Birds of Amer.* III. 191 Bewick's Wren. . . . [Also called] Song Wren.

Song and dance.

+**1.** A vaudeville act made up of singing and dancing. Also attrib.

1872 *Chicago Tribune* 13 Oct. 5/6 First week of the distinguished song and dance artists. **1880** E. JAMES *Negro Minstrel's Guide* 4 A two-hours' entertainment is quite enough, allowing . . . ten minutes or so each for song-and-dance, stump speech, instrumental solos [etc.]. **1887** *Courier-Journal* 19 Feb. 8/1 The 'Colored Society Ball' introduced a song and dance that is much more refined than most of those exhibitions are. **1895** *N.Y. Dramatic News* 23 Nov. 13/3 The first double song and dance team was comprised of Wash Norton and Ben Cotton.

2. A rigmarole; nonsense. *colloq.*[2]

1900 B. MATTHEWS *Confident To-Morrow* 9 And it ain't a song-and-dance I'm giving you either. **1908** McGAFFEY *Show-Girl* 15 That show . . . [is] a song and dance about this mental telepathy gag.

+**Song sparrow.** A sparrow (*Melospiza melodia*) of the eastern part of the country having a song of several notes; one of several geographic varieties of this bird. — **1810** WILSON *Ornithology* II. 125 [The] Song Sparrow, *Fringilla melodia*, . . . is fond of frequenting the borders of rivers, meadows, swamps. **1828** BONAPARTE *Synopsis* 108 The Song Sparrow . . . inhabits throughout the Union. **1850** *Knickerb.* XXXV. 459, I have availed myself of the first leisure hour . . . to fulfil my promise of calling your attention to the song-sparrow. **1880** *Harper's Mag.* June 70 There's the ringing voice of song-sparrow and the bell note of the thrush. **1917** *Birds of Amer.* III. 52/2 One form, the Alameda Song Sparrow (*Melospiza melodia pusillula*), is strictly limited to the salt marshes around San Francisco Bay.

+**Son of (fair) freedom.** A patriotic American. — **1768** in Buckingham *Newspaper Lit.* I. 149 The Sons of fair Freedom are rallied once more. **1798** in H. M. Brooks *Gleanings* IV. 71 Take Notice! Ye Sons of Freedom! **1842** *Lowell Offering* II. 42 Sons of Freedom! let not the true spirit of patriotism . . . be extinguished in your own [bosoms]. **1885** CRAWFORD *Amer. Politician* 18 'And the Irish and German votes,' added Vancouver, with that scorn which only the true son of freedom can exhibit in speaking of his fellow-citizens.

Son of liberty.

+**1. 1. a.** A patriotic American fighting for freedom from British rule, esp. a member of one of several loosely federated societies first organized to oppose the Stamp Act. **b.** In pl. and capitalized: One of these societies, or the societies collectively.

See also LIBERTY BOYS.

1766 in Buckingham *Newspaper Lit.* I. 32 On the common the Sons of Liberty erected a magnificent pyramid. **1768** [see LIBERTY HALL]. **1770** ADAMS *Diary Works* II. 243 [The] landlord . . . is a staunch, zealous son of liberty. **1787** TYLER *Contrast* III. i, I'm a true born Yankee American son of liberty. **1823** THACHER *Military Jrnl.* 14 His majesty's name . . . can have no charms with the sons of liberty. **1876** *Scribner's Mo.* Jan. 314/1 'The New York Journal' . . . was the sturdy and unpurchasable organ of the Sons of Liberty.

+**2.** *pl.* One of various Copperhead organizations during the Civil War: (see quotations).

1885 *Mag. Amer. Hist.* April 395/2 *Sons of Liberty*, a name assumed by certain secret societies whose purpose was the liberation of Confederate prisoners held at the North during the civil war. An alleged branch of the Knights of the Golden Circle. **1888** M. LANE in *America* 8 Nov. 15 *Sons of Liberty.* This organization, known by different names, developed in the West in 1862, about the time for the first draft. **1891** [see KNIGHTS OF THE GOLDEN CIRCLE].

+**Son of Seventy-six. 1.** A veteran of the Revolutionary War. **2.** A member of the American or Know-Nothing party; pl., the party itself. —

(1) **1862** Browne *A. Ward: His Book* 254 These brave sons of '76 took no part in the demonstration, but an honored bench was set apart for their exclusive use. (2) **1891** *Cent.* 5768/1 *Sons of Sires*, or *Sons of Seventy-six*, a name said to have been applied to or assumed by members of the American or Know-nothing party. **1894** C. Stickney *Know-Nothingism in R.I.* 4 In certain States we find promulgated orders and announcements of 'The Sons of '76,' and 'The Order of the Star-Spangled Banner.'

+**Son of Temperance. a.** *pl.* A fraternal and benevolent organization founded to afford mutual assistance among its members against the excessive use of alcoholic liquor. **b.** A member of this organization. — **1840** *Knickerb.* XXVIII. 145 The Sons of Temperance will hold their next celebration to-morrow. **1846** *Xenia Torch-Light* 2 April 4/1 The objection to the Sons of Temperance, that it is a Secret Society, loses all its force. **1890** Langford *Vigilante Days* (1912) 272 The circumstances of duress . . . ought not to impair his standing as a Son of Temperance. **1898** Westcott *D. Harum* xxiii, I'm a son o' temp'rance.

+**Son of the Sires.** =Son of Seventy-six 2. — **1855** (*title*), Sons of the Sires; A History of the Rise, Progress, and Destiny of the American Party. **1891** [see Son of Seventy-six 2].

+**Sonoma oak.** [f. *Sonoma* Co., Calif., f. Ind. place name.] 'An oak, *Quercus Kelloggii* . . . , of the mountains of Oregon and California' (*Cent.*).

+**Sonoranian.** [f. *Sonora*, a state in northwestern Mexico.] An Indian or Mexican from Sonora. — **1862** *Harper's Mag.* June 13/2, I . . . suddenly found myself close by a camp of Sonoranians. **1864** *Ib.* Oct. 560/2 Being thus left at the mercy of . . . roving bands of Apaches and Sonoranians.

+**Sons of America. 1.** A patriotic society during the Revolutionary period. **2.** (See quotation.) **3.** A patriotic and benevolent society founded about 1847. — (1) **1774** Fithian *Journal* I. 96 There were parties in Rooms made up, some at Cards; some toasting the Sons of America; some singing 'Liberty Songs.' (2) **1865** Richardson *Secret Service* 429 He belonged to a secret organization known as the Sons of America, instituted expressly to assist Union men . . . in escaping to the North. (3) **1892** *York County Hist. Rev.* 62/1 Born in this country, he is identified with the I.O.O.F. Encampment, and the Sons of America.

+**Sons of the Pilgrims.** A society, founded *c*1798, whose members were male descendants of the Pilgrim fathers of Plymouth, Massachusetts. — **1798** *Columbian Centinel* 26 Dec. 2/4 The Feast of the 'Sons of the Pilgrims.' **1799** *Ib.* 28 Dec. 1/4 The following are the Toasts given at the Feast of the 'Sons of the Pilgrims.'

+**Sons of the South.** =Blue lodge. — **1867** Dixon *New America* I. 21 A meeting of Sons of the South was called in Westport. **1883** Andreas *Hist. Kansas* 90/2 Secret lodges were organized under various names—'Social Band,' 'Friends' Society,' 'Sons of the South' [etc.].

+**Sons of Veterans.** A society, organized in 1879, consisting of sons of members of the Union forces in the Civil War. — **1884** *Boston Jrnl.* 6 Sept., Stirring speeches were made by . . . District Commander Atwood . . . and Mr. Chas. Penniman, Chief Mustering Officer of the Sons of Veterans of Minnesota. **1909** [see Camp *n.* 5].

Sontag. [f. Henriette *Sontag*, Ger. operatic singer (1806–54).] A knitted or crocheted jacket with long ends that cross over the front and fasten in the back. — **1863** A. D. Whitney *F. Gartney* xviii, Faith brought quickly, sontag, jacket and cloak. **1864** *Hist. North-Western Soldiers' Fair* 74 [Donations:] Mrs. Nolden, a sontag. Mrs. Howell, an opera shawl. **1900** Dix *Deacon Bradbury* 45 Did you hear what she said to Mrs. Delane about that worsted sontag she brought?

+**Sook, Sooky,** *n.* and *interj.* Also **suke, sukey. 1.** *n.* A cow or a sow. **2.** *interj.* A call to cattle or swine. — (1) **1838** Drake *Tales Queen City* 154 With a bellicose bellow, forwards and downwards went the old sukey. **1850** Garrard *Wah-To-Yah* xii. 160 The cows . . . looked quite different from the patient, chewing 'Suke' of the American farmer. **1899** Green *Va. Word-Book* 349 *Sooky*, name given to a female hog. (2) **1883** Sweet & Knox *Through Texas* 597 'Here, suke, suke!' And he . . . threw some of the grains [of corn] on the ground to inspire the hogs with confidence. **1892** *Dialect Notes* I. 237 *Suke.* Cows are often called by the word *sûk* or *sûki* (Kansas City). **1899** Green *Va. Word-Book* 349.

+**Sook cow,** *interj.* Also **suke cow, sookow.** =Sook 2. Also as noun used attrib. in fig. sense. — **1854** Harris *Sut Lovingood* 24 Yu mout jis' es well say . . . Suke cow tu a gal. **1897** *Amer. Anthropologist* X. 98 In Virginia and Alabama it [*sc.*, the call to a cow] becomes *sookow, sookow.* **1902** 'O. Henry' *Roads of Destiny* 156 Dis sook-cow kind of cheap sport gives me a pain. **1906** Pittman *Belle of Blue Grass C.* 176 'Sook Cow, Sook Cow,' called the milker.

+**Sooner.** [f. *soon* adv.]

1. a. *spec.* A person who occupied, or attempted to occupy, land in Oklahoma prior to the legal time set for occupancy of a given area. **b.** A person in any other area who makes prior or illegal settlement on land.

Cf. Eighty *a.* 3, note.

1890 *Congress. Rec.* 17 Jan. 657/2 We have recognized the fact that there are 'sooners' there. **1892** *Pall Mall Gaz.* 28 Sept. 7/1 One of these 'Sooners' got into the territory before the date for opening it up by the Presidential proclamation, by virtue of being an employee on a railroad which entered the territory. **1892** *San Francisco Chron.* 18 April, Annetta Daisy established her colony of young women sooners in 'F' county. **1893** *Phila. Inquirer* 21 Aug., The intention and attempt to keep the Sooners off the Cherokee strip . . . have come to grief. **1904** *N.Y. Ev. Post* 13 June 7 White 'sooners' . . . were trying to rob them [*sc.* Indians] of some of the most valuable mineral deposits on their reservation. **1911** Quick *Yellowstone Nights* 316 We powdered across the country like the first batch of sooners at a reservation openin'.

2. One who acts prematurely. *Obs.*

1890 *Columbus Dispatch* 7 May, The Governor is quite right in declining to be regarded as a sooner. **1892** *Boston Jrnl.* 2 May 4/7 The word 'Sooners' is a Southwestern descriptive term . . . gradually coming into general use in defining that numerous class of nervously excitable people who insist upon crossing bridges before they come to them.

+**Soonerism.** The activity of the sooners. — **1894** *Columbus Dispatch* 19 March, An important case growing out of the 'soonerism' at the Oklahoma opening will be given a hearing.

Soosy. A striped fabric of silk and cotton. {1621–} Also attrib. — **1733** *S.C. Gazette* 4 Aug., Just Imported, . . . beladine silk, . . . coarse soosees. **1741** *Ib.* 26 March, Just imported . . . Soosey and silk handkerchiefs. **1745** in Watson *Philadelphia* 179 Chain'd soosees, lemonees.

Soothing syrup. A syrup used to soothe children. {1896–} Also fig. and attrib. — **1861** *N.Y. Tribune* 26 Dec. 2/5 Don't fail to procure Mrs. Winslow's Soothing Syrup for children teething. **1872** 'Mark Twain' *Roughing It* 125 Soothing-syrup! Teething-rings! **1901** Churchill *Crisis* 246 When the worst comes, the Soothing Syrup men will rally for the Union.

+**Soot tea.** (See quot. 1877.) — **1842** [see Balmony]. **1877** Bartlett 627 *Soot-Tea*, a decoction of soot taken from a chimney, believed by some old grannies to be a sovereign remedy for the colic or cholera.

***Sooty,** *a.* In the specific names of birds. {1777–}

1813 Wilson *Ornithology* VIII. 145 Sooty Tern: *Sterna fuliginosa:* . . . its appearance at sea usually indicates the vicinity of land. **1872** Coues *Key to Birds* 331 Sooty Shearwater. Dark sooty brown. *Ib.* 345 Sooty Guillemot. No white on the wings. **1884** *Ib.* 580 *Canace obscura fuliginosa*, Sooty Grouse. **1891** *Boston Jrnl.* 21 Feb. 5/3 These birds were sooty petrels. **1917** *Birds of Amer.* III. 53/2 In southern Alaska . . . is the home of the Sooty Song Sparrow (*Melospiza melodia rufina*). *Ib.* 57/2 The Sooty Fox Sparrow (*Passerella iliaca fuliginosa*) . . . [winters] south along the coast to San Francisco.

Soph. {1661–} +Short for Sophomore. — **1778** Stiles *Diary* II. 277, I appointed Stevens a Soph. Waiter in the Hall. **1819** A. Peirce *Rebelliad* 9 Then rushed each Soph to battle driven. **1842** *Dartmouth* IV. 118 My Chum, a Soph, says he committed himself too soon. **1903** *N.Y. Times* 26 Sept. 5 [The freshmen's] progress was impeded by the 25 specially organized sophs.

Sophic, *a.* {1709–} +**1.** Sophomoric. ‖**2.** Pertaining to knowledge. — (1) **1853** in Hall *College Words* (ed. 2) 436 So then the Sophic army Came on in warlike glee. (2) **1898** *Rep. Bureau Amer. Ethnol. 1897–8* p. xlv, The sophic activities so highly developed among the tribes of the arid pueblo region.

***Sophister.** A junior or a senior in a college or university. *Obs.* (Cf. Junior sophister, Senior sophister.) — **1646** *Harvard Rec.* I. 25 All Sophisters & Bachellors . . . shall publiquely repeate Sermons in ye Hall whenever they are called forth. **1650** [see Questionist]. **1759** *Holyoke Diaries* 20 Officers of the Sophisters chose Valedictorian.

Sophomore. Also **sophimore, sophmore.** {1688, 1795}

+**1.** A second-year student in a four-year college or university.

[**1654** H. Dunster MS. (Harvard Archives), Orditurque Annus secundus 1628 quem dum transigunt, Sophomore dicuntur.] **1684** *Harvard Rec.* I. 77 Mr. Samuel Mitchell was . . . desired to undertake ye charge of ye class of ye Sophimores untill further order. **1710** *Ib.* 391 The Buttler [was] directed to put up his Name in the Buttery in the place assigned him among the Sophomores. **1779** E. Parkman *Diary* 176 His name was Charles Cutter, a soph-more. **1842** *Knickerb.* XIX. 433 We strongly suspect the freshman is as often victorious as the sophomore. **1893** Post *Harvard Stories* 4 Jack was a Sophomore then, but a pretty good sort of a Soph. **1912** Nicholson *Hoosier Chron.* 212 As a sophomore her fellows began to know her and take pride in her.

+**b.** A second-year student in a high school.

1906 Forum Jan. 363 High school pupils whose average age was about the same as that of the high school sophomores of to-day.

+**2.** Attrib. with *class, gown, room*, etc.

1765 Habersham *Letters* 51 He lately entered with honor the Sophmore Class. **1830** *Collegian* 252 The Sophomore Supper—with its thousand unmentionable associations—it is well perhaps to be silent upon. **1838** *U.S. Mag.* I. 152 Instead of mean black sophomore gowns, . . . the judges were dressed in stately scarlet and ermine. **1847** *Knickerb.* XXIX. 15, I well remember . . . the first recitation of my division during our sophomore year. **1871** Bagg *At Yale* 18 The two remaining sophomore rooms were enlarged. **1897** Flandrau *Harvard Episodes* 95 This fact is . . . of greater significance than any one . . . is likely to attach to the sophomore society.

+**Sophomoreship.** The condition of being a sophomore. — **1721** *Harvard Rec.* II. 455 The Moiety of £45 Sterling . . . [shall] be paid to him . . . as a Consideration toward reimbursing the charge of his Education in his Sophimorship. **1725** *Ib.* 525 Campbel [shall] be allowed . . . fourty pounds for this year of his sophimoreship.

+**Sophomoric,** *a.* Of or pertaining to a sophomore; having the characteristics of a sophomore; immature; bombastic; superficial. — **1837** *Harvardiana* IV. 22 Better to face the prowling panther's path Than meet the storm of Sophomoric wrath. **1850** *Knickerb.* XXXV. 213 Sophomoric wits on 'sets' grew sharp. **1881** Cable *Madame Delphine* 20 [They were] speculating upon the nature of things in an easy, bold, sophomoric way. **1904** *Springfield W. Repub.* 9 Sept. 8 From so sophomoric a preface a scholarly dictionary is not to be expected.

+**Sophomorical,** *a.* =prec. — **1839** *Knickerb.* XIV. 204 Its style . . . is labored and sophomorical, to the last degree. **1847** WELLS & DAVIS *Sk. Williams College* 74 [The composition] was rather Sophomorical. **1883** *Science* 27 July 113/2 The paper is decidedly sophomorical.

Sopsivine. A variety of apple. {sopsy-wine, 1764; sops in wine, 1860} — **1845** THOREAU *Journal* I. 371, I have carried an apple in my pocket tonight—a sopsivine, they call it. *c*1870 CHIPMAN *Notes on Bartlett* 429 *Sopsyvine*, a variety of apple much prized for its delicate flavor.—Connecticut. The name is clearly made from *Sops-in-wine*, a gilly-flower. **1899** A. BROWN *Tiverton Tales* 160 That was the 'sopsyvine,' its red fruitage fast coming on.

+**Sora.** Also **saurer, soree.** [Probably Indian.] The Carolina rail, *Porzana carolina.*

1705 BEVERLEY *Virginia* II. 37 The Shores . . . are also stor'd with . . . Snipes, Woodcocks, Saurers [etc.]. *c*1730 CATESBY *Carolina* I. 70 The Soree. . . . In Virginia . . . they are . . . much in request for the delicacy of their flesh. **1809** WILSON *Poems & Lit. Prose* I. 172 The Sora was in multitudes at Detroit. **1852** *S. Lit. Messenger* XVIII. 754/1, I never knew . . . what became of the sora after frost. **1894** TORREY *Fla. Sketch-Book* 217 The sora's call is familiar. **1917** *Birds of Amer.* I. 207/1 The Soras . . . remind one of very tiny dark-colored bantam hens.

attrib. **1877** BAGBY *Old Va. Gentleman* 11 Of fish-fries, barbecues, sailing-parties, sora and duck shooting, . . . I need not speak at length.

+**Sora rail.** =prec. Also comb. — **1835** AUDUBON *Ornith. Biog.* III. 251. **1856** *Porter's Spirit of Times* 6 Sept. 9/1 Sora-rail-shooting, is now to be had, wherever the bird is found.

***Sore eyes.** *spec.* +Trachoma. — **1805** CLARK in *Lewis & C. Exped.* III. (1905) 182 Sore eyes are common and maney [of the Indians] have lost their eyes. **1834** BAIRD *Valley Miss.* 86 Sore eyes may be mentioned as a prevailing disease of the western states. **1894** *Scribner's Mag.* May 606/2 Consumption, cancer, sore eyes, epilepsy . . . [are] at all times to be dreaded in these little hamlets [of Texas].

***Sorehead,** *n.* +A disappointed and disgruntled office-seeker or politician; also, generically, any person who is disgruntled. *slang.* — **1855** *Chicago W. Times* 29 March 4/7 The know nothing party has swallowed up the whigs, freesoilers, Burkites and soreheads. **1865** *Ore. State Jrnl.* 9 Sept. 2/1 The copperheads have . . . [induced] a sufficient number of 'soreheads,' to fill out a ticket, to bolt from the Union organization. **1904** CRISSEY *Tattlings* 292 These soreheads concluded that the time had come to elect a politician instead of a statesman. **1920** LEWIS *Main Street* 204, I guess if I had a woman like you I wouldn't be such a sorehead.

+**Sorehead,** *a.* Of a politician or office-seeker: Disappointed and disgruntled. — **1862** *Major Jack Downing* 26 Linkin laughed at it when I got thru, an sed it done very well for some sore-hed Dimmycrat. **1875** *Chicago Tribune* 22 July 1/5 The warrants are . . . in the hands of the Marshal, to the great mortification of certain sorehead politicians. **1885** *Wkly. New Mexican Rev.* 15 Jan. 4/4 Contrary to the prediction of not a few of the sore-head class, the most intense harmony and good feeling prevailed.

Sore shin. +A disease affecting the stem of a cotton plant. — **1855** *Fla. Plantation Rec.* 133 The cotton Still Ceepes diing like it had the Soar Shin. **1856** *Rep. Comm. Patents 1855: Agric.* 230 'Sore-shin,' is sometimes occasioned by a careless stroke of the hoe. **1883** SMITH *Geol. Survey Ala.* 547 Lice, flea-bugs, and sore-shin generally appear . . . when the cotton is young.

Sore skin. +A disease of the cotton or tobacco plant. — **1835** INGRAHAM *South-West* II. 282 Sometimes whole acres together, die with the 'rust,' 'sore skin,' or 'yellow fever.' **1909** WEBSTER 1996/2 S[ore] skin, a disease of the tobacco plant in which a section of the stem near the ground dries up so as to break the continuity of the sap flow.

Sorgho. Sorghum. {1760-} Also attrib. — **1857** H. S. OLCOTT *Sorgho & Imphee* 37 The sorgho is not a fast grower at first. *Ib.* 143 It is to the manufacture of sorgho spirit only that I shall refer. **1858** *Ill. Agric. Soc. Trans.* III. 525 No. 1, is pure Sorgho brandy. **1864** *Ohio Agric. Rep.* XVIII. 154 Corn potatoes and sorgho, [were] a poor half crop.

***Sorghum.**

*1. A genus of grasses introduced, esp. from Asia and Africa, into the United States; a plant of this genus, esp. *S. vulgare,* millet or Guinea corn, and *S. saccharatum,* Chinese sugar cane. Also collective and with specifying terms.

1860 DARLINGTON & THURBER *Weeds & Plants* 411 S[orghum nutans]. . . . Nodding Sorghum. Wood Grass. *Ib.* 412 S[orghum] cernuum. . . . Drooping Sorghum. Guinea Corn. **1862** *Rep. Comm. Patents 1861: Agric.* 293 There are really but two varieties of the sugar-cane, commonly called *Sorghum,* in cultivation in the northern States of this Union. **1868** *N.Y. Herald* 31 July 5/5 Sorghum is generally doing well in the West. **1890** *Rep. Secy. Agric. 1889* 19 The Chemical Division has also conducted . . . experiments looking to the manufacture of sugar from sorghum and sugar-beets. **1901** MOHR *Plant Life Ala.* 135 Various kinds of sorghum, known as durrha or kafir corn, millo maize, and pearl millet, . . . furnish green forage and hay crops.

+2. A molasses made from the juice of a saccharine sorghum.

1874 [see DEFECATOR]. **1888** *Century Mag.* Sept. 766/2 At home and abroad sorghum came to take the place of the vanished sugar. **1905** in

Dale & Rader *Okla. Hist.* (1930) 673 Some farmers making sorghum . . . promise me a jug full of sorghum in return for the picture when it is finished.

3. Attrib. and comb. with *boiler, cane,* etc.

1862 *Rep. Comm. Patents 1861: Agric.* 310 The sale of ordinary molasses and sirups has been reduced . . . about sixty per cent., simply by the supply of sorghum sirups. **1863** *Rep. Comm. Agric. 1862* 527 A specimen of sorghum wine patented by Mr. Myers has been subjected to analysis. **1870** *Dept. Agric. Rep. 1869* 530 Passmore & Wilhelm, of the sorghum works of Greenville, South Carolina, have been entirely successful in manufacturing syrup and sugar of superior quality from the black imphee. **1871** DE VERE 287 Among the minor details of the war that produced new terms, may be mentioned the word *sorghum pulling* or tugging. **1876** KNIGHT 2246/2 Sorghum-stripper, . . . a knife for stripping the blades from cane-stalks. See . . . *Sorghum-knife.* **1880** *Vt. Agric. Rep.* VI. 224 The sorghum industry has declined of late years. **1883** HOWELLS *Woman's Reason* xi, I've got the idea of a sorghum-planter that . . . is going to make somebody's fortune. **1885** *South Fla. Sentinel* (Orlando) 2 Sept. 2/2 There are three establishments in Kansas devoted to the manufacture of sorghum sugar. **1888** *Nation* 5 Jan. 2/2 Now the sorghum-boilers in Kansas are protesting against any meddling with the duty on sugar. **1890** *Rep. Secy. Agric. 1889* 20 The season proved too dry for the production of a crop of sorghum cane suitable for sugar-making

+**Sorghum molasses.** Molasses made from the juice of sorghum. — **1864** WHITMAN *Spec. Days* 54 The regular food [included] . . . once a week a ration of sorghum molasses. **1871** DE VERE 287 As the people of the South had always been fond of molasses stews, . . . the same [pulling and tugging] was now done with the sorghum-molasses.

***Sorority.** +1. The female members of a congregation. *Obs.* +2. A national or local society among women students of a college or secondary school. Also attrib. (Cf. FRATERNITY 2.) — (1) **1645** PAGITT *Heresiography* (1647) 86 The Synod of New-England maketh not only the fraternity but (as they speak) the sorority to be the subject of the . . . power of the keys. (2) **1900** *Dialect Notes* II. 14 Those societies of a social nature . . . are called . . . *fraternities* or *sororities.* **1900** *Harper's Mag.* Sept. 490 One saw many of those neat little sorority pins the American girl proudly brings home from boarding-school or college. **1924** CROY *R.F.D. No. 3* 13 The girls in Junction City . . . had their secret clubs, bridge games, chapters of sororities.

Sorosis. {1831-} +1. (See quot. 1895.) +2. A woman's club or association. — (1) **1873** ALDRICH *Marjorie Daw* 238, I would back our Club against the Sorosis. **1895** *Johnson's Univ. Cycl.* II. 349/1 In Mar., 1868, the first club exclusively for women, Sorosis, was founded . . . in New York city. (2) **1879** WEBSTER *Suppl.* 1579/2.

***Sorrel.** Any of various plants having sour juice, as the common sorrel, *Rumex acetosa,* or the wood sorrel of the genera *Oxalis* or *Xanthoxalis.*

1612 [see PURSLANE]. **1622** 'MOURT' *Relation* 62 We found heere in Winter . . . Sorrell, Yarow, [etc.]. **1784** *Amer. Acad. Mem.* I. 437 *Rumex.* . . . Sorrel. Common in old fields. June. **1806** *Lewis & Clark Exped.* VI. (1905) 210 The sorrel with an oval obtuse and ternate leaf has now put forth it's leaves. **1846** in Emory *Military Reconn.* 396 We also saw . . . the sorel (*oxalis stricta*) and lamb's quarter. **1889** DELAND *Florida Days* 196 There is . . . the hot red of flowering sorrel, or some tufted weeds, with yellow blossoms.

b. With specifying terms.

1737 BRICKELL *N. Carolina* 18 The Sallads are . . . French and English Sorrel, Purslain [etc.]. **1840** DEWEY *Mass. Flowering Plants* 103 R[umex] acetosella, Sorrel, or Field Sorrel, . . . appears everywhere over the dry, sandy fields that are neglected or untilled. **1901** MOHR *Plant Life Ala.* 481 *Rumex acetosella.* . . . Sand Sorrel. Canadian zone to Louisianian area. **1909** *Cent. Suppl.* 1242/2 Ladies' sorrel, *Oxalis stricta,* a delicate species . . . ranging throughout most of temperate North America east of the Rocky Mountains and introduced into Europe.

+**Sorrel top.** 'A derisive appellation for a red-haired person' (B. '77). — **1863** 'E. KIRKE' *Southern Friends* 58 'Har, you lousy sorrel-top,' said the trader to the red-faced and red-headed bar tender. **1884** 'CRADDOCK' *Where Battle Was Fought* 106 'Reg'lar sorrel-top,' drawled Dick. **1904** 'O. HENRY' *Roads of Destiny* 298 Thay don't raise 74-inch sorrel-tops with romping ways down in his precinct.

+**Sorrel tree.** 1. An ericaceous tree (*Oxydendrum arboreum*) with sour evergreen leaves. 2. The staggerbush, *Neopieris mariana.* — (1) **1687** CLAYTON *Va.* in *Phil. Trans.* XLI. 152 The Sorrel-tree . . . grows plentifully on the South-side of James River in Virginia. *c*1730 CATESBY *Carolina* I. 71 The Sorrel-Tree. The trunk . . . is usually five or six inches thick. [**1814** PURSH *Flora Amer.* I. 295 The leaves of a very pleasant acid taste, from which it has been called Sorrel-tree.] **1897** SUDWORTH *Arborescent Flora* 314. (2) **1909** *Cent. Suppl.* 1242/2.

+**Sorrel vine.** The vine sorrel, *Cissus trifoliata.* — **1891** *Cent.* 5777/3 *Sorrel-vine,* . . . a shrub . . . found in tropical America, reaching into Florida.

Sossle. (See SOZZLE *n.*)

+**Sotol.** S.W. [Sp., from Nahuatl.] Any one of various plants of the genus *Dasylirion.* Also attrib. — **1881** *Amer. Naturalist* XV. 874 The home of the sotol is Western Texas, Southeastern New Mexico and Northern Chihuahua. **1908** McDOUGAL *Bot. Features N.A. Deserts* 9 This is the typical sotol region.

+**Sots.** (See quot. 1902.) — **1817** *Niles' Reg.* XII. 165/2 The result was . . . that kind of rising called here 'sotts,' a Dutch term, I presume. **1902** CLAPIN 377 *Sots.* Yeast is so called, in Virginia and Pennsylvania.

Souchong. A fine variety of black tea, or a drink prepared from this. {1760–} In full *souchong tea.* — **1777** A. ADAMS *Familiar Lett.* 313, I feel as contented when I have breakfasted upon milk as ever I did with Hyson or Souchong. **1789** *Ann. 1st Congress* 168 On all souchong and other black teas, ten cents. **1849** G. G. FOSTER *N.Y. in Slices* 33 The respectable house of Wiggins & Winkle sells us . . . a catty-box of real Souchong. **1894** *Harper's Mag.* July 234/2 This is the flower of the souchong.

Soufflet. [Fr.] ?A collapsible brief case. — **1835** *Stimpson's Boston Directory* Cover, Orders received for . . . Gilchrist's Manifold Letter Copyer, Sermon Cases, and Attorney's Soufflets.

∗**Soul.** In special combinations. Usually slang or contemptuous.

Soul butter, pious and sentimental talk; *s. shark,* a preacher; *s. trap,* a grogshop; *s.-weeding,* a searching quiz or examination.

1884 'MARK TWAIN' *H. Finn* xxv, Music is a good thing, and after all that soul-butter and hogwash I never see it freshen up things so. **1898** HARPER *S. B. Anthony* I. 249 The country is full of these soul-sharks, men who haven't had brains enough to find pulpits or places in the free States. **1818** WEEMS *Letters* III. 225 This detestable *Soul Trap* was kept by one John Blackfoot. **1912** N. WOODROW *Sally Salt* 10 Lucy was apparently alarmed at the prospect of a soul-weeding.

Soul-driver. {1700} +One who took indentured servants, slaves, etc., from place to place to sell them; an overseer of slaves. Now hist. — **1774** *Amer. Hist. Review* VI. 77 Soul drivers . . . drive them [*sc.* servants and convicts] through the Country . . . untill they can sell them to advantage. **1818** *Mass. Spy* 4 Nov. (Th.), Two men, in the character of soul drivers, lodged in the jail for safe keeping, five negros. **1849** E. DAVIES *Amer. Scenes* 23 Two white men ('soul-drivers,' I suppose) were sauntering about in front of [the Negroes]. **1888** *Congress. Rec.* 2 May 3647/1 Today every old soul-driver of the South is a free-trader.

+**Soule(s).** A variety of wheat. In full *Soule(s) wheat.* — **1856** *Rep. Comm. Patents 1855:* Agric. 195 For the most part, we sow the 'Soule' wheat. **1868** *Mich. Agric. Rep.* VII. 424 The midge injured the variety known as the Soules wheat. **1874** *Rep. Comm. Agric. 1873* 220 All the varieties had stood the winter well—quite as well as the Soules and Bluestem.

+**Sou markee.** [Fr. *sou marqué.*] Orig., a French copper coin of low value that circulated to some extent in the United States; fig., anything of small value, a trifle. — **1826** *Mass. Spy* 5 July (Th.), Who the d——l would give a sumarkee to read the newspapers after breakfast? **1855** *Putnam's Mo.* April 410/1 The deacon'll save every soomarkee on't for the children. **1903** LEWIS *Boss* 181, I don't pony for a sou markee.

∗**Sound,** *n.*

∗**1.** A narrow stretch of water not a stream, as a strait or inlet.

1607 in *Amer. Speech* XV. 394/2 In ye large sounds neere the sea are multitudes of fish. **1769** CUTLER in *Life & Corr.* I. 20 The Sound was said to be frozen over near the West Chop of Homes' Hole. **1832** DUNLAP *Hist Amer. Theatre* 42 Having with consummate skill crossed the sound called the East river, he led the yet unmanageable mass of citizen soldiers beyond the reach of the enemy. **1883** *Rep. Indian Affairs* 151 A number of the Indians work in mills and logging camps on the sound. **1897** *Outing* XXX. 290/2 The shore of the Sound . . . and occasionally a guideboard, enable the touring novice to find his way.

+**2.** (See quotation.)

1881 INGERSOLL *Oyster-Industry* 248 Sounds, oysters grown in Staten Island sound, New York; especially an European brand.

∗**Sound,** *a.*

+**1.** Of currency: Possessing a relatively fixed or stable value. (Cf. SOUND MONEY.)

1841 TYLER in *Pres. Mess. & P.* IV. 85 The idea . . . of furnishing a sound paper medium of exchange may be entirely abandoned. **1844** *Lexington Observer* 25 Sept. 2/2 They embrace . . . a sound currency, emanating from the will, and upheld by the authority of the whole nation. **1903** ELY *Evolution Indust. Soc.* 482 The Fabians have been in favor of what is called with us sound currency.

+**2.** Holding sound views, esp. in politics; reliable as a politician or party man. *colloq.* (Cf. GOOSE *n.* 3).

1865 RICHARDSON *Secret Service* 34 The New Yorker was swift to explain that he was very 'sound,' favoring no compromise which would not give the slave holders all they asked. **1871** DE VERE 266 If he has been in political life the many . . . is carefully searched to find out if he is sound, that is, if he has always voted strictly with his party.

∗**Sounding.** ||(See quotation.) — **1804** C. B. BROWN tr. Volney *View* 174 Eddies or counter-currents, . . . aided by the depositions of the rivers, forms the muddy stratum or deposit, termed *soundings.*

+**Sounding boat.** A small boat used in taking soundings. — **1875** 'MARK TWAIN' *Old Times* v. 79 The pilot . . . goes out in the yawl provided the boat has not that rare and sumptuous luxury, a regularly devised 'sounding-boat.' *Ib.* 85 The paddle-wheel has ground the sounding-boat to lucifer matches!

+**Sound money.** Money having a stable value, esp. gold, or currency based on gold. Also attrib. — **1895** *Nation* 19 Dec. 438/1 He has astonished the friends of sound money. **1896** *Harper's Wkly.* 25 July 723/1

Sound-money Democrats are not hesitating as to their duty in the present crisis. **1913** LA FOLLETTE *Autobiog.* 209 A new heading for the paper [advocated]: . . . Sound money, a dollar's worth of dollar.

∗**Soup.** (Cf. BEAN SOUP, CLAM SOUP, etc.) Illustrated in attrib. and comb. uses only.

1. Designating articles used in making, serving, and eating soup.

1759 in H. M. Brooks *Gleanings* IV. 34 Tankards, soup-kettles, communion flaggons and cups. *c*1766 Soup spoon [see MARROW SPOON]. **1776** *Penna. Ev. Post* 27 April 212/1 Blue and white soup Turennes. **1779** *York Co., Va., Rec.:* Wills XXII. 28 April, 2 soup ladles. **1828** LESLIE *Receipts* 20 You may bake it either in a soup-plate, or in two small tin patty-pans.

2. In special combinations.

Soup bone, a bone, as a shin or knuckle, used in making soup or soup stock; *s. establishment,* a soup house or soup kitchen; *s. gravy,* gravy resembling soup; *s. herb,* an herb used in flavoring soup; *s. hole,* a hole in a marsh filled with mud and water of a souplike consistency; *s. piece,* a piece of meat suitable for use in soup.

1888 HARGIS *Graded Cook Book* 13 American Soup. One gallon cold water, one shank bone of veal, broken, one large beef soup bone. **1820** *Columbian Centinel* 12 Jan. 2/4 The Soup Establishment in Baltimore is spoken of as rendering the most extensive benefits. **1850** S. WARNER *Wide, Wide World* xxxviii, The soup-gravy poured over all would have met even Miss Fortune's wishes. **1923** WATTS *L. Nichols* 21 At his end of the stand, he presided over the onions, the green peppers, the bunches of dried soup-herbs [etc.]. **1911** *Essex Inst. Coll.* XLVII. 15 Little salt ponds or 'soup holes' . . . cover the marsh. **1902** L. RICHARDS *Mrs. Tree* 11 Direxia had been to market and had brought home the chops and the soup-piece.

Soup house. An establishment where soup is served to the poor at low cost or entirely free. {1861–} — **1809** BENTLEY *Diary* III. 412 A soup house is opened by subscription. **1837** *Niles' Nat. Reg.* 25 Feb. 416/3 The following is believed to be a correct statement of the number of persons supplied at four of the soup houses in Philadelphia. **1900** *Congress. Rec.* 17 Feb. 1900/1 The trusts and soup houses never prosper together.

+**Soup-house bill.** (See quotation.) — **1882** *Congress. Rec.* 5 Dec. 31/1 Is not the bill introduced by the gentleman from Pennsylvania commonly called the Soup-house bill? I refer to the bill for the establishment of soldiers' homes throughout the country.

Soup kitchen. =SOUP HOUSE. {1851–} — **1855** GLISAN *Jrnl. Army Life* 175 The City Council have established soup kitchens in various sections of [N.Y.]. **1869** HALE *Sybaris* 120 All our relief organizations, and all our soup kitchens, were but a poor apology for such a success as this. **1883** HOWELLS *Woman's Reason* xi, He saw her in a poverty that scarcely stopped short of the municipal soup-kitchen.

∗**Sour,** *n.* ||1. A facial expression manifesting discontent or bitterness. +2. (See quot. 1891 and cf. BRANDY SOUR, WHISKY SOUR.) +3. (See quot. 1902.) — (1) **1877** W. WRIGHT *Big Bonanza* 290 His face wears a calm, resigned, chronic 'sour.' (2) [**1889** *Pall Mall Gaz.* 20 June 3/2 Sours are made principally with whisky or brandy, or Santa Cruz rum.] **1891** *Cent.* 5785/1 *Sour,* . . . an acid punch. [Colloq.] (3) **1890** *Harper's Mag.* Oct. 708/2 He's so fond of sours. **1902** CLAPIN 377 *Sour,* used for pickles in parts of Pennsylvania. 'Pass the sour.'

∗**Sour,** *a.* In special combinations.

Sour beer, (see quotation); *s. bough,* a variety of apple; *s. clover,* (see quotation); *s. trefoil,* the wood sorrel, *Oxalis acetosella.*

1867 GOSS *Soldier's Story* 105 Another genius developed a process for converting Indian meal into beer, by souring it in water. And 'sour beer,' as it was termed, speedily became one of the institutions. **1853** FOWLER *Home for All* 146 The sweet and the sour Bough, ripe in July. **1915** ARMSTRONG & THORNBER *Western Wild Flowers* 262 Sour Clover. *Trifolium fucatum.* Cream-color. Spring, summer. Wash., Oreg., Cal. **1784** *Amer. Acad. Mem.* I. 446 Cuckow-Bread. Sour Trefoil. . . . An infusion of the leaves is an agreeable liquor in ardent fevers.

∗**Sour,** *v.* +intr. To sour on, to take a dislike to (a person or thing). — **1862** *Rocky Mt. News* (Denver) 20 Nov. (Th.), Guess the M.P. will 'sour' on William C. **1884** 'MARK TWAIN' *H. Finn* xix, But the duke kind of soured on him. **1898** WESTCOTT *D. Harum* xli, He's kind o' soured on the hull thing.

+**Sour-berry bush.** ?The small cranberry, *Oxycoccus palustris.* — **1847** PALMER *Rocky Mts.* (1904) 76 Occasionally there is a grove of quaking aspen, and a few sour-berry bushes.

Sourcrout. Also *sourkrout, sourkraut.* =SAUERKRAUT. {1617–} Also attrib.

1776 LEACOCK *Fall Brit. Tyranny* III. v, Don't leave me, and you shall have plenty of porter and sour-crout. **1806** *Balance* V. 25/1 Some of his neighbors might have spoken of him as . . . making excellent sour krout. **1857** 'MARK TWAIN' *Adv. Snodgrass* 38 The Dutch was friz to the sourkraut kegs.

||**b.** To look sourcrout at, to look at in a sour manner.

1846 CORCORAN *Pickings* 11 Here the Dutchman looked sourcrout at the tall, thin gentleman in the seedy black suit.

+**Sour gum. a.** =SOUR GUM TREE. **b.** =SOURWOOD. Also attrib. — **1785** MARSHALL *Amer. Grove* 97 Upland Tupelo-Tree, or Sour Gum. . . . The timber of this tree is . . . much used for hubs of wheels for waggons, carriages, &c. **1832** [see PIPPERIDGE]. **1885** M. THOMPSON *Byways & Bird*

Notes 118 The dogwood and sour-gum . . . flourish in fullest luxury of life and color. **1897** SUDWORTH *Arborescent Flora* 310, 311, 314.

+**Sour gum tree.** Any one of several trees of the genus *Nyssa*, as the tupelo and black gum. — **1857** GRAY *Botany* 162 *Nyssa*. Tupelo. Pepperidge. Sour Gum-tree. **1876** *Field & Forest* I. 66 The American Mistletoe . . . has been found growing on several Pepperidge or Sour-gum trees. **1891** COULTER *Bot. W. Texas* I. 151.

Sourkraut, Sourkrout. (See SOURCROUT.)

Sour mash. +Fermenting grain mash, or whisky made from this. Also attrib. — **1885** 'CRADDOCK' *Prophet* 150 Him an' me run a sour mash still on the top o' the mounting. **1894** ROBLEY *Bourbon Co., Kansas* 97 Ben said they run out of Polk County sour mash, and towards the last he had to chuck in some bay rum. **1902** CLAPIN 185 Another large group [of brands of whisky] is the 'sour-mash' family.

Sour orange. {1748} The bitter or Seville orange. — **1785** WASHINGTON *Diaries* II. 378 A few young Trees of the Civil or sower oranges in a box. **1812** STODDARD *Sk. Louisiana* 168 The Delta produces . . . sweet and sour oranges. **1836** *Knickerb.* VIII. 680 The wild sour orange . . . makes 'orangeade,' with good sugar.

+**Sour tupelo.** =OGEECHEE LIME. — **1810** MICHAUX *Arbres* I. 30 Nyssa capitata, *Sour Tupelo* (Tupelo à fruits aigres), dans l'Etat de Géorgie. **1832** BROWNE *Sylva* 220 The Sour Tupelo first makes its appearance on the river Ogeechee. **1884** SARGENT *Rep. Forests* 91. **1897** [see OGEECHEE LIME].

+**Sourwood.** A tree (*Oxydendrum arboreum*) common in the Allegheny region. Also attrib. — **1709** LAWSON *Carolina* 98 The Sorrel, or Sowr-Wood-Tree, is so call'd, because the Leaves taste like Sorrel. **1818** NUTTALL *N. Amer. Plants* 265. **1887** 'CRADDOCK' *Keedon Bluffs* 189 He clambered out of a clump of sour-wood shoots. **1896** POOL *In Buncombe County* 137 He cut me a whip from a sourwood. **1901** MOHR *Plant Life Ala.* 70 Among the tree growth of smaller size the sourwood . . . is most frequent.

*Souse. (See quot. 1895.) — **1805** *Pocumtuc Housewife* (1906) 6 Sausage, Ham, Souse, fried Pork and eggs . . . are always handy. **1839** *S. Lit. Messenger* VII. 39/2 Besides the animal figuring in part and in whole, . . . it may be traced in the stewed chine and souse. **1871** DE VERE 549 Souse, . . . often written sowce in New England and Virginia, means in Pennsylvania more generally pigs' feet. **1889** COOKE *Steadfast* 242 Sausages, head-cheese, and souse, were the matters in hand. **1895** *Dialect Notes* I. 394 Souse. . . . (1) Pigs' feet pickled or *soused* in brine. . . . (2) Pigs' ears and other parts as well as feet . . . either pickled or eaten fresh. . . . (4) The parts of the pig included in (2) and perhaps others, chopped or ground and potted.

*South, *n.**

1. The southern, esp. the present southeastern, part of the United States below the Mason and Dixon line. See also OLD SOUTH, SUNNY SOUTH.

1781 FRENEAU *Poems* (1786) 215 Cornwallis has manag'd . . . well in the South. **1832** *Congress. Deb.* 28 May 3155 The lofty and chivalrous spirit by which the people of the South have been heretofore distinguished. **1850** in A. C. Cole *Whig Party in So.* (1913) 174 We are heartily sick of this everlasting twaddle about the South—the South—that word of talismanic charm with southern demagogues. **1871** *Scribner's Mo.* II. 62 The colored population of the South. **1885** *Century Mag.* XXX. 280/2 White men of the South, what answer shall we, the intelligent, the cultured [etc.] . . . make to these men? **1902** BELL *Hope Loring* 4 In the South his business was conducted in a large and generous way.

+**b.** The Confederate States of America. Now hist.

1865 *Chicago Tribune* 15 April 1 The assassin . . . [shouted,] 'the South is avenged,' and then escaped from . . . the theater. **1880** *Harper's Mag.* July 260/2, [I] served the South during those four crucial years. **1898** PAGE *Red Rock* 50 Wherever a Southern woman stood during those four years, there in her small person was a garrison of the South.

+**2.** collect. The inhabitants of the southern states.

1796 [see NORTH]. **1837** *Diplom. Corr. Texas* I. (1908) 180 The North will be opposed and the South in favour of annexation. **1852** STOWE *Uncle Tom* xlv, Both North and South have been guilty before God. **1879** *Scribner's Mo.* June 306/1 We wonder if the South knows how hard it is making it for its friends. **1902** MEYER *Nominating Systems* 51 The party enthusiasm of the North greets that of the South.

*South, adv. +1.** =DOWN SOUTH. +**2.** To go south, (see quotation). — (1) **1834** C. A. DAVIS *Lett. J. Downing* 209 There warn't much in [nullification] . . . , but folks South thought there was. **1852** STOWE *Uncle Tom* xlii, A sister Emily . . . was sold South. **1898** PAGE *Red Rock* 526, I am going South to-night. (2) **1894** EGGLESTON in *Harper's Mag.* Feb. 470/2 The Dakota tribes believe that the soul, driven out of the body, journeys off to the south, and 'to go south' is, among the Sioux, the favorite euphemism for death.

South Americans. +(See quot. 1859.) *Obs.* — **1859** BARTLETT 430 *South Americans*, that branch of the American or Know-Nothing party which belongs to the South and favors slavery. **1860** *Harper's Mag.* May 860/2 The South Americans they have 23 votes, you know.

South Atlantic, *a.* +Belonging to the part of the United States extending from Delaware and Maryland south to Florida. — **1884** BLAINE *20 Years of Congress* I. 296 They had taken from the National Government its strongest fortress on the South-Atlantic coast. **1908** *S. Atlantic Quart.* Oct. 332 Gullah: a Negro Patois . . . spoken in the mainland and island regions, bordering the South Atlantic Seaboard.

Southbound. +A train bound for the south. In full *southbound train.* — **1885** JACKSON *Zeph* vi, I am going on the south-bound train.

1903 'O. HENRY' *Heart of West* 96 Passengers on the south-bound saw them seated together. **1909** — *Options* 273, I was on the south-bound, going to Cincinnati.

+**South Carolina.** *attrib.* Of or pertaining to the state of South Carolina. — **1853** in Stowe *Key* 68/2 The law with regard to the killing of runaways is laid down with . . . much clearness and precision by a South Carolina judge. **1859** *La Crosse Daily Union* 3 Nov. 4/3 The conflict . . . originated with the South Carolina Nullification. **1901** CHURCHILL *Crisis* 477 The South Carolina Campaign is a thing of the past.

+**South Carolinian.** A native or inhabitant of South Carolina.

1821 ROYALL *Lett. from Ala.* 137 She married a South Carolinian. **1862** MOORE *Rebellion Rec.* V, 11. 290, I was attacked at this place by . . . three regiments, composed of Kentuckians, Tennesseans, Georgians, Mississippians, Texans, and South-Carolinians. **1886** LOGAN *Great Conspiracy* 96 The Governor, the Congressional delegation, and other leading South Carolinians, met. **1906** BELL *C. Lee* 179 The whispers became nods and half-uttered words and mysterious signs which South Carolinians understood, but which mystified Mrs. Winchester.

attrib. **1856** MacLEOD *F. Wood* 45 He wrote . . . a review of South-Carolinian Governor Haynes' message in favor of Nullification. **1860** J. SHERMAN in *Sherman Lett.* 86 We have to meet . . . the movements of South Carolinian Disunionists.

Southdown. A short-wooled sheep or breed of sheep which originated in the South Downs of England. {1787-} Also attrib. — **1850** *Rep. Comm. Patents 1849: Agric.* 92 The Southdown and Tees-water are found more numerous than formerly. **1862** *Ib. 1861* 129 There are thousands of ewes . . . bred one season to either Southdown or Cotswold rams. **1870** *Rep. Comm. Agric. 1869* 384 Mr. A. F. Allen . . . has had for the last six years an average flock of 150 Southdowns and Leicesters. **1897** *Outing* XXX. 88/2 There is a barn for pure-bred Hampshire Down sheep, a large edition of the famous South Downs.

*South end. +The posteriors or buttocks. *colloq.* — **1883** 'MARK TWAIN' *Life on Miss.* iii, He bent stooping forward, with his back sagged and his south end sticking out far.

*Southern, *n.* +1.** =SOUTHERNER. +**2.** (See quotation.) — (1) **1834** CARRUTHERS *Kentuckian* I. 40 Those absorbing reveries [are] generally delightful in proportion to the goodness of the segar, which a southern knows so well how to enjoy. **1848** A. PRENTICE *Tour* 115 The annual migration of the southerns is very suggestive. (2) **1900** NELSON *A B C Wall St.* 17 Railroad stocks . . . are divided in distinctive groups, including the . . . Grangers, Southerns, Pacifics, and Local Transportations.

*Southern, *a.*

1. +**a.** Of Indians: Living in a southern region or in the southern states.

1684 *N.H. Hist. Soc. Coll.* VIII. 252 It [was] very necessary to entertain a number of southern Indians for soldiers. **1724** JONES *Virginia* 19 The Northern and Southern Nations might be managed by Missionaries from the Society. **1792** WASHINGTON *Writings* XII. 172 [They are] endeavoring to disaffect the four southern tribes of Indians towards this country.

+**b.** Of persons in general: Living in the southern states.

1789 *Ann. 1st Congress* 228 He did not mean to infer that the people of Massachusetts possessed any excellence over their Southern brethren. **1798** FESSENDEN *Orig. Poems* (1806) 56 With many a southern negro driver. **1803** J. DAVIS *Travels* 209 There was a perpetual conflict of opinions between these southern and northern men. **1851** *Knickerb.* XXXVIII. 550 Two stout 'Union men' . . . would go out of the way any day to catch a 'fugitive' for a 'Southern brother.' **1881** *Harper's Mag.* April 720/2 The Southern pupils, provided generously with money, . . . glanced with amusement at the attire of this girl from the Northwest. **1907** *St. Nicholas* May 619/2 He went there . . . in order to receive under his protection slaves who had succeeded in escaping from their Southern masters.

+**2.** Typical or characteristic of the southern states.

1836 *S. Lit. Messenger* II. 111/2 We have known a New Englander laugh at the Southern use of the word clever. **1862** BROWNE *A. Ward: His Book* 189 If what I've bin threw is 'Suthern hosspitality,' . . . I feel bound to observe [etc.]. **1884** *Century Mag.* July 398 The Klan disappeared from Southern life as it came into it, shrouded in deepest mystery. **1907** ANDREWS *Recoll.* 161 It was a generous southern meal.

+**3.** Located in the southern states.

1854 M. J. HOLMES *Tempest & Sunshine* 147 We will . . . pay a visit to Dr. Lacey in his southern home. **1887** *Century Mag.* May 111/1 Polly Ann had pounded the head of the hatchet on the handle—they have a natural tendency to part and go their separate ways in a Southern yard. **1911** PERSONS, etc. *Mass. Labor Laws* 23 In many . . . of the Middle and Southern mills, the hours are stated to have been even longer.

+**b.** Coming from the southwestern part of the United States.

1890 *Stock Grower & Farmer* 15 Feb. 6/4 Unless the price of southern steers is considerably under that of last season very few will be purchased for Montana.

*4. In specific names. **a.** Of trees and plants.

1813 MUHLENBERG *Cat. Plants* 96 *Fraxinus australis*, Southern ash. **1857** Southern buckthorn [see BUCKTHORN 2]. **1860** CURTIS *Woody Plants N.C.* 79 Southern Linn, (*T[ilia] pubescens*,) . . . is confined to the Lower Districts of the Southern States. **1868** *Amer. Naturalist* I. 639 The Southern Muscadine . . . is the *Vitis Rotundifolia* of Michaux. **1892** APGAR *Trees Northern U.S.* 184 *Abies Fraseri.* (Fraser's or Southern Balsam-fir.) . . . A rare, small tree, growing wild in the mountains, from Virginia south. *Ib. Taxodium distichum.* . . . (Southern or Bald Cypress.) . . . Wild from Maryland south. **1901** MOHR *Plant Life Ala.* 61 Southern crabapple (*Pyrus angustifolia*) frequent[s] the openings and borders of the woodlands. *Ib.* 87 The Southern shellbark or shagbark hickory is also abundant in these coves.

b. Of birds, fishes, etc.

1857 *Rep. Comm. Patents 1856: Agric.* 86 The Southern shrike, (*Lanius ludovicianus,*) . . . breeds largely in the prairie districts. **1874** COUES *Birds N.W.* 407 *Pediœcetes phasianellus.* . . . Southern Sharp-tailed Grouse. **1883** *Century Mag.* July 376/2 In portions of Virginia they are called chub, southern chub, or Roanoke chub. **1883** *Nat. Museum Bul.* No. 27, 455 *Notemigonus americanus.* Southern Bream; Shiner; Roach. **1917** *Birds of Amer.* III. 99 Loggerhead Shrike. *Lanius ludovicianus ludovicianus.* . . . [Also called] Southern Loggerhead Shrike; Southern Butcher Bird. *Ib.* 161/2 The Florida, or Southern, Yellow-throat (*Geothlypis trichas ignota*) is found in the southeastern United States. **1917** *Mammals of Amer.* 18/2 Southern Black-tailed Deer.—*Odocoileus columbianus scaphiotus.* . . . Southern California.

+**5.** In special combinations.

Southern brigadier, =REBEL BRIGADIER; *S. Congress,* the Congress of the Southern Confederacy; *S. Cross,* the battle flag of the Southern Confederacy; *s. Democrat,* a Democrat of the southern states; *s. fever,* a disease of cattle, transmitted by the cattle tick; *S. league,* one of the secret organizations formed in the South about 1860 to safeguard Southern interests; *S. measure,* a measure or bill in Congress favoring the South; *s. Methodism,* the Methodism prevailing in the South as a result of the separation in the Methodist Episcopal church over slavery in 1845; *S. side,* the side of the legislative chamber in the lower house of Congress occupied by members of the Democratic party; *S. Unionist, S. Union man,* a southerner who favored the Union cause during the Civil War; *s. Whig,* a southern member of the Whig party.

1886 POORE *Reminisc.* II. 272 The 'carpet-baggers' from the South were gradually being replaced by ante-bellum politicians and 'Southern brigadiers.' **1861** Moore *Rebellion Rec.* I. III. 95 Wm. C. Rives, a delegate from Virginia to the Southern Congress . . . , was called on . . . for a speech. **1866** in Fleming *Hist. Reconstruction* I. 66 The place which has so long been sacred to the 'Southern Cross.' **1900** *Congress. Rec.* 31 Jan. 1365/1 You can not discuss any question with a Southern Democrat . . . that he does not holler 'Nigger.' **1895** *Dept. Agric. Yrbk. 1894* 78 The losses from the Southern or Texas fever have been almost entirely prevented. **1861** in Logan *Great Conspiracy* 250 Senators entrusted with the representative sovereignty of the States . . . conceive a Conspiracy for the overthrow of the Government through the military organizations, . . . 'Committees of Safety,' Southern leagues, etc. **1854** BENTON *30 Years' View* I. 10/1 The non-slaveholding States . . . were successful in producing the compromise, conceived and passed as a Southern measure. **1866** in Fleming *Hist. Reconstruction* II. 243 This general remark applies more fully to Southern Methodism than to any other Southern ecclesiastical system. **1860** *Harper's Mag.* May 832/2 Mr. Lovejoy . . . advanced into the area, approaching the 'Southern side' of the House. **1866** *Ore. State Jrnl.* 15 Sept. 1/1 Convention of Southern Unionists. **1865** TROWBRIDGE *Three Scouts* 21, I believe Southern Union men are a humbug. **1855** in Hambleton *H. A. Wise* 76 The Southern Whigs very properly, refused to act as a party with such confederates.

+**b.** In adjectival compounds with *born, looking, made.*

1832 *Congress. Deb.* 28 May 3151 The prices of Southern made shoes could not be any higher than that of Northern made shoes in the same common market. **1853** STOWE *Key* 133/2 Various circumstances . . . from infancy conspire to degrade and depress the negro in the eyes of a Southern-born man. **1883** 'MARK TWAIN' *Life on Miss.* xxxiv, Lake Providence, La. . . . is the first distinctly Southern-looking town you come to.

+**Southern chivalry.** **1.** The chivalric manners and bearing of refined southern gentlemen. **2.** The aristocracy of the South. — **(1) 1857** [see DOLLAR 4]. **1868** *N.Y. Herald* 4 July 4/1 Here comes Wade Hampton, a gentleman from South Carolina, with all the Southern chivalry we were taught to admire some years ago. **(2) 1885** [see CHIVALRY *note*].

+**Southern colony.** A colony in the southern part of what is now the eastern United States. — **1724** JONES *Virginia* 18 These . . . are the Indians that make . . . such Disturbance in the Northern and Southern Colonies. **1774** HUTCHINSON *Diary & Lett.* I. 229 There are accounts from the south[er]n Colonies. **1789** *Ann. 1st Congress* 223 Previous to the late war we had a market in Nova Scotia, Newfoundland, and Canada, all the Southern Colonies, Europe, and Africa.

+**Southern confederacy.** **1.** A discussed or contemplated confederacy embracing the southern portion of the United States. *Obs.* **2.** *cap.* The Confederate States of America. Now hist. — **(1) 1788** MADISON *Writings* V. 80, I have for some time considered him as driving at a Southern Confederacy. **1837** *S. Lit. Messenger* III. 84 He regarded every attempt to unite the South, in support of a Southern President, as a prelude to the formation of a Southern Confederacy. **1860** ABBOTT *South & North* 307 The Southern confederacy shall again have its free North, and its slaveholding South, as now. **(2) 1863** WHITMAN *Nov. Boughs* (1888) 447 The Copperheads are getting furious, and want to recognize the Southern Confederacy. **1891** *Harper's Mag.* Dec. 46/2 If England had recognized the Southern Confederacy [etc.].

+**Southern corn.** A variety of Indian corn suited to the climate of the southern states. — **1820** *Columbian Centinel* 5 Jan. 4/5 Munson & Barnard . . . Offer for sale . . . 2000 bushels Southern Corn. **1856** *Rep. Comm. Patents 1855: Agric.* 166 Analysis of the Cob of 'Southern Corn,' a Red-colored Variety, grown near Cape May, New Jersey. **1874** *Rep. Comm. Agric. 1873* 414 It is more trouble to grow Southern corn [than sweet corn].

Southern country. +The southern part of the United States; the southern states. — **1789** *Ann. 1st Congress* 231 However slavery may be condemned in the Eastern States, it is impracticable to cultivate the Southern country without their assistance. **1836** *S. Lit. Messenger* II. 279 Everyone who is acquainted with the condition of society in our southern country, will bear witness [etc.]. **1852** EASTMAN *Aunt Phillis's Cabin* 50 Should the southern country become free . . . it will not be through the efforts of these fanatics.

Southern Empire. (See EMPIRE 1.)

Southerner. {1833-} +A native of the southern states. — **1828** *Western Mo. Rev.* II. 12 The Southerner, too, is such over the whole globe. **1860** OLMSTED *Back Country* 251 A great many of the 'Southerners,' as they are called here, are now traveling farther north. **1886** POORE *Reminisc.* II. 80 It was not uncommon to meet on Pennsylvania Avenue a defiant Southerner openly wearing a large Virginia or South Carolina secession badge. **1904** 'O. HENRY' *Roads of Destiny* 359, I believe I'm half Southerner by nature.

+**Southern gentleman.** A gentleman from the South. — **1789** *Ann. 1st Congress* 215 Suppose a member from Massachusetts was to propose an impost on negroes, what would you hear from the Southern gentlemen, if fifty dollars was the sum to be laid? **1852** EASTMAN *Aunt Phillis's Cabin* 27 Mr. Weston will stand for a specimen of the southern gentleman of the old school. **1884** [see CLAIM *n.* 1]. **1905** N. DAVIS *Northerner* 20 He has hurried off like a veritable Southern gentleman, an hour late, to keep [his engagement].

+**Southernism.** **1.** The qualities characteristic of southern culture or life. **2.** A word or expression peculiar to the southern states. — **(1) 1861** *N.Y. Tribune* 15 July (Chipman), Southernism has raised the standard . . . of social condition. [**1911** *Quarterly Reg. Panpresb. Chs.* (London) Nov. 479 New Orleans has its solid *Southernism* before, during, and since the war.] **(2) 1882** *Amer. Missionary* April 108 Aside from African features . . . and some Southernisms in voice and expression. **1886** *Academy* 11 Sept. 174/3 Prof. C. F. Smith of Nashville, read some interesting notes on 'Southernisms.'

+**Southern Methodist.** A member of the Methodist Episcopal Church, South. Also attrib. — **1846** *Jrnl. Gen. Conf. M.E. Church, S.* I. 105 Southern Methodists were enabled . . . to carry on . . . the ordinary operations of church enterprise. **1872** *Congress. Globe* App. 30 May 478/3 You belonged to the Southern Methodist Church? **1883** RITCH *Illust. N. Mex.* 57 The Baptists, Congregationalists and Southern Methodists have each a couple of clergymen on the ground. **1924** *Southwest Rev.* Oct. 89 The story of active service of Southern Methodist University . . . heartens every friend of humane culture in the state.

+**Southern pine.** =GEORGIA PINE. Also attrib. and transf.

1810 MICHAUX *Arbres* I. 17 *Southern pine* . . . et *Red pine* . . . dans les Etats du milieu et du nord. **1842** [see GEORGIA PITCH PINE]. **1852** *Harper's Mag.* Dec. 85* Jackson, the stalwart Hickory; Clay, the graceful Elm; Calhoun, the lofty, erect Southern Pine; all had gone before [Webster]. **1894** COULTER *Bot. W. Texas* III. 554. **1918** *Amer. Builder* April 83 Our Southern Pine products include . . . siding and flooring material.

b. Lumber obtained from this pine.

1900 BRUNCKEN *N. Amer. Forests* 70 Probably the extreme limit, however, for supplying the market with original southern pine on a large scale is fifty years.

+**c.** *Southern pine finch,* (see quotation).

1917 *Birds of Amer.* III. 49/1 The Pine-woods Sparrow of Florida and its northern variety Bachman's Sparrow, or Southern Pine Finch (*Peucœa æstivalis bachmani*) are striped Sparrows that are distinctly southern birds.

+**Southern rights.** Political rights, particularly with regard to slavery, which those in the South, prior to the Civil War, felt they had under the Federal Constitution. *Obs.* Also attrib. — **1851** *Harper's Mag.* June 129/1 A Convention of the Southern Rights Association assembled at Charleston, May 5. **1851** in Claiborne *Life Quitman* II. 135 The Southern-rights men will be ready to carry everything before them. **1852** *Whig Almanac 1853* 42/2 Candidate of the Southern Rights Party. **1865** PIKE *Scout & Ranger* (1932) 127, I heard nothing now, but clamor about 'Northern aggression,' and 'Southern rights,' wherever I went.

+**Southern-stater.** A native of the southern states. *Obs.* — **1849** *Knickerb.* XXXIV. 219 Speak of your Virginian, your South-Carolinian, and Southern-Staters in general; where are they? **1851** *Harper's Mag.* June 36/2 A Southern-stater, with a spanking wagon-team, and two grinning negroes behind, were new and strange elements in the life of a city.

+**Southern states.** The states in the southern part of the United States, esp. those south of Mason and Dixon's line and east of New Mexico. — **1776** *Jrnls. Cont. Congress* VI. 1039 Resolved, That two other magazines of ammunition . . . be formed, one in the eastern states, and one in the southern states. **1815** CAREY *Olive Branch* 282 The hardy and enterprizing Yankees pervade every bay, river, creek, and inlet of the southern states. **1864** *Wkly. New Mexican* 10 June 2/1 Very little money has been realized . . . from the cotton owned by the Southern or Confederate States. **1911** *Rep. Fisheries 1908* 307/2 The small-mouth bass . . . in the Southern states . . . is also called 'jumper.'

‖**Southernwise**, *adv*. In a manner favorable to the South. — **1862** *N.Y. Herald* 25 May (*Chipman*), I found them Southernwise inclined in sentiment and feeling.

⁂**Southernwood. a.** A shrubby European plant (*Artemisia abrotanum*) introduced into the United States. +**b.** =SAGE 2. — **1737** BRICKELL *N. Carolina* 20 The Pot-Herbs . . . [are] Dandelion, Wormwood, Southernwood. **1804** LEWIS in *L. & Clark Exped.* II. (1904) 68 The narrow bottoms of the Missouri producing little else but Hysop or southern wood and the pulpy leafed thorn. **1839** *S. Lit. Messenger* V. 751/2 Bachelor's hat with southernwood or old man, were conspicuous embellishments to almost every parterre. **1891** EARLE *Sabbath* 40 A large bunch of aromatic southernwood, or 'lad's-love,' . . . had been brought to meeting by the matron in the next pew. **1895** A. BROWN *Meadow-Grass* 240 Coming back to the southernwood, she took it in her arms.

⁂**Southland.** +**1.** The southern part of the United States; the southern states. +**2.** Southern California. — (1) [**1812** PAULDING *J. Bull & Bro. Jon.* 92 The farms usually called Southlands were principally settled by people who, having a great number of slaves, were great sticklers for liberty.] **1849** [see PRAIRIED *a.*]. **1880** TOURGEE *Bricks* 344 The colored man and the poor-whites of the South ought to . . . establish free schools and free thought and free labor in the fair, crippled, South-land. **1910** MCCUTCHEON *Rose in Ring* 4 The smile was creeping back into the haggard face of the Southland. (2) **1898** *Pomona Progress* 23 June, Santa Monica, determined to be one of the most progressive cities in the southland, has begun a campaign to rid the city of wooden or metal awnings.

Southlander. {1823-} +=SOUTHERNER. *Obs.* — **1812** PAULDING *J. Bull & Bro. Jon.* 92 The Southlanders . . . were a set of frank, jolly, hospitable, high-spirited fellows.

⁂**Southron.** +=SOUTHERNER. Also transf. — **1828** *Free Press* (Tarboro, N.C.) 9 Nov., I am a Republican in principle, and a Southron in feeling. **1831** AUDUBON *Ornith. Biog.* I. 110 When those [mocking birds] which had gone to the Eastern States . . . have returned, they are instantly known by the 'southrons,' who attack them on all occasions. **1859** A. VAN BUREN *Sojourn in South* 21 [Their] accent on many words bespeak them Southrons. **1878** *N. Amer. Rev.* CXXVI. 84 The Southron was a better fighter than the Northerner.

South Sea tea. =CASSINE 1. {1728-} Also attrib. — **1785** South-Sea Tea-Tree [see CASSINE 1]. **1813** MUHLENBERG *Cat. Plants* 18 *Ilex Cassena* (*vomitoria*) Cassena, South Sea tea. **1871** DE VERE 396 South-sea-tea or Yopon . . . occurs North and South.

+**South-southerly.** *local.* =LONG-TAILED DUCK. — **1813** WILSON *Ornithology* VIII. 93 This Duck is very generally known along the shores of the Chesapeake Bay by the name of South Southerly, from the singularity of its cry, something imitative of the sound of those words. **1875** *Fur, Fin & Feather* (ed. 3) 119 At the South it [the long-tailed duck] is called the South southerly. **1917** [see OLD *a.* 6].

⁂**Southward.** +The southern part of the United States; the southern colonies or states. *Obs.* — **1773** in Fithian *Journal* I. 41, I will let you know whenever I can hear anything related to your prospect of going to the southward. **1789** *Ann. 1st Congress* 230 Are there not other articles of trade of great moment to the southward? **1801** *Steele P.* I. 226 Mr. Porter . . . is absent to the Southward.

+**Southward Indians.** Indians dwelling south of a particular region, esp. those south of the Ohio River. *Obs.* — **1671** *S.C. Hist. Soc. Coll.* V. 341 Corne from time to time [is] taken out of the plantations by the Kussoe and other Southward Indians. **1725** in *Travels Amer. Col.* 114 If they were in Unity with the Southward Indians they should have no enemy. **1765** CROGHAN *Journal* (1904) 61 They brought an Account that the Southward Indians had come to the Lower Towns to War.

⁂ **Southwest.** +The southwestern part of the United States.

As in the case of Far West, the meaning of this term has shifted as the United States expanded.

1835 INGRAHAM *South-West* I. 73 We are at last in New-Orleans, the queen of the South-west. **1853** BALDWIN *Flush Times Ala.* 224 There is no greater error than that which assigns inferiority to the bar of the South-West. **1870** W. BAKER *New Timothy* 75 That very different operation known throughout the South-west as 'dipping snuff.' **1873** *Newton Kansan* 15 May 2/2 The A. T. & S. F. R. Road has already reached the southwest. **1880** *Cimarron News & Press* 21 Oct. 2/2 The broad plains of New Mexico at Springer . . . is the great pastoral region of the Southwest. **1913** BARNES *Western Grazing Grounds* 380 Arroyo. . . . Used in the Southwest generally to designate a dry wash.

attrib. **1860** *Harper's Mag.* Sept. 565/1 Captain H—— raved in true Southwest steamboat style for a few minutes.

Southwester. {1833-} **1.** *Naut.* A large waterproof hat having a large flap at the back to protect the head and neck in wet or stormy weather. {1845-} +**2.** *cap.* A native or inhabitant of the Southwest. — (1) **1840** DANA *Two Years* 439 We spring out of our berths, clap on a monkey-jacket and southwester, and tumble up the ladder. **1883** *Century Mag.* Oct. 947/1 The foaming crest . . . concealed for a moment the six oil-jackets and south-westers. (2) **1867** EDWARDS *Shelby* 231 Colonel Hooper rode to the front, taking with him Captain Lea, and some others of the Southwesters.

Southwesterly, *adv.* Southwestwardly. {1708-, as adj.} — **1755** L. EVANS *Anal. Map Colonies* 28 The same little broken Chain of Hills . . . continues South Westerly. **1849** *31st Congress 1 Sess.* H. R. Ex. Doc. No. 5, II. 883 The hills have a general course northeasterly and southwesterly. **1883** *American* VII. 168 The party now headed southwesterly for the Siberian coast.

⁂**Southwestern,** *a.* +Situated or living in the southwestern part of the United States. — **1794** *Ann. 3d Congress* 778 Mr. McDowell rose to correct what had fallen from Mr. Ames, as to the strength of the Indian nations on the Southwestern frontier. **1828** COOPER *Notions* II. 328 There is still another establishment [of Shaking Quakers], in one of the southwestern states. **1857** BENTON *Exam. Dred Scott Case* 47, [I] give two strong instances of action on slavery in that body [Congress]—Southwestern Territory, and original United States Territory. **1890** *Stock Grower & Farmer* 1 Feb. 3/2 The southwestern sheep owners must get a cross into their flocks that will make bigger and better mutton.

+**Southwesterner.** A native or inhabitant of the southwestern part of the United States. — **1860** WHITMAN *Leaves of Grass* 350 There shall be countless linked hands—namely, the Northeasterner's, and the Northwesterner's, and the Southwesterner's, and those of the interior. **1888** *Century Mag.* Feb. 502/2 The bulk of the cowboys themselves are Southwesterners.

⁂ **Sovereign.**

+**1.** The supreme governing power in a country or state.

[**1787** J. ADAMS *Defence of Constitutions* I. 26 The sovereign [in Switzerland] is the whole country.] **1829** JACKSON in Benton *30 Years' View* I. 164/1 These states, claiming to be the only sovereigns within their territories, extend their laws over the Indians. **1861** *Chicago Tribune* 19 July 1/2 None need be afraid that they will be held accountable for past opinions, . . . if they will now . . . acknowledge their allegiance to Virginia and her Confederate States, as their true and lawful sovereigns.

+**2.** An American voter or citizen.

1846 *Ind. Hist. Soc. Publ.* III. 412 This fact illustrates the situation of thousands of the future sovereigns of our beloved State. **1862** *N.Y. Tribune* 7 June (*Chipman*), [Nissen said that he] could not be forced to take an oath of allegiance to the Confederacy. . . . Instantly the 'sovereigns' in attendance pitched upon the audacious recusant. **1869** 'MARK TWAIN' *Innocents* 100, I am a free-born sovereign, sir, an American, sir.

+**b.** *To play the sovereign,* (see quotation).

1877 *Notes & Queries* 5th Ser. VIII. 186/1 In Western Pennsylvania, when a candidate for office puts on shabby clothes a short time before an election, drinks whiskey with everybody, and shakes hands with everybody, he is said to be 'playing the sovereign.'

+**Sovereigns of Industry.** (See quotation.) — **1877** BARTLETT 631 *Sovereigns of Industry*, a name assumed by artisans in the United States, who, by co-operative measures, endeavor to secure labor's products at cost, dispensing with middlemen.

Sovereign state. +One of the states in the Federal Union. — **1819** MARSHALL *Constitutional Opinions* (1839) 160 The defendant, a sovereign state, denies the obligation of a law enacted by the legislature of the union. **1847** *Whig Almanac 1848* 43/2 Shall we, the representatives of the Sovereign States of this Union . . . , precipitate this fearful struggle? **1861** *Chicago Tribune* 19 July 1/2 The sovereign state [Va.] proclaimed it [a second independence]. **1871** *Harper's Mag.* Dec. 51/1, I'll teach him . . . to go a-cavorting round coercing sovereign States of this Union.

⁂**Sovereignty.** +A state or statehood in the Federal Union; the authority possessed by a state in the management of its affairs. — **1799** *Ky. Resolutions* in Elliot *Debates* IV. (1836) 545 A nullification, by those sovereignties, of all unauthorized acts done under color of that instrument, is the rightful remedy. **1818** *Niles' Reg.* XIII. 298/1 Missouri and Illinois . . . will soon prefer their claims to sovereignty. **1846** MCKENNEY *Memoirs* I. 258 [President Jackson's] answer was, 'Sir, the sovereignty of the States must be preserved.' **1869** [see DIAMOND STATE].

+**Sowbelly.** Fat salt pork or bacon. *colloq.* — **1867** Goss *Soldier's Story* 205 My captor presented to me a generous slice of 'sow-belly.' **1876** CROFUTT *Trans-continental Tourist* 87 On the plains, bacon is called 'sow-belly.' **1917** J. A. MOSS *Officers' Manual* 485 Sow-belly, bacon.

Sow bug. {1750-} +(See quotation.) — **1883** *Harper's Mag.* Jan. 186/1 The common sow-bug (*idotæa*) often illumines the crevices and sea-weeds along our shores.

⁂**Sow thistle.** Any one of various plants of the genus *Sonchus.* — **1784** *Amer. Acad. Mem.* I. 474 Sowthistle. Blossoms purple. **1850** S. F. COOPER *Rural Hours* 106 It will be easy to name a number of these [weeds]:—such, for instance, as . . . the sow thistles; the chess. **1899** GOING *Flowers* 376 There is no month in the year in which one may not see the flowers of chickweed, sow-thistle and shepherd's-purse.

Sow-tit. *transf.* +The wild strawberry (*Fragaria vesca*) or a species of blackberry. — **1788** CUTLER in *Life & Corr.* I. 410 A white oak . . . [has a] cavity in the middle covered with sow-tits. **1893** *Amer. Folk-Lore* VI. 141 *Rubus villosus*, 'sow-tit' (teat). N.H.; Farrington, Conn.; Goshen, Conn.

Sozzle, *n.* {1823-} +A slattern; a state of disorder. *colloq.* — **1848** BARTLETT 321 *Sossle*, or *Sozzle*. A lazy or sluttish woman. Provincial in Connecticut. **1854** H. H. RILEY *Puddleford* 119 Mrs. Bird . . . was a great sozzle about home. **1866** A. D. WHITNEY *L. Goldthwaite* x, The woman . . . had always hated . . . anything like what she called a 'sozzle.'

Sozzle, *v.* {1836-, *dial.*}

+**1.** *tr.* To wash by splashing; to souse or douse. *colloq.* — **1845** JUDD *Margaret* I. 8 [Margaret] sat down and sozzled her feet in the foam. **1895** *Outing* XXVI. 393/2 We can just sozzle our faces here at the rain-water barrel. **1902** MCFAUL *Ike Glidden* 9 Ef yer call it thoughtlessness for a grown young man like him . . . ter sozzle my broody hen . . . with a pail o' water.

+2. *intr.* (See quot. 1848.)

1848 BARTLETT 321 *To Sozzle*, to loll; to lounge; to go lazily or sluttishly about the house. A term used by housekeepers in certain parts of Connecticut. 'This woman sozzles up her work.' **1885** JACKSON *Zeph* 44 He goes sozzlin' round, 'n' wastin' his time, 'n' gettin' out o' pocket.

Sozzling, *a.* **+1.** Becoming wet or soggy. **+2.** Slovenly, shiftless. *colloq.* — (1) **1852** *Knickerb.* XL. 183 Soiled and sozzling shirt-collars . . . stuck to such sap-heads as stirred in the sun. (2) **1878** COOKE *Happy Dodd* 368 'Tain't natur that a great lazy sozzlin' girl is one a woman will fellowship. **1911** *Dialect Notes* III. 547 Don't be so sozzling. [Neb.]

+Sozzly, *a.* (See quot. 1891.) — **1873** WHITNEY *Other Girls* xv, They grow helplesser all the time and the help grows sozzlier. **1891** *Cent.* 5790/2 *Sozzly*, sloppy; draggled; mentally flabby; shiftless. [New Eng.]

* Space.

+1. (See quotation.)

1877 BARTLETT 631 *Space*, floor. Second space, first floor. Massachusetts.

+2. a. *To be paid by space*, to be paid as a writer according to the amount of space occupied by one's writings. **b.** *On space*, on terms involving payment according to the space occupied by a writer's articles.

1893 PHILIPS *Making of Newspaper* 16 The special correspondents who send news by telegraph or post . . . are paid by 'space,' or at so much per column. **1894** SHUMAN *Steps into Journalism* 83 Articles by the beginner are nearly always submitted 'on space.' **1902** BANKS *Newspaper Girl* 202 If she is 'on space' [she] will soon find the editors with 'no work on hand to-day.'

+3. *attrib.* and *comb.* Of or pertaining to writing or drawing for a newspaper or periodical on space rates.

[**1887** *Westminster Rev.* Oct. 858 The standard of literary excellence in the news columns of the New York press has also been lowered by the general substitution of 'space writing' for the work of salaried reporters.] **1892** HOWELLS *Quality of Mercy* 116 He felt that as a space-man . . . his duty to his family required him to use every means for making copy. **1893** Philips *Making of Newspaper* 44 An ordinary 'space' reporter of today excels in cleverness the 'staff' special writer of twenty years ago. **1902** BANKS *Newspaper Girl* 207 [By] the 'guarantee space' system . . . a member of the staff is guaranteed a stipulated sum of money every week, and as much over that amount as he or she makes by writing at ordinary or special space-rates. *Ib.* 233 Space artists get paid two dollars a single-column cut.

Spaddle. (See quotation.) {1669} — **1835** TODD *Notes* 8 Jonathan . . . [uses] *spaddle*, for spade.

* Spade, *n.*

* 1. A shovellike instrument, usually having a flat oblong blade, which can be pushed into the ground with the foot.

1634 in WINTHROP *Hist.* (1853) I. 464 Spades and shovels. **1711** *N.C. Col. Rec.* I. 764, I am forced to work hard with Axe Hoe & spade. **1741** [see PIONEER *n.* 1]. **1864** *Harper's Mag.* Oct. 561/1 His spade stands ready to dig it, and his wheelbarrow to wheel it. **1885** CRAWFORD *Amer. Politician* 211 Enormous Irishmen . . . , armed with broad wooden spades, were struggling to keep the drifts from the pavement. **1902** *Harper's Mag.* May 943 You helped her win your little spade.

+2. A blade on the rotary wheel of a spader.

1864 *Ohio Agric. Rep.* XVIII. p. xxii, The result [of the operation of the spaders] may be taken as a fair average of what may be expected of the performance of the spades. **1876** KNIGHT 2252/1 The sharp-pointed spades . . . rotate in the direction in which the machine moves.

3. *attrib.* **a.** In sense 1 with *shovel.* **b.** In sense 2 with *wheel.*

1797 HAWKINS *Letters* 210, I want some nails, the spade shovel, hand saw [etc.]. **1874** KNIGHT 703/1 The ground-wheel *b* drives the spade-wheel.

* Spade, *v.* **1.** *To spade up*, to break up the soil of (a plot of ground) by digging and turning it over with a spade. **+2.** *To spade in*, to mix with the soil by digging. **+3.** *tr.* Of a spader: To break up (land). — (1) **1785** WASHINGTON *Diaries* II. 410 Began to spade up the Lawn in front of the Court yard. **1857** *Quinland* I. 184 Father and I spaded up the onion-bed after supper. (2) **1852** *Mich. Agric. Soc. Trans.* III. 185 Throw barnyard manure around them, and spade it in. (3) **1864** *Ohio Agric. Rep.* XVIII. p. xxi, This machine . . . [in] twenty-six and three-fourth days . . . spaded one hundred and sixty acres.

Spadefish. A fish shaped, or having a part shaped, like a spade. {1704-} — **1805** T. M. HARRIS *Journal* 116 A curious fish called the Spade-Fish . . . is furnished with a bony weapon projecting from the nose . . . like a narrow shovel. **1884** GOODE, etc. *Fisheries* I. 445 The Moon-Fish—*Chætodipterus Faber*. . . . In the northern parts of the Gulf of Mexico it is called the 'Spade-fish.' **1911** *Rep. Fisheries 1908* 307/1 ['Angelfish' is] applied to the moonfish, or spadefish . . . , from Florida to Charleston.

Spadefoot. {1891-} +One of various toads of the genus *Scaphiopus*, having a horny sheath adaptable to digging. {1901, of other toads} Also with specifying terms. — **1842** *Nat. Hist. N.Y.*, *Zoology* III. 66 Hermit Spade-foot. . . . In the neighborhood of Salem . . . they appear in great numbers. **1884** *Amer. Naturalist* XVIII. 1075 These spade-foots

remained in the shallow waters of this sink-hole. [**1899** *Zool. Soc. Proc.* (London) 790 On the American Spade-foot (*Scaphiopus solitarius*).]

+Spadefoot (or **Spade-footed**) **toad.** =prec. Also with defining terms. {1901, of other toads} — **1867** *Amer. Naturalist* I. 108 The Spade-footed Toads . . . are more uncertain in their appearance. **1884** *Ib.* XVIII. 1075 Near Trenton . . . there suddenly appeared a large colony of hermit spade-foot toads. **1891** *Cent.* 5376/1 *Scaphiopodinæ*, . . . a subfamily of *Pelobatidæ* . . . containing the American spade-footed toads.

Spader. {1647} +A machine provided with a rotary device for digging into and pulverizing land. — **1863** *Ill. Agric. Soc. Trans.* V. 255 If the rotary spader does not throw the steel clipper out of place. **1864** [see FOUR-HORSE *a.* 1]. **1874** KNIGHT 703/1 Other forms of spaders have blades thrust out and retracted as the machine advances.

+Spading fork. A flat- and broad-pronged fork for spading. — **1863** *Horticulturist* March, Advt. 15 New York Agricultural Warehouse [has for sale] . . . Spading Forks, Weeding Forks [etc.]. **1874** *Vermont Bd. Agric. Rep.* II. 272 The ground, however, may be kept mellow by the use of the cultivator and spading fork.

Spading-machine. =SPADER. — **1862** *Rep. Comm. Patents 1861: Agric.* 647 Spading-machines, Rotary. **1874** KNIGHT 702/2 Digging-machine, . . . a spading-machine for loosening and turning the soil.

Span, *n.* [Du.] +A pair of horses, mules, or donkeys, harnessed together as a team, and usually matched. {1828, in Canada} — **1769** *Boston Gaz.* 2 Oct. (Th.), Wanted, a Spann of good Horses for a Curricle. **1838** 'UNCLE SAM' in *Bentley's Misc.* IV. 41, I'd bet a span on 'em to a span of blind donkeys, you never seed any better. **1860** GREELEY *Overland Journey* 81 We were stalled until an extra span of mules was sent from the other wagon. **1885** *Wkly. New Mexican Rev.* 2 July 2/4 Col. Grayson . . . paid the Duncan boys $365 for a span of roadsters. **1899** TARKINGTON *Gentleman from Ind.* vii, There were . . . comfortable carryalls drawn by steady spans.

*Span, *v.* +(See quotations.) — **1828** WEBSTER, *Span*, to agree in color, or in color and size; as, the horses span well. (*New England.*) **1891** *Cent.* 5793/2 *Span*, . . . to be matched for running in harness; form a span. . . . (U.S.)

+Span, *adv.* [?f. the first element of *span-new*.] Entirely; completely. — **1843** STEPHENS *High Life N.Y.* II. 110 The men folks had on span white gloves. **1850** JUDD *R. Edney* 86 Her tire . . . was span-clean this morning. **1878** B. F. TAYLOR *Between Gates* 182 [The dresses] have been washed span-clean. **1887** *Lippincott's Mag.* Sept. 360 He got clean span away.

Spancel, *v.* {1610-} +(See quotation.) — **1859** BARTLETT 431 *To Spancel*, . . . to prevent a crab from biting, by sticking the point of a leg into the base of each movable claw.

+Spandy, *a.* Very good; new. — **1868** ALCOTT *Little Women* I. 126 My silk stockings and two pairs of spandy gloves are my comfort.

+Spandy, *adv.* Very; perfectly. — **1848** BARTLETT 322 *Span-clean, Spandy-clean*, very clean; perfectly clean. **1869** ALCOTT *Little Women* II. 11 The spandy-new kitchen never *could* have looked so cosy and neat. **1903** WIGGIN *Rebecca* 15 These [shoes] are spandy new I've got on, and they have to last six months.

+Span-fired-new, *a.* Brand-new. *colloq.* (Cf. BRAN-FIRE-NEW.) — **1843** STEPHENS *High Life N.Y.* II. 82 Jase was a going to send down his span fired new carriage to the Astor House, arter Lord Morpeth and I afore dinner time.

+Spang, *adv.* Directly; straight; smack; entirely. *colloq.* — **1843** 'CARLTON' *New Purchase* I. 173 She got three times right spang through it. *c*1845 *Big Bear Ark.* 158, I'm spang out of meat. *c*1875 BAGBY *Old Va. Gentleman* 304, I jumpt spang onto my seat. **1898** HARRIS *Tales of Home Folks* 18 [I'll] run right spang over you with my big gray. **1922** TARKINGTON *Gentle Julia* 199 New straw hat right spang the firs' warm day.

+Spangolite. [From Norman *Spang*, of Pittsburgh, Pa.] (See quotation.) — **1891** *Cent.* 5794/2 *Spangolite*, . . . a rare mineral occurring in hexagonal crystals of an emerald-green color, and having perfect basal cleavage. . . . It is found with cuprite in Arizona.

+Spang-up, *a.* Very good. *colloq.*[2] — **1879** *Harper's Mag.* Aug. 392 'A spang-up team' he called it.

* Spaniard.

1. a. A person of Spanish blood born in America; a Spanish American. **+b.** A Spanish-speaking person, often of mixed blood; a Mexican.

1775 ROMANS *Nat. Hist. Florida* 187 The principal fish . . . of which the Spaniards make up the bulk of their cargoes, is the red drum. **1808** PIKE *Sources Miss.* III. App. 8 The Spaniards think it more honorable to be agriculturists than mechanics. **1848** ROBINSON *Santa Fe Exped.* (1932) 40 The Spaniards who were to accompany us and drive the pack mules, were rather late in being on the ground. **1848** RUXTON in *Blackwood's Mag.* June 714*n.*, The Mexicans are called 'Spaniards' or 'Greasers,' (from their greasy appearance). **1900** *Congress. Rec.* 30 Jan. 1313/1 Why was it all right to take those 30,000 white people . . . , Frenchmen and Spaniards chiefly, without their consent?

2. In miscellaneous uses.

+a. =SPANISH DOLLAR. **+b.** A cigar. **+c.** A cloak or shawl.

1779 *N.J. Archives* 2 Ser. III. 703 Soft or paper dollars . . . now pass at the rate of near forty for one solid Spaniard at the city of Philadelphia. **1828** *Yankee* I. 328/2 Do they not smoke their spaniard? **1837** *S. Lit. Messenger* III. 227/1, [I] wrapped my spaniard about me, and once more essayed to imitate the gentleman in front.

*Spanish, n.

1. *collect.* Spaniards. {1660, rare}

1832 IRVING in P. M. Irving *Life W. Irving* III. (1863) 43 The levee . . . presents the most whimsical groups of people of all nations, castes, and colors—French, Spanish, half-breeds, creoles, mulattoes, Kentuckians, &c. **1846** ROBINSON *Santa Fe Exped.* (1932) 28 It is astonishing to see the heavy loads which the Spanish and Mexicans pile upon their jacks and mules. **1880** *Cimarron News & Press* 24 June 2/2 The famous Pecos Church, built by the Spanish in 1680, is near.

2. In miscellaneous uses.

a. =BLACK SPANISH. **b.** A fine flavor in a cigar. **c.** A kind of dance.

(a) 1850 BROWNE *Poultry Yard* 28 The cross between the pheasant-Malay and the Spanish produces a particularly handsome fowl. **(b) 1862** NORTON *Army Lett.* 46, I have been . . . drawing the Spanish out of my cigar. **1865** *Harper's Mag.* Dec. 134/1 Watching the floating wreaths of smoke, and wondering if some of the 'Spanish' had not . . . escaped unenjoyed. **(c) 1891** WELCH *Recoll. 1830–40* 377 The 'Spanish,' a rich, warm, seductive dance, suggestive of black and gold dresses with black lace flowing mantilla and fan.

*Spanish, a.

*1. Made or originated by Spaniards, or +by Spanish Americans: **a.** Of articles of food, drink, and smoking.

1624 *Va. House of Burgesses* 46 Wee retorne our humblest thankes unto his most excellent Ma[jes]tie for . . . the prohibition of all Spanishe Tobacco. **1646** *Plymouth Col. Rec.* XI. 51 All that are lycensed to retayle wines . . . [shall pay] upon euery gallon of spanish wine eight pence. **1711** *Boston News-Letter* 12 March 2/2 Good Brazil and Spanish Snuff. . . . To be Sold by Zabdiel Boylston. **1790** *Penna. Packet* 13 July 1/4 Jacob Beninghove . . . Has and always keeps . . . Spanish and other Segars. **1792** IMLAY *Western Territory* 118 Considerable quantities [of maple sugar] have been sent to the markets of Philadelphia and York, not inferior to the best clayed, French, and Spanish sugars. **1828** LESLIE *Receipts* 57 [Recipe for] Spanish Buns. **1836** CROCKETT *Exploits* 21 Corn husks, steeped in tobacco water, would make as handsome Spanish wrappers as ever came from Havanna. **1879** *Harper's Mag.* Dec. 26/2 A lesson in bechamel and Spanish sauces was then given. **1910** J. HART *Vigilante Girl* 84 He can confect the Spanish omelette in its variety.

b. Of utensils, tools, etc.

1655 *Essex Probate Rec.* I. 223, 2 spanish platters. *c*1692 *Essex Inst. Coll.* VIII. 18 Spanish Iorn bought of Capt. John Brown. **1714** *Boston News-Letter* 15 March 2/2 To be Sold by Publick Vendue or Outcry . . . Sundry broad Spanish Ribon and Flowered. **1744** *Md. Hist. Mag.* XXI. 245, 3 Black Spanish Leather Womens Shoes. **1847** *Santa Fe Republican* 23 Oct. 1/2 Spanish Blankets. . . . Shawls & Fancy Hdkfs. **1872** 'MARK TWAIN' *Roughing It* 42 The heels . . . were armed with great Spanish spurs.

c. Of coins or metals used as a medium of exchange.

See also SPANISH BIT,[1] SPANISH DOLLAR, etc.

1691 C. MATHER in *Mass. Bay Currency Tracts* 13 Our Countrymen . . . Refuse to accept . . . Paper-mony, as pay of equal value with the best Spanish Silver. **1694** Spanish gold [see ENGLISH *a.* 4]. **1720** *Amer. Wkly. Mercury* 12 Jan. 2/2 Spanish Plate.—8s. 6d. to 9s. per Ounce. **1764** *R.I. Col. Rec.* VI. 393 The keeper of the grand committee's office . . . [may give] silver and gold, at the rate of £7, for one Spanish silver milled dollar. **1829** COOPER *Wish-ton-Wish* iv, I paid thee . . . a Spanish piece of silver. **1840** Spanish shilling [see FIRST COST]. **1848** BARTLETT 139 *Fippenny Bit*, . . . in the State of Pennsylvania, the vulgar name for the Spanish half-real. **1854** *Harper's Mag.* April 588/1 Upon the board was displayed . . . the *lure* in the shape of Mexican dollars and Spanish doubloons, or 'ounces,' as they are called in [N. Mex.]. **1865** *Atlantic Mo.* May 534/1 Many's the Spanish half-dollar I've picked up myself among the kelp.

d. Of dances and games.

1826 FLINT *Recoll.* 366 If I could describe its Indian powwows, its Spanish fandangos [etc.]. **1837** Spanish dance [see COTILLION]. **1891** *Century Mag.* April 915 Spanish Monte [appeared to be] the favorite game.

2. Of people: Having Spanish blood or living among the Spanish or Spanish Americans.

1660 *Boston Rec.* 157 The Town Treasurer shall pay three pounds to Mis. Cooke for her services in curing the spanish Captives. **1704** *Boston News-Letter* 22 May 2/1 The Spaniards going all ashore leaving him & a Spanish Indian on board. **1836** EDWARD *Hist. Texas* 194 The Bexarian declaration embraced all the other Spanish settlers in the department. **1840** *Picayune* 3 Sept. 2/4 The real captain was a Spanish mulatto, who spoke broken English. **1848** ROBINSON *Santa Fe Exped.* (1932) 62 The Spanish Mexicans use no chairs, but sit upon the floor on a mat or carpet. **1880** CABLE *Grandissimes* 224 The Spanish-Creole master had often seen the bull. **1885** *Wkly. New Mexican Rev.* 12 Feb. 3/4 Captain Santiago Hubbell . . . was married to a Spanish lady of rank. *Ib.* 5 March 3/3 The ignorant peons of wealthy Mexicans . . . got their first idea of even the 'rocker' from the early Spanish explorers. **1913** LONDON *Valley of Moon* 136 This woman . . . must have lived much as the Spanish-Californians had lived in the old days.

3. Of live stock and poultry: Bred by Spaniards or by Spanish Americans.

See also SPANISH HORSE, SPANISH MERINO.

1805 PARKINSON *Tour* 295 The Americans have Spanish sheep, and sheep that have been in the West-Indies. **1810** *Steele P.* II. 630, I purchased three fine Spanish Rams of the very best Breed. **1850** KINGSLEY *Diary* 152 Several heads of wild or Spanish cattle . . . were in fine order. **1876** Spanish pony [see CALIFORNIA 2 b]. **1887** *Courier-Journal* 20 Feb. 4/2 A red Spanish cock, the property of Wright, . . . [weighed] four pounds nine ounces.

+4. Of or pertaining to acts or records of the Spanish government in respect to the old or to the present Southwest.

See also SPANISH (LAND) GRANT.

1812 *Ann. 12th Congress* 1 Sess. 1687 You may also guaranty . . . the confirmation of all such titles to land as are clearly sanctioned by Spanish laws. **1847** *Santa Fe Republican* 11 Dec. 1/4 The old Spanish decrees many of which are still in force, regarded them [the Indian pueblos] with especial favor. **1872** TICE *Over Plains* 182 Ex-Governor Gilpin . . . [owns] 2,250,000 acres, acquired by purchasing Spanish and Mexican concessions. **1880** *Cimarron News & Press* 9 Sept. 1/6 Spanish or Mexican titles to land for grazing or agriculture did not embrace a title to mineral land. **1884** *N. Mex. Terr. Rep.* 32 The old Spanish and Mexican archives . . . had been placed in my custody by Gov. Lew Wallace.

5. In the names of species or varieties of plants, fishes, insects, etc.

See also SPANISH BAYONET, SPANISH BEARD, etc.

1786 WASHINGTON *Diaries* III. 105 From this place to the Surface of the run at a turn of it by a spreading Spanish bush the rise is about 14 Inches. **1831** AUDUBON *Ornith. Biog.* I. 181 The wild Spanish Coffee. *Cassia occidentalis.* . . . It flowers through the summer, and grows chiefly in old fields, in the Southern States. **1901** MOHR *Plant Life Ala.* 686 *Gilia coronopifolia.* . . . Spanish Cypress. . . . Frequently cultivated for ornament, under the name 'Spanish larkspur.' **1880** *Nat. Museum Proc.* III. 292 The 'Spanish Flag' . . . is the most brilliantly colored large fish on the Pacific coast. **1836** HOLLEY *Texas* 106 Spanish flies . . . are common flies in Texas. **1888** GOODE *Amer. Fishes* 205 In this limpid pool were . . . the rainbow-fish, the Spanish-lady. **1818** DARBY *Emigrant's Guide* 63 The underwood, spice wood, Spanish mulberry . . . and other vines . . . [are] indicative of a productive soil. **1709** LAWSON *Carolina* 162 Spanish Oysters have a very thin Shell. **1760** WASHINGTON *Diaries* I. 146 Grafted and planted . . . 12 Spanish pairs. **1917** *Birds of Amer.* I. 246 Willet. *Catoptrophorus semipalmatus semipalmatus.* . . . [Also called] Spanish Plover; Stone Curlew. **1855** *Amer. Inst. N.Y. Trans. 1854* 590 Spanish spring wheat, (*Trigo candeal*) from Alicante . . . will doubtless succeed well as a winter wheat at the South.

6. In special combinations.

Spanish-Cuban war, =SPANISH AMERICAN WAR; *S. mine,* a mine in the Southwest originally worked under Spanish control; *S. mission,* a Protestant mission for Spanish Americans.

1900 *Congress. Rec.* 1 Feb. 1412/1 In a conversation, about the close of the Spanish-Cuban war, . . . he said [etc.]. **1883** RITCH *Illust. N. Mex.* 64 Bernalillo county contains some of the most valuable of these old Spanish mines. **1885** *Wkly. New Mexican Rev.* 4 June 1/5 Rev. Thomas Harwood . . . superintendent of the New Mexico Spanish mission.

+Spanish, *adv.* To walk Spanish, (see WALK *v.*).

Spanish America. That part of America once controlled by Spain, or in which Spanish is the principal language. — **1789** MORSE *Amer. Geog.* 480 The whites [in Mexico] are born in Old Spain, or they are creoles, that is, natives of Spanish America. **1856** *34th Congress. 1 Sess.* H. R. Ex. Doc. No. 135, 1. 42 A river . . . [making] what is called in Spanish America a cañon—that is, a river hemmed in by vertical walls. **1884** *N. Mex. Terr. Rep.* 33 For centuries it [N. Mex.] was a purely military government of a wild and remote province of Spanish-America.

+Spanish American, *n.* **a.** A native or citizen of a Spanish-speaking American country. {1866} **b.** A citizen of the United States of Spanish descent. — **1811** *Niles' Reg.* I. 14/2 The Creoles—Spanish Americans —i.e. the descendants of Spaniards born in this country. **1890** *Stock Grower & Farmer* 10 May 3/3 The upper and better class of our Spanish-Americans are good intelligent citizens.

+Spanish American, *a.* **1.** Of or pertaining to Spanish America, or to the citizens of Spanish descent, esp. those in the Southwest. **2.** Of or pertaining to the Spanish American War. — **(1) 1875** *Cimarron News & Press* 7 Aug. 3/2 Irwin, Allen & Co. sold for him 150 rams, selected from his flocks of thoroughbred Spanish American Merinos. **1885** *Wkly. New Mexican Rev.* 15 Jan. 4/4 The president in making appointments [must] pay due respect to our Spanish-American populace. **(2) 1900** *Congress. Rec.* 19 Jan. 992/1 The delay in the taking up and considering the pension applications of the Spanish-American soldiers.

Spanish American War. The war between Spain and the United States (1898–99). — **1899** *Pres. Mess. & P.* X. 602/1 Spanish-American War. In February, 1895, the natives of Cuba, being dissatisfied [etc.]. **1900** *Congress. Rec.* 15 Jan. 801/1 [From] the cannon on the gunboat Nashville . . . was fired the first shot in the Spanish-American war.

+Spanish bayonet. Any of several species of *Yucca,* esp. a rigid, short-trunked plant (*Yucca aloifolia*) of the Southwest. — **1843** *Knickerb.* XXII. 566 A few white flowers of the Spanish-bayonet . . . [looked] like sentries with white feathers. **1858** WARDER *Hedges & Evergreens* 33 The Spanish Bayonet has long stiff leaves. **1865** *Wkly. New Mexican* 18 Aug. 1/3 These Indians . . . eke out their supply of corn with mezcal, mesquite bean, [and] the fruit of the Spanish bayonet. **1893** *Harper's Mag.* April 763 Here [in Fla. were] . . . figs, and bananas, hedges of Spanish-bayonet, and a half-mile of orange walks. **1915** ARMSTRONG &

THORNBER *Western Wild Flowers* 40 Our Lord's Candle. Spanish Bayonet. *Yucca Whipplei.*

+**Spanish beard.** =SPANISH MOSS. — **1784** SMYTH *Tour* I. 372 Long and numerous filaments, here called *Spanish Beards*, . . . hang . . . from all the large branches of the lofty oaks. **1814** BRACKENRIDGE *Views La.* 42 The long moss, or Spanish beard begins to be seen below the Arkansas. **1836** EDWARD *Hist. Texas* 89, [I saw] vast quantities of moss, alias Spanish beard, in the lower parts of Texas.

+**Spanish bit.**[1] A silver coin valued at one-eighth of a Spanish dollar; a real. — **1683** *Penna. Col. Rec.* I. 85 The Gov[erno]r telleth Ch[arles] Pickering & Sam[ue]ll Buckley of their abuse to ye Governm[en]t, in Quining of Spanish Bitts and Boston money. **1738** W. STEPHENS *Proc. Georgia* I. 82 One Smith, . . . paying away a few Spanish Bits. *c*1782 JEFFERSON *Writings* I. 243 The tenth [of the dollar] will be precisely the Spanish bit, or half-pistareen.

+**Spanish bit.**[2] =MEXICAN BIT. — **1842** *S. Lit. Messenger* VIII. 466/1 [He stopped] his horse, with the aid of the unmerciful Spanish bit, in full career. **1877** ROE *Army Lett.* 180, I heard Kelly ordered to lead the horse to the sutler's store and fit a Spanish bit to her mouth. **1897** LEWIS *Wolfville* 150 You can't ride him with buckin'-straps an' a Spanish bit.

+**Spanish clover. 1.** =ALFALFA. **2.** =FLORIDA CLOVER. — (1) **1873** BEADLE *Undevel. West* 448 There at least is a patch of green, a tract grown up in alfalfa or Spanish clover. (2) **1889** VASEY *Agric. Grasses* 103 Richardsonia scabra (Mexican Clover; Spanish Clover; Florida Clover; Water Parsley [etc.].).

+**Spanish curlew.** The white ibis, *Guara alba.* (One of the species referred to in quot. 1791 is not identified with certainty.) — **1791** W. BARTRAM *Travels* 146 Both species are called Spanish curlews. **1813** WILSON *Ornithology* VIII. 43 White Ibis . . . are usually called Spanish Curlews. **1858** BAIRD *Birds Pacific R.R.* 684 *Ibis Alba.* . . . White Curlew; White Ibis; Spanish Curlew. . . . South Atlantic and Gulf States; straggling occasionally northward. **1917** *Birds of Amer.* I. 177/1 The old birds, which are popularly supposed to be of a different species, are usually referred to as 'Spanish Curlews' or 'White Curlews.'

Spanish dagger. One of several species of *Yucca*, esp. *Y. gloriosa.* {1866, in W. Indies} Cf. SPANISH BAYONET. — **1859** A. VAN BUREN *Sojourn in South* 108 A tall 'Spanish dagger' stood leaning its crested head against the veranda. **1890** *Stock Grower & Farmer* 5 July 5/2 Cattle have been compelled to eat cactus shrubs and Spanish daggers (Palmio) to keep from starving. **1901** MOHR *Plant Life Ala.* 47 The strange-looking Spanish dagger (*Yucca aloifolia*), an arborescent lily.

+**Spanish dollar.** A Spanish or a Spanish American silver coin worth eight reals; the value of such a coin.

See also SPANISH MILLED DOLLAR.

1684 *N.H. Hist. Soc. Coll.* VIII. 162 Spanish dollars of Seville and Mexico should pass at six shillings the piece. **1756** ROGERS *Journals* 14 Ten Spanish dollars were allowed to each man towards providing cloaths, arms, and blankets. **1790** MACLAY *Deb. Senate* 182 The average price of wheat, . . . when compounded, has seldom been equal to half a Spanish dollar per bushel. **1818** *Niles' Reg.* XV. 125/1 *Spanish Dollars* appear to be in great demand at this moment. **1852** [see HAMMERED *a.*]. **1894** LEAVITT *Our Money Wars* 34 In 1792, . . . people reckoned in pounds, shillings, and pence, and paid in Spanish dollars.

+**Spanish fever.**

1. =DENGUE. (Cf. BREAKBONE FEVER.)

1828 *Richmond Whig* 5 Aug. 2/3 (Th.), The Spanish fever, or 'Dengue,' . . . at once yields to a warm bath and hot tea.

2. An infectious disease among cattle transmitted by the cattle tick, *Margaropus annulatus;* Texas fever.

1858 *N.Y. Herald* 2 Oct. 5/3 Southern cattle communicate to those of Missouri a disease known as Spanish or Texas fever. **1870** *Rep. Comm. Agric.* 1869 409 In February, 1867, a sanitary measure was passed for the protection of cattle from the ravages of the Spanish fever. **1885** *Wkly. New Mexican Rev.* 26 Feb. 2/5 The railroads . . . can be instrumental in preventing the spread of contagious diseases and Spanish fever among cattle. **1898** *Dept. Agric. Yrbk.* 1897 240 Texas, or Spanish, fever . . . has more recently been called . . . splenetic fever.

+**Spanish horse.** A hardy breed of horse introduced by the Spaniards into the South and Southwest; a horse of this breed. — **1784** [see CHICKASAW 2]. **1807** SCHULTZ *Travels* II. 44 A Spanish horse, . . . about thirteen hands high, hardy, and full of mettle, . . . may almost be said to live by hard riding. **1837** IRVING *Bonneville* II. 144 The Spanish horses pass from hand to hand among the Indians, until they even find their way across the Rocky mountains. **1890** *Stock Grower & Farmer* 15 Feb. 5/2 The Spanish horse escaped in the wars with Mexico.

+**Spanish Indian,** *a.* {1871} **1.** Belonging to an Indian race of Spanish America. **2.** Of a language: Made up of Spanish and Indian. — (1) **1712** *Boston News-Letter* 18 Aug. 2/2 Ran-away. . . . A Spanish Indian man, named Peter. **1715** *Ib.* 9 May 2/2 Ran away from his Master, . . . a very likely Spanish Indian Lad. (2) **1899** *Atlantic Mo.* June 759/2 Men and women share in the possession of . . . the vitiated but musical Spanish-Indian patois of the Southwest.

+**Spanish (land) grant.** A land grant originally made by the Spanish government. — **1826** FLINT *Recoll.* 199 But it is not my intention to dip into the gulph of land-claims, . . . Spanish grants, confirmed claims [etc.]. **1865** *Wkly. New Mexican* 29 Sept. 1/4 In the Mesilla valley there are some Spanish Grants. **1870** [see PARCHMENT 4]. **1890** *Stock Grower & Farmer* 19 April 6/2 One of the greatest problems congress has had to do with in the past fifty years is the settlement of Spanish and Mexican land grants.

Spanish mackerel. {*a*1672} +**a.** One of several species of mackerel of the genus *Scomberomorus.* (See also MONTEREY (SPANISH) MACKEREL.) **b.** The chub mackerel. {1880} **1666** *Hist. Coll. S. Carolina* II. 13 Here are as brave Rivers as any in the World, stored with great abundance of . . . Spanish Mackrill. **1775** [see KINGFISH 1]. **1839** STORER *Mass. Fishes* 45 *Scomber colias,* . . . a rare species upon our coast, . . . is generally known by our fishermen as the 'Spanish Mackerel.' **1855** BAIRD in *Smithsonian Rep. 1854* 335 The spotted Cybium—Spanish Mackerel . . . *Cybium maculatum.* **1877** [see PLANKED *a.*]. **1903** T. H. BEAN *Fishes N.Y.* 397 The Spanish mackerel . . . is one of the choicest of our food fishes.

+**Spanish merino.** A breed of sheep introduced from Spain; a sheep of this breed. Also attrib. — **1802** F. L. HUMPHREYS *Life D. Humphreys* II. 346 A Gold Medal . . . [is] presented to you . . . for your patriotic exertions in introducing into New-England one hundred of the Spanish Merino breed of Sheep. **1863** RANDALL *Prac. Shepherd* 29 When the Spanish Merino came again into credit, this flock became a great favorite. **1890** *Stock Grower & Farmer* 8 March 7/2 Stock Sheep For Sale. . . . Improved with Spanish merino. **1893** G. W. CURTIS *Horses, Cattle* 238 The first importations of pure Spanish Merinos to the United States were soon lost sight of, through being mixed with other blood.

+**Spanish mill dollar.** =next. — **1781** *Essex Inst. Coll.* XXVI. 115, I received eight Spanish mill dollars. **1806** ORDWAY in *Jrnls. of Lewis & O.* 361 Frazer got 2 Spanish mill dollars from a squaw for an old razer.

+**Spanish milled dollar.** A Spanish dollar milled in Spain, current during the colonial period and later. — **1754** in C. Hazard *Thos. Hazard* 245 Received of Robert Haszard of South Kingstown . . . two Spanish Milled Dollars. **1773** FINLAY *Journal* 44 Two Shillings lawful money equal to 1/3 of a Spanish milled dollar. **1796** [see PAPER DOLLAR]. **1812** *Niles' Reg.* II. 77/1 Can we procure American coin or Spanish milled dollars? **1851** MITCHELL *Dream Life* 87 [He] seems to have great confidence in the value of Spanish milled dollars.

+**Spanish moss.** The black moss (*Tillandsia,* or *Dendropogon, usneoides*) forming tufts hanging upon trunks and branches of trees in the South. (Cf. MOSS 1 and SPANISH BEARD.)

1823 JAMES *Exped. Rocky Mts.* III. 220 The Spanish moss disappears northwardly of the 33d degree of north latitude. **1859** A. VAN BUREN *Sojourn in South* 167 The long Spanish moss does not hang so thick from the trees. **1883** 'MARK TWAIN' *Life on Miss.* xxxiv, Shade-trees [are] hung with venerable gray-beards of Spanish moss. **1904** STUART *River's Children* 63 Under festoons of gray Spanish moss . . . the little crafts sped lightly along.

b. Used as a stuffing for mattresses.

1834 *Visit to Texas* 126 The moss which we call Spanish moss . . . [we] use for stuffing mattresses. **1868** *Ore. State Jrnl.* 27 June 2/6 Spanish Moss for Mattresses. **1893** *Harper's Mag.* Feb. 385/1 There are more than sixty firms handling Spanish moss, which is used in mattresses and upholstering work.

+**Spanish needle(s).** A beggar-ticks (*Bidens bipinnata*) or a related species; the prickly achenes of these plants. — **1743** CLAYTON *Flora Virginica* 94 Bidens corona seminum retrorsum aculeata. . . . Spanish-needle. **1821** NUTTALL *Travels Arkansa* 29 The corn-fields . . . are so overrun with . . . seeds of different species of Bidens or Spanish-needles, as to prove extremely troublesome to woollen clothes. **1873** *Winfield* (Kan.) *Courier* 17 July 1/4 Sensations of exquisite joy . . . thrill through it like Spanish needles through a pair of tow linen trowsers. **1903** *Outlook* 7 Nov. 584, I picked off the cockle-burrs and Spanish needles I had collected during my day's tramping.

+**Spanish oak.** Any of the red oaks, as *Quercus borealis,* esp. in the South; the wood of any of these trees or an individual tree.

1671 *S.C. Hist. Soc. Coll.* V. 333 This Land bears very good . . . Spanish, & liue oak. **1681** *New Castle Court Rec.* 503 Beginning att a Corner marked spannish oake. **1733** *S.C. Gazette* 221/2 For all Distempers . . . take four Ounces of the Inside Bark of Spanish Oak. **1775** *Amer. Husbandry* I. 376 Red oak grows sometimes very large and lofty. . . . Spanish oak, more durable, is used sometimes in ship-building. **1797** HAWKINS *Letters* 106 The whole of the growth on this path scrub, black and small spanish oak. **1814** PURSH *Flora Amer.* II. 631 *Quercus falcata.* . . . A very large tree, commonly called Spanish Oak. In the southern states it is known by the name of Red Oak. **1832** BROWNE *Sylva* 267 [*Quercus falcata*] is said to have been called Spanish Oak by the first settlers. **1849** *New Eng. Farmer* I. 50 For durability, Spanish oak is much better than either red or post oak. **1901** MOHR *Plant Life Ala.* 87 The Spanish oak (*Quercus digitata* . . .) is at its best where the terraces merge into the lowland.

+**Spanish pistole. 1.** A Spanish gold coin valued at one-quarter of a doubloon, or about four dollars. **2.** ?A silver coin, possibly of Spanish American origin. — (1) **1693** SEWALL *Letter-Book* I. 137, I have sent you three and twenty Spanish Pistolls. **1745** FRANKLIN *Poor Richard's Almanac 1746* 2. (2) **1831** SLOCOMB *Amer. Calculator* 92 Coins which pass current in the United States [include] . . . an English Guinea, . . . a Spanish Pistole (Silver).

+**Spanish potato.** A variety of sweet potato. — **1765** ROGERS *Acct. N. Amer.* 139 This country also has a great variety of vegetables and fruits, as Spanish potatoes, pompions [etc.]. **1790** S. DEANE *Newengland Farmer* 224/2 We have had the Spanish potato, extremely prolifick, but fit only for cattle and swine. **1830** WATSON *Philadelphia* 718 Colonel A. J. Morris . . . told me that the potatoes used in his early life . . . were called Spanish potatoes. **1855** *Amer. Inst. N.Y. Trans. 1854* 421 There are several varieties of the Spanish or sweet potatoes, also of yams.

+**Spanish quarter. 1.** A Spanish coin worth one-fourth of a Spanish dollar. **2.** A section where Spanish-speaking people live. — (1) **1853** *Wkly. Oregonian* 13 Aug. (Th.), Levys, ninepences, Spanish quarters, pistareens [etc.]. **1857** *Harper's Mag.* March 549/2 Spanish quarters, eighths, and sixteenths of a dollar shall only be received by public officers at the rate of twenty, ten, and five cents. (2) **1872** POWERS *Afoot & Alone* 270, I entered the city [Los Angeles] near the little, old, mean called Spanish quarter, with its red-tiled adobes. **1890** *Internat. Ann., Anthony's Photogr. Bul.* III. 339 The baranca . . . [separates] the business part of the town [Santa Barbara, Calif.] from the 'Spanish Quarter.'

+**Spanish saddle.** A saddle used by Spaniards, esp. one of heavy and elaborate construction.

1827 COOPER *Prairie* xviii, A Spanish saddle, too, like a grandee of the Mexicos! **1847** PARKMAN in *Knickerb.* XXIX. 311 [His outfit] consisted of a plain black Spanish saddle. **1869** BRACE *New West* 96 The Spanish saddle is used, with high peaks before and behind, which is a great rest for a long ride. **1897** HOUGH *Story of Cowboy* 67 The Spanish saddles of the Southwest were often been heavily decorated with silver.

b. *Half Spanish saddle,* (exact description uncertain).

1873 Abbott *C. Carson* 288 Behold us, then, three of us, mounted in half Spanish saddles, with our rifles in front.

+**Spanish trefoil.** =ALFALFA. *Obs.* — **1843** TORREY *Flora N.Y.* I. 171 Lucerne. Spanish Trefoil. . . . Scarcely naturalized. **1868** GRAY *Field Botany* 101 Lucerne or Spanish Trefoil. Cultivated for green fodder, especially S. **1889** VASEY *Agric. Grasses* 84.

Spanish war. + =SPANISH AMERICAN WAR. — **1900** *Congress. Rec.* 8 Jan. 693/2. *Ib.* 30 Jan. 1308/1, I hope the Senator will not confuse in his mind . . . the cost of the Spanish war with the cost of the Philippine war.

Spanker. {1663-} +'A light cart suitable for rapid travelling' (O.E.D.). — **1831** in A. E. Lee *Hist. Columbus* I. 318 Our vehicle, which, in the dialect of the country was called a *spanker,* was intended for four persons.

+**Spanworm.** A larva of any geometrid. Also collective. (Cf. MEASURING WORM.) — **1820** *Amer. Farmer* I. 375/3 What can our obliging correspondents tell us about the . . . best method of destroying that dreadful plague of our orchards, the *span worm.* **1841** T. W. HARRIS *Rep. Insects Mass.* 330 The caterpillars of the *Geometrae* of Linnaeus, . . . or geometers, span-worms, and loopers, have received these several names from their peculiar manner of moving. **1874** *Rep. Comm. Agric. 1873* 163 The cotton caterpillar always moves like the span-worm or looper. **1892** KELLOGG *Kansas Insects* 61 The caterpillars . . . loop the body when walking, like a span worm.

Spar, *v.* {1657-} +*tr.* 'To aid (a vessel) over a shallow bar by the use of spars and tackles' (*Cent.*). Also absol. and as *vbl. n.* — **1843** TALBOT *Journals* 4 [We became] finally the prey of an insidious sand-bar, where after hours of sparring, . . . we again resume the slow ascent. **1872** *Harper's Mag.* March 542/2 She'll beach herself . . . if Boldman didn't spar her off good. **1872** 'MARK TWAIN' *Roughing It* 21 [I remember] sand-bars which we roosted on occasionally, and rested, and then got out our crutches and sparred over. **1883** *American* VI. 40 At low water, the vessel has often to be sparred over sand-bars.

+**Sparada.** [Of obscure origin.] A surf fish of the Pacific coast, *Cymatogaster aggregatus.* — **1891** *Cent.* 5796/1. **1896** JORDAN & EVERMANN *Check-List Fishes* 403 Sparada. Pacific Coast, from Port Wrangel, Alaska, to Todos Santos Bay.

＊**Spare.** +In the American game of bowling, the act of knocking down all the pins in two bowls. Hence *double spare,* a strike. — **1843** *Knickerb.* XXII. 327 He was never guilty of a 'spare.' **1879** *Daily News* (London) 2 Sept. 3/1 Younger people . . . sought out the American ten-pin alleys, . . . and, in striving for spares and 'double spares,' esteemed themselves far in advance of their wise elders. **1884** BUNNER in *Harper's Mag.* Jan. 299/2 Strikes and spares were less common.

Spare chamber. A bedroom not regularly used. Also attrib. Chiefly *New Eng.* — **1865** *Atlantic Mo.* March 299/1, I have put charming blue chintz curtains in the spare chamber. **1875** STOWE *We & Neighbors* 23 Certain brackets and lambrequins . . . are to adorn my spare chamber. **1896** WILKINS *Madelon* 141 She's tucked up nice and warm in my spare-chamber bed.

Spare room. A room not regularly used, esp. a bedroom. {spare bedroom, 1811} — **1837** *S. Lit. Messenger* III. 333 One of the third-story rooms we must keep for a spare room. **1855** *Knickerb.* XLVI. 380 They have stolen away into the spare-room, otherwise, parlor. **1857** VAUX *Villas* 201 The attic provides several spare rooms. **1893** 'THANET' *Stories* 12 It was . . . the sacred 'spare room.' **1904** A. DALE *Wanted: a Cook* 332 The wine-cellar was under the bed in the spare-room.

Spark, *v.* {1676-}

+**1.** *intr.* To engage in courtship; to 'neck.' *colloq.* Also quasi-*tr.* with *it.*

1787 TYLER *Contrast* II. ii, She promised not to spark it with Solomon Dyer while I am gone. **1813** PAULDING *Lay Sc. Fiddle* (1814) 192 A young man goes many miles to *spark.* **1866** LOWELL *Biglow P.* 2 Ser. p. lxxviii,

He'd sparked it with full twenty gals. **1875** CARLETON *Farm Legends* 54 Let's . . . spark it a while. **1890** CUSTER *Following Guidon* 314 Me and Eliza was mighty fond of each other, and off and on we was sparking.

+**2.** *tr.* Of a man: To court or make love to (a girl or woman). *colloq.*

1835 KENNEDY *Horse Shoe Robinson* II. 34, I'll be cursed if I wouldn't spark that little fusee myself. **1857** *Atlantic Mo.* I. 26/1 George . . . visited the farm-house for the laudable purpose of 'sparkin' Miss Sally. **1899** [see PAP²]. **1906** GUNTER *Prince in Garret* v, Isn't Ambigue sparking the actress?

+**Spark-arrester.** Any contrivance to prevent the escape of sparks from a locomotive. {1838} — **1835** *24th Congress 1 Sess.* H. R. Ex. Doc. No. 64, 24 Spark arrester, Alfred C. Jones, Portsmouth Va. **1856** in Brewster *Life J. D. Whitney* 158 The locomotive looked funny enough splashed with yellow clay from cow-catcher to spark-arrester. **1887** GEORGE *40 Yrs. on Rail* 31 Early engines were without spark arresters. **1905** *Forestry Bureau Bul.* No. 60, 29 The use of efficient spark arresters [should be required] on all locomotives.

+**Sparked-back.** *local.* The ruddy turnstone. — **1888** TRUMBULL *Names of Birds* 186 In Massachusetts . . . at Falmouth, [it is called] Sparked-back, Streaked-back, and Bishop Plover. **1917** *Birds of Amer.* I. 268 Ruddy Turnstone. *Arenaria interpres morinella.* . . . [Also called] Calico-jacket; Sparked-back; Streaked-back.

+**Sparker.** [f. SPARK *v.*] One who makes love to a member of the opposite sex. *colloq.²* — **1835** LONGSTREET *Ga. Scenes* 177 Come . . . all ye young sparkers, come listen to me. **1882** PECK *Sunshine* 169 These sparkers are looked upon by parents generally as a nuisance.

+**Sparking.** Courting; making love. Often *to go a-sparking.* — **1804** FESSENDEN *Orig. Poems* (1806) 77 She's courted been, by many a lad, And knows how sparking's done. **1807** IRVING, etc. *Salmagundi* xv. 396 He went a sparking among the rosy country girls. **1843** STEPHENS *High Life N.Y.* I. 47, I don't mean to say that Judy had anything agin sparking, in a regular way, on Sunday nights. **1864** NICHOLS *Amer. Life* II. 214 There is leisure for reading or 'sparking.' **1888** EGGLESTON *Graysons* xiii, I've promised the mare to one uv the boys to-night—to—to go a-sparkin' weth.

+**Sparkleberry.** =FARKLEBERRY. Also attrib. — **1860** CURTIS *Woody Plants N.C.* 87 Sparkleberry. . . . The fruit is black and small. **1897** SUDWORTH *Arborescent Flora* 312. **1908** CHAMBERS *Firing Line* viii, A superb butterfly . . . came flitting about the sparkleberry bloom.

＊**Sparrow.**

1. +**a.** Any of numerous American finches more or less resembling the English sparrow. ＊**b.** The English sparrow.

'In a strict sense the term "Sparrow" pertains to the species *Passer* only, represented in America only by the introduced House Sparrow, or so-called English Sparrow, and in this restricted sense we have no native American true Sparrows' (1917 *Birds of Amer.* III. 2).

1709 LAWSON *Carolina* 144 Sparrows here differ in Feather from the English. **1831** R. Cox *Adv. Columbia R.* 91, I saw plenty of wild geese, ducks, cranes, curlews, and sparrows. **1867** *Atlantic Mo.* March 278/2 There were sparrows and wrens. **1891** WILKINS *New Eng. Nun* 162 A sparrow pecked at some weeds piercing the snow-crust beside the door. **1903** [see COWBIRD 2]. **1917** *Birds of Amer.* III. 1 The Sparrows that breed on the farm have to content themselves early in the spring with seeds left from the preceding year.

+**2.** With qualifying terms in sense 1 a.

See also CHIPPING *ppl. a.* 1 (c); FOX SPARROW, GROUND SPARROW, etc. Bird books list several dozen different species.

1806 LEWIS & *L. & Clark Exped.* III. (1905) 309 A large brown sparrow, the bald Eagle and the beatiful Buzzard of the columbia still continue with us. **1811** WILSON *Ornithology* III. 76 [The] Yellow-Winged Sparrow, *Fringilla Passerina,* . . . inhabits the lower parts of New-York and Pennsylvania. **1839** AUDUBON *Ornith. Biog.* V. 336 Green-Tailed Sparrow, *Fringilla Chlorura.* **1858** Black-throated sparrow [see BLACK-THROATED *a.*]. **1870** *Amer. Naturalist* III. 631 Baird's Sparrow. *Centronyx Bairdii.* . . . Very little is known respecting its migrations or its distribution. **1881** *Ib.* XV. 872 Lenox, Berkshire county, . . . [gets] bay-winged and chipping sparrows . . . [before] Boston. **1917** *Birds of Amer.* III. 23 Vesper Sparrow. *Pooecetes gramineus gramineus.* . . . [Also called] Pasture Bird; Grass Sparrow; Ground-bird. *Ib.* 26/2 Bryant's Sparrow . . . [is] found in the salt marshes along the coast of California.

＊**Sparrow hawk.** +**a.** A small falcon (*Falco sparverius*) of North America. **b.** Any hawk or falcon of small size.

1612 SMITH, etc. *Virginia* I. 14 Sparrowhawkes . . . pray most vpon fish. **1709** LAWSON *Carolina* 138 The Sparrow-Hawk in Carolina is no bigger than a Fieldfare in England. **1805** LEWIS in *L. & Clark Exped.* I. (1904) 303 The small hawk, frequently called the sparrow hawk, . . . is common to most parts of the U. States. **1811** WILSON *Ornithology* IV. 57 The male Sparrow Hawk measures about ten inches in length, and twenty-one in extent. **1885** M. THOMPSON *Byways & Bird Notes* 68 Two sparrow-hawks were wheeling in small circles. **1917** *Birds of Amer.* II. 66 Sharp-shinned hawk. *Accipter velox.* . . . [Also called] Pigeon Hawk; Sparrow Hawk; Bird Hawk. *Ib.* 91/1 The Sparrow Hawk is the smallest and the most sociable of our Hawks.

Sparrow owl. Any one of various small owls, esp. one of the genus *Glaucidium.* {1831-} — **1891** *Cent.* 5799/1 *Sparrow-owl,* . . . any one of many small owls of the genus *Glaucidium.* Two occur in western parts of the United States. **1917** *Birds of Amer.* II. 106/1 Richardson's Owl. *Cryptoglaux funerea richardsoni.* . . . [Also called] Sparrow Owl.

Sparse, *a.* {1727-} +Of population or a settlement: Small and scattered; thin. {1863-} — **1827** SHERWOOD *Gaz. Georgia* 36 The land is poor and population sparse. **1838** *Diplom. Corr. Texas* III. (1911) 1219 The peculiar condition of our South Western frontier coast owing to the sparce population in that quarter. **1856** EMERSON *Eng. Traits* 63 A sparse population gives this high worth to every man. **1871** HOWELLS *Wedding Journey* 259 The village . . . grows sparser as you draw near the Falls of Montmorenci.

Sparsely, *adv.* In a scattered and thin manner {1800-}, +esp. in respect to the action of settling an area. {1863-} — **1796** MORSE *Univ. Geog.* I. 191 [Pitch pine] grows sparsely in the N. England and middle States. **1857** OLMSTED *Journey Texas* 365 The country . . . is sparsely settled. **1887** TOURGEE *Button's Inn* 54 Such comfortable lodging was rare in the sparcely-settled region where it stood.

Spartan Band. +A New York City Locofoco club of 1840. *Obs.* — **1840** *Daily Nat. Intelligencer* 5 Nov. 3/6 The Spartan Band (Locofoco) gave the Grinnell Club a drubbing.

Spat, *n.* {1823-} +A petty quarrel; a tiff. {1898} — **1804** *Repertory* (Boston) 27 April (Th.), The late spat between Mr. Pitt and Mr. W. Pulteney. **1871** STOWE *Sam Lawson* 33 They was pretty apt to have spats. **1887** *Courier-Journal* 6 May 6/3 The proceedings of the General Council were enlivened last evening by a spat between Mr. Stege . . . and Mr. H. C. Murrell.

Spat, *v.* {c1832-} +*intr.* To speak *up* and argue; to quarrel; to dispute. *colloq.* — **1809** KENDALL *Travels* III. 292, The women had not much to say in politics, though now and then they would *spat up.* **1848** BARTLETT 323 *To Spat,* to dispute; to quarrel. A low word. New England. **1885** BAYLOR *On Both Sides* 345 'The American ladies *spat* on all occasions, . . . I have read.' . . . 'We don't quarrel any more than any one else,' said Bijou, quite misunderstanding.

Spatter. {1797-} +*Thick as spatter(s),* or variant: Very thick or close. — **1823** *Daily Nat. Intelligencer* 1 May 1/4 *Spatter.* A comparative word, 'as thick as spatter.' **1851** JUDD *Margaret* (ed. 2) II. 246 They used to be thick as spatter when I was a boy. **1892** WILKINS *Young Lucretia* 156, I s'pose the berries are as thick as spatters. **1907** WHITE *Arizona Nights* 28 And outfits at that time were thicker'n spatter.

Spatterdash. A legging worn as a protection against water and mud. {1687-} — **1781-2** *Jrnls. Cont. Congress* XI. 584 Linen spatterdashes for soldiers. **1832** J. HALL *Legends of West* 173 His nether limbs were clad in long spatterdashes, reaching to the knee. **1889** *Century Mag.* April 826/2 [They] were dressed . . . with waistcoats and breeches and white gaiters, or spatter dashes.

+**Spatter-dock.** The yellow pond lily (*Nuphar advena*), or a related species. — **1857** GRAY *Botany* 23. **1872** *Amer. Naturalist* VI. 726 The more unpretending 'spatter-dock' or yellow pond-lily (*Nuphar advena*). **1915** ARMSTRONG & THORNBER *Western Wild Flowers* 156 Indian Pond Lily, Spatter-dock *Nymphaea polysepala* (*Nuphar*). . . . In quiet mountain ponds we find these yellow flowers, on stout stems standing up out of the water.

Spatterwork. (See quot. 1909.) — **1873** PHELPS *Trotty's Wedding* xviii, We had re-covered the pin-cushion, too, with gray spatter-work (oak-leaves and acorns) on cranberry silk. **1883** *Century Mag.* May 158/2 They can do spatter-work or worsted work, or paint plaques. **1909** WEBSTER 2003 *Spatterwork,* . . . a process of reproducing designs by laying them on a surface and spattering the exposed parts with a tinting fluid; also, a design, or designs, so made.

+**Spatula-fish.** (See quotation.) — **1781-2** JEFFERSON *Notes Va.* (1788) 6 [The Miss. R.] yields turtle of a peculiar kind, . . . spatula-fish of 50 lb. weight [etc.].

+**Spawn-eater.** A shiner or smelt, *Hudsonius hudsonius.* — [**1881** *Cassell's Nat. Hist.* V. 131 The Spawn-eater, or Smelt (*Leuciscus hudsonicus*), is a silvery fish . . . about three inches long, and occurs in Lake Superior.] **1896** JORDAN & EVERMANN *Check-List Fishes* 254 *Notropis hudsonius.* . . . Spawn-eater; Spot-tailed Minnow; Shiner. The Dakotas and Lake Superior to New York, and southward to South Carolina.

*****Speaker.**

+**1.** The presiding officer or chairman of a colonial legislative assembly or of the lower house of a state legislature. {*in English House of Commons}

1619 *Va. House of Burgesses* 16 It is fully agreed . . . That every man [pay] . . . one pound of the best tobacco . . . to be distributed to the Speaker. **1644** *Mass. Bay Rec.* III. 2 Mr. William Hawthorne was chosen Speaker for this Courte by ye howse. **1695** [see HOUSE OF BURGESSES]. **1714** *Boston News-Letter* 26 July 2/2 Our Governour (attended with several Gentlemen of Her Majesties Council; The Speaker, & several others of the Representatives of the Massachusetts-Bay) came here. **1775** [see HOUSE 2 a]. **1873** *Newton Kansan* 5 June 1/6 The Speaker of the Arkansas Legislature said [etc.].

+**2.** The presiding officer of the House of Representatives in Congress.

1789 *Ann. 1st Congress* 679 Mr. Goodhue moved to strike out twelve dollars, the pay assigned the Speaker, and insert ten. **1840** *Niles' Nat. Reg.* 20 June 253 The bill to establish a uniform rule of mileage . . . coming up in the order of the business on the speaker's table. **1886** POORE *Reminisc.* II. 470 John G. Carlisle . . . was elected Speaker. **1911** [see LOBBY *n.* 1].

+**3.** *Speaker of the house,* the presiding officer of a house of representatives, as in a state legislature or in Congress.

1792 CUTLER in *Life & Corr.* I. 483 The Speaker of the House sent the Marshal-at-Arms to summon the Committee. **1832** WILLIAMSON *Maine* II. 10 The Governor . . . could negative as many as thirteen of the Councillors chosen, and also the Speaker of the House. **1905** *McClure's Mag.* XXIV. 347 Aldrich became alderman, legislator, speaker of the house, congressman and, finally, senator.

+**4.** One who speaks for an Indian nation or tribe in a council. *Obs.*

1800 HAWKINS *Sk. Creek Country* 80 The opinion of Efau Haujo, . . . Speaker for the Nation in the National Council, [is given]. **1871** *Rep. Indian Affairs* (1872) 593 Each [division of the Creeks] had a principal and second chief, and a speaker of the council.

Speakership. {1653-} +The office of speaker in a state legislature or in Congress. Also attrib. — **1847** LOWELL *Biglow P.* 1 Ser. iv. 54 Now here wuz New England ahevin' the honor Of a chance at the Speakership showered upon her. **1881** *Ore. State Jrnl.* 15 Jan. 2/3 The hotels are quite lively with canvassing for the speakership. **1898** *Kansas City Star* 18 Dec. 2/5 The speakership race . . . has resolved itself into a Stephens and anti-administration fight. **1911** [see HALF NELSON].

*****Speaking.** +(See quots. 1863 and 1903.) *colloq.* — **1842** BUCKINGHAM *Slave States* II. 245 The farmers of the neighbourhood . . . had come in to attend 'the speaking,' . . . the rival candidates for the governorship being both here . . . 'in the field.' **1863** HOPLEY *Life in South* I. 57 Then came the 'speaking,' as the sermon was called. **1903** *Dialect Notes* II. 331 *Speaking,* a political meeting [s.e. Mo.]. 'There will be a speakin at the cross roads to-morrow and all the candidates will be there.'

+**Speaking leaf.** A piece of paper with writing or printing on it. *Obs.* In imitation of or to suggest Indian speech. — **1804** BURK *Hist. Virginia* I. 109 The whole people were astonished at the prophetic properties of 'the speaking leaf.' **1835** WHITTIER *Poetical Works* (1894) 498/1 Will he make his mark, that it may be known, On the speaking-leaf, that he gives the land?

Speaking trumpet. A trumpet used to increase the range of the voice. {1671-} — **1781** *Md. Hist. Mag.* VI. 312 Schooner Nautilus's Materials: . . . 1 Speaking Trumpet. 1 hand lead line. **1807** IRVING, etc. *Salmagundi* xii. 311, I dont much see the use of speaking-trumpets now-a-days. **1866** 'F. KIRKLAND' *Bk. Anecdotes* 397/2 The speaking-trumpet in Commander Cummings' hand was battered flat.

Speaking tube. A tube or pipe equipped for transmitting a speaker's voice from one floor, room, etc., to another. {1833-} — **1853** FOWLER *Home for All* 44 Speaking-tubes should generally open into closets. **1875** 'MARK TWAIN' *Old Times* v. 99, I flew to the speaking-tube and shouted to the engineer. **1907** ANDREWS *Recoll.* 233 There were speaking tubes from his table to his staff in adjoining rooms.

*****Spear,** *n.*[1] A long lance or thrusting weapon used by American Indians. Also attrib. — **1778** CARVER *Travels* 53, [I] advanced . . . close to the points of their spears. **1791** LONG *Voyages* 35 Dances among the Indians [include] . . . the spear dance. **1834** PECK *Gaz. Illinois* 52 Earthenware, arrow and spearheads, stone axes and mallets, and other antiquities, are found in various parts of the state. **1848** [see ARROW 1]. **1883** *Smithsonian Rep. 1881* 661 Spear and arrow heads have been found cached [near Windsor, Conn.].

*****Spear,** *n.*[2] *transf.* +A filament *of* hair. *Obs.* — **1852** STOWE *Uncle Tom* xxv, If they's to pull every spear o' har out o' my head it wouldn't do no good. **1853** G. C. HILL *Dovecote* 96, I'd no notion o' . . . gettin' my hair, every spear on't, pulled out o' my head.

*****Spear,** *v.* {1755-} +*tr.* To pierce (the stalk of a tobacco plant) with a pointed stick. Also *vbl. n.* — **1850** *Rep. Comm. Patents 1849: Agric.* 321 It may be put away in three different modes, by 'pegging,' 'spearing,' and 'splitting.' **1868** *Rep. Comm. Agric. 1867* 181 The plants should . . . be taken up and placed in small heaps of eight or ten plants, . . . to be speared in the field, and then carried on the sticks to the house.

+**Spearfish. 1.** =QUILLBACK. **2.** One or other species of large fishes of the genus *Tetrapturus.* — (1) **1882** *Nat. Museum Bul.* No. 16, 119. **1896** JORDAN & EVERMANN *Check-List Fishes* 238 *Carpiodes velifer.* . . . Spearfish; Sailfish; Skimback. Mississippi Valley and southwestward to Rio Grande and upper Missouri. (2) **1882** *Nat. Museum Bul.* No. 16, 420 *T[etrapturus] albidus,* Bill-fish; Spear-fish. **1896** JORDAN & EVERMANN *Check-List Fishes* 343 *Tetrapturus imperator.* . . . Bill-fish; Spear-fish. . . . West Indies; Cape Cod.

*****Spear grass.** +One of various species of pointed grasses, esp. the meadow grass, *Poa pratensis.* Also with specifying term. — **1747** FRANKLIN in *Amer. Jrnl. Science* IV. 359 The grass which comes in first, after ditching, is spear grass and white clover. **1814** BIGELOW *Florula Bostoniensis* 24 Spear grass or meadow grass is found in all situations. **1884** VASEY *Agric. Grasses* 94 *Poa pratensis.* (June grass, Kentucky blue grass, Spear grass). . . . It forms the principal constituent of pastures. **1901** MOHR *Plant Life Ala.* 384 *Poa chapmaniana.* . . . Chapman's Spear Grass. . . . In small tufts, stems erect.

Spearing. [Du. *spiering.*] (See quotations.) {ground spearing, 1838-} — **1884** GOODE, etc. *Fisheries* I. 612 Our Anchovy has recently been sold in considerable numbers in New York under the name 'Whitebait,' although the fishermen distinguish it from the true 'Whitebait,' the young of the herring, calling it 'Spearing.' **1896** JORDAN & EVERMANN *Check-List Fishes* 296 *Trachinocephalus myops.* . . . Ground Spearing; Lagarto. Tropical parts of the Western Atlantic, . . . and ranging on our Atlantic Coast to South Carolina. **1903** T. H. BEAN *Fishes N.Y.* 359

The common silversides, or spearing, lives in Gravesend bay almost all the year. **1911** [see SARDINE 1].

* **Spearman.** +(See quot. 1891.) Also with specifying term. — **1868** *Rep. Comm. Agric. 1867* 65 The Colorado bug or ten-lined spearman is reported to have produced poisonous effects on several persons who handled them incautiously. **1891** *Cent.* 5804/3 *Spearman*, . . . a book-name for any leaf-beetle of the genus *Doryphora*.

* **Spearmint.** The common garden mint, *Mentha spicata.* Also attrib. — **1784** *Amer. Acad. Mem.* I. 460 Spear Mint. . . . The leaves make an agreeable conserve. **1807** GASS *Journal* 103 There is in the bottoms a great quantity of spear-mint and currant bushes. **1873** BAILEY *Life in Danbury* 123 Two of the neighbors . . . gave him a half gallon of spear-mint tea. **1918** LINCOLN *Shavings* 236, I never can make out whether it's flavored with tansy or spearmint.

+**Spec.** [Short for *speculation.*] A commercial speculation or venture. {1824–} — **1794** J. ADAMS *Works* I. 469 Many merchants have already made a noble *spec.* of the embargo by raising their prices. **1829** *Va. Lit. Museum* 182 A man in our country lately found a lump of pure gold, and thinking I could make a *spec* by it, I purchased it. **1886** DALY *Nancy & Co.* 14 Made a pretty little pile by a nice little spec yesterday.

* **Special,** *n.*

+**1.** A special article or communication to a newspaper.

1867 *Ore. State Jrnl.* 19 Jan. 2/3 A Washington special says that [etc.]. **1894** SHUMAN *Steps into Journalism* 124 The typical 'special' is a long article making some pretentions to exhaustiveness. **1902** PHILLIPS *Woman Ventures* 94 [He helped] her quickly to gather the materials for her first 'special.'

+**2.** A free-lance writer for a newspaper.

1877 *Harper's Mag.* Dec. 48/2 The price paid to outsiders, or 'specials,' . . . is about eight dollars per column.

+**3.** In a store, restaurant, etc., a product which is specially featured.

1913 LONDON *Valley of Moon* 337 She had . . . persuaded the proprietor . . . to make a 'special' of her wares.

* **Special,** *a.*

+**1.** Of legislation: Having limited application.

1803 *Mass. Priv. & Sp. Statutes* p. iii. (Ernst), Private and special Acts of the Commonwealth. **1911** *Maryland Rep. 1910* 179 A special law is one that relates to particular persons or things of a class. **1917** *Corpus Juris* XII. 773/1 One who is active in procuring the adoption of a special or local statute may not question its constitutionality.

* **2.** Of persons: Appointed additionally or for a particular purpose.

1825 *Mass. Laws* X. 3 The Selectmen of the town of Charlestown . . . [shall appoint] special Police Officers . . . for the preservation of the peace. **1846** *Xenia Torch-Light* 2 July 2/4 Mr. Slidell . . . was sent as a Minister Plenipotentiary, and *not* as a Special Minister. **1890** *Stock Grower & Farmer* 15 Feb. 6/2 Special Indian agent Lewis thinks . . . to avert further difficulty. **1911** *Okla. Session Laws* 3 Legisl. 165 The office of Special Enforcement Officer is hereby established and created.

3. In special combinations.

Special assessment, a tax assessment in addition to what is usual; *s. deposit,* (see quotation); *s. election,* an election held at a time other than usual; *s. relief,* relief for the needy of a kind not usually given; *s. request,* a particular request; *s. supply,* (see quotation).

1875 *Mich. Gen. Statutes* I. (1882) 736 All special assessments shall . . . constitute a lien upon the respective lots. **1859** BARTLETT 432 *Special deposit,* a deposit made in a bank subject to the control of the depositor, and which is not made a part of the funds of the bank to be used by it in its business. **1866** *Wkly. New Mexican* 22 Dec. 2/2 One of the senators from San Miguel county having resigned, a special election was held. **1865** *Atlantic Mo.* Feb. 237/1 The immense collection of back pay, bounties, pensions, and prize-money . . . is Special Relief. **1898** FORD *Tattle-Tales* 129 You'll be saying next that to-night's arrangement was by 'special request.' **1893** CUSHING *Story of P.O.* 278 If the office is not upon a route, and is too far from one to make a change in it so as to have the carrier reach the new office, it is then supplied by what is known in the department as 'special supply.'

Special agent. An agent appointed or employed for a particular purpose. — **1855** HOLBROOK *Among Mail Bags* 26 A Special Agent relieved his pugnacious propensities by getting into a regular fight at the polls. **1880** *Harper's Mag.* March 553/2 Connected with the transmission of the United States mails are certain officials called 'special agents.' **1916** DU PUY *Uncle Sam* 9 The special agent examined both window pane and wall.

+**Special delivery.** Delivery of mail by special messenger ahead of the usual routine delivery schedule. Also attrib. and as adverb. — **1886** RITTENHOUSE *Maud* 368 Eliza brought me a special delivery letter from my good boy. **1909** STRATTON-PORTER *Girl of Limberlost* 327 If I'd put them special delivery on the morning train, she'd get them in the late afternoon. **1924** CROY *R.F.D. No. 3* 46 She sent it off with a special-delivery stamp.

+**Special partner.** One associated with others in carrying on a business but having only limited authority and liability. — **1828** KENT *Commentaries* III. 13 The special partners may receive an annual interest on the capital invested, provided there be no reduction of the original capital. **1839** MARRYAT *Diary in Amer.* 1 Ser. II. 251 In America, if a person

wishes to become a special partner (a sleeping partner) in any concern, he may do so to any extent he pleases. **1887, 1890** [see GENERAL PARTNER].

+**Special partnership.** (See quotation.) — **1859** BARTLETT 432 *Special Partnership.* A partnership limited to a particular branch of business, or to one particular subject.—*Judge Story.*

+**Special-request envelope.** An envelope upon which directions for return are printed. — **1893** *Congress. Rec.* 18 Feb. 1802/2 The issue of special-request envelopes has been going on ever since 1865. **1893** CUSHING *Story of P.O.* 380 There are more special request envelopes issued now than of any other kind.

Special session. =EXTRAORDINARY SESSION. — **1846** *Whig Almanac 1847* 10/1 Mr. Van Buren called a Special Session of Congress. **1900** *Congress. Rec.* 14 Feb. 1801/1 The governor, by force of public opinion, was forced to call the legislature in special session to pass this election law.

+**Special student.** (See quot. 1895.) — **1894** *Harper's Mag.* April 768/2 Yale has discouraged the attendance of 'special' students who are not graduates of any college nor pursuing any of the recognized courses for a degree. **1895** *Stand.* 1719/2 S[*pecial*] *student* (U.S.), a college student who is not a candidate for a degree, and who does not take the regular course.

* **Specie.**

1. Coined money or, in colonial times, one or more commodities used as money. {1671–}

1666 *Plymouth Laws* 149 All debtes shalbee payed in the specye for which a man dothe agree. **1676** *Conn. Rec.* II. 451 Men cannot discharge the country levy in the specia ordered by the Gen[era]ll Court. **1714** *Mass. Bay Currency Tracts* 100 If the Bills of the Bank of England it self were not looked upon as good as Specie, . . . the Credit of 'em would quickly come to nothing. **1792** *Ann. 2d Congress* 1007 Distressing drains of our specie may hereafter be experienced to pay the interest and redeem the principal of the purchased Debt. **1819** in Mackenzie *Van Buren* 156, I send you . . . $900 in Troy, Lansingburg, and Albany bills, which I wish you if possible to convert into specie. **1891** HARRIS in *Century Mag.* Feb. 563 Strapped around his body [was] a belt containing fifty dollars in specie. **1905** BELASCO *Girl of Golden West* (1925) I. 63, I keep the specie in an empty keg now.

2. Attrib. and comb. with *circulation, clerk, man,* etc.

1781 HAMILTON *Works* III. 114 This will give us, in specie-value, about fourteen millions of dollars. **1811** CLAY *Speeches* (1842) 33 The specie circulation of the United States is estimated by some calculators at ten millions of dollars. **1870** M. H. SMITH *20 Years Wall St.* 356 The bank employees are made up of numerous porters, messengers, check clerk, specie clerks, paying tellers [etc.]. **1875** *Chicago Tribune* 30 Sept. 1/4 He is a specie man. **1891** *Scribner's Mag.* Nov. 603/2 In these days of heavy gold shipments, the specie-room on the steamship is a very important institution.

+**Specie basis.** An amount of specie serving as a basis or reserve for paper money. Also fig. — **1832** D. WEBSTER *Works* 397 The general circulation has been extended too far for the specie basis on which it rests. **1840** [see CURRENCY 1 (b)]. **1863** LOWELL *Biglow P.* 2 Ser. vii. 180 To make a sneakin' truce Without no moral specie-basis.

+**Specie Circular.** *Hist.* An order issued at the instance of President Jackson in July, 1836, instructing officers of the Treasury to accept only gold and silver in payment for public land. — **1837** [see MINT DROP 1]. *a*1860 in Claiborne *Sam. Dale* 201 He took ground against the famous Specie Circular and the sub-treasury. **1894** LEAVITT *Our Money Wars* 69 Mr. Webster [in 1837] ascribed the distress to the interference of the Government with the currency, and to the 'Specie Circular.'

+**Specie dollar.** A coined dollar. — *a*1821 BIDDLE *Autobiog.* 238 State Island money [in Penna.] . . . soon depreciated to eight for one specie dollar. **1830** *Congress. Deb.* App. 13 April 114 A specie dollar in 1816, would purchase no more than half as much as a paper dollar will purchase at present. **1900** *Congress. Rec.* 1 Feb. 1385/2 The standard specie dollar . . . is the standard and medium by which other things . . . are redeemed.

+**Specie-paying bank.** A bank which redeemed its notes in specie. *Obs.* — **1818** *Niles' Reg.* XIV. 207/2 The incorporated banks of Maryland . . . whose bills are 12 per cent. below the paper of what are called specie-paying banks. **1845** *Big Bear Ark.* 143 It can boast of the only specie-paying bank in the State. **1875** *Chicago Tribune* 6 Oct. 4/4 The Whigs . . . proposed that the Government should receive in payment of public lands the notes of *specie-paying banks.*

Specie payment. Payment in coined money, esp. with reference to such payments by banks in redeeming their notes. {1845–} — **1816** A. GALLATIN *Writings* I. 691 The measure would have the double effect of assisting in resuming specie payments, and demonstrate to the British [etc.]. **1858** HOMANS *Cycl. Commerce* 131/2 The directors of the National Bank proposed to the State banks a resumption of specie payments on the 21st February, 1817. **1877** S. D. HORTON *Silver & Gold* (ed. 2) 180 The activity of Mr. Balch in promoting the Restoration of Specie Payment on the Bi-metallic basis, has a pleasant suggestion of prosperous augury.

Specific duty. A duty or tax assessed on goods according to quantity rather than value. {1930–} — **1789** *Ann. 1st Congress* 107, I shall not pretend to say that there ought not to be specific duties laid upon every one of the articles enumerated. **1818** *Ann. 15th Congress* 1 Sess. 1777 The Secretary of the Treasury was directed to report to Congress . . . [about] charging specific duties upon articles which are now charged with duties ad valorem. **1845** POLK *Diary* (1929) 23, I had recommended . . . the abolition of the minimum principle and specific duties.

∗ Speck.[1]

+1. A plant disease characterized by blasted seed grains, or speckled fruit or leaves.

1771 WASHINGTON *Diaries* II. 24 My Wheat every where being much Injurd. by the Speck or Spot. **1788** *Ib.* III. 372 This grain [wheat], however, and the Rye more so, is a good deal injured, by the speck. **1878** *Ill. Dept. Agric. Trans.* XIV. 126 The 'speck' . . . affects some few varieties [of fruit]. **1909** *Cent. Suppl.* 1247/2 *White speck of tobacco*, a disease on the leaves of tobacco producing small white spots caused by the fungus *macrosporium tabacinum*.

+2. (See quotations.)

1877 *Lyceum Nat. Hist. N.Y. Ann.* 1876 311 *Boleosoma Stigmœum*. . . . Known to boys and fishermen as *Speck*. **1891** *Cent.* 5808/2 *Speck*, . . . a percoid fish, *Ulocentra stigmœa* of Jordan, common in ponds of the hill-country from Georgia to Louisiana.

+3. *Not . . . a speck*, or variant: Not a bit, not in the least. *colloq.*

1843 HALIBURTON *Attaché* 1 Ser. I. ii, I didn't like it a spec. **1889** JEWETT *B. Leicester* 87, I s'pose you ain't kind of flaunted it a little speck. **1909** RICE *Mr. Opp* 26 Your talkin' won't bother me a speck.

+Speck.[2] [Du. *spek*, Ger. *speck*. A new borrowing.]

1. (See quot. 1886.)

1809 *Lancaster* (Pa.) *Jrnl.* 12 Sept., (Th.), He goes out almost every week to eat speck with the country folks. **1863** P. S. DAVIS *Young Parson* 47 You . . . eat the best of roast beef, while I have to put up with sauerkraut and speck. **1886** *Amer. Philol. Ass. Trans.* App. p. xii, 'Speck' is . . . the generic term applied to all kinds of fat meat.

+2. *Speck and applejees*, (see quotations).

1848 BARTLETT 321 *Spack* [ed. 2, *speck*] *and applejees*, . . . pork and apples, cooked together. An ancient Dutch dish made in New York. **1863** *Ladies' Repository* Jan. 55/2 'Speck and appeljees' is a slight modification of *spek en appeltjes* the name for fried pork and apples among the Hollanders.

Specklebelly. {1874-} **+1.** The white-fronted goose. **+2.** =GADWALL. **+3.** (See quotation.) — (1) **1874** COUES *Birds N.W.* 547 The 'Speckle-bellies,' as they are called in California, associate freely at all times with both the Snow and Hutchins' Geese. (2) **1888** TRUMBULL *Names of Birds* 24 Gadwall. . . . Though rather a rare visitant on Long Island, it is known (when it does appear) at Moriches as Speckle-Belly. **1917** *Birds of Amer.* I. 118. (3) **1891** *Cent.* 5808/3 *Speckle-belly*, . . . a trout or char, as the common brook-trout of the United States, *Salvelinus fontinalis*.

∗ Speckled, *a.*

1. In the names of animals, esp. fishes. {1797-}

1778 CARVER *Travels* 487 The Speckled Snake is an aqueous reptile about two feet and half in length, but without venom. **1814** MITCHILL *Fishes N.Y.* 406 Speckled Grunts. *Labrus fulvomaculatus*. . . . There are rows of yellow speckled stripes. **1842** *Nat. Hist. N.Y., Zoology* III. 14 Under the name of Speckled Turtle, this little animal [the spotted tortoise] is found throughout the Union. **1869** *Rep. Comm. Agric.* 1868 322 [It is] rank folly to allow so great a delicacy as the speckled brook trout (*Salmo fontinalis*) to become extinct. **1877** HODGE *Arizona* 39 They are well stocked with the real speckled mountain trout. **1888** GOODE *Amer. Fishes* 56 'Marsh Bass,' . . . and 'Speckled Hen' are other names applied to one or both species [of bass].

2. In the names of birds. {1668-}

1806 LEWIS in *L. & Clark Exped.* V. (1905) 136 Saw the speckled woodpecker. **1865** BURROUGHS in *Atlantic Mo.* May 521/1 The Winter-Wren . . . is one of those birds . . . that, like the Speckled Canada Warbler and the Hermit-Thrush, only the privileged ones hear. **1907** LILLIBRIDGE *Trail* 276 They were still there: sleepy brown mallards, . . . greyish speckled widgeon: these and others less common. **1912** N. WOODROW *Sally Salt* 11 That speckled thrush is three days earlier than usual. **1917** *Birds of Amer.* I. 158 *Anser albifrons gambeli*. . . . Speckled Brant.

+Speckled alder. The hoary alder, *Alnus incana*. — *a*1862 THOREAU *Maine Woods* 307 The speckled or hoary alder . . . abounds everywhere along the muddy banks of rivers and lakes. **1884** SARGENT *Rep. Forests* 165.

+Speckled-bill coot. Also **speckle-billed coot.** =SURF SCOTER. — **1888** TRUMBULL *Names of Birds* 103 At Stratford, [Conn., it is known as the] Speckled-Bill Coot. **1917** *Birds of Amer.* I. 151.

+Speckled trout. Any one of various trout, as the brook trout and the rainbow trout, having a speckled appearance. — **1805** [see MOUNTAIN TROUT]. **1857** HAMMOND *Northern Scenes* 43 He will not . . . take the speckled trout that we find in [northern N.Y.]. **1897** *N.Y. Forest, Fish, & Game Comm. 2d Rep. Salvelinus fontinalis*. . . . Brook Trout; Speckled Trout. **1902** HULBERT *Forest Neighbors* (1903) 60 Small, bright carmine spots . . . gave him one of his *aliases*, the 'Speckled Trout.'

∗ Spectacle.

∗1. *pl.* A pair of lenses in a frame adjusted to the eyes for improving the vision.

1737 FRANKLIN *Poor Richard's Almanac* 1738 1, I have just now unluckily broke my Spectacles. **1790** *Penna. Packet* 1 March 1/1 This Day, . . . Will commence the Sale of a Large and General Assortment of . . .

spectacles, ink pots, steel snuffers. **1820** *Columbian Centinel* 12 Jan. 4/4 The subscriber has received . . . an excellent assortment of best London made Spectacles. **1893** *Harper's Mag.* Feb. 455 Miss Sarey Mirandy readjusted her spectacles. **1922** TARKINGTON *Gentle Julia* 50 You or Herbert . . . used his spectacles to cut a magazine with, and broke them.

2. *attrib.* In the names of birds. {1783-}

1844 *Nat. Hist. N.Y., Zoology* II. 335 The Box Coot, Spectacle Duck, . . . is very common on the coast of New-York during the winter. **1917** *Birds of Amer.* I. 151 Surf Scoter. *Oidemia perspicillata*. . . . [Also called] Box Coot; Spectacle Coot; Butterboat-billed Coot.

∗ Spectacle case. A small case for spectacles. — **1789** [see CHIMNEY PIECE]. **1864** *Hist. North-Western Soldiers' Fair* 140 [Donations include] 2 jewel caskets, . . . 1 spectacle case. **1891** EARLE *Sabbath* 42 [She carried] in her lace-mitted hand . . . her spectacle-case and well-worn Bible.

+Spectacled eider. An Alaskan eider duck (*Arctonetta fischeri*) having eyes set in white plumage rimmed with black. — **1872** COUES *Key to Birds* 292 Spectacled Eider, . . . a whitish space round eye, bounded by black. **1883** *Nat. Museum Bul.* No. 27, 162. **1917** *Birds of Amer.* I. 145/1 The Spectacled Eider is essentially an Alaskan Duck.

‖**Spectacularity.** The quality of being spectacular. — **1883** HOWELLS *Woman's Reason* xii, The bare spectacularity of the keeping . . . must all be eloquent of a boarding-house. **1891** — *Imperative Duty* i, Boston . . . was not like Liverpool in a certain civic grandiosity, a sort of lion-and-unicorn spectacularity.

+Spectatorio. [From *spect*acle and *oratorio.*] A form of entertainment, devised by James Steele MacKaye (1842-94), which was to have combined oratorio, spectacle, pantomime, etc. Hence *spectatorium*, the building which was to have housed this production. — **1892** in P. MacKaye *Epoch* II. 337 A *Spectatorium* . . . is an entirely new species of building, invented and devised for the production of a new order of entertainment entitled a *spectatorio*. **1894** *Pittsburgh Dispatch* 28 Feb., Up to the day when work was abandoned upon the Spectatorium building, $850,000 had been sunk in the enterprise.

+Spectorama. (See quotation.) — **1898** *Chicago Inter Ocean* 23 Oct. 15/5 The Spectorama on Madison street reminds one of the dream of Steele Mackaye, both in the name and the delightful effects produced. Real water, real boats, are nicely blended with built-up fortifications, and these again blended with painted scene. The sinking of the Merrimac is a very interesting and picturesque exhibition.

+Spectral owl. =GREAT GRAY OWL. — **1884** COUES *Key to Birds* (ed. 2) 509. **1917** *Birds of Amer.* II. 105.

Spectrograph. {1891-} **+**An apparatus for photographing the spectrum. — **1884** *Amer. Acad. Proc.* XIX. 238 In July, 1876, several photographs of the spectrum of Vega were taken with an apparatus which Dr. Draper called the 'spectrograph.' **1889** *Internat. Ann., Anthony's Photogr. Bul.* II. 394 The color sensitiveness of the plate I find out with the aid of my Quartz spectrograph. **1893** *Nation* 16 Feb. 126/2 With the eleven-inch Draper spectrograph nearly a thousand photographs were taken.

∗ Speculator. One who speculates in trade or business. {1827-}

1778 HAMILTON *Works* VII. 560 The speculators in the city have been bidding against the commissaries. **1847** COYNER *Lost Trappers* 211 Several droves of cattle . . . have been taken to Oregon by speculators from Missouri. **1890** *Stock Grower & Farmer* 21 June 3/2 When you hear of a cattle speculator going broke, . . . it is generally one of these bum speculators whose knowledge of a cow is confined to the fact that it has four legs and a tail. **1901** MERWIN & WEBSTER *Calumet 'K'* 287 The young speculators were matching their wits against a great machine.

+b. =LAND SPECULATOR.

1790 [see DODGING]. **1803** J. DAVIS *Travels* 208 Mr. Paine . . . I suspect to have been what Americans call, A speculator in lands. **1857** [see EN-GROSS *v.* 1]. **1884** *Century Mag.* March 645/1 The lots on Capitol Hill were all bought up by speculators.

+c. =NEGRO SPECULATOR. *Obs.*

1852 STOWE *Uncle Tom* xx, I was raised by a speculator, with lots of others. **1863** 'E. KIRKE' *Southern Friends* 62 The dealer in negroes never applies the term 'trader' to himself; he prefers the softer word 'speculator.' **1899** CHESNUTT *Wife of His Youth* 85 Don't you remember Cicely —Cicely whom you sold . . . to the speculator?

∗ Speech. **+**Among the Indians, a communication relating to matters of concern to an entire tribe or nation. *Obs.* — **1690** SEWALL *Letter-Book* I. 110 Writt to Mr. Mather . . . enclosing the Print of the Maquas speeches. **1785** DENNY *Journal* 62 Three Shawanee Indians arrived with a speech from their nation. **1808** in *Niles' Reg.* II. 342/2 A Pottawattimie Indian had arrived at the towns, with a speech from the British.

+Speech belt. Among the Indians, a belt of wampum relating to a conference or council. *Obs.* — **1753** WASHINGTON *Writings* I. 28 The King . . . offered the French Speech-Belt which had before been demanded.

∗ Speeder. **+1.** (See quot. 1876.) **2.** One who rides or drives at a rapid rate of speed; a fast horse, etc. (1) **1847** *Knickerb.* XXX. 517 A few [girls] tend the 'warpers,' the 'spoolers,' and the 'speeders.' **1876** KNIGHT 2261/1 *Speeder*, (*Cotton-manufacture*,) a machine invented by Mason as a substitute for the bobbin and fly frame, by which slivers of cotton from the carding-machine are slightly twisted, and thereby converted into rovings. **1900** *Everybody's Mag.* I. 593/1 The 'speeder' . . . rolls two of the slubber's threads into one. (2) **1891** *Cent.* 5814/2 *Speeder*, . . . one who or that which moves with great swiftness, as a horse. **1893** *Columbus*

Dispatch 6 Sept., A certain good-fellowship has been established between the speeders and the city, and . . . confidence may be placed in the promises of the local wheelmen.

+Speedway. A road on which the speeding of harness horses is permissible; a road reserved for fast traffic; a race course for automobiles. — **1894** *Voice* 28 June, New England cities have millions of dollars to spend upon its uptown parks and speedways. **1903** *N.Y. Times* 16 Aug., The owners of rapid roadsters are devoting no inconsiderable portion of their summer leisure to spirited brushes on the new speedway. **1925** *Kansas City Star* 31 May 1/1 Here is how they finished . . . in the thirteenth annual 500-mile motor classic on the Indianapolis speedway yesterday.

*Speedwell.** Any one of various herbs of the genus *Veronica*, esp. *V. officinalis*. Also with specifying terms. (See also PURSLANE SPEEDWELL.) — **1791** MUHLENBERG *Index Florae* 159. **1818** *Mass. H. S. Coll.* 2 Ser. VIII. 169 Among those, that flower in June [are] . . . two species of veronica or speedwell. **1857** GRAY *Botany* 289. **1898** CREEVEY *Flowers of Field* 70 Marsh-speedwell. *Veronica scutellata.* . . . A delicate, tender plant. *Ib.* 338 Common Speedwell. *Veronica officinalis.* . . . Plants softly hairy, prostrate and creeping.

*Spell, n.**

1. A continuous stretch *of* weather, often of a specified kind. {1808–}
1705 *Boston News-Letter* 24 Dec. 2/2 Last Three Weeks we had a Spell of very good Weather. **1779** JEFFERSON *Writings* IV. 57 The spell of weather [was] the worst ever known within the memory of man. **1837** *S. Lit. Messenger* III. 229 We have had a spell of remarkably wet weather. **1892** *Courier-Journal* 1 Oct. 4/4 The general outlook was for a spell of warm and dry weather. **1904** PRINGLE *Rice Planter* 139 If a bad spell of weather should come she could not go out.

+b. Preceded by descriptive terms and freq. without the *of* phrase.
1740 T. SMITH *Journal* (1849) 268, I believe no man ever knew so winter-like a spell so early in the year. **1797** JEFFERSON *Writings* IX. 362 You wish to know the state of the air here during the late cold spell. **1824** MARSHALL *Kentucky* II. 319 [It] has yielded to the severity of winter spells of weather. **1892** *Nation* 4 Aug. 79/1 [In N.Y.] the mortality due to a 'hot spell' . . . [is] far less now than twenty years ago.

+2. A time or while. *colloq.*
1745 *Essex Inst. Coll.* XLVIII. 299, [I] continued in ye Trench a spell. **1841** GREELEY in *Corr. R. W. Griswold* (1898) 58, I've waited a spell to hear from you. **1889** *Harper's Mag.* Dec. 349/2 Why don't ye come and rest a spell with me? **1925** TILGHMAN *Dugout* 51 Maybe after you're rested up a spell and get strong you could go home.

+3. A period of being ill, out of sorts, or irritable; an attack of illness, indisposition, etc.
1806 W. PETTIGREW *Let.* 26 Nov. (Univ. N.C. MS.), My brother in law has had a Spell of Sickness but is recovered. **1869** STOWE *Oldtown Folks* 171 When Hepsy does get beat out she has *spells*, and she goes on awful. **1887** *Courier-Journal* 1 May 2/3 Witness said he has 'spells,' after which he is bright, but at other times dull and stupid. **1896** JEWETT *Pointed Firs* 21 She had also made dark reference to his having 'spells' of some unexplainable nature.

4. *By spells*, at intervals, now and then. {1821–}
1788 *Mass. Spy* 4 Sept. 3/2 It had . . . rained by spells for three days before. **1848** DRAKE *Pioneer Life Ky.* 152 By interrupted continuity, . . . in the commoner dialect, 'by spells,' I was the pupil of Master Braden. **1891** 'THANET' *Otto the Knight* 322 [She let] S'leeny go an' stay on the boat by spells to holp 'er.

+5. *A spell ago* (or *back*), some time ago. *colloq.*
1834 C. A. DAVIS *Lett. J. Downing* 346 Our folks . . . saw this a long spell ago. **1853** *Knickerb.* XLII. 653 'When?' 'A spell ago—an' more.' **1886** HOWELLS *Minister's Charge* 14, I don't know as you got a letter from me a spell back. **1917** FREEMAN & KINGSLEY *Alabaster Box* 48 There was another party looking at the place a spell back.

*Spell, v.¹** *tr.* To relieve (a person) by performing his work for a time. {1595, 1823} Also transf. ('Now *U.S.*' *O.E.D.*) — **1744** A. HAMILTON *Itin.* (1907) 7 He lighted every half mile and ran a couple of miles at a footman's pace, to 'spell the poor beast' (as he termed it). **1833** NEAL *Down-Easters* I. 119 Couldn't ye spell a feller, hey? **1889** HOWELLS *Annie Kilburn* 187 Don't you want I should spell you a little while, Miss Kilburn? **1921** PAINE *Comr. Rolling Ocean* 206 You can spell each other in two-hour watches.

*Spell, v.²**
+1. *tr.* To test (a person) in spelling.
1866 C. H. SMITH *Bill Arp* 171 He then spelt him right straight along on all sorts of big words, and little words. **1867** 'LACKLAND' *Homespun* 138 The hour arrived for us to be spelled round out of the little Walker dictionary.

+2. *To spell down*, to vanquish in a spelling contest.
1853 B. F. TAYLOR *Jan. & June* 259 The struggle is, to spell each other down. **1903** FOX *Little Shepherd* iv, [He] spelled them both down before the whole school.

+3. *To spell baker*, to play an unpleasant or difficult role. *colloq.*
1868 LONGFELLOW *Poetical Works* (1893) 504/1 If an old man will marry a young wife, Why then . . . he must spell Baker!

+Spellbinder. A political orator sent out chiefly during campaigns. — **1888** *N.Y. Tribune* 15 Nov. 6/1 A big and successful dinner was given at Delmonico's by the Republican Orators—'Spellbinders'—who worked during the recent campaign. **1897** *Scribner's Mag.* Oct. 517/2 The professor who patiently teaches his classes . . . to think straight, . . . serves his country better than a hundred 'spell-binders' in the last frantic days of a campaign. **1911** SAUNDERS *Col. Todhunter* 41 Emotional endowment . . . has made Missouri 'spell binders' long famous on the stump.

+Spellbinding. The speech-making of a spellbinder. — **1896** *N.Y. Wkly. Witness* 30 Dec. 13/1 He prayed to be permitted to try his hand at spellbinding.

*Speller.** ‖**1.** A seeker *after* something. **+2.** =SPELLING BOOK. — (1) **1796** PAINE *Writings* III. (1896) 217 John Adams . . . it is known was always a speller after places and offices. (2) **1864** WEBSTER 1269/2 *Speller*, . . . a book containing exercises in spelling; a spelling-book. **1881** *Harper's Mag.* Dec. 107/2 Mary still keeps the green-covered 'speller' in which she and Sam studied their lessons together. **1889** *Ib.* June 126/2 I'm a-goin' to put this 'ere letter in yo' speller.

*Spelling.**
*1.** Orthography as a subject of study. Also in ellipt. context.
1839 *Knickerb.* XIII. 190 Miss Peebles was 'in spelling,' soon after Jefferson became the chief servant of our 'free and enlightened citizens.' **1866** *Rep. Indian Affairs* 290 Reading, writing, spelling and ciphering . . . have been the chief exercises of the children.

+2. A spelling bee or spelling school. *Obs.*
1889 RILEY *Pipes o' Pan* 45 How her face used to look in the twilight As I tuck her to spellin'.

3. Attrib. with *class, club, fight, tournament.*
1871 EGGLESTON *Hoosier Schoolm.* 25 Hence the necessity for those long spelling-classes at the close of each forenoon and afternoon session of the school. **1882** THAYER *From Log-Cabin* 215 His two cousins . . . were members of his Spelling Club a few years before. **1876** 'MARK TWAIN' *Tom Sawyer* xxi. 170 There were reading exercises and a spelling-fight. **1871** EGGLESTON *Hoosier Schoolm.* 25 Time [elapsed] between the appointing of the spelling tournament and the actual occurrence of that remarkable event.

Spelling bee. A social gathering at which competitive spelling is the chief diversion. {1875} Also attrib. (This term seems to have come into use considerably later than either *spelling school* or *spelling match*. See *PMLA* LVI. 495 ff.) — **1875** *London Times* 16 April 4/4 The 'Spelling Bee,' a New England invention, . . . has made rapid strides over the country [i.e., the U.S.]. **1881** NEVIN *Vignettes of Travel* 154 Witness . . . the sweep of the praying-band or spelling-bee excitement from one ocean to the other. **1889** *Century Mag.* March 800/1 The Spellin' Bee wuz over.

Spelling book. A book designed for use by those learning to spell. {1677–} — **1746** FRANKLIN *Writings* II. 298 Please to send me . . . 6 doz. of Dyche's . . . Spelling Books. **1798** WEEMS *Letters* II. 101 There is an infinite demand among numerous Storekeepers of my acquaintance for *Spelling books.* **1817** [see COPYRIGHT 1]. **1878** STOWE *Poganuc People* 8 In she came, . . . dropping her knitting-work and spelling-book in her eagerness. **1925** BRYAN *Memoirs* 40 Webster's spelling book and McGuffey's reader . . . formed the basis of my education.

+Spelling match. A contest in spelling. — **1845** H. GREELEY in *PMLA* LVI. 501 It used to be the custom that the head of the first class and the next should choose sides for a 'spelling match.' **1857** E. STONE *Life of Howland* 17 To impart additional interest to the 'spelling match,' as it was called, the pupils were permitted in rotation to select and give out words to the class. **1889** RILEY *Pipes o' Pan* 133 Marindy read a letter 'bout . . . spellin'-matches, and huskin'-bees. **1902** G. M. MARTIN *Emmy Lou* 79 'Spelling match!' said Aunt Louise.

Spelling school. {1704 (Swift *Works* (1766) I. 14)} + =SPELLING BEE. — **1832** *Indiana Mag. Hist.* XV. 241 In the evening I appointed a spelling school at which I invited all the parents to attend. **1853** B. F. TAYLOR *Jan. & June* 256 Spelling Schools! Have you forgotten them? **1883** *Harper's Mag.* Sept. 643/1 We are in a fever about the Carnival, the paring bee, the spelling school, or whatever it is called.

*Spelt.** A variety of wheat, as *Triticum spelta* or *T. dicoccum*, valued chiefly for stock. Usually pl. — **1763** *Washington Diaries* I. 187 Sowed about a Peck of Spelts in Drills. **1789** MORSE *Amer. Geog.* 53 In Pennsylvania is a kind of grain called spelts, which grows much like wheat. **1806** LEWIS in *L. & Clark Exped.* IV. (1905) 121 The Grouse . . . feed on . . . the seeds of several species of spelts and wild rye. **1868** GRAY *Field Botany* 357 T[riticum] *Spelta*, Spelt. A grain rarely cult[ivated] in this country.

Spelter. Zinc. {1661–} Also attrib. — **1789** MORSE *Amer. Geog.* 227 Zinc or spelter, a semi-metal, and several other fossils and metals have been found in Connecticut. **1816** *Ann. 14th Congress* 1 Sess. 1874 The following articles shall be imported . . . free of duties; . . . zinc, teutenague, or spelter. **1861** *Army Regulations* 410 Spelter solder. **1879** *Scribner's Mo.* May 39/1 Many things they [thieves] hide under water, such as spelter and other metals. **1889** HOWELLS *Hazard of Fortunes* I. 60 Some red Japanese bird-kites were stuck down in the necks of spelter vases.

Spencer.¹ a. A close-fitting, short overcoat or jacket for men. {1796–} **b.** A garment for women made in imitation of this. {1803–} — **1803** CUTLER in *Life & Corr.* II. 115 Their fertile imaginations suggested a great number of uses besides that of cloaks and spencers. **1839** 'M. PENCIL' *White Sulphur P.* 108 A young lady . . . persists in wearing a red spencer every night. **1856** SIMMS *Charlemont* 374 By this time the old man had got on his spencer. **1907** ANDREWS *Recoll.* 24 On afternoons when I was to give a declamation, I dressed up in a blue broadcloth jacket, then called spencer.

+**Spencer.**[2] [Cf. SPENCER RIFLE.] A Spencer gun. {1904} — **1873** BEADLE *Undevel. West* 545 My horse, bridle, saddle, lariat, gun (a Spencer) and two Navajo blankets cost me two hundred dollars.

+**Spencer carbine.** = SPENCER RIFLE. — **1872** ROE *Army Lett.* 43, I was given a Spencer carbine to shoot (a short magazine rifle used by the cavalry). **1873** COZZENS *Marvellous Country* 208 We might see the 'brave boys in blue' . . . astonish them [the Indians] with their new Spencer carbines. **1923** J. H. COOK *On Old Frontier* 5, I had traded a pistol . . . for a Spencer carbine.

+**Spencer rifle.** A breech-loading magazine rifle of a type invented by C. M. Spencer (1833–1922). {1898–} — **1866** 'F. KIRKLAND' *Bk. Anecdotes* 660/1 Harris ordered the skirmish line forward, . . . with orders to silence the troublesome battery . . . with the aid of the Spencer rifle. **1868** *Ore. State Jrnl.* 19 Dec. 1/3 He had a trusty Spencer rifle with him. **1883** SWEET & KNOX *Through Texas* 38 Weapons of all sorts, from the murderous Spencer rifle to the soothing and medicinal pocket-flask.

*Sperling. local. +A young or immature herring. — **1884** GOODE, etc. *Fisheries* I. 550 The name 'Sperling,' employed by our own fishermen of Cape Ann to denote the young herrings. **1911** *Rep. Fisheries 1908* 311/1 'Sperling' and 'brit' denote differences in the age of the fish.

* **Spermaceti.** A waxlike, fatty solid which separates from the oil obtained from the sperm whale and certain other cetaceans; a candle made of this substance.

1678 *New Castle Court Rec.* 351 A parcell of spermas Citty. **1732** [see MANNA]. **1789** *Ann. 1st Congress* 147 On all candles of wax or spermaceti, per pound, six cents. **1829** WEEMS *B. Franklin* 16 Ben . . . [was] born to diffuse a light beyond that of tallow or spermaceti. **1891** CHASE & CLOW *Industry* II. 129 Spermaceti is used in making candles.

attrib. **1701** WOLLEY *Journal N.Y.* (1902) 47, I never heard of any Spermaceti whales, either catch'd or driven upon these Shores. **1749** *Boston News-Letter* 6 April, Sperma Ceti Candles, exceeding all others for Beauty, Sweetness of Scent when extinguished. **1760** Sperma-ceti Manufactory [see MANUFACTORY 1]. **1789** MORSE *Amer. Geog.* 260 Spermaceti works . . . were erected.

Sperm candle. A candle made of spermaceti. {1856–} — **1775** *Essex Inst. Coll.* XIII. 202 He heard sperm Candles were 3 s. **1839** BRIGGS *H. Franco* II. 143 Mrs. Brown's house was brilliantly illuminated with a sperm candle in each side light. **1870** M. H. SMITH *20 Years Wall St.* 494 The father-in-law of James F. Penniman . . . [was] a very wealthy trader in sperm candles and oil.

Sperm oil. Oil obtained from the head and blubber of the sperm whale. {1839–} — **1827** *Hallowell* (Me.) *Gaz.* 20 June 4/3 B. Wales Has just received Ground Rice; N. Rum; Sperm Oil. **1868** in Dana *Two Years* (1869) 468 She took and delivered at New London upwards of twenty-five thousand barrels of whale and sperm oil. **1883** *Century Mag.* July 326/2 Sperm oil was so dear as to be out of the reach of the poorer classes.

Sperm whale. (See quot. 1911.) {1839–} Also attrib. — **1834** *Congress. Deb.* 3 March 781 The increase or decrease . . . of the sperm whale fishery ought to depend on somewhat certain calculations. **1883,1887** [see PAN n. 6]. **1911** *Rep. Fisheries 1908* 316/2 Sperm whale (*Physeter macrocephalus*). . . . They are captured for their oil and spermaceti.

Sphagnum. A genus of mosses found in marshes, swamps, etc. {1753–}; the mossy substance of these plants. {1840–} Also attrib. — **1832** BROWNE *Sylva* 303 In all of them [*sc.* marshes] the surface is covered with a bed of sphagnum. **1885** *Outing* VII. 180/2 [The hollow] was carpeted with sphagnum moss. **1897** [see CRADLE HILL]. **1898** S. B. GREEN *Forestry in Minn.* 297 *Muskeg*, a term commonly applied to sphagnum swamps by the Indians and woodsmen of northern Minnesota. **1901** MOHR *Plant Life Ala.* 293 The flats bordering the swamps in the plain, are covered with peat mosses (Sphagnum) of various kinds.

*Sphinx. A hawk moth. {1753–} Also attrib. and with specifying terms. — **1854** [see HUMMING-BIRD MOTH]. **1876** *Vermont Bd. Agric. Rep.* III. 567 Another insect that sometimes does some damage to the potato crop is the Five spotted sphinx (*Macrosila quinque masculata*). **1879** *Scribner's Mo.* July 397/2 The Carolina sphinx—*Sphinx Carolina*—is a good example of this group. **1886** *Harper's Mag.* Nov. 877/1 Here in the twilight you may hear the hum of the sphinx-moth.

*Spice.

*1. A condiment derived from a tropical plant; also, collect., such condiments in general.

1633 *N.H. Prov. Papers* I. 71 Pd. Mr. Bole for 7 gallons of aq. vitae and spice. **1674** SEWALL *Diary* I. 3, 6d for spice &c. **1715** *Boston News-Letter* 19 Dec. 2/2 To be Sold . . . , all sorts of Fruit and Spice. **1751** *Boston Ev. Post* 23 Sept., Then season well with Pepper, Salt and Spice. **1803** *Austin P.* I. (1924) 89, 2 lb Spice. **1892** *York County Hist. Rev.* 53 The salesroom . . . carries a full line of family groceries, teas, coffees, spices.

+**2.** = SPICEBUSH 1 or 2.

1842 *Cultivator* IX. 82/2 Remove no logs; grub no spice; it costs too much. The bushes afford the finest amusement for fat cattle.

3. attrib. and comb. **a.** With *box, grater, mortar.*

1648 *Mayflower Descendant* X. 199 One spice morter & pestle. **1678** *New Castle Court Rec.* 362, 3 great spice greaters. **1852** ELLET *Pioneer Women* 37 It was usual with her to keep a supply of maple-sugar and cinnamon-bark in her spice-box.

b. In special combinations.

Spice bitters, s. oak, s. sweeting, s. tree, (see quotations).

1894 ROBINSON *Danvis Folks* 7 These 'ere spice bitters is compaounded of several nat'ral plants, but the main ingrejencies is fever-bush an' bayberry. **1807** C. SCHULTZ *Travels* II. 24 Natural fruit and forest trees, which I noticed on the banks of the Ohio: . . . black thorn, Jerusalem oak, or spice oak. **1850** *New Eng. Farmer* II. 359/2 There are several other varieties of apple under the name of Spice Sweeting. **1884** SARGENT *Rep. Forests* 120 *Umbellularia Californica.* . . . California Laurel. Spice Tree. . . . Rogue River valley, Oregon, south through the California coast ranges to San Diego county.

Spice apple. An aromatic variety of apple. {1611–} Also attrib. — **1764** *N.H. Hist. Soc. Coll.* IX. 152, 26th of March sat out 63 young apple trees . . . ; then 9 of ye spice apple. **1822** J. THACHER *Amer. Orchardist* 137 *Spice Apple.* . . . It appears to be peculiar to New Jersey. **1860** ANTHONY in Harper *S. B. Anthony* I. 199 The spice-apple tree is dead.

+**Spiceberry.** One or other of various aromatic shrubs, esp. the wintergreen. {1852, in Canada} — **1792** IMLAY *Western Territory* 216 There is a variety of shrubs in every part of the country, the principal of which are the myrtle and spice berry. **1871** DE VERE 404 The queen of them all is said to be the lovely, creeping snowberry . . . ; although others give the prize to the spice-berry. **1891** [see GROUNDBERRY]. **1897** SUDWORTH *Arborescent Flora* 306 *Eugenia procera.* . . . Red Stopper (Fla.). Spiceberry (Fla.).

+**Spicebush.**

1. The feverbush, *Benzoin aestivale.*

1770 WASHINGTON *Diaries* I. 409 The Growth, [is] Walnut, Cherry, Spice Bushes, etca. **1808** ASHE *Travels* 225 There were nine species of bark, spice, and leather wood bushes. **1842** *Amer. Pioneer* I. 349 They sometimes made use of the fresh roots of sassafras, or spice bush. **1856** BRYANT *Poetical Works* (1903) 185 The spice-bush lifts Her leafy lances. **1875** BURROUGHS *Winter Sunshine* 15 The red berries of the . . . spice-bush . . . shine in the sun like rubies and coral. **1901** MOHR *Plant Life Ala.* 101 The spice bush . . . form[s] the undergrowth and frequent[s] the openings.

2. One of various other plants: (see quotations).

1866 LINDLEY & MOORE *Treas. Botany* 821/2 *Oreodaphne californica* is a common tree in the mountainous parts of California, where it goes by a variety of names, such as Mountain Laurel, Spice-bush, Balm of Heaven. **1894** *Amer. Folk-Lore* VII. 89 *Aralia racemosa*, spice-bush, Hartford, Conn. **1896** *Ib.* IX. 180 *Calycanthus floridus*, spice-bush, Middleborough, Mass.

*Spice cake. A cake flavored with spice. — [**1643** WILLIAMS *Key* (1866) 122 *Sautáuthig* . . . is as sweet to them as plum or spice cake to the English.] **1872** ROE *Army Lett.* 54 Mrs. Hunt this moment brought a plate of delicious spice cake for our luncheon. **1902** L. RICHARDS *Mrs. Tree* 53 Ask Direxia to give you a spice-cake.

Spice mill. 1. (See quot. 1876.) {1862–} **2.** A factory in which spice is prepared for market. — (1) **1848** *Rep. Comm. Patents* 847 542 This cast iron grain, coffee and spice mill was invented . . . by a Mr. Swift. **1876** KNIGHT 2265/2 *Spice-mill*, a mill similar to a coffee or drug mill, for grinding spices. (2) **1893** *Harper's Mag.* April 664/2 Coffee and spice mills . . . are notable among the industrial establishments of [Brooklyn].

+**Spice root. 1.** The barren strawberry, *Waldsteinia fragarioides.* **2.** The dewdrop, *Dalibarda repens.* — (1) **1821** *Mass. H. S. Coll.* 2 Ser. IX. 149 *Dalibarda fragarioides*, . . . Spice-root, dry strawberry, [is indigenous in Vt.]. (2) **1833** EATON *Botany* (ed. 6) 120 *Dalibarda repens*, spice root, false violet. . . . Troy, rare.

+**Spice tea.** (See quot. 1871.) — **1856** CARTWRIGHT *Autobiog.* 25 We had sage, bohea, cross-vine, spice and sassafras teas. **1871** DE VERE 395 Spice-tea is . . . made from another laurel common at the South, the spice-bush (*Laurus benzoin*).

+**Spicewood.** = SPICEBUSH 1 and 2.

1756 KALM *Resa* II. 204. **1788** MAY *Jrnl. & Lett.* 66, [I am applying the leaves of spice-wood, soaked in vinegar. **1804** LEWIS & CLARK *Exped.* VI. (1905) 171 The buds of the Spicewood appeared. **1836** [see DOGBERRY]. **1856** A. CARY *Married* 260 We found ourselves in a green, quiet lane, bordered with cedars, and spicewood. **1885** M. THOMPSON *Byways & Bird Notes* 96 Go bite the bud of the spice-wood. **1903** BANKS *Round Anvil Rock* 159 Below ran a dazzling border of shrubs— . . . the red-bud, the spice-wood, the sweet-strife.

b. Attrib. with *berry, bottom, bush,* etc.

1785 MARSHALL *Amer. Grove* 174 *Laurus geniculata.* Carolinian Spice Wood Tree. **1789** Spicewood-berries [see BELLYACHE ROOT]. **1799** J. SMITH *Acct. Captivity* 23 The timber is white ash . . . and spicewood bushes. **1800** TATHAM *Agric. & Commerce* 61 Particularly cane-brake, sugar-tree, and spice-wood bottom. **1843** 'CARLTON' *New Purchase* I. 64 Tisn't nun of your spice-wood or yarb stuff, but the rele gineine *store* tea.

+**Spicewood tea.** = SPICE TEA. Also attrib. — **1818** [see DITTANY]. **1848** DRAKE *Pioneer Life Ky.* 86 [We] made spicewood tea with the syrup. **1852** ELLET *Pioneer Women* 40 She would relate interesting anecdotes . . . of the . . . 'spice-wood tea-parties.'

*Spicy, a. In the specific names of plants. — **1814** BIGELOW *Florula Bostoniensis* 191 *Conyza camphorata.* Spicy Conyza. **1817–8** EATON *Botany* (1822) 204 *Betula lenta*, spicy birch, cherry birch, black birch. *Ib.* 287 *Gaultheria procumbens*, spicy wintergreen.

* **Spider.**

*1. Any arachnid of the order Araneida.

1676 B. TOMPSON *Poetical Works* 50 Spiders and worms had drawn Their dungy webs. **1737** BRICKELL *N. Carolina* 159 The Spider is a poysonous Insect, which hurts by stinging. **1789** MORSE *Amer. Geog.* 62 Of the astonishing variety of Insects found in America, we will mention . . . [among others, the] Spider. **1832** WILLIAMSON *Maine* I. 172 Spider; several species, such as black, gray, . . . jumping, rose Spiders. **1872** POWERS *Afoot & Alone* 78 The sallow-looking soil . . . is full of unseemly toads, all manner of spiders [etc.]. **1907** *St. Nicholas* Sept. 1034/1 The Garden Spider and her Enemies.

+2. An iron frying pan or skillet, sometimes provided with long legs.

1790 *Penna. Packet* 1 March 3/3 William Robinson, Junr. . . . Hath for Sale . . . bake pans, spiders, skillets. **1831** [see DODGER 1]. **1833** A. GREENE *Life D. Duckworth* II. 63 There was, moreover, a three-legged spider. **1865** TROWBRIDGE *Three Scouts* 142 Mrs. Crumlett could not make very rapid progress cooking with one spider over a wood-fire. **1905** [see FRIED *a.*].

‖3. (See quotation.)

1823 DODDRIDGE *Logan* 25n., Spider is the Indian name for a cancer.

4. A light cart or phaeton. {1879–, in S. Africa} Also attrib.

1870 M. H. SMITH *20 Years Wall St.* 270 Men, who . . . are liable to be run into every minute and have their spider wagons dashed to pieces, find it necessary to have a cool brain and a steady hand. **1885** *Wkly. New Mexican Rev.* 12 March 4/2 Mr. Denent H. Smith has . . . bought Dr. Symington's 'spider.' **1895** *Outing* XXVII. 186/2 [He] found her spider standing in front of the door. **1903** BURNHAM *Jewel* 4 That tall one's a spider, and the other's a broom.

5. *attrib.* **a.** In the names of animals and plants. **b.** Designating foods cooked in a spider.

(a) **1850** *Conn. Public Acts* 5 It shall not be lawful in this State for any person to shoot . . . [any] spider-bird or wax-bird. **1869** *Rep. Comm. Agric. 1868* 317 The *Hippoboscidae*, or spider-flies, are found upon birds and animals. **1891** *Cent.* 5830/2 *Spider-bug*, a long-legged heteropterous insect of the family *Emesidæ, Emesa longipes*, somewhat resembling a spider. **1894** COULTER *Bot. W. Texas* III. 525 Spider bent grass . . . [is found in] low wet land, central Texas to Tennessee. **(b)** **1870** A. D. WHITNEY *We Girls* v, The flaky spider-cake, turned just as it blushed golden-tawny over the coals. **1920** LINCOLN *Mr. Pratt* 33 She'd been . . . giving 'em spider bread and dried apple pie for breakfast.

6. In special combinations.

Spider fashion, an arrangement like the three legs on some spiders (sense 2); *s. net*, a fine cloth like a spider's net; *s.-wheeled*, with wheels like those on a spider (sense 4).

1848 *Knickerb.* XVIII. 499 To this were yoked two tolerably good wheel-horses, and a third in what is technically called 'spider fashion,' that is, in front of the other two. **1807** IRVING, etc. *Salmagundi* iii, The recipe for a full dress is as follows: take of spider-net, crape, satin [etc.]. **1886** ROOSEVELT in *Century Mag.* July 338/2 There may be a crowd of onlookers in every kind of trap, from a four-in-hand drag to a spider-wheeled buggy drawn by a pair of long-tailed trotters.

Spider crab. A crab with long legs like those of a spider. {1710–} — **1865** in Harper *S. B. Anthony* I. 253 Meanwhile, let us break the legs of the spider-crab. **1879** *Scribner's Mo.* Sept. 648/1 The spider-crabs and horse-shoes occasionally pay them visits. **1883** *Nat. Museum Bul.* No. 27, 111 The Spider Crabs (*Libinia emarginata* and *dubia*,) are also used as bait, especially on the coast of the Southern States.

+**Spiderflower.** Any plant of the genus *Cleome*, or any of various plants of the genus *Tibouchina*, having long, thin stamens. — **1861** WOOD *Botany* 240 Spider Flower. . . . Herbs or shrubs. **1891** *Cent.* 5830/3 *Spider-flower*, . . . a plant of the former genus *Lasiandra* of the *Melastomaceae*, now included in *Tibouchina*. The species are elegant hothouse shrubs from Brazil, bearing large purple flowers. **1893** *Amer. Folk-Lore* VI. 138 *Cleome spinosa*, spider flower. West Va.

+**Spider lily. a.** The spiderwort. **b.** Any one of various other plants, as a plant of the genus *Hymenocallis*. — **1887** *Harper's Mag.* Feb. 351/1 The exquisite white spider-lily, nodding in clusters on long stalks. **1894** *Amer. Folk-Lore* VII. 103 *Tradescantia Virginica*, spider lily, N.Y., New Orleans, La. **1900** BAILEY, etc. *Stand. Cycl. Horticulture* III. 787/2 *Hymenocallis*. . . . Spider Lily. Sea Daffodil. Bulbous plants of about 30 species of the warm parts of the New World.

* **Spiderwort.**

1. A plant belonging to the genus *Tradescantia*, or to the family Commelinaceae.

[**1629** PARKINSON *Paradisus* 152 The soon fading Spider-wort of Virginia, or Tradescant his Spider-wort.] **1817–8** EATON *Botany* (1822) 488 *Tradescantia virginica*, spiderwort. . . . Cultivated in gardens. **1831** AUDUBON *Ornith. Biog.* I. 153 The plant . . . is usually called *Spider-wort*. **1869** *Amer. Naturalist* III. 163 The blue flowers of the Spiderwort are scattered over bluffs. **1894** TORREY *Fla. Sketch-Book* 81 Beside a similar road, . . . grew multitudes of violets, . . . and a fine profusion of spiderwort.

+2. (See quotation.)

1847 WOOD *Botany* 172 *C*[*leome*] *pungens*. Spiderwort. . . . A common garden plant, with curious purple flowers.

+**Spiegel iron.** [G. *spiegeleisen*.] A kind of pig iron containing a considerable amount of manganese, used in steel-making. {spiegeleisen, 1868–} — **1880** *Harper's Mag.* Dec. 61/1 From far above the now silent converter there tumbles a fierce rivulet of molten 'spiegel' iron. **1883** *Ib.* Aug. 334/1 A rill of snapping, scintillating spiegel-iron is let in. **1883** KNIGHT *Suppl.* 839/2 A spiegel iron in this country . . . made from the New Jersey Franklinite ore . . . has commenced to be universally used in place of the spiegel iron, thus far imported from Germany.

+**Spignet.** Variant of SPIKENARD 1. — **1891** *Cent.* 5831/2.

* **Spike,** *n.*

*1. A large, stout nail.

1609 HAKLUYT *Va. Richly Valued* 39 The Governour sent sawed plankes and spikes to the seaside, wherewith was made a piragua or barke. *a***1656** BRADFORD *Hist.* 263 [They] did intreat him to send a boat unto them, with some pitch, & occume, and spiks. **1789** *Ann. 1st Congress* I. 149 On nails and spikes, it was agreed to lay one cent per pound. **1888** SHERIDAN *Memoirs* I. 103, I have known them to empty in one night a keg of spikes in the storehouse in Yamhill.

b. The large-headed nail used in fastening a rail to a crosstie on a railroad track.

1854 *Penna. Agric. Rep.* 424 Three kegs railroad spikes, excellent article. **1866** 'F. KIRKLAND' *Bk. Anecdotes* 231/2 A young man . . . wrenched the spikes from four rails. **1869** *Ore. State Jrnl.* 15 May 2/1 The last rail was . . . nailed down with a spike of gold. **1883** KNIGHT *Suppl.* 839/2 The following table shows the amount of spikes to a mile of railroad.

2. The naillike metal point which protrudes from the sole of a lumberman's boot or of a baseball player's shoe.

1848 THOREAU *Maine Woods* 25 The spikes . . . which the lumberers wear in their boots to prevent their slipping on wet logs. **1898** *N.Y. Tribune* 23 April 9/3 He was in collision with Jennings and McGann, and his foot and legs were injured with their spikes. **1902** WHITE *Blazed Trail* 380 The spikes . . . failed to grip.

+3. The spikelike horn of a young deer.

1870 *Amer. Naturalist* IV. 190 Yet it is the first pair of horns only that are ever 'spikes' in a common *C. Virginianus*.

+**b.** Short for SPIKE BUCK.

1858 *Harper's Mag.* Oct. 615/2 A young 'spike' . . . made one plunge at the side of his now occupied antagonist.

+4. A small mackerel: (see quot. 1911).

*a***1884** in Goode, etc. *Fisheries* I. 298 Fish of this size are sometimes called 'Spikes.' **1911** *Rep. Fisheries 1908* 312/1 Small mackerel are known as 'spikes' (5 to 6 inches long), 'blinkers' (7 to 8 inches long), and 'tinkers' (9 inches long).

5. *attrib.* and *comb.* **a.** With *drawer, gimlet*, etc.

1633 *N.H. Prov. Papers* I. 77, 2 gunstock boryers, 1 spike gimblett, 2 hammers. **1847** *Rep. Comm. Patents 1846* 54 A spike machine has been patented this year. **1848** THOREAU *Maine Woods* 39 [The] operation was performed by sticking our two spike-poles into the ground in a slanting direction. **1876** KNIGHT 2266/2 *Spike-drawer*, a crow-bar with a claw for extracting spikes.

+**b.** Designating animals or the horns of animals.

1875 *Fur, Fin & Feather* (ed. 3) 119 The smaller species of loon I have heard variously called the spike-bill, the cape-race [etc.]. **1891** *Scribner's Mag.* Oct. 447/2 Usually, in a band of fifty cows, there would be three or four males, including possibly, one or two spike-bulls. **1902** HULBERT *Forest Neighbors* 239 The hound's fate had shown him what that spike antler could do.

Spike, *v.* {1624–} *To spike a gun* {1687–}, fig., to overthrow an argument or objection. — **1855** Hambleton *H. A. Wise* 322 The following letter . . . effectually spikes that gun. **1870** M. H. SMITH *20 Years Wall St.* 22 It was Mr. Bonner's policy to spike every gun that could be aimed against him. **1880** 'MARK TWAIN' *Tramp Abroad* 253 That spiked my gun. I could not say anything. **1887** *Courier-Journal* 21 June 2/6 The Republican gun is spiked.

+**Spike-bill.** *local.* **a.** =GREAT MARBLED GODWIT. **b.** =HOODED MERGANSER. — **(a) 1888** TRUMBULL *Names of Birds* 207 In New Jersey at Pleasantville (Atlantic Co.), . . . and Cape May City, [it is called] Spike-Bill, and less frequently, Spike-Billed Curlew. **1917** *Birds of Amer.* I. 241. **(b) 1888** TRUMBULL *Names of Birds* 74 At Detroit, [the hooded merganser is known as] Spike-Bill. **1917** *Birds of Amer.* I. 112.

+**Spike-billed curlew.** *local.* =SPIKE-BILL a. — **1888, 1917** [see SPIKE-BILL a].

+**Spike buck.** A young male deer in the stage of development in which the antler is a simple spike. (Cf. SPIKE *n.* 3.) — **1824** DODDRIDGE *Notes* 127 The spike buck, the two and three pronged buck, the doe and barren doe, figured through their anecdotes. **1842** *Nat. Hist. N.Y., Zoology* I. 113 In the first season . . . they are known as *spike bucks*. **1858** *Harper's Mag.* Oct. 619/2 An old buck is the least active, a spike buck is the fleetest. **1893** ROOSEVELT *Wilderness Hunter* 38, I killed a spike buck. **1916** WILSON *Somewhere* 309 What do they start but a little spike buck that has been down to a salt lick on the creek flat!

* **Spiked,** *a.* In the specific names of plants.

1789 MORSE *Amer. Geog.* 52 The spiked indian corn is of a similar kind. **1814** BIGELOW *Florula Bostoniensis* 90 *Epilobium angustifolium*. Spiked Willow herb. . . . A tall plant bearing a profusion of blue flowers. *Ib.* 222 *Myriophyllum spicatum*. Spiked water Millfoil. . . . It is frequently drawn up by the lines of anglers. **1817–8** EATON *Botany* (1822) 201 *Bap-*

tisia cærulea, spiked indigo-weed. *Ib.* 248 *Convallaria racemosa*, spiked solomon seal. **1833** *Ib.* (ed. 6) 99 *Clethra alnifolia*, spiked alder. **1839** in *Mich. Agric. Soc. Trans.* VII. 420 *Spartina cynosuroides*, Spiked saltgrass. **1888** *Boston Jrnl.* 6 Dec. 2/3 A native forage plant, called 'spiked clover,' is attracting attention in California. **1901** MOHR *Plant Life Ala.* 334 *Tripsacum dactyloides*. . . . Spiked Gama Grass. . . . Of some value for forage. *Ib.* 608 *Aesculus parviflora*. . . . Spiked Buckeye. . . . Highly ornamental.

‖**Spiked buck.** =SPIKE BUCK. — **1897** *Outing* Feb. 439/1 A strong, young, spiked buck came streaking through the Chênière with the howling pack close at his heels.

Spike grass. {1776 (Lee *Introd. Bot.* 347)} +One or other of several American grasses having large or conspicuous spikelets. — **1791** MUHLENBERG *Index Florae* 161 *Uniola*, Spike-grass. **1857** GRAY *Botany* 560 *Brizopyrum*. . . . Spike-Grass. Spikelets and numerous flowers compressed. **1885** HAVARD *Flora W. & S. Texas* 530 *Brizopyrum spicatum* (Spike Grass) . . . sometimes affords fair pasturage where hardly any other grass can be found.

+**Spikehorn.**

1. =SPIKE *n.* 3. Also attrib.
1857 HAMMOND *Northern Scenes* 189 He was a fine two year old buck, with spike horns. **1869** *Amer. Naturalist* III. 553 The first Spike-horn Buck was merely an accidental freak of nature. **1870** *Ib.* IV. 189, I shot on Louis Lake a buck with spike-horns, which was not a yearling, . . . but a *large* buck, of full age and size.

2. =SPIKE BUCK.
1870 *Amer. Naturalist* IV. 190 The spike-horn was shot just as deer were attaining the 'blue coat.' **1897** *Outing* XXIX. 439/2 The gamey spike-horn turned to bay. **1902** WISTER *Virginian* 405 [We] caught sight of a vanishing elk. . . . 'A spike-horn, wasn't it?' said I.

*Spikenard.

+**1.** An American herb (*Aralia racemosa*) the root of which is used for medicinal purposes. Also with defining term.
[**1640** PARKINSON *Theater of Plants* 1744/2 Virginia Spikenard.] **1778** [see PETTY MORRELL]. **1792** IMLAY *Western Territory* 208 Of herbs, &c. we have of the wild sort . . . hellebore, wolf's-bane, spikenard, &c. **1840** DEWEY *Mass. Flowering Plants* 13 Spikenard. . . . [The root] formerly was used in a bruised state upon wounds, and is still employed for some medicinal purposes. **1891** *Amer. Folk-Lore* IV. 148 *A. racemosa* we [in N.H.] generally called by the correct name, *Spikenard*, but we pronounced it with short i, as if Spicknard.

+**2.** With specifying terms: Any one of various other aromatic American plants, as the false spikenard or false Solomon's-seal, *Smilacina racemosa*.
1785 MARSHALL *Amer. Grove* 16 *Baccharis*. Plowman's Spikenard. **1843** TORREY *Flora N.Y.* II. 298 *Smilacina racemosa*. . . . Wild Spikenard. . . . Moist grounds, thickets, etc.: frequent. **1857** GRAY *Lessons Botany* 81 A compound raceme . . . [occurs] in the Goat's-beard and the False Spikenard.

+**Spikenard tree.** (See quotation.) — **1891** *Cent.* 5832/1 *A[ralia] spinosa*, the angelica-tree, has been called *spikenard-tree*.

Spiker. {1884} +**1.** ?A variety of oysters. +**2.** A railroad laborer who drives the spikes holding the rails to the crossties. — (1) **1842** 'UNCLE SAM' *Peculiarities* II. 5 The oysters you shall have with *my* money shall be spikers, fourteen to the dozen, and real, precious flabbers. (2) **1872** HUNTINGTON *Road-Master's Asst.* 32 Tall spikers usually set the spike leaning from them. **1887** *Scientific Amer.* 18 Jan. 389 There are 32 'spikers' to every five miles of track each man of whom drives 840 spikes a day.

Spike rush. Any sedge of the genus *Eleocharis*, in which the flowers grow in dense spikes. {1829–} Also with specifying terms. — **1843** TORREY *Flora N.Y.* II. 346 *Eleocharis palustris*. . . . Common Spike-rush. . . . Swamps and low grounds. *Ib.* 348 *Eleocharis obtusa*. . . . Obtuse-headed Spike-rush. . . . Bogs, and muddy borders of ponds and rivers. **1857** GRAY *Botany* 495. **1901** MOHR *Plant Life Ala.* 396 *Eleocharis cellulosa*. . . . Cellular Spike-rush. . . . *Eleocharis interstincta*. . . . Knotted Spike-rush.

+**Spiketail.**

1. a. =PINTAIL 1. +**b.** =SPIKE-TAILED GROUSE.
(a) **1888** TRUMBULL *Names of Birds* 38 *Dafila acuta*. . . . At Chicago, Spike-Tail, and less commonly Pike-Tail. **1890** [see SPINDLETAIL]. **1917** *Birds of Amer.* I. 128. (b) *Ib.* II. 27 Sharp-tailed Grouse. *Pediæcetes phasianellus phasianellus*. . . . [Also called] Northern Sharp-tailed Grouse; Spike-tail; Pin-tail.

2. =SPIKE-TAILED COAT. *slang.*
1894 HOWELLS *Trav. Altruria* vii, He says he isn't dressed for dinner; left his spike-tail in the city. **1905** *Brooklyn Eagle* 17 March, After the wedding he . . . sat around all day in his spike-tails.

+**Spike-tail coat.** =next. *slang.* — **1889** RILEY *Pipes o' Pan* 30 You'll have a little spike-tail coat an' travel with a show! **1890** McALLISTER *Society* 156 No one could send me my spike-tail coat as they call it at the South. **1904** LORIMER *Old Gorgon Graham* 62 If you'd given Sol the job of making over the earth he'd have . . . turned out something as correct as a spike-tail coat.

+**Spike-tailed coat.** A swallow-tailed coat; a dress coat. *slang.* — **1870** 'MARK TWAIN' in *Galaxy* May 721 Would we not miss a spike-tailed coat and kids? **1884** *Harper's Mag.* Sept. 514 You needn't worry about any spike-tailed coat or clerical tie. **1896** *Columbus Dispatch* 24 July 1 Captain Lloyd wore red, white and blue spike-tailed coat and the tall hat of Uncle Sam.

+**Spike-tailed grouse.** =SHARP-TAILED GROUSE. — **1891** *Cent.* 5832/1 *Spike-tailed grouse*, the sharp-tailed, sprig-tailed, or pin-tailed grouse, *Pediæcetes phasianellus* or *columbianus*.

+**Spike team.** A team of three animals so arranged that one precedes the other two. — **1848** BARTLETT 324 *Spike Team*, a waggon drawn by three horses, or by two oxen and a horse, the latter leading the oxen or span of horses. **1890** L. C. D'OYLE *Notches* 178, I got there with a loaded waggon, and a 'spike team'—three mules.

*Spile.¹ =PILE *n.*¹ Also comb. — **1655** *Suffolk Deeds* II. 158 The westerly side of the land & wharfe of Rich. Nortons and so along vp to the stake or spile standing on the west end of the sajd wharfe. **1720** *Mass. H. Repr. Jrnl.* II. 290 William Dummer . . . [is] to secure the East and West Heads of Castle-Island, . . . [by] driving in of Spiles, to be fill'd up with Stones. **1850** KINGSLEY *Diary* 99 A vote was taken to allow the directors to engage in a bargain or contract for spiles and timber for a dock. **1865** *Atlantic Mo.* April 393/1 By means of a spile-driver, an iron pipe . . . is driven down until it rests upon the solid rock. **1901** MERWIN & WEBSTER *Calumet 'K'* 196 A spile . . . projected waist high through the floor of the wharf.

*Spile.² Also †spoil. A small wooden peg used to stop the vent of a cask; a spigot. {1707–} Also fig.
1782 CRÈVECŒUR *Letters* 196 [They] employ themselves in . . . making bungs or spoyls for their oil-casks. **1824** *Mass. Spy* 18 Aug. (Th.), This, in the language of the proverb, is saving at the spoil, and losing at the bung-hole. **1830** *Va. Lit. Museum* 6 Jan. 479 Spile, 'a spigot.'

+**b.** The small wooden or metal spout used for conveying the sap from a maple tree to a pail.
1844 *Knickerb.* XXIII. 444 The clean white-pine buckets, . . . into which the sap drips from the spiles, are made expressly for this use. **1868** *Amer. Naturalist* II. 39 He remembers very distinctly making 'spiles' of its stems when tapping sugar-trees. **1898** N. E. JONES *Squirrel Hunters of Ohio* 22 The 'spiles' that conducted the water from the tree to the trough were made from sections of elder or sumac. **1904** ATHERTON *Rulers of Kings* 31 He was inserting the little nickel troughs called spiles into the trees of the maple orchard.

*Spill, v. *Stock exchange*. (See quotation.) — **1870** MEDBERY *Men Wall St.* 137 *Spilling stock*. When great quantities of a stock are thrown upon the market, sometimes from necessity, often in order to 'break' the price.

Spiller. Also **spilyard.** **1.** (See quot. 1705.) {1602–} **2.** A net or pocket for holding mackerel. {1891, attrib.} — (1) **1633** *N.H. Prov. Papers* I. 79, 1 old seane, 10 herring netts, 1 spiller. **1705** BEVERLEY *Virginia* IV. 74 They also fish with Spilyards, which is a long Line staked out in the River, and hung with a great many Hooks on short Strings, fasten'd to the main Line. (2) **1884** *Nat. Museum Bul.* No. 27, 998 Mackerel pocket or spiller. . . . The pocket was introduced into the mackerel-seine fishery in 1878 for holding the surplus catch which would otherwise spoil before being cleaned and salted.

*Spin, v. *To spin street yarn*, (see STREET YARN 2).

*Spinach. Also **spin(n)age.** A potherb (*Spinacia oleracea*), cultivated for its leaves, which are boiled and served as a vegetable; any other plant similarly used.
(a) **1709** LAWSON *Carolina* 77 The Spinage round and prickly. **1778** CARVER *Travels* 517 Gargit or Skoke is a large kind of weed, the leaves of which . . . resemble those of spinage in their colour and texture. **1843** *Cultivator* X. 73 Last year . . . we had spinnage and spring flowers. **1847** WOOD *Botany* 467 Spinage. . . . Native country unknown, but it has long been a common plant in gardens, and in some esteem as an esculent. (b) **1784** *Amer. Acad. Mem.* I. 431 [Chickweed] boiled when young . . . can hardly be distinguished from spring spinach. **1895** *Dept. Agric. Yrbk. 1894* 138 These soils . . . are rather light in texture for cabbage and spinach.

Spinal meningitis. A shortening of *cerebrospinal meningitis*. — **1873** *Winfield (Kan.) Courier* 10 April 2/2 A successful Wyandotte physician has cured every case of spotted fever (spinal meningitis) he has attended. *Ib.* 3/1 Spotted fever, (or Spinal Meningitis) has its appearance on Grouse Creek.

*Spindle.

*1. A metal rod serving as an axis about which something, as a grindstone, revolves.
1644 *Conn. Rec.* I. 460 A grinding stone w[i]th iron spindle & turne. **1779** *Narragansett Hist. Reg.* I. 97 Helped George mend a spindle for mill. **1812** *Niles' Reg.* II. 10/1 [The wire] then passes to cylinder which is set perpendicular, to revolve by a spindle like a millstone.

2. In a spinning machine, one of many rods by which the thread is twisted. {c1790–}
1813 *Niles' Reg.* V. 207/1 There are now running in Baltimore, or rather in the city and its vicinity, about 9,000 spindles. **1834** in Benton *30 Years' View* I. 416/2 That valley . . . has in it one hundred thousand spindles in operation. **1865** HOLLAND *Plain Talks* 183 [We] find all the spindles awhirr. **1911** PERSONS, etc. *Mass. Labor Laws* 55 New mills had been built by 1850 . . . estimated to operate nearly 220,000 additional spindles.

+b. *City of Spindles,* = SPINDLE CITY.
1875 *Chambers's Jrnl.* 13 March 172/1 Lowell, Mass., [is] the City of Spindles.

+3. An iron pole fixed on a rock as a guide to ships.
1819 *Stat. at Large* III. 535 For the spindle or buoys on the reef running from Cochney's Island . . ., and for that on the rock off the point of Fairweather Island, twelve hundred dollars [shall be appropriated]. **1829** *Ib.* IV. 345 Four hundred dollars for a spindle to be placed on Minot's Ledge [shall be appropriated]. **1904** *Hartford Courant* 19 Aug. 13 What this man was really doing was simply placing a spindle on Magazine Rock.

+4. The tassel of Indian corn. {1577–1750, a stalk or shoot of other grains}
1847 *Knickerb.* XXX. 239 The tall corn, whose spindles were high above your head. **1863** MITCHELL *My Farm* 66 The spindles begin to peep out from their green sheaths. **1871** *Amer. Naturalist* V. 245 The corn . . . sent forth a new tassel or spindle.

+5. A pine needle.
1865 G. W. NICHOLS *Story of Gt. March* 218 The roots of the trees are buried in the spindles and burrs which have fallen undisturbed for centuries. **1891** *Cent.* 5835/1.

6. In special combinations.
Spindle-fever, a fever causing one to waste away; *s. moth,* (see quot. and cf. SPINDLE WORM).
1861 *Harper's Mag.* Aug. 320/1 This *Gortyna Zea*—'Spindle-moth of the Corn'— . . . can only commit her injuries when the stalk is very young and tender. **1865** *Ib.* Nov. 705/2 She was took with a spindle-fever till her legs warn't no thicker than your thumb.

+Spindle City. Lowell, Mass. — **1858** *Scientific Amer.* 23 Jan. 153/1 The 'spindle city' is gradually resuming its steady hum of industry.

+Spindletail. = PINTAIL 1. — **1890** *Cent.* 4502/3 *Pintail,* . . . the pin-tailed duck, *Dafila acuta.* Also called, from the peculiarity of the tail, . . . *sharptail, spiketail, spindletail.* **1917** *Birds of Amer.* I. 128.

∗ Spindle tree. A shrub or tree of the genus *Evonymus.*
1785 MARSHALL *Amer. Grove* 29 [The capsules] spread open in three parts, disclosing their seeds after the manner of the Spindle Tree. **1884** SARGENT *Rep. Forests* 38 *Euonymus atropurpureus.* . . . Burning Bush. Wahoo. Spindle Tree. Arrow Wood. . . . Western New York, west to the valley of the upper Missouri river. **1891** COULTER *Bot. W. Texas* I. 57.

b. With specifying adjectives.
[**1713** *Phil. Trans.* XXVIII. 64 Virginia Spindle-tree with rough Fruit. **1771** J. R. FORSTER *Flora Amer. Septentr.* 11 *Evonymus Americanus.* Spindle tree, American.] **1781–2** JEFFERSON *Notes Va.* (1788) 38 Evergreen spindle-tree. *Euonymus Americanus.* **1785** MARSHALL *Amer. Grove* 43 *Euonymus carolinensis,* Carolinian Spindle Tree, . . . grows to the height of eight or ten feet. *Ib.* 44 *Euonymus latifolius,* Broad-leaved Spindle Tree.

+Spindle worm. The larva of a noctuid moth, destructive to Indian corn and other plants. Also attrib. — **1790** DEANE *New-Eng. Farmer* 148/1 *Top-worms,* or *spindle-worms,* a white worm . . . which eats off the stem of the [maize] plant. **1854** EMMONS *Agric. N.Y.* V. 243 *Nonagriadae.* . . . They are known by the common name of spindleworms. **1895** *Stand.* 1200/1 *Nonagrian,* . . . a noctuid moth of *Nonagria* or a related genus, as the spindleworm-moth.

Spinet.¹ A keyboard instrument in which the sound is produced by the striking of a single string by a quill. {1664–}
1752 in Singleton *Social N.Y.* 293 A good English spinet (Hitchcock's). **1763** JEFFERSON *Writings* I. (1892) 352, I am vastly pleased with her playing on the spinnette and singing. **1795** *Boston Gaz.* 13 July 3/3 An excellent well-tuned Spinnet. **1825** NEAL *Bro. Jonathan* II. 217 You forgot your spinet altogether one day. **1872** *Atlantic Mo.* March 330 It was the same with the spinet and the violin.

‖Spinet.² (See quotation.) — **1784** *Amer. Acad. Mem.* I. 484 *Lobelia.* . . . Spinet. Blossoms blue. In moist grass land.

Spinetail. A bird having sharp, pointed tail feathers {c1880–}, as +the spine-tailed swift or the ruddy duck. Also attrib. and with specifying term. — **1839** AUDUBON *Synopsis Birds* 33 *Chætura,* Spine-tail. *Ib., Chætura pelasgia,* American Spine-tail. **1884** COUES *Key to Birds* (ed. 2) 457 *Chæturinæ,* Spine-tail Swifts. *Ib.* 580 *Centrocercus.* . . . Spine-tail Grouse. **1917** *Birds of Amer.* I. 152 Ruddy Duck. *Erismatura jamaicensis.* . . . [Also called] Stick-tail; Spine-tail; Dip-tail.

+Spine-tailed swift. A swift having sharp, pointed tail feathers: (see quotations). — **1872** COUES *Key to Birds* 183 *Chæturinæ.* Spine-tailed Swifts. **1889** *Cent.* 908/2 The spine-tailed swifts [are] so called because the shafts of the tail-feathers project beyond the webs.

∗ Spinner.
Spinner of street yarn, (see STREET YARN 1).
∗1. One who spins cotton, wool, etc.; in later use, one who tends a spinning machine.
1725 *New-Eng. Courant* 18 Jan. 2/1 If therefore a School were set up in every Town, the Mistress whereof to be a good Spinner [etc.]. **1788** [see DAIRYWOMAN]. **1844** *Lowell Offering* IV. 169 The spinners watch the frames. **1891** CHASE & CLOW *Industry* II. 19 The spinner must 'look sharp' indeed.

2. (See quotations.) Also attrib.
1883 KNIGHT *Suppl.* 840/1 *Spinner,* . . . a trawling spoon-bait which revolves as it tows abaft the boat. A flanged attachment in connection

with a fish-hook to cause a lively motion of the hook and bait. **1895** *Outing* XXVI. 358 A 6–0 hook with a lively smelt wired to it spinner fashion.

∗ Spinning.
∗1. The action of making yarn from fibers of cotton, flax, etc., by hand or by machinery.
1720 [see sense 3]. **1732** FRANKLIN *Poor Richard's Almanac 1733* 12· Women for tea forsook spinning & knitting. **1848** [see DOUBLE *n.* 1]. **1876** INGRAM *Centennial Exp.* 394 Among the machines and implements of spinning . . . were some extremely valuable and interesting inventions.

+2. = SPINNING BEE.
1876 *Scribner's Mo.* Jan. 334/1 They had 'bees,' apple-cuts, huskings, quiltings, spinnings, . . . and plenty of weddings and christenings.

∗3. *attrib.* **a.** Designating places and establishments in which spinning is done.
1720 *Boston Rec.* 147 The Town will proceed to the choyce of a Comittee to consider ab[ou]t promoting of a Spinning School or Schools for the Instruction of the children of this Town, in Spinning. **1786** WASHINGTON *Diaries* III. 30 That square of my Botanical garden, adjoining to the Servants and spinning House. **1831** PECK *Guide* 158 Two or three spinning factories are in operation. **1845** KIRKLAND *Western Clearings* 39 In old Mr. Hicks' spinning-room she was in her element. **1865** *Atlantic Mo.* May 616/2 Workers . . . find employment in the spinning-mills. **1874** COLLINS *Kentucky* I. 226 [The legislature appropriates money to] erect a prison-house and spinning-walk for female convicts.

b. Designating machines and other devices used in spinning. {1678–}
1815 DRAKE *Cincinnati* 143, 23 cotton spinning mules and throstles . . . have been made. **1845** *Lowell Offering* V. 98 Here we have spinning jacks or jennies that dance merrily along. **1848** *Rep. Comm. Patents 1847* 65 Letters patent have also been granted for . . . improvements in spinning frames. **1869** *Mich. Gen. Statutes* I. (1882) 311 All spinning and weaving looms and apparatus. **1884** 'MARK TWAIN' *H. Finn* xxxiii, She took up the spinning-stick.

c. In miscellaneous combinations: (see quotations).
1832 TROLLOPE *Domestic Manners* II. 177 Once a year a day is fixed on which some member of every family in a congregation meet at their minister's house in the afternoon. They each bring an offering . . . of articles necessary for house-keeping. . . . These meetings are called spinning visits. **1839** KIRKLAND *New Home* (1840) 264 'Spinning money' is a looking-glass perhaps, or 'butter-money' a nice cherry table. **1845** *Lowell Offering* V. 268 We used to have sewing parties, . . . quilting matches, and spinning frolics. **1851** A. CARY *Clovernook* 45 As our spinning-girl Sally used to say.

+Spinning bee. A gathering of women for the purpose of spinning a large amount of material. — **1788** *Cumberland Gaz.* (Portland, Me.) 8 May, Spinning Bee. On the 1st inst. assembled at the house of the Rev. Samuel Deane of this town, more than one hundred of the fair sex. **1881** SCUDDER *Noah Webster* 15 Huskings and spinning bees made work and play shade into each other. **1904** *Sun* (N.Y.) 28 Aug. 4 The Martha Washington Benevolent Society . . . met at Sunset the other day for its annual spinning bee.

Spinning machine. A machine used for spinning thread. {c1790–} Also attrib. — **1788** [see CARDING MACHINE]. **1818** FLINT *Lett. from Amer.* 62 [Among] the manufacturing people of Pittsburg . . . [is] 1 Spinning Machine Maker. **1831** PECK *Guide* 199 There is a spinning machine in Bond county, of one hundred and sixty spindles. **1883** KNIGHT *Suppl.* 841/2 The Byewater spinning machine is remarkable as a continuous spinner in contradistinction to the intermittent work of the mule.

Spinning match. A contest in spinning. — **1769** *New-London* (Conn.) *Gaz.* 2 June 3/2 Three young Ladies met upon a Spinning-Match. **1880** *Harper's Mag.* Aug. 350/1 A spinning match took place at one of the school-houses.

∗ Spinning wheel. A device for spinning, consisting of a wheel which drives a spindle and is operated by hand or foot.
1644 *Conn. Rec.* I. 460 An Inventory of the Goods of Ephraim Huit: . . . 3 spinning wheels. **1702** SEWALL *Diary* III. 398 Two great Spinning Wheels, one small one for Linnen, and a Loom to weave it. **1835** AUDUBON *Ornith. Biog.* III. 235 The matron has cradled her babe, and betaken herself to the spinning-wheel. **1880** *Harper's Mag.* Aug. 350/1 Within the houses the women yet drive the spinning-wheel.

b. Attrib. and comb. with *factory, head, maker.*
1809 Spinning wheel maker [see CUTLER]. **1820** FLINT *Lett. from Amer.* 213 [In Cincinnati is] a spinning wheel factory. **1856** *Fla. Plantation Rec.* 519 Received . . . 1 Spining wheel head for Plantation.

∗Spinster. One who spins, esp. as a regular occupation. — **1640** *Essex Inst. Coll.* IX. 106 It is ordered . . . [that] brother ffogg doe enquire about fustean spinsters. **1785** MARSHALL *Amer. Grove* 35 Male Virginian Dogwood. . . . To its top, regular disposed shoots, our spinsters are often indebted for their distaffs.

∗ Spiny, *a.*
1. In the specific names of fishes, etc.
1897 *N.Y. Forest, Fish, & Game Comm. 2d Rep.* 244 *Chilomyterus schoepfii,* . . . Spiny Boxfish, . . . is found occasionally in small numbers from May to October in Gravesend Bay. **1884** GOODE, etc. *Fisheries* I. 780 The Spiny Lobster or Rock Lobster—*Panulirus interruptus.* **1883** *Nat.*

Museum Bul. No. 27, 411 *Eumicrotremus spinosus*. . . . Spiny Lumpfish.
. . . South to Massachusetts Bay.

2. In adjectival compounds.
1847 DARLINGTON *Weeds & Plants* 206 The Spiny-leaved Sow-thistle (*S[onchus] asper*) is frequently met with. **1882** *Nat. Museum Bul.* No. 16, 397 *Acanthopteri.* (The Spiny-rayed Fishes.)

Spir(a)ea. Any plant of the genus *Spiraea* of the rose family {1669–}, or a plant resembling these. Also with specifying terms.
1785 MARSHALL *Amer. Grove* 146 *Spiraea hypericifolia.* Canadian Spiraea. . . . This makes a very good appearance when in flower. **1814** BIGELOW *Florula Bostoniensis* 120 *Spiraea alba.* White Spiraea. Meadow sweet. . . . A slender shrub three or four feet high, bearing large, terminal bunches of white flowers. **1818** *Mass. H. S. Coll.* 2 Ser. VIII. 170 In August the eye is gratified with . . . the downy leaved spiraea. **1871** *Scribner's Mo.* II. 102/1 Spirea and hawthorn prickle with minute leaves adown their brown branches. **1894** *Outing* XXIII. 394/1 The pretty scarlet hibiscus, a kind of spirea. **1907** *St. Nicholas* June 762/1 The rose . . . was blushing in the hollow where the white spirea grows.

*****Spire. 1.** A tree, pole, or rod, esp. one used as a landmark. {1657–, the tapering top of a tree} ‖**2.** =SPEAR *n.*² — (1) **1688** *Southampton Rec.* II. 299 Running to the next corner to a little white oak spire about 20 pole. **1759** ROGERS *Journals* 156 We endeavoured to keep our wretched vessel by such paddles as we had made out of small trees, or spires split and hewed. **1782** *Southampton Rec.* III. 292 Then we received a piece of land . . . running west 26 degrees south 13 poles to a white oak spire. (2) **1868** ALCOTT *Little Women* I. 239 I'd do as much for our Jimmy any day if I had a spire of hair worth selling.

Spire grass. Any one of various grasses, reeds, or sedges. {1626–} — **1751** ELIOT *Field-Husb.* iii. 59 Our common Spire Grass . . . is a Hardy Grass, and is the best we have for Winter Feeding. **1820** *Plough Boy* I. 294 I could wish . . . that the Board of Agriculture . . . would recommend to scientific gentlemen . . . to examine the Spire Grass in their respective vicinities. **1831** PECK *Guide* 161 The English spire grass has been cultivated with success in the Wabash Country.

*****Spirit.**
1. Distilled alcoholic liquor. {1684–} Usually *pl.*
1663 *Plymouth Laws* 140 Noe liquors [shall] bee sold . . . that shall exceed in prise six shillings the gallon except it bee English speritts. **1726** SEWALL *Diary* III. 377 [She] saluted us very Courteously as we sat in the Calash and gave us Spirits. **1777** *Jrnls. Cont. Congress* IX. 929 Late useful discoveries for making molasses and spirits from the juice of corn stalks. **1820** CLAY *Speeches* (1842) 117 No other nation lets in so much of foreign spirits as we do. **1865** *Atlantic Mo.* Feb. 146/2 A slatternly 'carryall,' with a driver who reeks of bad spirit, keeps up uneasy communication with the outside world. **1890** [see HICKORY-WHIP *v.*].

b. *spec.* Rum. Usually *pl.*
1818 PALMER *Travels U.S.* 26 Rum is always called *spirits* in the United States. **1828** WEBSTER, *Spirit,* . . . the liquor distilled from cane-juice, or rum. We say, new spirit, or old spirit, Jamaica spirit, &c. **1830** PICKERING *Inquiries Emigrant* 93 Let him give out drams of whisky, 'Jamaica spirits,' (best rum).

+2. Attrib. with reference to American spiritualistic phenomena of the middle of the nineteenth century and later.
1852 Spirit world [see RAPPER]. **1854** (*title*), Spirit Advocate [Rockford, Illinois]. **1859** BARTLETT 434 *Spirit-land,* an expression which, in the cant of the rappers, means the abode of departed spirits, the other world. **1863** TAYLOR *H. Thurston* 112 Then there's sperut-raps, as they call 'em. **1864** NICHOLS *Amer. Life* I. 68 These lecturers, or spirit-speakers, are of both sexes. **1867** DIXON *New America* II. 162 He is ready to perform this miracle of Spirit-Act by letter, at any distance, for ten dollars. *a*1882 J. QUINCY *Figures of Past* (1883) 279, I am loath to borrow the word impressional from the vocabulary of spirit-mediums. **1883** *Century Mag.* Sept. 748/2 He ridiculed the spirit-lights, the voices, and the jugglery. **1887** *Courier-Journal* 18 Jan. 1/7, I have all my life greatly desired to see some spirit manifestations. **1896** S. A. UNDERWOOD (*title*), Automatic or Spirit Writing, with Other Psychic Experiences.

‖**Spirit crab.** A species of crab found on the keys of the Florida Reef. — **1871** *Harper's Mag.* June 28/1 The spirit-crabs reigned supreme on Loggerhead until the Bos'n took over some of our pet rabbits, the lop-ear kind.

Spirit duck. a. The bufflehead duck or the goldeneye duck. **+b.** (See quot. 1891.)
[**1785** PENNANT *Arctic Zool.* II. 558 Spirit Duck. . . . Inhabits North America, from Hudson's Bay to Carolina.] **1844** *Nat. Hist. N.Y., Zoology* II. 329 This little duck is known [as] . . . Butter-box, and Spirit Duck. *a*1862 THOREAU *Maine Woods* 322 *Fuligula albicola* (spirit duck or dipper), common. **1872** COUES *Birds N.W.* 577 Spirit Duck. . . . I have reason to believe that this Duck . . . nests in Northern Dakota. **1891** *Cent.* 5841/3 *Spirit-duck,* . . . any duck that dives at the flash of a gun or twang of a bow-string; a conjuring duck. **1917** *Birds of Amer.* I. 138 Golden-Eye. *Clangula clangula americana.* . . . [Also called] Copper-head; Cur; Spirit Duck. *Ib.* 140 Buffle-Head. *Charitonetta albeola.* . . . [Also called] Butter-back; Spirit Duck; Wool-head.

Spiritist. =SPIRITUALIST. {1865–} — **1858** *Brownson's Quart. Rev.* April 180 The dissatisfaction with Protestantism and the search after something better, manifested . . . by the Mormons, Swedenborgians, and

Spiritists, &c., are encouraging signs to the Catholic missionary. *c*1873 DE VERE *MS. Notes* 245 [They are called] *Spiritists* by those who consider Spiritualists too sacred a name for such people. **1896** *Pop. Science Jrnl.* L. 229 This condition finds its ideal fulfillment in the developing *seance* of the spiritist.

Spirit lamp. A lamp fed by alcohol. {1802–} — **1818** *N. Amer. Rev.* VII. 429 If the flame of a spirit lamp be brought in contact with a jet of steam, it disappears. **1858** HALE *If Yes & Perhaps* 127 His spirit-lamp blew up. **1885** CRAWFORD *Amer. Politician* 10 Teasing the flame of the spirit-lamp into better shape. **1920** HOWELLS *Vacation of Kelwyns* 82 Light the spirit-lamp under the coffee-pot.

+Spirit rapper. One who pretends to communicate with spirits by means of rapping. {1860–} — **1854** O. A. BROWNSON (*title*), The Spirit-Rapper; an Autobiography. **1859** BARTLETT 434 *Spirit-rapper,* a person, who . . . interprets raps produced by an unseen agency on tables, floors, etc., as messages from the other world. **1862** BROWNE *A. Ward: His Book* 45 Just so soon as a man becums a reglar out & out Sperret rapper he leeves orf workin.

+Spirit rapping.
1. *pl.* Rappings thought to be made by spirits.
Cf. RAPPING.
1852 *Harper's Mag.* Dec. 129/1 The spirit-rappings are again engrossing a lion's share of the talk. **1853** B. F. TAYLOR *Jan. & June* 226 Spirit Rappings.—Communications with the Spirit Land, 25 cents. **1887** HARRIS in *Century Mag.* Aug. 552/2 You'll be the wuss ha'nted mortal in this land, 'less in it's 'em that's got the sperrit-rappin's after 'em.

2. Communication with spirits attempted by rapping. {1854}
1862 LOWELL *Biglow P.* 2 Ser. vi. 164, I worked round at sperrit-rappin' some. **1872** EGGLESTON *End of World* 252 Clairvoyance and spirit-rapping would be great evils to the world.

Spirits (of) turpentine. The essential oil derived from turpentine. {spirit of turpentine, 1660–} — *c*1792 COXE *View U.S.* 305 The preparation of . . . spirits of turpentine . . . in North-Carolina and its vicinity, may be deemed a manufacture. **1819** *Amer. Farmer* I. 175 Spirits Turpentine, 40 *a* 45 cts. **1851** CIST *Cincinnati* 246 In this factory is consumed daily . . . three hundred and fifty gallons spirits turpentine. **1865** *Nation* I. 558 The chief business of Fayetteville is the shipment of tar, rosin, and spirits of turpentine down the river to Wilmington.

*****Spiritual,** *n.* **+1.** =SPIRITUAL WIFE. **+2.** =NEGRO SPIRITUAL. — (1) **1852** in *Putnam's Mo.* VI. 147/1 These extra wives are known by sundry designations—some call them '*spirituals.*' **1859** BARTLETT 434 *Spiritual,* a Mormon concubine. (2) **1866** *Harper's Mag.* May 775/1 Maum Rina flavored all her dishes with these 'spirituals,' as they are called among the negroes. **1867** HIGGINSON in *Atlantic Mo.* June 685/2 It seemed the simplest type of 'spiritual.' **1893** [see PLANTATION MELODY].

*****Spiritualistic,** *a.* **+** =SPIRITUALISTIC *a.* — **1858** *Sun* (Baltimore) 12 July 4/3 A Spiritual Funeral was held at Lowell lately, over the remains of J. B. Smith. Miss Emma Houston prayed, and the dead Smith spoke through her. **1859** BARTLETT 434. **1863** TAYLOR *H. Thurston* 113 Had the invitation to a spiritual *séance* been given by any one but Mrs. Waldo [etc.]. **1871** [see MEDIUM 2].

Spiritualism. {1831–} +The belief that departed spirits can communicate with the living through a 'medium,' by means of rapping and other manifestations. {1860–} — **1853** DIX *Transatlantic Tracings* 244 Every two or three years the Americans have a paroxysm of humbug— . . . at the present time it is Spiritual-ism. **1860** HOLMES *Professor* 15 Spiritualism is quietly undermining the traditional ideas of the future state. **1877** [see PRAYER CURE]. **1893** *Harper's Mag.* Feb. 346/1 Spiritualism . . . was a subject which earnestly and steadily held his attention.

Spiritualist. {1649–} +A believer in spiritualism. {1881–} Also attrib. — **1853** B. ALCOTT *Journals* 265 The Spiritualists' Convention . . . is sitting—or sleeping, rather—in the Masonic Temple. **1877** W. WRIGHT *Big Bonanza* 98 Being a spiritualist and having always the latest advices from the ghosts of the departed, in regard to mines, . . . O'Reilly did not find [etc.]. **1886** RITTENHOUSE *Maud* 374 Warren Chase, a spiritualist lecturer conducted the funeral services. **1896** *Pop. Science Mo.* Dec. 229 All present were ardent spiritualists.

Spiritualistic, *a.* {1852–} Pertaining to or concerned with spiritualism. {1865–} — **1882** HINSDALE *Pres. Garfield & Educ.* 79 Mr. William Denton, an itinerant spiritualistic and scientific lecturer and debater, occasionally visited the village. **1883** 'MARK TWAIN' *Life on Miss.* xlviii, A pilot . . . has been receiving a letter every week from a deceased relative, through a New York spiritualistic medium. **1887** [see MANIFESTATION].

Spiritual widower. A man separated from his wife. — **1872** POWERS *Afoot & Alone* 325 That queer Americanism 'grass widow,' is here supplemented by the other one, 'spiritual widower.'

+Spiritual wife. A wife married for eternity according to the principles of the Mormon church; loosely, an extra wife: (see also quot. *c*1870). — **1859** BARTLETT 434 *Spiritual wife,* . . . a Mormon extra wife or concubine. *c*1870 CHIPMAN *Notes on Bartlett* 434 *Spiritual Wife.* . . . So, as among the Millerites, 1843, in Athol, Mass.,—except that they claimed such a companion as *only* a 'spiritual' partner. 1842–3. **1872** MCCLELLAN *Golden State* 593 In the 'new revelation' provision is made for 'spiritual wives' for the saints.

‖**Spiritual wifery.** The practice of having spiritual wives. — **1870** BEADLE *Utah* 83 The apostolic dignitaries did not always agree among themselves, after the establishment of 'spiritual wifery,' in the distribution of female prizes.

＊Spit, n.¹

＊1. A sharp-pointed rod of metal or wood used for holding meat to be roasted before a fire. Also attrib.
1639 *Conn. Rec.* I. 444 A Inuentory of the goods and Cattle of John Brundish: . . . rostiron, spitt and frying pan. **1642** *Md. Archives* IV. 97 A p[air] of spitt-racks, 3 spitts. **1758** [see COOKMAID]. **1830** WATSON *Philadelphia* 350 They trained little bow-legged dogs, called spit-dogs, to run in a hollow cylinder, . . . by which impulse was given to a turnjack, which kept the meat in motion. *a***1918** G. STUART *On Frontier* II. 114, We roasted it [*sc.* a goose] on a spit over our camp fire.

2. A tongue of land projecting into water; a reef. {1673–}
1738 BYRD *Dividing Line* (1901) 36 The Virginia Commissioners contending . . . to begin [the dividing line] at the end of the spitt of sand. **1807** *Mass. H. S. Coll.* 2 Ser. III. 77 A spit . . . makes out from the west side. **1878** HARTE *Drift from 2 Shores* 33 You're that looney sort o' chap that lives alone over on the spit yonder, ain't ye?

Spit, n.² A light flurry. {1849–} Also attrib. — **1768** WASHINGTON *Diaries* I. 250 Cloudy and cold, with Spits of Snow. **1835** WYETH *Journal* 243 Fine sun in the forenoon but cloudy and snow spits in the afternoon. **1856** GLISAN *Jrnl. Army Life* 268 We have even had a few spits at this point. **1886** *Leslie's Mo.* Feb. 220/2 An occasional spit of snow dashes into his face. **1916** 'BOWER' *Phantom Herd* 266 Days of lowering clouds . . . brought nothing but exasperating little flurries of what Applehead called 'spit snow.'

＊Spit, n.³ In miscellaneous combinations: (see quotations). — **1887** *Courier-Journal* 21 June 1/1 The deadly explosives . . . turn out to have been innocent roman candles, fire-crackers and spit-devils. **1891** *Cent.* 5844/2 *Spit-bug*, . . . any spittle-insect. *Ib.* 5844/3 *Spitkid*, . . . *Naut.*, a spitbox.

＊Spit, v. 1. *tr.* To let fall (rain or snow). {1567–, *intr.*} **2.** *To spit cotton*, (see quot. 1899). — (1) **1773** *Md. Hist. Mag.* XV. 280 The wind is strong at N.E. & it spits Rain. **1835** WYETH *Journal* 243 Spit snow all day at night set in to snow. (2) **1866** LOWELL *Biglow P.* 2 Ser. p. xlvii, *To spit cotton* is, I think, American. **1899** GREEN *Va. Word-Book* 354 When one is very thirsty and his mouth dry the spittle white and sticky he is said to 'spit-cotton.'

+Spitball.
1. Paper chewed and made into a ball for use as a missile.
1846 *Knickerb.* XXVII. 410 [They] crooked pins, made pop guns, ejected spit-balls. **1854** SHILLABER *Mrs. Partington* 222 [Ike] chewed up a part of the paper into spit-balls. **1877** BURDETTE *Rise of Mustache* 312 That boy had been . . . soundly whipped for slapping three hundred and thirty-nine spit balls up against the ceiling. **1899** W. JAMES *Talks to Teachers* 92 The spitballs that Tommy is ready to throw.

2. *Baseball.* (See quot. 1909.) Also attrib.
Now not permitted in professional baseball.
1909 WEBSTER 2015/2 *Spitball.* . . . (Usually two words.) . . . A variety of pitched ball produced by moistening one side of the ball with saliva. **1912** MATHEWSON *Pitching* 20 Some spit-ball pitchers announce when they are going to throw a moist one by looking at the ball as they dampen it. **1913** A. E. CRAWLEY *Book of Ball* 44 The 'Spit-ball' . . . may (it is said) reverse its curvature.

Spitbox. A spittoon. {1833–} — **1827** SHERWOOD *Gaz. Georgia* 172 Keep a spit-box in each room. **1856** BAGBY *Old Va. Gentleman* 221 Through a puddle of . . . cigar stumps, broken spit-boxes, and pipestems, he wades to a bed. **1902** HARBEN *A. Daniel* 107, I could hit that spit-box better standin' than I kin over brother Tarver's legs.

+Spit curl. A small lock of hair, dampened and curled so as to lie flat on the forehead. *colloq.* — **1841** *Jamestown* (N.Y.) *Jrnl.* 29 July 4/2 Spit curls have gone out of vogue. **1857** [see BEAU *n.* 2]. **1884** *Century Mag.* June 282/2 Envy in spit-curls and jealousy in a false front held their tongues. **1903** WIGGIN *Rebecca* 31 On this occasion she formed what I must perforce call by its only name—a spit-curl—directly in the centre of her brow.

+Spite fence. A fence raised to spite a neighbor. — **1899** *Everybody's Mag.* I. 70/2 Meanwhile an ordinance was passed making the building of spite fences illegal. **1904** *Chicago Tribune* 21 Aug. 5 A 'spite fence' was hurried into place last evening separating the Commerce building from the Traders', the Imperial, and the Western Union buildings.

+Spittle bug, fly, insect. A froghopper (q.v.), which, in an immature stage, is found enveloped in a white froth. — **1882** *Vt. Agric. Rep.* VII. 77 Dr. Cutting spoke of the frog hopper, usually known as the spittle bug on grass. **1891** *Cent.* 5845/1 *Spittle-fly*, . . . a spittle-insect. **1921** *Conn. Agric. Exper. Sta. Bul.* No. 230, 330 The grass-feeding spittle-bug is protected from predaceous and parasitic enemies.

Spittle iron. ?An implement used in baking; a peel. {spittle, 1838–, *dial.*} — **1648** *Conn. Rec.* I. 507 An Inventory of the Estate of Thomas Newell: . . . one broiling iron, one cleaver, 1 spittle iron.

Spittoon. A receptacle for spit; a cuspidor. {1841–} — **1823** FAUX *Memorable Days* 218 No lump sugar, no brandy, no segars, no spitoons are seen at this hotel. **1852** BRISTED *Upper Ten Th.* 94 A small boy . . . escorted them up three flights of stairs into a room containing two small beds and a large spittoon. **1873** 'MARK TWAIN' & WARNER *Gilded Age* 223 The darky boy who purifies the Department spittoons—represents Political Influence. **1913** RILEY *Eccentric Mr. Clark* 176 A candle-box spittoon with a broken lamp-chimney in it.

+Spitz.¹ =SPITZENBERG APPLE. — **1875** BURROUGHS *Winter Sunshine* 151 You are company, you red-cheeked spitz, or you, salmon-fleshed

greening! *Ib.* 163 [It] can stand the ordeal of cooking, and still remain a spitz.

Spitz.² A dog of a small breed characterized by a pointed muzzle; a Pomeranian dog. {1845} In full *spitz dog*. — **1877** *Harper's Mag.* March 615/2 Especially is it desirable that the so-called Spitz dogs should be legislated out of existence. **1883** *Century Mag.* April 911/1 Madonna was occupied with a spitz, holding it one minute and pulling it by the tail the next. **1911** 'O. HENRY' *Rolling Stones* 181 Six burglars . . . bore away . . . a five-hundred-dollar prize Spitz dog.

+Spitzenberg apple. An apple of the Spitzenburg variety: (see next). Also *Spitzbergen apple.* — **1804** CUTLER in *Life & Corr.* II. 153 We had the Spitzbergen apple, from New York. **1809** IRVING *Knickerb.* III. i, His full-fed cheeks . . . were curiously mottled and streaked with dusky red, like a spitzenberg apple. **1845** *Knickerb.* XXVI. 584 We went to steal some Spitzenberg apples from Dean Williams.

+Spitzenburg, Spitzenberg. An apple of any of various red-and-yellow American varieties; a tree bearing such an apple. Also with defining term.
See also NEWTOWN SPITZENBURG.
*a***1817** [see HOLDEN (SWEETING)]. **1845** *Knickerb.* XXVI. 584 The Deacon was a tart man, and stingy of his Spitzenbergs. **1851** J. F. W. JOHNSTON *Notes N. Amer.* I. 166 The home of the Newtown pippin, the Spitzemberg, and other highly prized varieties—is on the Atlantic border, between Massachusetts Bay and the Delaware. **1856** *Rep. Comm. Patents 1855: Agric.* 291 The winter apples I prize most are the 'Jenetting,' 'Newtown' and 'Winter' Pippins, and 'Flushing Spitzenberg.' **1869** *Rep. Comm. Agric. 1868* 482 [He] names the Baldwin for dessert and cooking, the Spitzenburg for cooking. **1887** FREDERIC *Seth's Brother's Wife* 324 Go down 'n' git that sister o' yourn a Spitzenberg.

+Spizarinctum, Spizerinctum. [App. a fanciful formation on SPECIE.] Hard money; specie. *slang.* — **1845** HOOPER *Simon Suggs' Adv.* 40 A hundred and seventy dollars in the clear spizarinctum. **1869** *Overland Mo.* Aug. 128 In March, 1868, they [greenbacks] had gotten no farther west than Marshall [Tex.], and everywhere west of that, when a man named a price, he meant 'spizerinctums' (corrupted from *specie*). **1872** POWERS *Afoot & Alone* 125 [Texans] toss down their 'spizerinctums' with lofty contempt, to see them stagger and spin around on the counter.

Splash. {1736–} *Logging.* +A body of water suddenly released to carry down logs. Also attrib. — **1879** *Lumberman's Gazette* 23 Aug., Some of these . . . logs may possibly be moved by a splash. **1905** *Forestry Bureau. Bul.* No. 61, 49 *Splash*, to drive logs by releasing a head of water confined by a splash dam.

Splasher. {1848–} +A piece of oilcloth or a rug to protect a surface from splashings. — **1897** BRODHEAD *Bound in Shallows* 98 Did you notice the splasher? **1905** BELASCO *Girl of Golden West* (1925) II. 73 A washstand, backed by a 'splasher' of white oilcloth, is near the bed.

+Splatterdock. =SPATTER-DOCK. — **1813** WILSON *Ornithology* VIII. 30 [He] also eats the seeds of that species of nymphæ usually called splatter docks. **1832** KENNEDY *Swallow Barn* I. 262 Isaac Tracy . . . does not fling away five hundred pounds . . . to maintain his title to a bed of splatterdocks. **1889** *Harper's Mag.* May 860/2 Why . . . speak disparagingly of the yellow nuphar, our familiar splatter-dock?

Spleen, v. {a1629–} +*intr.* To feel angry or sick to one's stomach. — **1885** COOKE in *Congregationalist* (*Cent.*), It is fairly sickenin'; I spleen at it. **1889** *Steadfast* 198 [It] makes me spleen to think on it! **1902** WILSON *Spenders* 31, I spleened against it and let him know it.

＊Spleenwort. 1. Any fern of the genus *Asplenium*, or, loosely, of the genus *Athyrium*. Also with specifying terms. +**2.** A species of cactus. — (1) **1795** WINTERBOTHAM *Hist. View* III. 399. **1868** *Amer. Naturalist* II. 525 For the British Sea Spleenwort, Rock Spleenwort, Bristly Spleenwort, Black Spleenwort, we must content ourselves with . . . the Mountain, the Narrow-leaved and the Thelypteris-like Spleenworts. **1901** MOHR *Plant Life Ala.* 314–16 [Nine species listed]. (2) **1847** WOOD *Botany* 275 *C[ereus] Phyllanthus*. . . . Spleenwort. . . . From S. America.

+Splendiferous, a. [Modern coinage.] Magnificent; very striking. *jocular.* {1854} — **1837** BIRD *Nick* I. 226 At a close hug, a squeeze on the small ribs, or a kick-up of heels, he's all splendiferous. **1857** *Porter's Spirit of Times* 10 Jan. 299/3 Oh, it was splendiferous! **1882** SALA *Amer. Revisited* (1885) 151 A desire to appear 'splendiferous' and outshine all rival hotels.

+Splenic fever. A disease of live stock. — **1869** *Rep. Comm. Agric. 1868* 5 On the breaking out of the splenic fever at the halting places of Texas cattle. **1901** *Amer. Rev. of Reviews* XXIV. 309/2 The altitude . . . prevents the occurrence of splenic fever.

＊Splint. attrib. +Designating things made with flexible slips or strips of wood. — **1843** TORREY *Flora N.Y.* II. 183 Broom Hickory . . . [is] frequently used for making splint brooms. **1871** TAYLOR in *Life & Lett.* II. 564 An old-fashioned, highbacked splint-chair. **1887** WILKINS *Humble Romance* 220 There were a few poor attempts at adornment on the walls; a splint letter-case, a motto worked in worsteds. **1893** M. A. OWEN *Voodoo Tales* She ketch up all dem crows an' fling um inter er big splint bag.

+Splint basket. A basket made of long, flexible slips of wood. — **1866** A. D. WHITNEY *L. Goldthwaite* xi, Leslie had hanging upon her finger . . . [the] most graceful of all possible little splint baskets. **1884** 'CRADDOCK' *Tenn. Mts.* 92 An inverted splint-basket served as table. **1912** COBB *Back Home* 66 It was a fad of Aunt Dilsey's to bring one covered splint basket . . . under her dolman cape.

+Splint-bottom (arm)chair. A splint-bottomed (arm)chair. —
1876 'MARK TWAIN' *Tom Sawyer* vi, The master, throned on high in his great splint-bottom armchair, was dozing. **1892** *Harper's Mag.* Dec. 116 She'd sit in an old splint-bottom chair by the chimney all day long.

+Splint-bottomed, *a.* Of a chair: Having a bottom made of interwoven splints. — **1850** *Knickerb.* XXXVI. 73 She wiped out the seats of some splint-bottomed chairs with her calico apron. **1872** EGGLESTON *End of World* 235 [She] sat down in her splint-bottomed rocking-chair. **1883** [see ROCKER 3]. **1899** CHESNUTT *Wife of His Youth* 157 A couple of splint-bottomed chairs were fastened [on the cart] to accommodate Dinah and Cicely.

+Splint coal. Coal that is mined in long splints. — **1873** *Amer. Cycl.* IV. 726/2 Of the more highly bituminous coals the most valuable is the splint or block coal of N.W. Pennsylvania, Ohio, and Indiana.

∗ Splinter.

1. A thin lath.
*a*1649 WINTHROP *Hist.* I. 59 Mr. Sharp's house in Boston took fire, (the splinters being not clayed at the top).

2. A thin strip of wood used as a light. {1751–}
1791 W. BARTRAM *Travels* 468 Some take with them little fascines of fat Pine splinters for torches. **1831** [see FAT PINE 1]. **1873** COZZENS *Marvellous Country* 139 Bethinking himself of some pitch-pine which was in his luggage, he proceeded to light a splinter. *c*1908 CANTON *Frontier Trails* 39 He was . . . trying to light his pipe with a splinter.

+3. Used in mild oaths.
1840 SIMMS *Border Beagles* I. 197 By the splinters, you shall see how I shall drive. **1845** — *Wigwam & Cabin* 1 Ser. 49 Darn my splinters, said I . . . if I leave the lad.

∗ Split, *n.*

1. A strip of wood or cane formed by splitting. {1617–1837}
1796 HAWKINS *Letters* 20 The dies of the splits were good. **1800** — *Sk. Creek Country* 71 The rafters are near together, and fastened with splits. **1848** DRAKE *Pioneer Life Ky.* 94 The 'splits' were stripped up for eight or ten inches with a jack-knife. **1876** KNIGHT 2281/2 *Split*, . . . a ribbon of wood rived from a tough piece of green timber.

+2. (See quot. 1864.)
1864 DICK *Amer. Hoyle* (1866) 204 Whenever two cards of the same denomination . . . appear in the same turn, the dealer takes half the money found upon such card—this is called a 'split.' **1908** LORIMER *J. Spurlock* viii, One turn, high card to win, splits barred?

‖**3.** A cross *between* one thing and another.
1875 'MARK TWAIN' *Old Times* i. 19 You dash-dash-dash-*dashed* split between a tired mud-turtle and a crippled hearse-horse!

+4. a. *Full split*, full speed. **b.** *To go like split*, to go fast. *colloq.* or *slang.*
1834 C. A. DAVIS *Lett. J. Downing* 22, I arter him full split. **1842** *Ainsworth's Mag.* II. 555 We are flying, full split, with a locomotive, hot-pressed speed. **1845** S. SMITH *May-Day in N.Y.* 64 There was no end to the one hoss teams, haulin little carts, and goin like split all over the city.

+5. Attrib. and comb. in sense 1 with *basket, broom, roof,* etc.
1848 DRAKE *Pioneer Life Ky.* 94 We always used a split broom. **1880** *Scribner's Mo.* March 676/2 It was a split-seated chair, painted green. **1890** *Harper's Mag.* Jan. 282/1 [He shifted] his white oak split basket from one arm to the other. **1905** *Forestry Bureau Bul.* No. 61, 49 *Split roof,* a roof of a logging camp or barn made by laying strips split from straight-grained timber. . . . (N[orthern] F[orest].) **1906** LYNDE *Quickening* 11 Centering in the broad, low, split-shingled house at his back, it widened in front to the old-fashioned flower garden.

Split, *a.* {1648–} +Of various pieces of timber: Made by being split off from larger pieces. {1846–}
*a*1772 WOOLMAN *Journal* 204 [The houses] are built mostly of split plank. **1789** MORSE *Amer. Geog.* 198 This country abounds with . . . every species of split lumber manufactured from pine and oak. **1806** *Ann. 9th Congress* 2 Sess. 1124 They found an open log cabin, and a few huts of split boards. **1826** FLINT *Recoll.* 206 Scarcely has a family fixed itself, and enclosed a plantation with the universal fence,—split rails. **1857** HAMMOND *Northern Scenes* 257 The sloping roof [was] neatly covered with bark, in layers, like an old-fashioned roof, covered with split shingles. **1886** *Century Mag.* Nov. 21/2 The schools . . . were held in deserted cabins of round logs, as distinguished from the more aristocratic 'split logs.'

+b. Of firewood: Made by splitting up logs.
1814 BIGELOW *Florula Bostoniensis* 234 The wood [of pitch pine] . . . is chiefly used as a light fuel, under the form of 'split pine.' **1833** NEAL *Down-Easters* I. 1 They lay stretched out, heads and points, over the piles of split wood. **1835** HOFFMAN *Winter in West* I. 245 Presently, however, the landlord entered with an armful of burr-oak and split hickory.

∗ Split, *v.*
To split rails, (see RAIL *n.*[1] 2 a).

I. 1. *intr.* Of timber: To admit of being cleft by the stroke of an ax. {1846}

1785 MARSHALL *Amer. Grove* 46 The timber is used much for rails, splitting free. **1805** CLARK in *Lewis & C. Exped.* III. (1905) 279 We are much pleased to find that the [balsam] timber Splits most butifuly.

2. To move or go quickly {1868–}; to act with vigor. *colloq.*
1787 TYLER *Contrast* II. ii, I was glad to take to my heels and split home, right off. **1843** W. T. THOMPSON *Major Jones's Courtship* 22, I sot the niggers a drummin and fifin as hard as they could split. **1847** PALMER *Rocky Mts.* (1904) 69 Creighton wheeled and 'split' for the camp. **1876** MILLER *First Fam'lies* 165 Whiskey, quick! The gal is almost tuckered! Go! Split!

+3. To vote a split ticket. (Cf. sense 7.)
1851 HOOPER *Widow Rugby* 23 Never *split* in my life.

+4. To come out *even* in a division.
1892 *Chicago Herald* 16 June (E. J. Nichols). **1897** *Outing* Aug. 506/2 Georgia split even with North Carolina.

II. 5. *tr.* To make a furrow down (a ridge or middle) with a plow. {1807–}
1786 WASHINGTON *Diaries* III. 40, I therefore . . . split these Ridges again, by running twice in the same furrow. **1851** *Fla. Plantation Rec.* 373 Ploughs Runing around cotton and splitting cotton middles.

+6. To hollow *out* (a canoe).
1807 PIKE *Sources Miss.* II. App. 25 We cut down a small green cottonwood tree, and with much labor split out a canoe.

+7. To scratch (a political ticket); to vote for candidates of different parties on (a ballot).
1842 *Spirit of Times* (Phila.) 14 July (Th.), The cry is raised of 'Vote the whole ticket! Don't split your ticket!' **1848** *Knickerb.* XVIII. 515 Didn't Squire Great . . . split his ticket a couple of years since? **1877** BARTLETT 199 'Eel-skins,' judiciously distributed, are the most efficient instruments for 'splitting tickets.' **1905** *N.Y. Ev. Post* 17 Oct. 1 Plenty of talk is heard about intentions to split ballots.

+8. *Tobacco culture.* (See quotations.) Also *vbl. n.*
1850 *Rep. Comm. Patents* 1849: *Agric.* 321 'Splitting' tobacco . . . [is] simply splitting . . . the plant from the top to within a few inches of the bottom, before it is cut down for housing. **1909** *Cent. Suppl.* 1256/1 *Splitting,* . . . in harvesting tobacco, the cleaving of the stalk nearly to the base, with the purpose of 'hanging,' i.e. placing it astride a stick for curing.

+9. *To split the wind,* to run fast.
1856 *Porter's Spirit of Times* 27 Sept. 55/3 The veteran 'Columbus' . . . was there, and split the wind, showing the crowd that age had not crept into his heels.

+Split-bottom. 1. *attrib.* Designating chairs having bottoms made of split pieces of wood. **2.** *ellipt.* A split-bottom chair. — **(1) 1838** *S. Lit. Messenger* Jan. 28/1 At this log-house in the prairie . . . [were] split-bottom chairs, tin lamps [etc.]. **1866** W. REID *After the War* 61 A rather more airy hall still contained the old, split-bottom arm-chairs. **1889** *Harper's Mag.* Oct. 747/1 The boy hopped briskly over the rows of split-bottom chairs. **(2) 1839** *S. Lit. Messenger* V. 209/2 Nor had a windsor chair yet showed his rounded form among the old *split-bottoms,* with low seats and tall perpendicular backs.

+Split-bottomed chair. A chair having a bottom made of split pieces of wood. — **1843** *Amer. Pioneer* II. 444 [There were] four split-bottomed chairs. **1870** NOWLAND *Indianapolis* 85 This was one of a set of split-bottomed chairs presented to my father. **1904** GLASGOW *Deliverance* 516 The same basket of chicken feathers was in the sagging split-bottomed chair.

+Splitmouth (sucker). =CUTLIPS b. — **1882** *Nat. Museum Bul.* No. 16, 144 *Ouassilabia lacera,* . . . Split-mouth Sucker. **1884** GOODE, etc. *Fisheries* I. 614 The 'Rabbit-mouth,' 'Hare-lip,' 'Split-mouth,' or 'May Sucker' is found in abundance in many rivers of Tennessee. **1911** *Rep. Fisheries* 1908 317/1.

+Split-tail. 1. A cyprinid fish (*Pogonichthys macrolepidotus*) of California. **2.** =PINTAIL 1. — **(1) 1882** *Nat. Museum Bul.* No. 16, 223. **1883** *Ib.* No. 27, 486 The split-tail is 'singularly distinguished from our other *Cyprinidæ* by the great development of the upper lobe of the caudal and its rudimentary rays.' **(2) 1917** *Birds of Amer.* I. 128 Pintail. *Dafila acuta.* . . . [Also called] Split-tail.

Splitter.

1. One whose occupation is to split something open {1648–}, or off from something else.
See also RAIL-SPLITTER.
1800 *Mass. H. S. Coll.* VII. 248 The *splitter* then takes out the backbone, and splits them [the fish] completely open. **1817** PAULDING *Lett. from South* II. 176 There were four tavernkeepers, . . . a splitter of shingles, a speculator, and two non-descripts. **1861** *Harper's Mag.* March 460/1 The crew divide themselves into throaters, headers, splitters, salters, and packers. **1874** *Vermont Bd. Agric. Rep.* II. 744 The splitters and trimmers are termed the skilled workmen in slate making.

+2. (See quot. 1850.)
1850 S. WARNER *Wide, Wide World* xii, Splitters . . . were a kind of rich short-cake baked in irons, very thin and crisp, and then split in two and buttered. **1891** *Cent.* 5849/2.

+Split ticket. *Polit.* **a.** A ticket or ballot bearing names other than those nominated or recommended by a single party or party faction. **b.** A ballot cast by a voter who does not confine his votes to members of a single party.
Cf. SCRATCHED TICKET.
1836 in Mackenzie *Van Buren* 262, I was reproached by you for having voted a 'split ticket.' **1838** *N.Y. Advertiser & Exp.* 11 April 3/1 Look out for Split Tickets.—The Loco Focos in the 8th Ward, are playing this trick, for the purpose of smuggling in a Collector and Assessor. **1875** *Chicago Tribune* 4 Nov. 1/5 Besides the straight tickets thus disposed of, there were about 100 split tickets. **1885** *Mag. Amer. Hist.* April 396/2 A 'Split ticket' represents different divisions of a party. A 'Mixed ticket' combines the nominees of different parties. **1904** *N.Y. Ev. Post* 7 Nov. 2 To vote a split ticket, which is one for candidates of different parties, the voter should make a cross mark before the name of every candidate for whom he desires to cast a vote.

+Splitting knife. Any of several knives used for splitting fish, tobacco, etc. — **1634** [see COD HOOK]. **1722** *Broadside Verse* (1930) 115/2 [The] said Daniel still retain'd his splitting knife. **1820** *Amer. Farmer* I. 395 Split down the [tobacco] stalk . . . with a 'splitting knife.' **1885** *Harper's Mag.* Jan. 276/1 Iron rollers . . . roll or force the hides against a long splitting-knife.

Split-up. A breaking up *of* something; a discontinuance of association between persons. — **1837** *Diplom. Corr. Texas* I. (1908) 173 The questions of recognition and annexation will produce a general split up of the old democratic party. **1908** LORIMER *J. Spurlock* iv, I should have told her then about my split-up with the Governor.

+Splitworm. The larva of a small moth, *Phthorimaea operculella*. — **1899** *Dept. Agric. Yrbk. 1898* 122 Another new insect . . . is the so-called tobacco leaf-miner, or 'split worm.'

Splorum. [f. Sc. *splore* 'to show off.'] 'A splurging; great noise or fuss on slight occasion and with little effect' (B. '77).

Sploshy, *a.* Sloppy. {1905} — **1838** *N.Y. Advertiser & Exp.* 28 March 1/4 On Tuesday it was muggy and sploshy. **1881** *Harper's Mag.* Aug. 391 On horseback Rachel looks,—excuse the word but it expresses it,—sploshy.

+Splurge, *n.* [Imitative.]
1. An ostentatious display; a conspicuous effort or demonstration.
1830 SANDS *Writings* II. 179 What a splurge she makes! **1835** *Commercial Advertiser* (N.Y.) 13 Dec. (B.), Senator Benton was shining around, making what they call in Missouri a great splurge to get gold. **1858** *Harper's Mag.* Dec. 140/1 [He] opened the Bible, read his text, and, with a great flourish, made a *splurge* to begin his discourse. **1886** CHADWICK *Art of Batting* 6 The latter may excell in cutting a dash or making a showy splurge in odd games. **1911** *N.Y. Ev. Post* 7 Jan. Suppl. 3 Not a few manufacturers . . . are persuaded to make a splurge on their own account by sending their own special representative abroad.
b. *To cut a splurge,* to make a display; to show off.
[*c*1847 WHITCHER *BedottP.* 89 She tries to cut a spludge, and make folks think she's a lady.] **1897** *Chicago Tribune* 19 Sept. 37/1 Two shrewd young Hoosiers . . . came to Chicago in 1891 and cut a big splurge in monetary and real estate circles.
2. A sudden lunge.
1840 HOFFMAN *Greyslaer* II. 26 He caught my bullet in the back of his neck, gave a splurge, and was done for.

+Splurge, *v.*
1. *intr.* To brag.
1844 *Knickerb.* XXIII. 507 You'll see all their steam-ships and their sail-ships they splurge so much about, lying high and dry.
2. To show off; to make a display.
1845 *Big Bear Ark.* 54 The settlements is got too thick for 'em to splurge. **1855** *Chicago W. Times* 10 May 1/2 A young man named Charles Grandwell has been 'splurging' extensively in that town for some weeks. **1886** *Harper's Mag.* June 118/2 People . . . come here, buy or build expensive villas, splurge out for a year or two, then fail or get tired of it. **1923** WYATT *Invis. Gods* 15 Enos bought it . . . to splurge around and show off with.
b. To make ostentatious or violent physical movements; to splash.
1853 SIMMS *Sword & Distaff* (1854) 333 Ef you splurges about in that sort of style you'll resk mightily the security of all your fixins. **1887** T. STEVENS *Around World on Bicycle* I. 189, I don my gossamers . . . , and splurge ahead through the mud.

+Splurgy, *a.* Showy; ostentatious. — **1852** *Yale Tomahawk* May (Hall), They even pronounce his speeches splurgy. **1871** BUSHNELL in M. B. Cheney *Life Bushnell* 524 Great care [is] to be had of language—no hollow generalities, no splurgy matter. **1900** R. GRANT *Unleavened Bread* 221 It may be that I can introduce some of her and her daughter's splurgy and garish misconceptions without making myself hopelessly ridiculous.

∗Spoil, *n.*
1. The public offices to which a victorious political party has the power of appointments; political plunder; patronage. +Chiefly pl. {sing. 1770, *c*1789}

(*a*) **1812** *Mass. H. Rep. to Gov.*, The weaker members of the party . . . would be overlooked . . . ; whilst the more powerful would disagree in the division of the spoil. **1887** *Courier-Journal* 2 May 2/8 The office of Speaker . . . was never intended to be the spoil of a party.
(*b*) [**1830** J. S. JOHNSON in *Congress. Deb.* 2 April 299 The country is treated as a conquered province, and the offices distributed among the victors, as the spoils of the war. **1832** W. L. MARCY *Ib.* 24–25 Jan. 1325 If they [U.S. politicians] are successful, they claim, as a matter of right, the advantages of success. They see nothing wrong in the rule that to the victor belong the spoils of the enemy.] **1868** M. H. SMITH *Sunshine & Shadow* 477 To suit the soldiers who compose the home guard, who took care of the 'spoils,' filled the civil offices, [etc.] . . . General Grant's movements before Vicksburg were too slow. **1883** *Century Mag.* May 151/2 No party could now take its stand on the old doctrine of spoils with the least chance of success. **1905** *Psychological Bul.* 15 Dec. 395 Those who are contending for spoils and those who are contending for good government.

+2. Attrib. and comb. with *business, doctrine, hunter,* etc. See also SPOILSMAN, SPOILS SYSTEM.
1833 CLAY *Speeches* (1842) 303 The Senate . . . [was] where the spoils doctrine . . . was first boldly advanced in Congress. **1833** WHITTIER in Pickard *Life Whittier* I. 170, I should as soon think of worshipping the devil with the Manicheans, as to fall down and do homage to Andrew Jackson with the idolatrous 'spoils party' of the day. **1837** *Jamestown* (N.Y.) *Jrnl.* 15 Feb. 3/2 The spoil hunters must admit he holds an office under the government. **1883** *Century Mag.* Oct. 950/1 The spoils business, in fact, is one of the strongest proofs of the prevailing apathy. **1887** *Courier-Journal* 5 May 4/4 Responsible Democratic officials . . . [have been] accused of spoils-mongering in violation of law. **1905** *Forum* April 589 The system which has dragged the schools into spoils politics and fostered corruption.

∗Spoil, *v.* **+1.** *To be spoiling for lack of* (something), to be on edge or suffer for lack of something. **+2.** *To be spoiling for a fight,* etc., to be extremely eager for a fight, etc. — (**1**) **1861** Moore *Rebellion Rec.* I. III. 8 Youthful South Carolina . . . is literally 'spiling' for lack of [a fight]. (**2**) **1865** L. STEPHEN *Sk. from Cambridge* 67 We are in the condition which the Yankees call 'spoiling for a fight.' **1877** 'McCABE' *Hist. Great Riots* 148 It was an easy matter to detect the professional idler, . . . willing to do anything, and almost spoiling for a fight. **1893** *Nation* 16 Nov. 368/2 Dr. James Martineau . . . seemed still to be 'spoiling for an argument.' **1901** RIIS *Making of an American* 237 The man who is sober and minds his own business . . . will take the other side of the street when he sees a gang ahead spoiling for a fight.

+Spoilsman. One who shares in political spoils or supports the spoils system. — **1846** *Xenia Torch-Light* 11 June 1/7 Commend us to the vociferous leaders of the hard money faction, . . . for a fair specimen of the 'spoilsman,' one who always takes good care that his own broth is well seasoned. **1855** I. C. PRAY *Mem. J. G. Bennett* 411 It involves no objections beyond those which have been urged by spoilsmen. **1900** *Congress. Rec.* 14 Feb. 1791/2 When we spoilsmen . . . recommend some old soldier . . . to take one of these incompetents' places, it is said that we ought not to have that privilege. **1913** LA FOLLETTE *Autobiog.* 167 [Harrison] was not in favor with the spoilsman and the jobster.

+Spoils system. The practice of taking public offices from members of a defeated party and giving them to members of the victorious party.
1838 MAYO *Polit. Sk. Washington* 40 Mr. Jefferson . . . authorized a friend to compromise with the federalists for . . . a guarantee against the spoils system. **1855** I. C. PRAY *Mem. J. G. Bennett* 98 Compared with the bold-faced spoils system ruling at Washington now, the government was then a model of economy and purity. **1872** *Newton Kansan* 31 Oct. 4/3 It would not necessarily . . . cure the corruptions incidental to the 'spoils system' of party favoritism. **1882** *Nation* 9 Nov. 400/2 Abraham Lincoln was very much of their present way of thinking as regards the civil service and the abominations of the 'spoils system.' **1896** *Congress. Rec.* 7 Jan. 512/2, I dissent in toto from the low-down, disreputable spoils system that is defended here.

∗Spoke. *attrib.* Designating tools and establishments for making spokes and similar articles. — **1638** *Md. Archives* IV. 43 A spokeshave. **1759** in Chalkley *Scotch-Irish Settlement Va.* III. 54, 1 parcel of Welsh books; 1 spoke sheaver. **1856** *Mich. Agric. Soc. Trans.* VII. 84 Lewis Benham [exhibited] . . . spoke machine for turning irregular forms. **1884** *N.Y. Herald* 27 Oct. 2/1 For Sale or Exchange, . . . 1,700 acres . . . [with] Tongue and Groove Machines, Spoke Factory, &c.; all in operation.

‖Spondulick, *v. tr.* To enrich. *slang.* — **1871** *Billings' Farmer's Allminax* 4 Thou shalt not spondulick thyself with the dimes ov another.

+Spondulic(k)s. [Origin unknown.] Money; cash. *slang.* — **1856** M. THOMPSON *Plu-ri-bus-tah* 113 Spondulicks, or ye Tin. **1860** *Phila. Press* 5 Jan. (Chipman), Tights and tin, spangles and spondulicks were apparently in direct ratio to each other. **1884** 'MARK TWAIN' *H. Finn* xiii I'm derned if I'd live two mile out o' town . . . not for all his spondulicks. **1918** C. WELLS *Vicky Van* xvii, An' to her also Julie had passed the spondulicks.

∗Sponge.
∗1. A mop for cleansing the bore of a cannon after firing.
1628 *Va. House of Burgesses* 51 Wee doe intreate you to send us . . . ladles, spunges [etc.]. *c*1695 J. MILLER *Descr. N.Y.* 35 Spunges, ladles, worms, powder, and bullets . . . [should be provided] for the forces to be

raised in America. **1793** *Amer. State P.: Mil. Affairs* I. 45/2 Return of Ordnance and Military Stores deposited at Springfield, Massachusetts. . . . Sponges, for 4 pounders, 29; Lintstocks, 11 [etc.]. **1885** *Rep. Secy. War* III. 2 Principal articles procured by fabrication. . . . 16 sponges and rammers for 12-pounder mountain howitzer.

***2.** A soft, porous substance coming from certain aquatic animals, which absorbs liquids readily; one of the animals forming this substance.

1784 FRANKLIN *Autobiog.* 333, I marked my faults with a black-lead pencil, which marks I could easily wipe out with a wet sponge. **1868** *Amer. Naturalist* II. 306 Even the sponge is beautiful in such places and with such associations. **1881** INGERSOLL *Oyster-Industry* 243 A crawl or corral [is] made of upright stakes wattled together . . . to hold sponges while being cleaned. **1885** *South Fla. Sentinel* (Orlando) 1 July 4/1 There were over 60 lots of sponges on the wharf at Key West, Monday. **1902** G. M. MARTIN *Emmy Lou* 7 To copy digits until one's chubby fingers . . . ached, and then to be expected to take a sponge and wash those digits off, was strange.

3. *S.* A swampy surface or soil. {1890–}

1835 J. MARTIN *Descr. Virginia* 246 In this [surface of the Dismal Swamp] (sponge as it is called here) are imbedded innumerable old trees of juniper. **1842** BUCKINGHAM *Slave States* II. 489 The soft and yielding mass of decayed vegetable matter, with which this Dismal Swamp is chiefly covered, is called by the people living near it, Sponge. **1856** OLMSTED *Slave States* 157, I am aware of but a single attempt, as yet, to cultivate the sponge or true swamp soil.

4. Attrib. in sense 2 with *bar, fishery, glass, hook.*

1881 INGERSOLL *Oyster Industry* 248 *Sponge hook.*—The bent, two pronged iron tool at the end of a pole, with which sponges are gathered from the bottom. (Florida reefs.) **1883** *Nat. Museum Bul.* No. 27, 124 The American Sponge fishery is now a well-established industry of considerable importance. **1887** GOODE, etc. *Fisheries* v. II. 823 The sponge-glass as originally constructed consisted of a small, square, wooden box having a glass bottom. **1891** *Cent.* 5852/3 *Sponge-bar,* a sand-bar or rock bottom on which sponges grow. [Florida.]

Sponge bath. {1859} A bath in which the body is merely wiped off with a sponge or damp rag. — **1882** 'M. HARLAND' *Eve's Daughters* 106 His recommendation, in lieu of this wholesale 'dabbling,' was a daily sponge-bath quickly and lightly performed. **1893** *Harper's Mag.* Feb. 445 Maud Muriel . . . took a conscientious sponge-bath . . . and then went through her morning gymnastics.

Sponge cake. A kind of light, spongy cake. {1843–} — **1805** *Pocumtuc Housewife* (1906) 32. **1850** TYSON *Diary in Calif.* 66 Sponge-cake, and buttermilk, were spread out. **1920** ALSAKER *Eating for Health* 61 Desserts should be rather plain, such as gelatine, . . . fruit whip, plain cake like sponge cake, and ice cream.

Sponge-tree. {1760} (See quotation.) {1829} — **1891** *Cent.* 5853/1 *Sponge-tree,* an evergreen shrub or small tree, *Acacia Farnesiana,* . . . found in the United States along the Gulf of Mexico.

+**Spook,** *n.* [Du.] A ghost or specter. {1859–} Also attrib. — **1801** *Mass. Spy* 15 July (Th.), I fly so swift as any spoke. **1840** HOFFMAN *Greyslaer* II. 185 Be't you for sartain, or only your spook? **1884** *Lisbon* (Dak.) *Star* 31 Oct. 7/4 He was really run out of a fine position by spooks. **1896** E. HIGGINSON *Land of Snow Pearls* 160 You look just 's if you'd seen a spook! **1904** *Charleston News & Courier* 26 Oct. 9 'Spook dancing,' games, etc. played a prominent part.

+**Spook,** *v.* {1883, in S. Africa} *intr.* To go *about* as a spook; to play the spook. Also quasi-tr. — **1867** LOWELL *Poetical Works* (1896) 477/2 Yet still the New World spooked it in his veins. **1871** *N.Y. Tribune* 24 Feb. 1/5 Once he saw Toussaint L'Ouverture spooking about with an air of mournful majesty. **1893** LELAND *Memoirs* I. 10 The ghost . . . still 'spooks' about as of yore.

+**Spooky,** *a.* Suggestive of spooks; eerie. — **1883** *Harper's Mag.* Nov. 929/1 'Tis a spooky place, that grave-yard. **1888** ROE *Army Lett.* 382 At night . . . the dark, unoccupied building . . . seemed more spooky than ever. **1907** *St. Nicholas* May 633/1 It was decidedly too spooky for comfort.

***Spool,** *n.* A wooden, cylinderlike reel for holding sewing thread; such a reel and the thread upon it. {1861–} — **1817** PAULDING *Lett. from South* II. 7 About the mantelpiece . . . was an almanac, a comb-case, and several spools of cotton. **1852** STOWE *Uncle Tom* xv, I'll look your box over,—thimble, wax, two spools, scissors, knife, tape-needle. **1873** 'MARK TWAIN' & WARNER *Gilded Age* 29 It takes her a week to buy a spool of thread. **1902** *Sears, Roebuck & Co. Cat.* No. 112, 1115 We do not sell less than full 10-yard spools.

Spool, *v.* {1603–} +*intr.* Of corn: To sprout ears; to shoot. — **1786** WASHINGTON *Diaries* III. 89 The alternate rows of early Corn was Tassling and Spooling.

+**Spool cotton.** Cotton thread suitable for sewing. {1862} — **1839** BRIGGS *H. Franco* I. 28 He is the celebrated Mr. Bulbief, the importer of spool cottons. **1865** STOWE *House & Home P.* 160 The Portsmouth Steam Company makes white spool-cotton equal to any in England. **1881** *Rep. Indian Affairs* 384 Spool-cotton, 6 cord, Nos. 20 to 50.

***Spooler.** **1.** One who winds thread on spools. +**2.** A machine that winds thread on spools. — (1) **1826** G. POWERS *N.Y. Prison at Auburn* 28 The Spoolers and Bobbin-winders in this shop . . . are all invalids. **1898** HARPER *S. B. Anthony* I. 19 One of the 'spoolers' was ill. (2) **1847** *Knickerb.* XXX. 517 A few [girls] tend the 'warpers,' the 'spoolers' and the 'speeders.'

***Spoon,** *n.*

***1.** A utensil for use in eating, cooking, etc.

1622 'MOURT' *Relation* 101 The Inhabitants [gave us] . . . the spawne of Shads, which then they got in abundance, in so much as they gaue vs spoones to eate them. **1705** BEVERLEY *Virginia* III. 17 The spoons which they eat with, do generally hold half a pint. **1886** STOCKTON *Mrs. Lecks* 27 You'll have to take the beans in your hands, for we've got no spoons nor forks. **1904** GLASGOW *Deliverance* 136 Removing a speck of dust from the cream with the point of the spoon.

***b.** With distinguishing attributives.

See also HORN SPOON.

1640 *Conn. Rec.* I. 448 Goods and Cattell of James Olmestead: . . . 1 warmeing pan, 13 peuter spoones. **1661** *Essex Probate Rec.* I. 341, 2 pewter chamberpots, 6 Alcumy spoones. **1689** *Conn. Probate Rec.* I. 461 To my daughter Mabell I give . . . one silver spoone, & allso one silver porringer & goblet. **1775** *Essex Inst. Coll.* XIII. 186, 1 flesh Fork, 1 Iron spoon.

c. *Yale.* = WOODEN SPOON. {1824–, at Cambridge U.}

1864 *Harper's Mag.* Sept. 500/2 The 'Spoon' was attended by an audience of over three thousand. *Ib.,* At first the Spoon . . . was presented to the greatest glutton in the class.

2. *The spoons,* sentimental affection. {1860–, in related senses}

1846 *Spirit of Times* (N.Y.) 18 April 92/2 The girls are beautiful, with a very liberal allowance of 'the spoons,' as our friend Smith would say.

3. In phrases.

To be born with a silver spoon in one's mouth, to be born rich {1849–}; *that's a great spoon, to do business with a big spoon,* (see quotations). **1801** *Ann. 6th Congress* 905 It was a common proverb that few lawyers were born with silver spoons in their mouths. **1848** MITCHELL *Nantucketisms* 42 'That's a great spoon.' Good, promising. **1859** BARTLETT 437 'To do business with a big spoon,' is the same as to cut a big swathe.

4. Attrib. and comb. with *bread, corn bread,* etc.

1683 *Boston Rec.* 74 James Butler and William Paine . . . became surety to the town for Mathew Mabely, a spoonmaker. **1791** *Ky. Petitions* 184, I give and bequeath . . . one spoon strainer. **1864** *Harper's Mag.* Sept. 500/2 An essential requisite, too, in a Spoon man, in these days, is a full purse and a generous heart. **1879** A. D. WHITNEY *Just How* 41 Bring it to a very soft spoon-dough. **1898** *Kansas City Star* 18 Dec. 10/2 Splendid Sugar Bowls, Spoon Holders, Tea Pots. **1906** *Dialect Notes* III. 158 *Spoon corn-bread,* soft corn-bread served with a spoon. **1917** *Boston Ev. Globe* 17 April 12/5 (Ernst), Southern spoon bread.

Spoon, *v.* {1715–} +**1.** *intr.* To lie spoon-fashion with one or more persons. **2.** *tr.* To fit oneself snugly against (another person) while lying down. — (1) **1863** *Rio Abajo Press* 18 Aug. 1/3 Giving him a tremendous thump, I again requested him to 'spoon.' **1887** *Harper's Mag.* April 781/2 Two persons in each bunk, the sleepers 'spooning' together, packed like sardines. **1903** *Scribner's Mag.* June 704/2 With a heavy double blanket over you and a warm partner, with whom you can 'spoon,' you rarely sleep cold. (2) **1887** *Harper's Mag.* Dec. 49/2 'Now spoon me.' Sterling stretched himself out on the warm flag-stone, and the boy nestled up against him.

Spoonbill. {1678–}

+**1. a.** = SHOVELER. **b.** = ROSEATE SPOONBILL. **c.** = RUDDY DUCK.

1844 *Nat. Hist. N.Y., Zoology* II. 342 The Shoveller, or Spoonbill . . . is highly prized as affording delicate eating. **1846** THORPE *Myst. Backwoods* 128 The splendid spoon-bill decked the shallow places near the shore. **1858** BAIRD *Birds Pacific R.R.* 781 *Spatula Clypeata.* . . . Shoveller; Spoonbill. **1874** LONG *Wild-Fowl* 219 Spoonbills are seldom found in large numbers. **1891** *Cent.* 5855/1 *Spoonbill,* . . . the ruddy duck, *Erismatura rubida;* the broadbill. **1917** *Birds of Amer.* I. 175/1 Formerly the Spoonbills, or 'Pink Curlews,' as the Florida hunters know them, were extensively shot and their feathers shipped . . . [to be] made into fans.

+**2.** (See quotation.)

1891 *Cent.* 5855/1 *Spoonbill,* . . . the spoon-billed cat, or paddle-fish, *Polyodon spatula.*

+**3.** *attrib.* In the name of a fish.

1847 *Knickerb.* XXIX. 332 The shovel or spoon-bill fish is only found in the Alabama and its tributaries.

Spoonbill duck. {1813, *dial.*} +=SHOVELER. — **1789** MORSE *Amer. Geog.* 59 American Birds [which] have been enumerated [include] . . . Ilathera Duck, . . . Spoon bill ditto. **1861** *Calif. Statutes* 185 Spoonbill duck, and all other bill ducks, shall not be taken, killed, or destroyed. **1874** COUES *Birds N.W.* 570. **1917** *Birds of Amer.* I. 126.

Spoon-billed, *a.* In the specific names of birds and fishes. {1668–} — **1781–2** JEFFERSON *Notes Va.* (1788) 77 Spoon billed duck. **1883** *Nat. Museum Bul.* No. 27, 493 *Polyodon spathula.* . . . Spoon-billed Sturgeon. Ohio and Mississippi Valleys, generally abundant. **1891** *Cent.* 5594/3 *Shoveler.* . . . [Also called] spoon-billed duck, spoon-billed teal or widgeon. **1917** *Birds of Amer.* I. 152 Ruddy Duck. *Erismatura jamaicensis.* . . . [Also called] Spoon-billed Butter-ball.

+**Spoon-fashion,** *adv.* To lie (or *sleep*) *spoon-fashion,* to lie (or *sleep*) on one's side close to and facing the back of another person lying in the same position. *colloq.* — **1847** in Howe *Hist. Coll. Ohio* 442 The whole party crouched down together . . . lying spoon-fashion, with three heads one way and four the other, their feet extending to about the middle of their bodies. **1851** *Polly Peablossom* 168, I might have to sleep 'spoon fashion' with perhaps three. **1891** *Century Mag.* April 846 The squad or file of men slept 'spoon-fashion.'

+**Spoonfish.** =SHOVELFISH. — **1838** FLAGG *Far West* I. 107 Another singular variety found is the 'spoonfish,' about four feet in length, with a black skin, and an extension of the superior mandible for two feet, ... used probably for digging its food.

Spoon hook. A fishing hook baited with a spoonlike piece of metal that spins in the water. {spoon, 1851-} — **1858** *Harper's Mag.* Oct. 621/1 Picture to yourself ... a lad, ... trailing from the weather-side a line with a spoon-hook attachment. **1882** PECK *Sunshine* 90 The delegates divide their time catching sinners on spoon-hooks and bringing pickerel to repentance. **1894** *Outing* XXIV. 226/1, I once took a bass four inches long on a spoon hook.

+**Spoonhunt.** *local.* The mountain laurel or calico bush. — **1845–47** THOREAU *Journal* 435, I have watered ... the cornel and spoonhunt and yellow violet, which might have withered else in dry seasons. **1892** *Amer. Folk-Lore* V. 100 *Kalmia latifolia*, spoon-hunt. Mason, N.H.

+**Spoon tree.** (See quotation.) — **1770** FORSTER tr. Kalm *Travels* I. 360 The American evergreens are 1. *Ilex Aquifolium*, holly. 2. *Kalmia latifolia*, the spoon tree.

+**Spoon victuals.** *pl.* 'Food eaten with a spoon' (B. '77). {1880} Also transf. — **1777** *Penna. Ev. Post* 11 Feb. 73/2 Philip Clark ... has a remarkable way of throwing his head back when he eats spoon victuals. **1842** KIRKLAND *Forest Life* I. 89 Think of your own swimming oats, and as ye love not 'spoon vittles,' hasten. **1884** 'MARK TWAIN' *H. Finn* xxi, Meat first, and spoon vittles to top off on.

+**Spoonwood.** The wood of the mountain laurel (*Kalmia latifolia*), or the tree itself. — **1778** CARVER *Travels* 234 They fashion their spoons ... from a wood that is termed in America Spoon Wood, and which greatly resembles Box Wood. *Ib.* 507 The Spoon Wood is a species of the laurel. **1897** SUDWORTH *Arborescent Flora* 315.

+**Spoonwood ivy.** *local.* The sheep laurel. — **1892** *Amer. Folk-Lore* V. 100 *Kalmia angustifolia*, spoonwood ivy. Conn.

+**Spoops, Spoopsy.** (See quotations.) *slang.* — **1851** HALL *College Words* 291 At Harvard College, a weak, silly fellow, or one who is disliked on account of his foolish actions, is called a *spoops*, or *spoopsy*. **1860** *Yale Lit. Mag.* XXV. 192 (Th.), [If he] makes a dull recitation, he is denominated a regular 'spoops.'

***Sport.**
+**1.** Gaming.
1856 *Harper's Mag.* Dec. 60/1 The very words 'sport' and 'sportsmen' have been perverted from their old English significations to mean gaming and gamblers.

+**2. a.** A gamester or gambler. *colloq.*
1859 MATSELL *Vocabulum* 84 *Sport*, a gamester; a man fond of racing and gaming of all kinds. **1861** *N.Y. Tribune* 5 July (Chipman), The gamblers, or, as they are termed, the 'sports,' of the United States. **1873** MILLER *Amongst Modocs* 43 If I don't make the sports *ante*, my name ain't Boston.

+**b.** One who lives or acts in a flashy manner; a gay fellow.
1876 HARTE *Two Men of Sandy Bar* 91 Ye don't teach old sports like him new tricks. **1888** *Contemp. Rev.* Feb. 228 The police justices ... take very good care that 'the sports,' by which is meant those who like fast living, shall not suffer heavily when caught. **1900** GOODLANDER *Fort Scott* 26 The young bucks, or sports of the tribe, were pretty lively at times. **1920** LEWIS *Main Street* 274 He was nineteen now, tall, broad, busy, the town sport, famous for his ability to drink beer.

+**c.** One who lives up to the ideals of good sportsmanship. Usually *good sport.*
1905 A. ADAMS *Outlet* 295 We limited our losses at poker to so much an evening, ... taking our luck with a *sangfroid* which proved us dead-game sports. **1918** OWEN *Typewriting Speed* 85 It is better to be known by everyone as a 'fine girl' than a 'good sport.'

***Sporting.** *attrib.*
1. Designating various articles used in the sports of hunting, athletics, etc. {1728-}
1778 *N.H. Hist. Soc. Coll.* IX. 388 The Q[uarte]r Master to draw the sporting Cartridges as mentioned in Gen[era]l orders. **1843** *Knickerb.* XXI. 118 [He] saw a stranger in a sporting-jacket, with a dog and gun. **1856** *Porter's Spirit of Times* 25 Oct. 129/2 We are now prepared to attend to all orders which may be sent us for the purchase of ... sporting articles of every conceivable description. **1876** HABERTON *Jericho Road* 79 The Squire's gaze rested abstractedly upon a keg of sporting powder on the counter. **1881** *Ore. State Jrnl.* 1 Jan. 7 Leading All Others ... as a Sporting Rifle.

2. Designating publications or parts of publications that feature news of sports. {1793-}
1817 WEEMS *Letters* III. 185, I rejoice at the thought of the Sporting Magazine. **1873** F. HUDSON *Journalism* 341 The *Spirit of the Times* ... was the first weekly sporting paper published in the United States. **1883** WILDER *Sister Ridnour* 114 Augustus Asterbilt ... [was] reading a sporting journal. **1890** DAVIS *Gallegher* 90 It was nearly dusk ..., as he knew by the newsboys calling the sporting extras on the street below. **1909** *Dialect Notes* III. 399 Let me have the sporting section of that paper.

1915 *Lit. Digest* 21 Aug. 360/3 Bozeman Bulger ... contributes to the sporting page of the New York *Evening World*.

+**b.** Designating persons who edit or write for such publications.
1890 DAVIS *Gallegher* 212 The honor ... was given to Andy Spielman, the sporting reporter of the *Track and Ring*. **1895** *N.Y. Dramatic News* 9 Nov. 5/2 Advancing deferentially to the sporting editor [he] would say [etc.].

+**3.** Designating a place where gambling is done. *Obs.*
1878 BEADLE *Western Wilds* 46 He strayed into one of our sporting rooms.

Sporting gentleman. {1748} +A gambler. *Obs.* — **1835** INGRAHAM *South-West* II. 10 Two ... are professed 'black-legs'; or, as they more courteously style themselves, 'sporting gentlemen.' **1858** *Harper's Mag.* Jan. 279/1 In those 'flush times' the steamers swarmed with hoosiers, green-horns, and gamblers, the latter politely designated 'sporting gentlemen.' **1862** Moore *Rebellion Rec.* V. II. 285 They seemed to be of that class to which we apply the term 'sporting gentlemen.'

+**Sporting goods.** Clothing and equipment for different sports. — **1869** *Boyd's Business Directory* 500 John H. Mann, Importer and Dealer in Guns, Fishing Tackle, Gun Powder, and all Sporting Goods. **1887** *Courier-Journal* 11 Feb. 5/7 We have now the largest stock of Base-Ball and Sporting Goods of every description. **1903** *N.Y. Tribune* 20 Dec., Dealers in sporting goods say that they are receiving large orders for skees.

Sporting house. {1857-} +A house frequented by gamblers; a brothel. — **1891** *Cent.* 5857/3 *Sporting-house*, a house frequented by ... betting men, gamblers, and the like. **1894** STEAD *If Christ Came to Chicago* 5 The novice in the sporting house, as well as the hardened old harridan who drives the trade in human flesh, are herded together. **1895** *Stand.* II. 1737/1.

Sporting man. {1840-} +A gambler. *Obs.* — **1849** G. G. FOSTER *N.Y. in Slices* 27 'Sporting-man' is the title by which he prefers to be known in his profession. **1884** *Boston Jrnl.* 1 Nov. 2/3 A well-known sporting man wanted to put up $20,000 on Cleveland. **1897** *Ib.* 12 March 10/1 The sporting-man was $40 in the hole.

Sportsman. {1706–7-} +One who bets on horse races, etc.; a professional gambler.
1740 W. STEPHENS *Proc. Georgia* I. 606 The Sportsmen, as Yesterday, took a plentiful Cup in the Evening. **1833** J. STUART *Three Years N.A.* II. 160 He had found at the gambling-house that his fellow-traveller was a sportsman, ... a person who gives himself up to gambling as a profession. **1843** *Niles' Nat. Reg.* 30 Sept. 80/2 A Great Horse Race ... has set all the sportsmen agog. **1878** *Congress. Rec.* 27 March 2093/1 The adroit and sleight-of-hand Stebbins ... could handle a ticket as a sportsman would a playing-card.

+**Sposh.** Slush, mud. — **1845** *N.Y. Tribune* 25 Nov. (B.), The streets were one shining level of black sposh. **1877** BURROUGHS *Birds & Poets* 93 Yellow sposh and mud and water everywhere.

+**Sposhy,** *a.* Soft or wet. — **1842** *Yale Lit. Mag.* VIII. 96, I can't always decipher quail tracks—'specially in *sposhy* weather. **1884** JEWETT *Country Doctor* 22 There's a sight o' difference between good upland fruit and the sposhy apples that grows in wet ground.

*** Spot,** *n.*
*** 1.** A small piece or area *of* land. {-1811}
1637 *Essex Inst. Coll.* IX. 55 Roger Mory req. for a spott of ground. **1659** *Providence Rec.* II. 32 Sold ... a little Spott or Spots of meddow. **1779** *N.H. Hist. Soc. Coll.* VI. 320 It is a considerable spot of intervale. **1828** *Huntington Rec.* III. 332 [We] have sold to Moses Rolph Esqr. a spot of land adjoining his buildings. **1900** *Congress. Rec.* 9 Feb. 1667/2 There are spots here and there of irrigated land, where people can raise live stock.

2. A fungus disease of plants. {1852-}
1770 *Md. Hist. Mag.* XII. 366 If the spot keeps from it, it will be fine tob[acc]o. **1874** *Rep. Comm. Agric. 1873* 224 Other kinds [of wheat] ... were badly damaged by 'spot.'

+**3. a.** One of the conventional figures or pips on a playing card; a playing card with a designated number of such figures. *colloq.*
1843 STEPHENS *High Life N.Y.* II. 215 'Jest so,' sez I, a fli[n]gin down the ten spot o' clubs and the ace-o' diamonds. **1864** DICK *Amer. Hoyle* (1866) 457 Face cards, having but one spot, may be taken by a deuce or any other card having two or more spots. **1866** 'MARK TWAIN' *Lett. Sandwich Isl.* 13, I knowed it! took with a nine-spot! **1920** MULFORD *J. Nelson* x, I'm layin' down as fine a pair of four-spots as I've ever held.

+**b.** With the value in dollars designated by a number: A bank note, silver certificate, or the like. *colloq.*[2]
1848 LOWELL *Biglow P.* 1 Ser. ix. 135 He'd give a fifty spot right out. **1857** *Harper's Mag.* Sept. 568/2, I'll take that ten spot, if you please. **1896** J. LILLARD *Poker Stories* 244 But one single dollar remained of that five spot. **1908** LORIMER *J. Spurlock* 35, [I made] one boy unpin a ten-spot from the lining of his vest.

+**4.** One of various fishes, as the red drum (*Sciaenops ocellata*) or the sciaenoid food fish, *Leiostomus xanthurus*.
1879 KILBOURNE & GOODE *Game Fishes U.S.* 37/2 'Spot' is another name erroneously applied to this fish [the red drum], and which is the

property of a much smaller species of the same family, otherwise known as 'Lafayette,' or 'Cape May Goody.' **1882** G. C. EGGLESTON *Wreck of Red Bird* 23 They call croakers 'spot' in Virginia. **1885** *Harper's Mag.* Jan. 221/1 It might be a sheep's-head of three pounds, a spot (*Liostomus philadelphicus*) of five, or a tarpon of a hundred pounds. **1911** *Rep. Fisheries* 1908 316/2 Spot (*Leiostomus xanthurus*).... [It] is taken with hook and line and in gill nets.

5. *pl.* Goods at present cash prices. {**1890**}

1881 *Harper's Mag.* April 734/2 'Spots,' 'futures,' 'longs' and 'shorts' were unknown terms. **1893** *Congress. Rec.* 23 Jan. 778 In the New York market, futures were sold lower than spots.

6. In phrases. **a.** *In spots*, +at intervals; occasionally; in some respects.

1852 STOWE *Uncle Tom* xvi, Mammy has a kind of obstinacy about her, in spots. **1859** BARTLETT 437 A boatman on the Mississippi [said], ... 'I sleep in spots'; that is, at intervals, by snatches. **1900** *Congress. Rec.* 16 Jan. 867/1 It is found in spots, which is something like this war-time prosperity they have talked about.

+**b.** *To knock (the) spots off* (or *out of*), to whip thoroughly; to surpass. {**1888**}

1861 *Atlantic Mo.* June 747/1 [If] I had control of chain-lightning ..., I'd make it come thick and heavy, and knock spots out of Secession. **1884** 'MARK TWAIN' *H. Finn* xxi, [He] just knocked the spots out of any acting ever *I* see before. **1897** ROBINSON *Uncle Lisha's Outing* 34 If that don't knock the spots out'n all the dancin' ever I ever did see.

+**c.** *To go to the spot*, to be immediately effective; to satisfy completely.

1868 *Putnam's Mag.* I. 670/1, 'I hope that last corjul set you up?' 'Yes, Mr. Plunkitt, it went right to the spot.' **1923** NUTTING *Massachusetts* 241 Did ever a dish of apple dowdy go to the spot like that?

+**d.** *To get* (something) *down to a spot*, to get (something) down pat.

1886 CHADWICK *Art of Pitching* 69 A man who for years has been playing in one position, and who, in that position, has got everything down to a spot.

* **Spot,** *v.*

+**1.** *tr.* To blaze (a tree); to mark (a line) by blazing.

1718 *N.H. Probate Rec.* II. 58 One of the said lotts ... runs south-Easterly ... to a Beach tree spotted and numbered three. **1723** [see MARKING IRON]. **1792** BELKNAP *Hist. New Hampshire* III. 75 Where they find the land suitable for a road, the trees are spotted, by cutting out a piece of the bark. **1851** SPRINGER *Forest Life* 84 An experienced hand ... 'spots' the trees where he wishes the road to be 'swamped.' **1860** *Harper's Mag.* Feb. 300/1 We had struck the line which our friends had spotted as they past along. **1905** *Forestry Bureau. Bul.* No. 61, 30.

+**b.** To chip off a level place on (a railroad tie) for a rail.

1857 *Ill. Agric. Soc. Trans.* II. 434 Ties, like common fence posts, ... were spotted down. *Ib.* 437 Cross ties of size and quality for good fence posts—not hewed, but only spotted on the top.

+**2.** To recognize; to detect; to catch sight of. {**1868**-}

1848 JUDSON *Mysteries N.Y.* I. 116 To spot is to recognize—to mark. **1849** G. G. FOSTER *N.Y. in Slices* 15 The expertness acquired by the keepers of these shops in 'spotting' their man is truly wonderful. **1856** HARTE *Poems* (1871) 58 For thar isn't a man on the river as can't spot the place at first view. **1885** *Wkly. New Mexican Rev.* 15 Jan. 2/5 Mr. Twitchell went down to 'round up' the gang and was so far successful as to spot the leader. **1924** R. CUMMINS *Sky-High Corral* 34, I'm up spotting bear.

3. *intr.* To become spotty. {**1879**-}

1850 *Rep. Comm. Patents 1849: Agric.* 456 These varieties [of tobacco] *spot* better, and produce a finer leaf than any I have ever seen. When brought to perfection, the leaf is of a bright cinnamon color, having thousands of small white spots.... These spots it is that gives character to the tobacco, for without them the article is practically worthless.

+**4.** *tr.* To hit with a bullet.

1882 HARTE *Flip* 24 It's an even thing if she wouldn't spot me the first pop.

+**Spot cash.** Cash paid at once. Also as play title. — **1885** *Boston Transcript* 24 March 1/2 'Spot Cash' will hold the stage for the remainder of the week. **1888** *Boston Jrnl.* 20 July 5/1 Bismarck ... postponed his demand for spot cash. **1898** WISTER *Lin McLean* 6, I have most forgot the feel o' spot-cash. **1924** A. J. SMALL *Frozen Gold* 137 The amount of spot cash the Skagway agent happened to have in his possession.

+**Spot cotton.** Cotton on hand for immediate delivery. — **1887** *Courier-Journal* 17 Jan. 7/2 Spot cotton has declined ... in New York, while other American markets have been steady. **1900** NELSON *A B C Wall St.* 136 At the expiration of a future contract the cotton is delivered and becomes spot cotton.

+**Spotrump.** =HUDSONIAN GODWIT. — **1888** TRUMBULL *Names of Birds* 209 At North Scituate, Provincetown, and Chatham [Mass., it is called] Spot-Rump. **1917** *Birds of Amer.* I. 240.

* **Spotted,** *a.*

+**1.** Of trees or a trail: Blazed.

1828 SHERBURNE *Memoirs* 192 We could no longer find our way by our spotted trees. **1888** ROOSEVELT in *Century Mag.* June 204/1 Some furtrapper had chopped a deeper blaze than usual in making out a 'spotted line.'

2. In the specific names of plants, animals, birds, etc. {**1679**-}

Many more examples may be found in scientific books.

*c***1729** CATESBY *Carolina* I. 21 *Picus varius minimus*. The smallest spotted Wood-pecker. **1805** *Ann. 9th Congress* 2 Sess. 1103 We saw no animals that were not common in all the country of Louisiana, except the spotted tiger, and a few White bears. **1813** WILSON *Ornithology* VII. 60 *Tringa macularia*, Spotted Sandpiper.... This species is ... remarkable for perpetually wagging the tail. **1814** BIGELOW *Florula Bostoniensis* 161 *Geranium maculatum*. Spotted geranium or Cranesbill.... The root is perennial, very astringent, and useful for its medicinal properties. **1820** *Western Rev.* II. 356 *Silurus maculatus*.... Vulgar names Spotted, White, and Channel Catfish. **1860** *Harper's Mag.* Oct. 594/2 We drove through ... the clumps of white poplar and spotted alder. **1867** *Amer. Naturalist* I. 109 Other species of Frogs found in Massachusetts ... are the Spotted Frog, Marsh Frog, or Pickerel Frog (*Rana palustris* Le Conte); the second species of Spotted Frog [etc.]. **1868** *Ib.* II. 115 The Spotted-cricket ... appears simultaneously with the Black-cricket. **1884** GOODE, etc. *Fisheries* I. 199 The Spotted Sand Flounder, *Sophopsetta maculata*, ... [is] found from Bucksport, Maine, to Fort Macon, North Carolina. **1917** *Mammals of Amer.* 135 The Spotted Skunk and its relatives of the genus *Spilogale* are the smallest of the North American Skunks. **1917** *Ib.* 152 If one talks with hunters or ranchmen about Ocelots, the probability is that they will refer to them as Leopard Cats or Spotted Cats.

+**Spotted land.** (See quotation.) — **1845** *Congress. Globe* 4 Feb. 242/3 The lands of Missouri were called spotted lands: one strip was good, and another bad.

Spotter. {**1611**-}

+**1.** One who seeks out good spots of land.

1847 *Knickerb.* XXIX. 203 The soil is too thin and sandy to raise cotton, except in small and detached patches, on which the 'spotters' have settled.

+**2.** A detective, orig., a private detective hired to detect dishonesty among conductors on a train.

1876 *Scribner's Mo.* April 911/2 The stockholders and directors, the 'car-starters' and 'spotters,' ... were all embalmed in verse and immortalized in song. **1883** *American* VI. 333 A conductor ... had a private detective arrested for following him about, and the 'spotter' was fined ten dollars by a magistrate. **1898** HAMBLEN *Gen. Manager's Story* 309 Spotters were to be sent on the trains with them to see that they did not become familiar with the crews. **1903** HART *Actual Govt.* 570 It is almost impossible to get evidence against a liquor-seller without employing a spotter. **1917** SINCLAIR *King Coal* 197 He followed him for a while, desiring to get him where no company 'spotter' might interfere.

* **Spout.** +**1.** *spec.* A troughlike contrivance stuck into maple trees to drain off maple syrup. **2.** *To go up the spout*, to die. {*up the spout*, 'pawned, in a bad way,' 1853-} — (1) **1847** *Knickerb.* XXIX. 377 The little fellows are gathering at evening ... to see their elders split and whittle the sweet-smelling pine and bass-wood 'spiles' or 'spouts.' **1896** *Vt. Agric. Rep.* XV. 35 We want the bark all on the tree that it may hold the spout firmly in place. (2) **1862** *Point Pleasant* (Va.) *Reg.* June (B.), If they ever intend to apply such insulting epithets to us, ... they 'will go up the spout,' as surely as there is virtue in powder.

+**Sprague's lark, pipit.** [Isaac *Sprague*, Amer. illustrator (1811-95).] =MISSOURI SKYLARK. — **1875** *Amer. Naturalist* IX. 78 There is something I have not quite made out respecting the breeding range of Sprague's lark, *Neocorys Spraguei*. **1917** *Birds of Amer.* III. 171/1 The best known is Sprague's Pipit, called the Missouri Skylark, or sometimes the Prairie Skylark.

+**Sprangle.** A straggling cluster or ramification; branching rootlets. — **1839** *Jamestown* (N.Y.) *Jrnl.* 20 Nov. 1/4 The most I could git was two or three sprangles of little white things that I stirred up from the bottom of the plate. **1896** *Advance* 21 May 738/1 Skepticism has its roots and spreads its feeding sprangles chiefly in the affections and the will. **1898** *Ib.* 19 May 662/1 This [Philippine] archipelago lies upon the map a great sprangle of intermingled land and water.

+**Sprangly,** *a.* Scraggy, scrawny, spreading. Now *dial.* — **1840** HOFFMAN *Greyslaer* II. 25 Following hard on his trail along a hillside overgrown with short sprangly bushes, I saw [etc.]. **1886** *Leslie's Mo.* Oct. 503/1 We can command a view through their sprangly branches. **1895** JEWETT *Nancy* 245 There ain't much o' anything but fire-wood in the sprangly [...]. **1917** *Dialect Notes* IV. 417 'Sprangly bushes, like laurel.' [N.C. mts.]. Also Kan.

* **Sprat.** +**1.** (See quot. 1884.) +**2.** (See quotation.) — (1) **1884** GOODE, etc. *Fisheries* I. 277 *Rhacochilus toxotes* ... is called 'Alfione' at Soquel, 'Sprat' at Santa Cruz; elsewhere it is simply 'Perch.' **1911** [see PERCH 1 b]. (2) **1896** JORDAN & EVERMANN *Check-List Fishes* 283 *Opisthonema oglinum*.... Thread Herring; Machuelo; Sprat.... West Indian fauna, ranging regularly north to Florida and Carolina.

Sprat herring. +**1.** =SHAD.[1] +**2.** (See quotation.) — (1) **1814** MITCHILL *Fishes N.Y.* 454 Sprat Herring of New-York.... It is somewhat green about the heads, gills, and dorsal fin. **1884** GOODE, etc. *Fisheries* I. 579 Mitchill recognized seven species, to wit, ... the 'Sprat' Herring of New York, *C. indigena*; the 'Spring' Herring or 'Alewife,' [etc.]. (2) **1903** T. H. BEAN *Fishes N.Y.* 209 *Opisthonema oglinum*.... Thread Herring; Shad Herring; Sprat Herring.

Sprawl. Energy, spirit, activity. *dial.* {**1888**-, *dial.*} — **1833** NEAL *Down-Easters* II. 175 He may be one of our native New-Englanders who value themselves on their *sprawl*, as they term it. **1890** WIGGIN *Timothy's Quest* 107 Jabe Slocum ain't got sprawl enough to find out anythin' wuth knowin'. **1894** *Advance* 25 Oct. 24/1 Fact of it is neither of them had sprawl enough to disagree.

Sprawler. {1832-} *local.* +=HELLGRAMMITE. — **1891** *Cent.* 5860/3.

∗ Spread, *n.*

+1. A quilt or coverlet; also, a table cover. Cf. BED-SPREAD.

1836 GILMAN *Recoll.* (1838) 251 The bed-curtains and spreads were mostly patterns of gorgeous birds and trees. **1846** THORPE *Myst. Backwoods* 27 An enormously thick-leafed table, with a 'spread' upon it, attracted little attention. **1862** STOWE *Pearl Orr's Isl.* II. 4 The bed was draped with a white spread. **1905** *Springfield W. Repub.* 4 Aug. 10 When people speak of patchwork spreads they forget to mention dimity spreads.

+2. In a newspaper, an article given conspicuous treatment, as by display across two or more columns, or facing pages.

[**1858** HOLMES *Autocrat* 131 One gives a 'spread' on linen, and the other on paper—that is all.] **1877** *Harper's Mag.* Dec. 50/1 His remarkable ability is best seen when occasion arises for a 'spread.'

3. In billiards, a rebound of a cue ball from the object ball at a considerable angle from its former course.

1864 DICK *Amer. Hoyle* (1866) 418 Beginners . . . are apt to suppose that, to effect a 'spread,' it is necessary to hit the object ball far from the centre.

+4. (See quot. 1900.)

1879 WEBSTER *Suppl.* 1579/3 *Spread,* . . . the privilege of demanding shares of stock at a certain price, or of delivering shares of stock at another price, within a certain time agreed upon. **1885** *Harper's Mag.* Nov. 844/1 A 'straddle' . . . differs from the 'spread' in that the market price at the time of purchase is filled into the latter, while in the 'straddle' the price may vary from that of the market, by agreement or otherwise. **1900** NELSON *A B C Wall St.* 160 *Spread.* This is a double stock privilege which entitles the holder to the right to deliver or demand a certain amount of stock on specified terms, or grain price differences between different options, or between the same option in different cities, or between the put and call price.

+5. Jam, jelly, peanut butter, etc., suitable for spreading on bread.

1886 STOCKTON *Mrs. Lecks* 40 The one who gets the last biscuit will have somethin' of a little spread on it.

∗ Spread, *v.*

To spread the tiger, to spread wool over_(someone's) eyes, (see TIGER 2 b, WOOL).

+1. *reflex.* To exert oneself, to show off, to make a display, to brag. *colloq.* {1891-} Also *absol.*

1857 HAMMOND *Northern Scenes* 266 Cullen had promised, to use his own expression, 'to spread himself' in the preparation of this meal. **1860** HOLLAND *Miss Gilbert* 173 He sort o' stands around and spreads, and lets off all the big talk he hears. **1865** PIKE *Scout & Ranger* (1932) 149 The young folks [are] 'spreading' themselves, and full of glee, at the recitation. **1884** 'MARK TWAIN' *H. Finn* xxi, All through his speech, he howled, and spread around, and swelled up his chest. **1909** WASON *Happy Hawkins* 248 This afternoon he got to spreadin' himself about how much money the place handled.

+2. *tr.* To enter or record (an order, sentence, etc.), *on* or *upon* a permanent record. Also *fig.*

1845 COOPER *Chainbearer* xix, It will greatly aid the reader . . . if I spread on the record the language that passed between my late agent and . . . his confidant. **1894** ROBLEY *Bourbon Co., Kansas* 184 Councilmen Dimon, White and Drake caused the following order to be spread upon the minutes. **1910** *Atlantic Mo.* Feb. 231 Achievements in that field are naturally not spread on the record as are exploits in railway financiering.

∗ 3. *To spread out.* **a.** To have plenty of room; to feel relaxed and unconfined. **+b.** To expand the scope of one's operations. *colloq.*

(a) 1862 *Harper's Mag.* July 146/1 It is utterly impossible for a Californian to 'spread out' in such a complicated and thickly settled country. **(b) 1901** HARRIGAN *Mulligans* 158 He wanted to 'spread out,' but not in the sense of ostentation or extravagance. *Ib.* 159 Tom 'spread out.' He sold his Chicago possessions and invested the money . . . in Dakota farm lands.

+4. *To spread it on thick,* to exaggerate. *slang.*

1865 'MARK TWAIN' *Sketches* (1926) 172 Don't you think he is spreading it on rather thick?

∗ Spread eagle.

∗1. A representation of an eagle with outstretched wings, **+**as an emblem of the United States.

1846 DE SMET *Oregon Missions* 335 Let some efforts be made to rescue them . . . , lest, by guilty negligence, the last drop of aboriginous blood indelibly stain the fair fame of the Spread Eagle, under whose protecting wing they are said to live. *c*1870 CHIPMAN *Notes on Bartlett* 438. **1894** ALDRICH *Two Bites* 65 The Stars and Stripes, held in the claws of a spread eagle, decorated the editorial page.

+2. Bombast, boastfulness. Usually *attrib.*, with reference to high-flown patriotic oratory.

1858 *N. Amer. Rev.* Oct. 454 'The spread-eagle style' is chargeable only upon a certain class of writers. **1864** *Wkly. New Mexican* 15 July 2/2 There is no trifling and 'spread eagle' in his [Grant's] bearing and manners. **1883** ZEIGLER & GROSSCUP *Alleghanies* 290 The spread-eagle burst of oratory on the part of the fresh blossomed sprig of the law.

+b. A bombastic speech.

1861 *Harper's Mag.* Aug. 425/1 It was shortly after the Mexican war, and Barnes delivered himself of a 'spread eagle' on that . . . question. **1864** *Ib.* Jan. 281/1 The counsel for the plaintiff, who sometimes indulged in 'spread eagles,' was in the very climax of his rhapsody.

+3. =SPREAD *n.* 4. Also *attrib.*

1857 *Hunt's Merchants' Mag.* July 136 The buyer can call when he pleases, which would compel the 'spread eagle' operator to deliver. **1859** BARTLETT 438 *Spread Eagle.* This term is frequently used among stock speculators. **1870** MEDBERY *Men Wall St.* 86 One modification of this is the Spread Eagle, formerly a highly popular style of speculation with capitalists who had plenty of money and a wide-awake broker. **1910** *Encycl. Brit.* (ed. 11) V. 55/1 A combined option of either calling or putting is termed a 'straddle,' and sometimes on the American stock exchange a 'spread-eagle.'

+Spread-eagleism. Exaggerated laudation of the United States. {1877 (*Cent.*)} — **1859** G. F. TRAIN (*title*), *Spread-Eagleism. Ib.* p. ix, We cannot fasten an ism on him (except Spread-Eagleism). **1861** *Vanity Fair* 9 Feb. 70/1 [You] must learn to disuse much of your national Gasconade, Self-Conceit, Strut, . . . and in short, Spread-Eagleism of all kinds. **1884** *American* VIII. 212 The old-fashioned oration, though greatly abused by spread-eagleism. **1903** W. F. JOHNSON *Century of Expansion* 130 At the very moment when he was indulging in such spread-eagleism American ships were being fired upon at the mouths of American harbors.

∗Spreader. *Agric.* An implement for spreading hay or manure. — **1865** *Maine Agric. Soc. Returns 1864* 115 The hay tedder or spreader . . . tosses the hay about, opening it to the sun and the breeze. **1900** WEBSTER *Suppl.* 199.

∗Spreading, *a.* In the names of plants. — **1814** BIGELOW *Florula Bostoniensis* 171 *Hedysarum divergens,* Spreading Hedysarum. . . . Woods. August. **1833** EATON *Botany* (ed. 6) 47 *Atriplex patula,* spreading orache. **1840** DEWEY *Mass. Flowering Plants* 139 *H[elianthus] divaricatus.* Spreading Sunflower. . . . Rather showy. *a*1862 THOREAU *Maine Woods* 317 *Apocynum androsæmifolium* (spreading dogbane). **1891** *Cent.* 5861/2 *Spreading globe-flower,* a plant, *Trollius laxus,* growing in swamps in the northeastern United States.

+Spreading adder. =HOG-NOSE(D) SNAKE. — **1842** *Nat. Hist. N.Y., Zoology* III. 52 The Hog-nosed Snake . . . is also called Dead Adder, Spreading Adder, Hog-nose and Buckwheat-nose. **1904** STUART *River's Children* 91 Rattlers and copperheads, spreading-adders, moccasins, and conger-eels came up to the island.

Spreading frame. (See quot. 1876.) — **1850** *Rep. Comm. Patents 1849* 375, I claim . . . the treating of the lap after it comes from the 'spreading frame.' **1876** KNIGHT 2280/1 *Spreading-frame,* . . . a machine in which a number of stricks or slivers of flax are spread and conducted to a system of drawing-rollers, whereby they are united and drawn into one. **1891** CHASE & CLOW *Industry* II. 33 The 'spreading frame' . . . was much like it.

+Spreading viper. =SPREADING ADDER. — **1887** *Courier-Journal* 15 Feb. 6/6 Early in the fall the girl was playing in a field and was bitten on the arm by a spreading viper.

Spread-out, *a.* {1867-} +Not compact or densely settled; extended in operation or scope. — **1856** *Porter's Spirit of Times* 18 Oct. 115/1 City 'spread out' a good deal, streets very wide—houses far apart. **1887** *Nation* 20 Oct. 302/1 Nearly everybody was [financially speaking] 'spread out.'

∗Sprig. 1. A small nail or brad, usually wedge-shaped and headless. **+2.** =SPRIGTAIL DUCK. — (1) **1678** *New Castle Court Rec.* 363 A paper of spriggs. **1729** *Md. Hist. Mag.* VIII. 151 To 34 Quarries 7 sqrs. & 7 foot [of glass] Repaired and Spriggs, o..11..1. **1788** *Ky. Gazette* 31 May 2/3 Wood screws & sprigs. **1815** *Niles' Reg.* IX. 94/2 Spikes, nails, tacks and sprigs of all descriptions. (2) **1888** TRUMBULL *Names of Birds* 38 At Baltimore, Washington, [etc., it is known as] . . . Sprig-Tail; this being sometimes shortened to Sprig. **1895** *Outing* XXVI. 30/2 Sprig . . . are as wary as wild geese.

Sprigtail. {1676-}

+1. The pintail duck or the ruddy duck.

1768 WASHINGTON *Diaries* I. 254 Killd 2 Ducks, viz. a sprig tail and Teal. **1813-** [see PINTAIL 1]. **1887** *Courier-Journal* 23 Jan. 9/5 The mallards, sprigtail and bluebill are coming in immense numbers. **1917** *Birds of Amer.* I. 128 Pintail. *Dafila acuta.* . . . Other Names.—Male: Sprigtail; Split-tail [etc.]. *Ib.* 152 Ruddy Duck. *Erismatura jamaicensis.* . . . [Also called] Bristle-tail; Sprig-tail; Stick-tail.

comb. **1874** LONG *Wild-Fowl* 199 In sprigtail-shooting it is best to place the decoys to windward of the blind when circumstances will allow.

+2. The sharp-tailed grouse.

1891 *Cent.* 5862/3 *Sprigtail,* . . . the sharp-tailed or pin-tailed grouse, *Pediœcetes phasianellus columbianus:* more fully *sprig-tailed grouse.*

+Sprigtail duck. =SPRIGTAIL 1. — **1844** *Nat. Hist. N.Y., Zoology* II. 341 The Pin-tail, Sprig-tail or Winter Duck, is more common in the interior than along the coast. **1852** STANSBURY *Gt. Salt Lake* 323 *Dafila acuta.*—Sprig-tail Duck.

Sprigtailed, *a.* {1676-} In the names of birds. — **1872** COUES *Key to Birds* 39 A cuneate tail . . . is also called pointed, in contradistinction to rounded, as in the sprig-tailed duck. **1891** [see SPRIGTAIL 2]. **1917** *Birds of Amer.* II. 27 Sharp-tailed Grouse. *Pedioecetes phasianellus phasianellus.* . . . [Also called] Pin-tailed Grouse; Sprig-tailed Grouse; White Grouse.

+**Sprigtail grouse.** =SPRIGTAIL 2. — **1859** in F. Hall *Hist. Colorado* II. 522 Phil killed two sprigtail grouse.

***Spring,** *n.*

* **1.** A natural fountain or supply of water flowing from the ground, sometimes forming the source of a stream.

1612 SMITH, etc. *Virginia* I. 4 Many goodly brookes . . . are maintained by an infinit number of small rundles and pleasant springs. **1693** *Derby Rep.* 163 So up that spring to the est corner of insign riggs feild. **1736** *Va. Stat. at Large* IV. 520 All that intire tract, territory, or parcel of land, . . . bounded by and within the first heads or springs of the rivers Tappahanock, alias Rappahanock, and Quriough, alias Patomack. **1805** *Ann. 9th Congress* 2 Sess. 1077 There are creeks and springs of good water frequent. **1895** *Outing* Dec. 243/2 We were far south of the location of the spring. **1907** *St. Nicholas* July 791/1 Will looked around at . . . the little spring of clear water.

b. *pl.* A place or locality where there are mineral springs to which invalids and pleasure-seekers resort. {1849-}

1799 *Steele P.* I. 173, I have built a house . . . for the accommodation of company resorting to the Springs. **1818** FEARON *Sketches* 132 Many had returned from 'the springs,' as Balston and Savatoga [sic] are denominated. a**1882** in MCCABE *New York* 205 A lady going to the Springs takes from twenty to sixty dresses.

2. *attrib.* Designating localities or places near or connected with a spring or springs.

See also SPRING BRANCH, SPRING BROOK, etc.

1636 in *Amer. Speech* XV. 396/2 Downe the maine river into the Spring Swamp. **1681** *Ib.,* From thence with a direct line to the head of the spring slash. **1716** *Ib.* 396/1 To run across the Land of John Golightly over the spring bank. **1898** HARRIS *Tales of Home Folks* 53 Her voice came from the spring lot.

3. Designating things operated by, or making use of, mechanical springs.

See also SPRING BED, SPRING CARRIAGE, etc.

1644 *Harvard Rec.* I. 9 Spring Lock . . . 3 [s]. **1678** *New Castle Court Rec.* 362 One spring Playne a Rabbit Playne [etc.]. **1712** *Boston News-Letter* 10 Nov. 2/2 Mr. Joseph Essex . . . performs all sorts of New Clocks and Watch works, viz. 30 hour Clocks, . . . Spring Table Clocks, Chime Clocks [etc.]. **1789** WASHINGTON *Diaries* IV. 41 A number of Looms were at work with spring shuttles. **1847** BRYANT *Let. to F. Bryant* 5 May (MS.), I had a spring cart at 30 Warren Street. **1867** HARRIS *Sut Lovingood* 141 They moves like a cradil on cushioned rockers, ur a spring buggy runnin in damp san'.

4. Designating domestic animals born in the spring.

See also SPRING CHICKEN.

1657 *Essex Probate Rec.* I. 251 One Spring Calf, . . . foure piggs. **1684** *Essex Inst. Coll.* XXV. 154, 4 swine. 16 spring pigs. **1785** WASHINGTON *Diaries* II. 436 A Grey Spring Colt.

5. Designating natural phenomena, events, etc., occurring in the spring.

See also SPRING FEVER, SPRING TERM.

1815 DRAKE *Cincinnati* 58 In spring floods, boats laden with 200 barrels of flour, can descend from points . . . more than an hundred miles distant. **1849** EMMONS *Agric. N.Y.* II. 16 Spring snows are the poor man's manure. **1871** STOWE *Sam Lawson* 61 There's the spring house-cleanin' and the fall house-cleanin' to be seen to. **1884** W. SHEPHERD *Prairie Exper.* 216 The people, after the spring freshets, must content themselves with very little water. **1890** *Stock Grower & Farmer* 22 March 6/4 The stockmen had a meeting March 1st for the purpose of arranging ye spring roundup. **1923** HERRICK *Lilla* 258 She strained her arm lifting a barrel just in the busiest time of the spring planting.

6. In the names of plants, fishes, etc.

See also SPRING BEAUTY, BIRD, CRESS, etc.

1842 *Nat. Hist. N.Y., Zoology* III. 62 The Spring Frog . . . is that [species] usually eaten as a delicacy. **1850** Spring-salmon [see FALL SALMON]. **1859** BARTLETT 438 *Spring-keeper,* a salamander, or small lizard-shaped animal, found in springs and fresh water rivulets. **1883** *Nat. Museum Bul.* No. 27, 470 *Fundulus diaphanus.* . . . Spring Minnow; Barred Killifish. . . . Ponds and streams of the Eastern and Middle States. **1923** WYATT *Invis. Gods* 17 Spring star, yellow rose, bleeding heart . . . now dreamed their inscrutable futures.

7. In special combinations.

Spring beaver, the skin of a beaver taken in the spring; *s. butter,* =GRASS BUTTER; *s. clip,* a clip of wool taken in the spring; *s. dairy,* (see quotation); *s. fare,* (see quot. and cf. FARE *n.* 2); *s. goods,* goods for sale in the spring; *s. oil,* (see quotation); *s. still,* a whisky still at or near a spring.

1902 HULBERT *Forest Neighbors* 139 It would have made the pelt which the old fur-traders sometimes sold under the name of 'spring beaver.' **1852** *Knickerb.* XXXIX. 563 Where would be the yellowness of 'spring'

(usually denominated 'grass') butter? **1874** *Vermont Bd. Agric. Rep.* II. 410 Their spring clip . . . grows in the winter months. **1823** FAUX *Memorable Days* 129, I saw here a fine *Spring dairy;* that is to say, a dairy of stone built over a spring of pure cold water continually flowing through, and round it, so that the milk and cream-vessels may stand in water to prevent the butter from turning to stinking oil. **1891** *Cent.* 5864/2 Fishermen make about two fares of cod in a year, and the first or spring fare, which commences early in April, is of a superior quality. **1805** *State P.* (1819) V. 295 The said ship had on board a full supply of spring and summer goods. **1837** W. JENKINS *Ohio Gaz.* 457 Petroleum or spring oil rises with or near to the gas. **1869** TOURGEE *Toinette* (1881) 11 That's good whiskey, . . . made by an old Dutchman at a little spring-still up the country.

***Spring,** *v.*

‖**1.** *To spring to,* to turn to, to set to work.

1850 S. WARNER *Wide, Wide World* xl, Sam and Johnny found they must 'spring to,' as their leader said.

2. *To spring* (something) *on,* to bring (a thing) unexpectedly to the attention of a person or group, to surprise someone with (something). *colloq.* {spring upon, 1884-}

1876 'MARK TWAIN' *Tom Sawyer* xxxiv. 265 Why, old Mr. Jones is going to try to spring something on the people here to-night. **1890** S. HALE *Letters* 250 It was sprung on me at breakfast. **1896** *Internat. Typogr. Union Proc.* 37/1 He had something to spring on the union as soon as my back was turned.

+**Spring beauty.** Any one of various plants of the genus *Claytonia,* as *C. virginica,* that flower in the early spring. — **1821** *Mass. H.S. Coll.* 2 Ser. IX. 148 Plants, which are indigenous in the township of Middlebury, [Vt., include] . . . *Claytonia virginica.* . . . Spring beauty. **1863** *Rep. Comm. Agric.* 1862 158 These Claytonias . . . go by the name of 'Spring Beauty.' **1880** *Scribner's Mo.* May 101/2 A good sample of our native purslane is the Claytonia or spring beauty. **1915** ARMSTRONG & THORNBER *Western Wild Flowers* 122 Spring Beauty. *Claytonia lanceolata.* . . . A pretty little plant.

Spring bed. {1846} A bed having a framework or a mattress with sets of springs; a spring mattress. {1862} — **1858** *Mich. Agric. Soc. Trans.* IX. 508 A new spring-bed . . . was exhibited. **1869** J. R. BROWNE *Adv. Apache Country* 324 Spring beds invite the wayfarer to repose. **1881** *Ore. State Jrnl.* 1 Jan. 8 Edes & Durkee's Woven Wire Mattresses, the Best Spring Bed Ever Introduced in This City.

Spring beetle. Any beetle of the family Elateridae; a snapping beetle. {1835-} — **1835** J. DUNCAN *Beetles* 159 [They are called in the U.S.] skipjacks and spring-beetles, by which they are likewise known in England. **1861** *Ill. Agric. Soc. Trans.* V. 416 There is scarcely an individual . . . unacquainted with the 'Spring-beetles.' **1879** *Scribner's Mo.* Aug. 497/2 'Why do you call it a spring beetle?' I asked. 'It receives its name . . . from its habit of jerking or springing upward, and alighting on its feet, when it . . . has been thrown upon its back.'

Spring bird. Any one of various birds, as the horned lark, that appear early in spring. — **1760** T. SMITH *Journal* (1849) 273 The robin and spring birds came a week or ten days sooner than usual. **1824** [see HANGBIRD]. **1832** WILLIAMSON *Maine* I. 143 The Spring Bird is larger than a chipping bird, and is one of the very first to sing the vernal song. **1917** *Birds of Amer.* II. 212 Horned Lark. . . . [Also called] Wheat Bird; Spring Bird; Life Bird.

Springboard. {1866-} +**1.** (See quot. 1905.) +**2.** *local.* A light wagon or other vehicle. — (1) **1883** *Harper's Mag.* Jan. 200/2 These [mortise holes] were intended for the insertion of their iron-shod 'springboards.' **1905** *Forestry Bureau Bul.* No. 61, 49 *Spring board,* a short board, shod at one end with an iron calk which is inserted in a notch cut in a tree, on which the faller stands while felling the tree. (P[acific] C[oast] F[orest], S[outhern] F[orest].) (2) **1883** STEVENSON *Silverado Squatters* 174 A couple in a waggon, or a dusty farmer on a spring-board toiling over the 'grade' to . . . Calistoga.

+**Spring branch.** A branch or brook fed by a spring or by springs. — **1650** in *Amer. Speech* XV. 396/1 Bounded on the North East with a Spring branch or cove. **1738** in Chalkley *Scotch-Irish Settlement Va.* II. 374 Below ye mouth of a spring branch. **1826** T. FLINT *Recoll.* 192 [The settlement] is intersected with numerous spring-branches, around which there are always found clumps of trees. **1886** *Leslie's Mo.* Feb. 149/2 She'd better not take off them boots of hern to paddle her feet in the Spring branch.

+**Spring brook.** =prec. — **1852** MARCY *Explor. Red River* (1854) 30 In a few miles [we] found a spring-brook. **1857** *Porter's Spirit of Times* 3 Jan. 289/2 Any gentleman who has a spring, or spring-brook, such as supplies an ordinary dairy-house [etc.]. **1888** JEWETT *King of Folly Isl.* 132, I made an arrant out to the spring-brook to see if there was any cresses started.

Spring carriage. A carriage the box or frame of which rests upon springs. {1842-} — **1854** WHIPPLE, etc. *Explor. Ry. Route* I. 110 We concluded to abandon all the wagons except the light spring-carriage. **1884** BLAINE *20 Years of Congress* I. 402 He proposed . . . to levy duties . . . [upon] spring-carriages [etc.].

+**Spring chicken.**

1. A young chicken, usually one only a few months old.

1845 *Knickerb.* XXVI. 511 It consisted of a pair of spring chickens. **1877** *Harper's Mag.* Feb. 446/1 The bantams and the spring chickens . . . were clucking and picking in the grass. **1893** *Ib.* Feb. 453 The Old North had provided for its patrons that day roast beef, spring chickens, potatoes, and apple puddings. **1917** McCutcheon *Green Fancy* 22 'Ham and eggs, pork tenderloin, country sausage, rump steak and spring chicken,' said Mr. Bacon.

2. *transf.* A youthful or inexperienced person.

1879 Tourgee *Fool's Errand* 259, I'm no spring-chicken; and . . . I have never listened to more sound and convincing sense. **1893** 'Mark Twain' *P. Wilson* Introd., My remotest ancestors are but spring chickens compared with these robed and stately antiques. **1901** Harben *Westerfelt* 260 If I ever intend to [marry] . . . , I'll have to be about it, for I'm no spring chicken.

+**Spring creek.** A creek fed by a spring or by springs. — **1800** Hawkins *Sk. Creek Country* 57 A fine little spring creek joins on its right bank. **1904** White *Blazed Trail Stories* 76 They came to a glade through which ran a soggy, choked, little spring-creek.

+**Spring cress.** A variety of cress (*Cardamine bulbosa*), found in wet places in the eastern states. — **1817–8** Eaton *Botany* (1822) 177 *Arabis rhomboidea*, spring cress. **1843** Torrey *Flora N.Y.* I. 56 Spring Cress. . . . Wet meadows and about shady springs. The white-flowered form is common. **1869** *Amer. Naturalist* III. 130 Along streams in open woodlands, we may find the Spring Cress . . . , with large, white flowers.

Spring crop. A crop planted or available in the spring. Also transf. — **1816** *Niles' Reg.* X. 33/2 The process consists . . . in three successive fall plowings, winter fallows, and spring crops. **1825** Lorain *Pract. Husbandry* 145 The superficial cultivation for the spring crop, will have a powerfully destructive effect on such weeds. **1894** *Harper's Mag.* April 806/1 If she could have got outer bed and looked round at the spring crop of advertisements on her fences, she would hev struck somethin' worse.

+**Spring fever.** (See quot. 1859.) — **1859** Bartlett 438 *Spring fever*, the listless feeling caused by the first sudden increase of temperature in spring. It is often said of a lazy fellow, 'He has got the spring fever.' **1872** 'Mark Twain' *Roughing It* 398, I had the 'spring fever' and wanted a change. **1897** Stuart *Simpkinsville* 95 This [was] the annual mid-season's lull between spring fevers and green chinquapins. **1904** Stratton-Porter *Freckles* 41 Duncan accepted his wife's theory that it was a touch of spring fever, but Freckles knew better.

Springfield.

+**1.** *attrib.* Designating firearms made at the government armory at Springfield, Mass.

1813 *Niles' Reg.* IV. 87/2 [The] gun . . . is but one pound and a half heavier than the common Springfield gun. **1849** Parkman in *Knickerb.* XXXIII. 3 They carried slung from their saddles the excellent Springfield carbines, loading at the breech. **1872** Roe *Army Lett.* 43 They asked me to fire a heavy Springfield rifle—an infantry gun. **1888** J. D. Billings *Hardtack* 270 Plain smooth-bore Springfield muskets soon became Springfield rifles.

+**b.** *absol.* A Springfield gun.

1863 *Harper's Mag.* May 857/1 The sentinel carefully laid his bright 'Springfield' upon the ground. **1866** *Ib.* Aug. 407/1.

+**2.** *Springfield hickory,* the big shellbark (*Carya laciniosa*); *Springfield nut,* the nut of this tree or the tree itself.

1810 Michaux *Arbres* I. 21 *Springfield hickory* (Hickery de Springfield), autre dénomination donnée à cet arbre [shellbark hickory] dans cet endroit, peu éloigné de Philadelphie. **1814** Pursh *Flora Amer.* II. 637 [*Juglans*] *sulcata*. . . . It is called Thick Shellbark Hickory, Springfield or Glocester Nut. **1832** Browne *Sylva* 176 In the vicinity of Springfield, in Pennsylvania, . . . its fruit is called *Springfield nut*.

* **Springhead.**

* **1.** A fountainhead or source of a stream or pond.

1666 *Portsmouth Rec.* 133 John Almy Shall haue one ackre of land Nere adioyninge to the Birch Swamp buttinge one the salt water leuinge out the springe head. **1763** in *Amer. Speech* XV. 396/2 Beginning at a haw bush sapling at the spring head of the swan ponds. **1837** Williams *Terr. of Florida* 83 The following [shrubs] are found about spring heads, banks of rivers [etc.]. **1869** *Rep. Comm. Agric. 1868* 328 Close below a springhead dig a trench.

+**2.** (See quotation.)

1876 Knight 2290/2 *Spring-head*, a box, clutch, or connection at the point of contact of the outer ends of an elliptic spring.

+**Spring-heel.** A shoe in which the outsole is bent over a thickness of leather between the sole and the upper. In full *spring-heel shoe.* Also *spring-heeled* a. — **1790** *Penna. Packet* 5 Feb. 3/3 Nathaniel Prentiss [has] . . . Lined & bound spring-heel'd Pumps. **1887** *Courier-Journal* 6 Feb. 9/3 The figure . . . would have regarded with ineffable scorn . . . the ungainly but comfortable 'spring-heels.' **1887** *Ib.* 20 Feb. 9/4 Kid and Pebble Spring-heel Shoes by the hundreds.

+**Spring herring.** =Alewife. — **1839** Storer *Mass. Fishes* 114 Spring Herring . . . are still taken in some places in immense numbers. **1884** Goode, etc. *Fisheries* I. 579 Mitchill recognized . . . the 'Spring' Herring or 'Alewife.' **1911** *Rep. Fisheries 1908* 311/1.

+**Spring hole. 1.** A hole or pool of water at the source or along the channel of a stream. Also attrib. **2.** An air hole in ice. — (1) **1845** Kirkland *Western Clearings* 69 The pony didn't die in the spring-hole. **1869** *Rep. Comm. Agric. 1868* 329 Keep her a few days in a pool or spring-hole. **1869** W. Murray *Adventures* 49 No better fishing can be found than spring-hole fishing. **1902** White *Blazed Trail* 63 Muddy swamp and

spring-holes caused endless difficulty. (2) **1890–3** Taber *Stowe Notes* 35 The frost-formed spring-holes in the ice.

+**Spring house.** A small house built over a spring or brook for the purpose of keeping perishable foods cool. — **1755** in Chalkley *Scotch-Irish Settlement Va.* I. 445, 1 spring house, 18 feet long and 12 feet wide. **1805** Parkinson *Tour* 222 As to butter, the milk can only be kept in spring-houses. **1892** *York County Hist. Rev.* 75 For the preservation of goods, a spring house was built, through which is a running stream. **1911** Harrison *Queed* 174 Your course is . . . past the little springhouse.

Spring knife. {1815–} A pocketknife the blade of which is thrown or held out by a spring. — **1754** *S.C. Gazette* 8 Jan. 4/3 To Be Sold . . . spring and penknives. **1862** 'E. Kirke' *Among Pines* 193 Drawing, then, a large spring-knife from his pocket, he waved it above his head. **1876** 'Mark Twain' *Tom Sawyer* ix. 89 Potter took out a large spring-knife and cut off the dangling end of the rope.

Spring line. 1. A line securing the after part of a steamboat to a landing place. {spring, 1769} **2.** (See quotation.) — **1845** *Big Bear Ark.* 108 Uttering a grunt as he rose from fastening our 'spring line,' [he] answered. **1876** [see Head Line 2]. (2) **1876** Knight 2291/1 *Spring-line,* in a ponton-bridge, a line passing diagonally from one ponton to another.

+**Spring mackerel.** (See quot. 1890.) — **1818** *Amer. Monthly Mag.* II. 296 Spring Mackerel. This elegant fish is migratory. **1842** *Nat. Hist. N.Y., Zoology* IV. 101 The Spring Mackerel . . . appear[s] on our coast in the months of May and June. **1890** *Cent.* 3561/3 *Spring mackerel,* the ordinary commercial mackerel of good size and quality, sometimes technically named *Scomber vernalis:* distinguished from *fall mackerel.*

+**Spring-poor,** a. Of cattle: Poor or lean in spring after a hard winter. *colloq.* — **1868** *Iowa State Agric. Soc. Rep. 1867* 128, I do not believe in turning them out on watery grass to shift for themselves 'spring poor.' **1877** *Vermont Bd. Agric. Rep.* IV. 93 Under such treatment the stock literally came to grass in the spring, 'spring poor.'

Spring seat. {1862} +A seat resting on springs at the ends and suited for use on a wagon box or frame. — **1835** A. Parker *Trip to Texas* 30 [We] took a wagon, without any spring seats. **1893** Holley *Samantha at World's Fair* 527 If I'd had my way I'd had a good spring seat fixed onto that chariot. **1925** Benefield *Chicken-Wagon Family* 21 His wife continued sitting on the spring-seat staring ahead of her.

Springtail. {1797–} +Variant of Sprigtail 1. — **1870** *Amer. Naturalist* IV. 49 Pintail Duck. . . . By some it is called Spring-tail. **1917** *Birds of Amer.* I. 128 Pintail. *Dafila acuta.* . . . Other Names.—Male: Sprig-tail; . . . Sprit-tail; Spring-tail.

+**Spring term. 1.** The session of a court held in the spring. **2.** The school term which begins in the spring. — (1) **1771** *Copley-Pelham Lett.* 139 The tryal . . . must go to the spring term. **1864** *Wkly. New Mexican* 24 June 2/2 The fines . . . during the past spring terms, amounted to Eleven hundred and Fifteen dollars. (2) **1854** [see Chip-day]. **1904** Waller *Wood-Carver* 90 She is going to the district school during the spring term.

+**Spring vise.** (See quot. 1876.) — **1861** *Army Regulations* 467, [I have] inspected and approved . . . thirty-two ball-screws, thirty-two spring vices. **1876** Knight 2292/1 *Spring-vise,* . . . a small vise used for confining the main-spring of a gun-lock when the lock is to be taken apart.

Spring wagon. A wagon the bed of which rests on springs. {1794–} — **1854** Bartlett *Personal Narr.* I. 4 Ambulances, or spring wagons, for the transportation of surveying and astronomical instruments, and other purposes. **1880** *Scribner's Mo.* April 834/1 He went over for several days in his spring wagon. **1925** Bryan *Memoirs* 38 A spring wagon would take us to the lake.

Spring wheat. Wheat sown in the spring. {1766–} Also attrib.

1791 in Imlay *Western Territory* (1797) 479 He sows a little spring wheat on new land. **1825** Lorain *Pract. Husbandry* 279, I had never seen spring wheat grown before the year 1815. **1890** *Rep. Secy. Agric. 1889* 220 The spring-wheat States have taken the lead in increase of hay in the Western States for beef-making and dairying in place of exclusive wheat growing. **1920** *Dept. Agric. Yrbk. 1919* 124 Winter wheat . . . yields better than spring wheat.

* **Sprinkle,** *n.*

1. A light rain; a shower of rain.

1768 Washington *Diaries* I. 259 Lowering with some sprinkles of Rain. **1772** *Md. Hist. Mag.* XIV. 281 We had a little sprinkle of Rain last night. **1871** Eggleston *Hoosier Schoolm.* 60 There came up a little shower, hardly more than a sprinkle.

+**2.** *Smart sprinkle,* a considerable number or quantity. *colloq.*

1836 *Jamestown (N.Y.) Jrnl.* 20 April 1/1 There's been a smart sprinkle of bears about the settlement all spring. **1841** *Ib.* 26 May 2/3 We have a smart sprinkle of book makers.

Sprinkle, *v.* **1.** *tr.* To besprinkle (the head of a person) with water as a form of baptism. **2.** *tr.* To dampen (clothes) preparatory to ironing them. Also absol. — (1) **1729** Comer *Diary* (1893) 77 She was sprinkled 4 or 5 days before. **1864** Nichols *Amer. Life* I. 82 Some are sprinkled by the Presbyterians, some dipped by the Baptists. **1898** E. C. Hall *Aunt Jane* 159, I was sprinkled in infancy, and I j'ined the Presbyterian church. (2) **1865** A. D. Whitney *Gayworthys* 82 Huldah had been sprinkling. **1866** Lowell *Biglow P.* 2 Ser. p. lxxix, She is sprinklin' clo'es Agin to-morrer's i'nin'.

✳ **Sprinkler.**

+**1.** A machine for spraying or irrigating cotton plants to destroy insects.

1879 *Rep. upon Cotton Insects* (Dept. Agric.) 251 Mr. William T. Robinson, of Huntsville, Tex., has invented a machine that combines a sprinkler and duster, so that dry or fluid poisons may be applied. **1882** *Century Mag.* Jan. 477/1 The automatic sprinkler and the rotary dust-blower . . . are the largest and most complete tools.

+**2.** (See quot. 1905.) Also attrib.

1893 *Scribner's Mag.* June 708/1 In freezing weather the sprinkler is run, and . . . [one sees] immense sleigh-loads of logs passing down the road. **1902** WHITE *Blazed Trail* 68 They are supposed to serve . . . a variety of lunches up to midnight for the sprinkler men. **1905** *Forestry Bureau. Bul.* No. 61, 49 *Sprinkler,* a large wooden tank from which water is sprinkled over logging roads during freezing weather in order to ice the surface, (N[orth] W[oods], L[ake] S[tates] Forest.) *Ib., Sprinkler sleds,* the sleds upon which the sprinkler is mounted.

✳ **Sprinkling.**

1. The besprinkling of the head with water, as a form of baptism, in contrast to immersion. {1726}

*a*1656 BRADFORD *Hist.* 457 Ther fell out some differance aboute baptising, he holding . . . that sprinkling was unlawfull. **1738** [see DIPPING 1]. **1848** DRAKE *Pioneer Life Ky.* 194 Infant baptism, and sprinkling instead of immersion, were held to be unscriptural.

+**2.** (*Right*) *smart sprinkling,* = SPRINKLE *n.* 2.

1845 *Bangor Mercury* (Th.), A smart sprinkling of the inhabitants of Illinois are from New England. **1851** *Polly Peablossom* 111, I heerd a snort, and a roar, and a growl, and a right smart sprinklin' of fast travelin'. **1883** 'S. BONNER' *Dialect Tales* 81 An' ther' wuz even a pretty smart sprinklin' o' town folks.

3. *attrib.* Designating various articles or devices used for sprinkling water.

1858 HOLMES *Autocrat* 30 [He saw] a very dusty street, . . . and a man driving a sprinkling-machine through it. **1867** RICHARDSON *Beyond Miss.* 21 Navigating the Missouri, at low water, is like putting a steamer upon dry land, and sending a boy ahead with a sprinkling pot. **1896** *Harper's Mag.* April 812/2 [He] got a job at driving a sprinkling-cart.

+**Sprit-tail.** *local.* = PINTAIL 1. — **1891** *Cent.* 5867/1. **1917** *Birds of Amer.* I. 128 Pintail. *Dafila acuta.* . . . [Also called] Peak-tail; Sharp-tail; Sprit-tail.

✳ **Sprout.**

+**1.** A branch or mouth of a river. In proper name. *Obs.*

1758 *Essex Inst. Coll.* XVIII. 99 We cou'd get no further than . . . about a mile below ye upper Mohaak Sprout. **1801** *Hist. Review & Directory* I. 247 The Mohawk River empties itself at several mouths, called the *Sprouts.*

+**2.** A variety of potato.

1869 *Rep. Comm. Agric. 1868* 240 Michigan White Sprouts.

+**3.** *To put through a course of sprouts,* to put through a severe or exhaustive course of training. *colloq.* Also transf.

1851 M. REID *Scalp-Hunters* ii, See that he be put through a 'regular course of sprouts.' **1869** BARNUM *Struggles* 409 'Putting Barnum through a course of sprouts' . . . meant an examination . . . compelling him to disclose everything with regard to his property. **1897** *Outing* XXIX. 484/1 He put . . . [the dogs] through a course of sprouts which ultimately developed brilliant though erratic working qualities.

+**4.** In special combinations.

Sprout flow, s. water, the first flow of water over a rice field after sowing. **1856** OLMSTED *Slave States* 471 This is termed the 'sprout flow,' and the water is left on the field until the seed sprouts. **1856** in Commons, etc. *Doc. Hist.* I. 143 He drew off his 'Sprout Water' too rapidly, prostrating his rice to the ground.

+**Sprouting crab grass.** (See quotations.) — **1884** VASEY *Agric. Grasses* 37 In the Southern States, . . . there occurs a variety of this grass, called *Panicum proliferum,* var. *geniculatum,* or sprouting crab grass. **1909** *Cent. Suppl.* 309/2 *Sprouting crab-grass* . . . is liked by cattle but is hardly worthy of cultivation.

+**Sprouting hoe.** (See quot. 1800.) — **1800** TATHAM *Tobacco* 12 The sprouting hoe . . . is a smaller species of mattock that serves to break up any particular hard part of the ground. **1810** *Austin P.* I. (1924) 168. **1864** *Maine Agric. Soc. Returns 1863* 159 After the beds are thus burnt, . . . they are dug up with a common sprouting hoe.

+**Sprout land.** (See quot. 1874.) — *a*1862 THOREAU *Excursions* 230 In 'sprout-lands' they [*sc.* maples] seem to vie with one another. **1874** *Vermont Bd. Agric. Rep.* II. 493 In Massachusetts the 'sprout lands' . . . are those which have once been cultivated, but which have since been covered with trees in a natural way from roots remaining in the soil and from seed sown by the winds.

✳ **Spruce.**

1. A handsome, coniferous, evergreen tree or species of tree of the genus *Picea* or related genera. {1670–} Also collective.

See also BLACK SPRUCE, BLUE SPRUCE, etc.

1630 HIGGINSON *New-England* 7 There is also good . . . Spruce, Pines and Firre. **1665** *Plymouth Rec.* I. 81, [I did] lay out the same [a 50-acre

tract] begining att a smale spruce. **1751** BARTRAM *Observations* 27 We left it . . . to go up a hill covered with spruce. **1821** NUTTALL *Travels Arkansa* 13 The valley of the river is . . . rudely decorated with clumps of sombre evergreens, particularly the tall Weymouth pine and spruce. **1883** ZEIGLER & GROSSCUP *Alleghanies* 232 Tall conical firs, delicately tapering spruces interlocked their weeping branches. **1902** WHITE *Blazed Trail* 119 The young man had passed through a preliminary jungle of birch, cedar, spruce, and hemlock.

2. The wood or lumber of the spruce. {1853–}

1761 NILES *Indian Wars* II. 447 Mr. Haiselup . . . went up with his boat into the basin for a load of spruce. **1882** *Nation* 3 Aug. 87/3 Five-sixths of all the lumber manufactured in the State [of Maine] is spruce. **1897** F. C. MOORE *How to Build a Home* 21 Either spruce or hemlock makes fairly good floor-beams.

3. *attrib.* and *comb.* Designating the tree or parts of the tree used for various purposes.

*c*1618 *Mass. H. S. Coll.* 4 Ser. I. 241 These islands are all overgrowne with woods, as oak, walnutt, pine, spruce trees, hasell nutts, . . . and hurts in abundaunce. **1640** *New Haven Col. Rec.* 48 If any shall cutt a tree without leave where the spruce masts grow. **1784** CUTLER in *Life & Corr.* I. 101 Our ax-men . . . built us a very comfortable tent with spruce bark. **1792** BELKNAP *Hist. New-Hampshire* III. 265 In some of the new towns a liquor is made of spruce twigs, boiled in maple sap. **1828** SHERBURNE *Memoirs* 52, [I] broke off my arms full of fir and spruce boughs for my bed. *a*1862 THOREAU *Maine Woods* 193 Our Indian . . . used black spruce-roots to sew canoes with. **1873** ALDRICH *Marjorie Daw* 21 You know the kind of parlors in farmhouses on the coast, . . . [with] spruce branches in the chimney-place. **1892** HOWELLS *Quality of Mercy* 390 She possessed herself of the cushion, stuffed with spruce sprays.

+**4.** Designating places or regions where spruce prevails.

See also SPRUCE SWAMP.

1661 *Rowley Rec.* 115 All the meadow Commonly Called the Spruce meadow. **1759** ROGERS *Journals* 153 The water most of the way [was] near a foot deep, it being a spruce bog. **1817–8** EATON *Botany* (1822) 339 Lily orchis . . . grows from 4 to 6 inches high in the spruce woods on Catskill mountain. **1880** *Harper's Mag.* Aug. 344/2 There was . . . a rude timber assembly hall . . . erected in a spruce grove.

5. Designating things made or consisting of spruce.

1715 *Boston News-Letter* 29 Aug. 2/2 Good Spruce Ladders to be Sold . . . at five pence a Round. **1796** *Ann. 4th Congress* 2 Sess. 2701, 88 1-2 inches spruce spars, at 8 cents [were sold]. **1855** *Amer. Inst. N.Y. Trans. 1854* 394 He would lay a tight matched spruce floor. **1872** Spruce tubs [see BLACK ASH 2]. **1880** *Harper's Mag.* Aug. 398/2 The practiced hand, however, may work out the subtleties of the boat-builder's art in canvas and spruce strips. **1919** HOUGH *Sagebrusher* 99 He reached down silently to the stout spruce stick.

+**6.** In the names of animals and birds found in spruce forests.

See also SPRUCE GROUSE, SPRUCE PARTRIDGE.

1877 CAMPION *On Frontier* 131 [Of] 'spruce deer,' . . . a few small bands ranged high up the mountains. **1900** WEBSTER *Suppl.* 199/2 *Spruce bird,* . . . the white-winged crossbill (*Soxia leucoptera*). **1902** HULBERT *Forest Neighbors* 87 Spruce hens and partridges were scarce. **1917** *Birds of Amer.* III. 194 Winter Wren. . . . [Also called] Spruce Wren.

+**7.** In the names of insects injurious to spruce trees.

Cf. SPRUCE-BUD WORM.

1884 *Rep. Comm. Agric.* 374 My object . . . was to ascertain whether the spruce-bud tortrix . . . was concerned in the widespread destruction of spruce and fir. **1891** *Cent.* 5868/1 *Spruce bud-louse. Ib., Spruce cone-worm. Ib., Spruce leaf-hopper. Ib., Spruce plume-moth. Ib., Spruce saw-fly. Ib., Spruce timber-beetle.* **1900** WEBSTER *Suppl.* 199/2 *Spruce-borer,* . . . any one of several species of beetles, esp.: (*a*) A bark ambrosia beetle [etc.].

+**8.** In special combinations.

Spruce stumpage, spruce timber as it stands in the forest; *s. syrup,* a syrup in the making of which the leaves and branches of spruce are used; *s. wine,* (see quotation). **1896** *Vt. Agric. Rep.* XV. 83 Ten years of prolonged life may double the value of spruce stumpage. **1848** *Santa Fe Republican* 8 Aug. 1/2 All kinds of Groceries, Spruce and lemon syrrup. **1820** *Amer. Farmer* I. 335 Spruce Wine . . . is only a superior sort of white spruce beer.

✳**Spruce beer.** A beer made by boiling the leaves and small branches of spruce fir with sugar and molasses. {1706–} Also attrib. — **1766** STORK *Acct. E. Fla.* 44 The spruce fir here is quite a different tree from that to the northward, but answers the same end for making the spruce beer. **1814** PURSH *Flora Amer.* II. 640 The Black Spruce or Double Spruce is . . . the tree of which that wholesome beverage called Spruce Beer is made. **1865** WEED *Autobiog.* 6 The gingerbread and spruce-beer house . . . was kept quite at the upper end of the village. **1899** JEWETT *Queen's Twin* 45 The spruce-beer bottle was not yet in the well.

+**Spruce-bud worm.** (See quot. 1891.) — **1884** *Rep. Comm. Agric.* 378 The Reddish-Yellow Spruce-Bud Worm . . . was found to be very injurious to the white spruce. **1891** *Cent.* 5868/1 *Spruce bud-worm,* the larva of a tortricid moth, as *Tortrix fumiferana,* which eats the end-buds of the spruce in northeastern parts of the United States, especially in Maine.

+**Spruce duff.** (See quotations.) — **1878** *Pop. Science Mo.* XIII. 289 What is known among the woodsmen of Northern New York as 'spruce-duff' . . . is composed of rotten spruce-trees, cones, needles, etc. **1885**

Outing VII. 62/1 This forest-mould is composed of partially decayed leaves, logs, bark, cones and needles, and is spoken of generally as 'spruce duff' because found in greater quantities among the spruce trees.

+Spruce grouse. A grouse (*Canachites canadensis* or a related species) that frequents forests in the northern part of the United States. (See also FRANKLIN'S (SPRUCE) GROUSE.) — **1844** *Nat. Hist. N.Y., Zoology* II. 206 The Spruce Grouse. . . . The flesh . . . has a peculiar taste as if boiled in turpentine. **1888** ROOSEVELT in *Century Mag.* June 210/1 There were many grouse in the woods, of three kinds,—blue, spruce, and ruffed. **1893** — *Wilderness Hunter* 116 We stumbled across a family of spruce grouse.

+Spruce gum. The resinous exudation from a spruce tree or a balsam fir, used chiefly as chewing gum. — **1836** *Public Ledger* (Phila.) 21 May (Th.), The down east girls . . . [amuse] themselves . . . by chewing spruce gum. **1869** *Rep. Comm. Agric. 1868* 176 The seams [are] calked with spruce gum. **1897** *Outing* XXX. 584/2 We gathered and stored large bottles of spruce-gum for the small boys at home. **1907** *St. Nicholas* June 678/1 The little knicknack shop around the corner [sells] picture papers, spruce gum, needles and Malaga raisins.

Spruce partridge. (See quot. 1917.) {1744–, in Canada} — **1834** AUDUBON *Ornith. Biog.* II. 417 Those retired woods where the Spruce Partridges were to be found. **1844** [see CANADA GROUSE]. **1858** BAIRD *Birds Pacific R.R.* 622 Spruce Partridge. . . . Spruce forests and swamps of the Northern United States. **1895** *Outing* XXVII. 218/1 The spruce partridge abounds here. **1917** *Birds of Amer.* II. 15/1 There is no such bird as the Spruce Partridge. It is the Spruce Grouse (*Canachites canadensis*); but it is called Spruce Partridge in common parlance, to distinguish it from the Birch Partridge (Ruffed Grouse).

+Spruce pine. a. The bog spruce (*Picea mariana*) of the northeastern states. **b.** Any one of various American pines or hemlocks having light, soft wood.

1684 I. MATHER *Providences* (1856) x. 223 Passing through a thick swamp of spruce pine . . . , [the wind] laid all flat to the ground. **1743** [see FIR]. **1794** DENNY *Journal* 201 The timber [is] hemlock or spruce pine, and beech. **1805** LEWIS in *L. & Clark Exped.* II. (1904) 64 Some spruce pine of small size appears among the pitch pine. **1883** SMITH *Geol. Survey Ala.* 255 With it [beech] are associated . . . numerous spruce or swamp pines (*P. glabra*), and a few short-leaf pines. **1905** *Forestry Bureau Bul.* No. 60, 10 The hemlock (locally known as spruce pine) is its characteristic tree. *attrib.* **1886** *Outing* VIII. 60/2 One morning I entered a clump of bushes near a spruce-pine thicket.

+Spruce swamp. A swamp in which spruce is the prevailing growth. — **1652** *Essex Inst. Coll.* V. 266/2 Granted to James Standish the little spruce swamp lying neare his house. **1675** *Mass. H. S. Coll.* 4 Ser. VI. 308 [They] rested by the side of a spruce swampe. **1717** *Providence Rec.* XVI. 135, I give and bequeathe to my son Edward . . . a tract of Land . . . [bounded] on the west by . . . the spruce swamp. **1775** *Mass. H. S. Proc.* 2 Ser. II. 279 We Cross'd the pond and Came to . . . a Spruce Swamp Knee deep in mire.

*Sprung, a.

1. a. The worse for drink; tipsy. {1882–, *dial.*} **+b.** Slightly unbalanced mentally; crazy.

1833 A. GREENE *Life D. Duckworth* II. 176 He was seldom downright drunk; but was often all-firedly sprung. *a*1851 in Hall *College Words* 291 Many swallows make the fast man sprung. **1874** PINKERTON *Expressman & Detective* 168 Rivers is a little 'sprung' today. **1883** JEWETT *Mate of 'Daylight'* 143, I've sometimes thought he was a little sprung.

+2. = KNEE-SPRUNG *a.*

*a*1846 *Quarter Race Ky.* 96 'Chest foundered' and hairless, And 'sprung' though she be, She's . . . A good 'un to me. **1902** McFAUL *Ike Glidden* 138 He usually drove an old mare, blind of one eye, sprung in both forward legs.

Sprunt, v. {1601–} **+**To *sprunt up*, 'to bristle up; show sudden resentment' (*Cent.*). *colloq.*

*Spud.

+1. (See quotations.)

1871 *Amer. Inst. Mining Engineers Trans.* I. 378 A spud, as it is called, that is, a nail resembling a horseshoe nail with a hole in the head, is driven into the timbers. **1876** KNIGHT 2292/2 *Spud*, a spade-shaped implement, used in fishing for broken tools in a well. **1905** *Forestry Bureau Bul.* No. 61, 49 *Spud*, a tool for removing bark.

+2. *Archaeology.* A polished stone implement with a broad blade and a handle, formerly used by the Indians.

1896 *Rep. Bureau Amer. Ethnol. 1891–2* 109 The peculiar stones called 'spuds' . . . are usually of a comparatively soft material, carefully worked and polished. **1909** *Cent. Suppl.* 1259/3.

+Spudge, v. To *spudge up. colloq.* **1.** *tr.* To pay or fork over (money). **2.** *intr.* To brace up. — (1) *a*1855 J. F. KELLY *Humors* 386 The trio 'spudged up' the amount. (2) **1881** JEWETT *Country By-Ways* 49, I've wondered sometimes, myself, he didn't spudge up and be somebody. **1886** — *White Heron* 104, I'll spudge up and take right holt.

*Spunk. +To get (one's) *spunk up*, or variant: To become angry or to take courage. *colloq.* — **1834** *Jamestown* (N.Y.) *Jrnl.* 24 Dec. 3/1 My spunk is getting up a leetle about it. **1856** M. THOMPSON *Pluri-bus-tah* 147 How a Woman got her spunk up and left the country. **1873** *New-*

ton Kansan 27 Feb. 2/1 Philadelphia has got its spunk up. **1912** N. WOOD-ROW *Sally Salt* 38, I got my spunk up, and I says [etc.].

Spunk up, v. {1898, *Sc.*} *colloq.*

+1. *intr.* To pluck up courage or show one's spirit.

1840 HOFFMAN *Greyslaer* I. 61, I began to think that all sorts of luck hadn't left me, and I spunked up and looked about. **1892** *Harper's Mag.* Dec. 119 Then I spunked up. **1898** WESTCOTT *D. Harum* 202 An' then he spunked up some an' says, 'I don't give a darn.' **1906** *Springfield W. Repub.* 19 July 1 Congressman Sullivan has spunked up against Moran's plan for placing a mortgage on the democratic nomination for governor.

‖2. To make love *to* someone. (Cf. SPARK V. 1.)

*c*1849 NEAL *Beedle's Sleigh Ride* 21, I was spunking up to Sally Jones like all vengeance.

+3. *tr.* To encourage (someone) to a show of spirit.

1889 COOKE *Steadfast* 395 You stan' by the parson and spunk him up.

+4. To kindle or increase the intensity of (a fire).

1881 COOKE *Somebody's Neighbors* 264 He'd spunked up a fire. **1889** — *Steadfast* 124 [She was] puttin' on them cedar branches so's to spunk up the fire.

+Spunk water. Rain water that collects in cavities in stumps, used as a folk remedy in removing warts. Also attrib. — **1876** 'MARK TWAIN' *Tom Sawyer* 65 You got to go . . . to the middle of the woods, where you know there's a spunk-water stump. *Ib.*, Spunk-water, spunk-water, swaller these warts.

+Spun tobacco. Tobacco leaves rolled or spun into a cylindrical twist. — **1706** *Boston News-Letter* 14 Jan. 2/2 [There] will be exposed to Sale . . . twenty nine half Barrels of Leaf, and 40 Rolls of Spun Tobacco. **1748** *New Eng. Hist. & Gen. Reg.* IV. 176 She continues to sell the best Virginia Tobacco, Cut, Pigtail and spun, of all Sorts. **1803** *Lewis & Clark Exped.* VII. (1905) 235 Indian Presents [include]: . . . 50 lbs. Spun Tobacco.

+Spun truck. Spun thread or yarn. *colloq.* — **1851** HOOPER *Widow Rugby* 72 Jim Bell . . . had visited town, for the purpose of buying two bunches 'of No. 8, spun truck.' **1884** 'CRADDOCK' *Tenn. Mts.* 55 Her little all [included] . . . a few chickens, some 'spun-truck.' **1898** HARRIS *Tales of Home Folks* 367 She had gone to town with butter and eggs to exchange for some factory thread—'spun truck' Mrs. Pruett called it.

*Spur, n.

*1. A small device used on the heel of a rider for pricking the sides of a horse.

1654 *Essex Probate Rec.* I. 180 Sisers, spures, knife and Brasse wyer. **1715** *Boston News-Letter* 5 Dec. 2/2 English Boots half Jack and small, Tops and Spurs, . . . to be sold on reasonable Terms. **1822** *Ann. 17th Congress* 1 Sess. 324 Saddles, bridles, candle-wick, spurs, . . . [were] bought at Georgetown, at high prices. **1914** 'BOWER' *Flying U Ranch* 11 The bands of his spurs were . . . inlaid to the edge with beaten silver.

2. An offshoot of a mountain or range of mountains extending for some distance from the main mass or system. {1652–}

1737 in *Amer. Speech* XV. 397/1 In all eight hundred and twenty Poles to two white Oaks on a Spur of a Mountain. **1788** MAY *Jrnl. & Lett.* 27 A number of large hills (spurs, some call them). **1808** in *Niles' Reg.* XV. 49/2 Canals parallel to our mountains must necessarily cross the ridge or spur of the mountain which divides the waters of two primary rivers. **1873** MILLER *Amongst Modocs* 204 Paquita knew every dimple, bend or spur in these mountains now. *a*1918 G. STUART *On Frontier* I. 81 The mines were all deep gravel channels . . . on the mountain spurs and ridges.

b. An offshoot of a plain, plateau, body of timber, or mining lode. {1852–}

1851 M. REID *Scalp Hunters* xxxii, A spur of willows running out from the timber indicated the presence of water. **1852** MARCY *Explor. Red River* (1854) 122 The road crosses the southern spur of this plain. **1854** BARTLETT *Personal Narr.* I. 275 On a spur of the plateau, stood the village. **1860** GREELEY *Overland Journey* 21 Now belts and spurs of timber were seen. **1861** *Harper's Mag.* Jan. 161/2 The Comstock Lode was in a mass of confusion, . . . every body's spurs were running into every body else's angles.

+3. A hard, bony process at the end of a horn snake's tail. *Obs.* Also attrib.

1789 *Amer. Philos. Soc.* III. p. xxiii, The spur of his tail is so venemous, as to kill young trees. **1791** [see HORN SNAKE]. **1793** *Mass. H. S. Coll.* 1 Ser. III. 86 The jointed and spur snakes are sometimes met with.

4. A railroad that branches off from a main track or system. {spur of line, 1878} Also attrib.

1884 *Boston Jrnl.* 13 Sept., The Selectmen of Peabody have reserved their decision as to the location of a spur track from the Eastern Railroad freight yard. **1898** HAMBLEN *Gen. Manager's Story* 180 There was a way freight engine lying in a spur back of the station. **1923** J. H. COOK *On Old Frontier* 93 A spur of the road was built from Stringtown to the mines.

*Spur, v. +*Mining. tr.* To run into (an adjoining claim) with a spur or spurs. — **1861** *Harper's Mag.* Jan. 161/2 The Cedar Mill Company were spurring the Miller Company; the Virginia Ledge was spurring the Continuation; . . . and so on.

***Spurge.** One of various species of the genus *Euphorbia* or of several related genera. Freq. with specifying terms.

1791 MUHLENBERG *Index Florae* 170. 1817-8 EATON *Botany* (1822) 279. 1843 TORREY *Flora N.Y.* II. *Euphorbia corollata*, . . . is a favorite medicine among the western Indians. 1857 GRAY *Botany* 387 *E. maculata*. (Spotted Spurge.) . . . Gravelly open places, everywhere. *a*1862 THOREAU *Cape Cod* 101 The plants which I noticed here and there on the pure sandy shelf . . . were Sea Rocket, . . . Seaside Spurge [etc.]. 1891 *Cent.* 5870/2 *Ipecac-spurge, ipecacuanha-spurge.* . . . The root has an active emetic and purgative property.

+**Spurge nettle.** The tread-softly, a stinging weed (*Cnidoscolus stimulosus*). — 1847 DARLINGTON *Weeds & Plants* 289. 1901 MOHR *Plant Life Ala.* 594.

Spyglass. A small telescope or field glass. {1706-} — 1790 *Penna. Packet* 8 May 4/4 Thomas Seddon . . . has for Sale . . . Telescopes and spy glasses. 1806 LEWIS in *L. & Clark Exped.* V. (1905) 219, I halted and used my spye glass. 1840 OLMSTED *Lett. Astronomy* 376 A common spyglass will serve to give a distinct view. 1907 *St. Nicholas* July 849/1 Taking out a spy-glass we found that she was feeding the young robins.

Squab. {1640-} A young pigeon. {1694-} — 1831 AUDUBON *Ornith. Biog.* I. 326 The young Pigeons, or *squabs* as they are named, are violently hurried to the ground. 1850 S. F. COOPER *Rural Hours* 18 The young [pigeons], or squabs, as they are called, are in great request as a delicacy in spring. 1866 MOORE *Women of War* 155 [He] soon could take . . . a little broiled squab. 1885 *Weekly Sun* (N.Y.) 13 May 6/6 Capons and squabs are scarce.

‖**Squabblification.** A squabble; a quarrel. — 1837 BIRD *Nick* I. 218 You war in a squabblification!

Squad.

1. *Mil.* A small number of soldiers organized as a unit for drill or for some assigned duty {1649-}; a number of policemen assigned to a given task. (See also AWKWARD SQUAD.)

In the United States Army the squad is the basic unit in the infantry. 1757 WASHINGTON *Writings* I. 468 Divide your men into as many squads as there are Sergeants. 1804 *Lewis & Clark Exped.* I. (1904) 13 Each squad shall be devided into two Messes. 1861 *Army Regulations* 21 The captain will cause the men of the company to be . . . divided into four squads, each to be put under the charge of a non-commissioned officer. 1863 Moore *Rebellion Rec.* V. I. 70 The street was quite blockaded, when a squad of police appeared and the bulletin was removed. 1899 *Boston Transcript* 21 Aug. 10/6 A complete fantan layout and dominoes, cards, chips and dice cup were seized by the liquor squad in a raid. *attrib.* and *transf.* 1862 STRONG *Cadet Life W. Point* 115 Tom, Harry, and myself . . . just returned from the eleven, A.M., squad-drill.

b. *spec.* A band of guerrillas.

1835 SIMMS *Partisan* 14 Here and there only did some little partisan squad make a stand. 1855 — *Forayers* 209 The squad of St. Julien, after awhile, fell in with the wounded outlaw. 1865 TROWBRIDGE *Three Scouts* 23 It's only a little squad of guerillas.

+**2.** A number of persons working together in some athletic sport.

1903 *N.Y. Ev. Post* 7 Sept., The Yale football squad is expected to arrive at New Haven on Sept. 13. 1903 *N.Y. Times* 26 Sept. 7 Candidates for the rowing squad at Yale reported at the gymnasium this afternoon.

***Squadrant.** += SQUADRON 2. — 1665 *Groton Rec.* 14 Sergent James Parker Jam Knop and William Leaken were chosen . . . to determen the seuerall Squadrants and hom shall worke at each squadron succesiuly. 1707 *Cambridge Prop. Rec.* 255 The first Lott in ye Sixth Squadrant was layd out.

***Squadron.**

***1.** A body or detachment of men, esp. a subdivision of a cavalry regiment. {1702-} Also attrib.

1624 [see GENERAL MUSTER]. 1647 *New Haven Col. Rec.* 318 Thomas Lampson absent from one squadron trayninge. 1792 *Ann. 2d Congress* 80 There shall be raised a squadron of light dragoons. 1846 *Whig Almanac 1847* 20/1 Curtained by two squadrons in advance, [the army] moved steadily forward. 1862 Moore *Rebellion Rec.* V. II. 589 An hour before daylight a squadron of the brave Col. Allen's First Maine cavalry charged up the railroad. 1898 in R. A. Alger *Spanish-Amer. War* 93 The squadron of the 2d Cavalry . . . will be unloaded after the mounted squadron.

+**2. a.** A division of town land. **b.** A part of a town set apart as a unit for highway care; a school district.

See also SQUADRANT.

1653 *New Haven Rec.* I. 188 They will in the seuerall squadrons in their turnes worke at the makeing the damm. 1658 *Watertown Rec.* I. 1. The first lott shall begin at the north Squadron. 1665 [see SQUADRANT]. 1683 *Suffield Doc. Hist.* 100 All the Highwayes belonging to the Towne . . . should be divided into four squaderns. 1689 *Cambridge Prop. Rec.* 166 Each Squadron [shall] be so proportioned as that lots may not exceed four score Rods in length. 1724 *Ib.* 294 Voted that Andrew Bordman have his Rights Laid out to him on ye Northerly Side of ye Third Squadron on ye Lower Common. 1749 *Marlborough Rec.* (*Cent.*), Voted and chose a committee of seven men to apportion the school in six societies or squadrons, . . . taking the northwesterly corner for one squadron.

***3.** A part of a fleet; a detachment of warships.

1705 *Boston News-Letter* 14 May 2/1 We expect a Squadron of Men of War towards the Fall. 1780 *Heath P.* III. 87 The wind blowing fresh into the harbour prevented any part of . . . Ternay's squadron giting out. 1813 *Niles' Reg.* V. 280 A few days ago . . . it was believed at New-London, Decatur's squadron would put to sea during the night. 1861 *Chicago Tribune* 19 July 1/2 The Atlantic blockading squadron . . . consists of twenty-two vessels. 1899 J. R. SPEARS *Hist. Navy* V. 455 On July 10th, our squadron bombarded the city of Santiago. 1918 *Current Opinion* Oct. 222/3 Rear-Admiral Niblack is in command of Squadron Two of the American Patrol Fleet.

Squail. (See quot. 1889.) — 1859 MATSELL *Vocabulum* 85. 1889 FARMER 510/1 *Squail* (Cant), a drink.

Squall. {1719-} ‖A bad temper. — 1807 IRVING, etc. *Salmagundi* vi, The old gentleman came home in quite a squall; kicked poor Caesar the mastiff out of his way [etc.].

Squally, *a.* {1719-}

+**1.** *fig.* Threatening; dangerous; fearful; difficult. {1876} Often in phrase *to look squally.*

1814 IRVING in P. M. IRVING *Life W. Irving* I. (1862) 315 Affairs, I am afraid, are about to look squally on our Canadian frontier. 1834 C. A. DAVIS *Lett. J. Downing* 95 The times are now gittin pretty squally. 1873 BEADLE *Undevel. West* 339 Matters look squally here. 1896 HARRIS *Sister Jane* 262, Times were squally, I can tell you.

+**Squam.** [Anni*squam*, Mass., a fishing village.] (See quotation.) — 1891 *Cent.* 5874/2 *Squam*, . . . an oilskin hat worn originally by fishermen and deep-water sailors; a cheap yellow sou'wester.

+**Squam duck.** *local.* The eider duck. — 1844 GIRAUD *Birds of L.I.* 332 Eider Duck. . . . This species, so celebrated for the superior quality of its down, . . . is called 'Squam Duck.' 1917 *Birds of Amer.* I. 146.

+**Squanter-squash.** Also **isquouter-, squontersquash.** [Amer. Indian. Cf. *askútasquash,* s.v. SQUASH[1] 1.] = SQUASH[1] 1. *Obs.* — 1634 WOOD *New Eng. Prospect* 15 Muskmillions, Isquouterquashes, . . . and whatsoever growes well in England, growes as well there. *Ib.* 76 In Summer, when their [*sc.* the Indians'] corne is spent, Isquoutersquashes is their best bread, a fruite like a young Pumpion. 1672 JOSSELYN *New Eng. Rarities* 57 Squashes, but more truly Squontersquashes, a kind of Mellon, or rather Gourd. 1705 BEVERLEY *Virginia* II. 27 Squash, or Squanter-Squash, is their Name among the Northern Indians, and so they are call'd in New-York, and New-England.

+**Squantum.**[1] [See note.] Among the Indians of New England: A spirit: (see quotations).

'This name explains itself by the verb *musquantam* (he is angry,) and by Roger Williams's remark, ''They (the Narragansett Indians) will say, when an ordinary accident, as a fall, has occurred to somebody: *musquantam mánit* (God was angry and did it)'' ' (A. S. Gatschet in *Amer. Folk-Lore* XII. 211).

1630 HIGGINSON *New-England* 20 Their evill God whom they feare will doe them hurt, they call Squantum. 1654 JOHNSON *Wonder-w. Prov.* 226 Squantam is a bad Divel, and Abbamocho is their good Divell. 1674 JOSSELYN *Two Voyages* 132 They acknowledge a God who they call *Squantam,* but worship him they do not, because (they say) he will do them no harm.

+**Squantum.**[2] [*Squantum,* Mass.; see also quot. 1832.]

1. A name given to an annual celebration held near Boston, which includes ceremonies resembling Indian practices and the eating of sea food. Now hist. Also attrib.

1812 *Boston Gazette* 24 Aug. (Th.), The Squantum Celebration will be this day. . . . The antient celebrators of the Squantum Feast will be honored with the presence of . . . Caleb Strong and William Phillips. 1817 *Mass. Spy* 6 Aug. (Th.), An annual festival observed in the neighbourhood of Boston . . . is called the Feast of Squantum. 1832 GOODRICH *Syst. Universal Geog.* 106n., The feast of *Squantum* is held annually on the shore to the E. of Neponset Bridge, at a rocky point projecting into Boston Bay. . . . Squantum was the name of the last Indian female who resided there.

2. *local.* (See quots. 1883, 1902.)

The relationship of this sense to that preceding is not clear; it may be of independent origin.

1855 H. A. WISE *Tales for Marines* 21, I wish to all fired smash I was . . . hazin' round with Charity Bunker and the rest o' the gals at a squantum. 1882 GODFREY *Nantucket* 301 To visit Nantucket and not 'go on a Squantum' would be just as culpable [etc.]. 1883 in *Amer. Folk-Lore* XV. 259 The Squantum is a peculiar institution of this island (Nantucket), being an informal picnic on the beach-sands, where the dinner is made of fish and other spoils of the sea. 1902 *Ib.,* *Squántum,* a word still in use in Nantucket and some other parts of New England in the sense of 'a good time,' 'merry-making,' 'picnic party,' also 'a high old time.'

***Square,** *n.*[1]

1. In a town or city, an open area surrounded by buildings, as a park or a space formed by the intersection of streets. Often in proper names. {1687-}

See also COURTHOUSE SQUARE, PUBLIC SQUARE.

1698 THOMAS *Pensilvania* 5 There are also besides these Alleys and Lanes, several fine Squares and Courts within this Magnificent City [of Phila.]. 1759 FRANKLIN *Hist. Review Penna.* 433 The old Proprietor . . .

laid out five large Squares, one in each Quarter. **1781** [see BUTTON TREE 1]. **1859** BARTLETT 440 *Square.* In the city of New York this term is applied to the open spaces caused by the junction of several streets. 'Chatham square' and 'Franklin square' are triangles! **1924** CROY *R.F.D. No. 3* 1 There had been hitch racks around the Square, where the farmers tied their horses and mules.

+b. A central open area in an Indian town, used for public observances; also, the town itself or the inhabitants: (see quot. 1800).

1742 in *Travels Amer. Col.* 221 The Indians went into the Square to Dance. **1765** TIMBERLAKE *Memoirs* 65 [Among the Cherokees] the green corn dance . . . [is] performed in a very solemn manner, in a large square before the town-house door. **1800** HAWKINS *Sk. Creek Country* 53 The chiefs send out the women, and make them fish for the *square.* This expression includes all the chiefs and warriors of the town. **1840** IRVING in *Knickerb.* XVI. 345 At each corner of the square, there was an interval between the houses, for ingress and egress. **1907** HODGE, etc. *Amer. Indians* I. 364/1 The number [is not known] of their [*sc.* the Creeks'] towns (having a square for annual festivities) and villages (having no square).

+2. In a city, the area bounded by four streets; a block; also, on a street, the distance between one corner and the next.

1776 JEFFERSON *Writings* II. (1893) 106 Six whole squares of ground . . . shall be appropriated to the use & purpose of public buildings. **1784** *Maryland Jrnl.* 19 Oct. (Th.), Nine or ten lamps will abundantly lighten every square [in Baltimore]. **1827** in Commons, etc. *Doc. Hist.* IV. 127, I was going to take a walk a square or two. **1840** *Picayune* 9 Aug. 3/1 Comfortable rooms . . . only two squares above St. Mary market and the Levee. **1862** *Congress. Globe* 1 April 1483/2 These horse railroads carry passengers only a few squares as a general thing. **1923** WATTS *L. Nichols* 354 This machine . . . musta been th' len'th of four-five city squares off.

+3. The flower of the cotton plant with the three bracts enclosing it regarded as a unit. Also comb.

1842 in Bassett *Plantation Overseer* 163, I have cotten squairs too and three on a stalk. **1883** [see FORM *n.* 2]. **1906** HILGARD *Soils* 503 The writer found a 'patch' of cotton . . . almost devoid of 'squares' or 'blooms.' **1906** *Westminster Gaz.* 19 Dec. 2/1 The devastation caused by . . . the cotton aphis, the web-worm, and the square-borer.

+4. *Printing.* (See quot. 1876.)

1870 *Republican Rev.* 4 June 3/4 Advertisements will be published at the following rates, a *square* being equal to the space of one inch or ten lines of this letter. **1876** KNIGHT 2293/2 *Square,* . . . a certain number of lines in a column, of nearly equal height and width. **1877** *Harper's Mag.* Dec. 111/1 These newspaper people set an extraordinary value on their squares, as they call them.

+5. *Mining.* A sample of ore.

1885 *Wkly. New Mexican Rev.* 19 Feb. 4/1 The squares 3 x 5 inches . . . are sufficient to convince anybody that he has struck a bonanza.

Square, *n.*² +'Used colloquially for Squire' (Th.). Cf. SQUIRE *n.* — **1844** *Lowell Offering* IV. 52 The square will make you suffer for it. **1857** HOLLAND *Bay-Path* 65 Well, Square, I aint *guilty* of anything, as I know of. **1867** LOWELL in *Atlantic Mo.* Jan. 22 Wal, Square, I guess so.

* Square, *a.*

1. Open; direct. {1896}

1804 CUTLER in *Life & Corr.* II. 162 It was . . . a square fight between the all-important head man of the party and another who ranks as his second. **1873** HALE *In His Name* vi, [He] could not answer the square question put to him. **1892** *Congress. Rec.* 30 June 5658/2 This American Congress is here [to compose difficulties], if not by compromise, then by the square defeat of somebody and the honorable submission of the other side. **1917** MCCUTCHEON *Green Fancy* 19, I want to get a good square peep at a man who . . . is boob enough to come to this gosh-awful place.

+2. Full; complete. (See also SQUARE MEAL.)

1836 *Public Ledger* (Phila.) 25 March 1/1 [A subscription for] 1 square year, $20.00. **1854** *Congress. Globe* 19 May 1231/2 He has . . . a good square quarter of a century yet to devote to the welfare of his country. **1872** BAILEY *Folks in Danbury* 37 (Th.), I don't think she done a square day's work in two years. **1875** *Congress. Rec.* 20 March 107/1 Make it till half past five; that will make square hours.

+3. Of a horse's gait: Steady; even. Hence *square-gaited, square-pacer, square-trotter.*

1832 VIGNE *6 Mos. in Amer.* II. 8 The horse . . . is valuable according to his performances as a square or natural trotter, a pacer, or a racker. **1849** NASON *Journal* 52 There are what we call 'rackers,' and not square trotters. **1868** WOODRUFF *Trotting Horse* 79 He was a square-gaited horse as a trotter. *Ib.* 81 When a pacer is got to a square trot, he is to be kept at it by the nicest kind of handling. **1886** ROE *Army Lett.* 345 He is what we call a square pacer. **1907** WHITE *Arizona Nights* 294 Dimly could be seen the horses, their flanks swinging steadily in the square trot.

4. In special combinations.

+*Square feed,* substantial food; *squarehead,* a Scandinavian (*colloq.*; 'U.S. and Colonial' *O.E.D.*); +*s.-nut hickory,* =MOCKERNUT; *s. steel,* ? = GERMAN STEEL.

1873 BEADLE *Undevel. West* 708, [I] never tasted tea, coffee, flour-bread, meat or any one of the things we consider 'square feed' in Indiana. **1913** LONDON *Valley of Moon* 168, I'd like most to death to have just one go at

that squarehead Hansen. **1875** EMERSON *Trees & Shrubs Mass.* I. 222 The Mockernut Hickory . . . is also known by the name of the square-nut hickory. **1744** *Md. Hist. Mag.* XXI. 244, 3 ffaggotts German or Square Steel.

* Square, *v.*

1. *tr.* To pay (a bill); to meet (an obligation). {to square up, 1862-}

1821 QUITMAN in Claiborne *Life Quitman* I. 69, I paid my $25, squared my bill, and departed. **1914** S. H. ADAMS *Clarion* 15 Do what you can . . ., and I'll square the bills.

b. *absol.* To settle accounts. Used with *off* {1898 *dial.*}, *up.* {1904} Also *vbl. n.* and fig.

1834 SIMMS *Guy Rivers* I. 68 Now, to make up the score, and square off with the pedler. **1835** KENNEDY *Horse Shoe Robinson* I. 45 Squaring up, and smoothing off, and bringing out this and that shilling straight to a penny, dont come natural to me. **1884** 'MARK TWAIN' *H. Finn* xx, When he'd squared up there warn't nothing left but sixteen dollars. **1894** — *P. Wilson* xii, I'll square up with the proceeds of my raid.

2. To prepare or brace (one's self), as in readiness for action or self-defense. (Cf. sense 4.)

1823 COOPER *Pioneers* xxxiv, Square yourself, you lubber, square yourself, and we'll soon know who's the better man. **1847** ROBB *Squatter Life* 142 Tom squared himself for a yarn. **1864** 'MARK TWAIN' *Sk., New & Old* 165 He . . . squared himself to receive his assailants. **1893** *Harper's Mag.* March 643/1 With a look of determination on his face, [he] squared himself to write.

3. To place (someone) in satisfactory or amicable relations *with* some other person or group. Often *refl. colloq.*

1893 *Chicago Tribune* 24 April 2/5, I can square myself with my people and you can readily make it right with the Building Trades' Council. **1905** LINCOLN *Partners* 348 He can do more than anybody else to square you and me with Prissy and Tempy. **1910** J. HART *Vigilante Girl* 261 The sheriff will probably make at least a show of resistance in order to square himself with the Law-and-Order party.

4. *intr.* To assume a posture or an attitude of defense; to put one's self into the attitude of a boxer. {1820-} +With *off. colloq.* Also fig. (Cf. sense 2.)

1837 NEAL *Charcoal Sk.* (1838) 41 If he 'squares off' at a big fellow, he is obliged . . . to hit his antagonist on the knee. **1864** 'MARK TWAIN' *Sketches* (1926) 155, I ran against another man and he squared off for a fight. **1873** BEADLE *Undevel. West* 773 The bow appeared to be rearing up to square off at the midday sun. **1875** *N.Y. Herald* 17 April (B.), Mr. Fullerton . . . squared off with a vim . . . that sometimes makes victory half assured.

5. *Naut.* To sail *away* before the wind, with the yards squared. {1887-} Also quasi-tr. and fig. Also *to square off.*

1849 KINGSLEY *Diary* 57 The wind died away and soon sprung out from the South and [we] squared away before it. **1881** *Ore. State Jrnl.* 1 Jan. 2/4 When you got squared away before the wind, did you . . . return thanks to Providence? **1889** 'MARK TWAIN' *Conn. Yankee* 479, I didn't waste any time . . ., but squared away for business. **1901** ADE *40 Modern Fables* 151 The four Comrades squared away. It was to be a Gentleman's [card] Game. **1909** WASON *Happy Hawkins* 203 When she got squared away, she made 'em all get down an' scratch.

+b. *fig.* To take a new course; to reform.

1902 MCFAUL *Ike Glidden* 220 He was the brightest man in this section, and if he'd ever square away he'd be a smart man.

+6. Of cotton: To develop squares. (See SQUARE *n.* 3.)

1875 *Chicago Tribune* 2 July 7/2 The weather has been hot and moist enough to . . . cause the plant to form and square well.

+7. *To square back,* to turn back, to retrace one's steps.

1897 STUART *Simpkinsville* 16 Seen May Day first time on her way to church, an' looked after her—then squared back direct an' followed her.

+8. *To square it,* to live honestly, to reform. *colloq.*

1873 in W. Taylor *David* vii, Give a poor fellow a chance to square it for three months. **1883** 'MARK TWAIN' *Life on Miss.* lii, Lord give a poor fellow a chance to square it. **1903** HAPGOOD *Autobiog. of Thief* 25 Now that I have 'squared it' I see a good deal of my family.

* Square, *adv.*

+1. Completely; directly.

1862 E. W. Pearson *Lett. Port Royal* 103 His heart failed him and he backed square out. **1876** *Congress. Rec.* 5 July 4397/1 If the Senator from Vermont . . . does not like to vote square against [this bill] . . ., this is the right way to defeat it. **1880** 'MARK TWAIN' *Tramp Abroad* 152 [He] shot the dragon square in the center of his cavernous mouth. **1884** CABLE *Dr. Sevier* 352 In front of the 'Picayune' office he ran square against a small man. **1902** MCFAUL *Ike Glidden* 236 Hain't I bin a-runnin' my legs right square off this four days?

+b. With *out.*

1879 TOURGEE *Fool's Errand* 91, I told him square out what the matter was. **1882** THAYER *From Log-Cabin* 359, I guv him my life squar' out. **1883** *Harper's Mag.* Jan. 212/1, I tell him square out how it seemed to me. **1922** TARKINGTON *Gentle Julia* 213 There's no etiquette in coming right square out and asking how much it was.

+2. At a steady, even gait.

1868 WOODRUFF *Trotting Horse* 54 He will trot square again with the rollers on. *Ib.* 68 It is of no use to keep on in *hopes* that he will go square again.

Square dance. Any set dance, as a quadrille, in which the performers are so placed that they form a square. {1902-} Also attrib. — **1878** *Harper's Mag.* Jan. 303/2 Some moralists have drawn the line of danger at 'square dances.' **1901** WHITE *Westerners* 275 The performers might at once overlook the performance of the square-dance 'figures.' **1912** COBB *Back Home* 44 Strict church members . . . wouldn't let their children dance any dance except a square dance.

+Square deal. In card games, an honest, fair dealing or distribution of the cards; fig., a fair, honest treatment; an equitable arrangement of conditions. {1927-} — **1883** 'MARK TWAIN' *Life on Miss.* lii, Thought i had better give him a square deal. **1898** CANFIELD *Maid of Frontier* 88 It was a square deal, an' you all saw it. **1905** BELASCO *Girl of Golden West* (1925) I. 60 That ain't a square deal—he's cheating. **1919** [see NEW DEAL].

***Squarely,** *adv.* +Plainly; unequivocally. {1900} 'Chiefly *U.S.*' (*O.E.D.*). — **1860** in Victor *Hist. Southern Rebellion* I. 89 [This] means simply and squarely, that you intend either to rule or ruin this Government. **1872** *Congress. Globe* 17 April 2512/1 Until this truth was recognized the issue was not squarely made or the battles squarely fought. **1885** *Century Mag.* Feb. 511/1 He stands squarely upon observation, experience, induction. **1894** 'MARK TWAIN' *P. Wilson* xiii, Tom, tell me squarely—didn't he find any fault with you?

+Square meal. A substantial, satisfying meal. {1876-} — **1850** A. T. JACKSON *Forty-Niner* (1920) 12 Two square meals in town yesterday . . . put me out of face with my regular grub. **1869** A. K. McCLURE *Rocky Mts.* 30 The transition from the luxurious tables of the East to the 'square meals' of the West is, fortunately, gradual. **1893** PAGE *Red Rock* 76 He had not had a really square meal in two months. **1923** [see BUM *v.* 3].

Square-necked grain beetle. A grain beetle, *Cathartus gemellatus.* — **1895** *Dept. Agric. Yrbk. 1894* 290 An insect of some importance in the South is the square-necked or red grain beetle.

Square set. 1. A square dance. +**2.** *Mining.* A square frame used in timbering: (see first quot. 1896). Also attrib. — (1) **1824** DODDRIDGE *Notes* 131 The figures of the dances were three and four handed reels, or square setts, and jigs. (2) **1877** W. WRIGHT *Big Bonanza* 311 In the bottom of this opening or chamber are put down the sills for the first 'square-set' of timbers. **1896** SHINN *Story of Mine* 96 'Square sets' consist of short, square timbers, four to six feet long, mortised and tenoned at the ends so that they can be put together in a series of interlocked cribs and built up in a continuous row or block. *Ib.* 97 Dangers . . . were obviated by the proper use of the square-set timbers.

Square-shouldered, *a.* Having broad, straight shoulders; not round-shouldered. Also fig. — **1825** NEAL *Bro. Jonathan* II. 108 A dark, tall, square-shouldered man. **1904** STRATTON-PORTER *Freckles* 5 A broad, square-shouldered man was bending over some account-books. **1910** TOMPKINS *Mothers & Fathers* 244 There was something about her . . . square-shouldered and, above all, indomitably honest.

Square stern. A stern that is not round, or one without an overhang; a boat built with a square stern. Also attrib. — **1704** *Boston News-Letter* 30 Oct. 2/2 Capt. Lawrence . . . has took 2 Prizes on the Banks of Newfoundland, . . . the one a Pink of 130 Tons, the other a square Starn 240 Tons. **1754** *Georgia Col. Rec.* VI. 457 The Schooner Elizabeth . . . [is] a Square Stern Vessel of Fifteen Tons or thereabouts. **1873** *Rep. Comm. Fisheries 1872-3* 9 At Milwaukee, for a time, the most of the boats were the sloop-rigged 'Norwegians,' afterwards abandoned, and the square stern adopted. **1876** KNIGHT 2295/1 *Square-stern,* . . . a build in which the wing-transom is at right angles to the stern-post, in contradistinction to *round* stern.

+Square thing. The fair thing; the proper mode of procedure. Freq. *to do the square thing by* (someone). — *c*1860 H. PRESCOTT in *Casquet of Lit.* IV. 25/1 He had come to question . . . whether it was just the square thing to . . . shut her up all by herself. **1868** in *Congress. Rec.* 19 July (1894) 7692/2 Do the square thing by him [*sc.* the Indian] and he is a honey cooler. **1884** HOWELLS *Silas Lapham* 63, I tell you . . . it was a perfectly square thing. **1917** McCUTCHEON *Green Fancy* 304 If I get the stuff, I'll do the square thing by you.

Square timber. Timber that has been hewed square. {squared timber, 1577} — **1728** *Boston Rec.* 222 Twenty Shillings for Every Range that Shall haue the Quantity of Eight feet of Square Timber. *c*1790 COXE *View U.S.* 62 The produce, manufactures, and exports of Pennsylvania [include] . . . square timber, scantling, plank [etc.]. **1832** in Mackenzie *Van Buren* 240 These prisoners were in a house built of square timber. **1845** J. W. NORRIS *Chicago Directory* 125 Dealers in all kinds of Sawed Lumber, Square Timber, Shingles, Lath.

Square-toed, *a.* {1785-} Firm; direct; solid. {1795-, 'old-fashioned, formal, precise'} — **1854** *Knickerb.* XLIII. 439, I stand flat-footed, square-toed, hump-shouldered, upon the platform of free rights and true republicanism. **1884** NYE *Baled Hay* 11 [The letter] was manly and square-toed. **1887** HARDEN & SPAHR *Early Life Boone Co., Ind.* 350 He has been . . . a square-toed Democrat; never scratched his ticket with one exception.

+Squash.[1] [Of Algonquian origin.]

1. The gourd produced by any of various species of *Cucurbita* {1669-}; also, the plant producing this fruit. {1661-}

1643 WILLIAMS *Key* (1866) 125 *Askútasquash*, their Vine aples . . . the English . . . call Squashes. **1683** PENN *Let. Free Soc. Traders* 4 The Artificial Produce of the Country, is Wheat, Barley, Oats, Rye, Pease, Beans, Squashes [etc.]. **1705** BEVERLEY *Virginia* II. 17 The same Use is made also of . . . Vetches, Squashes, Maycocks [etc.]. **1778** CARVER *Travels* 37 The Winnebagoes raise . . . a great quantity of Indian corn, beans, pumpkins, squash, and water melons. **1819** *Plough Boy* I. 183 A squash, taken from the garden of Mr. Wm. Chouty, Londonderry, N.H. on the 2d inst. weighed 311 lbs. **1870** [see CUCUMBER 1]. **1914** E. STEWART *Lett. Woman Homesteader* 281, I have . . . found a kind of squash that can be raised here.

b. With specifying terms.

See also HUBBARD SQUASH, LONG-NECK(ED) SQUASH, etc.

1814 African squash [see BLUE *a.* 1 a]. **1818** *Mass. Spy* 11 Nov. (Th.), Upwards of ten tons of the best crook-necked winter Squashes. **1868** *Mich. Agric. Rep.* VII. 350 Thos. A. Parker, Detroit, [exhibited] 2 vegetable marrow squashes.

2. The flesh of such a gourd cooked as food.

1758 C. REA *Journal* 70, I've eat this Summer one meal of Squash, one of Turneps. **1789** MAY *Jrnl. & Lett.* 145 [We have] squash and string-beans without butter. **1846** G. D. WARBURTON *Hochelaga* 36 As you travel southward, there are many very original-looking dishes, with names as odd as their appearance, 'mush,' 'squash,' &c. **1872** POWERS *Afoot & Alone* 254 At dinner he plumped a spoonful of squash on his plate. **1902** 'O. HENRY' *Heart of West* 185 Hurry up with the fried squash, and the hot corn pone with sweet milk.

3. *attrib.* and *comb.* **a.** With *seed, shell, soup.*

1708 SEWALL *Diary* 11. 210 This day Mr. Belchar brings me Squash-Seeds from Dedham. **1725** *Lancaster Rec.* 238 They also found a paddle & some squash shells in one [wigwam]. **1751** J. BARTRAM *Observations* 62 We dined on Indian corn, and squash soop, and boiled bread.

b. In special combinations.

Squash beetle, a striped beetle (*Diabrotica vittata*) injurious to the leaves of the squash; *s.-borer,* a moth (*Melittia satyriniformis*), the larva of which bores into squash vines; *s. head,* a dolt (cf. PUMPKIN HEAD 2).

1867 *Amer. Naturalist* I. 163 The Squash Beetle . . . now attacks the squash plants before they are fairly up. **1891** *Cent.* 5878/1 *Squash-borer,* . . . the larva of an ægerian or sesiid moth . . . which bores the stems of squashes in the United States. **1817** *Yankee Traveller* 70 What are you about here (said he)—ye raggamuffins—ye squash-heads—ye pugnacious dogs.

Squash.[2] Short for MUSQUASH. *Obs.* — [**1678** PHILLIPS *New World of Words* (ed. 4), *Squash,* a little Creature in some parts of America, somewhat resembling an Ichnumon or Indian Rat. **1774** GOLDSMITH *Hist. Earth* III. 380 But the smell of our weasels, and ermines, and polecats, is fragrance itself when compared to that of the *squash* and the *skunk,* which have been called the Polecats of America.] **1796** MORSE *Univ. Geog.* I. 201 Another stinkard, called the Squash, is said . . . to be found in some of the southern states.

***Squash.**[3] A form of the game of rackets. {1886-, attrib.} Also attrib. — **1899** *N.Y. World* 8 Aug. 14/4 'Squash' . . . is a variation of the time-honored court tennis. **1908** SINCLAIR *Metropolis* 48 There were half a dozen squash-courts.

+Squash bug. An insect injurious to squash plants; spec., *Anasa tristis,* which feeds upon squash leaves. — **1846** WORCESTER 689/1 *Squash-Bug,* . . . a fetid insect destructive to squashes. **1865** STOWE in *Atlantic Mo.* Sept. 351/2 In the actual garden there are cut worms for every cabbage, squash-bugs for all the melons. **1870** WARNER *Summer in Garden* iv, Speaking of those yellow squash-bugs I think I disheartened them by covering the plants. **1882** *Vt. Agric. Rep.* VII. 69 Toads will eat the potato and squash bugs. **1925** HERRICK *Man. Injurious Insects* 262 The squash bug, distributed from coast to coast of the United States[,] is a well-known pest of cucurbits.

+Squash pie. A pie in the filling of which cooked squash is a principal ingredient. — **1805** *Pocumtuc Housewife* (1906) 24 Squash Pie with Raisins. **1854** CUMMINS *Lamplighter* 157 Let her stick to her cranberry-sauce and squash-pies. **1887** R. H. DAVIS *Silhouettes* 25 There was the cold squash pie ready to cut for breakfast. **1917** MATHEWSON *Second Base Sloan* 22, I ain' never eat any of that squash pie.

Squash vine. A squash plant. Also comb. {1750, in Barbados} — **1838** *Mass. Agric. Survey 1st Rep.* 57 This water, thus considerably charged with oil, he applies to his squash vines. **1883** *Wheelman* I. 353 They could hear the bees humming among the squash-vines out in the garden. **1909** *Cent. Suppl.* 1422/2 *Squash vine-borer,* the larva of an American sesiid moth, *Melittia satyriniformis,* . . . bores into and excavates the stems of squash-vines.

***Squat,** *n.*[1] ‖The place where a person has squatted or settled. — **1856** H. V. HUNTLEY *California* I. 196 There will be found nothing sufficiently persuasive to induce an American to 'vamose' his 'squat.'

+Squat, *n.*[2] [*Squatina.*] An angel fish of the genus *Squatina.* — **1884** GOODE, etc. *Fisheries* I. 675 *Squatina angelus.* . . . Angel-fish, Angelo or Squat. From San Francisco southward. Not rare. **1891** *Cent.* 5878/2.

***Squat,** *v.*

+1. *intr.* To settle on land, without legal title or payment of rent; to settle on public land, in accordance with regulations, with the intention of acquiring title. {1828-, in Australia, to take up pastoral land as a tenant of the crown; 1879}

[**1800** *Miss. Territorial Archives* (1906) 212, I wish also to be instructed for my Conduct towards those people, Squatting or establishing themselves upon the Public Lands.] **1829** MARRYAT *F. Mildmay* xxi, He was a Kentucky man, of the Ohio, where he had 'squatted,' as we say. **1859** HUNTER *Western Border Life* 67, I am the rightful claimant to these lands, having squatted here for the last six months. **1891** O'BEIRNE *Leaders Ind. Territory* 27/1 The Creek Indians . . . were at that time squatting in the Chickasaw Nation.

fig. **1903** ADE *People You Know* 70 If they squatted in a low-down Neighborhood, Mrs. Jump was ashamed to give her Address to Friends in the Congregation.

+b. Used with (*down*) *upon* or *on*. Also *fig.*

1813 PAULDING *Lay Sc. Fiddle* (1814) 207 They seem to have *squatted* down upon the public reputation, as they did upon the land. **1845** SIMMS *Wigwam & Cabin* 2 Ser. 127 They squatted down on the rich clay lands along the Edisto. **1855** GLISAN *Jrnl. Army Life* 225 Pre-emption right . . . [is] the title to mineral land conferred by virtue of having first 'squatted on it.' **1901** DUNCAN & SCOTT *Allen & Woodson Co., Kansas* 582 John Coleman squatted upon a piece of land in Owl Creek township.

fig. **1855** HOLBROOK *Among Mail Bags* 288 His chair was appropriated by a fatigued neighbor, who 'squatted' on the vacant territory, regardless of 'pre-emption' or pre-session.

+2. To sit and do nothing; to cease trying.

1836 *Crockett's Yaller Flower Almanac* 32 When you come to put in the scientific licks, I squat. a**1846** *Quarter Race Ky.* 118, I'll squat, and let Hooker do it.

+3. *tr. a. refl.* To establish one's self upon land as a squatter.

1809 IRVING *Knickerb.* III, viii, The Yankees . . . had the audacity to *squat* themselves down within the jurisdiction of Fort Goed Hoop. **1825** NEAL *Bro. Jonathan* I. 219 A person . . . had 'squatted' himself down, upon the vacant land.

+b. In passive construction with *on*, *upon*.

1857 *Lawrence* (Kan.) *Republican* 30 July 1 Nearly all the timbered claims within four or five miles are already squatted upon. **1860** GREELEY *Overland Journey* 65 To see a man squatted on a quarter-section of a cabin which would make a fair hog-pen . . . is enough to give a cheerful man the horrors. **1894** ROBLEY *Bourbon Co., Kansas* 48 A good part of these lands were squatted on by settlers.

+Squateree. (See SQUAT(T)EREE.)

+Squatment. A settlement; land occupied by squatting. {1887, the act of squatting on land} — **1835** *Knickerb.* VI. 176 Hawk-nosed speculators already rode . . . through the muddy, Virginia-fence lands of these squatments. **1860** *Chambers's Jrnl.* 21 July 39/2 The ghost of a squatter might prove a less unpleasant neighbour than the squatter himself, dispossessed of his *squatment*.

+Squat snipe. =SQUATTER 2. Also *squatting snipe*. — **1781–2** JEFFERSON *Notes Va.* 77 Besides these, we have The Royston Crow, . . . Squatting snipe [etc.]. **1888** TRUMBULL *Names of Birds* 176 In Connecticut at Milford, [*Tringa maculata* is called] Squat-Snipe; at Stratford, Squatter. **1917** [see SQUATTER 2].

+Squat tag. A form of the game of tag: (see quotation). — **1891** *Amer. Folk-Lore* IV. 222 Squat Tag. . . . Players . . . may escape being tagged by squatting down. This immunity is only granted to each individual a certain number of times, . . . and after his 'squats' are exhausted he may be tagged as in the ordinary game.

Squatter.

+1. One settling upon land to which he has no legal title; a person settling upon undivided public land, with the intention of establishing legal title. {1821–}

Quotations in the first group illustrate the use of this word as a term of condemnation or reproach.

(1) **1788** MADISON *Writings* V. 96 Their Constituents are only squatters on other people's land. **1824** BLANE *Excursion U.S.* 101 The Squatters are held by the landed proprietors in the greatest possible abhorrence. **1870** *Congress. Globe* 23 March 2173/3 If there is one term more than another which is opprobrious to our people, . . . it is the term 'squatter.'

(2) **1809** KENDALL *Travels* III. 161 *Squatters* are not peculiar to Maine. **1818** FEARON *Sketches* 224 These . . . remains until he . . . has realized a sufficiency to become a landowner;—or is expelled by the real proprietor. **1825** NEAL *Bro. Jonathan* I. 219 They had been 'smoking out a squatter.' **1836** *Jamestown* (N.Y.) *Jrnl.* 20 April 2/5 Mr. Senator Walker has introduced a bill . . . to give a preference in price on the purchase of public land to squatters. **1850** [see GOVERNMENT LAND]. **1871** *Rep. Indian Affairs* (1872) 183 And why are squatters continually seeking to encroach on Indian lands? a**1882** in McCabe *New York* 73 By the 1st of May, too, the squatters [on the west side of Manhattan] . . . will disappear. **1907** ANDREWS *Recoll.* 84 A registry of land claims has been established there by the squatters.

transf. **1841** *Knickerb.* XVII. 278 They amused themselves by calling the exclusives 'squatters,' 'preëmptioners,' etc.

+2. =PECTORAL SANDPIPER.

1888 [see SQUAT SNIPE]. **1917** *Birds of Amer.* I. 233 Pectoral Sandpiper. *Pisobia maculata.* . . . [Also called] Squat Snipe; Squatter; Krieker.

+3. Used in possessive in sense 1 to designate organizations or establishments formed by, or for the benefit or protection of, squatters.

1854 in W. E. Connelley *Stand. Hist. Kansas* I. 350 No person shall be protected by the Squatter's Association who shall hold in his own right more than one claim. **1877** JOHNSON *Anderson Co., Kansas* 110 In November, 1858, a Free State squatters' court was organized in the counties of Linn, Anderson and Bourbon, for the trial of contested land claims.

+4. *Attrib.* in sense 1 with *candidate, dodge, element*, etc.

1836 HILDRETH *Campaigns Rocky Mts.* 70 We descried a cluster of huts that we imagined might be a squatter settlement. **1838** *N.Y. Advertiser & Exp.* 11 April 3/1 Down with the *squatter* candidate. **1856** S. ROBINSON *Kansas* 11 A squatter meeting was held at Homsby & Ferril's store. **1860** G. W. Bungay *Bobolink Minstrel* 15 Douglas . . . tried the 'Squatter dodge,' And went for Kansas free. **1865** E. W. Pearson *Lett. Port Royal* 318 General Howard went to Edisto with the view of reconciling the squatter negroes with the claims of the former owners. **1871** DE VERE 659 Kansas . . . appears occasionally as *Squatter State*, from the pertinacity with which squatter-sovereignty was discussed there, and settlers poured in by the two contending parties. **1885** *Rep. Indian Affairs* 7 The present penalties of the law have no terrors for the squatter element.

+Squatter-butter. To go squatter-butter, (see quotation). *slang.* — c**1870** CHIPMAN *Notes on Bartlett* 439 Squatter-butter. To go 'squatter-butter,' is to slide down hill 'sitting on one's heels,' as more inoffensively the thing is expressed.—Eastern Massachusetts.

‖Squat(t)eree. A squatter's cabin. — **1843** 'CARLTON' *New Purchase* I. 101 Due east from the capitol about a furlong, was the squateree of uncle Tommy Seymour. *Ib.* 198 The squatteree was . . . built of small round saplings.

+Squatter law. A law or a system of law made by squatters for their own use and enforced by them. — **1857** DANA *Great West* 196 Squatter Laws. . . . Laws for the mutual recognition of land claims under their own restrictions were agreed to. **1873** BEADLE *Undevel. West* 76 The original squatters . . . enforced squatter law with blood-thirsty zeal.

+Squatter right. (See SQUATTER('S) RIGHT.)

+Squatter sovereign. A settler in a United States territory (so called in allusion to the doctrine of squatter sovereignty); an adherent of the doctrine of squatter sovereignty.

[**1848** CALHOUN *Works* (1854) IV. 498 The first half-dozen squatters would become the sovereigns, with full dominion and sovereignty over them.] **1855** (*title*), The Squatter Sovereign. [Atchison, Kan.]. **1861** in Logan *Great Conspiracy* 175 Those who are styled 'Squatter Sovereigns' give up their Territorial legislative policy. **1889** P. BUTLER *Recollections* 49 They had been flattered with the idea that if they would come to Kansas they should be 'Squatter Sovereigns.'

transf. a**1861** WINTHROP *Open Air* 284 When the road grew too hot for us, . . . we jumped over the fence into the Race-Course . . . and there became squatter sovereigns all day. a**1861** — *J. Brent* 79 The old fellow had deemed himself the squatter sovereign of that bleak and sere region.

b. Stephen A. Douglas.

1860 G. W. Bungay *Bobolink Minstrel* 72 Your little Squatter Sovereign Sha'nt be our King!

+Squatter sovereignty.

1. The right of settlers in a territory to make their own laws; popular sovereignty. Now *hist.* Also *attrib.*

Cf. POPULAR SOVEREIGNTY, note.

1854 *Congress. Globe* App. 9 May 586/2 It has been assumed that this bill embraces the principle of squatter sovereignty. **1857** *Lawrence* (Kan.) *Republican* 28 May 2 What a commentary is here on . . . the delusive theory of 'squatter sovereignty.' **1860** ABBOTT *South & North* 248 You avow a new principle, which, in language not very classical, you call 'Squatter Sovereignty.' **1878** BEADLE *Western Wilds* 371 The 'squatter sovereignty' doctrine of Stephen A. Douglas had suited his position. **1898** *Mo. So. Dakotan* I. 58 [A temporary government] would be a practical application for 'squatter sovereignty' in its best sense, and certainly preferable to lynch law.

2. The right of settlers to the lands upon which they have settled. Also *fig.*, and with allusion to the doctrine referred to in sense 1.

1855 *Knickerb.* XLV. 422 In that part of that beautiful state [Ill.] known as 'Egypt,' many of these wise men have exercised their 'squatter sovereignty' for the last forty years. **1858** *Ill. Agric. Soc. Trans.* III. 645 There are the sixty varieties of plant lice. . . . Their ideas of 'squatter sovereignty' conform to no true democratic or republican platform. **1866** C. H. SMITH *Bill Arp* 94 We became converted over to the doctrine of squatter sovereignty, and pitched our tents in the piney woods. **1868** *N.Y. Herald* 15 July 4/3 The railroad companies . . . will no longer occupy land under the feeble tenure of squatter sovereignty. **1892** *S. Dak. Hist. Coll.* I. 59 [A] surveyor general . . . [was] greatly needed when land-seekers preferred not to depend on the rights of 'squatter sovereignty.'

+Squatter('s) right. The claim of a squatter to the land upon which he settles. — **1873** BEADLE *Undevel. West* 417 This is not an 'Indian title,' so called, . . . not a 'squatter's right.' **1878** *Harper's Mag.* Jan. 197 The land had been claimed . . . by squatter rights. **1892** *S. Dak. Hist. Coll.* I. 61 He built a log cabin on land which he might hold by squatter's right until surer right came. **1898** *Mo. So. Dakotan* I. 16, I was shown a tract of unclaimed land . . . upon which I filed a squatter right, and subsequently improved and pre-empted it. **1904** *N.Y. Times* 15 Nov. 1 A valuable tract of land on the Chicago lake front . . . is claimed by Streeter under squatter rights.

∗Squatting, *n.* **+1.** The action of SQUAT *v.* 1. Also attrib. **+2.** (See quotation.) — (1) **1809** IRVING *Knickerb.* III. vii, This unceremonious mode of taking possession of *new land* was technically termed *squatting.* **1824** BLANE *Excursion U.S.* 101 This settling on land which belongs to another person, and clearing and cultivating it without leave, is called Squatting. **1839** MARRYAT *Diary Amer.* 1 Ser. II. 75 Squatting . . . is taking possession of land belonging to government and cultivating it. **1848** *Ib.* (rev. ed.) v. iii, The city of New Amsterdam was a mere Dutch squatting-place on their territories. (2) **1870** MEDBERY *Men Wall St.* 168 [He resorted] to what is known in street *argot* as 'squatting.' In other words, he dishonored his own contracts and entered upon a lawsuit to cover his duplicity.

Squatting, *a.* {**1871**} +Occupying land in the manner of a squatter. {**1887**} — **1839** IRVING in *Knickerb.* XIII. 317 The Yankees of Connecticut, those swapping, bargaining, squatting enemies of the Manhattoes. **1848** — *Knickerb.* (rev. ed.) v. iii, His first impulse was to . . . kick these squatting Yankees out of the country.

+Squatting snipe. (See SQUAT SNIPE.)

+Squaw. Also †squa. [Algonquian.] See also OLD SQUAW.

I. 1. An Indian woman or wife.
1634 WOOD *New Eng. Prospect* (1865) 109 If her husband come to seeke for his Squaw and beginne to bluster the English woman betakes her to her armes which are the warlike Ladle, and the scalding liquors. **1677** *Conn. Rec.* II. 310 The Court hath granted Wegucksesuck . . . a squa. **1732** HEMPSTEAD *Diary* 251, I went to Nahantie to the Indian Town to get a squaw to Botom chairs. **1797** *Mass. H. S. Coll.* 1 Ser. V. 55 One wigwam . . . is occupied by a negro and a squaw. **1820** in Morse *Rep. Indian Affairs* II. 37 An old negro . . . has a squaw for a wife. **1870** KEIM *Sheridan's Troopers* 211 Kidnapping another warrior's squaw is an offense which generally results in the death of the offending savage, if caught. **1905** [see MOCOCK].

b. Applied to white women.
See also WHITE SQUAW.
1642 LECHFORD *Plain Dealing* 49 When they [*sc.* Indians] see any of our English women sewing with their needles, or working coifes, or such things, they will cry out, Lazie *squaes!* **1879** *Cimarron News & Press* 20 Nov. 2/2 He spoke of Mrs. Price and Josephine Meeker heap brave squaws.

2. A womanish man, esp. an Indian.
1808 PIKE *Sources Miss.* 20, I directed my interpreter to ask how many scalps they had taken, they replied 'none;' he added they were all squaws. **1844** LEE & FROST *Oregon* 76 His daughter . . . , instead of getting a great warrior for a husband, had married herself to a squaw. **1855** KIP *Indian Council Walla Walla* (1897) 11 To be seen engaged in [menial tasks] . . . would procure for them [*sc.* Indian braves] the title of squaws.

3. Ellipt. for *squaw hitch,* (see sense 8).
1913 BARNES *Western Grazing Grounds* 368 There are an endless number of hitches used by western men, as the squaw, the stirrup, the bed and basco.

II. *attrib.* **4.** Designating creatures or things regarded as female or womanish.
1634 WOOD *New Eng. Prospect* 89 The Indians . . . bade her [*sc.* a mare caught in a deer trap] good morrow, crying out, what cheere, what cheere, Englishmans squaw horse. **1832** WILLIAMSON *Maine* I. 456 The proud Mohawks, afterwards called the Lenape, *squaw-fighters,* from the proverbial peace-making character of Indian females. **1901** RYAN *Montana* 93 You will never do squaw work for me again, little squaw?

5. Designating Indian women in stated capacities or relationships.
1707 SEWALL *Diary* II. 60∗ She sent then unto a French Priest, that he would speak unto her Squa Mistress. **1726** PENHALLOW *Indian Wars* 52 They withdrew the issue to the Squaw Widow. **1872** *Newton Kansan* 21 Nov. 2/4 Gillis used to be an Indian trader, and had a squaw wife. **1898** *Mo. So. Dakotan* I. 122 Walker Monroe's curiosity [was aroused] as to whether or no his blood might not be tainted with that of some squaw ancestor back in the old days.

6. Designating articles, etc., in some way identified with squaws.
1850 GARRARD *Wah-To-Yah* iv. 60 Out, pellmell, tore . . . the snarling squaw pets, to join the doggish revelry. **1873** ROE *Army Lett.* 89 A folded red squaw blanket [is] on the trunk. **1885** *Rep. Indian Affairs* 31 Their lack of knowledge in dress-making . . . makes them adhere to the old squaw costume. **1892** *S. Dak. Hist. Coll.* I. 56 The Indians . . . held . . . the eastward plains for cultivation, if any impulse to farming should possibly evolve from the squaw gardens of the untutored Sioux. **1894** *Outing* XXIV. 83/1 The short, choppy stepping of most squaw dances elsewhere. **1923** J. H. COOK *On Old Frontier* 52 Squaw-saddles were better than none at all.

7. In the specific names of plants.
See also SQUAW BUSH, SQUAW CORN, etc.
1891 *Cent.* 5879/1 *Squaw-berry,* . . . same as *squaw-huckleberry* [*Vaccinum stamineum*]. **1915** ARMSTRONG & THORNBER *Western Wild Flowers* 122 Miners's Lettuce. *Montia parviflora.* . . . It is also called Indian Let-

tuce and Squaw Cabbage. **1909** *Cent. Suppl.* 1261/2 *Squaw-carpet,* . . . same as *mahala-mats.* (California.) **1894** *Amer. Folk-Lore* VII. 102 *Trillium erectum,* squaw-flower, Ferrisburgh, Vt. **1909** *Cent. Suppl.* 544/1 *Xerophyllum tenax* . . . is the bear-grass of Lewis and Clark. Also called *squaw-grass* and *squaw-lily.* **1857** GRAY *Botany* 248 Deerberry. Squaw Huckleberry. . . . Dry woods, Maine to Michigan, and southward. **1891** *Cent.* 5879/1 *Squaw-mint,* . . . the American pennyroyal, *Hedeoma pulegioides.* (Rare.) **1829** EATON *Botany* (ed. 5) 433 *Vaccinium stamineum,* squaw whortleberry.

8. In special combinations.
Squaw campaign, (see quotation); *s. hitch,* a hitch used in fastening a pack on a horse.
1895 THWAITES ed. Withers *Chron. Border Warfare* 210 From the fact that this first American movement against the savages . . . resulted only in the capture of non-combatants, . . . it was long known as 'the squaw campaign.' **1903** A. ADAMS *Log of Cowboy* 32 He showed me what he called a squaw hitch, with which you can lash a pack single-handed.

+Squaw ax. A small ax or hatchet of a kind used by Indian women. — **1806** ORDWAY in *Jrnls. of Lewis & O.* 363 Excellent horses . . . they offer to Sell for a Squaw axe pr peace. **1832** *Louisville Directory* 104 [They stunned] the old Indian and squaw . . . by some smart blows with their squaw axes, (as the small axes are called usually handled by the squaws). **1844** GREGG *Commerce of Prairies* I. 203 The axe . . . is formed after the model of those clumsy hatchets known as 'squaw-axes' among Indian traders. **1896** *Harper's Mag.* April 707/1 A settler . . . fell on his captors . . . and slew them 'with a squaw-axe.'

+Squaw bush. 1. The red osier dogwood (*Cornus stolonifera*), or a related shrub. (The first quotation is probably in error.) **2.** (See quotation.) — (1) **1832** WILLIAMSON *Maine* I. 125 Indian Tobacco, called by the Natives 'Squaw-bush,' is a perennial herb, or shrub. **1894** *Amer. Folk-Lore* VII. 90 *Cornus stolonifera,* squaw-bush, Penobscot Co., Me. **1909** *Cent. Suppl.* 1261/2 *Squaw-bush,* . . . a name of *Cornus stolonifera, C. serica.* and *C. Canadensis.* (2) **1909** WEBSTER 2025 *Squaw bush. a.* The cranberry tree. *b.* A sumac of the western United States (*Rhus trilobata*), with unpleasantly scented trifoliate leaves.

+Squaw camp. A camp in which squaws and children live while the men are away hunting or fighting. — **1840** HOFFMAN *Greyslaer* I. 143 The 'Squaw Camp' of Thayendanagea [was] a lonely fastness where, in time of war, the women and children of his tribe were sequestered for safety. **1885** *Wkly. New Mexican Rev.* 18 June 1/4 Geronimo . . . , in order to mislead the troops and save the squaw camp, kept on with some twenty bucks.

+Squaw corn. A kind of maize (*Zea mays amylacea*) extensively cultivated by Indians. — **1824** DODDRIDGE *Notes* 90 How widely different is the large squaw corn . . . from the Mandan corn. **1873** COZZENS *Marvellous Country* 109 Near the lower end a few patches of squaw corn loomed up. **1914** E. STEWART *Lett. Woman Homesteader* 151 They had a small patch of land . . . on which was raised the squaw corn that hung in bunches from the rafters.

Squawfish. Any of various western fresh-water fishes of the genus *Ptychocheilus,* esp. *P. oregonensis.* {1888, in Canada} — **1896** JORDAN & EVERMANN *Check-List Fishes* 247 Squawfish. . . . Rivers of Oregon and Washington, . . . [and] California. **1911** *Rep. Fisheries 1908* 315/1 Sacramento pike . . . , a chub of the Sacramento and Columbia, . . . is also known as 'big-mouth' and 'squaw-fish.'

Squawk, *n.* +=NIGHT HERON. — **1872** COUES *Key to Birds* 269 *Nyctiardea,* Night Heron. Qua-bird. Squawk. **1897** *Kissimmee* (Fla.) *Valley Gazette* 2 June 1/4 A squawk, perched on one foot by a century plant, is serenely viewing the exhibit. **1917** *Birds of Amer.* I. 194.

Squawk, *v.* {1821-} **1.** *tr.* To cry *out* (something) in a harsh manner. **2.** *intr.* Of a thing: To make a raucous noise. **3.** To complain. *colloq.* — (1) *c*1849 WHITCHER *Bedott P.* xx. 208 The way she squawked it out was a caution to old gates on a windy day! (2) **1859** STOWE *Minister's Wooing* xix, That bedroom door squawks like a cat. **1869** 'MARK TWAIN' *Innocents* 43 A disreputable accordion that had a leak somewhere and breathed louder than it squawked. (3) **1875** HOLLAND *Sevenoaks* 239 He mustn't squawk an' try to git another feller to help 'im out of 'is bargain.

+Squaw man. 1. A non-Indian married to an Indian squaw. **2.** (See quotation.) — (1) **1866** *Rep. Indian Affairs* 91 White men . . . have located in the vicinity of the reservation, and are known as squaw men. **1888** ROOSEVELT in *Century Mag.* Oct. 832/1 Nowadays those who live among and intermarry with the Indians are looked down upon by the other frontiersmen, who contemptuously term 'squaw-men.' **1894** ROBLEY *Bourbon Co., Kansas* 155 Settlers on the Neutral Land married Cherokee women, thereby becoming 'squawmen'—legally Cherokees—and entitled to a 'headright.' **1904** *Cosmopolitan* Aug. 411 The Squaw-Man. An Idyl of the Ranch. (2) **1910** HODGE, etc. *Amer. Indians* II. 630/1 Squaw man (an Indian who does woman's work).

+Squawmash. Variant of QUAMASH. — **1806** LEWIS in *L. & Clark Exped.* III. (1905) 333 The natives . . . eat it [*i.e.,* whale blubber] either alone or with the roots of the rush, squawmash [etc.].

+Squawroot. Any one of various American plants, some of which have roots possessing medicinal or food value, esp. *Conopholis americana;* also, the root of one of these plants.
1815 DRAKE *Cincinnati* 85 Plants Useful in Medicine and the Arts. . . . *Actea racemosa*—squaw root, the *root* [etc.]. **1817-8** EATON *Botany* (1822) 369 *Orobanche uniflora,* squaw-root, . . . cancer-root. **1877** BARTLETT 131. **1891** *Amer. Folk-Lore* IV. 149 *Trillium erectum* we called [in N.H.] Squaw Root. **1901** MOHR *Plant Life Ala.* 674 *Apocynum cannabinum.* . . . Cana-

dian Hemp. . . . The root is . . . the 'squaw root' of the Choctaw Indians. **1910** HODGE, etc. *Amer. Indians* II. 630/1 Squawroot (in different parts of the country, *Trillium erectum*, the black and the blue cohosh, *Conopholis americana*, and other plants).

+Squaw sachem. Among certain Indian tribes, a woman chief; the wife of a sachem. Now hist.

1622 'MOURT' *Relation* 126 The Squa Sachim, or Massachusets Queene was an enemy to him. **1642** LECHFORD *Plain Dealing* 51 Commonly when he [*sc.* the sachem] dyes, the Powahe marryes the *Squa Sachem*, that is, the queene. **1716** CHURCH *Philip's War* 2 Among the rest he sent Six Men to Awashonks Squaw-Sachem of the Sogkonate Indians. **1761** [see SACHEMESS]. **1832** WILLIAMSON *Maine* I. 459 Their ancient chief . . . was a female and called a Squaw Sachem.

+Squaw vine. =PARTRIDGE BERRY 1 a. — **1850** S. F. COOPER *Rural Hours* 32 It was a perfect bed of the squaw-vine and partridge berry. **1892** *Amer. Folk-Lore* V. 98 *Mitchella repens*, squaw-vine. Parts of N.E. **1919** STURTEVANT *Notes on Edible Plants* 366 *Mitchella repens*. . . . Partridge-Berry. Squaw-Vine. . . . The insipid, red fruits are eaten by children.

+Squawweed. 1. =SCABIOUS b. **2.** The golden ragwort, *Senecio aureus*. — **(1) 1828** RAFINESQUE *Medical Flora* I. 167 [These plants] were known to the Northern Indians by the name of Cocash or Squaw-weed. **(2) 1848** BARTLETT 328 *Squaw-Weed*. (Lat. *senecio obovatus*.) A medicinal plant used for diseases of the skin. **1857** GRAY *Botany* 231 Golden Ragwort. Squaw-weed. . . . Common everywhere; the primary form in swamps. **1892** COULTER *Bot. W. Texas* II. 242.

+Squaw winter. A spell of wintry weather in the autumn. — **1874** B. F. TAYLOR *World on Wheels* 185 Those single-minded, grand old fellows . . . [had] kicked the light snow of 'squaw winter' from their Spanish-leather boots. **1903** A. ADAMS *Log of Cowboy* 361 This was but the squaw winter which always preceded Indian summer. **1912** N. WOODROW *Sally Salt* 297 Indian Summer . . . had been succeeded by the gusts and snow-flakes of Squaw Winter.

Squeaker. {1641–} +(See quot. 1900.) In full *squeaker crab*. — **1887** GOODE, etc. *Fisheries* V. II. 651 The lady crab, sand crab, or squeaker crab (*Platyonichus ocellatus*), . . . occurs on most sandy shores from Cape Cod to Mexico. **1900** WEBSTER *Suppl.* 200/1 *Squeaker*, . . . any crab that stridulates when irritated, as the American lady crab.

***Squeal,** *v.* **+1.** *intr.* To give up; to cry quarter. *colloq.*[2] **+2.** To speak. *slang.* — **(1) a1846** *Quarter Race Ky.* 45, I got his hed under my arm an I made him squeal immediantly. **1877** BARTLETT 797 *Squeal*, . . . to 'throw up the sponge.' **(2) 1880** *Cimarron News & Press* 8 April 1/5 Ef yer on the marry . . . , jist squeal an' we'll hitch.

Squealer. +1. =ROARER 1 a. Also transf. **2.** Applied to birds: (see quotations). {1854–} **+3.** A complainer. — **(1) 1837** [see RINGTAILED *a.*]. **1898** [see RINGTAIL 2]. **(2) 1877** BARTLETT 797 *Squealer*, (*Charadrius Virginianus*,) the Golden Plover. New England. **1881** *Century Mag.* May 100/1 When ready to leave the nest and face the world for itself, it [a young pigeon] is a squealer, or, in market parlance, a squab. **1888** TRUMBULL *Names of Birds* 91 Harlequin Duck, . . . known also as Squealer at Machias Port, Me. **(3) 1889** *Columbus Dispatch*, In nine cases out of ten, the editor gives the squealer more privileges in the way of reply than he is entitled to by equity. **1902** MCFAUL *Ike Glidden* 69 If it's anything I hate it's a squealer or a kicker.

+Squealing hawk. (See quotation.) — **1884** *Harper's Mag.* March 622 The red-tailed hawk . . . by some is called the squealing hawk.

+Squeamy, *a.* Squeamish. {1908–} Also comb. — **1836** GILMAN *Recoll.* (1838) 44, I feel so squeamy-like at my stomach. **1863** 'E. KIRKE' *Southern Friends* 76 Doan't be squeamy, gal; out with it. **1880** COOKE in *Harper's Mag.* Sept. 582/1 They'd eet so much sweet it kinder made 'em squeamy.

Squeeze, *n.* {1611–} *Exchange.* +An act or instance of applying pressure to the shorts, as by a minor corner. {1890–, financial pressure} — **1872** *Chicago Tribune* 23 Oct. 1/5 The Gold Room was treated to a slight sensation to-day in the shape of a 'squeeze' in cash gold, which was made as high as 3/8 per cent per diem for borrowing. **1891** *Boston Jrnl.* 1 Dec. 2/7 Corn was something of a surprise to-day to those who had expected a collapse in the November squeeze. **1923** W. H. HUBBARD *Cotton & Cotton Market* 396 The trade call these minor corners a '*squeeze*.' Such an operation differs from a corner in that the managers will always supply whatever contracts are wanted, but at a price.

Squeeze, *v.* {a1601–} **1.** *To squeeze out*, +to ruin by unscrupulous competition. **+2.** *Exchange.* To force (one who has sold short) to buy at a high price. Also *vbl. n.* — **(1) 1879** in Tarbell *Hist. Standard Oil Co.* I. 334 Has your company or corporation in conjunction with the railroads ever operated so[,] to 'squeeze out' . . . or injure any other refining company? **(2) 1885** *Harper's Mag.* Nov. 842/1 The bulls get a 'twist on the shorts' by artificially raising prices, and 'squeezing,' or compelling the bears to settle at ruinous rates. **1902** BELL *Hope Loring* 272 You squeezed me badly in '93.

***Squeezed,** *a.* +Made the victim of financial pressure of some sort; ruined; forced *out.* — **1875** DALY *Big Bonanza* (1884) 52 Squeezed? Have I lost everything? **1880** ROCKEFELLER in Tarbell *Hist. Standard Oil Co.* II. 325 This constitutes the only foundation for the oft-repeated expressions 'crushed out,' 'squeezed out,' and 'bulldozing.' **1900** NELSON *A B C Wall St.* 160 When shorts become frightened after having oversold and then are forced to violently bid up prices in competition with the owners of stocks they are said to have been squeezed.

Squeezer. {1611–} **+1.** *pl.* (See quot. 1891.) {Anglo-American Squeezers, 1880 (Hargrave *Hist. Playing Cards* 189)} **+2.** (See quotation.) — **(1) a1871** in Hargrave *Hist. Playing Cards* 334. **1888** *Amer. Humorist* (London) 15 Sept. (F.), The editor picked up his hand, slid the squeezers past his good eye, and began to softly whisper the Pirate King. **1891** *Cent.* 5880/2 *Squeezer* . . . *pl.*, a kind of playing-cards in which the face value of each card is shown in the upper left-hand corner, and can readily be seen by squeezing the cards slightly apart, without displaying the hand. **(2) 1920** HUNTER *Trail Drivers Texas* I. 297 Some cattlemen now employ a branding chute where an arrangement for holding the cattle while they are being branded is called a 'squeezer,' or 'snappin' turtle.'

+Squeteague. Also †**squeterg, squitteag.** [Narraganset Indian.] A weakfish, esp. the common species *Cynoscion regalis*. Also with specifying terms.

See also SQUETEE, SQUIT.

1803 *Mass. H. S. Coll.* 1 Ser. IX. 202 The fishes . . . are called the sheepshead, . . . mackerel, squeterg, grunters [etc.]. **1815** *Ib.* 2 Ser. IV. 289 The fish, common to this bay, are found at Wareham, such as . . . squitteag, scuppeag, . . . and alewives. **1884** GOODE, etc. *Fisheries* I. 365 *Cynoscion maculatum* . . . is of course in every respect very unlike a trout, and the name 'Spotted Squeteague' has been proposed for it. *Ib.* 367 The Silver Squeteague, *Cynoscion nothum*, . . . [is] of an uniform silvery hue. **1903** *N.Y. Ev. Post* 11 Sept., Buzzard's Bay now affords only small squeteague, where large ones once abounded.

+Squetee, Squit(t)ee. Variant of prec. — **1807** *Mass. H. S. Coll.* 2 Ser. III. 57 The squittee, or drummer, is taken in the Sound, but principally in the harbours and lagunes. **1848** BARTLETT 328 *Squeteague*, or *Squetee*, . . . a very common fish in the waters of Long Island Sound and adjacent bays. **1884** GOODE, etc. *Fisheries* I. 362 'Squit,' 'Succoteague,' 'Squitee,' and 'Chickwit' are doubtless variations of ['squeteague'].

***Squib.** A highly inflammable or explosive object, as a tube filled with gunpowder, used as a missile or a firework, or serving as a fuse.

1622 'MOURT' *Relation* 43 One of Francis Billingtons Sonnes . . . had got Gun-powder, and had shot off a peice or two, and made squibs. **1701** *Boston Rec.* 12 Nor shall any person hereafter fire or throw any Squib, . . . Rocket or Serpent, or other fireworks in any of the streets. **1779** *Essex Inst. Coll.* LII. 347 There were every where such crouds, such throwing of squibs & crackers that I could not pass to my lodgings. **1830** BRECK *Recoll.* 91 In the evening squibs and fireworks closed the fête. **1843** 'CARLTON' *New Purchase* II. 288 Log-guns done by boring solid trunks with a two-inch auger . . . were fired by means of an enormous squib, or slow match. **1881** RAYMOND *Mining Gloss*, *Squib*, a slow-match or safety-fuse, used with a barrel.

Squid, *n.* Any one of various cephalopod mollusks {1613–}, +as *Ommastrephes illecebrosa* or *Loligo pealii*, freq. used as bait; bait prepared from a squid. Also with defining terms.

1851 MELVILLE *Moby-Dick* 234 The food of the sperm whale—squid or cuttle-fish—lurks at the bottom of that sea. **a1862** THOREAU *Cape Cod* 107 Their bait was a bullfrog, or several small frogs in a bunch, for want of squid. **1881** *Amer. Naturalist* XV. 553 Professor Brooks describes and figures many of the stages in the development of the common squid, *Loligo pealii*. **1883** Short-finned squid [see SHORT *a.* 3 b]. **1912** DREISER *Financier* 12 That squid's a goner.

+b. =SQUID JIG.

1866 *Harper's Mag.* Nov. 720/2 The men and boys were meanwhile swinging their squids, and sending them . . . fifty yards into the surf. *Ib.* 722/1 Lloyd has got a squid through his foot.

+Squid, *v. intr.* (See quot. 1859.) — **a1859** in Bartlett 442 The bluefish is taken by squidding in swift tideways from a boat under sail in a stiffish breeze. **1859** BARTLETT 442 *To Squid*, to fish by trolling with a squid, either natural or artificial. **1894** *Outing* XXIV. 54/1 The fly-fisher scoffs at squidding.

Squid hound. The striped bass. {1812} — **1884** GOODE *Fisheries* I. 425 Large sea-going individuals are sometimes known in New England by the names 'Green-head' and 'Squid-hound.' **1911** *Rep. Fisheries 1908* 317/1.

+Squid jig. A device used in fishing for squid. Also *squid-jigger*. — **1861** *Harper's Mag.* March 459/1 These [squid] are caught by means of a 'squid-jig'—a piece of pewter run on a paper of hooked pins. **1876** KNIGHT 2295/2 *Squid-jigger*, a trolling-hook for catching squids for bait. **1884** *Nat. Museum Bul.* No. 27, 863 *Squid-jig*. . . . Made of 8 iron wire pins molded to lead sinker. **1911** *Rep. Fisheries 1908* 309/2 Cuttle-fish . . . are caught with a peculiar arrangement of hooks called a 'squid jig.'

Squiggle, *v.* (See quotations.) *colloq.* {1895–, *dial.*} — **1816** PICKERING *Vocabulary* 180 *To Squiggle*. To move about like an eel. Used in some parts of New England; but only in very familiar conversation. It is often used *figuratively* in speaking of a man, who evades a bargain. **1891** *Cent.* 5881/1 *Squiggle*, . . . to move about like an eel; squirm; wriggle. (Colloq., U.S.)

***Squill. a.** The bulb of the plant *Urginea scilla*, or the plant itself; a preparation made from this. {1652–} **b.** Any plant of the genus *Scilla*. — **1820** *U.S. Pharmacopœia* 185 Pills of Squill. **1829** EATON *Botany* (ed. 5) 383 *Scilla maritima*, squill. **1847** FIELD *Drama in Pokerville* 153 With a constant croup and no squills if it was taken this minute! **1857** GRAY *Botany* 469. **1875** CARLETON *Farm Legends* 78 Catnip, boneset, sirups, and squills.

‖**Squimmidge,** *v. intr.* To attempt, as if by wriggling or squirming, to escape. Also *vbl. n.* — **1898** WESTCOTT *D. Harum* ii, After a little more squimmidgin' he hauled out his wallet an' forked over. *Ib.* xl, She squimmidged some, but I wouldn't let her say 'No.'

+Squinch, *v. local* or *colloq.*² [Of obscure origin.]

1. *tr.* To screw up or squeeze.

1835 LONGSTREET *Ga. Scenes* 202 If I did'nt see that fellow wink, and that woman *squinch* her face, then hell's a dancing room. **1840** HALIBURTON *Clockmaker* 3 Ser. xi, How it will make her squinch her face, won't it?

2. To compress or squeeze together.

1843 STEPHENS *High Life N.Y.* 195 Harnsome gals . . . squinched themselves up to make room for me. **1909** CALHOUN *Miss Minerva* 200 [Ladies] got to squinch up their waists and toes.

3. *intr.* To shrink or flinch; to pinch or scrimp. Also *vbl. n.*

1843 STEPHENS *High Life N.Y.* II. 195 Wal, she squinched a trifle and gin a leetle start. *Ib.* 253, [I] poured the glass [of cider] down without squinchin. **1905** PHILLIPS *Social Secretary* 120, I reckon there's a lot of miserable pinching and squinching when the blinds are down.

+Squinch-eyed, *a.* Squint-eyed. Also *squinch-eye* attrib. *colloq.*²⁻ **1884** HARRIS *Mingo* 177 Mrs. Kendrick's brother . . . had been engaged [in China] in converting (to use a neighborhood phrase) the 'squinch-eyed heathen.' **1907** WHITE *Arizona Nights* 221 A little squinch-eye round-face with big bow spectacles came and plumped down beside me.

+Squinch owl. ? = SCREECH OWL. *local.* — **1884** HARRIS *Mingo* 31, I year de squinch-owl shiver'n' like he cole. **1896** — *Sister Jane* 132 Squinch-owl say of he comin'. **1902** MACGOWAN *Last Word* 54, I always believed a squinch-owl would do that!

Squinny, *v.* {1847-, *dial.*} *local.* +(See quotation.) — c**1870** CHIPMAN *Notes on Bartlett* 442 Squinny, to make a broad laugh.—New England.

Squint, *n.* {a1652-} +A narrowing of the eyelids; a screwing up of the eyes or face. (For the many different senses given this word by Americans, see G. Hempl in *Dialect Notes* I. 282-5.) — **1897** HOUGH *Story of Cowboy* 34 The bright sun causes him to hold . . . [his eyes] well covered with the lids, with a half squint to them. **1900** BACHELLER *E Holden* 118 When we . . . were on our way to the brook with pole and line a squint of elation had hold of Uncle Eb's face.

* Squint, *v.*

* 1. *intr.* To suggest, as by implication; to hint. {1768-} 'The fig. use of this word, whether verb or noun, is now obs. in Eng. but is still common in Am.' (Horwill). See also George Hempl, '*Squint and Squinny,' Dialect Notes* I. 282-5.

1806 J. Q. ADAMS *Diary* 38 It was advisable to *squint at it,* and to accustom the nations of Europe to the idea that we should claim it in future. **1900** *Congress. Rec.* 15 Jan. 837/2 We never proposed repudiation, or any act that squinted toward it. **1904** *N.Y. Ev. Post* 28 Oct. 7 They inspired some significant paragraphs in the daily papers, squinting at the possibility of a scandal.

+2. To make a shift; to get *along.*

1880 *Harper's Mag.* Sept. 619/2 In winter I haul logs, and in summer I haul mealers, and 'twixt the two I dew manage ter squint along.

3. To have an eye to something; to aspire to. {1642-1782}

1894 FORD *P. Stirling* 306 Now, we know what it means. You needn't deny it. You're squinting at the governorship yourself. **1902** RUSLING *Europ. Days* 343 A goodly Wesleyan chapel, . . . not ambitious to be called a church yet, but squinting that way.

Squinter. {1738-} +An eyeglass. *colloq.* — **1825** WOODWORTH *Forest Rose* I. i, *That* for the English dandy, . . . with his squinter!

* Squire, *n.* (Cf. ESQ., ESQUIRE.) A local dignitary in a village or a rural district {1676-}, +esp. a justice of the peace, a judge, or a lawyer. Also as personal title.

'The *squire* in an Eng. country district is usually both a landowner and a magistrate, but it is in the former rather than the latter capacity that he is given that name. In Am. the *squire* is primarily a justice of the peace, but the name is loosely given, most commonly as a title, to any prominent resident in a village' (Horwill).

[**1743** FRANKLIN *Writings* II. 232 We shall . . . discover in every little Market-Town and Village the 'Squire . . . [listening] to a Barber's News.] **1774** J. ANDREWS *Letters* 59 The parson as well as the Squire stands in the Ranks with a firelock. **1819** FLINT *Lett. from Amer.* 172 In cases where the squire is supposed to be remiss in the execution of his duty, the people sometimes interfere extrajudicially. **1839** LEONARD *Adventures* (1904) 198 A passport . . . must be renewed by the Alcalde or Squire in each district. **1848** *Knickerb.* XVIII. 379 Every body is a squire in these days. **1873** 'MARK TWAIN' & WARNER *Gilded Age* 17 'Squire' Hawkins got his title from being post-master of Obedstown. **1904** *Pittsburgh Gaz.* 29 Sept. 4 The trouble into which 'Squire Phelps of Stockbridge, Mass., has gotten himself by fining Hugh Gurney of the British embassy.

* Squire, *v.* +*tr.* To marry (someone) by a civil ceremony, without religious observance. With *together. colloq.* — **1892** *Advance* 16 June, I utterly forgot to utter a word of prayer over them. And so, . . . Mrs. Knowles was 'squired together' again.

Squir(e)arch. {1831-} +A justice or judge. — **1880** TOURGEE *Invisible Empire* xi, The slave-holder was also the squirarch and the legislator.

Squirm, *n.* A wriggle or contortion. {1883-} — **1839** *Havana (N.Y.) Republican* 21 Aug. (Th.), [The whale gave] a squirm, and roll'd over and over.

Squirm, *v.* {1691-} +*tr.* To fit or squeeze *into;* to utter with a squirm. — **1876** 'MARK TWAIN' *Tom Sawyer* xxi. 171 No matter what the subject might be, a brain-racking effort was made to squirm it into some aspect or other that the moral and religious could contemplate with edification. **1889** GUNTER *That Frenchman!* xxi, Here Zamaroff squirms out: 'Do I look like a man who would kill anything?'

‖Squirmulous, *a.* [f. SQUIRM *v.*] Writhing, wriggling, or twisting in the fashion of a reptile. — **1863** in Thornton 206, I'm a squirmulous vermiform wriggler.

Squirmy, *a.* {1885-} 'Having a squirming shape; crooked' (B.). — *a*1877 *N.Y. Times* (B.), It coils loosely and waveringly about the ground, as a huge snake might unfold it; in every respect, a squirmy piece of work.

* Squirrel.

* 1. Any one of various rodents of the family Sciuridae and allied families, +as the red squirrel and the gray squirrel of North America. Also collective and with specifying terms.
See also BLACK SQUIRREL, BURROWING SQUIRREL, etc.

1630 HIGGINSON *New-England* 10 Here are great store of Squerrels, some greater, and some smaller and lesser. **1666** ALSOP *Maryland* (1869) 40 The Hare, the Squirrel, . . . and several others . . . inhabit here in Maryland. **1726** *Braintree Rec.* 115 Voted, that the heads of said Birds, and squirrels, be brought in to one of the selectmen. **1749** in Chalkley *Scotch-Irish Settlement Va.* I. 40 [He] has not delivered in his crows heads or squirrels scalps, according to law. **1811** SUTCLIFF *Travels* (1815) 65 Broiled squirrels were served up at table. **1857** [see CHICKAREE]. **1891** *Cent.* 5882/3 *Federation squirrel,* the thirteen-lined spermophile, or striped gopher: so called in allusion to the thirteen stripes of the flag of the original States of the American Union. S. L. Mitchill, 1821. **1917** *Mammals of Amer.* 184/2 The food of Rock Squirrels consists of pinyon nuts, acorns, and juniper berries.

+2. a. A fish of the family *Holocentridae.* **b.** The serrano, *Diplectrum formosum.* (Cf. SQUIRREL FISH 2.)
c**1733** CATESBY *Carolina* II. 3 The Squirrel . . . is a good eating Fish. **1883** *Nat. Museum Bul.* No. 27, 503 *Diplectrum fasciculare.* . . . Squirrel.

3. Used in the names of games in which a player to be pursued is called the 'squirrel' {hunt the squirrel, 1742, transf.}; also, the player so called.

1787 TYLER *Contrast* II. ii, I know how to play hunt the squirrel, but I can't play anything with the girls. **1828** *Yankee* I. 131/2 'Hunt the Squirrel' was the favorite. **1896** *Peterson Mag.* Jan. 86/1 They played, 'Can't catch squirrel, hi diddle dee,' in which the 'squirrel' was enacted by a fair maiden.

+4. *Squirrel's jump,* fig., a short distance.
1838 *Knickerb.* XII. 506 Have you ever been as far as a squirrel's jump from it? **1856** *Harper's Mag.* XII. 570/2, I've never been a squirrel's jump *from* it.

5. *attrib.* **a.** In sense 1 with *broth, dog, hunting,* etc.
1789 MORSE *Amer. Geog.* 148 Squirrel hunting is a noted diversion in country places. **1805** PARKINSON *Tour* 305 Squirrel-shooting is a favourite diversion. **1808** ASHE *Travels* 241 The dinner [included] . . . a turreen of squirrel broth. **1844** EMERSON *Experience* Ess. 2 Ser., Western roads, which opened stately enough, . . . but soon became narrower and narrower, and ended in a squirrel-track. **1855** M. REID *Hunter's Feast* xix, A good squirrel-dog is a useful animal. **1869** STOWE *Oldtown Folks* 62 Squirrel-traps for us youngsters grew under his plastic hand. **1891** 'THANET' *Otto the Knight* 5 Marty Ann . . . was placing the squirrel stew on the table. **1907** *St. Nicholas* Aug. 901/2 It was a pretty, dainty girl in a blue velvet suit and hat, with a gray squirrel muff and tippet, that stood at last in the library door.

b. In the specific names of animals {1607-} and plants.
See also SQUIRREL CORN, SQUIRREL CUP, etc.

1842 *Nat. Hist. N.Y., Zoology* III. 72 The Squirrel Tree-toad . . . inhabits under logs and bark of decaying trees. **1890** WEBSTER 1398/2 *Squirrel grass,* . . . a pestiferous grass (*Hordeum murinum*) related to barley. **1891** *Cent.* 5882/3 *Squirrel-bot,* . . . a bot-fly, *Cutiterebra emasculator,* whose larvæ infest the genital and axillary regions of various squirrels and gophers in the United States. *Ib.* 5883/1 *Squirreltail,* . . . one of several grasses of the genus *Hordeum.* . . . In the United States, chiefly *H. jubatum,* but in California also *H. murinum,* there naturalized. **1900** WEBSTER *Suppl.* 200/1 *Squirrel frog,* a small American tree frog (*Hyla squirrilla*).

c. In special combinations.
Squirrel hold, a firm clutch like that of a squirrel on a tree; +*squirrel-picker,* ?one who eats squirrel meat or shoots squirrels (*contemptuous*).
1857 STROTHER *Virginia* 150, I am not to be stumped, nor yit to be called a squirrel-picker, by no set-up swell. **1858** HARRIS *Sut Lovingood* 152 He drapped ofen the hoss-rack, but hilt a squirrel-holt ontu the pole wif his paws and his feet, and hung back down.

+Squirrel corn. 1. A handsome wild herb of the genus *Dicentra,* having yellow tubers resembling kernels of Indian corn. **2.** (See quotation.) — (1) **1843** TORREY *Flora N.Y.* I. 46 Squirrel Corn. Turkey Corn. . . . Rather common in the western and northern counties. **1887** BURROUGHS in *Century Mag.* July 325 The more northern species, called 'squirrel corn' . . . , blooms in May. (2) **1915** ARMSTRONG & THORNBER *Western Wild Flowers* 170 *Bicuculla uniflora*, a diminutive alpine plant, of Bleeding Heart family. This is called Squirrel Corn and Steer's Head.

+Squirrel cup. The hepatica, *Hepatica triloba*. — **1850** S. F. COOPER *Rural Hours* 48 Perhaps it is this position [at the foot of trees], which, added to their downy, furred leaves and stems, has given them the name of squirrel-cups. **1880** *Harper's Mag.* Sept. 584/1 The squirrel cups . . . [lifted] soft gray buds and blooms of pink and purple from the dead leaves. **1894** ROBINSON *Danvis Folks* 223 Crushing unheeded a pink and purple colony of squirrel-cups, he crept up under cover of a stump.

Squirrel fish.

1. A grunt.

1803 SHAW *Gen. Zool.* IV. II. 439 Squirrel Sparus. *Sparus sciurus.* . . . Size of a common Perch: native of the American seas, where it is known by the name of the Grunt, or Squirrel-fish. **1842** *Nat. Hist. N.Y.*, *Zoology* IV. 86 The Squirrel-fish . . . appears to be but a casual visitor from the south. **1884** GOODE, etc. *Fisheries* I. 398.

2. The serrano or sandfish (*Diplectrum formosum*), or a related fish. (Cf. SQUIRREL 2 b.)

The first quotation may belong under senses 1, 3, or 4.
1867 LATHAM *Black & White* 122 The fisherman . . . [showed] me bastard snappers and squirrel-fish, the like of which I had never seen before. **1883** *Nat. Museum Bul.* No. 27, 447 Squirrel-fish; Serrano. . . . Atlantic coast of the United States from South Carolina to Florida. **1884** GOODE, etc. *Fisheries* I. 410 The Squirrel-fish is usually to be seen in the markets of Charleston.

+3. The sailor's-choice, *Lagodon rhomboides*.

1884 GOODE, etc. *Fisheries* I. 393 The 'Sailor's Choice' . . . [is known] at Brunswick, Georgia, as the 'Squirrel-fish.' **1903** T. H. BEAN *Fishes N.Y.* 562 [The sailor's choice] is also called pinfish, squirrel fish [etc.].

+4. (See quotations.)

1896 JORDAN & EVERMANN *Check-List Fishes* 338 *Holocentrus*. Squirrel-fishes. *Ib.*, *Holocentrus ascensionis*. Matejuelo; Squirrel-fish; Welshman; Soldado. Florida to St. Helena.

+Squirrel gun. A gun used, or suitable for use, in shooting squirrels. — **1875** *Fur, Fin & Feather* (ed. 3) 125 Then there are rural gunners . . . provided with quail and squirrel guns. **1883** SWEET & KNOX *Through Texas* 106 If we were to hint that we wanted to pay him, he would feel around for that squirrel-gun. **1902** *Munsey's Mag.* Jan. 503/1 Men armed with squirrel guns came from the back counties of Georgia to Chickamauga.

+Squirrel hake. A species of codling (*Phycis chuss*), or a related fish. — **1882** *Nat. Museum Bul.* No. 16, 799 *P*[*hycis*] *tenuis*, . . . Codling; White hake; Squirrel-hake. . . . North Atlantic, south to Virginia. **1897** *N.Y. Forest, Fish, & Game Comm. 2d Rep.* 246 Squirrel Hake. . . . It lives in the deeper water off shore. **1911** *Rep. Fisheries* 1908 311/1.

+Squirrel hawk. The ferruginous roughleg, *Buteo regalis*. Also *California squirrel hawk*. — **1858** BAIRD *Birds Pacific R.R.* 34 *Archibuteo Ferrugineus*. . . . California Squirrel Hawk. . . . This is one of the most handsome of the American Falconidæ. **1869** *Amer. Naturalist* III. 183 Occasionally a Squirrel Hawk . . . is seen sitting on the ground devouring one of these audacious burrowers. **1895** [see FERRUGIN(E)OUS a.].

Squirrel hole. A hole made or occupied by a squirrel. — **1851** *Zoologist* IX. 3298 There is a bird here [in Calif.] which lives in the squirrel-holes in the ground. **1869** DANA *Two Years* (new ed.) 447 This plain is almost treeless . . . and is filled with squirrel-holes, and alive with squirrels. **1904** WALLER *Wood-Carver* 9 [She thrust] her arm in the opening of a narrow squirrel-hole in the trunk [of a tree].

+Squirrel hunt. A hunt for squirrels. — **1840** *Niles' Nat. Reg.* 11 July 304/3 Squirrel hunt. . . . 21,000 squirrels were recently killed at Gratton, by two parties of sportsmen. **1841** CIST *Cincinnati* 170 An Arkansas editor . . . stated that he should attend a squirrel hunt. **1855** M. REID *Hunter's Feast* xix, To make a successful squirrel-hunt two persons at least are necessary.

Squirrel-hunter.

1. One who hunts squirrels.

*c***1790** FRENEAU *Poems* (1795) 426 No squirrel-hunter kills a deer. **1855** M. REID *Hunter's Feast* xix, The squirrel-hunter is often accompanied by a dog.

+2. *cap.* A member of the irregular volunteer Ohio militia summoned in 1862 for the defense of Cincinnati from attack by a Confederate force under Gen. Kirby Smith. Now hist.

1863 Moore *Rebellion Rec.* V. I. 77 Over one thousand squirrel-hunters from the neighboring counties . . . volunteered their services. **1864** *Ohio Agric. Rep.* XVIII. 163 He was killed on the cars last year, on his way to Cincinnati, as one of the celebrated Squirrel Hunters, to repel the then threatened rebel invasion of that city. **1874** COLLINS *Kentucky* I. 111/2 'Squirrel hunters' and volunteer militia from Ohio and Indiana . . . pour in from all directions.

*Squirreling. **+**The hunting of squirrels. Also attrib. — **1831** *Maysville* (Ky.) *Eagle* 5 July, Suppose we make a squirriling tour to the country today. **1843** 'CARLTON' *New Purchase* II. 188 Who's goin' squirrillin'?

Squirrel pie. A pie made of squirrel meat. {**1883**} — **1788** CUTLER in *Life & Corr.* I. 419 Dined . . . on venison steak and squirrel pie; very good dinner. **1857** STROTHER *Virginia* 79 'A squirrel pie,' said Boniface, . . . 'a fine squirrel pie.' **1893** *Harper's Mag.* April 791/1 There are the squirrel pies, with their flaky crust, and the corn fritters.

+Squirrel rifle. A small-bore rifle suitable for shooting small game. — **1834** NOTT *Novellettes* I. 56 They were differently armed and equipped . . . [with] old-fashioned muskets, squirrel-rifles, horse-pistols, and pocket-pistols. **1865** RICHARDSON *Secret Service* 272 The farmers . . . arrived by thousands with their shot-guns and their old squirrel-rifles. **1882** *Harper's Mag.* Feb. 477/1 In less than twenty minutes we had five hundred of Ohio's stalwart youths, . . . armed with squirrel-rifles. **1916** DUPUY *Uncle Sam* 7 Billy Gard, squirrel rifle on his shoulder, walked into the clearing.

+Squirrel shot. Shot suitable for squirrel-shooting. — **1803** C. PETTIGREW *MS. Let. to E.P.* (Univ. N.C. MS.), I wish you to fetch . . . 4 Lb. of good squirrel shot. **1850** LEWIS *La. Swamp Doctor* 44, I had upon a previous occasion missed killing a fine buck, owing to my having nothing but squirrel shot. **1872** EGGLESTON *End of World* 249 You heerd the buckshot and the squirrel-shot . . . a-rattlin' around.

Squirreltail grass. A weed of the genus *Hordeum* {1777–}, +esp. *H. jubatum*. Also *squirrel-tailed grass*. — **1814** BIGELOW *Florula Bostoniensis* 28 Squirrel tail grass . . . is remarkable for the length and fineness of its awns. **1840** DEWEY *Mass. Flowering Plants* 243 Squirrel-tailed Grass . . . is widely spread over North America. **1878** KILLEBREW *Tenn. Grasses* 225 *Hordeum Pratense*, Squirrel-Tail Grass, . . . is an annual. **1913** BARNES *Western Grazing Grounds* 272 Foxtail (*Hordeum*) and Squirrel Tail Grass.—The injurious effects of these grasses are entirely mechanical in their nature.

*Squirt, n.

1. An insignificant or contemptible person, esp. one who is pretentious in manner or dress. *colloq.* {1887, *dial.*}

'Chiefly *U.S.* and *dial.*' (*O.E.D.*).
1843 W. T. THOMPSON *Major Jones's Courtship* 160 *They* won't keep company with squirts and dandies. **1888** *Nation* 17 May 396/2 [If] Adams . . . had prosecuted criminally or sued civilly the young journalistic 'squirt' who . . . was calling him names [etc.]. **1922** SANDBURG *Slabs Sunburnt West* 72 Man is a poor stick and a sad squart.

+2. A showy or bombastic speech, recitation, or piece of writing.

1851 HALL *College Words* 292 At Harvard College, a showy recitation is denominated a *squirt*. **1872** HOLMES *Poet* 295 That sounds a little like what we college boys used to call a 'squirt.' **1876** TRIPP *Student-Life* 26 He couldn't have read a word, but, as luck would have it, did make a regular 'squirt' on another passage.

*Squirt, v.

1. +a. *intr.* (See quotation.) **b.** *tr.* To force (solid matter) into a desired shape or condition, as by sudden pressure. Also *vbl. n.*

(a) **1851** HALL *College Words* 292 *Squirt*, to make a showy recitation. (b) **1869** *Overland Mo.* III. 130 Swine's flesh, bread, sage, and other matters of nourishment and seasoning, [are] chopped fine, and then squirted out into links from the end of a sausage-gun. **1881** R. W. RAYMOND *Mining Gloss.*, *Squirting*, forcing lead by hydraulic pressure into the form of rods or pipes. **1904** *Elect. World & Engineer* 21 May 981/2 The plastic mass is then inserted in a press and forced through a small hole of requisite diameter, this process being the same as used in 'squirting' lamp filaments.

2. Used in combination with nouns.

Squirt can, an oil can with tapering spout, through which oil is forced when pressure is applied to the bottom of the can; +*s. clam*, =SOFT CLAM.

1902 *Amer. Inst. Elect. Engineers Trans.* XIX. 591 No part [of an engine] shall depend on squirt-can lubrication. **1887** GOODE, etc. *Fisheries* V. II. 581 In Long Island Sound and at New York it [*Mya arenaria*] is most spoken of as the 'long clam' and 'squirt clam.'

+Squirt gun. A syringe or other device for squirting liquid. Also *fig.* — **1803** FESSENDEN *Poetical Petition* 87 With glyster-pipe and squirt-gun There will be dev'lish deal of hurt done. **1806** *Balance* V. 150/3 Two paltry prints, (the Bee and the Albany Register) have opened their pop-guns, or rather squirt-guns, upon this gentleman. **1865** BURRITT *Walk to Land's End* 96 An instrument which American boys would call a squirt-gun is employed [at Reading, Eng.] in making the *macaroons*. **1894** HOYT *Texas Steer* (1925) III. 39, I won't be made the target for your squirt-gun of wit.

+Squirtiness. (See SQUIRTY a.)

+Squirtish, *a.* Given to display or ostentation in dress or manner. — **1847** ROBB *Squatter Life* 73 These squirtish kind a fellars ain't perticular hard baked. **1851** HALL *College Words* 292 *Squirtish*, showy; dandified.

+Squirty, *a. local.* (See second quotation.) Hence *squirtiness*. — **1851** HALL *College Words* 292 *Squirtiness*, the quality of being showy. *Ib.*, *Squirty*, showy; fond of display; gaudy. Applied to an oration which is full of bombast and grandiloquence; to a foppish fellow; to an apartment gayly adorned, &c.

+Squit. [?Shortened form of SQUETEAGUE.] The squeteague, *Cynoscion regalis*. — **1884** GOODE, etc. *Fisheries* I. 362 'Squit,' 'Succoteague,' 'Squitee,' and 'Chickwit' are doubtless variations of ['squeteague']. **1911** *Rep. Fisheries* 1908 317/1.

+Squitteag, Squit(t)ee. (See SQUETEAGUE, SQUETEE.)

+Squizzle, *v. colloq.* 1. *To let squizzle*, to let explode or go off. ‖2. To sizzle. — (1) *a***1861** WINTHROP *Open Air* 241 The recruit let squizzle and jist missed his ear. (2) **1890** *Detroit Free Press* 2 July, Think of an editor fairly 'squizzling' with the heat.

‖**Squmption.** ?A hurry. — **1851** *Polly Peablossom* 60 Hold on, fellers, don't be in such a squmption.

+**Squnch,** *v.* [Of obscure origin.] *intr.* (See quotation and cf. SQUINCH *v.* 2.) — **1877** BARTLETT 797 *Squnch*, to stoop or lie down; to squeeze one's self within the smallest compass.

‖**Squow.** ?A row or squabble. — **1862** E. W. Pearson *Lett. Port Royal* 70 It is a peculiar experience to be detective, policeman, judge, jury, and jailer, . . . —sometimes in cases of assault and battery, and general plantation *squows*,—then in a divorce case.

+**Sqush,** *v.* [Variant of *squash* v.] **1.** *tr.* To crush or mash. *colloq.*[2] **2.** *intr.* **a.** To collapse. **b.** To gush or squirt out. — (1) **1837** NEAL *Charcoal Sk.* (1838) 45 The next time I meet that chap, . . . I'll sqush it with my foot. **1905** *Dialect Notes* III. 21 Squush the bug. (2) **1884** 'MARK TWAIN' *Huck Finn* xxix, Blamed if the king didn't have to brace up mighty quick, or he'd 'a' squshed down like a bluff bank that the river has cut under. **1898** WESTCOTT *D. Harum* xxiv, When Polly Bixbee . . . puts that foot o' her'n *down* somethin's got to sqush. **1922** A. BROWN *Old Crow* 312 There were plenty [of peaches] to be . . . gobbled in the garden with the juice squshing over your white frock.

+**Squshy,** *a.* Soft and yielding. — **1891** *Century Mag.* Feb. 489 He reposes on three or four feather beds piled one upon another, a patchwork quilt being spread over the squshy mountain.

***Stab,** *v.* +*tr.* (See quot. 1883.) Hence *stabber.* — **1881** INGERSOLL *Oyster Industry* 249 *Stabber.*—One who opens oysters by sticking the knife in at the side, without previously breaking the shell. (Massachusetts and Rhode Island.) **1883** *Nat. Museum Bul.* No. 27, 221 The oyster is 'stabbed'; that is, instead of breaking the lips of the valves, the knife is entered at the side.

‖**Stabbist.** [*Stab* v. 'to strike' and *ist.*] One who stabs; a stabber. — **1871** DE VERE 658 The man of violence, who had heretofore been denounced as a murderer, now appeared before the charitable jury as a modest *stabbist*, or, at worst, called a formidable *strikist*.

***Stable.**

***1.** A building containing stalls, mangers, etc., in which domestic animals are kept. Also pl. in sing. sense.
1652 *Suffolk Deeds* I. 137 In the stable [are] one Rack & manger. **1731** *Phila. Ordinances* (1812) 17 No person . . . shall keep or stack any hay . . . except it be in a stable, or other secure house. **1846** COOPER *Redskins* viii, On one side of the hut there was a hog-pen and a small stable for a cow. **1905** VALENTINE *H. Sandwith* 33 Archy McSwords called me down to the stables.

b. *transf.* (See quotations.)
1886 *Harper's Mag.* July 175/1 The bicycle and tricycle stable was well patronized. **1904** *McClure's Mag.* April 661/1 Kelly and his 'stable,' as the retinue of rubbers and 'workout' boxers are known to the devotees of pugilism, had been at Ocean View.

2. *pl. Mil.* Duty at the stables; the bugle call for this. {**1885**-}
1873 ROE *Army Lett.* 109 It was afternoon stables and we rode around to the picket lines to watch the horses getting their grooming. **1894** WISTER in *Harper's Mag.* Sept. 509/2 At that moment 'stables' sounded, and the men ran out to form and march to their quarters.

3. Attrib. and comb. with *car, frock, guard,* etc.
1749 HEMPSTEAD *Diary* 528 Here is . . . a fine Stable House of Brick. **1790** *Penna. Packet* 9 April 2/2 Jesse Sharpless [sells] . . . stable halters. **1819** *Amer. Farmer* I. 66 Plough in your barn yard of stable manure. **1850** LEWIS *La. Swamp Doctor* 161 [The horses] had to trust the chances of a stray nubbin falling through the chinks of the stable loft. **1861** *Army Regulations* 83 In the cavalry, stable-guards form a separate roster, and count before fatigue. *Ib.* 488 Flannel shirt, drawers, stockings, and stable-frock—the same as now furnished. **1867** HOLMES *Guardian Angel* 370 The stable-keeper . . . offered the resources of his stable to the youth supposed to be in peril. **1869** ALCOTT *Little Women* II. 81 The stable-man lets her have horses cheap. **1890** *Stock Grower & Farmer* 11 Jan. 5/2 The patent stable-car alone delivered 48,000 car loads [to Chicago], which at twenty head to the car would amount to 960,000. **1896** *Cosmopolitan* XX. 391/2 In the stable lot . . . the grass was grazed so close that the geese could barely nip it.

Stabl(e)age. Care for a horse in a stable. *Obs.* — **1736** *Va. State P.* I. 227 To Stableage 19 Horses. **1779** in Summers *Ann. S.W. Va.* 282 Stablage with hay or fodder one night [10s.].

Stable boy. A boy or man who works in or about a stable. {**1729**-} — **1830** HOLMES *Poetical Works* (1899) 8/1 He shall think . . . Of the stable-boy's gathering numbers. **1851** *Harper's Mag.* Sept. 571/1 Throwing the reins to the stable-boy, . . . he helped out 'Miss Dinah.' **1898** ATHERTON *Californians* 104 The improvised groom, a sulky and intensely self-conscious stable-boy, led up the horses.

Stable call. *Mil.* The bugle call summoning to duty at the stables; the assembling of a troop for stable duty. — **1861** *Army Regulations* 39 In the cavalry, *stable-calls* immediately after reveille. **1886** MITCHELL *R. Blake* 132 The cavalry-man . . . rode away, humming gaily a doggerel verse set to the 'stable call.' **1889** *Century Mag.* April 900/2 Will you go down to stable-call and pick out a mount?

+**Stable fly.** A fly (*Stomoxys calcitrans*) found about stables. {**1910**} **2.** A related fly, *Muscina stabulans.* {**1910**} — (1) **1862** T. W. HARRIS *Treatise Insects Injur. Veget.* 16 The stinging stable-flies (*Stomoxys*). **1892** KELLOGG *Kansas Insects* 116 A cattle pest [from Europe] . . . bids fair to . . . be as troublesome as its nearly related pest, the well-known Stable Fly, or Cattle Fly. **1925** HERRICK *Man. Injurious Insects* 425 The stable fly . . . in this country is worst in the Southwest. (2) **1891** *Cent.* 5884/2 *Stable-fly,* . . . *Cyrtoneura stabulans*, common to Europe and North America.

+**Staboy, Stub(b)oy,** *v. tr.* To urge or encourage (dogs or other animals), as by calling 'staboy!' Also *fig.* — **1843** STEPHENS *High Life N.Y.* II. 141, I shook my bridle . . . , and stuboyed the old critter along. **1850** LOWELL *Poetical Works* (1896) 323/2 Like dogs let loose upon a bear, Ten emulous styles [of architecture] *staboyed* with care, The whole among them seemed to tear. **1900** *Sun* (N.Y.) 9 Nov. (*Dial. Notes* II. 347), Instead of offering a bounty for the heads of the wolves, he stubboyed them against the sheep.

+**Staboy, Stub(b)oy,** *interj.* Also **ste(e)boy, seeboy, suboy.** [?Contraction of *hist-a-boy* (cf. Emerson *Works* I. 322). Perh. *stuboy* under influence of *stoo* 'an exclamation used to urge on hounds.'] A call used to summon or arouse a dog or other animal. Also in fig. use.
1774 *Mass. Spy* 29 Dec. (Th.), Stu boy, Stu boy, seize 'em, Jowler. **1843** W. T. THOMPSON *Major Jones's Courtship* 55 The dogs started up sumthing. . . . 'Steboy; catch him!' ses he. **1845** HOOPER *Taking Census* 154 Sick, sick, si-c-k him, Bull—suboy! suboy! suboy! **1845** *Knickerb.* XXV. 172 Applause—hear! hear! and see-boy! from the Vampyres. **1848** LOWELL *Biglow P.* I Ser. vi. 74 Certain theologic dogmas, . . . when occasion offers, he unkennels with a *staboy*. **1884** A. A. PUTNAM *10 Yrs. Police Judge* 86 They stand off and say stee-boy to the constables. **1905** *Sun* (N.Y.) 15 Nov. (*Cent. Suppl.*), 'Stubboy, stubboy' . . . was the cry used in trying to force those obstinate beasts [*sc.* pigs] into the ways they should go.

***Stack,** *n.*

***1.** A pile of hay, straw, or grain in the sheaf.
1652 *Mass. Bay Rec.* III. 264 If any person of the age aforesaid shall . . . set on fire any outhowse, barne, stable, leantoo, stackes [etc.]. **1678** WILLIAMS *Unpublished Lett.* (1881) 60 His Stacks of hay . . . God sufferd not the Pagans to destroy. **1749** *N.J. Archives* I Ser. VII. 368 Edward Archer and one Elisha Clark . . . Set fire to the Stacks of Oats flax & Corn Stolks. **1845** KIRKLAND *Western Clearings* 63 The gradual completion of a stack and the final pointing out and thatching . . . is an operation in which we often find amusement by the hour. **1903** [see DRY *v.* 3].

2. A group of chimneys standing together; a single such chimney; a funnel of a steamship. {**1667**-} Also attrib.
1655 *Suffolk Deeds* II. 188 Hee shall not endanger or hurt the fowndation of the Stack of Chimnyes of the said Wm. Hudsons. **1701** *Boston Rec.* 11 To build a good Stack of brick Chimneys. **1843** 'CARLTON' *New Purchase* I. 107 The cabin . . . was as yet unchinked, undaubed and without its stack chimney. **1846** *S. Lit. Messenger* XII. 20/1 The blended masts and stacks of steamers there [in New Orleans] should be an emblem of union and harmony. **1893** PAGE in *Harper's Mag.* Dec. 7/1 The foundation of the old stack [of an iron furnace has been] uncovered.

3. A large quantity; a pile. *colloq.* {**1894**-, in Australia}
1870 'MARK TWAIN' *Sk., New & Old* 25 Never saw such a stack of them [*sc.* lightning rods] on one establishment. **1889** *Boston Jrnl.* 4 Feb. 4/1 Upon his desk rests a stack of bills.

+**4.** The part of a library in which the main collection of books is shelved. Also attrib.
1884 *Harper's Mag.* Nov. 828/1 The stack-rooms, in which the body of the collection . . . is packed. **1910** BOSTWICK *Amer. Pub. Library* 284 The relation of reading room to stack must be such as to make these [carriers] easily operable.

+**5.** *Dark* (or *black*) *as a stack of black cats,* very dark (or black).
1847 ROBB *Squatter Life* 65 All was dark as a stack of black cats. **1913** LONDON *Valley of Moon* 319 It's pretty still. . . . An' black as a stack of black cats. **1916** SANDBURG *Chicago Poems* 19 It is dark as a stack of black cats.

***Stack,** *v.* +**1.** To shuffle or arrange (cards) in such a way as to facilitate cheating. { =E. 'stock'} **2.** *To stack up,* {**1859**-} +to pile *up* one's poker chips; *fig.,* to measure *up* or turn out; to pile *up. colloq.* — (1) **1896** LILLARD *Poker Stories* 54 The cards were stacked and marked on the back, so that he didn't have any chance at all to win. (2) **1896** ADE *Artie* 10 He'd stack up, you know, an feel in his pockets and then he'd say: I'm forty-seven cents loser. *Ib.* 70 How does the old gentleman stack up? **1911** SAUNDERS *Col. Todhunter* 198 Old Bill Strickland, of Nineveh, somehow don't seem to stack up the right way against the Honorable Stephen K. Yancey. **1921** PAINE *Comr. Rolling Ocean* 71, I wish this trouble hadn't stacked up between us.

Stacker.

1. One who makes a stack of grain or hay. {**1757**-}
1769 WASHINGTON *Diaries* I. 338 Two, and sometimes three, Stackers will Stack as fast as it is cut. **1880** ALLAN-OLNEY *New Virginians* I. 150 None of the Virginians working for him were good stackers. **1924** CROY *R.F.D. No. 3* 39 One of the 'stackers' . . . stood by the blower.

+**2.** A machine or part of a machine which stacks straw or hay. {**1905**}
1864 *Ohio Agric. Rep.* XVIII. 61 The stacker may be easily and quickly raised or lowered, while the machine is in operation. **1891** GARLAND

Main-travelled Roads (1922) 12 The men . . . raised the long stacker into place. **1914** E. STEWART *Let. Woman Homesteader* 15 He couldn't run both the mower and the stacker.

+**Stack pole.** A pole used in building a haystack. — **1712** HEMPSTEAD *Diary* 12, I got Stack Poles & Stackt hay. **1754** *Ib.* 628 Adam carted out 2 ld. Stack poles. **1816** *Ann. 15th Congress* 1 Sess. 2456, I began by erecting . . . a signal . . . , in form of a tripod, made of a ladder and two stack-poles. **1891** READ *Emmett Bonlore* 343 He was almost as high as a stackpole, an' so slim.

*Stack yard.** A yard in which hay or grain is stacked. Also attrib. — **1684** *Essex Inst. Coll.* XXII. 3 All that marsh which we call the farr division neare the place called the stackyard. **1747** HEMPSTEAD 400, I was . . . fencing a Stackyard. *Ib.* 605, [I] carted up a L[oa]d of Stackyard poles & Stakes. **1833** *Trial E. K. Avery* 19 Within ten rods of a stackyard, I discovered the body of a female hanging to a stake. **1898** *Mo. So. Dakotan* I. 130 Out in the frosty morning with a half of a stackyard threshed at sunrise.

*Staddle.**

*1. A young tree or sapling.**
1679 *Conn. Rec.* III. 27 We marked a white oake stadle. **1729** HEMPSTEAD *Diary* 215, [I] Counted 100 Stadles Cut down by T. Wms. **1854** HAMMOND *Hills, Lakes* 29 Small saplings or 'staddles,' as my guide termed them, [were] cut first some six feet in length. **1877** COOKE *Somebody's Neighbors* 340 'Tain't so easy bending a white-oak staddle.

2. A platform upon which to cure hay {1729–}: (see also quot. 1848).
1774 *Brookhaven Rec.* 194 Every person that owned staddles on said beach should have liberty to take them away by the first of December next. **1809** KENDALL *Trav.* II. 177 To protect the stacks, they are either built upon high ground, or, if in the marshes, upon staddles or piles. **1848** LOWELL *Biglow P.* 1 Ser. 146/1 *Staddles*, stout stakes driven into the salt marshes, on which the hay-ricks are set, and thus raised out of the reach of high tides. **1911** *Essex Inst. Coll.* XLVII. 14 The staddles were about three feet above the marsh.

*Stadium.** A structure of tiers of seats enclosing an arena where athletic exercises or other public events are held. {1834} — **1900** *Scientific Amer.* LXXXIII. 361/1 The major axis of the Stadium will be fully 750 feet in length. **1905** *Harper's Weekly* XLIX. 1783 Harvard and Yale fought a brilliant contest in the Cambridge stadium for the season's championship. **1923** [see DASH 2].

Stadthouse. In regions of the United States formerly under Dutch influence, a town hall. Now hist. {1646–, of the Netherlands}
1666 *Md. Archives* II. 28 The Upper House do think fit . . . that Smith repay the Tobaccos next Year which he hath already received towards the building of the Great Stadt house. **1695** *N.Y. Hist. Soc. Coll.* I. 355 When he arrived he went to ye Stadt House. **1744** in *Penna. Mag.* I. 127 About 4 in the afternoon, the Company broke up, and from thence went to the Stadthouse. **1769** *Md. Laws* xiv. § 39 The stadt-house in the city of Annapolis is so much gone to decay that it is become necessary to build a new one, as well for the holding assemblies and provincial courts, as for providing safe and secure repositories for the public records. **1800** in Munsell *Ann. Albany* III. 119 Visit snuff manufactory, stadthouse. **1809** IRVING *Knickerb.* VII. vi, The sturdy Burgomasters called a public meeting in front of the Stadt-house.

*Staff.¹**

*1. A walking stick; a strong stick used as a weapon; a pole used for displaying a flag.**
1643 WILLIAMS *Key* (1866) 101 A Staffe is a rare sight in the hand of the eldest, their Constitution is so strong. **1736** *Boston Rec.* 139 The Others [shall be obliged] to carry a Staff with a Bill. **1856** SIMMS *Charlemont* 373 Give me that staff, my son, and your arm on the other side. **1907** *St. Nicholas* July 832/1 Up went our flag to the top of the staff.

*2. A constable's staff, used both as a weapon and as a badge of office. *Obs.**
1686 SEWALL *Diary* I. 162 The Constables were ordered this day to come and take new Staves.

‖**3. A stick attached to a fishing net.**
1823 COOPER *Pioneers* xxiii, He threw away the 'staff,' or 'stretcher.' *Ib.*, 'Staff, ho!' shouted the steward.

+**Staff.²** (See quotation.) — **1893** *Harper's Mag.* Feb. 478 The modern method of building by the use of iron . . . makes practicable the use of 'staff' for walls, a [plaster] composition light in weight, flexible to any form, and yet durable.

Staff officer. {1702–} +(See quotation.) — **1881** *Naval Encycl.* 770/2 *Staff-officer*, . . . an officer of the navy not exercising military command. **1891** *Cent.* 5887/1.

Staff tree. A tree or shrub of the genus *Celastrus* {1633}; +the false bittersweet, *C. scandens.* Also attrib. and with specifying term. — [**1771** J. R. FORSTER *Flora Amer. Septentr.* 11 *Celastrus bullatus.* Staff tree, elegant. Virginia.] **1785** MARSHALL *Amer. Grove* 28 The Staff-Tree. . . . The Corolla has five petals. **1813** Climbing Stafftree [see BITTERSWEET 2]. **1815** DRAKE *Cincinnati* 77 Forest of the Miami Country . . . [contains] Staff tree or bittersweet. **1849** EMMONS *Agric. N.Y.* II. 316. **1891** COULTER *Bot. W. Texas* I. 56 *Celastrineæ.* (Staff-tree Family.) Shrubs, with simple and undivided leaves.

*Stag.**

*1. A male deer.**
1663 *Harvard Rec.* I. 212 A stags head sent to England. **1743** [see MOOSE DEER]. **1820** *Amer. Antiq. Soc. Coll.* I. 72 A savage . . . killed several stags and wild goats. **1904** WALLER *Wood-Carver* 86 A stag and three does crossed the Pent Road.

2. A castrated bull. {1680–}
1744 HEMPSTEAD *Diary* 433, [I] carried my 2. 2 y[ea]r old Steers and Staggs to the common pasture. **1857** *Ill. Agric. Soc. Trans.* III. 428, I get my big plow and hitch on the stags. **1913** BARNES *Western Grazing Grounds* 180 Bulls . . . need their horns as a means of defense against steers or stags.

3. (See quotation.)
1848 BARTLETT 329 In the New York courts, a stag is the technical name for a man who is always ready to aid in proving an alibi, of course 'for a consideration.'

+**4.** Short for STAG PARTY. *colloq.²*
1904 *Brooklyn Eagle* 28 May 3 The Myrtle Fishing Club will have a stag at Hurman Hub's Park this evening.

+**5.** (See quot. 1905.) Also *to go stag.*
1905 N. DAVIS *Northerner* 213 'No man not escorting a lady'—a stag, you know—could go upon the floor. **1924** P. MARKS *Plastic Age* xix, Several of the brothers were going 'stag'; so he felt completely at ease.

+**6.** *attrib.* Designating social entertainments or activities organized for men only. *colloq.*
See also STAG DANCE, STAG PARTY.
1869 BOWLES *Our New West* 218 Our Mormon hosts took us . . . on a picnic excursion to Salt Lake,—a 'stag' picnic. **1886** POORE *Reminisc.* I. 311 Colonel Season . . . gave one of his famous 'stag' supper-parties. **1892** *Harper's Mag.* Jan. 252/1 A stag dinner is a good time that women would like to come to if they could. **1911** HARRISON *Queed* 185 Buck Klinker, returning from some stag devilry at the hour of two A.M. **1912** IRWIN *Red Button* 11 Tommy North . . . came home from a stag smoker drunk.

Stag beetle. Any of various beetles having mandibles resembling the horns of a stag, +esp. *Lucanus dama;* the horn beetle. {1681–} — **1778** [see HORN BUG]. **1809** *Amer. Acad. Mem.* III. 163 The larva or grub of the *Lucanus Capreolus* . . . is the Stag Beetle of New England. **1869** *Rep. Comm. Agric.* 1868 85 The larva of our native species, *Lucanus dama*, commonly known as the horn-bug, or stag-beetle, . . . is found in old decaying trunks and roots of trees.

+**Stagbush.** (See quotations.) Also with specifying term. — **1884** SARGENT *Rep. Forests* 94 *Viburnum prunifolium.* . . . Black Haw. Stag Bush. **1897** SUDWORTH *Arborescent Flora* 339 *Viburnum ferrugineum.* Rusty Stagbush.

+**Stag dance.** A dance performed or attended by men only. — **1843** *Amer. Pioneer* II. 61 If perchance a *fiddle* or a *jewsharp* was possessed by any of the inmates [of the fort], it was occasionally brought into requisition, and the monotony disturbed by the hilarity of a *stag dance.* **1855** *Yale Lit. Mag.* XX. 228 Seated in a circle in this place, which has been so often trampled by the 'stag-dance' of preceding classes, . . . are the present Graduates. **1873** [see LIGHTNING 2]. *a*1918 G. STUART *On Frontier* I. 82 On Saturday night the miners would get up a stag dance, there being very few women in camp.

*Stage.**

*1. A platform or other structure erected at a fishing place for drying and salting fish. Also transf.**
1633 *Mass. Bay Rec.* I. 104 Any swine [that] shall, in fishing time, come within a quarter of a myle of the stage . . . shalbe forfected to the owners of the s[ai]d stadge. **1676** *Southampton Rec.* II. 67 John Cooper of Southampton did . . . request my lycence that hee might have a priviledg . . . to erect small houses or stages for sawing and salting of such fish as shall bee taken. **1765** ROGERS *Acct. N. Amer.* 21 [They] spread it [*sc.* codfish] out . . . on a kind of stage raised with wattels, about two feet from the ground. **1817** BRADBURY *Travels* 122 Buffaloe skins . . . [are] placed on stages, erected both for this purpose [*i.e.,* dressing the skins] and to dry or jerk the flesh of animals cut into thin slices. **1828** SHERBURNE *Memoirs* 55 The men take the codfish from shore or to the stage, which is a kind of wharf, over which there is generally a shed.

2. A stagecoach. {1671–}
1772 in Fithian *Journal* I. 15, I had a letter wrote by the last stage. **1802** CUTLER in *Life & Corr.* II. 107 Messrs. Foster, Griswold, Goddard, Davenport, Read, and myself, hired a stage for ourselves at $3 1/2 each, for Baltimore. **1825** NEAL *Bro. Jonathan* I. 45 The 'stage' was a long, rough-built, heavy waggon. **1914** E. STEWART *Lett. Woman Homesteader* 3, I was twenty-four hours on the train and two days on the stage.

+**b.** An omnibus used within a city.
1855 M. THOMPSON *Doesticks* 41 Hereafter you may not mistake a Grand Street stage for a perambulating Circus wagon. **1882** MCCABE *New York* 157 In spite of the success of the elevated railways . . . the stages or omnibuses still manage to hold their own. **1912** J. MILNE *John Jonathan & Co.* 92 A fleet of motor-buses, which the New Yorkers call 'stages,' short for stage-coaches, meanders up and down [Fifth Ave.].

+**3.** The depth *of* water in a river; the level *of* water.
1805 CLARK in *Lewis & C. Exped.* III. (1905) 148 Several narrow chanels . . . pass through a hard black rock forming Islands of rocks at this Stage of the water. **1818** FEARON *Sketches* 461 If there is what is called 'a good

stage of water,' that is, if the waters of the Ohio are high, . . . boats will be taken by the stream. **1835** [see BURTHENSOME *a.*]. **1857** *Ill. Agric. Soc. Trans.* II. 4 Our general arrangements with the boats were . . . to be governed by the stage of water. **1875** 'MARK TWAIN' *Old Times* iv. 63 [The height of the bank] tells you the stage of the river. **1904** *N.Y. Ev. Post* 21 Jan. 2 Pittsburgh may have a forty-foot stage of water.

4. *attrib.* and *comb.* **a.** Designating animals, vehicles, and other equipment connected with travel by stage.

See also STAGE HORN, STAGE WAGON.

1761 *Essex Inst. Coll.* XI. 38 Large stage chair. **1767** *Ib.* LIII. 298 Mr. Boardman . . . goes regularly three Times a Week in the Stage-Chaise between Salem and Boston. **1792** *Ann. 2d Congress* 59 He shall provide for carrying the mail of the United States by stage carriages or horses. **1835** HOFFMAN *Winter in West* I. 78 By the light of the stage-lamps . . . I climbed to the coachman's box. **1838** *Mass. Agric. Survey 1st Rep.* 17 The number of stage and livery horses kept in the county cannot fall short of one thousand. **1850** S. F. COOPER *Rural Hours* 518 The stage-sleighs, with four horses and eight or ten passengers, perhaps, occasionally go and come over the ice at that season. **1860** GREELEY *Overland Journey* 264 The stage-mules are turned out to feed and rest. **1887** TOURGEE *Button's Inn* 52 She scanned the passengers who alighted one by one, as the glare from the stage-lanterns . . . fell upon them.

b. Designating persons or groups owning, operating, or otherwise concerned with stagecoaches.

See also STAGE COMPANY, STAGE-DRIVER, etc.

1825 NEAL *Bro. Jonathan* II. 445 Major Davison, the stage proprietor. **1843** 'CARLTON' *New Purchase* I. 17 So remarkably accommodating were the old-fashioned *accommodation* stages and stage owners. **1866** *Rep. Indian Affairs* 76 Two roads have been authorized . . . , one for the use of Thomas & Ruckel, a stage firm. **1882** SWEET & KNOX *Texas Siftings* 106 There are only nine stage robbers in jail at San Antonio. **1900** DRANNAN *Plains & Mts.* 390 Slade . . . used to be stage agent on the Overland road.

c. Designating routes, buildings, etc., used by or for the accommodation of stage travelers and stage animals.

See also STAGE HOUSE, STAGE OFFICE.

1845 *Xenia Torch-Light* 31 July 1/1, [There are] plenty of stage routes, well stocked and much traveled. **1847** D. P. THOMPSON *L. Amsden* 57 He had engaged to tend horses this winter at the stage-tavern. **1856** STOWE *Dred* II. 125 At the first stage-stand, [he] changed him [the horse] for a fresh one. **1860** G. T. CLARK *Diary* (MS.) 10 Drove down to a stage station to see if we could stay. **1874** B. F. TAYLOR *World on Wheels* 43 Dismantled stage barns . . . were sparsely sprinkled along the route. **1913** LONDON *Valley of Moon* 442 A combination of sickness and mischance found the stage stables short a driver.

d. Designating various events, activities, etc., connected with or involved in stage travel.

1807 IRVING, etc. *Salmagundi* iv, Famous fellow for running stage races—killed three passengers and crippled nine in the course of his practice. **1838** *Niles' Nat. Reg.* 29 Sept. 80/1 *Stage accident.* . . . The horses ran off at full speed. **1840** *S. Lit. Messenger* VI. 225/1, I had never before tried Virginia stage travelling in the winter. **1870** *Scribner's Mo.* I. 153 The stage-ride over the mountain is the grand feature of the journey. **1890** LANGFORD *Vigilante Days* (1912) 329, I'm afraid there will be a stage robbery to-night. **1912** RAINE *Brand Blotters* 165, I want to know what's being done about that Fort Allison stage hold-up.

e. In special combinations.

+*Stage connection,* a provision for continuing a journey by stage; *s. crazy,* fig., insane because of long riding in a stage; *s. time,* the time required for a given trip as made by stage.

1869 *Boyd's Business Directory* 62 Stage Connections: at Middleburgh for Gilboa, Moresville, Roxbury. **1893** *Nation* 23 March 220/1 He did not mind joltings in bullock-carts [in India] so long drawn out that they would have made most men stage-crazy. **1913** LONDON *Valley of Moon* 442 Billy . . . took the reins of six horses and drove a full load over the mountains in stage time.

5. Designating persons and things connected with the theater.

See also STAGE CARPENTER, DOOR, MANAGER.

1790 *Harvard Laws* 25 Any undergraduate [who] shall presume to be an actor in, a spectator at, . . . any stage-plays . . . [shall] be punished by a fine not exceeding ten shillings. **1807** IRVING, etc. *Salmagundi* i, 12 The stage-critics . . . censure an actor for a gesture he never made. **1832** DUNLAP *Hist. Amer. Theatre* 23 The slave dealers of Newport . . . probably thought a stage player a greater abomination than the kidnapper . . . of the miserable negro. **1855** WOOD *Recoll. Stage* 28 Mrs. Pownall . . . [was] long admired both as a stage vocalist and a concert singer. **1873** BEADLE *Undevel. West* 517 They are as much unlike the 'stage Indian,' and as much like a tribe of dark Caucasians as it is possible to conceive. **1887** *Courier-Journal* 13 Feb. 16/4 If he has to . . . [keep] its mother out of the way of the actors, scene shifters and other stage hands, his soul is filled with abiding gloom. **1888** WARNER *On Horseback* 116 His face was blackened to the proper color of the stage-darky. **1888** Stage entrance [see MASHER]. **1895** *Boston Transcript* 1 Jan. 5/7 A Continuous Stage Show from 1 to 11 P.M.

Stage carpenter. A carpenter employed in a theater or circus. {1856-} — **1846** *Chicago Jrnl.* 23 Dec. 3/2 Scenic Artist, L. G. Hager; Stage Carpenter, Geo. Wetsell. **1886** POORE *Reminisc.* II. 185 Spangler,

the stage-carpenter, was a chunky, light-haired . . . man. **1920** COOPER *Under Big Top* 120 A belligerent stage carpenter faced the animal trainer.

Stagecoach. 1. A coach that runs from one town to another, or others, according to a time schedule, for the purpose of carrying passengers, mail, and baggage. {1658-} +**2.** A social game. — (1) **1736** *R.I. Col. Rec.* IV. 527 Alexander Thorp . . . and Isaac Cusno . . . [requested] license to keep two stage coaches for the service. **1875** HARTE in *Scribner's Mo.* Dec. 248/1 The Wingdam and Sacramento stage-coach changed horses. **1902** WISTER *Virginian* 157, I changed from the saddle into a stage-coach. (2) **1892** *Nation* 24 Nov. 397/3 What happened on the demise of the Grand Prince resembled a game of 'stage-coach.' **1899** CHAMPLIN & BOSTWICK *Cycl. Games & Sports* (ed. 2) 679/1.

Stage company. 1. The occupants of a stagecoach. **2.** A company which owns and operates a line of stagecoaches. — (1) **1845** *Lowell Offering* V. 206 The stage company has to dine here or nowhere. (2) **1877** HODGE *Arizona* 206 These two stage companies employ four hundred horses, one hundred men, and fifty coaches. **1890** LANGFORD *Vigilante Days* (1912) 449 The whole subject was carefully investigated by the stage company.

Stage door. The theater entrance used by actors and workmen. {1778-} Also attrib. — **1761** *New York Post-Boy* 31 Dec., It will be taken as a particular Favour if no Gentleman will be offended that he is absolutely refus'd Admittance at the Stage Door. **1762** *Amer. Wkly. Mercury* 1 Feb., [To] Stage Door Keeper, 8 s. **1902** C. MORRIS *Stage Confidences* 167 These 'Johnnies' who hang about stage doors . . . are actuated by vanity, pure and simple.

Stage-driver. A man whose occupation is driving a stage. — **1790** *Ann. 1st Congress* 1822 He would exempt [from militia duty] the people called Quakers, . . . stage-drivers, and instructors of youth. **1811** SUTCLIFF *Travels* (1815) 111 The stage driver told us that . . . close by the place we then were at, his 4 horses suddenly stopped. **1857** UNDERHILL & THOMPSON *Elephant Club* 191 Sixth Avenue stage-driver affable. **1872** McCLELLAN *Golden State* 398 The stage-driver . . . is ceaseless in flinging right and left wads of newspapers at the door of every farm-house. **1904** *Automobile* 15 Oct. 428 Liverymen and stage drivers beat their horses into a lope.

Stage-driving. The occupation of driving stage. — **1856** STOWE *Dred* I. 108 [He] had tried his hand at stage-driving. **1894** WISTER in *Harper's Mag.* July 208/1 [He] had tried a little of everything; . . . saloons, stage-driving, marriage occasionally, and latterly mines.

‖**Stagee.** A small stagecoach. — **1833** *Md. Hist. Mag.* XIII. 343 We left in a stagee—a little two horse concern.

Stage fight. ‖A duel. — **1687** SEWALL *Diary* I. 175 After the Stage-fight in the even, the Souldier [went] Shouting through the streets.

Stage head. The head of a fishing stage or landing place. — **1677** HUBBARD *Narrative* II. 46 Coming too near the Stage Head, they presently found themselves in Danger of a Surprizal. **1692** *Mass. Hist. Soc. Proc.* 1 Ser. V. 37 He saw the said Burroughs . . . carry it from the stage-head to the door at the end of the stage. **1752** *Essex Inst. Coll.* XLVI. 117 The schooner May Flower . . . [was] well fastned to a stage head with sundry Fasts.

Stage horn. A horn used to announce the approach of a stagecoach. — **1825** NEAL *Bro. Jonathan* II. 112 A sound, like that of a stage-horn, arose from the valley. **1844** *Knickerb.* XXIII. 445 The stage horn is blown. **1884** 'CRADDOCK' *Where Battle Was Fought* 333 The cliffs began to echo the mellow resonance of the stage-horn.

Stage house. {1638} +A house of accommodation for stages and their passengers; an inn. Now hist. — **1772** ASBURY *Journal* I. 37 We came to the stage-house through much rain and bad roads. **1798** BENTLEY *Diary* II. 255, [I] left my Bundles & Papers behind in the care of the Bar keeper in the Stage House. **1825** WOODWORTH *Forest Rose* I. iii, Will you direct me to Major Butler's, who keeps the stage-house at the sign of the Spread Eagle? **1843** 'CARLTON' *New Purchase* I. 27 At all events we shall have a good breakfast at this fine looking stage-house. **1874** B. F. TAYLOR *World on Wheels* 18 He makes a sweep and comes about with a rattling halt in front of the stage-house. **1907** ANDREWS *Recoll.* 120 The stage-house was a two story building.

+**Stage line.** A line of stages operated on a schedule. Also attrib. — **1838** *Indiana H. Rep. Jrnl.* 23 Sess. 151 A stage line from Indianapolis to Evansville. **1860** HOLLAND *Miss Gilbert* 285 [He] rode rapidly off to the nearest stage-line station. **1867** [see FEEDER 2]. **1872** *Chicago Tribune* 17 Nov., The South Side theatres . . . have had the benefit of partially renewed horse car and stage line accommodations. **1907** *St. Nicholas* July 772/2 He had grasped the chance to take charge of one of the stations of the stage line flung across the desert to reach the new gold camps in southwestern Nevada.

*Stageman.** A stage-driver. {stagemanship, 1845} — **1776** FITHIAN *Journal* II. 185 With some difficulty however we urged the stageman—an execrable Tory—to proceed on to the ferry. **1835** in *S. Lit. Messenger* IV. 513/2 The blast of a stageman's horn broke my slumbers. **1860** GREELEY *Overland Journey* 201 Our stage-men . . . stood ready to repel the supposed depredator.

Stage manager. One who has charge of the stage during theatrical performances. {1817-} — **1832** DUNLAP *Hist. Amer. Theatre* 6 One man, or a company forming a co-partnership are lessees or proprietors, and the stage-manager and performers are hired. **1851** NORTHALL *Curtain* 33 The stage manager . . . has before him sundry parts, papers, and play bills. **1895** *N.Y. Dramatic News* 16 Nov. 3/2 Charles Stewart remains as stage manager and booking agent.

Stage office. The office of a stage line. (Cf. STAGE HOUSE.) — **1785** ELLICOTT in Mathews *Life A. Ellicott* 54, I went to the stage Office and took possession of my seat. **1829** ROYALL *Pennsylvania* II. 41 At taverns or stage-offices, (which are mostly the same thing,) there is a small share of attention. **1854** THOREAU *Walden* 128 Do they not talk and think faster in the depot than they did in the stage-office? **1879** STOCKTON *Rudder Grange* xvii, When I took our places at the stage-office, I inquired for David Dutton. **1910** J. HART *Vigilante Girl* 137 Fox came down to the stage office to bid his nephew farewell.

Stage passenger. A passenger on a stage. — **1827** McKENNEY *Tour to Lakes* 16, I am a stage passenger. **1886** HARTE *Snowbound* 201 Stanner tried to get up some sort of vigilance committee of the stage passengers to burn down Henniker's ranch out of spite.

+**Stage plank.** A landing place. — **1865** *Harper's Mag.* Feb. 400/2 She had noticed the sentinel passing to and fro at the shore-end of the stage-plank. **1875** 'MARK TWAIN' *Old Times* i, I would rather be the deck-hand who stood on the end of the stage-plank with a coil of rope in his hand.

Stage road. A road over which stages travel. Also attrib. — **1797** WEEMS *Letters* II. 70 Being off the Stage road, . . . I could not get to town in time for the mail. **1837** W. JENKINS *Ohio Gaz.* 103 Centerburg . . . [is] on the stage road from Mount Vernon to Columbus. **1898** *McClure's Mag.* X. 445 The second overland route . . . follows the Fraser River over an excellent stage road. **1904** 'O. HENRY' *Heart of West* 279 They spent the night at a stage road hostelry.

Stage room. {1642-} +Room for the erection of fishing stages; a room connected with a fishing stage. *Obs.* — **1628** *Mass. H. S. Coll.* 3 Ser. VIII. 164 More [ships] cannot well be there, for want of convenient stage room. **1713** *N.H. Probate Rec.* I. 711, I Give & Bequeath [to my sons] . . . my Stages Stage rooms, . . . moring places flakes flakrooms that was formerly mr. Phebeans.

Stage route. A route over which stages travel; the stage service maintained on such a route. — **1819** *Niles' Reg.* XVI. 4/1 The pecuniary receipts of the department . . . [cannot] defray the expenses of any considerable portion of the stage routes alone. **1854** M. J. HOLMES *Tempest & Sunshine* 115 They concluded to take the stage route to Lexington and Versailles. **1887** *Courier-Journal* 20 Feb. 4/1 Drifts have formed . . . along the stage routes.

Stage wagon. A wagon used for the transportation of passengers, mail, and freight; a stagecoach. {1761-} — **1763** *Md. Gazette* 3 Nov., The Subscriber . . . sent in the Stage Waggon from New Castle, a new Saddle. **1799** J. SMITH *Acct. Captivity* 73, [I] was carried in a stage waggon to Burlington. **1836** *S. Lit. Messenger* II. 245 The swiftness of the current forced the whole down the stream till the stage-wagon came to pieces. **1860** MORDECAI *Virginia* 275 The modes of conveyance were either by a stage-wagon, twice or thrice a week, or on horse-back with saddle-bags, or in a stick-chair.

+**Staggerbush.** A shrub (*Neopieris mariana*) which gives staggers to stock. — **1847** DARLINGTON *Weeds & Plants* 213 Maryland Andromeda. Stagger-bush. . . . The farmers . . . allege that it is injurious to *sheep*, when the leaves are eaten by them,—producing a disease called the staggers. **1898** CREEVEY *Flowers of Field* 512 Stagger-bush . . . is a fine shrub . . . thought to poison lambs and calves which browse upon its tender leaves.

+**Stagger grass.** 'The atamasco-lily, *Zephyranthes Atamasco*: so called as supposed to cause staggers in horses' (*Cent.*).

Staggerish, *a.* Intoxicated to the point of unsteadiness. *slang.* — **1737** *Penna. Gazette* 13 Jan. 2 He's Staggerish.

+**Staghorn coral.** Any of various corals of the genus *Acropora* which branch in such a way as to suggest antlers. — **1884** GOODE, etc. *Fisheries* I. 841 Among the true stony corals are the Stag-horn Corals (*Madrepora cervicornis, prolifera*, and *palmata*); the Brain Corals . . . , and many others.

Staghorn sumac(h). Also **stag's-horn sumach.** A kind of sumac (*Rhus typhina*) whose flower stalks and branches look somewhat like antlers. — [**1731** MILLER *Gard. Dict.* s.v. *Rhus*, Virginian Sumach, by some falsely called, The Stag's-horn-tree.] **1785** MARSHALL *Amer. Grove* 129 Stag's-horn Sumach . . . grows naturally in Virginia and Pennsylvania. **1813** MUHLENBERG *Cat. Plants* 32. *a*1862 THOREAU *Maine Woods* 314. **1898** CREEVEY *Flowers of Field* 481 Stag-horn Sumach. . . . The ends of the irregular branches, covered with a soft, velvety down, give the name stag-horn.

*Staging.** Driving, operating, or traveling in stages. Now hist. {1850- 'chiefly Anglo-Indian'} Also attrib. — **1840** *S. Lit. Messenger* VI. 381/2 He does not follow the sea nor staging. **1864** BROWNE in *Harper's Mag.* Oct. 563/1 [In] an ancient adobe building, . . . Mr. Banning carried on his staging and teaming operations. **1891** WELCH *Recoll. 1830-40* 133 The 'old staging days' . . . always revive their somnolent memories. **1894** *Outing* XXIV. 399/2 Stagin' in them days, stranger, was stagin'.

+**Stag party.** A party attended by men only. (Cf. STAG 4.) — **1856** *Knickerb.* XLVII. 407, I finally lose myself in a party of old bricks who . . . are keeping up a small stag-party . . . at the end of the room. **1867** *Atlantic Mo.* Jan. 60/1 An occasional fox-chase, horse-race, or a 'stag party' at some outlying tavern, formed the sum of their dissipation. **1884** *Lisbon* (Dak.) *Star* 20 June, Schurz and Logan were members of a select stag party at the house of a prominent Senator. **1923** HERRICK *Lilla* 109 Genial Uncle George . . . [slumped] into an obese and slipshod old age, with a taste for 'stag parties,' lodge room jokes, and cheap plays.

Stag's-horn sumach. (See STAGHORN SUMAC(H).)

---

*Stair.** A flight of steps. Usually pl. Also attrib.
1651 *Suffolk Deeds* I. 176, I frauncis smith of Boston Cardmaker have sold . . . the howse . . . and all the Appurtenances which thereunto did belong, doores stajres glasse &c. **1730-1** *Phila. Ordinances* (1812) 16 No stairs or passage up the loft. **1817** *Holyoke Diaries* 167 Began to mend Stair carpet. **1856** M. J. HOLMES *L. Rivers* xxx, 'Lena, half-way up the stairs, listened breathlessly for the result. **1897** HOWELLS *Open-eyed Conspiracy* xi, I got caught in a dark eddy on the first stair-landing. **1911** LINCOLN *Cap'n Warren's Wards* 256 He turned and strode toward the foot of the stairs.

+**b.** *To climb the golden stairs,* fig., to leave this life; to expire. *colloq.*
1883 in Ware *Passing English* 79/2 Edward's Folly Dramatic Company is reported as having climbed the golden stairs.

Stair-builder. A carpenter who specializes in building stairs. Also *stair-building.* {1900} — **1851** CIST *Cincinnati* 240 Stair Building. Three shops.—Eighteen hands; value of labor product, twenty-four thousand dollars. *Ib.* 260 Stair builders. **1886** J. A. PORTER *New Stand. Guide of Washington* 190 J. W. Boggs, Jr., Carpenter and Stair-Builder. **1892** *Nation* 11 Aug. 99/2 Two stairbuilders from Boston . . . could not work unless they had their union tickets changed.

Staircase. Orig. the case about a flight of stairs; later, the stairs themselves. {1624-}
1644 *Harvard Rec.* I. 4 An Account of the Glasse taken of Christopher Grant. . . . In the Turret 18 f[eet], Staire Case 8 f[eet]. **1704** S. KNIGHT *Journal* 53 The stair cases [were] laid all with white tile. **1763** [see PAPER *v.* 1]. **1852** STOWE *Uncle Tom* xxxix, The staircase that led to the garret, and even the passage-way to the staircase, was avoided by every one. **1880** *Harper's Mag.* May 873/2 Ascending the staircase, we enter the western picture-galleries. **1907** *St. Nicholas* Oct. 1097/1 Up the broad staircase came 'Brother Tom.'
attrib. **1863** A. D. WHITNEY *F. Gartney* xxvii, She heard . . . the staircase door closed and locked below. **1857** VAUX *Villas* 318 A large family bedroom . . . [is] easily accessible from the principal staircase hall. **1871** *Rep. Indian Affairs* (1872) 380 The New Mexico pueblos . . . [have] the staircase ladders on the outside. **1907** *St. Nicholas* Sept. 1017/2 Franky peered down into the empty staircase-well.

Stairway. A flight of stairs. {c1820-, transf.; 1872-}
1708 *Cambridge Prop. Rec.* 262 A Stairway for passage into ye S[ai]d Court house. **1749** *N.H. Probate Rec.* III. 754 We set off . . . [the] Stairways, and all Passage ways. **1812** *Niles' Reg.* I. 329/1 The stair-ways were immediately blocked up. **1892** GUNTER *Miss Dividends* 21 You must let me thank you again for the attention you showed me on the stairway. **1922** PARRISH *Case & Girl* 38 She calmly outgeneraled him again, . . . disappearing herself up the stairway with Miss Willis.

b. = FISHWAY.
1869 HALE *Sybaris* 54 You must take our friend out to see the fish go up his stairways.

+**Stait.** (See quotation.) *slang* or *cant.* — **1859** MATSELL *Vocabulum* 85 *Stait,* city of New-York.

*Stake, n.**
I. *1. A stout stick or post, driven into the ground, freq. used as a sign of ownership or as a boundary mark.
1639 *Conn. Hist. Soc. Coll.* VI. 6 Eury man shall sett a sufitiant stak with the to first leters of his nam towards the paling. **1655** *Charlestown Land Rec.* 135 A poplar tree being within 3 or 4 foot of the stake, or bound mark of this Ground. **1703** *Cambridge Prop. Rec.* 219 We pitched down two Stakes. **1820** *Mo. Intelligencer* 26 Aug. 3/5 He is guided chiefly by the blazed trees and stakes. **1850** *Huntington Rec.* III. 403 All persons [shall] be prohibited from putting down stakes in any of the harbors in the Town of Huntington to mark the lines of oyster beds, that will . . . obstruct fishing with nets. **1884** *Century Mag.* Nov. 59 If here truly was the lost mine, then was he too late; another set of stakes was in ahead of his!

+2. One of the crossed pieces of timber supporting the riders in certain fences, esp. rail fences. Also fig.
1671 *Portsmouth Rec.* 26 April 160 A Virginia ffence . . . Shallbe fower ffoot and a halfe high Stakt with Stakes halfe a foot above the fence. **1681** *N.H. Hist. Soc. Coll.* VIII. 65, I did see Thomas Every . . . strike William Cate with one of the stakes of the fence. **1789** [see RIDER 3]. **1797** [see FORK(ED) FENCE]. **1844** *Knickerb.* XXIV. 235 The yellow-hammer dodged round the stakes of the rail-fence. **1894** *Harper's Mag.* Oct. 713/1 'Mother Tyler' . . . was the 'main stake' in the 'Tyler fence.'

+**b.** *attrib.* In the names of different kinds of fences.
See also STAKE AND RIDERED FENCE, etc.
1850 *New Eng. Farmer* II. 68 On the same farm he also built a line of stake and board fence. **1868** BRACKETT *Farm Talk* 116 'Getting out fencing stuff?' 'Yes. I'm going to try some more of the stake and wire sort.' **1869** *Rep. Comm. Agric. 1868* 258 This form of thorn fence is similar to the old time 'herring-bone' rail and fence.

+3. A territorial division of the Mormon church.
[**1833** J. SMITH in Linn *Story of Mormons* 120 It is expedient in me that this Stake that I have set for the strength of Zion be made strong. **1839** *Ib.,* I have other places which I will appoint unto them, and they shall be called Stakes for the curtains, or the strength of Zion.] **1846** in Howe *Hist. Coll. Ohio* 283 This place [Kirtland] . . . they hold to be a *stake of*

Zion. **1870** BEADLE *Utah* 124 All the wealthy members were to follow him to western Pennsylvania, and establish a new 'stake' for the others to gather to! **1883** Schaff *Religious Encycl.* II. 1578 Every city, or 'stake,' including a chief town and surrounding towns, has its president.

+4. *To pull up stakes,* or variants: **a.** *fig.* To finish one's affairs in a place; to leave a place; to move. **b.** To remove boundary stakes put in the ground.

The suggestion that the *fig.* usage is in allusion to 'pulling up the stakes of a tent' (B. '59) is not supported.

1640 LECHFORD in De Vere 185, I am loth to hear of a stay [in New Eng.], but am plucking up stakes with as much speed as I may. *a*1658 BRADFORD *Hist.* 439 They of Hingam presumed to alotte parte of them [*i.e.*, meadow grounds] to their people, and measure & stack them out. The other pulled up their stacks, & threw them. **1703** SEWALL *Diary* II. 76 Went to my Bounds, asserted them, . . . then ordered Kibbe to pull up the Stakes. **1784** *Mass. H. S. Coll.* I Ser. I. 256 And so they plucked up stakes, and came over to this place to fix themselves here. **1817** PAULDING *Lett. from South* I. 83 When they have exhausted one hunting-ground, [the Indians] pull up stakes, and incontinently march off to another. **1894** ROBINSON *Danvis Folks* 140 She pulled up stakes an' went off somewhere. **1920** LEWIS *Main Street* 319 Course I've had thoughts of pulling up stakes and going West.

5. *To up stakes,* =sense 4 a. {1891}

1837 *Jamestown* (N.Y.) *Jrnl.* 6 Sept. 1/6 If we can't go according to that rule, then I say let everyman upstakes and go to Turkey or China. **1843** STEPHENS *High Life N.Y.* II. 40, I can up stakes, and go hum agin in the old sloop.

+6. a. *To set,* or drive, *stake(s),* originally, to place boundary stakes in the ground; *fig.,* to settle down.

1703 SEWALL *Diary* II. 76 Told Mr. Lynde's Tenants what my Bounds were . . . ; forwarn'd them of coming there to set any Stakes. **1854** SIMMS *Southward Ho!* 436 It seems to me to be good if we drive stakes and build our cabins here. **1906** *Outing* Feb. 605/2 After drifting about several years I finally drove stakes on the Spokane River.

+b. *To move stakes,* to change one's place of settlement.

1862 HARTE *Luck of Roaring Camp* 211 He built the shanty . . . lest titles should fall through, and we'd have to get up and move stakes farther down.

II. +7. Provisions or savings intended to last through a period when no other provisions or savings will be available; a grubstake.

1738 BYRD *Dividing Line* (1901) 178 [We] recommended to the men to manage this, their last stake, to best advantage. **1853** [see FLAT *adv.* 2]. **1863** *Rio Abajo Press* 21 April 1/1 Not finding any one . . . willing to donate or lend him another 'stake,' he had recourse to Dona Luiza. **1902** WHITE *Blazed Trail* 17, I ain't got no ticket. . . . I blows my stake.

+8. *To make a stake,* to accumulate enough money for living expenses or for capital; to make a fortune.

1873 BEADLE *Undevel. West* 510 It is a splendid country to travel through; a miserable poor one to stop in to make a 'stake.' **1891** C. ROBERTS *Adrift Amer.* 114 He had made a pretty good stake, and wanted to go east for the winter. **1898** POST *10 Years Cowboy* 56, I must make a stake first; a little one, anyway. **1923** 'BOWER' *Parowan Bonanza* 91, I thought if I made a real stake, . . . I could give you everything in the world you wanted.

∗ Stake, *v.*

I. ∗**1.** *tr.* To mark (land) with stakes. {−1523} Frequently with *out.* {−1710}

1624 Smith *Gen. Hist. Va.* VI. 232 We went to measure out the grounds, . . . and so we cast lots where euery man should lie, which we staked out. **1641** *Watertown Rec.* I. 1. 7 Abram Browne shall haue 4d. vpon the Acre for Surveying, Plotting, & Staking the severall Lotts vpon the two Plaines. **1715** *Md. Acts 1692–1715* (1723) 20 The Surveyor . . . [shall have] Fees and Rewards of laying out and staking the Towns and Lots. **1869** J. R. BROWNE *Adv. Apache Country* 493 He staked off his ledge. **1872** 'MARK TWAIN' *Roughing It* 334 When some roughs jumped the Catholic boneyard and started in to stake out town lots in it he *went* for 'em! **1890** *Harper's Mag.* June 140/2 [They] had staked out avenues and town lots.

+b. To mark (a line or route) with stakes.

1668 *Dedham Rec.* IV. 156 Lieft Fisher Joh: Haward and Sergent Fuller are deputed and empowered to laye out this way accordingly and stake or doole the same out as they shall Judge most equall. **1714** SEWALL *Diary* II. 435 Take Mr. Benjamin Mayhew with you . . . and Stake the Line between the Honble. Corporation and him. **1819** [see BLAZE *v.*¹ 2]. **1877** JOHNSON *Anderson Co., Kansas* 98 The route was staked out from Ohio City to Fairview.

+c. To mark off (a claim) with stakes. Freq. with *out, off.* Also *fig.* {1876}

1860 GEO. T. CLARK *Diary* (MS.) 14 Staked out some claims. **1879** *Scribner's Mo.* Oct. 811/2 Before the prospector began work he had 'staked out a claim' by putting up a conspicuous notice of the fact. **1898** ATHERTON *Californians* 13 In community with his brother-in-law, he staked off a claim. **1904** LONDON *Daughter of Snows* xiii, You staked that claim before he was dry behind the ears.

+d. *absol.* To settle down.

1872 DE VERE 184 Where he settles, there he stakes or sticks his stakes.

+2. a. *tr.* To provide (a fence) with stakes.

1655 *Suffolk Deeds* II. 149 Peleg heath shall make and mayntayne all ye fence where it is now staked Against the orchard. **1662** *Portsmouth Rec.* 116 All out fences . . . being sufishently staked and pould. **1866** *Rep. Indian Affairs* 249 A lawful fence shall be eight rails high, well staked and ridered.

b. To prop up (a haystack) with stakes.

1747 HEMPSTEAD *Diary* 487, I fenced 2 & staked and toppoled 2 more.

+3. To give (a person) a stake or grubstake.

1853 'P. PAXTON' *Yankee in Texas* 219 The jo-fired mean whelp wouldn't stake me. **1890** *Stock Grower & Farmer* 3 May 7/4 Several of these alleged Chinese doctors were 'staked' to go into business by Denver women of the demimonde, who saw a chance to make a speculation. **1894** 'MARK TWAIN' *P. Wilson* iv, Tom staked him with marbles to play 'keeps' with. **1917** McCUTCHEON *Green Fancy* 25 He staked her to a ticket to New York.

∗**4.** *To stake out,* to picket (an animal).

*a*1859 *Spirit of Times* (N.Y., B.), He got all his fixins for camping—his little wallet and tin cup, and a big lariat to stake out his mule. **1895** *Outing* XXVI. 403/1 We rode up as far toward the top of the ridge as we dared go and then staked out the ponies.

+Stak(e)age. The work of driving stakes in a channel. — **1792** *Ann. 2d. Congress* 1356 The stakeage of channels on the sea-coast . . . shall continue to be defrayed by the United States. **1854** PIERCE in *Pres. Mess. & P.* V. 263 Appropriations of this class were confined . . . to the construction of light-houses . . . and the stakage of channels.

+Stake-and-ridered fence. =next. — **1846** *Knickerb.* XXVII. 208 Already the 'stake and ridered' fence was beginning to enclose the cleared land. **1895** *Century Mag.* Aug. 625/2 The stake-and-ridered fences everywhere . . . would make following impossible.

+Stake-and-rider (fence). A fence having a rider supported by crossed stakes. — **1829** *Mass. Spy* 11 Feb. (Th.), [He met] a man in a lane with a stake-and-rider fence on each side. **1859** BARTLETT 443 *Stake and Rider,* a species of fence higher and stronger than a 'worm fence.' **1884** CABLE *Dr. Sevier* liv, Again they followed him, along a line of stake-and-rider fence. **1917** McCUTCHEON *Green Fancy* 100 He climbed over the stake and rider fence.

+Stake car. 'A platform car' (Chipman). — **1862** *N.Y. Herald* 18 March 2/1 In the rear was a stake car, upon which was loaded a quantity of furniture.

+Staked and ridered, *a.* **1.** Provided with a stake-and-rider fence. **2.** Of fences: Made with stakes and riders. (Cf. STAKE *v.* 2 a.) — (1) **1852** *Mich. Agric. Soc. Trans.* III. 333 The staked and ridered domicil, lopped over like some old lame hen. (2) **1855** *Chicago W. Times* 17 May 3/5 A whirlwind . . . scattered in every direction a strong 'staked and ridered' fence. **1879** *Scribner's Mo.* Nov. 135/2 An utter absence of fencing is preferable to the staked-and-ridered rail absurdity. **1901** HARBEN *Westerfelt* 271 The scarecrow in the cornfield beyond the staked-and-ridered rail fence looked like the corpse of a human being.

+Staked plain(s). [tr. of Sp. *llano estacado.*] **1.** A treeless plain or prairie. **2.** =LLANO b. Usu. *cap.* — (1) **1848** ROBINSON *Santa Fe Exped.* 67 The whole country may well be called, as some maps style it, a staked plain. (2) **1849** *31st Congress 1 Sess.* Sen. Ex. Doc. No. 64, 196 The Llano Estacado, or Staked Plain, . . . extends four hundred miles from north to south on the east side of the Rio Pecos. **1872** [see JORNADA]. **1913** BARNES *Western Grazing Grounds* 49 The staked plains were so called because . . . at a distance these yucca stalks are not unlike stakes.

Stake-driver. + =AMERICAN BITTERN. — **1814** *Mass. H. S. Coll.* 2 Ser. III. 101 Among the birds that are found here [in Lancaster, N.H.] are . . . stake-driver or bittern . . . ; wood-cock. **1888** [see POST-DRIVER 2]. **1917** *Birds of Amer.* I. 181/2 There comes to the ear only a single note closely resembling the driving of a stake, which can be heard from afar. Hence the name 'Stake Driver.'

+Stake notice. A notice of a mining claim affixed to a stake. — **1880** *Cimarron News & Press* 26 Feb. 1/5 Location stake notices were treated with contempt.

+Stake Prairie. =STAKED PLAIN(S) 2. — **1834** A. PIKE *Sketches* 42 This Stake Prairie is to the Comanche what the desert of Sahara is to the Bedouin.

+Stake rope. A rope used to stake out an animal. — **1871** DE VERE 130 Texans *twine* or *rope* a horse, . . . and then stake him out with a *stake-rope.* **1883** SWEET & KNOX *Through Texas* 63 Our stake-ropes [were] hung on the pommel. **1903** 'O. HENRY' *Roads of Destiny* 104 Lonny . . . sought Hot Tamales, placidly eating grass at the end of his stake rope.

Staky. (See quotation.) — **1877** BARTLETT 652 A staky horse is one that *jibbs,* or stands still when in harness.

+Stalk-borer. (See quot. 1909.) — **1884** *Rep. Comm. Agric.* 417 The Stalk-borer (*Gortyna nitela*) was often made the subject of complaint during the past summer. **1909** WEBSTER 2029/3 *Stalk borer,* the larva of a noctuid moth (*Papaipema nitela*), which bores in the stalks of the raspberry, strawberry, tomato, and other garden plants.

+Stalk-cutter. 1. One who cuts stalks. **2.** An implement for cutting cornstalks. Often *straw-* and *stalk-cutter.* (Cf. STRAW-CUTTER.) — (1) **1825** WOODWORTH *Forest Rose* I. iv, Here comes the stalk-cutters, and the apple-pickers, and the cider-grinders. (2) **1850** *Cultivator* ns. VII. 369 We stand much in need of some . . . cheap and effective straw and stalk cutters. **1868** *Mich. Agric. Rep.* VII. 346 C. E. Hutchinson, Cleveland,

O., straw and stalk cutter, hand power . . . ; G. E. Hutchinson, Cleveland O., straw, hay and stalk cutter, horse power. **1876** KNIGHT 2301/1.

+Stalk field. A field in which cornstalks are left standing. — **1845** *Cultivator* ns. II. 125/1 The stalk fields are the main dependance [sic] of half the farmers in the country for wintering the stock. **1871** EGGLESTON *Hoosier Schoolm.* 188 The stalk-fields . . . seemed to be peopled with terrors. **1885** *Rep. Indian Affairs* 93, 750 tons [of hay] . . . with the stalk-fields and other forage will be fair provision for the stock on hand.

∗Stall, n. +The berth of a locomotive in a roundhouse. — **1876** CROFUTT *Trans-continental Tourist* 42 The company have here . . . a round-house with six stalls. **1899** *McClure's Mag.* March 484 The engine . . . is put on the turn-table and sent into her stall.

∗Stall, v.

+1. intr. To come to a stop; to bog down. Also fig.

1807 JANSON *Stranger in Amer.* 172 His horses *stalled*, that is, they were for some time unable to drag the waggon through the worst places. **1848** BRYANT *California* iii. 36 The travelling has been very fatiguing to our oxen, the wagons frequently stalling in the mud-holes. **1857** CHANDLESS *Visit Salt Lake* 233 Twice he 'stalled' hopelessly, and had to send to the nearest farm for a yoke of cattle. **1921** PAINE *Comr. Rolling Ocean* 22 When things happened too fast, his mind stalled on a dead center.

+b. Of persons: To engage in obstructive activities; to loiter or hang about without acting. *colloq.*

1903 LEWIS *Boss* 23 [If] Big Kennedy shows up to stall ag'inst you, why I should say [etc.]. **1916** 'BOWER' *Phantom Herd* 194, I stalled around out there till my money gave out.

∗2. tr. To bring to a stop. Usually passive. {−1821}

'Now only *U.S.* or *dial.*' (O.E.D.)

1816 in Pickering 205 When a waggon has been broken down, or fast set in the clay or mud, so that it cannot be moved by the team, they say in the *Southern* States, that it is *stalled*. **1834** *Visit to Texas* 83 The mud was soft enough to mire or 'stall' our horses, as it is called. **1892** GUNTER *Miss Dividends* 231 The train is stalled, and the snow comes down faster and faster. **1907** [see COOK WAGON].

∗Stallion. An uncastrated male horse. — **1747** HEMPSTEAD *Diary* 481, I rid out to Parden Tabers to carry my mare to a Stallyon &c. **1787** WASHINGTON *Diaries* III. 155 A sorrell Stallion, a blaze face, 2 hind feet and off fore foot white. **1868** WOODRUFF *Trotting Horse* 61 It was the first time that a young stallion had appeared in public at that age. **1890** *Stock Grower & Farmer* 10 May 3/2 It is a sad commentary on New Mexico that so few stallions of merit are brought here for breeding purposes.

∗Stalwart. {c1470, 1891−} +(See quots. 1881, 1885.) — **1879** *Congress. Rec.* App. 26 April 89/2, I saw a great company of stalwarts approaching. **1881** *Nation* 16 June 415/2 The epithet 'Stalwart' . . . was first used by Mr. Blaine in 1877 to designate those Republicans who were unwilling to give up distrust of the South as a political motive. **1885** *Mag. Amer. Hist.* April 395/2 *Stalwart*, a Republican who stands by his party right or wrong. **1901** *McClure's Mag.* Dec. 152 [Platt] is merely a stalwart.

+Stalwartism. {1899} The principles of the Stalwarts. — **1879** *Nation* 27 Nov. 355/2 Stalwartism . . . includes indifference or hostility to civil-service reform, and a willingness to let 'the boys' have a good time with the offices. **1882** *Ib.* 16 Nov. 422/2 They have rejected President Arthur and Stalwartism; nor do they take more kindly to Mr. Blaine and Jingoism.

+Stalwartize, v. tr. To convert to the principles of the Stalwarts. — **1882** *N.Y. Tribune* 12 April, An attempt is being made . . . to stalwartize the Republican party, . . . convert its majority against its will from Garfield to Stalwart Republicanism. **1882** *Nation* 13 July 22/3 The Administration . . . has been [charged with] trying to 'stalwartize' the party by removals in the civil service.

∗Stamp.

1. a. An official impression or mark set upon papers or other objects signifying the prepayment of a tax {1694−}, esp. in connection with the Stamp Act. **b.** = REVENUE STAMP. {1802−}

1765 *Copley-Pelham Lett.* 36 Capt. Jacobson is just arrived with the stamps which has made so much noise and confusion among us Americans. **1766** [see PLAYBILL]. **1866** *Internal Revenue Guide* 272 The law requiring stamps upon conveyances, bonds, notes, etc., took effect Oct. 1st, 1862. **1875** *Chicago Tribune* 13 Sept. 5/3 It is this Gauger's duty also to see the packages emptied and the stamps destroyed. **1904** TARBELL *Hist. Standard Oil Co.* I. 32 Stocks in companies whose holdings were hardly worth the stamps on the certificates were sold all over the land.

+2. = HORSE STAMP.

1796 HAWKINS *Letters* 31 They have in the range a place called the stamp, where the horses have salt every spring, and here they gather of themselves.

+3. (See quotations.)

1848 BRYANT *California* xxi. 268 A tin coin issued by Captain Sutter circulates among them, upon which is stamped the number of days that the holder has labored. These stamps indicate the value in merchandise to which the laborer or holder is entitled. **1909** WEBSTER 2181/3 *Trading stamp*, a printed stamp, with a certain value, given as a premium by a dealer to a customer, and usable instead of money in procuring articles from the issuers of the stamps.

4. = POSTAGE STAMP 1. {1837−}

1861 *Chicago Tribune* 19 July 1/2 Stamps and stamped envelopes continue to be returned to the Post Office Department from discontinued offices. **1880** LAMPHERE *U.S. Govt.* 231/1 Officers of the fourth class . . . are allowed their box-rents and commissions on cancelled stamps. **1907** *St. Nicholas* May 670/2 *St. Nicholas* cannot start an exchange column for stamps and postal cards.

+5. a. A piece of fractional currency (q.v.). Now hist.

See also POSTAGE STAMP 2 and POSTAGE(-STAMP) CURRENCY, and cf. POSTAL CURRENCY.

1862 [see POSTAL CURRENCY]. **1866** WHITE in *Spectator* 9 June 634 Uneducated people . . . talk about 'having the stamps' or 'getting stamps,' where before the war they would have said 'change.' **1870** *Scribner's Mo.* I. 126 [He takes] a new ten-cent stamp from his porte-monnaie. **1903** HAPGOOD *Autobiog. of Thief* 21 He went to his father . . . and got a fifty cent 'stamp.'

+b. pl. Money, esp. paper money. Now *slang*.

1865 BOUDRYE *Fifth N.Y. Cavalry* 194 The paymaster . . . is relieving himself freely of 'stamps,' as the boys call his greenbacks. **1875** HOLLAND *Sevenoaks* 206 [It] must have cost the gallant Colonel a pile of stamps. **1882** MCCABE *New York* 161 If I had his stamps I wouldn't hang around nights to catch a five-cent fare. **1909** WEBSTER 2030/2.

6. A heavy iron pestle for crushing ore. {1674, 1875}

1867 *Wkly. New Mexican* 8 June 2/1 He has taken out about eight hundred tons of quartz and will commence work again as soon as the new stamps are up. **1871** RAYMOND *3d Rep. Mines* 341 The iron stamp consists of four parts. **1896** SHINN *Story of Mine* 82 The twenty-four stamps of the Pioneer Mill began to rise and fall upon Gold Hill ore. **1911** *U.S. Mineral Resources* (Geol. Survey) I. 711 Sorocco Mines [New Mexico]. . . . Equipment. 30 stamps, . . . 2 Dorr classifiers.

7. attrib. and **comb. a.** In sense 1 with *bill, distributor*, etc. **b.** In sense 4 or 5 with *book, box*, etc. **c.** In sense 6 with *gold*.

See also STAMP ACT, STAMP DUTY, etc.

(a) **1765** J. INGERSOLL *Lett. Stamp-Act* 11 The Stamp-Bill . . . has been preparing to lay before Parliament for taxing America. **1765** OTIS *Considerations Colonists* 27 The present palliative indeed seems to be appointing a number of influencial Americans to be *stamp* masters. **1765** ROWE *Diary* 88 A Great Number of people assembled . . . to see the Stamp Officer hung in Effigy. **1769** *R.I. Col. Rec.* VI. 591 Mr. Johnston . . . was appointed to the obnoxious office of stamp distributor. **1777** J. ADAMS *Familiar Lett.* 251 Ingersoll, the stamp man and Judge of Admiralty. (b) **1866** *Rep. Comm. Patents 1863* I. 531 Currency and Stamp Box. . . . The lid has clips or retainers on its inside for currency or stamps. **1869** J. H. BROWNE *Great Metropolis* 419 Within you observe the long lines of men and boys with money in their hands, earnest-faced, yet patient, waiting for their turn at the stamp-windows. **1873** PHELPS *Trotty's Wedding* v, They bought him a new stamp-book. **1893** CUSHING *Story of P.O.* 425 In Europe the stamp collection craze is much wilder than it ever was in this country. (c) **1876** RAYMOND *8th Rep. Mines* 293 The Quartz Hill mines have furnished during the year about one-third of the stamp-gold product of the county.

Stamp act. {1793−}

1. cap. The act of the British Parliament (1765) levying stamp duties on all paper, parchment, and vellum used in the American colonies. Now hist.

1765 *Duxbury Rec.* 333 The said meeting was to see whether or no the Town would . . . rest contented with the stamp act as it now stands. **1765** *Penna. Journal* 31 Oct., The Stamp act is feared to be obligatory upon us after the *First of November* evening. **1766** FRANKLIN *Writings* IV. 454, I congratulate you on the Repeal of that Mother of Mischief, the Stamp Act. a**1864** HAWTHORNE *Dr. Grimshawe* (1882) 102 There was a great deal of wisdom and knowledge . . . buried out yonder where my old father was put away, before the Stamp Act was thought of.

2. Any legislative act authorizing a stamp duty. {1793−}

1799 *Ann. 7th Congress* 2 Sess. 1435 They damned the house tax and the stamp act. **1806** FESSENDEN *Democracy Unveiled* I. 173n., The Federal stamp act having been obnoxious to the middling, and lower classes of the American people.

+Stampado. [Var. of STAMPEDO n.] **1.** ?The action of causing a stampede. **2.** A periodic meeting of trappers, Indians, etc. — (1) **1837** IRVING *Bonneville* II. 238 The night attack, the stampado, the scamper . . . will then exist but in frontier story. (2) **1847** COYNER *Lost Trappers* 235 Some two months are generally spent by all parties at one of those grand stampadoes.

Stamp duty. A duty collected by the sale of stamps or of articles bearing the impression of a stamp. {1704−} — **1765** HABERSHAM *Letters* 32 In respect to the stamp duty . . . that could be generally imposed on the Colonys. **1797** *Ann. 5th Congress* I. 331 Mr. W. Smith, from the Committee of Ways and Means, reported a bill for laying a stamp duty on vellum, parchment, and paper. **1872** *Newton Kansan* 29 Aug. 3/2 No stamp duties will be required.

+Stampedable, a. Subject to being stampeded. — a**1861** WINTHROP *J. Brent* 88 Every . . . wagon of the Mormon caravan was in its place. . . . Nothing stampedable there. **1888** *Advance* 19 Jan. 41 This pastor is not a stampedable sort of man.

+**Stampede,** *n.* [Mex. Sp. *estampida.*] {1859-}
See also the earlier STAMPEDO *n.*

1. A wild, headlong rush of animals, such as buffaloes, horses, and cattle. {1884}

1844 *Yale Lit. Mag.* IX. 262 Hast ever . . . *felt* the deep awe-inspiring silence, unbroken save by the thundering *stampede* of a herd of some thousand buffaloes? **1857** DAVIS *El Gringo* 391 As we were about hitching up, our animals treated us to a stampede. **1872** POWERS *Afoot & Alone* 126 We all leap to our feet, and hear the terrible cry, 'A stampede! a stampede!' *c*1908 CANTON *Frontier Trails* 9, I was awakened from a sound sleep by a deep, rumbling noise of a stampede.

b. A sudden fright that causes such a rush. Often *to take a stampede.* Obs.

1844 GREGG *Commerce of Prairies* II. 167 Their horses had taken a *stampede* and escaped. **1846** THORPE *Myst. Backwoods* 15 A stampede sometimes seizes the herd. **1846** SAGE *Scenes Rocky Mts.* xxx, One of our pack-horses, also, took the 'stampede,' and ran off with his entire load.

2. a. A precipitous rush of people. {1883} Also *fig.*

1846 LONGFELLOW in S. Longfellow *H. W. Longfellow* II. 69 There is a great 'stampede' on Parnassus at the present moment. **1847** FIELD *Drama in Pokerville* 132 Perhaps there wasn't the orfullest stampede down three pair of sta[i]rs that ever occurred in Michigan! **1884** *Century Mag.* Nov. 113 An old regular said to me regarding the stampede: 'That was the fault of the officers.' **1893** *Nation* 24 Aug. 140/3 Ward did not share the sanguine expectations of those converts who looked for an Anglican stampede into the Roman Church.

b. A movement of people toward a certain area, as a gold rush. {1859-}

1871 RAYMOND *3d Rep. Mines* 202 Rocky Bar . . . has suffered somewhat from the stampede to the bars of the Snake River. **1880** INGHAM *Digging Gold* 311 Stampedes were in order all over the State, to points wherever a new district was formed. **1908** BEACH *Barrier* 57 You must say nothing or it will start a stampede. **1923** 'BOWER' *Parowan Bonanza* 39, I hate boom stampedes that don't pan out.

c. Among delegates to a nominating convention, a sudden rush to support a particular candidate.

1888 M. LANE in *America* 8 Nov. 15 The first stampede occurred in the Democratic Convention of 1844, when James K. Polk received the nomination. **1897** METCALF *Great Fight* 354 There was a stampede at this time by States which changed their votes to Mr. Bryan.

3. Riotous confusion or excitement; a noisy outburst.

1848 COOPER *Oak Openings* II. 35 During the whole of that excited and tumultuous scene, which would probably now be termed a 'stampede,' . . . Peter had not stirred. **1862** McCLELLAN in *Own Story* 461 Everything quiet during the night; no firing and no stampede of any kind.

+**Stampede,** *v.* Also **stampedo.** {1868-}

1. *tr.* To cause a stampede among (animals); to frighten (an animal) into running.

1844 GREGG *Commerce of Prairies* II. 169 A party of Mexicans . . . *stampeded* and carried away, not only their own horses, but those of the Texans. **1851** GLISAN *Jrnl. Army Life* 91 His sudden action stampeded his pony, which ran off. **1864** *Wkly. New Mexican* 29 July 2/2 Five Indians . . . with a terrible whoop charged among the horses, stampeding and taking off with them twenty-four head. **1892** *S. Dak. Hist. Coll.* I. 62 A vast expanse of green prairie, where antelopes had never been startled, nor buffalos stampeded by a locomotive. **1923** [see MUSK HOG].

b. To cause a stampede among the cattle of (someone).

1848 *Blackwoods' Mag.* Nov. 593 The Chases . . . were stampedoed upon the waters of the Platte.

2. To cause excitement, confusion, etc., in (a community); to frighten.

1853 BREWERTON *With Kit Carson* (1930) 66 Some inexperienced mountaineer had given the alarm of Indians during his time of guard at night, or as Western men sometimes express it, 'stampeded the camp.' **1864** *Harper's Mag.* Oct. 560/2 The hostile Indians . . . believed they had at length stampeded the entire white population. **1893** *Congress. Rec.* App. 1 March 70/2 A successful draw in the Louisiana lottery . . . stampedes a community.

3. To cause (persons) to go precipitously in a certain direction; to drive out.

1862 Moore *Rebellion Rec.* V. 11. 497 The armies of the enemy were perfectly 'stampeded.' **1883** *N. Mex. Terr. Rep.* 84 Having succeeded in stampeding whatever rustler element there was abroad in the vicinity of the Black Range, . . . I pushed on in person to Las Cruces. **1887** in Gladden *Parish Problems* 313 Sometimes they have used exaggerated statements of doctrines . . . to stampede men into the kingdom of Heaven.

4. To leave (a place) hurriedly in a sudden fright.

1862 *N.Y. Tribune* 14 April 5/3 The owners of the principal buildings have stampeded the town.

5. a. To sway (a convention or other group) into a sudden, headlong action.

1884 *Boston Jrnl.* 11 July The convention refused to be stampeded. **1889** *Ib.* 7 March 2/4 Efforts of the Bears to Stampede the New York Market. . . . Checkmated by a Bull Operator. **1925** BRYAN *Memoirs* 161,

I was afraid that I would be accused of trying to stampede the convention.

b. To cause (a person) to act without sufficient consideration; to force into line. {1868-}

1890 C. KING *Sunset Pass* 56 Don't get stampeded. Just keep cool; watch and listen. **1903** *Atlantic Mo.* July 37 Such men must form fixed points in the civic mass, units of intelligence, not to be bribed nor stampeded.

6. *intr.* Of a person or group of persons: To rush *toward, to,* or *for* a certain place; to retreat suddenly. {1884} Also *vbl. n.* used attrib.

1849 *N.Y. Tribune* 12 June (B.), The Virginia Legislature, becoming frightened at the approach of the cholera, have finally stampeded toward the White Sulphur Springs. **1865** SABRE *Prisoner of War* 10, I gave what are termed in military parlance 'stampeding orders,' in hopes that by taking to the woods some of us might escape. **1873** *Newton Kansan* 12 June 2/3 The Syracuse colonyites are stampeding for Barton county. **1876** RAYMOND *8th Rep. Mines* 263 Among the miners who had 'stampeded' to Cedar were many of the best prospectors in the Territory. **1888** *Home Missionary* Dec. 362 Our comrades at the front, . . . hard-pressed often, and weary, but never stampeding.

b. Of a convention or its delegates: To act suddenly as with a common impulse, esp. to declare for a particular candidate with sudden action.

1887 *Courier-Journal* 21 Jan. 2/7 The first ballot showed how many had stampeded from Mr. Morton. **1894** *Congregationalist* 4 Oct., The New York Democratic convention at Saratoga last week surprised the public and perhaps itself by 'stampeding' for David Bennett Hill and nominating him for governor.

7. Of animals: To go into a stampede; to run headlong in disorder. {1879}

1859 MARCY *Prairie Traveler* xi, My entire herd of about two hundred horses and mules all stampeded in the night. **1881** *Cimarron News & Press* 17 March 1/4 Once fairly off, they will stampede twenty, thirty, and forty miles at a stretch. **1923** J. H. COOK *On Old Frontier* 43 The herd has stampeded.

+**Stampeder.** One who engages in a stampede (esp. in sense 2 b).
— **1862** *N.Y. Tribune* 5 May 3/2 The leader of the stampeders . . . was killed. **1877** W. WRIGHT *Big Bonanza* 284 The old hag . . . poled herself along in the rear of the stampeders with astonishing agility. **1884** *Century Mag.* Oct. 844/2 In the days of the stampeders and the toboggan trains, this was the only house on the trail. **1904** E. ROBINS *Magn. North* II. 142 When a group of returned stampeders came in, she sat down at a rough little faro-table.

+**Stampedo,** *n.* An early form of STAMPEDE. {1862} See also STAMPADO. — **1834** *23d Congress 2 Sess.* H. R. Doc. No. 2, 79 A stupid sentinel last night . . . alarmed the camp, and sent off in a *stampedo* the rest of the horses. **1836** HILDRETH *Campaigns Rocky Mts.* 84 The whole drove . . . commenced a grand *stampedo.* **1852** BRISTED *Upper Ten Th.* 62 Nearly a hundred slaves . . . had made a stampedo, as the Western men say.

+**Stampedo,** *v.* (See STAMPEDE *v.*)

＊**Stamper.** 1. A mill for crushing grain. 2. A post-office clerk who cancels postage stamps. {1850-} — (1) **1639** *Plymouth Col. Rec.* XII. 72 George Pollard and William Hiller . . . [are to] set vp . . . stampers to beate Indian Corne. **1651** *Providence Rec.* II. 58 James Leonard Shall have 25 acres of Land . . . as his home lot neere the Stampers. (2) **1893** CUSHING *Story of P.O.* 189 There are stamp clerks and stampers. **1894** *Columbus Dispatch* 19 Oct. 7/6 Charles Dowerman, night stamper at the Post Office, and Fred Groessle, carrier, are on the sick list.

+**Stamping ground.**

1. A place where animals, esp. horses, are accustomed to stamp. Also *transf.*

1786 in *Amer. Speech* XV. 396/1 Beginning about ½ mile So. of a place well known by the Stamping Ground. **1843** N. BOONE *Journal* 107 Passed . . . the stamping ground of countless hordes of [buffaloes]. **1870** W. BAKER *New Timothy* 176 It's with them fellows as it is with wild animals. You can just keep clear of them if you want, stay far out of their stamping-ground.

2. A place where a person is or was accustomed to go or stay; a favorite haunt. Frequently *old stamping ground.*

1836 H. R. HOWARD *Hist. V. A. Stewart* 70, I made my way from Milledgeville to Williamson County, the old stamping-ground. **1845** *Cincinnati Misc.* I. 126/1 The neighborhood of Pittsburgh . . . was the stamping ground, as the early settlers call it, of the Girtys. **1855** SIMMS *Forayers* 72 Fortunately, the region was a familiar one; his old stamping-ground, distinguished in his memory, by many a squirrel and 'coon hunt. **1886** *Outing* VIII. 318/2, I wonder when we shall see the old stamping-ground again? **1914** 'BOWER' *Flying U Ranch* 134 Back on the old stamping ground, are you?

＊**Stamping mill.** A mill for crushing ore. — **1775** in Deane *Correspondence* 322 The Stamping Mill is going. **1882** *Harper's Mag.* May 898/1 On the sides of this inlet are the great stamping-mills of the copper mines.

+**Stampler.** *Penna.* One favoring the federal stamp act of 1799. — **1799** *Ann. 7th Congress 2 Sess.* 1454 The unmeaning epithets of *Stamplers* and *Tories* were rudely applied to the friends of the government.

Stamp mill. =STAMPING MILL. {1749-} Also attrib. — **1869** BREWER *Rocky Mt. Lett.* 43 Buckskin . . . had three stamp-mills and perhaps twenty arastras for working the ore. **1883** [see SMELTER 2]. **1888** *Amer. Almanac* 275 Occupations of the People of the United States. . . . Quartz and stamp mill laborers, . . . Rag-pickers. **1910** J. HART *Vigilante Girl* 144 It's gin'ly coin to pay off fellers that work in the stamp-mills.

Stamp paper. Paper bearing a revenue stamp. {1765-} — **1766** HABERSHAM *Letters* 55 We have so far prevailed on the Sons of Liberty . . . that the Stamp Papers be issued to clear our Vessells. **1799** WEEMS *Letters* II. 113 If he . . . w[oul]d send an order on stamp paper he w[oul]d pay immediately. **1846** J. T. HUGHES *Doniphan's Exped.* (1907) 65 Gen. Kearny abolished the 'stamp paper' of the Government of New Mexico— 8 dollars per sheet.

+**Stamp tax.** A tax imposed by a stamp act. — **1797** *Ann. 5th Congress* I. 403 This stamp-tax was known to have taken a similar course at a former time. **1863** KETTELL *Hist. Rebellion* II. 645 A stamp tax upon all documents. **1900** *Congress. Rec.* 20 Feb. 1966/2 A petition . . . praying for the repeal of the stamp tax upon proprietary medicines, perfumeries, and cosmetics.

* **Stanchion.** +A framework attached to a stall, into which an animal's neck is put to limit its forward and backward movement. — **1868** BRACKETT *Farm Talk* 101 What do you think of slip stanchions? **1874** *Vermont Bd. Agric. Rep.* II. 515 In one stable I tie thirty-two head of cattle, using stanchions instead of chains, with an improved latch or fastener. **1896** *Vt. Agric. Rep.* XV. 72 The cows in general seem to like swinging stanchions much better than the stationary.

* **Stand,** *n.*

1. A small table on which to set something. {1686-}
1711 *Essex Inst. Coll.* IV. 187/1 My walnut tree table with two stands & pewter still. **1835** HOFFMAN *Winter in West* I. 118 The black walnut stand, upon which I am writing, occupies the centre of the room. **1911** VANCE *Cynthia* 81 Madame . . . agitated the small silver call bell on the bedside stand.

+**2.** A site or building suitable for business; a place of business. Also fig.
1776 *N.J. Archives* 2 Ser. I. 106 Its healthy pleasant and central situation . . . and old accustomed business render it [*sc.* an inn] a most commodious and profitable stand. **1796** WEEMS *Letters* II. 34 He has a most excellent stand in the main street. **1867** LOWELL *My Study Windows* 84 Their historians and biographers have succeeded to the good-will, as well as to the long-established stand, of the shop of glory.

+**b.** A place to stay.
1816 U. BROWN *Journal* II. 366 Not another Stand for 12 Miles. **1846** *Xenia Torch-Light* 23 July 4/1 Taverns, there were none; and their substitutes, 'stands,' in the phrase of the country, poor and far between.

+**c.** *Old stand*, the regular or usual place of business. Also fig.
1847 *Santa Fe Republican* 27 Nov. 2/2 Peacock and Co. have many rare things in their establishment of Del Gardo's old stand. **1866** *Ore. State Jrnl.* 23 June 4/1 J. F. Munz is still at the Old Stand. **1897** *Outing* XXX. 191/1 The outfit from Maine . . . was busy at the old stand. **1906** *Washington Post* 16 April 6 All the big and oppressive trusts are doing business at the old stand.

3. A stallion's performance as a breeder.
1797 *Steele P.* I. 151 As a covering horse I am of Opinion he would make a very good Stand.

+**4. a.** An elevated platform for a speaker; a pulpit, esp. one at a camp meeting.
See also MUSIC STAND 2.
1820 DEWEES *Lett. from Texas* 17 [They] came up to the camp ground with the determination of cutting down the stand. **1834** *Biblical Repertory* VI. 337 'A pulpit of wood,' or, as we generally term it, a *stand*, for the clergy was erected. **1840** *Niles' Nat. Reg.* LIX. 56/2 Upon the stand, general Harrison was welcomed to Dayton . . . by judge Crane. **1856** *Democratic Conv. Proc.* 68, I can not feel insensible to the honor you have done me, by thus unexpectedly calling me to the stand. **1890** H. M. FIELD *Bright Skies* 193 When I go back to 'the stand,' I look about [etc.].

b. At a race course, the elevated platform for the judges; also, a reviewing stand. {1615}
See also GRAND STAND, REVIEWING STAND.
1836 *Quarter Race Ky.* (1846) 17 There now arose a dispute as to whether they should run to or from the stand. **1842** *Niles' Nat. Reg.* LXIII. 103/3 From a stand erected on Main Cross street, Mr. Clay . . . reviewed a part of the procession. **1865** 'MARK TWAIN' *Sk., New & Old* 32 She'd . . . always fetch up at the stand just about a neck ahead. **1876** HOLMES *Poetical Works* (1895) 235/2 The old horse nears the judges' stand.

+**c.** The witness box in a court room.
1865 LOWELL *My Study Windows* 209 [Thoreau] had watched Nature like a detective who is to go upon the stand. **1898** PAGE *Red Rock* 566, I'll put you on the stand. **1922** PARRISH *Case & Girl* 316 Percival wouldn't go on the stand.

* **5.** A place where a hunter waits for game.
See also DEER STAND.
1831 AUDUBON *Ornith. Biog.* I. 340 The deer may be shot from the places called *stands* by the sportsman. *a*1841 HAWES *Sporting Scenes* I. 149 At the south-east corner of the lake, is built . . . a hiding place, or 'stand,' arranged out of old logs and fallen trees. **1874** LONG *Wild-Fowl* 143 You need not expect to shoot much until we get on a stand. **1897** *Outing* XXX. 127/1 This was probably as good a 'stand' as would be found in a day's run.

+**6.** A standing growth or crop.
1833 *Man. Sugar Cane* 12 Every joint sends up cane shoots, and thus contributes to a fuller stand of Cane than when the joints are farther apart. **1852** *Fla. Plantation Rec.* 62, I have a splendid stand of Corn. **1874** *Vermont Bd. Agric. Rep.* II. 205 We have succeeded in getting a good stand of grass. **1905** *Forestry Bureau Bul.* No. 60, 13 The proportion of sweet birch in the stand is large.

+**7.** *To get a stand*, (see quot. 1885.)
1885 ROOSEVELT *Hunting Trips* 274 Occasionally these panic fits make them [*sc.* buffaloes] run together and stand still in a stupid, frightened manner. . . . When they are made to act thus it is called in hunters' parlance getting a 'stand' on them. **1907** COOK *Border & Buffalo* 162 He got what is called a 'stand,' and killed thirty-seven of them.

8. (See quotation.)
1889 *Harper's Mag.* May 902/1 A large wooden shed, called 'The Stand,' without floor or weather-boarding, capable of covering, say, four thousand persons, stood near the centre [of a Ga. camp-meeting ground].

+**9.** On a theatrical tour, a stop for one or more performances.
See also ONE-NIGHT STAND.
1895 *N.Y. Dramatic News* 19 Oct. 11/1 Denver was the second stand of the week. **1900** *Everybody's Mag.* II. 583/2 The next 'stand' was Topeka. **1917** J. F. DALY *Life A. Daly* 195 Each of its 'stands' being supplied in turn with a play and a company strictly limited in the requirements of that piece.

* **Stand,** *v.*

I. +**1.** *intr.* Of a stallion: To cover.
1846 *Spirit of Times* (N.Y.) 18 April 94/1 Young Dread will stand this season at Watertown, Jefferson County, N.Y. **1880** *Cimarron News & Press* 25 March 3/3 The celebrated Stallion Sweeper will stand the coming season (three months) . . . at my ranch.

II. With prepositions. * **2.** *To stand for*, +to put up with; to tolerate; to acquiesce in. *colloq.*[2]
1896 ADE *Artie* 107 They say they can't stand for that kind o' work. **1903** FORMAN *Journeys End* iii, [They] tried to do me, but I wouldn't stand for it. **1921** PAINE *Comr. Rolling Ocean* 122, I can't stand for any rude language to my buddy.

+**3.** *To stand from under*, to avoid or escape (something). Cf. sense 4.
1857 *Chicago Times* 6 Oct., To enable me to stand from under the present crash, I shall offer my entire stock for the next 30 days at a great sacrifice.

III. With adverbs. +**4.** *To stand from under*, to avoid disaster; to get to a place of safety; to avoid responsibility. (Cf. sense 3.)
1861 *Cincinnati Commercial* 24 April (caption), Stand from Under. **1876** 'MARK TWAIN' *Punch, Brothers, Punch!* 16 You make up your mind that the earthquake is due; you stand from under, and take hold of something to steady yourself. **1904** *Boston Transcript* 11 June 18 Mr. Gompers carefully 'stood from under' by announcing that [etc.]. **1920** HOWELLS *Vacation of Kelwyns* 185 Brother Jasper was standing from under and letting him take the whole responsibility of dispossessing the Kites.

* **5.** *To stand off*, +to hold off; to induce (a person) to accept payment later; in bargaining, to hold out *for* some amount from (someone).
1878 BEADLE *Western Wilds* 38 He offered him fifty thousand for it, and the feller stood him off for seventy-five thousand. **1883** HAY *Bread-Winners* 274 Come, come, Sam, don't stand me off that way. **1897** *Boston Jrnl.* 25 Oct. 7/2 A Woman, Out Bicycling, Stands Off a Negro Highwayman. **1901** ADE *40 Modern Fables* 38 Doc was a Good Fellow, who could be Stood Off. **1925** TILGHMAN *Dugout* 89 Probably that old dug-out is the same one where your mother stood off the Indians.

+**6.** *To stand pat*, in poker to play a pat hand (q.v.); fig., to oppose change of any kind, esp. to oppose change in political matters. {1882}
[**1882** C. WELSH *Poker* 12 The gentleman . . . failed to better his hand. The other player stood pat.] **1884** 'CRADDOCK' *Where Battle Was Fought* 35 Then he drew one card, Estwicke standing pat. **1890** *Stock Grower & Farmer* 29 March 7/1 When it come to them two accomplishments he stood pat. **1894** FORD *P. Stirling* 384 To use a poker term, Peter was standing 'pat,' and wished no change. **1896** *Congress. Rec.* 28 Feb. 2268/2 Why should not the House 'stand pat,' as the Senate did? **1910** RAINE *B. O'Connor* 78 The 'ins' stand pat, but the 'outs' have always got a revolution up their sleeves.

+**b.** Hence *standpatter*, *standpat*, and *standpattism*.
1903 *Public Opinion* 8 Oct. 451/2 The father of 'stand pattism' himself could not find fault. **1904** *Boston Transcript* 16 Feb. 11/2 [Senator Hanna] was an avowed 'stand-patter' on the tariff; in fact, the author of the expression. **1904** *N.Y. Ev. Post* 20 June 7 The 'stand pat' idea, if it means

anything, means 'hands off the tariff.' **1910** *Boston Transcript* 18 Aug. 10/5 The standpats in Iowa have been licked. **1912** *Commoner* XII. 5 Illinois loses three dyed-in-the-wool stand-pat republicans in Cannon, McKinley and Rodenberg. **1913** LaFollette *Autobiog.* 415, I do not think the 'stand-patters' of the Senate understood what I was talking about.

+7. *To stand round*, to be on the alert.

1840 *Knickerb.* XVI. 205, I should have made more by *standing round;* i.e., watching the land-market for bargains. **1845** *Ib.* XXVI. 466, I knew him by the way they 'stood round' when he came along. **1853** *Turnover* 56 (Th.), She makes Armbus stand raound pooty well.

* 8. *To stand up.* **+a.** To go through a wedding ceremony; to act as a bridesmaid or best man at a wedding. *colloq.*

1842 *Amer. Pioneer* I. 314 They were married without any previous preparation of nice dresses, bride cakes, or bride maids—he standing up in a hunting dress, and she in a short gown and petticoat of homespun. **1859** in *Chicago Tribune* (1929) 10 Nov. VIII. 1/6 We had no one to stand up with us, as we wished to have a simple service. **1891** *Cent.* 5899/1 *To stand up with*, . . . to act as groomsman or bridesmaid to: as, I *stood up with* him at his wedding. (Colloq.) **1917** McCutcheon *Green Fancy* 344 Countess Mara-Dafanda . . . and Thomas Kingsbury Barnes 'stood up' with the happy couple.

+b. To hold up and rob.

1897 Lewis *Wolfville* 319 You don't want to go too close to stand-up your gent. **1897** Norris *Stories & Sk.* (1931) 146 That a girl should stand up a stage is extraordinary enough.

+c. *To stand up to* (or *and*) *be counted*, to take a strong or public stand.

1904 *Hartford Courant* 12 Aug. 10 Another democratic paper, the 'Sacramento Bee,' follows the example of the 'Chicago Chronicle' and stands up to be counted for Roosevelt. **1905** *N.Y. Ev. Post* 4 Jan. 6 Mr. Baldwin was ready to stand up and be counted.

+d. *To stand up to the rack*, (see RACK¹ 2 b).

* Standard. A measure of weight, quantity, or quality set by colonial or U.S. authority.

See also GOLD STANDARD, SILVER STANDARD.
1644 *New Haven Col. Rec.* 142 Rich: Miles, Witt Davis and Nicholas Elsey, shall see thatt all the measures in the towne be made according to the stander sent from the Bay. **1702** *N.C. Col. Rec.* I. 559 It was ordered there should be a standard of weights and measures sent for the use of the precinct. **1792** *Stat. at Large* I. 249 The standard for all gold coins of the United States shall be eleven parts fine to one part alloy. **1877** [see BIMETALLIC *a*.]. **1914** *Cycl. Amer. Govt.* III. 376/2 The Bureau of Standards . . . is charged with testing measuring instruments of all kinds, in order that they may conform to the public standards as defined by law and preserved at Washington.

*Standard-bearer. *spec.* **+**The presidential nominee of a political party; also, a vice-presidential nominee. — **1848** *N.Y. Herald* 6 May 4/1 It is on the old platform of principles, and for the good old cause, that the new standard-bearer is to be chosen. **1873** *Newton Kansan* 15 May 4/3 The standard-bearer of the Democracy, now wants the party to take the back track. **1900** *Congress. Rec.* 10 Jan. 746/1 The national convention . . . summoned Garret A. Hobart to be standard bearer with William McKinley.

Standard-bred horse. A horse having a standard pedigree or having a certain record of performance. — **1891** G. W. Curtis *Horses, Cattle* 82 In order to define what constitutes a standard-bred horse, . . . the following rules are adopted. . . . When an animal meets the requirements of admission and is duly registered, it shall be accepted as a standard-bred animal. **1903** A. Adams *Log of Cowboy* 236 They are strong on standard bred horses.

+Standard dollar. = STANDARD SILVER DOLLAR. — **1881** *Ore. State Jrnl.* 15 Jan. 2/3 The distribution of standard dollars from the U.S. mints during the month of December amounted to $1,807,481. **1885** *Wkly. New Mexican Rev.* 5 Feb. 2/3 The trade dollar . . . is not worth so much in domestic commerce as the standard dollar, which has less metal. **1887** *Stat. at Large* XXIV. 635 The trade-dollars recoined under this act shall not be counted as part of the silver bullion required to be purchased and coined into standard dollars.

Standard gauge. A railroad gauge of 4 feet 8½ inches, considered to be standard; also, a railroad of such a gauge. Also attrib. (See NARROW GAUGE 1, note.) — **1871** *Republican Rev.* 22 July 1/3 Statistics show that on the standard gauges more than four times of dead or non-paying weight are annually carried . . . to each ton of paying freight. **1881** *Chicago Times* 12 March 8/6 The company purposes constructing a standard-gauge railroad. **1887** *Courier-Journal* 25 Jan. 6/3 The entire line from Cairo, Ill., to Gatesville, Tex., is now standard gauge.

Standard gold. {1809-} **+**Monetary gold of a fineness specified by law—before 1837, eleven-twelfths fine; since 1837, nine-tenths fine. — **1792** *Stat. at Large* I. 248 Eagles—each . . . to contain two hundred and forty-seven grains and four eighths of a grain of pure, or two hundred and seventy grains of standard gold. **1834** *Ib.* IV. 699 Each eagle shall contain two hundred and thirty-two grains of pure gold, and two hundred and fifty-eight grains of standard gold.

+Standard gold dollar. A dollar, not necessarily coined, containing gold to an amount and fineness specified by law, which is used as the standard unit of value. (Cf. GOLD DOLLAR.) — **1876** in D. K. Watson *Hist. Amer. Coinage* 112 After that date [1834], owing to a reduction in the weight of gold required for the standard gold dollar, the silver dollar

was made to contain of fine metal almost precisely sixteen times that of the new gold dollar.

Standard silver. {1691-} **+1.** Monetary silver of a fineness specified by law—before 1837, slightly less than nine-tenths fine; since 1837, nine-tenths fine. **+2.** Short for STANDARD SILVER DOLLAR. — **(1)** **1792** *Stat. at Large* I. 248 *Dismes*—each . . . to contain . . . forty-one grains and three fifth parts of a grain of standard silver. **1837** *Ib.* V. 136 The melter and refiner shall execute all the operations which are necessary to form ingots of standard silver or gold. **1890** [see FREE SILVER]. **(2)** **1881** *Rep. Indian Affairs* 47 Amount earned . . . and paid in standard silver, $41,382.

+Standard silver dollar. The regular silver dollar, which was not coined between 1873 and 1878, as distinguished from the trade dollar. (Cf. BLAND DOLLAR.) — **1878** *Stat. at Large* XX. 25 An act to authorize the coinage of the standard silver dollar. **1900** *Congress. Rec.* 11 Jan. 771/1 There were in the United States in 1896 between five hundred and six hundred millions of standard silver dollars. *Ib.* 1 Feb. 1385/2, I have in my possession a standard silver dollar of the issue of 1798.

Standard time. **a.** A particular clock time adopted as standard by any agency. **+b.** One of the four clock times for the respective time belts of the United States, adopted by the railroads in 1883 and by Congress in 1918. — **1883** *Boston Transcript* 10 Nov. 9/6 The Standard Time for the running of Trains of this road will be changed to conform to the 'Eastern Standard Time.' **1887** George *40 Yrs. on Rail* 251 Among the many improvements of these later days of railroading must not be forgotten the adoption of the so-called standard time. **1918** *Stat. at Large* XL. 451 The standard time of the zone shall govern the movement of all common carriers engaged in commerce between the several States.

+Standee. **1.** One who is compelled to stand. *colloq.* **2.** (See quotation.) *Obs.* — **(1)** **1856** *Knickerb.* March 278 Occasionally the car is brought to a full stop, and the 'standees' are thrown against each other like alley-pins by a 'ten-strike.' **1895** *N.Y. Dramatic News* 16 Nov. 13/2 Many times through the day the sale of tickets had to be stopped, as the 'standees' were several rows deep. **1903** *N.Y. Sun* 29 Nov. 32 The standees were aware that to give up their places meant that they could never wedge into them again. **(2)** **1859** Bartlett 446 *Standee*, a standing bed-place in a steamer.

* Stander. **+**In deer-hunting, one who waits at a stand. — **1836** Gilman *Recoll.* (1838) 210 They were to scream behind them, and force the deer out to the standers. **1851** *S. Lit. Messenger* XVII. 46/1 When the deer is certainly coming, the stander experiences a degree of excitement which would scarcely be credited. **1886** *Leslie's Mo.* Sept. 376/2, I could . . . thus perhaps reach our next 'stander' before the deer could find a landing.

+Stand-in. An understanding; a 'pull.' *slang.* — **1870** *Food Jrnl.* 1 Nov. 523 The affair is settled amicably by a 'stand in,' which means that the purchaser shall pay the other, or others, a certain sum not to bid against him. **1908** McGaffey *Show-Girl* 89 My heart went out to him the minute he said he had a stand in with three city editors. **1923** *Dialect Notes* V. 222 He's got a stand-in 'ith the boss. [McDonald Co., Mo.]

* Standing, *a.* New Eng. **+**Of a church: Established. (Cf. STANDING ORDER.) — **1748** *N.H. Hist. Soc. Coll.* IX. 9 A Controversy was then subsisting whether they ought to be acknowledged as belonging by Right to the Standing Church.

Standing, *adv.* **+***To bring up standing*, to stop sharply; to bring to a sudden stop. (See also ALL-STANDING *adv.* 1.) — **1867** *Harper's Mag.* June 132/2 The Judiciary Committee . . . is not unfrequently brought up standing at the sage suggestions of one of its members. **1890** Custer *Following Guidon* p. v, The never tardy sound [of the bugle] . . . brought us up standing.

Standing collar. = STAND-UP COLLAR. — **1844** *Graham's Mag.* Jan. 48 The entirely new style of coats with standing collar. **1856** M. Thompson *Plu-ri-bus-tah* 220 Inaccessible his hat was, . . . And beneath it . . . towered his lofty standing collar. **1865** Pike *Scout & Ranger* (1932) 146 Forty or fifty stalwart men . . . were there, with checkered coats and what had been linen standing collars on heavy cotton shirts with no bosoms. **1912** Nicholson *Hoosier Chron.* 335 There are more standing collars in a Republican convention and more whiskers when the Prohibitionists get together.

+Standing cypress. A handsome perennial herb (*Gilia rubra*) of the South. — **1861** Wood *Botany* 569 Standing Cypress. . . . A splendid herb, . . . bearing at top a long . . . thyrse of scarlet red flowers. **1892** Coulter *Bot. W. Texas* II. 277.

Standing order. {1737-} **+**(See quot. 1909.) Also attrib. Now hist. Used humorously in first quotation but possibly alluding to other use. In the second quotation Presbyterian and Congregational have been confused. (Cf. CONGREGATIONALISM quot. 1878.) — **1823** Cooper *Pioneers* xv, I don't think that by nater they [*sc.* Episcopal clergymen] are as tonguey speakers . . . as the standing-order ministers. **1865** *Harper's Mag.* April 608/1 To pay taxes, for the support of the Presbyterian, or 'Standing Order.' **1909** Webster 2031/3 *Standing order*, . . . a term formerly used in Connecticut of the Congregational Church, the State church until 1818.

+Stand-off. *colloq.*

1. A postponement; credit.

1883 Harte *In Carquinez Woods* (1911) 28 You'd better make it a stand-off for twenty-four hours. **1896** *Typographical Jrnl.* IX. 236 Money of all kinds and colors was as plentiful as it is scarce today, and everybody had a 'standoff' at the corner.

2. Aloofness.

1885 D. D. PORTER *Incid. Civil War* 143 A kind of 'stand-off' between the army and the navy . . . prevented them from working in harmony. **1911** QUICK *Yellowstone Nights* 164, I don't take any high-an'-mighty stand-off from a lunkhead that's stole my melons.

3. A counterbalance.

1888 *Microcosm* Dec. 7 We are willing to allow this judicial estimate . . . to count as a stand-off against all the subsidized commendations. **1890** *Atlantic Mo.* Nov. 672/1 When therefore the lawyer hears the curses . . . of his impatient clients, the preferences of other clients . . . make a complete stand-off.

4. (See quot. 1895.)

1895 *Stand.* 1750/1 *Stand-off*, . . . a draw or tie, as in a game; a set-off; as, the contestants agreed to call it a stand-off. **1899** ADE *Fables in Slang* 103 That simply makes it a Stand-Off. **1904** *N.Y. Ev. Post* 6 Sept. 7 Rural Pennsylvania is very near a stand-off between the Republicans and the Democrats.

+Standpat, *n.* and *a.* **Standpatter.** (See STAND *v.* 6.)

Standpipe. {1850-} **+1.** An upright pipe through which oil is forced to be burned at the open end. **+2.** A water tower or supply pipe, esp. for equalizing pressure in a waterworks. — (1) **1875** *Chicago Tribune* 6 Nov. 2/5 A standpipe is erected a short distance off to consume the surplus and light the town. (2) **1882** *Wheelman* I. 17 It is the Roxbury stand-pipe. **1896** *Engineering Mag.* X. 1043 These stand pipes have been built in three main classes: a large wrought-iron or even wooden tank raised on a trestle; the same tank supported upon and enclosed by substantial masonry walls; . . . an immense wrought-iron or steel cylinder, filled with water from the ground up.

Stand-up collar. A collar that stands upright and does not fold over. {1813-} — **1860** HOLMES *E. Venner* vii, Some of the dashing young men in stand-up collars and extensive neck-ties . . . made quite free with the 'Madary.' **1861** *Army Regulations* 477 Stand-up collar to rise no higher than to permit the chin to turn freely over it. **1911** LINCOLN *Cap'n Warren's Wards* 153 The captain . . . donned spotless linen including a 'stand-up' collar.

+Stand-up law. *Conn.* An election law (1801-17) which required the electors to indicate their votes in certain elections by standing up. — **1817** *Niles' Reg.* XIII. 131/2 Many, if not all of the evils which wise and good legislators have sought to obviate by ballot-voting, have resulted from this 'stand-up law.' **1831** *Jamestown* (N.Y.) *Jrnl.* 23 March 2/4 Why did the people of Connecticut complain of the 'stand-up law' which formerly existed in that state?

Stanhope. A light, open buggy. {1825-} — **1830** HOLMES *Poetical Works* (1895) 8/2 He may . . . flourish the Stanhope gay. **1867** MELINE *Santa Fé & Back* 60 See the handsome turn-out of carriages, buggies, Stanhopes, and other pleasant things.

***Staple.*[1]** A piece of wire or other metal bent into a loop so that the two ends may be driven or otherwise secured in wood to hold a ring, bolt, etc. — **1678** *New Castle Court Rec.* 362, 5 door staples. **1740** W. STEPHENS *Proc. Georgia* I. 639 A Chain fixed in a Staple driven into the Floor. **1847** in Howe *Hist. Coll. Ohio* 188 Journeys were some times to be performed of 20 or 50 miles, for the sole purpose of having the staple of an ox-yoke mended. **1922** A. BROWN *Old Crow* 479 There was the horse, hitched to the staple in the corner of the barn.

***Staple.*[2]** **+1.** The quality or grade *of* tobacco. *Obs.* **2.** The fiber of cotton, often considered with respect to length, fineness, etc. {1825-} See also LONG-STAPLE COTTON, SHORT-STAPLE COTTON. — (1) **1728** *Bristol* (Va.) *Vestry Book* 41 In obedience to an act of assembly for the better Improveing the Staple of tobo it is ord'red that the parrish be Devided into precincts for Counting tobo plants. (2) **1825** *Austin P.* II. (1924) 1028 Cotton of a good staple would of course answer very well. **1891** CHASE & CLOW *Industry* II. 9 Small teeth . . . seize the staples and drag them between the rollers.

+Staple states. The southern states. *Obs.* — **1785** in *S. Lit. Messenger* XXVIII. 40/2 The giving Congress a power to legislate over the trade of the Union, would be dangerous in the extreme to the five Southern or staple States. **1837** CALHOUN *Works* III. 49 The staple States were wholly opposed to the protective system.

***Star.*

*1.** A representation of a star +used in the United States flag to represent one of the states in the Union.

1781 FRENEAU *Poems* (1786) 211 Bid the haughty Britons know They to our Thirteen Stars shall bend. **1805** *Ann. 9th Congress* 1 Sess. 34 Vessels bearing the variegated stripes and constellated stars of our Union had been sent to distant British ports. **1900** *Congress. Rec.* 24 Jan. 1130/1 Utah was given a star. . . . That star is a false star; it does not shine with the brilliancy and luster of its sister stars.

+2. A policeman. *Obs.*

1856 *Porter's Spirit of Times* 25 Oct. 133/3 One star had his peeper measured for a suit of mourning. **1859** BARTLETT 446 *Stars,* . . . The officers of the new police in the city of New York are so called from their badge, a brass star, which is required by law to be worn on the breast. **1866** *Harper's Mag.* Feb. 356/2 The star assuring Frankie that he would find his mother for him before long.

3. *attrib.* **a.** In the specific names of plants. {1758-} See also STAR ANISE, STAR FLOWER, etc.

1840 DEWEY *Mass. Flowering Plants* 87 C[ucubalus] *stellatus,* Star Campion, is a native of this country and State. **1847** Star cucumber [see CU-

CUMBER 2 b]. **1817-8** EATON *Botany* (1822) 469 *Solidago noveboracensis,* star golden-rod. . . . Grows plentifully along the banks of Connecticut river at the Northampton meadows. **1915** ARMSTRONG & THORNBER *Western Wild Flowers* 8 Star Zygadene, *Zygadenus Fremontii,* . . . grows among bushes, on hillsides and sea-cliffs along the coast.

+b. In special combinations.

Star buzzard, either of two species of hawks of the genus *Asturina* resembling the buzzard; *s.-nose,* = STAR-NOSE(D) MOLE; *s. tick,* (see quotation).

1884 COUES *Key to Birds* (ed. 2) 551 Star Buzzards. . . . A small group of handsome under-sized hawks, peculiar to America. **1842** *Nat. Hist. N.Y., Zoology* I. 14 The Star-nose burrows in moist places near the surface. **1863** *Ladies' Repository* Oct. 605/1 These ticks reappear, much larger in size and with a lustrous circle on their backs and are then called 'star-ticks,' or 'yearling-ticks.'

Star anise. A plant of the genus *Illicium* {1838-}, +esp. the poison bay (*I. floridanum*) of the southern states. Also with specifying term. — **1857** GRAY *Botany* 155 Section through the thickness of a leaf of the Star Anise . . . , of Florida, magnified. **1901** MOHR *Plant Life Ala.* 506 *Illicium floridanum,* Florida star anise.

+Star boarder. A boarder, usually of long standing, having, or regarded as having, special favors or privileges. Also transf. — **1897** *Boston Jrnl.* 16 Jan. 6/5, 'I'm afraid you are about to be dethroned.' The Star Boarder—'Why?' **1904** 'O. HENRY' *Roads of Destiny* 240 His salary, . . . sordidly speaking, ranked him star boarder at the Peek's. **1922** TARKINGTON *Gentle Julia* 113 The pill-boxes [for insects], . . . evidently contained star boarders, for they were pierced with 'breathing holes.'

+Star candle. A candle made of stearine, orig. for use in measuring luminous intensity. — **1848** *Rep. Comm. Patents 1847* 529, I now come to the star candles, made of the stearine. **1867** *Wkly. New Mexican* 2 May 1/2 Groceries & Provisions. . . . Sperm and Star Candles. **1873** BEADLE *Undevel. West* 573 With them were a number of star candles.

***Starch.** A preparation made from the carbohydrate of various plants and used chiefly for stiffening fabrics.

1712 in Felt *Customs New Eng.* 95 Very good starch, made in Boston by a starch maker lately from London, is for sale. **1792** *Ann. 2d Congress* 1025 Starch . . . [may] be placed among those [articles] which are rated at fifteen per cent. **1844** *Lowell Offering* IV. 169 These rooms . . . are disagreeably scented with the 'sizing,' or starch, which stiffens the 'beams,' or unwoven webs. **1884** NYE *Baled Hay* 207 To remove starch and roughness from flatirons, hold the iron on a large grindstone for twenty minutes or so.

b. Attrib. and comb. with *factor, factory, maker, mush.*

1711 *N.C. Col. Rec.* I. 764 Women [are] Soap makers Starch makers Dyes &c. **1841** CIST *Cincinnati* Advt., Soap and candle manufacturers, and starch factors. **1847** HOWE *Hist. Coll. Ohio* 477 [Cuyahoga Falls] contains . . . 1 starch factory. **1894** *Nation* LVIII. 451/3 To become proficient in the art of shooting fish, Indians have to live an entire month solely on starch-mush.

Stare-cat. (See quotation.) *colloq.*[2] *rare.* — **1859** BARTLETT 448 *Stare-Cat,* a woman or girl who amuses herself with gazing at her neighbors. A woman's word.

***Starfish.** Any one of various star-shaped echinoderms.

1672 JOSSELYN *New Eng. Rarities* 95 The Star Fish, having five points like a Star, the whole Fish no bigger than the Palm of a Mans hand. **1836** HOLLEY *Texas* 107 The great variety of marine animals such as star-fish, sunfish. **1883** *Nat. Museum Bul.* No. 27, 123 The two commoner species of Star-fish of the east coast (*Asterias vulgaris* and *Forbesii*), infest the oyster beds and occasion much destruction. **1911** *Rep. Fisheries 1908* 317/1 Starfish, a star-shaped animal . . . found all along the coast and known as 'five-finger,' 'sea-star,' 'star,' etc.

+b. *local.* The dollarfish, *Poronotus triacanthus.*

1884 GOODE, etc. *Fisheries* I. 333 The 'Butter-fish' of Massachusetts and New York, sometimes known . . . at Norfolk as the 'Star-fish,' is common between Cape Cod and Cape Henry.

Star flower. Any one of various plants having star-shaped flowers {1629-}, +as *Trientalis americana.* Also with specifying terms.

*c*1729 CATESBY *Carolina* I. 33 The Little yellow Star-Flower . . . grows plentifully in most of the open pasture lands in Carolina and Virginia. **1840** DEWEY *Mass. Flowering Plants* 133 Branched Star Flower. A very branching and spreading plant, . . . bearing a multitude of small white flowers. **1847** WOOD *Botany* 451 S[abbatia] *concinna.* . . . Elegant Star Flower. *Ib.,* S. *angularis.* . . . Angular-stemmed Star Fl. **1857** GRAY *Botany* 272 T[rientalis] *Americana.* . . . Star-flower. . . . Damp cold woods; common northward, and southward in the mountains. **1887** *Harper's Mag.* July 303/1 Star-flower, gold-thread, and anemones starred the woods. **1915** ARMSTRONG & THORNBER *Western Wild Flowers* 362 Star-flower. *Trientalis latifolia.* . . . Common names are Prairie Pointer . . . and American Cowslip.

Star grass. 'A name of various grass-like plants with starry flowers, or other radiate feature' (*Cent.*). {1796-} Also attrib. and with specifying term. See also WATER STAR GRASS.

1687 CLAYTON *Va.* in *Phil. Trans.* XLI. 158 Some call it ague-grass, others ague-root, others Star-grass. **1737** BRICKELL *N. Carolina* 22 Star-grass . . . is used with good Success in most Fevers in this Country. **1820**

Cottom's Va. & N.C. Almanack, Take of star grass roots . . . a spoon full. **1840** Long-leafed Star-grass [see LONG-LEAFED *a.*]. **1869** FULLER *Flower Gatherers* 127 The yellow flower is called the *Hypoxis*, or star-grass. **1898** CREEVEY *Flowers of Field* 222 Colic-root. Star-grass. . . . This plant grows from New England to Florida and in the mountains of Virginia.

✻**Starling.** +**a.** Any one of various American birds of the family Icteridae. (See also ORCHARD STARLING, RED-WINGED STARLING.) ✻**b.** The common European starling (*Sturnus vulgaris*), introduced into the United States. — *a*1676 WINTHROP in *Phil. Trans.* XII. 1065 The Ear is cloathed and armed with several strong thick Husks . . . defending it from . . . the Crows, Starlings and other Birds. **1811** WILSON *Ornithology* IV. 31, I was frequently entertained with the aerial evolutions of . . . great bodies of Starlings. **1850** S. F. COOPER *Rural Hours* 49 The red wing black-bird or starling, we have never seen in this county. **1880** CABLE *Grandissimes* 42 Clouds of starlings . . . rose from the high bulrushes. **1917** *Birds of Amer.* II. 237/1 The increase and spread of the Starling is due to its fecundity.

Star-nose(d) mole. The American button-nosed mole (*Condylura cristata*), having fleshy processes resembling a star at the end of the snout. — **1826** GODMAN *Nat. Hist.* I. 100 The Star-nose mole frequents the banks of rivulets, and the soft soil of adjacent meadows. **1859** WOOD *Illust. Nat. Hist.* I. 429 Radiated Mole, or Star-nosed Mole. . . . It is an inhabitant of Canada and the United States. **1871** *Amer. Naturalist* V. 314, [I] saw the star-nosed mole making . . . tracks and burrows [in the snow]. **1917** *Mammals of Amer.* 306/2 The tunnels of the Shrew Mole resemble those of the Star-nosed Mole more than those of others.

+**Star root.** The plant or root of a species of colicroot, *Aletris farinosa* or *A. aurea*; a medicinal preparation made of this. — **1743** CLAYTON *Flora Virginica* 38 *Hyacinthus caulenudo* [etc.]. . . . Stargrass & Starroot. **1789** *Amer. Philos. Soc.* II. p. xx, The root of *Aletris farinosa* . . . is called star-root. **1795** J. & E. PETTIGREW *MS. Let.* 5 April (Univ. N.C. MS.), I am about to use a method which I am in hopes will be of some benefit, which is starroot steipt in spirits. **1843** TALBOT *Journals* 29 External applications: . . . Star root, Rattlesnake plantain [etc.].

+**Star route.** [See quot. 1885.]

1. A mail route, other than a steamship, railroad, or rural delivery route, contracted for by the Post-Office Department.

1880 *Cimarron News & Press* 26 Feb. 2/3 The service on all star routes [shall] be reduced to one trip a week. **1885** *Mag. Amer. Hist.* April 395/2 Star Routes . . . are post-office routes which are not self-supporting, and are designated by asterisks in the 'Postal Guide'. The conditions of operating such routes are obviously favorable to peculation, and the term 'Star Route' was connected with highly disreputable official scandals from 1876 to 1884. **1900** *Congress. Rec.* 16 Jan. 865/2 It is a cheaper service to the Government than the star route. **1909** *Springfield W. Repub.* 16 Dec. 16 The post-office at Norwich has been served by a star route from Northampton.

2. Attrib. with *contractor, deficiency bill, service,* etc.

1876 *Congress. Rec.* 12 May 3050/2 The decrease in what is known as the star-route service will be $41,745. **1880** *Cimarron News & Press* 15 April 1/7 The president has approved the star route deficiency bill. **1882** *Nation* 10 Aug. 102/3 In the Star-route trial . . . Mr. A. C. Buell . . . testified as to his relations with Brady and Walsh. *Ib.* 30 Nov. 453/2 A creed . . . [which] permits its leading missionary to be . . . the passionate and even vituperative defender of the Star-route thieves . . . cannot enjoy considerable success in our time. **1886** POORE *Reminisc.* II. 454 General Garfield's friends afterward maintained that he had not alluded to the 'Star-route' contractors. **1896** *Columbus Dispatch* 20 Nov. 4 Stephen W. Dorsey, the once famous star route statesmen [*sic*], . . . is now in San Francisco. **1900** *Congress. Rec.* 17 Jan. 922/2 Star-route syndicates . . . secure a profit of nearly $150,000 per year on subcontracts.

+**Star-router.** One of those implicated in the star-route trials during the Garfield-Arthur administration. — **1882** *Nation* 30 Nov. 453/1 The Government is the party defrauded by the Star-routers. **1890** *Stock Grower & Farmer* 25 Jan. 4/2 The ex-star router has been particularly unfortunate of late years in all his business ventures.

+**Starry Banner.** =STARS AND STRIPES. — **1865** BOUDRYE *Fifth N.Y. Cavalry* p. iii, The Brave Boys . . . have heroically upborne the Starry Banner. **1865** RICHARDSON *Secret Service* 115 There, at last, thank God! was the old Starry Banner, flying in triumph over the Capitol. **1867** Goss *Soldier's Story* 50 Once again they were to be under the protecting folds of Liberty's starry banner.

+**Starry flounder.** The California flounder, *Platichthys stellatus.* — **1884** GOODE, etc. *Fisheries* I. 184 The Starry Flounder . . . is known, wherever found, as the 'Flounder,' all others being considered as Bastard or False Flounders. **1911** *Rep. Fisheries 1908* 56/1 The name flounder is variously applied to the flat fishes . . . known as 'American sole,' . . . 'starry flounder,' 'rough limanda' [etc.].

+**Stars and Bars.** The flag of the Confederate States of America; the battle flag of the Confederacy.

1862 in Moore *Rebel Rhymes* etc. (1864) 127 The Stars and Stripes, now so despised, Struck for the Stars and Bars. **1877** *Congress. Rec.* 3 March 2200/2 The bravest men that ever I saw under the 'stars and bars,' were . . . Union men until after the battles of the war began. **1894** *Ib.* 7 March 2689/2 No man who fought under the 'stars and bars' and failed has a word to say against giving deserved pensions to those brave men who

succeeded under the Stars and Stripes. **1912** *N.Y. Ev. Post.* 4 Jan. 4 Practically every relative he had was arrayed under the Stars and Bars.

+**Stars and Stripes.**

1. The flag of the United States.

1782 E. WATSON *Men & Times Revol.* (1861) 203 He . . . attached to the ship the stars and stripes. **1827** *Western Mo. Rev.* I. 195 The northern forests of Ohio have already seen the red cross of a hostile squadron giving place to the *stars and stripes.* **1888** SHERIDAN *Memoirs* I. 307 A small squad of men reached the top of Lookout and planted the Stars and Stripes on its very crest. **1923** *Imperial Night-Hawk* 29 Aug. 5/1 The Stars and Stripes, glorious emblem of freedom and liberty, has been torn to shreds at the hands of a mob.

b. (See quotations.) *Obs.*

1888 WHITMAN *Nov. Boughs* 407 In the slang of the New York common restaurant waiters a plate of ham and beans is known as 'stars and stripes.' **1917** J. A. Moss *Officers' Manual* 485 *Stars and Stripes,* beans.

2. *transf.* The United States.

[**1809** FRENEAU *Poems* II. 56 From the *Stars* and the *Stripes* you will mercy implore.] **1893** *Harper's Mag.* April 786/2 General Vallejo unhesitatingly gave his adherence to the Stars and Stripes. **1904** 'O. HENRY' *Roads of Destiny* 357 So the Stars and Stripes ain't landing any marines?

+**Star service.** The service to the public rendered by the star routes of the Post-Office Department. — **1877** *Congress. Rec.* 3 March 2224/1 The star service . . . is a service that does not yield much. **1880** *Ib.* 27 Jan. 548/2 The star service is the poor man's mail.

✻**Star-spangled,** *a.* Adorned or covered with stars, +esp. with reference to the flag of the United States; also, absol., =STAR-SPANGLED BANNER. — **1806** *Balance* V. 40/2 And pale beam'd the Crescent, its splendor obscur'd By the light of the star-spangled flag of our nation. **1861** NEWELL *Orpheus C. Kerr* I. 40 We raised the Star-spangled particular on the Post-office. *Ib.* 269 Yours, for the Star-Spangled, Orpheus C. Kerr. **1861** WHITTIER *Poetical Works* (1894) 334/1 What sets the roaring rabble's heel On the old star-spangled pennon?

+**Star-spangled Banner.**

1. =STARS AND STRIPES 1. Also transf.

1814 KEY in Delaplaine *F. S. Key* 169 O say does that star-spangled banner yet wave? **1832** DUNLAP *Hist. Amer. Theatre* 58 The first play performed in the United States under the protection of the flag, called proudly by Americans *the Star Spangled Banner,* . . . was 'the Countess of Salisbury.' **1863** *Rio Abajo Press* 23 June 4/1 Republicans, all parties, creeds, and their platforms are to-day enrolled under but one flag—the Star Spangled Banner. **1869** 'MARK TWAIN' *Innocents* 459 A robe swept down that was a very starspangled banner of curved and sinuous bars of black and white. **1894** *Congress. Rec.* 15 June 6385/2 Whenever an old soldier of the Confederacy comes up loyally to the support of the Union under the Star Spangled Banner, he will find the hand of fellowship extended to him. **1907** *St. Nicholas* July 831/1 How many of our boys of to-day know where and when the star-spangled banner was first raised?

attrib. **1886** D. L. BARTLETT *Lett. from Europe* 275 What would the Star Spangled Banner boys say to that?

2. The title of a patriotic poem written by Francis Scott Key in 1814 and set to music.

1862 *Mass. H. S. Proc.* 1 Ser. V. 374 A grandson . . . defended Fort McHenry at the time the 'Star-spangled Banner' was written. **1884** *Milnor* (Dak.) *Teller* 19 Sept., Fifty-two pretty American girls . . . enter a [German] town singing 'The Star-Spangled Banner.'

attrib. **1923** FAUX *Memorable Days* 392 Counsellor Jones and Key, of '*star-spangled banner*' fame, influence, and carry their honours almost as they please.

✻**Start,** *v.* +**1.** *intr.* To begin to go. ✻**2.** *To start in,* +to begin or set out. *colloq.* — (1) **1898** C. A. BATES *Clothing Bk.* No. 1279, That Boy . . . will have to start to school soon. (2) **1866** 'MARK TWAIN' *Sk., New & Old* 298 The showman drummed up his grit and started in fresh. **1923** HERRICK *Lilla* 28 She was finally reclothed according to city standards, and . . . 'started in' at high school in the big yellow brick building.

✻**Starter.**

+**1. a.** A lumberman who gets logs started in the spring. **b.** One who gets a quick start in a race.

1875 BURROUGHS *Winter Sunshine* 116 In the lumber countries, . . . starters are at work with their pikes and hooks starting out the pine logs on the first spring freshet. **1893** *Outing* XXII. 154/1 'Starters' . . . can start like a cannon-ball, literally outclassing, in all distances up to fifty yards, men who hold world's records in the hundred and two-hundred and twenty yard dashes.

+**2.** A foundation comb in a beehive.

1880 *Harper's Mag.* Oct. 778/1 Into the large frame there may be set eight little one-pound frames, each with its foundation 'starter.'

+**3.** *As a starter,* for a beginning, as a start. *colloq.*

1873 BEADLE *Undevel. West* 450 He gave me twenty drops of laudanum as a starter. **1892** *Courier-Journal* 2 Oct. 1/7, I've got $10,000 to bet now as a starter that Cleveland will carry the State. **1913** [see ORCHARDING 2].

+**Starting bar. 1.** (See first quot.) Also transf. **2.** (See quot. 1905.) — (1) **1876** KNIGHT 2310/2 *Starting-bar,* . . . a hand-lever for starting the valve-gear of a stream-engine. **1876** *Scribner's Mo.* Feb. 482/2 The fund subscribed was only the 'starting bar' which sets the train in motion.

(2) 1903 WHITE *Blazed Trail Stories* 36 The other man . . . seized the iron starting-bar and descended. **1905** *Forestry Bureau Bul.* No. 61, 38 *Gee throw*, a heavy, wooden lever, with a curved iron point, used to break out logging sleds. (N[orthern] F[orest].) Syn.: starting bar.

Starved rat. +The little chief hare (*Ochotona princeps*) of the Rocky Mountains region. — **1884** J. S. KINGSLEY, etc. *Stand. Nat. Hist.* V. 81 The miners and hunters in the West know these oddities as 'conies' and 'starved rats.' **1890** *Cent.* 3331/2 [The] starved rat . . . inhabits the mountains of the West as far south as New Mexico and Arizona.

*****Starwort.** One of various plants of different genera, as *Aster*, *Alsine*, etc., having flowers resembling stars. Also with specifying terms.

Cf. WATER STARWORT.

1640 PARKINSON *Theater of Plants* 132 The earlier and broad leafed purplish Starwort of Virginia. **1791** MUHLENBERG *Index Florae* 177. **1832** WILLIAMSON *Maine* I. 122 The Elecampane, or Starwort, grows 5 or 6 feet high . . . and its root is good for coughs. **1836** LINCOLN *Botany* App. 142 *Stellaria . . . longifolia*, (long-leafed starwort). **1861** WOOD *Botany* 657 *Callitrichaceæ*. Starworts. **1880** *Harper's Mag.* July 183 Purple ironweed, starwort, and golden-rod began again to show their friendly faces along the trail. **1898** CREEVEY *Flowers of Field* 170 Blazing-star. Devil's-bit. Unicorn-root. Drooping Starwort. *Chamaelirium Carolinianum.* **1901** MOHR *Plant Life Ala.* 499 *Alsine pubera*. . . . Soft Hairy Starwort. *Ib.* 500 *Arenaria lanuginosa*. . . . Spreading Starwort. *Ib.* 788 *Ionactis linariifolius*. . . . Pine Starwort.

+**Statal**, *a.* Of or pertaining to a state in the United States. *Obs.* — **1862** E. BATES in *Official Opinions Attorneys Gen.* X. 388, I have no knowledge of any other kind of political citizenship, higher or lower, statal or national. **1880** TOURGEE *Invisible Empire* xi, Public education flourished as a part of the statal economy.

*****State**, *n.*

I. +**1.** A British colony in America; one of the commonwealths making up the United States.

1634 *Mass. Bay Rec.* I. 117 When I shalbe called to giue my voice touching any such matter of this state, wherein ffreemen are to deale, I will giue my vote & suffrage [etc.]. **1776** A. ADAMS *Familiar Lett.* 204 Thus ends royal authority in this State [Mass.]. **1795** CLINTON in *Pub. Educ. City N.Y.* (1869) 21 The establishment of Common Schools throughout the state is happily calculated to remedy this inconvenience. **1814** *Niles' Reg.* VI. 393/1 This state is well intersected by many great rivers. **1883** *Gringo & Greaser* 1 Sept. 1/1 New Mexico has 1200 miles of railway,—more than the great commonwealth of Nevada which has been a state 19 years. **1910** *Okla. Session Laws* 3 Legisl. 2 Any resident taxpayer of this state, shall have a right to a hearing before the Supreme Court.

b. A representative or representatives of the authority of a state; a states attorney or a member of his staff; collectively, the government or inhabitants of a state. *To lose the state*, to lose the support of a majority of the voters in a state.

1787 *Constitution*, Done in Convention, by the unanimous consent of the States present. **1834** HONE *Diary* I. 114 We have lost the state, it is said, from the opposition of the Hicksites. **1894** 'MARK TWAIN' *P. Wilson* xx, Witness after witness was called by the State.

+**2.** *pl.* The United States; in later use, the older states, esp. those east of the Mississippi River, as contrasted with the unsettled or thinly settled West.

1777 J. ADAMS *Familiar Lett.* 301 The enemy are in possession of the Head of Elk, . . . in which they found a quantity of corn and oats belonging to the States. **1831** HOLLEY *Texas* (1833) 43 Sometimes . . . a white man from the States, who has become somewhat de-civilized, . . . is substituted. **1869** BOWLES *Our New West* 180 Food [in Colo. is] cheaper than in 'the States.' **1890** LANGFORD *Vigilante Days* (1912) 209 On his trip from the States, . . . an unfriendly gust had swept his only hat beyond recovery. **1900** DRANNAN *Plains & Mts.* 61 Col. Fremont had been detailed . . . to command an exploring expedition . . . [to] find a better route from the 'States' to California.

II. In attributive use.

The number of examples that might be shown here is very large. Only a few of the typical ones are included.

+**3.** Designating individuals or things serving in or relating to the military forces of a particular state.

See also STATE GUARD.

1777 *Vt. Hist. Soc. Coll.* I. 194 As to the quantity of state stores at Bennington it is quite out of my power to give you an account, at present. **1781** *Va. State P.* I. 492 He also recommends Lt: — Browne of the State Artillery as assistant Com: of Military Stores for the State. **1792** IMLAY *Western Territory* 49 When the State of Virginia conceded the country west of the Ohio to the United States, she reserved a tract of country . . . for those officers and soldiers which were called State troops. **1867** EDWARDS *Shelby* 397 General Shelby . . . galloped on to Booneville, . . . and invested the court-house, held by four hundred State militia. **1898** CANFIELD *Maid of Frontier* 116 He had seen blood spilled during his short life as a State soldier. **1911** PERSONS, etc. *Mass. Labor Laws* 277 A contractor for the erection of a state armory is violating the labor law by requiring his employees to work ten hours a day.

+**4.** Designating groups of persons functioning in connection with a state government or active in political matters affecting a state.

See also STATE BOARD, STATE CONVENTION.

1782 TRUMBULL *M'Fingal* 94 When in want no more in them [Congress] lies, Than begging of your State-Assemblies. **1787** *Constitution* vi, The Members of the several State Legislatures . . . shall be bound by Oath or Affirmation, to support this Constitution. **1840** *Niles' Nat. Reg.* 25 April 128/1 In 1836, Governor Noble was elected to the state senate. **1848** *Whig Almanac 1849* 6/2 The Hunkers . . . appointed a new State Central Committee, and in due time called another State Convention at Albany, which . . . chose the State Delegates to Baltimore. **1872** *Atlantic Mo.* March 387 The governor . . . will now probably control the next State delegation to the National Convention. **1892** *Vt. Agric. Rep.* XII. 142 The State House, . . . and also the County buildings [are] at Montpelier. **1904** *N.Y. Ev. Post* 6 Sept. 2 Information received by the Republican State Committee indicated that Mr. Bell, the Republican nominee for governor, was being cut by the farmers. **1911** PERSONS, etc. *Mass. Labor Laws* 219 The one place where we can meet both conditions now is in centralized state commissions for specific duties.

+**5.** Designating things relating to the finances or financial matters of a state.

See also STATE MONEY, STATE PAPER 1, etc.

1780 in *Travels Amer. Col.* 645 The State Warrants . . . of the first date should be drawn for to settle the priority of entry. **1784** *Conn. Acts & Laws* 219 [They] shall observe and follow the Directions of the Law relating to the gathering and collecting the State Rates. **1788** *Mass. Spy* 3 April 3/1 A considerable part of the State debt will shortly be extinguished. *a***1821** BIDDLE *Autobiog.* 237 With a Continental dollar you could purchase forty State dollars. **1837** PECK *Gaz. Illinois* 59 The Fund Commissioners are authorized to . . . [issue] state stock at a rate not exceeding six per centum per annum. **1838** *Indiana H. Rep. Jrnl.* 23 Sess. 101 A select committee [shall] be appointed to inquire into the expediency of authorizing a sale of state bonds redeemable in twenty years. **1840** *Niles' Nat. Reg.* 4 April 73/1 State security banks. . . . We hope to find the advantages anticipated from a system of free banking fully realized. *Ib.* 23 May 182/1 Mississippi state credit is in worse repute than that of any other in the union. **1844** *Indiana Senate Jrnl.* 29 Sess. 287 A select committee [shall] be instructed to inquire into the expediency of redeeming our State bonds . . . by giving . . . State scrip.

+**6.** Designating individuals serving a state in an official capacity.

See also STATE AUDITOR, STATE CLOTHIER, etc.

1789 MACLAY *Deb. Senate* 87 The State judges would be all sworn to support the Constitution. **1798** MANNING *Key of Liberty* 37 The State Senetors are more unknown. **1838** *Indiana H. Rep. Jrnl.* 23 Sess. 30 The act providing for the appointment of a State Geologist not having expired. **1850** *Western Journal* IV. 214 The New York Banking Law . . . requires the security . . . to be placed in the office of the State Comptroller. **1872** McCLELLAN *Golden State* 319 The State Surveyor-General being, ex officio, State Locating Agent, all the applicant has to do is to make application to him. **1881** *Mich. Gen. Statutes* I. (1882) 442 He shall pay over to the state inspector . . . all moneys received by him for inspection. **1900** *Congress. Rec.* 26 Jan. 1236/2 He started life at the lowest round . . . but never missed a step in its ascent, as the farm boy, . . . the State representative, . . . the ideal Vice-President of the United States. **1909** *Nat. Conservation Congress Proc.* 60 Forestry is most fortunate in having for its leader there the State Forester.

+**7.** Designating institutions maintained or carried on by a state in the public interest.

See also STATE LIBRARY, STATE PAPER 2, etc.

1791 *Phila. Ordinances* (1812) 83 An act to provide for completing the repairs of the wharf near the State Hospital. **1831** PECK *Guide* 256 One sixth part is to be . . . bestowed on a state college or university. **1840** *Niles' Nat. Reg.* 1 Aug. 342/3 A commission to inquire into . . . the practicability of a state asylum. **1862** *Rep. Comm. Patents 1861: Agric.* 271 In the experiment of the State farm of Massachusetts, the cost of the manure was forty dollars per acre. **1876** *Harper's Mag.* Dec. 155/1 The fertilizer control system introduced in Connecticut by the State Experimental Station is working very satisfactorily. **1892** *Vt. Agric. Rep.* XII. 114 The State Reform School is located there. **1897** *N.Y. Forest, Fish, & Game Comm. 2d Rep.* 130 Two of the parties . . . [had] built their cottages with timber cut from the adjoining State forests. **1904** State Park [see METROPOLITAN *a.*].

+**8.** Designating associations, societies, etc., that are state-wide in scope.

See also STATE SOCIETY.

1835 REED & MATHESON *Visit* II. 91 The State Association is the same species of meeting. **1840** *Niles' Nat. Reg.* 2 May 136/3 The annual meeting of the state temperance society have . . . elected the following officers. **1848** COOPER *Oak Openings* II. 214 A renowned annalist, whose information is sustained by the collected wisdom of a State Historical Society, does tell us that the enemy possessed both shores of Lake Erie in 1814. **1868** *Ore. State Jrnl.* 1 Aug. 2/3 The Oregon State Teachers' Association met to hold its eighth annual session. **1882** *Nation* 5 Oct. 281/1 The account given by Mr. Rogers, the President of the State Bar Association, . . . is far from encouraging. **1898** *Internat. Typogr. Union Proc.* 54/1, I look upon the State Union as a valuable auxiliary to the International Typographical Union.

+9. *pl.* Designating persons or things found in or typical of the eastern states as contrasted with the Far West. Also *state's.* (Cf. sense 2.)

1850 GARRARD *Wah-To-Yah* xv. 179 A skirt is worn a trifle shorter than the present States fashion. **1859** in F. Hall *Hist. Colorado* II. 520 My supply of State's grub short—two pounds bread, one pound coffee, one half pound salt. **1869** BOWLES *Our New West* 101 A 'States' horse cannot stand the hard riding and tough climbing. **1890** *Stock Grower & Farmer* 8 Feb. 3/2 The 'states farmers' [have] declared war against ranchmen.

10. In special combinations.

State badge, a device or symbol identified with a state; *s. boss,* one in a position of dominance or rulership in the political affairs of a state; *s. capital,* the seat of government of a state; *s. capitol,* the building in which a state legislature meets; *s. emancipation,* emancipation of slaves by state action (*Obs.*); *s. executive,* the governor of a state; *s. guardsman,* a member of a state guard; *s. lottery* {1775}, a lottery engaged in by a state to raise state funds; *s. patronage,* patronage consisting of the right to appoint officers in a state; *s. reservation,* a reservation for Indians in a state; *s. scholarship,* a scholarship awarded by the authorities of a state; *s. seal,* an engraved stamp adopted by a state for use on official documents.

1883 *Harper's Mag.* Oct. 712/1 The wolverine . . . is the State badge of Michigan. **1882** *Nation* 7 Sept. 194/2 They have already added one more State boss to their list. **1854** *Harper's Mag.* X. 135/1 The hero . . . has come up to the state capital on his first visit. a**1857** *Mich. Gen. Statutes* 1. (1882) 171 The board of state auditors are hereby authorized . . . to procure plans, drawings and estimates for a state capitol. **1853** STOWE *Key* 70/1 Such [slaveholders] are most earnest advocates for State emancipation. **1884** *Century Mag.* Feb. 583/2 There are few, if any, other State executives who would undertake [etc.]. **1906** *N.Y. Ev. Post* 14 Aug. 5 Bringing in the State guardsmen infuses new life into the monotony of the professional soldier's daily work. **1777** *Warren-Adams Lett.* I. 297 Dr. Jackson . . . is a Manager of the State Lottery. **1874** in Brewster *Life J. D. Whitney* 288 With state and federal patronage together, he controls the legislature easily. **1792** *Mass. H. S. Coll.* 1 Ser. I. 287 The whole Six Nations live on grounds, called the State Reservations. **1871** BAGG *At Yale* 38 Forty free State-scholarships were established. **1850** *31st Congress 1 Sess.* Sen. Ex. Doc. No. 74, x. § 8 The governor of the State shall make use of his private seal until a State seal shall be provided.

* State, *v.*

+1. *tr.* To allot or grant (land) *to* an individual or group. *Obs.*

1661 *Topsfield Rec.* 6 The aforsaid fiuehundred acres of land is stated to the inhabitants of the Town . . . to share in the said common. **1699** *Springfield Rec.* II. 78 The said land was first stated to the ministry In Springfeild.

+2. To establish (a road or way) by authority. *Obs.*

1674 *Conn. Rec.* II. 223 The Court . . . haue now seen cause to state the road thorow Nath: Hayden's quarter. **1692** *Ib.* IV. 68 There may be a roade stated between Conecticut Riuer and the upland. **1705** *Dedham Rec.* V. 340 We have layed out and stated a way from the East street up the Hill towards the house of James Fales four rods wide. **1724** *Cambridge Prop. Rec.* 281 Said Select Men have Nominated & appointed John Stedman and Solomon Prentice . . . to State passages thrû the Same.

+State aid. Aid given by a state to various projects within its borders carried on in the public interest. — **1856** OLMSTED *Slave States* 136 So, too, with regard to a line from Antwerp to Norfolk, (a proposition to grant State aid for establishing which, was the chief topic of public discussion in Virginia). **1895** *Dept. Agric. Yrbk. 1894* 87 Petitions asking for State aid in behalf of [agric. education] . . . were presented to the legislature. **1920** *3d Nat. Country Life Conf. Proc.* 139 'State aid' of this type . . . then becomes an immeasurable influence for the stimulation of local initiative.

+State auditor. A state official or member of a state board whose duty is to examine and certify accounts and claims against the state. — **1850** *Mich. Gen. Statutes* I. (1882) 57 The secretary of state, state treasurer, and commissioner of the state land office shall constitute a board of state auditors. **1864** *Ohio Agric. Rep.* XVIII. p. cii, The returns to the State Auditor should differ more widely than they are found to do from the census returns. **1911** *Okla. Session Laws* 3 Legisl. 198 The State Auditor shall, thereupon, issue public building bonds and deliver same to state treasurer.

+State bank. A bank that operates under a state charter. **1815** [see NATIONAL BANK 1]. **1841** in MacLeod *F. Wood* 74 Our nine hundred State banks . . . have been for years preying upon the vitals of the people. **1894** LEAVITT *Our Money Wars* 40 In 1811 the volume of money issued and circulated, by the old system of State banks, was $28,000,000. **1906** *N.Y. Ev. Post* 4 The wrecking of the Milwaukee Avenue State Bank of Chicago by its president.

b. Attrib. with *money, note, paper.*

1834 C. A. DAVIS *Lett. J. Downing* 39, I'll jist . . . let 'em go with that mess of 'State Bank Paper' already there. **1884** BLAINE *20 Years of Congress* I. 471 It had only increased the dangers of inflation by . . . the protection it afforded to the circulation of State bank notes. **1894** LEAVITT *Our Money Wars* 96 The State bank money had been a great nuisance.

State bed. A luxurious or richly ornamented bed. {1812–} Also transf. — **1839** KIRKLAND *New Home* (1840) 21 Around this state-bed, . . . all the men and boys I had seen below stairs were to repose. **1885** EGGLESTON in *Century Mag.* April 878/2 In the dwellings of the richer colonial gentry . . . there was a household idol, known as the state bed, very much adored, and kept shut up from vulgar eyes.

+State board. A board or group of state officials having charge of various matters of state concern.

1838 COLTON *Ind. Delineated* 45 The State Board . . . express their doubts whether it can be effected except by partial canalling. **1871** [see FAIR *n.*[1] 2 d]. **1903** E. JOHNSON *Railway Transportation* 410 The State board fixes the valuation of the entire railroad property within the State. **1911** PERSONS, etc. *Mass. Labor Laws* 185 The state board issues a pamphlet of the laws relating to school matters.

b. Such a board *of* a specified kind.

1845 *Xenia Torch-Light* 4 Dec. 2/5, I respectfully commend to your consideration the expediency of establishing a State Board of Education. **1873** *Newton Kansan* 14 Aug. 2/2 The Iowa State Board of Equalization closed their labors lately. **1877** State board of canvassers [see CANVASSER 1]. **1898** *Kansas City Star* 18 Dec. 4/3 Mr. Stanley . . . will recommend that the State board of pardons be abolished. **1911** *Okla. Session Laws* 3 Legisl. 42 There is hereby appropriated . . . the sum of forty-five thousand dollars . . . to be expended under the direction of the State Board of Agriculture. *Ib.* 107 [The following sum is appropriated] for the Deficiency in Available Funds Necessary for the Expense of the State Board of Health.

+State building. A building owned by a state, usually for carrying on administrative affairs. — **1835** HOFFMAN *Winter in West* I. 23 Upon this eminence . . . stands the capitol and state buildings. **1876** INGRAM *Centennial Exp.* 601 The procession entered the grounds and proceeded to the State building in the following order. **1893** *Harper's Mag.* April 708/1 More than twenty-one million dollars are invested in school-houses, State buildings, lands, and other property for educational purposes.

+State clothier. An officer who issued clothing, etc., to the troops of his state. *Obs.* (Cf. *Clothier general,* s.v. CLOTHIER 3.) — **1780** *N.H. Hist. Soc.Coll.* IX. 223 The regimental returns for Shous are to be Made to the State Clothier. **1782** *N.H. Comm. Safety Rec.* 299 He is to be accountable out of his pay as Sub or State Clothier.

+State convention. A convention or assembly, freq. of a political nature, of representatives from different parts of a state.

1779 *Amherst Rec.* 75 The calling a State Convention for the sole purpose of forming a new Constitution. **1812** JAY *Correspondence* IV. 362 The president of every county, State, or national convention should be a person fitted to receive and employ *authority.* **1842** *Niles' Nat. Reg.* 12 Feb. 384/2 A state convention is to be held . . . at Hartford, Conecticut, to adopt measures for laying before congress the claims of home industry. **1865** *Nation* I. 163 The colored people of Michigan recently held a State Convention. **1891** *World Almanac* 75/2 South-Carolina, Democratic 'Straight-out' State Convention . . . put a ticket in the field in opposition to the regular (Tillman) Democratic ticket. **1912** NICHOLSON *Hoosier Chron.* 73 She's . . . always . . . coming up to town to state conventions or federations.

+State court. A court forming a part of the judicial system of a state, as distinguished from a federal court. — **1789** MACLAY *Deb. Senate* 87 If any matter made cognizable in a Federal court should be agitated in a State court, a plea to the jurisdiction would immediately be put in. **1797** *Ann. 5th Congress* 388 Mr. Nicholas . . . doubted the right of the United States to tax the lawyers of the State Courts, as they were necessary in the State Governments. **1840** *Diplom. Corr. Texas* I. (1908) 445 The law of nations does not give jurisdiction to either the State or Federal courts farther than the same may be recognized by some enactment. **1912** NICHOLSON *Hoosier Chron.* 225 The doors of the state courts swing inward to any Hoosier citizen of good moral character who wants to practice law.

+Stated clerk. (See quot. 1909.) — **1831** PECK *Guide* 259 The Rev. John M. Ellis, of Jacksonville, . . . was stated clerk when the three Presbyteries were in one. **1871** *Harper's Mag.* July 315 The stated clerk lost his way when approaching the place on horseback. **1909** WEBSTER 2035/2 *Stated clerk,* in the Presbyterian churches of the United States, the secretary of a court.

+State Department. A federal department whose head is the Secretary of State and whose chief function is the conduct of the country's foreign affairs. Also attrib. — **1790** *Ann. 1st Congress* 1505 The resolution laid on the table yesterday, respecting the State Department, was taken up. **1846** POLK *Diary* (1929) 119, I had a full conversation with him [*sc.* Buchanan] on the subject of his transfer from the State Department to the Supreme Court bench. **1887** *American* XIV. 341 It is to be regretted that the State Department loses the services of so competent and 'level-headed' a chief. **1920** *Nation* CXI. 398/1 Under the State Department rules the press interview is deftly twisted inside out.

Stated preacher. A minister settled or established in a particular pastorate. {1752} — **1849** *Knickerb.* XXXIV. 89 We had the pleasure afterward to find . . . a 'stated preacher' of Sandy-Hill. **1858** WEED *Autobiog.* 18 There were neither churches nor 'stated preachers' in town. **1871** DE VERE 236 He becomes what in some churches is called a stated preacher.

+Stated preaching. Preaching at fixed or set times. — **1861** *Vanity Fair* 30 March 148/1 Twenty or thirty Sioux Indians . . . stated that they had adopted a number of customs in vogue among the whites, such as wearing pantaloons, . . . regular attendance upon 'stated preaching,' &c. **1863** *Harper's Mag.* May 858/1 A clergyman . . . heard that a portion of the country was without 'the stated preaching of the Gospel.'

+Stated supply. (See quot. 1861.) — **1860** *Harper's Mag.* July 194/1 The New School Meeting . . . 'sot under' Mr. Reuben Kenworthy, Stated Supply. . . . Stated Supplies are at liberty to go away whenever they get tired. **1861** *Contrib. Eccles. Hist. Conn.* 221 Stated supplies . . . [are] men employed to perform the duties of a pastor, but not inducted, in any appropriate way into the pastoral office.

+State election. An election held throughout a state for selecting state officers, including federal representatives. Also attrib. — **1798** MANNING *Key of Liberty* 38 In our State Elections for federal Representitives & Electors, . . . their was not halfe the peopel brought to act on either side. **1843** *Niles' Nat. Reg.* 176/3 There were all sorts of confusion in the political ranks prior to the state election on Tuesday last. **1890** *Stock Grower & Farmer* 1 Feb. 4/4 We would have state and national elections come together. **1911** *Okla. Session Laws* 3 Legisl. 225 The Governor shall . . . appoint a State Election Board.

+State fair. A fair at which prizes are awarded for the best farm and home products submitted by citizens of the state. — **1849** *Mich. Agric. Soc. Trans.* I. 17 Specimens of stock, seeds and fruits will be brought to our first State Fairs from adjoining States. **1861** *Chicago Tribune* 26 May 1/8, 10 small Lots in Brighton, near State Fair Grounds. **1870** NOWLAND *Indianapolis* 344 At the State Fair of 1869, he offered a fine side-saddle as a present to the second best lady equestrian. **1920** *3d Nat. Country Life Conf. Proc.* 14 They have . . . a school that takes prizes every few minutes at the state fair.

+State guard. The National Guard or militia force of a state; also, a portion of this force. — **1833** *Niles' Reg.* XLIV. 139/1 We the people, oversetting and nullifying the state guard by the way, who in vain attempted to keep us out. **1861** in Logan *Great Conspiracy* 364 Major-General John C. Fremont . . . has threatened . . . to Confiscate the property and Free the Negroes belonging to the members of the Missouri State Guard. **1898** PAGE *Red Rock* 232 Should they [*sc.* Negroes] plough when they were the State guard!

+State highway. A highway built or maintained by, or with the assistance of, state funds. Also attrib. (Cf. STATE ROAD.) — **1883** *Harper's Mag.* Aug. 335/2 Civilization has followed almost exactly the print of the moccasin in the State highway. **1895** *Dept. Agric. Yrbk. 1894* 507 For the maintenance of State highways, said commission shall contract with the city or town. **1911** *Okla. Session Laws* 3 Legisl. 221 A State Highway Department is hereby created and established.

+Statehood. The condition or status of a state. Also attrib. — **1868** *N.Y. Times* 8 June, Why indeed should the Federal Senate . . . be organized on the basis of an extinct statehood? **1885** *Congress. Rec.* 18 Dec. 303/1 This question is one . . . [of] breaking into Statehood without the consent of Congress. **1899** *Mo. So. Dakotan* I. 184 The greater part of the expense incident to the statehood movement of 1885 . . . was borne by Governor Mellette. **1925** BRYAN *Memoirs* 214 Illinois, assuming the responsibilities of statehood in 1818, held within her wide plains a wealth as great as any gold mine.

* Statehouse.

+1. The building in which the administrative affairs of a colony or state are carried on; the capitol of a colony or state.

A reputed 1638 example appears in the abstracts of colonial records in the *Calendar of State Papers, Amer. & W.I.* I. 268.

1666 *Md. Archives* II. 28 The Upper House do not think fit to repeal the act for building a State House. **1717** *Conn. Rec.* VI. 36 Six hundred fifty pounds . . . shall be improved towards a state house in Hartford. **1796** MORSE *Univ. Geog.* I. 620 A large state-house or capitol, has lately been erected on the hill [at Richmond, Va.]. **1814** [see COMMENCEMENT 2]. **1893** *Harper's Mag.* May 972/2 Disputes between the rival [parties] . . . threatened to culminate in a riot at the State-house in Topeka. **1912** NICHOLSON *Hoosier Chron.* 463 That bunch of lobbyists . . . was always gum-shoeing through the marble halls of the State House.

+2. An Indian council house. *Obs.*

1654 JOHNSON *Wonder-w. Prov.* 109 A State-house . . . covered round about, and on the top with Mats. **1666** *S.C. Hist. Soc. Coll.* V. 66 Before the Doore of their Statehouse is a spacious walke. **1751** GIST *Journals* 44 A Kind of State-House of about 90 Feet long, . . . in which they hold their Councils.

+3. Attrib. with *door, garden, lot, steeple.*

1676 *Virginia Mag. Hist.* I. 183 [He] presently drawes up his men before the state house door. **1791** *Phila. Ordinances* (1812) 83 It would contribute to the embellishment of the public walks in the state-house garden. **1846** *Xenia Torch-Light* 2 April 2/5 The State House lot has been surrounded by a picket-fence. **1876** INGRAM *Centennial Exp.* 656 The tolling of the new bell of liberty from the State House steeple.

+Stateite. [STATE *n.* 1 and *ite.*] One favoring the admission of New Mexico into the Union as a state. — **1871** *Republican Rev.* 25 Feb. 1/1 The Stateites imagine they have it all their own way about now, . . . but let the question be put to a vote of the people.

+State librarian. A person in charge of a state library. — **1850** *Ind. Hist. Soc. Publ.* III. 566, I have sent a copy of the record series from my own library, to the care of the State Librarian, for your inspection. **1881** *Mich. Gen. Statutes* I. (1882) 161 A State librarian shall be appointed by

the governor. **1907** *St. Nicholas* July 799/2 If I were a legislature and wanted to appoint a state librarian, I'd never appoint mother.

+State library. A library at a state capital, intended orig. for the use of state officers, but now in some states serving as the administrative headquarters of the state public library service. — **1833** *Niles' Reg.* XLIV. 114/2 The second story [will] . . . furnish a capacious room for the state library. **1872** McCLELLAN *Golden State* 398 The State library at the capital, Sacramento, contains about thirty thousand volumes. **1892** *Vt. Agric. Rep.* XII. 142 The State House, State Library, . . . and . . . County buildings [are] at Montpelier. **1912** NICHOLSON *Hoosier Chron.* 497 He dug diligently in the State Library preparing his case.

+State line.

1. The boundary line of a state.

1817 S. BROWN *Western Gazetteer* 56 More than one half of the village stands on the Ohio side of the state line. **1869** STOWE *Oldtown Folks* 355 These kidnappers always make for the New York State line. **1884** BLAINE *20 Years of Congress* I. 211 Fifty-five millions of American people . . . carry on their exchanges . . . without even the recognition of State lines. **1912** COBB *Back Home* 94 He was jayhawkin' back and forth along the State line.

2. The military force of a state enrolled for combat service.

1855 SIMMS *Forayers* 521, I will reserve Major Sinclair, whom I design to advance to a colonelcy in the state line, for a separate duty.

+State money. Money issued by a state prior to 1789; state notes circulating as currency. *Obs.* (Cf. GEORGIA CURRENCY, PENNSYLVANIA CURRENCY.) — **1781** *Va. State P.* I. 553 His employees having the choice of receiving Tobacco at the market price in lieu of State or Continental money. **1787** *Md. Jrnl.* 28 Sept. (Th.), Cash given for black and Continental State Money. **1866** C. H. SMITH *Bill Arp* 64 You allowed the members to exchange two hundred dollars of Confederate money for two hundred dollars of State money. **1882** in S. LEAVITT *Our Money Wars* 78 Indiana has generally had the best State money of any of the United States.

+State office. A public official position in or relating to the government of a state. — **1789** JEFFERSON *Writings* VII. 287 They have passed a bill rendering every person holding any federal office incapable of holding at the same time any State office. **1855** in MacLeod *F. Wood* 199 The election law . . . places the candidates for county offices on the same ballot with candidates for State offices. **1912** NICHOLSON *Hoosier Chron.* 246 From the way candidates are turning up for state office our fellows must think they have a chance of winning.

State paper. {1740- } **+1.** *collect.* Notes, serving as currency, issued by a state. *Obs.* **+2.** (See quot. 1891.) — (1) **1792** *Steele P.* I. 81 I mention this . . . that those who yet hold State paper may be upon their guard. **1822** *Ann. 17th Congress* 1 Sess. 323 It might have been had in Kentucky for three cents, State paper. (2) **1838** *N.Y. Laws* 246 The comptroller shall immediately thereupon . . . give notice in the state paper that [etc.]. **1850** *Mich. Gen. Statutes* I. (1882) 47 The Legislature shall not establish a state paper. **1891** *Cent.* 5912/1 State paper, . . . a newspaper selected, by or pursuant to law, for the publication of official or legal notices.

+State penitentiary. A penitentiary maintained by a state in accordance with state laws. — **1809** CUMING *Western Tour* 170 The publick buildings here [in Frankfort, Ky.], are a state-house, . . . the state penitentiary, and a government house. **1837** PECK *Gaz. Illinois* 148 The state penitentiary is located in Alton. **1903** Fox *Little Shepherd* xxv, Chad saw Morgan and Colonel Hunt loaded on a boat to be sent down to prison in a State penitentiary.

+State printer. A printer in charge of the public printing of a state. — **1800** *Steele P.* I. 191 They this day brought on the ballot for State printer. **1839** *Jamestown* (N.Y.) *Jrnl.* 23 Jan. 2/3 The bill to change the tenure of office of the state printer . . . was under discussion in the house. **1898** *Kansas City Star* 20 Dec. 5/4 We ought to pass a law reducing the fees of the state printer. **1911** *Okla. Session Laws* 3 Legisl. 287 It shall be the duty of the State Printer to prepare the plans and specifications for all public printing and binding.

State prison, State rights. (See STATE('S) PRISON, STATE('S) RIGHTS.)

+State road. A road surveyed and opened by state authority, as distinguished from a national, county, or private road. — **1809** CUMING *Western Tour* 183 A new state road crosses the river here. **1830** PAULDING *Chron. Gotham* 173 A great state road is to be laid out by the next legislature. **1895** *Dept. Agric. Yrbk. 1894* 507 All construction of State roads shall be fairly apportioned by said commission among the different counties.

Stateroom. {1660- }

+1. A small room on a passenger boat providing sleeping accommodations for one or more passengers.

[**1776** CUTLER in *Life & Corr.* I. 55 The cabins and state-rooms were spacious.] **1815** EVERETT *Journal* (Mass. Hist. Soc. MS.) 84 [We gave] an extra price of ten guineas for what was called an After cabin (a miserable stateroom). **1876** WHITNEY *Sights & Insights* I. 32 A man was going round . . . putting printed papers on all the pieces of luggage,—'Hold,' or 'State-Room,'—in big letters. **1922** PARRISH *Case & Girl* 239 You will stay in this stateroom until we get ready to let you out.

attrib. **1857** STACEY *Journal* 32 Her stateroom accommodations are very poor, the bunks being very small, and the staterooms of a size to match.

+2. = DRAWING-ROOM 3.

1867 DIXON *New Amer.* II. 291 On the Pennsylvania central line, a lady entered into my state-room. **1882** HOWELLS *Modern Instance* xxxviii, Halleck . . . went forward to the state-room that Marcia and Olive had occupied. **1903** ADE *People You Know* 32 Brad is making it Hand over Fist and wears $6 Shirts and rides in a State-Room on the Pullman. **1904** *N.Y. Times* 14 May 10 The train was made up of a dining car, a stateroom car, and five sleepers.

+State's attorney. Also †**state attorney.** An attorney, usually an elected official, who represents the state or county in judicial proceedings.

1779 *Mass. Province Acts* V. 1115 The selectmen . . . shall make application to the state's attorney. *Ib.*, After the legal charges of prosecution are paid, one fourth part shall be to the use of the state attorney. **1809** KENDALL *Travels* III. 251 There is, in Vermont, as in some of its fellow-republics, no attorney-general for the whole republic, but an attorney-general, or, as it is called, a *state's attorney*, for each particular county. **1871** EGGLESTON *Hoosier Schoolm.* 191 The 'prosecuting attorney' (for so the State's attorney is called in Indiana) had been sent for the night before.

+State senator. A member of the upper house of a state legislature. (Cf. SENATOR 2.) — **1842** BUCKINGHAM *E. & W. States* I. 18 While we remained at New York, the State senators were sitting daily, as a Court of Appeal, called technically a 'Court of Errors.' **1873** *Newton Kansan* 3 April 2/1 Wm. M. Tweed, of New York, State Senator of that State, resigned his seat in the house on the 27th. **1907** *St. Nicholas* July 798/1 Letters to the governor, state senators, and representatives must be written by herself.

+State's evidence.

1. Testimony in behalf of the state given by a participant in a crime, who seeks thereby to lessen his own punishment; one who supplies such testimony. Also transf.

1831 *Jamestown* (N.Y.) *Jrnl.* 2 Nov. 2/5 The state's evidence, though he may be despised, is not to be discredited, because of the enormity of the offences he discloses. **1890** LANGFORD *Vigilante Days* (1912) 300 Long John was admitted to testify under the rule of law regulating the reception of State's evidence. **1905** *Forum* April 532 The public accepted the articles as state's evidence, provided from motives of revenge or penitence.

2. *To turn state's evidence,* of an accomplice, to give evidence in behalf of the state in order to obtain leniency. {to turn Queen's evidence, 1865; to turn King's evidence, 1889} Also transf.

1796 A. BARTON *Disappointment* 86 Ye turn'd eenformer, and states-evidence, to get the ane half till yere sel. **1806** FESSENDEN *Democracy Unveiled* II. 105 Lyon, . . . by turning States' evidence, has brought out his friend Duane. **1870** 'F. FERN' *Ginger-Snaps* 285 And how they like to question them as to how women think and feel on such and such subjects, which information they can only obtain by their wives turning state's evidence. **1903** *N.Y. Tribune* 20 Sept., He was turning State's evidence and saving himself from punishment.

‖**Stateship.** = STATEHOOD. — **1884** *Milnor* (Dak.) *Teller* 21 Nov., One of these principles is the right of stateship.

+State society. A society that operates throughout a state. — **1835** [see COUNTY SOCIETY]. **1871** *Mich. Gen. Statutes* I. (1882) 613 It shall be the duty of the secretary of said state society to make and transmit to the secretary of state a report of the transactions. **1872** *Ill. Dept. Agric. Trans.* IX. 12 [We propose] to tender the Grounds and fixtures of the Macon County Agricultural Society, and make such additional improvements as the State Society requires.

+State sovereignty. a. Political supremacy possessed by a state in the management of its governmental affairs. **b.** In pre-Civil War debate, the doctrine that the individual states are essentially sovereign powers associated in voluntary union. Also attrib.

1811 *Ann. 12th Congress* 1 Sess. 2159 Our only hope of participating . . . in the rights and blessings of State sovereignty, is built upon the pleasing anticipation of becoming a part of the Mississippi Territory. **1815** *Niles' Reg.* VIII. 66/2 The theory of state sovereignty has assigned to each an equal power in the senate. **1833** *Md. Hist. Mag.* XIII. 272 In comes J. C. Calhoun at the head of the anti Tariff and the State Sovereignty parties. **1836** *S. Lit. Messenger* II. 184 One party . . . [favored dissolution of the Union], as necessary to prevent the destruction of State-sovereignty. **1866** 'F. KIRKLAND' *Bk. Anecdotes* 24/1 In that toast was presented the issue—liberty *before* Union—supreme State sovereignty. **1910** J. HART *Vigilante Girl* 284 John Tower had often declaimed against 'Federal centralism' and in favor of 'State sovereignty.'

State('s) prison. {1723-} +A prison maintained under state law by a state of the United States. {state prison, 1867, of Australia}

The form *state's prison* is regarded by the *O.E.D.* as American.

1797 F. BAILY *Tour* 289n., The Callibouse is the state prison. **1810** *Columbian Centinel* 3 Feb. 4/1 Samuel Benham . . . has been sentenced to ten years imprisonment and hard labor in the Vermont State Prison. **1877** HOWELLS *Out of Question* 44 It's the difference between three months in the House of Correction and ten years in the State's Prison. **1892** — *Quality of Mercy* 337 If you believe that his only chance of happiness on earth is to come home and spend the rest of his life in State's prison. **1918** LINCOLN *Shavings* 358 Do you cal'late I'll let my daughter marry a man that's been in state's prison?

attrib. **1839** *Knickerb.* XIV. 185 No one would believe the narrative of a state-prison convict. **1873** *Harper's Mag.* May 944/1 That the offices of the Canal Commissioners and State-prison Inspectors be abolished. **1875** BURNHAM *Three Years* 107 A stranger, . . . an ex-state prison bird, . . . thought he recognized him.

+State('s) rights. *pl.*

1. The body of political rights held to reside in the individual states; the principle of reserving to the states as much power as is possible under the Constitution.

Cf. text of the Tenth Amendment.

1798 *Ann. 5th Congress* 2022 The powers of our general Government are checked by State rights. **1811** CLAY *Speeches* (1842) 31 Let me inquire what they would have had those to do, who believed the establishment of a bank an encroachment upon state rights? **1864** *Ore. State Jrnl.* 30 April 3/1 The Copperheads want 'States Rights,' just what the rebels are fighting for. **1888** M. LANE in *America* 27 Sept. 15 *Centralization*, a tendency to concentrate all possible power under the national government in contradistinction to the doctrine of state's rights. **1900** *Congress. Rec.* 29 Jan. 1260/1 Secession and belief in States' rights, for which the South has always contended, precipitated the conflict. **1914** *Cycl. Amer. Govt.* I. 398/2 The conscription acts . . . of the Civil War period were opposed by the champions of state rights.

2. Attrib. with *man, member, plank,* etc.

1836 *S. Lit. Messenger* II. 686/2 The national-government-men contended that the states would have too much power—the states-rights-men that they would have just enough for protection. **1848** QUITMAN in Claiborne *Life Quitman* II. 13 The idea was first suggested in Congress by a state-rights member from Virginia. **1852** *Ib.* II. 164 What shall we of the strict state-rights school, what shall the 'Old Guard' do? **1856** *Democratic Conv. Proc.* 63, [I] expect soon to enter upon an active campaign . . . in advocacy of the glorious State Rights Platform. **1864** LOWELL *Writings* V. 157 The war plank would offend the one, the State Rights plank excite the suspicion of the other. **1888** *Century Mag.* May 58/1 Only a 'States Rights' ticket was voted for.

b. Used in or with the names of political parties.

1839 State Rights Republican school [see FEDERAL a. 1]. **1843** in Hambleton *H. A. Wise* 40 He stated . . . that John Tyler was nominated at Harrisburg, because of his States Rights Republican Whig principles, and that there was . . . a union of National Republicans and States Rights Whigs. **1854** BENTON *30 Years' View* I. 353/1 These extracts are valuable—for their precise definition and enumeration of the powers which . . . were really claimed for the States, by the State-Rights Republicans of that day. **1858** in Bartlett 290 There are two parties in the South, called 'National' and 'States-Rights' Democrats. **1862** in Logan *Great Conspiracy* 409 The leaders [in the South] . . . comprehend what was previously known as the State Rights Party. **1884** *Chicago Tribune* 15 May 7/3 Col. Phocion Howard . . . said he was . . . a State-rights Bourbon Democrat from away back.

+State tax. A tax levied by a state government as distinguished from a local or national tax. Also *collect.* — **1796** *Ann. 4th Congress* 2 Sess. 2694 The deficiency of the State tax has been hitherto supplied from the proceeds of vacant lands. **1801** *Spirit Farmers' Mus.* 268 [Twelve dollars] would pay the ministerial, the town, the county, or state taxes of a small farmer. **1849** CHAMBERLAIN *Ind. Gazetteer* 115 The whole State tax assessed in 1816, was $6,043.36.

+State ticket. (See quot. 1902.) — **1835** *Jamestown* (N.Y.) *Jrnl.* 4 Feb. 2/3 It was to save . . . the election of the regency state ticket, that these gentlemen stultified themselves. **1868** *Ore. State Jrnl.* 10 Oct. 1/6 The Republicans . . . have not nominated their State ticket yet. **1894** *Harper's Mag.* Jan. 318/1 The rest of the Republican State ticket was elected by 30,000 plurality. **1902** CLAPIN 385 *State ticket,* the list of candidates agreed upon by the leaders of a party for State's offices.

+State university. A university maintained by a state. — **1831** PECK *Guide* 256 Our sixth part is to be . . . bestowed on a state college or university. **1873** *Harper's Mag.* March 632/2 The State University has lately received a donation of forty-seven acres of land in Oakland. **1902** HARBEN *A. Daniel* 37 Just after being graduated at the State University he was admitted to the bar.

*** Station.** (See also EXPERIMENT, POLICE STATION.)

+1. A pioneer's residence; a plantation. *Obs.*

1677 HUBBARD *Narrative* II. 58 [At] Mount Desart, . . . his Peteroon used to keep his Winter Station. **1780** in *Travels Amer. Col.* 641 Three men were kild and scalped at Leva Todds Station the 27th. **1788** *Mass. Spy* 31 July 3/2 Col. James Robertson's son . . . was killed . . . within a few hundred yards of his father's station.

+b. A settlement of one family or several families, fortified against the attack of Indians or other enemies, esp. in Kentucky: (see also quot. 1833). Now *hist.*

1790 ASBURY *Journal* II. 82 We rode down to Blackmore's station. **1812** MARSHALL *Kentucky* 115 These stations, consisted of cabins built adjoining, . . . and at that time were sinonymous with forts. **1831** AUDUBON *Ornith. Biog.* I. 291 These emigrants [to Ky.] . . . had before them . . .

hundreds of miles to be traversed, before they could reach certain places of rendezvous called *stations.* **1833** J. HALL *Harpe's Head* 132 Every here and there a *station*—a rude block-house surrounded with palisades—afforded shelter to the traveller, and refuge, in time of danger, to all within its reach.

+2. A boundary mark. *Obs.*

1695 *Conn. Rec.* IV. 146 The north line of Stonington and the sowth line of Preston from station to station. **1736** *Smithtown Rec.* 310 Then layd out . . . a certain tract of land . . . running east thirteen degrees and a half south one hundred and thirty rods to the aforesaid white oak tree the first bound or station.

+3. A single church of the Methodist Episcopal denomination. Also attrib.

1844 Rupp *Relig. Denominations* 448 A leaders' meeting is composed of class leaders in any one circuit or station, in which the preacher presides. **1846** *Indiana Mag. Hist.* XXIII. 257 [He] was sometimes in circuits, and sometimes in the station and district work. **1910** *Census: Religious Bodies 1906* II. 432/2 The local church . . . may be a single station, or may include two or more congregations.

+b. Short for MISSION STATION.

See also MISSIONARY STATION.

1844 LEE & FROST *Oregon* 186 These pages relate to the work at the station, chiefly among the Indians of the Caclasco Village near it. **1883** WILDER *Sister Ridnour* 229 The converts . . . have been for many weeks at the station.

‖4. A shop or stand.

1855 *Harper's Mag.* X. 418/2 She stopped before a 'station' where hominy grits, buckwheat, flour, etc., were sold.

5. A regular stopping place for railroad trains {1830–} or other public conveyances; also, a building for the accommodation of the public and of the staff of the transportation system.

See also RAILROAD STATION, RAILWAY STATION.

1858 W. P. SMITH *Railway Celebrations* 147 When we left the Camden Station the rain was falling quite briskly. **1871** HOWELLS *Wedding Journey* 42 In a convenient place in the station hung a thermometer, before which every passenger, on going aboard the ferry-boat, paused as at a shrine. *a*1882 in McCABE *New York* 74 The better class of passengers using the cars, and the convenient and frequent recurrence of the stations, are all important factors in enhancing the growing popularity of the western district. **1922** TARKINGTON *Gentle Julia* 362 My trunk may come up from the station almost any time.

+b. A stopping place on a stage route. Also with defining term.

1859 GREELEY in Connelley *Stand. Hist. Kansas* I. 80 We left this morning, Station 17, on a little creek entitled Gouler. **1867** RICHARDSON *Beyond Miss.* 330 The ranches forty or fifty miles apart where passengers take meals, are termed 'home stations'; those where the coach only stops to exchange teams, 'swing stations.' **1890** LANGFORD *Vigilante Days* (1912) 252 This was the supper station.

+c. (See quotation.) Now hist.

1907 *St. Nicholas* May 619/2 He went there in order to establish a station on the Underground Railroad;—that is, in order to receive under his protection slaves who had succeeded in escaping from their Southern masters.

+6. *Mining.* (See first and third quotations.) Also attrib.

1877 W. WRIGHT *Big Bonanza* 307 A 'station' is the place of landing at each level of the mine. *Ib.* 443 The engineers, station-tender, pump-men, and the watchmen on the lower levels, all occupy positions to which are attached grave responsibilities. **1896** SHINN *Story of Mine* 223 A station is the office for the work done on that mining level, as well as the point where men stop and where freight is shipped or received.

7. *attrib.* **a.** In sense 5 with *ground, hack,* etc. **b.** In sense 5 b with *boss, building, proprietor.*

1857 *Mich. Gen. Statutes* I. (1882) 858 It shall be found expedient to use a common or joint station ground therein. **1863** 'G. HAMILTON' *Gala-Days* 42, I went into the station waiting-room to write a note. **1871** *Atlantic Mo.* Nov. 572 Copples, the former station-proprietor, had suffered amputation of the leg three times. **1872** 'MARK TWAIN' *Roughing It* 40 The station buildings were long, low huts, made of sun-dried, mud-colored bricks. *Ib.* 48 The station boss stopped dead still. **1897** *McClure's Mag.* Dec. 136, I left the lighted station-yard. **1903** *N.Y. Sun* 29 Nov. 11 Station wagons are very popular with many who live in the suburbs. **1905** PHILLIPS *Plum Tree* 273 He saw a man . . . hurriedly engage a station hack and drive away.

8. In special combinations.

Station hunting, the hunting of game by taking a position and causing the animal to be driven past; *s. point* {1859}, a point selected and marked, on a boundary, through which a line is, or may be, surveyed {1880}; *s. tree,* a tree established as a reference mark in defining a survey line.

1897 *Outing* XXX. 556/1 We kept to 'station-hunting,' there being less work about it. **1743** *N.J. Archives* 1 Ser. VI. 169 The station points on Hudson's & Delaware Rivers had been fixed in the year 1686. **1817** *Niles' Reg.* XII. 99/1 The deputy surveyors are required to note particularly . . . all corner or bearing trees, and all those trees which fall in the lines, called station, or line trees.

+Station agent. An agent in charge of a railway station; also, one in charge of a stage station. — **1855** *Ill. Agric. Soc. Trans.* II. 25 Your letter . . . suggests the active co-operation of this [railroad] company, through its station agents. **1887** GEORGE *40 Yrs. on Rail* 76 Superintendent Johnson had appointed me station agent. **1905** WIGGIN *Rose* 122 He was much too early for the train, which the station agent reported to be behind time. **1910** J. HART *Vigilante Girl* 203 He stopped at the stage station. . . . When the station agent looked to see [etc.].

+Station camp. A temporary camp erected by hunters or explorers. — **1820** DEWEES *Lett. from Texas* 17 Gabriel Martin, and five others with myself, left the station camp one morning. **1853** RAMSEY *Tennessee* 106 The party . . . formed a station camp upon a creek.

Stationed, *a.* {1735–} Of a Methodist clergyman: Serving a station; in charge of a station. — **1831** PECK *Guide* 67 The Methodists have a meeting-house, society, and stationed preacher. **1835** INGRAHAM *South-West* II. 162 A stationed minister, who regularly officiates. **1848** *Indiana Mag. Hist.* XXIII. 2 Five years he spent in our principal towns as a stationed preacher.

∗Stationer. One who sells stationery; in early use, sometimes a publishing bookseller. — **1684** STEERE *Monumental Memorial* t.-p., Printed . . . by Richard Pierce for James Cowse Stationer. **1788** *Mass. Spy* 3 April 4 Printed . . . by Isaiah Thomas, Printer, Bookseller and Stationer. **1851** CIST *Cincinnati* 175 Booksellers and stationers in the blank-book, pamphlet and job line. **1907** *St. Nicholas* Oct. 1098/2 Madeline mailed them right away to one of the stationers whom she knew.

Stationery. In attrib. uses designating articles sold by stationers, the establishments which sell them, etc. {1679–88–} — **1724** SEWALL *Letter-Book* II. 166, I hope . . . the Commissioners Minutes, and the disposal of Stationary Ware, are before now Received. **1771** FRANKLIN *Autobiog.* 267 You may make acquaintances, and establish correspondences in the bookselling and stationery way. **1819** *Plough Boy* I. 190, I called a few days since at Mr. D. K. Van Veghten's stationary store. **1879** STOCKTON *Rudder Grange* xviii, My wife got out her travelling stationery-box. **1882** McCABE *New York* 278 The northern part . . . is a favorite locality with the stationery trade.

Station house. {1833–}

1. The building at a railway station. {1838–}

1850 HAWTHORNE *Notebooks* (1932) 245 [The train] dashes along in front of the station-house, and comes to a pause. **1887** *Harper's Mag.* July 236/1 They looked out eagerly at . . . the unpainted wooden station-houses.

2. A police station; the lockup at a police station. {1836–}

1851 KINGSLEY *Diary* 176 The citizens were for takeing him out of the station house. **1877** McCABE *Hist. Great Riots* 55 Governor Carroll and General Herbert thereupon requested the police authorities to summon . . . all the policemen that could be spared from the station-houses. **1904** *McClure's Mag.* Feb. 373/2 The policeman . . . did not dare take him to the station-house.

+3. W. A hotel.

1862 'E. KIRKE' *Among Pines* 227 A large hotel, or station-house, and about a dozen log shanties made up the village. **1877** HALE *G. T. T.* 146 Here, on a level prairie, is a station-house, which is what people there call a hotel.

+b. W. A stopping place for stagecoaches.

1867 *Harper's Mag.* June 5/1 Station-houses along the road . . . have been constructed by the Overland Stage Company.

Station-keeper. {1846} The official in charge of a station on a stage line.

1860 GREELEY *Overland Journey* 75 The station-keeper is her second husband. **1867** DIXON *New America* I. 101 We heard from drivers and train-men of Jack Dunbar, the station-keeper. **1872** 'MARK TWAIN' *Roughing It* 39 A dozen solicitous inquiries after his health . . . [were made by] five or six . . . station-keepers and hostlers.

b. A station master on a railroad. {1846}

1865 RICHARDSON *Secret Service* 107 The station-keeper . . . was struck down and run over. **1894** WARNER *Golden House* xxiii, 'Quite a stranger in these parts, Mr. Delancy,' was the easy salutation of the station-keeper.

c. A man in charge of one of various types of stations, as a police station, a life-saving station, etc.

1887 *Courier-Journal* 31 Jan. 3/2 [The mule] played one of its circus-ring tricks on Station-keeper Pat Grimes. **1896** SHINN *Story of Mine* 233 The station keeper thought many of them would be torn to pieces. **1899** *Atlantic Mo.* Aug. 203/1 This was the coach sent to convey the station keeper's family home.

Station master. A man in charge of a railroad station. {1857–} — *a*1859 *N.Y. Tribune* (B.), A railroad station-master at Oakdale has absquatulated with funds belonging to the railroad. **1871** HOWELLS *Wedding Journey* 19 You are aware . . . of some one, conductor or station-master, walking the whole length of the train. **1901** *Munsey's Mag.* XXV. 749/2 The station master came up at a run.

Station platform. The platform at a railroad station. — **1882** McCABE *New York* 187 The station platforms [on the elevated railway] are black with a struggling crowd. **1902** WISTER *Virginian* i, The engine . . . pulled us up beside the station platform of Medicine Bow.

Station ship. A patrol vessel assigned to a naval station. {1758} — **1715** *Boston News-Letter* 30 May 2/2 His Majesties Ship the Rose . . . is to be the Station Ship for this Port. **1757** *Lett. to Washington* II. 184 Some French Privateers have been seen in the Mouth of the Bay & our Station Ship is gone out on the Cruise.

Statistician. One who collects and analyzes statistics. {1825-} — **1865** *Atlantic Mo.* Jan. 88/2 Acknowledgment is due to the well-known archæologist and statistician of New York, Mr. Valentine. **1900** *Congress. Rec.* 11 Jan. 774/1 Competent and reliable statisticians might be employed to investigate prices.

* **Stave,** *n.* One of the thin, narrow pieces of wood used to make the sides of a pail, cask, etc. Usually pl.
1647 in Shepard *Clear Sunshine* 28 All winter they sell Brooms, Staves, Elepots [etc.]. **1687** [see ASSIZE 2]. **1765** ROGERS *Acct. N. Amer.* 50 The chief commodities exported from this province [N.H.], are, masts . . . , staves, boards [etc.]. **1789** MORSE *Amer. Geog.* 149 Staves, hoops, and shingles, have been, and are still exported in large quantities. **1833** *Sketches D. Crockett* 146 He loaded a boat with staves. **1905** *Forestry Bureau Bul.* No. 63, 15 The lumber . . . is always in demand at good prices for match blocks, pail staves, and box boards.

‖**b.** ?A bar *of* lead for use in making bullets.
1683 *Doc. Hist. N.Y. State* III. 612 [R. Livingston agreed] to pay . . . Six Guns, fifty pounds of Powder, Fifty staves of Lead [etc.].

c. Attrib. and comb. with *machine, maker, oak*.
1776 *Jrnls. Cont. Congress* VI. 900 The sum of 966 2/3 dollars [shall] be paid to Colonel Moses Hazen, for his . . . joiners, coopers, and stave maker's tools. **1868** *N.Y. Herald* 3 July 10/3 Andrew Harper . . . was instantly killed . . . by being caught in a stave machine. **1897** SUDWORTH *Arborescent Flora* 151 *Quercus alba*. White Oak. . . . [Also called] Stave Oak (Ark.).

* **Stave,** *v.*
+**1.** *tr.* To drive with a hard blow.
1837 *Knickerb.* X. 408 [He had] stove two of his front teeth down his throat. **1837** NEAL *Charcoal Sk.* (B.), I'll stave my fist right through you. **1860** CLAIBORNE *Sam. Dale* 124, I staved the bayonet through his body.

2. *intr.* To proceed rapidly and vigorously; to hurry. {1819-, *Sc.* and *n. dial.* in similar senses}
1825 NEAL *Bro. Jonathan* II. 303 Our adventurers went, staving through Broadway, in Mr. Ashley's go-cart. **1828** SHERBURNE *Memoirs* 95 At length Ben came staving into the ward with his eyes wide open. **1858** *S. Lit. Messenger* XXVI. 122/1 The turkees git to gobblin, and the geese to cacklin, and the Guinea chickens to havin uv the hiccups all at the same time, hard as they can stave. **1880** 'MARK TWAIN' *Tramp Aboard* 368 Other pedestrians went staving by us with vigorous strides.

Stave bolt. A section of a log used for making staves. — **1869** *Boyd's Business Directory* 42 Burrowes & Lane, . . . Receivers and Forwarders of Lumber, Timber, Stave Bolts, &c. **1878** *Lumberman's Gazette* 26 Jan., Large quantities of stave bolts are being hauled in. **1885** *Rep. Indian Affairs* 206 [The Oneidas] obtain their living by farming and cutting stave-bolts, hoop-poles, and cord-wood.

Staver. {1876-, *dial.*} A vigorous, active person or animal. — **1860** HOLLAND *Miss Gilbert* 210 She's got one of the mothers—regular staver. **1868** WOODRUFF *Trotting Horse* 160, I drove the old stavers, Dutchman and Rifle. **1923** WATTS *L. Nichols* 8 Lizzie was a staver for work like her mother.

Staving, *a.* and *adv.* {1621} +Big, immense; excessively. — **1862** *N.Y. Tribune* 7 Feb. 5/6 A staving dram put him in a better humor. **1884** 'MARK TWAIN' *H. Finn* xv, This one was a staving dream. **1898** F. H. SMITH *C. West* 194 They was stavin' good to her. **1902** HARBEN *A. Daniel* 91 He got blind, stavin' drunk.

+**Stavy,** *a.* Tasting of the staves of a cask. — **1888** *Voice* 23 Feb., Stavy or woody butter from tubs made of green wood.

* **Stay,** *n.* pl. A form of corset. {1608-} Freq. *pair of stays.* — **1705** *Boston News-Letter* 9 July 2/1 They found on Board a flowered sattin pair of Stays. *a*1821 BIDDLE *Autobiog.* 69 A thick pair of new stays prevented her being crushed to death. **1867** DIXON *New America* II. 33 Our women . . . wear tight stays, thin shoes, and barrel skirts. **1891** WELCH *Recoll. 1830-40* 116 They did not shew those forced good forms which the tailor dressed American girl now exhibits; no pads, no stays, no palpitators.

* **Stay,** *v.*
I. **1.** *To stay dinner* (or *tea*), to stay to dinner (or tea). *Obs.*
1733 BYRD *Journey to Eden* (1901) 281, I stayed dinner with the good Colonel. **1796** A. BARTON *Disappointment* II. i, You shall stay tea first.

+**2.** *To stay put,* to stay in place; to remain where one is.
*a*1848 *Picayune* (B.), The levees and wharves of the First Municipality won't 'stay put.' **1893** *Harper's Mag.* Feb. 349/2 There was some talk, also, of the advantages . . . accruing to those who 'stay put' in this world. **1906** *Forum* July 88 It had classed him as a novelist and, in our expressive phrase, it wanted him 'to stay put.'

+**3.** *To come to stay,* to become permanent; to secure an established position.
1863 LINCOLN in E. McPherson *Polit. Hist. U.S. Rebell.* 336, I hope it [*sc.* peace] will come soon, and come to stay. **1888** *Pittsburg Bulletin* (F.),

In the realm of advertising, the illustration has evidently come to stay. **1904** *Hartford Courant* 24 June 10 The national convention came to stay in American politics seventy-two years ago.

II. With prepositions and adverbs. **4.** *To stay by,* +to stand by or stick with.
1883 'MARK TWAIN' *Life on Miss.* xxx, I stayed faithfully by him until his comedy was finished.

5. *To stay with.* +*a. local.* To marry. *Obs.* +*b.* To stick with or keep at (something) without regard for discouragements. *colloq.*
(a) **1833** A. GREENE *Life D. Duckworth* I. 35 He did not hesitate to pop the question, . . . whether she would 'stay with him.' (b) **1887** F. FRANCIS *Saddle & Moccasin* 177 But they couldn't bluff the old man off; he stayed with them. **1894** *Outing* XXIV. 342/2 A course which would in the end enable me to score my elk . . . was simply to 'stay with it.' **1907** LONDON *Road* 167 He could not run so fast as I, but he stayed with it.

Stay braid. A form of braid used for ornamenting stays. {1775} — **1759** *Newport Mercury* 26 June 4/3 To be sold by Jacob Richardson, . . . Stay Braid and Cord.

‖**Stay-by.** A stand-by. — **1899** *Voice* 7 June, The old stay-bys of the two old parties . . . have a bitter hatred for *The Voice*.

* **Stayer.** *local.* +(See quot. 1654.) *Obs.* — **1639** *Boston Rec.* 1 Philip Searle sen. and Jonathan Torry transfer their right of the halfe of the Nipmug Land . . . which did belong to the stayers. **1654** *Ib.* 51 The first goers or first setlers of Woodstock and the stayers, or other inhabitants of Roxbury.

Stay hook. 'A small hook stuck in front of the boddice for hanging a watch or etui upon' (Fairholt). {1771-} *Obs.* — **1743** in Earle *Costume Colonial Times* 240 Silver'd Stayhooks. **1762** *Ib.*, Plain Stay hooks.

* **Staying.** +**1.** Lodging for a night. +**2.** *attrib.* Lasting or paying a visit for some days. — (1) **1847** *Knickerb.* XXIX. 534 Can we have a staying here tonight? (2) **1832** TROLLOPE *Domestic Manners* II. 11 Above these rooms was a loft, . . . where I was told the 'staying company' who visited them, were lodged. **1889** *Century Mag.* April 840/2 Mrs. Herbert of Alexandria was often asked . . . to fetch a coach-load of her offspring for a 'staying-visit' to the Washingtons.

Stay lath. A lathlike board used to support something, or hold something in place. — **1863** RANDALL *Pract. Shepherd* 230 Single or wall racks . . . [are] attached to the walls by stay-laths.

‖**Stay-lathed,** *a.* Supported or held in place by stay laths. *Obs.* — **1845** COOPER *Chainbearer* x, The bent was stay-lathed. **1848** — *Oak Openings* I. 211 The whole [structure] was erect and stay-lathed, waiting only for the earth to be shovelled back into the trench.

+**Stay law.** A law establishing a moratorium on the payment of judgments or foreclosures. — **1846** *Knickerb.* XXVIII. 132 They will doubtless avail themselves of all manner of 'stay-laws.' **1868** *N.Y. Herald* 3 July 3/5 Mr. Ingersoll . . . characterized the proviso as a sort of stay law, or a confession that the government was not able to pay its debts. **1894** *Congress. Rec.* 24 Jan. 1349/1 Were it not for the stay law of Dakota, she would be . . . turned over to the manufacturers of Connecticut and Massachusetts under foreclosure of contract of mortgage.

Stay-maker. One whose trade is making stays. {1730-} *Obs.* — **1750** *Md. Hist. Mag.* XVII. 374 One John Pugsley, a Stay maker on the North Side of Severn, . . . was this Morning found dead. **1790** *Penna. Packet* 23 Sept. 4/4 S. Finlass, Stay-Maker, . . . makes all sorts of Stays in the neatest and newest fashion. *a*1821 BIDDLE *Autobiog.* 227 Then followed . . . other trades and professions, . . . plasterers . . . , brushmakers . . . , staymakers.

Steady habits. Habits that are staid and regular, +esp. as attributed to the people of Connecticut and other parts of New England. — (See also LAND OF STEADY HABITS.) — **1800** *Aurora* (Phila.) 23 Dec. (Th.), Steady Habits and Straight Waistcoats. **1806** *Intelligencer* (Lancaster, Pa.) 14 Jan. (Th.), A letter from a Gentleman in the State of Steady Habits to his friend in Newport, Rhodeisland. **1813** *Mass. Spy* 16 June (Th.), Troops were assembled, ready to repel any invasion of the soil of 'steady habits.' **1827** *Ib.* 4 April (Th.), [I cannot] banish from my mind the old steady habits of Massachusetts. **1864** *Harper's Mag.* March 450/1 It is . . . as vociferous in sounds of . . . industry as any place of its size in the good old State of steady habits.

* **Steal,** *n.*
+**1.** A corrupt transaction or deal, often of a political nature, highly remunerative to its perpetrators.
1872 *Daily Gazette* (Little Rock, Ark.) 1 April, Of all the swindles and steals that have ever been proposed or carried out in our State, this is the largest and boldest. **1886** *N. Amer. Rev.* July 88 The Broadway Surface Railroad job—or the 'Broadway steal,' as it is popularly termed—is the most conspicuous recent illustration of corporate and municipal corruption. **1900** *Congress. Rec.* 9 Feb. 1675/1 The enormous pension expenditure in this country is a stupendous abuse, a gigantic steal, an appalling extravagance.

+**2.** *Baseball.* An advance from one base to another without the assistance of a hit or an error.
1880 *Chicago Inter-Ocean* 29 June 8/3 Rowe obtained the next run on two safe hits, a steal and sacrifice hits. **1887** *Courier-Journal* 27 May 2/4 The base-running, too, was extraordinarily fine, Collins, Kerins, Browning and Werrick . . . accomplishing some daring steals. **1912** MATHEWSON *Pitching* 125 Two base runners start a double steal.

*Steal, v. *Baseball.* +*tr.* To reach (a base) without the assistance of a hit or an error. — 1868 CHADWICK *Base Ball* 26 When on the third base they will find many a good chance to steal home. 1875 *Chicago Tribune* 16 Sept. 8/4 He stole second at once. 1912 MATHEWSON *Pitching* 126 In 1911 the Giants led the National League by a good margin in stealing bases.

* **Steam.** *attrib.* and *comb.*

1. Designating boats operated by steam.

See also STEAMBOAT, STEAM FERRYBOAT, etc.

1814 FULTON in *Mag. Amer. Hist.* I. 618 On Saturday morning, 29th inst., the steam frigate was safely launched. 1856 HALE *If, Yes, & Perhaps* 155 By sledges to Port Leopold, and so by a steam-launch. 1857 DANA *Great West* 347 Vessels . . . are now for the most part taken up to New Orleans by steam tow-boats. 1901 MERWIN & WEBSTER *Calumet 'K'* 49 Can they have one or more steam barges at Monistogee?

2. Designating factories and other establishments making use of steam as power.

See also STEAM SAWMILL.

1817 S. BROWN *Western Gazetteer* 94 Three steam grist mills, and two steam paper mills. 1826 FLINT *Recoll.* 37 [You] contemplate the steam-manufactories, darting their columns of smoke aloft. 1827 DRAKE & MANSFIELD *Cincinnati* 66 No returns have been received [from] . . . 2 Steam Flour Mills. 1831 PECK *Guide* 307 Three steam and two copper distilleries. 1860 MORDECAI *Virginia* 44 A steam corn mill and several other steam engines have lately intruded themselves as near neighbors to the ancient and honorable stone house. 1866 *Rep. Indian Affairs* 92 A large and valuable steam lumber mill was erected on the reservation. 1875 *Chicago Tribune* 2 Nov. 1/1 Oriental Steam Laundry. We do Shirts, Collars, and Cuffs same as new. 1877 MCCABE *Hist. Great Riots* 68 The burning premises . . . proved to be the extensive steam planing mills and lumber yard of J. Turner & Cate. 1903 ADE *In Babel* 29 For ten years it had braced itself against the onsweeping rush of big machine-shops and steam-bakeries.

3. Designating tools, machines, etc., operated by steam.

See also STEAM CAR, STEAM CARRIAGE, etc.

1817 *Niles' Reg.* XIII. 224/1 A *steam pump* has been erected at Alexandria. 1852 *Whig Almanac 1853* 26/2 For steam-dredge and discharging scows for Atlantic Coast . . . $20,000. 1857 BORTHWICK *3 Years in Calif.* 80 The hills were easily cut down, and for this purpose a contrivance called a Steam Paddy was used. 1862 E. W. PEARSON *Lett. Port Royal* 117 I shall have . . . [the cotton] taken to Beaufort for the steam-gin. 1868 *N.Y. Herald* 20 July 4/1 But for the arrival of the Philadelphia steam fire engines [the fire] would probably have destroyed the entire village. 1883 *Harper's Mag.* June 75/2 When the wheat comes in it is unloaded from the cars, by the aid of steam shovels, into a hopper bin. 1887 *Courier-Journal* 7 May 5/8, I Want Agents To Sell . . . The Missouri Steam Washer. 1889 Steam excavator [see PADDY¹ 1 b]. 1905 *Forestry Bureau Bul.* No. 61, 49 Steam loader, a machine operated by steam and used for loading logs upon cars.

4. In special combinations.

Steam piano, = CALLIOPE; *s. radiator,* a device for radiating heat from pipes or coils filled with steam.

1895 *N.Y. Dramatic News* 5 Oct. 3/3 Two Johns, Phillips and McVicker, . . . brought up the rear like a steam piano. 1904 'O. HENRY' *Four Million* 153 Our romance has been a pallid thing of a marriage or two, a satin rosette kept in a safe-deposit drawer, and a lifelong feud with a steam radiator.

Steamboat, *n.*

1. A boat of considerable size, esp. one for river traffic, propelled by steam. {1814–}

1785 in T. Westcott *Life J. Fitch* 127, I have examined the Principles and construction of Mr. Fitche's Steamboat. 1812 *Niles' Reg.* II. 48/1 The exclusive right of Messrs. Livingston and Fulton to the navigation of the waters of this state by steam-boats [is] established. 1884 *Dakota Mission Conf.* (M.E. Ch.) *Minutes* 5 Sess. between pp. 68 and 69 Bells of all sizes for Churches, Factories, Academies, Steam-boats, Plantations, Locomotives, etc., constantly on hand. *a*1918 G. STUART *On Frontier* II. 31 The gold was . . . shipped down the river by steamboat.

+**2.** *transf.* **a.** (See quot. 1859.) *Obs.*

1819 [see HALF HORSE (AND) HALF ALLIGATOR 1]. 1835 HOFFMAN *Winter in West* I. 259 Come here, old fellow, and take your treat—you're a steamboat. 1859 BARTLETT 449 *Steamboat,* a term used at the West to denote a dashing, go-a-head character.

‖**b.** (See quotation.)

1841 BUCKINGHAM *America* II. 420 The vehicle which conveyed the family to church was called 'the Steam-boat,' from its great length, though drawn on four wheels and by a pair of horses. In it were seats for sixteen persons.

3. *attrib.* and *comb.* **a.** Designating mishaps suffered by steamboats.

1830 *Congress. Deb.* 6 April 739/1 Steam boat Accidents . . . from the explosion of boilers. 1869 *Atlantic Mo.* July 77/1, I was probably as happy as an itinerant mortal can be in this world of belated railway trains, steamboat explosions and collisions, and runaway stage-horses. 1880 *Harper's Mag.* Oct. 793/1 The summer of 1880 will be known in New York as that of steamboat disasters.

b. Designating individuals who work on or have to do with steamboats.

1838 *Niles' Nat. Reg.* 13 Oct. 112/2 The steamboat inspectors at Cincinnati . . . have condemned the boilers of several boats. 1840 *Knickerb.* XVI. 227 Come, gentlemen, 'fire up, fire up!' as the steam-boat engineer says. 1849 PARKMAN *Ib.* XXXIII. 4 In his former capacity of steamboat clerk he had learned to prefix the honorary *Mister* to every body's name. 1866 'F. KIRKLAND' *Bk. Anecdotes* 40/2 She and her husband, a Mississippi steamboat captain, occupied the middle front room. 1891 WELCH *Recoll.* 1830–40 155 There was a class of men in Buffalo of a race or type peculiar to themselves. . . . They were 'steamboat agents.' 1901 MERWIN & WEBSTER *Calumet 'K'* 289 Steamboat masters up at Duluth knew it.

c. In special combinations.

Steamboat basin, (see quotation); *s. canal,* a canal for use by steamboats; *s. gun,* a gun on a steamboat fired to announce its approach to a landing; *s. landing,* a place where a steamboat lands to discharge and take on freight, passengers, etc.; *s. lock,* a lock for facilitating steamboat traffic; *s. runner,* a solicitor for a steamboat; *s. wagon,* an unusually large or long wagon; *s. wood,* wood for firing the boiler or boilers of a steamboat; *s. yard,* a place where steamboats are built or repaired.

1837 PECK *Gaz. Illinois* 56 A steamboat basin, or harbor, is to be constructed . . . near the termination of the canal. 1835 HOFFMAN *Winter in West* II. 106 The steamboat-canal, . . . commencing two miles below Louisville, terminates at the wharfs of that flourishing city. 1845 SIMMS *Wigwam & Cabin* 1 Ser. 83 We had heard the steamboat gun the night before. 1845 *Big Bear Ark.* 87 We took a lounge down to the steamboat landing. 1838 COLTON *Ind. Delineated* 44 Contracts . . . have been made for the construction of a dam and steamboat lock. 1847 ROBB *Squatter Life* 101 A steamboat runner came to their aid. . . . 'Passage up the Missouri, sir?' inquires the runner. 1889 *Harper's Mag.* Aug. 390/2 The mountaineers . . . have come down to 'the settlements' . . . bringing in slow-moving, ox-drawn 'steamboat' wagons. 1833 *Sketches D. Crockett* 13 Was [the timber] corded up like steamboat wood? 1827 DRAKE & MANSFIELD *Cincinnati* 66 Three Steam-boat Yards, 200 hands.

+**Steamboat,** *v. tr.* To 'take in,' to swindle. *slang.* — 1864 *Harper's Mag.* Dec. 128/1 He has always boasted that *he* never was 'steamboated.'

+**Steamboat bug.** (See quot. 1891.) — 1876 *Field & Forest* II. 4 Among these [fish] I placed a . . . steamboat bug, *Belostoma grandis.* 1891 *Cent.* 5920/1 *Steamboat-bug,* . . . a water-beetle of large size, or otherwise conspicuous.

+**Steamboat coal.** (See quotation.) — 1891 *Cent.* 5920/1 *Steamboat-coal,* coal broken small enough to pass between bars set from 6 to 8 inches apart, but too large to pass between bars less than 5 inches apart.

Steam car. {1877–} +**a.** A railroad locomotive. *Obs.* +**b.** A car, or, in pl., a train, drawn by steam.

1836 *S. Lit. Messenger* II. 762/1 The steam boat and steam car, constitute . . . the great and characteristic powers of the age in which we live. 1846 *Congress. Globe* 6 Feb. 323 The iron horse (the steam-car) with the wings of the wind, his nostrils distended with flame, salamander-like vomiting fire and smoke. 1876 KNIGHT 2331/2 *Steam-car,* a car drawn by steam-power. 1891 WILKINS *New Eng. Nun* 381, I went on the steam-cars. 1903 FOX *Little Shepherd* v, 'Steam cars!' they cried. *attrib.* 1901 HEGAN *Mrs. Wiggs* 58 Me an' the childern was comin' on the steam-car train.

Steam carriage. A carriage drawn or driven by steam. {1824–} — 1787 in *Rep. Comm. Patents 1849* 574 A steam carriage, so constructed as to move by the power of steam, . . . for the purpose of conveying burdens without the aid of animal force. 1901 *Outing* XXXVII. 550/2 The electric and steam carriages as known at present are to all intents and purposes new commodities. 1907 *St. Nicholas* Aug. 927/1 You remember that in that century inventors were everywhere trying to make a steam-carriage.

+**Steam cotton press.** A press operated by steam for packing cotton into bales; a building where such presses operate. Also *attrib.* — 1827 in Commons, etc. *Doc. Hist.* I. 287, I found myself in a steam cotton-press house. 1864 NICHOLS *Amer. Life* I. 181 Next are seen . . . the tall chimneys of the numerous steam cotton-presses.

+**Steam doctor.** A doctor who treats all or most diseases with hot water and vapor baths. *Obs.* — [1833 NEAL *Down-Easters* I. 15 Some calls him the screw-augur doctor, and some the steam-augur doctor.] 1837 [see NEW SCHOOL 2]. 1851 *Polly Peablossom* 50, I made a 'pointment with Ike Hamberlin the steam doctor. 1872 EGGLESTON *End of World* 79 The steam-doctor . . . was the family physician.

Steam engine. An engine operated by steam. {1751–}

1787 CUTLER in *Life & Corr.* I. 205 It was my wish to visit the famous steam engine at Cranston. 1788 in *Rep. Comm. Patents 1849* 568 The said improvement . . . [is] called Rumsey's improvement upon Savery's machine, or steam engine. 1814 *Niles' Reg.* VII. 206/1 Her steam engine will possess a power equal to 100 horses. 1876 Raymond *8th Rep. Mines* 363 First of all, must be named the erection in Philadelphia, in 1794, of the first steam-engine in America. 1907 *St. Nicholas* Aug. 927/1 The piston was worked by a steam-engine. *attrib.* 1812 MELISH *Travels* II. 55 Professions exercised in Pittsburg: . . . watch-makers, button-makers, steam-engine-builders. 1819 MCMURTRIE *Sk. Louisville* 138 There are at this moment, in Louisville . . . one air foundry and one steam engine factory. 1849 CHAMBERLAIN *Ind. Gazet-*

teer 227 The principal manufactories [include] . . . steam engine manufactories.

Steamer.

1. A steamboat. {1825-}

1833 COKE *Subaltern's Furlough* i, One of these huge leviathans of the deep, an American steamer, darted past. **1893** 'MARK TWAIN' *£1,000,000 Bank-Note* 159, I remember the brag run of a steamer which I travelled in once on the Pacific. **1921** PAINE *Comr. Rolling Ocean* 202 This isn't a coal-burning steamer.

2. Attrib. with *fireman, landing, man, ticket.*

1866 'MARK TWAIN' *Lett. Sandwich Islands* 15 Steamer firemen do not live, on an average, over 5 years. **1885** *Century Mag.* Jan. 414/1 The adherent of the old régime stands in the way to every public privilege and place—steamer landing, railway platform, . . . everything. **1912** NICHOLSON *Hoosier Chron.* 510 You go right down . . . and buy a steamer ticket. **1914** STEELE *Storm* 193 The steamer-men had always come ashore in Old Harbor.

Steamer chair. A chair for use on the deck of a steamer. — **1886** BURNETT *Lord Fauntleroy* iv, The people . . . [had] come on deck to recline in their steamer-chairs and enjoy themselves. **1897** 'MARK TWAIN' *Following Equator* 26 [We] sat down on our steamer-chairs contented and at peace. **1905** 'O. HENRY' *Roads of Destiny* 141, 'I might as well tell you now, pardner,' said the Kid, sliding down low on his steamer chair.

+**Steamer day.** The day upon which a steamer leaves a particular place; formerly, esp. in San Francisco, the day upon which a steamer sailed for the States. Also transf. — **1851** HALL *Manhattaner* 20 Every day is steamer day just now. **1856** CURTIS *Prue & I* (1892) 104, I cannot avoid often going to the dock upon steamer-days. **1896** SHINN *Story of Mine* 254 The habit of squaring accounts on Monday has grown up among merchants, so that Monday is still called 'steamer day,' a phrase borrowed from pioneer San Francisco. **1910** J. HART *Vigilante Girl* 104 All bills had to be settled on 'Steamer Day' when the bi-monthly steamers sailed for the States.

+**Steamer night.** The night upon which a steamer reaches a particular place. — **1863** 'E. KIRKE' *Southern Friends* 234 It was again 'steamer night.' **1889** HARTE *Waif of Plains* vii, It was dark, but, being 'steamer night,' the shops and business places were still open.

+**Steamer trunk.** A small trunk suitable for use in a stateroom on a steamer. — **1891** *Scribner's Mag.* X. 513 A number of agile cabin-stewards . . . [were] bringing aboard an endless variety of steamer-trunks. **1895** CHAMBLISS *Diary* 26 Her list of articles, necessary for her comfort and pleasure on the voyage, should [include] . . . One steamer trunk. **1911** HARRISON *Queed* 92, I have one small one—a steamer trunk, as it is called.

+**Steam ferry.** A ferry operating by steam power. *Obs.* — **1842** Mc-Donogh *P.* 65 The steam ferry which runs from one side of the river to the other lands a short distance below my house. **1844** 'UNCLE SAM' *Peculiarities* II. 196 A steam ferry from a New York wharf conveys its passengers in four or five minutes to Brooklyn. **1884** 'MARK TWAIN' *Huck. Finn* xiii, Go for the steam-ferry.

+**Steam ferryboat.** A ferryboat propelled by steam. *Obs.* — **1836** *Niles' Nat. Reg.* 1 Oct. 80/2 The steam-ferry boat . . . ran down the boat gen. Jackson in the harbor of New York. **1855** *Knickerb.* XLVI. 271 The horse-boat . . . was in its turn displaced by the steam ferry-boat. **1876** 'MARK TWAIN' *Tom Sawyer* xxix. 218 The old steam-ferryboat was chartered.

Steam heat. Heat afforded by steam. {1822-} +used to warm a house, apartment, etc. — **1883** *Harper's Mag.* Sept. 533/1 The idea of a hotel set on these mountains, with electric lights [and] . . . steam heat, . . . is, we must admit, repellent. **1892** *York County Hist. Rev.* 91 A public house . . . contains 14 well lighted, ventilated and furnished rooms, heated throughout by steam heat. **1923** HERRICK *Lilla* 98 Every door was warped, and all the woodwork pulled apart under the steam heat, even the oak flooring.

+**Steam-heated,** *a.* Of a hall, building, etc.: Heated by steam. — **1884** *N.Y. Herald* 27 Oct. 2/2 Single Flats . . . ; halls steam heated. **1890** H. PALMER *Stories Base Ball Field* 223 Electric Lighted and Steam Heated Vestibuled Trains between Chicago, Council Bluffs, and Omaha. **1907** *St. Nicholas* Oct. 1135/1 The European pelicans . . . in the cold weather of winter have to be placed in a steam-heated building.

∗**Steaming.** +Traveling by steamboat. {1913} — **1836** *S. Lit. Messenger* II. 696 Steaming from Washington to Baltimore is an improvement upon that route at least. **1883** CRAWFORD *Dr. Claudius* 140 Miss Skeat also thought sailing much more poetic than steaming.

+**Steam propeller.** = PROPELLER 2. *Obs.* — **1845** J. W. NORRIS *Chicago Directory* 108 Steam Propellers from Oswego to Chicago. **1856** *Mass. Priv. & Sp. Stat.* X. 570 [A company is incorporated] for the purpose of running steam propellers between Nantucket and New York. **1874** *Rep. Comm. Agric.* 1873 147 Double-track railroads, canals vexed with steam-propellers, . . . and every other fancied boon obtained, she will still remain in comparative poverty.

Steam sawmill. A sawmill operated by steam. Also attrib. — **1819** McMURTRIE *Sk. Louisville* 138 There . . . [is] at this moment, in Louisville . . . 1 steam saw mill. **1835** HOFFMAN *Winter in West* I. 70 Parts of three bastions . . . may still be discovered among the piles of lumber in a steam saw-mill yard. **1857** *Lawrence* (Kan.) *Republican* 4 June 2 A large and powerful steam sawmill is on the way. **1910** *Boston Ev. Transcript* 11 June III. 3/5 The steam sawmills of the northern forest belt from Minnesota to Oregon are in considerable part Indian-manned.

Steamship. A ship propelled by steam. {1819-}

1790 JEFFERSON *Writings* V. (1895) 165 What is become of Rumsey & his steam-ship? **1815** *Niles' Reg.* IX. 76/2 *Steam ships!* A project is on foot, at New York, to build a vessel of 350 tons, to be propelled by steam. **1872** McCLELLAN *Golden State* 125 On the 28th of February, 1849, the pioneer steamship of the ocean line of American passenger ships . . . arrived at San Francisco from New York. **1907** *St. Nicholas* Aug. 928/2 The homely log propelled by rude paddles has become . . . the huge twin- or triple-screw steamship of to-day.

attrib. **1858** HALE *If, Yes, & Perhaps* 124 So, of the signals which fog-bells can give. . . . Or of signals for steamship-engineers. **1870** MEDBERY *Men Wall St.* 212 We have corruption in railway management, finesse in telegraph and steamship lines. **1893** *Harper's Mag.* May 893/1, I sell out of that steamship firm instanter.

+**Steam shipping.** Shipping carried on by means of steamships. — **1883** *Century Mag.* Sept. 693/2 Offices of railroad and mining companies, of steam and other shipping, . . . next center closest around the financial hub. **1901** *N. Amer. Rev.* Feb. 286 It is our steam shipping that has been aided.

+**Steam thresher.** A threshing machine operated by steam. Also attrib. — **1865** *Atlantic Mo.* XV. 730/2 Thirty steam-threshers only were required. **1895** GRAHAM *Stories of Foot-Hills* 173 Mose Doolittle . . . was about to purchase . . . 'a second-hand steam-thrasher.' **1906** *N.Y. Ev. Post* 21 July Suppl. 3 The steam thresher trusts have no hold on the conservative 'black' Amish settlements of Indiana.

+**Ste(e)boy,** *interj.* (See STABOY.)

∗**Steel.**

∗**1.** An artificially produced form of iron characterized by hardness and elasticity.

1705 *Boston News-Letter* 16 April 2/1 The said Foreign Ships may not bring in or Import any European Manufactories of Gold, Silver, Copper, Steel, Woolens, Silk or Linens. **1786** *Penna. Ev. Herald* 12 April 92/3 American blistered Steel, Warranted equal in quality to the best steel imported from England, to be sold. **1793** COXE *View U.S.* 145 About one half of the steel, consumed in the United States, is home made. **1898** *Boston Herald* 5 Jan. 8/2 (Ernst), Pile driving, however, was continued, as was . . . the unloading of steel and granite. **1909** *Indian Laws & Tr.* III. 422 For pay of second blacksmith, and such iron and steel and other materials as may be required, . . . one thousand dollars.

∗**b.** Any one of various articles made of steel.

1636 *Essex Probate Rec.* I. 5, 2 steels & Cinamon. **1678** *New Castle Court Rec.* 362, 2 steels to strike fire. **1790** *Penna. Packet* 1 March 1/1 This Day, . . . Will commence the Sale of . . . Brass pullies and sconces, chimney hooks, butchers steels [etc.]. **1843** [see FIRE TOOL].

2. *attrib.* and *comb.* passing into *adj.* **a.** Designating things made of steel.

1666 *Essex Inst. Coll.* XXV. 147 Seuerall broken & old steele bowes & pistoll. **1725** *New-Eng. Courant* 8 Feb. 2/2 An Iron Crow and a Steel Saw, and some other Tools were found. **1845** J. W. NORRIS *Chicago Directory* 112 Constantly on hand and for sale, . . . the most approved Steel Plows. **1887** GEORGE *40 Yrs. on Rail* 246 Steel rails are no longer an innovation, and steel sleepers are proving a happy experiment. **1896** *Sun* (N.Y.) 24 Aug. 1/1 (Ernst), The twelve vessels will constitute the first fleet of steel war ships ever gathered hereabouts. **1908** *Indian Laws & Tr.* III. 345 For steel tower for water tank, two thousand dollars. **1920** COOPER *Under Big Top* 112 A steelcable noose . . . was being fashioned for his neck.

b. Designating persons, appliances, etc., employed in making or working with steel.

1776 *N.J. Archives* 2 Ser. I. 77 The steel forge with six fires . . . will be compleated in June next. *a***1817** DWIGHT *Travels* IV. 487, 1 Steel factory, 20 tons, spinning wheels, 6,393. **1880** *Harper's Mag.* Dec. 57/2 The steel-melter . . . seizes a crucible, and . . . draws it, cherry red, to the surface. **1894** *Harper's Mag.* July 251/2 American steel-makers could turn out material of as excellent quality as that produced abroad. **1898** *Scribner's Mag.* XXIII. 311/2 'Will he take 'em back, though?' said the steel-worker. **1903** *McClure's Mag.* Dec. 195/2 The steel builder's employment leaves a man tired at night. **1906** LYNDE *Quickening* 300, I can have a place as a chemist with the steel people at Bethlehem.

Steel dust. {1760-} +A chalybeate medicinal preparation. — **1795** J. & E. PETTIGREW *Let.* 4 May (Univ. N.C. MS.), Also have been taking Steel Dust steept in Brandy for better than a week. **1856** [see PERUVIAN BARK].

+**Steelhead.**

1. Either of two trouts (*Salmo gairdneri* and *S. irideus*) of the Pacific coast region. Also attrib.

1882 *Nat. Museum Bul.* No. 16, 313 *Salmo gairdneri,* Steel-head; Hard-head. **1897** *N.Y. Forest, Fish, & Game Comm.* 2d Rep. 223 The steelheads now in the Aquarium were obtained in November, 1896, from the United States Fish Commission. **1911** *Rep. Fisheries* 1908 317/2 *Salmo* is represented by . . . the steelhead trout (*S. rivularis*).

2. *local.* = RUDDY DUCK.

1888 TRUMBULL *Names of Birds* 112 William Wagner, a well known Washington gunner, tells of hearing it called Water-Partridge and Steel-head, on the Patuxent River, Md. **1917** *Birds of Amer.* I. 153/1 They are extremely tough, hardy little birds and gunners know them by such names as Tough-head, Hard-head, Steel-head, etc.

Steel mill. {1772–} **1.** (See quot. 1876.) **2.** A plant where steel is made. — (1) 1647 *Essex Probate Rec.* I. 85 One Steele mill, 1 li. 10 s. **1836** DEWEES *Lett. from Texas* 207 This [corn] I ground in a steel mill, and divided my mite with him. **1876** KNIGHT 2367/2 *Steel-mill*, ... a mill with metallic grinding-surfaces, usually of steel, but sometimes of cast-iron. ... Coffee and spice mills are instances. (2) **1917** SINCLAIR *King Coal* 395 The citizens and workers of such industrial communities ... [as] the steel-mills of Pittsburg ... will find that they have neither peace nor freedom.

Steel trap. A trap having iron or steel jaws forced together by a strong steel spring or springs when the bait is disturbed. {1735–} Cf. SMART *a.* 2. — 1660 *Springfield Rec.* I. 270 Laurence Bliss is to pay for ye chaine of ye steele Trap. **1804** CLARK in *Lewis & C. Exped.* I. (1904) 214 He had put before me 2 of the Steel traps which was robed from the french a Short time ago. **1871** LEWIS *Poultry Book* 173 Fasten it to the treadle of a steel trap. **1913** SETON *Wild Animals at Home* 118 Only a week before he had set steel traps at a den where he chanced to find a pair of Badgers in residence.

Steelyard. Also †steeleyerd, stylyard. A device for weighing, consisting essentially of a properly graduated steel beam upon which weights are used as counterbalances. {stilliard, 1650; steelyard, a1790–} — **1639** *Md. Archives* I. 79 No man shall sell or receive any Tobacco or other goods by Steeleyerds or other weight. **1701** *Boston Rec.* 11 No Butcher shall ... weigh and sell any dead meat by stylyards. **1808** *Steele* P. II. 562 My steelyards are quite new and clear of rust. **1903** WHITE *Forest* 130 By and by he ... conducted me outside, where hung ponderous ornamental steelyards, on which in the old days the peltries were weighed.

✶Steep, *a.* +Of a price or amount: High, exorbitant, large. *colloq.* — **1856** *Knickerb.* XLVII. 362 He's too steep in his price, any way. **1865** *Congress. Globe* 27 Feb. 1131/3 They replied three dollars the hog. He rejoined, 'That is rather steep.' **1877** BAILEY *Folks in Danbury* 38 (Th.), Don't it strike you that $18 is pretty steep for these times?

Steeper. (See quot. 1876.) {1737–} — **1784** SMYTH *Tour* II. 60 This vessel, which is called the *steeper*, is filled with water. **1835** INGRAHAM *South-West* I. 273 It may remain in the first vat, called the steeper, from ten to fifteen hours. **1876** KNIGHT 2371/1 *Steeper*, a vat in which the indigo-plant is soaked for maceration, previous to soaking in the beating-vat.

+Steeplebush. The hardhack (*Spiraea tomentosa*) or a related species. — **1817–8** EATON *Botany* (1822) 478 *Spiræa tomentosa*, steeple-bush. **1821** *Mass. H. S. Coll.* 2 Ser. IX. 156 *Spiraea salicifolia*. White steeple bush. **1872** *Vermont Bd. Agric. Rep.* I. 276 *Spiræa Salicifolia*, Meadow Sweet, and *S. Tomentosa*, Steeplebush, are weedy shrubs of wet lands. **1887** BURROUGHS in *Century Mag.* July 328 The steeple-bush, or hard-hack, had more color.

Steeple house. A church. Used esp. by Quakers. {1644–} — [1837 BANCROFT *Hist. U.S.* II. 334 On the morning of a first-day, he [George Fox] was moved to go to the great steeple-house and cry against the idol.] **1877** WHITTIER *Poetical Works* 121/2 There are steeple-houses on every hand, And pulpits that bless and ban. **1883** *Harper's Mag.* Dec. 14/2 The Quakers stigmatized the Puritan churches as steeple-houses.

✶Steer.

✶1. a. A young ox, esp. a castrated one. **b.** Any male animal of the ox family suitable for beef.

1636 *Springfield Rec.* I. 158 None that have cowes, steeres, ... shall have under two akers apiece. **1739** W. STEPHENS *Proc. Georgia* I. 300 They brought home a large Drove of ... well-grown Steers. **1788** [see FATTING *a.* 2]. **1844** *Lexington Observer* 25 Sept. 2/7 Also, will be sold ... some fine Young Steers. **1899** [see FEED *v.* 1]. **1916** WILSON *Somewhere* 291 First she tried to make 'em chase steers on horseback.

2. *Attrib.* and comb. with *buyer, driver, herd*, etc.

1657 *Huntington Rec.* I. 9 Thriving young cattell, ... (the one halfe being in the stear kind). **1729** HEMPSTEAD *Diary* 215, [I] brot over a Steer Hide & Tallow from Thos. **1772** *Md. Hist. Mag.* XIV. 141, By the steer drivers send me 6 pair of Chain traces. **1890** *Stock Grower & Farmer* 4 Jan. 3/1 The country will be filled with steer buyers next spring. *Ib.* 8 Feb 4/1 Nat Skinner ... has made quite a hole in the steer herds. **1913** BARNES *Western Grazing Grounds* 33 There are two distinct ranges—the southern or breeding range, and the northern or finishing range, sometimes called the steer range.

✶Steerage. +Attrib. with *country, mess, officer*. — **1881** *Naval Encycl.* 776 *Steerage-officer*. An officer living or messing in the steerage. Steerage-officers in the U.S. navy are clerks, midshipmen, cadet-midshipmen, mates, ... and all officers ranking with ensign. **1889** *Cent.* 1307/3 *Steerage country* ..., the open space in the middle of a ... steerage of a man-of-war not occupied by berths or state-rooms. **1891** H. PATTERSON *Naut. Dict.* 364 *Steerage Mess*. This mess is composed of midshipmen, ensigns, clerks and mates.

✶Steerer. +A swindler's accomplice who directs or entices victims to a place where they are fleeced. *slang*. (See also BUNCO STEERER.) — **1875** *Chicago Tribune* 30 Oct. 5/6 The gamblers and their ropers, steerers, and hangers-on maintained a sort of rear guard near the main entrance. **1889** *Columbus Dispatch* 6 Sept., The place was full of players, who got there by means of 'steerers' sent out for the purpose. **1905** 'O. HENRY' *Strictly Business* 70 On a corner lounged a keen-eyed steerer for a gambling-house.

+Steering committee. A committee in a legislative assembly or other group that directs or prescribes the order in which business shall be considered. — **1887** *Courier-Journal* 6 Feb. 2/2 A steering committee upon the order of business for the remainder of the session was appointed. **1896** *Boston Jrnl.* 28 Jan. 10/6 Senator Gorman, Chairman of the Democratic Steering Committee of the Senate, has been sounding Senators. **1908** *N.Y. Ev. Post* (s.-w. ed.) 10 Dec. 3 The position carries with it the chairmanship of the Republican steering committee of the Senate, which determines all important legislation in the Senate.

+Steering oar. An oar by which a boat, esp. a broadhorn or river flatboat, is steered. — **1834** AUDUBON *Ornith. Biog.* II. 460 He at the steering oar hoped 'the black rascal' had broken his neck. **1840** DANA *Two Years* 266 They had no rudder or steering oar. **1850** LEWIS *La. Swamp Doctor* 58 Her steering-oar ... instead of projecting, as custom and the law requires, had swung round. **1884** 'MARK TWAIN' *H. Finn* xiii, They lost their steering-oar.

Steering paddle. A paddle used in steering a canoe or other small boat. — **1840** HOFFMAN *Greyslaer* I. 123 One of those, who held the steering-paddle, threw himself backward over the stern. **1904** WHITE *Silent Places* 39 Sam Bolton sat in the stern with the steering-paddle.

Stella shawl. A type of shawl. — **1856** *Porter's Spirit of Times* 4 Oct. 74/1 The 'Stella' Shawls became so common last season that they will hardly be worn by our *elegantes*, at present. **1895** A. BROWN *Meadow-Grass* 176 She snatched her stella shawl from the drawer.

Steller. [G. W. STELLER, Ger. naturalist (1709-1746).] +1. *Steller's jay*, a dark-crested blue jay (*Cyanocitta stelleri*) found in the western states. +2. *Steller's duck*, a species of eider duck found in Alaska. — (1) **1828** BONAPARTE *Ornithology* II. 44 The Steller's Jay is one of those obsolete species alluded to in the preface to this volume. **1917** *Birds of Amer.* II. 220/2 There are several slightly varying local forms of Steller's Jay in the Rocky Mountain section. (2) **1883** *Nat. Museum Bul.* No. 27, 162 *Cosmonetta stelleri*. Steller's Duck. ... Arctic and subarctic coasts.

✶Stem, *n.* In special combinations.

Stem clam, (see quotation); *s. crop*, =DITCH STONECROP; *s. wood*, the wood contained in the stem or trunk of a tree.

1859 BARTLETT 84 The Soft Clam, or Mananosay (*Mya arenaria*) ... has a long, extensible, cartilaginous snout, or proboscis, through which it ejects water; whence it is also called Stem-clam. **1840** DEWEY *Mass. Flowering Plants* 93 P[enthorum] sedoides. Virginia Stem Crop. ... A plant of no consequence; a native of this country. **1896** *Vt. Agric. Rep.* XV. 83 About 24 cubic feet per acre is added to the stem wood of the merchantable trees annually.

✶Stem, *v.*

+1. *tr.* To free (tobacco or tobacco leaves) of the fibrous stems and midribs. {1844–}

In the 1724 example *stem* and *strip* are confused.

1724 JONES *Virginia* 40 It lies till they have Leisure or Occasion to *stem* it (that is pull the Leaves from the Stalk) or *strip* it (that is take out the great Fibres). **1797** IMLAY *West. Terr.* (ed. 3) 248 This done, you stem the tobacco, or pull out the middle rib of the leaf. **1843** *Amer. Pioneer* II. 447 We had raised no tobacco to stem and twist. **1898** *Treasury Decisions Customs* II. 967 Persons who have qualified as dealers in leaf tobacco are ... permitted to strip or stem their tobacco—that is, they may divide the leaf in half and take out the middle.

2. To remove the stems from (grapes, currants, etc.).

1873 *Ill. Dept. Agric. Trans.* X. 61 [Grapes] were stemmed and mashed and put to ferment on the skins for forty-eight hours. **1891** WILKINS *New Eng. Nun* 2 After her currants were picked, she sat on the back door-step and stemmed them. **1907** WIGGIN *New Chron. Rebecca* x, Her aunt and her mother were stemming currants on the side porch.

Stemmer. ‖a. Best stemmer, tobacco most easily stemmed. **b.** A machine for stemming grapes, etc. — **1887** *Courier-Journal* 19 Jan. 8/1 For best stemmer, usually grown in the Henderson and Owensboro districts, $50 [was] awarded to Mr. Foster of Hartford, Ohio county. **1899** *Dept. Agric. Yrbk.* 1898 558 Crushers and stemmers [are] capable of working up 300 tons of grapes per day.

+Stemmery. *local*. (See quot. 1859.) — **1859** BARTLETT 450 *Stemmery*, a large building in which tobacco is stemmed. **1887** *Courier-Journal* 5 May 6/6 At the stemmeries ... gangs of negroes, big and little, male and female, may be seen dexterously snatching the stem from the leaf. **1897** KILLEBREW & MYRICK *Tobacco Leaf* 283 The work in the stemmeries goes on from November ... until June.

+Stem-winder.

1. A watch which is wound and set by a mechanism connected with the stem; also, the obtruding part of this mechanism.

1876 KNIGHT 2373/2 Some of the stem-winders are so constructed that [etc.]. **1882** RITTENHOUSE *Maud* 135 Such a darling watch, stem-winder, with the dear little black cord to suspend it by. **1904** E. ROBINS *Magn. North* II. 128 [He] keeps a holt o' the stem-winder.

2. *transf.* A person or thing of superior excellence. *colloq.*

1892 GUNTER *Miss Dividends* 68 Ain't he a stem-winder? **1900** NORRIS *Blix* 72, Here you are,—'The Strange Ride of Morrowbie Jukes'; and it's a stem-winder, too. **1902** 'O. HENRY' *Roads of Destiny* 190 There's a new bank-examiner over at the First, and he's a stem-winder.

+Stem-winding watch. =STEM-WINDER 1. — **1867** *Rep. Comm. Patents 1866* 1115 Either side of the case of the stem-winding watch is opened by pressure upon the head of the winding arbor. **1876** KNIGHT 2373/2.

+**Stenographer.** A shorthand-writer. — **1796** *Ann. 4th Congress 2 Sess.* 1607 He also adverted to the attempt at the last session to introduce a stenographer into the House, which failed. **1813** *Ann. 13th Congress 1 Sess.* 125 Under an order of the House directing stenographers to be admitted by the Speaker . . . the petitioner made application to be received as such. **1877** *Harper's Mag.* Dec. 51/2 In reporting large meetings, the number of stenographers on the staff is increased. **1923** HERRICK *Lilla* 179 She is an excellent typist and stenographer.

* **Step,** *v.* With adverbs and prepositions in colloq. and slang expressions.

1. *To step along,* to go along or about one's affairs.
1888 STOCKTON *Dusantes* 124 We'd better be steppin' along an' see what else Mr. Enderton an' Elizabeth Grootenheimer is doin'. **1888** JEWETT *King of Folly Isl.* 120 You can eat a couple or three o' them nuts and step along, for all I care.

* **2.** *To step down,* transf., +to retire from office, to vacate.
1890 *Stock Grower & Farmer* 3 May 3/2 If the bureau cannot do this, the members of it, the lunkheads, step down and resign.

+**3.** *To step lively,* to hurry.
1891 *Outing* Nov. 147/2 There was . . . the guard's admonition to 'step lively.' **1906** FREEMAN *By Light of Soul* 41 She was told to step lively on the trolley-cars.

* **4.** *To step out,* +to die; to disappear.
1844 *Yale Lit. Mag.* IX. 381 Of the other pieces, . . . which have been sent us, some will be found in the present number, . . . and the remainder have '*step out.*' **1851** *Polly Peablossom* 177 Ay, dead!—stepped out! **1868** BEECHER *Sermons* (1869) I. 175 There are many men belonging to business circles in New-York who 'step out.' **1902** MCFAUL *Ike Glidden* 277 That is why he stepped out when he did.

* **5.** *To step upon,* +to reprove or criticize (one) sharply.
1871 HOWELLS *Wedding Journey* 100 Abjectly I . . . try to give myself the genteel air of one who has not been stepped upon.

Stepladder. A short, portable set of steps, usually supported at the back by an adjustable hinged prop. {1751-} — **1846** MACKENZIE *Van Buren* 198 Van Buren's Air-Built Castle and Step-Ladders. **1884** ROE *Nature's Story* 413 She mounted the step-ladder. **1916** WILSON *Somewhere* 171 [She] fell off a stepladder.

+**Stepping mill.** A treadmill used as an amusement or as a means of discipline. — **1825** WOODWORTH *Forest Rose* I. i, The Gas-lights, and the Water-works, and the Fire-works, and the Stepping-mill, and all other places of amusement. **1831** ROYALL *Southern Tour* II. 24 When a slave displeases his master, he or she is sent to the Work House or Stepping Mill, as they work and grind alternately.

‖**Stereoptician.** One who operates a stereopticon. — **1887** *Evans* (Colo.) *Jrnl.* 26 Nov., The great stereoptician . . . showed over one hundred different views.

+**Stereopticon.** An improved type of projector or magic lantern. — **1876** KNIGHT 2376/2 *Stereopticon,* an instrument for exhibiting photographic pictures greatly magnified upon a screen or wall with stereoscopic effect. **1885** HOWELLS *S. Lapham* vii, I'd rather go out to . . . a lecture, if they've got a good stereopticon to give you views of the places. **1891** Stereoptican [*sic*] exhibition [see EXHIBITION 2]. **1907** *Pearson's Mag.* Jan., Advt., Moving Picture Machines. Stereopticons. You Can Make Big Money Entertaining the Public.

Stereotyper. One who makes stereotype plates. {1818-} — **1851** CIST *Cincinnati* 260. **1892** *Courier-Journal* 3 Oct. 5/5 A. H. Conn, a Stereotyper, Grows Despondent and Ends his Existence. **1907** GIVEN *Making a Newspaper* 27 In the mechanical department . . . there are three heads: the foreman of the composing room, the foreman of the stereotypers, and the superintendent of the pressroom.

+**Stern wheel.**
1. A large paddle wheel serving as a propeller at the stern of a steamboat.
1819 *15th Congress 2 Sess.* Doc. No. 78, 12 Double stern wheel for boats, December 10, John L. Sullivan, Boston. **1860** HOLMES *Professor* 365 She had neither side-wheel nor stern-wheel. **1886** *Outing* VIII. 159/2 There was then 'a flat-boat with a tea-kettle boiler and stern-wheel' plying on Lake Umbagog.

2. (*Stern-wheel.*) = STERNWHEEL BOAT.
1882 RITTENHOUSE *Maud* 73 You can count 6 or 8 queer flats, canoes, rafts, dug-outs, stern-wheels, skiffs, sail-boats and so on. **1884** 'MARK TWAIN' *H. Finn* xix, You couldn't tell nothing about her only whether she was a stern-wheel or side-wheel.

3. *attrib.* **a.** In sense 1 with *craft, steamer.* **b.** In sense: Petty; trifling; insignificant.
1856 OLMSTED *Slave States* 368 The boat I was in . . . was a stern-wheel craft. **1859** BARTLETT 450 The term is applied to any thing small, petty; as, a 'stern-wheel church.' **1862** LOWELL *Biglow P.* 2 Ser. i. 20 Nary social priv'ledge but a one-hoss, starn-wheel chaplin. **1864** *Ohio Agric. Rep.* XVIII. p. xxi, The lifting and shaking of the earth behind the machine keeps it in a constant flutter, like the water after a stern-wheel steamer.

+**Sternwheel boat.** A steamboat having a large paddle wheel at the stern as a propeller. — **1836** J. HALL *Statistics of West* 228 Observing . . . the long struggles of a stern wheel boat to ascend Horse-tail ripple. **1862** Moore *Rebellion Rec.* V. ii. 225 The Musselman, a small stern-wheel boat

we had with us, went alongside of her. **1887** *Courier-Journal* 15 Feb. 3/3 The New Orleans and Ouachita packet Corona is undoubtedly the fastest stern-wheel boat of her size afloat.

+**Stern-wheeler.** =*prec. colloq.* — **1855** *Harper's Mag.* Dec. 40/2 He got possession of a 'starn-wheeler,' and entered the 'pine-knot business.' **1883** 'MARK TWAIN' *Life on Miss.* lviii, We met massed acres of lumber-rafts coming down, . . . shoved swiftly along by a powerful stern-wheeler. **1884** HEDLEY *Marching through Ga.* 422 In its wake, . . . lazily floated one of the most diminutive stern-wheelers of the western river class.

Stevedore. A laborer employed in loading and unloading ships. (Cf. STOWADORE.) {1850-} — **1828** WEBSTER, *Stevedore,* one whose occupation is to stow goods, packages, &c. in a ship's hold. *N. York.* **1836** *Jamestown* (N.Y.) *Jrnl.* 9 March 1/5 Yesterday and the day before the stevedores and laborers on shipboard struck for higher wages. **1871** HOWELLS *Wedding Journey* 178 The stevedores . . . were putting the freight aboard. **1907** 'O. HENRY' *Heart of West* 85 We go into a shanty and sit on high stools among stevedores and boatmen.

* **Steward.**
+**1.** An official chosen to have charge of providing meals for the members of a colonial legislative assembly. *Obs.*
1648 *Mass. Bay Rec.* III. 122 There shalbe two of theire members chosen for stewards for that session of Court. **1649** *Ib.* 171 James Penn and Wm. Parkes were chosen stewards for this session.

* **2.** A college official in charge of the provision of food, and often of other matters of administration.
1650 *Harvard Rec.* I. 34 The Butler shall . . . shew them [*sc.* bills] to the Steward at his demand. **1709** *Ib.* 388 The Steward Proposes to allow two pounds and a half to a mess. **1766** in Peirce *Hist. Harvard* 221 There has been great neglect in the Steward in the quality of the Butter provided by him for many weeks past. **1851** HALL *College Words* 293 [To] the steward . . . is usually assigned the duty of making out the term-bills and receiving the money thereon; of superintending the college edifices with respect to repairs, &c. **1874** *Rep. Comm. Agric. 1873* 352 A brick boarding-house . . . [contains] accommodations for the steward and his family.

* **3.** A ship's officer who has charge of the stores and the serving of meals; a servant who directs the domestic affairs of a household.
1785 WASHINGTON *Diaries* II. 417 Brought home Mr. Thomas McCarty with whom I had agreed to serve me in the capacity of a Ho. Keeper or Household Steward at Thirty pounds pr. ann. **1794** *Ann. 3d Congress* 1427 The following petty officers . . . shall be appointed by the captains of the ships, . . . one steward, one cooper [etc.]. **1846** POLK *Diary* (1929) 103, I handed him $5 and directed the steward to give him refreshments.

Stewardess. {1631-} In the Methodist church, a female religious worker in a particular congregation. — **1844** LEE & FROST *Oregon* 217 The Rev. J. P. Richmond . . . and O. Lankton, stewardess, were appointed to return with Mr. Lee.

Stewpan. A pot or pan used for stewing. {1651-} — **1633** *N.H. Prov. Papers* I. 80, 1 stue pann, 1 jack [etc.]. **1711** *Essex Inst. Coll.* IV. 187/1 New stewpan & cover. **1833** J. HALL *Harpe's Head* 156 A fat opossum . . . he cut up, and placed in the stew-pan. **1891** WILKINS *New Eng. Nun* 226 Nicholas . . . prepared some porridge in a little stewpan. **1908** 'O. HENRY' *Options* 26 She got the graniteware stew-pan out of the . . . earthenware closet.

+**Stib.** *local.* [?By error for *stile.*] =DUNLIN. — [**1876** F. C. BROWNE in *Forest & Stream* 9 Nov. 212/3 *T. alpina.* Stile.] **1888** TRUMBULL *Names of Birds* 182 F. C. Browne gives Stib in his list of gunners' names at Plymouth Bay. **1891** *Cent.* 5941/1. *Stib,* . . . the American dunlin, purre, or ox-bird: a gunners' name. . . . (Massachusetts.) **1917** *Birds of Amer.* I. 237.

* **Stick,** *n.*
I. 1. A dash of liquor put into tea, lemonade, or the like. {1804-}
'Now *U.S.* and *colonial*' (*O.E.D.*).
1854 in E. C. Porter *Songs of Yale* (1860) 64 This lemonade it has no 'stick.' **1871** DAYTON *Last Days Knickerb. Life* 63 Their peaceful slumbers . . . were seldom disturbed, and then only by some party of youngsters who had put '*too strong a stick*' in their lemonade. **1904** PRINGLE *Rice Planter* 66, I went, carrying lunch and a bottle of homemade wine, with a stick in it for those who were to get wet.

+**2. a.** A grove of timber. **b.** *pl. fig.* The backwoods; a rural district. *colloq.*
(a) **1860** *Harper's Mag.* March 446/2 We just took lodgings for the night in the big stick. (b) **1917** COMSTOCK *Man* 67 He meant, should he come across Burke in 'the sticks,' to take him off for a bear hunt.

+**3.** A baseball bat. *colloq.* or *slang.*
1868 *N.Y. Herald* 4 Aug. 6/5 The Empire seemed out of practice with 'the stick.' **1894** *Chicago Record* 7 May 2/2 The visitors . . . won by good work with the stick at opportune times. **1912** MATHEWSON *Pitching* 3 He had his stick way down by the handle.

II. In various phrases and expressions.
See also CUT *v.* 25 j, SHARP STICK.

+**4. a.** *As many* (or *as much*) *as one can shake a stick at,* as many (or as much) as one would want.

1818 *Lancaster* (Pa.) *Jrnl.* 5 Aug. (Th.), We have in Lancaster as many Taverns as you can shake a stick at. **1833** A. GREENE *Yankee among Nullifiers* 42, I can buy as many, jest like it, as you can shake a stick at. **1843** *Amer. Pioneer* II. 156, I have almost as much matter on hand, as you can shake a stick at, but not time to digest it.

+**b.** *More than one can shake a stick at*, or variant: More than enough; more than one would believe.

1830 *Western Mo. Rev.* III. 356 His slang-curses were ultra Kentuckian on a ground of Yankee; and he had, says my informant, more of this, 'than you could shake a stick at.' **1850** MATHEWS *Moneypenny* 32 As for . . . every sort of knave and villain, there's more than you could shake a stick at in a whole day. **1851** *Polly Peablossom* 69 She got onto the whappinest, biggest, rustiest yaller moccasin that ever you shuck er stick at. **1884** HOWELLS *S. Lapham* i, You can . . . buy more farms than you can shake a stick at for less money than it cost to build the barns on 'em. **1900** BACHELLER *E. Holden* 179, I've seen 'im more times 'n ye could shake a stick at.

+**c.** *That can shake a stick at*, that can possibly compare with.

1843 STEPHENS *High Life N.Y.* II. 216, I never sot eyes on anything that could shake a stick at that.

5. *To up sticks*, to pull up stakes. {1854}

1839 *Knickerb.* XIV. 141 Why, in the name of common sense, do you not up sticks and off? **1877** *Harper's Mag.* Jan. 213/2 If any man tries hard words with me, I knocks him down, up sticks, and makes tracks.

∗ **Stick,** *v.*

1. *To stick a pin there*, +to make a note of (something).

1836 *Public Ledger* (Phila.) 1 Nov. (Th.), Why does money become scarce? Because the bankers cannot discount, says the merchant. Stick a pin there. **1850** *Commercial* (Wilmington, N.C.) 25 April 2/1 (Th. S.), Yesterday every one of Benton's annoying resolutions [was] voted down by the Senate. Stick a pin there. **1861** *Knickerb.* LVIII. 266 There are two of the Norman in New-England for one in the South. Stick a pin there—not that it's of any account, but the Chivalry insist on it.

2. *To stick up for*, to defend; to stand up for. {1887}

1837 LOWELL *Letters* I. 20, I shall always like him [Whittier] the better for 'sticking up' for old New England. **1843** STEPHENS *High Life N.Y.* II. 175, I take a shine to that poetry of your'n; . . . I'll stick up for it as long as I live.

3. *To stick out*, to be conspicuous. {1638}

'Now esp. *U.S. slang*' (*O.E.D.*).

1842 *Spirit of Times* (Phila.) 12 March (Th.), The humbug 'sticks out a feet.' **1846** *Knickerb.* XXVII. 123 As Mr. Parley observed of Langstaff's sermon on Balaam's ass: it was so plain that '*it stuck right out.*'

4. *To stick* (a person) *for* a certain amount, to impose on (a person) for a certain amount; to cause (a person) an unwise expenditure. *colloq.* {1895-}

*a***1848** in Bartlett 333 Very often is a client stuck for a heavy bill of costs, which he would have saved but for the ignorance of his attorney. **1857** *Knickerb.* XLIX. 279 Pedro stuck him for about two thousand dollars' worth. **1881** *Harper's Mag.* April 643/1 They stuck us for two seventy-five. **1904** *N.Y. Ev. Post* 27 May 6 The financial world will say that Uncle Sam is hard up, and that it will be no sin to stick him for the highest rate he can be made to stand.

5. *To stick it out*, to persevere to the very end. {1901}

1876 BOURKE *Journal* 28 July–8 Sept., Munson determined to stick it out and remain with the command. **1889** 'MARK TWAIN' *Conn. Yankee* 334 The proprieties required me to stick it out. **1914** ATHERTON *Perch of Devil* 83 She would stick it out if she yawned every tooth in her head loose.

+**6.** *To be stuck on*, to be captivated with; to be enamored of; to like. Often in negative. *colloq.*[2]

1886 *American* XIII. 14/2 A customer willing to give ten francs for it . . . [was] ridiculed . . . for having been 'stuck' on the canvas. **1887** *Courier-Journal* 29 Jan. 6/3 Mr. John Smith . . . would not believe him on oath. He had never been 'stuck' on him. **1894** *Harper's Mag.* Oct. 697/1 The Senator's stuck on a rich lady in Harlem. **1908** 'YESLAH' *Tenderfoot S. Calif.* 39 After you've carted a wilted bunch [of poppies] around for a few hours, you ain't much stuck on 'em.

Stickability. Capacity for perseverance. {1905-} — **1888** *Voice* 10 May, Stickability, says *The Farmer at Work*, is the most important ability a farmer can possess. **1897** *Boston Jrnl.* 11 Jan. 8/4, I have [stayed by the Bible] for the last 24 years, and have more stickability tonight than ever.

+**Stick-and-clay chimney.** A chimney constructed of sticks covered over by clay. — **1863** *Ladies' Repository* XXIII. 398/2 A 'stick and clay chimney' on the same ample scale lets out the smoke and lets in the rain. **1888** 'CRADDOCK' *Despot* 69 Blue and curling smoke . . . issued from the stick-and-clay chimney.

+**Stick-and-dirt.** *attrib.* Designating a fireplace or chimney constructed of sticks covered over by mud. — **1885** *Century Mag.* March 684 The huge 'stick-and-dirt' fire-place . . . [was] in perfect accord with the figures, the costumes, and the predicament. **1887** *Ib.* May 111/1 The water mirrored the Shinault cabin with its one wee window and 'stick and dirt' chimney.

+**Stick-and-mud.** *attrib.* =MUD-AND-STICK. — **1881** PIERSON *In the Brush* 309 It had a stick-and-mud chimney on the outside, and was without floor of any kind. **1891** *Scribner's Mag.* X. 316 A stick-and-mud chimney, would seem odd to the unaccustomed.

+**Stickback chair.** A chair with upright rods in its back. — **1783** *Narragansett Hist. Reg.* II. 314 The Sheriff . . . [shall purchase] Three good large Windsor or Stickback Chairs.

Stick ball. A kind of game. *Obs.* — **1824** *Nantucket Inquirer* 12 Jan. (Th.), No person shall play Foot-ball or Poke, Stick-ball or Swinger, within the compact part of the town of Nantucket.

+**Stick bug.** (See quotations.) — **1891** *Cent.* 5943/1 *Stick-bug*, . . . any orthopterous insect of the family *Phasmidæ*. . . . (Local.) **1894** *Harper's Mag.* Feb. 456/1 The form [of walking stick] . . . dubbed 'stickbugs' and 'prairie alligators,' our *Diapheromera femorata*.

+**Stick candy.** Hard candy made into sticks. — **1886** *Harper's Mag.* June 93/2 The 'stick' candy, which seems to be an indigenous American product, is of ordinary 'A' sugar. **1900** ADE *More Fables* 30 He never Foundered them on Stick Candy or Raisins.

+**Stick chair. 1.** A chair constructed of rods or sticks of wood. **2.** = STICK GIG. — **(1) 1843** 'CARLTON' *New Purchase* I. 61 The room contained . . . a table, 'stick chairs' and some stools. **(2) 1860** MORDECAI *Virginia* 275 The modes of conveyance were either by a stage-wagon, . . . or on horse-back with saddle-bags, or in a stick-chair. **1908** M. JOHNSTON *L. Rand* I, Coach and chaise, curricle and stick-chair, were encountered.

+**Stick chimney.** An outside chimney made of sticks, usually laid across each other, and held together and protected by mud or clay. — [**1835** in Ellet *Pioneer Women* 410 It had not the ordinary stick and round chimney common to log houses.] **1845** KIRKLAND *Western Clearings* 208 At one side was a stick chimney . . . finished on the top by the remnant of a stone Churn. **1871** EGGLESTON *Hoosier Schoolm.* 95 The stick chimney . . . made this a typical cabin. **1897** W. E. BARTON *Hero in Homespun* 7 [They] began life in a pole cabin . . . with a stick chimney.

∗ **Sticker.**

+**1.** A narrow slip of paper bearing a printed name that may be pasted on a ballot to facilitate scratching; a similar slip of paper for other uses.

1871 DE VERE 270. **1888** *Voice* 5 July, [Quotations] printed on *one* side of little slips of paper . . . to be gummed and used as 'stickers' . . . on newspaper wrappers [etc.]. **1890** *Congress. Rec.* 19 March 2394/1 Where was that 'sticker' stuck? Was it not upon the words 'For Congress?' **1907** *Springfield W. Repub.* 31 Oct. 16 The republican nominee, who failed to get his name on the ballot . . . , has decided that . . . he will make use of stickers to obtain election. **1911** *N.Y. Ev. Post* 6 Jan. 1 A telegraph company is obliged to accept a 'sticker' on a message intended to fix additional liability on the company in the event of delay . . . or non-delivery.

+**2.** A thorn or bur.

1898 ATHERTON *Californians* 231 Trennahan . . . plucked the 'stickers' from his trousers. **1899** *Going Flowers* 350 When the 'stickers' are at last picked or rubbed off, they fall to the ground.

+**Stick gig.** A light, two-wheeled carriage for one person. — **1825** *Catawba Jrnl.* 17 May, The subscriber . . . is now finishing, about $4,000 worth of work . . . , consisting of a Coachee, Chariotee, Phaeton, Panneled and Stick Gigs [etc.]. **1857** *Harper's Mag.* May 744/2 That hoss reminds me of a hoss that old Major Bulbous used to drive in that old stick gig of his'n. **1877** BAGBY *Old Va. Gentleman* 1 Once a month the lawyers, in their stick-gigs or 'single-chairs,' . . . jogged on to court.

+**Stick horse.** A stick used by children as a play horse. — **1896** WHITE *Real Issue* 71 So his lonely way was strewn with broken stick-horses.

∗ **Stickleback.** Any of numerous small fishes of the family Gasterosteidae. Often with specifying terms. (See also FOUR-SPINED STICKLEBACK.) — **1814** MITCHILL *Fishes N.Y.* 430 Two-spined Stickleback. *Gasterosteus biaculeatus.* . . . Caught in the salt water among the killifishes. **1860** *Harper's Mag.* March 488/2 A little fish . . . goes by the names of Stickleback, . . . Tittleback, and a few others. **1871** *Harper's Mag.* June 32 If you have seen 'sticklebacks' you will say, How alike they are! **1884** GOODE, etc. *Fisheries* I. 457 The ten-spined Stickleback, *Gasterosteus pungitius,* [is] . . . found also in fresh water. **1907** *St. Nicholas* Aug. 945/2 One stickle-back . . . we cannot keep with the others, because he kills them.

+**Stickpot.** 'A lath-pot for taking lobsters . . . constructed of laths or of any narrow strips of wood' (*Cent.*). — **1887** GOODE, etc. *Fisheries* V. II. 666 Other names by which they are known to the fishermen are . . . 'stick-pots,' and 'lath-coops.'

+**Stickseed.** Any plant having prickly or adhesive fruit, esp. one of the genus *Lappula*. Also with specifying terms. — **1843** TORREY *Flora N.Y.* II. 90 Broad-leaved Stickseed. . . . Borders of woods, along fences, and hill-sides. **1847** DARLINGTON *Weeds & Plants* 245 Narrow-leaved Stickseed. . . . The nutlets adhere to the coats of sheep and cattle. **1872** *Vermont Bd. Agric. Rep.* I. 285 Stickseed. . . . [The] seeds are armed with hooked or barbed prickles. **1893** *Amer. Folk-Lore* VI. 141 *Agrimonia Eupatoria,* stick seed; beggar's ticks. West Va.

+**Stick sulky.** =STICK GIG. — **1868** WOODRUFF *Trotting Horse* 137 Mr. Treadwill used to drive Lady Blanche on the road, in an old stick sulky.

+**Sticktight.** Any plant having prickly or adhesive fruit, esp. one of the genus *Bidens*; =BEGGAR-TICK(S) 1. — **1892** COULTER *Bot. W. Texas* II. 223 Common beggar-ticks. Stick-tight. . . . A coarse weed, common everywhere. **1894** *Amer. Folk-Lore* VII. 95 *Cynoglossum officinale*, stick-tights, Anderson, Ind. **1901** [see BEGGAR-TICK(S) 1]. **1917** FREEMAN & KINGSLEY *Alabaster Box* 146 You can't seem to shake 'em off, no more than them spiteful little stick-tights that get all over your clo'es.

+**Stick-to-itiveness.** Perseverance. *colloq.* — **1867** in Custer *Tenting on Plains* 520 Old Rover, with the stick-to-it-iveness of a fox-hound when once on a trail, was in for [etc.]. **1869** BARNUM *Struggles* 620 'Yankee stick-to-it-iveness' was always a noted feature of my character. **1887** GEORGE *40 Yrs. on Rail* 231 They devote their quick wit and their stick-to-ativeness to 'sponging' for a living.

+**Stickweed.** One of a number of American plants, esp. ragweed, *Ambrosia elatior*, or a species of *Aster*. Also with specifying term. Also attrib. and fig.
1743 CLAYTON *Flora Virginica* 102 Verbesina floribus corymbosis, foliis lanceolatis petiolatis. . . . White Stickweed. **1808** WEEMS *Washington* (1840) 6 He will . . . stand forth confessed in native stickweed sterility and worthlessness. **1870** *Amer. Naturalist* IV. 400 The universal 'stickweed' (*Actinomeris squamosa* [sic]) of the Great Valley was rare. **1894** *Amer. Folk-Lore* VII. 90 Actinomeris squarrosa, . . . wing-stem, stickweed, West Va. *Ib.* 91 Aster cordifolius, . . . Blue Devil, stick-weed, bee-weed, Fall Aster, West Va.

Stiff, *n.* {1680–}
+**1.** A corpse. *slang.* {1915}
1859 BARTLETT 450 A dead body, in the language of the 'resurrectionists,' is called a stiff. **1878** *Ind. State Jrnl.* (Indianapolis) 11 Dec. 1/5 There is no use bringing in little stiffs; the doctors won't buy them. **1903** HAPGOOD *Autobiog. of Thief* 304 The man goes to any large hospital, represents himself as a doctor and for twenty-five dollars can generally get a stiff. **1922** PARRISH *Case & Girl* 183 If he's there, he's a stiff all right.

+**2.** A rough or clumsy person; a bum; a tramp. *slang.* Freq. *big stiff.*
1896 ADE *Artie* 17 There I set like a big stiff for five hours. **1902** WHITLOCK *13th District* 381 You 'as afraid to see me, you big stiff. **1922** PARRISH *Case & Girl* 324 This is my graft, anyhow, and not one of you stiffs gets a penny of it unless I split with you.

✽**Stiff,** *a.* (See LIP.)
+**Stifftail.** *local.* =RUDDY DUCK. — **1888** TRUMBULL *Names of Birds* 112 In the vicinity of Philadelphia . . . and at Savannah, Ga., [it is called] Stiff-Tail. **1917** *Birds of Amer.* I. 152.

✽**Stile.** An arrangement of steps to allow a person to pass over a fence or wall. — **1636** [see GATE¹ 1]. **1708** *Boston Rec.* 79 Ordered that the Stile at the burying place . . . be taken down. **1883** *Harper's Mag.* Sept. 629/1 She crossed the stile and walked down the road.

✽**Still,** *n.* **a.** An apparatus for distilling liquids, esp. alcoholic liquor. **b.** A distillery.
1648 *Mass. H. S. Coll.* 4 Ser. VI. 68, I have even now sold my horse to James Oliver for 10l. to purchase the still. **1689** *Conn. Rec.* I. 506, I give my Still to Dr. Hastings. **1713** *Mass. H. S. Coll.* 6 Ser. V. 270, I have put two white chamber pots on bord with the still. **1790** *Steele P.* I. 65 The excise bill if it passes will subject all stills to the payment of 60 cents per Gall. duty annually upon the capacity of the still. **1843** *Amer. Pioneer* II. 163 A good still of one hundred gallons would purchase two hundred acres of land. **1845** JUDD *Margaret* I. 129 The 'Still,' or Distillery, was a smutty, clouted, suspicious looking building. **1888** *Scribner's Mag.* Jan. 22/2 Let us first look at the stills, those broad, black towers, under which the fire rages. **1888** [see MOUNTAIN DEW].
attrib. **1802** *Steele P.* I. 247 Did I not refer to you some time ago a complaint of the different manner in which 'still bottoms' are considered in relation to duty in Philada. & Baltimore? **1789** *Ann. 1st Congress* 217 As to the proposition for an excise to be levied at the still-head, I cannot vote for it. **1904** TARBELL *Hist. Standard Oil Co.* II. 91 As stillman, he was paid by the hour.

✽**Still,** *a.* ⸰Of fishing, baiting, etc.: Remaining in one spot. — **1859** BARTLETT 451 *Still-baiting,* fishing with a deep line in one spot, as distinguished from trolling. **1883** *Century Mag.* July 383/1 The Floridians . . . use a long rod or pole for still-fishing, skittering, and bobbing. **1888** GOODE *Amer. Fishes* 58 The angler finds them at the proper seasons equally eager for fly-hook, trolling-spoon, or still-bait.

+**Still alarm.** A fire alarm given without sounding the public alarm. — **1875** *Chicago Tribune* 6 Nov. 5/4 Engine Company No. 4 answered a still alarm at 6:30 o'clock yesterday. **1911** *N.Y. Ev. Post* 2 March 1 A still alarm brought Engine No. 65 to the scene.

✽**Stiller.**¹ One who distills. — **1693** *Boston Rec.* 215 Stillers [should remove] to such places where there feces may be carried into some Common Shoar or Drein. **1725** *New-Eng. Courant* 12 April 2/2 The Still-House of Mr. Hill, the Turpentine Stiller, was burnt down. **1834** CARRUTHERS *Kentuckian* I. 97, I thought in a minute about . . . the miller, and the blacksmith, and the stiller, talking politics.

Stiller.² {1608–} +One of several classes of steers being fattened for sale. — **1880** *Cimarron News & Press* 25 Nov. 2/4 The experienced buyer will tell you in a minute whether a 'grasser,' a 'stiller,' a 'straw-tramper,' a 'stabler,' or a field fed bullock is before him.

Still-fed, *a.* Of an animal: Fed with the refuse of a still. — **1850** *Annual of Sci. Discovery* 98 Much the larger share of this [oil] is of inferior lard, made of mast-fed and still-fed hogs.

✽**Still house.** A building where liquids, esp. alcoholic liquors, are distilled. {–a1734}

1687 BLOME *Isles & Terr. in Amer.* 34 [Making sugar cane] is dangerous . . . in the Still-House. **1716** *Boston Selectmen* 6 Charles Man's Petition to Sell as a Retayler at his Still-House. **1725** [see STILLER¹]. **1768** *R.I. Commerce* I. 258 The Still Houses have a stock 600 hhd. Molosses, and run of 6 hhd. a day. **1807** J. R. SHAW *Life* (1930) 106, I went to captain Hollowback's still house one day, . . . [and] called for a quart of Whiskey. **1891** *Century Mag.* April 895 The meetings over at the still-house voted him out.

+**Still-hunt,** *n.* A hunt for game in a quiet and stealthy manner; fig., the pursuit of any object by stealth or under cover.
1834 CROCKETT *Narr. Life* 29 Though the school-house might do for a still hunt, it wouldn't do for *a drive,* and so I concluded to wait until I could get him out. **1855** *Harper's Mag.* Oct. 599/2 Starting on a 'still hunt,' he coursed along the edge of the island. **1875** BURROUGHS *Winter Sunshine* 102 A still-hunt rarely brings you in sight of a fox. **1903** *Sun* (N.Y.) 15 Nov., In appearance the Baron is the typical titled foreigner supposed to be on a still hunt for the American heiress. **1918** W. E. CONNELLEY *Stand. Hist. Kansas* I. 289 The terrible 'still-hunt' was usually used.

b. *Polit.* Activity and scheming conducted in secret, or by underhand methods.
1885 *Mag. Amer. Hist.* April 396/1 *Still Hunt,* originally a sporting term, but applied during the campaign of 1876 to political methods conducted in secret, or under-handed methods. **1887** *Century Mag.* April 864/2 The Democrats of Sangamon now [1854] organized what is known in Western politics as a 'still-hunt.' **1897** *Congress. Rec.* 5 Jan. 480/1 It seems now that somebody is on a 'still hunt.'

+**Still-hunt,** *v.*
1. *intr.* To hunt by stalking the game.
1858 *Harper's Mag.* Oct. 615/2 An old woodsman . . . had been, without success, still-hunting. **1871** *N.Y. Laws* 1669 No person shall . . . still-hunt or set any trap. **1890** CUSTER *Following Guidon* 179 One of the number still-hunted, singling out his animal, and firing at long range so that the sound of the bullet did not disturb the herd.

2. *tr.* To stalk and kill (game) by stealth.
1877 C. HALLOCK *Sportsman's Gazetteer* 81 (Cent.), The best time to still-hunt deer is just before sunset, when they come down from the hills to drink. **1885** *Outing* VIII. 78/1, I was still-huntin' deer. **1906** *Munsey's Mag.* Jan. 475/2 Lacy, a seasoned sportsman at twenty-two, had still-hunted many a deer.

+**Still-hunter.** One who still-hunts. — **1831** AUDUBON *Ornith. Biog.* I. 335 We are now about to follow the *true hunter,* as the Still Hunter is also called. **1844** GREGG *Commerce of Prairies* II. 219 The 'still-hunter' must needs be upon his guard. **1886** *Harper's Mag.* June 63/1 Still-hunters . . . know the haunts of bear and deer, needing no dogs. **1905** *N.Y. Ev. Post* 9 Sept., The animals . . . are now the worthy prize of the skilled still hunter.

+**Still-hunting.** The action or practice of hunting game by stealth. Also attrib. — **1831** AUDUBON *Ornith. Biog.* I. 335 Still Hunting is followed as a kind of trade by most of our frontier men. **1845** *Knickerb.* XXV. 214 As to deer, fire-hunting, still-hunting, or up in the fork of a tree by night, . . . it is all one to Harry. **1885** *Outing* VII. 78/1 It's an old still-huntin' shanty. **1902** HULBERT *Forest Neighbors* 103 Her long hours of still-hunting had brought their rich reward.

+**Stilt sandpiper.** =LONG-LEGGED SANDPIPER. — **1872** COUES *Key to Birds* 253. **1917** *Birds of Amer.* I. 231/2 A Stilt Sandpiper among a number of Semipalmated Sandpipers is instantly noticed.

Stingaree. A sting ray. {stingareeing, c1870–} — **1836** HOLLEY *Texas* 107 The crab—crayfish—shrimp—and stingaree, a species of horsefoot, are the principal [crustaceans]. **1873** T. GILL *Cat. Fishes E. Coast N. Amer.* 34 *Tryzon centrura.* . . . Sting-ray; whip-ray; stingaree. **1882** G. C. EGGLESTON *Wreck of Red Bird* 24 The creature [is] . . . called by negroes and fishermen, and nearly every body else on the coast, stingarees. **1897** *Outing* XXIX. 231/2 The stingaree . . . which is as lively as a two-ton anchor.

✽**Stinging nettle.** Any plant of the family Urticaceæ having foliage covered with stinging hairs. — **1737** BRICKELL *N. Carolina.* 20 Stinging-Nettle, the Seed being brought from Europe, there being none found growing Spontaneous in North Carolina. **1872** *Amer. Naturalist* VI. 728 The canes [were] matted with thorny 'green brier' . . . and mixed with tall stinging nettles.

Sting nettle. {1822–7–} +(See quotation.) — **1899** GREEN *Va. Word-Book* 364 *Sting-nettle,* . . . the jelly-fish; also called *sea-nettle.*

+**Sting ray.** Also **stingare, stingry.** Any ray of the family Dasyatidæ or allied families. Also with specifying terms. {1881} Cf. STINGAREE. — **1612** [see PORPOISE.] **1745** E. KIMBER *Itinerant Observer* 11 The View is still more enchanting, by the sporting of the finny Race; the shining Mullet, . . . the Warrior Stingre with his redoubted Tail. **1791** W. BARTRAM *Travels* 67 These islands, abound with . . . Skate, Skipjack, Stingray. **1799** ELLICOTT in Mathews *Life A. Ellicott* 186 Along the Florida Reef . . . , a great abundance and variety of fish may be taken: such as . . . porgys, turbots, stingrys. **1842** *Nat. Hist. N.Y., Zoology* IV. 375 The Broad Sting Ray, *Pastinaca maclura,* . . . is found at Newport (R.I.). **1884** GOODE, etc. *Fisheries* I. 665 The Sting Ray, *Trygon centrura,* ranges farther to the north than any of the other species.

*Stink. *attrib.* In specific names: (see quotations). — 1897 SUDWORTH *Arborescent Flora* 298 *Rhamnus caroliniana.* . . . Indian Cherry. . . . [Also called] Stinkwood (La.). . . . Stink Berry (Nebr.). Stink Cherry (Nebr.). 1877 BARTLETT 647 *Squash-Bug.* . . . A small yellow bug, injurious to the vines of squashes, melons, and cucumbers. . . . In Connecticut, called a *stink-bug.* 1909 WEBSTER 396/1 Most of the species [*Chrysopa*] . . . are called *golden-eyed flies*, or, from their disagreeable odor, *stink flies.* 1894 *Amer. Folk-Lore* VII. 104 *Eragrostis major*, stinkgrass, Neb. 1884 GOODE, etc. *Fisheries* I. 610 The 'Mud-Shark,' *Dorosoma cepedianum*, . . . is known as the . . . 'Stink Shad' [in the Chesapeake region].

Stinkard. {c1600-} +(See quot. 1777.) *Obs.* Also *attrib.* — 1777 W. ROBERTSON *Hist. America* I. IV. 344 Among the Natchez . . . Some families were reputed noble. . . . The body of the people were considered as vile. The former were called Respectable; the latter the Stinkards. 1791 W. BARTRAM *Travels* 466 Those numerous remnant bands or tribes . . . generally speak the Stincard language.

*Stinking, *a.* In the names of animals, plants, and trees: (see quotations).
1765 ROGERS *Acct. N. Amer.* 262 The Skunk or Pole-Cat . . . is called by the Indians the Stinking Beast. 1795 WINTERBOTHAM *Hist. View* III. 395 Other poisonous plants, are . . . the Water Elder, . . . the Herb Christopher, . . . the Stinking Snakeweed [etc.]. 1843 TORREY *Flora N.Y.* I. 133 *Ptelea trifoliata.* . . . Swamp Dogwood. Stinking Ash. . . . On the shore of Lake Erie. 1884 Stinking cedar [see CEDAR 1 b]. 1884 *Rep. Comm. Agric.* 126 Stinking yew; Savin. A very rare evergreen tree, resembling the yew, growing in the northwestern part of Florida. 1897 SUDWORTH *Arborescent Flora* 293 *Æsculus glabra.* Ohio Buckeye. . . . [Also called] Stinking Buckeye (Ala., Ark.).

Stinkpot. {1665-} +The musk turtle. {1844-} Also *attrib.* — 1825 *Phila. Acad. Nat. Sciences Jrnl.* IV. 217 The *odorata* is generally known by the name of 'stink-pot,' from its musky odor. 1839 STORER *Mass. Reptiles* 210 The mud Tortoise . . . has a very disgusting odor, and is hence sometimes called stink-pot. 1884 GOODE, etc. *Fisheries* I. 154. [1903 *Nature* 1 Oct. 531/2 Fourteen Stink-pot Terrapins (*Cinosternum odoratum*), . . . from North America [have been added to the London zoo].]

Stinkweed. {1793-} +=JIMSON WEED. (The identity of the weed mentioned in the first quotation is in doubt.) — 1753 ELIOT *Field-Husb.* iv. 92 Not knowing the botanical Name of this Plant: from its ill and singular Quality, we call it Stink-Weed. 1804 C. B. BROWN tr. *Volney View* 69n., These banks . . . abound with the stramoneum (stink weed). 1843 TORREY *Flora N.Y.* II. 101 Jamestown- or Jimson-weed. Stinkweed. . . . An extract is kept in the shops, which is used in various spasmodic and painful diseases. 1894 [see JAMESTOWN LILY].

Stinted common. a. A common limited to the pasturage of a definite number of animals. b. A right to pasture so many animals on such a common. *Obs.* — 1638 *Charlestown Land Rec.* 71 Alsoe Three cows comons and a quarter, lying on the stinted comon without the Neck. 1642 *New Haven Col. Rec.* 82 The Neck shall be a stinted common for cattell. 1666 [see ENFEOFF].

Stinted pasture. =prec. *Obs.* {1700-} — 1681 *Charlestown Land Rec.* 192 The Committe Appointed to Oversee & manage Sundry matters relateing to the Stinted Pasture, Usually Called the Common, Lying without the neck of Land in this Town. 1685 *Ib.* 204 This return . . . [should] have preceeded this Last division of the Stinted pasture.

*Stir-, stem of *stir* v. +Comb. with *cake, net, pudding.* — 1838 *Knickerb.* XI. 16 Which will you have for dinner, John, 'taters or stir-pudding? 1845 KIRKLAND *Western Clearings* 168 Her husband . . . mixes stir-cakes for the eldest blue eyes to bake on a griddle. 1872 *Penna. Laws* 481 It shall not be lawful . . . to take, capture or destroy fish by . . . stir-nets.

Stirring off. +The action of making sugar from maple sap; sugaring off. — 1846 *Knickerb.* XXVII. 211 All . . . were there . . . to witness the grand 'stirring off.' 1881 *Harper's Mag.* April 649/2 The hot syrup . . . was poured into a large . . . kettle for the process of 'stirring off.'

+Stirring plow. An ordinary plow, as distinguished from a breaking plow (q.v.). — 1857 *Lawrence (Kan.) Republican* 28 May 3 Also a great variety of Stirring or Old Ground Plows. 1881 *Rep. Indian Affairs* 95, I have purchased for them . . . 10 stirring plows.

*Stirrup. A device suspended from a saddle to support a rider's foot. — 1686 SEWALL *Diary* I. 146 A Boy killed by a Horse at Rowley; foot hung in the Stirrup and so was torn to pieces. 1790 *Penna. Packet* 2 Feb. 4/1 To be Sold by Jesse Sharpless, . . . A quantity of plated and polished stirrups. 1846 THORPE *Myst. Backwoods* 177 Dangling on either side are the enormous wooden stirrups, looking like a huge pair of mallets. 1893 SANBORN *S. Calif.* 177 The stirrups are faced and edged with silver half an inch thick, elaborately chased and carved.

*Stitchwort. A chickweed of the genus *Alsine* (syn. *Stellaria*). — 1784 *Amer. Acad. Mem.* I. 446 Stitchwort. Blossoms in panicles; white. 1814 BIGELOW *Florula Bostoniensis* 110 Stitchwort. . . . Grows among the bushes. 1857 GRAY *Botany* 59.

*Stiver. Also †styver, stuyver. [Du. *stuiver*, †*stuyver*.] A Dutch coin worth one-twentieth of a guilder; the value of this coin. *Obs.*
American usage was independently influenced by the Dutch.
1676 *New Castle Court Rec.* 47 A horse and man to pay for passage [on the ferryboat] 2 gilders a man with out a horse 10 styvers. 1701 in Munsell *Ann. Albany* IV. 141 The assessment . . . [is] approved off, and laid 4½ stuyver upon ye pound. 1789 MORSE *Amer. Geog.* 349 Four white grains and three black ones, should pass for the value of a stiver or penny.

+b. The value of this coin (in *seawan* or *wampum*).
1680 *N.Y. Hist. Soc. Coll.* XLV. 7 One Thousand Eight hund[re]d forty eight Gilders tenn Stivers Sewant. 1701 in Munsell *Ann. Albany* IV. 125 Upon which assessment . . . is laid three stuyvers wampum upon the pound.

*Stock, *n.*

I. *1. *pl.* A device for punishing petty offenders by confining their feet, and sometimes their hands and neck also, in timbers suitably notched and hinged. Now hist.
1633 *Plymouth Col. Rec.* I. 12 John Hews & Jone his wife adjudged to sit in the stocks because the said Jone conceived with childe by him before they were publickely married, though in the time of contract. 1663 *Plymouth Laws* 141 Any Indian or Indians [who] shall be found drunke . . . [shall be] sett in the stockes. 1680 *N.H. Hist. Soc. Coll.* VIII. 14 [If he] shall refuse that fine, he shall be comitted to the stocks. 1730 *Huntington Rec.* II. 364 Paid to Samll smith Juner for hinges for the Stocks . . . 4 s. 6 d. 1789 MORSE *Amer. Geog.* 229 [Justices of the peace in Conn.] have cognizance of small offences, and may punish by fine, not exceeding forty shillings, . . . or sitting in the stocks. 1891 EARLE *Sabbath* 13 The first man who was sentenced to and occupied the stocks in Boston was the carpenter who made them.

+b. *pl.* A framework variously constructed used to hold or confine animals.
1854 BARTLETT *Personal Narr.* I. 16 The first step . . . was to construct a frame-work of timber, called the 'stocks,' . . . capable of containing a single mule. 1876 KNIGHT 2391/1 *Stocks*, . . . a frame in which refractory animals are held for shoeing or veterinary purposes. 1892 *York County Hist. Rev.* 5 The shop is . . . the only shop in town having kicking stocks.

*2. *collect.* The domestic animals on a farm or ranch.
In the first two examples stock may be used in the general sense of total belongings or property. (See also FARM STOCK, LIVE STOCK.)
1637 *Conn. Probate Rec.* I. 106 His howsing, Lands, stock and estate [are] to be disposed of to the benefitt of his Children. 1691 *Ib.* 393, I give to my wife . . . my House, Houselott & Stock. 1730 [see ENGLISH HAY]. 1790 DEANE *New-Eng. Farmer* 267/1 But the word *stock*, in this country, is commonly used by farmers to express only live stock, or the beasts that are kept upon a farm. 1814 J. TAYLOR *Arator* 173, I will take up and consider separately, the mode of managing each species of our domestic animals, usually comprised by the term 'stock.' 1887 *Courier-Journal* 4 May 4/5 Little valleys here and there . . . seem to afford an abundance of bunch grass for stock. 1925 TILGHMAN *Dugout* 74 In time he built a house and stable, and had accumulated stock.

b. Bees or chickens.
1831 PECK *Guide* 175 Bees are profitable stock for the farmer. 1845 HOOPER *Taking Census* (1928) 117 The old lady seemed delighted, thus to exhibit her feathered 'stock.'

3. Government obligations; bonds. {a1692-}
1790 *State P.* (1819) I. 17 The progress of publick credit is witnessed by a considerable rise of American stock abroad as well as at home. 1807 *Phila. Ordinances* (1812) 212 'The sinking fund,' to be applied to the purchase and redemption of the several species of stock. 1851 MELVILLE *Moby Dick* 81 People in Nantucket invest their money in whaling vessels, the same way that you do yours in approved state stocks.

4. a. *collect.* Shares, or certificates of ownership, in a business corporation. {1708-} b. *pl.* Shares of different types or of different corporations.
1808 *Steele Papers* II. 562, I will receive Cape Fear Bank stock at par. 1820 *Niles' Reg.* XVIII. 464/2 We are sorry to believe that jobbing in stocks begins to be something like a regular business in the United States. 1856 [see FANCY *n.* 2]. 1888 *Economist* 27 Oct. 3/2 The St. Paul has not challenged particular attention since the first effects of its passage of the dividend on the common stock were spent. 1894 WARNER *Golden House* xiv, There was a little improvement in his stocks, and his spirits rose. 1900 *Congress. Rec.* 12 Feb. 1731/1 The stock of the street-car company is worth four to one, and yet they are kicking about putting up protection for the motormen.

‖5. A hydrant or fire plug.
1833 *Niles' Reg.* XLIV. 420/2 A hose was attached to the stock at the corner of William street and Exchange Place.

+6. (See quotation.)
1891 *Cent.* 5955/1 *Stock*, . . . the proceeds of the sale of the catch of a fishing-trip; the net value of a cargo of fish (New Eng.).

+7. *To take stock in*, to have regard for or confidence in. *colloq.*
1870 'MARK TWAIN' *Sk., New & Old* 161 The chance 'theory' concerning seven-up is . . . calculated to inflict . . . pecuniary loss upon any community that takes stock in it. 1882 PECK *Sunshine* 275 The next time any party advertises that the world will come to an end, we shall take no stock in it. 1891 WILKINS *New Eng. Nun* 55, I don't take any stock in signs. 1912 NICHOLSON *Hoosier Chron.* 604 There's Morton Bassett, that I never took much stock in.

II. *attrib.* and *comb.* 8. Designating domestic animals kept for breeding purposes.
See also STOCK CATTLE.

1831 PECK *Guide* 173 Stock hogs . . . usually sell from one dollar to one dollar and fifty cents per head. **1852** *Mich. Agric. Soc. Trans.* III. 145 Another common error is the excessive use of stock bucks. **1862** *Rep. Comm. Patents 1861: Agric.* 387 Like most of the stock horses of his time, . . . he had to work hard in clearing up new land. **1869** *Ill. Agric. Soc. Trans.* VII. 451 A very large proportion of the supply since last spring, has been made up of little better than stock sheep. **1889** WARFIELD *Cattle-Breeding* 288 The stock bull should be of the highest merit.

9. Designating individuals or groups having to do with live stock.

See also STOCK-GROWER, STOCKHOLDER 2, etc.

1835 J. MARTIN *Descr. Virginia* 99 No more grain is raised than is sufficient to supply the country itself, and the travellers and stock-drovers who pass through it. **1868** *Rep. Comm. Agric. 1867* 214 'Stock raisers,' or 'stock producers,' . . . [are] distinguished from 'stock feeders.' **1871** *Republican Rev.* 27 May 1/3 M. Maloney of Goshen, Indiana, arrived here on Thursday, being sent ahead to employ stock drivers. **1873** BEADLE *Undevel. West* 229 There is still abundant room for farmers and stock-handlers. **1885** *Wkly. New Mexican Rev.* 29 Jan. 1/3 The San Miguel County Stock Association has selected five delegates to attend the meeting of the Territorial Association. **1888** ROOSEVELT in *Century Mag.* Feb. 507/1 At every shipping point . . . stock inspectors . . . jealously examine all the brands on the live animals or on the hides of the slaughtered ones. **1890** LANGFORD *Vigilante Days* (1912) 518 The only habitations of whites . . . were the log cabins of the stock tenders. **1894** *Harper's Mag.* April 676/2 'Crit' Marston, the young blue-grass stock-farmer, is a favorite throughout all that section. **1906** LYNDE *Quickening* 35 Your business was transacted with lean, lantern-jawed Jopheth Pettigrass, the Major's stock-and-farm foreman.

10. Designating activities related to the raising of live stock.

See also STOCK-RAISING.

1838 ELLSWORTH *Valley of Wabash* 42 The great profits of stock-farming will be readily perceived. **1856** *Rep. Comm. Patents 1855: Agric.* 260 The mangold-wurzel . . . [is] a most valuable root to raise for stock-feeding. **1860** GREELEY *Overland Journey* 15 The soil . . . is admirably fitted for stockgrowing. **1868** *Ill. Agric. Soc. Trans.* VII. 144, [I] am well acquainted with the history of stock-grazing in my State. **1873** BEADLE *Undevel. West* 495 Eleven warriors . . . had been down to the Comanche country on a stock stealing expedition. **1874** J. C. McCOY *Hist. Cattle Trade* 92 [The farm] is allowed to lay awaste, whilst its owner has turned to stock-driving. **1878** BEADLE *Western Wilds* 101 Stock-ranching is the principal occupation. **1924** CROY *R.F.D. No. 3* 53 They were members of 'pig clubs' [and] went to stock-judging shows.

11. Designating individuals having to do with the buying and selling of stocks and shares.

See also STOCKBROKER, STOCK DEALER 1, etc.

1848 ARMSTRONG *Stocks* 14 These kind [*sic*] of Stock operators by no means belong to the producing classes. **1859** WILMER *Press Gang* 149 The special subjects to which I would now call attention are the frauds perpetrated by . . . Stock gamblers. **1877** W. WRIGHT *Big Bonanza* 310 The progress of the cross-cuts . . . is always watched with great interest by all the 'mining experts,' 'stock sharps,' and mining men generally. **1882** McCABE *New York* 355 The manner in which these . . . stock swindlers . . . conduct their operations, is very simple. **1900** NELSON *A B C Wall St.* 151 To stock speculators liquidation means the voluntary or forced sale of long stocks.

12. In special combinations.

Stock chute, a chute or passageway through which live stock is driven aboard railway cars for shipment; *s. fence*, a fence sufficient to restrain large live stock, as cattle; *s. guard*, a strong deck guard or railing to safeguard cattle shipped on the deck of a boat; *s. hay*, hay from low grounds; *s. mark*, a mark of identification on live stock; *s. mill*, a mill in which feed for live stock is ground; *s. pen*, a pen or enclosure suitable for live stock; *s. round-up*, a bringing together of the live stock, esp. cattle, from a considerable area; *s. saddle*, a saddle of a type used by cowboys and stockmen. **1875** *Chicago Tribune* 11 Sept. 2/6 The stock chute and grain-elevator are familiar objects [in Nebraska]. **1873** *Winfield* (Kan.) *Courier* 7 Aug. 1/5 Many farmers who live in the creek bottoms have open pasture lots fenced with a stock or open post and rail fence. **1897** BRODHEAD *Bound in Shallows* 29 On the little main-deck, protected with a heavy stockguard, numbers of men lounged. **1882** *Maine Agric. Rep.* XXVI. 43 What would be the difference between a ton of English hay and what we call stock hay, or swale hay? **1799** in Rothert *Muhlenberg Co.* 44 Peter Lyons' stockmark; Two smooth crops and a nick under each ear. **1851** CIST *Cincinnati* 169 Stock mills, for grinding corn and cobs together, and other grain for feeding purposes. **1886** *Rep. Indian Affairs* 148 There are suitable stables, cribs, meat-houses, stock-pens, hay-ricks. **1885** *Wkly. New Mexican Rev.* 8 June 2/6 About 700 saddle horses are being used in the Watrous stock round-up. **1886** ROOSEVELT in *Century Mag.* July 340/1 A stock-saddle weighs thirty or forty pounds.

*✱**Stock, v.***

+1. *tr.* (See quot. 1828.)

1828 WEBSTER, *Stock*, . . . to supply with seed; as, to stock land with clover or herdsgrass. American farmers. **1863** MITCHELL *My Farm* 70 Shall I stock my land with grass, and sell hay?

+2. To provide (a plow or plowshare) with a stock.

1851 *Fla. Plantation Rec.* 354, 1 [slave] Stocking Ploughs and soforth. **1857** *Ill. Agric. Soc. Trans.* III. 489 [The plant-cutter] is made by stocking a plow share similar to a common plow.

+3. To issue shares or stocks in (a business enterprise).

1880 *Cimarron News & Press* 18 March 2/2 The Jicarilla placers, close by, have been stocked for just one million. **1889** 'MARK TWAIN' *Conn. Yankee* 281, I noticed . . . there was something the matter . . . so I stocked the business and unloaded. **1908** STEVENS *Liberators* 212 We can easily bond it for six millions and stock it for five millions.

Stockade, *n.* {1614; 1777-}

+1. A wall or palisade of upright tree trunks or other heavy timbers forming a defensive barrier in Indian warfare; a place protected by such a structure. Now hist.

1668 *Doc. Col. Hist. N.Y.* XII. 461 [Resolved that] the Souldiers (so farre as conveniently they may) be lodgd in the Forte & keep the Stockades vp in defence. **1761** NILES *Indian Wars* II. 421 It burnt a great hole in the logs of the stockade. **1797** F. BAILY *Tour* 371 Mr. Mackintosh was fortifying his plantation with a regular stockade, raised about twelve feet high, and formed of thick planks. **1806** *Ann. 9th Congress* 2 Sess. 1113 The lieutenant . . . has built himself some log-houses, and enclosed them with a slight stockade. **1885** *Century Mag.* Jan. 451 The settlers hastily fled with their families to a stockade in Stevensville. *a***1918** G. STUART *On Frontier* II. 69 The councils were held inside the stockade at Fort Sully.

attrib. and *comb.* **1835** HOFFMAN *Winter in West* II. 10 [Fort Crawford] was . . . a comfortable frame building, with a stockade fence around it, made with pickets. **1856** C. W. WEBBER *Tale of South Border* 39 (Bentley), Facing me, were three stockade-houses, or lesser 'ranchos.' **1885** *Rep. Indian Affairs* 178 Eleven buildings, stockade-built, round logs, and dirt roofs, were repaired.

+2. Such a palisade about a prison or a palisaded enclosure serving as a prison.

1865 KELLOGG *Rebel Prisons* 276 After death, the men were carried . . . inside the stockade. **1884** *Century Mag.* Feb. 584/1 [Convicts are] quartered in camps or herded in stockades convenient to their fields of labor. **1893** *Columbus Dispatch* 9 Jan., Two convicts . . . had carried out an eleven-foot ladder and a coil of hose, for the purpose of going over the stockade. **1917** [see BULL PEN 2].

attrib. **1865** S. ANDREWS *South since War* 307 The cook-house, . . . standing forty or fifty rods north of the northwestern corner of the stockade walls. **1865** *Atlantic Mo.* March 286/2 'Is it a pen?' . . . 'Yes, yours,' retorted one of the guard, with a grin,—'the Stockade Prison.'

+Stockade, *v. tr.* To protect with a stockade. {1811-} — **1677** *Doc. Hist. N.Y. State* I. 12 The Caiougos . . . intend next spring to build all their houses together and stockade them. **1755** Gist *Journals* 150 This Fort was composed of four Houses built by way of Bastions and the intermediate Space stockaded. **1847** Howe *Hist. Coll. Ohio* 377 They kept no sentry, and had neglected to stockade or set pickets around the blockhouse.

+Stockaded, *a.* Protected with a stockade. {1834-} — **1675** [see PALISADOED *a.*]. **1756** *Doc. Hist. N.Y. State* I. 478 At the Falls . . . a good Stockaded Fort is building, to defend that Pass. **1837** IRVING *Bonneville* II. 166 Fort Union, the distributing post of the American Fur Company, . . . was a stockaded fortress. **1857** *Atlantic Mo.* Nov. 94/2 The spot was the site of the old block house and stockaded fort.

+Stockade fort. A fort or fortified place having a stockade as part of its defenses. Now hist. — **1742** *Essex Inst. Coll.* XLV. 343 He was going to the Lake after his Powder-Horn and his gun, he had left at the Stockade Fort there. **1803** Lewis in *Jrnl. of L. & Ordway* 38 On the point formed by this creek and the river stands an old stoccade fort, now gone to decay. **1842** *Amer. Pioneer* I. 333 [They] began to build a kind of stockade fort with fence rails. **1892** M. A. JACKSON *Gen. Jackson* 3 For their protection the whites were compelled to build stockade forts. **1903** *N.Y. Tribune* 13 Sept., The colonel's daughter was born in a stockade fort.

*✱***Stockado.** +A stockade, or one of the timbers of which this is made. Obs. — **1675** *Conn. Rec.* II. 413 [The council advises Hartford and New Haven] to compleat and lyne their stockadoes and flanckers with a ditch. **1687** SEWALL *Diary* I. 194 Wednesday, Dorchester Company [comes] to shovel and carry stockados. **1724** in Temple & Sheldon *Hist. Northfield, Mass.* 200, I forgot to notice your suggestion about setting stockadoes around the Block-house. **1744** A. HAMILTON *Itin.* (1907) 87 [In Albany] they call them stoccadoes.

Stock board. {1850-} **+1.** A stock exchange. Also attrib. **+2.** A board of even width, as 8, 10, or 12 inches. — (1) **1865** *Harper's Mag.* Aug. 318/2 Three stock boards . . . were in full operation in San Francisco. **1869** J. H. BROWNE *Great Metropolis* 520 A charming Fifth avenue belle is soon to be led to the altar by a prominent member of the stock board. **1889** 'MARK TWAIN' *Conn. Yankee* 516 Sir Launcelot . . . was president of the stock-board. **1896** SHINN *Story of Mine* 189 The stock-board valuation put upon the two bonanza mines in that month was $160,000,000. (2) **1872** *Ill. Dept. Agric. Trans.* IX. 390 The roof is of stock boards, grooved on both edges.

Stock book. {1901-} +A book in which records are kept of transactions in stock or shares. — [**1835** COOPER *Monikins* ii, Love was a sentiment much too pure and elevated for one whose imagination dwelt habitually on the beauties of the stock-books.] **1860** HOLMES *E. Venner* ii, Some of the old families . . . [have] names written in all the stock-books of all the dividend-paying companies. **1887** *Courier-Journal* 6 May

3/1 They had been permitted to examine the stock books of the company.

+**Stockbridge.** [The name of a town in Massachusetts.] An Indian of a tribe of the Mahican (see quot. 1910); also, pl., the tribe. Also attrib. with *Indian.* — **1775** *Jrnls. Cont. Congress* II. 110 A number of Letters and speeches from the Chiefs of the Stockbridge Indians to the Congress . . . were laid before the Congress. **1838** VAN BUREN in *Pres. Mess. & P.* III. 429, I transmit for your consideration a communication from the Secretary of War, respecting a treaty before you with the Stockbridge and Munsee Indians. **1894** ROBLEY *Bourbon Co., Kansas* 7 These various tribes of New York Indians, consisting of the remnants of the Senecas, Onondagas, . . . Stockbridges, Munsees and Brothertowns, were called the 'Six Nations.' **1910** HODGE, etc. *Amer. Indians* II. 637 *Stockbridges*, a tribe of the Mahican confederacy, first known under the name Housatonic.

Stockbroker. One whose business is buying and selling securities. {1706-} — **1796** [see EXCHANGE BROKER]. **1854** [see MARK *n.*[1] 5]. **1900** *Congress. Rec.* 1 Feb. 1382/2 Every time the money market of New York is disturbed by the stock brokers and gamblers it is the duty of the Treasury of the United States to go to their relief.

+**Stock car.** A railway car for carrying live stock. Also *stock palace car.* — **1858** *Penn. R.R. Ann. Rep.* 14 The rolling stock [included] . . . 188 Eight-wheeled Stock Cars. **1871** DE VERE 356 It is to be hoped that the introduction of Stock Palace-Cars on some of the Northern roads will speedily lead to the adoption of more appropriate names [for passenger cars]. **1890** *Stock Grower & Farmer* 11 Jan. 5/2 Twenty years have elapsed since the first patent stock car was brought out. **1920** *3d Nat. Country Life Conf. Proc.* 12 They shot me across the country in a stock car.

Stock cattle. Cattle kept for breeding purposes. — **1857** BRAMAN *Texas* 70 The green was all wilted, . . . and the stock-cattle became reduced to old fog. **1880** *Cimarron News & Press* 19 Feb. 3/2 He has contracted for the delivery of 500 head of stock cattle from Andreas Sena. **1904** *Indian Laws & Tr.* III. 72 Two hundred and fifty thousand (250,000) dollars shall be expended in the purchase of stock cattle.

Stock company. {1827-}
1. A company of actors employed more or less permanently by the same management and usually having a central or home theater.
1839 *Chicago American* 30 Aug., As a stock company we consider it unsurpassed. **1855** WOOD *Recoll. Stage* 132 The receipts averaged $700 for eleven nights, with the regular stock company. **1895** G. KING *New Orleans* 270 The new enterprise offered all-year-round, legitimate drama, with a fine stock company of English players.
2. A joint-stock company or corporation. {1827-} Also attrib.
1877 *Vermont Bd. Agric. Rep.* IV. 54 All of these factories were built by stock companies. **1891** O'BEIRNE *Leaders Ind. Territory* 46/2 Then with J. J. McAllester, D. N. Robb, G. G. Randell and Will McBride, he formed a stock company known as the Choctaw Mercantile Co. **1905** *Outlook* 7 Oct. 471/1 Within the last two years there have been three exposures of gigantic stock-company frauds.

Stock dealer. +**1.** A person who deals in stocks or shares. {1902} **2.** A person who deals in live stock. {1885-} +**3.** (See quotation.) — **(1)** **1870** MEDBERY *Men Wall St.* 133 For stock-dealers are the keenest men in the civilized hemispheres. **(2)** **1877** BARTLETT 663 *Stock-Dealer*, a trader in farm stock; a cattle-dealer. **1892** *Scribner's Mag.* XI. 733/2 One of the first comers was an Illinois stock-dealer, . . . to whom is due the honor of originating the Kansas and Texas cattle-trails. **(3)** **1885** *Harper's Mag.* Jan. 280/1 The houses which sell these different component parts of a shoe are known as leather, stock, or finding dealers.

Stocker. {1641-} +A young beef steer or heifer to be used for breeding purposes until ready for butchering. — **1881** *Chicago Times* 1 June, Stockers and feeders were dull and weaker. **1890** *Stock Grower & Farmer* 22 Feb. 6/3 Your cattle men have depended either on making beef or selling stockers to the northern range. **1898** [see FEEDER 4 b].

Stock exchange. A building or part of a building where stocks and other securities are regularly bought and sold; an organized association of men engaged in buying and selling securities. {1773-} Also attrib. (See also NEW YORK STOCK EXCHANGE.) — **1856** *Porter's Spirit of Times* 13 Dec. 245/3 The failure of the great bear of the Stock Exchange has been the all-absorbing talk of the city men. **1882** *Nation* 20 July 41/1 Another section of the new law . . . was directed against a custom which all the banks having Stock Exchange accounts have safely practised for years. **1893** M. HOWE *Honor* 55 Mr. Archer . . . was driven to the stock exchange. **1908** HORNBLOW *Profligate* 77 Wall Street and the Stock Exchange . . . , the stronghold of frenzied financiers.

Stock farm. A farm devoted to stock raising. {1806-} — **1837** WETMORE *Gaz. Missouri* 54 On Lick branch there is a stock farm, on a large scale. **1848** *30th Congress 1 Sess.* Sen. Rep. No. 75, 29 Some five hundred head of beef cattle were taken from the government stock farm at Suscol to the Sacramento. **1892** *Vt. Agric. Rep.* XII. 138 Successful stock farms are rearing the finest bred horses the country has ever seen. **1912** NICHOLSON *Hoosier Chron.* 27, I own a stock farm near Lexington.

+**Stock gap.** =CATTLE GUARD 2. — **1865** in Fleming *Hist. Reconstruction* I. 19 Stock-gaps were out of order, and fences built across the track. **1887** *Courier-Journal* 21 Jan. 3/2 Wm. Lacy . . . lost his way and let his horse fall into a stock gap.

+**Stock-grower.** One who raises stock. — **1837** PECK *New Guide* 114 Some stock growers have monopolized the smaller farms till they are surrounded with several thousand acres. **1863** *Rio Abajo Press* 27 Jan. 2/1 This will be of great benefit . . . indirectly to grain and stock grower. **1884** *Rep. Comm. Agric.* 6 This Bureau has been directed . . . to collect such information as is valuable to the stock-grower.

Stockholder.
1. One who holds stock or shares in a stock company. {1753-}
1791 *Ann. 1st Congress* 1913 Gentlemen had been pleased to consider the proposed terms as giving an undue advantage to the stockholders. **1817** *Ann. 14th Congress* 2 Sess. 431 This penalty was no hold on the stockholders. **1888** *Economist* 20 Oct. 4/3 The stockholders are liable to the amount of their stock and 100 per cent more. **1913** LA FOLLETTE *Autobiog.* 418 Any federal judge should be disqualified from hearing . . . any case . . . against any road in which he was a stockholder.
2. The owner of cattle or live stock. {1819-, in Australia}
1796 HAWKINS *Letters* 31 At this season all the stockholders make a gathering. **1836** EDWARD *Hist. Texas* 87 Some stockholders insist that they would rather have it so.

Stockily, adv. With *built*: Sturdily or heavily built; thickset. — **1892** *Harper's Mag.* March 530/1 A pair of stockily built horses [were] . . . enjoying the river view over a trough of feed. **1898** *Ib.* April 710/1 General Grant [was] . . . not overweighted with flesh, but, nevertheless, stockily and sturdily built.

Stockinet. An elastic knitted fabric used chiefly for making underwear. {1824-} Also attrib. — **1784** *Mass. Centinel* 26 June 3/3 For Sale, a Variety of Goods, by wholesale, amongst which are . . . Herring Bone, Cotton Ribb, Stockinets [etc.]. **1813** *Ann. 13th Congress* 1 Sess. 39 Richard Ward . . . hath obtained . . . a machine for weaving stockings and stockinetts of all descriptions. **1890** (Advt., Ann Arbor, Mich., 1 March) One gross Seamless Stockinet Dress Shields to go at 10 cents a pair.

* **Stocking.** A close-fitting covering for the foot and leg.
1639 *Md. Archives* IV. 77 Old milld stockings. **1705** *Boston News-Letter* 8 Oct. 2/2 He has on . . . Russet coloured Stockings, and old Shoes. **1830** PICKERING *Inquiries Emigrant* 72 Stockings are hardly ever worn by the settlers in the woods in summer. **1887** PERRY *Flock of Girls* 34 The stockings were hung here and there upon little hooks. **1922** TARKINGTON *Gentle Julia* 2 Mrs. Atwater . . . let the stocking collapse flaccidly into the work-basket.
attrib. and *comb.* **1788** *Mass. Spy* 10 April 2/3 Our stocking weavers in Mulberryward and Germantown. **1812** MELISH *Travels* II. 55 Professions exercised in Pittsburg: . . . stocking-makers, taylors, printers, book-binders. **1883** RITTENHOUSE *Maud* 265 Did you know it by the muss it was in, and the stocking-bag on the floor?

Stocking basket. A basket in which a housewife keeps stockings to be mended. — **1868** A. D. WHITNEY *P. Strong* 150 'That's off my mind!' said mother, . . . turning the stocking-basket bottom up. **1878** STOWE *Poganuc People* 112 He had been known to upset all Mrs. Cushing's nicely arranged yarn-baskets and stocking-baskets. **1890** [see FEETING 2].

Stocking-weaving. The weaving of stockings. — **1723** *Amer. Wkly. Mercury* 10 Dec. 2/2 Mathew Burne of Chester County served John Camm two years . . . at Stocking weaving and other work. **1780** *N.J. Archives* 2 Ser. IV. 261 A sober man, understanding stocking weaving, will meet with great encouragement by applying to the Printer. **1818** DARBY *Emigrant's Guide* 259 Pottery is carried on in Birmingham. . . . [Also] silver plating, stocking weaving.

Stockjobber. a. A member of a stock exchange who deals in stocks on his own account. {1626-} +**b.** A stockbroker who purchases and sells stocks or shares for others. — **1793** FRENEAU *Poems* (1795) 434 Stock-jobbers fainted while they read. **1833** *Niles' Reg.* XLIV. 370/1 The 'black-leg,' in the gambling houses . . . more fairly takes the chances of the play, than the stock-jobber on 'change. **1887** *Courier-Journal* 19 Jan. 1/7 A man who said that he . . . was inspired by any stock-jobber, he could not properly reply to. **1911** HARRISON *Queed* 107 If a man became the greatest stock-jobber in the world, who would remember him after he was gone?

* **Stock-keeper.** +One who has charge of the live stock on a farm, ranch, or change station on a stagecoach line. — **1786** WASHINGTON *Diaries* III. 16 Frank, Stock keeper. **1867** DIXON *New America* I. 39 'The road is a little rough,' says one of the stock-keepers as we roll from his station into the black midnight.

Stock list. A list published by a stock exchange or in a newspaper giving pertinent information about stocks or shares. — **1850** *Harper's Mag.* Oct. 671/2 She will annoy you by looking over the stocklist at breakfast time. **1882** 'M. HARLAND' *Eve's Daughters* 405 [He] wants to glance at the telegraphic column, or the stock-list. **1883** [see LETTER BOOK].

* **Stock lock.** A lock in a wooden case suitable for use on an outer door, being operated from within by a bolt and from without by a key. *Obs.* — **1642** *Md. Archives* IV. 95, 2. stocklocks & 5 l of lead. **1718** *N.H. Hist. Soc. Coll.* IX. 422 Shipped . . . two Stock Locks. **1780** in Summers *Ann. S.W.Va.* 328 The door is to be . . . furnished with a good and sufficient stock lock.

Stockman. {1806-} A man who raises live stock. {1856-} Also attrib. — **1866** *Rep. Indian Affairs* 92 They will be occupied by stock men, hunters, and squaw men. **1881** HAYES *New Colorado* 146 The stockman . . . is pushing his ranches and flocks and herds out along the Arkansas. **1899** *Everybody's Mag.* I. 32/2 He looked like my old friend, 'Mormon

Joe,' only for the whiskers and the stockman clothes. **1913** BARNES *Western Grazing Grounds* 25 The stockmen of the West were a prodigal as well as a restless lot.

+**Stock-minder.** One who has charge of live stock on a farm or the open range. — **1856** *Fla. Plantation Rec.* 162, I Doant think that the Stock minder has don his duty. **1866** W. REID *After the War* 483 A negro ..., enjoying the title and dignity of stock-minder, was charged with the duty of ... herding it [the stock] on this open common. **1905** PRINGLE *Rice Planter* 239 The middle of the tract is a little cabin where my father's stock-minder used to live.

+**Stock note.** A note secured by stocks or bonds. — **1818** *Niles' Reg.* XIV. 3/1 The regular and irregular accommodation of the rest amounts to not less than Six Millions of Dollars; ... including certain things called stock notes. **1831** BENTON *30 Years' View* I. 194/2 [The U.S.] gave her stock note, bearing an interest of five per cent. per annum. **1840** BANCROFT *Hist. U.S.* III. 232 Philip V. of Spain took one quarter of the common stock, agreeing to pay for it by a stock-note.

Stock-owner. One who owns live stock; a stock-raiser. {1865-} **1817** S. BROWN *Western Gazetteer* 16 The borders of the Conecah are fast settling, especially by the poorer class of people, and stock owners. **1874** *Rep. Comm. Agric. 1873* 30 The losses in decrease in flesh and reduced vitality by neglect of stock-owners ... amount to many millions of dollars annually. **1884** W. SHEPHERD *Prairie Exper.* 125 If stock-owners are in power, they say to the small rancher, 'Fence your fields.'

+**Stock pea.** ?A variety of pea raised for feeding stock. — **1869** *Rep. Comm. Agric. 1868* 221 The lot intended for peanuts, say next year, has been seeded in stock peas this year. **1901** H. ROBERTSON *Inlander* 120 The fields ... were now luxuriant in stock-peas.

+**Stock-raiser.** One whose occupation is raising live stock. — **1836** EDWARD *Hist. Texas* 143 Should they also be *stock raisers*, grazing land shall be added to complete a *sitio*. **1891** O'BEIRNE *Leaders Ind. Territory* 162/1 He has been a farmer and stock-raiser since living in the Choctaw Nation. **1913** BARNES *Western Grazing Grounds* 33 In the phraseology of the western stock-raiser, there are two distinct ranges.

+**Stock-raising.**

1. The raising of live stock.

1800 HAWKINS *Sk. Creek County* 30 They have begun to settle out in villages for the conveniency of stock raising. **1847** *Santa Fe Republican* 10 Sept. 2/2 New Mexico ... possesses some great advantages from ... its adaption to stock and wool raising. **1900** *Congress. Rec.* 10 Jan. 730/1 An urgent necessity for the enlargement of the Navajo Indian Reservation ... to enable these Indians to support themselves by stock raising.

2. Attrib. with *business, country, county,* etc.

1847 HOWE *Hist. Coll. Ohio* 333 [Madison] is principally a stock-raising county. **1871** *Republican Rev.* 2 Sept. 1/3 The Indian Territory ... is one of the finest farming and stock-raising countries in North America. **1874** ALDRICH *P. Palfrey* xiii, I went into the stock-raising business with another man. **1883** *Gringo & Greaser* 1 Dec. 1/1 As a stock raising and farming region this portion of New Mexico is unexcelled in natural advantages. **1884** *N. Mex. Terr. Rep.* 17 A comprehensive report [shall] be made of the progress in mining, agriculture and stock-raising industries of the Territory.

+**Stock ranch.** A ranch devoted to stock-raising. — **1871** *Old & New* June 640/1 The Hacienda de Encarnacion ... was an 'estancia,' or stock-ranch. **1878** BEADLE *Western Wilds* 110 Stock-ranches ... appear devoid of life at this season. **1892** [see HUNTING GROUND].

+**Stock rancher.** =STOCK-RAISER. — **1867** *Harper's Mag.* June 20/1 Nestled in many valleys could be seen the houses of stock-ranchers.

+**Stock range.** A range suitable for live stock. — **1819** E. DANA *Geogr. Sk.* 190 These swamps afford the finest stock range imaginable, particularly for hogs. **1857** BRAMAN *Texas* 26 East of this stream ... is prairie, good soil, and fine stock range. **1896** SHINN *Story of Mine* 41 He might possibly have posted a mere notice on the 'stock range.' **1913** BARNES *Western Grazing Grounds* 382 Nester, a small farmer generally located within the limits of some stock range.

+**Stock ticker.** A telegraphic device which automatically prints stock quotations and other market news on a narrow strip of paper. {1899} **1886** *Boston Jrnl.* 17 July 2/3 The Stock Ticker. ... The exclusive right of the 'ticker' service in the [N.Y.] Stock Exchange ... has been a constant source of contention. **1912** DREISER *Financier* 61 There was as yet no stock-ticker and no telephone.

+**Stock train.** A train carrying live stock. (Cf. CATTLE TRAIN.) — **1859** BARTLETT 451 *Stock-train,* a train of railroad cars loaded with cattle. **1868** *Ill. Agric. Soc. Trans.* VII. 461 Express stock trains are provided, so as to avoid the necessity of change of cars. **1898** *McClure's Mag.* X. 403 You're wanted for a stock train.

+**Stock water.** Water for live stock. — **1842** *Cultivator* X. 37 Stock water is obtained in creeks, ponds and springs. **1869** *Rep. Comm. Agric. 1868* 259 There are many ditches ... which might be rendered more valuable could they be made to hold stock-water during a greater portion of the warmest season of the year. **1894** ROBLEY *Bourbon Co., Kansas* 159 Stock water was not so scarce. **1923** *Kansas City Star* 23 April Out in western Kansas ... the farmers depend upon deep wells for their stock water.

+**Stock-watering.** Increasing the number of stocks or shares in an enterprise without adding to its assets or resources. — **1870** MEDBERY *Men Wall St.* 158 Such occasional diversions as corners, money lock-ups, wholesale stock-watering, ... are the indications of forces with large reserves of strength. **1882** WELLS *Practical Economics* 69 All the injury

that has resulted from 'stock-watering' ... is relatively but as the 'small dust upon the balance.' **1913** LA FOLLETTE *Autobiog.* 459 It was inevitable that the years of stock-watering and promotion ... should bring ... financial distress and reaction.

Stockyard. {1802-} *pl.* +An extensive enclosed area having pens and shelters for cattle, hogs, etc., awaiting slaughter. Also attrib. — **1867** *Atlantic Mo.* March 332/2 Out on the flat prairie ... may be seen the famous 'Stock Yards.' **1879** *Diseases of Swine* 164 The stock-yards in Chicago are full of diseased animals. **1890** *Stock Grower & Farmer* 4 Jan. 4/2 W. H. Monroe ... has stock yards at Albany and big slaughter houses at Brighton, Mass. **1924** CROY *R.F.D. No. 3* 72 [She] carefully pulled out the stockyards paper.

+**Stogy.** Also **stoga, stogie.** [Cone*stoga*, Pa.]

1. A heavy, rough shoe or boot. Also attrib.

1847 PALMER *Rocky Mts.* (1904) 217, I paid for a pair of stoga shoes. **1866** 'F. KIRKLAND' *Bk. Anecdotes* 177/2 He hammered away at an immense 'stoga.' **1890** HOWELLS *Boy's Town* 76 Most of the fellows had stoga boots, as heavy as iron and as hard. **1894** CLARK *On Cloud Mt.* 135 I bet a hen ye fergot ... my winter stogies.

2. An inexpensive cigar, usually long and slender.

1893 *Dialect Notes* I. 237 *Stogies,* ... cheap cigars. **1906** 'O. HENRY' *Heart of West* 83, I have a pal ... that's been subsisting for years on cereals and short stogies. **1923** WATTS *L. Nichols* 25 The head of the establishment bestowed on him ... the latter-day equivalent of the parsley-wreath, a powerful Wheeler stogie.

+**Stomach tooth.** (See quot. 1889.) — **1875** R. H. DAVIS *Silhouettes* 240 He has one stomach-tooth almost through. **1880** *Harper's Mag.* Sept. 582/1 Cuttin' of his stomach teeth was the end o' him. **1889** BILLINGS *Nat. Medical Dict.* II. 594 *Stomach tooth,* canine tooth of lower jaw of first dentition, so called because of gastric disturbance frequently accompanying its eruption.

* **Stone.** *attrib.* (passing into *adj.*) and *comb.*

1. Designating implements wholly or chiefly of stone used by American Indians in early times. {a1728-, in general use}

1817 S. BROWN *Western Gazetteer* 57 We discovered ... several stone axes ... which unquestionably served as helves. **1821** NUTTALL *Travels Arkansa* 39 In digging [he] had discovered ... several stone pipes, and fragments of earthen ware. **1858** THOREAU *Maine Woods* 153, I picked up ... one broken stone chisel. **1867** H. LATHAM *Black & White* 82 Stone implements and stone mortars ... are still used by the Digger Indians to pound their roots in. **1871** *Republican Rev.* 18 March 1/3 It was pronounced to be a 'stone crow-bar,' formerly used by the old Aztec inhabitants of this country.

* **2.** In the specific names of plants.

1850 S. F. COOPER *Rural Hours* 125 The downy 'rabbit-foot,' or 'stone-clover,' the common red variety ... [are] introduced. **1797** IMLAY *Western Territory* (ed. 3) 270 The wild laurel ... grows in the woods without any cultivation: the same may be said of the stone laurel. **1855** C. A. HARRIS *Dict. Med. Term.* 192/2 *Cunila Mariana,* dittany; mountain dittany; stone-mint; a plant possessing stimulant, carminative, and aromatic properties. **1840** DEWEY *Mass. Flowering Plants* 60 *Rubus saxatilis.* Stone Raspberry. **1848** BARTLETT 335 Stone-Root, (*Collinconia* [ed. 1859; *Collinsonia*] *Canadensis*) a plant used in medicine.

3. In the specific names of birds.

See also STONE CURLEW, STONE SNIPE.

1917 *Birds of Amer.* I. 242 Greater Yellow-Legs. *Totanus melanoleucus.* ... [Also called] Stone-bird. *Ib.* 268 Ruddy turnstone. *Arenaria interpres morinella.* [Also called] Stone-pecker.

4. In the specific names of fishes.

See also STONE-ROLLER, STONE-TOTER.

1852 *Mich. Agric. Soc. Trans.* III. 228 Stone Carrier. These are knowing little fish. **1884** GOODE, etc. *Fisheries* I. 628 The Stone Cat.—*Noturus flavus.* This species reaches a length of about a foot. **1871** *Amer. Naturalist* IV. 719 The 'stone-cat-fish' were much more active, and shy. **1882** Stone lugger [see STONE-ROLLER 1 and 2]. **1883** *Nat. Museum Bul.* No. 27, 493 *Acipenser rubicundus.* ... Stone Sturgeon; Rock Sturgeon; Red Sturgeon. Mississippi Valley; Great Lakes, and northward.

5. In special combinations.

Stone cloth, cloth made wholly or chiefly of asbestos; *s. dog,* =CLAY DOG; *s. jacket,* a prison (slang); *s. paint,* paint the pigment of which occurs in a hard, stony form; *s. pasture,* stony ground used as pasture; *s. porcelain,* porcelain in the manufacture of which partially decomposed stone or granite is used; *s. road,* a road paved with stones; *s. salt,* rock salt; *s. scow,* a scow for transporting stones; *s. sloop,* a sloop for transporting stones; *s. wedge,* a wedge for splitting stones.

1829 *Va. Lit. Museum* 11 It is not ... our wish to interfere with the Virtuoso's taste for neck handkerchiefs and shirts of *stone cloth.* **1892** *N.J. State Geologist Rep.* 138 The low plain [south of Morristown is] ... equally rich in concretions, which are locally known as 'clay-stones,' 'clay-dogs,' 'stone-dogs,' etc. **1799** *Aurora* (Phila.) 21 June (Th.), Paragraphs an hundred times more obnoxious than those for which Abijah Adams was dressed in a stone jacket. **1842** *Nat. Hist. N.Y., Geology* II. 420 *Ochres and Stone paints.* Among the specular oxides, abundance of this material exists. **1869** STOWE *Oldtown Folks* 125, [I've] heerd that 'ere boy's screeches clear from the stun pastur'. **1881** *Harper's Mag.* Feb. 368/1 In stone porcelains America leads the world. **1850** *Western Journal*

IV. 75 In comparing the merits of stone and plank roads, the Judge says [etc.]. **1651** *Conn. Rec.* I. 223 If the said John Wenthrop Esqr shall discouer . . . mynes of . . . black lead, allom, stone salt, salt springs, or any other the lyke. **1737** J. HEMPSTEAD *Diary* 314, I was at home al day splitting & hewing peices for a Stone Scow. **1886** *Leslie's Mo.* Feb. 223/1 The harbor is . . . just large enough to store away three or four stone-sloops. **1772** *Md. Hist. Mag.* XIV 287 Yr. stone Wedges are not done.

+**Stone bee.** A gathering of neighbors for removing stones from a piece of land. *Obs.* — **1829** COOPER *Wish-ton-Wish* xix, The neighbors will not be backward at the stonebee. **1856** GOODRICH *Recoll.* I. 75 At Ridgefield we used to have 'stone bees,' when all the men of a village or hamlet came together with their draft cattle.

*✱**Stone boat.** +A flat-bottomed sled for transporting stones or other heavy objects for short distances. — **1855** WILLIS *Convalescent* 75 A *stone-boat* would run glibly over such shallow snow! **1862** *Ill. Agric. Soc. Trans.* V. 207 The winter apples . . . are drawn to the house on a *stoneboat*. **1898** WESTCOTT *D. Harum* 270 After this you'd better take your airin's on a stun-boat.

Stone-breaker. {1843-} +A machine for breaking or crushing stone. — **1869** *Rep. Comm. Agric.* 1868 355 The cost . . . [has been] reduced by the introduction of the 'Blake Stone-Breaker.' **1876** INGRAM *Centennial Exp.* 393 These rollers . . . are adapted for driving stone-breakers or other fixed machinery.

+**Stone bruise.** A painful bruise, usually on the foot, caused by a stone or other rounded object. Also *stone-bruised* a. — **1805** LEWIS in *L. & Clark Exped.* II. (1904) 290 We have a lame crew just now, . . . one with a bad stone bruise. **1898** *McClure's Mag.* X. 210 The water won't cure a stone-bruise. **1904** 'O. HENRY' *Roads of Destiny* 354 Five of my best staff-officers fell, suffering extremely with stone-bruised heels.

*✱**Stone coal.** A hard variety of mineral coal, as anthracite. {1708-} — **1773** in *Cincinnati Misc.* I. 254/1 We have a very great abundance of stone coal. **1804** CLARK in *Lewis & Clark Exped.* I. (1904) 58 At 3 Miles passed a Coal-Mine, or Bank of stone Coal. **1866** *Rep. Indian Affairs* 127 There are good indications of stone-coal and iron. **1882** *Econ. Geol. Illinois* II. 121 The stone coal of the lower Coal Measures extends under her surface.

Stone crab. {1713-} +A large edible crab (*Menippe mercenaria*) found along the southern coast of the United States. — **1709** LAWSON *Carolina* 161 The large Crabs, which we call Stone-Crabs, . . . are plentifully met withal. **1863** *Harper's Mag.* Aug. 356/2 People went to Beaufort . . . to eat stone-crabs and fish. **1884** GOODE, etc. *Fisheries* I. 773 The Stone Crabs generally live more or less buried beneath the bottom.

Stone cricket. (See quot. 1891.) — **1891** *Cent.* 5963/2 *Stone-cricket*, one of the wingless forms of the orthopterous family Locustidæ, living under or among stones and in dark places. . . . The commonest American stone-crickets belong to the genus *Ceuthophilus*. **1908** KELLOGG *Amer. Insects* 155 The genus *Ceuthophilus* . . . includes the various species of stone, or camel, crickets found all over the country.

Stone curlew. {1678-} +a. *local.* The willet, *Catoptrophorus semipalmatus.* +b. (See quotation.) — (a) **1835** AUDUBON *Ornith. Biog.* III. 510 The Semipalmated Snipe is known . . . from the Carolinas Southward . . . [as the] 'Stone Curlew.' **1888** TRUMBULL *Names of Birds* 165. **1917** *Birds of Amer.* I. 246 Willet. . . . Other Names. . . . Spanish Plover; Stone Curlew; Duck Snipe. (b) *Ib.* I. 177 The young birds [of the white ibis] before they assume the adult plumage are called 'Stone Curlews' by the fishermen.

*✱**Stonecutter.** A workman who carves or shapes stone for building or other purposes.

1694 *Boston Rec.* 81 William Mumford, stone cutter, became surety to the town, for Thomas Cumins. **1722** *New-Eng. Courant* 3 Sept. 2/2 One Gilcreese a Stone-Cutter, fell out of a Canoo in the Mill-Creek. **1794** BENTLEY *Diary* II. 79 The Committee gave an invitation to Levi Maxey, Stone Cutter, to assist in our Music. **1817** *Niles' Reg.* XII. 175/2 A small supply [of marble] has been received at Baltimore, by one of our stonecutters. **1902** HARBEN *A. Daniel* 95 Jeff Dukes . . . came directly towards them from a stone-cutter's shop near by.

+**Stone drag.** A broad plank or flat sled used in hauling stones or other heavy objects. — **1867** RICHARDSON *Beyond Miss.* 131 One family even rode triumphantly on a stone drag—a broad plank dragged over the ground by two horses. **1902** MCFAUL *Ike Glidden* 26 They attached him to a stone-drag.

Stone fence.

1. A fence made of stones. {1712- (Mortimer *Art Husb.* II. 2)}

1682 *Derby Rec.* 305 [Mr. Bowers] is to hav that part of ye fenc . . . next his hous namely ye stone fenc. **1707** *Boston News-Letter* 24 March 2/2 The Lynn-Spring Farme . . . contains 20 Acres inclosed with a Stone Fence. **1819** IRVING *Sketch Book* I. 63 [He] was a foremost man at all country frolics for husking Indian corn, or building stone fences. **1905** VALENTINE *H. Sandwith* 14 The stone-fence proved a handicap in the race.

+**2.** A mixed alcoholic drink, esp. whisky and cider. *slang.*

1843 *Ainsworth's Mag.* IV. 239 Anything in the shape of stone-fence will suit *my* fancy. **1873** BEADLE *Undevel. West* 227 In the towns the standard drink is whisky—'stone fence,' 'forty-rod,' and 'tarantula-juice.' **1910** [see HARD CIDER 1].

*✱**Stone house.** A house built of stone. Also attrib. — **1651** *Portsmouth Rec.* 58 There shalbe a stone house built for the more comfortable being of ould John Mott in the winter. **1749** HEMPSTEAD *Diary* 527 [There

is] a good Stone house at the ferry. **1817** U. BROWN *Journal* II. 371 [Shepherdstown] affords Many good Brick houses & some good Stone houses. a**1847** in Howe *Hist. Coll. Ohio* 357 John Knoop . . . came down the Ohio to Cincinnati, and cropped the first season on Zeigler's stone house farm.

+**Stoneite.** A follower of Barton Warren Stone (1772-1844), an evangelist who seceded (1803) from the Presbyterian church in the Kentucky revival and subsequently organized churches known simply as 'Christian.' (Cf. NEW LIGHT 1 b.) — **1824** R. H. BISHOP *Hist. Church Ky.* 130 The people of whom we propose to give a short sketch . . . have usually been called 'New Lights, or Stoneites.' **1847, 1856** [see MARSHALLITE].

Stonemason. One who shapes and lays stones in building. {1809-} — **1758** *Lett. to Washington* II. 269 Our Stone Masons has been Sick, . . . and our Stone Work is much Behind hand. **1809** CUMING *Western Tour* 223 Pittsburgh [has] . . . three stone masons; two book-stores. **1878** in Summers *Ann. S.W. Va.* 1558 We have . . . any number of carpenters, painters, shoemakers, tailors, brick and stone masons. **1907** *St. Nicholas* Oct. 1113/1 The plan generally followed is to keep the stone-masons, housesmiths, and plumbers one floor behind the iron-workers.

+**Stone mill. 1.** A mill in which grain is ground on burrstones instead of steel rollers. **2.** (See quotation.) — (1) **1838** FLAGG *Far West* I. 84 My attention was arrested by that series of substantial stone mills situated upon the shore immediately above. **1850** *Indiana Mag. Hist.* XII. 229 The first sermon [was delivered] . . . on the river beach, a little above the stone mill. **1898** YOUNG *Jessamine Co., Ky.* 188 There is an old stone-mill at Keene, which was built in 1794. (2) **1876** KNIGHT 2398/2 *Stone-mill*, a machine for breaking or crushing stone. . . . A machine for facing stone.

Stone pick. A pick made of, or for use on, stone. — **1854** *Penna. Agric. Rep.* 425 Silver Medal for best stone, clay and coal picks. **1883** ZEIGLER & GROSSCUP *Alleghanies* 16 The marks of stone picks may still be seen upon the soft feldspar.

Stone pile. A heap of stones or rocks. — c**1870** CHIPMAN *Notes on Bartlett* 452 *Stone-pile*, a heap of stones. **1873** *Newton Kansan* 23 Jan. 3/4 Glass house people should use more caution how they dispose of their stone piles. **1895** *Harper's Mag.* April 713/2 A stone-pile near at hand where they filled their pockets full of rocks.

Stone quarry. A quarry from which building stones are secured. {1601-} — **1823** JAMES *Exped.* I. 167 The stone quarry . . . was situate . . . an hundred yards below our cantonment. **1881** STODDARD *E. Hardery* 86 There had been a stone quarry started. **1903** *Chicago Chronicle* 11 April 1/1 Whether the tragedy at Gehre's stone quarry on March 10 . . . was due to accident or design was not proved.

Stone-quarrying. The quarrying of stone; a gathering of neighbors for such work. Also attrib. — **1859** A. CARY *County Life* 7 [The half holiday] was less welcome than as if it had brought a log-rolling, brush-burning, or stone quarrying with it. **1872** BRACE *Dangerous Classes N.Y.* 153 The few men there worked hard at stone-quarrying. **1893** *Harper's Mag.* May 947/2 The place supports three banks . . . a stone-quarrying company, and the inevitable brewery.

Stone-roller. +1. =HOG MOLLY 1. +2. (See quotations.) — (1) **1882** *Nat. Museum Bul.* No. 16, 130 *Catostomus nigricans*, Stone Roller, Hammer-head; Stone lugger. **1903** T. H. BEAN *Fishes N.Y.* 103 The stone roller has a peculiar physiognomy. (2) **1882** *Nat. Museum Bul.* No. 16, 149 *Campostoma anomalum*, Stone-roller; Stone-lugger. **1896** JORDAN & EVERMANN *Check-List Fishes* 243 *Campostoma*. . . . Stone-rollers. . . . *Campostoma anomalum*. . . . Stone-roller. . . . Central New York to Tennessee, Wyoming, and Texas.

Stone snipe. {1785-} +A long-legged American bird of the genus *Totanus*. Also with specifying adjective. — **1858** BAIRD *Birds Pacific R.R.* 731 Tell Tale; Stone Snipe. . . . A large and handsome species, abundant throughout the United States. **1872** COUES *Key to Birds* 258. **1917** *Birds of Amer.* I. 242 Greater Yellow-Legs. *Totanus melanoleucus.* . . . [Also called] Stone-bird; Stone Snipe; Yelper. *Ib.* 244 Yellow-Legs. *Totanus flavipes.* . . . [Also called] Little Stone-bird; Little Stone Snipe.

+**Stone-toter. a.** =STONE-ROLLER 1. **b.** An American cyprinoid river fish, *Exoglossum maxillingua.* **c.** The stone-lugger, *Campostoma anomalum.* — **1817** PAULDING *Lett. from South* II. 4 The most singular fish . . . is called the *stone-toter*, whose brow is surmounted with several little sharp horns, by the aid of which he *totes* small flat stones . . . in order to make a snug little circular inclosure for his lady. **1880** [see CUTLIPS a]. **1883** *Harper's Mag.* Dec. 103/2 The fishes known as stone-toters, or suckers, are so named from their habit of piling up pebbles into rude mounds, in which their eggs are concealed. **1903** T. H. BEAN *Fishes N.Y.* 104, 113.

*✱**Stone wall.**

*✱**1.** A wall, usually serving as a fence, made of stones.

1651 *Portsmouth Rec.* 54 The aforesayed Earl shall make fforty Rod of stone wall. **1671** *Portsmouth Rec.* 160 For Stone wall they Shall be fower foot and Six inchis high. **1754** HEMPSTEAD *Diary* 626 Mr. Swan . . . hath agreed with me to make Stonewall for 20s a Rod. **1845** *Knickerb.* XXVI. 509 The boundary of the road-side was formed commonly by a stone-wall. **1919** in *Maine My State* 287 They took the long slide and dashed against the stone wall.

+**2.** A title or nickname for General Thomas Jonathan Jackson (1824-63) of the Confederate army.

1862 Moore *Rebellion Rec.* V. II. 472 What a strange strength and confidence we all felt in the presence of the man, 'Stonewall' Jackson. **1866** C. H. SMITH *Bill Arp* 144 Wish old Stonewall had cotched these Harpers at their ferry. **1890** [see next].

+**Stonewall Brigade.** The brigade or troops commanded by Stonewall Jackson. — **1890** HENTY *With Lee in Va.* 107 Bee . . . shouted, 'Look, there is Jackson standing like a stone wall.' . . . Henceforth the brigade was known as the Stonewall Brigade, and their general by the nickname of Stonewall Jackson. **1892** [see PET LAMB 2].

+**Stonewall Guard.** A secret organization formed in the South after the Civil War to assist in maintaining white supremacy. *Obs.* — **1880** *46th Congress 2 Sess.* Sen. Rep. No. 693 p. xvii, The distrust of Democracy . . . was inspired during the days, when the 'Kuklux,' the 'White Brotherhood,' the 'Universal Empire,' and the 'Stonewall Guard' spread terror and desolation over the State. *Ib.* 400 The White Brotherhood, the Invisible Empire, and the Stonewall Guard.

Stoneware. A coarse potter's ware made of very siliceous clay or of a mixture of clay and flint or sand. {1683–} Also attrib. — **1759** *Newport Mercury* 8 May 3/2 To be Sold by Thomas Rodman, . . . House Lanthorns, Stone Ware, and White Stone Buttons. **1827** DRAKE & MANSFIELD *Cincinnati* 66 No returns have been received [from] . . . 2 Crockery and Stone ware Factories. **1891** *Scribner's Mag.* X. 348 Gentle Agnes Surriage may once have held this old stone-ware pitcher in her fair hand.

* **Stool,** *n.*

* **1.** A single seat without a back or arms, usually having three or four legs.
1639 *Conn. Rec.* I. 444 The goods and Cattle of John Brundish: . . . cushens, stooles & chaires. **1706** *N.H. Probate Rec.* I. 555 My Said wife [shall] have the one halfe of all my . . . beds, Wollen, Linnen, Chairs, Stools. **1841** COOPER *Deerslayer* xxv, Following the hunter into the cabin, she took a seat on a stool. **1891** WILKINS *New Eng. Nun* 82 She sat on a stool on the other side of the stove. **1922** TARKINGTON *Gentle Julia* 362 [She] sat upon a stool before the crackling fire.

2. The sill of a window. {1663–; now *obs.*}
1696 *Boston Rec.* 136 [He shall] Frame a Stoole and Cap for a window into said Doore case. **1897** F. C. MOORE *How to Build a Home* 100 The window trim shall be pilaster finish, with . . . 5½ inch rebated stool with apron.

+**3.** A bird, either real or artificial, used as a decoy. Also attrib.
1811 WILSON *Ornithology* IV. 84 Two or three live Crows being previously procured as decoys, or as they are called, *Stool-crows.* **1825** *Huntington Rec.* III. 522 No person [shall] be permitted to gun with macheanes or stools in sd Town. *a*1841 HAWES *Sporting Scenes* I. 199 Your man disposes the stool-birds to your leeward, and sails away to stir up flocks miles off. **1874** LONG *Wild-Fowl* 199 [They] decoy to mallard stools.

+**4.** (See quot. 1881.)
1881 INGERSOLL *Oyster-Industry* 249 *Stools,* material spread on the bottom for oyster spawn to cling to. **1883** *Nat. Museum Bul.* No. 27, 220 All shells, or other matters suitable for 'stools' or 'cultch,' are put on the shell-heaps on shore for subsequent use.

* **Stool,** *v.*

1. *intr.* Of wheat: To throw out lateral roots. {1790–}
1770 *Md. Hist. Mag.* XII. 360 Our Wheat . . . cannot stool or Branch. **1786** WASHINGTON *Diaries* III. 13 The last sowed wheat . . . was stooling very prettily. **1868** *Iowa State Agric. Soc. Rep.* 1867 433 The dry weather immediately following prevented its stooling out. **1889** *Lisbon Star* 8 Feb. 3/1 The stalks . . . are stooling out.

+**2.** *tr.* and *intr.* To entice (wild fowl) by means of a stool or decoy; of a bird, to come to a decoy.
*a*1841 HAWES *Sporting Scenes* I. 55, I'll tell you all about that . . . the next time we're stooling snipe together. **1874** LONG *Wild-Fowl* 209 Widgeon . . . stool well to almost any decoys.

+**Stool pigeon.**

1. A pigeon fastened to a stool or perch to serve as a lure for others.
1836 IRVING *Astoria* I. 137 One man . . . was used like a 'stool pigeon,' to decoy the others. **1871** DE VERE 211 The *Stool-Pigeon* . . . [literally] means the pigeon, with its eyes stitched up, fastened on a stool, which can be moved up and down by the hidden fowler.

2. A person serving as a decoy; now usually a police informer. *colloq.* {= E. 'nark'}
1850 *Congress. Globe* 18 July 1403/1 Sheltering this aggression, on the part of the United States, behind 'poor New Mexico,' who is only a stool-pigeon. **1864** R. B. KIMBALL *Was He Successful?* 133 (Th. S.), As to Onis and Tweed, auctioneers, they . . . lived by acting as stool-pigeons and cheating generally. **1901** FLYNT *World of Graft* 125 In New York City he [one who informs] is also called a Stool-pigeon. The 'profession' generally speak of him as a Squealer. **1910** WALCOTT *Open Door* 134 Rafferty . . . assured the chief that he would pass word to certain stool-pigeons to keep their eyes and ears open for trace of the missing canvas.

+**Stool-pigeoning.** (See quotation.) — *a*1848 *N.Y. Courier & Enquirer* (B.), 'Stool-pigeoning' is for an officer to arrest a party of doubtful or perhaps decidedly bad reputation on suspicion, and making him or her give up money or valuables to obtain liberty, when the officer would set the party free, and nothing would be heard by the public or any one else of the arrest, or anything else connected with it.

+**Stoop.** [Du. *stoep.*]

1. Formerly, a small porch with seats or benches; now, any small porch, veranda, or entrance stairway at a house door.
1755 *Essex Inst. Coll.* LII. 78 Houses of one Story & a Stoop to each. **1845** *Knickerb.* XXV. 127 No man can be found who will . . . run up and down one hundred and fifty 'stoops.' **1848** IRVING *Knickerb.* (rev. ed.) v. vi, They found him . . . smoking his afternoon pipe on the 'stoop,' or bench at the porch of his house. **1855** BRISTED in *Cambridge Ess.* 65 *Stoop* (the steps of a house) is pure and almost literal Dutch. **1893** HOLLEY *Samantha at World's Fair* 503, I went out onto the stoop and kinder put my hand out. **1911** [see DUTCH *a.* 1 b].

b. Steps over a fence; a stile.
1897 STUART *Simpkinsville* 135 The cordial relations . . . were still indicated by the well worn 'stoop' set in the dividing-fence between the two gardens.

2. Attrib. with *bench, door, line.*
1852 *Harper's Mag.* March 446/1 She gave him the message, standing at the stoop-door. **1885** EGGLESTON in *Century Mag.* April 876/2 Balconies on the roofs . . . afforded a cool and more private retreat than the stoop-benches. **1904** *N.Y. Ev. Post* 21 Nov. 2 Five Italian bootblacks were charged with 'keeping and maintaining bootblack stands within the stoop line without a licence.'

* **Stop,** *v.*

+**1.** *To stop off,* to interrupt one's journey for a brief stay at some intermediate point. *colloq.*
1855 *Knickerb.* XLVI. 604 He had 'stopped off,' he said, to see a friend. **1892** *Harper's Mag.* Feb. 437/2, I stopped off overnight to see about something for a friend. **1908** LORIMER *J. Spurlock* xii, We shall stop off fo' a visit in Canon City.

+**2.** *To stop over,* on a journey, to remain at a place after the departure of the regular conveyance, with the intention of proceeding by one going later. *colloq.*
1857 M. J. HOLMES *Meadow-Brook* xvi, We have stopped over one train. **1873** 'MARK TWAIN' & WARNER *Gilded Age* 218 You renewed your ticket after stopping over in Baltimore. **1922** DEPEW *My Memories* 220 Passing through Albany while he was governor, I stopped over to pay my respects.

+**Stop law.** A law placing limitations on proceedings against debtors. — **1820** *Ann. 16th Congress* 1 Sess. 1944 Pennsylvania speaks . . . of a stop law to prevent the sale of real and personal property in execution, unless it sells for two-thirds of its appraised value. **1832** CLAY *Speeches* (1842) 157 Stop laws and relief laws were adopted to save the people from impending destruction. **1854** [see PROPERTY 2].

+**Stop-over.** A stop at an intermediate point on a journey. Also attrib. — **1881** *Harper's Mag.* April 767/2 Stop-over tickets . . . give them the privilege of turning their stock out at any place for the winter, and then sending them on in the spring to market. **1885** ROE *Army Lett.* 334 The grand event of the stop-over was the champagne supper Captain Martin gave in our honor. **1893** SANBORN *S. Calif.* 97 The schedule of trains allows of convenient stop-overs. **1907** *Scribner's Mag.* July 121/2 They rarely inquire about interesting scenery on the way; stop-over privileges are not in demand.

Stopping-place. {1848} A place of temporary stay. — **1827** SHERWOOD *Gaz. Georgia* 37 *Camp c.* in the N.W. part of Warren . . . and well known as a stopping place. **1862** *Harper's Mag.* June 32/1 This house has been a favourite stopping-place for candidates for many years. *a*1918 G. STUART *On Frontier* I. 68 At our home in Iowa we had been a favorite stopping place for the circuit rider, as mother was an excellent cook.

Storage reservoir. A reservoir for storing up water. — **1876** RAYMOND *8th Rep. Mines* 91 For a supply of water during the dry season we rely almost exclusively upon our storage-reservoirs. **1882** McCABE *New York* 670 At this end of the bridge two large reservoirs are located, known as the Storage and 'High Service' reservoirs. **1893** SANBORN *S. Calif.* 89 The storage reservoirs . . . dot the valley and are used in irrigation.

* **Store.**

I. +**1.** A shop or other place of business where goods are kept for sale; a retail shop. {= E. 'shop'}
1721 *Amer. Wkly. Mercury* 16 March 2/2 At a Store under George Mifflins House . . . are several Sorts of English Goods to be sold. **1789** ANBUREY *Travels* II. 357 What are called shops in England, are here denominated stores. **1817** S. BROWN *Western Gazetteer* 54 There are within the precincts of the town . . . five taverns and seven stores. **1887** ALDEN *Little Fishers* xviii, The store by Crossman's made tobacco and liquor its chief trade. **1907** *St. Nicholas* May 617/1 Men must . . . labor hard in factories, or offices, or stores, and 'get along.'

+**b.** *To keep (a) store,* to have charge of a store as an owner or clerk.
1752 *Penna. Gazette* 25 June 4/3 Where Mr. Samuel Burge kept store. **1786** *Mag. Amer. Hist.* I. 242 A noisy Irishman . . . kept store at the Rapids. **1833** NEAL *Down-Easters* I. 27 A little dapper Bostonian . . . kept a store as they call it, where every shop is a *store,* . . . every stall a *factory,* and every goose a *swan.* **1873** 'MARK TWAIN' & WARNER *Gilded Age* 19 [The postmaster] 'kept store' in the intervals. **1904** *Cosmopolitan* May 88 He has 'kept store' in a country town.

‖2. (See quotation.)

1775 *Amer. Husbandry* I. 187 Every planter [in Penna.] has his pond at least, but generally a chain of them, on a brook, which always supplies fresh water; in these stores, as they call them, are kept the products of their river-fishing.

II. *attrib.* and *comb.* **+3.** Designating financial obligations, transactions, etc., involved in keeping or trading in a store.

1800 *Stat. at Large* II. 79 [For] storekeeper's salary, clerk hire, store rent. **1838** *U.S. Mag.* I. 37 The store price for each number will be $4.00 on white paper. **1843** *Knickerb.* XXII. 238 Obtaining mortgages on the farms for his store accounts. **1853** 'P. PAXTON' *Yankee in Texas* 76 A little money was sometimes to be found, if their store bill did not overrun their crops. **1856** *Mich. Agric. Soc. Trans.* VII. 811 The times of selling wheat at 44 cents per bushel to pay store debts have gone by.

+4. Designating articles or materials purchased at a store, as contrasted with those made or obtained at home.

See also STORE GOODS, STORE TEETH.

1840 *Knickerb.* XVI. 262, I felt an awe of young ladies in 'store clothes.' **1843** 'CARLTON' *New Purchase* II. 115, I fished with pin-hooks, and caught . . . more roach and gudgeon than the fellow with his store-hook with a barbed point! **1857** STROTHER *Virginia* 238 Nowadays, since these store-boots come in, . . . there hain't no distinctions; . . . everything w'ars boots now. **1863** P. S. DAVIS *Young Parson* 61 On the table: . . . one plate of 'store cheese,' and half a bread-basket of ginger crackers. **1873** 'MARK TWAIN' & WARNER *Gilded Age* 60 Hawkins fitted out his house with 'store' furniture from St. Louis. **1877** JEWETT *Deephaven* 196, I sends by them for what store stuff I want. **1877** BARTLETT 667 *Store Tea*, a term applied to the tea of China bought at the stores, to distinguish it from herb tea. **1884** 'MARK TWAIN' *H. Finn* xxi, You borry'd store tobacker and paid back niggerhead. **1891** Store pants [see GALLOWS *n.* 2]. **1900** ADE *More Fables* 28 People would see him there in his Store Suit.

+b. In adjectival compounds.

1883 ZEIGLER & GROSSCUP *Alleghanies* 91 Two good-natured-looking young men [were] dressed in . . . 'store-boughten' coats, and homespun pantaloons. **1901** WHITE *Westerners* 169 Old Mizzou . . . [had] a seven dollar suit of clothes, from which he suffered severely, because it was 'store made.'

+5. Designating individuals who own or work in stores.

See also STOREKEEPER, STOREMAN.

1844 'UNCLE SAM' *Peculiarities* II. 186 'A am not a common nigga.' . . . 'A store-porter?' **1845** *Big Bear Ark.* 34 The young store boys of the village became greatly interested. **1907** *St. Nicholas* Oct. 1106/2 He wondered how the store detectives worked to find a man who might be picking pockets in a great crowd. **1908** 'O. HENRY' *Options* 24, I want no millionaire store-proprietors climbing the fire-escape of my tenement-house.

+6. Designating parts or furnishings of buildings in which goods are sold.

1845 HOOPER *Taking Census* 166 We were making an entry of somebody's chickens at a store door in the village. **1880** CABLE *Grandissimes* 376 A large *porte-cochère* . . . [opened] upon the banquette immediately beside and abreast of the store-front. **1891** 'THANET' *Otto the Knight* 328, I are seekin' my own chile, thet I leff unner the store-counter. **1894** CHOPIN *Bayou Folk* 137, I been try settin' down still on de sto' gall'ry. **1896** WILKINS *Madelon* 123 He pointed towards the store-windows with a rosy glow of light. **1907** *St. Nicholas* Aug. 874/2 They cast anxious glances at the store clock.

+7. In special combinations.

Store hours, the hours during which a store is open; *s. street*, a street along which there are many stores; *s. ticket*, a ticket entitling one to make purchases in a store under certain conditions.

1857 *Knickerb.* XLIX. 40 A great moving we had, all being done of course after dark and after store-hours. **1879** WHITMAN *Spec. Days* 155 Fourth, Fifth and Third streets are store-streets. **1878** *Rep. Indian Affairs* p. xxxix, Formerly the Indians were imposed upon through a system of brass checks, tokens, and store-tickets.

Store boat. 1. A boat carrying supplies needed on an expedition. {1898–} **+2.** A boat carrying miscellaneous articles for sale. — **(1) 1797** *State P.* (1819) III. 144 Their store-boat arriving on the 28th [of January], they proceeded on the 31st for the Natchez. **1802** ELLICOTT *Journal* 20 The large store boat not being calculated for expedition, I left her with directions to follow. **(2) 1822** WOODS *English Prairie* 87 The master of the store-boat . . . had freighted his boat with store-goods and fruit. **1864** NICHOLS *Amer. Life* I. 169 Selling supplies to steamboats, and transferring passengers from the down to the up-river boats, is done on floating store boats, made fast to the shore.

+Store book. An account book in which transactions in a store or shop are recorded. — **1740** W. STEPHENS *Proc. Georgia* II. 20 [Upon] looking into the Store-Books, it was found there was a considerable Debt. **1898** PAGE *Red Rock* 446, I want to ax you,—is Mr. Spickit—'lowed to write 'whiskey' down in his sto'-book?

Store box. {1826} **+**A box in which goods are shipped to a store or shop. — **1880** N. BROOKS *Fairport Nine* 2 Spare barrels, store-boxes . . . were to be brought in. **1890** HOWELLS *Boy's Town* 133 When a boy had a coon, he had to have a store-box turned open side down to keep it in. **1904**

STRATTON-PORTER *Freckles* 69, I'll have Duncan get you a ten-bushel store-box the next time he goes to town.

+Store goods. Goods such as are usually sold in a store. — **1822** WOODS *English Prairie* 98 We had about 14,000 lbs. weight of store goods, on board the ark, to be left at this place [Cincinnati]. **1844** *Cincinnati Misc.* I. 5 He brought the flat boat which was loaded with his storegoods from the Ohio. **1874** WELLS *Practical Economics* 4 One sold his interest, however, to a firm in New York, and took his pay in store-goods.

∗Storehouse. a. A building or structure in which goods are stored. **+b.** = STORE 1.

1622 'MOURT' *Relation* 78 In the after-noone [we] carried vp our hogs-heads of meale to our common store-house. **1707** *Boston News-Letter* 27 Jan. 2/2 To be Sold . . . at his Store-House upon the Dock in Boston near the Swing-Bridge, Good Barbadoes Rum & Molasses. *c*1773 in *S. Lit. Messenger* XI. 139/1 Shops . . . are here called Store Houses. **1818** FLINT *Lett. from Amer.* 79, I observed . . . a court-house, a jail, a large store-house, and several taverns. **1877** JOHNSON *Anderson Co., Kansas* 63 About this time a store house was built and occupied by a merchant. *a*1918 G. STUART *On Frontier* I. 65 [The Indians] stored the acorns in little store-houses built upon poles about four feet from the ground.

Storekeeper.

1. One who has charge of stores belonging to or used by the army or navy. {1618–}

1654 *Md. Archives* 343 [Any] Storekeeper or Shipmaster . . . who shall Suffer Drunkeness . . . shall be lyable to the aforesaid fine. **1711** *N.J. Archives* 1 Ser. IV. 89 Capt[ain] Bond the storekeeper in New York Fort was . . . made one of [the] jury. **1817** *State P.* (1819) XII. 8 One Champion, who was a commissary in the late war, and store-keeper of ordnance. **1872** *Harper's Mag.* Dec. 95/2 His companions usually were William Selden, Treasurer of the United States, Cary Selden, his brother, store-keeper at the navy-yard, and sometimes Governor Gilmer. **1900** BENJAMIN *U.S. Naval Academy* 368 Uniforms [of the cadets] . . . must be obtained from the Naval Academy store-keeper.

b. One who keeps large quantities of goods in warehouses for others.

1671 *S.C. Hist. Soc. Coll.* V. 301 [The governor] desired that Mr. West the storekeeper for the proprietors should succeed him in the Governm[en]t. **1724** JONES *Virginia* 55 In all convenient Places are kept Stores or Ware-Houses of all Sorts of Goods, managed by Store-Keepers or Factors.

+2. A shopkeeper or merchant.

[**1741** P. TAILFER, etc. *Narr. Georgia* 107 Augusta . . . is principally, if not altogether, inhabited by Indian Traders and Store-keepers.] **1742** *Penna. Gazette* 13 Jan., [Franklin offers his goods to] country storekeepers. **1797** F. BAILY *Tour* 414 A storekeeper is the general denomination for such persons, and under this head you may include every one who buys and sells. **1841** *Knickerb.* XVII. 33 [They sent] the blacksmith to the legislature, in opposition to the store-keeper, who was 'too much of a gentleman.' **1886** STAPLETON *Major's Christmas* 83 Store-keepers come, too, with goods as fine as in Bankton. **1925** TILGHMAN *Dugout* 57, I just told the storekeeper's wife to put up a number one outfit.

3. In various industries, an employee having charge of stores or materials: (see also quot. 1875).

1875 *Chicago Tribune* 13 Sept. 5/3 A storekeeper . . . whose duty it is to record the time of emptying and filling every wash-tub. **1876** *N. Amer. Rev.* CXXIII. 300 A dishonest store-keeper at a distillery could allow two quick fermentations in the time the law prescribed for one. **1890** in Cooley *Railways of Amer.* 307 Everything in the nature of material, however small, directly or indirectly passes through the Store-keeper's books. **1900** *Engineering Mag.* XIX. 706 There should be push-buttons at each window with an annunciator at the store-keeper's desk [in a machine shop].

+Storekeeping. The keeping of a store or shop. Also *attrib.* and as *ppl. a.* — **1774** FITHIAN *Journal* I. 157 Mr. Potter took home my brother Amos with an intention . . . to learn him the Storekeeping business. **1843** 'CARLTON' *New Purchase* I. 105 If I could join him with a few hundred dollars in a little tanning, store-keeping, and *honest* speculation, we might gain . . . independence. **1901** *N. Amer. Rev.* Feb. 311 The store-keeping magnate shoots down his drunken tormentor.

Storeman. {1859–} **+**One who keeps a store or shop. {1862–, in Australia} — **1857** *Harper's Mag.* July 284/1 He tried the store-man in the way of barter. **1900** MUNN *Uncle Terry* 13 The storeman I sold 'em to never trusted me again.

+Store pay. Payment for produce or other articles by goods from a store instead of by cash. — **1845** COOPER *Chainbearer* xix, One pound sixteen, one-third store-pay, is the utmost farthin' I can offer. **1882** PECK *Sunshine* 137 They are . . . arranging facilities for transporting wheat worth forty cents a bushel in store pay, without railroads, to a market where the farmer realizes nearly a dollar a bushel in cash. **1891** WELCH *Recoll. 1830–40* 353 The workmen were to receive . . . only half cash, the remainder in trade—store pay, *i.e.*: in orders on the employers or other stores for such goods as they needed.

+Store teeth. Artificial teeth. *colloq.* or *humorous.* — **1891** 'THANET' *Otto the Knight* 1 Nobody on the plantation has such beautiful, white store teeth. **1901** *Emporia Gazette* 19 July, Stop weeping and wailing and wearing the enamel off your good store teeth.

+Store trough. A trough in which maple sap is stored temporarily in sugar-making. — *a*1797 [see CISTERN 2]. **1851** *Knickerb.* XXXVII.

377 He tramped [through the snow] . . . to bring the luscious juice to the 'store-trough.'

∗The American wood ibis, *Mycteria americana*. — **1709** LAWSON *Carolina* 145 Among them [*sc.* cranes] often frequent Storks, which are here seen, and nowhere besides in America, that I have yet heard of. **1791** [see GANNET]. **1805** CLARK in *Lewis & C. Exped.* III. (1905) 193 Emence numbers of fowls flying in every direction, Such as Swan, . . . Stalks [*sic*], white guls. **1917** *Birds of Amer.* I. 179/2 After the breeding season [in Florida] these Storks wander north as far as Pennsylvania and Michigan.

∗**Stork(s)bill.** A plant of the genera *Erodium* or *Pelargonium.* Also attrib. — **1817–8** EATON *Botany* (1822) 275 *Erodium ciconium,* stork-bill geranium. **1869** FULLER *Flower Gatherers* 70 All of the Stork-bills have this peculiarity. **1889** VASEY *Agric. Grasses* 102 Storksbill . . . is neither a grass nor a clover, but belongs to the geranium family. **1891** COULTER *Bot. W. Texas* I. 51.

∗ **Storm.** +In special combinations.
Storm coat, a coat for use in stormy weather; *s. dam,* a dam for confining surface water resulting from rains or snows; *s. porch,* a porch at the entrance to a house for protection in inclement weather; *s. quarters,* quarters for use in a storm; *s. shed,* a shed before an outer door for protection during inclement weather; *s. shield,* a barrier or protection against storms; *s. twister,* a tornado.
1830 WATSON *Philadelphia* 179, In the year 1749, I met with the incidental mention of a singular over-coat, worn by captain James as a storm coat, made entirely of beaver fur. **1890** *Stock Grower & Farmer* 15 March 7/1 The irrigating dam on upper Cherry Creek [in Colo.] . . . will be the finest if not the largest 'storm dam' in America. **1879** *Lumberman's Gazette* 15 Oct., Horses . . . should be protected at every much-used entrance, by storm-porches. **1883** 'MARK TWAIN' *Life on Miss.* iii, Three or four wigwams [were] scattered about the raft's level space for storm-quarters. **1920** LEWIS *Main Street* 81 Storm sheds were erected at every door. **1871** *Harper's Mag.* Sept. 631/2 The growth of living storm-shields along the line of the Kansas Pacific Railway . . . is only a matter of effort and time. **1904** *Sun* (N.Y.) 23 Aug. 1 The storm twister struck Willow Lakes about 9 o'clock.

Storm center. The central point in an area over which a storm prevails; also, fig., the focal point about which trouble gathers or revolves. — **1894** *Harper's Weekly* 7 April 315 It establishes a sort of Weather Bureau of disease, and . . . is to show . . . where the storm centres of communicable disease are. **1900** *Jrnl. School Geog.* June 230 The wind should be kept well on the starboard quarter, the effect of this being to carry the vessel constantly from the storm centre. **1904** CRISSEY *Tattlings* 246 The party general in a big campaign . . . must have a scent for landslides and storm centers.

+**Storm door.** An additional door, sometimes temporary, at an outer entrance for protection in severe or inclement weather. — **1878** E. B. TUTTLE *Border Tales* 29 The horses . . . broke loose from the stable, and begun gnawing the storm doors in front of the officers' quarters. **1899** *Mo. So. Dakotan* I. 145 The flapping of the storm door which Putnam had left open, the creaking . . . of the loose window sashes, . . . were deafening. **1907** M. C. HARRIS *Tents of Wickedness* 342 There was much matting of vines, many storm-doors [etc.].

+**Storm flag. 1.** One of the flags used as a signal of an approaching storm. **2.** (See quot. 1918.) — (1) **1881** *Naval Encycl.* 789/2. **1896** *Weather Bureau Bul.* No. 80, 7 Two storm flags (red with black centers), displayed one above the other, . . . announce the expected approach of tropical hurricanes. (2) **1918** FARROW *Dict. Milit. Terms* 588 *Storm flag,* in the United States army, the national flag, having 9 feet fly and 5 feet hoist. It is hoisted in stormy or windy weather, and is also to be used as a recruiting flag.

+**Storm house.** A structure, sometimes as a temporary addition before an outer door, for protection in stormy weather. — **1839** *S. Lit. Messenger* V. 8/2 The James Cropper in 1822 . . . was fitted with . . . a storm house over the wheel. **1887** *Harper's Mag.* Dec. 119/1 Two men . . . were bending down at the storm-house in front of her parlor-door.

Stormy petrel. Any one of various petrels, esp. *Hydrobates pelagicus.* {1776-} Also with specifying adjective. — **1813** WILSON *Ornithology* VII. 90 Stormy Petrel. . . . [These birds have] long been fearfully regarded by the . . . superstitious . . . as the foreboding messengers of tempests. **1858** BAIRD *Birds Pacific R.R.* 830 *Thalassidroma Melania.* . . . The Black Stormy Petrel. . . . Coast of California. **1883** [see MOTHER CAREY'S CHICKEN]. **1917** *Birds of America* I. 84.

∗**Story.** +A news article in a newspaper, or material for such an article. — **1892** *Harper's Wkly.* 9 Jan. 42/4 An estimate is made of how much space each 'story' will occupy. **1898** ATHERTON *Californians* 44 There's no 'story' in this. **1914** S. H. ADAMS *Clarion* 14 You wouldn't hardly expect me to kill the story.

∗**Stove.**
∗ **1.** An enclosed fireplace or furnace for warming or cooking purposes.
1702 SEWALL *Diary* II. 70 Mr. Dudley &c in their Chamber, where their Stove is. **1786** FRANKLIN in *Amer. Philos. Soc.* II. 57 Description of a new Stove for burning of Pitcoal, and consuming all its Smoke. **1844** *Lexington Observer* 25 Sept. 1/6 The subscriber has just received . . . Stoves of every description for sale low. **1896** JEWETT *Pointed Firs* 117 There was . . . a good enough stove so anybody could cook and keep warm in cold weather. **1918** ROOSEVELT in *Maine My State* 21 We had stoves to keep us warm in the bitter winter weather.

2. A foot-warmer or foot stove. {1716-}
1750 *New York Post-Boy* 19 Nov., Gentlemen and Ladies may cause their Stoves to be brought. **1772** A. G. WINSLOW *Diary* 39, I rode to & from meeting in Mr. Soler's chaise . . . & with a stove was very comfortable there. **1827** DRAKE & MANSFIELD *Cincinnati* 36 [The Humane Society] has procured . . . a moveable bed, with a stove for heating it.

3. *attrib.* and *comb.* **a.** With *brick, frame, hearth,* etc.
1789 *Boston Directory* 204 Weare, John, jun. carpenter & stove frame-maker, Eliot-street. **1850** JUDD *R. Edney* 18 Richard . . . sank into the rocking-chair . . . , with his feet bolstered on the clean and bright stove-hearth. **1851** CIST *Cincinnati* 192 [Of the] forty-four founderies, one-third . . . are mainly or entirely in the stove trade. **1863** *Horticulturist* June, Advt. 3 Greenwich Pottery established 1833. . . . Manufacturer of . . . Stove Brick, Fire Brick [etc.]. **1873** *Harper's Mag.* March 596/1 [I baked it] in the stove oven. **1886** *Century Mag.* May 591/2 Let us hope that the building . . . will contain collections from which Detroit's stove-molders, lithographers, and other artisans may gain ideas. **1894** ROBLEY *Bourbon Co., Kansas* 124 C. F. Drake occupied the east room for his stove and tin store.

b. In special combinations.
Stove cover, a stove lid; *s. glass,* (see quotation); *s. length,* a length short enough to go into the fire box of a stove; *s. lifter,* a metal contrivance for removing and replacing stove lids; *s. plate,* a cast-metal plate forming part of a stove; *s. stick,* a piece of stove wood; *s. truck,* (see quotation).
1861 NEWELL *Orpheus C. Kerr* I. 312 Though met by a perfect hail of turnips, stove-covers, and kindling-wood, the Mackerels went over the fence. **1889** *Cent.* 2531/1 Stove-glass, sheets of mica used in the fronts of stoves, etc. **1881** *Chicago Times* 16 April, The buyer decides to have it taken to him sawed into stove lengths. **1886** *Harper's Mag.* Nov. 835/1 We'll have a real egg and cinder flip with the hot stove-lifter in it when we get back. **1833** *Niles' Reg.* XLIV. 353/2 Messrs. Heermans, Rathbone & Co. sell annually 750 tons stove plates. **1888** GRIGSBY *Smoked Yank* (1891) 146 A little bundle of 'fat' pine, as much as a common stove stick would make, when split up fine, brought twenty-five cents in the prison. **1876** KNIGHT 2413/2 *Stove-truck,* . . . a truck employed in cannon-foundries for moving pieces of ordnance.

Stove lid. A round plate fitting into an opening in the top of a stove or range. — **1876** 'MARK TWAIN' *Tom Sawyer* i. 18 She could have seen through a pair of stove-lids just as well. **1898** *McClure's Mag.* X. 270 S'posin' that . . . you'd hear . . . some other woman's hands rattlin' the stove-lids around. **1922** TARKINGTON *Gentle Julia* 113 In a room in the cellar, . . . were loosely stored . . . rusted stove lids and flatirons.

Stovepipe. {1699-} +Short for STOVEPIPE HAT. Also attrib. — [**1851** *Illust. London News* XIX. 395/2 Every male who wears the present stove-pipe section head-gear.] *a***1861** WINTHROP *J. Brent* 209 Tall men and short, men hatted with slouched hats, wash-bowls, and stove-pipes. **1863** *Harper's Mag.* May 857/2 How changed from him we in the city knew, In stove-pipe beaver, and a long-tailed blue. **1886** POORE *Reminisc.* II. 210 Nye, picking up the crushed stove-pipe, said [etc.]. **1903** 'O. HENRY' *Roads of Destiny* 88 With impunity might the tenderfoot ventilate his 'stovepipe' or his theories of culture.

+**Stovepipe hat.** A tall, cylindrical silk hat. *colloq.* {1886-} — **1855** *Oregon Wkly. Times* 16 June (Th.), Know-Nothingism . . . was got up amongst 'stove-pipe hats' and patent black leather shoes. **1883** SWEET & KNOX *Through Texas* 401 A red-faced man [was] attached to an immense scarf-pin, and accompanied by a very tall stovepipe hat. **1907** ANDREWS *Recoll.* 66 When in the street [he wore] a light colored stove-pipe hat with wide black band.

+**Stove wood.** Wood suitable for use in a stove. — **1867** LOCKE *Swingin' Round* 159, I held a stick of stove wood suspended over his head. **1917** SINCLAIR *King Coal* 27 What had once been a picket-fence, now falling apart and being use l for stove-wood.

Stowadore. [By association with *stow* v.] A stevedore. — **1788** *Mass. Spy* 10 July 2/3 Stowadores.

Straddle, *n.* {1611-}
+**1.** The action of taking a noncommittal position on a question, esp. a political question; the position so taken.
1843 *Knickerb.* XXII. 233 These are . . . subjects for the straddle. **1883** *American* VI. 100 Expediency demanded a 'straddle' that could be explained either way. **1885** *South Fla. Sentinel* (Orlando) 2 Sept. 2/2 He thinks the Republican party has given its chance away by its straddle on the liquor question. **1894** *Voice* 18 Oct. 4/3 A [political] platform that is confessedly a straddle, framed for the very purpose of cheating. **1905** *Springfield W. Repub.* 1 Dec. 2 A compromise between free trade and protection that in America would be contemptuously characterized as a straddle.

2. (See quotation.)
1864 WEBSTER 1304/1 *Straddle,* . . . the position, or the distance between the feet, of one who straddles; as, a wide straddle.

+**3.** *Poker.* A doubling of the blind or ante.
1864 DICK *Amer. Hoyle* (1866) 177 If the dealer choose, he may, in turn double the straddle. **1887** KELLER *Draw Poker* 11 The next on his left may straddle his straddle. **1909** WEBSTER 93/2 The ante is usually twice the amount of the blind or of the last straddle.

+**4.** *Stock exchange.* (See quot. 1877.) {1902-}
1877 BARTLETT 667 *Straddle* . . . means a contract which gives the holder the privilege of calling for the stock at a fixed price, or of delivering

it at the same price to the party who signs the contract. **1883** *Harper's Mag.* March 598/2 [N.Y. brokers] always talked of 'margins' and 'puts' and 'calls,' and 'straddles.' [**1902** *Longman's Mag.* April 485 The lady's wealth is based on a successful Straddle, operated . . . in—Bristles—Hog's Bristles and Lard.]

✳**Straddle,** *v.*

+**1.** *tr.* To double the amount of (a blind).

1864 DICK *Amer. Hoyle* (1866) 177 The next player to the left may at his option straddle this bet. **1884** 'CRADDOCK' *Where Battle Was Fought* 34 Only knew vaguely that somebody was 'passing' or 'straddling the blind.' **1887** KELLER *Draw Poker* 21 The right to straddle the ante rests wholly with the player immediately to the left of the age.

+**2.** To take an equivocal position on (an issue or question). Also *absol.*

1884 *Boston Traveller* Aug., Mr. Hendricks has straddled almost every issue of recent years, . . . [but has] remained firm on the negro question. **1896** *Voice* 2 April 5/1 The Republican Party of '56 . . . did straddle the [slavery] question most magnificently. **1906** *N.Y. Ev. Post* 6 Dec. 8 Eleven Senators answered yes, four no, and four straddled. **1913** LA FOLLETTE *Autobiog.* 510 He deliberated . . . as to whether he would stand with the administration, supporting Taft . . . , or seek to identify himself with the Progressives—or straddle.

+**3.** *Stock exchange.* (See quotation.)

1900 NELSON *A B C Wall St.* 161 A speculator who has bought and is long of one stock, and sold and is short of another, has straddled the market.

+**Straddlebug.** A long-legged beetle. Also *attrib.* and *fig.* — **1833** *Niles' Reg.* XLIV. 152/1 This illustrious chieftain . . . has been so instrumental in bringing to a glorious and bloodless termination the war of the straddlebugs. **1865** 'MARK TWAIN' *Sk., New & Old* 31 If he even see a straddle-bug start to go anywheres, he would bet you how long it would take. **1872** *Newton Kansan* 5 Sept. 2/1 We think it well that the people . . . not see quite so much of the straddle-bug business carried on by a few.

Straddler. {1863-} +A politician who straddles an issue. — **1884** *Boston Traveller* Aug., Multitudinous attacks . . . are being made on the record as a straddler of Vice-Presidential Candidate Hendricks. **1896** MOE *Hist. Harvard* 37 Increase Mather . . . , like McKinley of Ohio, . . . never spent any time where he of right belonged, and was a straddler on the question of bimetalism.

✳**Straight,** *n.*

+**1.** *Poker.* A hand in which cards of different suits form a numerical sequence.

1864 DICK *Amer. Hoyle* (1866) 177 A Straight will beat two pairs. **1880** *Ib.* (ed. 13) 198 *Pat Hand.*—An original hand not likely to be improved by drawing, such as a full, straight, flush or pairs. **1903** 'O. HENRY' *Roads of Destiny* 210 He always would play jack, queen, king, ace, deuce for a straight.

+**2.** *The straight,* the truth. *colloq.*

1866 C. H. SMITH *Bill Arp* 35 You should git the straight of it from one who seen it with his eyes. **1900** DIX *Deacon Bradbury* 266 You've heard th' straight of it, Mr. Leavitt. **1902** LORIMER *Lett. Merchant* 271 No one except the Widow ever really got at the straight of Bud's conduct.

+**3.** *ellipt.* **a.** A regular party member. **b.** Straight liquor.

1887 *Courier-Journal* 20 Jan. 2/5 The 'straights' will caucus this evening. **1905** 'O. HENRY' *Trimmed Lamp* 242, I managed to soak in a little straight or some spilled Martini.

✳**Straight,** *a.*

+**1.** Genuine; undiluted.

1855 M. THOMPSON *Doesticks* 59 My glass of brandy, . . . [which] should have been 'straight,' was also surreptitiously diluted. **1859** *Harper's Mag.* Aug. 344/2, I am a little particular . . . that what I drink is the 'straight' article. **1879** TOURGEE *Fool's Errand* 28, I allers did like my liquor clar, —clar an' straight.

+**b.** Unmixed with or unaccompanied by anything else.

[**1865** VISCT. MILTON & W. B. CHEADLE *N.-W. Passage by Land* (1867) 33 As a Yankee would express it, they were geese and ducks 'straight.'] **1869** *Ill. Agric. Soc. Trans.* VII. 460 Sheep-growers or western shippers . . . scarcely ever send in good straight lots. **1869** BOWLES *Our New West* 135 We had to take our victual and drink 'straight,'—plain ham and bread and butter and black coffee. **1873** BEADLE *Undevel. West* 528 We lived on Navajo bread, coffee, and 'commissary butter,' straight. **1885** PATTEN *England* 51 The expression 'straight milk,' which I have used in describing the watering of London's milk supply, recalls to me the fact that I first heard it used by an American milkman. **1895** *N.Y. Dramatic News* 6 July 2/1 Trilby is the only 'straight' theatrical entertainment now left in New York.

+**c.** *Whisky* (or *Bourbon*) *straight,* undiluted whisky (or Bourbon), or a drink of this.

1862 *Harper's Mag.* Aug. 312/1 [The] primer was simply a gill of Bourbon straight. **1864** *Congress. Globe* 21 April 1786/2 From the impassioned tone of the gentleman from Illinois . . . one would suppose that he had been investing in whisky straight. **1879** *Scribner's Mo.* Oct. 931/1, I'd swallowed a glass o' whisky straight. **1914** STEELE *Storm* 59, [I] called for a 'whisky straight.'

+**2.** *Politics.* Made up only of persons who support uncompromisingly a party or a principle; of a person, strictly partisan.

1856 *N.Y. Courier & Enquirer* Sept. (B.), The present candidate of the straight Whigs for the Vice-Presidency. **1857** *N.Y. Times* 16 Oct. 2/6 The straight Republican Convention is to meet to-morrow. **1887** FREDERIC *Seth's Brother's Wife* 403 You mustn't allow that to lead you into the habit of thinking that all bolters are saints and all straight-party men devils. **1898** *Kansas City Star* 18 Dec. 5/7 The straight silver party . . . got only twenty-two out of the forty-five members of the legislature in Nevada. **1925** *Scribner's Mag.* Sept. 249/1 He's a good mixer and a straight Republican.

+**b.** Of votes: Cast in support of all the candidates of a single party.

1892 *Chicago D. News Almanac* 237 Readjuster and straight Republican votes, combined. **1904** *Brooklyn Eagle* 9 June 4 One unable to hold his straight party vote in his own city would be a calamity.

+**3.** Of flour: (see quotations).

1859 BARTLETT 454 *Straight,* . . . even or uniform in quality. A term used in commerce, and particularly among flour-dealers. **1883** *Harper's Mag.* June 78/1 Bakers . . . use what is known as 'wheat,' or 'straight' flour.

Straight ball. *Baseball.* +(See quotations.) — **1886** CHADWICK *Art of Pitching* 27 The 'straight ball' referred to being a ball over the plate and at the height called for. [**1912** MATHEWSON *Pitching* 14 Big League ball-players recognize only two kinds of pitched balls—the curve and the straight one.]

✳**Straighten,** *v.* +**1.** *tr.* To lay out (a person) in death. **2.** *To straighten out* {1900-}, +to put back in health. +**3.** *To straighten up,* to stand erect; fig., to adopt an honest course in life. — (1) **1860** HOLMES *E. Venner* xxx, And now Elsie's to be straightened,—the Lord have mercy on her poor sinful soul! **1875** in Fleming *Hist. Reconstruction* II. 206 If you dont leave this settlement with your negro children we will straten you. (2) **1873** BEADLE *Undevel. West* 34 A third was positive the Lake Region would straighten me out. (3) **1897** *Amer. Pediatric Soc. Trans.* IX. 168 After a series of such oscillations . . . he straightens up. **1908** J. WEBSTER *Four-Pools Myst.* xix, He wishes to straighten up and lead a respectable life.

+**Straight flush.** *Poker.* A hand in which all the cards are of the same suit and form a sequence. Also *fig.* — **1864** DICK *Amer. Hoyle* (1866) 182 The strongest hand you can get is a straight flush. **1884** 'CRADDOCK' *Where Battle Was Fought* 36 Casey laid his cards, a straight flush—ace, king, queen, jack, and ten of diamonds—upon the table. **1887** *Courier-Journal* 23 Jan. 15/7 It is only about fifteen years since straight flushes take precedence of four aces. **1903** MARCHMONT *When I was Czar* 239 This is no mere bluff I'm putting up: I hold a straight flush.

+**Straight-out,** *n.* One who gives undivided support to something; one who is usually a straight party man. — **1840** *Nashville Whig* 17 Aug. (Th.), Straight-Outs . . . are the representatives of a hardy race of honest log cabin pioneers, who, however ridiculed for their primitive manners, never fail to make their influence felt at the ballot-box. **1872** *Chicago Tribune* 13 Oct. 2/1 A sufficient number of Straight-outs can be bought to insure Indiana and New Jersey, and . . . New York.

+**Straight-out,** *a.* {1915}

1. Unqualified; open; unconcealed; real or genuine.

1848 W. ARMSTRONG *Stocks* 9 The Stock is to be delivered and paid for upon a certain day—these are sometimes termed straight out contracts. **1856** STOWE *Dred* II. 319 Anne was indignant—with that straight out and generous indignation which belongs to women. **1872** *Harper's Mag.* Oct. 795/1 In a straight-out husking match he'd bet on his aunt. **1898** *Kissimmee* (Fla.) *Valley Gazette* 18 Feb. 1/2 The failure of this bill to become a law means a straight-out fight for prohibition. **1912** DREISER *Financier* 57, I don't like it as well as I do the straight-out brokerage business.

2. Of a person or group of persons: Making no exceptions in the support of a party, principle, etc.; representing uncompromising members of a party.

1856 *N.Y. Commercial Adv.* May (B.), We feel what a blessed thing it is just now to be a straight out whig. **1866** GREGG *Life in Army* 249 Most [passengers] . . . were, or professed to be, of the straight-out, unterrified, and not-to-be-conquered class of secessionists. **1882** *Nation* 3 Aug. 85/1 The Virginia Straight-Out Republican Committee decided . . . not to call a State Convention. **1891** *World Almanac* 75/2 South-Carolina, Democratic 'Straight-out' State Convention . . . put a ticket in the field in opposition to the regular (Tillman) Democratic ticket.

3. Of a political ticket: Straight.

1888 BRYCE *Amer. Commw.* II. 11. 1. 269 The electors . . . give little thought to the personal qualifications of the candidates, and vote the 'straight out ticket.'

+**Straight poker.** A form of poker in which players do not draw to the hands originally dealt them. — **1864** DICK *Amer. Hoyle* (1866) 175 The Age does not use the term 'I pass,' as in Straight Poker. **1887** *Courier-Journal* 23 Jan. 15/7 Draw poker was evolved out of straight about the year 1845. **1894** ROBLEY *Bourbon Co., Kansas* 16 The rest of the time . . . they could play . . . straight poker. . . . They didn't draw.

+Straight ticket.

1. 'A ticket containing the regular nominations of a party, without change' (W. '79); the complete list of a party's candidates, formerly printed on a separate sheet, now in a column on the same sheet with other parties' candidates.

1860 *Harper's Mag.* Jan. 280/1 Old Henry . . . generally votes a 'straight ticket,' and is entirely opposed to taxes. 1870 *Congress. Globe* 24 May 3761/1, I do not suppose that ten per cent of the members of this body have voted what is called a straight ticket for a great number of years. 1891 O'BEIRNE *Leaders Ind. Territory* 147/1 He is, however, a member of the Progressive party and will continue to vote the straight ticket. 1904 *N.Y. Ev. Post* 7 Nov. 2 To vote a straight ticket, which is one to cover all the candidates of one party, the voter need only mark a cross in the circle set at the head of the ballot between the emblem and the name of that party.

2. A political ticket composed of members of a single party.

1872 *Newton Kansan* 10 Oct. 2/2 If the Republicans . . . think best to have a straight ticket, then let us have it.

+Straight whisky.

1. Undiluted or pure whisky.

Cf. STRAIGHT *a.* 1 c.

1865 'MARK TWAIN' *Sketches* (1926) 163 Calaveras possesses . . . 'straight' whisky that will throw a man a double somerset. 1877 W. WRIGHT *Big Bonanza* 64 Mr. Jones opened his house with two barrels of 'straight' whisky. 1890 HARTE *Waif of Plains* 127, I will take straight whisky. 1901 CHURCHILL *Crisis* 432 Now Stephen had never learned to like straight whiskey.

2. (See quotation.)

1877 BARTLETT 751 Straight Whiskey means the liquor upon which the excise duty has been paid.

*Strainer. A device for filtering or sifting. — 1687 SEWALL *Letter-Book* I. 46, [I] desire your sending me . . . before winter . . . 5 Duzen large Strainers. 1772 in *Travels Amer. Col.* 502 They afterwards put a Strainer made of Split Canes into the pot. 1878 *Vermont Bd. Agric. Rep.* 106, I would have the sap strained through a flannel strainer.

+Stram, *n.* A hard walk. *colloq.* — 1869 STOWE *Oldtown Folks* 568, I hed sech a stram this mornin'.

+Stram, *v. intr.* To walk or tramp in a forceful manner. *colloq.* — c1850 WHITCHER *Bedott P.* xxv. 306 [She] strammed right across the room and sot down. 1869 STOWE *Oldtown Folks* 142 You might jest as well give young turkey chicks to the old gobbler, and let him stram off in the mowin' grass with 'em.

Stramonium. The thorn apple, esp. the Jimson weed; the dried leaves of this plant. {1677–} — 1793 *Columbian Centinel* 26 Oct., Several children have very much injured themselves, by eating the seeds of Stramonium, or Thorn-Apple, commonly called Devil's Apple. 1827 *Md. Hist. Mag.* XVII. 257 Having got as comfortable nights sleep as my asthma and stramonium would allow, I sallied out after breakfast. 1849 *31st Congress 1 Sess.* Sen. Ex. Doc. No. 64, 103 [In the Cañon de Chelly] I noticed two or three hackberry trees, and also the *stramonium.* 1891 EGGLESTON in *Century Mag.* Feb. 550 Mrs. Farnsworth was under the frequent necessity of holding a platter of burning stramonium under his nose.

*Stranger.

+**1.** Used vocatively: One who is unknown to the speaker. *colloq.* Chiefly *W.*

1817 BIRKBECK *Notes Journey in Amer.* (1818) 85 A man . . . hailed me with the common, but to us quaint appellation of 'stranger.' 1831 *Louisville Pub. Advertiser* 17 Oct., Says he, Stranger, you're a beauty! 1848 BRYANT *California* App. 477 Look here, stranger, do you see this? 1897 LEWIS *Wolfville* 169 The fact is, stranger, this Jerry mule's a thief.

+**2.** (See quotation.)

c1845 *Big Bear Ark.* 121 A barrel of whiskey is called a 'stranger,' from the fact that it is brought from a distance, there being none made in the country.

+**Stranger's fever.** A fever suffered by persons residing for the first time in a new country; spec., yellow fever. *Obs.* — 1824 HODGSON *Letters from N.A.* I. 52 The *natives* . . . are generally exempt, after the age of from ten to fifteen years, from the yellow or stranger's fever. 1840 *Picayune* 24 Sept. 2/1 The Charleston Board of Health reports the death of twenty persons . . . —stranger's fever, four.

+**Strangite.** A follower of J. J. Strang (1813–56), who claimed the leadership of the Mormon church upon Joseph Smith's death. — 1847 HOWE *Hist. Coll. Ohio* 284 The Strangites maintain the original doctrines of Mormonism, and are located at this place [Kirtland] and Voree [Wis.]. 1870 [see GLADDENITE]. 1890 *Amer. Notes & Q.* V. 184/2 The sect which once lived on Beaver island, in Lake Michigan, were called Strangites.

*Strangler. +A local designation for a vigilante. — 1858 in H. H. Bancroft *Works* XXXVII. 619 Ned McGowan . . . he saw among the audience one of the damned stranglers. 1888 ROOSEVELT in *Century Mag.* May 43/1 During the preceding fall the vigilantes—locally known as 'stranglers,' in happy allusion to their summary method of doing justice—had made a clean sweep of the cattle country along the Yellowstone.

*Strap, *n.* **1.** A band attached to the bottom of a trouser leg and worn under the shoe. {1837–} **2.** A piece or loop of leather, suspended from the ceiling of a vehicle, to which standing passengers may hold. {1861–} — (1) 1837 *Harvardiana* III. 263 A Genius should . . . wear no straps to his pantaloons. 1841 *S. Lit. Messenger* VII. 564/2 Ever since . . . the invention of 'straps,' perhaps the most difficult thing on earth is to button a pair of *rather* short pants under your boots. 1872 EGGLESTON *End of World* 65 When a man comes to Clark township a-wearing straps to his breechaloons, . . . I suspicion him. (2) 1856 [see AISLE 3]. 1898 *Kansas City Star* 18 Dec. 4/2 The 'Great American Hog' . . . occupies two seats . . . while others stand and swing on the straps.

Strap, *v.* {1711–} +*tr.* To make penniless. Usually *p.p.* — 1857 *Nat. Intelligencer* Oct. (B.), No go. Lowndes is strapped. c1866 BAGBY *Old Va. Gentleman* 50 [He] plays 'poker' on the Mississippi, gets cheated, gets 'strapped.' 1893 *Outing* XXII. 118/2, I was 'strapped.' 1909 STRATTON-PORTER *Girl of Limberlost* 193 Have you forgot that the ditch and the road completely strapped me?

+**Strap game.** A kind of swindling game played with a strap. — 1847 *Knickerb.* XXIX. 281 He was accused of having 'come the strap-game' over a native. 1873 BEADLE *Undevel. West* 140 A score of 'smart Alecks' relieved of their surplus cash by betting on the 'strap game.'

Strap iron. {1833} +Iron in long, narrow strips. — 1870 KEIM *Sheridan's Troopers* 229 The blade is made of flint, or a piece of strap-iron. 1882 *47th Congress 1 Sess.* H. R. Ex. Doc. No. 216, 641 Sometimes only wooden rails are used, but generally they are faced with a light strap iron. 1918 *Essex Inst. Coll.* LIV. 197 On many early American railroads the rails were of strap iron spiked on wooden rails.

+**Strappet.** *local.* [Origin uncertain.] A strip *of* land. *Obs.* — 1655 *Springfield Rec.* I. 238 There is granted to John Lamb yt little strappet of land over ye river at ye hay place. 1665 *Ib.* II. 216 Japhett Chapin hath grannted unto him a Strappet of meddow on ye Mill River.

+**Strap rail.** A strip of flat iron formerly used as a railroad rail; also, the iron and the stringer to which it was attached. Also allusive. — 1874 B. F. TAYLOR *World on Wheels* 105 Years ago, he rode on a train of the old Toledo & Adrian Railway—strap-rail at that. 1887 GEORGE *40 Yrs. on Rail* 33 The strap-rails . . . in use on the Boston and Maine when I went on that road . . . were wooden rails on which strap iron was spiked. 1903 *N.Y. Ev. Post* 19 Sept. 5 The State built a road to Springfield in 1838 . . . with strap rails on wooden stringers.

+**Strap road.** A railroad constructed of strap rails. — [1861 N. A. WOODS *Prince of Wales in Canada* 357 The first part of the journey was over . . . a 'strap road,' one of the most unsafe varieties of railway ever used.] 1891 WELCH *Recoll. 1830–40* 28 It was an ordinary strap road, the moving power was one horse.

*Straw.

1. ?A case made of straw used in packing.

1810 *Columbian Centinel* 20 Jan. 3/5, 7 cases Dutch half-pint Tumblers, each containing 100 straws.

2. *ellipt.* =STRAW HAT. {1863–}

1849 LONGFELLOW *Kavanagh* 50 A milliner, who sold 'Dunstable and eleven-braid, open-work and colored straws.' 1883 [see FELT² 1].

+**3.** *collect.* Pine needles. *Obs.*

1856 OLMSTED *Slave States* 321 There were occasionally young long-leaved pines: . . . the leaves, or *straw*, as its foliage is called here, long, graceful, and lustrous. 1860 WHITMAN *Leaves of Grass* 162 The ground in all directions is covered with pine straw.

4. (See quot. 1883.) {1872}

1883 DE VERE in *Encycl. Brit.* (ed. 9) *Amer. Suppl.* I. 201/1 With the various *drinks* invented by Americans came into use the *straws*—slender tubes of wheat, grass, or even of glass—through which beverages are sucked up. 1890 *Amer. Notes & Q.* IV. 135 Whence the name sherry cobbler for that well-known beverage . . . sucked through a straw?

5. *To draw straws* {1691–}, to draw lots by making a selection from a number of straws of different length.

1888 *Amer. Humorist* (London) 27 Oct. (F.), My cousin and I were in at the death, and drew straws for the brush.

6. *attrib.* Designating things made of straw.

There is some question as to whether quot. 1773 should be included here. (See also STRAW BED, STRAW BONNET, etc.)

1773 *Holyoke Diaries* 80 Bought Straw Petticoat at Mrs. Cotnam's. 1809 *Ib.* 152 Hitty put down straw carpet in the entry. 1830 WATSON *Philadelphia* 176 The only straw wear was that called the 'straw beehive bonnet,' worn generally by old people. 1834 AUDUBON *Ornith. Biog.* II. 117 Having placed straw-baskets . . . , in which the female deposited her eggs. 1837 *S. Lit. Messenger* III. 689 We saw on either side of the river several Indian tents made of straw mats.

Straw bail. Insufficient or worthless bail. {1853} — c1844 R. H. COLLYER *Amer. Life* 12 Hundreds of rogues have been let out on bail of the most insignificant and irresponsible character; . . . and this practice is so very common as to procure the name of 'straw-bail.' 1873 MILLER *Amongst Modocs* 313 We tried 'straw' bail but the prosecuting attorney was too rigorous. 1890 LANGFORD *Vigilante Days* (1912) 479 Buckner was released on straw bail.

*Straw bed. A mattress filled with straw. — 1641 *Conn. Rec.* I. 444 Goods of Richard Lyman deceased: . . . 3 Couerlids, 4 blankets, 3 straw bedds. 1692 *Conn. Probate Rec.* I. 463, I giue to my gran child an Thomson . . . a strawe bead & stad to. 1777 in *Scribner's Mo.* XIX. 416/1 A

straw bed was at the bottom, a feather bed on that. **1897** *Outing* XXX.
387/2 The straw bed in the boat . . . proved comfortable.

✳ Strawberry.

✳ 1. The juicy, edible, red fruit of various species of *Fragaria*, +as the wild strawberry (*F. Virginiana*), or cultivated varieties of it; the plant that bears this fruit. Also with specifying terms.

1588 HARRIOT *Briefe Rep. Va.* D1 Straberries there are as good & as great as those which we haue in our English gardens. **1612** SMITH, etc. *Virginia* I. 12 During Somer there are either strawberries . . . or mulberries. **1686** SEWALL *Diary* I. 143 Eat Strawberries and Cream with Sister Longfellow at the Falls. **1709** LAWSON *Carolina* 103 The common red Mulberry . . . is the earliest [fruit] we have, (except the Strawberries). **1772** *Md. Hist. Mag.* XIV. 138 Coll Sharpe has sent the Alpine Strawberries & Vine Plants. *a*1817 Field Strawberry [see FIELD 5 b]. *a*1817 Meadow Strawberry [see MEADOW 5 a]. **1831** PECK *Guide* 139 The gooseberry, strawberry and blackberry grow wild and in great profusion. **1846** *Niles' Nat. Reg.* 13 June 240/2 Thirty to forty thousand baskets of strawberries are received daily in New York. **1863** A. D. WHITNEY *F. Gartney* xiii, I guess she'll like strawberries and cream. **1906** *Harper's Mag.* 885 She hulled strawberries until her fingers were dyed red.

2. *attrib.* **a.** Designating places where strawberries grow or are cultivated.

1627 in *Amer. Speech* XV. 398 Fifty acres of the same land lying and being a parte of the Strawberry bancke. **1835** BIRD *Hawks* II. 144 You robbed Elsie Bell's straw-berry patch. **1880** *Scribner's Mo.* Feb. 569/1 We realized the difference between a strawberry farm and a strawberry bed or 'patch,' as country people say.

b. In the names of various plants, varieties of fruits, insects, etc.

See also STRAWBERRY BASS, STRAWBERRY BUSH, etc.

1847 IVES *New Eng.Fruit* 45 *Strawberry Apple.*—This variety originated in New Jersey; it is an early winter fruit. **1854** EMMONS *Agric. N.Y.* V. 263 (*index*), Strawberry-bugs, 171. **1883** *Nat. Museum Bul.* No. 27, 461 *Pomoxys sparoides*. . . . Strawberry Perch. . . . This species . . . is esteemed as a food-fish. **1854** *Mich. Agric. Soc. Trans.* V. 208 Some of the more approved kinds [of potatoes] are . . . the White, Red, and Strawberry Pinks. **1915** ARMSTRONG & THORNBER *Western Wild Flowers* 158 [The] Strawberry Shrub . . . has many other names, such as Sweet Shrub, Carolina Allspice, Wineflower, etc. **1868** *Rep. Comm. Agric. 1867* 73 A saw fly or strawberry worm, *Emphytus maculatus*, . . . the larvæ of which eat the foliage of the strawberry plants.

c. In special combinations.

+*Strawberry moon*, the months of May and June; +*s. pincushion*, a pincushion resembling a strawberry; +*s. run*, (see quotation); +*s. Sunday*, a dish of ice cream covered with strawberries.

1916 THOBURN *Stand. Hist. Okla.* I. 68 The most noted conflict between the Cherokees and the Osages . . . took place at the Claremore Mound in 'the Strawberry Moon', in 1818. **1864** *Hist. North-Western Soldiers' Fair* 74 [Donations include] 5 strawberry pin cushions, . . . 12 bottles perfumery. **1891** *Cent.* 5272/2 *Strawberry run*, a run of fish in the season of the year when strawberries are ripe. . . . (Local.) **1904** DERVILLE *Other Side of Story* 277 Cool off for the night with 'chocolate Fridays,' 'strawberry Sundays,' and other popular concoctions.

+**Strawberry bass.** =CALICO BASS. — *a*1876 [see LAMPLIGHTER 3]. **1888** *Outing* July 307 Lake Canadarago has . . . rock and strawberry bass. **1911** *Rep. Fisheries 1908* 308/2.

+**Strawberry-blonde**, *a.* Reddish blond; red-headed: (see also quot. 1880). — **1880** *Scribner's Mo.* Feb. 575/2 In the vernacular of the farm the mulatto-girls are called 'strawberry blondes.' **1884** NYE *Baled Hay* 98 That is what is . . . sprinkling my strawberry blonde hair with gray. **1887** *Courier-Journal* 6 Feb. 12/2 Seventeen young women, with hair ranging from strawberry blonde to deep crimson, are seated . . . on a long platform.

+**Strawberry bush. a.** A shrub of the genus *Calycanthus*. **b.** An American spindle tree (*Evonymus americanus*) having bright red pods. — **1847** DARLINGTON *Weeds & Plants* 135 Carolina-allspice. . . . Strawberry-bush. . . . There are several species of this genus cultivated for the fragrance of their rather unsightly flowers. **1860** CURTIS *Woody Plants N.C.* 102 Strawberry Bush. . . . The fruit gives the plant a peculiar beauty, for which chiefly it is prized in shrubberies. **1893** *Amer. Folk-Lore* VI. 141.

+**Strawberry festival.** A sociable or similar gathering at which strawberries are featured. — **1863** *Boston Sun. Herald* 14 June 4/2 (Ernst), Strawberry festivals are the rage here just now. **1887** *Courier-Journal* 8 May 10/3 A strawberry festival and lawn fete . . . will be given June 3. **1902** McFAUL *Ike Glidden* 105 They had . . . strawberry fest'vals at the meetin'-house.

+**Strawberry Night.** At Harvard, a student festival. — **1893** POST *Harvard Stories* 134 The night before I left was Strawberry Night at the Pudding. **1897** FLANDRAU *Harvard Episodes* 114 There is Strawberry Night at the Signet, when the First Seven, from the Sophomore Class is taken in, . . . and Strawberry Night at the Pudding.

+**Strawberry party.** =STRAWBERRY FESTIVAL. — **1865** A. D. WHITNEY *Gayworthys* 25 This was a strawberry party. **1877** HALE *G. T. T.* 215 They had a Sunday-school picnic . . . , a strawberry party or some such entertainment. **1900** BACHELLER *E. Holden* 151 He came over one noon in the early summer . . . to tell us of a strawberry party that evening at the White Church.

+**Strawberry shortcake.** A shortcake or biscuit covered with sweetened strawberries, usually crushed or sliced. — **1865** A. D. WHITNEY *Gayworthys* 28 As she came into the out-room again, . . . [he was] eating strawberry shortcake. **1907** [see PUMPKIN PIE].

+**Strawberry tomato.** One of several species of ground cherry. — **1847** DARLINGTON *Weeds & Plants* 256. **1868** GRAY *Field Botany* 268 P[*hysalis*] *Alkekengi*, Strawberry Tomato. Cultivated from S. Eu[rope]. and running wild E[ast]. **1919** STURTEVANT *Notes on Edible Plants* 432 *P. lanceolata* . . . was among the strawberry tomatoes grown at the New York Agricultural Experiment Station in 1886.

✳ Strawberry tree. +**a.** =BEAR-BERRY 1. +**b.** A species of spindle tree. — **1785** MARSHALL *Amer. Grove* 11 Arbutus. The Strawberry Tree, or Bear-Berry. **1813** MUHLENBERG *Cat. Plants* 25 *Euonymus Americanus*, (burning bush, strawberry tree). **1838** S. PARKER *Tour Rocky Mts.* 202 A tree . . . which grows much in the form of the laurel or bay tree, but much larger, . . . has been called the strawberry tree. **1866** *Ill. Agric. Soc. Trans.* VI. 391 The Strawberry Tree, with its delicate foliage, green wood and beautiful berries.

+**Straw bid.** (See quotation.) — **1877** BARTLETT 669 *Straw Bid*, a bid for a contract which the bidder is unable or unwilling to fulfil.

+**Straw bidder.** One who makes a worthless bid. — **1876** [see next].

+**Straw bidding.** The action of making a worthless bid. *colloq.* — **1872** A. KENDALL *Autobiog.* 344 Thenceforward all 'straw-bidding' ceased. **1876** in Bartlett 669 The House post-office committee has agreed to report Luttrell's bill to prevent straw-bidding for mail contracts, and to punish straw-bidders when caught.

Strawboard. Paper board made from straw pulp. {1881} Also attrib. — **1850** *Rep. Comm. Patents 1849* 305 [The] said process is peculiar to the use of strawboard. **1862** *Harper's Mag.* June 135/1 He was making a personal examination of the straw-board shoes provided for those who have gone to be soldiers. **1923** HERRICK *Lilla* 269 Slawn glanced appreciatively over . . . the tinted strawboard walls and ceiling.

+**Straw bond.** A bond for which the sureties are worthless. — **1881** *Ore. State Jrnl.* 8 Jan. 1/2 He'd be dashed if any little jack-legged shyster could shove a straw-bond on him. **1899** in *Congress. Rec.* 25 Jan. (1900) 1169/2 [He] was let off on his own recognizance or straw bond, I have forgotten now which.

Straw bonnet. A bonnet made of woven straw. {1848} Also comb. — **1809** CUMING *Western Tour* 223 Pittsburgh [has] . . . eight straw bonnet makers. **1848** BURTON *Waggeries* 37 A full-grown girl in . . . an Angouleme straw bonnet, as big as a modern coal-scuttle. **1894** *Harper's Mag.* April 693/1 Something not unlike peace shone from the dim blue eyes under the poking rim of her straw bonnet.

+**Straw boss.** A subordinate boss. — **1894** CARWARDINE *Pullman Strike* 117 These employees . . . [having suffered] the continued oppression of the 'straw bosses,' . . . were in no condition to be trifled with by the Company. **1909** WASON *Happy Hawkins* 141 Omaha was supposed to be the straw boss; but he was too easy-goin'.

Straw braid. Braid made by plaiting straw. {1882} Also *strawbraider*, *straw-braiding*. — **1849** G. G. FOSTER *N.Y. in Slices* 99 The flygirls, the type-rubbers, the straw-braiders,—all the working girls from all parts of the City . . . have also found their sweethearts. **1864** *Harper's Mag.* Oct. 578/2 He laid all kinds of evil results at the door of straw braid. *Ib.*, It became customary for the straw braiders to take the bonnets they had made to the village. *Ib.*, Straw-braiding daily increased in importance as a branch of manufacture. **1875** STOWE *Deacon Pitkin's Farm* 50 Her straw braiding sold for a little more than that of any other hand.

Straw-cutter. A machine or instrument for cutting straw. {1790-} See also STALK-CUTTER 2. — **1845** *S. Lit. Messenger* XI. 755/1 A Yankee . . . had been through that country with a new-fangled patent straw-cutter. **1868** *Mich. Agric. Rep.* VII. 22 For tools, including straw-cutter, wagon-box, garden cultivator, &c., $25.85.

Straw foot. [In allusion to the alleged use of hay and straw to assist rustic recruits to distinguish between the right and left foot.] One of the alternate steps in marching. Hence *straw-foot* v. {1898, *dial.*} Also fig. and attrib. — **1851** *Knickerb.* XXXVIII. 79 But it was all 'hay-foot, straw-foot' with him. He knew as little of tactics as he did of politics. **1887** BILLINGS *Hardtack* 208 Scores of men . . . would 'hay-foot' every time when they should 'straw-foot.' **1911** SAUNDERS *Col. Todhunter* 98 You never got in a thousand miles of one of 'em, for all your 'heppin' and 'hay-foot' and 'straw-foot' drillin'.

✳ Straw hat. A hat made of woven straw. Also fig. — **1809** *Ann. 11th Congress* 2253 The annual amount of straw hats and bonnets made in the town of Wrentham alone is equal to one hundred thousand dollars. **1838** *S. Lit. Messenger* IV. 638/1 A gentleman's summer dress . . . [usually included] a home-made straw-hat. **1879** HOWELLS *Lady of Aroostook* 13 He took off his straw hat and fanned his face with it. **1922** TARKINGTON *Gentle Julia* 89 Looks like last year's straw hat to me.

Straw ride. {1856} +A pleasure ride taken by a group in a wagon or hayrack partially filled with straw. Also attrib. (Cf. HAY RIDE.) — **1881** DU CHAILLU *Land of Midn. Sun* II. 434 A custom which reminded me of the 'straw ride' parties common in the rural districts of the United States. **1895** *Outing* XXVI. 408/1 Invitations to sailing parties, straw rides or picnics are given verbally. **1905** 'O. HENRY' *Four Million* 131 Take her for a walk in the park, or a straw ride, or walk home with her from church.

Straw tick. A tick or mattress filled, or to be filled, with straw. — **1837** in Ellet *Pioneer Women* 421 We have filled straw ticks with the sweet smelling marsh hay. **1894** [see BUFFALO ROBE].

+**Straw town.** A town engaged in straw-plaiting. — **1864** *Harper's Mag.* Oct. 578/2 Among all the 'straw towns' of Massachusetts is a not very large yet quite enterprising one.

+**Straw vote.** An unofficial vote taken to indicate the probable outcome of an election or other issue. — **1891** *Cent.* 5982/3 *Straw vote*, a vote taken without previous notice, in a casual gathering or otherwise. **1904** *Boston Herald* 2 Nov. 1 A straw vote taken . . . among the Harvard faculty . . . gives Roosevelt a majority of 6 in a total vote of 66.

Strawworm. {1653} (See quotation.) — **1859** G. W. PERRY *Turpentine Farming* 107 Straw Worm . . . is to be found on the boughs of pines from the latter part of July during the remainder of the season.

* **Stray,** *n.* = ESTRAY *n.*
1643 *Boston Rec.* 73 In case they be not owned in 24 howers . . . , they shall be accounted and used as a stray. **1783** *Ky. Petitions* 69 A particular law respecting Strays. **1890** *Stock Grower & Farmer* 12 April 5/1, 12,049 head, from which was cut 118 head of strays belonging to members. **1907** WHITE *Arizona Nights* 112 There were present probably thirty men . . . here to pick up the strays inevitable to the season's drift.
attrib. **1836** H. R. HOWARD *Hist. V. A. Stewart* 114 One of our friends examines the stray-books regularly. **1837** WETMORE *Gaz. Missouri* 17 Our representatives . . . employ their energies on unimportant subjects of discussion, such as road-laws, stray-laws, &c. **1869** Stray brand [see CUT *v.* 20 h].

Stray, *v.* +*tr.* To separate the strays from (a herd). *colloq.* — **1869** *Overland Mo.* Aug. 126 They are obliged to stop and 'stray' the herd.

* **Streak,** *n.*
+**1.** A run *of* good or bad luck.
See also PAY STREAK.
1843 *Knickerb.* XXI. 303, I had 'struck a streak of bad luck.' **1865** 'MARK TWAIN' *Sketches* (1926) 205 There never was a bad James in the Sunday-school books that had such a streak of luck as this sinful Jim. **1889** MUNROE *Golden Days* 176 You can't never tell when a streak of luck is going to strike you in this business.

+**b.** *Baseball.* A run in hitting, winning, or losing.
1868 CHADWICK *Base Ball* 20 They got into what is called a 'streak of batting,' that is, one after another made good hits. **1910** Hitting streak [see HITTING]. **1912** MATHEWSON *Pitching* 233 But what's a new hat against a losing streak or a batting slump?

+**2. a.** *To start off like a streak* or variants: To go very fast. {1901}
Cf. STREAK *v.*
1839 *Knickerb.* XIII. 298, I see him yesterday afternoon . . . starting off like a streak, to go to Norridgewock. **1849** LANMAN *Lett. Alleghany Mts.* 89 The water wheeled my head round to the hole, and in I went quick as a streak. **1901** *Scribner's Mag.* April 501/1 We worked like streaks. **1920** SANDBURG *Smoke & Steel* 138 Maybe I will light out like a streak of wind.

+**b.** *To go a good streak*, to go at a good rate or pace.
1865 A. D. WHITNEY *Gayworthys* 141 She's going a good streak, ain't she?

+**c.** *To make a streak for*, to hasten towards (a place).
See also BLUE STREAK 2.
1875 HOLLAND *Sevenoaks* 60 [We'll] make a clean streak for the woods. **1909** WASON *Happy Hawkins* 280 She was in the habit of . . . gettin' it [food] into her in the shortest possible time, an' then makin' a streak for it.

3. *Streak of lightning* {1847}, +a drink of whisky.
Cf. CHAIN LIGHTNING 2, LIGHTNING 2.
1859 C. MACKAY *Life & Liberty* I. 169 'Ginsling,' 'brandy-smash,' 'a streak of lightning.'

* **Streak,** *v.*
+**1.** *quasi-tr.* To hasten; 'to light out.' *colloq.* or *slang.*
Cf. STREAK *n.* 2.
1834 C. A. DAVIS *Lett. J. Downing* 34, I streaked it round through New-Hampshire. **1837** *S. Lit. Messenger* III. 225 His companion was 'streaking it' down the street. **1860** *Harper's Mag.* March 447/1, I saw six Chippewa red-skins streaking it through the timber. **1910** McCUTCHEON *Rose in Ring* 119 Five terrified hoodlums were 'streaking it' in as many directions.

+**2.** *intr.* **a.** In same sense with adverbs.
1834 *New Monthly Mag.* XLI. 465 Away we 'streaked' at the rate of twelve miles an hour against the current. **1843** 'CARLTON' *New Purchase* I. 268 If he didn't make brush crack and streak off like a herd of buffalo! **1898** [see GOSH]. **1912** COBB *Back Home* 321 One hired livery stable rig after another went streaking by.

+**b.** Without adverbs.
a**1849** HILL *Yankee Stories* (B.), Blackstrap . . . [is] the sweetest drink that ever streaked down a gullet. **1897** *Outing* Feb. 439/1 A strong, young, spiked buck came streaking through the Chêniere.

* **Streaked,** *a.*
+**1.** *To look* or *feel streaked*, to look or feel alarmed, silly, uncomfortable, or irritated. *local.*
1815 HUMPHREYS *Yankey* 57 How streaked I feel all over! **1835** LONGSTREET *Ga. Scenes* 190 A limb . . . fetched me a whipe [*sic*] across the face, . . . giving me for the first time in my life a *sensible* idea of the Georgia expression, 'feeling streaked'; for my face actually felt as though it was covered with streaks of fire and streaks of ice. **1840** THOMPSON

Green Mt. Boys I. 141 You needn't look so streaked—we belong to the right party, you know. **1848** BURTON *Waggeries* 16 He felt considerable streeked at bein' roused out o' his mornin's nap for nothin'. **1878** BEADLE *Western Wilds* 416, I felt orful streaked, . . . but I knowed 'old blaze' had never failed yet.

2. In specific names. {1665–}
1782 CRÈVECŒUR *Letters* 129 Most common are the streaked bass, the blue fish [etc.]. **1820** RAFINESQUE in *Western Rev.* II. 51 Streaked-cheeks River-Bass. *Lepomis trifasciata*. . . . Found in the Ohio and many other streams. **1834** *S. Lit. Messenger* I. 97 The underwood is mostly streaked maple or elkwood. **1884** *Rep. Comm. Agric.* 336 During the past season the Streaked Cottonœur Leaf-beetle has done great damage in portions of Nebraska and Dakota.

+**Streakfield.** (See SCUTTLER.)

Streaky, *a.* {1670–} +Ashamed; confused. — **1845** *Big Bear Ark.* 43 That party did look streaky. **1848** *Family Companion* (B.), I never did feel so streaky and mean before.

* **Street.**
* **1.** *The street.* +**a.** A thoroughfare or a district of a city where financial business is conducted, esp. Wall Street in New York City; a money or stock market.
1854 'O. OPTIC' *In Doors & Out* (1876) 99 How does it happen, Joe, that you are in the street borrowing money? **1870** [see DEPRECIATED *a.*]. **1896** SHINN *Story of Mine* 157 Safe, steady pay ore produces no such flurry on the street.

+**b.** Those engaged in financial business in such a place.
1870 M. H. SMITH *20 Years Wall St.* 312 At least a thousand men . . . have startled the street by gigantic speculations. **1894** [see INSURANCE 2]. **1903** *N.Y. Times* 30 Aug., The Street has never received any direct information as to the identity of those now in control.

2. *attrib.* and *comb.* **a.** Designating various objects connected with a street or streets.
See also STREET CAR, STREET LAMP, etc.
1650 *Rowley Rec.* 66 This is that sid of the street fence which belongs to ther planting lots. **1737** *Boston Rec.* 184 The Street Dirt . . . might not be carried away into the Country. **1799** Street pipe [see PIPE *n.*¹ 5]. **1819** *Plough Boy* I. 51/3 Before the last ploughing [he] put on 700 horse cart loads of *street manure.* **1843** *Niles' Nat. Reg.* 1 July 279/1 Street Scraping Machine. **1867** RICHARDSON *Beyond Miss.* 50 A mechanic had sold a street-sprinkler. **1914** STEELE *Storm* 186 One street-light . . . had lived through.

b. Designating various persons and municipal organizations charged with the maintenance and safeguarding of the streets.
See also STREET-SWEEPER 1.
1789 *Phila. Ordinances* (1812) 75 [The] common councilmen shall . . . [do all] things, as the . . . street commissioners were . . . enabled by law to do. **1856** MACLEOD F. *Wood* 170 The Street Department . . . has charge of the opening, regulating and paving. **1880** CABLE *Grandissimes* 121 [She was] fortified against the street-watch with her master's written 'pass.' **1884** *Century Mag.* July 462/1 Already the whites . . . are giving them a share of the public employment, by making them street-cleaners, firemen, and policemen.

+**c.** In sense 1 with *advice, argot, broker*, etc.
1856 *Harper's Mag.* April 714/2 We have . . . seen a very laughable description of what is called a *Street-Broker*. **1870** MEDBERY *Men Wall St.* 31 The Commodore's 'pups,' as the merciless, cacophonic 'street' argot denominates the lightning friends of Vanderbilt, are making an ineffective rally. **1884** in Leavitt *Our Money Wars* 277 'The number of brokers in this city has increased immensely,' said an old-time 'Street' operator. **1894** WARNER *Golden House* vii, Have you heard any Street rumor? **1907** HARRIS *Tents of Wickedness* 22 Courtney . . . did not like 'street advice' either in stocks or morals.

+**Streetage.** **a.** ?Carriage along a street or streets. **b.** A charge for the use of street facilities. — **1866** *Md. Rep.* XXV. 87 The defendant . . . charged in addition to the usual freight . . . a further compensation for streetage to the foot of 6th street. **1884** *Reading Morning Herald* 17 April, There has been charged but a nominal sum on the Reading's business for streetage.

+**Street car.** { = E. 'tramcar'}
1. A public conveyance, chiefly for passengers, that runs through the streets on rails.
1862 TROLLOPE *N. America* I. 185 Omnibuses, or street cars working on rails run hither and thither. **1882** McCABE *New York* 239 Before the construction of the Elevated roads, the travel on the street cars was enormous. **1898** *Kissimmee* (Fla.) *Valley Gazette* 4 March 4/4 Electricity will do very well for propelling street cars on their smooth solid tracks. **1915** CAMPBELL *Proving Virginia* 108 So I shall bid you good-by and take a street car home.

2. Attrib. with *animal, conductor, driver*, etc. Also *fig.*
1870 *Rep. Comm. Agric. 1869* 372 Horse buyers [obtain] . . . street-car animals, and heavy dray or omnibus horses. **1873** *Newton Kansan* 15 May 1/5 It is proposed to introduce civil service reform among the uncivil street-car conductors. **1877** BURDETTE *Rise of Mustache* 132 He took his money, a ragged shinplaster and two street car nickels. **1885** *Santa*

Fé Wkly. New Mexican 30 July 4/6 Captain Hoover furnished him street car fare to the extent of two five case notes. **1892** *Courier-Journal* 2 Oct. 3/7 Dennis Knott, a street-car driver, ... noticed a man step on the front platform.

Street lamp. A lamp set up to illuminate a street. {1870–74} — **1799** C. B. BROWN *A. Mervyn* iv, The room's height and spaciousness were imperfectly discernible ... by gleams from a street-lamp. **1842** *Knickerb.* XIX. 118 A scrap of paper ... [was] being read over by the light of the street-lamp. **1883** *Century Mag.* July 326/1 The petroleum ... will be a valuable article for lighting the street lamps in the future cities of Ohio. **1907** LONDON *Road* 222 Under the light of a street-lamp was a [policeman]

+**Street railroad.** =next. *Obs.* or *obsolescent.* — **1859** *Ladies' Repository* Nov. 694/1 The problem of street railroads in Cincinnati has been solved. **1882** *Nation* 6 July 4/3 Governor Cornell has vetoed the bill to provide for the construction, maintenance, and operation of street-railroads in cities, villages, and towns. **1893** *Boston Jrnl.* 25 March 2/1 The New England Street Railway Company ... [was organized] to acquire various street railroads in New England.

+**Street railway.** The physical equipment, esp. the tracks and right of way, of a company operating street cars; such a company.

[**1861** *Chambers's Jrnl.* 29 June 416/1 The street railways of the American cities.] **1867** *Mich. Gen. Statutes* I. (1882) 908 The cars on the street railway of any company organized under this act, may be operated by steam, or by any power other than animal power. **1874** *Mass. Acts & Resolves* 348 'Street railway' shall be construed to mean a railroad or railway operated by animal power. **1880** *Cimarron News & Press* 15 July 3/3 While at Albuquerque ... he organized a company and secured a charter and concession for a street railway for freight and passengers. **1906** *Springfield W. Repub.* 7 Feb. 10 The cars on the street railway have been installed with electric searchlights.

+**b.** Attrib. with *car, company, franchise, president.*

[**1862** D. W. MITCHELL *Ten Yrs. U.S.* 265 If a poorly-dressed woman enter a crowded street-railway car, ... the young workman ... offers her his seat.] **1867** *Mich. Gen. Statutes* I. (1882) 909 Street railway companies may be organized under the provisions of this act. **1888** *N.Y. Herald* 13 May, May be the street-railway presidents never saw a starched shirt. **1902** *Harper's Mag.* May 890/1 Governor Rudd ... has been working like the devil over that street-railway franchise case.

Street-sweeper. **1.** One who cleans a street by sweeping it. {1848–} **2.** A long garment that drags in the street. **3.** A machine for sweeping the streets. — (1) **1815** in H. M. Brooks *Gleanings* IV. 82 Charles Hardy, Street Sweeper. **1848** JUDSON *Mysteries N.Y.* ii. 97 He is not fit for a street-sweeper. (2) **1855** *Chicago W. Times* 29 March 3/2 The ladies consider them [*sc.* bloomers] far more convenient than the street sweepers. (3) **1902** HARBEN *A. Daniel* 284 From the other direction came a gigantic concern looking like ... a metropolitan street-sweeper.

+**Street yarn.** **1.** *Spinner of street yarn,* a street gossiper. **2.** *To spin street yarn,* to gad about and gossip in the streets. — (1) **1816** *Mass. Spy* 6 March (Th.), [When I] see the yard covered with stumps, old hoops, and broken earthen[ware], I guess the man is a horse-jockey, and the woman a spinner of street-yarn. (2) *c*1848 WHITCHER *Bedott P.* xiv. 149 They say when she ain't a spinnin' street yarn, she don't dew nothin' but write poitry. **1864** NICHOLS *Amer. Life* I. 23 The young ladies ... 'spin street yarn.'

Stretch, n. Racing. The straightaway. (Cf. BACK STRETCH.) — **1868** WOODRUFF *Trotting Horse* 85 Her gait, ... when she darts up the stretch, is as square as ever was seen. **1903** *Public Ledger* (Phila.) 24 June 13/9 Mexoana ... took command in the stretch.

Stretch, v. **1.** *tr.* To *stretch out,* +to start moving, each vehicle falling into line. +**2.** *Baseball.* To play (a hit) for one or more bases further than it would normally permit. — (1) **1862** *Harper's Mag.* Sept. 449/1 At the command 'Stretch out!' each waggon falls into its appointed place, and ... we begin our march. *Ib.* 455/2 (2) **1897** *N.Y. Tribune* 9 Sept. 4/1 Clark ... was retired at second trying to stretch the hit. **1912** *Ib.* 15 Oct. (E. J. Nichols).

Stretcher. +An instrument that eases the fit of shoes, gloves, etc. — **1769** *Md. Hist. Mag.* XII. 280 The shoes ... had been on the Stretchers some months. **1885** *Harper's Mag.* Feb. 449/2 She was manipulating the ... pair of stretchers.

+**Strict construction.** (See CONSTRUCTION 1.)

+**Strict constructionist.** (See CONSTRUCTIONIST and cf. LOOSE CONSTRUCTIONIST.)

Strike, n.

1. a. A dry measure of from two pecks to four bushels. *Obs.* *b. By (the) strike,* leveled off, as by use of a strickle. *Obs.* {1674–}

1631 *N.H. Hist. Soc. Coll.* IV. 234 Both the English and Indian corne beeinge at tenne shillings a strike, ... we made laws to restraine the selling of corne to the Indians. **1639** *Md. Archives* I. 79 [Corn] shall not be Shaken at all but delivered by Strike. **1649** *Southampton Rec.* I. 59 The miller shall take but two quarts by strike vpon the vper part of the dishe for toll for one bushell of corne. **1859** BARTLETT 457 To sell by the strike, is not to heap up the article, as is usually done with potatoes, apples, etc., but to scrape off what is above the level of the top, as in selling grain, salt, or the like.

2. An organized and concerted action whereby workingmen stop work as an expression of discontent with their wages or working conditions. {1825–}

The earlier term was apparently *turnout.*

1810 *Trial of Journeymen Cordwainers N.Y.* 167 The society ... enforced obedience by decreeing what was called *a strike* against a particular shop that had transgressed. **1836** *Dialogue betw. Strike & Steady* 15 He was doing very well till the time of the strike last winter. **1872** [see LONGSHOREMAN]. **1890** *Boston Jrnl.* 11 Feb. 4/7 The great strike continues. **1900** *Congress. Rec.* 16 Jan. 875/1 The idea that the Democratic party ... are trying to create strikes and disturb business is ridiculous. **1913** LONDON *Valley of Moon* 182 If us teamsters keep on haulin' the mill-work the strike is lost.

b. On a strike, engaged in a strike.

1881 *Chicago Times* 14 May, The employés of the Grand Trunk car shops are on a strike for an advance in wages.

3. (See quot. 1864.) {1847, on Madeira Isl.}

1853 *Harper's Mag.* Nov. 761/2 [Juice] from cane first cut from the fields ... yields only indifferently well, and it seems as if a 'strike' would never be made. **1864** WEBSTER 1308/2 *Strike of sugar*. ... (*a.*) The act of emptying the teache, or last boiler, in which the cane-juice is exposed to heat, into the coolers. (*b.*) The quantity of the sirup thus emptied at once. **1887** *Century Mag.* Nov. 114/1 The 'strike' is now done.

+**4. a.** *Baseball.* (1) A turn at bat. *Obs.* (2) One of three counts against the batter, either called by the umpire or resulting from the batter's unsuccessful effort to hit the ball or to hit it fair.

See also FOUL STRIKE.

1845 in *Appletons' Ann. Cycl.* X. 77/2 Players must take their strike in regular turn. **1868** CHADWICK *Base Ball* 75 Mills called 'one strike' on him. **1891** [see BALL *n.*[1] 1 c]. **1912** MATHEWSON *Pitching* 12 It put me in the hole with the count two balls and one strike.

+**b.** In American bowling, the action of knocking all the pins down with one bowl.

1866 LOWELL *Biglow P.* 2 Ser. lix, To make a *strike* is to knock down all the pins with one ball, hence it has come to mean fortunate, successful. **1884** [see SPARE].

+**5.** A sudden success in finding rich ore or oil; any sudden financial success. {1895}

1855 H. HELPER *Land of Gold* 296, I may make a 'strike,' but that is mere speculation. **1868** *Putnam's Mag.* Jan. 25, I'll make a strike in Erie. **1883** *Century Mag.* July 329/1 Eager speculative men ... rushed in to share the profits of the big strike. **1897** *Boston News Bureau* 22 June, Leasing lands and sinking wells with the expectation of making a lucky strike. **1923** 'BOWER' *Parowan Bonanza* 12 Make that strike yet?

+**6.** A form of legislative blackmail in which a bill is introduced by a legislator merely for the purpose of getting paid to let the matter drop.

1885 *Century Mag.* April 824 The latter, technically called a 'strike,' is much the most common. **1903** HART *Actual Govt.* 135 Another method of influencing legislation is to introduce so-called 'strikes'—bills not intended to be passed, but to be bought or shaken off in some way.

+**7.** A quick movement by a fish as in taking the bait.

1894 *Outing* XXIV. 217/1 You'd never get a strike. **1897** *Ib.* XXX. 55/1 Discolored waters rippled with the 'strikes' of running fish.

8. Attrib. in sense 2 with *benefit, breaker, dues.*

1896 *Internat. Typogr. Union Proc.* 22/1, $48,087.18 ... [was] paid during the two years in strike and lockout benefits. **1904** *N.Y. Ev. Post* 4 Aug. 2 [Half of] the strike breakers are men who, having been idle for a time, simply wanted a chance to make a little ready money. **1913** LONDON *Valley of Moon* 8 Look at your brother, ... diggin' up extra strike dues to the union.

Strike, v.

The use of the participial form *stricken,* archaic in England but not uncommon in American English, is illustrated in the following quotations: **1790** WEBSTER in *Mass. Spy* 26 Aug. (Th.), I am not a little surprised at the revival of the word stricken, after being disused for centuries. **1820** *Mass. Spy* 15 Nov. (Th.), He had been stricken with a paralytick affection in July. **1864** *Ill. Agric. Soc. Trans.* V. 933, I wish to have one of those trees stricken from the list. **1902** *Independent* 29 May 1269 The provision for additional cadets was stricken out on a point of order.

I. +**1.** *tr.* To take down (tobacco) from the place where it has been curing. *Obs.*

1642 *Md. Archives* I. 153 No attachm[en]t ... may be layd upon Tobacco afore it be struck in Cask. **1678** *New Castle Court Rec.* 252 A forthy foott house of Tobbacco w[hi]ch was struck & Lay in bulke. **1784** SMYTH *Tour* II. 135 All that is within the house is struck or taken down.

+**2.** To print (paper money, hand bills, etc.). *Obs.* (See also sense 9 a.)

1759 FRANKLIN *Hist. Review Penna.* 99 The Assembly ... resolved to strike an additional Sum of 20,000 l. **1775** MORRIS in Sparks *Life G. Morris* 38 Each colony should strike for itself the sum apportioned by the Continental Congress. **1797** *Ann. 4th Congress* 2 Sess. 2045 For striking

Mediterranean passports, being done by a copper-plate, . . . [$]1,500. **1816** U. Brown *Journal* II. 146, [I] Gave him orders to strike me fifty Hand Bills.

+3. a. Of a line or course: To come out at; to meet. {1830-}

1798 *Mass. Mercury* 30 Oct. (Th.), Thence south, such a course as will strike William Negro's house. **1802** Ellicott *Journal* 179 The articles were then taken . . . up the lake to the point where our road from the hill struck it. **1863** A. D. Whitney *F. Gartney* xiv, A little side road . . . wound off from it, and struck the river again. **1890** *Congress. Rec.* 8 Aug. 8317/2 The water comes rapidly down [the Potomac R.] until it strikes tide water here at Georgetown.

+b. Of a person: To come upon or arrive at (a place); to hit upon (a trail, path, etc.); to happen upon or find (a thing or situation). {1893} Also fig.

1808 Pike *Sources Miss.* 134 In about five miles we struck a beautiful hill. **1838** *S. Lit. Messenger* IV. 114/2 Jest say Marion to her, and you strike the trail, she'l go on upon it. **1869** *Overland Monthly* Aug. 127 On the first good grass which they 'strike' they halt a few days. **1873** Cozzens *Marvellous Country* 77 After an hour or so they struck his trail. **1878** Pinkerton *Strikes* 53 The course taken by the regular tramp when he 'strikes a town,' as it is called, is to immediately hunt up the printing offices. **1881** Chase *Editor's Run in N. Mex.* 176 [Leadville, Colo.] is the highest point 'we've struck,' as they say here. **1906** *McClure's Mag.* Feb. 342 We seemed to have struck a late season.

+c. To meet or find (a person). *colloq.*

1886 *Congress. Rec.* 4 June 5253/1 He discovers in conversation with him, that he 'knew more about levees than any man he ever struck.' **1892** *Harper's Mag.* Aug. 404/1 You'll strike him at the office just now, if you'd like to see him. **1901** White *Westerners* 316 Struck Billy down the road a piece.

+4. To discover (a lead or pocket of ore); to hit upon (pay dirt). {1875-} Also fig.

See also Oil 2.

1835 Hoffman *Winter in West* II. 47, I hear that he has lately struck a lead. **1876** Bourke *Journal* 31 May, I succeeded in striking color; . . . [but] colors could be found on almost any stream near the mountains. **1884** Matthews & Bunner *In Partnership* 63 The young woman had refused to have anything to do with him for a long period; but he seems to have struck pay gravel about two days before my arrival. **1892** *Harper's Mag.* May 906/2 Water is struck at from 600 to 1200 feet.

+b. *To strike it,* to find a rich ore deposit; fig., to hit upon a profitable enterprise. Often *to strike it rich.*

1852 Clappe *Lett. from Calif.* 216 Every man wish to reach the bed-rock as quickly as possible, they sink a shaft . . . until they 'strike it.' **1869** J. R. Browne *Adv. Apache Country* 295 'Struck it rich!' 'Silver bricks!' and 'Pay rock!' hummed and drummed through the air. **1879** *Scribner's Mo.* Oct. 811/2 When the miner really 'strikes it,' . . . a house is built over the shaft. **1880** *Cimarron News & Press* 15 July 2/5 A miner is reported to have struck it rich over in the Taos mountains. **1899** *Harpers' Wkly.* 8 April 344/1 The lay-men struck it the first hole. **1905** Crothers *Pardoner's Wallet* 183 A dozen times he has 'struck it rich.'

5. *To strike camp,* ‖to make camp.

1846 Sage *Scenes Rocky Mts.* xi, It was midnight ere we arrived . . . and struck camp. *Ib.* xvii, [We] struck camp in a small grove of cottonwood.

+6. To induce (a person) to pay money on the promise of getting him votes, legislative favors, etc.

1859 Matsell *Vocabulum* 87 *Strike,* to get money from candidates before an election, under the pretense of getting votes for them; to borrow without intending to pay back. **1883** Landon *Wit & Humor* 345 He had a way of striking the politicians who wanted a favor out of the Governor. **1894** *Atlantic Mo.* Feb. 248/2 A legislator 'strikes' a corporation, . . . when he introduces some bill calculated to injure it directly or indirectly; his purpose being . . . to compel the corporation to buy him off.

+7. (See quotation.)

1891 *Cent.* 5991 *Strike,* . . . in the United States army, to perform menial services for an officer; act as an officer's servant: generally said of an enlisted man detailed for that duty.

II. In phrases with prepositions or adverbs. **8.** *To strike for,* +to aim at getting or attracting.

1867 Holmes *Guardian Angel* 32 Happening one day to see a small negro girl . . . in a flaming scarlet petticoat, she struck for bright colors in her own apparel. **1897** Howells *Landlord at Lion's Head* 365 He meant to strike for the class of Americans who resorted to those climates; to divine their characters and to please their tastes.

*9. *To strike off.* **a.** =sense 2. {1838-}

1775 *Jrnls. Cont. Congress.* III. 398 That the plates . . . be used for striking off and printing the above bills. **1857** *Lawrence* (Kan.) *Republican* 2 July 2 We shall . . . strike off a large edition.

b. To mark as being sold or allocated *to* someone.

1777 *Narragansett Hist. Reg.* II. 313 The above mentioned house is struck off the day above mentioned to Mr Silas Niles for 260 Dollars. **1816** U. Brown *Journal* I. 355 Lot No. 135 . . . was struck off to William Thompson Hays . . . for One Hundred Dollars. **1830** [see Country *n.* 2].

*10. *To strike out,* +in baseball, to fan out at bat.

1862 *N.Y. Sun. Mercury* 29 June (E. J. Nichols). **1868** Chadwick *Base Ball* 45 He is to be recorded on the score book as having struck out. **1907** *St. Nicholas* May 630/1 If I'd had a bat that was any good, I'd have knocked out a home run . . . instead of striking out the way I did.

*11. *To strike up.* **a.** To light (a fire), orig. with flint and steel. {without *up,* 1604-}

1758 *Essex Inst. Coll.* XII. 147 Rose this morning at 3 o'clock, ordered a fire struck up. **1828** Sherburne *Memoirs* 192 At length we concluded to strike up a fire.

+b. *passive.* (1) To be surprised, confounded, or unnerved. *colloq. Obs.* (2) To be attracted by someone.

(1) **1833** S. Smith *Life J. Downing* 230 At this I was a little struck up. **1843** Stephens *High Life N.Y.* I. 15, I never was so struck up in my life, as I was tu see her. *Ib.* 116, I was so struck up in a heap at seeing her in sich a fix. (2) **1884** Howells *Silas Lapham* 37 'Seem struck up on Irene?' asked the Colonel.

+Strike-out. *Baseball.* An out made by fanning the batter. — **1887** *Courier-Journal* 2 Feb. 8/3 A pitcher is not to receive an assist for a strike-out under the amended rules. **1917** Mathewson *Second Base Sloan* 246 But two strike-outs followed and averted calamity.

* Striker.

+1. a. One who does odd jobs for another.

1836 *Quarter Race Ky.* 20 [He] came and took the mare from his striker.

+b. One employed to do villainy; a ruffian; a runner employed by a real estate company, a gambling joint, etc.

1845 Hooper *Simon Suggs' Adv.* vi, Among her admirers was a young man named Eggleston—a sub-partner, or 'striker,' of the great Columbus Land Company. **1853** 'P. Paxton' *Yankee in Texas* 355 To each of these [he] gave the authority to enlist all the minor villains of their acquaintance . . . [to be] termed Strikers, and used but as tools. **1859** Bartlett 457 *Striker,* a bruiser; a ruffian. *a1871* *Country Merchant* 317 (De Vere), He was one of the most accomplished strikers, or barkers, as they are called, in the employ of the hells. **1893** *Harper's Mag.* April 712/2 Professional 'boomers,' with a retinue of surveyors and cappers and strikers, invaded the State.

+c. A political henchman, esp. one who seeks to effect a strike (sense 6).

c1855 *Sons of Sires* 90 The 'strikers' are a bold class of marauders, who 'come down' upon a candidate for a place . . . with threats that if he does not give it, they will be down upon him in the Primary Elections. **1873** Beadle *Undevel. West* 184, I had published a severe criticism of this Judge Smith. His 'strikers' now had me at Court as defendant. **1882** *Nation* 31 Aug. 171/1 The political striker sees his opening and begins to 'assess.' **1888** *Chicago Inter-Ocean* 2 Jan. 1/4 In the former [saloon were] . . . a number of political strikers and ward bummers. **1903** *N.Y. Ev. Post* 18 Nov. 8 The 'striker' for aid has become recognized as a distinct type of Congressional parasite.

+d. In the army, a soldier detailed as a servant to an officer. (Cf. Strike *v.* 7.)

1867 in Custer *Tenting on Plains* 558 Several Indians of a lower grade . . . seemed to act as strikers for the rest, attending to the cooking of the meat, and so on. **1885** Roe *Army Lett.* 336 Miller, our striker, . . . [must] make blinders with his hands back of Rollo's eyes so he will not see me jump to the saddle. **1897** Clover *Paul Travers' Adv.* 27 The lieutenant's 'striker' broiled [steaks] for supper. **1917** J. A. Moss *Officers' Manual* 485.

+2. *Baseball.* The batter. *Obs.*

1845 in *Appletons' Ann. Cycl.* X. 77/2 A player running home . . . can not make an ace if the striker is caught out. **1875** *Chicago Tribune* 15 July 5/5 O'Rourke, the first Boston striker, was put out on called strikes. **1887** *Outing* May 99/1 The new rule . . . gives a left-hand pitcher somewhat of an advantage over a right-hand one when opposed to a right-hand striker.

3. A workman on strike. {1850}

1865 in Commons, etc. *Doc. Hist.* IX. 101 These two congresses might adopt the same rule respecting strikers. **1878** Pinkerton *Strikers* 143 The strikers responded that no more trains were to be run over that road. **1923** Herrick *Lilla* 272, I'd been fighting the strikers same as the rest with hired thugs and all that.

+4. An apprentice engineer on a Mississippi steamboat.

1872 Eggleston *End of World* 171 It was natural enough that the 'mud-clerk' on the old steamboat Iatan should take a fancy to the 'striker,' as the engineer's apprentice was called. **1876** 'Mark Twain' *Old Times* i. 12 At last he turned up as apprentice engineer or 'striker' on a steamboat.

* String, *n.*

+1. A line *of* fence.

1794 Washington *Writings* XIII. 20 The string of fence . . . divides the upper from the lower fields. **1810** *East-Hampton Rec.* IV. 365 The string of fence near his house . . . fences the Nepeague meadows. **1854** *Mich. Agric. Soc. Trans.* VI. 177 The strings of fence will average eight and three-quarter rails high. **1903** A. Adams *Log of Cowboy* 17 On the Mexican side there was a single string of high brush fence.

+**2.** A whip. *Obs. slang.*

1839 KIRKLAND *New Home* (1840) 14 By some judicious touches of 'the string,' the horses are induced to struggle as for their lives. **1852** BRISTED *Upper Ten Th.* 30 And now the b'hoy . . . lays the string about fearfully.

+**3.** In certain games, a score or tally, or the number of turns at play.

1855 HOLBROOK *Among Mail Bags* 60 Just allow me twenty on a 'string.' **1879** WEBSTER *Suppl.* 1580/1 *String*, the number of points made, in a game of billiards. **1891** *Cent.* 5994/2 He made a poor string at first, but won.

+**4.** In certain games of billiards or pool, a line across the table over which a cue ball must pass after being out of play.

1864 DICK *Amer. Hoyle* (1866) 419 An imaginary line across the table at this point is the string. **1872** 'MARK TWAIN' *Roughing It* 336 Cheese it, pard; you've banked your ball clean outside the string.

+**5.** A restriction or condition attached *to* something. *colloq.*[2]

1888 *Battle Creek Wkly. Jrnl.* 15 Feb., Bob Ingersoll Says There Is a String to It. **1905** *N.Y. Ev. Post* 11 Aug. 6 The members of the committee have seen the folly of an investigation with a string tied to it. **1908** 'O. HENRY' *Options* (1916) 54, I've told you . . . my oral sentiments, and there's no strings to 'em.

+**6.** In miscellaneous senses.

a. A joke. **b.** (See quot. 1891.) **c.** A dozen traps set to catch wild animals. (a) **1851** BURKE *Polly Peablossom* 92 Of course Mabe was innocent of the 'string.' (b) **1875** *Chicago Tribune* 23 Nov. 7/3 [She] always had a full string at measuring-time. **1891** *Cent.* 5994/1 *String*, . . . in *printing*, a piece-compositor's aggregate of the proofs of types set by him, pasted on a long strip of paper. The amount of work done is determined by the measurement of this string. (c) **1900** DRANNAN *Plains & Mts.* 57 One dozen traps is called a 'string,' and it is considered one man's work, ordinarily, to 'tend a string.'

String, v. +*tr.* To fool or hoax (a person). Often with *along. slang.* — **1859** MATSELL *Vocabulum* 87 'String the bloke and pinch his honey,' humbug the man and get his money. **1894** HOYT *Texas Steer* (1925) II. 18 Somebody's been stringin' dat fellow. **1908** LORIMER *J. Spurlock* 219 What's your idea in stringing Lord Percy along?

+**String beans.** The unripe, edible pods of several varieties of beans; a plant producing such beanpods. — **1759** *Holyoke Diaries* 20 First Str[ing] Beans ys. year viz. C. W. Beans. **1865** *Nation* I. 239 A small patch of garden ground, planted with cabbages, string-beans, and tomatoes. **1891** WILKINS *New Eng. Nun* 167 She came down the mountain laden with green peas and string-beans.

Stringent, *a.* {1605-} +Of the money market: Tight. — **1870** MEDBERY *Men Wall St.* 69 Money is 'very active,' and the loan market 'stringent.' **1909** WEBSTER 2059/2.

* Stringer.

+**1.** A heavy timber laid lengthwise on a railroad track for the support of the rails.

1848 *Rep. Comm. Patents 1847* 72 One patent has been granted for improvements in . . . the manner of fastening it [*sc.* the rail] to the stringers. **1872** HUNTINGTON *Road-Master's Asst.* 37 Common spikes . . . act as so many wedges to split the stringers or rail-plates. **1903** E. JOHNSON *Railway Transportation* 34 Track with wooden stringer, surfaced with straps of iron.

+**2.** A tale or story concocted to hoax someone.

1850 in *Tall Tales of S.W.* (1930) 99 He never lacked assistance from his acquaintances whenever he had concocted a 'stringer.'

+**3.** A narrow, stringlike vein of ore.

1872 RAYMOND *4th Rep. Mines* 47 It is generally believed they [*sc.* pocket veins] are outlying 'stringers' of the main lode. **1896** SHINN *Story of Mine* 133 Their ledge . . . contained only a very low-grade ore that could not be milled at a profit after a few surface stringers were mined out. **1923** 'BOWER' *Parowan Bonanza* 282 They had gutted the rich vein and passed up tiny stringers that might lead to rich deposits.

4. A device, as a twig or cord, upon which fish are strung.

1893 *Outing* XXII. 88/2 Though he had several strikes, his stringer remained dry in his pocket.

Stringpiece. {1789-} + =STRINGER 1. — **1840** TANNER *Canals & Rail Roads* 261 *String pieces*, wooden rails upon which the iron bars of rail-roads are placed. **1883** *Harper's Mag.* Jan. 199 The track is rudely built and rickety, the rails being heavy strap-iron bolted on stringpieces.

* Strip.

1. A long, narrow piece *of* land, meadow, etc. {1816, in Africa; 1841-}

1638 *Essex Inst. Coll.* IV. 183/1 Hay . . . groweth vpon a stripp of ground nere to the pond. **1690** *Waterbury Prop. Rec.* 28 A strips [*sic*] that rune by the river to the mouth of the brooke. **1701** *Boston Rec.* 17 Samuell Sewall Esqr. & Hannah his wife grants unto the Town of Boston a certaine strip or Slip of Land. **1789** MORSE *Amer. Geog.* 458, 220,000,000 acres . . . to be sold for the discharge of the national debt; except a narrow strip of land. **1844** *Knickerb.* XXIII. 114 The Government . . . have laid out between them a strip of country forty miles in width. **1902** GOR-

DON *Recoll. Lynchburg* 98 The hands and their families are huddled on a strip of land over which the water is shallowest.

+**2.** *spec.* The Cherokee strip (q.v. under CHEROKEE 5).

1873 *Winfield* (Kan.) *Courier* 22 May 2/3 One Henry House, residing on the strip, about five miles south of this place [etc.]. **1890** *Stock Grower & Farmer* 29 March 4/1 The cattlemen in from the strip say that the wire fences have been cut.

Strip carpet. (See quot. 1845.) — **1843** *Lowell Offering* III. 90 [She] had not only the requisite pillow-case full of stockings before she was engaged, but also divers rag-mats and strip carpets. **1845** *Ib.* V. 255 A strip carpet . . . is made of the best remnants of old coats, and overcoats, and waistcoats, and the dark groundwork is relieved by strips of red and green and yellow flannel.

Stripe. {1626-} *Obs.*

1. =STRIP 1. *Obs.* {1801-}

1628 *Essex Inst. Coll.* IV. 181/2 Granted to Roger Mory a stripe of meadow conteyning tooe acres & an halfe. **1672** *Springfield Rec.* II. 241 Theres grannted him his three acres in a little strip or stripes between the meddow grannted Cornelius & Skipmuck. **1714** *Essex Inst. Coll.* XX. 179 The Committee . . . are ordered and Impowered to Sell and dispose of some small Pieces and Stripe of the Comon Lands. **1746** *N.H. Probate Rec.* III. 449, I also give her . . . a stripe of Land between the County road and Levets fence.

+**2.** A particular kind of political or religious opinion; a kind, sort, or race.

1850 GARRARD *Wah-To-Yah* viii. 109 The ox-driver . . . was of the same stripe as those to whom the scalps dangling from the Arapaho lance points, originally belonged. **1864** 'MARK TWAIN' *Sketches* (1926) 150 You'll not find a good many of *your* stripe in there! **1904** *N.Y. Times* 27 May 8 No Democrat of the Bryan-Hearst stripe could make headway in such an enterprise.

+**3.** *pl.* A prison uniform.

1887 *Courier-Journal* 29 Jan. 3/2 He changed his stripes for a suit of citizens' clothes. **1904** [see BALL AND CHAIN].

Striped, *a.* {1617-} In the specific or descriptive names of plants, animals, fruits, etc. {1629-}

Only a selection of examples is given here. See also the separate entries below.

1772 ROMANS in Phillips *Notes* (1924) 123 Those [river fish] peculiar to America are three Species of the Bream, . . . the Striped Bream [etc.]. **1790** DEANE *New-Eng. Farmer* 148/2 The *striped bug*, or yellow fly . . . eat[s] and destroy[s] the young plants of cucumbers, melons, squashes and pumpions. **1791** W. BARTRAM *Travels* 278 The striped lizard, called scorpion . . . I have already mentioned. **1842** *Nat. Hist. N.Y., Zoology* IV. 216 The Striped Killifish, *Fundulus fasciatus*, . . . abounds in all our salt-water creeks and bays. *Ib.* 251 The Striped Herring, *Clupea fasciata*, . . . is a rare but well defined species, occurring south of Cape Cod. **1856** *Rep. Comm. Patents 1855: Agric.* 103 The Striped Pale-green Caterpillar . . . [was] found upon the leaves of the cotton-plant, near Columbus, in Georgia. *Ib.* 273 The varieties of cane which have hitherto been most cultivated in Louisiana . . . are the 'Striped-blue Ribbon;' . . . the 'Yellow' [etc.]. *Ib.* 295 Of apples we have . . . the 'Striped Seek-no-further,' the 'Newton Pippin' [etc.]. **1869** *Amer. Naturalist* II. 598 Striped-back woodpecker (*Picoides dorsalis*). **1883** *Nat. Museum Bul.* No. 27, 479 *Minytrema melanops*. . . . Striped Sucker. . . . Sold in great numbers, though of inferior quality. **1884** GOODE, etc. *Fisheries* I. 316 The common Bonito of England, *Orcynus pelamys*, is what is here called the 'Striped Bonito.' **1917** *Birds of Amer.* III. 112 Black and White Warbler. . . . [Also called] Creeping Warbler; Striped Warbler.

+**Striped bass. a.** A serranoid fish (*Roccus saxatilis*, syn. *lineatus*), native to the Atlantic coast, but introduced on the Pacific. **b.** A white bass, *Lepibema chrysops*. — **1818** *Amer. Mo. Mag.* II. 295 The striped bass, of New-York, or Rock-fish, . . . is another excellent salt-water fish. **1820** *Western Rev.* I. 370 Golden-eyed Perch. *Perca chrysops*. . . . Vulgar names Rock fish, . . . Gold eyes, Striped bass, &c. **1838** *Mass. Zool. Survey Rep.* 38 *Labrax lineatus*—striped bass—at some seasons is brought into market in considerable quantities, and sold in the fresh state. **1848** *S. Lit. Messenger* XIV. 682/2 We consider the striped basse one of the finest game fish to be found in American waters. **1904** *N.Y. Times* 2 June 9 New Yorkers . . . stayed there all night to catch striped bass in the early morning. **1911** *Rep. Fisheries 1908* 317/1 In the North it [*Roccus lineatus*] is generally called the 'striped bass.' . . . The name is sometimes applied to the white bass (*Roccus chrysops*) of the Great Lakes region.

+**Striped maple.** An eastern maple (*Acer pennsylvanicum*) with striped bark; moosewood. — **1785** MARSHALL *Amer. Grove* 3 American Striped Maple. . . . The bark, especially of the young shoots, is beautifully variegated or striped. **1832** BROWNE *Sylva* 113 In many of the forests of Maine and New Hampshire, the striped maple constitutes a great part of the undergrowth. **1850** S. F. COOPER *Rural Hours* 461 Our striped maple is a great favorite with [the moose]. **1892** APGAR *Trees Northern U.S.* 85.

+**Striped pig.** A fictitious animal used as a sign of some surreptitious activity. *Obs.* Also *attrib.* — **1839** *Knickerb.* XIV. 429 A bookseller in Nassau-street announces a work in press, . . . giving a faithful account of the rise and overthrow of the sect of *striped pigs*. **1840** *Boston Transcript* 1 June 2/3 Kendall of New Orleans . . . has opened an exhibition of the 'striped pig' at his sanctum on Camp Street. **1846** *Spirit of Times* (N.Y.) 11 July 234/1 A '*Striped Pig*' *Arrangement*—Since the legislative Solons of Massachusetts have prohibited trotting and racing, the [race] courses have taken the name of 'pleasure grounds.'

+Striped snake. A garter snake, esp. *Thamnophis sirtalis.* — 1778 CARVER *Travels* 478 The Wall or House Adder, the Striped or Garter Snake. 1839 in Audubon *Ornith. Biog.* V. 601 The snake was the common and apparently innoxious Striped Snake. 1891 *Cent.* 5725/1.

+Striped squirrel. Any squirrel with stripes on its back, as the chipmunk. {1901} — 1796 MORSE *Univ. Geog.* I. 203 The Striped Squirrel is still less than the [red squirrel]. 1842 *Nat. Hist. N.Y., Zoology* I. 62 The Striped Squirrel . . . is well known under the various popular names of Hacky, Ground Squirrel, Chipping Squirrel, Chipmuck. 1888 [see GOPHER *n.* 3].

+Stripper. One seeking a land claim in the Cherokee strip. — 1893 *Columbus Dispatch* 15 Sept., Eager strippers swarmed to-day at the new booth established here last night.

Strong arm. {1606-} Violence; physical force; *strong-arm man,* a slugger. — 1828 J. HALL *Lett. West* 291 When a horse thief, a counterfeiter, or any other desperate vagabond, infested a neighbourhood, evading justice by cunning, or by a strong arm, . . . the citizens formed themselves into a 'regulating company.' 1836 HOLLEY *Texas* 322 This military council . . . distributed lots to the inhabitants, contrary to all law, but that of the *strong arm.* 1901 'FLYNT' *World of Graft* 17 One of the best illustrations of the indifference of the Chicago police force . . . is the freedom with which the 'hold-up' and 'strong-arm' men conduct their operations. 1903 [see KNOCKABOUT 2].

Strong bark. A tree of southern Florida and the West Indies (*Bourreria ovata*), from the bark of which a beverage is prepared. {1864} — 1884 SARGENT *Rep. Forests* 114 *Bourreria Havanensis.* . . . Strong Bark. Semitropical Florida, southern keys . . . ; in the West Indies.

+Stroud. [From *Stroud,* Eng.]
1. a. A coarse woolen material from which blankets and garments are made; a piece of this material. Also pl. in sing. sense. **b.** A blanket of this material made esp. for trade with Indians. **c.** A garment made of this material. Cf. DUTCH BLANKET.
1683 in C. H. Hunt *Life E. Livingston* 6 Four garments of Strouds. 1748 WEISER *Journal* 31, I made a Present to the old Shawonese Chief Cackawatcheky, of a Stroud, a Blanket [etc.]. 1755 *Lett. to Washington* I. 89, 2 pr. red Stroud, 6 blue Strouds. 1773 *Hist. Brit. Domin. N. Amer.* II. 83 Peltry of all kinds is purchased with . . . blankets, strouds, and wampum or conque-shell beads. 1816 McKENNEY *Memoirs* I. 309 Strouds are a blue cloth, six quarters wide, with a narrow cord about one inch from the selvage. 1822 Morse *Rep. Indian Affairs* II. 240 A stroud, which is a kind of short petticoat, ornamented round the bottom with red or jetted binding. 1871 *Rep. Indian Affairs* (1872) 459 Not a vestige of Indian costume—as blankets, leggings, strouds, &c.—comes into our schoolroom.
2. Attrib. with *blanket, coat, shirt.*
1683 in C. H. Hunt *Life E. Livingston* 7 Four Stroud-Coats and Two duffel-Coats. 1765 CROGHAN *Journal* (1904) 60, I gave him a Strowd Shirt, Match Coat [etc.]. 1772 in *Travels Amer. Col.* 553, I also gave him a Stroud Blanket flap.

+Strouding. The cloth of which stroud blankets are made. Also attrib. — 1814 BRACKENRIDGE *Views La.* 201 The merchandise . . . consisted of strouding, blankets, lead, tobacco [etc.]. 1827 McHENRY *Tour to Lakes* 255 She is dressed in a . . . blue strouding petticoat. 1840 HOFFMAN *Greyslaer* II. 9 A fillet of colewort leaves . . . was kept in its place by a strip of strouding torn from her own dress. 1886 *Century Mag.* Nov. 33/2 He and his sons gathered hazel-nuts enough to barter at the nearest store for a few yards of blue strouding such as the Indians used for breech-clouts.

‖Strychnine whisky. A grade of whisky thought to be poisonous. — 1860 *Harper's Mag.* Aug. 427/2 It was apparent that the man had died from the immoderate use of strychnine whisky.

Stuartia. [f. John *Stuart,* Marquis of Bute (1713-92).] A genus of American and Japanese shrubs of the family Theaceae or a plant of this genus. Also with specifying term. — 1831 AUDUBON *Ornith. Biog.* I. 91 I have placed them on a branch of Stuartia. *Ib.* 95 The White-flowered Stuartia. . . . A small tree, with smooth spreading branches. 1857 GRAY *Botany* 70. 1891 *Cent.* 6003/1 Two handsome white-flowered species, from the mountains of Virginia, Kentucky, and southward, are sometimes cultivated under the name of *stuartia.*

∗Stub, *n.*
+1. The butt or stump of a cigar or cigarette.
1855 M. THOMPSON *Doesticks* 133 Perhaps they expect us to smoke 'stubs,' like the newsboys. 1873 BEADLE *Undevel. West* 787 Even little darkeys watch for the 'old stubs' as they are thrown away. 1914 'BOWER' *Flying U Ranch* 187 He spat upon the burnt end of his cigarette stub from force of the habit that fear of range fires had built.
2. A short or stocky person.
1865 *Harper's Mag.* Dec. 133/2 In these . . . regions there dwells a stub of the law who is possessed of august presence. 1890 CURTIN tr. Sienkiewicz *With Fire & Sword* 514, I have something to say to this little stub of an officer.
+3. A counterfoil; the portion of a ticket detached and returned to the purchaser by a ticket-collector.

1876 *N. Amer. Rev.* CXXIII. 301 The shipment of large packages, for which check stubs representing only small amounts were retained. 1879 *Webster Suppl.* 1580/1 *Stub,* . . . the part of a leaf left in a check-book, after a check is torn out; the number and destination of the check are usually recorded on it. 1887 *Postal Laws* 91 Before returning the stubs, the calculations and footings should be reviewed and made correct. 1911 REEVE *Poisoned Pen* 303 'Number 156' Herndon noted as the collector detached the stub and handed it to her.

+4. In special combinations.
Stub ballot book, the book or pad remaining when ballots of a certain type are torn out; *s. hoe,* a hoe for grubbing up stubs; *s.-hunter,* one who searches for cigar or cigarette stubs; *s. scythe,* a scythe for use on stubble, a stubble scythe; *s. switch, s. tail, s. track,* (see quotations).
1911 *Okla. Session Laws* 3 Legisl. 229 The bundle of voted ballots and the stub ballot book, . . . shall be placed in the envelope labeled 'Voted Ballots.' 1870 EMERSON *Soc. & Solitude* 85 He is a graduate of the plough and the stub-hoe. 1869 'MARK TWAIN' *Innocents* 162 It wounds my sensibilities to see one of these stub-hunters watching me . . . and calculating how long my cigar will be likely to last. 1650 *Mayflower Descendant* X. 174 One spade one mattacke one holborne and stub syth. 1909 WEBSTER 2062 *Stub switch,* . . . a switch in which the track rails are cut off squarely at the toe and the switch rails are thrown to butt end to end with the lead rails. 1867 SIMMONDS *Dict. Trade* Suppl., *Stubtail, Stumptail,* names in North America for flour made out of damaged wheat and good wheat ground together. 1909 *Cent. Suppl.* 1287/2 The parallel tracks of the train-shed of a terminal station are *stub-tracks.*

∗Stub, *v.*
+1. *tr.* To strike (one's toe) against something while walking or running. {1897-}
1846 *Spirit of Times* (N.Y.) 25 April 100/1 In Yankee parlance, 'she stubbed her toe.' 1894 'MARK TWAIN' *Those Twins* i, If you can fix me so I can eat for two and only have to stub toes for one, I ain't going to fool away no such chance. 1908 J. WEBSTER *Four-Pools Myst.* x, They finally fell silent, with only an occasional imprecation as someone stubbed his toe.
+2. *intr.* To stump *about;* to go *along* heedlessly. *colloq.*
1878 B. F. TAYLOR *Between Gates* 241 An old whaler stubbing about estimated him [a whale] at sixty barrels. 1895 *Stand.* 1783/1 The boy stubs along to school.

+Stub-and-twist. 1. A firearm having a stub-twist barrel or barrels. Also attrib. **2.** (See quotation.) — (1) 1844 *Knickerb.* XXIII. 440 There, Peter, is a true 'stubb-and-twist.' 1861 *Chicago Tribune* 26 May 1/5 When finished the gun presents the appearance of a stub-and-twist rifle. (2) 1917 *Birds of Amer.* I. 152 Other names [of the ruddy duck are] . . . Paddy-whack; Stub-and-twist; . . . Dinky; Dickey; Paddy.

Stubbing hoe. A stub hoe. — 1660 *East Hampton Rec.* I. 180 The spade, houghes, wedges, & stubing houghes [of John Hand].

∗Stubble.
+1. The stump or lower part of sugar cane remaining when the crop is cut; sugar cane growing from these stumps. In full *stubble cane.*
1827 in Commons, etc. *Doc. Hist.* I. 214 Stubbles of Creole cane in new land mark the row. 1833 SILLIMAN *Man. Sugar Cane* 12 [Cane tops], when not reserved for planting, are suffered to remain on the field, for the protection of the stubble. 1856 *Fla. Plantation Rec.* 455 Plantin and Replanting stuble cane. 1897 *Kissimmee* (Fla.) *Valley* 19 May 1/4 Well cared for stubble will rattoon for three years in most parts of this state.
2. In special combinations.
Stubble crop, a crop of sugar cane that springs up from the stubble of the preceding crop; *s. plow,* (see quotation); *s. rye,* rye sown on stubble; *s.-shorn,* of sheep, shorn long so as to leave more wool than usual.
1881 *Chicago Times* 11 June 7/2 The sugar districts in this state [La.] report . . . Stubble crop good. 1876 KNIGHT 2431/1 *Stubble-plow,* . . . one for plowing *old* ground, so called; land which was lately in small grain, not in grass. In contradistinction to *sod-plow.* 1802 *Mass. H. S. Coll.* I Ser. VIII. 189 The first year, Indian corn; the second, hill rye; the third, stubble rye. 1866 *Maine Agric. Soc. Returns 1865* 157 This sheep was stubble shorn, which accounts for one staple being so much longer than the other.

Stubbling. {1872} +*Stubbling in,* (see quotation). — 1825 LORAIN *Pract. Husbandry* 129 The worst system of cultivation in common practice seems to be stubbling in; or annually putting in crops of small grain on stubble grounds.

+Stub book. A book or pad of stubs of checks, receipts, etc. — 1886 *Rep. Secy. Treasury* 700 Stub-books of stamps . . . [occupy] a very large and rapidly increasing space in the files-rooms. 1887 *Postal Laws* 91 The postmaster will continue to use what is left of the stub book. 1902 'O. HENRY' *Roads of Destiny* 191 Then the stub book of the certificates of deposit.

+Stub(b)oy, *interj.* (See STABOY.)

+Stub sho(r)t. (See quot. 1876.) — 1843 *Knickerb.* XXII. 446, I was flat on my back . . . by the camp-fire, . . . with the 'stub-shot' for a pillow. 1876 KNIGHT 2431/2 *Stub-short; stub-shot.* 1. The unsawed portion of a plank where it is split from the bolt or log. . . . 2. (*Turning.*) The portion by which an object to be turned is grasped.

∗Stuck, *a.* +*To be stuck on,* (see STICK *v.* 6).

*Stud.¹

+1. A studhorse or stallion.

1803 CUTLER in *Life & Corr.* II. 142 The famous white stud, an Arabian horse. **1845** *Knickerb.* XXVI. 368 A very large stud broke from the line. **1891** C. ROBERTS *Adrift Amer.* 183 He was a stud, and as fine a horse of his class as I ever saw.

+b. *To take the stud(s),* (see quot. 1830). *colloq.*

1797 *Penna. Mag.* VI. 111 Dont you think Mr Ashleys leading Strings may give way, if the Commy. should take the Studd. **1830** *Va. Lit. Museum* 6 Jan. 479 'To take the stud'—to be obstinate: originally applied to a horse that refuses to go on. **1900** HARRIS *On the Wing* 226, I'm a pretty good walker, but if I was to take the studs and lie down in the road, you'd have some trouble.

+2. = STUD POKER. Also *studhorse.*

1902 WISTER *Virginian* 24 'Any cyards going to-night?' . . . 'Stud and draw.' **1920** MULFORD *J. Nelson* ii, He's a travellin' eddicator in th' innercent game of draw—or was it studhoss, Nelson?

*Stud.² +The height of a room from floor to ceiling. — **1850** in J. Hawthorne *N. Hawthorne & Wife* I. 369 You cannot think how pretty the room looks, though with such a low stud that I have to get acclimated to it. **1886** E. S. MORSE *Jap. Homes* 63 These rooms were unusually high in stud.

*Studded, *a.* (See HIGH-STUDDED *a.,* LOW-STUDDED *a.*)

*Studding. +The height of a room or story in a house. — **1884** HOWELLS *Silas Lapham* iii, Lapham promptly developed his ideas of black walnut finish, high studding, and cornices.

+Student lamp. An adjustable lamp especially suitable for use by students. — **1873** 'G. HAMILTON' *Twelve Miles* 101 The fame of the German Student Lamp was noised abroad. **1880** TOURGEE *Bricks* 394 The student-lamp had been lighted before his story was ended. **1910** TOMPKINS *Mothers & Fathers* 147 Cora . . . drew their chairs up to the student lamp.

+Studfish. A killifish, *Xenisma stellifer* or *X. catenatum.* Also with specifying term. — **1882** *Nat. Museum Bul.* No. 16, 337 *Fundulus stellifer,* Spotted Stud-fish. **1896** JORDAN & EVERMANN *Check-List Fishes* 310 *Fundulus catenatus.* Studfish. Tennessee and Cumberland rivers and clear streams of the Ozark Mountains.

+Stud poker. Also **studhorse poker.** A form of poker differing slightly in the dealing and betting from other forms of the game. — **1864** DICK *Amer. Hoyle* (1866) 182 Stud Poker . . . , in all essential particulars, is like the other Poker games. **1884** W. SHEPHERD *Prairie Exper.* 77 The main trade of the town is at the bars of the saloons or at the tables of stud poker. **1891** C. ROBERTS *Adrift Amer.* 152 Every saloon had a gambling room, where poker, stud-horse poker, faro, . . . and a wheel of fortune were usually hard at it.

*Study, *n.* In special combinations.

Study bell, a bell that announces the beginning of a study hour or period; *s. club,* a club formed by those interested in study; *s. gown,* a loose wrapper or dressing gown worn in a study; *s. rent,* rent for a study in a college building.

*c*1764 in Woolsey *Hist. Disc. Yale* 54 The Seniors, however, are not to detain a Freshman more than five minutes after study-bell. **1871** STOWE *Pink & White Tyranny* 198 Then again, John, there's our old study-club. **1865** *Atlantic Mo.* Jan. 23/1 His long palm-leaved study-gown and tasseled velvet cap lent him a reverend appearance. **1655** in Quincy *Hist. Harvard* I. 463 The study rents . . . were discounted with Mr. Dunster.

*Study, *v.* To study up, (see quot. 1891). *colloq.* — **1880** 'MARK TWAIN' *Tramp Abroad* 412, I resolved to devote my first evening in Zermatt to studying up the subject of Alpine climbing. **1891** *Cent.* 6005/3 *To study up.* (a) To learn by special study or investigation; get up a knowledge of, as for a particular purpose or occasion. . . . (b) To seek or get a knowledge of by observation or consideration; observe or reflect upon critically; make up one's mind about.

Study hall. {1891-} In a school, a large hall or room reserved chiefly for studying. — **1846** E. Waylen *Reminiscences* 497 About eight the bell calls them to the study-hall, where half an hour is spent in exercises in English grammar. **1873** HOLLAND *A. Bonnicastle* 357 He never entered the study-hall without awakening a smile of welcome from the whole school.

Study hour. An hour or period during which pupils study. — **1873** TYLER *Hist. Amherst Coll.* 178 A legislative body, called the House of Students, enacted laws . . . for the better observance of study hours, etc., etc. **1888** *Detroit Free Press* 4 Aug. (F.), The High School girls kick against long study hours. **1907** *St. Nicholas* May 663/2, Duty calls with the voice of the bell, for study-hour.

Study lamp. A lamp especially suitable for use in a study. — **1830** *Collegian* 231 A rusty old study-lamp hung from the dingy ceiling. **1868** *Mich. Agric. Rep.* VII. 166 The gaily-attired moth . . . [flits] around our study-lamp. **1890** H. O. WILLS *Twice Born* 122, I went to bed to read by the light of a large study lamp.

Study room. A room in which one studies; a study. — **1837** *Knickerb.* X. 383 Our study-rooms were contiguous. **1882** MCCABE *New York* 466 The attic story is set apart for work and study rooms for those carrying on original researches. **1907** *St. Nicholas* Aug. 872/1 You look in the study room and I'll go upstairs.

*Stuff, *n.* +(See quotation.) — **1787** J. Q. ADAMS *Life New Eng. Town* 66 [She] has rather too much temper, or as it is called in New-England, too much *stuff.*

*Stuff, *v.*

1. *tr.* To deceive or hoax (a person). *slang.* {1859}

1840 in *Amer. Speech* XVI. 231/1 Alexander Stewart was committed to prison for *stuffing* Mr. James Brainard, of Colchester, Delaware county, with a gold watch at an expense to him of $30. **1861** *Harper's Mag.* Jan. 155/2 Here and there a loose man was caught by the button, and led aside behind a shanty to be 'stuffed.' **1894** FORD *P. Stirling* 319, I believe you are trying to stuff me.

+2. *tr.* To fill (a ballot-box) with fraudulent votes. *slang.*

1857 *Lawrence* (Kan.) *Republican* 28 May 1 The invading hordes . . . stuffed the boxes with illegal ballots. **1890** [see BALLOT-BOX 1]. **1917** SINCLAIR *King Coal* 115 He says you stuff the ballot-boxes.

Stuffer. {1611-} +1. = WATCH STUFFER. *slang.* +2. One who stuffs ballot boxes. *slang.* (See also BALLOT-BOX 3.) — (1) **1840** in *Amer. Speech* XVI. 231/1 'A stuffer' . . . persuaded Robert that he could not live here in York, without a watch. (2) **1875** *Chicago Tribune* 9 Nov. 2/4 The first thing to do was to use every means to bring the scoundrelly 'repeaters' and 'stuffers' to justice. **1910** J. HART *Vigilante Girl* 255 Tower always stands by his stuffers and plug-uglies, to give the Devil his due.

*Stuffy, *a.* New Eng. +Sulky, obstinate, bad-tempered. *colloq.* — **1825** NEAL *Bro. Jonathan* III. 289 Well then, if you're so stuffy about it. **1862** LOWELL *Biglow P.* 2 Ser. iii. 91 It's justifyin' Ham to spare a nigger when he's stuffy. **1890** *Dialect Notes* I. 20 *Stuffy,* sullen, obstinate, ill-humored. [New Eng.]

*Stump, *n.*

I. *1. The portion of a felled tree remaining in the ground, freq. used as an identifying object in a surveyed line or boundary or in constructing a stump fence.

1649 *Portsmouth Rec.* 346 From the Corner of the sayd ffence to the aforsayd Stump. **1678** *Providence Rec.* XIV. 15 The sayd Land is Bonded on the north westerne Corner with a black stump standing in the range of the aforesaid meadow. **1733** *Providence Rec.* IX. 67 Thence E 17 pole to a Chestnut Stump. **1784** in *Harper's Mag.* XLIII. 948/2 [One line of boundary is described as running to] a stump and stones where Daniel Harrington licked William Smith. **1815-16** *Niles' Reg.* IX. Suppl. 178/1 I observed . . . [a] strong substantial and durable fence, made of white pine stumps. **1886** [see PIG-TIGHT *a.*].

+2. A tree stump serving as a platform from which a speaker addresses an audience.

1775 in Moore *Songs & Ballads Amer. Rev.* 101 Upon a stump, he placed (himself,) Great Washington did he. **1808** *Ann. 10th Congress* 2 Sess. 766 This species of party insinuation was a mighty engine . . . on an election day, played off from the top of a stump. **1844** *Knickerb.* XXIII. 506 A western orator recently delivered himself of it from the summit of a sugar maple stump.

+b. *transf.* Any place or platform from which an audience may be addressed.

1816 *Ann. 14th Congress* 1 Sess. 1169 His arguments are better calculated for what is called on this side of the river *stump,* than for this Committee. **1838** [see MEAT BLOCK]. **1891** SWASEY *Early Days Calif.* 315 In politics he has been a power of commanding influence, whether in political oratory upon 'the stump' . . . or as a public journalist. **1913** LA FOLLETTE *Autobiog.* 340 It is one thing to talk of general propositions on the stump [etc.].

+3. (See quot. 1835.) *Obs.*

1835 TODD *Notes* 34 Candidates of doubtful principles are called *Stumps.* **1844** EMERSON *Poet Ess.* 2 Ser., Our stumps and their politics . . . are yet unsung.

+4. (See quotation.) *Obs.*

1851 HALL *College Words* 294 A *stump,* a bad recitation; used in the phrase, 'to make a stump.'

+5. A dare or challenge; a test or trial. *colloq.*

*a*1861 WINTHROP *J. Brent* 279, I'll take yer stump. **1871** A. D. WHITNEY *Real Folks* 24 It was a 'stump' again. That was all she called it; she did not talk piously about a 'cross.' **1894** *Advance* 18 Oct. 102/3 The bravest thing ye did was to refuse to run the risk fer a mere stump!

II. In phrases.

To whip the devil round a stump, (see DEVIL *n.* 5); *to talk (a)round a five-cornered stump,* (see FIVE-CORNERED STUMP).

+6. *To be up a stump,* to be in a perplexing situation or difficulty. *colloq.*

1829 KIRKHAM *Eng. Grammar* 206 [He will] soon be up a stump. **1876** 'MARK TWAIN' *Tom Sawyer* ii, Hi-yi! You're up a stump, ain't you? **1915** CAMPBELL *Proving Virginia* 149 I'm rather up a stump.

+7. *To take (to) the stump,* to go on a political speaking tour; to engage in political speech-making. Also *to go on the stump.*

1852 STOWE *Uncle Tom* xxiii, Why didn't you ever take to the stump? **1872** *Ku-Klux Klan Rep.* VII. 607, I ought to . . . take the stump for Seymour and Blair. **1884** *Lisbon* (Dak.) *Star* 31 Oct. 2/3 Henry Ward Beecher . . . has at last come out and taken the stump for Cleveland. **1904** *Sun* (N.Y.) 7 Aug. 1 [If someone] informed him that Chauncey M. Depew had turned Democrat and was going on the stump for Parker and Davis . . . , 'he wouldn't bat an eye.'

+8. In miscellaneous expressions.

From the stump, from the beginning; *to run against a stump*, to encounter a difficulty; *fooling round the stump*, beating about the bush; *to put to* (one's) *stumps*, to force to one's best efforts; *in* (or *at*) *the stump*, of timber, unfelled, standing, uncut.

1844 LEE & FROST *Oregon* 280 A house must be built from the stump in a few weeks. **1871** EGGLESTON *Hoosier Schoolm.* 50 Ralph Hartsook ran against a stump where he was least expecting it. **1880** *Scribner's Mo.* XIX. 428/2 Thar ain't no use in foolin' round the stump! **1890** McALLISTER *Society* 317, [I urged] them to show these Britishers what the Yankee could do when put to his stumps. **1902** WHITE *Blazed Trail* 243 Worth in the stump anywhere from sixteen to twenty thousand dollars. **1905** PRINGLE *Rice Planter* 153 It has been the habit of many to sell the wood to negroes at the stump.

9. *attrib.* and *comb.* **a.** In sense 2 with *campaign, man, material*, etc.

1832 FERRALL *Ramble* 244 Sundry 'stump orations' were delivered . . . for the enlightenment of the electors. **1834** BRACKENRIDGE *Recollections* 172 The term stump oratory is probably derived from the practice in early times of speaking from a stump or log of wood. **1840** KENNEDY *Quodlibet* 98 Agamemnon Flag . . . was the only stump man on the ticket. **1840** *Picayune* 21 Aug. 2/4 Speaker . . . Polk of Tennessee, used to do his own playing on these stump tours. **1852** HAWTHORNE *Blithedale Romance* vi, She was made . . . for a stump-oratress. **1862** LOWELL *Biglow P.* 2 Ser. v. 149 Excuse me for usin' a stump-phrase agin. **1867** LOCKE *Swingin' Round* 82 Pilin Billinsgate upon Billinsgate, usin Tennessee stump slang. **1879** *Congress. Rec.* 9 Dec. 35/2 Possibly it may be a part of the duty of Congress to furnish stump material of that kind, but I did not know it. **1888** BRYCE *Amer. Commonw.* I. i. x. 132n., The famous struggle of Mr. Douglas and Mr. Lincoln for the Illinois senatorship in 1858 was conducted in a stump campaign.

b. In special combinations.

Stump city, a town in a region where lumbering has left many tree stumps; *s. country*, cut-over lands in which tree stumps abound; *s. machine*, a stump-puller; *s.-stinger*, an insect resembling a wasp (see quotation); *s. swallow*, (see quotation); *s. yard*, a yard or enclosure where stumps abound.

1862 *Harper's Mag.* June 133/2 In one of the many stump cities for which Michigan is somewhat noted live two individuals [who are doctors]. **1896** *Home Missionary* July 129 Vast tracts of stump country [in Mich.] are as truly virgin soil as if the region had just been discovered. **1868** LOSSING *Hudson* 54 One of the stump-machines stood in a field near the road. **1849** LANMAN *Lett. Alleghany Mts.* 82 The stump-stinger is remarkable for having attached to the middle of his body a hard and pointed weapon, with which he can dig a hole one inch in depth in the body of even a hickory tree. **1917** *Birds of Amer.* III. 88 Tree Swallow. *Iridoprocne bicolor.* . . . [Also called] White-bellied Swallow; Stump Swallow; Eave Swallow. **1723** *New-Eng. Courant* 2 Dec. 1/2 For suppose . . . they should forget where they were, and order their Men . . . to *face about to the Stump-Yard*, or turn about to the Barn.

∗Stump, *v.*

+1. *tr.* To challenge or dare. *colloq.*

1766 J. ADAMS *Diary Works* II. 204 Keen . . . stumped Soule, the moderator, to lay down the money to prevent a tax upon the poor. **1825** NEAL *Bro. Jonathan* I. 317, I stump you, therefore, to pick up that are Bible—if you dare. **1882** THAYER *From Log-Cabin* 73, I stump you to do it. **1922** A. BROWN *Old Crow* 34, Turn in your money. I will mine. Stump you!

+2. To perplex, confuse, baffle. *colloq.* {1852–}

1812 PAULDING *J. Bull & Bro. Jon.* 129 John Bull was a little stumped when he saw Jonathan's challenge. **1840** *Picayune* 25 Aug. 2/2 The following . . . rather stumps us. **1889** 'MARK TWAIN' *Conn. Yankee* 322 [He would] chalk off mathematical nightmares . . . that would stump the angels themselves. **1910** [see DIRECTORY 2].

+3. (See quot. 1828.)

1828 WEBSTER, *Stump*, to strike any thing fixed and hard with the toe. (*Vulgar.*) **1891** *Harper's Mag.* Feb. 364/2 Mus' be powerful sorrowful ter set at home an' shed tears lest he mought hev stumped his toe on the road.

+4. *intr.* To make stump speeches; to electioneer in a political campaign. Also *to stump it*.

1838 BIRD *Peter Pilgrim* I. 114, I stumped through my district, and my fellow-citizens sent me to Congress! **1857** *Quinland* II. 176, I am empowered by my party to employ whom I like to 'stump it,' during the coming campaign. **1878** *N. Amer. Rev.* CXXVI. 275 [The government was] down in Carolina, stumping for Grant. **1905** *Springfield W. Repub.* 6 Oct. 8 That year he stumped in Maryland, Virginia, Michigan and throughout a long western trip.

+b. *tr.* To travel or canvass (a state or other area) in a speech-making political tour.

1856 in Rhodes *Hist. of U.S.* II. 232 There are about two hundred orators, great and small, now stumping Pennsylvania for Fremont. **1869** BROWNE *Great Metropolis* 637 She has stumped the West. **1884** R. GRANT *Average Man* 226, I stumped the State for Buchanan in '56. **1897** *Kissimmee* (Fla.) *Valley Gazette* 31 Dec. 2/1 Ex-State Treasurer Collins is said to have threatened to stump the state in the cause of his innocence.

+Stumpage.

1. Standing timber.

1835 *Knickerb.* V. 423 The folds of verse are too tender for such rough words as tariff, jobbing, cuts, stumpage, snags, sawyers, etc. **1854** S. SMITH *'Way Down East* 53 Major Grant . . . was returning home from Moosehead Lake, where he had been . . . to sell stumpage to the loggers. **1888** *Boston Herald* 13 Aug. 8/7 Options have already been secured on a large amount of Minnesota stumpage. **1902** WHITE *Blazed Trail* 98 Five million feet of timber, . . . at the price of stumpage' (standing trees) 'was worth ten thousand dollars.'

attrib. **1906** BELL *C. Lee* 318 He leased them the stumpage rights of Sunnymede.

2. The value or price of standing timber; a tax on cut timber: (see also quot. 1848).

1848 BARTLETT 341 *Stumpage*, the sum paid to owners of land for the privilege of cutting the timber growing thereon. **1870** *Congress. Globe* 21 March 2104/2 The American lumberman pays about $2 per 1,000 feet for stumpage, so called, upon the quantity he cuts. **1911** J. F. WILSON *Land Claimers* 107 With stumpage at six bits that's a scant eight hundred dollars.

attrib. **1884** *Rep. Comm. Agric.* 142 All stumpage laws should be repealed.

Stumper. {1731–}

+1. A question, problem, etc., which stumps or baffles one. *colloq.* {1855–}

1807 IRVING, etc. *Salmagundi* vi, Now this [a new dramatic reading] was 'a stumper.' **1862** 'E. KIRKE' *Among Pines* 74 That was a 'stumper' for the poor woman, who evidently did not understand one-half of the sentence. **1887** *Courier-Journal* 20 Jan. 4/5 The question was sort of a stumper.

+2. A stump speaker.

1849 *Knickerb.* XXXIV. 513 The best 'stumpers' are not always the best qualified for the business of the state. **1863** *Boston Sun. Herald* 30 Aug. 2/7 An Ohio stumper, while making a speech, paused in the middle. **1896** *Columbus Dispatch* 23 Sept., The secretary of the American Marine association . . . [wrote] to the Republican stumpers asking them to call special attention to the shipping plank.

+Stump-extractor. =STUMP-PULLER. — **1847** *Rep. Comm. Patents 1846* 94 Letters patent have been granted for improvements in . . . stump extractors. **1889** HOWELLS *Hazard of Fortunes* I. 105 Then somebody invented a stump extracter, and we pulled them out with a yoke of oxen.

+Stump fence. A fence made wholly or chiefly of tree stumps. — **1845** JUDD *Margaret* I. 138 They crossed the stump-fence into the herb-garden. **1880** *Scribner's Mo.* Feb. 508/2 Some timely genius arose and invented the stump puller and the stump fence. **1902** WHITE *Blazed Trail* 120 The twisted stump-fences about the most fertile farms of the north alone break the expanse of prairie.

Stumping. +The delivering of stump speeches. {1865–} Also attrib. — **1844** *Lexington Observer* 18 Sept. 2/3 Gen. Cass has started on a *stumping* excursion for Polk and Dallas. **1857** *Lawrence* (Kan.) *Republican* 28 May 3 Mr. Perrin made a speech of some length, rather in *stumping* style. **1875** *Chicago Tribune* 5 Oct. 2/3 There is very little stumping in Wisconsin this fall. **1900** *Congress. Rec.* 5 Feb. 1518/2 The President . . . in his stumping tour through the West . . . rejected that theory.

+Stump lot. A lot or enclosure in which stumps abound. — **1865** TROWBRIDGE *Three Scouts* 7 Around them were all the evidences of desolating war,—neglected fields, demolished fences, and orchards converted into stump-lots. **1873** BAILEY *Life in Danbury* 97, If every flying pang had been a drunken plow chased by a demon across a stump lot, I think the observer would understand my condition.

+Stump orator. A stump speaker. Freq. derogatory. — **1813** JEFFERSON *Writings* XIII. 281 Of this acrimony, the public papers of the day exhibit ample testimony, in the debates of Congress, of State legislatures, of stump-orators. **1852** STOWE *Uncle Tom* xxiii, You'd make a famous stump orator! **1888** FERGUSON *Experiences of Forty-Niner* 151 Over the hill . . . [lived] the Dutch blacksmith, politician, and stump orator.

+Stump-puller. A device or machine for pulling up tree stumps. — **1854** *Mich. Agric. Soc. Trans.* V. 505 The afternoon was spent in a trial of plows, a stump puller, and in general conversation. **1880** *Scribner's Mo.* Feb. 508/2 Some timely genius arose and invented the stump puller and the stump fence. **1888** *Scientific Amer.* 21 April 247 The John Cornelius Grub and Stump Puller.

+Stump speaker. One who makes stump speeches. — **1844** *Lexington Observer* 24 Aug. 3/1 The mendacity of the Locofoco press, and Locofoco stump speakers, has reached to such a degree, that [etc.]. **1869** BOWLES *Our New West* 41 Lieutenant-Governor Brass of Illinois . . . [is] a ready and most popular stump speaker. **1899** in *Congress. Rec.* 31 Jan. (1900) 1365/2 It was customary to hear Democratic stump speakers urge him . . . to cast in his political fortunes with his real friends.

+Stump speaking. The delivering of stump speeches; an occasion on which such speeches are made. — **1836** J. HALL *Statistics of West* 205 In the west . . . the practice of stump-speaking prevails. **1851** *Knickerb.* XXXVII. 285 There was a 'stump-speaking.' **1862** *Christian Banner* 23 July 1/1 Political stump speaking has infused deadly poison into the heart of the whole body politic. **1889** *Harper's Mag.* Sept. 554/2 Other occasions . . . were set apart for . . . militia musters, stump-speakings, county court day assemblages.

+Stump speech. A speech or harangue, usually of a political nature, of a type delivered orig. from tree stumps before backwoods audiences. — **1820** FLINT *Lett. from Amer.* 251 The harangues are called stump-speeches. **1857** *Quinland* II. 166 As for making stump speeches, I'm no hand at that. **1915** B. MATTHEWS in *Scribner's Mag.* June 757/2 A stump-speech was certain of a warm reception.

Stumptail. {1868-} **+1.** A contemptuous designation for depreciated bank notes. *Obs.* Also *stump-tail currency*. **2.** =*Stubtail* (see under STUB *n.* 4). — (1) **1861** *Chicago Tribune* 26 May 1/8 By a special arrangement to use Illinois Bills, (Stump-tail), I am able to sell the following list of Real Estate. **1879** *Congress. Rec.* 22 Feb. 1788/1 The country will go back to the wild-cat and the red-dog and stump-tail currency that we had before we established the national banks. **1888** KIRKLAND *McVeys* 236 Here the stranger lugged out . . . bills of all denominations and all kinds of banks, those being the days of 'stump-tail' currency. (2) **1867** [see STUB *n.* 4].

+Stump tree. (See quot. 1890.) — **1890** NEWHALL *Trees Northeastern Amer.* 190 Kentucky Coffee Tree, Stump Tree. G[ymnocladus] disicus. **1900** [see KENTUCKY COFFEE 2].

Stumpy, *a.* {1600-} **+**Abounding in stumps. — **1673** *Southampton Rec.* II. 253 All the meadow and mowing land . . . standing on the west side of the stumpy marsh. **1875** 'MARK TWAIN' *Old Times* iv. 71 We were shaving stumpy shores. **1897** *Outing* XXX. 328/2 We were passing a cabin surrounded by a few acres of stumpy pasture.

Stunt, *n.* [Of obscure origin.] **1.** A feat or performance, esp. of an athletic nature, that is unusual or done for effect: (see also quot. 1895). *colloq.* {1901-} **2.** *Stunt master,* (see quotation). — (1) **1895** *Dialect Notes* I. 400 *Stunt* . . . one of those convenient words which may be used in almost any connection . . . ; in general it is synonymous with 'thing' and may be used as variously. **1904** *Sun* (N.Y.) 8 Aug. 5 He took lessons in holding the life net . . . and the other stunts firemen are taught. **1924** CROY *R.F.D. No. 3* 57 'Josie, do a scene for us,' . . . 'Yes, do a stunt!' (2) **1891** *Amer. Folk-Lore* IV. 228 Stunt Master, or Follow the Leader is a game in which the leader endeavors to stunt the others; that is, perform some feat in which they are unable to follow him.

Stunt, *v.* **1.** *tr.* To stun. *colloq.* **2.** To surpass in doing stunts. — (1) **1845** HOOPER *Daddy Biggs' Scrape* (1928) 142 Some one an 'em would throw a long log o' wood . . . as nigh at me as they could guess, *to stunt the cat.* **1859** *S. Lit. Messenger* XXVIII. 144/2 We wuz ableeg'd to stunt him with rocks. (2) **1891** [see STUNT *n.* 2].

*Sturgeon.

*1. Any one of various ganoid fishes, usually of the genus *Acipenser,* found in both fresh and salt water.

1613 PURCHAS *Pilgrimage* 632 Jamestown [furnishes] . . . many commodities, as Furres, . . . Sturgeon. **1672** [see FROSTFISH 1]. **1725** *New-Eng. Courant* 3-10 July 2/2 Some evil minded Persons carry'd into the Presbyterian Meeting House there, a stinking Sturgeon of about 8 foot in Length. **1768** WASHINGTON *Diaries* I. 269 Dredgd for Sturgeon, and catchd one. **1846** *Spirit of Times* (N.Y.) 6 June 171/3 Mr. Thornton Stringfellow, 'hooked' a small sturgeon . . . which weighed 302 pounds. **1885** *South Fla. Sentinel* (Orlando) 29 April 1/9 Many remarkable stories have been told concerning the sagacity of the sturgeon.

+2. In special combinations.

+*Sturgeon extract,* (see quotation); *s. fishery,* the catching of sturgeon and the preparing of them for market; **+***s. pie,* a compost heap of which sturgeon form the chief ingredient.

1884 *Nat. Museum Bul.* No. 27, 1117 Sturgeon extract. . . . 'This is a novelty, and is what its name indicates, the extract of sturgeon meat, intended to be used for meat or fish sauces, soups, &c.' **1726** PENHALLOW *Indian Wars* 88 The Sturgeon fishery was also begun. **1841** *Farmers' Cabinet* (Phila.) V. 368 Sturgeon Pie. . . . Plough up a bank of earth, and place upon it half-a-dozen sturgeon [etc.].

*Style.

1. The manner in which a printing office or publishing house deals with certain details of editing and typography. Also attrib.

1871 RINGWALT, etc. *Amer. Encycl. Printing* 451 It is highly important for a compositor to thoroughly familiarize himself with the style of the office in which he is employed, as well as the style adopted for any special work. **1894** SHUMAN *Steps into Journalism* 41 One of the many revelations that come to the new recruit in journalism is the fearful and wonderful diversity of these 'styles.' **1908** (*title*), Chicago Daily News: Style-book. **1912** G. M. HYDE *Newspaper Reporting* 33 A paper that uses many capital letters is said to follow an *up* style, and a paper that uses small letters instead of capitals whenever there is a choice is said to follow a *down* style.

+2. *To put* (or *sling*) *on style,* to put on side. *slang.*

1864 *Rio Abajo Press* 5 July 1/3 [J. C. Frémont] was in command of the Department of Missouri, wherein he fizzled in generalship, and put on 'style' that was a scandal to American sentiment. **1875** 'MARK TWAIN' *Old Times* v. 83 Ours was a steamer where no end of 'style' was put on. **1875** [see MOKE 1].

+Suability. Liability to be sued; the state of being suable. Freq. in phrase *suability of states.* (Cf. ELEVENTH AMENDMENT.) — **1793** JAY *Correspondence* III. 454 The second object of inquiry now presents itself, viz., whether suability is compatible with State sovrignty. **1798** *Ann. 5th Congress* 483 An Act of the Legislature of the State of Kentucky, consenting to the ratification of the amendment of the Constitution of the United States . . . relative to the suability of States. **1806** WEBSTER

295/2 *Suability,* liability to be sued, subjection to civil process. **1838** *U.S. Mag.* I. 159 The first cycle of American nationality was rounded off before the Supreme Court pronounced any formidable judgment on constitutional law, save that which . . . asserted the suability of States.

Suable, *a.* (See quot. 1891.) {a1623-} 'Now chiefly *U.S.*' (*O.E.D.*). — **1810** MARSHALL *Writings on Constit.* 137 A state, then, which violated its own contract was suable in the courts of the United States. **1891** *Cent.* 6014/2 *Suable,* . . . capable of being or liable to be sued; subject by law to civil process.

Sub, *n.*

1. Short for *subaltern.* {1812-}

1756 WASHINGTON *Writings* I. 293, I would have you . . . Build Fort after Fort, leaving Garrisons in them . . . under command of a sub or Trusty Sergeant. **1855** *Knickerb.* XLV. 112 The bare idea . . . was extremely diverting to the hilarious sub. **1895** REMINGTON *Pony Tracks* 8 After some sarcasm by a jolly young sub, . . . we were again mounted and on the way.

2. Short for SUBSTITUTE *n.* {1830-} **a.** A substitute for military service.

1844 *Cincinnati Misc.* I. 72 The Advantage of getting 'a Sub.' **1866** 'F. KIRKLAND' *Bk. Anecdotes* 161/1 They were politely informed that the intended 'sub' was already a soldier.

+b. A printer serving temporarily in the place of another. Also attrib.

1876 *Scribner's Mo.* April 838/1 He consented finally to allow another printer to take his place in the 'Clarion' office—temporarily, and as his 'sub' only. **1895** *Stand.* 1788/2 *Sub-list,* . . . a list of the subs or substitute printers who are allowed to supply the places of regular compositors in an office without notice to the foreman or proprietor. **1896** *Internat. Typogr. Union Proc.* 44/2 In the meantime the Call office is overrun with subs.

c. In athletics, a player serving as substitute for a regular member of a team. {1896}

1889 *Trenton* (N.J.) *Times* 24 July (E. J. Nichols). **1894** *Outing* XXIV. 70/2 Only after much maneuvering can one eight get on the water without drawing the rival 'subs' to the spot. **1899** QUINN *Penna. Stories* 27 A sub was put in his place and the game started from the centre of the field once more. **1921** PAINE *Comr. Rolling Ocean* 5 Sure I'll run in a sub and you go lie down.

Sub, *v.* {1778-} **1.** *intr.* To act as substitute for a telegrapher. **+2.** (See quotation.) *colloq.* — (1) **1879** *University Mag.* (London) Nov. 589 At Cincinnati . . . [Edison] 'subbed' for the night men [i.e., telegraph operators]. (2) **1909** *Cent. Suppl.* 1289/2 *Sub,* . . . to subirrigate.

*Sub-, *prefix.*

*1. Designating persons of secondary or subordinate authority.

See also SUBAGENT, SUBCHIEF, etc.

1671 *Md. Archives* II. 322 An Act prohibiting . . . all Clerkes Sub Clerkes . . . to plead as an attorney. **1683** in Hough *Papers Pemaquid* 74, I do hereby Constitute and appoint you . . . to be Sub Coll[ecto]r and Receiver of the publiq Revenue. **1703** *Mass. Province Acts* VIII. 288 [The Council sent a message proposing] an establishment for a commissary-general and two sub-commissaries for the forces. **1838** *Mass. H. S. Coll.* 3 Ser. IX. 91 John Neptune is the lieutenant-governor or sub-sachem. **1848** in *Commons, etc. Doc. Hist.* I. 336, I have had many young men as sub-overseers on the place. **1848** BRYANT *California* iii. 43 Mr. Jacob, who had been appointed sub-captain of one of our divisions. **1883** *Harper's Mag.* Jan. 206/2 These Maine men are likely to become foremen, or sub-foremen. **1893** HALE *New Eng. Boyhood* 33 There was one headmaster, a sub-master, and two others, who were called ushers on the printed catalogue.

2. Designating organizations, assemblies, etc., subsidiary to, or forming parts or branches of, other organizations or groups.

See also SUBAGENCY, SUB-BAND, etc.

1800 *Aurora* (Phila.) 8 Jan. (Th.), They would recommend that the [Congressional] library be divided into several small apartments, for the purpose of holding Sub-Caucuses. **1844** RUPP *Relig. Denominations* 41 The East Sub-Synod, containing the following Presbyteries: Big Spring, Monongahela, The Lakes, Mansfield, Steubenville, Blairsville, Second Ohio. **1849** *31st Congress 1 Sess.* H. R. Ex. Doc. No. 5, II. 1014 The Dacotahs are subdivided among themselves into seven grand council-fires. **1881** *Chicago Times* 17 June, Regarding the formation of a pool, the report . . . recommends three sub-pools. **1896** *Pop. Science Mo.* 572 The bureau will be aided . . . by sub-bureaus. **1922** PARRISH *Case & Girl* 12 An answer appeared, . . . mailed from one of the sub-postoffices.

3. In special combinations.

Sub-bay, a bay constituting a division of a larger inlet; *subirrigation,* a method of irrigating below the surface; *subreport,* a report made as a preliminary to, or a part of, a more inclusive report; *subtrousers,* pl., drawers; *subzero,* of temperature, below zero.

1840 *Knickerb.* XVI. 213 We encamped in a quiet little sub-bay of this inlet, near Granite Point. **1880** *Cimarron News & Press* 19 Aug. 1/6 But sub irrigation for wheat would be too expensive. **1856** OLMSTED *Slave States* 292 The Second Auditor's General Report on Education . . . contains abstracts of sub-reports. **1890** *Columbus Dispatch* 11 July, Four inches of white canvass subtrousers was exposed. **1896** *Home Missionary* April 611 Our work has kept up . . . in spite of storms, blizzards, and sub-zero temperature.

Subagency. {1845} +A government Indian agency of subordinate rank. — **1834** *Stat. at Large* IV. 736 The limits of each agency and sub-agency shall be established by the Secretary of War. **1853** J. W. BOND *Minnesota* 209 The sub-agency of this tribe was removed . . . to Sandy Lake. **1881** *Rep. Indian Affairs* p. viii, On the Gila (where a sub-agency was established). **1900** *Rep. Geol. Survey 1898-9* IV. Pl. 44 Subagency of Southern Utes at Navajo Springs.

Subagent. {1863-}

+**1.** A government officer, subordinate to an Indian agent, stationed among the Indians. Also *assistant subagent.*

1818 *Stat. at Large* III. 428 All sub-agents [shall] receive five hundred dollars per annum. **1822** MORSE *Rep. Indian Affairs* I. 87 Indian superintendents, agents, sub-agents, and all other officers of government, who have to do with Indians . . . [should] be . . . members of one or other of these Education Families. **1849** WHITNEY in Brewster *Life J. D. Whitney* 105 You can have a place as assistant sub-agent at $2 per day. **1869** *Overland Mo.* III. 171 Hostilities had commenced with the murder of sub-agent Bolon.

2. An agent of an agent; a subordinate agent. {1863-} 'Spec. in *U.S. Law*' (O.E.D.).

1843-56 BOUVIER *Law Dict.* (ed. 6) II. 552/2 A sub-agent is generally invested with the same rights, and incurs the same liabilities in regard to his immediate employers, as if he were the sole and real principal. **1865** in Fleming *Hist. Reconstruction* I. 28 The Agents at Memphis, Little Rock, Vicksburg and Natchez, have delegated authority . . . , to Collect Confederate Cotton, to sub-Agents. **1892** *Current History* II. 81 The plan being to hold all steam-ship agents and sub-agents responsible for the cost of the returned ineligibles. **1909** *Md. Ct. Appeals Rep.* CXI. 252 The supervising engineer of a manufacturing company . . . has no implied authority to bind the company by employing sub-agents.

Sub-band. +A division of a band of Indians. — **1810** PIKE *Sources Miss.* I. App. 60 A young man . . . has recently taken the lead in all the councils and affairs of state of this sub-band. **1866** *Rep. Indian Affairs* 210 This sub-band of the Brulés still maintain a distinct organization.

Sub-base. {1826-} +**1.** (See quotation.) **2.** A secondary base of supplies. — (1) **1877** BARTLETT 676 *Sub-Base,* a mop or wash-board. Philadelphia. (2) **1903** *Science* 9 Oct. 478 After establishing a sub-base there [at Cape Sabine, Mr. Peary] will force his way northward.

Subcellar. An undercellar; a cellar beneath another cellar. Also attrib. — **1857** VAUX *Villas* 303 There is a sub-cellar under the whole house. **1877** *Harper's Mag.* Dec. 52/2 A squad of health-officers . . . inspecting the sub-cellar tenements of a poor neighborhood. **1906** *Springfield W. Repub.* 22 March 16 He knows a paper mill from the subcellar to the roof.

Subchief. {1858} +Among American Indians, a subordinate chief. — **1844** [see HALF *a.* 3]. **1877** *Rep. Indian Affairs* 17 The chief Spotted Tail agreed to visit in person the hostile camp, accompanied by 250 sub-chiefs and headmen. *a***1918** G. STUART *On Frontier* I. 182 It will probably be the cause of civil war among the Blackfeet for those killed were all sub-chiefs.

+**Subclothier.** An army official subordinate to the clothier general. *Obs.* (See CLOTHIER 3.) — **1780** *N.H. Hist. Soc. Coll.* IX. 238 The Sub Clother of the Troops in gerrison . . . will Make Returns to Head Quarters. **1781** *Va. State P.* I. 481 The sub-clothier, as he is styled by Congress, . . . is the proper officer thro' whose hands all issues of clothing should pass.

Subeditor. A subordinate or assistant editor. {1837-} — **1865** 'MARK TWAIN' *Sk., New & Old* 167 Our esteemed friend . . . walked into the office where we are sub-editor at a late hour last night. **1871** *Scribner's Mo.* I. 362 He was a sub-editor of a leading New York paper.

Subfactor. {1705-} +=SUBAGENT 1. — **1822** [see FACTOR 3]. **1822** *Missionary Herald* XVIII. 381 The sub-factor brought the goods to us.

+**Subfresh.** =next. Also collective. — **1850** [see CONDITION *n.*]. **1855** *Yale Lit. Mag.* XX. 103 Everybody happy, except Sub-Fresh, and they trying hardest to appear so. **1871** BAGG *At Yale* 62 And before the sub-Fresh has time to protest, he is rolling along in a hack. **1893** *Congregationalist* 21 Sept., Enrollment as freshmen or 'sub-fresh' in the City College.

+**Subfreshman.** A (prospective) student just below the rank of college freshman. Also attrib. — **1871** BAGG *At Yale* 51 The sub-Freshman is pledged to his society months before he approaches the college walls. **1896** J. B. Alden *Living Topics Cycl.* II. 264 [The College of the City of New York included] classical, scientific and mechanical subfreshman classes. **1905** *McClure's Mag.* June 125/2 The coaches . . . distribute them [*sc.* managerships] to sub-freshmen athletes. **1909** BREWSTER *Life J. D. Whitney* 72 When Josiah went away, he was not even a sub-freshman.

‖**Subgenation.** [L. *sub* 'under' and *genus* 'race.' Cf. MISCEGENATION.] The subjection of one race to another. — **1864** J. H. VAN EVRIE (title), Subgenation: the Theory of the Normal Relation of the Races; an Answer to 'Miscegenation.'

Subhead, *v. tr.* To supply a subhead for (newspaper material). — **1877** *Harper's Mag.* Dec. 45/2 One of them was heading and sub-heading cable dispatches from the seat of war.

+**Sub-Indian-agent.** =SUBAGENT 1. — **1847** PALMER *Rocky Mts.* 50 Here we met Dr. White, a sub-Indian agent. **1871** *Rep. Indian Affairs* (1872) 288 A. A. Henry, Sub-Indian Agent.

***Submarine,** *a.* Carried on under water; designed for use or operation under water. {1648-}

See also SUBMARINE BOAT, SUBMARINE CABLE, etc.

1785 JEFFERSON *Writings* V. 37, I remember to have heard of his [Bushnell's] submarine navigation during the war. **1798** *Amer. Philos. Soc.* IV. 303 General Principles and Construction of a Sub-marine Vessel. **1813** *Niles' Reg.* IV. 337/2 We would respectfully solicit the *pious men* to explain to us the difference between waging war with *sub-marine machines,* and with *aerial* destructive weapons. **1838** *N.Y. Advertiser & Exp.* 21 Feb. 2/2 Mr. Fulton . . . [set] forth his ability to blow up the largest of the enemy's ships by his Sub-marine Torpedoes. **1860** PRESCOTT *Telegraph* 179 The wires of a submarine telegraph. **1868** *Rep. Comm. Patents 1867* 1174/1 Submarine Plow. . . . To throw up the mud and sand and induce its removal by the current. *Ib.* 2439/1 *Submarine Explorer,* a diving-bell or lantern . . . used in examining sites beneath the surface of the water.

Submarine boat. A boat operated under water. Also *submarine torpedo boat.* {1880-} — **1807** JEFFERSON *Writings* XI. 328, I have ever looked to the submarine boat as most to be depended on for attaching [torpedoes and] . . . I am in hopes it is not abandoned as impracticable. **1864** *Scientific Amer.* XI. 183/1 A New Submarine Boat. The *Herald* . . . speaks of a new torpedo boat recently invented. **1885** *Ib.* LIII. 406/2 The accompanying engravings represent a submarine torpedo boat. **1899** *Marine Review* XX. 14/1 The inspection of the submarine torpedo boat Holland will take place . . . [in] the Potomac river. **1908** 'O. HENRY' *Options* 80 Motor-cars . . . hissed through the foaming waves like submarine boats on their jocund, perilous journeys.

Submarine cable. An insulated wire or strand of wires used for the transmission under water of telegraphic messages; the system using such wires. {1855-} Also attrib. Also *submarine telegraph cable.* — **1858** GLISAN *Jrnl. Army Life* 415 The most important news is the success of the Submarine Telegraph Cable. **1860** PRESCOTT *Telegraph* 176 Fig. 72 represents several kinds of submarine cable. **1876** KNIGHT 2507/1 The essential features of a submarine telegraph-cable are a wire or wires for conducting and a protecting compound. **1883** *Ib.* Suppl. 817/2 *Siphon Recorder,* a delicate recording instrument for the receiving end of submarine cables. **1900** *Congress. Rec.* 3 Jan. 641/1 Resolution of the Trades League of Philadelphia, Pa., favoring a competing submarine cable line between Cuba and the United States.

Submarine gun. A gun to be fired under water. Also *submarine sixteen-inch gun.* — **1818** [see BALL *n.*[1] 2]. **1876** KNIGHT 2439/1 An American submarine gun was shown at the French Exposition of 1867. **1887** *Courier-Journal* 4 Jan. 7/6 A submarine sixteen-inch gun, thirty feet long, . . . discharges a projectile weighing fifteen hundred pounds of gun-cotton.

Submissionist. One favoring or urging the policy of submission. {1828-} Usually a term of opprobrium.

+**1.** In the South, one favoring submission to the demands of the northern states in the controversies over nullification and secession. Now hist.

1834 *Savannah Georgian* 8 July 2/6 (Th. S.), The Nullifiers call us Submissionists. **1850** QUITMAN in Claiborne *Life Quitman* II. 45 Cheer on the faithful, strengthen the weak, disarm the submissionists with instructions. **1860** in Logan *Great Conspiracy* 248 The submissionists are routed, horse, foot, and dragoons. **1863** [see RECONSTRUCTIONIST]. **1913** A. C. COLE *Whig Party in So.* 189 The disunion men [c1851] . . . tried to discredit the Union movement in the eyes of Democrats by applying to it such epithets as 'Federalists,' 'Feds,' 'Submissionists,' . . . 'Coalitionists,' 'Dirt-eaters,' etc.

+**2.** In the North, one favoring submission to the demands of the South.

1861 HOLMES in Motley *Correspondence* I. 360 The Hunker, or Submissionist, or whatever you choose to call the wretch who would sacrifice everything and beg the South's pardon for offending it. **1864** MOTLEY *Ib.* II. 182, I had hoped . . . that they would have selected a Submissionist out and out, like Vallandigham or Seymour, but they were not quite such fools as that.

***Submit,** *v. Law.* +*tr.* To appeal (a case). —**1818** *Niles' Reg.* XIV. 48/2 On his apparent repentance, [he was] fined only $20, and discharged. He submitted the case.

+**Suboy,** *interj.* (See STABOY, *interj.*)

***Subscriber.**

+**1.** The undersigned. Also in colloq. use as a substitute for the personal pronoun.

1744 *S.C. Gazette* 9 Jan. 4/1 Run away some Time since from the Subscriber . . . an Indian Wench. **1767** in Commons, etc. *Doc. Hist.* I. 245 The one on which the subscriber lives has . . . a large apple orchard. **1821** [see FIRE COMPANY 1]. **1870** 'MARK TWAIN' *Screamers* 42 'Let us have Abraham for one of his names.' . . . 'Abraham suits the subscriber.'

+**2.** In the New York Stock Exchange, a nonmember broker allowed certain privileges on payment of a subscription fee. *Obs.*

1885 *Harper's Mag.* Nov. 842/2 A 'gutter snipe,' or 'curb-stone broker,' . . . does business mainly upon the sidewalk, and is supremely happy in the light and warmth of the Subscribers' Room or corridor when he can raise shekels sufficient to pay for them.

∗Subscription.

1. The price of a lottery ticket; a lottery.

1852 *S. Lit. Messenger* XVIII. 753/2 The process of collection resulted in his getting the price of one chance—the winner of the horse magnanimously paying his subscription. **1888** *Century Mag.* June 307/1 Nevertheless a 'subscription' had been opened for a handsome pair of cloisonné vases.

+2. Direct sale, by house-to-house methods, of books.

1866 *Ore. State Jrnl.* 23 June 3/4 The Photograph Family Record . . . Sold Only by Subscription. **1897** G. H. P. & J. B. PUTNAM *Auth. & Publ.* (ed. 7) 51 Books sold by subscription (that is, through canvassers).

+3. *To take up* (or *make*) *a subscription*, to collect a fund from a number of persons.

1866 H. PHILLIPS *Hist. Sk. Paper Currency* II. 168 To relieve the army a subscription was taken up by the ladies of Philadelphia. **1897** *Daily News* (London) 22 April 6/3 [Amer. sailor:] Let's make a subscription.

4. *attrib.* **a.** Designating institutions, occasions, etc., supported by subscription or arranged for subscribers. {1704-}

1776 Subscription Masked Ball [see MASKED BALL]. **1836** in Quincy *Hist. Harvard* II. 643 Arrangements ought to be made for a subscription dinner of Alumni and other friends . . . on the approaching Anniversary. **1868** G. G. CHANNING *Recoll. Newport* 170 Each winter, there were held 'subscription assemblies,'—the last one being Washington's birth-night ball. **1901** DUNCAN & SCOTT *Allen & Woodson Co., Kansas* 357 There were no school advantages [in Ky.] except subscription schools.

b. In special combinations.

Subscription agency, an office or establishment at which subscriptions are received; *s. price* {1886}, the price at which a periodical is sold to a subscriber {1891}; *s. purse,* a prize consisting of a sum of money raised by subscription. {1811}

1900 *Boston Directory* (Ernst), W. H. Guild, subscription agency. **1845** *Xenia Torch-Light* 31 July 2/5 The subscription price . . . is One dollar per annum. **1780** in Earle *Colonial Days N.Y.* 223 To be run for by women, a Holland Smock and Chintz Gown. . . . Country Subscription Purse of £50.

Subscription book. {1721-} +A book sold by house-to-house canvass. — **1868** *Ore. State Jrnl.* 13 June 3/2 Agents Wanted at once to canvass for the most popular Subscription Books of the season. **1886** *Harper's Mag.* Dec. 162/1 The sale of a successful subscription book is something unrivalled by that of any book in the trade. **1910** BOSTWICK *Amer. Pub. Library* 143 Librarians are regarded by the agents for subscription books as fair game.

‖**Subscriptioneer,** *v.* To sell a book or books by subscription methods or direct personal canvass. Also *vbl. n.* and *ppl. a.* — **1796** WEEMS *Letters* II. 29 It is a choice work for a subscriptioneering parson. *Ib.* 46 Subscriptioneer there and in its neighborhood. **1805** *Ib.* 310 In 18 hours subscriptioneering I obtained from the Legislature 100 subs. to Sydney.

‖**Subscriptionist.** A solicitor of subscriptions. — **1853** HAWTHORNE *Eng. Note-Books* I. 51, I wish . . . I had given the poor family ten shillings, and denied it to a begging subscriptionist, who has just fleeced me to that amount.

Subscription library. A library supported at least in part by subscription fees paid by those using it. {1808} — **1771** FRANKLIN *Autobiog.* 312, I set on foot my first project of a public nature, that for a subscription library. **1775** BURNABY *Travels* 112 A subscription library has been lately opened [in N.Y. City]. **1859** Trübner *Bibl. Guide to Amer. Lit.* p. cxiii, Of all those Subscription Libraries which bear the name 'Mercantile,' that of New York is foremost. **1877** [see INSTITUTE 2]. **1910** BOSTWICK *Amer. Pub. Library* 6 Subscription libraries . . . are 'public' in the sense that they are open to all on the same conditions, without discrimination.

Subscription list. A list of names of subscribers and the amounts subscribed. {1887}

1. For a periodical publication. Also *attrib.*

1834 *Jamestown* (N.Y.) *Jrnl.* 22 Jan. 2/2 The subscription list presents an increase of four and five hundred. **1880** [see INJUNCT *v.*]. **1895** WILLIAMS *Princeton Stories* 73 But that, like the *Nassau Lit.* and *Princetonian* subscription-list-game, had been played out. **1912** NICHOLSON *Hoosier Chron.* 92 The object . . . was frankly to aid the circulation manager's efforts to build up subscription lists in the rural districts.

2. For a specific undertaking, as a work of charity. {1887}

1878 *Harper's Mag.* March 609/2 No subscription list for a poor man . . . ever crossed the door-sill of the store. **1917** SINCLAIR *King Coal* 289 An agent of the 'Red Cross' . . . was feeding the hungry out of Mrs. Curtis's subscription-list.

‖**Sub-sermon.** A religious or moral essay. — **1845** POE in *Broadway Jrnl.* 13 Sept. 152 The work consists of twenty-four well-written and instructive essays, which from their brevity and character we may as well denominate sub-sermons or sermonoids.

Subsheriff. {1745} +An undersheriff. — **1671** *Md. Archives* II. 322 An Act prohibiting all sherriffes Subsherriffes or Deputy Sherriffes . . . to plead as an attorney. **1759** *Md. Hist. Mag.* XVIII. 154 Mr. William Outen, one of the Sub Sheriffs of Worcester. **1853** 'P. PAXTON' *Stray Yankee in Texas* 52 It was the sub-sheriff.

Subsidiary coin. A coin of one of the lower denominations {subsidiary coinage, 1863}, +as any nickel or bronze coin, or any silver coin lower in value than one dollar. Also collective. — **1886** G. EVANS *Illust. Hist. U.S. Mint* 151 Subsidiary Coins, in the United States silver coins of less denomination than the dollar, which have a nominal value exceeding their intrinsic or bullion value, and limited as legal tender to sums not exceeding five dollars. **1900** *Congress. Rec.* 11 Jan. 776/1 The Secretary of the Treasury is authorized . . . to coin the silver now held for their redemption into subsidiary coin.

∗Subsidy. Financial assistance given by a government or a quasi-governmental organization to a private enterprise. {1867-} Also attrib. and comb. — **1832** BENTON *30 Years' View* I. 238/2 Abuses [of the Bank of the U.S.] worthy of inquiry: . . . Subsidies and loans, directly or indirectly, to printers, editors, and lawyers, for purposes other than the regular business of the bank. **1881** *Harper's Mag.* March 550/2 Here and there a man . . . sells his power to politicians and subsidy-seekers. **1887** LOWELL *Lit. & Polit. Addresses* 187 They play their three-card trick as subsidies or as protection to labor. **1893** CUSHING *Story of P.O.* 147 The Subsidy Bill had provided for this advertising. **1893** *Harper's Mag.* April 712/1 County subsidies for railways and other public objects.

∗Subsist, *v. tr.* To make provision for; to maintain. {1683-} +With specific reference to Indians. — **1835** *Indian Laws & Tr.* II. 443 The United States also agrees . . . to remove the Cherokees to their new homes and to subsist them one year after their arrival there. **1840** *Pres. Mess. & P.* III. 626 In addition, we will be bound . . . to subsist them for one year after their arrival. **1866** *Rep. Indian Affairs* 83 Several of them . . . [were allowed] to visit the Dalles salmon fishery, that they might obtain salmon sufficient to subsist them until harvest. **1878** *Congress. Rec.* 19 Dec. 314/1 To subsist and properly care for the Apache and other Indians in Arizona and New Mexico . . . , $320,000.

∗Subsistence. Food or other means of sustaining life {1697-}, +as provided by the United States for the Indians. — **1866** *Rep. Indian Affairs* 89, I started for Fort Klamath to attend to the issuing of subsistence to the Snake Indians. **1881** *Ib.* p. xiii, The treaty with the Indians provides a specific amount of clothing, or subsistence to be furnished them. **1913** *Indian Laws & Tr.* III. 574 For subsistence and civilization of the Northern Cheyennes . . . , $85,000.

+Subsistence Department. In the United States Army, a staff department having charge of the procurement and issue of provisions. Now hist. — **1846** McKENNEY *Memoirs* I. 222 The duty of providing the rations for the emigrating Indians was referred to the Subsistence Department. **1861** *Army Regulations* 248 Ovens may be built or paid for by the Subsistence Department.

+Subsistence stores. *pl. Mil.* (See quot. 1891.) — **1861** in Kettell *Hist. Rebellion* I. 171 The subsistence stores . . . must last to include the 23rd inst. **1891** *Cent.* 6030/1 *Subsistence stores* . . . , the food-supplies procured and issued for the support of an army. The phrase also covers the grain, hay, straw, or other forage supplied for the sustenance and bedding of animals intended for slaughter. **1918** FARROW *Dict. Mil. Terms* 594.

Subsoiler.

1. A subsoil plow. {1852}

1851 BARRY *Fruit Garden* 50 The subsoiler follows in the same furrow and loosens . . . the lower part of the surface and a part of the subsoil. **1879** *Scribner's Mo.* Dec. 241/2 There are no implements equal to the plow and subsoiler.

+2. = RAZORBACK HOG.

1858 C. FLINT *Milch Cows* 362 The class of hogs usually denominated 'subsoilers,' with their long and pointed snouts, and their thin flabby sides. **1872** *Harper's Mag.* April 663/2 She told me it was a 'ridge-back'— a 'jumping alligator,' a 'sub-soiler.' **1899** CUSHMAN *Hist. Indians* 239 [The wild boar's] progeny were styled the 'racers, razor backs, subsoilers, jumpers, and rail splitters,' by the early white settlers.

‖**Substanche,** *v. tr.* To substantiate. *slang.* — **1838** *Lexington Observer* 7 July, He said he was only fending off the blows of her darned old rollin pin, that she could substanche.

‖**Substaquilate,** *v. tr.* To discomfit; to overwhelm. *humorous.* — **1842** *Ainsworth's Mag.* II. 151 You estimate I'm flummuxed; but I swear I'll substaquilate you *some* when the day is hot enough for it. *Ib.* 556 If you will all foller my steps to the polling windows, we'll substaquilate the loafing locofocoes in two twos.

Substation. A station or establishment subsidiary to a main or central station, as a subordinate police station, a branch post office, etc. {1901, for electricity}

1881 *Rep. Indian Affairs* 45 The temporary establishing of two substations for the police . . . resulted in the locking up of the offenders. **1890** *Rep. Postmaster-General* 44 It is hoped that . . . the system [of pneumatic tubes] may then be extended to the substations and post-offices of large cities. **1891** *Advance* 12 March, Substations at convenient distances for the issuance of rations. **1904** *Amer. Inventor* 1 March 104/3 This plant . . . has seven substations containing transforming machinery. **1922** W. AITKEN *Automatic Telephone Systems* I. 3 We have, therefore, a *sub-station* at the subscriber's office, which may consist of one, or a plurality of direct lines, or a small switchboard.

Substitute, *n.* One who, for a consideration, performs military service in the place of a conscript. Now hist. {1802-} — **1777** *Jrnls. Cont. Congress* IX. 1002 The laws which have been enacted in the State of Pensylvania, permitting the furnishing of substitutes to perform militia duty, have . . . tended . . . to encourage desertions from the continental army. **1865** *Congress. Globe* 24 Feb. 1083/2 [We have been] putting bounty jumpers into the army as substitutes, to desert from time to time. **1881–5** McCLELLAN *Own Story* 259 Out of these wholesale drafts grew the system of substitutes and bounties, which cost so many unnecessary millions to the country.

＊**Substitute,** *v. intr.* To serve in the place of another person. — **1888** *Advance* 15 Nov., The idea of substituting for Gertrude now thoroughly possessed her. **1907** *Springfield W. Repub.* 13 June 16 Miss Smith is substituting as teacher during the illness of Miss Sherman.

＋**Substitute broker.** One who makes a business of procuring substitutes for military service. Also *substitute-brokerage.* Now hist. — **1863** *Congress. Globe* 4 Feb. 714/3 As soon as it seemed to be understood that the government was determined to force men into the army . . . , these substitute brokers made their appearance. **1865** LOWELL in *N. Amer. Rev.* C. 541 We have had shoddy, . . . we have had substitute-brokerage, we have had speculators in patriotism. **1865** *Congress. Globe* 6 Feb. 612/2 A substitute broker, . . . the vilest of mankind, . . . is entitled to a fair trial. *Ib.* 614/3 These substitute brokers in the city of New York have a brokers' board and have regular meetings.

‖**Substruct,** *v. tr.* To build underneath, as a foundation. — **1850** EMERSON *Representative Men* 57 Metaphysics and natural philosophy expressed the genius of Europe; he [Plato] substructs the religion of Asia, as the base. *Ib.* 131 This seer of the souls [Swedenborg] substructs a new hell and pit, each more abominable than the last, round every new crew of offenders.

Subterranean railroad, railway. ＋=UNDERGROUND RAILROAD. — **1846** *Congress. Globe* 18 March 523/1 Amend the amendment by adding $50,000 for the perfection of the Bebb and Schenck subterranean railroad, on which to carry their odoriferous friends from Kentucky to Canada. *Ib.* 523/3, I am told that it [the amendment] proposes a subterranean railway for carrying the blacks from Kentucky to Canada.

＊**Subtreasurer.** ＋**1.** An assistant treasurer of the United States in charge of a subtreasury. Also as title. ＋**2.** *transf.* (See quotation.) — (1) **1837** *Congress. Deb.* 30 Sept. 1164/2, I should not feel authorized to appoint any number of 'new officers,' whether called sub-treasurers, or otherwise. **1845** *Xenia Torch-Light* 23 Oct. 2/6 One of them was . . . chosen by Mr. Van Buren as Subtreasurer of the city of New York. **1861** *N.Y. Tribune* 24 Aug. 3/2 Mr. Sub-Treasurer Cisco continues to receive a large number of applications for the new Treasury Notes. (2) **1838** *N.Y. Advertiser & Exp.* 20 Jan. 1/3 The Sub-Treasurers in St. Louis,—*this* is now the fashionable name for our Office-holders,—met in St. Louis, . . . to hold a Loco Foco meeting.

Subtreasury. ｛1901, in Sierra Leone｝
＋**1.** A branch of the United States Treasury maintained for the deposit and safekeeping of government funds; the building housing such a branch.
Established by acts of 1840 (repealed 1841) and 1846; abolished by an act of 1920.
1837 *Congress. Deb.* 30 Sept. 1164/2 The Secretary . . . [is] required to furnish this House with a statement of the number of sub-treasuries which will be required if the bill . . . should become a law. **1863** *Harper's Mag.* June 53/1 Unless he descended from the Sub-Treasury, and sought some business . . . , could he marry? **1882** McCABE *New York* 332 The Sub-Treasury, [is] a noble edifice of white marble. **1903** *Boston Herald* 19 Aug., The amount of gold delivered to the sub-treasury at San Francisco indicates that gold mining operations in Alaska have been profitable. **1920** *Stat. at Large* XLI. I. 654 The Secretary of the Treasury is authorized and directed to discontinue . . . such subtreasuries.

＋**2.** An independent, or branch, treasury system.
1837 CALHOUN *Works* III. 81 This proposed reorganization has been called a sub-treasury. **1845** *Whig Almanac 1846* 1 The Whig Party [is] Opposed to the Sub-Treasury, and all kindred devices to secure a distinctively Specie Currency to the Federal Office-Holders. **1858** HOMANS *Cycl. Commerce* 1765/2 The failures of many of these [banking institutions] during the years 1837–1842 led to the establishment, on the 6th August, 1846, of the Independent Treasury, or Sub-treasury. **1870** MEDBERY *Men Wall St.* 249 The gold-operators renewed their attack, and compelled the Sub-Treasury to vary its rates.

3. Attrib. with *bill, building, deposit,* etc.
1838 *Diplom. Corr. Texas* I. (1908) 312 The Sub-Treasury Bill is still under consideration in the Senate. **1840** *Niles' Nat. Reg.* 30 May 197/3 The remonstrance of the people of this state against the sub-treasury scheme . . . has caused the president of the United States to falter in his wicked purposes. **1846** *Whig Almanac 1847* 10/2 The cost of refitting the old Sub-Treasury vaults and safes is limited to $12,000. **1856** MACLEOD *F. Wood* 63 President Van Buren's Sub-Treasury system had succeeded to the United States Bank. **1866** *Ore. State Jrnl.* 21 April 2/1 The enemy seized upon the sub-Treasury deposits. **1870** MEDBERY *Men Wall St.* 77 A sub-treasury sale of gold may assist. **1889** *Century Mag.* April 810/2 [The] buildings . . . gave way to the old Custom-house and to the United States Sub-Treasury building of to-day.

＊**Suburb. a.** A place in an outlying part of, or adjacent to, a town or city; in pl., the environs. **b.** *spec.* A politically independent community, usually residential, located near, and economically dependent upon, a larger city. Also attrib. or appositive.

1640 *New Haven Col. Rec.* 34 As well without the towne as within the towne and the suburbs allso. **1662** *New Haven Rec.* I. 518 The veiwers of Fences . . . are as followeth: . . . for the Suburbs Quarter, John Allen, George Ross. **1794** *Phila. Ordinances* (1812) 86 The city of Philadelphia, or the suburbs thereof. **1837** PECK *New Guide* 178 There are . . . perhaps some others [*sc.* churches] in the city or suburbs. **1852** REYNOLDS *Hist. Illinois* 46 His plantation occupied the lower part of New Orleans, known as the 'suberb of St. Marigny.' **1880** CABLE *Grandissimes* 366 Doctor Keene tarried all night in suburb St. Jean. **1893** *Harper's Mag.* April 653/1 There lies the secret of the suburb, whose growth is only matched by a few cities, which are all in the West. **1918** SHACKLETON *Book of Phila.* 323 It [is] impossible to see where the city ends and the suburbs begin.

Suburban, *a.* Of or pertaining to a suburb or suburbs ｛a1625–｝, freq. with reference to methods of transportation between city and suburb.
1838 INGRAHAM *Burton* II. 58 Leaving this suburban quarter, they came into the open country. **1858** GLISAN *Jrnl. Army Life* 411 My agent in New York . . . was directed to invest [the funds] . . . in suburban real estate in Chicago. **1880** *Harper's Mag.* July 319/2 The narrator . . . [was] riding on a suburban railway. **1884** *Boston Jrnl.* 23 Dec. 2/3 Suburban trains carried full cars of passengers yesterday morning. **1893** *Harper's Mag.* April 653/1 Those who are married . . . are certain to settle in Brooklyn, or, in far fewer numbers, in the other suburban towns. **1911** Suburban line [see MOTORMAN].

Suburbanite. One who lives in a suburb. ｛1896｝ — **1890** *Advance* 20 Feb., Much dissatisfaction among suburbanites over the proposed [reduction in train speed]. **1894** *Harper's Mag.* June 160/2 A friend of the Drawer, a suburbanite, was greeted . . . with this choice specimen. **1904** *Amer. Inventor* 1 May 208/2 The motor . . . is marked O.K. and goes forth to carry the suburbanites, and be submissive to the careless motorman.

Subway. ｛1828–｝
1. An underground passage for vehicles or pedestrians. ｛1884–｝
1865 *Atlantic Mo.* Jan. 83/1 Central Park . . . [contains] four sub-ways for the passage of trade-vehicles across the Park, with an aggregate length of two miles.

＋**2.** A tunnel for a metropolitan railway; a metropolitan railway operating underground. ｛=E. 'underground'｝
1893 *Mass. Acts & Resolves* 1421 The said board is hereby authorized to lay out and construct a subway for street railway purposes. **1896** *Advance* 9 Jan. 47/2 On a recent Sabbath there was work going on every section of the subway. **1904** *Public Ledger* (Phila.) 5 Jan. 16 'The subway for mine' was the decision of every man, woman and child who had journeys to make [in the snowstorm]. **1919** SALTUS *Paliser Case* 67 In the subway, the following evening, Cassey saw a man eyeing her.

b. Attrib. with *commissioner, express, train, travel.*
1893 *Mass. Acts & Resolves* 1420 The mayor of the city of Boston shall appoint . . . three commissioners . . . to be known as the board of subway commissioners. **1903** *N.Y. Times* 2 Oct. 6 The long-haul passengers will elect to do their travelling on the swift subway trains. **1907** *Nation* 21 Nov. 474 The kind of book which is heard of for a season above the din of subway travel. **1911** BURGESS *Find the Woman* 15 He took a subway express to Times Square and, as was his wont, wandered down Broadway.

＋**Succahanah.** (See quot. 1687.) *Obs.* — **1687** CLAYTON *Va.* in *Phil. Trans.* XLI. 160 [The Indians] drink, I think, little besides Succahanah, that is, fair Water, unless when they can get Spirits . . . from the English. **1708** E. COOK *Sot-Weed Factor* 21, [I] soon got up, To cool my Liver with a Cup Of *Succahana* fresh and clear.

＋**Succession sale.** 'A sale of property to enable the heirs to divide the same' (B. '59). — **1858** *La. Democrat* 20 July (B.), At the succession sale of the slaves belonging to the minor heirs of S. A. and A. X. Baillie, . . . long sums were bid.

＊**Succory.** Chicory, or a plant of the chicory family. — **1737** [see ENDIVE]. **1814** BIGELOW *Florula Bostoniensis* 182 *Cichorium intybus.* Succory. . . . The large, blue flowers of this elegant plant are extremely common in pastures and road sides. **1885** HOLMES *Mortal Antipathy* v, Those eyes of his . . . [are] as blue as succory flowers.

＋**Succotash.** [Narraganset *misickquatash* 'an ear of corn.' Cf. Williams *Key* (1866) 40: '*Manusqussedash,* beanes.'] A dish consisting principally of corn and beans boiled together with or without meat.
1751 MacSPARRAN *Diary* 47 Mo[the]r dined with us upon Suckatash and Ham. **1778** CARVER *Travels* 263 Unripe corn . . . and beans . . . [are] boiled together with bears flesh. . . . They call this food Succatosh. **1823** THACHER *Military Jrnl.* 213 The landlady brought on the table a dish of succatash, boiled corn and beans. **1850** *New Eng. Farmer* II. 66 Winter Saccatash . . . is an excellent accompaniment to pickled pork, bacon, or corned beef. **1869** STOWE *Oldtown Folks* 157 The old woman . . . disclosed a smoking mess of the Indian dish denominated succotash,—to wit, a soup of corn and beans, with a generous allowance of salt pork. **1912** *Ladies' Home Jrnl.* Nov. 66/2 Meatless Menus. . . . Dinner: Tomato Soufflé, Tomato Sauce, Succotash, Lettuce and Egg Salad, Arrowroot Pudding, Coffee.

b. *Plymouth, Mass.* (See quotation.)

c1870 *Old Plymouth Receipts,* The soup of beans and the vegetables are then mixed with the water the fowl and beef were boiled in and salt and pepper added. Four quarts of hulled corn having been boiled soft and tender are added to the succotash.

c. (See quotation.)

1859 *Ill. Agric. Soc. Trans.* III. 503 The white succotash (a large, round bean,) is most excellent, green or dry.

+**Succoteague.** (See quotation.) — 1884 GOODE, etc. *Fisheries* I. 362 The name 'Squeteague' is of Indian origin, and 'Squit,' 'Succoteague,' 'Squitee,' and 'Chickwit' are doubtless variations of this name in different ancient and modern dialects.

* **Suck,** *n.*

1. A whirlpool. {1849–} Freq. in proper names.

1778 HUTCHINS *Va., Penna., Md., & N.C.* 32 The Whirl, or Suck continues rapid for about three miles. 1780 in *Amer. Speech* XV. 398/2 Thence along his lines . . . to his corner Maple by the Suck. 1805 CLARK in *Lewis & C. Exped.* III. (1905) 157 Some [were] to take over the canoes . . . to a place on the chanel below this bad whorl & Suck. 1838 *S. Lit. Messenger* IV. 220/2 The shoals of the Tennessee were to be passed, as well as the boiling suck, which even at this day is the terror of all navigators of that stream. 1890 *Scribner's Mag.* VIII. 611/1 [The Colorado River's] dashing current is torn up by . . . powerful whirlpools, sucks, and eddies.

attrib. 1792 in *Amer. Speech* XV. 398/2 Crossing a drain by the Suck Lick. 1816 *Ib.,* To a Beach and gum by the road side near the suckspring.

2. In various slang and colloq. applications.

a. A trick. *Obs.* **b.** A river. **c.** A whirling movement of air.

(a) 1847 *Knickerb.* XXIX. 281 The elongated countenance of the discomfitted gambler required no additional evidence to testify his appreciation of 'the suck.' **(b)** 1867 *Atlantic Mo.* April 804/2 Three great 'sucks,' as we call them here,—the Ohio, the Missouri, and the Mississippi,—drained out the land. **(c)** 1877 W. WRIGHT *Big Bonanza* 253 Fierce whirls and 'sucks' are formed in the lee of the mountain.

* **Suck,** *v. tr.* To deceive; to trick. {1806–, *dial.*} Usually with *in. slang.* — 1839 BRIGGS *H. Franco* I. 76 'Reg'larly sucked, Jack?' asked a young man who had been listening. 1840 *Picayune* 3 Nov. 2/4 Now don't you feel small at being so sucked in? 1855 BARNUM *Life* 26 '[The butchers will] get sucked in then,' I replied exultingly. 1874 EGGLESTON *Circuit Rider* 14 Whoever got aholt of them air nubbins would git sucked in.

* **Sucker,** *n.*

1. +**a.** Any of many fresh-water fishes of the family Catostomidae, having lips which suggest that they feed by suction. **b.** Any of several other fishes with a suckerlike mouth or a sucking organ. {1753–, of British fishes}

[1772 *Phil. Trans.* LXIII. 155 The fourth and last fish brought from Hudson's Bay is there called a Sucker, because it lives by suction.] 1775 FITHIAN *Journal* II. 82 We dined on fish, suckers, chups, & on venison. 1806 CLARK in *Lewis & C. Exped.* V. (1905) 22 With those nets they take the Suckers. 1832 *N.H. Hist. Soc. Coll.* III. 85 The Sucker differs from the Barvil in shape. 1857 *Ladies' Repository* July 445/1 Sucker is the name of a numerous species of fish, common in all our western waters. 1884 GOODE, etc. *Fisheries* I. 379 *Menticirrus undulatus* . . . is known as the 'Bagre' or 'Sucker.' *Ib.* 446 Very often, especially in the case of sharks, the fish to which the Suckers attach themselves become very much emaciated. 1904 *Springfield W. Repub.* 9 Sept. 10 As a boy he used to lie on the rocks, snare suckers, and swim in the pot holes.

comb. 1856 COZZENS *Sparrowgrass P.* 63, I could hear . . . the reverberations of the big oathes . . . that had been the running accompaniment to the sucker-fishing on the Nepperhan!

+**2.** With specifying terms.

Only a selection of these is given.

1814 MITCHILL *Fishes N.Y.* 458 Fresh-water Sucker, *Cyprinus teres,* . . . is extensively employed in the interior districts for food. 1820 RAFINESQUE in *Western Rev.* II. 302 Black-back Sucker. *Catostomus melanotus.* . . . Vulgar names Black sucker and Blue sucker. 1842 *Nat. Hist. N.Y., Zoology* IV. 202 The Large-scaled Sucker, *Catostomus macrolepidotus,* . . . appears to be a common species. 1884 GOODE, etc. *Fisheries* I. 614 Numerous other species . . . , belonging to the genera of *Moxostoma, Minytrema,* and *Placopharynx,* are found in the waters of the West and South, all going by the general names of Red Horse, White Sucker, and Mullet. 1903 T. H. BEAN *Fishes N.Y.* 689 The swordfish sucker is an inhabitant of warm seas, ranging northward to Cape Cod.

* **3.** (See quot. 1784.)

1775 ROMANS *Nat. Hist. Florida* 148 Now the first hoeing takes place, and suckers and worms begin to appear. 1784 SMYTH *Tour* II. 133 On the [tobacco] plants that have been topped young sprouts are apt to spring out, which are termed suckers, and are carefully and constantly broken off lest they should draw too much of the nourishment and substance from the leaves. 1850 *Rep. Comm. Patents 1849: Agric.* 320 The '*suckers*' ought to be pulled off when they get three or four inches long. 1904 GLASGOW *Deliverance* 125 The men worked . . . in the great fields, removing the numerous 'suckers' from the growing plants.

+**4.** *cap.* An Illinoisan. A nickname.

1835 HOFFMAN *Winter in West* I. 176 There was a long-haired 'hooshier' from Indiana, a couple of smart-looking 'suckers' from the southern part

---

of Illinois. 1841 [see SUCKER FISH]. 1901 CHURCHILL *Crisis* 152 The Tall Sucker was on the steps to receive them.

b. Attrib. with *boy, marketeer, office-seeker, style, woman.*

1842 *Knickerb.* XX. 298 You should have seen the 'Sucker' women marching to the drum, in martial order. 1845 *Ib.* XXV. 374 A Friend writing from Washington . . . gives us this pleasant sketch of a 'Sucker' office-seeker. 1847 ROBB *Squatter Life* 116 The sucker marketeer drew off a few paces, to be ready to run. 1857 *Ill. Agric. Soc. Trans.* III. 438 Those farms immediately on the river, with a soil of sandy loam that has been cropped in the usual Sucker style, viz: Corn and wheat . . . for twenty years, without fallowing, show that they need rest and manure. 1861 Moore *Rebellion Rec.* I. III. 101 Our Sucker boys are now on a grand 'whaling expedition.'

+**5.** A 'gull,' a person easily deceived and cheated; a fool. *colloq.*[2] Also attrib.

See also GONE SUCKER.

1836 *Quarter Race Ky.* (1846) 16 Old Tompkins has brought her here, and I like him for a *sucker!* 1873 *Newton Kansan* 3 April 2/1 Messrs. Prentice and Platte . . . are now in search of other suckers. 1890 H. PALMER *Stories of Base Ball Field* 28 The average ball-player of to-day would . . . disregard his captain's *request,* and look upon him as a 'sucker' for having made it. 1898 *Congress. Rec.* 20 Jan. 804/1 The gentlemen who form the platform[s] are always adroit enough to frame them so as to catch the 'suckers' on Election day. 1904 W. H. SMITH *Promoters* 11 A house full of gaping suckers who have paid a dollar and a half apiece. 1924 G. C. HENDERSON *Keys to Crookdom* 127 If he can get a list of all the victims of other bursted bubbles, he figures that they are exceedingly good prospects for his game. Thus has evolved the 'sucker lists.'

* **6.** One who allows himself to be maintained by the efforts of others; a parasite. {–1728}

1856 Dow *Sermons* III. (B.), I may mention those suckers belonging to the body loaferish, whose sole study appears to be to see how much they can get without the least physical exertion. 1863 NORTON *Army Lett.* 136, I don't know that he has but one [friend] in the company, and he is a sort of sucker. 1900 BACHELLER *E. Holden* 352 [He] spoke of a certain public man as a 'big sucker.' . . . To him a 'sucker' was the lowest and meanest thing in the world.

b. A corrupt political worker. *slang.*

c1855 in *Sons of Sires* 90 Under this system of Primary Elections, there have grown up a large class of men known in the slang of the city as 'suckers' and 'strikers.' *Ib.* 91 The man who does not wish to be known as taking money in person, puts into these nominating committees these 'strikers' and 'suckers,' and they notoriously sell their votes.

Sucker, *v.* Also **succour.** {1660–} *tr.* To remove suckers or shoots from (tobacco {a1661–}, corn, cotton, and sorghum).

1724 JONES *Virginia* 40 When it is grown up they . . . succour it [tobacco], or cut off the Ground Leaves. 1774 FITHIAN *Journal* I. 246 [Cotton] must be weeded . . . & suckered as Tobacco. 1786 WASHINGTON *Diaries* III. 82 The Corn had all been succoured. 1851 *Fla. Plantation Rec.* 374, 21 [slaves] Suckering Corn. 1862 *Ill. Agric. Soc. Trans.* V. 161 Part of the cane was suckered. 1908 M. JOHNSTON *L. Rand* xiv, I've wanted power ever since I went barefoot and suckered tobacco.

+**Sucker boot.** A kind of boot. — 1872 *Chicago Tribune* 9 Oct. 4/6 Another invoice of those Celebrated Hand-Made Sucker Boots.

+**Suckerdom. a.** Hard drinkers, regarded as a group. **b.** Illinois. — 1862 *N.Y. Tribune* 22 March 5/2 One distiller . . . would pay into the Treasury $1,200 a year, or $375,600 a year, if Suckerdom continued thirsty. 1863 *Harper's Mag.* Oct. 713/2 Of some of the localities in Suckerdom . . . the schoolmaster has been shamefully negligent.

* **Suckerel.** +(See quotations.) — 1883 *Nat. Museum Bul.* No. 27, 477 *Cycleptus elongatus.* . . . Missouri Sucker; Suckerel. . . . One of the most interesting of all the suckers. 1884 GOODE, etc. *Fisheries* I. 615 The 'Black Horse,' 'Gourd-seed Sucker,' 'Missouri Sucker,' or 'Suckerel' is found chiefly in the river channels of the Ohio and Mississippi.

Sucker fish. {1867–} +A species of sucker or fish of the sucker family. — 1841 STEELE *Summer Journey* 222 The people of Illinois obtained their nickname of suckers from the practice of going up the Mississippi when the spring opened for lead, which was the period of the annual voyage up the river of the Succar fish. 1893 *Chicago Tribune* 26 April 6/4 Their principal catch in those days were the buffalo, a species of sucker fish similar to that caught on a sandbar the other day.

‖**Suckerism.** *collect.* Illinoisans. — 1846 FARNHAM *Prairie Land* 97 We entered on the flood tide of Suckerism that was setting into the narrow, winding door.

+**Suckerland.** Illinois. A nickname. (Cf. SUCKERDOM b.) — 1860 *Harper's Mag.* March 567/1 The County of Jasper lies on the line between 'Hoosierdom' and the 'Suckerland.'

+**Sucker-mouth buffalo.** (See quotation.) — 1885 *Nat. Museum Proc.* VIII. 13 *Ictiobus bubalus,* . . . Sucker-mouth Buffalo, . . . can generally be distinguished [from other species of buffalo fish].

+**Sucker State.** Illinois. — 1845 in *Tall Tales of S.W.* (1930) 25 Judge Douglass . . . was a beardless youth of twenty years of age, freshly come amongst the people of the 'Sucker State.' 1868 *N.Y. Herald* 2 July 4/3 The Sucker State . . . will wheel into line. 1907 *Boston Transcript* 9 Nov. 11. 9.

Suckfish. {1753-1758} +**a.** =SUCKER 1 a. +**b.** (See quot. 1896.) — **1840** SIMMS *Border Beagles* II. 184 There's not a suckfish in Big Black that wouldn't laugh at this for gill-tackle. **1896** JORDAN & EVERMANN *Check-List Fishes* 491 *Caularchus mæandricus.* . . . Suckfish. Pacific Coast . . . , from Vancouver Island to Monterey.

Suck in. A deception. *colloq.* {1877, *dial.*} — *c***1849** PAIGE *Dow's Sermons* II. 316 (B.), Life is all moonshine—a monstrous humbug—a grand suck in.

Suckley. [Dr. George *Suckley,* Amer. surgeon and naturalist (1830-69).] +Used in possessive in specific names. — **1858** BAIRD *Birds Pacific R.R.* 848 *Larus Suckleyi.* . . . Suckley's Gull. . . . Pacific coast; Puget's Sound. **1869** *Amer. Naturalist* III. 126 Suckley's Salmontrout (*S[almo] Suckleyi*). . . . The first of this splendid salmontrout we met with were at the mouth of St. Regis Borgia creek, which flows down the east slope of the Cœur d'Aleñe Range.

+**Suckwick.** The leatherwood (*Dirca palustris*) or the basswood (*Tilia glabra*). — **1778** CARVER *Travels* 499 The Wickopick or Suckwick appears to be a species of the white wood.

+**Suction engine.** A fire engine with a suction pump. — **1830** *Mass. Laws* XI. 400 The number of enginemen shall not exceed fifty to every hydraulion or suction engine [etc.]. **1851** CIST *Cincinnati* 168 Each of these companies is provided with Fire and Suction Engines and Hose Reel. **1893** HALE *New Eng. Boyhood* 135 Every engine, therefore, which was good for anything, was a 'suction engine,' as it was called; that is, it was able to pump from a well, as well as able to throw water to an indefinite height.

*Sudden death. +Highly intoxicating liquor; cheap whisky. — **1865** 'MARK TWAIN' *Sketches* (1926) 163 Our reserve . . . we had . . . kept out of sight and full of chain-lightning, sudden death and scorpion-bile all day.

Suds, *v.* {*sud} *intr.* To make suds. — **1893** M. A. OWEN *Voodoo Tales* 5 An impertinent housewife had dared to affirm that her soap wouldn't 'suds.'

+**Sudsing.** Washing in suds; soaping. Also attrib. — **1843** STEPHENS *High Life N.Y.* II. 20, I'd gin myself a good sudsing in the wash hand basin. **1879** *Scribner's Mo.* Oct. 940/2 As soon as they begin to boil, remove them to the 'sudsing'-water. **1881** McLEAN *Cape Cod Folks* 167 A good poundin', and boilin', and sudzin', you need.

+**Sudsy,** *a.* Full of suds; produced by suds. Also transf. — **1866** *Harper's Mag.* Sept. 544/2 He's gone! across the sudzy sea. **1884** *Ib.* Sept. 528/2 We then bade adieu to . . . our string of washers still laving their linen in the sudsy stream. **1891** *Advance* 5 Nov., [He] raised his little shaven head Above the steaming, sudsy tub. **1901** *Munsey's Mag.* XXV. 394/2 There was a pleasant, sudsy cleanliness about the two little rooms.

Suffolk. A breed of swine or an animal of this breed. {1846-} Also attrib. — **1864** *Maine Agric. Rep.* IX. 28 Mr. Pratt . . . preferred a cross of the Suffolks. **1866** 'F. KIRKLAND' *Bk. Anecdotes* 448/1 [Upon] a letter envelope . . . was delineated the Goddess of Liberty standing upon a Suffolk pig, wearing the emblem of our country. **1893** G. W. CURTIS *Horses, Cattle* 324 American, or White Suffolk . . . is an undoubted descendant of the English York and Cumberland breeds.

***Suffrage.**
See also FEMALE SUFFRAGE, NEGRO SUFFRAGE.

1. Voting. {1665-} In phrase *right of suffrage.*
1790 MACLAY *Deb. Senate* 179 Ellsworth was even so absurd as to suppose if a man acquired the right of suffrage in one State, he had it in all, etc. **1840** *Niles' Nat. Reg.* 10 Oct. 96 (caption), Right of Suffrage. **1887** *Courier-Journal* 27 Jan. 1/5 The Senate proceeded . . . to investigate the allegations made by three residents of Washington county, Texas, as to their being . . . deprived of the right of suffrage. **1911** PERSONS, etc. *Mass. Labor Laws* 11 The New England Association of Farmers, Mechanics, and other Workingmen . . . [demanded] extension of the right of suffrage.

+**2.** The right of voting as a member of a nation or state. {1840}
1787 *Constitution* v, No State, without its Consent, shall be deprived of its equal Suffrage in the Senate. **1837** MARTINEAU *Society* III. 164 Foreigners of all ages may scoff at the self-confidence and complacency of young men who have just exercised the suffrage for the first time. **1873** *Republic* I. 54 Louisiana must be held to have been denied its suffrage. **1884** LOWELL *On Democracy* 4, I recollect hearing . . . that the doing away with the property qualification for suffrage twenty years before had been the ruin of the State of Massachusetts.

3. Attrib. in sense: Of or pertaining to female suffrage.
1886 *Harper's Mag.* Dec. 68/1 They had walked all the way to get me to sign the suffrage petition. **1911** *N.Y. Ev. Post* 14 Sept. (Th.) Whether or not the new woman Mayor would 'make good' was . . . of considerable importance to the future of the suffrage movement.

Suffragist. {1822-} =FEMALE SUFFRAGIST. {1914} Also attrib. — **1883** *American* VI. 7 The most persistent suffragist claims no more than this. **1887** *Voice* 3 Feb. 1/4 Suffragists make a mistake in asking for the ballot because they are women. **1898** *Mo. So. Dakotan* I. 62 The suffragist speakers are mistaken in coming into free Dakota, expecting to find 'women slaves.' **1911** VANCE *Cynthia* 85 [She betrayed] an advanced state of intelligence which, had Madame been twenty years younger, would certainly have made of her a militant suffragist.

***Sugar,** *n.*

I. ***1.** A sweet, crystalline substance derived chiefly from sugar cane, sugar beet, +or maple sap.
See also BEET-SUGAR, BROWN SUGAR, etc.
1649 *Suffolk Deeds* II. 227 He stands, engaged to pay . . . Twenty fiue pounds . . . odd money payable in Suger or Cotton next June. **1735** J. BROWNE *Letter Book* (1929) 15 Please to send by the bearer Mr. Hill halfe a doz. or halfe a Score loves of Single refined Sugar. **1778** CARVER *Travels* 262 The sugar which they have extracted from the maple tree. **1841** *Lowell Offering* I. 228 Father, the sugar has grained. **1897** *Outing* XXIX. 488/2 The flour, salt, sugar and coffee were carried in rubber-cloth bags.

+**b.** *To bring sugar in one's spade,* to make use of a courteous, pleasant manner in order to accomplish one's purpose.
1894 *Congress. Rec.* 25 Jan. 1383/1 When you seek to get your voucher approved, bring sugar in your spade, and nothing else.

2. a. =SUGAR MAPLE. ***b.** =SUGAR CANE.
(a) **1839** PLUMBE *Sk. Iowa* 62 The prairies are generally . . . surrounded with groves of . . . sugar, lynn, walnut, &c. **(b)** **1821** ROYALL *Lett. from Ala.* 140 Sugar and oranges grow in the same latitude.

II. *attrib.* and *comb.* **3.** Designating processes, places, articles, etc., concerned in the manufacture of sugar.
See also SUGAR-BOILER 2, SUGAR ESTATE, etc.
1749 *Doc. Hist. N.Y. State* I. 729 The production and Manufacture is . . . for nineteen years, Sugar baking and its refining. **1794** *Ann. 3d Congress* 635 There were only seventeen sugar-bakeries in the United States. **1834** AUDUBON *Ornith. Biog.* II. 464, I found a sort of large garret filled with sugar-moulds. **1839** Sugar coast [see sense 8]. **1852** *Fla. Plantation Rec.* 72 It would be a good plan to have the old Iron Screw Pin . . . run up into Sugar Rolers. **1870** STEPHENS *Married in Haste* 366 He held a sugar-crusher in one hand. **1876** KNIGHT 2452/1 *Sugar-sifter,* a machine for sorting grades of crushed or ground sugar according to fineness of grain. **1904** Sugar 'central' [see CENTRAL *n.* 2].

b. With specific reference to the making of maple sugar.
See also SUGAR BUSH, SUGAR CABINS, etc.
1848 D. P. THOMPSON *L. Amsden* 11 A body of three or four hundred straight, tall, and thrifty rock-maple trees . . . composed the sugar-place. **1853** *Harper's Mag.* March 562/1 Many a night-gathering is there before the blazing 'sugar-fires,' in comfortable wigwams, with odorous clean straw upon the 'ground'-floors. **1854** RILEY *Puddleford* 242 These March days, were 'sugar days.' **1871** DE VERE 206 The gatherings of young people in the beautiful groves to eat the warm sugar are practically but very prosaically called *sugar-licks.* **1886** *Harper's Mag.* June 92/2 A good many of us have helped in sugar frolics. **1896** *Vt. Agric. Rep.* XV. 35 [The sugar maker] will need to watch his opportunity to get his roads made about his sugar lot, and not spend the first week of the sugar season breaking roads.

4. Designating articles of food and drinks made with sugar.
1787 TYLER *Contrast* II. ii, Why, I was thinking then how I should contrive to pass this broken piece of silver—won't it buy a sugar-dram? **1805** *Pocumtuc Housewife* (1906) 32 Sugar Gingerbread. **1828** LESLIE *Receipts* 62 Sugar Biscuits. **1845** *Xenia Torch-Light* 31 July 4/3 He pledges himself that his . . . Sugar crackers and small cakes of all kinds shall be equal to any in the Western country. **1887** PERRY *Flock of Girls* 258 Bonbons fresh from Paris . . . [including] sugar robin's eggs.

5. Designating dishes and other containers for sugar.
See also SUGAR HOGSHEAD.
1764 *N.H. Hist. Soc.Coll.* IX. 156, [I sent] also lb 14 1/4 Sugar bag with it. *c***1766** *York Co., Va., Rec.: Wills* Inventories XXI, 2 Tea Pots, 1 Milk Pot and 1 Sugar Dish (earthen). **1783** E. PARKMAN *Diary* 298 Tin Tunnel. . . . A Shugar Bowl. **1812** STODDARD *Sk. Louisiana* 161 They were mostly engaged in sawing boards for sugar cases. **1840** *Picayune* 2 Sept. 2/2 A newspaper would be kept from their sight with more caution than sugar pot and sweetmeats. **1853** 'P. PAXTON' *Yankee in Texas* 401 A hundred . . . boats all lie with their bows . . . pointing to the . . . unwieldy sugar puncheons or countless coffee bags which they are about to engulf. **1877** BARTLETT 808 As busy as a negro in a sugar-cask. **1880** BURNETT *Old Pioneer* 9 After the sugar was molded into cakes or grained, it was carefully deposited in the black walnut 'sugar-chest.'

6. Designating means of transportation of sugar and places involved in such transportation.
1776 *Warren-Adams Lett.* I. 255 A large Sugar Ship from Jamaica . . . is taken and got into the vineyard in her way to Bedford. **1887** *Century Mag.* Nov. 108/1 Sugar-boats . . . carry supplies to the plantations on rivers and bayous. **1916** DU PUY *Uncle Sam* 72 You will be assigned to one of the great sugar ports.

7. Designating parts of sugar-maple trees, or sugar-maple trees in general.
See also SUGAR MAPLE, SUGAR TREE.
1816 U. BROWN *Journal* II. 233 A sugar stump in the Corn which we Imagine nearly south. **1826** COOPER *Mohicans* iv, The thief is leaning against the foot of the sugar sapling that you can see over them bushes. **1837** W. JENKINS *Ohio Gaz.* 285 The land lies rolling, and is covered with beech and sugar timber. **1843** 'CARLTON' *New Purchase* II. 303 Scamper away, you little grey gaffer, and peep from the dense foliage of that lofty sugar-top!

8. Designating persons concerned with the production, manufacture, or sale of sugar.

See also SUGAR-BAKER, SUGAR-BOILER 1, etc.

1839 in Stowe *Key* 41/1 The sugar-planters upon the sugar coast in Louisiana had ascertained that [etc.]. **1841** *Picayune* 10 June 2/3 Several dealers in sugar and sugar brokers were yesterday summoned before Recorder Bertus. **1876** KNIGHT 2446/2 [The] touch test . . . is a delicate test, requiring judgment, but is preferred to the saccharometer, where the 'sugar-master' is skillful. **1881** *Harper's Mag.* April 646 We met one of the largest sugar producers. **1891** Sugar 'Nabobs' [see COTTON STATE]. **1898** *Kansas City Star* 18 Dec. 15/2 Hop, Skip and Jump are . . . the pet sheep of . . . the children of Mr. Henry O. Havemeyer, the sugar king.

9. In the specific names of plants and trees.

See also SUGAR BEET, SUGARBERRY, etc.

1837 Sugar apple [see CUSTARD APPLE]. **1895** A. BROWN *Meadow-Grass* 100 Mrs. Pettis . . . had been holding a long conversation with young Mrs. Lamson on the possibility of doing over sugar-barberry. **1751** J. BARTRAM *Observations* 27 The timber was sugar birch, sugar maples, oak and poplar. **1891** COULTER *Bot. W. Texas* I. 63 *V[itis] rupestris*. . . . Sugar grape. . . . In the Valley of Devil's River and westward into the mountains of the Pecos. **1824** DODDRIDGE *Notes* 86 The sugar haws . . . were most esteemed. **1860** DARLINGTON *Weeds & Plants* 210 *V[accinium] Pennsylvanicum*. . . . Pennsylvanian Vaccinium. . . . Sugar Huckleberry. **1901** MOHR *Plant Life Ala.* 831 *Cucumis melo cantelupa.* Cantaloupe. Sugar Melon. **1856** *Porter's Spirit of Times* 18 Oct. 118/1 The sugar millet . . . is used for fattening cattle. **1893** Sugar pear [see SUGARBERRY 2]. **1905** in *Cent. Suppl.* 1295/3 Negro or Nantucket Sugar Pumpkin. The true old-fashioned black-warted, shelled pumpkin. **1894** COULTER *Bot. W. Texas* III. 494 *S[orghum] vulgare*, . . . widely introduced in cultivation, . . . includes the many varieties cultivated as sugar sorghum, Kaffir corn [etc.].

10. In special combinations.

Sugar crop, the crop of sugar cane; *s. ham*, sugar-cured ham; *s. money*, sugar used as a medium of exchange; *s.-nippers*, 'a tool for cutting loafsugar into small lumps' (*Cent.*); *s. rag*, a piece of cloth in which a little sugar is tied for an infant to suck on; *s. rolling*, the period or season when cane is crushed under the rollers of a cane mill; *s. snow*, a fall of snow when the maple sap is running; *s. state*, a state one of whose chief products is sugar; *s. tax*, a tax imposed on sugar; *s. time*, the time when the sap runs and maple sugar is made; *s. town*, a town in a district notable for the production of maple sugar.

1818 *Amer. Mo. Mag.* II. 317 The sugar crops are worth from 20 to 150,000 dollars a year. **1838** *N.Y. Advertiser & Exp.* 7 Feb. 3/3 The 'Sugar Hams' prepared by E. S. Miller . . . have been considered equal to any. **1691** *Mass. Bay Currency Tracts* 31 And why may not Paper-mony be as good as Tobacco-mony, Potato-mony, and Sugar-mony? **1790** *Penna. Packet* 1 March 1/1 This Day, . . . Will commence the Sale of a Large and General Assortment of . . . screw drivers, iron holders, sugar nippers. **1855** COOKE *Ellie* 203 Are you going . . . to make a sugar-rag for that baby up there? **1853** *Harper's Mag.* Nov. 763/1 To the children, 'sugar rolling' is composed of halcyon days. **1861** G. K. WILDER *Diary* (MS.) 6 March, It will be a 'sugar snow with a little more.' **1876** *Wide Awake* 174/1 Massachusetts . . . is not much of a sugar state. **1802** *Steele P.* I. 295 There should be no mistake about the payment of duty on the old stock of Sugar at the commencement of the Sugar tax. **1825** NEAL *Bro. Jonathan* I. 143 Ever seed a snarl o' black sneks thawin' out—in sugar time—under a pooty smart rock heap? **1831** *Harper's Mag.* April 644 A Sugar Town in the Green Mountains.

*Sugar, *v. intr.* (See also SUGARING.)

+1. To make maple sugar.

1872 *Vermont Bd. Agric. Rep.* I. 215 My brother . . . sugared in what we called the old sugar place.

+2. *To sugar off*, to make sugar from maple sap.

[**1836** TRAILL *Backwoods of Canada* (1846) 237 Those that sugar-off outside the house have a wooden crane fixed against a stump.] **1844** *Knickerb.* XXIII. 441 We will rendezvous about one o'clock, and in the afternoon help 'sugar off.' **1858** WEED *Autobiog.* 16 The transparent and delicious streaks of candy congealed and cooled in snow while 'sugaring-off.' **1872** *Rep. Vermont Bd. Agric.* I. 216 The syrup should be sugared off as soon as it has stood sufficient time to settle. **1893** HOLLEY *Samantha at World's Fair* 5 They had more'n two hundred maple trees, . . . and they had to sugar off every day. **1894** *Vt. Agric. Rep.* XIV. 135 Take all that is wanted for maple syrup or honey and sugar it off.

+b. To amount to; to measure up to (a given amount) after all allowances have been made.

1871 *Harper's Bazar* 13 March 163/3 It is estimated that his estate would 'sugar off,' as they say in Vermont, at about $200,000.

Sugar-baker. {1650} A sugar-refiner. {1688-} — **1725** *New-Eng. Courant* 13-20 Nov. 2/2 James Lubbuck Chocolate Grinder, . . . opposite to Mr. Smith's Shugar baker in Boston, sells the best Chocolate. **1795** *Ann. 3d Congress* 1086 As very little refined sugar is imported, the American sugar bakers would have a complete monopoly. *a***1855** J. F. KELLY *Humors* 229 A man well enough to do in the world, chief clerk of a 'sugar baker,' and receiving his twenty hundred dollars a year. **1883** *Century Mag.* Oct. 856/1 The old prison-like stone structure . . . [is] occupied by William Rhinelander & Sons, sugar-bakers.

Sugar beet.

1. A kind of beet cultivated for the sugar which is derived from its root. {1831-}

1817 [see MANGEL-WURZEL]. **1840** *Niles' Nat. Reg.* 7 March 16 The sugar beet is cultivated to some extent in this country. **1890** *Stock Grower & Farmer* 24 May 3/4 Root crops do particularly well, and the growing of the sugar beet will soon be one of our greatest industries [in N. Mex.]. **1908** *Indian Laws & Tr.* III. 331 To enable said Indians to engage in the raising of sugar beets and other crops, the sum of twenty-five thousand dollars.

2. Attrib. and comb. with *belt, leaf beetle*, etc.

1882 LATHROP *Echo of Passion* iv, Mr. Evans had not forgotten the younger man's opposition on the sugar-beet question. **1899** *Chicago Record* 31 Jan. 10/1 The great success of the experiment of sugar beet raising in Michigan . . . has led to the formation of six or eight . . . companies. **1900** *Congress. Rec.* 6 Feb. 1571/2 The western sugar-beet raiser was beginning to see a little farther than the end of his nose. **1909** *Cent. Suppl.* 713/3 Larger *sugar-beet leaf-beetle, Monoxia puncticollis.* *Ib.* 1295/3 *Sugarbeet belt*, . . . from southern New York and northern Pennsylvania to northern Nebraska and South Dakota, over large sections of Colorado, Utah, Wyoming, Montana, Idaho, Washington, and Oregon, and in California on the coast side. **1924** Sugar-beet leaf hopper [see LEAF HOPPER].

+Sugarberry.

1. = HACKBERRY 1. Also attrib. and with specifying adjective.

1843 [see BEAVER WOOD 2]. **1859** BARTLETT 186 *Hackberry*, . . . a small or middle-sized tree, with sweet and edible fruits as large as bird-cherries, . . . is also called Sugar Berry. **1869** *Amer. Naturalist* III. 407 Western Sugar-berry (*Celtis reticulata*). This tree is strictly limited toward the north-west by Snake and Columbia River. **1877** BURROUGHS *Birds & Poets* 95 Many times during the winter the sugar-berry tree was visited by a flock of cedar-birds. **1896** *Chicago Record* 17 Feb. 4/6 He laid the groundwork . . . by cutting a sugarberry sprout.

2. The shadbush, *Amelanchier canadensis*.

1893 *Amer. Folk-Lore* VI. 141 *Amelanchier Canadensis*, sugar pear. Orono, Me. Sugar berry. N. Woodstock, N.H.

Sugar bird. {1688-} +=EVENING GROSBEAK. — **1891** *Cent.* 6046/2 *Sugar-bird*, . . . a translation of the Indian name of the American evening grosbeak . . . , which is specially fond of maple sugar. (Local, U.S.) **1917** *Birds of Amer.* III. 2.

Sugar-boiler. **1.** A sugar-baker {1688-}; +one who boils maple sap for sugar. **2.** A boiler used in sugar-making. — **(1) 1789** *Boston Directory* 188 Ivers James, sugar-boiler. **1823** COOPER *Pioneers* xx, The sugar-boiler . . . was busy in his 'camp.' **1790** [see GRATE BAR]. **1815** *Niles' Reg.* VIII. 141/1 There are in Pittsburgh, three large and extensive air-founderies, where are cast . . . sugar boilers, iron boilers for distilleries, &c. **1856** *Rep. Comm. Patents* 1855: *Agric.* 284 A sugar-boiler that will make 30 gallons of syrup a day, may be purchased in Augusta for less than $60.

Sugar bush. {1822-} +A grove of sugar maples. — **1823** COOPER *Pioneers* xx, We will stop and see the 'sugar-bush' of Billy Kirby. **1842** KIRKLAND *Forest Life* II. 206 A sugar-bush means from two hundred to a thousand maple-trees, grouped here and there within the circuit of a mile or so. **1877** BURROUGHS *Birds & Poets* 109 The camp-fire in the sugarbush. **1904** WALLER *Wood-Carver* 51, I went with Aunt Lize and Uncle Shim over into the sugar-bush.

+Sugar cabins. *pl.* ?Any one of various settlements or camps at which sugar is or was made from sap. — **1756** *Lett. to Washington* I. 191 One at the Sugar Cabbins called Fort Littleton Commanded by Capt. Hanee Hamilton. **1758** *Post Journal* (1904) 249 We concluded to go within three miles of Kushkushking, to their sugar cabbins, and to call their chiefs there. **1765** CROGHAN *Journal* (1904) 124 We travelled . . . to a place called the Sugar Cabins.

+Sugar camp. a. In a sugar bush, the place where the sap is boiled. **b.** A sugar bush.

1808 PIKE *Sources Miss.* 49 The sugar camp near the stockade was where he made sugar. **1813** *Niles' Reg.* IV. 316/1 Many of our farmers have their 'sugar camp,' of three or four acres. **1829** *Va. Lit. Museum* 288 [The troughs] are removed to the temporary boiling house or *sugar-camp.* **1851** A. CARY *Clovernook* 115 He proposed building a little cabin in the edge of the sugar-camp. **1874** *Vermont Bd. Agric. Rep.* II. 734 Bright pictures of the sugar camp with the boiling sap come to mind. **1903** G. C. EGGLESTON *First of Hoosiers* 79 The 'sugar camp'—a vast grove of sugar maple trees—yielded all the sugar and molasses used.

attrib. **1807** in Marshall *Kentucky* (1824) II. 415 A line at right-angles will strike the head of Black's and Newman's sugar camp branch. **1845** *Lowell Offering* V. 268 We used to have sugar-camp parties in the woods. **1874** B. F. TAYLOR *World on Wheels* 71 It is . . . a full-grown maple, that gave down the sap for the sugar-camp kettle in your grandfather's time.

*Sugar cane.

*1. A grass (*Saccharum officinarum*), a principal source of manufactured sugar; a stalk of this plant; also, collect., a field of these plants.

1634 *Relation of Beginnings of Maryland* 21 We haue also . . . Sugar-Canes of our owne planting. **1788** in P. L. Phillips *Notes on B. Romans* 111 The land however, . . . was what is called high swamp; the soil of which was even strong enough for sugar canes. **1827** SHERWOOD *Gaz.*

Georgia 10 The sugar-cane has been in successful cultivation for several years. **1847** *Rep. Comm. Patents 1846* 291, I do not claim as my invention the combination of two sets of rollers to crush and re-crush sugar-cane. **1862** MOORE *Rebellion Rec.* V. II. 310 The advance was made . . . through sugar-cane. **1899** 'O. HENRY' *Roads of Destiny* 316 He overlooked fields of sugar-cane so vast that their farthest limits melted into the sky.

2. Attrib. and comb. with *bagasse, beetle, borer,* etc.

1856 *Porter's Spirit of Times* 15 Nov. 172/3 The refuse sugar-cane *bagasse* was being burnt up. **1859** BARTLETT 19 *Bagasse Furnace,* a furnace arranged to burn the sugar-cane stalks. **1867** *Atlantic Mo.* March 275/2 For beverage, we had . . . the delicious sugar-cane syrup, which we had brought from Florida. **1891** *Cent.* 6046/3 [The] *Sugar-cane beetle,* a scarabæid beetle, *Ligyrus rugiceps,* . . . damages sugar-cane in Louisiana by boring into the canes in the early spring. *Ib.,* [The] *Sugar-cane borer,* the larva of a crambid moth, *Chilo saccharalis,* . . . bores sugar-cane in the southern United States, the West Indies, and elsewhere. **1909** *Cent. Suppl.* 161/1 *Sugar-cane brand,* a disease of the leaves of sugar-cane caused by the smut, *Ustilago Sacchari.*

+**Sugar-cured,** *a.* Of ham or pork: Prepared with the use of sugar. {1897} — **1851** CIST *Cincinnati* 186 The firm of Stagg & Shays . . . does a heavy business in sugar-cured hams. **1864** *Hist. North-Western Soldiers' Fair* 106 [Donations include] 2 sacks sugar cured hams. **1881** [see DRY *a.* 7]. **1902** LORIMER *Lett. Merchant* 31 And when I started in the packing business it was all straight sailing . . . —just turning hogs into hog meat— dry salt for the niggers down South and sugar-cured for the white folks up North.

+**Sugar eat.** A party at which maple sugar or candy is served. — **1859** G. K. WILDER *Diary* (MS.) 7 April, I was invited to a party, a sugar eat. **1906** *Springfield W. Repub.* 7 Feb. 9 A number attended the moving picture entertainment and sugar-eat.

Sugar estate. A plantation devoted to the growing of sugar cane. {1796-} — **1818** *Niles' Reg.* XIII. 314/2 Negroes on the sugar estates of Louisiana are worth from 600 to 1000 dollars yearly. **1856** *Rep. Comm. Patents 1855: Agric.* 268 By the year 1803, there were no less than eighty-one sugar estates on the delta alone. **1888** [see COAST *n.* 1].

+**Sugar farm.** =prec. — **1818** DARBY *Emigrant's Guide* 10 On all those places, except the Vermilion, sugar farms and houses are at this time established to advantage. **1888** [see ORANGERY].

+**Sugar grove.** =SUGAR BUSH. — **1792** IMLAY *Western Territory* 136 [Settlement in this country] has expanded into fertile fields, blushing orchards, pleasant gardens, luxuriant sugar groves. **1860** HOLLAND *Miss Gilbert* 148 [She] marked the smoke slowly curling up from the sugar groves. **1874** *Vermont Bd. Agric. Rep.* II. 275 It is often the case in selecting a site for an orchard that we can take advantage of the shelter afforded by a hill or sugar grove.

Sugar-grower. One who grows sugar cane or sugar beets. {1844-} — **1869** *Rep. Comm. Agric. 1868* 55 The total number of sugar-growers was 747. **1892** *Courier-Journal* 2 Oct. 2/3 The Republicans had . . . taken fifteen million dollars a year for fifteen years, from the people to pay the sugar growers a bounty. **1900** *Congress. Rec.* 31 Jan. 1359/1 You will add to this list of opposers the sugar growers.

Sugar-growing, *a.* Producing sugar. {1856-} — **1816** *Niles' Reg.* X. 81/1 The representatives of the *sugar-growing* states insist on a certain duty upon that article. **1840** *Ib.* 2 May 132/2 The duties of 1816 . . . [are] essentially important to the sugar growing interests in the United States. **1856** *Rep. Comm. Patents 1855: Agric.* 268 Some few sections only of the sugar-growing parishes were favored even with occasional vernal showers. **1886** *Harper's Mag.* June 73/2 Texas, our other chief sugar-growing State.

Sugar hogshead. A hogshead used for storing and transporting sugar. — **1699** J. DICKENSON *God's Protecting Prov.* 33 We saw Sugar-Hogsheads. **1826** COOPER *Mohicans* xvi, A pretty degree of knighthood, sir, is that which can be bought with sugar-hogsheads! **1894** 'MARK TWAIN' *P. Wilson* xviii, [I] robbed de sugar hogsheads en grain-sacks on de wharf.

Sugarhouse.

1. a. A building in which raw sugar is made, or a sugar refinery {1600, in Africa; 1769-}; a building in which sugar is stored or sold. +**b.** A shed in which maple sap is boiled.

In the Revolutionary War sugarhouses in New York were used by the British as prisons for captured American soldiers and American civilians under suspicion.

1725 *New-Eng. Courant* 12 April 2/2 To be sold at Mr. James Smith's Sugar House . . . , Single Refined Loaf Sugar. **1778** *Jrnls. Cont. Congress* X. 74 The privates in New York have been crowded all summer in sugar houses. **1821** W. DALTON *Travels U.S.* 102 There being few farms in this part of the country without maple trees and sugar houses. **1881** *Harper's Mag.* April 650/2 If the grove is on a hill and the sugar-house is in a hollow, the sap as it is gathered is emptied into a 'flume.' **1886** *Ib.* June 80/2 These processes, in the old-fashioned plantation sugar-houses, are effected by what is known as a 'battery' of open pans or 'taches.'

+**2.** (See quot. 1803.)

1784 *S.C. Gazette* 6 Jan. 1/2 Delivers her [a slave] to the Warden of the Sugar-House, in Charleston. **1803** J. DAVIS *Travels* 90 The ladies of Carolina, and particularly those of Charleston . . . send both their men-slaves and women-slaves, for the most venial trespass, to a hellish-mansion, called the Sugar-house: here a man employs inferior agents to scourge the poor negroes.

3. Attrib. in sense 1 with *interior, syrup, yard.*

1856 *Porter's Spirit of Times* 15 Nov. 172/3 A roaring wood fire at one end of the room, three or four chairs, an old wooden table, a cot bedstead . . . and you have a sugar-house interior. **1881** STODDARD *E. Hardery* 168 I'm going to try for some real sugar-house syrup. **1883** Sugar-house yard [see CANE CART].

Sugarhouse molasses. A thin molasses which remains after the refining of cane sugar. {1890} — **1848** BURTON *Waggeries* 35 Encomiums on the sweets of married life were drowned in sugar-house molasses. **1886** POORE *Reminisc.* I. 39 Many of the passengers visited the bar to imbibe Holland gin and sugar-house molasses—a popular morning beverage.

Sugaring. {1740-}

+**1.** The making of sugar by boiling maple sap till it crystallizes; a social affair often accompanying this process; also, the time of the year when the sap is gathered and boiled up. Freq. with *off.*

[**1836** TRAILL *Backwoods of Canada* (1846) 237 The best rule I can give as to the sugaring-off, as it is termed, is to let the liquid continue at a fast boil.] **1842** KIRKLAND *Forest Life* II. 211 The process called 'sugaring off' . . . [is] not considered likely to be quite perfect without the aid of female hands. **1881** *Harper's Mag.* April 649/1 The women and children . . . no longer know the old-time delights of 'sugaring off.' **1896** *Advance* 23 April 607/1 The farmers are hardly getting to sugaring in dead earnest. **1903** *Atlantic Mo.* Sept. 383 The 'huskings' and 'sugarings-off' of the old-fashioned rural New Englander. **1904** WALLER *Wood-Carver* 30, I'll hev ter knit from now t'll sugarin'-off.

b. *Sugaring down,* crystallizing.

1850 S. F. COOPER *Rural Hours* 26 The syrup boils until on the point of graining, as it is called, or in rustic parlance, 'sugaring down.'

2. Bribery.

1902 WHITE *Blazed Trail* 117 The old-time logger found these two individuals susceptible to the gentle art of 'sugaring.'

3. Attrib. with *part, season, time.*

1835 THOMPSON *Adv. T. Peacock* 40 My boy, Jock, . . . was fourteen last sugarin'-time. **1862** *Rep. Comm. Patents 1861: Agric.* 262 The sugaring season is commonly in March. **1897** *Advance* 8 April 455/2, I don't know how it has been in the sugaring parts of Ohio.

Sugar interest. The sugar-planters, regarded as an economic and political group. — **1836** *Diplom. Corr. Texas* I. (1908) 170 This government . . . will not consent to see an independent slave holding community . . . presenting a formidable rivalry to the cotton and sugar growing interests of Louisiana and Mississippi and the whole south. **1843** *Niles Nat. Reg.* 15 July 3/7 The Tariff and the Sugar Interest. **1881** *Ore. State Jrnl.* 8 Jan. 4/2 He has always favored a tariff policy that protects the Louisiana sugar interest.

Sugar kettle. A kettle used in manufacturing maple or cane sugar. — **1843** STEPHENS *High Life N.Y.* II. 183 The folks . . . gin me three cheers that made the blood bile in my heart like maple sap in a sugar kittle. **1886** Z. F. SMITH *Kentucky* 505 These became known for the large sugar kettles manufactured at the former furnace for the planters of Louisiana.

+**Sugar kiss.** A piece of sugar candy. Also attrib. and fig. (Cf. KISS.) — **1839** [see PHILOPENA]. **1876** *Congress. Rec.* 25 July 4873/2 The conservatives of Portsmouth [Va.], . . . had printed tickets of the smallest possible size, on the thinnest paper, and by folding several in a large ticket and presenting it as their vote they succeeded in filling the ballot-boxes with over a thousand of these small tickets—sugar-kiss tickets as they are called.

Sugar land. Land noted for the number of sugar maples on it, or used for growing sugar cane. — **1692** *Va. State P.* I. 44 We marcht to the Suggar Land. **1814** *Niles' Reg.* VI. 393/1 In Louisiana are great quantities of the most valuable 'sugar lands' in the world. **1852** GOUGE *Fiscal Hist. Texas* 84 Texas . . . would have been under no necessity of cultivating . . . her sugar lands. **1883** SWEET & KNOX *Through Texas* 82 In the counties of Fort Bend, Wharton, Colorado, and Brazoria, there is a great deal of the finest sugar-lands in the world.

***Sugar loaf.** A solid loaf of refined sugar. Also attrib. and transf. — **1687** SEWALL *Letter-Book* I. 74 Send a barrell or two of shopp sugar and 3 or 4 sugar loves. **1740** *Mag. Amer. Hist.* I. 612, I hope sone to receive the ballance . . . in such goods as will answer, suger loaf at the rate you sent itt will not. **1850** *Rep. Comm. Patents 1849: Agric.* 149 Cotton.—There have been some new varieties of seed introduced in this section, the banana and sugar-loaf. **1889** *Century Mag.* April 841/1 If there were a 'sugar loaf' to crack, . . . it was the mistress of the house who brought her strength to bear on it.

+**Sugar lot.** =SUGAR BUSH. — **1841** *Lowell Offering* I. 225 Friend H. called to invite me to visit his sugar lot. **1859** *Harper's Mag.* July 278/1 The Judge learned that his applicant had been arrested for wantonly upsetting a churn of sap in his neighbour's sugar-lot. **1896** [see SUGAR *n.* 3b].

***Sugar-maker.** One who makes maple or cane sugar. — **1814** J. TAYLOR *Arator* 128 The early Kentucky settlers contended, that unless the sugar makers killed the sugar trees, it threw a portion of their labor out of employment. **1834** NOTT *Novellettes* I. 90 [He] took him for at least a Carolina rice-planter, or Louisiana sugar-maker. **1898** N. E. JONES *Squirrel Hunters of Ohio* 20 It was considered by the 'sugar-maker' as the announcement of the near approach of 'sugar weather.'

+**Sugar maple.** The rock maple (*Acer saccharum*), the source of the sap from which maple sugar is made, or a similar related species; a tree of such a species, or the wood of such a tree.

See also BLACK SUGAR-MAPLE.

[1731 MILLER *Gard. Dict.* s.v. *Acer*, There is another sort of Maple, which is very common in Virginia, and is known by the Name of the *Sugar Maple*.] 1751 J. BARTRAM *Observations* 27 The timber was sugar birch, sugar maples, oak and poplar. 1781-2 JEFFERSON *Notes Va.* (1788) 37. 1820 FLINT *Lett. from Amer.* 229 The sugar-maple . . . is used in making stocks for rifles. 1840 COOPER *Pathfinder* xviii, I had a cabin in a grove of sugar maples. 1853 *Harper's Mag.* March 562/1 Now are the 'sap-buckets' . . . got ready for the delicious juice of the sweet sugar-maple. 1892 *Vt. Agric. Rep.* XII. 120 [There is] a large supply of the sugar maple, making many valuable orchards.

attrib. 1791 *Amer. Philos. Soc.* III. 70 It has been a subject of inquiry whether the maple sugar might not be improved in its quality and increased in its quantity by the establishment of boiling houses in the sugar maple country. *Ib.* 77 It were to be wished, that the settlers upon the sugar maple lands, would spare the sugar tree in clearing their lands. 1844 *Knickerb.* XXIII. 506 A western orator recently delivered himself of it from the summit of a sugar-maple stump at a political barbacue.

+**Sugar-maple borer.** (See quotation.) — 1881 *U.S. Entomological Comm. Bul.* No. 7, 103 The sugar-maple borer, *Glycobius speciosus*, . . . bores for several inches into the trunks of healthy trees.

+**Sugar-maple tree.** =SUGAR MAPLE. — 1791 *Amer. Philos. Soc.* III. 64 The Sugar Maple-tree grows in great quantities in the western countries of all the middle states of the American Union. 1825 NEAL *Bro. Jonathan* I. 156 Don't know a pitch-pine hay-mow from a sugar maple-tree. 1847 HOWE *Hist. Coll. Ohio* 239 Ten miles below Findlay . . . are two sugar maple trees, 30 feet distant at their base, which, about 60 feet up, unite and form one trunk. 1903 G. C. EGGLESTON *First of Hoosiers* 79 The 'sugar camp'—a vast grove of sugar maple trees—yielded all the sugar and molasses used.

Sugar mill. A machine which presses the juice from sugar cane {1600-}; a factory in which sugar is made. — 1831 PECK *Guide* 79 Large drafts for sugar mills . . . are made upon the Cincinnati and Pittsburgh iron foundries. 1838 C. NEWELL *Revol. Texas* 87 The enemy attempted a sally in the night at the sugar-mill. 1867 L. BAKER *U.S. Secret Service* 502 The blaze lit up . . . the tumbled farm gear in the corner, ploughs, harrows, hoes, rakes, sugar-mills.

Sugar mite. {1796} Any one of various mites of the genus *Glyciphagus* which frequently infest unrefined sugar. — 1868 *Amer. Naturalist* II. 112 The Sugar Mite (*Acarus saccharinum*) is found in brown sugar. 1891 *Cent.* 6047/1.

+**Sugar orchard.** An orchard of sugar maples. — 1833 FLINT *D. Boone* 113 The contiguity of a salt lick and a sugar orchard . . . was a very desirable circumstance. 1871 EGGLESTON *Hoosier Schoolm.* 32 After he got over the fence to go through the 'sugar camp' (or sugar *orchard*, as they say at the East), he stopped and turned back. 1896 *Vt. Agric. Rep.* XV. 38, [I] would not pay any attention to the matter of pasturage in a sugar orchard.

+**Sugar party.** (See quotation 1871.) — 1871 DE VERE 206 Sugar-parties, during which the sap collected in large vessels is boiled down in the still wintry woods, amid much merriment and innocent mirth, are common from Vermont down to Western Virginia. 1907 HOWELLS *Through Eye of Needle* 65, I once went to a sugar party up in New Hampshire.

+**Sugar pine.**

1. Wild sago.

1848 DUNGLISON *Med. Lexicon* 80/1 Florida arrow root is derived from *Zamia integrifolia* or *Z. pumila*, Sugar pine.

2. A species of pine (*Pinus lambertiana*) found on the west coast.

1857 BORTHWICK *3 Years in Calif.* 188 The pine-trees are of an immense size. . . . The most graceful is what is called the 'sugar pine.' 1860 GREELEY *Overland Journey* 293 Yellow, pitch, and sugar (white) pine . . . once overspread the whole country. 1873 MILLER *Amongst Modocs* 70 Sugar-pines, tall as pyramids, on either hand as we rode up the trail. 1897 LEWIS *Wolfville* 285, I peels some sugar-pines, like I sees Injuns. a1918 G. STUART *On Frontier* I. 58 There were the lofty smooth-trunked sugar pines.

Sugar-planter. One who operates a sugar plantation. {1747-} — 1766 STORK *Acct. E. Florida* 61 The stock of a sugar planter is not only procured, but supported at vast expence. 1842 *Niles' Nat. Reg.* 14 May 176/3 (*caption*), Sugar Planters of Louisiana. 1888 *Congress. Rec.* 12 May 4040/1 If free trade is such a good thing, why not tear down the walls surrounding the Louisiana sugar-planter?

Sugarplum. {1608-} +The shadbush, *Amelanchier canadensis*. — 1832 BROWNE *Sylva* 216 In the northern section of the Union, it is called *Wild Pear Tree* and *Sugar Plum*. 1893 *Amer. Folk-Lore* VI. 141 *Amelanchier Canadensis*, sugar-plum. Vt.

Sugar-refiner. One whose business is the refining of sugar. {1688-} — 1724 *New-Eng. Courant* 15 June 2/1 Ran away from his Master Mr. James Smith, Sugar-Refiner, . . . a Negro Man named Sambo. 1802 *Steele P.* I. 294 Our Sugar refiners were too intelligent to have submitted to so palpable an injustice. 1879 BAGBY *Old Va. Gentleman* 232 What was

their petty thieving compared to the enormous pillage of the modern sugar refiner and the crooked-whiskey distiller?

Sugar refinery.

1. A factory for the refining of sugar. {1833-}

1803 *Ann. 8th Congress* 2 Sess. 1524 One sugar-refinery, said to make about two hundred thousand pounds of loaf sugar. 1827 DRAKE & MANSFIELD *Cincinnati* 66 No returns have been received: 1 Sugar Refinery. 1893 *Harper's Mag.* April 797/2 The Eastern sugar-refineries purchase the bones found scattered all over the plains, to be used in clarifying sugar.

‖**2.** The refining of sugar.

1803 *Ann. 8th Congress* 2 Sess. 1479 Congress made another provision for encouraging the domestic sugar refinery.

+**Sugar sand. 1.** A granular sediment, principally calcium malate and silica, which forms in the process of making maple sugar. **2.** A sandstone of a sugary or grainy texture. — (1) 1882 *Vt. Agric. Rep.* VII. 64 In the process of sugar making there was a point where it would combine with the lime, making 'sugar sand' or the malate of lime. 1908 *Franklin Inst. Jrnl.* Oct. 265. (2) 1890 J. CARLL *7th Rep. Oil & Gas Fields W. Penna.* 139 Drillers have certain terms—not classical, but expressive and well understood by the craft and by oil men generally—*sugar-sand, cloverseed* [etc.].

Sugar ticket. (See SUGAR KISS, quot. 1876, and cf. KISS-JOKE TICKET.)

Sugar tree. {1801-, in Africa and Australia}

+**1.** The sugar maple; a tree yielding a sap from which sugar can be made; the wood of such a tree.

See also BLACK SUGAR-TREE.

1705 [see HONEY TREE 1]. 1775 FITHIAN *Journal* II. 35, In this valley are many of the Sugar trees. 1821 NUTTALL *Travels Arkansa* 113 There is a maple in this country [of Arkansas] . . . which has not come under my notice, called the sugar-tree (though not, as they say, the *Acer saccharinum*). 1851 CIST *Cincinnati* 250 Our domestic veneers . . . are from black walnut, curled maple, cherry, sugar-tree, oak, ash, and apple. 1884 SARGENT *Rep. Forests* 48 *Acer saccharinum*. . . . Sugar Maple. Sugar Tree. a1918 G. STUART *On Frontier* I. 24 The bottom land . . . was covered with . . . oak, hard maple (the blessed sugar tree), and some other kinds.

+**2.** ?The honey locust: (see quotation).

1819 E. EVANS *Pedestrious Tour* 299 The sugar-tree produces a sweet pod, like that of a pea, and furnishes very nutritious food for swine.

+**3.** Attrib. in sense 1 with *bark, bottom, sapling, sugar*.

1775 FITHIAN *Journal* II. 57 Peggy . . . showed me their Sugar-tree bottom, out of which Mrs. Piper . . . makes yearly, plenty of sugar for her family's use. 1782 in V. B. Howard *Bryan Sta. Heroes* (1932) 144 Two beech trees and sugar tree saplin. 1783 in *Travels Amer. Col.* 667 The Inhabitants tan leather with beach tree bark they likewise find sugar tree bark will answer. 1843 'CARLTON' *New Purchase* I. 112 Mrs. Seymour entered the parlour with a cake of sugar-tree sugar in her hands.

+**Sugar trough.** A wooden trough used for collecting maple sap. Also transf. — 1779 *Mass. H. S. Proc.* 2 Ser. II. 453 Made Sugar Troughs and katchd some Sap. 1837 BIRD *Nick* I. 222 What should I do but see the old sugar-trough floating in the bushes. 1886 [see MAPLE 1]. 1898 N. E. JONES *Squirrel Hunters of Ohio* 22 The sugar-trough was a short trough two to four feet long made of some light wood.

+**Sugar trust.** A combination of owners of sugar refineries, exercising quasi-monopolistic control over the refining and selling of sugar. Usually specific. Also attrib. — 1888 *Congress. Rec.* App. 9 June 211/2 The next largest trust in the world is the 'sugar trust.' 1889 HOWELLS *Hazard of Fortunes* II. 116 We found competition gone and the whole economic problem in the hands of monopolies—the Standard Oil Company, the Sugar Trust, the Rubber Trust, and what not. 1894 *N.Y. Tribune* 10 June 1/3 E. R. Chapman . . . was the first witness before the Sugar Trust Investigating Committee today. 1910 PINCHOT *Fight for Conservation* 110 The Sugar Trust and the beef-packers . . . injure the average man without good reason.

∗**Sugar water.** +Maple sap. — 1824 DODDRIDGE *Notes* 250 A young man . . . brought over . . . a trough designed for holding sugar water. 1852 ELLET *Pioneer Women* 118 [She] had sent her negro woman to the woods for sugar water. 1876 KNIGHT 2496/2 In the West the liquid is called *sugar-water;* in the East, *sap*. 1890 HOWELLS *Boy's Town* 161 The boys began to go to the woods to get sugar-water, as they called the maple-sap.

+**Sugar wood.** The sugar maple; a grove of sugar maples. — 1809 A. HENRY *Travels* 68 A ridge, or mountain . . . is rocky, and covered with rock or sugar maple, or sugar-wood. 1890-3 TABER *Stowe Notes* 36, I was in the sugar-wood for some time.

Sugary. 1. A sugar factory. {1696} **2.** A place or camp in which maple sap is boiled in order to make sugar. {1840-, in Canada} — (1) 1873 *Newton Kansan* 24 April 1/6 A sugary working 500 tons of beets . . . was then thought quite extensive. (2) 1883 ALLEN *New Farm Book* 272 The primitive mode of arranging the sugary, is with large receiving troughs, (or much better, tanks,) placed near the fires.

Suggestive, a. {1631-} +Hinting at something improper; indecent. Hence *suggestiveness*. — 1889 GUNTER *That Frenchman!* xi, Her incomparable drolleries and naughtinesses, in some suggestive opera bouffe, some musical debauch. 1894 WARNER *Golden House* iii, Her judges were cosmopolitans who had seen the most suggestive dancing in all parts of the world. 1914 S. H. ADAMS *Clarion* 130 'The Nymph in the Nightie' . . .

[is] rotten with suggestiveness. **1925** *Scribner's Mag.* Oct. 4/2, I liked the story and found it neither smutty nor suggestive.

+Suggumug. [Of obscure origin.] (See quotation.) — **1784** *Amer. Acad. Mem.* I. 456 *Bixa.* . . . Bass Wood. White Wood. Suggumug. . . . Blossoms white. In woods. Not common. July.

*Suit. Also **suite.**

+1. A person's head *of* hair or set *of* whiskers or teeth.

1803 LEWIS in *Jrnls. of L. & Ordway* 61 Lorimier . . . is remarkable for having once had a remarkable suit of hair. **1845** JUDD *Margaret* I. 10 His laughter exposed a suite of fair white teeth. *Ib.* II. 216 The face of this gentleman was strikingly marked by a suit of enormous black whiskers. **1893** 'MARK TWAIN' *P. Wilson* ii, She had a heavy suit of fine soft hair. **1903** WIGGIN *Rebecca* 82 Cousin Cyrus . . . says I've got a splendid suit of hair.

2. (One's) *strong suit* {1742–}, *fig.*, one's special excellence; one's forte. {1898}

1865 'MARK TWAIN' *Sk., New & Old* 33 Jumping on a dead level was his strong suit. **1878** BEADLE *Western Wilds* 215 His strong suit then was abuse of Democrats as the proslavery party.

Suke, Sukey, *n.* and *interj.* (See SOOK, SOOKY *n.* and *interj.*)

Suke cow, *interj.* (See SOOK COW, *interj.*)

Sulky.

1. A light, two-wheeled carriage, with a seat for only one person. {1756–}

'Now used principally in America for trials of speed between trotting-horses' (*O.E.D.*).

1767 *Boston Gazette* 12 Feb. 4/2 (Ernst), A very neat sulkey. **1822** WEEMS *Letters* III. 340 If I had . . . a little light Sulky with delicate tall wheels [etc.]. **1836** W. O'BRYAN *Travels* 359 Sulky is a carriage on a pair of high wheels, room for only one to sit. **1877** *Harper's Mag.* Jan. 293/1 The doctor stepped into his sulky and drove off. **1903** *N.Y. Times* 25 Aug., Trained and shod in the modern manner and drawing the modern sulky.

2. *attrib.* **a.** Designating parts of a sulky. **+b.** (Passing into *adj.*) Designating farm implements supplied with one seat.

1800 WEEMS *Letters* II. 156, [I] was detained by accidental fracture of one of my sulky shafts. **1862** E. W. Pearson *Lett. Port Royal* 75 [He] retired, . . . incubating, like a hen, upon a sulky-box full of eggs. **1865** *Ill. Agric. Soc. Trans.* VI. 49 There were but two competitors, E. B. Skinner, driving a sulky plow [etc.]. **1868** *Iowa State Agric. Soc. Rep. 1867* 140 After the corn is up so that it can be rowed, . . . sulky-cultivators are used. **1872** *Newton Kansan* 22 Aug. 3/6 Agent for the sale of . . . Taylor Sulky Rake. **1876** KNIGHT 2452/1 *Sulky-harrow,* one having a wheeled carriage and seat for the rider. **1880** TOURGEE *Bricks* 451 The man sits up on a sulky-seat. **1881** *Rep. Indian Affairs* 95, I have purchased for them . . . 1 mower and sulky hay-rake.

+Sull, *v.* [?Back-formation from *sullen* a.] *intr.* To sulk or balk: (see also quots. 1902, 1906). Used principally of animals. *dial.*

1869 *Overland Mo.* III. 127 A mustang . . . will both 'sull,' (have the sulks) and 'buck.' **1891** THANET *Otto the Knight* 29 The ox, he sulled, . . . an' Jim jes' guv 'im one on the head. **1897** HOUGH *Story of Cowboy* 99 Again he stops still, 'sulling,' his ears back, but his legs braced stiffly. **1902** *Dialect Notes* II. 246 *Sull.* 1. To hold a position with imperturbable obstinacy and a total disregard of surroundings, as a possum, or a hog in a corner. 2. To be in a semi-comatose state through pain. Used only of animals. [s. Ill.] **1906** *Ib.* III. 159 *Sull.* 1. (Of an opossum.) To pretend to be dead. 'Just watch that possum sull.' 2. (Of a person.) To sulk. [n.w. Ark.]

Sulla. An herb of the pea family (*Hedysarum coronarium*); the French honeysuckle. {1818} — **1787** JEFFERSON *Writings* VI. 204, I had the honor of sending you, the last year, some seeds of the sulla of Malta, or Spanish St. Foin. **1788** WASHINGTON *Diaries* III. 322 The Seeds of Sulla were sown.

*Sulphur.

*1. A nonmetallic element, which occurs in nature either free or in combination; brimstone.

1674 *Cal. State P., Amer. & W.I.* VII. 581 [In] Maine . . . [are] lead, coals, sulphur, and other minerals. *c*1790 COXE *View U.S.* 75 In the settled parts of the states . . . [we have] sulphur, saltpetre. **1843** MARRYAT *M. Violet* iv, Sulphur and magnesia appear plentiful in the northern districts. **1891** *Boston Jrnl.* Nov., The men took with them . . . a lot of sulphur to burn in the hollow for the purpose of smothering the bees. **1909** *Nat. Conservation Congress Proc.* 58 Louisiana today produces more sulphur than any nation on earth.

2. Any one of many butterflies of the family Pieridae. Usually with specifying adjective. {1832–}

1891 *Cent.* 6052/2 *Sulphur.* . . . These butterflies are of some shade of yellow. *Ib.* 6052/3 *Colias philodice* of the United States is the clouded sulphur; *Callidryas enbule* is the cloudless sulphur. **1898** W. J. HOLLAND *Butterfly Book* 287 *Catopsilia agarithe,* . . . The Large Orange Sulphur. . . . The species occurs in the hot parts of the Gulf States, and is common throughout tropical America. **1904** KELLOGG *Amer. Insects* 446 Of the yellows, or sulphurs, . . . the dainty sulphur, *Nathalis iole* [is the smallest].

+3. *Sulphur and molasses,* a spring tonic corresponding to the brimstone and treacle of England.

1896 *Wkly. Witness* 2 Dec. 7/3 Our mother gave us lib'rally Of sulphur and molasses.

4. *attrib.* and *comb.* **a.** In sense 1 with *bluff, deposit, fire,* etc.

1775 in J. Hall *Sk. of West* II. 222 The agent shall not grant any lands adjoining . . . sulphur mines, knowing them to be such. **1792** in *Amer. Speech* XV. 398/1 About one mile above the Sulphur Lick. **1807** GASS *Journal* 38 We came to black sulphur bluffs. **1846** EMMONS *Agric. N.Y.* I. 301 A fact of considerable interest was reported to me, in regard to the efficacy of the milder sulphur waters in incipient phthisis. **1883** RITTENHOUSE *Maud* 258, I must wash my face with Glenn's sulphur soap. **1883** *Century Mag.* Oct. 812/2 Underneath these is a sulphur fire. **1883** *Gringo & Greaser* 1 Dec. 1/1 We have also gypsum (plaster of paris) beds, sulphur deposits and beds of kaolin or potters clay.

b. In specific names.

1884 COUES *Key to Birds* (ed. 2) 431 *M[yiodynastes] luteiventris.* . . . Sulphur-bellied Striped Flycatcher. . . . Central Am. and Mexico to Arizona. **1915** ARMSTRONG & THORNBER *Western Wild Flowers* 94 This plant [*Erigonum bakeri*] is quite pretty and conspicuous. . . . There are several other kinds of Sulphur Flower.

Sulphur-bottom. The blue whale (*Sibbaldus musculus*), having white or yellowish white spots on its belly. In full *sulphur-bottom whale.* {1924} — **1782** CRÈVECŒUR *Letters* 169 The sulpher-bottom, river St Lawrence, ninety feet long. **1883** [see FINBACK WHALE]. **1897** *Outing* XXX. 257/2 'A sulphur-bottom,' replied the captain's friend. **1911** *Rep. Fisheries 1908* 317/1 *Sulphur-bottom whale,* . . . the largest known cetacean, reaching a length of 100 feet.

Sulphur spring. A spring of water containing sulphurous compounds, or impregnated with sulphurous gases. {1813– (Hooker *Tour Ireland* I. 230)} Also *attrib.* — **1807** GASS *Journal* 101 A beautiful sulphur spring rises out of the bank. **1819** SCHOOLCRAFT *Mo. Lead Mines* 59 The sulphur springs in Jefferson county are sometimes resorted to by persons suffering from bilious complaints. **1877** HODGE *Arizona* 241 A series of hot sulphur springs are in the Sulphur Spring Valley. **1893** *Harper's Mag.* Jan. 206/2 There are sulphur springs near by.

*Sultan. The purple gallinule. Also *sultan gallinule.* {sultan-hen, 1882} — **1884** COUES *Key to Birds* (ed. 2) 675 *Ionornis.* . . . Sultan Gallinules. Hyacinths. . . . Plumage beautiful with rich blue, etc. **1891** [see SULTANA].

*Sultana. =SULTAN. {1837–, attrib.; 1840} — **1891** *Cent.* 6053/3 The American sultan is *Ionornis martinica.* . . . Also called *sultana.* **1898** *Kissimmee* (Fla.) *Valley Gazette* 28 Jan. 3/5 Plenty of squirrels, sultanas and water-fowl to be shot from canoe.

*Sum. **+**A quantity *of* tobacco, reckoned as the equivalent of an amount of money. {–1680, of other goods} — **1666** *Md. Archives* II. 136 The Governor and Councell are hereby impowered to Levy . . . such Sume or Sumes of Tobacco [etc.]. **1871** DE VERE 64 The term *Sums of Tobacco,* which is still occasionally met with in official papers, has its origin in the fact that for many generations, in old Virginia times, all taxes raised for the support of government officers, ministers, etc., were assessed in so many pounds of tobacco.

*Sumac(h). Also **sumack(e).** (See also SHOEMAKE.)

*1. Any one of various shrubs or small trees, esp. of the genera *Rhus* and *Toxicodendron;* also, the leaves or the wood of such a plant, used for kinnikinnick, dye, and other purposes.

1682 *Hist. Coll. S. Carolina* II. 34 Sumack growes in great abundance naturally. **1724** JONES *Virginia* 61 There grows Plenty of Sumack, so very useful in the Dying Trade. *a*1797 in Imlay *Western Territory* 147 The spout [for the discharge of maple sap] is generally made of the shumach or elder, which generally grow in the neighbourhood of the sugar-trees. **1822** WOODS *English Prairie* 219 Columbia-root, and sumack, and sassafras trees [are used in medicine]. **1835** IRVING *Tour on Prairies* 174 He had scented the smoke of mingled sumach and tobacco, such as the Indians use. **1872** TICE *Over Plains* 25 The undergrowth [in Kan.] is principally hazel and sumach. **1905** N. DAVIS *Northerner* 267 On one side lay . . . a tangle of vines lashing together the undergrowth of sumach and oak scrub.

b. With specifying terms.

See also POISON SUMAC, RED SUMAC(H), SMOOTH SUMAC(H), STAGHORN SUMAC(H).

1629 PARKINSON *Paradisus* 611 *Rhus Virginiana.* The Virginia Sumach, or Buckes horne tree of Virginia. **1721** Swamp sumach [see SWAMP *n.* 8]. **1784** *Amer. Acad. Mem.* I. 427 Hairy Sumach. Blossoms greenish white. Fruit scarlet. *Ib.,* Velvet sumach. Blossoms greenish white. Fruit in large, ovate, close panicles; crimson. **1785** MARSHALL *Amer. Grove* 129 Carolinian Scarlet-flowering Sumach . . . is a variety . . . having scarlet flowers. **1821** *Mass. H. S. Coll.* 2 Ser. IX. 155 Indigenous in the township of Middlebury [Vt.]: . . . *Rhus glabrum,* Sleek sumach. *Rhus copallinum,* Mountain sumach. **1897** SUDWORTH *Arborescent Flora* 275 Dwarf Sumach. *Ib.* 276 Western Sumach.

2. *attrib.* and *comb.* **a.** With *berry, bob, crop,* etc.

1630 HIGGINSON *New-England* 10 Sumacke Trees . . . yeeld a precious Gum called White Beniamen, that they say is excellent for perfumes. **1788** *N.Y. Packet* 8 April 2/1 It has long been a practice among the natives of this Continent to substitute the *sumach berry* for tobacco. **1854** THOREAU *Walden* 49, I dug my cellar . . . down through sumach and blackberry roots. **1881** *Harper's Mag.* Nov. 868/1 They are the fires of the sumac-gatherers. *Ib.* 868/2 The sumac crop is a very important source of revenue to [the 'mountain people']. *Ib.*, The leaves and twigs . . . bring a cent a pound at Winchester, where there is a large sumac factory. **1889** 'MARK TWAIN' *Conn. Yankee* 517 She charged a couple of church-wardens with willow-bark and sumach-tobacco for us. **1894** ROBINSON *Danvis Folks* 72 They saw the scarlet sumach bobs.

+**Sumarkee.** (See SOU MARKEE.)

Sumatra. Used attrib. of poultry and other products from the East Indian island or in some way associated with it. {1822-} — **1810** *Columbian Centinel* 17 Jan. 3/1 William Marston . . . has for Sale, Two hundred bags first quality Sumatra Pepper. **1854** *Penna. Agric. Rep.* 73 For superior Sumatra game fowls, . . . $2.00. **1892** Sumatra wrapper [see HAVANA 2]. **1907** BAILEY, etc. *Cycl. Amer. Agric.* II. 642/2 Sumatra tobacco (from seed saved under bag), grown in Connecticut valley under cover.

*** Summer,** *n.* (See also INDIAN SUMMER.) *attrib.*

*** 1.** Designating crops harvested in summer or other products identified with summer.

1640 *Conn. Rec.* I. 448, 30 bushl of sumer wheat. **1677** HUBBARD *Narrative* I. 82 They should be in great Want of Summer-fruits, *sc.* Beans and Squashes. **1680** *New Castle Court Rec.* 377 Sixty twoo schipples of sommer barly. **1709** Summer Cider [see LONGSTALK 1]. **1748** ELIOT *Field-Husb.* i. 14 Summer Wheat sowed with Barley is not apt to blast, and do well together; also Summer Rye and Oats. **1789** *Ann. 1st Congress* 133 It is scarcely possible to maintain our fisheries with advantage, if the commerce for summer fish is injured. **1794** *Mass. H. S. Coll.* 1 Ser. III. 197 The people make their summer butter. **1823** JAMES *Exped.* I. 192 Those [bison] skins which are obtained during this season are known by the name *Summer skins.* **1842** *S. Lit. Messenger* VIII. 199/2 He can make good summer candles from Castor Oil.

2. With reference to summer holidays. **a.** Designating activities, places, etc.

See also SUMMER COTTAGE, HOTEL, RESORT.

1880 *Harper's Mag.* Sept. 536/1 Summer boarding here can be had for one dollar per week. **1881** *Ib.* April 743/1, I have a sister . . . who has a summer home on Last Island. **1882** G. C. EGGLESTON *Wreck of Red Bird* 6 The planters . . . in the Summer . . . go off to little Summer villages in the pines to escape the fever. **1883** *Century Mag.* Sept. 695/2 Space also is wanting . . . to describe the summer towns by the ocean. **1892** *Vt. Agric. Rep.* XII. 136 Few sections can afford more attractions than this County for summer travel. **1893** *McClure's Mag.* I. 242/2 The camp was founded by Mr. Ernest Berkeley Balch as a summer camp for boys. **1897** *Chicago Ev. Post* 15 May, The question of summer tourist rates has been under consideration. **1909** *World To-day* Oct. 1014 A summer capital . . . means the town in which the President owns or hires a summer residence.

b. Designating persons.

See also SUMMER BOARDER, SUMMER TOURIST.

1886 *Leslie's Mo.* Feb. 203/1 Old Sampson don't like the Summer gentry. **1889** HOWELLS *Hazard of Fortunes* I. 135 She frankly gave up her house to the summer-folks (as they call them in the country). **1892** *Vt. Agric. Rep.* XII. 139 To these more prominent places may be added a multitude of . . . attractive homes to the summer guest. **1898** WESTCOTT *Harum* 286 Our friend had met quite a number of the 'summer people.'

3. In specific names: **a.** Of birds and animals.

See also SUMMER DUCK, SUMMER REDBIRD, etc.

1884 COUES *Key to Birds* (ed. 2) 373 *Peucæa æstivalis illinoensis*, Illinois Summer Finch. **1917** *Birds of Amer.* I. 220 Wilson's Phalarope-*Steganopus tricolor*. . . . Other Name.—Summer Phalarope. **1888** TRUMBULL *Names of Birds* 73 At Stonington, Conn., [the hooded merganser is called] Wood Sheldrake; at Essex, same state, Summer Sheldrake. [**1802** SHAW *Gen. Zool.* III. II. 551 Summer Snake, *Coluber Æstivus*. . . . Native of many parts of North America, residing on trees.] **1917** *Birds of Amer.* III. 126 Yellow Warbler. . . . [Also called] Summer Warbler.

b. Of plants and fruits.

See also SUMMER GRAPE, SUMMER HAW.

1890 *Amer. Naturalist* XXIV. 731 Summer Crooknecks appeared in our garden catalogues in 1828. **1817-8** EATON *Botany* (1822) 235 *Chenopodium scoparium*, summer cypress. **1737** Summer-Fox-grape [see FOX GRAPE]. **1847** IVES *New Eng. Fruit* 58 *Summer Frankreal.*—This very fine pear is of medium size. **1817-8** EATON *Botany* (1822) 361 *Neottia aestivalis*, summer ladies' tresses. **1856** *Rep. Comm. Patents: Agric.* 293 The summer varieties are the . . . 'Wine Apple,' 'Summer Pearmain,' and 'Leatherberry's Favorite.' **1817** W. COXE *Fruit Trees* 103 Summer Rose . . . is an apple of singular beauty and excellence.

4. In special combinations.

+*Summer normal*, a teachers' institute held in the summer (*colloq.*); *s. pasture*, a piece of land used in the summer as a pasture {1729- (Swift *Works* (1766-9) XVI. 234)}; *s. price*, a special price for summer patrons; +*s. range*, foraging at large by animals during the summer.

1898 CANFIELD *Maid of Frontier* 17 She had . . . been sent to . . . one 'summer normal,' an occasional institution intended for the development of teachers. **1637** *Dedham Rec.* III. 27 A certeyne quantety of yt medowe . . . shall become a somer pasture for milch Cowes. **1876** *N.Y. Tribune* 22 May 4/6 Summer prices will prevail at the Park Theater, where 'Uncle Tom's Cabin' will be produced tonight. **1831** PECK *Guide* 105 [Horses] find . . . herbage for the summer range.

***Summer,** *v.* +*To summer over*, to keep over summer. — **1872** *Vermont Bd. Agric. Rep.* I. 138 Do not be afraid of summering over a few tons of hay. **1896** *Vermont Agric. Rep.* XV. 39 In what way would you take care of the sugar that is intended to be summered over?

+**Summer boarder.** One who boards in a country place during the summer. Also attrib. — **1879** *Harper's Mag.* July 164 A few quiet summer boarders took shelter for a season's rest. **1887** *Nation* XLIV. 204/3 The 'summer-boarder' trade shall yield the highest amount of profit. **1920** HOWELLS *Vacation of Kelwyns* 132, I thought you were going to start a cooking-school for summer boarders.

+**Summer complaint.** Diarrhea of children during summer. *colloq.* — **1847** *Amer. Jrnl. Medical Sci.* XIV. 40 On the Endemic Gastro-follicular Enteritis, or 'Summer Complaint' of Children. **1880** *Harper's Mag.* Sept. 582/1 The summer complaint was dreadful prevalent that year.

Summer cottage. A cottage, usually in the country or at a summer resort, occupied during the summer. — **1840** *Knickerb.* XVI. 253 Mary's father had a summer-cottage in the neighborhood. **1894** HOWELLS in *Harper's Mag.* Feb. 371/1 The scene is in the summer cottage of Mr. and Mrs. Edward Roberts, in a Boston suburb.

+**Summer duck.** A duck associated in some way with the summer season, esp. the wood duck, *Aix sponsa.* {1885 (Swainson *Prov. Names Br. Birds* 158), of the garganey} — **1731** CATESBY *Carolina* I. 97 The Summer Duck. . . . They breed in Virginia and Carolina. **1775** SCHAW *Jrnl. Lady of Quality* (1921) 175 The beauty of the Summer-duck makes its death almost a murder. **1836** *Knickerb.* VIII. 680 It is a summer-duck, which swims with its body all under water. **1871** LEWIS *Poultry Book* 86 The Wood or Summer Duck . . . , one of the finest varieties we have, is easily reared and domesticated. **1917** *Birds of Amer.* I. 129.

+**Summerer.** One who spends the summer, or a part of it, at a resort or similar establishment. *colloq.* — **1881** H. J. WARNER *New Lett. Idle Man* 7 The first week of September brings with it everywhere else a hopeless collapse of 'Summerers.'

***Summer fallow.** (See FALLOW *n.* 1 b).

+**Summer false herring.** (See SUMMER HERRING 2.)

+**Summer flounder.** A large flounder of the Atlantic coast, *Paralichthys dentatus.* — **1814** MITCHELL *Fishes N.Y.* 390 [The] Flounder of New-York . . . is called the summer flounder. **1884** GOODE, etc. *Fisheries* I. 178 The Plaice, Summer Flounder, or Turbot Flounder . . . is, next to the Halibut, the most important flat-fish on the eastern coast. **1911** *Rep. Fisheries 1908* 308/2 The name ['chicken halibut'] is also incorrectly applied to the summer flounder.

+**Summer garden. 1.** A plot of ground devoted to the culture of plants during the summer. Also attrib. **2.** An outdoor refectory or amusement place, for use in summer. — **(1) 1868** GRAY *Field Botany* 79 *Pelargonium*, the Geranium, so-called, of house and summer-garden culture. **1901** CHURCHILL *Crisis* 451 Virginia and he would . . . descend to the bench on the lower tier of the summer garden. **(2) 1882** MCCABE *New York* 660 Castle Garden . . . was converted into a summer-garden, where refreshments were sold and indifferent concerts given. **1903** ADE *In Babel* 29 The Barclays never went to summer-gardens where malt drink is served.

+**Summer grape.** A sweet wild grape (*Vitis aestivalis*) of North America. — **1709** LAWSON *Carolina* 102 Two [kinds of fox grapes] . . . are called Summer-Grapes. **1771** WASHINGTON *Diaries* II. 46 The Summer grape of tolerable good taste. **1804** CLARK in *Lewis & C. Exped.* I. (1904) 68, I observe great quantity of Summer & fall Grapes. **1847** EMORY *Military Reconn.* 13 We find in the bottoms . . . summer grape. **1901** MOHR *Plant Life Ala.* 101 The vigorous summer grape . . . and the supple jack . . . ascend the highest trees without visible support below the lofty summits.

+**Summer haw.** The May haw or a related plant. — **1857** GRAY *Botany* 124 *C[ratægus] flava*, (Summer Haw.) . . . Sandy soil, Virginia and southward. **1868** — *Field Botany* 128 *C[rataegus] æstivalis*, Summer Haw of S. States. . . . Large red juicy fruit, pleasantly acid, used for tarts, &c.: ripe in summer. **1884** SARGENT *Rep. Forests* 83.

Summer herring. {1614-} +**1.** The hickory shad, *Pomolobus aestivalis.* +**2.** (See quotation.) Also *summer false herring.* **(1) 1814** MITCHILL *Fishes N.Y.* 456 Summer Herring of New-York . . . has a row of spots to the number of seven or eight. **1911** *Rep. Fisheries 1908* 311/1. **(2) 1820** *Western Rev.* II. 174 Summer False Herring. *Hyodon heterurus.* . . . A common species in the Ohio and tributary streams; it appears later than the following, whence it is called Summer-herring.

+**Summer hotel.** A hotel operated for summer visitors and residents. Also attrib. — **1852** *Harper's Mag.* Aug. 335/2 You lose your personal identity in a great summer hotel, as you would in a penitentiary. **1880** *Ib.* Sept. 496/1 The greater part of the active population was drafted to the service of the summer hotels. **1883** *Ib.* Sept. 533/1, 'I hear,' or 'Would you believe it?' or 'I was saying to my husband,' . . . is the floating coin of all summer-hotel piazzas. **1894** *Ib.* Nov. 341/2 They are called 'lakes' by the summer hotel-keepers.

***Summering.** The action or the manner of passing the summer. {-1675} Also attrib. ('Now *U.S.' O.E.D.*) — **1818** COBBETT *Year's Residence* I. 272 [The settler] would consequently set to work scratching up the earth, . . . after a long summering upon wild flesh. **1856** S. WARNER *Hills of Shatemuc* x, The young ladies' summering in the country had begun with good promise. **1880** *Harper's Mag.* July 168/2 The history of all summering-places is alike. **1894** FORD *P. Stirling* 175 My summering's over.

+**Summer kitchen.** An extra kitchen, built adjacent to a house, used for warm-weather cooking. Also attrib. — **1875** *Field & Forest* I. 28 Jim was tempted to steal . . . mutton-chops left for a moment on the summer-kitchen table. **1887** *Courier-Journal* 3 Feb. 3/6 For Rent—Two-story brick dwelling of 6 rooms, bathroom and summer kitchen. **1893** HOLLEY *Samantha at World's Fair* 158 Miss Gowdey wuz a-comin' to the World's Fair as soon as she made her rag-carpet for her summer kitchen.

+**Summer redbird.** =SUMMER TANAGER. — *c*1730 CATESBY *Carolina* I. 56 The Summer Red-Bird. . . . They are Birds of Passage, leaving Virginia and Carolina in Winter. **1781–2** JEFFERSON *Notes Va.* (1788) 76. **1831** AUDUBON *Ornith. Biog.* I. 232 The Summer Red Bird . . . feeds principally on insects. **1871** BURROUGHS *Wake-Robin* (1886) 78 The bluebird is not entirely blue; nor will the indigo-bird bear a close inspection, . . . nor the summer redbird. **1917** *Birds of Amer.* III. 81.

+**Summer resort.** A place frequented by visitors on summer holidays {1887–}; sojourn at such a place in the summer. Also attrib. Hence *summer resorter.* — **1854** BROMWELL *Locomotive Sk.* 93 Lewistown might become a more important place, even as a *summer resort.* **1857** *Appletons' Illustr. Hand-Bk. Amer. Trav.* 149/2 Saratoga has been for many years . . . the most famous place of summer resort. **1882** PECK *Sunshine* 125 He said he should at once begin . . . by boarding at a summer resort hotel. **1889** *Advance* 19 Sept., At Astoria the summer resorters distribute themselves to the various beaches. **1913** LONDON *Valley of Moon* 496, I saw from the car windows . . . hotels, springs, summer resorts, winter resorts.

+**Summer school.** A school holding sessions in summer; a school session held in summer. — **1871** EGGLESTON *Hoosier Schoolm.* 1 You might teach a summer school. **1878** *Harper's Mag.* March 502/1 The summer school provides him with a royal road to either chemistry, zoology, botany or geology. **1914** *Cycl. Amer. Govt.* III. 270/1 Nearly all summer schools lay special emphasis upon courses for teachers.

+**Summer squash.** One of various squashes which mature and are used in summer. Also attrib. — **1815** BENTLEY *Diary* IV. 346 A more free use has been made of the summer squash than ever before known. **1842** HAWTHORNE *Twice-told Tales* (1879) I. 224 Behind comes a 'sauceman,' driving a wagon full of new potatoes, . . . turnips, and summer-squashes. **1870** [see CROOKED-NECK(ED) *a.*]. **1902** FREEMAN in *Harper's Bazar* Sept. 766 There was nothing in her larder except a summer-squash pie.

+**Summer tanager.** A tanager (*Piranga rubra*) of the middle and southern states; the summer redbird. — [**1783** LATHAM *Gen. Synopsis Birds* II. 220 Summer T[anager]. *Muscicapa rubra*. . . . A little bigger than an House Sparrow. . . . Inhabits Carolina and Virginia in the summer.] **1884** COUES *N. Amer. Birds* 317. **1895** *Outing* XXVI. 69/2 The purple linnet . . . had vied with the summer tanager and the Carolina wren. **1917** *Birds of Amer.* III. 82/2 Because of his habit of eating honey-bees, the Summer Tanager has been given the name of Bee Bird.

Summer term. In a school or college, the final division of the academic year, coming to an end in the summer. — **1853** ROOT & LOMBARD *Songs of Yale* 4 Presentation Day is the sixth Wednesday of the Summer Term, when the graduating Class . . . are presented to the President as qualified for the first degree, or the A.B. **1854** [see MOUNTAIN DAY]. **1860** *Ann. Amherst College* 29 A legislative body, called the 'House of Students' was organized in this memorable Summer term of 1828. **1883** WILDER *Sister Ridnour* 132, I had just finished the Summer term in the city of West, and was glad to bid good-bye to the . . . furnace-like room under the French roof.

Summer tourist. A summer traveler; one making a pleasure trip in summer. Also attrib. — **1854** BROMWELL *Locomotive Sk.* 93 These are too much exposed to gossiping loafers to merit any considerable patronage from summer tourists. **1892** TORREY *Foot-Path Way* 31 The diapensia . . . is seldom seen by the ordinary summer tourist.

+**Summer yellowbird.** The yellow warbler, *Dendroica aestiva*. — **1791** W. BARTRAM *Travels* 290 P[arus] *luteus;* the summer yellow bird. **1810** WILSON *Ornithology* II. 111 [The] Blue-Eyed Yellow Warbler . . . [is the] Summer Yellow-bird [of] Bartram. **1844** *Nat. Hist. N.Y., Zoology* II. 99 The Summer Yellow-Bird . . . is a very common species in our State. **1917** *Birds of Amer.* III. 126.

‖**Sumsion.** [For *assumption* (1590).] =ASSUMPSIT *a.* Obs. — **1637** *Maine Doc. Hist.* III. 108, I desire that you will . . . binde them in a sumsion of money to performe their promyse.

*** Sun.**

*** 1.** In expressions fixing the time of day. **a.** *At* (or *by*) *sun,* with reference to the position of the sun in the sky; after sunrise. +**b.** *By sun,* before sunset. Now *dial.*

1637 *Essex Inst. Coll.* IX. 66 The keeper . . . [is] to take the Cattle at the pen at Sun halfe an hower highe. **1667** *Conn. Rec.* II. 73 This Court doth desire and require the Towne of Windsor to meet on Munday next, at ye meeting house, by sunn an hower high in the morning. **1700** SEWALL *Diary* II. 10 Came aboard about 2 hours by Sun, and landed at Mrs. Butler's Wharf before 3 p.m. **1771** WASHINGTON *Diaries* II. 27 Finishd the Wheat . . . abt. two Hours by Sun in the afternoon. **1827** McKENNEY *Tour to Lakes* 398 About two hours by sun, re-embarked. **1854** *Fla. Plantation Rec.* 111 The mill hands dont get to work before an hour be sun. **1882** BAILLIE-GROHMAN *Camps in Rockies* 218, I usually began fishing 'an hour by sun'—the trapper expression for an hour before sunset.

+**2.** =SUNFISH *n.* 1.

1807 GASS *Journal* 29 The fish here are generally pike, cat, sun, perch. **1896** BRUCE *Econ. Hist. Virginia* I. 113 There were in the waters of Virginia when first explored, grampus, . . . perch, tailor, sun [etc.].

+**Sunapee.** *attrib.* [*Sunapee* Lake, N.H.] Designating a species of char (*Salvelinus aureolus*) found in New Hampshire and Maine. —**1897** *N.Y. Forest, Fish, & Game Comm. 2d Rep.* 186 As the October pairing time approaches, the Sunapee fish becomes illuminated with the flushes of maturing passion. *Ib.* 188 The Sunapee saibling takes live bait readily. **1903** T. H. BEAN *Fishes N.Y.* 278 *Salvelinus alpinus aureolus.* . . . Sunapee Trout; Golden Trout; Silver Trout (Introduced).

Sunbonnet. A bonnet with an extended projection in front and, usually, a flounce or cape behind, worn by women to protect the face and neck from the sun. {1860–} (Cf. SHINGLE, SLAT SUNBONNET.) — **1824** DODDRIDGE *Notes* 116 They could . . . cover their heads with a sun bonnet made of six or seven hundred linen. **1855** *Knickerb.* XLVI. 87 My calico sun-bonnet, with its deep cape and ruffled front, hung for many a week upon the same peg. **1887** *Century Mag.* May 118/1 All Lum could see was the profile of her sun-bonnet. **1910** J. HART *Vigilante Girl* 122 Rows of gaunt and sunburnt women in sun-bonnets sat in rocking chairs.

Sunburst. {1816–} Jewels arranged in a piece after the fashion of a conventional representation of the sun and its rays. — **1878** ROE *Army Lett.* 189 An immense gold star with a diamond sunburst in the center was above her forehead. **1905** *N.Y. Times* 7 Jan. 14 The sunburst . . . consists of a large centre diamond with thirty smaller stones set in a double row around it.

+**Sunck, Sunk(e).** [Natick *sonksq, sonkusq* 'queen']. A female chief of an eastern Indian tribe. In full *sunck squaw.* Obs.

[**1662** *Brookhaven Rec.* 7 This writing, made . . . between Weany Sunk, squaw, Anabackus and Iackanapes, all of them residents of Shinecock.] **1663** *Southampton Rec.* II. 36 An agreement between the great Sunk squa Quashawam, and the Indians of Shinecock as followeth. **1676** *Conn. Rec.* II. 458 That ould peice of venum, Sunck squaw Magnus was slaine. **1797** B. TRUMBULL *Hist. Conn.* I. 347 A treaty was concluded between the United colonies and the six Narraganset sachems, and the sunk squaw or old queen of Narraganset. **1804** *Mass. Hist. Coll.* 1 Ser. IX. 83*n.*, Awaking one night, . . . and finding his sunck (queen) lying near another Indian, he . . . took his knife, and cut three strokes on each of her cheeks.

+**Sun-cured,** *a.* Cured or preserved by exposure to the sun's rays. — **1877** (advertisement), Old Judge Sun cured Virginia Smoking Tobacco. **1880** *Harper's Mag.* Aug. 351/2 Sun-cured salt-fish . . . was the favorite article of diet in the islanders' households. **1897** HOUGH *Story of Cowboy* 5 A cow, . . . if driven north and allowed to range on the sun-cured short grasses, . . . might increase [in weight] fairly by one-third.

+**Sundae.** (See SUNDAY *n.* 2.)

+**Sun dance.** Among the Plains Indians, a ceremonial dance performed in honor of the sun, freq. accompanied by public self-torture. — **1849** EASTMAN *Dahcotah* p. xxii, The *sun dance* is performed by young [Sioux] warriors who dance, at intervals of five minutes, for several days. **1882** *Rep. Indian Affairs* 39 The heathenish annual ceremony, termed the 'sun dance,' will, I trust, . . . be soon a thing of the past. **1894** *Harper's Mag.* Nov. 945/2 The sun-dance was one of the great religious and political events of the Sioux life. **1901** WHITE *Westerners* 68 This was indeed the young hero of the sun dance.

*** Sunday,** *n.*

1. In various colloq. or slang uses.

a. *A week of Sundays,* a very long time. {month of Sundays, 1850} **b.** (See quotation.) **c.** *To play Sunday on,* to pretend to be more virtuous or pious than (someone).

(a) **1843** STEPHENS *High Life N.Y.* II. 62 But it would take a week of Sundays to tell you all. (b) **1901** HARRIGAN *Mulligans* 86 They were all dressed in their Sunday's, as they called their best clothes. (c) **1902** WISTER *Virginian* 111 You and me and the boys have hit town too frequent for any of us to play Sunday on the balance of the gang.

+**2.** *l.c.* (Usually *sundae.*) A dish consisting of ice cream covered with fruit, syrup, nuts, etc. Often with defining terms.

Of obscure origin, but usually regarded as related to *Sunday.*

1904 *N.Y. Ev. Post* 21 May, The Sunday, so popular at the confectioner's, can be prepared at home. **1915** Ice-cream sundaes [see ICE CREAM 2]. **1921** TUCKER *Amer. English* 306 *Sunday,* sometimes misspelled 'sundae.' . . . Name said to have been first used, about 1897, at Red Cross Pharmacy, State Street, Ithaca, N.Y. **1922** TARKINGTON *Gentle Julia* 184, I'll take a chocolate sundae.

3. Attrib. with *best, comic, shoe, suit.*

1844 GREGG *Commerce of Prairies* I. 111 They were prepared, with clean faces . . . and their choicest Sunday suit. **1849** WILLIS *Rural Lett.* 325 Nature seems dressed and resting—every tree looking its 'Sunday best.' **1880** BURNETT *Old Pioneer* 11, I have seen young women, in going to public places, stop a short distance before reaching the place, take off their coarse shoes, and put on their 'Sunday shoes.' **1908** *Nation* 5 Nov. 426/2 We are familiar with the defence of the Sunday comic.

+**Sunday,** *v. intr.* To spend Sunday. *colloq.* or *journalistic.* — **1884** *Lisbon* (Dak.) *Clipper* 13 March, H. R. Turner Sundayed in Fargo. **1888** *Milnor* (Dak.) *Teller* 13 July 8/3 W. H. Pelton and Frank Hammond, two of Forman's jolly young men, Sundayed in town. **1909** RICE *Mr. Opp* 103 You read that Uncle Enoch Siller had Sundayed over at the Ridge.

+**Sunday-go-to-meeting,** *a.* =GO-TO-MEETING *a.* 1 and 2. {1894–} — **1841** S. *Lit. Messenger* VII. 646/2 [He discarded] his 'Sunday go-to-meetin'' broadcloth.' **1894** *Harper's Mag.* July 297/1 Uncle Reub . . . was standing on the door-sill in his Sunday go-to-meeting trousers, shirt, necktie, and suspenders, but without a coat. **1902** ALDRICH *Sea Turn* 199 The street wasn't what might be called a Sunday-go-to-meeting street, but the neighbors . . . lodged complaints.

+Sunday-go-to-meeting(s). One's best clothes worn on Sundays. *colloq. Obs.* Also fig. (Cf. GO-TO-MEETIN(G) *n.*) — **1837** NEAL *Charcoal Sk.* (1838) 193 [She] snips up all my Sunday-go-to-meetings to make jackets for the boys. **1841** *Jamestown* (N.Y.) *Jrnl.* 15 July 4/2 He dressed himself in his 'Sunday-go-to-meetings.' c**1849** PAIGE *Dow's Sermons* I. 265 Rig Virtue up in the best of Sunday go-to-meetings.

+Sunday scholar. A pupil in a Sunday school. — **1836** W. O'BRYAN *Travels* 32 We went to the Park, (an enclosed green before the city Hall,) to hear the Sunday Scholars sing. **1850** S. F. COOPER *Rural Hours* 130 We saw a little girl, one of the village Sunday-scholars, moreover, put her hand within the railing of a garden and break off several very fine plants. **1872** [see NEW SCHOOL PRESBYTERIAN 1].

Sunday school.

1. A school held on Sundays, usually in connection with a church and for religious instruction. {1783-}

1785 *Mass. Centinel* 27 Aug. 4 The Preparationalist cannot answer the enquiry but with the proposal for the institution of Sunday Schools. **1826** FLINT *Recoll.* 119 We had three efficient bible societies, and many sunday schools and associations of a like character. **1870** *Scribner's Mo.* I. 155 The house is occupied on Sunday by two Sunday-schools. **1892** M. A. JACKSON *Gen. Jackson* 78 He inquired of every visitor . . . how his colored Sunday-school was getting on. **1925** BRYAN *Memoirs* 450, I find his diversions to have been Sunday school, church, prayer meetings, . . . and at long intervals, a circus or an evening at the theater.

2. *attrib.* and *comb.* **a.** Designating places or things used by Sunday schools, or activities of Sunday schools.

1819 *Plough Boy* I. 30 The Sunday School-house at Baltimore, has been destroyed by fire. **1837** *Gaz. Illinois* 148 The basement furnishes . . . a Sunday school room. **1857** STROTHER *Virginia* 72 [She must] do as she was bid, like the good little girls in the Sunday-school books. **1862** NORTON *Army Lett.* 44, I had a little Sunday-school paper that I took out with me from camp. **1863** 'G. HAMILTON' *Gala-Days* 145, I remember their Sunday-school lessons. **1891** FREEMAN *New Eng. Nun* 126 She even began to sing as they went along, a Sunday-school tune. **1898** Sunday-school excursion train [see EXCURSION TRAIN]. **1906** BELL *C. Lee* 221 At Sunday-school picnics . . . Miss Sue Yancey . . . [went] around to the different tables. **1910** BOSTWICK *Amer. Pub. Library* 101 A class of library that has been or . . . should be greatly modified by the rise and extension of the free public circulating collection is the Sunday-school library.

b. Designating persons or groups of persons attending or associated with Sunday schools.

1820 FLINT *Lett. from Amer.* 214 Cincinnati has . . . four Sunday school societies. **1831** PECK *Guide* 4 The American Sunday School Union has had the most extensive influence. **1865** *Atlantic Mo.* May 628/2 A military commission . . . sentenced to the pillory an eminent Sunday-school teacher who had been convicted of the unlawful sale of whiskey. **1875** STOWE *We & Neighbors* 342, If *I*, who have had more education than our Sunday-school scholars, can't read a card like that, why, *they* could not. **1878** COOKE *Happy Dodd* 9 Mr. Fox, the Sunday-school superintendent, came in. **1880** *Harper's Mag.* May 951/1 A young lady . . . has a Sunday-school class of rather bright boys. **1883** 'MARK TWAIN' *Life on Miss.* liv, A bald-summited superintendent . . . had been a towheaded Sunday-school mate of mine.

∗Sundew. Any plant of *Drosera* or a related genus, having leaves covered with hairs that secrete shiny drops. Also with specifying adjective. — **1674** JOSSELYN *Two Voyages* 80 *Rosa-solis*, Sun-dew, moor-grass. **1784** *Amer. Acad. Mem.* I. 432 Sundew. . . . The juice will destroy warts and corns. **1868** *Amer. Naturalist* II. 107, I noticed the tiny leaves of the sun-dew, . . . each tipped with a glistening dew-drop. **1882** *Harper's Mag.* June 68 [We] gather the interesting sun-dews, especially the rare thread-leaved sun-dew (*Drosera filiformis*). **1898** A. M. DAVIDSON *Calif. Plants* 176 The curious pitcher plants and sundews . . . thrive on animal food.

∗Sundial. 1. A device for indicating the time of day by a shadow thrown on a dial. **+2.** The common lupine, *Lupinus perennis*. — (1) **1736** *Boston Selectmen* 316 The Committee . . . Be also Desired to order the New Painting the Sun Dials on the Town house. **1875** HOWARD *One Summer* iv, The pretty, sloping common, and old, old sundial in its centre. (2) **1840** DEWEY *Mass. Flowering Plants* 63 Sun Dial . . . has long been cultivated for ornament in gardens. **1871** BURROUGHS *Wake-Robin* (1886) 192 Lupine, or sun-dial, . . . makes the ground look blue from a little distance. **1892** *Amer. Folk-Lore* V. 94 *Lupinus villosus*, monkey faces; sun-dial. N. Ohio.

Sundown. (Cf. SUNUP.)

1. Sunset. {1620-}

'Chiefly *U.S.* and *Eng.* and *Colonial dial.*' (O.E.D.).

1712 in Sewall *Diary* II. 361n., Daughter Mary had a fitt about sun-down. **1784** ELLICOTT in Mathews *Life A. Ellicott* 23 About sun down we got to Jackson's. **1820** E. HOWITT *Selections from Lett.* 50 We reached Newburgh about *sun down*, as the American phrase is. **1842** BUCKINGHAM *Slave States* I. 499 They use the terms 'at sun-up,' and 'at sundown,' instead of sunrise, and sunset. **1879** TOURGEE *Fool's Errand* 57 It was nearly sundown. **1906** *Harper's Mag.* March 504, I reached the place about sundown on Friday evening.

+2. A hat with a wide brim.

1878 in *Amer. Speech* XIV. 78/2 The ladies who left for 'Camp Comfort' yesterday thoughtfully provided themselves with broad 'sundowns.' **1888** *Century Mag.* Sept. 769/1 Young faces of those days seemed . . . sweet and winning under wide-brimmed 'sundowns' or old-time 'pokes.'

3. Attrib. with *doctor, gun.*

1854 GLISAN *Jrnl. Army Life* 159 We reached Havana . . . just before the firing of the sun-down gun. **1904** DERVILLE *Other Side of Story* 42 A sundown doctor . . . [is] a doctor who practices his vocation after four o'clock, when he can leave his desk in some Government office.

+Sundrop(s). Any one of various plants of the genus *Kneiffia* of the evening-primrose family having flowers that open in daylight. Also with specifying term. — **1784** *Amer. Acad. Mem.* I. 438 Sundrop. They open about eleven o'clock. **1840** DEWEY *Mass. Flowering Plants* 47. **1901** MOHR *Plant Life Ala.* 638 *Kneiffia linearis.* . . . Pine-barren Sundrops.

Sunfish, *n.*

1. Any of many fishes, +esp. one belonging to the family Centrarchidae, abundant in streams and ponds in many parts of the United States.

Cf. SUN 2 and SUNNY.

[**1629** in Hutchinson *Coll. Papers Mass. Bay* 39 Myself and others saw a large round fish. . . . The mariners called it a sunne fish.] **1685** PENN *Further Acct. Penna.* 9 There is the Catfish, . . . Smelt, Sunfish, &c. **1709** LAWSON *Carolina* 157 Sun-Fish are flat and rounder than a Bream, and are reckon'd a fine-tasted Fish. **1784** FILSON *Kentucke* 26 Suckers, sunfish, and other hook-fish, are abundant. **1847** [see BILL-FISH]. **1888** *Outing* July 307 Lake Canadarago has . . . suckers, sunfish [etc.]. **1911** *Rep. Fisheries* 1908 315/1 Sacramento perch (*Archoplites interruptus*), a sun-fish of the Sacramento and an excellent food fish.

b. With specifying terms.

See also BLACK EYE 3, FRESH-WATER SUNFISH, LONG-EARED SUNFISH. **1814** Pond sun-fish [see PALE *a.* 1]. **1820** *Western Rev.* I. 376 Blue Sun-fish. *Icthelis cyanella.* . . . A small species hardly three inches, called Blue-fish or Sun-fish. **1839** STORER *Mass. Fishes* 170 *Orthogoriscus mola*, The short Sun Fish . . . is not a common fish in Massachusetts Bay. **1842** Great Sun-fish [see HEADFISH]. **1855** BAIRD in *Smithsonian Rep.* 1854 324 Banded Sun-Fish, *Pomotis chætodon*, . . . abundant in . . . Cape May county, New Jersey. *Ib.* 325 The Bass Sun-Fish. *Centrarchus pomotis.* . . . Found in muddy water, or where there was considerable cover. **1860** *Harper's Mag.* March 488/2 A still more beautiful fish, perhaps, is the other New York species of sun-fish, called the 'black-eared,' or *Pomotis apendix.*

2. A jellyfish or starfish. {1681}

1831 HOLLEY *Texas* (1833) 25 We amused ourselves . . . with dissecting some of those curious links, between the vegetable and animal kingdoms, called sunfish. **1859** BARTLETT 463 The Medusae, or Sea-Nettles, . . . about Boston harbor . . . are called *Sun-fish.* **1884** GOODE, etc. *Fisheries* I. 841 The Jelly-fishes, Sun-fishes, or Medusæ . . . are, at times, a source of great annoyance to the net fishermen.

+3. A method of bucking. (See next.)

1903 *Wide World Mag.* 548 A broncho named 'E.A.' . . . used a combination of 'sunfish' and 'twister.'

+Sunfish, *v. intr.* (See quotation.) — **1888** ROOSEVELT in *Century Mag.* April 854/2 [The bronco may] buck steadily in one place, or 'sunfish,'—that is, bring first one shoulder down almost to the ground and then the other.

+Sunfish (river) bass. (See quotation.) — **1820** *Western Rev.* II. 53 Sunfish River-bass, *Lepomis icthetoides*, . . . is found in the Kentucky and tributary streams. Vulgar names White Bass, or Sunfish Bass.

∗Sunflower.

‖1. = INDIAN FIG.

1737 BRICKELL *N. Carolina* 23 The Sun-Flower, the Indian-Figg, or Prickly-Pear, the Fruit of this Vegetable is frequently eaten.

∗2. Any one of various plants in some way popularly associated with the sun, esp. those of the genus *Helianthus*, in which the flower heads resemble representations of the sun and its rays.

1766 J. BARTRAM *Journal* 25 The last frost killed the . . . pea-vines, sun-flowers [etc.]. **1814** BRACKENRIDGE *Views La.* 63 Hunters tell of some curious plants on the Arkansas, amongst which are the common sun-flower, the bean, and the simblin. **1843** FRÉMONT *Exped.* 22 Many spots on the prairie are yellow with sunflower. **1851** *S. Lit. Messenger* XVII. 374/2 Yonder the prairie is golden with tall but miniature sun-flowers. **1867** DIXON *New America* I. 42 These sunflowers of the West are not the tawny gauds of our cottage gardens; . . . but little golden flowers. **1889** *Century Mag.* April 817/1 On the summit was a large sunflower.

3. With specifying adjectives.

[**1731** P. MILLER *Gardeners Dict.* (1735) s.v. *Corona Solis*, Common Perennial *or* Everlasting Sun-Flower.] **1784** *Amer. Acad. Mem.* I. 457 *Cistus.* . . . American Cistus. Little Sunflower. . . . In dry pastures. June. *Ib.* 478 *Ageratum.* . . . Meadow Sunflower. Blossoms yellow. *Ib.* 483 [The] Rough-Leaved Sun flower . . . is, in a considerable degree, astringent. **1814** BIGELOW *Florula Bostoniensis* 204 *Coreopsis trichosperma.* Tickseed Sun flower. . . . Flowers large, erect, yellow. **1817-8** Cone-disk sunflower [see CONEFLOWER]. **1832** S. J. HALE *Flora* 171 Sun-Flower, Dwarf. *Helianthus indicus.* . . . Exclusively indigenous to the Americas except two species in India and Egypt. **1840** DEWEY *Mass. Flowering Plants* 138 *H[elianthus] trachelifolius*, Wild Sunflower, . . . is the common sunflower of the woods and hedges.

4. Attrib. with *bed, calico, quilt*, etc., sometimes with reference to Kansas. (Cf. SUNFLOWER STATE.)

1840 *Picayune* 11 Oct. 2/4 Vast sunflower beds spread far and near around the spot. *a*1846 *Quarter Race Ky.* 84 [The girls] came pourin out of the woods . . . fixed out in all sorts of fancy doins, from the broad-striped homespun to the sunflower calico. *Ib.* 92 He gin 'em [the cards] the Sunflower 'shuffle,' and I the Big Greasy 'cut,' and pushed 'em back. **1846** *S. Lit. Messenger* XII. 597/2 Tell Patsy to put on the sun-flower quilt that your Miss Adaline Amelia made. **1898** *Internat. Typogr. Union Proc.* 62/1 During his visit to Kansas City, Mo., . . . he visited Sunflower Union No. 157.

+Sunflower oil. Oil derived from sunflower seeds. {1860} — *c*1770 *Amer. Philos. Soc.* I. 308 The sun-flower oil may prove equally valuable with the best Florence oil, for diet or medicine. **1819** *Plough Boy* I. 43 The sun-flower oil was a subject of conversation.

Sunflower seed. The seed of the common sunflower, used for poultry food and for the oil obtained from it. {1789-} Often collective. — *c*1770 *Amer. Philos. Soc.* I. 305 An essay on the expressing of Oil, from Sun-Flower Seed. **1807** GASS *Journal* 125 The people of these lodges have gathered a quantity of sun-flower seed. **1848** BRYANT *California* xi. 153 [We] made exchanges of small articles with the women for parched and pulverized sunflower and grass seeds.

+Sunflower State. Kansas. A nickname. — **1888** *Harper's Mag.* June 39/1 Her citizens affectionately speak of Kansas as the 'Sunflower State.' **1904** *Minneapolis Times* 7 June 6 There was danger for a time that the Sunflower state would grow a crop of pond lilies.

Sunglass. A burning glass. — **1806** CLARK in *Lewis & C. Exped.* IV. (1905) 236, I took with me . . . an Indian whome I hired for a Sun glass to accompany me as a pilot. **1840** OLMSTED *Lett. Astronomy* 32 A sun-glass . . . collects the solar rays into a small bright circle in the focus. **1844** *Knickerb.* XXIV. 188, I allude to shooting red squirrels with a lead-pistol, touched off with a sun-glass. **1891** *Cent.* 6060/3.

Sun hat. {1879-, in India} A hat with a wide, flexible brim, worn for protection under the sun. — **1881** RITTENHOUSE *Maud* 28 Of course I had to clap on Mama's cherry-sun-hat and pick bouquets in the yard at once. **1894** *Advance* 7 June, In summer she wore . . . a thin striped shawl and a 'sun-hat' tied down over her ears. **1900** MUNN *Uncle Terry* 197 [She sat] in front of a pretty cluster of small spruce trees, with the pail beside her and her sun-hat trimmed with ferns.

+Sun-jerked, *a.* Cured by cutting into strips and drying in the sun. (Cf. JERKED *a.*) — **1888** ROOSEVELT in *Century Mag.* Oct. 832/1 [He] shares his last bit of sun-jerked venison with you.

Sunk. (See SUNCK.)

*****Sunken,** *a.* In geographical expressions: Depressed; submerged; marshy.

1636 in *Amer. Speech* XV. 399/2 Westerly upon the rich neck otherwise upon sunken Marsh. **1653** *Ib.* 399/1 South East by East downe ye river to an oake tree by Sunken ground. **1738** BYRD *Dividing Line* (1901) 50 Within a Quarter of a Mile of the Dismal above-mention'd . . . the Ground began to be already full of Sunken Holes and Slashes. **1784** in *S. Lit. Messenger* XXVIII. 34/2 The vast quantities of naked and sunken grounds will point out some of the reasons for such extent. **1791** W. SARGENT *Diary* 12 We were halted by a swamp or sunken 'Prairie' in our Front.

b. Of grass: Growing in a swampy area.

1682 *Southold Rec.* I. 168 All the borders of meadows & krick thatch with the sunken grass at the mouth of Goose Kreek.

Sunken land. *S.* An area of low ground; a marsh. — **1647** in *Amer. Speech* XV. 399/1 Six hundred Acres of Land . . . bounded North Upon a parcell of Sunken Land. **1716** *N.C. Col. Rec.* II. 226 Samuel Charles has made a Survey of a Tract of Sunken Land and Swamp. **1785** *Md. Hist. Mag.* XX. 47 He did . . . attend him in making a Survey of a Lot or tract of sunken land.

+Sunken swamp. A low-lying marsh. — **1702** in *Amer. Speech* XV. 399/2 A part of ye parcell of Land . . . Beginning on ye Sunken Swamp att ye mouth of a branch. **1775** *Mass. H. S. Proc.* 2 Ser. II. 282 Round here was all a Sunken Swamp for a Great distance. **1779** *N.H. Hist. Soc. Coll.* VI. 315 Rocky mountains, sunken swamps and burning plains the whole of the way.

+Sunk hole. =SINK HOLE. *Va.* — **1751** in *Amer. Speech* XV. 399/2 Thence . . . to a Hiccory Standing near a Sunk Hole. **1834** *Ib.*, Thence . . . to a white oak on the East side of a sunk hole.

Sunk whale. A submerged dead whale. *colloq.* — **1883** *Nat. Museum Bul.* No. 27, 278 A toggle-iron of large proportions, intended to be used only in raising sunk whales (*Megaptera* sp.) principally.

+Sunny. =SUNFISH 1. — **1835** AUDUBON *Ornith. Biog.* III. 51 The sunny . . . swam to one side, then to another. **1870** *Amer. Naturalist* IV. 102 Since then it has been crowding out the old time 'Sunny' (*Pomotis aureus*). **1884** [see PUMPKIN SEED 2 a].

+Sunny South. The southern states. — **1846** *Spirit of Times* (N.Y.) 18 April 96/2 The wish of his heart should always be, peace and prosperity to the 'Sunny South.' **1863** LINCOLN in Logan *Great Conspiracy* 519 The Sunny South, too, in more colors than one, also lent a helping hand. **1889** CUSTER *Tenting on Plains* 215 Texas is in the 'Sunny South.'

+Sun pain. (See quotations.) — **1832** BAIRD *Valley Miss.* 73 A form of winter or relapsing intermittent fever; is 'periodical head-ache,' or

'Sun pain,' so called . . . from the well known fact, that the fit generally comes on . . . about sun-rise and seldom continues after sun-set. **1840** *Niles' Nat. Reg.* 20 June 247/1, I was very unwell with a violent cold in the head. . . terminated in intermittent neuralgia, or sun pain. **1855** DUNGLISON *Med. Lexicon, Hemicrania* . . . , pain, confined to one half the head, . . . at times, continuing only as long as the sun is above the horizon; and hence sometimes called *Sun-pain.*

+Sun perch. Any of various fresh-water fishes of the family Centrarchidae. (Cf. SUNFISH 1.) — **1804** LEWIS & CLARK *Exped.* VI. (1905) 174 In this lake there is also . . . Sunperch. **1852** *S. Lit. Messenger* XVIII. 680/1 He was a pretty good live parody on an enormous goggle-eyed sun perch. **1876** 'MARK TWAIN' *Tom Sawyer* xiv, They were back again with some handsome bass, a couple of sun-perch, and a small catfish. **1902** [see GRINDLE].

+Sunsetty, *a.* Suggesting a sunset. Rare. — **1870** A. D. WHITNEY *We Girls* i, We always thought it was a pretty, sunsetty name. **1886** PAGE in *Harper's Mag.* Jan. 306/1 Her arms so white, an' her face sort o' sunsetty.

Sunshade. A form of parasol. {1852-} Cf. SHADE *n.* 4. — **1842** *N.Y. Times* 22 March, Umbrellas, Parasols and Sun-shades . . . manufactured at Newark, N.J. **1881** *Harper's Mag.* April 731/2 Ladies . . . [were] halting under sun-shades to chat. **1912** *Drygoodsman's Handy Dict.* 60/2 Sunshade.—Anything used as a shield or covering from the sun's rays. A parasol with the handle hinged so that the expanded top may be adjusted to any desired angle.

+Sun shaft. A sunbeam or shaft of sunlight. — **1868** A. D. WHITNEY *P. Strong* 156 The maples were splendid in the sunshafts that shot through their bosoms. **1908** CHURCHILL *Mr. Crewe* xiii, He had but to beckon a shining Pegasus from out a sun-shaft in the sky.

Sunshine cake. A form of sponge cake. — **1888** HARGIS *Graded Cook Book* 362 [Recipe for] Sunshine Cake. **1891** RITTENHOUSE *Maud* 533 Pineapple ice in thin glass sherbet-cups, angel-food, kisses and sunshine cake. **1908** GALE *Friendship Village* 37 Mebbe one o' you'd stir up a sunshine cake.

+Sunsquall. A sea nettle or jellyfish. — **1859** BARTLETT 463 *Sun-Squall*, a term applied, on the coast of New England, to the Medusae, or Sea-Nettles. **1880** *Harper's Mag.* Sept. 503/2 The round, limpid jellyfish called the sun-squall, occurring sometimes almost numerously enough to stop the way of a boat. **1884** GOODE, etc. *Fisheries* I. 169 Jelly-fish, or sun-squalls . . . [are] abundant along the New England coast in summer.

+Sun trout. The squeteague. — **1884** GOODE, etc. *Fisheries* I. 362. **1911** *Rep. Fisheries* 1908 316/2 [The squeteague] is known as . . . 'gray trout,' 'sun trout,' 'shad trout,' 'sea trout,' and 'salt-water trout' in the Middle and South Atlantic states.

+Sun umbrella. A large sunshade. {1904} — **1861** *Cincinnati Commercial* 3 July, Great Bargains in . . . Parasols and Sun Umbrellas. **1866** A. D. WHITNEY *L. Goldthwaite* xi, Miss Craydocke appeared, walking across, under her great brown sun-umbrella, from the hotel. **1885** *Harper's Mag.* May 832/1 Our easels and large white sun-umbrellas soon became familiar objects on the yellow plains. **1898** M. LEONARD *Big Front Door* 31 A little girl came slowly up the street carrying a sun-umbrella.

Sunup. Sunrise. {c1882-} 'Local, chiefly *U.S.*' (*O.E.D.*).

1712 *Wyllys Papers* 377 Wee Set out by or before Sun up, for Wyndham. **1735** HEMPSTEAD *Diary* 295, I came away before Sun up. **1842** BUCKINGHAM *Slave States* I. 499 They use the terms 'at sun-up,' and 'at sun-down,' instead of sunrise, and sunset. **1872** BOURKE *Journal* 22 Nov., Broke camp at sun-up. **1891** RYAN *Told in Hills* 31 At sun-up tomorrow, Mrs. Genesee? **1901** *Scribner's Mag.* April 502/2 It was a dark kind of a sun-up, you know.

b. *From sunup to sundown*, or variants: From sunrise to sunset; all day long.

1826 COOPER *Mohicans* iv, One would think such a horse as that might get over a good deal of ground atwixt sun-up and sun-down. **1852** in Stowe *Key* 43/1 The result of a day's picking, from sun-up until sundown: . . . 4880 lbs. of clean-picked cotton from the stalk. **1873** MILLER *Amongst Modocs* 90 Why we should tear up the earth . . . from sun-up to sun-down . . . was to them more than a mystery. **1903** WIGGIN *Rebecca* 108, I could teach school from sun-up to sun-down if scholars was all like Rebecca Randall. **1904** *N.Y. Ev. Post* 11 June 4 Capable of working from sun-up to dusk.

+Supawn. Also **soupaan**, etc. [Cf. Natick *sapaen* 'softened.'] Boiled corn meal; mush. Also attrib. (See also SAPA(E)N.) — **1780** *N.J. Archives* 2 Ser. IV. 586 Those that eat Soupaan. **1809** IRVING *Knickerb.* 327 [The Van Brummels] were the first inventors of Suppawn, or Mush and milk. **1835** HOFFMAN *Winter in West* I. 121, I helped myself with an iron spoon from a dish of suppawn. **1857** *Harper's Mag.* March 461/2 The 'suppawn bell' . . . was the signal for all to eat their 'suppawn' or hasty-pudding, and prepare for bed. **1910** HODGE, etc. *Amer. Indian* II. 652/2 Supawn, [is] spelled also sepawn, sepon, supaen, suppaen, suppawn, etc., by earlier writers.

Supe. {1824-} *Theater.* A supernumerary. *slang.* {sup, 1885} — **1840** *Knickerb.* XVI. 359 Such men as these are nightly held up to indiscriminate ridicule, by the 'supes' of a theatre. **1864** 'MARK TWAIN' *Sketches* (1926) 133 The upper circles, with one accord, shouted, 'Supe! supe!' **1893** POST *Harvard Stories* 107 [At] the Boston Theatre . . . 'supes' were in demand.

*****Superintendency.** +An area under the direction of a superintendent of Indian affairs. — **1856** PIERCE in *Pres. Mess. & P.* V. 363, I herewith communicate to the Senate . . . two treaties recently negotiated by . . . the superintendent of Indian affairs for the northern superintendency. **1866** [see INDIAN AGENCY]. **1871** *Rep. Indian Affairs* (1872) 171 They receive the largest annuity (per capita) of any Indians in the superintendency.

* **Superintendent.**

* **1.** An officer or official who has control or oversight of some business, administration, or works. Often used in official titles.

1789 *Ann. 1st Congress* 389, I have had also transactions at the treasury whilst it was managed by a Superintendent of Finance. **1794** *Ann. 3d Congress* 1428 The said superintendents shall each receive, as a compensation, seventy dollars per month. **1812** *Boston Selectmen* 54 Charles Bulfinch Esq. was declared to be chosen Superintendent, & Mr. Jeremh. Bridge assistant Police officer. **1852** EASTMAN *Aunt Phillis's Cabin* 265 A superintendent of Irishmen, who were engaged on a Northern railroad, told him he did not hesitate to knock any man down that gave him the least trouble. **1864** in Young *Jessamine Co., Ky.* 186 Deputy Marshal and Superintendent of Colored Enlistment at Camp Nelson. **1876** RAYMOND *8th Rep. Mines* 225 The new superintendent has worked like a beaver since he assumed the management. **1900** *Congress. Rec.* 3 Jan. 631/2 Transmit to the Senate . . . a full copy of the report of R. H. Rosa, superintendent of logging on the Chippewa ceded lands in Minnesota. **1925** BRYAN *Memoirs* 47 The superintendent was the best Sunday-school superintendent I have ever known.

2. a. The name given by John Wesley to one of those ordained by him to serve as bishops among American Methodists. *Obs.*

1784 WESLEY in Southey *Life Wesley* II. 440, I have this day set apart, as a Superintendent, by the imposition of my hands and prayer, . . . Thomas Coke, . . . a Presbyter of the Church of England. **1785** T. COKE *Serm. Godhead Christ* Ded., To the Rev. Francis Asbury, Superintendent, the Elders, Deacons, and Helpers, of the Methodist Episcopal Church in America.

+**b.** A presiding elder in the Methodist church.

1909 WEBSTER 1362/2 Presiding elders [are] . . . now called district superintendents in the M.E. Church. **1912** in Sanford *Reports Committee on Judiciary, Meth. Epis. Ch.* 143 The Bishops in the Annual Conference appointed a Superintendent to preside over a District containing more than fifty pastoral charges.

+**3.** A conductor in charge of a train or an official in charge of some other form of transportation. *Obs.*

1835 BRECK *Recoll.* 275 'Make room for the ladies!' bawled out the superintendent. **1855** GLISAN *Jrnl. Army Life* 190 The Superintendent . . . put on a second engine to assist us over the heavy grades. **1869** J. R. BROWNE *Adv. Apache Country* 307 As most passengers desire to get an outside seat [on a stagecoach], . . . it is highly important that you should proceed at once to secure the favorable consideration of the superintendent.

+**4.** A superintendent of schools.

See also COUNTY SUPERINTENDENT.

1842 BUCKINGHAM *Slave States* I. 360 The Secretary of State [in La.] was made 'Superintendent of Education.' **1881** MCLEAN *Cape Cod Folks* 15, I wrote to the Superintendent of the Farmouth schools. **1911** PERSONS, etc. *Mass. Labor Laws* 186 Elasticity of method . . . is one of the great advantages in the issue of certificates by the superintendents in person.

+**5.** =SUPERINTENDENT OF INDIAN AFFAIRS.

1849 *31st Congress 1 Sess.* H. R. Ex. Doc. No. 5, II. 952 There are, nominally, five superintendents of Indian affairs, but two of these are local agents for particular tribes . . . and perform the duties of superintendents in addition to those of agents. **1867** *Wkly. New Mexican* 9 April 1/3 The Apache Indians (the Coyoteros) in 1864, desired to see Dr. Steck, the then superintendent. **1912** *Indian Laws & Tr.* III. 547 [For] the Indian school at Flandreau, South Dakota, and for the pay of Superintendent, sixty-one thousand five hundred dollars.

+**6.** A railroad administrative officer, as one in charge of a division.

1878 [see DIVISION n. 3]. **1885** *Wkly. New Mexican Rev.* 19 March 4/4 The superintendent of the roads running through Atchison, Kansas, raised an important point.

+**Superintendent of Indian affairs.** A public official in charge of Indian affairs for a certain area; since 1832, such an official responsible to the Commissioner of Indian Affairs in Washington. — **1757** *Lett. to Washington* II. 80 Edm[un]d Atkin his Majestys Agent & Superintendent of Indian Affairs in the Southern District of America. **1774** *Doc. Hist. N.Y. State* I. 767 Within the Department of Sir William Johnson His Majesty's Superintendant of Indian Affairs there are Twenty Five Thousand Four Hundred and Twenty Fighting Men. **1789** *Ann. 1st Congress* I. 40 The Superintendent of Indian Affairs for the Northern Department [shall] inform the Five Nations, the Hurons, and other Indian nations [etc.]. **1849** [see SUPERINTENDENT 5]. **1863** *Rio Abajo Press* 19 May 3/1 The Superintendent of Indian Affairs is not an officer of the Government of this Territory; he is rather an 'ambassador' to and from the Indian tribes.

+**Superintendent of Indian trade.** The former title of the chief of the national Indian bureau. — **1816** MADISON in McKenney *Memoirs* I.

18, I do appoint him [Thomas McKenney] superintendent of Indian trade.

+**Superintendent of schools.** A local, county, or state official in charge of the school system. — **1881** MCLEAN *Cape Cod Folks* 81 Such was the name given by the Wallencampers to Mr. Baxter, the superintendent of schools. **1883** *Harper's Mag.* Sept. 642/1 State Superintendent of Schools, John Akers (renominated). **1901** DUNCAN & SCOTT *Allen & Woodson Co., Kansas* 19 Watson Stewart was elected to the council . . . with the following county officers: . . . superintendent of schools; . . . surveyor [etc.]. **1914** *Cycl. Amer. Govt.* III. 270/2 The city superintendent of schools is usually chosen by a city board of education yearly.

* **Superior court.** {1597– (Skene *De Verb. Sign.* s.v. *Curia*)} +**a.** =SUPREME COURT 1. +**b.** In several of the states, an intermediate court between the lower and supreme courts.

1686 SEWALL *Diary* I. 118 [He] must be relieved by some Superiour Court, as Chauncery. **1695** *Topsfield Rec.* I. 90 Leiut Thomas Baker and Capt John How shall enter a complaint . . . at ye next seuperieur Court to be houlden at Ipswich. **1723** *New-Eng. Courant* 3 June 2/1 A Woman try'd at our Superiour Court for counterfeiting the Parchment Money of this Province, was brought in guilty. **1771** in *New Eng. Mag.* ns. XII. 352/2 The Superior or Circuit Court sits here twice a year. **1777** *Jrnls. Cont. Congress* IX. 918 Every commissioner before he sits in judgment shall take an oath to be administered by one of the judges of the supreme or superior court of the state. **1829** [see INFERIOR COURT]. **1845** *Xenia Torch-Light* 31 July 2/6 The Superior Court of Virginia shall say whether they are felons or not. **1906** *Springfield W. Repub.* 8 Nov. 2 The appellate division of the N.Y. supreme court (corresponding to our superior court). **1911** *Okla. Session Laws* 3 Legisl. 264 A superior court is created by operation of this act.

+**Supersedure.** The act of setting aside or superseding. — **1788** HAMILTON in *Federalist* lxxxi, An implied supersedure of the trial by jury. in favor of the civil law mode of trial. **1854** *La Crosse Democrat* 14 March 2/2 Was it [the Nebraska Bill] not a supersedure of [the Missouri Compromise]? **1894** *Forum* Feb. 683 No opportunity to vote out the Cabinet which had just come into power, by supersedure of the Wilcox ministry the day before, could possibly occur before May, 1894.

* **Supervisor.** A name given to any one of several different officials or officers: (see quotations).

1640 *Dorchester Rec.* 42 There shall be yeerely Chosen 2 officers by the name of supveysors of high wayes who shall ouer see and p'cure the makeing or amending such high wayes as are defectiue. **1693** *East-Hampton Rec.* II. 294 Thomas Chatfield was Chosen & appointed Supervizer in our Townes behalf of County Charges for this year. **1802** *Ann. 7th Congress* 1313 The collectors in each district shall prepare and transmit to their respective supervisors, correct lists of all lands. **1835** *Jamestown* (N.Y.) *Jrnl.* 21 Jan. 2/6 What the supervisors of the county have resolved accords much better with the sense of the community. **1846** *Mich. Gen. Statutes* I. (1882) 249 Each supervisor shall lay before the board of supervisors such copies of entries concerning moneys voted to be raised in his township, as shall be delivered to him. **1875** *Scribner's Mo.* July 268/2 The power [of local govt. in San Francisco] rests almost absolutely in a single body—the Board of Supervisors. **1891** O'BEIRNE *Leaders Ind. Territory* 51/2 Mr. Hampton was employed by Allington Telle, supervisor of census to take the census of the Senatorial district. **1905** *N.Y. Ev. Post* 11 Oct. 6 He had been a supervisor of his county for 16 years, and for 12 years chairman of the Board of Supervisors. **1907** *Springfield W. Repub.* 9 May 12 The school board voted that the office of supervisor of penmanship be discontinued. . . . Penmanship was not in itself distinctly educational, like drawing, manual training, music and the other departments over which there are supervisors.

+**Suppawn.** Variant of SUPAWN.

* **Supper.**

* **1.** The regular evening meal.

To some extent in recent years, *dinner* has displaced the word *supper* among those who eat their chief meal of the day in the evening.

1622 'MOURT' *Relation* 29 Wee got three fat Geese, and six Ducks to our Supper. **1676** SEWALL *Diary* I. 26 Supped at Mr. Smiths, good Supper. **1704** S. KNIGHT *Journal* 67, I stayed a day here Longer than I intended by the Commands of the Honble. Governor Winthrop to stay and take a supper with him. **1775** CRESSWELL *Journal* 104 Just as the Sun went down we stopped to get our Supper on some Dewberries. **1818** FEARON *Sketches* 44 A mechanic . . . [has] coffee with fish or meat for breakfast; a hot dinner; and tea (called supper) in the evening. **1842** BUCKINGHAM *Slave States* I. 468 At supper—for so the evening meal at seven o'clock is usually called—coffee is more frequently used than tea. **1863** HOPLEY *Life in South* I. 207 'Supper,' as the third and last meal is termed, is 'after dark,' all the year round. **1893** HOLLEY *Samantha at World's Fair* 535 Supper wuz all ready—or dinner, as they all called it. **1925** TILGHMAN *Dugout* 65 Fan lighted the lamp and began to prepare supper.

2. a. An evening meal eaten at a social gathering. **b.** An irregular meal eaten late in the evening, as a lunch after the theater.

1773 FITHIAN *Journal* I. 76 Whenever any person or Family move into a House, or repair a house they have been living in before, they make a Ball & give a Supper. **1792** BELKNAP *Hist. New-Hampshire* III. 263 In the evening a company of neighbours join in husking them [*sc.* the ears of corn that have been gathered], and conclude their labor with a supper and a dance. **1827** *Md. Hist. Mag.* XVII. 264 At half past 11 the President . . . handed my wife down to supper, and was followed by all the company. **1882** McCabe *New York* 210 Fashionable New York dearly loves these suppers. **1894** *N.Y. Herald* 3 Nov. 10/5 Supper was served at midnight. **1922** Tarkington *Gentle Julia* 163 You gave me the first dance and the last dance, and of course sitting together at supper, or whatever there is.

3. Attrib. with *bell, dance, party,* etc.

1770 Fithian *Journal* I. 9 About seven the supper Bell rings. **1825** Neal *Bro. Jonathan* I. 72 A new England supper-table . . . may be worth . . . half a dozen sweeps of our brush. **1848** Bryant *California* xxvi. 326 I attended a supper-party given this evening by Mr. Frank Ward. **1885** Baylor *On Both Sides* 64 'A supper-dance, then,' he stupidly insisted.

Supple-jack. {1725–} **1.** (Meaning uncertain.) +**2.** The woody vine, *Berchemia scandens:* (see also quot. 1834). +**3.** A jumping jack.

— (1) **1776** Cutler in *Life & Corr.* I. 55 They made us several presents of the small affairs in the cabins, . . . such as sweetmeats, cayenne-pepper, supple-jacks, cassada or bread. (2) **1812** Stoddard *Sk. Louisiana* 169 Most of the low lands are covered with underwood, vines, supple jacks, and cane. **1834** Audubon *Ornith. Biog.* II. 344 The Supple Jack is a species of Smilax extremely abundant in all the swampy portions of the Southern States. **1901** Mohr *Plant Life Ala.* 101 The slender-stemmed bullace grape, and the supple jack . . . ascend the highest trees without visible support below the lofty summits. (3) **1832** Kennedy *Swallow Barn* II. 19 He would . . . spring from the floor upwards, flinging out his arms and legs like a supple-jack. **1871** Whitman *Democ. Vistas* 30 Millions of sturdy farmers and mechanics are thus the helpless supple-jacks of comparatively few politicians. **1904** *N.Y. Times* 8 July 5 Those political supplejacks . . . go about with sanctimonious moan, saying: 'The President is wrong, but we must support the President.'

***Supply.** Attrib. with *association, boat, teamster,* etc. — **1840** Cooper *Pathfinder* II. 73 We shall lie in wait . . . to intercept their supply-boats. **1860** Greeley *Overland Journey* 55 Our route . . . was no longer encumbered with great army supply-trains. **1865** Cumming *Hospital Life* 160/1 The Supply Association is still in operation. **1865** Richardson *Secret Service* 241 Their retreat was a stampede, leaving behind great quantities of ammunition, . . . supply-wagons and ambulances. **1902** White *Blazed Trail* 67 One morning he came in from a talk with the supply-teamster.

+**Supreme Bench.** The United States Supreme Court. — **1845** Polk *Diary* (1929) 39, I had a right to nominate Judge Woodward to the Supreme Bench of the United States. **1870** *Nation* 6 Jan. 6/1 The President committed an act of very doubtful propriety . . . by nominating Mr. Stanton to the Supreme bench long before any actual vacancy existed. **1900** *Congress. Rec.* 5 Feb. 1520/2 No man who is fit to sit on the Supreme Bench . . . would tolerate that cheap demagogy for half a minute.

***Supreme court.** {1597– (Skene *De Verb. Sign.* s.v. *Curia*)} +**1.** In certain of the colonies and states, a court of general jurisdiction composed of a distinct body of judges, often exercising appellate jurisdiction; a session of such a court.

Freq. called *superior court* (sense a).

1709 *N.J. Archives* 1 Ser. III. 458 On search of the Docquet of Causes depending in the Supream Court of her Majestys Province of New Jersey, I find [etc.]. **1720** [see Grand juror]. **1732** Franklin *Poor Richard's Almanac 1733* 20 Supream Courts in Pennsilvania are held at Philadelphia. **1785** *Warren-Adams Lett.* II. 261 Mr. Dana is appointed one of the Judges of the Supreme Court [in Mass.].

+**b.** In New York, orig. a court of general jurisdiction, which also served with state senators as a court of impeachment and appeals; since 1869, a court subordinate to the court of appeals; a similar court in New Jersey.

*a*1817 Dwight *Travels* III. 277 The Governour, Chancellor, and Judges of the Supreme Court [of New York] . . . are constituted a Council. **1841** Tyler in *Pres. Mess. & P.* IV. 41 Alexander McLeod has been heard by the supreme court of the State of New York on his motion to be discharged from imprisonment. **1886** *Nevada Rep.* XIX. 342 The name 'supreme court' . . . in New York . . . is given to courts possessing similar jurisdiction to that given to the district courts in this state. **1914** *Cycl. Amer. Govt.* III. 532/1 The court of chancery [in N.J.] still stands as of equal dignity with the supreme court.

+**2. a.** *cap.* The highest court in the federal system of courts. Often *Supreme Court of the United States.*

1787 *Constitution* ii. § 2 The President . . . shall appoint . . . Judges of the supreme Court. **1789** *Ann. 1st Congress* I. 86, I nominate for the Supreme Court of the United States—For Chief Justice.—John Jay, of New York. **1816** *Ann. 14th Congress* 2 Sess. 357 Chief Justice and Associate Justices of the Supreme Court of the United States shall cease to be Judges of the Circuit Courts of the United States. **1869** in *Arena* XIV. 221 [Proposed amendment to Constitution.] No judge shall act as a member of the Supreme Court . . . after he shall have reached the age of seventy years. **1900** *Congress. Rec.* 30 Jan. 1294/2, I think it would be a wise thing to have a preliminary inquiry respecting . . . an independent building for the Supreme Court. **1906** *Indian Laws & Tr.* III. 209 Nothing herein shall apply to the intermarried whites in the Cherokee Nation whose cases are now pending in the Supreme Court of the United States.

+**b.** The highest court in the judiciary system of a state or territory. (Cf. sense 1 b.)

1789 Morse *Amer. Geog.* 180 The salaries of governor and justices of the supreme court [of Mass.], cannot be diminished. **1840** [see Circuit court 2]. **1872** McClellan *Golden State* 417 The Supreme Court of California consists of five judges. **1885** *Wkly New Mexican Rev.* 22 Jan. 1/3 The supreme court is doing good work. **1918** *Missouri Rep.* CCLXXIV. p. iii, Judges of the Supreme Court during the time of these reports [include] . . . Hon. Robert Franklin Walker, . . . Hon. James T. Blair.

3. Attrib. with *business, judge, justice,* etc.

1846 *Knickerb.* XXVIII. 360 The attorneys . . . in company of the supreme court judge and the 'side-judge,' take the opportunity of having a bit of fun. **1852** *Harper's Mag.* Dec. 4/2 Beneath the Senate Chamber is the Supreme Court room. **1884** *N.Y. Herald* 27 Oct. 4/6 Colonel William H. Rawle . . . was defeated for Supreme Court Justice in Pennsylvania two years ago. **1900** *Congress. Rec.* 8 Jan. 688/1, I for one think the Supreme Court library should be located in that room. **1925** Bryan *Memoirs* 74, I might expect Supreme Court business from outside counties.

Surah. A twilled silk fabric. {1881–} — **1886** *Delineator* Nov. 388 The latest combination for little girls' wear is almond-brown cashmere and cactus-red Surah. **1893** *Chicago Tribune* 26 April 8/6 Elegance in Surahs. Imported.

Sure cure. A certain remedy. Also attrib. — **1881** *Ore. State Jrnl.* 1 Jan. 7/3 No other preparation . . . will give such universal satisfaction as *Dr. Keck's Sure Cure For Catarrh.* **1890** *Stock Grower & Farmer* 26 April 7/1 A 'sure cure' for pullers. **1907** [see Patent n. 3].

+**Sure-enough,** *a.* Actual; genuine. *dial.* or *colloq.* — *a*1846 *Quarter Race Ky.* 112 It was a man with a sure-enough fence-rail. **1872** *Republican Rev.* 20 Jan. 2/2 We naturally supposed that we were going to have a sure enough circus. **1911** Quick *Yellowstone Nights* 129 By this time Mr. Elkins was a sure-enough cowman.

+**Sure thing,** *n.* A certainty; a thing upon which one cannot lose. *colloq.* Also attrib. — **1853** 'P. Paxton' *Yankee in Texas* 98 Instead of . . . permitting us to surround the beast, and make a sure thing of it; . . . he allowed the exuberance of his joy to evaporate in a yell. **1870** [see Point n. 7 a]. **1885** *Santa Fé Wkly. New Mexican* 31 Dec. 4/3 Every prospect holder in the district feels that he is banking his time and money on a sure thing! **1903** Hapgood *Autobiog. of Thief* 246 There are several kinds of sure-thing grafters.

+**Sure thing,** *adv.* Certainly. *colloq.* — **1896** Ade *Artie* 147 'Sure thing,' says he. **1904** *N.Y. Ev. Journal* 13 May 2 'Give us a box,' said Mr. Lehr. 'Sure thing,' said the man. **1921** Paine *Comr. Rolling Ocean* 44 Sure thing! They won't bother to look it up.

***Surf.** Used attrib. in the specific names of American birds, fishes, etc.

See also Surf bird, fish, scoter.

1883 *Nat. Museum Bul.* No. 27, 260 Hen Clam, Surf Clam, or Sea Clam. Florida and Gulf of Mexico to Labrador. **1813** Wilson *Ornithology* VIII. 49 *Anas perspicillata.* Black, or Surf Duck. . . . This duck is peculiar to America. **1885** *Nat. Museum Proc.* VIII. 134 The Development of the Viviparous Surf-Perches or Embiotocidae of the Pacific Coast. **1882** *Nat. Museum Bul.* No. 16, 294 *Hypomesus.* . . . Surf Smelts. . . . *H[ypomesus] pretiosus.* . . . Surf Smelt. . . . Pacific coast, from California northward. *Ib.* 933 *M[enticirrus] littoralis.* . . . Surf Whiting. . . . South Atlantic and Gulf coast.

Surface. {1611–} In attrib. uses.

1. Designating various things associated with mining ore on or near the surface.

1865 *Atlantic Mo.* March 311/1 The surface mines are usually nearly filled with leaves. **1869** J. R. Browne *Adv. Apache Country* 509 Did you ever see finer surface ore? **1871** Raymond *3d Rep. Mines* 77 Much of the surface dirt will not yield over a few cents per cubic yard. **1874** — *6th Rep. Mines* 20 This action of the water . . . has kept the surface-gravel in a ceaseless state of agitation. **1877** W. Wright *Big Bonanza* 73 The surface-diggings on the first-mentioned 1,400 feet.

+**2.** Designating things or actions connected with traffic on city streets.

1867 *Harper's Mag.* June 134/2 Soon afterward he was seen in company with George Lanman . . . , talking over some matter about a surface railroad. **1882** McCabe *New York* 238 There are thirty-two lines of street (or surface) railways traversing New York. **1893** *Harper's Mag.* April 652/1 Here come . . . the surface vehicles . . . of Manhattan. **1909** *N.Y. Ev. Post* (s.-w. ed.) 4 March 1 On streets leading to these ferries surface travel was blocked by heavily laden vehicles stalled.

+**Surface-boat.** A sink boat. — **1851** Lewis *Amer. Sportsman* 189 The Surface-boat. . . . This artful contrivance for the destruction of ducks we claim as entirely American. **1859** Bartlett 24 *Battery,* a sort of boat used for duck-shooting in the Chesapeake, in which the shooter lies below the surface of the water. It is also called . . . a Surface-boat, Coffin-boat, Sink, or Box.

+**Surface car.** A street car as distinguished from an elevated or subway car. — **1889** Howells *Hazard of Fortunes* II. 208 He stopped at the corner to wait for a surface-car. **1906** *N.Y. Globe* 13 Oct. 2 After arriving at the Grand Central Mrs. Norris took a surface car to her home. **1920** *Nation* 21 Feb. 223/2 The surface cars of Manhattan ceased to run for a week.

+**Surf bird.** A Pacific-coast shore bird, *Aphriza virgata.* — **1839** AUDUBON *Ornith. Biog.* V. 249 Townsend's Surf-Bird . . . was procured . . . on the shores of Cape Disappointment. **1883** *Nat. Museum Bul.* No. 27, 146 Surf Bird. . . . Pacific coast of America, from Alaska to Chili. **1917** *Birds of Amer.* I. 268/1 Ornithologists have been divided as to whether the Surf-bird should be considered a Plover or a Turnstone.

+**Surfer.** =SURF SCOTER. — **1876** *Forest & Stream* 9 Nov. 212/3 List of Gunner's Names for Birds and Wild Fowl obtained in Plymouth Bay, Mass.: . . . *Pelionetta perspicillata.* Surfer. **1917** *Birds of Amer.* I. 151.

+**Surf fish.** Any of numerous fishes of the family Embiotocidae, living chiefly off the California coast in shallow water. Also attrib. — **1882** *Nat. Museum Bul.* No. 16, 585 The Surf-fishes. . . . Fishes of the Pacific coast of North America, inhabiting bays and the surf on sandy beaches. **1884** GOODE, etc. *Fisheries* I. 276 The Surf-Fish Family . . . forms the most characteristic feature of the fauna of our Pacific coast. **1911** *Rep. Fisheries 1908* 313/1 The name 'perch' is also given . . . to the surf-fishes.

+**Surfman.** A member of the crew of a surfboat, esp. in the life-saving service. — *a*1878 *Harper's Mag.* LVI. 337/2 The beach will be patrolled by the surf-men every night. **1894** *Nation* LVIII. 473/3 The title story is a readable episode of the heroism of the surf-men belonging to an isolated life-saving station. **1903** *N.Y. Tribune* 4 Oct., The surfmen rowed ashore, and the bathing season was at an end.

Surf scoter. A N.A. sea duck, *Melanitta perspicillata.* {1835} — **1887** RIDGWAY *Manual N.A. Birds* 113 North America in general . . . ; accidental in Europe. . . . Surf Scoter. **1917** *Birds of Amer.* I. 152/2 The summer home of the Surf Scoter is in the Far North.

* **Surgeon.** A doctor of medicine, esp. one who practices surgery.
Cf. CHIRURGEON.
1623 in Bradford *Hist.* (1912) I. 344 The sirgion hath bin very large on his tongue concerninge my selfe. **1740** *S.C. Hist. Soc. Coll.* IV. 58 He begged him . . . to send them a Surgeon. **1774** FINLAY *Journal* 80 His business as a Surgeon makes it impossible for him to give the requisite attendance and attention to the Post office. **1839** *Jamestown* (N.Y.) *Jrnl.* 3 April 3/1 A Quack advertises that whoever uses his medicine will never need a physician or surgeon. **1870** *Republican Rev.* 9 April 8/3 John Symington, Physician and Surgeon, First door south of the Post Office. **1904** STRATTON-PORTER *Freckles* 354, 'I never handled a finer man,' said the surgeon.

+**Surgeon dentist.** A dental surgeon. *Obs.* — **1768** in H. M. Brooks *Gleanings* IV. 21 All Persons who have had false Teeth fixt by Mr. John Baker, Surgeon-Dentist. **1796** *Boston Directory* 245 Flagg, Josiah, surgeon dentist, No. 47, Newbury street. **1836** *Niles' Nat. Reg.* 29 Oct. 144/3 The surgeon dentist, Aldis Brainard, . . . was indicted for having as many wives as a sultan. **1851** *Knickerb.* XXXVII. 97 Dr. N. Dodge . . . [is] one of the most experienced, skilful, and popular surgeon-dentists in New-York.

+**Surgeon fish.** One of numerous fishes of the genus *Acanthurus* and of the family Acanthuridae. — **1871** *Harper's Mag.* July 191/2 The terror of all, the surgeon-fish, . . . boldly swims in every quarter, opening and shutting his lancet, threatening to bleed every thing that comes in his way. **1884** GOODE, etc. *Fisheries* I. 279 On the coast of Florida . . . occur two species of this family, *Acanthurus cœruleus* and *A. nigricans,* generally known as the 'Doctor-fish' or 'Surgeon-fish.' **1911** *Rep. Fisheries 1908* 317/1 Surgeon-fish (*Teuthis hepatus*). This is the Tang common from Carolina to Florida.

Surgeon-general. a. *Milit.* A high-ranking medical officer {1802-}; now, in the army, the chief of the Medical Department and, in the navy, the head of the Bureau of Medicine and Surgery. +**b.** In the federal or a state bureau of public health, the chief medical officer.— **1777** *Jrnls. Cont. Congress* VII. 162 There [shall] be a physician and Surgeon General with the main army. **1840** *Niles' Nat. Reg.* 14 March 26/1 The vice president communicated to the senate . . . a report from the secretary of war, covering a statement of the surgeon general in relation to sites for marine hospitals. **1869** *Boyd's Business Directory* 111 Governor's Staff [N.Y. State]— . . . Surgeon-General, Jacob S. Mosher, of Albany. **1881** *Harper's Mag.* May 866/1 Dr. William H. Watson, of Utica, now Surgeon-General of this State, . . . encouraged the patient. **1917** *Rep. Surgeon General, U.S. Navy* 16 The Surgeon General, as a member of the General Medicine Board, has participated in the work [for the Council of National Defense].

Surprise candidate. A little known person used as a stalking-horse in an election. — **1858** *National Intelligencer* 20 Sept., In a judicial district a 'surprise candidate,' scarce known as a awyer or to the people . . . , was run . . . to aid in breaking down one of two able and unobjectionable candidates for the Supreme Bench.

Surprise party. {1841} +An unannounced party given as a surprise to a person. Also fig. — **1859** REDPATH *Roving Editor* 86 Was he never at a husking, . . . a bee, a surprise party, a 'social'? **1870** *Nation* 13 Jan. 18/2 A man who does work of this kind is a public benefactor, and ought to have a 'surprise party.' **1901** MERWIN & WEBSTER *Calumet 'K'* 268 There's no telling what sort of a surprise party those railroad fellows may have for us. **1908** GALE *Friendship Village* 71 So Calliope Marsh's surprise party came about.

Surrey. +A four-wheeled, two-seated carriage, usually without a top, and sometimes with a cut-under bottom: (see also quot. 1896). Now hist.
Said to be an adaptation of a pleasure cart introduced into the United States in 1872, by J. B. Brewster & Co., from Surrey, England.

1895 HOWELLS *Day of Their Wedding* 32 There was . . . a rank of stately hacks and barouches, and light, wood-colored surreys and phaetons. **1896** *Cosmopolitan* XX. 420/1 The Hill locomotor . . . is a canopy-top surrey with two seats. **1899** S. HALE *Letters* 342 We drive when we choose, or are driven in a great surrey with two horses. **1903** *N.Y. Tribune* 27 Sept., When the President drives he prefers the 80-year old surrey which belonged to his father. **1907** LILLIBRIDGE *Trail* 105 He made his descent from the two-seated canvas-covered surrey in front of Bob Manning's store.

Surrogate. {1604-} +In New York, New Jersey, and a few other states, a judicial officer with jurisdiction over infants, the probation of wills, testaments, etc. — **1784** *N.J. Archives* XXIII. p. lxxi, An Act to Ascertain the Power and Authority of the Ordinary and his Surrogates. **1834** *Jamestown* (N.Y.) *Jrnl.* 22 Oct. 1/5 Who holds the office of Surrogate in this County? **1836** *N.H. Hist. Soc. Coll.* V. 45 In some few cases the files of original wills are imperfect, from the surrogates having neglected to transmit them. **1869** *Boyd's Business Directory* 89 County Officers. . . . Milton A. Fowler, Poughkeepsie, Surrogate. **1911** GOUVERNEUR *As I Remember* 12 Some of his decisions as Surrogate are regarded as precedents to this day.

+**Surround.** The action or process of surrounding wild animals and driving them toward the center of the circle. — **1833** CATLIN *Indians* I. 199 The plan of attack, which in this country is familiarly called a 'surround,' was explicitly agreed upon. **1843** FRÉMONT *Explor. Rocky Mts.* 27 The Indians had made a surround here. **1889** H. O'REILLY *50 Yrs. on Trail* 37 They go out after the buffalo . . . , make what is termed a surround[,] . . . then ride in a circle round them.

Surtout. A long overcoat. {1686-} Also attrib. — **1754** *S.C. Gazette* 1 Jan. 2/2 He had on when he went away, a blue surtout coat. **1787** JEFFERSON *Writings* VI. 170, I could only bring off as much as my coat and surtout pockets would hold. **1825** NEAL *Bro. Jonathan* I. 149 Such a piece of cloth . . . would have begun to see service, belike, in the shape of a loose great coat, or double-breasted surtout. **1852** *Knickerb.* XXXIX. 164 He wears a long surtout and a prodigious red-and-yellow silk pocket-handkerchief. **1882** HOWELLS *Modern Instance* xxii, The Squire's dress-coat, . . . fully revealed by the removal of his surtout, . . . was a trial to a fellow of Bartley's style.

* **Survey.**
1. The process or operation of determining the contour, dimensions, position, etc., of an area; the results of such a process; an area subjected to this process. {1610-}
See also GEODETIC SURVEY, GEOLOGICAL SURVEY.
1645 *New Haven Col. Rec.* 190 It was ordered that the survay may goe on. **1732** *Doc. Hist. N.Y. State* I. 383 There being no previous Survey to the Grants, their Boundaries are generally expressed with much uncertainty. **1753** HEMPSTEAD *Diary* 603, I was also . . . settling Surveys of Land &c. **1792** [see MAP *n.* 1]. **1811** *Ann. 12th Congress* 1 Sess. 2226 The said commissioners shall make out accurate plats of such surveys. **1890** *Stock Grower & Farmer* 8 March 5/3 While on the survey of one of the Texas railroads we had with us one of the meanest horses a man ever saw. **1905** *Indian Laws & Tr.* III. 136 To pay all expenses incident to completion of the survey, platting, and appraisement of town sites, . . . ten thousand dollars.

b. A subdivision of land established by such a survey.
1791 *State P.* (1819) I. 24 The powers . . . , which respect the sub-divisions of the districts into surveys . . . have likewise been carried into effect.

+**2.** 'A district for the collection of the customs, under the inspection and authority of a particular officer' (*Cent.*).
1791 *Ann. 2d Congress* 21 New Hampshire forms one survey of inspection [for the collection of excise].

Surveying compass. A compass made especially for surveying land. — **1722** HEMPSTEAD *Diary* 124, I Recd . . . 24 yds of wire to make a chain & ye Needle of a Surveying Compass. **1802** ELLICOTT *Journal* 137 An excellent surveying compass, corrected for the variation of the needle, was used in taking the courses.

Surveying party. A group of persons who work together in making a survey of land. — **1798** I. ALLEN *Hist. Vermont* 39 They were in the surveying party from New York under Captain Stephens. **1884** *Century Mag.* Oct. 874/1 Scott Braxton . . . had once crossed the Plains with a surveying party.

* **Surveyor.**
* **1.** One who surveys land, roads, mines, etc.; one trained to make land surveys.
See also COUNTY SURVEYOR.
[**1623** *Va. Stat. at Large* I. 125 Every privatt planters devident shall . . . be divided by the surveyor.] **1627** *Plymouth Laws* 29 Whatsoever the surveighers judge sufficient shall stand without contradiction or opposition. **1650** *Warwick Rec.* 92 Ordered that the Surveiors . . . shall have 4 pence an acher. **1705** *N.C. Col. Rec.* I. 614 The said surveyors [shall] be derected to take particular notice what lands or Plantations . . . may happen to be cutt off. **1753** *Georgia Col. Rec.* VI. 399 The Board ordered the Surveyor to lay out and put the said Henry Yonge in Possession of thirty seven Acres of Land. **1818** *Ann. 15th Congress* 1 Sess. 2589 The powers and duties of the surveyor for the lands . . . shall extend to the whole of the Alabama Territory. **1877** [see GOVERNMENT 5 c]. **1907** *St. Nicholas* May 618/1 He was an expert surveyor.

+2. In the colonies, an official charged with looking after and maintaining certain property, as a surveyor of highways, fences, cattle, etc. { * in general sense}

1634 *Cambridge Rec.* 10 John White is Chossen surveior to see the highways and streete kept cleane and in repair. **1636** *Essex Inst. Coll.* IX. 40 All our fences fformerly made shalbe sufficientlie repaired . . . as the surveiors shall approve of. **1656** *Portsmouth Rec.* 73 The survayers ar to se the Cattell boated. **1664** *Dorchester Rec.* 124 The day above sayd, chosen Surveyors of the high wayes. **1697** *Manchester Rec.* I. 76 Isack Whicher and John bishop was chosen seaveiers of fences and field Drivers. **1721** *Mass. H. Rep. Jrnls.* III. 159 There are no words therein, that tend to infringe the Office of Surveyor of the Woods. **1728** *Braintree Rec.* 126 The meeting then proceeded to chuse Surveyours of Clapboards & Shingles. **1737** *Boston Rec.* 190 Mr. Isaac Gridley [shall] be Surveyor of Hemp. **1770** in Summers *Ann. S.W. Va.* 97 Stoval Kettering is appointed Surveyor of the Road.

3. A customs officer, whose duties are to inspect weights, quantities, etc., of taxable merchandise, esp. merchandise brought into a port. {1709-}

1665 in *N.Y. State Lib. Hist. Bul.* No. 2, 168, I do further appoint you to bee Surveyor of Long Island. **1683** *N.H. Hist. Soc. Coll.* VIII. 159 Edward Randolph, Esq., . . . was constituted and appointed collector, surveyor and searcher of his Majesty's customs in New-England. **1760** *Holyoke Diaries* 47 The Surveyor [of the port of Salem] came with them. **1789** *Ann. 1st Congress* 619 Nor shall any foreign vessel enter or unlade but at those ports to which a collector, naval officer, and surveyor have been appointed. **1859** BARTLETT 91.

* Surveyor-general.

+1. A colonial official having control of other surveyors, or general oversight of some public property or undertaking. { * in general sense}

1645 *Mass. Bay Rec.* III. 41 To ye surveyor gennerall of ye ammunition. **1714** *Boston News-Letter* 13 Sept. 2/2 The Surveyor General of the Western District was arrived in Maryland. **1769** in *Boston Transcript* 28 Sept. (1911) III. 12 To his Excellency John Wentworth, Esq., Surveyor General of his Majesty's Woods Thro'out North America.

b. A principal surveyor of land.

1665 *N.J. Archives* I. 26 [We] constitute and appoint you our Surveyor generall of our said province of New Cesarea or New Jersey. **1717** *Ib.* IV. 289 The said Surveyor Generall . . . shall not Survey any lands within the Western Division without a Warrant from this board.

+2. A federal officer in charge of the survey of public lands in a particular area.

1790 *Ann. 1st Congress* 1719 Resolved, That a Surveyor General for the United States be appointed. **1803** *Ann. 8th Congress* 2 Sess. 1588 The powers of the Surveyor General extend only over the lands lying north of the river Ohio and above the mouth of the river Kentucky. **1835** JACKSON in *Pres. Mess. & P.* III. 132 Charges . . . may have been made to me against the official conduct of Gideon Fitz, late surveyor-general south of the State of Tennessee. **1873** *Newton Kansan* 13 March 2/1 The President has nominated C. A. Babcock as surveyor general of Kansas. **1900** *Congress. Rec.* 17 Feb. 1903/1 The surveyor-general of that State [Nevada] writes me that there are more inquiries for public land than there have been for years.

* Suspend, *v.* +*tr.* To bar (a student) from a class or school for a period of time. — **1818** in J. Maclean *Hist. College of N.J.* II. 175 This morning we suspended one student. **1871** BAGG *At Yale* 256 The combatants . . . who are caught are heavily 'marked' or even 'suspended.'

* Suspender. A band of material, usually one of a pair, passing over the shoulders to hold up a pair of trousers. {1830, 1841}

'Chiefly *U.S.*' (O.E.D.).

1810 *Mass. Spy* 23 May 3/2 Part of the buckle of his suspenders . . . [was] extracted from the wound. **1836** SIMMS *Mellichampe* xliii, Wait a bit, till I pull up my suspenders. **1840** KENNEDY *Quodlibet* 90 His corduroy trowsers had but one suspender to keep them up, this giving them rather a lop-sided set. **1872** 'MARK TWAIN' *Roughing It* 42 The man wore . . . no suspenders. **1907** *St. Nicholas* Sept. 998/1 The accepted summer style . . . [was] a cotton shirt, a pair of butternut trousers held by one suspender, and bare feet.

attrib. **1833** C. A. DAVIS *Lett. J. Downing* 149 The Gineral got in a way he has of twitchin with his suspender buttons. **1850** *Rep. Comm. Patents 1849* 166 Improved Machine for making Suspender Buckles.

Suspension bridge. A bridge in which the roadway is suspended from wire cables or chains extended between supports. {1821-} Also comb. — **1840** in Schuyler *Roeblings* 55 An Assistant for the construction of suspension bridges, who is competent for the task. **1847** *Rep. Comm. Patents 1846* 298 A timber foundation [is used] in place of stone . . . to support the pressure of the anchor chains or cables against the anchor masonry of a suspension bridge. **1869** *Boyd's Business Directory* 498 Suspension Bridge is 304 miles from Albany and is situated on Niagara river, two miles below the cataract. **1900** *Everybody's Mag.* II. 46/2 This greater efficiency has been made possible by recent progress in the art of suspension-bridge building.

Suspicion, *v. tr.* To suspect; to be suspicious of. Chiefly *dial.* {1637, 1863-}

'Now *dial.* (chiefly *north.*), *U.S.*, or *rare arch.*' (O.E.D.).

*a*1820 in *Cincinnati Misc.* I. 127 He broke out afresh, accusing me of suspicioning him of a wish to rob me. **1834** CARRUTHERS *Kentuckian* I. 22 I rather suspicion, stranger, that I've seen more Injins than your missionaries. **1872** EGGLESTON *End of World* 65 When a man comes to Clark township a-wearing straps to his breechaloons, . . . I suspicions him. **1885** *Wkly. New Mexican Rev.* 30 April 4/4 They still use 'suspicioned' at all points south of the latitude of Alton, Ill., and west of the Mississippi. **1894** ALDRICH *Two Bites* 185 You people up at the North here don't suspicion what we have been through. **1910** J. HART *Vigilante Girl* 149, I think he sort of suspicioned a hold up.

+**Susquehanna.** [Amer. Indian.] An Indian of an Iroquoian tribe formerly living on the Susquehanna River; also, pl., the tribe. Also attrib.

— **1612** SMITH, etc. *Virginia* I. 19 The people differ very much in stature, . . . some being very great as the *Sesquesahamocks*, others very little as the *Wighcocomocoes*. **1676** *New Castle Court Rec.* 39 If the Sasquehannos should aply to you for anything, you are to use them kindly. **1751** [see MOHAWK *n.* 1]. **1768** in C. Hazard *Thos. Hazard* 246 To the Company or proprietors of the Susquehannah Purchase . . . I hereby Certify [etc.].

* Sutler. One who follows an army and sells provisions to the soldiers.

1757 *Lett. to Washington* II. 195 Mr. Ramsay return'd . . . with resolutions to pursue the plan of Suttlers, Retailers, Commissary, and what not, for the Compleat and proper Accomodating Your Regiment. **1776** *Jrnls. Cont. Congress* IV. 113 General Schuyler [shall] be desired to encourage suttlers to attend the army in Canada. **1860** GREELEY *Overland Journey* 16 Army officers and sutlers for the forts far up the Missouri . . . are constantly arriving. **1873** COZZENS *Marvellous Country* 239 He had recently received the appointment of sutler to the U.S. Military Post of Fort Buchanan.

b. One who operates a sort of commissary or provision store for persons other than soldiers.

1827 McKENNEY *Tour to Lakes* 73 Nearly opposite to this castle . . . a sutler had established himself to hold commerce with the Indians. **1891** *Century Mag.* April 847 Prisoners . . . were allowed to purchase certain articles from the prison sutler.

+**Sutler('s) store.** A store operated by a sutler. — **1845** GREEN *Texian Exped.* 276 We had the privilege of buying brandy at the tienda, shop, a kind of sutler store. **1863** *Rio Abajo Press* 27 Jan. 3/1 Sutler Store, Albuquerque, New Mexico. **1887** [see GOSSIP MILL].

+**Suwarrow.**[1] [A. V. *Suwarrow* (Suvorov), Russian field marshal, 1729-1800.] A type of cavalry boot. In full *suwarrow boot. Obs.* — **1805** *Lancaster* (Pa.) *Jrnl.* 29 March (Th.), [Egbert Taylor advertises] Cossacks, Suwarrows, Back-straps, Fire-buckets [etc.]. **1834** BRACKENRIDGE *Recollections* 208 The captain . . . [was] dressed in a leathern doublet, blue broadcloth pantaloons, and Suwarrow boots. **1847** *Knickerb.* XXIX. 380 Their titles we invoke not; . . . nor eke of style, Of Wellington, Suwarrow, tasselled, lanced. **1860** *Harper's Mag.* Aug. 351/2 He bought himself a pair of Suwarrow boots, then [*c*1800] just coming into fashion in the Eastern cities.

+**Suwarrow.**[2] Also **suaro.** Corruption of SAGUARO. — **1864** *Harper's Mag.* Nov. 693/1 A difference of opinion exists as to whether the petayah is not a distinct species from the suwarrow. **1884** SARGENT *Rep. Forests* 90 *Cereus giganteus.* . . . Suwarrow. Saguaro. Giant Cactus. . . . A tall, columnar tree, 8 to 18 meters in height. **1894** *Garden & Forest* 22 Aug. 334/2 The Suwarro . . . dots the . . . mesas of southern Arizona.

+**Suz,** *interj. local.* (See quot. 1848.) — **1843** STEPHENS *High Life N.Y.* I. p. xi, *Dreadful suz*—'quite awful, sirs.' **1848** BARTLETT 345 *Suzz,* a common pronunciation of *sirs!* An exclamation much used in New England, as *sirs* is in Scotland. **1856** A. CARY *Married* 72 'Oh dear me suz!' she exclaimed on hearing the name of the attending physician. **1895** A. BROWN *Meadow-Grass* 178 'Dear me suz!' she wailed, 'Dear me suz!' **1906** — in *Harper's Mag.* Oct. 714 'My suz!' she breathed.

+**Swa(a)r.** [?Du. *zwaar* 'large.'] A large, medium-late variety of apple, of fine quality. Also fig. — **1847** IVES *New Eng. Fruit* 42 *Swaar.*—This is a large apple, the form round, somewhat flat. **1850** S. WARNER *Wide, Wide World* xxii, 'What a great monster!' 'That's a Swar; they ain't as good as most of the others.' **1875** BURROUGHS *Winter Sunshine* 140 Those late ripeners are the winter varieties—the Rhode Island greenings or swaars of their kind.

Swab. Any one of various devices used for cleaning, absorbing, or moistening, as a mop made with rope yarn. {1659-}

1653 *Boston Rec.* 114 Every howseholder shall provid a pole . . . with a good large swob at the end of it, to rech the rofe of his house to quench fire in case of such danger. **1787** CUTLER in *Life & Corr.* I. 243 The hostler is at the door, ready to take your horse, . . . rubs him down, then washes him with a swab and wipes him dry. **1868** BRACKETT *Farm Talk* 60 To destroy [caterpillars] . . . give them . . . a thorough soaking, by means of a brush or swab fastened on the end of a pole. **1876** KNIGHT 2465/2 *Swab.* . . . It is used by the molder to wet the parting edge before *drawing* the pattern, and also to moisten parts of the mold requiring repairs. **1883** *Nat. Museum Bul.* No. 27, 565 Tangle-Frame and Swabs for collecting marine animals having a spiny or otherwise roughened exterior, or bushy growths, especially on rocky bottoms where they cannot be reached by the dredge.

b. A similar implement used for taking up snuff and spreading it on the teeth and gums.

1860 E. COWELL *Diary* 106 The snuff box and swab were on the table, Mrs. Green and her friend 'chewing snuff' with devotion.

+**Swad.** [Of obscure origin.] A number or mass; a bunch. *slang.* Chiefly *New Eng.* — **1828** WEBSTER, *Swad*, . . . in New England, a lump, mass or bunch; also, a crowd. (*Vulgar.*) **1834** C. A. DAVIS *Lett. J. Downing* 35 There was a swod of fine folks. **1843** STEPHENS *High Life N.Y.* I. 152 It must have cost an allfired swad of money. **1869** *Overland Mo.* Aug. 131 A Texan never has a great quantity of any thing, but he has 'scads' of it, or . . . 'swads.'

✷**Swaddle.** A covering of lengths of cloth, wrapped about a newborn infant; swaddling clothes. {−1659} 'Now *U.S.*' (*O.E.D.*). — **1881** *Pop. Science Mo.* XIX. 146 Out-doors add no cap or shawl before October, and under no circumstances any swaddles or baby night-gowns. **1897** *Amer. Pediatric Soc. Trans.* IX. 14 The one reformation of delivering the child from the incarceration of the swaddle . . . was sufficient to entitle him to the plaudits of succeeding pediatrists.

+**Swaddle bill.** A kind of duck: (see quot. 1917). — **1709** LAWSON *Carolina* 151 Swaddle-Bills are a sort of an Ash-Colour'd Duck, which have an extraordinary broad bill, and are good meat. **1917** *Birds of Amer.* I. 126 Shoveller. *Spatula clypeata.* . . . [Also called] Shovel-bill; Swaddle-bill; Butter Duck.

✷**Swag.** A depression in the ground; a marshy place. {1856−} (Cf. SAG *n.* I.) — **1848** *Dollar Mag.* 475/2 'A Swag' is often met with in the Western country. **1869** *Overland Mo.* Aug. 103 In Texas . . . a 'swag' is a kind of hollow which seems to be peculiar to its prairies—narrow, shallow, and marshy and rush-grown at the bottom. *a*1908 In Handsaker *Pioneer Life* 75 They finally succeeded in rolling the log backward until they reached a low swag.

Swainson. [Wm. *Swainson,* Eng. naturalist (1789–1855).] +Used in possessive in the names of species or varieties of birds.

1858 BAIRD *Birds Pacific R.R.* 19 *Buteo Swainsoni,* . . . Swainson's Buzzard, . . . [is] more nearly related to a generic form of the Old World (typical *Buteo*) than any bird hitherto discovered inhabiting the continent of America. *Ib.* 252 *Helmitherus Swainsonii.* Swainson's Warbler. . . . South Atlantic States. **1869** *Amer. Naturalist* III. 31 Swainson's Thrush (*Turdus Swainsonii*). . . . Common at Cœur d'Aleñe Mission up to the 22d [of Sept.]. **1895** *Dept. Agric. Yrbk. 1894* 222 The food of Swainson's hawk . . . is of much the same character as that of the two preceding species. **1917** *Birds of Amer.* III. 85/2 The Mexican, or Swainson's, Cliff Swallow (*Petrochelidon lunifrons melanogastra*) . . . visits Arizona for [breeding]. *Ib.* 105/2 In western North America there is a smaller and darker form of [the warbling vireo] . . . , known as the Western, or Swainson's, Warbling Vireo (*Vireosylva gilva swainsoni*).

✷**Swale.** A hollow place {now chiefly *dial.*}, +esp. a marshy or moist depression in a level or rolling area.

1667 *Dedham Rec.* IV. 135 He may cutt in a place called the Swale, adjoyning to the Ceader Swampe. **1695** *Ib.* V. 235 Now there is a way drawen by Jonathan Gay to a swale or run of watter. **1792** *Mass. H. S. Coll.* I Ser. I. 273 The swamps and swails yield maple, black birch, ash, and some hemlock. **1827** COOPER *Prairie* viii, A swale of low land lay near the base of the eminence. **1853** *Mich. Agric. Soc. Trans.* IV. 158, I have drained wet swales that were not made wet by springs. **1878** HARTE *Drift from Two Shores* 15 She pointed to a shining film of water slowly deepening in a narrow swale in the sands. **1913** CATHER *O Pioneers!* 83 South of the hill, in a low, sheltered swale, surrounded by a mulberry hedge, was the orchard.

attrib. **1838** *Mass. Agric. Survey 1st Rep.* 19 Considerable quantities of fresh meadow or swale hay is cut. **1873** *Vermont Bd. Agric. Rep.* II. 189 [If] the lightest were swale grass, . . . I would cut it in June.

✷**Swallow,** *n.*[1]

✷**1.** Any bird of the family Hirundinidae, or a bird mistakenly identified with these birds. Also in *fig.* context.

1676 SEWALL *Diary* I. 31 Called at her House . . . to tell Mr. Fosterling's Receipt, i.e., A Swallows Nest (the inside) stamped and applied to the throat outwardly. **1789** MORSE *Amer. Geog.* 60 American Birds [which] have been enumerated [include the] . . . Redstart, Red winged Starling, Swallow. **1850** [see MOSQUITO HAWK 1]. **1920** HOWELLS *Vacation of Kelwyns* 138 A little swallow . . . fell out of the nest.

attrib. **1812** WILSON *Ornithology* V. 50 This place of repose [for chimney swallows] . . . is usually a large hollow tree open at top, trees of that kind, or *Swallow trees,* as they are usually called, having been noticed in various parts of the country. **1853** B. F. TAYLOR *Jan. & June* 132 They heaped the new hay into the empty 'mow' . . . up to the swallow-hole.

2. With specifying or descriptive terms.

See also BANK SWALLOW, BARN SWALLOW, etc.

1781–2 JEFFERSON *Notes Va.* (1788) 76 *Hirundo Pelasgia, Hirundo cauda aculeata Americana,* American swallow. **1858** BAIRD *Birds Pacific R.R.* 311 *Hirundo Thalassina.* . . . Violet-Green Swallow. . . . Rocky Mountains to Pacific. **1894** TORREY *Fla. Sketch-Book* 8 More than one little flock of tree swallows went over the wood. *Ib.* 65 White-breasted swallows straggling northward along the line of sand-hills.

3. *ellipt.* =SWALLOW FORK.

1636 *Plymouth Rec.* 1 William Pontuss [a] swallow cropt upon the [word omitted] and a snip cut out upon the outside of the right eare.

✷**Swallow,** *n.*[2] An amount, esp. of liquid, swallowed at once. {a single act of swallowing, 1822−} — **1833** *Md. Hist. Mag.* XIII. 353 Bought a few swallows of milk and paid a 4 pence for it. **1883** *Century Mag.* June 277/1 To live like an Arab, content with a few dates and a swallow from the gourd. **1904** LYNDE *Grafters* 24 The Honorable Jasper . . . took a swallow of water from the glass on the desk.

✷**Swallow,** *v. Polit. tr.* (See quotations.) — *a*1850 FORD *Hist. Illinois* 89 The easy, facile, credulous fool who was the victim of artful fascination, was said to be *greased and swallowed.'* A man . . . was 'swallowed' when he was made to act to suit the purposes of 'the intrigue,' whatever it might be.

+**Swallow fork. 1.** An earmark for stock, resembling the fork of a swallow's tail. Also *transf.* **2.** *Swallowfork coat,* =SWALLOW-TAILED COAT. — (1) **1636** *Plymouth Rec.* 1 Every mans marke of his Cattle. . . . Christopher Waddesworth a swallow forke. **1665** *Hempstead Rec.* I. 176 One hors black branded . . . with a swallow forke one the nere aere. **1746** *Va. Gazette* 9 Jan., A small Black and White Cow . . . is mark'd with a Crop in the right Ear and a Swallow Fork in the left. **1869, 1887** [see OVERSLOPE]. *a*1903 'O. HENRY' *Roads of Destiny* 370, I'll make a swallow-fork in your other ear. (2) **1912** COBB *Back Home* 308, I still remember his swallowfork coat and his white neckerchief.

Swallow's tail. + =SWALLOW FORK 1. — **1667** *Essex Inst. Coll.* XXXVII. 218 Richard Gardner his mark, a swallows taile on ye left ear and a half penny under ye right. **1715** *Topsfield Rec.* I. 189 Taken up by Nathaniel Borman . . . a stray Heifer; . . . a Swallows Tail cut out of both Ears. **1746** [see MARK *n.*[1] a]. **1845** [see FORK *n.* 3].

✷**Swallowtail.**

1. =SWALLOW FORK 1.

1636 *Plymouth Rec.* 1 Mr John Weekes a swallow tayle cut out on the left eare. **1644** *Md. Archives* IV. 288 John Price entred for the mark of his cattell . . . swallow-taile in the left eare & slitt the right eare.

2. =SWALLOW-TAILED COAT. {1835−}

1845 HOOPER *Taking Census* 175 Mr. Marks . . . [buttoned up] his blue swallow-tail. **1870** 'F. FERN' *Ginger-Snaps* 9 A great deal of dress, or undress, on the part of the ladies; much swallow-tail, and an exquisite bit of cravat and kid-glove, on the part of the gentlemen. **1909** 'O. HENRY' *Options* 258 Along comes a slumming-party . . . , all in swallowtails.

+**b.** *Polit.* (See quot. 1914.)

1875 *Nation* 1 April 218 In this city [New York, there are among Democrats] two sets of politicians known familiary as 'Short Hairs' and 'Swallow-Tails.' **1885** *Mag. Amer. Hist.* April 395/2 *Swallow Tails.* During the campaign of 1876 a considerable number of Democrats who moved in fashionable New York circles took an unprecedented interest in political affairs. **1914** *Cycl. Amer. Govt.* III. 464/1 *Swallow Tails,* a derisive term applied to men prominent in fashionable circles who have gained some influence in politics.

3. a. A swallow-tailed butterfly. {1749−, attrib.; 1819−} +**b.** The swallow-tailed kite, *Elanoides forficatus.*

1869 *Rep. Comm. Agric. 1868* 314 The swallow-tails . . . are among our largest and most common butterflies. **1917** *Birds of Amer.* II. 60/2 No other North American bird approaches the Swallow-tail in the grace and beauty of its flight.

4. *attrib.* **a.** In senses 2 and 2 b with *coat, Democracy, suit.* {1853−}

1847 LOWELL *Biglow P.* 1 Ser. iii. 36 Parson Wilbur sez he never heerd . . . Thet th' Apostles rigged out in their swaller-tail coats. **1882** MCCABE *New York* 167 The Manhattan Club . . . is the headquarters of what is known in New York as the 'Swallow Tail Democracy.' **1901** FITCH *Captain Jinks* 73 For a new Prince Albert and a swallow-tail suit.

b. In specific names. {1749−}

*c*1728 CATESBY *Carolina* I. 4 The Swallow-Tail Hawk. . . . They continue long on the wing, catching, as they fly, . . . other Insects. **1832** WILLIAMSON *Maine* I. 145 We suppose there are with us four [species of gulls including] . . . the swallow-tail Gull, or Medrake. **1883** *Science* I. 371/2 The American species of swallow-tail butterflies.

Swallow-tailed, *a.* {1697−}

1. Of the stern of a ship: Cleft.

1835 INGRAHAM *South-West* I. 27 Those short, stump-masted non-descripts, with swallow-tailed sterns, snubbed bows, and black hulls.

2. a. Of a coat: Having a cleft tail; having two pointed, tapering skirts. (See also SWALLOW-TAILED COAT.) **b.** Of a person: Wearing a swallow-tailed coat.

1841 *Knickerb.* XVII. 187 His coat was a swallow-tailed blue, with gilt buttons, stamped with some curious device. **1843** *Ib.* XXI. 120 The coat in question was . . . not swallow-tailed, but cut off remarkably square and broad just where it began to taper off. **1869** 'MARK TWAIN' *Innocents* 220 Young ladies and gentlemen . . . ate supper on board, bringing their swallow-tailed, white-cravatted varlets to wait upon them. **1889** GUNTER *That Frenchman!* viii, The crowd is swelled by the swallow-tailed gentry, the news having got to the clubs and cafés.

3. In the specific names of birds. {*a*1672−}

[**1771** *Encycl. Brit.* II. 540/2 The [*Falco*] *furcatus,* or swallow-tailed hawk, weighs about 14 ounces. **1781** LATHAM *Gen. Synopsis Birds* I. 60 Swallow-tailed F[alcon] . . . is a most elegant species. . . . This bird inhabits *Carolina.*] **1858** BAIRD *Birds Pacific R.R.* 857 *Creagrus Furcatus.* . . . The Swallow-tailed Gull. . . . California. **1872** COUES *Key to Birds* 211 *Nauclerus.* . . . Swallow-tailed Kite.

Swallow-tailed butterfly. Any one of various butterflies in which the hind wings have projections which suggest swallows' tails. {1743-} — **1883** *Century Mag.* Oct. 956/2, I watched the larva of the swallow-tailed butterfly through their different stages.

Swallow-tailed coat. A coat with a pair of pointed tails or skirts; a man's dress coat. {1882} — **1835** WILLIS *Pencillings* I. 235 He was dressed in an exceedingly well cut swallow-tailed coat. **1867** *Jamestown* (N.Y.) *Jrnl.* 12 July 1/5 Did you ever know me to be conscious whether a woman had on a shawl or a swallow-tailed coat? **1895** [see FULL DRESS].

∗**Swallowwort.** Any one of various plants, chiefly of the milkweed family. — **1737** [see OAK OF JERUSALEM]. **1784** *Amer. Acad. Mem.* I. 424 *Asclepias.* . . . Swallowwort. . . . Blossoms white. **1832** [see BUTTERFLY WEED].

+**Swaly,** *a.* [f. SWALE.] Marshy or swampy. — **1792** *Mass. H. S. Coll.* 1 Ser. I. 272 There are pretty large tracts of swaily or swampy land. **1874** *Vermont Bd. Agric. Rep.* II. 420 The Cotswolds are just the kind to improve springy, swaly pastures.

+**Swammock.** (See quot. 1863.) — **1863** *Rep. Comm. Agric.* 1862 63 Low hummocks . . . from the fact of their participating of the nature of hummocks and swamps, are sometimes termed swammocks. **1889** *Amer. Notes & Q.* III. 285 In Florida, the term *swampy hammock* (for a certain description of land), is sometimes abbreviated to *swam-mock*.

Swamp, *n.* {1691-}
'First recorded as a term peculiar to the N. American colony of Virginia, but prob. in local use before in England' (*O.E.D.*).

I. 1. A tract or area of low-lying ground, usually along streams or near lakes or lagoons, often marshy or overflowed in wet seasons, and supporting many trees or bushes. {1725-}
The examples in the second group show the difficulty of defining the word in precise terms.
(1) **1624** SMITH *Gen. Hist. Va.* IV. 163 Some small Marshes and Swamps there are, but more profitable than hurtfull. **1694** [see LABOR[1] 1]. **1716** CHURCH *Philip's War* 13 Philip and his gang . . . took into a Swamp. **1806** LEWIS in *L. & Clark Exped.* IV. (1905) 84 Sergt. Ordway brought me a specemine of a species of pine peculiar to the swamps and marshes frequently overflown by the tide. **1813** in *Maine My State* 317, I struggled on one day more, . . . climbing over water-falls and through tangled swamps. **1874** *Vermont Bd. Agric. Rep.* II. 547 Year after year the farmer gets bean poles, hop poles, fence rails, building timber and fire wood from such a swamp.
(2) **1775** ROMANS *Nat. Hist. Florida* 25 By *swamps* in general is to be understood any low grounds subject to inundations, distinguished from marshes in having a large growth of timber, and much underwood, canes, reeds, wythes, vines, briars, and such like, matted together. **1798** *Amer. Philos. Soc.* IV. 440 By a swamp, I exclusively mean a piece of ground, the surface of which is wet and soft, but which has a sound bottom. **1837** WILLIAMS *Florida* 89 The third kind of swamps are those spongy tracts, where the waters continually ooze through the soil, and finally collect in streams and pass off. **1875** TEMPLE & SHELDON *Hist. Northfield, Mass.* 21 Swamps.—As used by our fathers in the earliest times, this term did not necessarily denote marshy ground; but flat land which from its peculiar location had escaped the ravages of the annual fires set by the Indians, and was covered with an old growth of wood. **1890** *Cent.* 3689/2 In the United States, however, *swamp* is often used in the restricted sense of 'fresh-water marsh.'

2. = SWAMP LAND.
1671 *Springfield Rec.* II. 237 Thomas Mirrick hath grannted unto him two or three acres of . . . meddowish land & Swamp. **1740** *Georgia Col. Rec.* IV. 670 The American Dialect distinguishes Land into Pine, Oak and Hickory, Swamp, Savannah, and Marsh. **1784** SMYTH *Tour* II. 74 Another sort of ground, which lies low and wet, upon some of their rivers, . . . is called *swamp.*

II. *attrib.* and *comb.* **3.** Designating tracts of land situated in, or related to, swamps.
See also SWAMP LAND, SWAMP LOT.
1639 in *Amer. Speech* XV. 400/2 Southerly wth Swamp and Marsh Necks and Creekes. **1697** *Cambridge Prop. Rec.* 344 Four Rods of fence, Lyeing att the head of Samuel Hastings Swamp-meadow. **1750** in *Amer. Speech* XV. 400/2 A Certain parcell of Swamp Marsh or Sunken ground Lying Contiguous to his unpatented high Land. **1845** SIMMS *Wigwam & Cabin* 1 Ser. 15 A portion [of the forest] . . . was swallowed up in . . . a swamp-bottom, the growth of which consisted of mingled cypresses and bay-trees. **1848** *Rep. Comm. Patents* 1847 388 The rich swamp hammocks have not yet been tested in wheat.

4. Designating streams, roads, fences, etc., in swamps.
1651 in *Amer. Speech* XV. 401/1 To the Maine Swamp Upon the head of Ware river and down the said swamp runn and river. **1657** *Conn. Hist. Soc. Coll.* VI. 97 Thos men that haue ground in the medow: shall carey one the ffenc from the swamp fenc . . . to meett wth William Houghtens fenc. **1716** *N.C. Col. Rec.* II. 248 Swamp water goes down worse in winter than in Summer. **1726** in *Amer. Speech* XV. 400/2 Along the said Swamp-Branch to a white Logg. *a*1817 DWIGHT *Travels* IV. 176 The Northern [lake was] . . . encircled by a dismal border of swamp shrubbery. **1847** ROBB *Squatter Life* 76 He gone into de swamp road, massa.

5. Designating soil or kinds of soil found in swamps and often used as fertilizer.
1753 Swamp Mud [see COW YARD]. **1839** BUEL *Farmer's Companion* 47 Where the vegetable matter is deficient, blend with it quantities of peat or swamp earth. *Ib.* 73 Peat earth, or swamp muck, is vegetable food, in an insoluble state. **1848** *Rep. Comm. Patents* 1847 167 Mr. Poinsett expresses the opinion that it will succeed best in a rich swamp soil.

6. Designating persons who live in or near swamps.
See also SWAMP ANGEL 1, SWAMP FOX.
1776 Fithian *Journal* II. 249 Many straggling, impertinent, vociferous swamp-men were along this morning. **1832** SANDS *Writings* II. 298 Tacitus, speaking of some Swamp Democrat of his day, uses this verb intransitively. **1835** SIMMS *Partisan* (1854) 86 Thou art a better swamp-sucker than Ned Travis, and he born . . . in a bush and cradled in a bog. **1850** LEWIS *La. Swamp Doctor* 132 An infernal dog . . . jumped—like a swamp gal into a jar of pickles—into the ring of our felicity. **1867** EDWARDS *Shelby* 410 The 'higher civilization' folks from the North . . . [found] in him a specimen of the green Arkansas 'swamp-rat.' **1880** CABLE *Grandissimes* 29 They were . . . adventurous swamp-rangers, and . . . lively free-livers. **1890** Swamp-dweller [see PINELANDER].

7. Designating, or forming part of the names of, snakes, birds, and insects found in swamps.
See also SWAMP ANGEL 3, SWAMP BLACKBIRD, etc.
1709 LAWSON *Carolina* 130 Of the Swamp-Snakes there are three sorts, which are very near akin to the Water-Snakes. **1810** WILSON *Ornithology* II. 36 *Fringilla erythrophthalma* . . . is called . . . in Pennsylvania the Chewink, and by others the Swamp Robin. **1836** *Public Ledger* (Phila.) 21 May, The down east girls . . . [chew] spruce gum mingled as it frequently is with dirt, dead mosquitoes, and swamp flies. **1842** *Nat. Hist. N.Y., Zoology* III. 45 The Striped Snake, *Tropidonotus taenia,* . . . is known under various popular names, such as . . . Swamp Garter. **1844** *Ib.* II. 318 The Buff-Breasted Sheldrake. *Mergus Merganser.* . . . The female . . . is called Weaser, or Swamp Sheldrake. **1846** THORPE *Myst. Backwoods* 130 I'd be as musty as an old swamp moccasin. **1874** COUES *Birds N.W.* 394 Canada Grouse; Spruce Grouse. . . . [Also called] Spruce Partridge, Wood Partridge, Swamp Partridge. **1917** *Birds of Amer.* III. 50 Song Sparrow. *Melospiza melodia melodia.* . . . [Also called] Red Grass-bird; Swamp Finch.

8. In the names of plants and trees found in swamps.
The number of formations of this kind is large. Only a few are here illustrated. (See also SWAMP APPLE, SWAMP ASH, etc.)
1721 DUDLEY in *Phil. Trans.* XXXI. 145 The Poyson-Wood-Tree . . . is by some called the *Swamp Sumach.* **1751** Swamp-wire-Grass [see FOWL MEADOW]. **1754** ELIOT *Field-Husb.* v. 123 The Brush was . . . Swamp Button Wood, the most difficult to subdue of any Wood I know. **1786** WASHINGTON *Diaries* III. 34 Replaced . . . in my Shrubberies . . . 3 locusts, 1 Swamp red berry. **1813** MUHLENBERG *Cat. Plants* 53 *Magnolia glauca,* Swamp magnolia. **1814** BIGELOW *Florula Bostoniensis* 248 *Nyssa villosa,* Tupelo tree, Swamp Hornbeam, . . . grows in swamps. **1831** AUDUBON *Ornith. Biog.* I. 450 The plant on a twig of which two Nashville Warblers are represented, is usually called the *Swamp Spice.* **1834** *Ib.* II. 121 The Swamp Snowball . . . is found on the broken sandy banks bordering small water-courses. **1870** *Amer. Naturalist* IV. 216 The Swamp Blueberry (*Vaccinium corymbosum*) . . . is a very attractive shrub. **1888** *Century Mag.* Sept. 768/1 'A brilliant yellow' may be obtained by pouring boiling water upon other component parts of 'sassafras, swamp bay, and butterfly root.'

9. In special combinations.
Swamp broadcloth, (see quotation); *s. fever,* malarial fever; *s. grant,* a grant by the federal government to a state of the swamp lands within its borders; *s. island,* a piece of elevated land in a swamp; *s. law,* law such as swamp-dwelling backwoodsmen exercise, lynch law; *s. malaria,* malaria that prevails in swamps; *s. manure,* manure or compost made chiefly of swamp soil; *s. ore,* ferruginous mould or muck found in swamps; *s. tacky,* = MARSH TACK(E)Y.
1850 LEWIS *La. Swamp Doctor* 110, I donned a suit of 'swamp broadcloth,'—yellow linsey—which clove to my proportions as if it were an integral part of my frame. **1846** *Knickerb.* XXVIII. 431 And cured the good folks of all their complaints, from swamp-fever to phthisic. **1860** *Harper's Mag.* Feb. 401/2, 1,712,040 acres were approved to the several States under swamp grants. **1846** CHILD *Fact & Fiction* 195 They arrived at one of those swamp islands so common at the South. **1832** WILLIAMSON *Maine* II. 173 Nor would they very readily shrink from a 'trial by battle,' or by 'swamp-law,' which seemed to rest much upon the same principles. **1872** POWERS *Afoot & Alone* 44 It shall be in the spring, before the swamp malaria . . . has banished the whites to the uplands. **1796** *N.Y. State Soc. Arts* I. 252 Some of the swamp-manures will also produce good harvests of wheat. **1804** *Mass. H. S. Coll.* 1 Ser. IX. 256 There is another kind found in bogs and swamps, which the workmen call swamp or mud ore. **1836** SIMMS *Mellichampe* xliii, If you see that little bullet foot of a swamp-tacky freshly put down in the swamp or sand after mine, be sure the skunk's started.

Swamp, *v.* {1772-}
+**1.** *pass.* or *reflex.* To mire or bog down in a swamp; to take refuge in a swamp. *Obs.*
1646 *New Haven Col. Rec.* 270 Samuell Marsh . . . [was] seeking cowes, it being in the spring, yn catle being lyable to be swampt. **1654** in *Hutchinson Coll. Papers Mass.-Bay* 263 Ninnigret . . . had swampt him-

selfe and refused conference with us. **1814** BRACKENRIDGE *Views La.* 210 A poor ox . . . was swamped near the bank. **1821** FOWLER *Journal* 25 Some of our Horses . . . Ware Swamped with their loads.

+**2.** Used in mildly profane imprecations. *Obs.*

Cf. SWAN *v.* 1.

1764 HUTCHINSON *Hist. Mass.* 436 He has, in like manner, . . . I swamp, and I vum, for I swear, and I vow. **1776** *Battle of Brooklyn* I. iii, Swamp me, if I have not hove up a breast-work. **1815** HUMPHREYS *Yankey* 19 I shood never have swimmed to shore, to all atarnity I swamp it.

+**3.** *tr.* In logging operations, to make (a road) over which logs may be hauled; to clear an area of undergrowth or brush.

1851 SPRINGER *Forest Life* 84 An experienced hand . . . 'spots' the trees where he wishes the road to be 'swamped.' **1905** *Forestry Bureau. Bul.* No. 61, 50.

+**Swamp angel.**

1. A dweller in a swamp; also, transf., a member of a southern anti-Negro group.

1857 *Jrnl. of Discourses* V. 31 (Th.), Angels who would thus visit us are swamp angels,—they are filthy. **1876** *Congress. Rec.* 27 Dec. 384/1, If I were to credit what I hear, he was once known as a 'swamp angel.' **1890** *Ib.* 23 Jan. 804/2 'Jim' Liddell was there with his crowd of 'Swamp Angels' (for this badge was worn by them all—a green silk ribbon with 'Swamp Angel' on it).

2. *cap.* A Parrott gun used in the siege of Charleston, South Carolina, during the Civil War. *Obs.*

1865 *Atlantic Mo.* May 591/2 The War . . . has created . . . 'Swamp Angels' and thousand-pounders. **1871** DE VERE 117 Enormous projectiles [were] thrown into the city of Charleston by the Swamp Angel of General Gilmore, as his monster-gun in the swamps was ironically called. **1876** *Congress. Rec.* 19 May 3215/2 The Swamp Angel that hurled its ponderous shells into Charleston would destroy such an establishment from the open sea.

transf. **1865** *Harper's Mag.* Oct. 673/2 The striking letter . . . is a 'swamp angel' in the attack which is now opened upon the traditions of education. **1882** *Congress. Rec.* 13 Feb. 1106/2 That assertion . . . was a sort of 'swamp angel' shot from his mathematical battery.

3. *local.* The hermit thrush.

1865 BURROUGHS in *Atlantic Mo.* May 522/2 [The hermit thrush is usually found] in damp and swampy localities. On this account the people in the Adirondack region call it the 'Swamp Angel.' **1917** *Birds of Amer.* III. 234.

+**Swamp apple.** A gall found on some species of azalea; also, the plant itself. (Cf. HONEYSUCKLE APPLE.) — **1805** BENTLEY *Diary* III. 166 The young ladies furnished themselves with the Kalmia, swamp apples. **1846** *Zoologist* IV. 1281 The galls called swamp-apples . . . grow on the small twigs of the swamp-pink, or *Azalea viscosa.* **1860** DARLINGTON *Weeds & Plants* 214 These succulent excres[c]ences are much sought after by boys who call them 'swamp apples' and 'swamp cheeses.' **1881** *Harper's Mag.* March 526/1 Both he and his followers were covered with Pinxter *blummies*—the wild azalea, or swamp-apple. **1892** *Amer. Folk-Lore* V. 100 *Rhododendron nudiflorum*, swamp apple. E. Mass.

+**Swamp ash.** Any one of various ashes, as black ash and red ash, found in swamps. — **1815** DRAKE *Cincinnati* 83 The swamp ash . . . and aspen, seem to be confined to the more northern portions of this tract. **1819** SCHOOLCRAFT *Journal* 76 The other forest-trees and plants . . . composing the forest of White River [include]: . . . swamp-ash, (*fraxinus juglandifolia;*) white oak. **1842** Z. THOMPSON *Hist. Vermont* I. 211/2 The Black Ash . . . is commonly found growing . . . in and about swamps; and hence it is sometimes called *Swamp Ash.* **1889** [see JACK OAK].

+**Swamp blackbird.** =RED-WING(ED) BLACKBIRD. — **1794** *Amer. Philos. Soc.* IV. 108 Red-winged-maize-thief. [Note:] Commonly called, in Pennsylvania, the Swamp-black-bird. **1811** [see MAIZE THIEF]. **1895** *Outing* XXVII. 75/1 A huge flock of swamp blackbirds covered the ground.

+**Swamp chestnut oak.** (See quot. 1897.) — [**1801** MICHAUX *Histoire des Chênes* 6 Quercus prinus (palustris) Chêne chataignier, *Swamp's Chestnut Oak*]. **1832** BROWN *Sylva* 286 Farther south . . . it is called *Chesnut White Oak, Swamp Chesnut Oak,* and . . . *White Oak.* **1860** CURTIS *Woody Plants N.C.* 33 Swamp Chestnut Oak . . . has a straight split and shreds easily, and is therefore employed, especially by the negroes, in the making of baskets and brooms. **1897** SUDWORTH *Arborescent Flora* 156 *Quercus prinus.* Chestnut Oak. . . . Swamp Chestnut Oak (N.C.). *Ib.* 158 *Quercus michauxii.* Cow Oak. . . . Swamp Chestnut Oak (Fla.).

Swamper. {1884}

+**1.** One who lives in a swamp or swampy region.

1840 *Picayune* 20 Aug. 2/1 John Jones, Stephen Jones and Bill Sails, three notorious swampers, were arrested as dangerous and suspicious characters. **1856** *Harper's Mag.* Sept. 447/2 Joe Skeeters . . . is a thoroughbred swamper, and an occasional fisherman on the lake. **1891** *Boston Jrnl.* 9 April 2/3 [Alligator oil] has a high reputation among the swampers as a remedy for rheumatism.

+**2.** One who swamps or clears roads in lumbering operations.

1851 SPRINGER *Forest Life* 92 Next [come] the swampers, who cut and clear the roads through the forest to the fallen trees. **1880** *Lumberman's Gazette* 28 Jan. 1/3 A Wisconsin lumber-camp is divided into 'choppers,'

'sawyers' and 'swampers.' **1903** *Outlook* 7 Nov. 588 He had picked a quarrel with Ole Erickson, one of the swampers.

+**b.** A man of all work in a saloon.

1907 *Oregonian* 13 Oct. (Th.), He was a swamper in a saloon.

+**Swamp Fox.** General Francis Marion (1732–95), a celebrated South Carolina patriot and partisan leader during the Revolutionary War. — **1836** SIMMS *Mellichampe* p. v, The pursuit of the 'swamp fox' by Colonel Tarleton . . . follows closely the several authorities. **1900** *Congress. Rec.* 29 Jan. 1262/2 Marion, the 'Swamp Fox,' . . . and the other men who fought and continued to fight were hiding out.

+**Swamp grass.** Any one of various coarse grasses or rushes found in swamps. — **1845** FRÉMONT *Exped.* 206 Only the high swamp grass appeared above. **1881** *Rep. Indian Affairs* 144 Swamp grass and shrubbery are abundant. [**1907** C. HILL-TOUT *Brit. N. Amer., Far West* 119 The materials employed in the manufacture of this basketry are . . . various swamp grasses, of which the bulrush is the commonest specimen.]

+**Swamp hare.** =SWAMP RABBIT a. — **1891** *Cent.* 6098/3 *Swamp-hare*, a large, long-limbed hare or rabbit, *Lepus aquaticus*, inhabiting the fresh-water swamps and bayous of the southern United States.

+**Swamp hellebore.** =AMERICAN HELLEBORE. — **1751** ELIOT *Field-Husb.* iii. 66 Take the Roots of Swamp Hellebore, sometimes called Skunk Cabbage, Tickle Weed, Bear Root. **1814** [see POKEROOT]. **1874** [see INDIAN POKE].

+**Swamp hickory. a.** The bitternut hickory, *Carya cordiformis.* **b.** The water hickory, *C. aquatica.* — **1805** *Ann. 9th Congress* 2 Sess. 1090 The growth, on . . . the highest [places is] handsome oaks, swamp hickory, ash, grape vines, &c. **1832** BROWNE *Sylva* 170 Bitternut Hickory . . . in Pennsylvania . . . sometimes [is called] *Swamp Hickory.* **1884** [see BITTER *a.*]. **1912** COBB *Back Home* 306 He was tough as swamp hickory.

+**Swamp honeysuckle.** The azalea (*Azalea viscosa*) common in swamps in the East. — **1814** O. O. RICH *Amer. Plants* 23. **1835** BIRD *Hawks* I. 59 The swamp-honeysuckle shook its fragrant clusters. **1869** FULLER *Flower Gatherers* 59 The *Azaleas*, or *Swamp Honeysuckles*, are beautiful cousins of the Rhodora. **1901** MOHR *Plant Life Ala.* 653.

+**Swamp hook.** (See quot. 1905.) — **1877** *Lumberman's Gazette* 22 Dec., Swamp Hooks, Pevys, Skidding Tongs always on hand. **1902** WHITE *Blazed Trail* 53 The chain was fastened around one end by means of the ever-useful steel swamp-hook. **1905** *Forestry Bureau Bul.* No. 61, 50 *Swamp hook*, a large, single hook on the end of a chain, used in handling logs, most commonly in skidding.

+**Swamp huckleberry.** A species of huckleberry found in swamps or swampy regions. — **1800** J. MAUDE *Niagara* 8 The swamp huckleberry, a tall shrub like the alder. **1860** CURTIS *Woody Plants N.C.* 86 Swamp Huckleberry (*Vaccinium corymbosum*). . . . The berries are large, deep blue, subacid and pleasant, ripening in May and June. **1865** BURROUGHS in *Atlantic Mo.* May 520/2 That clump of Swamp-Huckleberry conceals three or four different songsters.

Swamping, *a.* [Cf. Eng. *swapping a.*] 'Very large; huge' (B.). — **1775** *Yankee Doodle* in *Poems of Amer. Hist.* (1908) 159/2 And there we saw a swamping gun, Large as a log of maple.

+**Swamp land.** Land, usually cultivable and fertile, in a swamp.

1663 *Conn. Hist. Soc. Col.* XIV. 433 One parcel of land . . . being Swamp land. **1701** *Providence Rec.* V. 125 A Certaine ffarme or tract of land Consisting of upland swampe land & Meadow land. **1791** W. BARTRAM *Travels* 95 This district consists of a vast body of rich swamp land, fit for the growth of Rice. **1850** *Whig Almanac 1851* 23/1 The necessary levees and drains to reclaim the swamp and overflowed lands. **1913** LONDON *Valley of Moon* 438 They followed the railroad west, through a region of swampland, to Davisville.

attrib. **1868** *N.Y. Herald* 2 July 3/2, These lands were obtained under the Swamp Land act. **1869** *Mich. Agric. Soc. Trans.* VII. 483 All swamp land scrip known as 'general scrip' shall be received in payment of all lands sold under the provisions of this act.

+**Swamp laurel.**

1. The sweet bay (*Magnolia virginiana*).

1743 CLAYTON *Flora Virginica* 83 *Magnolia Lauri folio,* . . . Swamp-Laurel. **1814** PURSH *Flora Amer.* II. 381 This species is known by the names of Swamp Sassafras, Sweet Bay, Swamp Laurel, and Beaver-wood. **1884** SARGENT *Rep. Forests* 20.

2. The bog kalmia, *Kalmia polifolia.*

1817-8 EATON *Botany* (1822) 325. **1847** WOOD *Botany* 374 Swamp Laurel. . . . A delicate shrub, 2½ high, found in swamps, &c. **1869** FULLER *Flower Gatherers* 138 The farmers around here call it 'Swamp-Laurel.'

+**Swamp lily.** One of various plants growing in low or swampy ground: (see quotations). {1814–, in Australia; 1902}

1737 BRICKELL *N. Carolina* 21 Another Weed, vulgarly called the *Swamp-Lillie,* . . . grows in the Marshes and low Grounds, and is something like our *Dock* in its Leaves. **1836** LINCOLN *Botany* App. 137 *Saururus . . . cernuus,* (lizard's-tail swamp-lily.) **1857** *Knickerb.* XLIX. 213 It was a swamp, with green slime, and the swamp-lily moving sluggishly above it. **1890** *Cent.* 3454/2 The American Turk's-cap or swamp-lily, *L[ilium] superbum,* . . . [is] found on low grounds at the north. **1891** *Ib.* 6098/3 *Swamp-lily,* . . . a plant of the genus *Zephyranthes.* **1909** WEBSTER 2090/3 *Swamp lily,* . . . a white-flowered species of *Crinum* (*C. angustifolium*) of the southern U.S.

+Swamp lot. A lot or plot of ground in a swamp. — **1677** *Hartford Land Distrib.* 92 The sayd parcell of land containes about Sixty acres, . . . abutting on the Swamp lotts on the west. **1692** *Ib.* 246 One parcell of land . . . abutteth west on a High way leading to the swamp lotts. **1715** *Harvard Rec.* II. 427 A Swamp-Lott in the West fields [shall] be Sold. **1880** *Harper's Mag.* June 70 Down in the moist green swamp lot the yellow cowslips bloom along the shallow ditch.

+Swamp maple. 1. =RED MAPLE. **2.** The Californian box elder, *Acer negundo californicum.* **3.** (See quotation.) — **(1) 1810** MICHAUX *Arbres* I. 28. **1869** STOWE *Oldtown Folks* 153 Here and there, a swamp-maple seemed all one crimson flame. **1907** *N.Y. Ev. Post* (s.-w. ed.) 4 April 6 In the moist lowlands where the skunk cabbage has its home the swamp maple puts forth its flowers. **(2) 1891** *Cent.* 6099/1 *Swamp-maple,* . . . *Negundo Californicum,* of the Coast Range in California. **(3) 1909** *Ib. Suppl.* 1304/2 *Swamp-maple,* . . . the silver maple. . . . The mountain-maple.

+Swamp milkweed. A common American milkweed, *Asclepias incarnata.* — **1857** GRAY *Botany* 353 *A[sclepias] incarnata.* (Swamp Milkweed.) . . . Milky juice scanty. **1882** *Century Mag.* May 153/2 The only species of our milkweed . . . that we would recommend for the wild garden are the swamp milkweed . . . , the four-leaved milkweed . . . , and the butterfly weed. **1892** COULTER *Bot. W. Texas* II. 265.

+Swamp oak. Any one of various oaks found in swamps, as the swamp white oak and the pin oak.

1681 *New Castle Court Rec.* 503, 40 perches to a corner marked swamp oake. **1766** J. BARTRAM *Journal* 22 The east banks being . . . full of live and swamp-oaks. **1814** BIGELOW *Florula Bostoniensis* 226 The wood of the swamp oak is strong, heavy, and flexible, easy to split. **1897** SUDWORTH *Arborescent Flora* 152 *Quercus lobata.* . . . California White Oak. . . . Swamp Oak (Cal.).

attrib. **1790** DENNY *Journal* 144 March through beech and swamp oak land.

+Swampoodle. *local.* A low-lying or poor section of a town or city. *slang. Obs.* — **1871** *Congress. Globe* 15 April 718/1 Passengers . . . will be left out here at this part of the city [of Washington] that . . . is known as Swampoodle. **1894** *Congress. Rec.* App. 1 Aug. 1117/2 A part of that city [Kansas City, Kansas] . . . at one time the suburbs of old Kansas City, Mo., . . . was made up of what you would call here [in Wash.] 'swampoodle.'

+Swamp owl. (See quots. 1917.) — **1853** *Harper's Mag.* Nov. 771/1 With night came . . . the screech of the swamp-owl. **1892** HARRIS *On Plantation* 72 He was imitating the cry of the swamp owl. **1917** *Birds of Amer.* II. 101 Short-eared Owl. *Asio flammeus.* . . . [Also called] Swamp Owl. *Ib.* 103 Barred Owl. *Strix varia varia.* . . . [Also called] Swamp Owl.

+Swamp pine. Any one of various pines, as the loblolly pine and the slash pine, found in wet or swampy regions. Also with specifying terms.

[**1731** P. MILLER *Gardeners Dict.* (1735) s.v. *Abies,* Species . . . to be found in the English Gardens . . . [include] *Pinus; Americana, palustris.* The Swamp Pine.] **1743** CATESBY *Carolina* II. p. xxii, The Swamp Pine grows on barren wet land. **1785** MARSHALL *Amer. Grove* 102 *Pinus Tæda,* Virginian Swamp, or Frankincence Pine, . . . grows to a pretty large size. **1851** SPRINGER *Forest Life* 41 This difference is accounted for by . . . the tardiness with which the swamp Pine matures. **1897** SUDWORTH *Arborescent Flora* 26 *Pinus tæda.* Loblolly Pine. . . . Swamp Pine (Va., N.C.). *Ib.* 31 *Pinus heterophylla.* . . . Cuban Pine. . . . Swamp Pine (Fla., Miss., Ala., in part). **1914** E. STEWART *Lett. Woman Homesteader* 7, I have a grove of twelve swamp pines on my place.

+Swamp pink.

1. An azalea, esp. *A. viscosa,* found in wet or swampy regions.

1784 *Amer. Acad. Mem.* I. 416 American Honeysuckle. Swamp Pink. . . . Common in low, swampy land. June. **1814** BIGELOW *Florula Bostoniensis* 52 Wild honeysuckle. Swamp pink. . . . A fine flowering shrub, very common among the brushwood in low land. **1892** *Amer. Folk-Lore* V. 100 *Rhododendron nudiflorum,* swamp pink. Parts of N.E. **1894** *Harper's Mag.* Nov. 920/1 The low, marshy meadow Where pale swamp-pinks blow.

2. (See quotations.)

1898 CREEVEY *Flowers of Field* 85 Swamp Pink. *Helonias bullata.* . . . A pretty plant, found from New Jersey southward to Virginia. **1909** WEBSTER 2090.

+Swamp prairie. =WET PRAIRIE. — [**1791** W. SARGENT *Diary* 12 We were halted by a swamp or sunken 'Prairie.'] **1895** G. KING *New Orleans* 44 The rush-covered banks of to-day extended then into vast swamp prairies.

+Swamp rabbit. a. A rabbit, *Sylvilagus aquaticus,* frequenting wet or swampy places. **b.** =MARSH RABBIT. — **1845** LYELL *Second Visit* I. 228, I had heard much of the swamp-rabbit, which they hunt near the coast in South Carolina and Georgia. **1875** *Fur, Fin & Feather* (ed. 3) 136/1 The 'swamp rabbit' inhabits the heavy timbered woodlands and river bottoms. **1917** *Mammals of Amer.* 291/1 The Swamp Rabbit dwells among the bogs, swamps, and bottom-lands.

+Swamp rose. A wild, clambering rose, *Rosa carolina,* found in swamps. Also *swamp Pennsylvanian rose.* (The identity of the species in the first quotation is not certain.) — **1785** MARSHALL *Amer. Grove* 135 *Rosa palustris,* Swamp Pennsylvanian Rose . . . [rises] to the height of four or five feet. **1814** [see ROSE 2]. **1860** CURTIS *Woody Plants N.C.* 89. **1902** *Outing* June 272/2 The Carolina or swamp rose . . . is well known.

+Swamp sassafras. The sweet bay, a species of magnolia, *M. virginiana.* — **1785** MARSHALL *Amer. Grove* 83 Small Magnolia, or Swamp Sassafras, . . . grows naturally in low, moist, or swampy ground. **1814** PURSH *Flora Amer.* II. 381 *Magnolia longifolia* . . . is known by the names of Swamp Sassafras, Sweet Bay, Swamp Laurel, and Beaver-wood. **1832** [see BEAVER WOOD 1].

+Swamp Spanish oak. =PIN OAK 1. — **1810** MICHAUX *Arbres* I. 25 *Swamp Spanish oak,* . . . dans les Etats de Pensylvanie et de Maryland. **1832** BROWNE *Sylva* 278 [*Quercus palustris*] is called . . . Swamp Spanish Oak, in Pennsylvania. **1894** COULTER *Bot. W. Texas* III. 417.

+Swamp sparrow. A fringilline sparrow (*Melospiza georgiana*) related to the song sparrow and found in swamps in the South and East. — **1811** WILSON *Ornithology* III. 49 [The] Swamp Sparrow, *Fringilla Palustris,* [frequents] . . . the immense cypress swamps and extensive grassy flats of the southern states. **1831** AUDUBON *Ornith. Biog.* I. 331 The shores and such flat sand-bars as are overgrown with grasses and rank weeds along the Mississippi . . . are the resorts of the Swamp Sparrow. **1872** COUES *Key to Birds* 138 Swamp Sparrow, . . . a common inhabitant of low thickets, swamps and marshes. **1917** *Birds of Amer.* III. 54.

+Swamp warbler. Any one of various American warblers found in swamps. Also with specifying terms. — **1865** BURROUGHS in *Atlantic Mo.* May 521/2, I have met here many of the rarer species, such as . . . the Blue-Winged Swamp-Warbler. **1884** COUES *Key to Birds* (ed. 2) 291 *Protonotary.* . . . Golden Swamp Warblers. **1917** *Birds of Amer.* III. 156 Connecticut Warbler, *Oporornis agilis.* . . . [Also called] Swamp Warbler.

+Swamp white oak. An oak found in the East (*Quercus bicolor*); also, the overcup oak (*Q. lyrata*) and the cow oak (*Q. michauxii*). — **1725** *Cambridge Prop. Rec.* 314 We have Settled ye Line . . . to a Swamp white Oak tree mark'd. **1785** MARSHALL *Amer. Grove* 120 Swamp White Oak . . . becomes a pretty large spreading tree. **1832** BROWNE *Sylva* 283 The swamp white oak is a beautiful tree more than 70 feet in height. **1897** SUDWORTH *Arborescent Flora* 155 Overcup Oak. . . . Swamp White Oak (Tex.). *Ib.* 158 Cow Oak. . . . Swamp White Oak (Del., Ala.).

+Swamp willow. =PUSSY WILLOW. — **1795** WINTERBOTHAM *Hist. View* III. 399 Among the native and uncultivated plants of New-England, the following have been employed for medical purposes: . . . Stinging nettle, . . . Swamp willow. **1814** BIGELOW *Florula Bostoniensis* 239 Swamp Willow. . . . A small tree, common in low, moist grounds. **1899** GOING *Flowers* 54 All the earliest tree blossoms, poplar, swamp-willow, elm, and red maple, come out of buds which contain flowers only.

+Swamp wood. a. (See quot. 1668.) *Obs.* Also attrib. **b.** Wood, as firewood, cut from trees in a swamp. **c.** Trees that grow in a swamp; a wood of such trees.

(**a**) **1666** *Plymouth Rec.* 87 On the south side and east side of the said land [I have] bounded it with a swamp wood tree. **1668** *Boston Rec.* 41 A white swamp wood [is] by some called a plumb tree. (**b**) **1670** *Essex Inst. Coll.* XLII. 47 Marshall Skery hath liberty to Cutt . . . swampe wood w[ha]t he needeth. **1683** *Cambridge Prop. Rec.* 158 We found Cutt seuerall heapes of green Swamp wood. (**c**) **1814** J. TAYLOR *Arator* 208, [I] cleared and drained some acres of springy swamp, closely covered with swamp wood. **1851** HALL *Manhattaner* 150 A thick swamp wood on our left, and the turbid Mississippi at our right.

Swampy, *a.* Low-lying; marshy; boggy; situated in a swamp. {1697–}

1649 *Providence Rec.* II. 21 John Jones . . . Sold vnto George Shepard . . . a peece of low Swampey land. **1691** *Essex Inst. Coll.* V. 93/1 That remaining part of fifti foure acres & a quarter . . . [is] upland & Swampie Land. **1716** CHURCH *Philip's War* 31 [He] took into the Woods and Swampy thickets. **1807** IRVING, etc. *Salmagundi* xvi. 421 Others . . . stroll along the borders of a little swampy brook. **1891** WELCH *Recoll. 1830–40* 131 Long stretches of these swampy roads were bridged over by what are known as 'Corduroy Roads.' **1905** PRINGLE *Rice Planter* 184 Every swampy low spot . . . is beautiful with . . . the white iris, or flag.

*Swan, *n.* One or other of several American species of birds of the genus *Cygnus.*

See also AMERICAN SWAN.

1588 HARRIOT *Briefe Rep. Va.* D2 In winter great store of Swannes & Geese [are found]. **1674** *Cal. State P., Amer. & W.I.* VII. 581 [In] Maine . . . the islands and woods yield . . . swans, geese, brants [etc.]. **1778** CARVER *Travels* 55 Great numbers of fowl frequent also this Lake and Rivers adjacent, such as storks, swans, geese, brants, and ducks. **1807** GASS *Journal* 159 The party did not . . . have good luck, having killed only a swan and three ducks. **1883** *Harper's Mag.* Oct. 714/1 Wild duck and geese (and sometimes swans) are found at times in great abundance on the very margin of the [Great Salt] lake. **1917** *Birds of Amer.* I. 164.

+Swan, *v.*

1. *I swan,* I swear. Chiefly an exclamation of surprise. *dial.*

1823 *Mo. Intelligencer* 20 May (Th.), I swan it is. **1838** *Poor Will's Almanack 1839,* And Turkeys as fat as the *dickens,* I never did see such, I swan. **1846** COOPER *Redskins* v, Oh! it isn't gold then—I swan! **1877** 'MARK TWAIN' *Punch, Brothers, Punch!* 33, I swan you've took me mighty unexpect. **1891** GARLAND *Main-travelled Roads* (1922) 108 This must be a surprise party. Wal, I swan! **1917** FREEMAN & KINGSLEY *Alabaster Box* 117 But, I swan! you can't tell that girl nothing.

b. *I swan to man,* a strengthened or intensified form of the preceding, euphemistically used for 'I swear to God.'

1841 *Jamestown* (N.Y.) *Jrnl.* 24 June 1/3 Well, I swan to man, if old Tyler hain't made a fool of himself. **1865** *Atlantic Mo.* June 672/1, I swan to man! natur' was too much for me this time. **1905** LINCOLN *Partners* 7, I swan to man . . . if she didn't stand on the front steps and watch me.

2. *intr.* To swear. *rare.*

1836 DUNLAP *Mem. Water Drinker* (1837) I. 103 Trusty vowed and *swan'd* that he had not come so far for nothing. **1858** *Harper's Mag.* July 277/2 The whining Yankee . . . swans that Butler County is the leetle eend of nothin' whittled eout to a pint.

Swanney. By Swanney, variant of *I swanny*. (Cf. next.) — **1861** *Harper's Mag.* March 462/2 'She's parted her cable, by Swanney!' ejaculated Cap'n Clap.

+Swanny, *v.* [Var. of SWAN *v.*] *I swanny,* I swear. *dial.* — **1839** *Salem Advertiser* 18 Sept. 3/2 (Th.), 'Didn't I tell you Van Buren was not the man?' 'Yes you did, I swanny.' **1843** STEPHENS *High Life N.Y.* II. 132, I swanny, it eenamost made me boo-hoo right out. **1865** *Harper's Mag.* Feb. 325/1, I swanney, their mother does give 'em such dinners Sundays.

Swan shot. Large shot used in shooting swan and other wild fowl. {1719-} — **1639** *New Haven Col. Rec.* 26 Every one that beares armes shall be . . . furnished . . . [with] 4 pound of pistol shott or swan shott at least. **1675** *Essex Inst. Coll.* VIII. 40 One pistole . . . [was] Loaded with Gunpowder and three swann Shot. **1726** PENHALLOW *Indian Wars* 96 The corporal of the troops . . . had five swan-shot in his body. **1788** *Mass. Spy* 10 April 2/2 Wightman . . . was shot through the heart with two balls and three swan shot. **1855** SIMMS *Forayers* 197 'Swan-shot as I live,' said the major.

Swanskin. A fine kind of flannel. {1694-} Also attrib. In full *swanskin flannel.* — **1744** *Md. Hist. Mag.* XXI. 245, 6 Yards Fine Swan Skin Flannel. **1761** *Newport Mercury* 28 April 4/3 Just Imported . . . And to be sold, . . . by John Bours, . . . white and striped swanskin. **1904** CHURCHILL *Crossing* 64 He wore jauntily a swanskin three-cornered hat.

Swap, *v.*

+1. *tr.* To cheat in a trade; also, *absol.,* to rob. Also with *off. colloq.*

1880 HARRIS *Uncle Remus* iv, Den Brer Fox know dat he bin swop off mighty bad. **1888** FERGUSON *Experiences of Forty-Niner* 61 The Crows would rob, or 'swap' as they called it. **1898** HARRIS *Tales of Home Folks* 159 Come, watch me swap him out of his eye teeth.

+2. *To swap lies,* to converse; to tell stories. *colloq.*

1835 LONGSTREET *Ga. Scenes* 233 He begged me . . . to go home with him and swap lies that night. **1864** 'MARK TWAIN' *Sketches* (1926) 143 I have been visiting the Board of Brokers . . . and swapping lies with them. **1887** *Courier-Journal* 6 May 2/2 After supper Gov. Knott . . . and Treasurer Tate sat out in front of the little hotel and began to 'swap lies.' **1902** LORIMER *Lett. Merchant* 217 Most men dropped into Lem's store of an evening, because there was n't any other place to go and swap lies.

b. *To swap stories* (*yarns, words,* etc.), to converse; to tell stories; to exchange confidences, secrets, etc.

1887 *Harper's Mag.* Jan. 222/1 Step out here, an' less me 'n' you swap a few words. **1888** *Scribner's Mag.* Jan. 24/1 The older men . . . stayed at home and swapped stories. **1897** STUART *Simpkinsville* 152, I s'pose you and Mis' Carroll 've been swappin' confidences about garden-truck. **1904** CRISSEY *Tattlings* 412 We didn't swap family secrets for a long time. **1911** BURGESS *Find the Woman* 55 Just a crowd of good fellows that meet every night to swap yarns.

+3. *No time to swap knives,* or variant: No time to change tactics or plans.

1871 in Collins *Kentucky* I. 218 It was 'no time for swapping knives.' **1875** 'MARK TWAIN' *Old Times* vi. 120 It was no time to 'swap knives.' **1884** — *H. Finn* xxxii, There warn't no time to swap knives.

+4. *To swap* (a)*round,* to move from one place or subject to another. *colloq.*

1873 'MARK TWAIN' & WARNER *Gilded Age* 307 Husband says Percy'll die if he don't have a change; and so I'm going to swap round a little and see what can be done. **1892** — *Amer. Claimant* 205 So the chat would swap around to some other subject.

+5. *To swap ends,* to buck. *colloq.*

1879 *Scribner's Mo.* Oct. 888/1 Tony's mule performed the evolution known as 'swapping ends.'

+Swar. (See SWA(A)R.)

Swarming, *a.* In the specific names of insects. — **1876** *Field & Forest* I. 81 Caloptenus spretus, the swarming grasshopper, singularly confirms this law. **1884** *Rep. Comm. Agric.* 413 A Swarming Mite. . . . In May, specimens of one of the almost omnivorous species of the mite-genus . . . were sent.

+Swartwout, *n.* An embezzler. In allusion to Samuel Swartwout, who absconded in 1838 after embezzling more than a million dollars. Also attrib. — **1845** *Xenia Torch-Light* 23 Oct. 2/4 McNulty, soon after his defeat, joined the Swartwout church. **1853** W. ISHAM *Mud Cabin* 159 And have they no Swartwouts of their own here [in England]?

+Swartwout, *v.* [Cf. prec.] *intr.* To abscond with embezzled money. — **1840** *Knickerb.* XVI. 480, [I] live in daily fear of being compelled to 'absquatulate,' or 'Swartwout.' **1845** *Xenia Torch-Light* 31 July 2/5 How natural that the representatives of those who have . . . 'Swartwouted' . . . should compliment a man who proved recreant to . . . his party!

1886 POORE *Reminisc.* I. 128 He 'Swartwouted' (to use a word coined at the time) to avoid a criminal prosecution.

+Swartwouter. =SWARTWOUT *n.* — **1844** *Spirit of Times* (Phila.) 22 Aug. (Th.), 'An English Swartwouter.'—W.S.W., clerk in a Birmingham bank, absconded.

+Swartwouting. Embezzlement. — **1839** *Daily Mercury* (New Bedford) 18 Sept. (Th.), Considerable excitement prevailed at Cincinnati, in consequence of the real or supposed Swartwouting [by a bank cashier]. **1841** CIST *Cincinnati* 176 More Swartwouting. **1876** *Trial W. W. Belknap* 47 'Swartwouting' is equivalent to embezzlement and official peculation.

Swash. +A channel or inlet between sand banks or between a sand bank and the shore. {=E. 'swatch,' 1626-} Also attrib.

1681 in *Amer. Speech* XV. 401/1 Downe the side of James river . . . to a marked willow tree in a small swash. **1740** *S.C. Hist. Soc. Coll.* IV. 77 There was water Enough in the Swash opposite the Castle for the Boats to pass. **1785** WASHINGTON *Diaries* II. 399 We . . . examined a Gut, or swash, through which it is supposed the Navigation must be conducted. **1869** *Bee* (New Orleans) 17 May (De Vere), It is said they took refuge in the swash behind the house. **1885** *Century Mag.* March 742/2 The *Minnesota,* taking the middle or swash channel, steamed up halfway between Old Point and Newport News.

Swat, Swot. A blow. *colloq.* {a1800-, *dial.*} Also fig. — **1848** BARTLETT 347 *Swot,* a violent slap or blow with the open hand. **1894** *Outing* XXIV. 417/2 One 'swat' from his mighty fore-paw . . . may send a man into the happy hunting grounds. **1903** *N.Y. Sun* 4 Dec. 2 In the course of his speech he gave what some of the diners regarded as a swat for the President in the short ribs.

Swath. +To cut a swath, (see CUT *v.* 25 k).

+Sway-back, *a.* Of an animal: Having a sagged back. {s.-backed, 1680-} Also absol. — **1866** 'MARK TWAIN' *Lett. Sandwich Isl.* (1938) 16 Molokai lay like a homely sway-back whale on the water. **1874** *Vermont Bd. Agric. Rep.* II. 402 The buckskin McClellan was a regular hollow or sway back. **1913** BARNES *Western Grazing Grounds* 384 Swaybacks.—Animals whose backs are unusually bent or swayed.

Swear, *v.*

1. *To swear off,* to abjure or forswear, as the use of strong drink. {1896-}

1853 STOWE *Key* 91/2 Well, after all, I suppose, Mr. Legree, you wouldn't have any objections to swarin' off? **1885** *Outing* Oct. 55/1 It's the fashon to 'swear-off' on New Year's. **1902** LORIMER *Lett. Merchant* 148 He wasn't one of those elders who would let a fellow dance the lancers if he'd swear off on waltzing.

+2. *To swear out,* to cause (a warrant) for arrest to be issued by making a charge upon oath; to cause a warrant to be issued on (a certain charge).

1895 *Denver Times* 5 March 8/5 During the scuffle, Miss Alderfer . . . saw the 'black jack' up his sleeve, . . . and as a result, swore out the concealed weapons charge. **1898** HAMBLEN *Gen. Manager's Story* 236 The president [of the railroad] . . . swore out warrants for the arrest of all the members of the committee. **1912** *Times* (London) 19 Oct. 5/6 The warrant was 'sworn out' by the girl's mother at Minneapolis.

+Swearword. A word used in profanity. {1893-} — **1883** A. M. GOW *Primer of Politeness* 58 A youth who mixed his conversation with many swear-words. **1891** *Boston Jrnl.* 3 March 2/3 A long rest from it had permitted a large stock of swear-words to gather. **1898** *Kansas City Star* 21 Dec. 2/5 The answer was a 'swear word.'

Sweat. In special combinations.

Sweat bee, any one of various small bees, esp. of the genera *Andrena* and *Halictus*; *s. collar,* a sweat pad for a horse collar; *s. hole,* =SWEAT HOUSE; *s. lining,* the sweat band of a hat; *s. lodge,* a lodge or tepee in which an Indian takes a sweat bath; *s. mill,* a small hand mill for grinding grain; *s. rag,* a pocket handkerchief, *colloq.*; *s. weed,* a species of rose mallow; *s. work,* hot work. *colloq.*

1894 *Veg., Physiol. & Path. Bul.* (Dept. Agric.) No. 5, 79 The sweat bees of the genus *Halictus* and *Andrena.* **1850** SAWYER *Way Sketches* 107 The harness light, but new and strong, with sweat collars fastened to the main collars. **1806** LEWIS in *L. & Clark Exped.* V. (1905) 61 During the time of his being in the sweat hole, he drank copious draughts of a strong tea of horse mint. **1876** KNIGHT 2706/2 The ventilator for hats consists of a hole in the crown, and a head-band supported at a certain distance from the sweat-lining. **1850** GARRARD *Wah-To-Yah* ii. 35 A few steps from the outside was a 'sweat lodge' . . . into which the medicine men enter before performing their sacred duties. a**1847** in Howe *Hist. Coll. Ohio* 188 Prior to the year 1800, many families used a small hand-mill, properly called a *sweat-mill.* **1843** 'CARLTON' *New Purchase* I. 73 This luxury, however, was used only as 'a sweat rag,' and not as 'a nose-cloth.' **1817-8** EATON *Botany* (1822) 305 *Hibiscus virginicus,* sweat weed. **1852** WATSON *Nights in Block-House* 37 We're goin' to have some sweat-work afore mornin'.

Sweatband. A leather or leatherlike band stitched around the inside of the crown of a hat as a protection against sweat. — **1891** *Pall Mall Gaz.* 28 Sept. 2/3 An American chemist . . . threatens us with lead-poisoning from the 'sweat-band.' **1898** *Mo. So. Dakotan* I. 106 Beneath the sweat band of every union made hat you will find a little square piece of paste board. **1908** 'O. HENRY' *Options* 190 [We] put on the clean collars we brought along inside the sweat-bands of our hats.

+**Sweat board.** A device used in gambling. *Obs.* — **1849** *Knickerb.* XXXIV. 253/1 [The lad] must . . . give bonds not to . . . frequent oyster-cellars, . . . billiard-rooms, sweat-boards [etc.]. **1865** *Nation* I. 371 He was recently the owner of a 'sweat-board,' a singular gambling instrument. **1867** Goss *Soldier's Story* v, Fifty to seventy venders of beans, . . . together with small gamblers with sweat-boards, sat on the ground.

Sweat box. 1. A place of confinement {1888-}; +spec., a place in which a prisoner is questioned. **2.** An extremely hot room or place. — (1) **1888** BILLINGS *Hardtack* 148 Some were put into what was known as the sweat-box. This was a box eighteen inches square, and of the height of a man, into which the culprit was placed to stand until released. **1901** 'FLYNT' *World of Graft* 102 They put him in the sweat-box, made him cough, an' you know the rest. **1910** WALCOTT *Open Door* 88 The patrol-wagon is drawing up at the door now, and we'll have a date for the sweat-box this afternoon. — **(2) 1895** *Pop. Sci. Monthly* XLVI. 345 The sick half-brother sighed when sympathetic visitors crowded around his sweatbox. **1897** *Chicago Tribune* 10 July 1/4 The upper gallery, commonly known as the 'sweat box' in regular theaters.

Sweat cloth. {1894-} +(See quot. 1872.) *Obs.* — **1850** W. RYAN *Adv. Calif.* 126 Several [gamblers] had brought roulette-tables, 'sweat-cloths,' and dice, and banks were immediately established on every available spot. **1872** DE VERE 329 The sweat-cloth, a cloth marked with figures, and used by gamblers with dice.

Sweat house. +A hut, cavern, lodge, or booth in which sweat baths are taken, esp. by Indians; also, the process of taking a sweat bath. {1898}
1731 *Bristol* (Va.) *Vestry Bk.* 54 Walthur Childes & Robert Tucker [procession] . . . up Deep Creek to the sweathouse. **1804** LEWIS in *L. & Clark Exped.* I. (1904) 365, 3 pieces of scarlet one brace in each, which had been left as a sacrifice near one of their swet houses. **1873** BEADLE *Undevel. West* 559 Their physicians treat this disease with the sweat-house. a**1918** G. STUART *On Frontier* II. 43 At the conclusion of this dance the participants take an emetic and then go to the sweat house.

∗**Sweating.**

+**1.** Torturing to obtain a confession; putting one charged with or suspected of a crime through the third degree: (see also quot. 1824). Also attrib.
1824 in J. Hall *Sk. of West* (1835) I. 222 The torture of sweating, . . . that is, of suspension by the arms, pinioned behind the backs, brought a confession. **1890** *Boston Jrnl.* 10 April 2/3 It is curious that in London and New York at the same time there should be a serious revolt against the 'sweating system.' **1904** *Cincinnati Enquirer* 21 Oct. 4 He confessed, under sweating, that he broke into several offices.

2. In special combinations.
Sweating coop, =SWEAT HOUSE; *s. kiln,* a crude drying booth used by Indians; *s. lodge,* =SWEAT HOUSE; *s. weed,* any one of various rose mallows found in the East.
1751 J. BARTRAM *Observations* 33 [The conjurers' tents] differ from their sweating coops, in that they are often far from water, and have a stake by the cage. **1806** LEWIS in *L. & Clark Exped.* IV. (1905) 14 The natives . . . eat these berrys when . . . dryed in the sun or by means of their sw[e]ating kilns. **1848** PARKMAN in *Knickerb.* XXXII. 52 The ashes of some three hundred fires were visible . . . together with the remains of sweating lodges. **1843** TORREY *Flora N.Y.* I. 114 *Hibiscus Virginicus.* Virginian Hibiscus. Sweating-weed. . . . Borders of salt marshes on the north side of Long Island.
Sweating house. =SWEAT HOUSE. *Obs.* {1664-} — **1705** BEVERLEY *Virginia* III. 51 In every Town they have a Sweating-house, and a Doctor is paid by the Pubiick to attend it. **1791** J. LONG *Voyages* 47 A sweating-house is prepared with six long poles fixed in the ground. **1847** COYNER *Lost Trappers* 52 A vapor bath, or sweating house, is 'a hollow square, of six or eight feet deep, formed against the river bank, by damming up, with mud, the other three sides, and covering the top completely, except an aperture about two feet wide.'

+**Sweatshop.** A room or shop in which employees work long hours under unsanitary conditions for insufficient wages. Also attrib. — **1895** *Westminster Gaz.* 2 Nov. 2/3 All but fifteen of the 385 wholesale clothing manufacturers in New York have made goods made in 'sweat shops.' **1901** HARRIGAN *Mulligans* 162 Sweatshop troopers are paid but little. **1911** ROLT-WHEELER *Boy with Census* 317 Any of these sweatshop jobbers will give [work] to them. **1914** *Cycl. Amer. Govt.* III. 464/1 A number of states require that all sweatshops be licensed.

Swede. The rutabaga. {1812-} Also *Swede turnip.* (See also SWEDISH TURNIP.) — **1822** WOODS *English Prairie* 215 Swede turnips but little known here. **1835** SHIRREFF *Tour* 58 Some good crops were seen, more especially Indian corn and Swede turnip. **1856** *Rep. Comm. Patents 1855: Agric.* 262 The Swedes were transplanted in drills August 4th. **1863** RANDALL *Pract. Shepherd* 239 That acre does very poorly that does not produce 500 bushels of Swedes.

Swedenborgian. A believer in the religious teachings of Emanuel Swedenborg (1688-1772) of Sweden. {1810-} — **1802** CUTLER in *Life & Corr.* II. 114 In the evening the Swedenborgian preached in the Hall. **1821** WELBY *Visit N. Amer.* 177 We have lately attended services at the churches of the Anabaptists, the Swedenborgians, &c. **1868** BEECHER *Sermons* (1869) I. 123, I am . . . a Swedenborgian. **1900** *Scribner's Mag.* Sept. 369/1 Mrs. Lowell was also a Swedenborgian.

Swedes iron. [Prob. ad. Du. *zweeds(ch) ijzer.*] Iron obtained from Sweden. Also attrib. — **1704** *Boston News-Letter* 3 July 2/2 There's a parcel of Spanish and Swedes Iron to be Sold. **1790** [see GERMAN STEEL]. **1881** *Century Mag.* Nov. 134/1 Nothing had given him more delight than . . . to discuss with him . . . the economy of 'Swedes iron' nails.

Swedish, *a.* In special combinations.
Swedish bitters, (see quotation); *s. clover,* a species of clover introduced into this country from Europe and valued for forage; *S. Nightingale,* Jenny Lind (1820-87), of Stockholm, a celebrated singer; *S. steel,* steel from Sweden or made by a Swedish process.
1890 BILLINGS *Nat. Medical Dict.* II. 629/1 *Swedish bitters,* compound tincture of aloes. **1855** Swedish clover [see ALSIKE]. **1855** BARNUM *Life* 296 This speculation . . . must prove immensely profitable, provided I could engage the 'Swedish Nightingale' on any terms within the range of reason. **1897** *Outing* XXX. 278/1 This tubing is made from ingots of Swedish steel.

Swedish turnip. The rutabaga. {c1791-} — **1806** MacMAHON *Amer. Gard. Cal.* 427 The Swedish turnep, or *Roota Baga,* as it is called, . . . requires to be sown in a different season. **1847** WOOD *Botany* 171 Swedish Turnip. . . . Cultivated like the common turnip; but . . . conceded by farmers to be inferior in value.

+**Sweenied,** *a.* Suffering from or affected by sweeny. — **1871** *Rep. Indian Affairs* (1872) 554 The three mules were thin, one of them lame in the right shoulder, 'sweenied.'

+**Sweeny.** Also **swinny.** [App. f. G. dial. *schweine* 'emaciation.'] Atrophy of the muscles of the shoulder in a horse. Also transf. and fig. — **1832** KENNEDY *Swallow Barn* II. 22 He professed to cure the colt's distemper, sweeny, and other maladies. **1866** C. H. SMITH *Bill Arp* 128 Thar was nary one but what had the dyspepsy or the swinny. **1872** MORRELL *Flowers & Fruits* 114 A few such purchases would give my pocketbook the swinny. **1892** *York County Hist. Rev.* 50 Hanes' Liniment is positively the . . . Most Sure and Certain Cure for . . . Sweeney, Scratches, Bruises in animals.

∗**Sweep.** +**a.** An elastic pole or lever arranged to give assistance in pounding Indian corn in a mortar. *Obs.* +**b.** One who takes care of the rooms of college students. *Obs.* +**c.** A triangular plowshare used in the shallow cultivation of row crops.
(a) 1824 DODDRIDGE *Notes* 141 The sweep was sometimes used to lessen the toil of pounding grain into meal. **1852** REYNOLDS *Hist. Illinois* 144 A sweep is prepared over the mortar, so that the spring of the pole raises the piston, and the hands at it force it so hard down on the corn, that after much beating, meal is manufactured. **(b) 1846** *Yale Banger* 10 Nov., A Freshman by the faithful sweep, Was found half buried in soft sleep. **1853** Root & Lombard *Songs of Yale* 12 A College Sweep went dustily 'round, Plying his yellow broom. **(c) 1852** *Fla. Plantation Rec.* 65, [I] sent back the six sweeps. **1854** *Ib.* 104 Swepes 35, corn plowes 20.

Sweeping day. A day upon which the sweeping in a household is done. — **1882** *Century Mag.* Oct. 828 [She] lef' sweepin'-day out o' the almanic, washed dishes in cold water. **1889** *Ib.* June 180 Friday . . . was general sweeping-day at Mrs. Dansken's.

∗**Sweepings.** *pl.* +(See quot. 1871.) *slang. Obs.* — **1868** *Putnam's Mag.* I. 668/2 The sweepin's of the post-office is about three thousand a-year. **1871** DE VERE 264 *Sweepings* are more exclusively the side-earnings of lucrative offices.

+**Sweep-rake (reaper).** (See quot. 1883.) — **1876** *Vermont Bd. Agric. Rep.* III. 610 The sweep-rake reaper is now so perfect a machine that it will reap grain so badly lodged that it is with difficulty that it can be mown with a scythe. **1883** KNIGHT *Suppl.* 876/1 *Sweep Rake,* the rake that clears the table of a self-rake reaper. **1910** *Encycl. Brit.* (ed. 11) XIII. 108/1 An American invention known as the sweep rake was introduced . . . into England in 1894.

∗**Sweet,** *a.*

1. In the names of, or with reference to, plants and trees.
1787 *Amer. Acad. Mem.* II. II. 156 Sugar Tree or sweet Maple . . . ; very beneficial to the country. **1832** WILLIAMSON *Maine* I. 107 The former [black elder], called 'Sweet Elder,' has handsome blossoms. **1845** DE SMET *Oregon Missions* 117 The sweet onion . . . bears a lovely flower resembling the tulip. **1850** *Rep. Comm. Patents 1849: Agric.* 156 In wettish flat lands, several varieties of *Panicum crus-galli* . . . grow vigorously, not unfrequently mixed with *cyperus repens,* sweet coco, or nut grass. **1850** SAWYER *Way Sketches* 31 There is some sweet poplar on the island. **1867** Sweet coltsfoot [see COLTSFOOT 2]. **1873** BEADLE *Undevel. West* 641 A species of milky weed, with tough, stringy root, in taste resembling the 'sweet hickory' the boys used to pull and chew. **1894** *Amer. Folk-Lore* VII. 96 *Melissa officinalis,* . . . sweet Mary, lemon-lobelia (pronounced lobely), N.E. **1913** BARNES *Western Grazing Grounds* 57 The forage is greatly augmented by the great sage family, especially the sweet sage or 'winter fat' (*Eurotia lanata*). **1915** *Dept. Agric. Bul.* No. 209, 14 *V[itis] monticola* (sweet mountain grape): Texas. . . . [Vine] rather small; good grower.

2. In special combinations.
Sweet drinking, the drinking of sweetened liquors; *s. girl graduate,* a complimentary or jocular way of referring to a girl who has just graduated; *s. marten, s. scents,* (see quotations); *s. sixteen,* the age of sixteen banteringly regarded as the most desirable for a girl or woman; *s. soap,* fragrantly scented soap of superior quality or mildness; *S. South,* a complimentary term for the South; *s. toddy,* toddy that is unusually sweet; *s. trade,* confectionery. *colloq.*

1847 ROBB *Squatter Life* 57 On the last visit, good cause was given for an end being put to any more 'sweet drinking.' **1882** Sweet girl graduate [see PATENT INSIDES]. **1840** EMMONS *Mass. Quadrupeds* 41 The Marten . . . [emits] rather an agreeable odor, and is hence termed the sweet Marten. **1794** *Ann. 3d Congress* 1472 There shall be levied . . . [on all] preparations or compositions, commonly called sweet scents, . . . 5 per cent. ad valorem. **1833** NEAL *Down-Easters* I. 155 All women wish to be, 'Sweet sixteen.' **1892** *Harper's Mag.* May 936/2 Strongly scented sweet soap of a marbleized reddish color lay wrapped in tin-foil. **1859** WILMER *Press Gang* 69 He left the 'Quaker City,' and removed further toward the 'Sweet South.' **1867** HARRIS *Sut Lovingood* 138 She sed tu the gals, 'Sweet toddy, huggin, dancin, an' huggers in 'bundunce.' **1899** A. BROWN *Tiverton Tales* 31 Betsy Marden's darter Ann rode down to the poor-house t'other day with some sweet trade.

Sweet bay. {1716–} **a.** = SMALL MAGNOLIA. **b.** = RED BAY. — **1766** J. BARTRAM *Journal* 29 On it grew great magnolia, sweet-bay, live-oak, palms. **1806** *Ann. 9th Congress* 2 Sess. 1116 Bailing it, from time to time, upon sweet bay leaves, restores its sweetness. **1857** GRAY *Botany* 16. **1897** SUDWORTH *Arborescent Flora* 201 *Persea borbonia.* Red Bay. . . . [Also called] Sweet Bay (Fla.).

+Sweet birch. One or other species of birch, esp. *Betula lenta,* found in the East. — **1785** MARSHALL *Amer. Grove* 18 *Betula nigra.* Black, or Sweet-Birch. . . . A large tree, often rising to the height of fifty or sixty feet. **1884** SARGENT *Rep. Forests* 162. **1897** SUDWORTH *Arborescent Flora* 141 *Betula occidentalis.* Cañon Birch. . . . [Also called] Sweet Birch (Idaho). **1905** *Forestry Bureau Bul.* No. 60, 13 The proportion of sweet birch in the stand is large.

+Sweet bough. A variety of apple or apple tree. — **1850** *Rep. Comm. Patents 1849: Agric.* 281 Of summer apples, the best and most productive are the early-harvest and early sweet-bough. **1875** BURROUGHS *Winter Sunshine* 161 Whether the pippin and sweetbough bear or not, the 'punctual birds' can always be depended on. **1906** *Harper's Mag.* April 667 He halted under the sweet-bough and gave one branch a shake, and then . . . he crossed the sward to . . . the wall.

Sweet clover. Any one of various clovers, esp. bokhara clover. — **1868** WHITTIER *Poetical Works* (♦894) 260 A drowsy smell of . . . white sweet-clover, . . . Comes faintly in. **1892** *Amer. Folk-Lore* V. 94 *Trifolium pratense,* 'real sweet clover.' Mass. and parts of Me.

+Sweet corn. a. Indian corn in the milk or roasting-ear stage. **b.** Any one of several varieties of Indian corn the kernels of which are rich in sugar.
1646 *Mass. H. S. Coll.* 4 Ser. VI. 334 Wequash Cooks brother tooke from him . . . 2 bushell of sweet corne. **1677** WINTHROP in *Phil. Trans.* XII. 1067 The Indians have another sort of Provision out of this Corn, which they call Sweet-Corn. **1808** [see BUFFALO 5]. **1842** *S. Lit. Messenger* VIII. 582/1 They now pull much of their corn while it is in the milk, and dry it carefully in the sun: it is then called 'sweet corn.' **1894** *Vt. Agric. Rep.* XIV. 45 Is there any more nutrition in sweet corn than in other kinds? *attrib.* **1882** *Maine Bd. Agric. Rep.* XXVI. 17 Good corn stalks . . . with plenty of sweet corn meal to go with them will make butter that will bring the highest prices. **1903** 'O. HENRY' *Roads of Destiny* 364 Cigarettes rolled with sweet corn husk were as honey to Buck's palate; . . . [but] he never could learn to roll a cigarette.

✳Sweetening. +Molasses, sugar, or sweetmeats. *colloq.* (Cf. LONG, SHORT SWEETENING.) — **1851** *Polly Peablossom* 165 Both of them took seats by the fire; the table between them, and liquor and sweetenin' plenty. **1860** OLMSTED *Back Country* 241 [She] had taken pains to boil in some sweetenin' (molasses) on my account. **1878** COOKE *Happy Dodd* 290 They set on the sweetenin' fust. **1905** *Dialect Notes* III. 97 *Sweetnin',* sugar, molasses, syrup.

Sweet fern. {1787–}
+1. a. Any one of various ferns of the genus *Dryopteris.* **b.** A small shrub (*Comptonia asplenifolia*) having fernlike leaves. **c.** = POLYPOD(Y).
1654 JOHNSON *Wonder-w. Prov.* 81 The sweet Ferne, whose scent is very strong so that some herewith have beene very nere fainting. **1778** CARVER *Travels* 504 Juniper, Shrub Oak, Sweet Fern, the Laurel [are native shrubs]. **1832** WILLIAMSON *Maine* I. 118 *Sweet-fern* is much smaller and of less notoriety, than the Rose-bush, though its leaves are wholesome in diet-drink. **1869** [see BAYBERRY 2]. **1896** JEWETT *Pointed Firs* 213 The darker green of the sweet-fern was scattered on all the pasture heights. **1909** WEBSTER 2093/1 *S[weet] fern,* any of several buckler ferns (*Dryopteris*).

2. Attrib. with *bush, cigar, couch, mattress.*
1814 PURSH *Flora Amer.* II. 635 The Sweet-fern Bush rises to about three or four feet high. **1869** ALCOTT *Little Women* II. 358 Tommy Bangs will smoke sweet-fern cigars under the bed-clothes. **1877** *Harper's Mag.* Feb. 454/2 Laying himself at length upon Nikomis's sweet-fern mattress, he began a leisurely account of his adventures. **1886** *Outing* IX. 102/1 Then to our sweet-fern couch we crept and dreamed away.

Sweet flag. An herb (*Acorus calamus*) that grows in water and in marshy places. {1796–} Also attrib. — **1784** *Amer. Acad. Mem.* I. 435 Sweet Flag. Spicewort. The roots and blossoms are aromatic and pungent. **1804** ORDWAY in *Journals of Lewis & O.* 99 He found Callimous (sweet flag we call it) opposite where we camped. **1878** STOWE *Poganuc People* 217 You can find some of them sweet-flag 'graters' if you want. **1919** STURTEVANT *Notes on Edible Plants* 23 Sweet Flag. . . . The rhizomes are used by confectioners as a candy.

+Sweet gum.
1. A North American tree (*Liquidambar styraciflua*), the copalm.
1700 *Md. Hist. Mag.* XIX. 367, 127 acre Sur[veyed] . . . for Samuell Baker Lyeing betwixt rumley & delph Creek begun at a bounded sweet gum. **1789** *Amer. Philos. Soc.* III. p. xviii, Dysentery has been cured by the bark and gumm of . . . Sweet-gum; . . . Hounds-tongue. **1806** *Ann. 9th Congress* 2 Sess. 1141 [In the vicinity of the Washita there are] three kinds of ash, . . . sweet gum, black gum [etc.]. **1897** W. E. BARTON *Trouble at Roundstone* 144 The sweet gum was glorious in its autumn dress. **1906** [see BLACK GUM 2].
b. The gum exuded from a cut or bruise on this tree.
1896 HARRIS *Sister Jane* 26 She came to my house the other day, with her little brother, hunting sweet-gum.
2. Attrib. with *ball, corner tree, leaf,* etc.
1709 LAWSON *Carolina* 95 The sweet Gum-Tree, so call'd, because of the fragrant Gum it yields in the Spring-time, upon Incision of the Bark, or Wood. **1835** *Survey of Property* Nov., (Pettigrew P.), To a littel sweet Gum corner Tree. **1850** LEWIS *La. Swamp Doctor* 150 How learnedly we discoursed upon 'yarbs,' and 'kumfrey tea,' and 'sweet gum sav'! **1866** C. H. SMITH *Bill Arp* 61, I found Dick ploughing away down in a field close by a sweet-gum swamp. **1887** *Harper's Mag.* Dec. 72/2 He had found . . . a sweet-gum ball and a pine cone. **1909** RICE *Mr. Opp* 122 There's some pretty sweet-gum leaves.

+Sweetleaf. A tree (*Symplocos tinctoria*) found in the South. — **1814** PURSH *Flora Amer.* II. 451 *Hopea tinctoria* . . . is known by the inhabitants under the name of Sweet-leaf. **1832** BROWNE *Sylva* 167 The Sweet Leaf is common in Virginia. **1883** [see JUNIPER 1].

+Sweet locust. = HONEY LOCUST a. — **1832** BROWNE *Sylva* 161 The Sweet Locust belongs peculiarly to the country west of the Alleghanies. **1884** SARGENT *Rep. Forests* 59.

+Sweet magnolia. The sweet bay (*Magnolia virginiana*) of the Atlantic coast region. — **1878** WHITMAN *Spec. Days* 123 These perennial blossoms and friendly weeds [include] . . . sweet magnolia, milk-weed, wild daisy. **1897** [see BEAVER TREE].

✳Sweet oil. Any mild oil that is edible. — **1705** *Boston News-Letter* 10 Dec. 4/2 To be Sold in Boston. . . . Sweet Oyl, Indigo, Brasilet, Cocoa. **1790** *Penna. Packet* 1 Jan. 4/1 E. Dutilh & Wachsmuth . . . Have for Sale . . . Sweet oil in hampers. **1812** *Niles' Reg.* II. 86/2 Sweet and castor oil is made in great abundance on the sea coast of Georgia. **1889** HOWELLS *Hazard of Fortunes* I. 104 He thought it was sweet-oil.

+Sweet pepper bush. Any one of various species of *Clethra* having fragrant flowers. — **1836** LINCOLN *Botany* App. 88 *Clethra.* . . . Sweet pepper-bush. **1860** CURTIS *Woody Plants N.C.* 100 Sweet Pepper-Bush . . . Grows near damp places. **1901** MOHR *Plant Life Ala.* 652 Sweet Pepper Bush. . . . Common in the Coast plain on swampy banks of pine-barren streams.

+Sweet potato.
1. A vine (*Ipomoea batatas*), or its farinaceous root valued as food.
1750 J. BIRKET *Cursory Remarks* 9 They have . . . abundance of . . . the Sweet Potatoe. **1797** MORSE *Amer. Gazetteer* s.v. *Kentucky.* Sweet potatoes are raised with difficulty. **1823** JAMES *Exped.* III. 140 Sweet potatoes are produced in great perfection in many parts of the Arkansa territory. **1890** *Stock Grower & Farmer* 22 Feb. 8/4 Sweet potatoes yield from 250 to 300 bushels to the acre [in the Pecos valley]. **1916** THOBURN *Stand. Hist. Okla.* I. 260 In such fields they raised crops of corn, beans, squash, melons, sweet potatoes and a few other vegetables.

2. *attrib.* Designating various foods prepared from sweet potatoes.
1828 LESLIE *Receipts* 21 Sweet Potato Pudding. **1829** FLINT *G. Mason* 19 There was no . . . deficiency of custards, delicious sweet potatoe pies, and various wild fruits. **1867** Goss *Soldier's Story* 227 A friend gave me . . . wheat bread and sweet potato soup. **1877** BARTLETT 686 *Sweet Potato Pone,* sweet potatoes, flavored with spices, and baked in a tin pan.

3. In special combinations.
Sweet-potato beetle, any one of various beetles that eat the leaves of sweet potatoes; *s. patch,* a patch of sweet potatoes; *s. rot,* a rot which affects sweet potatoes.
1861 *Ill. Agric. Soc. Trans.* V. 432 The 'Sweet Potato Beetle' . . . depredates upon the leaves and stems of sweet potatoes. c**1862** BAGBY *Old Va. Gentleman* 84 There is a wagon-way which runs in a straight line by the sweet-potato patch. **1890** *Rep. Secy. Agric. 1889* 420 The special subjects under investigation in the laboratory have been . . . sweet-potato rot, pear blight, peach yellows.

Sweet scabious. 1. A European plant, *Scabiosa atropurpurea,* introduced into the United States. {1796–} **+2.** A plant of the genus *Erigeron.* — **(1)** **1817–8** EATON *Botany* (1822) 449. **1868** GRAY *Field Botany* 178 Sweet Scabious, or when with dark purple or crimson flowers called Mourning Bride. **1913** BRITTON & BROWN *Illustrated Flora* III. 440 Sweet Scabious. White-top. . . . Kentucky and Missouri. **(2)** **1828** RAFINESQUE *Medical Flora* I. 162 *Erigeron Philadelphicum.* . . . Vulgar Names—Skevish, Scabish, Sweet Scabious [etc.]. **1898** CREEVEY *Flowers of Field* 242 Daisy Fleabane. Sweet Scabious. *E[rigeron] annuus.* . . . The flowers have many long, fine rays.

⁕ **Sweet-scented**, *a.* In the specific names of plants.
1785 MARSHALL *Amer. Grove* 152 *Thuya odorata*, American Sweet-scented Arbor Vitae, . . . [has] an agreeable or sweet scent, when bruised. **1795** WINTERBOTHAM *Hist. View* III. 392 Sweet-scented crab apple-tree. **1814** BIGELOW *Florula Bostoniensis* 59 *Viola blanda*. Sweet scented white violet. . . . Flowers white with purple veins at bottom. **1843** TORREY *Flora N.Y.* I. 131 *Rhus aromatica*. Sweet-scented Sumach. . . . Dry rocky hills and gravelly banks. **1884** SARGENT *Rep. Forests* 72 *Pyrus coronaria*. . . . American Crab. Sweet-scented Crab. . . . Often planted for ornament.

+**Sweet-scented shrub.** A shrub having exceptionally fragrant flowers or leaves, esp. the strawberry bush of the genus *Calycanthus*. — **1786** WASHINGTON *Diaries* III. 53 Planted . . . 6 of the Sweet scented, or aromatic shrubs in my Shrubberies. **1859** BARTLETT 7 The 'sweet-scented shrub' . . . is also known as Carolina Allspice, the bark and wood having a somewhat spicy flavor. **1893** *Amer. Folk-Lore* VI. 141 *Calycanthus floridus*, sweet-scented shrub. . . . E. Mass.

Sweet-scented (tobacco). A variety of tobacco the leaves of which have an especially agreeable odor. Also attrib. — [**1666** *Essex Rev.* XVII. 133 One hogshead of Sweet-sented tobacco, lodgd in Cornwall.] **1690** *Va. State P.* I. 25 The sweet scented Tobacco of this Colony may be improv'd. **1724** JONES *Virginia* 40 There are two Sorts of Tobacco, viz. Oroonoko the stronger, and Sweetscented the milder. **1764** WASHINGTON *Diaries* I. 201 Trimmed up 52 heads of Tobo. at Creek Quarter for Sweet scented Seed. **1800** TATHAM *Tobacco* 4 The different species of the genus have been in former days distinguished in Virginia by the names of Oronoko, sweet scented, and little Frederic.

Sweet-scented vernal grass. An Old World grass (*Anthoxanthum odoratum*) introduced into the United States. {1796–} — **1793** *N.Y. State Soc. Arts* I. 181. **1814** BIGELOW *Florula Bostoniensis* 8 Sweet scented vernal grass . . . when partly faded, is exceedingly fragrant. **1855** BROWNE in *Amer. Inst. N.Y. Trans. 1854* 620. **1878** KILLEBREW *Tenn. Grasses* 199 Sweet-scented Vernal Grass . . . possesses rather poor qualities as a pasture grass.

+**Sweet sucker. a.** A chub sucker, *Erimyzon oblongus.* **b.** = GOURDSEED SUCKER. — **1884** GOODE, etc. *Fisheries* I. 614 The 'Chub Sucker,' 'Sweet Sucker,' or 'Creek-fish' is one of the most abundant and widely diffused of the Suckers. **1911** [see MISSOURI SUCKER].

+**Sweet viburnum.** The sheepberry, *Viburnum lentago.* — **1843** TORREY *Flora N.Y.* I. 305 Sweet Viburnum. . . . The fruit is rather palatable, especially after having been frozen. **1861** WOOD *Botany* 398 Sweet Viburnum. . . . A common tree-like shrub, in rocky woods. **1892** APGAR *Trees Northern U.S.* 114.

⁕ **Sweet william. a.** A pink (*Dianthus barbatus*) introduced into the United States from Europe. +**b.** The scarlet lychnis, *Lychnis chalcedonica.* — **1737** [see PINK² 1]. **1810** M. DWIGHT *Journey to Ohio* 34 On the first mountain, I found some Sweet Williams. **1892** *Amer. Folk-Lore* V. 93 *Lychnis chalcedonica*, sweetwilliam. Weathersfield, Vt. **1907** *St. Nicholas* Oct. 1067 Sweet-william, four-o'clocks . . . and things All bordered 'round with box.

⁕ **Swell**, *n.* An area or extent of rising land. {with qualifying phrase, 1764–; absol., 1792–}
'Orig. with qualifying phr., e.g. *swell of ground*, which is still usually felt to be necessary by English writers; the absol. use is specially American' (*O.E.D.*).
1808 PIKE *Sources Miss.* II. App. 3 The extensive prairies . . . [are] gently diversified by the rising swells. **1832** WILLIAMSON *Maine* I. 20 Skirting these waters and the streams that enlarge them, are innumerable vallies, swells, and ridges. **1872** TICE *Over Plains* 33, I went to the southwest of the town, which stands upon a considerable swell. **1889** MUNROE *Golden Days* 88 It occupied a commanding position on a grassy swell a few hundred yards back from the river.

Swell-, stem of *swell v.* {1817–} In special combinations.
Swell-butted, s. shark, (see quotations); *s.-skull whisky*, = BUSTHEAD. *slang.*
1905 *Forestry Bureau Bul.* No. 61, 50 *Swell butted*, as applied to a tree, greatly enlarged at the base. **1891** *Cent.* 5436/1 *S*[*cyllium*] *ventricosum* is the swell-shark, a small voracious species found on the Pacific coast from California to Chili. **1867** HARRIS *Sut Lovingood* 233 She fotch a glass bottil ove swell-skull whiskey outen the three-cornered cupboard.

+**Swelled neck.** Goiter. *Obs.* — **1832** BAIRD *Valley Miss.* 74 Goiter, or 'swelled neck,' once prevailed on the upper waters of the Ohio. **1863** RANDALL *Pract. Shepherd* 152, I never have applied any remedy whatever for 'swelled neck.'

+**Swellfish.** Any one of various fishes capable of inflating the body; a puffer or globefish. — **1807** *Mass. H. S. Coll.* 2 Ser. III. 55 The puff fish, or swell fish, or bellows fish, is a cartilaginous fish. **1839** STORER *Mass. Fishes* 169 *T*[*etraodon*] *turgidus.* . . . The Swell Fish. . . . This very curious fish . . . receives its name from its power of inflating itself. **1897** [see PUFFER 1]. **1911** *Rep. Fisheries 1908* 317/1 Swell-fish (*Tetraodontidae*).—The different species are known as . . . 'puffers,' 'swell-toad,' etc.

+**Swell front.** A house front that is rounded or curved. — **1848** N. DEARBORN *Boston Notions* 350 The building is of brick, with an imposing agreeable swell front projecting twelve feet. **1871** HOWELLS *Wedding Journey* 58 A humble three-story swell-front up at the South End is no longer the place for me. **1886** *Century Mag.* May 243/1 In the central house, the 'swell front' and domed roof of which make it somewhat more pretentious than the wings, are feather and fan palms.

+**Swell head.** A person inordinately conceited or vain. Also jocose and attrib. — **1845** HOOPER *Simon Suggs' Adv.* iv, As for the present directory, they're all a pack of d——o swell-heads. **1852** *Congress. Globe* App. 29 April 519 The hard-fisted yeomanry of the country . . . pay to the swell-head aristocracy of Virginia from one third to one half of their labor in the shape of rent. **1873** C. GORDON *Boarding-School Days* 35 Where's Bullock and Gracie?—don't see them with you swell-heads lately.

+**Swelltoad.** = SWELLFISH. — **1878** *Nat. Museum Proc.* I. 366 *Chilomycterus geometricus.* Swell-toad. . . . Sold by small boys as curiosities. **1911** [see SWELLFISH].

⁕ **Swift.**
1. Any of several small birds of the family Apodidae {1668–}, +esp. the chimney swift. Also with specifying terms.
1839 AUDUBON *Ornith. Biog.* V. 419 [The] American Swift . . . inhabits the Rocky Mountains. **1849** — *Western Jrnl.* 129, I saw fifteen or twenty swifts. **1858** BAIRD *Birds Pacific R.R.* 141 *Panyptila melanoleuca*, White-throated Swift. . . . The prevailing color of the upper parts is of a sooty black. **1917** *Birds of Amer.* II. 175 The Black Swifts in Nevada . . . were 'perfectly silent.'

+**2.** Short for SWIFT LIZARD. {1530–, a newt}
1842 *Nat. Hist. N.Y., Zoology* III. 33 The Brown Swift . . . is also called the Brown Scorpion, and its activity has doubtless suggested the name of Swift. **1887** CUSTER *Tenting on Plains* 122 The lizards the Texans call swifts . . . also haunted the tangles of the moss.

+**3.** Short for SWIFT FOX.
1877 CAMPION *On Frontier* 132 Of foxes there were . . . many 'swifts'—the last-mentioned a species of fox I have rarely met with. **1881** CHASE *Editor's Run in N. Mex.* 86 The prairies [near Cimarron] still abound with antelope, swift, . . . and coyote. **1897** HOUGH *Story of Cowboy* 42 At these red or tawny blotches which lie about over the landscape the coyotes are feeding, then the foxes and swifts.

+**Swift fox.** The kit fox, *Vulpes velox.* — **1869** *Amer. Naturalist* III. 476 Visiting a steel trap which I had set . . . I was surprised to find in it a Swift Fox. **1917** *Mammals of Amer.* 77/1 The Kit, or Swift Fox, . . . is a much smaller animal than the Red and Gray Foxes.

Swift lizard. A swift-running lizard, +esp. the fence lizard. {1802} Cf. SWIFT 2. — **1778** CARVER *Travels* 489 The Swift Lizard is about six inches long, and has four legs and a tail.

+**Swift witness.** ?A witness who is eager to testify. — **1857** *Lawrence (Kan.) Republican* 11 June 3 [A] lady appeared at the police court yesterday, with a bundle of hair in her hands as 'swift witness' against one Mary Bolle. **1884** BLAINE *20 Years of Congress* I. 383 The stories told by many of these swift witnesses were on the surface absurd.

⁕ **Swill.** Attrib. and comb. with *barrel, collector*, etc.
1741 *Boston News-Letter* 12 Feb. 2/1 Taken up by John Morey, Esq. . . . a Swill-Pale, otherwise called a Hog-Pale. **1843** 'CARLTON' *New Purchase* I. 102 Swiney becomes wholly savage and loses all reverence for corn-cribs and swill-tubs. **1869** M. STOWE *Oldtown Folks* 469 Miss Krissy Pike still went on reporting the wasteful excesses she had seen in the minister's swill-barrel. **1872** BRACE *Dangerous Classes N.Y.* 154 The life of a swill-gatherer, or coal-picker, or *chiffonnier* in the streets soon wears off a girl's modesty. **1874** *Vermont Bd. Agric. Rep.* II. 512 In said basement I have . . . also a swill-room. **1912** DREISER *Financier* 128 Butler could be made official swill-collector.

+**Swill boy.** (See quotation.) — **1859** BARTLETT 467 *Swill-Boys*, a gang of New York rowdies.

+**Swill milk.** Milk from cows fed on the refuse from distilleries. Also attrib. — **1858** C. FLINT *Milch Cows* 208 The nefarious traffic in 'swill-milk,' or milk produced from cows fed entirely on 'still-slops.' **1887** *Science* 1 Ser. X. 72 Parties who produce swill-milk for sale in large cities find swill to be the cheapest food for the production of milk. **1894** FORD *P. Stirling* 72 The press began, too, a crusade against the swill-milk dealers.

⁕ **Swim**, *v.* +*tr.* (See quot. 1864.) — **1790** S. DEANE *New-Eng. Farmer* 16/2 Swimming the barley before it is sowed, will in great measure prevent [mixture of oats]. **1864** WEBSTER 1339/2 *Swim*, . . . to immerse in water that the lighter parts may swim; as, to *swim* wheat for seed.

+**Swimming hole.** A place in a stream used for swimming. — **1867** [see CRICK]. **1883** SHIELDS *S. S. Prentiss* 21 It was one of the delights of the boys to bathe in the swimming-holes of Fairchild's Creek. **1906** LYNDE *Quickening* 58 His lip curled stiffly at the thought of a girl . . . dividing the sovereignty of . . . the swimming-hole . . . with him.

+**Swimming market.** A buoyant market. — **1870** MEDBERY *Men Wall St.* 138 *Swimming market*, the opposite of a sick market. **1885** *Harper's Mag.* Nov. 841/2 He . . . has a 'swimming market' when all is buoyant. **1900** NELSON *A B C Wall St.* 161.

Swimming pool. A pool of water for swimming. {1932} — **1899** *Scribner's Mag. Advt.* 26/2 There is a sombre marble swimming pool, where the water is tempered according to season. **1924** *Lit. Digest* 25 Oct. 24/1 A great majority of the States have passed and have in operation regulations governing the use and care of swimming pools.

Swindle. {1852–}
+**1.** The charge for something. *slang.*
1835 *Knickerb.* V. 146, [I] desired to know what the swindle would be for a new set of buttons. **1853** *Harper's Mag.* Aug. 424/1 After 'dickering' some time with the long-legged door-keeper, he disbursed 'the swindle,' as he called it,—a quarter of a dollar. **1871** DE VERE 576 When he [a

Western man] wishes to know what he has to pay, he asks, What's the damage? or, not so charitably, What's the swindle?

2. Anything that is less than advertised or less than it appears to be. {1882}

1866 HOWELLS *Venetian Life* 4 Let us take, for example, that pathetic swindle, the Bridge of Sighs. **1869** 'MARK TWAIN' *Innocents* 48 'This thing's a swindle!' 'What's a swindle?' 'Why, this watch.'

∗ Swine.

∗1. Any animal of the hog kind. Usually pl.

1622 'MOURT' *Relation* 48 [The two grampuses] were some fiue or six paces long, . . . and fleshed like a Swine. **1637** *Plymouth Laws* 58 All Swine . . . shalbe sufficiently ringed. **1687** *East-Hampton Rec.* II. 207 All swine that goe in the Towne or Limits thereof unyoaked are poundable. **1709** LAWSON *Carolina* 80 Our Stocks of Horses, Cattle, Sheep and Swine multiply. **1798** I. ALLEN *Hist. Vermont* 276 A swine is said to be the only animal that is found from pole to pole, capable of contending with rattlesnakes. **1861** *Ind. Bd. Agric. Rep. 1859–60* 285 One [disease], among swine, has . . . been made the object of special investigation. **1883** ALLEN *New Farm Book* 477 Swine are profitable in connection with a dairy or orchard.

2. *attrib.* and *comb.* **a.** With *breeder, drover,* etc.

1640 *Conn. Rec.* I. 445 Abraham Fynch, when he deceased . . . [had] four swyne shoots. **1696** *Groton Rec.* 115 Chosed for town ofcers . . . swinerd Eleazer Green. **1778** E. PARKMAN *Diary* 79 Breck trades with two swine drovers, and buys two shoats for me. **1874** *Rep. Comm. Agric. 1873* 439 No swine-breeder or pork-raiser will deprive his stock of this important auxiliary [the beet crop]. **1879** *Diseases of Swine* 198 Hogs frequently die of cholera or swine-pox.

b. In the specific names of plants.

1833 EATON *Botany* (ed. 6) 110 *Coronopus didyma,* swine's cress. . . . Charleston, S.C. **1791** MUHLENBERG *Index Florae* 176 *Hyoseris,* Swine-succory. **1836** LINCOLN *Botany* App. 185 Swine thistle. *Sonchus.*

∗ Swing, *n.*

1. A contrivance in which one may swing. {1687–}

1846 *29th Congress 1 Sess. H. R. Ex. Doc. No. 140,* 1210 Swing for exercise, Joel H. Ross, New York, August 26, 1845. **1832** McCABE *New York* 448 A few steps north of the swings is 'The Carousel.' **1909** CALHOUN *Miss Minerva* 34 In a very short time he was sitting again facing Billy in the swing.

2. A dance with a swinging movement.

1847 *Santa Fe Repub.* 1 Oct. 2/3 Beginning like a Country Dance it [the Coonie] changes to an Indian swing. **1865** PIKE *Scout & Ranger* (1932) 149 The 'swing' was rendered with such a hearty good will, . . . that I almost wished I was a dancer myself.

+3. *Swing* (a)*round the circle,* a political tour. Cf. SWING *v.* 3.

1902 PHILLIPS *Woman Ventures* 121 Marlowe found that he must leave town on Wednesday night to go with the President on a short 'swing round the circle.' **1905** *Springfield W. Repub.* 6 Oct. 1 Will the appropriated money be available for campaigning swings around the circle?

+4. In herding, the position occupied by the outriders. Also *attrib.*

1903 ADAMS *Log of Cowboy* 28 The main body of the herd trailed along, . . . guarded by outriders, known as swing men. *Ib.* 91, Quince Forrest . . . rode in the swing on the branded side of the cattle.

∗ Swing, *v.*

+1. *intr.* (See quot. 1851.) Also with *out.*

1851 HALL *College Words* 296 At several American colleges, the word *swing* is used for coming out with a secret society badge. . . . Generally, *to swing out* signifies to appear in something new. **1871** BAGG *At Yale* 143 Old graduates seldom 'swing out' except on special occasions.

+2. *tr.* To bring around; to manage; to control.

1873 'MARK TWAIN' & WARNER *Gilded Age* 405 You will find we can swing a two-thirds vote. **1875** HOLLAND *Sevenoaks* 156, I don't b'lieve I can swing it! **1883** *Century Mag.* Oct. 895/2 Jake Runckel can swing that ward like a dead cat. **1896** WHITE *Real Issue* 13 [Each] told how some precinct could 'be swung into line' by a little work. **1902** [see CORNER *n.* 6]. **1917** FREEMAN & KINGSLEY *Alabaster Box* 62 But it's going to be a good thing for the creditors, if she can swing it.

+3. *To swing round the circle,* to make an extended political tour of the country. Also *transf.* and as *vbl. n.*

1877 WRIGHT *Big Bonanza* 227 This [trip] surpasses any 'swinging round the circle,' political or otherwise, that has ever been done in the United States. **1887** *Chicago Tribune* 2 Oct., President Andrew Johnson originated the phrase 'swinging round the circle' on the occasion of his famous tour to Chicago . . . in September, 1866. **1910** *N.Y. Evening Post* 29 Oct. 2 To stem the rising tide against him, Col. Roosevelt is to swing around the circle in Brooklyn to-night.

Swing-, stem of *swing v.* {1791–} +Designating a swinger team or one of the animals composing it. — **1869** Swing-steer [see LEAD *a*]. **1888** *Century Mag.* Nov. 159/2 Mules had to be there, 'wheelers,' 'swing team,' and 'leaders.' **1895** Swing mule [see LEAD MULE 2]. **1910** J. HART *Vigilante Girl* 147 Snorting with fear, they bounded forward against the swing horses.

Swing bridge. A drawbridge that swings to one side. {1791} — **1707** *Boston News-Letter* 27 Jan. 2/2 To be Sold . . . by Mr. William Clark

Merchant, at his Store-House . . . near the Swing-Bridge, Good Barbadoes Rum [etc.]. **1794** *Mass. H. S. Coll.* 1 Ser. III. 246 A Swing bridge was a conveyance over the Town dock.

Swing-clear. 'A woman's gown, tight at the neck, and falling to the ankles, not fitted to the figure, and swinging clear of the ground' (B. '77).

+Swinge cat. A 'singed cat.' — **1835** LONGSTREET *Ga. Scenes* 219 For all you see him in these fine clothes, he's a *swinge*-cat—a darn sight cleverer fellow than he looks to be. **1840** *S. Lit. Messenger* VI. 506/2 She's a *swinge*-cat, arn't she?

Swinger. +'In the West, the name given to the middle horses in a team of six' (De Vere).

Swingfelter. Also **Swingfielder.** (See SCHWENKFELDER.)

+Swing ferry. ?A ferry directed across a stream by a cable. — **1873** BEADLE *Undevel. West* 758 We traveled northwest . . ., crossing the Klamath River by a 'swing-ferry' soon after daylight. **1878** — *Western Wilds* 327 When the swing ferry had landed them on the west bank [of the Wabash], . . . the boy climbed out of the rear of the wagon-box.

Swing gate. {1774–} + =SWINGING GATE *a.* — **1769** *Southampton Rec.* III. 262 The owners of the said land do obligate themselves to make and maintain good and sufficient swing gates, and those persons that do use . . . said highway are carefully to shut the gates. **1791** *Huntington Rec.* III. 160 He petitions the Trustees to Grant him toleration to Run a water fence . . . Down to the Channel, with his erecting and keeping a Good & Convenient Swing Gate.

Swinging bridge. {1892} **+1.** =SWING BRIDGE. **+2.** =FLOATING BRIDGE 1. — (1) **1705** *Boston News-Letter* 8 Oct. 2/2 To be Sold by Mr. William Clarke, . . . near the Swinging-Bridge upon the Dock in Boston, a parcel of the best Jamaica Sole-Leather. (2) **1890** *Cent.* 4219/2 These [oyster] houses are . . . kept in constant communication with the wharf by means of a swinging bridge.

Swinging door. A door that may be pushed open from either direction, swinging shut when released. {1843– (*Ainsworth's Mag.* IV. 436)} — **1805** D. McCLURE *Diary* (1899) 62 It was a long building . . . with a swinging door at each end. **1887** *Trial H. K. Goodwin* 20 The door was always open, except that this was a swinging door.

Swinging gate. +**a.** A gate that opens and shuts by swinging; a swing gate. **b.** A gate that may be pushed open in either direction. — **1688** *East-Hampton Rec.* II. 219 To Mr Baker Mending ye swinging Gate, 0–02–6. **1735** *Ib.* IV. 7 Benjamin Osbourne . . . [has] liberty for to set up . . . a swinging gate. **1865** *Atlantic Mo.* Jan. 6/1 The swinging gate communicated with the burial-ground. **1894** ALDRICH *Two Bites* 56 The narrow counter . . . [was] divided in the centre by a swinging gate.

+Swinging harness. In a fire station, harness that may be swung up, ready to be dropped on a horse when needed. — **1889** BRAYLEY *Boston Fire Dept.* 317 The commissioners made arrangements with the patentee of the Speedy swinging-harness to use it in this department.

+Swingletail. The thresher shark. — **1832** [see MAN-EATER 1]. **1842** *Nat. Hist. N.Y., Zoology* IV. 349 The Thresher Shark . . . is known here under the various popular names of Thresher, Fox Shark and Swingletail. **1911** *Rep. Fisheries 1908* 316.

+Swingle tow. =SWINGLING TOW. — **1836** *Knickerb.* VIII. 47 Imagine the swingle-tow of the farmer to have been profusely lodged on a tree. **1855** *Amer. Inst. N.Y. Trans. 1854* 343 Good crops of potatoes have been grown under swingletow, upon a grass sod.

∗Swingletree. =SINGLETREE 1. Now *rare.* — **1774** *Md. Hist. Mag.* XVI. 30 The Stallions . . . Broke my Swingle Tree, snapped one of my Traces. **1832** KENNEDY *Swallow Barn* I. 23 A sickly-looking wagon . . . droops its rusty swingle-trees. **1874** [see PINE brush]. **1920** HOWELLS *Vacation of Kelwyns* 96 They had vainly tugged at the swingletree.

+Swingling tow. (See quot. 1828.) — **1828** WEBSTER, *Swingling-tow,* the coarse part of flax, separated from the finer by swingling and hatcheling. **1843** STEPHENS *High Life N.Y.* II. 173 A son of the President of these United States ought to be noticed for what's inside of his head, and not for such an eternal swad of swinglin-tow as that are.

Swing plow. **a.** A plow without a fore wheel. {1733–} **b.** 'A reversible or sidehill plow' (W. '09). — **1805** PARKINSON *Tour* 493 A few of the swing or Rotherham ploughs are used. **1822** WOODS *English Prairie* (1904) 203 They plough with a light swing-plough, and use two horses. **1870** *Rep. Comm. Agric. 1869* 319 In the matter of swing plows, it can scarcely be said that any decided and unusual stride has been made during the year.

+Swing pole. A well sweep. — **1818** FORDHAM *Narr. Travels* 157 The swing pole and bucket are forever out of order.

+Swing rope. The rope used to suspend a load across the back of a pack animal before securing it with the pack rope. — **1894** WISTER in *Harper's Mag.* April 783/2 The rolls were made, balanced as side packs, and circled with the swing-ropes. **1902** — *Virginian* 488 He would teach her how to loop and draw the pack-ropes, and the swing-ropes on the pack-saddles.

+Swing station. *W.* A station on a stage line where teams are changed. — **1867** *Ore. State Jrnl.* 27 April 4/1 At the swing station at Duck Lake . . . the stage started out at 8 P.M. **1869** McCLURE *Rocky Mts.* 178 Not one half of the 'swing-stations' . . . had so much as a single gun of any kind . . . to defend the stock.

Swipe, *v.* {1829–} +*tr.* To steal. *colloq.* {1900} — **1890** BARRÈRE & LELAND (1897) II. 316/2 *Swipe, to* (American), . . . to appropriate. **1896** *Boston Jrnl.* 24 Nov. 6/5 The kid who swiped my pie at the picnic said the same thing. **1911** VANCE *Cynthia* 174 They won't think no more of takin' it away from you'n they would of swipin' candy off'n a sick kid.

∗Swiss, *a.*

1. Originating or made in Switzerland. {a1700–}

1864 *Hist. North-Western Soldiers' Fair* 109 [Donations include] 8 prs. of children's drawers, elegantly trimmed, 2 Swiss muslin aprons. **1891** WELCH *Recoll. 1830–40* 175 Ladies' Swiss watches from Geneva . . . were as stylish then as ladies' diamond solitaires [*sic*] are now. **1897** *Outing* XXX. 377/1 It is not a bad plan to take a few yards of Swiss mull, in case insects prove troublesome.

2. In the specific names of birds and trees.

1828 BONAPARTE *Synopsis* 298 The Swiss Plover, *Charadrius helveticus,* . . . inhabits the north of both continents. **1832** BROWNE *Sylva* 256 This poplar is indigenous to North America, though very rare, and is called Virginian poplar and Swiss Poplar. **1892** APGAR *Trees Northern U.S.* 173 *Pinus cembra.* . . . Swiss Stone-pine. . . . Forms a regular cone; branches to the ground.

∗Switch, *n.*

1. *Railroads.* The movable rail or rails and the apparatus connected with them, used to shunt a car or train from one track to another {1797–}; the place where such rails are fixed; +a side track.

1835 *Mass. Laws* XIII. 461 It shall be the duty of the corporation . . . to enter the said Boston and Lowell rail-road, by . . . proper turn-outs or switches. **1868** [see FROG 3]. **1873** *Newton Kansan* 29 May 2/2 It has now 495 miles of track besides switches. *a*1882 in McCabe *New York* 190 On we go, slowly at first, over the tangle of switches. **1900** *Congress. Rec.* 2 Feb. 1448/2 Is the track to be a switch, or a part of the main line of the road? **1904** *N.Y. Times* 11 May 3 The rule is to maintain a six-mile speed when entering a switch. **1918** *Essex Inst. Coll.* LIV. 337 The tower operated about thirty switches.

+**b.** *To open a switch,* to set a switch so as to shunt a car to another track.

1898 *McClure's Mag.* X. 212/1 A conductor . . . opened the switch.

+**2.** A quantity of long hair bound together at one end, worn by women with their natural hair.

1873 *Newton Kansan* 29 May 1/6 [She] hides these lines by a chaotic and formless mass of . . . rats and switches. **1882** RITTENHOUSE *Maud* 129 Wanted a lock of my hair (which he did not get though I thoughtfully offered him a piece of Mama's new switch.) **1887** WILKINS *Humble Romance* 75, I've got a switch, an' done up my hair like other women.

3. *attrib.* and *comb.* **a.** In sense 1 with *ball, engineer,* etc.

1860 EMERSON *Conduct of Life* 275 The switchman at the railway intersection, the farmer in the field, . . . ascribe a certain pleasure to their employment. **1878** PINKERTON *Strikers* 152 A militiaman, . . . while sitting on the cow-catcher, particularly noticed the position of the switchball. **1883** FULTON *Sam Hobart* 169 They were placed in the switch-houses. **1889** SALMONS *Burlington Strike* 355 They went out on a strike, being joined by the switch engineers and firemen. **1892** *Harper's Mag.* Dec. 80 He saw the station agent running down the tracks with the red switch-light. **1903** *N.Y. Ev. Post* 30 Dec. 3 A slight blaze occurred in an elevated road switch tower.

b. In the specific names of plants.

1884 SARGENT *Rep. Forests* 134 *Carya porcina.* . . . Switch-bud Hickory. . . . Dry hills and uplands; common. **1845** *Big Bear Ark.* 132 They circled about among the switch-cane and priscimmon bushes a long time.

Switch, *v.* {1611–}

+**1.** *tr.* To turn (a car, train, etc.) on to another track by means of a switch. {= E. 'to shunt'}

1861 in G. H. Putnam *Memories of Publisher* 421 [Each car carried in white letters the caution:] not to be switched under penalty of death. **1879** *Scribner's Mo.* Nov. 23/2 This road has also cabin cars . . . which it will switch off at any station. **1891** C. ROBERTS *Adrift Amer.* 60 The car that I was in was switched out of the train and left in the yard there. **1903** *N.Y. Ev. Post* 17 Sept. 1 At Hagerstown the train was switched from the Cumberland Valley Railroad to the Norfolk & Western.

+**b.** *intr.* Of a railroad line or train: To branch or turn off at a switch. Also fig.

1875 L. F. TASISTRO tr. Comte de Paris *Civil War Amer.* I. 230 Two branches of the Alexandria and Lynchburg line switch off to enter the Valley of Virginia. **1887** DALY *Railroad of Love* 72 The track is ever smooth and straight, 'Tis only when the coupling breaks, Or we switch off, we seal our fate. **1905** *N.Y. Ev. Post* 27 Dec. 3 The freight was switching to this track as the passenger train was leaving it.

+**2.** *fig.* **a.** *tr.* With adverb or adverbial phrase: To move or shift (a thing or action) to another place or in another direction. {1897}

1860 HOLMES *E. Venner* xvii, Good ministers . . . [sometimes] contrive to switch off their logical faculties on the narrow side-track of their technical dogmas. **1883** SHIELDS *S.S. Prentiss* 82 When the banks got into operation, the road was quietly 'switched off,' and left the bank in full sway. **1895** *Advance* 5 Sept. 331/3 He was the life of every company . . . setting the pace for all conversation and switching it at will from one topic to another. **1911** HARRISON *Queed* 53 Suppose it popped into his head some day to switch all that directness and concentrated energy in some other direction.

+**b.** *intr.* and *tr.* To turn or move *off, in,* etc.

1869 'MARK TWAIN' *Innocents* 432 We had all intended to go by diligence to Damascus, and switch off to Baalbec. **1890** BARRÈRE & LELAND (1897) II. 317/1 *Switch in,* . . . to bring in expeditiously, to introduce with promptness, and execute with despatch. **1898** WESTCOTT *D. Harum* xli, Did I ever tell you . . . how Lawyer Staples come to switch round in that there railroad jangle last spring?

+**c.** Without adverb or adverbial phrase: To exchange.

1897 *Columbus Dispatch* 18 June 5/2 An opportunity presented itself to 'switch' the bottles.

+**3.** *I'll be switched,* I'll be doggoned.

1838 *U.S. Mag.* I. 427, I'll be switched if I do. **1850** WATSON *Camp-Fires Revol.* 313, I'll be switched if it took away the cold feeling from me. **1881** RITTENHOUSE *Maud* 4, I'll be switched if I'd get married if I couldn't be called 'Little Wifey.' **1920** LEWIS *Main Street* 182, I'll be switched if I'll stand for your thinking I'm nothing but a dollar-chasing ——.

Switchback. {1888} +A railroad track that follows a zigzag course to lessen the grade up a hill. — **1863** *Harper's Mag.* Sept. 465/1 We descend from our high elevation by gravity, changing our direction at various points by means of what is called a Switch-back. **1873** 'MARK TWAIN' & WARNER *Gilded Age* 445 There will have to be a branch track built, and a 'switch-back' up the hill. **1880** *Harper's Mag.* July 194/2 The railroad first using a very bold and ingenious 'switch-back' now runs through a tunnel.

Switchboard. An apparatus for connecting and combining electric circuits. {1884–} — **1887** *Trial H. K. Goodwin* 63 The switch-board, as I understand it, is a contrivance by which the subscribers to a telephone are put into communication with each other. **1895** *N.Y. Dramatic News* 9 Nov. 4/2 An elaborate system of electric lighting has been installed, . . . and the switchboard is a formidable affair. **1912** MCMEEN & MILLER *Telephoning* 612 Private branch exchanges most used in connection with automatic offices employ manual switchboards.

+**Switchel.** [Origin unknown.] A drink of molasses and water, often seasoned with vinegar and ginger, and sometimes with rum. — **1790** FRENEAU *Poems* (1795) 375 For such attempts men drink your high-proof wines, Not spiritless switchel and vile hogo drams. **1801** *Spirit Farmers' Mus.* 267 Drink Switchel—that is, Molasses or Maple sugar mixed with water. **1846** *Xenia Torch-Light* 6 Aug. 1/3 The captain . . . [offered] the refreshment of 'switchell' (a liquor composed of new rum, molasses, ginger and water). **1903** S. H. WARD *Life G. H. Hepworth* 7 This drink . . . [was] the popular switchel, made of molasses, a dash of vinegar, 'a spice of ginger,' or nutmeg, and water from the well.

+**Switch engine.** An engine used for switching. — **1867** *Jamestown Jrnl.* 28 June 3/2 Mary Haycroft was knocked down by a switch-engine. **1883** [see EMPTY 2]. **1913** LONDON *Valley of Moon* 127 They heard the switch engines puffing in the railroad yards.

+**Switch grass.** ||**1.** =QUACK GRASS. **2.** A western panic grass, *Panicum virgatum.* — (1) **1839** BUEL *Farmer's Companion* 232 The quack, switch, or witch grass, a variety of the fiorin. (2) **1889** VASEY *Agric. Grasses* 28 Switch Grass . . . forms a large constituent of the native grasses of the prairies. **1895** *Dept. Agric. Yrbk. 1894* 430 *Switch grass* . . . has powerful creeping rootstocks.

∗Switzer. A person from Switzerland. — **1612** SMITH, etc. *Virginia* II. 90 We imploied one William Volda (a Switzer by birth). **1713** *N.C. Col. Rec.* II. 24 A swiss nobleman . . . came here to settle a colony of Switzers and Palatines. **1805** D. MCCLURE *Diary* (1899) 35 His wife was a Switser.

∗Swivel. A gun or cannon mounted on a pivoted rest. {1748–} In full *swivel gun.* {1712–}

1725 *New-Eng. Courant* 3 May 2/1 The Mary-Woodley, with . . . 2 Swevil Guns, and several small Arms, was at Curracoa. **1745** POTE *Jrnl. Captivity* 4 We discharged one Cannon and one Swivel. **1778** *Essex Inst. Coll.* LII. 5 From the shore there came off a small boat . . . armed with swivels. **1832** CATLIN *Indians* I. 20 We had on board . . . three or four eight-pound swivels. **1871** [see PUNT GUN]. **1883** *Nat. Museum Bul.* No. 27, 320 *Swivel-guns.* . . . Used in discharging gun-harpoons and explosive lances for fastening to and killing whales.

+**Swivel chair.** A chair that turns on a swivel. — **1860** HOLMES *Professor* 37 The swivel-chair spins round with me. **1884** HOWELLS *S. Lapham* i, He continued, wheeling round with his leather-cushioned swivel-chair. **1911** HARRISON *Queed* 312 Queed leaned back in his swivel chair.

Swob. (See SWAB.)

+**Swod.** (See SWAD.)

∗Sword. A hand weapon having a long blade with a sharp edge. — **1622** 'MOURT' *Relation* 13 Sixteene men were set out with every man his Musket, Sword, and Corslet. **1645** [see MOOSE 2]. **1746** *N.H. Probate Rec.* III. 449, I also give him . . . my best fiarlock gun and my sword. **1861** *Army Regulations* 467 [I have] inspected and approved . . . sabres or swords, accoutrements, &c.

∗Sword-bearer. +(See quot. 1841.) **1841** HARRIS *Insects Mass.* 131 One more grasshopper . . . belongs to the genus *Conocephalus,* and . . . bears the specific name of *ensiger,* the sword-bearer, from the long, straight, sword-shaped piercer of the female. **1904** KELLOGG *Amer. Insects* 153.

Sword cane. A hollow cane that conceals a sword. {1837} — **1843** 'CARLTON' *New Purchase* II. 294 Why does so large and able bodied a man ask for a guard, and in addition to his sword-cane? **1895** *Columbus Dispatch* 19 March 1/6 The latter drew the steel blade of his sword cane and made a lunge at his assailant.

*Swordfish. 1. A marine fish (*Xiphias gladius*) having a long sword-like beak. **2.** A garfish. — **(1) 1793** *Mass. H. S. Coll.* 1 Ser. III. 119 There are but few towns so well supplied with fish of all kinds as Wellfleet; among which are some that are uncommon, such as the sword-fish and cramp-fish. **1832** WILLIAMSON *Hist. Maine* I. 162 The Swordfish . . . has been seen off Mount Desert and other places. **1884** GOODE, etc. *Fisheries* 1. 336 The Sword-fish . . . ranges along the Atlantic coast of America from Jamaica . . . to Cape Breton. **(2) 1815** DRAKE *Cincinnati* 141 Perch, pike, eel, yellow-cat and sword-fish are most esteemed. **1911** *Rep. Fisheries* 1908 310 Gar-pike . . . [is often called] 'swordfish.'

Swordtail. {1858-} + =SWORD-BEARER. — **1891** *Cent.* 6119/2 *Sword-bearer.* . . . Also called *swordtail.*

Swot. (See SWAT.)

+Swow, *v. I swow*, I declare. A mild oath. — **[1790** *Mass. Spy* 30 Dec. 1/1 In one village you will hear the phrase 'I snore,'—in another 'I swowgar.'] *c*1815 PAULDING *Amer. Comedies* (1847) 34 By gum, that's jist what I want yow to tell me, I swow. **1843** STEPHENS *High Life N.Y.* I. 104, I swow, Miss Miles, you look as harnsome as a full blown rose. **1886** STAPLETON *Major's Christmas* 38 It's Freckles, I swow.

+Swyneyed, *a.* [f. SWEENY.] Atrophied in the shoulder. In quot. *fig.* — **1861** *Harper's Mag.* Aug. 421/2 A lot of spavined, ring-boned, . . . swyneyed, split-hoofed, . . . pollevilled politicians.

*Sycamore. +a. The buttonwood or plane tree, esp. *Platanus occidentalis* and *P. orientalis;* the wood of this tree. Also with specifying terms. **b.** Occasionally in the South, esp. in North Carolina, the planer tree.

1709 LAWSON *Carolina* 100 The Sycamore, in these Parts, grows in a low, swampy Land, by River-sides. **1734** [see ILEX]. **1774** in PEYTON *Adv. Grandfather* (1867) 127 The forest of Kentucky consists of . . . gum, sycamore, maple [etc.]. **1804** LEWIS in *L. & Clark Exped.* I. (1904) 83 The country around is generally divided into prairies, with little timber, . . . and that consisting of cottonwood, mulberry, elm, and sycamore. **1834** BAIRD *Valley Miss.* 42 The sycamore is the prince of the western forests. **1850** *New Eng. Farmer* II. 142 The Buttonwood, or American Sycamore, is every where well known in New England. **1884** SARGENT *Rep. Forests* 130. **1897** SUDWORTH *Arborescent Flora* 183 Planera aquatica, . . . Sycamore (N.C.). *Ib.* 206 *Platanus racemosa*. . . . California Sycamore.

attrib. **1815** *Niles' Reg.* VIII. 135/1 We were desirous to see the effect of sinking large Sycamore gums as low down as we could force them. **1888** *Century Mag.* Sept. 770/1 A favorite lamp . . . was a saucer of lard with a dry sycamore ball floating in the midst of it.

*Sycamore tree. + =SYCAMORE a. — **1750** T. WALKER *Journal* 56 I Blazed several Trees in the fork and marked T W on a Sycomore Tree. **1816** U. BROWN *Journal* II. 221 We now set the Compass at a Sicamore tree standing on the East bank of the River. **1848** *Santa Fe Repub.* 15 Jan. 4/2 A new sort of sycamore tree made its appearance here; . . . [with] a leaf resembling our maple. **1903** *N.Y. Herald* 8 March (Ernst), The hubs are one with the wheels, the whole fashioned from circular slices from oak or sycamore trees.

+Sydney duck. [f. *Sydney*, Australia.] On the Pacific coast, a disreputable person. *Obs.* — **1872** [see HOUND 2]. **1873** MILLER *Amongst Modocs* 120 When you call a man a 'Sydney duck' it is well understood that you mean blood. **1880** BURNETT *Recollections* 342 The immigrants from Australia consisted in part of very bad characters, called 'Sydney Ducks.'

Sylvania. (See PENNSYLVANIA note.)

Sympathetic strike. A labor strike by one group of workmen called to promote the success of a strike by another group of workmen. {1901} — **1895** *Chicago Strike of 1894* 133 The general managers have organized in a way to compel or to 'force sympathetic strikes.' **1903** JOHNSON *Railway Transportation* 399 The purpose of this 'sympathetic strike' was to tie up the railway business of the country.

*Symphony. Attrib. with *concert, orchestra.* — **1881** *Harper's Mag.* May 804/2 In 1861 . . . the famous Symphony concerts were begun [in

N.Y.]. **1895** *Scribner's Mag.* XVII. 384/1 Mr. Arthur Nikisch resigned his position at the head of the Boston Symphony orchestra in . . . 1893.

*Synagogue. A building used by Jews primarily for religious purposes. — **1773** E. STILES *Literary Diary* I. 354 [At] the Synagogue . . . I saw Rabbi Carigal. **1832** DUNLAP *Hist. Amer. Theatre* 40 Their synagogue was in Mill-street, near Broad-street. **1847** [see BANKING-HOUSE]. **1898** CAHAN *Imported Bridegroom* 4 Just comin' from the synagogue, papa.

Syndicate, *n.* {1624-} A business organization which buys newspaper stories, photographs, etc., and sells them for simultaneous, or nearly simultaneous, publication in a number of newspapers and magazines. (Cf. *newspaper syndicate business* under NEWSPAPER 2 c.) — **1887** *Harper's Mag.* Feb. 484/1 Syndicates . . . purvey a vast variety of literary wares, chiefly for the Sunday editions of the city journals. **1914** S. S. MCCLURE *My Autobiography* 168, I launched the syndicate November 16, 1884.

Syndicate, *v.* {1610-} *tr.* To arrange for simultaneous publication of (a story, article, etc.) in a number of newspapers or magazines. — **[1889** *Pall Mall Gaz.* 20 Feb. 6/2 Mr. W. F. Tillotson . . . first acclimatized in this country the American system of 'syndicating' fiction.] **1891** 'M. O'RELL' *Frenchm. in Amer.* 240 Dr. Talmage syndicates his sermons. **1914** S. S. MCCLURE *Autobiography* 168 The first thing I syndicated was a two-part story by H. H. Boyesen.

*Synod. An assembly of the clergy of a particular church or denomination; esp., in Presbyterian churches, the court above the presbytery.

*c*1646 *Boston Rec.* 189 A synod was held this yeare at Cambridg. **1667** *Conn. Rec.* II. 70 The decission thereof should be referred to a Sinod or Councill of Messengers of churches. **1725** *New-Eng. Courant* 3 July 2/2 It is humbly desired that the Honoured General Court would . . . [call] the several Churches in the Province to meet by their Pastors and Messengers in a Synod. **1775** FITHIAN *Journal* II. 131, I left home this morning by eight; on my second journey, by order of synod. **1796** [see CLASSIS 2]. **1837** PECK *Gaz. Illinois* 172 A theological seminary, under patronage of the Presbyterian Synod of Illinois is about to be established at this place. **1883** [see CALL 1].

Syringa. =MOCK ORANGE 2. {1664-} See also SERINGA. — **1785** MARSHALL *Amer. Grove* 99 *Philadelphus inodorus*, Carolinian Scentless Syringa, . . . is said to grow naturally in Carolina. **1832** [see MOCK ORANGE 2]. **1897** *McClure's Mag.* X. 63 The air was fragrant with wild syringa. **1915** ARMSTRONG & THORNBER *Western Wild Flowers* 208 *Philadelphus Californicus* . . . looks very much like the familiar garden Syringa.

Syrphus fly. Any of numerous flies of the genus *Syrphus.* {1834-} — **1867** *Amer. Naturalist* I. 223 The larva of the Syrphus-fly . . . devours immense quantities [of plant lice]. **1879** *Ib.* XIII. 260 Certain syrphus-flies . . . have succeeded in producing certain flowers corresponding to their tastes. **1888** *Insect Life* I. 7 The descriptions of the Syrphus fly . . . will sufficiently enable its recognition in all stages.

*Syrup, Sirup, *n.* A thick sweet liquid; in sugar refining, the liquid of the sugar solution at one stage in boiling down. Also transf.

1695 SEWALL *Diary* 1. 408, I went to Capt. Daviss and fetched some Trecle Water and Syrup of Saffron. **1725** [see BROWN SUGAR]. **1816** *Ann. 14th Congress* 2 Sess. 1187 Syrup or juice of the maple,—cents the gallon [shall be the duty]. **1833** SILLIMAN *Man. Sugar Cane* 33 The largest [kettle] is called the *grande*, . . . the third the *syrup*. **1850** *Rep. Comm. Patents 1849: Agric.* 413 The sirup used in claying may be regenerated by evaporation. **1880** *Vt. Agric. Rep.* VI. 113 For syrup boil down [sap] immediately to the proper consistency. **1889** *Opelousas* (La.) *Democrat* 2 Feb. 2/3 Outside of Louisiana they usually call syrup molasses.

Syrup, *v.* {1619-} *+To syrup off*, in making maple sugar, to remove from the pan or evaporator the syrup resulting from the preliminary boiling of the sap. — **1872** *Vermont Bd. Agric. Rep.* I. 216 One should make it a point to syrup off quite often.

T

Ta, *n.* and *v.* (See quotation.) — *c*1870 CHIPMAN *Notes on Bartlett* 468 *Ta, ta-ta, taw,* ordure, dung; to ease one's self. Eastern New England. Used mostly by, and to children.

Tab. {1607-} +*To keep tab* (*on* or *upon*), or variant: To keep track (of); to check on. — **1888** *Mo. Republican* 15 Feb. (F.), [As] the conductor . . . did not keep tab on the party Maloney travelled free. **1896** ADE *Artie* 91 He kept tab on her every minute. **1904** *N.Y. Ev. Post* 26 Nov., 'We see so many people that it's hard to keep tab,' remarked the platform guard. **1911** HARRISON *Queed* 118 He kept the most careful sort of tabs upon himself.

Tabby.[1] A thick taffeta silk. {1638-} Also attrib. — **1639** *Md. Archives* IV. 77, 7. yds. tabbie. **1711** *Boston News-Letter* 29 Oct. 2/2 To be Sold, . . . Tabbys, blew Linnen, Kentins. **1731** *Md. Hist. Mag.* XIX. 289 One pair of white Tabby Stays according to the Inclosed measure. **1762** *Newport Mercury* 7 Sept. 3/2 To be sold By Gideon, John & Edward Wanton, . . . white water'd tabby. **1842** HAWTHORNE *Notebooks* (1932) 96 The governor in black velvet, and his lady in crimson tabbey.

Tabby.[2] Also †**tappy.** A concrete made by mixing lime, shells, gravel, and water. {1836-} Also attrib. — **1775** *S.C. Hist. Mag.* VI. 91 [The Council of Safety ordered that Fort Lyttelton be repaired with] tappy **1802** ELLICOTT *Journal* 267 That part [of Frederica] lying immediately on the water . . . was defended by a small battery of tabby work. **1833** SILLIMAN *Man. Sugar Cane* 46 The walls [of the draining rooms] are all constructed of tabby. **1847** *Knickerb.* XXIX. 455 The borders of the beds are made of 'tabby.' **1885** EGGLESTON in *Century Mag.* April 874/2.

Tabellion. *Tabellion public,* a public scrivener or notary. *Obs.* {1656-} — **1654** *Suffolk Deeds* II. 122 This publique Instrument of procuration or letter of Atturney . . . beefore mee frederick Ixem Notary and Tabellion public admitted and sworne. **1752** *Boston Ev. Post* 16 Oct., William Winter, Notary and Tabellion Publick. **1793** *State P.* (1819) I. 117 Assheton Humphreys, notary and tabellion publick, in and for the commonwealth of Pennsylvania.

** Tabernacle.*

1. A meeting place {1693-}, esp. among nonconformist groups {1768-}: (see also quot. 1909).

1745 *Georgia Col. Rec.* VI. 139 The Petitioners . . . are willing by joint Labour among themselves to erect a Tabernacle. **1846** MACKENZIE *Van Buren* 189 [At] the great Anti-Texas-annexation meeting . . . Albert Gallatin presided in the Tabernacle, Broadway, New York. **1877** *Providence Press* 26 Jan. (B.), The tabernacle prepared for Moody and Sankey at Boston was dedicated last night . . . in the presence of 5,000 people. **1909** WEBSTER 2103/1 *Tabernacle,* . . . a place of worship; . . . now, esp., a church with a very large auditorium.

+2. *cap.* The Mormon Tabernacle in Salt Lake City, Utah.

1852 *Harper's Mag.* Dec. 121/2 The Mormons . . . have finished their *Tabernacle.* **1888** ROE *Army Lett.* 386 We have been to see the tabernacle, with its marvelous acoustic properties. **1892** GUNTER *Miss Dividends* 206 Mormons . . . have come to the Tabernacle from the south and the north, the east and the west.

** Table,* *n.*

*1. An article of furniture having a flat top supported on legs.

1639 *Conn. Rec.* I. 444 Goods and Cattle of John Brundish: . . . a boxe, a small cubbert & a table. **1746** *N.H. Probate Rec.* III. 439 My said Wife [is] to have the Round tabel and two Chairs. **1856** M. J. HOLMES *L. Rivers* 199 She found John Jr. listlessly leaning upon the table with his elbows. **1922** *Sears, Roebuck & Co. Cat.* No. 145, 791/3 Table has top 24×38 inches.

b. A table at which a séance is conducted by spiritualists.
1855 WILLIS *Convalescent* 52, I should have liked to consult some 'table' (in a warm room), as to whether his spirit thought posthumous renown worth while.

*2. A flat, elevated stretch of land; a plateau. {-1634; 1869-}
1710 *Va. Mag. Hist.* V. 12 The Table of pines is accounted 10 miles from Currotuck Inlett and 20 from Cape Henry. **1815** DRAKE *Cincinnati* 72 In the upper table on which Cincinnati is built, a joint of the backbone of one of these species was found. **1848** *30th Congress* 1 *Sess.* Sen. Ex. Doc. No. 23, 43 The rocks rise in abrupt masses on either side; on the west terminating in a level table, capped with a sheet of lava. **1895** *Outing* XXVII. 16/2 These are but tables upon which the mountain ranges rest.

3. a. *To lie on the table,* of a bill or resolution, to be deferred for consideration. {1817}

1744 *N.J. Archives* 1 Ser. VI. 191 The House of Representative . . . would not commit it [a bill], but ordered it to lie on the table. **1790** *Steele P.* I. 62 After some debate the motion was ordered to lie on the Table untill next monday.

b. *To lay* (a bill, resolution, etc.) *on the table,* to postpone consideration of (a bill, etc.). {1860 (*Philol. Soc. Trans.* X. 142)}
1837 HONE *Diary* I. 274 The famous sub-treasury bill . . . was *laid on the table.* **1856** *Mich. Agric. Soc. Trans.* VII. 23 After some discussion the whole matter was laid on the table. **1923** H. M. ROBERT *Parliamentary Law* 63 It is in order for a mere majority to lay on the table the questions that have not been disposed of.

+c. *To take from the table,* to take up again for consideration.
1839 *Indiana H. Rep. Jrnl.* 23 Sess. 190 Bill No. 54 . . . was taken from the table and read a second time.

4. *attrib.* and *comb.* **a.** Designating things used to cover a table.
See also TABLECLOTH, TABLE COVER.
1640 *Conn. Rec.* I. 450 The Estate of the said Will' Spenser: . . . sheets and tabell lynen. **1649** *Ib.* 501 The estate of Mr. Thomas Hooker: . . . 4 table carpetts, window curtaines [etc.]. **1779** *York Co., Va., Rec.:* Wills XXII. 28 April, 12 table mats. **1845** *Xenia Torch-Light* 23 Oct. 3/2 Linen Table Damask and Diapers. **1856** *Mich. Agric. Soc. Trans.* VII. 64 Nall . . . [exhibited] 1 velvet table spread. **1883** *Rep. Indian Affairs* 360 Table oil-cloth.

b. Designating articles used at a dinner table.
See also TABLE BELL.
1643 *New Haven Col. Rec.* 89 She stole a table napkin. **1759** *Newport Mercury* 26 June 4/3 Imported . . . , Porringers, Table-spoons, Pint and Quart Pots [etc.]. **1824** in Z. F. Smith *Kentucky* 394 Some clap-boards . . . served for shelves for the table furniture. **1841** *Knickerb.* XVII. 39 The messenger . . . now presented to the breast of Mr. Cram the sharp points of a two-pronged table fork. **1861** *Chicago Tribune* 19 July 1/9 Genteel Furniture, Crockery Ware, Table Cutlery, Plated Ware, &c. **1894** REMINGTON in *Harper's Mag.* March 524/1 The fact that a man . . . uses his table-knife as though it were a deadly weapon counts very little.

c. Designating foods or drinks eaten at or suitable for eating at the table.
1678 *New Castle Court Rec.* 312 Hee [is] to haue for a meals meat & Table beer 2 gilders. **1770** *Boston Gaz.* 15 Jan. (Th.), Table fish. **1817** W. COXE *Fruit Trees* 100 Juneting, or Jenneting, . . . ls the earliest table apple of our country. **1871** Table bird [see DORKING].

d. In sense 1 b with *mover, rapper,* etc.
1852 *Harper's Mag.* Dec. 129/1 [The biologists'] province . . . does not as yet extend into the spirit world. Not so, however, of the rappers and table-movers. **1857** *Quinland* I. 181n., The editor of the Quinland papers . . . cannot be claimed as a believer, nor as an unbeliever in 'table-rapping.' **1865** LOWELL *Letters* I. 345 A lost poem of Pindar's, from which I translate by direct inspiration of a scholiast turned table-tipper. **1893** *Harper's Mag.* Feb. 377/1, I could not ring a bell when there was none to ring, as spirits do in table-rappers' closets.

*Table, *v.* +*tr.* To postpone action on (a bill, resolution, etc.) by laying it on the table. (Cf. TABLE *n.* 3b.) — **1849** *Whig Almanac 1850* 22 Senator Westcott tried to table the bill, but failed: it became law. **1887** *Courier-Journal* 21 Jan. 3/2 At the afternoon session the House resolution . . . was tabled. **1916** THOBURN *Stand. Hist. Okla.* II. 715 [The bill] was sent to the council where it was considered, amended, and finally tabled.

Tableau. {1699-} ‖A stretch of mesa or table-land. — **1849** *31st Congress* 1 *Sess.* Sen. Ex. Doc. No. 64, 72 Our route lay through a shallow valley—a succession of them, bounded by tableau or rounded hills.

Table bell. A small bell which stands on a table and is used to summon attendants. {1832- (*Chambers's Jrnl.* I. 236)} — **1779** *York Co., Va., Rec.:* Wills XXII. 28 April, 2 table bells. **1854** CUMMINS *Lamplighter* 186 Mr. Graham . . . so far forgot his usual politeness as to drown her voice in the violent ringing of the table-bell.

*Table board. **1.** A table top or table. *Obs.* {a1603-} +**2.** Board without lodging. — (1) **1644** *Conn. Rec.* I. 460 The Goods of Ephraim Huit: . . . one table board & forme. **1678** *N.H. Probate Rec.* I. 220, I give to ye s[ai]d Rich[ar]d Joce . . . ye Table-Board & Joyn-stooles. **1845** JUDD *Margaret* I. 11 The room also contained the table-board, block, and rag-bottom chairs. (2) **1883** HOWELLS *Woman's Reason* viii, People must find table-board at some of the neighboring houses. **1898** PAGE *Red Rock* 113 Captain Stevenson Allen . . . had applied to her for table-board.

***Tablecloth.** A cloth for covering a table, esp. a dining-room table. — **1640** *Conn. Rec.* I. 449 The goods and Cattell of James Olmestead: . . . two shorte Table Cloathes. **1747** *N.H. Probate Rec.* III. 507, I give her two Course table Cloths and four Course napkins. **1889** *Century Mag.* April 883/2 Milly Robinson appeared, with a freshly ironed tablecloth upon her arm. **1907** *St. Nicholas* Aug. 873/1 Once he laid down his fork and began tracing patterns on the table-cloth with his thumb nail.

Table cover. A cover for a table not used, or not in use, for eating. {1851-} — **1841** *Lowell Offering* I. 181 The white bed spreads and table covers . . . were equal, if not superior to those of English manufacture. **1876** *Wide Awake* 121/2 What Aunt Lesbia does not see is the pinch which Paty gives Rick's hand under the border of the table-cover. **1906** [see BUREAU 1 c].

+**Table girl.** A girl who serves people eating at a table. — **1877** HOWELLS *Out of Question* 15 Our table girls teach school in the winter and are as good as anybody. **1898** *McClure's Mag.* X. 208 A table-girl . . . serves you at a way-side café.

Table-land.
1. An elevated region of more or less flat land usually free of tree growth; a plateau. {1697-}
1826 COOPER *Mohicans* xxii, The younger is detained among the women of the Hurons, whose dwellings are but two short miles hence, on a table land. **1834** PECK *Gaz. Illinois* 372 Turkey River rises in the table lands west of the Mississippi. **1848** BRYANT *California* iii. 42 The trail is smooth and hard, running over the high table-land of the prairies. **1873** BEADLE *Undevel. West* 481 We turn south-west, rising by successive 'benches' to a vast barren table land. **1902** WISTER *Virginian* 306 The Virginian . . . came into a high tableland, beyond which the mountains began in earnest.

+**2.** A mesa with steep sides.
1843 *Knickerb.* XXII. 161 Some are perched like watch-towers on the elevations or table-lands of the mountains. **1873** ARNY *Items regarding N. Mex.* 26 The Pablo Montoya Grant . . . is agreeably diversified by . . . a great number of mesas or table-lands of moderate size. **1877** HODGE *Arizona* 168 The table-lands where the Moquis live are from two hundred to five hundred feet high.

3. Without article: Elevated ground, usually level. {1869}
1827 SHERWOOD *Gaz. Georgia* 186 The soil is diluvial, or what may be termed table-land. **1837** WILLIAMS *Florida* 8 There are many extensive tracts of table land, hammock and swamp. **1849** *31st Congress 1 Sess.* Sen. Ex. Doc. No. 64, 210 We found ourselves upon very high rolling table land. **1881** *Cimarron News & Press* 24 Feb. 1/6 About one-half . . . is mountain land and the balance, the eastern half, prairie or table land.

+**Table-mountain pine.** A pine (*Pinus pungens*) having cones covered with knobs. — **1810** MICHAUX *Arbres* I. 16 *Table mountain pine,* . . . seule dénomination . . . dans la haute Caroline du nord. **1892** APGAR *Trees Northern U.S.* 177 Table-Mountain Pine. . . . New Jersey and southwestward, along the mountains.

Table plain. A table-land or plateau. — **1835** WILLIS *Pencillings* I. 166 A graceful slope . . . swells up to a broad table plain on the mountain. **1844** GREGG *Commerce of Prairies* I. 160 Most of the high table-plains afford the finest grazing in the world, while, for want of water, they are utterly useless for most other purposes.

***Tacamahac.** Also **tacmahacca.** The balsam poplar (*Populus tacamahaca*, syn. *balsamifera*); the resin of this tree. In full *tacamahac tree.* — [**1739** MILLER *Gardeners Dict.* (ed. 3) II. Addenda s.v. (*O.E.D.*), The Tacamahaca. This Tree grows spontaneously on the Continent of America.] **1785** MARSHALL *Amer. Grove* 107 Balsam, or Tacamahac-Tree. . . . The buds abound with a glutinous resin, which is the tacamahacca of the shops. **1843** TORREY *Flora N.Y.* II. 216 Balsam Poplar. Tackamahac. . . . Banks of rivers and borders of swamps. **1897** SUDWORTH *Arborescent Flora* 130.

***Tack.** A small, sharp nail usually with a flat head. Also attrib. — **1759** *Newport Mercury* 26 June 4/3 Imported . . . , Tacks and Brads of all sizes. **1813** *Niles' Reg.* IV. 294/2 We have tons of nails, cut or drawn, with spikes, brads, sprigs and tacks. **1864** *Wkly. New Mexican* 10 June 2/2 Thomas Blanchard . . . invented the tack machine. **1907** *St. Nicholas* June 729/2 A small tack here and there will keep the paper from slipping.

+**Tack hammer.** A light hammer for driving tacks. {1890, in Australia} — **1865** *Atlantic Mo.* June 736/2 If she absolutely cannot get a tack-hammer with a claw on one end, she can take up carpet-nails with an iron spoon. **1882** PECK *Sunshine* 40 Then he calls for a tack-hammer. **1904** W. H. SMITH *Promoters* 15 You can drive a fortypenny nail into an oak plank with a tack hammer.

***Tackle,** *n.* Football. **1.** The act of tackling a runner. {1901-} +**2.** One of the two linesmen playing next to the guards; the position played by such a player. — (1) **1876** in P. H. Davis *Football* 462 A tackle is when the holder of the ball is held by one or more players of the opposite side. **1893** POST *Harvard Stories* 22 A Yale full-back is not apt to miss a clear tackle in the open. (2) **1893** CAMP *College Sports* 100 The two [players] next the ends . . . were called 'tackles.' **1899** QUINN *Penna. Stories* 22 A series of attacks on the centre and tackles . . . slowly but surely brought the ball up the field. **1920** [see FUMBLE v.].

***Tackle,** *v. tr.* To harness (an animal); to hitch up (a carriage). {1787-} Also absol. Also with *up, in.*
1714 SEWALL *Diary* II. 432 Our Horses were forced to leap into the Sea. By that time had tackled them was duskish. **1722** *New-Eng. Courant* 17 Dec. 1/1 May not Coaches be tackled to convey them [infirm people] to the publick Worship? **1804** ORDWAY in *Jrnls. of Lewis & O.* 141 They tackled one [dog] to day which carried about 80 weight with ease. **1849** NASON *Journal* 53, I thought the horse was not properly tackled in. **1884** *Century Mag.* July 452/1 Solon, he used to tackle up and . . . go after 'em in the mornin'. **1891** *Harper's Mag.* Sept. 579/2 She wants to know if one of the men shall tackle up a team horse.

***Tackling.**
1. The harness of a draft animal. *Obs.* {c1645-} Also in fig. context.
1641 *Conn. Rec.* I. 65 Fower of the better sorte of Oxen or Horsses, with tacklin, shall not be valued at aboue 4s. xd. the day. **1641** *Ib.* 443 The goods of Richard Lyman deceased: . . . a Cart & plow & tacklin belonging to them. **1711** *Boston News-Letter* 15 Oct. 2/2 Two good Cart Horses, Trucks and Tackling to be Sold. **1775** J. ADAMS *Familiar Lett.* 55 My mare, being galled with an ugly buckle in the tackling, suddenly flinched. **1843** STEPHENS *High Life N.Y.* II. 223 That aint a primin tu what I mean tu du, if you and I can only agree tu draw in the same tacklin.

2. The gear of a loom.
1684 *Conn. Probate Rec.* I. 356, I give to my son Joseph both my Looms with all the Tackling. **1756** in Chalkley *Scotch-Irish Settlement Va.* III. 344 One loom and all the takelings and utensils to her belonging.

+**Tacky, Tackey,** *n. S.* [Of obscure origin.]
1. An unkempt or ill-conditioned horse.
See also MARSH TACK(E)Y, SWAMP *n.* 9.
1800 TATHAM *Agric. & Commerce* 81 You are thus asked (in local phrase and expression) to *truck* or *trade* for a horse, a cow, or a little *tackie,* &c. **1835** SIMMS *Yemassee* I. 130 [He was] mounted upon the little ambling pony, or tacky. *a*1846 *Quarter Race Ky.* 146 Mac mounted a piney-wood-tacky. **1884** *Century Mag.* Jan. 444/2 The scrubby little 'tackeys' still taken in the marshes along the North Carolina coast are descendants of the wild horses of the colony.

2. A neglected person; a poor white.
[**1835** SIMMS *Partisan* (1854) 187 As if it wasn't curse enough to be bleareyed without having every dirty field-tackey whickering about it.] **1861** M. B. CHESNUT *Diary from Dixie* 58 They were sandhill tackeys, . . . not very anxious to fight with anything, or in any way. **1887** HARRIS in *Century Mag.* Aug. 549/1 All his time . . . was devoted to the work of improving and elevating the tackies. **1896** *Peterson Mag.* Jan. 85/1 One need not look for refinement in a 'tacky.'

3. Attrib. with *race, word.*
1836 *Quarter Race Ky.* (1846) 16 One hundred dollars . . . is enough for a little tacky race like this. **1851** *Polly Peablossom* 174 It'll be 'the old quarter tackey word.' **1865** M. B. CHESNUT *Diary from Dixie* 401 She was a perfect specimen of the Sandhill 'tackey' race.

+**Tacky,** *a.* [Cf. TACKY *n.* 2.] Dowdy; showing lack of good taste; common. *colloq.*
1883 RITTENHOUSE *Maud* 262 Two little cards (with his name printed on them in gilt. Tackey? Ugh! **1887** *Harper's Mag.* Dec. 39/1, I tell you it's downright tackey as it is. **1893** *Advance* 22 June, I feel especially sorry for Grace, she looks so tackey in her shabby dress. **1925** BENEFIELD *Chicken-Wagon Family* 311 The rather tacky and shabby shame-ride was now nearly over.

b. *Tacky party,* a party at which the guests dress up in ridiculous clothes.
1904 *Charlotte Observer* Sept. 1/2 A tacky party was given at the home of Mrs. G. W. Smithson.

+**Taconic system.** [*Taconic* Mts., a branch of the Green Mts.] (See quotations.) — **1888** *Amer. Jrnl. Science* Dec. 427 'Taconic system' is only a synonym of the older term 'Lower Silurian,' as this term was used by geologists generally twenty . . . years since. **1891** *Cent.* 6143/1 *Taconic system,* . . . in *geol.,* rocks of Lower Silurian age (or Cambrian, in part . . .), more or less metamorphosed, formerly supposed by some geologists to constitute a distinct system.

+**Tad.** [Cf. dial. *toad* in similar senses.]
1. (See quotations.)
1845 *Cincinnati Misc.* I. 240 Among a certain class in the eastern cities, . . . the word *Tad,* is applied to *one who don't nor won't pay.* **1851** HALL *College Words* 297 At Centre College, Ky., there is a society . . . composed of the very best fellows of the College, calling themselves Tads. **1890** CUSTER *Following Guidon* 213 These youths [although graduates of West Point] were called 'tads' and 'plebes,' and treated in a half-contemptuous manner by officers [until] . . . they had been in a fight.

2. A person, esp. a small child.
1877 BARTLETT 688 *Little tads,* small boys. *Old tads,* graybeards, old men. **1896** ADE *Artie* 98 Oh, he's a great old tad. **1904** NESBIT *Trail to Boyland* 49 That handle has been broken since he was just a tad.

***Tadpole,** *n.* +**1.** A Mississippian. A nickname. +**2.** The hooded merganser. — (1) **1845** *Cincinnati Misc.* I. 240 The inhabitants of . . . Mississippi [are called] Tadpoles. **1888** WHITMAN *Nov. Boughs* 406 Those from . . . Mississippi . . . [were call'd] Tad Poles. (2) **1888** TRUMBULL *Names of Birds* 75 Another name [for the hooded merganser] . . . commonly heard among the 'crackers' of St. Augustine is Tadpole. **1895** RIDGWAY *Ornith. Illinois* II. 191 Hooded merganser. . . . [Also called] Moss head; Tow-head; Tadpole, etc. . . . *Hab.* All of North America. **1917** *Birds of Amer.* I. 112.

‖**Tadpole**, a. Premature. — **1862** E. W. Pearson *Lett. Port Royal* 62 Hunter's action . . . seemed to me very like the tadpole resolution in 'Festina Lente.'

* **Taffeta.** Also †**taffety, taffity.**

* **1.** In early times, a plain-woven, glossy silk fabric; in recent times, a fine silk fabric having a luster; a garment made of this.

a**1649** WINTHROP *Hist.* II. 273 The captain gave every one of them an eln of black taffeta for a mourning robe. **1667** SANFORD *Letter Book* 45 If you please to Send in . . . taffety & other Silk to the Value of 10 l. **1733** *S.C. Gazette* 282/1 Just Imported, . . . taffitys, porses, black gorgerans. **1764** *Md. Hist. Mag.* X. 41 Eight yards of India Crimson Tafferty [shall be purchased] for Lining. **1828** [see FAN *n.*¹ 2]. **1886** BYNNER *A. Surrige* 210 To think of my having on this old taffeta. **1904** A. DALE *Wanted: a Cook* 24 She wore an exquisite little dinner dress of pink taffeta.

2. Attrib. with *gown, hat, purse, scarf.*

1642 *Md. Archives* IV. 94 A taffeta purse with a parcell of silk, thread, & buttons. **1654** *Essex Probate Rec.* I. 200, 1 tafetie Scarfe, 6 s. **1807** IRVING, etc. *Salmagundi* ix, My aunt . . . put on her pompadour taffeta gown. **1914** *Lady's Pictorial* 4 July, Advt. p. v, Soft Taffeta Hat.

Taffy.

1. a. An unpulled hard candy; toffee. *Obs.* {**1817**-}
+**b.** A pulled hard candy made usually of molasses and certain other ingredients.

1848 BARTLETT 348 *Taffy,* a kind of candy made of molasses, flour, and butter, baked in a pan. New York. **1864** WEBSTER 1348/3 *Taffy,* a kind of candy made of molasses boiled down and poured out in shallow pans. **1882** RITTENHOUSE *Maud* 63 Then we made some splendid taffy, and pulled it till it was white and glistening. **1888** HARGIS *Graded Cook Book* 500 Taffy. . . . Put in granite kettle and boil without stirring. Test in cold water. When done spread on buttered plates. **1907** *St. Nicholas* July 790 Caramels or taffy, whichever one liked best; . . . You only *asked,* you did not have to *buy.*

+**2.** Flattery; cajolery. *colloq.*

1879 *Congress. Rec.* 15 April 462/1, [I wish to prevent them from] denouncing me as the coadjutor of the South, distributing 'taffy' to the South. **1895** GRAHAM *Stories Foot-Hills* 155 'Oh, taffy!' she said, looking at him coquettishly. **1904** *Buffalo Commercial* 2 Sept. 4 Watson the Populist takes no taffy from the democrats.

3. Attrib. and comb. in sense 1 with *bake, pull, pulling.*

1877 PHELPS *Story of Avis* 31 There were twenty-five candy-pulls and taffy-bakes in that town that winter. **1883** RITTENHOUSE *Maud* 159 We're going to have a taffy pull at our Y.P.T.A. Friday night. **1888** *Tattler* (Baltimore) Dec. 3/1 The taffy pulling club . . . has been resumed again by the young girls of this city.

Tafia, Taffia. Also **taffy, taffieo.** A rumlike spirituous liquor. {**1793, 1799**}

1775 ADAIR *Indians* 260 The French Alebahma Garrison had been . . . supplied pretty well with corrupting brandy, taffy, and decoying trifles. **1781** *Va. State P.* I. 517 A Bottle of Taffier [is] at my Elbow. **1812** STODDARD *Sk. Louisiana* 304 In the neighbourhood of that city [New Orleans] were also twelve distilleries for making taffia. **1880** CABLE *Grandissimes* 113 Come, gentlemen, a little tafia will do us good. **1895** G. KING *New Orleans* 75 A woman . . . had taken too much tafia.

attrib. **1779** in *Travels Amer. Col.* 620 We dined and got some taffieo drink.

* **Tag**, *n.* +A label to be attached to a box, piece of goods, etc. (See PINE TAG, PRICE TAG.)

1835 *Stimpson's Boston Directory* (cover advt.), Tags for Dry Goods put up in boxes of 1000. **1866** *Jamestown* (N.Y.) *Jrnl.* 1 June 3/5 [The patent tags] are better than the linen tags and cost only half as much. **1895** *Dept. Agric. Yrbk. 1894* 67 These tags enable the consumer to learn whether the meat which he is buying has been inspected. **1911** *Okla. Session Laws* 3 Legisl. 250 Any person who shall counterfeit or use the counterfeit of a tag . . . shall be guilty of a misdemeanor.

+**b.** *Tag day*, a day during which tags are sold to secure money for charitable purposes.

1909 *Washington Post* 20 Feb. 3 Monday has been designated as 'tag day' in Alexandria, and the proceeds will be used to improve the children's playgrounds. **1923** *Kansas City Star* 23 April 3/2 The George Birmingham Memorial Society will have a tag day Saturday.

+**Tag**, *v. tr.* In certain games, to touch (a person). — **1891** *Amer. Folk-Lore* IV. 222 One player, who is 'it,' attempts to tag, or touch, one of the other players. **1924** C. WARDLAW *Fundamentals of Baseball* 44 It is often necessary to slide back to first in order to avoid tagging by the first-baseman.

+**Tag alder.** Any of several American alders. — [**1891** *Lancet* 3 Oct. 772/1 Tag alder.] **1894** *Amer. Folk-Lore* VII. 98 *Betula pumila,* tag alder, Minn.

Tagtail. {**1681**-} +(See quot. 1864.) — **1834** C. A. DAVIS *Lett. J. Downing* 311 You are surrounded by such a raft of snuffle-nose, scabby set of tag-tails, that I can't have nothin more to do with you. **1864** WEBSTER 1348/3 *Tag-tail,* . . . a person who attaches himself to another against the will of the latter; a dependent; a sycophant; a parasite.

* **Tail**, *n.*
* **1.** The rear end *of* a wagon.

1844 GREGG *Commerce of Prairies* II. 21 The two front wagons are driven up, side by side, with their 'tails' a little inclined outward. **1853** SIMMS *Sword & Distaff* (1854) 71 They crowded together at the tail of the wagon. **1870** NOWLAND *Indianapolis* 166 The two old men were placed in the tail of the wagon. **1920** HOWELLS *Vacation of Kelwyns* 128 The man had untethered two colts from the tail of the wagon.

2. In special combinations.

Tail band, t. chain, (see quotations); *t. digging, t. flume,* a digging or flume serving as an outlet; *t. hold,* a sitting-down position (*jocular*); *t. hook,* a hook used by anglers; *tail vise,* (see quotation).

1890 HOWELLS *Boy's Town* 90 The kite . . . had to be hung, with belly-bands, and tail-bands; that is, with strings carried from stick to stick over the face and at the bottom. **1905** *Forestry Bureau Bul.* No. 61, 50 *Tail chain,* a heavy chain bound around the trailing end of logs as a brake, in slooping on steep slopes. (N[orth] W[oods].) **1867** *Wkly. New Mexican* 23 Feb. 1/3 [They] had to make tail-diggings of about 160 feet in length to draw off the water. **1882** *47th Congress 1 Sess.* H. R. Ex. Doc. No. 216, 99 The mine . . . is provided with a large dump-house, reservoir, and lengthy tail flumes. **1878** BEADLE *Western Wilds* 459 Suddenly the walker's breath gave out and he took 'tail hold.' **1888** GOODE *Amer. Fishes* 8 Use a 'tail-hook' to avoid the risk of losing the minnow without gaining the Perch. **1864** WEBSTER 1349/2 *Tail-vise,* a small hand-vise, with a tail or handle to hold it by.

* **Tail**, *v.*
+**1. a.** *tr.* To catch by the tail (a deer that is in the water or otherwise hampered) in order to kill it with a knife. **b.** To upset or throw (a bull or pony) by grasping its tail and tripping or turning it about.

1839 HOFFMAN *Wild Scenes* 61 A man that can't tail a deer, oughtn't to hunt him. **1895** REMINGTON *Pony Tracks* 95 Mr. Bailey . . . in the next instant 'tailed' and threw the bull as it was about to enter the timber. **1897** LEWIS *Wolfville* 203 Tailin' a pony . . . [is] ridin' up from the r'ar an' takin' a half-hitch on your saddle-horn with the tail of another gent's pony, an' then spurrin' by an' swappin' ends with the whole outfit,— gent, hoss, an' all.

+**2.** To ease (a heavy load or a heavily loaded wagon) *down* a steep hill. *colloq.* (Cf. TAILING 2.)

1851 *Harper's Mag.* Sept. 518/1 In this manner the load is 'tailed down' steeps where it would be impossible for the 'tongue oxen' to resist the pressure of the load.

+**3.** *To tail up,* to assist (a cow) to escape from a bog by pulling or lifting on its tail; to force (a cow) to stand up by twisting its tail.

1868 *Iowa State Agric. Soc. Rep. 1867* 129 Shelter and good feeding is a sure preventive [for hollow horn], and much cheaper than 'tailing them up' or taking off their hides toward Spring. **1913** BARNES *Western Grazing Grounds* 122 There she was 'tailed up' and got onto her feet. **1920** HUNTER *Trail Drivers Texas* I. 299 A 'bog rider' is the cowboy who 'tails' up the poor cows which get stuck in the mud.

Tailender. {**1908**-} +A baseball team in the last place in league standing. *colloq.* — **1887** *Chicago Inter-Ocean* 7 May (E. J. Nichols). **1904** *Post Express* (Rochester) 17 Aug. 4 This year baseball is a failure in Rochester; . . . the club is a hopeless tail-ender.

+**Tail fly.** *Angling.* The fly at the end of a leader. — **1869** W. MURRAY *Adventures* 67 For the tail fly I noosed on a brown hackle. **1883** [see POLKA *n.*¹ 2]. **1899** VAN DYKE *Fisherman's Luck* 44 He does not . . . tear the tail-fly out of the fish's mouth.

+**Tail gate. 1.** A gate or barrier in the tailrace of a water mill; in a canal lock, the lower gate. **2.** The tailboard of a wagon, or a similar part of a railroad car. — **(1) 1853** *S. Lit. Messenger* XIX. 665/1 Bethink you of a fish sailing around the tail-gate of a country-mill. **1875** KNIGHT 1341/1 The head-gate and tail-gate [of a canal lock], . . . with the sidewalls, inclose the lock-chamber. **(2) 1868** *Ore. State Jrnl.* 28 Nov. 2/3 The whole charge . . . [passed] through the tailgate of the wagon. **1897** HOUGH *Story of Cowboy* 178 The cook unfastened the tail-gate of his wagon. **1909** WEBSTER 2106 *Tail gate,* . . . a heavy wooden panel pivoted to the end of a railroad car to form an incline from the car bottom to the rails.

+**Tail house. a.** (See quot. 1881.) **b.** A building housing the discharge ends of oil-condensing apparatus. — **1881** RAYMOND *Mining Gloss., Tail-house, tail-mill,* the buildings in which *tailings* are treated. **1888** *Scribner's Mag.* Jan. 22/2 This tail-house, or receiving house [for oil], was a favorite haunt of hers.

Tailing.

1. The lighter and less valuable parts of grain removed in the milling process. {**1764**-} Usually pl.

1787 WASHINGTON *Diaries* III. 277 The other hands were cleaning the tailings of wheat. c**1856** in Bassett *Plantation Overseer* 29 The Overseer must see them [*sc.* oxen] well provided with straw, tailing, and coarse flour. **1886** *Century Mag.* May 46/2 The lowest grade [of flour] comes from the tailings of the middlings-purifying machines. **1890** *Stock Grower & Farmer* 15 March 6/4 From the 'tailings' or leavings he fed fifteen head of horses.

+2. (See quotation and cf. TAIL *v.* 2.)

1792 BELKNAP *Hist. New-Hampshire* III. 106 Some of the cattle are placed behind it [the load]; a chain . . . attached to their yokes is brought forward and fastened to the hinder end of the load, and the resistance which is made by these cattle checks the descent. This operation is called *tailing*.

3. The refuse or debris resulting from the washing of ground ore. {1864-} Usually pl.

1850 A. T. JACKSON *Forty-Niner* (1920) 18 Worked out the claim and before I moved the Tom, tried some of the rocker tailings. **1872** *Harper's Mag.* Dec. 24/1 It issues from beneath the heavy stamps a grayish, sparkling, thin mud, and . . . passes off under the name of 'tailings,' leaving the gold-dust amalgamated. **1893** M. HOWE *Honor* 43 The tailing mill, . . . the remnants of metal, or tailings, which could not be utilized at the mine, were made use of. *a*1918 G. STUART *On Frontier* I. 89 Shallow gulches . . . would not afford any place for sluices to dump tailings. *fig.* **1876** MILLER *First Fam'lies* 226 He now found that the entire end of his father's name had been . . . worn or torn away, and hid or covered up forever in the tailings. **1889** MUNROE *Golden Days* 268 Come in and take a smile to wash the tailings out of your throats.

b. Attrib. with *assay, company, dump, mill.*

1860 *Harper's Mag.* April 616/1 Numberless are the 'tailing companies,' whose labors are confined to washing by a more careful method the 'tailings' or refuse. **1876** RAYMOND *8th Rep. Mines* 106 The mine of Sierra Buttes Company . . . crushed 49,821 tons of ore, yielding $356,420—a little over $7.15 per ton, exclusive of the tailing-assay of $3.76 per ton. *Ib.* 186 The silver or tailings mill has not undergone any change worth noticing. **1923** 'BOWER' *Parowan Bonanza* 46 He showed me a piece of rock no better than you can pick up on any tailing dump in Goldfield.

∗ Tailor.

∗1. One whose occupation is to make or repair clothes.

1626 *Plymouth Laws* 28 No handy-craftsman of what profession soever as taylors shoemakers carpenters . . . shall use their science or trades . . . for any strangers or foreigners. **1704** *Boston News-Letter* 7 June 2/2 A Young man, . . . of a middle Stature, . . . by occupation a Taylor, he's said to be gone. **1796, 1800** [see HABIT-MAKER]. **1888** *Amer. Almanac* 275. **1920** HOWELLS *Vacation of Kelwyns* 47 He was well enough dressed, but by the clothier rather than the tailor.

2. Any one of various fishes {1880-, in Australia}, +esp. the fresh-water tailor and the salt-water tailor.

1676 GLOVER *Va.* in *Phil. Trans.* XI. 625 In the Creeks are great store of small fish, as Perches, Crokers, Taylors, Eels, and divers others. **1709** LAWSON *Carolina* 158 The Taylor is a Fish about the bigness of a Trout, but of a bluish green colour, with a forked Tail. **1743** CATESBY *Carolina* II. p. xxxii, Sea Fish [of Carolina include] . . . Taylor, Smelt. **1859** BARTLETT 469 *Tailor*, a fish resembling the shad, but inferior to it in size and flavor. **1903** T. H. BEAN *Fishes N.Y.* 446 Some of the many names applied to this widely distributed fish are . . . salt-water jack (southern states), tailor (Chesapeake bay), whitefish (Hudson river).

+Tailor bee. Any one of various leaf-cutting bees. — **1867** *Amer. Naturalist* I. 373 The interesting habits of the Leaf-cutting, or Tailor-bee (*Megachile*), have always attracted attention. **1873** *Harper's Mag.* March 595/2 Peggy rolled out her paste reflectively, and lined a deep pan as daintily as the tailor-bee lines her nest with a rose leaf.

Tailoress. A woman tailor. {1654-} — **1723** *New-Eng. Courant* 15 April 2/1 The Callico was found to be of the same sort with some which Mrs. Sacum, a Tayloress living in the House, had lately been at work upon. **1796** *Boston Directory* 231 Bushley Mary, tayloress. **1836** WESTON *Visit* 63 In New York, gentlemens' trowsers, vests, and summer dresses, are all made by females, who are called tailoresses. **1888** *Amer. Almanac* 275 In [the census of] 1870, seamstresses were included with tailors and tailoresses.

+Tailor herring. The fall herring or mattowacca, *Pomolobus mediocris.* — **1883** *Nat. Museum Bul.* No. 27, 476 Hickory Shad; Tailor Herring; Fall Herring. . . . This is a comparatively poor fish; yet it is largely sold by unprincipled persons as the true shad. **1911** *Rep. Fisheries 1908* 312/1 Mattowacca . . . is called . . . 'tailor shad,' 'tailor herring,' and 'fresh-water tailor' in the Potomac.

+Tailor shad. =prec. — **1884** GOODE, etc. *Fisheries* I. 608 In the Potomac the species is called the 'Tailor Shad,' or the 'Fresh-water Tailor.' **1911** [see TAILOR HERRING].

Tailor('s) shop. A shop kept by a tailor. — **1827** DRAKE & MANSFIELD *Cincinnati* 65 Thirty-five Tailors' and Clothiers' Shops. **1884** *Century Mag.* Aug. 546/2 The daily walk of the Marquis began and ended at the Broadway tailor-shop. **1904** *N.Y. Ev. Post* 4 Feb. 2 A window of the tailor shop.

+Tail sluice. *Mining.* (See quot. 1877.) — **1871** RAYMOND *3d Rep. Mines* 85 This tail-sluice cost $55,000, and has been exceedingly profitable. **1877** BARTLETT 611 A *tail-sluice* is a sluice below other sluices through which the earth and water passes.

∗ Take, v.

I. 1. *tr.* To get behind or up into (a tree). {1618}

1835 SIMMS *Yemassee* II. 168 The foresters took their tree when necessary, as well as their enemies. **1847** L. COLLINS *Kentucky* 195 Both parties then took trees, and the fight was obstinately continued. **1853** 'P. PAXTON' *Yankee in Texas* 30 To all appearance the bear had . . . taken a tree.

2. *intr.* To freeze. {1877, in Canada (B. '77)}

1871 *Scribner's Mo.* II. 458 The rivers are beginning to 'take' or freeze.

+3. Short for *to take into camp,* (see CAMP *n.* 2).

1880 *Chicago Inter-Ocean* 11 June 8/1 They Take Troy, The Chicago Club Does Vanquish the Nine of That Classic Village.

II. In phrases.

For additional phrases, such as *to take the back track, to take the floor,* see BACK TRACK 2, FLOOR 2 b, RAG *n.* 2 a, SHINE *n.* 4, 5, SHOOT *n.* 7, STUMP *n.* 7.

+4. *To take and,* to proceed to.

1836 *S. Lit. Messenger* II. 388/2 If you do so I will take and tell father. **1865** *Atlantic Mo.* April 501, I'd take an' citify my English. **1876** 'MARK TWAIN' *Tom Sawyer* i, I'll take and bounce a rock off'n your head.

+5. *To take the hair,* to scalp.

1858 PETERS *Kit Carson* 215 The common expression now in use is that they proceeded to 'take the hair' of their victims.

+6. *To take a hand in,* to participate (in).

1874 EGGLESTON *Circuit Rider* 60 The new-comers 'took a hand' in all the sports. **1880** *Harper's Mag.* March 623/1 General Jackson . . . 'took a hand in' as soon as he could, by calling Mr. Eaton to the cabinet.

∗7. *To take hold.* **a.** To apply one's self; to become active. {1868-}

'*Dial.* and *U.S.*' (O.E.D.).

1830 N. AMES *Mariner's Sk.* 72 Whenever religion called in the aid of form and display, the women 'took hold' more naturally and entered into the details more devoutly than men. **1830** S. SMITH *Life J. Downing* 66 They took hold in good earnest and turned off more business in two days, than they had done in a month before. **1897** [see HUMP *v.*]. **1918** LINCOLN *Shavings* 238 Captain Hunniwell . . . [made] occasional references to the wonderful manner in which young Phillips had 'taken hold' at the bank.

+b. With *of:* To take under one's control; to manage. {1897}

1876 RAYMOND *8th Rep. Mines* 222 Men taking hold of their camp will have to spend a considerable amount of money before they can expect to recoup their investment. **1903** WIGGIN *Rebecca* 12 She takes hold of housework better than I do.

III. With adverbs. **8.** *To take back* {1674-}, +to withdraw or retract (a word, assertion, or statement). {1873}

1775 A. ADAMS *Familiar Lett.* 86, I had . . . made some complaints of you, but I will take them all back again. **1850** *Congress. Globe* 12 April 721/2, I take it all back—the whole of it. **1891** RYAN *Told in Hills* 319 That man is no horse-thief. Take it back.

∗9. *To take in.* **+a.** To visit as a part of a journey; to attend (a dance, entertainment, etc.); to inspect.

1755 *Essex Inst. Coll.* LII. 80 In our way by the Skuylkill rd. took in ye prop[rieto]rs Gardens. **1880** 'MARK TWAIN' *Tramp Abroad* 42 An owl . . . come from Nova Scotia to visit the Yo Semite, and he took this thing in on his way back. **1886** *Outing* IX. 59/1 The driver strongly advised me to 'take in' the *baile* to be given by the La Noria Goose Club tomorrow night. **1890** *Stock Grower & Farmer* 22 March 5/2 Then the party took in a Wichita hog killing. **1896** NORRIS *Stories & Sk.* (1931) 211 Sometimes [he] 'takes in' the races, or balloon jumps or high dives. **1906** *Springfield W. Repub.* 4 Oct. 5 American visitors to London would do well to 'take in' some of the lesser-known auction-rooms.

+b. (1) Of a school: To begin. (2) To teach (school).

1876 'MARK TWAIN' *Tom Sawyer* xx, She could hardly wait for school to 'take in,' she was so impatient to see Tom flogged. **1894** *Amer. Missionary* Sept. 324 Here, not quite two years up, we, in the dialect of the country [Miss.], 'took in school.'

c. To accept (work) to be done in one's own home for pay {1832-}; to serve meals to (boarders).

1879 *Harper's Mag.* Dec. 43/1 The women 'take in washin'.' **1892** *Ib.* May 874/1 Jane had used to take in sewing before her hands were diseased. **1896** HARRIS *Sister Jane* 65 The reason you was keeping the gal was because you wanted to take in boarders. **1896** — in *English Illus. Mag.* June 243/2 She supplemented the meagre income . . . by taking in weaving.

∗10. *To take up.* **∗a.** To occupy or settle on (land); to claim (a piece of public land) in accordance with the land laws; to make claim to (a mine).

1662 *Va. Stat. at Large* II. 95 Any person having taken up land deserted before the making of this act . . . , shall not . . . be outed of possession. **1672** *Doc. Col. Hist. N.Y.* XII. 498 They desired me to take them vp sume land. **1674** *Penna. Archives* 1 Ser. I. 33 Permission is hereby granted to Mr. Fopp Outhout for to take vp a certaine peice of land for himself and his heires. **1718** *Mass. H. Rep. Jrnl.* II. 92 The Committee [are] to be paid for their Services by those who Take up Lots. **1733** BYRD *Journey to Eden* (1901) 288 We crost a narrow Branch of the River into a small Island, not yet taken up. **1824** DODDRIDGE *Notes* 104 Our people had become . . . accustomed to the mode of 'getting land for taking it up.' **1826** FLINT *Recoll.* 56 The land had been, as the phrase is, 'taken up.' **1870** [see GULCH MINE]. **1885** *Santa Fé Wkly. New Mexican* 1 Oct. 4/3 Moore had taken up a ranch. **1896** SHINN *Story of Mine* 37, I took up five claims. **1903** W. E. CURTIS *True A. Lincoln* 17 Josiah took up a homestead in what is now called Harrison County.

b. To seize and hold (a runaway slave or indentured servant). *Obs.* {1596-, in general sense}

1704 *Boston News-Letter* 17 July 2/2 There is a Negro man taken up supposed to be Runaway from his Master. **1771** FRANKLIN *Autobiog.* 252, I was suspected to be some runaway servant, and in danger of being taken up on that suspicion. **1852** in Stowe *Key* 179/1 Had on, when taken up, a pair of blue cotton pants, . . . a new cotton shirt [etc.].

c. To make (a collection). {1908-, *Sc.*}

1849 E. DAVIES *Amer. Scenes* 42 While they were singing Brother such-a-one would 'take up the collection,'—a phrase which seems to indicate a greater degree of preparation on the part of the people than our 'make a collection.' **1870** M. H. SMITH *20 Years Wall St.* 323 If a child is born to one of the Board, it is common to take up a penny collection as a present. **1909** WASON *Happy Hawkins* 191 They took up a purse of eighteen hundred dollars.

+d. 'To call on a student to rehearse a lesson' (1856 Hall *College Words*).

e. Of a school, etc.: To begin.

1876 'MARK TWAIN' *Tom Sawyer* xiii, The bell for school to 'take up' tinkled faintly. **1878** *Scribner's Mo.* XV. 653/1 Meanwhile the 'animal show' at the appointed time 'took up,' as the country people expressed it. **1903** Fox *Little Shepherd* iii, When school 'took up' again Chad was told to say them aloud in concert with the others.

+f. To gather (honey); to ravage (a hive) for honey.

1880 *Harper's Mag.* Oct. 777/1 This fearless being, however, knew only one way to 'take up the honey,' viz., to brimstone the bees, killing every one. **1884** ROE *Nature's Story* 226 If a hive is to be emptied and the bees destroyed, or a bee tree to be cut down, the act is described as 'taking up' the hive or tree.

+11. *To take up for*, to stand up for. *local*.

1878 *Scribner's Mo.* XV. 769/2 To Amanda's surprise her father took up for Mark. *Ib.* XVI. 627/2 It was a shame for . . . Mr. Whittaker to take up for Bonamy.

*Taker-up. +One who takes up land or a piece of property. *Obs.* — **1662** *Va. Stat. at Large* II. 95 The former act . . . reserved to the first taker up his rights to take up land in another place. **1729** *Baltimore Rec.* p. xi, Such Taker-up or Purchaser [must] build and finish . . . such House as in this Act is before limited. **1745** *Ib.* p. xviii, There are several Sums of Money due from Takers-up of Lots in the said Town.

*Talk, *n.*

+1. A powwow or conference among or with Indians; a message or speech sent to or received from them.

1725 in *Travels Amer. Col.* 102, I was come with a great talk from all the beloved men of the English. **1784** in Ramsey *Tennessee* 305, I have received a Talk from the Cherokee nation, greatly complaining of trespasses daily committing against them. **1807** in *Niles' Reg.* II. 342/2 The enclosed *talk* which has been industriously spread among them needs no comment. **1870** KEIM *Sheridan's Troopers* 30 The council 'talk' resulted in a treaty.

‖2. *To be on talk*, to be under discussion.

1838 AUDUBON in *Harper's Mag.* XLI. 674/1 Just such an expedition is now *on talk*.

+3. *That's the talk*, that's right, that's the stuff. *colloq.*

1857 *Lawrence Republican* 11 June 2 Good, good, that's the talk. **1876** 'MARK TWAIN' *Tom Sawyer* ix, 'That's the talk,' said Injun Joe.

*Talk, *v.*

1. *intr.* To discuss a matter; to speak plainly or to the purpose. *colloq.* Also *fig.*

1865 TROWBRIDGE *Three Scouts* 138 If you'd like to say about eight hundred for this one, then we'll talk. **1883** HAY *Bread-Winners* 149 Now you're talkin'. **1911** SAUNDERS *Col. Todhunter* 109 Money's all that talks.

+2. To parley; to have a conference. (Cf. TALK *n.* 1.)

1868 *Harper's Mag.* Feb. 302/2 He told him that it was Pawnee-Killer and some other Sioux chiefs, who were anxious to 'talk.'

3. In phrases.

To talk (a)round a five-cornered stump, (see FIVE-CORNERED STUMP); *to talk turkey*, (see TURKEY 4 b.)

a. *To talk to death*, +to prevent the passage of a bill or other legislative measure by continuing discussion of it until the time of adjournment is reached. Also *transf.*

1884 *Boston Herald* 17 Jan., Its danger is that it may be talked to death. **1886** ALTON *Among Law-Makers* 62 The committee would run a great risk of being talked to death. **1908** STEVENS *Liberators* 304 The opponents of the measure undertook to talk them to death.

+b. In miscellaneous phrases.

To talk against time, to forestall an undesirable event by talking until a particular time; *to talk baby*, to talk as to a baby; *to talk sailor*, to speak in nautical terms; *to talk shop*, to talk of one's special interests or work {1888}; *to talk stand*, (see quotation); *to talk straight*, to tell the truth; *to talk the bark off a tree*, to talk incessantly and persistently.

1838 *Democratic Rev.* I. 44 A minority, however small, . . . may determine to 'talk against time.' **1869** LOWELL *My Study Windows* 82 Don't shake that rattle in our faces, nor talk baby to us any longer. **1881** *Cen-*

tury Mag. Nov. 126/2, [I] could talk sailor like an 'old salt.' **1854** EMERSON *Lett. & Soc. Aims* 88 We never 'talk shop' before company. **1871** BAGG *At Yale* 594 To 'talk stand' . . . is, to make the rank and recitation-marks of various men a topic for extended conversation. **1864** E. W. Pearson *Lett. Port Royal* 250 Mr. Tomlinson talked very 'straight' to Pompey. **1891** *Outing* Nov. 137/1 The sort of cover that tempts one to halt and 'talk the bark off a tree.'

4. With adverbs. **a.** *To talk up* {1719-}, +to talk freely or boldly *to*, to discuss.

1843 STEPHENS *High Life N.Y.* II. 190, I talked right up to him, as a free-born American ought tu. **1882** T. D. PRICE *Diary* (MS.) 6 Feb., J. H. Keller to see me in afternoon and talk up his troubles. **1884** *Vt. Agric. Rep.* VIII. 30 The subject . . . was talked up quite extensively.

+b. *To talk back*, to answer back, to indulge in back talk. *colloq.* Also *talking back*.

1869 'MARK TWAIN' *Innocents* 112 There was no 'talking back,' no dissatisfaction about over-charging, no grumbling about anything. **1874** — *Sk., New & Old* 203 An' when dey talk' back at her, she up an' she says, 'Look-a-heah!' **1887** BILLINGS *Hardtack* 144 Some of the more common ways [of showing disrespect] were to 'talk back,' in strong unmilitary language.

Talkee-talkee. {1808-} ‖A talkative person. — **1877** *Harper's Mag.* Dec. 38/1, I am only giving to these talkee-talkees the right to bully me.

Talking irons. =SHOOTING IRON. *humorous* or *colloq.* — **1843** HALIBURTON *Attaché* 1 Ser. ii, I jist hops out of bed . . . and outs with my talkin' irons, that was all ready loaded.

+Talking machine. 1. A phonograph. **2.** The sound-producing mechanism of a talking doll. — **(1)** **1891** *Appletons' Ann. Cycl. 1890* 709/1 In 1886 J. S. Taintor, working along the lines followed by Mr. Edison, produced a talking machine, which was called the *graphophone*. **1907** *St. Nicholas* May 637/1 It does not sound a bit like any talking-machine I ever heard. **1924** CROY *R.F.D. No.* 3 54 [The farmers] had talking machines, radio sets. **(2)** **1897** STUART *Simpkinsville* 110 The little talkin'-machine inside it has got out o' fix.

*Tall, *a.*

+1. Denoting something regarded as superlative or unusual, exaggerated, remarkable, extravagant, etc. *colloq.*

1834 in Mackenzie *Van Buren* 253 Our brethren in Oneida are all 'with one accord united'—look out for a tall majority in O. **1852** WATSON *Nights in Block-House* 110, I had a tall opinion of him ever after I heard of it. **1866** LOWELL *Biglow P.* 2 Ser. xi. 232 Democ'cy needn't fear The tallest airthquakes we can git up here. **1902** WISTER *Virginians* 338 Editors immediately reared a tall war out of [the event].

b. *quasi-adv.* Handsomely, proudly, or boastfully. *colloq.*

1842 *Knickerb.* XIX. 221 One of the striking peculiarities of our people is the disposition to talk tall. **1846** THORPE *Myst. Backwoods* 131 Well, I will walk tall in varmint and Indian; it's a way I've got. **1869** STOWE *Oldtown Folks* 72 You're the fust one . . . that's got into college, and I'm 'mazing proud on't. I tell you I walk tall.

2. Applied to plants that grow high. {1812- (Withering *Brit. Plants* III. 646)}

1806 SHECUT *Flora Carolinæensis* I. 106 Yellow flowered Horse Chesnut, or Tall Buck Eye, or Deers Eye, . . . a native of the western parts of Pennsylvania and Virginia. **1814** BIGELOW *Florula Bostoniensis* 66 *Chenopodium hybridum*. Tall Goosefoot. . . . Wastes and rubbish. July. Annual. **1843** TORREY *Flora N.Y.* I. 325 *Liatris spicata*. . . . Tall Button-Snakeroot. **1860** CURTIS *Woody Plants N.C.* 60 Tall Gallberry, (*I*[*lex*] *coriacea*) . . . grows in similar situations with the preceding. **1901** MOHR *Plant Life Ala.* 480 *Dondia linearis*. Tall Sea-blite. . . . Seacoast from South Carolina to Florida.

+Tall feed. (See quot. 1848.) *colloq. Obs.* — **1848** G. E. ELLIS *Let.* (Bartlett MS.), [I have heard] *tall feed*—as high grass. **1863** RANDALL *Pract. Shepherd* 371, I might have imagined that it [*sc.* hoofrot] was caused by 'tall feed.'

*Tallow. (See also BAYBERRY TALLOW.)

*1. The fat of an animal.

See also BUFFALO TALLOW.

1675 *Conn. Rec.* II. 385 The Councill doth grant Mr. Wm. Jones liberty to transport ten pownds worth of hides and tallowe. **1737** *Mayflower Descendant* X. 87 He [shall] further Render to my Said Wife . . . what Tallow She Shall have Occasion of for hir use. **1801** *Hist. Review & Directory* I. 110 The produce of North Carolina is . . . lumber, tallow, raw hides. **1835** HOFFMAN *Winter in West* I. 133 [Among] articles of Indian produce, . . . were large cakes of deer's tallow, about the size of an ordinary cheese. **1899** [see LYED CORN].

2. *attrib.* and *comb.* **a.** With *chandlery, cup, house*, etc.

1767 *Charlestown Land Rec.* 232 From Capt. Sheaffes Tallow House . . . to the So Corner of Flucker's Chaise House is 180 Feet. **1815** *Niles' Reg.* VIII. 141/2 There are . . . 6 tallow chandleries [in Pittsburgh]. **1841** CIST *Cincinnati* Advt., Evan Todhunter, Tallow renderer, Factory on Deer Creek. **1875** *Scribner's Mo.* July 266/1 [San Francisco] was no less uninviting . . . [with] a few hide and tallow warehouses on the beach. **1876** KNIGHT 2484/1 *Tallow-cup*, a lubricating-device for journal-boxes, etc., in which tallow is employed as the lubricant.

b. In the specific names of plants and fruits.

See also TALLOW NUT, SHRUB, TREE.

1875 BURROUGHS *Winter Sunshine* 153 The tallow apple . . . sheds water like a duck. **1884** SARGENT *Rep. Forests* 28 *Byrsonima lucida.* . . . Tallow-berry. Glamberry. Semi-tropical Florida, on the southern keys. **1901** MOHR *Plant Life Ala.* 834 *Sapium sebiferum.* Tallow-berry Tree. Coast plain. **1835** SIMMS *Partisan* (1854) 387 The prisoners . . . had been made to file into the groves of tallow bushes. **1909** *Cent. Suppl.* 1317/3 *Tallow-weed,* . . . a native forage plant, *Tetraneuris linearifolia,* of southern and western Texas. . . . Its name is due to its remarkable fattening quality.

*Tallow candle. A candle made of tallow. — **1731** J. SECCOMBE *Father Abbey's Will* xii, A rusty Lamp, Two Quarts of Samp, And half a Tallow Candle. **1785** WASHINGTON *Diaries* II. 452 In order to try the difference between burning Spermaciti and Tallow Candles I took one of each. **1838** [see GOURD 2]. **1891** *Century Mag.* Feb. 495 By the light of pine knots and sputtering tallow candles the mill workers have conned the primer.

*Tallow chandler. One whose occupation is making or selling tallow candles. *Obs.* — **1681** [see CLOTH-WORKER]. **1769** *Phila. Ordinances* (1812) 29 If any . . . tallow-chandler, within the said city . . . shall [etc.]. **1818** FLINT *Lett. from Amer.* 62 Manufacturing people of Pittsburg: . . . 4 Tallow Chandlers. **1852** *Harper's Mag.* Jan. 146/1 He concluded to choose some other occupation; and he finally determined upon that of a tallow chandler.

Tallow dip. A candle made by repeated dippings of a wick into melted tallow. In full *tallow-dip candle.* — **1857** STROTHER *Virginia* 212 The bare log walls, and the cold, yawning fire-place, were made dimly manifest by the rays of a single tallow dip. **1888** [see DIP *n.* 1]. *a*1918 G. STUART *On Frontier* I. 32 This was still the era of tallow-dip candles for lighting.

+Tallow hunt. A hunt for buffalo in order to obtain tallow. — **1821** NUTTALL *Travels Arkansa* 182 The Osages had now returned to their village from a tallow hunt.

+Tallow nut. =HOG PLUM 1. — **1791** W. BARTRAM *Travels* 94 These shelly ridges have a vegetable surface of loose black mould, very fertile, which naturally produces . . . Tallow-nut, or Wild Lime, and many others. **1884** SARGENT *Rep. Forests* 34 Wild Lime. Tallow Nut. . . . Common and reaching its greatest development in Florida on the west coast.

+Tallow shrub. A wax myrtle of eastern North America. — **1770** FORSTER tr. *Kalm's Trav.* I. 192 Candleberry Tree, Bayberry-bush, [or] Tallow shrub. **1789** ANBUREY *Travels* II. 300 [The candles] were made from the berries of a tree, which is called the tallow shrub. **1911** *Boston Transcript* 27 May 11. 3/7 The early English settlers called this plant [the bayberry] the 'Candleberry tree,' and the Swedes called it the 'Tallow-shrub.'

Tallow tree. Any one of various trees that produce vegetable tallow, esp. *Sapium sebiferum,* introduced into the southern states from China as a shade tree. {1704–} — **1814** PURSH *Flora Amer.* II. 608 *Stillingia sebifera.* . . . On the sea-coast of South Carolina; originally a native of China. . . . Known by the name of Tallow Tree. **1847** EMORY *Military Reconn.* 62 The trees chiefly cotton-wood, a new sycamore, mezquite, pala (the tallow tree of our hunters;) a few cedars, and one or two larch. **1857** *Rep. Comm. Patents 1856: Agric.* 138 [Fish crows] are fond of many kinds of berries, such as the cassena, Holly, and the tallow-tree. **1886** *Harper's Mag.* July 293/1 The long rows of tallow-trees . . . shaded an unpaved street. **1901** MOHR *Plant Life Ala.* 595.

*Tally, *n.*

+1. *Baseball.* A score, or a total of scores.

1868 CHADWICK *Base Ball* 46 *Tally.*—This term applies to the total score of the single innings played, or of the even innings, or of the totals at the close of the match. **1875** *Chicago Tribune* 29 July 5/4 [They] were only two tallies behind at the beginning of the ninth inning.

2. In special combinations.

Tally-keeper, one who keeps count of the votes cast in an election; *t. list,* a list of persons voting at an election; *t. pole,* a stick to which a beaver trap is affixed; *t. table,* a table or chart.

1875 *Chicago Tribune* 3 Nov. 2/2, 100 more votes had been counted by the judges than were numbered on the cards of the tally-keepers. **1856** DOUGLAS in *34th Congress 1 Sess.* Sen. Rep. No. 34, 11 The judges shall open and count the votes, and keep two corresponding tally-lists. **1889** *Harper's Mag.* Jan. 238/1 Trap and sticks being in place, the tally-pole is moved in parallel with the bank and lightly anchored below the surface of the water. **1885** *Missionary Herald* May 181 An ingenious tally-table is presented, which shows at a glance to which of the seven Congregational Benevolent Societies each church has contributed within the year.

*Tally, *v.* *Baseball.* **+**tr. and intr. To bring in (a run); to score. *colloq.* — **1875** *Chicago Tribune* 24 Aug. 5/6 A furious overthrow by Beals at second . . . tallied three unearned runs. **1903** *N.Y. Times* 18 Aug., The home players tallied only five times during the entire contest.

Tally board. {1849–} **+1.** *Naut.* A board containing instructions sent along with a tailblock to a shipwrecked vessel. **+2.** (See quot. 1905.) — (1) **1882** *Harper's Mag.* Feb. 372/1 The whip . . . is drawn on board with a pulley-block, . . . and a tablet, or tally board. (2) **1901** MERWIN-WEBSTER *Calumet 'K'* 11 The red-headed young man . . . came in, tossed a tally board on the desk, and said that another carload of timber had come in. **1905** *Forestry Bureau Bul.* No. 61, 50 *Tally board,* a thin smooth board used by a scaler to record the number or volume of logs.

Tallyho. {1756–} **1.** A large coach or stage. {a fast stagecoach, 1831–} Also attrib. **+2.** (See quot. 1901.) — (1) **1882** McCABE *New York* 260 In the summer of 1876, the 'Tally-ho,' the first four-in-hand coach, made its appearance in Fifth avenue. **1887** *Courier-Journal* 8 May 17/7 The air was chilly to those who rode on the four-horse tally-ho coach and all who were in open carriages. **1904** *System* April 249 Both the street railway and railroad will be relieved by automobile and tallyho service. (2) **1893** *Harper's Mag.* Jan. 287/1 They were . . . easily amused with picture-books, and accustomed not to play auction or tally-ho while their parents read and wrote. **1901** *Dialect Notes* II. 149 Tally-ho, a game like hare and hounds.

Tallyman. {1654–} One who tallies or keeps a count, as of votes, branded calves, or log measurements. {1889–} — **1867** [see COUNTER[1] 2]. **1888** ROOSEVELT in *Century Mag.* April 862/1 The tally-man shouts out the number and sex of each calf. **1897** HOUGH *Story of Cowboy* 166 A 'tally man,' to keep record of the calves branded at each outfit, has been appointed . . . to serve as general clerk of the round-up. **1905** *Forestry Bureau Bul.* No. 61, 50 *Tally man,* one who records or tallies the measurements of logs as they are called by the scaler. (N[orthern] F[orest].)

+Tally sheet. A sheet on which a tally is kept, esp. one used in keeping a record of votes cast. — **1887** *Courier-Journal* 7 May 3/3 The tally sheets of the counties gratuitously distributed at the convention . . . were a great convenience to delegates. **1889** *Century Mag.* Feb. 622/1 The growing disposition to tamper with the ballot-box and the tally-sheet. **1911** *Okla. Session Laws* 3 Legisl. 77 Such special election commissioner . . . shall receive . . . the ballots, ballot boxes, . . . tally sheets, stamps, pen, ink, pencils [etc.].

Tally stick. A stick on which a series of notches form a record of time or of transactions. {1897} — **1830** *Va. Lit. Museum* 526/2 A 'negro boy, with a tally stick was a statesman complete in his school.' *a*1861 WINTHROP *Canoe & Saddle* 153 [The Indian squaw] told my grandfather that he had been gone many years;—she could not tell how many, having dropped her tally-stick in the fire by accident that very day. **1895** W. J. HOFFMAN *Beginnings of Writing* 140 Several tribes of Indians, in California, employed a variety of tallysticks to record transactions in business.

Talma. [François Joseph *Talma,* French tragedian (1763–1826).] A large cape or loose, short cloak. — **1855** M. THOMPSON *Doesticks* 61 'Oberon' was not so objectionable (being a gentleman,) in a talma and plaid pantaloons. **1860** MORDECAI *Virginia* 357 The beau who struts beside his chamber-maid, is attired in a talma or shawl. **1870** M. H. SMITH *20 Years Wall St.* 274 They wear in their office, hats, heavy chignons, grecian bends, and talmas, thrown over their shoulders, which gives them an untidy and bunchy look. **1894** *Stat. at Large* XXVIII. 531 [There shall be levied on] jackets, talmas, ulsters, or other outside garments for ladies' and children's apparel, . . . fifty per centum ad valorem.

+Tamale. [Amer. Sp. from Nahuatl *tamalli.*] A highly seasoned article of food made of corn meal and minced meat, and usually wrapped in a corn husk. (See also HOT TAMALE.)

1854 BARTLETT *Personal Narr.* I. 107 Tamaules are minced meat, rolled up in corn shucks, and baked on coals. **1884** *Boston Jrnl.* 16 Feb. 2/2 A queer article of food, known as 'tamales,' is sold in the streets of San Francisco. **1913** LONDON *Valley of Moon* 104 They were seated around the table in the kitchen . . . making a cold lunch of sandwiches, tamales, and bottled beer.

b. Attrib. and comb. with *eater, wagon.*

1900 *Boston Transcript* 22 Aug. 11/4 A valiant Bostonian . . . promptly established a champion record as a tamale-eater, consuming three hot tamales in swift succession. **1908** 'YESLAH' *Tenderfoot S. Calif.* 79 At almost every street corner in Los Angeles, you'll find little tamale wagons standing.

+Tamarack. [Algonquian.]

1. a. Any of several larches, esp. the red larch of the North. **b.** One of the lodgepole pines of the West, esp. *Pinus contorta.*

1805 CLARK in *Lewis & C. Exped.* III. (1905) 66 The Mountains which we passed to day much worst than yesterday the last excessively bad & thickly Strowed with falling timber & Pine Spruce fur Hackmatak & Tamerack. **1821** *Mass. H. S. Coll.* 2 Ser. IX. 153 Plants, which are indigenous in the township of Middlebury [Vt., include] . . . *Pinus pendula,* Tamarack. **1835** HOFFMAN *Winter in West* I. 169 A tall pine or two lifted its sweeping cone above the tapering tamaracks around. **1867** HOLMES *Guardian Angel* 86 In place of the larger forest-trees which had covered them stood slender tamaracks, sickly, mossy. **1873** MILLER *Amongst Modocs* 2 Column upon column of storm-stained tamarack . . . have rallied here. **1897** SUDWORTH *Arborescent Flora* 23 Twisted Pine. . . . Tamarack (Cal.). *Ib.,* Lodgepole Pine. . . . Tamarack (Wyo., Utah, Mont., Cal.). **1916** [see MUSKEG].

2. Attrib. with *breeze, log, pole, root.*

1842 KIRKLAND *Forest Life* I. 30 Corn-cribs and pig-sties . . . are made of slender tamarack poles, which need no cost of sawing. **1853** J. W. BOND *Minnesota* 362 [He took up] a residence with the other 'Bachelors' in a house of tamarac logs. **1869** *Rep. Comm. Agric. 1868* 176 Frames of canoes . . . are afterwards covered with its bark, sewed with spruce or tamarack (*Larix*) roots. **1894** *Outing* XXIV. 94/1 By vigorous working of three paddles we got up a 'tamarack breeze' that carried us rapidly along.

+Tamarack pine. =TAMARACK 1 b. — **1891** *Cent.* 6174/1 *Tamarack-pine,* . . . same as *tamarack,* 2 [*Pinus murrayana* and *P. contorta*].

1897 SUDWORTH *Arborescent Flora* 23 *Pinus murrayana*, . . . Lodgepole Pine. . . . [Also called] Tamarack Pine (Cal.). **1909** WEBSTER 2110.

+**Tamarack swamp.** A swamp where tamaracks grow. — **1835** HOFFMAN *Winter in West* I. 169 You generally find a tamarack swamp the favourite covert of [bears]. **1853** J. W. BOND *Minnesota* 26 Frequently the lake opens at one end into a tamarac swamp. **1902** HULBERT *Forest Neighbors* p. xiii, The tamarack swamp showed golden yellow in October.

⁎**Tamarind.** A tropical tree (*Tamarindus indica*) having an acid, pulpy fruit; the fruit of this tree. — **1795** *Columbian Centinel* 21 Jan. 3/3 At Joseph Callender's Store . . . may be had . . . A few boxes Muscadel Raisins, . . . A few pots excellent Tamarinds. **1850** TYSON *Diary in Calif.* 20 The pomegranate, the tamarind, the date, . . . were scattered around in rich profusion. **1866** MOORE *Women of War* 133 On the other [side were] boxes of tea, coffee, soft crackers, tamarinds [etc.].

⁎**Tamarisk.** +Erroneously used for TAMARACK. Also attrib. — *a*1817 [see HACKMATACK 1]. **1842** *S. Lit. Messenger* VIII. 657/1 Opposite was a very extensive and almost impenetrable tamarisk swamp.

⁎**Tambour.** A kind of embroidery done on embroidery hoops; a kind of lace made by embroidering coarse net. {1778–} Also attrib. — **1781** in H. M. Brooks *Gleanings* IV. 52 Isaac Greenwood . . . makes Flutes, . . . Tea-Boards, Bottle-Stands, Tamboy [*sic*] Frames. **1789** *Md. Hist. Mag.* XXI. 240 She was . . . adorn'd with Pink Sattin Tambour muslin. **1820** *Boston Advertiser* 12 May 2/6 (Ernst), Tambour cotton. **1893** *Chicago Tribune* 23 April 44/4 Irish Point, Colbert, Renaissance, and Tambours $1.50, $1.25, and $1.00.

⁎**Tambourine.** A small, drumlike musical instrument with loose metallic disks around the rim. — **1807** IRVING, etc. *Salmagundi* v, Then the whole band opened a most tremendous battery of drums, fifes, tambourines, and trumpets. **1835** LONGSTREET *Ga. Scenes* 134 The band consisted of three performers on the violin, one on the clarionet, one on the tamborine, and one on the triangle. **1880** CABLE *Grandissimes* 247 Snatching a tambourine from a bystander as he entered, the stranger thrust the male dancer aside.

⁎**Tame**, *a.*

+**1.** Of grass or hay: Grown by cultivation; not wild.
1838 ELLSWORTH *Valley of Wabash* 39 It is very desirable . . . to get the tame grasses . . . set as soon as possible. **1863** RANDALL *Pract. Shepherd* 259 Some farmers . . . [make] enough 'tame hay' to give their sheep one feed a day. **1898** *Mo. So. Dakotan* I. 45 Corn stalks, oats in the bundle, millet, hay and other tame fodders are also found to be much richer in sugar and other flesh forming properties. **1906** *Daily Chronicle* (London) 28 Nov. 6/7 In America they call it 'tame grass,' we call it 'hay.'

+**2.** Of pasture: Having tame grass.
1857 *Ill. Agric. Soc. Trans.* II. 382 Where tame pasture is resorted to something more needs be done. **1898** *Mo. So. Dakotan* I. 46 As soon as eastern tame pastures are sufficiently formed to receive stock at all.

+**3.** Of land: Improved by cultivation.
1887 BUCK, etc. *Handbk. Med. Science* V. 9/2 The careful pioneer . . . had his corral . . . where the land had become 'tame.'

+**Tammanial**, *a.* Of or pertaining to the Tammany Society of New York. *Obs.* — **1791** J. PINTARD in *Amer. Daily Reg.* (N.Y.) 16 May, Before them was borne the Cap of Liberty; after following seven hunters in Tammanial dress. **1793** in G. Myers *Hist. Tammany Hall* 10 At Tammanial Hall in Broad street. **1812** *Columbian Centinel* 2 Dec. 2/3 The Ticket which prevailed was at first denounced by the Ohio Madisonians as 'Mongrel'—'Clintonian'—and 'Tammanial.'

+**Tammany.**
This was the name of a Delaware chief, *Tamanen*, *Tammenund*, or *Tammany*, who flourished about 1683. References to him for that year may be found in: *Penna. Archives* I. 62; Wm. Penn *Works* (1782) IV. 305.

1. *St. Tammany*, a patron saint of America, canonized facetiously about 1770. *Obs.*
See also TAMMANY SOCIETY.
1771 W. EDDIS *Lett. from Amer.* 115 The Americans on this part of the continent have . . . a Saint. . . . The first of May is . . . set apart to the memory of Saint Tamina. **1776** LEACOCK *Fall Brit. Tyranny* III. vi, Our shepherds . . . are celebrating our glorious St. Tammany's day. **1779** *N.J. Archives* 2 Ser. III. 293 The piece for celebration of the festival of St. Tammany . . . may not be much relished by our moral readers. **1789** *N.Y. Daily Gaz.* 14 May 470/3 Last Tuesday, being the 12th inst. (or the 1st of May old stile) was the anniversary of St. Tammany, the Tutelar Saint of America. **1791** *Augusta* (Ga.) *Chron.* 7 May 2/3 (Th. S.), The memory of St. Tammany. **1816** TUCKER *Lett. from Va.* 144 'By St. Tammany' said he, 'he died like a martyr.'

b. *Sons of St. Tammany*, the members of several patriotic societies loosely associated during the Revolutionary period; in later usage, =sense 3. *Obs.*
1773 *Penna. Mag.* XXV. 446 You are requested to meet the children and associates Sons of Saint Tammany at the house of Mr. James Byrnes to dine together and form such useful charitable plans for the relief of all in distress as shall be agreed upon. **1782** *Ib.* XXVI. 210 The Constitution of the New Jersey Society of the Sons of St. Tamminy No. 1. **1785** WASHINGTON *Diaries* II. 371 Received and accepted an invitation to dine with the Sons of Saint Taminy [in Richmond, Va.]. **1790** *N.Y. Journal* 11 May 3/3 To-morrow . . . the annual feast of St. Tammany will be celebrated by the Sons of St. Tammany & Columbian Order, at their wigwam on the banks of the Hudson. **1846** *Congress.*

Globe App. 1 July 1041, I was told that the sons of St. Tammany had degenerated into old hunkers, barnburners, and office-seekers.

c. The name of a parish in Louisiana.
1813 in Brackenridge *Views La.* 281 Lake Ponchartrain in the parish of St. Tammany, in the state of Louisiana.

2. *King Tammany*, a variant of *St. Tammany*. *Obs.*
1772 *Penna. Chronicle* 4 May 63/2 A number of American Gentlemen, Sons of King Tammany, met . . . to celebrate the Memory of that truly noble Chieftain. **1782** FRENEAU *Poems* (1786) 308 The Prophecy of King Tammany.

3. A fraternal and benevolent society of New York City, developed out of one of the earlier patriotic societies; the political club identified with this society.
Tammany has been a Democratic organization, associated at first with the early Democratic-Republican party, later with the Democratic party.
1790 *N.Y. Daily Gaz.* 13 April 351/2 To the Independent Electors of the City of New-York. . . . [Signed] Tammany. **1790** MACLAY *Deb. Senate* 206 The sons of *Tammany* had a grand parade through the town in Indian dresses. . . . There seems to be some kind of scheme laid of erecting some kind of order or society under this denomination, but it does not seem well digested as yet. **1839** *Jamestown* (N.Y.) *Jrnl.* 23 Jan. 3/2 A change has come over the spirit of Tammany. **1872** *Atlantic Mo.* Jan. 126 The overwhelming defeat of Tammany in the November elections shows what may be done towards redeeming a city from misgovernment. **1894** *Voice* 1 Feb., All the laws, good and bad, are . . . misexecuted by Tammany. **1925** BRYAN *Memoirs* 126 Mr. Richard Croker, the leader of Tammany, played an important part in this matter.

4. **a.** A member of the New York Tammany Society elected to office. **b.** *pl.* =sense 3. *Obs.*
1819 *Niles' Reg.* XVI. 224/1, 46 republicans, 39 federalists and 41 'Tammanies.' **1821** [see BUCKTAIL 1]. **1837** *Jamestown* (N.Y.) *Jrnl.* 26 April 2/4 Of the seventeen aldermen, the Whigs have twelve and the Tammanies five.

5. *attrib.* **a.** Designating actions, things, etc., associated with Tammany.
1807 IRVING, etc. *Salmagundi* xiii. 335 Mortars should be placed on the battery which . . . might be charged with newspapers, Tammany addresses, &c. **1868** *N.Y. Herald* 2 July 4/1 This Democratic Convention . . . takes possession of the Tammany wigwam. **1872** *N.Y. Herald* 22 Aug. 6/4 The Tammany robberies . . . [are] trifling in comparison with the old revenue robberies. **1895** *N.Y. Dramatic News* 16 Nov. 2/4 The return of the Tammany ticket in triumph this year certainly goes to show that the populace prefers to be ruled by this institution. **1903** Tammany coat lapel [see BUTTON *n.* 5]. **1905** *N.Y. Ev. Post* 16 Dec. 8 A very good young man whose goodness permeates a Tammany stronghold.

b. Designating persons or groups of persons connected with the New York Tammany Society.
1834 *Boston Transcript* 5 April 2/2 He is at present engaged . . . in fighting for the Whigs against the Tammany aristocracy. **1868** *Ore. State Jrnl.* 31 Oct. 2/2 The Tammany men attempted to drive them back into line. **1872** *Atlantic Mo.* May 642 If Mr. Thomas Nast could have died when the Tammany Ring did [etc.]. **1872** *Newton Kansan* 3 Oct. 4/2 R. H. Dana, Jr., says of the Tammany candidate [etc.]. **1884** *Boston Jrnl.* 11 Oct. 2/3 The Tammany braves are having barbecues. **1885** Tammany member [see ANTI- *prefix* 3]. **1890** *Boston Jrnl.* 1 July 4/1 Richard Croker . . . is to be entertained this week by the Tammany sachems. **1896** DODD *On the Broads* 110 Think of . . . our Tammany leaders turned into the Forty Immortals!

+**Tammany Hall.** Any of the successive buildings which have served as headquarters of Tammany.
The present Tammany Hall was built in 1867–8. (Cf. TAMMANIAL *a.* quot. 1793.)
1812 *N.Y. Ev. Post* 6 July 3/2 At a meeting of citizens held, in pursuance of public notice, at Tammany Hall [etc.]. **1832** [see DEMOCRACY 2]. **1868** *N.Y. Herald* 7 July 4/1 Outside Tammany Hall . . . a surging mass of humanity congregated. **1882** MCCABE *New York* 306 Tammany Hall stands on the North side of East Fourteenth street. **1924** *Atlantic Mo.* Sept. 315/1 This Tammany Society still lives and owns the structure known as Tammany Hall.

b. =TAMMANY 3.
1880 *Scribner's Mo.* Oct. 863/1 Ex-Governor Lucius Robinson, . . . diverted many votes . . . from the ticket of Tammany Hall, the local organization most powerful in the neighborhood. **1908** STEVENS *Liberators* 284 When their district workers could get no information as to how the laboring people were voting; . . . then Tammany Hall became alarmed.

+**Tammanyite.** A member or supporter of Tammany. — **1882** *N.Y. Tribune* 5 April, A resolution striking the names of the Tammanyites from the caucus roll. **1883** *Century Mag.* July 469/2 Tammanyites and Tildenites . . . would hereafter work together in harmony. **1903** *Nation* LXXVI. 469/3 The Tammanyite starts in with energy and enthusiasm, as indifferent as Light-Fingered Jim himself to nice ethical considerations.

+**Tammany Society.** =TAMMANY 3. Also *St. Tammany Society*.
1787 *N.Y. Journal* 3 May 3/1 Tuesday last, being St. Tammany's Day (the Tutelar Saint of America) the St. Tammany Society of this City

held their Anniversary Meeting, at the Wigwam at Halls. **1791** in *Mass. Col. Soc. Pub.* XXVI. 411 The 12th [Oct.] . . . was observed as a Centuary Festival by the Tammany Society. **1813** *Niles' Reg.* IV. 75/2 Tammany Society or Columbian Order. **1830** *Jamestown* (N.Y.) *Jrnl.* 26 May 2/5 The new party . . . assail . . . the Masonic Society and Tammany Society. **1872** *Harper's Mag.* April 686/1 The Tammany Society, or Columbian Order, is doubtless the oldest purely self-constituted political association in the world. **1882** McCABE *New York* 307 The 'Tammany Society, or Columbian Order.'

+Tammany Tiger. The symbol of the New York Tammany Society.
— **1871** NAST in *Harper's Wkly.* XV. 1056 (*caption*), The Tammany Tiger Loose.

Tammy. a. A kind of woolen, or cotton and woolen, cloth, often with a glazed finish. {1665–} Also attrib. **b.** A piece of this cloth.

1638 *Md. Archives* IV. 75 Goods of Thomas Cullamore: . . . an old black tammie suite & cloake. **1661** *Essex Probate Rec.* I. 344 A peece of stuff and a peece of tammie. **1754** *S.C. Gazette* 28 May 3/2 Wooddrop & Douxsaint have just imported . . . durants and tammies. **1790** [see DU-ROY]. **1811** *Niles' Reg.* I. 46/1 Tammies . . . can only be made of wool long enough to be *combed*. **1866** *Maine Agric. Soc. Returns 1865* 152 This in the days of tammy warp, was considered the best worsted warp wool produced.

Tam-o'-shanter. A round, soft, flat-topped cap, much wider on top than in the headband. {1884–} Also attrib. — **1887** *Harper's Mag.* March 602/2 She had run in to get a wrap and a Tam-o'-Shanter cap. **1905** RICE *Sandy* 33 Instead of the tam-o'-shanter she wore a big drooping hat of brown. **1920** LEWIS *Main Street* 16 Carol [was] youthful in a tam-o'-shanter of mole velvet.

Tamp, v. {1819–} +*tr.* To pack by ramming or tapping. {1909} Also fig. Also *ppl. a.* and *vbl. n.* — **1834** *Jamestown Jrnl.* 12 Nov. 1 He has all the accomplishments of Lord Bolingbroke, tamped into the mold of nature. **1872** HUNTINGTON *Road-Master's Asst.* 54 In tamping, it is customary to tamp the ties their entire length. **1880** *Cimarron News & Press* 19 Aug. 1/5 The lecturer then showed . . . [a glass chimney] with tamped adobe. **1888** SHERIDAN *Memoirs* I. 26 The floor was dirt compactly tamped.

*Tan. =TANBARK. Also attrib. — **1639** *Essex Inst. Coll.* V. 167 The land is granted him to make tan pitts. **1755** HEMPSTEAD *Diary* 660, I was . . . carting Tann from Nathan Douglass's to mend the Highway. **1835** *Knickerb.* V. 214 The black . . . cast a fresh handful of tan upon the ashes in the fire place. **1874** COLLINS *Kentucky* I. 514 The First Tannery was a very small one—a tan trough—made by Capt. James Estill . . . in the spring of 1780. **1896** NORRIS *Stories & Sk.* (1931) 26 How the Girl had come into the opium den underneath the tan-shop in St. Louis Place Bandy never knew.

Tanager. Any one of various tropical American birds of the family Thraupidae, some of which, as the scarlet tanager, have brilliant plumage. {1614–}

'Few of these numerous brilliant birds are actually known as *tanagers* except in technical treatises. Those to which the name is chiefly given are the few species which are conspicuous in the woodlands of the United States' (*Cent.*). See also LOUISIANA, SCARLET, SUMMER TANAGER.

1842 BUCKINGHAM *Slave States* II. 153 The exquisitely beautiful bird called the tanager . . . is about the size of our English thrush. **1862** [see GROSBEAK]. **1886** *Harper's Mag.* Nov. 872 A tanager flits by as though to fire the foot-lights. **1917** *Birds of Amer.* III. 78 It is the song of a Tanager.

Tanbark. The bark of certain trees, especially oaks, used in tanning leather; spent bark from tan pits. {1799} Also attrib.

1840 POE *Works* (1902) IV. 131 You have only to stroll along, . . . until you see tan-bark in the street, and a knocker wrapped up in buck skin. **1849** *31st Congress 1 Sess.* H. R. Ex. Doc. No. 5, II. 1144 A large number of the men found employment this summer in getting out tan-bark. **1883** ZEIGLER & GROSSCUP *Alleghanies* 286 Justice is no less likely to preside in pristine purity within battered, worm-eaten doors, above a tan-bark floor, . . . than within frescoed ceilings, stone walls and chiseled columns! **1903** *Smart Set* I. 140/1 She had ridden her first horse over the tanbark of Durland's. **1905** *Forestry Bureau Bul.* No. 61, 32 In gathering tanbark, the section of bark taken from the butt of the tree before felling it [is called the butt cut].

+b. Used in fig. phrases concerning the devil or hell, to indicate great haste or activity. *colloq.*

1851 *Polly Peablossom* 153, I'll larrup you worse nor the devil beatin' tan-bark! **1902** WHITE *Blazed Trail* 192 Old Morrison he's as busy as hell beatin' tan-bark.

+Tanbark oak. Any oak producing tanbark, as the rock chestnut oak or an evergreen species (*Lithocarpus densiflora*) of the Pacific coast. — **1883** SMITH *Geol. Survey Ala.* 296 On the high lands or extensive table-lands [is found] . . . *Q. Prinus*, (the mountain or tan-bark oak.) **1886** *Harper's Mag.* June 55/1 On the summits one sees the tan-bark oak. **1905** [see JAYHAWK *v.* b]. **1913** LONDON *Valley of Moon* 526 Trees and vines had conspired to weave the leafy roof— . . . lofty tan-bark oaks, scaled and wrapped and interwound with wild grape and flaming poison oak.

+Tan bay. The loblolly bay (*Gordonia lasianthus*) of the southern states. — **1884** SARGENT *Rep. Forests* 25 Tan Bay. . . . The bark, rich in

tannin, was once occasionally used, locally, in tanning leather. **1897** SUD-WORTH *Arborescent Flora* 273.

+Tandem. [Of obscure origin.] A kind of linen cloth. Also *tandem Hollands. Obs.* — **1741** *S.C. Gazette* 26 March, Just imported . . . wide garlix, tandem Hollands [etc.]. **1745** [see PRUNELLA]. **1758** *Newport Mercury* 19 Dec. 4/2 George Hazard . . . has to sell . . . Yard-wide Tandems.

*Tangent. +(See quot. 1895.) *colloq.* — **1888** KIRKLAND *McVeys* 147 [They] knew the radius of every curve, and the length of every straight stretch ('tangent'). **1895** *Stand.* 1839/1 Tangent, . . . a straight stretch of railway-track.

*Tangle, v. +*tr.* To add spirituous liquor to (water); to spike. *slang. Obs.* — **1835** KENNEDY *Horse Shoe Robinson* I. 256 Some water, Mr. Musgrove, and it will not come badly to my hand if you can tangle it somewhat. **1840** — *Quodlibet* 126 Bring us a tumbler of water—tangle it.

+Tanglefoot.

1. Strong drink, esp. that of an inferior quality. In full *tanglefoot whisky. slang. Obs.*

1859 MATSELL *Vocabulum* 89 Tangle-foot, bad liquor. **1867** HARRIS *Sut Lovingood* 113, I got two for one boots, an' old tangle-foot whisky enuf tu fill 'em. **1884** *Gringo & Greaser* 1 Jan. 2/3 A bottle of tanglefoot supplies the place of Mumm's best dry. *a*1918 G. STUART *On Frontier* 265 Each dispenser of liquid refreshments had the formula for making 'tanglefoot:'—a quantity of boiled mountain sage, two plugs tobacco steeped in water, box cayenne pepper, one gallon water.

attrib. **1864** *Congress. Globe* 20 Dec. 85/2 Take about a gallon of first-rate whiskey,—not any of the tanglefoot article.

2. *fig.* Something which makes one stumble. Also attrib.

1893 *Advance* 28 Sept., The tangle-foot complications in which it was sure to involve its defenders. **1908** W. R. HEARST in *Westminster Gaz.* 2 Oct. 5/1 The deeper he sinks into the tangle-foot of corruption and contradiction.

3. =HOBBLEBUSH.

1894 *Amer. Folk-Lore* VII. 90 Viburnum lantanoides, . . . tangle-foot, N.H.

+Tangle-footed, a. a. (See quot. 1859.) **b.** Awkward; stumbling. *slang. Obs.* — **1859** MATSELL *Vocabulum* 89 Tangle-footed, Drunk. **1888** *Voice* 27 Dec., Republican lies . . . are nearly always of this tanglefooted variety, which trip up and throw themselves by their absurdity and self-contradiction.

Tangle-leg. {1880–, *dial.*}

+1. *pl.* =HOBBLEBUSH.

1817–8 EATON *Botany* (1822) 510 Hobble-bush, tangle-legs. . . . Stem very flexible and crooked. **1860** CURTIS *Woody Plants N.C.* 91 Tangle-Legs. . . . The branches . . . form well secured loops for tripping the feet of inexperienced wayfarers.

+2. =TANGLEFOOT 1. In full *tangle-leg whisky. slang. Obs.* {strong beer, 1880–, *dial.*}

1864 *Ore. State Jrnl.* 12 Nov. 3/1 Little 'tangle-leg' was consumed. **1867** HARRIS *Sut Lovingood* 129 Onder a deckload ove tangle-laig whiskey. **1882** BAILLIE-GROHMAN *Camps in Rockies* 6 But my men and I knew too much of Western 'tangle-leg' and its vile poisonous qualities.

+3. *fig.* Intoxication.

1875 *Billings' Farmer's Alllminax* 22 Thare iz no fluid known to mortal man, that haz got more bakbone, and less tangle leg, in a quart ov it, than good, old 1776, Egg Nogg.

Tangle-legged, a. (See quotation and cf. TANGLE-LEG 3.) — *a*1856 in Hall *College Words* (ed. 2) 461 We give a list of a few of the various words and phrases which have been in use . . . to signify some stage of inebriation: . . . jug-steamed, tangle-legged [etc.].

Tanglewood. A region of thick, bushy woods. Also attrib. — **1853** N. HAWTHORNE (*title*), Tanglewood Tales, for Girls and Boys. **1863** MITCHELL *My Farm* 158 Within this tangle-wood, I have set a few graft-lings upon a wild-crab. **1894** *Advance* 26 April, [The bird] scuttled off in a wild panic through the thick tanglewood.

*Tan house. A house or building in which hides are tanned. — **1649** in Commons, etc. *Doc. Hist.* I. 188 He keeps Weavers, and hath a Tan-house. **1747** *Southampton Rec.* III. 113 John Foster Jr. shall have liberty to set up a tan house by the pond side. **1802** *Mass. H. S. Coll.* 1 Ser. VIII. 151 The other buildings are a rope-walk, a tan-house, a number of barns, and six windmills. **1843** 'CARLTON' *New Purchase* I. 91 You can't scarcely miss the path to the tan house.

Tank, n. {1616–}

1. A natural pond. {1678; 1825–, *dial.*} Chiefly W.

1869 *Overland Mo.* Aug. 130 A 'tank' in Texas is a pond of fresh water. **1890** *Amer. Antiquarian* July 201 The surface is smooth sandstone, with here and there great hollows filled with rain-water. These places are called 'tanks' by the ranchmen. **1896** *Dialect Notes* I. 426.

2. In special combinations.

Tank engine, t. locomotive, (see quotations); *t. room,* a room in a cheese factory where there are tanks or vats for milk; *t. rowing,* rowing for instruction and practice in a tank; *t. station,* (see quotation); *t. steamship,* a steamer having tanks for the transportation of liquids in bulk; *t. vessel,* a tank steamship; *t. water,* (see quotation).

1864 WEBSTER 1353/1 *Tank-engine,* a locomotive which carries the water and fuel it requires, thus dispensing with a tender. **1876** KNIGHT 2488/2 *Tank-locomotive,* . . . one having a tank or tanks enabling it to carry a supply of water sufficient for its own consumption without a tender. **1868** *Mich. Agric. Rep.* VII. 230 The tank-room is 14 by 14 feet, and two stories high. **1902** CORBIN *Amer. at Oxford* 148 To teach our oarsmen the rudiments of the stroke we resort to months of the galley-slavery of tank-rowing. **1895** *Stand.* 1839/2 T[ank]-*station*, . . . a railway-station at which there is a tank for supplying water to the locomotives. **1891** *Scribner's Mag.* Oct. 608/2 The tank steamship, for carrying oil in bulk, is an American invention. **1869** *Causes Reduct. Tonnage* (1870) 80 The Atlantic Works had recently invented a tank vessel for the carriage of molasses in the bulk. **1895** *Stand.* 1839/2 T[ank]-*water*, the watery matter that remains in the tank or vat in which fat or lard is rendered.

Tank, *v.* {1863-} +*tr.* (See quotation.) — **1874** J. C. McCoy *Hist. Sk. Cattle Trade* 59 Many thousands of stock cattle . . . were sold . . . to be 'tanked;' that is, the hide, horns, and hoofs taken off, and the balance of the carcass placed in a tank and rendered, or steamed; the tallow obtained, the balance was thrown away.

Tankage. {1866-} +The residue of slaughterhouses and rendering plants dried and used as manure and feed. Also attrib. — **1886** *Scientific Amer.* LV. 149/1 A new drier [is] adapted for drying . . . tankage, sewage, clay, fertilizers, etc. **1898** *Engineering Mag.* XVI. 112/1 The receiving tanks, . . . each receiving the cooked garbage, called tankage, from four digesters. **1924** CROY *R. F. D. No. 3* 64 On one wall [was] . . . a large calendar got out by a Chicago tankage company.

* **Tankard.** A one-handled drinking vessel, usually of pewter or silver. — **1638** *Md. Archives* IV. 48, 1. pewter tankerd. **1707** *Boston News-Letter* 17 Feb. 2/2 Stolen . . . A large Tankard with a Coat of Arms. **1761** *Essex Inst. Coll.* XLVIII. 96 To be sold . . . , tankards and cans, tea and table spoons. **1847** LONGFELLOW *Poetical Works* (1893) 78/1 Evangeline . . . Filled, till it overflowed, the pewter tankard with home-brewed Nut-brown ale. **1906** BELL *C. Lee* 307 She held in one hand . . . a large silver tankard engraved.

Tank car. (See quot. 1876.) {1904-} — **1874** KNIGHT 457/2. **1876** *Ib.* 2488/2 *Tank-car*, . . . a large tank mounted on a platform-truck, for carrying petroleum or other liquid. **1883** *Century Mag.* July 332/2 It transfers its oil to tank cars on the Philadelphia and Reading Railway. **1904** TARBELL *Hist. Standard Oil Co.* I. 23 Tank cars for carrying in bulk had been invented.

+**Tank drama.** (See quot. 1891.) — **1891** *Cent.* 6180/2 *Tank drama*, a sensational or cheap melodrama in which water is employed in the scenic effects as in representing a rescue from drowning. (Theatrical slang.) **1895** *N.Y. Dramatic News* 9 Nov. 9/1 The melodrama, a Dark Secret, . . . was the first of the tank dramas and a very big success. **1898** *Scribner's Mag.* XXIII. 505/2 'Real tubs' [as properties on the stage] lead straight to the 'tank drama.'

Tanking. +(See quotations.) — **1891** *Cent.* 6181/1 *Tanking*, . . . the operation or method of treating in tanks, as fish for the extraction of oil, by boiling, settling, etc. **1905** *Forestry Bureau Bul.* No. 61, 51 *Tanking*, the act of hauling water in a tank, to ice a logging road. (N[orthern] F[orest].)

* **Tanner.** One whose occupation is to tan hides.
1624 SMITH *Gen. Hist. Va.* v. 187 The Governour . . . set some that professed themselues Tanners, to make tryall of their skill. **1709** LAWSON *Carolina* 167 Tanners, Taylors, Weavers, and most others, may . . . thrive very well in this Place. **1790** *Penna. Packet* 1 May 1/1 Wanted by the Tanners of Philadelphia, a large quantity of . . . Birch and Beach Bark. **1812** MELISH *Travels* II. 55 The professions exercised in Pittsburg will show the rapid progress that society has made here: . . . glass-makers, glass-cutters, looking-glass-makers, tanners. **1897** [see FINE-HAIR]. **1904** TARBELL *Hist. Standard Oil Co.* I. 10 The second well in the immediate region was drilled by a Titusville tanner.
attrib. **1864** 'PENNIMAN' *Tanner-Boy* 17 Ulysses [Grant], the tanner-boy, had a mind of his own.

Tanner's bark. The bark of various trees, esp. oaks, used by tanners. {1731-} — **1722** *New-Eng. Courant* 29 Oct. 2/2 A House full of Tanner's Bark, a Smoke House and a Work-house were burnt down. **1789** [see POTTER'S CLAY]. **1808** in *Niles' Reg.* XV. 57/2 Let us look at the rich productions of our interior country: . . . Hides, tallow, beeswax; . . . Pot and pearl ashes, tanners' bark.

Tanner's oil. Oil of a kind used by tanners. — **1779** *N.J. Archives* 2 Ser. III. 58 To be sold, . . . tanners oil by the barrel. **1790** *Penna. Packet* 1 March 3/3 William Robinson, Junr. . . . Hath for Sale, . . . Lamp and tanners oil. **1845** *Xenia Torch-Light* 31 July 3/6 J. W. & W. W. Cooper . . . keep a general assortment of Leather, &c., . . . Tanner's Oil, Tanner's & Courier's Tools.

* **Tannery.** A place where tanning is carried on. {1736-} — **1788** CUTLER in *Life & Corr.* I. 407 Nottingham township [has] . . . fine gardens, mills, tannery, etc. **1812** *Emporium Arts & Sci.* (Phila.) I. 70, I recorded the 867 tanneries, 491 distilleries [etc., in N.Y. State]. **1873** [see OIL MILL]. **1882** LATHROP *Echo of Passion* xiii, Perhaps Mr. Evans . . . had turned off on to the tannery road. **1902** HARBEN *Abner Daniel* 31 My hosses is hitched up ready to haul a load o' bark to the tannery.

* **Tanning.** The process or business of converting hides into leather.
1630 HIGGINSON *New-England* 10 Sumacke Trees . . . are good for dying and tanning of Leather. **1695** *Huntington Rec.* II. 169 Whome soever peeleth any standing trees for bark for their use of tanning . . . shall forfit five shillings for every tree found so peeled. **1750** *Georgia Col. Rec.* VI. 360 The Lot before mentioned was well water'd for tanning. **1859** [see HOLLY BAY]. **1889** MUNROE *Golden Day* 8, I've follered tannin' fer a trade.

attrib. **1738** *N.H. Probate Rec.* II. 735, I give to my Son . . . all the Hides & Leather & Tanning Tools. **1778** *Essex Inst. Coll.* XLIII. 127 My said Grandson . . . [shall] have my Tan house and Tan yard with all the appurtenances & utensils for the Tanning Business. **1855** *Knickerb.* XLV. 14 The skins of minks, wood-chucks, and squirrels . . . [emerged] from a cheese-box, used as a tanning-vat.

* **Tansy. a.** Any one of various plants of the genus *Tanacetum*, as *T. vulgare.* **b.** A plant resembling or confused with this. Also with descriptive or specifying adjective.

1698 THOMAS *Pensilvania* 21 Most sorts of Saladings . . . [as] Mint, Tanzy, Wormwood. **1709** LAWSON *Carolina* 77 Our Pot-herbs and others of use . . . [are] Columbines, Tansey, Wormwood, Nep [etc.]. **1805** CLARK in *Lewis & C. Exped.* II. (1904) 126, I also observed wind [wild] Tanzey on this little river in great quantities. **1892** Crisp-leaved tansy [see CRISP(ED) a.]. **1918** LINCOLN *Shavings* 236, I never can make out whether it's flavored with tansy or spearmint.

attrib. **1809** CUMING *Western Tour* 179 [I refrain] from everything which might have the smallest tendency towards keeping up the heat of the blood, with the exception of the tansey bitters at May's lick. **1858** *S. Lit. Messenger* XXVI. 123/2 Tried to git a tansy dram befo I eet. **1894** ROBINSON *Danvis Folks* 246 It was told . . . by the rank tansy bed.

+**Tansy mustard.** An herb (*Descurainia pinnata*) having leaves like those of the tansy. — **1857** GRAY *Botany* 36 Tansy Mustard. . . . Penn. and Ohio to Wisconsin, and southward and westward. **1891** COULTER *Bot. W. Texas* 1. 16 Tansy mustard. . . . One of the most common of western mustards.

+**Tan-toaster.** *local.* (See quotation.) — **1873** C. THAXTER *Isles of Shoals* (1885) 69 I never could understand . . . what they mean by calling a great gale or tempest a 'Tan toaster.'

* **Tan vat.** A vat or trough in which hides are placed in a solution of tannic acid. — **1658** *Boston Rec.* 148 The complaint of greatt anoyance by tan Fatts of Mr. Batts. **1713** HEMPSTEAD *Diary* 24 In foren[oon] I Trimed T: Trumans Tan fatt. **1775** DEANE *Correspondence* 254 They take a piece of Ticklenburgh . . . and put it in a tan-vat until it has the shade of a dry or fading leaf. **1824** DODDRIDGE *Notes* 143 The tan vat was a large trough sunk to the upper edge in the ground. **1884** HARRIS *Mingo* 128 Ef the calf's fat, the ole cow ain't got much choice betwixt the quogmire an' the tan-vat.

Tan work. A tannery. *Obs.* — **1800** *Columbian Centinel* 4 Jan. 3/1 The tan-works of Samuel Henshaw . . . have been consumed by fire. **1819** FLINT *Lett. from Amer.* 125 The manufactures [of Cincinnati include] . . . a tan-work, a glass-house, and a white-lead factory.

Tanyard.

1. A tannery. {1711-}
1666 *Md. Archives* II. 24 Neither are there men to be found that are of Ability to set up a Tanyard. **1701** *Boston Rec.* 14 No person [shall] suffer their . . . Tann yards, to lie open where there is a well celler. **1796** HAWKINS *Letters* 19 Russel has been . . . about to set up a tanyard at Etowwah. **1804** *Doc. Hist. N.Y. State* II. 1183 [In] a large tan-yard . . . is manufactured a large quantity of leather. **1891** O'BEIRNE *Leaders Ind. Territory* 109/1 In 1856 the subject of this sketch ran a tan yard east of Boggy Creek.

+**2.** In slang or colloq. phrases.
Big dog of the tanyard, (see BIG DOG); *bully of the tanyard,* the cock of the walk; *to draw to a shoestring and obtain a tanyard,* (see DRAW *v.* 7 b).
1845 W. T. THOMPSON *Chron. Pineville* 18 The doctor could not but feel himself, to use one of his own polished expressions—'bully of the tanyard.'

+**Taos whisky.** Whisky of a kind made in the vicinity of Taos, New Mexico. *Obs.* — **1850** GARRARD *Wah-To-Yah* xviii. 211 We were under the influence of the harmony of nature, tobacco, and Taos whisky. **1851** M. REID *Scalp Hunters* xxv, There was plenty of . . . Taos whiskey, in the encampment. **1888** J. J. WEBB *Adventures* 119 A bottle of taos whiskey and *aguardiente* were set out.

* **Tap,** *n.*

1. (See quotation.)
1864 WEBSTER 1353/3 *Tap*, . . . the piece of leather fastened upon the bottom of a boot or shoe in tapping it, or in repairing or renewing the sole or heel.

+**2.** *pl. Mil.* A signal on a drum or bugle at which all lights in soldiers' quarters must be extinguished. Also used at the close of a soldier's burial.
1862 NORTON *Army Letters* 50 At 9 o'clock the 'taps' are beaten and all lights must be extinguished. **1884** *Century Mag.* Feb. 497/2 After taps . . . Slocum and Sheridan were in the habit of hanging a blanket over the window, and then lighting their lamp and pursuing their studies. **1919** HOUGH *Sagebrusher* 300 'Blow "Taps,"' he ordered of the bugler near by.

* **Tap,** *v.*[1]

1. *tr.* To pierce (a sugar-maple tree) in order to draw off its sap. {1694-, in general sense}
1792 IMLAY *Western Territory* 117 The men generally . . . tap the trees. **1818** *Amer. Jrnl. Science* I. 366 Maple-trees tapped for sugar. **1862** [see AUGER 1]. **1896** *Vt. Agric. Rep.* XV. 35 Tap with a one-half inch or seven-sixteenths inch bit.

+**2.** To drain off water from (a lake or stream) for a canal or for irrigation.

1829 J. Mactaggart *Three Years* II. 35 The Americans make a great boast of having proposed the daring plan of *tapping* Lake Erie, as they say, to feed their great canal. **1866** *Rep. Indian Affairs* 110 For irrigation, either the Gila or Salinas may be tapped at any convenient point.

+**3.** (See quot. 1864.)

1850 A. T. Jackson *Forty-Niner* (1920) 8 'Texas Bill' tapped one of the banks for two thousand dollars and won on the first pull. **1864** Dick *Amer. Hoyle* (1866) 456 In this game [monte], the limit is the bank, the player having the right, at any time, to bet the whole amount, which is called 'tapping the bank.'

4. To open up (a vein of mineral).

1871 Raymond *3d Rep. Mines* 268 It is the intention of the owner to tap the vein by a tunnel. **1877** W. Wright *Big Bonanza* 35 A tunnel was then started to tap the ledge on which the old shaft was supposed to have been sunk.

5. To cut in secretly or surreptitiously on (a telegraph or telephone line) so as to overhear messages. {1897-}

1878 Pinkerton *Strikers* 199 The strikers certainly had some experienced telegraphers . . . capable of tapping the line. **1886** Poore *Reminisc.* II. 109 Every wire in the country was 'tapped' and its contents made a matter of record. **1895** *Chicago Strike of 1894* 404, I took with me an operator and an apparatus for tapping the wires at any point.

* **Tap,** *v.*²

1. *tr.* To repair (a boot or shoe) by putting on a tap, or piece of leather, as a half sole. {1818-, *dial.*} Also absol.

1746 Hempstead *Diary* 453, I tapt & nailed Jont. Pierpoints Shoes. **1781** *Narragansett Hist. Reg.* I. 284 Tapped a pair of shoes. **1852** Mitchell in *Knickerb.* XL. 149 There is also the shoemaker . . . who 'taps' for half the city price. **1894** Robinson *Danvis Folks* 103, I'd rather tap tew pair o' boots.

‖**2.** (See quotation.)

1894 *Outing* XXIV. 347/2 He decided that the coon only tapped that tree, that is started up but jumped down and continued on its course.

+**Tapadera.** [Sp., 'a cover.'] (See also Tapidaro.) A leather cover for a stirrup serving to protect one's foot in riding through underbrush. Also attrib. — **1844** Gregg *Commerce of Prairies* I. 213 The estribos or stirrups are usually made . . . of bent or mortised wood, . . . over which are fastened the tapaderas or coverings of leather to protect the toes. **1879** *Cimarron News & Press* 20 Nov. 3/4 New Saddler Shop. . . . Stirrups, Tapaderos, Saddle Bags, etc. **1910** J. Hart *Vigilante Girl* 197 She looked, from the peak of her conical sombrero to the *tapadera* points trailing from her stirrups to the ground, the personification of equestrian grace.

+**Tap-borer.** (See quot. 1876.) — **1633** *N.H. Prov. Papers* I. 79 Tapp boarers 4. **1759** *Newport Mercury* 26 June 4/3 Imported . . . , Box Pullies and Pins, Gimblets and Tapborers. **1845** Judd *Margaret* I. 36 Above these hung proof-glasses, tapborers, a measuring-rod, and decanting-pump. **1876** Knight 2495/1 *Tap-borer*, a tapering boring-instrument for making spigot or bung holes in casks.

* **Tape.**

***1.** A narrow strip of linen or cotton material, used chiefly on wearing apparel.

1633 *N.H. Prov. Papers* I. 73 He sent me from the Isle of Sholes . . . 6 knotes of tape. **1759** *Newport Mercury* 26 June 4/3 Imported . . . Worsted Caps, striped Tapes [etc.]. **1803** *Austin P.* 1. (1924) 89, 1 Doz Wide tapes. **1898** [see Dolman].

2. Attrib. and comb. with *binding, lace, needle*, etc.

1655 *Essex Probate Rec.* I. 204 Inventory of the estate of widow Alice Ward: . . . tape binding, 2 s.; pins & needles & thred, 2 s. [etc.]. **1711** *Springfield Rec.* II. 41 Twenty one silke tape laces at 9 pence the lace. **1845** *Lowell Offering* V. 202 Here is a fragment of the pink apron which I ornamented so tastefully with 'tape trimming.' **1852** Stowe *Uncle Tom* xv, Two spoons scissors, knife, tape-needle.

+**Tape grass.** An aquatic plant (*Vallisneria spiralis*) having leaves suggestive of tape. — **1817-8** Eaton *Botany* (1822) 505 Tape grass. . . . In the river Hudson from Waterford to the Highlands. **1840** Dewey *Mass. Flowering Plants* 190 [Our] Tape Grass . . . was considered by Michaux a distinct plant from that of Europe. **1894** Coulter *Bot. W. Texas* III. 421.

Tapeline. A tape or strip of strong cloth or steel marked off in linear dimensions and used for measuring. {1893-} Also transf.

1841 Webster II. 752/2 *Tapeline*, a painted tape, marked with inches, &c., and inclosed in a case, used by engineers in measuring. **1878** B. F. Taylor *Between Gates* 144 What if we meet somebody on the tape-line of a road between! **1887** *Century Mag.* Sept. 697/2 Behind the locker . . . was an ordinary 100-foot tape-line. **1896** *Internat. Typogr. Union Proc.* 64/1 Tape line, 50¢.

+**b.** *To doctor the tapeline*, to impair the accuracy of a tapeline.

1877 W. Wright *Big Bonanza* 428 'Doctoring the tape-line' is a trick that strolling miners have sometimes been known to perform, when the opportunity was found.

Tape measure. =Tapeline. {1907-} — **1845** *Lowell Offering* V. 254 Do they have . . . tape-measures, and finger-nail brushes? **1876** [see Pocket scales]. **1906** Pringle *Rice Planter* 360, [I] took my tape measure and found it was fully thirteen inches long.

Tapestry carpet. A carpet made of threads upon which a design is printed or dyed before the fabric is woven. — **1852** *Knickerb.* XXXIX. 165 Her house is after the usual city pattern—[with] . . . tapestry-carpets, very soft, arabesque pattern, quite showy. **1854** 'O. Optic' *In Doors & Out* (1876) 125 Why couldn't she have . . . a tapestry carpet, and velvet draperies at the windows? **1891** Chase & Clow *Industry* II. 46 In tapestry carpets a pile is made as in Brussels, but only a single thread is used in texture, instead of the five or six which are run through the Brussels.

Tapeworm. {1752-} *local.* +A short, narrow ticket employed as a device for controlling votes: (see quotations). Also attrib. In full *tape-worm ticket. Obs.* — **1875** *Congress. Rec.* 27 Feb. 1890/2 The 'tape-worm' ticket . . . is three inches in length, one-sixteenth of an inch in width. **1878** *Ib.* 6 Feb. 804/2 'Tape-worm tickets' . . . were given to a certain class of voters, and as they were put into the ballot-box the employers of the voters could easily tell whether such tickets were voted or not. **1882** *Ib.* 2 June 4460/1 'The tape-worm' . . . had to be voted as given.

+**Tapidaro, Tapidero.** =Tapadera. {1897} — **1872** 'Mark Twain' *Roughing It* 175 It was a Spanish saddle, with ponderous *tapidaros*. **1873** Miller *Amongst Modocs* 45 The man . . . stretched his long legs in the tapideros. **1916** 'Bower' *Phantom Herd* 25 The tapideros were almost Mexican in their elaborateness.

Tapioca. A farinaceous food prepared from cassava starch and much used in puddings. {1707-}

1790 *Penna. Packet* 10 May 2/1 Tapioca For Sale By William Delany Druggist. **1817** *Holyoke Diaries* 167 Bought 59 lb Tapiocha for $3.54. **1867** [see Farina 1]. **1911** White *Bobby Orde* x, It was the season of . . . apple-tapioca and Brown Betty.

attrib. **1864** Moore *Women of War* 326 Make . . . a tapioca pudding. **1876** M. F. Henderson *Cooking* 322 Tapioca Jelly. . . . Soak the tapioca for four or five hours in the water.

+**Tappahannock.** A variety of early winter wheat. In full *Tappahannock wheat. Obs.* — **1868** *Rep. Comm. Agric. 1867* 349 The 'Tappahannock' is named as the only variety that ripened side by side with the white Mediterranean. **1870** *Ib. 1869* 245 Tappahannock wheat has been widely distributed by the Department since the spring of 1862.

Tapping. +The boring of holes or cutting of boxes in sugar-maple trees to obtain sap.

1791 in Imlay *Western Territory* (1797) 471 Tapping or boring . . . with screw augers from half to one inch, according to the size of the tree. *a*1797 *Ib.* 145 A single tree has not only survived, but flourished, after 42 tappings in the same number of years. **1857** *Quinland* I. 52 The 'tapping' of the trees, the gathering of the sap, . . . were exceedingly laborious. **1898** N. E. Jones *Squirrel Hunters of Ohio* 19 The evidence shown in the wood made into lumber after many years *'tapping'* for *'sugar water'* (not sap), is not significant of injury or decay.

attrib. **1872** *Vermont Bd. Agric. Rep.* I. 214 The metallic or tin spout is a great improvement on the old wooden spout used after the tapping iron. **1900** Bacheller *E. Holden* 95 Then came tapping time in which I helped carry the buckets.

* **Tar,** *n.*

***1.** A thick, black or dark-colored, viscous substance, obtained by the distillation of wood, coal, etc.

1610 *Estate of Va.* 54 [Virginia] yeeldeth abundance of wood, as Oake, Wainscot, . . . Cedar and Firre; which are the materials of soape ashes, . . . of pitch and tarre [etc.]. **1640** *Conn. Rec.* I. 114 Richard Lyman hath the like liberty . . . for the making pitch and tarr. **1705** *Boston News-Letter* 25 June 1/2 They took a small Sloop . . . loaded with Pitch and Tarr. **1777** Cresswell *Journal* 268 More Tar and Pork is exported from Carolina than Virginia. **1832** Browne *Sylva* 232 To procure the tar, a kiln is formed in a part of the forest abounding in dead wood. **1865** *Nation* I. 558 The chief business of Fayetteville is the shipment of tar, rosin, and spirits of turpentine down the river to Wilmington. **1915** Tarkington *Penrod* 256 It was the stickiest tar Penrod had ever used for any purposes whatsoever.

+**2.** *Tar and feathers*, a coating of tar smeared upon a person and then covered with feathers.

1775 Fithian *Journal* II. 25 [He] is now in great fear, & very humble, since he hears many of his townsmen talking of tar and feathers—these mortifying weapons. **1789** *Md. Hist. Mag.* XVIII. 311 It was hinted that a Coat of Tar and Feathers, would be given him as a reward for his Services. **1834** *S. Lit. Messenger* I. 87 If he remained longer, he was in danger of tar and feathers. **1853** Simms *Sword & Distaff* (1854) 149 We dressed [the Dutchman] in tar and feathers at Monk's Corner, for stealing cattle. **1925** Benefield *Chicken-Wagon Family* 310 That's the stuff; give 'em the tar and feathers.

+**3.** *To knock the tar out of*, to beat unmercifully. *colloq.*

1923 *Dialect Notes* V. 212 *Knock the tar out of*, . . . to beat senseless. [McDonald Co., Mo.]

4. *attrib.* and *comb.* **a.** Designating things out of which tar is distilled, or equipment or places connected with making tar.

1668 *Plymouth Rec.* I. 100 Land . . . lying on the southeast syde . . . by John Rickards Tar pitts by a swamp syde. **1707** *N.J. Archives* 1 Ser. XI. 24 No person . . . shall presume to Cut, Fell, or Destroy any Pitch-Pine Trees, or Tar-Trees. **1723** Tarr Bucket [see FORCED *a.*]. **1798** *Wilmington* (N.C.) *Gazette* 22 Feb., A Water Lot, 66 2-3 feet in front, with the tar shed &c. thereon. **1890** *Congress. Rec.* 23 June 6393/2 Burn some North Carolina tar-knots. . . . That will destroy your malaria.

b. Designating substances containing tar, esp. for medicinal purposes.

1748 H. ELLIS *Hudson's Bay* 200 The only powerful and prevailing Medicine, was Tar-Water. **1820** *U.S. Pharmacopœia* 253 Tar Ointment. **1882** RITTENHOUSE *Maud* 128, I'm taking . . . lemons, troches, tar drops, and still I croak. **1891** *Cent.* 6187/3 *Tar bandage*, an antiseptic bandage made by saturating a roller bandage, after application, with a mixture of 1 part of olive oil and 20 parts of tar. **1898** *Kansas City Star* 18 Dec. 5/2, 25 boxes Tar Soap, 12 bars . . . 25¢. **1907** *Putnam's Mag.* July 482/1 A whole house covered with tar paper . . . sat complacently upon a hay wagon.

c. Designating persons engaged in making tar. Hence, *tarburner*, a nickname for a rustic southerner.

1791 WASHINGTON *Diaries* IV. 164 The lower down [the country] the greater number of Tar makers are there. **1808** *Norfolk* (Va.) *Gazette* 16 March 2/4 (Th. S.), According to the arithmetick of the ignorant 'Tar-burners,' [this] would amount to eleven hundred and fifty dollars.

✳ Tar, *v.*

1. *tr.* To punish (a person) by smearing tar upon his body.

1774 J. ADAMS *Familiar Lett.* 12 Pote . . . railed away at Boston mobs, drowning tea, and tarring Malcom. **1865** *Atlantic Mo.* Feb. 192/1 The poem covers the whole Revolutionary period: . . . mobs, tarring, feathering, and smoking Tories.

+2. *To tar and feather*, to punish (a person) by smearing him with tar and feathers. (See TAR *n.* 2.)

In group (2) the verb *tar* is not subject to inflection. (See TAR AND FEATHERING).

(1) **1773** FINLAY *Journal* 23 An informer would get tar'd and feather'd. **1794** *Ann. 4th Congress* 2 Sess. 2852 A party of men . . . seized, tarred and feathered him, cut off his hair, and deprived him of his horse. **1836** E. L. JOHNSTON *Recoll. Ga. Loyalist* 44 If a Tory refused to join the people, he was imprisoned, and tarred and feathered. **1857** *Lawrence* (Kan.) *Republican* 28 May 1 A free state man . . . had been taken into Missouri, tarred and feathered and sold at auction to a negro. **1903** 'O. HENRY' *Roads of Destiny* 367, I was telling him about the fun we had tarring and feathering that faro dealer at California Pete's layout!

(2) **1840** *Niles' Nat. Reg.* 9 May 160/2 Some white persons . . . , hearing that a white girl was living with two black boys, caught the lads and tar and feathered their head.

+Tar and feathering. The action of tarring and feathering a person. Also attrib. with *party.* — **1809** IRVING *Knickerb.* IV. iv, The enemy . . . were represented as a gigantic, gunpowder race of men, . . . exceedingly expert at boxing, biting, gouging, tar and feathering. **1864** TROWBRIDGE *Cudjo's Cave* 39 Now, where's your tar-and-feathering party? **1890** *Century Mag.* Dec. 307 We ain't a tar-and-feathering party.

+Tar and Turpentine State. =TURPENTINE STATE. — **1856** *Harper's Mag.* May 854/2 He lost his way among the pine woods that abound in that tar and turpentine State. **1876** INGRAM *Centennial Exp.* 734 He spent his youth in the good old 'Tar and Turpentine State.'

✳Tarantula. +A large, hairy, American spider of the family Aviculariidae, as the common southwestern species, *Eurypelma hentzii.* {1871, in W. Indies} — [**1794** MORSE *Amer. Geog.* 597 Scorpions and tarantulas are found here [in Dutch Guiana] of a large size and great venom.] **1814** BRACKENRIDGE *Views La.* 59 In the southern parts, both the scorpion and the tarantula exist. **1835** A. PARKER *Trip to Texas* 152 The tarantula . . . looks like a large brown spider, as big as the palm of the hand. **1872** 'MARK TWAIN' *Roughing It* 164 They brought in great store of prodigious hairy spiders—tarantulas. **1923** J. H. COOK *On Old Frontier* 28 There were plenty of tarantulas, centipedes, and scorpions.

+Tarantula hawk. Any large wasp of the genus *Pepsis.* — **1878** B. F. TAYLOR *Between Gates* 198 The tarantula hawk . . . pounces upon his victim and makes a needle-cushion of him. **1909** WEBSTER 2114/3.

+Tarantula juice. Straight whisky: (see also quot. 1873). *slang.* *Obs.* — **1861** *Harper's Mag.* Jan. 147/2 Little to drink, except old-fashioned tarentula-juice, 'warranted to kill at forty paces.' **1873** BEADLE *Undevel. West* 393 That [whisky] which is smuggled in is the vilest compound known to the trade, familiarly called 'tarantula juice.' **1886** F. W. GREEN *Notes on N.Y.* 28 The sweetly simple whiskey straight, 'Old Bourbon,' . . . is also called . . . Tarantula juice.

+Tarantula-killer. =TARANTULA HAWK. — **1867** *Amer. Naturalist* I. 137 The large, red-winged 'Tarantula Killer' . . . is, as far as I know, the largest of the dauber group. **1899** *Cambridge Nat. Hist.* VI. 105 P[epsis] formosus, . . . is called in Texas the tarantula-killer.

✳ Tar barrel. A barrel for holding tar.

1673 *Plymouth Laws* 170, 15 Gallons beer measure shalbe a settled Gage for Tarr barrells. **1709** *Boston Rec.* 91 Mr Isaiah Tay & Mr Jonas Clark are desired to provide conveniencyes for the ready placeing and fireing a Tarr barrell on ye Beacon. **1854** SIMMS *Southward Ho!* 63 He fired a beacon of tar-barrels. **1902** HARBEN *A. Daniel* 249 Half a dozen big bonfires made of dry-goods boxes, kerosene and tar barrels . . . were blazing along the main street.

+b. *To have one's head in a tar barrel*, to be in a fix.

1834 CARRUTHERS *Kentuckian* I. 63 Pete had his head in a tar barrel sure enough.

+c. *As busy as a bee in a tar barrel*, or variant: Very busy.

1859 [see BEE[1] 1 b]. **1889** COOKE *Steadfast* 197, I've been busier'n a bee in a tar-barrel ever sence the folks come home.

+Tar-Boiler. =TARHEEL. — **1845** *Cincinnati Misc.* I. 240 The inhabitants of . . . N. Carolina [are called] Tar-boilers. **1888** WHITMAN *Nov. Boughs* 406 Those from . . . North Carolina . . . [were called] Tar Boilers.

✳Tardy, *a.* Late for a meeting, appointment, etc. — **1638** *Md. Archives* I. 16 Mr. Greene amerced for tardie appearing. **1843** *Yale Lit. Mag.* VIII. 240 We were 'tardy' at our *matins.* **1901** G. M. MARTIN *Emmy Lou* 10 His tardy and clattering arrival had been a daily happening. **1905** *Springfield W. Repub.* 28 April 9 In all his career he never missed a rehearsal nor was tardy.

✳ Target, *n.* **a.** An object to be aimed at in shooting practice. {1757-} **+b.** A signal attached to a railroad switch to indicate whether it is open or shut. Also attrib.

(a) **1704** S. KNIGHT *Journal* 39 On training dayes The Youth divert themselves by Shooting at the Target, as they call it, (but it very much resembles a pillory). **1806** LEWIS in *L. & Clark Exped.* V. (1905) 30 [The Chopunnish Indians'] amusements . . . consist principally in shooting their arrows at a bowling target made of willow bark. **1902** [see CHUG *n.*]. (b) **1883** KNIGHT *Suppl.* 810/1 These are turned by the target-man by means of a hand-lever. *Ib.*, A common form at ordinary switches is an upright pivoted lever with target on top. **1904** *Chicago Tribune* 18 Aug. 3 The passenger train had the right of way, and the 'target' was against the freight train.

Target, *v.* {1611-} **+**tr. To have a favorable target at (a switch). — **1893** *Columbus Dispatch* 17 Nov., The crews of both trains claim to have had the crossing targeted.

+Tarheel. A native of the pine barrens, esp. of North Carolina; a North Carolinian. A nickname. — **1864** *Southern Hist. Soc. P.* II. 232 A poor, starving Tar Heel at Elmira [prison]. **1869** *Overland Mo.* III. 128 A brigade of North Carolinians . . . failed to hold a certain hill, and were laughed at by the Mississippians for having forgotten to tar their heels that morning. Hence originated their cant name, 'Tar-heels.' **1872** POWERS *Afoot & Alone* 39 The Tar-heels haven't no sense to spare. **1884** *Encycl. Brit.* (ed. 9) *Amer. Suppl.* I. 199/1 In pineries [in the South], . . . the population is far superior to the *tar heel*, the nickname of the dwellers in barrens. **1903** *N.Y. Tribune* 20 Sept., The men really like to work, which is all but incomprehensible to the true 'tar heel.'

✳ Tariff, *n.*

✳1. A schedule of duties imposed by law upon imports; collect., the duties thus imposed; a law imposing such a schedule of duties.

See also BLACK TARIFF, HORIZONTAL TARIFF and cf. COMPROMISE b. The quotations in the first group that follows illustrate the early use of the full term *tariff of duties.* The second group shows the more elliptical use now common.

(1) **1814** *Ann. 13th Congress* 2 Sess. 1971 The proper measure is undoubtedly a new regulation of the tariff of duties. **1837** JACKSON in *Pres. Mess. & P.* III. 299 Many powerful interests . . . succeeded in obtaining a tariff of duties bearing most oppressively on the agricultural and laboring classes of society.

(2) **1816** *Ann. 14th Congress* 1 Sess. 1674 A statement of the general principles for reforming the tariff of the United States. **1830** S. SMITH *Life J. Downing* 98 The Portland Advertiser has been blowin away lately and praising up the tariff. **1833** A. GREENE *Yankee among Nullifiers* 16 You know what my opinion has hitherto been in relation to State Rights and the unconstitutionality of the Tariff. **1836** *Diplom. Corr. Texas* I. (1908) 152 She would soon complain of and be oppressed by high Tariffs and other Northern measures. **1852** GOUGE *Fiscal Hist. Texas* 141 In the ten years Texas existed as an independent Republic, it had no less than seven distinct tariffs. **1883** WELLS *Practical Economics* 111 A high tariff, under present conditions, therefore, necessarily means low wages. **1906** *Nation* 9 Aug. 112 The Secretary of the Treasury is always planted with both feet on a tariff which it is a sacrilege to revise.

+b. *Tariff for revenue* (*only*), a tariff to raise revenue, not to protect industry.

See also REVENUE TARIFF and cf. PROTECTIVE TARIFF. **1830** *Congress. Deb.* 27 Jan. 84/1 Suppose, Sir, the New England gentlemen were now to join the South in going back to a tariff for revenue. **1880** in McKee *National Conventions* (1901) 183 The Democrats of the United States [declare] . . . a tariff for revenue only.

+c. *Tariff of abominations,* (see quotations).

[**1833** CALHOUN *Works* (1856) II. 217 The act of 1828, that 'bill of abominations,' as it has been so often and properly termed.] **1902** D. R. DEWEY *Financial Hist. U.S.* 180 The tariff act of 1828 represented the high-water mark of protective legislation before the Civil War; it was generally condemned, and derisively termed the 'Black Tariff' and the 'Tariff of Abominations.'

2. A duty on a particular commodity, constituting an item in the general tariff schedule.

1890 *Stock Grower & Farmer* 1 March 5/3 The difficulty was largely over the proposed tariff on carpet wools. **1892** *Courier-Journal* 3 Oct. 5/7, I shall surely not vote against any amendment to our laws imposing a triple tariff on imported convict-made goods.

+3. *spec.* A schedule of rates or charges made by a railroad; an item in such a schedule; a fare. {a1751–1838 in general sense}

1868 *Rep. Comm. Agric. 1867* p. viii, These monopolies have combined, in their tariff of rates, to discriminate unfairly against farm products. **1881** [see FAST FREIGHT LINE]. **1903** E. JOHNSON *Railway Transportation* 255 Packing-house products from the central West to the Atlantic seaboard were habitually charged from five to ten cents per hundred pounds less than the published tariffs. **1904** *N.Y. Ev. Post* 18 June, The 'fares' . . . are not passenger tariffs, but cargoes of fresh or salted fish.

4. *attrib.* and *comb.* **a.** In sense 1 with *act, bill*, etc.

1821 J. Q. ADAMS *Memoirs* V. 309 The revival at the next session of Congress of Mr. Baldwin's tariff bills. **1824** *Ann. 18th Congress* 1 Sess. 2142 This falling off [of revenue] . . . cannot well be attributed to Tariff legislation. **1830** *Congress. Deb.* 29 April 859/2 Restrictions [were] imposed by the tariff States upon the commerce of the planting states. **1845** POLK in *Pres. Mess. & P.* IV. 401 The intention of Congress, expressed in a proviso to the tariff act itself, that [etc.]. **1882** *Nation* 31 Aug. 166/1 At a Boston session of the Tariff Commission Mr. H. O. Houghton . . . gave some novel reasons for objecting to any reduction of the twenty-five per cent. duty on books. **1890** *Boston Jrnl.* 22 Oct. 2/4 The gerrymandered Eighth Congressional District . . . was one . . . that the 'tariff reformers' depended on to help them control the House of Representatives. **1903** HART *Actual Govt.* 7 The coast of the ocean fronts and the Great Lakes is divided into 120 tariff collection districts. **1904** Tariff wall [see MIDDLE STATES].

+b. In sense 3 with *sheet*.

1898 *Boston Herald* 23 Jan. 14/3 (Ernst), There are indications that tariff sheets are being secretly shaved.

Tariff, *v.* {1756–} *tr.* To put a duty on (goods): (see also quot. 1828). {1864–} — **1828** WEBSTER, *Tarif*, to make a list of duties on goods. **1832** WATSON *Hist. Tales N.Y.* 86 We tariff *goods*, but put no restraint on men. **1893** McKINLEY in *Columbus Dispatch* 8 June [A protective tariff] which shall tariff every foreign product which we can produce. **1900** *Nation* LXX. 352/3 [If Philippine] products cannot be tariffed in our ports, why, Republicans are determined [etc.].

+Tariff convention. A convention or meeting for consideration of problems connected with tariff legislation. — **1831** HONE *Diary* I. 41, I attended the tariff convention this morning. **1842** *Niles' Nat. Reg.* 2 April 80 Alabama Tariff Convention.

+Tariffite. One who supports or favors a protective tariff. — **1830** *Western Mo. Rev.* III. 376 She is a true tariffite, a hearty and staunch advocate for the genuine American system. **1835** [see CONSOLIDATIONIST]. **1903** *Nation* LXXVI. 467/1 Mr. Chamberlain . . . follows in the footsteps of William McKinley, as the latter did in those of Lord George Bentinck and the other tariffites of sixty years ago.

+Tariff man. One who favors or advocates a protective tariff. — **1824** *Ann. 18th Congress* 1 Sess. 2025 'Be of good cheer,' ye tariff-men; in the end you will triumph. **1830** S. SMITH *Life J. Downing* 98, I want you to be particular to put me up as a Tariff man. **1870** [see INFLATIONIST].

+Tariff plank. A party's declaration of policy on tariff, as expressed in the party platform. — **1884** *Boston Jrnl.* 6 June, The phrase on the tariff plank, that duties shall be placed on imports not for revenue only, elicited a round of applause. **1892** *Ib.* 1 Aug. 2/7 Cleveland and the Tariff plank. **1894** [see PLANK *n.* 3].

+Tariff question. The controversial question concerning tariff legislation arising from the conflict of interests between different sections of the country. — **1824** *Ann. 18th Congress* 1 Sess. 2359 When are we to have enough of this Tariff question? **1833** *Knickerb.* I. 186 What is the reason why our country is convulsed from north to south by the Tariff Question? **1884** *Boston Jrnl.* 31 Dec. 2/2 This is the nub of the tariff question. **1904** *N.Y. Ev. Post* 27 June 7 On the tariff question . . . there will be a sharp difference of opinion between the White House group and the leaders at the other end of the avenue.

Tariff reform. {1903–} +Reform intended to reduce high tariff duties. Also attrib. — **1885** CRAWFORD *Amer. Politician* 228, I am a tariff reform man. **1904** *N.Y. Ev. Post* 19 Nov. 4 In England 'tariff reform' means just the opposite of what it does with us. There the reform contemplated is a higher tariff.

Tar kiln. A kiln for extracting tar from wood, coal, etc.: (see also quot. 1877). {1755–} — **1665** *Springfield Rec.* II. 218 There is granted . . . Tenne acres of land . . . a little beyond where the Tar kilne was. **1766** in *Travels Amer. Col.* 484 We saw several Smokes . . . which we were told by our Pilot was as many Tar Kilns. **1837** WETMORE *Gaz. Missouri* 281 He became initiated in . . . an acquaintance with whiskey and tar-kilns. **1877** BARTLETT 694 *Tar-Kiln*, a conical heap of wood made and burned for obtaining tar. North Carolina. **1894** *Dialect Notes* I. 334 *Tar kiln*, place where tar is tried out of pine knots.

Tarlatan. A kind of thin, stiff muslin; a garment made of this. {1727–41–} Also attrib. — **1844** *Lexington Observer* 25 Sept. 1/6 Tarlatan Muslin . . . will be sold. **1852** STOWE *Uncle Tom* xviii, I was just dying to know whether you would appear in your pink tarlatan. **1901** FITCH *Captain Jinks* 141 She is gowned in a billowy mass of white tarlatan.

+Tarnal, *n.* A noun use of TARNAL *a.* — **1825** NEAL *Bro. Jonathan* I. 104 What *could* possess you tho', neighbour Lijah, for to come over

here, *in* that 'ere tarnal? **1844** 'UNCLE SAM' *Peculiarities* II. 88 'Old Virginny' is the finest song on the 'tarnal. **1890** *Buckskin Mose* 135 By the 'Tarnal! I nev'r met one as has.

Tarnal, *a.* [Contraction of ETARNAL *a.*] *slang.* 'Chiefly *U.S.*' (*O.E.D.*).

1. Used as an intensive: Darned; damned. {a1821, 1828, *dial.*}

1787 TYLER *Contrast* III. i, There was . . . such a tarnal blaze with the lights, my head was near turned. **1825** NEAL *Bro. Jonathan* II. 50, I say its a 'tarnal shame for you to be takin' a nap. **1845** KIRKLAND *Western Clearings* 71 [The Indians] are such tarnal thieves! **1866** 'F. KIRKLAND' *Bk. Anecdotes* 592/1 Here, take the tarnal thing; I can see through it! **1897** ROBINSON *Uncle Lisha's Outing* 203 Wal, it does beat Sam Hill what tarnal luck I du hev.

+2. = ETARNAL *a.* 1.

1821 DODDRIDGE *Backwoodsman & Dandy*, Why, Sir, the tarnal appearance of the country was, that it was all wild woods, and full of deers, and bears.

+Tarnal, *adv.* Very; darn. *slang.* — **1775** *Broadside Verse* (1930) 141/2 They say he's grown so tarnal proud [etc.]. **1848** BURTON *Waggeries* 17 The ship drifted on tew a korril reef, and rubbed a tarnal big hole in her plankin'. **1897** ROBINSON *Uncle Lisha's Outing* 81, I'm a tarnal good mind to shake ye, so I be.

+Tarnally, *adv.* Everlastingly; very much. *slang.* — **1787** TYLER *Contrast* III. i, I am sure where I sat it smelt tarnally of brimstone. **1827** J. BERNARD *Retrosp.* 241 May I be 'tarnally starved down for mutton broth, if [etc.]. **1900** MUNN *Uncle Terry* 168, I shall be most tarnally grateful.

+Tarnation, *n.* [Suggested by TARNAL *a.* Cf. *t. nation* s.v. NATION *a.* b, quot.1809.] A euphemism for *damnation. colloq.²* Also as interj. and intensive. — **1787** TYLER *Contrast* v. i, Tarnation! That's no laughing matter though. **1801** G. HANGER *Life* II. 151 The Americans say, Tarnation seize me. **1840** *S. Lit. Messenger* VI. 735/1 Tarnation seize me if I don't riddle you with buck-shot. **1907** C. D. STEWART *Partners* 115, There was a tarnation of mud in things.

+Tarnation, *a.* [Cf. prec.] Used as an expletive or intensive: All-fired; blamed; damned. *colloq.²* — [**1784** W. WILSON in *Mem.* (1796) 47 They only came to look at the 'tarnation Tories' from Canada.] **1823** THACHER *Military Jrnl.* 432 The tarnation fools . . . call it a chapeau. **1836** GILMAN *Recoll.* 43, I want nothing but to get out of this *tarnation* basket. **1851** *Polly Peablossom* 51 But the tarnation critters wouldn't budge a peg. **1890** FREDERIC *Lawton Girl* 368 It's a tarnation sight better than being bullied by a warder in Auburn State's prison. **1908** FREEMAN *Shoulders of Atlas* 172 Everybody has something on her mind unless she's a tarnation fool.

+Tarnation, *adv.* [See prec.] All-fired; darned. *colloq.²* — **1787** [see RATTLE *n.* 4]. **1846** *Spirit of Times* (N.Y.) 25 April 100/1 The Yankees consider themselves 'tarnation spry.' **1890** GUNTER *Miss Nobody* vi, People . . . don't call me 'my *good* man,' for they know I'm a tarnation *bad* one when I'm riled. **1917** COMSTOCK *The Man* 4 Travelling is tarnation bad.

Taro. A starchy tuberous plant (*Colocasia esculenta*); the rootstock of this plant. {1779–} Also attrib. — **1838** S. PARKER *Tour Rocky Mts.* 345 Taro . . . is frequently eaten for bread with no other preparation except roasting. **1850** COLTON *Deck & Port* 333 A few taro-leaves [are] thrown in, and on this the taro itself and meat.

Tarpaulin.

1. Canvas made waterproof by being coated with tar or paint; a sheet of this. {1605–}

1632 *Va. Stat. at Large* I. 175 Boates [shall] be . . . fitted with a grating and a trapaulinge. **1702** *Essex Inst. Coll.* XLII. 161 Inventory of Ship Providence . . . 2 Tarpolines, Twelve Water Caske [etc.]. **1827** COOPER *Red Rover* II. 206 Wilder urged . . . the females to seek their rest beneath a little canopy of tarpaulings. **1890** CUSTER *Following Guidon* 73 A huge tarpaulin of very thick canvas . . . was spread over the large tent. **1914** E. STEWART *Lett. Woman Homesteader* 166 The tarpaulin was spread on the ground for us to eat from.

2. Attrib. with *hat, northeaster*.

1838 *Yale Lit. Mag.* III. 9 A large tarpaulin North Easter was the covering of my head. **1839** BIRD *Robin Day* 4 An old beldam who used to wear a sailor's tarpaulin hat and pea-jacket.

Tarpon. A large game fish (*Tarpon atlanticus*) common on the coast of Florida. {1685–, in W. Indies} — **1775** ROMANS *Nat. Hist. Florida* App. p. lii, The fish caught here are . . . tarpom, bonita, cavallos [etc.]. **1889** *Scribner's Mag.* Aug. 156/1 Probably no less than one hundred tarpon have been killed with the rod and reel. **1911** *Rep. Fisheries 1908* 317/2 Tarpon . . . is caught on hooks and in seines.

+Tarring and feathering. = TAR AND FEATHERING. — **1774** HUTCHINSON *Diary & Lett.* I. 164 The committee for tarring and feathering blamed the people for doing it. **1823** TUDOR *Life J. Otis* 506 The strange punishment of tarring and feathering . . . occurred but twice in Boston. [**1861** *Illust. London News* 17 Aug. 152/1 The Southern chivalry have nobler game before them now than the tarring and feathering of defenceless individual Northerners.] **1925** BENEFIELD *Chicken-Wagon Family* 304 We don't count tarring and feathering as violence.

＊Tarry, *n.*

＊1. The act of tarrying. *Obs.* {–a1578}

1725 *Maine Doc. Hist.* X. 282, I must neglect my Role if your Hon[ou]r Doe oblige my tarry. **1778** *New Eng. Hist. & Gen. Reg.* XXX. 319, I am informed . . . that your ill health will not permit your tarry long after him.

2. A sojourn; a short stay. {–1589, 1817}

'Now chiefly *U.S.*' (*O.E.D.*).

1770 *Boston Rec.* 8 [The troops are] obliged for the protection of the Inhabitants to keep up a military Watch during their tarry. **1786** CUTLER in *Life & Corr.* II. 273 We shall endeavor to . . . make provisions for a much longer tarry . . . in the neighborhood of the mountain. **1836** LONGFELLOW in S. Longfellow *H. W. Longfellow* I. 232, I intend, . . . after a few days' tarry, [to] start for home. **1883** *Wheelman* I. 431 The ferry-man steers his craft towards the place that invites a tarry.

* **Tarry,** *v. intr.* To remain in a place; to linger; to stay a while.

'Now chiefly *literary* in Gt. Brit., still *colloq.* in U.S.' (*O.E.D.*).

1704 S. KNIGHT *Journal* 9, I vissitted the Reverd. Mr. Belcher . . . and tarried there till evening, in hopes ye post would come along. **1756** J. ADAMS *Diary Works* II. 11 Tarried at my uncle Webb's. **1778** CUTLER in *Life & Corr.* I. 68, I returned to our old quarters and tarried the night. **1849** NASON *Journal* 85 Tarried here one week. **1876** 'MARK TWAIN' *Tom Sawyer* iii, Tom came up to the fence . . . hoping she would tarry yet awhile longer. **1899** GREEN *Va. Word-Book* 383.

* **Tarrying.** + = BUNDLING. *Obs.* — **1775** BURNABY *Travels* 144 A very extraordinary method of courtship, . . . sometimes practised amongst the lower people of [Mass.], . . . is called Tarrying. **1815** *Reviewers Reviewed* 34 Neither your *grave* or *gay* [British] authorities on the subject of 'bundling' and 'tarrying' are worthy of criticism.

* **Tart.** A small pie, often without an upper crust, filled with fruit, jelly, or the like. — **1676** TOMPSON *Poetical Works* 70 A tribe of female hands, but manly hearts Forsake at home their pastry-crust and tarts To knead the dirt. **1746** [see PIE¹ 1]. **1854** M. J. HOLMES *Tempest & Sunshine* 335 Tarts, or 'little pies' as she called them, were her special favorites. **1907** *St. Nicholas* July 854/2 All the jellies, pies and tarts, . . . Sold under that crowded street.

* **Tartan.** A Scottish plaid woolen cloth. Also attrib. — **1761** [see PLAID]. **1820** *Columbian Centinel* 5 Jan. 3/1 Thomas Furber . . . Offers for sale . . . Tartan Plaids.

Tartar emetic. A poisonous white salt, used as an emetic and sudorific. {1704–} — **1780** FRANKLIN in W. Pepper *Medical Side B. Franklin* 80, I give it you here, in exchange for your receipt of tartar emetic. **1815** *Niles' Reg.* IX. 94/2 Tartar emetic . . . [is] to be found in our druggists' shops. **1852** REYNOLDS *Hist. Illinois* 264 The remedies to cure the billious fever and ague . . . were tartar-emetic, calomel and jalap and peruvian barks.

* **Tartarian,** *a.* In the names of plants and grains. {1805–} — **1838** *Mass. Agric. Survey 1st Rep.* 33 The Tartarian, or as some call it, the Horse-Mane Oat, from the grain hanging together on one side of the panicle, is sometimes cultivated. *Ib.*, The Tartarian, or smaller kind of buckwheat, has been recently introduced into the country. **1846** BROWNE *Trees Amer.* 73 The Tartarian Maple . . . attains a height of forty or fifty feet. **1892** APGAR *Trees Northern U.S.* 115 Tartarian Honeysuckle . . . [is] occasionally trimmed to a tree-like form.

+ **Tarve.** [Origin uncertain.] (See quot. 1859.) *Obs.* — **1848** COOPER *Oak Openings* I. 24 This helve has no tarve to 't, to my mind. **1859** BARTLETT 473 *Tarve*, a turn, bend, curve.

+ **Tarweed.**

1. Any of several resinous, glandular plants of California, esp. of the genera *Madia* and *Grindelia.*

1872 McCLELLAN *Golden State* 167 Blackberries, salmonberries, tarweed, . . . and wild mustard abound all over the coast, valleys, and hillsides. **1894** *Amer. Folk-Lore* VII. 92 *Hemizonia pungens*, . . . tar-weed, Cal. *Ib.*, *Madia sativa*, . . . tar-weed. **1903** NORRIS *Responsibilities of Novelist* 142 The reek of the tar-weed on the Colorado slopes. **1915** ARMSTRONG & THORNBER *Western Wild Flowers* 538 Common Madis, Tarweed. *Madia elegans.* . . . Pretty flowers, with hairy stems.

2. The waxweed, *Cuphea petiolata.*

1893 *Amer. Folk-Lore* VI. 142 *Cuphea petiolata*, tar weed. West Va.

Tasajo. [Sp.] **1.** Jerked beef. {1783–, in Sp. Amer.} ‖**2.** (See quotation.) — (1) **1838** 'TEXIAN' *Mexico v. Texas* 77 The whole company . . . [had nothing] except some raw *tassajo*, or jerked beef. **1851** M. REID *Scalp Hunters* xxvi, Our tasajo was all eaten, and we began to hunger. (2) **1872** POWERS *Afoot & Alone* 159 Few and far between were bunches of that strange mountain shrub, the tasajo.

+ **Tasimeter.** [Gr. *tasis* 'stretching' and *meter.*] 'An instrument devised by Edison for detecting minute changes of pressure and thereby small variations in temperature' (*Cent.*).

* **Task. a.** *S.* An amount of work formerly demanded of a slave. Also attrib. +**b.** *S.* A measure of land fixed in terms of the time needed to work it. *Obs.*

(a) **1839** KEMBLE *Residence in Ga.* 28 In the part of Georgia where this estate is situated, the custom of task labour is universal. **1903** PRINGLE *Rice Planter* 41 All the work in this section is based on what was the 'task' in slavery times. (b) **1850** BURKE *Reminisc. Georgia* 117 If a person is asked the extent of a certain piece of land, he is told it contains so many tasks. **1853** SIMMS *Sword & Distaff* (1854) 317 We have . . . twenty-five niggers, and all, I reckon, able to hoe a task. **1862** E. W. Pearson *Lett. Port Royal* 78 Tirah had planted a task of cow-pease for the Government.

+ **Tasked hand.** *S.* A slave who worked by the task. *Obs.* — **1856** OLMSTED *Slave States* 435 It is the driver's duty to make the tasked hands do their work well.

* **Tassel,** *n.*

+**1.** The inflorescence of a corn plant or other grain.

*a*1649 WINTHROP *Hist.* II. 277 [Caterpillars] eat up first the blades of the stalk, then they eat up the tassels, whereupon the ear withered. **1765** ROGERS *Acct. N. Amer.* 165 [Of wild oats or rice:] Its tossel resembles oats, but the kernel is more like rice. **1785** WASHINGTON *Diaries* II. 409 The tassel . . . had got too dry for the farina to impregnate the grain. **1847** DRAKE *Pioneer Life Ky.* 52 The air becomes redolent with the peculiar odor of the tassels. **1901** CHURCHILL *Crisis* 443 He would watch for hours the tassels stirring over the green fields of corn.

+**b.** *In tassel*, (of corn) in the stage of having tassels.

1774 FITHIAN *Journal* I. 207, I was not a little Surprised to see Corn out in Tassel. **1903** *Atlantic Mo.* July 84 The corn was in tassel now, and rustled softly in the fields.

* **2.** A pendent ornament made of bunched threads or cords.

1705 BEVERLEY *Virginia* III. 6 The [Indian] Conjurer . . . [wears] his Girdle, the Bottom of this is likewise fring'd with Tassils for Ornament Sake. **1841** BACHE *Fire-Screen* 14 She was sewing tassels on a rich bead bag. **1914** 'BOWER' *Flying U Ranch* 12 The reins of braided leather with horsehair tassels made Happy Jack's eyes greedy with desire.

* **Tassel,** *v.* +*intr.* Of corn: To bloom or form tassels. Also with *out.* — **1774** [see SILK *n.* 2 b]. **1785** WASHINGTON *Writings* XII. 227 [Indian corn] should be kept clean and well worked . . . till it shoots and tassels at least. **1843** *Amer. Pioneer* II. 83 Corn, if planted, grows a foot high, tassels out and dies. **1887** WILKINS *Humble Romance* 29 His corn tasselled out . . . as soon as anybody's.

Tassel flower. a. A tropical Asiatic herb, *Emilia flammea.* {1885} +**b.** A perennial herb (*Brickellia umbellata*) of the West. — **1836** LINCOLN *Botany* App. 83 *Cacalia . . . coccinea*, tassel-flower; from the East Indies. . . . The flowers of a scarlet colour. **1863** 'G. HAMILTON' *Gala-Days* 10 The scarlet tassel-flower utterly refuses to unfold his brave plumes. **1868** GRAY *Field Botany* 194 S[enecio] *sonchifolia*, Tassel-Flower: cult[ivated] as a summer annual, from India. **1909** WEBSTER 2116/3 *Tassel flower*, . . . an asteraceous plant (*Coleoanthus grandiflorus*) of the western United States.

+ **Tassel-worm.** 'An early generation of the boll-worm, or corn-ear worm, which feeds on the tassels of maize in the southern United States' (*Cent.*).

+ **Tasso.** [Cf. La. Fr. *tasseau* 'jerked beef.'] = TASAJO 1. *rare.* — **1841** *S. Lit. Messenger* VII. 77/2 The evening banquet of gumbo, tasso, and beef, in every variety of form, was shortly served up by their attendants.

+ **Taste.** [Origin unknown.] A kind of narrow silk ribbon. Now *local.* — **1788** *Ky. Gazette* 28 June 2/3 Hugh M'Ilvain, Is now opening at his Store in Lexington . . . An Assortment of Goods: . . . Taste and garters [etc.]. **1845** JUDD *Margaret* I. 132 The third [beautiful girl] led down from the skies the brilliant Planet Venus, by a bridle or blue taste tied about one of its rays. *a*1889 in *New Haven Palladium* 18 April, If . . . Mrs. S. has any taste she will oblige me by sending me half a yard, no matter of what color, so it be not black. **1899** GREEN *Va. Word-Book* 384.

+ **Tata.** *S.W.* The head of some group; an Indian agent; *tata grande*, Great Father. Also attrib. — **1838** 'TEXIAN' *Mexico v. Texas* 16 The Tata padre and the strange gentleman . . . drove away with great speed towards the *rancho*, or village of Larza. **1870** *Republican Rev.* 21 May 3/1 We wish these statements sent to our 'Tata Grande,' and let the Government know our wishes. **1885** *Wkly. New Mexican Rev.* 12 March 3/6 The head chiefs and warriors of the Mescaleros and Jicarillas told your correspondent that he was the first 'tata,' father or agent, who protected them against the encroachment of settlers.

Tater. [Colloq. shortening of POTATO.] Now illiterate.

1. = POTATO 1. {1839–, dial.}

1759 *Essex Inst. Coll.* XIX. 126 There we Dined upon codfish and taters. **1775** in Pusey *Road to Ky.* 42 [We] there Suplid our Selves With Seed Corn & irish tators. **1838** *Poor Will's Almanack 1839* And then there's the gravy and *tatur.* **1917** COMSTOCK *The Man* 89 What's a matter o' a hen o' two an' a sack o' taters when lined up agin that fever spell?

2. Attrib. with *barrel, hill, patch.*

1845 *Big Bear Ark.* 22 Them ar 'Indian mounds' ar tater hills. **1847** LOWELL *Biglow P.* 1 Ser. iii. 34 He draws his furrer ez straight ez he can, An' into nobody's tater-patch pokes. **1902** HARBEN *A. Daniel* 198, I got up on the head of a tater-barrel behind the counter.

Tatting. a. A kind of knotted lace. **b.** The action of making this. {1842–} Also attrib. — **1862** NORTON *Army Lett.* 74, I whittled out a tatting needle and made a rivet of the bullet. **1869** ALCOTT *Little Women* II. 44 Two matrons . . . discussing Woman's Rights and making tatting. **1873** PHELPS *Trotty's Wedding* xx, The President of the Tatting Club shuddered under her soft blue veil. **1893** HOLLEY *Samantha at World's Fair* 150 Six new complete suits of under-clothes made, all trimmed off elaborate with tattin'.

* **Tat(t)ler.** +A long-billed, limicoline bird of the genus *Totanus* or allied genera. Also with specifying terms.

[**1831** J. RICHARDSON, etc. *Fauna Bor.-Amer.* II. 388 *Totanus semipalmatus*, Semipalmated Tatler.] **1839** PEABODY *Mass. Birds* 370 Bartram's Tattler . . . is considered a great luxury. **1844** *Nat. Hist. N.Y., Zoology*

II. 250 The Varied Tatler . . . appears with us about the middle of May. **1858** BAIRD *Birds Pacific R.R.* 734 [The] Wandering Tatler . . . ranges over an immense extent of locality. **1874** COUES *Birds N.W.* 503 In most parts of the West, between the Mississippi and the Rocky mountains, this Tattler, commonly known as the 'Prairie Pigeon,' is exceedingly abundant during the migrations. **1892** A. E. LEE *Hist. Columbus Ohio* I. 17n., Yellow-legged snipe, or tattler . . . common in autumn on western rivers. **1917** *Birds of Amer.* I. 244 Yellow-legs. . . . [Also called] Lesser Long-legged Tattler.

+**Tattletale.** One who tells tales or secrets. — **1888** 'CRADDOCK' *Despot* 429, I'd strangle that tattle-tale with a mighty good will. **1902** C. MORRIS *Stage Confidences* 165 'Mean thing' and 'tattle-tale' brought sobbing little maids to the teacher's arms. **1925** BENEFIELD *Chicken-Wagon Family* 210 A tattletale is a person of no account whatsoever.

***Tattoo.** (See quotations.) — **1881** *Naval Encycl.* 802/2 *Tattoo,* the evening drum-beat before 'piping down.' **1891** *Cent.* 6198/2 *Tattoo,* . . . in United States men-of-war, a bugle-call or beat of drum at 9 P.M.

+**Taushent.** (See TORSHENT.)

+**Tautog.** Also **tautaug, tatogue,** etc. [Narraganset *tautauog,* pl. of *tautau* 'blackfish.'] An edible fish (*Tautoga onitis*) of the Atlantic. Also collect.
1643 WILLIAMS *Key* (1866) 138 Of Fish and Fishing. . . . *Taut-auog,* sheeps-heads. **1750** J. BIRKET *Cursory Remarks* 31 An ill natured Scold at the ferry house . . . gave us Potatoes & Tatogue. **1775** BURNABY *Travels* 121 Fish are in the greatest plenty and perfection, particularly the tataag or black-fish. **1802** *Mass. H. S. Coll.* I Ser. VIII. 191 A few tautaug are caught in Town Cove. *a*1841 HAWES *Sporting Scenes* I. 37, I once crossed over to Faulkner's island, to fish for tautaugs, as the north side people call black fish. **1911** *Rep. Fisheries 1908* 317/2 In New Jersey, [it is called] 'blackfish,' 'tautog,' and 'chub.'

***Tavern.**
***1. a.** A public house where wine and other liquors are sold to be consumed on the premises. **b.** An inn or hotel: (see quot. 1817).
1624 Smith *Gen. Hist. Va.* III. 44 There remained neither taverne, beere house, nor place of reliefe. **1647** *R.I. Col. Rec.* I. 185 Each Towne shall have power to allow Tavernes, Alehouses, and Victualling houses within its own precincts. **1708** *Boston News-Letter* 15 March 2/2 A Large Dwelling House fit for a Tavern . . . to be Lett. **1734** *Harvard Rec.* I. 141 If any scholar shall unnecessarily frequent Taverns . . . he shall be punished. **1784** SMYTH *Tour* I. 49 Inns, taverns, ordinaries, and public-houses . . . are all in one, and are known by the appellation of the names here, are synonymous terms. **1810** *Columbian Centinel* 31 Jan. 4/1 During the recent year 74 persons were licenced to keep taverns; and 74 licences were granted for petty groceries, including 8 ordinaries. **1817** [see INN]. **1833** FLINT *D. Boone* 11 [Before] a large log building . . . a sign creaked in the wind, conspicuously lettered 'Store and Tavern.' **1891** *Fur, Fin, & Feather* 157/2 Hotels are scarce [in the hills in n.w. Ga.], although most of the towns have each one or more 'taverns.' **1905** WIGGIN *Rose* 155, I was over to the tavern to-night.

2. Attrib. and comb. with *bar, hunter, keeper,* etc.
1715 *Boston News-Letter* 31 Jan. 2/2 A House and Land . . . in the Tenure of William Skinner Tavern-Keeper. **1827** COOPER *Red Rover* I. 11 Some half dozen notorious tavern-hunters, were, however, the sole fruits of all their nods of recognition. **1834** *S. Lit. Messenger* I. 85, I have seen and chatted with all sorts of people, . . . down to the tavern porter and the country laborer. **1840** MATHEWS *Politicians* I. ii, Gudgeon is friendly to tavern-license. **1852** STOWE *Uncle Tom* xl, Others were some of Legree's associates at the tavern-bar of a neighboring city.

***Taverner.** A tavern-keeper. *Obs.* — **1715** *Mass. H. Rep. Jrnl.* I. 71 There being no Taverner in the said Town. **1723** *Boston Rec.* 174 If the Person . . . be a Tavernor Inholder or Retailer He Shal forfeit his Recognizance. **1760** J. ADAMS *Diary* Works II. 85 An artful man . . . [may] multiply taverns and dram shops, and thereby secure the votes of taverner and retailer, and of all.

Taw. {1709-} +*At long taw,* at a distance. *S.* — **1854** *Fla. Plantation Rec.* 113, I dislike to speak at long taw. **1884** HARRIS *Mingo* 248 That's what I call courtship at long taw.

+**Tawkee.** Also **tawho,** etc. [Algonquian.] =TUCKAHOE 1. — **1725** in Nelson *Indians of N.J.* 78 The families gather the first-fruits of roots, which grow in swamps, not unlike nuts, called *Tachis.* **1772** FORSTER tr. Kalm *Travels* I. 389 This Taw-ho seems to be the same with what the Indians in Carolina call *Tuckahoo.* **1877** BARTLETT 695 *Tawkee.* . . . The name was adopted by the Swedes. **1910** HODGE, etc. *Amer. Indians* II. 711/2 *Tawkee.* . . . The word . . . is derived from *p'tukwi,* or *p'tukqueu,* in the Delaware dialect of Algonquian, signifying 'it is globular.'

***Tawny, n.** A dark-skinned person. {1660-} Applied to an American Indian. *Obs.* — **1693** C. MATHER *Wonders Invis. World* (1862) 75 The Tawnies . . . have watered our Soil with the Blood of many Hundreds of our Inhabitants. **1707** SEWALL *Diary* II. 59* One of the Fierce *Tawnies* looked in, with a Gun ready to Fire upon them. **1797** *Spirit Farmers' Mus.* 85 While blood stain'd tawnies drop the hatchet, And scour the wilderness to catch it.

***Tawny, a.**
***1.** Having a brown color. Applied to an Indian. *Obs.* Also transf.

1707 SEWALL *Diary* II. 60* She travelled with her Tawny Guardians all that night. **1806** *Balance* V. 187/2 We should like to be informed by some of the wisest of these our tawny brethren. **1839** *Jamestown* (N.Y.) *Jrnl.* 18 Sept. 2/1 He intends this autumn to go again that long journey to see his tawny sister [adopted by Indians].

2. In specific names.
1817-8 EATON *Botany* (1822) 304 *Hemerocallis fulva,* tawny day-lily. **1826** GODMAN *Nat. Hist.* II. 111 The tawny American marmot, or Richardson's marmot, is nearly of the size of [Franklin's marmot]. **1828** BONAPARTE *Synopsis* 76 The Tawny Thrush, *Turdus mustelinus,* . . . inhabits all North America. **1842** *Nat. Hist. N.Y., Zoology* I. 85 The Tawny Meadow-Mouse. *Arvicola rufescens.* . . . I venture to consider this animal as new. **1917** *Birds of Amer.* III. 200/2 The Tawny Creeper . . . occurs on the Pacific coast from Sitka, Alaska, to the Santa Cruz Mountains, California.

***Tax, n.**
***1.** A compulsory charge, usu. in the form of money, made upon persons or property to meet the costs of public services or government: (see also quot. 1766).
See also DIRECT TAX, INCOME TAX, etc.
1639 *Plymouth Laws* 68 Every Township shall have liberty to . . . make levyes rates and taxes for their towne's charges. **1654** *R.I. Col. Rec.* I. 288 We have almost forgotten what tythes are; yea, or taxes, either to Church or Commonweale. **1766** FRANKLIN *Writings* IV. 446 By taxes, they [*sc.* the Amer. colonists] mean internal taxes; by duties, they mean customs. **1796** *Ann. 4th Congress* 2 Sess. 2706 This head will comprise a variety of taxes . . . upon merchant traders, and mechanics. **1812** in Young *Jessamine Co., Ky.* 85 The trustees . . . shall have power to levy a tax on the real property in said town. **1870** *Congress. Globe* 28 June 4923/2 The tax on sugar is a greater oppression . . . than the tax on sales.

2. Attrib. and comb. with *abstract, assessor, bill,* etc.
1720 *Mass. H. Rep. Jrnl.* II. 284 A Petition . . . Complaining of the Proceedings of the Court . . . in their Nulling Three Tax-Bills by them made . . . [was] Sent up. **1737** *Boston Rec.* 178 We have . . . Two Hundred and Twenty People more in Our Tax books, whom Our Assessors thought not Rateable for their Poverty. **1765** HABERSHAM *Letters* 49 No Private Person (unless for Sums provided for in the Tax Laws) [was] to have more than £100. **1816** *Ann. 14th Congress* 1 Sess. 809 [The people of Maine] are called upon by your tax-gatherers. **1837** W. JENKINS *Ohio Gaz.* 69 This township . . . has entered on the tax list 21,000 acres of land. **1847** *Knickerb.* XXIX. 203 He was inn-keeper, grocer, tax-receiver and justice of the peace. **1863** E. W. Pearson *Lett. Port Royal* 129 One of the tax-commissioners . . . read both proclamations. **1877** *Mich. Gen. Statutes* I. (1882) 366 The register of deeds . . . shall transcribe such tax abstracts. **1880** 'MARK TWAIN' *Tramp Abroad* 150 A most prodigious fire-breathing dragon . . . made more trouble than a tax-collector. **1902** ALDRICH *Sea Turn* 248 Nobody had suspected how rich he was—not even the tax assessors.

***Tax, v.** +*tr.* To charge (a person) a certain price; to fix as a charge. *colloq.* — **1848** BARTLETT 351 *To Tax,* to charge; as, 'What will you tax me a yard for this cloth?' i.e. what will you charge for it, or what is the price of it? *c*1849 WHITCHER *Bedott P.* xx. 218 [Jabe Clark] said 'twas woth double the money he taxed; but seein' he was tradin' with the clargy, he wouldent charge but half-price. **1907** *Dialect Notes* 219.

+**Taxable.** One who or that which is subject or liable to taxation. {1861-} — **1662** *Mag. Amer. Hist.* XI. 39 Every householder and freeman . . . should take up ten shillings per poll . . . for every taxable under their charge. **1733** *Md. Hist. Mag.* XV. 218 The said overseer [shall] warn half of Hyde's taxables . . . to work on aforesaid roads. **1770** *N.H. Prov. Papers* VII. 257 If any one honest taxable in the Province is comforted in one penny thus saved to him . . . I do Rejoice at the vote. **1821** JEFFERSON *Writings* I. 47 [Franklin] was for their voting, in all cases, according to the number of taxables. **1904** *Newark Ev. News* 24 Aug. 6 A readjustment of local taxables [has been] recently completed by the city Board of Assessors.

+**Tax certificate.** A certificate issued or to be issued at a tax sale certifying that the purchaser is entitled to a tax deed on a given piece of land upon the fulfillment of certain conditions. — **1878** *Wis. Supreme Ct. Rep.* XLIV. 489 Tax certificates issued to a county cannot be transferred by it without an assignment in writing. **1883** *Ill. Rev. Statutes* 1307/1. **1900** *Okla. Supreme Ct. Rep.* X. 279 A tax certificate represents an interest in real estate.

+**Tax deed.** A deed to land bought at a tax sale. — **1861** *Mich. Acts* 178 An act to authorize the Auditor General to execute second tax deeds, in certain cases. **1872** *Ill. Laws* 52 [The] affidavit shall be delivered to the person authorized by law to execute such tax deed.

+**Tax-dodger.** One who avoids paying taxes by resorting to one device or another. — **1876** *Nation* XXII. 202/2 The 'tax-dodger' is one who, finding that the rate of taxation in Boston is too high for his means, flies, with his wife and children to some rural town. **1885** CRAWFORD *Amer. Politician* 281 The migration of the 'tax-dodgers' took place on the last day of April; they will return on the second day of December. **1894** *Congress. Rec.* App. 29 Jan. 277/1 There are tax dodgers under any system which may be inaugurated.

Taxidermist. One whose business is the preparation and preservation of the skins of dead animals, as by stuffing and mounting them in such a manner as to suggest the living animals. {1851-} (Not in the 1828 ed. of Webster available to us.) — **1841** WEBSTER 757/1 *Taxidermist,* a person skilled in preparing and preserving the skins of animals, so as to represent their natural appearance. **1849** LONGFELLOW *Kavanagh* 70 The taxidermist presented himself, coming from an inner room. **1882** GODFREY *Nantucket* 264 [Professions include] Taxidermists.

+**Tax land.** Land taken over by the state for nonpayment of taxes. — **1882** *Mich. Gen. Statutes* I. 1258 Any person may purchase any parcel of the unsold state tax lands now held by the state.

Taxpayer. One who pays a tax or taxes. {1816–, excludes 'local rate-payers'} — **1832** *Congress. Deb.* 23 Jan. 1623 They of the South were the tax payers. **1853** *Inaugural Addresses Boston Mayors* II. 22 A subject which possesses . . . interest to every water taker and tax payer in the City . . . [is] wastefulness in the use of water. **1866** *Internal Revenue Guide* 282 A delinquent tax-payer proposes . . . to pay the tax found due, with the assessed penalty. **1874** GLISAN *Jrnl. Army Life* 458 [Alcohol] fills our hospitals, almshouses and prisons, and costs the sober, industrious taxpayers of the country millions upon millions of dollars. **1916** WILSON *Somewhere* 355, I says that's the best way out of it, being myself a heavy taxpayer.

Tax-paying, a. Of a person: Paying taxes. — **1832** *Congress. Deb.* 4 April 2390 As a representative of the tax paying people of the South, I must ask, . . . what becomes of the excessive heavy amount of revenue? **1851** *Inaugural Addresses Boston Mayors* I. 403 The sale [of the Public Gardens] would cause discontent and unhappiness to a very large number of tax paying citizens. **1894** *Harper's Mag.* Feb. 392 There are, indeed, no poor resident, tax-paying, voting citizens.

+**Tax sale.** A sale of property, usually at auction, for delinquent taxes. Also attrib. — **1857** BRAMAN *Texas* 94 In the States of Ohio and Illinois . . . the greatest number of tax-sales have been made. **1879** *Mich. Pub. Acts* 16 The auditor general of this state . . . is hereby authorized to execute a second deed upon tax-sale certificates.

+**Tax title.** A title acquired under a tax sale. — **1831** PECK *Guide* 320 Purchasers for taxes, now offer and sell quarters [of land] thus held by tax-titles. **1865** E. W. Pearson *Lett. Port Royal* 319 Charleston lawyers . . . didn't see how to get around our tax-titles.

+**Taylorism.** A modified Calvinism taught by Nathaniel William Taylor (1786–1858), professor of theology at Yale. Now hist. (Cf. NEW HAVEN.) — **1848** in *Scribner's Mo.* XIX. 60/2 Colonel Webb wrote a paragraph . . . saying we had 'no sympathy with independent Taylorism.' **1884** Schaff *Religious Encycl.* III. 2306/1 An elaborate system, which . . . powerfully affected theological thought and preaching in America, . . . was called 'Taylorism.'

+**Taylorite.** One who accepts the doctrines of Taylorism. — **1867** DIXON *New America* II. 308 In the Congregational Church . . . there arose endless divisions, including Millenialists, Taylorites, and the strange heresy of the Perfectionists.

T cart. A light, open wagon for four passengers, the body of which is shaped somewhat like a T. *Obs.* {1873–} — **1883** CRAWFORD *Dr. Claudius* 269 Silas B. Barker junior drew up to the steps of the hotel in a very gorgeous conveyance, called in America a T-cart, and resembling a mail phaeton in build. **1888** KIRK *Queen Money* 185 [As] Otto was both a lover and connoisseur of horses . . . [he asked] his aid in purchasing a T-cart. **1894** B. MATTHEWS in *Harper's Mag.* Sept. 590/1 Did he drive a T-cart too?

Tea.

1. The dried and prepared leaves of the tea plant or a drink made from these. {1655–}

See also BALM-TEA, HERB TEA, etc.

1732 FRANKLIN *Poor Richard's Almanac 1733* 12 Women for tea forsook spinning & knitting. **1772** ANDREWS *Letters* 11 Each [had] an hundred and odd chests of the detested Tea. **1802** [see INTERNAL a.]. **1840** *Niles' Nat. Reg.* 4 July 288/3 The people of the United States consume about eight million pounds of tea per annum. **1903** FREEMAN *Wind in Rose-Bush* 142 She looked ill, and could not take even the toast and tea which Sophia had prepared for her.

b. The tea plant. {1663–}

1872 *Harper's Mag.* Dec. 151/1 In Georgia the culture of tea is being undertaken with good promise of success.

2. A meal or social entertainment at which tea is served. {1738–}

1771 A. G. WINSLOW *Diary* 2, I repeated [a little of the sermon] to her yesterday at Tea. **1840** HONE *Diary* II. 4 After tea I had retired to my room. **1888** ROE *Army Lett.* 386, I am not very enthusiastic over the prospect of crowded rooms, daily receptions and 'teas,' and other affairs of more formality. **1902** C. MORRIS *Stage Confidences* 203 Their lunches, dinners, teas, dances, . . . [give] occasion for glorious display. **1907** HARRIS *Tents of Wickedness* 347 Tea was always at seven.

3. *attrib.* and *comb.* **a.** With *farmer, furniture, glass,* etc.

1732 FRANKLIN *Writings* II. 185 With some of the Money of the Tea-Furniture I have bought a Set of Knitting-Needles. **1775** FITHIAN *Journal* II. 86 We have no *tea,* Sir—nor tea-women—you will say then we have no *scandal,* nor *slander,* nor *calumny,* nor *match-making.* **1790** *Penna. Packet* 6 Jan. 3/3 Tea-Warehouse, . . . Where is now selling, . . . A few dining setts of China. **1838** Tea society [see PRESIDENTESS]. **1863** A. D. WHITNEY *F. Gartney* xix. 201 This very afternoon she sat in the southwest tea-parlor. **1872** MCCLELLAN *Golden State* 336 Herr Schnell . . . arrived with a small colony of Japanese tea-farmers and founded a colony. *Ib.* 337 It is almost beyond a doubt that tea-raising in California will yet prove a success. **1874** COLLINS *Kentucky* I. 143/1 [The] Maysville *Bulletin* [was]

issued . . . on small tea wrapping paper, 12 by 16 inches—being refused . . . a permit to purchase regular white paper. **1898** CAHAN *Imported Bridegroom* 121 Jealousy . . . of the empty tea-glasses . . . , of the whole excited crowd.

b. In expressions relating to tea or the tax on tea as a source of friction between Great Britain and the American colonies.

See also TEA PARTY b, TEA-SPILLER.

1773 in *Niles' Reg.* XLIV. 421/2 The tea ship being arrived, every inhabitant who wishes to preserve the liberty of America is desired to meet at the state house. **1775** HUTCHINSON *Diary & Lett.* I. 505, I was threatened by the Tea mobs. **1775** *Jrnls. Cont. Congress* III. 370 Tuesday [shall] be assigned for the consideration of the memorials of the Tea-holders. **1781** PETERS *Hist. Conn.* (1829) 293 [To] exert themselves . . . in favour of the Bostonian tea-merchants. **1830** *Jamestown* (N.Y.) *Jrnl.* 5 May 2/2 What if our fathers had . . . called the excitement of the Stamp Act a humbug and of the Tea Tax a forlorn hope of disappointed office seekers? **1883** *Century Mag.* Sept. 648/2 The little town . . . showed . . . spirit on the tea question.

c. In special combinations:

Tea-and-coffee splash, a social gathering at which tea and coffee are served; *t. bincum,* (see quotation); *t. doings,* a kind of tea or the leaves, roots, etc., used in making it; *t. drink, t. entertainment,* a tea party; *t. nut,* tea seed; *t. paper,* paper in which tea is packed; *t. sauce,* sauce eaten at tea; *t. train,* a train carrying tea; *t. waiter,* a tea tray.

1889 *Boston Jrnl.* 28 March 2/3 Rural towns in Pennsylvania indulge in what they call a 'tea and coffee splash.' **1837** WILLIAMS *Florida* 100 Of this [sc. wild thyme] is made the Tea Bincum, which immediately cures the Dangue. **1859** *Knickerb.* LIII. 318 Instead of 'store-tea' they had only saxifax tea-doin's, without milk. **1869** FULLER *Flower Gatherers* 34 We were soon seated around him, and a merrier tea-drink no one could have desired. **1785** ELLICOTT in Mathews *Life A. Ellicott* 37 My Assistant . . . and myself had a Tea Entertainment, at which the Principle Ladies of the Place attended. **1850** *Rep. Comm. Patents 1849: Agric.* 403 As my chief object . . . is to cultivate and increase the tea-nut, it will be a year or two perhaps before I attempt to convert the leaf into tea. **1857** GRAY *Botany* 199 The poorest printing-paper and grocers' tea-paper are very good for [a portfolio for botanical specimens]. **1845** KIRKLAND *Western Clearings* 90 [They are] amassing in leafy baskets the rich remainder [of the strawberries], . . . to dry in the burning sun for next winter's 'tea-saase.' **1874** TAYLOR *World on Wheels* 37 At Omaha, . . . I saw . . . the tea-train from the Celestial Kingdom. **1827** Will M. Pettigrew, *Pettigrew P.* (Univ. N.C. MS.), I give and bequeath to Mary Catherine Williams . . . one large Tea waiter.

Tea bell. A bell rung as a summons to tea. — **1836** *Knickerb.* VIII. 418 It was nearly time for the tea-bell to ring. **1864** *Md. Hist. Mag.* XXI. 300 As soon as the tea bell rung he left, as it was his first watch. **1890** R. H. DAVIS *Silhouettes* 97 Presently the cracked tea bell would ring, and he would go in to eat a small slice of cold, soggy pie, washed down with a glass of cold water.

+**Teaberry.** The wintergreen (*Gaultheria procumbens*), or its fruit. — **1858** HOGG *Vegetable Kingdom* 482 *Gaultharia procumbens* . . . [is] called Tea-berry and Mountain Tea. **1866** [see DEERBERRY].

Tea caddy. A small box for tea. {1837–} — **1790** *Penna. Packet* 7 Dec. 3/3 Joseph Anthony, Junior, . . . Has Imported . . . Tea cadies, cannisters and salts. **1810** [see DRESSING CASE 1]. **1896** JEWETT *Pointed Firs* 80 She gave into my hand an old flowered-glass tea-caddy.

Tea cake. A kind of light cake eaten at tea. {1892–} — **1832** CHILD *Frugal Housewife* 71 There is a kind of tea cake still cheaper. **1863** 'E. KIRKE' *Southern Friends* 236 [I'll come] before the tea cakes are cold. **1904** [see CUNNING a.].

✻ Teacher.

1. One who gave instruction in religion; +spec., in the early Congregational churches of New England, a person appointed to give such instruction; a preacher. *Obs.*

1642 *Suffolk Deeds* I. 35 The dwelling house of the Reverend Teacher Mr. John Cotton in Boston aforesaid. **1659** *Ib.* III. 344 Thomas Mount did desier our Teacher mr. Cotton and myself to be present. **1693** (*title*), Cases of Conscience concerning Evil Spirits Personating Men. . . . By Increase Mather, . . . Teacher of a Church at Boston in New England. **1720** D. NEAL *Hist. New-Eng.* I. 211 Mr. William Brewster [died], Teacher of the Church of New-Plimouth. **1788** FRANKLIN *Autobiog.* 347, I rather approv'd his giving us good sermons compos'd by others, than bad ones of his own manufacture, tho' the latter was the practice of our common teachers.

+**b.** In the Christian Science church, a person prepared and authorized to give class instruction in Christian Science to qualified applicants.

1896 M. B. EDDY *Miscellaneous Writings* 92 The teacher of Christian Science needs continually to study this textbook [i.e., *Science and Health*].

✻ 2. One who gives general instruction, as in a school.

See also SCHOOL-TEACHER.

1837 PECK *New Guide* 221 The Academic Institute is designed to . . . elevate the profession amongst the teachers in Cincinnati. **1865** [see EDUCATOR] **1877** *Rep. Indian Affairs* 47 One [boy] who was with the teacher last year has made considerable progress in reading, writing, and simple arithmetic. **1891** *Univ. Chicago Official Bul.* No. 1, 11 Lecturers and

Teachers . . . shall be classified as follows: (1) The Head-Professor. **1920** HOWELLS *Vacation of Kelwyns* 121 She added to the teacher, 'Nelly, I guess if we don't hurry we shall be late for tea.'

‖**Teacherly,** *a.* Of or pertaining to a teacher in a church. — c1680 HULL *Diaries* 173 Mr. John Norton . . . continued with us three years and upward . . . ; laboring in God's work, and joined in a teacherly office with us.

+**Teachers' institute.** An assembly of the teachers in a state, county, etc., for discussing the problems and methods of teaching. Also *teachers' state institute.* — **1837** in S. N. Sweet *Teachers' Institutes* 14 *Resolved,* That in the opinion of this community, Professor Sweet, the founder of Teachers' Institutes, or Temporary Normal Schools, is entitled to the gratitude of all the lovers of science and friends of improvement. **1847** B. ALCOTT *Journals* 195 The Teachers' Institute . . . gave me an opportunity to see what the State is doing for the rising generation. **1868** *Ore. State Jrnl.* 18 July 2/6 Teachers and others coming from a distance to attend the Teachers' State Institute. **1883** *Century Mag.* June 197/2 A general dissemination of proper knowledge among teachers . . . might perhaps be done through the normal schools and teachers' institutes. **1906** [see INSTITUTE 3].

+**Teaching elder.** An elder, as in the colonial Congregational churches, exercising teaching or pastoral functions: (see quot. 1889). — **1642** *Harvard Rec.* I. 42 All the magistrates . . . together with the teaching elders of the six next adjoyning townes. **1735** in C. Hazard *Thos. Hazard* 226 We the Subscribers, Teaching Elders or Pastors of the first gathered . . . Church in Boston New England. **1887** EGGLESTON in *Century Mag.* April 908/2 The 'teaching elders,' or ministers, of whom most churches in the first years of the colonies had two, occupied the highest seat behind the pulpit. **1889** *Cent.* 1864/3 In churches of the Presbyterian order the pastor of a church is technically called the *teaching elder,* as distinguished from the *ruling elders,* commonly called simply *elders,* who are a body of laymen.

+**Tea clam.** (See quotations.) — **1881** INGERSOLL *Oyster-Industry* 249 Tea-clam.—The quahaug, *Venus mercenaria* of small size. **1883** *Nat. Museum Bul.* No. 27, 234 Smaller sizes . . . , when about one inch in diameter, are called 'tea-clams.'

Tea fight. A tea party. *humorous. slang.* {1849–} — **1837** NEAL *Charcoal Sk.* (1838) 77 If you go to a tea-fight, the people are always tumbling over your trotters. **1855** HOLBROOK *Among Mail Bags* 365 An out-of-the-way incident . . . gave new life to the Sewing Society, and its auxiliary 'tea-fights.' **1875** [see BIB 2].

+**Tea junketing.** A tea or tea party. *Obs.* — **1820** IRVING *Sketch Book* No. 7, 116 Mrs. Lamb . . . would give little hum-drum tea junkettings to some of her old cronies. **1852** *Harper's Mag.* July 185/1 There was to be a tea-junketing.

Teakettle. A kettle in which water is boiled for making tea. {1705–}
1744 FRANKLIN *Writings* II. 267 You do not lose the pleasing Sight nor Use of the Fire, as in the Dutch stoves, but may boil the Tea-Kettle, [etc.]. **1790** *Penna. Packet* 1 March 3/3 William Robinson, Junr. . . . Hath for Sale . . . Iron Castings, consisting of, tea kettles, bake pans [etc.]. **1815** *Niles' Reg.* IX. 35/2 Stills, tea kettles and other vessels of copper, with a great variety of tin ware, are made in abundance. **1896** JEWETT *Pointed Firs* 88 You just sly out and set the teakittle on again. **1922** [see DIPPER 2].
attrib. **1871** BAGG *At Yale* 173 The 'Tea-Kettle' society, established in the class of '53, . . . has left nothing behind it save the announcement of its birth in the Lit. **1886** *Outing* VIII. 159/2 There was a flat-boat with a tea-kettle boiler.

*****Teal.** Any one of various river ducks, +as the bluewing and the green-winged teal (qq.v.). Also with specifying term.
1610 *Estate of Va.* 30 The riuers . . . are couered with . . . teal, wigeons, hearons, bitters. **1637** MORTON *New Canaan* 68 Teales, there are of two sorts, greene winged, and blew winged. **1701** WOLLEY *Journal N.Y.* 40 They have great store of wild-fowl, as . . . Cranes, Geese, Brants, Ducks, Widgeon, Teal and divers others. **1792** IMLAY *Western Territory* 95 There is a variety of wild-fowl in every part of this State, particularly teal, and the summer duck. **1806** LEWIS in *L. & Clark Exped.* IV. (1905) 152 The larger species [of divers] are about the size of the teal. **1887** RIDGWAY *Manual N.A. Birds* 93 Western America . . . ; east, casually or irregularly, to Mississippi Valley. . . . *A*[*nas*] *cyanoptera.* Cinnamon Teal. **1894** *Harper's Mag.* Aug. 457/1 Only darkness can end the miseries of the poor little teal coming home to their marsh.

*****Team,** *n.*
1. Two or more draft animals, or one such animal, along with the implement or vehicle drawn. {1675–}
1640 *Conn. Rec.* I. 58 The Court . . . haue graunted to ech Teeme a hundred acres of plowing grownd. **1681** *Huntington Rec.* I. 287 Meny yt have wells, doe fech of ye watter of ye brooks some with their teams & sume with horses for theire use. **1709** in Sheldon *Hist. Deerfield, Mass.* I. 367 Hinsdell driving his teem from Northampton loaded with apple trees . . . was met by two Indians. **1771** CUTLER in *Life & Corr.* I. 35 The teams, with our goods, set out this morning for the Hamlet. **1807** *Ann. 10th Congress* 1 Sess. 2039 He was . . . employed sometimes as a wagoner, driving a team to and from Baltimore. **1885** [see FIREBREAK]. **1903** LOOMIS *Cheerful Americans* 43 By 'a team' I mean a horse and buggy. . . . In Connecticut . . . a team is anything you choose to call one.

*****2.** Draft animals used together.

c1644 *Mass. H. S. Proc.* 2 Ser. VIII. 14 Teemes for carriage may be hired. **1754** WASHINGTON *Writings* I. 55 We got but ten [wagons] . . . , and some of those so badly provided with teams, that the soldiers were obliged to assist them up the hills. c1816 D. McCLURE *Diary* (1899) 191 He had . . . a team of one yoke of oxen. **1892** M. A. JACKSON *Gen. Jackson* 223 The teams were especially shod for the purpose. **1925** TILGHMAN *Dugout* 5 By Christmas time they paid for their team and wagon.
transf. **1868** *Ill. Agric. Soc. Trans.* VII. 444 [A train of 88,761 cars would require] a 'team' of locomotives twenty-five miles in length.

+**b.** *To drive too much team,* to go beyond one's capabilities. *colloq.*
1842 *Cultivator* IX. 193/3, I should have accomplished all this, . . . but I undertook to drive *too much team.*

3. The vehicle drawn by a draft animal or animals. *New Eng.* {1688}
1779 PARKMAN *Diary* 151 Mr. Nathan Maynard junr. goes to Boston for Breck and carries in his Team Mr. Eli Forbes' Trunk. **1806** *Mass. Laws* 4 March 65 For each . . . team of burthen, drawn by one beast, [the toll is] sixteen cents. **1848** THOREAU *Maine Woods* 12 Here was . . . a stock . . . brought home in the wagon-box, or a corner of the Houlton team. **1904** *Hartford Courant* 11 July 13 (*caption*), Young Woman Thrown from a Team and Hurt.

+**b.** *Double team,* a vehicle for two draft animals.
1846 WHITCHER *Bedott P.* i. 25 A mess o' men in a double team . . hysted us out.

+**4.** A grandiose term for an individual of superior endowments. Usually *whole team,* and often with various embellishments as *the whole team and the dog under the wagon. colloq.*
1843 STEPHENS *High Life N.Y.* II. 193, I tell you what, he's a hull team, and a horse to let. **1852** WATSON *Nights in Block-House* 142 Lew Whetzel was a whole team at shootin'. **1866** LOWELL *Biglow P.* 2 Ser. p. lxi, He's a whole team and the dog under the wagon. **1892** *Harper's Mag.* Feb. 439/1 She says I'm a team in myself, with a little dog under the wagon. **1911** LINCOLN *Cap'n Warren's Wards* 170 Mother's the whole team and the dog under the wagon!

+**5.** A pack of dogs that hunt together. *Obs.*
1844 FEATHERSTONHAUGH *Slave States* 111/2 They maintained stout *teams* of dogs until the hunting season commenced. **1851** *Polly Peablossom* 126, I had long promised myself the pleasure of following a good 'team' of dogs through these unexplored wilds.

+**6.** Baseball. A nine.
1868 *N.Y. Herald* 24 July 7/4 They had, however, a 'team' to contend with which . . . is one of the toughest combinations in the fraternity [of baseball players]. **1887** *Courier-Journal* 27 May 2/4 The victory sent the Kentucky team to third place in the race for the pennant. **1910** *Spalding's Base Ball Guide* 361 'No game' shall be declared by the umpire if he terminates play in accordance with Rule 22, Sec. 3, before five innings are completed by each team.

7. Attrib. and comb. with *driver, harness, leader,* etc.
1841 *Knickerb.* XVII. 26 He was not by any means so heavy or muscular as the team-driver. **1852** BRISTED *Upper Ten Th.* 125 Did you ever notice the whiffle-trees of my team-trotting-wagon? **1871** *Rep. Indian Affairs* (1872) 285 Now they are capable of cutting and making team-harness for the agency teams. **1876** KNIGHT 2501/2 *Team-shovel,* an earth-scraper. A scoop drawn by horses or oxen, managed by means of handles, and used in removing earth. **1890** HARTE *Waif of Plains* 91 Clarence had been allowed to bestride one of the team leaders postillionwise, and was correspondingly elevated.

*****Team,** *v.* (See also DOUBLE-TEAM *v.,* TEAMING.) +intr. and *tr.* To work as a teamster; to transport or haul with a team. — **1841** EMERSON *Self-reliance* Ess. 1 Ser., A sturdy lad from New Hampshire or Vermont, . . . who *teams* it, *farms* it, *peddles,* . . . is worth a hundred of these city dolls. **1865** *Atlantic Mo.* April 390/2 The farmers back of the Creek prefer bringing their horses down and teaming oil to working the land. **1903** LONDON *Valley of Moon* 307, I've teamed there [in Oakland, Calif.] most of my life.

+**Team boat.** (See quot. 1876.)
1816 *Niles' Reg.* X. 414/1 The team boat . . . is 62 feet long and 42 feet wide, and propelled by eight horses. **1821** W. DALTON *Travels U.S.* 8 We returned in a team boat. **1876** KNIGHT 2501/2 *Team-boat,* . . . a ferryboat whose paddles are worked by horses on board. **1895** *Forum* May 378 The 'team-boat,' or ferry-boat propelled by horse power, actually ran for some time in competition with steam ferries.
attrib. **1820** *Columbian Centinel* 12 Jan. 3/1 A Team Boat ferry connects the travel with the eastern shore opposite.

Teaming. {1733–} Cf. TEAM *v.* +**1.** The conveying of commodities by means of a team. Also *attrib.* +**2.** (See quotation.) — (1) **1778** *N.H. Hist. Soc. Coll.* IX. 286 The price of teaming and all land Transportation Shall not exceed the rate of five twelveths of a Continental dollar. **1818** *Essex Inst. Coll.* VII. 99/1, I was employed . . . in teaming between Bedford & Boston. **1871** *Ill. Agric. Soc. Trans.* VIII. 229 Were I following the business of teaming, with but one span of horses, . . . I should [etc.]. **1909** *Springfield W. Repub.* 25 Feb. 16 There is birch, beech and maple enough within a teaming distance of Orange. **1913** LONDON *Valley of Moon* 501, I seen the fellow with the teamin' contract for the pavin'-stone quarry. (2) **1876** KNIGHT 2501/1 *Teaming,* . . . a certain mode of manufacturing work, which is given out to a boss, who hires a gang or team to do it, and is responsible to the owner of the stock.

Team play. Play in which members of a team co-operate for a desired end. Also *team player*. — **1886** CHADWICK *Art of Batting* 7 The practical effect of all this is to destroy a batsman's ambition to excel as a 'team player' in batting. **1890** *N.Y. Ev. Post* 13 June (E. J. Nichols).

+**Teamster.** One who drives a team.
1777 *N.H. Comm. Safety Rec.* 88 The Committee delivered the Several Teamsters. **1817** *N. Amer. Rev.* IV. 183 We there sat down to table with teamsters. **1856** DERBY *Phoenixiana* 15 These gentlemen, with one hundred and eighty-four . . . teamsters, chainmen, rodmen, etc., made up the party. **1897** HOUGH *Story of Cowboy* 37 Early teamsters . . . crossed the plains, freighting to Denver in the days before the railroads. **1925** TILGHMAN *Dugout* 3 They worked as teamsters and on the railroad construction camp and hunted some.
attrib. **1850** GARRARD *Wah-To-Yah* xxvi. 304 Only a green teamster train.

Teamwork. 1. (See quot. 1828.) {1886, *dial.*} **2.** Co-operative work by individual members of an athletic team, who subordinate their own interests to the success of the group. **3.** Work of which different people do different parts. — **(1) 1828** WEBSTER, *Team-work*, . . . work done by a team, as distinguished from personal labor. *New England.* **1872** *Vermont Bd. Agric. Rep.* I. 513 All kinds of heavy team work are done to advantage in winter. **(2) 1886** *Outing* June 365/1 All three of the college nines were . . . weak in their team-work together to a more or less extent. **1891** *Harper's Wkly.* XXV. 291/1 The strongest feature of the nine is its excellent team-work. **(3) 1887** H. CAMPBELL *Prisoners of Poverty* 26 [Others preferred] to send out what is known as 'team work,' [shirt] flaps being done by one, bosoms by another, and so on.

Tea party. A social entertainment at which tea is served. {1778–}
1787 TYLER *Contrast* I. 1, I cannot charge myself with ever having discredited a tea-party by my silence. **1833** J. STUART *Three Years N.A.* I. 476 Tea-parties . . . are very common in the United States. **1886** H. D. BROWN *Two College Girls* 7 Edna, however, had made no active resistance to the present tea-party. **1905** 'O. HENRY' *Roads of Destiny* 135 But no barehanded scrapping, like ladies at a tea-party, for me.

+**b.** *Boston Tea Party*, the coming together of citizens disguised as Indians and the throwing overboard of the cargoes of three tea ships in Boston Harbor in 1773.
1840 *Picayune* 24 Oct. 2/4 Died in Boston. . . . Mr. Wm. Pierce, aged 96 years—one of the few survivors of the celebrated Boston Tea Party. **1874** O. W. HOLMES *(title)*, A Ballad of the Boston Tea-Party.

Tea plant.
1. Any one of various Asiatic tea-producing plants introduced into the United States. {1727–41–}
1803 CUTLER in *Life & Corr.* II. 145 Every part was crowded with trees and plants from the hot climates, . . . the tea-plant in full perfection. **1812** *Ann. 12th Congress* 1 Sess. 2178, I take the liberty of sending you an account of the progress I have made in the introduction of the *tea plant*. **1850** *Rep. Comm. Patents 1849: Agric.* 403, I have a variety of both black and green tea-plants. **1890** *Rep. Secy. Agric. 1889* 29 The same tests have been made with the tea plant, the coffee plant [etc.].

+**2.** Any one of various American wild plants whose leaves can be used in making a beverage somewhat like tea.
1809 KENDALL *Travels* II. 143 Where the pine only is found, the ground beneath is nearly bare, sustaining but dwarfish plants, such as the partridge-berry, sometimes called the tea plant and Indian tea. **1894** *Amer. Folk-Lore* VII. 96 Lantana, sp., tea-plant, Louisiana.

Tear, *n.* {1611–} +A spree or frolic. In phrase *to go on a tear. slang.* — **1849** G. G. FOSTER *N.Y. in Slices* 24 A grand 'tear' is to be held in that large and rather aristocratic-looking cellar across the way. **1875** HARTE *Tales of Argonauts* 11 My girl Jinny's jist got back from a little tear up at Robinson's. **1920** LEWIS *Main Street* 389 Her and couple of other skirts bought a whole case of whisky and went on a tear.

*‖*Tear, *v.* **1.** *To tear round*, to rush about with impetuosity. *colloq.* {tear about, 1779–} **2.** *To tear along*, to pull along. — **(1) 1844** *Knickerb.* XXIV. 587 Some would 'tear round,' throw over the benches, etc. **1857** *Quinland* I. 304 [The] 'hired girl,' is also in the kitchen, tearing round, like mad, among the pots and kettles. **1869** STOWE *Oldtown Folks* 174 It's no use tearin' round gen'lly. **(2) 1852** BRISTED *Upper Ten Th.* 25 He tears along behind him a sleigh, . . . furnished with an ancient and fragmentary buffalo.

+**Tear-blanket.** Any one of various prickly plants: (see quotations). — **1835** LATROBE *Rambler in N.A.* I. 213 We found . . . abundance of green-briar or tear-blanket as it is familiarly called. **1859** BARTLETT 473 *Tear-coat*, or *tear-blanket*, . . . [the] Angeli[c]a tree, so called because its prickles tear the coats of hunters, or the blankets of Indians, in passing. **1897** SUDWORTH *Arborescent Flora* 265 *Xanthoxylum clava-herculis*. Prickly Ash. . . . Wait-a-bit, Tear-blanket (Ark.).

+**Tear-coat.** =prec. — **1859** [see prec.].

*‖*Tearer. +Something exceptional, as an elaborate party or a violent storm. — **1835** *S. Lit. Messenger* I. 357/2 A real tearer—a regular turnout—been preparing a fortnight. **1892** S. HALE *Letters* 275 The storm increased as day went on, and by noon was a regular tearer.

Tea rose. Any one of various garden roses having a scent supposedly similar to that of tea. {1850–} Also attrib. — **1852** STOWE *Uncle Tom*

xxvii, Topsy . . . [held] up a half-blown tea rose-bud. **1863** TAYLOR *H. Thurston* 56 A shelf inside the southern window held some tea-roses in pots. **1912** N. WOODROW *Sally Salt* 44 The skin was of the exquisite, pale, pinkish yellow of the tea-rose.

*‖*Tear-round. A spree or frolic. *colloq.* — **1872** HARTE in *Atlantic Mo.* March 350 Maybe ye'd all come over to my house to-night and have a sort of tear-round.

*Teasel. Also teazel. One or other species of *Dipsacus*, esp. *D. sylvestris*, the wild teasel; the dried flower heads of *D. fullonum* used to dress cloth. Also attrib. — **1791** MUHLENBERG *Index Florae* 162. **1843** TORREY *Flora N.Y.* I. 320 *Dipsacus sylvestris*. . . . Wild Teasel . . . Fields, road-sides, etc.; naturalized in many places. A native of Europe. **1891** CHASE & CLOW *Industry* II. 40 The wiry sharp fine hooks or awns, of the thistleheads, known as teazels, which are imported from France. **1901** MOHR *Plant Life Ala.* 746.

+**Tea-spiller.** A participant in the Boston Tea Party. *humorous. Obs.* — **1837** PHILLIPS in C. Martyn *W. Phillips* 96 Certainly we sons of the tea-spillers are a marvellously patient generation! **1895** *Advance* 8 Aug. 192/1 Would the old tea spillers and Puritan parents know themselves now?

Tea table. A table used in serving tea. {1688–} Also attrib. — **1712** *Boston News-Letter* 16 June 2/2 The ladies may have their choice of silks, fine Tea Tables &c. **1731** in Singleton *Social N.Y.* 381 The Ceremony of the Tea-Table . . . is look'd upon as a Point of great Importance. **1788** *Ky. Gazette* 31 May 2/2 A Large & General Assortmen of Goods. . . . Tea table ketches . . . Turners tools & wheel-irons. **1842** KIRKLAND *Forest Life* I. 185 The difficulty was obviated by the arrival of a handsome tea-table, borne by two young men. **1907** *St. Nicholas* May 629/1 Susie . . . pulled out her little tea-table.

Tea tree. {1760–} +The yaupon or a related species, the leaves of which are used as a substitute for tea. — **1785** MARSHALL *Arbust. Grove* 26 Ever-green Caffine, Yapon, or South-Sea Tea-tree . . . grows naturally in Carolina and some parts of Virginia. **1836** HOLLEY *Texas* 88 The Yawpan or tea tree deserves a special notice. **1841** W. KENNEDY *Texas* I. 100 Among the latter [*i.e.*, shrubs], may be enumerated . . . red bud, hog wood, the yawpan or tea tree [etc.].

Tea water. {1693–} *local.* +Water, regarded as exceptionally pure, obtained from a deep well in New York City. *Obs.* Also attrib. — **1870** M. H. SMITH *20 Years Wall St.* 34 'Tea water' was expensive. **1871** *Scribner's Mo.* II. 44 Better be a tea-water man's horse, in New York, than a portrait painter anywhere.

+**Tea-water pump.** *local.* (See quot. 1885.) *Obs.* — **1832** DUNLAP *Hist. Amer. Theatre* 39 Nearly opposite the place where Queen-street ended in Chatham-road, was the celebrated tea-water pump. **1885** *Century Mag.* April 886/1 The famous well from which pure water was carted into New York to be sold in the street was known as the 'tea-water pump.' **1889** *Ib.* April 858/2 Into the punch went . . . lime-juice, water from the old tea-water pump.

+**Tea weed.** =MEADOWSWEET. — **1852** *Mich. Agric. Soc. Trans.* III. 197 My timber is generally oak, with some hickory, indigo weed, tea weed. **1874** *Vermont Bd. Agric. Rep.* II. 775 Common upon flowers of many kinds, especially those of the meadow-sweet or tea-weed.

+**Tea wheat.** A variety of wheat alleged to have originated from some stray seed found in a shipment of tea. Also *China tea wheat. Obs.* (Cf. CHINA WHEAT.) — **1832** J. MACGREGOR *British America* II. 315 The kind of seed-wheat generally sown . . . [is] known by the distinction of 'tea-wheat.' **1862** *Ill. Agric. Soc. Trans.* V. 197 China Tea Wheat . . . was said to have been taken from a chest of black tea some fifteen years since, by a gentleman in Rensalaer [*sic*] county, New York. **1868** *Iowa State Agric. Soc. Rep. 1867* 141 The first seed wheat I bought in Iowa (in 1853) was called Red River, and when it was grown I recognized at once the Tea wheat of New York.

Teazle burr. {1821–} +(See quotation.) — **1869** BRACE *New West* 301 One of the great plagues throughout California to the cattle-breeder, is a species of mullen—the teazle-burr.

Technic. {1798–} +A technical term or expression. *Obs.* — **1826** FLINT *Recoll.* 86 We began to pull the boat up the stream, by a process, which, in the technics of the boatmen, is called 'bush-whacking.' **1855** *Knickerb.* XLV. 438, [The mare] has a new disease—the staggers,' perhaps. . . . I don't know as 'staggers' is the technic.

Technical, *a.* {1617–} In special combinations.
Technical judge, (see quotation); *t. school*, a school in which the major emphasis is placed upon the teaching of such subjects as engineering; *t. training*, training in technical and mechanical arts.
1822 *Ann. 17th Congress* 1 Sess. 75 One may take an expansive view of a subject, and base his decision upon truth and justice; another may be, what is sometimes called a *technical judge* . . . , and confine himself in all decisions to the forms of judicial proceedings. **1893** GILMAN *University Problems U.S.* 306 There is no reason to fear that the distinctive 'college' will be disprized, as technical schools increase in numbers and in excellence. **1904** *Atlantic Mo.* Nov. 606 West Point is not a school aiming to fit men for a given technical training.

+**Technological school.** A school in which technology is taught. — **1883** *Harper's Mag.* Aug. 327/2 Many graduates from the technological schools of Boston . . . work in these [car] shops. **1914** [see PROFESSIONAL SCHOOL].

*Tedder. +A machine for stirring and spreading hay, to promote its drying. — **1868** *Mich. Agric. Rep.* VII. 223 There are important advantages in the use of the tedder for machine-cut grass. **1883** *Harper's Mag.* Oct. 789/1 The click of the mowing-machine, the rapid sweep of the tedder, and the horse-rake, foretold a new epoch in agriculture. **1888** *Vt. Agric. Rep.* X. 18 [He] mows clover in the afternoon and the next forenoon sets the tedder to work.

+Teenty, *a.* Also **teensy.** Very tiny or small. *colloq.* Also with *tointy, taunty.* — **1843** STEPHENS *High Life N.Y.* II. 227 A little teenty tointy handful of wood keeps 'em warm as blazes. **1863** *Harper's Mag.* Dec. 112/2 A pretty little teenty-taunty babe as ever you see. **1881** M. J. HOLMES *Madeline* 136 Only that little, teenty thing? **1894** *Harper's Mag.* Feb. 429 You were six months old—a little teenty baby. **1902** HARBEN *A. Daniel* 197 Then Jimmy's young wife come with her little teensy baby.

+Teest. [Of obscure origin.] (See quotations.) — *a*1870 CHIPMAN *Notes on Bartlett* 473 Teest, an anvil used by planishers of tinned plate.—Mass. **1876** KNIGHT 2504/1 *Teest,* a stake or small anvil used by sheet-iron workers.

Teeter, *n.* **+1.** The spotted sandpiper, *Actitis macularia.* Also attrib. **2.** A seesaw. {titter, 1884-, *dial.*; 1887-} — (1) **1842** [see TILT-UP 1]. **1844** *Nat. Hist. N.Y., Zoology* II. 247 It is better known among the people by the name . . . of Teeter and Tilteep, from its often repeated grotesque jerking motions. **1885** M. THOMPSON *By Ways & Bird Notes* 53 So accentuated is this light seesaw movement of one of the lesser sandpipers, that the bird is called 'teeter-snipe' by the country folk. **1895** *Outing* XXVII. 69/2 The 'teeter' is fat and well flavored. **1917** *Birds of Amer.* I. 249 Spotted Sandpiper. . . . [Also called] Teeter-peep; Teetertail; Teeterer. (2) **1863** *Harper's Mag.* Aug. 343/2 Teeters to jump on, rings to swing by. **1883** in *Pat. Off. Gazette* XXVI. 302/2 In a teeter, the stands A, having inclined post *a,* that are connected on top [etc.].

+Teeter, *v.*
1. *intr.* To walk or move in a swaying, unsteady, or mincing manner. {titter, *a*1618-}
1843 STEPHENS *High Life N.Y.* II. 231, I teetered up tu her a tiptoe. **1855** *Knickerb.* XLV. 31 The ill-conditioned chair was teetering to-and-fro. **1878** B. F. TAYLOR *Between Gates* 152 You walk . . . with the tiptoe feeling with which you used to teeter into church at prayer-time. **1916** 'BOWER' *Phantom Herd* 1 Fat old squaws . . . teetered tirelessly round and round in their queer native dances.

2. To seesaw. {titter, *a*1825-, *dial.*}
1846 WORCESTER 728/2 *Teeter,* . . . to seesaw on a balanced plank, as children [do]. **1857** UNDERHILL & THOMPSON *Elephant Club* 173 [We] 'teetered' in happy sport upon the same board. **1869** *Overland Mo.* III. 109 She is . . . contented to teeter for hours on a plank by the woodpile.

+Teeter board. A seesaw. Also attrib. and transf. — **1855** *Knickerb.* XLVI. 88 We were having a grand time with our 'teeter-boards up on the highest fence. **1894** *Congress. Rec.* App. 6 June 915/1 The moneyed men could work the financial 'teeter' board to suit their pleasure. **1909** *Springfield W. Repub.* 2 Dec. 3 Lord Rosebery's brilliant teeterboard speech, protesting against the budget and at the same time against its rejection by the House of Lords.

+Teeter-totter, *v. intr.* To seesaw. {titter-totter, *a*1825-} — **1888** RILEY in *Voice* 21 June, [In] the lane . . . we used to 'teeter-totter.' **1907** *Black Cat* June 25 He called back to the figure teter-tottering with the bowing of the log it rode.

Teethbrush. A brush for the teeth. *Obs.* {1651-} — **1781** in H. M. Brooks *Gleanings* IV. 52 Teeth-Brushes, and Teeth-Powder, which when used will recommend itself. **1790** *Penna. Packet* 19 April 4/2 John Murduck . . . has likewise for Sale . . . teeth brushes, &c. **1810** *Columbian Centinel* 17 Jan. 3/5 Samuel Kidder, jun. . . . has received per the late arrivals from London Teeth Brushes. **1875** HOLLAND *Sevenoaks* 15 Buxton . . . may advance [in the care of its paupers] to some economical form of teeth-brushes.

+Teetotaciously, *adv.* =TEETOTALLY *adv. colloq.*[2] — *a*1859 *N.Y. Spirit of Times* (B.), I won't swear, 'cause it's wicked; but if he wasn't, I hope to be teetotaciously chawed up!

Teetotal, *a.* Denoting or having reference to entire abstinence from alcoholic drinks. {1834-} — **1837** FEATHERSTONHAUGH *Canoe Voyage* II. 342 One of them asked him, 'if there was no tea-total society in the neighbourhood.' **1849** WILLIS *Rural Letters* 173 After two days of the pendulum life at Washington, . . . I turned once more toward the teetotal zone, ('temperate' will scarce express it,) and was in Philadelphia. **1855** BARNUM *Life* 335 Among other signers to the teetotal pledge was the famous comedian.

Teetotaler. One who abstains entirely from alcoholic drinks. {1834-} — **1835** E. C. DELAVAN in J. Pearce *Life J. Livesey* I. p. cxii, Our people by thousands are becoming *teetotallers.* **1846** CORCORAN *Pickings* 130 A glance at it [his round, ruddy face] would shame a Grahamite or teetotaller out of his abstinence principles. **1887** CUSTER *Tenting on Plains* 247 One of the staff, now a teetotaler, made himself of his past . . . by the present of a wooden faucet. **1925** BRYAN *Memoirs* 351 He told them that we had always been teetotalers.

Teetotally, *adv.* Totally; entirely. *colloq.* {1839-} — **1807** WEEMS *Letters* II. 361, I am now . . . wholly, solely, & tetotally absorbed in Wayne's business. **1843** 'CARLTON' *New Purchase* I. 175 There I was tetotally lost! **1894** *Congress. Rec.* 15 June 6380/2, I am teetotally opposed to pensions of that kind. **1907** HARRIS *Tents of Wickedness* 172 He's lost teetotally the little Christianity that he ever had.

+Telautograph. (See quot. 1883.) — **1883** KNIGHT *Suppl.* 880/1 *Telautograph,* an electrical device for transmitting autographs, or copying designs. . . . The possibility of deception and the impossibility of automatic unquestionable record . . . are removed, it is said, by the employment of telautography. **1893** *Boston Jrnl.* 30 March 7/1 A number of

newspaper men and invited guests witnessed an exhibition of Prof. Elisha Gray's telautograph. **1897** *Boston Rec.* 12 Aug. 1/6 Telautograph . . . renders possible the transmission of handwriting, in fac-simile, by wire.

Telegram. A message sent by telegraph. {1855-} Also attrib. — **1852** *Albany Ev. Jrnl.* 6 April (B.), Our friend . . . would have them 'held and firmly bound' to speak, write, print, and telegraph, *Telegram,* instead of any two words signifying the same thing. **1866** [see FLAG *n*.[2] 1]. **1883** SWEET & KNOX *Through Texas* 26 The Galveston Board has its telegram-blanks lithographed by the hundred. **1897** [see OFFICE BOY]. **1924** CROY *R.F.D. No. 3* 233 Josie had expected that they would have to go to the railroad station, the 'depot'—it was the way her father had always sent telegrams.

Telegraph.
1. A device for transmitting messages to a distance. {1794-}
[**1798** *Ky. Laws* II. 12 All advertisements . . . which shall be published in the . . . Kentucky Telegraphe, . . . shall be as good and valid in law as if they had been published in the Kentucky Gazette or Herald.] **1807** *Mass. H. S. Coll.* 2 Ser. III. 74 A line of telegraphs extends from Boston, and terminates at the West Chop.

b. Such an apparatus making use of electric current, as a Morse telegraph. {1797-, with descriptive adj.}
See also ELECTRIC, FIRE ALARM, MAGNETIC TELEGRAPH.
[**1858** LONGFELLOW in S. Longfellow *H. W. Longfellow* II. 361 Standing in the office I hear the click! click! of the telegraph.] **1860** BUCHANAN in *Pres. Mess. & P.* V. 621 The telegraph was silent respecting these contradictions. **1885** *Harper's Mag.* Aug. 351/1 Later on, the railroad and telegraph, inevitable even here, met scant welcome. **1898** *Mo. So. Dakotan* I. 72 All proposed laws . . . concerning railroads, telegraphs, telephones, [etc.] . . . should be submitted to the people for approval.

2. A telegram. Now *dial.* {1857-}
1850 D. WEBSTER *Letters* (1902) 392, I recd. your Telegraph last eve. **1886** STAPLETON *Major's Christmas* 85 Mr. Charles was ill when the telegraph was sent him. **1898** WESTCOTT *D. Harum* xlii, This here telegraph wouldn't 'a' ben sent.

3. Attrib. with *clock, dispatch, head,* etc.
1873 *Republic* I. 19 Among these measures [is] . . . the breaking up of the telegraph monopoly. **1876** KNIGHT 2511/2 *Telegraph-clock,* an arrangement by which time is signaled to a number of different apartments in a building or to several buildings. **1877** *Harper's Mag.* Dec. 44/1 Occasionally a telegraph messenger dived into the entrance of a building. **1882** PECK *Sunshine* 119 He is the telegraph manager. **1883** *Harper's Mag.* Oct. 790/1 The telegraph strike has had the good result of promoting intelligent reflection. **1887** Telegraph system [see OPERATE *v.* 2]. **1887** FREDERIC *Seth's Brother's Wife* 336, I got a telegraph dispatch from him. **1892** *Aberdeen* (S.D.) *Sun* 24 Nov. 2/3 Women never read the huge telegraph-heads of a newspaper. **1893** Philips *Making of Newspaper* 16 Certain excellent local newspapers . . . pay for telegraph-tolls not more than one hundred dollars a week.

+Telegraph blank. A printed form on which the words of a telegram are to be written. — **1893** Philips *Making of Newspaper* 99 Mr. Slawson . . . struck out the formal matter in the heading of the telegraph blank. **1914** GERRY *Masks of Love* 172 His hand, suddenly vigorous, drew a telegraph-blank toward him.

+Telegraph company. A company of business associates who operate a telegraph line or lines. — **1859** *N.Y. Tribune* 13 Aug. (Chipman), No party has any such preferential rights over the lines of the American Telegraph Company. **1872** *Newton Kansan* 12 Dec. 2/1 Telegraph companies are liable for failure or delay in the transmission or delivery of messages. **1905** *Indian Laws & Tr.* III. 155 Two hundred dollars for cable anchorages of two telegraph companies . . . is discretionary with the Secretary of the Interior.

+Telegraph editor. On a newspaper staff, one who receives and edits news received by telegraph. — **1875** C. F. WINGATE *Views & Interviews* 195 Have been continuously employed on the *Missouri Republican* . . . [as] telegraph editor, political writer &c. **1894** SHUMAN *Steps into Journalism* 108 While the city editor is the autocrat of the news within a radius of 100 miles, the telegraph editor is boss of the rest of the world. **1923** [see NEWSROOM b].

Telegrapher. {1795-} A telegraph operator. {1865-} 'In Am. the form *telegrapher* is preferred to the Eng. *telegraphist*' (Horwill). — **1851** CIST *Cincinnati* 51 Telegraphers, 7. **1878** PINKERTON *Strikers* 199 The strikers had some experienced telegraphers in the society. **1910** J. HART *Vigilante Girl* 376 This was the room of the man who filled the manifold offices of station-master, ticket-agent, express-agent, . . . and telegrapher.

Telegraph instrument. A device for sending or receiving telegraph messages. — **1876** KNIGHT 2512/1 *Telegraph-instrument,* a moving mechanical device used in the electric circuit. **1897** FLANDRAU *Harvard Episodes* 111 [He beat] a preliminary tattoo, that sounded like the clicking of a telegraph instrument. **1906** BELL *C. Lee* 169 From a shed at one end came the clicking of a telegraph instrument.

Telegraph line. A system of communication over which telegrams are sent. {1858-} — [**1830** *Boston Advertiser* 17 Oct. 2/5 (Ernst), Telegraph line. The public is respectfully informed that a new line of stages by the above name is established between this city and Hartford.] **1849** *Mich. Gen. Statutes* I. (1882) 944 The owner of any land through which said telegraph line may pass, and railroad corporation on whose right of way the same may be constructed, having first given consent. **1884**

BLAINE *20 Years of Congress* I. 507 An Act had been passed . . . to aid in the construction of a railroad and telegraph line from the Missouri River to the Pacific Ocean. **1904** W. H. SMITH *Promoters* 40 Thousands of miles of new telegraph lines [will be] necessary and they'll be our meat, every mile of 'em.

+Telegraph man. A man who has charge of a telegraph office; a sender of telegrams. — **1864** DALY in *A. Daly* 65 The telegraph man . . . keeps a grocery. **1879** *Scribner's Mo.* Sept. 653/2 'Come, Dickie, come, that's a dear,' whispered the telegraph man coaxingly. **1890** LANGFORD *Vigilante Days* (1912) 315 Hayes Lyons, telegraph man and roadster. **1901** McCUTCHEON *Graustark* 56 Your aunt and I went at once to the telegraph man and implored him to tell us the truth.

Telegraph office. An office or station at which telegraphic communications are sent and received. {1858-} — **1837** J. R. PARKER Broadside (Ernst), Telegraph office. **1862** McCLELLAN in *Own Story* 311, I started at once for the telegraph-office. **1904** 'O. HENRY' *Cabbages & Kings* (1916) 120 Felipe would anchor the navy and hang about the little telegraph office.

Telegraph operator. One employed to send or receive telegrams. — **1858** W. P. SMITH *Railway Celebrations* 67, 260 firemen, 210 watchmen, 34 telegraph operators. **1899** CHESNUTT *Wife of His Youth* 38 Among [the Negroes] . . . there were lawyers and doctors, teachers, telegraph operators, clerks, milliners and dressmakers. **1906** BELL *C. Lee* 188, I am telegraph operator there six months in the year.

+Telegraph road. A road along which a telegraph line is built. — **1867** CRAWFORD *Mosby* 192 [We] took the old telegraph road to within a mile of Stafford Court House. *a*1892 in M. A. Jackson *Gen. Jackson* 379 [Gen. Jackson] seemed gazing intently on the enemy's line of battle on the old telegraph road.

+Telegraph station. =TELEGRAPH OFFICE. — **1839** *Knickerb.* XIV. 187 A recent excursion . . . [extended] from New-Brighton to the telegraph station. **1862** Moore *Rebellion Rec.* V. II. 186 The substance . . . I put into a despatch, to be forwarded to the nearest telegraph-station. **1894** ROBLEY *Bourbon Co., Kansas* 67 Early in March, 1857, Governor Geary sent his resignation in a letter to St. Louis, the nearest telegraph station. **1905** 'O. HENRY' *Roads of Destiny* 129 There were telegraph stations ahead.

Telegraph wire. (See quot. 1876.) {1875-} — **1848** *Knickerb.* XXXI. 455 The wrecks of hundreds of little urchins' high-soaring 'hopes,' . . . [hang] on all the telegraph-wires. **1876** KNIGHT 2512/2 *Telegraph-wire,* . . . the road by which the electric current passes from one station to another, the metallic communication between stations, also connecting instruments, battery, and ground. **1907** *St. Nicholas* May 654/1 [I] have noticed a great many cobwebs on the grass, . . . and even the telegraph wires.

Telephone, n. {1835-}

+1. An instrument of a type devised by Alexander G. Bell, consisting of a transmitter and receiver so combined and connected as to transmit and receive sounds. {1879-}

1876 BELL in *Amer. Acad. Proc.* XII. 7 The telephones so constructed were placed in different rooms. **1880** *Harper's Mag.* Oct. 723/1 The use of the telephone [in Chicago] is far more general and effective than in New York. **1891** WELCH *Recoll. 1830-40* 423 We now have for daily convenience . . . the telephone. **1923** DUTTON *Shadow on Glass* 7 Instead he reached for the telephone once more.

2. *attrib.* **a.** Designating messages, sounds, etc., communicated by telephone.

1878 VIVIAN *Notes Tour Amer.* 35 At a telephone concert . . . the songs were sung at New York, and we heard them almost as clearly and distinctly at Saratoga as if but a few feet . . . separated us from the singers. **1878** EDISON in *N. Amer. Rev.* May 535 Were . . . our telephone-conversation automatically recorded, we should find the reverse of the present status of the telephone. **1893** *Harper's Mag.* April 808/1 He received a telephone call to the effect that one of his patients had become alarmingly worse.

b. Designating physical equipment, apparatus, etc., used in the operation of the telephone.

1880 *Cimarron News & Press* 24 June 2/1 Las Vegas wants a telephone exchange. **1885** *Wkly. New Mexican* 12 Feb. 4/3 The top barbed wire of the fence [is used] for the telephone line. **1887** *Trial H. K. Goodwin* 60 The subscribers . . . were connected with the telephone office. **1900** *Everybody's Mag.* II. 407/2 The telephone wires . . . are strung on poles or buried in subways. **1903** *McClure's Mag.* Nov. 101/2 He strolled to the telephone-closet. **1907** FIELD *Six-Cylinder Courtship* 29 Strangle that young devil at the telephone desk until he looks dead. **1909** 'O. HENRY' *Options* 261, I hurried to a telephone-booth and rang up the Telfair residence. **1920** COOPER *Under Big Top* 122 People were . . . running and climbing trees and telephone poles.

c. In special combinations.

Telephone frank, the privilege of using a telephone system free of charge; *t. girl,* a woman telephone operator; *t. number,* the number assigned to a given subscriber's instrument or instruments in a telephone system; *t. system,* a number of telephones and the organization controlling and connecting them.

1913 LA FOLLETTE *Autobiog.* 209 Prohibit the acceptance by public officials of railroad passes, . . . express, telegraph and telephone franks. **1897** L. RICHARDSON (*title*), The Telephone Girl. **1907** HARRIS *Tents of Wickedness* 33, 'I don't get her,' she murmured, as if Leonora was a tele-

phone number. **1881** RITTENHOUSE *Maud* 22 [We have a] telephone system, new Opera House, . . . street-cars soon to be running, and we are altogether citified.

Telephone, v. intr. To communicate by telephone. {1899-} — [**1880** *Times* (London) 22 Sept. 7/6 Mr. Bell . . . has succeeded in telegraphing, or rather 'telephoning,' along a beam of light.] **1881** *Chicago Times* 4 June, Mr. Smith . . . telephoned immediately to headquarters about the matter. **1894** HOWELLS in *Harper's Mag.* Feb. 371/2, I telephoned at once for Dr. Lawton to come instantly. **1923** DUTTON *Shadow on Glass* 29, I telephoned to her, after I called you.

Telescope, n.

1. An optical instrument for viewing distant objects. {1648-}

1721 *Mass. H. S. Coll.* 4 Ser. II. 165 There is a pretty good Quadrant and Telescope in the College about four miles from this. **1764** in Peirce *Hist. Harvard* 287 For Astronomy, we had before been supplied with Telescopes of different lengths. **1851** CIST *Cincinnati* 274 A good chemical and philosophical apparatus, . . . comprising a telescope with a reflector of six and one-fourth inches aperture. **1884** *Century Mag.* June 284/1 Cap'n Poinsett . . . was taking down the path in his pea-jacket, with his brass telescope tucked under his arm.

+2. A traveling bag consisting of two cases of which the larger slips over the smaller.

1896 *Chicago Tribune* 28 June 4/1 A set of the best safe-boring tools were put into a 'telescope' for the Ohio job. **1912** NICHOLSON *Hoosier Chron.* 81 Dan Harwood attained to a freshman's dignity at New Haven, . . . arriving with his effects in a canvas telescope.

Telescope, v. {1861-}

+1. *intr.* Of railroad cars: To crash into each other in the manner of sliding tubes in a telescope. {1881-} Also *vbl. n.*

1872 *Amer. R. R. Jrnl.* 20 April 493 Telescoping. . . . Car raised up and sent through the advancing car, after the manner of a closing telescope. **1877** HOLMES *Poetical Works* (1895) 139/2 They telescoped like cars in railroad smashes. **1887** GEORGE *40 Yrs. on Rail* 245 Telescoping has become almost unknown. **1887** *Courier-Journal* 5 Jan. 1/2 (*caption*), A Entire Express Train Telescopes Into a Freight Stopped in a Curve.

+2. *tr.* To force together (railroad cars, etc.) in the manner of the sliding tubes of a telescope; to smash (a railroad car) in this way. Also *transf.* and *vbl. n.*

[**1876** *World* V. 14 No one has ever yet been killed in a Pullman, in which, says its inventor, you can never be 'telescoped.'] **1881** *Chicago Times* 18 June, A freight of thirty loaded cars . . . collided with the other train, telescoping and completely wrecking several of the cars. **1889** *Boston Jrnl.* 11 April 6/4 (*caption*), A Private Sleeping Car Telescoped by a Locomotive.

Tell, n. {1742-} [Var. of *tale*.] +An account, explanation. *dial.* — **1795** DEARBORN *Columbian Grammar* 134 Improprieties, commonly called Vulgarisms, . . . [include] By his tell for By his tale. **1815** HUMPHREYS *Yankey* 43 He is a leetle twistical, according to their tell. **1889** COOKE *Steadfast* 386 Here's your sellery ain't half-paid, at least, that's the tell.

*Tell, v. +*To tell* (one) *good-bye,* to say good-bye to. *colloq.* — **1872** EGGLESTON *End of World* 128 You aren't going without telling me good-bye? **1883** HAY *Bread-Winners* 297 'Will you tell me good-by?' he asked. **1906** *Atlantic Mo.* Aug. 176 A dozen of my students were gathered there to tell me good-by, and two of them . . . were inviting me to a mountain trip with them.

* Telltale.

+1. A yellowlegs or tattler.

1813 WILSON *Ornithology* VII. 57 This species and the preceding . . . are detested [by duck gunners] and stigmatized with the names of the greater and lesser tell-tale, for their faithful vigilance in alarming the ducks with their loud and shrill whistle. **1835** AUDUBON *Ornith. Biog.* III. 244 Along the sea shore . . . [were] marbled Godwits, Tell-tales, and other species. **1867** *Amer. Naturalist* I. 109 Ornithological Calendar for April. . . . 10th to 20th.—During this time appear the Hermit Thrust, . . . the Tell-tales. **1917** *Birds of Amer.* I. 244/1 'Tattler' and 'Tell-tale' are also popular names for [the greater yellowlegs].

2. Any one of various mechanical contrivances for indicating some fact or condition not otherwise easily apparent. {1832-} Also *attrib.*

1851 MELVILLE *Moby-Dick* 262 The cabin-compass is called the tell-tale. **1876** KNIGHT 2525/2 *Tell-tale compass.* . . . A compass is suspended overhead in the cabin. The face of the card is downward, so that it is visible from below, and enables the captain to detect any error or irregularity in steering. **1881** *Chicago Times* 4 June, An ingenious machine, called the 'tell-tale,' . . . registers the speed of trains, when and where they stop, and how long.

+Telltale godwit. =next. — **1813** WILSON *Ornithology* VII. 57 Tell-tale Godwit, or Snipe, . . . [is] detested [by duck gunners]. **1823** JAMES *Exped.* I. 266. **1917** *Birds of Amer.* I. 242 Greater Yellow-legs. . . . [Also called] Tell-tale Godwit; Yellow-shins; Winter Yellow-legs.

+Telltale sandpiper. The greater yellow-legs, *Totanus melanoleucus.* — **1823** JAMES *Exped.* I. 4 Among other birds [we] saw . . . the tell-tale sandpiper. **1870** *Amer. Naturalist* IV. 547 Tell-tale Sandpiper (*Gambetta melanoleuca*). . . . Early in May, . . . these birds in company with other *Scolopacidæ* arrive in the neighborhood of Trenton, New Jersey.

* **Temperance.**

I. 1. Moderation in the use of alcoholic liquor; total abstinence. {see TEMPERANCE SOCIETY}

1827 (*title*), Annual Report of the Executive Committee of the American Society for the Promotion of Temperance. **1837** W. JENKINS *Ohio Gaz.* 153 Temperance prevails universally among the inhabitants; and no ardent spirits are sold in the town. **1864** [see GOOD TEMPLARS]. **1889** RILEY *Pipes o' Pan* 214 A passel o' the boys . . . got To talkin' Temperance left an' right.

II. *attrib.* and *comb.* **2.** Designating places of public entertainment where alcoholic liquors are not sold or served. *Obsolescent.*

1833 COKE *Subaltern's Furlough* i, Many hotels have 'temperance house' inscribed in large gilded letters over the door or sign. **1837** W. JENKINS *Ohio Gaz.* 107 [Chester] contains about 1,200 inhabitants, 2 stores and 1 *Temperance* tavern. *Ib.* 198 Gambier contains 3 stores, a printing office, and a temperance hotel. **1843** *Knickerb.* XXII. 85 Let . . . the Temperance-halls and root-beer *perambulatories* make answer.

3. Designating social gatherings and other meetings where alcoholic liquors are not served or where temperance is promoted.

1840 *Niles' Nat. Reg.* 23 May 192/3 The reverend Mr. Kirk . . . suggested the project for holding a temperance convention composed of delegates from all parts of the world to which the reformation has extended. **1845** *Lowell Offering* V. 249 We . . . proceeded to the grove on Gorham street, to await the coming of the procession . . . of those engaged in the Temperance festival. **1860** HOLMES *E. Venner* vii, Is this to be a Temperance Celebration, Mrs. Sprowle? **1880** *Congress. Rec.* 1 May 2938/1 [Mr. Simonton] holds temperance mass-meetings in his district, every month. **1881** RITTENHOUSE *Maud* 5, I received a note from Eugene asking me to go to the Temperance Dance. *Ib.* 6 Elmer . . . said he asked Mabel, second choice, to the Temperance picnic.

4. Designating parties, speeches, and other media promoting moderation in, or abstinence from, the use of alcoholic liquors.

1844 *Lexington Observer* 25 Sept. 3/5 Gen. Flournoy will make a Temperance address. **1855** in Hambleton *H. A. Wise* 254 A certain per cent. may be assessed to be expended in promoting the success of the Temperance party. **1872** 'MARK TWAIN' *Roughing It* 184 We tried to trade him off . . . for second-hand tombstones, old iron, temperance tracts—any kind of property. **1873** BEADLE *Undeveloped West* 402 This radical temperance platform in this latitude excited our astonishment. **1877** *Harper's Mag.* Dec. 146/2 So long as temperance statistics and temperance legislation confound the grog-shop and the hotel, . . . so long the temperance reformers will continue to hazard their effort. **1910** C. HARRIS *Eve's Husband* 189 The last time I was ever behind the scenes in his political life was during the temperance campaign.

5. In special combinations.

Temperance drink, =SOFT DRINK; *t. pledge,* a pledge to exercise temperance in the use of alcoholic liquors; *t. revival,* a revival of interest in temperance; *t. state,* a state in which temperance laws are in force.

1869 J. H. BROWNE *Great Metropolis* 327 A large number remain open, pretending to sell nothing but 'temperance drinks.' **1833** *New Eng. Mag.* Aug. 137 The Temperance Pledge. **1905** LINCOLN *Partners* 6 The temp'rance revival is the reel thing, though; folks signin' the pledge as if 'twas catchin', like the measles. **1884** W. SHEPHERD *Prairie Exper.* 166 Two men . . . had been raised in severely temperance States.

+**Temperance lecturer.** One who lectures in behalf of moderation in, or abstinence from, the use of alcoholic drinks. — **1847** ROBB *Squatter Life* 58 Sich a mixtur' . . . is temptin' to temperance lecturers. **1861** BROWNE in *Vanity Fair* 12 Jan. 15/2, I arterwards learned he was a temperance lecturer. **1883** *Harper's Mag.* Aug. 460/2 Those old-fashioned temperance lecturers who aroused their energies with a good 'nip of brandy.'

Temperance meeting. A meeting of those opposed to the sale and use of intoxicating liquors. — **1841** *Cultivator* VIII. 163, I witnessed . . . a very large temperance meeting at which I saw 'female influence' fully exerted in a most glorious cause. **1881** RITTENHOUSE *Maud* 17 Went to the Temperance Meeting last night with Emma and Mabel. **1902** WISTER *Virginian* 454 Once I had to sleep in a room next a ladies' temperance meetin'.

Temperance society. A society made up of those pledged to temperance in the use of alcoholic liquors. {1836-} — **1831** (*title*), Report of the American Temperance Society. **1871** [see LIQUOR LAW]. **1923** STANARD *Richmond* 144 A Temperance Society is born [c1840] in Richmond whose pledge seems to presage the death knell of the free punch-bowl at the Governor's Mansion.

+**Temper screw. 1.** A link connecting the walking beam and the cable of the drilling apparatus used in boring deep wells. **2.** (See quotation.) — (1) [a1864 GESNER *Coal, Petrol.* (1865) 28 The Temper Screw . . . serves to regulate the descent of the drill, without the inconvenience of lengthening the rope at short intervals.] **1883** *Century Mag.* July 330/1 The 'temper-screw' . . . lowers the drilling apparatus inch by inch as it goes down. (2) **1876** KNIGHT 2529/1 *Temper-screw,* . . . a *set*-screw for adjustment. One which brings its point against a bearing or an object.

* **Temple.**[1]

+**1.** Among American Indians, a ceremonial structure, as a medicine lodge.

1814 BRACKENRIDGE *Views La.* 72, I saw . . . in an open space before the temple or medicine lodge, an enclosure about six feet square. **1840** [see MEDICINE HOUSE].

+**2.** A place of worship among Mormons.

1843 MARRYAT *M. Violet* xxxix, In 1836, an endowment meeting, or solemn assembly, was called, to be held in the temple at Kirkland. **1848** PARKMAN in *Knickerb.* XXXII. 97 They began . . . [to] sound a lamentation over the loss of their great temple at Nauvoo. **1882** WAITE *Adv. Far West* 137 These marriages are always performed in their sacred and secret Temple, in a singular manner, and are called 'Sealings.' *attrib.* **1844** GREGG *Commerce of Prairies* I. 320 A large lot . . . known as the 'Temple Lot,' upon which the 'Temple of Zion' was to have been raised,—has lately been 'profaned,' by cultivation. **1852** *Harper's Mag.* Dec. 121/2 A wall fifteen feet high . . . is to surround the temple grounds.

* **Temple.**[2] +(See quot. 1876.) — **1850** *Rep. Comm. Patents 1849* 224 What I claim as my invention . . . is making the temples of spectacles . . . hollow or tubular. **1876** KNIGHT 2529/1 *Temple,* . . . one of the bars on the outer ends of the spectacle bows by which the spectacles are made to clasp the head of the wearer.

Temple spectacles. Spectacles with side bars that clasp the temples. *Obs.* {1762-} — **1744** *Md. Hist. Mag.* XXI. 252 One pair Temple Spectacles. **1832** WATSON *Hist. Tales N.Y.* 154 In early olden time they had not the art of using temple spectacles.

* **Ten.** *ellipt.* +A ten-dollar bill. — **1845** SOL. SMITH *Theatr. Apprent.* 23 [He] began counting out tens, twenties, and fifties. **1874** B. F. TAYLOR *World on Wheels* 196, I give her a 'ten' sometimes. **1905** 'O. HENRY' *Trimmed Lamp* 171 He drew out his 'roll' and slapped five tens upon the bar.

+**Ten-acre lot.** A lot measuring ten acres; any relatively large lot. — **1671** *S.C. Hist. Soc. Coll.* V. 284 Tenn acre lotts . . . are laid out to them. **1850** S. WARNER *Wide, Wide World* xxxix, The wheat in that ten-acre lot . . . ought to be prostrated too. **1902** ALDRICH *Sea Turn* 232 The old gentleman was swinging across the ten-acre lot on his way to the house.

* **Tenant.** One who occupies a piece of land, a house, an apartment, etc., owned by another.

1647 *Conn. Rec.* I. 152 If the said debttor can then presently procure a Chapman or Tenant, that can giue to the creditor or creditors satisfaction . . . , he shall haue the first refusall thereof. **1712** SEWALL *Letter-Book* II. 5, I am willing that the Tenant be allowed something Towards the Repair of the Buildings. **1728** [see LANDLORD 1]. **1796** *Ann. 4th Congress* 2 Sess. 2709 A tax of this nature . . . must, under the operation of a permanent system, finally fall entirely upon the tenant. **1855** [see HOLLAND 2 c]. **1872** BRACE *Dangerous Classes N.Y.* 47 The fact that tenants must forever be 'moving' in New York, is a preventive of some of the worst evils among the lower poor. **1902** W. J. GHENT *Our Benevolent Feudalism* 50 Something more than every third farm in the United States is operated by a tenant. *attrib.* **1845** *Xenia Torch-Light* 4 Dec. 1/1 The improvements consist of a number of ordinary tenant houses, barns.

Tenant farmer. A farmer who operates a farm owned by another. {1860} — **1900** *Everybody's Mag.* II. 596/1 More than half of it was raised by 'tenant farmers' . . . white and black. **1920** [see FARM *n.* 4 d].

Tenant farming. Farming done by tenants. {1887-} — **1861** *Ill. Agric. Soc. Trans.* IV. 203 On the greater part of this farm are the usual indices of tenant farming. **1913** LONDON *Valley of Moon* 432 He got on the subject of tenant farming.

+**Ten-cent.** *attrib.*

1. Of fractional currency, coins, and stamps: Worth ten cents.

1846 CORCORAN *Pickings* 26 He only gave me thirteen of these (ten cent pieces) in change. **1864** Ten-cent bill [see FIVE-CENT BILL]. **1873** EGGLESTON *Myst. Metrop.* 158 The joyful keys and the cheerful ten-cent coins lay in his pocket. **1903** HAPGOOD *Autobiog. of Thief* 17 He only had a ten-cent stamp. **1920** HOWELLS *Vacation of Kelwyns* 130 From one pocket he brought forth a small wad of greenish paper worth twenty-five cents; from another a ten-cent note.

2. Priced or sold at ten cents; consisting of ten cents.

1860 M. J. HOLMES *Maude* 26 Dr. Kennedy . . . [bought] for Hannah a ten-cent calico apron. **1875** C. F. WINGATE *Views & Interviews* 97, I also think it possible that New York might well sustain a ten cent daily paper. **1905** VALENTINE *H. Sandwith* 182 Allusions to Buchanan's 'ten-cent wages' clashed with accusations that Fremont was in league with the pope. **1908** 'O. HENRY' *Roads of Destiny* 60, I expected to have to typewrite about two thousand words of notes-of-hand, liens, and contracts, with a ten-cent tip in sight. *transf.* **1890** *Congress. Rec.* 2 July 6932/1 A ten-cent supervisor takes the place of the President of the United States.

3. *Ten-cent store,* a five and ten cent store. (See FIVE *a.* 2.)

1901 H. ROBERTSON *Inlander* 118 The sleepers in the grass-grown churchyard . . . had been removed elsewhere, to make room for the thriving innovation known as the 'Ten Cent Store.' **1911** HARRISON *Queed* 203, I bought them at a ten-cent store on Sixth Avenue when I was twelve years old.

+Ten-cent Jimmy. (See quot. 1856.) Also transf. — **1856** *Congress. Globe* App. 5 Aug. 1169/2 Mr. Buchanan . . . was at one time an advocate of . . . low tariffs and low wages, till he came to be called, as he perhaps deserved to be, 'Ten-Cent Jimmy.' **1864** *Congress. Globe* 12 May 2260/1 Why, Mr. Speaker, I had no idea there were so many ten-cent 'Jimmys' on the intensely loyal side of the House. **1874** *Ib.* 15 Jan. 667/2 A distinguished statesman . . . [once] said that it would be just as well to have wages ten cents a day, provided the purchasing power of ten cents was equal to what a dollar was then, . . . and I believe that he obtained by that remark the *sobriquet* of 'Ten-cent Jimmy.'

*** Tench.** **+1.** An American fresh-water fish resembling the European tench, probably a dace. *Obs.* *** 2.** A European cyprinoid fish (*Tinca tinca*) introduced into U.S. rivers and lakes. — (1) **1637** MORTON *New Canaan* 91 There are in the rivers, and ponds, very excellent . . . Roches, Perches, Tenches, Eeles, and other fish. **1750** T. WALKER *Journal* 35 The Inhabitants enjoy plenty of fine fish, as . . . Carp, Rocks, Fat-Backs which I suppose to be Tench. (2) **1883** *Nat. Museum Bul.* No. 27, 490 Tench. . . . Introduced into the United States by the U.S. Fish Commission.

*** Tend,** *v.* **+1.** *local.* To tend out (on), to attend. **2.** To tend to business, to pay attention to one's own affairs, or to an immediate task. {1901} — (1) *a*1877 in Bartlett 698 An auction sale is advertised in our columns to-day. . . . Country merchants should tend out. **1890** *Dialect Notes* I. 22 One 'tends out on' church. (2) **1880** 'MARK TWAIN' *Tramp Abroad* 39, I got to 'tend to business. **1902** LORIMER *Lett. Merchant* 294 He was tending to business so strictly that he didn't see me bearing down on him. **1917** MCCUTCHEON *Green Fancy* 68 They came here like any one else, paid their bills regular, 'tended to their own business, and that's all.

*** Tender.**[1] +Money or other things that may be legally offered in payment. Often *common* or *lawful tender.* {1883-} Also fig.
See also LEGAL TENDER.
1739 W. DOUGLASS *Discourse Currencies* 20 France never made their State Bills a common Tender. **1764** HUTCHINSON *Hist. Mass.* I. 27 Indian corn . . . was made a tender in discharge of all debt. **1777** *Jrnls. Cont. Congress* VII. 36 That it be recommended to the legislatures of the united States, to pass laws to make the bills of credit, issued by the Congress, a lawful tender. **1857** E. STONE *Life J. Howland* 101 Paper money was . . . made lawful tender. **1903** WHITE *Forest* 24 Strange, suggestive words and phrases . . . [are] coined into the tender of daily use.
attrib. **1781** A. ADAMS *Familiar Lett.* 390 A repeal of the obnoxious tender act has passed the [Mass.] House and Senate. **1786** HUMPHREYS, etc. *Anarchiad* (1861) 20 Cheat heaven with forms, and earth with tender-laws.

*** Tender.**[2] *Football.* +A backfield man. *Obs.* — **1874** *Boston Transcript* 16 May 2/5 The McGill and Harvard foot-ball eleven . . . are as follows: . . . Harvard—W. R. Tyler, Lombard and Goodrich (tenders) [etc.].

+Tenderfoot, *n.* [Cf. TENDER-FOOTED *a.*]
1. A newly arrived immigrant in the West; an inexperienced or young person. Orig. *W.*
1875 *Chicago Tribune* 21 Aug. 5/6 'Tender-feet,' or raw miners. **1879** *Cimarron News & Press* 20 Nov. 3/2 A tenderfoot can sling his heels higher at a baile than the average old timer. **1890** CUSTER *Following Guidon* 172 The frontiersman had then, as now, a great 'despise,' as they put it, for the tenderfoot. **1903** *N.Y. Times* 30 Aug., A large number of the very best discoveries were made by tenderfeet who didn't know gold unless stamped with the American eagle.
2. A cow recently brought into a country.
1887 *Scribner's Mag.* Oct. 508/1 'Pilgrim' and 'tenderfoot' were formerly applied almost exclusively to newly imported cattle.
3. *attrib.* passing into *adj.* Inexperienced; belonging to or consisting of tenderfeet.
1888 *San Francisco Wkly. Bul.* (F.), The boys were of the tenderfoot kind. **1891** *Harper's Mag.* July 204/2 His pony . . . [will] slide down a bank which would make our tenderfoot hair stand on end. **1907** PEARY in *Harper's Mag.* Feb. 338 The arrival of this supply of fresh meat created a very agreeable impression . . . upon the 'tenderfoot' members of the expedition and crew.

+Tenderfoot, *v.* To tenderfoot it, to go about as a tenderfoot. — **1886** HOWELLS *Minister's Charge* 260 His wife wanted to go to Europe a while, and kind of tender foot it round for a year or two in the art-centres over there.

Tender-footed, *a.*
1. Of animals: Having tender or sore feet. {1682, 1690}
1844 GREGG *Commerce of Prairies* II. 94 Most of mine being a little tender-footed, I engaged Mexican *herreros* to fit them out in their own peculiar style. *c*1857 *Kit Carson's Own Story* (1926) 68 During our march, from snow and travelling over rocks our cattle became very tender-footed.
+2. *fig.* Of persons: Lacking experience; timid; sensitive. *slang* or *colloq.*
*a*1850 FORD *Hist. Illinois* 219 Rebellious, free-thoughted, independent little leaders, in the slang language of the day, are called 'tender-footed democrats.' **1854** *N. Amer. Rev.* July 189 My friends were tender-footed, and did not wish to denounce the Nebraska infamy. **1865** PIKE *Scout*

& *Ranger* (1932) 156 A good many Kentuckians are a little tender-footed now; they don't like to come out against the Union. **1883** 'MARK TWAIN' *Life on Miss.* xxvii, Each tourist . . . went home and published . . . a book which was usually calm, truthful, reasonable, kind; but which seemed just the reverse to our tenderfooted progenitors.

+Tenderloin.
1. a. (See quot. 1828.) **b.** In beef, pork, etc., a strip of tender meat on either side of the vertebral column; a cut of this. Also transf.
1828 WEBSTER, *Tenderloin*, a tender part of flesh in the hind quarter of beef. [Probably an inexact definition.] **1832** COOPER *Memoirs of a Nullifier* (1860) 28 A rib there, a slice of the tenderloin somewhere else. **1851** CIST *Cincinnati* 281 The tender-loins, usually two pounds to the hog, after affording supplies to families, who consume probably one half of the product, are sold to the manufacturers of sausages. **1880** 'MARK TWAIN' *Tramp Abroad* 572 The long white bone which divides the sirloin from the tenderloin still in its place. **1909** STERNBERG *Life Fossil Hunter* 10 We were rarely out of antelope meat, and even now my mouth waters at the thought of the delicious tenderloin.
2. a. In New York City, a police precinct originally west of Broadway between Twenty-third and Forty-second streets, affording to the police opportunities for graft. **b.** A district in any city noted for its night life, or for its vice and police corruption.
1887 *Harper's Mag.* March 500/2 His precinct is known as the 'Tenderloin,' because of its social characteristics. **1900** *Boston Transcript* 13 Oct. 32/2 Under Tammany arrangements, new tenderloins have been established on the west side of [N.Y.]. **1903** *San Francisco Argonaut* 2 Nov. 273 Its tenderloin [*i.e.*, of Portland, Ore.] is extensive and worse than anything in San Francisco. **1920** SANDBURG *Smoke & Steel* 30 The segregated district, the Tenderloin, is here no more.
3. attrib. a. In sense 1 with *steak.* **b.** In sense 2 with *district, experience.*
(a) **1883** *Southern Hist. Soc. P.* XI. 84 Tenderloin steaks are tough behind iron gratings. (b) **1898** *Voice* 6 Jan. 4/3 If laws generally suitable to a city do not suit some slavic, Polish, or other quarter, or some 'tenderloin' district, the local police must pass upon those laws, . . . and give a 'liberal' enforcement. **1909** FITCH *City* (1925) II. 168 Ask any detective with tenderloin experience.

+Ten-dollar, *a.* Of paper currency and coins: Worth ten dollars. — **1807** *Ann. 10th Congress* 1 Sess. 429, One, a ten dollar note, was returned on my hands. **1825** J. NEAL *Bro. Jonathan* I. 221 For a ten dollar bill . . . Peters would have set fire to it. **1861** *Chicago Tribune* 19 July 1/8 Lost— . . . a Lady's Portmonnaie, containing a Ten Dollar Gold Piece, and sixty-five cents in change. **1916** PORTER *David* 24 A ten-dollar gold-piece!

*** Tenement.**
*** 1. a.** A house or dwelling place. **+b.** = TENEMENT HOUSE.
1655 *Charlestown Land Rec.* 133, [I] have sould . . . A certaine Hous or Tenement with A Garden by it. **1732** *S.C. Gazette* 21 Oct., A House . . . to be Let: . . . likewise a Tenement . . . with a good Kitchen and Store. **1832** [see ONE-STORIED *a.*]. **1840** *Picayune* 10 Sept. 3/3 Wanted. A tenement of two or three stories, convenient to the business part of the Second Municipality. **1859** *La Crosse Daily Union* 8 Nov. 2/2 His home is among the squalid tenements of the Five Points. **1898** *Kissimmee* (Fla.) *Valley Gazette* 11 Feb. 1/4 The [building] was joined on the east by a three story tenement. **1923** HERRICK *Lilla* 67 She mingled freely with the other pickers, chiefly girls from the factory tenements in Chicago.
2. attrib. a. In sense 1a with *lot.* **b.** In sense 1b with *attic, building, district.*
(a) **1713** *Mayflower Descendant* XI. 181 To my Son Nathaniel . . . my Teniment Lott and my wood Lott. (b) **1860** *Harper's Mag.* March 546/2 A fire broke out in a six-story tenement building in . . . New York, occupied by about twenty families. **1880** *Ib.* June 26/1 Some working-women in New York, . . . may be [inured] to hunger and the dismalness of tenement attics. **1882** MCCABE *New York* 37 The great infantile mortality occurs in the tenement districts.

+Tenement house.
1. A dwelling house or building divided into separate apartments which are rented out to different families; esp. such a building with certain facilities, such as water-closets, shared by several families; an apartment building occupied by persons of the poorer classes of a city. {1884-}
For the purposes of legal contracts and enforcement of city regulations, *tenement house* has been given technical definitions in certain statutory provisions.
1859 BARTLETT 476. **1861** WINTHROP *C. Dreeme* 78 A court, . . . serving as a well to light the rear range of a tenement-house. **1873** ALDRICH *Marjorie Daw* 69 They chose to halt at the small, shabby tenement-house by the river. **1882** MCCABE *New York* 562 The tenement houses . . . are hot-beds of disease. **1894** *Harper's Mag.* Jan. 275/2 Fully a third of its people live in tenement-houses. **1910** PERSONS, etc. *Mass. Labor Laws*

276 What are the powers of the Commissioner of Labor relative to tenement houses?

2. Attrib. with *children, district, home,* etc.

1868 *N.Y. Herald* 1 July 6/5 The case which we reported ... reveals in a striking manner the evils of the tenement house system. **1870** 'F. FERN' *Ginger-Snaps* 119, The cheap and comfortable boarding houses ... [are] a refuge to the working-girl from the horrors of their tenement-house home. **1891** *Scribner's Mag.* Nov. 566 The majority of them [naval apprentices] come from the tenement-house districts of cities. **1894** Tenement-house regulation [see FOOD]. **1923** WATTS *L. Nichols* 225 No more Fresh-Air-Farm picnics for tenement-house children.

Ten-footer. *spec.* +A room or house only ten feet long; a small place. — **1854** 'O. OPTIC' *In Doors & Out* (1876) 119 Though she had been brought up in a ten footer in an obscure street, she earnestly desired to become what is technically called a 'lady.' **1867** *Atlantic Mo.* April 485/2 He had previously rented a 'ten-footer' with two rooms in it. **1872** HOLMES *Poet* 26 [Near] the district school-house ... [was] Ma'am Hancock's cottage, never so called in those days, but rather 'ten-footer.'

Ten-foot pole. A pole ten feet long; +a typical or figurative measure of that length. — **1738** BYRD *Dividing Line* (1901) 52 We found the ground moist ... insomuch that it was an easy matter to run a ten-foot pole up to the head in it. **1848** MITCHELL *Nantucketisms* 41 Can't touch him with a ten-foot pole. **1868** *Ib.* He is distant, proud, reserved. **1884** HOWELLS *Silas Lapham* v, Do you suppose a fellow like young Corey ... would touch mineral paint with a ten-foot pole? **1902** WISTER *Virginian* 469 Then Providence makes use of instruments I'd not touch with a ten-foot pole.

Ten-hour. Attrib. with reference to a working day of ten hours. {1905} Cf. EIGHT-HOUR.

1840 VAN BUREN in *Pres. Mess. & P.* III. 602 The President of the United States ... directs that all such persons, whether laborers or mechanics, be required to work only the number of hours prescribed by the ten-hour system. **1852** (*title*), Address of the Ten-Hour State Convention, Held in Boston, Sept. 30. **1853** in Persons *Mass. Labor Laws* 76 [They had been deputed] to visit the eastern states and help forward the Ten Hour Movement. **1871** *Ib.* 124 You may anticipate Executive approval if you enact a ten-hour law. **1905** *McClure's Mag.* XXIV. 349 They'd agreed to buy an eleven-hour road and they wouldn't take a ten-hour road. **1911** PERSONS, etc. *Mass. Labor Laws* 71 In this two weeks' interval Butler and the ten-hour issue entered together what may thenceforth fairly be called the political arena.

Ten-lined, *a.* +Of a potato bug: Having ten stripes marking its body. — **1868** *Rep.Comm. Agric. 1867* 65 The Colorado bug or ten-lined spearman is reported to have produced poisonous effects on several persons who handled them incautiously with naked hands. **1876** *Vermont Bd. Agric. Rep.* III. 574 We now come to the chiefest agent among insects in the destruction of the potato, the famous ten-lined potato beetle.

+Tennessean, *n.* and *a.* (See TENNESSE(E)AN.)

+Tennessee. [Cherokee.] A river and a South Central state. Used attrib.

1. Designating varieties of fruits, vegetables, etc.

1827 *Western Mo. Rev.* I. 82 The kinds of cotton which are chiefly cultivated, are Louisiana, green seed, or Tennessee, and recently Mexican. **1855** *Amer. Inst. N.Y. Trans. 1854* 594 Indian Millet ... [is called] 'Tennessee rice.' **1856** Tennessee Milam [see KENTUCKY 4 b]. **1890** *Amer. Naturalist* XXIV. 738 In 1884 there appeared in our seedsmen's catalogues, under the name of Tennessee Sweet Potato Pumpkin, a variety very distinct.

2. Designating things made in, or coming from, Tennessee. Also absol.

1827 COOPER *Prairie* iv, I scorn to slander even a Tennessee shot-gun. **1839** *S. Lit. Messenger* April 272/2 Tennessee *shin-plasters* were rejected. **1845** HOOPER *Simon Suggs' Adv.* 53 That light-yaller bottle tho', ... that's Tennessee! **1857** *Harper's Mag.* Aug. 423/2 In a dream ... I had swallowed my big Tennessee wagon, and the great pole stuck out of my mouth. **1859** *Ib.* April 688/1 The 'Tennessee Platform' ... opposes the idea of disunion, but advocates retaliation for what the South considers her wrongs. **1860** *Ib.* Sept. 571/2 A gallon of No. 1 gin, and ... a gallon of Tennessee brand.

3. Designating persons in or from Tennessee.

1833 Tennessee ranger [see RANGER 1 b]. **1895** G. KING *New Orleans* 244 On the summit of the parapet stood the corps of Tennessee sharpshooters.

+Tennesse(e)an, *n.* A native or resident of Tennessee; a soldier from Tennessee.

1815 *Niles' Reg.* VII. 373/1 Glory to ... the hardy and gallant Tennesseeans, Kentuckians and Louisianians. *c*1836 CATLIN *Indians* II. 158, I have shared the genuine cottage hospitality of ... the easy, affable and sociable Tennesseean. **1853** *S. Lit. Messenger* XIX. 465/1 The Bostonian looks down upon the Virginian—the Virginian on the Tennesseean. **1862** Moore *Rebellion Rec.* V. ii. 591 At the time the Tennesseeans fired there was not a man of my regiment in sight. **1900** *Congress. Rec.* 6 Feb. 1568/1 Did not we Tennesseans expel the Cherokees?

b. Sometimes distinguished by the specifying adjectives *East* and *West*.

1818 JACKSON in *Ann. 15th Congress* 2 Sess. App. 20 Jan. 2175, [I] advised you of the appeal I had made to the patriotism of the West Tennes-

seans. **1845** SOL. SMITH *Theatr. Apprent.* 184 He got rid of any further inquiries from the anxious West Tennesseans. **1846** POLK *Diary* (1929) 128 He had not been in my office or at the President's mansion, ... except once for a few minutes ... in company with Hon. John Blair and some other East Tennesseeans.

+Tennesse(e)an, *a.* Of or pertaining to Tennessee. — **1853** McCONNEL *Western Char.* 269 Its dye a favorite 'Tennessean' brownish-yellow. **1869** 'MARK TWAIN' *Sk., New & Old* 50 The paragraphs, ... into whose cold sentences your masterly hand has infused the fervent spirit of Tennessean journalism, will wake up another nest of hornets. **1891** *Cent.* 6232/2.

+Tennessee warbler. A small warbler (*Vermivora peregrina*) of the eastern states. — **1811** WILSON *Ornithology* III. 83 [The] Tennesee Warbler ... I first found ... on the banks of Cumberland river. **1858** BAIRD *Birds Pacific R.R.* 258 Tennessee Warbler. ... Eastern United States to the Missouri. **1892** TORREY *Foot-Path Way* 7 Then I saw him, facing me, showing white under parts. A Tennessee warbler!

* Tennis.

1. A game played with rackets and a ball on an unenclosed court, usually outdoors; =LAWN TENNIS. {1888-}

1883 *Harper's Mag.* Nov. 815/1 Well-disposed lawns, across which ... the harmless missiles of tennis make their abrupt flights. **1894** FORD *P. Stirling* 17 Croquet ... is becoming very *passé* ... being replaced by a new game called tennis. **1907** *St. Nicholas* May 601/1 We can beat Hammond at anything—foot-ball, base-ball, tennis.

2. Attrib. with *cap, club, court,* etc.

1882 *Wheelman* I. 55 A tennis-lawn ... is seldom far removed from the smoke of the town. **1885** BAYLOR *On Both Sides* 171 There was the usual *entourage* of such places,—a windmill, a tennis-court, hammocks. **1892** RITTENHOUSE *Maud* 550 He's going to select my tennis shoes for me. **1893** *Harper's Mag.* March 494 Long porches crowded with ease-taking men and women in flannels and tennis caps and russet slippers and gossamer gowns. **1894** *Ib.* June 156/1 The champion player in our tennis club.

* Tenon saw. Also **tenant saw.** A fine saw for making tenons. — **1642** *Md. Archives* IV. 94 One tenant saw a hand saw. **1794** [see COMPASS 2]. **1898** *Mo. So. Dakotan* I. 57 This operation was successfully performed by Dr. Phillips with no further implements at hand than a large butcher's knife and a small tenon-saw.

* Tenor. +In colonial Massachusetts, the value of a piece of paper money. Now hist. (See also NEW TENOR, OLD TENOR.) — **1716** *Mass. H. Rep. Jrnl.* I. 114 That the Bills be of the same tenour with those that are already emitted.

+Tenpenny (bit). A pistareen. — **1835** TODD *Notes* 7 A tenpenny, or pistorine, passing in most Western States for 13 pence, [has] an eagle with the figures 10 beneath it. **1841** *Knickerb.* XVII. 187 The chain ... was terminated by three seals, three keys, and a ten-penny bit.

Tenpin. {1807}

1. *pl.* A bowling-alley game similar to ninepins except that ten pins are used.

1830 PICKERING *Inquiries Emigrant* 15 Almost every tavern keeps a bowling-alley, where the idle resort to play at tenpins (nine pins having been prohibited by law!). **1853** *Harper's Mag.* March 437/1 There is no lack of ten-pins. **1873** *Ib.* May 951/1 There exists among certain reputable members of the Legislature of Texas a laudable desire to extirpate from the State that bane of society—ten pins. **1897** NORRIS *Stories & Sk.* (1931) 240 A sort of combination of tenpins and golf and marbles.

+b. *Tenpin alley,* a bowling alley where this is played.

1835 NICKLIN *Letters Va. Springs* 23 The means of amusement at the Warm Springs, consist of a bagatelle table ..., a ten-pin alley [etc.]. **1847** *Santa Fe Repub.* 1 Oct. 2/3 Another Billiard Room and Ten Pin Alley will soon be opened. **1886** POORE *Reminisc.* I. 62 Ten-pin alleys were abundant [in Washington].

+c. *To roll tenpins,* to play at tenpins.

1852 BRISTED *5 Years in Eng. Univ.* I. 60 Our Columbia [College] boys roll ten-pins and play billiards. **1872** *Newton Kansan* 5 Sept. 4/1 A Texas German ... lost $12 rolling ten-pins.

2. *sing.* One of the pins used in the game.

1851 MELVILLE *Moby-Dick* 25 The savage ... sets up this little hunch-backed image, like a tenpin, between the andirons. **1870** 'MARK TWAIN' *Sk., New & Old* 155 Riley would tell all about ... setting up ten-pins. **1906** *Harper's Mag.* May 839 One of the green hands was swept from his feet like a tenpin.

+3. Attrib. and comb. with *ball, rolling.*

1840 *Picayune* 29 July 2/1 [With] billiard playing, ten pin rolling, eating, smoking [etc.] ... some of our friends are enjoying rare times at the watering places. **1895** *Outing* XXVI. 444/1 You rush to the bottom like a ten-pin ball sent spinning down its alley.

+Ten-plate stove. A stove designed to radiate a great deal of heat by exposing ten plates of metal to the air. — **1830** WATSON *Philadelphia* 198 Ten plate stoves when first introduced, though very costly, and but rudely cast, were much used for kitchens and common sitting rooms. **1833** J. HALL *Harpe's Head* 125 The front door opened into a bar-room, in the centre of which was placed a large ten-plate stove. **1841** BACHE *Fire-Screen* 12 The little ten-plate stove looked battered and rusty.

Ten-pound court. A small-claims court. *Obs.* — **1687** *Mass. H. S. Coll.* 4 Ser. V. 162, I am ... willing to serve God, my king and his subjects, in as low a place as Judge of the £10 Court in the least county of this Colony. **1812** IRVING *Knickerb.* Acct. Author, He might have risen . . . to be . . . a justice in the ten-pound court.

+Ten-rail fence. A rail fence having ten rails. — [**1835** *Knickerb.* VI. 178 She could leap a ten-rail Virginia-fence, like a deer.] **1859** *La Crosse Daily Union* 15 Oct. 4/5, I kin jump a ten-rail fence. **1867** EDWARDS *Shelby* 143 The infantry were concealed in a deep, dry ditch, directly behind a huge, new ten-rail fence.

+Ten spot. (See SPOT *n.* 3 b.)

+Ten-strike. **1.** *Tenpins.* A bowl that knocks down all ten pins; a strike. **2.** Any completely successful stroke or act. *colloq.* — (1) **1844** *Spirit of Times* (Phila.) 10 Aug. (Th.) The first five balls were each ten strikes. **1850** HAWTHORNE in Bridge *Pers. Recoll.* iii, I may calculate on what bowlers call a ten-strike. **1899** CHAMPLIN & BOSTWICK *Cycl. Games & Sports* (ed. 2) 109/1 If a player makes a ten-strike, the pins may be set up again. (2) **1851** HALL *College Words* 298 *Ten-strike*, at Hamilton, a perfect recitation, ten being the mark given for a perfect recitation. **1887** *Courier-Journal* 13 Feb. 7/5 His first ten-strike was made when he took a suit for a share of the property involved. **1911** HARRISON *Queed* 190 That little scientist I made you a present of last year has made me a ten-strike.

+Ten-striker. Among Confederate soldiers, a contemptuous name for the shirker who boasted but would not fight. — **1869** *Overland Mo.* III. 128 Some boasted that one Southerner could 'whale' ten Yankees. Lieutenant J. W. Boothe, of the Seventh Texas Battalion, I am told, first applied to this sort the phrase 'ten-strikers', which became immensely popular in that State.

Ten-striped, *a.* **+=TEN-LINED** *a.* — **1869** *Mich. Agric. Rep.* VII. 170 The results of my observations on the Ten-striped Potatoe Beetle, for the year 1868. **1877** *Vermont Bd. Agric. Rep.* IV. 108 Say gave it the scientific name *Doryphora decem-lineata*, or the Ten-striped Spearman.

* Tent.¹

* 1. A portable shelter or lodge of canvas, skins, or the like. **1654** JOHNSON *Wonder-w. Prov.* 38 At Charles Towne . . . they pitched some Tents of Cloath. **1738** BYRD *Dividing Line* (1901) 90 It was hardly possible to find a level large enough . . . whereupon to pitch our tent. **1777** *Jrnls. Cont. Congress* IX. 912/2 Every State shall . . . constantly have ready for use . . . a due number of field pieces and tents, and a proper quantity of arms. **1836** W. O'BRYAN *Travels* 37 In the summer, or about Autumn, the Methodists hold their protracted meetings sometimes in the open air, where the people erect tents (generally in a wood). **1862** STRONG *Cadet Life W. Point* 138 Two tall forms . . . issued from the opposite tent. **1891** *Cent.* 6234/2 Tents are also used in towns to shelter large occasional assemblies, as the spectators at a circus or the audience at a political or religious gathering. **1902** [see FAIR *n.*¹ 2]. **1925** TILGHMAN *Dugout* 58 The good lady was then living in a tent.

2. A stand or pulpit at an open-air camp meeting. {1678–, *Sc.*} **1801–3** J. LYLE *Diary* (MS.) 35 Then word was given that Mr. Burke would preach at the tent or stand.

3. *attrib.* and *comb.* **a.** In sense 1 with *bedstead, circus, lot,* etc. **1750** T. WALKER *Journal* 59 [We] got tent Poles up, and were just stretching a Tent. **1758** HEMPSTEAD *Diary* 701, I was . . . mending up the fence of the Tent Lot. **1773** in Singleton *Social N.Y.* 83 [Joseph Cox from London] makes all sorts of . . . field and tent beadsteads and furniture. **1846** MAGOFFIN *Down Santa Fé Trail* 6 [Our tent] was made in Philadelphia by a regular tent-maker of the Army. **1847** PARKMAN in *Knickerb.* XXIX. 392 Drive down the tent-pickets hard. **1862** Moore *Rebellion Rec.* V. II. 156 The desolated, hard-trodden ground, and a few tent-stakes, remain to tell the story. **1877** *Harper's Mag.* Jan. 301/2 We have nothing but Thomas's orchestra and the opera . . . to console us for the loss of . . . the tent circus. **1895** *N.Y. Dramatic News* 9 Nov. 12/1 Year after year the American tent shows grow bigger and better.

* Tent.² A deep red Spanish wine with low alcoholic content. *Obs.* Also attrib. — **1686** *Conn. Rec.* III. 408 Every butt or pipe of Sherry, Sack, Malaga, . . . Tent and Alicant, twenty shillings. **1769** in H. M. Brooks *Gleanings* IV. 39 To be sold . . . , Canary, Malaga, Tent, sweet and other wines. **1797** *Wilmington* (N.C.) *Gazette* 16 Feb., Sherry in quarter-casks, and Tent Wines of a superior flavor.

+Tent caterpillar. Any of several gregarious caterpillars which spin large webs on trees, esp. the larva of the moth *Malacosoma americanum.* Also with specifying terms. — **1854** EMMONS *Agric. N.Y.* V. 236 To eradicate completely the tent caterpillar, it will be necessary to give attention to the wild cherrytrees. **1868** *Mich. Agric. Rep.* VII. 168 The tent caterpillar . . . has become very greatly decreased in numbers. **1884** *Rep. Comm. Agric.* 412 These . . . appeared to be closely allied to, if not identical with, the common Apple-tree Tent-caterpillar . . . of the Eastern States. **1898** S. B. GREEN *Forestry in Minn.* 301 *Tent-caterpillars*, caterpillars that build silky-like tents on trees and other plants.

Tented, *a.* **1.** Of a place: Covered with tents. {1604–1773} **+2.** *Tented meeting,* a camp meeting. — (1) **1833** LONGFELLOW *Poetical Works* 591/1 In tented field and bloody fray, An Alexander's vigorous sway And stern command. **1847** *Santa Fe Repub.* 20 Nov. 2/1 Illinois and Missouri may well be proud of their citizens who have been in the tented field. **1871** *Rep. Indian Affairs* (1872) 261 Headsmen of the tribe . . . [received] me in their tented camp. (2) **1898** N. E. JONES *Squirrel Hunters of Ohio* 131 Protracted, tented, or camp-meetings increased, following the settlements, and becoming very popular with preachers and people.

+Tented wagon. A covered wagon. — **1848** BRYANT *California* i. 14 Long trains of oxen . . . pulling huge tented-wagons, were moving about the streets.

+Tenter. One who lives in a tent. {1907} — **1846** *Indiana Hist. Mag.* XXIII. 409 The eating hours were the same as those of the tenters. **1888** *Harper's Mag.* Oct. 801/1 The pretty girl of our civilization, who pushes into the canvas home of the tenters.

+Tent fly. A piece of canvas serving as a roof for a tent, or used as a temporary shelter. (Cf. FLY *n.*³ 1.) — **1849** T. T. JOHNSON *Sights Gold Region* 169 The tent-fly is a second roof usually erected over the tent. **1865** KELLOGG *Rebel Prisons* 96, [I] found only one living of the thirteen who were under that one tent fly a few days ago. **1887** BILLINGS *Hardtack* 362 The gallant old veteran setting the example, by taking only a tent-fly, which was pitched over saplings or fence rails. **1920** [see FLY *n.*³ 1].

+Tent pin. A stake or pin driven into the ground to which the ropes of a tent are fastened. — **1807** Pike *Sources Miss.* II. App. 24 We found the next morning many tent-pins made of wood, different from any in that country. **1854** BARTLETT *Personal Narr.* II. 306 [We] broke up one of the wheels for tent-pins. **1889** *Century Mag.* Oct. 868/2 Jael drove the tent-pin through his head and fastened it to the ground.

+Tent town. A town consisting of tents. — **1878** BEADLE *Western Wilds* 103 Along the track west of it had sprung up five tent-towns.

+Ten up. (See quot. 1885.) — **1841** *Week in Wall St.* 29, I will send you in a check for 'ten up,' and the rest we will arrange tomorrow. **1885** *Harper's Mag.* Nov. 842/2 Brokers demand 'ten up,' or a deposit of ten per cent.

+Tepee. Also †teebee, tepe, etc. [Dakota *tipi.*]

1. An Indian lodge or wigwam. **1835** FEATHERSTONHAUGH *Canoe Voyage* I. 338 Here, also, were their spring teebees, which they inhabit at that season. **1846** SAGE *Scenes Rocky Mts.* xvi, The term *tepor,* or *tepe,* . . . [becomes] the only one by which a lodge is known. **1849** EASTMAN *Dahcotah* xxii, The messenger enters the wigwam (or *teepee,* as the houses of the Sioux are called) of the juggler. **1866** *Wkly. New Mexican* 1 Dec. 1/3 Kaneatche . . . withdrew to the mountains having lost his tepees and a large amount of his Camp equipage. **1876** BOURKE *Journal* 15 March, Their tepis were large, conical tents of canvass obtained at the Agencies and elk and buffalo skins, procured by the chase. **1903** A. ADAMS *Log of Cowboy* 149 [The camp] had contained nearly a hundred lean-tos, wickyups, and tepees. **1925** TILGHMAN *Dugout* 15 She went back to where Bear Claw's tepee had stood.

2. Attrib. with *cloth, cover, pole, trail.* **1869** *Amer. Naturalist* II. 648 [We] follow upon the dim road or the tepe trail over the broad prairie. **1877** *Rep. Indian Affairs,* Tepee cloth should be discontinued, and . . . log or frame houses should be substituted. **1890** CUSTER *Following Guidon* 6 The hides [were] dressed for robes or tepee covers. **1899** *Mo. So. Dakotan* I. 175 Indians . . . had cut and peeled teepe poles.

+Tequila. [From *Tequila,* Mexico.] A spirituous drink made from the maguey. — **1882** *Harper's Mag.* Dec. 47/1 You may find *mescal* and *tequila*—the two varieties of intoxicating liquors distilled from the maguey, or aloe—to drink. **1892** *Dialect Notes* I. 252 *Tequila,* a seductive Mexican alcoholic drink, made from the *sótole.* **1894** *Harper's Mag.* Feb. 351/2 Between various cigarettes, the last drink of tequela, and the drying of our clothes, we passed the time.

* Term.

1. In schools, a division of the school year; a semester or quarter: (see also quot. 1891). {1678–} Also attrib. **1766** in Peirce *Hist. Harvard* 246 In term-Time no scholar shall go out of Cambridge, unless upon some very special occasion. **1826** *Harvard Laws* 8 Stipends . . . shall be charged to the students in their term bills. **1863** HOPLEY *Life in South* I. 186 The school 'terms' usually begin in September and February. **1891** *Univ. Chicago Official Bul.* No. 1, 12 Each quarter shall be divided into two equal terms of six weeks each. **1920** *3d Nat. Country Life Conf. Proc.* 43 The Rosenwald Fund . . . [was] devoting its energies to . . . the lengthening of rural-school terms.

+2. *spec.* The space of time for which a public official is elected to office. (See also SHORT TERM.) **1793** WASHINGTON in *Pres. Mess. & P.* I. 138 Since the commencement of the term for which I have been again called into office, no fit occasion has arisen [etc.]. **1797** *Ann. 5th Congress* 470 Joseph Anderson, appointed a Senator by the State of Tennessee, for the remainder of the term which the late Senator William Blount had drawn, . . . produced his credentials. **1830** HONE *Diary* I. 15 If Jackson succeeds for another term, it will be owing to the difficulty of agreeing upon his successor. **1886** ALTON *Among Law-Makers* 13 The terms of the Representatives begin at twelve o'clock, noon. **1913** LA FOLLETTE *Autob.* 320 Another term, with another legislature, would securely ground and bulwark self-government in Wisconsin.

Terminal. {1656, 1831–}

+1. *Railroad.* The end of a railroad line, usually including the switches, sheds, etc., also pl.; a town at the end of a railroad. **1888** *Boston Jrnl.* 7 Aug. 3/2 The Canadian Pacific Road . . . has purchased extensive dock property and terminals at Windsor, opposite Detroit. **1898** *Engineering Mag.* XVI. 67 The capacity of a railroad is the capacity of its terminals. **1904** *Atlantic Mo.* March 363 The train neared the tangled net-work of the city terminal. **1909** WEBSTER 2130/3 *Terminal,* . . . a town lying at the end of a railroad.

+2. *transf.* The end of something, as a telegraph wire or a bridge, or the place where something ends.

1897 *Boston Globe* 29 Aug. (Ernst), The arbitrage broker required only a private wire . . . with terminals as near as possible to the exchanges in the two cities. **1904** *N.Y. Ev. Post* 29 Dec. 6 The traffic problem presented by the Manhattan terminal of the Brooklyn Bridge. **1912** IRWIN *Red Button* 93, I have an option on the Hudson Terminal and a mortgage on the Singer Building.

*Terminer. *Court of oyer and terminer,* (see COURT 3 l).

*Terminus. The end of a railroad; the town in which a railroad line ends. {1836-} — **1848** LONGFELLOW in S. Longfellow *H. W. Longfellow* II. 137 Long walk with my brother Stephen to the railway terminus on the sea-shore. **1872** TICE *Over Plains* 12 The General Superintendent . . . had provided for us an extra train to take us to Waterville, the present terminus of the road.

Tern.

1. Any of the several gull-like birds of the genus *Sterna* and allied genera, esp. *S. hirundo.* {1678-}

1823 JAMES *Exped.* I. 31 The terns appear to be attracted hither by great numbers of a species of phryganea. **1894** *Youth's Comp.* 22 Nov. 562/4 Scores of terns hovered overhead.

2. With specifying terms.

Only a selection is given. See also BRIDLED TERN, CASPIAN TERN, etc.

1813 Lesser tern [see LESSER *a.*]. **1835** AUDUBON *Ornith. Biog.* III. 366 The Arctic Tern is found with us on the eastern coasts of the United States only . . . in autumn. **1844** *Nat. Hist. N.Y., Zoology* II. 298 The *Big* or *Common Tern* appears in great numbers along our coast. **1887** RIDGWAY *Manual N.A. Birds* 47 *H[ydrochelidon] nigra surinamensis* (Gmel.). American Black Tern.

*Terrace. A level, artificially made surface on naturally sloping ground. — **1774** FITHIAN *Journal* I. 130 This Terrace is made along the Front of the House, and ends by the kitchen. **1863** MITCHELL *My Farm* 46 The terrace was a wilderness of roses, lilacs, and unclipped box. **1896** WILKINS *Madelon* 21 Burr was clearing the snow from the stone steps over the terraces.

Terra cotta. {1722-} *attrib.* Designating objects made of hard-baked pottery. {1868-} — **1866** A. D. WHITNEY *L. Goldthwaite* viii, The sprays of some light, wandering vine that sprung from a low-suspended terra cotta vase between. **1869** Terra cotta pipes [see PIPE *n.*[1] 5]. **1876** INGRAM *Centennial Exp.* 281 Messrs. Galloway & Graff . . . made a very beautiful display of their art and horticultural terra-cotta ware, in the shape of statuary, vases, flower boxes, etc. **1893** 'MARK TWAIN' *P. Wilson* i, Terra-cotta pots in which grew a breed of geranium.

+Terrapin. Also †**terrapine, tarapin, tarapen, turpin.** [Algonquian. Cf. Abnaki *toarebe.*]

1. a. Any of several edible turtles of the family Testudinidae, living in fresh or brackish water, esp. the diamondback turtles of the genus *Malaclemys;* loosely, any land or fresh-water turtle. **b.** One of these turtles used as food.

See also TORUP, WOOD TERRAPIN.

1672 JOSSELYN *New Eng. Rarities* 34 The Turtle that . . . is called in Virginia a Terrapine. **1705** BEVERLEY *Virginia* III. 14 Their Food is Fish and Flesh of all sorts, and that which participates of both; as . . . a small kind of Turtle, or Tarapins. **1738** BYRD *Dividing Line* (1901) 215 We catcht a large terrapin in the river. **1784** SMYTH *Tour* I. 338 These animals are called here *Tarapens.* **1825** *Phila. Acad. Nat. Sciences Jrnl.* IV. 211 *E. centrata,* is the animal so well known here by the name of 'Terrapin.' **1844** 'UNCLE SAM' *Peculiarities* II. 199 The fowl and game (including terrapins, or land-tortoises), were in sufficient abundance. **1886** POORE *Reminisc.* I. 524 Terrapin, oysters . . . were furnished in profusion. **1904** *Green Bag* March 163 He had landed two terrapins.

2. *attrib.* **a.** In sense 1 with *egg, farm,* etc.

1772 in *Travels Amer. Col.* 517 The women danced the Snake dance, the leader haveing her legs Covered with Turpin shells . . . filled with small stones on purpose to make a noise. **1825** PAULDING *J. Bull in Amer.* 16 There was a very suspicious dish on the table, which they called terrapin soup. **1839** *S. Lit. Messenger* V. 376/2 Jane . . . proposed that 'they should all go the next day to hunt terrapin eggs.' **1853** SIMMS *Sword & Distaff* (1854) 188 Besides, she makes a first-rate terrapin stew. **1910** J. HART *Vigilante Girl* 88 The diamond-back costs almost as much in Baltimore as it would if terrapin farms were carved out of the dryest plains of western Texas.

b. *fig.* Designating things regarded as similar to terrapins in drawing within themselves or in making slow progress.

1809 *Ann. 10th Congress* 2 Sess. 1003 Is the Chinese, or Terrapin system [of commerce], as it is called, to be enforced? **1812** in *Harper's Encycl. U.S. Hist.* IX. 51/2 There's Porter and Grundy and Rhea, . . . Who draw their six dollars a day, And fight bloody battles *on paper!* Ah! this is true Terrapin war! **1847** ROBB *Squatter Life* 113 Boys, that terrapin team will arrive to night on the other side of the river with the message.

+Terrell grass. (See quot. 1891.) — **1891** *Cent.* 6246/3 Terrell grass, a species of wild rye, or lyme-grass, *Elymus Virginicus,* a coarse grass, but found useful for forage in the southern United States: so named from a promoter of its use. **1901** MOHR *Plant Life Ala.* 388.

Territorial, *a.* {1625-} +Of or pertaining to a territory of the United States.

1. In respect to appointees, law, etc.

1802 *Ann. 7th Congress* 1 Sess. 1101 [It is] the interest of the United States to obtain some further security against an injurious sale, under the Territorial or State laws, of lands sold by them to individuals. **1807** *Ann. 10th Congress* 1 Sess. 593 The French had not been enough attended to in the Territorial appointments. **1814** BRACKENRIDGE *Views La.* 99 The territorial governor [of Mo.] acts as well in the capacity of a general agent for the United States, as in that of civil magistrate. **1836** JACKSON in *Pres. Mess. & P.* III. 253 Governor Call [of Florida] . . . as commander in chief of the Territorial militia had been temporarily invested with the command. **1857** BENTON *Exam. Dred Scott Case* 116 The remission of the slavery question in Territories to the Supreme Court of the United States, by appeals from the Territorial Courts. **1870** *Republican Rev.* 16 April 3/4 The Republican Review . . . advocates the payment of the Territorial debt. **1877** JOHNSON *Anderson Co., Kansas* 172 Then the citizens applied to the Territorial Legislature, at its session in 1861, for a charter of incorporation. **1888** BRYCE *Amer. Commw.* I. i. xiii. 167 There are also eight Territorial delegates, one from each of the Territories, . . . not yet formed into States.

2. In respect to things that exist within a territory.

1867 *Wkly. New Mexican* 11 May 2/1 Attempt to break open the Door of the Territorial Library. **1884** *N. Mex. Terr. Rep.* 10 Thanks are due to most of the Territorial press for supplying . . . their newspapers. **1894** *Harper's Mag.* July 318/1 Blueblossom . . . boomed herself like other new Territorial towns.

+Territorial fair. An exhibition of agricultural and other products sponsored by a United States territory. — **1872** RAYMOND *3d Rep. Mines* 287 The Territorial fair . . . was a striking exhibition of the wealth and progress of Colorado. **1890** *Stock Grower & Farmer* 19 July 3/2 For several years the territorial fair has been plodding along without startling success.

+Territorial government. A government set up for a territory of the United States.

1804 *Ann. 8th Congress* 1 Sess. 1062, I believe the Territorial government, as established by the ordinance of the Old Congress, best adapted to the circumstances of the people of Louisiana. **1822** *Ann. 17th Congress* 1 Sess. 225 The Senate . . . proceeded to the consideration of the bill to establish a Territorial government for the Territory of Florida. **1850** FILLMORE in *Pres. Mess. & P.* V. 75 Congress having just passed a bill providing a Territorial government for New Mexico, I do not deem it advisable [etc.]. **1907** ANDREWS *Recoll.* 80 All the offices under the territorial government are bought by votes in favor of the bill.

b. *First grade of territorial government,* a territorial government having an elected legislature; *second grade of territorial government,* a territorial government conducted entirely by federal appointees.

1818 *Niles' Reg.* XIV. 48/2 A majority of the votes in Michigan territory is *against* the second grade of territorial government. **1831** PECK *Guide* 327 In 1789, the first grade of territorial government was organized, and called the 'Western Territory.'

Territorialize, *v.* {1818-} +*tr.* To reduce (a state) to the condition of a territory. — **1869** *Congress. Globe* App. 1 April 437/2 What bill? The bill to territorialize the State of Mississippi?

*Territory.

+1. Land or country lying outside the states, but belonging either to a state or to the federal government. {* in general sense}

See also LOUISIANA TERRITORY, NORTHWEST TERRITORY, WESTERN TERRITORY.

1787 *Constitution* iv. § 3, The Congress shall have Power to dispose of and make all needful Rules and Regulations respecting the Territory or other Property belonging to the United States. **1792** *Ann. 2d Congress* 1034 The Territory ceded by the State of North Carolina to the United States . . . is bounded as described. **1818** *Niles' Reg.* XV. 116/1 Calculate the immense extent of unappropriated territory . . . which stretches into the north-westernmost angle of the United States. **1845** [see MISSOURI COMPROMISE LINE]. **1900** *Congress. Rec.* 5 Feb. 1500/1 That part of the decision which says that the only constitutional purpose for which we can acquire territory is to make new States has never been controverted.

+2. a. A particular area of the country not yet admitted to the Union as a state, but organized under an act of Congress with some degree of self-government; the government or people of such an area. **b.** In some cases, as with New Mexico between 1846 and 1850, such an area not yet organized with any degree of self-government.

1787 in W. M. West *Source Book Amer. Hist.* 488 Be it ordained by the United States in Congress Assembled that the said territory for the purposes of temporary government be one district. **1816** [see DELINQUENT *n.*]. **1833** JACKSON in *Pres. Mess. & P.* III. 35 The survey [was] made in pursuance of the fourth section of the act of Congress of the 4th July, 1832, authorizing the survey of canal routes in the Territory of Florida. **1847** *Santa Fe Repub.* 10 Sept. 2/3 Ex-Gov. Armijo, Archulette and Ortize are at El Paso, waiting until they deem it safe to return to this Territory. **1858** [see ENABLING BILL]. **1885** *Wkly. New Mexican Rev.* 8 Jan. 4/3 The first case . . . was an old criminal case, territory vs. Donariano Lopez. **1905** *Springfield W. Repub.* 1 Sept. 2 The people of Arizona are so hostile to a merger with New Mexico that they are now content to remain a territory for an indefinite period.

+**3.** With specifying names, in sense 2 a.

1799 J. ADAMS *Works* IX. 41 The organization of the government of the Mississippi territory . . . should perhaps be mentioned to Congress. **1857** *Lawrence* (Kan.) *Republican* 28 May 1 The Lawrence Republican Is published every Thursday Morning, at Lawrence, Kansas Territory. **1873** *Newton Kansan* 2 Jan. 2/1 Dr. James Wright . . . has been appointed Superintendent of Indian affairs for Montana Territory.

+**4.** = INDIAN TERRITORY 2.

1874 ALDRICH *P. Palfrey* vi, What might not happen to them, among the desperate white men and lawless savages, out there in the territory?

+**5.** The area assigned to or normally traversed by a traveling salesman.

1903 *Windsor Mag.* Sept. 409/1 His line was jewellery, and his territory was the middle west. **1904** CRISSEY *Tattlings* 88 This young reformer . . . had invaded a competitor's territory and put in his own goods.

Tertium Quid. {1724-} +=QUID. *Obs.* — **1806** *Balance* V. 11/2 He was a deserter, and had either joined the federalists, or the tertiumquids. **1914** *Cycl. Amer. Govt.* III. 529/2 Tertium Quid was the term applied to the faction led by John Randolph, in Jefferson's administration.

Tertulia. [Sp.] An evening party or ball. {1785-, in Spain} — **1827** *Md. Hist. Mag.* XVII. 262 At night we went to the Tertullia, an assembly so called in imitation of the Spaniards. **1844** KENDALL *Santa Fé Exped.* II. 155 At night a tertulia or party, was given to the Mexican officers. **1910** J. HART *Vigilante Girl* 223 He is the master of ceremonies of the *tertulia*, or ball.

+**Tesquite.** [From Mex. *tequesquite*.] (See quotation.) — **1859** BARTLETT 476 *Tesquite*, an alkaline efflorescence of considerable value which exudes from the earth around many of the lakes, ponds, and marshy grounds in New Mexico, California, and Arizona.

+**Tessellated darter.** A small, brilliantly colored fish (*Boleosoma olmstedi*) of the eastern states. — **1883** *Nat. Museum Bul.* No. 27, 465 Tessellated Darter. Great Lake region; Eastern United States from Massachusetts to Georgia. **1897** *N.Y. Forest, Fish, & Game Comm. 2d Rep.* 241.

Test, *v. tr.* To try the quality, validity, etc., of (something); to subject to proof or a trial of some kind. {tested, 1603-; 1760-}

'Before 1800 chiefly in pa. pple.; the simple vb. was considered by Southey as an Americanism' (*O.E.D.*).

*a***1799** WASHINGTON (W. '28), Experience is the surest standard by which to test the real tendency of the existing constitution. **1815** JEFFERSON *Writ.* (1830) IV. 260 They have not the means of testing the statements. **1871** RAYMOND *3d Rep. Mines* 335 These lodes have not been tested by the repeated and continuous milling of the ore raised from them. **1914** 'BOWER' *Flying U Ranch* 29 Irish tested his tongs as he had been told to do.

* **Tester.** A canopy over a bed; the headboard supporting this. Also attrib.

1762 ELIAKIN SMITH *Acct. Bk.* (MS., Forbes Lib., Northampton, Mass.), Bedstead with tester and false post. **1807** IRVING, etc. *Salmagundi* xiv. 376 Old-fashioned bedsteads, with high testers; massy clothes-presses [etc.]. **1848** JUDSON *Mysteries N.Y.* II. 49 The open door . . . showed the white counterpane and neat tester of a bed. **1904** GLASGOW *Deliverance* 483 He sat in the shadow beside the tester bed.

+**Tester bar.** A mosquito bar. — **1850** COLTON *Deck & Port* 122 If by good fortune your tester-bar keeps out the musquito, you fall into the hands of a still worse enemy in the shape of the flea.

Testimonial benefit. A benefit (q.v., sense 1) given as a testimonial of esteem. — **1875** *Chicago Tribune* 25 Aug. 7/4 Grand Testimonial Benefit to B. H. Grover. **1895** *N.Y. Dramatic News* 9 Nov. 2/4 A young Spanish lady named Villardel was about to receive a testimonial benefit.

Test oath. a. An oath the taking of which is a test of one's sentiments or loyalty. {1715-} +**b.** = IRONCLAD OATH. Also attrib.

1775 *S.C. Hist. Soc. Coll.* III. 42 The form of a test-oath, proposed by Robinson's party. **1857** *Lawrence* (Kan.) *Republican* 13 Aug. 2 At the second general Territorial election the ballot-box was hedged about by degrading test oaths. **1866** J. SHERMAN in *Sherman Lett.* 271 The very moment the South will agree to a firm basis of representation, I am for general amnesty and a repeal of the test oaths. **1871** *Harper's Mag.* June 150/2 It is an important feature of the bill, as passed by the Senate, that the test oath to be taken by jurors in the United States is retained. **1882** *Nation* 6 July 2/2 The term 'officer' must include members of Congress, as is shown . . . by the employment of the same term in the Test-Oath Act.

Test paper. {1827-} +(See quot. 1891.) — **1841** *Penna. Rep.* (Wharton) VI. 291 No doubt must remain as to the handwriting of the test paper. **1850** BURRILL *Law Dict.* (1860) II. 522/2 *Test Paper*. In practice. A paper or instrument shown to a jury as evidence. A term used in the Pennsylvania courts. **1891** *Cent.* 6253/1 *Test-paper*, . . . a document allowed to be used in a court of justice as a standard of comparison for determining a question of handwriting.

+**Test pit.** A shallow pit or hole made by a prospector in searching for or testing a mineral deposit. Also fig. — **1882** *Harper's Mag.* May 897/2 The prospectors sink a well, which they call a 'test pit.' **1896** *Atlantic Mo.* May 606/2 Sinking test-pits through layers of crusted consciousness into depths of fiery nature.

+**Test run.** A proof or milling of a given amount of ore for determining its yield. — **1876** RAYMOND *8th Rep. Mines* 302 A test-run made upon about three tons showed it to contain 51 ounces of silver and 41 per cent. of lead per ton. **1880** *Cimarron News & Press* 3 June 2/4 Jack Burroughs, the man who made a 'test run' with the Sperry mill, . . . passed the winter in London.

+**Test vote.** A vote, often informal, as an indication of sentiment. — **1856** *Porter's Spirit of Times* 8 Nov. 168/1 The intention . . . [is to] ridicule the mania for taking test votes in railroad cars, steamboats and everywhere else. **1864** *Wkly. New Mexican* 24 June 2/2 This is considered a test vote. **1870** MEDBERY *Men Wall St.* 14 The Stock Exchange . . . on a test vote . . . could only muster fifty-two members.

Tête-à-tête. {1697-} +A sofa or settee for two persons, usually one enabling its occupants to face each other. — **1864** WEBSTER 1368/3. **1876** KNIGHT 2541/2. **1899** *Boston Traveller* 25 July, It is more than [a] tete-a-tete, larger than a canape.

+**Tewksbury Winter Blush.** A variety of apple. *Obs.* — **1817** W. COXE *Fruit-Trees* 156 Tewksbury Winter Blush. This apple was brought from the township of Tewksbury in Hunterdon county, New-Jersey. **1849** *New Eng. Farmer* I. 90 *Tewksbury Winter Blush.*—Very small and beautiful.

+**Texan,** *n.*

1. A native or inhabitant of Texas.

1838 C. NEWELL *Revol. Texas* 27 The Texans were gallantly led to the charge by their commander, John Austin. **1865** RICHARDSON *Secret Service* 99 A Texan on board the boat was very bitter against Governor Houston. **1894** [see CANVAS-COVERED *a.*]. **1923** J. H. COOK *On Old Frontier* 53 In our outfit was . . . a large, hungry-looking Texan.

2. *pl.* Texas cattle.

1868 *Ill. Agric. Soc. Trans.* VII. 138 We also put five cows and a buffalo with some Texans about the 20th of June. **1878** BEADLE *Western Wilds* 438 In the early days the Kansas Legislature set apart the width of one township, . . . along which Texans might be driven to the Pacific Railroad. **1890** *Stock Grower & Farmer* 1 March 3/4 Rules for Shipping Texans.

‖**3.** The language or vernacular of Texas people.

1877 HALE *G. T. T.* 41 The English talk of American dialect, as if I spoke Texan, or could; or as if a Carolinian could speak Yankee.

+**Texan,** *a.* Of or pertaining to what is now the state of Texas.

1835 DEWEES *Lett. from Texas* 157 A part of the Texan army . . . marched over on the San Antonio river. **1848** *Santa Fe Repub.* 22 Jan. 4/1 The detachment . . . consisted of the Greys and a few Texan colonists. **1895** *Outing* XXVI. 390/2 Arthur Whipple's 'Deacon,' and Mr. Carrington's 'Comanche,' a Texan pony, are also promising animals.

b. In the specific names of animals and plants.

1859 BARTLETT 218 Jackass Rabbit. (*Lepus callotis*.) . . . It is known also by the names of Mule Rabbit, Texan Hare, and Black-tailed Hare. **1890** *Cent.* 4347/1 Peba, or Texan Armadillo (*Tatusia novemcincta*). **1894** *Harper's Mag.* Feb. 457 The Texan Walking Stick, *Diapheromera denticrus*. **1897** SUDWORTH *Arborescent Flora* 248 *Zygia flexicaulis.* . . . Texan Ebony.

+**Texan Ranger.** = TEXAS RANGER. *Obs.* — **1848** ROBINSON *Santa Fe Exped.* 69 At Mier we saw a Mexican shot by the Texan Rangers. **1864** NICHOLS *Amer. Life* I. 212 It is only by keeping a large force of Texan rangers . . . upon the frontier that the settlements are safe. **1867** *Wkly. New Mexican* 2 March 1/4 The fame and splendid horsemanship of the Texan Ranger were too much for Bryant.

+**Texan Republic.** The republic (1836-1845) established by the citizens of Texas after their declaration of independence from Mexico. — **1842** *Picayune* 4 Jan. 1/6 The Texans . . . represented . . . their object was to invite the New Mexicans to unite themselves to the Texan Republic.

+**Texas.** [Sp., from Caddo *techas* 'allies.']

1. A Caddo (q.v.), or an Indian of a Caddoan tribe: (see quot. 1910). In full *Texas Indian.*

[**1818** LUIS DE ONIS in *State P.* (1819) XII. 31 He wrote to the viceroy, informing him that the Texas Indians possessed great attachment to the Spaniards.] **1822** MORSE *Rep. Indian Affairs* II. 373 Indian Tribes between Red River, and Rio del Norte. . . . Texas. **1858** *Texas Almanac 1859* 130 The State of Texas . . . set apart twelve leagues of land, upon which the Texas Indians to be settled by the U.S. Government **1910** HODGE, etc. *Amer. Indians* II. 738/2 *Texas*, a name variously applied by writers, but most commonly used by the Spaniards, from whom French and English writers borrowed it, to designate the Hasinai tribes of Angelina and upper Neches valleys, Texas.

2. A range of staterooms immediately behind or beneath the pilot house.

1857 OLMSTED *Journey Texas* 27 To this Texas, inveterate card-players retire on Sundays. **1893** *Harper's Mag.* Jan. 167 Most of the large boats have the big square pilot-house on top of the 'Texas.' **1907** STEWART *Partners* 207, I had the texas all to myself.

b. 'The elevated gallery, resembling a louver or clear-story, in a grain-elevator' (*Cent. Suppl.*).

3. *attrib.* and *comb.* **a.** Denoting persons and things living in or characteristic of Texas.

1836 EDWARD *Hist. Texas* 240 It is a certain part of the Texas inhabitants, who have proved to be the unprovoked and *unnecessary aggressors*. **1853** 'P. PAXTON' *Yankee in Texas* 50 He was with his family, all his household gods, and a Texas wagon, filled with what . . . was literally 'plunder,' drawn by those miserably slow oxen. **1877** BEARD *K.K.K. Sketches* 36 The large bridle-bits, Texas spurs, and other appendages of a cavalry outfit . . . were carefully muffled. **1881** C. M. CHASE *Editor's Run in New Mex.* 118 They are honest, old-fashioned people, hardshelled Baptists, speak the Texas dialect with 'that,' 'whar,' 'befo,' etc., in the broadest style. **1884** Texas rancher [see PRINCE 1 a]. **1885** *Wkly. New Mexican Rev.* 25 June 3/6 These are Texas herds which came in via the Pecos trail recently.

b. In the specific names of plants and trees found in Texas.

See also TEXAS BLUE GRASS.

1877 BARTLETT 790 New Orleans Moss. (*Tillandsia usneoides.*) . . . Also called Texas Moss, as it is equally abundant in that State. **1885** HAVARD *Flora W. & S. Texas* 458 Other shrubs deserving mention are: The Trefoil Barberry . . . ; the well known Texas Persimmon (*Diospyros Texana*). **1901** Texas white oak [see PIN OAK b]. **1907** *Springfield W. Repub.* 22 Aug. 6 The fields are dotted with clumps of white golden coreopsis, called the Texas star.

c. In the specific names of birds found in Texas.

1878 *Nat. Museum Proc.* I. 119 The nests . . . are . . . readily distinguishable from those of the Texas Thrasher and Mocking-bird. **1917** *Birds of Amer.* II. 145/2 The Texas Woodpecker shows the ruling characteristic of its family in its choice of food.

4. In sense 2 with *deck, hall, tender*.

1875 'MARK TWAIN' *Old Times* i. 11 A fanciful pilot-house, all glass and 'gingerbread,' perched on top of the 'texas deck.' *Ib.* i. 31 Here was . . . a tidy, white-aproned, black 'texas-tender,' to bring up tarts and ices and coffee. **1884** — *H. Finn* xii, Away down through the texas-hall we see a light!

5. In special combinations.

Texas annexation, the annexation of Texas as a state of the United States in 1845; *T. cow*, a cow of the old longhorn breed once common in Texas; *T. insurrection*, the revolt (1835-6) of Texas against Mexico; *T. line*, the boundary line of Texas; *T. longhorn*, an animal of the ox kind belonging to an early breed found in Texas; *T. Lullaby*, a song often sung by cowboys in their efforts to keep their herds quiet; *T. money*, warrants or promissory notes issued by the Republic of Texas; *T. murrain*, = TEXAS FEVER 2; *T. pony*, a pony, as a mustang, of a kind commonly used in Texas; *T. question*, the question of the annexation of Texas to the United States; *T. rig*, the costume worn formerly by Texas cowboys; *T. trail*, the Chisholm cattle trail from Red River Station on the Red River to Abilene, Kansas.

1845 *Xenia Torch-Light* 31 July 3/1 The National Treasury is open to any and all demands made as the price of Texas Annexation. **1875** *Cimarron News & Press* 7 Aug. 4/4 Texas cows, $12 to $16 per head. **1847** *Whig Almanac 1848* 5/1 The Texas Insurrection, the open and ostentatious drumming up of men, munitions and money throughout the Southwest . . . —are all matters of public history. **1882** *N. Mex. Terr. Rep.* (1884) 96 Three men . . . were driving them [*sc.* cattle] towards the Texas line. a**1918** G. STUART *On Frontier* II. 178 None of our cattle were Texas long horns. **1923** J. H. COOK *On Old Frontier* 17 All . . . [were] singing the melody known as the 'Texas Lullaby.' **1840** *Picayune* 8 Sept. 2/3 Texas money is worth 22 cents and improving. **1866** *Ill. Agric. Soc. Trans.* VII. 222 Another pest . . . is the 'Texas fever,' 'Spanish fever,' or 'Texas murrain,' as it is variously known. **1883** RITTENHOUSE *Maud* 206 Last night on the front porch Elmer said, 'The Texas pony is yours.' **1844** *Whig Almanac 1845* 4/1 Sixty-odd Thousand votes [were] thrown away on the Birney or Abolition ticket—every one opposed to Polk's views on the Texas Question. **1853** 'P. PAXTON' *Yankee in Texas* 18 Joe was in full Texas rig. **1881** *Cimarron News & Press* 17 March 1/4 The well-known old Texas trail was infested with hostile Indians.

+**Texas blue grass.** A grass (*Poa arachnifera*) valued for pasturage and hay. — **1885** HAVARD *Flora W. & S. Texas* 530 Other grasses highly prized for pasture or hay . . . [include] Texas Blue Grass . . . native on the prairies of the Brazos. **1889** VASEY *Agric. Grasses* 64 Texas Blue Grass . . . was first described by Dr. John Torrey in the report of Captain Marcey's exploration of the Red River . . . , as having been found on the headwaters of the Trinity. **1894** COULTER *Bot. W. Texas* III. 546.

+**Texas cattle.** Cattle raised in Texas, esp. a breed or variety of long-horned cattle found in early times in Texas. Also attrib. — **1857** BRAMAN *Texas* 72 The Texas cattle are descendants, with few crosses, from the old Mexican stocks, and they are well adapted to the country. **1867** *Illinois Revised Statutes* (1883) 136 An act to prevent the importation of Texas or Cherokee cattle into the state of Illinois. **1880** *Cimarron News & Press* 13 May 1/6 Texas cattle are being rapidly improved by the introduction of blooded bulls from the states. **1880** *Ib.* 17 June 1/4 Ogallala [Neb.] is the natural terminus of the Texas cattle trail. **1893** G. W. CURTIS *Horses, Cattle* 220 Although known as 'Texas Cattle,' the same race extends throughout Mexico, and has been pretty well scattered through the more northern and western territories of the United States.

+**Texas Compromise.** In the joint resolution of Congress providing for the annexation of Texas (1845), the stipulation that slavery should be prohibited in any new states to be formed in Texan territory north of the Missouri Compromise line (q.v.), and that the slavery question should be decided for itself by every such state to be formed south of that line. Also attrib. — **1848** POLK in *Pres. Mess. & P.* IV. 608 The Territory of Oregon lies far north of 36°30′, the Missouri and Texas compromise line. **1857** BENTON *Exam. Dred Scott Case* 102 The Texas Compromise of 1845 omits it [the word 'forever'], and not by accident.

+**Texas fever.**

1. An extreme desire to go to Texas. *Obs.*

Cf. CALIFORNIA FEVER 3.

1825 *Austin P.* II. (1924) 1020 The emigrating, or Texas *fever* prevails to an extent that your *wishes* would no more than anticipate. **1878** *Ill. Dept. Agric. Trans.* XIV. 146 The Texas fever has called away a number.

2. = SPANISH FEVER 2. {1902}

1866 [see TEXAS 5]. **1870** *Ill. Agric. Soc. Trans.* VII. p. xii, The prevalence of Spanish or Texas fever . . . in this State during the summer of 1868. **1885** *Santa Fé Wkly. New Mexican* 3 Sept. 3/7 The reported breaking out of Texas fever among the domestic cattle at Crosson's ranch . . . is followed to-day by more serious reports. **1895** *Dept. Agric. Yrbk. 1894* 70 Carcasses of animals affected with . . . pneumonia, Texas fever, and similar diseases would be considered fit for food if the carcasses show no signs of emaciation. **1913** BARNES *Western Grazing Grounds* 294 Texas Fever . . . is not general over the West.

b. *Texas-fever tick*, a cattle tick (*Margaropus annulatus*), which transmits the parasite causing Texas fever.

1913 BARNES *Western Grazing Grounds* 135 An inspector of the Bureau of Animal Industry . . . looks the stock over carefully for evidences of disease, especially Texas fever ticks and mange.

Texas millet. (See quots. 1858, 1889.) — [**1858** SIMMONDS *Dict. Trade Products* 377/2 Texas Millet, the *Sorghum cernuum*, a prolific breadcorn cultivated in the tropics.] **1889** VASEY *Agric. Grasses* 25 *Panicum Texanum* (Texas Millet). . . . In some localities it is known as river grass; in others as goose grass, from its being supposed to have been introduced by wild geese. **1901** MOHR *Plant Life Ala.* 346.

+**Texas Panhandle.** A narrow strip of Texas in the extreme northern part of the state between New Mexico and Oklahoma. — **1894** *McClure's Mag.* III. 107/1 Old Dad Morrison . . . used to have his headquarters on Buck Creek, Briscoe County, in the Texas Panhandle. **1902** MACGOWAN *Last Word* 382 Mr. Lord was a cattle baron in the Texas Panhandle. **1905** *Forestry Bureau Bul.* No. 65, 7 The Red Beds Belt is named from the geological formation prevailing in western Oklahoma and the eastern part of the Texas 'Pan Handle.'

+**Texas Ranger.** **1.** A member of a body of armed Texans, originally Indian-fighters and preservers of order on the frontier, and later active as soldiers. (Cf. RANGER 1 b.) **2.** A member of the mounted police of the state of Texas. — (1) **1846** *Whig Almanac 1847* 19/1 Capt. Samuel Walker, at the head of a small company of Texas Rangers, left Point Isabel. **1872** POWERS *Afoot & Alone* 132 The Texas rangers . . . never had time to find the Yankees. **1907** ANDREWS *Recoll.* 163 We were under charge of Colonel Wharton and a detachment of his regiment, the Texas Rangers. (2) **1911** *Everybody's Mag.* Sept. 354/1 Two Texas rangers faced Antonio Carrasco and his seventeen thieves sometime in December of 1910.

+**Texas saddle.** A heavy stock saddle usually having a high cantle, a high knobbed pommel, and two cinches. — **1877** MINTURN *Travels West* 36 A Texas saddle . . . comes high up in front, where the lasso is fastened. **1898** CANFIELD *Maid of Frontier* 5 The enormous load of Texas saddle, gun, blanket. **1923** J. H. COOK *On Old Frontier* 5, I had purchased . . . a good second-hand Texas saddle for $5.

+**Texas steer.** A steer raised in Texas or one of a long-horned Texas variety. — **1865** *Wkly. New Mexican* 8 Sept. 2/3 The stock, (Texas steers) corralled about seven miles below Las Cruces, . . . became badly frightened. **1890** *Stock Grower & Farmer* 12 April 6/3 It was no uncommon sight to see from 5,000 to 10,000 long-horned Texas steers in a drove on the trail.

+**Texian,** *n.* [Cf. KENTUCKIAN *n.*, MISSOURIAN, etc.] = TEXAN *n.* 1. Also *Texasian, Texican.*

'An official variant of the word Texan which enjoyed wide popular usage during the ten years of the Republic of Texas. . . . After the Civil War a new generation allowed the old spelling to fall into disuse—much to the disgust of many old Texians' (Adams & Coleman *Dict. Amer. Hist.* V. 257/2).

1836 EDWARD *Hist. Texas* 64 Nature has distributed her favors, as regards wood and land to the Texasians, in a peculiar manner. **1843** N. BOONE *Journal* 183, I also received a copy of your letter . . . , apprising me of the movements of Col Ryburn, and other Texians. **1862** CUMMING *Hospital Life* 38/1 We met some very nice young Texians, who were delighted to see us. **1910** J. HART *Vigilante Girl* 47 North agin South—a Yankee agin a Texican!

+**Texian,** *a.* = TEXAN *a.* — **1836** in Mackenzie *Life Van Buren* 306 A fertile paradisaical piece of Texian land . . . [has been promised] to every American citizen . . . who will sally forth to capture it from the Mexican republic! **1837** *Diplom. Corr. Texas* I. (1908) 270 The passengers were transferred on board of a Texian armed schooner called the Brutus. **1843** Texas Republic [see FRONTIERMAN]. **1848** *Santa Fe Repub.* 31 Aug. 2/1 We would now inform our Texian friends, that it is not necessary to send us a Judge nor a District Attorney to settle our affairs.

Textbook. {1730-} A book specially prepared to serve as a basis for instruction, as in a school course. {a1855-}

1828 in Quincy *Hist. Harvard* II. 560 Another committee has been instructed to take measures for lessening the price of text-books. **1865** *Atlantic Mo.* March 367/2 Text-books for schools and colleges were prepared. **1883** *Harper's Mag.* June 154/2 There was no book on [organic chemistry] . . . quite satisfactory as a text-book. **1923** HERRICK *Lilla* 225 I'll just have to go back to selling text-books, rotten text-books, for kids who hate 'em!

attrib. **1849** CHAMBERLAIN *Ind. Gazetteer* 60 Text books in the collegiate course, when procured from the text-book library, will cost about $2.00 per annum. **1916** THOBURN *Stand. Hist. Okla.* II. 713 [There was] a small flurry of excitement over an alleged school textbook scandal.

* **Thank,** *v.* +*Thank fortune!* ejaculatory phrase of thankfulness. *colloq.* — **1845** KIRKLAND *Western Clearings* 44 'Who has Phebe Penniman got tacked to her?' 'Nobody, thank fortune!' said his mother. **1886** *Harper's Mag.* June 98/1 She was in her own coupé, thank fortune!

* **Thanksgiving.**

1. a. The public expression of thanks, in special observances, for divine favor; a day set apart for this. {1641-} +**b.** The American holiday of Thanksgiving Day.

1632 *Mass. Bay Rec.* I. 96 The Court . . . hath appoyncted the 13th day of this present moneth [June] to be kept as a day of publique thanksgiuing throughout the seuerall plantacions. **1676** in Evans *Amer. Bibliography* I. 40 The Council have thought meet to appoint and set apart the 29th day of this instant June, as a day of solemn Thanksgiving and praise to God. **1715** SEWALL *Diary* III. 64 The day for reading the Order for the Thanksgiving according to the usual custom. **1778** CUTLER in *Life & Corr.* I. 73 This day [Dec. 30] appointed by Congress as a day of Thanksgiving through the United States of America. **1824** *Niles' Reg.* XXVII. 144/2 Thursday, the second day of December next, is to be observed as a day of thanksgiving in Massachusetts. **1863** LINCOLN in G. W. Douglas *Amer. Book of Days* 589, [I] invite my fellow citizens . . . to set apart and observe the last Thursday of November next as a day of thanksgiving and praise to our beneficent Father who dwelleth in the heavens. **1887** WILKINS *Humble Romance* 53 Are you coming over to our house Thanksgiving? **1904** *Boston Herald* 24 Nov. 6 There are five states in which the state governments have not made Thanksgiving a legal holiday.

‖**2.** A blessing or grace said in connection with a meal. *Obs.*

1650 *Harvard Rec.* I. 35 Neither may any Schollar rise from his place or goe out of the Hall at Meal-times before thanksgiving bee ended.

3. Attrib. with *celebration, dinner, eve,* etc.

1712 SEWALL *Diary* II. 364 Made a good Thanks-giving Sermon from PS. 116.9. **1788** *Mass. Centinel* 30 July 155/3 Cato . . . [and] one of his brethren of colour . . . were staggering home from a frolic on a thanksgiving eve. **1830** S. SMITH *Life J. Downing* 50 What did I see but one of the grandest thanksgiving dinners you ever laid your eyes on? **1849** *Knickerb.* XXXIV. 556 This is *Thanksgiving Night.* **1871** STOWE *Sam Lawson* 2 There were in Oldtown no parties or balls, except, perhaps, the annual election, or Thanksgiving festival. **1878** B. F. TAYLOR *Between Gates* 278 Think of a single vine in Yuba County bearing . . . squash . . . equal to the manufacture of two thousand Thanksgiving pies. **1887** ALDEN *Little Fishers* xxii, I will give you a chicken myself for the Thanksgiving time. **1903** *Boston Herald* 19 Aug., Colonial teas, Thanksgiving celebrations and other occasions . . . seek to recall the early history of New England.

Thanksgiving day. A day of public thanksgiving for divine blessings {1704}; +spec., *cap.,* an American holiday, proclaimed by the president annually since 1863, designated for this purpose.

First observed by the Plymouth colony in 1621; proclaimed for the nation by Washington in 1789.

1674 JOSSELYN *Two Voyages* 214, I returned to Boston again, the next day being Thanksgiving day. **1707** SEWALL *Diary* II. 206 Thanks-giving-day, very serene, moderate, comfortable Wether. **1781** PETERS *Hist. Conn.* (1829) 142 Those religionists preach damnation to all people who neglect to attend public worship twice every Sabbath, fasting and thanksgiving day. **1836** *S. Lit. Messenger* II. 746 As ever I hope to eat pumpkin pie thanksgiving day, that's no English trader. **1880** *Cimarron News & Press* 18 March 2/3 The great East river bridge will be opened to traffic by next Thanksgiving day. **1904** *Public Ledger* (Phila.) 24 Nov. 4 There were national Thanksgiving Days before the Civil War, but it was Lincoln who made the Thanksgiving Day for the nation a custom.

+**Thanksgiving turkey.** A turkey served as a traditionally appropriate part of a Thanksgiving dinner. — **1853** *Knickerb.* XLII. 540, I pass the Deacon's house, on my way to the paternal mansion, to eat the thanksgiving-turkey. **1870** KEIM *Sheridan's Troopers* 108 The 'thanksgiving turkey' . . . weighed thirty pounds dressed. **1907** *St. Nicholas* July 792/1 No mallard duck or Thanksgiving turkey ever tasted so good.

+**Thank-you-ma'am.** Also **thank-you-marm.** A slight obstruction or defect, as a hollow, ridge, or drain, in or across a road. *colloq.* Also transf. — **1849** LONGFELLOW *Kavanagh* 56 The driver called them [*sc.* hollows in the snow] 'thank-you-ma'ams,' because they made everybody bow. **1867** HOLMES *Guardian Angel* 166 Life's a road that's got a good many thank-you-ma'ams to go bumpin' over. **1895** WIGGIN *Village Watch-Tower* 198 'Life' Lane was . . . just the man to . . . drive the three horses through ruts and 'thank-you-ma'ams.' **1906** *N.Y. Ev. Post* 24 May 1 The settling of the tunnel shield, and a consequent sagging of the tube in spots was the defect which Mayor McClellan so dramatically exposed, when in fact . . . these 'thank you marms' were first noticed by the tunnel engineers two years ago and fully reported to the board.

* **That,** *pron.*

+**1.** *At that,* even so, into the bargain. *colloq.*

1830 *Mass. Spy* 28 July (Th.), The march was now hurried on, yet slow at that, for I could not walk fast. **1850** MATHEWS *Moneypenny* 12 Had to take [the mare] or get none, and to buy her, at that. **1880** 'MARK TWAIN' *Tramp Abroad* 489 We must have made fully a mile and a half an hour, and it was all downhill, too, and very muddy at that. **1897** *Amer. Pediatric Soc. Trans.* IX. 73 The infant was underfed, and did not receive the correct food at that.

+**2.** *That's so,* that is true. *colloq.* Also *that is so; that so?*

1857 *Knickerb.* XLIX. 86 One of the quaintest, quietest, most musical, and most engaging forms of acquiescence is in the new and popular phrase of 'That's so,' which is working its way into common parlance. **1876** *Congress. Rec.* 3 Aug. 5134/1 That is so. That is what the Chair has ruled. **1891** RYAN *Pagan* 93 'That so?' she said.

3. In various other colloq. expressions.

That is a fact, that is certainly true; *that's the how,* that is the way of it (local); *that's right,* an expression of approval; *that's too bad,* an expression of sorrow or sympathy regarding a misfortune.

1836 WESTON *Visit* 59 'That is a fact,' and 'no mistake,' are continually used to give effect to an assertion. A Yankee, for instance, says, 'He is a smart fellow, and that's a fact,' or, 'and no mistake.' **1838** DRAKE *Tales Queen City* 36 'Squire Daggett would fine you ever so much, for swearing so wicked;—that's the how. **1905** *N.Y. Ev. Post* 7 April 2 The President's address was frequently interrupted with applause and cries of 'That's right.' *Ib.* 12 Oct. 1 When told of Mathews's suicide, he started, turned pale, and exclaimed: 'My God, my God; that's too bad.'

* **Thatch.**

1. a. The material, as reeds, straw, etc., used in thatching. +**b.** Any one of various tall, coarse grasses, esp. of the genus *Spartina,* common along the north Atlantic coast of the United States. Cf. CREEK THATCH.

1622 'MOURT' *Relation* 70 Some of our people being abroad, to get and gather thatch, they saw great fires. **1695** *Providence Rec.* VI. 156 That Parcell of Meadow marsh & thatch . . . belongeth to me. **1704** *Ib.* V. 224 [The] Cove is a place of Salt Grass called Thatch. **1797** [see BENT GRASS 2]. **1863** MITCHELL *My Farm* 49, I gave them [*sc.* bees] a warm shelter of thatch. *a*1918 G. STUART *On Frontier* I. 65 On this they would put thatch and cover with mud mortar.

2. Attrib. with *bank, cove, grass,* etc.

1704 *Providence Rec.* XI. 90 Care might be taken for the orderly Cutting of the thatch Grass. **1711** *Ib.* XVI. 66, I give . . . my share of thach Cove. **1718** *N.H. Probate Rec.* I. 532 A Peice of Marsh & Thatch Ground Lyeing by the Boare's Head. *Ib.* II. 73, I give to Collo. George Vaughan . . . ye marsh and the thach bank of Crooked lane. **1746** *Ib.* III. 362, I Give unto my son . . . two thach shares. **1841** *Huntington Rec.* III. 379 [This Indenture] doth convey a certain piece of thatch meadow.

+**Thatch bed.** A tract or area on which thatch grass grows. *Obs.* — **1682** *Providence Rec.* XV. 238 Sume kare may bee taken Consarning the thach beeds. **1703** *Ib.* V. 63 Ye sd thatch Bedds are in Comon. **1757** *Smithtown Rec.* 407 On the beach thatch bed we allow six acres and sixteen rods for one lot. **1841** *Huntington Rec.* III. 379 All the several thatch beds & meadow within the said bounds . . . [are conveyed] unto Jacob Scudder.

* **Thatcher.** One who thatches. *Obs.* — **1630** *Mass. Bay Rec.* I. 74 Brickelayers, sawers, and thatchers shall not take aboue 2s. aday. **1666** *Groton Rec.* 18 Wages for those who did attend the thatcher.

* **Thaw,** *v.* +*To thaw out,* to free from the effects of cold; to become warm. Also transf. and fig. — **1785** CUTLER in *Life & Corr.* II. 228 This cold snowy winter has considerably cooled my zeal, but when I get thawed out, in the spring, perhaps it may return. **1835** INGRAHAM *South-West* I. 33 When vessels in their winter voyages . . . become coated with ice, . . . they seek the genial warmth of this region [the Gulf Stream in the latitude of Baltimore] to 'thaw out,' as this dissolving process is termed by the sailors. **1896** [see GIANT POWDER]. **1910** McCUTCHEON *Rose in Ring* 177 He could save us a lot of trouble if he'd thaw out and hand over some of the money he's hiding.

* **Theater, Theatre.**

***1.** A building erected or adapted for dramatic presentations.

1733 *New Eng. & Boston Gaz.* 1 Jan. (Odell), The *New Theatre* in the building of the Hon. Rip Van Dam, Esq., was opened with the comedy of the *Recruiting Officer.* **1789** MACLAY *Deb. Senate* 43, I received a ticket from the President . . . to use his box this evening at the theater. **1832** DUNLAP *Hist. Amer. Theatre* 22 In the year 1760, Douglass . . . opened the theatre in Southwark, which remained the only theatre of the metropolis of Pennsylvania until . . . 1791. **1890** RYAN *Told in Hills* 174, I heard an actor spoutin' . . . in a theatre at Helena. **1920** COOPER *Under Big Top* 118 Ed Warner, general agent of a circus, and myself stood in the wings of a theater in Denver.

2. Attrib. with *bee, floor, manager,* etc.

1851 HALL *Manhattaner* 33 The clerk is at his bowling, or his billiards, or in theatre parquet. **1875** *Chicago Tribune* 15 Aug. 15/5 Seats may be secured at the theatre office daily. **1891** H. CROSBY *Conformity to World* 22 If a theatre-manager should now advertise only pure plays, he would soon have a empty house. **1895** *N.Y. Dramatic News* 6 July 5/3 Handsome Mlle. Troja is a warmly regarded entertainer on the American theatre roof. **1895** *Stand.* 1868/3 *Theater-floor,* an inclined floor in a public building, as a lecture-hall, affording a better view of the platform from rear seats. **1897** FLANDRAU *Harvard Episodes* 268 Returned 'theatre bees' came there to scramble eggs and drink beer.

+**Theater party.** A social entertainment consisting largely of attendance at a theater; a group of people who go to the theater together. — **1883** *Century Mag.* Sept. 787/1 This city . . . some novelists will have it . . . has no more interesting social life than is shown in a report of . . . Mrs. Dash's theater party. **1893** POST *Harvard Stories* 108, I had a seat right under a box where there was a theatre-party. **1907** A. THOMAS *Witching Hour* (1925) I. 110 In the same theater party a girl's got to listen —or leave the box.

＊**Theodolite.** An instrument used by a surveyor for measuring angles. — **1644** *Md. Archives* IV. 279 A theodulite a brass universall Sun-diall. **1790** *Penna. Packet* 29 April 2/1 At 3 o'clock in the Afternoon will be Sold . . . A new improved Theodolite with Telliscope complete. **1837** [see FISHING POLE]. **1877** W. WRIGHT *Big Bonanza* 109 The theodolite had been left standing on the bank.

Theological school. =next. — **1807** in *Union Theol. Sem. Va. Centennial Cat.* (1907) 7 The head of the theological school must be the president of Hampden-Sidney College. **1883** *Century Mag.* July 456/2, I had rather hear from you the fruits of your studies than your complaints of the parties, which, I suppose, is a necessary consequence of living in a theological school. **1909** *Religion & Life* Pref. Note, This volume comprises addresses made by members of the teaching community of the Meadville Theological School.

+**Theological seminary.** A divinity school; a school in which students are trained in theology. — **1810** in *Union Theol. Sem. Va. Centennial Cat.* (1907) 7 It was chiefly from a regard to a theological seminary lately established at this place that I was induced to accept the presidency of Hampden-Sidney College. **1847** WEBSTER 635/2 *Junior,* . . . one in the first year of his course at a theological seminary. **1877** *Harper's Mag.* March 563/1 He had in the theological seminary cultivated a native talent . . . for the purpose of illuminating prayer and psalm books. **1915** *Current Opin.* Feb. 113/1 His reportorial preconception of theological seminaries got a jolt.

+**Thermal belt.** A limited area on the sloping side of a mountain in which the vegetation escapes, at least in part, frost damage. Also *thermal zone.* — **1862** *Rep. Comm. Patents 1861: Agric.* 146 The beautiful phenomenon of the 'Verdant Zone' or 'Thermal Belt' exhibits itself upon our mountain sides, commencing about three hundred feet vertical height above the valleys. **1883** ZEIGLER & GROSSCUP *Alleghanies* 192 Horticulturists are just beginning to appreciate the advantages of the thermal or 'no frost' zone.

Thermal deposit. A deposit of material resulting from volcanic action or the eruption of hot matter from the earth. — **1871** *Scribner's Mo.* II. 15/1 Around these immense thermal deposits, the country . . . is filled with boiling springs.

Thermal spring. =HOT SPRING. {1800-} — **1821** NUTTALL *Trav. Arkansa* 216 Many thermal springs . . . are seen boiling out of the side of the hill. **1843** *Nat. Hist. N.Y., Geology* I. 104 The thermal springs at Bath, Virginia, . . . have nearly the same geological relations as those of New-York. **1854** BARTLETT *Personal Narr.* II. 25 We crossed the valley to examine some thermal springs.

Thermal zone. (See THERMAL BELT.)

+**Thermolamp.** A device for supplying illumination by the use of inflammable gas. — **1802** *Med. Repository* V. 474 The theory of the Thermolamp . . . merely consists of exposing . . . any thing that contains carbon and phlogiston, to a high heat, in a close apparatus. **1805** SILLIMAN *Jrnl. Travels* (1812) I. 237 It is the same thing with the thermo-lamp of which you have heard much in America.

Thermometer. An instrument for ascertaining temperatures. {1633-} — **1721** *Mass. H. S. Coll.* 4 Ser. II. 165, I know of no Thermometer nor Barometer in [Boston]. **1789** *Mass. Spy* 20 Aug. 3/2 The Thermometer stood yesterday . . . at 92 degrees. **1820** *Columbian Centinel* 15 Jan. 3/1 James W. Burditt . . . has for sale Thermometers of various sizes and prices. **1890** *Stock Grower & Farmer* 19 July 4/3 Reliable thermometers in Atchison have registered from 102 to 104 today. **1907** *St. Nicholas* July 780/1 When the thermometer . . . registers four degrees below zero at noon it means cold weather.

+**Theses collector.** (See quot. 1814.) *Obs.* — **1759** *Holyoke Diaries* 20 Theses Collectors, (John) Lowell, (John) Warren. **1814** *Harvard Laws* 35 The president, professors, tutors, annually, sometime in the third term, shall select from the junior class a number of theses collectors, to prepare theses for the next year.

Thespian society. A society of amateur actors and actresses. — **1845** SOL. SMITH *Theatr. Apprent.* 36, I never knew any good to come from Thespian societies. **1848** *Santa Fe Repub.* 8 Jan. 4/3 Thespian Society.— A society of this kind has been formed in our town. **1863** MASSETT *Drifting About* 21 A lot of young students started a Thespian Society.

Thibet. (See TIBET.)

+**Thick-bark(ed) juniper.** The alligator juniper (*Juniperus pachyphloea*) of the southwestern United States. — [**1857** *Rep. Explorations*

Pacific R.R. (War Dept.) IV. 142 On the Zuñi Mountains, Western New Mexico, . . . is the thick-barked Juniperus.] **1885** HAVARD *Flora W. & S. Texas* 503 Thick-bark Juniper . . . furnishes . . . a yellow, aromatic, transparent balsam. **1897** SUDWORTH *Arborescent Flora* 99.

+**Thick-billed guillemot.** (See quot. 1917.) — **1835** AUDUBON *Ornith. Biol.* III. 142 The Foolish Guillemot . . . lays only a single egg, which is the case with the Thick-billed Guillemot also. **1873** [see GUILLEMOT]. **1917** *Birds of Amer.* I. 27 Brünnich's Murre. *Uria lomvia lomvia.* . . . [Also called] Thick-billed Guillemot; Thick-billed Murre. . . . Similar to common Murre . . . ; bill, shorter and stouter.

＊**Thicken,** v. +**1. a.** *intr.* Of ice: To continue to freeze so as to become increasingly thick. **b.** *tr.* To increase the population of (an area). **2.** *To thicken up,* +to become angry. *colloq.* — (1) **1808** PIKE *Sources Miss.* 42 Ice in the river thickening. **1814** BRACKENRIDGE *Views La.* 116 It is perhaps good policy in our government . . . to thicken the frontier, and to suffer the intermediate space to fill up gradually. (2) **1841** COOPER *Deerslayer* iii, You're not thick'ning up about a small remark, I hope. **1844** '*UNCLE SAM*' *Peculiarities* I. 161, I don't thicken up without calculation.

＊**Thicket.** A dense growth of shrubs, bushes, or small trees. — **1612** SMITH, etc. *Virginia* I. 35 A myle from Orapakes in a thicket of wood, hee hath a house. **1723** *New-Eng. Courant* 21 Oct. 2/2 One of them being in a Thicket of Bushes, with a Deer-Skin Bag ty'd to his Side, the other . . . took it for a Deer. **1789** MORSE *Amer. Geog.* 381 Deer are seen through the thickets. **1836** in *Jrnl. Southern Hist.* I. 367, I have been . . . wandering about in pine thickets—cane thickets, and all sorts of thickets. **1907** *St. Nicholas* July 791/1 They broke through a thicket into an open space set with grand trees.

+**Thick-joint.** A variety of tobacco. *Obs.* — *c*1775 BOUCHER *Glossary* p. l, In *twist-bud, thick-joint, bull-face, leather-coat,* I'd toil all day. **1784** [see THICKSET 2].

Thickset. 1. A strong cotton cloth resembling velveteen. *Obs.* {1756-} Also attrib. +**2.** A variety of tobacco. *Obs.* — (1) **1714** *Boston News-Letter* 8 March 2/2 To be Sold . . . very good Thicksetts of all colours. **1762** *Essex Inst. Coll.* XLIX. 277 Had on . . . a Pair of Snuff-colour'd Thickset Breeches. **1809** [see JEAN I]. (2) **1784** SMYTH *Tour* II. 129 There are seven different kinds of tobacco, . . . named . . . Thickjoint, Shoe-string, Thickset [etc.].

+**Thick shellbark hickory.** The king nut, *Carya laciniosa.* — **1810** MICHAUX *Arbres* I. 20 *Thick shell-bark hickery,* . . . nom donné dans les Etats de l'ouest où elle est le plus souvent confonde avec le vrai *Shell bark Hickery.* **1819** E. DANA *Geogr. Sk.* 237 Growing in the Attacapas and Opelousas region [are] . . . water hickory, thick shell bark hickory. **1897** [see KING NUT].

＊**Thimble.**

＊**1.** A caplike covering worn over the end of the finger in sewing.

1649 *Conn. Rec.* I. 497 The Estate of Mr. William Whiting: . . . thimbles, boxes, kniues [etc.]. **1711** *Springfield Rec.* II. 42 Three dozen & one of thimbles at 2d ye thimble. **1845** *Knickerb.* XXV. 444 On one [needle] . . . was my aunt's steel thimble. **1907** *St. Nicholas* July 801/2 'Willis Hunter,' she declared, springing up and sending her thimble and spool flying.

+**b.** In the names of games.

1782 DALRYMPLE *Journal* 36 We have diverted ourselves playing . . . hide the thimble. **1833** *Sketches D. Crockett* 49 Plays which had been fashionable when their grandmothers were girls, such as Sell the Thimble . . . were called up and wearied out.

+**2.** A short piece of metal tubing attached to the under side of the barrel of a muzzle-loading gun for securing the ramrod.

1835 LONGSTREET *Ga. Scenes* 227 The thimbles were made, one of brass, one of iron, and one of tin. *a*1918 G. STUART *On Frontier* I. 33 From two to four small pieces of iron or brass tubing [were] called thimbles.

3. In special combinations.

Thimble bell, a small ornamental bell resembling a thimble; *t. belt,* a belt having loops for cartridges; *t. bibb,* a cock or faucet resembling a thimble; *t. blackberry,* a blackberry having fruit shaped like a thimble; *t. fish, t. flower,* (see quotations); *t. party,* a sewing party; *t. skein,* a conical sheath for the spindle of an axle; *t. thrift,* petty thrift.

1899 CUSHMAN *Hist. Indians* 501 The monotonous tinkling and rattling of the thimble bells and terrapin shells [in the dance] could be heard. **1901** *N. Amer. Rev.* Feb. 231 The thimble belt, used only by the Americans, is still preferred to the cartridge pouches of the others. **1897** F. C. MOORE *How to Build a Home* 124 Supply with hot and cold water through ⅜-inch flange and thimble bibbs. **1883** *Century Mag.* Sept. 681/2 The tall thimble blackberries grew in abundance. **1885** J. S. KINGSLEY, etc. *Stand. Nat. Hist.* I. 93 One of the most abundant medusæ at times in the neighborhood of the Florida Keys is a Discophore, called by naturalists *Linerges,* and known to fishermen there as the 'thimble-fish.' **1840** DEWEY *Mass. Flowering Plants* 140 R[udbeckia] laciniata. Often called Thimble Flower, from the length and size of the cone-part of the flower. **1906** *Springfield W. Repub.* 7 Feb. 5 The women of Christ church will hold a thimble party. **1865** *Chicago Tribune* 10 April, Manufacturers of Leonard's Patent Seamless Thimble Skeins. **1910** C. HARRIS *Eve's Husband* 286 [In] women's characters . . . penuriousness . . . has been reduced . . . to a sort of thimble thrift.

+**Thimbleberry.** Any one of various American raspberries or black-berries having fruit shaped like a thimble. — **1814** BIGELOW *Florula Bostoniensis* 121 Black raspberry. Thimbleberry.... Fruit black, sprightly and pleasant to the taste. **1853** *Harper's Mag.* April 582/2 The thimbleberry is a large and luscious species of raspberry, destitute of briars. **1897** *Outing* XXX. 552/1 [We] eat the thimble-berries on its banks for dessert. **1920** HOWELLS *Vacation of Kelwyns* 161 They would not find any thimbleberries on that road.

Thimble-eye. {1867–} + = next. — **1884** GOODE, etc. *Fisheries* I. 303 The Chub Mackerel, ... or, as it is called, the 'Thimble-eye,' ... closely resembles in general appearance the common Mackerel. **1911** *Rep. Fisheries* 308/1.

+**Thimble-eye(d) mackerel.** = CHUB MACKEREL. — **1815** *Lit. & Phil. Soc. N.Y. Trans.* I. 422 Thimble eyed, bull eyed, or chub mackerel. (*Scomber grex.*)... Comes occasionally in prodigious numbers to the coast of New-York in autumn. **1884** GOODE, etc. *Fisheries* I. 304 The 'Thimble-eye Mackerel,' or 'Mixed Mackerel,' were very plentiful from 1826 to 1830. **1897** *N.Y. Forest, Fish, & Game Comm. 2d Rep.* 236 Thimble-Eye Mackerel ... in 1896 ... abounded in all the little creeks.

+**Thimbleweed.** 1. An American plant of the genus *Anemone.* 2. Any one of various plants of the genus *Rudbeckia.* — (1) **1833** EATON *Botany* (ed. 6) 19 *Anemone virginiana*, wind-flower, thimble weed. **1843** TORREY *Flora N.Y.* I. 8 Thimble-weed.... One of the numerous plants supposed to possess the power of curing the bite of the rattlesnake. **1893** *Amer. Folk-Lore* VI. 136 *Anemone Virginiana*, thimble-weed. West Va. (2) **1848** BARTLETT 354 *Thimble Weed* ... is one of the herbs prepared by the Shakers, and is used in medicine for its diuretic and tonic properties.

+**Thin grass.** Any one of various plants of the genus *Agrostis* having unusually thin panicles. Also with specifying term. — **1814** BIGELOW *Florula Bostoniensis* 22 *Trichodium laxiflorum*, Thingrass, ... is readily known by its very thin, spreading, capillary panicle. **1843** TORREY *Flora N.Y.* II. 442 *Agrostis laxiflora....* Thin-grass.... Old fields and exsiccated swamps: very common. **1857** GRAY *Botany* 543 *A. elata.* (Taller Thin-Grass.) ... Swamps, New Jersey and southward.... *A. perennans.* (Thin-Grass.) ... Damp shaded places. **1901** MOHR *Plant Life Ala.* 76 Thin grass (*Agrostis perennans*) with its weak, decumbent stems, occurs [in the 'rock houses' of the Warrior table-land].

***Think,** *v.* + *To think up,* to decide upon, devise, or arrive at by thinking. *colloq.* — **1855** STOWE *Tales New Eng. Life* 79, I have got to think up presents for everybody. **1885** *Century Mag.* Jan. 350/1, I believe she is thinking up another poem. **1912** WASON *Friar Tuck* xxvii, [We] called Badger-face Prometheus every time we could think up an excuse.

***Third,** *a.*

+**1.** *ellipt.* = THIRD BASE.
1858 *Chadwick Scrapbook* (E. J. Nichols). **1891** *Cent.* 6294/1 *Third,* ... in base-ball, same as *third base.* **1904** BARBOUR *Sch. & Coll. Sports* 191 The 'hit-and-run' play may also be used when there is a man on third and a run is badly needed. **1917** MATHEWSON *Second Base Sloan* 246 The Billies caused consternation by ... advancing a man to third on a sacrifice and an error.

||**2.** *To play third fiddle,* to occupy an inferior position. *colloq.* (Cf. SECOND FIDDLE.)
1866 'MARK TWAIN' *Lett. Sandwich Islands* 9 America ... is out in the cold now, and does not even play third fiddle to this European element.

+**3.** In special combinations.
See also the separate entries which follow, esp. THIRD TERM.
Third classman, in the United States Naval Academy, a student in his second year; *t. clerk,* on a river steamboat, a clerk ranking below the first and second clerks; *t. strike,* in baseball, the final strike permitted a batter; *t. termer,* one holding, or aspiring to hold, the presidency for the third time; *t.-termery,* something suggesting, or partaking of the nature of, a third term; *t.-termism,* devotion to or advocacy of a third term.
1888 DORSEY *Midshipman Bob* 128 His class-mates backed him to a man, ... and even the third-classmen were divided. **1883** 'MARK TWAIN' *Life on Miss.* xxxvii, Among the forty-seven wounded were the captain, chief mate, second mate, and second and third clerks. **1886** CHADWICK *Art of Pitching* 15 Batsmen frequently find opportunities to punish the mere swift pitching by quick wrist-play batting long before the third strike is called from it. **1912** *N.Y. Herald* 13 June 3/7 (Ernst), A third termer [T. Roosevelt]. **1890** *Cincinnati Commercial-Gaz.* 30 June, There would be no thirdtermery in it, as he [Cleveland] had not two consecutive terms. **1896** *Sun* (N.Y.) 2 Sept. (Ernst.), Third termism.

+**Third base.** *Baseball.* The base to the pitcher's right as he faces the home plate; the playing position centering on this base. — **1845** in *Appletons' Ann. Cycl.* XXV. 77/2 A ball knocked outside the range of the first or third base is foul. **1880** N. BROOKS *Fairport Nine* 24 At the third base he was perhaps the very best in all Fairport. **1897** *Outing* May 202/2 Ward and Gunter have left vacant the positions of short-stop and third base. **1912** [see CALL *v.* 5 d].

+**Third baseman.** *Baseball.* A player stationed at third base. — **1868** CHADWICK *Base Ball* 34 The third baseman has the most important and arduous task to perform of the three positions. **1875** *Chicago Tribune* 22 Aug. 9/3 Charley Smith, in past years third baseman of the Atlantics. **1897** [see OUTFIELDER].

Third class. {1839–}
+**1.** The classification of United States mail which includes printed matter other than newspapers and periodicals. Also attrib.

1863 *Stat. at Large* XII. 705 The third class embraces ... all pamphlets, occasional publications, books, ... maps, prints, engravings, ... cards, ... seeds, cuttings, bulbs, [etc.]. **1879** *Ib.* XX. 361 (in margin) Second, third, and fourth-class matter containing writing, etc. **1894** Third class rate [see CLIPPING 2].

2. Attrib. in general sense: Poor, inferior.
1866 *Rep. Indian Affairs* 288 The soil is extremely light and divided into ridges of sand and marsh, ... which may be called third-class farming land. **1902** *Harper's Mag.* May 879/1 It is too late to make a third-class student of me.

+**Thirdling law.** (See quotation.) Now hist. — **1862** *Harper's Mag.* April 715/1 A law of the State [of Georgia] at that time, called a thirdling law, allowed a man to pay one-third of a judgment against him in cash.

Third party. {1818–}
+**1.** *Polit.* A party organized as an independent rival of the two major parties, often in the interest of specified reforms.
1801 F. AMES *Works* (1854) II. 138 There are but two divisions of party in the United States; and he is a very weak or very presumptuously vain man, who can think of organizing a third party, that shall rule them both. **1815** *Niles' Reg.* IX. 188 The *third* party in that state [Pa.] have not one member we believe, in either branch. **1884** *Century Mag.* Nov. 132 The formulation of these 'third-parties' ... is on the whole a public misfortune. **1914** [see QUID].

+**2.** Attrib. with *candidate, gentry, movement,* etc.
1806 FESSENDEN *Democracy Unveiled* II. 158 The Third Party gentry of Pennsylvania ... have made violent news-paper attacks on most of their quondam friends and associates. **1840** Third-party project [see PENNY 3 a]. **1868** *N.Y. Herald* 10 July 6/5 Van Buren ... took the field as a third-party candidate on his independent free-soil Buffalo platform. **1884** *Century Mag.* Nov. 150 The only 'third party' movement of note has been captured by a 'politician' who repudiates civil service reform. **1887** *Boston Jrnl.* 23 Aug. 5/4 Some of the well-meaning people who have gone daft upon third party prohibition may not understand it. **1892** *Courier-Journal* 2 Oct. 2/2 A Small Third-Party Rally.

||**Third partyism.** Advocacy or support of a third party. — **1845** *Xenia Torch-Light* 31 July 3/3 The editor of the Voice of Freedom ... [has] manfully renounced his third partyism.

Third term. An additional term of office for a candidate who has already served two terms. +With reference to the presidency of the United States. Also attrib. — **1833** *Niles' Reg.* XLV. 202/2 A late preposterous suggestion that president Jackson may be induced to stand for a third term of the presidency. **1875** *Courier-Journal* 4 May 3/2 The Third-Term Business. **1888** BRYCE *Amer. Commonw.* II. ii. xlix. 103 In those [states] which do not [limit the governor's re-eligibility] there seems to exist no tradition forbidding a third term. **1892** WALSH *Lit. Curiosities* 114 In 1879 ... the Grant third-term movement was started. **1912** *Lit. Digest* XLV. 892 The nation's interpolation: 'I shall not be a (successful) candidate for a third term.'

Third tier. In a theater, a third balcony or gallery, formerly sometimes set aside especially for prostitutes. — **1870** O. LOGAN *Before Footlights* 537 It is within my own recollection that the hideous abomination known as the 'third tier' was in existence in our theatres. **1878** DALY in J. F. Daly *A. Daly* 249 There is a 'Nigger Heaven' (as the third tier is called in Troy) here.

Thirstland(s). A region of arid lands. {1895–, in Africa} — **1889** FARMER 532/1 The region of extinct lakes and inland seas of Southern Nevada and South-eastern California is the great *thirstland* of the continent. **1899** GOING *Flowers* 153 The running mesquit of Arizona and the alkali-grass of the plains help to hold in place the shifting soils of the great thirst-lands.

Thirteener. {1762–} Something or someone left over: (see quot. 1891). — **1849** MELVILLE *Redburn* 56 They were all chosen but me; ... I was a thirteener. **1891** *Cent.* 6295/2 *Thirteener,* ... in whist, the last card of a suit left in the hands of a player after the other twelve have been played.

+**Thirteen fires.** In Indian speech, the original thirteen states of the Federal Union. *Obs.* — **1789** in Cist *Cincinnati* (1841) 213 The chief ... wished to be informed ... whether the thirteen fires had sent me hither. I ... spread before them the thirteen fires, which I had in a flag then in my camp. **1847** HOWE *Hist. Coll. Ohio* 142 Their people ... determined to make a permanent peace with the 'Thirteen Fires,' as they called the federal states.

+**Thirteen states.** The original states making up the Federal Union. Also *thirteen original (or united) states.* — **1776** *Decl. Independence,* The unanimous Declaration of the thirteen united States of America. **1806** *Ann. 9th Congress* 1 Sess. 558 The true territory of the United States, ... the good old United States—part of Georgia, of the old thirteen States—where citizens have been taken, not from our ships, but from our actual territory. **1851** *Harper's Mag.* July 274/1 He would never consent that there should be one foot of slave-territory beyond what the old Thirteen States had. **1886** ALTON *Among Law-Makers* 10 The people of the thirteen original states were represented in the House by sixty-five members.

+**Thirty-six thirty.** The degree of latitude agreed upon in the Missouri Compromise as that north of which no slave state except Missouri would be formed from the Louisiana territory. — **1857** BENTON *Exam. Dred Scott Case* 150 Northern men who would not agree to spread slavery over the broad expanse of all that half of California, New Mexico, and

Utah, which lies south of 36°30'. **1865** PIKE *Scout & Ranger* (1932) 105 We pushed on . . . to the famous line of 36°30'.

***Thistle.**

***1.** Any one of various prickly plants, usually of the family Carduaceae.

1671 in Alvord & Bidgood *Trans-Allegheny Region* 192 [Ground was] grown up with . . . small prickly Locusts and Thistles to a very great height. **1737** BRICKELL *N. Carolina* 22 Sarsaparilla, White Hellebor, several sorts of Thistles, Fern, Male and Female, Liquorice. **1805** LEWIS in *L. & Clark Exped.* II. (1904) 263 [We] saw a great abundance of the common thistle. **1894** ALLEN *Ky. Cardinal* ix, Everything is an impenetrable thicket of weeds and vines—blackberry, thistle, ironweed [etc.]. **1914** E. STEWART *Lett. Woman Homesteader* 108 In one window was an old brown pitcher, cracked and nicked, filled with thistles.

2. In special combinations.

Thistle-digger, t.-leaved salvia, (see quotations); *t.-plume*, (see quotation); *t. poppy*, a prickly poppy; *t. sage*, (see quotation); *t. spud*, a tool for uprooting thistles. {1896}

1876 KNIGHT 2251/2 The thistle-digger is a pronged tool, intended to catch the root below the crown, and then pry out the plant. **1898** A. M. DAVIDSON *Calif. Plants* 146 There is another Salvia, the big chia, or the thistle-leaved Salvia. **1891** *Cent.* 6297/1 *Thistle-plume*, a plume-moth *Pterophorus carduidactylus*, whose larva feeds on thistle-heads. **1915** ARMSTRONG & THORNBER *Western Wild Flowers* 162 Thistle Poppy. Milk Thistle. *Argemone hispida*. . . . This grows in dry places. *Ib.* 450 Thistle Sage, Persian Prince. *Salvia carduacea*. . . . The plants when they are crushed give out a rather heavy smell of sage. **1891** CHASE & CLOW *Industry* II. 41 Farmers . . . carry a narrow, chisel-edged thistle-spud to cut them [*s.c.*, teazels] instead.

+**Thistle bird.** A goldfinch. — **1808** WILSON *Ornithology* I. 21 [Goldfinches] pass by various names . . . such as Thistle-bird, Lettuce-bird. **1893** *Scribner's Mag.* June 763/1 'Thistle bird' is another name that he bears. **1917** *Birds of Amer.* III. 15 The habit of feeding on thistles . . . has given the species the common name of 'Thistle Bird.'

+**Thlack.** *S.W.* =TLACO. — *a***1892** in *Dialect Notes* I. 252 Two thlacks are equivalent to two and a quarter cents of our money.

+**Thomas('s) elm.** [David *Thomas*, of New York State.] The rock elm (*Ulmus racemosa*) of the eastern states. — **1843** TORREY *Flora N.Y.* II. 166 *Ulmus Racemosa*. . . . Thomas's Elm. White Elm. . . . Banks of rivers in the western part of the State; rather frequent. **1846** BROWNE *Trees Amer.* p. x/1 **1897** SUDWORTH *Arborescent Flora* 182 Cork Elm. . . . Thomas Elm (Tenn.).

+**Thom(p)sonian,** *n.* [Dr. Samuel *Thomson*, of Massachusetts (1769–1843).] A believer in or practitioner of the Thomsonian system of medicine. Now hist. — **1848** DUNGLISON *Med. Lexicon* 833/1 The Thompsonians are Botanic Physicians. **1850** COLTON *3 Years Calif.* 61 The Indians here are practical Thomsonians or Hydropathists; they sweat for every kind of disease. **1864** NICHOLS *Amer. Life* I. 364 There are . . . chronothermalists, Thompsonians, Mesmerists [etc.].

+**Thom(p)sonian,** *a.* Of or pertaining to a system of medicine characterized by the use of vegetable preparations and steam baths. Now hist. — **1832** (*title*), Thomsonian Recorder [Cincinnati]. **1859** BARTLETT 477 *Thompsonian Doctor*, a physician who follows the Thompsonian practice; also called Steam Doctor. **1877** *Ib.* 702 *Thomsonian System*, a peculiar treatment of diseases, so named from its inventor.

+**Thom(p)sonianism.** The Thomsonian medical system. Now hist. — **1847** *S. Lit. Messenger* XIII. 567/1 There are Medical Schools in Winchester and the City of Richmond; and there are rumors of others founded not only upon the approved principles of Medical Science, but also upon those of Thompsonianism and quackery. **1894** *Outing* XXIV. 332 Dr. Reed, do you believe in the mind cure—Thompsonianism—metallic tractors?

***Thong.** A narrow strip of hide used as a cord or strap. Also attrib. — **1676** *Conn. Rec.* III. 500 Disbursements for . . . thongs, neck cloths, pins, needles. **1790** *Penna. Packet* 2 Feb. 4/1 To be Sold by Jeffe Sharpless, at his Saddle Manufactory, . . . Best crops and thong whips. **1805** LEWIS in *L. & Clark Exped.* II. (1904) 376 For nails . . . we substitute throngs [*sic*] of raw hide which answer verry well. **1867** *Amer. Naturalist* I. 287 An elegant arrow-case . . . is slung by a thong. **1916** THOBURN *Stand. Hist. Okla.* I. 265 Each player used a pair of long-handled racquets or ball sticks, having a cup-shaped loop of thinly scraped hickory, loosely laced with buckskin thongs, at the end.

+**Thorite.** [*Thor* and *ite*.] (See quot. 1909.) *Obs.* — **1899** *Boston Transcript* 20 July 12/7 The final trials of thorite will take place within a few weeks. **1909** *Cent. Suppl.* 1344/3 *Thorite*, . . . an explosive of the ammonium-nitrate class once experimented with as a bursting charge for shell.

***Thorn.** In special combinations.

Thorn cane, a walking cane made of a thorn plant; *t. locust*, the common North American honey locust; *t. plum*, any one of various species of hawthorn; *t. walk*, a walk bordered by thorn bushes.

1807 IRVING, etc. *Salmagundi* xv. 393 [He carried] a gold-headed thorn cane, bequeathed him by his uncle John. **1893** *Amer. Folk-Lore* VI. 140 *Gleditschia triacanthus*, the common locust. N.Y. **1897** SUDWORTH *Arborescent Flora* 216 *Cratægus crus-galli*. Cockspur. . . . Thorn Plum (Me.). *Ib.* 219 *Cratægus coccinea*. Scarlet Haw. . . . Thorn Plum (Me., Vt., N.Y.). *Ib.* 230 *Cratægus tomentosa*. Black Haw. . . . Thorn Plum. **1887** FREDERIC *Seth's Brother's Wife* 368 Samantha met her, half-way down the thorn walk.

***Thorn apple.**

***1.** Any one of various plants of the genus *Datura*, as *D. stramonium*.

*c***1770** *Amer. Philos. Soc.* I. 384 An account of the effects of the Strammonium, or Thorn-Apple, by Benjamin Rush, M.D. **1802** DRAYTON *S. Carolina* 63 Thorn apple, (*Datura tatula*,) grows near dung hills, and other loose rich high grounds. **1857** GRAY *Lessons Botany* 100 Take, for example, the flower of the Stramonium or Thorn-Apple. **1893** F. DANA *Wild Flowers* 104 Thorn-Apple. Jamestown-Weed. . . . The plant . . . was introduced into our country from Asia.

+**2.** Any one of various haws or their fruit.

1817 S. BROWN *Western Gazetteer* 322 The plants and shrubs [include] . . . pennyroyal, thorn apple, wild hops. **1844** LEE & FROST *Oregon* 89 The natural fruit of this valley is much the same . . . as that upon the Clatsop Plain . . . , with the addition of wild cherries, red and black, and the thorn-apple. **1881** *Amer. Naturalist* XV. 151 The larva of this Longicorn beetle infests what we call thorn apple or red haw. **1897** SUDWORTH *Arborescent Flora* 215–6, 219, 230.

***Thornback.** One of various skates or sticklebacks found in the United States. — **1674** *Cal. State P., Amer. & W.I.* VII. 581 [In] Maine . . . there are infinite quantities of fish, such as bass, . . . smelts, thornback, eels, herrings, capelin. **1806** [see SKATE *n.*¹]. **1903** T. H. BEAN *Fishes N.Y.* 343 In Great South Bay the four spined stickleback is called thornback.

***Thorn bush.** Any one of various bushes, esp. of the genus *Cratægus*, that bear thorns. Also attrib. — **1699** *Essex Inst. Coll.* XXXVI. 66 Whear a stump stands . . . vpon the northerly sied of the thorn bushes. **1759** *Newport Mercury* 8 May 1/1 Plough it in, and harrow it . . . with a Thorn-bush Harrow. **1784** *Amer. Acad. Mem.* I. 450. **1818** *Amer. Jrnl. Science* I. 369 June 3. . . . Thorn-bush (*Cratægus coccinea*) in flower. **1897** SUDWORTH *Arborescent Flora* 216, 219.

+**Thorntail snake.** =HORN SNAKE. *Obs.* Also *thorn-tailed snake.* — **1778** CARVER *Travels* 486 The Thorn-Tail Snake . . . receives its name from a thorn-like dart in its tail. **1836** EDWARD *Hist. Texas* 76 One will meet with . . . a speckled snake, or a thorntailed snake.

***Thorn tree.** Any one of various spiny trees, as a hawthorn or honey locust. — **1817–8** EATON *Botany* (1822) 255. **1852** WATSON *Nights in Block-House* 214 He provided himself with a stout switch, taken from a thorn-tree. **1895** *Atlantic Mo.* July 61 The thorn-tree before me was perhaps fifteen feet high.

***Thorny,** *a.* In the names of various plants and shells having thorns or spines. — **1847** DARLINGTON *Weeds & Plants* 180 *Spinose Xanthium*. Thorny Clot-bur. . . . This execrable weed . . . is becoming naturalized in many portions of our country. **1859** BARTLETT 200 In the West and South it [*sc.* the honey locust] is called the Thorny Locust. **1869** *Amer. Naturalist* III. 464 Here also abound not only many smaller molluscous animals . . . , but the Thorny Conch (*Melongena corona*).

+**Thorogummite.** [f. *thorium* and *gummite*.] A hydrous silicate of uranium and thorium. — **1889** *Amer. Jrnl. Science* 3 Ser. Dec. 481 We name this mineral *thoro-gummite*, because it is a gummite in which the water has been replaced by the thorite molecule. **1891** *Cent.* 6301/1 *Thorogummite* . . . occurs with gadolinite and other rare minerals in Llano county, Texas.

+**Thorough-brace. 1.** One of a number of strong leather straps supporting the body of a passenger vehicle, as a stagecoach. Also attrib. **2.** A stagecoach. *Obs.* — (1) **1837** MARTINEAU *Society* II. 175 The thorough-brace broke, and we had to walk. **1886** *Leslie's Mo.* June 744/1 His wedding trip was made in a 'thorough brace' coach. **1894** ROBINSON *Danvis Folks* 19 Dr. Wead, watching the bent figure from the height of his sulky-seat, rocking on its leathern thorough-braces, remarked. (2) **1886** *Leslie's Mo.* Dec. 722/1 The mustangs looked worse than the thorough-brace itself.

+**Thorough-braced,** *a.* Built with or supported on thorough-braces. — **1869** J. R. BROWNE *Adv. Apache Country* 445 Scouts were sent out all over the town of Aurora to secure the best wheeled vehicle . . . , preference to be given to a thorough-braced ambulance of Concord manufacture. **1884** JEWETT *Country Doctor* 19 The old-fashioned thorough-braced wagon.

***Thoroughfare.**

1. A strait or other body of water affording a passage for boats or ships {1699-}; +spec., a river or waterway connecting two lakes or bays. {1896, in Canada}

1699 in *Amer. Sp.* XV. 402/2 Three thousand acres of Land . . . in Accomack County on the sea side . . . bounded . . . by a Thorowfare then by a great bay or Sound unto a gutt. **1724** *Ib.* 403/1 A Beach . . . on the side of a hill by the thorough fair of the Broad Run under the foot of the Biscake Mountain. **1804** C. B. BROWN tr. Volney *View* 18 All their thoughts tend, like the great thoroughfares, their rivers, to the Gulph of Mexico. **1848** THOREAU *Maine Woods* 35 After one mile of river, or what the boatmen call 'thoroughfare,'—for the river becomes at length only the connecting link between the lakes,— . . . we entered the North Twin Lake . . . , and steered across for the river 'thoroughfare,' four miles distant. **1895** *Outing* XXVI. 484/1 Mr. Iselin sent Captain Haff down among the 'thorofares' of the Maine Islands.

+**b.** (See quotation.)

1878 C. HALLOCK *Sportsman's Gazetteer* (1883) p. xi/2 *Thoroughfare*, a strait of water, or neck of land connecting two bodies of water, habitually traversed by wild fowl in migrating or passing to and from their feeding-grounds.

+2. (See quot. 1859.)

1730 in *Amer. Sp.* XV. 403/1 Opposite to the lower Gap or Thoroughfare of the aforementioned Blew Ridge. . . . At a place called the meeting house by a gap or thoroughfare of the mountains. **1859** BARTLETT 477 *Thoroughfare,* a low gap between mountains; as, 'Thoroughfare gap' in Fauquier county, Virginia. 'Thoroughfare mountain.' Southern.

3. Attrib. in sense 1 with *branch, creek, gut, run.* Sometimes as proper name.

1700 in *Amer. Sp.* XV. 403/1 Bounded on Each Side with the said Piscataway Creek and a Gutt, Called a Thoroughfare gutt running on the Lower Side of the Sd. three acres of woods. **1725** *Ib.* 403/1 Crossing the Thoroughfair branch of Ceadar run, to a red Oak. **1751** *Ib.* 453 Along the said Marsh Side to the Mouth of a Creek commonly called and known by the Name of the Thoroughfare Creek. **1765** *Ib.* 403/2 At Three White Oaks standing on The South Side of Hughes's Thoroughfare Run.

+Thoroughgoer. A person or thing of a superior or thoroughgoing type. — **1895** *Outing* XXVI. 388/1 [The polo ponies] are such thoroughgoers in the field that it is difficult to say this or the other is best. **1897** STUART *Simpkinsville* 155 [The widow is] a reg'lar business thorough-goer, she is.

+Thoroughwort. Any one of various species of *Eupatorium,* esp. the boneset, *E. perfoliatum.* — **1814** BIGELOW *Florula Bostoniensis* 190 *Eupatorium perfoliatum,* Thoroughwort, Boneset, . . . has acquired great medicinal reputation. **1887** WILKINS *Humble Romance* 280 There were . . . the great white corymbs of thoroughwort. **1906** A. BROWN in *Harper's Mag.* Oct. 712 [To] the boggy place . . . she came in all warm seasons of the year for one thing or another: the wild marsh-marigold, . . . thoroughwort, and the root of the sweet-flag.

+Thoroughwort tea. Tea prepared from the leaves of one or other species of thoroughwort. — **1863** RANDALL *Pract. Shepherd* 150 The tonic contained in half a dozen teaspoonfulls of . . . thoroughwort (*Eupatorium perfoliatum*) tea, has an excellent effect. **1877** *Vt. Dairymen's Ass. Rep.* VIII. 54 He had a cow which he thought he cured by dosing with thoroughwort tea. **1887** WILKINS *Humble Romance* 84, I'll hev to fix me up some thoroughwort tea.

Thousand. *Typog.* (See quotation.) — **1865** *Harper's Mag.* Dec. 10/1 A 'thousand' is not that number of letters, but the space occupied by a thousand of the letter m.

+Thrasher.¹ [Var. of Eng. dial. *thrusher, thresher* (a thrush), modified in U.S. by the influence of THRASHER.²] Any of several American birds of the family Mimidae, related to the mocking bird; esp. a bird of the genus *Toxostoma.*

1810 WILSON *Ornithology* II. 84 The Thrasher is a welcome visitant in spring. **1877** *Harper's Mag.* April 662/1 [The catbird] brings forth sounds as mellow and as powerful as those of the thrasher and mocking-bird. **1903** *Atlantic Mo.* July 31 In the copses the thrasher chants and trills.

+b. With specifying terms. (See also BROWN THRASHER.)

1898 APGAR *Birds U.S.* 64 The Curve-billed Thrasher . . . of Mexico and New Mexico has been found in Texas. **1917** *Birds of Amer.* III. 183 California Thrasher *Toxostoma redivivum.* . . . Coast and interior valleys of California. *Ib.* 175 On the sagebrush plains, or the ragged desert mountains of the West, the Sage Thrasher makes its home.

*Thrasher.² (See THRESHER.)

Thrashing machine. (See THRESHING MACHINE.)

*Thread. *attrib.*

1. Designating things made of linen or, sometimes, of cotton thread.

1637 *Md. Archives* IV. 76, 5. dozen of thread points. **1645** *Essex Inst. Coll.* L. 326, 1 pr. white knit thrid gloves. **1759** *Newport Mercury* 26 June 3/2 Just Imported, . . . Mens Cotton, Thread, and Worsted Hose. **1864** *Hist. North-Western Soldiers' Fair* 83 [Donations include] 1 boy's thread jacket.

2. Designating things used in handling thread.

1820 *Columbian Centinel* 5 Jan. 2/6 For Sale, . . . Thread Cases and Purses. **1864** *Hist. North-Western Soldiers' Fair* 162 [Donations include] 1 thread holder, 2 doll cushions.

3. In the specific names of fishes, animals, and plants.

See also THREADFISH, THREAD HERRING.

1896 JORDAN & EVERMANN *Check-List Fishes* 335 Polynemidæ. The Threadfins. **1817–8** EATON *Botany* (1822) 397 *Podostemum ceratophyllum,* thread-foot. . . . Attached to rocks and large loose stones in shallow waters. **1868** *Boston Soc. Nat. Hist. Proc.* XII. 100 On a Thread Worm (*Filaria anhingæ*) infesting the Brain of the Snake-bird.

Thread-and-needle. +Attrib. with *merchant, shop, store.* — **1839** BRIGGS *H. Franco* I. 128 Her part of the proceeds . . . set her up in an elegant thread and needle store in the Bowery. **1844** *Knickerb. Mag.* XXIV. 34 You may hear a thread-and-needle merchant counting up his charges. **1882** McCABE *New York* 270 Dry goods are exhibited in the modest thread and needle shops.

Threadfish. 1. =THREAD HERRING 1. **2.** A carangoid fish, *Alectis ciliaris.* **3.** Any fish of the family Polynemidae. — **(1)** **1842** *Nat. Hist. N.Y., Zoology* IV. 265 The Spotted Thread Herring . . . has also the names of Thread Herring and Thread-fish, in allusion to its last filamentous dorsal ray. **(2)** **1883** *Nat. Museum Bul.* No. 27, 500 *Blepharis crinitus.* . . . Thread-Fish. **1897** *N.Y. Forest, Fish, & Game Comm. 2d Rep.* 239 Thread-Fish . . . is occasional in summer in Gravesend Bay. **(3)** *a***1884** in Goode,

etc. *Fisheries* I. 279 The Thread-fish is rather common at Pensacola in summer. **1884** GOODE, etc. *Ib.,* The Thread-Fish Family—Polynemidæ.

+Thread herring.¹ 1. A species of herring (*Opisthonema oglinum*), of which the last ray of the dorsal fin is long and slender. **2.** A gizzard shad. — **(1)** **1842** [see THREADFISH 1]. **1855** BAIRD in *Smithsonian Rep. 1854* 349 The Thread-Herring. . . . A few specimens were caught in the bay. **1890** [see MENHADEN]. **(2)** **1884** GOODE, etc. *Fisheries* I. 610 In North Carolina [the mud shad is known] as the 'Hairy-back' or the 'Thread Herring.'

*Thread lace. Lace made of linen thread. Also attrib. — **1634** *Mass. Bay Rec.* I. 126 Noe person . . . shall hereafter make or buy any apparell, . . . with any lace on it, siluer, golde, silke, or threed. **1776** *N.J. Archives* 2 Ser. I. 195 Silk and thread lace, peelongs, persians. *a***1817** DWIGHT *Travels* I. 443 Silk and thread lace have been manufactured in Ipswich by women and children with better success. **1860** HOLMES *E. Venner* xiii, I don't believe you men know . . . whether a lady wears a ninepenny collar or a thread-lace cape worth a thousand dollars. **1881** M. J. HOLMES *Madeline* 140 The dreaded Mrs. Noah, in rustling black silk and a thread lace collar, sat sewing.

Thread stocking. A stocking made of thread, esp. of linen. {*c*1665-} — **1678** *New Castle Court Rec.* 350, 3 Payer of threed stockings. **1761** in H. M. Brooks *Gleanings* IV. 29 Silk, worsted, cotton, and thread Stockings. **1789** *Steele P.* I. 32 There is a pair of thread stockings . . . for Bob. **1838** *S. Lit. Messenger* IV. 638/1 [In summer a gentleman wore] thread or cotton stockings.

*Three, *a.*

+1. *Baseball.* **a.** With *bagger, base (hit), baser,* in reference to the number of bases made by a runner on a hit.

1871 *N.Y. Herald* 23 Aug. 8/4 Wolters also made a brace of beautiful 'three bases.' **1879** *Spirit of Times* 23 Aug. I, Three-base hit. **1881** *N.Y. Herald* 13 July 9/3 Daily led off with a beautiful three-baser, and was followed with . . . a three-bagger by Esterbrook.

+b. *Three strikes,* the number of strikes allowed the batter.

1878 *De Witt's Base-Ball Guide* 83 Should he fail to strike at or hit the next good ball 'three strikes' must be called.

2. Comb. with adjectives in *-ed* in the specific names of plants, fishes, etc.

1770 FORSTER tr. Kalm *Travels* I. 55 *Gleditsia triacanthos,* the honey locust tree, or three thorned acacia, [grows] in the same soil. **1814** MITCHILL *Fishes N.Y.* 449 Three-fingered Polyneme. *Polynemus tridigitatus.* **1818** *Mass. H. S. Coll.* 2 Ser. VIII. 168 Among our herbaceous wild plants, the first that appear are the delicate claytonia, the graceful three-lobed hepatica [etc.]. **1842** *Nat. Hist. N.Y., Zoology* IV. 98 The Banded Ephippus. *Ephippus faber.* . . . The popular names of Three-tailed Sheepshead, and Three-tailed Porgee, were given them . . . in allusion to their prolonged dorsal and anal fin. **1843** TORREY *Flora N.Y.* I. 207 *Potentilla tridentata,* Three-toothed Cinquefoil. **1876** C. V. RILEY *Potato Pests* 100 The Three-Lined Potato-Beetle, (*Lema trilineata,* Oliv.).

Three-ball game. A billiard game in which three balls are used. — **1869** 'MARK TWAIN' *Innocents* 186 We have never seen anybody playing the French three-ball game yet. **1880** *Cimarron News & Press* 3 June 1/5 He didn't play anything but a three ball game.

Three-card. *ellipt.* +=next. Also attrib. and fig. — **1887** LOWELL *Writings* II. 187 [They] play their three-card trick as subsidies or as protection to labor. **1898** CANFIELD *Maid of Frontier* 109, I've seen low-down greasers playin' three-card, . . . but never any decent white men. **1920** SANDBURG *Smoke & Steel* 175 Pickpockets, yeggs, three card men.

+Three-card monte. A gambling game in which three cards, previously identified, are dexterously thrown face down on the table to deceive the player who bets upon the position of one of them. Also attrib. — **1854** PARKER in Weiss *Life T. Parker* II. 134 Three-card-monte men, and gambling-house keepers. **1873** BEADLE *Undevel. West* 140 'Smart Alecks' relieved of their surplus cash by betting on the . . . 'three-card monte.' **1899** *Everybody's Mag.* I. 176/1 Their father at one time was as bad a scamp as ever drew pistol or played three-card monte on the plains of the wild West.

+Three-cent coin. A coin valued at three cents. — **1852** *Republic* (Wash., D.C.) 10 April, Three Cent Coins.—The treasurer of the mint . . . is prepared to exchange three cent pieces for gold. **1866** *Wkly. New Mexican* 18 Aug. 1/4 At Philadelphia . . . the nickel three and five cent coins, can be had in exchange for gold and silver coins.

+Three-cent piece. 1. A coin worth three cents, composed of silver and copper. **2.** A similar coin composed of copper and nickel, authorized in 1865 and discontinued in 1890. Also *three-cent nickel piece.* — **(1)** **1851** *Stat. at Large* IX. 587 No ingots shall be used for the coinage of the three-cent pieces herein authorized, of which the quality differs more than five thousandths from the legal standard. **1857** *Ladies' Repository* Feb. 97/2 Your patriot whose heart feels most at home down in his pocket, keeping company there with his three-cent pieces and quarters. **(2)** **1865** *Stat. at Large* XIII. 517 There shall be coined at the mint of the United States a three-cent piece, composed of copper and nickel. **1882** McCABE *New York* 243 A three-cent piece . . . will get in between other change which we hand to a customer. **1890** Three-cent nickel piece [see THREE-DOLLAR].

+Three-dollar, *a.* Pertaining to a gold coin authorized in 1853. — **1858** J. H. HICKCOX *Amer. Coinage* 56 Three Dollar gold coins were coined . . . under an act passed in 1853. **1873** *Stat. at Large* XVII. 426 The gold coins of the United States shall be a one dollar-piece; . . . a three-dollar piece [etc.]. **1890** *Ib.* XXVI. 485 The coinage of the three-dollar gold piece, . . . and the three-cent nickel piece [shall] be . . . prohibited.

+**Three-foot (or -feet) gauge.** A railroad gauge three feet wide or a road of this width. — **1871** *Republican Rev.* 22 July 1/3 To carry the same number of passengers on the three-feet gauge, we require . . . less than one half the total weight of the train on the standard gauge. **1885** *Santa Fé Wkly. New Mexican* 6 Aug. 4/6 The road is a three-foot gauge.

+**Three-fourths hand.** =THREE-QUARTER HAND. — **1865** [see HALF-HAND 1].

Three-minute, *a.* Of horses: Capable of trotting a mile in three minutes. — **1833** *Knickerb.* I. 160 The present Mrs. S. admired his three minute roan. **1868** WOODRUFF *Trotting Horse* 41 A three-minute trotter in England is about as scarce an article as a two-thirty horse is here. **1874** *Vermont Bd. Agric.* II. 211 They are able to ride in grand carriages with their three minute blacks hitched thereto.

Three-month, *a.* +Of certain Civil War soldiers: Enlisted for only three months. — **1861** *Chicago Tribune* 26 May 1/3 So shameful has been the treatment of many of the three month volunteers, that most of them will certainly return home as soon as their terms expire. **1881-5** McCLELLAN *Own Story* 53 The time of the three-months regiments was now rapidly expiring.

+**Three-quarter hand.** One whose labor is rated at three-fourths of the value of that of a full hand. — **1856** [see HALF-HAND 1].

+**Three-rail fence.** A rail fence made up of three rails. — **1666** *East-Hampton Rec.* I. 250 A three raile fence shalbe sufficient in all comon fences. **1681** *Ib.* II. 102 Thomas Bee doth . . . maintaine a soficient three raile fence one the beach.

+**Three-sheet.** A poster composed of three sheets. — **1895** *N.Y. Dramatic News* 30 Nov. 8/2 The bronze statues, who haven't washed up for eleven weeks, look like a three-sheet in nine colors. **1908** McGAFFEY *Show-Girl* 128 They will leave Flossie, the belle of the village, waiting at the gate any time a burlesque three-sheet shows up on the side of the blacksmith shop.

+**Three-shift system.** A system of rotating land with three crops. (Cf. FOUR-SHIFT SYSTEM.) — **1814** TAYLOR *Arator* 126 Those tied by habit to the rotation of corn, wheat and pasture, or the three shift system, object [etc.]. **1819** 'AGRICOLA' *Ess. Agriculture* 22 The system of tillage which has generally been pursued under the name of the three-shift system, has also tended greatly to the destruction of our lands.

Three-toed, *a.* {1752-} In the specific names of birds. {1772} — **1839** PEABODY *Mass. Birds* 338 The Three-toed woodpecker, *Picus tridactylus*, . . . is distinguished by . . . that peculiar formation of the feet from which it derives its name. **1844** *Nat. Hist. N.Y., Zoology* II. 313 The Kittiwake, or Three-toed Gull, *Larus Tridactylus*, . . . is a northern species. **1917** *Birds of Amer.* I. 257 Golden Plover. *Charadrius dominicus dominicus*. . . . [Also called] Green Plover; Three-toed Plover; Whistling Plover.

Three-twenty-nine. +(See quotation.) — **1885** *Mag. Amer. Hist.* April 396/2 *Three-Twenty-Nine* (329).—During the presidential campaign of 1880 these numbers were chalked by Democrats on every wall and door-step, and fence in the land. Mr. Garfield, the Republican candidate, had been charged with having received as a bribe $329 worth of Credit Mobilier stock.

Three up. {1851} A kind of card game. — **1834** NOTT *Novellettes* I. 40 They could indulge in three up, old sledge, whist, or loo. **1840** *S. Lit. Messenger* VI. 294/2 The crowd was . . . playing cards; whist, loo, three-up, and all fours.

∗**Thresher, Thrasher.**

∗**1.** One who threshes grain.

1752 HEMPSTEAD *Diary* 592, I rid out to carry D(inner) to the Threshers. **1899** GARLAND *Boy Life on Prairie* 170 There were always three men who went with the machine and were properly 'the threshers.'

2. A threshing machine. {1884-}

1844 *Lexington Observer* 25 Sept. 2/7 At the same time and place will be sold . . . a Thresher and Power, an Ox-cart, and a Six Horse Wagon. **1853** B. F. TAYLOR *Jan. & June* 114 The spring array of life was . . . bound in the sheaf to fade upon the floor of the thresher. **1865** *Atlantic Mo.* June 731/2 The telegraph, the reaper, the thresher . . . have all come since that day. **1881** *Rep. Indian Affairs* 39 [There is] but one thrasher at the agency. **1914** E. STEWART *Lett. Woman Homesteader* 133 Clyde has taken the thresher on up the valley to thresh for the neighbors.

∗**Threshing floor.** A hard level floor on which grain is threshed. {-1697, 1805} — **1770** FORSTER tr. *Kalm's Travels* I. 223 In the middle was the threshing floor, and . . . in the loft or garret they put the corn which was not yet threshed. **1788** WASHINGTON *Diaries* III. 381 Began to lay . . . the part for the threshing floor. **1831** PECK *Guide* 150 Few of our farmers have barns or threshing-floors. **1900** HANDSAKER *Pioneer Life* 31 He did not have sufficient level ground on which to have a threshing floor.

Threshing, Thrashing, machine. A machine for separating grain from straw or husks. {1797-} — **1775** ROMANS *Nat. Hist. Florida* 178 In England the people were breaking their heads for the invention of a threshing machine no longer than four years ago; when the same machine had been . . . commonly used in New York and Pennsylvania, near fifty years. **1790** WASHINGTON *Diaries* IV. 72 Called . . . on the Baron de Polnitz, to see the operation of his (Winlaw's) threshing machine. **1842** M. CRAWFORD *Journal* 20 He has a thrashing machine and a grinding mill all under one roof driven by water power. **1871** *Rep. Indian Affairs* (1872) 356 A thrashing-machine, under the supervision of the farmer, would be of almost inestimable value to the Indians. **1910** GARLAND

Other Main-Travelled Roads 253 She pointed at a thrashing-machine in the field.

∗**Thriftily,** *adv.* +Flourishingly. — **1865** BURRITT *Walk to Land's End* 215 Two of the largest and oldest California pines are growing most thriftily in these gardens. **1874** *Vermont Bd. Agric. Rep.* II. 305 He had had trees apparently get over it, and grow thriftily and be good trees. **1894** *Amer. Missionary* Sept. 330 The seed . . . is growing thriftily.

∗**Thrifty,** *a.* In a healthy condition; vigorous; flourishing. {-1707, 1886; now *dial.*} — **1741** *R.I. Col. Rec.* V. 35 A white pine tree . . . does not appear to be a very thrifty tree; it is something crooked. **1760** *Huntington Rec.* II. 447, I have two Little daughters thrifty and well. **1836** *Knickerb.* VIII. 47 Marion's Battle-ground . . . [is] covered with young and thrifty evergreens. **1881** *Amer. Naturalist* XV. 34 In thrifty twigs, one year old, the pith is yellowish white. **1904** *Newark Ev. News* 13 June 6 The plants already above ground appear to be thrifty.

+**Thrip.** *S.* [Short for *threepence*.] The English threepenny piece; a coin of little value. {*threpps*, 'three-pence,' a1700} — **1834** SIMMS *G. Rivers* II. 108 He rewarded [him] with a *thrip* (the smallest silver coin known in the southern currency—the five cent issue excepted). **1845** W. T. THOMPSON *Chron. Pineville* 180 [He] dropped the thrip into the drawer. **1884** HARRIS *Mingo* 176 He never ceased to higgle over a thrip. **1904** CHURCHILL *Crossing* 257 Kentucky can go to the devil, . . . and not a thrip do they care.

Thrips. Also *erron.* **thrip.** *a.* Any of numerous small insects of the order Thysanoptera. **b.** In loose usage, any small injurious insect. {1658-} — **1858** *Mich. Agric. Soc. Trans.* IX. 226 The *Thrips* . . . seem but as little specks. **1863** *Horticulturist* XVIII. 296 Dusting the vines with lime . . . keeps the thrip down to a moderate number. **1884** ROE in *Harper's Mag.* Aug. 446/2 Thrips and slugs met their deserved fate. **1925** HERRICK *Man. Injurious Insects* 413 The Greenhouse Thrips. *Heliothrips hæmorrhoidalis*. . . . This species of thrips probably occurs in most of the greenhouses in this country.

+**Throat-rattler.** A drink *of* liquor. *slang.* — **1837** *Harvardiana* III. 238, I was obliged to down with a throat-rattler of West India.

+**Throatroot.** A species of avens, as *Geum virginianum*. — **1784** *Amer. Acad. Mem.* 454 Water Avens. Throatroot. Cureall. . . . The root is powerfully astringent. **1789** *Amer. Philos. Soc.* III. p. xix, In New-England a species of Geum, *water-avens, throat-root, cure all*, is an esteemed remedy for ulcretated [sic] sore-throat. **[1884** W. MILLER *Dict. Names of Plants* 200/1 *Geum virginianum*, Throat-root, White Avens.]

∗**Throstle.** A machine for spinning cotton, wool, etc. {1825-} Also attrib. and comb. — **1815** DRAKE *Cincinnati* 143 [In] six years . . . 23 cotton spinning mules and throstles . . . have been made. **1832** CLAY *Speeches* (1842) 185 In this country women and girls spin with the throstle and superintend the power loom. **1859** *Rep. Comm. Patents* 1858 I. 654 Improvement in spindles for throstle spinning. **1891** CHASE & CLOW *Industry* II. 22 As a rule, the twist, to form the *warp* . . . , is throstle-spun.

∗**Throttle.** *ellipt.* =next. {1903-} — **1876** KNIGHT 2564/1. **1887** *Courier-Journal* 6 May 3/4 [He] has been engaged by the Ferry Company to handle the throttle on the Shallcross during the coming excursion season. **1901** [see FIRE SHOVEL].

Throttle valve. In a steam engine, a valve for regulating the supply of steam. {1824-} Also fig. — **1813** [see CYLINDER 1]. **1869** 'MARK TWAIN' *Innocents* 111 The Old Travelers . . . open their throttle-valves, and how they do brag and sneer. **1874** B. F. TAYLOR *World on Wheels* 76 Now is your time to . . . see how an engine acts when the throttle-valve is wide open. **1883** FULTON *Sam Hobart* 222 Then opening the throttle-valve his engine sprang forward so violently as to break the connection with the train.

Through, *n.* (See quotation and cf. *to cut a swath*, under CUT *v.* 25 k.) {1796, *dial.*, 'a slip or width of corn which a set of reapers, &c. drive before them at once'} — **1859** BARTLETT 477 *Through*, is used in the West for swathe, or the cut of the cradle through grass or grain. Like 'swathe,' it is also used figuratively; as, 'What a through he cut!' i.e. what a swell!

∗**Through,** *a.*

+**1.** Of or pertaining to railroad or other traffic beyond intermediate or local stops. **a.** Of traffic, passengers, mail, etc.: Going or extending to a destination beyond local or intermediate stops. {1861-} Also comb.

1837 *Jamestown* (N.Y.) *Jrnl.* 26 July 2/2 The chief object is to prevent the detention of the through-going mail. **1842** *Phila., Wilmington, & Balt. R.R. 4th Rep.* 8 (Ernst), Through passengers. **1849** *Whig Almanac 1850* 19/1 On Mr. Whitney's route there would be scarcely any but *through*-business. **1855** HOLBROOK *Among Mail Bags* 137 At Ogdensburg, all matter for New York was put into a 'through bag,' which was . . . not to be opened until its arrival in New York. **1860** GREELEY *Overland Journey* 385 Said company . . . [should] carry a daily through-mail each way. **1867** *Ore. State Jrnl.* 5 Jan. 1/1 The only through traffic at present consists of mail and cargo. **1874** PINKERTON *Expressman & Detective* 12 On the morning of the twenty-sixth of April, 1858, the messenger from Atlanta . . . turned over to him the through pouch. **1887** GEORGE *40 Yrs. on Rail* 35 Even when tickets began to creep into use, they were at first sold only to through passengers.

+**b.** Of a ticket or baggage check: Allowing transportation to a given destination without further purchase or re-checking.

1845 *Boston Transcript* 29 Nov. 3/2 Through tickets may be obtained for Montreal. **1858** Through baggage Checks [see BAGGAGE-CHECK]. **1870**

B. ALCOTT *Journals* 410 The price of a through ticket to San Francisco . . . is $130. **1888** [see TICKET *n.* 6].

+**c.** Of a car or train: Carrying through traffic; moving without change or delay. {1884–}

1846 *Boston Traveller* 2 July, Through trains from Boston. **1879** BURDETTE *Hawkeyes* 128 You don't have to change; you get into a through car whichever route you take. **1880** *Cimarron News & Press* 26 Feb. 3/2 Through passenger trains are now being run on a schedule time of 20 miles an hour. **1922** TARKINGTON *Gentle Julia* 350 The arrival of a 'through express,' stirred him from his torpor.

+**d.** Of railway rates: Charged for through traffic.

1847 DOGGETT *U.S. R.R. Guide* Sept. 94 (Ernst), Through fare—from Savannah to Montgomery . . . $19.50. **1887** *Courier-Journal* 11 Jan. 2/1 The joint through rates . . . are made by two or more railroad companies between points on their respective roads.

+**e.** Of a route or line: Conducting traffic beyond local stops to a distant destination.

1861 J. DAVIS *Lett., Papers, & Sp.* V. 169 This comparatively short line would give us a through route from north to south in the interior of the Confederate States. **1873** 'MARK TWAIN' & WARNER *Gilded Age* 203 Harry had a way of casually mentioning Western investments, through lines, the freighting business. **1887** *Courier-Journal* 11 Jan. 2/2 Freight going from New York to San Francisco may pass over the various lines of road, making up a through line for perhaps half their regular rates. **1909** *Boston Herald* 17 Dec. 4/4 A through route from Boston by way of the great lakes to the west and northwest.

+**2.** Of cattle: Driven or shipped beyond local places.

1884 *Harper's Mag.* July 297/2 The latter receives most of the 'through Texans,' the old cows, and the 'scrubs' and 'culls' from the better lots. **1890** *Stock Grower & Farmer* 12 April 4/4 The local owners [in Colo.] banded together for a vigorous opposition to the use of their ranges for common trails and bed grounds for these through herds.

+**Through baggage-master.** A baggage-master who checks the baggage of through passengers. — **1855** HOLBROOK *Among Mail Bags* 97 Accompanying the night express trains there were also 'through baggage-masters,' so called.

Through cut. A water channel cut through land separating two bodies of water. (Cf. CUT *n.* 1 a.) — **1871** *Scribner's Mo.* II. 501 The level over which the Suez 'through-cut' from sea to sea has been constructed. **1898** PAGE *Red Rock* 350 Farther back is a through-cut to the Bend.

+**Through freight. a.** Material sent by freight that goes to its destination supposedly without change, reshipment, or the like. Also attrib. **b.** A freight train that carries such goods. Also attrib. — **1853** *Boston Ev. Traveller* 10 May 2/8 (Ernst), Through freight Lines to Philadelphia. **1875** *Chicago Tribune* 11 Sept. 3/4 'Through freight' meant freight that went through a half dozen sets of hands, and was transferred and re-transferred. **1879** [see FREIGHT *n.* 4]. **1900** GARLAND *Eagle's Heart* 316 The train, being a 'through freight,' ran almost as steadily as a passenger train.

‖**Through-other,** *v. tr.* To confuse. — **1862** *Harper's Mag.* Dec. 100/1, I expect, if I am ever so happy as to reach heaven, to be completely through-othered with the folks I shall meet and miss.

* **Throw,** *v.*

I. +**1.** *tr.* To give (one's vote or support), sometimes with a view to upsetting a delicate balance or deadlock. {1890}

1844 PHILLIPS in W. P. & F. J. Garrison *W. L. Garrison* III. 99 No one can take office, or throw a vote for another to hold office. **1888** BRYCE *Amer. Commonw.* I. i. v. 55*n.*, These [votes] have in the last two elections . . . been all thrown for the Democratic candidate. **1909** *N.Y. Ev. Post* (s.-w. ed.) 1 March 2 Mr. Root's utterances will influence many doubting politicians to throw their support to the Governor.

+**2.** To lose (a game or contest) deliberately.

1868 WOODRUFF *Trotting Horse* 263 It was . . . very unjust to charge Mr. Nodine with throwing the race. **1890** H. PALMER *Stories Base Ball Field* 144 Certain players, a year or two later, were accused and convicted of a plot to 'throw' certain championship games. **1912** COBB *Back Home* 56 This here next heat is goin' to be throwed.

3. In miscellaneous senses: (see quotations).

1847 RUXTON *Adv. Rocky Mts.* (1848) 256 To 'throw a buffalo in his tracks,' which is the phrase for making a clean shot, he must be struck but a few inches above the brisket. **1848** W. ARMSTRONG *Stocks* 6 [When money is scarce] people . . . withdraw their investment by throwing their Stocks upon the market. **1870** M. H. SMITH *20 Years Wall St.* 121 Vanderbilt has never been 'thrown' since he commenced his stock speculations. **1895** *Harper's Mag.* Feb. 348/2 There was but one thing left—to throw the switch before the express, due in two minutes, whirled past. **1897** FLANDRAU *Harvard Episodes* 132, I don't suppose the creature thought I was throwing a fit like that just for exercise. **1902** WILSON *Spenders* 30 He could throw the diamond hitch with his eyes shut—I reckon by the time he was nine or ten. **1921** MULFORD *Bar-20 Three* xv, You got plenty of gall, comin' down here an' throwin' a gun on me.

II. With adverbs. ***4.** *To throw down.* *colloq.*[2] +**a.** To discard (a friend or associate). +**b.** To pull (a gun) *on* a person.

(**a**) **1896** *Typographical Jrnl.* IX. 281 He was 'thrown down' by his party and he secured the nomination of the Democrats, but was defeated. **1913** BIGGERS *7 Keys to Baldpate* xiii, He'll throw you down some day. (**b**) **1898** CANFIELD *Maid of Frontier* 183 [He] threw his pistol down on Chisolm at three feet distance.

***5.** *To throw in,* +to contribute; to join partnership. {to throw in one's lot with, 1867–}

1904 PRINGLE *Rice Planter* 61 The whole family unite and 'trow een' to make up the sum necessary to bring the wanderer home. **1919** HOUGH *Sagebrusher* 184 They'll all throw in together and help you build an extra cabin. **1923** J. H. COOK *On Old Frontier* 125 He said . . . he should be glad to have me 'throw in' with him as a partner.

***6.** *To throw off.* +**a.** = BAR *v.* +**b.** Faro. (See quotation.) +**c.** To toss off (a drink).

(**a**) **1829** in Commons, etc. *Doc. Hist.* I. 235 Hoes still in Groces field, two ploughs throwing off before them. (**b**) **1864** DICK *Amer. Hoyle* (1866) 208 When a dealer, by a preconcerted plan, allows a player to win, he is said to throw off the game. (**c**) **1873** HARTE *Mrs. Skagg's Husbands* 6 He threw off his liquor with a single dexterous movement of head and elbow, and stood refreshed.

+**7.** *local.* *To throw off on.* **a.** To belittle. **b.** To avoid; to ignore.

(**a**) **1876** 'MARK TWAIN' *Tom Sawyer* xxv. 193, I ain't going to throw off on di'monds. **1904** *Charlotte Observer* 27 July 4 Charlotte can no longer throw off on Lincolnton for being behind the times. (**b**) **1894** HARTE *Bell-Ringer of Angel's* 52 It looks mighty like ez if ye was throwing off on Sofie and me on account of what I said. **1896** HIGGINSON *Land of Snow Pearls* 193 It was considered quite proper for a young man and a young woman to 'go together' for months, or even years, and for one to 'throw off' on the other, when attracted by a fresher face, with no explanation or apology.

8. *To throw out.* +**a.** To stop cultivating (land). +**b.** To reject (a vote) as invalid. +**c.** *Baseball.* To put (a runner) out on base by a throw.

(**a**) **1856** OLMSTED *Slave States* 241 [They] 'threw out,' to use their own phrase, so much of the land as they had ruined. **1904** PRINGLE *Rice Planter* 63, I have decided to throw out three of my fields. (**b**) **1877** JOHNSON *Anderson Co., Kansas* 78 On the canvass of the vote the probate judge threw out all the returns except the Shannon precinct. (**c**) **1880** *Brooklyn Eagle* 10 Oct. (E. J. Nichols).

***9.** *To throw up,* +to bring up or mention repeatedly *to* someone as a challenge or taunt.

1870 'MARK TWAIN' *Sk., New & Old* 276 He would . . . let on to be studying algebra by the light of a smouldering fire, so that all other boys might have to do that also, or else have Benjamin Franklin thrown up to them. **1872** EGGLESTON *End of World* 152 Julia had throwed up to him that he had been dismissed from School. **1884** NYE *Baled Hay* 219 Do not throw it up to us that we are weird and pixycal.

Throw-in. {1898–} *Baseball.* +A throw from the outfield to an infielder. — **1881** *N.Y. Herald* 23 July (E. J. Nichols).

* **Thrush.**

***1.** Any of numerous passerine birds of the family Turdidae; any one of various birds similar to the true thrushes.

1612 SMITH, etc. *Virginia* I. 15 There are . . . thrushes, and diuerse sorts of small birds. **1674** *Cal. State P., Amer. & W. I.* VII. 581 [In Maine & N.H.] the islands and woods yield . . . pigeons, thrushes, turtle-doves [etc.]. **1709** LAWSON *Carolina* 142 The Thrushes in America, are the same as in England, and red under the Wings. *a*1817 [see CATBIRD]. **1882** *Vt. Agric. Rep.* VII. 69 There are many small birds, as the blue bird, the thrush, etc., that should not be molested. *a*1918 G. STUART *On Frontier* II. 125 Heard a thrush or mountain mocking-bird at our camp in Eighteen Mile coulee.

2. With qualifying terms.

See also BROWN, FERRUGINOUS, FOX-COLORED, etc., THRUSH.

1805 LEWIS in *L. & Clark Exped.* II. (1904) 140 [The white-rumped shrike] is about the size of the blue thrush or catbird. **1810** WILSON *Ornithology* II. 88 [The] Golden-Crowned Thrush, *Turdus Aurocapillus,* . . . is also a migratory species, arriving in Pennsylvania late in April. **1839** New York Thrush [see NEW YORK 2 d]. **1917** *Birds of Amer.* III. 174 Sage Thrasher. *Oreoscoptes montanus.* . . . Other Name.—Sage Thrush. *Ib.* 177 Catbird. *Dumetella carolinensis.* . . . [Also called] Black-capped Thrush.

+**3.** *Thrush blackbird,* (see quotations).

1891 *Cent.* 6317/3 Thrush-blackbird, the rusty grackle. **1917** *Birds of Amer.* II. 263 Rusty Blackbird. *Euphagus carolinus.* . . . [Also called] Thrush Blackbird; Rusty Oriole.

Thule. (Variant of TULE.)

Thumb latch. A latch opened by pressing a lever with the thumb. {1801} — **1761** *Essex Inst. Coll.* XLVIII. 96 To be sold . . . hinges, thumb latches, hammers. **1850** *Rep. Comm. Patents 1849* 444 Patents have been granted for improvements in thumb latches. **1908** 'O. HENRY' *Strictly Business* 10, I can show you only the dark patch above the cast-iron handle . . . [made by] gloved hands too impatient to finger the clumsy thumb-latch.

Thumb-nail. {1604–} A small or brief sketch. In full *thumb-nail sketch.* {1900–} Also attrib. — **1852** HALE in *Sartain's Mag.* Jan. 39

The Old and the New, Face to Face. A Thumb-Nail Sketch. **1911** SAUNDERS *Col. Todhunter* 125 A full-length 'character-cartoon' of the Colonel [was] surrounded by 'thumb-nail' impressions of his face and bodily pose.

+**Thumb paper.** A card, paper, etc., used by school children to keep their thumbs from soiling the lower inner parts of the pages of their books. — **1865** *Wkly. New Mexican* 6 Jan. 2/4 Thumbpapers are among the first practical lessons in economy and cleanliness taught [children]. **1871** EGGLESTON *Hoosier Schoolm.* 187 Hannah . . . [held] out a little note folded like an old-fashioned thumb-paper. **1888** — *Graysons* viii, Fervid little love-notes . . . were folded like the 'thumb-papers' that served to protect their books.

+**Thumb tack.** A steel tack with a broad, flat head for pressing into soft boards or the like with the thumb. {1908} — **1884** RITTENHOUSE *Maud* 278 [He] coolly left me to put the thumb-tacks in my picture by myself. **1918** OWEN *Typewriting Speed* 111 Stick three or four thumb-tacks in the base to keep up your papers.

✻**Thumper.** +(See quotation.) — **1828** COOPER *Notions* II. 327 All that one hears concerning Thumpers and Dunkers, and other enthusiasts, is grossly caricatured.

✻**Thumps.** +In animals, a disorder consisting of spasmodic contractions of the diaphragm. — a**1846** *Quarter Race Ky.* 137 [The dog was] breathing like a horse with the thumps. **1866** *Iowa State Agric. Soc. Rep. 1865* 363 Called by some the cholera, but what I think was inflammation of the lungs, and is generally called the thumps, or heaves. **1890** *Spec. Rep. Diseases Horse* (Bureau Animal Indust.) 134 Thumps is produced by the same causes which produce congestion of the lungs.

✻ **Thunder.**

+**1.** An expressed policy; an argument; vigor or force.

1838 D. WEBSTER *Works* I. 427 Another will exclaim, 'That won't do; that's not my thunder.' **1856** E. G. PARKER *Lesson of '76* 15 No party owns the Revolution. . . . No party can say 'that's my thunder.' No, it is the thunder of America. **1877** *N.Y. Tribune* (B.), Whatever thunder there can be in the present Southern policy [of Pres. Hayes], it is not the thunder of those Republicans who oppose it.

2. Used in various phrases as a type of comparison or as a mild oath. {1709–10, 1842}

1826 *Mass. Spy* 23 Aug. (Th.), The bull roared like thunder! **1850** GARRARD *Wah-To-Yah* iv. 65 At other times, he . . . interpolated with *Thunder strike you* in Cheyenne. **1861** NEWELL *Orpheus C. Kerr* I. 346 Why the thunder don't somebody shoot that unnatural dog! **1883** *Wheelman* I. 363, I was as mad as 'thunder.' **1910** FRANCK *Vagabond Journey* 383 'I'm American,' . . . 'The thunder you are! . . . So 'm I.'

+**b.** *In thunder*, introduced with *why*, *what*, etc. {1894–, in Australia}

1841 GREELEY in *Corr. R. W. Griswold* (1898) 94 Why in thunder did you go off on Saturday without seeing me? **1865** *Atlantic Mo.* June 670/2 What in thunder do you pester me so about this cow for? **1890** *Buckskin Mose* 246 How in thunder could he go to the wood-pile while the door was locked?

+**c.** *By thunder*, a strong, yet not profane, oath.

1843 *Yale Lit. Mag.* IX. 79 Wal! You're considerable of a critur now, you are, by thunder! **1870** M. H. SMITH *20 Years Wall St.* 309 'Am I Governor of New York?' 'No, by thunder! Thurlow Weed is.'

+**d.** *Go to thunder*, go to hell.

1848 N. AMES *Childe Harvard* 82 A voice . . . replied, 'Please, go to thunder!' **1856** M. J. HOLMES *L. Rivers* 278 John Jr. bade her 'go to thunder.' **1894** *Outing* XXIV. 125/2 'You go to thunder!' I yelled at him.

+**e.** *To give* (or *catch*) *particular thunder*, to give (or catch) hell.

1851 [see PARTICULAR *a.*]. **1875** *Chicago Tribune* 21 Sept. 8/4 If the rations happen to be short, the squaw catches particular thunder.

+**Thunder-and-lightning snake.** The milk snake, or a related species. — **1842** *Nat. Hist. N.Y., Zoology* III. 39 The Milk Snake . . . is called Chicken Snake, Thunder and Lightning Snake, House Snake, and Chequered Adder. **1891** [see THUNDER SNAKE 1]. **1907** *St. Nicholas* July 845/1 Another of its many local names is 'thunder-and-lightning snake,' but I cannot imagine why so gentle a serpent should be so named.

+**Thunderation,** *n.* and *interj.* Used for emphasis. — **1845** W. T. THOMPSON *Chron. Pineville* 181, I'll blow 'em all to everlastin' thunderation. **1856** 'MARK TWAIN' *Adv. Snodgrass* 23 Thunderation. It [the 'iron horse'] wasn't no more like a hoss than a meetin house. **1884** HARRIS *Mingo* 233 Why, what the thunderation! **1911** SAUNDERS *Col. Todhunter* 17 What in thunderation is the matter, suh?

+**Thunderation,** *adv.* Used as an intensive. — **1836** *Crockett's Yaller Flower Almanac* 21, I don't know as I can say he was so all darned thunderation fat. **1852** BENNETT *Mike Fink* 28/1 And all fur your good, too, ef you warn't so thunderation blind you couldn't see it.

Thunderbird. {a1827–} +Among certain Indians, a mythical bird supposed to cause thunder. — **1875** PARKMAN in *N. Amer. Rev.* Jan. 40 The thunder-bird is offended, and all thunder-storms are occasioned by his anger. **1888** GOODE *Amer. Fishes* 266 According to the Indians, they had been struck by the Thunder-bird, which, with its companion, the Lightning-fish, causes many of the phenomena in that region. **1898** *Amer. Folk-Lore* XI. 140 In the beginning of the world the crow had the voice of the thunderbird.

+**Thunder bug.** (See quotation.) — **1837** WILLIAMS *Florida* 71 Horse Fly.—*M(usca) equi*. Of these there are five kinds—1st. the large black, called thunder bug, an inch long.

+**Thunder cap.** A great billow of a cloud. — **1877** *Harper's Mag.* Jan. 297/1 All day long great 'thunder caps' had rolled their still and solemn heights of rounded pearl and shadow upward. **1912** N. WOODROW *Sally Salt* 146 Look at the thunder-caps on the horizon.

✻**Thunderer.** +Anything exceptional of its kind. — **1857** *Harper's Mag.* Nov. 727 [The panther] was a thunderer, I tell ye. **1872** *Ib.* Aug. 348/1 Dick talked and vociferated, slashed his rod in the water, hooked a 'thunderer' and let him get away.

+**Thunder gust.** A thunderstorm accompanied by strong wind. {1817} Cf. GUST.

1733 FRANKLIN *Poor Richard's Almanac 1734* 11 Wind southerly, thunder-gusts. **1774** FITHIAN *Journal* I. 165 Last Evening was the first thunder Gust we have had this Season. **1816** U. BROWN *Journal* II. 155 Detained there 'till Evening by a great Thunder Gust. **1845** *Knickerb.* XXV. 302 A thunder-gust came up, and . . . filled every gully and ravine with foaming waters. **1886** *Harper's Mag.* July 282/2, I have yet to see . . . the bushes that some thunder gusts would not prostrate into the mud.

attrib. **1832** KENNEDY *Swallow Barn* I. 156 It was a blasted thunder-gust mill, and not worth a man's while to be fooling about it with hi corn. **1879** B. F. TAYLOR *Summer-Savory* 42, I think a man might . . . make a respectable lightning-rod of himself, and cheat those modest peripatetics with thunder-gust bayonets out of a bargain.

+**Thunderhead. 1.** A large head, as a whale's head. In allusive context. **2.** A massive, round cloud with bright, white edges, appearing before a thunderstorm. {1861} — (1) **1851** MELVILLE *Moby-Dick* 365 Throw all these thunder-heads overboard, and then you will float light and right. (2) **1853** B. F. TAYLOR *Jan. & June* 74 Three Macbeth-ish 'thunder-heads' lay lurking sullenly in the North-west. **1902** WHITE *Blazed Trail* 365 The huge thunder-heads gathered and flashed and grumbled. **1916** PORTER *David* 164 The massing of the thunderheads in the west meant more than just a shower.

+**Thunder-pumper.** *local.* **a.** The fresh-water drumfish. **b.** The American bittern. — **1884** GOODE, etc. *Fisheries* I. 370 In the Southern States the name 'Drum' predominates; that of 'Thunder-pumper,' also used for the bittern, . . . is heard along the Mississippi River. **1891** *Cent.* 6321/3 *Thunder-pumper.* . . . 1. The American bittern. . . . 2. The croaker or sheepshead, *Haplodinotus grunniens*.

+**Thunder snake. 1.** The milk snake or a related species. (See also THUNDER-AND-LIGHTNING SNAKE.) **2.** (See quotation.) — (1) [**1800** LAMB *Letters* (1935) I. 219 There is an exhibition quite uncommon in Europe, . . . a live rattlesnake, . . . whip-snakes, thunder-snakes, pig-nose-snakes, American vipers.] **1853** [see CHAIN SNAKE]. **1875** *Field & Forest* I. 30, I observed . . . a reptile which proved to be the Chain, or Thunder snake. **1891** *Cent.* 5725/1 *Thunder-snake, thunder-and-lightning snake.* . . . The name probably means no more than that these, like a good many other snakes, crawl out of their holes when it rains hard. (2) *Ib.* 6321/3 *Thunder-snake,* . . . the little worm-snake, *Carphiophis* (formerly *Celuta*) *amœna*, common in the United States: apparently so called because forced out of its hole by a heavy shower.

+**Thusly,** *adv.* Thus. *humorous.* {1893} — **1865** *Harper's Mag.* Dec. 133/2 It happened, as J. Billings would say, 'thusly.' **1870** *N.Y. Commercial Adv.* Jan. (Chipman), Things must not be allowed to continue thusly. **1891** RYAN *Pagan* 196 Why is this thusly, Mrs. Krin?

✻**Thwart saw.** A crosscut saw for sawing timber. *Obs.* — **1633** *N.H. Prov. Papers* I. 78, Received from Mr. Card, 2 old roaps, . . . 1 broken hand-saw, 1 thwart-saw [etc.]. **1654** *Essex Probate Rec.* I. 198, 1 hand saw . . . 2 thwart Sawes.

✻**Thyme.** A plant of the genus *Thymus*. — **1709** LAWSON *Carolina* 77 Our pot-herbs and others of use . . . [are] Lambs Quarters, Thyme, Hyssop [etc.]. **1792** IMLAY *Western Territory* 207 Of herbs, &c. we have of the wild sort . . . thyme, Indian leaf, rosemary. **1895** 'CRADDOCK' *Mystery Witch-Face Mt.* 237 The beautiful green beetle . . . hovered about the beds of thyme.

Tiarella. [mod. L. diminutive of *tiara*.] A plant belonging to a small genus (*Tiarella*) of saxifragaceous herbs. Also attrib. — **1871** *Scribner's Mo.* II. 470 Tiarella leaves just tipped with claret color. **1890** *Harper's Mag.* April 709/1 The soft, light plumes of tiarella are waving there.

Tibet, Thibet. A heavy fabric made of goat's hair or an imitation of this; a lighter fabric made of wool; also, a garment made of such cloth. {1827–} — **1854** *Penna. Agric. Rep.* 97 Miss Isabella A. Slaymaker . . . exhibited a specimen of thibet made of turkey feathers. **1891** *Cent.* 6326/2 Tibet, thibet. **1891** FREEMAN *New Eng. Nun* 90 An' I had a good thibet; there was rows an' rows of velvet ribbon on it. **1907** WIGGIN *New Chron. Rebecca* x, She couldn't decide whether to wear her black merino or her white thibet.

✻ **Tick.**

✻**1. a.** Any of numerous bloodsucking arachnids of the order Acarina. **b.** Any of certain two-winged insects that suck blood from animals and birds.

1737 BRICKELL *N. Carolina* 165 The Tick is a . . . kind of Louse. . . . There are two sorts, viz. the Dog, or large Tick, and the small or Sea Tick. **1775** CRESSWELL *Journal* 79 Ticks . . . get on you by walking in the Woods in great numbers. **1804** CLARK in *Lewis & C. Exped.* I. (1904) 51 The Mosquitoes and Ticks are noumerous & bad. **1880** *Cimarron News & Press* 26 Feb. 2/5 This dip kills Ticks, Lice, and all parasites. **1917** COMSTOCK *Man* 8 Why folks is as thick as ticks up here.

+**2.** *As full as a tick*, very full.

1822 *N.J. Almanac 1823*, Though of love I'm *as full as a tick*.

+**Ticker.**¹ (See quot. 1851.) *slang. Obs.* — **1836** *Harvardiana* III. 123 If any 'Ticker' dare to look, A stealthy moment, on his book. **1851** HALL *College Words* 301 *Ticker*, one who recites without knowing what he is talking about.

Ticker.² {1828-} +A telegraphic machine that prints off market quotations or other news on paper tape or ribbon. Also attrib. — **1882** MCCABE *New York* 338 Thanks to these 'tickers,' . . . men can watch the market, and buy and sell, miles away from the Stock Exchange. **1885** *Wkly. New Mexican Rev.* 7 May 3/2 The ticker service was partially restored this morning. **1894** *Voice* 20 Sept., In every saloon which boasts a ticker are to be found men who will register a bet to any amount. **1902** WILSON *Spenders* 407 For two days he clung to the ticker tape as to a life line.

✳ **Ticket,** *n.*

I. 1. A slip of paper or cardboard bearing evidence that the holder is entitled to some service or privilege. {1673-}

1637 *Essex Inst. Coll.* IX. 40 He may have [5 acres of land] laid out when he hath a ticket from me that he hath paid me. **1663** [see BOLT *n.*¹ 1]. **1682** *Plymouth Rec.* I. 171 Serjeant harlow . . . [shall] Graunt Ticketts according to Law in such Case provided unto such as are Nessesitated to travell on the Lords day. **1790** *Columbian Centinel* 9 Oct. 31/2 Whole and quarter Tickets in the Monthly State Lottery, may be had of David West. **1832** DUNLAP *Hist. Amer. Theatre* 14 Gentlemen and ladies that choose tickets may have them at the new printing office in Beaver-street. **1861** *N.Y. Tribune* 16 Dec. 6/4 Throughout the South . . . the change was invariably made in tickets. **1879** B. F. TAYLOR *Summer-Savory* 206 On the Cincinnati and Sandusky railroad . . . the conductor gives no check, but takes your ticket, . . . and passes on. **1882** MCCABE *New York* 415 Robert Greene escaped from the second tier of cells by using a forged visitor's ticket. **1907** *St. Nicholas* June 734 After he'd lunched, He thrust out a ticket and had it punched.

b. A playing card.

1870 RAE *Westward by Rail* 187 The card-dealer calls upon him to return the 'ticket.'

II. *Polit.* +**2.** A sheet of paper bearing the names of several candidates, nominated usually by a single political party; such a sheet used as a ballot; the list of candidates appearing on such a sheet, or, commonly since 1888, one of the lists in a column on a blanket ballot.

1711 [see sense 5 a]. **1755** in Franklin *Hist. Review Penna.* 403 Every one votes . . . as privately as he pleases, the Election being by written Tickets folded up and put into a Box. **1777** in W. T. Read *Life & Corr. G. Read* 275 The election was . . . held at Newark by a very few people and [I] have just seen a ticket. *a*1821 BIDDLE *Autobiog.* 330, I was surprised . . . to find my name on the ticket to be run as Senator. **1846** *Mich. Gen. Statutes* I. (1882) 138 The ballot shall be a paper ticket. **1875** HOLLAND *Sevenoaks* 28 Mr. Belcher's ticket for town officers . . . was unanimously adopted. **1903** *Evanston* (Ill.) *Press* 11 April, Several of the friends of Mr. A. W. Kimball have . . . urged him to consent to allow his name to be placed on the ticket.

+**b.** A ballot for or against some proposition.

1876 *Harper's Mag.* Dec. 159/1 A voter came up and asked for a ticket against the school tax.

+**3.** *collect.* The group of party candidates selected for a given set of offices.

1764 in W. B. Reed *Life J. Reed* I. 36 The Calvinists and the Presbyterians . . . I believe to a man assisted the new ticket. **1789** MADISON *Writings* V. 330 The Western ticket . . . is supposed to have prevailed. **1806** *Balance* V. 135/2 In New-York—three distinct tickets are nominated. **1840** *Picayune* 15 Aug. 2/1 The Whigs have elected their entire ticket. **1882** *Nation* 6 July 4/2 The ticket is considered a strong one, and likely to succeed. **1917** SINCLAIR *King Coal* 386 The Supreme Court handed down a decision which unseated him and the entire ticket elected with him.

transf. **1910** *Springfield W. Repub.* 21 April 14 The broad church ticket was successful in a stubborn contest over the election of delegates to the Episcopal triennial general convention.

+**4.** With specifying terms in either sense 2 or 3.

See also DEMOCRATIC, FUSION, GENERAL, MIXED, PARTY, SCRATCHED, SPLIT, STATE, STRAIGHT TICKET.

1800 JEFFERSON *Writings* X. 159 If the *city* election of New York is in favor of the republican ticket, the issue will be republican. **1827** in Mackenzie *Van Buren* 173 It is probable that the Jackson ticket will be elected. **1856** M. J. HOLMES *L. Rivers* 416 The whole American ticket was defeated at Laurel Hill. **1866** 'F. KIRKLAND' *Bk. Anecdotes* 57/1 He held a War ticket, and the presiding member of the board of selectmen . . . refused permission for him to vote. **1910** C. HARRIS *Eve's Husband* 138, I have determined to run on the anti-liquor ticket against Clancy Drew.

5. In phrases. +**a.** *To carry a ticket*, to elect the candidates on a ticket.

1711 *Penna. Hist. Soc. Mem.* X. 438 Chester carried their ticket entire. **1835** C. P. BRADLEY *I. Hill* 35 They carried their ticket by a small majority.

+**b.** *To run ahead of one's ticket*, or variants: To get more votes than the other candidates on one's ticket.

1846 *Xenia Torch-Light* 2 April 2/3 He ran ahead of every Whig on the ticket in Preble County. **1904** *N.Y. Ev. Post* 29 Sept. 3 Even the most optimistic admit that it [the state ticket] will run behind the national ticket. **1910** *Ib.* 23 Nov. 8 [Mr. Wilson] ran 35,000 ahead of his ticket.

+**c.** *The head of a ticket*, the candidate whose name appears at the top of a ticket; the candidate for the most important office represented on a ticket.

1884 *N.Y. Herald* 7 June 5/2 [The Democrats] can easily win with Tilden's name at the head of their ticket. **1888** *Chicago Inter-Ocean* (F.), The head of the ticket is one of the most vulnerable men who figured in Southern politics in the carpet-bag era.

+**d.** *To put a ticket in the field*, to nominate a group of candidates, esp. in response to an independent movement.

1891 *World Almanac* 75 South-Carolina, Democratic 'Straight-out' State Convention . . . put a ticket in the field in opposition to the regular (Tillman) Democratic ticket. **1904** *Omaha Bee* 16 Aug. 3 The talk of putting a new ticket in the field was due to the fact that the national populist leaders were fearful that the fusion populists would fail to put the electoral ticket in the field. **1913** [see BOLT *v.* 3].

III. 6. Attrib. and comb. in sense 1, esp. in respect to railroad tickets.

1816 *N. Amer. Rev.* III. 434 A ticket dinner will be provided. **1851** *Polly Peablossom* 107 The fine arts might impel him to play any character but that of 'ticket-seller.' **1857** *Harper's Mag.* Feb. 400/1 There was a mail-train . . . which the ticket-master informed me would land me in New York at half-past six. **1865** *Ib.* May 816/1 [He] asked me to await his return while he crowded to the ticket-window and procured tickets for both. **1868** *Ore. State Jrnl.* 12 Dec. 1/5 When the General and his companions passed into the Theater, not even the ticket-taker knew of his presence. **1887** GEORGE *40 Years on Rail* 34 Frequently, a pine box in open air by the side of the track served as the ticket case, and was the only landmark for a station. **1888** *Interstate Commerce Comm. 2d Rep.* 44 Ticket brokers or 'scalpers' . . . deal in unused coupons of through tickets, . . . in the unused portion of excursion tickets [etc.]. **1888** *Boston Jrnl.* 11 Dec. 1/4 Rates Reduced by Ticket Scalping and Commissions. **1895** *N.Y. Dramatic News* 19 Oct. 10/4 Two cars [were] filled with managers and friends of the late George Tyson, the ticket speculator.

Ticket, *v.* {1611-}

+**1.** *pass.* To be issued a ticket for accommodations on a train, boat, etc.; to be booked *through to* a place.

1842 LONGFELLOW in S. Longfellow *H. W. Longfellow* I. 415 To borrow the expression of a fellow-traveller, we were 'ticketed through to the depot.' **1852** *Boston Traveller* 24 Dec. 3/2 Passengers ticketed through from New York to Cincinnati. **1859** A. VAN BUREN *Sojourn in South* 17 I was soon 'ticketed' and aboard [the steamer]. **1882** PECK *Sunshine* 165 They thought they were ticketed through to the other place.

+**b.** *absol.* To supply tickets *to* specified places.

1882 *Kansas City Jrnl.* 19 Feb., We ticket directly to every place of importance.

+**2.** *tr.* To give a ticket or invitation to (someone).

1860 *Ladies' Repository* May 267/1 There was to be a great ball, and Mrs. Locke's girls were to be ticketed.

+**Ticket agent.** A railroad employee who sells tickets. (See also GENERAL TICKET AGENT.) — **1871** HOWELLS *Wedding Journey* 159 [They bought] tickets . . . of the heartiest imaginable ticket-agent. **1887** GEORGE *40 Yrs. on Rail* 76 C. C. Wheeler . . . [was] ticket agent. **1916** DU PUY *Uncle Sam* 201 The ticket agent thought he remembered selling the man . . . a ticket to Chicago.

+**Ticket book.** 1. An official book of ballots. 2. A book of railroad tickets. — (1) **1888** *Nation* 19 Jan. 46/2 A full set of ticket-books is to be provided at each polling-place before the polls are opened. (2) **1903** E. JOHNSON *Railway Transportation* 152 The original buyer . . . must sign his name on the last page of the ticket-book.

Ticket box. {1878} +**1.** A place for selling tickets. +**2.** A box for the deposit of tickets. — (1) **1851** *Polly Peablossom* 104 Tom Placide was dealing out in the Ticket Box. (2) **1898** *N.Y. Tribune* 13 May 11/2 Mr. Hoy is supposed to stand near the ticket-box and see to it that the pasteboards are dropped into the box.

+**Ticket-chopper.** An employee of a city transportation system in charge of a ticket-chopping machine. *colloq.* — **1898** C. B. DAVIS *Borderland of Soc.* 90 She took up with a ticket-chopper on the elevated road. **1903** *N.Y. Ev. Post* 21 Nov. 2 The ticket chopper then placed a newspaper over the mouth of his box and refused to take any more tickets.

Ticket-holder. *spec.* One who holds a lottery ticket. — **1863** HALE *If, Yes, & Perhaps* 15 The money that was gained in the combination was to be given by lot to two ticket-holders. **1882** MCCABE *New York* 550 The managers of the various lottery schemes . . . do not intend to pay any prizes to ticket holders.

+**Ticket office.** An office where tickets are sold. — **1835** INGRAHAM *South-West* I. 221 A noisy crowd was gathering around the ticket-office. **1839** *Boston Almanac* 71 Lowell Rail Road. . . . Ticket Office at the Depot. **1871** HOWELLS *Wedding Journey* 44 They reached the ticket-office on Broadway, whence they could indefinitely betake themselves to the steamboat an hour or two before her departure. **1903** E. JOHNSON *Rail-*

way Transportation 148 Ticket offices are located in the most central sections of the large cities.

+**Ticket peddler.** One who hands out party tickets at a polling place to be cast as ballots. Now hist. — **1872** *Chicago Tribune* 6 Nov. 1/6 There were the usual congregations of ticket-pedlers and candidates, serving their country and themselves. **1875** *Ib.* 3 Nov. 2/1 In the Fourth Precinct there was no excitement whatever, except an occasional exchange of courtesies between ticket-peddlers. **1903** LEWIS *Boss* 59 Go for the blokes with badges—th' ticket-peddlers.

Ticket room. {1895} 1. A room where a voter gets his ballot. 2. A room where railroad tickets are kept. — (1) **1888** *Century Mag.* Dec. 312/2 The voter receives his ballots from a sworn official of the State in a room called the 'ticket-room,' which only one voter is allowed to enter at a time. (2) **1907** LILLIBRIDGE *Trail* 172 Within the station itself the shirt-sleeved agent surreptitiously locked the door to the ticket-room.

+**Ticket scalper.** A person who buys railroad tickets, esp. unused return tickets, for resale at less than the established rates. Now hist. (Cf. SCALPER 3.) — **1880** *Congress. Rec.* 14 June 4521/1 Thomas P. Mills [was] a ticket-scalper of Indianapolis. **1903** *N.Y. Times Sat. Rev.* 26 Sept. 656 The ticket scalpers have deterred the railways from selling low-rate tickets to stimulate special travel.

Ticking. Also †**ticken, tyking.** The material of which bedticks are made. {1649-}
1645 *Essex Inst. Coll.* L. 336, 4 yards of yard wide tyking, 16s. **1711** *Boston News-Letter* 26 Nov. 2/2 A small Feather Bed, the Ticking old, a New Bob Wigg, . . . and several other things were taken out of the House of Edward Weaver. **1847** *Santa Fe Repub.* 17 Sept. 2/4 Staple and Fancy Dry Goods . . . consisting of 20 Bales Brown Domestics, . . . Tickings [etc.]. **1903** [see HAIR MATTRESS].

b. *attrib.* Designating things made of this fabric.
1704 *Boston News-Letter* 8 May 2/2 He ript a small stript Ticking-bolster. **1714** *Ib.* 9 Aug. 2/2 [The runaway] has on . . . stript Ticken Breeches, a new Castor Hat. **1725** *New-Eng. Courant* 1 Feb. 2/2 She went away with a black Grisset Gown . . . and a Pair of Ticken Shoes, with red Heels. **1754** *S.C. Gazette* 28 May 3/1 Samuel Kynaston has just imported from London . . . dimity and ticken Pockets [etc.].

+**Tickle grass.** The rough bent or hair grass (*Agrostis hiemalis*), or one of various other American grasses. — **1832** WILLIAMSON *Maine* I. 124. **1840** DEWEY *Mass. Flowering Plants* 234 *T[richodium] laxiflorum*, Tickle-grass, . . . forms a handsome turf. **1857** [see FLYAWAY GRASS]. **1894** *Amer. Folk-Lore* VII. 104 *Panicum capillare*, tickle-grass, West Va., Neb. **1915** BAILEY *Cycl. Horticulture* 1500/2 *H[ordeum] jubatum*, Squirrel-tail Grass, called . . . Tickle-Grass in Nev. **1924** CROY *R.F.D. No. 3* 30 The hated barbed ticklegrass was stuffed down trousers.

+**Tickle match (grass).** (See quotations.) — **1819** *Niles' Reg.* XVII. 143/2 Two elegant imitations of ladies Leghorn hats . . . [were made] from a grass common in the vicinity of Hartford, . . . commonly known as *ticklematch* grass. **1819** *Plough Boy* I. 199 A grass, commonly called *Tickle match*, has lately been used for making hats, by some ladies of Hartford.

+**Tickle mouth.** (See quot. 1819.) — **1819** *Amer. Farmer* I. 280 It is known, generally among our farmers, by the name of 'tickle mouth'—although some call it 'wire grass.' [**1833** *Veg. Subst. Materials of Manuf.* 162 (*O.E.D.*), A species of grass growing spontaneously in that part of the United States [Conn.], and popularly known by the name of tickle-moth.]

Ticklenburg. A coarse linen cloth. {1696-} Also attrib. — **1741** *Boston Ev. Post* 16 Nov., Ticklin-burghs and Ozenbrigs. **1776** *N.H. Hist. Soc. Coll.* IX. 264 Ticklenburgs & Ozenbu[r]gs shall not be sold wholesale, at a higher Rate. **1830** WATSON *Philadelphia* 174 Poor labouring men wore ticklenberg linen for shirts, and striped ticken breeches.

Tickler. {1680-}
+**1.** A small flask or bottle for liquor. *slang.*
1809 WEEMS *Marion* (1833) 162 [The old man held] up a stout tickler of brandy. **1841** *Picayune* 10 Jan. 2/2 The 'Rackinsaw' man had a 'pint companion' or 'tickler' with him which he wanted filled with whiskey. **1889** *Harper's Mag.* Aug. 388/2 The tickler was a bottle of narrow shape, holding a half-pint—just enough to tickle.

+**2.** A person having some exceptional quality. *slang. Obs.*
1834 *Knickerb.* III. 34, I've a notion of Jinny—she's a real ticlur. **1843** STEPHENS *High Life N.Y.* I. 135 He was a tickler, though, at trapping mushrats and shooting foxes.

+**3.** A memorandum book, as an account book giving ready information on debts.
1839 BRIGGS *H. Franco* I. 74, I don't see that I have got your first name down in my tickler. **1891** NICHOLS *Business Guide* (ed. 28) 244 *Tickler*, a book containing a memoranda of notes and debts arranged in the order of their maturity.

+**4.** (See quotation.)
1905 CALKINS & HOLDEN *Art Mod. Advertising* 351 A tickler is any small piece of printed matter sent out to keep open a prospective sale on the part of the inquirer.

+**Tickle weed.** =AMERICAN HELLEBORE. — **1751** ELIOT *Field-Husb.* iii. 66 Take the Roots of Swamp Hellebore, sometimes called Skunk Cabbage, Tickle Weed, Bear Root.

+**Tick nation.** (See quotation.) *jocular.* — **1859** BARTLETT 478 *Tick Nation.* A name given to regions in which ticks abound, and, as the

grasses and sandy soil infected by them are peculiar to the poorer parts of the country, it is sometimes used as a term of reproach.

+**Tickseed sunflower.** Any large-rayed plant of the genus *Bidens*. — **1817-8** EATON *Botany* (1822) 250 *Coreopsis tripteris*, tickseed sunflower. **1838** DEWEY *Mass. Flowering Plants* 140 *C[oreopsis] trichosperma*, Tickseed Sunflower, . . . bears large, yellow flowers. **1909** WEBSTER 2156/1.

*Ticktack.** +A contrivance for making a rattling sound on a window or door. — **1884** RITTENHOUSE *Maud* 288, I formed plan after plan to frighten them. Finally a 'tick-tack' was decided on. **1902** McFAUL *Ike Glidden* 9 An' then ter come an' rig one o' them plaguey tick-tacks on ther window.

+**Tick trefoil.** A plant of the genus *Desmodium*. — **1857** GRAY *Botany* 99 Tick-Trefoil. . . . ([Pod] roughened with minute hooked hairs by which they adhere to the fleece of animals or to clothing). **1901** MOHR *Plant Life Ala.* 88 Tick-trefoils . . . afford the only pasturage to live stock.

Tidal wave. {1830-} *fig.* +A progressive movement of overwhelming force. {1895} — **1875** 'MARK TWAIN' *Sk., New & Old* 213 A great tidal wave of grief swept over us all when Joan of Arc fell at Waterloo. **1882** *Nation* 9 Nov. 391/1 The so-called tidal wave of 1874 was only a lively ripple compared with this overwhelming flood. **1892** WALSH *Lit. Curiosities* 1053 *Tidal Wave*, an American political figure of speech, applied to an election in which the winning party is returned with an overwhelming and unprecedented majority.

Tiddle, v. +*intr.* To move with small, mincing steps. — **1881** HOWELLS *Modern Instance* x, Mr. Macallister, a slight little straight man, . . . tiddled farcically forward on his toes.

+**Tiddledies, Tiddlies.** Also **tiddledy (or tiddly) benders.** *pl.* [Of obscure origin.] *To run tiddlies*, or variants: (see quot. 1877 and cf. KITTLY-BENDERS). Also *fig.* — **1877** BARTLETT 704 Boys say, 'run tiddlies,' *i.e.* run over ice after it has begun to break up on a sheet of water. **1888** *Boston Jrnl.* 17 Dec. 3/6 Running tiddledies, or 'tiddledy-benders,' is a great test of character. **1902** LORIMER *Lett. Merchant* 70 You had the old man running tiddledies. **1909** *Cent. Suppl.* 1349/3 Tiddly-benders.

*Tide.
+**1.** A rising of the water in a river at a time of heavy rains; a flood or freshet.
1781-2 JEFFERSON *Notes Va.* (1788) 9 In common winter and spring tides it [the Ohio R.] affords 15 feet water to Louisville. **1897** BRODHEAD *Bound in Shallows* 104 A hope of early fall 'tides' began to enliven the loggers' conversation. **1903** FOX *Little Shepherd* iii, In the spring, . . . the 'tides' came.

+**2.** (See quotation.)
1817 *Ann. 14th Congress* 2 Sess. 1008 In speaking (in the phraseology of the country) of the tides in the Currituck, and the other sounds and inland waters with which it is connected, a regular periodical ebb and flow of the waters is not to be understood, but that change which is produced by the action of a strong and constant wind in driving the water from one sound to another.

3. *attrib.* **a.** Designating areas overflowed by tides.
See also TIDELAND.
1675 *Essex Inst. Coll.* LVI. 308 Seven acres more of tide meadow. **1770** Tide marsh [see BANK *v.*¹ 2]. **1789** ANBUREY *Travels* II. 274 A cave or well, formed by nature, . . . is called the tide well, in allusion to its ebbing and flowing. **1796** *Ann. 4th Congress.* 2 Sess 2694 All tide-swamps, not generally affected by the salts or freshes, of the first quality, are rated at six pounds per acre.

b. Designating various structures or contrivances for use with tidewater, as for controlling or utilizing it.
See also TIDE MILL.
1803 *Ann. 7th Congress* 2 Sess. 406 The first, if not all their docks, were to be tide docks. **1808** *Niles' Reg.* XV. 54/2 It would be necessary to place the tide lock as far out as possible. **1818** *Ib.* XIII. 312/2 *Tide or Gill nets* . . . obstruct the passage of the fish. **1862** *Rep. Comm. Patents 1861: Agric.* 345 The drainage should receive attention immediately after the embankment and tide-gate. **1864** WEBSTER 1383/3 *Tide-wheel*, a water-wheel so constructed as to be moved by the flow of the tide. **1891** *Cent.* 6331/1 *Tide-predictor*, . . . an instrument for calculating the times and heights of high and low water.

c. In animal and plant names.
1877 C. HALLOCK *Sportsman's Gazetteer* (1883) 244 These big fellows [weakfish] are designated as 'tide-runners.' **1914** STEELE *Storm* 330 We walked back slowly, cutting along the margin of the tide-grass.

d. In special combinations.
Tide navigation, salt-water navigation; *tiderace*, a strong current or rough water caused by the movement of the tide; *t. rip*, an unevenness or roughness in the sea caused by the action of the tide {1875}; *t. spring*, a spring in which the water ebbs and flows, like a tide; *t. stream*, a tidal river {1875}; *t.-surveyor*, a customhouse official in charge of tidewaters. {1684-}
1791 WASHINGTON *Diaries* IV. 167 [Wilmington] is at the head of the tide navigation. **1883** *Harper's Mag.* Aug. 375/1 These numerous tide-races often make the St. Lawrence a rough passage for small craft. **1830** N. S. WHEATON *Journal* 518 We are now on George's Bank, and surrounded with tide-rips, having precisely the appearance of those at the mouth of a river. **1838** FLAGG *Far West* II. 222 From this remarkable *tide-spring* until we reach the Grand Tower, the face of the country has a depressed and sunken aspect. **1795** *Essex Inst. Coll.* LIV. 101 To compensate for any supposed inconveniences that may attend a tide stream. **1774** *Doc.*

Hist. N.Y. State I. 760 The Custom House officers [include] . . . Tide Surveyor and Three Tide Waiters.

Tideland. **1.** Land that is covered and uncovered by the flow and ebb of the tide. +**2.** *Tideland spruce,* the Sitka spruce, *Picea sitchensis.* — (1) **1802** DRAYTON *S. Carolina* 61 Oat grass. (*Avena Caroliniana.*) Grows in rich tide lands. **1829** SHERWOOD *Gaz. Georgia* (ed. 2) 251 Tide lands, and Island swamp of light mellow soil, appears [*sic*] to claim a preference for cane culture. **1881** [see DIKE *n.*¹ 2]. **1900** *Congress. Rec.* 20 Feb. 1999/2 We hold the tide lands in such territory for the future States to be created out of them. (2) **1884** SARGENT *Rep. Forests* 206 Tide-Land Spruce. . . . A large tree of great economic value, . . . reaching its greatest development . . . near the mouth of the Columbia river.

Tide mill.

1. A mill operated by the action of the tide. {1796–}

1640 *Essex Inst. Coll.* V. 169/2 Captane Traske hath leave to sett up a tyde myll upon the North River. **1793** *Mass. H. S. Coll.* I Ser. III. 121 We have for grinding it into meal, five wind-mills, and one tide-mill. **1843** *Nat. Hist. N.Y., Geology* II. 251 The white clay . . . occurs on West Neck . . . below the first tide-mill. **1883** *Century Mag.* Oct. 847/1 Some half a dozen tide-mills . . . varied the scene.

+**2.** (See quotations.)

1828 WEBSTER, *Tide-mill,* . . . a mill for clearing lands from tide-water. **1891** *Cent.* 6331/1 *Tide-mill,* . . . a water-pumping station operated by a tide-wheel, used to pump water over a dike.

Tidewaiter. A customhouse official whose duty was to meet arriving ships and enforce upon them the observance of customs regulations. Now hist. {1699–} — **1773** *Broadside Verse* (1930) 53 At Salem, near Boston . . . , Mr. Nathaniel Diggadon, Tidewaiter [was drowned]. **1840** *Niles' Nat. Reg.* 1 Aug. 339/1 The tide-waiter . . . got hold of the cook's axe. **1881** *Reinbeck* (Iowa) *Times* 9 June 1/5 The officeholders, from Cabinet officer to tidewaiter, had been assessed three times.

Tidewater.

1. a. Water brought into a given area by the action of the rising tide. {1799–} +**b.** Water, as of a given area or in specified streams, which is affected by the tide; a region or area in which water is affected by the tide.

In sense b often used with specific reference to eastern Virginia.

1772 *Va. Stat. at Large* VIII. 564 The extension of the navigation of James river . . . will be greatly promoted by cutting a canal, through the falls, from Westham to the tide water. **1785** *Md. Hist. Mag.* XX. 43 The mud bank on the outside of the Channel is always covered with tide water at common tides. **1789** *Amer. Philos. Soc.* I. 358 The first place proposed to be viewed, was the ground between the tide waters of Apoquiniminck and Bohemia. **1834** *S. Lit. Messenger* I. 92/1 Within a few miles of the tide water of a majestic stream . . . , bituminous coal of a good quality . . . has been found. **1857** *Harper's Mag.* March 434/1 All the swamps bordering the southern tide-water present the same characteristics. **1889** *Century Mag.* Feb. 602/1 Long 'tidewaters' . . . ran up to the very foot of the wooded hills. **1904** *N.Y. Sun* 21 Aug. 4 He aspires to be the Republican boss of the Old Dominion, from mountains to tidewater.

2. *attrib.* **a.** Designating regions situated on tidewater or affected by tides.

1832 KENNEDY *Swallow Barn* I. 179 There are very few villages in the tide-water country of Virginia. **1835** *S. Lit. Messenger* I. 662 Soft, fragile, dovelike females . . . claim their home only in the tranquil and affectionate hearths of tide-water Virginia. **1868** *Rep. Comm. Agric. 1867* p. x, The whole tide-water area . . . is endowed with a climate peculiarly adapted to market gardening. **1873** BEADLE *Undevel. West* 316 In the swamp and tide-water lands . . . are found one-half of the Chinese. **1884** *Century Mag.* April 825/2 Mr. Jones . . . [has] one of those thin, mournful faces common to tide-water Maryland. **1897** *Outing* XXIX. 438/1 The great tide-water wilderness of trembling prairie and treeless sea-marsh.

b. Designating bodies of water affected by tides or supplying navigable routes from inland to the sea.

1835 J. MARTIN *Descr. Virginia* 40 A tide water river, or more correctly a bay, the Chowan, gradually widens. **1840** *Niles' Nat. Reg.* 16 May 167/2 It is but a reasonable pride, then, with which we now hail the completion of the Tide Water canal. **1862** *Rep. Comm. Patents 1861: Agric.* 207 The principal dependence for hay . . . [was] upon upland meadow and the embankment of the marshes, which bordered the tide-water streams.

+**Tidewater spruce.** ?Tideland spruce. — **1884** *Rep. Comm. Agric.* 142 Tide-water Spruce.—This variety grows 200 feet high and 8 to 10 in diameter.

+**Tidingman.** =TITHINGMAN. — **1703** *Groton Rec.* 123 [Certain persons were chosen] for tiding men. **1846** *Knickerb.* XXVIII. 466 He had been watched by a 'tiding-man' at church. **1857** *Harper's Mag.* Aug. 427/2 A grave personage, known as a 'tiding-man,' . . . coolly informed Mr. Otis that he was arrested for travelling on the Sabbath. **1878** STOWE *Poganuc People* 63 They're goin' clean agin everything—Sunday laws and tiding man and all.

Tidy. {a1634–} An ornamental covering or antimacassar, esp. a piece of fancywork, for an article of furniture, as a chair. {1861–} Also attrib. — **1850** *Knickerb.* XXXVI. 255 There is one cane-seated rocking-chair, . . . the back of which is covered with an unapproachable netting of spotless white, called a 'tidy.' **1868** *Mich. Agric. Rep.* VII. 356 Wm. Keith, Detroit, [exhibited a] tatting tidy cover. **1880** *Harper's Mag.* Oct.

656/1 [She] carries home an embroidered 'chair-back'—the more dignified name that she gives nowadays to her 'tidy.' **1892** WILKINS *Young Lucretia* 249 She's been talkin' about goin' to get a tidy-pattern. **1913** WHARTON *Custom of Country* 114 How'd they expect her fair young life to pass? . . . Knitting tidies for church fairs?

+**Tidytips.** (See quotations.) Also with specifying term. — **1891** *Cent.* 6331/3 *Tidytips,* a Californian composite plant, *Layia* (*Callichroa*) *platyglossa;* a showy plant with bright-yellow rays, frequently cultivated as a half-hardy annual. **1915** ARMSTRONG & THORNBER *Western Wild Flowers* 554 Yellow Tidy-tips, *Blepharipappus elegans* (*Layia*), Yellow, Spring, California. . . . Very pretty flowers.

*✱**Tie,*** *n.*

+**1.** =RAILROAD TIE.

1853 *La Crosse Democrat* 4 Oct. 2/5 The contract [has been let] for furnishing the whole of the ties required for the road. **1871** *Republican Rev.* 16 Sept. 1/4 The ties for seventy miles were all [laid]. **1894** *Outing* XXIV. 123/2 We were swinging over the ties where the woods bordered the railroad. **1918** *Essex Inst. Coll.* LIV. 196 The track . . . was laid on ties of split granite.

+**2.** Attrib. with *chopper, contract, contractor,* etc.

1883 *Wheelman* I. 338 Old Tie City . . . [had] perhaps one hundred cabins inhabited by tie choppers and their families. **1883** SWEET & KNOX *Through Texas* 264 One big Irish tie-spiker sent her a bottle of whiskey. **1885** *Wkly. New Mexican Rev.* 2 July 4/1 The tie gang is now being gathered up at Alamosa, Pueblo and Denver. **1891** O'BEIRNE *Leaders Ind. Territory* 35/2 John R. Davis . . . had the tie contract in the Choctaw Nation. *Ib.* 195/2 He is also tie contractor for the M. K. & T. **1897** BRODHEAD *Bound in Shallows* 47 Some tie-makers . . . were working the timber off a tract of land. **1900** *Congress. Rec.* 10 Jan. 754/2 The cutting of tie and bridge timber for the construction of railroads in the Indian Territory.

*✱**Tie,*** *v.*

I. +**1.** *tr.* To supply (the roadbed of a railroad) with ties.

1875 *Chicago Tribune* 8 July 5/5 The funds already raised will grade, bridge, and tie the road. **1883** *Local News* (West Chester, Pa.) II. No. 234, 1 Forty miles of road . . . had to be rebuilt entirely, graded, tied.

II. With adverbs in various colloq. expressions. +**2.** *To tie in,* to join closely by, or as if by, tying.

1842 *Amer. Pioneer* I. 274 A pair of buckskin leggins, . . . made to fit the leg and tie in at the ankle with the moccasins.

+**3.** *To tie out,* to take out and tie (mail matter) in separate bundles.

1893 CUSHING *Story of P.O.* 56 The postmasters at distributing points like Sisson should 'tie out' the little packages of letters intended for offices on the radiating routes.

4. *To tie up.* **a.** To moor a boat to the shore; of a vessel, to be moored or fastened. {1886–}

1846 *S. Lit. Messenger* XII. 20/2 At night we tied up again. **1895** G. KING *New Orleans* 85 These contraband boats used to tie up at a tree on the river bank. **1907** LONDON *Road* 187 We tied up to the bank. *fig.* **1876** *Fur, Fin & Feather* Sept. 144/1 Cutchogue, Long Island, . . . is a good place to 'tie up to' for any one fond of fishing and fowling.

+**b.** To delay or stop.

1887 GEORGE *40 Yrs. on Rail* 140 A snow-storm . . . tied us up until we were six days making the run. **1896** [see PLANT *n.* 1]. **1907** *Springfield W. Repub.* 10 Oct. 16 Traffic west of Springfield was tied up until about midnight.

+**c.** To join forces *with;* to attach oneself *to.*

1903 *N.Y. Ev. Post* 5 Dec. 1 When a representative has a navy yard in his district, . . . [he can] make business for that yard . . . by tying up with the other navy yard representatives on the committee. **1904** *Indianapolis News* 21 June 6 The assurance that Captain New is to have a good post may be the reason that so many fellows want to tie up to him.

III. With prepositions in various colloq. expressions. +**5.** *To tie to,* to rely upon; to identify one's interests with.

1859 BARTLETT 479 *To Tie to.* In Western phraseology, a man who 'will do to tie to,' is one who can be relied upon, an honest man. **1872** EGGLESTON *End of World* 173 Tell him not to tie to the serious-looking young fellow. **1909** *N.Y. Ev. Post* (s.-w. ed.) 13 Sept. 5 The college must offer in its faculty men whom students can tie to, men who can evoke personal devotion and enthusiasm.

+**6.** *To tie into,* to go to work upon, to take to task.

1902 WHITE *Blazed Trail Stories* 71 Just tie tight into her and keep her hustling. **1912** WASON *Friar Tuck* xiv, They girded up their loins, and tied into him a little harder.

IV. 7. In combination with nouns.

Tie post, a hitching post; *t. rail,* a rail or railing to which horses are hitched; *t. strap,* (see quotation); *t. string,* a string attached to a blanket, dress, etc., for tying it to something.

1861 *Harper's Mag.* Feb. 424/2 He alighted, . . . carelessly throwing the reins over a tie-post. **1924** MULFORD *Rustlers' Valley* vi, Matt . . . led Pete to the tie rail. **1876** KNIGHT 2567/2 *Tie-strap,* (Saddlery,) a long strap having a buckle and chape on one end, used as an extra strap to a bridle for tying. **1897** *Outing* XXX. 379/1 A rubber blanket, . . . with tie-strings at the four corners, can be made into a first-rate shelter.

+Tie game. A game in which the final scores of the opposing sides are equal. — **1868** CHADWICK *Base Ball* 46 A tie game occurs whenever the score is even at the close of the even innings played. **1880** *Chicago Inter-Ocean* 7 June 6/2 The tie game of yesterday was played off to-day.

+Tienda. *S.W.* [Sp.] A shop or store. — **1844** KENDALL *Narr. Santa Fé Exped.* II. 38, I saw . . . the detestable Salezar, standing in front of a small *tienda*, or store. **1884** HARTE *On Frontier* 139 A part of the shanty was used as a *tienda* or shop. **1885** — *Maruja* 60, I met him outside the tienda on the highway.

＊Tier, *n.*[1] (See also THIRD TIER.) +A row, range, or series of contiguous lots, townships, states, or counties.

1693 *Hartford Land Distrib.* 212 One [parcel of land] lyeing in the Same Teere of lotts abutting on a High way. **1703** *Derby Rec.* 283 His lott is . . . in ye middle teer. **1733** *Waterbury Prop. Rec.* 144 The teers to be laid out Shall Run North and South. **1824** in Cox *Recoll. Wabash Val.* 18 The land is sold in tiers of townships. **1849** CHAMBERLAIN *Ind. Gazetteer* 154 Marion, Pleasant and Lafayette [townships], lie in the first tier. **1860** *Congress. Globe* 19 Dec. 139/3 They constitute the first tier of the border slave States. **1873** BEADLE *Undevel. West* 41 How few Americans realize the comparative greatness of that tier of States just west of the Mississippi. **1904** *N.Y. Ev. Post* 7 Nov. 2 Any defection in the northern end of the State will be more than offset by the big Republican majorities in the lower tier of counties.

Tier, *n.*[2] {1633-} *New Eng.* +A child's pinafore or apron covering the whole front of the dress. (Cf. TIRE *n.*) — **1846** WORCESTER 740/2 *Tier*, . . . a child's apron. **1865** WHITNEY *Gayworthys* 73 She took care of Say; put on her long-sleeved tyers when she sent her out to play. **1892** WILKINS *Young Lucretia* 33 It was Fidelia's white tier. **1902** *Dialect Notes* II. 254 Even among the older people, 'cricket' has mostly given place to 'footstool,' and 'tier' to 'apron.'

‖Tier, *v. tr.* To arrange (freight) in tiers. — **1889** *N.Y. Produce Exch. Rep.* 301 Lightermen shall not . . . be required . . . to tier or pile their freight on the docks.

＊Tierce. A measure of varying size, but usually about forty gallons; a cask or vessel intermediate in size between a hogshead and a barrel.

1666 SANFORD *Letter Book* 21 The other tearse and Barrell wanted 3 2/4 of full. **1701** [see PIPE *n.*[2] 1]. **1787** *Md. Gazette* 1 June 3/2 A few Hogsheads of Tobacco, Tierces, or half Tierces of Rice, can be taken on freight, if offered immediately. **1846** MCKENNEY *Memoirs* I. 22 It was customary to pack the supplies in water-proof tierces. **1902** LORIMER *Lett. Merchant* 132, I never saw one that liked a drummer's jokes more than an eighth of a cent a pound on a tierce of lard.

attrib. **1850** *Rep. Comm. Patents 1849: Agric.* 426 Tierce Middles, Strips, and all pickled meats for domestic use, have been in singularly bad demand.

＊Tie rope. +A short rope used by cowboys for tying together the feet of lassoed cattle. — **1890** *Stock Grower & Farmer* 4 Jan. 5/2 Tom Davenport . . . had lost his tie rope. **1923** J. H. COOK *On Old Frontier* 19 With one of the 'tie-ropes' which he always carried tucked under his belt, [he] 'hog-tied' the bull.

+Tierras. *pl.* [Sp.; pl. of *tierra* 'earth.'] *Mining.* Inferior ore, esp. that containing sand or earthy matter: (see quot. 1881). Also attrib. — **1874** RAYMOND *6th Rep. Mines* 397 Tierras yielded (estimated) 3 per cent. **1876** — *8th Rep.* 9 Number of tons tierras-ore roasted. *Ib.* 17 A new tierras-furnace will take its place. **1881** — *Mining Gloss.*, *Tierras*, . . . fine dirt impregnated with quicksilver ore, which must be made into adobes before roasting.

Tie-up. {1714-}

+1. A place where cows and oxen are tied up for the night. Also attrib.

1851 SPRINGER *Forest Life* 82 At the further end of the 'tie-up' he thinks he hears a little clattering noise. **1882** *Maine Agric. Rep.* XXVI. 50 The farmers throw the dressing out of the tie-up windows. **1894** *Vt. Agric. Rep.* XIV. 112 Think you she will rest until the cob-webs are swept from the tie-ups?

+2. A stoppage of work or operations because of a strike, accident, etc.

1889 *Scientific Amer.* LX. 32/3 In the event of a 'tie-up,' or strike, these street boxes would be used. **1904** *N.Y. Tribune* 29 Oct. 1 An accident to one of the motor cars caused a tie-up of the southbound trains. **1920** COOPER *Under Big Top* 227 Add to all this the handicaps of weather, of railroad tie-ups [etc.].

+Tiff. (See quotations.) — **1814** BRACKENRIDGE *Views La.* 148 The porter's ore, or galena, has always adhering to it, a sparry matter, which the miners call tiff. **1819** SCHOOLCRAFT *Mo. Lead Mines* 70 Tiff, cawk, and sulphate of barytes, are therefore one substance, consisting of the earth barytes united to the sulphuric acid.

＊Tiger.

+1. Any one of various American animals, of the cat family, as the cougar.

1709 LAWSON *Carolina* 119 Tygers are never met withal in the Settlement; but are more to the Westward. **1735** *Ga. Hist. Soc. Coll.* II. 43 We saw . . . four tigers and six bears. **1797** HAWKINS *Letters* 86 The tygers killed his hogs, cattle and sometimes horses. **1817** S. BROWN *West-*

ern Gazetteer 14 On the ridges, and in the swamps, there were a great many bear, deer, and tigers. **1858** [see LEOPARD 1]. **1894** EGGLESTON in *Century Mag.* April 849 The panther was long called a 'tyger' in the Carolinas, and a 'lyon' elsewhere.

+2. The game of faro. *slang.* Also attrib.

To buck the tiger, (see BUCK *v.*[2] 3).

1845 HOOPER *Simon Suggs' Adv.* 55 Of these tables the 'tiger' claimed three—for faro was predominant in those days. **1849** G. G. FOSTER *N.Y. in Slices* 47 The groggeries and tiger dens . . . were in quite a flutter for several hours. **1870** NOWLAND *Indianapolis* 198 In one of the back rooms . . . was a tiger's lair. **1890** [see LEOPARD 2]. **1896** LILLARD *Poker Stories* 87 The unsophisticated young tiger hunter had something on his mind.

+b. *To fight the tiger,* to play against the bank in faro; to gamble. Also *to spread the tiger.* *slang.*

1847 *Santa Fe Repub.* 17 Sept. 2/3 Have you seen the *Elephant,* or fought the *Tiger?* **1853** 'P. PAXTON' *Yankee in Texas* 183 All the rogues is thar fer some reason or nother— . . . some to stock a jury, and a pile to 'spread the tiger' and play poker. *a*1877 *N.Y. Commercial Adv.* (B.), Strange, isn't it, that so many countrymen who come to New York to 'see the elephant' will go and fight the tiger. **1886** WARNER *Pilgrimage* 220 While the majority of the vast encampment reposes in slumber, some resolute spirits are fighting the tiger.

+3. A howl or yell concluding a round of cheering.

1856 *Knickerb.* XLVIII. 288 We summon you to the Inlet. . . . (Terrific cheers and a tiger.) *a*1859 *Boston Ev. Gaz.* (B.), In 1826, the [Boston Light] Infantry visited New York . . . ; and while there the Tigers at a public festival . . . astonished the Gothamites by giving the genuine howl. It pleased the fancy of the hosts, and gradually it became adopted on all festive and joyous occasions, and now 'three cheers and a tiger' are the inseparable demonstrations of approbation in that city. **1876** MILLER *First Fam'lies* 179 'Three cheers for Sandy!' They were given with a tiger. **1905** *Springfield W. Repub.* 3 Nov. 12 As he arose the company gave three rousing cheers and a 'tiger.'

+4. (See quotations.)

1864 WEBSTER 1384/1 *Tiger,* . . . a pneumatic box or pan used in sugar-refining. **1876** KNIGHT 2568/1 *Tiger,* (*Sugar*), a tank having a perforated bottom, through which the molasses escapes. **1881** RAYMOND *Mining Gloss., Tiger.* . . . A tool for supporting a column of bore-rods while raising or lowering them.

+5. a. The Tammany political organization. (See TAMMANY 3 and TAMMANY TIGER). **b.** Short for BLIND TIGER. *colloq.*

1903 *N.Y. Times* 1 Oct. 8 For when we let the Tiger into the City Hall we put him in control of pretty much the entire City Government. **1905** *Dialect Notes* III. 70 The abbreviated form 'tiger' is beginning to be used [in n.w. Ark.].

6. In special combinations.

Tiger frog, =LEOPARD FROG; *t. rug,* a rug made of a tiger's skin; *t. triton,* (see quotation).

1842 *Nat. Hist. N.Y., Zoology* III. 62 The Marsh Frog, *Rana palustris,* . . . is called, in various districts, Pickerel Frog, and also Tiger and Leopard Frog. **1904** A. DALE *Wanted: a Cook* 8 We placed the tiger-rug, with the real tiger-head, . . . by the fireplace. **1842** *Nat. Hist. N.Y., Zoology* III. 83 The Tiger Triton. (*Triton tigrinus.*) . . . It is occasionally found in decayed hollow trees. It resembles, in some respects, the S[alamandridæ] *subviolacea.*

Tiger cat. {1699-} +A western wild cat or lynx. Also attrib. and transf. — **1806** CLARK in *Lewis & C. Exped.* IV. (1905) 113 Capt Lewis [has] a Tiger cat skin [coat]. **1834** A. PIKE *Sketches* 14 Imagine, also, here and there a lonely tiger-cat, lying crouched in some little hollow. **1879** [see MOSS AGATE]. **1886** BURNETT *Lord Fauntleroy* xi, A hefty un she was,—a regular tiger-cat.

Tiger lily. Any one of various lilies having spotted, orange-colored flowers. {1824-} — **1836** LINCOLN *Botany* App. 111 [*Lilium*] *tigrinum,* (tiger lily.) . . . A very showy plant, of easy culture. **1890** HOWELLS *Shadow of Dream* I. vii, The sun . . . shone through clumps of tiger-lilies. *a*1918 G. STUART *On Frontier* II. 227 There were tiger lillies, Maraposa lillies [etc.].

Tiger skin. {1895-} +The skin of any one of various American animals formerly known as tigers. — **1734** *Georgia Col. Rec.* III. 93 Left by him, . . . as a Token of Friendship, . . . One Tyger Skin, & Six Buffalo Skins. **1797** HAWKINS *Letters* 229. **1854** WHIPPLE *Explor. Ry. Route* I. 75 Juan Septimo brought for us several excellent robes of wild-cat or tiger skin.

＊Tight, *a.* +1. Of a bargain or contest: Involving little profit; closely contested. *colloq.* +2. Of a person: Stingy, parsimonious. — (1) **1828** WEBSTER, *Tight,* . . . close; hard; as a tight bargain. **1848** BARTLETT 356 The Loco-focos may succeed in electing Cass, but they will have a tight match to do it. **1867** 'LACKLAND' *Homespun* 243 Writs, summons, capiases, . . . fly from hand to hand like ballots at a tight election. (2) **1828** WEBSTER, *Tight,* . . . close; parsimonious; saving; as a man tight in his dealings. (*In common use in America.*) **1843** STEPHENS *High Life N.Y.* I. 135 It aint common that you'll find a lazy shack of a feller very tight about money. *c*1847 WHITCHER *Bedott P.* ix. 90 Tim Crane was so tight he fairly begrudged the air he breathed.

Tight, *adv.* {1680-} +With verbs of motion: Quickly; with great haste. *colloq.* — **1837** [see BIRCH TREE]. **1867** GOSS *Soldier's Story* 185 'Captin Sherman' . . . was making for Macon as 'tight as he can come.'

1894 'MARK TWAIN' *P. Wilson* xviii, I jumped on his hoss en took out for de river as tight as I could go.

+**Tight place.** A close place; a difficulty or embarrassment. *colloq.* — **1841** *Jamestown* (N.Y.) *Jrnl.* 31 March 2/4 It speaks of his being in a tight place. **1852** BRISTED *Upper Ten Th.* 186 Thus he would . . . shave through tight places on rough and crowded roads. **1880** 'MARK TWAIN' *Tramp Abroad* 248 But truly this was the tightest place I ever was in. **1910** TOMPKINS *Mothers & Fathers* 298 Next time I get into a tight place, . . . I'll give him a little exhibition of how Clingy Vine behaves under those circumstances.

Tight rope. A rope drawn taut upon which an acrobat performs. {1801–}

1840 *Picayune* 27 Sept. 2/1 A sweet girl . . . is to dance the tight rope. **1855** WOOD *Recoll. Stage* 287 In the autumn of 1822 an arrangement was made with the celebrated equestrian, Hunter, . . . for an exhibition of feats on the tight-rope. **1869** *Atlantic Mo.* July 83/2 The Polish lady . . . walked on a tight-rope from the floor of one end of the museum up to the roof of the farthest gallery. **1902** LORIMER *Lett. Merchant* 211 The fellow on the tight-rope . . . [must] keep his feet on the wire all the time and travel straight ahead.

b. *Tight-rope walker*, one who walks or performs on a tight rope.

1869 *Atlantic Mo.* July 83/2 This tight-rope walker was one of the most exemplary, domestic little bodies imaginable. **1891** EARLE *Sabbath* 37 The unhappy would-be tight-rope walker . . . [wished] he had at least broken his arm instead of his father's hat.

★ **Tile.**

★ **1.** A thin, usually rectangular piece of burnt clay, concrete, etc., used for roofing or for paving or lining walls, fireplaces, etc.

1630 HIGGINSON *New-England* 7 We are setting a Bricke-Kill on worke to make Brickes and Tyles for the building of our Houses. **1704** S. KNIGHT *Journal* 53 The Hearth is of Tyles. **1794** COXE *View U.S.* 25 Bricks, tiles . . . are tending to greater perfection, and will soon . . . throw foreign goods of the same kind entirely out of the market. **1879** *Scribner's Mo.* Dec. 246/2 Tile can be bought at moderate prices. **1905** N. DAVIS *Northerner* 243 They could see the motionless figure of the man lying . . . upon the cold tiles.

+**2.** Short for TILEFISH.

1893 *Worthington's Mag.* I. 150 The Tile should be obtainable in numbers equal to the cod.

3. Attrib. and comb. with *earth, factory, fence*, etc.

1654 JOHNSON *Wonder-w. Prov.* 209 Lime, Brick, and Tilemakers . . . are orderly turn'd to their trades. **1757** *Huntington Rec.* II. 443, [I] do hereby Bind & oblige my self . . . to Make and Maintain a good tile fence. **1845** *Knickerb.* XXV. 447 There was the tile-hearth and the diminutive pair of tongs. **1901** HEGAN *Mrs. Wiggs* 115 How would you like to go up to the tile factory, and learn to do decorating?

+**Tilefish.** [From generic name *Lopholatilus* and the tilelike appearance of the brilliantly colored fish.] A marine food fish (*Lopholatilus chamaeleonticeps*) of the eastern coast; by extension, a fish of the family Branchiostegidae: (see quot. 1911). Also attrib. — **1881** in *Rep. Comm. Fisheries* IX. 34 One of the tile-fish taken in the morning was boiled for dinner and served with egg sauce. **1884** GOODE, etc. *Fisheries* I. 360 The Fish Commission steamer . . . was dredging upon the 'Tile-fish Ground.' **1892** *Courier-Journal* 1 Oct. 6/5 The object of the expedition is the search for the tile fish. **1911** *Rep. Fisheries 1908* 317/2 Tilefish (*Latilidae*). . . . The California species (*Caulolatilus princeps*) is also known as the 'whitefish' and 'blanquillo.'

★ **Tillage land.** Land suitable for tillage. — **1662** *Hempstead Rec.* I. 104 [They] have all tred the rates from meeado land to bee levied vpon improved tilidge land and catell. **1681** *Essex Inst. Coll.* I. 156/2 Laid out lotts for tillage land. **1792** *Mass. H. S. Coll.* 1 Ser. I. 272 The tillage lands will produce on an average twenty-five bushels of Indian corn per acre. **1817** [see PLAIN LAND].

Tillandsia. +Any one of various tropical and subtropical American plants, chiefly of the genus *Tillandsia*, of the pineapple family (Bromeliaceae), as the Spanish moss, *Dendropogon* (syn. *Tillandsia*) *usneoides*. Also with specifying term. — **1785** MARSHALL *Amer. Grove* 155 Carolinian Tillandsia. This is a parasite plant. **1857** *Rep. Comm. Patents 1856: Agric.* 67 In the deep shade of cypress swamps . . . the sombre drapery, formed by the hanging tillandsia, gives them a dark and sad appearance. **1884** *Harper's Mag.* March 601/2 Morning-glory, jasmine, water-lily, sparkle among the green of vines and the gray of tillandsia.

+**Till-tapper.** One who robs tills. Also *till-tapping.* — **1893** *Columbus Dispatch* 14 Nov., The firm has been a loser by persistent till-tapping. *Ib.*, the camera lens caught automatically with the photographs of the till-tappers imprinted on the instantaneous plate. **1903** *N.Y. Times* 7 Oct. 8 Their rank [among criminals] will be about that of tilltappers and pickpockets.

★ **Tilt.** +**1.** =LONGSHANKS. +**2.** =TILT-UP 2. — (1) **1813** [see LONGSHANKS]. **1844** *Nat. Hist. N.Y., Zoology* II. 266 The Lawyer . . . is known under the various popular names of Tilt, Stilt, Longshanks. (2) **1891** *Cent.* 6339/1 A simple tilt is a lath or narrow board with a hole bored through one end. . . . An improved tilt consists of an upright with an arm. . . . Also called *tilter, tilt-up,* and *tip-up.*

Tilter, *n.* {1630–} +**1.** A seesaw. +**2.** A swaying motion. +**3.** = TILT-UP 2. — (1) **1727** COMER *Diary* (1893) 17 As I was playing a child-

ish play on a tilter with one Power Merit . . . , I fell. (2) **1833** NEAL *Down-Easters* I. 173 A lawyer . . . [with] a tilter in his walk. (3) **1891** [see TILT 2].

+**Tilter,** *v.* To seesaw or sway up and down. *colloq.* — **1825** NEAL *Bro. Jonathan* III. 271 The cursed pistol . . . was tiltering too, as if it were just ready to go off, at every jump. **1845** JUDD *Margaret* I. 105 A bobolink clung tiltering to the breezy tip of a white birch. **1895** WIGGIN *Village Watch-Tower* 36 Butterflies . . . perch on the . . . stalks and tilter up and down in the sunshine.

Tilt hammer. A heavy hammer raised by mechanical means and allowed to drop upon the object being worked. {1773–} Also attrib. — **1750** *Md. Hist. Mag.* II. 380 One Plateing Forge, working with two Tilt Hammers. **1812** *Ann. 12th Congress* 1 Sess. 2075 [They have] erected . . . steel furnaces, and tilt hammer forges, for manufacturing iron and steel. **1852** *Harper's Mag.* July 149/1 Such is the incessant and intolerable clangor and din produced by the eighteen tilt hammers. **1894** *Ib.* Jan. 422/1 Before James Nasmyth's great invention of the steam hammer, trip or tilt and helve hammers had been the forging tools.

+**Tilt pan.** (See quotation.) — **1833** SILLIMAN *Man. Sugar Cane* 38 [The plan of evaporation] consists in the use of the *Bascule pan* of the French, . . . known also to American refiners by the name of *tilt pan.*

+**Tilt-up. 1.** The spotted sandpiper, *Actitis macularia.* **2.** In fishing, a device placed over a hole in the ice in such a position that it will be tilted, as a signal, by the pull of a fish on the line. — (1) **1842** *Nat. Hist. N.Y., Zoology* I. 247 The Spotted Sand-Lark . . . is known . . . [as] *Teeter* and *Tiltup*, from its often repeated grotesque jerking motions. **1917** *Birds of Amer.* I. 249 Spotted Sandpiper. . . . [Also called] Tip-up; Tilt-up; . . . from its nervous habit of constantly tilting its body. (2) **1891** [see TILT 2]. **1899** VAN DYKE *Fisherman's Luck* 128 [A] 'tilt-up' . . . consists of two sticks fastened in the middle, at right angles to each other.

★ **Timber.**

★ **1.** Trees collectively; the wood of growing trees; +a forest or wood.

1627 *Plymouth Laws* 29 Neither fire wood nor other timber . . . for building or fencing . . . is to be felled or caryed off. **1700** *Waterbury Prop. Rec.* 203 Eyght acers of swamp and upland on ye brook above Langtons timber. **1706** *Va. State P.* I. 101 One Maurice Jones . . . hath comitted diverse great Wastes . . . upon the said land, by falling of Timber, grubbing up of Trees [etc.]. **1792** in *Young Jessamine Co., Ky.* 49 [He] shot him in the arm and ran off into the timber. **1805** in *Young Jessamine Co., Ky.* 69 The timber is white ash, hickory, hackberry. **1835** LATROBE *Rambler in N.A.* II. 219 These Prairies abound with the thickest and most luxuriant belts of forest, or as they are called 'timbers.' **1842** *S. Lit. Messenger* VIII. 63/1 The dwellings [of settlers] are . . . often placed . . . in some sequestered nook of 'timber.' **1894** *Harper's Mag.* March 518/1 The animal was about to enter the thick timber. **1901** DUNCAN & SCOTT *Allen & Woodson Co., Kansas* 9 They found about four hundred lodges of Osage Indians encamped in the timber. **1902** HARBEN *Abner Daniel* 89 It will take a quarter of a million investment to market a half-million-dollar bunch of timber.

+**b.** *Fallen timber*, (see quotation).

1824 DODDRIDGE *Notes* 85 Those places where shortly before the settlement of the country, the timber had been blown down by hurricanes . . . were called the 'fallen timber.'

+**2.** A person or persons considered with respect to his or their qualifications for specified responsibilities; human material. *colloq.*

1831 in Mackenzie *Van Buren* 227 There is but little first rate timber in the democratic ranks. **1878** STOWE *Poganuc People* 30 Zeph is about the last timber I'd expect to make a 'Piscopal on. **1894** *Congress. Rec.* 20 June 6604/1, I do not want to see all the presidential timber in the Democratic party destroyed. **1914** *Emporia Gazette* 13 Jan., He is everlastingly . . . N.G. as gubernatorial timber.

+**3.** *To give* (a horse) *the timber*, to apply the switch or whip to a horse. *slang. Obs.*

1809 WEEMS *Marion* (1833) 192 Giving their horses 'the timber,' [they] flew back upon our main body. **1834** WAKEFIELD *Hist. of War* 63 He suddenly wheeled his horse to the right-about, and giving him timber left them. **1834** *S. Lit. Messenger* I. 182, I did give him the timber—Flying Childers was nothing to him.

+**4.** *To break for high timber*, or variants: To depart in haste and without ceremony. Also in allusive contexts. *slang.*

1836 PECK *New Guide* 115 To employ his [the frontier pioneer's] own figures, he 'breaks for the high timber,' 'clears out for the New Purchase.' **1845** SOL. SMITH *Theatr. Apprent.* 29, I stored my pockets with provisions, and 'broke for high timber.' **1850** GARRARD *Wah-To-Yah* xix. 233 It's time to break fur timber, sure. **1877** BEARD *K.K.K. Sketches* 166 The panic-stricken darkies broke across the landscape with a yearning desire for tall timber that was eloquently depicted on every motion of the supple limbs. **1910** J. HART *Vigilante Girl* 75, I'm afraid a lot of them'll take to the tall timber.

5. *attrib.* (passing into *adj.*) and *comb.* **a.** Designating objects made or consisting of timber.

See also TIMBER RAFT.

*c*1621 in Earle *Sabbath* 1 A timber fort both strong and comely, with flat roof and battlements [served as a meeting place]. **1646** Timber fensinge [see ESTRIPP]. **1721** *Manchester Rec.* I. 151 Ye select men shall bueld a timber pound. **1818** Timber rail roads [see RAILROAD *n.* 1]. **1852** MITCHELL *Dream Life* 86 A high timber gate, opens upon the scattered pasture lands of the hills. **1870** 'O. OPTIC' *Field & Forest* 67 Here's plenty of timber sticks. **1879** *Mich. Gen. Statutes* I. (1882) 552 [Any mill-owner who] shall knowingly manufacture into lumber, shingles, timber-pickets or posts, any log, spar, or shingle-bolt not his own, . . . shall be deemed guilty of a misdemeanor.

b. Designating tracts or areas covered, or partially covered, with timber.

See also TIMBER BELT, TIMBERLAND.

1628 *Plymouth Col. Rec.* XI. 5 They leave all great Tim(ber) swamps for common use. **1663** in *Amer. Speech* XV. 404/1 An irregular Tract of Land Known by the name of Timber slash in Henrico County. **1836** *Quarter Race Ky.* 22 [He] was, as they brag in the timber districts, twenty foot in the clear. **1836** EDWARD *Hist. Texas* 49 Have I not seen hogs, taken from the timber bottoms, . . . [weigh] upwards of three hundred and fifty pounds each. **1837** *Jamestown* (N.Y.) *Jrnl.* 23 Feb. 2/2 Not more than one third of what is called a timber township [in Maine] is covered with pine timber. **1845** KIRKLAND *Western Clearings* 125 There would be timber-patches that looked at first no bigger than your hand. **1846** COOPER *Redskins* vi, The whole property, mills, taverns, farms, timber-lot and all fall in to young Hugh Littlepage. **1852** M. REID *Boy Hunters* xxxiv, There are the 'timber prairies' where trees grow in 'mottes' or groves. **1856** *Porter's Spirit of Times* 27 Dec. 269/1 Certainly the birds must have suffered as severely on the prairie as they could possibly in a 'timber country.'

c. Designating persons who have to do with timber.

See also TIMBER THIEF, and *timber cruiser* in sense d below.

1775 ROMANS *Nat. Hist. Florida* App. p. xxx, The hunters and timber-cutters . . . burn the woods to clear them of under-wood. **1898** N. E. JONES *Squirrel Hunters of Ohio* 223 The 'timber inspector' failed to 'hold up' several thousand Canadian robbers, who were engaged in floating American timber across the line. **1901** *Boston Ev. Globe* 2 Dec. 12/2 (Ernst), Timber dealers always talk of a large piece of mahogany or oak as a log. *Ib.* 227 The timber pirates [were found] responsible for most all the calamities from fire which have befallen the timber lands of [Minn.].

d. In special combinations.

Timber camp, a camp of those engaged in timbering operations; *t. cart*, (see quotation); *t. clock*, ?a wooden or New England clock; *t. cruiser*, one who walks over a tract or area and estimates the amount of timber on it; *t. drive*, =DRIVE *n.* 5 b; *t. farm*, a farm situated in a timbered region; *t. grouse*, (see quotation); *timberheels*, (see quotation) *colloq.*; *t. landing*, =LANDING 2 b; *t. opening*, a natural opening in a wooded region; *t. shoot*, (see quotation); *t. wheel*, (see quotation); *t. wolf*, the large gray wolf of the northern United States and Canada; **t. worm*, (see quotation).

1879 *Scribner's Mo.* Nov. 21/1 We came across occasional timber camps. **1883** KNIGHT *Suppl.* 894/2 *Timber Cart*, . . . a high wheeled cart for drawing timber. The timber, after the cart is driven over it, is raised to the axle by crank-gearing and tackle. **1820** HALL *Lett. from West* 194 In Goshen . . . he will find a land abounding in cheese and timberclocks. **1902** HULBERT *Forest Neighbors* 138 The timber cruiser laughed at him, and lay down to sleep again. *a***1861** WINTHROP *Open Air* 23 The head-driver of a timber-drive leads a disorderly army, that will not obey the word of command. **1857** *Rep. Comm. Patents 1856: Agric.* 104 This meadow-mouse . . . in timber-farms . . . is doubtless as great a pest . . . as the prairie species. **1891** *Cent.* 6340/2 *Timber-grouse*, . . . any grouse of wood-loving habits, as the ruffed grouse, the pine-grouse, or the spruce-partridge. **1877** BARTLETT 706 *Timberheels*, a headlong fellow careless in walking. **1791** W. BARTRAM *Travels* 312 The log or timber landing is a capacious open area. **1845** *Xenia Torch-Light* 31 July 1/1 Many an emigrant . . . [had] 'dotted down' in the midst of the timber-openings. **1884** *Rep. Comm. Agric.* 172 One of these models represented the timber-shoot, or lade, adown which timber can be sent. **1905** *Forestry Bureau Bul.* No. 61, 42 *Logging wheels*, a pair of wheels, usually about 10 feet in diameter, for transporting logs. . . . Syn.: big wheels, katydid, timber wheels. **1891** *Cent.* 6340/2 *Timber-wolf*, . . . the ordinary large gray or brindled wolf of western parts of North America, *Canis lupus occidentalis*. Though by no means confined to wooded regions, this wolf is so named in antithesis to *prairie-wolf* (the coyote). **1885** *Library Mag.* April 292/2 [The ivory-bill's] principal food is a large flat-headed timber-worm, known in the South as *borer* or *saw-worm*.

+**Timber belt.** A belt or strip of timbered country or of timber. — **1862** *Ill. Agric. Soc. Trans.* V. 212 Along side of a timber belt it would be different. **1872** TICE *Over Plains* 15 The view is bounded by the timber belt along that stream. **1889** MUNROE *Golden Days* 92 Our adventurers made their slow way after leaving the timber belt of the bottom lands.

+**Timber claim.** A claim to public land secured upon condition that the claimant plant and cultivate a specified acreage of trees upon the land. — **1857** *Lawrence* (Kan.) *Republican* 4 June, Timber claims . . . may be purchased on better terms than in any place of equal distance from Lawrence. **1884** *Rep. Comm. Agric.* 337 Most of the timber-claims in the counties named have been taken from six to ten years ago. **1890** *Stock Grower & Farmer* 8 Feb. 2/2 The largest stock of Forest Trees for Timber Claims in the world.

+**Timber doodle. 1.** A form of spirituous drink. *slang. Obs.* **2.** (See quotation.) — **(1) 1842** DICKENS *Amer. Notes* 26 There, too, the stranger is initiated into the mysteries of . . . Sherry-cobbler, Timber Doodle, and other rare drinks. **1844** 'UNCLE SAM' *Peculiarities* I. 161 Give me a hold-fast, or a timber-doodle. **1873** *Punch* 17 May 201/2 Any description of beverage possessing the properties of American 'timberdoodle.' **(2) 1891** *Cent.* 6340/1 *Timberdoodle*, . . . the American woodcock, *Philohela minor*. [Local, U.S.]

+**Timbered country.** A timbered or wooded region. — **1807** GASS *Journal* 153 Acorns . . . are signs of a timbered country not far distant. **1834** PECK *Gaz. Illinois* 215 It is a timbered country, undulating, and broken. **1883** HOWE *Country Town* (1926) 8, I believed that the writers lived in a heavily timbered country.

+**Timbered land.** Land covered with timber. {1887-} — **1722** *Amer. Wkly. Mercury* 17 May 4/2 Two Plantations . . . both containing about 700 Acres of very rich well-water'd and timber'd Land. **1797** HAWKINS *Letters* 112 Continue on a blind tract thro' hilly loch timbered land and down a stream. **1817** BIRKBECK *Notes Journey in Amer.* (1818) 116 We are so taken, with the prairies we have seen . . . that no 'timbered' land can satisfy our present views. **1847** LANMAN *Summer in Wilderness* 170 The best and most fertile soil in Michigan is that designated by the title of timbered land.

+**Timberland.** Land that is well wooded, esp. with marketable timber. — **1654** *Suffolk Deeds* II. 55 Howses fence or gardens, Tymber Lands broaken & vnbroaken as whatsoeuer elce Appertenances. **1816** U. BROWN *Journal* II. 233 This Line Cuts away . . . Considerable of Their Timber Land. **1884** *Rep. Comm. Agric.* 138 A code of laws was passed making provision for securing the rights of property in timber-lands. **1909** *Indian Laws & Tr.* III. 403 All merchantable timber on said lands returned and classified by said commission as timber lands shall be sold and disposed of by the Secretary of the Interior.

+**Timber line. 1.** In cold or mountainous regions, the line above which timber does not grow. Also transf. **2.** The boundary line of a timbered tract. — **(1) 1867** *Harper's Mag.* June 17/2 A high mountain range divided into innumerable peaks, all of which tower above the timber-line. **1881** CHASE *Editor's Run in N. Mex.* 182, I had a feeling, too, of being *locked up*, far away in the Rocky mountains, almost above timber line. **1901** RYAN *Montana* 72 The top of his head had got above timber line and glistened in the sun of early summer. *a***1918** G. STUART *On Frontier* II. 116 The top of the range is above timber line. **(2) 1904** STRATTON-PORTER *Freckles* 20 The Boss showed him around the timber-line.

+**Timber pine.** Any one of various pines the wood of which is valued as timber. — **1817** S. BROWN *Western Gazetteer* 10 Between the Mobile and the Perdido, the soil is thin, timber pine, loblolly bay, cypress. **1877** JEWETT *Deephaven* 156 No such timber-pines nowadays.

Timber raft. A raft of logs. {1853, in Canada} — **1819** *Plough Boy* I. 7 The experiment of towing timber-rafts, on our northern waters, . . . is about to be tried. **1875** 'MARK TWAIN' *Old Times* iv. 68 Down came a swarm of prodigious timber-rafts from the head waters of the Mississippi. **1883** — *Life on Miss.* iii, The river from end to end was flaked with coal-fleets and timber-rafts. **1889** MUNROE *Golden Days* 228 The miner had helped navigate great timber rafts down the Ohio.

+**Timber thief.** One who cuts and sells timber which is the property of another, esp. of the state or national government. — **1878** *Rep. on Forestry* (Forest Service) I. 9 Too often the forest history of our most valuable woodlands would be a record of the doings of timber-thieves. **1893** *Garden & Forest* VI. 511/2 Timber-thieves have been cutting on the public domain. **1904** STRATTON-PORTER *Freckles* 208 You've kept the timber-thieves out of this lease.

***Timber tree.** A tree the wood of which is valuable as building material. — **1628** *Plymouth Col. Rec.* XI. 4 Timber trees were excepted [against use for firewood] for the owners of the ground. **1781** PETERS *Hist. Conn.* (1829) 187 The ash, elm, beech . . . are the chief timber trees of this province. **1832** WILLIAMSON *Maine* II. 28 All timber trees upon the crown lands . . . were reserved for the use of the royal navy. **1883** SMITH *Geol. Survey Ala.* p. vi, Next follows a list of the botanical and common names of the characteristic timber-trees.

***Time,** *n.*

I. +**1. a.** An unexpired period of compulsory service, orig. of indentured servants. *Obs.* **b.** The time of a slave who is permitted to seek outside employment on condition that he pay a stipulated amount to his owner. *Obs.*

1705 *Boston News-Letter* 5 Nov. 2/1 This Young man wrote to Mr. Samuel Carpenter, and other Quakers of Philadelphia, . . . who came forthwith to Virginia, and bought his time & brought him to Philadelphia last year. **1715** *Ib.* 2 May 2/2 A North British Mans Time for Seven years to be disposed of by Simon Slocum. **1769** *Boston Gaz.* Nov. (Th.), To be sold for five Years, The Time of a hearty young Man, who is a good Sailor. **1843** *Missouri Reporter* 28 Jan. (Th.), I have for sale a very likely yellow woman . . . [with] between five and six years to serve. The balance of her time will be sold very low. **1865** *Atlantic Mo.* April 509/1 He was the slave of a gentleman who allowed him to buy his time.

+**2.** *Baseball.* (See quotations.)

1878 *De Witt's Base-Ball Guide* 79 When the umpire calls 'time,' play shall be suspended until he calls 'play' again. **1910** *Spalding's Base Ball Guide* 349 'Time at Bat' is the duration of a batter's turn against the pitcher until he becomes a base runner.

II. In colloq. phrases. **4.** *On time.* **a.** Of a transaction in securities: Arranged to take place at some time, at the price then current, in the future. {1766}

1841 *Week in Wall Street* 80 Stocks sold on time, are seldom delivered. **1848** ARMSTRONG *Stocks* 10 One result of these methods of operating on time is, that a person . . . may realize the advance upon a much larger amount than he is able to buy for cash. **1859** BARTLETT 255 '*Long*' means when a man has bought stock on time, which he can call for at any day he chooses. **1885** *Harper's Mag.* Nov. 848/2 Sales are either for *cash* . . . or on *time*, usually three, ten, thirty, or sixty days.

+b. With reference to buying or selling in general: To be paid for, in whole or in part, at a later time or in installments.

1846 *Spirit of Times* (N.Y.) 6 June 170/3 But I never recovered my hat, and since then I have been buying 'em on time! **1855** *Chicago Times* 16 Jan. 2/5 Port wine . . . will be sold very low and on time to responsible parties. **1920** SANDBURG *Smoke & Steel* 50 They go to an installment house and buy a bed on time.

c. At the time set or expected; punctually. {1890, in Australia; 1892–}

1848 DURIVAGE & BURNHAM *Stray Subjects* 30 S'pose you never heard of burying a man on time! **1874** PINKERTON *Expressman & Detective* 79 He got to the station 'on time.' **1893** 'MARK TWAIN' *£1,000,000 Bank-Note* 16 They'll be here on time. **1905** ATHERTON *Travelling Thirds* 139 The train arrived on time.

5. *To have a time*, to pass through a period of exceptional activity, difficulty, excitement, etc.

1847 DRAKE *Pioneer Life Ky.* 65 On such occasions mother always had a 'time on't,' for there must be many extras on the table. **1857** [see CORN-STEALER]. **1882** RITTENHOUSE *Maud* 149, I've had a 'time' with Mr. Blauvelt.

* b. To have a time of a designated nature.

'To have a good time (= a time of enjoyment) was common in Eng. from *c*1520 to *c*1688; it was app. retained in America, whence readopted in Britain in 19th c.' (*O.E.D.*). See also GOOD TIME.

1834 C. A. DAVIS *Lett. J. Downing* 35, I had a real time there for a week. **1856** OLMSTED *Slave States* 82, I was having a very good time with her, when her father came in and told her she was 'troubling the gentleman.' **1888** *Boston Jrnl.* 30 June 2/4 The editor . . . will hardly have as big a time as he expected. **1903** 'O. HENRY' *Roads of Destiny* 369 We'll have the highest old time y u ever saw.

c. *Not to have much of a time*, not to have a pleasant time of it.

1898 WESTCOTT *D. Harum* 14 Mis' Perkins don't hev much of a time herself.

* 6. *By time*, +a mild oath or ejaculation.

1847 LOWELL *Biglow P.* 1 Ser. ii. 15 By Time, ses he, I *du* like a feller that aint a Feared. **1865** TROWBRIDGE *Three Scouts* 351 By time, don't that taste good!

+7. *Why* (or *what*) *in time*, why (or what) on earth.

1849 *Corr. R. W. Griswold* (1898) 250 Why in Time don't you come our way and see the boys? **1898** N. BROOKS *Boys of Fairport* 201 What'n time are you fellers up to? **1918** LINCOLN *Shavings* 191 Why in time . . . didn't you tell me right out that 'twas Mrs. Armstrong's brother you had in mind?

+8. *To make a time*, to make a demonstration or fuss *over* or *about* something.

1888 *Boston Jrnl.* 31 July 2/5 She doesn't weep at the parting or make any time over it. **1901** *N. Amer. Rev.* Feb. 228 No other troops made such a time about water as the Americans.

+9. *To bring* (or *call*) *to time*, to call to account; to take in hand.

1890 CUSTER *Following Guidon* 31 [The bouncer's] duties consist in bringing to time people who neglect to pay their bill. **1894** RITTENHOUSE *Maud* 572 She guys him, and calls him to time sharply, laughing the most infectiously jolly laugh right afterward.

10. In miscellaneous phrases. (See also BEAT *v.* 3 b.)

On a time, on a drunken spree; *to run like time*, to run rapidly; *up to time*, up to standard; *to take* (a laborer's) *time*, to begin a record of (a laborer's) working time, as a basis for pay; *in with the times*, in harmony with the times; *for all the time*, always.

*a*1855 J. F. KELLY *Humors* 185 The captain, being on a *time*, dashed into a meeting-house. **1864** 'E. KIRKE' *Down in Tenn.* 118 The current was running 'like time.' **1869** 'MARK TWAIN' *Innocents* 58 They were always up to time—they could outrun and out last a donkey. **1876** HABBERTON *Jericho Road* 10 Go below and tell the mate to take your time. **1894** CABLE *J. March* xl, Just that Yankee's being here . . . has pulled my wits together . . . because he's in with the times. **1902** G. C. EGGLESTON *D. South* 273, I wish you would keep her there 'for all the time.'

III. **11.** In special combinations.

Time alarm, (see quotation); *t. belt*, one of the four longitudinal belts or strips, approximately fifteen degrees wide, into which the United States is divided for standardizing time; *t. bet*, a bet on the time necessary for a horse to run a certain distance; *t. bill*, a bill payable at a specified future date; *t. candle*, (see quotation); *t. check*, a check or certificate showing the time an employee has worked; *t. deposit*, a deposit in a bank for a definite length of time; *t. draft*, a draft payable at a specified time; *t. locker*, a bank vault provided with a time lock; *t. register*, (see quotation); *t. watch*, a stop watch.

1876 KNIGHT 2572/2 Time-alarm, an audible notice at the expiration of a set time. **1894** *Amer. Annual Photography* IX. 22 In each of these time-belts, the standard time is one hour faster than in the adjoining time-belt on the West. **1868** WOODRUFF *Trotting Horse* 235 Time-bets were made upon the Lady. **1851** CIST *Cincinnati* 90 This House deals very extensively . . . in time bills on N. Orleans. **1876** KNIGHT 2573/1 Time-candle, one in which the size and quality of the material and the wick are so regulated that a certain length will burn in a given time. **1901** MERWIN & WEBSTER *Calumet 'K'* 128 He leaves the job just as quick as we can make out a time-check. **1851** CIST *Cincinnati* 90 Their policy of taking *time* deposits and allowing eight and ten per cent. interest . . . [has] attracted public attention. **1863** 'E. KIRKE' *Southern Friends* 224 Our banks requiring two home names on time drafts, I have to beg you to honor a small bill at one day's sight. **1905** 'O. HENRY' *Roads of Destiny* 142 His little tin safe is as good as the time-locker in the First National Bank of Laredo. **1855** HOLBROOK *Among Mail Bags* 102 The 'time register'—a book in which each clerk is required to enter his name and the time of his arrival at and departure from the office. **1856** *Porter's Spirit of Times* 25 Oct. 129/2 We are now prepared to attend to all orders . . . for the purchase of . . . fishing apparatus, time-watches and sporting articles of every conceivable description.

* Time, *v.* Baseball. +*tr.* (See quotation.) — **1867** CHADWICK *Base Ball Reference* 139 To time a ball well is to hit it . . . in such a manner as to send it in the very direction you want it to go. . . . The pace of the pitching must be taken into consideration in timing the swing of the bat.

+Time card.

1. A card on which there is a time-table or schedule.

1873 *Newton Kansan* 24 April 3/2 The new time card . . . allows the conductors . . . to lay over here. **1904** *Booklovers Mag.* May 663 On every large railway system there is a train not scheduled on the time-card.

2. A card for keeping a record of hours worked or the time of a worker's arrival or departure.

1891 *Cent.* 6342/2. **1898** *Engineering Mag.* XVI. 41 Each workman perforates a five-minute time-card for each job on which he is employed. **1901** MERWIN & WEBSTER *Calumet 'K'* 11 My time cards for the first years figured up four hundred and thirty-six days.

+Time clock. A clock having a device for recording the time of arrival and departure of employees or the time at which something is done. — **1887** GEORGE *40 Yrs. on Rail* 56 [He] pulled a wire leading to a time-clock. **1923** WATTS *L. Nichols* 62 He came every morning promptly, registered his arrival on the time-clock.

Timekeeper. {1686–} One who keeps track of the time employees work. {1851–} — **1870** NOWLAND *Indianapolis* 274 McPherson was employed . . . as a clerk and timekeeper. **1892** *Courier-Journal* 3 Oct. 3/3 Mr. Needy . . . is now a time-keeper of a gang of laborers. **1902** LORIMER *Lett. Merchant* 36, I raised his salary, and made him an assistant time-keeper and checker.

Time lock. (See quot. 1876.) {1908–} — **1869** *Rep. Comm. Patents* II. 224/2 Time-Lock. . . . The combination of the shaft [etc.]. **1876** KNIGHT 2573/2 Time-lock, a lock having clock-work attached, which . . . prevents the bolt being withdrawn when locked, until a certain interval of time has elapsed. **1903** 'O. HENRY' *Roads of Destiny* 169 [The vault] fastened with three solid steel bolts, . . . and had a time-lock.

Timist. {1613–} +(See quotation.) — **1884** *Independent Almanac* 18 Only a small company [of Adventists], called 'Timists,' now venture to fix a definite time for the advent.

+Timothy. [f. *Timothy* Hanson, an early (*c*1720) grower of this grass.]

1. A meadow grass (*Phleum pratense*) valued for forage.

1747 FRANKLIN *Writings* II. 313 What [grass seed] you gave me is grown up and proves mere Timothy. **1787** CUTLER *Life & Corr.* I. 288 [N. J. farmers] begin, however, to sow some quantity of herd's-grass seed, which they call Timothy. **1807** GASS *Journal* 127, [I] saw no clover or timothy, as I had seen on the Missouri and Jefferson river. **1879** TAYLOR *Summer-Savory* 13 The timothy smelled sweet in the sun. **1923** [see BLACK-EYED *a.* 2].

b. = TIMOTHY HAY.

1889 VASEY *Agric. Grasses* 56 An inferior hay, called salt hay, . . . is worth about half as much per ton as Timothy or redtop.

2. Attrib. with *field, head, seed*, etc.

1784 *Penna. Gazette* 17 March 3/2 Timothy seed. **1843** 'CARLTON' *New Purchase* I. 168 [We] told tales, . . . tickled folk's ears with timothy heads, . . . chased girls going to the spring for water. **1847** *Cultivator* ns. IV. 159 I broke a piece for wheat, which was a stiff timothy sod. **1856** *Rep. Comm. Patents 1855: Agric.* 254 Timothy, with us, is generally sown . . . by means of a Timothy sower attached to the drill. **1884** ROE *Nature's Story* viii, The mowing machine would be used in the timothy fields.

+Timothy grass. = TIMOTHY 1. — **1751** ELIOT *Field-Husb.* iii. 57 Herd-Grass (known in Pennsylvania by the name of Timothy-Grass). **1804** J. ROBERTS *Penna. Farmer* 49 Timothy Grass . . . makes the best hay. **1884** BURROUGHS *Fresh Fields* 185 [As] Timothy grass . . . is an American grass, it seems to be quite unknown among English and Scotch farmers. **1909** BIGELOW *Retrospections* I. 9 [On] a few stalks of timothy grass . . . I would string as many raspberries as would suffice for my dinner.

+**Timothy hay.** Hay made from timothy grass. — **1772** *Penna. Gazette* 16 April 4/3 (Ernst), Timothy and blue grass hay to be sold. **1816** U. BROWN *Journal* 11. 356 A great deal of grain & Timothy hay [is] made in this Valley. **1885** *Rep. Indian Affairs* 67 They all cut more or less wild grass in addition to what timothy hay is herein enumerated.

+**Timothy meadow.** Meadowland sown with timothy grass. — **1786** *Penna. Ev. Herald* 12 April 89/1 To be Sold . . . thirty acres of timothy meadow. **1831** PECK *Guide* 160 By this process, timothy meadows may be made and preserved. **1863** *Rep. Comm. Agric.* *1862* 80 His own and his neighbor's old and well-established timothy meadows . . . had that year yielded a good crop of cheat.

∗**Tin.**

∗**1.** A well-known malleable metal in appearance resembling silver; a commercial form of this.

1637 MORTON *New Canaan* 85 Mines of Tinne are likewise knowne to be in those parts. **1780** *Va. State P.* I. 397 Colo[nel] Muter will be pleased to prepare proper requisitions on Mr. Armstead for nail-rods and tin. **1850** [see FIRE INSURANCE COMPANY]. **1902** LORIMER *Lett. Merchant* 94 A big drought . . . began driving the canners in to the packing-house quicker than we could tuck them away in tin.

+**b.** A professional man's sign.

*c*1845 PAULDING *Amer. Comedies* (1847) 108, I've had my tin up in gilt letters for two months.

2. *attrib.* (passing into *adj.*) and *comb.* **a.** Designating articles made of tin plate.

See also TIN BUCKET, TIN CAN, etc.

1678 *New Castle Court Rec.* 361 A Piggin & A Tinne paile. **1776** Tin fish kettle [see FISH KETTLE]. **1825** NEAL *Bro. Jonathan* I. 90 As if he were sounding a charge with . . . a tin-whistle. **1840** *Knickerb.* XVI. 238 Among the innumerable little tin signs in Wall-street, [was] one which bore the name of Brothers Tuck. **1863** Tin-baker [see BAKER 2]. **1873** *Winfield* (Kan.) *Courier* 7 Aug. 1/7 He passed over the edge of the roof, with twenty feet of tin gutter hitched to him. **1883** *Harper's Mag.* Dec. 111/1 Each member carried some article of feminine necessity—a bird-cage, . . . a tin cake canister. **1896** Tin growler [see GROWLER 2]. **1907** *St. Nicholas* June 729/1 For the receivers, secure two empty tin baking-powder boxes.

b. In special combinations.

Tin coat, a short, close-fitting coat; *tinmonger*, a dealer in tin or tinware; *t. store*, a store in which tinware is sold; *t. tag*, a tag of tinned iron used as an identification mark on cattle; *t. trader*, =TIN PEDDLER; *t. wagon*, a wagon in which a tin peddler conveys his wares, used attrib.; *tin wedding*, the tenth anniversary of a marriage, used attrib.

1856 'MARK TWAIN' *Adv. Snodgrass* 9 Then some soldiers with bob-tailed tin coats on (high water coats we used to call 'em in Keokuk) come in. **1893** — *P. Wilson* i, The chief tinmonger's noisy notice to the world. **1866** *Ore. State Jrnl.* 23 June 4/1 Eugene City Stove and Tin Store. **1885** *Wkly. New Mexican Rev.* 15 Jan. 2/6 On left sides slit in right ear, tin tag in left. **1812** PAULDING *J. Bull & Bro. Jon.* 93 When he [a Southerner] was taken in, he was sure to pummel the tin-trader. **1827** *Western Mo. Rev.* I. 85 The tin wagon, pit-coal-indigo, wooden nutmeg, and wooden clock missionaries find the harvest beginning to fall short. **1863** *Harper's Mag.* Nov. 856/2 Mr Jones's people made him a tin-wedding visit on the tenth anniversary of his marriage.

Tin bucket. A bucket, esp. a small one, of tinned iron, often used as a dinner pail. Also attrib. — **1839** 'M. PENCIL' *White Sulphur P.* 84 Suspended from the ceiling, were tin buckets, hosiery, baskets, . . . and numerous other trifles. **1856** M. J. HOLMES *Homestead* vi. i, The little 'tin bucket' . . . serves the treble purpose of dinnerpail, washbowl, and drinking cup. **1890** *Congress. Rec.* 12 May 4576/1 Fancy brings before me now that long line, the 'tin-bucket brigade' of railroad laborers.

Tin can. A can made of tinned iron. — **1770** WASHINGTON *Diaries* I. 442, I was to . . . give them a Quart Tinn Can. **1851** CIST *Cincinnati* 171 Among other things produced was a tin can of water crackers. **1888** *Outing* May 102 The fools, like empty tin cans, are found everywhere. **1920** SANDBURG *Smoke & Steel* 63 You jazzmen, bang . . . drums, traps, banjoes, horns, tin cans.

+**Tin cart.** A cart in which a tin peddler conveys his wares. Also attrib. — **1858** *Harper's Mag.* May 722/2 They were presently provided with a vehicle of the tin cart species for the passengers. **1887** WILKINS *Humble Romance* 12 The tin-cart had been put up in the hotel stable.

+**Tinclad (gunboat).** A vessel planked or otherwise protected by light armor from rifle fire. — **1864** *Amer. Annual Cycl. 1863* 680/1 The flotilla on the Mississippi . . . [included] 33 'tinclads,' so called from being less heavily plated than [ironclads]. **1874** COLLINS *Kentucky* I. 125 Morgan crosses . . . , although resisted by . . . the tin-clad gunboat in the river above. **1887** *Scientific Amer.* LVI. 263/3 [Eads] converted . . . seven transports into what were called 'tinclads,' or musket-proof gunboats. **1899** *Boston Globe* 4 June 28/8 The term 'tin-clad' . . . is not remotely connected with the white metal but signifies rather boats heavily planked with oak for the purpose of protecting them somewhat from ravages of bullets.

Tin cup. A cup made of tinned iron or tin plate. — **1805** [see HOWEL]. **1874** EGGLESTON *Circuit Rider* 217 She persuaded her father to buy half-a-dozen tin cups. **1881** *Rep. Indian Affairs* p. xxxv, This year the Carlisle school has shipped to forty-two Indian agencies 8,929 tin cups, coffee-boilers [etc.]. **1907** STEWART *Partners* 204, [I drank] a big tin-cup full of black coffee the first thing in the morning.

∗**Tinder box.** A box for holding tinder used in kindling fires. — **1638** *Md. Archives* IV. 48, 1. tinder box & steele. **1759** *Newport Mercury* 26 June 4/3 Imported, . . . Pistol Tinder-boxes, English Pack-thread. **1840** COOPER *Pathfinder* I. 55 Take the flint and tinder-box, creep along the bank, and light a fire at that spot. **1886** POORE *Reminisc.* I. 108 The lucifer match-box . . . superseded the large tin tinder-box with its flint and steel.

Tinhorn. +A person, esp. a pretentious or flashy one, of little real substance; spec., one who gambles with low stakes. Also attrib. or as adj. *slang.* — **1885** *Wkly. New Mexican Rev.* 26 Feb. 4/2 We have been greatly annoyed of late by a lot of tin horn gamblers and prostitutes. **1887** F. FRANCIS *Saddle & Moccasin* 225 The tin-horns were there in a body, with a few stacks of chips, playing light. **1902** W. J. GHENT *Our Benevolent Feudalism* 171 What is colloquially known as 'tin-horn' gambling has advanced by leaps and bounds. **1920** [see PIKER[2] b].

∗**Tinker.** +**a.** A small mackerel approximately two years old. +**b.** (See quot. 1891 and cf. next.) — (a) **1848** BARTLETT 356 *Tinker*, small mackerel. New England. **1864** *Boston Soc. Nat. Hist. Proc.* X. 67 The fishermen divide the mackerel into four classes, according to their size, . . . 'large,' 'second size,' 'tinkers,' and 'blinks.' **1886** *Scientific Amer.* LIV. 352/3 Mackerel may be so plenty as to be almost given away, as . . . recently, during the early run of young mackerel or 'tinkers.' (b) **1891** *Cent.* 6347/2 *Tinker*, . . . the chub-mackerel.

+**Tinker mackerel.** The chub mackerel or a related species. (Cf. prec.) — **1884** GOODE, etc. *Fisheries* I. 304 A considerable school of these fish [the chub mackerel] . . . were taken in company with the Tinker Mackerel. *Ib.*, The Tinker Mackerel, S[comber] *pneumatophorus*, is known as 'Mackerel,' 'Easter Mackerel,' . . . and 'Little Mackerel.' **1911** *Rep. Fisheries 1908* 309/1 Chub mackerel (*Scomber japonicus*) . . . is also called . . . 'tinker mackerel.'

+**Tin kitchen.** An oven made of tin for roasting meat before an open fire. — **1828** WEBSTER, *Kitchen*, . . . a utensil for roasting meat; as, a tin kitchen. **1838** FLAGG *Far West* II. 46 A huge lumbering baggage-wagon, around which dangled . . . dutch-ovens and tin-kitchens, cheese-roasters and bread-toasters. **1868** G. G. CHANNING *Recoll. Newport* 161 There were no 'tin kitchens' then to dry up the birds . . . ; but roasting was done on a long spit. **1899** A. BROWN *Tiverton Tales* 243 ' 'Milia,' said aunt Ann suddenly, looking down over her glasses at the tin kitchen.

∗**Tinman.** A dealer in tinware, a tin peddler; a tinsmith. — **1782** *Royal Gaz.* (Charleston, S.C.) 13 July 3/1 His stock in Trade [includes] . . . Tin Man's Tools. **1796** *Boston Directory* 261 King, Henry, tinman, Prince street. **1829** SANDS *Writings* II. 57 They actually appointed a subcommittee [including a] . . . pot-bellied tinman. **1887** WILKINS *Humble Romance* 11 The tinman came down with astonishing alacrity from his first price.

+**Tinmouth.** **a.** The crappie, *Pomoxis annularis*. **b.** The calico bass, *P. sparoides*. — **1888** [see BRIDGE PERCH]. **1903** T. H. BEAN *Fishes N.Y.* 463 Other names of local application are barfish, bitter head, tinmouth, sac-a-lait [etc.].

Tin pan, *n.*

1. A pan made of tinned iron.

1806 *Austin P.* I. (1924) 102, 1 doz. Tin pans. **1848** *30th Congress 2 Sess. H. R. Ex. Doc. No. 1*, 57 About two hundred men were at work . . . washing for gold, some with tin pans, some with close woven Indian baskets. **1872** BRACE *Dangerous Classes N.Y.* 204 Drawing out a good-sized tin pan full of boiled corn-meal. **1917** MATHEWSON *Second Base Sloan* 160 The clattering, tinkling wagon hung with tin pans and dippers and plates and dustpans.

+**2.** *Tin-pan revival*, ?a religious revival marked by noisy enthusiasm.

1902 HARBEN *A. Daniel* 178 Sister, that's the trouble with these tin-pan revivals.

Tin-pan, *v.* To serenade (someone) with the beating of tin pans and similar noise-makers. *colloq.* — **1885** *South Fla. Sentinel* (Orlando) 22 July 1/6 The parties were tin-panned Monday night.

+**Tin peddler.** A peddler who sells tinware. — **1812** *Beauties of Bull-us* 53 [The] 'feather-merchants, rag-men, tin-pedlars, and horse-jockies' of *Connecticut* are almost to a man *democrats*. **1837** *U.S. Mag.* I. 34 Here is a tin-pedler, whose glittering ware bedazzles all beholders. **1887** WILKINS *Humble Romance* 2 She went over to the pantry, and whispered to her mistress that it was the tin-peddler. **1918** RIDEOUT *Key of Fields* 262 Old Eph Bucklands, the tin peddler, carted me round Canada and New England on his cart.

+**Tin-peddling.** The occupation of a tin peddler; hence any sharp activity regarded as characteristic of the shrewd Yankee peddlers. — **1837** *S. Lit. Messenger* III. 414 Mr. Hardin . . . is represented . . . to have 'hit at cod-fishery, wooden nutmegs and tin peddling.' **1883** EGGLESTON *Hoosier School-Boy* 99 Ignorant and pretentious men, . . . wanderers from New England, who had grown tired of clock-peddling, or tin-peddling, . . . would get places as teachers.

Tin-plate worker. A tinsmith. {1720-} — **1729** *Boston Selectmen* 193 The Select men Executed a Lease to Benjamin Bunker Junr. of Boston, Tin plate worker. **1789** *Boston Directory* 177 Bradley Josiah, tin-plate-worker. **1809** CUMING *Western Tour* 222 Pittsburgh [has] . . . seven coppersmiths, tinplate workers, and japanners. **1851** CIST *Cincinnati* 51 Occupations, Trades, and Pursuits. . . . Telegraphers 7, Tin-plate workers 7.

Tin roof. A roof made of tinned iron. — **1827** SHERWOOD *Gaz. Georgia* 174 The proprietors pledge themselves to furnish it as cheap as a tin roof. **1875** *Chicago Tribune* 26 July 5/7, I find it [*sc.* paint] a slow drier, which is . . . no objection, especially on tin roofs, where there is expansion and contraction to contend with. **1903** [see EXTENSION 3].

Tin shop. The shop of a tinsmith. {1850– (Mayhew *London Labour* I. 372/1)} Also attrib. — **1827** DRAKE & MANSFIELD *Cincinnati* 65 Nine Tin and Coppersmith shops. **1876** HABBERTON *Jericho Road* 130 A tinshop apprentice . . . dropped at the bench with a groan. **1881** *Rep. Indian Affairs* p. xxxiv, The articles manufactured and job work done by apprentices in the harness, shoe, tin, and blacksmith shops have netted the school, $776.62.

Tinsmith. A worker in tin plate. {1858–} — **1812** MELISH *Travels* II. 55 Professions exercised in Pittsburg: . . . copper-smiths, tin-smiths, silver-smiths. **1861** *N.Y. Tribune* 19 Nov. 8/1 In a vacant lot . . . tinsmiths had dumped a heap of refuse tin. **1892** *York County Hist. Rev.* 33 The individual members of the firm . . . are practical and experienced tinsmiths and sheet metal workers.

+Tintinnabulation. [From L. *tintinnabulum* 'bell.'] The ringing, pealing, or jingling of bells; a sound or series of sounds suggestive of this. {1883} — **1831** POE *Bells* i, The tintinabulation that so musically swells From the bells. **1853** *La Crosse Democrat* 6 Dec. 2/5 The last tintinabulation of the last funeral bell is drowned by the clattering of hurrying feet. **1877** BURROUGHS *Birds & Poets* 25 The bobolink [has] . . . the qualities of hilarity and musical tintinnabulation.

+Tintype.
1. A photographic positive taken on a thin iron plate. {1894–}
1864 E. W. Pearson *Lett. Port Royal* 243 You will probably in due course see the tin-types of Rose and Demus. **1892** *York County Hist. Rev.* 81 Another feature is made in taking all kinds of photographs, whether in- or out-door, tin-types [etc.]. **1919** *Maine My State* 18 (*caption*), Theodore Roosevelt on His First Maine Vacation. From an Old Tintype.
2. Attrib. and comb. with *album, gallery, man, taker.*
1880 HOWELLS *Undiscovered Country* 3 That round table . . . with its subscription literature and its tin-type albums. **1880** *Scribner's Mo.* July 362/1 The tin-type man is driven to distraction with business. **1883** *Harper's Mag.* May 818/1 Third Street . . . [abounds] in small restaurants, markets, and 'tin-type' galleries. **1903** 'O. HENRY' *Roads of Destiny* 212 Old man Billfinger, an educated tintype taker.

Tinware. Articles made of tin plate. {1850– (Mayhew *London Labour* I. 392/1)} Also attrib. — **1758** REA *Journal* 26 Rogers . . . got considerable baggage, Iron, Copper and Tinware with other Household Furniture. **1820** FLINT *Lett. from Amer.* 213 Tin ware manufactories, 6. **1851** CIST *Cincinnati* 215 Japaned[,] Ornamental, and Pressed Tin Ware.— There are four establishments manufacturing these articles. **1868** *Ore. State Jrnl.* 20 June 4/3 J. Ward & Co. [have] purchased the entire interest of Wheeler & Ward in the Stove and Tin Ware Business. **1895** *Outing* XXVI. 449/1 We heard a fall, a rattle of tinware, a slight splash.

+Tiny herring. A name given by Mitchill to a herring of the Atlantic coast, perhaps the fall herring, *Pomolobus mediocris.* — **1814** MITCHILL *Fishes N.Y.* 452 Tiny Herring. *Clupea pusilla.* About six inches long.

* Tip, *n.*
+1. The top of a hat crown; a piece of stiffening material pasted to this on the inside.
1864 WEBSTER 1387/3 *Tip,* . . . the lining of the top of a hat;—so called among hatters. **1876** KNIGHT 2578/2 *Tip,* . . . a circular piece of scale or paste board pasted on the inside of a hat crown to stiffen it. **1891** *Cent.* 6349/3.
+2. (See last quotation.)
1868 CHADWICK *Baseball* 17 Two hands were put out on tips. *Ib.* 18 The last two hands being put out on 'tips'—viz., foul balls just touching the bat and bounding sharply into the catcher's hands.
3. *attrib.* and *comb.* **+a.** In sense 1. **+b.** In the names of insects injurious to the terminal buds of plants.
(a) **1876** KNIGHT 2579/1 *Tip-paper,* a variety of paper of a rigid quality, made for lining the tips or insides of hat-crowns. **1876** INGRAM *Centennial Exp.* 385 The Eickenmeyer Hat Blocking Machine Company exhibited . . . a tip-stretcher. (b) **1891** *Cent.* 6351/3 *Tip-worm,* . . . the larva of a gall-fly, *Cecidomyia vaccinii,* which works in the terminal buds of the cranberry-vine. **1905** *Forestry Bureau Bul.* No. 66, 20 The tip-borer . . . , in the larval form, destroys the terminal buds of the leading shoots and dwarfs the young pines.

* Tip, *v.*[1] *Baseball.* **+To tip out,** of a batter, to be put out as the result of striking the ball a glancing blow, deflecting it so slightly that the catcher is still able to catch it. — *c***1858** A. G. Spalding *Base Ball* 61 Our first man took the bat; tipped out. **1868** CHADWICK *Base Ball* 95 Williams . . . began by tipping out.

* Tip, *v.*[2] **1.** *To tip one's hat,* to raise or touch the hat in greeting or salutation. **+2.** *To tip the scales at* (a given number of pounds), to weigh. *colloq.* — (1) **1881** RITTENHOUSE *Maud* 18 Nearly ran over little WmSn at the P.O. and he solemnly tipped his hat. **1898** C. A. BATES *Clothing Bk.* No. 1261 He isn't afraid to tip his hat to any one. (2) **1884** *Harper's Mag.* June 111/2 Single fish often tipping the scales at from five to seven pounds. **1893** *St. Louis Globe-Dem.* Oct., She tips the scales at 150 pounds.

Tip-. The stem of TIP *v.*[2] Used in the names of vehicles and other objects that tip or tilt in discharging their loads or contents. {1852–} — **1891** *Cent.* 6350 *Tip-car,* . . . on a railroad, a gravel-car or coal-car pivoted on its truck, so that it can be upset to discharge its load at the side of the track; a dump-car. **1877** BARTLETT 798 *Tip-Cart,* a two-wheeled vehicle,

so constructed as to 'dump' its load by tipping up the forward end of the body. **1876** KNIGHT 2579/1 *Tip-sled,* a dumping-sled. **1879** *Scribner's Mo.* July 346/2 There's the tip-trough, but it's down-stairs.

+Tip bound. *Baseball.* ?A ball hit or tipped by the batter so that it is barely deflected from its course and is caught by the catcher on the first bound. — **1868** CHADWICK *Base Ball* 80 Hatfield . . . was disposed of handsomely on a tip-bound.

+Tip foul. *Baseball.* =FOUL TIP. — **1874** *Chicago Inter-Ocean* 7 July 5/1 Schafer was given a life on an easy foul muffed by Malone, and then retired on a tip-foul to the same player.

+Tippecanoe. [Native place name.]
1. Gen. William Henry Harrison (1773–1841); also, pl., his political followers. A nickname alluding to his victory in the battle of Tippecanoe (1811). *Obs.*
[**1835** *Jamestown* (N.Y.) *Jrnl.* 25 March 1/2 Many, very many who have been the zealous supporters of the 'hero of New Orleans,' are ready to unite heart and hand in support of the hero of Tippecanoe.] **1840** *N.Y. Daily Express* 9 April 2/2 The Tippecanoes have a pow-wow tonight. **1840** [see LOG CABIN 3 b]. **1885** *Mag. Amer. Hist.* April 396/2 Tippecanoe. a nickname of William Henry Harrison, ninth President of the United States.
2. *Tippecanoe and Tyler too,* a rallying cry used by the Whigs in the campaign of 1840 in which William Henry Harrison and John Tyler were the Whig candidates for president and vice-president. Also attrib.
1842 *Congress. Globe* App. 11 Jan. 128/3 [These] facts . . . will make those political fanatics—those 'Tippecanoe and Tyler too' politicians, feel [etc.]. **1864** NICHOLS *Amer. Life* I. 43 There was a great 'Tippecanoe' and Tyler too mass-meeting at Saratoga. **1885** *Mag. Amer. Hist.* April 396/2 'Tippecanoe and Tyler too' was the refrain of a popular song during the Log Cabin and Hard Cider campaign. *a***1918** G. STUART *On Frontier* I. 28 Ben, who was an ardent Whig, said . . . 'Even the birds are saying, "Tippecanoie-oo and Tyler-too-oo-oo." '
3. *attrib.* Designating partisans of General Harrison, songs honoring him, or things named after him.
1840 *Congress. Globe* App. 2 April 376 [They could] sing a few Tippecanoe songs, and then what a soul-stirring time they had of it! **1840** *Kentucky Rifle* 31 Oct., Old father Adam or uncle Moses . . . [would] be wholehog *Tippecanoe Boys.* **1841** *Picayune* 1 April 2/5 A man of genius in Philadelphia has invented a new culinary mixture which he calls Tippecanoe soup. **1843** *S. Lit. Messenger* IX. 651/1 First, there was to be 'the marshal, on horseback'—then 'the Tippecanoe clubs' from here, there and all over; then the 'distinguished strangers.'

+Tipple. A device for tipping and thus unloading coal cars; a place where such cars are weighed and unloaded. Also attrib. — **1880** *Harper's Mag.* Dec. 55/1 Noisy cars . . . rush down the 'incline,' bang against the 'tipple,' and discharge their contents . . . into the waiting boat or barge below. **1886** *N. Amer. Rev.* Aug. 181 The law allows a check weighmaster on each tipple. **1917** SINCLAIR *King Coal* 134 The tipple-boss reappeared.

* Tippling house. A house or shop where intoxicating liquors are sold. — **1639** *Mass. Bay Rec.* I. 270 Thom: Gray, for . . . keeping a tippling house . . . was censured to bee severely whiped. **1737** W. STEPHENS *Proc. Georgia* I. 20 There were Abundance of unlicenced Tippling Houses in all parts of the town. **1806** *Balance* V. 288/3 A man who kept a tippling house, asked his neighbor what he should put upon his sign.

Tippling shop. =prec. {1755–} — **1809** WEEMS *Marion* (1833) 48 Young vagabonds . . . in a log tippling shop, with a tickler of brandy before them! **1839** *Indiana H. Rep. Jrnl.* 23 Sess. 246 The committee of ways and means [shall] be directed to inquire into the expediency of levying a direct tax of . . . six dollars on every tippling shop, otherwise called coffee houses. **1873** *Newton Kansan* 7 Aug. 2/1 Emporia has more wholesale tippling shops . . . than any other western city.

+Tippy. A fop or dandy. *slang. Obs.* Also transf. — *a***1800** in *Spirit Farmers' Mus.* 262 He is called the 'dandy,' by one party, and the 'tippy' by another. **1804** *Balance* III. 153/3 A smirking race, called, in fashion's vocabulary 'Tippies,' re-assumed whiskers. **1843** STEPHENS *High Life N.Y.* I. 107, I don't see as there's much difference between our gals there in Weathersfield . . . and these York tippies that go out all furbeloned off in thin silks and satins.

+Tipteer, *v. intr.* (See quot. *c*1870.) *slang. Obs.* — *c***1849** PAIGE *Dow's Sermons* I. 208 You see a gentleman tipteering along Broadway, with a lady wiggle-wagging by his side, and both dressed to kill. *a***1870** CHIPMAN *Notes on Bartlett* 481 *Tipteer,* to promenade, to show off, to strut, to walk mincingly.

Tip-up.
+1. A device used in fishing to show when a fish has been hooked; a tilt-up (sense 2).
1880 *Harper's Mag.* March 517 With baited lines and tip-ups set, we waited. **1892** *Outing* March 439 The upper ends of the lines . . . [are] affixed to what are termed 'tip-ups.'
+2. a. The spotted sandpiper, *Actitis macularia.*
1848 BARTLETT 356 *Tilt-up,* or *Tip-up,* the popular name of the Sandpiper. **1889** *Cent.* 2201/2 From its habit of balancing the body as if on a pivot . . . [it is] called *teetertail* or *tip-up.* **1900** *Congress. Rec.* 30 April 4872/2 The kingfishes and the little tip-up were seen upon the shores of the river.

1917 *Birds of Amer.* I. 250/1 The Spotted Sandpiper . . . is popularly nicknamed 'Teeter' or 'Tip-up,' from its nervous habit of constantly tilting its body.

+b. *Yellow tip-up, tip-up warbler,* (see quotation).

1917 *Birds of Amer.* III. 150/1 This tilting or waving of the tail up and down . . . has given [the palm warbler, *Dendroica palmarum*] the names Tip-up Warbler and Yellow Tip-up.

*Tire, *n.* +A pinafore or apron that protects the dress. (Cf. TIER *n.²*) — **1846** WORCESTER 742/2. **1848** LOWELL *Biglow P.* 1 Ser. p. xiii, Welldrilled urchins, each behind his tire, Waited in ranks the wished command to fire. **1867** HOLMES *Guardian Angel* 30 The child untied her little 'tire.' **1896** POOL *In Buncombe County* 262 They were washed and combed and put into red 'tires' and white sunbonnets.

Tire, *v. tr.* To put a tire upon (a wheel); to furnish with tires. {1909} Also *ppl. a.* {tyred, 1884-} — **1770** *Md. Hist. Mag.* XII. 351 The Cart wheels . . . I Believe are not tier'd. **1771** *Ib.* XIV. 137 A pair of Cart wheels . . . are made & allmost tired. **1805** in *Amer. Pioneer* II. 232 The goods here are drawn in carts with very high wheels, which are never *tired* nor the axles *ironed.* **1890** *Electrical Rev.* XVI. x. 2/2 The tread may be turned down like the tread of a steel-tired wheel.

+**Tire-shrinker.** A machine for decreasing the size of wagon and carriage tires. — **1857** *Ill. Agric. Soc. Trans.* II. 171 J. L. Warfield's tire shrinker appeared . . . likely to prove a useful instrument. **1868** *Iowa State Agric. Soc. Rep.* 1867 420 We have invented . . . Sandgreen's combined shears, tire-shrinker and punch. **1881** *Rep. Indian Affairs* 442.

+**Tissue ballot.** (See quot. 1885.) Also attrib. — **1879** *Congress. Rec.* App. 23 June 120/1 If my friend takes position behind the literal term 'onion skin' or 'tissue ballots,' I do not know whether they were used in Williamsburgh County or not. **1885** *Mag. Amer. Hist.* April 396/2 *Tissue ballots,* ballots printed on thin paper so that a single voter can deposit a number of them at one and the same time without detection. Tissue ballots are believed to have been invented in North Carolina in 1876. **1903** HART *Actual Govt.* 75 The 'tissue ballot' system allows a voter to put in a handful of tickets at once.

+**Tiswin.** [Sp. *tecutn, tejuino,* from Nahuatl.] An intoxicating liquor made by the Apache Indians. Also attrib. — **1877** *Rep. Indian Affairs* 162 'Tiswin' . . . they manufacture from corn, and whiskey [is] obtained from traders. **1881** *Ib.* 11 There have been several Indians wounded . . . at Tis-win parties. **1891** *Century Mag.* March 655/1 The apache intoxicant 'tizwin' . . . [is] beer made from fermented corn.

+**Tithable.** {1828} One who is subject to payment of tithes. *Obs.* (Cf. next.)

1653 *Va. House of Burgesses* 88 Northampton County—500 Tithables. **1697** *Va. State P.* I. 52 Several Loose & vagrant persons, That have not any Settled Residence, do too Comonly enter themselves singly, and not in any house Keepers' List of Tithables. **1701** *N.C. Col. Rec.* I. 544 Whatsoever Charge shall accrue for and towards the building of the aforesaid Church, . . . [shall] be levied . . . upon the Tythables of the Precinct. **1787** *Ky. Petitions* 111 The settlements of Limestone do not contain . . . more than one hundred and fifty Tithables. **1829** *Va. Lit. Museum* 462/1 Nearly one half of the 'male tithables' paid but a hundredth part of the taxes. **1893** *Nation* LVI. 309/2 The population of a Virginian county a hundred and forty years ago was probably considerably more than three times as great as its number of tithables.

+**Tithable person.** =prec. *Obs.* — **1654** *Va. Stat. at Large* I. 388 Certaine arrears by overcharging of tithable persons in some counties is now in question. **1677** *New Castle Court Rec.* 127 You are . . . Required to take a true & exact List of all the Tydable persons from 16 to 60. **1713** *N.C. Col. Rec.* II. 11 These are therefore to impower you . . . to collect and receive of every Tythable person in the precinct of Chowan twenty pence. **1796** MORSE *Univ. Geog.* I. 627 The poor, unable to support themselves, are maintained by an assessment on the titheable persons in the parish.

*Tith(e)man. (See TITHINGMAN.)

*Tithing. A minor administrative unit consisting typically of ten households; a square mile of land. *Obs.* — a**1647** GORGES *Briefe Narration* 48 Four Tything Men . . . shall give account to the Constable of the parish of the demeanour of the House holders within his Tything. **1737** W. STEPHENS *Proc. Georgia* I. 58, I had long since . . . called for Lists of the several Inhabitants in each Tything. **1741** *Ga. Hist. Soc. Coll.* II. 107 Ten of the said inhabitants . . . having petitioned the said Oglethorpe . . . for one tithing of land together, being a mile square. **1744** MOORE *Voy. Georgia* 97 Every ten houses make a tithing, and to every tithing there is a mile square.

*Tithingman. +In various of the American colonies, a local officer of the peace; later, in New England, an official enforcing the observance of the Sabbath and the keeping of order at divine service. Also *tithman.* Now hist.

Sometimes definitely identified with the unit called the *tithing.* *Tithman* (1639), rendered in Bacon's *Laws of Maryland at Large* (1765) as *tythingman,* occurs in the text of an act which was never passed.

1639 *Md. Archives* I. 54 The Lord of every Mannour . . . [shall] appoint some Inhabitant . . . to be tithman of that Mannour. a**1647** GORGES *Briefe Narration* 48 Every parish [shall have] one Constable and four Tything Men. **1680** *Dedham Rec.* V. 98 Tithinge men Choosen for the year insuinge as Foloweth. **1721** *Conn.* VI. 277 Be it enacted . . . That each town at their annual meetings . . . shall choose two or more Tything Men in each parish or society for divine worship within said town. **1765**

T. BACON ed. *Maryland Laws at Large* A2 A Tything-man in each Manor, a Constable in each Hundred, a Sheriff and Coroner in the County. **1781** PETERS *Hist. Conn.* (1829) 236 From the governor down to the tithing-man, . . . they will aid smugglers. **1828** *Yankee* I. 199/2 What a farce to keep up the show of tithingmen and police-officers in a town where such things [injuries to property] are repeated every day with impunity. **1895** HART in *Forum* May 377 The interference with Sunday travel by the tithingmen of the Puritan Connecticut towns.

+**b.** (See quotation.)

1682 *Plymouth Col. Rec.* XI. 253 In each towne where Indians doe reside euery tenth Indian shalbe chosen by the Court of Assistants or said ouerseer yeerly whoe shall take the Inspection care and oursight of his nine men and present theire faults [and] Misdemenors to the ouerseer which said ouerseer shall keep a list of the Names of the said Tithing Men.

Titi. {1866-, in N. Zeal.} +The ironwood tree (*Cliftonia monophylla*), or any one of various trees resembling this. Also with specifying adjectives. — **1837** WILLIAMS *Florida* 89 These galls are usually covered with titi and other andromedas. **1883** [see JUNIPER 1]. **1897** SUDWORTH *Arborescent Flora* 277 *Cyrilla racemiflora.* Ironwood. . . . Red Titi (Fla.). *Ib.,* *Cliftonia monophylla.* . . . Titi. . . . Black Titi (Fla.). *Ib.* 314 *Oxydendrum arboreum.* . . . Sourwood. . . . Titi (S.C.).

Titlark. {1668-} +=PIPIT b. Also with specifying adjective. (See also BROWN TITLARK, PRAIRIE TITLARK.) — **1844** *Nat. Hist. N.Y., Zoology* II. 76 The American Titlark . . . frequents in preference rocky shores and the banks of streams. **1858** [see MISSOURI SKYLARK]. **1894** TORREY *Fla. Sketch-Book* 38 Behind me are sharp cries of titlarks.

+**Title paper.** A deed to property. Usually pl. — **1805** *Ann. 8th Congress* 2 Sess. 1122 [They] had the best right imaginable to put faith in the authenticated documents and title papers presented to them. **1816** U. BROWN *Journal* I. 273 Nicholas Orrick Esqr. would be likely to give information respecting the title papers of Lot No. 100. **1861** *Army Regulations* 157 Complete title papers, with full and exact maps, plans, and drawings of the public lands purchased . . . will be . . . filed in the Bureau of the Corps of Engineers.

+**Titman.** The smallest pig in a litter; hence, transf., a man stunted physically or mentally. *colloq.* Also attrib. — **1818** FESSENDEN *Ladies Monitor* 113 But vanity oft prematurely calls, Her titman-votaries to your *baby-balls* Where tiny belles, and Lilliputian beaux, . . . Strut round the hall. **1854** THOREAU *Walden* 117 We are a race of tit-men, and soar but little higher in our intellectual flights than the columns of the daily paper. **1900** GARLAND *Eagle's Heart* 101 This yer little man must be the tit-man. **1903** *Dialect Notes* II. 334 *Titman,* the smallest of a litter of pigs. In the North 'runt.' [s.e. Mo.]

+**Tlaco.** *S.W.* [Sp.] A small copper coin having the value of one-eighth of a real. (Cf. THLACK.) — **1863** *Rio Abajo Press* 21 April 1/2 When I want something more substantial, not a tlaco will they care.

*To, *prep.*

*1. At.

To home, (see HOME *n.* and *adv.* 6); *sick to the stomach,* (see SICK *a.* 1 b).

a. *To work,* at work. *colloq.* {1888, *dial.*}

1776 *Mass. H. S. Proc.* 2 Ser. II. 304 [We] met some people to work on the High: Way. **1834** C. A. DAVIS *Lett. J. Downing* 116, I have been to work on it ever since we was at the Rip-Raps. **1858** *Rome Sentinel* Sept. (B.), Men were to work on each side of where the boiler passed.

b. *To once,* at once. *dial.* {1901, *dial.*}

1843 STEPHENS *High Life N.Y.* I. 58 All to once somebody hit me a slap on my shoulder. **1859** *Knickerb.* LIII. 206, I reckon . . . [she liked] *me,* too, but not to-once, I expect. **1899** JEWETT *Queen's Twin* 171, I never saw such a sight o' moths to once.

*2. With. +Indicating the crop planted on land. *colloq.*

1862 *Ill. Agric. Soc. Trans.* V. 154 The land . . . [was] mostly planted to potatoes. **1874** *Vermont Bd. Agric. Rep.* II. 493 Dr. Warder recommends that the farmers of Ohio plant one fourth of their farms to timber forests. **1884** *Vt. Agric. Rep.* VIII. 355 Last year [I] planted an acre to Sanford corn.

+**3.** Included or involved in. Often *that is all there is to it.* *colloq.*

1888 DORSEY *Midshipman Bob* 230 There's just this to it: if you'll go to any place [etc.]. **1898** DELAND *Old Chester Tales* 245 Well, that was all there was to it. **1914** CASTLE *Mod. Dancing* 44 Simply *walk* as softly and smoothly as possible. . . . This is the One Step, and this is all there is to it.

*Toad. In special combinations: (see quotations). — **1877** BARTLETT 708 Toad-Grunter, the toad-fish, so called from the noise it makes. **1886** *Forest & Stream* XXVII. 382/3 In those days [1869–72] the golden plover was quite as often called 'toadhead' as 'green plover.' **1784** *Amer. Acad. Mem.* I. 456 *Nymphaea.* . . . Yellow Water Lily. Toad Lily. . . . In ponds and rivers. **1877** BARTLETT 708 Toad-Sticker, a term for a sword, almost universal among our soldiers during the late war.

Toadfish. Any one of various ugly marine fishes {1642–, in S. Amer.} +as the oyster fish (*Opsanus tau*) and the common puffer (*Sphoeroides maculatus*) of the Atlantic coast. Also with defining terms.

1624 SMITH *Gen. Hist. Va.* II. 28 The Toadefish . . . will swell till it be like to burst, when it commeth into the ayre. **1709** LAWSON *Carolina* 158 Toad-Fish are nothing but a Skin full of Prickles, and a few bones. **1814** MITCHILL *Fishes N.Y.* 463 Toad-fish. *Lophius bufo.* . . . An inhabitant of our salt water. *Ib.* 473 [The] Puffer . . . is called in some places, *toad-fish,* because his back is mottled with yellow and dark somewhat like that of a toad. **1842** *Nat. Hist. N.Y., Zoology* IV. 170 The Two-spined Toad-fish, *Batrachus celatus*, . . . is usually found on muddy bottoms. **1896** JORDAN & EVERMANN *Check-List Fishes* 466 *Thalassophryne*. . . . Poison Toad-fishes. **1903** T. H. BEAN *Fishes N.Y.* 646 Other names . . . [for the sea raven] are rock toadfish and deep water sculpin.

*Toadflax. Any one of various plants, chiefly of the genus *Linaria*, having showy yellow flowers; ranstead; butter and eggs. Also attrib. — **1784** *Amer. Acad. Mem.* I. 464 *Antirrhinum*. . . . Toad flax. Blossoms purple. **1845** JUDD *Margaret* I. 19 Wait till the flowers is gone, they wouldn't be worth more'n your toad-flax and bean vines. **1886** *Harper's Mag.* July 285 An atom of down floating above the yellow toad-flax flowers. **1915** ARMSTRONG & THORNBER *Western Wild Flowers* 474 Toad Flax. *Linaria Canadensis*.

Toad plantain. (See quot. 1778.) *Obs.* — **1778** CARVER *Travels* 517 Toad Plantain resembles the common plantain, only it grows much ranker. **1836** EDWARD *Hist. Texas* 42 Then there are the herb varieties . . . [such as] the rattle-snake plantain, the toad plantain.

+Toad's-sorrel. =SHEEP SORREL a. — **1892** *Amer. Folk-Lore* V. 102 *Rumex acetosella*, toad's sorrel. Stratham, N.H.

*Toasting iron. An iron used for toasting bread. *Obs.* — **1642** *Md. Archives* IV. 97 A gridiron & a tosting iron. **1651** *Essex Probate Rec.* I. 127. **1783** PARKMAN *Diary* 298 Toasting Iron 1/6.

* Tobacco. Freq. abbrev. **tobo, toba, tob.**

I. *1. The leaves of the tobacco plant, cured and pre-pared for immediate use or as an article of commerce.

See also CAKE-TOBACCO, CHEWING TOBACCO, etc.

1607 in Smith *Works* (1910) p. xliii, We satt . . . seeing their Daunces, and taking Tobacco. **1698** THOMAS *Pensilvania* 25 Their Merchandize chiefly consists in . . . Furs, Tobacco. **1701** WOLLEY *Journal N.Y.* (1902) 41 Amongst Provisions I may reckon Tobacco, of which they are ob-stinate and incessant Smoakers. **1770** *Md. Hist. Mag.* XIII. 54, I Have not had any offer for my tobo. **1821** COOPER *Spy* i, I find it very difficult to procure that quality of tobacco . . . to which I have been accustomed. **1899** CUSHMAN *Hist. Indians* 497 The ancient Chickasaws . . . [buried] with the corpse, if a man, his . . . pipe and tobacco. **1916** WILSON *Some-where* 286 Her trained fingers began to combine paper and tobacco.

*2. A tall annual plant of the genus *Nicotiana*, cultivated for its leaves.

See also INDIAN TOBACCO.

1607 in Smith *Works* (1910) p. xliii, He sowes his wheate, . . . tobacco, pompions [etc.]. **1682** *Hist. Coll. S. Carolina* II. 34 Tobacco doth here grow very well, and is nearer to the nature of the Spanish Tobacco than that of Virginia. **1707** [see ENGLISH WHEAT]. **1797** IMLAY *Western Terri-tory* (ed. 3) 246 When the tobacco is about 4 or 5 inches high, they weed it. **1821** NUTTALL *Travels Arkansa* 101 The cultivation of . . . tobacco, indi-go, hemp, and wine . . . [is] without the aid of artificial soils or manures. **1867** RICHARDSON *Beyond Miss.* 18 Thriving corn and tobacco concealed the rich jet-black soil. **1904** GLASGOW *Deliverance* 129 If you were any-body else and didn't injure my tobacco—yes.

II. *attrib.* and *comb.* 3. Designating containers for to-bacco.

1643 WILLIAMS *Key* (1866) 72 Generally all the men throughout the countrey have a Tobacco-bag, with a pipe in it, hanging at their back. **1658** *Md. Archives* I. 371 An act Concearning the Gage of Tobacco Hogs-heds. *Ib.*, Several Complaints have bene made . . . of the vnreasonable Size of Tobacco Caske. **1763** W. TRENT *Journal* 88 He had seen an Indian with the skin of Captain Robertson's arm for a tobacco pouch! **1775** *Essex Inst. Coll.* XIII. 186, 1 Tobacco jar. **1833** CATLIN *Indians* I. 115 A piece of the 'castor,' which it is customary amongst these folks to carry in their tobacco-sack to give it a flavour.

4. Designating persons having to do with tobacco.

See also TOBACCO-PLANTER, TOBACCO-ROLLER.

1653 *Suffolk Deeds* I. 324 Twentye five poundes . . . [were] payed by Thomas Watkins of Boston Tobacco maker. **1807** J. R. SHAW *Life* (1930) 74 A certain militia-man by the name of Everman, a tobacco spinner, . . . lived in Lancaster. **1812** BENTLEY *Diary* IV. 97 Mr. Nathan Pierce . . . came [into Newburyport] . . . in the business of a Tobacco Manu-facturer. **1835** *S. Lit. Messenger* IV. 197/2 The tobacco grower was an original Virginian to the back-bone. **1840** HONE *Diary* II. 46 This Glent-worth had been appointed . . . to the office of tobacco inspector. **1840** *Picayune* 13 Sept. 3/1 The same Mac . . . [is] well known to the Western country Tobacco Traders. **1848** *Rep. Comm. Patents 1847* 428, I was in-duced, by the advice of . . . a distinguished tobacco factor in New Or-leans, to lay it before the public. **1856** MACLEOD *F. Wood* 45 In June, 1832, [he] started for himself as a tobacco dealer in Pearl street. **1862** *Harper's Mag.* June 38/1 Madeleine turned to discover the nationality of her companions—an uproarious set of tobacco-feoffs for the most part. **1872** *Atlantic Mo.* Jan. 18 Isham Randolph was the name of this tobacco lord. **1880** *Harper's Mag.* June 36/2 We think again of the tobacco workers.

5. Designating things that have to do with tobacco as a commercial product.

See also TOBACCO FACTORY.

1654 *Suffolk Deeds* II. 93 The sajd tobacco bills of lading to be taken for ye vse & in the name of mr. John Samson. **1780** *N.J. Archives* 2 Ser. IV. 559 He carries on the Tobacco Manufactory in Trenton. **1809** FRENEAU *Poems* I. 137 This box . . . Has been unfilled a week or more, And curses the tobacco store. **1835** MARTIN *Descr. Virginia* 140 Lynchburg . . . has long been the largest tobacco market in the world. **1864** *Maine Agric. Soc. Returns 1863* 164 The writer has been a close observer of tobacco sales for several years. **1869** Tobacco emporium [see CIGAR 3]. **1883** *Har-per's Mag.* July 260/2 The tobacco business furnishes the sum-maker some wonderful rows of figures.

6. Designating land or areas upon which tobacco is cul-tivated or is the prevailing crop.

See also TOBACCO PLANTATION.

1659 *Southold Rec.* I. 86 The Tobacco lands . . . hee lately exchanged with Samuell King for his meadowe in the Indian neck. *Ib.* 87 Other par-cell of woodland in Oyster ponnd Lower neck in the Tobackow ground. **1772** in *Amer. Speech* XV. 404/2 Two Hundred and thirty Acres of rich Tobacco woodland. **1820** *Amer. Farmer* I. 394 The tobacco planter was under the necessity of robbing all the rest of his farm, to keep up the fer-tility of his *tobacco lots*. **1872** *Atlantic Mo.* Jan. 26 The capital of Virginia was . . . surrounded by an expanse of dark green tobacco-fields. **1880** To-bacco belt [see COTTON 4 g]. **1885** HOWELLS *Silas Lapham* xiv, Anybody who had ever lived off a tobacco country could tell him better than that. **1902** G. C. EGGLESTON *D. South* 89 Let's ride to the tobacco new grounds at once.

7. Designating things that relate to the use of tobacco as money.

See also TOBACCO MONEY.

1662 *Md. Archives* I. 445 Which money shall pass in discount of tobacco debts at 2d. per lb. **1705** *Va. State P.* I. 97 Such notes shall be received in all tobacco payments. **1733** *Md. Hist. Mag.* XIX. 303, [I must] pay at the Rate of ten shillings per Cent. for the Tobacco Fee. **1760** WASHING-TON *Diaries* I. 136 Gave Captn. Cawsey's Skipper . . . 1 Tobo. Note.

8. Designating boats or aggregations of boats used in transporting or shipping tobacco.

1709 LAWSON *Carolina* 88 We lie near at hand to . . . sell our Provisions to the Tobacco-fleets. **1745** E. KIMBER *Itinerant Observer* 29 They have also a Kind of Sloops, clumsily built, which may be called Tobacco Drug-gers. **1777** HUTCHINSON *Diary & Lett.* II. 132 The tobacco ship was taken by four sailors only. **1781** *Va. State P.* I. 451 He had proceeded up James River thus far, in search of canoes of the kind-need[ed], viz 'Sound tobacco canoes.' **1792** POPE *Tour S. & W.* 23 At Night one of Mr. Craig's Tobac-co Boats . . . passed us.

9. Designating various actions, procedures, etc., associat-ed with the production and use of tobacco.

See also TOBACCO-CHEWING.

1824 *Congress. Deb.* 15 April 2324 The effect of this measure [the tariff bill] on the cotton, rice, and tobacco-growing States will be pernicious in the extreme. **1838** KENNEDY *Rob of Bowl* I. 191 But the townspeople are scarce better in this quickness to censure—especially such as look to the tobacco viewing. **1868** *Rep. Comm. Agric. 1867* 182 But a better plan . . . [is to] unite it with Messrs. Bibb & Company's patent tobacco 'firing and curing apparatus.' **1871** *N.Y. Tribune* 2 Feb. 3/2 For many years, my attention . . . has been called to the necessity of a change of base, in the matter of tobacco-spitting. **1882** *Wheelman* I. 93 [They] smoke the room blue, and themselves into the 'blues,' from chronic tobacco-poisoning and dyspepsia. **1904** GLASGOW *Deliverance* 161 It'll have to lie over till after tobacco cutting.

10. In special combinations.

Tobacco bed, a seed bed in which tobacco plants are grown; *t. beetle*, (see quotation); *t. cancer*, a cancer attributed to the excessive use of tobacco; *t.-chewer*, one who chews tobacco; *t.-grater*, (see quotation); *t. hoe*, a hoe used in cultivating tobacco; *t. horse*, (see quotation); *t. knife*, a sharp blade, hinged to a support, for cutting or shaving tobacco; *t. law*, a law making a levy of a quantity of tobacco; *t. seconds*, pl., tobacco plants of second-rate or inferior quality; *t. shed*, a shed in which tobacco is cured; *t. shrub*, (see quotation); *t. tag*, a small metal tag, bearing a trade name or trademark, placed on plug tobacco; *t. tax*, a tax levied upon tobacco; *t. twist*, a piece of twisted tobacco; *t. warehouse*, a warehouse in which to-bacco is stored; *t. weed*, a perennial herb (*Elephantopus tomentosus*) of the southeastern states (cf. ELEPHANT('S) FOOT); *t. wheel*, (see quotation).

1819 *Amer. Farmer* I. 62 We have been dreadfully annoyed in our *To-bacco beds*, by a small black insect, called the fly. **1891** *Cent.* 6362/3 *Tobac-co-beetle*, a cosmopolitan ptinid beetle, *Lasioderma serricorne*, . . . a pest in many manufactories and warehouses in the United States. **1884** NYE *Baled Hay* 142 Ben Hill died, after suffering intolerable anguish from to-bacco cancer, caused by too much smoking. **1881** *Ore. State Jrnl.* 1 Jan. 3/5 A lady wants to know why the railroad companies do not provide special cars for tobacco-chewers, as well as for smokers. **1876** KNIGHT 2583/1 *Tobacco-grater*, a machine for grinding tobacco into small pieces suitable for smoking in pipes. **1790** *Penna. Packet* 14 April 3/2 William Perkins, Blacksmith, Makes and sells . . . the best kind of corn or tobacco hoes. **1849** *Amer. Farmer* V. 185/2 A 'Tobacco horse' is nothing more than three small sticks nailed together so as to form a triangle, each side being three or four feet long. **1875** KNIGHT 929/2 [By] a hinged knife working . . . like a tobacco-knife . . . the fuse . . . is cut off. **1729** *Md. Hist. Mag.* VIII. 71 This Vestry according to the Directions of the Tobac-co Law proceed to lay out the parish. **1769** *Va. House of Burgesses* 205 The Acts . . . prohibiting the tending of Tobacco-seconds. **1887** CABLE in *Century Mag.* March 666/2 They could . . . have walked quietly across the village green to the forlorn tobacco-shed that 'Mian had given them for a school-house. **1885** HAVARD *Flora W. & S. Texas* 472 First observed as a native plant north of the Rio Grande, is the beautiful Tobacco-Shrub (*Nicotiana glauca*). **1908** 'O. HENRY' *Roads of Destiny* 54 His dollars had appeared as but tin tobacco-tags. **1887** *Courier-Journal* 8 Jan. 4/3 The repeal of the tobacco tax is among the expedients . . . [for abolishing] surplus revenue. **1823** JAMES *Exped.* I. 141 His [Indian] auditors . . . were presently highly wrought up by the sight of two or three little mounds of tobacco twist. **1775** *Jrnl. Cont. Congress* II. 219 The surface of the earth, in long used tobacco warehouses and their yards, . . . is particularly and strongly impregnated with Nitre. **1894** *Amer. Folk-Lore* VII. 92 *Elephantus tomentosus*, tobacco weed, devil's grandmother, W. Va. **1876** KNIGHT 2585/2 *Tobacco-wheel*, a machine by which leaves of tobacco are twisted into a cord.

+**Tobacco barn.** =TOBACCO HOUSE. — **1877** BAGBY *Old Va. Gentleman* 3 Where is your plank to come from, and your logs for new cabins and tobacco barns? **1880** TOURGEE *Bricks* 28 You had better give Nimbus the empty house near the tobacco-barn. **1907** [see NIGHT RIDER 2].

Tobacco-chewing. The chewing of tobacco. {1878–} Also attrib. and as adj. — **1834** *Jamestown* (N.Y.) *Jrnl.* 12 Nov. 2/1 Your eye can't help but rest on a plump, tobacco chewing, jolly looking fellow. **1870** TOMES *Decorum* 59 It is the belief of some dentists that . . . tobacco-chewing, is favorable to the preservation of the teeth. **1883** 'MARK TWAIN' *Life on Miss.* xxii, By and by we entered the tobacco-chewing region. **1898** *McClure's Mag.* X. 216 A yellowish streak [in his beard] from the chin down, [was] evidence of many years of tobacco-chewing.

+**Tobacco crop.** The yield of tobacco in a particular season. — **1847** ROBB *Squatter Life* 133, [I asked] what'ud be the probable amount of the old man's tobaccer crop this season. **1852** *Harper's Mag.* Sept. 532/1, I will neither wear what they make [in New Eng.], nor eat what they raise, so long as my tobacco crop will enable me to get my supplies from *Old* England. **1885** BAYLOR *On Both Sides* 208 The result was recorded in . . . tabulated expositions of the imports, exports, cotton-, tobacco-, and corn-crops of the United States for about fifty years.

+**Tobacco factory.** A factory in which various kinds of chewing tobacco, smoking tobacco, snuff, etc., are made. — **1827** DRAKE & MANSFIELD *Cincinnati* 65 Three Tobacco and Snuff Factories. **1856** MACLEOD *F. Wood* 45 He was sent to Richmond to take charge of a large tobacco factory in that city. **1879** *Scribner's Mo.* June 220/2 In Richmond, the tobacco factories and warehouses were so many hospitals and prisons.

+**Tobacco fly.** Either of two hawk moths, *Protoparce quinquemaculata* and *P. sexta.* (Cf. TOBACCO WORM.) — **1807** JANSON *Stranger in Amer.* 339 Many planters . . . knew of no remedy against the devastation produced by the '*tobacco-fly.*' **1850** *Rep. Comm. Patents 1849: Agric.* 459 The horn-worm is deposited on the smooth or upper surface of the leaf in an egg by the tobacco-fly. **1904** GLASGOW *Deliverance* 126 It was . . . mid-August—the time of the harvest moon and of the dreaded tobacco fly.

+**Tobacco hill.** A mound or heap of soil in which a tobacco plant grows; the plant itself. — **1763** WASHINGTON *Diaries* I. 183, 170 Tobo. Hills. **1785** in Commons, etc. *Doc. Hist.* I. 131, I have one hundred and sixty thousand Corn hills . . . and also sixty thousand Tobo. hills. **1792** POPE *Tour S. & W.* 62 They plant their Corn in Holes at an unequal, tho' never greater Distance than Tobacco Hills, from one another.

Tobacco house. {1611–} +**a.** A structure in which tobacco is stored during the curing process. **b.** A concern dealing in tobacco.

1652 *Southold Rec.* I. 17 The Neck over against the east side of the Tobacco house in Oysterpound Meadows. **1714** *N.C. Col. Rec.* II. 123, My lodging for the best part of my time in this Government was in an old Tobacco house. **1797** [see HANGER[2] 1]. **1808** *Ann. 10th Congress 2* Sess. 141 [The tobacco] must either remain in the tobacco houses of Virginia and Maryland, or go to rot in the King's warehouses at London. **1887** *Courier-Journal* 13 Jan. 8/5 Mike Billings . . . was apprehended at Levy's tobacco house, in Portland. **1900** WINCHESTER *W. Castle* 166, I was traveling for a large tobacco house.

attrib. **1691** *Va. State P.* I. 27, I have searched in such places as it was suspected ye broad-arrow was unduly putt on ye toba. house-doores. **1760** WASHINGTON *Diaries* I. 134, [I] set a course for the head of the drain that Runs into my Meadow which leaves in the Tobo. House Field. **1775** J. ADAMS in *Warren-Adams Lett.* I. 115 Coll. Harrison of Virginia . . . is very confident that they are making large Quantities [of saltpeter] from Tobacco House Earth in his Colony.

+**Tobacco Indians.** *pl.* The Tionontati, an Iroquoian tribe allied with the Hurons. So called because of their large fields of tobacco at the time (1616) when they were first visited by white men. (Cf. TOBACCO NATION.) — **1854** SCHOOLCRAFT *Information resp. Indian Tribes* IV. 203 The Eries and Petuns, or Tobacco Indians, who were Wyandots, had been pursued and slaughtered mercilessly in West Canada.

Tobacco juice. The secretion ejected from the mouth of a person chewing tobacco. — [**1834** MARRYAT *P. Simple* xiv, There were spitting-pans placed . . . that they might not dirty the planks with the tobacco-juice.] **1852** STOWE *Uncle Tom* xi, The long legged veteran . . . walked up to the advertisement, and very deliberately spit a full discharge of tobacco juice on it. **1884** *Century Mag.* March 654/2 A host of constituents . . . throng the gaunt lodgings of the Senator, spitting tobacco juice on his floor. **1904** GLASGOW *Deliverance* 156 Look at . . . the hands knotted by toil and stained with tobacco juice.

+**Tobacco money.** Tobacco used as money; money with which to purchase tobacco. — **1691** *Mass. Bay Currency Tracts* 31 Why may not Paper-mony be as good as Tobacco-mony, Potato-mony, and Sugar-mony? **1834** CARRUTHERS *Kentuckian* II. 202 The buckles which their fathers wore in the days of 'tobacco-money.' **1862** NORTON *Army Lett.* 124 $42 for postage and tobacco money.

+**Tobacco Nation.** =TOBACCO INDIANS. — **1867** PARKMAN *Jesuits in N. Amer.* 426 The Wyandots . . . are descendants of the ancient Hurons, and chiefly of that portion of them called the Tobacco Nation.

***Tobacconist. a.** One who sells or manufactures tobacco. {1657–} ***b.** A user of tobacco. — **1678** *Boston Rec.* 123 George Wardnr. Coatch maker not admitted into ye Colony, Nichelas Wardnr Tobacconist. **1724** *New-Eng. Courant* 6 Jan. 1/1, I had in View, a Reformation of that rude and unmannerly Practice, that the generality of Tobacconists are chargeable withal, viz. of obtruding their Smoke and Filth upon all Companies. **1819** *Amer. Farmer* I. 167 Get some waste Tobacco from the Tobacconist. **1904** *N.Y. Ev. Post* 6 Aug., [The Indian woman's] image formerly advertised the tobacconist's shop.

* **Tobacco pipe.**

* **1.** A pipe for smoking tobacco. Also attrib.

c1618 STRACHEY *Virginia* 31 There is a clay which the Indians call assequeth, whereof they make their tobacco pipes. **1685** [see EARTHENWARE]. **1769** *Mass. Gazette* 18 May 2/3 Tobacco Pipes made here, equal in goodness to any imported, . . . [for sale] at their Factory at New-Boston. **1809** A. HENRY *Travels* 252 [There] is a rock of great length . . . entirely composed of a *pièrre à calumet*, or stone used by the Indians for making tobacco-pipe bowls. **1877** *Harper's Mag.* Feb. 454/1 The old lady . . . derived . . . consolation from a view of these ghastly mementos, dully illumined by the lurid glow from the bowl of her tobacco-pipe.

+**2.** =INDIAN PIPE.

1840 DEWEY *Mass. Flowering Plants* 108 Tobacco Pipe . . . is a singular and handsome plant. **1845** JUDD *Margaret* I. 143 She found . . . the curious mushroom-like tobacco-pipe.

+**Tobacco plantation.** A plantation devoted to raising tobacco. — **1676** GLOVER *Va.* in *Phil. Trans.* XI. 627 [They are] so intent on their Tobacco-Plantations that they neglect all other more Noble and advantageous improvements. **1775** BURNABY *Travels* 5 The road is exceedingly pleasant, through some of the finest tobacco plantations in North-America. **1861** *Vanity Fair* 8 June 271/1 Then I've got . . . four tobacco-plantations.

+**Tobacco-planter.** A farmer who raises tobacco on a large scale. — **1775** *Amer. Husbandry* I. 66 Those who have dealings with London . . . are the tobacco and rice planters. **1791** WASHINGTON *Diaries* IV. 180 It bids fair to be a large town . . . which is settling very fast by Tobacco planters. **1808** *Steele P.* II. 535 The owner seemed sanguine in his expectation of selling [slaves] for that sum to some of the Tobacco Planters in Granville. **1867** DIXON *New America* II. 2, I have heard [the phrase] . . . among the tobacco-planters of Richmond.

+**Tobacco-roller.** The driver of a rolling hogshead in which tobacco was conveyed to market. *Obs.* — **1835** LONGSTREET *Ga. Scenes* 125 Just beyond these went three tobacco-rollers. **1856** OLMSTED *Slave States* 361 All quiet housekeepers were kept in a state of excited alarm during the seasons when the tobacco-rollers were in town. **1860** MORDECAI *Virginia* 331 The *tobacco roller*, as the driver (often the owner) was called, sought no roof for shelter, during his journey.

+**Tobacco root. 1.** (See quotations.) **2.** =BITTER-ROOT. — **(1) 1845** FRÉMONT *Exped.* 135, I ate here, for the first time, the *kooyah*, or tobacco root, (*valeriana edulis*,) the principal edible root among the Indians. **1919** STURTEVANT *Notes on Edible Plants* 589 Tobacco Root. Valerian. Ohio to Wisconsin and westward. **(2) 1864** *Chambers's Encycl.* VI. 109/2 [*Lewisia*] *rediviva* . . . is called *Tobacco Root* because, when cooked, it has a tobacco-like smell. **1890** *Cent.* 3429/3.

+**Tobacco screw.** A screw used in pressing tobacco. — **1832** *Louisville Directory* 174 Jacob A. Horning . . . is prepared to execute . . . tobacco screws. **1853** *La Crosse Democrat* 27 Sept. 1/2 Oil and Tobacco Screws.

Tobacco stalk. The stem of the tobacco plant after the leaves have been removed. {1704–} — **1659** *Md. Hist. Mag.* VIII. 31 [He] took tobacco stalks and beat his servants. **1807** IRVING, etc. *Salmagundi* xvii. 448 It was not worth a tobacco-stalk. **1899** [see CATON CHIMNEY].

+**Tobacco stick.** A small stick upon which tobacco is hung to cure in a tobacco house. — **1676** GLOVER *Va.* in *Phil. Trans.* XI. 635 They hang them up by the pegs on Tobacco-sticks. **1776** CRESSWELL *Journal* 166 About 600 men appeared under-armed, with Tobacco sticks in general. **1800** TATHAM *Tobacco* 26 These are termed the *tobacco sticks;* and their use is to hang the tobacco upon. **c1866** BAGBY *Old Va. Gentleman* 48 He must make partridge-traps out of tobacco-sticks.

Tobacco tongs. Small tongs or tweezers for taking up a live coal to light a tobacco pipe. *Obs.* {1669–} — **1648** *Md. Archives* IV. 406 One payre Shott-molds, & pr. Tob: Towngs. **1711** *Springfield Rec.* II. 42 Eight tobacca tonges at 6 pence a peace. **1783** E. PARKMAN *Diary* 298.

+**Tobacco worm.** The larva of the tobacco fly which feeds on the leaves of the tobacco plant. — **1737** BRICKELL *N. Carolina* 168 The Tobacco-worm . . . has two sharp horns on its Head. **1789** MORSE *Amer. Geog.* 62 Of the astonishing variety of Insects found in America, we will mention the Glow Worm, . . . Tobacco Worm [etc.]. **1848** *Rep. Comm. Patents 1847* 168 The tobacco worm was the subject of complaint. **1899** GOING *Flowers* 218 [This] caterpillar has a great and evil reputation throughout the South, where it is known as the tobacco-worm.

+**Tobin bronze.** [John A. *Tobin*, U.S. Navy (*c*1875).] A bronze resistant to corrosion in salt water and hence useful in naval construction. — **1891** *Franklin Inst. Jrnl.* July 54 The Ansonia Brass and Copper Company . . . [are] the sole manufacturers of Tobin Bronze. **1893** *Outing* XXII. 147/1 The fin is of Tobin bronze. **1909** *Cent. Suppl.* 168/1 *Tobin bronze*, an alloy . . . composed chiefly of copper, zinc, tin, iron, and lead, in varying proportions.

Tob(o), Toba. [Abbrev. of TOBACCO.] (For examples see TOBACCO 1 and 7, TOBACCO HILL, HOUSE, TONGS.)

Toboggan, *n.* [Canadian Fr. *tobagan*, from Algonquian.] A light, narrow sled made of a long, thin piece of wood turned up at front; used for transporting articles over the snow or for coasting. Also attrib.

[**1829** G. HEAD *Forest Scenes* 64 After leaving Fredericton there was no town . . . at which the required articles could be procured: namely, a couple of tobogins, a tobogin bag [etc.].] **1884** *Century Mag.* Oct. 844/2 In the days of the stampeders and the toboggan trains, this was the only house on the trail. **1886** *Boston Jrnl.* 14 Dec. 2/4 The dealers . . . have been exhibiting toboggans for Christmas gifts. **1891** *Outing* XXIX. 584 Adown the long inclines they glide, . . . Toboggans o'er the snow. **1894** FORD *P. Stirling* 317, I wonder what the papers will say . . . if a governor gives toboggan parties?

Toboggan, *v. intr.* To coast or slide down a slope on a toboggan. {1863–, in Labrador} Also fig. and transf. — [**1879** WEBSTER *Suppl.* 1582/1 *Toboggan*, to slide down hill over the snow, on a toboggan. (*Colloq. Canada.*)] **1887** *Advance* 30 June, Europe is . . . tobogganing straight towards bankruptcy. **1890** *Boston Jrnl.* July, At Ipswich Neck the visitors are tobogganing down the steep grassy slopes on the . . . bottom of an old dory.

Tobogganing. The sport of coasting on a toboggan. {1874–} Also attrib. — [**1856** I. L. BIRD *Englishwoman in Amer.* 264 Balls, and moose-hunting, and sleigh-driving, and 'tarboggining.'] **1882** *Harper's Mag.* April 697/2 This sort of snow-shoeing is said to excel coasting or even tobogganing. **1887** *South Fla. Sentinel* (Orlando) 9 Feb. 1/7 For the first time in my life I have seen tobogganing. **1905** RICE *Sandy* 183 The ice-house . . . recalled a thrilling tobogganing experience.

+Toboggan slide. A steep incline or slide for coasting on toboggans. — **1886** *Boston Jrnl.* Nov., The Edmunds and Myrrhline toboggan slides remain unimpaired. **1893** HOLLEY *Samantha at World's Fair* 286 Inventions . . . of all kinds, from a toboggan slide . . . to a stock car.

+Tod. Short for TODDY. *colloq.* — **1797** C. PRENTISS *Fugitive Ess.* 67 Whether thou exercisest thy power in the full bowl of *punch*, . . . or the circling mug of *tod.* **1856** *Porter's Spirit of Times* 6 Sept. 7/2 Bring us a couple of 'stiff tods' out here. **1893** POST *Harvard Stories* 106 With 'tod and tobac.' the party disposed itself about the room.

Toddy. {1620–} A beverage consisting essentially of a spirituous liquor and sweetened water; a glass or drink of this. {1786–} — **1771** in *New Eng. Mag.* ns. XII. 347/2, I got very intimate after drinking plentifully of punch, toddy and wine. **1808** ASHE *Travels* 241 The poor woman . . . made a large bowl of drink called *toddy*, composed of sugar, water, whiskey, and peach-juice. **1896** HARRIS *Sister Jane* 210 Few things suited him better than a long toddy and a brisk game of cards. **1925** TILGHMAN *Dugout* 7 Let me fix you a toddy.

Toddy-ladle. {1858–} 'A name applied to the American aloe, *Agave Americana*, the juice of which makes pulque, a drink analogous to toddy' (*Cent.*).

Toddy stick. A small stick for stirring toddy; a muddler. — **1840** *Picayune* 4 Oct. 2/5 A 'toddy stick' is as spirit-stirring an article as any poet can boast. **1865** *Atlantic Mo.* May 597/1 Old Boody stirs with an appetizing rattle of the toddy-stick. **1867** 'LACKLAND' *Homespun* 179 [The landlord] was twirling the toddy-stick in his customer's punch at the bar.

*Toe, *n.* In special combinations.

Toe hold, a slight hold on something with the toes; *t. itch,* an itching inflammation that affects the toes; *t.-nippers,* nippers for trimming the toes of sheep and other animals; *t.-scorcher,* a twinge of the gout (*humorous*); *t. weight,* a small mass of metal attached to the hoof or shoe of a trotting horse to modify its gait.

1880 'MARK TWAIN' *Tramp Abroad* 379 One man's toe-hold broke and he fell! **1925** BASSETT *Plantation Overseer* 184 Probably refers to the 'toe itch,' due to excessive rain. **1863** RANDALL *Pract. Shepherd* 362 The principal operator or foreman seats himself in a chair . . . [with] the powerful toe-nippers . . . within his reach. **1827** *Hallowell* (Me.) *Gaz.* 20 June 4/2 4/2 Its most exquisite sensation arises upon the departure of the *toe-scorcher.* **1901** *Scribner's Mag.* April 422/1 A trotting dandy who sported ankle-boots and toe-weights, pulled up before him.

Toe, *v.* {1607–} In colloq. phrases.

+1. *To toe off,* in knitting, to diminish the stitches at the toe of (a stocking or sock) and so complete it. Also *vbl. n.*

1856 M. J. HOLMES *Homestead* II. iii, [She] was toeing off the stocking only that morning commenced. **1876** WHITNEY *Sights & Insights* I. 21 It is the 'toeing off' that is the satisfaction, after all, even whilst you knit the stocking. **1904** WALLER *Wood-Carver* 36 Ther ain't nothin' more ter learn but 'toein' off.'

+2. *To toe in* (or *out*), to turn the toes *in* (or *out*) in walking. Also *vbl. n.*

1877 BARTLETT 710 *To toe in,* to turn in the toes. **1891** WELCH *Recoll.* 1830–40 116 That peculiar turn of the foot called 'toeing in' which in the white girl would be called 'pigeon toed.' **1894** *Vt. Agric. Rep.* XIV. 120 Avoid a horse which toes in or toes out.

+3. *To toe up,* to toe the mark.

1901 MERWIN & WEBSTER *Calumet 'K'* 226, If he doesn't toe up, I'll get one and send him the bill.

Toe calk. (See quot. 1876.) — **1859** *Rep. Comm. Patents 1858* I. 525 Certain indentations are made in the rolls to correspond to the toe-calk. **1876** KNIGHT 2585/2 *Toe-calk*, a prong or barb on the toe of a horse's shoe, to prevent slipping on ice or frozen ground. **1881** *Rep. Indian Affairs* 442.

Toenail. **1.** The nail of a toe. {1852– (s.v. *Ingrowing* vbl. sb.)} Also fig. **+2.** An alcoholic drink. *slang. Obs.* — (1) **1841** *Knickerb.* XVII. 407 All the young ladies were on the very toe-nail of curiosity. **1856** KANE *Arctic Explor.* I. 132 Bonsall was minus a big toe nail and plus a scar upon the nose. (2) *c*1844 R. H. COLLYER *Amer. Life* 7 Various fancy mixtures called, 'Toenails, Bowel Ploughers, Corn Cobs, Eye Snappers,' are retailed.

Toggle, *v.* {1875–} +*tr.* To secure or make fast by means of a toggle or toggles. Also *fig.* — **1836** *Knickerb.* VIII. 207 Has the devil toggled you at last? **1853** KANE *Grinnell Exped.* 83 Each man . . . has a canvas strap . . . fastened to the tow-line; or, nautically, . . . 'toggled to the warp.' **1899** *Outing* XXX. 229/1 In the *Mab* and other canoes employing this device, the stick is toggled at one end to the rudder yoke.

+Togue. *local.* [Canadian Fr. from Algonquian.] =NAMAYCUSH. Also attrib. — **1864** *Maine Agric. Rep.* IX. 132 [The whitefish] will live where the trout will, especially the lake trout, or 'togue.' **1876** *Fur, Fin & Feather* Sept. 145/1 These are called togue trout, and some are said to weigh twenty pounds. **1884** GOODE, etc. *Fisheries* I. 486 The 'Togue' or 'Tuladi' of the Maine and New Brunswick Indians and lumbermen . . . [has] been honored with a distinct binomial. **1911** *Rep. Fisheries 1908* 311/2.

*Toilet. *attrib.* Designating articles used in dressing or in a dressing room. {1660–}

1800 TATHAM *Agric. & Commerce* 87 Articles of fabric . . . chiefly attended to in the functions of household manufactures [include] . . . napkins, towels, toilet-cloths. **1803** BOWNE *Life* 175 We went to a room where they keep their work for sale,—pocket-books, pin balls, toilette cushions [etc.]. **1836** GILMAN *Recoll.* (1838) 207 The bride's chamber . . . was neatly set off with white curtains and toilet cover. **1840** Toilet powders [see FLORIDA WATER]. **1860** E. COWELL *Diary* 148 Two large, and elegant toilet bottles with perfume. **1864** *Hist. North-Western Soldiers' Fair* 158 [Donations include] 1 pair night dress cases, 1 pair toilet mats. *Ib.* 168 [Donations include] 1 set fancy toilet ware.

Toilet article. An article such as soap, perfume, a comb, etc., used in making one's toilet. — **1868** *Mich. Agric. Rep.* VII. 351 Frederick Stearns, Detroit, [exhibited] perfumery toilet articles. **1893** *Harper's Mag.* Jan. 202/1 [On] the table . . . was spread out a profuse array of toilet articles, all of ivory or crystal. **1904** [see DRESSER¹ 2, second quot.].

Toilet table. A table provided with toilet articles. {1794–} — **1773** Singleton *Social N.Y.* 83 [Joseph Cox from London] makes . . . commode dressing and toilet-tables. **1838** INGRAHAM *Burton* II. 194 Two strips of carpeting, . . . one lying by the bedside, the other before the tall, half-moon toilet table. **1879** STOCKTON *Rudder Grange* iii, She made a toilet-table . . . neat and convenient. **1923** WATTS *L. Nichols* 222 Ordering another consignment of ivory pyraline toilet-table furnishings.

+Tola, Tolle. *S.W.* Short for ATOLE. *Obs.* — [**1846** *Sage Scenes Rocky Mts.* xxi, A kind of gruel (*tolle*) made by stirring a few handfuls of flour into boiling water or milk.] **1881** C. M. CHASE *Editor's Run in N. Mex.* 215 For supper, tola, or roasted corn, ground into meal, boiled into a mush, and served with goat's milk and tortillas.

Tole, *v.* Variant of TOLL *v.*

*Tolerance. +(See quot. 1905.) — **1898** PINCHOT *Adirondack Spruce* 6 A provisional scale of tolerance is as follows. *Ib.* 30 Black Cherry stands about midway in the scale of tolerance among the trees in the Park. **1905** *Forestry Bureau Bul.* No. 61, 24 *Tolerance*, the capacity of a tree to endure shade.

Tolerant, *a.* {1784–} +(See quot. 1905.) — **1898** PINCHOT *Adirondack Spruce* 5 A selection forest is usually composed of species tolerant of shade. **1905** *Forestry Bureau Bul.* No. 61, 25 *Tolerant*, Capable of enduring more or less heavy shade.

*Toleration. *local. spec.* +A tax or license for taking clams or oysters. Also attrib. — **1796** *Smithtown Rec.* 129 Any person not an inhabitant . . . taking Soft shelled clams within the limits of said Town shall pay six pence for every bushel as toleration for taking the same. **1881** *Oyster-Industry* 249 *Toleration*, license to gather oysters or operate beds; paid by every individual annually. (Brookhaven, Long Island.) The money paid is called a *Toleration fee.*

*Toll, *n.*

*1. A proportion of grain taken by a miller as a charge for grinding.

1637 *Plymouth Laws* 56 Mr. John Jenney . . . shall have a pottle of Corne toule upon every bushell for grinding the same. **1725** *Boston Rec.* 197 A Law to prevent the abuse of Millers in Boston upon the Inhabitants in taking Toll. **1817** S. BROWN *Western Gazetteer* 49 The miller takes one eighth part of the grain for toll. **1877** W. H. BURROUGHS *On Taxation* 17 Their grists are ground for the same . . . tolls.

+b. A proportion of timber taken by a mill-owner for sawing it into lumber.

1779 *N.J. Archives* 2 Ser. III. 76 Plenty of timber would be brought to the said mill to be sawed for toll.

∗2. A charge made for the privilege of passing over a bridge or road.

1641 *Mass. Bay Rec.* I. 333 The tole of Mr. Mayhews bridge is referd to the Governour. **1668** *Providence Rec.* III. 121 Mr Roger Williams shall Receaue Tole of all strangers which shall heareafter passe ouer the Bridge at wapwaysitt. **1848** *Mich. Gen. Statutes* (1882) I. 919 No farmer shall be required to pay any toll for the use of said road by himself or persons in his employ. **1907** *St. Nicholas* Aug. 875/2 [They] walked out on the bridge a way, Roy standing treat for the tolls.

3. In special combinations.

Toll bin, ?a bin holding a miller's share or toll of the grain he has ground; *t. board,* a sign announcing the rate of toll; *t. gin,* a cotton gin for public use upon payment of a toll; *t.-tax,* a charge for the use of a public thoroughfare.

1884 HARRIS *Mingo* 230, I was in-about up to my eyes in the toll-bin. **1807** IRVING, etc. *Salmagundi* iv, Bridge over the Passaic—rate of toll—description of toll-boards. **1896** *54th Congress 2 Sess.* H. R. Doc. No. 267, 357 With the subdivision of farms an almost new industry was developed in the way of toll gins. **1880** *Harper's Mag.* Aug. 354/1 Every county in Pennsylvania is yoked down to civilization by a 'pike' and toll taxes.

∗ Toll, Tole, *v.*

+1. *tr.* To lure or decoy (wild creatures) for the purpose of capturing or killing them.

*a*1835 in Audubon *Ornith. Biog.* IV. 8 An instance in which I had toled to within a space of from forty to seventy yards off the shore a bed of certainly hundreds of ducks. **1847** LEWIS in Youatt *Dog* 90 In this simple branch of education, within the comprehension of any dog, consists the almost incredible art of toling the canvass-back. **1893** ROOSEVELT *Wilderness Hunter* 280 A bear carcass will toll a brother bear to the ambushed hunter better than almost any other bait.

fig. **1864** *Harper's Mag.* April 616/2 When there ain't nothing else to toll you off from your work it's always flowers. **1867** *Ib.* Aug. 283/2 My man . . . said, from the talk among them, it was Jackson's intention to toll Pope across the Rapidan.

+2. *intr.* To admit of being lured or decoyed.

*a*1835 in Audubon *Ornith. Biog.* IV. 7 The Black-heads toll the most readily, then the Red-heads. **1847** LEWIS in Youatt *Dog* 90 The canvass-back toles better than any other duck.

+Toll bait. Bait cut or ground up for throwing into the water to toll or attract fish. — **1870** *Amer. Naturalist* IV. 516 The 'tole-bait' consists chiefly of menhaden ground very fine. **1887** GOODE, etc. *Fisheries* v. II. 594 In the old style of mackerel fishing, . . . clams were chopped up (often with a mixture of menhaden) and sprinkled overboard as 'toll-bait.'

Toll bridge. A bridge at which a toll is charged for crossing. {1790-} Also attrib. — **1773** FITHIAN *Journal* I. 47 Expence at Toll-Bridge /2. **1810** M. DWIGHT *Journey to Ohio* 9 The Deacon & his family complain most bitterly of the gates & toll bridges. **1893** *Scribner's Mag.* June 755/2 It may be the interest on my toll-bridge stock. **1911** *Okla. Session Laws* 3 Legisl. 142 The board of county commissioners . . . is hereby authorized and empowered to acquire by purchase . . . all the rights . . . in the operation of any toll-bridge in the said county.

+Tolle. (See TOLA.)

∗Tol(l)er. +Something used to lure game. Also attrib. — *a*1835 in Audubon *Ornith. Biog.* IV. 7 Most persons on these shores have a race of small white or liver-coloured dog, which they familiarly call the *toler* breed, but which appear to be the ordinary poodle. **1874** LONG *Wild-Fowl* 72 For deep-water ducks, three or four decoys as tolers may be set out to leeward.

Toll gate. A gate on a road or at a bridge or ferry where a toll is collected for passing. {1773-} Hence *toll-gate keeper.* — **1797** *Phila. Ordinances* (1812) 138 The toll-gates at the ferry on the said river. **1807** IRVING, etc., *Salmagundi* ii, [He] even hinted at the expediency of erecting a toll-gate there. **1856** GOODRICH *G. Go-ahead* 48 James Grinnel, son of the toll-gate keeper. **1883** ZEIGLER & GROSSCUP *Alleghanies* 84 At the commencement of the ascent stands a primitive toll-gate. **1905** VALENTINE *H. Sandwith* 5 Uncle Billy was the toll-gate keeper.

∗Toll-gatherer. One who collects tolls. — **1799** BROWN *A. Mervyn* iii, Scrupulous honesty did not require me to . . . awaken the vigilance of the toll-gatherer. **1809** *Ann. 10th Congress* 2 Sess. 1841 It shall be lawful for them to appoint such, and so many toll-gatherers as they shall deem necessary. **1878** JACKSON *Travel at Home* 333 It is a toll-road, and the toll-gatherer takes minute reckoning of all he can see, passing the door.

∗Tol(l)ing. +The luring or decoying of ducks, fish, etc. Also attrib. — *a*1835 in Audubon *Ornith. Biog.* IV. 6 The usual mode of taking these birds has been . . . by *toling,* . . . an operation by which the ducks are sometimes induced to approach within a few feet of the shore. **1847** LEWIS in Youatt *Dog* 90 The toling season continues about three weeks from the first appearance of the ducks. *a*1888 ATWOOD in Goode *Amer. Fishes* 180 The present mode of catching mackerel by drifting and tolling with bait did not come into general use until 1812.

+Tollon. (See TOYON.)

Tolman. +A variety of apple. Also attrib. and in possessive. — **1822** J. THACHER *Amer. Orchardist* 139 *Tolman sweeting.* . . . It is held in much estimation for family use during the autumn. **1849** *Mag. of Horticulture* IX. 162 Tolman's Sweeting . . . is one of the most common sweet apples to be found in our markets. **1875** BURROUGHS *Winter Sunshine* 155 Now you have got a Tolman sweet. **1903** [see NORTHERN SPY].

∗Tom.

+1. =LONG TOM 2. Also attrib. {1890, in Australia}

1852 WHITMORE *Diary* 28 June, Helped the boys make dam across the Knaka Creek. Put in thier [*sic*] tom and carried dirt. **1856** *Harper's Mag.* Oct. 594/2 A stream of water . . . is led through wooden flumes to the 'tom heads.' **1876** MILLER *First Fam'lies* 127 Limber Tim looked to the left at a lot of picks and pans, and tom irons, and crevicing spoons, that lay up against the wall.

+2. In specific names and in phrases: (see quotations).

1834 AUDUBON *Ornith. Biog.* II. 539 Lincoln's Finch. . . . I named it *Tom's Finch,* in honour of our friend [Thomas] Lincoln, who was a great favourite among us. **1862** *Harper's Mag.* Feb. 373/1 Tar and feathers and the torch were freely used [in the Whisky Insurrection], and the violence employed was in a manner personified, and called *Tom the Tinker.* **1885** *Mag. Amer. Hist.* April 396/2 *Tom, Tip, and Ty,* a party motto common in Ohio during the 'Hard Cider' campaign of 1839. 'Tom' Corwin was running for the governorship of the State, while 'Tippecanoe' (Harrison) and Tyler were the Whig candidates on the Presidential ticket.

+Tomahawk, *n.* Also **tamahauke,** etc. [Algonquian Indian.] (See also TOMHAWK.)

1. A club or hatchetlike weapon or tool used by the Algonquian Indians of the eastern United States. {1718-}

1612 SMITH, etc. *Virginia* I. 44 *Tomahacks,* Axes. **1634** WOOD *New Eng. Prospect* (1865) 66 *Tamahaukes* be staves of two foote long and halfe long, and a knob at one end as round and bigge as a footebale. **1648** *Md. Archives* IV. 359, 3 hoes & a little Tomahawke. **1701** WOLLEY *Journal N.Y.* 38 They dig their ground with a Flint, called in their Language *tom-a-heakan.* **1744** *Mass. H. S. Coll.* VII. 183 They likewise throw their tomahawk (or little hatchet) with great certainty. **1807** *Ann. 10th Congress* I Sess. 582 What kind of tomahawks were these? . . . They were such as were generally used for shingling. *a*1817 DWIGHT *Travels* I. 118 The well known Tomahawk, or war-club, . . . [was] in shape not unlike a Turkish sabre, but much shorter and more clumsy. . . . Since the arrival of the English, they have used fire-arms . . . [and] a small battle-axe, to which they have transferred the name of Tomahawk. **1888** FERGUSON *Experiences of Forty-Niner* 86 A red devil brained him with a stone tomahawk. *a*1918 G. STUART *On Frontier* II. 73 Treaties were forgotten; guns and ammunition brought forth, tomahawk and scalping knife sharpened and . . . they again took the war path.

2. In phrases. **a.** *To bury the tomahawk,* or variants: To cease hostilities; to conclude peace.

Cf. *to lay down* (or *bury*) *the hatchet* (HATCHET *n.* 2 c).

[**1705** BEVERLY *Virginia* III. 27 They use . . . very ceremonious ways in concluding of Peace, . . . such as burying a Tomahawk.] **1765** [see sense b]. **1775** ADAIR *Indians* 315 We in a few days packed up a sufficient quantity [of presents], to bury the tomahawk which the French had thrust into their unwilling hands. **1808** PIKE *Sources Miss.* 86 The two nations had laid aside the tomahawk at my request. **1815** *Niles' Reg.* IX. 75/1 The northwestern Indians . . . have met our commissioners, . . . with a sincere desire of planting the tomahawk. **1848** *Congress. Globe* 18 Jan. 193/1 Will the time never come when we may honorably bury the tomahawk? **1865** in Thoburn *Stand. Hist. Okla.* I. 334 The tomahawk shall be forever buried.

b. *To take up the tomahawk,* or variants: To begin hostilities; to go on the warpath.

Cf. *to take up the hatchet* (HATCHET *n.* 2 d).

1765 TIMBERLAKE *Memoirs* 33 The bloody tommahawke, so long lifted against our brethren the English, must now be buried deep, deep in the ground, never to be raised again. **1775** ADAIR *Indians* 239, I persuaded the Choktah to take up the bloody tomohawk against those perfidious French. **1807** C. SCHÜLTZ *Travels* I. 101 Certain overtures . . . had been made to them by some hostile Indians, 'to take up the tomahawk against the United States.' **1812** *Niles' Reg.* II. 5/2 Every savage . . . may be expected to unbury the tomahawk. **1823** JAMES *Exped.* I. 163 He turned ι is back upon his nation, in consequence of their raising the tomahawk upon our citizens.

c. *To play tomahawk,* (see quotation).

1844 POE *Works* (1902) VI. 20 By 'playing tomahawk' he referred to scalping, brow-beating and otherwise using-up the herd of poor-devil authors.

3. In special combinations.

Tomahawk dance, an Indian dance in which tomahawks were used or displayed; *t. entry,* =TOMAHAWK IMPROVEMENT; *t. face,* a hatchet face; *t. right,* (see quotation); *t. settler,* a settler who has made a tomahawk improvement or who has a tomahawk right to a piece of public land.

1856 EMERSON *Works* V. (1903) 87 They have no Indian taste for a tomahawk-dance. **1842** *Amer. Pioneer* I. 312 One tract, a few miles above Marietta, is still known as 'Wiseman's bottom,' after the man who made a 'tomahawk entry' at that place. **1862** 'E. KIRKE' *Among Pines* 248 [The Abolitionists have] long, lean, tommerhawk faces. **1824** DODDRIDGE *Notes* 100 At an early period of our settlements an inferior kind of land title denominated a 'tomahawk right' . . . was made by deadening a few trees near the head of a spring, and marking the bark of some one, or more of them with the initials of the name of the person who made the improvement. **1788** CUTLER in *Life & Corr.* I. 425 Stopped and breakfasted at a little clump of houses on the Indian side. They were tomahawk settlers.

+Tomahawk, v. [f. prec.] tr. To strike or kill with a tomahawk. {1815-, fig.; 1829-}

1711 N.C. Col. Rec. I. 813. The Baron de Graftenried . . . was still alive but supposed only reserved for a more solemn execution, to be tomahawked and tortured. **1783** Travels Amer. Col. 672 The Indians had broken to the Station and were tomahawking the Women. **1812** MARSHALL Kentucky 144 When about to be tomahawked by one Indian, another saved her life. **1899** CUSHMAN Hist. Indians 440 Sixteen warriors . . . were led out and, in cold blood, tomahawked.

fig. **1869** Overland Mo. III. 111 [He] sharpens his bill with great gusto and tomahawks a bit of fruit. **1898** Milwaukee Sentinel 12 Jan. 6/2 There is also a disposition manifested on the part of some to tomahawk him.

+Tomahawk improvement. A casual improvement such as the girdling of a few trees or the planting of a little corn made in order to secure a preemption claim to government land; the place so improved. — **1803** Steele P. I. 374 There were many Tomahawk-Improvements. **1824** in J. Hall Sk. of West (1835) I. 194n., Those who wished to secure favourite tracts of land, chose to buy the tomahawk improvements, rather than quarrel with those who had made them. a**1847** HOWE Hist. Coll. Ohio 377 Below the garrison, was an old 'tomahawk improvement' and a small cabin.

+Tomahawking. The use of a tomahawk or tomahawks in attacking or fighting. Also transf. and attrib. — **1835** BIRD Hawks I. 120, I'll allow you to be a complete master of the science of tomahawking, skinning, and scalping. **1839** IRVING in Knickerb. XIII. 318 They lived by hunting and fishing, and recreated themselves occasionally with a little tomahawking and scalping. **1883** Harper's Mag. Feb. 423/1 After a great deal of tomahawking and scalping . . . , the united forces . . . crushed the Tuscaroras.

+Tomahawk pipe. (See quot. 1860.) Obs. — **1835** HOFFMAN Winter in West I. 245 The frontiersman, knocking the ashes from his tomahawk-pipe, passed me a flask of old Ohio whiskey. **1848** Ladies' Repository June 165 Next the tomahawk pipe of peace passed around, each taking his whiff in turn. **1860** DOMENECH 7 Yrs. in Deserts N. Amer. II. 272 The Comanches, in Texas, . . . have tomahawk-pipes (small hatchets, the head of which is made hollow like the bowl of a pipe, and the handle perforated in its whole length to serve for a tube).

Tom-and-Jerry. [Names of the two chief characters in Pierce Egan's Life in London (1821).] **1.** A hot drink of sweetened and spiced rum or punch beaten up with eggs. +**2.** A coat or overcoat. — (1) **1845** GREEN Texian Exped. 368 These very men . . . now want, one a 'sherry cobbler,' one a 'Tom and Jerry.' **1876** MILLER First Fam'lies 116 The cinnamon-headed dealer of drinks put . . . Scheidam schnapps in a Tom and Jerry. **1904** MACKAYE Panchronicon 248 Give me a Scotch high-ball. No? . . . Hot Tom and Jerry, then. (2) **1838** Knickerb. XII. 313 The intruder . . . [was] wrapped to the throat in a shaggy Tom-and-Jerry.

Tomato.
1. The fruit, usually large and rounded, of a widely cultivated plant (Lycopersicon esculentum) of South American origin; also, the fruit of any of various related species. {1604-}

See also CHERRY TOMATO, STRAWBERRY TOMATO.

1781-2 JEFFERSON Notes Va. (1788) 40 The gardens yield musk-melons, water-melons, tomatas, okra [etc.]. **1842** KIRKLAND Forest Life I. 52 The tomato has hitherto been considered heathenish and abominable. **1891** WELCH Recoll. 1830-40 76 But never a tomato, as they were considered poisonous at that time. **1912** N. WOODROW Sally Salt 80 The clear little artificial stream, its sides bordered with . . . tomatoes turning red in the midsummer sun.

b. pl. Cooked tomatoes put up in cans or jars.

1859 JACKSON in M. A. Jackson Gen. Jackson 128 Yesterday I went into the kitchen and sealed some jars of tomatoes. **1885** H. H. JACKSON Zeph iii, There's cold turkey and veal, . . . an' a can o' tomatoes.

2. attrib. and comb. **a.** Designating foods prepared from tomatoes.

1805 Pocumtuc Housewife (1906) 39 Tomato Soy. **1832** CHILD Frugal Housewife 114 Tomatoes Pie.—Tomatoes make excellent pies. **1867** Common Sense Cook Book 29 Tomato Sauce.—If fresh, put six in a stewpan [etc.]. **1878** Amer. Home Cook Book 28 Tomato Soup. **1883** Harper's Mag. Aug. 461/2 [She] must stimulate herself with some cress and onion and tomato salad.

b. In special combinations.

Tomato cushion, a cushion, probably a pincushion, suggestive of a tomato; t. gall, (see quotation); t.-nosed, having a large red nose; t. patch, a small piece of ground planted in tomatoes; t. pincushion, a pincushion made to resemble a tomato; t. vine, the stalk of the tomato plant.

1864 Hist. North-Western Soldiers' Fair 117 [Donations include] 1 pr. infant's shoes, 6 tomato cushions. **1891** Cent. 6371/3 Tomato-gall, . . . a gall made upon the twigs of the grape-vine in the United States by the gall-midge Lasioptera vitis: so called on account of its resemblance to the fruit of the tomato. **1867** HARRIS Sut Lovingood 21 'Yu'se counted yerself five times, Mister Lovingood,' said a tomato-nosed man in ragged overcoat. **1892** RITTENHOUSE Maud 555 We were hunting a ball in the tomato-patch back of the stop-net. **1903** WIGGIN Rebecca 37 She ran up the back-stairs to put . . . a red tomato-pincushion on Rebecca's bureau. **1876** 'MARK TWAIN' Tom Sawyer i. 18 [She] looked out among the tomato vines and 'jimpson.'

+Tomato can. A can of tinned iron in which cooked tomatoes are sealed for preservation. Also attrib. — **1883** HOWELLS Woman's Reason xvii, A few slatternly goats . . . wandered over the dismal expanse, as if to crop the battered tomato-cans. **1897** Forum Feb. 742 If these fits [of terror] once become customary, [the criminal] . . . usually ends his life in the lowest class of the outcast's world,—the 'tomato-can tramp class.' **1916** [see CAN n. 2].

+Tomato worm. A tobacco worm. So called when found on a tomato plant. — **1868** Mich. Agric. Rep. VII. 167 In many parts of Michigan, the tomato worm—larvæ of the Sphinx quinqua-maculata—have been frightfully abundant. **1892** [see CLOTHESMOTH].

✳Tombs. pl.
+1. The New York City prison. colloq.

1840 Picayune 27 Aug. 2/3 Poor Chapman . . . is in the 'Tombs,' charged with false swearing at an election. **1853** Harper's Mag. March 558/2 They will grow up Short Boys, Rowdies [etc.], . . . vibrating between the Five Points, the Tombs, the Hospital, and the Penitentiary. **1890** H. O. WILLS Twice Born 34, I was in the Tombs . . . , waiting for trial. **1903** N.Y. Ev. Post 22 Aug., The magistrate decided to hold him for trial, and he was committed to the Tombs.

+2. Used attrib. with lawyer, shyster, to designate a lawyer without professional ethics or reputation, as one preying upon defendants in such lower courts as the police court in the Tombs.

1852 BRISTED Upper Ten Th. 207 Kelly the carrier, And Lynch the Tombs lawyer, a pleader well known. **1870** M. H. SMITH 20 Years Wall St. 87 If a man goes to a pettifogger or tombs' lawyer for advice, instead of a reputable lawyer, people laugh at him for his pains. **1881** Phila. Record No. 3473, 4 One of the worst abuses in the most depraved days of New York City was the prevalence of the Tombs shyster.

Tomcod. {1883} +**a.** Any one of various small fishes of the genus Microgadus; a frostfish. +**b.** local. The kingfish, Menticirrhus saxatilis. +**c.** A rockfish (Sebastodes paucispinis) of the California coast. — **1722** New-Eng. Courant 1 Oct. 1/2 Some Fishermen in Boston made me pay Two Pence for the Sight of a Tom-Cod instead of a Maremaid. **1802** Mass. H. S. Coll. 1 Ser. VIII. 199 In the harbour, and on the coast, are haddock, tom-cod, pollock [etc.]. **1880** Nat. Museum Proc. III. 146 The names used by the fishermen . . . [include]: Meron, Tom-cod, Jack-fish. **1884** GOODE, etc. Fisheries I. 223 The Pacific Tom Cod . . . [is] found in California. Ib. 375 The King-fish, also known . . . as the 'Tom-cod' on the coast of Connecticut, . . . ranges from Cape Ann south at least as far as . . . Florida.

+Tom fuller. Also tom-ful-la. (See quot. 1916.) — **1848** Ladies' Repository Sept. 275 Some were beating corn for tomfuller, (a kind of hominy). **1863** Ib. Oct. 603/2 The chief article of food was tom-ful-la, a coarse preparation of sour hominy, of which they are very fond. **1916** THOBURN Stand. Hist. Okla. I. 262 The fermented hominy which was known as 'tah-fula' (corrupted into the English 'tom fuller') was the national dish of the Choctaws.

+Tomhawk. Also tomhog, etc. Variants of TOMAHAWK n. — **1716** CHURCH Philip's War 24 A great surly look'd fellow took up his Tomhog, or wooden Cutlash. **1758** Post Journal 228 The Indians . . . lay with their guns and tomhocks on all night. **1788** FRENEAU Poems (1795) 89 The North American Indians . . . [decorate the corpse of a warrior] with bows, arrows, tomhawks [etc.]. **1821** DODDRIDGE Backwoodsman & Dandy, Next I larned to shoot the bow and arrow, throw the tomhok, and handle the rifle.

+Tom pung. [Corruption of TOBOGGAN or the Algonquian source of this.] =PUNG 1. — **1801** Spirit Farmers' Mus. 243 That fam'd town, which sends to Boston mart, The gliding Tom Pung, and the rattling cart. **1825** COOPER L. Lincoln xix, Polwarth drove into the little courtyard . . . with all those knowing flourishes . . . which, in the year 1775, were thought to indicate the greatest familiarity with the properties of a tompung.

+Tomtate. The redmouth grunt, Bathystoma rimator. — **1896** JORDAN & EVERMANN Check-List Fishes 385 Tom-tate; Red-mouth Grunt.

Tomtit. Any one of various small birds, as the chickadees. {1709-} — **1709** LAWSON Carolina 145 The Tom-Tit, or Ox-Eyes, as in England. **1796** MORSE Univ. Geog. I. 211 Tom Teet. Parus atricapillus. Cutler. **1843** 'CARLTON' New Purchase I. 123 In vain do flocks of black-birds and robbins, and tom-tits rise! **1872** Harper's Mag. Nov. 810/2 Frogs, crayfish, tomtits, ground-squirrels—all . . . went in [the stew] without question. **1904** T. E. WATSON Bethany 21 The tom-tit flies here and there.

✳Ton. A measure of weight of varying signification, usually either the long ton (2240 pounds) or, especially in the United States and in British colonies, the short ton (2,000 pounds). — **1658** Suffolk Deeds III. 137 The summe of Six Tonnes fiue hundred weight of Good and merchantable barr Iron. **1777** [see NAIL ROD]. **1866** Internal Revenue Guide 104 On Steel made directly from muck-bar, blooms, slabs, or loops, [there is] a tax of three dollars per ton. **1876** INGRAM Centennial Exp. 673 They were mostly heavy cart horses, some of them magnificent animals, weighing a ton and over. **1910** Appleton's New Pract. Cycl. VI. 222/2 In the domestic commerce of the U.S. it is customary to reckon . . . 2,000 lb. to the ton . . . , and this usage in some of the states has received the sanction of law.

+Tong. [Chinese.] An association or secret organization among the Chinese in the United States. (Cf. HIGHBINDER 2.) — **1883** Harper's Mag. 831/1 This burial-place . . . is parcelled off by white fences into enclosures for a large number of separate burial guilds, or tongs, as the

Fook Yam Tong [etc.]. **1906** *N.Y. Ev. Post* 13 Feb. 14 The police . . . thought the war of the tongs had broken out afresh.

+**Tonger.** (See quot. 1881.) — **1881** INGERSOLL *Oyster-Industry* 249 *Tonger*, one who procures oysters by the use of tongs. **1887** *Courier-Journal* 1 May 15/5 The tongers are jubilant having received better prices than ever before from their commission merchants.

+**Tonging.** The taking of oysters with tongs. Also attrib. — **1869** *Rep. Comm. Agric. 1868* 342 The Baltimore department . . . reports an annual average of eleven million bushels, taken in the legitimate way of dredging and tonging. **1884** *Nat. Museum Bul.* No. 27, 220 The majority of the 'tonging' canoes employ one man and a boy. **1887** GOODE, etc. *Fisheries* v. II. 525 Certain richer tracts . . . form centers of tonging-work. **1911** *Rep. Fisheries 1908* 313/1 Oysters are obtained by dredging, raking, and tonging.

+**Tongman.** =TONGER. — **1881** INGERSOLL *Oyster-Industry* 249. **1887** GOODE, etc. *Fisheries* v. II. 525 In midwinter, when the heavy planters are busy marketing their crops, the tongmen are idle. **1891** W. K. BROOKS *Oyster* 140 They are exposed to the depredations of both tongmen and dredgers.

⁎ **Tongs.** *pl.*

⁎ **1.** Any one of various implements having two bars or legs so hinged or attached at one end as to be useful in grasping and holding objects.

1633 *N.H. Prov. Papers* I. 80 Tongues, bellows and andirons of each 1 pr. **1689** *Conn. Rec.* I. 468 Two payre of Andirons, Tongs, fire pen. **1707** *N.H. Probate Rec.* I. 552 Lett hear have tooungs: shovel and other Ieron. **1832** WILLIAMSON *Maine* I. 283 Nothing of his household-stuff remaining but an old pot, a pair of tongs, and a couple of cob-irons. **1902** [see FIRE STICK 1].

2. A long-handled implement having two rakelike or basketlike jaws used to grapple oysters or crabs and bring them to the surface. (See also OYSTER TONGS.)

1811 SUTCLIFF *Travels* (1815) 129 These instruments, which are called tongs, are opened wide when the heads are let down from the boats. **1881** INGERSOLL *Oyster-Industry* 245 Nippers, tongs having at the end not a rake head with many teeth, but only one tooth, or a very few teeth, so as to act as pincers. **1911** *Rep. Fisheries 1908* 309/2 Crabs . . . are caught with . . . hand lines, spears, and tongs.

+**3.** *local.* (See quotations.) *Obs.*

1845 JUDD *Margaret* I. 34 The boys dressed in 'tongs,' a name for pantaloons or over-alls. *a***1847** in J. S. Hall *Book of Feet* 138 This continued until long trowsers were introduced, which they called *tongs*.

⁎ **Tongue.** In special combinations.

Tongue cattle, cattle that work beside the tongue of a vehicle; *t. distemper*, a disease which affects the tongues of cattle; *t. hounds*; (see quotation); *t. oxen*, oxen that work beside the tongue of a vehicle; *t. patriot*, a patriot given to speech-making; *t. trap*, a verbal snare; *t.-whacking*, a tongue-lashing; *t. worm*, a wormlike parasite which when adult inhabits the frontal sinuses of dogs and wolves.

1851 SPRINGER *Forest Life* 106 The tongue cattle, pressed by the leaders, . . . threw the teamster under the runner. **1820** *Plough Boy* I. 270 Several of my cattle having been severely afflicted with the distemper now prevalent, called the *Tongue Distemper*. **1875** KNIGHT 931/2 The jaws between which the hinder end of a tongue is inserted . . . in a wagon are called tongue-hounds. **1851** SPRINGER *Forest Life* 104 It would be impossible for the 'tongue oxen' to resist the pressure of the load. **1806** *Balance* V. 5/2 Economy of time was one of those strings on which formerly our tongue-patriots were constantly harping. **1835** KENNEDY *Horse Shoe Robinson* I. 77 We hold in despise all sorts of contwistifications—either by laying of tongue-traps, or listenings under eaves of houses. **1896** *Godey's Mag.* Feb. 166/2 Is the deaf child expected to learn his lesson of self-control sooner than the hearing child who has the double shock of the tongue-whacking and the—other kind? **1897** *Dept. Agric. Yrbk. 1896* 161 The Tongue worm is found encysted in the viscera of cattle, sheep, and other animals, . . . and when eaten by dogs . . . inhabits the nasal cavities.

Tongue and groove, *v. tr.* To dress or finish (a plank or board) so as to leave a tongue or tenon on one edge and a groove on the other. {grooved and tongued, 1823} Also as adj. — **1773** *Bristol* (Va.) *Vestry Bk.* 238 A Dwelling House [shall] be built . . . [with] Good flouring Plank, well Tong'd & Groved. **1833** SILLIMAN *Man. Sugar Cane* 46 On each side of the centre wall, are two floors of tongued and grooved boards. **1897** MOORE *How To Build a Home* 15 The sheathing should be tongued and grooved and planed on one side.

⁎ **Tonnage.** *attrib.* +Designating a train or car for freight as distinguished from passengers. *Obs.* — **1858** W. P. SMITH *Railway Celebrations* I. 92 Equipment of the Marietta and Cincinnati Railway. . . . For Passenger Trains, 24; For Tonnage Trains, 24; making a Total of 48 Locomotives. **1862** *N.Y. Herald* 11 June 1/2 We took . . . three passenger and fifty tonnage cars.

Tonsorial artist. A barber. Now *Obs.* except in humorous use. — **1884** *Lisbon* (Dak.) *Star* 15 Aug., Geo. Pickard, the popular tonsorial artist, . . . will return to business in a week or two. **1892** *York County Hist. Rev.* 5 J. G. Cupit, Tonsorial Artist, 224½ West Market St. **1910** *Daily News* (London) 15 Dec. 6 American 'tonsorial artists' are furious at the popularity of the safety razor.

Tony, *a.* Stylish, fashionable. *colloq.*² '*U.S. and Colon.*' (*O.E.D.*). — **1879** R. GRANT *Little Tin Gods* 9 We the magnificent leaders of fashion

Fresh from a dinner and tony as possible. **1890** *Atlantic Mo.* Feb. 240/1 Mrs. Branner ought to be 'tony' enough for her. **1907** C. D. STEWART *Partners* He might be a down-river gambler. Some of them are pretty tony gentlemen.

⁎ **Tool.** Any one of various instruments used for performing manual operations.

1622 'MOURT' *Relation* 89 All our tooles againe . . . were taken in the Woods. **1699** *N.H. Probate Rec.* I. 442, I give and bequeath to my beloved wife . . . all my tools yt I now work with. **1755** *Lett. to Washington* I. 162, I should be glad to know . . . what I am to provide For the Expedition such as Tools, Pack Sadles [etc.]. **1822** *Ann. 17th Congress* 1 Sess. I. 87 It is the practice of many . . . to exempt . . . some part of the property of a debtor from execution; . . . [such as] the tools of a mechanic. **1883** *Rep. Indian Affairs* 151 The boys are taught . . . to become proficient in the use of tools. **1920** LEWIS *Main Street* 318 You looked at the tools on the glass shelves in Father's office.

Toot. {tout, 'a drinking bout, a drinking match,' 1790} *On a toot*, on a spree. *slang.* — **1877** BARTLETT 711. **1891** *Century Mag.* Nov. 54 Grubbsy's went off on a toot. **1899** 'LYNCH' *High Stakes* xxxii (F. and H.), I'd never 'a' carried 'em . . . if I 'adn't been on a regular toot for the last week.

Tooter. {1620-} +**1.** One who proclaims loudly. +**2.** A hotel runner or a circus barker. (Cf. TOUTER.) — (1) **1863** *Rio Abajo Press* 19 May 2 The nameless party's tooter speaks confidently of the success of its, nominee. (2) **1886** *Harper's Mag.* Aug. 417/2 The wharf . . . was alive with vehicles and tooters for the hotels. **1897** ROBINSON *Uncle Lisha's Outing* 297 Noisiest of all were the tooters, vociferously proclaiming the wonders of the side shows.

⁎ **Tooth.**

1. In the specific names of plants.

1817-8 EATON *Botany* (1822) 215 *Caltha flabellifolia*, tooth-leaf cowslip. **1813** MUHLENBERG *Cat. Plants* 32 [*Viburnum*] *dentatum* (arrow-wood), tooth-leaved [mealy tree]. **1785** MARSHALL *Amer. Grove* 160 *Viburnum dentatum*, Tooth-leaved Viburnum, or Arrow Wood. This grows naturally in moist places. **1784** *Amer. Acad. Mem.* I. 471 *Aeschynomene.* . . . Tooth-podded Bean. **1817-8** EATON *Botany* (1822) 263 *Dentaria diphylla*, tooth root, trickle, pepper-root.

2. In special combinations.

Tooth bar, a bar in an oyster dredge; *t. carpenter*, a dentist (*humorous*); *t.-filler*, an instrument used by a dentist in filling teeth; *t. mug*, ?a mug used when cleaning the teeth.

1891 *Scribner's Mag.* X. 471 No one is allowed to use a dredge for catching oysters with a longer tooth-bar than thirty-two inches. **1873** *Newton Kansan* 15 May 1/5 Yankee tooth carpenters stand (and charge) high in Europe. **1867** COZZENS *Sayings* 67 The little steel instrument . . . looked very much like a dentist's tooth filler. **1907** *St. Nicholas* Aug. 870/1 [He] was able to stand off the enemy with a tooth-mug filled with water.

+**Toothache bush.** A prickly ash of the genus *Zanthoxylum*. — **1817-8** EATON *Botany* (1822) 519 *Zanthoxylum fraxineum*, prickly ash, toothache bush. **1839** in Audubon *Ornith. Biog.* V. 436 Once only I saw it [the nest] lower, on the toothach bush, *Xanthoxylum*. **1859** BARTLETT 483 *Toothache Bush*, . . . Prickly Ash; so called from its pungent properties, made sensible when applied to an aching tooth.

+**Toothache grass.** S. A tall grass (*Ctenium aromaticum*) having a dense and much-awned, one-sided spike. — **1837** WILLIAMS *Florida* 82 Tooth-ache Grass . . . affects the breath and milk of cows. **1901** MOHR *Plant Life Ala.* 124 Toothache grass . . . [has a] stout aromatic rootstock deeply buried in the compacted sand.

+**Toothache tree.** A tree, as the prickly ash, allegedly of use in cases of toothache. — *c***1729** [see PELLITORY]. **1775** ROMANS *Nat. Hist. Florida* 22 Tooth ach tree, with white spines almost an ash leaf. **1802** DRAYTON *S. Carolina* 6 Their soil is of very sandy nature; producing . . . tooth-ache tree, prickly pear. **1897** SUDWORTH *Arborescent Flora* 265.

Toothbrush. 1. A brush for cleaning the teeth. {1651-} Also attrib. +2. (See quotation.) — (1) **1790** *Penna. Packet* 7 Dec. 3/3 Joseph Anthony, Junior, . . . Has Imported . . . Chess-men, cribbage boxes, tooth brushes. **1825** NEAL *Bro. Jonathan* II. 131 Out of six or eight, who made use of the *publick* tooth brush, only one used it, as if he knew what it was for. **1888** *Century Mag.* Sept. 769/2 Bristle tooth-brushes were replaced with twigs of the dog-wood. **1910** J. HART *Vigilante Girl* 34 If a moustache is worn, it must be of the toothbrush kind. (2) **1913** MORLEY *Carolina Mts.* 170 When a mountain woman refers to her 'toothbrush' the snuff-stick is what she means.

⁎ **Toothed,** *a.* In specific names: (see quotations). — **1817-8** EATON *Botany* (1822) 512 *Viola dentata*, toothed violet. **1821** *Mass. H. S. Coll.* 2 Ser. IX. 149 Plants . . . indigenous in the township of Middlebury [Vt., include] . . . *Cymbidium odontorhizum*, Toothed coral. **1842** *Nat. Hist. N.Y., Zoology* IV. 266 The River Moon-eye . . . is known under the popular names of Herring, River Herring, and *Toothed Herring*. **1843** TORREY *Flora N.Y.* I. 54 *Arabis dentata*. . . . Toothed Wall Cress. . . . A rather common species in the western States. *Ib.* II. 342 *Cyperus dentatus*. Toothed Galingale . . . Sandy swamps, Long Island.

Tooth instrument. 1. An instrument, as a hackle, having teeth. 2. Any one of various instruments used by dentists. — (1) **1732** *S.C. Gazette* 8 Jan., [The piece of hemp] now remains to be heckled, or passed thro' divers tooth Instruments. (2) **1787** *Md. Gazette* 1 June 1/3 Amputating, trepaning, pocket, and tooth instruments.

Tooth paste. A paste used in cleaning the teeth. Also attrib. — **1848** DUNGLISON *Med. Lexicon* 851/2 T[ooth] Paste, Dentifricium. **1881** *Ore. State Jrnl.* 15 Jan. 5/4 Slaven's Cherry Tooth Paste. **1883** *Century Mag.* July 410/1 The people rally to hear . . . the tooth-paste orator in nights of financial hypertrophy. **1924** *Scribner's Mag.* Dec. 647/1 [He] took the labels from tubes of tooth-paste, and pasted them on tubes of shaving cream.

* **Toothpick.**

+1. A bowie knife or dagger. *colloq.*
See also ARKANSAS *n.* and *a.* 6, CALIFORNIA TOOTHPICK.
1848 COOPER *Oak Openings* II. 43 We got our own tooth-picks. **1861** LOWELL *Biglow P.* 2 Ser. i. 22 He drawed toothpick on me. **1910** J. HART *Vigilante Girl* 135 He loaned him his toothpick.

+2. A native of Arkansas. A nickname. *Obs.*
1872 *Harper's Mag.* Jan. 317/2 Below will be found a careful compilation of the various nicknames given to the States and people of this republic: . . . Arkansas, Toothpicks.

3. *attrib.* Designating slender, sharp-pointed objects.
1880 'MARK TWAIN' *Tramp Abroad* 245 [Lucerne offers] to the eye a heaped-up confusion of red roofs, quaint gables, dormer windows, tooth-pick steeples. **1891** WELCH *Recoll.* 1830–40 179 A white two-pointed collar coming up and over the chin and lapping, called 'tooth-pick collars.' **1895** *Outing* XXVII. 6/1 A girl . . . gave me the go-by for a patent medicine drummer with tooth-pick shoes.

+Tooth saw. (See quot. 1876.) — **1868** *Ore. State Jrnl.* 31 Oct. 2/2 He is engaged with a company in New York in the manufacture of Brown's patent adjustable tooth saws. **1876** KNIGHT 2596/1 *Tooth-saw.* The dental saw is a fine frame-saw, used for cutting off the natural teeth for the attachment of pivot teeth; for sawing between teeth; or for sawing off the wires of artificial teeth to detach them from the plate.

Tooth wash. A liquid for cleaning the teeth. Also attrib. — **1871** 'MARK TWAIN' *Sk., New & Old* 261 He tendered me a tooth-wash atrocity of his own invention. **1878** *Decorum* 307 Use no tooth-washes nor powders whatever. **1889** 'MARK TWAIN' *Conn. Yankee* xx. 241 He could head off a company of travelers who would be rare customers for prophylactics and tooth-wash.

* **Toothwort.** Any one of various plants having toothlike parts, or used as a remedy for toothache, esp. a plant of the genus *Dentaria*. (Cf. PEPPERROOT.) — **1792** *Western Territory* 208 Of herbs, &c. we have of the wild sort . . . colewort, ground-pine, tooth-wort. **1843** TORREY *Flora N.Y.* I. 58 *Dentaria laciniata.* Common Tooth-wort. . . . Rich shady soils, particularly along rivers. **1857** [see PEPPERROOT]. **1890** *Cent.* 4566/3 P[*lumbago*] *scandens*, a trailing white-flowered species, is native to the south of Florida, . . . and known . . . as *toothwort*, from the use to which its caustic leaves and roots are put.

* **Tooting.** +A characteristic sound made in breeding time by pinnated grouse. Also attrib. — **1810** in Wilson *Ornithology* III. 109 This noise . . . is termed *tooting*, from its resemblance to the blowing of a conch or horn from a remote quarter. **1835** AUDUBON *Ornith. Biog.* III. 100 To the Gulls [mud flats or sandy beaches] are what the scratching or tooting grounds are to the Pinnated Grous.

* **Top,** *n.*

+1. *pl.* The upper parts of stalks of Indian corn cut off for use as fodder.
1724 [see BLADE *n.* 1]. **1811** *Agric. Museum* I. 240 [I was] informed of the advantages of using the tops of Indian Corn as rye straw. **1894** *Vt. Agric. Rep.* XIV. 42 The stalks are divided into . . . the tops, or topfodder (cut off above the upper ear)[,] the husks or shucks, and the butts. **1906** PRINGLE *Rice Planter* 369 Jim is cutting tops of the oldest corn.

2. *pl.* The best beef cattle in a herd. {1831–, of sheep}
1911 QUICK *Yellowstone Nights* 97, I sent Wallace . . . into a yard of feeders in Montana to pick out a trainload o' tops.

3. *attrib.* (passing into *adj.*) and *comb.* +**a.** Designating various vehicles that have tops.
See also TOP BUGGY, TOP-BUGGY WAGON, TOP WAGON.
1770 *Mass. Gazette* 23 April 3/2 (Ernst), Top chaises. **1780** ASBURY *Journal* I. 392 The sun is so violent, that . . . I could not stand it, were it not for the top-carriage. **1868** *N.Y. Herald* 18 July 1/2 Fine Top Gig For Sale. **1897** HOWELLS *Open-eyed Conspiracy* v, To issue from the railway station in the midst of those buoyant top-phaëtons and surreys, with their light-limbed horses is to be thrilled.

b. In special combinations.
Top fire, a fire in the tops of standing timber; *t. fodder,* =TOP *n.* 1; *t. leather,* a piece of leather used for boot tops; *t. minnow,* any one of various small fishes of the family Poecillidae that feed on the surface of sluggish waters in the South; *t. onion,* the tree onion, *Allium cepa bulbellifera; t. rail,* the rail at the top of a rail fence; *t. saw,* in a sawmill, the upper one of a pair of circular saws; *t. sergeant,* (see quotation) *colloq.; t.-shelfer,* a person of the highest rank (*colloq.*); *t. washing,* the washing of the topsoil in gold-mining; *topworks,* the brain (*slang*); *t. worm,* =SPINDLE WORM.
1900 BRUNCKEN *N. Amer. Forests* 109 There is something horrible in the slow, steady approach of a top fire. **1894** Top-fodder [see sense 1]. **1858** HOLMES *Autocrat* 20, I always feel as if I were a cobbler, putting new top-leathers to an old pair of boot-soles and bodies. **1883** *Nat. Museum Bul.* No. 27, 471 *Gambusia patruelis.* . . . Top Minnow. . . . Southern United States, from Virginia to Texas. **1871** *Rep. Comm. Agric.* 1870 223 The

top onion . . . produces perfect offspring, or bulbs, on the flower stalks. **1832** KENNEDY *Swallow Barn* I. 250, I have read . . . of ladies . . . seated . . . on the top-rail of a fence. **1876** KNIGHT 2597/2 The top-saw is a little in advance or rear of the under one. **1917** J. A. MOSS *Officers' Manual* 485 Top Sergeant—first sergeant. **1882** BAILLIE-GROHMAN *Camps in Rockies* 9 The frontiersman calls them, as we have heard, 'top-shelfers;' they are accompanied by their servants from England. **1850** AUDUBON *Western Jrnl.* 211 These diggings . . . were completely riddled; first by the top washing, and 'dry' washing of the Mexicans. **1838** INGRAHAM *Burton* II. 102 You will find a comrade of mine behind the rock a little cracked in the topworks. **1790** DEANE *New-Eng. Farmer* 148/1 *Topworms,* or *spindle-worms,* a white worm resembling a grub, found in the hose, or socket of a plant of maize, which eats off the stem of the plant, and renders it unfruitful.

* **Top,** *v.*

* **1.** *tr.* To cut off or otherwise remove the top: **a.** Of the tobacco plant.
1688 CLAYTON *Va.* in *Phil. Trans.* XVII. 982 They top their Tobacco, that is, take away the little top-bud. **1724** JONES *Virginia* 40 When it is grown up they top it, or nip off the Head. **1792** [see PRIME *v.*²]. **1864** *Maine Agric. Soc. Returns* 1863 160 When the plant is large enough to top, the leaves nearest the ground are to be broken off.

b. Of cotton, sugar cane, or turnips.
1774 FITHIAN *Journal* I. 246 [Cotton] must be top'd & suckered as Tobacco. **1862** *Ill. Agric. Soc. Trans.* V. 160, I hauled in [*sc.* sugar cane] into the barn and stripped and topped it. **1873** T. D. PRICE *Diary* (MS.) 25 Nov., Topped turnips and put in cellar.

c. Of Indian corn.
1791 in Imlay *Western Territory* (1797) 477 He sows his turnips, tops his indian corn, and blades it for the cattle. **1803** LEWIS in *Jrnls. of L. & Ordway* 40 The people began to top ther corn and collect ther fodder. **1850** S. F. COOPER *Rural Hours* 344 Some farmers 'top' the stalks, that is to say, cut off the upper half.

2. *To top off with,* to put on top of; to finish up or round off with. *colloq.* {1870–}
1787 CUTLER in *Life & Corr.* I. 231 Her hair . . . [is] topped off with a wire skeleton . . . covered with black gauze. **1837** IRVING *Bonneville* I. 105 The braves [were] . . . painted and decorated, and topped off with fluttering plumes. **1872** HOLMES *Poet* 44 He has topped off his home training with a first-class foreign finish. **1909** WASON *Happy Hawkins* 158 Then to top off with, I'd blown in about a month's wages.

Top-boot. A boot having a top of white, light-colored, or brown leather; a high boot. {1813–} — **1768** in Peyton *Adv. Grandfather* (1867) 17, I found my heavy top-boots of immense service also. **1841** *Knickerb.* XVII. 366 Our country doctor, . . . with cocked-hat and top boots, . . . always affected the old style of dress. **1898** [see SHEEPSKIN 1].

+Top buggy. A buggy having a top, esp. one that may be readily raised or lowered. — **1863** *Boston Auditor's Rep.* 1862–3 115 New Top Buggy for use of Superintendent, $275. **1896** HARRIS *Sister Jane* 298 Turning, I saw a light two-horse top-buggy,—a vehicle that was rare enough in these parts to attract attention. **1913** LONDON *Valley of Moon* 73 She had been buggy-riding before, but always . . . in a top-buggy, heavy and dingy.

+Top-buggy wagon. A light wagon having a top over the driver's seat. — **1849** *Knickerb.* XXXIV. 266 She started with her husband in an ordinary 'top-buggy' wagon.

Top crop. {1889} **1.** That part of a cotton crop obtained from the top and latest maturing part of the plants. **2.** *Top-crop rock,* in mining, an outcrop. — (1) **1854** *Fla. Plantation Rec.* 97 The top crop of cotton will be short. (2) **1895** *Advance* 19 Dec. 910/3 And it ain't top-crop rock, anyhow.

+Top cross. (See quot. 1909.) — **1890** *New Breeder's Gaz.* (Chicago) 28 March (*Cent.*), A filly with three top crosses or a horse with four top crosses can be registered. **1894** *Vt. Agric. Rep.* XIV. 105 The basis of registration . . . most generally accepted is . . . five top crosses of Thoroughbred sires. **1909** WEBSTER 2172/1 *Top cross,* . . . a cross in which superior or pure-bred breeds or individuals (usually males) are mated with inferior stock; a generation of ancestors in which one parent has superior qualities; the product of such a cross.

Top crust. The crust on the top of a pie or other pastry. — **1856** S. F. BATEMAN *Self* I. ii, Like the meat-pies they gave the boys at boarding-school,—all top-crust, and nothing inside. **1869** STOWE *Oldtown Folks* 340 Custard pies, apple pies, Marlborough-pudding pies,—pies with top crusts, and pies without. **1879** A. D. WHITNEY *Just How* 35 Fit the top-crust on again nicely.

+Top dirt. *Mining.* Topsoil; surface soil. — **1852** CLAPPE *Lett. from Calif.* 214 In many places the surface soil, or in mining phrase, the top dirt, pays when worked in a long-tom. **1857** BORTHWICK *3 Years in Calif.* 120 The miners talk . . . of stripping off so many feet of 'top dirt' before getting to 'pay dirt.' **1876** RAYMOND *8th Rep. Mines* 96 The top dirt has been entirely stripped.

* **Top-heavy,** *a.* +Of the audience in a theater: Distributed principally in the upper, lower-priced seats, with a small attendance on the main floor. — **1895** *N.Y. Dramatic News* 2 Nov. 18/1 Lansing Theatre . . . Human Hearts, 14; top-heavy house. *Ib.* 7 Dec. 10/3 In Old Kentucky had a top-heavy house in the evening at the Olympic.

Topknot. {1686–} +A scalp. *Obs.* — **1837** BIRD *Nick* I. 92 It's time you war tryin your hand at an Injun top-knot. **1844** KENDALL

Santa Fé Exped. II. 57 [Kirker] did not scruple to kill any of the lower order of Mexicans . . . and pass off their top-knots for those of true Apaches. **1850** GARRARD *Wah-To-Yah* xiii. 168 Mind the time we 'took' Pawnee 'topknots' away from the Plattes?

+Topknot quail. The California quail. — **1877** HODGE *Arizona* 223 Two others are similar to the top-knot quail of California. **1917** *Birds of Amer.* II. 8.

+Top-mounter. In a troupe of acrobats performing together, the one who mounts to the highest position. — **1895** *N.Y. Dramatic News* 14 Dec. 14/3 The top-mounter of the Athos troupe skipped away during the Chicago engagement. **1896** *Ib.* 11 July 12/3 Willie Milette, the top-mounter of the Milette brother act, made a mis-cue . . . and fell heavily.

+Top notch. The highest point or degree of excellence. *colloq.* Also attrib. — **1833** S. SMITH *Life J. Downing* 203 [To] ride awhile in one [wagon] without any cover to it, finny-fined off to the top notch, . . . [is] enough to tucker a feller out. **1898** C. A. BATES *Clothing Bk.* No. 1520 They are . . . the top notch of style. **1917** MCCUTCHEON *Green Fancy* 190 He telegraphed last night for four top-notch people to join us.

+Topnotcher. A person or thing of the highest quality. *colloq.* — **1899** ADE *Fables in Slang* 164 They told him he ought to go after the Top-Notchers. **1903** *Kan. State Bd. Agric. Rep. 1901-2* 64 There are not a sufficient number of 'top-notchers' to go around, the result being . . . the use of many inferior specimens [of cattle].

Topographical engineer. A topographer; an engineer skilled in topographic surveying and mapping. Also attrib. — **1816** *Ann. 14th Congress* 1 Sess. 1852 The general staff shall [include] . . . three topographical engineers. **1840** VAN BUREN in *Pres. Mess. & P.* III. 559 A communication from the Secretary of War . . . is accompanied by documents from the military and topographical engineer bureaus. **1897** DANA *Recoll. Civil War* 62 James H. Wilson . . . was serving as chief topographical engineer and assistant inspector.

Topping, *a.* {1681-} *New Eng.* +Domineering or boastful. — **1885** WILKINS in *Harper's Mag.* March 595/1 He was awful toppin' at first. **1899** JEWETT *Queen's Twin* 217 Child'n has too hard a time now,—all the responsibility is put on 'em since they . . . get to be so toppin' an' knowin'.

+Top-pole, *v. tr.* To finish off (a fence or wall) with a pole placed on top. — **1737** HEMPSTEAD *Diary* 317, I top poled the fence. **1753** *Ib.* 608 Staked & Toppoled ye fen(ce). **1868** BRACKETT *Farm Talk* 118 If you have a wall, it must be well top-poled.

+Top stick. A stick of wood placed on top in a wood fire. (Cf. BACK-STICK.) — **1852** *Knickerb.* XXXIX. 203 The log has been placed; the 'back-log' has surmounted it; the 'top-stick' crowns the apex. **1853** B. TAYLOR *Jan. & June* 189 Back-stick, fore-stick, top-stick, and super-structure, all [were] in their places.

+Top-tail, *v. intr.* (See quot. 1891.) — **1839** *Knickerb.* XIII. 385 'There she top-tails! there she blows!' added he, . . . after taking a long look at the sporting shoal. **1891** *Cent.* 6389/1 *Toptail*, . . . to turn the tail up and the head down, as a whale in diving.

Top-thresh, *v. tr.* To thresh the top or best-developed grains of (wheat, etc.). — **1874** *Vermont Bd. Agric. Rep.* II. 222, I would recommend the plan of top-threshing some of the best grain for seed.

+Top wagon. A wagon having a top or cover. — **1852** BRISTED *Upper Ten Th.* 205, I have a top-wagon. **1876** *Vermont Bd. Agric. Rep.* III. 158 We must breed a class of horses . . . of a size sufficient not to be *dwarfed* by a top wagon with the top *up.* **1884** ROE *Nature's Story* 294 He hastened to harness Thunder to his light top-wagon.

+Top-work, *v. tr.* (See quot. 1898.) Also *ppl. a.* — **1882** *Maine Agric. Rep.* XXVI. 342 The Bourassa . . . does well top-worked on a strong stock. **1898** S. B. GREEN *Forestry in Minn.* 301 *Top-worked*, said of trees that are grafted or budded at some distance above the ground.

* Torch, *n.*

* 1. An illuminating device that can be carried in the hand. Also transf.

See also LIGHTWOOD, PINE, PITCH-PINE TORCH.

1684 I. MATHER *Providences* (1856) p. ii, A Corps, with attending Torches, [was] brought to his Bedside. **1840** HOFFMAN *Greyslaer* I. 122 The torches . . . would enable them to fix the buck at gaze. **1876** [see FIRE HORN]. **1923** DUTTON *Shadow on Glass* 172 It may be the mere flash of an electric torch.

2. *attrib.* **a.** With *basket, boy, dragon, fishing.*
1875 'MARK TWAIN' *Old Times* vii. 129 The forecastle [was] lit up with the red glare of the torch-baskets. **1884** *Nat. Museum Bul.* No. 27, 1029 Torch-dragon. An open-work basket of hoop-iron, having an iron handle . . . which is attached to a wooden handle. . . . In this a fire or blaze is built when torching sperling (small herring). **1889** Torch-fishing [see FIRE FISHING]. **1889** BRAYLEY *Boston Fire Dept.* 363 [He] was a member of Deluge Engine Company No. 3 of that town as a torch-boy.

b. In specific names: (see quotations).
1854 EMMONS *Agric. N.Y.* V. 269 (*index*), *Phanaeus,* or Torch-beetle. **1890** *Cent.* 4496/2 *Pitch-pine,* . . . in America, *Pinus rigida,* . . . found from New Brunswick to Georgia. . . . Also called *torch-pine.*

Torch, *v.* {1847, *dial.*} +*tr.* To catch (fish, etc.) by using torch-light. Also *vbl. n.* — **1839** STORER *Mass. Fishes* 111 [The] scarcity [of herring] has been attributed by the fishermen to *torching* them at night. **1884** [see TORCH *n.* 2 a]. **1887** GOODE, etc. *Fisheries* v. II. 502 'Torching' . . . is practiced principally by negroes. **1896** *Boston Transcript* 21 Nov. 20/1 The boats [of the herring fleet] . . . are engaged in 'torching' herring.

*Torchlight. 1. Short for TORCHLIGHT PROCESSION. **2.** *attrib.* Designating organized public demonstrations, often of a political nature, carried on by torchlight. {torchlight ball, 1884} — (1) **1848** S. HALE *Letters* 2 It was a splendid procession, to which the Free-Soil Torch-light of last Wednesday was a miserable small '*sizzle.*' (2) **1865** *Ore. State Jrnl.* 13 May 2/1 The Democrats at their great torch-light demonstration . . . packed around a transparency. **1868** *Ib.* 17 Oct. 2/4 The Republicans had an immense torchlight display last night. **1876** INGRAM *Centennial Exp.* 656 The torchlight parade . . . had served only to increase the excitement for the Fourth. **1878** DALY in J. F. Daly *A. Daly* 255 Next week we are to have a torchlight turnout of the Mystic Knights of Mornus.

Torchlight procession. A parade, usually a political demonstration, consisting of torchbearers or carried on by torchlight. — **1844** *Lexington Observer* 3 Aug. 3/3 The Whigs of Louisville have . . . a great Torchlight Procession this evening. **1861** MCCLELLAN in *Own Story* 175 Last night the German division gave a grand torchlight procession and serenade. **1901** WHITE in *McClure's Mag.* Dec. 150 This money, which the lobbyist used to spend at Albany, is now spent for torch-light processions and picnics.

Torchwood (tree). {1601-} A tree of the genus *Amyris.* {1866} — **1833** *Niles' Reg.* XLIV. 394/1 The torchwood tree . . . burns bright like lightwood; and in combustion emits a pleasant odour resembling frankincense. **1880** *Lib. Universal Knowl.* VI. 65 There are [in Florida] splendid flowering magnolias, . . . palmetto, mangrove, torchwood. **1884** SARGENT *Rep. Forests* 33 *Amyris sylvatica.* . . . Torch Wood. . . . Wood very heavy, exceedingly hard and strong.

*To rights. (See RIGHT *n.* 4.)

*Torment. *spec.* Hell. — **1852** STOWE *Uncle Tom* xviii, I'm gwine to torment. . . . I's gwine straight to torment.

*Tormented, *a.* *New Eng.* +Confounded; darned. *colloq.* — **1825** NEAL *Bro. Jonathan* I. 138 They hadn't•come such a tormented long piece. **1866** LOWELL *Biglow P.* 2 Ser. Introd. p. lix, *Tormented:* euphemism for damned, as, 'not a tormented cent.'

* Tornado.

1. *** a.** A violent storm in the tropical Atlantic; a hurricane or a squall. +**b.** In the central U.S., a whirling wind, accompanied by a funnel-shaped cloud, which moves in a narrow path and freq. does great damage.
1752 *Md. Hist. Mag.* XVIII. 24 A tornado blew down the house of John Grove. **1817** S. BROWN *Western Gazetteer* 148 The tornadoes to which the country is subject, will not admit of the houses being carried up several stories. **1862** 'E. KIRKE' *Among Pines* 220 Not three hundred yards in our rear, had passed the Tornado. **1916** [see COLLEGE 3].

2. Attrib. with *cellar, character, insurance, track.*
1815 *N. Amer. Rev.* II. 58 The strength of the wind, and its tornado character, was principally felt . . . between New-London and Newbury-port. **1891** SWASEY *Early Days Calif.* 15 In some portions of the West these tornado tracks are termed 'windrows.' **1898** C. B. DAVIS *Borderland of Soc.* 92 Wait till you marry and can't get even a tornado insurance company to put a cent on your frizzled self. **1905** *Springfield W. Repub.* 19 May 7 Inhabitants of the 'new country' in Oklahoma are digging 5000 tornado cellars.

‖Tornadoish, *a.* Characteristic of a tornado. — **1889** *Columbus Dispatch* 16 Jan., The storm is going out of the United States across Lake Superior and . . . we will escape . . . its powerful warm, wet, tornadoish right [hand].

+Tornillo, Tornilla. *S.W.* [Sp., 'screw.'] =SCREW-POD MESQUITE; also, the bean of this plant. — **1844** GREGG *Commerce of Prairies* II. 78 In the immediate vicinity of El Paso there is another small growth called *tornillo* (or screw-wood), so denominated from a spiral pericarp. **1847** RUXTON *Adv. Rocky Mts.* (1848) 174 The mezquite is now becoming scarce, the tornilla or screw-wood taking its place. **1858** *Harper's Mag.* Sept. 464/1 The Mojave rancherias are surrounded by granaries filled with corn, mesquite beans, and tornillas. **1873** ARNY *Items regarding N. Mex.* 21 Pecan and walnut with considerable hackberry, mesquit, manzanilla and tornillo, were found. **1892** *Dialect Notes* I. 195 *Tornillo.* . . . The beans are used as food by men and animals.

Torop(e). (See TORUP.)

* Torpedo, *n.*

* 1. Any one of various fishes of the family Torpedinidae, noted for their power of transmitting electric shocks, as the crampfish (*Tetranarce occidentalis*); a related fish having a similar property. Also with specifying term.
1794 *Mass. Hist. Soc. Coll.* III. 199 The cramp fish . . . possesses the properties of the torpedo, being capable of giving a smart electrical shock. **1860** PRESCOTT *Telegraph* 37 The torpedo is occasionally found in the waters surrounding Cape Cod. **1896** JORDAN & EVERMANN *Check-List Fishes* 222 *Tetranarce californica.* . . . California Torpedo. Coast of California. **1911** *Rep. Fisheries 1908* 314/1 Ray (*Raiæ*).—A general name given to a large group of fishes found on all our coasts. They are also called 'skates,' 'torpedoes,' 'devil-fishes,' etc.

+2. Any one of various devices for blowing up enemy ships by an explosion in the water. {1868-}
See also AMERICAN TORPEDO.
1807 IRVING *Salmagundi* xiii, The Society have . . . invented a cunning machine, a *Torpedo,* by which the stoutest line-of-battle ship . . . may be

caught napping. **1864** NORTON *Army Lett.* 212 The steamers Maple Leaf and General Hunter have been blown up by torpedoes. **1886** *Harper's Mag.* June 25/1 It is probable that the auto-mobile torpedo for our new navy will be an American invention. **1898** *Boston Ev. Globe* 25 Feb. 2/3 (Ernst), The term ['mine'] is generally applied to such torpedoes as are fixed in a particular place.

+3. *Mil.* An explosive shell hidden in the ground or other places and designed to go off at the tread or touch of an enemy.

1863 Moore *Rebellion Rec.* V. I. 3 The rebels have been guilty of the most murderous and barbarous conduct in placing torpedoes within the abandoned works, ... in carpet-bags, barrels of flour, etc. **1867** CRAWFORD *Mosby* 274 Lieutenants I. and Y. placed torpedoes in the road between Piedmont and Markham. **1907** [see FATIGUE PARTY].

4. A small firework which explodes when thrown with sufficient force against a hard surface. {1831–}

1852 *Knickerb.* XXXIX. 380 Unruly boys played pranks upon him: slipping torpedoes under his feet. **1872** BRACE *Dangerous Classes N.Y.* 164 She joined a company of poor working-girls, who earned their living by manufacturing children's torpedoes. **1920** HOWELLS *Vacation of Kelwyns* 165 He did not, in fact, much mind ... being broken of his morning nap by the torpedoes and fire-crackers which the three boys exploded.

+5. An explosive charge set off to open up an oil well or to start the flow of oil.

1886 [see GO-DEVIL 4]. **1889** 'MARK TWAIN' *Conn. Yankee* 275 When an oilwell ceased to flow, they used to blast it out with a dynamite torpedo.

+6. *Railroad.* A contrivance placed on a track to serve as a signal to an engineer by exploding under the wheels of the locomotive.

1900 *Everybody's Mag.* II. 444/2 Another device that is useful in giving warning to engineers at points unprovided with fixed signals, or in case of fogs which obscure such signals, is the torpedo.

7. *attrib.* and *comb.* **a.** In senses 2 and 3 with *bureau, catcher, corps,* etc. **b.** In sense 1 with *fish.* **c.** In sense 4 with *trade.* **d.** In sense 5 with *man.*

(a) 1813 *Niles' Reg.* IV. 365/2 In a little while, we hope to hear of a *Torpedo Corps.* **1877** KNIGHT 2602/1 *Torpedo-catcher,* a forked spar or boom extending under water, ahead of a vessel, to displace or explode torpedoes. **1883** *Century Mag.* Sept. 732/1 The tide stands high off the torpedo station. *Ib.* Nov. 132/1 He had been on duty in the 'torpedo bureau.' **1889** in *N.Y. Pub. Lib. Bul.* XLIV. 116 Lt. Moore 22 Inf. ... has been taking course of torpedo instruction at Willet's Point. **1891** *Cent.* 6392/2 In the United States a torpedo-school for the navy has been established at Newport, Rhode Island, and for the army at Willet's Point, New York. **(b) 1825** NEAL *Bro. Jonathan* I. 29 It would appear as if she had been lying in wait, like a torpedo-fish, in the water, for an opportunity to set people tingling. **(c) 1868** *N.Y. Herald* 6 July 9/4 The Torpedo Trade ... is prosecuted in the town of Southold. **(d) 1883** *Century Mag.* July 330/2 The 'torpedo man' is one of the interesting personages of the oil regions.

Torpedo, *v.* {1771–2–} **+tr.** To clear out or start flowing (an oil well) by exploding a torpedo (sense 5). Also *ppl. a.* and *vbl. n.* — **1873** HOWELLS *Chance Acquaintance* vi, He treats me very gingerly, as if I were ... an inflammable naiad from a torpedoed well. **1883** *Century Mag.* July 330/1 When a well fails it is usually 'torpedoed' to start the flow afresh. **1893** *Columbus Dispatch* 1 Aug., A success in the oil well at this place is assured as shown by the result of torpedoing last evening.

+Torpedo boat. A boat from which torpedoes are launched. {1884–} Also *comb.* — **1810** FULTON *Torpedo War* 44 It would be difficult for a Torpedo boat to depart from any port of America, and return without being detected. **1866** W. REID *After the War* 60 Near the iron clad lay some of the cigar-shaped torpedo boats. **1886** *Harper's Mag.* June 25/2 [There is] a new type of vessel, called torpedo-boat catchers, whose primary duty is to destroy the torpedo-boats of the enemy. **1904** 'O. HENRY' *Roads of Destiny* 356 It wouldn't hurt to have a couple of cruisers and a torpedo-boat destroyer, too.

+Torrey. [John *Torrey,* Amer. botanist (1796–1873).] Used attrib. and in possessive in the specific names of plants. — **1843** TORREY *Flora N.Y.* II. 62 *Pycnanthemum Torrei.* Torrey's Pycnanthemum. ... Dry rocky hill-sides, near Kingsbridge on the Island of New-York. **1897** SUDWORTH *Arborescent Flora* 19 *Pinus torreyana.* ... Torrey Pine. *Ib.* 102 *Tumion taxifolium.* ... Florida Torreya. ... Torrey Tree (Fla.).

+Torreya. [See prec.] A plant of the genus *Torreya;* the stinking cedar of Florida (*T. taxifolia*), or the California nutmeg (*T. californica*). Sometimes with specifying terms. — **1897** SUDWORTH *Arborescent Flora* 102 *Tumion californicum.* ... California Torreya. **1901** MOHR *Plant Life Ala.* 34 The Torreya ... and the Florida yew ... present similar striking instances of a strange localization.

+Torshent. Also **toshance, torsh,** etc. *New Eng.* [See quot. 1802.] The youngest child in a family. — **1802** J. FREEMAN in *Mass. H. S. Coll.* 1 Ser. VIII. 97 The Indians of New England had ... [a] word, which in the dialect of the Nauset Indians was *taushents.* It has been adopted by the descendants of the English in many parts of the Old Colony of Plymouth, and is applied as a term of endearment. **1888** L. G. MORSE *Chezzles* 36 Bob ... is your father's torshent, and the little Barnes girl is her father's; every one in Nipsit calls her little Torsh Barnes. **1890** *Dialect Notes* I. 75 The youngest child of a family is called a 'tortience.' South

Yarmouth, Mass. ... 'That's my toshuns' = that's my youngest. **1912** *Yarmouth Register* 29 Nov., I have heard 'toshance' ... in quite recent years.

+Tortience. (See TORSHENT.)

+Tortier. [Corruption of TORTILLA.] = next. — **1884** *Gringo & Greaser* 1 Jan. 2/3 [We] munch our tortiers and sheepmeat on the wing.

Tortilla. [Sp., 'little cake.'] A flat, round cake baked of corn meal. {1699–, in Sp. Amer., etc.} — **1831** PATTIE *Personal Narr.* 42 She then brought forward some tortillas and milk. **1854** *Harper's Mag.* April 584/2 The 'United States Hotel' [in Santa Fe provided] ... *frijoles* and *tortillas.* **1873** COZZENS *Marvellous Country* 59 Tortillas are ... moulded by the hands into a kind of pancake, and baked. **1898** CANFIELD *Maid of Frontier* 189 The tortillas and 'cabritas' ... had been eaten.

Tortle, *v.* {turtle, *a*1756–} *intr.* To move steadily, in the manner of a turtle. — **1836** CROCKETT *Exploits* 33, I am now on my journey, and have already tortled along as far as Little Rock. **1844** NEAL *Peter Ploddy* 148 Get up and tortle home the straightest way there is. **1856** *Knickerb.* XLVIII. 284 As we tortled along over the sand, I begun to notice a couple walking just before.

*Tortoise.

*1. Any reptile of the order Chelonia; a turtle or terrapin. Also with specifying term.

See also ALLIGATOR, BOX, LAND TORTOISE.

1624 Smith *Gen. Hist. Va.* I. 17 Here are many Tortoises. **1763** in W. Roberts *Nat. Hist. Florida* 101 They have ... tortoises of five several kinds. **1839** STORER *Mass. Reptiles* 209 E[mys] *insculpta,* ... the wood Tortoise, ... remains a long time out of the water. **1911** *Rep. Fisheries 1908* 317/2.

2. In special combinations.

Tortoise beetle, any one of various tortoise-shaped leaf beetles of the family Chrysomelidae {c1711–}; *t. spike,* a pointed weapon used by a turtler for piercing the shell of a tortoise. **1837** WILLIAMS *Terr. of Florida* 64 The tortoise spike is one inch and a half long. **1854** EMMONS *Agric. N.Y.* V. 265 (index), *Cassida,* or Tortoise-beetle.

Tortoise-shell(ed) butterfly. Any one of various mottled butterflies of the family Nymphalidae. {1782–} — **1845** JUDD *Margaret* II. 215 A yellow-breeched bee and a tortoise-shelled butterfly were quietly together feeding upon [a thistle]. **1854** EMMONS *Agric. N.Y.* V. 209 *Vanessa urticæ.* Tortoise-shell Butterfly. ... I am unable to say whether this is a common species in this State, or not.

Torup, Torop(e). ?Variant of TERRAPIN. — **1613** WHITAKER *Good Newes from Va.* 42, I haue caught with mine angle ... the Torope or little Turtle. **1894** *Critic* 27 Oct. 268 Farmers and sailors call the big 'snapper' the torup or torop.

Tory. {1646–}

1. a. A member of the Tory party. {1705–} Also transf.

+b. In the conflict between the American colonies and England, and in the Revolution: An American partisan of the cause of the British crown; a loyalist. Now *hist.*

In some examples there may be connotations, referable to British usage, of either (1) lawlessness or (2) political conservatism.

1769 *Boston Gaz.* 24 April 3/2 Keep your Rights out of Sight, and you may have any Thing you please. A Tory. **1775** *Penna. Ev. Post* 1 July 278/1 The Whigs and Tories at Georgia are disputing with each other. **1781** *Va. State P.* I. 494 The destruction of the Works at the Lead Mines, are an object the Tories have in view. **1823** THACHER *Military Jrnl.* 285 They are continually exposed [c1780] to the ravages and insults of infamous banditti, composed of royal refugees and tories. **1864** 'PENNIMAN' *Tanner-Boy* 17 [The bitterness of some Canadians toward the United States] is owing to the fact that among their forefathers were to be found many of the Tories of the American Revolution. **1902** S. G. FISHER *True Hist. Amer. Revol.* 10 Those colonists who were opposed to the rebellion ... never fully accepted the name Tory, either in its contemptuous sense or as meaning a member of the Tory party in England.

+2. A person regarded as disloyal; a traitor.

Applied to the New England opponents of the War of 1812 and, in the Confederate States, to sympathizers with the Union. *Old Tory,* as applied to Federalists, apparently implied previous loyalist sympathies or activity.

1809 *Ann. 10th Congress* 2 Sess. 1333 The Old Tories and Federalists of the North ... are not much worse [about violating the embargo acts] ... than the young Tories and Democrats of the South. **1812** *N.Y. Ev. Post* 28 Oct. 2/4 The war-hawks of that vicinity ... began abusing him with the usual slang of Federalist, old Tory, &c. **1818** FEARON *Sketches* 139 Federalists, [are] called also 'Tories.' **1862** *Southern Confederacy* (Atlanta, Ga.) 3 May (Th.), The other prisoners were all sharp, intelligent-looking men, no hard-looking cases like Yankee prisoners, and East Tennessee Tories usually are. **1866** W. REID *After the War* 402 Ef you fetch any d——d tories heah, that went agin their State, and so kin take the oath, ... 'twill soon be too hot to hold 'em.

+3. *attrib.* **a.** Designating various phenomena relating to loyalist activities.

1769 *Boston Gaz.* 11 Dec. 2/2 The Printer ... closes this Tory ... article, with this beautiful sneer! Glorious Patriotism! **1776** *Penna. Ev. Post* 23 March 148/2 Donald McDonald, Esq.; lately created Brigadier-

General in the Tory Army. **1780** STEELE *P.* I. 8 We have been surrounded by Tory-Insurrections.

b. Designating persons of Tory principles or persons active in the loyalist cause. *Now hist.*

1775 *Penna. Ev. Post* 12 Dec. 570/1 Colonel Scott . . . has taken several Tory prisoners. **1806** FESSENDEN *Democracy Unveiled* II. 161 How many a Tory renegadoe, You've rais'd . . . Above the Whigs of seventy-six. **1857** *Lawrence Republican* 11 June 1 The tory Taneys of that age adjudged the declaration 'unconstitutional.' **1881** *Harper's Mag.* April 720/2 She comprehended the especial aristocracy of Tory families. **1883** ZEIGLER & GROSSCUP *Alleghanies* 29 The Cherokees . . . , associated with tory guerrillas, engaged in many acts of bloody violence.

+Tory bud. (See TORY WEED.)

Toryess. +A woman loyalist. — **1777** FRANKLIN *Writings* VII. 24 She is a *Toryess* as well as you, and can as flippantly call *Rebel*.

Toryish, *a.* {1681–} +Sympathetic to the cause of the loyalists. *Now hist.* — **1860** HOLMES *E. Venner* vii, [Among the guests were] the Vaughans, an old Rockland race, . . . Toryish in tendency in Revolutionary times.

Toryism. {1682–} +The principles of the loyalists; sympathy with the cause of the British crown. *Now hist.* — **1771** J. ADAMS *Diary* Works II. 266 John Chandler, Esq. of Petersham, . . . gave us an account of Mr. Otis's conversion to Toryism. *Ib.* 437 We are yet in Philadelphia, that mass of cowardice and Toryism. **1838** INGRAHAM *Burton* II. 57 Now, major, be careful you are not converted to toryism on the ride. **1838** BRYCE *Amer. Commw.* III. VI. ciii. 468 The Anglican Clergy were prone to Toryism.

+Tory weed. A coarse plant of the genus *Cynoglossum;* the hound's-tongue. Also *tory bud.* — **1836** EATON *Botany* (ed. 7) 269. **1863** RANDALL *Pract. Shepherd* 142 The large and small Hounds-tongue, or Tory-weed . . . and the wild Bur-marigold . . . are peculiarly injurious to wool. **1876** J. E. TODD *John Todd* 24 After a time [he] returned with some leaves of a plant called 'tory weed.' **1894** *Amer. Folk-Lore* VII. 95 *Cynoglossum officinale*, tory-bud, N.Y.

+Toshance. (See TORSHENT.)

*Toss, *v.* 1. *To toss the feather,* to throw a feather into the air to test the wind. 2. *To toss* (oars), 'to throw up the blades of the oars and hold them perpendicularly, the handles resting on the bottom of the boat: a salute' (*Cent.*). Also *absol.* — (1) **1832** CATLIN *Indians* I. 25 Mons. Chardon 'tossed the feather' (a custom always observed, to try the course of the wind). (2) **1888** DORSEY *Midshipman Bob* 101 They slipped into their places, 'tossed,' their oars, . . . and 'gave way.' **1891** *Harper's Wkly.* XXXV. 714/4 'Toss!' and with one graceful sweep the long oars rise in salute.

Toss 'em boys. +(See quotations.) — *c*1775 BOUCHER *Glossary* p. l, At dinner, let me . . . toss 'em boys, and belly bacon see. **1800** *Ib.*, *Toss 'em boys;* chickens: so called, it is supposed, because . . . [they are] run down with . . . [a dog set on] by the phrase *Toss 'em boys.*

‖**Tossomanony.** ? = HOMINY. — *a*1797 in Imlay *Western Territory* (ed. 3) 382 Corn . . . was then in the milk, and in that stage when the Indians prepare it for tossomanony.

‖**Totage.** [f. TOTE *v.*] The carrying of burdens. — **1886** *Boston Herald*, The burro, that patient little beast of general totage.

Total abstinence.

1. The principle or practice of complete abstention from the use of intoxicants. {1853}

1831 H. FINN *Amer. Comic Ann.* 76 Medicine or no medicine, we go for total abstinence. **1833** *New Eng. Mag.* V. 137 Among other means . . . adopted in aid of the Temperance cause . . . is a *pledge of total abstinence.* **1879** *Harper's Mag.* June 141/1 The old way was that of aiming at temperance rather than at total abstinence. **1904** KITTREDGE *Old Farmer* 172 Mr. Thomas's satire on the husking was written when the agitation for total abstinence was at its height.

2. Attrib. with *convention, movement, reform, society.*

1835 REED & MATHESON *Visit* I. 284 [In addition to] the usual Temperance Society . . . is 'The Total Abstinence Society,' whose pledge extends to 'wine, cordials, and strong beer.' **1865** *Atlantic Mo.* Jan. 54/1 He might be invited to attend a Total Abstinence Convention. **1872** BRACE *Dangerous Classes N.Y.* 67 The 'Total Abstinence Reform' in this country . . . was one of the happiest events that ever occurred in the history of the working classes. **1883** *Century Mag.* Sept. 783/1 The improvement among educated people in the drinking customs of society is . . . [not due] to any of these extreme total abstinence movements.

‖**Total abstinent.** A total abstainer. — **1882** *Harper's Mag.* Sept. 633/2 They are total abstinents.

+Tote, *n.* [f. TOTE *v.*] The position of being carried. — **1867** GOSS *Soldier's Story* 260, I've told yer four times to bring that gun ter a tote.

+Tote, *v.* Also **toat.** [Of obscure origin.] *colloq.* Chiefly *S.*

1. *tr.* To carry; to transport or haul.

1677 in *Virginia Mag.* II. 168 [Certain men were] commanded to goe to work, . . . and mawl and toat railes. **1769** *Boston Gaz.* 7 Aug. 3/2 The next Morning he was toated on board the Rippon, in a Canoe. **1775** in Pusey *Road to Ky.* (1921) 44 We are obliged . . . to toate our packs. **1836** GILMAN *Recoll.* (1838) 50 Fayther . . . wants Master Richard's horse to help tote some tetters. **1883** *Harper's Mag.* Jan. 207/1 John Chinaman . . . totes kegs of water . . . up and down the rough declivities. **1905** *Forestry Bureau Bul.* No. 61, 51 Tote, to haul supplies to a logging camp. (N[orthern] F[orest].) **1920** [see GOPHER HOLE 1].

transf. and *fig.* **1837** *Knickerb.* IX. 263 He 'toted' a wheel-barrow with cake and ale . . . throughout the city. **1883** 'MARK TWAIN' *Life on Miss.* xxviii, You've got to admire men that deal in ideas of that size and can tote them around without crutches.

b. *To tote plunder,* to carry or fetch baggage or personal belongings.

1835 HOFFMAN *Winter in West* II. 124 Help yourself, stranger, . . . while I tote your plunder into the other room. **1848** BURTON *Waggeries* 93 His 'plunder' was toted from the Astor before daybreak. **1869** BARNUM *Struggles* 97, I reckon they's totin' that plunder off to get ready for a dance.

2. To lead or conduct (persons).

1807 IRVING in P. M. Irving *Life W. Irving* I. (1862) 189 At Baltimore . . . I was *toted* about town and introduced to everybody. **1852** STOWE *Uncle Tom's Cabin* v, Will you wait to be toted down river, where they kill niggers with hard work and starving? **1924** MULFORD *Rustler's Valley* iii, I don't need no safe conduct, an' you might as well know that ain't why I'm totin' you along with me.

3. To wear; to carry regularly as a part of one's clothing or equipment.

1823 QUITMAN in Claiborne *Life Quitman* I. 85 The belles . . . 'tote' their fans with the air of Spanish señoritas. **1883** SWEET & KNOX *Through Texas* 13 They said that he 'always went heeled, toted a derringer, and was a bad crowd generally.' **1909** WASON *Happy Hawkins* 311, I didn't take kindly to that, 'count o' there not bein' any handy place to tote a gun.

4. *intr.* To go.

1862 LOWELL *Biglow P.* 2 Ser. i. 16 Tote roun' An' see ef ther's a featherbed (thet's borryable) in town. **1865** *Atlantic Mo.* April 387/1 Nothing would do but to tote down here to the Crik and make his fortin.

5. *To tote fair,* to take one's just portion of a burden; to play square.

1866 C. H. SMITH *Bill Arp* 147, I don't think you tote fair. **1883** *Gringo & Greaser* 1 Sept. 1/2 Some of our exchanges are clipping from the *Gringo & Greaser* without credit. . . . Tote fair, brethren. **1896** *Current Hist.* VI. 865 The trust maintained a regular force of inspectors to keep all the members of the pool 'toting fair.'

+Tote bag. A canvas bag for carrying miscellaneous articles. — **1900** in *Notes & Q.* 10 Ser. II. 162/1 The Watson Tote Bag . . . best thing for hunting, tramping and fishing trips, for carrying coat, camera, blankets, lunch, &c.

+Tote-load. 'As much as one can carry. Southern' (B. '59).

+Totem, *n.* Also **totam.** [Of Algonquian origin.] Among the American Indians, something, as a species of animal or plant, associated with and identifying a specific group of persons, or, loosely, an individual; also, the group so designated, or a representation or symbol of the identifying object.

'Irregularly derived from the term *ototeman* of the Chippewa and other cognate Algonquian dialects, . . . of which *ote* is the grammatic stem' Hodge.

[**1609** P. ERONDELLE tr. Lescarbot *Nova Francia* 178 Memberton . . . carrieth hanged at his neck . . . a purse . . . within which there is I know not what as big as a small nut, which he saith to be his devil called Aoutem.] **1791** J. LONG *Voyages* 86 [Each Indian has] his *totam*, or favourite spirit, which he believes watches over him. **1809** A. HENRY *Travels* 305 In the Algonquin tongue, a *totem* . . . is in the nature of an armorial bearing. **1841** COOPER *Mohicans* xxvi, The Hurons are boasters . . . ; their 'totem' is a moose. **1860** WHITTIER *Poetical Works* (1894) 74/2 Very mournful, very wild, Sang the totem of my child. **1901** WHITE *Westerners* 336 A brave arose from among us arose and took the sacred totem, the great Turtle, from the lodge of his chief.

attrib. **1892** *Rep. Comm. Educ. 1891–2* 890 The [Tchuktchi] women have their faces covered with totem marks. **1896** W. S. PHILLIPS (*title*), Totem Tales.

transf. and *fig.* **1890** HOWELLS *Boy's Town* 132 The fox was the emblem (*totem*) of the Democrats in the campaigns of 1840 and 1844. **1891** *Century Mag.* April 935 Most of us don't belong to the same totem with Jesus.

b. *Totem pole,* a pole covered, as by carving or painting, with totemic symbols, usually placed before an Indian house.

1909 *Cent. Suppl.* 1362/3 Totem-poles are used by the Indians of the coasts of Alaska and British Columbia.

+Totem, *v. tr.* To apply, as by painting or tattooing, (a totem symbol). — **1892** *Rep. Comm. Educ. 1891–2* 890 Some [Tchuktchi men] have a small mark or figure totemed on their cheek.

+Totemic, *a.* Of or pertaining to totems. {1865–} — **1846** SCHOOLCRAFT *Notes on Iroquois* 79 It will be necessary to go back, and examine . . . the curious and intricate principles of the Totemic Bond. *Ib.* 81 What was true of the totemic organization of the Senecas, was equally so of the Mohawks. **1875** PARKMAN in *N. Amer. Rev.* CXX. 39 The existence of totemic clans [among the Thlinkets], designated by birds and animals, . . . is thoroughly Indian.

+Totemism. Also **totamism.** The customs and traditions connected with the use of totems. {1870–} — **1791** J. LONG *Voyages* 87 This idea of destiny, or, if I may be allowed the phrase, 'totamism,' . . . is not confined to the Savages. **1908** *Amer. Anthropologist* Oct. 559 Clan totemism is . . . obviously only a higher development of personal totemism.

+**Toter.** [f. TOTE v.] (See quot. 1891 and cf. STONE-TOTER.) — 1891 *Amer. Notes & Q.* VI. 190 Roads . . . over which the supplies for the camps are carried, are always called 'tote roads,' and the teamsters are called 'toters.' 1895 *Century Mag.* July 478/2 Every one of the hundreds of logging-camps . . . over all parts of our great Maine woods . . . [is] furnished with its separate 'tote road,' 'tote team,' and 'toter.'

+**Tote road.** A road for the transportation of supplies, as to a lumber camp. — a1862 THOREAU *Maine Woods* 222 The Indian was greatly surprised that we should have taken what he called a 'tow' (i.e. tote or toting or supply) road, instead of a carry path. 1891, 1895 [see TOTER]. 1911 QUICK *Yellowstone Nights* 329 They had come by the old 'tote road' to the deserted lumber-camp.

+**Tote team.** A team for hauling supplies to a lumber camp. Hence *tote teamster*. — 1895 [see TOTER]. 1902 WHITE *Blazed Trail* 84 The tote teamster drove his hay-couched burden to Beeson Lake. 1913 EMERSON *R. Fielding at Snow Camp* 153 Men had to drag the tote teams instead of horses.

+**Toting.** The action or activity of carrying. Also attrib. — a1862 [see TOTE ROAD]. 1887 'CRADDOCK' *Keedon Bluffs* 165 He could not refuse his assistance in a mere matter of 'toting.' 1904 PRINGLE *Rice Planter* 115, I am sitting on Vareen bank watching the 'toting.'

+**Tottlish,** a. Unsteady; infirm. *colloq.* — 1835 *Knickerb.* VI. 6 [She was obliged] to steady her tottleish bark with the paddle. 1849 LANMAN *Lett. Alleghany Mts.* 51 The rock started from its tottlish foundation. 1893 *Harper's Mag.* April 763/1 She must . . . sit still, for their tottlish craft was only a dugout.

* **Touch,** n.

+**1.** (See quotation.)

1823 *New Eng. Farmer* II. 85/3 [New York City] has been much amused with a low tripod-kind of a hat, made of fine beaver, and worn by our Bang-ups. Some call them the *Touch*, others the *Gape and Stare*, the real name is the Bolingbroke.

+**2.** In negative comparisons: Something nearly equivalent to another thing. *colloq.*

1835-7 HALIBURTON *Clockmaker* I Ser. iii. 20 A school come out of little boys . . . [is] no touch to it. 1843 STEPHENS *High Life N.Y.* I. 152, I never did see a table so set off. . . . Cousin Beebe's warn't a touch tu it. 1846 FARNHAM *Prairie Land* 23 The bugs ain't a touch in *hyur* to what they be in yander.

+**3.** Used attrib. with reference to the ability to use the typewriter without watching the keyboard.

1897 in *Story of Typewriter* (Herkimer Co. Hist. Soc., 1923) 113 Omaha has become the storm center of the commotion over the touch method of typewriting. 1915 *Lit. Digest* 21 Aug., Advt. p. i, Great numbers were so-called touch writers—yet there has hardly been a single one who hasn't doubled or trebled his or her speed and accuracy. 1918 OWEN *Typewriting Speed* 147 Do not try to apply the touch system . . . until you have thoroughly mastered it.

* **Touch,** v.

To touch bottom, (see BOTTOM n. 5).

+**1.** *intr.* To make an attempt *to* do something; to make a beginning. *colloq.*² *Obs.*

1831 S. SMITH *Life J. Downing* 136 He dared Mr Ingham out to fight. . . . But Mr Ingham wouldn't touch to, and told him he was crazy. 1843 STEPHENS *High Life N.Y.* I. 49, I won't make up, nor touch tu. 1865 TROWBRIDGE *Three Scouts* 53, I never will touch to do another stroke of work in your house. 1867 S. HALE *Letters* 23, I didn't touch to unpack the trunks.

2. *tr.* Of frost: To injure (a plant).

1837 ꞏHERWOOD *Gaz. Georgia* (ed. 3) 79 Frost . . . touched the corn and cotton. 1887 WILKINS *Humble Romance* 267, I left 'em out last year, an' they got touched. 1895 JEWETT *Nancy* 9, I've got them pears well covered, but I expect they may be touched.

3. With adverbs. **a.** *To touch off,* to ignite (an explosive or inflammable substance) by applying a flame to it. {1907}

1884 'MARK TWAIN' *H. Finn* xxviii, It does seem most like setting down on a kag of powder and touching it off.

b. *To touch up.* {1715-} 1. To present or describe (a person, etc.), freq. in an unfavorable or ridiculous light. +2. *Baseball.* To hit the balls delivered by (a pitcher).

(1) 1870 'MARK TWAIN' *Sk., New & Old* 240, I might es well touch him up a little at the same time and make him ridiculous. 1904 *Minneapolis Times* 10 June 6 G. S. Pease of the Anoka Union touches up R. C. Dunn to the extent of nearly a column in the last issue of his paper. (2) 1887 *Chicago Inter-Ocean* 9 May 3/5 King pitched a splendid game and, though touched up lively at times, was especially effective at critical points of the game.

Touchback. *Football.* (See quot. 1899.) — 1893 CAMP *College Sports* 92 [When the ball is kicked behind the line by the enemy] it is called a 'touchback.' 1899 CHAMPLIN & BOSTWICK *Cycl. Games & Sports* (ed. 2) 342/2 A *Touchback* is made when the ball in possession of a player guarding his own goal is declared dead by the Referee, any part of it being on, over, or behind the goal line, provided the impetus which sent it to or across the line was given by an opponent. 1908 in P. H. Davis *Football* 498 The ball . . . becomes dead and shall count as a touchback to the defenders of that goal.

Touchdown. a. The act of touching the ball to the ground back of the opposing team's goal line. {1864, in Rugby} +b. The score resulting from possession of the ball behind the opponents' goal at the time the ball is declared dead. — 1876 in P. H. Davis *Football* 462 A match shall be decided by a majority ot touchdowns. 1899 CHAMPLIN & BOSTWICK *Cycl. Games & Sports* (ed. 2) 342/2 A *Touchdown* is made when the ball in possession of a player is declared dead by the Referee, any part of it being on, over, or behind the opponents' goal line. 1920 *N.Y. Times* 7 Nov. IX. 2/4 The Crimson got the jump at the start with a touchdown resulting from a fumble.

* **Touch-me-not.** Any plant of the genus *Impatiens*; a jewelweed. {1650~} — 1782 *Amer. Philos. Soc.* III. 224 The orange colour employed by the Indians, is obtained . . . from the plant called *Touch-me-not*. 1843 *Amer. Pioneer* II. 451 We had . . . to chop down the nettles, the waterweed, and the touch-me-not. 1880 [see MOURNING a.]. 1904 GLASGOW *Deliverance* 32 Now I'm planting zinnias, and touch-me-nots.

+**Touch-monk.** (See quotation.) — 1875 *Fur, Fin & Feather* (ed. 3) 119 The smaller species of loon I have heard variously called the spikebill, the cape-race, the touch-monk [etc.].

+**Tough,** n. A ruffian; a hoodlum. — 1884 MILLER *Memorie & Rime* 9 Another 'tough' . . . helped them hustle me in. 1889 RITTENHOUSE *Maud* 483, I have 51 pupils and four or five of them are toughs. 1911 ROLT-WHEELER *Boy with Census* 334 The boy noted a number of halfgrown toughs, hoodlums, and trouble-makers generally.

* **Tough,** a.

+**1.** Disposed to cause trouble; vicious; rough.

1884 MILLER *Memorie & Rime* 9 This is a tough town! 1896 ADE *Artie* 23 Some o' them was dead tough and the others was hams. 1916 SANDBURG *Chicago Poems* 46 He married a tough woman.

+**2.** Imposing hardship or difficulty *on* (a person, etc.).

1890 *Stock Grower & Farmer* 8 March 4/2 The recent blizzard . . . was pretty tough on range cattle. 1901 WHITE *Claim Jumpers* 256, I've been a little tough on you occasionally.

+**3.** Designating a species of ironwood: (see quotations).

1813 MUHLENBERG *Cat. Plants* 24 Bumelia tenax, Ironwood, silvery-leaved, (tough) Car[olina]. 1897 SUDWORTH *Arborescent Flora* 318 Bumelia tenax. . . . Tough Buckthorn (S.C.).

+**Tough,** v. *tr.* **1.** With *it.* To undergo hard conditions; to rough it. **2.** ?To tax the ability of (a person); to stump. — (1) 1830 *Mass. Spy* 27 Jan. (Th.), Judy, with whom he had toughed it three years. 1854 S. SMITH *Down East* 331 We had toughed it out five or six weeks. 1897 *Outing* XXIX. 423/1 Guess we could tough it. (2) 1843 'CARLTON' *New Purchase* I. 127 If you win, which a will sort a tough you though, you may [etc.].

+**Toughhead.** *local.* =RUDDY DUCK. — 1888 TRUMBULL *Names of Birds* 111 To some at Martha's Vineyard, [the name of the ruddy duck is] Tough-Head. 1889 *Cent.* 2718/1.

* **Toughness.** +Roughness; propensity to violence or crime. — 1895 *Pilgrim Missionary* June 11/1 You have gained a very good idea of the toughness of these mining towns.

+**Tough nut.** A person stubborn or otherwise difficult to deal with; a tough customer. *slang.* — 1862 E. W. Pearson *Lett. Port Royal* 81 There are a great many men of twenty-five to forty, 'tough-nuts' many of them.

Toupee. A sectional wig used to cover a bald top of the head; a wig. Also transf. in quot. 1835. {1862} — 1835 in *S. Lit. Messenger* IV. 89/2 One twists a yellow bandanna round his head for a night cap, while another puts on . . . a black velvet toupee. 1863 'M. HARLAND' *Husks* 149 Mr. Bond . . . wears false teeth and a toupee. 1900 *N.Y. Journal* 25 March 28 (Ernst), Toupees for Gentlemen, made to fit partially or entirely bald heads.

Tourist.

1. One making a pleasure trip. {c1800~}

1832 KENNEDY *Swallow Barn* I. 6, I entered Richmond between hawk and buzzard—the very best hour, I maintain, out of the twenty-four, for a picturesque tourist. 1872 TICE *Over Plains* 193 These bell-weather-led tourists were people without any taste. 1885, 1894 [see HEALTH-SEEKER]. 1920 *Lit. Digest* 17 Jan. 31/1 The detour, the abomination of the motoring tourist, is necessary.

2. *attrib.* and in *possessive.* With *agency, book, guide, line.*

1882 GODFREY *Nantucket* 29 Those interested in the game [of baseball] are referred to E. K. Godfrey, of the Tourists' Agency. 1883 'MARK TWAIN' *Life on Miss.* xxvii, A glance at these tourist-books shows us that . . . the Mississippi has undergone no change. 1898 *Boston Herald* 23 Jan. 14/4 (Ernst), When the Southern Pacific established its tourist line out of Washington it was found [etc.]. 1924 CUMMINS *Sky-high Corral* 15 You cut me down because you leased eighty acres of Hay Fork Meadow to that measley tourist guide to fence for horse feed.

Tourmaline. A semi-precious, colored mineral, used as a gem and for polarizing apparatus. {1759-} — 1857 DANA *Mineralogy* 189 Dark brown tourmalines are obtained at Orford, N.H. 1880 *Harper's Mag.* Nov. 880/2 There is no such vein of tourmaline as that which runs through 'Clark's Ledges' in the West Village.

Tournure. {1748-} A pad or frame worn by women in order to extend the skirts; a bustle. {1874-} — [1843 *Yale Lit. Mag.* IX. 15 They were old-fashioned in every sense of the word; . . . and touranours and flounces were things unheard of.] 1845 *Knickerb.* XXVI. 428 Any lady who wears a tournure composed of feathers . . . acts injudiciously. 1878 *Decorum* 286 Small light hair-cloth tournure.

Tout, *n.* {1718–} **a.** One who secures, by such improper means as spying at training quarters, information concerning a horse race. {1865–} +**b.** (See quot. 1909.) — (a) **1887** *Courier-Journal* 6 May 5/2 The efforts of touts to learn the condition of Goliah, Pendennis and the other cracks in Lucky Baldwin's string have been fruitless. **1894** *Columbus Dispatch* 4 April, One man was . . . a race track tout. (b) **1909** WEBSTER 2177/3 *Tout,* . . . one who gives a tip on a race horse for an expected compensation, esp. in hopes of a share in any winnings;—usually contemptuous.

✳**Tout,** *v.* **1.** *intr.* To solicit votes. {1891, in Australia} **2.** *intr.* and *tr.* (See quotations.) — (1) **1881** *Nation* XXXII. 397 It has never occurred to him that people would be disposed to see him 'tout' at Albany. **1894** FORD *P. Stirling* 358 'Hear him talk,' jeered one of the crowd, 'and he touting round the saloons to get votes.' (2) **1909** WEBSTER 2177/3 *Tout,* . . . to act as a tout; to tout, or give a tip on, a race horse. *Ib.,* *Tout,* . . . To give a tip on (a race horse) to a better with the expectation of sharing in the latter's winnings.

Touter. A solicitor of customers {a1754–}; one who solicits votes. — **1881** *Nation* XXXII. 397 Mr. Arthur, the Vice-President, is exciting a great deal of indignation . . . by his performances at Albany as a touter for votes for his friend. **1888** LOWELL *Lit. & Polit. Addresses* 211 Between the two a conscientious voter must feel as the traveller . . . felt between the touters of the two rival hotels.

✳**Tow.**[1]

✳**1.** The fiber of flax or hemp, prepared for spinning; the shorter fibers, separated from the longer and finer by hackling; a cloth spun from this material.
1646 *Conn. Probate Rec.* I. 16, 13 lb. of towe, 6 s. **1732** FRANKLIN *Poor Richard's Almanac 1733* 1 She cannot bear . . . to sit spinning in her Shift of Tow. **1824** DODDRIDGE *Notes* 113 The bosom of this dress served as a wallet to hold . . . tow for wiping the barrel of the rifle, or any other necessary for the hunter. *a*1842 *Indiana Mag. Hist.* XV. 231 The hackle pulled out was called tow and was spun into coarse thread and woven into coarse cloth.

b. (See quotation.)
1891 *Cent.* 6405/1 *Tow,* . . . in *heckling,* a quantity of hemp fibers sufficient for spinning a yarn 160 fathoms long.

2. *Attrib.* and *comb.,* sometimes in allusion to the appearance of tow, with *card, comb, comforter,* etc.
1642 *Essex Inst. Coll.* L. 237 Hand carte, 5 s.; 2 towe comes, 5 s. **1643** *Conn. Rec.* I. 456, 2 pairre tow sheets. **1655** *Essex Probate Rec.* I. 201 A pair of tow cards, 1 s. **1739** *Boston News-Letter* 18 Oct., An Indian Lad . . . had on . . . an old tow Shirt. **1838** *Knickerb.* XII. 325 His serene head [was] overshadowed by a vast canopy of a tow-hat. **1840** *Niles' Nat. Reg.* 29 Aug 407/3 Schuyler . . . sent one hundred young men dressed in tow frocks. **1850** JUDD *R. Edney* 450 Bronze-faced and tow-headed Wild Olive boys . . . were there. **1897** *Scribner's Mag.* XXII. 728/2 On top . . . are four or five thicknesses of coarse blankets and 'tow comforters.'

Tow.[2] {1600–}
1. A line of boats or rafts being towed. {1883–}
1862 *N.Y. Tribune* 15 Feb. (Chipman), Our progress had been slow . . . on account of the heavy tows which some of our army steamers had to carry. **1887** *Harper's Mag.* Feb. 336/2 A tug is dragging along a tow of old rafts. **1897** *Outing* xxx. 120/1 The tow consisted of thirty-four boats towing four abreast.

2. In special combinations, sometimes with allusion to *tow* v.
Tow boy, a boy who drives the draft animals along a towpath; *tow car,* (see quotation); *tow cord,* a towrope; *tow horse,* a horse used in towing, esp. along a canal; *towline,* (see quotation); *tow master,* an employee of a canal transportation company whose duty is to supervise the making up of tows; *tow road,* ?a logging road; *tow steamer,* a tug.
1887 *Century Mag.* Aug. 493/1 The Patriarch stepped ashore and arranged for an extra team of mules and a tow-boy. **1908** *Stand.* 1908/2 *Tow-car,* a street railway-car drawn by a grip- or motor-car; trail-car. **1805** CLARK in *Lewis & C. Exped.* II. (1904) 46 We proceeded on [the river] verry well with the assistance of the Toe Coard. **1865** *Harper's Mag.* April 571/1 It requires as much judgment to drive tow-horses up the Alleghany as to pilot a steamboat down the Mississippi. **1891** *Cent.* 6407/1 *Tow-line,* . . . in *whaling,* the long line which is attached to the toggle-iron or harpoon, and by means of which the whale is made fast to the boat. **1887** *Century Mag.* Aug. 487/2 It is the business of the towmaster to see that all the expected boats are accounted for, in proper places, and that the whole tow is well made up. *a*1862 THOREAU *Maine Woods* 287 Polis detected . . . what he called a 'tow' road, an indistinct path leading into the forest. **1831** HOLLEY *Texas* (1833) 20, I took my seat . . . while waiting for the *tow steamer,* to conduct us to the mouth of the Mississippi.

Towboat. **a.** A boat used for towing other boats or barges: (see also quot. 1880). {1860} +**b.** (See quotation.) — (a) **1815** *Mass. Laws* 595 Hereby is granted to John L. Sullivan . . . the exclusive right to Connecticut river within this Commonwealth, for the use of his patent steam tow boats. **1838** *Niles' Nat. Reg.* 10 Nov. 176/2 The tow-boats . . . , at New Orleans, are in constant employment, bringing up fleets from sea. **1880** *Harper's Mag.* Dec. 54/2 Pittsburgh is the home of 130 tow-boats of a pattern incomprehensible to Eastern eyes, for they do not 'tow' but push. **1903** E. JOHNSON *Railway Transportation* 33 The capital employed in transportation is far greater than in the days of the stage-coach and the towboat. (b) **1836** W. O'BRYAN *Travels* 294 Tow-boats are large boats with decks; these are tied to, and towed by the Steamers; sometimes one or more each side.

+**Towboating.** The piloting or operation of a towboat. — **1887** *Courier-Journal* 7 Feb. 3/3 Theodore Brooks . . . will try his hand at towboating this season.

+**Towboat man.** A man in charge of, or working on, a towboat. — **1879** *Scribner's Mo.* Nov. 46/2 The usual expression of pilots and towboat men was not that a vessel 'went to sea.'

+**Tow cloth.** A coarse fabric spun from tow. Also attrib. — **1706** *Boston News-Letter* 18 Nov., The uppermost [jacket is] . . . lined with brown linen called western Tow-cloth. **1746** *Ib.* 17 July, A Negro Man Servant . . . had on . . . a good Tow cloth Shirt. **1809** KENDALL *Travels* II. 26 Large quantities of linen and *tow-cloth* are made in interior towns for exportation. **1866** A. D. WHITNEY *L. Goldthwaite* x, I want some tow-cloth to sew on immediately.

✳**Towel.** A cloth used for various purposes, esp. for wiping something dry. Also attrib. (See also HICKORY TOWEL.) — **1638** *Md. Archives* IV. 46, 4. towells & 1. pillowber. **1800** TATHAM *Agric. & Commerce* 87 The articles of fabric which are chiefly attended to in the functions of household manufactures, are . . . napkins, towels, toilet-cloths, &c. **1876** KNIGHT 2604/1 *Towel-rack,* a frame or rod on which to hang towels. **1907** *St. Nicholas* Aug. 920/1 Sidney's mother says that . . . the cost of . . . half a dozen towels, and a cake of sand soap should be added.

✳**Tower.** *Railroad.* +A tall structure containing controls governing switches or signals. Also attrib. (See also SIGNAL TOWER.) — **1900** *Everybody's Mag.* II. 442/2 The tower from which the traffic entering and leaving the Grand Central Station in New York city is directed, is located just outside the station itself. **1905** *N.Y. Ev. Post* 16 Oct. 3 The tower operator . . . discovered the bar of iron wedged beside the rail.

+**Towerman.** *Railroad.* An employee who works in a switch tower. — **1895** [see ROUNDHOUSE b]. **1908** *Atlantic Mo.* Nov. Advt. 42 A powerful statement of the causes of our railroad accidents, [was] written by . . . a tower man of long experience.

✳**Tower mustard.** Any one of various rock cresses of the genus *Arabis.* Also with specifying adjective. — **1817–8** EATON *Botany* (1822) 495. **1847** WOOD *Botany* 166 Smooth Tower Mustard. . . . Shores of Lake Superior, W. to the Rocky Mts. **1898** CREEVEY *Flowers of Field* 279 Tower-mustard. *A. perfoliata* is the tallest species.

+**Towhead.**
1. *local.* A shoal, indicated by a white ripple or foam in the water; a small island made by alluvial accumulations, often having a tufted appearance caused by plant life.
1829 CUMINGS *Western Pilot* 7 There are . . . a great number of tow-heads and sand-bars. **1836** J. HALL *Statistics of West* 26 Sometimes they [*sc* islands in the Ohio R.] are mere sandbanks, covered with thick groves of the melancholy willow. . . . The term *tow-head,* is significantly applied . . . by the boatmen. **1879** BISHOP *4 Months in Sneak-Box* 317 These little, low islands, covered with thickets, are called tow-heads. **1884** 'MARK TWAIN' *H. Finn* xii, A towhead is a sand-bar that has cottonwoods on it as thick as harrow-teeth.
2. A person, esp. a child, with white or whitish hair.
1830 ROYALL *Southern Tour* I. 92 One insolent little tow-head . . . came in upon parole. **1902** WHITE *Blazed Trail* 45 'Get out of that, you big tow-head!' he cried [to the Swede].
3. = HOODED MERGANSER.
1888 TRUMBULL *Names of Birds* 75 The name Tow-Head . . . was heard in one of our Southern States. **1917** *Birds of Amer.* I. 112.

+**Tow(head) deer.** ?A white-tailed deer. — *a*1846 *Quarter Race Ky.* 44 We killed a mitey fine tow hed deer. *Ib.* 45, I wuz tellin the fellars 'bout Reub.'s eatin a hole tow deer.

+**Towhee (bird).** [Imitative.] Any one of various finches, chiefly of the genus *Pipilo;* the chewink. Also with specifying terms. (See also ABERT'S TOWHEE, CAÑON TOWHEE.)
*c*1729 CATESBY *Carolina* I. 34 The Towhe-bird . . . is about the size of, or rather bigger than a Lark. **1810** [see BULLFINCH]. **1858** BAIRD *Birds Pacific R.R.* 512. **1878** *Nat. Museum Proc.* I. 419 [The] Long-clawed Towhee . . . is a common constant resident of the valleys and foot-hills. **1917** *Birds of Amer.* III. 62 [The] Chestnut-crowned Towhee . . . has the peculiar trait of running along the ground when he is surprised.

+**Towhee-bunting.** =prec. — **1810** WILSON *Ornithology* II. 35 [The] Towhe Bunting . . . is a very common, but humble and inoffensive species. **1867** *Amer. Naturalist* I. 435 What would Mr. Endicott say if I should affirm . . . that the Towhe Bunting . . . nests in low trees? **1903** *N.Y. Ev. Post* 12 Sept., Still another shy visitor . . . was the chewink, or towhee bunting, whose cheerful cry announced his presence every morning.

+**Tow-hook.** (See quotation.) — **1876** KNIGHT 2604/2 *Tow-hook,* an artilleryman's hook, used in unpacking ammunition-chests.

✳**Towing.**
+**1.** Fishing by means of a net dragged through the water by a boat; the catch obtained by such fishing. Also attrib.
1775 ROMANS *Nat. Hist. Florida* App. p. vii, Spanish mackerel and Barrows are also often caught towing. **1883** *Nat. Museum Bul.* No. 27, 566 Towing Nets for collecting free-swimming marine vertebrates at the surface, or at intermediate depths between the surface and the bottom. **1889**

Smithsonian Rep. 1887 II. 135 The surface towings he obtained are very rich in interesting forms. **1891** *Cent.* 6406/3.

2. The moving of a vessel, etc., by pulling or pushing. Also attrib. {1611–}

1806 *Ann. 9th Congress 2 Sess.* 1110 The current of the river is gentle, and the banks favorable for towing. **1814** BRACKENRIDGE *Views La.* 203, [I was] obliged to abandon oars and poles, and take the towing line. **1882** *Harper's Mag.* Jan. 166/1 [On] all Western streams towing means pushing. **1889** *Century Mag.* March 713/2 In 1869 the Harvey towing-torpedo created no little stir. **1901** STILLMAN *Autobiog. Journalist* I. 48 We went by train to Albany, where we took deck passage on a towing steamer for New York.

+Tow linen.

1. A fabric made of spun tow.

1779 *N.J. Archives* 2 Ser. III. 154 [A] blue long elk saddle cloth, lined with tow linen [was stolen]. **1792** *Ann. 2d Congress* 1000 Great quantities of . . . tow linens . . . are made in the household way. **1843** *Amer. Pioneer* II. 454 Pioneers found it to their advantage to wear tow linen and eat skim milk. **1900** H. ROBERTSON *Red Blood & Blue* 132, I've got a suit of tow-linen that the ladies think irresistible.

2. Attrib. with *apron, pantaloons, robe*, etc.

1812 PAULDING *J. Bull & Bro. Jon.* 98 He wore . . . a pair of tow linen trowsers. **1843** 'CARLTON' *New Purchase* I. 63 [She gave] her heated and perspiring face a last wipe with the corner of her tow-linen apron. **1845** F. DOUGLASS *Narrative* 26, I was kept almost naked—nothing on but a coarse tow linen shirt reaching only to my knees. **1881** *Chicago Tribune* 8 July 11/3, I was supplied every year with . . . two pairs of tow-linen pantaloons. **1889** 'MARK TWAIN' *Conn. Yankee* 28 They and the women . . . wore a coarse tow-linen robe that came well below the knee, and a rude sort of sandal.

*Town. (See also BOOM TOWN, COLLEGE TOWN, etc.)

I. *1. A group of houses and buildings constituting a recognized community; a legally organized local government for such a community; +spec., chiefly in New England, a local administrative unit exercising self-government through a town meeting; a township. (See also POST TOWN.)

In the specific sense, a *town*, in later use, is essentially a rural unit, which may or may not include a village or villages.

1628 *Plymouth Laws* 29 Those grounds which are nearest the town . . . shall be used by the whole. **1658** *Portsmouth Rec.* 361 A pearsall of Land containinge Six acres Lijnge withine the boundes of portsmouth towne. **1704** *Conn. Rec.* IV. 474 The said tract of land shall . . . be an intire township and town of itselfe. **1834** *N.H. Hist. Soc. Coll.* IV. 101 The length of the town is about thirteen miles. **1891** *Cent.* 6407/1 *Town*, . . . in a few of the States, a municipal corporation (not formed of one of the subdivisions of a county, but having its own boundaries like a city) with less elaborate organization and powers than a city. **1906** CHURCHILL *Coniston* 49 The town of Coniston, it must be explained for the benefit of those who do not understand the word 'town' in the New England sense, was a tract of country about ten miles by ten, the most thickly settled portion of which was the village of Coniston, consisting of twelve houses.

b. collect. The people of a town (in the specific sense), the voters, or the representatives governing it.

1634 *Watertown Rec.* I. 1. 1 One of them . . . shall keep the Records and Acts of the Towne. **1660** *Oyster Bay Rec.* I. 1 The towne have given unto Daniell Whithead a swamp. **1710** SEWALL *Letter-Book* I. 391 The Town augmented the Master's Salary to One Hundred pounds per annum. *c*1870 CHIPMAN *Notes on Bartlett* 486 *Town*, . . . the body of legal voters within a township.

+c. An administrative division of a county; =TOWNSHIP 1 b.

1870 *Rep. Comm. Agric.* 1869 398 County commissioners are the fence-viewers in counties [in Minn.] not divided into towns. **1891** *Cent.* 6407/3 The townships of Wisconsin are more often called *towns*.

+2. A local community of Indians.

See also INDIAN TOWN.

1638 *Mass. H. S. Coll.* 4 Ser. VI. 251 With Onkace at his towne Monahiggin, a great number mingled. **1676** [see KING 1]. **1725** in *Travels Amer. Col.* 98 [He] took away what Skins he could get from the people of the Town. **1798** HAWKINS *Letters* 316 If any white man behaved himself in a way disagreeable to the chiefs, . . . he would immediately remove him from the town. **1844** GREGG *Commerce of Prairies* II. 259 With some tribes, and particularly among the lower classes of the Creeks, they are inclined to settle in 'towns,' as they are called,—making large fields, which are cultivated in common, and the produce proportionally distributed. **1907** HODGE, etc. *Amer. Indians* I. 364/2 At present the Creek Nation in Indian Ter. is divided into 49 townships ('towns'), of which 3 are inhabited solely by negroes.

+3. A collection of prairie-dog burrows.

1810 PIKE *Sources Miss.* 156n., The Wishtonwish of the Indians . . . reside on the prairies of Louisiana in towns or villages. **1847** RUXTON *Adv. Rocky Mts.* (1848) 283 The hawk and the eagle . . . watch their towns, and pounce suddenly upon them. **1902** *Dept. Agric. Yrbk. 1901* 258 In old towns many holes are abandoned, so that it is difficult to ascertain how many animals live in a stated number of holes.

II. *attrib.* and *comb.* 4. Designating pieces of land or improvements situated in, maintained by, or otherwise associated with towns.

See also TOWN COMMON, TOWN LOT, etc.

1635 *Essex Inst. Coll.* IV. 91/2 In regard to the towne pastures. **1659** *Charlestown Land Rec.* 71 The east end . . . extends to the Towne way. **1685** Towne Dock [see COVE 1 c]. **1750** *Baltimore Rec.* 27 They have order'd the Town fence to be made up. **1771** *Huntington Rec.* II. 508 We Do order and Direct Doctor Wiggins to have Jonah Woods house at swego or some other Remote place and not in the Town Spott. **1825** *Austin P.* II. (1924) 1063, I wish you to make out the Town Tract in Brooks deed. **1873** *Newton Kansan* 3 April 3/2 Workmen have commenced putting a fence around the town park.

5. Designating officials, employees, or other persons identified with towns or townships.

See also TOWN CLERK, TOWN CRIER, etc.

1636 *Essex Inst. Coll.* IX. 17 By the town representative Its ordered that [etc.]. **1654** *Springfield Rec.* I. 233 Thomas Stebbins should be the Towne mesurer. **1699** *Braintree Rec.* 41 Mr. Nathaniel Eells Came to Braintree as their Town Schoolmaster. **1797** *Mass. H. S. Coll.* 1 Ser. V. 48 The defendants issued a warrant, under pretence of authority of town assessors. **1857** E. STONE *Life J. Howland* 113 He was appointed town auditor. **1859** *Harper's Mag.* Oct. 708/1 One Deacon Tinker held the post of town miller. **1865** *Wkly. New Mexican* 23 Dec. 2/4, I have resigned my license as Town Auctioneer. **1870** *Rep. Comm. Agric.* 1869 398 The [value of the fence is] . . . to be determined by a majority of the town supervisors.

6. Designating debts, taxes, etc., of towns or townships.

See also TOWN CHARGE, TOWN ORDER 2.

1637 *Essex Inst. Coll.* IX. 57 Chosen for the making of a country rate of 45£–12s.–ood. and also 10£ for a towne rate. **1649** *Southampton Rec.* I. 57 Mr. Richard Smyth & Thomas Halsey shall make a levy of 18d vpon every 50 lb. lott for the satisfying of towne debts. **1780** PUTNAM in *Memoirs* 145 The Town Bounties ware to be taken into consideration . . . and charged as wages. **1857** *Mass. Acts & Resolves* 727 Let preference, then, be given to our own State scrip in the investment of our school and sinking funds—selecting next our county, city and town bonds.

7. Designating groups of townspeople or their representatives, or meetings held by such groups.

1647 *R.I. Col. Rec.* I. 197 The head officer of the Towne, at the next Towne Court, shall enquire of damages. **1649** *Portsmouth Rec.* 42 Thomas Cornell, Richard Bordin, [and] Phillip Shearman are Chosen to make up the towne Counsell. **1724** Town-Congregation [see CONGREGATION]. **1754** *Duxbury Rec.* 320 Mr. William Brewster and Mr. Samuel Seabury, [were chosen] as a town committee, to go and acquaint Mr. Turner of the Town's proceedings. **1788** *Mass. Spy* 3 April 3/2 Rhodeisland Town Conventions, on the Federal Constitution.

8. Designating persons, ideas, and objects identified with towns or cities rather than with the country.

1722 *New-Eng. Courant* 3 Sept. 2/1 The Buyers will be oblig'd to return the Stones to the Peach-Merchant, . . . to prevent the Town-Gardiners from spoiling his Trade for the future. **1852** REYNOLDS *Hist. Illinois* 149 Streets, and other *town* notions were observed in the building of the place. **1885** 'CRADDOCK' *Prophet* 240, I ain't keerin' much fur the new sher'ff, 'kase he air a town man, an' don't know me. **1910** McCUTCHEON *Rose in Ring* 245 Jenison town property was to be found in no less than five cities.

+9. Designating persons or activities concerned with the planning of new towns.

See also TOWN COMPANY 2.

1826 FLINT *Recoll.* 59 A kind of speculation, almost peculiar to this country, that is to say, town-making. **1891** *Harper's Mag.* Aug. 485/2 The Western town-boomer is a silky man and wide between the eyes. **1895** Town-platting [see BOOM n.² 2 b].

Town-at, *interj.* (See TOWN-HO *interj.*)

+Town ball. A ball game resembling baseball. — **1878** *De Witt's Base-Ball Guide* 15 Nearly forty years ago, a species of base-ball, known as 'Town Ball,' was in vogue in Philadelphia. **1898** J. Fox *Kentuckians* 215, I told you I had got it playing town-ball.

*Town book. The record book of a town. Obs. — **1635** *Watertown Rec.* I. 1 The towne Clarke shall have six pense for every Lott of land that he shall Inroll in the Towne Booke. **1660** *Portsmouth Rec.* 95 Each towne shall prouide a towne booke, where in thay shall Record the Euidences of the lands by them Impropriated. **1720** SEWALL *Letter-Book* II. 120 'Twill be contrary to the Agreement solemnly made Twenty years ago, and Recorded in the Town-Booke.

Town-bounds. *pl.* The limits of a town or township. **Obs.** — **1655** *Portsmouth Rec.* 67 To forewarn Nuport inhabitants for falling any timber in ower Towne boundes. **1672** *Conn. Rec.* II. 178 A plantation on the east of their town bownds. **1698** *Conn. Hist. Soc. Coll.* VI. 252 The Land bought . . . as an Adition to ye toun Bounds . . . [shall] be laid acording to the disbursments of etch person.

Town charge. {1619} An expense to a town; spec., a person supported by a town. — **1671** *Portsmouth Rec.* 159 James Parker . . . is in Such a distempered Condition that he is now licke to become a Towne Charge. **1710** *Boston Rec.* 64 A Committee [shall] be chosen to advise & consider of Some proper Methodes to prevent damage by the Sea's wast-ing away ye neck & to prevent the growth of a Town charge there. **1894** ROBINSON *Danvis Folks* 291 She hain't goin' tu be no taown charge!

* **Town clerk.** In the local government of a town, an official serving as a secretary. — **1634** *Watertown Rec.* I. 1. 1 [The] Towne Clark . . . shall keep the Records and Acts of the Towne. **1723** *Amer. Wkly. Mercury* 26 Sept. 3/1 The Town Clerk [shall] cause the same Freedom to be handsomely Ingrosed on Parchment. **1770** *Boston Rec.* 20 The Town Clerk [shall] be directed not to give out Copies or deliver any of the Original Papers respecting the late horred Massacre. **1834** *Niles' Reg.* XLVI. 190/1 The whole anti-Jackson ticket for common council and town clerk. was carried by a small majority. **1905** [see MODERATOR 1].

Town clock. In a town, a public clock. {1779} — **1668** *Boston Rec.* 44 Richard Taylor is ordred. to haue £5. p an. for his takeinge care of the towne clocke. **1776** FITHIAN *Journal* II. 196 So near is New York that I can hear the Town Clocks distinctly from my Chamber. **1860** HOLMES *E. Venner* vii, An old miser . . . gave the town clock.

Town common. In a town or township, land owned in common and reserved for pasturage or other purposes. Also *town's common*. Often pl. — **1658** *New Haven Col. Rec.* 254 He had rockes laid out instead of land, w[hi]ch he understands since are towne commons. **1670** *Plymouth Rec.* I. 118 To Restraine the eregulare Improvement of the Townes Comons. **1704** *Providence Rec.* V. 182 Bounded . . . on ye west End with ye Townes Comon. **1779** *Ky. Petitions* 49 [A tract of] two acre tending lotts . . . was to be given up the next year for the use of a Town and Town common's.

Town company. +**1.** The militia company of a town. +**2.** A group of persons organized or incorporated to establish a town. — (1) **1723** *New Eng. Courant* 4 Feb. 2/2 The Town-Company of English, and a considerable Number of Indians under Arms attended at his Funeral. (2) **1860** in Johnson *Anderson Co., Kansas* 170 [We have] organized ourselves into a town company, under the general incorporation act of the territory. **1877** JOHNSON *Ib.* 62 A town company . . . at once made arrangements for sending a colony from Louisville to the new town. **1894** ROBLEY *Bourbon Co., Kansas* 71 A 'Town Company' had already . . . formed a 'curbstone' organization.

Town crier. In a town, an official who calls out proclamations and other public announcements. {1602–} — **1640** *Boston Rec.* 55 For towne Crier, William Courser. **1792** BENTLEY *Diary* I. 381 They have ordered the Town Crier to give notice. **1800** *Constitutional Telegraph* 8 Aug., Frequent applications [are] being made to the Town-Cryer, to proceed through the streets in search of Children that have strayed. **1882** GODFREY *Nantucket* 66 Another custom to which the town clings with wonderful tenacity . . . is the employment of 'town criers.'

Towney. (See TOWNY.)

+**Town farm.** A poor farm maintained by a town or township. — **1880** *Harper's Mag.* Dec. 86/2 She would rather have taken her children to the town farm. **1882** *Wheelman* I. 10 The city of Roxbury . . . purchased it for a town-farm. **1899** JEWETT *Queen's Twin* 225 Her nearest neighbor . . . wished her to go to the town farm.

* **Town hall.** A hall or building used for the public business of a town, or as a place of assembly. Also attrib. — **1825** NEAL *Bro. Jonathan* I. 125 It was . . . after a time a sort of town-hall. **1875** EMERSON *Lett. & Soc. Aims* 107 Jenny Lind . . . complained of concert-rooms and town-halls, that they did not give her room enough to unroll her voice. **1882** McCABE *New York* 369 The head quarters of the watch were at the Town Hall. **1900** DIX *Deacon Bradbury* 221 There was no jail in town, but there was a strong room . . . in the little town-hall building.

+**Town-ho,** *interj.* Also **town-ho, townor, townor.** (See quotations.) — **1791** *Mass. H. S. Coll.* 1 Ser. III. 154 *Townor* . . . is an Indian word, and signifies that they have seen the whale twice. **1848** MITCHELL *Nantucketisms* 40 *Town-at*, exclamation when a whale is seen. **1851** MELVILLE *Moby-Dick* 269 Town-Ho . . . [is] the ancient whale-cry upon first sighting a whale from the mast-head, still used by whalemen in hunting the famous Gallipagos terrapin.

* **Town house.**

* **1.** = TOWN HALL.
1657 *Boston Rec.* 134 A committee [was chosen] to consider of the modell of the towne house, to be built. **1718** *Brookhaven Rec.* 109 Ye Towne at thare owne cost & charge hath ingaged to Repaire what building the sd. Phillips [a minister] hath made for his perticeler convenience joyneing to ye Towne house. **1819** E. DANA *Geogr. Sk.* 76 The town . . . [has] an elegant market house, with a town house in the second story. **1867** 'LACKLAND' *Homespun* 197 The chief centre of all attraction in the village is the town-house, where are to be seen the various articles of female ingenuity and industry. **1907** *Dialect Notes* III. 203.

+**b.** A house, as a parsonage, supplied at the expense of a town. *Obs.*
1672 *Huntington Rec.* I. 186 The towne hous or parsonadge hous and land and fence.

+**2.** In an Indian town, the building in which public business is conducted. *Obs.*
1725 in *Travels Amer. Col.* 108 About Eight of Clock at Night I went to the Town House. **1765** TIMBERLAKE *Memoirs* 32 The [Cherokee] townhouse, in which are transacted all public business and diversions, . . . has all the appearance of a small mountain at a little distance. **1800** HAWKINS *Sk. Creek Country* 34 The townhouse is an oblong square cabin. **1819** *Niles' Reg.* XVI. Suppl. 101/2 The singer has proclaimed, with his song, on the top of the Town House, 'Hayan wah, Yauth caunu.'

attrib. **1765** TIMBERLAKE *Memoirs* 65 The green corn dance [among the Cherokees is] . . . performed in a very solemn manner, in a large square before the town-house door.

3. A house in town; a city residence, as opposed to a country house. {1825–}
1803 WEEMS *Letters* II. 264 A Town house & a Country house . . . shall be thine. **1838** COOPER *Home as Found* i, He sent orders to his agent to prepare his town-house in New York. **1907** *St. Nicholas* Aug. 901/2 [They] admitted that he was at his town house.

+**4.** A town poorhouse.
*c*1870 CHIPMAN *Notes on Bartlett* 486 *Town-house*, an almshouse.—Conn. **1889** COOKE *Steadfast* 28 Just as soon as the road settled she should 'cart her off to the town-house.'

+**5.** 'The town prison; a bridewell' (*Cent.*).

Townie. (See TOWNY.)

* **Town land.** +Land within the jurisdiction of, or belonging to, a town; a common. Also *town's land*. Also attrib. — **1639** *Boston Rec.* 1 This booke was bought . . . for the entrying of the Towne Lands and other weighty bussinesses. **1651** *Suffolk Deeds* I. 115 Twenty fyve foote southward next the townes land. **1670** *Braintree Rec.* 9 The towne land meadow and upland should be disposed off by the Selectmen then in being. **1738** *Brookhaven Rec.* 141 All that I request of you . . . is one acre & half of land joining to me, of the town land.

Town library. A library belonging to or situated in a town. — **1713** *Boston News-Letter* 8 June 2/2 All Persons that . . . can give Notice of any of the Town Library; or other things belonging to the Town-House in Boston, before the late Fire: are desired to Inform the Treasurer. **1749** FRANKLIN *Writings* II. 390 The House [shall] be furnished with a Library (if in the Country, if in the Town, the Town Libraries may serve). **1809** [see DISTRICT SCHOOL]. **1912** NICHOLSON *Hoosier Chron.* 101 Basset . . . was imparting information that might have been derived from a local history of the town library.

+**Town limits.** *pl.* The boundaries of a town. — **1658** *Oyster Bay Rec.* I. 40 Wee have Comitted ye Draught of our Towne Limitts [to John Underhill]. **1855** MITCHELL *Fudge Doings* I. 130 But two house-raisings have been known within the town-limits in the last three years. **1907** *St. Nicholas* July 821/2 They got beyond the town limits, and out of Tin Star's control.

+**Town line.** The boundary line of a town. — **1645** *Suffolk Deeds* I. 67 Gregory Stone of Cambridge granted unto Nathaniell Sparhawke . . . two Acres of Meddowe . . . lying by Cambridge towne line. **1788** [see RANGE *n.* 4]. **1840** *Knickerb.* XVI. 206 Such searching of trees for town lines!

+**Town lot.** A parcel of land within a town or on the site of a future or proposed town; an area of common land owned by a town. Also attrib. — **1671** *S.C. Hist. Soc. Coll.* V. 284 We were forced to grant them towne lotts. **1713** *Providence Rec.* XVI. 131 To makeing and maintaining fence in the Town Lott, [£]o4. **1737** *S.C. Hist. & Gen. Mag.* XIII. 9, I will give unto such Minister a Town-Lott and 10 Acres of Land back. **1821** NUTTALL *Trav. Arkansa* 111 Town-lot speculations have already been tried at the Cadron. **1860** *Harper's Mag.* Oct. 581/1 Town lot speculators striving to have the Capitol elsewhere than at St. Paul. **1902** HARBEN *A. Daniel* 290 Why, another railroad would make my town-lots bound up like fury.

Town major. A military, executive, or other officer in a town {1676–} — **1775** *Boston News-Letter* 16 Nov. 1/2 All those . . . who chuse to depart the town, may give in their names to Captain James Urquhart, Town Major. **1784** HUTCHINS *Hist. Narrative La. & W. Fla.* 17 The people . . . [decided to send] three deputies to General O'Riley, viz. Messieurs Grandmaison town-major, La Friniere attorney-general, and De Mazant. *a*1821 BIDDLE *Autobiog.* 151 Captain Bowen . . . was appointed Town Major.

Town marshal. +**1.** In colonial times, a town official having various duties, as to levy and collect fines. +**2.** A police officer or policeman in a town. — (1) **1683** *Derby Rec.* 132 Ye fines [are] to be to the town marshall. (2) **1903** *N.Y. Sun* 16 Nov. 1 The town marshal arrested him on a charge of murder. **1910** McCUTCHEON *Rose in Ring* 51 He's got some of the town marshal's men with 'im now.

+**Town meeting.**

1. A formal assembly of the voters in a town for the transaction of public business; also, collect., the voters thus assembled. {1878} Freq. with descriptive or defining terms. Cf. MARCH MEETING.
1636 *Salem Rec.* I. 16 At a generall Court or towne meeting of Salem held the second of . . . May A[nn]o 1636. **1698** SEWALL *Diary* I. 474 Anniversary Town-Meeting . . . : I, being present, am chosen Moderator. **1723** *New-Eng. Courant* 11–18 March 2/2 Monday last . . . [was] the Annual Town-Meeting for chusing Town-Officers for the Year ensuing. **1768** *Essex Inst. Coll.* LIV. 192 The afore-mentioned Town-Meeting was convened upon the Petition of Ninety-two of the Freeholders. **1825** [see MODERATOR 1]. **1891** *Harper's Mag.* June 111/1 It is only there [in New England] that the most democratic institution of our race—the town meeting —is the basis of the government of the State.

b. Used in singular without article, chiefly after prepositions.
1737 E. PARKMAN *Diary* 9, It was Town Meeting. **1809** KENDALL *Travels* I. 16 The towns, in town-meeting, elect their own town-officers, and may recover a fine on refusal to serve. **1859** HALE *If, Yes, & Perhaps* 188

This standing in a double queue at town-meeting several hours to vote was a bore of the first water.

2. Attrib. with *book, day, man,* etc.

1683 *Southold Rec.* I. 129 Stephen Bayly [shall] be the Town Clark to keep the Town meeting book. **1766** J. ADAMS *Diary* Works II. 185 Cleverly will become a great town-meeting man. **1845** *Lowell Offering* V. 268 It was customary for some girl to give a party . . . on town-meeting-day evening. **1857** Town-meeting resolves [see PUBLIC OPINION]. *a*1862 THOREAU *Maine Woods* 235 The Anglo-American . . . ignorantly erases mythological tablets in order to print his hand-bills and town-meeting warrants on them.

Town officer. An official in a town or township (**1737**–, an excise official); + a selectman. — **1705** *Boston News-Letter* 19 March 2/2 Boston, Monday the 12th Instant, being the Annual Election-day of Town Officers. **1741** W. STEPHENS *Proc. Georgia* II. 213 Getting Messieurs Jones and Parker together, with the Town-officers all convened, we made some Progress in looking over the long List of Defaulters in the Guard-Duty (so long complained of) and appointed another Day a Week hence, to go through with all. **1834** *Jamestown* (N.Y.) *Jrnl.* 12 Feb. 2/6 A Meeting . . . will be held at the Schoolhouse . . . for the purpose of nominating suitable persons to be supported for town officers. **1895** *Dept. Agric. Yrbk. 1894* 506 County commissioners and city and town officers having the care of and authority over public roads and bridges. **1911** PERSONS, etc. *Mass. Labor Laws* 339 Municipal or town officers grant the licenses.

Townor, *interj.* (See TOWN-HO *interj.*)

Town order. +**1.** An ordinance passed by a town or township. +**2.** A draft on the treasury of a town or township. — (1) **1659** [see BLACKBIRD]. **1691** *Boston Rec.* 206 Selectmens instructions and towne orders were not considered of for want of time to doe it. **1719** *Ib.* 138 It [shall] be Left to ye Sel[ect]men to draw up a Town order relating to ye marking Baggs, Sent to mill. (2) **1833** *Niles' Reg.* XLIV. 347/1 If I do not get a town order for your board, I must make a journey to Portland.

+**Town plat.** An area or patch of ground belonging to or occupied by a town; a town site; the plan of such an area or patch of ground. Also attrib. — **1723** *Waterbury Prop. Rec.* 121 A committe perticularly to settle the old Town platt Lotts. *a*1817 DWIGHT *Trav.* II. 335 The town-plat is originally distributed into lots, containing from two to ten acres. **1850** *Mich. Gen. Statutes* I. (1882) 431 When application is made to alter or vacate any town or village plat, . . . any person or persons interested may . . . oppose the same.

+**Town plot.** =TOWN PLAT. — **1637** *Watertown Rec.* I. 1. 4 Those Freemen of the Congregation shall build and dwell upon their Lotts at the Towne plott. **1703** *Conn. Rec.* IV. 446 A committee for the stating of the town plott and laying out the lotts. **1877** HALE *G. T. T.* 72 At one time he owned half of the original town plot.

Town pump. A public pump in a town. — **1702** *Boston Selectmen* 28 Mr. John Barnet [shall] take the Care of geting a gutter paved to co[n]vey the wast watter from the Town pump. **1834** HAWTHORNE *Twice-told Tales* (1879) I. 126 The millmen resolved to . . . refresh him with an ablution at the town-pump. **1908** 'O. HENRY' *Options* 16 Is it a continued story, or an account of the unveiling of the new town pump in Whitmire, South Carolina?

Town's common, land, meeting. (See TOWN COMMON, LAND, MEETING.)

Townsend. [J. K. *Townsend,* Amer. naturalist (1809–51).] +Used in possessive in the specific names of birds.

1887 RIDGWAY *Manual N. A. Birds* 452 Chester County, Pennsylvania (only one specimen known). . . . *S[piza] townsendii.* Townsend's Bunting. **1839** AUDUBON *Ornith. Biog.* V. 149 Townsend's Cormorant. *Phalacrocorax Townsendi.* **1869** *Amer. Naturalist* III. 34 Townsend's Flycatcher (*Myiadestes Townsendii*) . . . was pursuing insects from bush to bush in a small prairie. **1874** COUES *Birds N.W.* 93 *Myiadestes Townsendii.* . . . Townsend's Flycatching Thrush. . . . Middle and Western Provinces of the United States. **1917** *Birds of Amer.* III. 57/2 In western North America . . . [is] Townsend's Fox Sparrow (*Passerella iliaca townsendi*). **1839** AUDUBON *Ornith. Biog.* V. 336 Townsend's Mocking Thrush, *Turdus Townsendi,* . . . [is] cinereous brown above. **1887** RIDGWAY *Manual N.A. Birds* 572 Western United States (in mountains), north to British Columbia, east to and including Rocky Mountains (casually to Illinois). . . . *M[yadestes] townsendii.* Townsend's Solitaire. *Ib.* 434 Pacific coast, breeding from southern Alaska (British Columbia?) to Unalashka; south, in winter, to southern California. . . . *P[asserella] iliaca unalaschcensis.* . . . Townsend's Sparrow. **1839** AUDUBON *Ornith. Biog.* V. 249 Townsend's Surf-Bird, *Aphriza Townsendi,* . . . was procured by Dr. Townsend on the shores of Cape Disappointment. *Ib.* 36 Townsend's Warbler . . . was procured about the Columbia River.

+**Townsendia.** [David *Townsend* (1787–1858), of Pennsylvania.] A genus of western plants of the thistle family; a plant belonging to this genus. — **1871** *Amer. Naturalist* V. 65 There appears [in Colo.] . . . a real beauty, which, as it yet lacks an English name, may bear its Latin one, Townsendia (*T. sericea*). **1872** TICE *Over Plains* 64 Here were . . . white and purple *Anemones;* the gaudy *Gaillordia aristata* . . . ; the white *Townsendia* [etc.].

Town sergeant. A town official charged with various duties, as the collection of taxes. (See also SERGEANT 1.) — **1649** *Portsmouth Rec.* 42 Thomas Gorton is chosen towne Sargiant. **1650** *Providence Rec.* II. 53 [The] Town-Sergeant shall collect the Rate. **1676** *Ib.* XV. 151 James Olny [was chosen] Towne sergeant.

* **Township.**

1. +**a.** *New Eng.* A local area or political unit governed by means of a town meeting; the jurisdiction of a New England town.

1635 *Watertown Rec.* I. 1. 1 Two Hundred Acres of vpland . . . shalbe reserved as most convenient to make a Township. **1682** *Braintree Rec.* 20 Every proprietor in the Towne of Brantry . . . shall have & injoy all his owne lands & proprieties in the Towne ship of Brantry. **1712** *Ib.* 76 The Petition of the Town of Milton about the blew hill lands . . . Petitioned to ly within there Township. **1789** ANBUREY *Travels* II. 261 Most of the places you pass through in Connecticut are called townships . . . which are not regular towns as in England, but a number of houses dispersed over a large tract of ground. **1828** COOPER *Notions* I. 94 Each township, as parishes, or *cantons,* are here called, has the entire control of all the routes within its own limits. **1884** [see HAYWARD]. **1903** *N.Y. Times* 24 Sept. 7 Last spring the Legislature passed a bill making two townships out of the present township of Norwalk.

b. Elsewhere, as in the states of the Northwestern Territory, a similar political unit having somewhat more limited powers of self-government. (See also POST TOWNSHIP.)

In states surveyed into geographical townships (see sense 2 below), the political township is usually based upon the geographical one.

1769 *Phila. Ordinances* (1812) 26 No waggon, wain or cart . . . within the district of Southwark, or the townships of Moyamensing or Passyunk, shall travel . . . on any of the paved parts of the said city. **1808** *Austin P.* I. (1924) 150 Seth Hunt Esqr. lately of the district of St. Genevieve and Moses Austin to the Township of Breton did enter into an agreement. **1846** *Mich. Gen. Statutes* I. (1882) 261 Debts owing by a township . . . shall be apportioned in the same manner as the personal property of such township. **1888** BRYCE *Amer. Commonw.* II. 11. xlviii. 240 The words 'town' and 'township' signify [in Ill. and other western and northwestern states] a territorial division of the county, incorporated for purposes of local government.

+**2.** One of the regular tracts into which public land is surveyed.

'An "original surveyed township" or "congressional township" . . . should be distinguished from both the "civil township" and the "school township" which may or may not coincide with the thirty-six square mile tracts' *Cycl. Amer. Govt.* III. 544/2.

1768 in B. P. Smith *Hist. Dartmouth* 36 The Deputy Surveyor . . . offered his assistance to look out the township and survey it. **1780** *Ann. Register 1779* 9 The Settlement of Wyoming consisted of eight townships, each containing a square of five miles. **1836** *Diplom. Corr. Texas* I. (1908) 67 The lands are regularly surveyed into Townships, sections, etc. **1891** *Amer. Notes & Q.* VI. 264 In Maine, the unsettled lands are surveyed into townships. . . . When the Maine township becomes settled, it receives a name, and organizes a local 'plantation' government. **1909** WEBSTER 2178/3 In Maine, New Hampshire, and Vermont there are unorganized subdivisions of the county called townships, which are simply tracts of land laid off by the State authorities.

b. Under the public-land ordinance of 1785, one of the tracts, approximately six miles square (containing thirty-six sections) in area, into which the public lands of the United States were divided before sale was permitted.

See also CONGRESSIONAL TOWNSHIP, FRACTIONAL TOWNSHIP, and cf. SECTION 1.

1785 *Jrnls. Cont. Congress* XXVIII. 378 There shall be reserved the lot N 16, of every township, for the maintenance of public schools, within the said township. **1815** DRAKE *Cincinnati* 129 Cincinnati is built upon one entire and two fractional sections . . . in the fourth township. **1860** [see PAPER CITY]. **1902** WHITE *Blazed Trail* xxii, You can give no receipt for any land in these townships.

3. *attrib.* +**a.** With *division, high school, insurance company,* etc.

1647 *Watertown Rec.* I. 1. 12 The Land giuen in lieu of the Towneship; is not a Just satisfaction for the Townshipp Land. **1814** *Niles' Reg.* V. 321/2 Our very intelligent principal surveyor . . . has been running township lines. **1816** *Ib.* X. 81/1 Paltry, contracted, contemptible *township-politics* . . . are frequently discovered by some members of our national legislature. **1816** *Ind. Constitution* ix. § 2 It shall be the duty of the General Assembly, as soon as circumstances will permit, to provide, by law, for a general system of education, ascending in a regular gradation from township schools to a State University. **1883** *Ill. Revised Statutes* 660 Any township insurance company . . . [may] receive into its said organization one or more adjoining congressional or political townships. **1885** *Harper's Mag.* Sept. 553/1 The admirable system of township division . . . was the natural precursor of the planting of the township organization. **1914** *Cycl. Amer. Govt.* III. 260/3 The township high school has been organized to bring secondary education nearer to all pupils of the public schools.

+**b.** Designating officials, or groups of officials, concerned with township administration.

1837 *Knickerb.* X. 408 He led up before the township justice of the peace a hope-inspired damsel. **1838** *Indiana H. Rep. Jrnl.* 23 Sess. 114 [It shall be] the duty of the township treasurer to divide and distribute the school funds. **1842** *Niles' Nat. Reg.* 29 Jan. 352/3 Moneys paid by the township collectors to the trustees of districts in townships. **1851** CIST *Cincinnati* 335 Longworth is a supernumerary township trustee. **1852** *Ind. Hist. Soc. Publ.* III. 615 This organization is under the control and supervision of the township educational board.

Town site. +A tract of land set apart by legal authority for the location of a town, esp. one surveyed and laid out with streets and lots. Also attrib. — **1831** PECK *Guide* 8 Having no connection with the business of land speculation or of town sites [etc.]. **1869** [see ALKALI LAKE]. **1880** INGHAM *Digging Gold* 232 The General Land Office . . . contains much of history in regard to the town-site controversy. **1896** *Critic* 31 Oct. 270/1 We have made a plan of Trilby Townsite, Pasco Co., Fla.

* **Townsman.**

+1. *New Eng.* =SELECTMAN. *Obs.*
1634 *Cambridge Rec.* 11 Whatsoever these Townsmen . . . shall doe . . . sha[ll] stand in as full force as if the whole To[wn] did the same. **1651** *Maine Doc. Hist.* IV. 12 Per me Humphrey Chadburne tounes man & recorder for the toune of Keterey. **1705** *Boston News-Letter* 19 March 2/2 There was Chosen to Serve as Select or Townsmen, Timothy Clark, . . . and Joseph Prout. *a*1817 DWIGHT *Travels* I. 243 The inhabitants choose, not exceeding seven men, . . . to be Selectmen, or Townsmen, to take care of the order, and prudential affairs of the town.

* **2.** One admitted to citizenship in a town.
1638 *Watertown Rec.* I. 1. 5 The rest of the Townesmen . . . shall haue their Farmes out of the Freemens Common. **1653** *Boston Rec.* 113 Mr. Pighogg, a Chururgeon, is admitted a Townsman. **1666** *Brookhaven Rec.* 17 [We] doe hereby assigne . . . said tract of land . . . unto our ancient and loving ffriends, the Townes men of Southampton.

3. A citizen or resident of a college town, as opposed to a student or teacher. {1768-}
1650 *Harvard Rec.* I. 33 The Steward shal in no Case permit any Students . . . to expend or bee provided for themselves or any Townsmen any extraordinary Commons.

Townspeople, Town people. {1648-} In a college town, the citizens, as distinguished from students and teachers. — **1887** *Lippincott's Mag.* Aug. 295 These performances were very attractive to old graduates and town-people. **1895** WILLIAMS *Princeton Stories* 228 Nearly everyone in the little city, students, faculty and townspeople, were New Englanders by blood or birth.

Town treasurer. An official charged with keeping the public funds of a town. — **1652** *Portsmouth Rec.* 19 The which acoumpt is to be giuen unto the Towne Tresurer. **1726** *Boston Rec.* 205 The Select-men [shall] be Impowred to Draw upon the Town Treasurer the Sum of Three Pence upon the pound. **1857** E. STONE *Life J. Howland* 114 [In] 1818 . . . he was elected town treasurer.

Towny. Also **towney.** {1828-} +A citizen of a college town, as distinguished from a student or a teacher. *College slang.* — **1853** *Yale Lit. Mag.* XIX. 2 (Th.), The genus . . . which custom here has named 'Townies.' **1869** W. T. WASHBURNE *Fair Harvard* 54 (Th.), One beholds the conscious 'towney' on his evening promenade. **1887** *Lippincott's Mag.* 738 When, however, a cheap play or concert is 'broken up' by the students [at Amherst], the townies find it hard to be reconciled to the loss of their evening's entertainment.

+Towpath. A path beside a canal, used by men or animals drawing boats. {1876- (*Encycl. Brit.* IV. 785/2)} Also attrib. — **1788** WASHINGTON *Diaries* III. 361 The Canal at the head was accomplished . . . and a tow path on the Maryland side for some distance below. **1827** McKENNEY *Tour to Lakes* 50 These horses trot along the *tow path*, as it is called. **1848** *Indiana Gen. Ass. Doc. 1848-9* 11. 144 This division of work . . . embraces . . . two guard locks, and a road and tow path bridge. **1886** STAPLETON *Major's Christmas* 297 Nancy . . . [advanced] to the edge of the tow-path. **1904** CRISSEY *Tattlings* 387 We started him out as the 'tow-path candidate.'

+Tow string. A string or rope made of tow. Also attrib. and fig. — **1806** *Balance* V. 5/3 Our worthy old friend . . . sometimes wears a tow string round his hat. **1856** STOWE *Dred* I. 186 She is one of the tow-string order of women. **1876** MILLER *First Fam'lies* 234 He held an old bull-dog by a tow-string. **1892** *Harper's Mag.* March 649/2 What was known as the 'tow-string survey' offered him an excellent opportunity for the display of his peculiar talents.

+Tow trousers. *pl.* Trousers made of tow cloth. — **1767** *Va. Gazette* 11 June, Michael Murray, an Irishman, . . . had on . . . tow trousers. **1845** [see SKILTS]. **1856** A. CARY *Married* 184 This sturdy and independent looking youth wore . . . a muslin shirt, tow trousers, and leather suspenders.

* **Toy.**

* **1.** An article prized not for its intrinsic value but as an ornament; a trinket. +Freq. an article of trade with the Indians.
1623 BRADFORD *Hist.* (1912) II. 345*n*., The Duch on one side and the French on the other side . . . doe furnish the savages, not with toyes and trifles, but with good and substantial commodities. **1674** in Alvord & Bidgood *Trans-Allegheny Region* 220 They took from him some toys which hung in his eares. **1737** BRICKELL *N. Carolina* 105 [From the fruit of] the Bead-Tree . . . are made Bracelets, and several other Toys. **1820** *Amer. Antiq. Soc. Coll.* I. 72 We presented them with . . . several little toys for their wives.

* **2.** A child's plaything.
1801 *Ann. 7th Congress* 2 Sess. 1226 Articles paying twelve and a half per cent. ad valorem. . . . Whips and canes, toys, lampblack. **1865** *Atlantic Mo.* Feb. 187/1 Not a snug valley [in Conn.] . . . but rattles with the manufacture of . . . tin pans and toys, hats, garters [etc.]. **1890** [see ROOT BEER].

3. Attrib. in sense 2 with *automobile, cannon,* etc. {toyman, etc. 1707-}
1796 *Boston Directory* 232 Butler, Mary, crockery and toy shop. **1854** CUMMINS *Lamplighter* xiv, Willie . . . undertook to tell her what he knew of the veteran toy-dealer [Santa Claus]. **1863** 'G. HAMILTON' *Gala-Days* 396 He tricks out toy-engines and knick-knacks. **1887** PERRY *Flock of Girls* 12 Her ignorant little hands had seized upon a toy cannon. **1899** CHAMPLIN & BOSTWICK *Cycl. Games & Sports* (ed. 2) 377/1 The Grace Hoops sold at toy stores are usually covered with velvet or colored cloth. **1907** *St. Nicholas* Aug. 882/2 The sandwiches stood in individual toy automobiles, which were the favors.

Toy book. A children's book. {1865} — **1801** WEEMS *Letters* II. 177, I sell the Primers & toy books wholesale at great discount. **1850** MITCHELL *Lorgnette* I. 195 Her toy-books are well selected.

Toy dog. {1863} A small dog. — **1806** LEWIS in *L. & Clark Exped.* V. (1905) 178 [Barking squirrels] will generally set and bark at you . . . , their note being much that of the little toy dogs.

+Toyon, Tollon. [ad. Mex. Sp. *tollon.*] An evergreen shrub (*Heteromeles arbutifolia*) of the Pacific coast; the California holly. — [**1848** G. BENTHAM *Plantæ Hartweg.* 307 Photinia arbutifolia, *Toyon* incolarum.] **1876** BREWER, etc. *Botany Calif.* I. 188. **1884** SARGENT *Rep. Forests* 84 Toyon. Tollon. California Holly. . . . Wood . . . susceptible of a beautiful polish.

* **Trace,** *n.*[1]

* **1.** A tug, usually a leather strap or chain, forming part of the harness of a draft animal.
1651 *Mayflower Descendant* X. 162 A Cartrope & trace & Coller. **1783** in Summers *Ann. S.W. Va.* 377, 25 lbs. [shall] be allowed Thomas Read for a horse bridle, collar, harnes, & traces. **1834** CARRUTHERS *Kentuckian* I. 102 The saddles were stuck on the shoulders of the animals, like . . . a pair of haims to hitch traces to. **1887** *Century Mag.* Sept. 706/1, I've cast two shoes on the leader and broken a trace. **1904** WALLER *Wood-Carver* 12 [The driver] was busy with the horses—putting on the check-rein, testing the traces.

2. In fig. and colloq. phrases.
To force into the traces, to force into regular or humdrum work; *to break a trace,* to exert oneself to the utmost; *to get one leg over the traces,* to get slightly out of line with the interests of one's party or group; *to work in the traces,* to work or proceed in a regular or uniform manner.
1824 IRVING *Tales of Traveller* I. 203 He was too fond of my genius to force it into the traces. **1845** *Big Bear Ark.* 101 You must marry that gal and no mistake, or brake a trace! **1871** *Harper's Mag.* Dec. 155/2, I may have got one leg over the traces, but I was in the harness all the while. **1881** in McCabe *New York* 129 This whole system was founded on . . . the tendency of every voter to work in the traces, and vote for any man ostensibly nominated by the party.

3. In special combinations.
Trace buckle, in saddle-making, a long, heavy buckle used in attaching a trace to a tug; *t. leather,* leather such as is used in making traces.
1855 *Knickerb.* XLV. 199 They sew together long pieces of almost unmatchable trace-leather 'for tandems.' **1868** *Mich. Agric. Rep.* VII. 353 Geo. Washer, Romeo, [exhibited] 1 trace buckle (Fillmore patent).

* **Trace,** *n.*[2] +A string of ears of Indian corn, the husks of which are plaited together. — **1678** *Phil. Trans.* XII. 1066 The common way (which they call Tracing) is to weave the Ears together in long traces by some parts of the Husk left thereon. **1753** E. CHAMBERS *Cycl. Suppl.* s.v. *Tracing,* These traces of corn they hang up within doors.

* **Trace,** *n.*[3] +A path, trail, or road in a forest or wilderness made by the passage of men or animals.
1783 in *Travels Amer. Col.* 668 On the trace to Boons station they were fired on. **1802** *Ann. 7th Congress* 1 Sess. 1322 They shall travel in the trace or path which is usually travelled. **1851** *S. Lit. Messenger* XVII. 571/1 The 'trace' is growing a frequented highway. **1886** Z. F. SMITH *Kentucky* 7 By following its trodden roads, or 'traces,' . . . which the buffaloes made from their grazing fields and brakes, they found [etc.]. **1904** CHURCHILL *Crossing* 77 They were going off up the trace toward mother's.

b. Preceded by a descriptive or specifying term.
See also BUFFALO TRACE.
1807 in Pike *Sources Miss.* 11. App. 24 [We] took the large Spanish beaten trace for the Arkansaw river. **1831** WITHERS *Chron. Border Warfare* 285 [They guarded] the Ohio river and the 'wilderness trace,' to cut off parties of emigrants removing to that country. **1870** NOWLAND *Indianapolis* 14 Berry's Trace crossed that of Whetzell's.

* **Trace,** *v.* +*tr.* To form (ears of Indian corn) into traces by plaiting their husks. Also as *vbl. n.* and with *up.* — **1678, 1753** [see TRACE *n.*[2]]. **1884** *Vt. Agric. Rep.* VIII. 285 The ears thus selected should be 'traced up' and hung away to dry. *Ib.* 351 Corn traced and hung in a dry, airy place will cure well and seldom fail at planting time.

Trace chain. A chain used as a trace for a draft animal. {1844-} — **1815** *Niles' Reg.* IX. 94/2 Trace chains and other chains. **1865** *Harper's Mag.* July 170/2 With trace-chains, secured by padlocks around their necks, [they] were fastened to each other. **1910** J. HART *Vigilante Girl* 141 Then, with a jingle of bells, a creaking of whiffle-trees, and a clanking of trace-chains, the wagons fared on.

*Tracer. +1. An inquiry sent from one place to another to locate the whereabouts of a person or thing. **+2.** (See quotation.) — **(1) 1884** *Century Mag.* May 159/1 (*title*), A Tracer for J[ohn] B[urroughs]. **1887** *Postal Laws* 399 Inquiries or tracers regarding registered packages . . . must receive immediate attention. **1902** LORIMER *Lett. Merchant* 282 She strikes me as a young woman who's not going to lose a million dollars without putting a tracer after it. **(2) 1888** *Scientific Amer.* LIX. 217/1 Nearly all the great roads employ a corps of what are known as 'lost car searchers' or 'tracers.'

‖Traceway. A trace or trail. — **1857** *Ladies' Repository* April 235/2 'There,' pointing to what had once been a traceway, 'that will take you down to the river.'

* Track, n.

I. 1. The footprints, marks, etc., left by Indians in passing. {* in general sense}
1637 *L. ss. H. S. Coll.* 4 Ser. VI. 163 They had that day . . . discovered the track & footing of a party of Indians. **1692** *Va. State P.* I. 44 We Ranged about to see if we could find ye tract of any Indians. **1705** *Boston News-Letter* 12 March 2/2 The Fort encompassed 3 quarters of an acre of ground . . . , wherein were 12 Wigwams but no Enemy; neither the discovery of any Tracks seen. **1757** *General Orders* 21 When any Discovery of The Enimy Be Made Either By Track Sight or Firing of Small Arms the Commanding offi[ce]rs . . . [are] immediately to Send one Man or More.

2. An extent or tract of land. {1687–}
1676 in *Amer. Speech* XV. 405/1 Everie man may be taxed according to the tracks of Land they hold. **1695** *Topsfield Rec.* 92 Ye Towne granted a small track of land to set a barne on. **1778** CARVER *Travels* p. xiv, The accounts here given of the various nations that inhabit so vast a track of it . . . will furnish an ample fund of amusement. **1875** *Amer. Naturalist* 385 The vegetable life of Illinois presents many points of general interest . . . [on] the broad, level tracks of moist land so often bordering the large streams.

3. The line over which railway cars pass; a railroad road-bed. {1805–}
'Now *U.S.*' (*O.E.D.*). (See also CAR TRACK, DOUBLE TRACK *n.*, SINGLE TRACK *n.*)
1846 *Xenia Torch-Light* 2 April 1/3 Along some places, the track of the road was used for boats instead of cars. **1872** TICE *Over Plains* 69 For two and a half miles up the canyon the track for a narrow-gauge railroad is graded. **1897** *Kissimmee* (Fla.) *Valley* 3 March 2/4 The pike crosses the tracks just beyond a curve. **1917** MATHEWSON *Second Base Sloan* 123 Wayne got to walking across the tracks and up the line a ways.

+4. The tread or transverse distance between the two wheels of a vehicle.
1850 *Western Journal* IV. 96 This distance will, therefore, vary in different sections of the country according to the usual 'track' of wagons.

+5. = RACE TRACK. {1887–}
1852 BRISTED *Upper Ten Th.* 228 A barouche and four does not differ more from a trotting wagon . . . than an American race-course from an American 'track.' **1893** *Outing* May 99/1 The sulkies and tracks were primitive affairs. **1898** [see PIKER²].

II. In phrases. **+6.** *To make tracks*, to depart in haste, to hurry. *colloq.*
1832 KENNEDY *Swallow Barn* II. 63, I'll be bound I make tracks! **1845** KIRKLAND *Western Clearings* 201 The rising sun of the next morning saw Elliott 'making tracks' for Templeville. **1884** WEED *Autobiog.* 610, I advise you . . . to make tracks for that tall timber. **1907** WHITE *Arizona Nights* 138 Make tracks. Come in to Buck Cañon.

+7. *To plumb a track*, to follow out a road or track. *colloq.*
1844 M. C. HOUSTOUN *Texas* (1845) 230 *Plumbing the track*, the Texan term for tracing a road, is, at all times, a slow and tedious operation. **1892** *Country Church* (Buckland, Mass.) 16 March, When Old Rover took one track and plumbed it through, he holed the game.

+8. *In one's tracks*, on the spot where one is at the moment; at once; immediately. *colloq.*
1845 HOOPER *Taking Census* 179, I'll die in my tracks fust. **1866** LOWELL *Biglow P.* 2 Ser. p. xlviii, *In his tracks* for *immediately* has acquired an American accent, and passes where he can for a native. **1883** HARTE *In Carquinez Woods* 180, I'd only to bring you in range of that young man's rifle, and you'd have dropped in your tracks.

+9. *To fly the track*, to depart from or leave a usual or prescribed course. Usually *fig.*
1847 *Congress. Globe* 4 Feb. 322/2, I had been accused of flying the track on the creed of the Democratic party. **1852** J. B. JONES *Col. Vanderbomb* 167 There is no chance for any of our men, unless they fly the track, and leave the old party lines. **1880** 'MARK TWAIN' *Tramp Abroad* 510 He is disposed to fly the track and avoid the implacable foe. **1910** C. HARRIS *Eve's Husband* 85 No man ever gets too old to fly the track in some way.

+10. *To cover (up) one's tracks*, to conceal one's actions or motives.

1865 RICHARDSON *Secret Service* 57 In corresponding, I endeavored to cover my tracks as far as possible. **1878** *Masque of Poets* 244 Whatever else he lacks, He has the art of covering up his tracks.

+11. *To lose track of*, to fail to keep up with or follow the course of.
1871 EGGLESTON *Hoosier Schoolm.* 83 May be God lost track of my father when he come away from England. **1894** *Outing* XXIII. 387/1 Day after day passes in precisely the same manner . . . until one loses all track of the days of the week. **1907** LILLIBRIDGE *Trail* 271 We got too far apart and lost track of each other.

+12. *To jump the track*, of a railway car, to leave the rails. Also *fig.*
1872 *Harper's Mag.* Dec. 152 The ladies' car on an express train on the Paducah and Elizabethtown Railroad jumped the track. **1888** *Economist* 27 Oct. 10/3 There were a good many instances of 'jumping the track' during the week. **1904** *Newark Ev. News* 14 June 5 Trolley car 415 . . . jumped the track midway between the Frank Creek and the Pennsylvania Railroad meadow shops.

13. In various other phrases.
To beat (someone) *out of his track*, to force (someone) from his course; *to yield the track to*, to give way or submit to; *to keep out of* (someone's) *tracks*, to avoid (someone); *to go back on one's tracks*, to give up one's intentions.
1833 FLINT *D. Boone* 28 He was remarkable for the backwoods attribute of *never being beaten out of his track*. **1847** FIELD *Drama in Pokerville* 41 Mr. Busby Case . . . had entirely yielded the track to his formidable rival. **1847** ROBB *Squatter Life* 122 He'd better keep out of my tracks. **1878** STOWE *Poganuc People* 158 He'll put it through, though; he won't go back on his tracks.

14. In special combinations.
Track athletics, (see quotation); *t. dog*, a dog that hunts by scent; *t. force*, a group of workmen employed to keep railroad tracks in repair; *t. man*, one employed to work on a railroad track, a track walker {1893}; *trackmaster*, one in charge of a section of railroad track; *track meet*, an athletic meeting comprising contests in various track sports; *t. path*, a towpath; *t.-rider*, a jockey; *t. season*, the season suitable for track athletics; *t. sport*, sports engaged in upon a track; *t.-sprinkler*, (see quotation); *trackwalker*, one employed to walk at regular intervals over a railroad track to see that it is in proper order.
1890 *Century Mag.* June 204/2 'Track athletics' are walking, running, jumping [etc.]. **1858** *Harper's Mag.* Oct. 614/1 The 'track-dog' is unloosed. **1866** *30th Congress 2 Sess.* H. R. Rep. No. 34, 1026, I found the road in bad condition; the track force had been over two weeks at work repairing. **1881** *Chicago Times* 30 April, Track men and mechanics now in employment on the road. **1866** in Fulton *Sam Hobart* 103 The trackmaster failed to ascertain the fact. **1904** *Cap & Gown* (Chicago) IX. 215 Track Meets and Scores, 1903 . . . Second Annual Interscholastic Meet, at Marshall Field. **1785** WASHINGTON *Diaries* II. 396 No track path can be had in a navigation thus ordered. **1891** *Harper's Mag.* Aug. 372/1 We should scarcely credit the mechanical possibility of some of the positions the track-rider can assume. **1899** QUINN *Penna. Stories* 218 That was the way things were when the track season opened. **1905** *Outing* XLVI. 490/1 Track and field sport has been working out its own spontaneous solution. **1848** BARTLETT 362 *Track-Sprinkler*, a contrivance recently invented in Providence, R.I., and now in use on the railroads in that State, for sprinkling railroad tracks. **1889** *Scribner's Mag.* VI. Advt. 29 (*Cent.*), The chapters . . . describe the work of the railroad man from president to track-walker.

* Track, v.
+1. a. *tr.* To soil or mark (a floor, etc.) with tracks. Freq. with *up*. **b.** To bring (snow or mud) into a place on one's feet. Freq. with *in*.
(a) 1832 *Jamestown* (N.Y.) *Jrnl.* 1 Aug. 3 The gardens and roads about the city were 'tracked up' with [rats and mice]. **1836** GILMAN *Recoll.* (1838) 127 Miss Neely, one buckra woman want for track up all de clean floor. **1869** STOWE *Oldtown Folks* 21 Don't come in to track my floor. **(b) 1866** *Harper's Mag.* Jan. 271/2 The snow had been tracked in till it lay pretty thick on the floor. **1878** STOWE *Poganuc People* 9 Sweep out that snow you've tracked in. **1901** MERWIN & WEBSTER *Calumet 'K'* 117 There's going to be a law passed about tracking mud inside the railing.

‖2. To provide (a region) with railroad tracks.
See also DOUBLE-TRACK *v.*, SINGLE-TRACK *v.*
1846 *Niles' Nat. Reg.* XX. 64/2 We would compete with England for the supplies which the continents of Europe and Asia will soon require, of railroad iron—besides tracking our own 'wilderness' with iron highways in all directions.

+3. *intr.* In walking, to place one foot in the same straight line with the other.
1857 GLISAN *Jrnl. Army Life* 382, I observed to-day that he does not 'track' (step his hind foot straight after the fore one). **1897** HOUGH *Story of Cowboy* 34 His feet, in the vernacular of the range, do not 'track,' but cross each other way.

+Trackage. The collective tracks of a railroad or railroad system; *trackage charge*, a charge for the use of a railway line by another company. — **1884** *Morning Herald* (Reading, Pa.) 17 April, Our general agent has, therefore, advanced this trackage charge. **1892** A. E. LEE *Hist.*

Columbus, Ohio II. 314 [With] the improvement in the trackage and rolling stock . . . [the] street-railway service] promises to be equal . . . to that of any city of equal population in the Union. **1903** *Booklovers Mag.* Nov. 517 The trackage on the New York division had already been increased to four lines of rails.

+Track-clearer. (See quot. 1876.) — **1859** *Rep. Comm. Patents 1858* I. 433 Improvement in Track Clearers for Mowing Machines. **1864** *Ohio Agric. Rep.* XVIII. 70 Take the lever in one hand and track-clearer in the other, bear down on the lever [etc.]. **1876** KNIGHT 2608/1 *Track-clearer.* 1. (*Railway.*) *a.* A cow-catcher in front of, or bars extending down from the front frame of the locomotive, to push objects from the track. *b.* A track-sweeper to remove snow. . . . 2. (*Harvesting.*) A triangular frame on the outer end of the cutter-bar of a mowing or reaping machine to draw the grain toward the cutter.

+Track hound. A hound that hunts and follows a track by scent. — **1865** *Jamestown* (N.Y.) *Jrnl.* 13 Jan. 4/1 No more flying fugitives, white men or negroes, shall be followed by track hounds. **1888** *Century Mag.* May 42/2 We retraced our steps, intending to return on the morrow with a good track hound. **1893** ROOSEVELT *Wilderness Hunter* 45 The cowboy and our one trackhound plunged into the young cottonwood.

+Tracklayer. 1. One employed in laying a railroad track. {1888} 2. (See quot. 1876.) — (1) *a*1861 WINTHROP *Open Air* 234 'Wanted, experienced track-layer!' was the word along the files. **1876** CROFUTT *Trans-continental Tourist* 96 These boards mark the track which was laid by the track layers of the Central Pacific Company in *one day*. **1897** *Atlantic Mo.* Jan 25/2 The demand for track-layers opened new fields of labor. (2) **1876** KNIGHT 2608/1 *Track-layer,* . . . a carriage provided with apparatus for placing the rails in their proper positions . . . as the machine advances.

+Tracklaying. The laying of the rails on a railway line. {1900} — *a*1861 WINTHROP *Open Air* 234 Track-laying was the business on hand. **1872** HUNTINGTON *Road-Master's Asst.* 11 There is no remedy for some of the defects of poor track-laying. **1890** *Stock Grower & Farmer* 21 June 5/1 Track-laying on the Pecos Valley railroad commenced this week, and will be pushed rapidly.

Traction. {1615-} +Attrib. with reference to city transportation systems. — **1897** *Kissimmee* (Fla.) *Valley Gazette* 31 Dec. 1/5 A trolley car on the Schuylkill Valley Traction Company line at Norristown, Pa. was held up by four highwaymen. **1903** *Boston Transcript* 20 Aug., Plans are being worked out for the consolidation of the traction systems of this city. **1904** *N.Y. Tribune* 27 March 12 The reservoir broke, flooding paper mills and tying up railway and traction lines.

+Tractor.

1. *pl.* A pair of pointed bars, one of brass and one of steel, supposed to give relief by electricity or magnetism when drawn over swollen or rheumatic parts of the body. {1801-} Usu. *metallic tractors* {1798-} or (after the inventor, Dr. Elisha Perkins (1741-99), of Norwich, Connecticut) *Perkins's tractors*. *Obs.*

1796 *Aurora* (Phila.) 29 March (Th.), [Notice of] Metallic Tractors. **1800** *Lancaster* (Pa.) *Jrnl.* 20 Dec. (Th.), The Turkey-cock and Tractors. **1804** *Balance* 10 Jan. 9 (Th.), There are Perkins's Tractors. They will cure everything. **1885** WHITTIER *Writings* VI. 314 Jacob Perkins, in drawing out diseases with his metallic tractors, was quite as successful as modern 'faith and mind' doctors.

2. (See quot. 1909.) {1901-}

[**1900** HISCOX *Horseless Vehicles* 41 A number of [vehicles] . . . were built extending over the time from 1830 to 1840, carriages, omnibuses and tractors being seen on the roads about London.] **1909** *Cent. Suppl.* 1366/2 *Tractor.* . . . 2. A traction-engine for use on streets and highways. Such tractors may be used to drag loaded vehicles, to drag plows in a gang, or to haul artillery-wagons and field-pieces. 3. The frame and steel rope by which a gang of plows is drawn across a field by a traction-engine. **1924** H. CROY *R.F.D. No. 3* 183 Many men came to sell him things—tractors, trucks, riding plows.

+Tractoration. The use of metallic tractors. *Obs.* — **1803** T. G. FESSENDEN (*title*), Terrible Tractoration! **1861** HOLMES *Medical Essays* 9 Homœopathy has not died out so rapidly as Tractoration.

+Tractoring, *a.* Using metallic tractors. In allusive use. *Obs.* — **1803** FESSENDEN *Terrible Tractoration* 132 You'll confound the tractoring folks By Haygarth's tale.

+Tractorize, *v.* {1817} *intr.* and *tr.* To use metallic tractors; to attract by the use of metallic tractors. Also *ppl. a.* In allusive use. *Obs.* — **1803** T. G. FESSENDEN (*title*), A Poetical Petition against Tractorising Trumpery. **1803** — *Terrible Tractoration* 104 A spruce young patent-monger Contrives to wheedle simple ninnies, And *tractorise* away *our* guineas.

Tract society. A society for distributing religious literature, usually in the form of tracts. Often in the names of particular societies. {1816} — **1760** J. ADAMS *Diary Works* II. 97, I should be very sorry to see the Tract Society dissolved. **1820** FLINT *Lett. from Amer.* 214 Cincinnati has . . . two tract societies, (one of them for distributing Bibles and tracts amongst boatmen on the river). *c*1865 'MARK TWAIN' *Sk., New & Old* 73 You can use it to better purpose . . . in charities, and in supporting tract societies. **1885** BAYLOR *On Both Sides* 221, I am the agent of the American Tract Society, madam.

*Trade, *n.*

1. Commodities or produce used in barter. {1883-}

*a*1656 BRADFORD *Hist.* 153 This ship had store of English-beads (which were then good trade). **1800** TATHAM *Agric. & Commerce* 81 Such a one wishes to give you trade for your horse. **1847** PALMER *Rocky Mts.* 127 The value of fourteen dollars in trade would buy an ordinary horse.

+2. A business deal or transaction involving barter. *colloq.* See also HORSE TRADE.

1772 in *Travels Amer. Col.* 533 He would not give them such a good Trade as the people of the Puckantallahassie did. **1802** *Steele P.* I. 250, I Could not make that trade with James Smith. **1883** HARRIS *Mingo* 137 Teague wore the air of awkward, recklessly, helpless independence which so often deceives those who strike the Mountain men for a trade. **1903** A. ADAMS *Log of Cowboy* 331 Our foreman thought he could effect a trade for a serviceable wagon.

+b. *To make trade,* to barter. *Obs.*

1823 I. HOLMES *Account* 215 If a farmer goes to a country shopkeeper with flour, beef, mutton, &c. the common question is—'Will you make trade?'

+c. *Polit.* A deal or bargain; the making of deals.

1888 *Century Mag.* Dec. 313/2 We should be rid at one stroke . . . of 'deals' and 'dickers' and 'trades' at the polls. **1910** [see DICKER *n.*² 1 b].

3. *attrib.* and *comb.* Designating things and places involved in trade with American Indians.

1633 *N.H. Prov. Papers* I. 73 The intermixing of all the trade goods in my care. **1668** *N.H. Hist. Soc. Coll.* III. 216 Ye sayd Capt. did at the very first tyme of settling ye Trade house aforesaide loade four Indians with Liquors. **1881** *Rep. Indian Affairs* 30 Two other Indians of the tribe are preparing to open trade stores. **1892** *Harper's Mag.* Feb. 373/2 They are the relics of the fur company's stock of those famous 'trade guns.'

+4. In special combinations.

Trade boom, a period of unusual activity in trade; *t. journal,* a paper published in the interest of a particular trade or business; *t. rat,* a pack rat which leaves articles in exchange for those it carries away; *t. school,* a school in which trades are taught, used attrib.; *t. vehicle,* a commercial vehicle.

1925 *Scribner's Mag.* Oct. 69/1 What we call a 'trade boom' would undoubtedly be facilitated by abnormally easy credit. **1902** NORRIS *Pit* ix, What do I own all these newspapers and trade journals for? **1912** WASON *Friar Tuck* xxiv, Either the pack-rat reformed into a trade-rat, or else he sold out his claim to a trade-rat. **1889** *Century Mag.* Jan. 403/1 When the trade-school course is finished . . . , he is to enter a workshop as a 'junior' [mechanic]. **1865** *Atlantic Mo.* Jan. 83/1 Central Park . . . contains . . . four sub-ways for the passage of trade-vehicles across the Park.

*Trade, *v.*

+1. *tr.* To obtain or dispose of by barter. Also with *off*.

1636 *Conn. Rec.* I. 1 Henry Stiles . . . had traded a piece with the Indians for Corne. **1793** *Mass. H. S. Coll.* 1 Ser. III. 1 Good crops of corn and rye, which they trade off for spirituous liquors. **1802** *Steele P.* I. 250 [I] have not traded the mare away yet. **1855** 'P. PAXTON' *Capt. Priest* 54 A girl has just arrived with a pot of butter to trade off for 'store-pay.' **1899** JEWETT *Queen's Twin* 183 He wouldn't trade him for no coon dog he ever was acquainted with.

+b. *Polit.* To make (political support or offices) the object of political bargaining.

1856 *Harper's Mag.* Nov. 847/2 The judgeships are, therefore, constantly 'traded off.' . . . Friends of John Doe for sheriff are told that A. B. and C. D. . . . will vote for their candidate, if they in return will vote for Richard Roe for judge. **1902** MEYER *Nominating Systems* 57 It often happens that his wishes are ignored, forgotten, or traded, before they can find a faithful expression.

+2. *To trade out,* to take commodities (to the amount of a sum due).

*c*1847 WHITCHER *Bedott P.* xi. 109, I make a practice o' lettin' on 'em *trade* it out. **1853** B. F. TAYLOR *Jan. & June* 95 The wife was going in to help her husband 'trade out' a portion of the proceeds of the wheat. **1874** in Leavitt *Our Money Wars* 189 When we demand our specie, we are . . . told to 'go to the store and trade it out'!

+Trade dollar. A dollar of 420 grains of standard silver, authorized in 1873 and discontinued in 1887.

'So called because coined expressly for use in *trade* with Asia' (W. '79).

1873 *Stat. at Large* XVII. 427 The silver coins of the United States shall be a trade-dollar, a half-dollar [etc.]. **1882** *Congress. Rec.* App. 16 May 303/2 The Bland dollar . . . is worth in the market some twenty cents more than the trade-dollar. **1890** *Harper's Mag.* June 144/1 My trade dollar dropped without a sound into his desolate pocket. **1907** *Springfield W. Repub.* 7 Nov. 1 The trade dollar, coined formerly for use in foreign trade, was actually of more value in bullion than the standard dollar, but was subject to discount.

attrib. **1887** *Courier-Journal* 17 Feb. 1/6 The House to-day insisted upon its amendments to the Senate Trade-dollar Bill.

*Trader.

*1. One who engages in trade, esp. among the Indians. See also FUR TRADER, INDIAN TRADER 1.

1695 *Mass. Province Acts* I. 238 Hucksters and traders of the town shall not . . . buy of the market people. **1721** *New-Eng. Courant* 21 Aug. 4/1 Some of their Young Men being called Dogs by the English Traders, could not forbear taking some of their Rum. **1789** *Boston Rec.* X. 171

The Boston Directory. Containing, A List of the Merchants, Mechanics, Traders, and others of the Town of Boston. **1827** [see ENGLISH *n.* 2]. **1881** *Rep. Indian Affairs* 41 The same was true with the trader's store. **1918** [see CAPTAIN I b].

+**2.** = NEGRO TRADER. *Obs.*

See also SLAVE TRADER.

1724 in A. Benezet *Caution to Gt. Britain* (1767) 22 Our Traders came on board to-day. **1852** STOWE *Uncle Tom* xi, The enlightened, cultivated, intelligent man . . . supports the system of which the trader is the inevitable result. **1869** TOURGEE *Toinette* (1881) 150 He hoped they would go into the hands of traders so that you might never see them again.

+**3.** A horse kept for trading.

1902 McFAUL *Ike Glidden* 66 All prosperous people there keep a 'driver' and a 'trader.'

Trade(s)-union. A union or organization of workers in a trade or trades, formed to promote their interests. {1835–}

Now less common than *labor union* or simply *union*.

1836 HONE *Diary* I. 210 A set of vile foreigners . . . establish trades-unions, and vilify Yankee judges and juries. **1875** [see HOODLUMISM]. **1885** *Century Mag.* April 822 His political future depends . . . upon the skill and success with which he cultivates the good-will . . . of certain bodies and knots of men (such as compose a trade-union, or a collection of merchants in some special business). **1921** [see ORGANIZE *v.* 2 b].

b. Attrib. with *house, leader, meeting, secretary.*

1836 *Dialogue betw. Strike & Steady* 3, I had to go to a Trades Union meeting. . . . Nothing would do but I must stop in with them, at 'the Trades Union House.' **1911** PERSONS, etc. *Mass. Labor Laws* 115 One of its members, Edward H. Rogers, a trade union leader, made some half-hearted recommendations. *Ib.* 230 A prominent trade union secretary had never heard of the state inspector of health.

Trade(s)-unionism. The system of trade-unions. — [**1875** *N. Amer. Rev.* Jan. 215 [A British economist] investigates at length . . . the theory . . . of trades-unionism.] **1887** FREDERIC *Seth's Brother's Wife* 203 A new civilization has substituted for individual patronage and beneficence the thanks-to-nobody trade-unionism of universal conceit and rivalry. **1911** PERSONS, etc. *Mass. Labor Laws* 106 Trade Unionism was strong enough to maintain a Workingmen's Assembly.

Trade(s)-unionist. A member of a trade-union. {1869– (Fawcett *Pol. Econ.* 233)} — [**1837** *U.S. Mag.* I. 75 Gen. Waddy Thompson . . . saw in the Trades Unionists and the mechanics of the north the two great moving forces of the abolition cause. **1875** in C. Evans *Hist. United Mine Workers* I. 74 If these men are criminally guilty, so are you—so is every trade unionist in the land. **1911** PERSONS, etc. *Mass. Labor Laws* 227 Legislators, as well as trade unionists and others originating labor legislation, . . . have become convinced of the necessity for enforcement by special inspectors.

* **Trading.**

I. 1. Swapping; bartering.

1835 LONGSTREET *Ga. Scenes* 27, I didn't care about trading. **1848** ROBINSON *Journal Santa Fe Exped.* (1932) 46 There was almost a continual trading going on between our men and the Indians in the way of barter. **1882** BAILLIE-GROHMAN *Camps in Rockies* 91 'Trading' . . . is the favourite amusement of your genuine Western man.

+**2.** *Polit.* = LOGROLLING 2.

1880 [see DICKERING *n.* b]. **1892** WALSH *Lit. Curiosities* 1057 Trading . . . is the name of a peculiarly insidious form of political treachery. **1902** MEYER *Nominating Systems* 59 It also presents the opportunity of dropping the candidate of first choice upon one plea or another, if 'trading' or 'logrolling' accompanied by personal advantage should make this expedient.

II. Attrib. and comb., esp. with reference to bartering with Indians. **3.** Designating commodities, articles, etc., used in trading.

See also TRADING CLOTH.

1642 *Md. Archives* IV. 99 Such goods as doth belong to the estate of Mr. Adams [include:] . . . some trading fish[h]ooks in a small lether bagg, . . . 3 trading axes. *a*1656 BRADFORD *Hist.* 409 A Dutch man . . . , having good store of trading goods, came to this place. **1733** *S.C. Gazette* 3 March, Indian Trading Guns. **1742** *Boston Rec.* 312 A great part of the Personal Estate with their Trading Stock and Faculty in the Countrey Towns is not Exhibited. **1758** Trading Kettle [see GUNFLINT I]. **1821** FOWLER *Journal* 72 [The Spanish Creoles'] whole trading equipment in the U.S. would not sell for fifty dollars. **1856** KANE *Arctic Explor.* II. 79 He can easily reach the Esquimaux of Etah Bay, and may as easily seize upon the sledge-dogs, rifle, and trading-articles.

4. Designating vessels used in trading.

1705 *Boston News-Letter* 9 July 2/1 Two Trading Sloops were returned to Port Royal from the Spanish Coast. **1738** W. STEPHENS *Proc. Georgia* I. 156 An Indian Trading Boat Arrived. **1791** W. BARTRAM *Travels* 63 Our captain knew it to be the trading schooner from the stores on St. John's. **1836** IRVING *Astoria* II. 199 The tribes from the northern coast . . . [were] noted for their attempts to surprise trading sloops. **1870** 'O. OPTIC' *Field & Forest* 13, I procured my rifle, . . . which old Matt had purchased on board a trading steamer for my use. **1883** 'MARK TWAIN' *Life on Miss.* xxviii, We should have passed . . . occasional little trading-scows, peddling along from farm to farm, with the peddler's family on board.

5. Designating places where trading is carried on.

See also TRADING HOUSE, TRADING POST.

1755 L. EVANS *Anal. Map Colonies* 10 The situation of Indian Villages, trading Places, the Creeks [etc.]. *a*1817 DWIGHT *Travels* III. 68 Except a small trading village . . . , the township is distributed into plantations. **1847** PARKMAN in *Knickerb.* XXX. 235 It was a little trading fort, belonging to two private traders. *a*1861 WINTHROP *J. Brent* 138 A cattle-shed, house, and trading-shop surrounded three sides of the square. **1873** *Newton Kansan* 3 April 3/2 The country people who make this their trading point ask [etc.]. **1883** *Century Mag.* Oct. 845/2 [Violent change] goes unremittingly on in the oldest trading quarters.

6. Designating journeys undertaken for trading purposes, or routes followed on such journeys.

1775 ADAIR *Indians* 396 [He] set off along the trading path, trusting to his heels. **1791** W. BARTRAM *Travels* 227 In these large canoes they descend the river on trading and hunting expeditions. **1850** GARRARD *Wah-To-Yah* x. 130 The mountaineer deems it not good that he should be alone, and . . . a trading tour to the Indian lodges, often results in his returning a quiet, contented Benedict. *a*1861 WINTHROP *Canoe & Saddle* 51 The Klickatats . . . had just arrived at Nisqually, on their annual trading trip.

7. Designating groups of traders.

1791 W. BARTRAM *Travels* 24 The trading company here received and treated me with great civility. **1837** IRVING *Bonneville* I. 66 He was on his way . . . with reinforcements and supplies for . . . trading parties beyond the mountains. **1845** FRÉMONT *Exped.* 163 Trading caravans . . . may hereafter traverse these . . . inhospitable regions. **1871** Trading-trains [see MORMON 5].

Trading cloth. Cloth of a kind used chiefly by traders in barter with the Indians. *Obs.* {1672–} Also attrib. — **1638** *Mass. H. S. Coll.* 4 Ser. VI. 571 Occasion presentinge to me for a parcell of Dutch tradinge cloth. **1658** *Southold Rec.* I. 440, 3 yards ½ Tradeinge cloath. **1681** *Jamaica Rec.* I. 181 Henery Foster of Jemaicae . . . did in the yeare 1681 pay by order of the constable and overseares a trading cloath coat and som Rom.

+**Trading house.** A house in which barter trade with the Indians is carried on.

1637 *Mass. H. S. Coll.* 4 Ser. VI. 215 He came from a trading howse which Plymouth men haue at Qunnihticut. **1725** *N.J. Archives* I Ser. V. 109 My proposall is . . . Tradeing-houses to Supply the Indians. **1791** W. BARTRAM *Travels* 18, I sat off early in the morning for the Indian trading-house. **1802** ELLICOTT *Journal* 189 Latitude 30°21'30'', where there was formerly a trading house. **1870** NOWLAND *Indianapolis* 59 The first log cabin trading-house was established here, in the winter of 1821. **1902** WHITE *Conjuror's House* 38 The great trading-house attracted his attention, with its narrow picket lane leading to the door.

+**Trading post.** A place where a trader or a group of traders carries on barter trade with the Indians. (Cf. POST *n.³* 2.) — **1796** HAWKINS *Letters* 15 The land . . . has been recommended . . . as proper for a trading post. **1837** IRVING *Bonneville* II. 241 A fortified trading post was to be established on the Columbia. **1860** GREELEY *Overland Journey* 194 There are . . . two or three trading-posts, somewhat frequented by Indians of the Snake tribe. *a*1918 G. STUART *On Frontier* II. 145 The two houses were connected with a bastion like those used at the early trading posts.

+**Trading stamp.** A printed stamp or coupon given away with a purchase as a premium, and redeemable, in sufficient quantities, for merchandise. Also transf. Used attrib. — **1898** *Kissimmee* (Fla.) *Valley Gazette* 11 Feb. 1/4 A bill placing a privilege tax of $500 on trading stamp agencies . . . was vetoed by the governor. **1904** *Brooklyn Standard Union* 30 Aug. 6 A Brooklyn man admits he got his naturalization papers for 50 cents and a few drinks and cigars, but the trading-stamp brand of citizenship is going to be withdrawn from the market pretty suddenly.

+**Traditionate,** *v. tr.* To indoctrinate or teach by tradition. *rare.* Also *ppl. a.* — **1856** G. A. SMITH in *Jrnl. of Discourses* III. 282 (Th.), They have been traditionated to run over a great quantity of ground, and to not half cultivate it. **1862** YOUNG *Ib.* IX. 193 Had we been brought up and traditionated to burn a wife upon the funeral pile, we should [do it]. **1924** F. S. HARRIS *Scientific Research* 12 He was so traditionated in the old theories and treatments that he did not finally abandon them until 1552.

* **Trail,** *n.*

I. ***1.** The indications, as trampled grass or broken bushes, left on the ground by the passage of a person or an animal. {chiefly of scent}

1758 WASHINGTON *Writings* II. 82n., Within 2 miles of Fort Duquesne [he] came upon a few fresh trails making inwards. **1808** PIKE *Sources Miss.* 233 Came on a trail of appearance of 200 horses. **1827** COOPER *Prairie* xvii, The broad trail the party had made through the thicket. **1848** PARKMAN in *Knickerb.* XXXI. 438 Shaw and Henry . . . had found . . . the recent trail of about thirty horsemen. **1883** *N. Mex. Terr. Rep.* 112 Next morning [I] struck the trail of the Indians going south.

+**2.** A more or less permanent path or rude road made by the repeated passage of people or animals. {1894, in Canada}

1807 GASS *Journal* 237 We went off the path or trail. **1835** HOFFMAN *Winter in West* I. 130 A trail . . . is an Indian footpath, that has been travelled perhaps for centuries. **1846** THORPE *Myst. Backwoods* 84 In their wanderings about the prairies, they will leave trails, worn like a long-travelled road. **1873** MILLER *Amongst Modocs* 86 Others . . . would take the single deep-cut trail that led to The Forks. **1896** *Putnam's Mag.* Jan. 78/1 Trails, rather than roads, connected one log-house with another. **1907** *St. Nicholas* Oct. 1142/1 The mountains are honeycombed with trails which early prospectors and railroad builders have made.

b. With defining terms, as in proper names.

See also BUFFALO TRAIL, CATTLE TRAIL, etc.; MORMON TRAIL, OREGON TRAIL, SANTA FE TRAIL.

1849 in *Knickerb.* XXXIII. 111 The Pawnees and the Camanches began a regular series of hostilities on the Arkansas trail. **1856** GLISAN *Jrnl. Army Life* 347 His orders were to proceed to a point on the Big Bend trail, some twelve miles from here. *c*1857 *Kit Carson's Own Story* (1926) 30 We followed the Spanish trail that leads to California. **1858** in F. Hall *Hist. Colorado* II. 519 [We] took the old Ute trail with cart and one yoke of cattle. **1860** GREELEY *Overland Journey* 22 The great California trail . . . keeps along the highest 'divides.' **1897** HOUGH *Story of Cowboy* 7 The Long Trail . . . now crowded to the West.

+3. *W.* A track commonly followed by cattle; *on the trail,* (see quot. 1888).

1880 *Cimarron News & Press* 17 June 1/4 Cow-boys . . . will immediately start some thirty thousand head on the trail. **1888** ROOSEVELT in *Century Mag.* April 849/2 Cattle, while driven from one range to another, or to a shipping point for beef, . . . [are] said to be 'on the trail.' **1890** *Stock Grower & Farmer* 19 April 4/1 There are now on the trail and in transit by rail nearly as many . . . cattle as there were at this time last year. *c*1908 CANTON *Frontier Trails* 6 Our cattle were now well broken to the trail.

+4. In figurative use.

1833 COKE *Subaltern's Furlough* xv, Though the Yankees are so notoriously inquisitive, . . . [I never felt] annoyed by their asking such prying questions, generally leading them 'considerably on the wrong trail,' as they would say. **1834** CARRUTHERS *Kentuckian* I. 23 You are off the trail for once in your life. *Ib.* I. 25 He couldn't keep me on the trail,—I was for ever slipping into Yankee Doodle. **1844** LEE & FROST *Oregon* 97 Now the facts in the premises lie upon the opposite side of the '*trail.*' **1889** MUNROE *Golden Days* 82 Whenever I follow up the trail of one of these yarns I fetch up, sooner or later, against the name of Tedder. **1895** *Outing* XXVI. 452/1 My friend . . . decided to have some sport in the mountains before he took the long steel trail for New York. **1895** REMINGTON *Pony Tracks* 43 He 'struck the long trail to the kingdom come,' as the cowboys phrase it.

5. In phrases.

For other phrases, see CUT v. 25 l, STRIKE v. 3 b, TRASH v.²

To break trail, to make a road or path; *to hit the t.,* to set out *to* a place; *to make t.,* to proceed on a journey; *to ride t.,* to ride over trails in gathering up cattle; *to take the t.,* to set out *for.*

1904 WHITE *Silent Places* 181 The bending figure of the man breaking trail, his head low. **1897** *Outing* XXX. 374/1 Men can pass out the church door, shoulder their packs of general cussedness, and unconcernedly hit the trail to the lower [regions]. **1894** *Harper's Mag.* Feb. 359/2 We 'made trail fast' for the Neuearachie ranch. **1902** WISTER *Virginian* 105 All spring he had ridden trail. **1850** GARRARD *Wah-To-Yah* viii. 105 Old Kurnel Price wanted some one to take the trail for the States on express.

II. *attrib.* and *comb.* **6.** Designating persons making or following trails, esp. persons or groups employed on cattle trails.

1856 *Porter's Spirit of Times* 6 Sept. 2/2 We find 'the Trail-taker's' shanty, where we are to rest this evening. **1885** *Wkly. New Mexican Rev.* 5 March 2/3 Little hopes of driving cattle north or west this season are entertained by the trail men there. **1890** *Stock Grower & Farmer* 21 Jan. 6/3 Trail bosses bronzed from exposure . . . are familiar sights. *Ib.* 19 April 3/3 Cattle inspectors of New Mexico were holding up trail herders for one and one-half cents per head. **1891** *Harper's Mag.* Nov. 884/1 There was little more than the trail-cutters' path to mark what had been determined as the 'right of way.' **1893** ROOSEVELT *Wilderness Hunter* 419 The riders of a huge trail-outfit from Texas . . . abandoned themselves to a night of roaring and lethal carousal. **1903** A. ADAMS *Log of Cowboy* 121 This boundary river on the northern border of Texas was a terror to trail drovers. **1907** WHITE *Arizona Nights* 52 He collected a trail crew. **1923** J. H. COOK *On Old Frontier* 39 Mr. Roberts informed me that I was to be one of his trail waddies.

+7. In sense 3 with *broken, cattle, cinch,* etc.

1885 *Wkly. New Mexican Rev.* 18 June 1/3 The trail herds in Colfax county must go forward or turn back at once. **1887** *Scribner's Mag.* II. 509/1 Common [cowboy] terms are . . . *trail-cattle, trail-cinch.* **1888** ROOSEVELT in *Century Mag.* April 849/2 More important than herding is 'trail' work. **1903** A. ADAMS *Log of Cowboy* 121 At this and lower trail crossings on Red River, the lives of more trail men were lost. *Ib.* 296 The cattle were well trail-broken.

* Trail, *v.*

+1. *tr.* (See quotation.)

1828 WEBSTER, *Trail,* . . . in *America,* to tread down grass by walking through; to lay flat; as, to *trail* grass.

+2. *intr.* To troll.

1857 TOMES *Amer. in Japan* 308 Another cluster of fishing-boats was . . . trailing for fish. *a*1862 THOREAU *Maine Woods* 176 My companion trailed for trout as we paddled along.

3. With adverbs. **+a.** *To trail in,* to go or come in. **b.** *To trail through,* (see quotation).

(a) **1875** *Fur, Fin & Feather* (ed. 3) 112/1 Light and drink; drop off and trail in. **1907** WHITE *Arizona Nights* 234 With exultant cackles of joy they'd trail in, reachin' out like quarter-horses. (b) **1906** *N.Y. Ev. Post* 27 Oct. Saturday Suppl. 1, I determined to have the sheep 'trailed through' to Nebraska, which, in Western parlance, means driving them overland.

+T rail. A railway rail, a section of which has the shape of a T. Also *fig.* — **1837** *Civil Engineer* I. 39/2 The pattern . . . is by American engineers called the inverted T rail. **1855** HOLBROOK *Among Mail Bags* 172 The locomotive of a mail train upon one of the Western railroads was thrown from the track by a 'T' rail. **1880** *Boston Soc. Nat. Hist. Memoirs* 14 The edge is rendered stiff by its shape, which in section is much like that of a T-rail of a railroad. **1883** *Century Mag.* Nov. 87 That is the sort of T-rail I am. That young gentleman voted agin me, on the ground I wasn't high-toned enough.

+Trail car. 'A street railway-car which is not furnished with motive power, but is designed to be pulled or trailed behind another to which the power is applied' (*Cent.*).

* Trailer.

+1. One skilled in following a trail; a guide or scout.

1855 SIMMS *Forayers* 252 He's the 'Trailer,' and a mighty good scout. **1870** KEIM *Sheridan's Troopers* 63 As an additional measure to secure success, by the employment of proper guides and trailers, the General opened negotiations with the Osage and Kaw tribes. **1894** *Outing* XXIV. 440/2 Another is a phenomenal trailer and reader of 'sign.' **1904** WHITE *Silent Places* 59 The expert trailers took pains to obliterate the most characteristic indications of their stay.

transf. **1890** DAVIS *Gallegher* 128 The 'trailer' for the green-goods men who rented room No. 8 in Case's tenement, had had no work to do for the last few days.

+2. a. = TRAIL CAR. {1900–} **b.** (See quotation.)

(a) **1890** *Columbus Dispatch* 5 Aug., The line is to start with five motor cars for winter service, with some 'trailers' for excursion business. (b) **1891** *Cent.* 6421/2 *Trailer,* . . . an old style of vessel employed in mackerel-fishing about 1800 . . . [having] outriggers or long poles on each side, . . . to the ends of which were fastened lines.

* Trailing, *a.* **+**In the specific names of plants.

1784 *Amer. Acad. Mem.* I. 413 *Cuscuta.* . . . Trailing Cockspur. . . . Borders of brooks and ditches. **1813** MUHLENBERG *Cat. Plants* 91 *Salix prostrata,* Trailing willow. *Ib.* 93 *Juniperus prostrata,* Trailing juniper. **1833** EATON *Botany* (ed. 6) 48 *Azalea procumbens,* trailing honeysuckle. Whitehills. **1840** DEWEY *Mass. Flowering Plants* 67 *L[espedeza] prostrata.* Trailing Clover. **1878** COOKE *Happy Dodd* 347 A profusion of trailing pine had been stored away in the barn cellar, before frost came. **1899** GOING *Flowers* 251 The lycopodiums, . . . under the names of 'ground-pine,' 'club-moss,' or 'trailing-evergreen,' are familiar to almost every one who has summered in New England. *Ib.* 269 Those cousins of the ferns which look so confusingly like evergreens . . . have received the names of 'ground-pine' and 'trailing-hemlock.'

+Trailing arbutus. The Mayflower or ground laurel, *Epigaea repens.* — **1785** MARSHALL *Amer. Grove* 42 Trailing Arbutus . . . grows naturally upon northern hills, or mountains. **1868** BEECHER *Norwood* 20 Pete, I want some trailing-arbutus; where does it blossom earliest? **1883** *Wheelman* I. 276 The trailing arbutus perfumed the air, and the wild pink blushed in the shadow. **1903** J. K. SMALL *Flora Southeastern U.S.* 890.

+Traill. =next. — **1891** *Cent.* 6421/2. **1892** TORREY *Foot-Path Way* 9 The phœbe-like cry of the traill was to be heard constantly from the hotel piazza.

+Traill's flycatcher. [T. S. *Traill,* British writer on scientific subjects (1781–1862).] A flycatcher (*Empidonax trailli*) of western North America. — **1831** AUDUBON *Ornith. Biog.* I. 236 Traill's Fly-Catcher. *Musicapa Traillii.* . . . This is a species . . . closely allied to the Wood Pewee. **1870** *Amer. Naturalist* IV. 539 Traill's Flycatcher . . . [is] a very restless, wild bird, remaining among the topmost branches of tall trees. **1917** *Birds of Amer.* II. 209/1 A variety of Traill's Flycatcher is found in eastern North America.

+T railroad iron. Iron used for T rails. — **1845** *Xenia Torch-Light* 4 Dec. 1/4 The usual T railroad iron, as imported into this country under the present tariff, costs not less than $2,000 per mile for the duty.

Trail rope. {1899} A rope tied to a horse and allowed to drag while the animal grazes. — **1848** PARKMAN in *Knickerb.* XXXI. 3 A long trail-rope was wound round poor Pauline's neck. **1851** M. REID *Scalp Hunters* xviii, We ran our animals out on their trail-ropes to feed.

* Train, *n.*

‖1. = TRAIN-BAND. *Obs.*

1713 *Boston News-Letter* 2 March 2/2 They are hereby Ordered . . . [to] apply themselves to Mr. Humphrey Huchenson Pay Master and Fire-worker to the Train here.

*2. *Mil.* A body of artillery with men, vehicles, and supplies; a supply outfit for an army unit.

See also BAGGAGE TRAIN.

1757 *Lett. to Washington* II. 94 A large Body of French and Indians, with a train of Artillery, were actually marched from Fort Du Quesne. *Ib.* 172 The Enemy Set down before Fort Wm. Henry with an Army . . . and train of 35 ps. of Cannon and six Mortars. **1849** *31st Congress 1 Sess.* Sen.

Ex. Doc. No. 64, 173 Our 'train,' consisting of eighteen wagons, one six-pounder iron gun and a travelling forge, each drawn by six mules. **1861** *Army Regulations* 110 The train of a division marches with the train of general head-quarters. **1881-5** McCLELLAN *Own Story* 551 [The army's] trains, administration services, and supplies were disorganized or lacking. **1887** CUSTER *Tenting on Plains* 16 The divisions of cavalry, . . . breaking the last line the enemy attempted to form, charged upon their artillery and trains.

*3. A number of wagons or pack animals proceeding in line. Now hist.

See also EMIGRANT TRAIN a, MULE TRAIN, PACK TRAIN.

1806 *N.Y. Ev. Post.* 7 Sept. 2 [He] had beaten his way from Syracuse to this city by 'trains and turnpike.' **1827** [see ROLLING PRAIRIE]. **1837** IRVING *Bonneville* I. 35 The unusual sight of a train of waggons, caused quite a sensation among these savages. **1847** *Santa Fe Repub.* 27 Nov. 2/4 Mr. McCarty . . . arrived . . . via Bent's Fort with a train for their house. **1857** DAVIS *El Gringo* 208 The train of pack-mules is generally led by a . . . *mulera;* the train is called an *atajo.* **1864** *Wkly. New Mexican* 27 May 2/2 Trains are daily arriving from the states heavily loaded with all kinds of dry goods. **1884** HARRIS *Mingo* 190 He was brought to the little village of Rockville in chains in a speculator's train, . . . consisting of two Conestoga wagons and thirty or forty forlorn-looking negroes. **1900** GOODLANDER *Fort Scott* 5 This freight would be . . . started out from there in regular trains of wagons hauled by oxen.

4. A number of railway cars, coupled together and usually drawn by an engine. {a1824-}

In early use freq. *train of cars.*

1833 *Niles' Reg.* XLIV. 99/1 Two engines are now in successful operation . . , and their continual passing and re-passing each other, with their trains of cars, . . . afford a spectacle at once highly novel and interesting. **1867** CRAWFORD *Mosby* 36 Volunteers from the Border and Gulf States were arriving by every train of cars. **1887** STOCKTON *Hundredth Man* viii, Mr. Crisman was coming in the evening train. **1907** *St. Nicholas* Aug. 920/2 What is it that enables a railroad bridge looking like a spider web to hold an enormously heavy locomotive and train?

+5. (See quot. 1848.)

1835 HOFFMAN *Winter in West* I. 178 At last a *train* and a couple of carioles drove up to the door. [**1848** BARTLETT 362 *Train,* . . . a peculiar kind of sleigh used for the transportation of merchandise, wood, &c., in Canada.]

6. Attrib. and comb. in sense 3. a. With *air signal, hold-up, load,* etc.

1876 *Ill. Dept. Agric. Trans.* XIII. 318 Strawberries and peaches began to go northward by the train load. **1898** *B. & M. R.R. Ann. Rep.* 10 (Ernst), All the Company's passenger cars and passenger locomotives have been equipped with the train air signal. **1903** KILDARE *My Mamie Rose* 176 The train-yard, where the freight trains were made up. **1904** 'O. HENRY' in *McClure's Mag.* April 611 His estimate of the pleasures of train robbing will hardly induce any one to adopt it as a profession. **1907** WHITE *Arizona Nights* 89 [He] was killed finally in the train hold-up of '97.

b. Designating persons employed on, or otherwise associated with, railroad trains.

See also TRAIN BOY, TRAIN-DISPATCHER, etc.

1879 STOCKTON *Rudder Grange* vii, The train-agent . . . began to declare that he would not have the fellow in his car. **1894** WISTER in *Harper's Mag.* Aug. 386/2 The train conductor, the Pullman conductor, the engineer, and fireman abandoned their duty. **1896** FREDERIC *Damnation of T. Ware* 265 The money that bought the vote was put up by the smartest and most famous train-gambler between Omaha and 'Frisco. **1903** ADE *In Babel* 347 Don't buy nothin' of the train butcher. **1904** 'O. HENRY' in *McClure's Mag.* April 617/1 As to the train crew, we never had any more trouble with them than if they had been so many sheep. **1910** RAINE *B. O'Connor* 11 The young woman in Section 3 had glimpsed a bevy of angry train officials. **1925** *Scribner's Mag.* Oct. 372/1 The Secretary, important as a train-starter, sat at a table under a huge white score-sheet.

.* Train, *v.*

+1. *intr.* To associate *with* (or *along of*). colloq.

1871 HAY *Pike Co. Ballads* 22 It gravels me like the devil to train Along o' sich fools as you. **1891** *Cent.* 6421/3. **1896** ADE *Artie* 180 Most o' them West Side boys I started in to train with got to be dead tough. **1907** *Methodist Rev.* Nov. 984 He does not train with the extreme radical theologians.

+2. *local.* To romp or 'carry on.'

1877 BARTLETT 717 Almost peculiar to girls in New England. 'She's an awful one to train.' **1889** HOWELLS *Hazard of New Fortunes* I. 205 Oh, I guess you love to train!

Train-band. A company of civilians trained for emergency military service. Now hist. {1630-}

1646 *Harvard Rec.* I. 26 Neither shall any without Licence of the overseers of the Colledge bee of the Artillery or traine-Band. **1683** *Boston Rec.* 162 One man out of each Compa. of the traines bands should take the care . . . of the water Engine. **1721** *New-Eng. Courant* 9 Oct. 2/2 The several Clerks of the Train-Bands made a Strict Enquiry at all the Houses within their respective Beats. **1788** BENTLEY *Diary* I. 194 The

Militia both Train band & Alarm list appeared this day. **1837** HAWTHORNE *Twice-told Tales* (1879) II. 217 The English colors were displayed by the standard-bearer of the Salem trainband.

Train boy. {1883} +A boy employed to sell candies, periodicals, etc., on a train. — **1869** *Atlantic Mo.* July 73/2 [He] prevailed upon me to be his train-boy. **1871** HOWELLS *Wedding Journey* 88 The train-boy . . . passed through on his many errands with prize candies, gum-drops, pop-corn, papers and magazines. **1883** 'MARK TWAIN' *Life on Miss.* xxix, Cheap histories of him were for sale by train-boys. **1899** MUIRHEAD *Baedeker's U.S.* p. xx, The incessant visitation of the train-boy . . . renders a quiet nap almost impossible.

+Train-dispatcher. A railroad official who issues orders controlling the movements of trains. — **1857** *Mich. Gen. Statutes* I. (1882) 863 No person shall be employed as an engineer, train dispatcher, fireman, . . . or other servant upon any railroad . . . who uses intoxicating drinks. **1887** *Courier-Journal* 7 May 5/3 He will have control of all train dispatchers and operators on the line. **1890** *Opelousas* (La.) *Democrat* 8 Feb. 2/5 A train dispatcher . . . never gets a chance to be romantic. **1910** HART *Vigilante Girl* 376 The man . . . filled the manifold offices of station-master, . . . train-despatcher, and telegrapher.

Traineau. Also **traino.** A sledge drawn by animals. {1676-} — **1835** [see JUMPER¹ 1]. **1838** INGRAHAM *Burton* I. 96 Neither *burline, traineau,* nor *carriole* can move the length of a rosary till the road is somewhat broken up by heavy sleds. **1899** CATHERWOOD *Mackinac Stories* 55, I have brought the mail . . . with my traino—you know the train-au-galise —the birch sledge with dogs.

*Trained band. *Obs.* =TRAIN-BAND. — **1637** *Dedham Rec.* III. 30 Abraham Shawe Clarke of our trayned band Daniell Morse Sariant, & Philemon Dalton are apoynted. **1683** *N.J. Archives* 1 Ser. XIII. 75 The Bill for setleing the Train'd Bands or Militia . . . was presented to the Governor and Councill. **1720** D. NEAL *Hist. New-Eng.* I. 142 The Trained Bands were divided, some refusing to follow the Colours which had a Cross.

Trained nurse. A nurse who has completed a course of training. {trained hospital nurse, 1899} — **1888** *Boston Jrnl.* 15 Sept. 2/4, I'm one of the leading trained nurses of New Orleans. **1907** *St. Nicholas* May 594/1 Mrs. Sims . . . [had] been a teacher herself out in Indiana before she came to New York to be a trained nurse. **1922** TARKINGTON *Gentle Julia* 59 She was joined by her invalid sister, Aunt Harriet, with a trained nurse.

* Trainer.

*1. A member of a train-band. Now hist. {1581-2}

1841 *Knickerb.* XVII. 276 The gentler sex . . . exhibit their patriotism . . . by unwearied running after the 'trainers.' **1848** BARTLETT 362 *Trainers,* the militia when assembled for exercise. **1855** BARNUM *Life* 21 No sooner did I hear the words 'halt,' 'ground arms,' than I approached the 'trainers' with my decanter.

2. One who trains animals for contests. {1659-}

1868 WOODRUFF *Trotting Horse* 115 The flat-race trainers first began to fit horses for steeple-chase running. **1883** *Harper's Mag.* Aug. 342/2 The success of Mr. Lorillard's horse is to be attributed in no small degree to his American trainer, Pincas. **1893** [see RUBBER 2].

3. One who trains athletes.

1904 *McClure's Mag.* April 659/1 He was a prize-fighter out for his morning run with his trainer.

Train hand. A man, as a brakeman, employed on a train. {1894} — **1883** *Harper's Mag.* Aug. 458/1 She could learn nothing from the train hands. **1898** *McClure's Mag.* X. 358 There was no one with me except the train hands and the engineer. **1902** MACGOWAN *Last Word* 15 The various train-hands . . . were called in.

* Training. Military drill required of civilians; a general muster for such drill.

See also GENERAL TRAINING.

1624 [see GENERAL MUSTER]. **1641** *Mass. Bay Rec.* I. 332 Mr. Tynge, the Treasurer, is freed from ordinary trainings. **1744** *N.J. Archives* 1 Ser. VI. 195 The Captain may deliver out such Arms, &c. at the time of Training, as are in his Charge. **1819** FLINT *Lett. from Amer.* 175 The officers of the United States' Militia . . . attend trainings, voluntarily and gratuitously. **1857** *Quinland* I. 102 Never had he seen a training, to which his father and the neighbours were obliged to go every year. **1894** ROBINSON *Danvis Folks* 145 Captain Peck . . . in his biggest military voice, usually reserved for trainings, gave the order.

b. Attrib. and comb. with *band, close, clothes,* etc.

1667 *Charlestown Land Rec.* 165 Nine pole and three foote . . . reaches to the trayning close. **1684** *Plymouth Rec.* I. 179 Soe to the northerly end of the training green. **1706** SEWALL *Diary* II. 162 Col. Noyes invites me to his Training Dinner. **1792** BELKNAP *Hist. New-Hampshire* III. 286 Men capable of bearing arms, from forty to sixty years of age, and who are exempted from the training band, are called the alarm list. **1843** STEPHENS *High Life N.Y.* II. 149 A hull swad of fellers, some on 'em in training clothes, and some on 'em with cocked hats on, went into a leetle room.

Training camp. A camp in which men are trained for military service; a camp at which athletes train in preparation for contests. Also attrib. — **1894** ALDRICH *Two Bites* 216, I don't fancy he heard a gun fired, unless it went off by accident in some training-camp for recruits. **1913** LONDON *Valley of Moon* 405 They would . . . rub each other down in training camp style.

Training day. The day on which training or general muster took place. Now hist. {1676-} Also attrib.

1633 *Mass. Bay Rec.* I. 109 Any trained solder . . . absent from traineing, vpon their traineing dayes, . . . shall forfect Vs. **1677** *Huntington Rec.* I. 229 Being a Training daye apoynted and Consented vnto By the whole Companie. **1704** S. KNIGHT *Journal* 39 Their Diversions . . . are on Lecture dayes and Training days mostly. **1787** TYLER *Contrast* III. i, He was afraid of . . . shooting irons, such as your troopers wear on training days. **1825** [see GO-TO-MEETING a. 2]. **1856** GOODRICH *Recoll.* I. 86 The two great festivals [in Conn. c1800] were Thanksgiving and 'trainingday'—the latter deriving, from the still lingering spirit of the revolutionary war, a decidedly martial character. **1878** COOKE in *Harper's Mag.* Sept. 578/1 As for . . . training-day gingerbread, and pot-pie, she was simply wonderful.

+**Training field.** The field on which training was performed, freq., Boston Common. *Obs.* — **1670** *Charlestown Land Rec.* 187 From Shepie into the Training field, the way is Eleven foot. **1713** *Duxbury Rec.* 219 He will grant as much of his land to the town of Duxbury, . . . to be a perpetual Common for a training field. **1776** [see GUN HOUSE]. **1800** *Mass. H. S. Coll.* 1 Ser. VI. 235 They assigned as a training field, what is now called the Common.

Training ground. =prec. *Obs.* {1864-} — **1644** *Dedham Rec.* III. 108 Granted to the Feofees for ye free School in Dedham . . . a percell of the Training ground. **1845** *Knickerb.* XXVI. 367, I was on the trainingground again. **1857** *Quinland* I. 118 They arrived at the 'training ground.'

Training place. {1884} =TRAINING FIELD. *Obs.* — **1638** *Watertown Rec.* I. 1. 5 The two Faires at Watertowne . . . shalbe Kept upon the Trayning Place. **1669** *Boston Rec.* 48 The select men [shall] assigne a place for a house lot for him . . . , prouided it be noe place of ye Common or training place.

Training school. A school in which students are given special training, usually of a vocational or technical character. {1829-} Also fig. — **1870** 'F. FERN' *Ginger-Snaps* 168 'A good mistress' . . . is yet perfectly seraphic at the idea of being at the head of a training-school for servants, the remainder of her natural life. **1882** *Nation* 30 Nov. 463/3 Teachers' training-schools should be managed in a somewhat more liberal spirit than most of them at present are. **1885** *Rep. Indian Affairs* 8 They should be sent to those training-schools so distant that they would not likely attempt to run away. **1894** WARNER *Golden House* xx, The greater part of his property . . . was to go to endow a vast training-school, library, and reading-room on the East Side.

Training ship. A ship on which boys are trained for naval service. {c1860-} — **1890** *Congress. Rec.* 5 Aug. 8170/1 The Monongahela is now . . . being repaired for a training-ship. **1907** *St. Nicholas* July 812/2 After serving for many years as a training-ship, she is reduced to the humble duty of store-ship at Guantanamo.

+**Training table.** The table at which members of an athletic team eat while in training. Also attrib. — **1893** POST *Harvard Stories* 260 He hardly talks at all at the training table. **1897** *McClure's Mag.* X. 167 He had declined the training-table dinner and a half-dozen other invitations. **1903** ADE *People You Know* 59 We keep about 40 at the Training Table all of the time.

Train man.

1. A member of a train-band. *Obs.* {1654}

1642 *Conn. Rec.* I. 75 The Clarke . . . shall giue in to the deputyes . . . an exacte list of all the Trayne men.

+**2.** (*Trainman.*) A man employed on a railway train; any member of a train crew.

1877 McCABE *Hist. Great Riots* 48 These motives have been misunderstood, and in a great degree produced the present troubles amongst our trainmen. **1892** GUNTER *Miss Dividends* 60, I saw a dozen trainmen . . . on the platform. **1905** RICE *Sandy* 283 A trainman out at the Junction gave us a clue.

+**Train master.**

1. The man in general charge of a wagon train. Now hist. **1860** GREELEY *Overland Journey* 52 How can a competent train-master . . . overlook the policy of this? **1883** *Rep. Indian Affairs* 314 The last train numbered sixty-nine wagons and the same number of Indian drivers, with one white train-master. **1890** LANGFORD *Vigilante Days* (1912) 352 'We have none to spare,' said the train master.

2. The railroad official in charge of train operations on a division or subdivision of a line.

1880 *Cimarron News & Press* 9 Sept. 3/2 Mr. Frank Fulton, train master on this Division, . . . gave the following information concerning the damage. **1900** *Everybody's Mag.* II. 586/2 The train-master opens the door and announces that the train will arrive in five minutes. **1907** *N.Y. Ev. Post* (s.-w. ed.) 21 Jan. 4 The trainmasters . . . superintend the trainmen.

*Train oil. Oil obtained from whales or fish.

1637 MORTON *New Canaan* 87 Greate store of traine oyle is mayd of the livers of the Codd. **1686** [see FISH OIL]. **1742** *Md. Hist. Mag.* XX. 179 Send me six Barrels of Good Blubber and Two Barrells of Train Oil. **1824** *New Eng. Farmer* II. 353 Some people have recommended the application of *train oil* to the tree. c**1866** BAGBY *Old Va. Gentleman* 47 Drinking train-oil does not necessarily turn a man into an Eskimo.

+**Train-robber.** One who robs trains or the passengers on trains. — **1887** *Courier-Journal* 21 Jan. 5/6 A Crank or a Train-robber? **1894** *Scribner's Mag.* May 605/1 The mantle of charity might be stretched enough

to cover the ex-train-robber. **1908** 'O. HENRY' *Options* 52 It wouldn't be at all a disingenuous idea for a train-robber to run down into this part of the country to hide.

Train shed. A structure covering railroad tracks, usually at a station. — [**1892** *Pall Mall Gaz.* 21 Nov. 7/3 The great iron and glass portal [in Phila.] . . . will constitute the most extensive railway train-shed in existence.] **1898** *Boston Herald* 12 Aug. 4/7 (Ernst), A number of passenger cars were shunted into the trainshed. **1922** TARKINGTON *Gentle Julia* 350 A clanging and commotion in the train-shed outside . . . stirred him from his torpor.

Train time. The time at which a train is scheduled to leave or to arrive. {1892} — **1877** ROE *Army Lett.* 163 From then on to train time, Hal was patted and petted and given dainties. **1902** 'O. HENRY' *Roads of Destiny* 158 At ten minutes to train time every man was at his post.

Train-wrecker. One who wrecks, or attempts to wreck, a railroad train. {train-wrecking, 1885} — **1887** GEORGE *40 Yrs. on Rail* 84 My experience with trainwreckers has been limited. **1909** [see DERAIL v.].

*** Trammel.** An implement used in a fireplace to support pots and other vessels used in cooking.

Now local *Eng.* and *U.S.* (*O.E.D.*).

1639 *Conn. Rec.* I. 444 A Inventory [includes] . . . Tramels, tongs, fier pan, bellowes. **1703** *N.H. Probate Rec.* I. 502, I give unto Mary my Beloved Wife, . . . my best Iron Pot, Iron Kettle, tromell. **1783** E. PARKMAN *Diary* 300 Tramels and Hooks in ye Kitchen. **1861** STOWE *Pearl Orr's Island* I. 56 Those were the days of the genial open kitchen fire, with the crane, the pot-hooks, and trammels. **1889** COOKE *Steadfast* 13 Pothooks and trammels hung from nails in the chimney corners.

attrib. **1641** *Essex Probate Rec.* I. 14 One trevet, a tramell chayne, 5s. **1735** J. HEMPSTEAD *Diary* 296 The Trammel Stick . . . slipt off the Cross Barr & spilt a pot of boyling water.

Tramp, *n.* One who tramps about seeking work; an idle, thieving vagrant who goes from place to place. {1664-} — **1875** *Chicago Tribune* 1 Sept. 4/6 Recent accurate estimates place the number of 'tramps,' or wandering, idle, vicious characters, in the State of Massachusetts at 40,000(?). **1891** in B. S. Heath *Labor & Finance Revol.* p. xxiii, For the first time in our national history [i.e., in 1873], we heard of the tramp! **1925** BRYAN *Memoirs* 96, [I was] defeated in a thesis contest by a classmate who had once been a tramp.

*** Tramp,** *v. tr.* To thresh (wheat) by having horses or oxen trample upon it. Also with *out. Obs.* — **1855** T. D. PRICE *Diary* (MS.) 13 Sept., Tramped 8 doz. [sheaves] of wheat. **1860** *Ib.* 17 Aug., Threshed out wheat with horses, tramped out 15 doz. for seed. **1900** HANDSAKER *Pioneer Life* 30 We were all engaged in threshing grain by 'tramping' it out with horses and oxen.

+**Trampage.** Tramping; the habit or condition of a tramp. — **1894** *Advance* 3 May (*O.E.D.*), A menace, a nuisance all along the line of their trampage. **1897** *Plantation Missionary* (Oberlin, O.) Dec., The poor [may be] rescued from pauperism, trampage and crime.

+**Trampdom.** The state or condition of a tramp or tramps; the domain or sphere of tramps. — **1895** *Century Mag.* Oct. 945/1 The love of liquor brings more men and women into trampdom than anything else. **1896** *Pop. Science Mo.* L. 253 There is another class . . . who would be placed on the border land of trampdom.

Trampish-looking, *a.* Having the appearance of a tramp. — **1890** *N.Y. Sun* Feb., The depot policeman was shoving a trampish-looking man out of the place. **1895** *Ram's Horn* (Chicago) 25 May 10/3 Seven trampish looking men went forward to seek Christ.

||**Trampoose,** *n.* A tramp or trudge. *Obs.* — **1840** COOPER *Pathfinder* I. 118, I was with him in one of his trampooses.

+**Trampoose,** *v.* [Of obscure origin.] **1.** *intr.* To tramp or trudge about. *slang. Obs.* **2.** *tr.* To traverse or trudge through. *slang. Obs.* — (1) **1725** *New-Eng. Courant* 22 Feb. 1/2 It would save the latter the Toil and Disgrace of trampoosing thro' all the Streets and Lanes in the Town to sell their Pork, Butter, Eggs. **1815** HUMPHREYS *Yankey* 160, I landed near to Dover, and seed such strange sights, trampoosing Ingland over. **1845** *Big Bear Ark.* 44 So we trampoosed along down the edge of the swamp. (2) **1828** ROYALL *Black Book* II. 287 The ladies and myself trampoozed the whole of it. **1845** S. SMITH *J. Downing's Lett.* 37 The next morning . . . I trampoosed the city from one end to 'tother.

+**Trampoosing.** Tramping or trudging about. *slang. Obs.* {tramboozing, 1798} — **1840** HOFFMAN *Greyslaer* II. 30 What good has it done us, all this trampoosing and paddling hither and thither in this eternal wilderness? **1842** *S. Lit. Messenger* VIII. 146/2 With their trampoosing through the woods, and their 'fire hunts,' . . . it would have taken a regiment of sentinels to check the stragglers. **1866** *Harper's Mag.* June 136/2 He gave vent to the wish that . . . [they would] 'put a stop to this eternal trampoosin.'

Tramp printer. A printer who goes from place to place, never working long in any one job. {1895-} — **1873** *Newton Kansan* 20 March 3/2 A tramp printer and dead beat of the deepest dye, registered here as T. W. Ritchie, from Missouri. **1878** PINKERTON *Strikers* 55 Probably one of the greatest night rendezvous for tramp-printers in this country is at the Battery, in New York city. **1898** [see FREE LUNCH].

Tramway. {1825-} +A system of transportation consisting essentially of a cable or cables from which cars are suspended. — **1870** *Overland Monthly* Dec. 516/2 The ore extracted from the Brown is brought down on an aerial tramway. **1871** RAYMOND *3d Rep. Mines* 318 All the ore will be sent to the base of the mountain by the tram-way.

+**Trans-Alleg(h)anian,** *n.* and *a.* **1.** *n.* One dwelling west of the Allegheny Mts. *Obs.* **2.** *adj.* Situated or lying west of the Allegheny Mts. — (1) **1774** J. ADAMS *Diary Works* II. 401, I went to the Baptist Church, and heard a trans-Alleghanian, a preacher from the back parts of Virginia. **1794** JEFFERSON *Writings* VI. (1895) 516 Make friends with the trans-Alleghanians. (2) **1814** *Ann. 13th Congress* 1 Sess. 1422 Even then the trans-Alleganean wilderness was rustling with the preparation of the savage. **1826** MITCHILL *Discourse on Jefferson* 25 The order of an intendant [at New Orleans] had . . . thrown our citizens inhabiting the trans-alleghanian lands into serious alarm.

+Trans-Alleghany. *attrib.* Designating regions situated west of the Allegheny Mts. — **1838** *S. Lit. Messenger* IV. 294 The trans-alleghany country thus appears to have been the city of refuge of those early times. **1873** *Harper's Mag.* March 572/2 The subdivision adopted in the revision of the Constitution of Virginia in 1829-30 into the Trans-Alleghany, Valley, Middle, and Tide-water districts proved a fertile source of discontent.

Transatlantic, *a.* {1779–} +Coming from, situated in, or pertaining to, a region beyond the Atlantic as viewed from the United States. — **1782** JEFFERSON *Writings* III. (1894) 193 To suggest a doubt . . . whether nature has enlisted herself as a cis- or trans-Atlantic partisan. **1809** IRVING *Knickerb.* I. v, The trans-atlantic visitors acquired an incontrovertable [*sic*] property therein. **1843** *Knickerb.* XXI. 54 We are like our trans-atlantic neighbors. **1891** *Harper's Wkly.* 19 Sept. 705/1 The aristocrats [of Salem] were proud of their transatlantic ancestries.

+Transboard, *v. tr.* To transfer from one ship to another. *Obs.* — **1807** BARLOW *Columbiad* 38 Barks after barks the captured seamen bear, Transboard and lodge thy silent visitors there. **1899** *Scribner's Mag.* July 69/1 The boat . . . for this [postal] service . . . is equipped with spacious mail-rooms, chutes for transboarding sacks [etc.].

Transcendental, *a.* {1668–} Transcending experience. {1798–} Used esp. of the New England school of philosophic thought of which Brook Farm (1841-47) was the outgrowth. Also *absol.* — **1842** EMERSON *Miscellanies* 329 It is well known . . . that the Idealism of the present day acquired the name of Transcendental, from the use of that term by Immanuel Kant. **1883** *Harper's Mag.* July 307/1 The Transcendental illumination died away into the light of common day. **1887** CABOT *Memoirs Emerson* I. 248 The transcendental was whatever lay beyond the stock notions and traditional beliefs to which adherence was expected because they were generally accepted by sensible persons.

Transcendentalism. {1803–} +The teaching or philosophy of Emerson and others who regarded the interrogation of the subjective consciousness as the best approach to the study of objective realities. — **1838** in W. P. & F. J. Garrison *W. L. Garrison* II. 204 The Unitarian . . . calls it Transcendentalism. The Calvinist . . . calls it Perfectionism. **1841** *Niles Nat. Reg.* LX. 240/3 Transcendentalism is making quite a sensation in some places. **1876** *N. Amer. Rev.* Oct. 468 Boston and its immediate neighborhood . . . really made up the kingdom ruled by Transcendentalism. **1887** CABOT *Memoirs Emerson* I. 248 The Boston or New England Transcendentalism had . . . no very direct connection with the transcendental philosophy of Germany.

Transcendentalist. {1803–} +An adherent of New England transcendentalism. — **1838** LONGFELLOW in S. Longfellow *H. W. Longfellow* I. 306 He is something of a Transcendentalist, and a friend of Emerson. **1842** DICKENS *Amer. Notes* 26 There has sprung up, in Boston, a sect of philosophers known as Transcendentalists. **1893** *Harper's Mag.* May 849/1 [Lowell] shared in the efforts of the Transcendentalists to enlarge the bounds of spiritual freedom.

Transcontinental, *a.* That extends or passes across a continent. {1883–, in Australia} Also *fig.* — **1853** *Harper's Mag.* Feb. 550/2 A company, embracing the wealthiest of New York capitalists, [was proposed] to construct a trans-continental railroad. **1880** *Cimarron News & Press* 3 June 2/5 This line and the St. Louis and San Francisco . . . have provided for building the remaining portion of the great trans-continental line. **1889** 'MARK TWAIN' *Conn. Yankee* 279 She pulled out . . . and got her train fairly started on one of those horizonless transcontinental sentences of hers. **1900** *Congress. Rec.* 23 Jan. 1104/1 About this time, the fall of 1861, the transcontinental telegraph line reached Salt Lake. **1910** J. HART *Vigilante Girl* 368 The transcontinental railway was making the first of the gigantic leaps by which it was to cross mighty mountain ranges and span the continent.

Transfer. {1674–}
+1. *ellipt.* =TRANSFER TOBACCO. *Obs.*
1800 TATHAM *Tobacco* 80 All under that weight are considered to be *transfer*, or parcels which may be transferred to make full hogsheads.

+2. A ferry boat for trains. In full *transfer boat.*
1882 *Uncle Rufus & Ma* 52 We ferried over in a transfer-boat, and in due time arrived at the Town of Mandan, D.T. **1883** RITTENHOUSE *Maud* 187 It was a delightful trip—the sun was just coming up as we crossed the river on the transfer. [**1888** *Daily News* (London) 10 Dec. 6/8 The transfer boat Maryland was conveying a section of a train from Washington to Boston across the Haarlem River, at midnight.]

+3. A ticket given with or without extra cost to a passenger on a street car or other medium of transportation, entitling him to change to another conveyance and continue his journey on another route. Also *fig.*
1892 S. HALE *Letters* 269, I mounted a cable, took a transfer [etc.]. **1901** G. ADE *40 Modern Fables* 46 If she wanted that kind of an Article around the House she had better pull the Rope and ask for a Transfer. **1908** 'YESLAH' *Tenderfoot S. Calif.* 81 He'll . . . tell her to ask for her transfer when she pays her fare.

+4. A certificate enabling a pupil to transfer from one school to another.
1911 PERSONS, etc. *Mass. Labor Laws* 199 He presented a transfer from the East Boston parochial school.

+5. *attrib.* and *comb.* **a.** Designating a check or draft drawn by the Secretary of the Treasury at the time of the removal of public funds to state banks by President Jackson. *Obs.*
1834 C. A. DAVIS *Lett. J. Downing* 213 The game they had been playin most at latterly was . . . showin how to use the '*transfer checks*' and '*contingent drafts*,' so as to puzzle folks in time and need. **1834** BENTON *30 Years' View* I. 409/1 The difference between a transfer draft and a treasury warrant was a thing necessary to be known by every man.

+b. Designating vehicles used in transferring passengers and goods to and from railway stations, or persons employed in this work.
1870 MEDBERY *Men Wall St.* 167 [In] theatrical and operatic magnificences, in ferry-boats and transfer-coaches, . . . Mr. Fisk has obtained a splendor of reputation which will make him forever memorable. **1892** GUNTER *Miss Dividends* 48 He almost misses the last transfer omnibus. **1899** ADE *Fables in Slang* 188 He would be arranging for her Baggage with the Transfer Man. **1909** *Forward* (Phila.) 2 Oct. 317 In the place stood a depot hack with an omnibus behind, and a transfer wagon on the other side.

+Transfer company. A draying company, esp. one that transfers passengers, trunks, etc., to and from railway stations. — **1896** *N.Y. Dramatic News* 18 July 4/2 It will give the names of all the . . . transfer companies. **1901** RYAN *Montana* 86 When a reliable man was needed by the transfer company . . . , it was Overton to whom was given the responsibility. **1908** *N.Y. Ev. Post* 4 Aug. 2 The wagons of the transfer companies are lined up on the outside, delivering more trunks.

+Transfer note. A note, serviceable in commercial transactions, issued to a tobacco planter for tobacco deposited in a warehouse. *Obs.* — **1748** *Md. Gazette* 23 Nov., He will . . . furnish each Inspection in the respective counties with Transfer Notes. **1784** SMYTH *Tour* II. 138 The last [bad tobacco] is immediately committed to the flames, and for the first [good tobacco] he receives a Transfer note, specifying the weight, quality, &c.

+Transfer ticket. =TRANSFER 3. — **1861** *Mass. Acts & Resolves* 521 The city of Boston . . . shall establish the terms and conditions on which commutation transfer, or exchange tickets shall be issued. **1900** *Everybody's Mag.* II. 192/1 The object of the remarkable transfer ticket of which we give a photograph is the proper identification of the holder, to prevent the abuse of the transfer privilege.

+Transfer tobacco. (See quot. 1800.) *Obs.* — **1740** *Va. State P.* I. 234 The said Anderson is very much Involved in debt, and . . . the Transfer Tobacco will be subject to the Discharge thereof. **1800** TATHAM *Tobacco* 84 *Transfer* tobacco is that collection in leaf, bundle, or hand, which arises from the aggregate stock of remnants which remain from hogsheads that are reduced by wastage and refusal beneath the standard weight of . . . what is commonly termed, a *crop*, hogshead.

Transfusionist. One who believes in or practices blood transfusion. — **1889** *Pop. Science Mo.* April 808 The early transfusionists reasoned . . . that the blood is the life.

Transient, *n.* {1652–}
+1. One who passes through a place; one who stays at a hotel or boarding house for a short time only.
1748 in Earle *Curious Punishments* 41 The officer shall take the said transient forthwith to some public place in this town and . . . whyp him twenty strypes well layd on his naked back. **1877** HOWELLS *Out of Question* 28 This is the parlour of the 'transients,' as they call them,—the occasional guests. **1897** — *Landlord at Lion's Head* 70 When the farm became a boarding-house, . . . people paid ten dollars a week, or twelve for transients. **1917** MCCUTCHEON *Green Fancy* 289 Three or four 'transients,' had great cause for complaint about the service.

+2. A steamboat not belonging to a regular line or not having a fixed route.
1893 'MARK TWAIN' *P. Wilson* i, The big Orleans liners stopped for hails only, or to land passengers or freight; and this was the case also with the great flotilla of 'transients.'

Transient, *a.* {1607–}
+1. Of a guest at a hotel or boarding house: Staying for a short time.
1818 FEARON *Sketches* 44 Boarding at a moderately respectable house is 8 dollars a week, for what is termed 'a transient man.' **1851** *Knickerb.* XXXVIII. 179 [Hamilton House] has been crowded by delighted boarders, permanent and transient. **1887** WARNER *Their Pilgrimage* vi, Occasionally transient guests appear with flash manners. **1906** *Springfield W. Republican* 9 Aug. 16 They will then rent apartments with or without board to transient and permanent guests.

+b. *transf.* Designated or designed for those wishing hotel accommodations for a brief period.
1884 'CRADDOCK' *Where Battle was Fought* 40 The 'elevator boy' knew the number of Estwicke's room on the transient floor. **1891** *Fur, Fin, &*

Feather 185/1 The transient rate for travelers at the Hilsabeck Hotel in Springfield is $1 a day. **1903** *N.Y. Ev. Post* 19 Oct. 3 Charles F. Rogers will build a 12-story transient hotel at E. 27th Street.

+**2.** Of newspapers or other printed matter: Not mailed regularly or in quantities, as by the publishers, but occasionally and individually.

1841 *Lowell Offering* I. 245 The clerk asked her if it was a transient paper. **1852** *Harper's Mag.* V. 693/1 The postage on all transient matter must be prepaid by stamps or otherwise. **1857** *Ib.* Feb. 403/1 The prepayment of postage on transient printed matter has been made compulsory.

+**Transient advertisement.** A newspaper advertisement that appears for a short time only. Also *transient advertising.* — **1857** *Lawrence* (Kansas) *Republican* 28 May 1 All transient advertisements must be paid for in advance. **1868** *Ore. State Jrnl.* 8 June 1/1 Legal and Transient Advertising. For first insertion, Three Dollars per square. **1904** *Friends' Intelligencer* (Phila.) 15 Oct. p. ii, For transient advertisements, 5 cents per line. For longer insertion reduced rates.

+**Transisthmian,** *a.* Crossing or extending across an isthmus, esp. the isthmus of Panama. {1902} — **1885** CLEVELAND in *Pres. Mess. & P.* VIII. 328 The construction of three transcontinental lines of railway . . . has been accompanied by results . . . [which] increase our interests in any transisthmian route which may be opened. **1899** *Boston Jrnl.* 28 Nov. 4/1 Senator Frye's long and earnest advocacy of an American transisthmian canal is now very near its fulfillment.

*Transit. 1.** An instrument used by surveyors for measuring horizontal angles. {1843-} Also attrib. 2. (See quotation.) — (1) **1800** EL-LICOTT *Journal* App. 45 We had . . . a transit and equal altitude instrument. **1860** *Harper's Mag.* Feb. 291/2 There was a tent, a tripod, a compass, and a transit. **1880** *Cimarron News & Press* 18 March 3/2 Mr. Warner has been on the A. T. & S. Fe surveys through Arizona, as transitman. **1891** *Cent.* 6432/2 Most transits read only to the nearest minute of arc. (2) **1895** E. CARROLL *Principles Finance* 303 Transit, a custom-house warrant or pass.

+**Trans-Mississippi.** The region beyond the Mississippi as viewed from the eastern states. Also attrib. — **1883** *Century Mag.* Nov. 142/1 If the President was to attempt to reach the Trans-Mississippi at all, . . . he should move on at once. **1885** [see ADDITION 2]. **1900** *Congress. Rec.* 5 Feb. 1527/1 If [Jefferson] . . . had not been [president in 1803] we never would have had the trans-Mississippi country.

+**Trans-Missouri,** *a.* Lying, extending, or operating west of the Missouri River. — **1883** *Harper's Mag.* Nov. 943/2 Statistics show a well-ascertained increase of moisture in the trans-Missouri country. **1897** *Chicago Ev. Post* 15 May, The chairman . . . at once called a meeting of the transmissouri lines, to be held at St. Louis next Wednesday. **1903** E. JOHNSON *Railway Transportation* 244 Agreements [were] entered into . . . by the roads which formed the Trans-Missouri Freight Association.

*Transom.** +**1.** A window above a door. +**2.** A seat at the side of a cabin or stateroom aboard a ship. — (1) **1880** HEALY *Lett. & Leaders* I. 141 Get a step ladder to reach over the 'transom.' **1897** [see FANLIGHT 1]. **1908** LORIMER *J. Spurlock* 16 Sappho . . . tried to climb over the transom. (2) **1851** MELVILLE *Moby Dick* 88 To my astonishment, he sat down again on the transom very quietly. **1883** CRAWFORD *Dr. Claudius* ix, He sat down on the transom.

Transparency. A device, inscription, picture, etc., illuminated by a light placed behind it {1807-}, formerly carried in political processions or used for advertising purposes.

1813 *Niles' Reg.* V. 145/1 On this occasion some very elegant and appropriate transparencies were exhibited. **1840** *Niles' Nat. Reg.* 9 May 154/1 In front of the transparency was painted a likeness of general Harrison. **1863** TAYLOR *H. Thurston* 217 Transparencies gleamed before ice-cream saloons, and gas-lamps burned brilliantly at the corners. **1875** *Chicago Tribune* 8 Oct. 5/2 A vast procession . . . moved through the principal streets with banners, and transparencies, and wagons, in which were represented the leading departments of manufactures. **1894** [see LOTTERY OFFICE]. **1902** WHITLOCK *13th District* 159 There was a company of railroad men—at least their transparencies said they were railroad men—wearing overalls, and swinging lighted lanterns.

*Transpire,** *v.* +*intr.* To occur or happen. {1810-} — **1775** A. ADAMS *Familiar Lett.* 91 There is nothing new transpired since I wrote you last. **1805** CLARK in *Lewis & C. Exped.* II. (1904) 127 Nothing remarkable had transpired at camp in my absence. **1806** LEWIS in *L. & Clark Exped.* IV. (1905) 24 Nothing transpired today worthy of notice. **1850** N. KINGSLEY *Diary* 163 The place will seem odd . . . when you return to see the changes that have transpired. **1871** BURROUGHS *Wake-Robin* (1886) 75 On a bank of club-moss, . . . I recline to note what transpires.

Transplanter. (See quotations.) {1855-} — **1828** WEBSTER, *Transplanter,* . . . a machine for transplanting trees. **1909** *Cent. Suppl.* 1370/1 Transplanter, a horse-power machine used in setting out tobacco or other field plants.

*Transportation.**

+**1. a.** Means of conveyance. **b.** The cost or expenses of transport. **c.** (See quot. 1909.)

1853 McCONNEL *Western Char.* 163 He furnished his own 'transportation,' and selected his own encampment. **1890** *Wis. Hist. Soc. Prospectus,* Upon any gift to the Society, transportation will be cheerfully paid. **1894** *Outing* XXIV. 234/2 Transportation is furnished for the horses of mounted officers. **1909** *Cent. Suppl.* 1370/2 Transportation, . . . railway tickets or other permits for travelling.

+**2.** *attrib.* Designating persons, things, etc., having to do with conveying persons or things from one place to another.

1819 QUITMAN in Claiborne *Life Quitman* I. 36, I went to the agent of a train of transportation-wagons. **1823** in McKenney *Memoirs* I. 299 About nine years ago, I was appointed transportation agent for the United States at St. Louis. **1862** *Harper's Mag.* Sept. 561/2 On Monday . . . the last of our army, with the transportation train, crossed the White Oak swamp. **1883** GOODE *Fishery Industries U.S.* 67 The use of steamships and steam machinery; the construction of refrigerating transportation cars, . . . are forms of activity only attainable by government aid. **1887** GEORGE *40 Years on Rail* 56 Dunlap was assistant superintendent, or what was then called transportation-master. **1905** *N.Y. Ev. Post* 25 Jan. 7 If the transportation interests can induce Mr. Roosevelt to withdraw his idea of an extra session, the victory will be with them.

*Trap,** *n.*[1]

*1.** Any one of various devices for catching and, frequently, killing animals.

See also BEAR-TRAP 1, BEAVER TRAP, etc.; also STEEL TRAP. *Smart as a steel trap,* (see SMART *a.* 2).

1633 *Plymouth Laws* 33 [A bounty shall not be given] except to such as . . . shall set themselves by traps or other engines to take the [wolves]. **1654** JOHNSON *Wonder-w. Prov.* 225 Bever, Otter, and Moose they catch with Traps also. **1780** *Narragansett Hist. Reg.* I. 175 Fixed my cage traps. **1807** GASS *Journal* 26 One of our men went to visit some traps he had set. **1847** RUXTON *Adv. Rocky Mts.* (1848) 235 The beaver . . . very foolishly puts his leg into the trap, and is a 'gone beaver.' **1918** MULFORD *Man from Bar-20* 23, I was just as happy as a bobcat in a trap.

2. A light carriage on springs. {1806-7-}

1773 in J. L. Peyton *Adv. Grandfather* (1867) 28 Fetch these in your 'trap.' **1894** FORD *P. Stirling* 18 Watts was promptly bestowed on the front seat of the trap. **1912** NICHOLSON *Hoosier Chron.* 187, I gathered up a beautiful two-seated trap with a driver.

+**3.** =TRAP NET.

1888 GOODE *Amer. Fishes* 216 The Tunny is taken in large nets, . . . similar in many respects to the so-called 'traps' of Seconnet River in Rhode Island. **1911** *Rep. Fisheries 1908* 315 Sea bass . . . are caught with hand lines, and in pounds and traps.

+**4.** *pl.* The group of percussion instruments in an orchestra; *trap drummer,* a musician who plays a drum and other instruments at the same time.

1903 *Medical Record* 14 Feb. 268/1 Trap-drummer's neurosis: A Hitherto Undescribed Occupation-disease. . . . The man's occupation was to beat a drum by the operation of a pedal which is manipulated with right foot, while with his hands he plays the other drum, triangle, and the various traps. **1920** SANDBURG *Smoke & Steel* 63 You jazzmen, bang . . . drums, traps, banjoes.

5. In special combinations.

Trap bait, a piece of bait placed in a trap; *t. cage,* a device for catching and confining birds; *t. catch,* the number of fish, etc., taken in traps or trap nets; *t. dialect,* trappers' jargon or speech; *t. fishery,* a fishery employing trap nets; *t. hook,* a hook which, by springing when the bait is taken, secures the fish; *t. land,* land on which trapping is carried on; *t. light,* a light to lure insects into a trap; *t. log,* (see quotation); *t. match,* a trap-shooting contest; *t. pile,* a pile of wood for a fish trap; *t. tree, t. weir,* (see quotations).

1856 KANE *Arctic Explor.* I. 356 The foxes seem tired of touching our trap-bait. **1831** AUDUBON *Ornith. Biog.* I. 279 No sooner does it [the painted finch] make its appearance than trap-cages are set. **1894** *Youth's Comp.* 22 Nov. 562/4 For some weeks past our trap-catch, both of eels and lobsters, had greatly diminished. **1850** COLTON *Deck & Port* 392 They looked at our frowning battery with a wonder for which their trap dialect had no expression. **1883** GOODE *Fishery Industries U.S.* 27 The New England Pound and Trap Fishery. **1883** *Century Mag.* April 899, I discard all trap-hooks . . . as only adapted for the capture of land animals. **1751** in *Amer. Speech* XV. 405/1 A Tract containing 1000 Acres, lying . . . on the South Side by Mr. Gibson's Trap Land. **1896** *54th Cong. 2 Sess.* H. R. Ex. Doc. No. 267, 331 Mally . . . made extensive experiments with trap lights for the moths. **1843** *Amer. Pioneer* II. 445 The trap logs [of a log cabin] are those of unequal length above the eave bearers, which form the gable ends, and upon which the ribs rest. **1895** *Outing* XXVII. 67/1 Experts . . . may be seen at any important trap-match. **1910** *Haines* (Alaska) *Pioneer Press* 18 March 3/3 Stephen Rose . . . was in Haines last Saturday making arrangements to get trap piles for the Columbia Canning company. **1905** *Forestry Bureau Bul.* No. 61, 25 Trap tree, a tree deadened or felled at a time when destructive bark beetles will . . . enter the bark. . . . The bark is peeled and exposed to the sun, burned or buried, . . . to destroy the insect. **1891** *Cent.* 6443/2 *Trap-weir,* a trap-net.

Trap, *n.*[2] =TRAP ROCK. {1794-} Also attrib. — **1835** POE *Works* (1914) IV. 16 He informed us all about internal fires and tertiary formations; . . . about quartz and marl; about schist and schore; about gypsum and trap. **1849** *31st Congress 1 Sess.* H. R. Ex. Doc. No. 5, III. 584 The trap islands . . . are occasionally worn very smooth and finely marked with 'drift scratches.' **1851** Ross *In New York* 16 The paving stones . . . are square blocks of *Trap,* a species of rock resembling granite, though much harder. **1862** DANA *Manual Geol.* 66 The trap hills of Connecticut . . . have a long talus of broken stone. **1876** COZZENS *Ariz. & New Mex.*

106 Stumbling . . . over stones and masses of trap, that have been precipitated from the vast heights above us.

Trap, *n.*³ (See TRAPS.)

* Trap, *v.*

+1. *intr.* To set traps for animals; to take animals by the use of traps. {1894}

1806 ORDWAY in *Journals of Lewis & O.* 391 Three frenchmen . . . have been trapping as high as the river Roshjone but have made out but poorly. **1832** WYETH *Journal* 171 Crossed by fording to the other side of the river intending to . . . trap up three streams. **1852** WATSON *Nights in Block-House* 30, I was fotched up right in among 'em, and taught some of the best of 'em how to shoot and trap. **1890** RYAN *Told in Hills* 176 An Indian can always get that much if he is not too lazy to hunt or trap. **1916** EASTMAN *From Deep Woods* 57 My immediate kindred hunted all kinds of game, and trapped and fished as well.

* 2. *tr.* To catch in a trap or traps. {–1530; 1860} Also fig.

1828 NEAL *R. Dyer* 65 They had sworn to trap their pray [*sic*] alive, and to bring it off with the hide and the hair on. **1848** RUXTON *Life Far West* i, Many's the time I've said I'd strike for Taos, and trap a squaw. **1885** [see BEAVER 1 b].

+3. To set traps or use traps to take animals in (a place).

1834 A. PIKE *Sketches* 33 Lewis . . . had entered a little narrow cañon, which had never been trapped, because a man could not ride up it. **1837** IRVING *Bonneville* II. 192 A range of country is 'trapped,' by small detachments from a main body. **1841** CATLIN *Indians* II. 251 They assume the right . . . of hunting and trapping the streams and lakes. **1847** *Santa Fe Repub.* 20 Nov. 2/4 Mr. Kirker . . . remained for a period of eight years, trapping the Rio Gila every winter.

+4. *Baseball.* To catch a ball after it has hit the ground.

1892 *Chicago Herald* 16 May (E. J. Nichols). **1912** MATHEWSON *Pitching* 181 A Boston batter tapped one to Merkle which I thought he trapped.

Trapball. An old game in which the ball is thrown into the air from a device called a *trap* {1658–}; also, the ball used in this game. — **1713** SEWALL *Diary* II. 388 The Spout . . . [was cleared] by thrusting out a Trap-Ball that stuck there. **1834** *S. Lit. Messenger* I. 181 A high trotting, rawboned devil . . . made the old man bound like a trapball. **1859** ELWYN *Glossary* 19 *Trap-ball* was not common, but sometimes seen. *c*1866 BAGBY *Old Va. Gentleman* 49 [He] cut up his father's gum shoes, to make trap-balls, composed of equal parts of yarn and india-rubber.

Trap dike. A mass of trap rock in a fissure. {1842–} — **1843** *Nat. Hist. N.Y., Geology* IV. 295 The existence of trap dykes upon the immediate borders of the district, show that the dynamics of igneous agency have not entirely slumbered. **1875** BOURKE *Journal* 25 May, We saw . . . what I took to be a trap dyke. **1885** *Outing* VII. 67/1 The mountain has split down to unknown depths and separated, displaying an immense trap-dike.

Trapdoor spider. Any one of various spiders which make nests with hinged lids at the top, suggestive of trap doors. {1826–} — **1876** *Field & Forest* I. 75 The Trap-Door Spider.—A fine specimen of this wonderful spider was received . . . from Mr. M. B. Wever, of Edgefield County, S.C. **1885** *Wkly. New Mexican Rev.* 18 June 4/6 Large trap door spiders are occasionally found.

+Trap fishing. Fishing by means of a line of baited hooks, sunk in the water and anchored in place. — **1877** BARTLETT 718 *Trap-Fishing* . . . is now much practised on our coast.

+Trap line. 1. ?A line used in trap fishing. **2.** The filament in a spider web that ensnares the prey. — (1) **1647** *Conn. Rec.* I. 478 Goods att Totokett of the sd Tho: Fenners: . . . 11 traplines. (2) **1889** McCOOK *Amer. Spiders* I. 134 The trapline of the Labyrinth spider differs . . . in being composed of several threads instead of a single line. **1907** *St. Nicholas* July 848/1 The architect, with fore feet clasping what we call the 'trap line,' [is] waiting for some night-flying insect to strike the snare.

+Trap net. (See quot. 1876.) {1904–} — **1865** *Mich. Acts* 717 The size of the meshes of all the lead of pound or trap nets, used in the waters of this State, shall not be less than five inches in extension, knot to knot. **1876** KNIGHT 2617/1 *Trap-net*, a fishing-net in which a funnel-shaped piece leads the fish into a pound from which extrication is not easy.

Trapper. One who sets traps for animals {1768–}, usually in order to secure their furs.

1821 FOWLER *Journal* 61 Started the trappers under the Command of Slover. **1833** WYETH *Oregon* 57 We found them a body of white men called *trappers*, whose occupation is to entrap the beaver and other animals that have valuable furs. **1847** LONGFELLOW *Poetical Works* (1893) 92/2 Into this wonderful land, at the base of the Ozark Mountains, Gabriel far had entered, with hunters and trappers behind him. **1881** *Ore. State Jrnl.* 1 Jan. 8/1 Attention! Hunters! Trappers! Farmers! I will pay more than any one else in Eugene . . . for Hides, Furs and Deerskins. **1902** HULBERT *Forest Neighbors* 116 There are trappers who say that a Canada lynx is a fool and a coward.

* Trapping. +Attrib. and comb. with *canoe, company, depot,* etc.

1806 CLARK in *L. & Clark Exped.* V. (1905) 329 Those men are on a trapping expedition. **1837** IRVING *Bonneville* I. 224 In company with Campbell's convoy, was a trapping party of the Rocky Mountain Company. *Ib.* II. 241 Part of the goods, thus brought out, were . . . to supply the

trapping companies and the Indian tribes, in exchange for their furs. **1842** *S. Lit. Messenger* VIII. 64/1, I shaped my course to the nearest trapping dépot and soon obtained a new outfit and supply. **1853** RAMSEY *Tennessee* 105 [They] built two boats and two trapping canoes.

+Trapping ground. The area selected by a trapper or trappers for the setting of traps for game. — **1837** IRVING *Bonneville* I. 118 Those doughty rivals . . . started off for the trapping grounds to the northnorthwest. **1847** RUXTON *Adv. Rocky Mts.* (1848) 235 Having determined the locality of his trapping-ground, he starts to the mountains. **1903** WHITE *Forest* 207 The Ojibway family . . . searches out new trappinggrounds, new fisheries.

Trappist. A monk of a branch of the Cistercian order noted for extreme asceticism. {1836–} — **1814** BRACKENRIDGE *Views La.* 290 A boy brought up here . . . can never be fit for any thing but a Trappist. **1847** L. COLLINS *Kentucky* 142 The Trappists . . . were a body of religious monks who devoted themselves to fasting and praying and lived retired from the world. **1891** *Cent.* 6443/2.

+Trappy, *a.* {1883–} Of a horse: Having a quick, short, high gait. — **1872** *Vermont Bd. Agric. Rep.* I. 207 Cross a large, roomy, strong-boned, coarse mare with a smooth, stylish, trappy little horse. **1894** *Vt. Agric. Rep.* XIV. 100 The Vermonter . . . wants a smart, trappy horse. **1902** McFAUL *Ike Glidden* 108 Ben had a nice, smooth, slick mare, what wuz trappy and smart.

Trap rock. Any of various dark igneous rocks. {1813–} — **1834** in *Atlantic Mo.* XXVI. 490 The former [East Rock] towers most naked and pointed; almost an entire mass of dark, *trap* rock. **1849** *31st Congress 1 Sess. Sen. Ex. Doc.* 64, 109 A protrusion of trap rock . . . could be seen. **1897** *Kissimmee* (Fla.) *Valley Gazette* 31 Dec. 4/7 All along the Palisades the trap rocks and boulders are seen most smooth where the mountains of ice and sand passed over them. **1918** *Essex Inst. Coll.* LIV. 314 They seem to be of trap rock, and cleft from a large round boulder.

Traps. {1813–} +1. (See quot. 1870.) *Obs.* ||2. =TRUCK *n.*¹ 1. — (1) **1870** MEDBERY *Men Wall St.* 138 *Traps,* an almost obsolete phrase for broken fancy stocks, depreciated railroad securities, etc. **1885** *Harper's Mag.* Nov. 842/2 Sometimes the broker or operator is caught by 'traps,' or worthless securities. (2) **1875** WINANS *Reminiscences* 69, I couldn't afford it unless you would take your pay in 'Traps.'

Trap shooter. One who engages in trap shooting. {1899} — **1875** *Fur, Fin & Feather* (ed. 3) 24 The Trap-Shooters' Referee, a Compilation of the Rules for Pigeon Shooting.... Charles Suydam, Publisher. **1891** *Ib.* March 184/1 In Taney county, where they are . . . too remote from the trap-shooter to bring him with his nets, there are a few small flocks [of wild pigeons].

Trap shooting. The sport of shooting at pigeons, etc., released from a trap. {1892} — **1875** *Fur, Fin & Feather* 118 Bogardus, Champion Wing-Shot of America, uses Orange Lightning [powder] for Trap-Shooting.

* Trash, *n. collect.*

* 1. a. Strippings, refuse, or impurities resulting from or found during the processing of various products. (See also CORN TRASH.) **b.** A low grade of tobacco leaf.

1834 in Commons etc. *Doc. Hist.* I. 281 Under the name of trash, they [*sc.* sugar canes from which juice has been expressed] are carried away to serve as fuel. **1852** *Fla. Plantation Rec.* 83 The Cotton that I have Saved is Verry Nice Cotton and Clear of Trash. **1881** INGERSOLL *Oyster Industry* 249 Trash, all cullings, small oysters, refuse, etc., thrown over from the oyster gathering on to idle ground. **1909** *Cent. Suppl.* 1355/2 The leaves [of white Burley tobacco] are thus classified: lowest two, 'fliers'; next two, 'common lugs' ('trash' apparently the same).

+2. Broken ice mixed with water.

1856 KANE *Arctic Explor.* I. 342 Warped about one hundred yards into the trash.

3. A person lacking claim to social position. *contemptuous.* {1604–, a worthless person}

See also POOR WHITE TRASH, WHITE TRASH, and cf. POOR WHITE, note. **1862** LOWELL *Biglow P.* 2 Ser. iv. 126 Mason wuz F. F. V., . . . But t'other wuz jes' New York trash. **1872** *Harper's Mag.* March 547/2 It's what sech trash is got to come to. **1876** W. M. FISHER *Californians* 53 The original note of patronising contempt for the 'yellow trash' is dying off.

+4. Attrib. and comb. in preceding senses or in general sense of 'rubbish' with *barrel, basket, cleaner,* etc.

1772 *Md. Hist. Mag.* XIV. 281 Two Trash hgds [of tobacco] . . . are not yet sold. **1784** SMYTH *Tour U.S.* II. 135 The whole [is] covered with trash tobacco, or straw. **1864** WEBSTER 1407/1 *Trash-ice,* crumbled ice mixed with water. **1866** W. REID *After the War* 492 The horizon was blue and misty with the columns of smoke from the trash-gangs on the plantations. **1882** *Century Mag.* Feb. 563/2 Trash-cleaners, for saving the waste or total loss of storm-beaten cotton, . . . cannot now be made fast enough to supply the demand. **1885** CABLE *Dr. Sevier* 143 He must be expected to come fishing them out of their hole, like a rag-picker at a trash-barrel. **1895** *Dialect Notes* I. 395 Trash-basket, waste-paper basket. N.Y. City.

Trash, *v.*¹ *tr.* **a.** To remove dry leaves from (sugar cane). {1793–, in Brit. colonies} Also *vbl. n.* **b.** To free (seed cotton) of refuse. — **1833** B. SILLIMAN *Man. Sugar Cane* 14 Neither the cutting up of Suckers, nor the trashing of Cane is practised [in La.]. **1847** *Fla. Plantation Rec.* 311 Old george grind, old Billy and Barracks trash Cotton in gin house. **1848** BARTLETT 364 *To trash the cane,* is to strip off the dry leaves. **1886** *Har-*

per's Mag. June 78/2 As the canes grow they must be well weeded and 'trashed,' i.e., all dry, dead leaves removed.

Trash, *v.²* {1610-} +To cover up or conceal (a trail). ('Prob. a term of the French trappers' *O.E.D.*) — **1859** BARTLETT 487 *To Trash a Trail*, an expression used at the West, meaning to conceal the direction one has taken by walking in a stream, or, in fact, taking to water in any way.

‖**Trashed,** *a.* Characterized by the presence of waste or impurities. — **1852** *Fla. Plantation Rec.* 83 The Cotton . . . will be a Little trashed now owing to the Catterpillar Eating of it.

Trashy, *a.* {a1620-}
1. Of literature: Of cheap, poor quality. {1868-}
1835 *Knickerb.* V. 120 The trashy productions, of course, had the best chance of being perused. **1855** I. C. PRAY *Mem. J. G. Bennett* 217 The age of trashy novels, of more trashy poems, of most trashy quarterly and weekly literature is drawing to a close. **1876** *Portland Transcript* May (F.), Beware of the cheap, trashy romances.

+**2.** Of persons: **a.** Of poor physical constitution. **b.** Of inferior social standing.
1852 STOWE *Uncle Tom* xxxi, Stout fellers last six or seven years; trashy ones get worked up in two or three. **1862** 'KIRKLAND' *Among Pines* 167 He regarded the white man as altogether too 'trashy' to be treated with much ceremony.

+**3.** Of land: Covered with refuse, as the waste and discarded matter from an earlier season.
1861 *Ill. Agric. Soc. Trans.* IV. 250 The wheat drill . . . is designed to do this work rapidly and perfectly, on ground however rough and trashy. **1905-6** *Trade Catalogue* (Cent. Suppl.), The high curve of the beam prevents fouling in trashy land.

+**Travail.** [Fr. *travail*, used in Canada to indicate the space for the horse between the shafts of a vehicle.] A crude vehicle used by Indians, consisting of two poles which, dragged as shafts by an animal, support the load on a frame or basket; the basket or a similar device carrying the burden. — **1847** PARKMAN in *Knickerb.* XXX. 287 Several dozen of these curious vehicles, called, in the bastard language of the country *travaux*, were now splashing together through the stream. **1849** — *Oregon Trail* 146 Margot . . . was couched in the basket of a *travail*. **1876** BOURKE *Journal* 8-22 Sept. 886 Our wounded . . . [rested] on 'travaux' constructed from the tepi poles and buffalo-robes of the Indian village. **1889** *Century Mag.* Jan. 339/2 'Richard's himself again,' ready . . . to drag the *travaux*.

+**Travee, Travée.** [f. Canadian Fr. pron. of Fr. *travail*.] =TRAVAIL. — **1846** SAGE *Scenes Rocky Mts.* xi, Dogs, harnessed to travées, had their part to perform. **1850** GARRARD *Wah-To-Yah* iii. 53 The animals, with the lodge-pole *travees* (drays), jogged along. **1857** *Harper's Mag.* Oct. 647/1 The working horses were led up, ready to be harnessed into the travées.

***Travel,** *n.* The number of persons or vehicles journeying to or past a given point; {1830} +tourists, collectively; the distance traveled. — **1852** REYNOLDS *Hist. Illinois* 283 The travel on the road from the Ohio to Kaskaskia increased. **1892** *Vt. Agric. Rep.* XII. 136 At Fairlee Lake something is done in the way of attracting this travel. **1903** E. JOHNSON *Railway Transportation* 174 If each car carrying the mails be taken as a unit, the 'annual travel' or car mileage aggregated 302,613,325.

***Travel,** *v.* (See also FACE *n.* 1 a and RECORD 4 a.) *intr.* Of an animal: To remove to new ground; to move on while browsing. — **1839** MARRYAT *Diary in Amer.* 1 Ser. I. 199 Bears . . . do not come down to the shores, (or travel, as they term it here,) until the huckleberries are ripe. **1877** C. HALLOCK *Sportsman's Gazetteer* 88 If the deer is 'travelling,' as it is called, one has to walk much faster.

+**Travelers' Aid (Department, Society).** An organization, or a department, which extends aid to travelers in need of help. — **1895** *Y.W.C.A. Rep.* 1894 5 Travelers' Aid Department. Miss P. L. McIlvaine, North-Western Depot. **1911** *Rep. Travelers' Aid Soc. N.Y.C.* No. 6, 5 The Travelers' Aid Society was incorporated under the laws of the State of New York in January, 1907. **1921** *National Travelers Aid Bul.* IV. Nov.-Dec. 3/2 They were . . . obviously leaving the responsibility entirely to the Travelers Aid.

***Travel(l)ed,** *a.* +Of a road or place: Used or frequented by travelers. — **1843** FRÉMONT *Exped.* 163 [To Fort Hall] along the *travelled* road from the town of Westport, . . . is 1,323 miles. **1874** *Vermont Bd. Agric. Rep.* II. 658 If the hill is heavy clay, it may be much improved, . . . by covering the traveled portion with gravel or sand. **1882** HARTE *Flip* 106 [The dawn came with] voices in the traveled roads and trails.

***Travel(l)er.**
See also COMMERCIAL TRAVEL(L)ER. The spelling *traveler*, characteristic of modern American usage, was entered by Webster in his edition of 1828.
+**1.** An itinerant preacher.
1813 ASBURY *Journal* III. 346 The increase . . . in preachers seventy-nine; but of these there are only thirty-three travellers.
2. A bird migrating or making a long flight.
1874 LONG *Wild-Fowl* 21 Frequently in spring continuous shooting may be had at 'travellers.'
+**3.** *Traveler's check*, 'A check issued by a banker and payable by any of the correspondents of the issuing banker' (W. '09).

Travel(l)er's-delight. +(See quotation.) — **1892** *Amer. Folk-Lore* V. 94 *Apios tuberosa*, traveller's delight. New Albany, Miss.
***Travel(l)er's-joy.** Any one of various species of *Clematis*, +esp. the virgin's-bower, *C. virginiana*. — **1784** *Amer. Acad. Mem.* I. 458 Traveller's Joy. Virgin's Bower. Blossoms white. **1841** *S. Lit. Messenger* VII. 37/1 Nor did I refuse a helping hand to the traveller's joy and jessamine. **1892** *Amer. Folk-Lore* V. 91 *Clematis Virginiana*, traveller's joy; wild hops, N.H.

***Travel(l)ing,** *n. attrib.*
1. Designating articles and equipment designed for or used by travelers. {1669-}
See also TRAVEL(L)ING BAG, CARRIAGE 2, OUTFIT.
1761 *Va. Gazette* 16 Jan., Directions for making a Travelling-Umbrella, which may be carried without the least Inconvenience. **1790** *Penna. Packet* 11 Dec. 3/2 Imported, . . . Travelling port folios and paper cases. **1803** ELLICOTT in Mathews *Life A. Ellicott* 209 [My] copying machine . . . is not larger than a common travelling desk. **1835** *Stimpson's Boston Directory* (cover), James Dyer, Manufacturer . . . [of] Travelling Cases. **1842** KIRKLAND *Forest Life* I. 18 My travelling-basket . . . was supplied with two or three capacious note-books. **1854** *Penna. Agric. Rep.* 97 Their very handsome riding saddle and russet traveling trunk. **1870** STEPHENS *Married in Haste* 369 Sterling found a traveling-flask in the basket. **1897** *McClure's Mag.* X. 54 Mrs. Ennis was writing as usual . . . , the traveling-inkstand at her elbow.

b. Designating articles of clothing designed for or worn in travel. {1844-}
See also TRAVEL(L)ING CAP, SUIT.
1782 J. ADAMS *Diary Works* III. 297, I had on my travelling gloves. **1871** HOWELLS *Wedding Journey* 136 He hands her travelling-shawl after one [bride] she springs from the omnibus into her husband's arms. **1878** *Decorum* 285 Velvet is not fit for a traveling-hat. **1887** HARRIS in *Century Mag.* XXXIV. 544/1 A gentleman wrapped in a long linen traveling-coat was pacing restlessly up and down the platform.

2. In special combinations.
Travel(l)ing card, a card issued to a member of a local union who is about to go elsewhere; *t. fee*, an allowance or remuneration for traveling expenses; *t. song*, a song or chant sung by Indians making a journey.
1874 *Internat. Typogr. Union Proc.* 14 Subordinate Unions cannot require members to pay for traveling cards. **1733** *Harvard Rec.* II. 607 Mr. Goffe [is] to have the travelling fees. 2s. for ten miles. **1808** *Cuming Western Tour* 411 After singing their war songs . . . they marched off against the frontiers of Virginia, . . . singing the travelling song.

***Travel(l)ing,** *a.*
1. Of establishments or facilities: Moved from place to place; portable. {1827-}
1780 *Va. State P.* I. 376 They have but one Travelling Forge and that without tools. **1831** PECK *Guide* 60 Some [boats] have travelling stores. **1883** *Harper's Mag.* June 137/1 The travelling circus . . . had journeyed on and left her. **1900** *Everybody's Mag.* 591/2 Also there are 'travelling gins' on wheels, that proceed from place to farm to farm, as the travelling thrashing machines go about in a Western wheat district. **1910** BOSTWICK *Amer. Pub. Library* 108 Traveling libraries are simply collections of books sent to communities, associations, or individuals for circulation. **1920** COOPER *Under Big Top* 5 The ton of coal . . . will be consumed in the big traveling ranges.

2. Of persons: Journeying from place to place, as itinerant practitioners of a trade or profession. {1619-20-}
See also TRAVEL(L)ING AGENT, MAN, etc.
1798 HAWKINS *Letters* 303 The Indians . . . view every traveling party as intruders on their lands. **1840** HOFFMAN *Greyslaer* I. 130 You don't take the chap for a horse-thief, do you? He's more like some travelling cobbler. **1847** S. BRYANT *MS. Letter* 16 March, We have occasionally . . . an exhibition from some travelling showman. **1851** *N. Amer. Miscellany* I. 93/1 We trust that the managers of the Collins Line . . . [will be] more careful of the interests of the travelling public. **1895** WIGGIN *Village Watch-Tower* 72 She disowned her daughter . . . fer alienatin' the 'fections of a travelin' baker-man. **1907** *St. Nicholas* May 633/2 They were able to recognize the unmistakable form of their old enemy, the traveling photographer.

3. Of mechanical devices: Moving or sliding, as in a fixed course. {1835-}
See also TRAVEL(L)ING CARRIAGE 1.
1850 *Rep. Comm. Patents 1849* 361, I claim . . . the combination of the double travelling hearth with a blast furnace. **1876** INGRAM *Centennial Exp.* 355 A railroad supported on one side by heavy cast-iron pillars . . . carries a travelling platform. **1909** *Cent. Suppl.* 1371/3 Traveling staircase. See *escalator.*

4. In special combinations.
Travel(l)ing camp, a camp of roving Indians; *t. connection*, in the Methodist Episcopal church, the body of traveling preachers; *t. maid*, a woman servant attending a traveler; *t. ring*, a ring, moving freely on a support, used in the performance of gymnastic exercises; *t. stone*, (see quotation).
1837 IRVING *Bonneville* II. 202 Captain Wyeth . . . passed some months in a travelling camp of the Flatheads. **1846** *Indiana Mag. Hist.* XXIII. 270 He subsequently joined the traveling connection, and filled some im-

portant charges in the Pittsburg conference. **1905** N. DAVIS *Northerner* 321 Milly Ann . . . was to go . . . as a traveling maid. **1897** *Outing* XXX. 182/2 The use of chest-weights, the traveling-rings and punching-bag, may be taken to develop different groups of muscles. **1877** WRIGHT *Big Bonanza* 38 Traveling stones . . . were almost perfectly round. . . . When scattered . . . on a table . . . they immediately began traveling toward a common centre.

Travel(l)ing agent. An itinerant salesman; a representative traveling for his employer. — **1865** KELLOGG *Rebel Prisons* 399 We shall sell this work by traveling agents exclusively. **1881** RITTENHOUSE *Maud* 4 His traveling agent at New Orleans is holding on to it and corn is rising every day. **1887** *Courier-Journal* 2 Feb. 6/1 Herman Holmes, Travelling Agent of the Louisville and Nashville, . . . was in the city yesterday. **1894** ALDRICH *Two Bites* 215 Among the travelling agents for the Savonarola Fire Insurance Company was a young man by the name of Brett.

Travel(l)ing bag. A satchel or valise for carrying the clothes, etc., of a traveler. {1862} Also attrib. — **1836** GILMAN *Recoll.* (1838) 18 He . . . called the little boy who held the travelling bag a 'black-faced nigger.' **1865** *Chicago Tribune* 10 April 1 Chicago Traveling Bag Manufactory. . . . Traveling Bags, Haversacks, &c. **1873** PHELPS *Trotty's Wedding* xiv, Down came her best travelling-bag, of umber-colored morocco. **1922** TARKINGTON *Gentle Julia* 148 Noble had chanced to see Mr. Atwater driving down Julia's Street . . . , a travelling bag beside him.

Travel(l)ing cap. A cap for wear by a traveler. {1814- (A. Mathews *Mem. C. Mathews* II. 337)} — **1790** *Penna. Packet* 2 Jan. 4/2 Trimmings for . . . Gentlemens Travelling Caps. **1839** *Knickerb.* XIII. 213 [Mosquitoes are kept] off by gauze nets, both for the hat, or travelling cap, by day, and the bed at night. **1871** HOWELLS *Wedding Journey* 74 The principal speaker was a tall person, wearing a silk travelling-cap. **1907** HARRIS *Tents of Wickedness* 14 'Too civil by half,' returned her father, adjusting his travelling cap.

Travel(l)ing carriage. 1. A wheeled support for a gun. {1834-47} **2.** A horse-drawn vehicle of substantial construction for long-distance travel. {1798} — **(1)** **1777** *Essex Inst. Coll.* XIII. 132 Transport from Hull the Eighteen Pounder with its traviling Carridge. **1797** *Ann. 4th Congress* 2 Sess. 2144 Heavy guns and howitzers on travelling carriages . . . with a well-armed militia, . . . would be a sufficient protection. **(2)** **1834** CARRUTHERS *Kentuckian* I. 8 A handsome travelling carriage . . . was moving at a brisk rate. **1860** M. J. HOLMES *Cousin Maude* 83 A large traveling-carriage stopped at the gate.

✲**Travel(l)ing man.** +A commercial traveler selling to retailers. — **1884** *Graceville* (Minn.) *Transcript* 25 Aug., A brace of suspicious looking men . . . held up a traveling man. **1896** *Harper's Mag.* June 160/2 The travelling man had impressed upon the night porter of the hotel the importance of calling him.

+**Travel(l)ing minister.** An itinerant preacher. — **1741** HEMPSTEAD *Diary* 384 Traveling ministers . . . in Some places promote the withdrawing from the Settled ministers & Set up Separate meetings. **1846** *Indiana Mag. Hist.* XXIII. 397 A man who is too old to learn watchmaking or any other business . . . can never succeed in the whole work of a traveling minister. **1848** *Ib.* 2 That same territory . . . contains . . . more than 2,000 local preachers, besides the traveling ministers.

+**Travel(l)ing outfit.** A supply of clothing or equipment for travel. — **1886** RITTENHOUSE *Maud* 377 Both milliner and dress-maker thought they were doing my traveling out-fit. a**1918** G. STUART *On Frontier* I. 218 They had six good horses, but very little in the shape of a traveling outfit.

Travel(l)ing preacher. An itinerant minister; a preacher, esp. a Methodist, who travels from congregation to congregation; a circuit rider. {1789-} — **1775** ASBURY *Journal* I. 124 At this meeting we admitted F.P. T.F. and J.H—y as travelling preachers. **1844** Rupp *Relig. Denominations* 447 A local preacher generally . . . [preaches] without any temporal emolument, except when he supplies the place of a travelling preacher. **1874** EGGLESTON *Circuit Rider* 252 The incessant activity of a traveling preacher's life did not allow Morton much opportunity for . . . society.

+**Travel(l)ing salesman.** =TRAVEL(L)ING MAN. — **1885** *South Fla. Sentinel* (Orlando) 1 July 3/3 B. F. Harn, the popular traveling salesman, . . . will leave in a few days. **1892** *Harper's Mag.* Feb. 439/1 I've met travelling salesmen before. **1902** McFAUL *Ike Glidden* 133 A traveling salesman named Carson made a visit to Blueberry Falls about once every three weeks.

Travel(l)ing suit. A suit of clothes designed for, or appropriate for, wear during travel. — **1867** A. J. EVANS *Vashti* xxvii, Elsie was waiting to clothe me in my travelling-suit. **1894** WARNER *Golden House* xxiii, He ran against . . . a man in a pronounced travelling suit, grip-sack and umbrella in hand. **1907** *St. Nicholas* July 798/2 Willis [was] in her stylish dark traveling suit and hat.

Travel-worn, *a.* Exhausted by travel; shabby or disreputable in appearance because of travel. — **1837** IRVING *Bonneville* I. 67 Both men and horses were . . . much travel-worn. **1880** *Harper's Mag.* March 542/1 [I] had several minutes' view of a number of travel-worn linen dusters. **1888** *Ib.* Sept. 494/2 From all that elegant crowd of travellers he . . . picked us out, the only two in the least disreputable and travel-worn.

✲**Traverse.**

✲**1.** The act of passing over or crossing, esp. with reference to a body of water.

1733 BYRD *Journey to Eden* (1901) 309 He being oblig'd to make a traverse, we cou'd reach no farther than 4 Miles. **1808** PIKE *Sources Miss.* 189, I determined to attempt the traverse of the mountain. **1839** BRIGGS *Harry Franco* I. 198 If you choose to join me, we will work a traverse, and get ashore. a**1862** THOREAU *Maine Woods* 175 We crossed a broad

bay, . . . [and] made what the voyageurs call a *traverse*. **1903** WHITE *Forest* 159 The traverse was accomplished.

+**2.** A sled made with a board extending over two or more sets of runners. Also attrib.

In this sense possibly a corruption of *travois* or a related form. Cf. **1930** *Amer. Speech* V. 420: 'Travois, two or more sleds fastened together by means of a plank bolted to them.'

1886 *Boston Globe* 20 Dec., The man who doesn't own a toboggan, [or] a traverse . . . , stands a good chance of getting through the winter without an accident policy. **1887** *Courier-Journal* 6 Jan. 2/6 Twenty boys were coasting down South Main street on a traverse sled.

3. In special combinations.

Traverse line, a line in a traverse survey {1900}; *t. map,* a map showing points determined by a traverse survey or traversing; *t. table* {1669-}, (see quotation).

1739 STEPHENS *Proc. Georgia* I. 440 Due Observance was had, in running the traverse Lines. **1901** *Dept. Agric. Yrbk. 1900* 121 It is almost impossible to carry on the soil survey except through the co-operation of State institutions which will undertake to make a traverse map. **1864** WEBSTER 1407/3 *Traverse-table,* . . . (Railways), a platform with one or more tracks, and arranged to move laterally on wheels, for shifting cars, etc.; a traverser.

+**Travois, Travoy,** *n.* [Corruption of TRAVAIL.]

1. =TRAVAIL.

1847 K. CARSON in Cody *Wild West* 349 The Klamaths . . . prevented his body from falling into our hands by drawing it away on a travoi. **1876** BOURKE *Journal* 28 July-8 Sept., [He] says he will stick with the column if he has to be hauled on a travois. **1890** *Harper's Mag.* Aug. 383/1 Dogs, hastily hitched to the dust-raising travois, dragged the wondering pappooses. a**1918** G. STUART *On Frontier* II. 20 One of the squaws exercising much ingenuity in fixing up a travois, made the injured man comfortable.

2. A go-devil or sled used for dragging logs.

1878 *Lumberman's Gazette* 2 Feb. 87 The haul . . . is too long to use travoys. *Ib.* 9 Feb., The 'travoy' is kept busy on short hauls.

3. Attrib. in senses 1 and 2 with *dray, fashion, pole,* etc.

1891 *Harper's Mag.* Dec. 32/1 He came and hitched the required number of horses to her mother's travois poles beside her tent. **1901** WHITE in *Munsey's Mag.* (Eng. ed.) XXV. 387/2 The travoy road is in the process of construction. **1902** — *Blazed Trail* 52 A number of pines had been felled out on the ice, . . . and left in expectation of ice thick enough to bear the travoy 'dray.' **1903** — *Blazed Trail Stories* 49 The scaler swung leisurely down the travoy trail. **1907** COOK *Border & Buffalo* 207 Not a lodge-pole had been dragged travois-fashion to here, but from here a travois trail started northeast toward Fort Sill.

+**Travoy,** *v. tr.* To transport by means of a travois (sense 2). Also *vbl. n.* — **1878** *Lumberman's Gazette* 2 Feb. 86 Travoying can be carried on to good advantage. **1902** WHITE *Blazed Trail* 13 When Nolly and Fabian had travoyed the log to the skidway, they drew it with a bump across the two parallel skids.

✲**Trawl.**

+**1.** (See quot. 1860.)

1860 WORCESTER 1536/2 *Trawl,* . . . a line, sometimes a mile or more in length, with short lines and baited hooks suspended from it at frequent intervals;—now much used in fishing for cod, haddock, and mackerel. *Gilbert.* **1880** *Harper's Mag.* Aug. 351/1 A trawl . . . was sunk so as to rest on the bottom, buoyed at both ends and left there. **1896** JEWETT *Pointed Firs* 52 It was her brother's trawl, and she meant to just run her eye along for the right sort of a little haddock. **1914** STEELE *Storm* 71, I shook a thumb at the tubs of baited trawl.

2. Attrib. and comb. with *anchor, buoy, line, roller.*

1876 KNIGHT 2621/1 *Trawl-roller,* a roller . . . over which the trawls are drawn into the boat. **1884** *Nat. Museum Bul.* No. 27, 756 Trawl anchor. . . . Used for anchoring trawl-lines, boats, and nets. *Ib.* 965 Trawl-buoy. Five glass balls . . . covered with netting, and lashed around a series of cork floats strung on a staff. *Ib.* 915 Cod trawl-line. . . . It is made up in 'tubs' or parts.

✲**Trawler.** +A person engaged in fishing with a trawl line; a vessel used in fishing with a trawl line. — [**1864** WEBSTER 1408/1 *Trawler,* . . . one who, or that which, trawls.] **1880** *Harper's Mag.* Aug. 340/1 In other departments [of fishing] there were . . . trawlers, draggers, . . . and the bankers before mentioned. **1884** *Nat. Museum Bul.* No. 27, 715 In the foreground is a Grand Bank cod-trawler being towed out of the [Gloucester] harbor by a steam tug.

✲**Tray.** A flat or shallow utensil used esp. for carrying plates and dishes. Also comb.

1622 'MOURT' *Relation* 35 In the houses [of Indians] we found wooden Boules, Trayes & Dishes [etc.]. **1652** *Mass. H. S. Coll.* 4 Ser. VII. 63 My wife desiarith Mistris Lake to get hur a dusen of trays. **1676** B. TOMPSON *Poetical Works* 49 The dainty Indian Maize was eat . . . out of wooden Trayes. **1790** *Penna. Packet* 7 Dec. 3/3 Joseph Anthony, Junior, . . . Has Imported . . . Snuffers, snuffer trays and inkstands. **1855** GLISAN *Jrnl. Army Life* 13 A waiter . . . unfortunately capsized a tray full of this beverage on Captain Graham's shoulders. **1912** NICHOLSON *Hoosier Chron.* 101 A maid placed on the table . . . a tray, with a decanter and glasses.

+**Treacle-berry.** (See quot. 1672.) *Obs.* — **1634** WOOD *New Eng. Prospect* (1865) 15 There bee . . . Treacleberries, Hurtleberries, Currants.

1672 JOSSELYN *New Eng. Rarities* 45 Treacle Berries, having the perfect tast[e] of Treacle when they are ripe.

Treadmill. A device for producing rotary motion by the weight of men or animals stepping on an inclined plane or the steps of a revolving cylinder or wheel. {1822-} Also transf. — **1831** PECK *Guide* 196 Ox tread mills, on the inclined plane, and horse mills by draught, are very common. **1849** in Hall *College Words* (1856) 159 The treadmill . . . might be a useful appendage to a college, not as a punishment, but as a recreation for 'digs.' **1884** 'CRADDOCK' *Where Battle Was Fought* 865 You have interests away from this little treadmill of a town.

+**Tread softly.** =SPURGE NETTLE. — [**1814** PURSH *Flora Amer.* II. 603 *Jatropa stimulosa* . . . ruins the Negroes' feet when they tread upon it; from which it is known by the name of Tread-softly.] **1894** COULTER *Bot. W. Texas* III. 397 Tread softly. Spurge nettle. . . . Sandy plains along the Rio Grande.

* **Treasure.** In special combinations.

Treasure bag, a bag in which a housewife keeps scraps and oddments of cloth, lace, etc.; *t. coach,* a stagecoach transporting treasure from a gold mining region (*Obs.*); *t. ship,* a ship bringing gold from the west coast of the United States to the United States treasury. (*Obs.*)

1887 ALDEN *Little Fishers* xv, [With] some pieces of lace from her mother's old treasure bag, she meant to make herself a bonnet. **1880** INGHAM *Digging Gold* 288 Only one treasure coach has ever been robbed. **1862** MOORE *Rebellion Rec.* V. II. 145, I directed that an armed revenue cutter should proceed to sea to afford protection to . . . the California treasure-ships.

+**Treasure box. 1.** A strong box or receptacle on a stagecoach in which valuables, esp. gold from mining camps, were carried. **2.** A box in which an individual keeps things that are treasured. — (1) **1880** INGHAM *Digging Gold* 288 Failing to unlock the treasure-box, . . . one [of the robbers] hit upon the plan of blowing it open with gunpowder. **1890** LANGFORD *Vigilante Days* (1912) 527 There's no treasure-box aboard. **1893** *Chicago Tribune* 24 April 3/1 Among the articles of greatest historical value . . . [is] the treasure-box, a memento of the attack on the Redding and Alturas Stage in 1892. (2) **1881** STODDARD *E. Hardery* 20 She picked up the miniature . . . and carefully locked it away again in its ebony treasure-box. **1907** *St. Nicholas* July 813/1 His 'ditty-box' . . . is the sailor's work-basket, writing-desk, treasure-box, and camp-stool all in one.

* **Treasurer.**

+**1.** An officer in charge of the finances of an American colony, county, town, city, or state.

See also COUNTY TREASURER.

*a***1649** WINTHROP *Hist.* I. 76 At this court an act was made expressing the governor's power, etc., and the office of the secretary and treasurer, etc. **1707** *Boston Rec.* 41 Joseph Prout . . . is chosen to Serve as Treasurer. **1769** *Conn. Rec.* XIII. 273 The Treasurer . . . [shall] pay out of the public treasury to said Buel one hundred pounds. **1802** *Phila. Ordinances* (1812) 102 The treasurer of the corporation of the city of Philadelphia shall be appointed as heretofore. **1845** *Xenia Torch-Light* 31 July 2/6 The loco-foco treasurer of Fairfield County . . . has been proved . . . to be a defaulter. **1879** *Calif. Constitution* v. § 17 A Treasurer, an Attorney-General, and a Surveyor-General shall be elected at the same time. **1911** *Okla. Session Laws* 3 Legisl. 133 The treasurer shall . . . have the power to appoint one or more deputies.

+**2.** An officer of the United States Treasury Department in charge of all government funds and disbursements.

1777 *Jrnls. Cont. Congress* VII. 40 The continental treasurer [shall] be empowered and directed to borrow money on the loan office certificates. **1790** HAMILTON *Works* VII. 52 The treasurer of the United States shall be the receiver of all payments for sales at the general land-office. **1834** JACKSON in *Pres. Mess. & P.* III. 112 The power of Congress to direct in what places the Treasurer shall keep the moneys in the Treasury . . . is unlimited. **1900** *Congress. Rec.* 16 Jan. 876/1 This Treasurer of the United States walks in and fills the coffers with free money that they may lend it at a high rate of interest.

3. The custodian of the funds of a theatrical or operatic company; a box-office ticket-seller.

1844 *Gem of Prairie* 29 June, The evening is set apart for the Benefit of the gentlemanly Treasurer, Mr. W. H. Hough. **1870** O. LOGAN *Before Footlights* 174 'Mr. Ryely in?' I asked of the treasurer at the box-office. **1896** *N.Y. Dramatic News* 4 July 14/1 The affairs of the Summer Tour Opera company . . . are in a sad state, the treasurer of the company having decamped some time Tuesday night.

* **Treasury.**

+**1.** The public funds of an American colony, county, state, etc.; the place where these are kept, or the governmental department having charge of them.

1640 *Portsmouth Rec.* 17 The charges about the Mill shall be borne by the Treasurie. **1775** *Jrnls. Cont. Congress* III. 471 Samuel Adams moved . . . that a sum be advanced from the treasury. **1836** CROCKETT *Exploits* 26 The Land office, the Post office, and the Treasury itself, may all be drained. **1900** *Congress. Rec.* 16 Jan. 876/2 We pay them [the bankers] interest upon their bonds that lie in our Treasury. **1913** *Stat. at Large* XXXVIII. I. 251 The Secretary of the Treasury . . . shall designate not less than eight nor more than twelve cities to be known as Federal reserve cities.

2. *attrib.* and *comb.* Designating things pertaining to the treasury of an American colonial town or to the United States treasury.

1646 *Portsmouth Rec.* 33 Gorge Parker shall be quitted of the tresury pay for his land. **1659** *Ib.* 89 Mr. Briges hath the tresury cow with all hir increase for thre years. **1801** *Steele P.* I. 217, I have now to acknowledge the receipt of the Treasury draft No. 3241 for $48.60. **1833** JACKSON in *Pres. Mess. & P.* III. 13 The purchase money was . . . simply added to the Treasury deposit. **1843** *Niles' Nat. Reg.* 29 July 340 A Treasury Report . . . has at last been published. **1894** *Harper's Mag.* Feb. 480/1 The President's message . . . estimated a Treasury deficit for the current year of $28,000,000.

3. In special combinations.

Treasury agent, an agent appointed to dispose of United States government securities; *t. bill,* a bill in Congress relating to the United States treasury; *t. certificate,* a certificate of indebtedness issued by the treasury of the United States; *t. greenback,* =GREENBACK 1; *t. ring,* a clique of politicians particularly interested in congressional legislation affecting the United States treasury; *t. shinplaster,* =SHINPLASTER 1.

1842 *Niles' Nat. Reg.* 16 July 307/2 T. F. Robinson, Esq. of Harrisburg Pa. has been appointed as treasury agent of the U. States. **1846** POLK *Diary* I. 368, I feared . . . that both the Treasury Bill & the reduction of the tariff would be postponed. **1791** *Ann. 2d Congress* App. 1071 There were Treasury certificates issued in exchange for Loan Office settlement certificates. **1862** *N.Y. Tribune* 30 May 3/4 He has plenty of Treasury 'green-backs,' but he very prudently never spends any of them. **1868** *N.Y. Herald* 6 July 6/4 The Treasury ring are working like beavers to get Sherman's Funding bill acted upon. **1838** *Jamestown* (N.Y.) *Jrnl.* 18 July 1/6 The new 'money bill' or act, authorizing a new issue of Treasury shinplasters, . . . has been vetoed.

Treasury board. {1855-} +A board, consisting originally of five congressmen, established by the Continental Congress in 1776 to serve chiefly as a ways and means committee. *Obs.* — **1776** *Jrnls. Cont. Congress* VI. 1038 Two members [shall] be added to the committee appointed on the 17 October for the better regulating the Treasury Board. **1778** *Ib.* X. 28 One million of dollars [shall] be emitted under the direction of the Treasury Board. **1787** JEFFERSON *Writings* VI. 128 This has prevented the treasury board from remitting any money to this place.

+**Treasury Department.** The financial department of the United States government, now having the Secretary of the Treasury at its head. Also *attrib.* — **1784** *Jrnls. Cont. Congress* XXVI. 357 A motion of the delegates of Massachusetts, to revise the institution of the treasury department, . . . was read a first time. **1833** JACKSON in *Pres. Mess. & P.* III. 8 To the Treasury Department is intrusted the safe-keeping and faithful application of the public moneys. **1863** *Stat. at Large* XII. 711 Secretary of the Treasury . . . may provide for the . . . issue [of fractional notes] . . . in the treasury department building. **1900** *Congress. Rec.* 14 Feb. 1794/2 The Treasury Department of the United States . . . will figure for untold hours to disallow every cent that does not come within the red tape of that organization.

Treasury note. {18th cent.}

+**1.** A note or interest-bearing certificate issued by the treasury department of a colony.

1756 *Lett. to Washington* I. 202 The Treasurer . . . is hereby required to pay the same in Treasury Notes. **1778** *Ann. S.W. Virginia* 988 Francis Hopkins was guilty of passing Treasury Notes knowing the same to be bad. **1894** LEAVITT *Our Money Wars* 13 In 1723, Pennsylvania . . . issued treasury notes, and kept them in use until 1773.

+**2.** A currency bill or note issued by the Treasury Department of the United States government. Also *attrib.*

The first notes of this kind were issued to meet the expenses of the War of 1812, and many issues subsequently appeared. (Cf. GREENBACK 1.)

1812 *Stat. at Large* III. 767 The said treasury notes . . . shall be every where received in payment of all duties and taxes laid by the authority of the United States. **1842** *Whig Almanac* 1843 35/2 A Loan Bill, Treasury Note Bill, and Provisional Tariff were passed, to preserve the Treasury from dishonor. **1858** BUCHANAN in *Pres. Mess. & P.* V. 522, $9,684,537.99 were applied to the payment of the public debt and the redemption of Treasury notes. **1890** *Stat. at Large* XXVI. 289 The Secretary of the Treasury is hereby directed to . . . issue in payment for such purchases of silver bullion Treasury notes of the United States. **1911** VANCE *Cynthia* 78 He smoothed the Treasury note out between his fingers.

+**b.** Such notes issued by the Republic of Texas or the Southern Confederacy. *Obs.*

1836 *Diplom. Corr. Texas* I. (1908) 71 We have concluded to adopt the plan of issuing treasury notes. **1852** [see MOUNTED RANGER]. **1861** *Vanity Fair* 27 April 195/2 The treasury notes of the Confederate States have at the end the Goddess of Liberty in starry drapery.

Treasury scrip. +Scrip issued by the United States treasury. — **1849** *31st Congress 1 Sess.* H. R. Ex. Doc. No. 5, II. 1178 The ninth section of the act . . . gives bounty land or treasury scrip, at the claimant's option, to non-commissioned officers . . . who served in the late Mexican war. *Ib.*, The act of March 3, 1849, prohibits the issue of treasury scrip.

Treasury warrant. {1834-} +**a.** A land warrant issued by the treasury of a state. In full *treasury land warrant.* (Cf. LAND WARRANT 1.) +**b.** A warrant for the payment of money into or from the United States treasury. — **1784** *Ky. Petitions* 73 [The] House did . . . pass a Resolution forbidding the issuing any Treasury Land warrants. **1784** FILSON *Kentucke* 37 Treasury warrants were afterwards issued, authorizing their possessor to locate the quantity of land mentioned in them. **1834** C. A. DAVIS *Lett. J. Downing* 217 Pieces of paper all full of figerin, and some on 'em marked . . . 'Treasury Warrants.'

* **Treaty.**

+1. A formal meeting of representatives of the United States and Indian tribes looking to the drawing up of an agreement to govern future relationships. *Obs.*

1776 *Jrnls. Cont. Congress* IV. 348 The 20th day of July [shall] be fixed on for holding a treaty . . . with the Indians. **1776** [see CHEROKEE 4 (1)]. **1788** PUTNAM in *Life & Corr. Cutler* I. 377 Congress had promised them a treaty, which was to have been holden about this time.

+2. A formal contract relating to peace, land purchases, indemnities, etc., entered into by representatives of the United States government and Indian tribes.

1789 *Ann. 1st Congress* 40 The treaty [was] entered into by the said Commissioners Plenipotentiary and the sachems and warriors of the Wyandot, Delaware, Chippawa, and Ottawa nations of Indians. **1827** MCKENNEY *Tour to Lakes* 479 The United States agreed to assemble the Chippeway tribe upon Lake Superior during the present year, in order to give full effect to the said treaty. **1849** *New Mexican* 28 Nov. 2/3 It is folly . . . to think of securing peace and quiet by making treaties with these Indians. **1894** [see CHEROKEE 1]. **1912** *Indian Laws & Tr.* III. 539 For fulfilling treaties with Senecas of New York: For permanent annuity . . . , six thousand dollars.

3. *Attrib. and comb.* with *breaking, fund, line, party.*

1797 HAWKINS *Letters* 148 The line run between the Indians and the white inhabitants . . . [was] for the express purpose of ascertaining a line of accommodation for the white settlers who were then over the treaty line. **1842** *S. Lit. Messenger* VIII. 578/2 We were often visited by deputations and treaty parties of the many wilder tribes of Indians. **1865** *Wkly. New Mexican* 3 March 1/4 They compel the people . . . to make a detour of one hundred and fifty miles to avoid these marauding, treaty-breaking savages. **1871** *Rep. Indian Affairs* (1872) 306, I would recommend . . . a pro rata division of the Klamath and Modoc treaty-funds for employés and annuities.

+Treaty-ground. A place designated for holding a treaty conference with Indians. *Obs.* — **1836** *Knickerb.* VII. 588 The treaty-ground was forty miles above Fort Howard. **1846** MCKENNEY *Memoirs* I. 75 We had arrived at the treaty ground, and were waiting to give time for . . . many Indians to come.

+Treaty Indian. An Indian belonging to a tribe which has signed a treaty with the United States. *Obs.* Hence *non-treaty Indian.* — **1877** CAMPION *On Frontier* 8 Though 'treaty Indians,' [they] had a well-served reputation of being . . . horse-thieves. **1877** *Rep. Indian Affairs* 12 The three chief leaders of all the non-treaty Indians, agreed to go upon the reservation with their several bands.

+Treaty-making power. The power or authority to make treaties. — **1796** WASHINGTON *Writings* XIII. 178 It is thus that the treaty-making power has been understood by foreign nations. **1870** *Nation* 10 Feb. 86/1 An amendment may readily be such as most materially to affect our foreign relations, . . . as in the treaty-making power. **1900** *Congress. Rec.* 19 Jan. 980/2 The President is a part of the treaty-making power, but not the whole of it.

Treble viol. A stringed musical instrument played with a bow and having a treble pitch. {1611–} — **1655** *Essex Probate Rec.* I. 224 A treble violl, 10s. **1853** FELT *Customs New Eng.* 45 [Musical instruments] used in a few of our earliest families, were the spinet, virginal, and treble viol.

* **Tree,** *n.*

1. In phrases with *of*: * **a.** *Tree of life,* +the American arbor-vitae, *Thuja occidentalis.*

[**1712** *Phil. Trans.* XXVII. 423 American Tree of Life, *Thuya.*] **1785** MARSHALL *Amer. Grove* 151 *Thuya.* Arbor vitae, or Tree of Life.

b. *Tree of liberty* {1837–, in France}, a tree regarded as a symbol of freedom; the elm. Also *fig.*

Cf. LIBERTY TREE.

1765 *Universal Mag.* XXXVII. 376/2 The great tree at the south part of the town [Boston is] . . . known by the name of the Tree of Liberty. **1781** HUTCHINSON *Diary & Lett.* I. 147 He had been harrassed . . . , his house plundered, and himself drove to their Tree of Liberty, and forced to a resignation. **1841** *Lowell Offering* I. 359 The little Pilgrim band . . . planted with a careful hand, The sacred Tree of Liberty. **1868** BEECHER *Norwood* 328 We are agreed, then, the elm is the Tree of Liberty.

‖**c.** *Tree of friendship,* a tree symbolic of friendship.

1846 BROWNE *Trees Amer.* 507 [About 1722] a deputation of Indians came to their newly-settled minister, . . . requesting permission to plant [two elms] . . . before his door, as a mark of their regard, or as the 'Tree of Friendship.'

2. *Up a tree.* **+a.** *fig.* In a difficult or embarrassing position.

1825 NEAL *Bro. Jonathan* I. 112 If you don't, says I, I'm up a tree, says I. **1845** S. SMITH *J. Downing's Lett.* 36 So there I found I was up a tree again. **1911** SAUNDERS *Col. Todhunter* 110, I'm up a tree in the matter of campaign expenses.

+b. *fig.* In the position of a spectator.

1835 LONGSTREET *Ga. Scenes* 230 It may be funny, . . . but it looks mightily like yearnest to a man up a tree.

3. *attrib.* **a.** In the names of plants that are relatively large or treelike.

1847 WOOD *Botany* 376 R[hododendron] *arborescens.* . . . Tree Azalea. . . . Flowers large, rose color. **1848** *Rep. Comm. Patents 1847* 129 The tree corn is highly recommended by some. **1821** *Mass. H. S. Coll.* 2 Ser. IX. 154 *Populus grandidentata,* Tree poplar. **1894** *Amer. Folk-Lore* VII. 95 *Nicotiana glauca,* . . . tree tobacco, Santa Barbara Co., Cal. **1869** FULLER *Flower Gatherers* 139 Do you mean this tree-tulip, sir? **1817–8** EATON *Botany* (1822) 344 *Lycopodium dendroideum,* tree-weed. **1785** MARSHALL *Amer. Grove* 157 *Vaccinium arboreum.* Winter, or Tree Whortle-Berry. . . . The fruit is small, ripening late in autumn.

b. In the names of birds, animals, etc., that live in or frequent trees.

1844 *Nat. Hist. N.Y., Zoology* II. 160 The Tree Bunting, *Emberiza Canadensis,* . . . is a northern bird. **1893** ROOSEVELT *Wilderness Hunter* 355 On the walls were nailed the skins of . . . raccoons, wild cats, and the tree-civet. **1872** COUES *Key to Birds* 45 The crural feathers are . . . sometimes long and flowing, as in . . . our tree-cuckoos. **1870** *Amer. Naturalist* IV. 126 A specimen of the Brown Tree Duck, *Dendrocygna fulva,* was . . . presented by Mr. N. B. Moore to the Smithsonian Institution. **1897** BLANCHAN *Bird Neighbors* 84 White-breasted Nuthatch (*Sitta carolinensis*). . . . Called also Tree-mouse. **1806** *Balance* V. 265/1 It was nothing, as he afterwards expressed himself, but 'a —— tree-peck.' **1835** AUDUBON *Ornith. Biog.* III. 176 At Indian Key, I observed an immense quantity of beautiful tree snails. **1822** WOODS *English Prairie* (1904) 289 Tree-squirrels are of two or more sorts, and are eaten here. **1892** TORREY *Foot-Path Way* 182 Beside these tree swallows there are purple martins, barn swallows, . . . and chimney swifts.

c. In special combinations.

Tree agent, one who sells young trees; *t. culture,* the culture, or the study of the culture, of trees; *t. day,* a day upon which a college class plants a tree as a memorial; *t. looker,* (see quotation); *t. man,* =*tree agent; t. molasses,* =MAPLE SYRUP; *t. peddler,* =*tree agent; t. ripe,* ripened on a tree; *t. scraper,* a utensil for scraping turpentine, etc., from the trunk of a tree; *t. warden,* one having supervision over trees.

1879 STOCKTON *Rudder Grange* xii, I invited the tree-agent to get down out of the tree. **1883** *Rep. Indian Affairs* 249 Tree culture, . . . one teacher. **1906** *Boston Transcript* 9 June 1. 3/5 Tree Day has by honored tradition been the one great fete day which Wellesley aims to keep entirely to herself. **1913** *Dialect Notes* IV. 28 Tree looker, . . . a timber estimater, cruiser, etc. **1879** STOCKTON *Rudder Grange* xiii, Happenin' to look over to old John's, I saw that tree-man there. **1880** *Harper's Mag.* Sept. 582/1 We'd hed buckwheats an' tree molasses for breakfast that day. **1861** *Ill. Agric. Soc. Trans.* IV. 511 The regular Nurseryman does not make a large profit out of him, whatever the tree peddler may do. **1872** *Vt. Bd. Agric. Rep.* I. 72 There is a time in the life of a fruit when its growth is complete, —when it will receive nothing further from the tree. It is then tree-ripe. **1856** *Mich. Agric. Soc. Trans.* VII. 54 D. O. & W. S. Penfield . . . [exhibited] 3 tree scrapers. **1910** *Springfield W. Repub.* 8 Dec. 3 One of the things to be seriously considered by tree wardens is the disturbing intelligence that the gypsy moth is making its way into the western counties.

Tree, *v.* {1650–}

+1. *tr.* To cause (a hunted animal) to take refuge in a tree. Also *absol.*

1733 BYRD *Journey to Eden* (1901) 304 In our way to this place we treed a Bear. **1786** WASHINGTON *Diaries* III. 5 Found a fox . . . and after running it very indifferently and treeing it once, caught it. **1832** KENNEDY *Swallow Barn* I. 91 It was as good as a dozen dogs treeing an opossum. **1889** CUSTER *Tenting on Plains* 181 The dog treed the coon. **1895** *Outing* XXVI. 439/2 The old man advised that we should wait till the dogs treed.

+b. *fig.* To stump, corner, or catch (a person). {1859–}

1834 CARRUTHERS *Kentuckian* I. 97, I thought I would tree him next time. **1841** COOPER *Deerslayer* vi, We've fairly tree'd the scamps. **1875** 'MARK TWAIN' in *Lotus Leaves* 28, I had the Unabridged and I was ciphering around in the back end, hoping I might tree her among the pictures. **1881** *Harper's Mag.* May 884/1 Though not exactly able to tree him, . . . [they] did go on about the prospect of the old bachelor . . . being caught at last.

+2. *intr.* To take refuge behind a tree when fighting or skirmishing in wooded country. Also *refl.* and *p.p.*

1756 *Doc. Hist. N.Y. State* (1849) I. 477 Lieut. Blair . . . behaved like a brave Soldier; for being wounded the first Fire, he begged his Men to Tree all. **1841** B. DRAKE *Life Tecumseh* 58 The remainder of the party, who were near by, returned the fire, and all of them 'treed.' **1852** WATSON *Nights in Block-House* 141 The Indians treed themselves. **1886** Z. F. SMITH *Kentucky* 296 Crist and Crepps stood over him, keeping the Indians *treed,* while the release was made.

3. Of an animal: To climb a tree for safety when hunted. {a1700–}

1769 WASHINGTON *Diaries* I. 321 Chased the above fox for an Hour and 45 Minutes when he treed again. **1833** J. HALL *Harpe's Head* 230 [The raccoon's enemies] took care to prevent him from again treeing. **1899**

JEWETT *Queen's Twin* 187 Soon as the coon trees, you'll hear the dog sing, now I tell you.
fig. **1853** 'P. PAXTON' *Yankee in Texas* 325 The hangers on about town do not run to see, but, according to their vernacular, 'tree' in the first store or 'grocery' convenient.

Tree box. 1. The common bushy box used for hedges. **2.** A box-like wooden frame for protecting a tree, esp. when it is young. — **(1) 1785** WASHINGTON *Diaries* II. 360 Received . . . an equal number of cuttings of the Tree Box. **1858** WARDER *Hedges & Evergreens* II. 240 Where a moderate or low hedge is needed, . . . nothing can be better than the Tree-box. **(2) 1876** 'MARK TWAIN' *Tom Sawyer* ii. 27 [Tom] sat down on the tree-box discouraged. **1896** HARRIS *Sister Jane* 157, I looked back and saw him whittling away with his pocket knife on the tree-box.

+**Tree claim.** =TIMBER CLAIM. — **1885** *Santa Fé Wkly. New Mexican* 10 Dec. 2/5 The ruling . . . leaves the settler the right to take either a pre-emption or a homestead in addition to his 'tree claim.' **1892** *Aberdeen & Brown Co.* (S. Dak.) *Illustrated* 5 Exclusive of tree-claims, there are under cultivation in the county 600,000 acres of land.

+**Tree coral.** A branching coral, as madrepore. — **1871** *Harper's Mag.* June 28 On the confines of this channel may be seen in clear water a perfect forest of coral—tree-coral, we call it, on account of its great size. **1884** *Nat. Museum Bul.* No. 27, 821 Contents of ditty-box: 1 broken dory-compass; 1 spray of tree coral; 1 bunch of buttons. **1891** *Cent.* 6453/3.

+**Tree cranberry.** The high or bush cranberry, *Viburnum opulus.* (Cf. CRANBERRY TREE.) — **1846** BROWNE *Trees Amer.* 353 The edible-fruited guilder rose or tree-cranberry . . . [is] found from York to Canada. **1866** LOSSING *Hudson* 35 Here and there among the rocks . . . the tree-cranberry appeared.

+**Tree cricket.** Any one of various whitish American crickets of the genus *Oecanthus.* — **1859** *Amer. Cycl.* VI. 63/1 They form the genus *œcanthus,* and are called tree or climbing crickets. **1868** *Amer. Naturalist* II. 333 During this month the Tree-cricket, *Œcanthus niveus* . . . , lays its eggs in the branches of peach trees. **1877** *Vermont Bd. Agric. Rep.* IV. 154 The tree cricket . . . is sometimes very troublesome to the raspberry.

+**Tree fish.** A rockfish of the Pacific coast, *Sebastocarus serriceps.* — **1884** GOODE, etc. *Fisheries* I. 263 Wherever this species [of rock cod] receives a distinctive name, it is known as the 'Tree-fish,' an appellation originating with the Portuguese at Monterey. **1911** *Rep. Fisheries 1908* 314/2.

Tree frog. Any one of various tailless, leaping amphibians, usually of the family Hylidae, commonly found in trees. {1802–} Freq. *green tree frog.* — **1738** CATESBY *Carolina* II. 71 The Green-Tree Frog . . . was of a bright grass green. **1785** CUTLER in *Life & Corr.* II. 229 Dr. Hill says the tree-toad, or tree-frog as he calls it, is peculiar to North America, and to some few places in the North of Europe. **1806** LEWIS in *L. & Clark Exped.* V. (1905) 87 A smal green tree-frog [on the upper Clearwater]. **1854** HAMMOND *Hills, Lakes,* etc. 154 Just listen to the tree-frog, how merrily he pipes all along the shore. **1907** M. C. DICKERSON *Frog Book* 126 The Green Tree Frog, *Hyla cinerea,* . . . is found in the southern United States.

＊**Treenail.** Also **trennell, trunnell,** etc. A round, hard-wood pin used in fastening timbers together, as in erecting log and frame houses.
1645 *Conn. Rec.* I. 473, 6000 Trunnells, 500 of Iron, part att Frances Homes, part att Mr. Tappings, the rest in a grapnell lying att the Waterside. **1675** *Mass. H. S. Coll.* 4 Ser. VII. 42 The vessell cast away was buillt with pyne, cedar, or such like wood. Not a trennell in hir. **1796** *Ann. 4th Congress* 2 Sess. 2791 White oak trennails, [were sold] at 60 cents per 100. **1852** WATSON *Nights in Block-House* 16 The palisades were strengthened and kept in their places by stout ribbons or wall-pieces, pinned to them with inch tree-nails on the inside. **1897** MOORE *How to Build a Home* 90 All sills, girts, and posts are to be securely framed into each other, mortised and fastened, with hard-wood pins or treenails.
attrib. **1799** WASHINGTON *Writings* XIV. 233 The partition fence . . . may be taken away and applied to that fence, and to the trunnel-fence on the Mill road. **1851** CIST *Cincinnati* 228 Plug, Bung, and Tree Nail Factory.—Employs eight hands; product, twelve thousand dollars.

Tree onion. A variety of onion, esp. *Allium cepa bulbellifera,* which produces a cluster of bulbs at the summit of the stems. {1832–} — **1840** DEWEY *Mass. Flowering Plants* 210 *A[llium] proliferum,* Tree Onion. . . . A native of the West Indies; rarely cultivated. **1859** *Ill. Agric. Soc. Trans.* III. 507 The tree onion is grown from seed bulbs, which form on the top of the stalk. **1919** STURTEVANT *Notes on Edible Plants* 31 *A[llium] canadense.* Tree Onion. Wild Garlic. . . . It is found throughout northern United States and Canada.

Tree planter. a. One who plants or sets out trees. +**b.** *Tree Planters State,* Nebraska. — **(a) 1858** WARDER *Hedges & Evergreens* 224 The people of whole neighborhoods are becoming tree-planters. **1864** *Ohio Agric. Rep.* XVIII. App. 50 A nurseryman will . . . soon learn that it is better to pinch the tips of the laterals . . . and produce the true desideratum for the tree-planter. **(b) 1895** *Neb. Laws* 441 Nebraska shall hereafter in a popular sense be known and referred to as the 'Tree Planters State.'

Tree poppy. A California shrub (*Dendromecon rigidum*) having large yellow flowers. — [**1866** LINDLEY & MOORE *Treas. Botany* 392/2 *Dendromecon,* literally Tree Poppy, is a most appropriate name, the plant having all the aspect and character of the poppy tribe, combined with a woody stem and branches.] **1898** A. M. DAVIDSON *Calif. Plants* 108 In some parts of the state, tree poppies flourish on mountain sides or in sandy washes. **1915** ARMSTRONG & THORNBER *Western Wild Flowers* 166 [The] Tree Poppy . . . is a handsome and decorative shrub, both in form and color.

Tree primrose. The common evening primrose, *Oenothera biennis.* — [**1629** PARKINSON *Paradisus* 264 *Lysimachia lutea siliquosa Virgiana.* The tree Primrose of Virginia. **1785** MARTYN *Rousseau's Bot.* (1794) xix. 256 Tree Primrose, a Virginian plant. . . . The corolla is a fine yellow.] **1814** BIGELOW *Florula Bostoniensis* 90 Tree primrose. . . . This plant, originally American, is now naturalized, and very common throughout Europe. **1840** DEWEY *Mass. Flowering Plants* 47 Tree Primrose. . . . Found in fields, and flowers from June to September.

Tree sparrow. {1770–} +=CANADA SPARROW. — **1810** WILSON *Ornithology* II. 123 [The] Tree Sparrow, *Fringilla Arborea,* . . . frequents sheltered hollows, thickets, and hedgerows, near springs of water. **1850** S. F. COOPER *Rural Hours* 414 The tree-sparrow is one of the largest and handsomest of its tribe. **1875** BURROUGHS *Winter Sunshine* 27 Every tangle and overgrown field or lane swarmed with . . . Canada or tree-sparrows. **1917** *Birds of Amer.* III. 40 The Tree Sparrow . . . [sings] real songs in real winter weather.

+**Tree sugar.** (See quot. 1859.) — **1859** BARTLETT 488 *Tree-Sugar,* sugar made from the Maple-tree. Western. **1886** Z. F. SMITH *Kentucky* 697 The ministers . . . traversed the Wilderness Path in Indian file, living upon biscuit, broiled bacon, dried beef, and tree sugar.

Tree toad, *n.* =TREE FROG. {1855–} — **1778** CARVER *Travels* 489 Among the reptiles of North America there is a species of the toad termed the Tree Toad, which is nearly of the same shape as the common sort, but smaller and with longer claws. **1830** PICKERING *Inquiries Emigrant* 95 There is a singular kind of toad, called a tree-toad, on account of its being mostly seen on trees, up which it climbs. **1899** *Mo. So. Dakotan* I. 165 They were content to spend their days . . . listening as evening approached, to the orchestra of beetles and tree toads. **1906** *Harper's Mag.* Feb. 391/1 [Panthea sat] on the porch steps throughout the long droning of the tree-toads in the yard.

‖**Tree toad,** *v. intr.* To make a noise resembling that of a tree toad. Also *vbl. n.* — **1866** A. D. WHITNEY *L. Goldthwaite* x, They tree-toaded, they cat-called, they shouted, they cheered. *Ib.* vii, What a 'howl' was, superlative to 'tree-toading,' 'owl-hooting,' and other divertisements, did not appear.

＊**Trefoil.**
＊**1.** Any one of various plants of the genus *Trifolium.* Also *attrib.*
1760 WASHINGTON *Diaries* I. 148 Began to prepare a Small piece of Ground . . . to put Trefoil in. **1786** CUTLER in *Life & Corr.* II. 264 The two species of trefoil undoubtedly are native, for they abound in new settlements in the eastern, southern, and western parts of New England. **1804** J. ROBERTS *Penna. Farmer* 26, I then sowed . . . broad cast, at the rate of six pounds of clover, and four pounds of trefoil seed per acre. **1834** PECK *Gaz. Illinois* 34 Of the trefoil, or clover, there is but little cultivated. **1919** STURTEVANT *Notes on Edible Plants* 575 *T[rifolium] involucratum.* Trefoil. Western North America. This clover is eaten by the Digger tribes.

2. With specifying terms: (see quotations).
1847 WOOD *Botany* 231 *Desmodium Canadense.* . . . Bush Trefoil. . . . Rather common in woods. **1814** BIGELOW *Florula Bostoniensis* 168 *Trifolium arvense,* Field trefoil, . . . is exceedingly common in roads and dry fields.

3. *attrib.* In the specific names of plants.
1885 HAVARD *Flora W. & S. Texas* 458 The Trefoil Barberry (*Berberis trifoliata*), [is a] low evergreen bush with glaucous, spiny leaves, yellow blossoms, and red, palatable berries. **1901** MOHR *Plant Life Ala.* 99 *Ptelea trifoliata* (trefoil hop tree).

＊**Trembler.** +(See quotation.) — **1847** EMORY *Military Reconn.* 70 They [Indians in valley of Gila R.] were supposed by some to be the Cayotes, a branch of the Apaches, but Londeau thought they belonged to the Tribe of Tremblers, who acquired their name from their emotions at meeting the whites.

＊**Trembling,** *a.* In special collocations: (see quotations.) — **1897** SUDWORTH *Arborescent Flora* 128 *Populus tremuloides,* Aspen. . . . [Called] Trembling Aspen (Iowa). **1834** PECK *Gaz. Illinois* 368 *Trembling Lands.* . . . On Rock river . . . is a tract of country for thirty or forty miles in extent . . . made up of alternate sand ridges covered with shrubs and quagmires, and swamps, that *shake* for some distance around when the traveler attempts to pass over them.

＊**Trencher.** A plate or platter, usually of wood, upon which food was cut up or served. Now *hist.*
1637 *Md. Archives* IV. 70 One trencher. **1685** *Harvard Rec.* I. 78 [There] shall be allowed to the Butler thirty shillings on account of washing the trenchers. **1709** LAWSON *Carolina* 99 The Maple, of which we have two sorts, is used to make Trenchers, Spinning-wheels, &c. **1778** CARVER *Travels* 499 Trenchers [of bass wood] . . . wear smooth, and will last a long time. **1824** [see NOGGIN 1]. **1885** E. EGGLESTON in *Century Mag.* April 881/2 From pewter plates or wooden trenchers the first-comers ate without forks.

+**b.** (See quotation.)
1889 *Harper's Mag.* Jan. 238/2 The next binds his [beaver] trap to a flat stone 'about the size of a teakettle,' opens the jaws, and arranges the 'trencher,' as the pan is called, pressure on which springs the trap.

Trenton limestone. *Geol.* A limestone formation of a type exemplified at Trenton Falls, N.Y. {1854-} — **1843** *Nat. Hist. N.Y., Geology* III. 38 At Fort-Plain, . . . the change from Birdseye to Trenton limestone is perfectly abrupt. **1890** *Cent.* 3457/3 *Trenton limestone*, a rock of Lower Silurian age, finely exhibited at Trenton Falls, New York.

+**Trestlework.** A structure, as a railway bridge, supported by trestles. Also transf. and attrib. — **1848** *Knickerb.* XVIII. 153 The thick tresselwork of an hundred Lombardy poplars screened it from the profane gaze of the passer-by. **1863** F. MOORE *Rebellion Rec.* V. I. 29 A force from Gen. Sherman's command . . . destroyed several pieces of trestle-work on the Mississippi Central Railroad. **1870** LOGAN *Before Footlights* 205 The rebel General Lyon . . . had closed communication between Louisville and Nashville, by burning an important trestlework bridge on the road. **1896** SHINN *Story of Mine* 210 Nothing better can be found in the way of concrete illustration than the . . . trestle works, machinery, and all.

Trial balance. In double-entry book-keeping, a balance arrived at by comparing the sum of all the debits with that of all the credits. Also in allusive context. — **1838** *U.S. Mag.* I. 42 He becomes familiar with the various account books, . . . with trial balances, balance sheets [etc.]. **1847** A. LAWRENCE *Diary & Corr.* 242 The early business habits you acquired are . . . to be carried forward till the footing up of the account, and the trial-balance presented to the Master at his coming. **1884** CABLE *Dr. Sevier* 59, I should begin to take a trial-balance off the books. **1902** LORIMER *Lett. Merchant* 96 [They] spend the evenings . . . hunting up the eight cents that they are out on the trial balance.

+**Trial judge.** A judge who presides at the trial of a case. — **1896** *Internat. Typogr. Union Proc.* 11/1 The trial judge has publicly expressed his lack of confidence in his construction of the statute.

+**Trial justice.** A justice of the peace or other subordinate magistrate empowered to try certain types of cases. — **1869** *Mass. Acts & Resolves* 556 Whoever, without a written license . . . , takes any trout . . . , shall forfeit and pay a fine of twenty-five dollars for every such offence, to be recovered before any trial justice. **1906** *Ib.* 676 Police, district and municipal courts and trial justices shall have jurisdiction of offences arising under the provisions of this act.

+**Trial sermon.** A sermon delivered by: **a.** A ministerial candidate seeking ordination. **b.** A minister complying with an invitation extended him by a congregation that is considering engaging him. — **1801-3** J. LYLE *Diary* (MS.) 98 Mr. Stuart preached his trial sermon before ordination. **1863** P. S. DAVIS *Young Parson* 9 The Rev. Petit Meagre had accepted an invitation to preach a 'trial sermon' before the Gainfield congregation.

* **Tribe.** +A body of American Indians bound together by consanguinity, common customs and ceremonies, and language or dialect. Also transf.

1723 *Amer. Wkly. Mercury* 5 Sept. 2/1, I do observe with Pleasure the Appearance of so many of the Sachems and Chief Captains of your Tribes. **1812** *Salem Gazette* 5 June 3/3 The Warriors of the Democratic Tribe will hold a powow at Agawam on Tuesday next. **1872** TICE *Over Plains* 13 [The Kickapoos] have a system of public schools and good school houses, where all the children of the tribe are educated. **1885** *Rep. Indian Affairs* 33 In years gone by, before the Government assumed a guardianship over the Indians, . . . continual war with neighboring tribes . . . prevented increase in population with many tribes. **1913** *Indian Laws & Tr.* III. 557 There shall be deposited . . . the sums of which the said tribe may be entitled.

* **Tributary.** A stream that contributes to or flows into a larger stream or lake. {1846-} — **1831** HOLLEY *Texas* (1833) 54 The whole of this eastern section of Texas is very well watered by the above mentioned rivers and their tributaries. **1836** J. HALL *Statistics of West* 59 The great road . . . pursues the valley of one of these tributaries. **1884** [see MUSK TORTOISE]. **1902** WISTER *Virginian* 311 This creek received tributaries and widened, making a valley for itself.

* **Trick.**

+**1.** A small article or one of little worth; a personal belonging or effect. Usually pl.

1869 *Overland Mo.* III. 131 In Texas you never have *things* in your house, or *baggage* on your journey, but 'tricks.' **1884** MONTEITH *Parson Brooks* 21 What was there left to ask the world for except a little store tricks 'terbacky,' 'kofee'? **1906** 'O. HENRY' *Trimmed Lamp* 77 Here's a little trick I picked out for you on my way over.

+**2.** A child, young woman, or animal. *colloq.* Usually *little trick.*

1887 *Century Mag.* May 113/1 We uns played tergether w'en we wuz little tricks. **1890** *Stock Grower & Farmer* 29 March 7/1 Down in the Panhandle . . . I used to ride a little trick named Dandy. **1904** HARBEN *Georgians* 99 He had . . . a beautiful young daughter, the purtiest trick I ever laid my eyes on.

+**3.** A device used in conjuring; a conjure bag. {1910} Also attrib.

1893 M. A. OWEN *Voodoo Tales* 209 The aunties searched under every doorstone for 'tricks.'

+**Trick doctor.** A conjurer or sorcerer. — **1889** BRUCE *Plantation Negro* 116 The trick doctor . . . employs the arts of the Obeah practitioners . . . with the arts of the Myal. **1898** PAGE *Red Rock* 161 The trick-doctor . . . bowed himself off.

+**Triddler.** *local.* =PECTORAL SANDPIPER. — **1888** TRUMBULL *Names of Birds* 176 Pectoral Sandpiper. . . . Known also to some Atlantic City gunners as Triddler. **1917** *Birds of Amer.* I. 233.

Triennial (catalog). +A college catalogue or list of alumni issued every three years. — **1847** J. MITCHELL *Reminisc. College* 198 The Triennial Catalogue becomes increasingly a mournful record . . . to survivors. **1860** *Songs of Yale* 84 By no means fail to come to Yale . . . And shine in the Triennial. **1890** HOLMES *Over Teacups* 28 The class of 1829 at Harvard College, of which I am a member, graduated, according to the triennial, fifty-nine in number.

* **Trier.** A tool or implement used in testing or sampling something. {1797-} — **1855** 'P. PAXTON' *Capt. Priest* 241 We left our friend . . . with his hand raised and prepared to plunge his trier into the puncheon. **1882** PECK *Sunshine* 103 Van took a butter tryer and lifted it out. **1901** *Dept. Agric. Yrbk.* 1900 237 These samples are drawn by means of a 'trier,' or clover-seed sampler, which is thrust through the bag, allowing the seed to run out at the open end of the trier.

Trigger. {1621-}

+**1.** *Quick on (the) trigger*, quick at pulling the trigger in shooting; fig., impetuous, quick to act. {1905-}

1808 WEEMS *Lett.* II. 377, I trust that all your Aids will be quick on the trigger. **1853** SIMMS *Sword & Distaff* 76, I was afear'd he'd be too quick on trigger. **1865** *Harper's Mag.* July 157/1 To be 'quick on the trigger' is their greatest boast. **1873** BEADLE *Undevel. West* 371 He is reported 'so quick on trigger,' that all the other 'shootists' in the country have an awe of him. **1884** 'CRADDOCK' *Where Battle Was Fought* 47 You are quick on the trigger.

2. In special combinations.

Trigger eye, fig., a sharp eye; *t. file-fish*, (see quotation); *t. itch*, eagerness to use a gun.

1837 NEAL *Charcoal Sk.* (1838) 63 He agreed to keep his trigger eye on the dog. **1814** MITCHILL *Fishes N.Y.* 467 Trigger file-fish. *Balistes sufflamen.* . . . Is said to shed his scales almost immediately after he is taken out of water. **1914** 'BOWER' *Flying U Ranch* 154 The man who feels the trigger-itch had better throw his gun away.

* **Trim,** *n.* +'The visible woodwork or finish of a house, as the baseboards, door- and window-casings, etc.' (*Cent.*). — **1884** *N.Y. Ev. Post* 14 April (*Cent.*), 972 No wood having been used in construction except for floors, doors, and trim. **1887** *Harper's Mag.* May 935/1, I was just thinking of . . . a rug on a bare floor, a trim of varnished pine. **1897** MOORE *How to Build a Home* 60 The owner should require the architect to furnish details of the trim.

* **Trim,** *v.* To trim one's corners, (see CORNER *n.* 4 b).

* **Trimmer.** +A dishonest or unscrupulous lawyer. *colloq.* — **1891** S. M. WELCH *Recoll.* 1830-40 293 There was an *esprit de corps* of reliability and honor in their practice; excluding such characters as are known as 'Shysters,' 'Tombs Lawyers,' 'Trimmers,' and lawyers guilty of 'sharp practice.'

+**Trimountain,** *n.* and *a.* Also **trimontane.** With reference to Boston, Mass. **1.** *n. pl.* A group of three hills. **2.** *adj.* Having, or related to, three hills. — (1) **1838** HAWTHORNE *Twice-told Tales* II. 10 From this station, . . . Gage may have beheld his disastrous victory on Bunker Hill (unless one of the tri-mountains intervened). (2) **1840** — *Works* XII. 219 The dusk has settled heavily upon the woods, the waves, and the Trimountain peninsula. **1851** WORTLEY *Travels in U.S.* 62 [Boston] is not only called the Granite City, but the Trimountain City. **1885** *Century Mag.* Feb. 511/2 It has required some independence for . . . a trimontane poet to be a progressive and speculative thinker.

* **Trinket.** A small ornamental or fancy article such as was used in trade with the American Indians. Also attrib.

1756 *Lett. to Washington* II. 21 As to Silver Trinkets for Wrists & Arms, they were never given but to the Chief Warrior of the Party. **1823** JAMES *Exped.* I. 166 [The Indians] brought jerked deer meat, mockasins, &c. to exchange for their favourite drink, and for trinkets. **1846** COOPER *Redskins* iv, Our original plan was to travel in the character of immigrant trinket and essence peddlers. **1881** *Rep. Indian Affairs* 142 The policy at that time pursued towards them . . . [was to purchase] innumerable trinkets, which were of no value to them. a**1918** G. STUART *On Frontier* II. 51 When a man takes an Indian girl he is expected to leave a good horse, some blankets, and trinkets at her father's lodge.

+**b.** (See quotation.) *Obs.*

1859 MATSELL *Vocabulum* 92 Trinkets, bowie-knife and revolver.

* **Trip.**

+**1.** *To get a trip*, of a steamboat, to get enough freight, passengers, etc., to justify a run.

1883 'MARK TWAIN' *Life on Miss.* xxiii, This calm craft would go as advertised, 'if she got her trip.'

+**2.** (See quotation.)

1891 *Cent.* 6485/2 *Trip*, . . . in the fisheries, the catch, take, or fare of fish caught during a voyage; the proceeds of a trip in fish.

+**3.** Time, occasion. *colloq.*

1902 WHITE *Blazed Trail* 188, I guess I'll let you off this trip. **1902** WISTER *Virginian* 243 He ain't got religion this trip.

+**4.** In special combinations.

Trip book, (see quotation) *local*; *t. card*, a card giving route information for cyclists; *t. wagon*, a wagon or car used for hauling ore in a mine.

1891 *Cent.* 6486/1 *Trip-book*, . . . a book in which the account of a voyage of a fishing-vessel is made up, showing the shares belonging respectively to the vessel and the crew. (Massachusetts.) **1897** *Outing* XXX. 492/2 These trip-cards . . . have been adopted by many other clubs for the information of riders. **1874** RAYMOND *6th Rep. Mines* 405 The chargers can take the ore in quantities to suit. A trip-wagon, holding one charge, is generally used.

+**Trip and twitch.** A hold or maneuver in wrestling. Also transf. — **1746** *N.H. Hist. Soc. Coll.* II. 88 He tried his strength, and skill, in his favorite mode of 'trip and twitch.' **1876** *Congress. Rec.* 8 Aug. 5302/2 In this body, . . . there is none of that trip and twitch by which legislation is jerked through so quickly that you cannot see it go.

+**Trip hammer**, *n.* A heavy machine hammer which is raised by mechanical means and allowed to fall by gravity. {1831-} Also attrib. — **1781** PETERS *Hist. Conn.* (1829) 199 Anchor making is done by water and trip hammers. *a*1817 DWIGHT *Travels* II. 15 Here he [Hon. Hugh Orr] built a shop; and set up the first trip-hammer in this part of the country. **1883** *Harper's Mag.* Nov. 825/2 Another machine . . . makes complete cuts by means of systems of chisels acting on the trip-hammer principle. **1922** PARRISH *Case & Girl* 251 His heart [was] beating like a trip-hammer.

+**Trip-hammer**, *v. tr.* To beat with a trip hammer. In fig. sense. — **1867** *Harper's Mag.* Aug. 345/2 So to speak, I wasn't trip-hammered. I was taken through the rollers.

+**Triple play.** *Baseball.* A play during which three men are put out. — **1870** *De Witt's Base-Ball Guide* 42 The remarks concerning double and triple plays will apply to the third baseman. **1885** CHADWICK *Art of Pitching* 140 Whenever three players are put out by the fielders after a ball has been pitched to the bat, and before it is again sent to the bat, a triple play is made. **1889** CAMP *College Sports* (1893) 177 Triple plays are also possible, although seldom made.

Triplet. {1656-} +**1.** (See quot. 1864.) **2.** *Baseball.* A three-base hit. — (1) **1864** DICK *Amer. Hoyle* (1866) 177 *Triplets* are three cards of the same denomination, and rank higher than two pairs. **1887** KELLER *Draw Poker* 14 Full Hand—(Triplets accompanied by a pair). . . . A full hand beats a flush. (2) **1883** *Chicago Inter-Ocean* 9 June 3/1 In the seventh and ninth innings Radbourne hit for a triplet and a four-bagger, each productive of runs. **1893** [see DOUBLE *n.* 5].

Tripletail. A large marine fish, *Lobotes surinamensis.* {1803-} Also with specifying term. — **1884** GOODE, etc. *Fisheries* I. 444-5 The Tripletail of the New York market, *Lobotes surinamensis*, . . . is also called by various authors the 'Black Triple-tail.' **1896** JORDAN & EVERMANN *Check-List Fishes* 380 Flasher; Triple-tail; Dormeur. Atlantic Coast from Cape Cod to Surinam. **1911** *Rep. Fisheries 1908* 310/2.

*∗**Tripper.** +(See quot. 1891.) — **1882** MCCABE *New York* 244 The 'trippers,' as those men are called who only run three-quarters of a day, get $1.50. **1891** *Cent.* 6488/2 *Tripper*, . . . a street-railroad conductor or driver who is paid according to the number of trips which he makes, or who is employed to make special trips, as in the place of others who are laid off for any cause.

+**Trip slip.** (See quot. 1891.) — **1876** *Scribner's Mo.* April 910/2 The conductor, when he receives a fare, will immediately punch in the presence of the passenger, A blue trip slip for an 8 cent fare. **1891** *Cent.* 6488/3 *Trip-slip*, a slip of paper in which the conductor of a horse-car punches a hole as record of each fare taken.

*∗**Trivet.** Also †treavett, trevit. A stand, used in cooking over a fire, as a support for a pot, kettle, etc. — **1635** *Essex Probate Rec.* I. 5 A treavett a fier shovell and tongs. **1711** *Essex Inst. Coll.* IV. 187/1, I give to my Cousin Anne Williams . . . My brass Skimmer & Trevet to warm plates on. **1814** *Niles' Reg.* V. 318/1 By the New-York Hardware Manufactory, . . . improved andirons with trevits [are made]. **1888** EGGLESTON in *Century Mag.* Aug. 532/1 She got up to set the pot of coffee back on the trivet.

+**Triweekly**, *n.* A newspaper issued three times a week. — **1851** CIST *Cincinnati* 74 These are all dailies, tri-weeklies and weekly reissues of dailies. **1872** *Ill. Dept. Agric. Trans.* 136 Papers Published. . . . 1 triweekly, with circulation of 300. **1884** S. N. O. NORTH *Hist. Newspaper Press* 111 The *Spy* ran as a tri-weekly.

Triweekly, *a.* and *adv.*
+**1.** *adj.* Operating three times a week. {1903-}
1832 *Amer. State P.: Post Office* 348 The line of stages . . . has been increased from a bi-weekly to a tri-weekly line to Eastville. **1865** *Ore. State Jrnl.* 18 Nov. 1/2 From this point (Celilo), there is uninterrupted navigation, and daily or tri-weekly steamers running. **1877** HODGE *Arizona* 204 It is a tri-weekly route, and is made in eight days from San Diego to Mesilla.
2. *adv.* Three times a week.
1837 PECK *Gaz. Illinois* 180 The mail . . . arrives here tri-weekly. **1877** JOHNSON *Anderson Co., Kansas* 98 The mail was carried . . . at first only once a week, on a small mule, but soon after tri-weekly, in a two-horse hack. **1884** *Harper's Mag.* July 300/1 A line of . . . coaches has been established, leaving tri-weekly.

Troculus. {trochilus, 1579-; 1615-} ?+A water thrush. — **1672** JOSSELYN *New Eng. Rarities* 7 The Troculus, a small bird, black and white, no bigger than a Swallow. **1674** — *Two Voyages* 100 Other sorts of Birds there are, as the Troculus, Wag-tail, or Dishwater, which is here of a brown colour.

*∗**Trojan.** +A native or inhabitant of Troy, New York. — **1824** *Microscope* (Albany, N.Y.) 22 May 43/1 (Th.), Ye dull-minded Trojans . . . you must now hide your diminished heads. **1833** COKE *Subaltern's Furlough* xiv, The gallant 'Trojans,' as the inhabitants call themselves,

were partaking of the New York panic. **1888** *Troy* (N.Y.) *Daily Times* 25 Aug., Among the Trojans who went to the state firemen's convention at Cortland was Orange S. Ingram.

Troll, *n.* {1705-} A line or lure used in trolling. {1869} — **1886** *Leslie's Mo.* XXI. 742/2 We will . . . just drop a troll overboard without any sinker. **1894** *Outing* XXIV. 367/1 You had better throw out the trolls now.

*∗**Troll**, *v.¹ intr.* To fish by trailing the line after a boat. {1606-, in related senses} (See also TROLLING.¹) — **1835** HOFFMAN *Winter in West* I. 27 The skiff from which we trolled approached the margin. **1856** [see NEW YORK SHINER]. **1888** GOODE *Amer. Fishes* 108, I trolled with rod, reel and spinner.

Troll, *v.²* +To bring *up* (fish) with a trawl net or trawl line. (See also TROLLING.²) — **1884** GOODE, etc. *Fisheries* I. 291 When the Mackerel are t[r]olled up from twelve or fifteen fathoms below the surface their stomachs are often full of bait.

Trolley, Trolly.¹ (See quot. 1891.) {a1700-} Also attrib. with *lace.* — **1759** *Boston Gazette* 13 Aug., Indian Ginghams, white Callico, Cape Lace, black Bone Lace, and Trolly ditto. **1775** SINGLETON *Social N.Y.* 247 Henry Wilmot, in Hanover Square, sells . . . minionet, thread, trolly and Dutch laces. **1891** *Cent.* 6497/2 *Trolley, trolly*, . . . in *Eng. lacemaking*, lace the pattern of which is outlined with a thicker thread, or a flat narrow border made up of several such threads.

Trolley, Trolly.² {1823-}
+**1.** A device for collecting electric current from a wire; a trolley pole.
1890 *Amer. Notes & Q.* IV. 275 A motorneer is the man who rides on the front of an electric car and handles the trolly, which runs on the wires overhead. **1902** SLOANE *Stand. Electrical Dict.* s.v., Trolleys are principally used on electric railroads.
b. A pulley running on an overhead rope or track.
1901 MERWIN & WEBSTER *Calumet 'K'* 99, I see, . . . you're going to run it over on a trolley.
+**2.** A trolley car, or a railroad on which such cars are operated.
[**1891** *Month* LXXIII. 24, I jumped off the trolley.] **1907** *St. Nicholas* Aug. 883/1 The five o'clock trolley from Putney dropped a boy at the Fairport station. **1923** WATTS *L. Nichols* 28 Towards noon the family trade arrived whether in carriages or by the trolley.
3. Attrib. in sense 2 with *crowd, franchise*, etc. {1891-}
1893 'THANET' *Stories Western Town* 136 All day . . . the crooked pole slips up and down the trolley wire, as the yellow cars rattle. **1897** *Voice* 16 Sept. 5/5 In Greenwich, Conn., . . . the people . . . are able to ride in a trolley stage-coach that needs no rails for its operation. **1904** A. SURBRIDGE *Confessions of Club Woman* 81 After that there were trips to parks and trolley-rides and carriage drives. **1905** *McClure's Mag.* XXIV. 346 Now for the 'trolley crowd'; what have they done with it? **1906** QUICK *Double Trouble* 138 You know the talks we've had with the fellows about this trolley franchise. **1921** Trolley system [see ELECTRICAL ENGINEER].

+**Trolley car.** An electric car or tram. Also attrib. — **1895** *Pop. Science Mo.* April 758 The lazy barges will perhaps rival in bustle the trolley car on land. **1896** *N.Y. Tribune* 4 Sept. 7/4 It is proposed . . . to conduct . . . a hasty tour of the city, . . . ending possibly with a trolley-car party to Mount Vernon. **1908** *Springfield W. Repub.* 3 Sept. 16 Potato bugs on the rails stalled eight trolly cars laden with excursionists. **1914** [see NETWORK *v.*].

+**Trolleyize**, *v. tr.* To convert (a tramway) into an electric trolley railroad. — **1895** *Pop. Science Mo.* April 751 Every species of tramway spins its overhead wires and becomes trolleyized.

Troll(e)y lace. (See TROLLEY.¹)

+**Trolley line.** A line of electric street or interurban cars. — **1895** *Stand.* 1935/1. **1899** ADE *Fables in Slang* 16 The Local Editor . . . was playing Pin-Pool with the Superintendent of the Trolley Line. **1916** [see OWL CAR].

+**Trolley pole.** a. A pole placed along a street or way to support a wire for a trolley line. b. (See quot. 1895.) — **1894** *Harper's Mag.* June 4/1 The new town . . . has seen fit to . . . erect red trolley poles on the most exclusive streets. **1895** *Stand.* 1935/1 T[rolley]-*pole*, a pole, on a trolley-car, carrying the trolley-wheel.

*∗**Trolling.¹**
1. The act or the practice of fishing from a boat by trailing line and bait in the water. {1651-7-, in related senses}
1850 S. F. COOPER *Rural Hours* 42 Pickerel . . . are caught in summer, by 'trolling,' a long line being thrown out and drawn in from the stern by the fisherman. **1856** *Porter's Spirit of Times* 4 Oct. 77/2 In the Adirondack country, lake-trout trolling is still to be had. **1873** *Rep. Comm. Fisheries* I. 248 The usual method of taking them [sc. bluefish] with the line is by drailing or trolling. **1886** *Outing* VIII. 160/1 Trolling with a minnow also brings the capture of some large fish.
2. Attrib. with *bait, hook, rig*, etc.
1857 HAMMOND *Northern Scenes* 57 Nobody in them days tho't of sich contrivances as trollin'-rods, reels, and minny-gangs. **1883** Trolling bait [see PROPELLER 3]. **1883** *Century Mag.* July 382/2 Most of the Florida bass are taken with the hand-line and trolling-spoon. **1891** *Cent.* 6497/3 *Trolling-hook*, . . . a fish-hook used in trolling. **1892** *Courier-Journal* 2 Oct. 17/8, I immediately sent to Seattle for a Siwash or Indian salmon trolling rig.

Trolling.[2] The act or practice of fishing with a trawl net, +or a trawl line. — **1884** GOODE, etc. *Fisheries* I. 320 [The Long-finned Tunny] is taken by trolling.

Trolling line. {1701} +A fish line trailed after a boat. — **1801** MORRIS in Sparks *Life G. Morris* III. 140, I took with a trolling line above fifty [trout and perch in Lake George]. **1857** HAMMOND *Northern Scenes* 208 We threw out a trolling line as we passed up the lake; but we caught no trout. **1875** *Chicago Tribune* 30 Aug. 7/2 Fishing with a trolling line on horseback is a novel sport. **1901** MERWIN & WEBSTER *Calumet 'K'* 281 Somebody on the tug had fished it out with a trolling line.

+**Troll line.** =TRAWL I. — a**1888** in Goode *Amer. Fishes* 195 The smack fishermen of Charleston catch a few on troll-lines during . . . spring and early summer. **1911** [see POUND NET].

Trollope. [Frances Milton *Trollope* (1780–1863), Eng. author of *Domestic Manners of the Americans* (1832).] +(See quotations.) — **1834** C. D. ARFWEDSON *United States* II. 177 Whenever an individual in a playhouse happens, when seated in the boxes, to turn his back towards the pit, or, occupying a front seat, to put his feet on the benches, (a want of decorum severely censured by Mrs. Trollope) a general outcry of 'Trollope, Trollope!' is heard from every part of the house. **1846** LEVINGE *Echoes fr. Backwoods* II. 73 If a man attempts to take off his coat, or to sit upon the edge of the boxes, turning his back to the audience, there is an immediate cry of 'Trollope, Trollope, turn him out.'

Trollopise, *v.* [See TROLLOPE.] +*tr.* To ridicule or criticize as crude or unrefined. — **1838** A. BELL *Men & Things* (1862) 210 They now stand in awe, under a dread, as they say, of being *Trollopised.*

Trolly. (See TROLLEY[1] and TROLLEY.[2])

Trombone. A musical wind instrument made of brass, with either sliding tubes or pistons {1724-}; also, a performer on such an instrument. {1848} — **1828** *Yankee* June 199/1 Let Mr. Phillips call to mind the three rounds of applause with which the . . . green curtain, and the growl of the trombone were received. **1851** NORTHALL *Curtain* 35 The Trombone was inordinately fond of pork and beans. **1854** M. J. HOLMES *Tempest & Sunshine* 53 They contented themselves by lustily blowing their trombones. **1891** *Cent.* 6498/1 *Trombone.* . . . It is now a regular constituent of the orchestra and of the military band. For the latter it is sometimes made with valves or keys instead of a slide.

+**Trompillo.** [Sp.] A nightshade, *Solanum elaeagnifolium.* — **1885** HAVARD *Flora W. & S. Texas* 512 Trompillo. . . . One of the most common of weeds in all valleys of Southern and Western Texas. **1892** *Dialect Notes* I. 253 *Trompillo.* . . . The berries . . . are used for curdling milk.

* **Troop.**

*1. a. A body of soldiers; armed forces. Usually pl. b. A body of cavalrymen or troopers.

a**1656** BRADFORD *Hist.* 20 The rest of ye men yt were in greatest danger, made shift to escape away before ye troupe could surprise them. **1658** *Plymouth Laws* 116 It is enacted . . . that a troop of horse well appointed . . . shalbe raised. **1678** *Conn. Rec.* III. 11 This Court [examined] whither the former immunities were stated upon the Troop as a Troop or upon those whoe were the first listers. **1707** [see FOOT COMPANY]. **1781** *Md. Hist. Mag.* III. 110 The troops were obliged to draw corn in lieu of Meal on the Eleventh. **1885** *Harper's Mag.* Sept. 609/2 'Boots and saddles' has been sounded, and the troops stand near their fluttering guidons. **1918** [see MUSTER MASTER].

2. In special combinations.

Troop beating, a drumbeat signal for the marching of troops; +*t. boot,* a cavalry boot; *t. kitchen,* a kitchen for the preparation of food for troops; *t. train,* a train carrying soldiers. {1893}

1757 *General Orders* 66 The off[ice]rs & Men of ye 35th 60th & Independent Companys . . . To Peraid at Troop Beating In order To March To Albany. **1885** CUSTER *Boots & Saddles* 107 He wore troop-boots reaching to his knees. **1924** *Scribner's Mag.* Dec. 645/2 Some wops wear white caps and hang around the troop kitchens. **1877** McCABE *Hist. Great Riots* 37 The special troop train would not go to Wheeling without orders from Vice-President King.

Trooper. A soldier in a cavalry troop; a horse soldier. {1690-} — **1654** [see FOOT COMPANY]. **1778** *Jrnls. Cont. Congress* X. 312 For each trooper a pair of boots . . . to be furnished out of the public stores. **1865** BOUDRYE *Fifth N.Y. Cavalry* 68 Having gathered his troopers together, Kilpatrick addressed them a few words of cheer. **1903** *Chicago Chronicle* 11 April 1/2 The cub is led along a trail by a trooper on horseback and then a few hours later the dogs are put on the scent.

+**Troop fowl.** *local.* =FLOCKING FOWL. — **1876** *Forest & Stream* 9 Nov. 212/3 *Fulix marila.* Troop fowl. **1891** *Cent.* 6498/2 *Troop-fowl,* the American scaup . . . (Massachusetts.) **1917** *Birds of Amer.* I. 135.

Troopial, Troupial. Any bird of the family Icteridae, as the bobolink. {1825-, in S. Amer.} Also with specifying terms. (See also BULLOCK'S TROUPIAL, YELLOW-HEADED TROOPIAL.) — **1839** AUDUBON *Ornith. Biog.* V. 1 The refreshed travellers . . . listen attentively to the notes of the Red-and-White-winged Troopial. **1846** *29th Congress 2 Sess.* H. R. Ex. Doc. No. 41, 437, I, however, obtained a beautiful male specimen of the troopial. **1881** Hooded troupial [see HOODED *a.*]. **1893** *Scribner's Mag.* June 771/1 [In the names] meadowwink, reed-bird, rice-bird, troopial, we have a brief summary of his [the bobolink's] habits.

Trooping. *attrib.* Of or pertaining to the activities of horse soldiers or troopers. {trooping horse, 1647} — **1664** *Plymouth Col. Rec.* XI. 185 Noe Trooper . . . shall att any time put away or dispose of his Trooping horse unless hee haue some other horse that is approued. **1680** *Conn. Rec.* III. 63 There is much disorder especially after traineing and trooping

dayes. **1745** *N.H. Probate Rec.* III. 237, I give unto my Son . . . the Gun & Pistols & trooping furniture that he hath rid with. **1747** *Ib.* 507, I give and bequeath unto my brother John Odlin all my trooping Clothes.

* **Trophy.** Something taken as spoils or as a symbol of victory in war; something won as a prize, representing victory in a competition.

1805 CLARK in *Lewis & C. Exped.* III. (1905) 170 This is the first Instance I ever knew of the Indians takeing any other trofea of their exploits off the dead bodies of their Enimies except the Scalp. **1858** VIELÉ *Following Drum* 232 Some trophies were secured from the camp, consisting of robes, head-dresses, ponchos etc. **1873** *Newton Kansan* 3 July 2/1 The War Department will send to West Point from the Ordnance Bureau as a trophy of the late war, the first gun fired in the late war. **1886** [see PITCHED BALL]. **1907** *St. Nicholas* July 815/1 There are trophies and prizes for individuals and for crews.

b. Attrib. with *race, room.*

1895 WILLIAMS *Princeton Stories* 254 Come down to-morrow and we'll show you the Trophy-room and all. **1897** *Outing* XXX. 227/1 The occasional sailor has no chance in the trophy races.

Trophy cress. =next. — **1891** *Cent.* 6500/1.

Trophywort. A plant of the nasturtium family, Tropaeolaceae. {1866, in S. Amer.} — **1847** WOOD *Botany* 199 Tropæolaceæ.—Trophyworts. . . . The fruit of the following species [the Indian cress or nasturtium, *T. majus*] is pickled and used as a substitute for capers. **1891** *Cent.* 6500/2 *Trophy-wort,* . . . the Indian cress, *Tropæolum.*

Tropic bird. Any one of various birds of the genus *Phaëthon.* {1681-} Also with specifying adjectives.

1709 LAWSON *Carolina* 150 Tropick-Birds are a white Mew, with a forked Tail. **1731** *Essex Inst. Coll.* XLII. 237 Trophick Birds . . . are very rare in this part of ye World. **1835** AUDUBON *Ornith. Biog.* III. 442 The Tropic Bird, *Phaeton Aethereus.* **1871** *Harper's Mag.* July 188/2 The frigate-bird and the tropic-bird swoop down, skim the long undulating masses of weed, and find choice morsels there. **1883** *Nat. Museum Bul.* No. 27, 166 Yellow-billed Tropic Bird. *Ib.* 167 Red-billed Tropic Bird. **1917** *Birds of Amer.* I. 89/1 Imagine to yourself a beautiful Dove with two central tail-feathers sweeping out behind to a distance of a foot and a half, and you will have a fairly correct mental picture of the Tropic-bird.

* **Trot,** *n.* a. A trotting race. {1891-} +b. *College slang.* A literal translation of a text.

(a) **1856** *Porter's Spirit of Times* 25 Oct. 128/2 Nothing would have given the lovers of the trotting turf more pleasure than to witness a trot of three miles. **1868** *N.Y. Herald* 4 July 5/6 Great interest has been manifested here today in a trot at the Mystic Riding Park. **1905** RICE *Sandy* 215 Nelson wants the fellow to drive for him at the fall trots. (b) **1891** *Cent.* 6501/2. **1893** POST *Harvard Stories* 235 The mucker was put in the middle of the room with the 'trot'; the students . . . followed the translation in their Greek texts. **1924** MARKS *Plastic Age* 299, I'm talking about the copying of math problems and the using of trots.

* **Trot,** *v.*

1. *tr.* Of a seated person: To jog (a child) on one's knee; to move (one's knee) with a regular up-and-down motion.

1853 HAWTHORNE *Works* IV. 223 He had trotted him on his knee when a baby. **1873** HOLLAND *A. Bonnicastle* viii, She sat alone, trotting her knees, looking into the fire, and knitting. **1887** A. J. WILSON *At Mercy of Tiberius* 79, I trotted her on my knee.

2. To cause (a person or thing) to move, as if at a trot; to bring forward or move into a designated place or position. {to trot out, 1838-}

a**1855** J. F. KELLY *Humors* 288 [They] were about trotting him forth to the Mayor's office. **1864** *Rio Abajo Press* 22 March 2/3 As the escape of the prisoners . . . was a consequence of his [the jailer's] negligence, we hope our authorities will trot him through. **1884** *Gringo & Greaser* 1 Feb. 1/2 A nuncio is visiting Uncle Sam's kingdom to inquire into the policy and feasibility of moving the Holy See to the U.S.! Trot it right over, Leo. **1887** *Nation* 10 March 211/3 [Verdi] never cared to be 'trotted about' as a curiosity.

+3. *College slang.* 'To use a "pony" or some similar means in studying' (*Cent.*).

Troth. +Used in possessive to designate an early-ripening variety of peach. — **1866** *Rep. Comm. Agric. 1865* 192 The Troth's Early Red . . . has for years held the position of the earliest market variety. The Hale's Early ripens at least two weeks in advance of the Troth's.

Trot-line. A long line, fitted with shorter lines with baited hooks, for catching bottom fish; a trawl line. {trat line (in similar sense), 1894-, local or dial.} — **1835** AUDUBON *Ornith. Biog.* III. 123 A trot-line is one of considerable length and thickness, . . . varying according to the extent of water, and the size of the fish you expect to catch. **1860** OLMSTED *Back Country* 166 The 'Doctor' returned from 'a hunt,' . . . with no game but a turtle, which he had taken from a 'trot line.' **1883** [see CRAB *n.*[1] 4]. **1891** *Cent.* 6501/3 The trot-line takes catfish and other bottom-fish.

* **Trotter.** (See also RAW TROTTER.)

*1. A horse that trots, esp. one trained to compete in trotting matches.

1747 *N.J. Archives* 1 Ser. VII. 59, I keep 4 good trotters. **1772** *Md. Hist. Mag.* XIV. 278, I shall dayly Expect Molly . . . if you Chuse to Ride y[ou]r Trotter so far. **1833** C. A. DAVIS *Lett. J. Downing* 170 He ought to put on the lead some Albany trotters. **1853** BALDWIN *Flush Times Ala.* 97 The horse, a nick-tailed trotter, Tom had raffled off. **1888** CABLE *Bonaventure* 160, I can tell you the best time of every celebrated trotter in this country. **1910** J. HART *Vigilante Girl* 231, I don't think the flood waters could move rapidly enough to overtake these fast trotters of yours.

2. *Natural trotter*, a horse that trots without having been trained to do so.

1776 *Penna. Ev. Post* 26 March 154/2 A Dark Brown Coloured Horse . . . a natural trotter. **1799** PARMENTER *Hist. Pelham, Mass.* 488 Also entered by Said Hamilton a Horse Colt . . . Neatral troter [*sic*]. **1832** VIGNE *6 Mos. in Amer.* II. 8 The horse in the United States is valuable according to his performances as a square or natural trotter, a pacer, or a racker. **1893** G. W. CURTIS *Horses, Cattle* 62 Bellfounder, the 'Norfolk Trotter,' . . . was a natural trotter.

* **Trotting.**

+**1.** Participation in a trotting match; the racing of trotters.

1846 *Spirit of Times* (N.Y.) 11 July 234/1 The legislative Solons of Massachusetts have prohibited trotting and racing. **1857** *Porter's Spirit of Times* 3 Jan. 290/2 The *Spirit*, still, will treat of stakes, and trotting. **1883** [see RUNNING TRACK].

2. Attrib., chiefly with reference to trotting as a sport. {1840-}

a**1846** *Quarter Race Ky.* 49 Out slides that eternal torment, Bill Sikes, in his new trotting sulky. **1856** *Porter's Spirit of Times* 15 Nov. 172/2 There are other men who see the benefit a trotting-park would be to our city. **1858** WILLIS *Convalescent* 373, I must have the room of another letter . . . to tell you of the trotting-races and cavalcades. **1860** in *Wisconsin Alumni Mag.* (1929) April 226 The fences and the buildings are nearly completed, wells dug and a trotting course laid out. **1866** W. REID *After the War* 99 The roads were alive with a gaily-dressed throng, . . . wending their way . . . in Northern trotting buggies. **1868** WOODRUFF *Trotting Horse* 175 The accomplishment of this feat in harness caused a vast amount of interest and excitement among trotting-men. **1882** McCABE *New York* 270 Trotting stables and theatres are near neighbors. **1883** Trotting cross [see FOUNDATION 3]. **1892** J. P. QUINN *Fools of Fortune* 556 For many years in the Northeastern States the trotting meeting was the recognized form of sport. **1893** *Outing* XXII. 98/1 The perfect trotting track of the present time is built by its inventor, Mr. Seth Griffin.

3. In special combinations.

Trotting record, a race record made by a trotting horse; *t. register*, a register of trotting horses.

1883 *Harper's Mag.* Oct. 716/2 [The Ky. Trotting-horse Breeders' Assn.] have . . . established of late a Trotting Register of their own. **1893** SANBORN *S. Calif.* 96 Not the kite-shaped track of new-made trotting records and pneumatic tires.

* **Trotting horse.** A horse that trots, esp. one taking part in trotting races. Also comb. — **1856** *Mich. Agric. Soc. Trans.* VII. 276 Trotting horses shall be tested in harness, by going at least one mile and repeat. **1858** HOLMES *Autocrat* 40 Wherever the trotting horse goes, he carries in his train brisk omnibuses, lively bakers' carts, and therefore hot rolls, the jolly butcher's wagon [etc.]. **1883** *Harper's Mag.* Oct. 716/2 The Kentucky Trotting-horse Breeders' Association offer at their annual meeting in the fall only colt stakes and purses. **1912** NICHOLSON *Hoosier Chron.* 390 It doesn't do a newspaper any good to speak of Dan Patch as a trotting-horse.

Trotting match. A race in which trotting horses are driven. {1840-} — [**1834** in A. Mathews *Mem. C. Mathews* IV. 303 One thing he witnessed [in the U.S.] which much surprised him,—a trotting-match between two horses in harness . . . in three *two-mile heats*.] **1841** *Picayune* 25 Sept. 2/1. **1858** WILLIS *Convalescent* 375 The excitement of the morning, I soon found, was to be the trotting-match between Ethan Allen and Hiram Drew. **1864** NICHOLS *Amer. Life* I. 393 There are every year . . . trotting-matches for horses. **1893** HOWELLS *Coast of Bohemia* 1 The trotting-matches had begun.

+**Trotting turf.** The ground used in a trotting match; hence, fig., the institution of trotting races. — **1856** [see TROT *n.*1 a]. **1868** WOODRUFF *Trotting Horse* 64 There is no question in my mind about his ability to have beaten any thing that has yet appeared upon the trotting-turf. **1893** *Outing* May 98/2 Glancing at the kings and queens of the trotting turf, . . . the most memorable events of the trotting turf will pass in review.

Trottoir. A paved walk along a street; a sidewalk. {1804-} Now rare. — **1835** INGRAHAM *South-West* I. 111 Every individual upon the 'trottoirs' was hurrying. **1851** HALL *Manhattaner* 38 Descending from buildings and street-names, we jump to the pavement and trottoirs. **1879** WHITMAN *Spec. Days* 129, [I] possess to some extent a personal and saunterer's knowledge of . . . the broad trottoirs of Pennsylvania avenue in Washington.

* **Trouble.** +**1.** Disorderly festivity. *colloq.* **2.** *To look for* (or *seek*) *trouble*, to run the risk of involving one's self in disagreement, difficulty, or danger, by adopting some course of activity. *colloq.* — (1) **1884** BUCKLAND *Sk. Social Life India* 66 A day of rest comes in between each day of pleasure, or 'trouble' as the Yankees more rightly call it. **1897** FLANDRAU *Harvard Episodes* 313 There is always more or less, what is technically known as 'trouble' in Claverly [Hall] and its vicinity on Class Day afternoon. (2) **1901** MERWIN & WEBSTER *Calumet 'K'* 134 We've got to build the belt gallery—and we'll have no end of a time doing it if the

C. & S.C. is still looking for trouble. **1905** *N.Y. Ev. Post* 29 Aug. 2 In the possible chance of rounding up all who might be seeking trouble, the police temporarily sequestered and searched 140 Chinamen.

+**Trouble man.** (See quot. 1909.) — **1889** *Cassell's Family Mag.* 410/1 What the Americans call 'Trouble-men.' **1909** *Cent. Suppl.* 1381/3 *Trouble-man*, . . . an expert, familiar with the working of any apparatus or process, who is able to locate the cause of 'trouble' (unsatisfactory operation) and remedy it.

* **Trough,** *n.*

* **1.** A vessel or receptacle used for any one of various purposes, as to hold water or food for domestic animals. Also transf.

See also FEEDING TROUGH, HORSE TROUGH, etc.

1655 *Essex Probate Rec.* I. 204 Wood and a troft and pales, 3s. **1790** *Phila. Ordinances* (1812) 120 No person whatever shall set . . . any trough, or other vessel in any public street. **1806** LEWIS in *L. & Clark Exped.* III. (1905) 353 The Culinary articles of the Indians in our neighbourhood consist of wooden bowls or throughs, baskets, wooden spoons and woden scures or spits. **1857** *Ill. Agric. Soc. Trans.* II. 382, I teach them to drink coppered milk, feeding ten or twelve together in a trough. **1901** HOBART *John Henry* 95 She crawled into her wraps and we left the mob just as all hands were paddling off to the ice-cream trough.

* **2.** A channel or conduit for the passage of liquid. 'Now *dial.*' (O.E.D.).

1689 SEWALL *Diary* I. 276 Notwithstanding the Hilliness of the Country, no Troughs are used to carry it [the water] over Valleys. **1714** *Boston Rec.* 103 The Comon usage of Conveying Watter by Troughs, or Gutters from the Eves of Houses in this Town . . . hath been a great annoyance. **1883** *Harper's Mag.* April 692/2 From the upper stories of these Cheeseries were long wooden gutters . . . , and along these troughs trickled a never-ceasing rill of the ripened and matured article.

* **3.** A cut, hollow, or valley.

1748 WASHINGTON *Diaries* I. 11 The Trough is (a) couple of Ledges of Mountain Impassable running side and side together for about 7 or 8 Miles. **1845** FRÉMONT *Exped.* 167 The river still continued its course through a trough or open cañon. **1884** *Harper's Mag.* Feb. 364/1 The Columbia River is there . . . compressed into 'dalles,' or long, narrow, and broken troughs.

+**4.** In the making of maple sugar, a receptacle for catching and holding the sap of the maple tree.

1796 HAWKINS *Letters* 24 They use small wooden troughs, and earthen pans to ketch the sap. **1817** PAULDING *Lett. from South* I. 155 The only traces of human agency are the incisions of the sugar maple, and the little troughs at the foot of the tree. **1881** *Harper's Mag.* April 649/2 The sap was collected in troughs each about three feet long.

5. *Mining.* (See quot. 1876.)

1850 KINGSLEY *Diary* 122 Stoped down to day and made a panning trough to pour quicksilver from the riffler into. **1876** KNIGHT 2630/2 *Trough*, . . . a *frame, vat, buddle*, or *rocker* in which ores or slimes are washed and sorted.

+**6.** *To walk up to the trough, fodder or no fodder* and variants: To accept one's responsibilities or one's lot.

Cf. RACK1 2 b.

1843 STEPHENS *High Life N.Y.* II. 45 If that don't bring him up to the trough, fodder or no fodder, I don't know what will. **1871** EGGLESTON *Hoosier Schoolm.* 43 Walk up to the trough, fodder or no fodder, as the man said to his donkey.

Trough, *v. intr.* (See quotation.) — **1835** AUDUBON *Ornith. Biog.* III. 377 When the waves run high, you may see them [brown pelicans] 'troughing,' as the sailors say, or directing their course along the hollows.

Troupe, *n.* [New borrowing from Fr., but cf. *troop* sb. in O.E.D.] A company or band, esp. one of performers or entertainers. — **1825** *N.Y. Ev. Post* 6 Dec. 2 The whole troupe were equally excellent. **1860** [see OPERA 3 a]. **1884** NYE *Baled Hay* 85 Here . . . he finds the electric light, and bicycles, and lawn mowers, and Uncle Tom's Cabin troupes. **1917** J. F. DALY *Life A. Daly* 162 It was utterly distasteful to him to be what he called a 'janitor manager,' opening the door for independent troupes and locking it after each disappeared.

Troupe, *v. tr.* To travel as a member of a troupe of entertainers. Also *vbl. n.* — **1900** *Everybody's Mag.* II. 586/2 One hesitates to say which impresses a novice in 'trouping' the most—the seeming omnipotence of the manager, or the social sets into which the travelling troupe divides itself. **1925** COOPER *Lions 'n' Tigers* 33 He was a menagerie superintendent, she a trainer of lions, tigers and elephants. But they troupe no more.

Trouper. An actor or performer belonging to a troupe. {1929} — **1900** *Everybody's Mag.* II. 585/2 That phrase was the inspiration of some tortured 'trouper.' **1912** VANCE *Destroying Angel* vi, I'm as superstitious as any trouper in the profession.

Troupial. (See TROOPIAL.)

* **Trouser, Trowser.** Usually pl. A garment for men, covering the loins and legs, with a separate division for each leg. {1681-}

1732 *S.C. Gazette* 20/1 Stolen . . . an old Ebo Negro Man; . . . had on a blue Negro Cloth Frock, and new Oznaburgh Trowsers. **1820** [see FATIGUE JACKET]. **1838** *U.S. Mag.* I. 152 Mr. Taney is the first Chief Justice of these United States, who ever so far departed from precedent, . . . as to give judgment in trowsers! **1900** GARLAND *Eagle's Heart* 162 A few of the younger ones wore a sort of rude outside trouser of leather called 'chaps.' **1922** TARKINGTON *Gentle Julia* 152 He decided to return to his room and brush the affected portion of his trousers.

b. Frilled or trimmed drawers, reaching down to the ankles, worn by girls and women. *Obs.* {1821–}

1835 HOFFMAN *Winter in West* I. 200 Here you might see a veteran officer in full uniform balancing to a tradesman's daughter still in her short frock and trowsers.

Trousseau. The outfit of clothes and other personal articles of a bride. {1833–} — **1863** 'M. HARLAND' *Husks* 100 Vic. and I are about to settle our trousseaux. **1895** G. KING *New Orleans* 68 The last shipment of girls sent by the mother country . . . , intended as wives only for young men of established character and means, . . . are known as 'les filles à la cassette,' from the little trunk or cassette, containing a trousseau, given each one by the Company.

∗Trout.

I. ∗1. Any one of certain fishes of the genera Salmo, +Salvelinus, and Cristivomer; also, any one of various other game fishes. Freq. sing. in generic or collective sense.

For details on the use of the word in various parts of the country, see Farmer p. 541.

1588 HARRIOT *Briefe Rep. Va.* D3 There are also Troutes: Porpoises: Rayes. **1637** [see PIKE *n.*[1] 1]. **1685** BUDD *Penna. & N.J.* 80 In the said River and Cricks are many other sorts of good Fish . . . some of which are Cat-fish, Trout, Eales [etc.]. **1709** LAWSON *Carolina* 158 Trouts . . . are in the Salts, and are not red within, but white. **1772** ROMANS in P. L. Phillips *Notes B. Romans* (1924) 123 The Rivers have . . . the Chab or Chevin, here Miscalled a Trout. **1831** PECK *Guide* 47 The streams . . . are alive with trout and other fish. **1842** *Nat. Hist. N.Y., Zoology* IV. 26 In Carolina, . . . [the growler] passes under the name of trout. **1876** *Wide Awake* III. 143/2 Antoinette . . . suddenly landed the trout in the bottom of the boat. **1883** *Century Mag.* July 376/2 [Black bass] are known in different sections of our country as bass, perch, trout, chub, or salmon. **1884** *Century Mag.* April 908/1 The name of 'trout' is also applied . . . to a salt-water fish called 'squeteague.' **1902** [see FEEDING GROUND 3].

b. With specifying or qualifying terms. {1661–}

Many other examples of these can be found in fish books. See also BLACK TROUT, BROOK TROUT, etc.; also BLUE-BACKED *a.*, DEEP-WATER, etc.

1879 *Scribner's Mo.* Nov. 17/1 A white-meated fish . . . was known to them [Mich. hunters] as 'Crawford County trout.' **1884** *Nat. Museum Bul.* No. 27, 1067 'Ocean-trout.' (Sea-herring.) **1884** GOODE, etc. *Fisheries* I. 362 In the Southern Atlantic States it [the squeteague] is called 'Grey Trout.' *Ib.* 367 The Silver Squeteague . . . [is] called at Charleston the 'Bastard Trout.' *Ib.* 475 The Black spotted Trout . . . is known as the . . . 'Black Trout,' 'Silver Trout,' etc., in the mountains. **1909** *Cent. Suppl.* 1381/3 *Coast Range trout, Salmo irideus,* found in coastwise streams of the western United States.

∗2. One or more of these fish cooked for food.

1838 HAWTHORNE *Notebooks* (1932) 31 Breakfast between four and five, newly caught trout . . . —truly excellent. **1885** *Outing* VII. 76/1 Then comes supper, consisting of trout, fried potatoes, tea, and 'slapjacks.'

II. *attrib.* and *comb.* **3.** Designating places or establishments in which trout are bred or reared or are taken.

See also TROUT BROOK, TROUT STREAM.

*a***1841** W. HAWES *Sporting Scenes* I. 189 A scow, chiefest for a trout-pond. **1850** LEWIS *La. Swamp Doctor* 90 You'll never want vensun or a good trout-hole while I'm in the swamp! **1867** *Harper's Mag.* Dec. 48/1 Caledonia Creek, a natural trout-ground a score of miles south of the city of Rochester. **1869** *Rep. Comm. Agric. 1868* 328 A fountain capable of filling constantly a two-inch pipe will sustain a trout preserve. **1882** LATHROP *Echo of Passion* iv, A streamlet, alternately flowing in bright shallows, . . . and lost in deep trout-pools. **1891** *Cent.* 6503/3 *Trout-farm,* . . . a place where trout are bred and reared artificially.

∗4. Designating articles of equipment used in fishing for trout.

1857 *Knickerb.* XLIX. 57 Take your trout-pole in one hand. **1869** W. MURRAY *Adventures* 118 The trout-pail was bottom up, and the contents lying about almost anywhere. **1872** *Harper's Mag.* Nov. 809/1 His hat, garnished with trout flies, fell off and went floating down the current. **1919** HOUGH *Sagebrusher* 309 The strap of her trout creel [was] cutting deep into the shoulder of her sweater.

5. Designating products of trout, or trout of an indicated size or condition. {1910}

1869 *Rep. Comm. Agric. 1868* 327, [I] sold about five hundred thousand impregnated trout spawn. **1870** *Amer. Naturalist* IV. 434 No trout raiser should purchase his five hundred or more trout eggs unless he has plenty of good water. **1896** *Vt. Agric. Rep.* XVI. 127 Millions of trout fry find the way from the hatchery to our streams and ponds annually. **1907** Trout fingerling [see FINGERLING].

6. Designating persons breeding or taking trout. {1894–}

See also TROUT FISHER(MAN).

1870 *Amer. Naturalist* IV. 434 This screen or box . . . is a most convenient and labor saving contrivance for the trout breeder. **1870** Trout

raiser [see sense 5]. **1883** *Advance* 25 Oct., One of our most genial and great-hearted California troutmen.

7. In specific names: **a.** Of fishes.

See also TROUT PERCH.

1820 RAFINESQUE in *Western Rev.* II. 52 Trout River-Bass. *Lepomis Salmonea.* . . . Vulgar names White Trout, Brown Trout, Trout Pearch, Trout Bass [etc.]. **1890** *Cent.* 4474/1 *Trout-pickerel,* the banded pickerel, *Esox americanus.* **1814** MITCHILL *Fishes N.Y.* 442 Trout Pike. (*Esox salmoneus.*) . . . Length eight or nine inches, and figured somewhat like the eel. **1891** *Cent.* 6503/3 *Trout-shad,* . . . the squeteague.

b. Of plants.

1892 *Amer. Folk-Lore* V. 96 *Begonia maculata,* trout begonia. Bedford, Mass. **1894** *Ib.* VII. 101 *Erythronium Americanum,* trout-flower (local) N.Y. **1909** *Cent.* 729/2 *Trout-lily,* the yellow dog-tooth violet or adder's-tongue, *Erythronium Americanum.*

Trout brook. A small, fresh-water stream in which trout are found. — **1847** LANMAN *Summer in Wilderness* 115 We found the bed of our pilot's trout brook without a particle of water. **1865** WHITTIER *Poetical Works* (1894) 402/1 We fished her little trout-brook. **1897** *Outing* XXX. 324/2 In this place one can . . . trace . . . the trout-brook to its source.

Trout fisher(man). One who fishes for trout. — **1852** *Harper's Mag.* May 843/2 The early-trout fishers upon the south-shore of the Island, were bandaged in pea-coats. **1856** SIMMS *Charlemont* 364, I'm the sleepy trout-fisherman! **1882** LATHROP *Echo of Passion* x, He strode off towards the stream, entirely forgetting the usual elaborate approaches of a trout-fisher.

Trout fishing. The activity or amusement of fishing for trout. {1653} Also attrib. — **1807** IRVING *Salmagundi* xi. 279 Trout-fishing was my uncle's favorite sport. **1846** *Knickerb.* XXVIII. 176 It was exceedingly pleasant . . . to find himself . . . bound to the trout-fishing grounds of Sullivan county. **1888** *Voice* 12 April, Lake George has greatly improved as a trout-fishing resort since the system of annual restocking began. **1902** WISTER in *Harper's Mag.* Feb. 466/1 He discoursed for a while about trout-fishing.

+**Trout perch. 1.** The small-mouthed black bass, *Micropterus dolomieu.* **2.** The sand roller, *Percopsis omiscomaycus.* — (1) **1820** [see TROUT 7 a]. **1883** *Century Mag.* July 376/2 In North and South Carolina they [black bass] are variously known as trout, trout-perch, or Welshman. (2) **1883** *Nat. Museum Bul.* No. 27, 472 The trout-perch spawns in spring.

Trout stream. A fresh-water stream containing trout. {1751} (Fielding *Amelia* III. xii)} Also attrib. — **1843** *Knickerb.* XXI. 41 The effect produced [by] . . . the torches . . . glistening from the trout-streams—may be better imagined than described. **1883** *Harper's Mag.* Oct. 705/1 Very pleasant they were, those saunterings . . . in the trout-stream cañons that surrounded the Lucern Territory. **1913** LONDON *Valley of Moon* 476 Through Del Norte and Humboldt counties they went . . . whipping innumerable trout streams, and crossing countless rich valleys.

∗Trowel. A tool consisting of a flat or rounded blade fitted with a handle. — **1644** *Essex Inst. Coll.* L. 333 One daubinge truell & a parcel of old Iron, 2s. 6d. **1759** *Newport Mercury* 26 June 4/3 Imported . . . and to be sold by Jacob Richardson, . . . Stone and Plaistering Trowels. **1854** CUMMINS *Lamplighter* 504 Drawing forth a pair of gardening-gloves and a little trowel, she employed herself for nearly an hour among the flowers. **1905** N. DAVIS *Northerner* 319 She spent the days . . . in the garden, with . . . her trowel in her hand, making piteous pretense at work.

+**Trowel bayonet.** (See quot. 1876.) — **1876** KNIGHT 2631/1 *Trowel-bayonet,* a bayonet resembling a mason's trowel, used as a weapon, and as a light intrenching-tool, or as a hatchet when detached from the rifle. **1877** McCABE *Hist. Great Riots* 71 The rifles were all equipped with the trowel bayonet, a terrible-looking weapon, which may be used, either to stab as a regular bayonet or to cut as a sabre, with deadly effect. **1884** *Century Mag.* May 137/2 Each man had protected himself by earth thrown up with his trowel bayonet.

Trowel(-)hoe (plough). (See quotations.) — **1814** J. TAYLOR *Arator* 96 These furrows are made by . . . a plough called a trowel hoe, made one third larger than usual, with a coulter on the point, and a mould board on each side. *Ib.* 104 The large trowel-hoe-plough with its two mould boards, splits the summit of the fallow ridge, and throws its earth and manure into the two furrows made on each side by the preceding plough.

+**Trowsaloons.** *pl.* [*Trousers* and pant*aloons.*] Pantaloons or trousers. *humorous.* — **1827** *Beacon* (Norfolk, Va.) 13 Oct. 2/2 (T.H.S.), [One shot] glanced and passed through the trowsaloons of the Jackson man.

Troy. [*Troy, N.Y.*] +**1.** *Troy coach,* a coach of a type built in Troy, New York. +**2.** *Troy laundry,* a laundry using equipment manufactured in Troy, New York. — (1) **1834** *Western Mo. Mag.* II. 589 Here is the Harrodsburg stage driving up, and an elegant affair it is—a new Troy coach, of the latest construction, drawn by four fine horses. (2) **1900** *Everybody's Mag.* II. 37/2 Four barbers' shops had been established, and what is more extraordinary, half a dozen 'Troy' laundries and a bath-house had also sprung into existence.

∗Troy weight. A weight or standard of weight formerly used for various commodities but now restricted to precious metals. Also *quasi-adv.* — **1642** *Suffolk Deeds* III. 62 Received . . . of Edward Jackson Nayler . . . forty seven ounces ¼ ⅛ of Silver plate troy weight. **1678** *New Castle Court Rec.* 361 A set of troy weights. **1705** *Boston News-Letter* 15 October 2/2 There is now Published [in] Mr. Clough's Almanack for

1706 . . . the difference between Troy and Averdupoize Weights. **1848** Bryant *California* App. 474 In five weeks . . . he had $17,000, or upwards of ninety pounds troy weight, of gold dust.

+Truant officer. An officer charged with investigating the absence of children from school. — **1872** [see next]. **1895** *Denver Times* 5 March 8/2 The lad intended to shoot the truant officer, he said. **1911** Persons, etc. *Mass. Labor Laws* 181 The truant officer finds that no certificate has been issued from the central office.

Truant school. (See quot. 1872.) {1882–} — **1872** Brace *Dangerous Classes N.Y.* 348 The Massachusetts system of 'Truant-schools'— that is, Schools to which truant officers could send children habitually truant—does not seem so applicable to New York. **1901** Riis *Making of American* 314 As for a truant school, the lack of one . . . compelled the sending of boys, who had done no worse harm than to play hooky on a sunny spring day, to a jail with iron bars in the windows.

*Truck, *n.*¹

*1. Commodities used in trade. {–1770}

1638 *Md. Council Proc.* 73 Question . . . the persons so offending together with all such truck as you shall find with them. **1674** in Jillson *Dark & Bl. Ground* 17 They got ye English mans snapsack with beades, knives and other petty truck in it. **1736** J. Browne *Letter Book* (1929) 40, I will pay them in Rum, hoops, Cydar or some other truck, in a Short time or Money in Six Months. **1776** *Jrnls. Cont. Congress* V. 852 One bundle of Indian truck, containing coarse hats, shirts &c., . . . to George Measam Superintendent of Stores. **1833** Neal *Down-Easters* I. 24 What'll ye give [for] a thousand—*cash?* . . . Or truck out o' the store at cash prices. **1866** C. H. Smith *Bill Arp* 53 This bill . . . ought to exasperate all those patriotic citizens who hold their truck for higher prices.

+2. *local.* Medicine.

c**1775** Boucher *Glossary* p. l., Till now ne'er *crazy*, in my bones no pains, I *never took no truck*, nor doctor's *means*. **1835** Longstreet *Ga. Scenes* 210 Oh, they gin' her a 'bundance o' truck . . . ; and none of 'em holp her at all. **1850** Lewis *La. Swamp Doctor* 45 No 'drap,' [of liquor] 'cept in doctor's truck, should ever come on their plantation. **1856** Cartwright *Autobiog.* 49 He had seen me take out a phial, in which I carried some truck that gave his sisters the jerks.

+3. Vegetables; garden produce. (See also Garden truck.)

1805 Parkinson *Tour* 161, I thought nothing in the farming-line likely to be profitable, except . . . what in that country is called truck,—which is garden produce, fruits, &c. c**1849** Wanamaker in Appel *Biog. Wanamaker* 20 We can raise as good truck out here as they do about your city. **1873** Beadle *Undevel. West* 707 People were living on what they could not sell, to wit: corn-bread, potatoes and 'green truck.' **1895** *Dept. Agric. Yrbk. 1894* 26 Such soils are naturally adapted to the forcing of early 'truck' and vegetables.

+4. Applied depreciatively to a person. Also collect.

1815 Humphreys *Yankee* 77 A bad truck—all in tatters. Without a copper or a cent. **1860** Holmes *Maude* 61 Some low lived truck or other that they called 'Janet.' **1890** Wiggin *Timothy's Quest* 97 They ain't any common truck ter be put inter 'sylums 'n' poor-farms.

+5. *collect.* Articles of any sort; stuff.

In English dialect use, only with depreciative force, 'odds and ends, rubbish, trash.'

1822 J. Woods *English Prairie* (1904) 345 Plunder and truck include almost everything. **1845** W. T. Thompson *Chron. Pineville* 40 They had brought [change] with them to purchase . . . rum and tobacco, and such other 'truck' as their necessities called for. **1855** Bristed in *Cambridge Ess.* 72 In some places . . . *truck* [expresses] every commodity that can be subjected to the process of *toting*. **1890** Custer *Following Guidon* 109 'All kinds of truck,' to use the phrase with which the Western man designates a variety of possessions, was heaped in the big army-wagon. **1901** *Emporia Gazette* 19 July, Sears, Roebuck and Montgomery Ward will sell thousands of dollars' worth of truck which should be sold in Emporia.

6. *attrib.* **a.** In sense 1 with *axe, kettle, knife.* **+b.** In sense 3 with *crop, grower, soil.*

See also Truck cloth, farm, farmer, etc.

(a) **1638** *Md. Council Proc.* 76, I have seised: . . . 2. truck kettles . . . 5. dozen of truck-knives . . . 6. large truck-axes. (b) **1895** *Dept. Agric. Yrbk. 1894* 132 The heavy grass and wheat lands will produce three or four times as great a yield of truck as the truck soils do. *Ib.* 133 Soils having over 10 or 12 per cent of clay are too heavy and too retentive of moisture for the early truck crops. **1897** *Kissimmee* (Fla.) *Valley Gazette* 1 Dec. 2/1 His long experience as a truck grower here will, we hope, make his advice valuable to our readers.

Truck, *n.*² {1611–}

1. A cart used for transporting heavy loads; a dray. {1774–}

1701 *Boston Rec.* 12 No cart, Dray, Trucks or Sled . . . shall be suffered to pass through any of the streets . . . but with a sufficient driver. **1748** Hempstead *Diary* 511, I was at home all day Making a New Tongtree for the Trucks. **1847** Field *Drama in Pokerville* 173 The conception of a ready loaded truck . . . despatching a 'cord' [of wood] for every shoulder load, appears not to have entered the head of either wood dealer or captain. **1886** Stockton *Hundredth Man* i, If a truck arrived with some heavy merchandise, John . . . would proceed to the sidewalk. **1904** *Min-*

neapolis Times 8 June 6 A roadway for stone trucks, garbage wagons and other disagreeable things on wheels.

b. A cart or wagon used for conveying the ladders used by firemen.

1855 M. Thompson *Doesticks* 287, [I] got run over by two hose-carts, and a hook and ladder truck. **1885** *South Fla. Sentinel* (Orlando) 22 July 3/1 The truck of the Hook and Ladder Company was shipped from the factory.

c. A hand-propelled barrow, cart, or wagon used to transport baggage about a railroad station.

1879 Burdette *Hawkeyes* 98 If the baggageman runs over him with a truck, he says 'Huh!' **1904** Lynde *Grafters* 14 Pending the chalking-up of its arriving time on the bulletin board, the two men sat on an empty baggage truck and smoked.

+2. 'A group of two, three, or more pairs of wheels in one frame, for supporting one end of a railway-car or locomotive' (*Cent.*).

1850 *Rep. Comm. Patents 1849* 327 Brake levers have been placed between the trucks of a car. **1872** Huntington *Road-Master's Asst.* 35 If track is ½ or ¾ of an inch too wide, then, of course, the trucks have an excessive side-motion. **1907** London *Road* 24 The tramp, snugly ensconced inside the truck, . . . has the 'cinch' on the crew.

3. *Attrib.* and comb. with *builder, team.*

See also Truck-driver, frame, horse, etc.

1879 Howells *Lady of Aroostook* 11 They entangled themselves in knots of truck-teams and hucksters' wagons and horse-cars. **1894** Carwardine *Pullman Strike* 81, I shall give you some prices paid . . . Car-builder $13.00. Truck builder .90. Truck labor .31.

Truck, *v.* **1.** *tr.* To convey by truck; to cart. {1809–} **2.** *intr.* To work as a trucker. (See Trucker.²) — (1) **1748** Hempstead *Diary* 505 Joshua Truckt Stones for Samuel Gardiner yesterday & to day. **1878** *Lumberman's Gazette* 6 April, Build a tramway . . . on the log road made for trucking logs to the streams on snow. (2) **1901** *Scribner's Mag.* XXIX. 427/1 [I worked at] trucking in a factory for awhile. **1907** *Black Cat* 3 June, I been truckin' fer you . . . eighteen years.

+Truck cloth. =Trucking cloth. *Obs.* — **1637** *Md. Council Proc.* 57 Shipped for the Isle of Kent . . . ; three pieces of blew truck cloth. **1642** *Md. Archives* IV. 100, 10. yards ½ of blew truck cloth.

Truck-driver. A man employed in driving a truck. {1907} — **1892** Crane *Maggie* (1896) 31 He became a truck driver. **1898** *McClure's Mag.* X. 363 Phelps has got a notion of fishin' up all sorts of canallers, an' truck-drivers, an' sendin' 'em out to fire for me. **1901** Harrigan *Mulligans* 13 Tom . . . went to work as a truck-driver for a large dry-goods firm.

*Trucker.¹ +A truck farmer. — **1868** *Norfolk* (Va.) *Jrnl.*, The Truckers in this neighborhood. **1887** J. E. McGowan *Chattanooga & Tenn.* 35 The fruiters, farmers and truckers have now more capital for their business. **1897** *Kissimmee* (Fla.) *Valley Gazette* 1 Dec. 2/3 A portion of this column is to be devoted to the interests of the farmer and trucker. **1911** Jenks & Lauck *Immigration Problem* 83 The truckers and small fruit growers are doing exceptionally well.

Trucker.² (See quotation.) {1878–} — **1880** *Scribner's Mo.* Oct. 862/1 The better class of population is found among the 'truckers,' or the men employed in the city as porters, messengers or drivers.

+Truck farm. A farm which produces garden truck for market. — **1866** *Notes & Q.* 3 Ser. IX. 323/1 A truck garden, a truck farm, is a market-garden or farm. **1877** *Field & Forest* II. 160 The insect is . . . somewhat injurious on 'truck farms,' as it destroys all kinds of vegetables. **1882** McCabe *New York* 664 The country for miles around New York abounds in market gardens and truck farms. **1905** *Springfield Wkly. Repub.* 15 Sept. 5 In the neighborhood of many large cities there are extensive truck farms, on which cauliflower is grown for home consumption.

+Truck farmer. One who operates a truck farm. — **1877** 'A. Douai' *Better Times* (1884) 7 The truck-farmers from Virginia down to Florida. **1884** *Rep. Comm. Agric.* 289 There are a number of species usually concerned in the work which the truck farmer generally puts to the account of 'the cut-worm.' **1900** Garland *Eagle's Heart* 99 He came under the head of a 'nester' or 'truck farmer,' who was likely to fence in the river somewhere. **1903** *N.Y. Ev. Post* 27 Nov. 6 Until 1898 all the land included in these limits was still cultivated by truck farmers.

+Truck farming. The operation of truck farms. Also attrib. — **1870** *Rep. Comm. Agric. 1869* 447 Truck Farming in New Jersey. **1891** *N.-Y. Weekly Witness* 22 April 2/2 Truck-farming is defined as the production of green vegetables on tracts remote from market. **1901** Mohr *Plant Life Ala.* 134 This industry of truck farming is carried on most extensively on the Coast plain. **1923** Watts *L. Nichols* 9 The truck-farming career, as they pursued it, was . . . stocked with daily urgencies.

Truck frame. The frame of a railway truck. (Cf. Truck *n.*² 2.) — **1850** *Rep. Comm. Patents 1849* 164, I claim the shapes and combinations of the truck frame pieces. **1903** Johnson *Railway Transportation* 50 The construction of cars with a capacity of 50 tons or more has been facilitated by the large use of steel, both in the truck-frames and in the body of the car.

+Truck garden. 1. A truck farm. **2.** A vegetable garden. — (1) **1866** Lossing *Hudson* 394 From the road . . . stretch away numerous 'truck' gardens, from which the city draws vegetable supplies. **1884** *Harper's Mag.* April 712/1 The electric messages fly from house-keeper to market-man over wide cow pastures and truck gardens. **1913** London *Valley of Moon* 517 Squares, oblongs, and narrow strips . . . displayed the thousand hues of green of a truck garden. (2) **1900** Dix *Deacon*

Bradbury 3 His glance wandered off to . . . the orchard and the glowing truck-garden. **1923** HERRICK *Lilla* 256 There was the truck garden on the farther side of the ranch house.

+**Truck gardening.** The raising of vegetables. — **1890** *Boston Jrnl.* 12 April 2/4 During their two years' residence they have done all of their own work and truck-gardening.

Truck horse. A horse used to draw a truck. — **1856** *Porter's Spirit of Times* 4 Oct. 81/2 Our truck horses, whose labors are very fatiguing, . . . come from their work, and as soon as unharnessed, go to the trough. **1873** W. MATHEWS *Getting On in World* 10 As well might . . . the truck-horse [hope] to rival Dexter in fleetness. **1891** S. FISKE *Holiday Stories* (1900) 21 What does it cost to keep a truck-horse?

+**Truck house.**
1. A building used as a store for trading with the Indians. Now hist. Also attrib.

1720 *Mass. H. Rep. Jrnls.* II. 236 It would be very much for the Interest of the Government . . . if there were set up . . . a few Truck-houses, where the Indians might be supplied at reasonable Rates, with what they want. **1734** *Ib.* XII. 32 The said Committee carried up the Votes for a Truck-Master to manage the Truck Trade at the Truck House above Northfield. **1753** FRANKLIN *Writings* III. 163 If you can procure and send me your truckhouse law, and a particular account of the manner of executing it, . . . you will much oblige me. **1832** WILLIAMSON *Maine* II. 200 The Indian trade at the truck houses was revised.

2. A building used to house fire trucks.

1904 *Baltimore News* 18 May 6 He wished to erect a Fire-Department truckhouse on the little grass plot.

***Trucking.** +Truck farming. Used attrib. — **1897** *Jrnl. Fine Arts* (Phila.) June, About one half [of the grounds] is used for trucking and pasture purposes.

+**Trucking cloth.** Cloth used in trade. *Obs.* Also attrib. — **1638** *New Haven Col. Rec.* 4 Twelve coates of English trucking cloath. **1659** *Essex Probate Rec.* I. 28 A blewe Trucking cloth blanckett. **1674** *Mass. H. S. Coll.* I. 152 [Indians] buy of them for clothing a kind of cloth, called duffils, or trucking cloth, . . . made of coarse wool. **1682** *Mass. H. S. Coll.* 4 Ser. V. 63 [They] have sent their good mother . . . bonnets, truckingcloth, and other things mentioned.

+**Trucking farm.** =TRUCK FARM. — **1865** *Nation* I. 209 Free nigger labor may do on a trucking farm.

+**Trucking house.** =TRUCK HOUSE 1. Now hist. — **1631** *N.H. Hist. Soc. Coll.* IV. 240 One man . . . fell lame by the way, and . . . [stopped] at a trucking house. **1633** *Mass. Bay Rec.* I. 108 There is liberty graunted to Mr. John Winthrop, Junr., & to his assignes, to sett vp a trucking howss vpp Merrymak Ryver. **1668** *N.H. Hist. Soc. Coll.* III. 214, [I went] to the Trucking house of Capt. Richard Walderne . . . to make enquiry . . . concerning the killing of an Englishman. **1755** in E. Arber *Eng. Garner* II. 619 There shall be a Trucking House in every Plantation, whither the Indians may resort to trade.

+**Trucking stuff.** Articles used in trade with the Indians. *Obs.* — **1619** *Va. House of Burgesses* 5 The Indians refusing to sell their Corne, those of the shallop . . . tooke it by force, . . . given [*sic*] them satisfaction in Copper, Beades, and other trucking Stuffe. **1624** *Ib.* 33 We were to give to [the Indians] . . . clothes and truckinge stuffe we esteemed of more worth then their corne. **1674** *Mass. H. S. Coll.* 1 Ser. I. 159 To this end they must be furnished with such Indian trucking stuff, as may be suitable.

***Truckle-bed(stead).** A low bed which, when not in use, can be pushed under a higher bed. — **1661** *Essex Probate Rec.* I. 341 In the Hall, a bedstead & a trucklbedsted, with a fetherbed. **1679** *Essex Inst. Coll.* XXXVII. 98 A truckle bedstead, a fether bed with the pillowes, blanketts & coverlid. **1745** HEMPSTEAD *Diary* 444 He was a Sleep in the Truckle bed. **1850** JUDD *R. Edney* 19 Two little children, snugly asleep in their truckle-bed.

+**Truckman.**[1]
1. One who drives a truck.

1787 CUTLER in *Life & Corr.* I. 306 By them . . . licensing retailers, taverns, carters, truckmen, are regulated. **1832** H. B. STOWE in C. E. Stowe *Life H. B. Stowe* 57 The truckman carried all the family baggage to the wrong wharf. *a***1882** in McCabe *New York* 143 The scene is full of a brief amusement—hack-drivers, truckmen, omnibus drivers, swearing vehemently at each other. **1917** MATHEWSON *Second Base Sloan* 126 By common consent the truckmen left their vehicles at the far end of the platform.

2. One of a body of mounted horsemen taking part in public ceremonies.

1833 *Jamestown* (N.Y.) *Jrnl.* 3 July 2/2 Next came a sturdy cavalcade of 300 well-mounted truckmen in uniform white frocks and blue cockades, five abreast. **1858** HOLMES *Autocrat* 348 The Governor came, with his Light-horse Troop And his mounted truckmen, all cock-a-hoop.

+**Truckman.**[2] (See quotation.) — **1864** WEBSTER 1419/2 *Truckman*, . . . one who does business in the way of barter or exchange.

Truck master. {1907} +In colonial times, a man appointed to have charge of trade with the Indians. *Obs.* — **1637** MORTON *New Canaan* 159 Two truckmasters were chosen; wages prefixed. **1640** *New Haven Col. Rec.* 43 Mr. Gregson shall be Truck ma[ste]r of this towne . . . to truck with the Indians for venison. **1700** SEWALL *Diary* II. 10 Mr. Turfrey is made . . . Truck-master with the Indians, in stead of Capt. Hill. **1734** [see TRUCK HOUSE 1]. **1767** HUTCHINSON *Hist. Mass.* II. 318 The charge of

trading houses, truckmasters, garrisons, and a vessel employed in transporting goods was deducted.

+**Truck patch.** A patch of ground on which vegetables are grown.

1824 DODDRIDGE *Notes* 109 Every family . . . had another small enclosure containing from half an acre to an acre, which they called a 'Truck patch.' In which they raised corn, for roasting-ears, pumpkins, squashes, beans, and potatoes. **1847** DRAKE *Pioneer Life Ky.* 28 He and I went into the 'truck-patch,' and pulled off all the young cucumbers. **1857** *Ill. Agric. Soc. Trans.* II. 313 Lawyers and doctors, with merchants and mechanics, had what was then termed their 'truck patches,' if not regular farms. **1870** NOWLAND *Indianapolis* 196 He helped twenty-eight families to roll logs, burn brush and clear a garden, or 'truck patch,' as it was commonly called. **1900** DRANNAN *Plains & Mts.* 137 The Pimas were very kind to us . . . , often taking us out to their truck patches and pulling nice, large melons for us.

Truckster. One who deals in small articles; a shopkeeper. {1868, in pejorative sense} — **1843** *Knickerb.* XXII. 291 Chairs, tables, bureaus, bedsteads, and pictures . . . [are] daily exposed for sale in the windows of the trucksters or on the counters of the auctioneers. **1894** FORD *P. Stirling* 45 [Peter] would sometimes stop and chat with people—with a policeman, a fruit-vender, a long-shore-man or a truckster.

+**Truck trade.** Bartering; the exchange of commodities. — **1720** *Mass. Bay Currency Tracts* 357 Were this Truck Trade at an end, and the Trader Sold all for Money, . . . I should think it a more proper time to propose such Laws. **1734** [see TRUCK HOUSE 1]. **1832** WILLIAMSON *Maine* II. 202 A vessel, the Snow, was likewise built, for the protection of the coasting and truck trade.

+**Truck wagon.** A heavy truck; a dray. — **1805** *Lewis & Clark Exped.* VII. (1905) 106 They had Some difficulty with their truck waggons as they broke Sundry times. **1857** *Ill. Agric. Soc. Trans.* II. 361 Truck wagons, the wheels being made of large sycamore logs, sawed off, were frequently used. **1878** COOKE *Happy Dodd* 169, I don't want to hire a big truck-wagon. **1897** *Outing* XXX. 352/2 Our camping outfit was packed upon a truck-wagon.

Truck wheel. {1825} A wheel for a truck of any kind, or a wheel of similar type. — **1756** HEMPSTEAD *Diary* 664, I putt a pr of Box's into my new Truck whell. **1805** LEWIS in *L. & Clark Exped.* II. (1904) 165, I set six men at work to p[r]epare four sets of truck wheels with couplings, toungs and bodies. **1857** *Lawrence* (Kan.) *Republican* 28 May 3 Rolling Cutters and Clasps, Gauge Wheels, Truck Wheels, and other plow fixtures. **1861** *Army Regulations* 407.

+**Trudeau's tern.** [Jean Baptiste *Trudeau*, explorer and Indian trader (1748–1827).] (See quotations.) — **1839** AUDUBON *Ornith. Biog.* V. 125 Trudeau's Tern. . . . This beautiful Tern . . . was procured at Great Egg Harbour in New Jersey, by my . . . friend, J. Trudeau, Esq. of Louisiana. **1887** RIDGWAY *Manual N.A. Birds* 41 Casual on Atlantic coast of United States (New Jersey). *S[terna] trudeaui.* Trudeau's Tern.

‖**Trudgeon.** One who trudges; a child. — **1814** IRVING in P. M. Irving *Life W. Irving* I. (1862) 308, I have allowed the little Major to . . . go to the country with his wife and little trudgeons.

True-blue, *a.* {1672–} *Polit.* Dependable, sound. {1705–, in more general sense} — **1787** TYLER *Contrast* (1790) II. ii, I am a true blue son of liberty, for all that. **1831** S. SMITH *Life J. Downing* 133 You cant get any kind of an office at Washington, unless you are a true blue genuine democratic republican. **1835** HONE *Diary* I. 142 There are some difficulties in the way, such as a double set of delegates from Pennsylvania, true-blue both, but hating each other. **1865** KELLOGG *Rebel Prisons* 310 He sang the following 'true blue' Union song.

+**True grit.** Ground grain of a certain quality. Used in allusive context or in transf. sense. Also attrib. — **1840** KENNEDY *Quodlibet* 127 After the Middlings, come the True Grits. . . . Wheat are nature's noblemen. **1846** *Knickerb.* XXVIII. 63 We don't like to leave a real true-grit American, . . . among a lot of cowardly Diegos.

+**True Wesleyan church.** (See quot. 1846.) — **1844** RUPP *Relig. Denominations* 484 Statistics of the True Wesleyan Church. **1846** *Indiana Mag. Hist.* XXIII. 262 He was in what is very improperly called, the 'True Wesleyan Church,' the organization effected by Scott, Lee and others, who erroneously supposed the Methodist Episcopal Church to be pro-slavery.

***Trumpet.**
***1.** A metal wind instrument used specially in military activities.

1687 *Conn. Rec.* III. 431 All Captains . . . [shall] provide for their companies and troops, . . . trumpets, trumpeters and banners. **1714** *Boston News-Letter* 18 Oct. 2/2 The Regular Forces Marching after His Excellency, . . . with Hoboys and Trumpets before them. **1835** BIRD *Hawks* I. 45 Remember the bugles and trumpets, blasting up for the charge of cavalry. **1895** G. KING *New Orleans* 70 Its bells began a chime of welcome, joining in with the fifes, drums, trumpets, and singing.

2. =SPEAKING TRUMPET. {1696–}

1793 *Amer. State P.* (1819) I. 128 We saw a sloop . . . bearing down upon us, . . . sent five armed men on board of us, who rendered an account by trumpet, that the vessel was laden with coffee and cotton. **1838** COOPER *Homeward B.* xxxii, The English captain . . . held a trumpet; but neither of the two commanders used his instrument, the distance being sufficiently near for the natural voice. **1868** G. G. CHANNING *Recoll. Newport* 201 After a little hesitation, he handed me the trumpet; and . . . the boat aimed for the shore.

3. An ear trumpet. {1774-}

1865 *Atlantic Mo.* Jan. 24/1 Here, speak into my trumpet.

+4. *S. pl.* The yellow trumpetleaf, *Sarracenia flava.*

1857 GRAY *Botany* 24 Trumpets.... Bogs, Virginia and southward. **1891** *Cent.* 6509/1. **1898** CREEVEY *Flowers of Field* 36 A larger pitcher-plant ... is *Trumpets* ..., with a large, drooping, yellow flower.

5. Attrib. with *ash, blossom, gourd,* etc. Freq. in the specific names of plants.

See also TRUMPET CREEPER, FLOWER, etc.

1890 Trumpet milkweed [see TRUMPETWEED]. **1891** *Cent.* 6509/1 *Trumpet-creeper.*... More often, but less specifically, called *trumpet flower,* sometimes *trumpet-vine* and *trumpet-ash.* **1891** *Harper's Mag.* March 544/2 Purple and white passion-flowers ... and the scarlet trumpet blossom ... [were] flaring over the staked and ridered rail-fence. **1901** MOHR *Plant Life Ala.* 831 *Lagenaria vulgaris clavata,* Trumpet Gourd. Louisianian area. **1910** C. HARRIS *Eve's Husband* 32, I began to take a sad, weeping-willow joy in the heartiness of the white hyacinths, narcissuses and pale trumpet lilies.

+Trumpet creeper. A vine (*Campsis radicans*) having trumpet-shaped flowers. — **1834** *Western Mo. Mag.* II. 574 The sides [are] ornamented with beautiful bunches of the trumpet-creeper. **1853** 'P. PAXTON' *Yankee* 58 From the branches of every tree, the trumpet-creeper ... suspended her crimson coniform cups. **1888** WARNER *On Horseback* 132 We saw beautiful wild trumpet-creepers in blossom, festooning the trees. **1904** STRATTON-PORTER *Freckles* 145 The trumpet-creepers were flaunting their gorgeous horns of red-and-gold sweetness.

*Trumpeter.

*1. One who plays a trumpet.

*a***1656** BRADFORD *Hist.* 281 Rasier ... was accompanied by a noyse of trumpeters, and some other attendants. **1724** *New-Eng. Courant* 7 Dec. 2/1 Thirty-two Principal Barbers of this Place, assembled at the Golden Ball, with a Trumpeter attending them. **1842** *Life in West* 43 Our trumpeter seems to be out of sorts and out of tune. **1880** CABLE *Grandissimes* 247 Now a fresh man ... revived the flagging rattlers, drummers and trumpeters.

+2. = TRUMPETER SWAN.

1709 LAWSON *Carolina* 146 Of the Swans we have two sorts; the one we call Trumpeters; because of a sort of trompeting Noise they make. **1835** J. MARTIN *Descr. Virginia* 484 There are two kinds [of swans] ... ; the trumpeter is the largest. **1874** LONG *Wild-Fowl* 230 Their notes ... resemble greatly those of a trumpet; and because of this peculiarity of note the name 'trumpeter' was given them. **1917** *Birds of Amer.* I. 168/2 The reason for the rapid decrease of the Trumpeter is not far to seek.

‖**3.** (See quotation.)

1836 *S. Lit. Messenger* II. 541 The trumpeter creeps to her high perched nest. *Ib. note,* The greater wood-pecker.

+Trumpeter swan. An American wild swan noted for the loudness of its call. — **1834** NUTTALL *Manual Ornith.* II. 371 The length of the Trumpeter Swan is about 70 inches. **1853** *Harper's Mag.* Nov. 769/1 Here [in La. swamps] you may see the red flamingo, the egret, the trumpeter-swan. **1874** LONG *Wild-Fowl* 227 The *cygnus buccinator,* or trumpeter swan, the largest of its kind, and most common to the valley of the Mississippi. **1917** *Birds of Amer.* I. 167 The Trumpeter Swan, the largest of North American wild fowl, represents a vanishing race.

+Trumpet flower. Any one of various plants having trumpet-shaped flowers, esp. the trumpet creeper. {1731-(Miller *Gard. Dict.* s.v. *Bignonia*)}

*c***1730** CATESBY *Carolina* I. 65 The Trumpet-Flower. These Plants climb upon Trees; on which they run a great height; and are frequently seen to cover the dead trunks of tall trees. **1784** *Amer. Acad. Mem.* I. 465 *Bignonia.*... Trumpet-Flower. Yellow Jasmine.... On the borders of fields, and in open woods. **1835** BIRD *Hawks* I. 140 Sitting down under an arbour of honey-suckle and trumpet-flowers, [she] indulged herself in a long fit of weeping. **1872** POWERS *Afoot & Alone* 96 There were the most execrable, scratching thickets of dewberry creepers, trumpet-flowers, elders, and all manner of brambles. **1893** *Scribner's Mag.* June 798/1 Vines of wild grape and scarlet trumpet-flower swaying and blooming among them.

+Trumpet-flowered, *a.* Having flowers shaped like trumpets. — **1785** MARSHALL *Amer. Grove* 80 *Lonicera caroliniana.* Carolinian scarlet Trumpet-flowered Honeysuckle. [**1857** HENFREY *Elem. Botany* 353 The Trumpet-flowered climbers form striking features of American forests.]

+Trumpet gall. (See quot. 1891.) — **1891** *Cent.* 6509/3 *Trumpet-gall,* a small trumpet shaped gall occurring commonly upon grape-vines in the United States. **1908** KELLOGG *Amer. Insects* 470 Trumpet-galls on leaves of California white oak.

Trumpet honeysuckle. An American honeysuckle (*Lonicera sempervirens*) with red or orange flowers. — [**1731** MILLER *Gardeners Dict.* s.v. *Periclymenum,* Trumpet Honeysuckle.... We have but one species of this Plant at present, viz.... Virginian Scarlet Honeysuckle.] **1781-2** JEFFERSON *Notes Va.* 38. **1843** TORREY *Flora N.Y.* I. 296 Scarlet or Trumpet Honeysuckle.... Borders of swamps, and on bushy hill-sides. **1898** CREEVEY *Flowers of Field* 454 [The] Trumpet Honeysuckle ... is wild from Connecticut southward.

+Trumpetleaf. Any one of several varieties of pitcher plant of the genus *Sarracenia.* Also with specifying terms. — **1861** WOOD *Botany* 222 *S. Gronovii.* Trumpet-leaf.... In swampy pine woods, Va. to Fla. and

La. **1869** FULLER *Flower Gatherers* 187 Another species, very common in the Southern States, is the *Gronovii* or *Trumpet Leaf,* which is small at the base, swelling gradually toward the throat like a trumpet. **1901** MOHR *Plant Life Ala.* 530 *Sarracenia rubra.*... Red-flowered Trumpet-leaf or Pitcher Plant. *Ib., Sarracenia flava.*... Yellow Trumpet-leaf.

+Trumpet vine. An American vine having large, red, trumpet-shaped flowers; the trumpet creeper. — **1709** [see SCARLET *a.* 1 a]. **1883** *Peterson's Ladies' Nat. Mag.* June 460/2 The great porch in front ... [was] destitute of railing or ornament, but the creeping trumpet-vine. **1897** GLASGOW *Descendant* 15 Upon the rail-fence the dripping trumpet-vine hung in limp festoons, yellow and bare of bloom.

+Trumpet-vine seed-worm. 'The larva of a tortricid moth, *Clydonopteron tecomæ,* which lives in the seed-pods of the trumpet-creeper' (*Cent.*).

Trumpetweed. {1866-} +Any one of several American plants, esp. the joe-pye weed and the wild lettuce. Also with specifying terms. — **1833** EATON *Botany* (ed. 6) 142 *Eupatorium purpureum,* trumpet weed, purple thorough-wort, joe-pye. **1850** *New Eng. Farmer* II. 12 The Trumpet Weed, and the New England Aster, having fine, sweet-scented, aromatic flowers, attract many insects. **1890** *Cent.* 3422/3 *Wild lettuce.*... In America, *Lactuca Canadensis.* Also called *trumpetweed* and *trumpet-milkweed.* **1901** MOHR *Plant Life Ala.* 761 Spotted Trumpet-weed. Queen of the Meadow.... Low Trumpet-weed. **1913** BRITTON & BROWN *Flora N.A.* III. 357.

Trunched, *a.* Short and thick. *dial.* {trunch, *dial.*} — **1787** CUTLER in *Life & Corr.* I. 267 But how were my ideas changed, when I saw a short trunched old man [Benjamin Franklin] in a plain Quaker dress.

+Truncheon snake. ?A short, thick snake: (see also quot. 1736). Also with descriptive term. — **1709** LAWSON *Carolina* 126 Red-back'd Snake. Black Truncheon Snake. [Etc.] **1736** CATESBY *Carolina* II. 45 *Vipera fusca.* The Brown Viper.... They are found in Virginia and Carolina, in the last of which Places they are called the Trunchion Snake.

Trunchy. Thick, stocky. *dial.* {trunch, *dial.*} — **1778** *Md. Journal* 21 July (Th.), A thick, trunchy fellow, with short light hair, and grey eyes. **1789** *Ib.* 21 April (Th.), Strayed or stolen, a trunchy well-set bright-bay horse.

*Trundle(-bed). = TRUCKLE-BED(STEAD). — **1640** *Conn. Rec.* I. 450 On[e] trundell bedd and blankett. **1783** E. PARKMAN *Diary* 299 Trundle bed and bolster. **1851** C. CIST *Cincinnati* 202 E. Rowe ... manufactures bedsteads, patent and common, including trundles. **1851** *Knickerb.* XXXVII. 139, I was to sleep in a trunnel-bed, that was run underneath my uncle's bed in the day-time and then out at night. **1904** GLASGOW *Deliverance* 311, I've known him for sixty years and slept in a trundle-bed with him as a baby.

*Trunk.

*1. A chest or box, esp. a container in which clothing or other property of a traveler is transported.

1640 *Conn. Rec.* I. 449 The goods and Cattell of James Olmestead: ... diuers smale things in a trunke. **1742** *Md. Hist. Mag.* XX. 177 You will send me the Contents of the Inclosed Invoice of Goods packed up in a good strong Trunk well matted and corded. **1837** *Diplom. Corr. Texas* (1908) I. 271 One of the passengers, Taylor, had his trunks broken open ... and 497 dollars together with other property taken. **1922** TARKINGTON *Gentle Julia* 362 My trunk may come up from the station almost any time.

2. a. A trough or other passageway, usually made of boards, for water {1610-}; a floodgate or sluice.

1704 *Boston Rec.* 38 [A] Stone drain ... [frees] the Street from the Usual annoyance with water & mire by the Often Stoppage & breaking of the Small wooden Truncks or drains. **1784** WASHINGTON *Diaries* II. 291 The trunk, which conveys the water to the wheel ... [is] in bad order. **1856** in *Commons,* etc. *Doc. Hist.* I. 120 Trunk-minders undertake the whole care of the trunks. **1860** MORDECAI *Virginia* 59 A small stream ... passed in a trunk through Byrd's Warehouse. **1903** PRINGLE *Rice Planter* 8 Each field has a very small flood-gate (called a trunk), which opens and closes to let the water in and out.

+3. *pl.* Short, close-fitting breeches or drawers, freq. worn by athletes.

1883 *Pall Mall Gaz.* 26 July 7/1 Captain Webb attempted his perilous feat of swimming Niagara Rapids.... He wore a pair of silk trunks. **1889** GUNTER *That Frenchman* xi, Black-velvet trunks cover his [the wrestler's] hips and thighs. **1894** *Harper's Mag.* Aug. 341/1 The use of tights or 'trunks' by bathers will not be allowed.

4. *attrib.* **a.** In sense 1 with *check, manufactory, nail,* etc.

1858 *Texas Almanac* (advt.), Hughes' Saddle, Harness and Trunk Manufactory. **1860** HOLLAND *Miss Gilbert* 293 Cheek was ... led to the trunk-room of the lodging-hall. **1874** B. F. TAYLOR *World on Wheels* 58 He has ... shown his ticket and his trunk check, and asked if this is the right train. **1891** *Cent.* 6511/2 *Trunk-nail,* ... a nail with a large, ornamental, convex head, used for trunks and for cheap coffins. **1904** WALLER *Wood-Carver* 47, I used, as a boy, to ride on the trunk-rack of the old Hornet, holding by the leathern straps.

b. With specific reference to trunk-line railroads.

1851 CIST *Cincinnati* 312 Here are four trunk roads. **1861** *Chicago Tribune* 19 July 1/9 Great Reduction in Freight and Fares to Montreal, Quebec [etc.].... by Grand Trunk Railway of Canada. **1884** *Congress. Rec.* 10 Dec. 163/1 Here are eight or ten ... great trunk railroads running eastward from Chicago to the New York market. **1893** *Harper's*

Mag. Feb. 382/1 [New Orleans] is the seaport terminus of several great trunk railway lines and supply depot for Texas, the Southwest, Mexico, and Central America.

+**c.** In special combinations.

Trunkback, =TRUNK TURTLE; *t. cabin,* in a ship, a cabin partly above and partly below the upper deck; *t. loo,* (see quotation); *t. rod,* a fishing rod made in sections, to permit of convenient packing. **1883** GARMAN *Reptiles N. Amer.* p. vi, 'Trunk-backs' or 'Leather-backs,' *Sphargis,* are the largest [of the sea turtles off coasts of Fla.]. **1886** *Outing* VIII. 11/2 In the second class I put regular decked vessels . . . which have trunk cabins. **1849** W. BROWN *America* 4 These men live partly . . . by stealing trunks from passengers, which they call *playing at Trunk loo.* **1893** *Outing* XXII. 121/2 Trunk rods made to pack in small space often have six or seven [joints].

Trunkfish. Any one of various fishes of the family Ostraciidae, having box-shaped bodies with bony plates. Also with specifying terms. {1804-} — **1818** *Amer. Monthly Mag.* II. 328 *Ostracion Sex-cornutus;—* Six-horned Trunk-Fish; with six horns, two in front [etc.]. **1839** STORER *Mass. Fishes* 176 *Ostracion Yalei. . . .* Yale's Trunk Fish. **1869** *Amer. Naturalist* III. 467 The surf rolled up a fine living specimen of the odd-looking trigonal Trunk-fish (*Lactophrys camelinus*), sometimes called Cow-fish. **1884** GOODE, etc. *Fisheries* I. 170 The Trunk Fishes, *Ostraciontidæ,* are occasionally taken on our coasts, especially to the south of Cape Hatteras.

Trunk line.

1. A main line of a railroad, as distinguished from a branch or local line {1861-}, +esp. one of the principal routes between the Atlantic seaboard and the Middle West.

1851 CIST *Cincinnati* 311 The railroad is a costly structure . . . —its true and legitimate use is the extended trunk line between great points. **1870** *Republican Rev.* 24 Sept. 3/3 What Albuquerque looks to . . . is the completion of the main trunk line of railroad from the East, through here to the Pacific. **1878** PINKERTON *Strikers* 215 The Pennsylvania Railroad, like other great trunk lines, had sorely felt the iron hand of the general stagnation of business. **1903** E. JOHNSON *Railway Transportation* 56 First through or trunk lines in the United States were those built to connect the Atlantic seaboard with the Great Lakes and the Ohio River. **1918** [see FEEDER 2 b.]

2. Attrib. with *company, fare-agreement,* etc.

1868 *Rep. Comm. Agric. 1867* 109 The location of the main trunk-line railroad from the northern lakes to the Gulf of Mexico has advanced the price of lands generally 20 per cent. **1883** *N.Y. Chr. Union* Aug. 30 The monopolistic 'railroad trunk-line fare-agreement.' **1887** *Courier-Journal* 6 May 3/1 The New York, Ontario, and Western railroad became a member of the Trunk-line Passenger Association. **1903** E. JOHNSON *Railway Transportation* 56 Comprised within this trunk-line territory is a distinct subdivision of lines whose business consists chiefly of transporting anthracite coal. The larger part of this coal is mined and transported by other than the trunk-line companies.

Trunk-maker. One whose business it is to make trunks. {a1704-} — **1700** *Boston Rec.* X. 81 Joseph Lowle, Cooper, and William Crow, trunk maker, became sureties to the town, for Exercise Connant. **1815** *Niles' Reg.* VIII. 141/2 There are [in Pittsburgh] . . . 3 trunk makers; 2 gun smiths. **1841** *Knickerb.* March 258 The rest [of the articles] . . . , if not claimed in due season, . . . will be sold to the trunk-makers. **1898** *Kansas City Star* 18 Dec. 1/3 N. M. Freling is a trunk maker.

+**Trunk-minder.** On a rice plantation, one who controls the flow of water through a trunk to the field. — **1856** in Commons, etc. *Doc. Hist.* I. 120 Trunk-minders undertake the whole care of the trunks. **1904** PRINGLE *Rice Planter* 80 Foreman, trunk minder, and hands were all . . . sure it could never make a crop, being mill-threshed seed.

Trunk turtle. A leatherback turtle, *Dermochelys coriacea.* {1697-} — [**1743** CATESBY *Carolina* II. 40/1 *Testudo arcuata.* The Trunk Turtle. I never saw one of these Turtle.] **1834** AUDUBON *Ornith. Biog.* II. 372 The Trunk Turtle, which is sometimes of an enormous size, and which has a pouch like a pelican, reaches the shores latest. **1884** GOODE, etc. *Fisheries* I. 147 The so-called 'Leather Turtle,' or 'Luth,' or 'Trunk Turtle' . . . occurs sparingly all along our Atlantic coast.

Trunnel(1). (See TREENAIL.)

*Truss. Attrib. and comb. with *maker* {1776}, *span, tie, work.* — **1796** *Boston Directory* 288 Trott George, tobacconist and truss maker, South Bennet street. **1813** *Niles' Reg.* III. 323/1 Upon the tops of these posts are truss ties extending the whole length of the bridge. **1876** INGRAM *Centennial Exp.* 340 The unprecedented length of truss spans make[s] this structure an especial object of interest to the engineering profession. **1884** *Harper's Mag.* Nov. 826/2 A triple-arch roof supported by iron truss-work.

+**Truss bridge.** A bridge in which support is secured by the use of trusses or frames of wood or metal. Also with defining proper name. — [**1840** *Civil Eng. & Arch. Jrnl.* III. 125/2 On the Pottsville and Sunbury Railway, in Pennsylvania, the wood for small truss bridges, for crossing roads [etc.].] **1847** *Rep. Comm. Patents 1846* 95 By long use and repeated strains the various parts of a truss bridge are loosened and weakened, and the bridge becomes unsafe. **1875** *Chicago Tribune* 11 Sept. 2/5 [A part of the Santa Fé line] has stone culverts, and the streams are spanned by Howe truss bridges. **1907** *St. Nicholas* Aug. 919/2 The bridge is what is known as a 'truss' bridge, like most railroad and highway bridges.

Truss(ing) hoop. A hoop used for forcing into position the staves of a barrel {trussing hoop, 1688}; an adjustable iron hoop or band fastened around a mast or spar. {truss hoop, 1867} — **1654** *Essex Probate Rec.* I. 198 Trussing hoopes, 2s.; 2 Cresses, 2s. 6d. **1851** CIST *Cincinnati* 226 His salerooms are depots also of truss hoops.

*****Trust,** *n.*

1. Used in place names. *Obs.*

1700 *Md. Hist. Mag.* XX. 189 Harrises Trust, 300 acr Sur. the 5 August 1684 for William Harris. *Ib.* 193 Hathaways Trust, 150 acr Sur. the 28 of March 1685 for John Hathaway. **1700** *Ib.* XXI. 345 Cockeys Trust, 300 acr Sur the 8 of Aprill 1696.

2. *Hist. collect.* The board of trustees in whose hands was placed the government of the colony of Georgia, 1732-52. Cf. TRUST LAND 1 and *trust lot* in sense 6 below.

1739 W. STEPHENS *Proc. Georgia* I. 314 All [cattle] found without any Mark, were to be judged unquestionably to belong to the Trust. **1741** *Ib.* II. 216 And I was with good Reason grown averse to any more retailing work at the Stores, more especially knowing the Trust's opinion therein, which nothing should occasion us to vary from. **1741** *Georgia Col. Rec.* VI. 4 The Trust upon the Same being duly represented, will Order such a Grant to be made.

3. A conveyance, or a deed making conveyance, to a person or persons, of property to be held for the benefit of another, sometimes in order to secure the payment of a debt. Freq. *deed of trust.*

1825 *Austin P.* II. (1924) 1098 The land deeded in the Trust . . . reverts to said Pettus on the payment of the forty Mules. **1831** PECK *Guide* 247 The land on which the buildings are erected . . . is held by a deed of trust. **1869** TOURGEE *Toinette* (1881) 309 The deed of trust . . . might yet be declared valid. **1898** PAGE *Red Rock* 223 Hiram Still held Dr. Cary's notes secured by deed of trust on the whole Birdwood estate.

4. An organization or co-operating group of companies by means of which control is exercised over the policies of technically independent or competing business establishments, for the elimination of competition, the control of prices, etc. {1887-}; also, a large company practically monopolizing its field.

Variously applied to agreements and pools, as well as organized combinations; in narrow sense, used to designate an organization of trustees issuing certificates in exchange for stock in the companies to be controlled. (Cf. OCTOPUS.)

1877 WANAMAKER in Appel *Biog. Wanamaker* 137 Why should not individual ownership be permitted to grow peaceably and equally with industries that are bunched into trusts? **1888** LOWELL *Lit. & Polit. Addresses* 217 The principle [of excessive protection] . . . is the root also of Rings, and Syndicates, and Trusts, and all other such conspiracies for the artificial raising of profits. **1890** *Boston Jrnl.* 15 Sept. 2/3 If the Alabama farmers who have formed a cotton 'corner' can indicate where their tactics differ in principle from those of the much berated 'trusts,' they should hasten to enlighten a curious people. **1896** *Advance* 6 Feb. 185/2 The trusts, whose superstructures are erected on the principle of unfairness. **1900** NELSON *A B C Wall St.* 162 Trusts generally work for smaller profits than individuals. **1913** LONDON *Valley of Moon* 253 When the boats catch too much fish, the trust throws them overboard.

b. With restricting terms. Also transf. See also SUGAR TRUST.

1888 *Congress. Rec.* 9 June App. 211 The most gigantic and merciless 'trust' today is the coal-oil trust. *Ib.* 31 Aug. 4526/1 Take the Standard Oil trust, the whisky trust, the cotton-seed-oil trust, . . . and various coal trusts. **1888** *Cosmopolitan* Oct. 445/2 By . . . guaranteeing to each club a monopoly of its territory, a base-ball 'trust' is created. **1888** *Economist* 10 Nov. 5/3 The most active securities in the Chicago market at present are those associated with the Gas Trust. **1900** *Congress. Rec.* 15 Feb. 1851/1 The civil-service 'trust' . . . have erected a 'machine' under those rules that would startle Tweed himself.

5. *Trust and savings bank;* a name frequently given to a general banking institution, usually a state bank.

1888 *Economist* I. 1/1 Illinois Trust and Savings Bank. . . . Foreign Exchange and Cable Transfers, Circular Letters of Credit for Travelers.

6. In special combinations.

Trust bond, a bond issued by a group of trustees; +*t.-buster,* one who attacks and tries to break up trusts (*colloq.*); +*t. lot,* a piece of land belonging to the trustees of the colony of Georgia; *t. member,* in a communistic society, a member holding, as if in trust, a part of the total property; *t. money,* money placed in the hands of a trustee, to be administered for a beneficiary; +*t. patent,* a patent issued to an Indian, as record of the allotment of a portion of land to be held in trust for twenty-five years; +*t. plank,* a plank in a political platform dealing with the regulation of trusts; +*t. scrip,* paper promises circulated as money; *t. stock,* (see quotation).

1888 *Economist* 27 Oct. 8/3 It was reported that the latter company would soon issue $16,000,000 of 5 per cent. trust bonds to provide for the Georgia Central purchase and other requirements. **1903** *Chicago Chronicle* 11 April 2 Mr. Knox is surprising everybody by his zeal as a trust-buster. **1739** W. STEPHENS *Proc. Georgia* I. 469, I proposed it to

Mr. Jones to send down a few German Families to work on the Trust Lots there. **1835** HOFFMAN *Winter in West* I. 80 The German Rapp has . . . successfully raised a community, who labour in common, and own all their property only as trust-members of a corporation. **1868** M. H. SMITH *Sunshine & Shadow* 31 Widows and orphans who had left trust money in his hands lost their all. **1909** *Indian Laws & Tr.* III. 389 [For] delivery of trust patents, so far as allotments shall have been selected under said act, ninety thousand dollars. **1925** BRYAN *Memoirs* 125 The trust plank was given second place of importance. **1862** G. K. WILDER *Diary* (MS.) 23 May, [We received] from 16–18 in specie, 23–25 in Trust scrip. **1900** NELSON *A B C Wall St.* 17 The Industrial group [of stocks] . . . includes the so-called Trust stocks, representative of industrial enterprises.

✻**Trust,** *v.* **1.** *To trust out,* to sell (goods) on credit {without *out,* 1678}; to deposit (money). *colloq.* **2.** *To trust* (someone) *for* (something), to allow (someone) to purchase (something) on credit. *colloq.* {1648} — (1) **1833** S. SMITH *Life J. Downing* 184, I sold nigh upon a half a bushel for cash, and trusted out most three pecks besides. **1881** COOKE *Somebody's Neighbors* 181 You don't think I ever see a copper o' her cash, do ye? It's trusted out to a bank. (2) **1862** BROWNE *A. Ward: His Book* 117 [They] git trustid for a soot of black close & cum out to lectur at 50 dollers a pop. **1867** D. R. LOCKE *Swingin' Round* 75 The wretch who is post master at the Corners . . . only last nite refused . . . to trust me for postage stamps.

+**Trust certificate.** A document describing and defining the extent of the possessor's proprietorship in a trust; an official statement issued by a trust attesting the right of the holder to participate, in consideration of stock deposited by him, in the divided profits. — **1888** *Economist* 20 Oct. 8/3 Yesterday there was a still further advance in the Trust certificates, based on higher prices in New York. **1898** *Kansas City Star* 21 Dec. 1/3 [The] court ordered the Standard Oil company to . . . show whether the Standard had paid dividends to the holders of the trust certificates.

+**Trust company.** A company specifically empowered to act as a trustee: (see esp. quot. 1903). Often in titles of banking institutions. — **1834** *Jamestown* (N.Y.) *Jrnl.* 29 Jan. 2/3 You may not, from the but recent existence of the Trust Company, have as perfect a knowledge of their powers and operations. **1839** *Merchants' Mag.* I. 274 N. A. Trust & B'king Co. . . . Howard Trust & B'king Co. **1888** *Economist* 3 Nov. 5/3 The Merchants' Loan and Trust Company . . . has openly declared in favor of the gas bonds. **1903** HART *Actual Govt.* 489 The other kind of bank is the trust company, which has developed within the last 20 years. Such companies undertake the administration of large transactions, such as the refunding of a corporate loan or the amalgamation of corporations; they act as trustees and investors for estates; and most of them receive deposits, subject to check, although none of them have any privilege of note issue.

Trustee, *n.* {1647–} (Cf. OVERSEER.)

1. One of various public officials. +**a.** An official having governing powers of general scope, as a selectman in a town or a councilman in a city.

1662 *Maine Hist. Soc. Coll.* 2 Ser. IV. 246 Resolved by the Trustees of Fardin [etc.]. **1682** [see OVERSEER 1]. **1791** *East-Hampton Rec.* IV. 269 If any person shall cut any beach grass on any of the beaches belonging to this town without liberty from the trustees [etc.]. **1827** DRAKE & MANSFIELD *Cincinnati* 50 This instrument vests the municipal power of the city in a City Council, which is to consist of three Trustees. **1851** *Iowa Code* 40 The trustees are empowered to call meetings of the township. **1900** GOODLANDER *Fort Scott* 65 Years later he was trustee of Scott Township.

b. An officer of a superior court.

1709 *Md. Hist. Mag.* IV. 384 March Court 1709. March the Eleven The Trustees again were present.

c. A local official charged with a limited responsibility, esp. one administering the educational affairs of a school township. {1846–}

1800 *Md. Laws* II. lxv, The trustees of the poor in the several counties in this state in which poor-houses have been established . . . [may] keep any number of out-pensioners, not exceeding ten in any one county at one time. **1831** PECK *Guide* 245 Each [school] district may become a corporate power, to a limited extent, and the voters were authorized to appoint trustees to manage the concern. **1871** EGGLESTON *Hoosier Schoolm.* 72 So he found himself speaking crabbedly to the daughter of the leading trustee. **1902** G. M. MARTIN *Emmy Lou* 66 The trustees were coming this day to visit the school.

+**2.** *Hist.* One of the board of trustees governing the colony of Georgia.

1741 *Ga. Hist. Soc. Coll.* II. 115 John More McIntosh who had the care of the trustees stores . . . , issued corn-kind, such as was rotten. **1742** in *Travels Amer. Col.* 224 The Spaniards . . . had killed two of the Trustees' Serv[an]ts. **1789** MORSE *Amer. Geog.* 453 A corporation, consisting of 21 persons, was constituted by the name of trustees, for settling and establishing the colony of Georgia.

3. One of the administrative officials controlling the property and directing the policy of an organization, esp. a corporation not for profit. {1902} +**a.** An official of a school or college.

1705 BEVERLEY *Virginia* IV. 31 Their Majesties granted a Power to certain Gentlemen, and the Survivors of them, as Trustees, to build and establish the College by the Name of *William* and *Mary* College. **1722** in Clap *Annals Yale-Coll.* 34 Upon just Ground of Suspicion of the Rector or Tutor's Inclination to Arminian or Prelatic Principles, a Meeting of the Trustees shall be called. **1780** *N. J. Archives* 2 Ser. IV. 199 As the Subscriber has been solicited and encouraged by several of the Trustees of the Academy of Newark and others, he intends opening a School in Newark. **1807** *Ann. 10th Congress* 1 Sess. 1206 The petition of the Board of Trustees of the University of Vincennes. **1846** *Knickerb.* XXVIII. 10 That the whole plan of education should be under the control of such a board of Trustees, is a defect in the constitution of American colleges. **1879** *Scribner's Mo.* Dec. 206/1 It is not the intention of the trustees of the Johns Hopkins to collect a large library. **1911** HARRISON *Queed* 223 How could he ever do anything, with a lot of moss-backed trustees tying his hands?

+**b.** An official of an organized religious society or congregation.

N.Y. Laws 1804–6 393 It shall be lawful for the mayor, aldermen and commonalty of the city of New-York, to pay to the trustees of the Roman catholic congregation . . . the like sum as was paid to the other congregations [for the support of free schools]. **1844** Rupp *Relig. Denominations* 447 The trustees have charge of all the church property, to hold it for the use of the members of the Methodist Episcopal Church. **1900** *Congress. Rec.* 3 Jan. 630/1 Also, a bill . . . for the relief of the trustees of the Round Hill Methodist Episcopal Church South. **1903** *Evanston* (Ill.) *Press* 11 April, Mr. Kedzie was for many years a trustee of the Congregational church.

+**c.** An official of the communistic society at Brook Farm.

1842 in Codman *Brook Farm* 14 The Chairman of the General Direction shall be presiding officer in the Association, and together with the Direction of Finance, shall constitute a Board of Trustees, by whom the property of the Association shall be managed. **1897** *McClure's Mag.* X. 193 Before he [Charles A. Dana] had been there [at Brook Farm] many weeks he was elected a trustee.

4. A person or corporation intrusted with the administration of property for the benefit of another. {1653–}

1714 *Mass. Bay Currency Tracts* 74 The said Trustees disclaiming all Right and Property in any Mortgage or Conveyance to them by virtue of their Trusteeship. **1795** *Ann. 4th Congress* 2 Sess. 2585 The proprietors of all the lands . . . have conveyed the same to trustees for a Federal City. **1848** *Whig Almanac 1849* 46/2 The trustees of the magnetic telegraph patents agreed with O'Rielly in 1845 that he should build certain lines. **1888** *Economist* 20 Oct. 1/1 [The] Illinois Trust and Savings Bank . . . acts as Executor and Trustee for Estates, individuals and corporations.

+**b.** *local.* A person in whose hands another person's property is attached in a trustee process.

[**1708** *Mass. Province Acts* I. 630 Such attourny, factor, agent or trustee, . . . shall be admitted to defend the suit on behalf of his principal. **1758** *Ib.* IV. 168 Be it . . . enacted, That where no goods or effects of such absent or absconding person in the hands of his attorney, factor, agent or trustee . . . can be come at so as to be attached [etc.].] **1799** *Mass. Supreme Ct. Rep.* III. 558 The plaintiff, a creditor of Martin, summoned Welles, one of the underwriters, as trustee of Martin. **1810** D. C. WHITE *Compendium Laws Mass.* 1268 In this state there is a process given by statute, in imitation of the Foreign Attachment of the English law; whereby a creditor may attach any property or credits of his debtor in the hands of a third person. This third person is called in the English law, the *garnishee:* in our law he is called the *trustee.* **1883** HOWELLS *Woman's Reason* ix, [The paper] makes a personal appeal to me, in the name of the Commonwealth of Massachusetts, to become your trustee.

Trustee, *v.* {1818–} *local.* +*tr.* To attach the property of (a debtor) in the hands of a third person; to make (a third person) a trustee in a trustee process. — **1879** WEBSTER *Suppl.* 1582/3. **1883** HOWELLS *Woman's Reason* ix, You don't say you never was trusteed before? **1902** McFAUL *Ike Glidden* 38 Yer know if I want ter trustee any one I have ter send ter Debtor's.

+**Trustee process.** Legal attachment without seizure, in the interests of a creditor, of a debtor's properties in the hands of a third party; garnishment. — **1810** W. C. WHITE *Compendium Laws Mass.* 1268 In what cases, and against whom, a trustee process will lie. **1833** L. S. CUSHING (*title*), A Practical Treatise on the Trustee Process, or Foreign Attachment of the Laws of Massachusetts or Maine; with . . . the Statutes of the Eastern States on that Subject. **1891** *Cent.* 6513/3.

Trust fund. Money or other valuables placed in trust. {1838– Bell *Dict. Law Scot.* 1008)} — **1862** *Harper's Mag.* Aug. 337/1 Mr. Pennington has a considerable practice as a lawyer. . . . He has, as a consequence, many trust funds. **1872** TALMAGE *Sermons* 291 The heroes of this country are fast getting to be those who have most skill in swallowing 'trustfunds.' **1900** *Congress. Rec.* 3 Feb. 1474/2 The committee may be advised as to the trust funds of the various nations in the Indian Territory.

✻**Trusting.** +The use of credit in place of cash payment. — **1704** S. KNIGHT *Journal* 42 Their Goods [are rated] according to the time and spetia they pay in: viz. Pay, mony, Pay as mony, and trusting. **1720** *Mass. Bay Currency Tracts* 318 If Ten per Cent Interest are allow'd by Law for Book Debts, it wou'd certainly put an effectual stop to Trusting among all Wise and Honest Men.

Trust land. +**1.** Land belonging to the board of trustees governing the colony of Georgia. (Cf. TRUST *n.* 2.) **2.** Reservation lands held in trust as Indian property by the federal government. — (1) **1738** W. STE-PHENS *Proc. Georgia* I. 67 Jones the Surveyor came at Mr. Bradley's Call, in order to run out some of the Trust-Land for the Germans to work on. (2) **1857** in *36th Congress 1 Sess.* H. R. Rep. 648, 172 The trust lands . . . [include] the eastern part of the Delaware lands. **1866** *Rep. Indian Affairs* 262 The '*trust lands*' are nearly all sold.

* **Trusty.** +A convict regarded as trustworthy and hence eligible for special duties and extra privileges. — **1889** *Century Mag.* Jan. 448/1 The 'trusties' are often domesticated upon ranches near the town, and apparently are unwatched. **1897** NORRIS *Third Circle* 23 [The Chinamen] get all the yen shee . . . and make it into pills and smuggle it into the cons over at San Quentin prison by means of the trusties. **1907** LONDON *Road* 91 My pal . . . had been promptly appointed a trusty of the kind technically known as 'hallman.'

* **Try,** *v.*

+**1.** *To try* (a play) *on a dog*, to test the effectiveness of (a play) by performing it before a provincial audience before bringing it to the metropolitan stage. *colloq.* {1889–}

1888 *Sporting Times* (B. and L.), 'Bootle's Baby' will on the 7th of May be produced somewhere in the provinces. This is what the Americans call trying it on a dog.

***2.** *To try out.* +**a.** To experiment with or test (a person, thing, etc.) in order to determine value.

1888 *Judge* 29 Dec. 190/1 Tried Out by Fire. **1899** *New York Jrnl.* 30 July 34/6 Britain will try out heavy motor wagons. **1909** *Springfield W. Repub.* 4 March 14 Mr. Alexander tried the choir out. **1922** Z. GREY *To Last Man* 199, I reckon we'd better try it [a plan] out, for a while.

+**b.** (See quotation.)

1891 *Cent.* 6515/1 *To try out,* . . . to separate, as fat or grease from a substance roasted, boiled, or steamed: as, the grease *tries out* of ham in cooking.

+**c.** To come forward as a candidate, esp. in competition for a place on an athletic team.

1909 *N.Y. Ev. Post* (s.w. ed.) 25 Feb. 7 Because of the small number of men trying out for winter track practice, Coach Moakley has issued another call for candidates.

3. *To try up* {1776–}, to render or melt down.

1694 *N.C. Col. Rec.* I. 419 [She] tryed up three Barrell of oyle out of the whale. **1805** CLARK in *Lewis & C. Exped.* I. (1904) 374 We had him [a bear] skined and divided, the oile tried up & put in Kegs for use. **1847** *Fla. Plantation Rec.* 211, 1 [slave], Easter, trying up fat.

+**Try-house.** A shed or other structure in which whale oil is extracted from blubber, or lard or a similar substance is rendered. — **1792** *Mass. H. S. Coll.* III. 157 The blubber was brought home in large square pieces, and *tried* or boiled in try-houses. **1895** *Century Mag.* Aug. 575/1 The men and their wives and children begin to come up the crooked road by the clump of willows, past the try-house.

+**Trying kettle.** The pot or receptacle used for trying out blubber. — **1848** in Bryant *California* App. 464 The furnaces are of the simplest construction—exactly like a common bake-oven, in the crown of which is inserted a whaler's trying-kettle.

Try-pot. =prec. — **1836** F. L. HAWKS *Uncle Philip's Conversa. about Whale Fishery* 267 [They] cut the blubber before it is thrown into the try-pots. **1851** MELVILLE *Moby Dick* 547 A crowd of her men were seen standing round her huge try-pots.

Try-works. The apparatus for extracting whale oil from blubber. {c1825} Also attrib. — **1792** *Mass. H. S. Coll.* 1 Ser. III. 157 Vessels from sixty to eighty tons were employed, and the oil boiled out in the try works at sea. **1840** DANA *Two Years* 187 They moored ship, erected their try-works on shore, . . . and commenced operations. **1869** *Overland Mo.* III. 42 The try-work fires were kindled. **1883** *Nat. Museum Bul.* No. 27, 300 Model of try-works common to all whaling vessels. [**1898** F. T. BULLEN *Cruise 'Cachalot'* 11 Her deck was flush fore and aft, the only obstructions being the brick-built 'try-works' in the waist.]

+**Tsuppitch salmon.** (See quotation.) — **1878** *U.S. Nat. Museum Proc.* I. 72 *Salmo Tsuppitch.* Tsuppitch Salmon. Black Trout of Lake Tahoe.

* **Tub.**

***1.** An open vessel or low cask, usually of wood.

1644 *Conn. Rec.* I. 460 An Inuentory of the Goods of Ephraim Huit [includes:] . . . tubbs, pales [etc.]. **1712** *Boston Rec.* 94 The . . . Inhabitts are with all Convenient Speed to provide themselves with Ladders and Tubbs of water. **1817** BRADBURY *Travels* 286n., Hollow trees were . . . used by the first settlers as tubs to hold grain. **1880** *Vt. Agric. Rep.* VI. 116 [Mr. S. K. Quimby] buys and sells large quantities of sugar, some in tubs and some stirred or granulated, in barrels. **1916** WILSON *Somewhere* 142 He told her she was strong as a horse and ought to be doing a tub of washing that very minute.

b. (See quotation.)

1881 INGERSOLL *Oyster Industry* 249 *Tub.*—I. Long Island measure for selling oysters, holding somewhat less than a bushel. . . . II. Chesapeake measure; is similar to the above, but twice as capacious.

2. Attrib. with *churn, factory, filterer,* etc.

1850 *Rep. Comm. Patents* 1849 180 The cylindrical dash works, with the ordinary upright tub-churn A. **1863** *Rep. Comm. Agric.* 1862 136 [The juice] is then passed, while hot, through three tub filterers. **1884** *Nat. Museum Bul.* No. 27, 731 *Tub-lamp,* tin lamp to hang on side of trawl-

tub while 'baiting-up' in the hold of a haddock vessel. **1891** WILKINS *New Eng. Nun* 130 A man in Waterbury had told him that there was a tub factory in Bassets. **1892** *Vt. Agric. Rep.* XII. 156 Nice tub sugar or cakes [sell] at eight to fifteen cents per pound.

+**Tube well.** (See quot. 1876.) — **1876** KNIGHT 2645/2 *Tube-well,* an iron pipe of small diameter, pointed, and having a number of lateral perforations near the end, driven into the earth by a small pile-driver hammer until a water-bearing stratum is reached. **1884** *Gringo & Greaser* 1 Feb. 2/1 Messrs. Houck and Morrow have gone to Las Lunas and Albuquerque to buy casing &c. for some tube wells.

+**Tub mill.** A grain mill for which a tub wheel supplies the power. — **1775** CRESSWELL *Journal* 66 He has got a small tub mill. **1824** DODD-RIDGE *Notes* 143 Our first water mills were of that description denominated tub mills. **1858** *Harper's Mag.* Jan. 174/2 There was a tub-mill belonging to the mountaineer's establishment. **1924** J. W. RAINE *Land of Saddle-Bags* 80 When a man lives on a branch or a prong of the creek, . . . he puts him in a tub mill, and lets the water grind fer him.

Tub wheel. (See quot. 1876.) {1851–} — **1815–16** *Niles' Reg.* IX. Suppl. 182/2 Many mill owners have laid aside their tub wheels. **1821** *Mass. H. S. Coll.* 2 Ser. IX. 128 The water, in the ordinary manner, is thrown on six *tub-wheels,* . . . placed in the bottom of the vault. **1876** KNIGHT 2650/1 *Tub-wheel,* a form of water-wheel which has a vertical axis and radial spiral floats, which are placed between two conical cases attached to the axis.

***Tuck,** *n.* +*To take the tuck out of,* fig., to take the toughness, stamina, or determination away from (one). *slang.* — **1878** 'MARK TWAIN' *Punch, Brothers* 87 We had an iron-clad chicken that ought to have been put through a quartz mill until the 'tuck' was taken out of him, and then boiled till we came again. **1882** PECK *Sunshine* 296 The incident seemed to take all the tuck out of him. **1910** *N.Y. Ev. Post* 10 Nov. 1 The sight of a wounded man lying on the pavement seemed to take the tuck out of the mob.

***Tuck,** *v.* *To tuck it on to* (a person), to raise the price to or overcharge (a person). — **1877** BARTLETT 722 That horse is not worth half what you gave for him. The dealer has tucked it on to you pretty well.

+**Tuckahoe.** [Algonquian Indian.]

1. One of several vegetable foods used by Indians, esp. the floating arum and the Virginia wake-robin.

1612 SMITH, etc. *Virginia* I. 22 In Iune, Iulie, and August, they feed vpon the rootes of Tocknough, berries, fish, and greene wheat. **1662** *Va. Stat. at Large* II. 140 The poore Indians whome the seating of the English hath forced from their wonted conveniencies of . . . gathering tuckahoe, . . . cuttyemnions or other wild fruites. **1671** OGILBY *America* 196 Their peculiar roots are the tockawaugh, good to eat [etc.]. **1770** FORSTER tr. Kalm *Travels* II. 389 To judge by these qualities, the Tuckahoo may very likely be the *Arum Virginicum.* **1815** *Lit. & Phil. Soc. N.Y. Trans.* I. 163 The tuckahoe (or tawkee, as Kalm supposes) was probably a native of this state. **1816** *Mass. Spy* 23 Oct. (Th.), The name of Tuckahoe is supposed to be of Indian origin. **1883** *Amer. Naturalist* XVII. 972 Tuckahoe —a representative name for all round or tuberous esculent roots. **1910** HODGE, etc. *Amer. Indians* II. 831.

2. (See quot. 1848.)

1817 PAULDING *Lett. from South* I. 112 The people [west of the Blue Ridge] call those east of the mountains Tuckahoes. **1835** HOFFMAN *Winter in West* II. 204 The Tuckahoes and Coheese of Virginia, on either side of the Blue Ridge, respectively complimenting each other with as much amiability as do John Bull and Monsieur Jean Crapeau. **1848** BARTLETT 366 The term *tuckahoe* is often applied to an inhabitant of Lower Virginia, and to the poor land in that section of the State. **1855** WHITMAN *Leaves of Grass* 16 Growing among black folks as among white, Kanuck, Tuckahoe, Congressman, Cuff, I give them the same.

+**Tuck comb.** =TUCKING COMB. — **1824** *Mo. Intelligencer* 8 May 3/3 Tortoise Shell, Tuck and Side Combs. **1870** EGGLESTON *Queer Stories* 63 Sukey's way of doing up her hair in a great knot, behind, with an old-fashioned tuck comb, was not pretty. **1886** *Amer. Philol. Ass. Trans.* 42 Redding-comb . . . is the opposite of tuck-comb.

***Tucker,** *n.*

+**1.** *Mad as tucker,* extremely angry. *colloq.*

1846 *Spirit of Times* (N.Y.) 9 May 125/2 Old Bill got mad as 'tucker' because the boys left him.

+**2. a.** A round dance or game in which one player, without a partner, directs the movements of the others until, in a general shift, he manages to secure a partner for himself. **b.** The partnerless player.

1881 RITTENHOUSE *Maud* 25 It was a tucker and I danced it with Mr. B. . . . Just then the tucker swung me. **1883** *Ib.* 266, I was green with jealousy . . . when we were dancing the tucker and he promenaded with Lizzie when he might have done it with me. **1891** *Harper's Mag.* Jan. 216/1 'This ain't fair,' he said, taking the 'Tucker' by the arm. **1898** M. LEONARD *Big Front Door* 123 Frank Hazeltine actually induced Aunt Marcia to take part in 'Tucker.'

3. An attachment to a sewing machine for making tucks in cloth.

1882 PECK *Sunshine* 84 A sewing machine, complete, with cover, drop leaf, hemmer, tucker [etc.]. **1920** *Sears, Roebuck & Co. Cat.* No. 141D, 517 The set [of sewing machine attachments] consists of one tucker, one ruffler, one shirring blade.

+**Tucker,** v.

1. tr. To tire, weary, or exhaust (a person or thing). Usually with out. colloq.

1833 S. SMITH Life J. Downing 204 If this aint enough to tucker a fellow out I dont know what is. **1836** Knickerb. VII. 21 There's no sich thing as tuckering out his raal white shark. **1883** JEWETT Mate of 'Daylight' 39 He aint been sick enough to tucker them out, seems to me. **1920** B. CRONIN Timber Wolves 40, I got a friend hereabouts that tuckers me when I'm along this way.

2. passive. To be worn out or exhausted. colloq.

a**1848** in Bartlett 366 We sot and sot, and waited for her, till we got eenamost tuckered out. **1866** Harper's Mag. Feb. 406/2 Won't yer ride, Mister? You look tuckered. **1904** CHURCHILL Crossing 265 They had two niggers— . . . and they were tuckered, too, for a fact. **1907** G. M. WHITE Boniface to Burglar 134, 'I can't, I'm tuckered,' he gasped.

+**Tuckering,** a. Exhausting, wearying. colloq. — **1893** HOLLEY Samantha at World's Fair 304 Some of the snortin' and prancin' of the horses of the Ocean . . . wuz meant, I spoze, to represent how awful tuckerin' it is for humanity to control the forces of Nater.

+**Tucket** (corn). [Prob. from Algonquian.] Green corn; ?a particular variety of corn. — **1856** Mich. Agric. Soc. Trans. VII. 528 The committee notices other samples: . . . Wm. Knowles, bushel tucket corn. Good sample. **1858** Harper's Mag. May 763/1 [In] a certain barrel in the barn . . . , he had made . . . frequent deposits of green corn, of the diminutive species called tucket. **1871** DE VERE 39 The tucket, as the green ear is called as long as it is soft and milky, is quite a delicacy to some palates.

∗**Tucking.** +**1.** The whole twist and tucking, the entire group or company. slang. (Cf. KIT 3 d.) **2.** Tucking bush, (see quotation). — (1) **1835** LONGSTREET Ga. Scenes 124 No man's to make a grab till all's been once round— . . . then the whole twist and tucking of you grab away, as you come under. (2) **1890** SHIELDS, etc. Big Game N. Amer. 88 Large patches of 'tucking-bushes,' or dwarf juniper, which grow about breast-high, with strong branches stiffly interlaced.

+**Tucking comb.** A comb worn by women to keep the hair in place. — **1822** Receipt by Daniel McDowell 11 April (Pettigrew P.), Mr. Pettigrew Bot of D McDowell one tucking Comb at $4.50. **1884** HARRIS Mingo 247 'Icabod,' said Miss Jane, scratching her head with the long teeth of her tucking-comb, 'you're too old to be made a tool of.' **1895** Outing XXVII. 11/2 He stopped and held up a gold-tipped tucking comb.

+**Tuft-eared squirrel.** S.W. A large tree squirrel having long and noticeably tufted ears. — **1867** Amer. Naturalist I. 355 The most characteristic, as well as most abundant species of Squirrel, is the Tuft-eared (Sciurus Abertii), discovered by Dr. Woodhouse in the San Francisco Mountains. **1917** Mammals of Amer. 175/1 The Tuft-eared Squirrel is characteristic of the stately yellow pine forests.

Tufted, a. In the names of birds having a tuft of feathers on the head. {1770-} — **1832** NUTTALL Manual Ornith. I. 236 Tufted Titmouse. Parus bicolor. . . . The third and pointed, like that of the common Blue Jay. **1850** COLTON Three Years Calif. 361 The quail, or tufted partridge, abounds in California, and is a delicious bird.

Tufted duck. A duck having a tufted head {1768-}, +esp. the American ring-necked duck. — **1813** WILSON Ornithology VIII. 60 [The] Tufted Duck: Anas fuligula; . . . is a plump, short bodied Duck; its flesh generally tender, and well tasted. **1835** AUDUBON Ornith. Biog. III. 259 In shape, the Tufted Duck, or Ring-bill, . . . resembles the Scaup or Flocking Fowl, but is plumper and more rounded. **1874** LONG Wild-Fowl 16 In the deep water varieties, . . . I shall treat of the . . . tufted duck, and buffle-head or butter ball.

Tuft grass. A grass that grows in tufts or clusters. Also comb. — **1859** H. VILLARD Pike's Peak Gold Fever (MS.) 24 The elevations were covered with tuft grass. **1897** Outing XXX. 250/1 A rugged, slightly hilly and coarse, tuft-grass grown stretch of open country is all that is requisite.

+**Tufting button.** 'A style of button used in upholstery' (Cent.). — **1882** Rep. Indian Affairs 450. **1884** FORNEY Car-Builder's Dict. (Cent.).

∗**Tug.**

+**1.** A rope or leather thong. Also tug rope.

1805 LEWIS in L. & Clark Exped. I. (1904) 369 The white perogue . . . [was] refitted in a few minutes with some tugs of raw hide and nales. **1852** WATSON Nights in Block-House 60 While the Indians were binding Kenton with tugs, Montgomery came in view. **1852** J. REYNOLDS Pioneer Hist. Illinois 236 They often pack their meat . . . by running a tug rope through each piece. **1891** Century Mag. March 774/2 We began by eating the rawhide tug ropes and parfleches. **1910** W. M. RAINE B. O'Connor 159.

2. A small but powerful steamer built for towing purposes. {1817-}

1844 M. C. HOUSTON Texas (1845) 153 The steamer proved to be the 'Swan' a tug. **1880** 'MARK TWAIN' Tramp Abroad 130 She was a tug, and one of very peculiar build and aspect. **1906** PRINGLE Rice Planter 418 There was a tug coming down the river bringing him a new flat.

b. Attrib. with load, office, skipper.

1883 'MARK TWAIN' Life on Miss. xlviii, He 'wouldn't give a d—— for a tug-load of such rot.' **1901** MERWIN & WEBSTER Calumet 'K' 290 There were a bad few days, with tales of . . . risks run that supplied roundhouse and tug-office yarn spinners with stories. **1906** N.Y. Ev. Post (Sat. Suppl.) 18 Aug. 1 The characters of tug skippers and their crews vary widely.

Tug boat. +**1.** (See quotation.) **2.** =TUG 2. {1832-} — (1) **1830** PICKERING Inquiries Emigrant 31 On board the steam tug-boat (a boat tugged along by a steam boat) for Albany. (2) **1861** MCCLELLAN in Own Story 205 Charter or buy . . . tug-boats for transportation of men and supplies. **1888** Scribner's Mag. Jan. 21/2 We thread our way among the tug-boats, the scows, . . . and other land-lubber craft. **1895** G. KING New Orleans 300 In the river the shipping, tug-boats, and gun-boats, floated down the current in flames.

+**Tuladi.** [Algonquian.] The namaycush or a variety of this. — **1884** GOODE, etc. Fisheries I. 486 [The] 'Tuladi' of the Maine and New Brunswick Indians and lumbermen [is a variety of lake trout]. **1911** Rep. Fisheries 1908 311/2 In different localities the individuals . . . are known by the local names 'salmon trout,' 'namaycush,' 'togue,' 'tuladi.'

+**Tulare.** **1.** Tules or a region overgrown by these. **2.** pl. (See quot. 1910.) In full Tulares Indians. — (1) **1836** PARKER Trip to West & Texas 266 (Bentley), Below the town . . . the land dips away to the river pastures and tulares. **1845** FRÉMONT Exped. 237 We afterwards found them to be fires, that had been kindled by the Indians among the tulares, on the shore of the bay. (2) **1848** 30th Congress 1 Sess. Sen. Rep. No. 75, 53 We undertook to cross the mountains nearly east, into the San Joaquin valley, and through the Tulares (Bullrush) Indians. **1910** HODGE, etc. Amer. Indians II. 835/2 Tulares, a band, probably of the Olamentke, formerly living on the N. coast of San Francisco bay, Cal., but nearly extinct in 1853.

+**Tule.** Also tula, thulé. S.W. [Sp. f. Nahuatl tollin, 'rush.']

1. Either of two large bulrushes of the genus Scirpus found in overflowed marshy regions.

1838 'TEXIAN' Mexico v. Texas 249 It was a little Jacal, or cabin, . . . thatched over with tule, a kind of rushes that grow in the swampy bottoms of the Rio Bravo. **1847** HENRY Campaign Sketches 24 Their residences are . . . nothing more than sheds . . . thatched with a long grass which grows in the marshes, called 'tula.' **1850** J. L. TYSON Diary in Calif. 54 The shores [of the Sacramento R.] were flat and marshy, being overgrown with thulé, a kind of light cane. **1898** CANFIELD Maid of Frontier 203 A hut . . . roofed with 'tules,' which are water flags, dried and tough. a**1918** G. STUART On Frontier I. 98 They had to wade in water among the tules up to their armpits.

2. A region or tract overgrown by tules.

1852 Knickerb. XXXIX. 224, I determined to penetrate the tule and look them up. **1872** MCCLELLAN Golden State 171 The land upon the west and east sides, being low, is overflowed to a great extent, forming tule and swamp. **1887** Boston Jrnl. 22 April 2/4 At Davisville, Cal., the wild geese gather in immense numbers on the farms adjoining the tules. **1893** Advance 2 Feb., The early settlers found that the tule made excellent farming land, if the water could be kept off in the winter.

3. Attrib. with boat, farm, hut, etc.

1848 BRYANT California xxx. 360 The tule-boat consists of bundles of tule firmly bound together with willow withes. When completed, in shape it is not unlike a small keel-boat. **1850** KINGSLEY Diary 100 Our boat went out back in the tula swamp. **1869** HARTE Luck of Roaring Camp 220 Stretches of 'tule' land fertilized by its once regular channel and dotted by flourishing ranchos are now cleanly erased. **1873** MILLER Amongst Modocs 363 The few remaining Modoc warriors now returned to their sage-brush plains and tule lakes. **1876** — Unwritten Hist. 284 We . . . sailed on little mountain lakes with grass and tule sails. **1883** Century Mag. May 9/1 The Indians . . . [tore] off the clothes of the sick lying helpless in the tents or tule huts on the beach. Ib. Aug. 515/1 They took the tule roofs off the little houses. **1888** SHERIDAN Memoirs I. 49 The pots [were] filled with camas and tula roots—but not an Indian was to be seen. **1891** A. WELCKER Wild West 64 A cabin on a swampy tule farm. **1907** WHITE Arizona Nights 165 We all set to building a tule raft like the others.

b. In specific names: (see quotations).

1897 Kissimmee (Fla.) Valley 26 May 3/3 Remarkable in many ways, the tule gnat of the far West is the most curious for its almost total lack of weight. **1915** ARMSTRONG & THORNBER Western Wild Flowers 2 Arrowhead. Sagittaria latifolia. . . . The tubers are edible and hence the plant is often called Tule Potato and they are much eaten by the Chinese in California. **1891** Cent. 6525/2 Tule-wren, a kind of marsh-wren, . . . Telmatodytes palustris, var. paludicola, which abounds in the tule-marshes of California.

+**Tule marsh.** A marsh overgrown with tules. — **1850** TYSON Diary in Calif. 54 The country is cut up with 'sloughs,' and extensive thulé marshes are the consequence. **1860** GREELEY Overland Journey 344 The residue [of Calif. land is] . . . either ruggedly mountainous . . . or absorbed in the tule marshes which line the San Joaquin. **1889** MUNROE Golden Days 84 The San Joaquin [drained] the vast tulé marshes of the south. **1909** Nat. Conservation Cong. Proc. 112 The great tule marshes of the West were white with the nesting multitude [of herons].

∗**Tulip.** Any one of various plants of the genus Tulipa, or the flower of such a plant.

1682 ASH Carolina 13 [Planters'] Gardens also begin to be beautified and adorned with . . . The Rose, Tulip, Carnation and Lilly, &c. **1777** CUTLER in Life & Corr. I. 63 Planted out in my borders . . . Tulips, Persian Iris, . . . and Peonies. **1815** Lit. & Phil. Soc. N.Y. Trans. I. 172 Our Dutch forefathers . . . introduced . . . wall flowers, tulips, imperial flowers, the white lily. **1890** [see NASTURTIUM]. **1907** *St. Nicholas* June 762/1 I heard the breezes telling how the tulip kissed the rose.

Tulip-bearing, a. Producing flowers resembling tulips. {1786 (s.v. *Tulipiferous*)} Used in designations for the tulip tree and the evergreen magnolia. — **1705** BEVERLEY *Virginia* II. 25 The fine Tulip-bearing Laurel-Tree . . . keeps Blossoming and seeding several Months together. **1784** FILSON *Kentucke* 47 Here also is found the tulip-bearing laurel-tree, or magnolia, which has an exquisite smell. **1818** FORDHAM *Narr. Travels* 153 The live poplar, or tulip-bearing tree, of which canoes are made, . . . grow to a prodigious size. **1846** BROWNE *Trees Amer.* 24 *Liriodendron tulipifera*, Tulip-bearing Liriodendron.

+**Tulip laurel**. The evergreen magnolia, *Magnolia grandiflora. Obs.* — **1765** ROGERS *Acct. N. Amer.* 120 Here [in Va.] is the large tulip laurel, the bark of whose roots, in intermitting fevers, has been found to answer all the purposes of the famous Peruvian Bark. **1766** STORK *Acct. E. Florida* 47 The magnolia, tulip-laurel, tupelow-tree, are all beautiful. **1797** IMLAY *Western Territory* (ed. 3) 270 Among the laurels the preference should be given to the tulip laurel (magnolia), which is not known in Europe.

+**Tulip poplar**. =next. — **1843** TORREY *Flora N.Y.* I. 28 Tulip Tree. Tulip Poplar. . . . The bark is a stimulating tonic and diaphoretic. **1860** MORDECAI *Virginia* 105 A fine tulip poplar . . . marks the corner where his house stood. **1897** SUDWORTH *Arborescent Flora* 198 Tulip-tree. . . . [Also called] Tulip Poplar (Del., Pa., S.C., Ill.).

Tulip tree. +A large deciduous North American tree (*Liriodendron tulipifera*) having tulip-shaped flowers. {1731– (Miller *Gard. Dict.* s.v. *Tulipfera*)} — **1705** BEVERLEY *Virginia* II. iv. 25 The large Tulip-Tree, which we call a Poplar [perfumes the woods]. **1771** *Copley-Pelham Lett.* 159 The Tulip Trees are plenty with you. **1802** ELLICOTT *Journal* 286 [The] tulip tree . . . is improperly called *poplar* in the middle states. **1886** MITCHELL *R. Blake* 374 They had turned into the bridle-path . . . and followed it under tulip-trees and over grass-lands. **1915** E. ATKINSON *Johnny Appleseed* 83 Johnny went . . . through a belt of woods that was honey-sweet with blossoming tulip-trees.

+**Tullibee**. [Canadian Fr.] A species of whitefish found in the Great Lakes. — [**1822** in Morse *Rep. Indian Affairs* II. 31 A fish called . . . by the English and French 'Telibees,' not equal to, but greatly resembling, the white fish.] **1888** GOODE *Amer. Fishes* 93 Tautog, chogset, . . . tullibee . . . are among the best. **1896** JORDAN & EVERMANN *Check-List Fishes* 289 Tullibee; Mongrel Whitefish. Great Lakes, Lake of the Woods, and northward. **1910** HODGE, etc. *Amer. Indians* II. 835/2.

+**Tulpehocken**. =FALLAWATER. *Obs.* — **1857** E. J. HOOPER *Western Fruit Book* 35 Fallowater, or Fallenwalder, or Apple of the Fallen Timber, called, also, Tulpehocken, from the creek of that name. **1867** WARDER *Pomology* 495 Tulpehocken. . . . A native of Pennsylvania, where it is a great favorite; extensively cultivated through the West.

Tumble, *n.* {1634–} +**1.** (See quotations.) **2.** *To take a tumble*, to change one's mode of behavior; to turn over a new leaf. *colloq.* — (1) **1809** KENDALL *Travels* II. 133 The vats [for obtaining salt] . . . stand from two to six feet from the ground, on piles or *tumbles*. a**1870** CHIPMAN *Notes on Bartlett* 490 *Tumble*, a cock (of hay); a heap. New London County, Conn., July, 1871. (2) **1884** NYE *Baled Hay* 48 Brace up . . . and take a tumble.

✳**Tumble**, *v. intr.* +To understand, 'get wise to' (someone or something). *slang.* — **1859** MATSELL *Vocabulum* 92 *Tumbled*, Suspected; found it out. **1880** *Cimarron News & Press* 23 Dec. 1/7 O blow the fever! Can't you tumble to nothin'? **1889** *Opelousas* (La.) *Democrat* 2 Feb. 3/4 I didn't tumble worth a cent. **1903** ADE *People You Know* 40 Father often spoke of a Second Cousin who had been in Congress until the District tumbled to him.

+**Tumble beetle**. =next. — **1860** *Ladies' Repository* XX. 265/1 The tumble beetle in vain tries to roll its little ball up a hill.

+**Tumble bug**. Any one of various scarabaeid beetles which fashion dung into balls to serve as depositories for their eggs. — **1805** PARKINSON *Tour Amer.* 362 There is a kind of beetle, called a tumble-bug, which in the summer forms a cave in the earth. **1890** *Harper's Mag.* Mar. 651/2 A 'tumble-bug' . . . put in an appearance, and commenced his loud humming round the soldier's head. **1916** 'MARK TWAIN' *Mysterious Stranger* 44, I suppose he could not be insulted by Ursula any more than the king could be insulted by a tumble-bug.

+**Tumble over**. A toy so weighted at the bottom that it always assumes an upright position. — **1895** *Outing* XXVI. 380/1 She stood there with two-thirds of her weight at the bottom of her fin, like one of those lead-weighted, pith 'tumble-overs,' with which we played when children.

✳**Tumbler**.

1. A cylindrical or barrel-shaped drinking vessel or glass, originally one with a rounded or pointed bottom so that it could not be put down until empty. {1664–}
1678 *New Castle Court Rec.* 322 One silver tumbler markt AW. **1725** SEWALL *Letter-book* II. 189 One small Tumbler, One Thimble and Three broken pieces of Silver. **1788** *Kentucky Gazette* 28 June 2/3 Hugh M'Ilvain, Is now opening at his Store in Lexington; . . . An Assortment of Goods. . . . Tumblers, decanters and vinegar cruets. **1807** *Boston Gazette* 8 Oct. 3/2 Ten cases half pint tumblers, for sale. **1897** 'THANET' *Missionary Sheriff* 123 He passed the tumbler to Harned, who shook his head.

+**2.** =DUNKER.
1796 MORSE *Univ. Geog.* I. 281 Tumblers . . . perform baptism, . . . by putting the person, while kneeling, head first under water. **1867** DIXON *New America* II. 184 The Tunkers . . . are also called Tumblers, from

one of the abrupt motions which they make in the act of baptism. **1883** Schaff *Religious Encycl.* III. 2401.

+**3. a.** =TUMBLE BUG. **b.** The pupa of a mosquito.
1807 IRVING *Salmagundi* xv. 403 That indefatigable insect, called the tumbler, . . . the only industrious animal in Virginia, . . . works ignobly in the dirt. **1859** *New Amer. Cycl.* VIII. 317/1 They are changed into pupæ, called tumblers from the manner in which they roll over and over in the water by means of the fin-like paddles at the end of the tail.

4. Attrib. with *dam, light, quilt*.
1779 *N.J. Archives* 2 Ser. III. 184 A tumbler dam was erected . . . sufficient to vent the water in the time of great freshes. **1877** in McCabe *Hist. Great Riots* 307 When the tumbler lights were started on the stand where the speakers of English were expected, the crowd surged forward in a lazy way toward the stand. **1895** A. BROWN *Meadow-Grass* 181 Where's that piece o' chalk you had when you marked out your tumbler-quilt?

+**Tumble turd**. =TUMBLE BUG. *colloq.* and *vulgar.* — **1737** BRICKELL *N. Carolina* 161 The Tumble-turds, are a Species of the Beetles, and so called, from their constant rowling the Horsedung (whereon they feed) from one place to another, 'till it is no bigger than a small Bullet. **1748** CATESBY *Carolina* App. 11 *Scarabœus pilaris Americanus.* The Tumble-Turds. This is the most numerous and remarkable of the Beetle kind of any in North America.

+**Tumbleweed**. Any one of various branching plants whose globular tops become detached from the roots and are tumbled about by the winds. — **1887** *Amer. Naturalist* XXI. 929 A nearly spherical plant body . . . at the end of the season breaks away at the root, thus forming a tumbleweed. **1888** *Century Mag.* Jan. 453/2, I secured a 'tumble-weed' or 'rolling-weed,'—one of those globular perennials of the plains that . . . goes rolling around over the prairies at the mercy of the blast. **1899** *Mo. So. Dakotan* I. 176 The tired oxen trudged crowding angrily when the plow hung in an uncut red root and hauling wearily to escape a spreading tumble weed. **1925** TILGHMAN *Dugout* 79 The bones they strewed were white and dry, and the doorway choked with drifted sand and tumbleweed.

✳**Tumbling**. Attrib. or as adj. with *box, dam, mustard*. — **1760** WASHINGTON *Diaries* I. 139 Dogue Run carried of[f] the Tumbling Dam of my Mill. **1876** KNIGHT 2652/2 *Tumbling-box*, . . . a cylindrical or barrel-shape vessel, . . . mounted on an axis so as to be revolved by a winch or pulley. **1915** ARMSTRONG & THORNBER *Western Wild Flowers* 98 There are other Tumble-weeds, such as Tumbling Mustard, *Sisymbrium allissimum* and *Amaranthus albus*, not of this family.

+**Tump**, *v. local.* [See next.] *tr.* (See quot. 1848.) *Obs.* — **1848** BARTLETT 366 *To Tump.* . . . It means to draw a deer or other animal home through the woods, after he has been killed. . . . Used in Maine. **1855** HALIBURTON *Nature & Human Nat.* 116 A man passed the north barrack gate, tumping . . . an immense bull moose on a sled.

+**Tumpline**. Also **trumpline**. [Algonquian.] (See quot. 1848.) — **1796** *Captivity of Mrs. Johnson* 66, I was a novice at making canoes . . . and tumplines, which was the only occupation of the squaws. **1848** BARTLETT 367 *Tumpline*, a strap placed across the forehead to assist a man in carrying a pack on his back. Used in Maine, where the custom was borrowed from the Indians. [**1888** *Harper's Mag.* Aug. 380/1 Each with her axe bends and plods along under a back-load of wood suspended by a trumpline across the forehead.] **1903** WHITE *Forest* 25 Tump-lines welter in a tangle of dimness.

✳**Tumulus**. +=MOUND 2. — **1765** J. BARTRAM *Journal* 7 Saw a middling sized Indian tumulus, 20 feet diameter and 6 or 8 foot high. **1802** ELLICOTT *Journal* 134 Those mounds or tumuli, are generally square and flat on the top. **1823** JAMES *Exped.* I. 55 Tumuli, and other remains of the labours of Indians . . . , are remarkably numerous about St. Louis. **1847** SQUIER & DAVIS *Ancient Monum. Miss. Valley* 139 In connection more or less intimate with the various earthworks already described, are the Tumuli or mounds.

✳**Tuna.**[1] The tuna cactus or its fruit. Also attrib.
1609 HAKLUYT *Va. Richly Valued* 145 The Indians . . . fed upon Tunas and rootes of the fields. **1722** COXE *Descr. Carolana* 74 Tunas [are] a most delicious Fruit, especially in hot Weather. **1848** BRYANT *California* xxxiii. 391 The blood-red *tuna*, or prickly-pear, looked very tempting. **1877** CAMPION *On Frontier* 304 Bucks, squaws, and papooses, all [were] engaged in gathering their tuna harvest. **1895** GRAHAM *Stories of Foot-Hills* 44 You can go up the bank there and pick some tunas.

+**Tuna.**[2] [Amer. Sp., from Sp. *atún* 'tunny.'] A fish of the family Thunnidae; a tunny (q.v.). — **1884** JORDAN in Goode, etc. *Fisheries* I. 319 The names 'Spanish Mackerel,' 'Skipjack,' and 'Tuna' are also sometimes applied to [the California bonito]. **1896** — & EVERMANN *Check-List Fishes* 340 *Thunnus thynnus.* . . . Tunny; Horse-mackerel; Great Albacore; Tuna. Cape Cod and off all coasts; north to England, Newfoundland, San Francisco, and Japan.

+**Tuna cactus**. Any one of various prickly pears of the genus *Opuntia* found in tropical parts of the United States. (Cf. PRICKLY-PEAR CACTUS.) — **1875** BOURKE *Journal* 30 May, A plant, plentiful in this country [along the South Cheyenne R.], called the nopal, or Tuna cactus, . . . is employed with success to clarify water for drinking purposes. **1893** *Garden & Forest* 11 Oct. 429/2 The Candle-Cactus . . . and a large Tuna Cactus are the most conspicuous plants. **1898** A. M. DAVIDSON *Calif. Plants* 189 The prickly pear, or tuna cactus, so common in Southern California on dry hillsides and sandy wastes.

+Tune book. A book containing hymn tunes. — **1848** *Ladies' Repository* VIII. 286 We advise all our Churches, east and west, to patronize our new and excellent tune-book. **1879** B. F. TAYLOR *Summer-Savory* 116 I see the long tune-books fluttering along the top of the gallery as they opened them to the tune. **1887** *Nation* 19 June 427/1 A hymn and tune-book for Congregational use.

Tuning fork. A small steel instrument having two prongs and giving off, when struck, a musical tone of a particular pitch. {1799-} — **1773** in E. Singleton *Social N.Y.* 294 [Rivington had] tuning-forks, harpsichord and spinet hammers [etc.]. **1851** MITCHELL *Dream Life* 97 He draws out his tuning fork, and waits for the parson to close his reading. **1880** E. JAMES *Negro Minstrel's Guide* 4 Pitch-pipes and tuning forks, 50 cts.

+Tunker. =DUNKER. Also attrib.
1789 MORSE *Amer. Geog.* 324 They appear to be humble, well-meaning christians, and have acquired the character of the *Harmless* Tunkers. **1826** FLINT *Recoll.* 40 The Tunkers, with their long and flowing beards, have brought up their teams in woods late in autumn. **1844** RUPP *Relig. Denominations* 93 All the 'Tunker churches' in America sprang from the church of Schwartzenau in Germany. **1864** *Commonwealth* (Boston) 19 Aug., John Kline, an aged Tunker preacher . . . , has been assassinated solely for being a good Anti-Slavery Unionist. **1878** *N. Amer. Rev.* CXXVI. 255 Near at hand was the meeting-house of a sect of German-Quakers—Tunkers or Dunkards, as they are differently named.

+Tunket. A euphemism for *hell. colloq.* — **1871** *Scribner's Mo.* II. 630 What in tunket are you making such a to-do about it for? **1894** CLARK *On Cloud Mt.* 24 Things is so contrariy in this Western country. A feller'd better be in Tunket any day. **1918** FREEMAN *Edgewater People* 226 What in tunket possessed you?

∗Tunnel.
1. A subterranean passage for a canal or railroad; an adit or a mine consisting of an adit. {1782-}
1835 HOFFMAN *Winter in West* I. 73 The Pennsylvania Canal . . . flows on an aqueduct over the Alleghany, and, passing through a tunnel of a few yards in length, locks into the Monongahela. **1856** *Porter's Spirit of Times* 22 Nov. 194/2 The chief paying tunnels at Monte Cristo, are the . . . 'Bigelow,' and 'Crandall.' **1867** SHINN *Story of Mine* 195 A mining country that contains high mountains and short, steep ravines is well adapted to tunnels. **1910** *Springfield W. Repub.* 8 Dec. 16 A second of the four [engines] was at once set hauling trains east-bound through the tunnel.

2. Attrib. and comb. with *borer, claim, mining,* etc.
1828 WEBSTER, *Tunnel-pit,* a shaft sunk from the top of the ground to the level of an intended tunnel, for drawing up the earth and stones. **1856** *Porter's Spirit of Times* 22 Nov. 194/2 Tunnel mining at Monte Cristo is also said to be particularly successful. **1872** *Harper's Mag.* Dec. 30 Here we notice a 'tunnel claim,' a slight excavation made into the rock, with a few timbers put up before it. **1876** KNIGHT 2656/1 *Tunnel-borer,* . . . a ram, operated by compressed air, for making excavations through rock. **1883** *Century Mag.* Oct. 823/2 A tunnel-way for passengers connects the whole.

3. In special combinations. {1610-}
Tunnel fungus, t. roof, (see quotations); *t. sieve,* a tunnel- or funnel-shaped sieve; *t. skirt,* a skirt shaped somewhat like a tunnel.
1817-8 EATON *Botany* (1822) 258 *Cyathus striatus,* tunnel fungus. . . . On the earth and fallen branches in woods late in autumn. **1887** EGGLESTON in *Century Mag.* April 901/1 A 'tunnel roof'—that is, a roof sloping on all four sides to a point in the middle—with a belfry perched on the apex from which the bell-rope dangled to the floor in the very center of the assembly. **1863** *Rep. Comm. Agric. 1862* 135 A tunnel sieve may be used for conducting the juice from the spout of the mill to the filterers over the pan. **1870** A. D. WHITNEY *We Girls* ix, Gathers and gores, tunnel-skirts and barrel-skirts.

∗Tunny. Any one of various fishes of the family Thunnidae or of genera resembling *Thunnus.* Also with specifying adjectives. (Cf. TUNA.') — **1839** STORER *Mass. Fishes* 47 *Thynnus vulgaris.* The Common Tunny. **1879** WEBSTER *Suppl.* 1561/2 *Horse-mackerel,* . . . the American tunny (*Orcynus secundi-dorsalis*), found on the coast from Newfoundland to Florida. **1884** GOODE, etc. *Fisheries* I. 320 In addition to the Striped Bonito, which is, properly, a Tunny, there are two other small Tunnies—the Long-finned Tunny, *Orcynus alalonga,* and the Silver-spotted Tunny, *Orcynus argentivittatus.* **1896** JORDAN & EVERMANN *Check-List Fishes* 340.

+Tupelo (tree). [Creek Indian.] Any one of various trees of the genus *Nyssa,* as the black or sour gum. Also with specifying term.
c**1730** CATESBY *Carolina* I. 41 The Tupelo Tree. . . . The Grain of the Wood is curled and very tough, and therefore very proper for Naves of Cart-wheels, and other Country-Uses. **1785** MARSHALL *Amer. Grove* 97 *Nyssa sylvatica.* Upland Tupelo-Tree, or Sour Gum. **1816** W. DARBY *Geogr. Descr. La.* 130 The tupeloo is known in Louisiana by the popular name of olive. **1876** HALE *P. Nolan's Friends* ix, Swamp oak and tupelo were all around her. **1900** HOWELLS in *Scribner's Mag.* 367/2 He wished to show me a tupelo-tree.
attrib. **1765** in Stork *Acct. E. Florida* 79 The low lands are partly cypress and tupeloo swamps. **1888** CABLE in *Century Mag.* Jan. 347/1 The tupelo-gums were hiding all their gray in shimmering green. **1917** *House Beautiful* March 246 Tupelo flooring does not splinter or sliver.

∗Turban. A cloth, usually of a bright color, worn as a headdress by Indians and Negroes. — **1836** GILMAN *Recoll.* (1838) 26 Chloe, with a turban of superior height . . . , stood behind her chair with the basket of keys. **1838** *S. Lit. Messenger* IV. 466/2 The chiefs were equipped in their warlike costumes— . . . their guns by their sides, and feathers in their turbans. **1848** BRYANT *California* iv. 52 A turban; a soiled damask dressing-gown . . . ; buckskin leggins and moccasins, composed the dress of Ki-he-ga-wa-chuck-ee. **1863** E. W. Pearson *Lett. Port Royal* 192 All her wool [was] carefully concealed by an enormous turban. **1893** *Harper's Mag.* Feb. 442 Zoe, brilliant in a new scarlet turban in honor of the occasion, was stirring the syrup.

Turban handkerchief. A handkerchief suitable for wear as a turban. — **1836** C. GILMAN *Recoll.* (1838) 101 Mamma and I and our friends had been busy the day previous in cutting the turban-handkerchiefs. **1870** 'F. FERN' *Ginger-Snaps* 169 A most excellent colored woman, in a family of my acquaintance, . . . refused to wear the colored turban-handkerchief at the request of her mistress.

Turbine wheel. A form of water wheel, driven by a moving stream of water and usually operating on a vertical shaft. — **1860** EMERSON *Conduct of Life* 181 There is faith . . . in machinery, in the steam-engine, galvanic battery, turbine-wheels, sewing machines. **1880** *Harper's Mag.* July 318/2 [An Irishman was] looking at the water-works at Fairmount, and the great turbine wheels. **1891** *Scribner's Mag.* X. 19 All attempts at propulsion . . . by turbine wheels, pulsometers, ejectors or by pumps—have failed.

∗Turbot. Any one of various large flounders resembling the European turbot, as the sand flounder. {1555-, in W. Indies} Also with specifying term.
1616 SMITH *New England* 29 [There were] whales, Grampus, Porkpisces, Turbut, Sturgion, [etc.]. **1630** *Mass. H. S. Coll.* 1 Ser. I. 120 Also heere is abundance of herring, turbut, sturgion, cuskes, hadocks, mullets, eeles; crabbes, muskles, and oysters. **1772** ROMANS in P. L. Phillips *Notes B. Romans* (1924) 125 [A Spaniard] during Six Weeks made up a Cargo of Two Thousand Arobas of Red and Black Drum Fish, dry'd and Salted, Besides Several hundred Turbots. **1802** ELLICOTT *Journal* 255 Along the Florida Reef, and among the Keys, a great abundance and variety of fish may be taken: such as . . . porgys, turbot, stingrys. **1842** *Nat. Hist. N.Y., Zoology* IV. 301 The Spotted Turbot . . . is considered as a delicate article of food. **1911** *Rep. Fisheries 1908* 310/1 The family of flounders is composed of the turbots . . . , the halibuts . . . , the plaices . . . , and probably the soles.

Tureen. A deep, covered, and usually oval dish for holding liquids, esp. soup, at the table. {1706-} — **1761** in Singleton *Social N.Y.* 147 Very fine silver chased turene, dish and spoon. **1787** *Ky. Gazette* 24 Nov. 2/3 Samuel Blair, Has for sale, . . . frying pans, tureenes, tin ware. **1806** *Austin P.* I. (1904) 104 Articles Wanted from Orleans [include] . . . Cups, Saucers, Tureens, Tea Potts. **1903** Fox *Little Shepherd* xvii, At the head sat Mrs. Dean, with a great tureen of calf's head soup in front of her.

∗Turf.
∗1. The matted surface or sward of grass-land; also, a slab of sod cut from this.
1633 *Mass. Bay Rec.* I. 108 Serieant Perkins shall carry 40 turfes to the ffort, as a punishmt for drunkenes. **1678** *Boston Rec.* 118 Noe person whatsoever . . . [shall] digg or carry away any Turfe . . . vnlesse it be at Fox hill. **1701** *Ib.* 15 No person . . . shall hereafter break, digg, or carry away, any of the Sord, Turf, or Earth of or belonging to the common. **1833** *Foreign Miss. Chron.* (Pittsburgh) I. 75 Fencing can be done with stone, turf, or hedges. **1890** *St. Nicholas* May 556/2 Many a good in-field for base-ball has no turf on it, and is called a 'scalped' field.

b. Attrib. with *grass, house, hovel, knife.*
1820 *Columbian Centinel* 12 Jan. 4/6 On the premises is . . . [a] Chaise-House, Turf-House, . . . and other Out Buildings. **1848** *Rep. Comm. Patents 1847* 386 We have very little turf grass. **1854** THOREAU *Walden* 315 There came a hundred men . . . with many car-loads of ungainly-looking farming tools, sleds, . . . turf-knives, spades. **1879** HOWELLS *Lady of Aroostook* 66 'Now, if you were taking some nice girl with you!' . . . 'To those wilds? To a redwood shanty in California, or a turf hovel in Colorado?'

∗2. A sod or parcel of turf used as a symbol of ownership. *Obs.* Freq. in phrase *(by) turf and twig.*
1654 *N.C. Col. Rec.* I. 18 Actual possession was solemnly given to them . . . in delivering them a turf of the earth with an arrow shot into it. **1654** *Suffolk Deeds* II. 92 Possession was giuen & deliuered vnto ye said Symon Lynde of all ye afore mentioned Estate & turfe & twig [delivered]. **1684** *Huntington Rec.* I. 390 John finch senr . . . gave the sd. Edward higby possession by braking a twig and diging a turfe. **1689** *Ib.* II. 55 The within mentioned bill of sale was delivered possession by turf & twigg. **1729** HEMPSTEAD *Diary* 213, [I] Recd Possession of that & the other Lot by Turff & Twig.

3. The track or course over which horse-racing takes place; the racing world. {1755-}
1798 *Steele P.* I. 159 He is much thought of by all the good Horse Breeders and Gentlemen of the Turff who have seen him. **1840** *Picayune* 26 Aug. 2/3 In England the match is noticed as characteristic of Yankee spirit on the turf. **1893** *Harper's Mag.* April 659/1 Such *nouveaux riches* as a millionaire chewing-gum manufacturer, the leading jockey of America, his most ambitious rival on the turf [etc.].

b. Attrib. with *amusement, exchange,* etc. {*c*1802–}

1868 WOODRUFF *Trotting Horse* 293 If they were [always at their best], the turf-prophets could select the winners more often than they do. **1875** *Courier-Journal* 6 May 4/4 The grand opening . . . promises an entertainment not before equaled in the turf history of this country. **1885** *Weekly New Mexican Rev.* 9 April 4/6 Magdalena has a sporting association for turf amusements. **1898** *Kansas City Star* 19 Dec. 3/1 Many Records Reduced by the Turf Stars of 1898. **1902** WILSON *Spenders* 49 Young Bines played the deal from soda card to hock at Lem Tully's Turf Exchange.

* Turkey.

+1. A large, wild, North American bird (*Meleagris gallopavo*).

1607 in Smith *Works* (1910) I. p. xli, We found an Ilet, on which were many Turkeys. **1698** THOMAS *Pensilvania* 13 There are an Infinite Number of Sea and Land Fowl, of most sorts, viz. . . . Turkies, . . . Pheasants, Partridges. **1701** WOLLEY *Journal N.Y.* 40 They have great store of wildfowl, as Turkys, Heath-hens, Quails, Partridges, Pigeons. **1788** J. MAY *Journal & Lett.* 72 Our luck has been heretofore to have good provisions—the best of bread, fine venison, and turkeys—when we pleased. **1804** CLARK in *Lewis & C. Exped.* I. (1904) 64 Deer and turkeys in great quantities on the bank. **1891** O'BEIRNE *Leaders Ind. Territory* 209/2 In these parts deer, turkey and beaver are plentiful.

* b. A domesticated variety of this bird.

*c*1618 STRACHEY *Virginia* 26 Howses of stone, tame turkyes and monkyes, supposed at Peccartcanick. **1785** *Huntington Rec.* III. 130 No person shall Let his Turkeys Ramble in his neighbours enclosure without one wing being cut. **1831** PECK *Guide* 173 It is no uncommon thing for some farmer's wives to raise three or four hundred fowls, besides geese, ducks, and turkies, in a season. **1904** GLASGOW *Deliverance* 48 A flock of turkeys had settled to roost along its twisted boughs.

transf. **1880** CABLE *Grandissimes* 19 The proudest old turkey in the theater was an old fellow whose Indian blood shows in his very behavior.

* c. The cooked flesh of this bird or the dressed fowl to be used for food, esp. for festive occasions as Thanksgiving and Christmas.

1716 SEWALL *Diary* III. 100 Writt to Mr. Parris at Rice's, eat Roast Turkey near Strawberry-Hill. **1787** B. H. YOUNG *Jessamine Co., Ky.* (1898) 32, I invite you . . . on Christmas day to partake of a big dinner of turkey and oysters. **1851** MELVILLE *Moby Dick* 97 These presents were [like] so many Christmas turkeys. **1871** DAY *Knickerb. Life* (1897) 213 The Yankee Thanksgiving, with its turkey, cranberry sauce, mince, pumpkin, apple pie, and cider, found favor with the dames of Knickerbocker proclivities. **1898** *Kansas City Star* 18 Dec. 1/3 John J. Valentine . . . has instructed Charles R. Teas . . . to present every employee . . . who is a married man or the supporter of a family a turkey. **1907** HARRIS *Tents of Wickedness* 227 She had assimilated the oyster-soup, the turkey [etc.].

+2. *fig.* Easy money or advantage; the 'gravy'; pompous or high-flown speech. *slang.*

1873 *Ill. Agric. Dept. Trans.* X. 14, I do not . . . [oppose] the colleges in their legitimate work, but I do object to the *turkey* being all on the College side. **1888** *Washington Critic* (F.), 'What . . . does locum tenens mean, Tim?' . . . 'Why, that's turkey for *pro tem.*, of course.'

+3. *Lumbering.* (See quotations.)

1893 *Scribner's Mag.* June 715/2 [With] his 'turkey,' a two-bushel bag in which he carries his belongings, strung over his shoulder, the shanty boy starts . . . for town. **1905** *Forestry Bureau Bul.* No. 61, 52 *Turkey,* a bag containing a lumberjack's outfit. To 'histe the turkey' is to take one's personal belongings and leave camp. (N[orth] W[oods], L[ake] S[tates].)

+4. In colloquial phrases.
See also JOB'S TURKEY.

a. *To say turkey,* to speak pleasantly, to remind or speak plainly; *to say turkey to* (one) *and buzzard to* (another), to give (one) the advantage over (another); *not to say pea-turkey,* not to say a thing.

1846 *30th Congress 1 Sess.* H. R. Ex. Doc. No. 41, 502 The Indian replied, 'You never once said turkey to me.' **1862** *Harper's Mag.* June 33/1 He vaulted on his horse, and was out of sight before the astonished Boniface could 'say turkey' about his bill. **1896** *Congress. Rec.* 22 Dec. 409/2 That is a sort of civil service that says 'turkey' to every Democrat and 'buzzard' to every Republican. **1899** *Ib.* 25 Jan. App. 108/1 Why do these professed champions of liberty insist on saying 'turkey' to the Filipinos and 'buzzard' to the negroes? **1909** *Dialect Notes* III. 356 She never said pea-turkey to me about it.

b. *To talk turkey,* to talk affably, to say pleasant things; *to talk turkey to,* to address with the utmost plainness and frankness.

*c*1840 in Haliburton *Traits Amer. Humor* I. 79, I was plagy apt to talk turky always when I get sociable, if it was only out of politeness. **1919** HOUGH *Sagebrusher* xiv, Do you know when he got rattled he began to talk Dutch to me? Well, I talked turkey to him.

c. *Month of turkeys,* October.

1876 HALE *P. Nolan's Friends* x, The Americans found them in this 'month of turkeys,' as they called October.

d. *To walk turkey,* of a ship, to pitch and roll.

1888 *San Fran. W. Examiner* 22 March (F.), The north wind commenced to make the Yaquina walk turkey, standing her up on either end alternately and rolling her both ways at once.

5. *attrib.* and *comb.* **a.** In sense 1 and 1 b with *butcher, drumstick,* etc.

See also TURKEY CALL, DANCE, etc.

1827 COOPER *Prairie* iii, Their natures have greatly changed if they too are not both dreaming of a turkey-hunt or a court-house fight at this very moment. **1838** *S. Lit. Messenger* IV. 232 Besides the dwelling-house, there are the negro-quarters, corn-cribs, . . . turkey-house. **1845** *Big Bear Ark.* 118 The 'Turkey Runner' who is also a bee and still hunter, sallies forth in quest of a drove. **1850** BROWNE *Poultry Yard* 165 There are turkey butchers of whom you may buy the half or a quarter of a bird. **1851** *S. Lit. Messenger* XVII. 660/1 My passion for, and all the skill I possess in Turkey hunting, grew out of my association with two gentlemen nearly of my own age. **1853** 'P. PAXTON' *Yankee in Texas* 117 You hear of turkey sign, bear sign, hog sign, cow sign, Indian sign, etc. **1860** HOLMES *Professor* 60 Our landlady and her daughter and the bombazine-clad female . . . are of the turkey-drumstick style of organization. **1872** ROE *Army Lett.* 35 The turkey galantine was perfect, and . . . was composed almost entirely of wild goose!

b. In geographical names.

1662 *Dedham Rec.* IV. 44 The wood upon Tirkie Iland that is fitt for the making of charcole. **1845** *Cincinnati Misc.* II. 100 The women and their children came from Columbia to Turkey Bottom to scratch up the bulbous roots of the bear-grass. **1854** *La Crosse Democrat* 14 Feb. 2/3 Situated on the Turkey river.

c. In the names of plants.

1791 MUHLENBERG *Index Florae* 174 *Arabis,* Turkey-pod. **1843** Turkey Corn [see SQUIRREL CORN 1]. **1898** A. M. DAVIDSON *Calif. Plants* 46 Turkey-weed . . . is sticky, prickly, and ill-scented.

d. In special combinations.

Turkey-buster, a gun for shooting turkeys (*humorous*); *t. dog,* a dog useful in hunting turkeys; *t. dream,* a day dream or brown study; *t. gnat,* a small black fly (*Simulium meridionale*) common in the Mississippi valley region; *t. hound,* a turkey dog; *t. match,* a shooting match at which turkeys serve as targets and prizes; *t. raffle,* an occasion upon which a turkey is raffled off; *t. roan,* (see quotation and cf. TURKEY EGG); *t. roosting,* a turkey hunt in which wild turkeys are shot while roosting; *t.-shooter,* one adept at shooting turkeys; *t. snake,* (see quotation); *t. time,* the time in the autumn when turkeys are usually hunted; *t. tribe,* a tribe of southern Indians belonging to the Creek confederacy; *t. yelper,* a small instrument used by hunters for imitating the cry of turkeys.

1869 J. R. BROWNE *Adv. Apache Country* 462 Chiv he looked black, but Pop had his turkey-buster well in hand. **1895** *Outing* XXVI. 231/1 This setter, Blank, was an excellent turkey dog. **1845** HOOPER *Simon Suggs' Adv.* 53 A body would suppose him to be asleep, or in a 'turkey dream' at least. **1891** *Cent.* 6536/2 *Turkey-gnat,* a small black fly, *Simulium meridionale,* which attacks poultry in the southern and western United States. **1831** AUDUBON *Ornith. Biog.* I. 5 A slow turkey-hound has led me miles before I could flush the same bird. **1863** 'E. KIRKE' *Southern Friends* 49 About a hundred men, women and children were . . . witnessing a 'turkey match.' **1875** WINANS *Reminiscences* 77 As a Turkey Raffle was in progress we were invited to participate in the sport. **1893** G. W. CURTIS *Horses, etc.* 160 [Among the shorthorns] we find . . . red and white in all grades as to size and arrangement of spots—red roan, white roan, . . . and speckled or 'turkey' roan. **1877** CAMPION *On Frontier* 233 The diversion of turkey-roosting, as it is called, is not without its attractions for the sportsman. **1869** T. W. HIGGINSON *Army Life* 11 Some steady old turkey-shooter hit the mark. **1791** J. LONG *Voyages* 160 The turkey snake . . . takes its name from its voice which resembles the note of a wild turkey. **1846** *Spirit of Times* (N.Y.) 6 June 174/3 When 'turkey time' came, in the fall, the boys in the shop enjoyed plenty of 'turkey,' and no mistake. **1800** Turkey tribe [see TURKEY DANCE]. **1895** *Outing* XXVII. 231/2 Matt drew from his pocket a 'turkey yelper' and began to call.

+Turkey buzzard.

1. A blackish brown vulture (*Cathartes aura septentrionales*) found chiefly in the southern states.
Cf. BUZZARD 3.

1672 JOSSELYN *New Eng. Rarities* 12 The Turkie Buzzard, a kind of Kite, but as big as a Turkie. **1709** LAWSON *Carolina* 138 The Turkey-Buzzard of Carolina is a small Vulture, which lives on any dead Carcasses. **1799** WELD *Travels* 112 In the lower parts of Virginia, and to the southward, are great numbers of large birds, called turkey buzzards. **1806** LEWIS in *L. & Clark Exped.* IV. (1905) 260 We saw some turkey buzzards this morning. **1894** B. TORREY *Florida Sketchbook* 36, I look up from my paper to see a turkey buzzard sailing majestically northward. *a*1917 in *Birds of Amer.* II. 57/1 The food of the Turkey Buzzard is mainly carrion, but it also eats snakes, toads, and probably rats.

transf. **1857** STROTHER *Virginia* 66 Ha, you ole turkey-buzzard!

b. The figure of an eagle used on the one-cent piece. *derisive.*
Cf. BUZZARD DOLLAR.

1861 *Vanity Fair* 9 March 117/1, I remember, . . . in 1858, . . . how bitterly you laughed at the Turkey-Buzzard stamped on the cent coin of that date.

2. Attrib. with *dance, fashion.*

1845 GREEN *Texian Exped.* 134 Among their other dances they have one called the zopilote, or turkey-buzzard dance. **1854** HARRIS in *Spirit of Times* (N.Y.) 448/1 Thar was dad's bald head, for all the yearth like a peeled onion, a bobbin up an' down, an' the honets sailin' an' a circlin' round, turkey buzzard fashion.

+**Turkey call.** The cry of a turkey; an imitation of this; *turkey-call quill,* a device used to produce the imitation cry. — **1873** *Forest & Stream* 2 Oct. 123/1 A turkey-call is easily imitated by using the hollow bone of the leg or wing of the same. **1886** Z. F. SMITH *Kentucky* 330 Indians, by answering his turkey-call, lured him nigh to death. **1900** DRANNAN *Plains & Mts.* 35 Uncle Kit . . . loaned me his turkey-call quill.

*__Turkey carpet.__ A handmade, one-piece carpet finished to resemble velvet and made in Turkey or in the Turkish manner. — **1647** *Essex Probate Rec.* I. 66, 1 old Turky carpet. **1784** *Mass. Centinel* 26 June 3/2 Will be sold, by publick Vendue . . . Eight Day Clocks, Turkey and Wilton Carpets. **1836** *Jamestown* (N.Y.) *Jrnl.* 20 April 1/6 Now they must have turkey carpets from the cellar to the garret. **1869** STOWE *Oldtown Folks* 325 Turkey carpets is that kind, you know, that lies all up thick like a mat.

+**Turkey dance.** A ceremonial dance practiced by certain American Indians. *Obs.* — **1800** HAWKINS *Sk. Creek Country* 76 The pin-e-bungau, (turkey dance,) is danced by the women of the turkey tribe. **a1820** in *Western Rev.* II. 161 There are a number of other dances, such as the . . . Turkey dance, the new corn dance, the pipe dance, &c.

Turkey egg. The egg of a turkey {1718-}; +in pl., freckles. Often used in comparisons. Also attrib. — **1856** *Harper's Mag.* XIII. 446/2 Ely Reed is a turkey-egg mulatto. **1857** STROTHER *Virginia* 129 You are getting as fat as partridges. . . . And as freckled as turkey eggs. **1871** STOWE *Sam Lawson* 63 You must be sure to save the turkey-eggs. **1890** *Harper's Mag.* Dec. 139/1 His nose was kind o' wide, an' jest a mash o' freckles, like a turkey egg. **1899** GREEN *Va. Word-Book* 405 His face is covered with turkey-eggs.

Turkey feather. The feather of a turkey; used by Indians for ornamentation or for tipping arrows. {1767-} — **1624** SMITH *Gen. Hist. Va.* II. 30 We haue seene some vse mantels made of Turky feathers. **1705** BEVERLEY *Virginia* III. 60 They fledged their Arrows with Turkey Feathers, which they fastned with Glue made of the Velvet Horns of a Deer.

+**Turkey gobbler.** A turkey cock. — **1833** J. S. JONES *Green Mt. Boy* I. v, I feel about as grand as a large-sized turkey-gobbler, when his hen is settin'. **1865** *Atlantic Mo.* June 736/1 A humming-bird can . . . build a nest as efficiently as a turkey-gobbler and hatch her eggs. **1886** MITCHELL *R. Blake* 309 'A man who does not respect his own individuality of opinion is like'—'A turkey-gobbler in a hail-storm.'

+**Turkey hunter.** One who hunts turkeys. — **1846** THORPE *Myst. Backwoods* 62 The implements of the turkey-hunter are few and simple. **1851** *S. Lit. Messenger* XVII. 660/2, I was reckoned . . . good material for making a turkey hunter out of. **1895** *Outing* XXVII. 231/1 Nearly every negro man and boy on the plantation came up to have a look at the famous turkey hunter.

+**Turkey oak. a.** An oak (*Quercus catesbaei*) found chiefly in the sandy barrens of the South. **b.** A red oak (*Q. rubra*) found in the southern states.

1709 LAWSON *Carolina* 92 Turkey-Oak is so call'd from a small Acorn it bears, which the wild Turkeys feed on. **1797** PRIEST *Travels* 11 My landlord . . . tells me they have ten species of oak; viz, . . . spanish, turkey, chesnut, . . . and live oak. **1832** BROWNE *Sylva* 276 [The flowers] are very sweet, and form a delicious food for squirrels and wild turkeys; hence the tree is sometimes called Turkey Oak. **1884** SARGENT *Rep. Forests* 151. **1901** MOHR *Plant Life Ala.* 96 The turkey or barren oak and the blue jack . . . are frequent companions of the long-leaf pine.

Turkey oil stone. (See quot. 1891.) — **1761** in H. M. Brooks *Gleanings* IV. 26 Files of all Sorts, freezing Punches, Turkey Oyl Stones. **1790** *Penna. Packet* 7 May 3/3 Imported and to be Sold by John Wood, Clock and Watch Maker, . . . Turkey oil stones, emery, pumice and rotten stones. **1806** *Ann. 9th Congress* 2 Sess. 1123 The stone in the bed of the river . . . was of the hardest flint, or of a quality resembling the Turkey oil stone. **1825** *Columbian Centinel* 5 Jan. 4/3, 2000 lbs. Hindostan Oil Stones, a superior article to the common Turkey Oil Stone, and much cheaper. **1891** *Cent.* 6536/3 *Turkey-stone,* . . . a very fine-grained silicious rock. . . . It is used with oil for sharpening small cutting-instruments. It is commonly called *Turkey oil-stone,* as it comes from the interior of Asia Minor.

Turkey pea. +**a.** (See quot. 1891.) +**b.** The harbinger-of-spring, *Erigenia bulbosa.* +**c.** (See quot. 1915.) — **1891** *Cent.* 6536/3 *Turkey-pea.* 1. Same as *squirrel-corn.* . . . 2. The hoary pea, *Tephrosia Virginiana.* . . . (Southern U.S.) **1892** *Amer. Folk-Lore* V. 97 *Erigenia bulbosa,* turkey-pea. **1915** ARMSTRONG & THORNBER *Western Wild Flowers* 332 Turkey Peas. *Orogenia linearifolia.* White. Spring. Northwest and Utah. A quaint little plant, only about three inches high, with a tuberous root, spreading, slanting stems, and smooth leaves, all from the root.

+**Turkey pen.** A pen for turkeys, esp. one in which wild turkeys are trapped. Also attrib. — **1843** *Amer. Pioneer* II. 57 In respect to turkey pens, as they were called, the more southern pioneers constructed them as above described by Mr. Whittlesey. **1855** 'P. PAXTON' *Capt. Priest* 164 It was a huge turkey-pen, in which were confined at least an hundred fine, fat birds. **1857** *Harper's Mag.* May 748/1 He rose, and, entering a log building hard by that looked like a turkey pen, he commenced pegging away merrily at a pair of shoes. **1872** *Ib.* Aug. 352/2 The walls, built of logs, turkey-pen fashion, were only partially chinked with moss.

Turkey red. {1789-} Cotton cloth of a bright, permanent red color. {1880-} — **1835** LONGSTREET *Ga. Scenes* 57 'Have you any Turkey-red?' said Mrs. S. **1882** 'M. HARLAND' *Eve's Daughters* 71 Cushions covered with Turkey red [were] on chairs and floor. **1890** *Century Mag.* Dec. 303 These were carefully packed away in a barrel covered with turkey-red.

+**Turkey roost.** A place near a residence where tame turkeys roost; a place in the forest where wild turkeys customarily roost. (Cf. PIGEON ROOST, ROOST 1.) — **1867** CRAWFORD *Mosby* 83 Hen and turkey roosts were robbed. **1883** HOWE *Country Town* (1926) 22 Usually Jo and I . . . roamed the country . . . visiting turkey roosts a great distance in the woods.

+**Turkey shoot.** A shooting match at which turkeys or turkeys' heads were the targets. — **1845** JUDD *Margaret* I. 62 Its succedanea . . . were a turkey shoot the next day, and a ball. **1873** C. GORDON *Boarding-School Days* 232 Do you remember . . . the great field back of the gray church, where the turkey-shoots used to come off? **1898** FREDERIC *Deserter* 81 The farther of the two was now so far away that he seemed a mere dark speck, like the object seen from the gun-line of a turkey shoot.

Turkey stone. {1607-} =TURKEY OIL STONE. {1816-} — **1803** *Lewis & Clark Exped.* VII. (1905) 233 Camp Equipage [includes]: . . . 1 lb. Turkey or Oil Stone. **1817** S. BROWN *Western Gazetteer* 130 There is a kind of argillaceous composition, resembling oil-stone or turkey-stone, but too brittle for flints. **1891** [see TURKEY OIL STONE].

+**Turkey tail (fan).** The tail of a turkey prepared for use as a fan. — **1839** *S. Lit. Mess.* V. 375/2 The more useful and enduring turkey-tail fan had not given place to the delicate pink and white plumage of these aquatic birds. **1851** HOOPER *Widow Rugby* 84 Betsy dodged behind the wild turkey-tail which she carried by way of a fan. **1896** HARRIS *Sister Jane* 232 Her turkey-tail fan, which she always carried with her on occasions of moment, was swinging in the adjoining pew.

+**Turkey trot.** A fast trot similar to that of a turkey. — **1839** *S. Lit. Messenger* V. 377/1 May-be I didn't set up a high turkey trot, and peeled it like thunder. **1895** REMINGTON *Pony Tracks* 187 He would run me off the plantation at a turkey-trot if I did shoot.

+**Turkey vulture.** =TURKEY BUZZARD. — **1823** JAMES *Exped.* I. 4 At evening we heard the cry of the whip-poor-will; and among other birds saw . . . several turkey vultures. **1883** *Amer. Naturalist* XVII. 830 The olfactories of a turkey vulture . . . can alone serve its purpose in the discovery of food. **1917** *Birds of Amer.* II. 56/1 The Turkey Vulture is ugly to the last degree.

*__Turkey wheat.__ Indian corn. *Obs.* — **1674** JOSSELYN *Two Voyages* 73 Maze, otherwise called Turkie-wheat, or rather Indian-wheat, because it came first from thence. **1751** MACSPARRAN *Diary* 58 We have but 51 Bushels of good, and 5 Ditto, of Hog Corn, exclusive of the Turkey wheat. **1800** BENTLEY *Diary* II. 342 At Mr. Ingersoll's I obtained a specimen of the Turkey Wheat, which is the true zea or Maize.

Turkey wing. 1. The wing of a turkey +used as a brush. +**2.** *attrib.* Designating a fan or brush consisting of the wing of a turkey. — **(1) 1871** STOWE *Sam Lawson* 4, 'I'll sweep up the coals now,' he added, vigorously applying a turkey-wing to the purpose. **1896** E. HIGGINSON *Land of Snow Pearls* 60 She dropped the turkey-wing with which she was polishing the stove. **(2) 1888** *Century Mag.* Sept. 769/2 Turkey-wing fans and fans of peacock feathers supplanted those of a more . . . elaborate design. **1904** M. E. WALLER *Wood-carver* 140 [She] 'redded up,' as she says, the hearth with the turkey-wing brush.

+**Turkey wing plow.** A plow the shape of which suggests a turkey's wing. — **1854** *Mich. Agric. Soc. Trans.* V. 53, 1 turkey wing plow.

*__Turkey work.__ Turkish tapestry work, or work imitative of this. *Obs.* In attrib. use. — **1642** *Md. Archives* IV. 98 A turkie-work carpet. **1678** *New Castle Court Rec.* 361, 6 Turkey worke Covers for Chayres. **1711** *Essex Inst. Coll.* IV. 187/1 Two doz. chairs, viz. Twelve Turkey work, six leathern & six canvas.

*__Turkish,__ *a.* Brought from or originating in Turkey, or made in the Turkish manner.

1833 *Niles' Reg.* XLIV. 37/1 Turkish Barley. The New York Daily Advertiser notices the arrival at that port of nine thousand bushels of barley from Constantinople. **1855** BROWNE in *Amer. Inst. N.Y. Trans. 1854* 589 Turkish flint wheat, from Mount Olympus, in Asia, a fall variety, with rather large, long, flinty berries, . . . has proved itself both hardy and prolific in the Middle States. **1886** MITCHELL *R. Blake* 42 The room . . . was luxuriously comfortable with a heavy-piled Turkish carpet and easy-chairs. **1902** ALDRICH *Sea Turn* 145 A silver half-dollar slipped from his trousers pocket and rolled along a strip of inlaid flooring not covered by the Turkish rug. **1907** *St. Nicholas* May 589/1 'She's my chum,' explained Jo, putting out one bare foot to fish about under the bed for her Turkish slippers.

b. *Turkish captivity,* captivity by Algerian pirates to obtain ransom money. *Obs.*

Cf. TURK'S RATE.

1674 *Boston Rec.* 192 This sab: we had a pub: collection for Edward Howard of Boston, to redeeme him out of his sad Turkish captivity.

Turkish bean. (See quotation.) — **1894** EGGLESTON in *Century Mag.* April 849 The beans that were found here were called 'Turkish-beans' by the first Dutch and Swedish writers on America.

*__Turk's cap. 1. a.__ A garden lily, *Lilium martagon.* {1672-} +**b.** The American swamp lily, *L. superbum.* **2.** A globular cactus (*Cactus melocactus*) having a fez-like cap with red flowers. {1829-} — **(1) 1836**

LINCOLN *Botany* App. 111 Turk's cap, . . . petals reflexed so as to give the corolla the appearance of a turban. **1869** FULLER *Flower Gatherers* 176 Uncle John told us there was a lily in his garden called 'The Turk's Cap,' a very showy member of the family. **1890** *Cent.* 3454/2 The American Turk's-cap or swamp-lily, . . . found on low grounds at the north. (2) **1847** WOOD *Botany* 275 Turk's Cap. Melon Thistle. . . . This remarkable plant appears like a large, green melon, with deep furrows and prominent ribs. **1891** *Cent.* 6537/1.

+**Turk's cap lily.** =TURK'S CAP 1 b.— [**1884** W. MILLER *Dict. Names of Plants* 213/2 Great American Turk's-Cap Lily.] **1891** *Cent.* 6537/1. **1898** CREEVEY *Flowers of Field* 170 Turk's-cap Lily . . . is one of the handsomest gifts of the flower kingdom.

Turk's head. {1725-} +a. (See quotation.) +b. =TURK'S CAP 1 b.— (a) **1854** WHIPPLE, etc. *Explor. Ry. Route* I. 102 There are . . . various kinds of Echino cactus, the most conspicuous being that named Wislizenus, and sometimes called the 'Turk's Head.' (b) **1892** *Amer. Folk-Lore* V. 104 *Lilium superbum*, nodding lilies; Turk's head. Mass.

Turk's Island salt. Salt obtained from Turk's Islands, south of the Bahamas. *Obs.* — **1779** *N.J. Archives* 2 Ser. IV. 45 Turk's Island and Lisbon Salt to be sold in any quantity. **1821** *Cape-Fear Recorder* 14 April, 3500 bushels Turks Island Salt. **1849** *31st Congress 1 Sess.* Sen. Doc. No. 64, 202 From the specimens that I saw, I should imagine it to be . . . equal to the best Turk's island salt.

+**Turk's money.** =next. — **1684** *Huntington Rec.* I. 384 Thos men how war bee hind of the payment of the: turkes money: ar now to pay the remaindar in Speshy.

+**Turk's rate.** (See quot. 1887.) *Obs.* — **1684** *Huntington Rec.* I. 384 Thos men . . . are behind of the turks Ratte. **1887** *Huntington Rec.* I. 383 *n.*, The 'Turks Rate' was a term used to denote a tax levied by the British Government to provide funds for ransoming prisoners taken by Algerian pirates in the Mediterranean Sea and other waters.

*∗**Tu(r)meric.** A powder made from the underground, rootlike stems of an East Indian herb which is used as a condiment, a dye, etc. — **1651** *Mayflower Descendant* X. 202 Cloves nuttmeggs Turmericke . . . Safforon a little of all; a box. **1682** *S.C. Hist. Coll.* II. 34 Drugs—Jallop, Sassaparilla, Turmerick, Sassafras, Snake-root and divers others. **1810** *Columbian Centinel* 10 Jan. 3/1 Have now landing for sale . . . 479 bags Circuma, or Tumerick. **1867** COZZENS *Sayings* 15 Then they add a little salt, sometimes tumeric for color.

∗**Turn,** *n.*

1. An attack or spell of illness, depression, or the like. {1859}

1745 HEMPSTEAD *Diary* 443 My Daughter Minor hath had a very sharp Turn of the Colick. **1775** A. ADAMS *Familiar Lett.* 97 Jonathan is the only one . . . in the family who has not had a turn of the disorder. **1843** *Amer. Pioneer* II. 375 In the fall he had a pretty sharp turn of fever and ague. **1863** 'M. HARLAND' *Husks* 18, I have a 'blue' turn now and then. **1892** WILKINS *Young Lucretia, etc.* 57 She ate some sassage-meat an' had a little faint turn.

2. (See quot. 1800 and 1890.) {1886-, *dial.*}

1800 TATHAM *Tobacco* 25 A turn signifies such a quantity as each person respectively can carry upon his shoulder or in his arms. **1859** BARTLETT 491 *Turn of Meal*, a quantity of grist sent to mill. Tennessee. **1879** *Scribner's Mo.* Aug. 564/2 There are yet living those who . . . might testify concerning certain 'turns' of fire-wood, conveyed by night . . . to a particular bell-tent. **1890** *Dialect Notes* I. 70 *Turn*, a turn of wood . . . is an arm-load, a cart-load, or any other quantity that can be transported at one return. **1896** READ *Jucklins* 173 The next day I took a 'turn' of corn to the water mill.

+**3.** *Faro.* **a.** (See quot. 1864.) **b.** *To call the turn*, (see quot. 1889). Also fig. and as *vbl. n.*

(a) **1864** DICK *Amer. Hoyle* (1866) 207 The two cards drawn from the dealer's box—one for the bank and the other for the player, which thus determine the events of the game, constitute a turn. **1901** JAMES *Sacred Fount* 44 The gentleman close to her . . . offered us the face of Guy Brissenden, as recognizable at a distance as the numbered card of a 'turn.' (b) **1889** *Cent.* 2144/2 After each turn new bets are made for another, down to the last three cards of the pack; the only betting allowed after this is on 'calling the turn,' or guessing which will show first. **1894** WISTER in *Harper's Mag.* May 907/2 You've called the turn on me. **1898** *N.Y. Journal* 17 Aug. 6/6 He called the turn on all of them.

+**4.** A transaction involving the buying and selling (or vice versa) of securities, or the profit so made; any business transaction or chance to make money.

1870 MEDBERY *Men Wall St.* 78 This neat profit is called a 'turn.' *Ib.* 96 They had made 'the turn' simply as an accommodation. **1872** BRACE *Dangerous Classes N.Y.* 38 The boys of the street . . . preferring to make fortunes by lucky and sudden 'turns,' rather than by patient and steady industry. **1898** WESTCOTT *D. Harum* 355 If I was where I could watch the market, I'd mebbe try to make a turn in 't 'casionally. **1913** WHARTON *Custom of Country* 449 The sum his wife demanded could be acquired only by 'a quick turn.'

5. 'In *furriery*, a bundle of five dozen skins' (*Cent.*). {1897}

∗**Turn,** *v.*

I. 1. To invert (a turtle) in order to render it helpless and prevent it from escaping. {∗in general sense}

1682 ASH *Carolina* 28 The Seamen or Turtlers . . ., getting between them and the Sea, turn them on their Backs, from whence they are unable ever to rise. **1837** WILLIAMS *Florida* 64 The turtle hunters . . . turn them on their backs, where they remain safely till they are conveyed away. **1885** *Lisbon* (Dak.) *Star* 18 Sept. 6/1 Now is the time to 'turn' the great reptile, if you want to use her flesh for food.

II. In phrases.

+*To turn the double corner*, (see CORNER *n.* 4 a); +*to turn up missing*, (see MISSING 2).

*∗**2.** *To turn back*, to backslide.

1801-3 J. LYLE *Diary* (MS.) 94 All who fell there were either religious people or children of religious parents (except Jonathan Parish who is turned back).

3. *To turn down.* {1601-} +a. To overcome or disqualify (a contestant) in a spelling contest.

1876 'MARK TWAIN' *Tom Sawyer* vi, He took his place . . . in the spelling class, and got 'turned down,' by a succession of mere baby words. **1903** G. C. EGGLESTON *First of Hoosiers* 45 The successful speller was said to have 'turned down' all who had failed, and was entitled to take his place above them in the line.

+**b.** (See quot. 1891.) *colloq.*

1891 *Cent.* 6538/2 *To turn down*, . . . to snub; to suppress. **1894** *Congress. Rec.* 10 Aug. 8393/2 As soon as any one of these parties or societies . . . has shown signs of anarchy, communism, or oppression, . . . such parties have been turned down and relegated to their proper place.

+**c.** To refuse or deny.

1897 *Boston Jrnl.* 14 Jan. 7/6 Secretary Olney was turned down by the Senate . . . in his effort to have the vote on the extradition treaties . . . reconsidered. **1899** *Chicago Record* 7 Jan. 8/1 Requests for repairs . . . were 'turned down.' **1907** LONDON *Road* 3 Something to eat was a hard proposition. I was 'turned down' at a dozen houses.

4. *To turn flukes.* **a.** Of a whale: To raise the tail and make a perpendicular dive. {peaking the flukes, 1839} **b.** *transf.* To go to bed. *Naut. slang.*

1839 *Knickerb.* XIII. 381 When the 'school' turn flukes, and go down, the flag is to be struck, and again displayed when they are seen to ascend. **1851** MELVILLE *Moby-Dick* 21 It's getting dreadful late, you had better be turning flukes—it's a nice bed.

*∗**5.** *To turn in.* +a. To enter with vigor upon some activity; to work energetically.

1822 WOODS *English Prairie* (1904) 345, I calculated to sell my creature there, and then when I got home, to turn in and earn some money to get me another. **1862** McCLELLAN in *Own Story* 530, I have no command at present . . . and have merely 'turned in' on my own account to straighten out whatever I catch hold of. **1882** *Harper's Mag.* Sept. 601/1 Best of attention. Two leading doctors turned in on me.

+**b.** To deliver; to give.

1844 FEATHERSTONHAUGH *Slave States* 81 He is 'to turn in' 15 gallons of *bar* (bear) oil, the current value of which is one dollar per gallon. **1891** F. W. ROBINSON *Her Love & His Life* IV. x, You will turn in the cash by wholesale. **1896** *Boston Jrnl.* 30 Dec. 2/8 A citizen . . . promptly turned in an alarm of fire from the nearest box. **1903** A. ADAMS *Log of Cowboy* 12 A number of different rancheros had turned in cattle in making up the herd.

*∗**6.** *To turn loose.* +a. To fire or discharge (a gun) freely.

1851 A. T. JACKSON *Forty-niner* (1920) 59, I hadn't gone forty feet away when he turned loose his gun. **1903** A. ADAMS *Log of Cowboy* 206 Somebody . . . turned his gun into the air.

+**b.** To open fire with a gun. *colloq.* Also transf.

1868 *All Year Round* 31 Oct. 491/2 It was etiquette to tell him [an armed man] to 'turn loose.' **1903** A. ADAMS *Log of Cowboy* 137 The chief could not speak a word of English, but . . . when I turned loose on him in Spanish, however, he instantly turned his horse. **1907** WHITE *Arizona Nights* 14, I made up my mind that when the star was darkened I'd turn loose.

+**c.** To break loose from the customary restraints upon conduct; to cut loose. *colloq.* Also reflexive.

Cf. CUT *v.* 25 h.

1880 *Scribner's Mo.* March 771/1 Once arrived in New Sharon, the herder, or 'cow-boy,' . . . 'turns loose,' as he calls it, and . . . becomes a spendthrift, a drunkard, a gambler, a libertine. **1883** 'MARK TWAIN' *Life on Miss.* iii, Lay low and hold your breath, for I'm 'bout to turn myself loose!

7. *To turn on* {1833-}, in faro, to begin a 'turn' by displaying a card from the pack.

a**1846** *Quarter Race Ky.* 78 'Very well,' said I, placing a ragged Indiana dollar behind the queen—'turn on.' He turned, and the king won for me.

*∗**8.** *To turn out.* **a.** To go on strike. {1825-}

1806 in *Commons*, etc. *Doc. Hist.* III. 74, I must turn-out.

+**b.** To put (land) out of cultivation. Also *ppl. a.*

1814 J. TAYLOR *Arator* 107 The phrase 'the land is killed and must be turned out,' has become common over a great portion of the United States. **1856** OLMSTED *Slave States* 373 The greater part, even of these once rich low lands, that had been in cultivation, were now 'turned out,' and covered, either with pines, or broom-sedge and brushwood. **1879**

TOURGEE *Fool's Errand* 35 The overseer . . . accomplished all his employer required, by 'turning out' from year to year portions of the plantation. **1883** SMITH *Geol. Survey Ala.* 445 Such turned-out lands will produce well if Japan clover cover them one or two years.

+c. To keep (a schoolmaster) from entering a school by fastening the door; to drive (a schoolmaster) from a school by force; to bar out.
Cf. TURNOUT 3.
1835 LONGSTREET *Ga. Scenes* 78 The boys . . . are going to turn out the schoolmaster to-morrow. **1857** *Quinland* I. 274 He says I must look out for the large boys, or they will knock me down and drag me out of the school-house, which they call 'turning-out' the master.

+d. To pour out.
1864 in M. Todd *Life S. Jex-Blake* [In America] they ask if they shall 'turn out the tea.'

+e. To release the logs of (a boom).
1905 WIGGIN *Rose* 60 The boom above the falls would be 'turned out,' and the river would once more be clear.

∗9. *To turn over*, to deliver (property); to yield ownership or control of (something).
1637 *Dedham Rec.* III. 32 Ezechiell Holliman Requireing consent of our society to turne over his Lott. **1882** 'MARK TWAIN' *Life on Miss.* App. A, As soon as the *Susie* reached Troy she was turned over to General York. **1910** J. HART *Vigilante Girl* 322 This weapon he impounded, and turned it over to the custody of the court-room clerk. **1925** W. L. CROSS *Life Sterne* I. 175 Robert Dodsley had just turned over the management of his business to his brother.

+10. *To turn up jack*, to tear up jack. (See JACK *n.*[1] 7 a.)
1828 *Yankee* I. 227/1 Everything is pell-mell, helter-skelter, pig-corn, baskets, and all are upside-down; or as they have it, they 'turn up jack.'

11. In miscellaneous other phrases.
∗*To turn Hudson*, (see quotation); *to turn the Bible*, to use (a Bible suspended from a freely turning key ring supported on the finger tips of two persons) as a means of fortune-telling; *+to t. the paunch*, (see quotation).
1865 *Harper's Mag.* April 619/2 Application was made to several leading bear houses to 'turn Hudson'; that is to say, to buy it for cash from the cornering party, and to sell it back to them on buyer's option. **1887** EGGLESTON *Graysons* i, In gossip and banter the time went by, until some one proposed to 'turn the Bible.' **1891** *Cent.* 6538/3 *To turn the paunch*, to vomit; disgorge, as fish. (New Eng.)

Turn-, stem of TURN *v.* Used in combinations.
+*Turn row*, a row or area sufficient for a row at which teams turn in cultivating a crop; *t. skin* {1831-}, a renegade Indian; *t. stick* {1813}, a stick used in weaving; *t. vise*, a screw vise.
1885 CRADDOCK *Prophet* 3 A young man . . . came to a meditative halt in the turn-row. **1873** MILLER *Amongst Modocs* 104, I do protest against taking these Indians—turn-skins and renegades— . . . as representative Indians. **1873** BEADLE *Undevel. West* 578 By a leathern loop at each end, is suspended a 'turn-stick,' about the size of one's wrist. **1646** *Essex Probate Rec.* I. 49, 1 turne vice.

Turnabout. {1833-} +A merry-go-round. — **1889** *Harper's Mag.* Sept. 560/1 Here were found the hundreds of neat stalls . . . , the high swings and the turnabouts.

Turndown. {1849-} *Euchre*. (See quotation.) — **1864** DICK *Amer. Hoyle* (1866) 64 *Turn Down*, the trump card which is turned face downward on the talon by the dealer, after all have passed.

Turned-(a)round, *a.* Confused; in doubt or error as to one's whereabouts. — **1877** R. I. DODGE *Plains of Gt. West* 46 To me, Detroit is always in Canada, and New Orleans always on the right bank of the Mississippi, because I happened to be 'turned round' when I first arrived in those cities. **1880** 'MARK TWAIN' *Tramp Abroad* 119, I could see the dim blur of the windows, but in my turned-around condition they were exactly where they ought not to be.

∗Turner.[1] One whose occupation is the fashioning or shaping of objects of wood or other materials by the use of a lathe. — **1654** JOHNSON *Wonder-w. Prov.* 209 Turners, Pumpmakers, and Wheelers . . . are orderly turn'd to their trades. **1711** *Boston News-Letter* 28 May 2/2 The Smith's Shop in Newbury-Street Boston next to Matthias Smith Turner; is to be Lett. **1776** *Penna. Ev. Post* 23 March 149/1 A Turner of Brass is likewise wanted. **1851** CIST *Cincinnati* 245 Warner B. Mahone, turner in general, . . . executes balustrades of any and every pattern.

Turner.[2] A performer of gymnastic exercises, esp. a member of a society of Germans or German Americans organized for such activity. {1865, in Europe} — **1859** BARTLETT 491. **1866** RICHARDSON *Secret Service* 139 Three companies are made up of German Turners—the most accomplished of gymnasts. **1871** DE VERE 141 A *Turner* . . . has become literally what Americans call an 'institution.' **1904** *Indianapolis News* 27 June 5 It was largely due to the activity of the turners that physical training had become so general in educational institutions.

∗Turning. Attrib. with *arbor, mill, row*, etc.
1790 *Penna. Packet* 7 May 3/3 Imported and to be sold by John Wood, Clock and Watch Maker, . . . turning arbors, gravers and scorpers. **1837** JENKINS *Ohio Gaz.* 314 [Morgan] contains . . . 1 turning shop, 1 blacksmith shop, 1 cabinet shop [etc.]. **1839** *Knickerb.* XIII. 346 He clambered up on the top [of the locomotive] with a turning screw in one hand, and . . . commenced screwing down the valves. **1844** *Knickerb.* XXIV. 184 The uplifted arm of Labor . . . meets his eye everywhere, in the paper-

mill and grist-mill, and . . . turning-mill. **1885** *Century Mag.* Aug. 503/1 In a light wind at a turning-stake the jib has a marvelous fashion of gaining several lengths by turning the boat closely and sharply around the stake. **1890** *Dialect Notes* I. 66 *Turning row*, a row unplanted in a corn or tobacco field, where the horses turn around in plowing.

Turning lathe. A machine for turning wood or other material to be worked. {1794-} — **1795** *Ann. 3d Congress* 1404 The works consist of . . . two turning lathes for dies, and a boring machine. **1853** J. W. BOND *Minnesota* 125 There is also a turning-lathe attached [to the mill]. **1884** HARRIS in *Century Mag.* Nov. 120 He managed to earn a precarious living with his turning-lathe.

Turning machine. A heavy machine lathe or a machine used in boot-making. — **1849** CHAMBERLAIN *Ind. Gazetteer* 429 There are on the east fork of the White Water and its tributaries . . . one foundry and several turning and carding machines, all driven by water. **1876** KNIGHT 2660/2 *Turning-machine*, . . . one for turning boot-legs after the seams have been sewn and rolled.

Turning out. {1711-} **+1.** A strike. **+2.** *attrib.* Designating the action of releasing logs in a boom. — **(1)** **1825** *Congress. Deb.* App. 21 Nov. 18/1 There were on three occasions, mutinous combinations among the mechanics and laborers, or 'turning out,' as they term it, for an increase of wages. **(2)** **1905** WIGGIN *Rose* 29 Thousands of logs lay quietly 'in boom' until the 'turning out' process, on the last day of the drive, should release them.

Turning-over. {1842-} +A critical condemnation. *colloq.* — **1895** *N.Y. Dramatic News* 9 Nov. 2/3, I don't think I ever heard such a 'turning over' extended to a production.

+Turning plow. A plow that turns a furrow slice; a moldboard plow. — **1850** *Rep. Comm. Patents 1849: Agric.* 313, I throw two furrows, one on each side, with one or two-horse turning-ploughs. **1873** *Winfield* (Kan.) *Courier* 12 June 3/2 The winter wheat was sown on corn stubble and plowed in with a turning plow last September. **1899** *Caddo* (Okla.) *Herald* 24 Feb. 1/6 Chilled turning plows.

Turning table. =TURNTABLE 1. {1839} — **1865** *39th Congress 2 Sess.* H. R. Rep. No. 34, 1026 Turning-table at Trenton full of mud; had to be rewalled. **1902** HARBEN *A. Daniel* 301, I was over at Darley a-walkin' along the railroad nigh the turnin'-table.

Turning-up. {1628-} (See quotation.) — **1800** TATHAM *Tobacco* 77 Turning-up, is a technical term which signifies the act of replacing the tobacco in the hogshead after it has passed the inquest of inspection.

∗Turnip.
∗1. The edible root of either of two species of *Brassica* (*B. rapa* and *B. napobrassica*) or of a similar plant; also, the plant.
See also INDIAN, PRAIRIE, etc., TURNIP and cf. GREEN TOP, RUTABAGA.
1610 *Estate of Va.* 13 What should I speake of . . . parsneps, carrets, turnups, which our gardens yeelded with little art and labour. **1685** BUDD *Penna. & N.J.* 31 Garden Fruits groweth well, as Cabbage, . . . Parsneps, Turnups, Oynions. **1714** SEWALL *Diary* III. 22 Carried them a Bushel Turnips. **1769** in Chalkley *Scotch-Irish Settlement Va.* III. 109 To wife, all cleared land where house stands to clear land for turnips where they last grew. **1804** J. ROBERTS *Penna. Farmer* 204 Feeding with turnips makes the horse's coat fine, and cures the grease. **1839** PLUMBE *Sk. Iowa* 30 Wheat, potatoes, turnips, all kinds of vegetables, clover, timothy, and also all sorts of tame grass, grow most luxuriantly. **1905** PRINGLE *Rice Planter* 195 Turnips . . . are a very important winter crop for us.

2. These roots cooked and prepared as food.
1758 C. REA *Journal* 70, I've eat this Summer one meal of Squash, one of Turneps, one of Potatoes & one of Onions & no more. **1835** IRVING *Tour on Prairies* I. 272 Boiled beef and turnips, and an earthen dish to eat them from! **1878** *Amer. Home Cook Book* 87 Send around mashed turnips with the meat. **1891** WILKINS *New Eng. Nun* 176 It was quite true that he could smell the roasting turkey, and the turnip and onions, out there.

3. *attrib.* and *comb.* **a.** With *barrel, feed, greens*, etc. Sometimes in place names.
1663 *Essex Inst. Coll.* XX. 79 From the heape of stones Southeasterly to a red oake marked on foure Sides Standing near turnup Swampe. **1666** *Md. Hist. Mag.* I. 74 Four hundred acres of Land . . . Lying on the North Side of Turnep Creek in Sassafrax River. **1725** *New-Eng. Courant* 18 Dec. 2/1 [He was] carelessly looking into the Turnip Yard, when several Indians [fired] upon him. **1770** *Md. Hist. Mag.* XIII. 70 Pray write to Mr. Thos. Philpot for a turnep slicer. **1773** in Fithian *Journal* I. 40 His turnip-patch and corn-gardens seem . . . to have put on a fresh bloom. **1793** *Holyoke Diaries* 128 First turnip tops Cut. **1804** J. ROBERTS *Penna. Farmer* 24, [I] sowed turnip-feed, broad cast, every day. **1826** FLINT *Recoll.* 79 On this journey in the middle of March, turnip-greens were brought to the table. **1884** 'MARK TWAIN' *H. Finn* vi, I laid it across the turnip-barrel.

b. In the names of plants resembling turnips. {1786-}
See also TURNIP CABBAGE.
1909 *Cent. Suppl.* 1462/1 The bulbous panic grass, *Panicum bulbosum*, native in cañons from Texas to Arizona and in Mexico, . . . [has a stem with] a bulbous base (hence called *turnip grass*). **1890** *Cent.* 4301/3 Varieties of the parsnip . . . [include] the round or turnip, and the student. **1847** DARLINGTON *Weeds & Plants* 54 Black Turnip-radish. Spanish Radish. . . . The tender fleshy *root* of this plant is an universal favorite at table.

c. In the names of insects infesting or attacking turnips. {1816-}

See also TURNIP FLY. Other examples may be found in insect books and dictionaries.

1854 EMMONS *Agric. N.Y.* V. 263 (*index*), Turnipeaters, 129, 135. **1868** *Amer. Naturalist* II. 164 The Turnip-butterfly (*Pontia oleracea*) . . . lays its eggs the last of [May].

Turnip cabbage. 1. The kohlrabi. {1765-} **2.** The rutabaga. — **1890** *Cent.* 3311/1 *Kohlrabi*, . . . the turnip-stemmed cabbage, or turnip cabbage, *Brassica oleracea*, var. *gongylodes* (*caulo-rapa*). **1909** WEBSTER 2218 *Turnip cabbage*, . . . the rutabaga.

Turnip fly. a. A flea beetle infesting turnips. {1733-} **b.** The adult of the cabbage maggot, *Pegomyia brassicae*. — **1790** DEANE *New-Eng. Farmer* 148/2 The *turnip fly*, a well known winged insect, . . . eats the seed leaves of turnips. **1856** *Rep. Comm. Patents 1855: Agric.* 262 The first sowing was almost destroyed by the turnip-fly, and the second by grasshoppers. **1889** *Cent.* 238/2 *A*[*nthomyia*] *brassica*, is the cabbage-fly; *A. trimaculata* and *A. radicum* are turnip-flies. **1890** WEBSTER 1554/1 *Turnip fly*, . . . the turnip flea.

Turnout. {1688-}

1. A strike of workmen. {1834-}

1806 in Commons, etc. *Doc. Hist.* III. 74 In a little time there came a turn-out to raise the wages upon boots. **1875** *Chicago Tribune* 30 Sept. 2/4 In case of a turnout or strike in any other mill or mills in Fall River, we will continue at our work . . . as if no such strike or turnout had occurred.

b. A striker. {1826-}

1846 in Persons, etc. *Mass. Labor Laws* (1911) 46 They wanted none of the turn-outs from the Middlesex.

2. a. On a railroad, a siding, switch, or loop permitting a train to pass another train. {1824-} Also *attrib.*

1829 *Western Mo. Rev.* III. 23 A single Railway or one set of tracks, with suitable turn-outs, . . . will cost from 7 to $8000 per mile. **1846** *Congress. Globe* 28 Jan. 266 [Both locomotives] had gone beyond the turn-out place. **1872** HUNTINGTON *Road-Master's Asst.* 42 It requires considerable skill and judgment to lay a good turn-out. **1900** *Congress. Rec.* 12 Feb. 1727/2 The Capital Traction Company . . . [shall be required] to lay down an underground electric railway, with the necessary switches and turn-outs in the City of Washington.

b. A branch or side road; a wide section in a narrow road to enable vehicles to pass each other.

1844 FEATHERSTONHAUGH *Slave States* 104 When a tree falls on the narrow forest road, the first traveller that passes is obliged to make a circuitous track around it. . . . These circuitous tracks are known by the name of *turn-outs*. **1855** SIMMS *Forayers* 502 He had . . . looked heedfully at every cross-road and turn-out. **1874** *Vermont Bd. Agric. Rep.* II. 662 Our roads are cramped down to mere lanes, requiring turn-outs like railroads. **1905** *Forestry Bureau Bul.* No 61, 52 *Turnout*, a short side road from a logging-sled road, to allow loaded sleds to pass. (N[orth] W[oods], L[ake] S[tates].)

3. The act of ejecting or excluding; +spec., the action of students in preventing a schoolmaster from entering the school building, as by fastening the door.

Cf. TURN *v.* 8 c and BARRING-OUT.

1834 SIMMS *Guy Rivers* I. 276 He had been advised of the contemplated turn-out of all the squatters from the gold region. **1835** LONGSTREET *Ga. Scenes* 78 The boys always conceive a holiday gained by a 'turn out,' as a sole achievement of their valor.

4. Attrib. with *path, station, track.*

1835 J. MARTIN *Descr. Virginia* 92 Every quarter of a mile, the canal is widened to 60 feet for turnout stations. **1850** *Western Journal* IV. 93 A single track of plank, eight feet wide, with an earthen turn-out track beside it, of twelve feet, will, in almost all cases, be sufficient. *Ib.* 94 This imperfect double track, even without any turn-out path between, worked better than its original state.

Turnover. {1611-}

1. A small pie or tart made with a single layer of paste, half of which is turned over the filling as a top crust. {1798-}

1850 *Knickerb.* XXXV. 82 There was relief only in eating our Sunday 'turn-overs' and nut-cakes-and-cheese. **1886** *Harper's Mag.* Nov. 834/1, I doubt if we should bring better appetites . . . than Binns had when grinning over his apple turnover. **1905** LINCOLN *Partners* 4 'Turnovers' [were] arranged cob-house fashion under a glass cover.

2. *Polit.* A shift of votes from one party to another.

1895 *Forum* Oct. 160 It represents, of course, no very sweeping change of opinion—no very considerable turnover of votes. **1903** *N.Y. Times* 16 Aug., The best-informed sentiment of Union County is looking for a Democratic turnover there this fall.

+**3.** = TURNING PLOW.

1901 HARBEN *Westerfelt* 59 He hain't drawed a bow in two weeks, an' has been plough in' a two-hoss turnover.

* **Turnpike,** *n.*

* **1.** A turnstile for excluding animals from a way or passage. *Obs.*

1764 *Boston Selectmen* 57 Capt. Henshaw is desired to get Turn pikes fixed in Hog alley agreable to a Vote of the Town.

2. A tollgate or similar contrivance for the collection of tolls on a road or way. {a1678-} Now *hist.*

1785 *Va. Stat. at Large* XII. 76 The said commissioners . . . may set up and erect . . . one or more gates or turnpikes across the roads. **1796** MORSE *Univ. Geog.* I. 457 One [petition] . . . was, to establish a turnpike on the road between Norwich and Providence. **1809** *Ann. 10th Congress* 2 Sess. 1841 It shall be lawful for them thereafter to erect and fix such and so many gates or turnpikes . . . as shall be necessary and sufficient to collect the tolls. **1829** *Va. Lit. Museum* 16 Dec. 418 Originally when tolls were taken, a turnpike was placed upon the footpath. **1874** COLLINS *Kentucky* I. 537 A turnpike road, or road on which turnpikes (i.e. *toll-gates*) are established by law.

3. A road originally built or maintained by a turnpike company or another agency empowered to collect tolls; a substantially built, through road, often one with a rounded surface. {1748-}

1799 *Va. Stat. at Large* ns. II. 227 The opening of a turnpike from the said Emmen's mill across the South mountain. **1817** BROWN *Western Gazetteer* 292 [Two roads] are sixteen feet wide and elevated about three feet like our turnpikes. **1836** J. HALL *Statistics of West* 272 A Macadam turnpike from Covington to Georgetown and Lexington . . . is now constructing. **1862** MOORE *Rebellion Rec.* V. II. 473 A single Federal battery was boldly thrown over the stone bridge on the turnpike. **1894** ALDRICH *Two Bites* 141 We reached the junction of the Green Lodge road and the turnpike. **1909** J. W. WILKINSON *Pract. Agric.* 271 In Missouri they [sc. macadam roads] are frequently called gravel roads, while in Tennessee and Kentucky they are designated as pikes or turnpikes.

b. Used in comparisons.

1802 *Ann. 7th Congress* 1 Sess. 759 They have all travelled the same road; it is as plain as a turnpike. **1891** *Harper's Mag.* Dec. 49/1 My course lay before me as straight as a turnpike.

c. Used without article to indicate surface material or construction characteristic of turnpike roads.

1843 'CARLTON' *New Purchase* I. 29 There we emerged into a piece of superb turnpike. **1882** *Wheelman* I. 11 The route lay over worn turnpike, the worst of all roads for a bicycler, except unmitigated sand.

+**4.** A small cake of meal, scalded and allowed to ferment; used to raise bread.

1850 S. WARNER *Wide, Wide World* xiv, I am scalding this meal with it to make turnpikes. **1850** *Knickerb.* XXXVI. 83 The old aunt . . . had borrowed some little yellow cakes, called *turnpikes*, and used, I believe, for some purpose or other in baking bread.

5. *attrib.* and *comb.* **a.** In senses 2 and 3 with *bridge, corporation, crossing*, etc.

1796 *Mass. Acts & Resolves* 8 [There] shall be a Corporation by the name of 'The First Massachusetts Turnpike Corporation.' **1803** ASBURY *Journal* III. 121 On Saturday we found heat, and dust, and turnpike-gates, (twelve in seventy-five miles) as usual. **1826** FLINT *Recoll.* 88 The stillness of the forest had not been broken by the shouting of turnpike-makers. **1834** in *Atlantic Mo.* XXVI. 334 The common roads are nearly all *ridged up*, turnpike fashion; and are as good as our turnpikes. **1844** LEE & FROST *Oregon* 203 The current from the two opposite sides . . . [heaps] up the water mid-channel, in a turnpike form. **1844** *Indiana Senate J.* 29 Sess. 272 The State of Indiana hereby gives to said company . . . the use of the present turnpike grade, in getting on and off from said bridges. **1846** *Xenia Torch-Light* 23 April 2/1 This sum is to be raised from . . . tolls, fines, and water rents, collected on the canals, railroad and turnpike stock. **1847** HOWE *Hist. Coll. Ohio* 159 The road . . . passed through the site of Lancaster, at a fording about 300 yards below the present turnpike bridge. **1851** MITCHELL *Dream Life* 88 The Squire has been in his day, connected . . . with Turn-pike enterprise, which the rail-roads of the day have thrown sadly into the background. **1862** F. MOORE *Rebellion Rec.* V. II. 69 The Twenty-second Massachusetts went out on the railroad and took up several hundred feet of the track, following up the road to the turnpike-crossing.

+**b.** In sense 4 with *cake, emptins.*

1843 STEPHENS *High Life N.Y.* II. 78 Her face begun to swell and puff up, like a baking of bread wet up with turnpike emptins. **1850** S. WARNER *Wide, Wide World* xiv, Turnpike cakes—what I raise the bread with.

+**Turnpike,** *v. tr.* To build (a road) in the manner of construction characteristic of turnpike roads. {1903} Also *vbl. n.* and *ppl. a.*

[**1806** WEBSTER 320/1 *Turnpike*, to form or erect a turnpike.] **1817** *Ann. 14th Congress* 2 Sess. 860 [This road] is generally turnpiked, and by incorporated companies, who own the road. **1830** PICKERING *Inquiries Emigrant* 35 In some of these new towns, the streets are as yet only ridged or 'turnpiked,' in the centre. *Ib.* 68 They are . . . ploughing the sides . . . with a kind of large shovel, having a handle (called a scraper) and a yoke of oxen, the dirt is drawn into the centre and rounded, which is called 'turnpiking.' **1835** J. MARTIN *Descr. Virginia* 139 The Richmond road is now being turnpiked to Chilton's. **1861** *Ill. Agric. Soc. Trans.* IV. 202 There were worked streets, back-furrowed or turnpiked, . . . traversing the fields.

+**Turnpike company.** A group of persons organized to construct or to control the use of a turnpike road or roads. — **1806** *Balance* V. 37/1

Those for the incorporation of turnpike companies occupy many pages. **1845** *Xenia Torch-Light* 31 July 4/3 The stockholders of the Dayton, Xenia and Washington Turnpike Company . . . [shall pay] $5 on each share. **1866** *Internal Revenue Guide* 133 Any railroad, canal, turnpike [etc.] . . . company . . . shall be subject to . . . a tax.

Turnpiker. {1896} +**1.** One who travels on a turnpike. +**2.** (See quotation.) — (1) **1812** *Boston Gazette* 27 Aug. (Th.), The heroes, who were to have mounted the heights of Abram, are yet in the garb of turnpikers. (2) **1819** *Niles' Reg.* XVI. 440/1 A mob of Irishmen, calling themselves *turnpikers*, armed with axes, mattocks, &c. . . . in an ruffian-like manner demanded toll.

Turnpike road. =TURNPIKE *n.* 3. {1745-}
1774 HUTCHINSON *Diary & Lett.* I. 165 The longest way the road is generally equal to the turnpike roads here; the other way rather rough. **1793** COXE *View U.S.* 206 A great and expensive turnpike road has been commenced by Pennsylvania, leading directly westward towards Pittsburg. **1796** MORSE *Univ. Geog.* I. 556 Lancaster . . . stands on Conestoga creek, 58 miles, as the new turnpike-road now runs, a little northwest from Philadelphia. **1814** *Niles' Reg.* V. 307/2 A turnpike road, being raised three feet above the level of the water, will . . . admit a depth of nine feet water, in the canal. **1874** COLLINS *Kentucky* I. 56 The Maysville and Lexington Turnpike road . . . was overplowed. **1886** LOGAN *Great Conspiracy* 280 From Alexandria . . . runs a fine turnpike road to Fairfax Court-House.
attrib. **1834** JACKSON in *Pres. Mess. & P.* III. 65 The former appropriation is . . . in express violation of the principle maintained in my objections to the turnpike-road bill.

+**Turnplow.** =TURNING PLOW. Also attrib. — **1854** *Fla. Plantation Rec.* 104, I think you will nead about 10 turnplowes. **1856** *Ib.* 518 Received 12 turn plough points from Mr. George Jones. **1907** T. F. HUNT *Forage & Fiber Crops* 352 The land having been plowed with an ordinary mold board or turn plow, the field is made up into alternate beds.

*Turnsole. The Indian heliotrope (*Heliotropium indicum*), or an allied plant. — [**1731** P. MILLER *Gardeners Dict.* (1735) s.v. *Heliotropium*, Blue American Turnsole, with Clary Leaves. *Ib.*, Blue American Turnsole, with narrower Clary Leaves.] **1817-8** EATON *Botany* (1822) 303.

Turnstile. A device consisting of an upright fixture with horizontal arms turning about it, for preventing the passage of animals, or controlling or measuring the passing of persons, through an entrance or other passage. {a1643-} Also comb. — **1839** BIRD *Robin Day* 15 The new president . . . had [been] seen . . . crossing the street to a turnstile, which led into the schoolhouse green. **1850** JUDD *R. Edney* 12 He came to the covered bridge, and entering by the narrow 'turn-stile,' found a breathing-place from the storm. **1876** INGHAM *Centennial Exp.* 606 The report of the turnstile-keepers placed the total at 83,540. **1899** *N.Y. Journal* 7 Feb. 4/2 Turnstiles have been put in at several of the gates.

Turnstone. Any one of various shore birds {1674-}, +esp. the ruddy turnstone (*Arenaria interpres morinella*) and the black turnstone (*A. melanocephala*). Also attrib. and with specifying adjectives.
1731 CATESBY *Carolina* I. 72 The Turn-Stone, or Sea-Dottrel . . . flew on Board us [near the coast of Florida] and was taken. **1839** PEABODY *Mass. Birds* 361 The Turnstone, *Strepsilus interpres*, derives its popular name from the habit of turning over stones with the bill and sometimes the breast, to find insects and worms beneath them. **1858** BAIRD *Birds Pacific R.R.* 702 *Strepsilas Melanocephalus*. Black Turnstone. . . . Western North America. **1891** *Cent.* 6543/1 Plover-billed turnstone. **1917** *Birds of Amer.* I. 267 The Surf-birds and Turnstones constitute the family *Aphrizidæ* of the order of Shore Birds. . . . The Turnstone subfamily includes two species. *Ib.* 270/1 The Black, or Black-headed, Turnstone (*Arenaria melanocephala*) averages a trifle smaller than the Ruddy Turnstone.

Turntable.
1. *Railroad.* A revolving platform with a track or tracks, for turning or reversing the position of a locomotive or car. {1838-} Also attrib.
1835 *Mass. Laws* XIII. 455 The respective proprietors . . . shall severally have the right to unite any rail-road . . . with the rail-road of said corporation, . . . by turntables or otherwise. **1868** *Ill. Agric. Soc. Trans.* VI. 318 There is also ample provision made for the engines, water-tanks, wood-yards, turn-tables. **1898** *McClure's Mag.* X. 521/1 Three locomotives had been run into the turn-table pit.
2. Any one of various revolving devices similar to a railroad turntable. {1865-} Also attrib.
1881 *Mich. Gen. Statutes* I. (1882) 407 Such bridge . . . shall have a draw or turn-table therein for the purpose of opening the same. **1893** *Nation* 13 July 28/3 At the Columbian Fair there is a turn-table stack of official publications. **1920** *Ladies' Home Jrnl.* May 66 These springs furnish the motive power . . . to the turntable or mandrel [of the phonograph].

+**Turnus (butterfly).** A northern variety (*Papilio glaucus turnus*) of the tiger swallowtail, a large, yellow, black-striped butterfly common in the United States. — **1890** WEBSTER 1455/3 The tiger swallowtail, or turnus . . . , and the zebra swallowtail, or ajax . . . are common American species [of swallowtail]. **1904** KELLOGG *Amer. Insects* 449 The tiger swallowtail, or Turnus butterfly . . . , is another common species, with a striking 'negro' form.

+**Turnverein.** [Ger.] A club or society of turners. Also attrib. — **1856** DERBY *Phoenixiana* 236 The organ alluded to has been disposed of to a member of the Turn-verein Association. **1871** DE VERE 141 Their clubs, or *Turn Vereine*, as they begin to be called even by many who are ignorant of German, exercise a most salutary influence on the people. **1905** *N.Y. Ev. Post* 13 May 4 Turnvereins came to this country about as soon as Germans did.

*****Turpentine.**

*****1. a.** A viscous oleoresin obtained from coniferous trees, esp. pines. **b.** =SPIRITS (OF) TURPENTINE.
1634 WOOD *New Eng. Prospect* 17 The Firre and Pine bee trees that . . . doe afford good masts, good board, Rozin and Turpentine. **1694** SEWALL *Letter-Book* I. 142, I have sent you . . . five Barrels of Turpentine. **1706** *Boston Rec.* 50 Mr. Samuell Plummer . . . [is] to be Veiwer & Surveyor of Cask made for Tar Pitch, Tur[p]entine & Rosin. **1784** SMYTH *Tour* II. 73 The pine barren . . . bears the pine tree, and some other useful plants naturally, yielding good profit in pitch, tar, and turpentine. **1809** *Phila. Ordinances* (1812) 115 No person shall distil or boil any turpentine or oil, . . . unless . . . in a completely fire proof building. **1890** HOWELLS *Boy's Town* 128 [Fire-balls] were made of cotton rags wound tight and sewed, and then soaked in turpentine.

2. *attrib.* and *comb.* Designating people, processes, establishments, etc., connected with making and selling turpentine.
See also TURPENTINE BARREL, FARMER, etc.
1799 *Wilmington Gazette* 12 Dec., Two Turpentine Stills. **1834** *S. Lit. Messenger* I. 29 'We keep it,' said one of the colonists, 'for *handy-work*, when there is no farming, or turpentine-gathering.' **1856** OLMSTED *Slave States* 338 There are very large forests of this tree [*Pinus palustris*] in North and South Carolina, Georgia, and Alabama; and the turpentine business is carried on, to some extent. **1857** *Harper's Mag.* May 751/1 There are the same interminable pine forests, boxed and scarified by the turpentine-gatherers. **1862** 'E. KIRKE' *Among Pines* 64 Bidding the turpentine-getter a rather reluctant 'good-by,' I rode on into the rain. *Ib.* 190 A half-hour found me near one of the turpentine distilleries. **1906** BELL *C. Lee* 243 At the turpentine plant at Schoville, . . . my engineer found them ladling out the crude turpentine by hand. *Ib.* 282 It was . . . a tract she intended leasing to some orchard turpentine factors in Jacksonville.

b. Designating areas associated with the gathering or distilling of turpentine.
See also TURPENTINE FARM, ORCHARD, STATE.
1848 *N.Y. Tribune* 22 May (B), From Petersburgh I railed it through the North Carolina pitch, tar, turpentine, and lumber country. **1848** in *Commons, etc. Doc. Hist.* I. 197 Burn over turpentine land. **1856** OLMSTED *Slave States* 325, I was now fairly in the Turpentine region of North Carolina. **1858** THOREAU *Maine Woods* 125, I have been into the lumberyard, and . . . the turpentine clearing. **1888** *Fort Smith Tribune* Feb. (F.), He came originally from the clay-eating and turpentine district of South Carolina. **1892** *Pall Mall Gaz.* 15 Nov. 2/3 The Florida convicts . . . were mostly put to work in the turpentine woods.

3. In special combinations.
Turpentine ball, a torch or other means of illumination consisting of a ball of some substance soaked in turpentine and then set on fire; *t. gin,* inferior gin or whisky; *t. moth,* (see quotation); *t. pine,* =LONG-LEAF PINE 1; *t. spirits,* inferior spirits or liquor; *t. torch,* a torch consisting of the heartwood of a turpentine pine.
1885 *Santa Fé Wkly. New Mexican* 9 July 4/2 Santa Fe celebrated the 4th. . . . All business ceased at noon, and in the evening there were bonfires, fireworks and turpentine balls. **1855** 'P. PAXTON' *Capt. Priest* 53 The odor of 'New England' and 'Turpentine Gin' that pervaded the atmosphere . . . induces me to suppose, that nothing like Maine law was recognized in the establishment. **1891** *Cent.* 6543/3 *Turpentine-moth,* any one of several tortricid moths whose larvæ bore the twigs and shoots of pine and fir, causing an exudation of resin and killing the twig. . . . *R[etinia] comstockiana* and *R. frustana* are common in the United States. **1897** SUDWORTH *Arborescent Flora* 30 *Pinus palustris,* Longleaf Pine. . . . [Also called] Turpentine Pine (N.C.). **1775** ADAIR *Indians* 307 Those turpentine spirits did not inebriate him, but only inflamed his intestines. **1850** LEWIS *La. Swamp Doctor* 62 The remainder [carrying] large turpentine torches, we prepared to make our descent upon the camp-meeting.

Turpentine barrel. A barrel made especially tight and secure for holding turpentine. — **1862** 'E. KIRKE' *Among Pines* 100 The foreman . . . seated himself on a turpentine barrel. **1904** TARBELL *Hist. Standard Oil Co.* I. 12 Turpentine barrels, molasses barrels, whiskey barrels . . . were added to new ones made especially for oil.

+**Turpentine farm.** =TURPENTINE ORCHARD. — **1867** H. LATHAM *Black & White* 124 They led our cavalry in file through the woods, along the paths which lead among the turpentine farms. **1897** *Kissimmee* (Fla.) *Valley* 23 June 2/8 A turpentine farm is to be conducted on the land secured.

+**Turpentine farmer.** One who operates a turpentine orchard. — **1856** OLMSTED *Slave States* 350 The majority of what I have termed turpentine-farmers . . . [are] small proprietors of the long-leaved pine forest land. **1896** *Pop. Science Mo.* Feb. 471 When a turpentine farmer speaks of his *crop* he means ten thousand boxes. **1906** BELL *C. Lee* 196 Let's see what I have to sell my turpentine farmers.

+**Turpentine orchard.** A pine forest or extent of forest from which turpentine is obtained. — **1856** OLMSTED *Slave States* 339 If we enter, in the winter, . . . a 'turpentine orchard,' we come upon negroes engaged in making boxes, in which the sap is to be collected the following spring. **1865** *Nation* I. 651 [He] had a turpentine orchard containing a hundred thousand boxes. **1884** SARGENT *Rep. Forests* 518 Their owners oftener . . . employing them [negroes in N. Carolina] in turpentine orchards than in the cotton-fields.

+**Turpentine State.** North Carolina. A nickname. — **1850** M. REID *Rifle Rangers* vi, The danger is, we may stick in the Turpentine State. **1867** *Trübner's Amer. Lit. Rec.* Aug. 41/1 North Carolina [is known] as The Old North or Turpentine State. **1907** *Boston Transcript* 9 Nov. II. 9.

***Turpentine tree.** A tree, esp. a pine, that yields turpentine. — **1708** *Springfield Rec.* II. 376 It was voted to restraine the boxing of Turpentine Trees within the inmost Comons. **1867** *Harper's Mag.* May 746/2 Turning from the main road into the first by-path that presented itself, he was soon wandering . . . among the turpentine-trees. **1872** POWERS *Afoot & Alone* 32 The very lowest classes . . . subsist chiefly by renting turpentine trees.

+**Turpentine weed.** Any one of various herbs, as various species of *Silphium*, which possess, or are thought to possess, some of the characteristics of turpentine. — **1819** *Western Rev.* I. 95 Among the most remarkable and singular [plants of Ky. is] . . . *Silphium therebinthaceum*, Turpentine weed. [**1885** *Girl's Own Paper* Jan. 171/1 The compass plant —variously known, also, as the pilot weed, polar plant, and turpentine weed—is a vigorous perennial.] **1913** BARNES *Western Grazing Grounds* 236 In the southwest and on some of the ranges in the northern regions there is a little green weed (*Guttierrezia*) known locally as snakeweed, fireweed, turpentine weed.

+**Turpentine whisky.** Moonshine whisky of a low grade. *Obs.* (Cf. PINE TOP.) — **1869** *Overland Mo.* III. 130 'Pinetop' is a kind of mean turpentine whisky of North Carolina. **1877** BARTLETT 124 *Clay-Eaters*, otherwise *Dirt-Eaters*, a miserable set of people inhabiting some of the Southern States, who subsist chiefly on turpentine whiskey.

***Turquoise.** +A variety of the true or oriental turquoise found in the Southwest. Also attrib. — **1880** *Cimarron News & Press* 23 Dec. 1/4 [The Spaniards] obtained immense amounts of silver and gold and turquoise. **1882** *47th Congress 1 Sess.* H. R. Ex. Doc. No. 216, 323 Many ancient turquoise workings are found in the neighborhood [of Tombstone, Ariz.]. **1885** *Weekly New Mexican Rev.* 16 April 3/6 Capt. John Gray has purchased the old Castillian turquoise mine, and today set four men at work.

***Turret.**

*1. A small tower forming a part of, or constituting an addition to some part of, another building.

1647 *Watertown Rec.* I. 1. 21 A turrett added vnto the schoolehowse. **1691** *R.I. Col. Rec.* III. 576 The Newport township [shall] have full power to build a turret upon the Court House in Newport. **1713** *Narragansett Hist. Reg.* III. 276 A committee . . . [are to examine] defects of the Terret or Bellfary on the Meeting House. **1838** HAWTHORNE *Note-Books* I. 201 The house on the eastern corner of North and Essex Streets [Salem], supposed to have been built about 1640, had, say sixty years later, a brick turret erected, wherein one of the ancestors of the present occupants used to practice alchemy. **1885** *Harper's Mag.* Feb. 457 Turrets, sharp points, blunt points, triangles, irregular quadrangles, are devices resorted to in the upper stories.

attrib. **1706** *Hist. Digest Press Mass.* (1911) 369 [They] destroyed the biggest part of the Covering of the Terret boards. **1712** *Boston News-Letter* 10 Nov. 2/2 Mr. Joseph Essex . . . performs all sorts of New Clocks and Watch works, viz. 30 hour Clocks, . . . quarter Chime Clocks, Church Clocks, Terret Clocks.

+2. (See quotation.)

1876 KNIGHT 2665/1 *Turret.* . . . (*Railway*.) The elevated central portion of a passenger-car, whose top forms an upper story of the roof, and whose sides are glazed for light and pierced for ventilation.

***Turtle.**[1]

*1. Any one of various reptiles, esp. the aquatic species, of the order Chelonia, having a short, broad body enclosed in a bony or horny shell.

1613 WHITAKER *Good Newes from Va.* 42, I haue caught with mine angle, . . . the Toropoe or little Turtle. **1672** JOSSELYN *New Eng. Rarities* 34 The Turtle that lives in Lakes . . . is called in Virginia a Terrapine. **1744** A. HAMILTON *Itin.* (1907) 107 They have a diversion here [in N.Y.] very common, which is the barbecuing of a turtle. **1789** MORSE *Amer. Geog.* 287 Black turtle, crabs and oysters . . . the sea, rivers, and creeks afford in great abundance. **1836** HOLLEY *Texas* 102 Both hard and soft shell turtle are numerous in all the rivers and bayous especially near their mouths. **1894** EGGLESTON in *Harper's Mag.* Feb. 467/1 The young man in the white blanket coat asked if we would like a Red River turtle. **1907** *St. Nicholas* July 843/1 Farther out, the commotion among the rushes or the swaying stems of the arrow-heads reveal the plodding course of turtles.

b. The flesh of these prepared as food.

1670 D. DENTON *Brief Descr. N.Y.* 7 They eat likewise Polecats, Skunks, Racoon, Possum, Turtles, and the like. **1761** *Holyoke Diaries* 51 Dined upon turtle at Colonel Pickman's. **1880** SALA in *Daily Tel.* (Lond.) 26 Feb. 5/6 The once affluent Southerners . . . who once delighted to entertain their guests on chicken gumbo, venison, turtle, [etc.].

+2. a. A crude form of submarine invented by David Bushnell (c1742–1824). Now hist.

Cf. AMERICAN TURTLE.

1813 JEFFERSON *Writings* XIII. 263 Bushnel's Turtle is mentioned slightly [in Clarke's sketches of U.S. naval history]. **1876** *Wide Awake* III. 140/1 Paddle, paddle, toward the river-bank came the Turtle, David Bushnell's head rising out of its shell.

+b. A ship used in the Civil War.

1897 C. A. DANA *Recoll. Civil War* 37 It was Admiral Porter's fleet of ironclad turtles, steamboats, and barges. . . . First came seven ironclad turtles and one heavy armed ram.

3. Attrib. and comb. in sense 1 with *entertainment, hunter, meat*, etc.

1769 Singleton *Social N.Y.* 370 Contiguous to the Garden there is a very good Long Room convenient for a Ball or Turtle Entertainment. **1837** WILLIAMS *Florida* 64 The turtle hunters often find them at their nests, and turn them on their backs. **1851** HALL *Manhattaner* 59 [Some mosquitoes] are dainty, and associate only with fat people whose nightmares are based upon turtle steaks and oyster pies. **1879** BISHOP *4 Months in Sneak-box* 272 We landed by a large turtle-pen, near which was a deserted grass hut, evidently the home of the turtle-hunter during the 'turtle season.' **1885** *Lisbon* (Dak.) *Star* 18 Sept. 6/1 In days of the garrison turtle meat was a welcome item in the subsistence department.

4. In special combinations.

Turtle-back scale, a common brown scale that infests orange trees; *turtle-peg harpoon*, a harpoon or long pole having a detachable peg or point used in harpooning turtles; *turtle step*, a slow, deliberate step.

1884 *Rep. Comm. Agric.* 355 In Florida [this insect] destroys . . . the common 'Turtle-back scale.' **1884** *Nat. Museum Bul.* No. 27, 873 Turtle-peg Harpoon. A dart or harpoon about two inches long. . . . Used on the southern coast for the capture of turtles. **1877** HABBERTON *Jericho Road* 7 Lively, boys, lively! Trot along! 'Taint no time to try the turtle-step.

***Turtle.**[2] +=next. — **1631** *N.H. Hist. Soc. Col.* IV. 246 They were all turtles, as appeared by diverse of them wee killed flying. *c*1729 CATESBY *Carolina* I. 24 The Turtle of Carolina . . . is somewhat less than a Dove-house Pigeon. **1789** MORSE *Amer. Geog.* 60 Tropic bird. Turtle of Carolina. Water wagtail.

***Turtle dove.** +=MOURNING DOVE. — **1674** *Cal. State P., Amer. & W.I.* VII. 581 [In] Maine . . . the islands and woods yield swarms of birds, . . . turtle-doves, swans, geese [etc.]. **1709** LAWSON *Carolina* 142 Turtle Doves are here very plentiful. **1808** IRVING, etc. *Salmagundi* xx. 541 The turtle-dove, the timid fawn, . . . joy in the sequestered haunts of nature. **1877** HODGE *Arizona* 223 The most common of the birds of Arizona are . . . turtle doves, . . . and numerous quantities of vultures. **1917** *Birds of Amer.* II. 46.

Turtle feast. A dinner at which the main dish is turtle; a festive occasion featuring a turtle dinner. {1753–} — **1775** BURNABY *Travels* 65 There are several houses pleasantly situated upon East river, near New York, where it is common to have turtle-feasts. **1785** WASHINGTON *Diaries* II. 445, I went up to Alexandria . . . to a Turtle feast. **1822** in Mackenzie *Van Buren* 187 We had a turtle feast at Cruttenden's about eight or ten days since.

+**Turtle frolic.** =prec. — **1750** in *Amer. Speech* XV. 231/1 Had an Invitation to day to Go to a Turtle Frolick with a Comp[an]y of Gent[leme]n and Ladies. **1771** *Holyoke Diaries* 76 Turtle frolick. Invited. Didn't go. **1787** CUTLER in *Life & Corr.* I. 205, I received a polite invitation from Governor Bowen . . . to join them in a Turtle frolic. **1886** BYNNER *A. Surriage* xv, There was a turtle-frolic at Cambridge, whither the company repaired in chairs and chaises.

Turtlehead. +Any one of various American plants of the genus *Chelone.* (Cf. BALMONY and SNAKEHEAD 1.) — **1857** GRAY *Botany* 285 *Chelone,* Turtle-head. Snake-head. . . . The corolla resembling in shape the head of a reptile. **1898** CREEVEY *Flowers of Field* 158 Snake-head. Turtle-head. . . . This plant grows often very high, usually 2 to 3 feet. **1904** STRATTON-PORTER *Freckles* 283 Milk-weed, golden-rod, iron-wort, fringed gentians, cardinal flowers, and turtle-head stood on the very edge of the creek.

Turtler. One who catches turtles. {1697–} — **1682** ASH *Carolina* 28 The Seamen or Turtlers sometimes turn 40 or 50 [turtles] in a night. **1775** ROMANS *Nat. Hist. Florida* App. p. xxx, Turtlers and wood-cutters . . . frequent this coast from Providence. **1837** WILLIAMS *Florida* 64 A good turtler, will take from ten to twenty in a day.

Turtle soup. Soup of which turtle meat, esp. that of the green turtle (*Chelonia mydas*), is the chief ingredient. {1763–} — **1815** in H. M. Brooks *Gleanings* IV. 129 Turtle Soup. Two Green Turtles will be served up. **1883** *Harper's Mag.* Aug. 463/1, I think turtle soup is almost as good as mock turtle. **1911** *Rep. Fisheries 1908* 310 *Green turtle.* . . . —The flesh of this turtle forms the basis of the well-known turtle soup.

Turtle soup bean. A variety of bean. — **1849** EMMONS *Agric. N.Y.* II. 280. **1856** *Rep. Comm. Patents 1855: Agric.* 287, I have tried the 'Turtle-soup Bean' you sent me, and find it very productive.

+**Tuscaloosa.** [*Tuscaloosa*, Alabama.] 1. *Tuscaloosa roarer*, (see quotation). *Obs.* 2. A kind of liquor. *Obs.* — (1) **1822** *Amer. Beacon* (Norfolk, Va.) 6 Sept. 4/1 (Th. S.), The bargemen . . . are divided into classes, such as Tuscaloosa Roarers, Alabama Screamers, Cahawba Scrougers, and the like gentle names. (2) **1835** HOFFMAN *Winter in West* I. 47 A venison steak and flask of old Tuscaloosa . . . gave cordiality to the meeting.

+**Tuscarora.** [Amer. Indian.]

1. An Indian of an Iroquoian tribe first encountered by Europeans in what is now eastern North Carolina; also, in pl., the tribe itself. Also collective.

1713 *N.C. Col. Rec.* II. 2 An order from ye Governm[en]t of New Yorke to Caution ye Tuscaroras ag[ains]t going to warr w[i]th ye English here. **1726** PENHALLOW *Indian Wars* 79 Col. Barnwell went in pursuit of another nation, called the Tuskarorahs. **1840** COOPER *Pathfinder* i, There must be Oneidas or Tuscaroras near us, Arrowhead. **1894** ROBLEY *Bourbon Co., Kansas* 7 These various tribes of New York Indians, consisting of the remnants of the Senecas, Onondagas, Cayugas, Tuscaroras, Oneidas, St. Regis, Stockbridges, Munsees and Brothertowns, were called the 'Six Nations.' **1910** HODGE, etc. *Amer. Indians* II. 842 The Tuscarora . . . possessed in early times the 'country lying between the sea shores and the mountains, which divide the Atlantic states.'

attrib. **1709** LAWSON *Carolina* 163 Craw-Fish, in the Brooks, and small rivers of water, amongst the Tuskeruro Indians, . . . are found very plentifully. **1713** *N.C. Col. Rec.* II. 2 He doe have and take to his own use three Tuscaroro men. *Ib.* 23 The Fund given by the Assembly of Virginia is insufficient to furnish the pay and provisions of such a number of men as can in prudence be ventured to attack the Tuscaruro Towns. **1803** *Indian Laws & Tr.* III. 703 The Indians composing the Tuscarora nation, have . . . requested the concurrence of the General Assembly of the State, to enable them to lease or demise . . . the residue of their lands.

2. A variety of Indian corn. *Obs.* Also attrib.

1856 *Rep. Comm. Patents 1855: Agric.* 162 [There is] generally some appreciable quantity of this element [oil], the 'Tuscarora,' the 'White-flour,' and the 'Wyandotte' being among the exceptions. *Ib.* 166 Analysis of the Ashes of the 'Tuscarora' Corn-cob.—This corn was grown . . . in Massachusetts.

+**Tuscarora rice. 1.** (See quotation.) **2.** A wild aquatic grass, *Zizania aquatica*, the edible grains of which somewhat resemble rice. — **(1) 1830** WATSON *Philadelphia* 616 Mrs. Sybilla Masters . . . went out to England in 1711–12, to make her fortune abroad by the patent and sale of her 'Tuscarora rice.' . . . It was her preparation from our Indian corn, made into something like our hominy. **(2) 1843** TORREY *Flora N.Y.* II. 416 Tuscarora Rice. Water Oats. Indian Rice. . . . The grain of this plant is a favorite article of food among the Indians.

+**Tusk.** =CUSK. *Obs.* Also attrib. — **1802** BENTLEY *Diary* II. 431 Many tusk are taken, and an abundance of Cod, & particularly Haddock. **1814** *Mass. H. S. Coll.* 1 Ser. III. 118 The salmon trout, pickerel, eel, and cusk, or tusk, are the most plenty. **1884** GOODE, etc. *Fisheries* I. 233 The name 'Tusk,' used for this fish in Newfoundland, is now never used in the United States, although it seems to have been in use a century ago, a well-known fishing ground in the Gulf of Maine being known as the 'Tusk Rock.'

+**Tuskee.** [Amer. Ind.] 'The prairie turnip, *Psoralea esculenta*' (Cent.).

+**Tusks.** *ellipt.* The Tuscaroras. *Obs.* — **1713** *N.C. Col. Rec.* II. 26 [The traders] engaged to go so strong & to march so far wide of the Tusks, as not to be in danger of any attack. **1714** *Ib.* 140 He is further advised that ye said Order is passed Since ye Tusks Articled w[i]th ye Governm[en]t.

+**Tusk shell.** Any one of various mollusks, esp. of the genus *Dentalium*, having a shell resembling the tusk of an elephant. — **1861** *Smithsonian Rep. 1860* 222. **1881** INGERSOLL *Oyster-Industry* 249 Tusk-Shell, a species of the *Dentalium*. (Pacific coast.) **1884** GOODE, etc. *Fisheries* I. 703 This mollusk . . . occurs all along the northern Pacific coast of America, and is known to Americans as the 'Tusk-shell.'

*Tussock.** A small clump or hillock of grass, sedge, etc. {1607–} Also in plural as a place name.

1658 *Providence Rec.* XIV. 212, I give unto ye said Jeremiah Roades all that marsh, Meaddow or Tusekes that lieth on both sides of ye River. **1714** *Duxbury Rec.* 97 Up said brook until it comes to a creek that leads to the place called the Tussocks. **1785** WASHINGTON *Diaries* II. 365 Had the Roots, shrubs . . . and tussics of broom Straw . . . raked of[f] and burnt. **1834** NOTT *Novellettes* I. 35 We could only get along by stepping, and often jumping, on *tussocks*, which afforded but a narrow and insecure footing. **1898** *Atlantic Mo.* Oct. 494/2 It seemed well within the range of probability that the same changes which had brought in one lover of sedgy tussocks and button-bushes should have attracted also another.

attrib. **1848** *Rep. Comm. Patents 1847* 157, I have no longer any doubt of the tussac grass being freely introduced within a short period. **1877** *Vermont Bd. Agric. Rep.* IV. 148 Tussock moths, *Orgyia antiquaoc*, . . . [are] reddish brown.

Tussocky, *a.* Abounding in tussocks. {1805–} Also fig. — **1662** *Providence Rec.* XV. 90 There is laid out . . . [a] Necke of land . . . [bounded by] the swamp and tussikie places lying on the west. **1684** *Ib.* XIV. 79 [I] make over & confirme unto my son . . . a percell of Boggy or Tussichey Meaddow. **1867** 'LACKLAND' *Homespun* 219 Of really tough and tussocky obstacles he has his full share to contend with.

*Tutor,** *n.*

1. a. One assigned to instruct undergraduates. +**b.** A faculty member at Harvard College. Now hist. +**c.** 'In U.S. colleges, a teacher subordinate to a professor, usually appointed for a year or a term of years' (*Cent.*). *Obsolescent.* **d.** In recent practice in some American universities, an instructor who tutors in a particular subject a group of pupils assigned to him.

1646 *Harvard Rec.* I. 25 [Students] shall . . . bee ready to give an account to their tutours of their profiting. **1687** *Harvard Rec.* I. 81 Ordered by the Rector & Tutors, that Rogers be appointed the Colledge Butler. **1707** SEWALL *Diary* II. 183, I go to Cambridge and carry Joseph a small piece of Plate to present his Tutor with. **1719** *Mass. Col. Soc. Publ.* VI. 186 It Is thought Needful . . . to have a Resident Rector, who with one Tutor may be Sufficient to Instruct the Students. **1790** *Harvard Laws* 13 The Freshman Class shall attend the Tutor who teaches Latin. **1817** *N. Amer. Rev.* Nov. 147 The officers of the University are, at present, twenty Professors, two Tutors [et al.]. **1851** HALL *College Words* 304 In the American colleges, tutors . . . have a share, with the president and professors, in the government of the students. **1895** [see NEW ENGLANDISM]. **1905** W. WILSON in E. M. Norris *Story of Princeton* 245 The tutor will bring out and strengthen the individual characteristics of each man.

*2.** A private teacher who instructs children in a family or who coaches college students.

1771 FRANKLIN *Autobiog.* 266 A West India captain, who had a commission to procure a tutor for the sons of a gentleman at Barbadoes, . . . agreed to carry him thither. **1803** J. DAVIS *Travels* 18 Can you passively submit to be called School-master by the children? . . . No. Then you will not do for a private tutor. **1838** *U.S. Mag.* I. 386 A young man from Massachusetts . . . had been engaged to go to Georgia in the capacity of a family tutor. **1871** BAGG *At Yale* 687 He should get his 'fit,' too, at one of the large preparatory schools; not at some little academy, or, worst of all, at the hands of a private tutor. **1903** WISTER *Philosophy Four* 23 Bertie and Billy had colonial names (Rogers, I think, and Schuyler), but the tutor's name was Oscar Maironi.

Tutor, v. +*intr.* To act or serve as a tutor; to study under a tutor. — **1892** *Nation* 11 Aug. 116/2 Graduate . . . of experience wishes to tutor for the September examinations. **1897** FLANDRAU *Harvard Episodes* 93. *Ib.*, I didn't know anybody was tutoring in that course this year. **1900** MUNN *Uncle Terry* 55, I tutored some, read law, and was admitted to the bar. **1921** PAINE *Comr. Rolling Ocean* 99 He tutored for Princeton and flunked in freshman year.

Tutti-frutti (ice cream). A kind of ice cream in which chopped fruits are mixed. — **1876** M. F. HENDERSON *Cooking* 313 Tutti Frutti. When a rich vanilla cream is partly frozen, candied cherries, English currants, chopped raisins, . . . or any other candied fruits chopped rather fine, are added. **1919** FRANDSEN & MARKHAM *Manufacture Ice Cream* 110 Tutti Frutti Ice Cream . . . Colored pineapple cubes are now used to a considerable extent.

+**Tuxedo.** [*Tuxedo* Park, N.Y., a fashionable resort and country club.] A tailless dinner jacket less formal than a full dress coat; a suit of which such a jacket forms a part. Also attrib. — **1894** B. MATTHEWS in *Harper's Mag.* Sept. 589/1 There were a few men in sacks and cut-aways; but the most of them had dressed for the occasion, some . . . with the black cravat and the hybrid jacket which is known as a 'Tuxedo coat.' **1899** ADE *Fables in Slang* 130 Now she began to see . . . the Kind that wears . . . a jimmy little Tuxedo at Night. **1902** S. HALE *Letters* 374 The young men in Tuxedos, four-in-hands, panamas. **1906** *Harper's Mag.* July 310 No white male citizen should sit at dinner there unless clothed . . . at least in the smoking-jacket known to us as a Tuxedo.

*Twain.** +In river navigation, two fathoms. Used in various phrases, as *mark twain*. — **1863** 'MARK TWAIN' in Paine *Biog. Mark Twain* I. 221 I want to sign my articles . . . 'Mark Twain.' It is an old river term, a leadsman's call, signifying two fathoms—twelve feet. **1867** RICHARDSON *Beyond Miss.* 22 Every minute or two, he reports, in drawling sing-song, . . . 'F-i-v-e feet,' 'Quarter less t-w-a-i-n,' (a quarter fathom less than two fathoms,) 'M-a-r-k twain,' 'N-o bottom.' **1875** 'MARK TWAIN' *Old Times* ii. 39 M-a-r-k three! Quarter-less-three! Half twain! Quarter twain! M-a-r-k twain!

Twankay. A variety of green tea. {1840–} — **1830** S. H. COLLINS *Emigrant's Guide* 156 Hyson skin and twankay we purchase for 3s. 4d. **1839** *Knickerb.* XIII. 231 How nicely is it [tea] adapted, by its delicately varying shades, to every especial palate! . . . There is Twankay.

*Twayblade.** +**a.** An American species of the orchidaceous genus *Liparis*, having two leaves springing from the root. *b.** The species *Listera* or +an American species of this genus. — **(a) 1817–8** EATON *Botany* (1822) 347 *Malaxis liliifolia*, twayblade. . . . I have seen hundreds in flower at one time along the north side of Pinerock, New Haven. **1840** DEWEY *Mass. Flowering Plants* 201 Twayblade. . . . Wet woods; June. a**1862** THOREAU *Maine Woods* 182, I have also received *Liparis liliifolia*, or tway-blade, from this spot. **(b) 1884** W. MILLER *Dict. Names of Plants* 140/1 Tway-blade, American, *Listera convallarioides*. **1907** *St. Nicholas* Aug. 940/1 Only mention can be made of the other groups: . . . the *Listera*, also called twayblade; . . . *Calypso*, whose pouched lip once grouped it with the lady's slipper.

Tweed. A rather thick, rough-surfaced, woolen cloth; a garment made of this. Freq. pl. {1847–} Also attrib. — **1865** *Chicago Tribune* 10 April 1 Tweeds and Kentucky Jeans! at Field, Benedict & Co's. **1877** *Rep. Indian Affairs* 470 Tweed plaid. **1883** *Century Mag.* July 376/1 He now stood, clad in a quiet fishing suit of gray tweed. **1905** N. DAVIS *Northerner* 7 His energy, his tweeds, his accent seemed, collectively and severally, a personal affront.

+**Tweedian,** *a.* [See next.] Characteristic of the rule of the Tweed Ring. — **1878** *N. Amer. Rev.* Nov.-Dec. 491 Our fellow-citizens of the South . . . are resolved not to submit to Tweedian government.

+**Tweedism.** [W. M. *Tweed*, N.Y. political boss (1823–78).] The rule of the Tweed ring; boss control of similar character. — **1881** *Harper's Mag.* Jan. 201/1 Tweedism was not rampant in those days.

+**Tweed Ring.** [See prec.] The group comprising W. M. Tweed and his associates, who, from 1858 to 1871, controlled the municipal government of New York City. Now hist. — **1882** MCCABE *New York* 297 It was the chief means used by the Tweed Ring in carrying out their stupendous frauds. **1894** S. LEAVITT *Our Money Wars* 154 In 1871, the Credit Mobilier at Washington, and the Tweed Ring at New York, were exposed.

+**Tweeg.** [Amer. Indian.] The hellbender. — **1825** *Amer. Jrnl. Science* XI. 278 *Menopoma Alleghaniensis.* . . . Tweeg. . . . The Menopoma always resides in the water. **1891** *Cent.* 6549/2.

Tweeled, *a.* Variant of TWILLED *a.*

Tweeling. A twilled fabric. {1839–} — **1777** *Essex Inst. Coll.* XLIX. 106 Sold . . . tweeling at 2s.

+**Tweezer.** *local.* The American merganser, *Mergus americanus.* — **1888** TRUMBULL *Names of Birds* 65 Another [name for the American merganser] . . . is heard at Shinnecock Bay . . . , viz.: Tweezer.

+**Tweezer bird.** The kingfisher. — *a*1862 THOREAU *Maine Woods* 207, I heard a . . . kingfisher (tweezer bird), or parti-colored warbler, and a night-hawk.

Twelfth cake. A cake used in the celebration of Twelfth Night. {1774–} — **1745** in Singleton *Social N.Y.* 303 Twelfth Cakes sometime the beginning of the winter.

Twelve Apostles. *pl.* +One of the governing bodies of the Mormon church. (Cf. APOSTLE 2.) — **1861** REMY *Journey to Gt.-Salt-Lake City* II. 51 There are three high-priests, presidents. . . . Then come twelve travelling councillors, who are no other than the twelve apostles, or special witnesses to the name of Jesus Christ throughout the world. *a*1918 G. STUART *On Frontier* I. 50, I lived a month with one of the 'Twelve Apostles' and his family.

+**Twelveite.** (See quot. 1890.) — **1847** HOWE *Hist. Coll. Ohio* 284 The Mormons . . . [are] now divided into three factions, viz.: the Rigdonites, the Twelveites, and the Strangites. **1890** *Amer. Notes & Q.* V. 184 The main body of Mormons are some times called *Twelveites,* probably as being followers of the Twelve Apostles.

*✶***Twelve men.** +In colonial Massachusetts, a town-governing body. — **1636** *Dorchester Rec.* 21 One acre . . . the sayd Bray is to haue upon Condition he remaynne in the Plantation, . . . and not to alienate it without app[ro]bation of the Twelue men. **1637** *Essex Inst. Coll.* IX. 50 A towne meeting of the 12 men appoynted for the busines thereof.

Twelve-pounder. A cannon which uses twelve-pound shot. {1800–} Also attrib. — **1757** *General Orders* 52 The Artilery is To Send Two Brass Twelve Pounders to ye Ground Barrear. **1775** in Sparks *Corr. Revolution* I. 43 The two row-galleys carrying a twelve-pounder each, . . . to lay in the river. **1837** in Trumbull *Autobiog.* 306, I found you . . . directing a long twelve pounder to be loaded. **1862** in Moore *Rebellion Rec.* V. II. 171 Lieut. Avery, of the marine artillery, with three of Wiard's twelve-pounder boat-howitzers, . . . accompanied the expedition.

Twelve-rowed, *a.* +Of Indian corn: Characterized by ears having twelve rows of kernels. — **1838** *Mass. Agric. Survey 1st Rep.* 25 The Dutton or Sioux corn, a twelve-rowed variety, has likewise ripened in favorable locations. **1849** EMMONS *Agric. N.Y.* II. 264 Twelve-rowed Canada corn . . . is esteemed by the Vermont farmers. **1888** *Vt. Agric. Rep.* X. 30 He had tried both the 8 and the 12-rowed, and had decided that for him the 12-rowed was the better.

*✶***Twenty.** +**1.** A twenty-dollar gold piece or bill. **2.** A tract of land comprising twenty acres. ‖**3.** *Like twenty,* an intensive. — (1) **1845** SOL. SMITH *Theatr. Apprent.* 23 He began counting out tens, twenties, and fifties, to the amount of three hundred dollars. **1877** W. WRIGHT *Big Bonanza* 148 The gentleman had closed his hand upon the three 'twenties' and held them above his head while submitting to the search. **1910** J. HART *Vigilante Girl* 82 The miners . . . used to toss twenties on the stage. (2) **1899** *Mo. So. Dakotan* I. 198, I bought this 'twenty' of timber. (3) **1839** *S. Lit. Messenger* V. 377/2 Lord, how scared she was—she jumped and kicked and hollared like twenty.

+**Twenty-cent piece.** A coin of the value of twenty cents. Now hist. — **1875** *Stat. at Large* XVIII. 479 The twenty cent piece shall be a legal tender at its nominal value for any amount not exceeding five dollars in any one payment. **1878** *Ib.* XX. 47 From, and after the passage of this act, the coinage of the twenty cent piece of silver, by the Government of the United States [shall] be, and the same is hereby prohibited. **1882** C. B. LEWIS *Lime-kiln Club* 113 We took advantage of a cloudy day to pass a twenty-cent piece off fur a quarter.

+**Twenty-deck poker.** (See quots. 1857 and 1887.) Also attrib. — *a*1846 *Quarter Race Ky.* 66 [Officers were] all going it like forty at twenty-deck poker. **1857** *Hoyle's Games* (Amer. ed.) 289 Twenty-Deck Poker . . . is played and governed precisely in the same manner that 'Bluff' is, with the exception that only twenty cards are used. **1858** *S. Lit. Messenger* XXVII. 353/2 Pruce was the best Twenty-Deck Poker player Draymanne had ever met. **1887** *Courier-Journal* 23 Jan. 15/7 Twenty-deck poker came first in the order of time, when all the cards below the ten were discarded from the pack. Only four could play it.

+**Twenty-dollar gold piece.** A gold coin of the value of twenty dollars. — **1867** RICHARDSON *Beyond Miss.* 58 They would cancel the debt from pockets burdened with twenty-dollar gold pieces. **1900** *Congress. Rec.* 12 Feb. 1710/1 If you melt a twenty-dollar gold piece into a nugget the money functions of that piece would be destroyed. **1912**

NICHOLSON *Hoosier Chron.* 218 Her friend never forgot to send her a Christmas gift—once a silver purse and a twenty-dollar gold piece.

+**Twenty-five-cent piece.** =QUARTER DOLLAR. — **1875** *Stat. at Large* XVIII. 478 The twenty-five cent piece shall be a legal tender at its nominal value for any amount not exceeding five dollars in any one payment. **1891** *Boston Jrnl.* 25 Sept. 2/3 He kissed a silver twenty-five cent piece and threw it as far as he could out upon the sea.

Twenty-four-pounder. A cannon which fires twenty-four-pound shot. {1684–} Also attrib. — **1776** A. ADAMS *Fam. Lett.* 138 The continual roar of twenty-four pounders, and the bursting of shells . . . realize a scene of which we could form scarcely any conception. **1861** *Army Regulations* 460, I hereby certify that I have . . . inspected and proved twenty twenty-four pounder iron cannon.

Twenty-four-pound shot. *collect.* Shot which weighs twenty-four pounds. — **1825** NEAL *Bro. Jonathan* III. 380 A place which it was quite impossible for anything to get into, or out of . . . till a few twenty four pound shot did both.

Twenty-one. +A form of cassino in which a score of twenty-one points wins. — **1852** A. T. JACKSON *Forty-Niner* (1920) 159 'Twenty-one,' 'Rondo,' and 'Fortune Wheels' are the banking games, and they play poker and 'Brag' for big stakes. **1891** SWASEY *Early Days Calif.* 87 At private houses the game of twenty-one was most in vogue. **1896** SHINN *Story of Mine* 23 Old Billy Williams, of Carson Valley, . . . came into Johntown with the card game of 'Twenty-one.'

Twenty-penny nail. A nail which cost twenty pence a hundred; a nail 4 inches in length. — **1715** *Boston News-Letter* 25 April 2/2 To be Sold by Mr. Jonathan Belcher at his Store-house in Boston, . . . Nails 4d, 6d, 8d, 10d, 20d. **1879** *Scribner's Mo.* Nov. 52/1 Oak wedges [are] driven into the lower ends of the pins, with twenty-penny nails to keep the pins steady. **1887** *Courier-Journal* 2 May 4/7 On top of an extra heavy load of buckshot a twenty-penny nail was dropped.

Twenty-pounder. {1861–} A cannon firing shot weighing twenty pounds. Also attrib. — **1862** NORTON *Army Lett.* 120 A battery of twenty-pounders was dealing death to the enemies of our country. **1888** P. H. SHERIDAN *Memoirs* I. 295 At first our nerves were often upset by the whirring of twenty-pounder shells dropped inconsiderately into our camp at untimely hours of the night.

Twenty-shilling bill. A bill of the value of one pound. {1855–} **1705** *Boston News-Letter* 12 Nov. 1/2 One Thomas Odell a chief Contriver and Actor in Counterfeiting of the Twenty Shilling Bill of Credit on this Province.

Twid-line. [Of obscure origin.] ? A heavy cord suitable for flying a kite. — **1844** *Knickerb.* XXIV. 258 In his hand is a great ball of twine containing three skeins of 'twid-line.'

Twiffler. ? An earthen dish. (Cf. MUFFIN 1.) — **1820** *Columbian Centinel* 12 Jan. 3/6 An extensive assortment of Crockery, Glass, and China Ware, viz. . . . Twifflers and Muffins [to be auctioned off]. **1843** in *Ill. State Hist. Soc. Jrnl.* XXXIV. 310 For plates, twifflers, and muffins [we pay] 4s. 2d. per score. *Ib.* 320 Bring with you some pots, viz., cups, twifflers, dishes, &c.

‖**Twig,** *n.*¹ A blow with a twig or stick. — **1774** FITHIAN *Journal* I. 87, I took him by the hand and gave him four or five smart twigs.

Twig, *n.*² {*a*1800–} A 'pull' at a container of liquor; a draught. — **1825** NEAL *Bro. Jonathan* I. 54 For . . . a 'twig o' cider' a piece, [the people] put up the frame for the owner, in a frolick.

✶ **Twig,** *n.*³

1. A switch or rod used in punishing children. {*pl.*, a birch rod, 1736–}

*a*1841 HAWES *Sporting Scenes* II. 50 Everybody knows what a twig is. It is built of hickory—willow,—that's poor, and breaks easy,—cowhide, dressed leather, twisted eel-skin, or plaited horse-hair.

+**2.** Attrib. and comb. in the names of insects and diseases injurious to twigs.

1909 *Cent. Suppl.* 1301/3 Twig beetle, a twig-borer. **1889** *Cent.* 587/1 *Pear-blight,* an epidemic disease attacking pear trees, also known as *fire-blight,* and when affecting the apple and quince as *twig-blight.* **1891** *Ib.* 6551/3 Twig-borer, one of numerous small beetles which bore the twigs of trees, as the ptinid *Amphicerus bicaudatus,* which infests the grape and the apple in the United States. **1874** *Dept. Agric. Rep.* 1873 153 The twig-girdler, *Oncideres cingulatus.* . . . The insects girdle the twig before depositing their eggs. **1891** *Cent.* 6551/3 Twig-pruner, a longicorn beetle of the genus *Elaphidion.* The larvæ of the parallel twig-pruner, *E. parallelum,* live in the twigs of . . . forest and fruit-trees in the northern United States.

Twig, *v.*¹ {1725–} **1.** *tr.* To take a pull at. *slang. Obs.* **2.** *Nautical.* To pull. {*dial.,* in general sense} — (1) **1809** WEEMS *Marion* (1833) 162 [He] twigg'd the tickler to the tune of a deep dram. (2) **1840** DANA *Two Years* 233 The mate then took his place between the knight-heads to 'twig' the fore.

+**Twig,** *v.*² (See quotation.) *slang.* — **1887** *Lippincott's Mag.* July 100, I take my club-mates around to see my new friend, and, if the general opinion be favorable, proceed to 'twig' him, or, in plain English, to ask him to join my fraternity.

+**Twig broom.** A broom made of hemlock twigs. — **1851** JUDD *Margaret* (ed. 2) I. 10 In one corner stood a twig-broom. [**1863** HAWTHORNE *Our Old Home* 194 There was a much greater variety of merchandise: . . . twig-brooms, beehives, oranges, rustic attire.]

+**Twig bug.** =STICK BUG. — **1891** *Cent.* 5943/1 *Diapheromera femorata* . . . is also called *twig-bug, twig-insect.*

+**Twig goldenrod.** (See quotation.) — **1817–8** EATON *Botany* (1822) 468 *Solidago viminea*, twig golden-rod.... Flowers numerous.

Twig rush. Any rushlike plant of the genus *Cladium*. {1836–} Also with specifying term. — **1843** TORREY *Flora N.Y.* II. 366 *Cladium mariscoides*.... Smooth Twig-rush.... Bog meadows and borders of ponds. **1894** COULTER *Bot. W.Texas* III. 476 Twig-rush.... With ovoid or oblong spikelets of several loosely imbricated scales. **1901** MOHR *Plant Life Ala.* 410.

***Twilled,** *a.* Of fabrics: Having the diagonal lines or ridges characteristic of twill. — **1803** *Austin P.* (1924) I. 84, 4 yd Twild flannels. **1812** *Niles' Reg.* II. 8/2 Two of the most useful articles of woolen manufacture are the plain man's tweeled blanket... and the plain man's tweeled kersey. **1840** DANA *Two Years* 288 Several of us clubbed together and bought a large piece of twilled cotton which we made into trousers and jackets. **1853** *La Crosse Democrat* 4 Oct. 4/6 Ready-Made Clothing.... Plain and Twilled Sheep Gray Cloth. **1869** ALCOTT *Little Women* II. 328 I want some twilled silesia.

+**Twinberry. 1.** A North American honeysuckle of the genus *Lonicera*. **2.** The partridge berry. **3.** The fruit of any one of these plants. — **(1) 1821** *Mass. H. S. Coll.* 2 Ser. IX. 158 Plants, which are indigenous in the township of Middlebury, [Vt., include]... Clott-bur, Twinberry, Prickly ash [etc.]. **1839** in *Mich. Agric. Soc. Trans.* VII. 422. **(2)** [**1836** TRAILL *Backwoods of Canada* (1846) 184 The plant is also called winter-green, or twin-berry.] **1871** DE VERE 402 In the New England States... it [the partridge-berry] is often called *twin-berry*, from its uniformly double scarlet-berry. **(3) 1869** *Rep. Comm. Agric. 1868* 178 Among them [*sc.* small fruits] may be noted red and black currants,... twinberries [etc.].

+**Twin boat.** (See quotations.) — *c***1816** REES *Cycl.* XXXV. s.v. Steam-engine, In 1811 and 1812 two steam-boats were built... as ferryboats for crossing the Hudson river.... These boats are what are called twin-boats; each of them being two complete hulls united by a deck or bridge. **1876** KNIGHT 2667/1 *Twin-boat*, a boat or deck supported on two parallel floating bodies, which are placed some distance asunder.

+**Twin Cities.** Minneapolis and St. Paul, Minnesota. A nickname.— **1883** *Harper's Mag.* June 73/2 The twin cities... emulate each other in metropolitan airs. **1904** *Chicago Tribune* 21 Aug. 1 Tornado Sweeps the Twin Cities.

***Twine.**

1. String or cord composed of two or more strands twisted together.

1655 *Essex Probate Rec.* I. 216 Twyne & cotten yarne. **1752** FRANKLIN *Electrical Experiments* (1769) 112 To the end of the twine, next the hand, is to be tied a silk ribbon. **1789** *Hist. Congress* (1834) 302 Duty... on twine, or pack thread, 100 cents per 112 lbs. **1815** *Niles' Reg.* VIII. 141/2 Three large and extensive rope walks... make all kinds of rope, twine and cordage. **1909** 'O. HENRY' *Strictly Business* 131 The lone button was the size of a half-dollar, made of yellow horn and sewed on with coarse twine.

2. Attrib. and comb. with *cutter, holder, sheet,* etc.

1658 *Southold Rec.* I. 438, 8 lbs of twine sheets & other lynnen in a chest. **1707** *Boston News-Letter* 24 Feb. 2/2 A Manuscript... was rowled up together, and tyed about with a Twine Thre[a]d. **1789** *Boston Directory* 180 Caswell and Tyler,... twine-spinners. **1848** *Rep. Comm. Patents 1847* 83 Some of these patents are for fire escapes, twine stands for counters, cigar machines. **1876** KNIGHT 2668/1 *Twine-cutter*, a blade or knife on a table, stand, or counter, to cut twine when tying packages. *Ib. Twine-holder*, a box or case to hold a ball of twine on a counter. **1894** WARNER *Golden House* xxiii, He was going with nothing, humiliated, a clerk in a twine-store.

+**Twine-binding,** *a.* Tying harvested grain into sheaves. Also *twine-binder*, a machine which does this. — **1885** *Rep. Indian Affairs* 47 There are twelve twine-binding harvesters... owned by members of the tribe. **1902** *Scientific Amer. Suppl.* 20 Dec. 22546/3 He [Marquis L. Gorham] would have done much to solve the problem of a practical twine binder. *Ib.*, He [William Deering] established twine binding machines as the grain harvesters of the time.

Twine factory. A factory that produces twine. Also attrib. — **1805** *Holyoke Diaries* 147 Twine factory burnt at 11 P.M. **1872** BRACE *Dangerous Classes N.Y.* 356 Twine-factories... reveal the same state of things [*i.e.*, employment of children]. **1911** PERSONS, etc. *Mass. Labor Laws* 144 Several doctors in twine and cordage factory towns have suggested... [a] relation between wet-room conditions and morals.

+**Twinflower.** A plant of the genus *Linnæa*, which produces flowers in pairs. Also attrib. — **1817–8** EATON *Botany* (1822) 338 *Linnaea borealis*, twin-flower:... branches erect, each bearing 2 flowers. **1843** TORREY *Flora N.Y.* I. 295 Two-flowered Linnaea, or Twin-flower.... Moist shady woods, and in swamps. **1845** JUDD *Margaret* I. 8 She got running mosses, twin-flower vines, and mountain laurel blossoms. **1869** FULLER *Flower Gatherers* 87 It was a little flower... [called] 'Twin-flower.' **1892** TORREY *Foot-Path Way* 218 Enough that the twin-flower and the star-flower each obeys its own law.

***Twinkler.** *pl.* ‖Spectacles. slang or *facetious*. — **1830** *Collegian* 96 A slender man.... With black-rimmed twinklers on a Roman nose.

+**Twinleaf.** The herb *Jeffersonia diphylla*, each leaf of which is divided into two leaflets; rheumatism root. — **1817–8** EATON *Botany* (1822) 321 Twin leaf.... Leaves in pairs. **1843** TORREY *Flora N.Y.* I. 34 Twin-leaf. Rheumatism-root.... Sometimes employed as a remedy in chronic rheumatism. **1863** *Rep. Comm. Agric. 1862* 157 One of these

plants..., named by a botanist in honor of President Jefferson,... is commonly known as the 'twin leaf.'

+**Twin States.** North and South Dakota. — **1899** *Mo. So. Dakotan* I. 184 Mr. Mellette [was] Governor of Dakota territory... until the admission of the twin states November 2nd.

***Twirl,** *v.* *Baseball*. +*tr.* and *intr.* To pitch. — **1883** *Chicago Inter-Ocean* 26 June 2/2 Shaw, the Detroit's Eastern acquisition, twirled the sphere with his left hand to excellent purpose. **1921** *N.Y. Times* 2 Oct. IX. 1/1 No Homers for Ruth, but he Twirls a Little.

Twirler. {1808–} *Baseball*. +A pitcher. — **1883** *Sporting Life* 15 April 2 (E. J. Nichols). **1887** *Courier-Journal* 20 Feb. 9/1 He says the new pitching rules are a failure, and will kill all twirlers. **1890** H. PALMER *Stories Base Ball Field* 45 All have been great twirlers in their day. **1917** MATHEWSON *Second Base Sloan* 225 'Red'... was working out near by in company with three other twirlers and two catchers.

***Twirling.** *Baseball*. +Pitching. — **1898** *Outing* June 308/2 Miller continues to do effective twirling for Michigan.

***Twist,** *n.*

+**1.** Tobacco formed into a thick rope; a rope *of* tobacco. {1818–} Also attrib.

1748 WEISER *Journal* 32, I made a Present to the old Shawonese Chief... [of] a large twist of Tobacco. **1753** WASHINGTON *Diaries* I. 46, I gave him a String of Wampum, and a twist of Tobacco. **1804** CLARK in *Lewis & C. Exped.* I. (1904) 172 The Chief on board askd. for a twist of Tobacco. **1833** *Sketches D. Crockett* 74, I pulls my twist out of t'other pocket and gives him a chaw. **1862** *Statutes at Large* XII. 463 On tobacco, cavendish, plug, twist, fine cut, and manufactured of all descriptions... [there shall be a tax of] thirty cents per pound. **1900** *Dept. Agric. Yrbk. 1899* 430 This leaf... is particularly well adapted to plug fillers and plug and twist wrappers. **1925** TILGHMAN *Dugout* 32 Ballard was shredding up several huge bunches of tobacco twist, into their large bean kettle.

***2.** Thread formed by twisting two or more filaments together.

1759 *Newport Mercury* 26 June 4/3 Imported... and to be sold by Jacob Richardson,... Silk and Hair Buttons and Silk Twist. **1861** STOWE *Pearl Orr's Island* I. 37 Roxy says she never see nothin' so rotten as that 'ere twist we 'v' been a-workin' with. **1896** *Godey's Mag.* Feb. 222/2 The cost of findings for a waist... [including] twist, $2.09.

+**3.** A place at which a stream bends or curves.

1792 in *Amer. Speech* XV. 406/1 Crossing said Creek twist. **1819** *Ib.*, Crossing the river twist to a white Oak and dogwood.

b. A curve in the configuration of rough country.

1909 WASON *Happy Hawkins* 36, I reckon they'll bring 'em around the twist an' down this cañon.

4. The twisted end of an early form of cartridge.

1835 LONGSTREET *Ga. Scenes* 160 Handle cartridge!... You done it wrong end foremost, as if you took the cartridge out of your mouth, and bit off the twist with the cartridge box.

5. A piece of paper twisted into a spill to serve as a fire lighter.

1874 B. F. TAYLOR *World on Wheels* 202 Ticket 104,163 was worth—well—about a twist for a cigar-lighter!

6. In phrases. **a.** *The whole twist and tucking*, the whole kit and caboodle. **b.** *A twist on the shorts*, exaction of a high price for stock or commodities sold short.

(a) 1835 LONGSTREET *Ga. Scenes* 124 Then the whole twist and tucking of you grab away, as you come under. **(b) 1870** MEDBERY *Men Wall St.* 138 Twist on the shorts. A clique phrase used where the shorts have undersold heavily, and the market has been artificially raised, compelling them to settle at ruinous rates. **1885** *Harper's Mag.* Nov. 842/1 He groans lustily when the bulls get a 'twist on the shorts' by artificially raising prices, and 'squeezing,' or compelling the bears to settle at ruinous rates.

***Twist,** *v.* +**1.** *Twist me*, a mild imprecation. **2.** *To twist the tail of*, to get the better of; to annoy. — **(1) 1834** CARRUTHERS *Kentuckian* I. 29 Twist me, if I didn't feel as if I was about to be nicked. **(2) 1902** 'O. HENRY' *Roads of Destiny* 259 [He] twisted the tail of a Connecticut insurance company that was trying to do business contrary to the edicts of the great Lone Star State.

+**Twist bud.** A variety of tobacco. — **1800** BOUCHER *Glossary* p. l, In *twist-bud, thick-joint, bull-face, leather-coat*, I'd toil all day.

***Twisted,** *a.*

1. (See quotation.)

1776 FITHIAN *Journal* II. 165 In the next Congregation... all domestic affairs seem 'twisted'; this is a new phrase for female sluttery.

2. In the specific names of plants.

1833 EATON *Botany* (ed. 6) 391 *Viola amoena*, twisted violet.... Moist woods. Flowers odorous. **1817–8** — *Botany* (1822) 513 *Viola obliqua*, twisted-wing violet.... Flowers with purple and yellow veins. **1820** in Morse *Rep. Indian Affairs* II. 34 'Twisted wood'... resembles the bitter sweet,... and is sweet and palatable, when boiled.

Twisted (branched) pine. {1866} +A pine of the Pacific coast (*Pinus contorta*); the shore pine. — **1869** *Amer. Naturalist* III. 409 Twisted Pine (*Pinus contorta*). I first met with this pine at the last base of Mullan's Pass. **1892** APGAR *Trees Northern U.S.* 177 Twisted-branched Pine... has an irregular shape, and crooked branches. **1897** SUDWORTH *Arborescent Flora* 23.

+**Twisted stalk.** A plant of the genus *Streptopus*, having a slightly twisted stem, or an orchid of the genus *Spiranthes*. — **1857** GRAY *Botany* 474 Twisted-Stalk.... S[*treptopus*] *amplexifolius*.... Cold and moist woods, Northern New England. **1890** *Harper's Mag.* April 709/2 The twisted-stalk hangs its rosy cups. **1894** *Amer. Folk-Lore* VII. 101 *Spiranthes gracilis*, twisted stalk, West Va.

***Twister.**
1. a. *Bowling.* A ball delivered with English. +**b.** *Baseball.* A pitcher; a curved ball. **c.** *Football.* A punt with English on it. Used attrib.
(a) **1858** *S. Lit. Messenger* XXVII. 351/1 'Twisters' he rarely indulged in; but sent his ball with the force of a catapult, and the certainty of an arrow ... straight to the left quarter of the Centre-Pin. (b) **1887** *Courier-Journal* 20 Feb. 9/1 Stearns wants to trade Corkhill for the big twister. **1888** *Reach's Base Ball Guide*, [Charles Getzein] pitched his puzzling twisters and curves in the Northwestern League. (c) **1895** WILLIAMS *Princeton Stories* 186 But just then the 'varsity full-back made a long 'twister' punt.
2. A device by means of which a part of the body may be painfully twisted.
1892 *Columbus Dispatch* 24 May, One of the highwaymen ... confessed his guilt after being tortured with 'twisters' and hot coals.
+**3.** A tornado. *colloq.*
1897 *Strand Mag.* Sept. 266/1 Kansas ... is a favourite spot of the 'twisters,' as the Westerners playfully term their windy enemy. **1902** W. M. DAVIS *Elem. Phys. Geog.* (Th. S.), Violent local storms ... are often called cyclones, or prairie twisters, in the Mississippi Valley.

+**Twistical,** *a.* Twisted, crooked, tortuous. *literary and fig.* {1890 (Jas. Hogg in *Harper's Mag.* Feb. 449/1)} — **1806** FESSENDEN *Democracy Unveiled* II. 114 Certain sages, learn'd and *twistical*, ... Have prov'd what's wonderful. **1824** R. B. PEAKE *Americans Abroad* 1 You are but an underlin', tho' you are so uppish and twistical. **1835** *Jamestown* (N.Y.) *Jrnl.* 26 Aug. 1/5 Quakers [are] ... right in everything, except politics—there, always twistical. **1855** 'P. PAXTON' *Capt. Priest* 233 He was rather twistical or so.

+**Twistified,** *a.* =TWISTICAL *a.* {twistification, 1835} — **1835** BIRD *Hawks* I. 254 The path is astonishing twistified, and not fit for horse. **1872** *Newton Kansan* 17 Oct. 4/3 [The Republicans] repudiate his twistified explanations now.

+**Twistify,** *v. tr.* To twist or curve. Also *vbl. n.* used attrib. — **1843** STEPHENS *High Life N.Y.* I. 148 There was the fat nigger a twistifying his whip-lash round the horses' heads. *Ib.* II. 22, I stopped to twistify my dicky down a trifle. **1845** *Cincinnati Misc.* 167, I knew ... an individual in Western Pennsylvania, who possessed this twistifying talent in high perfection.

Twisting machine. A machine which twists strands of fiber into rope or cord. — **1815** DRAKE *Cincinnati* 143 Twisting machines and cotton gins, have been made. **1891** *Cent.* 6556/3 *Twisting-machine*, a machine for twisting rope and cordage; a rope-machine.

***Twit,** *v.* +*To twit on facts*, to taunt or tease with charges based on fact. — **1867** F. H. LUDLOW *Little Brother* 268 You've no idea, Uncle Teddy, that you're twitting on facts; but you hit the truth there. **1905** CROTHERS *Pardoner's Wallet* 127 In the work of creating a condition of peace and good will among men the Christian nations have not gone very far. But why twit on facts?

***Twitch,** *v. Lumbering.* + *tr.* (See quots. 1848, 1905.) — **1838** HALIBURTON *Clockmaker* 2 Ser. xiii. 187 He is a giant ... and can twitch a mill-log as easy as a yoke of oxen can. **1848** BARTLETT 367 *To twitch*, to draw timber along the ground by a chain. Used by lumbermen in Maine. **1905** *Forestry Bureau Bul.* No. 61, 41 *Skid*, ... to draw logs from the stump to the skidway, landing, or mill. ... Syn.: snake, twitch.

Twitch grass. =COUCH GRASS. {1707–} Also attrib. and fig. — **1690** *Waterbury Prop. Rec.* 28 Up the brooke above twich gras medow. **1790** DEANE *New-Eng. Farmer* 230/2 *Quitch-Grass*, called also Witch-Grass, Twitch-Grass ... , a most obstinate and troublesome weed. *a*1861 WINTHROP *J. Brent* 243 Daughters ought to stick closer 'n twitch-grass to their fathers, and sons to their mothers. *c*1870 CHIPMAN *Notes on Bartlett* 38. **1871** *Harper's Mag.* July 295 That jungle is a twitch-grass—a Canada thistle.

+**Twitteration.** Twitter. *humorous.* — **1840** HALIBURTON *Clockmaker* 3 Ser. iii, When they struck up our blood-stirrin' national air, it made me feel all over in a twitteration. **1843** STEPHENS *High Life N.Y.* I. 242 'Oh, say only jest one thing more, and I shall be ez happy ...' sez he, all in a twitteration.

***Two,** *a.* (See also FORWARD TWO.)
No two ways about it, (see WAY).
I. *absol.* +**1.** A two-year old beef.
1890 *Stock Grower & Farmer* 19 April 4/4 Maisch & Driscoll ... deliver at this point 2,000 head of twos, and as many threes as they find.
2. *In two twos*, in a brief time; quickly. {1882}
1838 HALIBURTON *Clockmaker* 2 Ser. xiv. 211 The press can lash us up to a fury here in two twos any day. **1844** 'UNCLE SAM' *Peculiarities* II. 74 I outs with my brushes, begs a stout shingle, and paints the colt's portrait in two twos.
+**3.** For *two*, very, extremely.
1890 CUSTER *Following Guidon* 121, I took hold of his chain and yanked him down, and Dixie was 'mad with me for two.'

II. In combination. **4.** With nouns to form attributive nouns.
1743 *Md. Hist. Mag.* XX. 371 Inch & ½ & two Inch Rope a whole Coil of each. **1760** *Essex Inst. Coll.* XLVI. 254 To be sold. ... A Two-Mast Boat. **1782** CRÈVECŒUR *Letters* 204 A species of what we call here the two-thorn acacia ... yields the most valuable timber we have. **1814** *Niles' Reg.* V. 330/1 A penny biscuit and a 2 copper candle. **1839** KIRKLAND *New Home* 289 Miss Arethusa was a strapping damsel, in a 'two-blues' calico, and a buff gingham cape. **1848** RUXTON *Life Far West* i, He'd a nor-west capote on, and a two-shoot gun rifled. **1856** OLMSTED *Slave States* 43 Turn it under, as soon as possible after the sowers, with a 'two-shovel plow' (a sort of large two-shared cultivator). **1876** BOURKE *Journal* 28 July–8 Sept., Our Indians said it was called 'two days' grass because if a tired, hungry pony got a belly-full of it, he would be able to keep up two (2) days longer. **1897** MOORE *How To Build a Home* 12 They should be constructed of ... 'two-man' stone (requiring two men to handle it). **1903** LEWIS *Boss* 42 We stopped before a grocery. It was a two-store front, and of a prosperous look. **1910** BOSTWICK *Amer. Pub. Library* 41 The allowance of two books, known as the 'two-book system,' originated in an effort to stimulate the circulation of nonfiction. **1913** MULFORD *Coming of Cassidy* 90 Longhorn ... was being shot to pieces by a two-gun man.

5. With nouns to form compound nouns.
1844 *Knickerb.* XXIII. 51 The signal would be the report of a two-pounder which the captain carried on his quarter-deck. **1873** *Harper's Mag.* March 639, I had loaded the two-shooter as soon as I got it. **1879** TOURGEE *Fool's Errand* 33 An old family ... had erected the usual double log-house (or 'two-decks-and-a-passage,' as it is still called). **1891** WELCH *Recoll.* 1830–40 376 At the balls and parties the popular figures in dancing, were the 'Contra Dances,' viz.... 'Two Sisters,' 'Hulls' Victory.' **1892** *Harper's Mag.* Jan. 268/2 The worn 'two-ply' in the centre of the well-scrubbed boards gave a hint of comfortable color underfoot. **1904** *N.Y. Tribune* 27 March 1 Summoned by the dreaded 'two nines,' the signal used only in extreme need, every fireman and every piece of apparatus available fought for hours yesterday an ugly blaze. **1905** *Forestry Bureau Bul.* No. 61, 42 *Logging sled*, the heavy double sled used to haul logs from the skidway or yard to the landing. (N[orthern] F[orest]). Syn.: twin sleds, two sleds, wagon sled.

6. With other numerals to make attributive nouns.
1865 *Atlantic Mo.* May 636/1 Six two-hundred pounders and seventeen one hundred-pounders were burst during the siege of Charleston. **1868** WOODRUFF *Trotting Horse* 41, I find that a three-minute trotter in England is about as scarce an article as a two-thirty horse is here. **1903** ADAMS *Log of Cowboy* 237 He was certain it was better than a two-ten clip.
b. With *by.* (Cf. TWO-BY-FOUR.)
1893 *Congress. Rec.* 13 Dec. 211/1 Men call him a crank, and all the little two by seven newspapers and all the little two by nine politicians in the country jump onto him. **1911** HARRISON *Queed* 236 This little two-by-twice grammar school ... tries to pass itself off for a college.
7. With adjectives in -*ed*.
1760 WASHINGTON *Diaries* I. 135 Fitted a two Eyed Plow Instead of a Duck Bill Plow. **1812** *Niles' Reg.* II. 408/1 Sixty dollars for the best two toothed ram lamb of the fine wooled breed. **1832** TROLLOPE *Domestic Manners* I. 54 We saw ... a brick church, which, from its two little peaked spires, is called the two-horned church. **1849** CHEEVER *Whale & His Captors* 85 The mincer, with a two-handled knife, slashes it nearly through into thin slices, which just hang together. **1854** CUMMINGS *Lamplighter* iii, A small and very narrow yard ... stretched along the whole length of a decent two-storied house. **1862** *Ill. Agric. Soc. Trans.* V. 692 Many men ... are compelled to make ... 'Shanghai' or 'Bloomer' fences (two-boarded fences). **1890** HOWELLS *Boy's Town* 83 Two-cornered cat was played by four boys: two to bat, and two behind the batters to catch and pitch. **1891** in B. S. Heath *Labor & Finance Revol.* p. xl, We traveled in our own conveyance, which consisted of a two-seated carriage and a spirited team of handsome bays.
b. In the specific names of plants and insects.
1889 VASEY *Agric. Grasses* 28 Two-edged Panic Grass ... frequently occurs in neglected and poor land in sufficient quantity to afford considerable grazing for stock. **1843** TORREY *Flora N.Y.* I. 295 Two-flowered Linnaea, or Twin-flower. ... Common in the northern and western counties. **1847** DARLINGTON *Weeds & Plants* 393 *Distichous Hordeum*. Two-rowed Barley. ... This species ... is preferred by many farmers in Pennsylvania. **1892** KELLOGG *Kansas Insects* 42 Two-striped locust ... [has] 'two lateral, yellowish stripes from the head to the extremities of the wing-covers.'

+**Two-bagger.** *Baseball.* =next. — **1881** *N.Y. Herald* 13 July 9/3 Schenck ... scored on a two-bagger by Reipslaugher. **1887** *Courier-Journal* 27 May 2/4 Both Wolf and Cross lined out splendid two-baggers when the bases were crowded. **1922** SANDBURG *Slabs Sunburnt West* 75 They begin the game, they knock it for home runs and two-baggers; the pitcher puts it across.

+**Two-base hit.** *Baseball.* A hit which enables the batter to reach second base safely. — **1874** *N.Y. Sun* 24 July (E. J. Nichols). **1880** N. BROOKS *Fairport Nine* 184 Ned made a fine two base hit which brought Watson home amidst great excitement. **1910** *Spalding's Base Ball Guide* 383 The Summary shall contain: ... The number of two-base hits, if any, made by each player.

+Two-baser. Baseball. =prec. — **1874** Chicago Inter-Ocean 14 July 5/1 [He] was credited with four base hits, including one two-baser. **1875** Chicago Tribune 24 Aug. 5/6 Hines followed with a clean two-baser, bringing both Warren and Glen home.

+Two bits. pl.
1. Twenty-five cents. colloq. (Cf. BIT n. 3, FOUR BITS.)
1730 COMER Diary (1893) 117, I saw peach trees in ye blossom and many delightful varieties. Cost me two bitts. **1846** FARNHAM Prairie Land 97 Two bits ain't much anyhow. **1866** W. REID After the War 489 Some wanted a pound or two of sugar; others a paper of needles or a bar of soap, or 'two bits worth o' candy.' **1890** Stock Grower & Farmer 1 Feb. 4/4 We would abolish gambling in futures, if we had to tax to the tune of 'two-bits,' every bushel of grain sold in that way. **1907** LONDON Road 28 I wonder if that beautiful young Frenchwoman would remember . . . the laugh I gave her when I uttered the barbaric phrase, 'two-bits.'
2. Attrib., usually in sing., with cigar, club, country, etc.
1802 DRAYTON S. Carolina 215 Hence the origin of this society; which, from the contributions, being a sum of money called two bitts, became known by the appellation of the two bitt club. **1873** Harper's Mag. May 799 Thompson's Two-bit House, Front St., bet. Main and Madison. **1875** Scribner's Mo. July 274/2 There are two classes of saloons where these midday repasts are furnished—'two bit' places and 'one bit' places. **1877** W. WRIGHT Big Bonanza 360 A man one day sauntered into a two-bit saloon and called for a drink of whiskey. **1884** NYE Baled Hay 9 A little two-bit novelette that has never been published. **1901** WHITE Westerners 281 The two . . . passed over brimming little glasses of 'forty rod' and jingled two-bit pieces into the drawer. **1902** LORIMER Lett. Merchant 197 Smoked two-bit cigars and wore a plug hat. **1904** N.Y. Ev. Post 12 Feb. 5 Out in the 'two-bits' country, on the other side of the Rocky Mountains, it is still possible to pass Confederate paper money if the swindler goes about in a cool, nonchalant way.

Two-bushel (corn-)basket. A basket which can hold two bushels. — **1739** Boston Selectmen 227 The Country People's Selling coal in Baskets commonly called Two Bushel Baskets . . . is not only Contrary to Law, but also the said Baskets are Seldom found to Contain two Bushels. **1852** Knickerb. XXXIX. 203 There is the big two-bushel corn-basket of chips.

+Two-by-four. 1. A board measuring two inches by four. **2.** Attrib. in sense: Of trifling size. — (1) **1884** NYE Baled Hay 23 The managing editor of the mill lays out the log in his mind, and works it into dimension stuff, shingle bolts, slabs, edgings, two by fours. **1916** 'BOWER' Phantom Herd 77 The whole row of shack-houses . . . had no backs; bald behind as board fences, save where two-by-fours braced them from falling. (2) **1897** 'THANET' Missionary Sheriff 13 'That how she makes a living?' 'Yes—little two-by-four bakery.' **1900** Congress. Rec. 14 Feb. 1804/2 No small-bore, two-by-four, radical politicians can hurt that great court. **1917** McCUTCHEON Green Fancy 45 You'd be surprised to know how many great generals we have running two by four farms.

+Two-cent. attrib. Sold for two cents; of the value of two cents.
1859 WILMER Press Gang 42 The Express was a two-cent cash paper. **1864** Weekly New Mexican 27 May 1/4 The new two cent piece . . . resembles, as much as anything can, a gold coin. **1875** C. F. Wingate Views & Interviews 57 It saw in New York a city of sufficient population to warrant the experiment of a two-cent newspaper. **1883** J. S. DYE Coin Encycl. 1137 No change whatever was made in this coinage down to 1873, when, by act of Congress, the issue of the Two Cent Bronze Piece was discontinued. **1883** RITTENHOUSE Maud 226 To-day the 2-cent stamp-law goes into operation.

+Two-center. A cigar that sells for two cents. — **1834** Boston Post 6 Aug. 2/2 Durant was in the habit of peddling water for rum-traps, and taking his pay in two-centers. **1883** H. J. WARNER New Lett. Idle Man 21 'Two-centers' are really made of tobacco and are not bad.

Two-colored, a. {1648-} In the specific names of trees and plants. — **1813** MUHLENBERG Cat. Plants 96 Two-coloured ash. Ib. 87 Q[uercus] discolor, Two-coloured oak. **1817-8** EATON Botany (1822) 515 Viola bicolor, two coloured violet. . . . Petals white, the lower ones spotted with yellow.

+Two-dollar. attrib. Receiving two dollars; of the value of two dollars; priced at two dollars.
1793 Ann. 2d Congress 788 The miserable two-dollar men who were raised for a six months' service—their fate is too well known. **1830** BRECK Recoll. 102 Two lines of stages were kept up . . . in opposition at a two-dollar fare. **1884** WELLS Practical Economics 211 The Government collected . . . three dollars for every one that was obtained during the last year of the two-dollar tax. **1886** STAPLETON Major's Christmas 216 She examined the two-dollar bill he offered. **1900** NELSON A B C Wall St. 131 Two-Dollar Broker, a member of the Stock Exchange who executes orders for fellow-members for a commission of $2 per hundred shares. **1903** ADE People You Know 110 He wanted to parlee a $2 Silver Certificate and bring home enough to pay the National Debt. **1913** LONDON Valley of Moon 524 'That's the trouble with two-dollar-a-day men.' 'With two-dollar-a-day heads.'

+Two-eyed berry. The partridge berry. — **1832** WILLIAMSON Maine I. 128 Another [plant], called Two-eyed berry, is wild, and its fruit has two dimples, or eyes, and in other respects it resembles a chequerberry.

Two-fisted, a. **a.** Clumsy, awkward. {1859} **+b.** Able to fight with both fists; strong, vigorous. — **1774** FITHIAN Journal I. 223 [He]

appointed a sturdy two fisted Gentleman to open the Ball with Mrs. Tayloe. **1852** STOWE Uncle Tom xvii, Phineas had been a hearty, two-fisted backwoodsman. **1855** I. C. PRAY Mem. J. G. Bennett 104 'Mother,' bawled out a great two-fisted girl one day. **1874** Vermont Bd. Agric. Rep. II. 596 He was, as we say sometimes, a 'great, two-fisted, green, awkward fellow.' **1920** WILSON Somewhere 133 No meal can ever be like breakfast to them that's two-fisted.

Two-forty.
+1. Two minutes and forty seconds, the former trotting record for a mile. Also allusive.
1855 Knickerb. XLV. 634, I commenced, therefore, the process of sliding my legs out from under him—not, to be sure, at a pace of two-forty—but imitating more the speed of the snail. **1856** S. Lit. Messenger XXIII. 455 Then there were the jockies all whirling around At 'two-forty' or less and scarce touching the ground. **1866** GREGG Life in Army 102 Our lieutenant-colonel spurred his fine cream-colored steed, moving forward . . . at the rate of two-forty on a plank road.
b. A horse that attains this speed; a person who moves rapidly.
1856 Harper's Mag. XII. 620/2 He knew men by their horses, and designated them thus—. . . 'The bird that trots the two-forty.' **1866** J. KENNAWAY On Sherman's Track 243 When a lady is inclined to go ahead she is spoken of sometimes as 'a two-forty.'
c. Used adverbially in sense: Very fast.
1904 WALLER Wood-Carver 132 He's going it two-forty a minute.
2. Attrib. with gait, horse, move, etc.
1851 Knickerb. XXXVII. 279 It is only the steam-whistle of the iron-horse on the Hudson River rail-road, rushing into the Great Metropolis, at a 'two-forty' pace. **1855** M. THOMPSON Doesticks 20, I had introduced . . . a team of 'two-forty' reindeers. **1863** 'E. KIRKE' Southern Friends 194 That woman is running him to the devil at a two-forty gait. **1863** NORTON Army Letters 138 Nothing but a 2:40 horse . . . would do me. **1896** Advance 26 March 450/3 Get a two forty move on you, Nags!

Two-headed snake. =DOUBLE-HEADED SNAKE. {t.-h. worm, 1752-} — **1778** CARVER Travels 487 The Two-Headed Snake . . . was found about the year 1762, near Lake Champlain, by Mr. Park, a gentleman of New England. **1789** MORSE Amer. Geog. 61 The Two Headed Snake. Whether this be a distinct species of snakes intended to propagate its kind, or whether it be a monstrous production, is uncertain. **1806** ASHE Travels II. 287 We called the following at least to our attention. Rattle Snake, . . . Two Headed Ditto, Copper Headed Ditto.

+Two-hole-cat. (See TWO-OLD-CAT.)

Two-horse. attrib. Designating plows and vehicles drawn by two horses. {1798-}
1782 CRÈVECŒUR Letters 109, I saw . . . Andrew holding a two-horse plough, and tracing his furrows quite straight. **1829** FLINT George Mason 17 The children . . . were packed . . . into a two-horse wagon. **1837** W. JENKINS Ohio Gaz. 365 Pleasantville is supplied daily by a two horse coach mail. **1850** in Glisan Jrnl. Army Life 44, I was delighted to perceive coming along the road, in a two-horse ambulance, a couple of gentlemen. **1857** Lawrence Republican 28 May 3, I shall send . . . a large assortment . . . of my extra Two Horse Moldboard Breakers. **1872** Atlantic Mo. March 330 The newly married pair started from The Forest . . . in a two-horse chaise. **1875** Chicago Tribune 20 Sept. 8/3 The present cars have seven-eighths of the seating-capacity of the two-horse conductor-car. **1877** JOHNSON Anderson Co., Kansas 98 The mail was carried . . . in a two-horse hack. **1898** PAGE Red Rock 321 A two-horse carriage . . . stood near a fence at some little distance.

Two-horse team. A team consisting of two horses. — **1885** Century Mag. Sept. 762 Thirty wagons also, counting two two-horse or mule teams as one, will be allowed to transport such articles as cannot be carried along. **1920** HOWELLS Vacation of Kelwyns 225 Do you know where Professor Kelwyn could get a two-horse team to move his things over?

Two-leaved, a. {1610-} **1.** In the specific names of trees and plants: Having twin leaves. **2.** Of a table: Having two leaves, i.e., movable boards or planks. — (1) **1785** MARSHALL Amer. Grove 102 Pinus virginiana, Two-leaved Virginian, or Jersey Pine. **1813** MUHLENBERG Cat. Plants 58 Bignonia crucigera, Two-leaved Trumpet-flower. (2) **1850** Rep. Comm. Patents 1849 307 The table may be simultaneously and together turned down . . . so as to cause the table to have the advantages usually possessed by a common two leaved table.

Two-miler. A horse that competes in two-mile races. — **1846** Spirit of Times 18 April 91/1 But talking about 'two milers,' Portsmouth was certainly the best of modern times.

+Two-old-cat. Also two-hole-cat. A ball game in which there are two batters. (Cf. ONE-OLD-CAT.) — **1850** Knickerb. XXXV. 84 [We] never indulged in a game of chance of any sort in the world, save the 'baseball,' 'one' and 'two-hole-cat,' and 'barn-ball' of our boyhood. **1906** Harper's Mag. Oct. 779, I recalled a certain game of two-old-cat that I had played one July day years ago in the open lot at home.

+Two (pipe) scatter (shot)gun. A double-barrelled shotgun. (Cf. SCATTER GUN.) — **1886** Milnor (Dak.) Teller June, Guess I'll go for the galoot with the two-scatter shotgun. **1889** FARMER 544/2 Two Pipe Scatter Gun.

Two-pole chain. A measuring chain two poles or rods long. — **1790** Penna. Packet 10 May 4/3 John Sparhawk . . . Has For Sale . . . two-pole chains. **1800** ELLICOTT Journal App. 48 [We had] two two-pole chains of the common construction.

Two-seater. {1906–} A vehicle having two seats for passengers. — **1891** BUNNER *Zadoc Pine* 172, I climbed into his 'two-seater,' and sat behind, talking to Mrs. Tom.

Two-Seed. *ellipt.* + =next. Used attrib. — **1844** *Indiana Mag. Hist.* XXII. 407, I promised to try to shew that the two seed doctrine was a hethan [*sic*] opinion. **1872** MORRELL *Flowers & Fruits* 72 There was an organization of some ten or twelve members . . . under the pastoral care of Daniel Parker, of 'two-seed' notoriety.

+**Two-Seed Baptist.** A Seed Baptist (q.v. under SEED 7). Also *Two-Seed-in-the-Spirit Predestinarian Baptist.* — **1893** *Census Bul.* No. 375, 38 The Old Two-Seed-in-the-Spirit Predestinarian Baptists . . . are not in fellowship with the Regular or Missionary, nor with the Primitive or any other body of Baptists. *Ib.* 39 Many of the Two-Seed Baptists are strongly opposed to a paid ministry. **1919** *Census: Religious Bodies 1916* II. 151/2 In their church government the Two-Seed Baptists are thoroughly independent.

Two-spot. +**1.** A two of any suit of cards. **2.** An insignificant person. *colloq.*² **3.** A two-year prison term. *colloq.*² +**4.** A two-dollar bill. *colloq.* — (1) **1885** *Narragansett Hist. Reg.* III. 213 We were shown a play-card, the two-spot of clubs. **1897** GUNTER *Don Balasco* vii Señor Balasco builds up in his vivid imagination a palace of cards that will someday fall down and crush him as fatally as if each two-spot were a great marble column. (2) **1896** ADE *Artie* 50 You're nothin' but a two-spot. (3) **1901** FLYNT *World of Graft* 184 They convicted me at last and I got a two-spot. (4) **1904** 'O. HENRY' *Roads of Destiny* 305 We get the heelers out with the crackly two-spots, and coal-tickets.

Two-step. A ballroom dance having a sliding step in 2/4 or march time; a musical composition to which this dance is performed. {1900–} — *c*1895 NORRIS *Vandover* (1914) 191 Almost every number was a waltz or a two-step, the music being the . . . popular airs of the day set to dance music. **1899** CHESNUTT *Wife of His Youth* 25 The pianist had struck up a lively two step. **1912** NICHOLSON *Hoosier Chron.* 427 The newest two-step struck up.

Two-story. *attrib.* Designating buildings having two floors or stories. {1880–}
1796 *Aurora* (Phil.) 15 April (Th.), That certain one-story Frame shop in front, and Two Story Frame messuage. **1803** *Steele P.* I. 395 A tolerable two Story House with the Frames now ready to put up. **1837** MARTINEAU *Society* II. 252 A dozen artisans of one town . . . [are] rearing each a comfortable one (or, as the Americans would say, two-story) house. *a*1862 THOREAU *Maine Woods* 162 His house was a two-story white one with blinds. **1883** 'MARK TWAIN' *Life on Miss.* xxxviii, It is easy to describe it: . . . big, square, two-story frame house, painted white. *a*1918 G. STUART *On Frontier* I. 56 We stopped at a large two-story hotel.

b. *transf.* Designating other objects having an appearance similar to that of a two-story building.
1828 *Yankee* July 227/1 A motherly quantity of lusty pumpkin and coalpit or two-story apple platter pies are provided. **1834** CARRUTHERS *Kentuckian* I. 19 He wore a large two-story hat. **1866** RICHARDSON *Secret Service* 38 We took a two-story car of the Baronne street railway. **1882** SWEET & KNOX *Texas Siftings* 10 He has a two story iron-bound trunk . . . which he checks through to the next town.

Two-thirds rule. +A rule, enforced in national conventions since 1832 but now abolished, requiring a candidate to secure two thirds of the delegates' votes at a Democratic convention for nomination. — **1868** *N.Y. Herald* 10 July 6/3 The two-thirds rule is a beauty. **1882** *Nation* 27 July 63/1 The Georgia Democrats, in their State Convention, on the 19th inst., abandoned the 'time-honored' two-thirds rule. **1911** WILSON in R. S. Baker *Woodrow Wilson* III. 299, I feel very strongly that the two-thirds rule is a most undemocratic regulation, and puts us at a particular disadvantage as compared with the Republicans.

Tycoon. {1863–} +One who occupies a dominant position in politics, business, etc. Also *humorous.* — **1861** HAY *Lincoln & Civil War* 12 Gen. Butler has sent an imploring request to the President to be allowed to bag the whole nest of traitorous Maryland legislators. This the Tycoon . . . forbade. **1861** *N.Y. Tribune* 19 Oct. 4/3 No Tammany candidate has a shadow of a chance for election unless he has the Tycoon's indorsement. **1886** *Outing* IX. 164/1 The tycoon of the baggage car objected to handling the boat.

+**Tyee (salmon).** [Chinook jargon.] =CHINOOK SALMON. — **1881** *Amer. Naturalist* XV. 177 As vernacular names of definite application, the following are on record: Quinnat—Sacramento salmon, tyee salmon. **1902** JORDAN & EVERMANN *Amer. Food Fishes* 151 Chinook Salmon. . . . Other names by which this fish is known are quinnat salmon, . . . tyee, tchaviche, and tschawytscha.

+**Tyler grippe.** A form of influenza that was widespread about the time John Tyler became president in 1841. *Obs.* Also *fig.* — **1845** *Xenia Torch-Light* 23 Oct. 2/1 Mr. A. died of the Tyler-grip, and, politically speaking, has gone to decay. **1858** *Santa Fe Gazette* 22 May 2/3 For a week past an epidemic similar in its symptoms to what was known in the States some years ago as the 'Tyler Grippe' has prevailed in this city. **1891** WELCH *Recoll. 1830–40* 35 That severe and virulent form of Influenza, which appeared soon after the elevation of John Tyler to the Presidency, when he abandoned his party platform and principles, . . . was named in grim satire, the Tyler Grippe.

+**Tylerism.** [John *Tyler* (1790–1862).] The political practices and methods of President Tyler; the followers or supporters of President Tyler. *Obs.* — **1844** *Lexington Observer* 9 Oct. 2/4 The Transfer of Tylerism.—The rumor . . . that Mr. Tyler . . . was to have a foreign appoint-

ment . . . as a consideration for his transfer of the Tyler party to the cause of Polk and Dallas. **1859** WILMER *Press Gang* 46 When the presidential election came off, . . . the *Philadelphia Evening Mercury*, and all the other organs of Tylerism found it necessary to change their tune.

+**Tylerize,** *v. intr.* To forsake the party or side to which one owes office or allegiance as President Tyler did. *Obs.* Also *ppl. a.* — **1865** *Nation* I. 227 The Democratic party . . . might either assail and unseat the Administration, or else persuade the Executive to 'Tylerize.' **1866** 'F. KIRKLAND' *Bk. Anecdotes* 601 His enemies hinted that he had gone over to the enemy—in fact, been Tylerized.

＊**Tympanites, -is.** + =BLOATING *vbl. n.* — **1890** *Stock Grower & Farmer* 22 Feb. 6/2 Acute Tympanitis . . . occurs very rarely among cattle grazed on the range country. **1913** BARNES *Western Grazing Grounds* 286 There are but three diseases among western range cattle which can be considered general: Big jaw (actinomycosis), bloating (tympanites) and black-leg.

＊**Type.**

1. A small block of metal having at one end a raised letter, figure, etc., for use in printing. {1713–} Also collective.
1771 FRANKLIN *Autobiog.* 273, I was to take with me . . . the letter of credit to furnish me with the necessary money for purchasing the press and types. **1846** LYELL *Second Visit* II. 336 [Harper's] manufacture their own types and paper. **1852** *Perrin Ky. Pioneer Press* 28 The click of his rifle is succeeded by that of his types. **1876** INGRAM *Centennial Exp.* 298 The radiating arms vary in thickness and are bevelled at the part where the type are fixed. **1902** DE VINNE *Practice of Typography* 107 Large types need thick leads; small types, thin leads.

‖**b.** *To put the types on,* (see quotation).
1849 WILLIS *Rural Lett.* 94 'To put the types on to' a man, is to send the constable to him with a printed warrant.

2. *attrib.* and *comb.* **a.** In sense 1 with *distributing, foundry.* **b.** With reference to the parts or the work of a typewriter.
1809 JEFFERSON *Writings* XII. 295 The foundation of printing . . . is the type-foundry. **1876** KNIGHT 2676/1 Type-distributing machines have frequently been invented as companion machines to those for composing. **1886** *Science* 17 Sept. 252/2 The type-bar of a type-writer is connected with its key. **1893** *Nation* 6 July 10/3 Writing . . . concerning a typewritten document . . . , I half apologetically used the word typescript.

Type-casting machine. A machine that casts type. Also *type-casting and setting machine.* — **1864** NICHOLS *Amer. Life* I. 381 By the use of type-casting machines a workman can cast ninety brevier types a minute. **1876** KNIGHT 2674/1 Type Casting and Setting Machine, one which makes its type from matrixes [etc.]. **1895** *Current History* V. 961 The Lanston Monotype . . . [is] both a type-setting and a type-casting machine.

Type-founder. One who makes type. {1801–} — **1797** WEEMS *Letters* II. 84 A letter was written . . . containing an order on Mr. Baine the Type Founder for some money. **1810** HOWLAND in E. M. Stone *Life J. Howland* 186 Strike the type-founder, the printer and the manufacturers of paper and parchment, out of the system, and what would become of the republic of letters? **1898** *Internat. Typogr. Union Proc.* 53/2 On May 1, 1897, attended open meeting of Chicago typefounders.

Typer. (See quotations.) *colloq.* {1915–} — **1892** *Boston Jrnl.* 27 May 4/7 For 'typewriter' (the machine) say 'typer.' **1909** *Cent. Suppl.* 1393/3 Typer, a type-writer. . . . A person who uses a type-writer.

Typesetter. One who sets type; a compositor. {1867–} — **1833** *Niles' Reg.* XLIV. 375/2 The legislature of Georgia have passed a law, forbidding the employment of any slave or free person of color, as a compositor, (type setter) in any printing office in that state. **1868** *Ore. State Jrnl.* 21 Nov. 1/5 The old type setters of the office prefer his manuscript above that of any other editor. **1900** *Congress. Rec.* 18 Jan. 963/1, I have always been friendly . . . to the typesetters' union.

Typesetting. The setting of type preparatory to printing. {1867–} Also attrib. — **1857** *Quinland* I. 99 [He] practised type-setting for three months. **1865** *Atlantic Mo.* May 616/2 They were taught the truly feminine, . . . as well as intellectual art, of type-setting. **1896** *Internat. Typogr. Union Proc.* 43/2 The piece system applied to typesetting, especially on machine work, has a tendency to cause men to overwork. **1899** HALE *Lowell & His Friends* 178 There entered the foreman of the type-setting-room.

Typesetting machine. A machine that sets type for printing. {1888–} — **1864** NICHOLS *Amer. Life* I. 265 There are type-setting machines. **1896** *Internat. Typogr. Union Proc.* 27/1 The rapid introduction of typesetting machines . . . has proved a constant menace to the stability of our organizations. **1909** *Scientific Amer.* 26 June 482/1 Nearly everyone is . . . familiar with the type-setting machines that are in daily use in our large newspaper and printing offices.

+**Type-sticker.** A compositor or typesetter. *colloq.* — **1842** GREELEY in *Corr. R. W. Griswold* (1898) 105 You will keep [this lecture] out of the dirty hands of all type-stickers, for the present. **1873** *Newton Kansan* 16 Jan. 2/1 He soon became an expert type-sticker. **1896** *Typographical Jrnl.* IX. 298 Charley was a 'type-sticker.'

Typewriter.

+**1.** A machine for writing by means of type characters similar to those of printers. {1899–}
1876 KNIGHT 2677/1 The Sholes type-writer has attained more popularity than any with which the writer is acquainted. **1885** HOWELLS *Silas*

Lapham 478 He's got me a typewriter, so that I can help myself a little. **1923** DUTTON *Shadow on Glass* 76 The only thing that seemed to have caused it was the typewriter.

2. A typist. {1887–}

1884 *N.Y. Herald* 27 Oct. 7/2 Situation Wanted—By Lady, Rapid Stenographer, and typewriter. **1893** 'THANET' *Stories* 135 Tilly Louder came home from the Lossing factory (where she is a typewriter). **1902** WISTER *Virginian* 93 The day of women typewriters had as yet scarcely begun to dawn.

3. Attrib. and comb. with *brush, cabinet, copy, girl.*

1884 HOWELLS *Silas Lapham* 24, I want you should put these in shape, and give me a type-writer copy to-morrow. *Ib.* 293 The type-writer girl had lingered. **1902** BANKS *Newspaper Girl* 155, I took my typewriter brush out, as though to wash it in the kitchen sink. **1918** M. B. OWEN *Typewriting Speed* 115 The typewriter cabinet is one of the things that should receive attention.

+**Typewriting machine.** A typewriter. — **1881** *X-Y-Z Guide* (N.Y.) Oct. 161 For sale . . . a type writing machine. **1890** *Stock Grower & Farmer* 22 March 6/2 The squeals of hogs . . . were drowned by the rumble of Barbour's type-writing machine. **1902** BANKS *Newspaper Girl* 8, I would be bidden . . . to return and write on my typewriting machine all about the things I had seen and heard.

+**Typo.** A typographer or printer. *colloq.* {1880–} — **1816** *Mass. Spy* 7 Aug. (Th.), [Printers] will confer a favour on a brother typo [by publishing an advertisement of a runaway apprentice]. **1844** *Gem of Prairie* 29 June, Mr. Hough, being, by profession, a brother *typo*, we feel under some obligations to give him 'a puff.' **1872** *Chicago Tribune* 21 Oct. 7/3 Governor Warmouth . . . became a typo in the St. Louis *Republican* office. **1901** DUNCAN & SCOTT *Allen & Woodson Co., Kansas* 614 He had begun his life here as a typo on the *Advertiser.*

Tyrant.** + =next. Also *tyrant king bird.* — *c1730** CATESBY *Carolina* I. 55 The Tyrant . . . pursues and puts to flight all kinds of Birds that come near his station. **1789** MORSE *Amer. Geog.* 60 The Hangbird. . . . Turkey. Wild Turkey. Tyrant. **1852** MITCHELL *Dream Life* 116 A tyrant king-bird . . . dashes down assassin-like, upon some home-bound, honey-laden bee.

Tyrant flycatcher. Any one of various flycatchers of the family Tyrannidae. {1783–, in Amer.} — **1810** WILSON *Ornithology* II. 66 [The] Tyrant Flycatcher . . . is the *Field Martin* of Maryland and some of the southern states, and the *King-bird* of Pennsylvania and several of the northern districts. **1869** *Rep. Comm. Agric. 1868* 88 Thirty specimens of this species were taken from the stomach of a king bird, or tyrant flycatcher. **1917** *Birds of Amer.* II. 189 The Tyrant Fly catchers are exclusively American birds.

+**Tyrotoxicon.** (See quot. 1886.) — **1886** *Scientific Amer.* 21 Aug. 112/3 About a year ago, Dr. Victor C. Vaughan, of the University of Michigan, succeeded in isolating from some samples of cheese . . . a highly poisonous ptomaine, which he named tyrotoxicon.

U

+**Uchee.** =EUCHEE. Also attrib. — **1744** MOORE *Voy. Georgia* 145 They had also turned their cattle over the river, some of which had strayed away and eat the Uchee's corn twenty miles above the Ebenezer. **1746** *Georgia Col. Rec.* VI. 170 [They] had petitioned the Trustees to obtain for them a Tract of Land said to belong to the Uchee Indians. **1800** HAWKINS *Sk. Creek Country* 34 Some Uchees have settled with them [the Shawnees]. **1851** DRAKE *Indians N.A.* 16 The *Uchees* are said to speak a primitive language.

Uehre. Variant of EUCHRE *n.*

Ugly. {1755-} +The quality of ugliness. *colloq.* or *dial. Obs.* — **1835** LONGSTREET *Ga. Scenes* 63, I want to get in the breed of them sort o' men to drive ugly out of my kin folks. **1845** HOOPER *Taking Census* (1928) 121 The *ugly's* out on her wuss nor the smallpox!

+**Ulicon.** Also **ulken, ulichan.** Variant of EULACHON. — **1807** GASS *Journal* 187 In the afternoon some of the natives came to visit us, and brought some of the small fish, which they call Ulken. **1849** A. ROSS *Adv. Oregon River* (1904) 108 A small fish resembling the smelt or herring, known by the name of ulichan. **1880** *Lib. Universal Knowl.* I. 205 All the early navigators and explorers . . . have spoken of the immense numbers of salmon, cod, halibut, mullet, ulicon, etc.

***Ulster.** A long, loose overcoat, sometimes girded with a belt. {1878-} Also attrib. — **1879** B. F. TAYLOR *Summer-Savory* 108 Yonder is a man in an Ulster duster. **1894** *Harper's Mag.* Feb. 486/2, I should put on my cap and ulster and go out and stand guard over them! **1922** TARKINGTON *Gentle Julia* 361 Papa's . . . taken his ulster.

Ultra, *a.* {1817-} Extreme. +With reference to persons associated with or to attitudes adopted toward Negro slavery. — **1838** *N.Y. Advertiser & Exp.* 10 March 4/4 Ultra-abolitionism, and many other ultraisms of the day, are merely commented on. **1860** ABBOTT *South & North* 313 We will suppose that the ultra slaveholders of the extreme South . . . resolve to break off from the Union. *a***1882** WEED *Autobiog.* 98 Dr. Backus, an earnest Whig, was no less earnest in his opposition to the ultra 'one-idea abolitionism' of his brother-in-law.

Umbrel(l). Colloq. variant of UMBRELLA. {1857-} — **1816** U. BROWN *Journal* II. 151, [I] never was as wet in my Clothing, through Great Coat umbrell & all. **1835** REED & MATHESON *Visit* I. 75 You shall have a good buffalo and *umbrel,* and nothing will hurt you. **1898** WESTCOTT *D. Harum* ii, I had my old umbrel'—though it didn't hender me f'm gettin' more or less wet.

Umbrella.

1. A device consisting of a collapsible frame covered with a fabric and used as a protection against rain or the sun. {1634-}
1745 E. KIMBER *Itinerant Observer* 13 [The people of Georgia] scorn Umbrellas and Musketto-Nets, as Jamaican and Carolinean Effeminacies. **1796** WELD *Travels* (1800) I. 251 Those that could make it convenient with their business always walked with umbrellas to shade them from the sun. **1830** WATSON *Philadelphia* App. 52 The first umbrellas he ever knew worn, was by the British officers, and were deemed effeminate in them. **1853** FELT *Customs New Eng.* 112 The umbrella was not used much by our ancestors before the peace of independence. **1898** WESTCOTT *D. Harum* vi, He was glad to be spared the discomfort of going about . . . with hand-bag, overcoat, and umbrella. **1922** TARKINGTON *Gentle Julia* 100 Passing by an umbrella which stood in a corner, [he] went out.

+**2.** Short for UMBRELLA TREE.
1775 BURNABY *Travels* 12 They are likewise adorned and beautified with . . . flowering poplars, umbrellas, magnolias. **1801** *Hist. Review & Directory* I. 147.

3. Attrib. and comb. with *bonnet, manufacturer,* etc.
1781 *Salem Gazette* 3 July, He makes and mends Umbrella Sticks in the best Manner. **1795** *Boston Gaz.* 7 Sept. 3/3 John Foley's Umbrella & Oil-Cloth Manufactory. **1830** ROYALL *Southern Tour* I. 36 These silly women, . . . when the Convention was about to meet, fabricated these large umbrella bonnets, which they named Convention-bonnets. **1842** *Niles' Nat. Reg.* 14 May 174/2 Mr. Buchanan presented a petition of the umbrella manufacturers of Philadelphia. **1877** HOWELLS *Out of Question* 44 Yonder goes an umbrella-mender. **1902** HARBEN *A. Daniel* 9 As fer them umbrella-pans to ketch the drip [on a hat-rack], he said they was fancy spit-boxes.

b. In the names of plants and trees whose leaves or foliage suggest an umbrella. {1798-}
1784 *Amer. Academy Mem.* I. 423 Dogsbane: Umbrella Weed. Blossoms white, striped with red. Borders of woodland. **1817-8** EATON *Botany* (1822) 478 *Splachnum ampullaceum,* umbrella moss. **1846** BROWNE *Trees Amer.* 10 The Umbrella Magnolia. . . . The leaves are eighteen or

twenty inches long. **1897** SUDWORTH *Arborescent Flora* 270 *Melia azedarach umbraculifera,* Umbrella China-tree.

Umbrella grass. {1884-} +Any plant of the genus *Fuirena.* Also with specifying term. — **1817-8** EATON *Botany* (1822) 284 *Fuirena squarrosa,* umbrella grass. **1894** COULTER *Bot. W. Texas* III. 472 Umbrella-grass. . . . The leaves have well-developed blades. **1901** MOHR *Plant Life Ala.* 404 *Fuirena scirpoidea.* . . . Rush-like Umbrella Grass.

Umbrella maker. One whose occupation is making umbrellas. {1793-4-} — **1796** *Boston Directory* 245 Foley, John, umbrella maker, Court street. **1861** *Vanity Fair* 13 April 180/1 Four umbrella-makers have been arrested. **1888** *Amer. Almanac* 275 Occupations of the People of the United States. . . . Umbrella and parasol makers, . . . Upholsterers.

+**Umbrella tree.** A magnolia or species of magnolia, *Magnolia tripetala.* — **1738** CATESBY *Carolina* II. 80 The Umbrella Tree. . . . The leaves . . . grow in horizontal circles, representing somewhat the appearance of an Umbrella. **1785** MARSHALL *Amer. Grove* 84 The Umbrella Tree . . . grows pretty frequent in Carolina, and some parts of Pennsylvania. **1814** PURSH *Flora Amer.* II. 381 Umbrella-tree; in the mountains they call it Elk-wood. **1832** BROWNE *Sylva Amer.* 213 The Umbrella Tree is first seen in the southern part of the state of New York. **1903** FOX *Little Shepherd* ii, Here and there was a blossoming wild cucumber and an umbrella-tree with huger flowers and leaves.

+**Um-hum,** *interj.* Also **umhu, uh-huh,** etc. A colloquial expression of assent or of continuing attention to what is being said. {imhm, imphm, *Sc.* 1870-} — **1839** MARRYAT *Diary* II. 36 There are two syllables—*um, hu*—which are very generally used by the Americans as a sort of reply, intimating that they are attentive, and that the party may proceed with his narration. **1883** CABLE *Dr. Sevier* 57 'Umhum,' said Sam. **1909** STRATTON-PORTER *Girl of Limberlost* 410 'Umhu!' assented Polly. **1923** VANCE *Baroque* 47 'Think so?' 'Uh-huh.'

***Umpire.** Baseball. +**1.** A person chosen or appointed to make decisions and to see that the rules of play are observed during a game. The system indicated in quotation 1856 has long been obsolete. +**2.** *Umpire-in-chief,* an umpire having superior jurisdiction. — (1) **1856** *Porter's Spirit of Times* 6 Dec. 229/1 In [baseball] matches, an umpire is chosen on each side, and a referee to decide, when the umpires cannot agree. **1886** CHADWICK *Art of Batting* 73 One of the rules governing the selection of an umpire applies with equal force to the choice of **a** captain of a nine. **1910** *Spalding's Base Ball Guide* 374 The umpires are the representatives of the League. (2) *Ib.,* The Umpire-in-Chief shall take position back of the catcher.

*****Un-.** A negative prefix used with adjectives.
Only a few of the more unusual or more interesting examples are illustrated.
Unbroken, not cultivated; *unfixed,* open to persuasion, undecided in thinking or voting; *unparted,* (see quotation); *unscratched,* voted straight; *unsuit,* unfitting; *unwestern,* not characteristic of the West.
1872 TICE *Over Plains* 30 There are still immense stretches of unbroken prairie, covered with a luxuriant growth of wild grass. **1902** E. C. MEYER *Nominating Systems* 42 They will bribe, with promise of office, employment, or fat job, or with cash in hand, so many of the 'unfixed' members as may be needed to effect their purpose. **1886** G. EVANS *Illus. Hist. U.S. Mint* 150 *Unparted Bullion.*—Gold containing silver or silver containing gold which has not been subjected to the parting operation. **1867** D. R. LOCKE *Swingin' Round* 73 To vote, ez wunst they did, a tikkit all unskratched. **1704** in W. S. Perry *Hist. Coll. Amer. Col. Church* I. 135 Aspersed with the most unsuitest imputations as if I had been raising sedition or rebellion. **1843** *Knickerb.* XXI. 56 This is a cruel, unmanly, unwestern sport, and should be scorned by the forester.

*****Unabridged,** *a.*

1. Not abridged or shortened, +esp. of Webster's dictionary.
*a***1861** WINTHROP *J. Brent* 100 Their 'dixonary,' as Shamberlain called it, of rascality is an unabridged edition. **1890** WIGGIN *Timothy's Quest* 85 She was perched on a Webster's Unabridged Dictionary. **1908** LORIMER *J. Spurlock* 126, I came across the unbound sheets of a tremenjous big book, bigger than an unabridged Webstah.

+**2.** *absol.* An unabridged dictionary, usually Webster's.
1860 HOLMES *Professor* 56 Hurry up that 'Webster's Unabridged!' **1875** 'MARK TWAIN' in *Lotus Leaves* 28, I had the Unabridged and I was ciphering around in the back end, hoping I might tree her among the pictures. **1902** HARBEN *Abner Daniel* 58 Well, the unabridged does not furnish it.

Unacclimated, *a.* Not adjusted physically to a particular climate. {1852-} Also absol. — **1826** FLINT *Recoll.* 302 The biennial visits of this pestilence . . . [sweep] off multitudes of unacclimated poor. **1869** *Rep. Comm. Agric. 1868* 39 It is reported from Fayette County, Texas, that

Spanish fever only prevails among unacclimated animals. **1883** *Century Mag.* July 425/2 The fatality of the epidemics [of yellow fever] was principally among the unacclimated. **1894** *Outing* XXIV. 152/2 It was a beautiful prospect to the unacclimated Yankee.

+**Unaker.** (See quotations.) *Obs.* — **1744** in *Dict. Nat. Biog.* (1889) XX. 300/1 The material [for making china-ware] is an earth, the produce of the Cherokee nation in America, called by the natives *unaker.* **1881** *Harper's Mag.* Feb. 358/1 Wedgwood . . . made arrangements for a regular supply of 'unaker' or Pensacola clays. [**1885** *Encycl. Brit.* XIX. 641/1 The clay, which was called 'unaker,' was brought from America, and was probably an impure kind of kaolin.]

+**Un-American,** *a.* Not characteristic of America. — **1817** BIRKBECK *Notes Journey in Amer.* (1818) 28 Ninety marble capitals have been imported at vast cost from Italy, . . . and shew how *un*-American is the whole plan. **1860** HOLMES *Professor* 359 To hang about his birth-place all his days, . . . is a most un-American weakness. **1880** *Harper's Mag.* Aug. 347/1 Middleton set down [the incident] to a discouraged listlessness characteristic of a place in the very un-American condition of not looking forward. **1913** LONDON *Valley of Moon* 426 Everything seemed un-American.

+**Unappropriated land.** Land not sold to, or possessed by, an owner; land not set aside for a particular purpose. — **1717** *Mass. H. Rep. Jrnl.* I. 196 A Petition . . . praying that 600 Acres of Land . . . may be laid out in some Unappropriated Land of this Province. **1780** in *Pres. Mess. & P.* III. 59 Unappropriated lands which may be ceded or relinquished to the United States by any particular State . . . shall be disposed of for the common benefit of the United States. **1807** *Ann. 10th Congress* 1 Sess. 11 An act authorizing the State of Tennessee . . . to settle the claims to vacant and unappropriated lands. **1836** *Mich. Gen. Statutes* (1882) I. 37 Five entire sections of land . . . from any of the unappropriated lands . . . are hereby granted to the state for the purpose of completing the public buildings.

Unassimilable, *a.* Not capable of being assimilated. — **1873** E. H. CLARKE *Sex in Educ.* 23 Our girls revel in those unassimilable abominations. **1900** *Congress. Rec.* 30 Jan. 1303/1 There is no possibility that we should ever admit to an equal participation in our Government these Asiatic people . . . so utterly unassimilable to ourselves.

***Unavailable,** *a.* +Not available as a political candidate. (Cf. AVAILABLE *a.*) — **1888** BRYCE *Amer. Commw.* II. III. lxx. 558 The larger delegations hold meetings to determine their course in the event of the man they chiefly favour proving 'unavailable.' **1904** *N.Y. Ev. Post* 26 Oct. 6 He now comes forward with an elaborate statement to show that h is not 'Odell's candidate,' that Mr. Odell regarded him as unavailable.

+**Unbank,** *v.* [1] *tr.* To deprive a bank of its functions as a financial institution. Used with reference to the second bank of the United States. *Obs.* — **1834** CALHOUN *Works* II. 363 We must . . . use a bank to unbank the banks, to the extent that may be necessary. **1854** BENTON *30 Years' View* I. 434/1 [Mr. Calhoun's] frequent expression was, that his plan was to 'unbank the banks.'

Unbank, *v.* [2] {1842} +*tr.* To free or clear (a fire) from the material used in banking it. — **1890** *Scientific Amer.* 17 May 315/3 The first duty of an engineer . . . is to ascertain how many gauges of water there are in his boilers. Never unbank or replenish the fires until this is done.

+**Unbankable,** *a.* Not suitable for depositing in a bank. — **1855** *Knickerb.* XLV. 469 Kin you let me have four hundred and fifteen dollars, unbankable money? **1890** GILDERSLEEVE *Essays & Studies* 55 All the gold that France has paid, or can pay, were a poor exchange for the treasure of German idealism, unbankable as it is.

***Unbleached,** *a.* Not bleached. +Used of Negroes. *slang* or *humorous.* *Obs.* — [**1865** J. C. HOTTEN *Slang Dict.* 264 *Unbleached American,* the new Yankee term for coloured natives of the United States.] **1867** CRAWFORD *Mosby* 360 Word came that a detachment of . . . unbleached Yankee Cavalry, had been dispatched from Washington. **1872** DE VERE 281 In familiar intercourse, he [the Negro] appeared . . . humorously as an unbleached American.

***Unbury,** *v.* +*tr.* To *unbury the tomahawk,* to begin war. Usually with reference to Indians. *Obs.* — **1811** *Niles' Reg.* I. 311/2 Certain deputations from the northern tribes lately visited the southern Indians to induce them to unbury the tomahawk. **1812** *Ib.* III. 57/2 Thus have they been induced to sign their own death warrants by unburying the tomahawk against the whites. **1813** *Ib.* IV. 76/2 The society are ready to unbury the tomahawk whenever their country's good requires it.

***Unbutton,** *v.* *fig.* +*tr.* To kill. Also *to unbutton the collar of.* *slang.* *Obs.* — **1834** CARRUTHERS *Kentuckian* I. 20, I think no more of taking my jack-knife and unbuttoning the collar of a Creek Injin, than I would of takin the jacket off a good . . . bell-wether. **1845** SIMMS *Cabin & Wigwam* 64, I had but one shoot, and if I didn't onbutton him in that one, it would be a bad shoot for poor Lucy.

Unchartered bank. A bank not having a charter. — **1812** *Niles' Reg.* II. 19/2 Those planters . . . who should place confidence in the paper of unchartered banks. **1822** FLINT *Lett. from Amer.* 283 At the time when this happened, the people had just become jealous of unchartered banks.

+**Unchinked,** *a.* Of logs or cabins: Unprovided with chinking or daubing. — **1819** *Niles' Reg.* XVII. 30/2 A year ago there were only 'five or six unchinked cabins' on the town plot. **1843** 'CARLTON' *New Purchase* I. 107 As to the cabin it was as yet unchinked, undaubed, and without its stack chimney. **1890** LANGFORD *Vigilante Days* (1912) 213 They were confined in a small, half-roofed, unchinked cabin. **1905** *Forestry Bureau Bul.* No. 67, 80 There are over a hundred cabins without door, floor, window, or chimney, built, pen like, of unchinked logs.

***Uncle.**

1. A term of familiarity, affection, or respect used in addressing or referring to a man, usually elderly, unrelated to the speaker. {1793-} '*Local* and *U.S.*' (*O.E.D.*).

1813 in *Amer. ntiq. Soc. Proc.* ns. XIX. 26n., Bring your plots and your intrigues, uncle Tim, And let's all be tories together. **1831** J. FOWLER *Tour New York* 52, I was a little surprised on the gentleman approaching us, to find him address him by the familiar appellation of 'uncle.' **1845** HOOPER *Taking Census* 165 Uncle Kit was sixty years old, we suppose, but the merriest old dog alive. **1855** BARNUM *Life* 69n., My father's name was Philo, but as it was the custom to call everybody in those parts uncle or aunt, deacon, colonel, captain, or squire, my father's general title was [Uncle Phile]. **1906** *N.Y. Ev. Post* 7 May 6 [Mr. Cannon's] quaintness of manner, homely and Lincoln-like humor, have given him that title of 'Uncle' which goes only to the beloved among statesmen.

transf. **1847** EMERSON *Representative Men* 74 Plain old uncle as he [Socrates] was, . . . the rumour ran, that [etc.].

+**b,** Applied to Negroes, esp. an elderly slave or servant. Also *unkey.*

1830 S. P. HOLBROOK *Sketches* 111 In many families, however, the children are taught to address the older servant as *uncle* or *auntee,* and this is sometimes more than a form of speech. **1850** WEIR *Lonz Powers* 32 Old Uncle Ned,—every family in Kentucky has some old family servant bearing this endearing title. **1861** W. H. RUSSELL *My Diary* I. 144 We passed through the market [at Charleston, S.C.], where the stalls are kept by fat negresses and old 'unkeys.' **1873** 'MARK TWAIN' & WARNER *Gilded Age* 78 The Hawkins hearts [had] been torn to see Uncle Dan'l and his wife pass from the auction-block into the hands of a negro trader. **1883** *Harper's Mag.* Oct. 728/2 The negro no longer submits with grace to be called 'uncle' and 'auntie' as of yore.

+**2.** = UNCLE SAM.

1857 *Lawrence Republican* 25 June 1 [The states] may *play* sovereign as long as their gracious Uncle shall think it safe for the little ones to amuse themselves. **1867** *Atlantic Mo.* March 328/2 This was the work of our common Uncle, and Chicago does not boast of it.

+**Uncle Abe.** Abraham Lincoln. An affectionate nickname. — **1860** [see OLD ABE]. **1867** GOSS *Soldier's Story* 128, I suppose you know that Uncle Abe is coming down this way to set you all free. **1886** LOGAN *Great Conspiracy* 613 In response to the loud and jubilant cries of 'Lincoln!' 'Lincoln!' 'Abe Lincoln!' 'Uncle Abe!' and other affectionate calls, . . . he appeared at an open window.

Uncleared, *a.* {1637-} Of land: Not cleared of trees. {1772-} — **1744** MOORE *Voy. Georgia* 97 These uncleared lots are a nuisance to their neighbors. **1823** JAMES *Exped.* I. 82 Uncleared lands [were sold at] from two to ten or fifteen dollars per acre. **1856** SIMMS *Charlemont* 149 The route . . . conducted them . . . [through] an uncleared woodland tract.

+**Uncle Jonathan.** = BROTHER JONATHAN 1. — **1800** *Aurora* (Phila.) 14 July (Th.), I have heard that uncle Jonathan and some of the rest of 'em say [etc.].

+**Uncle Sam.** ['U.S.': see note.]

Often ascribed to the facetiousness of acquaintances of Samuel Wilson (1768-1854), of Troy, New York, a member of a slaughtering firm supplying provisions to the army in the War of 1812; the initials 'U.S.,' stamped on barrels, are said, without conclusive proof, to have been jocularly interpreted as standing for 'Uncle Sam' Wilson, as inspector. Albert Matthews (1908 *Amer. Antiq. Soc. Proc.* ns. XIX. 21-65), after examining the evidence, discards this explanation in favor of the simpler one assuming merely the expansion of the initials 'U.S.' into 'Uncle Sam.'

1. The government of the United States; the people of the United States. A nickname.

See also U. SAM.

1813 *Troy Post* 7 Sept. 3/3 'No ill luck stir[r]ing but what lights upon Uncle Sam's shoulders,' exclaim the Government editors. [**1838** Bentley's *Misc.* IV. 40 (title), Uncle Sam's Peculiarities.] **1857** *Lawrence* (Kan.) *Republican* 9 July 2 Kansas—The youngest and smartest child in Uncle Sam's family. **1862** NORTON *Army Lett.* 109, I can get along first-rate on Uncle Sam's rations. **1884** *Harper's Mag.* June 48/1 To cheat Uncle Sam in revenue matters is regarded as a . . . venial sin. **1906** *N.Y. Ev. Post* 9 May 8 The railroads which Uncle Sam is to bestow upon his Philippine wards.

2. Gen. Ulysses S. Grant. A nickname.

1866 W. F. G. SHANKS *Personal Recoll. Dist. Generals* 117 The patriotic friends of the general have given this name several facetious variations, such as 'Uncle Sam,' 'Unconditional Surrender,' and 'United We Stand.' **1884** BLAINE *20 Years of Congress* I. 356 The initials of his name were seized upon. . . . He was 'Uncle Sam.'

3. In possessive combinations. Chiefly *humorous.*

See also UNCLE SAM'S FARM, UNCLE SAM'S MEN.

1821 *Niles' Reg.* XXI. 199 Those who live upon the treasury, or expect to become rich by *plucking* 'Uncle Sam's' great grey goose. **1834** C. D. ARFWEDSON *United States* II. 91 On the Mississippi, these snag-boats are technically called Uncle Sam's tooth-pullers. **1838** *N.Y. Advertiser & Exp.* 10 Jan. 2/1 Uncle Sam's Shin Plasters (Treasury notes) one and one quarter per cent below Paper Money. **1863** LINCOLN in E. McPherson *Polit. Hist. U.S. Rebell.* 335 Nor must Uncle Sam's web feet [the navy] be forgotten. **1871** DE VERE 263 The *lobby* and the *rings* are said to be bent upon filling their purses at *Uncle Sam's crib*, as the National Treasury is often called.

+**Uncle-Sam-ish,** *a.* Characteristic of the United States of America. — **1844** tr. Sealsfield *North & South* 105 The idea of commencing the cochineal business . . . was so perfectly Uncle Sam-ish.

+**Uncle Sam's farm.** The territory of the United States; spec., the public land. — **1861** LOWELL *Biglow P.* 2 Ser. 18 A spotteder, ring-streakeder child the' warn't in Uncle Sam's Holl farm. **1884** *Lisbon* (Dak.) *Star* 20 June, The stream of western immigration . . . will soon spread over all there is left of Uncle Sam's farm worth taking.

+**Uncle Sam's men.** Men employed in some capacity by the United States government. — **1813** in *Amer. Antiq. Soc. Proc.* ns. XIX. 34 A recent battle . . . between what are called in this part of the country [near Lansingburg, N.Y.], *Uncle Sam's Men* and the *Men of New-York.* **1826** ROYALL *Sketches* 165 In Washington . . . , I met with 'uncle Sam's' men, as they call themselves. **1893** *Harper's Mag.* Feb. 462/1 Uncle Sam's men, with a-plenty o' greenbacks.

+**Uncle Samuel.** [Humorous var. of UNCLE SAM.] = UNCLE SAM 1. — **1816** 'FIDFADDY' *Adv. Uncle Sam* 11 Behold said Thomas [Jefferson], how mine Uncle Samuel hath fought in times past against John Bull. **1846** *Spirit of Times* (N.Y.) 6 June 177/1 The monotony of this place has been relieved . . . by the drilling of 'Uncle Samuel's' 'web feet,' . . . that came here from the squadron. **1873** *Newton Kansan* 27 Feb. 2/1 Some of the Mormons . . . think they can whip 'Uncle Samuel.'

+**Uncle Tom.** [The Negro hero of Harriet Beecher Stowe's antislavery novel *Uncle Tom's Cabin* (1851–2).] Used as the root of several words coined by adding suffixes: (see quotations). — **1853** in T. S. Perry *Life F. Lieber* 257 Our papers have coined a word—*Uncle-Tomitude*—to sneer at the sympathy with the African. **1853** *Putnam's Mo.* Jan. 99/2 India, and Mexico, and South America, have yet to be Uncle Tomitized. *Ib.* 100/1 One of our newspaper critics compares the Uncle Tomific, which the reading world is now suffering from, to the yellow fever.

Unconditional surrender. Surrender without condition or stipulation of any sort {1844–8–}; also, a nickname of Gen. U. S. Grant. — **1862** GRANT *Memoirs* I. 255 No terms except an unconditional and immediate surrender can be accepted. I propose to move immediately upon your works. **1864** *Harper's Mag.* March 568/1 If that butter don't outrank old Unconditional Surrender by a great sight, then I'll never draw trigger on another reb! **1866** [see UNCLE SAM 2].

+**Unconditional Union man.** In the campaign of 1864, a supporter of the administration; a member of the National Union party professing the ideal of 'the unconditional maintenance of the Union.' — **1864** *Rio Abajo Press* 12 April 1/3 The Unconditional Union Men of this Territory are respectfully requested to send Delegates to a Territorial Convention.

Unconstitutional, *a.*

1. In the colonial period: Not in accord with the recognized principles of government. {1765–}

1743 in *Ga. Hist. Soc. Coll.* II. 92 Every grant or tenure of theirs [*sc.* of the trustees] . . . was contrary to the charter, and an illegal and unconstitutional reserve. **1782** *Boston Rec.* 284 If . . . the breach of this Clause as well as others is to be tried on Issue at Law, . . . we conceive it to be unconstitutional.

+**2.** Under the United States government: At variance with the provisions of the Federal Constitution of 1787.

1790 P. HENRY in *Life, Corr. & Speeches* (1891) III. 415 If, then, the act of cession is unconstitutional, can congress derive any right under it? **1792** HAMILTON *Works* VII. 60 There appears, therefore, no room to say that the bill is unconstitutional. **1806** *Balance* 22 April 127/1 He accused Mr. Madison of unconstitutional views in wishing to draw from the Treasury . . . public monies. **1837** CALHOUN *Works* III. 57 The State of South Carolina . . . declared the act to be unconstitutional, and as such null and void. **1890** *Stock Grower & Farmer* 31 May 3/3 The meat inspection law has been declared unconstitutional by the supreme court of the United States. **1895** *Supreme Ct. Rep.* CLVIII. 635 It is elementary that the same statute may be in part constitutional and in part unconstitutional.

Unconstitutionality. The quality of being unconstitutional; legal action resulting in the setting aside of a law because of this. {1850–} +Esp. with reference to the Federal Constitution of 1787. — **1782** *Boston Rec.* 283 These Circumstances . . . are sufficient to demonstrate its Unconstitutionality in the Mode of Proceedure should it [an act for more effectual observance of the Sabbath] be adopted. **1795** WASHINGTON *Writings* XIII. 73 Any further sentiment now on the unconstitutionality of the measure would be received too late. **1833** A. GREENE *Yankee among Nullifiers* 16 You know what my opinion has hitherto been in relation to State Rights and the unconstitutionality of the Tariff. **1846** L. SPOONER (*title*), The Unconstitutionality of Slavery. **1894** *Columbian Dispatch* 6 June, Judge Ricks' decision seems to prepare the way for the departure of the law from the statute books by the pathway of unconstitutionality.

‖**Unctuate,** *v. tr.* To treat with an unguent. — **1851** *Harper's Mag.* March 494/2 The hair much unctuated, as is the custom of the land, was adorned with a pendant fringe of black silk.

Unculled, *a.* Of a crop +or of woodlands: Not sorted or picked over; not freed from refuse or inferior timber. {1667–, in general sense} — **1661** *Md. Hist. Mag.* VIII. 7 They found two more hogsheads with ground leaves and unculled tobacco. **1892** *Vermont Bd. Agric. Rep.* XII. 121 In the value of its timber and unculled wood lands, Essex County is ahead of many other Counties.

Uncultivatable, *a.* Of land: That cannot be cultivated. — **1870** *Putnam's Mag.* Sept. 290/1 The land . . . [is] perfectly uncultivatable.

Uncurrent, *a.* Of notes or other money: Not in circulation; not generally accepted: (see also quot. 1835). {1601–} — **1819** in Mackenzie *Van Buren* 153, I send you . . . two sealed packages containing . . . Uncurrent notes $1750. **1832** *Louisville Pub. Adv.* 11 Sept., Uncurrent bank notes bought at low rates. **1835** TODD *Notes* 26 The notes of those banks without agents in large cities, are called *uncurrent.* **1838** *N.Y. Advertiser & Exp.* 6 Jan. 3/2 Uncurrent Money—There is no change in the rate of uncurrent notes. **1870** MEDBERY *Men Wall St.* 153 He saw an opportunity for making something by buying uncurrent money between the United States and Canada.

+**Undemocratize,** *v. tr.* To make undemocratic. — **1876** *N. Amer. Rev.* Oct. 255 Its consequence was to undemocratize the Democratic party and secure its final defeat.

***Under,** *adv.* +*To go under,* (see GO *v.* 34); +*to stand from under,* (see STAND *v.* 4).

***Under,** *prep.* Used in special phrases.

For many such phrases see the object nouns; e.g., *under the* (or *God's*) *canopy,* (see CANOPY).

Under the doctor, under the care of a physician {1898}; *u. paddle,* by paddling; *u. par* {1755–}, +below accepted standards of ethics or morals; *u. saddle,* of a horse, bearing a saddle.

1846 MAGOFFIN *Down Santa Fé Trail* 135 He has been under the Doctor for some time. **1880** *Harper's Mag.* Aug. 401/2 From twenty to thirty miles per day may be comfortably made under paddle. **1856** CARTWRIGHT *Autobiog.* 114 He located and went into land speculations and got under par as a good man. **1857** *Mich. Agric. Soc. Trans.* VIII. 707 Some [were] under saddle, others attached to gigs.

Underbearer. A funeral attendant who assists in the carrying of the coffin, as distinguished from a pallholder. Now hist. {1755–, now *dial.*} Cf. PALLBEARER. — **1700** SEWALL *Diary* II. 9 Mr. Cook was at the funeral. The under-bearers were honest men. **1714** *Ib.* III. 11, I and the President went next the Corps. Had underbearers. **1774** CUTLER in *Life & Corr.* I. 45 Eight ministers were appointed as pall-bearers, and four under-bearers, or porters. **1885** EGGLESTON in *Century Mag.* July 394/1 The 'underbearers' . . . carried the coffin [in funerals in the Amer. colonies], walking with their heads and shoulders covered with the pall-cloth.

Underbed. {1648–} A mattress used under a feather bed. — **1725** Kidder *Exped. Lovewell* (1865) 93 A feather bed and under bed and bed furniture. **1778** *N.H. Hist. Soc. Coll.* IX. 108 We have cut up all the sheets, table cloths, underbeds [etc.]. **1868** G. C. CHANNING *Recoll. Newport* 254 The bed or under-bed of straw was laid on cords, and the feather bed above.

+**Underbill,** *v. tr.* To bill (goods) at less than the proper measure or amount. Also *vbl. n.* — **1872** *Chicago Tribune* 20 Nov. 4/4 A committee of the Chicago Board of Trade appointed to investigate the abuse of the 'underbilling' of grain when shipped in bulk by rail have made a report. *Ib.*, The shippers at interior points have thus been tempted to 'underbill' the quantity or weight in order to save railroad freights. **1888** *Boston Jrnl.* 13 April 3/3 The Interstate Commerce Commission has been investigating quite extensively the matter of underbilling. **1889** *Advance* 17 Jan., The bribing of a railroad servant to underbill goods or in some other way to give an advantage to a shipper.

+**Underbit.** A mark cut in the lower side of the ear of an animal, as a sign of ownership. Also transf. {under bytted, 1555, 1899–, *dial.*; underbit ear, 1901, *dial.*} Cf. OVERBIT. — **1837** *Knickerb.* X. 408 The young bridegroom boasted that he had taken an 'under bit out of his left ear.' **1872** MORRELL *Flowers & Fruits* 96 It was released, with a crop and underbit in the right and a swallow-fork in the left. **1899** *Caddo* (Okla.) *Herald* 3 March 3/3, I sow underbit left and split underbit right.

+**Underbrush,** *n.* In a forest, the shrubs and low trees forming the undergrowth. {1888–} — **1775** *Essex Inst. Coll.* L. 107 The fire ran among the leaves & dry underbrush for upwards of a mile. **1805** LEWIS in *L. & Clark Exped.* I. (1904) 299 The underbrush is willow, red wood, . . . the red burry, and Choke cherry. **1870** KEIM *Sheridan's Troopers* 302 Suddenly a crashing of underbrush was heard not more than twenty feet off. **1904** GLASGOW *Deliverance* 47 The dogs . . . started a rabbit once from the close cover of the underbrush.

+**Underbrush,** *v.* [From prec.] *tr.* To clear (land or a forest) of underbrush. Also fig. — [**1865** P. B. ST. JOHN *Snow Ship* vi, A thorough good chopper, after the land is underbrushed, will, in eight days, on an average, fell the trees.] **1896** *Home Missionary* Jan. 461 The minister . . . begins to underbrush and cut down the giant sins that have grown.

Undercharge. (See quot. 1864.) — **1843** *P.O. Laws & Reg.* II. 23 If the postage which the deputy postmaster is asked to refund, was added by him, as an undercharge, . . . he may . . . refund the excess of postage. **1864** WEBSTER 1438/3 *Under-charge,* a charge less than is usual or suitable.

+**Underclassman.** A student in one of the lower classes in a school or college; a freshman or sophomore. Also attrib. — **1871** BAGG *At Yale* 490 Under-class men and graduates can enjoy much that is beyond the reach of others. **1895** WILLIAMS *Princeton Stories* 51 Some of the fellows . . . slipped way down in their chairs in the same purposely reckless manner of under-classmen days. **1896** F. COHEN & E. BOYD *Vassar* 53 Other much prized delicacies which tantalize the underclassmen as they pass by. **1904** *N.Y. Ev. Post* 4 May 4 In Cambridge—unless we are underclassmen—we walk more slowly than in New York.

+**Under cleets.** *pl.* A dance or dance step. *Obs.* or *local.* — **a1846** *Quarter Race Ky.* 178 When my time came [in the dance], therefore, I . . .

commenced . . . 'Pete Jonson's knock,' 'the under cleets,' and other refined steps.

Underclothes. *pl.* **a.** Smallclothes or trousers. **b.** Clothing to be worn under other clothing; underwear. {1884} — **1835** BIRD *Hawks* I. 19 The ornaments of his outward man . . . consisted of under-clothes of some white summer-stuff, a frock of blue cloth [etc.]. **1855** MITCHELL *Fudge Doings* I. 47 She supplies her cook with cast-off under-clothes. **1891** *Harper's Mag.* Oct. 808/2 You should see my under-clothes.

Undercurrent. {1683-} *Mining.* +A shallow receptacle into which water is diverted from a sluice, with the object of catching the finer material. — **1876** RAYMOND *8th Rep. Mines* 95 The company has this season added a series of under-currents near the point where the washings empty into the river.

Undercut, *n.* {1859-} +(See quot. 1905.) — **1883** *Harper's Mag.* Jan. 201/1 In about an hour the undercut had approached the heart of the tree. **1905** *Forestry Bureau Bul.* No. 61, 52 *Undercut*, the notch cut in a tree to determine the direction in which the tree is to fall, and to prevent splitting.

＊**Undercut,** *v.* +*tr.* To make an undercut in (a tree). Hence *undercutter.* — **1851** SPRINGER *Forest Life* 52 A smaller tree is undercut and lodged against it. **1893** *Atlantic Mo.* Feb. 197/2 They were 'under-cutting' the tree on the side toward which they wanted it to fall. **1905** *Forestry Bureau Bul.* No. 61, 52 *Undercutter*, a skilled woodman who chops the undercut in trees so that they shall fall in the proper direction.

+**Under dog.** The loser in a dog fight; fig., a person in a position of inferiority, esp. a victim of misfortune or injustice. — **1879** B. F. TAYLOR *Summer-Savory* 140 It smells of old geographies and . . . readers with ragged edges like the ears of 'the under dog' in the fight. **1897** J. L. SULLIVAN in *Westminster Gaz.* 9 Sept. 7/1 Give the under dog a chance. **1901** *N. Amer. Rev.* Feb. 317 It is not sympathy with the under dog merely as under dog that moves Mark Twain; for the under dog is sometimes rightfully under.

Underdrain, *v. tr.* To drain (ground) by underground drains or trenches. {1832} Also *vbl. n.* {1805} — **1838** *Mass. Agric. Survey 1st Rep.* 88 We have done considerable at underdraining our low and wet grounds to very great advantage. **1858** *Ill. Agric. Soc. Trans.* III. 368 It remains only to say a word about the mode of this under-draining or short-hand plowing. **1879** *Harper's Mag.* June 135/2 Other minor improvements have been made, such as the underdraining of a low tract. **1899** *Dept. Agric. Yrbk. 1898* 318 If a road . . . is not underdrained in all wet spots, this should be the first work done.

Underdress. {1785} **a.** =UNDERCLOTHES a. **b.** A garment, as a petticoat, worn under another dress, or made to appear as if covered by another dress. {1861-} — **1835** BIRD *Hawks* II. 50 He was a tall man, with a French military coat of white cloth. . . . Instead of a white underdress, however, he had on breeches of broad blue and white stripes. **1848** *Ladies' Repository* VIII. 130 [The Falls] presented the appearance of a rich under-dress of white gracefully covered with a delicate emerald gauze.

＊**Underfoot,** *adv. fig.* +In the way. *colloq.* — **1891** *Harper's Mag.* June 62/1 He muttered something about children being underfoot and staring at such times.

Underfur. The fine, soft fur under the longer hairs of the coat of an animal; an undercoat. — **1877** *Field & Forest* II. 150 This close under-fur . . . is the clothing that enables the musk ox to withstand the inclemency of an Arctic winter. **1902** HULBERT *Forest Neighbors* (1903) 21 [The beavers'] bodies were . . . covered with thick, soft, grayish under-fur, which in turn was overlaid with longer hairs of a glistening chestnut-brown.

Underglaze. The surface of pottery before the glazing process has been applied; decoration applied to pottery before the glaze. {1882} Also *attrib.* or *as adj.* {1885} — **1880** *Harper's Mag.* Nov. 905/2 The painting or under-glaze is essentially different from the process I have just tried to describe. **1881** *Ib.* May 835/2 Miss McLaughlin painted the first successful piece of blue underglaze on white ware. *Ib.*, The adaptation of colors, suitable firing for underglaze decoration, were . . . matters of vital importance. **1884** [see OVERGLAZE *n.*].

+**Undergo.** (See quotation.) *colloq.* — **1875** HOLLAND *Sevenoaks* 123 They were blue undergoes—in other words, blue flannel shirts.

Undergraduate. In a college or university, a student who has not yet taken a degree. {1630-} Also *attrib.* or *as adj.* {1654-} — **1725** C. MATHER *Diary* II. 810 There is doubtless a Number, even of the undergraduates, whose prayers may help. **1837** *Laws Yale College* 11 The undergraduate students shall be divided into four distinct classes. **1847** *Knickerb.* XXX. 13 When I was an under-graduate in —— College, 'Protracted Meetings' were all the rage. **1899** E. E. HALE *Lowell & Friends* 141 The Greek-letter societies have it in their power to do a good deal to tone up the undergraduate conscience. **1904-5** [see APPOINTMENT 2 b].

＊**Underground.** +Short for UNDERGROUND RAILROAD. — **1852** STOWE *Uncle Tom* vii, I know the way of all of 'em,—they makes tracks for the underground.

Underground forest. +(See quotation.) — **1890** *Cent.* 3727/1 Under the action of prairie fires it [*sc.* mesquite] is reduced to a low shrub, developing then an enormous mass of roots, locally known as *underground forest*, of great value as fuel.

+**Underground line.** =UNDERGROUND RAILROAD. — **1852** STOWE *Uncle Tom* viii, The gal's can carried on the underground line up to Sandusky or so. **1853** *Knickerb.* XLII. 454, I have been said to be a conductor on the under-ground line.

Underground railroad. +An informally organized chain of antislavery 'stations' for the shelter of slaves being conducted or assisted to escape to the free states or to Canada. Now hist.

1842 *N.Y. Semi-Weekly Express* 28 Sept. 1/5 We passed 26 prime slaves to the land of freedom last week. . . . All went by 'the underground railroad.' **1860** *Richmond Enquirer* 21 Dec. 4/1 (Th.), [The Republican party insists that] slavery, where it now exists, shall be surrounded by a cordon of free States, infested by Abolitionists, libe.ty-shriekers, underground railroads, and border ruffians. **1861** *N.Y. Tribune* 29 Jan. 5/2 There has been, for a long time, an active and well-organized underground railroad at [Leavenworth, Kan.]. **1865** *Atlantic Monthly* April 505/1 My father combined the two functions of preaching in a New England college town and ticket-agency on the Underground Railroad. **1899** CHESNUTT *Wife of His Youth* 201 The underground railroad seemed to have had its tracks cleared and signals set for this particular train. **1907** *St. Nicholas* May 619/2 Others have said that he went there in order to establish a station on the Underground Railroad.

attrib. **1857** *Lawrence* (Kan.) *Republican* 11 June 2 He is . . . charged with being in correspondence with underground railroad directors. **1861** in O. J. Victor *Hist. Southern Rebellion* I. 227/2 Certain States . . . added to the insult of the passage of Personal Liberty bills, Underground Railroad operations, not only in the Border States. but the entire South.

Underground railway. **1.** A railroad operating underground. {1834-6-} +**2.** =UNDERGROUND RAILROAD. Now hist. — **(1)** **1868** *N.Y. Herald* 5 Aug. 7/5 A bill was passed . . . incorporating the New York Central Underground Railway Company. **(2)** **1871** DE VERE 278 Before the abolition of slavery the Underground Railway had become quite an important feature in Northern efforts to aid escaping slaves. **1903** FOX *Little Shepherd* xiv, The underground railway was busy with black freight.

Underground route. + =UNDERGROUND RAILROAD. — **1883** *Harper's Mag.* Aug. 331/1 The Rev. Robert W. Oliver . . . helped a number of fugitive slaves to freedom by the underground route.

Undergrowth. *collect.* Shrubs and small trees growing under and about tall trees or other large plants. {1600-} — **1666** *Conn. Rec.* II. 52 This Court . . . doe desire that there may be some provision agreed on in each Towne for ye subdueing of vndergrowth and shrubs neer the townes. **1785** WASHINGTON *Diaries* II. 337 Began to grub and clear the undergrowth in my Pine Grove on the Margin of Hell hole. **1880** *Harper's Mag.* Aug. 333/1 The buttonwood trees . . . must, with the undergrowth of blackberry vines and wild-rose bushes, have hidden me from sight.

＊**Underhew,** *v.* +*tr.* (See quotation.) — **1841** WEBSTER II. 855/1 *Underhew*, to hew a piece of timber which should be square, in such a manner, that it appears to contain a greater number of cubic feet than it really does. *Haldiman* [*sic*].

Underhold, *n.* (and, perhaps, *adv.*). A wrestling hold in which one man grasps the other below the arms. — **1835** LONGSTREET *Ga. Scenes* 62 Before Billy could recover his balance—Bob had him 'all under-hold.' The next second, sure enough, 'found Billy's head where his feet ought to be.' **1880** N. BROOKS *Fairport Nine* 116 Tom Tilden . . . invited the captive to a rough-and-tumble wrestle, no tripping, underhold, and no biting nor pulling hair.

＊**Underhole,** *v.* +*tr.* or *intr.* 'To cut away or mine out the lower portion of a coal-seam or a part of the underclay so as to win or get the overlying coal. (Penn. anthracite region.)' (*Cent.*).

+**Underkeel,** *n.* An earmark cut on the under side of the ear of an animal. *Obs.* (Cf. OVERKEEL *n.*) — **1677** [see CROP *n.* 3]. **1693** *N.C. Col. Rec* I. 388 Diana ffoster records her marke an under keele and over keele on the right ear and a cropp and 3 slitts on the left ear. **1713** *Ib.* II. 108 One . . . Cowe marked on the Right Eare with a Cropp and on the left with an under Keel. **1773** in Summers *Ann. S.W. Va.* 596 It is ordered that his Mark be Recorded a small fork in the Right ear an under keel in the left ear.

+**Underkeel,** *v. tr.* To mark with an underkeel. *Obs.* — **1648** *Md. Archives* IV. 379 One blackish pyed browne Cow . . . slit on the left eare & underkeeld. **1653** *Ib.* X. 304 Robert Jones his mark for Cattle and hogs viz The Right Eare Swallow forked and the Left Eare Underkeeled. **1681** *New Castle Court Rec.* 448 Twoo Cropps and underkeeld on ye Left Eare.

Underlayer. A substratum. {1896-} — *a*1877 *Phila. Times* (B.), We found . . . a large underlayer of black-jack of too poor a quality to work.

Underline, *v.* {1721-} *tr.* To give advance notice of the production of (a play) by listing it below the advertisements of the current attraction {1900} — **1861** *Chicago Jrnl.* 25 June, At the theatre this evening there is a new piece underlined. **1895** *N.Y. Dramatic News* 14 Dec. 16/4 Underlined for the coming week are: Grand opera house, Charley's Aunt; Walnut street theatre, Sidney Drew. **1912** T. R. SULLIVAN *Heart of Us* 75 Ives . . . reminded himself of this, upon seeing for the first time his new play 'underlined.'

Underpinners. *pl.* Legs. {1861, supports or props} — **1859** BARTLETT 493 *Underpinners*, the legs, which in English flash language are called pins.

＊**Underpinning.**
＊**1. a.** Material or construction used for supporting or strengthening a building. **b.** *?local.* The foundation of a wooden building.

1666 *Groton Rec.* 18 Carting clay & stone for dawing the wall & underpinning. **1723** *New-Eng. Courant* 29 April 2/1 The old Man . . . fell down with his Head against the Under-Pinning of the House. **1789** *Mass. Spy* 16 July 3/4 A new frame of a barn, uncovered, . . . was taken by a whirl-wind from its underpinning. **1804** *Ib.* 19 Dec. (Th.), You will discover a vacuum in the underpinning of the house, which is of brick. **1872** *Congress. Globe* 22 May 3759/2 We found the underpinning of the . . . [Executive Mansion], if I may so call it, all its underwork, in a state of extreme rottenness. **1890** *Southern Californian* (Lordsburg) 2 Oct. 3/1 It is easier to lay the foundation at the first, than, after the building is up, to put in underpinning.

+2. *transf.* Legs. *colloq.*[2]
[**1848** Durivage & Burnham *Stray Subjects* 102 A brace of legs . . . formed the underpinning to a long slabsided body, of otherwise generous proportions.] **1852** Bennet *Mike Fink* 13/2 Nothing like long under-pinins fur travel. **1857** Hammond *Northern Scenes* 167 The old buck . . . made them things [scars] on my underpinin'. **1895** *N.Y. Dramatic News* 5 Oct. 6/1 Do cigarette girls at work wear their dresses decollete at the bottom and show their underpinning?

+Under rake. *R.I.* (See quot. 1890.) — **1879** *R.I Acts & Resolves* Jan. Sess. 180 Nothing in the next preceding section shall be construed to prevent any citizen of this state from taking oysters in Point Judith ponds . . . by a certain instrument . . . known by the name of an under-rake. **1890** *Cent.* 4046/1 *Under-rake,* a kind of oyster-rake, used mostly through holes in the ice, with handle 15 to 20 feet long, head 1 to 2 feet wide, and iron teeth 6 to 10 inches long.

***Underrun,** v. tr.* To haul in, free of the catch, and reset (a trawl). {1883-, of Canada} — **1880** *Harper's Mag.* Aug. 351/1 [He] 'underran' it, that is drew up one end, passed it over his boat, taking off the fish, and baiting the hooks anew, and paid it out at one side as he took it in at the other. **1896** Jewett *Pointed Firs* (1910) 56, I just made one stop to underrun William's trawl till I come to jes' such a fish's I thought you'd want.

Undershot, *a.* Of a wheel or a mill: Driven or operated by the passage of water underneath. {1610-} Also *absol.* {1759} — **1705** *Penna. Hist. Soc. Mem.* IX. 233 After it has passed through the saw-mill it comes to the corn-mill, an undershot, and grinds very well. **1755** L. Evans *Anal. Map Colonies* 21 Each [stream] is about large enough to turn an under-shot Grist Mill. **1877** *Harper's Mag.* Jan. 213/2 Sawyer Grundy could have taken him with one hand and tossed him over the undershot wheel.

Underskirt. A skirt worn under another skirt; a petticoat {1861-}; a foundation skirt over which an overskirt or drapery is worn. — **1872** *Picayune* 2 April, Ladies' Underwear— . . . fine muslin underskirts, ten-tuck. **1873** A. D. Whitney *Other Girls* 15 Nobody really looked down to see that the underskirt was the identical black brilliantine that had done service all the spring. **1883** [see OVERSKIRT].

***Understanding.** slang.* **a.** A foot or leg. {1828-} **b.** Something worn on the foot or leg, as a shoe or a part of a shoe. {1822-} In both senses usually pl. or collective.
1833 A. Greene *Yankee among Nullifiers* 107 We were obliged to mingle feet with feet, in the usual manner in which the *understandings* of people are thrust together in those villanously short vehicles. **1840** [see NULLI-FIER 2]. **1843** Stephens *High Life N.Y.* II. 58 She had on a short petti-coat that showed a purty considerable chunk of understandings. **1850** D. Dudley *Pictures of Life* 140 Having lost a sole in the mud . . . I stepped into a shop to get my understanding renewed. **1858** D. K. Ben-nett *Chronology N.C.* 107 The young man put in two not very feminine understandings, and by the force of gravity lowered the salt to one peck, or less. **1861** *Ill. Agric. Soc. Trans.* IV. 399 A bed . . . which any one may walk on with dry 'understanding' in the worst of weather. **1881** McLean *Cape Cod Folks* 151 What—poor, wanderin' creeturs—if your understandin's should give out!

***Undertake,** v. +intr.* (See quot. 1891.) — [**1786** *Boston Rec.* 293 The names of the Persons who are willing to Undertake the charge of Funerals.] **1891** *Cent.* 6599/3 *Undertake,* . . . to manage funerals, and arrange all the details for burying the dead. (Colloq.)

***Undertaker.**

1. One who takes leadership or initiative, or otherwise actively participates in the planning or the conduct of an enterprise {1615-}; one who assumes, by agreement, certain responsibilities on behalf of another, as for a government; a contractor. Now rare or *Obs.* {1602-}
1627 in Bradford *Hist.* 272 Articles of agreemente betweene ye collony . . . and William Bradford, Captein Myles Standish . . . and shuch others as they shall thinke good to take as partners and undertakers with them. **1636** *Dedham Rec.* III. 23 Euery man of our societye shall p[er]forme one dayes worke in the same [mending a swamp], or otherwise to paye unto ye sayd undertakers . . . 2s: 6d: towards ye same worke. **1645** *Suffolk Deeds* I. 62 Georg Ruggles of Braintre granted unto Richard Leader in behalfe of the Companie Undertakers of the Yron worke twenty Acres of land. **1653** *Lancaster Rec.* 24 The intrest of Harmon Garrett & such others as were first vndertakers or haue ben at great charges there, shalbe made good. **1708** *Boston Rec.* X. 153 The Ancient undertakers & builders of ye Sd Out wharfes are in ye Sd report represend as delinquents. **1785** Wash-ington *Diaries* II. 378 One Richd. Boulton, a House joiner and under-taker, recommended to me.

b. A publisher. *Obs.* {1697-1823}

1706 *Boston News-Letter* 4 March 4/2 The Undertaker would be enabled to Print a Sheet instead of half a Sheet. **1723** *New-Eng. Courant* 13 May 2/2 The Undertaker, William Price, desires all Gentlemen to be speedy in their Subscriptions. **1787** J. Adams *Works* IX. 552, I doubt whether any of these undertakers will proceed.

2. One who makes a business of arranging and conduct-ing funerals and preparing the dead for burial. {1698-}
1810 Lambert *Travels* (1813) II. 181 A few months before the yellow fever raged in that city [Charleston, S.C.], in 1807, an undertaker made his appearance, which was so great a novelty to the inhabitants that he was obliged to explain what was meant by the term undertaker in an ad-vertisement. **1869** *Boyd's Business Directory* 237 E. Ayers, Furnishing Undertaker, Ready-Made Coffins of all kinds, Burial Robes and Shrouds always on hand. **1882** McCabe *New York* 233 The personal attendance of an undertaker is worth from $1 to $50. **1922** Tarkington *Gentle Julia* 265 She'd find fault with the undertaker at her own funeral.

Undertone. {1806-} **1.** A state of subnormal elasticity or resili-ency. **2.** (See quotation.) — **(1)** **1872** H. W. Beecher *Yale Lect. Preach-ing* I. 199, I have sometimes had a whole month of undertone, because I let go and ran clear down. **(2)** **1891** *Cent.* 6600/2 *Undertone,* . . . the color of a pigment when seen in very thin layers on a white or light-colored surface. Also—*(a)* A low, subdued color: as, gray undertones. *(b)* A tone of color seen through and giving character to other colors: as, there was a subtle undertone of yellow through the picture.

Undervest. An undershirt. {1813-} — **1854** J. E. Cooke *Va. Comedians* I. 18 She is clad in the usual child's costume of the period, namely, a sort of half coat—half frock . . . ; an embroidered undervest. **1862** *N.Y. Tribune* 28 June 1/2 An officer of the 19th Massachusetts was 'iron clad' with a patent undervest. **1881** *Ore. State Jrnl.* 1 Jan. 4 Ladies Under Vest[s], . . . Ladies Pebbled Button Shoes [etc.].

+Underwaist. A waist worn beneath another garment. — **1857** in A. Allan *Life P. Brooks* I. 209 Thick winter underwaists and socks. **1870** 'F. Fern' *Ginger-Snaps* 264, I don't speak of my cambric underwaist, ir-retrievably torn down the back. **1906** Freeman *By Light of Soul* 333 Maria had a beautiful neck showing above the lace of her underwaist.

Underwear. Underclothing; clothing worn next the skin. — **1872** *Picayune* 2 April, Ladies' Underwear—Best merino undershirts, fine fin-ish; . . . fine French corsets. **1889** *Harper's Mag.* Aug. 485/1 When his suit of clothes wore out, he used to borrow mine, . . . leaving me in the office alone with my thoughts and a suit of very 'near' under-wear. **1908** 'Yeslah' *Tenderfoot S. Calif.* 14 All I had in that blamed trunk of mine was some peek-a-boo underwear and drop stitched stockings.

***Underwood.** Small trees or shrubs growing beneath tall-er trees.
1634 Wood *New Eng. Prospect* 15 It being the custome of the Indians to burne the wood in November, . . . it consumes all the underwood, and rubbish. **1671** *S.C. Hist. Soc. Coll.* V. 309 The woods [are] so cleare of . . . underwoods that a man may ride his horse a hunting. **1718** *Essex Inst. Coll.* XLIV. 147 One plantation clear Grounde, orchards, houses, Gar-dens, woods, underwoods, water and water cources. **1784** Cutler in *Life & Corr.* I. 102 The ground [was] covered with an underwood of moose bush. **1882** *Century Mag.* May 153/2 Does not our wild-gardener know the American dogwood (*Cornus florida*), giving such a dash of snow-white here and there to our under-woods? **1905** *Forestry Bureau Bul.* No. 61, 26 In a two-storied forest . . . the shorter trees form the *underwood,* or *lower story.*

Underwriter. {1616-} One who insures. {1622-} — **1721** in Wat-son *Philadelphia* 721 An insurance officer at his office, where he will pro-vide competent underwriters to assure any sum applied for. **1840** *Niles' Nat. Reg.* 7 March 11/1 By Mr. Wright, from the board of underwriters of New York, remonstrating against any alteration in the laws. **1889** *Century Mag.* Feb. 566/1 A somewhat desultory inspection has been main-tained . . . for the purpose of informing the underwriters. **1915** *Lit. Digest* 21 Aug. 367/2 A roof constructed strictly according to the Barrett speci-fication . . . is classified as non-inflammable by fire underwriters.

***Undivided,** a.* Of property, esp. land, belonging to a group of set-tlers: Not allotted to individual owners. *Obs.* — **1666** Sanford *Letter Book* 10 Two yearleinge Weathrs one ould Rame Five this yeare Ewe Lames . . . one weathr Lame undevided. **1679** *Waterbury Prop. Rec.* 7 If thes Lands herein exprest fall short of this devetion then too be made up by any undevided lands. **1708** *Suffield Doc. Hist.* 157 Every Mine, or Mines yt do . . . appear to be in any undivided land, . . . shall be se-questred. **1817** *N. Amer. Rev.* V. 313 The lake is owned in 70 undi-vided shares by the assignees of the original settlers of the town.

+Unearned run. *Baseball.* A run scored because of an error on the part of the side scored against. (Cf. EARNED RUN.) — **1875** *Chicago Trib-une* 16 Sept. 8/4 The Athletics made four unearned runs by the errors of McMullin, Meyerle, and Fulmer. *Ib.* 24 Aug. 5/6 The Bostons . . . were sent to bat and scored four unearned runs.

Unfair competition. Business competition effected by unethical methods and involving infringement of the rights of a competitor or of the public. (Cf. FAIR COMPETITION.) — **1896** *Ill. Appellate Court Rep.* LXIV. 478 An injunction to prevent the fraudulent use of resemblances to trade-marks, or to stop unfair competition in business. **1909** H. D. Nims *Law Unfair Business Competition* 2 Unfair competition . . . exists wherever unfair means are used in trade rivalry. **1917** W. H. Stevens *Unfair Competition* 244 Until unfair competition is eliminated it is doubt-ful whether the trust problem will be solved.

Ungraded, *a.* {1884-} +Not laid out in, or brought to, proper gradients. Used esp. of roads. — **1845** JUDD *Margaret* I. 33 The roads rough, ungraded, and divided by parallel lines of green grass. **1879** BIRD *Lady's Life Rocky Mts.* 219 Golden City . . . is ungraded, with here and there a piece of wooden sidewalk. **1885** *Atlantic Mo.* April 467/1 These roadways, [are] ungraded, unsewered, and unpaved.

+**Ungranted land.** Land that has not been granted to an individual owner. *Obs.* {1828-, in Australia} — **1715** *Mass. H. Rep. Jrnls.* I. 62 All the ungranted land lying between the two rivers and the frontier towns. **1798** I. ALLEN *Hist. Vermont* 111 It was thought good policy . . . to raise a sufficient revenue out of the property confiscated and the ungranted land. **1834** *N.H. Hist. Soc. Coll.* IV. 217 Between Hillsborough . . . and New Boston . . . lay a large tract of ungranted land.

+**Unhandselled,** *a.* Untouched, unimproved. *Obs.* — **1837** EMERSON *Works* I. (1903) 99 Not out of those on whom systems of education have exhausted their culture, comes the helpful giant to destroy the old or build the new, but out of unhandselled savage nature. **1848** THOREAU *Maine Woods* 70 Here was no man's garden, but the unhandselled globe.

Unhitch, *v.* {1622-} *tr.* To untie (a horse, etc.) from a vehicle, post, etc. {1706-, rare} — **1862** TAYLOR *At Home & Abroad* 2 Ser. II. 91 The younger children unhitched and watered the horses. **1894** *Outing* XXIV. 216/2 Mac and I unhitched and fed old Bald Face. **1920** HOWELLS *Vacation of Kelwyns* 141 Emerance went forward to unhitch the horse from the post.

＊**Unicorn.** + =COLICROOT 2. *Obs.* — **1784** *Amer. Acad. Mem.* I. 435 Unicorn . . . is said to be useful in chronic rheumatism. **1795** WINTERBOTHAM *Hist. View* III. 397 Adder's tongue, *Convallaria bifolia.* Unicorn, *Aletris farinosa.*

+**Unicorn plant.** Any one of various North American plants, esp. *Martynia louisiana,* the fruit of which ends in a long curved beak. — **1817-8** EATON *Botany* (1822) 349 Unicorn plant. . . . Fruit somewhat gourd-like, with one long horn. **1843** TORREY *Flora N.Y.* II. 318 Unicorn-plant. . . . The root is a popular tonic and anthelmintic. **1869** FULLER *Flower Gatherers* 170 The country people usually know it as 'The Blazing Star' or 'Unicorn Plant.' **1901** MOHR *Plant Life Ala.* 733 *Martynia louisiana.* . . . Unicorn Plant. . . . Central Pine belt. Waste places.

+**Unicorn root. a.** The colicroot. **b.** The devil's bit (*Chamælirium luteum*) or its root. — **1817-8** EATON *Botany* (1822) 166 False aloe, unicorn root, false star grass, . . . [is used] as a moderate cathartic. **1847** WEBSTER 1204/3 *Unicorn-root,* a popular name of two plants, viz. *Chamælirium Carolinianum,* to which this name was first applied, and *Aletris farinosa,* . . . ; both used in medicine. **1901** MOHR *Plant Life Ala.* 436 *Chamaelirium luteum.* . . . Devil's Bit; . . . The root, called 'starwort,' or 'unicorn root,' is used medicinally.

＊**Unicorn's horn.** +The devil's bit. (Cf. UNICORN ROOT b.) — **1840** DEWEY *Mass. Flowering Plants* 205 *Helonias dioica.* Blazing Star. Devil's Bit, Unicorn's Horn; . . . wet situations on hills. **1891** *Cent.* 6615/3.

+**Unicycle.** A vehicle having one large wheel. — **1869** *Velocipede* (N.Y.) April 76 Hemming's Unicycle or 'Flying Yankee Velocipede.' **1882** *Wheelman* I. 213/1 Her horse took fright at a unicycle (popularly known as a wheelbarrow). **1883** KNIGHT *Suppl.* 913/1 *Unicycle,* a one-wheeled vehicle for propulsion by foot-power.

+**Unicyclist.** A performer who rides on a one-wheeled vehicle. — **1881** *Sells Bros. Show Bill,* Celebrated Russian Bicyclists, Unicyclists, and Roller Skaters.

Uniform, *n.* A distinctive style of dress worn by all the members of a group, as students, soldiers, etc. {1748-} — **1790** *Harvard Laws,* No Student shall appear, within the limits of the College, or town of Cambridge, in any other dress, than in the uniform belonging to his respective Class, unless he shall have on a night gown, or such an outside garment, as may be necessary, over a coat. **1799** WASHINGTON *Writings* XIV. 148 It is predicated, first, on the supposition, that the uniform for the different grades of officers is conclusively fixed. **1894** *Outing* XXIV. 392/2 The respective States supplying the uniform, as is now done in the case of the various divisions of the National Guard. **1902** BANKS *Newspaper Girl* 107 Handing me an order for that amount on the cashier, and bidding me buy a 'uniform' with it . . . , he bade me farewell.

＊**Uniform,** *v.* +*tr.* To dress or put in uniform. — **1861** NORTON *Army Lett.* 12 We are to be uniformed and equipped immediately. **1884** *Harper's Mag.* April 752/1 At one of their gatherings in 1789, there was a company of 'School-boy Federalists' to the number of 250, uniformed in blue and white. **1902** *Munsey's Mag.* XXVI. 504/2 He established an élite cavalry corps and uniformed it in the most dazzling creation.

Unimproved land. Land not in use, esp. land not in use for agricultural purposes. — **1698** *Conn. Rec.* IV. 253 Twentie five acrs. of unimproved land. **1757** *Essex Inst. Coll.* XLIV. 344 A tract of unimproved Land . . . of about 80 acres. **1815** DRAKE *Cincinnati* 53 The prices of good unimproved land, are between fifty and one hundred and fifty dollars per acre. **1881** *Mich. Gen. Statutes* (1882) I. 391 Commissioners shall also have power to lay out and establish highways on section lines, through uninclosed and unimproved lands.

＊**Union,** *n.*

+**1.** A number of American colonies or states united into one national confederation; a projected association of this sort; the United States.

1754 *Mass. H. S. Coll.* 3 Ser. V. 27 A motion was made that the Commissioners deliver their opinion whether a Union of all the Colonies is not at present absolutely necessary for their security and defence. **1775** JEFFERSON *Writings* IV. 251 A committee of Congress is gone to improve circumstances, so as to bring the Canadians into our Union. **1813** *Niles' Reg.* IV. 189/2 While the enemy is supplied . . . with the provisions of the middle states, . . . the eastern section of the union is really in want of bread! **1862** LINCOLN in Kettell *Hist. Rebellion* II. 638 My paramount object is to save the Union, and not either to save or destroy slavery. **1885** CRAWFORD *Amer. Politician* 334 The imminent danger was that the nonelection of the candidate from the West would produce a secession of the Western States from the Union. **1910** J. HART *Vigilante Girl* 88 The Lone Star Republic . . . was not yet admitted to the Union when I was born.

+**b.** A soldier of the Union army. *colloq.*

1874 'MARK TWAIN' *Sk., New & Old* 204 When de Unions took dat town, dey all run away an' lef' me all by myse'f.

c. The Northern, as distinguished from the Confederate, states. *Obs.*

1880 *Harper's Mag.* Aug. 364/2 'Most of these mountaineers were stanch toh the Union,' said the Virginian with a shrug. **1893** *Ib.* Dec. 20/1 Before the huzzas over the returning armies of the Union had died away in the North, the soldiers of the other army . . . [were] trying to build up again the waste places of their States.

2. A labor or trade union. {1833-}

1836 *Dialogue betw. Strike & Steady* 4 My objection to your Union is, that you wish to use the very compulsion, you will not yourselves endure. **1863** *Boston Jrnl.* 10 May 4/6 The newly formed union of floor-layers . . . met at 987 Washington Street last evening. **1883** *Century Mag.* July 470/1 We ask ourselves what the unions have done toward raising the rate of wages. **1917** SINCLAIR *King Coal* 195 They had him in Sheridan when the union first opened headquarters.

b. One of various other organizations designed to help or protect workers.

1855 COOKE *Ellie* 29 Ellie had often taken these articles to good Mrs. Brown, at the 'Seamstress' Union,' where work was given to poor needlewomen. **1880** *Harper's Mag.* June 27/2 They appeal in vain for consideration, . . . unless they find the Union which is an implacable litigant for them.

3. *attrib.* and *comb.* Designating religious principles, activities, etc., relating to more than one sect.

1834 PECK *Gaz. Illinois* 203 There are three lawyers, . . . a good English school, a Sunday school and Bible class, conducted on union principles. **1852** *Knickerb.* XXXIX. 55 By the large scale of charities, I refer to . . . aid to political enterprises, Union committees, and purchase of ten per cent. bonds of western railways. **1877** JOHNSON *Anderson Co., Kansas* 253 A union Sabbath school was organized at the same place during the same spring [1860]. **1878** COOKE *Happy Dodd* 15 These were not the days of Union lessons, or Sunday-school papers, or helps.

+**4.** Designating persons who espoused the Union cause during the Civil War.

1861 in McClellan *Own Story* 148 Send detachments of a sufficient number of men to the different points in your vicinity where the elections are to be held, to protect the Union voters. **1864** TROWBRIDGE *Cudjo's Cave* 326 [He] saw nothing . . . revolting in the idea of extorting a secret from a hated Union woman by means of the lash. **1865** LOWELL *Writings* V. 254 The rumors which . . . the people believed on the authority of reliable gentlemen from Richmond, or Union refugees whose information could be trusted. **1903** Fox *Little Shepherd* xx, Crittenden, in the name of union lovers and the dead Clay, pleaded with the State to take no part in the fratricidal crime. **1907** ANDREWS *Recoll.* 201 At a dinner at the home of Madame Le Vert, an authoress and Union lady of Mobile, . . . Generals Carr, Totten, and Smith were also guests.

+**b.** Designating men in the Union forces.

1863 Moore *Rebellion Rec.* V. I. 32 A train of cars on the Memphis and Ohio Railroad, laden with a company of Union troops, . . . was this day captured by a large force of rebel cavalry. **1865** *Atlantic Mo.* March 285/1 Drake Talcott, a Union prisoner, marched with other prisoners to Danville. **1866** in *Sherman Lett.* (1894) 273 'Union Scouts' (alias Confederate jayhawkers and deserters) two years after kidnapped me.

+**c.** Designating abstractions, places, organizations, etc., pertaining to the Federal Union during the Civil War.

1862 *Rep. Ind. Affairs* 28 A strong Union sentiment was found to exist among the Indians [in Okla.]. **1866** CARPENTER *At White House* 43 He was improving his first opportunity to go over to the Union lines, when he was taken prisoner. **1885** *Century Mag.* April 934/1 During the passage of the Union fleet she was secured to the river-bank. **1892** *York County Hist. Rev.* 33 He is now a member of the Union Veteran League, No. 65, of York. **1895** G. KING *New Orleans* 314 A Union constitutional convention was held, and a Union constitution of the state adopted, a Union legislature elected.

5. Designating sentiments, places, etc., pertaining to a labor union or unions.

1874 *Internat. Typogr. Union Proc.* 14 Infringement on Union principles in the job department does not affect the hands in the news department. **1896** *Ib.* 43/1 Machines [have been introduced] into every union town in the state. **1898** *Mo. So. Dakotan* I. 106 Hats are made in union factories and in scab factories. **1904** *McClure's Mag.* Feb. 370/1 Many stores, restaurants, and saloons display placards in their windows advertising the fact that they are strictly union shops. **1911** M. W. Ovington *Half a Man* 98 Strong organizations in the South . . . send men North with union membership, who easily transfer to New York locals. **1913** London *Valley of Moon* 198 They're all union-bustin' to beat the band.

6. Designating business enterprises or activities participated or engaged in jointly by different organizations.

1888 *Economist* 10 Nov. 6/2 Union Stock Yards stocks sold at 110. **1901** Ade *40 Modern Fables* 224 Farmers . . . come out of the Union Station carrying . . . Shoe Boxes full of Lunch. **1905** *Forestry Bureau Bul.* No. 61, 52 *Union drive*, a drive of logs belonging to several owners, who share the expense pro rata. (N[orthern] F[orest].)

7. In special combinations.

Union anaconda, =Anaconda; *u. ball,* (see quotation); *u. cockade,* a cockade signifying loyalty to the Federal Union; *u. garment,* a garment having the upper and the lower portions in one piece; *U. labor party,* a political party, organized at Cincinnati in 1887, that espoused the cause of labor; *u. leather,* (see quotation); *u. pope,* (see quotation and cf. Pope 1); *U. States,* the United States; *u. undergarment,* an undergarment the upper and the lower parts of which are in one piece.

1861 Newell *Orpheus C. Kerr* I. 312 Surrender to the Union Anaconda and the United States of America. **1844** *Lowell Offering* IV. 90 There was to be a 'Union ball'; or an assembly in which the 'different classes' should meet. **1798** Dunlap *André* p. viii, Bland . . . [is] in the uniform of a Captain of horse—dress, . . . a horseman's helmet on the head, decorated as usual, and the union cockade affixed. **1904** *Nation* 21 Jan. 51 [Overalls are] what would be called nowadays a 'union garment,' lacking the sleeves. **1891** in B. S. Heath *Labor & Finance Revol.* p. xxxvi, The proceedings of this convention . . . have gone into the history of the Union Labor party there organized. **1885** *Harper's Mag.* Jan. 279/2 'Union' leather designates a combination of oak and hemlock tannage. **1823** Tudor *Otis* 29 [The factions of 'Pope Day'] had what was called an *Union Pope,* when the two parties, after great preparations, met with their pageants, and . . . proceeded to make a common bonfire. **1852** in Stowe *Key* 60/2 [The reality of slavery would be made clear] if Christians would unite, not to destroy the Union States, but honestly to speak out. **1896** *Godey's Mag.* Feb. 218/2 Union undergarments of silk or wool are often substituted.

Union, *a.* +Loyal to the United States, or to the Union cause during the Civil War. — **1845** Hooper *Taking Census* (1928) 120 Bless your union soul, little squire. **1863** Boudrye *Fifth N.Y. Cavalry* (1868) 339 An oyster man . . . Was Union on the York, but Secesh on James river. **1881** J. W. Buel *Border Outlaws* 62 He was my child and Union to the core. **1883** Bagby *Old Va. Gentleman* 148 His auditors [were] in doubt whether he was Union or secesh, or simply a crank.

+**Union army.** An army or the military forces of the United States during the Civil War. — **1866** 'F. Kirkland' *Bk. Anecdotes* 376 Colonel Bailey . . . [believed] that their capture or destruction would involve the destruction of the Union army. **1893** *Harper's Mag.* April 706/1 Not less than 30 per cent. of its electors have fought in the Union armies. **1925** Tilghman *Dugout* 74 Ira had served in the Union army.

+**Union card.** A card attesting the owner's membership in a labor union. — **1874** *International Typogr. Union Proc.* 84 The International Typographical Union shall issue . . . a card, with appropriate designs, to be called the 'Union Card.' **1902** Wilson *Spenders* 340, I can show you people all right that won't ask to see your union card. **1925** Bryan *Memoirs* 463 A man with a 'Union Card' now sits as an adviser to the President.

+**Union cause.** The cause of preserving the Union. — **1862** Greeley in Logan *Great Conspiracy* 432 There is not one . . . intelligent champion of the Union Cause who does not feel that every hour of deference to Slavery is an hour of added and deepened peril. **1885** *Century Mag.* April 923/1 It is necessary . . . to be able to comprehend not only the immediate results to the Union cause, but the whole bearing of the fall of New Orleans on the Civil War. **1890** Langford *Vigilante Days* (1912) 415 Early in the Summer of 1861 he espoused the Union cause.

+**Union church.** A church the services and activities of which are not confined to one sect. — **1847** Howe *Hist. Coll. Ohio* 204 Washington . . . has 1 Lutheran, 1 Presbyterian, 1 Methodist, 1 Union and 1 Catholic church. **1904** Tarbell *Hist. Standard Oil Co.* I. 35 It was not long . . . before there was a church, a union church.

+**Union depot.** A railroad depot that serves two or more lines. — **1862** *Dinsmore's R.R. Guide* No. 101 All changes by this route, from New York to the Mississippi river, made in union depots. **1879** Burdette *Hawkeyes* 18 About two o'clock in the afternoon Mr. Thumbledirk dropped in at the Union depot. **1883** *Wheelman* April 31/1 The depot at Reading . . . was once famous as being the first Union depot of any importance. **1922** Parrish *Case & Girl* 333 The shadow phoned in from the Union depot that Hobart had just purchased two tickets for Patacne.

+**Unioner.** An adherent of the Union cause during the Civil War. *Obs.* — **1879** Tourgee *Fool's Errand* 99, I first heard of it in the mountains of East Tennessee, as instituted for self-protection and mutual support among the sturdy Unioners there in those trying times.

Union flag. {1634-} +**1.** The flag of the federated American colonies during the Revolutionary War. (Cf. Rattlesnake flag.) +**2.** During the Civil War, the flag of the United States as distinguished from that of the Confederate states. — **(1) 1776** *Penna. Ev. Post* 28 May 266/2 The Union Flag of the American States waved upon the Capitol. **(2) 1861** Norton *Army Lett.* 14 He had a big fuss with the boys who put up a Union flag near his house. **1866** 'F. Kirkland' *Bk. Anecdotes* 222/2 Those Union flags fluttered along the fringe where fifty rebel guns were kenneled.

1887 Custer *Tenting on Plains* 219 The girl had known of a Union flag in the State House, held in derision and scornfully treated by the extremists.

Unionism. {1845-} +Advocacy of, or loyalty to, federal union between states. — **1861** Cox *8 Yrs. in Congress* 23 In this work no one gave to General Millson more effective aid than Sherrard Clemens, of Wheeling, . . . whose Unionism never wavered. **1879** Tourgee *Fool's Errand* 125 The instincts of what was termed 'Unionism' . . . led them to affiliate somewhat coolly with the party of reconstruction. **1883** *American* VI. 92 The obstinate Unionism of the mountaineer farmers.

Unionist, *n.* {1799-}

+**1. a.** A supporter of the Federal Union of the United States. Esp. with reference to the efforts at nullification by South Carolina. *Obs.*

1830 D. Webster *Works* III. 259, I am a unionist, and, in this sense, a national republican. **1832** J. Q. Adams *Memoirs* VIII. 513 All the Jackson party, and the Unionists of South Carolina, voted against the consideration. **1833** *Niles' Reg.* XLIV. 20/1 All legal proceedings [may] be thus arrested in the district by the peaceful action of the unionists in their elective character.

b. A supporter of the Union cause during the Civil War.

1861 *N.Y. Tribune* 26 Nov. 4/5 It was the cowardice of the Unionists of the South that created the seeming unanimity there for Secession. **1865** *Nation* I. 109 Anybody might tell that you're no Unionist. **1888** *Century Mag.* Dec. 277/2 When the rebellion broke out he was an ardent Unionist. **1890** G. A. Henty *With Lee in Va.* 185 Although the Unionists were the majority, the party of sympathizers with the South was a strong one.

c. (See quotation.)

1888 M. Lane in *America* 8 Nov. 15 *Unionists.*—The name assumed by the Woolly-heads after the split in the old Whig party in 1850. Also the name of the party that met at Baltimore and nominated Everett and Bell in the campaign of 1860.

2. One who belongs to a union church.

1837 W. Jenkins *Ohio Gaz.* 416 The public buildings [include] . . . six houses of public worship, one belonging . . . to the unionists.

3. A member of a trade union. {1834-}

1883 *Century Mag.* Oct. 906/2 A lot of bad eggs among the strikers—not the unionists proper, . . . intend to go through some of the principal houses. **1898** *Scribner's Mag.* XXIV. 108/2 While the Unionist was talking to the sweater, I walked between the close lines of machines. **1906** *Outlook* 9 June 784/1 The non-union shop from which unionists are completely excluded . . . [is] very strongly represented [in the U.S.].

Unionist, *a.* {1816-} +Loyal to the Union cause during the Civil War. *Obs.* — **1863** Digby *6 Mos. Federal St.* II. 187 The *Atlantic Monthly,* the great New England Review, is very . . . staunchly Unionist, and more or less anti-slavery. **1865** *Atlantic Mo.* April 441/2 He found us thorough Unionist.

+**Unionite.** [*Unionville,* Penn.] A silicate of alumina and lime occurring in various crystalline forms. — **1849** Silliman in *Amer. Jrnl. Science* 2 Ser. VIII. 384 Unionite . . . in general appearance . . . somewhat resembles scapolite or spodumene. **1873** *Amer. Philos. Soc. Proc.* XIII. 374 Silliman described it under the name of *unionite.*

Unionization. The organization of workers into a trade union. — **1896** *Internat. Typogr. Union Proc.* 30/2, I am sure there would be little to gain in its unionization. **1918** *World's Work* XXXV. 486 The issue of the strike being once more unionization.

Unionize, *v.* {1841-} *tr.* To bring under trade union rules or principles; to organize into a trade union or unions the workers of (a place). {1903-} Also as *ppl. a.* — **1890** *Columbus Dispatch* 18 Nov., It has been decided by the Trades Council . . . to unionize all work in the building trades. **1900** *Amer. Rev. of Reviews* XXI. 651 New England papers [report] that nearly every 'unionized' town in that section has now the eight-hour day for building trades workmen. **1914** Atherton *Perch of Devil* 58 Although she . . . is so tyrannically unionized . . . , yet ability and talent make good as always.

+**Union League. 1.** A secret political organization among the newly freed Negroes just after the Civil War. *Obs.* Also attrib. (Cf. Loyal League.) **2.** A northern society established in 1862 to promote the Union cause. — **(1) 1867** in Fleming *Hist. Reconstruction* II. 18 You should organize into a Union League and Republican Clubs. **1872** Powers *Afoot & Alone* 21 From his [a freedman's] tattered breast fluttered a Union League badge, a bit of ribbon worth five cents, for which he said he expended a dollar. **1893** Page in *Harper's Mag.* Dec. 22/1 The negroes were enrolled by the carpetbag leaders in what was known as the Union League. **(2) 1863** in H. W. Bellows *Hist. Sk. Union League Club N.Y.* 37 The Union League . . . shall be [formed] to discountenance and rebuke by moral and social influences all disloyalty to the Federal Government. **1894** S. Leavitt *Our Money Wars* 117 In a speech before the Union League of New Providence, N.J., November 9, 1863, Dr. Townsend went over the question [of currency reform].

Union man. {1871-}

+**1.** One who places his loyalty to the Federal Union above that to any state or section; a member of one of various parties purporting to support the Union.

Cf. Unionist 1, Unconditional Union man.

1837 Sherwood *Gaz. Georgia* (ed. 3) 245 None but 'Union men reside in it,' i.e. Union men in contradistinction to States' right men or nullifiers. **1851** *Knickerb.* XXXVIII. 550 Two stout 'Union men,' who would go out of the way any day to catch a 'fugitive' for a 'Southern brother,' were driving in a gig. **1859** S. Cox *8 Yrs. in Congress* 68 The gentleman undertakes to acknowledge that I am a Union man. **1868** *Ore. State Jrnl.* 25 July 2/1 What Union man can vote for him? **1898** PAGE *Red Rock* 39 Dr. Cary and Mr. Bagby, both strong Union men, had been chosen.

+b. During the Civil War, one supporting the Northern states; a Union soldier.

1861 *Chicago Tribune* 26 May 1/3, 2,500 Secession troops are stationed there, for the express purpose of overawing the Union men. **1862** F. Moore *Rebellion Rec.* V. II. 167 He professed to be a Union man. **1865** KELLOGG *Rebel Prisons* 259 The Doctor of my ward was a Georgian, a fine fellow, and a Union man. **1867** EDWARDS *Shelby* 107 He warred upon the cavalry because they took but few prisoners among the Union men. **1879** *Scribner's Mo.* July 380/1 During that conflict, he was a Union man, a general in the Federal army and the provisional governor of a Southern state.

2. = UNIONIST 3.

1896 *Internat. Typogr. Union Proc.* 27/2 He would have nothing to say or do with the Union or Union men. **1900** *Congress. Rec.* 18 Jan. 954/2 The union men in the Government Printing Office claim that if this amendment is adopted the work will be done by nonunion men. **1916** WILSON *Somewhere* 168 A union man nowadays would do just enough to keep within the law.

Union meeting. **+a.** A religious meeting participated in by people of different sects. **+b.** Among Shakers, a meeting for social intercourse and fellowship. — **1871** DE VERE 246 It is gratifying to think . . . how triumphantly the fraternal love among all Christians has been proven by the Union meetings held in all the States. **1884** Schaff *Relig. Encycl.* III. 2169/2 Meetings are held [by the Shakers] . . . for social converse, called 'Union Meetings.'

+Union party. a. In South Carolina, the political party composed of those who opposed the nullifiers. *Obs.* **b.** A group of Union soldiers. *Obs.* **c.** A political party supporting the Union cause; *spec.*, during the campaign of 1864 and later, the Republican party including those War Democrats who favored vigorous prosecution of the war. *Obs.*

(a) **1831** J. Q. ADAMS *Memoirs* VIII. 449 Mr. James Blair, a member of the House of Representatives from South Carolina, . . . is of what they call the Union party. **1833** *Niles' Reg.* XLIV. 33/2 The 'union party,' also opposed to the protective system, appear fully satisfied. **1846** MANSFIELD *Winfield Scott* 231 The name of the party of the majority was known as the nullification party, and that of the minority as the Union party. (b) **1863** Moore *Rebellion Rec.* V. I. 42 The Union party retired to a house in the neighborhood, from which they fought the rebels six hours. (c) **1866** *Ore. State Jrnl.* 30 June 1/2 The great Union party . . . shall continue to administer the Government it preserved. **1867** in Fleming *Hist. Reconstruction* II. 44 Unfortunately for us, poor proscribed members of the Union party, these military men have too much influence with our ignorant black population. **1867** *Congress. Globe* 16 Feb. 1445/2 This bolting convention of radicals at Cleveland was condemned . . . by the great mass of the Union party.

+Union people. Those who favored the Union cause during the Civil War. Now hist. — **1865** KELLOGG *Rebel Prisons* 51 Among them were many Union people whose unmistakable expressions of sympathy did us much good. **1888** SHERIDAN *Memoirs* I. 124 Considerable apprehension was felt by the Union people lest the State [California] might be carried into the Confederacy. **1907** ANDREWS *Recoll.* 155 At Pikeville we were in the midst of Union people who wanted to take the oath of allegiance.

+Union Republican. A member of the Republican party who gave staunch support to the war policy of President Lincoln. Now hist. Also attrib. — **1867** *Congress. Globe* 12 April 835/3 [These offices] were filled by Mr. Lincoln with good, responsible, reliable Union Republicans. **1868** *N.Y. Herald* 2 July 8/4 The Union republicans of Richmond county have elected Messrs. Wagner, Webster and Seaman. **1886** LOGAN *Great Conspiracy* 599 The victory of the Union-Republican Party at this election was an amazing one.

+Union-Saver. (See quot. 1914.) — **1860** G. W. Bungay *Bobolink Minstrel* 38 A Union Saver, brush in hand, Once made the tour of this broad land. **1914** *Cycl. Amer. Govt.* III. 594/1 *Union Saver*, the element of the Whig party during the two decades preceding the Civil War, which advocated compromising measures in dealing with slavery.

+Union school. (See quot. 1852.) *Obs.* — **1852** *Ind. Hist. Soc. Publ.* III. 615 Union, or graded schools, for the terms are synonymous, are simply the schools of a given township, village or city, classified and arranged according to the attainments of the pupils. **1867** *Ore. State Jrnl.* 12 Jan. 2/3 In Michigan every town of 3,000 inhabitants is required to establish a Union school for both sexes.

+Union soldier. A soldier who served on the Northern or Union side during the Civil War. — **1864** 'PENNIMAN' *Tanner-Boy* 99 Only a short distance off was a large body of well-armed rebel troops, ready, it was reported, to turn back on the entering Union soldiers at a given signal. **1900** *Congress. Rec.* 19 Jan. 1004/2 On behalf of the Union soldier of the North, the East, and the West I say we owe our thanks. **1920** LEWIS *Main Street* 16 Carol and Kennicott found prints [of] . . . whiskered Union soldiers in slant forage caps and rattling sabers.

+Union ticket. 1. A ticket supporting candidates of different political views. **2.** The ticket of the Constitutional Union party, or of any one

of various other organizations or parties purporting to support the Union. **3.** = UNION CARD. — (1) **1813** *Mass. H.S. Coll.* 2 Ser. II. 176 [In] the years 1809 and 1812 . . . a union ticket prevailed. **1850** LOWELL *Letters* I. 188 I shall vote the 'Union' ticket (half Free-soil, half Democrat). (2) **1862** KETTELL *Hist. Rebellion* I. 37 The election was still further complicated by the nomination of a Union ticket, at the head of which was placed John Bell of Tennessee, while Edward Everett of Massachusetts was its candidate for the Vice-Presidency. **1866** RICHARDSON *Secret Service* 31 The newspapers of the city, with a single exception, were disloyal, but the Union ticket was elected by a majority of more than three hundred. **1868** *Ore. State Jrnl.* 8 June 2/4 In Washington county the whole Union ticket is elected by an increased majority. (3) **1891** 'THANET' *Otto the Knight* 19, I went to two or three cities, but I couldn't get work, having no union ticket.

Unitarian, *n.* One who maintains the doctrine of Unitarianism. { 1687– } — **1822** WOODS *English Prairie* (1904) 318, I think they style themselves Unitarians. **1834** in *Atlantic Mo.* XXVI. 489, I scanned him sharply—he being the first Unitarian professed, that I had ever seen. **1883** *Century Mag.* July 457/1 Am not sure with regard to the propriety of one who thinks himself an Unitarian.

Unitarian, *a.* Of or pertaining to the Unitarians or to Unitarianism. { 1687– } — **1824** LONGFELLOW in S. Longfellow *H. W. Longfellow* I. 52, I presume he has frequently mentioned to you our little Unitarian Society at Bowdoin. **1832** KEMBLE *Journal* I. 224 Throughout all the northern states, and particularly those of New England, the Unitarian form of faith prevails very extensively. **1879** HOWELLS *Lady of Aroostook* 93 He had, several years earlier, forsaken the pale Unitarian worship of his family. **1894** — in *Harper's Mag.* 823/1, I stood on the Promenade at Portland with the kind young Unitarian minister.

Unitarianism. The doctrine of those who affirm the unipersonality of the deity { 1698– }; +esp. the doctrine of the New England Congregational churches which followed Channing and others in the early nineteenth century. — *a*1817 DWIGHT *Travels* I. 511 At the present time, Unitarianism seems to be the predominating system [in Boston, Mass.]. **1822** EMERSON in *Century Mag.* XXVI. 454/1 Meantime Unitarianism will not hide her honours. **1852** EASTMAN *Aunt Phillis's Cabin* 136 There is Unitarianism, that faith that would undermine the perfect structure of the Christian religion. **1914** *Lit. Digest* 24 June 1549/1 Some signs are seen of narrowing the old cleavage between New England Unitarianism and Congregationalism.

* United, *a.* In special combinations.

United Baptists, (see quotation); *U. Brother*, one of the United Brethren in Christ; *U. Nations*, = FIVE NATIONS; *u. ranger*, a ranger on the side of the United States; *U. Republic*, the United States.

1889 P. BUTLER *Recollections* 253 'Hardshell' Baptists . . . wish to be known as Old Baptists, or United Baptists, for they allege that they are the lineal descendants of the United Baptists, and that the Missionary Baptists have apostatized. **1871** EGGLESTON *Hoosier Schoolm.* 121, I don't know whether you're a Hardshell . . . or a United Brother, or a Millerite. **1745** *Penna. Col. Rec.* V. 8 We were inclinable to speak to the Indians of the United Nations separately. **1857** *Ill. Agric. Soc. Trans.* II. 362, I was a private united ranger during the year 1813. **1832** DUNLAP *Hist. Amer. Theatre* 36 [Boston] now holds but a third place in the scale of political importance among the cities of the United Republic.

United Brethren.

1. Brethren united in Christian faith.

[**1692** C. MATHER *Blessed Unions* (title-page), A most happy union, has been lately made between those two eminent parties in England, which have now changed the names of Presbyterians, and Congregationals, for that of United Brethren.] **1702** — *Magnalia* (1853) II. 75 The difference, as to this matter, between a Presbyterian and a Congregational man (who are nevertheless 'united brethren') is this.

+2. The Moravians. Also *Old United Brethren.*

1753 in *Memorial of Monuments Erected by Moravian Hist. Soc.* (1860) 67 [We are] confirmed in the choice we have made of one of the United Brethren to be our minister. **1822** *Ann. 17th Congress* 1 Sess. 234 Mr. Brown, of Ohio, said . . . he was unable to give an estimate . . . of the value of the property in Ohio, possessed by the United Brethren. **1844** Rupp *Relig. Denominations* 692 This denomination . . . is distinguished from the Old United Brethren or Moravian Church, by the additional phrase of 'In Christ.' **1876** *Moravian Hist. Soc. Trans.* I. 11 The Nazareth congregation of the United Brethren presented us with a room in the old stone mansion.

+3. A denomination which was organized in Maryland in 1800 under the leadership of the Rev. P. W. Otterbein and Martin Boehm. In full *United Brethren in Christ.* (Cf. OTTERBEIN METHODIST.)

[**1800** in Drury *Hist. Church United Brethren in Christ* 183 Von Die Vereinigte Bruederschaft zu Christo.] **1822** *Discipline United Brethren in Christ* (1895) 70 They there united themselves into a society, which bears the name of 'The United Brethren in Christ'; and elected William Otterbein and Martin Bœhm as superintendents or bishops. **1834** PECK *Gaz. Illinois* 91 In McLean County is a society of United Brethren, or as some call them, Dutch Methodists. **1884** Schaff *Religious Encycl.* III. 2422/2 In the year 1800, at one of these conferences, these scattered societies were organized into one body; and the name 'United Brethren in Christ' was adopted as the official title of the denomination thus formed. **1919**

Census: Religious Bodies 1916 II. 696 The polity of the United Brethren is similar to that of the Methodist Episcopal Church.

+United Colonies. a. The New England colonies of Massachusetts Bay, Plymouth, Connecticut, and New Haven which bound themselves together in 1643 for protection against the Indians, French, and Dutch. *Obs.* **b.** The colonies or states which united against Great Britain at the opening of the Revolutionary War. *Obs.*

(a) **1643** *Plymouth Laws* 309 They all be and henceforth bee called by the Name of *The United Colonies of New-England.* **1676** I. MATHER *K. Philip's War* (1862) 102 The Commissioners of the united Colonies sat at Boston, in the latter end of September. **1682** M. RAWLINSON *Narr. Captivity* Pref. 1 The Narrhagansets quarters . . . were the second time beaten up by the Forces of the united Colonies. (b) **1775** *Mass. H. S. Coll.* 3 Ser. V. 75 We acquainted you yesterday from whence we came, and by whose authority; namely, by the authority of the Twelve United Colonies dwelling upon this island of America. **1776** C. CARROLL *Jrnl. Visit to Canada* (1845) 40 Saw two frigates . . . building for the service of the United Colonies. **1823** J. THACHER *Military Jrnl.* 36 This day [in 1775] is devoted to a Public Fast throughout the United Colonies.

United States. {1617–, the Netherlands} Cf. U.S.

I. +1. The republic or Federal Union of North America. At first regarded as plural, the term is now usually construed as singular.

1776 *Jrnls. Cont. Congress* VI. 865 Resolved, That the inhabitants of Canada, captivated by the United States, . . . be released and sent home. **1792** *Ann. 2d Congress* 1019 The United States already, in a great measure, supply themselves with nails and spikes. **1810** PIKE *Sources Miss.* 97 The crime was committed long before the United States assumed its authority, and . . . no law of theirs could affect it. **1836** DEWEES *Lett. from Texas* 193 A part of us went down to Harrisburg . . . for the purpose of bringing up a couple of cannons, which had been sent to this place by our brethren of the United States. **1863** HALE *If, Yes, & Perhaps* 207 'United States' had picked you out first as one of her own confidential men of honor. **1885** CRAWFORD *Amer. Politician* 211 The United States are only an institution after all. **1900** *Congress. Rec.* 20 Feb. 2004/2 In its constitutional meaning the term 'United States' relates entirely to the States forming the Federal Republic. **1917** *Lit. Digest* 12 May 1395/2 The United States is prepared for sacrifices as great as the British and French people have already made.

+2. The English language as written and spoken in the United States. *colloq.*

1879 BURDETTE *Hawkeyes* 248 There should be a law compelling railroad people to speak United States. **1895** GRAHAM *Stories of Foot-Hills* 166 Ricardo don't understand United States. **1900** *Congress. Rec.* 5 Feb. 1516/2 Suppose the appointee is simply a good American citizen who speaks only good 'United States.'

+b. *To talk United States,* to use plain and forceful language; to be American. *colloq.*

1883 *Harper's Mag.* Sept. 561/1 The architects are still sometimes exhorted, to 'talk United States.' **1898** HAMBLEN *Gen. Manager's Story* 134 If he made any disparaging comments . . . , I vowed to myself that I'd talk United States to him if I lost my job by it.

II. *attrib.* **+3.** Designating establishments created, fostered, or maintained by the United States government.

1827 DRAKE & MANSFIELD *Cincinnati* 80 United States Land-Office. **1840** *Diplom. Corr. Texas* I. (1908) 470, I have in my possession a certified copy of an indictment found against him by the Grand Jury for the United States Court. **1865** *Atlantic Mo.* Feb. 233/1 For three years I had been a thorough believer in the United States Sanitary Commission. **1893** *Harper's Mag.* Feb. 464 'N' you offered us the United States Mint for 'em even so, th' ain't for sale.

+4. Designating soldiers or parts of the military forces of the United States government. Also *U.S.*

See also UNITED STATES ARMY.

1840 *Boston Transcript* 14 April 2/3 Company A of the 1st Regiment of U.S. Artillery . . . will leave this city. **1845** *Xenia Torch-Light* 31 July 2/2 A party of U.S. troops arrived from Governor's Island. **1859** MATSELL *Vocabulum* 93 *U.S. cove,* a soldier; a man in the employ of the United States. **1865** PIKE *Scout & Ranger* (1932) 24 Captain Ross, the sub agent, and Captain Plummer, commanding the United States regulars, at the post, had mistaken us for Baylor's men, and had accordingly prepared a vigorous defense. **1881** *Harper's Mag.* May 811/2 The male chorus is supplied by United States soldiers. **1900** *Congress. Rec.* 11 Jan. 787/2 Second Lieut. Arthur W. Orton Thirty-ninth Infantry, United States Volunteers, to be first lieutenant.

+5. Designating titles, laws, etc., relating to lands belonging to or claimed by the United States government.

1846 POLK *Diary* (1929) 61 He was authorized to say that I had asserted the United States title to Oregon up to 54°40′. **1849** CHAMBERLAIN *Indiana Gazetteer* 281 Digby had bought the town site at the United States land sale at a little more than Congress price. **1916** EASTMAN *From Deep Woods* 14 He had taken up and improved [the farm] under the United States homestead laws.

+6. Designating money, securities, etc., issued by the United States government. Also *U.S.*

See also UNITED STATES BOND.

1852 *Whig Almanac 1853* 27/2 All unsatisfied military land warrants . . . may be surrendered, and assignable United States scrip, payable in public lands, issued therefor. **1865** KELLOGG *Rebel Prisons* 277 From one to three dollars in U.S. money was the price for being permitted to carry out a dead body. **1865** *Atlantic Mo.* XV. 209/2, I was safe as the owner of an annuity based upon United States securities. **1889** *Century Mag.* Feb. 556/2 The rapidly increasing popularity of the United States notes, or greenbacks, . . . [induced] Congress to grant, a wide extension of the authority to issue them.

+7. Designating persons living in or serving the United States. Also *U.S.*

1857 DAVIS *El Gringo* 300 The United States Attorney for New Mexico is obliged to make the circuit of the Territory twice a year. **1859** *U.S. cove* [see sense 4]. **1885** *Wkly. New Mexican Rev.* 16 April 1/2 Sheriff Romulo Martinez is to be United States Marshall. **1916** C. A. EASTMAN *From Deep Woods* (1929) 10 Father showed him his papers as a United States citizen.

+8. Designating objects or things owned by, or otherwise associated with, the United States government. Also *U.S.*

See also UNITED STATES MAIL.

1859 MATSELL *Vocabulum* 93 *U.S. plate,* fetters; handcuffs. **1867** Goss *Soldier's Story* 144 Every batch of prisoners sent into the 'pen' were accompanied by a spy in U.S. blue. **1874** ALDRICH *P. Palfrey* vii, The speaker was a gaunt, sunburnt man, with deer-skin leggings, fringed at the seams and gathered at the waist by a U.S. belt. **1876** WARNER *Gold of Chickaree* 367 A mutual friend of all the parties had laid the United States flag down in her drawing room as a floorcloth, to be trodden under foot. **1888** *Century Mag.* Nov. 159/1 The army wagon, the big blue wagon, the six-mule wagon, the U.S. wagon, Was blessed or was cursed. **1898** PAGE *Red Rock* 503 Three men in United States uniform stood in the doorway.

+9. Designating terms used by people in the United States.

1895 A. O. MYERS *Bosses & Boodle* 39 The word Boss is a United States word, belonging solely to our language. It was taken from an old Dutch word, Baas, meaning a master workman or superintendent.

+United States Army. The army maintained by the United States government. Also *U.S. Army.* Also attrib. — **1836** *Diplom. Corr. Texas* I. (1908) 104, I sometime ago addressed a letter to General Gaines of the United States Army on the subject of the Indians of our frontier. **1870** *Republican Rev.* 29 Oct. 2/1 The U.S. Army officers in New Mexico. Their kindness to Catholic Missionaries. **1881** *Harper's Mag.* Jan. 232/2 [The] little cook at last enlisted in the United States army. **1917** *Lit. Digest* 2 June 1712/2 Maj.-Gen. John J. Pershing . . . is the youngest of his rank in the United States Army.

+United States Bank.

1. One or other of two banks chartered by Congress in 1791 and 1816; also, a continuation of the latter bank. Now hist. (Cf. NATIONAL BANK 2.)

1819 McMURTRIE *Sk. Louisville* 116 Upon the location of a Branch of the United States Bank here, . . . these same lots . . . rose to 800 dollars per foot. **1833** GOUGE *Paper-Money & Banking* (1835) 19/2 One year before the expiration of the charter of the United States Bank, and two years before the commencement of the war with Great Britain, the Bank mania raged in Pennsylvania. **1841** *Picayune* 31 Jan. 2/3 Resumption in Philadelphia. . . . Numerous persons were seen gathering in front of the U.S. Bank. **1900** *Congress. Rec.* 17 Jan. 915/2 The old United States Bank, of which Nick Biddle was president. **1913** A. C. COLE *Whig Party in So.* 25 Jackson's war on the United States Bank stirred up general excitement throughout the country.

2. *attrib.* **a.** In sense 1. **b.** In sense: Issued by a national bank.

1837 in Mackenzie *Van Buren* (1846) 178 The amount of payments to the Morris Canal and United States Bank Agency, as I am informed, would be about $12,000,000. **1845** *Ib.* 236 Before the summer was over, however, Mr. Webb bolted from the democratic party on the United States bank question. **1852** GOUGE *Fiscal Hist. Texas* 97 The money . . . consisted of United States Bank post-notes. **1886** *Leslie's Mo.* Jan. 68/2 He was stripped of chains and . . . great rolls of United States Bank notes.

+United States bond. A bond issued by the United States government. Also *U.S. bond.* — **1841** *Jamestown (N.Y.) Jrnl.* 7 April 1/2 Let Congress pass a law authorizing the issue of U.S. Bonds having 20 yrs. to run. **1870** M. H. SMITH *20 Years Wall St.* 318 The fellow went up to the safe, took one hundred thousand dollars of United States bonds, . . . and has never since been seen. **1900** *Congress. Rec.* 17 Jan. 906/1 We heard a distinguished Senator from Vermont say to the Senate with great solemnity, 'If you pass this bill, you will sell no more United States bonds except at a great discount.'

+United States Grant. Gen. U.S. (*i.e.,* Ulysses Simpson) Grant (1822–85). A nickname. — **1866** W. F. G. SHANKS *Personal Recoll. Dist. Generals* 117 'United States Grant' is an appellation much more common than Ulysses S. Grant.

United Statesian. A citizen of or dweller in the United States. {1892–} — **1892** *Nation* LV. 433/3 A recent writer in the London *Notes and Queries* . . . insists on the name United Statesians as best fitting dwellers in the United States. **1916** *Nation* CII. 74 The protest . . . of the Canadians against the habit which the Unitedstatesians have of arrogating to themselves the name American.

+**United States mail.** Mail in the care of the United States Post Office. Also *U.S. mail.* Also attrib. — **1837** *Jamestown* (N.Y.) *Jrnl.* 26 July 2/2 On either side of the car is painted in large letters, 'United States Mail Car.' **1846** HUGHES *Diary* 85 Capt. Reid . . . brought U.S. mail. **1855** in *Pres. Mess. & P.* V. 322 An act making appropriations for the transportation of the United States mail, by ocean steamers and otherwise.

United States of America. = UNITED STATES I.
1776 *Battle of Brooklyn* I. iv, My dear General, the great, the important day advances; big with the fate of empire, in the united States of America. **1789** *Ann. 1st Congress* 1 Sess. 17 It appeared that George Washington, Esq. was elected President, and John Adams, Esq., Vice President of the United States of America. **1806** FESSENDEN *Democracy Unveiled* I. 121n., Freedonia is a cant phrase, which certain small poets or prosaic scribblers . . . would have us adopt as an appellative to designate the United States of America. **1876** in Ingram *Centennial Expos.* 87 To the United States of America, through Congress, we are indebted for the aid which crowned our success. **1917** in Scott *Wilson's Foreign Policy* 274 The Imperial German Government has committed repeated acts of war against the Government and the people of the United States of America.

+**Unit rule.** (See quotations.) — **1884** *Century Mag.* Nov. 125 A device called the 'unit rule,' whereby the whole vote of the delegation is thrown by a majority of its members. **1914** *Cycl. Amer. Govt.* III. 594/1 *Unit Rule.* This rule is in vogue in Democratic national conventions. . . . Instructions are given to delegates by the state conventions to vote as a unit.

***Universal, a.**[1] +*Universal Yankee nation,* a term applied to the United States, the North, or New England. — **1830** *Mass. Spy* 6 Jan. (Th.), It will probably light up a smile in the features of 'the universal Yankee nation' [New Eng.]. **1860** *Richmond Enquirer* 1 May 1/5 (Th.), It is the universal custom of the universal Yankee nation to vaunt itself, and boast of its glorious triumphs. **1881** *Harper's Mag.* March 628/2 If any nation can afford to laugh good-naturedly at itself for some things, it is the universal Yankee nation.

+**Universal, a.**[2] Universalist. — **1840** *Niles' Nat. Reg.* 8 Aug. 368/3 The rev. Mr. Smith, late minister of the Universal church in Hartford, Connecticut, and the rev. Mr. Whittaker, . . . have both declared their solemn convictions that Universalism is not a scripture doctrine. **1868** W. C. FOWLER *Eng. Language* 122 Classification of Americanisms. . . . Ungrammatical expressions, disapproved by all; as, . . . *Universal preacher* for Universalist preacher.

Universal (compulsory) education. The provision of free school instruction for all children, freq. with attendance required by law. — **1867** *Nation* V. 192/1 Universal compulsory education is at first costly, but it is, in the long run, the truest economy. **1873** *Republic* I. 34 Its receipt by any State [is] conditioned on the support of free schools for universal education.

Universal Empire. +A secret organization in the South after the Civil War similar in purpose to the Ku-Klux Klan. — **1880** *46th Congress 2 Sess.* Sen. Rep. No. 693, p. xvii The distrust of Democracy . . . was inspired during the days when the 'Kuklux,' the 'White Brotherhood,' the 'Universal Empire,' and the 'Stonewall Guard' spread terror and desolation over the State.

Universaler. {Universaller, 1626} +A member of the Universalist church. *colloq.* — **1846–51** WHITCHER *Bedott P.* ix. 87, I don't care if he is a Universaler nother. **1867** *Harper's Mag.* Aug. 408/2 The old Universaller was not entirely sure but that there might be [some catch in it].

+**Universalian, a.** Relating to theological universalism. — **1837** W. JENKINS *Ohio Gaz.* 357 Perrysburg . . . has . . . three houses for public worship, (methodist, presbyterian, and universalian). *Ib.* 457 The religious sects in this county are composed of the presbyterian, . . . universalian, and christians, or free-will baptists. **1853** E. G. HOLLAND *Mem. J. Badger* (1854) 205 [Calvinism's] bold premises were the foundation of the plea of its opposite extreme—the Universalian statement.

Universalism. The theological doctrine that all souls will be saved and that good will ultimately triumph. {1805–} — **1828** SHERBURNE *Memoirs* 142 My faith in Universalism fled like the baseless fabric of a vision. **1844** Rupp *Relig. Denominations* 724 Universalism was introduced into the United States as a distinctive doctrine, by John Murray. **1878** *N. Amer. Rev.* CXXVI. 330 Universalism . . . adopts the theological method diluted by sentimental considerations.

Universalist, n. One who believes in the ultimate salvation of all people {1626–}; +a member of a sect or denomination maintaining this view or, in pl., such a sect. — **1786** BENTLEY *Diary* I. 36 Attended the association at Cape Ann . . . so much agitated by the controversy between Mr. Forbes, & J. Murray the Universalist. **1801** *Hist. Review & Directory* II. 39 A new sect has lately started, called the Universalists. **1844** Rupp *Relig. Denominations* 653 Those who formed a distinct sect were more frequently denominated Universalists than Restorationists. **1898** HARPER *S. B. Anthony* I. 5 Daniel became in later years, a thorough Universalist.

Universalist, a. {1819–} +Belonging to, or representing, the denomination made up of Universalists. — **1846** *Indiana Mag. Hist.* XXIII. 279 He became a miserable backslider, and is now an unhappy Universalist preacher. **1847** HOWE *Hist. Coll. Ohio* 348 The village contains . . . 1 Universalist church. **1870** *Nation* 27 Jan. 59/1 In Maine, at the end of 1868 there were forty Universalist clergymen. **1877** W. WRIGHT

Big Bonanza 33 A. B. Grosch, a Universalist clergyman of considerable note, and editor of a Universalist paper at Utica, New York.

***University.**
*1. An institution giving graduate instruction and granting degrees in its various departments.
In the United States the term is usually applied to educational institutions that have graduate or professional schools but it is often used loosely of a college.
1650 *Conn. Rec.* I. 555 They may bee fitted for the Vniversity. **1679** *Harvard Rec.* I. 39, I give, and bequeath unto the Colledg, or University . . . the summe of one thousand pounds. **1785** J. ADAMS *Works* IX. 530 He is anxious to study some time at your university [Harvard] before he begins the study of the law. **1829** J. SPARKS *Corresp. Bancroft & Sparks* 136 It is a great mistake, however, to call any of our institutions by the name of Universities. They are neither such, nor ever can be, without a radical change. **1884** *Critic* 10 May 216/2 Some of our universities, so called, have not the full complement of faculties. **1920** HOWELLS *Vacation of Kelwyns* 88, I ought to resign my position in the university.

b. A building or buildings housing, or formerly housing, a school or university.
1808 ASHE *Travels* 13, I saw an old brick building called *the university,* in which the scholars had not left a whole pane of glass. **1835** in *S. Lit. Messenger* IV. 198/1 The University is a collection of brick buildings, forming a square; on one side are the residences of the faculty.

+c. (See quotation.)
1856 HALL *College Words* (ed. 2) 472 *University,* . . . at some American colleges, a name given to a university student.

2. Attrib. and comb. with *campus, course,* etc.
1868 *Rep. Comm. Agric. 1867* 331 A 'University Fund' of $300,000 had been realized. **1869** *Ib. 1868* 140 Students enter upon the university course with a certain preparation and self-confidence as the result of this brief term of study. **1872** HOLMES *Poet* 23 The soil of the University town is divided into patches of sandy and of clayey ground. **1895** *Univ. Nebraska Calendar 1895–6* 33 The Experiment Station Farm . . . [is] northeast of the University campus and connected with it by electric cars. **1905** *Forestry Bureau Bul.* No. 62, 36 There are four classes—public school lands, university lands, asylum lands, and county school lands. **1922** *Who's Who in Amer.* XII. 702/2 Claxton, Philander Priestley, univ. provost.

+**University settlement.** An institution maintained by university people for social uplift among the underprivileged in a large city. Also attrib. — **1892** *Philanthropy & Social Progress* 92 There ought to be . . . a University Settlement in each considerable neighborhood of every great city. **1894** B. MATTHEWS in *Harper's Mag.* June 33/2, I was on my way to the University Settlement to look you up. **1901** *Univ. Settlement Rep.* (Chicago) 13 The officers and teachers of the University Settlement Day Nursery Association present to interested friends its first biennial report.

+**Unleached (wood) ashes.** Ashes that have not been leached, used as fertilizer. — **1804** in J. Roberts *Penna. Farmer* 111 Are leeched or unleeched ashes most beneficial as a manure? **1850** *Rep. Comm. Patents 1849: Agric.* 318 This manure should be composed of half a bushel of unleached ashes. **1884** L. F. ALLEN *New Amer. Farm Bk.* 81 Eight bushels of unleached wood ashes.

***Unload, v.** *tr.* and *absol.* To sell; to get rid of by sale. *colloq.* {1876} — **1876** HARTE in *Scribner's Mo.* XI. 853 There's a dozen men, as you and me know, that we could unload to to-morrow. **1884** *Boston Jrnl.* 15 March 2/3 There is a flavor of reviving an excitement in order to unload oil lands. **1894** *Vt. Agric. Rep.* XIV. 94 It is a speculation to unload a horse at many times his value. **1901** MERWIN & WEBSTER *'Calumet K'* 30 They're going to make a mighty good try at unloading it on him and making him pay for it. **1916** 'BOWER' *Phantom Herd* 69 He blew in here temporarily hard up and wanting to unload.

+**Unlocated land.** Public land the limits and boundaries of which have not been surveyed and recorded. — **1776** JEFFERSON *Writings* (1893) II. 80 The idea of Congress selling out unlocated lands has been sometime dropped. **1780** HAMILTON in Bancroft *Hist. U.S.* X. 412 The confederation should provide certain perpetual revenues, . . . which, together with the duties on trade and the unlocated lands, would give congress a substantial existence. **1792** IMLAY *Western Territory* 13 A land office was opened by the state, granting warrants for any quantity of unlocated land.

Unlotted, a. {1758–} +Of land: Owned by a colonial town and not allotted to individual owners. With *out. Obs.* — **1637** *Dedham Rec.* 33 Ther are about 16: acres of land Remayne lying at the Southermost corner of the mydle playne as yet unlotted out. **1673** *Braintree Rec.* 15 The Towne of Boston still retaining the right and power of allotting and disposing of all these lands to ytickler [i.e., particular] persons yt are yet vnlotted out.

+**Unmailable, a.** Not suitable for mailing; concerned with matter unsuitable for sending through the mail. — **1874** *Official Postal Guide* p. xvii, Such matter must be forwarded to the Dead-Letter Office, marked as 'unmailable.' **1893** CUSHING *Story of P.O.* 249 No such feeling of resignation can surround the letters handled in the Unmailable and Property Division. **1896** *Columbus Dispatch* 17 Dec. 7 Inquiries have been made of the department as to the correct treatment of registered articles . . . found to be unmailable.

***Unmarked,** *a.* Of domestic live stock: Unprovided with a mark or brand of ownership. {1651} — **1659** *Plymouth Laws* 124 [Anyone who neglects to mark his horses] shall forfite five shillings . . . for every horse found unmarked. **1695** *N.C. Col. Rec.* I. 454 Ordered that noe p[er]son hunt or kill any unmarked Cattle in the neck of land lying upon Ruscopannock River. **1747** *Ga. Col. Rec.* VI. 184 All unmarked Cattle becomes the Property of him that can lay hold of them.

Unmentionables. *pl.* Trousers. *Obs.* {1836-} — **1830** *Mass. Spy* 6 Jan. (Th. 478), The man in 'Varmount,' who, disdaining all machinery, took himself up by the waist bands of his unmentionables. **1847** FORD *Hist. Illinois* 94 The leather breeches strapped tight around the ancle, had disappeared before unmentionables of more modern material. **1881** RITTENHOUSE *Maud* 17, I'm making Robin . . . some unmentionables.

Unorganized, *a.* {1690-} +**1.** Of a county or other area: Not having local governing officers or not formally organized as a government. +**2.** Characterized by the presence of nonunion working men. — (1) **1850** FILLMORE in *Pres. Mess. & P.* V. 67 The governor of Texas . . . dispatched a special commissioner with full power and instructions to extend the civil jurisdiction of the State over the unorganized counties of El Paso, Worth, Presidio, and Santa Fe. **1861** *Mich. Gen. Statutes* I. (1882) 195 All the taxes levied in such unorganized county . . . shall be expended within the limits of such unorganized territory. **1873** *Ib.* 270 The governor [shall] appoint marshals to take the census in the unorganized territory not otherwise provided in this act. (2) **1896** *Internat. Typogr. Union Proc.* 27/2 Complaints were frequent from other parts of the state on account of the unorganized condition of Rochester.

* **Unpleasantness.** +The Civil War. Freq. in phrase *the late unpleasantness.*

1868 *Congress. Globe* 14 Feb. 1174/1 Leaving out of view 'the late unpleasantness.' *Ib.* 9 July 3880/2 The rebel generals . . . think the 'little unpleasantness' did not amount to much, after all. **1872** *Harper's Mag.* Feb. 479/1 During our 'late unpleasantness' a 'convalescent hospital' was established . . . in Nashville. **1882** *Congress. Globe* 1 June 4418/1 We know the history of the recent 'unpleasantness,' as I will call it,—well, 'war,' gentlemen say. **1891** *Ib.* 29 Jan. 1981/2, I always deplore the recalling on the floor of Congress of the history of the past 'unpleasantness.' **1903** *Congress. Directory* (58th Congress Extraord. Sess.) 4 [He] was a private soldier during the 'late unpleasantness' on the losing side.

transf. **1903** *N.Y. Times* 19 Sept. 3 The only soldier to be killed from Orange during the late unpleasantness with the Filipinos. **1905** *N.Y. Ev. Post* 28 Jan. 5 The sting of the late unpleasantness, the blizzard, has declined almost to a memory.

***Unprotected,** *a.* Not protected or favored by a tariff. — **1820** *Ann. 16th Congress* 2 Sess. 2311 The unprotected state of American manufactures. **1871** GROSVENOR *Protection* 117 Unless we can import foreign gas, the makers and gas-fitters must also be classed as unprotected. **1885** CRAWFORD *Amer. Politician* 225 We both agree in saying that it is great nonsense to leave iron unprotected.

+**Unreconstructed,** *a.* **1.** Not reconciled to the results of the Civil War. Also absol. **2.** (See quotation.) — (1) **1869** *Nation* 25 March 221/2 Butler's Committee on Reconstruction reported in favor of extending . . . the time during which an 'unreconstructed' Southerner may retain his Government employment. **1884** 'CRADDOCK' *Where Battle Was Fought* 5, 'I thank the Federal army for nothing,' declared the unreconstructed, bitterly. (2) **1891** *Cent.* 6640/1 *Unreconstructed,* . . . not yet reorganized as a State of the Union: applied to seceded States after the civil war.

+**Unreconstructed rebel.** A former Confederate who has not accepted as permanent the conditions imposed upon the South after the Civil War. — **1877** LONGFELLOW in S. Longfellow *H. W. Longfellow* III. 277 A letter from Mr. ——, of Washington, a fierce and 'un-reconstructed' rebel. **1894** *Outing* XXIV. 280/1 We made our way . . . to the tavern kept by an unreconstructed rebel. **1897** in W. C. Church *U.S. Grant* 346 The feeling against the President was heightened by the appearance, at the doors of Congress, of what were known as 'unreconstructed rebels' arrogantly demanding to be admitted.

Unrope, *v.* {1883-} *tr.* 'In some parts of the United States, to unharness' (*Cent.*). — **1883** *Phila. Times* 30 July (*Cent.*), The horse was unroped from the wagon and turned loose.

+**Unscalped,** *a.* Not scalped. Used esp. of Indians. — **1726** PENHALLOW *Indian Wars* 37 We found seven dead upon the spot: six of whom we scalped, and left the other unscalped. **1890** *Buckskin Mose* 163 The unscalped Indian is supposed . . . to hold a higher rank in the Happy Hunting grounds . . . than the one who has lost his hair.

Unseated, *a.* {1775-} +Of land: Unsettled; not occupied. *Obs.*

1662 *Va. Stat. at Large* II. 98 The greatest part of the country [will be left] unseated and unpeopled, noe man knowing how or of whome either to purchase or take lease. **1724** [see UNSETTLED *a.*]. **1816** U. BROWN *Journal* II. 357 Makes Search after James Gilmore, Collector of the Direct Tax on unseated Lands for the years 1815 & 1816. **1842** *Pres. Mess. & P.* IV. 125 The States of Maine and Massachusetts . . . are the joint proprietors of the unseated lands. **1877** W. H. BURROUGHS *On Taxation* 208 In Pennsylvania, prior to 1844, . . . unseated lands, that is lands unoccupied or vacant, were alone liable to be sold for taxes.

***Unsettled,** *a.* +Not occupied by settlers. {1869-} Also *unsettledness.* — c**1695** J. MILLER *Descr. N.Y.* 20 There is something to be said in excuse hereof, that is, the unsettledness of the country for a long time. **1724** *Penna. Assembly Acts* I. 102 Exempting . . . all unsettled Tracts or Parcels of Land, That is to say, such Tracts of Land as . . . are unseated. **1789** MORSE *Amer. Geog.* 218 A traveller . . . even in the most unsettled parts of the state, will seldom pass more than two or three miles without finding a house. **1816** U. BROWN *Journal* I. 272 Thence 16 Miles through an Ugly hilly unsettled Country in the night to the Town of Bath. [**1859** CORNWALLIS *Panorama New World* I. 154 Those occupying runs in the then 'unsettled' districts.]

***Unspotted,** *a.* In the specific names of fishes. {1804-} — **1842** *Nat. Hist. N.Y., Zoology* IV. 324 The Unspotted Balloon-fish. *Diodon fuliginosus.* **1897** *N.Y. Forest, Fish, & Game Comm. 2d Rep.* 230 *Lucius masquinongy immaculatus.* . . . The examples of unspotted mascalonge received at the Aquarium were from Chautauqua Lake, New York. **1903** BEAN *Fishes N.Y.* 628 *Chilomycterus fuliginosus.* Burfish; Unspotted Balloonfish.

Unterrified, *a.* {1609-}

+**1.** Rock-ribbed; staunch; unswervingly loyal. Applied, freq. derisively, to the Democratic party and to Democrats. *Obs.*

1832 S. SMITH *Lett. J. Downing* (1860) 169n. (Th.), Mr. Van Buren was taken up by the 'unterrified Democracy' to run as Vice-President on the ticket of 'old Hickory.' **1839** *Congress. Globe* App. 15 Feb. 185, I take leave to say that I too am an unterrified Senator of the unterrified Commonwealth of Virginia. **1840** *Atlas* (Boston) 12 Nov. 2/3 And if any of the 'unterrified democrats' can answer this question it would confer a particular favor on a Real Hard Ciderite. **1848** *Wilmington* (N.C.) *Commercial* 2 Sept. 2/1 (Th.S.), The 'unterrified democracy' are very hard [pushed] to understand the character of the Oregon Bill. **1861** *Knickerb.* Dec. 560 A primary meeting of one of our 'unterrified' wards. **1866** *Congress. Globe* 19 May 2699/1 [Andrew Johnson's] traducers charge that he actually suffered unterrified Democrats to stand around him, listening to his speech. **1890** *Congress. Rec.* 12 Feb. 1253/1 The Democracy has always . . . stood rockribbed and unterrified for . . . the eternal principles of truth and justice.

2. *absol.* Democrats.

1853 *Wkly. Oregonian* 8 Jan. (Th.), A great portion of the unwashed, as well as the 'unterrified' left the hall. **1866** *Ore. State Jrnl.* 5 May 3/1 The 'unterrified' meet here to-day to 'liquor up'—and make nominations.

Untimbered, *a.* {1606-} +Not wooded. — **1805** LEWIS in *L. & Clark Exped.* II. (1904) 74 An untimbered Island [is] situated in the middle of the river. **1808** PIKE *Sources Miss.* App. II. 8 The vast tract of untimbered country . . . lies between the . . . Missouri, Mississippi, and the western Ocean. **1905** *Indian Laws & Tr.* III. 149 Untimbered lands so purchased are not susceptible of cultivation.

+**Unvented brand.** A brand which has not been nullified by a sale brand. (Cf. VENT *v.*) — **1844** GREGG *Commerce of Prairies* I. 186 Should they by chance discover any *unvented* brand, they immediately set to work to find some one with a branding-iron of the same shape, by which the beast is at once claimed.

+**Unwashed democracy.** The common people. *contemptuous. Obs.* — **1848** DURIVAGE & BURNHAM *Stray Subjects* 177 A score of loafers from the 'unwashed democracy' had got together for the purpose of seeing a live President. **1882** *Congress. Rec.* 9 March 1750/1 If that shirt has been on that fellow these whole twelve years, I think he would be a good representative of the unwashed Democracy.

Unwhisperables. *pl.* Trousers. *slang. Obs.* {1863-} — **1837** *Knickerb.* March 288 [He could] see about procuring himself a new pair of unwhisperables from his host. **1843** *Amer. Pioneer* II. 373 His borrowed gun, . . . together with his 'unwhisperables,' was bathed in anything but blood! **1848** BURTON *Waggeries* 75 Mr. Brattle dressed himself in a new bright blue coat, . . . and a pair of large and showy unwhisperables.

***Up,** *a.* Of or pertaining to travel upstream, or proceeding upward or uptown. {1784-} — **1824** *Catawba Journal* 30 Nov., Up freights will be insured at one fourth of one per cent on their value. **1872** HARTE in *Atlantic Mo.* March 349 The upstage was stopped at Granger's. **1879** BAGBY *Old Va. Gentleman* 232 The up-cargo . . . afforded good pickings. **1882** McCABE *New York* 182 The up stations [on the elevated railroad] are on the east side of the streets. **1883** 'MARK TWAIN' *Life on Miss.* li, On this up trip I saw a little towhead (infant island) half a mile long.

* **Up,** *adv.*¹

Up to the (*last*) *notch,* (see NOTCH *n.* 5 b).

1. Of a ship: Bound *for* (a place).

1705 *Boston News-Letter* 26 Feb. 2/2 Two sloops are up for Barbadoes. **1839** *S. Lit. Messenger* V. 7/1 Orders . . . for a large cargo . . . to any one agent may not be sufficient to complete the cargo of a ship 'up' for the very place. **1851** KINGSLEY *Diary* 177 Some vessels . . . are now up for Panama. **1870** LONGFELLOW *Poetical Works* (1893) 471/2 [I was] on board the Swallow, Simon Kempthorn, master, Up for Barbadoes, and the Windward Islands. **1874** B. F. TAYLOR *World on Wheels* 138 The steamer Nile [was] . . . 'up' for the City of the Straits.

2. Exhausted or run out; all over. *colloq.* {1838-}

The jig is up, (see JIG 1).

1787 JEFFERSON *Writings* VI. 322 Are we to suppose the game already up. **1877** HARTE *Story of Mine* (1896) 95 Don't you see the whole thing will be up before he gets here?

3. Running *for* an office; in court, before a judge. *colloq.*

1835 LONGSTREET *Ga. Scenes* 234 If you're up for any thing you need'nt be mealy-mouthed about it. **1898** *Scribner's Mag.* XXIII. 273/2, I had to . . . give him [the policeman] my last dollar to fix him, or else he'd have run me in, and I've been up three times this week.

+**4.** With *south, north, east:* In the (south, north, east.) *colloq.*

Cf. Down east *adv.*

1835-7 Haliburton *Clockmaker* 1 Ser. viii. 51, I've been away up south, a speculating in nutmegs. *a***1870** Chipman *Notes on Bartlett* 494 *Up North*, used instead of North, *n.*, and adverbially. **1906** Lynde *Quickening* 209 Money is tighter than a shut fist—up East.

+**5. a.** Of a player in poker: In the position of having staked an amount equal to the ante. **b.** Of money: At stake.

1844 J. Cowell *Thirty Years* 94 The dealer makes the game, or value of the beginning bet, and called *the anti* . . . and then everybody stakes the same amount, and says, '*I'm up.*' **1867** 'Mark Twain' *Sk., New & Old* 32 But as soon as money was up on him he was a different dog; his under-jaw'd begin to stick out like the fo'-castle of a steamboat.

+**6.** *Baseball.* At bat.

1862 *N.Y. Sun. Mercury* 13 July (E. J. Nichols). **1909** Barber *Double Play* 208 The fourth man up chose a ball to his liking and sliced it down the first-base line. **1912** Mathewson *Pitching* 23, I was the first man up and started the eighth inning with a single.

7. With *to.* {1785-} +In poker, incumbent upon (a player) to make a bet; hence, in general use, incumbent upon. *colloq.²*

1896 Ade *Artie* 11 Up to me—see! **1900** Norris *Blix* 151 It's up to you. **1921** Paine *Comr. Rolling Ocean* 110 It's up to me to stay as dry as a covered bridge.

+**8.** *(To be) up against* (something), to be confronted with or faced by (something); *to be up against it,* to be faced with difficulties; to have a hard time. *colloq.* or *slang.*

1896 Ade *Artie* 7, I saw I was up against it. **1904** Atherton *Rulers of Kings* 25 He felt himself up against the barren rocks of life. **1915** *Emporia Gazette* 23 April, Our good friend Borah is up against a hard proposition.

* **Up,** *adv.²*

For *to ante up, to break up,* etc., (see Ante *v.* 1, 2, Break *v.* 21, etc.); *to go up in the air,* (see Go *v.* 16); *up to the eyes, up to the handle, up to the hub* (see Eye 3, Handle *n.* 1, Hub 2).

***1.** Used to modify a verb omitted but understood. Freq. in nautical usage. {1829-}

For *up jib, up stakes, up sticks* (see Jib 2, Stake *n.* 4, Stick *n.* 5). **1775** in Johnston *N. Hale* 152 He up Anchor and went round forthwith. **1841** Cooper *Deerslayer* xix, Let's up kedge, old fellow, and move nearer to this point. **1843** Haliburton *Attaché* II. 263 If ever . . . she begins that way, up hat and cut stick, double quick. **1884** 'Mark Twain' *H. Finn* xl, Then we up-steam again, and whizzed along after them.

***2.** In phrases.

+**a.** *Up and dust,* =*to get up and dust* (q.v. under Dust *v.* 1). *colloq.* +**b.** *Up to the minute,* up to date. Also as adj.

(a) 1877 Bartlett 728 *Up and dust.* Hurry! Move fast! **(b) 1909** Wason *Happy Hawkins* 322 They had stopped for over a month with his friends in England, an' was posted up to the minute. **1922** Sandburg *Slabs Sunburnt West* 5 There are sidewalks polished with the footfalls of . . . greased mannikins, wearing up-to-the-minute sox.

* **Up,** *prep.* Used in phrases.

For *up chamber, up the flume, to be up a stump, up a tree,* and *to send up the river,* see the nouns.

+**1.** *Up creek,* to an ignominious or crushing defeat.

To row up Salt Creek (see Salt creek b).

1843 'Carlton' *New Purchase* I. 261 Happily, my complimentary neighbour had no wish for that pleasant little excursion—'up crick,' and no further disturbance ensued.

+**2.** *Up garret,* up into, or up in, the garret.

1775 *Essex Inst. Coll.* XLVIII. 48 Stevens ordered us out of our Chamber . . . & so we moved up garret. **1845** Judd *Margaret* II. 344 You will find . . . in the bottom of my chest, up garret, five dollars and a quarter. **1862** G. Hamilton *Country Living* 206 Only an old cage thrust away up garret under the eaves. **1899** Wilkins *Jamesons* 88 Jest old andirons like mother keeps up garret.

+**3.** *Up Green River,* (see quotation and cf. Green River 1).

1871 De Vere 200 The mountaineers in the wilder parts of the Southwest . . . say they send a man *up Green River,* when they have killed him.

+**4.** *Up Salt River,* (see quotation).

To row up Salt River, (see Salt river 2).

1842 'Uncle Sam' *Peculiarities* I. 89 When the Yorker was quite 'up Salt River'—decidedly intoxicated—he went to sleep.

* **Up-,** *prefix.* Used to form nouns.

Upbring, upbringing (*slang*); *up-comer,* a steamboat moving upstream; *upswing,* (see quotation).

1898 *Advance* 5 May 609/1 Carl showed his 'up bring' for the first time when he deposited the cherry stones on the carpet under his chair! **1847** Field *Drama in Pokerville* 175 In the mean time, round the point below, sweeps the up-comer . . . moving over the water like a rushing fire-

palace. **1897** *Boston News Bureau Summary* 13 Dec. 2/3 The upswing . . . a slow gain in prices.

+**Up and coming,** *a.* Energetic; capable; aggressive or pushing. *colloq.* — **1848** D. P. Thompson *L. Amsden* 78, I saw a little *up-and-coming* sort of a fellow . . . fairly scare from the ground a fellow . . . as big as two of him. **1889** Jewett in *Harper's Mag.* Dec. 146/2 Can't you hear just how up an' comin' it was? **1894** Wilkins *Pembroke* 50 If you'd kept your family on less meat, and given 'em more garden-stuff to eat Barney wouldn't have been so up an' comin'. **1912** Nicholson *Hoosier Chron.* 391 Farmers are up and coming I can tell you.

+**Up-and-comingness, Up-and-a-comingness.** Enterprise; readiness. *colloq.²* — **1890** *Advance* 24 April, There is about our Methodist brethren . . . an up-and-a-comingness . . . that is delightful. **1899** Howells *Ragged Lady* 59 The *chef* bore their mirth stoically, but not without a personal relish of the shoeman's up-and-comingness.

Up-and-down, *a.* {1616-} +Direct or straightforward; outright or downright. *colloq.*

See also *right up and down* under Right up *adv.* 2.

1837 *Knickerb.* X. 379 He was remarkable for his independence and fearlessness; for his up-and-down dealing. **1856** Stowe *Dred* I. 10 We had a real up-and-down quarrel. **1867** 'Lackland' *Homespun* 159 Many a young fellow . . . would gladly exchange all his acquired readiness in translating the Greek and Latin poets for the practical up-and-down knowledge of a respectable selectman. **1869** Stowe *Oldtown Folks* 291 Miss Debby was a well-preserved, up-and-down, positive, cheery, sprightly maiden lady. **1896** *Peterson Mag.* Jan. 94/2 The two women folks . . . finally had an up-and-down row.

* **Up and down,** *adv.* +Directly; without attempt at concealment. *colloq.* (See also *right up and down* under Right up *adv.* 2). — **1854** 'O. Optic' *In Doors & Out* (1876) 30, I told her, up and down, that she was not what she used to be. **1886** Alton *Among Law-Makers* 274, 'I will recognize the higher authority of the Constitution.' That is what . . . [the President] told . . . [Congress], up and down!

‖**Upasian,** *a.* As deadly as the upas tree. — **1841** *Niles' Nat. Reg.* 17 July 320/3 The New Orleans Advertiser . . . speaks of that city suffering under the blasts of the upasian winds, the forerunners of epidemic disease, unless they are driven back by the south winds. They blow from the northeast.

+**Up boat.** A river boat moving upstream. — **1857** Willis *Convalescent* 154 The 'up-boat' . . . reaches Poughkeepsie . . . a few minutes before the 'down-boat' touches at the same place.

* **Upbound,** *a.* +Of a steamboat: Moving upstream. — **1884** 'Mark Twain' *H. Finn* xii, Up-bound steamboats fight th big river in the middle.

Upcountry, *n.*

1. The part of a country situated inland or away from the seaboard; the interior. *colloq.* {1688; without article, 1837-, of India and Australia}

'As adv. and adj. the phrase is current in English dialects . . . , but the general 19th century use originated partly in India and partly in the United States; from *c*1875 it has also been employed in, or with reference to, Australia, South Africa, etc.' (O.E.D.).

1817 Weems *Letters* III. 176, I have a number due in the up country. **1827** Sherwood *Gaz. Georgia* 51 Eatonton [contains] . . . one of the finest houses of worship in the up country. **1865** S. Andrews *South since War* 207 All these low-country districts are filled with negroes from the up-country. **1887** *Harper's Mag.* April 666 The spring and fall freshets . . . brought down . . . fleets of flat boats from the 'up-country.'

2. Attrib. (passing into adj.) with *editor, flat-bottomed boat, Indian,* etc. {1835-}

1810 Weems *Letters* III. 27 Not thinking the little up country post offices safe, . . . I thought it my duty to you to concentrate all my monies into good drafts. **1831** Peck *Guide* 61 You may see 20 or 30 steamboats, with their bows . . . projecting over an 'up country' flat-bottomed boat. **1861** *New Haven Palladium* 30 Nov. (Chipman), As the up-country editor [said, etc.]. **1866** Lowell *Biglow Papers* 2 Ser. Introd. p. vi, I imagined to myself such an upcountry man as I had often seen at anti-slavery meetings. **1867** 'Lackland' *Homespun* 216 In a good many up-country parishes, it is esteemed rather effeminate to pay much attention to letters. **1885** *Wkly. New Mexican Rev.* 23 April 1/4 An up-country paper has it that the appointment of G. E. Lyons as inspector of hides . . . gives the highest satisfaction to stockmen. **1899** Jewett *Queen's Twin* 5 There's a path leadin' right over to it that . . . belonged to the up-country Indians.

Upcountry, *adv.* Into or in the interior. *colloq.* {1864-, in India} — **1815** Humphreys *Yankey* 40 Afore I was born he moved up country, into the back parts. **1853** 'P. Paxton' *Yankee in Texas* 54 He was great upon speculation, usually spending one third of his time in expeditions 'up country' in search of silver mines. **1883** Howells *Woman's Reason* xv, One girl . . . writes for two or three papers up-country, and out West. **1907** White *Arizona Nights* 36, I'll march you up country and see that Geronimo gone.

+**Up-creek.** *attrib.* Designating something that comes down a creek. — **1864** *Harper's Mag.* Dec. 58/2 At the point of the bluff where the up-creek mud ran into . . . the mud of the town.

+**Upgrade,** *n.* A slope upward; an incline upward. {1892} — **1873** Beadle *Undevel. West* 257 Forty miles of staging over boulders and rocky up-grade. **1883** *Century Mag.* Nov. 130/2 Our locomotive proved unable to take us over a slight up-grade. **1893** Sanborn *S. Calif.* 87, I have no taste for overtaking runaway mules on a steep and interminable up-grade. **1923** WATTS *L. Nichols* 314 The steady up-grade to the North Hill [was] accomplished without incident.

+**Upgrade,** *adv.* Upward on an incline. — **1893** *Outing* XXII. 133/2 The twelve miles up-grade to Alto station . . . consumed just three hours' time. **1916** 'BOWER' *Phantom Herd* 44 They can lope a horse upgrade without falling off backwards.

Up-head. *attrib.* +Of or pertaining to a person or animal holding the head erect. Also *up-headed* a., *up-header*. {*up-headed, 'having upright horns,' *dial.*} — **1845** GREEN *Texian Exped.* 224 They seemed to know that we were Texians . . . from our national *up-head* appearance. **1875** *Ill. Dept. Agric. Trans.* XIV. 210 [The Siamese swine] had a fine, high-bred, up-headed style, especially in their walk. **1893** *Dialect Notes* I. 334 *Upheader*, horse that holds his head high. Applied figuratively to men. [N.J.]

***Upholster,** *n.* A dealer, esp. one dealing in clothing, furniture, and small goods; one who repairs such articles; an upholsterer. *Obs.* — **1651** *Suffolk Deeds* I. 189, I Edward Tyng of Boston in New England Vphoulster, . . . [have sold] All that my wharfe in the sajd Boston. **1682** *Boston Rec.* X. 72 Ebenezer Savage, upholster, became surety to the town for John Burder and his family.

+**Upholster,** *v.* [f. *upholsterer* or *upholstery*.]

1. *tr.* To cover (a piece of furniture) with fabric, stuffing, etc.; to equip (something) with such furniture. Also fig. Also *ppl. a.* {1873–}
1853 LOWELL *Fireside Trav.* (1864) 45 The dull weed upholstered the decaying wharves. **1882** MCCABE *New York* 184 The cars . . . though neatly upholstered and decorated are not as ornamental as those of the Sixth avenue line. **1902** BANKS *Newspaper Girl* 255 He took one of the upholstered chairs near me. **1918** *Essex Inst. Coll.* LIV. 212 The seats were arranged in the present manner and upholstered in black haircloth.

2. *intr.* To make coverings of fabric, as for furniture; to stuff cushions, etc.
1861 STOWE *Pearl Orr's Isl.* I. 21 Miss Roxy and Miss Ruey . . . could upholster and quilt.

3. *fig. tr.* To equip (a person) with clothes. *humorous.* {1890–, in other fig. senses; 1926}
1873 'MARK TWAIN' & WARNER *Gilded Age* 300 It had cost something to upholster these women. **1883** 'MARK TWAIN' *Life on Miss.* xxx, Women and girls . . . upholstered in bright new clothes. **1897** FLANDRAU *Harvard Episodes* 305 Celestial companies of maidens . . . floated past Beverly, in the wake of panting but determined ladies richly upholstered.

Upholsterer. One whose business is to cover chairs and other furniture with fabric, to put in or renew cushions, etc. {1613–} — **1717** *Boston Selectmen* 29 Sam[ue]ll Gifford from London Upholster . . . [was] warned to depart. **1790** *Penna. Packet* 1 Jan. 1/2 John Mason, Upholsterer, . . . has for sale and makes Sacking Bottoms of the best kind. **1851** CIST *Cincinnati* 210 Forgey, Warren & Co., manufacture glue, curled hair for upholsterers' use, also dress bristles, etc. **1914** ATHERTON *Perch of Devil* 22 [Ida] divided her day between . . . the upholsterer, and the bargain counter.

Upholsterer bee. A bee that uses pieces cut from leaves or petals in making its cell. {1830–} — **1843** CHILD *Lett. New York* (1846) 255 The upholsterer-bee had a perfect cutting instrument, ages before scissors were invented. **1867** *Amer. Naturalist* I. 162 This little upholster bee carpets her honey-tight apartment.

Upholstery. *collect.* The fabric-covered surfaces of furniture, cushions, etc. {1649–} Also *attrib.* — **1796** F. BAILY *Tour* 102 The New-England men . . . bring them turnery ware, upholstery, home-made linens and cloths. **1869** *Boyd's Business Directory* 749 G. L. & J. B. Kelty & Co. . . . Importers of Upholstery Goods, Lace and Muslin Curtains. **1880** *Harper's Mag.* June 25/2 Workers on upholstery, fringes, feathers, and millinery goods. **1887** I. ALDEN *Little Fishers* ix, I'm your friend and fellow-labourer and partner in the cabinet business, and the upholstery line.

***Upland.**
***1. a.** High ground; an area or piece of high ground. **b.** An area or stretch of high ground rising from low land near a body of water. ('Chiefly *local* and *U.S.*' O.E.D.)
1635 *Watertown Rec.* I. I. 1 Agreed . . . that two Hundred Acres of upland nere to the Mill shalbe reserved . . . to make a Towneship. **1656** *Mayflower Descendant* X. 25, I William Bassett . . . Doe freely Surrender and give up all my . . . landes . . . both uplands and meddow lands unto my two sonnes. **1702** *Providence Rec.* XI. 71 He may change 5 acres of Meaddow in ye 2nd devision, & to take up 10 acres of upland in lue of it. **1775** ROMANS *Nat. Hist. Florida* 283 A few spots of hammock or upland, are found on this island. **1812** STODDARD *Sk. Louisiana* 125 The seventh is composed of the more elevated grounds, commonly called uplands. **1857** *Ill. Agric. Soc. Trans.* III. 410 They commenced making farms . . . on the upland of Monroe county. **1918** SANDBURG *Cornhuskers* 10 Listen to six mockingbirds Flinging follies of O-be-joyful Over the marshes and uplands.

+**2.** = UPLAND(S) COTTON. Sometimes pl. Also attrib. {1880}
1819 *Niles' Reg.* XVII. 9/2 Bengal cotton . . . heretofore paid the same duty as uplands. **1824** *Shipping & Commercial List* 31 July (Pettigrew P.), A lot of 300 bales of Upland was sold at 14¾ cents, cash. **1838** *U.S. Mag.*

I. 385 The species of cotton first introduced, known in commerce by the name of upland, adheres to every part of its seed with great tenacity. **1864** *Maine Agric. Soc. Returns 1863* 48 The great cotton dearth . . . has caused that production to go up from 9 cents for middling Uplands . . . to 90 cents.

3. *attrib.* and *comb.* Designating crops grown on upland ground. {1639–}
See also UPLAND GRASS, UPLAND RICE, UPLAND(S) COTTON.
1634 WOOD *New Eng. Prospect* 10 These Marshes . . . bring plenty of Hay, of which the Cattle feed and like, as if they were fed with the best up-land Hay in New-England. **1772** *Md. Hist. Mag.* XIV. 279 Our upland Oates are Low. **1785** in *S. Lit. Messenger* XXVIII. 40/1 The effect of it on upland corn has been favourable.

4. Designating pieces or tracts of elevated land. {1610–}
See also UPLAND PRAIRIE.
1637 *Essex Inst. Coll.* IV. 114/1 Will[ia]m woodbery . . . is to have a p[ar]cell of marshe . . . and soe much of vpland ground at the other end. **1639** *N.H. Prov. Papers* I. 138 All the inhabitants of the towne of Exeter shall [have] their uplands lotts for planting laid outt. **1682** *Conn. Rec.* III. 102 They have granted to sayd Rutham, one acre, . . . at the price of other upland feilds. **1832** *N.H. Hist. Soc. Coll.* III. 205 Hay of good quality is cut upon the upland farms. **1866** *Maine Agric. Soc. Returns 1865* 107 Sheep changed from dry upland pastures to low, moist, luxuriant pastures, are very likely to suffer. **1880** *Harper's Mag.* June 65/1 Down the upland slope, . . . the blinding drift . . . speeds in its wild caprice. **1925** in *Amer. Speech* XV. 296 There is also an accumulation of humus on some of the upland flats, which are known as pocosons.

5. In specific names. **a.** Of plants and trees.
See also UPLAND WILLOW OAK.
1825 Upland beech [see RED-HEARTED a.]. **1901** MOHR *Plant Life Ala.* 370 *Agrostis intermedia.* . . . Upland Bent Grass. . . . Eastern Tennessee, Alabama, Louisiana, and Texas. **1857** GRAY *Botany* 187 *E. sessilifolium,* (Upland Boneset.) . . . Copses and banks, Massachusetts to Ohio. **1860** DARLINGTON *Weeds & Plants* 211 *A[rctostaphylos] Uva-ursi,* . . . Bearberry. Upland Cranberry. **1819** SCHOOLCRAFT *Mo. Lead Mines* 29 Plants from which colours have been extracted for dyeing . . . [are] shumac, upland dock, and smartweed. **1897** SUDWORTH *Arborescent Flora* 113 *Hicoria ovata.* . . . Shagbark (Hickory). . . . Upland Hickory (Ill.). **1720** DUDLEY in *Phil. Trans.* XXXI. 27 Maple Sugar is made of the juice of the Upland Maple, or Maple Trees that grow upon the Highlands. **1785** MARSHALL *Amer. Grove* 123 *Quercus rubra montana.* Upland Red Oak. . . . The timber is generally worm eaten, or rotten at heart. **1840** DANA *Two Years* 415 Being of the short, tough, upland spruce, it bent like whalebone. **1836** WOOD & BACHE *Dispensatory* 544 *Rhus glabrum* . . . , called variously smooth sumach, Pennsylvania sumach, and *upland sumach.* **1785** MARSHALL *Amer. Grove* 97 *Nyssa sylvatica.* Upland Tupelo-Tree, or Sour Gum. This grows naturally in Pennsylvania. **1801** MICHAUX *Histoire des Chênes* 5 *Quercus obtusiloba,* *Upland White-Oak.* **1788** MAY *Jrnl. & Lett.* 48 To cure the rheumatism, take the bark of upland or red willow.

b. Of animals.
See also UPLAND PLOVER.
1891 *Cent.* 6660/3 *Upland moccasin,* a venomous serpent of the southern United States. **1917** *Birds of Amer.* I. 247 Upland Plover. *Bartramia longicauda.* . . . [Also called] Bartram's Plover; Upland Sandpiper; Uplander.

6. In special combinations.
Upland bird, a bird frequenting elevated or inland areas; +*u. flake,* (see quotation); +*u. planter,* a planter whose land is inland and higher than the tidewater area.
1869 *N.J. Acts* 831 It shall not be lawful . . . to destroy any upland birds whose principal food is insects. **1889** *Cent.* 2250/1 *Upland flake,* a flake for drying codfish, built permanently upon the shore. It differs from the ordinary pattern in not being movable. **1843** *Knickerb.* XXI. 223 The upland planters . . . are too poor to make a show.

Uplander. {1699–} + = UPLAND PLOVER. — **1888** TRUMBULL *Names of Birds* 172 [At] Salem, Mass., Pasture Plover; at Provincetown, Uplander. **1917** *Birds of Amer.* I. 247 Upland Plover. *Bartramia longicauda.* . . . [Also called] Uplander.

Upland grass. Grass growing on elevated ground or upland. — **1649** *New Haven Col. Rec.* I. 429 Allso some upland grase . . . where it maye be some haye maye be cutt. **1764** HUTCHINSON *Hist. Mass.* I. 480 The natural upland grass of the country commonly called Indian grass, is poor fodder. **1824** *Catawba Journal* 16 Nov., A Silver Cup was also awarded to Dr. Stephen Fox, for the best lot of upland grass.

+**Upland Indian.** An Indian living inland; spec., an Indian of one of the Algonquian tribes of New England and New York, as a Mohegan. *Obs.* — **1656** *Mass. H. S. Coll.* 4 Ser. VII. 75, I feare nothing soe much as warres with our Indianes about vs, who stands ready to encounter with the vpland Indianes. **1716** CHURCH *Philip's War* 27 Some . . . [were] Narraganset Indians, and some other Upland Indians, in all about 300. [**1790** UMFREVILLE *Hudson's Bay* 56 In the month of March, the Upland Indians assemble on the banks of a particular river or lake, the nomination of which had been agreed upon by common assent.]

+**Upland plover.** A sandpiper (*Bartramia longicauda*) of the eastern states. Also comb. — **1832** WILLIAMSON *Maine* I. 147 The upland Plover is larger than a robin. **1882** GODFREY *Nantucket* 157 In September, . . . upland plover make their appearance on various parts of the island. **1917** *Birds of Amer.* I. 248/1 Upland Plover shooting is now becoming a thing of the past, under the protection of Federal Law.

+**Upland prairie.** A level, treeless area of elevated ground. — **1817** S. Brown *Western Gazetteer* 45 There are two kinds of these meadows— the river and upland prairies. **1836** *S. Lit. Messenger* II. 354 Not long after we began to catch glimpses of the upland prairies. **1872** Tice *Over Plains* 17 The soil is deep and rich, even on the upland prairie.

+**Upland rice.** Rice of a kind that can be grown on elevated land without irrigation. — **1772** Franklin *Writings* VIII. 21, I send you enclosed a small box of Upland Rice, brought from Cochin China. **1827** Sherwood *Gaz. Georgia* 10 Upland or dry culture rice is raised here. **1847** Darlington *Weeds & Plants* 370 There are several varieties of cultivated Rice; some, called Upland or Mountain Rice, usually awnless.

+**Upland(s) cotton.** Short-staple cotton of a variety grown in the uplands of the southern states. — **1819** *Niles' Reg.* XVII. 9/1 Hitherto our cottons, sea island and upland, . . . have been subject to a specific duty. **1839** *Diplom. Corr. Texas* III. (1911) 870 She possesses . . . River bottom land better adapted to the cultivation of upland cotton than any other part of the habitable Globe. **1863** *Ladies' Repository* XXIII. 637/1 It is short staple or upland cotton, and is worked by East Tennessee and Georgia refugees. **1867** *Harper's Mag.* Aug. 349/1 A bale of uplands cotton. **1910** *Dept. Agric. Yrbk.* 57 Several new types of Upland cotton . . . introduced from Mexico and Central America . . . have now become as productive and as uniform as any of the United States Upland varieties that are being tested in the same places.

+**Upland willow oak.** The bluejack (*Quercus cinerea*), an oak of the southern states. — **1801** Michaux *Histoire des Chênes* 6 Quercus cinerea. . . . *Upland Willow Oak.* **1860** Curtis *Woody Plants N.C.* 37 Upland willow oak . . . affords a fine yellow dye. **1901** [see BLUEJACK 2].

+**Uplift.** {1885–}

1. Elevation; lifting up.

1844 Willis *Poems* 12 His brow Had the inspired up-lift of the king's. [**1890** Stanley *In Darkest Africa* I. 413 There was uniform uplift and subsidence of the constantly twirling spear blades.]

b. *spec.* An upheaval; a lifting or rising of the surface of the earth.

1853 Kane *Grinnell Exped.* 128 The false horizon, which I had selected as an index of the uplift, rose as it receded from the sun. **1878** Whittier *Poetical Works* (1894) 163/2 Broad meadows belted round with pines, The grand uplift of mountain lines! **1882** *47th Congress 1 Sess.* H.R. Ex. Doc. No. 216, 619 The assumption of an uplift or elevation of the Sierra Nevada Mountains, subsequent to the gravel epoch. **1886** *Harper's Mag.* June 50/1 We had set our faces towards the great Appalachian uplift. **1923** J. H. Cook *On Old Frontier* 105 Gullies cut into both sides of this channel-bed through a little high uplift of country.

2. *fig.* Spiritual elevation; the improvement and ennobling of the mind. {1885–}

1873 Holland *A. Bonnicastle* 22 It is impossible that he could know what an uplift he gave to the life to which he ministered. **1913** W. Wilson *New Freedom* 218 Every one of the great schemes of social uplift . . . is based, when rightly conceived, upon justice.

attrib. **1912** G. M. Hyde *Newspaper Reporting* 236 One of these is the 'up-lift run' for cub reporters—a round of philanthropic news sources to teach them the business of reporting before they become cynical.

b. *On the uplift,* improving.

1904 *N.Y. Ev. Post* 11 June, The summer season is on the uplift, and the outlook is for record-breaking crowds.

‖**3.** A curb or low wall.

1896 Ade *Artie* 183 Mamie sat with him on the stone uplift dividing the park driveway from the slope toward the water.

‖**Up-offering.** An offering up. — **1829** Cooper *Wish-ton-Wish* v, Mark was on the point of making . . . an up-offering of thanks, when Whittal Ring broke rudely into the room.

Upper, *n.*

1. In a boot or shoe, the part above the sole; a vamp. {1845–} Also attrib.

1844 *Cincinnati Misc.* I. 54 My boots . . . have been twice half-soled, and the uppers wont stand it any longer. **1876** Knight 2684/1 *Upper-machines,* . . . those for cutting out or preparing the uppers of boots or shoes. **1886** Mitchell *R. Blake* 197 The rain-butt was right under the window where I used to cut out uppers.

+**b.** *pl.* 'Separate cloth gaiters to button above the shoes over the ankle' (*Cent.*).

+**c.** *To walk on one's uppers,* to wear shoes with holes in the soles; *on one's uppers,* poor or destitute. *colloq.* {1905–}

1891 *Fur, Fin & Feather* 195 An old pair in which one is just ready 'to walk on his uppers,' . . . will serve admirably after they have been half-soled and had the heels straightened. **1891** *Cent.* 6661/2 *To be on one's uppers,* to be poor or in hard luck: referring to a worn-out condition of one's shoes. **1896** Ade *Artie* 106 Two years ago he was on his uppers and now he's got money to burn. **1917** McCutcheon *Green Fancy* 275 The 'ingrates' were in New York, on their 'uppers.'

+**3.** A log or piece of lumber of superior grade.

1877 *Lumberman's Gaz.* 24 May 357/1 There are about 100,000 feet [of lumber] on dock, mostly uppers.

✶**Upper,** *a.* Situated on more elevated ground; farther inland or upstream; farther north.

✶**1.** Of a place, area, or district.

1692 *Conn. Rec.* IV. 67 Upon the motion of . . . the gent[leme]n of the upper townes, . . . there were sent a captaine with fifty men (to guard those upper townes). **1708** *Va. State P.* I. 118, [I] ordered one in ye upper parts to take 12 men and range our frontiers. **1733** *Md. Hist. Mag.* XV. 209 The upper hundred of Potapsco is divided by order of court by the Court road. **1879** *Harper's Mag.* June 77/1 That's in the upper village.

✶**b.** Of a part of a geographical or political unit. In proper names.

1831 Royall *Southern Tour* II. 35 It appears to be a harbor for people, obnoxious to the laws, and is divided into *Upper Hog Thief, Lower Hog Thief,* and *Middle Hog Thief.* **1832** Browne *Sylva* 247 The French of Canada and of Upper Louisiana give it the name of Cotton Tree. **1848** Polk in *Pres. Mess. & P.* IV. 589 Foreign commerce to a considerable amount is now carried on in the ports of Upper California.

2. Of a body, or a part of a body, of water. {1778}
See also Upper river.

1789 Morse *Amer. Geog.* 46 The upper waters of the Patomak . . . are yet to be cleared of their fixed obstructions. **1813** *Niles' Reg.* V. 65/1 The expected movements of the northwestern army . . . very naturally produce much enquiry for the geography of that portion of North-America lying on the Upper Lakes. *a*1817 Dwight *Travels* II. 193 At this time he had reached a place, just below the Upper-narrows. **1835** Hoffman *Winter in West* I. 242, I left Boyd's Grove, bound for the Upper Mississippi. **1865** *Ore. State Jrnl.* 5 Aug. 1/1 The steamer Yellowstone . . . arrived from Fort Benton yesterday, making the quickest trip on the record on the Upper Missouri. **1899** Cushman *Hist. Indians* 429 For the first time the English were now in possession of the upper Ohio.

3. In special combinations.

Upper bench {1649–*a*1675}, the people occupying the front bench in a Quaker meeting; *u. cabin,* a cabin on an upper boat deck; *u. coal,* (see quotation); *u. Indian,* an Indian living in an upland region; +*u. keel,* a mark of ownership cut on the upper side of the ear of an animal (cf. Overkeel *n.*); *u. marshal,* a marshal of superior authority; +*U. Peninsula,* the part of Michigan directly adjoining the state of Wisconsin, bounded principally by Lake Superior and Lake Michigan; *u. people,* people living inland or on uplands.

1873 'Mark Twain' & Warner *Gilded Age* 280 You are as solemn as the upper bench in Meeting. **1834** Baird *Valley Miss.* 335 Such boats are always advertised as having 'upper cabins.' **1840** *Knickerb.* XV. 105 About a foot from the bottom of every vein, there is a layer of earth. . . . This divides it into 'foot-coal' and 'upper coal.' **1825** Austin *P.* II. (1924) 1210 Will a war at this time with the upper Indians have a tendency to stop emigration? **1773** in Summers *Ann. S.W. Va.* 607 His Mark is ordered to be recorded a Swallow Fork in the right ear a Crop in the Left Ear and an Upper Keel. **1658** *New Plymouth Laws* 119 When the upper Marshall shall have occasion to levy any fine or fines [etc.]. **1863** *Mich. Gen. Statutes* I. (1882) 146 The election for all state and county officers in the Upper Peninsula, shall be held on the Tuesday succeeding the first Monday in November. **1725** in *Travels Amer. Col.* 107 We had an Acco[un]t of the ffrench Indians doing some damage to the upper People.

Upper berth. In a building, boat, or railroad coach, the higher of two bunks or beds placed one over the other; the top bed. — **1894** F. M. Crawford *Upper Berth* 14 Sad-coloured curtains half-closed the upper berth. **1897** *Outing* XXX. 62/1 There were two 'upper berths' in case the river entered unbidden. **1917** J. Husband *Story of Pullman Car* 29 The upper berth might be closed in the day time and also serve as a receptacle for bedding.

+**Upper classman.** A member of one of the upper classes in a college or school; a junior or senior. — **1871** Bagg *At Yale* 70 Only a few upper-class men will be found there. **1896** *Boston Herald* 15 Aug. 1/7 (Ernst), Abusing new cadets by upper class men is so mean and cowardly . . . that severe punishment should not be necessary for its prevention. **1899** Williams *Stolen Story* 195 After luncheon he leisurely floated up to the campus again, with a bunch of upper-classmen about him.

✶**Upper crust.** *collect.* +In any society, the group claiming, or generally accorded, the highest social rank, as by virtue of family or wealth; also, a member of such a group. *colloq.* {1896} Also attrib. or as adj.

1835–7 Haliburton *Clockmaker* 1 Ser. xxviii. 274 It was none o' your skim-milk parties, but superfine uppercrust real jam. **1841** *Jamestown* (N.Y.) *Jrnl.* 24 June 1/3 Sam is kind of naturally set down as one of our upper crust. **1850** Judd *R. Edney* 218 Who are they but mangy skipjacks, half-baked upper crusts? **1891** Wilkins *New Eng. Nun* 124, I've got a little feelin', ef I ain't one of the upper crust. **1912** Nicholson *Hoosier Chron.* 503 She considered herself unassailably a member of the upper crust of the Hoosier aristocracy.

✶**Upper house.** The superior branch of a bicameral legislative assembly, +as a colonial or state council or senate, or the Senate of the United States. — **1666** *Md. Archives* II. 20 The Upper House do think that the 1400 lb. powder . . . [is] very necessary to be provided. **1709** *Mass. H. S. Coll.* 3 Ser. VII. 69 Two Gentlemen of the upper house . . . were ordered to confer with me about it. **1718** *Mass. H. Rep. Jrnl.* II. 62, [I] recommended . . . when the Upper and Lower House are divided in their Sentiments that a Conference be immediately appointed. *a*1817

DWIGHT *Travels* I. 270 The Legislature [of Conn.] is formed of two Houses; the Council and Representatives: customarily called the Upper and Lower Houses.

∗**Upper lip.** +*To keep a stiff upper lip*, (see LIP).

Upper river. *spec.* +That part of the Mississippi River between Cairo and St. Louis. Also attrib. — **1876** 'MARK TWAIN' *Old Times* ii. 33 What is called the 'upper river' (the two hundred miles between St. Louis and Cairo, where the Ohio comes in) was low. **1883** — *Life on Miss.* lvii, In all these Upper-River towns, one breathes a go-ahead atmosphere. **1896** — in *Harper's Mag.* Aug. 346 We was four days getting out of the 'upper river.'

+**Upper ten.**

1. Short for UPPER TEN THOUSAND. *colloq.* {1860-}

*a*1848 *N.Y. Herald* (B.), The seats for the first night are already many of them engaged . . . by the very cream of our 'upper ten.' **1851** NORTHALL *Curtain* 126 So many of the most prominent leaders among the 'upper ten' of New York society were involved in the preliminary arrangements. **1861** MOORE *Rebellion Rec.* I. III. 79 The whole city of New York, men, women, and children, the upper ten and the b'hoys, assembled in one dense and shouting multitude. **1882** MCCABE *New York* 313 Invitations are eagerly sought after by the Upper Ten. **1891** [see FOUR HUNDRED].

2. Attrib. with *ball, element, idea, lady.*

1851 ROSS *In New York* 173 The upper-ten lady made a commendable effort to escape. **1857** GUNN *N.Y. Boarding-Houses* 43 The *Herald* . . . can not be dispensed with on account of its winter reports of upper-ten balls. **1862** LOWELL *Biglow P.* 2 Ser. 99 Now this I thought a fees'ble plan, . . . Suitin' the Nineteenth Century an' Upper Ten idees. **1867** *Atlantic Mo.* May 556/1 Germans who are heavy bankers or stock-brokers . . . soon become absorbed into the 'upper-ten' element of New York society.

+**Uppertendom.** The world of the upper ten. *colloq.* {1887} — **1851** *S. Lit. Messenger* XVII. 180/1 We love to meet . . . [at] the soiree of a fresh aspirant for the honors of Upper Tendom. **1855** M. THOMPSON *Doesticks* 131, I did go to a ball for the benefit of the poor—a two-dollar commingling of upper-tendom with lower-twentydom. **1863** HAWTHORNE *Our Old Home* 330 In America, . . . all the girls, whether daughters of the uppertendom, the mediocrity, the cottage, or the kennel, aim at one standard of dress and deportment. **1902** FITCH *Captain Jinks* 245 The Uppertendom have been entrancingly kind to me.

+**Upper ten thousand.** The people belonging to the highest social class; the aristocracy. *colloq.* {1861-} (Cf. FOUR HUNDRED.) — **1844** WILLIS in *N.Y. Ev. Mirror* 11 Nov. 2/1 At present there is no distinction among the upper ten thousand of the city. **1850** MITCHELL *Lorgnette* I. 111, I have been set down as a caterer to the tastes of those who are facetiously termed by the Sunday Journals . . . 'the upper Ten Thousand.' **1882** MCCABE *New York* 320 With the Upper-Ten-Thousand it is made the occasion of displaying the wealth and style of the family.

+**Uppowoc.** Also **apooke.** [Virginian *uppôwoc, uhpooc.*] Tobacco. *Obs.* (Cf. POKE *n.¹*) — **1588** T. HARRIOT *Briefe Rep. Va.* C3 This *Uppôwoc* is of so precious estimation amongst them, that they thinke their gods are maruelously delighted therwith. *c*1618 STRACHEY *Virginia* 121 There is here great store of tobacco which the salvages call apooke.

+**Upraise.** Mining. A steep shaft driven upward. *colloq.* — **1876** RAYMOND *8th Rep. Mines* 158 A drift . . . has been run through the . . . ground, and an upraise commenced. **1882** *47th Congress 1 Sess.* H. R. Ex. Doc. No. 216, 98 At the end of this [tunnel] they are pushing an up-raise, finding the rock a little softer as they go up. **1896** SHINN *Story of Mine* 224 An 'upraise' is the beginning of a winze started on a level and carried upward toward the next higher level. **1900** GARLAND *Eagle's Heart* 234 All the talk was of 'pay-streaks,' 'leads,' 'float,' 'whins,' and 'up-raises.'

∗**Upright**, *n.* +1. (See quotation.) +2. A kind of fly hook. {1892} 3. A piano with the frame mounted vertically, as opposed to a grand piano. {1860} — (1) *a*1870 CHIPMAN *Notes on Bartlett* 495 *Upright*, a leg. Western U.S. (2) **1878** NASH *Oregon* 135 The lawyer put on a 'black palmer' and a 'blue upright.' (3) **1891** *Cent.* 6662/1. **1891** S. FISKE *Holiday Stories* 118 The baby grands nestled between the larger instruments. The uprights looked . . . out of place.

∗**Upright**, *a.*

∗**1.** Mounted vertically; operated in a vertical position.

1820 *Columbian Centinel* 19 Jan. 3/3 G. Graupner & Co. . . . will sell off . . . London made Piano Fortes, among which is an elegant Upright Cabinet Piano with 6 octaves. **1853** J. W. BOND *Minnesota* 125 The mill near the upper landing runs one upright and one circular saw.

∗**2.** In the specific names of plants.

1817-8 EATON *Botany* (1822) 290 *Geum strictum*, upright avens. **1843** TORREY *Flora N.Y.* II. 98 *Calystegia spithamœa*, Upright Bindweed. . . . [Grows in] dry woods and copses; not common. **1814** BIGELOW *Florula Bostoniensis* 106 *Monotropa Morisoniana*. Upright Birdsnest. . . . A white plant. . . . Woods. June, July. **1813** MUHLENBERG *Cat. Plants* 48 *Prunus Pennsylvanica borealis*, Upright Cherry Tree. *Ib. Cornus stricta*, Upright dogwood. *c*1730 CATESBY *Carolina* I. 57 *Cistus Virginiana, flore & odore Periclymeni*. . . . The Upright Honysuckle . . . is a Native of Virginia and Carolina. **1843** TORREY *Flora N.Y.* I. 84 Upright St. Peter's Wort. . . . [Grows in] sandy swamps. *Ib.* 95 Upright Sand-wort. . . . *Arenaria stricta*. . . . [Grows] on rocks and in barren places, particularly on the banks of rivers and lakes. **1814** BIGELOW *Florula Bostoniensis* 162

Oxalis stricta. Upright Wood Sorrel. . . . Common about the borders of fields and cultivated grounds.

∗**Uprise.** +1. *Mining.* =UPRAISE. 2. (See quotation.) *colloq.* — (1) **1876** RAYMOND *8th Rep. Mines* 174 Fifty feet in from the mouth of the tunnel an uprise was made, which finally ran into wall-rock. (2) **1891** *Cent.* 6662/2 *Uprise*, . . . rise; development; advance; augmentation, as of price or value.

∗**Uprising.** An insurrection. +Often with specific reference to Indians. — **1851** CIST *Cincinnati* 313 The next great effect will be, the general up-rising of the labor class in agriculture. **1885** *Wkly. New Mexican Rev.* 16 April 4/1 This spring has been hidden from the world since the uprising of the Pueblo Indians [in 1680]. **1890** LANGFORD *Vigilante Days* (1912) 490 Governor Green Clay Smith had requested me . . . to convey to Colonel Howie . . . the news of a reported Indian uprising **1916** EASTMAN *From Deep Woods* 118, I found to my surprise that the press still fostered the illusion of a general Indian uprising.

+**Up-river**, *a.* and *n.*

1. *adj.* Going upstream; living in or situated in a place farther upstream. {1877-}

1836 *S. Lit. Messenger* II. 698/1, I had never imagined that any thing half so grand . . . awaited us on our up-river jaunt. **1852** *Knickerb.* XL. 278 We commend this fact to the consideration of our 'up-river' correspondent. **1857** CHANDLESS *Visit Salt Lake* 1, I passed a few days there, waiting for an up-river boat. **1871** BAGG *At Yale* 7 The 'up-river' ministers . . . had appealed to the Legislature . . . to prevent the establishment of the school at New Haven. **1915** *Lit. Digest* 4 Sept. 467/1 The second stampede of the Klondikers from up-river points.

2. *n.* A region or area situated farther upstream.

1902 WHITE *Blazed Trail* 143 If the men from up-river come by, . . . don't act mysterious. **1907** LONDON *Road* 153, I had come down from 'up river' some time before.

+**Up-river**, *adv.* Toward the source of a river; farther upstream. {up the river, 1650-} — **1848** THOREAU *Maine Woods* 83 Only a few axe-men have gone 'up river,' into the howling wilderness which feeds it. **1887** *Harper's Mag.* April 667/1 Logs were usually cut and hauled in summertime to the banks of streams, often a long distance 'up-river.' **1893** *Harper's Weekly* 16 Dec. 1211/2 Day and night it poured, upriver and down. **1902** WHITE *Blazed Trail* 123 They're getting this stuff out up-river first.

∗**Upset.** ‖A summary or digest. — **1841** GREELEY in *Corr. R. W. Griswold* (1898) 102 Having got the right sort of a letter from Burleigh, I have set right down and written you an upset of it.

Upset price. At a public sale or auction, a minimum price set by the seller or the auctioneer. {1814-} 'Orig. *Sc.* and *U.S.*' (*O.E.D.*). — [**1834** *Spectator* 8 Nov. 1066/1 The price at which land [in the U.S.] is . . . sold, varies from the upset price to many pounds sterling per acre.] **1848** BARTLETT 372 At public auctions an article is sometimes 'set up,' or 'started,' by the auctioneer at the lowest price at which it can be sold. This is called the *upset price.* **1917** J. F. DALY *Life A. Daly* 306 Bouton tried to protect some of the 'extra illustrated' books relating to the stage by putting an 'upset price' upon them.

∗**Upshoot. 1.** A movement upward; a rush upward. +**2.** *Baseball.* An upward-curving pitched ball. — (1) **1866** ALGER *Solitudes* 25 A palm, in its resistless upshoot, cleaving altar and image. **1888** *Advance* 14 June 383 The averages of the depth of water in the great lakes run in cycles of nine years each—that is, there is a downshoot for nine years and then an upshoot for the same period. **1898** *Columbus Dispatch* 29 March 12/4 The upshoot of flame was well forward. (2) **1885** CHADWICK *Art of Pitching* 14 It is essential to change the direction of the curve . . . from an 'up-shoot' to a 'down-shoot.' **1907** *St. Nicholas* June 720/1 The umpire . . . could throw an 'up shoot' and a 'snake curve' and never half try.

Upstairs. An upper story. {1884-} — **1872** EGGLESTON *End of World* 19 They say, he has all up-stairs full of books. **1880** in Appel *Biog. Wanamaker* 104 [Furniture stock added occupying the upstairs. **1898** *Kissimmee* (Fla.) *Valley Gazette* 14 Jan. 3/4 Mr. Slater has rented the upstairs at Mrs. Cannons and will spend the winter here. **1914** STEELE *Storm* 57, I went ashore with some of the men to a place called 'Schlinsky's up-stairs.'

+**Upstander.** An upright post or handle bar on a sledge. — **1856** KANE *Arctic Explor.* II. 98 It has two standards, or, as we call them, 'upstanders.' **1903** PEARY in *McClure's Mag.* Feb. 419/2, I had scarcely time to seize the upstanders when my dogs were off.

∗**Upstart.** +A member of a new religious sect. — **1837** JENKINS *Ohio Gazetteer* 307 The principal religious denominations are methodists, presbyterians, baptists, friends, and *Upstarts*, of which the methodists are the most numerous.

Upstream, *a.* Situated in, or lying or moving in the direction of, the upper part of a stream. {1838-}

1815-6 *Niles' Reg.* IX. Suppl. 164/2 Heavy scantling laid so close together as to be water tight, is extended up the river, with their up stream ends bolted to the rocks. **1826** COOPER *Mohicans* iii, They call this upstream current the tide. **1842** *Amer. Pioneer* I. 70 Steam-boats seem almost to say, we will do your up-stream business for nothing, if you will give us your down-stream business. **1847** ROBB *Squatter Life* 59 No sooner did they git it [a new town] again' . . . , than they wagon'd from Cincinnate and other up-stream villages, a pacel of fellers to attend the shops. **1901** *No. Amer. Rev.* Feb. 186 The 'up-stream' wolf . . . felt compelled to put his intervention upon the untenable ground that he was injured by the soiling of the waters.

+b. Proceeding in the face of opposition.

1847 in *Boston Pub. Lib. Bul.* May (1900) 177, I do not wish any upstream measure taken to supply funds.

Upstropelous, *a.* Obstreperous. *dial.* {upstrapelous, *dial.*} — *c*1840 J. NEAL *Beedle's Sleigh Ride* 18 Miss Jones, you're gettin' upstropulous. **1901** JEWETT *Tory Lover* 106 Along he come like some upstropelous poppet an' give me a cuff side o' my head.

+Uptown, *n.* The higher part of a town or city; the residential area. **1844** *N.Y. Ev. Mirror* 12 Nov. 2/2 'Up-Town' and 'Down-Town.'— We see that these names of the different halves of the city are becoming the common language of advertisements, notices, etc. **1853, 1856** [see DOWN TOWN *n.*]. **1884** *Century Mag.* March 681/1 The fathers of the city . . . thought that sandstone was good enough for 'up-town.' **1891** WELCH *Recoll. 1830–40* 27 It was a Saturday afternoon play-ground for the youngsters from up-town.

+Uptown, *a.* Situated in, or proceeding toward or coming from, the upper part, or the fashionable or residential area, of a town or city.

1838 STEPHENS *Travels Greece* I. 83 Even I, . . . a quondam speculator in 'up-town lots.' **1840** *N.Y. Daily Express* 3 April 2/2 About 9 o'clock a procession from the 10th and other up town wards marched down Center street. **1851** CIST *Cincinnati* 91 It enjoys the . . . advantage of being a convenient place of deposit for . . . up-town customers. **1880** CABLE *Grandissimes* 401 That social variety of New Orleans life now distinguished as Uptown Creoles. **1882** MCCABE *New York* 52 The steady uptown movement of the population . . . will no doubt be greatly accelerated by the elevated railroads. *Ib.* 160 An up-town stage of the same line was passed. **1905** N. DAVIS *Northerner* 108 Carmichael . . . is Falls's uptown manager.

Uptown, *adv.* In, into, or to the higher part {1855–}, or the residential or the fashionable area, of a town or city.

1802 J. COWLES *Diary* 65 Mama went uptown today. **1833** *Niles' Reg.* XLIV. 177/2 The property-holders, up-town, would have the site of the building a mile or so from the present chief seat of business. **1850** MITCHELL *Lorgnette* I. 37 Our man of fashion has then one position up-town, and quite another in Wall street. **1883** *Harper's Mag.* Nov. 945/1 We took a Broadway car up-town. **1893** M. HOWE *Honor* 21 The fashion of New York in its rapid flight up town has found no pleasanter dwellings. **1904** *Critic* May 405 Since Dr. Rainsford came to New York 40 churches below 20th Street have moved uptown. **1917** MATHEWSON *Sec. Base Sloan* 57 They parted, agreeing to meet uptown at noon.

Up-with-the-times, *a.* Up-to-date. *colloq.* — **1893** SANBORN *S. Calif.* 4, I know of bright people who actually carried their favorite matches from an eastern city to Tacoma, . . . only to find the best of everything in that brilliant and up-with-the-times city.

+Urban. A city dweller. — **1891** *Cent.* 6666/1. **1896** *Vt. Agric. Rep.* XVI. 123 Vermonters are learning that scenery has economic value, and urbans of wealth are gaining footholds all over her fair domain.

Urbaniste. A medium large variety of pear. — **1851** BARRY *Fruit Garden* 308 *Urbaniste* (Beurre Picquery of the French). A large, melting, buttery pear, a tardy bearer on the pear, but succeeds well on the quince. **1863** *Horticulturist* XVIII. 262/2 Of Pears, [we may mention] Bartlett, Belle Lucrative, . . . Louise Bonne de Jersey, Urbaniste. **1913** *Stand.* 1817/2.

Urbanite. A resident of a city. {1927} — **1897** *Advance* 29 April 542/1 They will capture streets . . . , will say to urbanites and suburbanites, 'Stand and deliver.'

Urbanization. The transformation of a rural area or population by the development of characteristics of urban or city life. {1904–} — **1888** *Advance* 8 March 152 One of the most remarkable characteristics of the time is 'the urbanization of the country.'

∗Urchin. =URSON. *Obs.* — **1736** GYLES *Mem. Captivity* 26 Our . . . Urchin is about the bigness of a Hog of six Months old. [see URSON].

Urette. A fertilizer: (see quotation). — **1839** BUEL *Farmer's Companion* 72 Urette is animal urine, absorbed and rendered dry by mixture with calcareous earth.

∗Urim and Thummim. [Exod. 28–30.] +In the Book of Mormon, two sacred objects: (see quot. 1843). Said by Joseph Smith to have been found by him with the plates of the Book of Mormon and used by him in translating. — **1830** J. SMITH *Book of Mormon* (1920) [5] There were two stones in silver bows and these stones, fastened to a breastplate, constituted what is called the Urim and Thummim. **1843** CASWALL *Prophet of 19th Cent.* 77 The mystic Urim and Thummim . . . appeared in the form of two transparent stones, set in the rim of a bow, like a pair of spectacles, and fastened to a golden breastplate. **1867** DIXON *New America* I. 239 You may smile at Joseph's gift of tongues; his discovery of Urim and Thummim (which he supposed to have been a pair of spectacles!)

Urson. The Canada porcupine, *Erethizon dorsalus.* {1774–, in Canada} — **1796** MORSE *Univ. Geog.* I. 201 The Urchin, or Urson, . . . is commonly called Hedgehog or Porcupine, but differs from both those animals.

Ursuline. A member of an order of Catholic women occupied principally with teaching and nursing. {1693–} Also attrib. — **1812** *Niles' Reg.* I. 345/2 The speaker laid before the house a petition of the Urseline Nuns at New-Orleans. **1895** G. KING *New Orleans* 69 Then came the nineteen Ursulines, in their choir mantles and veils, holding lighted candles.

+U.S. [Abbrev. for UNITED STATES.] The United States of America.

Examples of the attributive use of *U.S.* are under UNITED STATES 4, 6, 7, 8, and in separate entries beginning *United States;* e.g., UNITED STATES ARMY.

1796 HAWKINS *Letters* 31 He was during the Revolution War attached to the armies of the U.S. and made some contributions in aid of them. **1842** 'UNCLE SAM' *Peculiarities* I. 42 The military are for a minute obstructed by . . . a dirty cart carrying the mail of 'U.S.'—Uncle Sam or United States. **1860** in *Vanity Fair* III. 269/1 His brother, Colonel Fuss, Trained up by old U.S. Tore down your dirty flag. **1917** *St. Louis Globe-Democrat* 6 April 1/4 (*headline*), Marked Change Toward U.S. is Seen in Berlin.

+U.S.A. Abbrev. of UNITED STATES OF AMERICA and of UNITED STATES ARMY. — [**1828** SHERBURNE *Memoirs* 68 On the forehead of some of her [a ship's] carved images, the letters U.S.A. were carved.] **1848** *Santa Fe Repub.* 24 Aug. 2/1 Maj. Weightman, Pay Master U.S.A. arrived in this city a few days since. **1881** *Naval Encycl.* p. iv, In several departments of the work Colonel George A. Woodward, U.S.A., has assisted by contributions and editorial supervision. **1898** *Lit. Digest* XVII. 592 The Slayton Electric Caster Co., Ltd., 25 Pearl St., Tecumseh, Mich., U.S.A.

+U. Sam. Abbrev. for UNCLE SAM 1. — **1814** *Columbian Centinel* 3 Dec. 2/5 U. Sam pays his soldier-servants in Paper Money . . . which the poor fellows . . . sell at a loss from 20 to 30 dollars in a hundred.

∗Use, *n.* +*To have no use for,* or variants: To dislike or distrust. {1903} — **1872** *Harper's Mag.* June 158/2 He was an obstinate fellow, . . . and, moreover, he 'had no use for' the defendant any way. **1883** *Harper's Mag.* Jan. 282/1 As far as he was concerned, he 'didn't have use for no Yankees.' **1906** CHURCHILL *Coniston* 373 Miss Duncan had no use for a heroine without a heart-ache. **1921** PAINE *Comr. Rolling Ocean* 11, I felt acquainted with you . . . though you seemed to have no great use for me.

∗Use, *v.*

∗1. *intr.* To make frequent visits; to resort. Now rare or local.

'Latterly *dial.* . . . and *U.S.*' (*O.E.D.*).

1770 WASHINGTON *Diaries* I. 424 On this Creek many Buffaloes use. **1833** J. HALL *Harpe's Head* 152 Yes, I use about here some. **1839** *S. Lit. Messenger* V. 377/1 These bears . . . are using about in the cornfields. **1884** 'MARK TWAIN' *H. Finn* vi, If he didn't quit using around there she would make trouble for him. **1924** RAINE *Land of Saddle-Bags* 98 In the mountains we hear 'The sheep uses under the clifts,' or 'The turkeys use in the wheat-patch.'

2. *To use up.* **a.** To kill. *colloq.* {1785} Also transl., fig., and *ppl. a.*

1832 J. HALL *Legends of West* 38 It's a mercy, madam, that the cowardly *varments* hadn't *used you up,* body-aciously. **1840** *Picayune* 9 Aug. 2/4 Henry McCann, found used up on the levee. **1846** THORPE *Myst. Backwoods* 131, I've seen trout swallow a perch, and a cat would come along and swallow the trout, and perhaps . . . the alligators use up the cat. **1860** G. W. BUNGAY *Bobolink Minstrel* 71 If once Dug. gets astride of that, He is a used-up man. **1887** GEORGE *40 Yrs. on Rail* 193 The engines and coaches were badly used up. **1900** GARLAND *Eagle's Heart* 64, I used up Clint Slocum because I had to.

b. To exhaust or wear out physically, as by overexertion. {1850–}

1833 *Md. Hist. Mag.* XIII. 321, I started the next morning by 4 for this place, . . . which I reached about 10 in the night, pretty much used up. **1845** S. SMITH *J. Downing's Lett.* 29 [Moving] has used me up worse than building forty acres of stone wall. **1886** H. D. BROWN *Two College Girls* 69, I am completely exhausted when I come out of Professor Powers's class. . . . It just uses me up. **1908** FREEMAN *Shoulders of Atlas* 230 Mrs. Whitman's none too strong, and when anything goes against her she's all used up.

+c. To subject to thoroughgoing discussion or unfavorable criticism. Also *vbl. n.*

1839 KIRKLAND *New Home* 253 After tea the poor Brents were completely 'used up' to borrow a phrase much in vogue with us. **1844** *S. Lit. Messenger* X. 720/2 Each and every one of the Magazines in question, gave Mr. 'Oppodeldoc' a complete using-up. **1848** POE *Works* (1902) XIII. 169 The various criticisms, in which we have been amused (rather ill-naturedly) at seeing Mr. Lowell 'used up.'

+Used-to-be. Someone or something past its period of power or influence; a has-been. *colloq.* — **1853** B. F. TAYLOR *Jan. & June* 206 [They] consign them [*sc.* poets] to that grand receptacle of dilapidated 'has beens' and despised 'used-to-be's—the old garret. **1911** LINCOLN *Cap'n Warren's Wards* 237 One of 'em's a used-to-be, and the other's a never-was.

+Usee. *Law.* 'A person for whose use a suit is brought in the name of another. (Rare.)' (*Cent.*)

Ush, *v.* {a1824, *dial.*} +*intr.* To act as usher. *humorous.* — **1890** *Harper's Mag.* Dec. 160/2 The six gentlemanly cow-boys . . . swore that whoever should prove to be the lucky man, the others would ush for him at the ceremony. **1910** *Ib.* March 613/1 Man alive, you've crossed half a continent to 'ush' at that wedding!

* **Usher.**

* **1.** In a school, an assistant or subordinate teacher. Now hist.

1710 *Boston Rec.* 65 We are of opinion the worke of that School do's necessarily require the Attendance of a master and an Usher. **1729** *Boston Rec.* 4 Voted that there be Alowed the Sum of Eighty Pounds for another Usher of the Said School. **1852** MITCHELL *Dream Life* 124 There is one big student . . . who you would like to see measure strength with your old usher. **1893** HALE *New Eng. Boyhood* 33 There was one head-master, a sub-master, and two others, who were called ushers on the printed catalogue, but were never so called by the boys.

2. An employee, in a theater, a restaurant, etc.; or a member in a church, who conducts persons to their places.

1868 DICKENS in M. Dickens & G. Hogarth *Lett. C. Dickens* II. 380 He met one of the 'ushers' (who show people to their seats) coming in with Kelly. **1870** O. LOGAN *Before Footlights* 309 At a Washington theatre . . . a nervous individual . . . [asked] if the usher 'wouldn't light that gasburner?' **1873** *Harper's Mag.* May 949/2 We were received at the [church] door by ushers in dress-coats and white ties. **1892** *Ib.* Feb. 426/1 Whoever is eating at one of the tables will see the ushers standing about like statues until a customer enters the door. **1897** FLANDRAU *Harvard Episodes* 15 'They' who so frequently wore little crimson usher's badges at the games. **1900** S. HALE *Letters* 355, [I] burst upon the mourners assembled, . . . instead of being sorted out . . . by Russell Sullivan and other devout ushers.

+**b.** *spec.* A man, usually an intimate friend of the bride or the bridegroom, serving in this capacity at a wedding.

1895 *Outing* XXVII. 181 He sent the young lady a beautiful Colport cup and saucer, . . . at the same time breathing a prayer that Elliott would not ask him to be usher. **1902** HARBEN *A. Daniel* 130 She's always said she wanted a lot of bridesmaids and ushers and decorations. **1923** WIGGIN *My Garden of Memory* 379 Four of the bride's summer friends were the ushers.

+**Using-ground.** An area frequented by game. — **1893** *Harper's Mag.* Oct. 681 The 'using-grounds' of the coveys [of quail] are generally known or suspected by the farmer who is fond of shooting.

Using up. (See USE *v.* 2 c.)

+**U.S.N.** Abbrev. for *United States Navy.* — **1862** MOORE *Rebellion Rec.* V. II. 177 All our fleet, (except the Pittsburgh,) under Commodore Davis, U.S.N., . . . was under way. **1881** *Naval Encycl.* p. v, List of Contributors and Articles. Ammen, Daniel, Rear-Admiral U.S.N.

+**U. States.** Abbrev. of UNITED STATES. *rare.* — **1837** PECK *Gaz. Illinois* 132 The possible destiny of the U. States as a nation of a hundred millions of freemen . . . is an august conception.

+**Utah.** Also **Yuta, Eutaw,** etc.

1. = UTE.

[**1720** in *Archæological Inst. Papers* V. 183 En que doi quenta . . . de la Jornada que acauaua de ejecutar en poz de la Nazion Yutta y Cumanche.] **1808** PIKE *Sources Miss.* 222 Well the Utahs are Indians also? **1837** IRVING *Bonneville* II. 216 Both the Shoshonies and the Eutaws conducted themselves with great propriety. **1844** GREGG *Commerce of Prairies* I. 300 The *Yutas* (or *Eutaws,* as they are usually styled by Americans) are one of the most extensive nations of the West. **1855** SCHOOLCRAFT *Information resp. Indian Tribes* V. 498 Tribes of Utah Territory. . . . Eutahs of New Mexico . . . 50 [lodges]. **1856** DERBY *Phoenixiana* 48 Oh! we gin them fits, The Ingen Utahs.

2. *attrib.* **a.** Designating persons belonging to, or groups composed of, the Utes.

1822 FOWLER *Journal* 122 The Indeans . . . Ware of the utaws nation. **1837** IRVING *Bonneville* II. 213 This was a band of Eutaw Indians, who were encamped higher up on the river. *Ib.* 219 A pert little Eutaw wench . . . had been taken prisoner . . . by a Shoshonie. **1850** TAYLOR in *Pres. Mess. & P.* V. 33, One [treaty was] negotiated with the Navajo tribe . . . , and the other with the Utah tribe.

b. Designating places and things connected with Utah Lake or the territory of Utah: (1) In general sense. (2) In specific names.

(1) **1848** BRYANT *California* xi. 159 The 'Utah Outlet,' the channel through which the Utah Lake empties its waters into the Salt Lake. **1857** *Congress. Globe* 24 Feb. 289/3 Many California emigrants have disappeared on the Utah route. (2) **1884** *Nat. Museum Bul.* No. 27, 488 *Squalius atrarius.* . . . Utah Mullet; Chub of Utah Lake.

+**Utahan.** A native or resident of Utah. — **1855** WHITMAN *Leaves of Grass* 58 Not only the free Utahan, Kansian, or Arkansian.

+**Ute.** Also **Yute.** [Amer. Indian.] (See also UTAH.)

1. a. An Indian belonging to a group of primitive, warlike Shoshonean tribes formerly occupying a large territory in Colorado, Utah, and New Mexico. **b.** An Indian of another western or southwestern group, as a Piute.

1850 GARRARD *Wah-To-Yah* xix. 217, I'd been hyar afore, tradin' liquor to the Yutes. **1865** [see PLAINS INDIAN]. **1890** *Stock Grower & Farmer* 10 May 5/2 Within a radius of 250 miles of Gallup, N.M., there are . . . the Navajos, Zunis, Apaches, Supais, Hualapais, Utes and Pueblos. **1905** *Field Columbian Museum Publ.* No. 103, 62 Tribal divisions prevail among the Cheyenne . . . Ute, . . . Cheyenne Sioux [etc.].

2. Attrib. with *commission, Digger, squaw.*

1850 GARRARD *Wah-To-Yah* xix. 223 You mind, Louy, my Yute squaw. **1876** SIMPSON *Rep. Explor. Utah* 460 These mixed bands are known as the Diggers, and commonly called Snake Diggers and Ute Diggers. **1882** *Rep. Indian Affairs* 149 The Ute commission failed to have the lands surveyed and allotted in severalty to those who came and remained.

* **Utensil. a.** A vessel or implement for use in cooking or similar domestic operations. **b.** A tool or piece of equipment employed in some branch of the useful arts. {1604–}

1650 *Harvard Rec.* I. 32 The necessary provisions of fuell, reparations of outworn utensils. **1676** *Boston Rec.* 100 Make use of John Courcers house & utensells for brewings. **1733** *Ib.* 62 Voted, That there be a Committee Chosen . . . to prepare Carriages, and all utensils necessary for compleatly Mounting the Cannon. **1787** *Salem Mercury* 28 April, A number of ladies . . . assembled at the Parsonage-house, with their spinning-wheels and other utensils of industry. **1854** BARTLETT *Personal Narr.* I. 272 We observe that the *olla,* or earthen pot, . . . is almost their only domestic utensil. **1877** *Rep. Indian Affairs* 46 No clothing, blanket, tent, implement, or utensil of any kind has been issued at this agency for nearly two years.

‖**Uthlecan.** [Amer. Indian.] The eulachon, *Thaleichthys pacificus.* — **1836** IRVING *Astoria* II. 79 A small kind of fish, . . . called by the natives the uthlecan, . . . made its appearance at the mouth of the [Columbia] river. *Ib.*, The sturgeon makes its appearance in the river shortly after the uthlecan.

* **Utility.**

See also *public utility* (under PUBLIC *a.* 10).

1. In a theatrical company, the playing of minor parts; also, an actor assigned these roles. {1803– (A. Mathews *Mem. C. Mathews* I. 359)}

1845 SOL. SMITH *Theatr. Apprent.* 71, I told him . . . that I was willing to engage for *utility.* **1870** O. LOGAN *Before Footlights* 177 'What are utility people?' 'The utilities are the persons who present a letter—announce that "my lord, the carriage waits"; and sometimes do the heavy business.' **1891** *Cent.* 6678/2 A supernumerary . . . is said to have gone into the 'utility,' when he has a part with words given him.

2. *attrib.* passing into *adj.* **a.** In sense 1 with *boy, business, people.* {1879–} +**b.** *Utility corporation,* a corporation operating a public utility.

(a) **1870** O. LOGAN *Before Footlights* 99 The utility people are a step higher on the ladder [than the supernumeraries]. *Ib.* 177 There's nothing degrading in doing the heavy—the utility-business, is there? **1892** *Courier-Journal* 2 Oct. 22/5 The comedian [spoke] with as much gravity as he used to assume when . . . utility boy in old Ben De Bar's company. (b) **1908** STEVENS *Liberators* 187 The franchises of the principal city utility corporations . . . were about to expire.

Utilization. A using or turning to account: (see also quot. 1841). {1881–} — **1841** WEBSTER II. 894/2 *Utilization,* a making profitable; a gaining. **1853** LOWELL *Fireside Trav.* (1864) 63 Dr. K. was President of the University then, a man of genius, but of genius that evaded utilization.

Utricularia. A bladderwort; a plant of the genus *Utricularia.* {1753–} — **1818** *Mass. H. S. Coll.* 2 Ser. VIII. 170 In August the eye is gratified with . . . the leafless utricularia. **1863** HIGGINSON *Out-Door Papers* 278 The slender Utricularia, a dainty maiden whose light feet scarce touch the water.

Uvularia. {1706} +An herb of the genus *Uvularia;* a bellwort. {1829–} — **1818** *Mass. H. S. Coll.* 2 Ser. VIII. 168 At the same time appear the blossoms of the alder, hazel, and poplar; soon after those of the uvularia or bellwort. **1850** S. WARNER *Wide, Wide World* xl, Wild columbine, the delicate corydalis, and more uvularias, which she called yellow bells. were added to her handful.

V

*V. The twenty-second letter of the alphabet.

1. *Double V*, an earmark on live stock.

1674 *Portsmouth Rec.* 283 The Eare-marke . . . is a double V on the left Eare.

+2. A five-dollar bill. Also attrib.

1837 *Jamestown* (N.Y.) *Jrnl.* 23 Aug. 2/3 Blacklegs are broken and reputable young men begin to perceive the necessity of saving their V's. **1848** LOWELL *Biglow P.* 1 Ser. vi. 103, I vow my holl sheer o' the spiles wouldn't come nigh a V spot. **1859** *Harper's Mag.* April 621/1 The stable-keeper had taken the 'V' from a grocer close by. **1883** BEADLE *Western Wilds* 614 [One] can buy good land right alongside o' mine now for a V an acre. **1912** *Boston Transcript* April (Th. S.), This morning while looking through an old suit I found the V I thought I'd lost.

Vaca. *S.W.* [Sp.] A cow. — **1846** MAGOFFIN *Down Santa Fé Trail* 91 They are inhabited by rancheros as they are called, who attend solely to raising of vacas. **1897** HOUGH *Story of Cowboy* 26 Even cattle are sometimes called *vacas*, though this is not usual.

+Vacant lot. A lot on which no building stands. — **1648** *New Haven Col. Rec.* 95 He shall build a dwelling house vpon it, . . . so it may not lye as a vacant lott. **1856** OLMSTED *Slave State* 406 The burying-ground was a rough 'vacant lot' in the midst of the town. **1885** HOWELLS *Silas Lapham* x, The frying of the grasshopper in the blossomed weed of the vacant lots on the Back Bay is interspersed with the carol of crickets. **1907** *St. Nicholas* June 718/1 'The only good place . . . is over there,' pointing to the vacant lot.

Vacate, *v.* {1643–} **+1.** *intr.* To spend a vacation. *colloq.* **2.** *tr.* To cause the occupants of a house to move from (it). — (1) **1836** *Knickerb.* VII. 15 Ned and I were vacating . . . at his father's charming residence. **1885** *Advance* 23 July 476 One thing he [a Chinaman] can never learn and that is how to vacate. (2) **1904** *N.Y. Ev. Post* 14 May 7 His system of vacating unlivable houses is less drastic. He does not summarily turn families out.

*Vacation. **+**A period of relaxation from one's customary occupation. { =E. 'holiday'} Also attrib. — **1844** *Lowell Offering* IV. 237, I wish they would have a vacation in 'dog days'—stop the mills and make all the girls rest. **1859** DANA (title), To Cuba and Back. A Vacation Voyage. **1882** LATHROP *Echo of Passion* i, They had but just come to Tanford, to spend the first vacation which the young chemist . . . had allowed himself since his marriage. **1925** TILGHMAN *Dugout* 95 Harriet had gone away for a brief vacation.

Vacationer. {1904} **+**One who is on a vacation from business or other occupation. — **1890** *Advance* 28 Aug., The 'swallows homeward fly,' and so, by sea and land, do vacationers and tourists. **1898** *Atlantic Mo.* LXXXII. 491/1 It did my vacationer's heart good to see men so cheerfully industrious. **1905** *Springfield W. Repub.* 28 July 2 Any vacationer may easily extend the bounds of his knowledge by drinking in what the natives may have to tell him.

Vacationing. Taking a vacation. — **1896** *Advance* 27 Aug. 273 Despite hard times, people will go vacationing.

Vacationist. {1885–} **+**=VACATIONER. — **1888** *Nation* XLVI. 391/3 What the vacationist takes as the extreme medicine of his constitution, is their daily food. **1905** *Springfield W. Repub.* 18 Aug. 14 This summer in particular [Lake Sunapee] has seen a great number of local vacationists.

Vacationless, *a.* Without a vacation. — **1891** *Advance* 25 June, I dislike to go away leaving people vacationless who deserve an outing more than I do. **1911** HARRISON *Queed* 202 The Colonel . . . gave an account of his vacationless summer.

Vaccination. Inoculation with vaccine as a preventive of smallpox. {1800–} — **1801** JEFFERSON *Writings* X. 303, I am happy to see that vaccination is introduced, and likely to be kept up, in Philadelphia. **1815–6** *Niles' Reg.* IX. Suppl. 182/1 When vaccination was struggling on to establish itself here, there were more people by far, who disbelieved its efficacy in preventing small pox, than there were who had confidence in its power. **1860** EMERSON *Conduct of Life* 27 The depopulation by cholera and small-pox is ended by drainage and vaccination. **1898** *Kansas City Star* 18 Dec. 4/2 All school children and all school teachers in Lincoln county must have a certificate of vaccination before attending school Monday morning.

Vaccine. {1803–} Any substance used to inoculate people against some disease; esp., =next. {1846–} — **1813** *Ann. 12th Congress* 2 Sess. 1336 The President of the United States . . . [is] authorized to appoint an agent to preserve the genuine vaccine. **1912** *Bureau Animal Industry* Circ. 190, 331 His vaccine contains living bacilli of bovine origin. **1917** *Public Health Rep.* No. 19, 687 The change in the antitoxins, serums, and such products as typhoid vaccine is a gradual chemical deterioration.

Vaccine matter. A preparation of the virus of cowpox, used in vaccination. {1799–} — **1803** LEWIS in *L. & Clark Exped.* VII. (1905) 278 I would thank you to forward me some of the Vaxcine matter. **1835** J. MARTIN *Descr. Virginia* 75 There are numerous applications for vaccine matter. **1904** *Indian Laws & Tr.* III. 38 For pure vaccine matter and vaccination of Indians, five thousand dollars.

Vaccinium. Any species of the genus *Vaccinium*, the blueberries; a plant of this genus. {1706–} Also with specifying terms. — **1785** MARSHALL *Amer. Grove* 157 *Vaccinium corymbosum.* Cluster-flowered Vaccinium. . . . The fruit is of a dark purplish colour when ripe, and of an agreeable acid taste. **1837** WILLIAMS *W. Florida* 142 The land rises into hills and ridges of light sand, scattered over with shrub pines and vacciniums.

+Vacher. [F.] A cowboy. Now rare. — **1826** FLINT *F. Berrian* 39 Then we traversed the belt of *vachers* and shepherds, with their blanket-capotes, [etc.]. **1841** *S. Lit. Messenger* VII. 245/2 The camp is in motion, and the vachers (herdsmen) are standing around the fire. **1848** BARTLETT 373 *Vacher*, . . . the stock or cattle keeper on the prairies of the Southwest.

*Vachery. A cattle farm. {–1650} — **1818** DARBY *Emigrant's Guide* 76 Many of the richer planters on the Teche, Vermilion, and other agricultural districts, have stock farms, or as they are termed in the country, 'vacheries.' **1831** PATTIE *Personal Narr.* 123 He had established a vacherie on the river Membry where he kept stock. **1846** THORPE *Myst. Backwoods* 14 Among the *vacheries* of New Spain, they [cattle] are killed for their skins alone.

+Vacquero. =VAQUERO. — **1871** HARTE *East & West Poems* 50 Skins grew rosy, eyes waxed clear, Of rough vacquero and muleteer. **1891** *Amer. Notes & Q.* VI. 198 The vacquero lassoes the one [horse] desired with his lariat.

Vacuum pan. A pan used to boil down syrup, by formation of a vacuum. {1839–} — **1833** SILLIMAN *Man. Sugar Cane* 72 Two vacuum pans . . . will each refine . . . two and a half tons per day. **1858** *Ill. Agric. Trans.* III. 523 The vacuum pan is most esteemed in sugar making. **1883** 'MARK TWAIN' *Life on Miss.* xlviii, Run the molasses . . . through the granulating pipe to condense it; then through the vacuum-pan to extract the vacuum. **1902** LORIMER *Lett. Merchant* 71 A man can't have his head pumped out like a vacuum pan.

+Vag. [Abbrev. of *vagrant* or VAGABOND.] A vagrant. *slang.* — **1895** *Denver Times* 5 March 1/3 'Which are the vags and which is the jury?' asked Judge Cowell this morning. **1896** ADE *Artie* 58 Say, Miller, am I a vag?

*Vagabond. A vagrant; a disreputable person. — **1661** *New Plymouth Laws* 130 If any . . . vagabonds shall come into any towne of this Government the marshall or Constable shall apprehend him or them. **1771** *Phila. Ordinances* (1812) 39 It shall . . . be lawful to and for the said watchmen . . . to apprehend all night-walkers, . . . vagabonds and disorderly persons. **1880** CABLE *Grandissimes* 308 There was a gathering of boys and vagabonds at the door of a gun-shop.

‖Vagarist. [f. *vagary* and *ist.*] One given to vagaries; a faddist. — **1888** *Voice* (N.Y.) 24 May, The Prohibition party are now free from that suspicion of being vagarists, which led to the invention of the word crank.

*Valance. A cloth border hanging down from the canopy of a bed, or, in later use, from the top of a window frame. — **1638** *Md. Archives* IV. 48, 4. bedd curtaines & vallence. **1691** SEWALL *Letter-Book* I. 118 Buy my wife . . . Six yards and ⅓ for the Vallens. **1744** *Md. Hist. Mag.* XXI. 252 Each Curtain 4 Vallons 4 foot Longe. **1876** KNIGHT 2688/1 *Valance*, a *lambrequin*, or drooping curtain hiding the curtain-rods of a window.

‖Valda. [Sp. *falda.*] (See quot. 1876.) — **1871** HARTE *Luck of Roaring Camp* 228 But I . . . soon prepared myself to take a boat to the lower 'valda' of the foot-hills. **1876** — in *Scribner's Mo.* XI. 560 His first impression was that it was the *valda* or a break of the stiff skirt of the mountain as it struck the level plain. **1877** — *Story of Mine* (1896) 1 It was a sterile waste bordered here and there by arable fringes and valdas of meadow land.

*Vale. A valley. — **1666** in *Amer. Sp.* XV. 406 To a marked white oak standing in a vale near the Mouth of a Creek. **1770** WASHINGTON *Writings* II. 308 The vail (through which this creek runs) . . . appears to be wide. **1804** C. B. BROWN tr. Volney *View* 33 Towards the vale of the Ohio, there are many remarkable hills. **1880** *Harper's Mag.* Dec. 49 At the foot of two great valleys of the Alleghany and Monongahela, at the head of the greater vale of the Ohio, Pittsburgh gathers . . . crude wealth.

Valediction. {1614–} (See quot. 1851.) — **1749** *Holyoke Diaries* 10 Valediction presented by Sr. Whipple. **1851** HALL *College Words* 308 *Valediction*, a farewell; a bidding farewell. Used sometimes with the meaning of *valedictory* or *valedictory oration*.

+**Valedictorian.** The student of a college or high school, usually the one of highest academic standing in his class, who delivers the valedictory oration at the graduation of his class. — 1759 *Holyoke Diaries* 20 Officers of the Sophisters chose Valedictorian. 1847 WEBSTER 1224/3 *Valedictorian*, the student of a college who pronounces the valedictory oration at the annual commencement. 1852 *Harper's Mag.* Aug. 335/1, [I was] pointed out, to the classes just entered, as the valedictorian. 1871 BAGG *At Yale* 146 General Russell, the valedictorian of that class, is its reputed founder. 1893 'THANET' *Stories Western Town* 99 Tommy himself, as the valedictorian, [was] occupying the centre of the picture in his new suit of broadcloth. 1903 *N.Y. Ev. Post* 14 Sept., He was graduated from Hamilton College as valedictorian.

+**Valedictory.**

1. Short for VALEDICTORY ORATION.
1779 *N.J. Archives* 2 Ser. III. 670 The six undergraduates pronounced orations, . . . Stephan Renselaer the valedictory in English. 1817 PAULDING *Lett. from South* I. 64, I was obliged to write his valedictory. 1861 *Harper's Mag.* Oct. 642/1 The valedictory . . . was very much applauded. 1893 'THANET' *Stories Western Town* 99 Tommy's valedictory scored a success that is a tradition of the High School, and . . . [it was] printed in both the city papers.

b. The privilege of delivering the valedictory.
[1830 *Collegian* 118, I was thinking you were in the Senior Class; at any rate, when you do leave, I suppose you'll carry the day in the Valedictory of course.] 1843 STOWE *Mayflower* 36 They say that your son is going to have the valedictory in college. 1868 BEECHER *Norwood* 165 The whole town hoped, when young Cathcart entered Amherst College, that he might 'take the Valedictory.' 1893 'THANET' *Stories Western Town* 96 Tommy's father . . . thinks everything of his getting the valedictory, and Tommy, he worked nights studying to get it.

c. A scroll or manuscript containing a valedictory address.
1893 *Harper's Mag.* Feb. 461 The blue bow on my valedict'ry is purty faded.

2. An address delivered or printed by one leaving a public office or a private position.
1824 MARSHALL *Kentucky* II. 199 President Washington, published his valedictory; in which he declined further service. 1843 *Niles' Nat. Reg.* 11 March 31 The Speaker, at one o'clock, delivered his valedictory. 1863 LINCOLN in Barnes *Mem. T. Weed* 433 Your valedictory to the patrons of the Albany 'Evening Journal' brings me a good deal of uneasiness. 1893 G. SMITH *United States* 296 John A. Andrew also, the great war governor of Massachusetts, said in his valedictory of January the 4th, 1866, that the natural leaders of the South . . . would resume their influence and their sway.

Valedictory address. a. An address delivered by a member of the faculty, or person of eminence, to a graduating class. {1829} **b.** =VALEDICTORY ORATION. — 1838 *S. Lit. Messenger* IV. 480/1 A Valedictory Address, delivered to the Students of the University of North Carolina. 1847 *Ib.* XIII. 568/1 Among the closing exercises of William and Mary was the usual Valedictory Address from the Faculty to the Students,— delivered this year, by Judge Beverley Tucker. 1852 *Harper's Mag.* Aug. 335/1 Then, when the long list was called, and the degrees had been conferred, came my turn—'the valedictory addresses.' 1905 *Springfield W. Repub.* 28 June 2 Baccalaureate sermons and valedictory addresses are once more the order of the day.

Valedictory oration. {1651} An oration delivered by the student of highest standing in a college or high school class at the graduation exercises of that class. — [1670 *Mass. H. S. Coll.* 4 Ser. I. 13 Our class declaimed their last declamations upon ye four languages Hebr. Gr. Lat. Eng. and ye 5 senses with an oration salutatory and valedictory.] 1705 SEWALL *Diary* II. 134 Mr. Hutchinson in his valedictory Oration Saluted the Justices of the Superior Court. 1779 *N.J. Archives* 2 Ser. III. 670 Valedictory oration in English, by Aaron Woodruff of Princeton, [etc.]. 1847 *Knickerb.* XXIX. 16 His valedictory oration . . . was an able defence of the maxim that 'What man has done, man *can* do.' 1925 BRYAN *Memoirs* 330 Mr. Bryan was first in his class and delivered the valedictory oration.

Valenciennes (lace). Lace manufactured, or similar to that manufactured, at Valenciennes, France; a petticoat trimmed with this lace. {1717-} Also attrib. — 1866 A. D. WHITNEY *L. Goldthwaite* i, The perfectly gloved hand . . . upheld a bit of extravagance in Valenciennes lace and cambric. 1882 RITTENHOUSE *Maud* 84 Mrs James says she'll make my graduating dress, quite too charming—India mull and Valenciennes-lace. 1897 STUART *Simpkinsville* 139 The widow Carroll, always a woman of her own mind, had *begun* with the Valenciennes ruche. 1904 'O. HENRY' *Strictly Business* 21 Get the property man to bind it up with a flounce torn from any one of the girls' Valenciennes.

*∗ **Valentine.**

1. A letter or card of ornamental design sent to a friend on St. Valentine's Day. {1824-}
1845 *Knickerb.* XXV. 126 Once before we wrote you a Valentine, in which we advised an old bachelor to get married. 1855 HOLBROOK *Among Mail Bags* 370 Then arose the manufacture and merchandise of Valentines. 1897 STUART *Simpkinsville* 199 Her brother held a pile of valentines in his hand. 1902 G. M. MARTIN *Emmy Lou* 23 Emmy Lou was sure of that, so grateful did she feel she would be to anyone sending her a valentine.

b. *Comic valentine*, a valentine consisting usually of a cartoon, representing a supposed type of some class or occupation, and a set of satiric verses.
1855 M. THOMPSON *Doesticks* 195 It seems to be a time which many a man takes advantage of to revenge some fancied slight from scornful lady, by sending her one of those scandalous nuisances, misnamed 'comic Valentines.'

c. *College.* (See quotation.)
1900 *Dialect Notes* II. 68 *Valentine*, official written communication from secretary of faculty, generally of warning or dismissal.

2. A variety of string bean. In full *valentine bean.*
1850 *Rep. Comm. Patents 1849: Agric.* 158 [Some peas are] speckled, like the valentine bean. 1859 *Ill. Agric. Soc. Trans.* III. 503 Early yellow six-weeks and early Valentine (long red mottled,) are excellent for snaps.

∗ **Valerian.**

∗**1.** Any species of the genus *Valeriana.*
1781-2 JEFFERSON *Notes Va.* (1788) 36, I shall confine myself too to native plants. . . . Seneca rattlesnake-root. *Polygala Senega*. Valerian. *Valeriana locusta radiata.* 1792 IMLAY *Western Territory* 209 Roots [growing in Kentucky include] . . . Ipecacuanha . . . Valerian . . . Ginseng. 1857 GRAY *Botany* 175 *Valeriana*. Valerian. . . . Perennial herbs, with thickened strong-scented roots.

2. A drug derived from the rootstock of the common valerian, *Valeriana officinalis*. {1794-}
1804 J. ROBERTS *Penna. Farmer* 66 A strong decoction of valerian and assafoetida may be given every three hours. 1882 'M. HARLAND' *Eve's Daughters* 236 She has swallowed 'quarts' . . . of valerian and hyoscyamos.

+**3.** (See quotations.)
1894 *Amer. Folk-Lore* VII. 100 *Cypripedium acaule*, valerian, Franconia, N.H. 1899 *Animal & Plant Lore* 115 *Cypripedium acaule*, the stemless lady's-slipper, is called valerian from its supposed efficacy in nervous disorders.

∗**Valet.** A man's body servant. — 1835 INGRAHAM *South-West* I. 88 He is a slave—about seventeen years of age, . . . placed at my disposal as *valet* while I remain here. 1893 M. HOWE *Honor* 259 With the assistance of his valet, she got her husband upstairs and into his bed.

Valet de chambre. =prec. *Obs.* {1646-} — 1791 WASHINGTON *Diaries* IV. 149 My equipage and attendance consisted of a Charriot . . . ; —my Valet de Chambre, two footmen. 1825 J. Q. ADAMS *Diary* 351 The General's valet-de-chambre . . . took the baggage.

Valinch, Velinche. (See quot. 1847.) {1823-} — 1847 WEBSTER 1224/3 *Valinch*, a tube for drawing liquors from a cask by the bung-hole. 1876 KNIGHT 2696/2 *Velinche*, . . . a tube open at both ends, the lower orifice being so contracted that while the finger is closed upon the upper end, liquid will not issue from the lower. 1877 BARTLETT 731.

Valise. Also **valeece.**

1. *Mil.* A cloth or leather case, usually strapped to a saddle, used to hold the kit of a soldier. {1833-} Also attrib.
1781 *Va. State P.* I. 467 They will furnish . . . Valeeces, pads, Swords, Caps & Halters. 1813 *Niles' Reg.* III. 296/1 Leather velises, 2,000. 1840 *Niles' Nat. Reg.* 8 Aug. 366/1 Each dragoon [is] to furnish himself with . . . a good saddle, bridle, mail pillion, and valise. 1876 KNIGHT 2688/1 A valise-saddle is placed on each off-horse of an artillery-carriage.

2. A piece of hand luggage; also, formerly, a bag that might be fastened to a saddle. {1633-}
'Now chiefly *U.S.*' (O.E.D.).
1797 JEFFERSON *Writings* IX. 360 Your impatience to receive your valise and its key was natural. 1819 VAN BUREN in Mackenzie *Van Buren* 183, I send by the boat my valice. 1821 COOPER *Spy* iv, The pedler officiously assisted to . . . fasten the blue cloak and vallise to the mail straps. 1855 BARNUM *Life* 44 His valise was fastened behind the saddle. 1870 RAE *Westward by Rail* 55 If a portmanteau forms part of it [luggage], the portmanteau must be spoken of as a 'valise.' 1888 STOCKTON *Dusantes* 97 The baggage of my party . . . consisted only of a few valises . . . and a package containing two life-preservers. 1900 MUNN *Uncle Terry* 282 Albert . . . found that the valise had disappeared.
attrib. 1876 KNIGHT 2688/1 *Valise-lock*, a small trunk-lock. 1899 *Scribner's Mag.* XXV. 63/1 Minor experiments were also tried with . . . two kinds of valise equipment.

∗ **Valley.**

∗**1.** A long depression between hills or stretches of high ground.
1612 SMITH, etc. *Virginia* I. 2 Here are mountaines, hils, plaines, valleyes, rivers and brookes all running most pleasantly into a faire Bay. 1683 *Providence Rec.* XIV. 50 Twelve Acors of it is Layd out in a Valley, on pautuckett River. 1733 BYRD *Journey to Eden* (1901) 308 The Ground was uneaven, rising into Hills, and sinking into Valleys great part of the way. 1823 JAMES *Exped.* I. 37 From the cultivation of the rich vallies and fertile plains of the west, a great production . . . must find a market here. 1903 *Atlantic Mo.* July 25 The Ceriso is not properly mesa nor valley, but a long healed crater.

b. The inhabitants of a valley.
1881 STODDARD *E. Hardery* 288 All the valley came, . . . and for once the roomy, rambling old parsonage was none too large.

+2. With reference to specific rivers or geographic areas. Often with specifying phrases.

1831 PECK *Guide* 51 We will make a hasty survey of that portion of the lower Valley which borders on the Mississippi. **1833** J. HALL *Harpe's Head* 9 A solitary horseman might have been seen slowly winding his way along a narrow road, in that part of Virginia which is now called the Valley. **1845** *S. Lit. Messenger* XI. 582/1 The steam power of the [Miss.] 'Valley' might be expanded, in case of war. **1847** *Whig Almanac 1848* 33/2 The imperishable principle set forth in the ever-memorable Ordinance of 1787 . . . [has] been the fundamental law of human liberty in the great Valley of the Lakes, the Ohio and Mississippi. **1854** BENTON *30 Years' View* I. 262/2 A separate and distinct bank . . . would save to that city, and to the Valley of the Mississippi . . . the command of their own moneyed system.

3. *attrib.* **a.** With *bottom, country, floor,* etc.

1845 *S. Lit. Messenger* XI. 584/2, I propose to show . . . how all the Valley States . . . may be benefitted, by restoring the commerce of the country to its natural channels. **1850** FOOTE *Virginia* 377 The call of General Greene for aid . . . aroused the Valley-men to come out of their quiet abode, with the habiliments of war. **1864** TAYLOR *H. Thurston* 373 The elms . . . had grown up since the valley-bottom was cleared. **1885** 'CRADDOCK' *Prophet* 10 Did they live in thar life-time up hyar in the Big Smoky, or in the valley kentry? **1891** *Scribner's Mag.* X. 465 A turbid stream, entering a valley trough, . . . deposits some of its earthy load. **1894** *Harper's Mag.* Sept. 622/1 There are main roads and there are wagons to use upon them, but they are both 'valley improvements.' **1919** HOUGH *Sagebrusher* 143 The main body of the forest lay three thousand feet above the valley floor.

b. In the specific names of birds and trees.

See also VALLEY QUAIL.

1905 *Forestry Bureau Bul.* No. 66, 33 Valley mahogany, western service-berry, buffalo berry, and dwarf maple have, without doubt, come down from the Rocky Mountains. **1897** SUDWORTH *Arborescent Flora* 152 *Quercus lobata.* . . . Weeping Oak (Cal.). Valley Oak (Cal.). **1887** RIDGWAY *Manual N.A. Birds* 192 C[*yrtonyx*] *californica vallicola,* Valley Partridge.

Valley land. Land at the bottom of a valley or a piece of such land. — **1866** A. D. WHITNEY *Leslie Goldthwaite* iv, Their road . . . wound for a time through the low, wet valley-lands. **1883** SMITH *Ala. Geol. Survey* 426 West of the town of Florence, in the great bend of the river, is the largest body of valley land in the county. **1893** 'CRADDOCK' in *Harper's Mag.* Dec. 83/1, I ain't settin' store on the valley lands I seen whenst I went ter the wars. **1910** J. HART *Vigilante Girl* 113 It was no longer marsh but rich valley land.

+Valley quail. (See quots. 1917.) Also with specifying term. — **1874** COUES *Birds N.W.* 439 Valley Quail of California.—*Lophortyx californica.* . . . It is abundant from the Columbia River to Cape Saint Lucas, on the plains and in the valleys. **1883** *Century Mag.* Aug. 484/1 Our partridges (viz. Bob White, the Mountain, Valley, and Massena quails, etc.) may be distinguished among American *Gallinæ*, by the foregoing characters. **1917** *Birds of Amer.* II. 8 The California quail . . . is known commonly in California as the Valley Quail . . . ; but ornithologists now recognize two subspecies, the California Quail and the Valley Quail (*Lophortyx californica vallicola*). *Ib.* 9 Gambel's Quail. *Lophortyx gambeli.* . . . [Also called] Arizona Quail; Gambel's Valley Quail.

+Valley tan. A kind of whisky manufactured by Mormons in the West. — **1868** WATERS *Life among Mormons* 59 Some of the stuff distilled in this country . . . [is] known as 'Valley Tan.' **1872** 'MARK TWAIN' *Roughing It* 74 He had been drinking . . . the exclusively Mormon refresher, 'valley tan.' **1890** LANGFORD *Vigilante Days* (1912) 272 The entire party joined in a pledge of amity over a bottle of 'Valley Tan.'

+Valparaiso oak. W. =MAUL OAK. — **1884** SARGENT *Rep. Forests* 146 Live Oak. Maul Oak. Valparaiso Oak. **1897** SUDWORTH *Arborescent Flora* 164 *Quercus chrysolepis.* . . . Valparaiso Oak (Cal.).

*Value, *v.* To value (one's self) *on* (someone), or variant: To recommend one's self to someone. Also without reflexive. *Obs.* — **1716** *Essex Inst. Coll.* XLII. 351 As to what he hath in your hands or any ones Elce or any wages or prize money due to him have valued my Selfe upon you. **1760** *Mass. H. S. Coll.* 2 Ser. II. 230 On your arrival there, value yourself on some gentle[ma]n of honor, integrity, and good substance. **1766** ROWE *Diary* 115 The master Capt. Smith values on me.

+Vamo(o)se, *v.* [Sp. *vamos* 'let us go, come.'] *colloq.* Orig. S.W.

1. *intr.* To depart. {1859-}

1848 *N.Y. Mirror* May (B.), I couldn't stand more than this stanza, . . . and I accordingly vamosed. **1868** *Ore. State Jrnl.* 18 July 1/6 The young Lieutenant vamoosed at the next stopping place. **1890** J. JEFFERSON *Autobiog.* 77 When she realized the fact that I was about to 'vamoose' she got up quite a little scene. **1903** HAPGOOD *Autobiog. of Thief* 43, I passed the leather to Jack, who 'vamoosed.'

2. *tr.* To depart from (a place). Freq. in phrase *to vamoose the ranch,* to depart, scatter.

1847 GEARY in H. M. Tinkcom *John White Geary* 29 The Indians had vamosed the country during the fighting. **1847** McH. E. RIPLEY *Rough & Ready Annuls* 245 (Bentley), On the morning after I wrote the letter to father . . . they stacked their arms and colors and 'vamoosed the ranch.' **1857** *Oregon Weekly Times* 1 Aug. (Th.), Another pair of jail-birds have vamosed the log jail at Jacksonville. **1866** C. H. SMITH *Bill Arp* 98 These functionaries very prudently vamosed the ranche to avoid their

too numerous friends. **1903** A. ADAMS *Log of Cowboy* 86 Before you could say Jack Robinson, our dogies had vamoosed the ranch and were running in half a dozen different directions.

*Vamp. **+**(See quot. 1876.) — **1845** WHITTIER *Poetical Works* (1894) 358/1 Now shape the sole! now deftly curl The glossy vamp around it. **1876** KNIGHT 2680/2 *Vamp,* the part of a boot or shoe-upper in front of the ankle seams. **1885** *Harper's Mag.* Jan. 280/1 The upper is found to consist . . . in the case of a button boot, of a 'vamp' to cover the front part of the foot [etc.].

Vampire trap. In a theater, a trap door through which a player can disappear. {1893} — **1845** SOL. SMITH *Theatr. Apprent.* 63 Down I went through the trap-door (it was what actors call a Vampire trap).

Van, *n.*

1. A covered truck or dray, used for transporting goods. {1829-}

1869 'MARK TWAIN' *Innocents* 167 The tall van, plastered with fanciful bills and posters, . . . follows the band-wagon. **1872** C. KING *Mountaineering in Sierra Nev.* 213 The great van rocked, settled a little and stuck fast. **1879** *Harper's Mag.* June 66/1 Large vans [are] piled high with crates of berries.

+2. Lumbering. (See quots. 1893 and 1905.)

1893 *Scribner's Mag.* June 710/2 There is the dealing out of tobacco and clothing to the men from the camp supply-chest, called the 'Van.' **1902** WHITE *Blazed Trail* 39 That stuff doesn't come here. . . . She goes to the 'van.' **1905** *Forestry Bureau Bul.* No. 61, 52 *Van,* the small store in a logging camp in which clothing, tobacco, and medicine are kept to supply the crew. N[orth] W[oods], L[ake] S[tates] Forest].

3. *attrib.* **a.** In sense 1 with *driver, man.* **+b.** In sense 2 with *bill, book, goods.*

(a) **1886** *Outing* April 65/1 In passing other vehicles . . . always take plenty of room; leaving 'shaving to half an inch' to . . . van-drivers and coachmen of accoucheur physicians. **1901** CHURCHILL *Crisis* 390 He locked the lid when the van man handed him the key. (b) **1902** WHITE *Blazed Trail* 61 His wages were twenty-five dollars a month, which his van bill would reduce to the double eagle. *Ib.* 196 He would have to figure on blankets, harness, . . . [and] van-goods. *Ib.* 218 Thorpe looked through the ledger and van book, and finally handed the man a slip.

+Van, *v.* I van (you), I swear. Used as a mild imprecation. *Obs.* — **1790** *Mass. Spy* 30 Dec. (Th.), In one village you will hear the phrase 'I snore,'—in another, . . . 'I van you, I wunt do it.' **1815** HUMPHREYS *Yankey* 97, I can hardly hold my hair on, I van.

+Van Burenism. [Martin Van Buren (1782–1862), eighth president of the United States (1837–41).] *Polit.* The methods or principles of Martin Van Buren and his followers. *depreciatory. Obs.* — **1840** *N.Y. Daily Express* 4 March 2/3 Disseminating the pernicious heresies of Van Burenism. **1846** MACKENZIE *Van Buren* 308 This was Van Burenism in 1836, and it is unchanged.

+Vandevere. A variety of apple. — **1786** WASHINGTON *Diaries* III. 24 Adjoining the cross walk, are 2 Apple trees taken from the middle walk in the No. Garden—said to be Vandiviers. **1849** *New Eng. Farmer* I. 90 *Vandevere.*—Medial size, roundish, mostly red. **1859** ELLIOTT *Western Fruit Book* 113 Vandevere. . . . American. Native of Delaware. **1875** BURROUGHS *Winter Sunshine* 155 Now a Vandevere or a King rolls down from the apex above.

+Vandue, Vandew, Vandoo. Phonetic variant of VENDUE *n.* — **1680** *Huntington Rec.* I. 262 [The] lot was formerly in the teniur or ocopation of trustam hoges and sould to the above sd. finch at a vandue. **1726** *Smithtown Rec.* 81 After 6 hours they are to be sold at a vandue for the charge being payed, one horse one shilling for pounding. **1835–7** HALIBURTON *Clockmaker* 1 Ser. xxvii. 262 Is it a vandew, or a weddin, or a rollin frolic, or a religious stir, or what is it? **1860** HOLMES *E. Venner* vii, I don't mean to set *her* up at vaandoo. **1900** STOCKTON *Afield & Afloat* 361 Next week there is to be a sale of the personal property—a 'vandoo' we call it out here.

Vandyke. A wide collar attached to a woman's dress. {1755–69} — **1783** in Griswold *Republican Court* (1856) 25 [The handkerchief] must be pinned up to the top of the shoulders, and quite under the arm, as you would a girl's vandyke. **1843** *Lowell Offering* III. 92 Cousin Mary would sit and wait for him . . . , with her pink calico gown on, and a white vandyke. **1879** B. F. TAYLOR *Summer-Savory* 116, I see green calashes and vandykes and hats of beaver.

*Vane.

*1. A revolving device placed on top of a building to show which way the wind is blowing; a weathercock.

1698 *East-Hampton Rec.* II. 445 A vane and stake and spikes for ye Meeting hous [etc.]. **1765** *Holyoke Diaries* 29 Weight of the Vane of Harvard 15¾ lb. **1842** *Knickerb.* XX. 569 There was another big vane on Mr. ——'s barn. **1882** McCABE *New York* 168 Its tall spire is surmounted by a gilt-wreathed vane in the shape of a game chicken.

*2. A sail of a windmill. Also attrib.

1724 *New-Eng. Courant* 14 Dec. 2/2 The Planters . . . are no small Sharers in this unhappy Accident, having the Vanes of their Mills blown off. **1761** *Holyoke Diaries* 23 Vane boards hung to Season. **1876** KNIGHT 2781/2 The vane . . . swings around so as to feather, or present its edge to the wind until it again comes into its former position.

Vane man. The man who carries the target in surveying. — **1806** *Ann. 9th Congress* 2 Sess. 1001 Josias Thompson . . . [was] authorized to employ two chain-carriers . . . as well as one vaneman.

Vanilla.

1. a. A species of climbing orchid found in tropical America, esp. *Vanilla planifolia*, from which the flavoring extract is derived. {1698–} **b.** The wild vanilla, *Trilisa odoratissima*.

1763 in W. Roberts *Nat. Hist. Florida* 96 The shore . . . [is] cloathed with . . . vanilla, moho, and cabbage-trees. 1835 Simms *Yemassee* II. 58 The dried leaves of the native and finely odorous vanella . . . diffused a grateful perfume upon the gale. 1877 *Rep. Comm. Agric. 1876* 69 The vanilla is a climbing plant.

2. The flavoring extract derived from the pods of *Vanilla planifolia*. {1728–}

1806 Lewis in *L. & Clark Exped.* III. (1905) 319 The mace vineller and other sweetsmelling spices might be employed with equal advantage. 1856 *Rep. Comm. Patents 1855: Agric.* p. xxiii, The amount of vanilla imported and consumed in this country . . . is believed to exceed 5,000 pounds. 1875 Stowe *We & Neighbors* 298 Here's the French mustard, and here's the vanilla, and the cloves is here. 1907 *St. Nicholas* May 670/1 Flavor the rest with one-half teaspoon of vanilla and almond to taste.

3. Attrib. with *bean, chocolate, extract*.

See also VANILLA PLANT.

1864 Stowe *House & Home* P. 263 He who buys Baker's best vanilla-chocolate may rest assured that no foreign land can furnish anything better. 1874 B. F. Taylor *World on Wheels* 96 There is something in the snuff. . . . It is a vanilla bean. 1893 *Harper's Mag.* Feb. 457 They's a spoonful o' v'nilla extrac' in my cake if they's a drop, for I dash it in by eye.

+**Vanilla grass.** Holy grass, *Hierochloë borealis*. — 1857 Gray *Botany* 574. 1884 Vasey *Agric. Grasses* 55 Vanilla or Seneca grass . . . is very sweet-scented and is often used to perfume drawers, &c.

Vanilla plant. {1753–} +**a.** The wild vanilla, *Trilisa odoratissima*. **b.** The vine of the true vanilla. — (a) 1857 Gray *Botany* 185 L[iatris] *odoratissima*, Vanilla-plant. . . . Leaves exhaling the odor of Vanilla when bruised. 1901 Mohr *Plant Life Ala.* 768 *Trilisa odoratissima*, . . . Vanilla Plant. . . . Carolinian and Louisianian areas. (b) 1877 *Rep. Comm. Agric. 1876* 69 Wild vanilla . . . has no relation whatever to the vanilla-plant that produces the fragrant pods of that name.

Vanist. 'One of the New England Antinomians, about 1637: so called from Sir Henry Vane, governor of Massachusetts Bay Colony in 1636' (*Cent.*).

+**Vanite.** A follower of Martin Van Buren (1782–1862). Also attrib. — 1838 *Lexington Observer* 9 May, The Vanite leaders at Richmond give it up. 1839 in *Corr. R. W. Griswold* (1898) 28 He will do now for a 'Vanite' of the first water.

‖**Vanjack.** =prec. — 1840 *Log Cabin Song Book* 52 The great Twenty-Second is coming, And the Vanjacks begin to look blue.

‖**Vanocrat.** =VANITE. — 1840 *Log Cabin Song Book* 43 He makes the Vanocrats look rather slim.

Vantoon. =VINGT ET UN. Also allusive. — 1839 Briggs *Harry Franco* I. 33 He exclaimed, 'vantoon,' and without more ceremony, he caught up a little heap of sixpences and shillings, and rose up from the table. 1888 Perrin *Ky. Pioneer Press* 35 By 'vantoon' it is presumed that he meant the old French game of cards, *vingt-un*.

Vapor bath. A structure used by Indians for steam baths. {1719–, in general sense} — 1833 Catlin *Indians* I. 186 In their sudatories, or vapour-baths, . . . steam is raised by throwing water on to heated stones. 1852 Marcy *Explor. Red River* (1854) 116 Small structures, consisting of a frame-work of slight poles, bent into a semi-spherical form, and covered with buffalo-hides . . . are called medicine-lodges, and are used as vapor-baths.

∗**Vapory,** *a.* ‖Inclined to low spirits or 'the vapors.' — 1771 J. Adams *Diary Works* II. 269 Thirty people have been here to-day, they say;—the halt, the lame, the vapory, hypochondriac, scrofulous, &c. all resort here.

+**Vaquero.** Also **vachero.** *W.* [Sp.] A cowboy, esp. one of Mexican nationality.

See also VACQUERO.

1837 Irving *Bonneville* II. 142 The vaqueros, or Indian cattle-drivers, have also learnt the use of the laso from the Spaniards. 1849 Audubon *Western Jrnl.* 146 The Rancho 'La Sone' . . . [was] a miserable cluster of mud jacals and surly Mexican vacheros. 1873 Miller *Amongst Modocs* 11 My dress was . . . a sort of cross between an Indian chief and a Mexican vaquero. 1889 Munroe *Golden Days* 36 Long trains of pack-horses . . . were urged forward by gaudily-dressed vaqueros. 1896 Shinn *Story of Mine* 55 The cries and maledictions of the Mexican *vaqueros* were terrific. 1912 Raine *Brand Blotters* 177 Farnum's vaqueros will pay my debt in full.

attrib. 1844 Gregg *Commerce of Prairies* I. 214 The shanks of the vaquero spurs are three to five inches long, with rowels sometimes six inches in diameter. 1877 Harte *Story of Mine* (1896) 203 Having caparisoned himself and charger in true vaquero style, . . . [he] put a sombrero rakishly on his curls.

Vara. *W.* **1.** A linear measure, usually about 33 inches. {1674–, of Spain and Sp. Amer.} Also attrib. **2.** A stick or cane used as an emblem of authority. — (1) 1831 Dewees *Lett. from Texas* 139 One labor shall be composed of one million square varas. 1853 *Alta Californian* 15 Feb., Fifty Vara Lots. . . . One Hundred Vara Lots. 1869 Browne *Adv. Apache Country* 259 This palatial edifice occupies a square of several hun-

dred varas, and is perhaps the largest and most imposing private residence in Arizona. 1910 J. Hart *Vigilante Girl* 153 In the centre of the walled enclosure was a great plaza or rectangle of open ground, some two hundred varas square. (2) 1864 *Weekly New Mexican* 27 May 2/1 Each vara is silver mounted, and has the name of the pueblo it is intended for engraved on the head, together with the name of President Lincoln.

∗**Variable,** *a.* In the specific names of plants. — 1803 Lambert *Descr. Genus Pinus* 22 *Pinus variabilis*. Variable-leaved Bastard Pine. . . . The Americans employ it for its tar and pitch. 1817–8 Eaton *Botany* (1822) 465 *Solidago altissima*, variable golden-rod.

∗**Variate,** *v.* {–1770} *intr.* To grant. — 1816 Pickering 191 To *Variate.* A friend has reminded me, that this is a favourite word with a few of our clergymen, in the following expression, which is used in their prayers: '*Variate of* thy mercies according to our circumstances and wants.' 1836 L. Matthews *Lectures* 130 We sometimes . . . hear *missionate, variate, betrustment*, and *bestowment*, in conversation or prayer.

∗**Varied,** *a.* +**1.** *Varied bunting*, a bunting (*Passerina versicolor*) allied to the painted bunting, and found in the S.W. +**2.** *Varied creeping warbler*, the black-and-white warbler. — (1) 1844 *Nat. Hist. N.Y., Zoology* II. 157 The Varied Bunting . . . has been noticed in Georgia, Kentucky, Alabama, Louisiana, Florida and New-Jersey. 1917 *Birds of Amer.* III. 74/2 The Varied Bunting is of accidental occurrence in Michigan. (2) *Ib.* 112 Black and White Warbler. . . . Other Names.— . . . Striped Warbler; Varied Creeping Warbler.

+**Varied thrush.** A conspicuously marked thrush (*Ixoreus naevius*) of the Northwest and Alaska. — 1839 Audubon *Ornith. Biog.* V. 284. 1858 Baird *Birds Pacific R.R.* 219 *Turdus* (*Ixoreus*) *Naevius*, Varied Thrush. . . . This strongly marked species in general appearance bears a close resemblance to the American robin. 1867 Coues in *Essex Inst. Proc.* V. 312 Varied Thrush. This Pacific species has at length been authenticated as a straggler in New England. 1917 *Birds of Amer.* III. 241/1 The Varied Thrush is driven down from the high mountains by the snows of winter.

Variegated, *a.* {a1661–} In the specific names of plants and animals. {1783–} See also VARIEGATED GOBY. — 1778 Carver *Travels* 456 There are five sorts of squirrels in America; the red, the grey, the black, the variegated, and the flying. 1840 Dewey *Mass. Flowering Plants* 214 *Trillium pictum*. Painted or Variegated Wake Robin. 1851 *S. Lit. Messenger* XVII. 568/2 The flower . . . is a species of milkweed, and is called . . . the variegated euphorbia.

+**Variegated goby.** (See quotations.) — 1814 Mitchill *Fishes N.Y.* 379 Variegated Goby. *Gobius viridipallidus*. . . . Is about two inches and a half long. 1842 *Nat. Hist. N.Y., Zoology* IV. 160. 1855 Baird in *Smithsonian Rep. 1854* 339 The variegated Goby. . . . A few specimens only of this rare fish were taken in the grass along the beach of the river.

∗**Variety.**

1. *pl.* Miscellaneous small articles for sale.

1857 *Lawrence* (Kan.) *Republican* 18 June 3 Here you will find the best stock of drugs, medicines, notions and varieties we know of in Kansas.

2. *pl.* The name of a theater.

1849 *Picayune* 7 Dec. 3/2 Placide's Varieties. . . . The new Theatre . . . will be opened . . . December 8th. 1860 E. Cowell *Diary* 76 We went to the Varieties in the evening. A good house. 1867 Meline *Santa Fé & Back* 2 Every little place must have its 'Metropolitan,' its 'Varieties,' and its 'saloons.'

3. *attrib.* **a.** In sense 1 with *basket*. **b.** In sense 2, designating performances of a mixed sort, including singing, dancing, juggling, and brief plays. {1886–}

(a) 1868 A. B. Condict *P. Eckert* 54 As she was quite old enough now to earn her own living, she should start out with a 'variety basket,' as she termed it. (b) 1868 *Ore. State Jrnl.* 17 Oct. 3/1 Variety Troupe.—This troupe gave an entertainment at the Court House on last Thursday. 1872 *Chicago Tribune* 9 Oct. 10/7 There were other but smaller places of amusement devoted to variety-business and vaudeville, the loss of which . . . was a gain to the city. 1882 McCabe *New York* 579 The performances are of the blood-and-thunder order, interspersed with 'variety acts' of a startling description. 1883 *Chicago News* 17 Sept. 3/3 Hyde and Behman's Specialty Consolidation in a strong variety bill. 1884 Matthews & Bunner *In Partnership* 30 Cal. Jardine's Monster Variety and Dramatic Combination on the Road. 1886 James *Bostonians* 190 A little variety-actress . . . lived in the house. 1887 *Courier-Journal* 8 May 17/2 The topical song comes from the variety stage. 1895 *N.Y. Dramatic News* 6 July 3/3 The excise commissioners have refused a renewal of the saloon license formerly held by the variety dives. 1908 Beach *Barrier* 53 Saloon and variety house—seven bartenders, that's all.

+**Variety shop.** =VARIETY STORE. — 1824 'Singleton' *Lett. South & West* 84 One indication of a new country is that the shops are variety-shops; each one keeping piece-goods, groceries, cutlery [etc.]. 1861 Winthrop *Open Air* 220 But there were parting gifts showered on the regiment, enough to establish a variety-shop.

Variety show. A theatrical performance including acts of varied character, as singing, dancing, acrobatic feats, and short plays. {1891–} Also attrib. — 1882 Sweet & Knox *Texas Siftings* 38 Do you think I am the advance agent of a variety show? 1884 *Century Mag.* March 688/2 Both these somewhat famous churches have become theaters of the 'variety show' sort. 1894 Matthews in *Harper's Mag.* Jan. 223/2 There's a comic opera at the Garden Theatre, with a variety show up in the roof garden afterwards. 1901 Flynt *World of Graft* 69, I found him in Scollay Square gazing interestedly at a dwarf dressed up as a policeman in the hallway of a variety show.

1902 CLAPIN 178 *Farce-comedy*, a play in which the characters are taken by variety-show 'artists,' who introduce their specialties, generally in the form of songs, dances, etc.

+Variety store. A store keeping a wide variety of articles for sale; a general store.

1790 *Columbian Centinel* 15 Sept. 4/2 To be sold, at J. Brazer's Variety-store, . . . Holland Gin, of the best kind in cases. **1793** BENTLEY *Diary* II. 46 There are several gentlemen of the Law in the Street & several variety stores. **1822** *Amer. Beacon* (Norfolk, Va.) 19 Jan. 2/5 (Th. S.). **1839** KIRKLAND *New Home* 163 Henry Beckworth . . . was glad to accept a situation as clerk in the comprehensive 'variety-store' of his cousin. **1864** *Harper's Mag.* Oct. 565/1 His favorite advice to all who contemplated visiting the Territory was to take with them plenty of . . . [such] articles as might be purchased in bulk at the selling out of any extensive variety store. **1879** B. F. TAYLOR *Summer-Savory* 138 The variety store of a hundred years ago, where needles and crowbars, goose-yokes and finger-rings, liquorice-stick and leather are to be had for cash or 'dicker'? **1884** *Harper's Mag.* Nov. 888/1 One of them walked gauntly down to the post-office in the corner of the variety store.

Variety theater. A theater which presents variety shows. — **1879** BISHOP *4 Months in Sneak-Box* 172 He became an actor in such plays as 'Black-eyed Susan' in one of the variety theatres in Philadelphia. **1887** *Courier-Journal* 2 Feb. 5/4 [He] has gradually sunk out of sight since shooting the proprietor of a variety theatre in Kansas City a couple of years ago. **1895** *N.Y. Dramatic News* 20 July 5/1 The best people in all the leading communities of the United States have become constant patrons of variety theatres.

Varioloid. A mild form of variola or small pox. {1843-} Also fig. — **1828** WEBSTER, *Varioloid*, the name recently given to a disease resembling the small pox. **1860** EMERSON *Conduct Life* 114 Is egotism a metaphysical varioloid of this malady? **1889** CUSTER *Tenting on Plains* 49, I not being afraid of contagion, having had varioloid.

Various-leaved, *a.* In the specific names of plants and trees. {1822-}

1813 MUHLENBERG *Cat. Plants* 52 *Tilia heterophylla*, Various-leaved Lime Tree. *Ib.* 87 *Quercus heterophylla*, . . . Various-leav'd Oak. *Ib.* 93 *Populus heterophylla*, . . . Various-leaved poplar. **1814** BIGELOW *Florula Bostoniensis* 201 *Aster diversifolius*. Various leaved Aster. . . . This species is remarkable for the gradation of its leaves. **1843** TORREY *Flora N.Y.* I. 160 *Phaseolus diversifolius*. Various-leaved Kidney-bean. . . . Common on sandy shores, particularly in the neighborhood of New-York. *Ib.* 242 *Myriophyllum heterophyllum*. Various-leaved Water Milfoil. . . . Ponds and slowly flowing streams; common in the western part of the State.

Variously, *adv.* {1627-} At various times. — **1892** A. E. LEE *Hist. Columbus, Ohio* I. 756 Samuel Perkins . . . kept a barber shop variously under the National Hotel and the Clinton Bank.

∗Varmint. Also **varmin(g)**, **varmit**, etc. [Var. of VERMIN.]

1. A person viewed unfavorably. *colloq.* {1773-} Freq. used of Indians.

1826 COOPER *Mohicans* xiii, We threw up a work of blocks, to keep the ravenous varments from handling our scalps. **1836** *Crockett's Yaller Flower Almanac* 20 The Colonel is a curis varmunt. **1852** WATSON *Nights in Block-House* 18 The red varmints want his hair bad. **1904** LOVETT *R. Gresham* 15 Just because I told him to get extry wood for the kitchen, the spiteful little varmint sasses me by filling the fireplace so full that you can't stay in the room.

2. Any animal or other living thing. Generally disparaging. *colloq.* {1823-, dial.}

1828 J. HALL *Lett. from West* 297 He gave his foe [a bear cub] a mortal shot, or to use his own language, 'I burst the varment.' **1839** *S. Lit. Messenger* V. 432/1 The rascally old varmin pokes up t'other paw and begins to crawl up. **1856** *Porter's Spirit of Times* 20 Sept. 38/2 Why, massa, dat 'tarnal varmit hab fooled me bad. **1888** WARNER *On Horseback* 96 That he was . . . a monstrous old varmint, Big Tom knew by the size of his tracks. **1904** PRINGLE *Rice Planter* 65 The 'varmint' is a dog, somebody's treasure, so that it cannot be convicted.

3. Used as a collective term in senses 1 and 2.

1835 IRVING *Tour on Prairies* 177 These beavers . . . are the knowingest varment as I know. **1844** FEATHERSTONHAUGH *Slave States* 41, I put myself under his direction, listening to the interesting stories he related about 'varmint,' as he called panthers, wild cats, and bears. **1848** BURTON *Waggeries* 22 There's sea varming enough in all conscience, sitch as oysters, and clams, and quahogs, and muscles, and crabs, and lobsters. **1853** 'P. PAXTON' *Yankee in Texas* 57 There was, to be sure, a kind of path . . . kept open . . . by such of the 'varmint' as could crawl through the cane and under the briers. **1867** *Wkly. New Mexican* 11 May 2/3 A fight lately . . . resulted in the early demise of half a dozen of the red varment.

4. Attrib. in sense 2 with *dog, skin.*

1873 BEADLE *Undevel. West* 352 The old style wooden pins, hung full of gears and 'varmint' skins. **1897** *Outing* XXX. 553/1 A sheepman willingly gives one hundred dollars for a good 'varmint dog' and often numbers six to a dozen in his pack.

+Varmounter. =VERMONTER. *dial.* — **1825** J. NEAL *Bro. Jonathan* II. 280 A downright Varmounter . . . is talking about his knowledge of women. **1834** *Vermont Free Press* 7 June (Th.), A Varmounter never uses

a dog. **1839** in *Corr. R. W. Griswold* (1898) 23 Do the Varmounters patronize, pay up, and let you *live?*

∗Varnish. A liquid, resinous preparation which, spread over a surface and dried, serves to protect it. Also attrib. and transf.

1748-9 FRANKLIN *Exper. on Electricity* 32 The gilding . . . [was] varnish'd over with turpentine varnish. **1787** JEFFERSON *Writings* VI. 302 He has contrived a varnish, also, for lining biscuit barrels, which preserves the biscuit good. **1833** SILLIMAN *Man. Sugar Cane* 25 If the alcoholic solution is evaporated to dryness, the gluten is left as a transparent varnish. **1869** *Boyd's Business Directory* 857 William Tilden & Nephew, Manufacturers of Varnishes. **1884** WELLS *Practical Economics* 161 Varnish-makers, . . . when alcohol could be purchased at from 50 to 60 cents per gallon, used it in large quantities. **1907** *St. Nicholas* July 747/1 Honey-bees fill all the cracks in their home and smear the interior . . . in a manner similar to a painter's use of putty, paint and varnish.

∗Varnisher. One whose business is varnishing. — **1685** *Boston Rec.* X. 78 Thomas Wyborne and Stephen Sergeant became surety to the town for Joseph Hill, varnisher. **1888** *Amer. Almanac* 275/1 Occupations of the People of the United States . . . Painters and varnishers.

Varnish tree. {1843-} +The poison sumac, *Toxicodendron vernix.* — [**1758** *Phil. Trans.* L. 448, I suppose he means by this rue varnish-tree, the Carolina pennated Toxicodendron.] **1785** MARSHALL *Amer. Grove* 130 *Rhus-Toxicodendron Vernix.* Varnish-Tree, or Poison Ash. . . . This is allowed to be the same with the true Varnish-tree of Japan. **1789** *Amer. Philos. Soc.* III. p. xxi.

Varsity. {1846-} *attrib.* Designating athletic teams or activities representing a university or persons or places connected with such teams or activities. {1888} — **1891** *Outing* Dec. 241/1 The 'varsity captain whistled a lively air. **1893** POST *Harvard Stories* 292 The day was beautiful and the water perfect, a most unusual combination for the 'Varsity race day. **1897** *N.Y. Journal* 5 Sept. 41/4 Captain Garrett Cochran will marshal a small army of gridiron warriors on the 'varsity athletic ground. **1898** *Outing* June 305/1 The nine . . . makes various trips to neighboring colleges, but always without the flourish and excitement generally attendant upon similar trips by 'varsity nines. **1902** BELL *Hope Loring* 79 Jermyn and Laflin Van Tassel . . . had won the goal of Hope's ambition, as well as their own, by being on the 'Varsity football team.

Varying hare. {1781-} +The American hare, *Lepus americanus.* — **1856** *Porter's Spirit of Times* 18 Oct. 113/1 The great varying hare, which turns white in winter, is no longer to be found in our state. **1872** *Harper's Mag.* Dec. 30 We find the 'varying hare' assuming at this season his white winter coat. **1917** *Mammals of Amer.* 278/1 The Varying Hare changes his coat twice a year, in spring and autumn.

‖Varysome, *a.* Changeable. — **1836** DUNLAP *Mem. Water Drinker* (1837) I. 80 Why she's more and more varysome:—one day pale, and another day red

‖Vastate, *v. tr.* To make unsusceptible. — **1892** HOWELLS in *Harper's Mag.* March 608/1 That long passion of his early youth, which seemed to have vastated him before he came there. He was rather proud of his vastation.

∗Vastation. +Purification by destruction of evil impulses. Also transf. — **1850** EMERSON *Representative Men* 132 He was let down through a column that seemed of brass, . . . that he might descend safely among the unhappy, and witness the vastation of souls. **1853** *S. Lit. Messenger* XIX. 603/2 That vastation with which Bolus invited you, Ben, was . . . a lesson and a warning to your amiable credulity. **1887** J. ELLIS *New Christianity* 290 Spirits [are] preparing for heaven, or undergoing vastation. **1892** [see VASTATE *v.*].

∗Vat. Also **†fatt.** A vessel designed to hold liquids used in brewing, tanning, and other processes. Also transf.

1647 *Suffolk Deeds* I. 88 Wm. Hudson of Boston Junior granted unto Tho: Dudley . . . his brew house . . . with all the Coppers fatts & brewing vessells. **1656** *Conn. Rec.* I. 286 Nor shall any person . . . set any of their fatts in tann hills or other places wheare the . . . Leather put into tann in the same, shall or may take any vnkinde heates. **1713** HEMPSTEAD *Diary* 23, I work'd at T Truman's & Ebe al day. finished his fatt. **1794** HUMPHREYS *Industry* 10 Press the fair apples till the vats o'erflow. **1806** *Ann. 9th Congress* 2 Sess. 1113 The leaves of those trees . . . are changed in the dyer's vat from the woods. **1846** MELVILLE *Typee* 233 He might be seen with his whole body fairly reeking with the perfumed oil of the nut, looking as if he had just emerged from a soap-boiler's vat. **1878** *Vermont Bd. Agric. Rep.* 78 My first experience in handling a vat of milk was in the month of April. **1885** *Harper's Mag.* Jan. 276/1 To 'drench,' however, the hides are placed for six or eight hours in vats filled with a dissolved excrement. **1902** LORIMER *Lett. Merchant* 93 They've run me through the scalding vats here till they've pretty nearly taken all the hair off my hide.

Vat man. In paper-making, the man who takes the pulp from the vat and molds it into sheets. {1839-} — **1790** *Penna. Packet* 27 March 4/3 Wanted, A Journeyman Paper-Maker, who is a good Vatman, and capable of making best kinds of Writing Paper.

Vaudeville. {1739-}

1. A light play or playlet containing songs and humorous or satirical episodes. *Obs.* {1833-} Also transf.

[**1828** LONGFELLOW in S. Longfellow *H. W. Longfellow* I. 139 The play was what the French call a *vaudeville*, a genteel kind of farce interspersed with songs.] **1842** *Chicago American* 5 Sept., Friday evening Sept. 9, will be enacted the Petit Comedy . . . after which the laughable vaudeville of the Lottery Ticket. **1851** NORTHALL *Curtain* 113 Operas, Vaudevilles, and the everlasting Ravel Family, occupied the theatrical saloon. **1861** LOWELL *Writings* V. 52 The weak policy of the Executive [is] in allowing men to play at Revolution until they learn to think the coarse reality as easy and pretty as the vaudeville they have been acting.

+2. A type of theatrical entertainment consisting of a number of short acts by singers, dancers, actors, etc.

See also CONTINUOUS *a.* and COMBINATION 4.
1872 *Chicago Tribune* 9 Oct. 10/7 There were other but smaller places of amusement devoted to variety-business and vaudeville. **1919** SALTUS *Paliser Case* 28 In vaudeville with acrobats and funny men and little suppers to follow.

+b. A theater presenting vaudeville; a vaudeville show.

1895 *N.Y. Dramatic News* 16 Nov. 13/1 The Election day performances at the vaudevilles were largely patronized. **1909** 'O. HENRY' *Options* 297 The first turn of the vaudeville being not yet over, we left to find a telephone.

3. Attrib. in sense 2 with *artist, bill, business,* etc.

1894 *Chicago Tribune* 22 April 33/3 Sam T. Jack's Creole company . . . will be the week's attraction at the Empire Theater in a burlesque and vaudeville bill. **1896** *N.Y. Dramatic News* 4 July 9/2 Another advantage about the vaudeville business is that those who are in it can control the deadheads. **1903** HAPGOOD *Autobiog. of Thief* 18 How I grew to love the vaudeville artists with their songs and dances, and the wild Bowery melodramas! **1912** NICHOLSON *Hoosier Chron.* 377 When they had a vaudeville show last winter she did the best stunts of any of 'em. **1908** 'O. HENRY' *Strictly Business* 19 'Mice Will Play' had a . . . successful run in New York for ten weeks—rather neat for a vaudeville sketch.

Vaudeville theater. A theater devoted to vaudeville. — [**1864** *Chicago Post* 19 Jan. 4/2 It is just such a place as is wanted in all cities, a neat, cosy vaudeville and variety theatre.] **1868** *Chicago Republican* 10 July, Vaudeville Theatre—Under this name, Arlington Hall will be reopened on Monday evening with a company of musical, gymnastic, and vocal abilities. **1901** *Munsey's Mag.* XXV. 716/1 They all received notes from Lanse asking them to come to a certain up town vaudeville theater. **1911** BURGESS *Find the Woman* 9 Joe and his friend left a vaudeville theater in shocked disgust at the row of vulgar, half-clad females, who were performing a suggestive burlesque.

Vaudou(x). (See quotations and cf. VOODOO *n.*) {1864–, in Hayti} — **1820** *Western Carolinian* 26 Sept., For sometime past, a house in the suburb T—— . . . has been used as a kind of temple for certain occult practices and the idolatrous worship of an African deity, called *Vandoo* [sic]. **1871** DE VERE 108 *Vaudoux,* a French term, designating a certain form of worship and the object of this worship alike, introduced from the Island of Santo Domingo.

*Vault.

*1. A burial chamber, usually partly or wholly underground, and originally vaulted.

1717 *Boston Selectmen* 28 Liberty is granted to Mr. Elias Callender to make a Vault in the Old burying place. **1753** *Md. Hist. Mag.* XVIII. 30 The Body of the Honourable Daniel Dulaney, . . . was honourably interred in a Vault prepared for that purpose. **1835** POE *Works* (1914) I. 180 She turned her glassy eyes from the earth to heaven, and . . . [fell] prostrate on the black slabs of our ancestral vault. **1882** MCCABE *New York* 233 When a body is deposited in a vault, an engraved copper plate is usually procured.

2. A privy. {1617–1700}
1779 *Essex Inst. Coll.* XLVI. 338 They [are to] Provid proper Volts and order the filth Covred. **1805** ORDWAY in *Journals of Lewis & O.* 163 We dug a vault 100 yds abo[ve] the huts in order to make or keep the place healthy.

*3. a. An underground room used as a cellar or storehouse for liquor and other commodities. **+b.** An underground room strongly walled and provided with heavy doors and complicated locks, used for storing money or valuables. Also *fig.* (Cf. BANK VAULT.)

(a) 1830 BRECK *Recoll.* 30 He placed in a vault all his large and valuable stock of old madeira. **1882** MCCABE *New York* 36 The business edifices have generally two cellars below the pavement, with vaults extending out under the street. **(b) 1841** *Diplom. Corr. Texas* III. (1911) 1284 He gave me a package . . . to be placed in the vaults of the Bank. **1853** *Rep. Comm. Patents 1852* I. 306 Improved Burglar-Proof Plates for Doors, Safe-Vaults, Vaults, etc. **1882** MCCABE *New York* 298 Beneath the rotunda is an extensive basement arranged in a series of vaults, in which are kept the coins, notes and bonds belonging to the general government. **1884** BLAINE *20 Years of Congress* I. 429 From customs, an increasing revenue was already enriching the Government vaults. **1893** M. HOWE *Honor* 123 He made over the contents of the great vaults beneath the counting-house to the receiver. **1898** WESTCOTT *D. Harum* 137 Everything had been put away, the safe and vault closed, and Peleg had departed with the mail.

4. Attrib. with *brick, cover, door, floor.*

1848 *Rep. Comm. Patents 1847* 247 Several specimens of vault brick were shown, exceedingly light and porous. **1876** KNIGHT 2694/1 *Vault-cover,* a lid over a hole through a pavement. **1902** 'O. HENRY' *Roads of Destiny* 35 Sometimes there was ten, fifteen, or twenty-thousand dollars

in sacked silver stacked on the vault floor. *Ib.* 38 With one hand he closed and locked the vault door.

+Vaux's swift. (See quot. 1917.) — **1887** RIDGWAY *Manual N.A. Birds* 303 Western United States (chiefly Pacific coast), north to British Columbia. . . . *C[hætura] vauxii.* Vaux's Swift. **1917** *Birds of Amer.* II. 178/2 Vaux's Swift (*Chætura vauxi*) is the western representative of the Chimney Swift.

+V.C. (See quotation.) *Obs.* — **1881** M. HARDY *Through Cities & Prairie Lands* 150 Here and there we decipher an English name, and, beneath, the information: 'Died by the hands of the V.C.' . . . The V.C. means the Vigilance Committee, who, in the early, lawless days, executed justice swift and sure upon proven criminals.

*Veal. A calf, or the flesh of a calf, as an article of food. — **1648** *Md. Archives* IV. 388 ffor a Beefe, A ueale & other necessaries for his Buriall. **1689** SEWALL *Diary* I. 294 Had very good Bacon, Veal, and Parsnips. **1743** MACSPARRAN *Diary* 10 We had for Dinner a Breast of ye best Veal I ever saw in ys Country. **1816** U. BROWN *Journal* II. 220, [I] saw an old Doe . . . full as heavy as a Veal of 4 weeks. **1898** WESTCOTT *D. Harum* 147 Jim brought three or four veals into town one spring to sell.

Vealy, *a.* {1769–} +Youthful, imperfect, immature. Also *vealiness.* — **1890** *Columbus Dispatch* 17 July, A vealy medical-school graduate, whose employment is an insult to intelligent people. **1895** *Stand.* 1995/2 *Vealiness,* . . . want of maturity. **1907** *Outlook* 19 Jan. 80/1 The sylvan thief shared our vealy homage with moonlighters, smugglers [etc.].

+Veery. The tawny thrush, *Hylocichla fuscescens.* — **1845** JUDD *Margaret* II. 187 Deep in the forest [there are] olive-backs, veeries, oven-birds. **1865** BURROUGHS in *Atlantic Mo.* May 522/1 The Hermit-Thrush, the Wood-Thrush, and the Veery (*Turdus Wilsonii*) are our peers of song. **1892** TORREY *Footpath-Way* 5 The vesper sparrow, the veery, and a host of other friends were singing about the hotel. **1917** *Birds of Amer.* III. 228/1 The Veery is essentially a bird of the deep woods and the 'silent places.'

Vega. *S.W.* An extensive plain or valley. {1645, in Spain} — **1850** TAYLOR *Eldorado* vii, The grass on the vega before the house was still thick and green. **1856** WHIPPLE, etc. *Explor. Ry. Route* I. 62 The valley spreads out into a wide vega covered with an abundance of grama. **1887** *Courier-Journal* 6 Feb. 12/3 We descended into wide grassy plains called 'vegas.'

*Vegetable. Illustrated in attrib. and comb. uses only.

1. Designating persons or things having to do with selling or preparing vegetables, or things made from products of the vegetable kingdom.

1876 KNIGHT 2695/1 *Vegetable-flannel,* a fabric made of a fine fiber obtained from the leaves of the *Pinus sylvestris.* *Ib.* 2694/2 *Vegetable-chopper,* one for cutting roots, etc., for stock. **1897** F. C. MOORE *How to Build a Home* 40 Spontaneous ignition . . . is exceedingly liable in the case of linseed-oil or of any of the vegetable-oils. **1904** *N.Y. Tribune* 17 July 8 Now even many rural districts are as dependent on the beef packer, the vegetable canner, . . . as the veriest cockney. **1906** 'O. HENRY' *Four Million* 16 Pennies saved . . . by bulldozing the grocer and the vegetable man. **1924** *Sears, Roebuck & Co. Cat.* No. 148, 840 Fruit and Vegetable Press. Made of steel.

b. Designating persons and things connected with the use of vegetable products in medicine.

1840 DEWEY *Mass. Flowering Plants* 110 Indian Tobacco . . . operates as a violent emetic, and is the dangerous medicine of many who are called vegetable doctors. **1841** *Picayune* 8 Sept. 2/5 This genius has found out that Irish potatoes make the most valuable vegetable pills at present known. **1876** *Billings' Farmer's Allminax* 8 The Vegetabel Bitters Man.

2. In the specific names of plants.

1845 LINCOLN *Botany* 40 Some of them [plants] flourish in the most dry and sandy places, exposed to a burning sun; as the *Stapelia,* sometimes called the *vegetable camel.* **1829** EATON *Botany* (ed. 5) 234 *Habenaria bracteata,* vegetable satyr. **1868** GRAY *Field Botany* 158 *Trichosanthes colubrina,* Snake-Cucumber or Vegetable Serpent, a tall climber.

Vegetable-cutter. (See quot. 1876.) — **1854** *Penna. Agric. Rep.* 392 Best vegetable cutter. **1876** KNIGHT 2694/2 *Vegetable-cutter,* one for slicing or chopping roots or leaves, as potatoes, cabbage, etc. **1877** *Harper's Mag.* Feb. 430/1 French scalloped knives and vegetable cutters of various patterns can be obtained at any house furnishing store.

Vegetable garden. A garden in which vegetables for the table are grown. — **1887** *Outing* X. 12/1 Back of its hacienda is a fine orchard and vegetable garden. **1891** WILKINS *New Eng. Nun* 121 Some were miniature vegetable gardens. **1898** *Century Mag.* Jan. 337/1 May I tell him . . . about your vegetable garden?

Vegetable oyster. {1882–} +An herb (*Tragopogon porrifolius*) the edible roots of which have a fancied resemblance to oysters in taste. — **1817–8** EATON *Botany* (1822) 488 *Tragopogon porrifolium,* vegetable oyster, goat-beard, salsify. **1859** BARTLETT 307 Oyster-plant . . . is also called the Vegetable Oyster. **1868** *Mich. Agric. Rep.* VII. 350 Thos. A. Parker, Detroit, [exhibited] 12 roots vegetable oysters. **1915** ARMSTRONG & THORNBER *Western Wild Flowers* 574 Salsify . . . has many common names, such as Jerusalem Star, Nap-at-noon, and Vegetable Oyster.

Vegetarianism. The doctrine and practice of abstaining from eating meat. {1861–} — **1851** DUNGLISON *Med. Lexicon* 896/2 *Vegetarianism,* . . . a modern term, employed to designate the view that man . . . ought to subsist on the direct productions of the vegetable kingdom and totally abstain from flesh and blood. **1857** GUNN *N.Y. Boarding-Houses* 183 At the time of our sojourn in his Boarding-House he devoted himself, almost exclusively, to Vegetarianism. **1880** *Harper's Mag.* June 28/1 Their vegetarianism does not immediately prepossess one by its apparent effects. **1893** *Missionary Herald* LXXXIX. 480 [He] was greatly offended because he was told that vegetarianism had no saving merit.

*Veil. A thin gauze or netlike covering for the face. — **1840** *Picayune* 2 Sept. 2/4 The creole ladies . . . [walk] the streets with veils instead of bonnets. **1857** *Lawrence Republican* 11 June 3 Curtis . . . says that the wearing of veils permanently weakens many naturally good eyes **1894** 'MARK TWAIN' *P. Wilson* vii, She would raise her veil and betray her face. **1922** TARKINGTON *Gentle Julia* 352 She was veiled in two veils.

*Vein.

*1. A strip or stretch of land, esp. one having a designated character. {−1693}
1624 SMITH *Gen. Hist. Va.* IV. 144 Most plantations were placed stragglingly and scatteringly, as a choice veine of rich ground inuited them. **1817** S. BROWN *Western Gazetteer* 13 Good oak land in small veins.

+2. A stretch, strip, or extent of timber. *Obs.*
1671 *S.C. Hist. Soc. Coll.* V. 333 A mile from the River side you will finde A veine of pines. **1800** HAWKINS *Sk. Creek Country* 20 These fifteen miles [of river bank] is waving, with some good oak in small veins. *a*1862 THOREAU *Maine Woods* 215 White and red pines . . . [grow] in 'veins,' 'clumps,' 'groups,' or 'communities.'

3. A current of wind. {1867−}
1792 BELKNAP *Hist. New-Hampshire* III. 24 The next day a whirlwind . . . directed its course toward the east, in a vein of near half a mile wide. **1842** *Amer. Pioneer* I. 260 An extraordinary vein of wind had crossed the lake a few miles above this place, and marked its way with fearful destruction. **1860** MAURY *Phys. Geog. Sea* xv, A vein of wind . . . forms a current in the air as remarkable as that of the Gulf Stream is in the sea.

Vein matter. The metallic material constituting a vein of ore. — **1871** RAYMOND *3d Rep. Mines* 19 The vein-matter is a crystalline limestone. **1877** W. WRIGHT *Big Bonanza* 466 So long as they . . . have a good width of 'vein-matter' they are not utterly cast down. **1896** SHINN *Story of Mine* 93 The whole body, constituting what miners call a vein, or vein matter, is lodged in a system of fissures.

Velinche. (See VALINCH.)

+Veloce. A velocipede. *Obs.* Also comb. — **1869** *Velocipede* (N.Y.) 31 It was found very difficult to construct a veloce sufficiently steady. **1896** *Godey's Mag.* April 348/1 The winter season is not favorable to veloce-riding.

Velocipede.
1. a. A dandy horse or hobby horse. *Obs.* {1819−1839}
b. An early form of bicycle. {1849−}
1828 *Holyoke Diaries* 179 Joshua came home on the Volocipede. **1868** *Mich. Agric. Rep.* VII. 389 *Resolved*, That the premiums on velocipedes be referred to the business committee. **1896** *Godey's Mag.* April 348/2 Youngsters ride down Fifth Avenue with their school-books strapped in front of their velocipedes.

2. Attrib. and comb. with *principle, riding, wise.*
1834 *Jamestown* (N.Y.) *Jrnl.* 26 Feb. 2/6 It is on the velocipede principle, but an improvement on those hitherto seen. **1869** BUSHNELL *Women's Suffrage* 178 He sings velocipede-wise, turning the crank himself. **1896** *Godey's Mag.* April 348/1 Schools for the instruction of velocipede-riding are being opened.

Velocipeding. The riding of a velocipede. {1886} — **1869** *Velocipede* (N.Y.) 21 April, Velocipeding is a hopeful sign of progress. **1883** *Wheelman* I. 401 The revival of velociping, the advent of the modern bicycle, in this country was in the latter half of 1877.

Velveret. An inferior kind of velvet, having a cotton back. {1769−} — **1776** *Penna. Ev. Post* 18 Jan. 3/1 Spotted and plain velverets, womens black velvet, Leghorn hats [etc.]. **1784** *Mass. Centinel* 19 May 3/3 Will be sold, by publick Vendue, . . . Figured Velverets, . . . Manchester Checks, Russia Sheetings. **1797** *Ann. 4th Congress* 2 Sess. 1870 [The lot] is composed of . . . silks, corduroys, velveretts, &c.

*Velvet.
*1. A closely woven fabric, usually of silk but sometimes of cotton, having a thick short pile on one side.
1758 *Newport Mercury* 19 Dec. 4/2 George Hazard . . . has to sell . . . cotton velvet, Cotton Velvet Shape [etc.]. **1793** *Mass. Spy* 16 May 3/3 New goods imported this Spring include: . . . Cassimere, Velvet, corduroy, [etc.]. **1822** *Ann. 17th Congress* 1 Sess. I. 319, 316 yards cords and velvets $210.14. **1887** WILKINS *Humble Romance* 387 'Now I've cut this velvet bias.' 'For the land's sake, don't mind anything about the velvet.'

2. *attrib.* and *comb.* a. With adjectives in *-ed.* {1611−}
1843 TORREY *Flora N.Y.* I. 179 *Desmodium viridiflorum.* Velvet-leaved Desmodium. . . . Sandy copse on . . . Long Island. **1850** *Rep. Comm. Patents 1849: Agric.* 181 There is but little difference in the time of ripening of the following varieties [of wheat], . . . the velvet-bearded, the red-chaff bald, the crate.

*b. In the specific names of plants.
1898 *Dept. Agric. Yrbk. 1897* 504 The velvet bean [is a widely grown forage crop] for Florida orange groves. **1849** EMMONS *Agric. N.Y.* II. 142 Velvet-chaff Bald. . . . Chaff greenish brown and dotted without beard or awns. **1892** *Amer. Folk-Lore* V. 93 *Abutilon Avicennæ,* . . . velvet-weed. Quincy, Ill.

c. In special combinations.
Velvet cream, a cream puff; *v. ore,* (see quotation).
1814 *Amer. Mineral. Jrnl.* I. 261 Argillaceous Iron stone . . . is generally nodular, in concentric layers, between two of which it occurs crystallized in minute crystals of a blackish brown, known by the name of velvet ore. **1863** A. D. WHITNEY *F. Gartney* xiv, Aunt Faith's . . . 'vanity cakes,' or 'velvet creams,' were no sooner disposed of than there surely came a starvation interval of sour biscuits [etc.].

+Velvet ant. (See quot. 1891.) — **1748** CATESBY *Carolina* App. 13 *Formica villosa coccinea.* The Velvet Ant. . . . [Except] the thorax, . . . the whole body and head resembled crimson velvet. **1891** *Cent.* 6715/1 *Velvet ant,* a solitary ant, of the family *Mutilidae;* a spider-ant; so called from the soft hairy covering.

Velvet cork. Cork bark of the best quality; a cork made from this. {velvets, 1830} — **1727** *Boston News-Letter* 2 March 2/2 Choice good Velvet, and other good Corks, to be Sold. **1776** *Essex Inst. Coll.* XLIX. 100 Sold by order . . . 12 bbls. best velvet corks, at 4 s. per gro[ss]. **1889** *Cent.* 1267/2 Velvet cork . . . is of a pale-reddish color and not less than an inch and a half thick.

Velvet duck. {1678−} +The white-winged scoter, *Melanitta deglandi.* — **1844** *Nat. Hist. N.Y., Zoology* II. 337 The White-winged Coot . . . is described in the books under the name of Velvet Duck. **1858** BAIRD *Birds Pacific R.R.* 805 The difference of the American Velvet Duck from the European . . . consists in the greater extension of the feathers of the forehead over the bill. **1917** *Birds of Amer.* I. 150 White-winged Scoter. . . . Other Names.—Velvet Scoter; Velvet Duck.

+Velvet grass. A coarse European grass (*Holcus lanatus*) naturalized in the United States. — **1840** DEWEY *Mass. Flowering Plants* 242 Velvet Grass . . . [is] a grass little desired by animals. **1889** VASEY *Agric. Grasses* 50 Velvet grass; Velvet Mesquite. . . . The seed has been in market many years. **1894** *Amer. Folk-Lore* VII. 104 *Holcus lanatus,* . . . old white top, feather-grass, velvet-grass, West Va.

Velvet leaf. {1707−} + = MORMON-WEED. — **1843** TORREY *Flora N.Y.* I. 113 Velvet leaf. . . . Introduced from India, and now abundantly naturalized in the middle and southern States. **1872** *Ill. Dept. Agric. Trans. 1871* p. ix. **1880** *Scribner's Mo.* May 101/2 In my section an annoying weed is *Abutilon,* or velvet-leaf.

+Vendue, *n.* [Du. *vendu.*]
1. A public sale or auction. {1748, 1806, in W. Indies} Often *at* (or *by*) *vendue.*
See also PUBLIC VENDUE, VANDUE.
1704 S. KNIGHT *Journal* 52 Mr. Burroughs went with me to Vendue where I bought about 100 Rheem of paper. **1757** FRANKLIN *Writings* III. 408, I stopt my horse lately where a great Number of People were collected at a Vendue of Merchant goods. **1775** HUTCHINSON *Diary & Lett.* I. 557 My property which was at Milton, sold at *vendue.* **1784** *Belknap P.* II. 169 Gov. Belcher's Letter-Books . . . were sold at Russell's vendue for waste paper. **1817** PAULDING *Lett. from South* II. 165 His farm is soon to be sold at vendue. **1897** HOWELLS *Landlord at Lion's Head* ii, [We must] have a vendue, and sell out everything . . . , and let the State take the farm. **1908** *Atlantic Mo.* Feb. 175 One of the treasured resources of the country banker has been the public auction—or 'vendue,' the Easterner might call it.

b. (See quotation.) *Polit. slang.*
1885 *Mag. Amer. Hist.* May 495/1 *Vendue,* . . . a shameless assignment of offices to the highest bidders.

2. Attrib. and comb. with *bill, charge, crier,* etc.
1678 *New Castle Court Rec.* 314 The Purchazers were obliged to pay all the vendu Charges etc. **1774** HUTCHINSON *Diary & Lett.* I. 222 The Vendue Bill, he said, was long before. **1790** *Penna. Packet* 1 Jan. 1/1 Vendue Sales. At Elijah Weed's Ferry. **1799** *Aurora* (Phila.) 10 April (Th.), By profession he is a vendue crier. He said he would cry the vendue in spite of the Standing Army. **1809** *Steele P.* II. 610 The Board of Directors would have approved of your taking the Vendue Notes. **1855** *Harper's Mag.* X. 853/1 The bow was bid off by a by-stander, who sold it to him at 'a quarter's' advance over the vendue-price!

+Vendue, *v. tr.* To sell by vendue. *Obs.* — **1764** OTIS in Tudor *Life J. Otis* 32, I was only to act in my profession as a lawyer, and not as a merchant or factor, to settle accounts and vendue goods. **1804** FESSENDEN *Orig. Poems* (1806) 164 Have pretty nymphs expos'd to sale, And ladies vendued off by tale.

+Vendue master. An auctioneer; one in charge of a vendue. *Obs.* — **1677** *New Castle Court Rec.* 53 The Pl[ain]t[iff] demands of the def[endan]t as Vendu Master of the Land & houses of Capt John Carr the sume of 1962 gilder ten stivers. **1708** *R.I. Col. Rec.* IV. 49 There shall be a vendue allowed in the town of Newport, and a vendue master chosen and engaged by the townsmen. **1761** GLEN *Descr. S. Carolina* 33 There is . . . a Receiver-general of the Quit-rents, a Vendue Master, and Naval Officer. **1787** *Ga. State Gazette* 10 Feb. 3/2 (Th. S.), Robert Montfort announces that he has been appointed a Vendue-Master for the town of Savannah. **1832** DUNLAP *Hist. Amer. Theatre* 49 This was the place for auctioneers, then called vendue-masters, to cry and sell their wares.

+Vendue store. A store or market in which goods are sold at or by vendue. *Obs.* — **1774** *Penna. Packet* 19 Sept. 1/3 He is removed to his new vendue-store. **1790** *Ib.* 1 Jan. 1/1 The subscriber having met with success in establishing his Vendue Store in New-Jersey, returns his most grateful thanks. **1798** *S.C. Superior Ct. Rep.* (Bay) I. 103 The goods were in a vendue store, a common market, a public place known and established in law.

Veneer. A thin layer of fine wood used to cover inferior wood. {1702-} Also attrib. and comb. — **1851** Cist *Cincinnati* 250 Henry Albro . . . has recently put up new veneer and saw mills. **1876** Knight 2701/1 *Veneer-planing Machine*, an implement for smoothing veneered and other surfaces. **1883** *Harper's Mag.* Sept. 565/1 Mr. Cady's veneer work is shown in a house of red brick and brown sandstone. **1904** Stratton-Porter *Freckles* 331 They would instruct the company to reserve enough of the veneer from that very tree to make the most beautiful dressing-table they could design.

+**Veneerer.** A workman who applies or fits veneer. — **1863** Hale *If, Yes, & Perhaps* 14, I was at work as a veneerer in a piano-forte factory at Attica.

Venetian blind. A window shade made of wooden slats arranged in such a manner that they may be turned to admit or exclude air and light. {1794-} — **1770** *Jrnls. Cont. Congress* VIII. 430 There is due to the commissioners of claims, for a pair of Venetian blinds, . . . the sum of 32 dollars. **1815** Drake *Cincinnati* 134 Painting, papering, and Venetian blinds, are executed in a firm and handsome style. **1899** Chesnutt *Conjure Woman* 196 The Venetian blinds . . . were partly closed on account of the heat. **1907** *St. Nicholas* Oct. 1045/2 It could be folded up like a Venetian blind and carried under the arm of a man.

Venetian window blind. =prec. {1769-} — **1828** Webster s.v. *Window-blind*, Venetian window-blinds are now much used in the United States. *a*1846 *Quarter Race Ky.* 110 Take a large stick . . . and rake it violently down a Venetian window-blind. **1907** *St. Nicholas* Sept. 1045/2 It was made of many parallel sticks, something on the principle of a Venetian window-blind.

Venire. {1665-} +A group of persons legally summoned to serve as a jury; a group from which a jury is selected. — **1807** *Ann. 10th Congress* 1 Sess. 391 The names of the *venire*, summoned in pursuance of the *venire facias*, . . . were accepted by the prisoner, and sworn. **1905** N. Davis *Northerner* 217 We had a special venire of sixty, county men most of them.

+**Venire man.** One summoned in making up a venire; a juryman or prospective juryman. — **1776** *Va. House of Delegates Jrnl.* 17 Oct., The several venire-men and witnesses attending for the trial of criminals [shall] be discharged. **1808** *Ann. 10th Congress* 2 Sess. 914 They therefore recommend that a further compensation be allowed to the witnesses and *venire men*. **1895** *Wkly. Examiner* (San Francisco) 5 Sept. 2/1 Sheriff Whelan's deputies had apparently summoned most all of the veniremen from the foreign sections of the city. **1907** *Springfield W. Repub.* 13 May 6 The summoning of the special veniremen in the case of William D. Haywood.

* **Venison.**

* **1.** The flesh of a deer, or of some other animals, hunted and killed for food.

1622 'Mourt' *Relation* 37 There was thrust into an hollow tree, two or three peeces of Venison. **1701** Sewall *Diary* 11. 44, I sent Mr. Increase Mather a Hanch of very good Venison. **1788** May *Jrnl. & Lett.* 104 Breakfasted at Fort Littleton, . . . on fine coffee, loaf-sugar, venison, shad, and smoked shad. **1805** Lewis in *L. & Clark Exped.* II. (1904) 284, I prevailed on him to . . . eat tolerably freely of our good venison. **1887** 'Craddock' *Keedon Bluffs* 47 It was at last done, and placed on the table with the platter of venison and corn dodgers. **1925** Tilghman *Dugout* 21 Then he began to fry bacon and fresh venison.

2. Attrib. and comb. with *bag, broth, cutlet*, etc.

1643 *New Haven Rec.* 84 Martha Malbon . . . [consented] to goe in the night to the farmes with William Harding to a venison feast. **1709** Lawson *Carolina* 28 We found here good Store of . . . Hickerie-Nuts, which they beat betwixt two great Stones, then sift them, so thicken their Venison-Broath therewith. **1835** Hoffman *Winter in West* I. 247, I left my landlady turning some venison cutlets and grilled grouse. **1836** Gilman *Recoll.* (1838) 212 One had dropped his red cap, another his venison-bag. **1894** Robley *Bourbon Co., Kansas* 26 Dodger and hoecake generally were mixed with eggs, venison gravy and milk.

+**Venison bird.** =Canada jay. — **1885** *Outing* VII. 75/1 The venison birds fill the woods with their peculiar cry.

Venison ham. The thigh of a deer, used as food. — **1775** Romans *Nat. Hist. Florida* 331, I purchased some bear, bacon and venison hams of them. **1824** Blane *Excursion U.S.* 145 Dried venison hams . . . are very good eating. **1831** Peck *Guide* 162 Fresh venison-hams . . . are a delicious article. **1899** Cushman *Hist. Indians* 528 He stood on the toes of his shoes to reach the venison ham.

+**Venison hawk.** =Venison bird. — **1889** *Internat. Ann., Anthony's Photogr. Bul.* II. 223 About our door the venison hawks came flitting.

Venison steak. A slice of venison cut for frying or broiling. — **1788** Cutler in *Life & Corr.* I. 419, [I] dined . . . on venison steak and squirrel pie; very good dinner. **1833** J. Hall *Harpe's Head* 214 Before the master of the house . . . were venison steaks, then fried ham. **1886** Roosevelt in *Outing* April 9 Before long the venison steaks were frying or broiling over the mass of glowing coals. *a*1918 G. Stuart *On Frontier* II. 138 Good hot coffee and venison steak and flapjacks.

* **Vent,** *n. S.W.* +(See quotation.) Also attrib. — **1887** *Scribner's Mag.* II. 508/2 Words used in connection with . . . life on the plains: . . . *dewlap*, a cut in the lower part of the neck; *vent*, a brand announcing sale. **1922** P. A. Rollins *Cowboy* 236 The vent brand ordinarily was a facsimile of the seller's ownership brand, though it might be reduced in size.

* **Vent,** *v.* +*tr.* To nullify an ownership brand on (an animal) by adding a sale brand. — **1844** Gregg *Commerce of Prairies* I. 186 It [is] impossible for persons not versed in this species of 'heraldry,' to determine whether the animal has been properly *vented* or not.

Venta. {1610-} *S.W.* =Vent *n.* — **1844** Gregg *Commerce of Prairies* I. 186 Every one marks him [a horse] with a huge hieroglyphic brand, which is called the *fierro*, and again, upon selling him, with his *venta*, or sale-brand. **1857** Davis *El Gringo* 206 When an animal is sold the old marks are obliterated with another brand called the *venta*, and in the absence of this the sale is not a valid one. **1888** H. H. Bancroft *Works* XXXIV. 572 All horses found in the possession of any one without the *venta*, that is to say, sale mark, . . . should be restored to the owners.

+**Venus('s) flytrap.** An insectivorous plant (*Dionaea muscipula*) that grows wild on the coast of the Carolinas. — [**1777** *Ann. Register* 1775 II. 93/1 A description of a newly discovered Sensitive Plant, called *Dionæa Muscipula*, or Venus's Fly-trap.] **1802** Drayton *S. Carolina* 70 Venus's fly trap . . . grows near the sea shore road on the borders of North Carolina. **1838** *S. Lit. Messenger* IV. 577/1 A good instance of the possession of this power, by a plant, is afforded in the Venus flytrap. **1884** *Harper's Mag.* Nov. 841/1 The Venus fly-trap . . . is a popular attraction. **1899** *Going Flowers* 300 The Venus's fly-trap . . . shuts up on him [the fly] and crushes him.

+**Venus('s) pride.** =Bluet 1. — **1784** *Amer. Acad. Mem.* I. 409 Venus Pride . . . spreads over pastures and fields, in large beds, and gives them a white appearance. **1829** Eaton *Botany* (ed. 5) 246 *Houstonia cærulea*, venus' pride, forget-me-not. **1894** *Amer. Folk-Lore* VII. 90 *Houstonia cærulea*, . . . Venus's pride, Stonington, Conn.

Veranda, Verandah.

1. A roofed gallery or piazza extending along the front or one of the sides of a building, esp. a private residence or hotel. {1711-}

1829 B. Hall *Travels in N.A.* III. 140 What gives Charleston its peculiar character, however, is the verandah, or piazza, which embraces most of the houses on their southern side. **1839** *S. Lit. Messenger* V. 751/1 It was a snug commodious building . . . with a pretty varandah. **1857** Vaux *Villas* 99 The *veranda* is perhaps the most specially American feature in a country house. **1873** Beadle *Undevel. West* 403 We find quarters at the inevitable 'double log-house' hotel with open porch, veranda and multitudinous additions. **1884** *Century Mag.* Sept. 796 At a shady end of the veranda, are seen the railroad king, . . . the Texas rancher, and the Pennsylvania iron prince. **1902** White *Conjuror's House* 7 The head Factor of all this region paced back and forth across the veranda of the factory.

2. Attrib. with *floor, pillar, porch, step.*

1852 Stowe *Uncle Tom* xxiii, The two brothers ran up the veranda steps. **1857** Vaux *Villas* 72 It will not probably be convenient to inclose entirely a veranda-porch at any season of the year. **1869** *Rep. Comm. Agric. 1868* 204 There is no . . . climbing plant that can excel [honeysuckle] . . . as a covering for veranda pillars. **1898** Westcott *D. Harum* xxxv, David . . . [leaned] forward to drop his cigar ash clear of the veranda floor.

Verandahed, *a.* {1823-} Abounding in verandas. — **1893** *Critic* 16 Nov. 316/2 The verandahed South is the home of the open-air *trouvère*.

* **Verbena.** Any one of various plants belonging to the genus *Verbena*, largely native to the United States. Also attrib.

1833 S. J. Hale *Flora* 257. **1848** Bryant *California* ii. 28 Among the flowers and plants which I have noticed to-day, are the verbena and the indigo-plant. **1868** Beecher *Norwood* 81 He went out by the window, where he could see the verbenas and . . . the rows of gladiolus. **1889** Deland *Florida Days* 35 The white galleries with scarlet geraniums and verbenas . . . have a look of absolute cleanliness. **1895** McClelland *St. John's Wooing* 141 The westering sun, slanted across the plain . . . , showing the brightness of cactus and verbena blossoms. **1907** *St. Nicholas* May 626/1 It had . . . bright verbenas with borders of sweet-smelling pinks.

+**Verdant zone.** =Thermal belt. — **1862** *Rep. Comm. Patents 1861: Agric.* 146 The beautiful phenomenon of the 'Verdant Zone' or 'Thermal Belt' exhibits itself upon our mountain sides, commencing about three hundred feet vertical height above the valleys, and traversing them in a perfectly horizontal line . . . like a vast green ribbon upon a black ground.

* **Verderer,** *a.* ‖A ranger. — **1893** *Columbus Dispatch* 24 Aug., Mounted police and Forest verderers look on with benign smiles.

* **Verdigris.** Also **verdigrease.** A green or greenish-blue substance obtained by the action of acetic acid on copper; basic acetate of copper. — **1752** *Va. Gazette* 22 May (*advt.*), Just imported . . . by the subscriber in Williamsburg, . . . Verdigrease, Yellow oaker [etc.]. **1800** *Columbian Centinel* 12 Feb. 3/1 Verdigreace prepared for Vessel's Bottoms an excellent substitute for copper. **1836** *Public Ledger* (Phila.) 25 March 1/2, 300 lbs Verdigris. **1876** 'Mark Twain' *Tom Sawyer* x. 96 A pin's brass. It might have verdigrease on it.

+**Verdin.** [Fr., 'yellowhammer.'] A small, yellow-headed titmouse (*Auriparus flaviceps*) of the Southwest. — **1881** *Amer. Naturalist* XV. 217, I will now describe the nest and eggs of another minute species of the titmouse family, the verdin or yellow-headed titmouse. **1903** *Atlantic Mo.* July 103 The same fretful verdin was talking about something with the old emphatic monotony. **1917** *Birds of Amer.* III. 218 The Verdin makes use of his home not only during the summer to raise a family, but he often uses it in winter as a sleeping place.

+**Vergaloo.** Also **virgalieu, bergaloo,** etc. [Fr. *virgou-leuse.*] A variety of pear; the White Doyenné, of French origin. Also attrib.
1806 WEBSTER 341/2 *Vergaloo.* a very rich pear. **1839** BUEL *Farmer's Companion* 269 It is as easy to cultivate the vergaleu as it is the choke pear. **1845** DOWNING *Fruits Amer.* 378 Virgalieu, of New York. . . . Virgaloo, Bergaloo, of some American gardens. **1877** BARTLETT 734 *Virgalieu Pear.* So called in New York. . . . It is the *Doyenné Blanc* of French authors, the *Butter Pear* of Philadelphia, and the St. Michael of Boston.
   b. *Black Virgalieu,* an American variety of pear; the Sheldon (*Stand.* 1913).
   Verge staff. ? On a river steamer, the forward jack staff, carrying the insignia of the line. *Obs.* — **1873** 'MARK TWAIN' & WARNER *Gilded Age* 43 [They] tried to make friends with a passenger-bear fastened to the verge staff. **1875** 'MARK TWAIN' *Life on Miss.* vii. 127 Every outward-bound boat had its flag flying at the jack-staff, and sometimes a duplicate on the verge-staff.
   +**Veriscope.** [L. *verus* 'true' and *scope.*] A trade name of an early form of moving picture. Also attrib. — **1897** *Columbus Dispatch* 2 July, There remain but three more exhibitions of the veriscope. **1898** *Boston Transcript* 25 April 5/7 Veriscope Pictures of Corbett-Fitzsimmons Contest.
   +**Veritism.** [Coined by Hamlin Garland, Amer. author (1860–1940).] Realism. Also *veritist, veritistic,* a. — **1894** *Nation* LIX. 53/2 Veritism is the name by which devils are to be cast out, and the artist himself is to be a veritist. **1894** GARLAND in *Forum* Aug. 690 My own conception is that realism (or veritism) is the truthful statement of an individual impression corrected by reference to the fact. *Ib.,* The veritist chooses for his subject not the impossible, not even the possible, but always the probable. *Ib.* 693 The critic cannot distinguish between the entirely fictitious characters of the veritistic novel and characters drawn from life.
   Vermicelli soup. Soup containing vermicelli. {1769–} — **1840** *N.Y. Daily Express* 15 Jan. 2/2, I took everything that come, even the soup full of worms—and they called it wormy-shilly soup too. **1850** TYSON *Dairy in Calif.* 85 Our first course consisted of vermicelli soup. **1876** M. F. HENDERSON *Cooking* 84 Vermicelli Soup is made exactly as macaroni soup, only the vermicelli is not cut.

* **Vermilion.**
   1. A red pigment used as a cosmetic {1600–}, +esp. by Indians.
   *c***1622** J. PORY *Descr. Plymouth Col.* 51 Their head they annoynt with oil mixed with vermillion. **1642** LECHFORD *Plain Dealing* 50 In time of rejoycing, they paint red, with a kind of vermilion. **1740** W. STEPHENS *Proc. Georgia* I. 556 They were a Body of lusty, lively Fellows, with all their Faces most dismally painted with Vermillion and Blue. **1809** HENRY *Travels* 247 The men were almost entirely naked, and their bodies painted with a red ochre, procured in the mountains, and often called *vermilion.* **1825** NEAL *Bro. Jonathan* II. 123 There was a savage lustre in his little snaky eyes; a treble portion of the portentous colour—vermillion—over his face. **1870** KEIM *Sheridan's Troopers* 168 [The war chief] was specially illuminated with a coating of vermilion.
   +**b.** Used in trade with Indians or as presents to them.
   1756 *Lett. to Washington* I. 363 Vermillion—at 7/ [per ounce]. **1797** HAWKINS *Letters* 78, [I] sent to each of them a package of vermilion. **1806** LEWIS in L. & *Clark Exped.* V. (1905) 25 We gave the young men who had delivered us the two horses this morning some ribbon, blue wampum and vermillion. **1848** BRYANT *California* iv. 47 We carried some vermilion and beads along with us for presents.
   c. (See quotation.)
   1843 MARRYAT *M. Violet* ii, I will send the vermillion to my young warriors, they will paint their faces and follow me on the war-path. . . . When a chief wishes to go to war, he sends to his warriors some leaves of tobacco covered with vermilion. It is a sign that they must soon be prepared.
   2. Attrib. and comb. with *paint, -tinted.*
   1848 BRYANT *California* iii. 39 He was rouged with vermilion paint. **1916** EASTMAN *From Deep Woods* 79 The Sioux belle was . . . holding over her glossy uncovered braids and vermilion-tinted cheeks a gaily colored silk parasol.

* **Vermin.** *collect.* (See also VARMINT.)
   * **1.** Destructive animals.
   'Now, except in *U.S.* and *Austr.* . . . , almost entirely restricted to those animals or birds which prey upon preserved game' (*O.E.D.*).
   1616 SMITH *New England* 30 Fitches, Musquassus, and diuerse sorts of vermine, whose names I know not. **1674** In Alvord & Bidgood *Trans-Allegheny Region* 212 They travell still towards the sun setting great store of game, all along as turkes deere, ellkes, beare, woolfe and other vermin very tame. **1705** BEVERLEY *Virginia* IV. 63 All the troublesome Vermine, that ever I heard any Body complain of, are either Frogs, Snakes, Musketa's, Chinches, Seedticks, or Red-worms, by some call'd Potato-lice. **1832** KENNEDY *Swallow Barn* I. 163 The negroes still consider it the finest place in the whole country to catch vermin, as they call [raccoons, opossums, and rabbits].
   attrib. **1705** BEVERLEY *Virginia* IV. 72 They have another sort of Hunting, which is very diverting, and that they call Vermine Hunting. . . . They find Abundance of Raccoons, Opossums, and Foxes.
   * **2.** Offensive insects, esp. those parasitic upon man.

1819 *Amer. Farmer* I. 46 Respecting the cleansing of poultry-houses from vermin, or chicken-lice. **1882** MCCABE *New York* 241 The majority of these vehicles are dirty, badly ventilated, and full of vermin. **1885** *Rep. Indian Affairs* 155 All of the buildings here save two are very old adobe, inhabited by snakes and vermin.
   +**Vermont.** [Fr. 'green mountain.'] The name of a New England state. Used attributively and absolutely. **1.** *attrib.* Designating horses raised in Vermont. **2.** Vermont gray, (see quotation). **3.** *absol.* Vermont horses. — **(1) 1858** VIELÉ *Following Drum* 35 The term 'Vermont horses' was . . . most potently realized in the possession of a pair of dapple greys worthy of the horse-flesh reputation of their . . . State. **1892** *Vt. Agric. Rep.* XII. 115 The farmers of this County . . . are giving more attention to raising . . . Vermont Morgans, so noted for their powers of endurance and staying qualities. **1894** *Ib.* XIV. 93 Vermont horses have always been in good demand for road purposes. **(2) 1884** *Century Mag.* Feb. 519/2 The 'tag-locks' and pulled wool were mostly worked up in the neighboring small factories into . . . the then somewhat famous 'Vermont gray,' which was the common cold-weather outer clothing of New England male farm folk. **(3) 1885** HOWELLS *Silas Lapham* i, I don't ride behind anything but Vermont; never did.
   +**Vermonteer.** =next. *Obs.* — **1782** FRENEAU *Poems* (1903) II. 181 The Sage who took the wrong sow by the ears, And more than kingdoms claimed for Vermonteers. **1798** I. ALLEN *Hist. Vermont* 57 So consequential were the Vermonteers, that an application for offensive operations came at the same time from different colonies. **1801** *Hist. Review & Directory* II. 346 Great numbers of the *Vermonteers* bring their produce here.
   +**Vermonter.** A native or resident of Vermont.
   See also VARMOUNTER and prec.
   1787 HAMILTON *Works* VII. 6 The peace found the Vermonters in a state of actual independence. **1833** *Niles' Reg.* XLIV. 345/2 A six foot Vermonter lately entered a store . . . in search of employment. **1849** KINGSLEY *Diary* 35 The senate passed a verry pleasant evening to night by listening to a yarn from Mr Stuart about a Vermonter going to Philadelphia. **1868** *N.Y. Herald* 4 July 4/4 Whatever course may be adopted by the delegates from New Hampshire in the Convention to-day will probably be followed by the Vermonters. **1898** *Mo. So. Dakotan* I. 3 It has been said that we do not hear much of Vermonters at home.
   +**Vermontese,** *n.* A Vermonter; Vermonters collectively. — **1798** I. ALLEN *Hist. Vermont* 262 You ask me if the Vermontese are good agriculturists? **1806** FESSENDEN *Orig. Poems* 97n., Hamilton was a Vermontese. **1823** COOPER *Pilot* I. ix. 115 Those loose-flapped gentlemen [whom] they call Vermontese and Hampshire-granters . . . finished two thirds of my company. **1845** *Knickerb.* XXVI. 583 We should be pleased to hear these lines applauded by the Vermontese.
   +**Vermontese,** *a.* Resident in Vermont; characteristic of Vermont. — **1798** I. ALLEN *Hist. Vermont* 280 Our Vermontese house-wives are not a little vain of their knowledge in making home-made wines. *a***1811** HENRY *Camp. Quebec* 209 In a conversation with the Vermontese gentleman. **1833** *Knickerb.* II. 247, I was apprehensive, that I had offended him by recurring . . . to the Vermontese pronunciation of such words as *home* and *stone.*
   +**Vernaculate,** *v.* **1.** *tr.* To name in the vernacular. **2.** *intr.* (See quotation.) — **(1) 1887** *N.Y. Semi-Weekly Tribune* 15 July (*Cent.*), Very large Antwerp 'patches,' as they are vernaculated by the average fruit-grower. **(2) 1895** *Stand.* 2003/2 *Vernaculate,* . . . to use vernacular language.
   Vernal grass. =SWEET-SCENTED VERNAL GRASS. {1762–} Also *sweet vernal grass.* — **1821** *Mass. H. S. Coll.* 2 Ser. IX. 146 Plants, which are indigenous in the township of Middlebury, [Vermont, include] . . . Sweet vernal grass. **1850** S. F. COOPER *Rural Hours* 125 Among the native plants of this kind are . . . several useful kinds of fescue-grass, and poa, one of which has something of the fragrance of the vernal-grass.
   * **Veronica.** =SPEEDWELL. — **1784** *Amer. Acad. Mem.* I. 465 Foxglove . . . has been mistaken for Paul's Betony, a speci s of the *Veronica.* **1818** *Mass. H. S. Coll.* 2 Ser. VIII. 169 Among those, that flower in June, the most interesting are . . . two species of veronica or speedwell. **1875** *Amer. Naturalist* IX. 388 With these charming plants are found blue lobelias, purplish or blue veronicas [etc.]. **1910** *Nation* 2 July 485/2 The tall spikes of erect veronica.

* **Vervain.**
   See also BLUE VERVAIN.
   * **1.** Any plant of the genus *Verbena,* growing wild or in gardens. Also with specifying adjectives.
   1737 BRICKELL *N. Carolina* 22 Vervine is very common here, being Spontaneous. **1814** BIGELOW *Florula Bostoniensis* 148 *Verbena urticifolia.* Nettle leaved Vervain. . . . A weed of no beauty. **1839** in *Mich. Agric. Soc. Trans.* VII. 422 Nettle-leaf vervain. **1840** DEWEY *Mass. Flowering Plants* 173 *Verbena angustifolia.* . . . Narrow-leafed Vervain. . . . Rocky grounds; June. **1843** TORREY *Flora N.Y.* II. 52 *Verbena spuria.* Procumbent Vervain. . . . Sandy fields in the suburbs of New-York and near Albany. **1865** *Atlantic Mo.* Jan. 5 The Doctor . . . [toiled] pretty vigorously at his medicinal herbs, his catnip, his vervain, and the like. **1875** BURROUGHS *Winter Sunshine* 138 Rag-weed, vervain, golden-rod, burdock . . . —how they lift themselves up as if not afraid to be seen now!
   2. In the specific names of other plants.
   1814 BIGELOW *Florula Bostoniensis* 189 *Eupatorium Verbenæfolium.* Vervain leaved Eupatorium. . . . The name is taken from the resemblance of the leaves to the upper ones of the officinal Vervain. **1817–8** EATON

Botany (1822) 446 *Salvia verbenac[e]a*, vervain sage. **1901** MOHR *Plant Life Ala.* 702 *Salvia verbenacea.* . . . Vervain-leaf Sage. . . . Sparingly naturalized on the coast of South Carolina.

+**Vesper bird.** =VESPER (SPARROW). — **1858** *Atlantic Mo.* Oct. 595/1 The usual resorts of the Vesper-bird are the pastures and the hayfields. **1871** BURROUGHS *Wake-Robin* (1886) 27 Like the vesper-bird, she, too, nests in the open, unprotected places, avoiding all show of concealment. **1884** COUES *Key to Birds* 364 *Passerculus gramineus.* . . . Grass Finch. Bay-winged Bunting. Vesper-Bird.

+**Vesper mouse.** =WHITE-FOOTED (PRAIRIE) MOUSE. — **1857** S. F. BAIRD *Mammals N. Amer.* 455 A striking feature of the North American vesper mice . . . is their diminutive size compared with the South American. **1891** *Cent.* 6739/2.

+**Vesper (sparrow).** =GRASS FINCH. Also with specifying term. — **1865** *Atlantic Mo.* XV. 515/1, I suspect . . . that the high pasture-lands begot the Vesper-Sparrow. **1892** TORREY *Foot-Path Way* 5 The vesper sparrow, the veery, and a host of other friends were singing about the hotel. **1917** *Birds of Amer.* III. 24 The Oregon Vesper is smaller than the Vesper.

* **Vessel.**

* **1.** A hollow utensil for holding liquids or other substances; a container for foods.

1654 JOHNSON *Wonder-w. Prov.* 15 When beholding their Vessells, which they had set before them, the Indian[s] knocking them were much delighted with the sound. **1701** *Boston Rec.* 9 Ordered that no person or persons, do presume hereafter to carry fire . . . but in a warming pan or other safe vessell. **1807** GASS *Journal* 37 All the party . . . took with them all the kettles and other vessels for holding water. **1912** *Sears, Roebuck & Co. Cat.* No. 124, 1022 [The] Daisy Fireless Cooker . . . is fitted with two high grade gray enameled vessels.

* **2.** A ship. Also attrib.

*a*1656 BRADFORD *Hist.* 395 Monsier de Aulnay . . . having before gott some of ye cheefe yt belonged to ye house abord his vessell. **1723** *Amer. Wkly. Mercury* 12 Feb. 3/2 The Guard le Coasts of Martineque have taken ten Vessels belonging to New England. **1845** *Cincinnati Misc.* I. 224 The first vessel navigation on Lake Erie, under the American flag, was the sloop Detroit. **1873** 'MARK TWAIN' & WARNER *Gilded Age* 49 The weight careened the vessels over toward each other.

b. *Vessel of war*, a warship.

1775 JEFFERSON *Writings* IV. 244 The New-Englanders are fitting out light vessels of war. **1830** COOPER *Water Witch* III. 146 The streak of white paint, dotted with ports, which marks a vessel of war, became visible to the naked eye. **1885** *Century Mag.* April 924/1 My plan . . . was as follows: To fit out a fleet of vessels-of-war with which to attack the city.

Vest. {1613-}

1. A jacketlike garment worn by men in military service.

1643 *Plymouth Laws* 326 If any man shall . . . come without his armes or with defective armes [he] shall forfaite for every trayneing day as followeth— . . . For want of a vest, VI *d.* For want of bandelires, VI. *d.*

2. A sleeveless garment reaching to the waist, worn by women. {1851-, of a knitted undergarment}

1806 LEWIS in *L. & Clark Exped.* IV. (1905) 186 When this vest is woarn the breast of the woman is concealed.

3. A sleeveless garment reaching to the waist, worn under a coat by men; a waistcoat. {1666-}

1809 FRENEAU *Poems* II. 31 The arrows . . . tore a passage through his vest, But bounded from his solid chest. **1838** *S. Lit. Messenger* IV. 59/2 His pantaloons and vest were of white—the former of the finest cassinet. **1866** 'F. KIRKLAND' *Bk. Anecdotes* 341 His dress was new, and of the most elegant make, broadcloth coat and pants, and a white satin vest. **1902** LORIMER *Lett. Merchant* 172 The Doctor stuck one hand in over the top of his vest.

b. *Pull down your vest*, (see quots. 1877 and 1892).

*c*1877 in *Burton's Events of 1875-76* (B.), The latest flash saying with which we are blest Is to tell a man quietly, 'Pull down your vest.' **1877** BARTLETT 502 *Pull down your Vest*, a curious flash expression of recent origin, without meaning. It is heard on all occasions . . . ; yet no man can tell whence it came. **1892** WALSH *Lit. Curiosities* 923 *Pull down your vest*, an American colloquialism, meaning, originally, 'Attend to your own business,' but now used as a mere senseless exclamation.

4. Attrib. and comb. with *back, coat, maker*.

1811 *Niles' Reg.* I. 292/1 A note of any manufactures . . . might be an useful addition to the communication; particularly of . . . strong woolen vest-back cloths; woolen or worsted lining stuffs. **1823** *Mass. Spy* 3 Dec. (Th.), He found him asleep, took from his vest pocket the key. **1850** W. MILES *Journal* (1916) 24 One had his last coat stolen—another his only vest coat. **1863** *Horticulturist* Dec. Advt. 4 We solicit the patronage of . . . Vest and Pantaloon Makers.

Vestibule, *n.* {1623-}

1. A hall between the entrance and the main interior rooms of a building. {1730-}

1818 J. TRUMBULL in *Autobiog.* 269 Stairs nine feet and lighted from the dome, mount on the right and left of the vestibule. **1872** *Chicago Tribune* 14 April 5/3 The entrance of the main vestibule is by a sort of parte [sic] cochere. **1893** *Harper's Mag.* April 683/2 [People] see life and judge Washington from a herdic, or in the vestibule of the hotels. **1922** TARKINGTON *Gentle Julia* 254 Florence stepped into the sheltering vestibule.

+**2.** (See quot. 1900.) {1889}

'Orig. *U.S.*' (*O.E.D.*).

1890 *Railways of Amer.* 246 A perfectly enclosed vestibule of handsome architectural appearance [runs] between the cars. **1900** *Everybody's Mag.* II. 444/2 One railway device that has increased the safety of passengers is the 'vestibule,' which connects coaches by a closely fitting covered hood over the platforms. **1901** MCCUTCHEON *Graustark* 17 Again, in Ohio, they met in the vestibule.

+**3.** Attrib. with *express train, Pullman train, sleeper.* {1889-}

1887 GEORGE *40 Yrs. on Rail* 243, I saw the vestibule Pullman train ready to start. **1889** *Congress. Rec.* 28 Feb. 2467/2 You might as well compare the stage-coach and the vestibule express train. **1890** *Stock Grower & Farmer* 12 April 7/4 Through Pullman vestibule sleepers from Los Angeles to Chicago.

+**Vestibule,** *v. tr.* To provide (a railroad car) with a vestibule. {1896} — **1891** *Cent.* 6741/2 *Vestibule,* . . . to provide with a vestibule. **1898** *Boston Herald* 21 April 9/5 Commissioner Goodwin inquired if it was the intention to have all the closed cars vestibuled.

+**Vestibuled,** *a.* Provided with vestibules. {1898} — **1890** H. Palmer *Stories Base Ball Field* 222 [The] Cincinnati, Hamilton, & Dayton R.R. [has] . . . the only Pullman Perfected Safety Vestibuled Train Service with Dining Car between Cincinnati, Indianapolis, and Chicago. **1894** *Congress. Rec.* 8 Aug. 8326/2 [The present building] bears no more relation to the building that should succeed it than a freight caboose bears to a vestibuled palace car. **1903** E. JOHNSON *Railway Tranportation* 48 The idea is as old as 1852, when a man by the name of Waterbury designed vestibuled car.

+**Vestibule(d) train.** A train the cars of which are vestibuled. {1896} — **1887** GEORGE *40 Years on Rail* 243 On this vestibule train are all the luxuries and conveniences a millionaire could desire at home. **1891** *Boston Jrnl.* 11 Feb. 2/3 Every vestibuled train arriving at Charleston is crowded. **1898** *Boston Herald* 19 April 2/1 (Ernst), South Carolina's 'Jim Crow car law' provides that the act shall not apply to . . . through vestibule trains. **1903** A. J. BEVERIDGE *Russian Advance* 7 You may now board a vestibuled train of sleeping-cars at Port Arthur.

Vesting. Cloth for making vests. {1851-} — **1813** *Niles' Reg.* IV. 295/1 For the best and handsomest fancy vesting, of cotton, . . . a premium of a piece of plate or its value, forty dollars. **1837** *Jamestown* (N.Y.) *Jrnl.* 16 May 1/5 Vestings . . . were manufactured at Nantucket. **1865** *Chicago Tribune* 10 April 1 Vestings . . . at Low Prices.

Vest pattern. An allowance of material for a vest; vesting. — **1804** *Austin P.* I. (1924) 108, 1 Vest Pattern, [$]1.75. **1818** DARBY *Emigrant's Guide* 259 Cotton and woollen cloth is also made e tensively, consisting of blankets, vest patterns [etc.]. **1867** *Ore. State Jrnl.* 25 May 4/1 The one that sells the most 'twixt now and Christmas, gets a vest pattern as a present.

* **Vestry.**

1. The body of members of a Protestant Episcopal church, or a smaller group vested with the administration of the affairs of the church. {*a*1672-}

1662 *Va. Statutes at Large* II. 102 Each county court shall appoint and order the vestrys of each parish . . . to appoint certaine dayes betweene Easter and Whitsunday to goe the said processions. **1705** BEVERLEY *Virginia* IV. 28 The Busness of these Church-Wardens, is to see the Orders, and Agreements of the Vestry perform'd. **1720** *Amer. Wkly. Mercury* 6 Oct. 1/2 The Humble Address of the Rector, Church Wardens and Vestry of Trinity Church in the City of New York in America. **1724** JONES *Virginia* 66 The Vestries consist of the Minister, and twelve of the most substantial and intelligent Persons in each Parish. **1741** *Md. Hist. Mag.* VIII. 359 This Vestry agreed to pay Simon Duffe for the work he agreed with this Vestry to do in the Church in Annapolis. **1775** *Ib.* 140 The Vestry agree that the Play house be fitted up for a place of divine worship. **1863** P. S. DAVIS *Young Parson* 211 [You] may be glad enough if I do not yet have you before the vestry to testify in the case. **1885** E. INGLE *Local Institutions Va.* 64 Once in every four years the vestry, by order of the county court, divided the parish into precincts, and appointed two persons in each precinct to 'procession' the lands.

* **2.** A meeting of the vestry.

1695 *Va. State P.* I. 49 At a Vesterye held ye 6th daye of Maye, 1695, St. John's parish. **1769** WASHINGTON *Diaries* I. 335 Went to an intended vestry at ye cross Roads.

* **3.** A room in which the vestments, records, etc., of a church are kept, and in which clergy and choir put on their robes; also, a room in a church edifice used for various church functions.

1865 A. D. WHITNEY *Gayworthys* 289 She reached the vestry just vacated by the Sunday School children, out now for their short 'nooning.' **1887** FREEMAN *Humble Romance* 362, I peeked into the vestry, an' saw 'em both.

4. Attrib. with *book, hour, house*, etc.

1704 *N.C. Col. Rec.* I. 597 [The clerk is] to keep the Vestry journal and to attend the Vestry at their meetings. *Ib.* II. 11 T'was then to be entred in the Vestry Book. **1725** *Md. Hist. Mag.* VII. 279 The present Church Wardens agree with any proper Workman for the new Covering the shed of the Vestry house with feather edged Cyprus Plank. **1768** *Ib.* X. 133 All Vestrymen or Church Wardens absenting themselves at Vestry Hours . . . shall be fined without a reasonable excuse at the Discretion of the Vestry. **1870** 'F. FERN' *Ginger-Snaps* 146 She don't . . . go to bed at dark, save on vestry-meeting nights.

Vestryman. A member of a vestry. {1614–} — **1695** *Va. State P.* I. 49 There was a little controversy between our Vestry men & me about our Church Glebe. **1741** *Boston Rec.* 289 He is now a Vestry Man in the Church of England. **1848** *Knickerb.* XVIII. 308 The vestry-men in particular deemed him just the man of all others to fill the pulpit. **1894** *Harper's Mag.* Feb. 486/1 The senior warden and four vestrymen are Valleyites.

+**Vestry room.** =VESTRY 3. — **1753** in Odell *Annals N.Y. Stage* I. 69 Mr. Tuckey [shall] have the Use of . . . the Vestry Room two Nights in the Week for the Teaching of his Singing Scholars. **1819** *Niles' Reg.* XVII. 60/1 A number of clergymen, of different denominations, met in the vestry room of St. Paul's Church. **1862** *Harper's Mag.* Dec. 127/1 We entered the vestry room, . . . and from thence passed up to the pulpit.

* **Vetch.**

* **1.** Any plant of the genus *Vicia*, esp. *Vicia sativa*, freq. cultivated for use as fodder or as a fertilizer.

1705 BEVERLEY *Virginia* II. 17 The same Use is made also of . . . Vetches, Squashes, Maycocks, Maracocks, Melons [etc.]. **1790** *Amer. Acad. Mem.* II. 1. 179 Many vegetables, as clover, peas, beans and vetches, help to fertilize exhausted feelds [*sic*]. **1817** BRADBURY *Travels* 326 The emigrant . . . should take with him . . . a small quantity of lucerne, saintfoin, and vetches. **1866** *Maine Agric. Soc. Returns* 148 The improved tillage of the hills, the production of vetches [etc.] . . . has changed to a great extent its character. **1878** JACKSON *Travel at Home* 366 There are sixteen varieties of vetch which grow in one small piece of table-land between the Colorado Springs Hotel and the railroad station. **1901** MOHR *Plant Life Ala.* 135 Vetch (*Vicia sativa*), cowpeas, and bur clover . . . will yield crops for soiling in the earliest days of spring.

2. With specifying terms. Applied also to plants of other genera.

See also MILK VETCH.

1817-8 EATON *Botany* (1822) 275 *Ervum hirsutum*, creeping vetch. **1843** TORREY *Flora N.Y.* I. 154 *Vicia americana*. American Vetch. . . . Moist shady places. *Ib.* 173 *Phaca neglecta*. Bastard Vetch. . . . Gravelly banks of rivers and lakes. **1847** WOOD *Botany* 220 V[icia] *Caroliniana*. . . . Carolinian Vetch. . . . Flowers pale-blue, the banner tipped with deep purple. **1887** *Amer. Naturalist* XXI. 710 Chickling Vetch, *Lathyrus sativus*, . . . was included among American vegetables by Burr in 1863. **1901** MOHR *Plant Life Ala.* 577 *Vicia hirsuta*. . . . Hairy Vetch. . . . Naturalized coast of New England to New Jersey.

* **Vetchling.** A plant or species of the genus *Lathyrus* of small beanlike herbs. Also with specifying terms. — **1784** *Amer. Acad. Mem.* I. 473. **1843** TORREY *Flora N.Y.* I. 157 *Lathyrus maritimus*. Sea-side Vetchling. Beach Pea. . . . Sandy sea-coast of Long Island. *Ib., Lathyrus ochroleucus*. Cream-Colored Vetchling. . . . Shady hill-sides and banks of streams.

* **Veteran.**

* **1.** A soldier of long service.

1787 in Ramsey *Tennessee* 392 A body of about fifteen hundred veterans, embodied themselves to rescue their governor . . . out of the hands of the North-Carolinians. **1864** EDWARDS *Shelby* 472 War worn veterans feeding for days on beef without salt or bread.

+**2.** An ex-soldier; one who has served in an American war.

1798 DUNLAP *André* (pref.), The Author has gone near to offend the veterans of the American army who were present on the first night. **1838** *S. Lit. Messenger* IV. 796 When the revolutionary pension-law was enacted, a majority of the war-worn veterans had travelled . . . beyond the reach of human reward. **1884** *Boston Jrnl.* 6 Sept., The whole affair . . . will long be remembered as a bright spot in the lives of these veterans who went forth in the hour of need to save that which was dearer than life to them, their country and their flag. **1912** COBB *Back Home* 38 Saturday . . . was also Veterans' Day, when the old soldiers were the guests of honor of the management. **1906** *N.Y. Ev. Post* 29 Jan. 1 A guard of honor, selected from the ranks of the Spanish war veterans here. **1924** F. J. HASKIN *Amer. Government* 401 In the wake of the World War there came the problem of the treatment . . . of the disabled veterans of that great conflict.

+**3.** (See quotation.)

1877 BARTLETT 733 *Veteran*, a term applied during the late civil war to soldiers, who, at the termination of the period for which they had enlisted, enlisted again.

4. An experienced player on an athletic team.

1880 *N.Y. Herald* 23 Aug. 9/4 Youthful players . . . are rarely to be depended upon throughout a season, to contend against veterans. **1882** *Nation* 6 July 9/3 Ten of the sixteen men who rowed to-day pulled in the race of 1881—five 'veterans' in each boat. **1902** BELL *Hope Loring* 172 That famous game [was] destined to be . . . played over from every youngster with his first pigskin to veterans with broken noses.

+**5.** (See first quotation.) Also attrib.

1905 *Forestry Bureau Bul.* No. 61, 26 *Veteran*, a tree over 2 feet in diameter breasthigh. *Ib., Veteran forest*, a forest of veteran trees.

+**Veteran camp.** The Confederate veterans of a community organized as a society. (Cf. CAMP *n.* 5.) — **1896** *N.Y. Dramatic News* 4 July 16/2 Benefits of various kinds will be given for several of the Confederate veteran camps. **1904** [see CAMP *n.* 5].

+**Veteranize,** *v.* **1.** *intr.* To re-enlist. Now rare. **2.** *tr.* To make veteran as by long service or by re-enlistment. — **(1) 1875** W. T. SHERMAN *Memoirs* I. 395 We were much embarrassed by a general order of the War Department, promising a thirty-days furlough to all soldiers who would 'veteranize'—viz., reënlist for the rest of the war. **1891** *Columbus Dispatch* 7 Oct., They were the first to veteranize, and this signified a good deal at the time. **(2) 1880** LAMPHERE *U.S. Govt.* 92/1 Soldiers of this class . . . who received only $300 cannot receive additional bounty, unless they became veteranized. **1893** *Johnson's Univ. Cycl.* I. 355/2 The proportion was at first a little over three pieces for 1,000 infantry, but as the latter became more veteranized this was reduced to about two pieces.

Veteran soldier. {1611–} =VETERAN 2. — **1808** *Ann. 10th Congress* 1 Sess. 2081 An application from a veteran soldier on the subject of his bounty land. **1891** in M. A. Jackson *Memoirs* 638 Old veteran soldiers gathered in groups and discussed incidents of life around the camp-fire on the battlefield when with their old commander.

Veterinarian. One whose profession is the medical or surgical treatment of sick animals. {1646–} — **1868** WOODRUFF *Trotting Horse* 372 A great deal of vagueness and uncertainty . . . has long existed, even among the most advanced veterinarians. **1890** *Stock Grower & Farmer* 25 Jan. 7/2 The veterinarians . . . have lately raised . . . a hubbub about it. **1906** *McClure's Mag.* Feb. 357 The veterinarian had been obliged to shoot five of the little animals as infected with glanders.

Veterinary. =prec. {1861–} — **1898** FORD *Tattle-Tales* 45 You will have the veterinary see the cob at once. **1916** WILSON *Somewhere* 326 The veterinary opposed a masterly silence to this majority diagnosis.

Veterinary surgeon. =VETERINARIAN. {1802–} — **1857** *Porter's Spirit of Times* 3 Jan. 291/2 Veterinary surgeons have, of late, introduced the use of chloroform in performing surgical operations upon horses. **1873** *Winfield* (Kan.) *Courier* 18 Jan. 3/1 The acknowledged best Veterinary Surgeons of the west having experience in the treatment of epizootic claim that [etc.]. **1903** BURNHAM *Jewel* 219 Zeke was as anxious as his master to get the veterinary surgeon.

Veto, *n.* {1629–} The right vested in the chief executive, esp. the president or the governor of a state, to nullify acts passed by a legislative body. {1792–, of continental governments} (Cf. POCKET VETO.) — **1812** *Lit. & Philos. Repertory* (Middlebury, Vt.) April 28 We cannot, therefore, approve of the use of the terms *veto* and *mania;* although we must allow, that much grosser instances of the same species of impropriety have been often noticed by us. **1837** PECK *New Guide* 227 The governor . . . exercised his right of *veto* in relation to the removal of a county seat. **1884** *Boston Jrnl.* 6 Sept., The Governor's veto of the Five-cent Fare bill. **1894** S. LEAVITT *Our Money Wars* 221 The Act of February 28, 1878, monetized the silver dollar over the veto of the President.

Veto, *v.* {1706–} +*tr.* Of the President: To nullify (an act of legislation). — **1837** MARTINEAU *Society* II. 210 Mr. Monroe vetoed the bill authorising the collection of tolls for the repair of the Cumberland road. **1842** *Whig Almanac 1843* 30/1 In the year 1832 he had vetoed the bill for a re-charter of the Bank of the United States. **1880** *Harper's Mag.* July 316/1 Immediate Deficiency, both Houses, April 29; vetoed by the President, May 4. **1894** S. LEAVITT *Our Money Wars* 58 Congress . . . rechartered the National Bank in 1832. Jackson vetoed the bill.

+**Vetoer.** An executive who vetoes. — **1888** *N.Y. Wkly. Tribune* 24 Oct. 1 (*Cent.*). **1892** *Columbus Dispatch* 27 Sept., Cleveland's record as a vetoer of pension bills has given him . . . an unsavory reputation among the ex soldiers.

+**Veto message.** The message of a President or the governor of a state, informing a legislative body of his rejection of a bill and his reasons therefor. — **1836** *Jamestown* (N.Y.) *Jrnl.* 6 April 1/5 In General Jackson's Veto Message the use of Foreign Capital was denounced as dangerous to Liberty. **1840** *Niles' Nat. Reg.* 11 April 96/3 Governor McNutt recently transmitted a veto message to the legislature of Mississippi. **1868** *N.Y. Herald* 27 July 4/2 Mr. Johnson, in his late veto messages, . . . takes the ground that the State governments under which said States have been readmitted into Congress are illegal and void. **1914** *Cycl. Amer. Govt.* III. 613/2 If Congress adjourns *sine die* within the period and thus prevents the President from sending his veto message, the bill does not become law.

+**Veto power.** The power vested in a chief executive to veto legislation. Also transf. — **1838** MAYO *Polit. Sk. Washington* 13 [The president] has the further power . . . under the protecting Ægis of the veto power to prevent the restoration of the treasury deposites to the legitimate control of the Legislature. **1856** *Democratic Conv. Proc.* 24 We are decidedly opposed to taking from the President the qualified veto power, by which he is enabled . . . to suspend the passage of a bill. **1873** *Harper's Mag.* April 744/1 The veto power of the Mayor [is] to be the same as that of the Governor. **1887** *Courier-Journal* 6 May 1/3 He could not indorse many things which Mr. Cleveland had accomplished by his use of the veto power. **1904** *N.Y. Ev. Post* 19 Jan. 6 His bid is evidently for a veto power.

+**Vetticost.** (See FETTICUS.)

Vevay. Attrib. with *straw hat*. — **1829** FLINT *G. Mason* 72 George and the boys concluded to try their skill upon the coarser manufacture of Vevay straw-hats.

+**V flume.** A flume shaped like a V. — **1896** SHINN *Story of Mine* 119 In 1866 or 1867 experiments were made . . . with a simple form of trough that has since been adopted in every mountainous region of the Pacific coast—the famous V-flume.

Viameter. A device to be attached to a wheel of a vehicle to indicate distance traveled. {1831-} — 1847 EMORY *Military Reconn.* 56 The viameter for measuring distances, heretofore attached to the wheel of the instrument wagon, was now attached to the wheel of one of the small mountain howitzers. 1854 *33d Congress 1 Sess.* H.R. Ex. Doc. No. 129, II. 111. 27 Abandoning our wagons, except a light vehicle to which was attached the viameter . . . , we packed upon mules our collections. 1856 in *So. Dak. Hist. Coll.* I. 438 The viometer makes the distance 310 miles.

Viburnum. {1731-} +Any one of various American shrubs or plants belonging to the family Caprifoliaceae. — 1785 MARSHALL *Amer. Grove* 162 *Viburnum alnifolium.* Alder-leaved Viburnum. 1814 BIGELOW *Florula Bostoniensis* 71 The different species of Viburnum are fine flowering shrubs. 1892 APGAR *Trees Northern U.S.* 113.

*Vice.[1] (See VISE.)

*Vice.[2] +Attrib. and comb. with *boss, crusader, grafter.* — 1903 STEFFENS in *McClure's Mag.* Nov. 89 In New York, Croker has failed signally to maintain vice-bosses whom he appointed. 1904 *Ib.* April 587/1 No wonder Minneapolis, having cleaned out its police ring of vice grafters, now discovers boodle in the council! 1915 *Scientific Amer.* 30 Jan. 98/3 The Puritan conception of life, like that of vice-crusaders, suffragettes, and most crusaders, scorns all trifling with its weighty realities.

*Vice-admiral. 1. A naval officer ranking next to an admiral; a vessel commanded by such an officer. 2. A civil officer exercising jurisdiction in a prescribed district. *Obs.* {a1618-} — (1) a1649 WINTHROP *Hist.* I. 32 We were forced to take in some sail to stay for the vice-admiral, which was near a league astern of us. 1706 *Boston News-Letter* 6 May 4/2 Our Forts at Nevis, Maul'd their Ships, and kill'd their Vice Admiral. 1776 *Jrnls. Cont. Congress* VI. 954 Resolved, . . . That the rank of the naval officers be to the rank of officers in the land service, as follows: Admiral as a General, Vice Admiral [as a] Lieutenant General [etc.]. 1864 *38th Congress 2 Sess.* H. R. Ex. Doc. No. 1, p. xxiv, In recommending, therefore, that the office of vice-admiral should be created, and the appointment conferred on Rear-Admiral David G. Farragut, I but respond . . . to the voice and wishes of the naval service. (2) 1717 *N.J. Archives* 1 Ser. IV. 306 Robert Hunter . . . [was appointed] Gov[erno]r in cheif of the Province of New Jersey, New York and the Territories . . . and Vice Admiral of the same.

+Vice-presidency. The office of Vice-president of the United States. — 1816 *Daily Nat. Intelligencer* 9 April 1/1 The Nomination of candidates for the Presidency and Vice Presidency by the Republican Congressional Meeting, appears to have received the approbation of a large majority of the Republican party. 1840 *Niles' Nat. Reg.* 1 Aug. 337/1 Vice presidency—withdrawal of Wm. R. King, as a candidate. 1868 *N.Y. Herald* 25 July 3/3 General Hancock . . . Was Not a Candidate for the Vice Presidency. 1900 *Congress. Rec.* 17 Feb. 1899/2, I am not a candidate for the Vice-Presidency of the United States.

*Vice-president. +The government official ranking next to the President of the United States.

1787 *Constitution* ii. § 4 The President, Vice-President and all civil officers of the United States. 1798 *Ann. 5th Congress* 493 The Electors of President, and Vice President . . . shall respectively distinguish the person whom they desire to be President, from the one they desire to be Vice President. 1803 *Constitution: 12th Amendment,* The electors shall meet in their respective states, and vote by ballot for president and vice-president. 1889 *Century Mag.* April 813/1 The mayor and corporation called to congratulate the Vice-President. 1925 BRYAN *Memoirs* 101, [I] have letters which I received from him [Gov. Altgeld] afterward suggesting the possibility of my receiving the nomination for Vice-President.

+Vice-presidential, *a.* Pertaining to the vice-presidency of the United States. — 1854 BENTON *30 Years' View* I. 45/1 Mr. Calhoun was the only substantive vice-presidential candidate before the people. 1884 CABLE *Dr. Sevier* 341 Those little round, ribbanded medals, with a presidential candidate on one side and his vice-presidential man Friday on the other. 1900 *Congress. Rec.* 17 Jan. 915/2 Being publicly notified that I am out of the Vice-Presidential race would have been somewhat humiliating.

Viceroy. 'The archippus, a handsomely colored American butterfly, *Basilarcha archippus'* (*Cent.*). — 1881 S. H. SCUDDER *Butterflies* 103 The caterpillar of the Viceroy signifies its displeasure at any disturbance by tossing the head upward.

+Vicissitous, *a.* Vicissitudinous. — 1865 BURRITT *Walk to Land's End* 165 A city set upon such a hill could not have been hidden in the vicissitous experiences of a nation. 1892 *Columbus Dispatch* 9 June, All of them reach their affluence . . . along the same vicissitous road.

Victoria. {1846-} +(See quotations.) *Obs.* — 1872 in G. W. Curtis *Horses, Cattle* 310 The family of pigs known as Victorias originated with Col. Frank D. Curtis, Kirby Homestead, Charlton, Saratoga Co., N.Y. 1893 *Ib.* 312 Victorias [are] . . . a new breed produced within the last decade, by a judicious blending of the blood of four different breeds— Poland-China, Chester-White, Berkshire and American or White Suffolk.

*Victualer. 1. One who supplies victuals. *Obsolescent.* 2. A vessel carrying provisions. — (1) 1636 *Plymouth Laws* 47 If any such thing can be proved it [shall] be esteemed a misdemeanor punishable in the said victualler. 1705 *Charlestown Land Rec.* 169 This Indenture made . . . [between] Eleizer Phillips, victualar, . . . and Eleizer Bateman, house Wright. 1836 *Knickerb.* VII. 44 One was 'a dealer in paper,' the other a 'victualler.' 1851 CIST *Cincinnati* 277 We owe this exhibition to the pub-

lic spirit of Vanaken and Daniel Wunder, John Butcher, J. & W. Gall, . . . among our principal victualers. (2) 1778 *Essex Inst. Coll.* 174 The armed Victuallers arranged in order guarded the right & left side of the fleet & 2 frigates brought up the van.

*Victualing house. An inn or tavern. *Obs.* — 1633 *Plymouth Laws* 35 That none be suffered to retale wine . . . except it be at some inne or victualling house. 1662 *Md. Archives* 447 There is a necessity of alloweing and Keeping Victualling howses for the Entertaynm[en]t of all persons. 1745 *Georgia Col. Rec.* VI. 129 He had taken upon him to impower Thomas Goodale of Augusta aforesaid to continue keeping a publick victualling House.

Vienna bentwood. *attrib.* Designating furniture of a type made in, or supposed to have been made in, Vienna. — 1876 *Scribner's Mo.* April 809/2 Even chairs so ostentatiously bare and matter-of-fact as . . . the Vienna bent-wood chairs, cost as much as some to be found in the fashionable shops. 1887 *Courier-Journal* 3 May 3/8 So as to include the manufacture and sale of Vienna Bent-wood Furniture.

*View, *v.*

*1. *tr.* To inspect, lay out, or survey (something) officially, usually in behalf of a colony or town. Now hist.

With reference to: a. Fences. b. Boundaries and roads. c. Land.

(a) 1636 *Watertown Rec.* I. 1. 2 If any trespase be done by great Cattle the fence shalbe viewed. 1658 *Dedham Rec.* IV. 2 Men apointed to view Fences in the remote fields as followeth. (b) 1646 *Portsmouth Rec.* 34 The line may be viwed & layed out betwene Nuport and this towne. 1733 *Penna. Col. Rec.* III. 521 Any five of them, should view and lay out by Course and Distance, a Convenient high road. 1803 in A. E. Lee *Hist. Columbus, Ohio* I. 312 [A commission was appointed to] view . . . [a road] from . . . Franklinton to Springfield. 1874 COLLINS *Kentucky* I. 514 The First Road ordered to be 'viewed' and opened, by Lincoln county court, was from Lincoln Court House . . . to Boonesborough, in the fall of 1783. (c) 1658 *Dedham Rec.* IV. 1 Lieft. Fisher Peter woodward & Nath: Coaleburne [were chosen] as a committee to view the said parcell. 1671 *Brookhaven Rec.* 28 At a towne meeting it was voeted . . . to goe and vew the medoes at unkechauge. 1718 *Mass. H. Rep. Jrnls.* II. 32 A Committee, to go to Cambridge, this Day [is to] view and consider the most convenient place whereon to erect an additional Building to Harvard Collge.

+2. To punish. *slang. Obs.*

1798 I. ALLEN *Hist. Vermont* 35 All civil and military officers who had acted under authority of the Governor or Legislature of New York, were required to suspend their functions on pain of being viewed. 1840 THOMPSON *Green Mt. Boys* I. 40, I shall vote to have him *viewed.*

*Viewer.

*1. In colonial times, one appointed to view or inspect (something) officially. *Obsolescent.*

With reference to: a. Fences. b. Tobacco. c. Weights and measures, wood, shingles. d. Corn or grain. e. Cattle.

(a) 1639 *Dorchester Rec.* 39 The order for fence last made is found defectiue in regard of the veiuers having but 3 s. a day for seeing the fence sufficient. 1692 *Southampton Rec.* II. 313 Francis Sayre chosen viewer of the fences belonging to the great and little plain. 1714 in Temple & Sheldon *Hist. Northfield, Mass.* 134 One-half of said fence to be accounted as Public Fence, and the whole to be under the viewers for the security of the Great Meadow. 1828 WEBSTER, *Viewer,* in New England, a town officer whose duty is to inspect something; as, a viewer of fences, who inspects them to determine whether they are sufficient in law. (b) 1640 *Md. Archives* I. 97 Any one that will may demand a veiwer to veiw any Tobacco wherein he hath . . . interest. 1666 *Md. Archives* II. 67 Then a Member of the howse motions Concerning the appoynting Viewers in each County for the Viewing of Tob[acco]. 1677 *New Castle Court Rec.* 94 The Court have this day appointed Cornelis Post to bee viewer & packer of Tobbacco in this Towne. (c) 1646 *New Haven Rec.* 275 Bro. Davis & bro Phillip Leek chosen viewers of measurs, as bushels, &c. 1711 *Boston Rec.* 75 Jabez Negus & Capt Thomas Barnerd are chosen to Serve as . . . Veiwers of Shingle. 1712 *Ib.* 90 Veiwers of wood within the Town of Boston [shall] be Allowed one peny pr Cord. 1713 *Plymouth Rec.* II. 78 Vewers of lumber or measurers of bords and Timber Are Samuel Harlow and Jacob Mitchel. 1730 *Boston Rec.* 19 Officers for Rumny Marsh Chose Vizt . . . John Indicott, Edward Moberly, . . . Surveyors of Board &c, & Viewers of Shingles. (d) 1654 *New Haven Rec.* II. 98 There shall be a viewer of corne. 1689 in Munsell *Ann. Albany* II. 105 Anthony Lespinard was appointed by ye mayor and aldermen to be veiwer of corn in this citty. 1744 *Md. Hist. Mag.* XXI. 243 Mr. Carrington sold the Corn at more than valued by the viewers. (e) 1689 *Portsmouth Rec.* 240 George Brownel, John Anthony and William Coggeshall are chosen viewers of cattle.

+2. One appointed to survey, report on, or mark out a prospective street or road.

1805 *Phila. Ordinances* (1812) 110 On the return of the viewers reporting in favour of opening any street, the court shall appoint twelve . . . freeholders. 1834 in Nicolay & Hay *A. Lincoln* I. 119n., [We] respectfully request your honorable body to appoint viewers to view and locate a road from Musick's ferry on Salt Creek. 1873 *Winfield* (Kan.) *Courier* 11 Jan. 3/3 Viewers report on the county road of T. H. Alley was presented and adopted.

+Viga. *S.W.* [Sp.] A beam or rafter. *Obs.* — 1844 GREGG *Commerce of Prairies* I. 284 [Rooms which are] still covered with the *vigas* and joists, remaining nearly sound under the *azoteas* of earth. **1854** *33d Congress 1 Sess* H. R. Ex. Doc. No. 129, II. III. 20 Magnificent pines are found . . . , such as are considered in this country to afford the best and most durable timber for 'vigas' (beams or rafters) of houses. **1863** *Rio Abajo Press* April 14/3 Ernst stated that he had . . . found the deceased in the act of carrying off a viga, the property of prisoner. **1873** BOURKE *Journal* 21 March, The entire work was of limestone, laid in an adobe cement, the vigas being of cottonwood.

∗ Vigilance.

+1. Committee of vigilance. a. = VIGILANCE COMMITTEE 1. **b.** = VIGILANCE COMMITTEE 2.

(a) **1837** MARTINEAU *Society* II. 139 He was brought to trial by the Committee of Vigilance; seven elders of the presbyterian church at Nashville being among his judges. *c*1851 in Stowe *Key* 189/2 The committees of vigilance [were exhorted] to increased activity in ferreting out all persons tinctured with abolitionism in the county. (b) **1851** *Harper's Mag.* Sept. 559/1 A large number of the most valuable citizens organized themselves into a Committee of Vigilance, for the purpose of securing the punishment of criminals. **1856** in H. H. Bancroft *Works* XXXVII. 185 You are hereby required to surrender forthwith the possession of the county jail. . . . [Signed] Committee of Vigilance.

+2. Attrib. with association, police.

See also VIGILANCE COMMITTEE, VIGILANCE MAN.

1851 in H. H. Bancroft *Works* XXXVI. 469 The courts under the new criminal organization are fast superseding the want of a vigilance association. **1887** *Ib.* 373 Mrs. Hogan . . . was seized by the Vigilance police and brought to the Committee rooms.

+Vigilance committee. (See also V. C.)

1. a. In the South, an organization of citizens using extralegal means to control or intimidate Negroes and abolitionists and, during the Civil War, to suppress loyalty to the Union. Now hist.

1835 GARRISON in W. J. & F. J. Garrison *W. L. Garrison* I. 519 The slave States . . . have organized Vigilance Committees and Lynch Clubs. **1851** in Stowe *Key* 189/1 The Vigilance Committee . . . required him to renounce his Abolition sentiments. **1860** ABBOTT *South & North* 286 Your 'vigilance committee' have ordered your post-masters not to distribute these [abolition newspapers] to their subscribers. **1865** PIKE *Scout & Ranger* (1932) 134 Vigilance committees were organized in every town and village [in Texas], and their motto was: 'No mercy to traitors,' meaning those who were true to their country and the old flag.

b. In the North, an organization designed to aid fugitive slaves. Now hist.

1851 B. ALCOTT *Journals* 244 The Vigilance Committee met at Timothy Gilbert's rooms. . . . Several volunteers volunteered to beat the streets for protecting fugitives from being arrested during the night. **1852** in Stowe *Key* 51/2 There was no Vigilance Committee at the time,—there were but anti-slavery men.

2. A voluntary association of men professing to supplement the efforts of the police and the courts in maintaining order, punishing crime, etc. Chiefly *W.* Also attrib.

1851 *Whig Almanac 1852* 19/1 The prevalence of crime in San Francisco led to the formation of a voluntary association . . . called the Vigilance Committee. **1856** *Harper's Mag.* XIII. 840/1 From *California* we have intelligence that the San Francisco Vigilance Committee was formally disbanded on the 18th of August, having been in active operation just three months. **1859** L. WILMER *Press Gang* 219 A mob, composed chiefly of foreigners, and calling itself a 'Vigilance Committee,' in June, 1858, took possession of the municipal government of New Orleans. **1869** J. R. BROWNE *Adv. Apache Country* 426 My companion entertained me with . . . his adventures as a police-officer during the Vigilance Committee excitement at Aurora. **1892** GUNTER *Miss Dividends* 84 You think Vigilance Committees right? **1904** 'O. HENRY' *Heart of West* 270 When a thousand citizens had arrived and taken up claims they . . . appointed a vigilance committee. **1916** THOBURN *Stand. Hist. Oklahoma* I. 314 Apparently, the Vigilance Committee of the Choctaws and Chickasaws antedated by several years the organization and operation of the Ku Klux Klan.

+Vigilance man. = VIGILANTE. *Obs.* — **1887** H. H. BANCROFT *Works* XXXVI. 314 It was not law and government that the vigilance men complained of, but the lack of these. **1892** GUNTER *Miss Dividends* 85 The best citizens of these places were Vigilance men.

Vigilant, *n.* { 1822- } **+** = VIGILANTE. — **1867** in H. H. Bancroft *Works* XXXVI. 703 In no instance did any of the many lawless characters arrested by the vigilants ever fire a pistol in their own defence. **1887** H. H. BANCROFT *Works* XXXVI. 18 The result [of the election] did not seem to indicate that the Vigilants, as I shall take the liberty of calling the men of vigilance, were sustained by the people. **1895** S. R. HOLE *Little Tour in Amer.* 67 A fight occurred there yesterday between vigilants and horse-thieves. **1920** R. M. JONES *Later Periods Quakerism* II. 581 William C. Faber and Joseph Ricketson . . . were co-labourers with the abolitionists and with the 'Vigilants' or underground committees.

∗Vigilant, *a.* +Belonging or pertaining to a vigilance committee. *Obs.* — **1824** *Mo. Intelligencer* 12 Feb. (Th.), We hate what are called vigilant men; they are a set of suspicious, mean spirited mortals, that dislike fun. **1856** in H. H. Bancroft *Works* XXXVII. 643 You are hereby appointed . . . to take charge of the vigilant police force which will be detailed to preserve the public peace.

+Vigilant committee. = VIGILANCE COMMITTEE. — **1873** *Newton Kansan* 13 Feb. 2/3 Threats of vigilant committees . . . have started the vicious crowd eastward.

+Vigilante. [Sp.] A member of a vigilance committee. Chiefly *W.* or *S.W.*

1867 RICHARDSON *Beyond Mississippi* 487 The power [in Montana] has vested in the 'Vigilantes,' a secret tribunal of citizens. **1869** *Atlantic Mo.* July 80/2 The vigilantes . . . had come down to the levee [in Cairo, Ill.], two or three hundred strong, armed, equipped, and determined to make the wretch surrender. **1884** *Century Mag.* Dec. 194 The second was reputed to be decidedly a 'bad' man, an old-time Virginia City vigilante. **1910** J. HART *Vigilante Girl* 286 He also taunted him with having declined to issue writs of habeas corpus to release men who, like himself, had been imprisoned by the Vigilantes.

b. Attrib. and comb. with *justice, red tape, work.*

1890 LANGFORD *Vigilante Days* (1912) 90 In the name of Vigilante justice [some men] committed crimes which on any principle of ethics were wholly indefensible. **1897** HOUGH *Story of Cowboy* 320 All the leaders were willing to admit that they had had enough of *vigilante* work for the time. **1910** J. HART *Vigilante Girl* 273 With some difficulty he cut the Vigilante red tape sufficiently to obtain for them a pass.

+Vigilanter. = VIGILANTE. *Obs.* — **1873** *Newton Kansan* 13 Feb. 3/3 The vigilanters extend from Dodge City to Pueblo. *c*1900 R. L HALE *Log of Forty-Niner* 120 The 'Vigilanters' were a law unto themselves, ferreting out criminals, and meting out punishments severe and sudden.

+Viginial crop. A crop produced in twenty years. Used esp. with reference to slave-breeding. *Obs.* — **1832** C. J. FAULKNER *Sp. Va. Legislature on Slave Population* (Chipman), Shall society suffer that the slaveholder may continue to gather his viginial crop of human flesh? **1848** W. H. CHANNING *Mem. W. E. Channing* I. 84 Not then, either, had speculators discovered how to postpone the destructive effects of slave cultivation, by breeding children, like cattle, for the south-west market, and replenishing exhausted coffers by the profits of the 'vigintial crop.'

∗Vigneron. Also **vineron.** A cultivator of grape vines; a vineyardist. *Obs.* — **1628** *Va. House of Burgesses* 48 The Vignerons that have beene sent over have spent their tyme heere to small purpose. **1698** THOMAS *Pensilvania* 16 Excellent Grapes . . . being daily Cultivated by skilful Vinerons. **1773** *Md. Hist. Mag.* XV. 60, I may expect my Vignerons by the 1st Ships.

+Vigorite. (See quot. 1884.) *Obs.* — **1879** WEBSTER *Suppl.* 1584/2 *Vigorite,* . . . a preparation of nitroglycerine used in blasting. **1884** KNIGHT *Suppl.* 928/1 *Vigorite,* a nitro-glycerine explosive, manufactured at Marquette.

+Vigors. [N. A. *Vigors,* a British naturalist (1785–1840).] **1.** *Vigors's warbler,* (see quot. 1891). **2.** *Vigors's vireo,* = sense 1. **3.** *Vigors's wren,* (see quotation). — (1) **1831** AUDUBON *Ornith. Biog.* I. 153 Vigors's Warbler. *Sylvia Vigorsii.* **1891** *Cent.* 6820/3 *Vigors's warbler,* . . . the pine-creeping warbler as mistaken for another species. (2) **1832** NUTTALL *Man. Ornith.* 318 Vigor's Vireo. *Vireo Vigorsii.* . . . An individual of this very rare bird was shot by its discoverer many years ago on an island in Perkiomen creek, in Pennsylvania, and has never been seen since by any naturalist. (3) **1917** *Birds of Amer.* III. 192 In the coast region of middle California is Vigors's Wren (*Thryomanes bewicki spilurus*).

+Vilfa. A variety of pasture or forage grass. *Obs.* Also with specifying term. — **1843** TORREY *Flora N.Y.* II. 438 *Vilfa vaginæflora.* Hidden-flowered Vilfa. . . . Sandy arid fields and barren hill sides. **1857** *Ill. Agric. Soc. Trans.* II. 494 The vilfa is a general favorite, both for grazing and for hay.

∗Village.

∗1. a. A settlement in the country smaller than a town. **+b.** Such a settlement incorporated and governed by local officials.

1638 *Charlestown Land Rec.* 3 Eight score acres of land . . . , bounded on the east by Boston line, and on the north by Lynne villiadge. **1680** *Conn. Rec.* III. 57 [They asked] that they might have liberty (they having obteyned consent of New Haven) to become a village. **1705** *Ib.* IV. 527 [The inhabitants may] make rates . . . within the bounds of the said villiadge . . . , for the maintenance of their minister. **1812** *Niles' Reg.* II. 382/1 Major-general Van Rensselear arrived in this village yesterday morning. **1883** in Bryce *Amer. Commw.* II. II. xlviii. 240 A minimum population of three hundred, occupying not more than two square miles in extent, may by popular vote become incorporated [in Ill.] as a 'village.' **1916** PORTER *David* 170 You'll have to call me 'The Old Man of the Mountain,' as they do down in the village.

+2. An encampment or community, often temporary, of Indians.

1720 in J. Winsor *Miss. Basin* (1895) 142 Villages of the Chactas or Flat Head Indians. **1805** CLARK in *Lewis & C. Exped.* I. (1904) 247 Some of our Men go to See a War Medeson made at the Village. **1837** IRVING *Bonneville* I. 98 A *village* of Indians, in trappers' language, does not always imply a fixed community; but often a wandering horde or band. **1883** *Rep. Indian Affairs* 6 The Indians live together in villages during the winter months and remove to their fields during the summer. **1916** EASTMAN *From Deep Woods* 52 The college grounds covered the site of an ancient village of mound-builders.

+3. _W._ An aggregation of burrows of prairie dogs.
Cf. Dog town.
1774 in Peyton _Adv. Grandfather_ (1867) 121 One of the singular and interesting sights on my route was the villages of the Prairie dogs. **1814** Brackenridge _Views La._ 239, I happened on a village of barking squirrels, or prairie dogs. **1872** Tice _Over Plains_ 144 Out on the vast Plains, . . . the only towns and villages are those of the prairie dog.

4. Attrib. (passing into adj.) and comb. in sense 1 with _academy, bank, bookstore,_ etc. (See also next.)
1863 Norton _Army Lett._ 140 When I left home there was a young lady teaching in the village academy. **1889** Munroe _Golden Days_ 4 A first-class passage . . . swallowed all but a few dollars of the modest sum . . . in the village bank. **1881** _Mich. Gen. Statutes_ I. (1882) 562 They may appeal . . . to the city council or to the village board of trustees, or village council. **1907** Andrews _Recoll._ 165, I obtained permission to send to the village bookstore for a copy of Shakespeare. **1908** White _Riverman_ 32 I'll just get along and bail the boys out of that village calaboose. **1891** _Harper's Mag._ June 112/1 Such a restoration would involve the surrender of village charters. **1818** Paulding _Backwoodsman_ 21 To village church poor Basil bent his way. **1820** _Hillsborough_ (N.C.) _Recorder_ 6 Sept., A fire engine, of the class denominated village engines, may be purchased in Philadelphia for 200 dollars. **1920** Howells _Vacation of Kelwyns_ 106 Her cooking could be ignored in the supplies of canned foods and of baker's bread from the village grocery. **1757** _Waterbury Prop. Rec._ 190 Ye meeting . . . was to Consider about Remeasuring our Lands & also of Disposing of ye village Land. **1746** _Ib._ 164 The Setling the line between Woodbury and Waterbury Against the Village Lots has Altered the Highwayes there. **1840** _Jamestown_ (N.Y.) _Jrnl._ 5 Feb. 2/5, I know not as there is any one system of education in operation, so well calculated to improve the mind, as a village lyceum. **1886** _Century Mag._ May 212/1 A characteristic instance of that way of village-planning which I have already spoken of as peculiarly American. **1812** Marshall _Kentucky_ 110 These are the _village rights._ **1874** Howells _Chance Acquaintance_ 38 Under the porch of the village store some desolate idlers . . . had clubbed their miserable leisure.

Village school. A school conducted in a village. Also attrib. and comb. — **1818** Fessenden _Ladies Monitor_ 124 Learning should never pose a woman's head, . . . Whose wealth and beauty sanction higher aims, Than those of village-school instructing dames. **1848** _Knickerb._ XVIII. 64 Among my early recollections of the primitive days of Stokeville, the Village School is the most vivid. **1855** Barnum _Life_ 179 He had recently lectured them for permitting their children to speak . . . at an exhibition of the village-school. **1893** J. Auld _Picturesque Burlington_ 96 In 1813 three of the town districts were consolidated into what was called the 'Village School District,' which was organized the following year.

+**Vim.** [L., 'strength,' 'vigor.'] Force, energy, dash. Also as _adv._ — **1843** _Yale Lit. Mag._ VIII. 406 He would have acted out his real nature with all the _vim_ and pathos which heroes always manifest in like circumstances. **1850** Lewis _La. Swamp Doctor_ 51 Sudden he thought of his spurs, so he ris up, an' drove them _vim_ in his hoss's flanx. **1866** _Congress. Globe_ 15 Jan. 241/3, I am indebted to it [a journey across the plains] for the vim with which I am now enabled to nail his charges to the floor. **1903** A. Adams _Log of Cowboy_ 307 The morning was cool, every one worked with a vim.

Vinaigrette. A small box or bottle containing aromatic vinegar or some other strong-smelling substance. {1811–} — **1852** Stowe _Uncle Tom_ xvi, Mammy, you shall take my vinaigrette. **1884** 'Craddock' _Where Battle Was Fought_ 237, I think she has a vinaigrette, and I've signalized the occasion by getting up a headache. **1893** M. Howe _Honor_ 76 [On] a low table . . . were placed a lamp, her work-basket, her silver vinaigrette, and a vase of white roses.

* **Vine.**
* **1.** A climbing plant bearing grapes; a grapevine.
1622 'Mourt' _Relation_ 10 They found it to be a small neck of Land; . . . all wooded with Okes, Pines, . . . Vines, some Ash, Walnut. **1676** Glover _Va._ in _Phil. Trans._ XI. 629 In the Woods there are abundance of Vines, which twine about the Oaks and Poplars. **1743** Catesby _Carolina_ App. p. xxii, _Vitis._ The Vine. Grapes are not only spontaneous in Carolina, but all the northern parts of America, from the latitude of 25 to 45. **1785** Marshall _Amer. Grove_ 164. **1831** Peck _Guide_ 138 The indigenous vines are prolific, and produce excellent fruit. **1877** _Rep. Indian Affairs_ 36 Fruit-trees and well-kept vines are not unusual.

* **2. a.** The stem of a climbing or trailing plant. **b.** Any one of various climbing or trailing plants. {_dial.,_ 'any trailing plant, esp. a fruit-bearing one,' 1888–}
Sense b is marked '_U.S._' by the O.E.D., being very rare and local in English dialect use.
1753 Eliot _Field-Husb._ iv. 91 There is a Weed which grows in wet Meadows, and is something like the . . . Vines of Pease. **1785** Washington _Diaries_ II. 361 Seed of a cluster of Red Berrys which looks pretty, and if I recollect right grows on a vine. **1786** _Ib._ III. 116 [They shifted] the tops of the vines from side to side as they hoed. **1817–8** Eaton _Botany_ (1822) 180 _Aristolochia sipho,_ birthwort. . . . A very high running vine, with large leaves: flowers yellowish-brown. **1847** _Knickerb._ XXIX. 197 Of vines, the white and yellow jasmine, the woodbine, and the bamboo are the most frequent. **1854** _Harper's Mag._ IX. 272/2 He saw what appeared to be a great many fine-looking _muskmelons_ on the vines. **1884** Rittenhouse _Maud_ 301 From the hot-house came . . . rustic stands of

trailing vines. **1910** _Atlantic Mo._ Feb., Advt. 48 The trailing vines over the porch.
3. With specifying terms.
See also Alleghany, Balloon vine, Blackberry vine, etc.
1629 Parkinson _Paradisus_ 564 The Virginia Vine . . . beareth small Grapes without any great store of iuice therein. **1708** E. Cook _Sot-Weed Factor_ 19 When sturdy Oaks, and lofty Pines Were level'd with Musmillion Vines. **1731** Miller _Gardeners Dict._ s.v. _Vitis,_ The Virginian Vine or Common Creeper. **1785** Marshall _Amer. Grove_ 165 _Vitis Labrusca._ Wild American Vine. . . . The berries or grapes . . . [are] of an acerb disagreeable taste. **1844** Welby _Poems_ (1867) 163 Sweet jasmine vines, their wreaths were looping Around her bower. **1896** Harris _Sister Jane_ 6 Beyond the door was the window . . . , and a few inches farther the honeysuckle vine hung its fragrant curtain.

* **4.** attrib. and comb. **a.** In the names of insects injurious to vines.
Only a selection of examples is given. American dictionaries contain names of other species. (See also Vinedresser 2.)
1854 Emmons _Agric. N.Y._ V. 268 (index), _Ips,_ or Vine-beetle. **1829** _Va. Lit. Museum_ 169 The names of _pucuron, vine fretter, cabbage louse_ &c. have been employed by naturalists to denominate some of [these insects]. **1854** Emmons _Agric. N.Y._ V. 218 _Sphinx vitis._ Vine Hawkmoth. Wings margined with red, and marked with yellow stripes. **1852** T. W. Harris _Treatise Insects Injur. Veget._ 199 In the autumn the vine-hoppers desert the vines. **1854** Emmons _Agric. N.Y._ V. 270 (index), _Philampelus,_ or Vinelover. **1862** T. W. Harris _Treatise Insects Injur. Veget._ 512 Fir Saw-Fly.—Vine Saw-Fly.—Rosebush Slug.

b. In special combinations.
+_Vine fruit,_ a fruit or berry growing on a vine; _v.-grower,_ one who grows grapes {1835, of ancient Greece}; _v.-planter,_ a vine-grower; +_v. rake,_ (see quotation).
1705 Beverley _Virginia_ IV. 56 They have several Roots, Herbs, Vine-fruits, and Sallad-flowers peculiar to themselves. **1856** _Rep. Comm. Patents 1855: Agric._ 261 The small expense of planting vineyards, in Cuyahoga county, literally astonishes the vine-growers of the southern part of the State. **1741** W. Stephens _Proc. Georgia_ II. 185 Grapes now ripening apace, our Vine-Planters began to pride themselves, in setting a good Value on what Stock they had. **1876** Knight 2710/2 _Vine-rake,_ an implement for pulling sweet-potato or other vines off from the ridges preparatory to the digging of the ground.

* **Vinedresser. 1.** One whose business or duty it is to cultivate or train and prune grapevines. +**2.** (See quotation.) — (1) **1812** _Niles' Reg._ II. 181/1 They have consequently given orders to their vine dresser, to propagate and cultivate this kind with avidity, in the company's vineyard. **1862** _Rep. Comm. Patents 1861: Agric._ 516 The slightest indication of frost . . . should keep the vine-dresser on the alert to watch the temperature. **1899** Going _Flowers_ 243 Among those borne by the grape the vine-dresser finds every gradation. (2) **1891** _Cent._ 6758/2 _Vine-dresser,_ . . . the larva of a sphingid moth, _Ampelophaga_ (_Darapsa_ or _Everyx_) _myron._ It cuts off the leaves of the vine in the United States, and also sometimes severs half-grown bunches of grapes.

* **Vinegar.**
* **1.** A sour liquid resulting from the acetic fermentation of wine, cider, or some other juice, used for preserving or seasoning food.
1649 _Conn. Rec._ I. 497 An Inventory of the Estate of Mr. William Whiting. . . . Oyle, soape, vinegar. **1709** Lawson _Carolina_ 110 Of this sort [of peach], we make Vinegar. **1817** _Holyoke Diaries_ 166 Strong vineagar & spirit & water frozen in closet by the chimney. **1884** F. E. Owens _Cook Book_ 414 [Recipe for] Cough Syrup. One pint best vinegar [etc.].
2. Preceded by descriptive or defining term.
See also Cider vinegar.
1662 _Essex Probate Rec._ I. 391 Wine viniger, 1 li.; ould caske, 10 s. **1861** Jackson in M. A. Jackson _Gen. Jackson_ 194, I received . . . a bottle of blackberry vinegar from the Misses B——. **1875** _Chicago Tribune_ 27 Sept. 1/2 White wine vinegar celebrated for its purity, strength and palatableness. **1882** F. E. Owens _Cook Book_ 291 Honey Vinegar. . . . Clover Bloom Vinegar. _Ib._ 292 Apple Vinegar. . . . Potato Vinegar. . . . Currant Vinegar. **1889** Beet-root vinegar [see Beetroot 2].
3. In attributive use.
a. Designating fruits and plants from which vinegar is made. {1677} See also Vinegar tree. ***b.** Designating vessels or containers for vinegar. **c.** Designating establishments in which vinegar is made or sold. {1842} **d.** Designating foods and other preparations made with vinegar.
(a) **1709** Vinegar-Peach [see Indian peach]. [**1797** _Encycl. Brit._ (ed. 3) XVI. 228/1 [The] Virginian sumach, or vinegar plant, grows naturally in almost every part of North America.] **1895** _Outing_ XXVI. 394/1 Branches of reddening vinegar cherries and sprays of sweet fern. (b) **1747** Franklin _Exper. on Electricity_ 5 This is best done by a vinegar cruet. **1867** Harris _Sut Lovingood_ 92 Pickil crocks, perserves jars, vinegar jugs, . . . all mix'd dam permiskusly. **1874** B. F. Taylor _World on Wheels_ 166 He looked as if he had been getting those features all ready to be poured . . . into a vinegar-barrel. (c) **1851** Cist _Cincinnati_ 251 Vinegar Factories.—This is a business of comparatively recent establishment. **1883** Peck _Boy_ 41 His breath smelled all the time like in front of a vinegar store, where they keep yeast. (d) **1868** _Ore. State Jrnl._ 8 Aug. 3/3 Dr. Walker's Vinegar Bitters is a perfect Renovator of the System. **1876** M. F. Hen-

DERSON *Cooking* 306 Vinegar Candy.... Three cupfuls of sugar, half a cupful of vinegar [etc.]. **1884** F. E. OWENS *Cook Book* 185 [Recipe for] Vinegar Pie. **1907** ANDREWS *Recoll.* (1928) 202 During the short time I was at Galveston, I saw sliced tomatoes served with rum instead of vinegar dressing.

+**Vinegarroon, Vinegerone.** [Sp. *vinagre* 'vinegar.'] A whip scorpion, esp. a large species (*Mastigoproctus giganteus*) regarded as venomous. Also fig. — **1891** *Cent.* 6758/3 *Vinegerone* . . . : so called on account of the strong vinegar-like odor of an acid secretion noticeable when the creature is alarmed. **1900** WEBSTER *Suppl.* 229/1. [**1914** *Blackwood's Mag.* July 123/1 His late breaking-in, the lengthy vacation [etc.], . . . keep the 'vinegarone' in his [a bronco's] composition.]

Vinegar tree. (See quot. 1891 and cf. STAGHORN SUMAC(H).) — [**1874** LINDLEY & MOORE *Treas. Botany* 1350/2 Vinegar-tree, *Rhus typhina*.] **1891** *Cent.* 6758/3 *Vinegar-tree,* . . . the stag-horn sumac, *Rhus typhina,* the acid fruit of which has been used to add sourness to vinegar.

+**Vine maple. 1.** A small tree (*Acer circinatum*) of the Pacific Northwest, the stems of which are often prostrate. Also attrib. **2.** (See quotation.) — **(1) 1872** [see SEQUOIA]. **1873** MILLER *Amongst Modocs* 21 It was a vine-maple thicket. **1874** GLISAN *Jrnl. Army Life* 480 The Coast Range . . . is covered with evergreen forests . . . intermixed at places with white maple, vine maple, Oregon alder, balsam tree. **1892** APGAR *Trees Northern U.S.* 88 Round-leaved or Vine Maple.... A small tree or tall shrub . . . ; cultivated; from the Pacific coast. **(2) 1909** *Cent. Suppl.* 770/1 *Vine-maple,* . . . the Canada moonseed, *Menispermum Canadense.*

***Vinery. 1.** A structure, as a glasshouse, for the cultivation of grapes. {1789-} +**2.** *collect.* Vines. — **(1) 1851** BARRY *Fruit Garden* 253 Culture of foreign Grapes in cold vineries. **1852** *Horticulturist* VII. 94, I respond with pleasure to your wishes respecting the description and management of the cold vinery, erected two years ago, . . . by my employer J. C. Green, Esq. *Ib.* 219 By having one end of the vinery . . . terminated by an enclosed shed. **(2) 1883** *Century Mag.* Sept. 729 Latticed porticoes . . . , overgrown with masses of vinery—feign romance rather than [realism]. **1895** *Outing* XXVI. 445/1 Its ruins . . . are overgrown with vinery and bushes.

***Vineyard.**

***1. A plantation of grapevines.**

1619 *Va. House of Burgesses* 10 Be it enacted . . . that every householder doe yearly plante and maintaine ten vines, untill they have attained to the arte & experience of dressing a vineyard. **1771** *Md. Hist. Mag.* XIII. 174, I shall plant what Layers & Cuttings I have in my Vineyard. **1863** *Horticulturist* XVIII. 374/1 The progress in vineyards near Bloomington is a very good one. **1884** W. SHEPHERD *Prairie Exper.* 127 There are many large vineyards cultivated by Chinese coolies. **1923** HERRICK *Lilla* 36 Across the road was a large vineyard.

2. Used as a place name.

1647 *Suffolk Deeds* I. 86, I Thomas Paine sonne of Thomas Paine . . . doe now make choise of Thomas Mayhew now of the Vineyard in N: England merchant . . . & Jane his wife . . . to be my Guardians. **1720** *Providence Rec.* XVI. 351, I Give and bequeathe to my beloved Daughter . . . my four Rights in an Jsland Called the vinyard. **1782** CRÈVECŒUR *Letters* 164 At the Vineyard . . . they are equally well situated for the fishing business. **1902** *R.I. Hist. Soc. Coll.* X. 396 Vineyard, an island in the Pawtuxet River.... [It] is still known by its original name.

3. Attrib. with *can, cart, society.*

1713 SEWALL *Diary* II. 404, I had spilt a whole Vineyard Cann of water just before we went to Bed. **1813** *Western Gleaner* (Pittsburgh) I. 31 The attempts, however, made by the American Vineyard Society near Philadelphia . . . deserve the greatest praise. **1838** FLAGG *Far West* II. 140 The same implements of husbandry and the arts which a century since were seen in France, are now seen here [Kaskaskia, Ill.]; the very vehicle they drive is the vineyard-cart.

+**Vineyarding.** The cultivation of grapevines. — **1870** *Congregationalist* 19 May (*Cent.*), Profits of vineyarding in California.

+**Vineyardist.** One who cultivates grapevines. — **1848** *Rep. Comm. Patents 1847* 199 A French wine maker and vineyardist came from Kentucky, where he had long been living. **1868** *Iowa State Agric. Soc. Rep.* 1867 199 Mr. Seevers . . . gave the whole matter into the hands of Mr. Amos Kemble, a practical horticulturist and vineyardist of this city. **1885** *Advance* 9 July 443 Many of the large vineyardists manufacture wine on their own account. **1897** L. H. BAILEY *Prin. Fruit-Growing* 291 Careful vineyardists are able to continue the practice [of girdling] year after year without apparent injury to the vine.

Vingt et un, Vingtun. A card game in which the individual player tries to secure cards approaching as nearly as possible, but not exceeding, twenty-one in total value. {vingt-un, 1804-; vingt-et-un, 1853-} — See also VANTOON. — **1808** C. SCHULTZ *Travels* II. 61 Whenever there is a ball given by even the most rigid and superstitious of the catholics, there is always one room set apart for gambling. *Vingt-un* is the game. **1833** J. STUART *Three Years N.A.* II. 160 Brag and *vingt-un* are the games which are generally played. **1872** *Harper's Mag.* Dec. 95 Many of these establishments had club-rooms attached, where members of Congress and others amused themselves with brag, vingt-et-un, and whist. **1888** *Scribner's Mag.* Jan. 27/1 Sometimes, when Si lost too much at vingt-et-un, he borrowed of his sister.

+**Vining,** *a.* Of a plant: Growing in the manner of a vine; twining. — **1804** LEWIS in *L. & Clark Exped.* VI. (1905) 148 The vining honesuckle which bears a red flour is also common to the Illinois. **1806** CLARK *Ib.*

IV. (1904) 13 The Vineing or low brown berry, a light brown berry rather larger and much the Shape of a black haw. **1897** *Voice* 4 March 5/3 The vining maples twined in so close . . . that we had to get right in the water and follow up the stream.

***Vinter.** =next. *Obs.* — **1671** *Plymouth Laws* 287 Nor shall any vinter or Tavern gain more than eight pence . . . more than it cost them by the Butte or Cask. **1683** *Boston Rec.* X. 73 John Winge, vinter, became Surety to the town for Joshua Bradburne, horne breaker.

***Vintner.** A wine merchant. *Obs.* — **1648** *Mass. Bay Rec.* II. 253 The vintners of Boston . . . expressed their desires for an abatement upon the imposition . . . layed upon such as sell wine by retayle. **1715** *Boston News Letter* 23 May 2/2 Mary Mason Wife of Mr. Alexander Mason . . . , Vintner, . . . Departed and Elop'd from her said Husband. **1734** in Earle *Colonial Days N.Y.* 214 The Consort will begin precisely at six o'clock in the house of Robert Todd vintner.

Violative, *a.* Tending toward, constituting, or causing violation. {1878} ('Chiefly *U.S.*' *O.E.D.*) — **1856** PIERCE in *Pres. Mess. & P.* V. 407 No act shall remain on its statute book, violative of the provisions of the Constitution. **1891** *Nation* 24 Dec. 495/2 Four of the judges held that the act was violative of the amendments, and therefore invalid. **1914** *Supreme Ct. Rep.* CCXXXVIII. 371 The Grandfather's Clause is not violative of the Fifteenth Amendment.

+**Violent Whig.** A member of a group opposed to the Federalists at the end of the American Revolution. Now hist. (Cf. LIBERTY BOYS.) — **1872** *Harper's Mag.* April 692/2 The Liberty Boys, or 'Violent Whigs,' as they were called, [constituted the Anti-Federalists].

***Violet,** *n.* A plant or flower belonging to, or resembling plants or flowers belonging to, the genus *Viola.*

See also BIRD'S-FOOT VIOLET, BLUE VIOLET, etc.

1612 SMITH, etc. *Virginia* I. 12 Many hearbes in the spring time there are . . . as Violets, Purslin, Sorrell, &c. **1683** *Mass. H. S. Coll.* 4 Ser. V. 113 We take strawberry-leaves, five-finger, violet, columbine, black-brier leaves, sorrel,—of each, a like quantity boiled in spring water. **1792** IMLAY *Western Territory* 207 Every part of the country abounds in . . . marshmallows, violets, roses of different sorts, &c. **1815** *Lit. & Phil. Soc. N.Y. Trans.* I. 172 Our Dutch forefathers . . . introduced . . . lily of the valley, ladies' rose, violet, and gold flower. **1841** *Lowell Offering* I. 203 You can find plenty of violets near by the rose bushes. **1883** *Harper's Mag.* Aug. 428/2 The buttercup, the dandelion, and the ox-eyed daisy [are] displacing the anemone and violet. **1922** TARKINGTON *Gentle Julia* 56 The widower came, holding out to her a votive cluster of violets, a pink rose among them.

***Violet,** *a.* In the specific names of plants.

1814 BIGELOW *Florula Bostoniensis* 171 *Hedysarum violaceum.* Violet Hedysarum. **1817-8** EATON *Botany* (1822) 371 *Oxalis violacea,* violet wood-sorrel. **1833** SILLIMAN *Man. Sugar Cane* 10 The third and last, principal variety is the Violet Cane. **1840** DEWEY *Mass. Flowering Plants* 74 *O[xalis] violacea.* Sheep Sorrel. Violet Sorrel.... Blossoms in May, in fields. **1843** TORREY *Flora N.Y.* II. 518 *Aster concolor.* Racemed Violet Aster.... Dry sandy soils, Queens county, Long Island. **1901** MOHR *Plant Life Ala.* 524 *Iodanthus pinnatifidus.*... Violet Rocket.... Alleghenian to Carolinian area.

Violet-green, *a.* In the specific names of birds. — **1839** AUDUBON *Ornith. Biog.* V. 148 Violet-green Cormorant, *Phalacrocorax Resplendens,* . . . the most beautiful hitherto found within the limits of the United States. **1858** Violet-Green Swallow [see SWALLOW *n.*[1] 2].

***Violin.** (See also FIRST VIOLIN and cf. FIDDLE.)

***1. A well-known stringed musical instrument played with a bow.**

1735 in Singleton *Social. N.Y.* 297 The Songs, Violins and German Flute by private Hands. **1771** FRANKLIN *Autobiog.* 234 When he played psalm tunes on his violin . . . it was extremely agreeable to hear. **1792** BENTLEY *Diary* I. 418 For the first time in this place the Clarionet, & violin, introduced into Church Music. **1829** ROYALL *Pennsylvania* I. 103 You hear the violin or Piana Fort, of an evening, almost in every house. **1885** ROE *Army Lett.* 339 We have two violins . . . , oboe, and bassoon, the latter instrument giving the deep organ tones. **1916** PORTER *David* 2 There were . . . two violins with their cases, and . . . scattered sheets of music.

2. Attrib. with *bow, bridge, contest, string.*

1759 *Newport Mercury* 26 June 4/3 Imported . . . and to be sold by Jacob Richardson, . . . best Roman Violin Strings. **1773** in Singleton *Social N.Y.* 294 [Rivington had] violin bows, the Giardini sort. **1835** *Simpson's Boston Directory* Advt. 14 Musical Instruments, Viz.... Violin Bridges and Pegs, Pitch Pipes, Music Paper. **1872** *Atlantic Mo.* Jan. 23 The prominence assigned to the violin contest . . . explains the frequent allusions to it in the early memorials of Virginia.

Violinist. A performer on the violin. {c1670-} Cf. FIDDLER 1. — **1844** HONE *Diary* II. 231 The party at dinner [included] . . . Ole Bull, the celebrated Norwegian violinist. **1887** BILLINGS *Hardtack* 69 There was probably not a regiment in the service that did not boast at least one violinist, one banjoist, and a bone player in its ranks. **1907** *St. Nicholas* June 715/1 He thought the world of Fritzi and had set his heart on making her a great violinist.

Violoncellist. A performer on the violoncello. {1835-} — **1884** *American* VIII. 94 Our own clever violoncellist, Mr. Hennig.

Violoncello. A stringed instrument resembling the violin but considerably larger and tuned to a lower range. {1724-} — **1773** in Singleton *Social N.Y.* 295 [Rivington had] the best Italian strings for violins; violoncellos; genuine German wire for harpsichords. **1818** [see FIDDLE 1]. **1888** CABLE *Bonaventure* 28 You have your pipe or cigar, your flute or violoncello.

Viometer. (See VIAMETER.)

＊Viper.

＊1. Any one of various venomous, supposedly venomous, or repulsive snakes.

Often construed as excluding rattlesnakes and other pit vipers, which are sometimes included in the viper family.

1709 LAWSON *Carolina* 133 Of those we call Vipers, there are two sorts. . . . One is reckon'd amongst the worst of Snakes, for Venom. **1791** W. BARTRAM *Travels* 274 There are many other species of snakes in the regions of Florida and Carolina, as . . . two or three varieties of vipers. **1827** WILLIAMS *W. Florida* 28 The rattlesnake, moccasin, and viper, are all dangerous snakes, and highly poisonous; but they are very rare. **1888** [see FLATHEAD *n.* 2].

2. With specifying or limiting terms.

See also *Blowing viper* (under BLOWING *ppl. a.* 1), WATER VIPER.

1736 CATESBY *Carolina* II. 44/1 The black Viper . . . is short and thick, of slow Motion. *Ib.* 45 *Vipera fusca.* The Brown Viper. . . . They are found in Virginia and Carolina. **1859** BARTLETT 99 Copperhead. (*Trigonocephalus contortrix.*) . . . It has various other popular names, as Copperbelly, Red Viper, Red Adder. **1890** *Cent.* 4518/3 *Pit-viper,* . . . a venomous serpent of the family *Crotalidæ,* as a rattlesnake; a pit-headed viper. **1891** *Ib.* 5333/1 *Sand-viper,* . . . a hog-nosed snake. . . . (Local, U.S.)

3. Used attrib. with *fish, mouth,* to designate a deepwater fish (*Chauliodus sloani*) of the Atlantic Ocean.

1743 CATESBY *Carolina* II. App. 19 *Vipera Marina,* the Viper-Mouth. This Fish is eighteen inches in length. **1891** *Cent.* 6763/1 *Viper-fish,* . . . a deep-sea fish of Mediterranean and Atlantic waters.

＊Viper's bugloss. A weed (*Echium vulgare*) of European origin. — **1814** BIGELOW *Florula Bostoniensis* 47 Vipers Bugloss. . . . Spikes . . . [bear] a row of crowded purplish flowers. **1843, 1847** [see BLUEWEED 1]. **1889** *Cent.* 712/1 The viper's-bugloss, *Echium vulgare,* . . . [has] rough leaves.

+Vireo. [L., a species of bird: (see sense 1, quot. 1917).]

1. Any one of various small American birds constituting the family Vireonidae.

1834 AUDUBON *Ornith. Biog.* II. 287 The Vireos quench their thirst with the drops of dew or rain that adhere to the leaves or twigs. **1868** BEECHER *Norwood* 130 The vireo, in the tops of the elm, hushed its shrill snatches. **1880** *Harper's Mag.* June 79 Pert little vireos hop inquisitively about you. **1917** *Birds of Amer.* III. 102 Vireos are sometimes called Greenlets; the Latin word *Vireo* means 'I am green.'

2. With descriptive or specifying terms.

Only a few examples are included. See also BELL'S VIREO, *Brotherly-love vireo* (under BROTHERLY *a.* 2), etc.

1839 AUDUBON *Ornith. Biog.* V. 432 Solitary Vireo, *Vireo solitarius.* **1856** CASSIN *N. Amer. Birds* Pl. 24 The Black-headed Vireo, *Vireo atricapillus.* **1866** *Auk* III. 111 *Vireo solitarius alticola,* . . . Mountain Solitary Vireo. . . . This new form may be easily distinguished from *solitarius* by its larger size. **1887** RIDGWAY *Manual N.A. Birds* 478 Southern California, Arizona, New Mexico, western Texas, and northwestern Mexico. . . . *V. vicinior.* Gray Vireo. **1917** *Birds of Amer.* III. 111 The Texas Vireo (*Vireo belli medius*) is found in southwestern Texas.

+Vireosylvia. [mod. L. *vireo* (see prec.) and *sylvia* 'forest.'] A genus of large vireos having a relatively slender bill. — **1871** BURROUGHS *Wake-Robin* (1886) 59 The vireosylvia is classed among the fly-catchers by some writers. **1891** *Cent.* 6764/1.

+Virgalieu. (See VERGALOO.)

Virgilia. a. The yellowwood (*Cladrastis lutea*), formerly referred to the genus *Virgilia.* **b.** The Kentucky coffee tree. — **1846** BROWNE *Trees Amer.* 192 *Cladrastis tinctoria,* The Virgilia, or Yellow-Wood. **1883** *Harper's Mag.* April 732/1 On this third lawn is a collection of magnolias, a fine specimen of virgilia, a tall tulip-tree, [etc.]. **1897** SUDWORTH *Arborescent Flora* 255 *Gymnocladus dioicus.* . . . Coffeetree. . . . Virgilia (Tenn.).

＊Virgin, *n.* and *a.*

I. *n.* **1.** Used in possessive in names of plants.

See also VIRGIN'S-BOWER.

1873 *Harper's Mag.* April 752 Lilacs, laburnums, virgin's-grace, And passion-flower in blue and lace. **1888** CABLE *Bonaventure* 7 They came under the spell of . . . that grass ribbon they call jarretière de la vierge,—the virgin's garter.

II. *attrib.* passing into *adj.* **2.** Of various substances: Occurring in nature in a pure state; unworked, or subjected to only slight working. {1611–}

1775 *Jrnls. Cont. Congress.* III. 456 Committee for inquiring after Virgin Lead . . . appointed. **1789** MORSE *Amer. Geog.* 37 This river is remarkable for the abundance of virgin copper that is found on and near its banks. *Ib.* 265 There is a silver mine at Phillipsburg, which produces virgin silver. **1891** *Cent.* 6764/3 *Virgin clay,* in industrial arts, . . . clay that has never been molded or fired, as distinguished from the ground substance of old ware, which is often mixed with it. **1893** SANBORN *S. Calif.* 155 [He] has perfected a machine which expresses the 'virgin oil' without cracking a single pit or stone.

3. Of an area, region, etc.: Unused or unworked by man; unfished. {1851–}

1827 COOPER *Prairie* i, A few sought the mines of the virgin territory. *Ib.* xi, Aquatic birds . . . were pursuing their customary annual journey from the virgin lakes. **1879** *Scribner's Mo.* Nov. 22/2 It was virgin water; no fly had heretofore been cast on it. **1893** *Harper's Mag.* March 601 The air was filled with delicate wild odors, a fragrance which is like no other—the breath of a virgin forest. **1916** EASTMAN *From Deep Woods* 173 On Rainy Lake, . . . I found the true virgin wilderness, the final refuge, . . . of American big game.

4. Of land: Untilled; not yet brought into cultivation. {1744–}

1830 WATSON *Philadelphia* 718 When our forefathers began to work this virgin soil, they found it very productive. **1869** *Rep. Comm. Agric. 1868* 18 [The present practice] will doubtless continue in vogue till our virgin wheat lands are run over by pioneers. **1884** *Century Mag.* Jan. 435/2 Virgin land was without any known limit, and the climate was congenial.

5. In special combinations. (See also DIP *n.* 6 b.)

+*Virgin cane,* the small cane, *Arundinaria tecta; v. dance,* +a ceremonial dance performed by young men within a circle of Indian maidens.

1863 *Ill. Agric. Soc. Trans.* V. 866 The smaller variety or perhaps species [of cane] . . . was called the Virgin Cane. **1847** LANMAN *Summer in Wilderness* 106 There had been a Virgin Dance.

Virginia. Also †**Virginny.** [L. fem. name. Used with allusion to Queen Elizabeth as the 'Virgin Queen.'] A name applied orig. to a vaguely defined region along the eastern coast of North America, and later to an area between the present states of Maryland and North Carolina, or to the colony or state of Virginia, formerly including West Virginia. (See also OLD VIRGINIA.)

I. 1. Tobacco produced in Virginia; American tobacco.

[**1624** Smith *Gen. Hist. Va.* IV. 126 There are so many sofisticating Tobaco-mungers in England, were it neuer so bad, they would sell it for Verinas, and the trash that remaineth should be Virginia.] **1872** HAWTHORNE *S. Felton* (1883) 301 [A] German pipe . . . puffed out volumes of smoke, filling the pleasant western breeze with the fragrance of some excellent Virginia.

+2. English as spoken in Virginia.

1825 NEAL *Bro. Jonathan* I. 179 Why do you talk 'Virginny'—that vile gibberish?

II. In attributive use.

Cf. VIRGINIAN *a.* In the separate entries which follow sense 12, forms with *Virginian* are included with those with *Virginia.*

3. Designating mineral products or veins.

See also VIRGINIA COAL.

1676 GLOVER *Va.* in *Phil. Trans.* XI. 627, I have seen several Rings of Virginia stones, which in my judgment have equalled Diamonds in lustre. **1877** W. WRIGHT *Big Bonanza* 53 This vein is known as the Virginia lead or Virginia croppings. **1895** M. A. JACKSON *Gen. Jackson* 633 The pedestal is of Virginia granite.

4. Designating persons living in or coming from Virginia, or groups consisting of Virginians or operating in Virginia.

See also VIRGINIA LINE c.

1697 in W. S. Perry *Hist. Coll. Amer. Col. Church* I. 20 Sir Edmund prevailed with his Virginia friends . . . to make as good compositions with the Governors of the College as they could. **1724** H. JONES *Virginia* 38 The Virginia Planters readily learn to become good Mechanicks in Building. **1757** *Md. Gazette* 22 Sept., Thomas Frazier . . . getting into some Dispute in a Tavern with an Officer of the Virginia Regiment, the Officer gave him a Blow. **1768** in *S. Lit. Messenger* XXIII. 37 By the Virginia Company of Comedians On Friday the 3d of June will be presented The Beggar's Opera. **1808** WEEMS *Washington* (1840) 42 The Virginia Rangers discovered signs of Indians. **1817** WEEMS *Letters* III. 196 Mr. Bertrand was as conceited a Virginia Fop as ever squeezed himself out at the little end of a horn. **1839** BIRD *Robin Day* 56 They were beef-eating Britons and not fever and aguy Virginee Yankees. **1855** COOKE *Ellie* 113 Mr. Sansoucy, the son of a Virginia Huguenot, was a man of twenty-five or thirty. **1856** BAGBY *Old Va. Gentleman* 220 In his personal appearance, the Virginia editor vibrates between positive gentility and absolute shabbiness. **1881** *Harper's Mag.* April 732/1 Her Virginia husband, with his English descent, would call her 'Eugenia' instead of 'Eugénie.'

5. Designating foods or food products found in, or characteristic of, Virginia.

See also VIRGINIA HAM.

1774 J. HARROWER *Diary* 76 He brought . . . with him four Barrells Virginia Pork. **1817** PAULDING *Lett. from South* I. 196, I confess to [liking] the Virginia venison. **1832** *Louisville Pub. Adv.* 3 March, 50 barrels superfine Virginia family flour . . . for sale. **1844** FEATHERSTONHAUGH *Slave States* 161 Virginia bread . . . is made up into so many forms, and is so white, and light, and excellent, that it is impossible . . . to make a bad repast. *c*1866 BAGBY *Old Va. Gentleman* 68 He will be able to give his friends . . . a dish of real old Virginia 'Bacon and Greens.' **1897** *Voice* 9 Sept. 7/3 Virginia picklet is made of four heads of cabbage, chopt fine, and a quart of white onions.

6. Designating implements or other equipment used in, or characteristic of, Virginia.

1790 *Penna. Packet* 31 May 3/4 Nicodemus Loyd, . . . has now for sale, . . . large Virginia hoes, suitable to hoe rice or tobacco. **1807** *Goss Journal* 209 This lodge is built much after the form of the Virginia fodder houses. **1849** WIERZBICKI *California* 47 They are getting out from $1500 to $2,000 per week, working with mercury in the Virginia rocker. **1866** RICHARDSON *Secret Service* 186 A long caravan of old-fashioned Virginia wagons . . . passed through town yesterday.

7. Designating attitudes, customs, dances, etc., characteristic of the people of Virginia.

See also VIRGINIA REEL, OLD VIRGINIA BREAKDOWN and cf. VIRGINIANISM.

1796 WEEMS *Letters* II. 39, I hope you have not . . . lost sight of the Virginia fondness for pretty binding. **1803** J. DAVIS *Travels* 379 Pat Hickory could tire him at a Virginia Jig. **1825** NEAL *Bro. Jonathan* I. 88 Will you never break yourself pray of these abominable Virginia habits? **1869** *Atlantic Mo.* July 72/2 When I executed my 'Juba' dance, or in company with others performed the Virginia Walk-around, these honest Germans would . . . rush precipitately into the middle of the street.

8. Designating political factions, principles, etc., associated with Virginia.

1833 *Congress. Deb.* 24 Jan. 1338 Whenever the doctrines of 'State rights,' as insisted upon by the Virginia school, are acted out, they must necessarily end in nullification and State rebellion. **1843** in Hambleton *H. A. Wise* 41 He intended contempt and derision of 'Virginia abstractions,' or of a strict construction of our glorious Federal Constitution. **1855** *Ib.* 183, I see nothing inconsistent with those unchanged and unchangeable principles of state rights Virginia republicanism which I have always cherished. **1913** A. C. COLE *Whig Party in So.* 65 Even should Tyler, as a state rights man and a 'Virginia abstractionist,' offer opposition . . . it would be but to detach himself from the great body of the Whig party. **1914** *Cycl. Amer. Govt.* III. 622 *Virginia Dynasty*, a name given by opponents of Virginia's domination of national affairs to the men from Virginia (Jefferson, Madison, Monroe) who filled the presidency from 1801 to 1825.

9. Designating bodies of persons representing, in various capacities, the people of Virginia.

1841 *Niles' Nat. Reg.* 30 Jan. 336/2 The Virginia annual conference of the Methodist Episcopal church commenced its session . . . yesterday. **1855** in Hambleton *H. A. Wise* 38 All the above named gentlemen, together with the entire Virginia delegation in Congress, will support Mr. Wise. **1855** *Ib.* 187, I do not understand the Virginia American party to be in favor of either. **1861** F. MOORE *Rebellion Rec.* I. iii. 40 In the Virginia Convention, . . . Mr. Carlisle suggested that a . . . committee should be sent to Montgomery. **1862** McCLELLAN in *Own Story* 349 The resolutions of the Virginia legislature . . . give positive assurance that our approach to Richmond involves a desperate battle. **1881** *Nation* 2 June 379/2 The Virginia Readjuster Convention meets to-day.

10. In names of animals, birds, fishes, etc.

See also VIRGINIA DEER, NIGHTINGALE, etc.

1884 *Nat. Museum Bul.* No. 27, 633 The Virginia Blackfish is believed by Professor Cope to be a distinct species, which he has designated as *G. brachypterus*. **1917** *Birds of Amer.* III. 63 Novels have been written in which the Virginia Cardinal and the Kentucky Cardinal . . . have given a tone of aristocratic elegance. [**1706** PHILLIPS *New World of Words* (ed. 6), *Virginia-Frog*, a kind of Frog that is eight or ten times as big as any in England, and makes a noise like the bellowing of a Bull.] **1839** MARRYAT *Diary in Amer.* 1 Ser. II. 172 There is no want of handsome equipages, many four in hand (Virginny long tails). **1881** INGERSOLL *Oyster Industry* 248 *Soft Oyster.*—The 'Virginia plant,' or southern oyster (Staten Island sound), as distinguished from the 'hard' native oyster. **1897** *N.Y. Forest, Fish, & Game Comm. 2d Rep.* 317 Popular synonyms [for the bob-white]: . . . Virginia quail; partridge or colin. **1895** *Century Mag.* Aug. 626/2 The Virginia red fox had already fashioned Lead [a dog]. **1724** JONES *Virginia* 42 Their Pork is famous, whole Virginia Shoots being frequently barbacued in England. **1609** in Smith *Works* (1910) p. c, I tould him of the Virginia squirills which they say will fly.

11. In names of plants or varieties of plants, or their fruits.

Many other examples may be found in Parkinson's *Paradisus* and *Theater of Plants*. (See also VIRGINIA CORN, VIRGINIA CREEPER, etc.)

1843 TORREY *Flora N.Y.* I. 102 *Silene Virginica*. Virginia Catchfly. . . . Sometimes employed in the Western States (where it is common) as an anthelmintic. **1825** LORAIN *Pract. Husbandry* 203 The ears of the Virginia gourdseed are not very long. **1781–2** JEFFERSON *Notes Va.* (1788) 39 Virginia hemp. *Acnida cannabina.* **1901** MOHR *Plant Life Ala.* 486 *Polygonum virginianum.* . . . Virginia Knotweed. . . . Ontario, southern New England, west to Nebraska, south to Florida, Louisiana, Arkansas, and Missouri. **1839** *Mich. Agric. Soc. Trans.* VII. 408 *Gaura biennis.* Virginia loosestrife. **1801** *Hist. Review & Directory* I. 144 Virginia Marshmallow, *Napæa hermaphrodita.* **1784** *Amer. Acad. Mem.* I. 410 *Plantago.* . . . Virginia Plantain. In grass land. Not common. **1672** JOSSELYN *New Eng. Rarities* 45 Salomons-Seal, of which there is three kinds; the first common in England, the second, Virginia Salomons-Seal. **1848** BARTLETT 366 *Tuckahoe.* . . . The Virginia truffle. A curious Vegetable, sometimes called

by the name of Indian bread, or Indian Loaf, found in the Southern States.

b. Of trees or shrubs or their fruit.

See also VIRGINIA MULBERRY (TREE), PINE, WINTERBERRY.

1811 SUTCLIFF *Travels* (1815) 273 He gave us a taste of his cyder, made from a species of apple, called the Virginia Crab. **1839** AUDUBON *Ornith. Biog.* V. 71 The nest was in a low, thick, and stunted Virginia juniper. **1856** *Rep. Comm. Patents 1855: Agric.* 293 The best apples for this region are the 'Early Harvest,' 'Virginia May,' 'Virginia Red,' 'June Red,' [etc.]. **1860** DARLINGTON *Weeds & Plants* 131 C[ratœgus] cordata. . . . Washington Thorn. Virginia Thorn. . . . It makes a handsome hedge, but not a very substantial one.

c. Designating tobacco, or varieties of tobacco, produced in Virginia.

See also VIRGINIA TOBACCO, VIRGINIA WEED.

1859 *Harper's Mag.* April 611/1 While he vigorously executed the Virginia reel, they devoted themselves to 'Virg'nia twist.' **1866** MOORE *Woman of War* 506 A young lady of the city made him a present in the form of a pretty bag filled with 'Virginia fine cut.' **1867** J. O. PHISTER *Mason County Tobacco* 14 If you were to get the Virginia or Clarksville seed . . . and cure by fire as they do, you would make the same kind of tobacco. **1871** *Atlantic Mo.* Nov. 566 The circle enjoyed itself socially,—taciturnity and clouds of Virginia plug reigning supreme. **1878** DALY in J. F. Daly *A. Daly* 250 The little tobacco shop . . . where you invested Santa Claus's money that fatal Christmas in your first & last plug of Virginia Honey-Comb.

12. In special combinations. Chiefly *U.S.*

Virginia-bred, reared in Virginia; *V. code*, the legal code effective in Virginia; *V. coupon cases*, (see quotation); *V. dynasty*, a name given by their political opponents to Jefferson, Madison, and Monroe, all from Virginia, who as presidents of the United States dominated national affairs from 1801 to 1825; *V. gap*, an opening in a range of Virginia hills or mountains; *V. mud*, muddy soil in Virginia; *V. patent*, the land granted to the Virginia Company; *V. poorhouse*, (see quotation); *V. post*, the mail from Virginia; *V. race horse*, a race horse bred in Virginia; *V. resolve*, a resolution passed by a legislative body in Virginia.

1854 COOKE *Va. Comedians* I. 46 When the Virginia-bred youths . . . called them 'ridiculous,' the young ladies, their companions, took Mr. Effingham's part. **1865** *Ore. State Jrnl.* 18 Nov. 2/5 One of the civil courts sentenced a negro to be whipped under the old Virginia code. **1889** *Cent.* 841/2 *Virginia coupon cases*, the generic name under which are known a number of suits determined by the United States Supreme Court in 1884, enforcing a Virginia statute which declared coupons on bonds of that State receivable in payment of State taxes, notwithstanding the repeal of that statute. **1812** *Columbian Centinel* 7 Nov. 2/3 Those who pourtrayed the characters and exposed the plots of the *Virginia Dynasty*, understood their men, and were Oracles of truth. **1823** COOPER *Pioneer* xvi, You must go into the Virginy gaps, if you want them [sc. wild turkeys] now. **1884** *Century Mag.* Nov. 108 Nothing except 'Virginia mud' ever took down my ideas of military pomp quite so low. *a*1656 BRADFORD *Hist.* 55 Sundrie Honbl: Lords had obtained a large grante from ye king, for ye more northerly parts of that countrie, derived out of ye Virginia patente. **1910** J. HART *Vigilante Girl* 31 There are so many Southerners in the custom-house that people call it the 'Virginia poorhouse.' **1745** *Md. Gazette* 30 Aug., By the Virginia Post of Wednesday Last, among other articles of News in the public Prints, we have the following. **1809** *Ann. 10th Congress* 2 Sess. 1045 Really, one of these boats chasing a fast sailing vessel, was something like a snail chasing a Virginia race horse. **1882** BANCROFT *Hist. Formation U.S. Const.* II. 16 The Virginia resolve, that the national legislature should be composed of two branches, passed without debate.

+Virginia coal. Coal mined in Virginia. — **1790** *Penna. Packet* 1 Jan. 4/2 Just Arrived by the Mary Ann, . . . Virginia coal. . . . Copper in sheets and bottoms. **1819** *Plough Boy* I. 8 A constant supply of Liverpool, and Virginia Coal, for family and smith's use. **1888** *Congress. Rec.* 12 May 4040/2, I am a free-trader . . . but not in Virginia coal.

+Virginia Company. (See COMPANY 1 a.)

Virginia corn. Indian corn; a variety of Indian corn. — **1624** Smith *Gen. Hist. Va.* IV. 564 Whatsoeuer is said against the Virginia Corne, they finde it doth better nourish than any prouision is sent thither. **1649** *Perfect Descr. Va.* 4 Their Maize or Virginia Corne . . . yeelds them fiue hundred for one. **1770** *Md. Hist. Mag.* XIII. 72, I have a great deal of soft Corn at all the Plantations where the Virginia Corn was Planted. **1835–7** HALIBURTON *Clockmaker* 1 Ser. xvi. 133 Oatmeal . . . tante even as good for a horse as real yaller Varginy corn.

Virginia creeper. An American climbing vine (*Parthenocissus*, syn. *Ampelopsis*, *quinquefolia*); the woodbine or American ivy. {1704–} Also *Virginian creeper*.

1785 MARSHALL *Amer. Grove* 59 *Hedera quinquefolia*. American Ivy, or Virginian Creeper. This hath a climing stem, attaching itself to any neighbouring support. **1843** TORREY *Flora N.Y.* I. 148. **1850** S. F. COOPER *Rural Hours* 90 Many a time our little friend, perched on a waving branch of the Virginia creeper, would sing his sweetest song. **1874** ALDRICH *P. Palfrey* ii, The house . . . [was] covered by a network of vines, honeysuckle and Virginia creeper. **1885** HAVARD *Flora W. & S. Texas* 459 Of vines, we have the Poison Ivy, . . . the Virginian Creeper, and several Grapes. **1904** GLASGOW *Deliverance* 15 The Virginia creeper covering the old brick walls had wreathed them in memories as tenacious as itself.

+**Virginia currency.** Coin or other forms of money current in the colony of Virginia. Freq. used adverbially. — **1754** WASHINGTON *Writings* I. 80 Regimentals . . . were not to be bought for less Virginia currency, than British officers could get for sterling money. **1758** *Lett. to Washington* II. 277, I have sent Mr. Gist £300. Virginia Currency, to supply them with any thing that he may find in Virginia. **1788** [see CURRENCY 2]. **1801** WEEMS *Letters* II. 164 The doz. I took with me on last tack, I retailed at 3/9 Virginia Currency.

+**Virginiad.** *Hist.* A period of five years between celebrations of the landing at Jamestown, Virginia. — **1807** in *S. Lit. Messenger* XXIV. 311/1 *Resolved*, That there be a quinquennial Festival kept at James Town . . . [and] That each portion of five years be called a Virginiad. **1857** *Ib.* 311/2 The first 'Virginiad' of five years rolled by and found the country on the eve of a war with Great Britain.

Virginia deer. The white-tailed deer, esp. the common eastern species, *Odocoileus virginianus.* Also *Virginian deer.* — [**1781** PENNANT *Hist. Quadrupeds* I. 104 Virginian Deer with slender horns.] **1823** James *Exped.* I. 262 *Cervus Virginianus*—Virginian deer. **1917** *Mammals of Amer.* 8/2 *Virginia Deer, or White-tailed Deer.* . . . The middle and eastern United States and Canada. *Northern Virginia Deer.* . . . Northern part of United States and southern Canada west to Rockies.

+**Virginia fence.**

1. A snake or worm fence; fencing of this kind. Also *Virginia rail fence* and *Virginian fence.*

See also VIRGINIA WORM FENCE.

1671 *Portsmouth Rec.* 160 For post and rayles it Shall be of the Same hight of the Virginia ffence. **1790** DEANE *Newengland Farmer* 92/1 A Virginia fence . . . [is] made by lapping the ends of rails or poles on each other, turning alternately to the right and left. **1823** *New Eng. Farmer* II. 21 After getting your posts and boards together build your fence crooked, or in the manner of 'Virginia fence.' **1842** *Lowell Offering* II. 129 He had surrounded his fields and pastures with stone walls, in lieu of Virginian, stump, brush, and board fence. **1864** NORTON *Army Lett.* 293 There were miles of Virginia rail fence. **1887** BILLINGS *Hardtack* 155 The wandering shote, the hen-roosts, the Virginia fence and the straw-stack came to be regarded in a sense as the perquisites of the Union army. **1909** *Dialect Notes* III. 410 *Crooked fence*, a Virginia fence.

attrib. **1835** *Knickerb.* VI. 176 Hawk-nosed speculators already rode beside lawyers through the muddy, Virginia-fence lands of these squatments.

b. In comparisons or in allusive context.

1837 *Baltimore Commercial Transcript* 5 Oct. 2/2 (Th.), [Mr. Adams said] that gentleman's marks were always so very crooked—zigzag—like what yankee boys termed a Virginia fence. **1838** FLAGG *Far West* II. 44 The traveller . . . describes with his route a complete Virginia fence. **1850** *Knickerb.* XXXVI. 380 [Jenny Lind] doesn't 'shake' like a windy sliver on a chesnut-rail of a 'Virginia fence' in the country; she *sings.* **1865** TROWBRIDGE *Three Scouts* 96 No use of yer denying what's as plain as daylight through a Virginny fence.

2. In slang phrases alluding to the shifting course of an intoxicated person. **a.** *To make (a) Virginia fence,* or variant.

1737 *Penna. Gazette* 13 Jan. 2 He makes [a] Virginia Fence. **1774** J. ANDREWS *Lett.* 21 A few steps further, another [man] came running, as the only expedient to avoid making *Virginia fences.* **1835** *Knickerb.* V. 205 All made 'Virginia fence,' but all made out to find the way aloft. **1867** LOWELL *Biglow P.* 2 Ser. p. lix, *Virginia fence, to make a:* to walk like a drunken man.

b. *To walk (like a) Virginia fence.*

1831 *Georgian* (Savannah) 22 Jan. 2/5 (Th. S.), I saw lots of fellers [in N.Y.] walking Virginia fence, and some at the corners holdin up a post. **1877** BARTLETT 734 The phrase 'to walk like a Virginia fence' is applied to a drunken man.

+**Virginia ham.** A ham cured and aged according to methods followed in Virginia; a ham from a razorback hog. Also *Virginian ham.* — **1824** *Shipping & Commercial List* 31 July (Pettigrew P.). **1833** *Md. Hist. Mag.* XIII. 295 We had Virginian ham—turkey—roast beef [etc.]. **1849** *Knickerb.* XXXIV. 181 Very much anhungered, [we] draw out a fragrant Virginia ham, red as a cherry, sweet, juicy. **1858** WILLIS *Convalescent* 415 It is this healthful exercise, probably, with perhaps some little flavor from their nut-eating and rooting, which gives the fame to the 'Virginia ham.' **1908** LORIMER *J. Spurlock* 207 First there was a chicken gumbo soup, and then cold boiled Virginia ham.

+**Virginia-ism.** = VIRGINIANISM 1. — **1825** NEAL *Bro. Jonathan* I. 46 Only break yourself, will you, of those execrable Virginia-isms— . . . I *reckon—jist* [etc.].

Virginia ivy. = VIRGINIA CREEPER. Also *Virginian ivy.* {1629-} — **1743** CLAYTON *Flora Virginica* 60. **1856** *Harper's Mag.* XIII. 57/1 Virginian ivy and the splendid ecremocarpus draped the walls. **1872** *Ib.* Jan. 225/2 Virginia ivy, rooted wherever it found protection, clambered over its face [*i.e.* of the cliff].

+**Virginia line. a.** The aristocracy of Virginia. **b.** The Virginia division of the Continental forces in the Revolution. **c.** The boundary line of the state of Virginia. — **1779** HAMILTON *Works* VII. 576 Some folks in the Virginia line, jealous of his glory, had the folly to get him arrested. **1790** *Ann. 1st Congress* 1685 The engrossed bill to enable officers and soldiers of the Virginia line . . . to obtain titles to certain lands. **1792** *Ann.*

2d Congress 1036 These were to be located within a district bounded northwardly by the Virginia line.

+**Virginia money.** Virginia currency; money circulated in Virginia. Also *Virginia paper money.* Also used adverbially. — **1757** *Lett. to Washington* II. 36 The Owner woud not Take Virginia Paper money at more than Maryland. **1777** *Jrnls. Cont. Congress* VII. 43 There is due to Abraham Simons, for the hire of Ludwick Neal's wagon, in the service of the Virginia light horse, the sum of £15, Virginia money, equal to 50 dollars. **1834** *Pres. Mess. & P.* III. 96 The troops, it seems, were paid off in Virginia money, which is below *par* in our State, and this just on the eve of the election.

Virginia mulberry (tree). = RED MULBERRY. Also *Virginian mulberry (tree).* — [**1731** P. MILLER *Gardeners Dict.* s.v. *Morus,* The broad-leav'd Virginian Mulberry. *Ib.,* The large-leaved Virginian Mulberry.] **1785** MARSHALL *Amer. Grove* 93 *Morus rubra.* Large-leaved Virginian Mulberry Tree. This grows common in many parts of North-America. **1846** BROWNE *Trees Amer.* 457. **1897** SUDWORTH *Arborescent Flora* 186 *Morus rubra,* Red Mulberry. . . . Common names [include] . . . Black Mulberry (N.J., Pa., W.Va.), Virginia Mulberry Tree (Tenn.), Murier Sauvage (La.).

∗**Virginian,** *n.* [*Virginia* and *-an.*] +A white resident or white native of Virginia. {1797-}

All the evidence for this word in the sense of an Indian inhabiting Virginia is British.

1634 in C. C. Hall *Narr. Early Md.* 38 By noone we came before Monserat, where is a noble plantation of Irish Catholiques whome the virginians would not suffer to live with them because of their religion. **1654** *N.C. Col. Rec.* I. 18 If you think good to acquaint the States with what is done by two Virginians born, you will honor our country. **1755** in Franklin *Works* (1887) VII. 97 No notice had ever been given of their wanting any more carriages, than the Virginians and Marylanders had undertaken to furnish. **1782** CRÈVECŒUR *Letters* 58 Europeans submit insensibly to these great powers, and become . . . Pennsylvanians, Virginians, or provincials. **1825** NEAL *Bro. Jonathan* I. 245 The Virginians are called Buckskins. **1894** ALDRICH *Two Bites* 171 Is Mr. Flagg a Virginian, or a Mississippian, or a Georgian? **1910** McCUTCHEON *Rose in Ring* 122 Dick Cronk . . . was a revelation to the young Virginian.

Virginian, *a.*

Cf. VIRGINIA II. Other examples of the use of *Virginian* may be found in the separate entries of attrib. compounds of *Virginia* which precede and follow this entry.

1. Of persons: Identified in some way with Virginia.

1612 SMITH, etc. *Virginia* II. 104 For the honorable and better sort of our Virginian adventurers, I think they vnderstand it as I have writ it. **1624** SMITH *Gen. Hist. Va.* V. 197 In the moneth insuing . . . arrived the second ship; . . . in her came two Virginian Women . . . to be married to some would haue them. **1826** COOPER *Mohicans* i, They had recently seen a chosen army . . . only saved from annihilation by the coolness and spirit of a Virginian boy [Washington]. **1835** HOFFMAN *Winter in West* I. 48 A perfect treasure, in the shape of a genuine Virginian negro, must not be forgotten. **1838** HAWTHORNE *Twice-Told T.* (1879) II. 50 A Virginian planter . . . had come to Massachusetts on some political errand. **1870** EMERSON *Soc. & Solitude* 243 The troop of Virginian infantry that had marched to guard the prison of John Brown ask leave to pay their respects to the prisoner. **1893** 'MARK TWAIN' *P. Wilson* i, Pembroke Howard . . . was another old Virginian grandee with proved descent from the First Families.

2. Of places or areas: Touching upon or constituting, wholly or partly, Virginia.

1612 SMITH *Works* (1910) opp. p. 384 The Virginian Sea. **1666** B. TOMPSON *Political Works* 106 [He] espousing the Virginian Land. **1884** *Century Mag.* April 805/1 This shining, white mansion, screened by trees on the city side, . . . [looked] out from its southern windows across the placid Potomac to the red Virginian hills.

3. With reference to personal traits: Typical of the people of Virginia; characteristic of Virginia.

1839 *S. Lit. Messenger* V. 313/1 Didst ever visit . . . this land . . . where still Virginian hospitality delights to linger? **1840** IRVING *Wolfert's Roost* 251 My Virginian love for anything of the equestrian species predominated. **1845** *Knickerb.* XXVI. 334 The Virginian type of negro character therefore has come to prevail throughout the slave states, with the exception of some portions of Louisiana and Florida.

4. In specific names. **a.** Of plants.

Only a selection of examples is included. The earliest examples occur in British books as in Parkinson's *Paradisus.* (See also VIRGINIAN DOGWOOD.)

1785 MARSHALL *Amer. Grove* 80 *Lonicera virginiana.* Virginian scarlet Honeysuckle. *Ib.* 107 *Populus heterophylla.* Virginian Poplar-Tree. **1836** LINCOLN *Botany* App. 123 *Penthorum . . . sedoides,* Virginian orpine, . . . stem branching, angled. **1846** BROWNE *Trees Amer.* 368 The Virginian Date Plum, when grown under favourable conditions, sometimes attains a height of sixty or seventy feet.

b. Of birds and other animals.

1823 JAMES *Exped.* I. 262 *Strix . . . Virginiana*—Virginian-eared owl. **1835** AUDUBON *Ornith. Biog.* III. 170 Besides man, the enemies of the Mallard are the White-headed Eagle, . . . the Virginian Owl . . . , and the snapping turtle.

Virginian dogwood. The flowering dogwood (*Cynoyxlon floridum*), the state flower of Virginia, or a related species. — [**1725** BRADLEY tr. Chomel *Family Dict.*, *Virginian-Dogwood*, a Tree of the natural growth of Virginia, about the size of the common Cherry-Tree, blossoming early in the Spring.] **1785** MARSHALL *Amer. Grove* 35 *Cornus alterna*. Alternate branched, or Female Virginian Dogwood. **1796** MORSE *Univ. Geog.* I. 190 Flowering Trees and Shrubs in the United States. . . . Pigeonberry (*Cissus sicyoides*)—Virginian Dogwood (*Cornus florida*) [etc.].

Virginia nightingale. =VIRGINIAN NIGHTINGALE. — [**1688** *Phil. Trans.* XVII. 995 Of Virginia Nightingale, or red Bird, there are two sorts.] **1744** MOORE *Voy. Georgia* 117 There are also a great number of small birds, of which . . . the red bird, or Virginia nightingale, the mocking bird, . . . and the rice bird were the chief. **1806** LEWIS in *L. & Clark Exped.* V. (1905) 111 The beak is reather more than half an inch in length, and is formed much like the virginia nitingale. **1820** F. WRIGHT *Soc. & Manners in Amer.* 333 The Virginia nightingale, his feathers all crimson with fine black marks on his head, has a singularly melodious song. **1917** *Birds of Amer.* III. 63 Cardinal. . . . Other Names.—Cardinal Grosbeak; . . . Virginia Nightingale.

Virginianism. +**1.** A word, phrase, or manner of expression characteristic of the English spoken in Virginia. +**2.** The mode of life characteristic of society in Virginia. — **(1) 1836** *S. Lit. Messenger* II. 111 We knew a vagrant word-catcher to have in his list of Virginianisms *Good bye t'ye*, a phrase purely Shakespearian. **(2) 1848** *Ib.* XIV. 635/1, I did not come to the State to see northern improvements, . . . but to get a glimpse of the genuine, unsophisticated, old Virginianism.

Virginian nightingale. =CARDINAL GROSBEAK. {1668–} — **1798** *Monthly Mag.* May 331/2, I noticed several kinds of birds . . . peculiar to the North-American continent, viz. the Virginian nightingale; . . . the American robin, larger than ours; and the blue variegated jay. **1842** BUCKINGHAM *Slave States* I. 156 The mocking-bird, and the red bird or Virginian nightingale, are each inhabitants of these woods. **1896** BRUCE *Econ. Hist. Virginia* I. 119 Much more interesting was the cardinal or red bird, which was always described as the Virginian nightingale.

+**Virginia paper money.** (See VIRGINIA MONEY.)

Virginia partridge. (See quot. 1917.) {1783–} Also *Virginian partridge*. — **1813** Wilson *Ornithology* IX. (*index*), Virginian Partridge. **1852** MARCY *Explor. Red River* (1854) 13, I observed . . . the Virginia partridge (*Ortyx Virginianus*). **1871** *Mich. Gen. Statutes* I. (1882) 583 No person shall kill or destroy, or attempt to kill or destroy, any colin or quail, sometimes called Virginia partridge. **1917** *Birds of Amer.* II. 2 Bob-White. *Colinus virginianus virginianus*. . . . [Also called] Virginia Partridge. . . . Northerners call him Quail; Southerners, Partridge.

+**Virginia pine. a.** =LOBLOLLY PINE. **b.** =JERSEY PINE. **c.** = GEORGIA PINE. Also *Virginian pine*, *Virginian swamp pine*. — **1775** BURNABY *Travels* 80 It becomes beautifully covered with Virginian pine. **1785** MARSHALL *Amer. Grove* 102 *Pinus Tæda*. Virginian Swamp, or Frankincence Pine. This grows to a pretty large size. *Ib.*, *Pinus virginiana*. Two-leaved Virginian, or Jersey Pine. This is generally of but low growth, but divided into many branches. **1890** *Cent.* 4496/2 *Virginian pine*, an old name of the long-leafed pine. **1897** SUDWORTH *Arborescent Flora* 26 *Pinus tæda*. Loblolly Pine. . . . Virginia Pine.

+**Virginia poke.**[1] **1.** =POKEWEED. Also *Virginian poke*. **2.** =INDIAN POKE. — **(1)** [**1731** P. MILLER *Gardeners Dict.*, *Phytolacca*; . . . American Nightshade, . . . commonly call'd Virginian Poke or Porke Physick.] **1769** STORK *Descr. E. Florida* 19 *Phytolocca octandra* . . . in Mexico, like Virginia poke. **1840** DEWEY *Mass. Flowering Plants* 100 Poke, or Virginia Poke, or Poke Weed . . . is a favorite food of robins and other birds. **(2) 1909** WEBSTER 2287/1 *V[irginia] poke*, . . . the Indian poke, or false hellebore.

+**Virginia poke.**[2] (See quotation.) *colloq.*[2] — **1887** *Century Mag.* 549/1 He gave the cards a Virginia poke whenever it came his turn to cut them; that is to say, he pushed one card out of the middle of the pack, and put it at the back.

+**Virginia rail.** A long-billed wading bird (*Rallus virginianus*) similar to, but smaller than, the king rail. Also *Virginian rail*. {1914, in Canada} — [**1785** LATHAM *Gen. Syn. Birds* III. 228 *Rallus Virginianus*, Virginian Rail.] **1813** WILSON *Ornithology* VII. 109 [The] Virginian Rail . . . spreads over the interior as far west as the Ohio. **1828** BONAPARTE *Synopsis* 334 The Virginia Rail . . . inhabits throughout North America; extending its migrations far to the north. **1844** *Nat. Hist. N.Y.*, *Zoology* II. 261 This little mud-hen, or Virginian Rail, is found . . . chiefly along . . . fresh water streams and morasses. **1874** COUES *Birds N.W.* 538 The Virginia Rail extends across the continent. **1911** in *Birds of Amer.* (1917) I. 203/1 The King Rail closely resembles the Virginia Rail except in size.

+**Virginia rail fence.** (See VIRGINIA FENCE 1.)

+**Virginia redbird.** The Virginia nightingale or cardinal grosbeak. Also *Virginian redbird*. — **1810** WILSON *Ornithology* II. 40 [Cardinal grosbeaks] are generally known by the names Red-bird, Virginia Redbird, . . . and Crested Red-bird. **1874** COUES *Birds N.W.* 172 *Cardinalis Virginianus*. Cardinal Grosbeak; Virginian Redbird.

+**Virginia reel.** An American country-dance corresponding to the English Sir Roger de Coverley; a musical piece accompanying such a dance; also, the dancers.

1817 PAULDING *Lett. from South* I. 151 One of the favourite Virginia reels is, 'Fire in the mountains, run, boys, run.' **1839** 'M. PENCIL' *White Sulphur P.* 84 The order of the dance is two cotillions, then a waltz, the Spanish dance, or Virginia reel, being generally the finale. **1864** LOWELL *My Study Windows* 167 There were . . . persons who seemed to think this as simple a thing to do as to lead off a Virginia reel. **1884** MATTHEWS & BUNNER *In Partnership* 189 There was a pause, which was filled by the strains of a Virginia reel. **1896** WILKINS *Madelon* 33 A smothered titter ran down the files of the Virginia reel. **1920** LEWIS *Main Street* 75 Carol got them into a waltz and a Virginia Reel.

+**Virginia Resolutions.** *pl.* A set of resolutions drawn up by James Madison and passed in 1798 by the legislature of Virginia, declaring the Alien and Sedition Laws to be unconstitutional, and laying down a strict-constructionist interpretation of the relative powers of the states and the national government. (See also *Kentucky and Virginia Resolutions*, under KENTUCKY 6.) — **1854** BENTON *30 Years' View* I. 139/1 The third resolve of the Virginia resolutions of the year 1798. **1886** LOGAN *Great Conspiracy* 18 The famous Kentucky Resolutions of '98 touching States Rights . . . were closely followed by the Virginia Resolutions of 1799 in the same vein by Madison.

+**Virginia seedling. a.** A variety of strawberry. **b.** A variety of grape. — **1853** FOWLER *Home for All* 140 The Virginia seedling is an early variety [of strawberry]. **1864** *Ohio Agric. Rep.* XVIII. 25 A premium of $20 shall be offered for the best three samples of pure Ohio wine, made from the Catawba, Virginia Seedling or Delaware grape.

+**Virginia silk.** (See quotations.) Also *Virginian silk*. — [**1629** PARKINSON *Paradisus* 444 *Periploca recta Virginiana*. Virginian Silke. . . . It came to me from Virginia, where it groweth aboundantly.] **1891** *Cent.* 5630/1 *Virginia silk*, the silk-vine, *Periploca Græca:* so called from the silky tuft of the seed.

Virginia snakeroot. A birthwort (*Aristolochia serpentaria*) of the eastern states; the root of this, or a preparation made from it. {1694–} Also *Virginian snakeroot*. — **1743** CLAYTON *Flora Virginica* 112 (*index*), Virginy-Snake-root. **1791** *Amer. Philos. Soc.* III. 114 Virginian Snake-root. **1796** *Hodge's N.C. Almanack* 46 For the Putrid Sore-Throat—Take of . . . Virginia snake root, the roots of aromatick calamus and wild valerian, . . . each one ounce. **1819** E. DANA *Geogr. Sk.* 85 Of the Herbaceous Indigenous productions, trees, and shrubberies of natural growth, divers species . . . are useful in medicine and the arts; such as the *Actea racemosa*, or squaw root, Virginia snake root [etc.]. **1898** CREEVEY *Flowers of Field* 381 Virginia Snakeroot. *Aristolochia serpentaria*. . . . The root has medicinal stimulant properties.

+**Virginia's warbler.** [Named by Baird for Mrs. W. W. Anderson.] The Rocky Mountain warbler, *Vermivora virginiae*. — **1860** BAIRD *Birds N. Amer.* p. xi, *Helminthophaga virginiae*, Virginia's Warbler. . . . N[ew] M[exico]. **1874** COUES *Birds N.W.* 51 Virginia's Warbler. . . . Southern Rocky Mountain region.

+**Virginia thyme.** A mountain mint (*Pycnanthemum virginianum*) or a related species. Also *Virginian thyme*. Also with specifying terms.

1814 BIGELOW *Florula Bostoniensis* 146 Virginia thyme . . . [has a] taste like pennyroyal. **1817–8** EATON *Botany* (1822) 415 *Pycnanthemum linifolium*, virginian thyme. **1829** *Ib.* (ed. 5) 352 *Pycnanthemum virginicum*, narrow-leaf virginian thyme. **1840** DEWEY *Mass. Flowering Plants* 182 Virginia Thyme. **1843** TORREY *Flora N.Y.* II. 64 *Pycnanthemum linifolium*. Narrow-leaved Virginian Thyme. . . . Moist thickets and exsiccated swamps. **1901** MOHR *Plant Life Ala.* 698 *Koellia flexuosa*. . . . Virginian Thyme. . . . The herb known as 'mountain mint' or 'Pycnanthemum' is used medicinally.

Virginia tobacco. Tobacco produced in Virginia. Also *Virginian tobacco*. {1694–} — **1655** *Suffolk Deeds* II. 191 Verginia tobacco at fower pence per pownd to be deliuered at Boston. **1705** *Va. State P.* I. 98 It will oblige the Planters to make only that which is good, whereby the reputation of the Virginia tobacco will be again advanced. **1748** *New Eng. Hist. & Gen. Reg.* IV. 176 She continues to sell the best Virginia Tobacco, Cut, Pigtail and spun, of all Sorts. **1817–8** EATON *Botany* (1822) 362 *Nicotiana tabacum*, virginian tobacco.

+**Virginia wake-robin.** The green arrow arum, *Peltandra virginica*. Also *Virginian wake-robin*. — **1770** FORSTER tr. Kalm *Travels* I. 125 The Virginian Wake robin, or *Arum Virginicum*, grows in wet places. **1883** *Smithson. Rep. 1881* 690 This name [Tuckahoe] . . . belonged to all esculent bulbous roots used by the Indians, among which are these: *Orontium aquaticum*, Golden Club, and *Pentandria virginica*, Virginia Wake Robin. **1891** *Cent.* 6807/1 *Virginian wake-robin*, the arrow-arum, *Peltandra undulata*.

+**Virginia weed.** Tobacco. Also *Virginian weed*. *colloq.* — **1821** COOPER *Spy* iii, He took from his mouth a large allowance of the Virginian weed. **1833** COKE *Subaltern's Furlough* xv, Several of his guests were enjoying 'a *drink*' and a mouthful of *the Virginia weed*. **1845** *S. Lit. Messenger* XI. 667/1 Left . . . only with the sweet companionship of the 'Virginia weed,' what 'strange vagaries' did my imagination pursue!

Virginia wheat. a. Indian corn. (Cf. INDIAN WHEAT 1.) **b.** Wheat grown in Virginia. — **1651** Hartlib *Legacy* (1655) 36 The hill where their Corn is planted, called Virginia-Wheat. **1688** *Phil. Trans.* XVII. 978 English Wheat (as they call it, to distinguish it from Maze, commonly called Virginia Wheat). **1709** *Essex Inst. Coll.* VIII. 19 In the Weare Hows . . . [were] 500 butchells of Vorginiy Whet, . . . 203 butchells of Engen Corn.

+**Virginia winterberry.** The black alder, *Ilex verticillatus*. Also called *Virginian winterberry*. — **1785** MARSHALL *Amer. Grove* 110 *Prinos verticillatus*. Virginian Winter-Berry. The inner bark of this shrub is very good to make poultices of for ripening tumors. **1891** *Cent.* 6943/3 The winterberry especially so named is *I. verticillata*, otherwise called *black alder*, sometimes distinguished as *Virginia winterberry*.

+**Virginia worm fence.** =Virginia fence. Also in fig. or allusive context. — **1809** Cuming *Western Tour* 34 Two very beautiful red foxes playfully crossed the road . . . leaping with ease a Virginia worm fence above six feet high. **1839** Mayo *Polit. Sk. Washington* 39 A meandering course, sometimes familiarly illustrated by the homely figure of 'a Virginia worm fence.' **1868** *Ore. State Jrnl.* 21 Nov. 1/5 Greeley can lay Virginia worm-fences in ink faster than any other editor in New York city.

*****Virgin's-bower.**

*****1.** Any one of various plants of the genus *Clematis,* +esp. the American species, *C. virginiana.* Also with specifying terms.

[**1771** J. R. Forster *Flora Amer. Septentr.* 25 *Clematis viorna.* Virgin's bower, violet.] **1817–8** Eaton *Botany* (1822) 241 *Clematis virginica,* virgin's bower. . . . Climbing. **1843** Torrey *Flora N.Y.* I. 6 *Clematis Virginiana.* Virginian Virgin's Bower. . . . Common in thickets, and along fences and stone walls. *Ib.* 7 *Clematis Verticillaris.* Whorl-leaved Virgin's Bower. . . . Northern and western parts of the State. **1878** Jackson *Travel at Home* 372, I have not yet spoken of the white clematis,—virgin's bower, as it is called in New England. **1885** Havard *Flora W. & S. Texas* 459 Of vines, we have . . . the Texas Virgin's Bower, a pretty climber with long-feathered fruit. **1898** Creevey *Flowers of Field* 443 Common Virgin's bower. . . . The plant has a very wide range, from New England southward and westward.

+**2.** The American wistaria, *Wistaria frutescens.*

1866 *Land We Love* (Charlotte, N.C.) May 80 Virgin's Bower. . . . Flowers purplish blue, pea-shaped.

Vis-à-vis. {1753–} +=Tête-à-tête. — **1851** Cist *Cincinnati* 202 Dressing bureaus, sociables, and *vis-à-vis* are sure to catch the visitor's eye, and to open the visitor's purse. **1891** *Cent.* 6768/2.

*****Vise, Vice.**

*****1.** A gripping or holding appliance having movable jaws regulated by a screw.

1669 *York Deeds* II. 69 The Smyths shopp with bellows, anvell, beckorne, vice, sledg hammer & some ould irons. **1738** *N.H. Hist. Soc. Coll.* II. 80 [A committee was also appointed] to procure an anvil, bellows, vice, sledge-hammer and tongs, fit for the work of a blacksmith. **1797** *Essex Inst. Coll.* LIV. 110 My nail machine consists of a cutting lever of the common form, . . . two vices & two hammers. **1801** *Ann. 7th Congress* 2 Sess. 1225 Articles paying twelve and a half per cent. ad valorem. . . . Anvils, vises and printing type. **1881** *Rep. Indian Affairs* 442 Vises, carpenter's, parallel, 4-inch jaw.

2. Attrib. with *anvil, bench, clamp.*

1678 *New Castle Court Rec.* 267 A vyce Clamp. **1851** Melville *Moby Dick* 518 The one grand stage where he enacted all his various parts so manifold, was his vice-bench; a long rude ponderous table furnished with several vices. **1859** *Rep. Comm. Patents 1858* I. 580 Improved Vise-Anvil for Repairing т Rails.

+**Visible admixture.** A mixture of races resulting in obvious Negroid features. Also attrib.— **1831** *S.C. Ct. Appeals Rep.* (Bailey) II. 558 Where there is a *distinct* and *visible* admixture of negro blood, the individual is to be denominated a mulatto, or a person of color. **1868** *Congress. Globe* 13 May 2452/2 The whole question of the 'visible admixture' law . . . is one of the most . . . characteristic chapters in modern Democratic history. **1870** *Ib.* 23 Feb. 1510/2 The Democratic party [in Ohio] endeavored to exclude [from citizenship] what are called 'visible admixture' persons—persons who had a visible admixture of black blood.

*****Visit,** *n.* +A chat or talk. — **1890** *Harper's Mag.* Dec. 147/2, I've had a real nice visit with you . . . an' I wish I could ask you to stay longer.

*****Visit,** *v.* +*intr.* To talk or chat. Also *vbl. n.* — **1887** Wilkins *Humble Romance* 319 You an' Mis' Wheat can visit a little while. **1888** Grigsby *Smoked Yank* xxv, Thought two soldiers would enjoy visiting together. **1898** Deland *Old Chester Tales* 75 You can eat it while I get out and visit with the minister.

*****Visitation.** +(See quot. 1851.) — **1650** *Harvard Rec.* I. 28 There shall bee three weeks of visitation yearly . . . between the tenth of June & the Commencement. **1766** *Holyoke Diaries* 29 To warn ye Cambridge School. Master of the Visitation of his School. **1851** Hall *College Words* 279 It was customary, in the early days of Harvard College, for the graduates of the year to attend in the recitation-room on Mondays and Tuesdays, for three weeks, during the month of June, subject to the examination of all who chose to visit them. This was called . . . the *Weeks of Visitation.*

Visite. **1.** A woman's cape or short cloak. *Obs.* {1852–} **2.** Short for *carte de visite.* Used attrib. — (1) **1850** Mitchell *Lorgnette* I. 23 The heavy visites, in this spring-like season, are worn with a languid air. **1863** 'G. Hamilton' *Gala-Days* 27 He sees the . . . visite put upon your shoulders. (2) **1891** *Internat. Ann., Anthony's Photogr. Bul.* IV. 302 A stereoscope camera . . . can be used to make . . . 24 visite negatives.

*****Visiting.** Attrib. and comb. with *costume, hour, pass,* etc. {1709–}

1850 *Harper's Mag.* Dec. 144/1 The figure on the right represents a Visiting Costume. **1866** A. D. Whitney *L. Goldthwaite* i, Here and there [was] a finishing of lovely, lace-like crochet, done at odd minutes, and for 'visiting-work.' **1875** Stowe *We & Neighbors* 36 It will be a grand summer visiting place at their house in Newport. **1877** *Rep. Indian Af-*

---

fairs 50 It is urged that refusal to grant visiting-passes will involve individual hardships. **1897** *Scribner's Mag.* XXII. 384/1 Formal visiting-hours were ignored in the village of Sewanee.

Visiting card. A calling card. {1782–} — **1790** *Penna. Packet* 8 May 4/4 Thomas Seddon . . . has for Sale . . . Message cards and visiting cards. **1854** *Penna. Agric. Rep.* 363 Visiting cards and pen drawing, Charles R. Fraily. **1891** Welch *Recoll. 1830–40* 195 Provided with a pack of 'visiting cards,' as they were then called, [they were] all ready at nine o'clock. **1908** 'O. Henry' *Options* 64 Your regular engraved Tuesdays-and-Fridays visiting-card wouldn't have a louder voice in proclaiming your indemnity than this here currency.

*****Visitor.** One appointed to inspect or supervise a college or other school; a college overseer or trustee. — **1650** *Harvard Rec.* I. 28 In Case any of the Sophisters . . . bee found insufficient . . . in the Judgment of any three of the visitors being overseers of the Colledge they shall bee deferred to the following Year. **1712** *Md. Archives* XXIX. 159 This Committee . . . pray the House to consider whether the present Governors and Visitors of the ffree School apply the Money arising by Virtue of such Duties according to the Act for that Purpose made. **1742** Peirce *Hist. Harvard* 194 The General Court alone have such a sovereign power; and are the Visitors of the said College. **1829** *Va. Lit. Museum* 95 The following exercises took place [at the Univ. of Va.], . . . in the presence of the Rector and Visiters, and a numerous assemblage of the public. **1900** *Outlook* Aug. 795/1 The executive head of the University is the chairman of the faculty, who is elected annually by the Board of Visitors.

*****Visor, Vizor.** +The stiff forepiece of a cap. — **1847** Parkman in *Knickerb.* XXIX. 504 The water dropped from the vizors of our caps, and trickled down our cheeks. **1875** Holland *Sevenoaks* 34 He held in his hand a fur cap without a visor. **1911** Lincoln *Cap. Warren's Wards* 2 He was a big man, . . . wearing a cloth cap with a visor.

Visualist. {1903–} +a. One whose memory retains visual images better than other kinds. +b. One who forms mental pictures of sounds, abstractions, etc. — **1895** *Pop. Science Mo.* April 731 Charcot . . . classified people into 'visualists'—those whose recollections were chiefly of things seen, who had to read a name in order to remember it; 'audists' [etc.]. **1902** *Amer. Jrnl. Psychol.* XIII. 544 The visualist probably proceeds more from the standpoint of the object and the enumeration of qualities.

+**Vitascope,** *n.* An early form of moving pictures or the machine which took them. *Obs.* — **1896** *Chicago Record* 4 July 7/3 The vitascope is sure to amaze and delight all who visit the popular-price theater. **1897** *Pop. Science Mo.* Dec. 180 In some forms of apparatus, such as the vitascope, . . . the shutter is omitted. **1899** *Ib.* Nov. 68 The principle is similar to that of the biograph or the vitoscope [*sic*], in which the quick to-and-fro motions of the spark are received on a sensitive film.

‖**Vitascope,** *v.* [f. prec.] *tr.* To take moving pictures of (a place). *colloq.²* — **1896** *N.Y. Dramatic News* 11 July 10/2 Niagara having been vitascoped, Coney Island has now fallen before the camera.

Vixen sister. +(See quotation.) — **1883** *Harper's Mag.* Feb. 425/1 After the union of the States . . . the political conduct of South Carolina was so imperious and so unreasonable that she was not uncommonly known as . . . the 'vixen sister.'

Vly. Also **vlaie.** *local.* [Du. dial. *vlei* 'valley.'] {vlei, 1849–, in S. Africa} A swamp or marsh. Also attrib. Usually in place names. (Cf. Fly *n.¹*) — **1832** Dunlap *Hist. Amer. Theatre* 41 From the Fly or Vly Market, Maiden-lane commenced, exceedingly narrow. **1877** Bartlett 734 *Vly,* . . . in New York, a swamp, a marsh. **1885** *Century Mag.* Oct. 914 From Seventy-second street to the hollow known in the old maps as 'Marritje David's Vly,' . . . the river banks are bold. **1904** Chambers in *Harper's Mag.* May 933/1 Have you reason to believe that an attempt has been made to fire the Owl Vlaie?

‖**Vocabulation.** The use or choice of words. — **1891** Eggleston *Faith Doctor* 162 A mind . . . felicitous in vocabulation and ingenious in the construction of sentences.

*****Voice.**

*****1.** A vote. *Obs.*

1638 *Md. Archives* I. 6 Came John Langford . . . and desired to revoke his voice. **1648** *Ib.* I. 222 Walter Pakes appointeth ffrancis Posey Proxie for himselfe and his uoyces. **1776** J. Adams *Works* IX. 376 A motion is made, and carried by a majority of one voice. **1796** Morse *Univ. Geog* I. 329 A convention . . . ratified the constitution without a dissenting voice.

2. *Voice of the people,* the collective opinion or will of the people.

1867 *Congress. Globe* 15 March 117/3 Building the foundation upon the voice of the people. **1900** *Congress. Rec.* 31 Jan. 1365/2 The voice of the people finds expression through the ballot box.

Volcano. {1613–} +a. An alcohol lamp. +b. (See quot. 1889.) — (a) **1861** Winthrop *C. Dreeme* 160, I'll run down and get Mr. Stillfleet's volcano and stew-pan to catch the Blue-Pointers. (b) **1889** *Cent.* 2245/2 *Fizgig,* a firework, made of damp powder, which makes a hissing or fizzing noise when ignited; in one form called by boys a *volcano.*

+**Volley ball.** (See quot. 1896.) — **1896** *Physical Ed.* V. 50/1 During the past winter Mr. W. G. Morgan of Holyoke, Mass. has developed a game in his gymnasium which is called Volley Ball. . . . The play consists in keeping a ball in motion over a high net, from one side to the other, thus partaking of the character of two games,—tennis and hand ball. **1916** J. N. Bancroft *Hdbk. Athletic Games* 463 The court for volley ball must be outlined by distinct lines at least two inches wide.

+**Voltaire.** A chair having a low seat and a high back. *Obs.* — 1870 TOMBES *Decorum* 97 It is not becoming to throw themselves at once on the sofa and stretch out their legs, or into the Voltaire or easy-chair.

Volunteer. One who enters upon military service of his own free will. {1618-} — 1654 *New Haven Col. Rec.* II. 55 The wrighting wch he and John Chapman was bringing along the coast to raise volunteeres to goe against the Duch. 1704 *Boston News-Letter* 24 April 2/2 His Honour . . . immediately caused the Drum to beat for Voluntiers, under the Command of Capt. Wanton. 1777 in Sparks *Corr. Revol.* I. 361 The deficiency in our regulars can no way be supplied so properly as by enlisting volunteers. 1836 JACKSON in *Pres. Mess. & P.* III. 234 The volunteers raised in Arkansas and Missouri . . . should have been called on before any other requisition was made upon Tennessee. 1898 *Kansas City Star* 18 Dec. 2/4 Private Will Litchfield of Kansas City . . . will sail for Manila next week to join his comrades of the Twentieth Kansas volunteers.

Volunteer company. A military company made up of volunteers. — 1812 *Niles' Reg.* III. 45/2 Volunteer companies . . . are rolling to the frontiers, in force sufficient to look down opposition. 1846 *Ib.* 4 July 288/1 Three volunteer companies, numbering about 300 men have already arrived here. 1884 *Century Mag.* April 822/2 He became the captain of a volunteer company.

+**Volunteer crop.** A crop that comes up and grows spontaneously. — 1857 GLISAN *Jrnl. Army Life* 387 Many of the farmers depend on their volunteer crops for two years in succession. 1883 *Century Mag.* Oct. 804/1 What are called volunteer crops, sowing themselves, give good yields for the first, second, and even third year after the original planting. 1893 SANBORN *S. Calif.* 159 In California even the hoe is not needed, for 'volunteer crops' come up all by themselves.

+**Volunteer fire company.** A company of fire-fighters made up of volunteers. — 1841 *Picayune* 22 April 2/5 Volunteer Fire Company, No. 1. The members of this Company are requested to attend an extra meeting on Friday evening next. 1880 *Harper's Mag.* July 208/2 Several of the members belonged to the volunteer fire-companies, then [in 1842] in the height of their glory. 1901 [see FIRE COMPANY 1].

+**Volunteer fire department.** A fire department the personnel of which is made up of volunteers. — 1876 INGRAM *Centennial Exp.* 662 Parade of Volunteer Fire Department. 1883 [see FIRE DEPARTMENT]. 1919 *Maine My State* 320 He was chief engineer of the Volunteer Fire Department of Portland.

+**Volunteer State.** Tennessee. A nickname. — 1853 RAMSEY *Tennessee* 116 Thus early did the 'Volunteer State' commence its novitiate in arms. 1898 *Congress. Rec.* 1 July 6575/1 Tennessee was once called the Volunteer State, and that is the general name it goes by in our country to-day.

+**Voodoo,** *n.* Also **voudou.** [African *vodu.*]

1. A system of defensive, amatory, or soothsaying charms, spells, secret rites, etc., practiced by so called conjurers, witch doctors, etc., among Negroes and Creoles; also, a spell or charm of this kind.

See also VAUDOU(X) and cf. HOODOO *n.*
1880 CABLE *Grandissimes* 90 Do this much for me this one time and then I will let voudou alone as much as you wish. 1884 *Lisbon* (Dak.) *Star* 20 Sept., The Voudoos of Louisiana . . . were recently viewed at the funeral of a negress, one of the Queens of Voudoo. 1902 G. C. EGGLESTON *D. South* 216, I'll put a Voodoo on anybody I ever heahs a callin' you a ole maid, Miss Mony.

2. A sorcerer or witch; one who practices voodooism.
1880 *Picayune* 20 May, The fool spends all her money to do us harm, thinking she is a voudou. 1888 *Century Mag.* Dec. 297/2 There was then in that city an aged negress claiming to be a Voodoo. 1906 BELL *C. Lee* 235 'It is the voodoo!' whispered Flower.

3. Attrib. with *dance, doctor, land,* etc.
1872 POWERS *Afoot & Alone* 101 One day I went with Tookey to visit an old crone who was reputed to be a Voodoo priestess. 1885 *Boston Jrnl.* 17 Aug. 2/4 Intelligent house servants . . . are frequently found under the influence of some withered old mummy of a voudoo doctor. 1897 GUNTER *S. Turnbull* 277 Jemima's only seen a Voodoo dance before! 1902 LORIMER *Lett. Merchant* 267, I reckon she'd have called herself a clairvoyant nowadays, but then she was just a voodoo woman. 1904 STUART *River's Children* 74 They told amazing mammy-tales of voudoo-land and the ghost country.

+**Voodoo,** *v.* Also **voudou.** *tr.* To bewitch or put a spell upon (someone) by the arts of voodooism. (Cf. HOODOO *v.*) — 1880 CABLE *Grandissimes* 242 Maybe, too, it is true as he says, that he is voudoued. 1906 BELL *C. Lee* 199 They think the baby is bewitched,—that he has been voodooed.

Voodooism. Also **voudouism.** The body of beliefs and practices making up voodoo. — [1871 *Notes & Q.* 4 Ser. VII. 210/2 What is Voodonism [*sic*]?] 1880 *Picayune* 20 May, Finding that no affidavit could be made for voudouism. 1911 HARRISON *Queed* 276 You must go to the voodooism of the savage black.

*∗**Vote,** *n.*

1. An enactment, resolution, or proceeding. *Obs.* {1641-}
1656 *Braintree Rec.* 7 A vote passed att a publike meeting about the common. 1720 *Amer. Wkly. Mercury* 3 Nov. 2/1 An Abstract of the Votes of Assembly. 1721 *Mass. H. Rep. Jrnl.* III. 1 Votes of the Honourable House of Representatives of His Majesties Province of the Massachusetts-Bay, in New England.

+**2.** *To dodge a vote,* to fail to vote through motives of evasion; *to get out the vote,* to see that all those entitled to vote do so.
1846 *Congress. Globe* 20 July 1118/1 [It has been suggested] that I dodged the vote. 1905 *Springfield W. Repub.* 10 Nov. 3 No one outside the inner councils knows what it costs Tammany to get out the vote.

3. In special combinations.
Vote-broker, one who buys and sells votes; *v.-buyer,* one who purchases votes; *v.-buying,* the purchasing of votes; *v.-distributor,* ?one who hands out tickets or ballots at an election; *v.-dodger,* one who, for ulterior motives, avoids voting; *v.-getter,* one who is successful in getting votes; *v.-getting machine,* a political clique or faction designed to secure votes; *v.-monger,* one who deals or traffics in votes; *v.-recorder,* (see quotation).
1875 *Chicago Tribune* 11 Nov. 4/2 The gentlemen . . . must be prepared to meet a powerful influence in his behalf,—the influence of the gamblers, confidence-men, thieves, roughs, plug-uglies, and vote-brokers. 1890 *Nation* 10 April 287/3 The vote-buyers were thrown out of business. 1905 *McClure's Mag.* XXIV. 342 Some men who talked to me of their vote-buying, knew . . . that it was a shameful practice. 1877 *Harper's Mag.* Sept. 614/1 If I had continued in active political life, I might have risen to be vote distributor or fence viewer, or selectman. 1852 J. W. BOND *Minnesota* 293 A wily sort of politician in Indian tactics, it seems, like some of our own vote-dodgers. 1906 *Springfield W. Repub.* 1 Nov. 3 He is also a strong campaigner, and has proved himself a vote-getter. 1892 *Courier-Journal* 3 Oct. 3/3 Mr. Needy . . . was made a victim of the vote-getting machine. 1887 *Amer. Missionary* July 195 [Negroes are] made tools of by wily politicians among the whites, and by corrupt vote-mongers among themselves. 1876 KNIGHT 2715/1 *Vote-recorder,* an apparatus in which, by an impulse given by each member of a body at his desk, upon the 'aye' or 'no' lever or button, the indication is made at the clerk's or president's desk, and the record counted or sum shown.

*∗**Vote,** *v.* +*tr.* To cause to vote. Also *transf.* — 1859 BARTLETT 98 They are treated with good living and liquors, and at a proper day are taken to the polls and 'voted,' as it is called, for the party. 1884 NYE *Baled Hay* 217, I believe they vote people there who have been dead for centuries 1904 *N.Y. Ev. Post* 8 Nov. 1, 25 men were in line in many places, and they were voted at a rate of nearly one a minute.

*∗**Voting.** Attrib. with *blank, machine, member,* etc. {1846-} — 1855 Hambleton *H. A. Wise* 212 Does this not restrict the free exercise of the voting power? 1864 *Ore. State Jrnl.* 17 Sept. 2/2 We have quite a number of distinguished lobby members at Salem, at present, who will be able to give the 'voting members' any quantity of advice. 1883 *Wheelman* I. 464 The corresponding secretary will send to each member . . . a voting-blank for a chief consul, and one representative. 1888 *Century Mag.* 312/2 The voter . . . passes alone to the 'voting-room,' where he deposits his ballot. a1906 J. S. GARLAND *New Eng. Town Law* R.I. 119 The town council of any town . . . may . . . order the discontinuance of said voting-machines for said election.

+**Voting list.** A list of the names of those entitled to vote in a particular ward or precinct. — 1859 HALE *If, Yes, & Perhaps* 187, [I told] Dennis that he might use the record on the voting-list. 1872 *Atlantic Mo.* Jan. 128 In Brooklyn voting-lists have been stolen by sworn officials for the purpose of enabling them to effect a fraud in the election. 1889 *Century Mag.* Feb. 626/2 Might it not be practicable to forbid the board to enter upon the voting-lists the name of any man . . . habitually violating the law?

+**Voting precinct.** =ELECTION DISTRICT. — 1872 *Chicago Tribune* 9 Oct. 1/6 About 200 voting precincts heard from. 1883 *Century Mag.* July 397 Expert politicians, so distributed over the city as to operate at canvasses and elections in every ward and voting precinct. 1911 *Okla. Session Laws* 3 Legisl. 75 The county election board of any county . . . shall furnish each voting precinct . . . with three ballot boxes.

+**Voyageur.** [Fr.] A man, usually a French Canadian or half-breed, engaged in transporting people or goods in the Northwest; a boatman. Also attrib.
1809 A. HENRY *Travels* 18 My canoes were three times unladen, and . . . carried on the shoulders of the *voyageurs.* 1837 IRVING *Bonneville* I. 25 The voyageurs or boatmen were the rank and file in the service of the trader. 1881 *Harper's Mag.* Jan. 231/2, 'I think we shall have snow again tomorrow,' said old Antoine in his voyageur dialect. 1900 *Jesuit Rel. & Allied Doc.* LXV. 272 For many years,—since at least 1660,—the fur trade had been illegally carried on by wandering Canadian trappers and voyageurs, who were commonly termed *coureurs de bois,* 'wood-rangers.' 1902 HULBERT *Forest Neighbors* 136 With all the skill of the *voyageurs* of old, [they] cooked their scanty supper, and made their bed of balsam boughs.

Vulgate. {1728-} +Common or everyday speech. — 1854 COOKE *Va. Comedians* I. 75 'Here's a pretty mess,' returned the pompous gentleman, descending to the vulgate. 1883 D. H. WHEELER *By-Ways of Lit.* 176 There is always 'a free and easy' vulgate for the street, the market, and the fireside.

*∗**Vulture.**

+**1. a.** The American turkey buzzard, *Cathartes aura.* **b.** The California condor, *Gymnogyps californianus.*
1672 JOSSELYN *New Eng. Rarities* 10 The Gripe, which is of two kinds, the one with a white Head, the other with a black Head, this we take for

the Vulture. **1806** CLARK in *Lewis & C. Exped.* IV. (1905) 79 Shannon and Labiesh brought in to us today a Buzzard or *Vulture* of the Columbia which they had wounded and taken alive. **1850** BURKE *Reminisc. Georgia* 135 The most useful bird in all the South, is the buzzard, more properly called the vulture. **1898** CANFIELD *Maid of Frontier* 130 The wonderful Texan sky was . . . speckled here and there by black dots of wings of the slow-moving vultures. **1916** THOBURN *Stand. Hist. Oklahoma* I. 346 After removing a few choice pieces that were desired for the day, [they] left the rest for vultures and wolves.

+**2.** *Vulture buzzard*, the common buzzard or vulture (*Cathartes aura*); *vulture eagle*, (see quotation).

1846 *Knickerb.* XXVII. 252 A huge vulture-buzzard, with wide-extended wings, sailed slowly by. **1869** *Amer. Naturalist* III. 480 Among these have been seen [in the Colorado Valley] the strange Vulture-eagles (*Polyborus Audubonii* and *Craxirex unicinctus*), . . . and the quaint Wood Ibis.

+**Vum,** *n.* A use of the expression *I vum.* — **1881** *Harper's Mag.* Jan. 249 Darius was piqued, and he said, with a *vum*, 'I'll pay for the wood, if *you'll* send it hum.'

+**Vum,** *v.* [From *vow.*] *intr.* To vow; to swear. *colloq.* Usually *I vum.*

1785 *Mass. Spy* 13 Oct. 2/2 We all must dreadful mindful be That we must fight for liberty And vum we'll 'fend it, if we die. **1839** *Havana* (N.Y.) *Republican* 21 Aug. (Th.), I vum I cant contrive who *you* be. **1858** HOLMES *Autocrat* 296 But the Deacon swore (as Deacons do, With an 'I dew vum,' or an 'I tell *yeou*'). **1899** A. BROWN *Tiverton Tales* 316 Young Nick muttered, 'Well, I vum!' beneath his breath. **1904** M. E. WALLER *Wood-Carver* 149 Uncle Shim was stupefied into an open-mouthed 'I vum!'

b. *To be vummed*, to be darned or dog-goned. *colloq.*

1881 M. J. HOLMES *Madeline* 282 'She'd be vummed,' the indignant old lady said, 'if she would not write to Lucy herself if Guy did not quit such doin's.'

+**Vumper,** *v. intr.* =VUM *v. Obs.* — **1815** HUMPHREYS *Yankey* 70, I don't care a cent for you and all your close, I vumpers.

W

+**Waahoo.** =WAHOO²; also, a medicinal preparation made from this shrub. — **1843** TORREY *Flora N.Y.* I. 141 From this shrub [Indian arrow] is prepared the '*Wa-a-hoo,*' a quack medicine of some reputation. **1857** GRAY *Botany* 81 E[*uonymus*] *atropurpureus,* Burning-Bush. Waahoo. . . . Ornamental in autumn, by its copious crimson fruit. **1866** *Ill. Agric. Soc. Trans.* VI. 391 W.10 wants a Waahoo, so common in our groves? **1870** *Amer. Naturalist* IV. 215 The Waahoo . . . with its crimson drooping fruit.

+**Wabana.** [Amer. Indian.] (See quot. 1886.) — **1827** McKENNEY *Tour to Lakes* 322 It was announced that a wabana would be danced. **1886** Z. F. SMITH *Kentucky* 385 The wabana is an offering to the devil, and, like some others, the green-corn dance, for example, winds up with a feast.

+**Wabash,** *n.* [Amer. Indian.] The name of one of the northern tributaries of the Ohio River. Used attrib. — **1789** *Ann. 1st Congress* 80 The Governor of the Western Territory has made a statement to me of the reciprocal hostilities of the Wabash Indians, and the people inhabiting the frontiers bordering on the river Ohio. **1838** ELLSWORTH *Valley of Wabash* 46 It produced 120 bushels to an acre, and this on 'Wabash poor land,' which had supported successive exhausting crops without manure.

+**Wabash,** *v.* slang. [f. prec.] **1.** *tr.* (See quotation.) **2.** ?To throw in the Wabash River. **3.** (See quotation.) — (1) **1837** *Chicago Theol. Sem. Home Missions Coll.* 23 Jan., My wife says she feels that we have got thoroughly *Wabashed* [attacked by bilious fever on the banks of the Wabash]. (2) **1839** *Logansburg* (Ind.) *Herald* 17 Sept., Two men at Vincennes, suspected of overzealousness in the cause of Abolitionism, were recently taken out of their beds, severely scourged, Wabashed, and coated with indelible paste, as a remembrancer of their evil doings. (3) **1859** BARTLETT 498 *To Wabash.* 'He's *Wabashed,*' meaning he is cheated, is an expression much used in Indiana and other parts of the West.

Wabble, Wobble, *v.* {*ppl. a.,* 1657; 1677-} +**1.** *intr.* (See quotation.) *Obs.* +**2.** *tr.* To crumple *up.* — (1) **1848** BARTLETT 374 *To Wabble,* in the Western States, to make free use of one's tongue; to be a ready speaker. (2) **1870** A. D. WHITNEY *We Girls* vi. 95 Kitchens are horrid when girls have . . . left the dish-towels dirty, and the dish-cloth all wabbled up in the sink. **1884** *Harper's Mag.* June 88/1 The great point is to keep the net straight, and not all tangled and wobbled up.

⁕ **Wad.**

1. A small plug of tow, cloth, or paper used in charging a gun. {1667-} Also attrib.

1776 *R.I. Col. Rec.* VII. 605 Nicholas Power, for gun carriages, junk, wads, plank, &c. **1830** BRECK *Recoll.* 23 [The pistol] went off, hit him with the wad in the temple, and killed him on the spot. **1876** KNIGHT 2717/2 *Wad-punch,* a tubular steel punch used for cutting gun-wads, etc. **1911** WHITE *Bobby Orde* xi, In the bunks themselves lay powder canisters, shotbags, wad-boxes.

+**2.** A roll of bills. *colloq.²* {1899-}

1814 *Niles' Reg.* VII. 205/2 He then rammed both hands into his trowsers' pockets, and drew out handfulls of notes ruffled into *wads.* **1856** *Harper's Mag.* XIII. 307/1 The bundle . . . proved to be a wad of one-dollar notes. **1895** *N.Y. Dramatic News* 26 Oct. 5/3 He was 'held up' on Thursday evening, and relieved of his 'wad.' **1902** C. MORRIS *Stage Confidences* 223 Will you take this 'wad' and go . . . out of my life forever?

+**3.** A 'chew' or portion *of* tobacco.

1844 *Knickerb.* XXIV. 71 He chews the precious weed inordinately; always keeping a large wad of tobacco upon the right side of his mouth. **1898** WESTCOTT *D. Harum* xvii, Mr. Harum . . . replenished his left cheek with an ample wad of 'fine-cut.'

⁕ **Wadder.** A popular term for a division of the madderwort family. — **1863** *Rep. Comm. Agric.* 159 We were near passing over the Madderwort family with its 'cleavers,' and 'bedstraws,' and 'wadders'—useful enough in the arts and sciences, but of little application to our subject.

Wadding. {1627-}

1. Cotton, paper, etc., used for padding, quilting, etc. {1734-}

1727 *Boston News-Letter* 29 June 2/2 To be Sold, . . . All sorts of European Goods, Consisting of . . . Blankets, Wadings [etc.]. **1802** CUTLER in *Life & Corr.* II. 113, I presented him a specimen of wadding for Ladies' cloaks. **1836** *Jamestown* (N.Y.) *Jrnl.* 28 Sept. 1/3 The bodies of these vehicles are covered with alternate coats of sheet iron, buffalo skins and paper wadding. **1850** MITCHELL *Lorgnette* I. 30 Our hero patronizes a fashionable tailor, and sets off a coat, by dint of slight wadding, capitally well.

2. (See quot. 1876.)

1876 KNIGHT 2717/1 *Wadding,* . . . loosely woven stuff used by tailors. **1882** *Rep. Indian Affairs* 414.

+**Waddy.** W. A cattle-rustler. — **1897** HOUGH *Story of Cowboy* 279 A genuine rustler was called a 'waddy,' a name difficult to trace to its origin. **1912** RAINE *Brand Blotters* 45, I'm a waddy and a thief, but you're going to protect me for old times' sake.

⁕ **Wade,** *v. colloq.* +**1.** *To wade into,* to attack vigorously. +**2.** *To wade in,* to 'go to it,' to 'get busy.' — (1) **1872** POWERS *Afoot & Alone* 130 We waded into 'em, and skinned 'em out mighty sudden. **1904** STRATTON-PORTER *Freckles* 365 You waded single-handed into a man almost twice your size. (2) **1883** *Albany* (Tex.) *Echo* 12 December, Build a Chinese wall around Coleman County, put all the fence-cutters inside it, furnish them with wire fence and nippers, and tell them to wade in.

Wader. {1673-} **1.** Any long-legged shore bird. {1771-} **2.** *pl.* High rubber boots, used by anglers. {1841-} — (1) **1813** Wilson *Ornithology* IX. 72 The Phalaropes constitute one of the links between the Waders and the Web-footed tribes. **1860** EMERSON *Conduct of Life* 34 Ducks take to the water, eagles to the sky, waders to the sea margin. **1870** *Amer. Naturalist* II. 227 The sea-side ornithology of New England [consists of] four or five groups . . . : shore birds or waders; sea-birds or swimmers. (2) **1894** *Outing* XXIV. 123/1 When we reached the snipe ground we removed our boots and . . . pulled on our waders. **1897** *Ib.* XXX. 63/1, I open the door again and step forth in my stocking feet to get my waders.

Wade river. =WADING RIVER. *Obs.* — **1728** *Brookhaven Rec.* 118 Layd oute a highway from the Olde man's . . . to the wade River.

⁕ **Wading.** Attrib. with *shoe, stocking, water.* — **1791** WASHINGTON *Diaries* IV. 156 [They] jumped into the River as soon as the Batteau was forced into wading water. **1884** *Nat. Museum Bul.* No. 27, 801 Wading-shoes with hob-nails. . . . Made especially for anglers. *Ib.,* Black rubber wading-stockings. Made of a good quality of rubber cloth. . . . Used by anglers.

Wading bird. =WADER 1. {1867-} — **1858** BAIRD *Birds Pacific R.R.* 706 Northern Phalarope. . . . One of the handsomest and most graceful of the wading birds. **1865** *Atlantic Mo.* Feb. 187/1 Their moss-grown remains . . . are as unmistakable as the footprints of the huge wading bird in the red sandstone. **1883** *Harper's Mag.* Oct. 714/1 The brackish marsh-lands are the haunt of curlews, avocets, plovers, and other wading birds.

⁕ **Wading place.** A ford. {1598} — **1627** in *Amer. Sp.* XV. 407/1 Abutting Northerly upon a small marshe towards the wading place. **1683** *Conn. Rec.* III. 331 To the place where the Common Road or Wading place over the said River is. **1724** *Talcott P.* 27 [We] came to a great stone at the wading place where the road cut the river. **1781** *Narragansett Hist. Reg.* I. 281 Went in swimming at Robert's wadeing place.

Wading river. ?A river or a place in a river that can be waded. *Obs.* — **1644** *R.I. Col. Rec.* I. 82 William Almy, and John Roome . . . are to have lande at the wading river. **1659** *Portsmouth Rec.* 383 Land . . . lyinge in the farme of the aforesaid Thomas Hazard and adjoyneinge unto the wadeing or mill river. **1664** *Brookhaven Rec.* 12 The feede and timber of all the lands, . . . from the ould manes to the wadeing river. **1720** *Ib.* 112 Voted . . . that Mr. Sills foreworn Nathaniel Dayton from fencing & improveing any further the Towne's lande along the clift, at the wadeing River.

⁕ **Wafer.**

1. A small disk of paste used for sealing letters. {1635-}

1711 *Mass. H. S. Coll.* 6 Ser. V. 240 Get some wafers; send the enclosed presently. **1794** *Steele P.* I. 121 After reading [your letter] . . . I put a wafer in it and gave it to the Colonel. **1820** *Columbian Centinel* 8 Jan. 1/1 Thomas Wells . . . intends to keep for Sale a good assortment of Books, . . . Wafers, Pocket Books. **1852** *Harper's Mag.* V. 275/1 A fellow-student . . . saw the Kentuckian . . . take from his pocket a slip of paper, and proceed to affix the same, with the aid of wafers, to the street door.

⁕**2.** A thin disk of cake or bread; a cracker.

1815 in H. M. Brooks *Gleanings* IV. 129 All kinds of Cakes, Wafers, French Rolls, &c. furnished at the shortest notice. **1848** THOREAU *Maine Woods* 62 After whetting our appetite on some raw pork, a wafer of hard bread, and a dipper of condensed cloud or water-spout, we . . . began to make our way up the falls.

3. *transf.* A somewhat round spot or disk.

1853 KANE *Grinnell Exped.* (1856) 236 Deck covered in with black felt, the frozen condensation patching it with large wafers of snow. **1897** *Outing* XXIX. 543/1 The Dalmatian, or 'coach dog,' white with black wafers stuck all over him.

4. Attrib. and comb. in senses 1 and 2 with *biscuit, cake, iron,* etc.

1643 *Conn. Rec.* I. 455 A Inventory of the goods of Tho. Scott: . . . a iron to make wafer caks. **1796** *Boston Directory* 261 Joyce, Joseph, inkpowder and wafer maker, Bridge's lane. **1832** *Boston Herald* 29 May 4/4 The error arose from our letter being wafer-torn where the figures were written. **1850** E. P. BURKE *Reminisc. Georgia* 178 Within I found . . . kettles, spiders, Dutch ovens, wafer-irons, and every thing else one could think of. **1876** M. F. HENDERSON *Cooking* 72 Wafer Biscuits. . . . These wafers are exceedingly nice to serve with a cheese course, or for invalids to eat with their tea.

+**Wafer ash. 1.** The hop tree, *Ptelea trifoliata.* **2.** Bark from the root of this tree used in making a tonic, or the tonic itself. Also attrib. — (1) **1884** SARGENT *Rep. Forests* 31 Hop Tree. Shrubby Trefoil. Wafer Ash. **1897** SUDWORTH *Arborescent Flora* 267. (2) **1872** EGGLESTON *End of World* 140 She should have a corn-sweat and some wafer-ash tea. *Ib.* 140 The wafer-ash would cause a tendency of blood to the head, and thus relieve pressure on the juggler-vein. Cynthy Ann . . . set the wafer-ash to draw.

Wafer box. A box for wafers (sense 1). — **1816** *Mass. H. S. Coll.* 2 Ser. VII. 119 These tacks are chiefly used by saddlers, . . . cabinet-makers, and also for wafer-boxes. **1861** *Army Regulations* 167 To each office table is allowed one inkstand, . . . one sand-box, one wafer-box.

Wafer card. An extremely thin calling card. — **1896** *Godey's Mag.* Feb. 220/1 The wafer card has only one thing to recommend it, and that is, that a greater number of cards may be compressed into a small space.

+**Waffle.** [Du. *wafel.*]
1. A cake somewhat like a pancake but usually crisper and baked in a waffle iron.
1817 BIRKBECK *Notes Journey in Amer.* (1818) 64 Waffles (a soft hot cake of German extraction, covered with butter). **1832** WATSON *Hist. Tales N.Y.* 125 The regale . . . was expected as matter of course, to be chocolate supper and soft waffles. **1848** *Ladies' Repository* VIII. 68 Then, as you may suppose, I feel tired, and I get something to eat, say a cup of tea and a waffle. **1857** *Knickerb.* XLIX. 98 Coffee and milk-toast, waffles and honey, disappeared . . . like magic. **1870** D. MACRAE *Amer. at Home* I. 291 The Americans are all fond of molasses; using them regularly at breakfast and supper to their buckwheat cakes and waffles. **1887** *Century Mag.* Nov. 16/2 A procession of little darkies [at Mount Vernon, Va.] . . . supporting plates of hot batter-cakes, muffins, Sally Lunns, rice waffles. **1906** DELAND in *Harper's Mag.* June 84 Before she could reply, Sarah came in with hot waffles.

2. Attrib. with *frolic, maker, mould.*
1744 in Earle *Colonial Days N.Y.* 216 We had the wafel-frolic at Miss Walton's talked of before your departure. **1864** 'MARK TWAIN' *Sketches* (1926) 139 His face was pitted like a waffle-mould. **1883** 'S. BONNER' *Dialect Tales* 93 As a waffle-maker she possessed a gift beyond the common.

+**Waffle iron.** A utensil for making waffles, consisting of two patterned iron griddles hinged together. Also fig. and attrib. — **1794** *S. Carolina State Gaz.* 30 Aug. 1/2 (Th.S.), Woffle irons [advertised]. **1828** LESLIE *Receipts* 71 Heat your waffle-iron. . . . Shut the iron tight, and bake the waffle on both sides. **1866** C. H. SMITH *Bill Arp* 115 Didn't the rebellion just close right up . . . like shutting up a pair of waffle-irons? **1889** 'MARK TWAIN' *Conn. Yankee* 385 One of the commonest decorations of the nation was the waffle-iron face. **1896** HARRIS *Sister Jane* 58 Why, Mandy, where in the world did you find the waffle-irons?

+**Waffle party.** A party at which waffles are served. — **1808** in *Scribner's Mag.* II. 183/1 They are going to have a fine waffle party on Tuesday. **1882** *Harper's Mag.* April 666/1 She tells him of 'little waffle parties' formed by her intimates.

***Wage,** *n.* Payment for work performed. Used attrib. in sing. or pl. — **1874** *Florida Plant. Rec.* 201 My only regret is that we had not planted 50 acres of cotton with wages hands. **1898** *Kansas City Star* 18 Dec. 2/1 The ultimate outcome of the labor movement . . . will be the destruction of the wage system. **1904** PRINGLE *Rice Planter* 62 The two families who are moving to town carry off four young girls who are . . . very necessary to the cultivation of my 'wages fields.' **1906** LYNDE *Quickening* 310 His father was deep in the new wage scale submitted by the miners' union. **1911** PERSONS, etc. *Mass. Labor Laws* 206 The other woman has likewise a special duty, inspecting for violations of wage schedules in textile factories.

***Wage,** *v.* intr. and tr. To wager. {–1742} — **1815** HUMPHREYS *Yankey* 110 *Wage,* or wager, to bet. **1825** NEAL *Bro. Jonathan* II. 55 Oh, my shins!—oh—oh!—they're pootely barked, I wage. **1876** TRIPP *Student-Life* 18 Do something splendid on the mathematics and the 'orals,' and I will wage any thing you will pass clear.

+**Wage worker.** One who works for wages; a wage-earner. Also transf. — **1876** *Mass. Labor Statistics 7th Rep.* 9 Wage Workers from whom Schedules were received. . . . Oysterman, Oyster Opener, Packer (of merchandise). **1892** *Courier-Journal* 2 Oct. 16/3 Twice as much paper . . . will be required in making the new stamps, thus affording employment to many more wage-workers. **1899** GOING *Flowers* 19 These insect visitors, however, are respectable wage-workers. **1904** *Boston Transcript* 11 June 18 The speaker went further than was necessary in his effort to do justice to the wage-worker.

+**Waggletail.** (See quotations.) colloq. — **1859** BARTLETT 498 *Waggletail,* the larva of the mosquito, etc.; also called a wiggler. a**1870** CHIPMAN *Notes on Bartlett* 498 *Waggletail* . . . wheel-insect.

+**Wagh,** *interj.* Also **wa.** An exclamation imitative of Indian speech. — **1791** J. LONG *Voyages* 164 *Wa! Wa!* or Oh! oh! replied the Savage, but what is the warrior tied up for? **1848** RUXTON *Life Far West* i, I ar' a trapper, marm, a mountain-man, wagh! **1850** GARRARD *Wah-To-Yah*

xiii. 166 Thar's two or three in this crowd—wagh!—howsomever, the green is 'rubbed out' a little.

***Wagon,** *n.*
***I. 1.** A stout, four-wheeled vehicle used for transporting heavy goods. Formerly freq. in military use.
1694 *Jamaica Rec.* I. 425 The waggen and harrow [are] for boath thier uses & boath to maintain eaquell charge. **1757** *Lett. to Washington* II. 74 I have sent from this place nine Waggons which will be sufficient to bring to Lancaster the following Ammunition. **1788** FRANKLIN *Autobiog.* 394 We found the general at Frederictown, waiting impatiently for the return of those he had sent thro' the back parts of Maryland and Virginia to collect waggons. **1796** WEEMS *Letters* II. 43 From Alexandria I can daily get opportunities to send them by the waggons to those places. **1841** *Picayune* 31 Aug. 2/1 A number of waggons, belonging to Mr. Ward, of Roacheport, passed through that town on Tuesday last. **1881–5** MCCLELLAN *Own Story* 415, I therefore determined to send the heavy guns . . . over the Chickahominy during the night, with as many of the wagons of the 5th corps as possible. **1907** *St. Nicholas* July 776/1 From outside there came . . . the creaking of wagons, and the noise of a driver's eloquence hurled at weary mules.

+**2.** A carriage or other light vehicle seating a few passengers.
1799 WELD *Travels* 15 The carriages made use of in Philadelphia consist of coaches, chariots, chaises, coachees, and light waggons. **1815** SUTCLIFF *Travels* p. xi, The open carriages described in this plate, are called waggons. **1829** B. HALL *Travels in N.A.* I. 106 At last we obtained a guide, who undertook to carry us in a one-horse waggon, as it is called, but which we should call a light cart. **1831** PECK *Guide* 124, I have brought two waggons, or carriages, to this country [Ill.], which were made in Litchfield, Connecticut. **1848** *Knickerb.* XXXI. 84 The Doctor was driving out in thoughtful mood the other day in a one-horse wagon. **1861** STOWE *Pearl Orr's Isl.* I. 7 A one-horse wagon, in which two persons are sitting. **1899** MUIRHEAD *Baedeker's U.S.* p. xxx, *Wagon,* carriage. **1904** D. CONWAY *Autobiog.* 196 They appeared in a handsome wagon, all in pretty gowns.

3. A strong vehicle used to transport emigrants and their property to new locations in the West.
1810 M. DWIGHT *Journey to Ohio* 19 Where we stopt to bait yesterday, we found another waggon. **1813** *Salem Gazette* 1 Oct. 3/3 A convoy of wagons, with families and house-hold furniture, from Nantucket, left Falmouth on Monday last, for Ohio. **1842** *Diplom. Corr. Texas* III. (1911) 1883 Upwards of 100,000 emigrants have gone into the country since Oct. last from the United States and 5000 wagons have crossed the Sabine this winter. **1877** JOHNSON *Anderson Co., Kansas* 153 In 1860 . . . they came in a wagon, drawn by a pair of oxen. **1880** *Harper's Mag.* LXI. 187/2 In such a caravan there would be, perhaps, one hundred wagons. **1890** HARTE *Waif of Plains* 7 The rear wagon creaked, swayed, and rolled on slowly and heavily. **1894** CHOPIN *Bayou Folk* 147 [Désirée] had been purposely left by a party of Texans, whose canvas-covered wagon . . . had crossed the ferry. a**1918** G. STUART *On Frontier* I. 44, I took him [a dog] up on the footboard of the wagon, where he lay part of the time, all the way to California.

+**4.** A baby carriage.
1847 [see sense 8]. **1868** A. D. WHITNEY *P. Strong* 139 It is an understood point that though you bring a basket as big as a baby's wagon [etc.]. **1887** CABOT *Mem. Emerson* II. 282 (O.E.D.), The whole town assembled, down to the babies in their wagons.

+**5.** A vehicle used to convey arrested persons to a police station. colloq. { = E. 'prison van'}
1891 *Boston Transcript* 8 May 5/2 A man . . . attacked the officer, and it required considerable clubbing to keep him quiet until the wagon arrived. **1902** MACGOWAN *Last Word* 334 If there hadn't been two of us on the job there'd have been murder done getting him in the wagon.

II. *attrib.* and *comb.* **6.** Designating persons having to do with wagons, or places or activities concerned with making wagons.
1781 *Va. State P.* I. 495 Waggon Conductors 5s. or 25 lbs. Tobacco. **1867** *Atlantic Mo.* Feb. 228/1 When quite young, he was apprenticed to a wagon-painter. **1872** TICE *Over Plains* 11 Atchison . . . [has] two wagon manufactories. **1884** W. SHEPHERD *Prairie Exper.* 141 A boy of eighteen attaches himself, say to a blacksmith, wheelwright, and waggon repairer. **1890** *Rep. Secy. Agric. 1889* 27 The relation of various industries to forest supplies has been made the subject of inquiry, especially that of . . . the carriage and wagon manufacture.

7. Designating ways made by, or suitable for, the passage of wagons.
1793 in Summers *Ann. S.W. Va.* 840 Gordon Cloyd appointed overseer of the road from top of Brushy Mountain to the wagon ford on Back Creek. **1845** SIMMS *Wigwam & Cabin* 1 Ser. 75, I suddenly caught a glimpse of an opening on my right, a sort of wagon-path. **1849** *31st Cong. 1 Sess.* Sen. Ex. Doc. No. 64, 135 We left Algadones for Santa Fe, . . . taking . . . the usual wagon-route between the two places. **1865** *Ore. State Jrnl.* 18 Nov. 1/4 By building a wagon portage . . . the stream is again struck at a navigable point.

8. Designating parts of wagons, or things used with or on wagons.

1800 TATHAM *Agric. & Commerce* 87 Farming Linen; comprehending sacks, waggon-cloths, winnowing sheets, &c [are manufactured in the U.S.]. **1810** *Austin P.* I. (1924) 168, 500 Wagon fellows. **1815** *Niles' Reg.* VIII. 59/2 They committed this act in retaliation for injuries received from the waggoners at fort Mitchell, having been used roughly with their waggon whips. **1847** EMERSON *Poems* 238 [They] let the world's affairs go by, Awhile to . . . mend his wicker wagon-frame. **1868** *Mich. Agric. Rep.* VII. 347 Brockway and Leaverens, Galesburg, [manufactured the] wagon skean and carriage axles. **1875** *Fur, Fin & Feather* 105 Their avoirdupois will go steadily up while the wagon-springs settle steadily down. **1887** CUSTER *Tenting on Plains* 364 The clank of the wagon-chains . . . sounded like thunder in the ears of the anxious, expectant men. **1891** *Century Mag.* Feb. 594 A carpet-bag—not the Northern variety of wagon-curtain canvas, but the regular old-fashioned carpet kind. **1899** *Mo. So. Dakotan* I. 176 [He] put the off ox over the wagon handle. **1901** CHURCHILL *Crisis* 99, 'I reckon I know,' said Brent, bringing down his fist on the wagon board.

9. Designating races in which horses draw light wagons, or the horses participating in such races.

1857 *Porter's Spirit of Times* 3 Jan. 292/2 Thus were disposed of the pretensions of the great wagon trotter. **1868** WOODRUFF *Trotting Horse* 265 After that wagon-race, Flora was deemed the mistress of any thing out in that way of going. *Ib.* 362 In a week after the time-race, Dexter trotted his first wagon-match with Gen. Butler.

10. In special combinations.

Wagon bonnet, w. breast, (see quotations); *w. bridge,* a bridge suitable for the passage of wagons; *w. company,* a company carrying on transportation by wagons; *w. distance,* the distance within which wagoning is feasible; *w. gait,* the gait at which a wagon is usually driven; *w. hoop,* =WAGON BOW; *w. office,* a business office of a system or line of transportation by wagons; *w. outfit,* an outfit employing wagons; *w. service,* postal service in which wagons are used; *w. sled, w. soldier,* (see quotations); *w. sugar,* sugar which at one stage of its manufacture is emptied into wagons or trucks; *w. tar,* tar used on a wagon; *w. tobacco,* tobacco brought to market by wagon; *w. work,* parts, materials, etc., for wagons.
1830 WATSON *Philadelphia* 176 The 'wagon bonnet' . . . was deemed to look, on the head, not unlike the top of the Jersey wagons. **1881** RAYMOND *Mining Gloss., Wagon-breast,* a breast into which wagons can be taken. **1900** *Congress. Rec.* 15 Jan. 802/1 It proposes to extend to June 3, 1902, the time for completing the construction of a wagon and motor bridge across the Missouri River. **1825** *Nat. Intelligencer* 8 July 2/4 The wagon company [of Santa Fé adventurers] will proceed separately, and under a different organization. **1901** WHITE *Westerners* 144 With the erection of a stamp mill, within wagon distance, they [quartz leads] become valuable. **1845** SIMMS *Wigwam & Cabin* 1 Ser. 33 The dull travelling wagon-gait at which he himself was compelled to go was a source of annoyance to him. **1891** *Scribner's Mag.* Sept. 309/1 A blanket is hung in the doorway, or the cotton from the wagon-hoops will serve, and there is the dugout home. **1829** ROYALL *Pennsylvania* I. 16, I sent a box of books to the waggon office, to be conveyed to Messrs. Johnson and Stockton. **1895** REMINGTON *Pony Tracks* 1 Before accepting an invitation to accompany an Indian commission into the Northwest I had asked the general quietly if this was a 'horseback' or a 'wagon outfit.' **1893** CUSHING *Story of P.O.* 38 The 'regulation wagon service' is performed in some forty of the chief cities of the country. **1905** *Forestry Bureau Bul.* No. 61, 42 *Logging sled,* the heavy double sled used to haul logs from the skidway or yard to the landing. (N[orthern] F[orest]) Syn.: twin sleds, two sleds, wagon sled. **1917** J. A. MOSS *Officers' Manual* 485 *Wagon-soldier*—light or field artilleryman. **1892** *Mod. Lang. Notes* Nov. 394 The mass [of syrup] thus reduced is emptied into wagons and run into a hot room, where it is allowed to crystallize slowly; this process is generally followed for all sugars except first sugars . . . and they are often called *wagon sugar.* **1890** LANGFORD *Vigilante Days* (1912) 121 There stood, on the bank . . . , a sign-post with a rough-hewn board nailed across the top, with the following intelligence daubed with wagon-tar thereon. **1819** *Amer. Farmer* I. 135 Fine wagon Tobacco sold yesterday, for $14. **1790** *Penna. Packet* 31 May 3/4 Nicodemus Loyd . . . has now for sale, . . . plough irons and waggon-work.

Wagon, *v.*

+1. *tr.* To transport or convey by wagon. *Obs.*

1755 WASHINGTON *Writings* I. 187 The quantity is too great for the present consumption, and to wagon it up can never answer the expense. **1782** JEFFERSON *Notes Va.* (1788) 24 The ore is first waggoned to the river. **1819** SCHOOLCRAFT *Mo. Lead Mines* 58 Goods are now wagoned over from St. Genevieve. **1857** STROTHER *Virginia* 152, I'll wagon licker and provis'ons for 'em for nothing. **1895** 'CRADDOCK' *Mystery Witch-Face Mt.* 62 In the fall of the year the folks would kem wagonin' their chestnuts over ter sell in town.

2. *intr.* To travel by wagon; to transport goods by wagon. {1606}

1794 DENNY *Journal* 199 The French had opened the Indian path . . . and wagoned considerably upon it. **1884** 'CRADDOCK' *Tenn. Mts.* 144 He hev determinated ter break up an' wagon across the range ter Kaintucky. **1889** CUSTER *Tenting on Plains* 445 We, encumbered with blankets, packs and arms, had no mind to walk when we could 'waggon.' **1907** 'CRAD-

DOCK' *Windfall* 103, I can't figure out how the lady managed to stay so stiff and starched . . . , waggoning down from the mountain.

Wagonage. **a.** Conveyance or transport by wagon. *Obs.* {1609-}
+b. Money charged, or paid, for conveyance by wagon. *Obs.* — **1755** *Lett. to Washington* I. 141, [I] desire you will send about one Thousand Pounds more to pay Waggonage and for Pork. **1757** WASHINGTON *Writings* I. 491 The amount of waggonage and other charges of transporting these provisions . . . will exceed the whole cost of the provisions. **1779** JEFFERSON *Writings* IV. 51 Wagonage, indeed, seems to the commissariat an article not worth economising. **1816** *Ann. 14th Congress* 1 Sess. 113 It became necessary to use four distinct lines of transportation . . . at an expense of wagonage estimated at . . . not less than four hundred and fourteen thousand dollars. **1845** *Cincinnati Misc.* 125 The high rates of wagonage across the mountains, led many persons early . . . to engage in the taking up in keel-boats . . . various articles.

Wagon bed. The body of a wagon. {1893, *dial.*} (Cf. BED n. 2.) — **1847** PALMER *Rocky Mts.* (1904) 95 All articles liable to damage, from coming in contact with the water, should be piled on the top of the wagon bed. **1879** BURDETTE *Hawkeyes* 73 There was even thirty-seven bushels of apples in the wagon bed. **1897** *Outing* XXX. 551/2 The Eel River has a summer flow measuring no greater depth than reached our wagon-bed. **1920** HOWELLS *Vacation of Kelwyns* 225 They saw a man lying on his back under the wagon-bed.

Wagon body. =prec. — **1768** in Chalkley *Scotch-Irish Settlement Va.* I. 458 Credit by one wagon body at 6/. **1805** ASBURY *Journal* III. 201 We had [in Ohio] a beach-swamp, mud up to the hubs, stumps as high as the wagon-body. **1865** *Atlantic Mo.* April 404/1 [He] watched them float away . . . in a wagon-body whose wheels and horses were . . . nearly submerged. **1916** PORTER *David* 26 Together they aided his father to climb into the roomy wagon-body.

+Wagon boss. W. A man in charge of a wagon train. — **1873** BEADLE *Undevel. West* 98 Our 'wagon-boss,' absolute monarch of a train while on the road, rejoiced in the name of John Monkins. **1888** *San Francisco W. Examiner* 23 Feb. (F.), I gave instructions to the wagon boss, and the long bull-team moved away. **1901** *Kansas H. S. Coll.* VII. 49 One wagon boss blacksnaked him, after which indignity he sought a friend.

+Wagon bow. (See quot. 1876 and cf. Bow 4.) — **1844** GREGG *Commerce of Prairies* II. 287 Some give their lodges a round wagon-top shape, as those of the Osages, which commonly consist of a frame of bent rods, resembling wagon-bows [etc.]. **1876** KNIGHT 2719/1 *Wagon-bow,* an arched-shaped slat with its ends planted in staples on the wagon-bed sides. Used to elevate the tilt or cover. **1891** SWASEY *Early Days Calif.* 163 They took some of our wagon-bows, which were made of hickory, and bent them into an oblong shape.

Wagon box.
1. The metal thimble or skein on the end of a wagon axle. *Obs.* (Cf. CART BOX.)
1790 *Penna. Packet* 2 Jan. 3/3 The Subscriber hath for Sale at his House . . . cart and waggon boxes of all sizes. **1815** *Niles' Reg.* IX. 94/2 Waggon boxes and hollow ware of all kinds. **1856** *Mich. Agric. Soc. Trans.* VII. 52 Cowing & Co. . . . [exhibited] specimens of wagon boxes.

+2. The body of a wagon. Also attrib. (Cf. Box n.² 5.)
1848 THOREAU *Maine Woods* 12 [Here was] a stock selected with what pains and care and brought home in the wagon-box. **1887** *Century Mag.* May 116/1 Polly-Ann saw Lum's wagon-box boat on the sand. **1890** LANGFORD *Vigilante Days* (1912) 118 One of this latter company . . . was drowned while attempting to cross the river in a poorly constructed boat, made out of a wagon-box. a**1918** G. STUART *On Frontier* II. 158 Mrs. Annie Boyd came driving into Bozeman with six small children in the wagon box.

+Wagon boy. **1.** A wagoner or teamster. **2.** (See quot. 1885.) — **(1)** **1836** *S. Lit. Messenger* II. 78 Seek them who will, they have no joys For mountain lads, and Wagon-boys. **1883** FULTON *Sam Hobart* 143 He looked at the weeping women and tear-dimmed eyes of the wagon-boys. **(2)** **1840** *Niles' Nat. Reg.* 12 Sept. 1/3 All the counties contiguous, both in Ohio and Pennsylvania, poured out their thousands to hear Ohio's favorite wagon boy.] **1847** *Whig Almanac 1848* 32/1 At the time the 'Wagon Boy' was first sent to the Legislature by the good people of Warren, he found a law on the statute-book providing for the punishment of certain offences by public whipping. **1885** *Mag. Amer. Hist.* May 495/1 *Wagon boy.*—The popular nickname of the Hon. Thomas Corwin, of Ohio. In his youth he earned his living by driving a team on a Kentucky farm.

Wagon-builder. One who builds wagons. {1850-} — **1786** WASHINGTON *Diaries* III. 137 Caleb Hall . . . was a compleat Wheel right, Waggon builder, and Plow and Hurdle maker. **1892** *York County Hist. Rev.* 63 Eckenrode & Koller, Wagon Builders.

+Wagon camp. A place where a wagon train is encamped. — **1854** WHIPPLE, etc. *Explor. Ry. Route* I. 79 Having sent messengers to the wagon camp, . . . we recrossed Colorado Chiquito. **1856** OLMSTED *Slave States* 359 An equally picturesque scene with that of the wagon camp was a collection of these boats, moored at night under the steep river bank. **1867** CRAWFORD *Mosby* 193 We started out to find the wagon-camp.

Wagon cover. A waterproof cloth or canvas of considerable size, used to protect persons or goods in a wagon. {1832-} — **1779** *N.J. Archives* 2 Ser. III. 408 Others now in the service, have in their possession waggons, horses, tents, waggon covers, forrage bags, etc. **1848** BRYANT *California* ii. 29 The numerous white tents and wagon-covers . . . represent a rustic village. **1897** HOUGH *Story of Cowboy* 198 It's yore own fault . . . lettin' that wagon cover blow off. *a*1918 G. STUART *On Frontier* I. 96 Like all the people who practise treachery, they feared it, and not knowing what might be inside the wagon covers, declined [a parley].

*∗**Wagoner**. Also **waggoner**. One engaged in hauling with a wagon. Also appositive. — **1662** *Plymouth Laws* 136 In case any master Carrier or wagoner shall have cause to suspect any such goods may bee concealled in any cask or sacke amongst other goods [etc.]. **1757** *N.Y. State Doc. Hist.* I. 523 Six Waggoners . . . were carrying Capt. Gage's Baggage to the Fort. **1788** WASHINGTON *Diaries* III. 440 Doctr. Craik . . . came down this afternoon to visit Waggoner Jack. **1807** *Ann. 10th Congress* I Sess. 2303 He was . . . employed sometimes as a wagoner, driving a team to and from Baltimore. **1897** HOUGH *Story of Cowboy* 38 One improvident wagoner . . . found himself with a broken axletree and no timber near except some cottonwoods.

Wagon factory. A place where wagons are made. — **1827** DRAKE & MANSFIELD *Cincinnati* 65 Eight Carriage and Wagon Factories. **1891** O'BEIRNE *Leaders Ind. Territory* 48/1 Mr. Frinzell . . . opened the first blacksmith and wagon factory in the county. **1901** *Harper's Mag.* Dec. 211/1 Miles and his partner were driving to the wagon-factory.

Wagon gate. A gate for the passage of wagons. — **1879** STOCKTON *Rudder Grange* xii, There was a wagon-gate at one side of the front fence. **1900** DIX *Deacon Bradbury* 221 The other sleigh turned in at the wagon-gate.

Wagon grease. A heavy grease for use on wagons. Also transf. — **1862** BROWNE *A. Ward: His Book* 49, [I] had a lot of sweet-scented wagon grease on my hair. **1882** SWEET & KNOX *Texas Siftings* 69, [I] actually captured a lot of wagon-grease, and a dozen monkey-wrenches.

Wagon guard. *Mil.* A force detailed to guard a wagon or wagon train. — **1852** WATSON *Nights in Block-House* 229 The wagon-guard had also been attracted by the firing. **1862** NORTON *Army Lett.* 39 [H.] will go as a wagon guard.

Wagon harness. Harness suitable for a horse or mule that pulls a wagon. (Cf. BUGGY HARNESS.) — **1781** *Va. State P.* I. 483 In establishing manufactures of waggon-harness, I have fixed one at Charlottesville. **1858** *Mich. Agric. Soc. Trans.* IX. 316 The committee would also recommend a premium to No. 92 a Wagon Harness, exhibited by Ward Gazlay. **1883** *Rep. Indian Affairs* 177 This year we are making . . . 100 sets of wagon harness.

*∗**Wagon horse.** A horse suitable for pulling a wagon. (Cf. BUGGY HORSE.) — **1760** WASHINGTON *Diaries* I. 129, [I] found one of my best Waggon horses . . . with his right foreleg mashed to pieces. **1800** *Steele P.* I. 185 They have lost one or two of their waggon Horses this fall. **1853** SIMMS *Sword & Distaff* (1854) 121 The wagon-horses were hidden in the woods.

Wagon house. A house or building for a wagon. {1660–} — **1773** in Fithian *Journal* I. 39 Whitehead has built a waggon house for his coach. **1812** *Niles' Reg.* II. 165/1 He then went to his waggon house and hanged himself. **1879** STOCKTON *Rudder Grange* xviii, I built several barns, wagon-houses, and edifices of the sort on my place.

Wagoning. Transporting, conveying, or traveling by wagon. {1865–} Also attrib. — **1782** in Summers *Ann. S.W. Va.* 770 He ought to be paid . . . for one day waggoning. **1808** in *Niles' Reg.* XV. 57/1 It pays for waggoning 300 miles, [$]5.00. **1843** 'CARLTON' *New Purchase* I. 118 Here he was brought up to the wagoning business. **1857** CHANDLESS *Visit Salt Lake* 264 Waggoning through the settlements . . . and thence 'packing' to California. **1861** *Ill. Agric. Soc. Trans.* IV. 373 In wagoning we can load to suit the strength of our team.

+**Wagon-ironing.** Providing or repairing the ironwork of a wagon. — **1864** *Ore. State Jrnl.* 10 Dec. 3/5 Luckey Bros., Are prepared to do all kinds of Blacksmithing, Horseshoeing, Wagon Ironing, etc. **1892** *York County Hist. Rev.* 61 Wagon ironing is done with special attention paid to horseshoeing.

Wagon-jack. (See quot. 1876.) — **1856** *Mich. Agric. Soc. Trans.* VII. 510 Best wagon jack, $0.50. **1876** KNIGHT 2719/2 *Wagon-jack*, one [*i.e.*, a jack] for lifting the wheels of a wagon clear of the ground.

*∗**Wagon-maker.** One who builds wagons. — **1820** FLINT *Lett. from Amer.* 213 Coach and waggon makers, 9 Work shops, 33 Workmen. **1887** *Courier-Journal* 25 Jan. 4 The wife of M. Iseman, a wealthy wagon-maker and real estate owner, to-day filed suit for divorce. **1901** DUNCAN & SCOTT *Allen & Woodson Co., Kansas* 595 Lumber was obtained for a new school house, but . . . the greater portion of it was 'jayhawked' by a wagon maker who had a shop near by.

Wagon-making. The making of wagons. — **1849** CHAMBERLAIN *Ind. Gazetteer* 132 There is also . . . a two story work shop . . . in which wagon making is carried on. **1869** *Overland Mo.* III. 10 In North Carolina, . . . wagon-making, coopery, and other sorts of hard-handed industry, were in noisy blast. **1891** O'BEIRNE *Leaders Ind. Territory* 38/2 His father pursued his trade of wagon making at Doaksville.

Wagon master. One in charge of wagons or a wagon train. {1645–1688} — **1757** WASHINGTON *Writings* I. 492 The commissary used to act as wagon-master. **1812** *Ann. 12th Congress* I Sess. 2260 The Quartermaster General [shall] be authorized to appoint a principal wagon master. **1862** *Harper's Mag.* Sept. 449/1 The wagon-master is an all-important personage, whose authority is little less than that of a captain's upon shipboard. **1916** THOBURN *Stand. Hist. Oklahoma* I. 328 Teamsters and wagon-masters, mounted upon mules from the wagon teams, beat a hasty retreat.

Wagon-mastership. The office or position of a wagon master. — **1850** GARRARD *Wah-To-Yah* v. 76 Buchanan . . . , in the pride of wagon-mastership, directed and superintended.

+**Wagon mound.** A mound or hillock resembling the top of a covered wagon. As a place name. *Obs.* — **1846** MAGOFFIN *Down Santa Fé Trail* 78 The 'wagon mound' . . . derives its name from its resemblance to the top of a covered wagon. **1888** J. J. WEBB *Adventures* 149 The first day we drove to a camp a few miles from Wagon Mound, and stayed all night.

Wagon road. A road suitable for the passage of wagons. {1884–} Also attrib. 1738 *Md. Hist. Mag.* XV. 219 The old Indian Road . . . intersects the waggon road. **1796** in Imlay *Western Territory* (1797) 515 These two roads are very good waggon-roads. **1824** DODDRIDGE *Notes* 187 The horse paths, along which our forefathers made their laborious journies . . . , were soon succeeded by waggon roads. **1888** CABLE *Bonaventure* 55 Under his trudging feet was the wagon-road along the farther levee of the Teche. **1905** COLE *Early Oregon* 39 One had a wagon road project across the Cascade mountains. **1925** BRYAN *Memoirs* 285 We found the distance by wagon road some 85 or 90 miles.

+**Wagon saddle.** A saddle for use on a draft animal ridden by the driver. *Obs.* — **1785** WASHINGTON *Diaries* II. 438 A Waggon Saddle and Gier for 4 Horses. **1843** N. BOONE *Journal* 210 One of the Mules of Co. H. was drowned and two wagon Saddles lost. **1851** HOOPER *Widow Rugby* 121 Save me his years for skearts to my old wagin saddle.

+**Wagon seat.** A seat, usually detachable, for use on a wagon body. (Cf. SPRING SEAT.) — **1852** STOWE *Uncle Tom* x, Haley, drawing out from under the wagon-seat a heavy pair of shackles, made them fast around each ankle. **1895** *Outing* XXVI. 5/1 Heck piled the wraps and bags . . . upon the wagon seat. **1919** HOUGH *Sagebrusher* 86 That's him settin' on the wagon seat up with Wid Gardner.

+**Wagon sheet.** =WAGON COVER. — *a*1846 *Quarter Race Ky.* 176 I histed the waggin-sheet, and looked out at him. **1888** ROOSEVELT in *Century Mag.* April 852/1 For bedding, each man has two or three pairs of blankets, and a tarpaulin or small wagon-sheet. **1914** E. STEWART *Lett. Woman Homesteader* 109 [Over] fresh, sweet pine boughs, . . . was spread a piece of canvas that had once been a wagon sheet.

+**Wagon shop.** A shop where wagons are made. — **1849** CHAMBERLAIN *Ind. Gazetteer* 175 There are in the county . . . two wagon shops. **1877** JOHNSON *Anderson Co., Kansas* 178 Harvey Springer opened a wagon shop in 1859. **1897** *Atlantic Mo.* May 589/2 There is a sleigh and wagon shop a couple of miles out of the village.

+**Wagon show.** A show that travels in a wagon or wagons. — **1895** *N.Y. Dramatic News* 6 July 3/2 The Keystone colossal circus . . . started from the East end as a wagon show. **1907** STEWART *Partners* 236 Stubbs . . . told me not to go into the show business . . . ; he said it took the constitution of a horse, especially with a wagon show.

+**Wagon team.** A wagon and the draft animals that pull it. — **1811** SUTCLIFF *Travels* (1815) 286 He employs upwards of 50 waggon teams. **1852** WATSON *Nights in Block-House* 229 Captain John Brady, taking with him a wagon-team and guard, went himself and procured what [supplies] could be had. **1873** *Newton Kansan* 12 June 3/3 Several of the bloods of Dodge City . . . seized upon a wagon team belonging to a negro and cavorted with it about town.

Wagon tire. The tire of a wagon wheel. +Freq. in phrase *as cold as a wagon tire. colloq.* Also attrib. — **1832** J. HALL *Legends of West* 88 If the man was as cold as a wagon tire, . . . she'd bring him to. **1836** *Quarter Race Ky.* (1846) 18 You'll lay him out cold as a wagon-tire. **1842** *Nat. Hist. N.Y., Geology* II. 292 The iron is tough and soft, and is very much employed . . . for wagon tires. **1851** CIST *Cincinnati* 187 The bottom [is] of six inch timber, and bound with nineteen iron wagon-tire hoops, of 4½ by ¼ inches.

+**Wagon trace.** =next. — **1821** NUTTALL *Travels Arkansa* 164 [We] had, at last, the unexpected satisfaction of entering upon, and pursuing the wagon trace. **1852** MARCY *Explor. Red River* (1854) 88 We started on, keeping the old wagon trace through the timber for eight miles.

Wagon track. A track or trace made by the passage of a wagon or wagons; a wagon road. {1850–} — **1854** SIMMS *Southward Ho!* 268 A single wagon-track led through the wood to the river from his house. **1887** *Century Mag.* March 736/2 There was a wide wagon-track leading from Nordhoff a few miles into the mountains. **1920** HOWELLS *Vacation of Kelwyns* 94 The wagon-track lost its distinctness and dwindled into two parallel ruts.

+**Wagon trail.** =prec. — **1848** BRYANT *California* ix. 126 Following the wagon-trail we left the river about nine o'clock. **1879** *Scribner's Mo.* Nov. 134/2 The different fields are divided only by wagon trails or little belts of furrowed earth. **1912** N. WOODROW *Sally Salt* 147 A shaded lane . . . led them eventually into the river road, a rough wagon trail, winding through the trees.

Wagon train.
1. A train of wagons carrying provisions and other supplies for a military force. {1810–}
1813 F. L. CLAIBORNE in J. F. Claiborne *Sam. Dale* 90 Lieutenant Colonel Ross . . . will proceed . . . to Liberty, where he will meet a wagon-train from Natchez. **1863** Moore *Rebellion Rec.* V. I. 35 A skirmish occurred near Morning Sun, Tenn., between the guard of a Union wagon-train . . . and a body of rebel cavalry. **1897** *Outing* XXIX. 491/1 Every day a bicyclist was detailed to follow immediately in rear of the wagon train.

+**2.** A number of wagons traveling together while transporting goods and settlers into a newly settled region, esp. the West. Also attrib.

1849 PARKMAN in *Knickerb.* XXXIII. 111 A wagon train, with some twenty Missourians, came out from among the trees. 1860 GREELEY *Overland Journey* 23 One great wagon-train was still in corral with its cattle feeding and men lounging about. 1868 *N.Y. Herald* 11 July 5/4 The towns of Ellsworth and Hays are likely to be permanent settlements, as there is a wagon train trade *in transit* that will hold them together. 1878 *Harper's Mag.* Jan. 202/2 Near him an emigrant wagon train have halted. 1913 LONDON *Valley of Moon* 22 They recollected a wagon-train of Oregon settlers that'd been killed by the Modocs four years before.

Wagon way. A road or track made by or suitable for the passage of wagons. {1764-} — 1694 *Mass. H. S. Coll.* 4 Ser. I. 107 Ye way is generally good, being all of it waggon way. 1846 *Knickerb.* XXVII. 52 Without the pasture grounds . . . there is a wagon-way knee deep with mud. 1883 ZEIGLER & GROSSCUP *Alleghanies* 82 The only wagon-ways to this point are across these ranges.

Wagon yard. A place for the accommodation of transient wagon teams and teamsters. {1827-} — 1815 *Austin P.* I. 248 You will . . . see that . . . all strange horses, and Cattle are kept from the wagon and stable yards. 1862 Moore *Rebellion Rec.* V. II. 285 The wagon-yard, wagons, ambulances, etc., were destroyed. 1902 HARBEN *A. Daniel* 212 He went to a public wagon-yard and hitched his horse to one of the long racks. 1925 BENEFIELD *Chicken-Wagon Family* 43 'Where is the nearest wagon-yard?' Mr. Fippany demanded of the proprietor.

* **Wagtail.** +Any one of various American birds that bob their tails as they walk, esp. the oven bird and the water thrushes of the genus *Seiurus.* Also with specifying terms. — 1868 *Amer. Naturalist* II. 181 Audubon placed them [*i.e.,* water thrushes] among his *Motacillinæ,* or wagtails. 1882 *Century Mag.* Jan. 360/1 Our two wagtails are our most brilliant warblers. 1917 *Birds of Amer.* III. 156 The Kentucky Warbler, like many other ground birds, . . . bobs his tail in that peculiar manner which has given them the vernacular name of Wagtail—he is the Kentucky Wagtail.

+**Wagtail warbler. 1.** A water thrush. Also with specifying term. **2.** (See quotation.) — (1) 1884 COUES *Key to Birds* (ed. 2) 309 *Siurus nævius.* Wag-tail Warbler. *Siurus motacilla.* Large-billed Wagtail Warbler. (2) 1917 *Birds of Amer.* III. 149 Palm Warbler. *Dendroica palmarum palmarum.* . . . [Also called] Wagtail Warbler; Tip-up Warbler.

+**Wahconda.** An Indian term for their god or supreme being. *Obs.* — 1823 JAMES *Exped.* I. 184 They have ample cause to return thanks to the great Wahconda or Master of life. 1830 *Western Mo. Rev.* III. 563 Maize, squashes, melons, and beans they supposed they had received as direct gifts from the Wahcondah, or Master of Life.

+**Wahoo.**[1] [Creek *ûhawhu.*] The cork or wing elm (*Ulmus racemosa* or *U. alata*) or one of various trees of other genera similar to these. Also attrib. (See also WHAHOO.) — 1802 DRAYTON *S. Carolina* 65 [The] *wahoo,* affords a pliable bark, which when stripped, and soaked in water, is made sometimes into strings and ropes. 1832 BROWNE *Sylva* 308 The Wahoo is a stranger to the Middle and Northern States. 1837 WILLIAMS *Florida* 11 South of Fort King, the Big swamp, Long swamp and Wahoo swamp present large bodies of first rate sugar lands. 1873 *Newton Kansan* 27 March 1/7 One ounce of wahoo (winged-elm) bark, added to a quart of pure whiskey . . . is very excellent in dyspepsia. 1883 ZEIGLER & GROSSCUP *Alleghanies* 49 A tree called the wahoo, grows here as well as on many of the ranges.

+**Wahoo.**[2] [Dakota *wanhu.*] =BURNING BUSH 1. (See also WAAHOO.) — 1884 SARGENT *Rep. Forests* 38 *Euonymus atropurpureus.* . . . Burning Bush. Wahoo. 1903 N. H. BANKS *Round Anvil Rock* 158 The bright wahoo with its graceful cluster of flame-coloured berries.

* **Wain.**

* **1.** A large open vehicle, usually having four wheels, for carrying heavy loads.
1648 *Conn. Rec.* I. 508 An Inventory of the Estate of Thomas Nowell. . . . Item, waine, wheeles, expinns, cops and pin. 1846 FARNHAM *Prairie Land* 218 The creaking wain came slowly in from the sunny fields. 1872 DE VERE 565 *Wain,* the old and obsolete form of wagon, is still in daily use in some parts of the United States, e.g. in the peninsula east of the Chesapeake. 1893 *Harper's Mag.* Feb. 447 And then one by one, with a jerk and a creak, the great wains started on again.

2. Attrib. and comb. with *body, head yoke, load.*
1635 *Essex Probate Rec.* I. 5, 2 wayne bodys, 16 s. 1648 *Ib.* 112 Two waine head yoakes, . . . two sling yoakes. 1881 *Ore. State Jrnl.* 1 Jan. 6/3 And even one appreciative hearer may bring forth a wain-load of golden sheaves to bless and crown his harvest hour.

* **Wainscot.**

* **1.** An oak supplying wood of a superior quality; a board or plank made of this. *Obs.*
1610 *Estate of Va.* 54 The country yeeldeth abundance of wood, as Oake, Wainscot, Walnut tres. 1612 SIMMONDS *Proceedings* 86 They made clapboard, wainscot, and cut down trees against the ships comming.

* **2.** Wooden panelwork covering the wall, or the lower part of the wall, of a room.
*a*1649 WINTHROP *Hist.* 74 The charge was little, being but clapboards nailed to the wall in the form of wainscot. 1771 *Copley-Pelham Lett.* 147, I will speak to Capt. Joy about the wainscot in the Painting Room. 1875 *Scribner's Mo.* Dec. 345/2 The wainscot or dado, the wall-paper, the frieze and the cornice, all these must make an agreeable impression upon the eye.

3. Attrib. with *chair, chest, desk,* etc.
1654 *Essex Probate Rec.* I. 200 A wenescot Chest & a sea chest. 1674 *Essex Inst. Coll.* XXXVII. 98 A wenscot chaire 5 sh. 1714 *Boston News-Letter* 17 May 2/2 To be Sold./. . . Wainscot Desks, Tables, Glasses, Book Cases &c. 1748 in *N.H. Hist. Soc. Coll.* V. 37 [Fire] run up the deal wainscot stairs into the loft. 1765 in Chalkley *Scotch-Irish Settlement Va.* I. 495 A partition across the house of punch and pennel work, with a wainscoat door in the same.

* **Waist.**

1. a. A bodice or blouse. {1816-} 'Chiefly *U.S.*' (*O.E.D.*). **b.** 'An undergarment worn specially by children, to which petticoats and drawers are buttoned' (*Cent.*).
1864 *Hist. North-Western Soldiers' Fair* 113 [Donations include] 2 child's waists. 1887 CUSTER *Tenting on Plains* 134 One of my hurried toilets was stopped short one morning, by the loss of the waist of my riding-habit. 1917 *Sears, Roebuck & Co. Cat.* No. 135, 551 Handsome Flaxon Finish Checked White Dimity. Desirable for waists.

2. Attrib. with *hand, pattern, ribbon.*
1852 EASTMAN *Aunt Phillis's Cabin* 180 Don't you want . . . a waist ribbon, or some candy? 1887 *Courier-Journal* 8 May 2/7 Wanted . . . Experienced Waist Hands, also a good Draper. 1898 *Kansas City Star* 20 Dec. 10/5 A waist pattern for $2.98.

* **Waistcoat.**

* **1.** A short garment for the upper part of the body, worn by women, usually beneath an outer gown. *Obs.*
1639 *Md. Archives* 80 To a maid Servant [shall be given] one new petty coat and wast coat. 1649 *Ib.* IV. 518 Thomas Pasmore . . . [bought] soe much red cotton bayes or cloth as made his . . . wife . . . a wastcoate. 1689 *Conn. Probate Rec.* I. 506, I give to Nathaniel Dickinson's wife my black wascoat, & Cloth wascoat with silver lace.

* **2.** A man's sleeveless garment for the upper part of the body, worn under a coat or jacket; a vest.
1640 *Conn. Rec.* I. 453 The Inuentory of Tho. Johnson [includes:] . . . a redde wascoat, a perre of start ups. 1710 SEWALL *Letter-Book* I. 387 He brought me . . . one Muzlin Waste-coat. 1790 *Harvard Laws* 36 All undergraduates shall be clothed in coats of blue gray, and with waistcoats and breeches of the same colour. 1819 *St. Louis Enquirer* Sept. 15 (Th.), Look in the bureaus and trunks of modern men of fashion and see the number of coats, waistcoats, pantaloons, &c. 1887 CUSTER *Tenting on Plains* 292 They knew that he had sewed some bills in his waistcoat. 1912 NICHOLSON *Hoosier Chron.* 207 He swung round . . . , fumbling in his waistcoat for a match.

* **Wait,** *v.*

* **1.** *To wait on* (or *upon*). **a.** To escort. {-1713}
1704 S. KNIGHT *Journal* 9 My Kinsman, Capt. Robert Luist, waited on me as farr as Dedham. 1853 COZZENS *Prismatics* 84 There was Fanny, accompanied by Mr. Bullwinkle, whom she had asked to wait upon her. 1887 WILKINS *Humble Romance* 67 She wondered, should she go to evening meeting, whether he would wait on her home.

+**b.** To court (a lady).
1877 BARTLETT 735 *To wait upon,* to pay attention to a lady with a view to matrimony. 1880 *Harper's Mag.* Oct. 690/1, He was waiting on that pretty Becket girl. 1887 WILKINS *Humble Romance* 160 Benny Field was waiting on Jenny. 1898 — *People of Our Neighborhood* (1901) 59 He never waited on her, never spoke to her.

+**2.** *To wait around,* to wait about; to remain at a place in expectation of some occurrence.
1895 M. HALSTEAD *Hundred Bear Stories* 57 It grew sort of monotonous waiting around. 1899 WILLIAMS *Stolen Story* 175, I suppose they're waiting around till it stops raining.

Wait-a-bit. {1785-, in S. Africa} **1.** =PRICKLY ASH 1 c. Also attrib. **2.** The greenbrier, *Smilax rotundifolia.* — (1) 1889 FARMER 550/1 *Wait-a-Bit Trees,* a facetious term given to a kind of bush. 1897 SUDWORTH *Arborescent Flora* 265 *Xanthoxylum clava-herculis.* Prickly Ash. . . . Wait-a-bit, Tear-blanket (Ark.). (2) 1892 *Amer. Folk-Lore* V. 104 Wait-a-bit. E. Mass.

+**Wait bill.** In theatrical parlance, a poster or bill announcing in advance a performance or appearance. — 1896 *N.Y. Dramatic News* 4 July 12/3 Several months ago we put up a few 'wait' bills in these cities, and the size of the audiences [this week] in both places was evidence that the people heeded the instructions.

* **Waiter.**

* **1.** A customs officer. *Obs.*
1648 *Mass. Bay. Rec.* II. 247 A deputy or deputies . . . shall be as searchers or waiters in severall places. 1692 in Munsell *Ann. Albany* II. 121 William Shaw, searcher and waiter of this port doth exhibit an information to this court. 1775 *S.C. Hist. Soc. Coll.* III. 89 John Moggride (one of the waiters in the service of the customs) . . . [shall] be forthwith seized and apprehended.

* **2. a.** A groom or body servant. **b.** One who waits on table, esp. in a public eating house or college dining room.
1734 *Harvard Rec.* I. 146 The waiters . . . shall receive the Plates and Victualls at the Kitchen Hatch, & carry the same to the severall tables. 1777 *N.J. Archives* 2 Ser. I. 543 A genteel footman and waiter, understands the care of horses well. 1788 *Mass. Spy* 29 May 3/4 A consider-

able number of the respectable inhabitants of Princeton, consisting of 37 gunners and their waiters, spent the day past in hunting. **1834** in *Atlantic Mo.* XXVI. 491 White waiters . . . make me feel awkward. **1851** *Harper's Mag.* Aug. 386/2 At this hotel was an admirable specimen of an American female waiter and housemaid. **1883** *Ib.* Aug. 469/1 [His works] reveal the fact of the most confidential relations between Jenkins and an enormous number of ladies' maids, hair-dressers, waiters, and flunkies. **1896** *Chicago Tribune* 28 June 4/1 Gerbach used to be a waiter in a West Side restaurant. **1910** J. HART *Vigilante Girl* 287 The waiters brought them the morning papers, and both were soon absorbed in their perusal. *attrib.* **1865** *Atlantic Mo.* May 539 Derrick went as waiter-boy, so's to get across seas.

3. A serving tray. {1738–, a salver, small tray} Now *local.*

1770 *Md. Hist. Mag.* III. 146 We will not hereafter . . . cause to be imported . . . Waiters, and all Kind of Japan Ware. **1839** *S. Lit. Messenger* V. 752/1 A demure looking damsel manifested herself, holding a neat waiter, on which was a covered saucer. **1857** *Harper's Mag.* May 848/2 To lug heavy waiters, piled with porcelain, . . . is not a movement of grace or agility. **1876** MILLER *First Fam'lies* 176 The woman . . . walked as carefully as if she had been bearing a waiter of wine. **1893** *Harper's Mag.* Feb. 456/2 The clink of the high goblets against the silver waiter, [was] reminiscent of a by-gone and more prosperous period. **1911** HARRISON *Queed* 25 Creamed potatoes, . . . two rolls, . . . coffee, . . . [were] arranged on a shiny black 'waiter.'

+**Waiter girl.** A girl who waits table, esp. in a restaurant or hotel dining room. Freq. *pretty waiter girl.* Also attrib.

1861 E. S. COWELL *Diary* 393 The conduct of the 'waiter girls' with the frequenters of the place is simply shocking. **1868** *Putnam's Mag.* April 438/1 The woman knows very well what 'pretty waiter-girls' are. **1869** J. H. BROWNE *Great Metropolis* 326 Concert-saloons, with pretty 'waiter-girl' attachments, . . . had their origin and earliest impetus here [in N.Y.]. **1875** *Scribner's Mo.* July 277/1 In the slang vernacular, . . . a 'pretty waiter girl' is a 'beer-slinger.' **1890** *Harper's Mag.* Oct. 654/2 One of the waiter-girls in the dining room was found never by any chance to know anything. **1902** WHITE *Blazed Trail* 183 Dozens of 'pretty waiter girls' served the customers.

＊**Waiting.** Household service, esp. service at table. — **1860** E. COWELL *Diary* 157 The dinner, here is homely, but very good, only the waiting is very primitive. **1884** *N.Y. Herald* 27 Oct. 7/3 A Young Strong Girl, lately landed, to do general housework or chamberwork and waiting.

Waiting boy. A man or boy who waits upon his employer; a male servant. {1864} —｜ **1811** SUTCLIFF *Travels* (1815) 276 [He] was employed about the house as waiting boy. **1835** LONGSTREET *Ga. Scenes* 208, I've often hearn o' women . . . following their True-love to the wars, bein' a watin'-boy to 'em. **1881** TOURGEE *'Zouri's Christmas* iii, Occasionally Peter had been allowed to go with 'Marse Ben' on a hunt instead of his regular waiting-boy.

Waiting list. A list, usually arranged in order of application, of persons waiting for admission to some privilege or position. Also transf. — **1897** *Outing* XXX. 347/2 The Michaux Club is composed of two hundred members, with a large 'waiting list.' **1913** LAFOLLETTE *Autobiog.* 227 It is certain that there were others on the waiting list who wanted the Senatorship.

＊**Waiting maid.** A maidservant. Also attrib. — **1643** *Md. Archives* IV. 224 She contracted not to serve him otherwhere then . . . in the condition of a waiting maid to his Lady or his daughters. **1837** *S. Lit. Messenger* III. 692 [Nor] is there any good reason why provincial phraseology should not be put into the lips of provincial people as well as . . . waiting-maid phrases into those of an abigail. **1853** SIMMS *Sword & Distaff* (1854) 479 You shill hev . . . a nice little waiting-maid servant of your own. **1881** M. J. HOLMES *Madeline* 77 No, not mamma, but Miriam, the waiting-maid we left in Boston.

＊**Waiting man.** A manservant. {–1585} — **1716** CHURCH *Philip's War* 31 Capt. Church promised him . . . he should not be Sold out of the Country, but should be his waiting man. **1773** FITHIAN *Journal* I. 62 At twelve she sent the waiting Man to know . . . what I would choose for Dinner. **1839** *S. Lit. Messenger* V. 752/1 A repetition of raps . . . quickened the steps of Mr. Singlesides' sedate waiting-man. **1883** CABLE *Dr. Sevier* 69 The speaker ceased as the mulatto waiting-man appeared at the open door.

Waiting room. A room, esp. in a public place such as a railroad station, provided for those who have to wait. {1683–} — **1863** 'G. HAMILTON' *Gala-Days* 42, I went into the station waiting-room to write a note. **1899** in *Congress. Rec.* 10 Jan. (1900) 748/2 He was borne in an unconscious state to the waiting room of the depot. **1906** *N.Y. Ev. Post* 17 May 7 Connecting with the main waiting room is the concourse, a covered assembling place over 100 feet wide.

＊**Waiting woman.** A woman servant. — **1838** COOPER *Homeward B.* xxiv, I intermated as much to Mrs. Sidley and t'other waiting-woman. **1863** 'G. HAMILTON' *Gala-Days* 42 At the station we inquired of the waiting-woman concerning it.

＊**Waitress.** A maidservant; a woman who waits at table. {c1586, 1834–} — **1787** TYLER *Contrast* II. ii, There is a little lump of flesh and delicacy that lives at next door, waitress to Miss Maria. **1875** [see PARLOR GIRL]. **1906** *N.Y. Herald* 5 March 14 A competent girl as waitress and to take charge of parlor floor; private family.

＊**Wake,** *v.* +To wake snakes, (see SNAKE *n.* 6); +*to wake* (*up*) *the wrong passenger,* (see PASSENGER 1).

＊**Wake-robin.**
+**1. a.** The arrow arum, *Peltandra virginica.* **b.** The jack-in-the-pulpit (*Arisaema triphylla*), or a related plant. **c.** Any one of various species of *Trillium.*

*c*1711 J. PETIVER *Gazophylacii Nat.* I. i, In South Carolina . . . it Flowers in June and July, and is called by them Wake-Robin. **1778** CARVER *Travels* 519 Wake Robin is an herb that grows in swampy lands. **1784** *Amer. Acad. Mem.* I. 487 Arum. . . . Cuckowpint. Dragon-root. Wake-Robin. **1819** *Amer. Farmer* I. 109 Our indians also made use of the root of a vegetable which . . ., Kalm says, is the *arum virginicum,* or wake robin. **1832** [see DRAGON-ROOT]. **1840** DEWEY *Mass. Flowering Plants* 213 *T[rillium] erectum.* Wake Robin. Very common in the woods in May. **1850** S. F. COOPER *Rural Hours* 80 Some are called nightshades; others wake-robins. **1871** BURROUGHS *Wake-Robin* (1886) p. vi, [For a title] I cast about for a word thoroughly in the atmosphere and spirit of the book, which I hope I have found in 'Wake-Robin,'—the common name of the white Trillium. **1913** LONDON *Valley of Moon* 482 She seemed a flower, with her small vivid face irresistibly reminding Saxon of a springtime wake-robin.

2. With specifying adjectives.
1821 *Mass. H. S. Coll.* 2 Ser. IX. 157 Plants . . . indigenous in the township of Middlebury [Vt., include] . . . *Trillium cernuum,* Nodding wake-robin. *Trillium pictum,* Smiling wake-robin. **1839** in *Mich. Agric. Soc. Trans.* VII. 421 *Trillium erectum.* False wake-robin.

+**Wake-up.** *local.* The flicker. — **1844** *Nat. Hist. N.Y., Zoology* II. 192 This species . . . is called High-hole, Yucker, Flicker, Wake-up and Pigeon Woodpecker. **1850** *Conn. Public Acts* 5 It shall not be lawful . . . to kill . . . [the] wake-up or high-hole. **1893** *Scribner's Mag.* June 773/2 The flicker has a long array of names, . . . like flicker, clape, wake-up, . . . derived from his notes.

+**Wakiup.** =WICKIUP 2. — **1874** ALDRICH *P. Palfrey* vii, On one side of an impetuous stream . . . lay a city of tents, pine-huts, and rude brush wakiups. **1890** LANGFORD *Vigilante Days* (1912) 208 The Temple of Justice was a wakiup of brush and twigs.

+**Wakon.** [Sioux *wakan.*] Among certain Indian tribes, the supreme life-giving and all-pervading power; a spirit, or the representation of a spirit. — **1778** CARVER *Travels* 381 The Chipeways call this being Manitou or Kitchi-Manitou; the Madowessies, Wakon or Tongo-Wakon, that is, the Great Spirit. **1809** A. HENRY *Travels* 299 They believe . . . in the spirits, gods, or manitos, whom they denominate wakons. *c*1837 CATLIN *Indians* II. 166 On the surface of the rocks, [are] various marks and their sculptured hieroglyphics—their wakons, totems, and medicines.

+**Wakon bird.** [Prec. and *bird.*] A bird held in veneration by some Indians: (see quots.). — **1778** CARVER *Travels* 472 The Wakon bird, as it is termed by the Indians, appears to be of the same species as the birds of paradise. **1789** MORSE *Amer. Geog.* 60 The Wakon-bird . . . is nearly the size of the swallow.

＊**Walk,** *n.*
＊**1.** A pasture used by cattle or sheep. *Obs.*
1644 *New Haven Col. Rec.* 150 The Mohegin Indians have done much damage to them by setting their traps in the walke of their cattell. **1645** *Ib.* 227 It was propownded that noe calues goe in the cowes walke, namely the cowes & ox pasture. **1658** *Dedham Rec.* IV. 3 The limits of each of these mens worke is to burne the ground according to the limits of each of the heards walke. **1674** *Portsmouth Rec.* 181 A Committee . . . [is] to Consider Some way to prevent the driveinge of Sheep on the Common and therby removeinge them from their wonted walke.

+**2.** (See quotation.)
1705 BEVERLEY *Virginia* IV. 208 Besides this Division into Counties, and Parishes, . . . two other Sub-divisions . . . are subject to the Rules and Alterations made by the County-courts; namely into Precincts or Burroughs, for the Limits of Constables; and into Precincts or Walks, for the Surveyors of High-ways.

3. On top of a house, a short, level space arranged for walking, somewhat like the captain's bridge on a ship.
1775 *Holyoke Diaries* 88n., A fine walk on the top . . . commands the prospect of the whole Island. **1876** *Wide Awake* III. 17/2 On Aunt Eliza's house-top was 'a walk,' an appendage to every mariner's home.

+**4.** (See quotations and cf. WALKING PURCHASE.)
1809 KENDALL *Travels* II. 282 Lands were sometimes to be measured by *walks* performed against time. **1901** P. FOUNTAIN *Great Deserts* 118 The Indians . . . sold it [*sc.* land] by the 'walk.'

+**5.** (See quotation.)
1877 BARTLETT 736 *Walk.* As 'Ladies' Walk,' 'Gentlemen's Walk,' *i.e.* a privy. This absurd piece of squeamishness is common at hotels and at railroad-stations.

6. In phrases. ＊**a.** *To take a walk,* +to depart, to get out.
1871 'MARK TWAIN' *Sk., New & Old* 248 The first time he opened his mouth and was just going to spread himself his breath took a walk. **1881** — in *Century Mag.* Nov. 37 They sing out, 'Oh, dry up!' 'Give us a rest!' 'Shoot him!' 'Oh, take a walk!' and all sorts of such things. **1888** *Chicago Herald* (F.), Mr. Berry [the employer] concluded to make a change and Tascott [the employee] took a walk.

+**b.** *To win in a walk,* to win without much effort. *colloq.*
1903 LEWIS *Boss* 138 He won in a walk.

* **Walk,** *v.*
To walk one's chalks or *(the) chalk,* (see CHALK *n.* 3 b).

+**1.** *To walk out,* to go on strike.
1894 CARWARDINE *Pullman Strike* 37 The men passed the word from one to another to 'walk out,' which they did orderly and deliberately.

+**b.** *To walk out on,* to desert.
1896 *Typographical Jrnl.* IX. 232 The Review, Republican daily, 'walked out' on the St. Louis platform.

2. *To walk over,* to act without regard for; to override. *colloq.*
1852 STOWE *Uncle Tom* xvi, St. Clare wouldn't raise his hand, if every one of them walked over him. **1908** WHITE *Riverman* 10 Are you going to let that old high-banker walk all over you?

3. *To walk round.* +'To walk round a person is to gain the advantage of him' (B. 77).
1859 HALIBURTON *Sam Slick's Wise Saws* 20 My ambassadors may not dance as elegantly as European courtiers, but they can walk round them in a treaty.

+**4.** *To walk Spanish.* **a.** To walk on tiptoes under compulsion, because of being held up by the seat of the trousers; hence, to proceed in a gingerly or cautious manner or under force; to depart under compulsion. Also *transf.* **b.** To force (someone) to move in such a manner.
1825 NEAL *Bro. Jonathan* II. 450 'Talk English, my boy—or'—'Or what, father?' 'Or walk Spanish.' **1834** *Louisville Pub. Adv.* 6 Aug., Friend Josiah laid his tongue in his cheek, and 'walked Spanish.' **1845** *Big Bear Ark.* 148 The turkis they put and wawks Sphanish, which means a turki trot. **1847** LOWELL *Biglow P.* 1 Ser. ii. 24 To take a feller up jest by the slack o' 's trowsis An' walk him Spanish clean right out o' all his homes an' houses. **1856** CURTIS *Prue & I* (1892) 57 She'll make you walk Spanish, Jonathan Bud. **1890** J. JEFFERSON *Autobiog.* 104 If in his presence we had dared talk Greek we should certainly have walked Spanish. **1890** *Voice* 14 Aug., [They] were hustled out of the country on an hour's notice, made to 'walk Spanish' in fact. **1920** LINCOLN *Mr. Pratt* 257 He moved then, 'walking Spanish,' like the boy in the school-yard.

+**Walk-along-Joe.** A dance similar to a walk-around. — **1862** 'E. KIRKE' *Among Pines* 283 Jim danced breakdowns, 'walk-along-Joes,' and other darky dances.

Walk-around. {1886} +A dance, or part of a dance, of Negro origin in which the dancers move in a large circle. Also *fig.*
See also WALK-ROUND.
1869 *Atlantic Mo.* July 72/2 We were constrained, however, to forego our jig and Walk-around. **1878** BEADLE *Western Wilds* 403 We danced about on unsteady footing, attempting an 'Ethiopian walk-around' on the heaving deck. **1882** PECK *Sunshine* 30 After the synod of Hayes and Sherman had bounced him from the Custom House for dancing the great spoils walk around. **1889** CUSTER *Tenting on Plains* 237 Out there they can have all the 'walk-arounds' and 'high jinks' they choose. **1897** F. NORRIS *Third Circle* 59 Miss Starbird . . . promised Shorty the first 'walk-around' in the 'Grand Ball.'

+**b.** The music for such a dance as performed on the stage.
1888 B. MATTHEWS *Pen & Ink* 153 'Dixie' was composed in 1859, by Mr. Dan D. Emmett, as a 'walk-around' for Bryant's minstrels. **1895** *Century Mag.* Oct. 958/2 Mr. Emmett . . . composed the walk-around the next day.

* **Walker.** **1.** A bird or insect which walks. {1817–} **2.** A floor walker. — (1) **1854** EMMONS *Agric. N.Y.* V. 142 Phasmidae. The insects of this family (*Ambulatoria,* the walkers) are distinguished by the undeveloped state of the wings, or by their total absence. **1872** COUES *Key to Birds* 44 It is among the Cursores, or walkers, and especially wading birds, that the crus is most naked. **1879** *Scribner's Mo.* Aug. 499/1 These sections are called . . . the walkers (*Orthoptera ambulatoria*), and the jumpers (*Orthoptera saltatoria*). (2) **1882** *Harper's Mag.* Oct. 760/2 As I walked down the shop one of the individuals popularly known as 'walkers' approached me.

* **Walking.** Illust. in attrib. uses only.

1. Designating articles of dress adapted to use by persons walking. {1806–}
1854 CUMMINS *Lamplighter* xxx, To change her slippers for thick walking-boots occupied a few minutes only. **1868** *N.Y. Tribune* 7 July 3/1 The latest styles of walking suits appearing on our streets may be pronounced very 'nobby.' **1874** ALDRICH *P. Palfrey* iv, Like a brave modern knight in an English walking-coat. **1878** *Decorum* 272 This dress . . . should differ from the ordinary walking-costume. **1882** 'M. HARLAND' *Eve's Daughters* 50 One can be trimly and becomingly arrayed in linen or gingham morning and walking-gowns. **1889** *Century Mag.* March 782/1 She was one day at Daniel & Fisher's, the great dry-goods store of the camp, looking at walking-jackets.

2. In special combinations.
Walking board, a board placed along each side of a boat, enabling crew members to walk back and forth; *w. engine,* an engine having a walking beam; *w. funeral,* a funeral at which people do not ride in carriages but walk; *w. plow,* a plow behind which the plowman walks.

1855 *Harper's Mag.* Dec. 29/2 The crew, divided equally on each side, took their places upon the 'walking-boards,' extending along the whole length of the craft. **1849** W. BROWN *America* 3 The ponderous looking steamers, with the walking engines and large pulpits high on the decks. **1877** JEWETT *Deephaven* 221 We had never seen what the people called 'walking funerals' until we came to Deephaven. **1868** *Iowa State Agric. Soc. Rep. 1867* 161 [The] ground [is] plowed and harrowed, . . . and cultivated with riding and walking-plows.

+**Walking beam.** An oscillating beam for the transmission of power: **a.** In a steamboat. **b.** In a device for drilling. {a1864, in Canada} — (a) **1845** *Knickerb.* XXV. 63 Some [passengers] . . . climbed up the chain and up the machinery to the walking-beam. **1861** VICTOR *Hist. Southern Rebellion* I. 215/2 Another [shot] passed between the smoke-stack and walking-beam of the engine. **1884** *Harper's Mag.* July 270/1 The walking-beam . . . drives the side-wheels. (b) **1865** *Harper's Mag.* April 573/2 The walking-beam is a heavy horizontal piece of timber, supported in the centre by a Samson-post. **1883** *Century Mag.* July 329/2 A huge rude walking-beam . . . gives the motion to a stout cable, passing over a pulley at the top of the derrick. **1904** TARBELL *Hist. Standard Oil Co.* I. 116 Creaking walking-beams sawed the air from morning until night.

+**Walking boss.** A foreman. — **1891** *Harper's Mag.* Nov. 888/1 Hence the presence of Dan Dunn, his walking boss or general foreman. **1902** WHITE *Blazed Trail* 25, I'm walkin'-boss there.

Walking cane. A walking stick. {1699–} — **1810** *Columbian Centinel* 6 Jan. 3/3 Lately received . . . 200 doz. Walking Canes. **1856** M. J. HOLMES *L. Rivers* 53 Poking a black baby's ribs with his walking cane, . . . he mounted his favorite 'Firelock,' and . . . rode off. **1897** STUART *Simpkinsville* 44 He hastily proceeded to raise his walking-cane.

Walking-cane chair. A chair that can be collapsed and carried conveniently. — **1846** *Spirit of Times* (N.Y.) 18 April 94/2 On hand, walking-cane chairs—the Neplus Ultra of convenience to the invalid pedestrian.

‖**Walking chalk.** =WALKING PAPERS. — **1896** E. HIGGINSON *Land of Snow Pearls* 97, I'll give him his walking-chalk when he comes tonight.

Walking cultivator. (See quot. 1876.) — **1869** *Rep. Comm. Agric. 1868* 417 Field No. 3 . . . [was] cultivated but once, when about a foot high, with a five-toothed walking cultivator. **1876** KNIGHT 2721/1 *Walking-cultivator,* one in which the operator walks behind, as distinguished from the *riding* or *sulky* cultivator.

+**Walking delegate.** An official of a labor union who sees that union rules are enforced and that membership is kept up, and who presents grievances to employers. — **1892** HOWELLS *Quality of Mercy* 131 She decided that he must be a walking-delegate, and that he had probably come on mischief from some of the workpeople in her father's employ. **1895** *Chicago Strike of 1894* 277 There would be no grievance committees to report to, and the work of the agitator, organizer, walking delegate, or whatever he is called, would be at an end. **1898** DUNBAR *Folks from Dixie* 209 [Then] had come the visit of the 'walking-delegate' for the district, and his command to the men to 'go out.' **1911** *N.Y. Ev. Post* 11 March 1 It was said that a walking delegate had ordered [the strike].

Walking dress. A costume appropriate for walking. {1822–} Also *attrib.* — **1753** WASHINGTON *Diaries* I. 63, I put myself in an *Indian* walking Dress. **1878** *Decorum* 274 Many prefer using the walking-dress length. *a*1882 in McCabe *New York* 204 Walking dresses cost from $50 to $300.

Walking fern. **1.** A club moss. {1829} +**2.** (See quot. 1891.) — (1) **1814** PURSH *Flora Amer.* II. 654 *L[ycopodium] alopecuroides* . . . is known by the name of *Walking Fern.* (2) **1843** TORREY *Flora N.Y.* II. 494 *Antigramma rhizophylla.* . . . Walking-fern. . . . Moist rocks, generally on limestone. **1861** WOOD *Botany* 821 *Antigramma,* Walking Fern. **1891** *Cent.* 6809/2 *Walking-fern,* a small tufted evergreen fern, *Camptosorus rhizophyllus,* native of eastern North America.

Walking leaf. {1659–} +**1.** =WALKING FERN 2. **2.** An insect of the family Phasmatidae, having something of the appearance of a leaf. {1826–} — (1) **1817–8** EATON *Botany* (1822) 188 *Asplenium rhizophyllum,* walking leaf. **1857** GRAY *Botany* 593 Walking-Leaf. . . . *C[amptosorus] rhizophyllus.* . . . Fronds evergreen, . . . tapering above into a slender prolongation like a runner, which often roots at the apex and gives rise to new fronds, and these in turn to others; hence the popular name. (2) **1872** HOLMES *Poet* 281 Insect it is,—*phyllum sissifolium,* the 'walking leaf,' as some have called it.

+**Walking orders.** *pl.* =next. — **1835** CROCKETT *Tour* 170 He got his walking orders, and Taney was taken into his place.

+**Walking papers.** *pl.* Notice of dismissal; discharge. Also *transf. colloq.* — **1825** WOODWORTH *Forest Rose* 1. iv, As for the bumpkin, her lover, he must take his walking papers. **1850** LEWIS *La. Swamp Doctor* 71 [He] has quite a retired life of it, as my uncle the postmaster remarked about his own situation, when the department gave him his walking-papers. **1862** McCLELLAN in *Own Story* 465, I have no idea that I will be with this army more than two or three weeks longer, and should not be surprised any day or hour to get my 'walking-papers.' **1887** STOCKTON *Hundredth Man* xxxi, What kind of man he must be which Miss Gay and Mrs. Justin had to give his walkin' papers to. **1907** *St. Nicholas* Oct. 1116/1 She gave Tin Star his walking papers.

+**Walking purchase.** A particular purchase of land, the extent being determined by a walk. (Cf. WALK *n.* 4.) — **1756** FRANKLIN *Writings* X. 185 It is said by many here that the Delawares were grossly abused in the Walking Purchase. **1895** J. WINSOR *Miss. Basin* 239 A scandalous act of Thomas Penn . . . had asserted inordinate claims by virtue of what was known as the 'Walking Purchase.'

Walking shoe. A stout, durable shoe suitable for extensive walking. {1850–} — 1815 in H. M. Brooks *Gleanings* IV. 102 He will keep constantly for sale . . . a Composition, with which he cleans Ladies' Walking Shoes. 1868 *Mich. Agric. Rep.* VII. 353 R. H. Fyfe, Detroit, [exhibited] 1 pair ladies' summer walking shoes. 1882 'M. HARLAND' *Eve's Daughters* 61 The latter objection [of enlarging the feet] obtains to stout walking-shoes with broad toes and low heels.

* **Walking staff.** A walking stick. *Obs.* — 1686 *Narragansett Hist. Reg.* III. 104, 4 prs. Gloves & Walking staff. 1782 TRUMBULL *M'Fingal* (1785) 55 Like spears at Brobdignagian tilting, Or Satan's walking-staff in Milton. 1848 IRVING *Knickerb.* (rev. ed.) VI. ix, [He] gave one of his bravest officers a severe admonishment with his walking-staff.

* **Walking stick.**

* **1.** A stick or cane carried while walking.
1709 LAWSON *Carolina* 99 There is another sort, which we call red Hickory . . . ; of which Walking-Sticks, Mortars, Pestils, and several other fine Turnery-wares are made. 1781 *Salem Gazette* 3 July, Gentlemen may be supplied with neat walking Sticks. 1851 MELVILLE *Moby Dick* 111 [Such a settee] was . . . much better than those garden-chairs which are convertible into walking sticks. 1872 HOLMES *Poet* 94 Sometimes you'll find a bit of a pond-hole in a pasture, and you'll plunge your walking-stick into it. 1889 JEWETT in *Harper's Mag.* Dec. 106/2 [Strangers] were detained by eager vendors of flowers and orange-wood walking-sticks. 1922 TARKINGTON *Gentle Julia* 371 He flourished a new walking-stick and new grey gloves.

2. An insect of the family Phasmatidae, having a long, slender body. {1760–}
1854 EMMONS *Agric. N.Y.* V. 142 The insects of this family (*Ambulatoria*, the walkers) . . . are commonly called walkingsticks. 1879 *Scribner's Mo.* Aug. 499/1 It is called the walking stick,—*Spectrum femoratum.*

+**Walking ticket.** = WALKING PAPERS. *colloq.* — 1835 CROCKETT *Tour* 162 He received his walking ticket. His services were no longer required. 1839 *S. Lit. Messenger* V. 378/1 The girl . . . gave him what was politely called in those parts 'a walking ticket.' *c*1850 WHITCHER *Bedott P.* xxv. 307 If ever you dew it agin you'll git your walkin'-ticket on short order. 1889 *Boston Jrnl.* 26 Jan. 2/3 His action would no doubt have been the same if President Cleveland had not given Mr. West his walking ticket. 1898 *Scribner's Mag.* XXIV. 313/2 Last week when the old man come round I looked to see you git a walking ticket.

Walkist. One who participates in walking matches. {1879–} — *a*1870 CHIPMAN *Notes on Bartlett* 499 Walkist. One who walks as a trial of skill.—Newspapers. 1883 in A. E. Lee *Hist. Columbus, Ohio* 638 Unlike the modern 'walkist' who has so many miles and one lap, these lines have all lap and no miles.

+**Walkout.** A strike. — 1888 *Chicago Inter-Ocean* (F.), The walk out of brewery employés, decided upon at last night's meeting of the union, was considerable of a fizzle. 1896 *Internat. Typogr. Union Proc.* 27/2 A dispute had arisen between the foreman and the men, culminating in a walkout by the men. 1919 *New Solidarity* (Chicago) 18 Jan. 1/1 The date . . . contemplated as the day for a general strike, or walk-out.

+**Walk-round.** = WALK-AROUND. — 1861 *Temple Bar* May 199 The 'Jim Crow dance' . . . soon gave place to better tunes . . . and 'walk rounds.' 1862 'E. KIRKE' *Among Pines* 147 About twenty 'gentleman and lady' darkies joined, two at a time, in a half 'walk-round' half breakdown. 1892 *Harper's Mag.* Jan. 251/1 The darkies try to see which can put on the most style in a kind of walk-round. 1895 *Century Mag.* Oct. 958/1 His work with the caravan was to sing songs, chiefly darky songs, accompanied by 'hoe-downs' and 'walk rounds.'

+**Walkway.** A sidewalk. — 1792 *Essex Inst. Coll.* VII. 37 John Saunders jr. . . . agrees to pave the Walk Way in front of his Father's Estate. 1816 BENTLEY *Diary* IV. 405 A walkway for the first time has been raised in the principal streets in the eastern part of the Town. 1904 *N.Y. Ev. Post* 14 May 5 A space . . . sufficient to provide each house with a walkway to the rear.

* **Wall,** *n. attrib.* and *comb.*

1. In general sense with *maker, scraper, tint.*
1754 HEMPSTEAD *Diary* 626, I rid out in the foren[oon] to fodder the Cattle & to see after the wall makers. 1884 *Century Mag.* April 807/2 The whole effect of carpet, furniture, and wall-tints is exceedingly rich and warm. 1891 *Cent.* 6812/2 *Wall-scraper*, . . . a chisel-edged tool for scraping down walls preparatory to papering.

2. Designating articles, utensils, etc., hung on or set into a wall. {1688–}
1880 *Scribner's Mo.* April 921/1 The family comb . . . occupied a convenient wall-pocket at one side of the small kitchen mirror. 1891 *Cent.* 6810/3 *Wall-clock*, . . . a clock made to be hung upon the wall. *Ib.*, *Wall-desk*, . . . a form of folding desk attached to a wall at a convenient height above the floor. 1893 *Harper's Mag.* Jan. 202/1 There were no souvenirs, or photographs of friends; there was not even a wall-calendar. 1901 MERWIN & WEBSTER *Calumet 'K'* 19 A wall lamp, set in a dull reflector, threw shadows into the corners.

* **Wall,** *v. tr.* and *intr.* To roll (the eyes) in such a way as to show the whites; of the eyes, to roll in this manner. *S.* {–1821} 'Now only *U.S.*' (*O.E.D.*). — 1845 HOOPER *Taking Census* 161 Hit kept a wallin' its eyes and a moanin'. 1847 in *Tall Tales of S.W.* (1930) 196 'Yas' (sez Wat, a-wallin a red eye to'ards the bed). 1883 *Amer. Philol. Ass. Trans.* 55 *Wall the eyes.* . . . I can remember this as a very common way among the little negroes in South Carolina of showing displeasure, and expressing

impudence, when they did not dare say anything. 1903 'O. HENRY' *Roads of Destiny* 96 Look at his [the horses'] eyes a wallin' and his tail a-wavin'. 1907 *Ib.* 119 It walled its great eyes almost humanly toward Kearny and expired.

+**Wallawalla.** [Amer. Indian.] **1.** An Indian of a small tribe of the Pacific Northwest. Also attrib. **2.** The language spoken by this tribe. — (1) 1807 GASS *Journal* 205 We then set out from Wal-la-wal-la river and nation. 1843 MARRYAT *M. Violet* ii, His leggings and mocassins were sewn with the hair of the Wallah Wallahs. 1850 G. HINES *Voyage* 167 Our motley party proceeded in high glee, alternately conversing in the English, Chenook, and Walla-Walla languages. 1866 *Ore. State Jrnl.* 5 May 1/2 The Walla Walla's and the Snakes . . . are all made voters by the Senator's constitutional amendment. (2) 1850 G. HINES *Voyage* 31 Mr. Perkins . . . applied himself to the acquirement of the Walla-Walla.

Wall cress. Any herb of the genus *Arabis* {1796–}; an herb of a genus similar to *Arabis*. Also with specifying term. — 1829 EATON *Botany* (ed. 5) 110 *Arabis sagittata*, wall cress. 1843 TORREY *Flora N.Y.* I. 55 *Arabis laevigata.* Smooth Wall Cress. . . . In rocky woods and on banks of rivers.

* **Walled,** *a.* Of an eye: Deficient in color or form. *colloq.* {–1705, of a horse's eye} — 1888 EGGLESTON *Graysons* xix, Rather under-sized, and with one eye a little walled.

+**Walled lake.** A shallow lake, occupying a depression in the surface of glacial drift, surrounded by embankments of boulders and similar matter. — 1868 *Amer. Naturalist* II. 143 [In] stories of the 'walled lakes' of Iowa . . . the wondrous handiwork of a departed race of men is described, consisting of walls of huge stones encircling the lakes like that of an artificial fish-pond.

* **Wallet.**

* **1.** A bag for holding provisions and supplies.
1738 BYRD *Dividing Line* (1901) 226 Every man took care to pack up some buffalo steaks in his wallet. 1821 DODDRIDGE *Backwoodsman & Dandy*, Our wallets were filled with cakes and good jirk. 1880 *Harper's Mag.* Sept. 539/2 Mr. Farjuice alone sat apart, . . . eating the corn-dodgers and bacon out of his wallet.

+**2.** A pocketbook or flat container for carrying money or important papers in the pocket. {1913–}
1834 C. A. DAVIS *Lett. J. Downing* 39, I out with my seal-skin wallet. 1880 *Harper's Mag.* June 28/1 This wholly objectionable person . . . opens a well-filled wallet. 1914 STEELE *Storm* 150, I took two five-dollar bills from my wallet and put them in his hand.

* **Wall-eye.** +**1.** = WALL-EYED PIKE. +**2.** A fish (*Hyperprosopon argenteus*) of the Pacific coast. Also *wall-eye surf fish.* +**3.** = next.— (1) 1876 *Fur, Fin & Feather* Sept. 163/1 All along the Minnesota Division are numerous clear lakes and ponds, teeming with . . . 'wall-eyes' or pike-perch, tarred-perch [etc.]. (2) 1884 GOODE, etc. *Fisheries* I. 278 Wall-eye Surf-fish. . . . This species is usually known as the 'Wall-eye,' in allusion to the great size of its eyes. (3) 1891 *Cent.* 6811/1 *Walleye*, . . . the alewife, or wall-eyed herring.

+**Wall-eyed herring.** The alewife, *Pomolobus pseudoharengus.* — 1884 GOODE, etc. *Fisheries* I. 580 *C. vernalis* is known . . . on the Albemarle River as the 'Big-eyed' Herring and the 'Wall-eyed' Herring.

+**Wall-eyed pike.** A fresh-water food fish (*Stizostedion vitreum*) common in the Great Lakes and the upper Mississippi. — 1869 *Rep. Comm. Agric. 1868* 330 The commission has . . . distributed many millions of shad spawn, but failed in efforts to obtain that of . . . the wall-eyed pike. 1873 *Mich. Gen. Statutes* I. (1882) 581 Nothing in this act shall be construed as prohibiting . . . any person from catching mullet, suckers, redsides, wall-eyed pike, or sturgeon. 1898 *Mo. So. Dakotan* I. 79 Our piscatorial friends are just at the present time enjoying rare sport in hauling out catfish, perch, wall-eyed pike, &c., from the Big Sioux.

* **Wallflower.** Any one of various plants of the genus *Cheirinia*, esp. *C. cheiri.* Also with specifying adjective. — 1737 BRICKELL *N. Carolina* 22 Strawberries are in such Plenty in the Season, that they are Feeding for Hogs; Narcissus, Daffodil, Snow-Drops, Wall-Flowers, Bloodwort [etc.]. 1847 WOOD *Botany* 169 E[*rysimum*] *Arkansanum.* Yellow Phlox. False Wall-Flower. . . . A fine plant with large, showy flowers, resembling the wall-flower. *Ib.* 170 C[*heiranthus*] *Cheiri.*—Wall-Flower. . . . A popular garden flower, admired for its agreeable odor and its handsome corymbose clusters of orange or yellow flowers. 1880 R. H. DAVIS *Silhouettes* 50 Back of these houses stretched trim gardens, gay with dahlias and yellow wall-flowers. 1898 A. M. DAVIDSON *Calif. Plants* 175 A goodly number of wild flowers, including the wallflower.

Wall moss. Any one of various mosses growing on walls. {1855–} — 1791 MUHLENBERG *Index Florae* 183 *Bryum*, Wall-moss. 1890 *Cent.* 3436/2 *Yellow wall-lichen* (commonly *wall-moss*), *Parmelia parietaria.*

Walloon. 1. ?Heavy cloth or leather imported from Belgium or the neighboring regions. +**2.** (See quotations.) +**3.** (See quot. 1917.) — (1) 1794 STEELE *P.* I. 118, I have also sent you some Cloth & such trimmings as I cou'd get—there is no Walloon of the Colour to be had. *Ib.* 120 There is no Buff Walloon in Town, but I presume the Durants will answer any purpose that Walloon would. (2) 1868 BANCROFT *Hist. U.S.* II. 279 They were chiefly Walloons, Protestant fugitives from Belgian provinces. 1891 *Cent.* 6811/3 *Walloon*, . . . in America, especially colonial New York, one of the Huguenot settlers from Artois, in northern France, etc. (3) 1873 BEADLE *Undevel. West* 771 [We] were soon surrounded by extensive flocks of ducks and wild geese, with occasionally a gull or walloon. 1917 *Birds of Amer.* I. 12 Loon. *Gavia immer.* . . . [Also called] Ember-Goose; Walloon; Ring-necked Loon.

* Wallow. +A place to which animals resort for rolling or wallowing; a depression in the earth caused by this activity, or resembling the hollows caused by wallowing. Also in place name. {1882-, in Canada, etc.}

See also BEAR-, BUFFALO, HOG WALLOW.

1786 in *Amer. Speech* XV. 175/2 To include a Spring Called the Elk Wallow. **1796** *Ib.* 407/1 To four Chesnuts in the head of a deep Wallow by a water Slip. **1827** WILLIAMS *W. Florida* 27 But it is in the wallows, large mud holes among the rushes, that the alligator appears herself. **1838** *S. Lit. Messenger* IV. 221/2 A bear was started from his wallow. **1876** J. A. ALLEN *Amer. Bisons* 65 These wallows thus become characteristic marks of a buffalo country. **1902** WISTER *Virginian* 332 That sorrel has gone in there by the wallow.

attrib. **1787** in *Amer. Speech* XV. 407/2 At white oak & red oak near a wallow Hole. **1882** BAILLIE-GROHMAN *Camps in Rockies* 37 All three [saddle blankets] were well soaked in the copper-coloured wallow water.

Wall paper. Paper, usually ornamental, pasted over walls and other interior surfaces; paper hangings. {1862-}

1845 J. W. NORRIS *Chicago Directory* 107 Carpets, Rugs, Floor Oil Cloths, Wall Paper, And many other articles in the house furnishing line. **1871** HOWELLS *Wedding Journey* 27 Here stood the half demolished walls of a house, with a sad variety of wall-paper showing in the different rooms. **1892** *York County Hist. Rev.* 100 Glazing is done and wall papers carried in stock. **1905** WIGGIN *Rose* 98 A pale pink-flowered wall-paper for the bedroom in the new home.

attrib. **1827** DRAKE & MANSFIELD *Cincinnati* 65 Two Wall Paper Factories, 9 hands. **1885** *Santa Fé Wkly. New Mexican* 6 Aug. 4/7 A facsimile of the last 'wall-paper' edition of the Vicksburg Daily Citizen, issued July 2, 1863, ... is sent out printed on modern style wall-paper as a supplement to that enterprising journal the Chicago Herald.

Wall piece. 1. A cannon designed to be mounted on a wall, as of a fortress. {1774-} 2. A crosspiece of wood reinforcing and supporting the vertical stakes of a palisade. — (1) **1755** ROGERS *Journals* 6, I embarked ... in four battoes, mounted with two wall-pieces each. **1779** *Essex Inst. Coll.* XLIX. 111 Sold ... 2 wall pieces, at £9. (2) **1852** WATSON *Nights in Block-House* 16 The palisades were strengthened and kept in their places by stout ribbons or wall-pieces, pinned to them with inch tree-nails on the inside.

Wall rock. +1. (See quotation.) +2. *Mining.* The rock which constitutes the wall of a vein. — (1) **1859** BARTLETT 499 *Wall Rock,* granular limestone, used in the building of walls. (2) **1876** RAYMOND *8th Rep. Mines* 86 The hardness of the wall-rock has proved an obstacle to successful mining. **1879** *Harper's Mag.* Sept. 512 Much of the way [is] half hidden underneath the edge of the 'wall rock.' **1883** BEADLE *Western Wilds* 582 The enclosing rocks, known in reference to the vein as 'wall rock,' ... are somewhat more simple in construction.

+Wall Street.

1. In lower Manhattan in New York City, a street (the site of a wall built by the Dutch in the seventeenth century) in which are located some of the principal financial institutions of New York; the financial center of the United States; by extension, the financial interests of the United States.

1806 *Balance* V. 228/1 Walking thro' Wall street yesterday morning, I saw a large crowd. **1841** *Week in Wall St.* p. ix, In the expressive language, of Wall-street, he has himself been 'flunked.' **1848** *Knickerb.* XXXII. 273 Something had gone wrong in Wall-street. **1868** *N.Y. Herald* 27 July 4/2 Wall street is in a confident ... mood again. **1883** *Century Mag.* Oct. 850/2 Within five or ten minutes' walk of Wall street and of South street ..., it was yet entirely removed from business. **1890** *Congress. Rec.* 5 June 5608/1 'Wall street' is a term supposed to suggest conscienceless greed for and criminal methods to obtain money. **1918** LINCOLN *Shavings* 288 Where is he now? Out somewhere where he don't belong, fightin' and bein' killed to help Wall Street get rich.

2. *attrib.* **a.** Designating members of the financial community of Wall Street, or persons in some way associated with it.

1836 *Jamestown* (N.Y.) *Jrnl.* 16 March 1/2 A company—Wall street brokers and speculators—are the applicants for the loan to the New York and Erie Railroad. **1853** J. BALDWIN *Flush Times Ala.* 86 Terms of payment which a Wall-street capitalist would have to re-cast his arrangements to meet. **1868** *N.Y. Herald* 7 July 6/4 The 'honesty' of our New York politicians of both parties ... is the honesty of our Wall street rings. **1870** M. H. SMITH *20 Years Wall St.* 27 The richest men in New York are Wall Street operators. **1887** *Courier-Journal* 8 Jan. 5/3 Mr. Gladstone never ... twisted the tails of the Wall-street bulls. **1893** *Chicago Tribune* 25 April 12/1 With gold at a premium, ... the speculators, or ... Wall street sharks, would have been in clover. **1903** *N.Y. Ev. Post* 19 Sept., The disrespectful term of 'Wall Street farmer' ... embraces a large number of people who would not know the condition of a wheat or cotton field if they saw it.

b. With *method, note-shaving, office,* etc.

1848 W. ARMSTRONG *Stocks* 14 Such persons [who raise or depress stock at their sovereign wills] are termed in Wall-street phrase for the time being, the king of the street. **1862** *N. Amer. Rev.* July 113 This Wall-Street note-shaving life is ... a very peculiar field. **1870** O. LOGAN *Before Footlights* 173 Men have the whole field of labor before them, from Wall

street speculation down—or up—to boot-blacking. **1873** 'MARK TWAIN' & WARNER *Gilded Age* 120 The two young men ... went down to the Wall street office of Henry's uncle. **1888** E. W. KIRK *Queen Money* 467 He had always, he declared, had some curiosity to see a Wall Street panic. **1892** GUNTER *Miss Dividends* 188 All the rest .. [had] fallen victims to his imported Wall Street methods. **1911** *N.Y. Ev. Post* 14 Sept. (Th. S.), The wealthy banker, straight from downtown by the 'Wall Street subway special' hobnobs with the office-boy for once.

+Wall-Streeter. [f. prec.] A member of the financial community of Wall Street; a financier. — **1885** *Wkly. New Mexican Rev.* 15 Jan. 2/2 The Wall streeters and money changers want less money that they may have a better chance to grind the borrowers.

‖**Wall-sweep clock.** A wall clock with a long pendulum. — **1873** BEADLE *Undevel. West* 449 A great grinning demon, top-ornament to an old Spanish wall-sweep clock. **1878** — *Western Wilds* 42 The old wall-sweep clock struck nine in a loud, aggressive tone.

+Wall tent. A tent with vertical walls or partitions of cloth. Also attrib. — **1842** *S. Lit. Messenger* VIII. 409/1, I had previously ripped a wall-tent and converted it into a sail. **1861** *Army Regulations* 236 Wall-tent flies. Wall-tent poles and pins, sets. **1864** NORTON *Army Lett.* 238, I have my wall tent nicely floored and a jolly fireplace in it. **1887** BILLINGS *Hardtack* 50 The Hospital or Wall tent is distinguished from those already described by having four upright sides or walls. **1903** 'O. HENRY' *Rolling Stones* 86 The big wall tent for provisions showed the camp was intended to be occupied for a considerable length of time.

* Walnut.

I. *1. a. The fruit or nut of a walnut tree. **b.** = WALNUT TREE 1. {1600-}

1609 HAKLUYT *Va. Richly Valued* (1846) 131 There are also in Florida great store of Walnuts, and Plummes, Mulberries, and Grapes. **1612** SMITH, etc. *Virginia* I. 10 Of walnuts there is 2 or 3 kindes. **1703** *Cambridge Prop. Rec.* 127 [We] Markd a Walnutt & three Black Oaks. **1789** DENNY *Journal* 132 A great deal of poplar, walnut, locust, cherry, shellbark hickory and black oak. **1817** FORDHAM *Narr. Travels* 119 In the Woods there are great quantities of Grapes, Walnuts, Hickory Nuts, and Parsimins. **1872** McCLELLAN *Golden State* 331 Walnuts grow in every county in the state. **1922** TARKINGTON *Gentle Julia* 296 There were apples and cider and cake, with walnuts, perfectly cracked.

*2. The wood of a walnut tree or trees.

1612 SMITH, etc. *Virginia* I. 10 The wood that is most common is Oke and Walnut. **1637** MORTON *New Canaan* 63 Walnut: of this sorte of wood there is infinite store. **1869** *Rep. Comm. Agric. 1868* 15 The museum has been partly filled with absolutely dust-proof cases of solid walnut. **1883** 'MARK TWAIN' *Life on Miss.* xliii, There's one thing ... which a person won't take in pine if he can go walnut; and won't take in walnut if he can go mahogany. ... That's a coffin.

+3. *ellipt.* A walnut grove or walnut timber.

1897 BRODHEAD *Bound in Shallows* 165 Would there be anything wrong in me selling the walnut and building me a house?

+4. *local.* A hickory nut.

1894 EGGLESTON in *Century Mag.* April 850 About Lake George, I find 'shuck' used ... for the outer covering of the hickory-nut—called here and in some other Northern districts 'walnut.'

II. *attrib.* and *comb.* **+5.** Designating areas where walnut trees are, or formerly were, the prevailing growth.

1659 *Hempstead Rec.* I. 75 There is Granted vnto Josias Forman, the walnut hollow, and the cherry-tree hollow. **1816** U. BROWN *Journal* I. 148 The Walnut-planes ... are Dry rich Land without any Timber or wood growing on the same. **1855** WHITTIER *Poetical Works* (1894) 396/2 Mine the sand-rimmed pickerel pond, Mine the walnut slopes beyond. **1883** SMITH *Geol. Survey Ala.* 468 A loose walnut prairie land makes up a small proportion of the country about Faunsdale.

6. Designating articles made of walnut. {1840-}

1670 *Doc. Col. Hist. N.Y.* XII. 476 If you can conveniently send me what Walnut Beames you can for my Chimney pieces. **1681** *New Castle Court Rec.* 515 The P[lain]t[iff] declares for a small blake walnut Chest with Lock & Key. **1779** *York Co., Va. Rec. Wills* XXII. 28 April, Walnut chairs. **1837** *S. Lit. Messenger* III. 174 The angler spread a cloth on the walnut table. **1845** *Knickerb.* XXV. 446 Here too was the tall walnut 'secretary,' which when shut looked like the half of a steep-roofed house. **1851** CIST *Cincinnati* 245 Warner B. Mahone ... [executes] walnut and maple banisters. **1876** *Scribner's Mo.* Feb. 585/2 Strips of ogee walnut molding can be fastened on the sides and base. **1885** *Wkly. New Mexican Rev.* 29 Jan. 4/1 The presents at the wedding [included]: ... Fine walnut bed-room set.

7. Designating foods or candies in the making of which walnuts are used. {1769-}

1861 *Vanity Fair* 23 March 134/2 That person [produced] ... walnut pickles, cold corned beef, hard-boiled eggs. **1882** RITTENHOUSE *Maud* 75 The thoughtful GWRC had his pockets full of creams, cocoanuts, walnut creams and all sorts of French candies. **1904** GLASGOW *Deliverance* 501, I declare, if she ain't been making walnut cake again.

8. In special combinations.

Walnut log, a section of a walnut tree used as firewood; *w. milk,* a milky, oily liquid obtained from crushed walnuts; *w. pill,* a pill made from the leaves or hulls of a walnut tree or its nuts; *w. shuck,* the shell of a walnut; *w. spire,* a walnut sapling; *w. wood,* firewood obtained from walnut trees.

1867 LOWELL *Biglow P.* 2 Ser. p. lxxvii, The wa'nut logs shot sparkles out Towards the pootiest. *c*1618 STRACHEY *Virginia* 119 The inhabitants seeth a kind of million [melon], which they put into their walnut-milke, and so make a kynd of toothsome meat. **1837** WETMORE *Gaz. Missouri* 290 The only medicine within reach of the settlers was a small parcel of walnut pills. **1837** *Yale Lit. Mag.* II. 220 (Th.), He thumped round the deck like a cat shod with walnut shucks. **1703** *Derby Rec.* 327 Capt: Ebenezer Johnson's division of land . . . [is] bounded . . . att ye Southerly corner with a walnut spire. **1707** SEWALL *Diary* II. 178 A great Storm of Snow; yet Dan Bayley breaks through, and brings us a Load of Walnut Wood.

Walnut bark. The bark of a walnut tree. — **1788** MAY *Jrnl. & Lett.* 73 Till then I intend to live on board ship, which I like better than the little cabins covered with walnut bark. **1807** IRVING, etc. *Salmagundi* x, [At] Chamouny—[there is a] floating bridge made of pine logs fastened together by ropes of walnut bark. **1821** *Amer. Jrnl. Science* III. 167 Walnut bark makes the most permanent yellow for dying cloth. **1852** STOWE *Uncle Tom* xi, A little walnut bark has made my yellow skin a genteel brown.

+Walnut fern. (See quotation.) — **1824** DODDRIDGE *Notes* 149 A kind of fern which from its resemblance to the leaves of walnut, was called walnut fern, is another remedy [for snake bite].

Walnut grove. A grove of walnut trees. — **1836** EDWARD *Hist. Texas* 52 Walnut groves are plentifully scattered throughout the prairies. **1848** *Knickerb.* XVIII. 64 [The school] was buried in a walnut grove that skirted the western border of the town. **1883** *Century Mag.* Oct. 818/2 [The road] winds and turns, past knolls of walnut grove.

+Walnut moth. Any one of various moths the larvae of which feed on walnut leaves. Also *regal walnut moth*. — **1854** EMMONS *Agric. N.Y.* V. 238 *Ceratocampa regalis*. . . . Regal Walnut-moth. **1879** *Scribner's Mo.* July 396/1 It is the regal walnut moth, . . . and a perfect beauty. **1892** KELLOGG *Kansas Insects* 98 Walnut moth (*Datana angusii*). . . . Infesting walnut and hickory; large, blackish caterpillars, feeding on the leaves.

* Walnut tree.

* 1. a. Any one of various trees of the genus *Juglans*. **+b.** = SHAGBARK HICKORY.

Cf. BLACK-WALNUT TREE, ENGLISH WALNUT.

1610 *Estate of Va.* 54 The country yeeldeth abundance of wood, as Oake, Wainscot, Walnut tres. **1634** WOOD *New Eng. Prospect* 16 The Wallnut tree is something different from the English Wallnut, being a great deale more tough, and more serviceable. **1698** *Boston Rec.* 233 [The line is to run] from a Walnut tree in the parting line between sd. Cheevers and Col. Shrimptons land. **1703** *Providence Rec.* V. 150 A walnut tree Marked for a Northeasterne Cornner of the bulke of the said land. **1792** POPE *Tour S. & W.* 46 Notwithstanding the natural Sterility of Soil from Pensacola almost to the Tallipoosee River, . . . Walnut Trees grow to their usual Height. **1805** PARKINSON *Tour* 374 There are walnut-trees in great numbers. **1895** GRAHAM *Stories of Foot-Hills* 5 A row of leafless walnut-trees stretched their gaunt white branches above the road.

2. Attrib. with *girdler, hill, press, wood.*

1649 *Perfect Descr. Va.* 5 Choice Walnut-tree-wood . . . is transported by them if Tobacco is not their full lading. **1659** *Topsfield Rec.* 5 Wee have rune the six miles Extent . . . Vnto a hill Comonly Called by the name of Wallnut tree hill. **1771** *Md. Hist. Mag.* XIV. 136 It was in the Walnut tree press wh[ich] stood in the Passage between the two Houses. **1854** EMMONS *Agric. N.Y.* V. 263 (index), Walnuttree girdlers, 123.

Waltz, *v.* {1794–} **+***tr.* To transport or convey (something heavy or clumsy). *colloq.* — **1884** 'MARK TWAIN' *H. Finn* iii, They've got to waltz that palace around over the country wherever you want it. **1901** MERWIN & WEBSTER *Calumet 'K'* 197 He'd call the men off just the same, and leave us to waltz the timbers around all by ourselves.

* Wamble-cropped, Womble-cropped, *a.* Upset; squeamish. *dial.* {–a1610} 'Now *U.S.*' (*O.E.D.*) — **1798** *Mass. Spy* 5 Sept. (Th.), I feel a good deal womblecropped about dropping her acquaintance. **1835–7** HALIBURTON *Clockmaker* 1 Ser. xxiii. 216 It makes me so kinder wamblecropt when I think on it, that I'm afeared to venture on matrimony at all. **1843** STEPHENS *High Life N.Y.* I. 44, I got back to the sloop and turned in awfully womblecropped. **1898** WESTCOTT *D. Harum* xxviii, I dunno 's I ever see the old man more kind o' womble-cropped over anythin'.

+Wammikin. [See WANGUN.] (See quotations.) — **1878** *Scribner's Mag.* XV. 150 The drive is accompanied by what is called a wammikin, consisting of a raft of square timber or long logs on which is built a comfortable shanty. **1910** HODGE, etc. *Amer. Indians* II. 903 Wammikan, a raft of hewed logs, upon which is constructed a shanty, provided with cooking and sleeping arrangements.

+Wampee. [Algonquian.] An aquatic plant: (see quotations). — **1802** DRAYTON *S. Carolina* 8 [Here grow] quantities of wampe (a species of arum). **1910** HODGE, etc. *Amer. Indians* II. 904/2 Wampee, a name used in parts of the Southern states for the pickerel-weed (*Pontederia caudata*).

+Wampum. Also **wampom, wampam,** etc.

1. Short for WAMPUMPEAG. Now hist.

1647 WINTHROP in R. C. Winthrop *Life J. Winthrop* II. 361 The wampom which he received for me never came to my hands. **1702** C. MATHER *Magnalia* (1853) I. 558 This wampam . . . is made of the shell-fish which lies upon the sea-coast. **1789** MORSE *Amer. Geog.* 349 Wampum was, at this time [*c*1670], the principal currency of the country. **1808** PIKE *Sources Miss.* 74 He informed me that a string of Wampum, had been sent among the Chipeways. **1847** PARKMAN in *Knickerb.* XXIX. 313 Several large necklaces of wampum hung on his breast. **1894** LEAVITT *Our Money*

Wars 1 Indian money or wampum was used in New England almost universally, as late as 1635.

b. Preceded by a term denoting color.

1644 *Mass. H. S. Coll.* 4 Ser. VI. 377, I had rather haue white wampam, then bad blew at 6 a peny. **1674** GOOKIN *Ib.* 1 Ser. I. 152 Black and white wompom . . . is of most esteem among them. **1748** WEISER *Journal* 24 Hired a Cannoe; paid 1,000 Black Wampum for the loan of it. **1808** BARKER *Indian Princess* II. i, Powhatan . . . presents her with a string of white wampum. **1851** SCHOOLCRAFT *Information resp. Indian Tribes* I. 88 It appears from ancient documents . . . that about 1640, three beads of purple or blue wampum, and six of white wampum were equivalent to a styver or to one penny English.

2. Attrib. and comb. with *band, bead, braid,* etc.

See also WAMPUM BELT, WAMPUM SNAKE.

1796 HAWKINS *Letters* 30 He gave half a pint of salt, or 3 strans of mock wampum beads a basket. **1820** EASTBURN & SANDS *Yamoyden* 197 She wrought the glittering wampum band. **1835** HOFFMAN *Winter in West* I. 171 Take into consideration the variously coloured calico dresses and wampum ornaments in which the females had arrayed themselves. **1840** HOFFMAN *Greyslaer* I. 14 A tomahawk [was] secured in the wampum sash of the latter. **1841** WHITTIER *Poetical Works* (1894) 11/2 There the fallen chief is laid, . . . girded with his wampum-braid. **1847** PARKMAN in *Knickerb.* XXIX. 590 Calico shirts, red and blue blankets, . . . wampum necklaces, appeared in profusion.

+Wampum belt. A belt made of wampum, often arranged in mnemonic figures or shapes, and used in ratifying treaties, confirming alliances, etc. — **1676** B. TOMPSON *Poetical Works* 91 All up in Wampam Belts, most richly drest. **1726** PENHALLOW *Indian Wars* 129 The Canada tribes . . . had sent a letter (as they said) with two wampum belts. **1809** WEEMS *Marion* (1833) 22 The Cherokees . . . sent on a deputation with their wampum belts and peace-talks to bury the hatchet. [**1865** J. G. HODGINS *Hist. Canada* 101 Wampum belts were the official records of alliance, and in the hands of a chief, were the ratification of treaties of friendship.]

+Wampumpeag. Also **wampumpeage, wampampeak,** etc. [Narraganset *wampompeag*.] Shell beads used by the Indians as ornaments and serving as a medium of exchange in early colonial Indian trade. Now hist.

1627 in Bradford *Hist.* 273 Ye above-said parties are to have . . . ye whole stock of . . . wampampeak, hatchets, knives, &c. that is now in ye storre. *c*1680 HULL *Diaries* 216 The king's commissioners . . . accepted crowns of wompum-peage from [the Indian sachems]. **1723** *New-Eng. Courant* 4 Feb. 2/2 The Narragansets have a Crown among them made of Wampumpeeg. **1764** HUTCHINSON *Hist. Mass.* I. 458 The Naragansets . . . were the most curious coiners of the wampompeag, and supplied the other nations with money, pendants, and bracelets. **1894** LEAVITT *Our Money Wars* 2 The aborigines of New England had a true money in wampum . . . called *wampum-peage*, meaning strings of white beads.

+Wampum snake. The hoop snake, *Abastor erythrogrammus.* — **1736** CATESBY *Carolina* II. 58 The Wampum Snake . . . receives its name from the Resemblance it has to Indian Money called Wampum. **1775** BURNABY *Travels* 18 Several snakes of this country [Va.] are harmless and beautiful; such as the black snake, the wampum-snake, . . . and some others. **1791** W. BARTRAM *Travels* 273 They seem to be a species, if not the very same snake which in Pennsylvania and Virginia, are called wampom snake. **1808** ASHE *Travels* 243 We called the following to our recollection: . . . green snake, wampum snake.

+Wamus. Also **waumus, warmus,** etc. [Du. *wammes*.] (See quot. 1847.) — **1805** *Lancaster* (Pa.) *Intelligencer* 12 Nov. (Th.), I got up, and found that my waumus was bloody, which I had not observed before. **1841** *S. Lit. Messenger* VII. 525/1 His long, matted locks overhung the back of a red flannel *warm-us*. **1847** HOWE *Hist. Coll. Ohio* 254*n.*, The '*warmus*' is a working garment, similar in appearance to a 'roundabout,' but more full, and being usually made of *red* flannel, is elastic and easy to the wearer. **1872** EGGLESTON *End of World* 40 Instead of a coat he wore that unique garment of linsey-woolsey known in the West as wa'mus (warm us), a sort of over-shirt. **1892** *Dialect Notes* III. 592 *Wammus*, a coat-like jacket worn by men in such work as threshing wheat. (Western Indiana.)

* Wandering, *a.* In the specific names of insects and birds: (see quotations). — **1832** WILLIAMSON *Maine* I. 172 Spider; several species, such as black, gray, wandering, garden, water, jumping, rose Spiders. **1835** AUDUBON *Ornith. Biog.* III. 555 The Wandering Shearwater, *Puffinus Cinereus,* . . . frequently uses its feet to support itself on the surface, without actually alighting. **1858** BAIRD *Birds Pacific R.R.* 734 *Heteroscellus brevipes,* . . . This species ranges over an immense extent of locality. **1917** *Birds of Amer.* II. 87/1 Duck Hawk. Other Names [include] . . . Wandering Falcon.

+Wangun. Also **wangan, wanigan.** [Abnaki *waniigan* 'a trap.'] (See quot. 1910 and cf. WONGEN, WAMMIKIN.)

1848 BARTLETT 377 *Wangan.* (Indian.) In Maine, a boat for carrying provisions. **1860** *Harper's Mag.* XX. 451 Behind each regiment of logs follows the wangan—a small boat or barge with a canvass awning stretched over it, and the cook and supplies. **1902** WHITE *Blazed Trail* 323 Outside, the cook and cookee were stowing articles in the already loaded wanigan. **1910** HODGE, etc. *Amer. Indians* II. 910 *Wanigan,* a receptacle in which small supplies or a reserve stock of goods are kept; also a large chest in which the lumbermen of Maine and Minnesota keep their spare clothing, pipes, tobacco, etc. Called also *wongan*-box, and spelled *wangun* and *wangan*. (2) A boat used on the rivers of Maine for the transportation of the entire personnel of a logging camp, along with the tools of the camp and provisions for the trip. . . . (3) A place in a lumber camp where accounts are kept and the men paid.

attrib. **1907** *Black Cat* June 19 Abe, limping about, bustled over to an ancient Wangan-chest, relic of his father's river-days. **1908** WHITE *River Man* 131 The ground had now hardened so that a wanigan boat was unnecessary.

b. Stores and provisions.

1907 *Scribner's Mag.* Jan. 2/1 Now load up with the bundles and boxes, the tent, . . . the provisions—all that stuff that is known as . . . 'wangan' in Maine.

+Wankapin. [Algonquian.] (See quot. 1891 and cf. YONKAPIN.] — **1832** KENNEDY *Swallow Barn* 232 The heirs of Swallow Barn . . . are hereafter to be pestered with this fine garden of wankopins and snake-collards. **1891** *Cent.* 6816/1 Wankapin, . . . the water-chinkapin.

＊Want, *n.* +=WANT AD. *colloq.* — **1855** BARNUM *Life* 143 My eyes were running over the columns of 'Wants' in the New York 'Sun.' **1856** MACLEOD *F. Wood* 42 [He] began to study the column of 'wants.' **1897** *Scribner's Mag.* XXII. 459 'Wants' bring in a large, sure income directly.

＊Want, *v.*

+1. *tr.* With a clause as object: To desire (that someone do something). Now *dial.*

1745 BRAINERD *Journal* (1902) 19 They replied, 'They wanted Christ should wipe their hearts quite clean.' **1833** NEAL *Down-Easters* I. 80, I want you should give me a letter o' recommend to Pheladelphy. **1882** THAYER *From Log-Cabin* 347 Everybody wants you should answer him. **1920** HOWELLS *Vacation of Kelwyns* 188 Want I should drive ye home?

2. *(I) want to know,* (see KNOW *v.* 2).

3. *To want of,* to want or need with. *colloq.* {1828}

1855 *Knickerb.* XLV. 136 What do you want of salt? **1884** 'MARK TWAIN' *H. Finn* xxxv, What do we want of a saw? **1914** ATHERTON *Perch of Devil* 246 What does he want of two cottages?

+Want-ad. A notice in a newspaper stating that something is wanted. In full *want advertisement*. (Cf. AD.) — **1887** *Courier-Journal* 12 Jan. 5/3 The World is treating Mr. Conkling as it treats its circulation and its 'want' advertisements upon occasion. **1897** *Scribner's Mag.* XXII. 459 (*caption*), Calling for Answers to 'Want Ads.' **1922** SANDBURG *Slabs Sunburnt West* 45 If you get lost try a want ad.

+Wantage. (See quot. 1828.) — **1828** WEBSTER s.v., *Wantage*, deficiency; that which is wanting. **1889** *N.Y. Produce Exch. Rep.* 256 Inspectors and Gaugers shall make a detailed return . . . of each lot inspected, showing . . . the gauge, wantage, proof, and number of proof gallons.

+Wantage rod. A gauged rod used in determining the wantage of a cask, etc. — **1861** *Ill. Agric. Soc. Trans.* V. 166 Our other implements, except the saccharometer, gauge-rod and wantage-rod, were the common utensils. **1886** *Harper's Mag.* July 215/1 Inspectors and gaugers . . . must make their returns . . . in accordance with the straight gauge rod, wantage rod, the hydrometer used by the government.

Want column. A column in a newspaper taken up with want ads. {1901-} — **1884** NYE *Baled Hay* 239 The want column of the Chicago *News* . . . has the following: 'Twelve "frightful examples" wanted, to travel with Scott Marble's new drama and appear in the realistic barroom scene of the "Drunkard's Daughter."' **1898** *Scribner's Mag.* XXIII. 596/2 There are groups of men who study closely the 'want-columns.' **1903** 'O. HENRY' *Rolling Stones* 36 [We] found J. Conyngham Binkly leaning against the want column of a newspaper.

Wapiti. [Algonquian.] The North American stag or elk, *Cervus canadensis.* {1817-} Also with specifying term.

1827 W. BULLOCK *Journey* p. xxi, A pair of the gigantic elk, or wappetti (nearly the size of horses), ranged through the meadows. **1842** *Nat. Hist. N.Y., Zoology* I. 119 The American Stag . . . is called . . . *Wapiti, Grey Elk* and *Round-horned Elk.* **1882** *Century Mag.* Aug. 517/2 The museum possesses already fine examples . . . of the wapiti. **1893** ROOSEVELT *Wilderness Hunter* 161 The wapiti is, next to the moose, the most quarrelsome and pugnacious of American deer. **1917** *Mammals of Amer.* 4 Western Wapiti. *Cervus canadensis occidentalis.* . . . Darker in coloration. Extreme western North America.

attrib. **1846** W. G. STEWART *Altowan* I. 127 The Wapati stag, still careful of his growing horns, was seen bounding from his covert. *Ib.* II. 53 The Wapati deer, commonly called the elk among the Americans, has a sharp, though loud cry.

+Wappato. Also *wapato*, etc. [Algonquian.]

1. The bulbous root of either of two species of arrowhead (*Sagittaria latifolia* or *S. cuneata*) used as food by the Indians in the Oregon region.

1805 CLARK in *Lewis & C. Exped.* III. (1905) 196 This root they call *Wap-pa-to* . . . has an agreeable taste and answers verry well in place of bread. **1831** R. COX *Adv. Columbia R.* 76 Below the rapids we also got a quantity of excellent roots, called by the Indians *wappittoo.* **1855** *Amer. Inst. N.Y. Trans.* 1854 453 A root used largely by the Indians, near the mouth of the Columbia, was called (40 years ago) *wapato.* **1872** DE VERE 401 In Oregon the Chinook Indians live largely on an edible bulb called *Wapatoo.*

attrib. and *comb.* **1805** CLARK in *Lewis & C. Exped.* III. (1905) 229 Several Indians followed him & soon after a canoe with *Wapto* roots, & Liquorice boiled. *c*1836 CATLIN *Indians* II. 113 'Wapito diggers,' [are] instruments used by the women for digging the wapito, a bulbous root, much like a turnip.

2. (See quotations.)

1888 *Puget Sound Gazetteer* July 12/1 Canvasback ducks . . . on the Columbia river . . . get an excellent flavor from the wapato, a sort of white water lily, upon the roots of which they feed. **1910** HODGE, etc. *Amer. Indians* II. 913 The Chippewa name *wápato* has been applied to some plant called rhubarb.

Wapper-jaw. Also **whopple-jaw,** etc. A crooked jaw or misshapen mouth {a1825, *dial.*}; +a protruding under jaw. *colloq.* — **1877** BARTLETT 746 *Whapper-Jaw,* a protruding under-jaw; so *whapper-jawed.* **1886** HOWELLS *Minister's Charge* 421 Her whopper-jaw twitching with excitement, and her eyes glaring vindictively upon Lemuel. **1891** *Cent.* 6818/1 *Wapper-jaw.* **1893** M. A. OWENS *Voodoo Tales* 219 He wuz de mos' uglies' man in de worl', wid er whopple-jaw an' er har'-lip.

Wapper-jawed, *a.* Also **whopper-jawed,** etc. Having a thin or crooked jaw, or a misshapen mouth {*dial.*}; +=JIMBERJAWED *a. colloq.* Also transf. — **1836** DUNLAP *Mem. Water Drinker* (1837) I. 65 His chin with the parts adjacent, assumed the appearance vulgarly called wapper-jaw'd. **1849** LOWELL *Writings* IX. 12 Fancy an heir that a father had seen born well featured and fair, turning suddenly wry-nosed, clubfooted, . . . wapper-jawed. **1860** T. PARKER in *Life & Corr.* (1863) II. 428 This sheet is ruled as whopper-jawed as some women cut their bread. **1877** BARTLETT 746 *Whapper-jawed.* **1884** NYE *Baled Hay* 60 Peculiarities of old traditions still linger . . . and are forked over to posterity like a wappy-jawed teapot or a long-time mortgage.

＊War.

I. ＊1. A conflict, in a series of engagements, carried on between armed forces representing nations or parts of nations.

1639 WILLIAMS *Letters* (1874) 134 That you would please to ratify that promise made to them after the wars, viz.; the free use of the Pequot country for their hunting. *a*1656 BRADFORD *Hist.* 232 This his death was one ground of the Pequente warr which followed. **1765** CROGHAN *Journal* 139 Southern Indians . . . are always at war with the northward Indians **1814** *Columbian Centinel* 18 June 2/3 The southern war-hirelings say the Administration will continue the War. **1848** *Congress. Globe* 2 March 418/2 The late war with Great Britain was unpopular with the blue-light Federalists. **1866** *Wkly. New Mexican* 11 Aug. 1/3 The balance of the funds will be devoted to preparing a home for the orphans and childless, resulting from the next war with England. **1919** *World's Work* Feb. 370/1 The outworn, discredited grab-bag diplomacy . . . caused this war.

b. =CIVIL WAR b. Also *War between the States.*

1861 *Chicago Tribune* 26 May 1/9, I, Samuel M. Fassett, Photographist, . . . Will Continue to Take Those Fine Plain Photographs For the Low sum of One Dollar, During the War. **1863** *Ladies' Repository* XXIII. 128/2 The emancipation Proclamation of President Lincoln makes an era . . . in the history of the war. **1883** 'MARK TWAIN' *Life on Miss.* xlv, In the South, the War is what A.D. is elsewhere; they date from it. All day long you hear things 'placed' as having happened since the War; or 'du'in' the War,' or 'befo' the War.' **1900** H. ROBERTSON *Red Blood & Blue* 283 Since the war between the States, until now, the Stars and Stripes had been rarely seen in the town.

c. In various transferred senses with defining terms.

See also BROAD SEAL WAR, *Buckshot war* (under BUCK-SHOT *n.* 3).

1887 *Courier-Journal* 30 Jan. 2/1 Louisville was enveloped in a London fog last night, a foretaste of what England will probably send us when the Cod-fish War begins. **1898** *Fox Kentuckians* 11 A feud . . . had broken out afresh. It was called the Keaton-Stallard 'war' in the mountains.

2. In phrases. (See also the separate entries.)

+War of Iniquity, =WAR OF 1812; +*w. of the gauges,* the controversy concerning the merits of standard gauge and narrow gauge in railroad track (*humorous*); +*W. of the Revolution,* =REVOLUTIONARY WAR.

1813 *Columbian Centinel* 7 April 2/2 Mr. Gallatin's second attempt to obtain cash to carry on the War of Iniquity, has confirmed him that the money holders are determined to let his Loan alone. **1854** *La Crosse Democrat* 14 Feb. 2/5 It is hoped that the war of the gauges is ended. **1847** *Whig Almanac* 1848 2 The number of our countrymen slain in that lamentable Mexican War . . . is equal to one-half of the whole of the American loss during the seven years' War of the Revolution.

II. *attrib.* and *comb.* Senses 3 through 6 refer chiefly to phases of Indian warfare.

＊3. Designating arms, weapons, or similar equipment for use in war.

See also WAR CLUB, WAR HATCHET.

1742 in *Travels Amer. Col.* 224 [He] could discover nothing but their Tracts and one of their War Sticks. **1799** J. SMITH *Acct. Captivity* 12 Each warrior had a tomahawk, spear or war-mallot in his hand. **1804** ORDWAY in *Journals of Lewis & O.* 109 Each of those Musicians had War hoop . . . made of thickest buffelow hides dressed white covered with thin Goat Skin dress[e]d white & ornamented with porcupine quills & feathers. **1844** LEE & FROST *Oregon* 178 The war-stone . . . is a smooth stone, nearly round, and about two inches in diameter, strongly enclosed in a piece of elk-skin.

∗b. Designating sound-producing devices used in war. {war drum, 1593–}

1775 ADAIR *Indians* 388 He is degraded, by taking from him his drum, war-whistle, and martial titles. **1797** F. BAILY *Tour* 367 The *war bells* . . . are formed of a hollow nut, about as big as one's fist, in which was a stone, which made a hollow dismal sound. **1900** DRANNAN *Plains & Mts.* 113 The war-drum, or what the Comanches call 'a tum-tum,' was made of a piece of hollow log . . . , with a piece of untanned deerskin stretched over one end.

∗c. Designating clothing or other property used in war.

See also WAR BAG 1, WAR BELT, etc.

1820 *Western Rev.* II. 48 The war budget is then hung in front of the door of the person that carried it on the march. **1842** *S. Lit. Messenger* VIII. 701/2 Their sacred war gourds, containing the teeth of the drumhead fish, were left on the ground. **1845** SIMMS *Wigwam & Cabin* 1 Ser. 131 But the blood of Connattee is not upon the war-shirt of Selonee. **1865** PIKE *Scout & Ranger* (1932) 123 Many had friends . . . who came after them with wagons; refusing to let them ride their war ponies. **1876** BOURKE *Journal* 10 June, The first thing to be done was to erect their war lodges of saplings covered over with blankets and shreds of canvass. **1881** *Harper's Mag.* April 675/2, I had my War Jacket on when [my picture was] taken, but I wear white man's clothes. **1883** 'MARK TWAIN' *Life on Miss.* App. D, It contains all my medicines, and my war-plumes. **1895** REMINGTON *Pony Tracks* 50, The Sibley tepees or the 'white man's war tents,' as the Indians call them.

d. Designating boats or vessels used in war. {1777– (Robertson *Hist. Amer.* (1778) I. 376)}

See also WARSHIP, WAR STEAMER.

1836 IRVING *Astoria* II. 248 Old Comcomly had beheld . . . the arrival of a 'big war canoe' displaying the British flag. **1869** *Causes Reduct. Tonnage* (1870) 61 [The nation should secure] available means for the prompt construction of war-vessels. **1883** 'MARK TWAIN' *Life on Miss.* xxvi, Several of the boat's officers had seen active service in the Mississippi warfleet.

4. Designating places associated with war or war councils, or journeys undertaken with hostile intent.

See also WAR GROUND and cf. WARPATH, WAR ROAD, WAR TRAIL.

1772 in *Travels Amer. Col.* 551 After he had Smoked with me he went to the head war Cabin where he Called two warriours to him. **1788** *Steele P.* I. 22 That he be instructed to hold the said Treaty at the upper War-ford on French Broad River. **1805** LEWIS in *Ann. 9th Congress* 2 Sess. 1072 The Minetares . . . have extended their war excursions as far westerly as that nation. **1808** PIKE *Sources Miss.* 32 Near a war encampment, I found a painted buckskin. **1847** RUXTON *Adv. Rocky Mts.* (1848) 227 A war-expedition was also talked of to that settlement. **1918** *Nation* 7 Feb. p. xii/1 One of the first things the Government did after entering the war was to . . . compel all ships plying to ports in the war zone to insure their men.

5. Designating sounds or calls associated with war. {1810–}

See also WAR CRY, WAR SHOUT, etc.

1775 ADAIR *Indians* 2 The general name they give us in their most favorable *war-speeches*, resembles that of a contemptible, heterogeneous animal. **1833** FLINT *D. Boone* 94 The captives, terrified by the war yell of their sentinels, added their screams of apprehension. **1846** *Knickerb.* XXVII. 210 The wild war halloo no longer awoke the echo of the woods. **1847** *Ib.* XXX. 48 Raise up the hatchet from the dust, . . . Sound the war-slogan!

6. Designating persons, groups of persons, or deities, considered with respect to their participation in war. {1610–}

See also WAR CAPTAIN, WAR CHIEF, etc.

1775 ADAIR *Indians* 384 The common number of an Indian war company, is only from twenty to forty. **1808** BARKER *Indian Princess* I. iv, Sure 'tis our war-god, Aresqui himself, who lays our chiefs low! **1898** *Kansas City Star* 19 Dec. 1/5 Following are the names of the members of the entertainment committee who received the war heroes.

7. Designating expenditures and other financial provisions for war needs. {1815–}

See also WAR CLAIM, WAR DEBT.

1801 *Steele P.* I. 219 My war office, or War accounts, for Rations, and house rent, and fire wood, I send on to the Secretary of War. **1865** *Atlantic Mo.* Jan. 81/1 Specie [disappeared] from circulation under the pressure of our unparalleled war-expenses. **1869** *Mich. Gen. Statutes* (1882) I. 183 Whatever portion of said amount he is not able to so invest . . . , he shall then use in the payment of the war loan bonds. **1875** *Ib.* 181 Such loan shall be known as the 'War Bounty Loan of the State of Michigan.' **1884** BLAINE *20 Years of Congress* II. 201 The free-traders point to the destructive effect of the war tariff of 1812. **1898** *Internat. Typogr. Union Proc.* 74/2 The war revenue bill . . . provided that a one-cent stamp should be placed on all telegraphic messages. **1898** *Amer. Rev. of Reviews* Sept. 322/2 Newspapers were required to bear the . . . expense of fire, marine, accident, and war insurance.

8. Designating writings or similar productions concerned with war or brought into being under war conditions.

See also WAR BOOK, WAR SONG 2.

1865 JAMES in *Atlantic Mo.* March 266 Were they not better than that stupid war-correspondence in the 'Times'? **1865** *Atlantic Mo.* May 589/1 We have had no such war-poetry, nor anything like it. **1866** CARPENTER *At White House* 82 The clergyman here alluded to his having left with the private secretary a war-sermon which he had lately preached. **1868** BAGBY *Old Va. Gentleman* 190 His assistants . . . were the local editor, J. Marshall Hanna . . . and the editor of the 'leaded minion' or war column, P. H. Gibson. **1873** F. HUDSON *Journalism* 365 Crowds would then surround the office, as in the days of modern war bulletins. **1896** *Typographical Jrnl.* IX. 263 Selling 'war' dailies at 25 and 50 cents a copy, he next entered a district printing concern. **1896** *Godey's Mag.* Feb. 182/1 The instrument . . . imitates horses' hoofs with . . . untiring fidelity in all war-plays.

9. In special combinations.

War crop, a planting of a nature calculated to meet wartime conditions; +*W. Democracy, collect.*, the War Democrats (q.v.); +*w. drink*, a liquid preparation drunk by Indians as preparation for war; +*w. hireling*, =WAR HAWK 1 b; *w. leader*, +among the Creek Indians, a warrior serving as a leader under the 'great warrior'; +*w. lock*, =SCALP LOCK; ∗*w. man*, + =WAR HAWK 1 b; *w. map*, a chart or plan showing the location of battles and military events; +*w. name*, (see quotation); *w. parade*, +(see quotation); *w. physic*, (see quotation); +*W. President*, a president holding office during a war, esp. Abraham Lincoln; +*w. shark*, =WAR HAWK 1 b; *w. star*, (see quotation); *w. stores*, provisions for use in war; +*w. town*, among the Creek Indians, a town set apart for war ceremonials; +*w. trace*, =WARPATH 1.

1862 *N.Y. Tribune* 28 June 8 He has planted a 'war crop' consisting of . . . twenty acres in potatoes, and half an acre in the Texas Mosquit or Musketo Grass. **1864** in Logan *Great Conspiracy* 576 We are told . . . of a War Democracy . . . found in the Union ranks bearing arms in support of the Government. **1833** FLINT *D. Boone* 158 [All] drank the war-drink, a decoction of bitter herbs and roots, for three days. **1814** War-hireling [see sense 1]. **1775** ADAIR *Indians* 30 Every one of their war-leaders must also make three successful *wolfish campaigns*. **1841** COOPER *Deerslayer* ix, Where does he wear his hawk's feather? . . . Is it fast to the war-lock, or does he carry it above the left ear? **1814** *Columbian Centinel* 11 June 2/4 The War-men in Washington appear determined to have some more blood shed before Peace takes place. **1866** CARPENTER *At White House* 55 The positions of the respective forces were traced on the war maps. **1800** HAWKINS *Sk. Creek Country* 70 All who go to war, and are in company, when a scalp is taken, get a war name. **1833** CATLIN *Indians* I. 191 A party of Crows . . . [were] galloping about and yelping, in what they call a war-parade, *i.e.* in a sort of tournament or sham-fight, passing rapidly through the evolutions of battle, and vaunting forth the wonderful character of their military exploits. **1800** HAWKINS *Sk. Creek Country* 79 They have in their shot bags, a charm, a protection against all ills, called the war physic. **1886** LOGAN *Great Conspiracy* 644 The early beams of the morrow's sun touched . . . the lifeless remains of the great War-President and Liberator. **1813** *Columbian Centinel* 1 Sept. 2/1 The whole [story] has been published, republished, and swallowed as matter of fact by our war sharks. **1890** J. JEFFERSON *Autobiog.* 322 A 'war star' . . . was the technical term given by the old legitimate stars and actors to satirize those self-lighted luminaries who had flickered during the national strife and who had gone out after the cessation of hostilities. **1775** ADAIR *Indians* 380 Each gets a small bag of parched corn-flour, for his war-stores. *Ib.* 178 Malakhe, the late famous chieftain of the Kowwetah head war-town of the lower part of the Muskohge country. **1842** *Amer. Pioneer* I. 77 The war trace at that time, between the northern and southern tribes, was along the south branch of Potomac.

+**War bag. 1.** =BUDGET 1. **2.** A bag containing supplies, money, etc.; a duffel bag. Also *transf.* — (1) **1820** *Western Rev.* II. 48 After the action is over, each person returns his war bag to the commander of the party. (2) **1897** A. H. LEWIS *Wolfville* 33 S'pose you-alls gropes about in your war-bags an' sees. I'm needin' of a drink mighty bad. **1902** WHITE *Blazed Trail* 26 That's the "turkey"—' he explained, 'his war bag.' **1908** McGAFFEY *Show-Girl* 197, I plant one century in my war bag [*i.e.*, stocking] and get seven to two on the next with the other three. *a*1918 G. STUART *On Frontier* I. 233 Best suits packed in the bottom of our 'war bags.'

War belt. {1798}

+**1.** Among the North American Indians, a belt of wampum used as a means of conveying a declaration of war or summoning or winning help in the conduct of a war. Now *hist.*

'The tradition is that the Iroquois declared war by sending a belt painted red, but that this was more than figurative language is uncertain. On the other hand a belt was sometimes carried by a messenger to call out warriors from the allied or subject tribes of the Six Nations' (Adams & Coleman *Dict. Amer. Hist.* V. 395/1).

1776 in Ramsey *Tennessee* 149 The Cherokees had received the warbelt from the Shawnese, Mingo, Taawah and Delaware Nations. **1779** G. R. CLARK *Sk. Campaign Illinois* 45, I presented them with a Peace & [a] War Belt, and told them to take their choice. **1809** *Ann. 10th Congress* 2 Sess. 1402 The Indians, to whom the war-belt has been sent . . . with an invitation to them to take up the tomahawk against us. **1818** *Niles' Reg.* XIV. 208/2 The war belt is said to have passed through the Winebago, Sack, Fox, and Kickapoo tribes. **1835** SIMMS *Yemassee* II. 97 [He] had been persuaded to visit the neighboring tribes . . . with the war-belt, and a proposition of a common league against the English settlements. **1847** LANMAN *Summer in Wilderness* 17 Captain James Clarke, . . . when about to be murdered by a council of Indians . . . , threw the war-belt in the midst of the savages, with a defying shout.

2. A belt worn by a warrior in which he carries his weapons. {1798}

1841 CATLIN *Indians* II. 222*n.*, He then slowly drew from his war-belt, his scalping-knife.

+**War bird.** A golden eagle. So called because Indians wore the feathers in war bonnets. — [**1836** TRAILL *Backwoods of Canada* 289 [An Indian squaw] adorned with the wings of the American War-bird.] **1855** LONGFELLOW *Hiawatha* 120 Then began the greatest battle . . . That the war-birds ever witnessed.

***Warble,** *v.* +*intr.* (See quot. 1890.) Also *vbl. n.* with descriptive term. — **1880** 'MARK TWAIN' *Tramp Abroad* 289 The famous Alpine *jodel* . . . was that sort of quaint commingling of baritone and falsetto which at home we call 'Tyrolese warbling.' **1890** WEBSTER 1626/3 *Warble,* . . . to sing with sudden changes from chest to head tones; to yodel.

Warbler. {1611–}

+**1.** Any one of numerous small, insect-eating birds of the family Compsothlypidae. {1773–, of birds of the family Sylviidae}

1835 AUDUBON *Ornith. Biog.* III. 177 Some of the Warblers had begun to think of removing farther south. **1862** *N.H. Laws* 2609 If any person shall . . . take, kill or destroy any of the birds called . . . linnets, fly-catchers or warblers; . . . he shall forfeit . . . the sum of one dollar. **1907** *St. Nicholas* May 648/2 Whether the bird to be sketched be the laziest heron or the most animated warbler it is always best to sketch its changing position or flying away. **1917** *Birds of Amer.* III. 111 As a rule the Warblers are birds of beautiful plumage.

2. With descriptive or specifying terms.
Only a selection of examples is included. Many more are given in dictionaries and books on birds. See also under specifying terms (BAY-BREASTED *a*, BLACKBURNIAN *a*. and *n.*, etc.) and under separate headings (AUDUBON'S WARBLER, CERULEAN WARBLER, etc.) for various species.

1811 WILSON *Ornithology* III. 63 Black and Yellow Warbler. *Sylvia Magnolia*. . . . This bird I first met with on the banks of the Little Miami. *Ib.* 119 *Sylvia rara*.—Blue Green Warbler. . . . The blue green warbler is four and a half inches long. **1831** AUDUBON *Ornith. Biog.* I. 255 The Azure Warbler, *Sylvia Azurea*, . . . arrives in the lower parts of the State of Louisiana. **1839** *Ib.* V. 464 Green Black-Capt Warbler, *Sylvia Mitrata*, . . . arrives in the woods of the Columbia, where it takes up its summer residence. **1839** PEABODY *Mass. Birds* 311 The Particolored Warbler, *Sylvia Americana*, . . . comes in May and returns in October. **1844** *Nat. Hist. N.Y.*, *Zoology* II. 95 The Black-poll or Black-headed Warbler . . . is highly useful in destroying canker-worms and other noxious insects. **1858** BAIRD *Birds Pacific R.R.* 268 *Dendroica occidentalis*, Western Warbler. . . . Pacific coast. **1870** *Amer. Naturalist* IV. 396 A number of species of birds, mostly wood-warblers (*Dendrœca* and other *Tanagridœ*) have an east and west, as well as a north and south migration. **1878** *Nat. Museum Proc.* I. 407 *Myiodioctes pusillus*, . . . *pileolata*.—Californian Black-Capped Green Warbler. **1917** *Birds of Amer.* III. 120/1 If any bird names itself from its preference for a special home-site, this bird [the Nashville warbler] certainly names itself the Birch Warbler.

***Warbling,** *a.* In the specific names of birds. {1783–, of non-British birds} (See also WARBLING VIREO.) — **1812** WILSON *Ornithology* V. 85 Warbling Flycatcher: *Muscicapa melodia*. . . . It is often heard among the weeping willows and Lombardy poplars of the city. **1844** *Nat. Hist. N.Y.*, *Zoology* II. 123 The Warbling Greenlet. *Vireo gilvus*. . . . This musical little bird reaches us from tropical America about the beginning of May.

+**Warbling vireo.** A sweet-singing vireo, *Vireo gilvus*. — **1839** PEABODY *Mass. Birds* 299 The Warbling Vireo . . . [is] so unwearied in its various and animated warble, that it is one of the chief attractions of a summer day. **1858** *Atlantic Mo.* Oct. 600/1 The notes of the Warbling Vireo have been described by the words, 'Brigadier, Brigadier, Bridget.' **1877** *Harper's Mag.* April 657/1 The lovely warbling vireo . . . fastens its neat pensile nest low down on the ends of the twigs. **1917** *Birds of Amer.* III. 105/1 The Warbling Vireo seems to be especially fond of tall shade trees growing along village streets.

+**War bonnet.** Among various groups of Indians, a ceremonial head-covering ornamented with eagle feathers. — **1845** FRÉMONT *Exped.* 134 Indians . . . with the long red streamers of their war bonnets reaching nearly to the ground. **1870** [see EAGLE FEATHER]. **1890** CUSTER *Following Guidon* 112 War-bonnets, with the eagle feathers so fastened that they stood out at right angles when worn, and extended from the head to the heels. *a*1918 G. STUART *On Frontier* I. 128 They wager everything they possess on this game; horses, blankets, belts, war bonnets [etc.].

War book. A book written about war or produced in time of war. {1916} — **1809** WEEMS *Marion* (1833) p. iii, I never dreamed of such a thing as writing a book; and least of all a *war book*. **1924** HOLT *60 Yrs. a Publisher* 104 Another fashion was . . . in war books.

+**War captain.** =WAR CHIEF 1. — **1709** LAWSON *Carolina* 174 Some one of the Nation . . . is appointed by their King, and War-Captains, to make these Songs [for their feasts]. **1744** MOORE *Voy. Georgia* I. 108 [They] have been ordered by their chief war captain, in case they saw any ship come in, not to shew themselves. **1803** [see CAPTAIN 4]. **1840** *S. Lit. Messenger* VI. 191/2 The same rule applies to a war-captain or

leader, who fails. **1871** *Rep. Indian Affairs* (1872) 392 The officers consist of a governor, . . . war captains, lieutenants, and constables.

War chief. {1800}

+**1.** The military leader of an Indian village, tribe, or other group.

1775 ADAIR *Indians* 292 The war-chiefs and beloved men were grown very poor. **1820** MORSE *Rep. Indian Affairs* II. 132 The whole authority [is] placed in the hands of the war chiefs. **1833** FLINT *D. Boone* 159 The leading war-chief marched first, carrying their medicine bag, or budget of holy things. **1849** EASTMAN *Dahcotah* xviii, To every village there is also a *war-chief*, and as to these are ascribed supernatural powers, their influence is unbounded. **1871** *Rep. Indian Affairs* (1872) 573 Each town had its chiefs (civil and war chiefs) and its lawmakers. **1885** *Century Mag.* May 13/2 A Sioux war-chief . . . sits all day with wife and child to be stared at by the passing multitude.

+**2.** A war-time president of the United States.

1813 *Steele P.* II. 704 The proferred mediation of the Emperor of Russia has been acceded [*sic*] to by our War Chief.

War chieftain. =WAR CHIEF 1. — **1844** *Knickerb.* XXIV. 241 The Tek-a-ri-ho-ge-a, or war-chieftain of the confederate nations, represented the dome, and was upheld and supported by forty-eight sachems. **1775** ADAIR *Indians* 130 All their prophets, priests, old warriors and war chieftains, before they enter on their religious duties, and while they are engaged in them, observe the strictest abstinence.

War claim. A demand for compensation for losses suffered in war. Also attrib. — **1865** *Wkly. New Mexican* 29 Sept. 2/3 War claim Agents, Santa Fe. **1893** *McClure's Mag.* Oct. 382/1 It had been put forward as being the most meritorious of these southern war claims.

War club. A primitive weapon used by Indians. {1845 (Coulter *Adv. Pacific* 196)}
Cf. CASSE TÊTE, TOMAHAWK *n.* 1.

1776 in Rauck *Boonesborough* 251 The war club we got was like those I had seen of that nation [*i.e.*, the Shawanese]. **1792** PUTNAM *Memoirs* 274 A War Club also [was found] with a very extreordinary [*sic*] spike in the head of it. **1808** PIKE *Sources Miss.* 28 One of their war clubs . . . [was] made of elk horn and decorated with inlaid work. **1843** *Amer. Pioneer* II. 109 The Indians . . . left a war club in a conspicuous place . . . which is their mode of letting their enemies know that war is begun. **1870** KEIM *Sheridan's Troopers* 230 The war-club has now almost been abandoned. **1916** EASTMAN *From Deep Woods* 94 Another held his stone war-club over a policeman's head.

+**War College. 1.** *Naval War College*, a college for giving advanced instruction to experienced U.S. navy officers. **2.** (*Army*) *War College*, a similar institution for senior army officers. — (1) **1894** *Naval War College Abstract of Courses* 3 The summer course at the Naval War College began on the 13th of June. (2) **1903** ROOSEVELT in *Laying Cornerstone Army War College Bldg.* 9 The Secretary of War [took] . . . the first practical step toward giving the Army a war college.

War correspondent. One who contributes news and information directly from the scene of war to a newspaper or periodical. {1891} — **1870** MAVERICK *Raymond & N.Y. Press* 256 The 'war correspondents' who had been sent out to the battle-fields to represent the newspapers of New York throve and grew famous. **1889** 'MARK TWAIN' *Conn. Yankee* 536, I had war correspondents with both armies. **1898** R. H. DAVIS in *Scribner's Mag.* Aug. 133/2 Horse dealers . . . led their ponies up and down before the more or less knowing eyes of dough-boy officers and war correspondents.

War council. A council of war (q.v. under COUNCIL *n.* 4). — **1775** ADAIR *Indians* 156 The Chikkasah war-council . . . [condemned] two pretended friends to death. **1825** NEAL *Bro. Jonathan* III. 360 He would stand by Savage, in the war council at night; and listen to him. **1835** SIMMS *Yemassee* II. 1. 3 It was a moment of gloomy necessity, that which assembled the chief defenders of the fortress to a sort of war council. **1884** *Century Mag.* April 805/1 There have been [in the White House] . . . war councils that flashed forth orders . . . which moved great armies.

War cry. A loud yell or whoop uttered by Indians to encourage fighters or to confuse an opponent. {1748, in S. Amer.}

[**1757** BURKE *Europ. Settlem. Amer.* I. II. iv. 187 Setting up a most tremendous shout, which they call the war cry, they pour a storm of musquet bullets upon the enemy.] **1775** ADAIR *Indians* 158 They instantly answered the war-cry. **1808** BARKER *Indian Princess* III. ii, Never did my tongue raise the war cry, and the foe appeared not. **1837** IRVING *Bonneville* I. 89 They put up tremendous war-cries and advanced fiercely. **1858** VIELÉ *Following Drum* 220 Thinking . . . that it was the dreaded war-cry of the Camanches . . . I prepared to rush to a pantry.

***Ward.**

I. ***1.** A subdivision, for administrative or other purposes, of a town or city, or a similar local unit.
See also POLICE-JURY WARD.

1636 *Plymouth Laws* 40 You shall faithfully serve in the office of a Constable in the ward. **1744** MOORE *Voy. Georgia* 97 Every forty houses in town make a ward. **1883** *Century Mag.* Aug. 581/2 Every grog-shop in the ward was his recruiting station. **1925** BRYAN *Memoirs* 74 The Congressional District to which I was moving was Republican; . . . so was . . . the ward in which I expected to live.

b. With specifying numbers.

1807 Seventh Ward [see WARD POLITICIAN]. **1838** in Mayo *Polit. Sk. Washington* 38 The officers of the Revenue Department, residing in the Fifth Ward, are requested to meet. **1881** *Bridgeport* (Conn.) *Municipal Reg.* 7 Councilmen. First Ward. Herman Gauss, [etc.]. **1898** *Kansas City Star* 18 Dec. 2/5 Cleary is the only man in the Third Ward who, last spring, voted for Frank Sebree for mayor.

+**c.** 'A territorial division in the Mormon Church for purposes of ecclesiastical government. It is the administrative unit, with an executive head called a bishop' (*Cent. Suppl.*).

2. A division of a hospital or similar institution. Also with specifying terms. {1749-}

1850 LEWIS *La. Swamp Doctor* 118 Patrick . . . took refuge in a large bathing-tub full of water, which, fortunately for him, stood in the ward. **1863** WHITMAN *Spec. Days* 27, [I] went thoroughly through ward 6. **1869** TOURGEE *Toinette* (1881) 327 With a heart heavy with fearful forebodings she went to the receiving ward. **1884** RITTENHOUSE *Maud* 315 The best wards [in the asylum] are carpeted brightly. **1905** *N.Y. Herald* 2 Sept. 8/3 If he were here the verdict would be:—'The psychopathic ward for his!'

∗**3.** A person in the control, or under the protection, of another. +With reference to the relationship of the Indians to the United States government.

1866 *Rep. Indian Affairs* 126 These poor and ignorant wards of the nation. **1877** *Ib.* 17 Sitting Bull and his adherents are no longer considered wards of this government. **1880** *Cimarron News & Press* 1 July 2/2 The Indians are by law wards of the government.

II. *attrib.* **4.** In sense 1. **a.** Designating institutions, etc., belonging to or characteristic of wards or ward political life. {1844-}

See also WARD MEETING, WARD POLITICS, etc.

1807 IRVING, etc. *Salmagundi* xv. 409 Dabble was now very frequent . . . in his visits to those temples of politicks, popularity and smoke, the ward porter-houses. **1818** FEARON *Sketches* 145 Shameful conduct and persecuting spirit [were] manifested by the Federal Judges, at the late ward election. **1818** *Niles' Reg.* XIV. 174/2 The portion of the $180,000, which, on the ward system, they will pay for the education of the poor as well as of their own children, will not be as much as they now pay for their own alone. **1825** in Brayley *Boston Fire Dept.* 154 One set of men complained of the ward power in the firewards to command. **1833** *Niles' Reg.* XLIV. 183/2 A curious suit was recently tried in one of the ward courts of New York. **1840** in Mackenzie *Van Buren* 255 [They sent desperadoes] here to be dressed up in the committee-rooms, and to vote at all the ward polls, if possible! **1868** *N.Y. Herald* 10 July 6/3 Sixth Ward Tactics Used in the National Convention. **1892** *Courier-Journal* 2 Oct. 16/2 Ward lines have no place in the school system.

∗**b.** Designating individuals representing wards or active in the political life of wards.

See also WARD HEELER, WARD POLITICIAN.

1864 *Mich. Gen. Statutes* I. (1882) 126 When any person shall apply to the inspectors of an election, excepting special elections for ward officers [etc.]. **1872** *Chicago Tribune* 17 Oct. 2/3, I do not mean any person in responsible management, but the ward-chaps, and those who run for the Legislature and expect no higher. *Ib.* 18 Oct. 4/3 Nor is the fact that a ward-bummer is in favor of suppressing the Rebellion . . . any proof that he will not steal the city's money if he gets a chance. **1885** *Atlantic Mo.* April 467/1 These roadways . . . the ward statesman regards with tender solicitude as furnishing a large . . . field of operations in the line of contracts. **1892** *Courier-Journal* 3 Oct. 3/3 The ward-workers began trying to dictate what day laborers should be employed. **1894** FORD P. *Stirling* 318, I'm a ward boss, and my place is in saloons. **1903** LEWIS *Boss* 86, I'm a ward-leader of Tammany Hall.

c. Designating groups of persons (or their meeting places) or organized bodies representing wards or concerned with ward activities.

See also WARD COMMITTEE.

1882 MCCABE *New York* 124 The immense Irish population . . . controls the primary meetings, the ward conventions, and even the greater political bodies. **1883** HAY *Bread-Winners* 247 There was not an Irish laborer . . . but knew his way to his ward club as well as to mass. **1911** CUBBERLEY in Monroe, etc. *Cycl. Educ.* I. 95/1 The school department [of Alleghany, Pa.] is under a Board of Controllers of 90, subdivided into 15 ward boards of 6 members each, elected by wards for three-year terms.

5. In sense 2 with *matron.* {1886}

1863 CUMMING *Hospital Life* 69/1 The food is brought from the kitchen to them, and distributed by a ward matron.

+**6.** In sense 1 c with *assembly room, teacher.*

1878 BEADLE *Western Wilds* 332 The ward teachers had reported every case of real or supposed heresy. *Ib.* 348 Bishop Warren was . . . thanking the Mormon 'Lord,' in the ward assembly rooms.

+**War dance,** *n.*

1. Among the Indians, a ceremonial, or a ceremonial dance, in celebration of victory or in preparation for war {1886, of New Zeal.}; also, a dance imitating or representing actual warfare, or imitating an Indian war dance.

1711 *N.C. Col. Rec.* I. 813 The Baron de Graffenried . . . was still alive but supposed only reserved for a more solemn execution, to be tomahawked and tortured at their first publick War Dances. **1723** *Amer. Wkly. Mercury* 31 Oct. 4/1 The 6 Mohawks . . . at their Request had a War Dance, in order to march the Night following. **1748** WASHINGTON *Diaries* I. 7 We had a War Daunce. **1786** DENNY *Journal* 71 After they had gone through several of their common dances they prepared for a war-dance. **1808** PIKE *Sources Miss.* 49 The Yanctongs and Susitongs . . . had commenced the war-dance. **1819** E. EVANS *Pedestrious Tour* 151 In their war dances, they imitate every part of an engagement: the onset, retreat of the enemy, pursuit. **1846** W. G. STEWART *Altowan* I. p. xvii, The profound stillness . . . was broken by the startling sound of a *Winebago war-dance.* **1848** ROBINSON *Journal Santa Fe Exped.* (1932) 34 These [Pueblo] Indians had the day before taken four Nebajo scalps, and were now celebrating the war dance. **1892** in *S. Dak. Hist. Coll.* I. 53 [The Sioux's] war dance had ceased, and the grass dance soon must go. **1904** M. KELLY *Little Citizens* 225 Patrick, his face and hands daubed with ink, was executing a triumphant war-dance.

b. Such a dance performed as a public entertainment.

1768 *N.Y. Journal* 7 April, The Cherokee Chiefs and Warriors . . . have offered to entertain the Public with, the War Dance. **1877** JOHNSON *Anderson Co., Kansas* 138 In the winter of 1860 these Indians gave a 'war dance' in Garnett, which was novel to our people. *c***1910** *Program Polar Star Open Air Theater, N.Y.,* 7 & 8 June, Chief Wolf Wanna will . . . finish with a masterous War dance typical of his people.

2. In transferred or figurative use. {1883}

1776 TRUMBULL *M'Fingal* (1785) 15 [Yankees instructed British troops in] the true war-dance of Yanky-reels, And manual exercise of heels. **1873** MILLER *Amongst Modocs* 144 Sometimes they have a six-shooter war dance in the streets. **1885** *Wkly. New Mexican Rev.* 19 March 2/3 The Albuquerque Journal is still performing a war dance with a knife in one hand and a bottle in the other. **1903** ADE *People You Know* 109 The Friend would compel him to put on his Low-Front and go out to a War-Dance and meet a Bunch of Kioodles.

+**War-dance,** *v. intr.* To jump up and down or indulge in other actions resembling those of an Indian war dance. — **1894** *Outing* XXIV. 446/2 Bond an' the Injun sorter war-danced round it fur quite a spell. **1895** *Ib.* XXVI. 441/2 We swung the fire-sticks and war-danced wildly around the fight.

+**Ward committee.** A group of persons representing the party organization in a ward.

1807 IRVING *Salmagundi* xi. 267 The secretaries of the ward committees strut about looking like wooden oracles. **1861** *N.Y. Tribune* 19 Dec. 5/3 They attempted to violently seize Mr. Heinrich of the Ward Committee. *a***1882** in McCabe *New York* 127 He saw that the party organization was composed primarily of Precinct Committees, Ward Committees, and the City Committee. **1922** MERRIAM *Amer. Party System* 71 Each of the forty-eight Ward Committees [in Phila.] . . . chooses two members of the City Committee.

War debt. A debt incurred by a government for the carrying on of a war. — **1865** *Nation* I. 386 The Reconstructing State Convention of Alabama has pronounced against the repudiation of the war debt of the state. **1880** in B. S. Heath *Labor & Finance Revol.* 29 They craved fifteen hundred millions of interest spoil, and drew it with the war debt. **1924** *Lit. Digest* 9 Feb. 20/2 The whole subject of war debts should undergo a new process of accountancy.

+**War Democrat.** One of the Democrats of the North who supported the policies of the administration during the Civil War. — **1863** *Chicago Tribune* 7 Jan. 2/2 We have yet to see the 'copperhead' journal that is not filled, day after day, with articles bitterly denunciatory of the President, his Cabinet, the Republican Party, the War Democrats, and the Abolitionists. **1864** *Ore. State Jrnl.* 22 Oct. 2/2 The copperheads assembled in town last Saturday . . . to behold the anomaly of a 'War Democrat,' in the person of B. F. Hayden. **1866** CARPENTER *At White House* 307 The field was open to the War Democrats to put down this rebellion by fighting against both master and slave. **1868** *Ore. State Jrnl.* 3 Oct. 1/5 Senator Doolittle is a rampant Democrat—an apostate War Democrat. **1896** *Congress. Rec.* 24 March 3159/1 As a War Democrat I voted for General Grant, the nominee for the Presidency in 1868.

∗**Warden.**[1] (See also CHURCHWARDEN, DEPUTY WARDEN.)

1. Any one of various local or municipal officers of varying powers and responsibilities. +**a.** In Rhode Island, a town officer similar to a justice of the peace.

See also HEAD WARDEN.

1662 *Providence Rec.* XV. 88 To the Warden or Deputty Warden of The Towne of Prouidence. **1672** *R.I. Col. Rec.* II. 467 The said elected and engadged persons shall be called Wardens. **1842** *R.I. Constitution* x. § 7, The towns of New Shoreham and Jamestown may continue to elect wardens as heretofore.

+**b.** A representative or an official of a ward.

1763 J. ADAMS *Diary* Works II. 144 Selectmen, assessors, collectors, wardens, fire-wards, and representatives, are regularly chosen [by the Caucus Club] before they are chosen in the town. **1789** MORSE *Amer. Geog.* 428 Charleston was . . . divided into 13 wards, who choose as many wardens, who, from among themselves, elect an intendant of the city. **1822** *Boston Charter* § 3 It shall be the duty of such warden to preside at all meetings of the citizens of such ward.

c. One of several officials in Philadelphia with responsibilities including the supervision of the night watch. Now hist.

1771 *Phila. Ordinances* 36 Jacob Winey, Moore Furman, and Joshua Humphreys, gentlemen, . . . are hereby styled wardens. **1789** *Ib.* 74 The city wardens . . . [and] the commissioners . . . shall no longer continue in office.

d. An official of the port of Philadelphia. {1538-, in general sense} Also *board of wardens*.

See also PORT WARDEN.

1805 *Phila. Ordinances* (1812) 112 The wardens of the port of Philadelphia, shall be authorised . . . [to] determine the extent or distance which . . . the owner or owners of lots or ground extending to the said river Schuylkill . . . may build wharves therein. **1811** MEASE *Philadelphia* 70 The governor is authorized to appoint annually, one master Warden and six assistants, with power to use a seal, and to appoint a clerk. *a***1821** BIDDLE *Autobiog.* 226 Twentieth [in the parade came] wardens of the port. **1914** *Cycl. Amer. Govt.* III. 654/1 In the United States, there is a board of wardens of the port of Philadelphia.

+e. 'The chief officer of a borough in Connecticut' (*Cycl. Amer. Govt.* III. 654/1).

1841 *Conn. Public Acts* 7 The Warden and Burgesses of said Borough shall have power to form and continue an additional Fire Company for the further protection of the property of said Borough. **1904** *Hartford Courant* 18 Aug. 9 No other democrat in town can carry the borough for warden.

∗2. An official in charge of a prison.

1827 *Conn. Statute Laws* 162 The said warden shall have the entire controul and management of the said prison. **1882** MCCABE *New York* 413 The Tombs is in charge of a Warden. **1893** *Harper's Mag.* Feb. 483, I'm goin' to take you to the warden. **1907** LONDON *White Fang* 299 The guard . . . lied about him to the warden.

+3. = FIREWARDEN, FIREWARD.

1852 *Conn. Public Acts* 60 All persons who shall be engineers or wardens of any fire department . . . [shall] be exempt from serving as jurors. **1905** *Bureau of Forestry Bul.* No. 60, 28 The ranger or warden could do much work on the trails when there was no danger from fires.

+4. An official responsible for the enforcement of laws protecting game; a fish or game warden. {game warden, 1912, in S. Africa}

See also FISH, FISHING, MOOSE WARDEN.

1870 *Dept. Agric. Rep. 1869* 520 The State commissioners on the fisheries recommend . . . the appointment of . . . a board of wardens for each river basin. **1883** GOODE *Fishery Industries U.S.* 83 It was impossible for any warden under the statute of the State of Maine to approach him.

∗Warden.² An old variety of pear. Also attrib. — **1649** *Perfect Descr. Va.* 14 The Governour in his new Orchard hath 15 hundred fruit-trees, besides his Apricocks, . . . Quinces, Wardens, and such like fruits. **1676** GLOVER *Va.* in *Phil. Trans.* XI. 628 There are some sorts of Pears . . . ; I have seen the Bergamy, Warden, and two or three other sorts. **1709** LAWSON *Carolina* 109 The Warden-Pear here proves a good eating Pear; and is not so long ripening as in England. **1759** *Holyoke Diaries* 20 Grafted ye Pear tree with Warden Ciens.

War Department. {1789 (*Despatches from Paris* II. (1910) 179)} +The military division of the executive branch of the United States government, under the charge of the Secretary of War; the Department of War or its headquarters.

1789 *Ann. 1st Congress* 369 We may then go to the consideration of the War Department and the Department of Foreign Affairs. **1815** *Niles' Reg.* IX. 37/2 Military land warrants . . . will, as usual, be issued gratis at the War Department. **1840** *Diplom. Corr. Texas* I. (1908) 446 The subject of the Indian relations between the two countries has been referred to the War Department. **1854** CUMMINS *Lamplighter* 264 [She] asked to be introduced to the member of the war department, as she styled Lieutenant Osborne. **1874** ALDRICH *P. Palfrey* xv, I got a letter this morning from the War Department. **1918** *Lit. Digest* 19 Jan. 16/1 The supply machinery of the War Department has been inadequate.

attrib. **1866** MCCLELLAN in *Own Story* 221 The entire establishment . . . was removed to the War Department building, without my knowledge. **1892** HART *Formation of Union* 144 The War Department bill passed August 7.

+Ward heeler. *Polit.* A hanger-on of the party leader in a ward. *colloq.³* Also attrib. — **1888** *N.Y. Herald* 4 Nov. 9/4 A band succeeded them and preceded a lot of ward heelers or 'floaters in blocks of five.' **1895** ROBINSON *Men Born Equal* 49 The usual municipal ring of worthless 'ward heelers'—an Irishman to poll the Irish vote, and a German for the German vote. **1906** QUICK *Double Trouble* 188 Entering at the door came . . . one or two hulking mustachioed citizens of the ward-heeler type. **1912** H. CROLY *M. A. Hanna* 114 He used to go to the business men of his ward, and try to persuade them . . . that they, the taxpayers, and not the ward heelers, should rule the city.

Wardmaster. A man in charge of a hospital ward: (see also quot. 1777). {1883} — **1777** *Jrnls. Cont. Congress* VII. 163 The business of the Wardmaster shall be to take care of the Arms, Accoutrements, and cloathes of the sick and wounded. **1862** CUMMING *Hospital Life* 24/2, I

had a slight quarrel with our ward-master. **1866** MOORE *Women of War* 249 The plan . . . was to make daily an inspection tour, . . . inquire into any cases of neglect, omission, or inattention on the part of ward-masters or hired nurses.

+Ward meeting. *Polit.* A meeting of the party members or party workers of a ward. — **1806** *Balance* V. 362/1 The sentiments . . . have met the approbation of the several federal ward meetings. **1844** *N.Y. Wkly. Tribune* 21 Sept. 5/2 Hon. H. C. Murphy of Brooklyn recently edified a Loco-Foco Ward Meeting in that City. **1865** *Ore. State Jrnl.* 9 Sept. 1/5 He never stayed out till eleven o'clock to a 'ward meeting.' **1883** HAY *Bread-Winners* 247 Hardly a millionaire . . . knew where the ward meetings of his party were held.

War dog. +1. An American favoring or supporting the War of 1812. A term of abuse. *Obs.* 2. A seasoned, experienced fighter; a veteran. — (1) **1813** *Columbian Centinel* 23 Oct. 2/1 His reward from the War-dogs will be, that he will be hurled from office without concern or ceremony. **1814** *Ib.* 29 June 2/3 'Apathy'—is the cry of the War-Dogs, in all directions. (2) **1825** COOPER *L. Lincoln* viii, A great war-dog is that old man, your honour. **1895** REMINGTON *Pony Tracks* 33 'Stand 'em off,' replies the war-dog.

+Ward politician. *Polit.* One who takes part in the political activities of a ward. Also with specifying numbers. — [**1807** IRVING *Salmagundi* iv. 84 He, however, maintained as mysterious a countenance as a Seventh Ward politician.] **1860** *Harper's Mag.* June 94/2 'A house-breaker or a ward politician,' thought I. . . . 'Why, Sir, they call me master of the ward.' **1867** *Atlantic Mo.* Feb. 163/1 Atwater was a ward politician, and never forgot a name. **1890** H. O. WILLS *Twice Born* 111, I believe the meanest of all devils, and worse than all thieves on earth, is the low 'ward politician.' **1904** *N.Y. Ev. Post* 27 July 2 The new chairman is a magnificent ward politician of much native ability and considerable personal magnetism.

+Ward politics. *pl.* The political activities and interests of a ward; participation in such activities. — **1883** *Century Mag.* Aug. 581/2 He had been a little alarmed at the sudden irruption of such men as Farnham and his associates into the field of ward politics. **1894** FORD *P. Stirling* 187 Don't you find ward politics very hard? **1923** HERRICK *Lilla* 103 He's quite a figure in ward politics.

+War dress. The costume worn by Indians engaged in war. Also fig. — **1724** JONES *Virginia* 5 The Seneca Indians in their War Dress may appear as terrible as any of the Sons of Anak. **1825** NEAL *Bro. Jonathan* II. 16 He had been sent by the prophet with a command . . . for Eagle to put on his war-dress. **1837** IRVING *Bonneville* I. 7 He was writing . . . in a, large barrack room, fancifully decorated with Indian arms, and trophies, and war dresses. **1850** MITCHELL *Lorgnette* I. 52 They have made all manner of paragraphs about her shape, her tears, and her war-dress. **1887** *Century Mag.* May 51/1 The war-dress of these warm-weather warriors [*sc.* Apaches] . . . is not so resplendent in buckskin and beads.

∗Wardrobe. A movable closet or special container for clothes. {1794-}

1841 BACHE *Fire-Screen* 29 Drawers, wardrobes, and bandboxes, yielded up their gay contents. **1874** ALDRICH *P. Palfrey* xvii, [He] took down his overcoat from a shelf in the black-walnut wardrobe. **1882** MCCABE *New York* 658 The large basement room contains a number of wardrobes, with locks and keys. **1910** TOMPKINS *Mothers & Fathers* 53 Every time Edy rocked there was a screaking protest from the wardrobe.

+b. *Wardrobe trunk*, a trunk having space to hang garments, and drawers or compartments for other articles.

1923 WATTS *L. Nichols* 242 Wardrobe-trunks and hat-boxes were haled from the attic.

Wardroom.

1. On a warship, the quarters, often specifically the messroom, assigned, with certain exceptions, to commissioned officers above the rank of ensign. {1801-}

In quot. **1856** *wardroom* appears to refer to the room occupied by an individual officer.

1827 COOPER *Red Rover* I. 197 The dining apartment of the secondary officers; or, as it was called in technical language, the 'ward-room.' **1838** HAWTHORNE *Notebooks* (1932) 28 Going down below stairs, you come to the ward-room, a pretty large room, round which are the state-rooms of the Lieutenants. **1856** HALE *If, Yes, & Perhaps* 169 It seems almost wrong to go into Mr. Hamilton's wardroom, and see how he arranged his soap-cup and his tooth-brush. **1883** HOWELLS *Woman's Reason* xi, He got himself with difficulty out of Fenton's door into the wardroom.

+2. *Polit.* A room used for meetings or political activities of a ward.

1872 HOLMES *Poet* 218 When they become voters, if they ever do, it may be feared that the pews will lose what the ward-rooms gain. **1889** BRAYLEY *Boston Fire Dept.* 154 The inhabitants had been warmed to the matter by the patriotic harangues in the ward-rooms.

3. *attrib.* **a.** In sense 1 with *boat, country, ladder*, etc. {1850} +**b.** In sense 2 with *politician*.

(*a*) **1814** *Niles' Reg.* VI. 36/1 The ward room officers of the Constitution will recollect to have heard Dr. Jones frequently spoken of during the cruise. **1841** *S. Lit. Messenger* VII. 762/1 The wardroom boat was called away and manned. **1881** *Naval Encycl.* 834/1 *Wardroom-country*, the open space between the state-rooms in the wardroom. **1882** *Harper's Mag.* Feb. 480/1 Passed Assistant Surgeon P—— . . . astonished the wardroom mess with: 'Oh, H——, you are straining at a gnat, and swallowing a camel!' 1866 'F. KIRKLAND' *Bk. Anecdotes* 370 While descending the ward-room ladder, the captain of the gun directly opposite was struck full upon the face by an 18-pounder shot. 1891 *Cent.* 5940/3 The cabinsteward, wardroom-steward, steerage-steward, and warrant-officers' steward are petty officers charged with providing for their several messes and keeping the apartments in order. (b) 1872 HOLMES *Poet* 323 The sting which would be fatal to a literary *débutante* only wakes the eloquence of the pachydermatous ward-room politician to a fiercer shriek of declamation.

+**Ward school.** One of a number of city schools located in different wards. — 1818 *Niles' Reg.* XIV. 174/1 Neither the people, nor their representatives, would agree to the plan of assessment on the wards for the expenses of the ward schools. 1852 *Harper's Mag.* Dec. 129/1 Their statues are not among us . . . to quicken the soul-springs of our ward-school boys. 1898 *Kansas City Star* 18 Dec. 4/3 Since the children of farmers have not the advantage of the high school, or even of the ward schools of the cities, they should be given better opportunities in the district school. 1904 STRATTON-PORTER *Freckles* 15 They sent me out to the nearest ward school as long as the law would let them.

+**Ward('s) willow.** (See quotations.) — 1897 SUDWORTH *Arborescent Flora* 119 *Salix wardi.* . . . Ward Willow. 1901 MOHR *Plant Life Ala.* 465 Ward's Willow. . . . District of Columbia west to Missouri, south to western Florida and Indian Territory.

*** Ware.**[1] (See also WEIR(E).) A barrier or obstruction placed in a stream, as a fence of brush for catching fish; an enclosure for catching fish.

1622 'MOURT' *Relation* 102 We found many of the Namascheucks . . . fishing vppon a Ware which they had made on a River. 1709 LAWSON *Carolina* 157, I never saw but one [lamprey], which was large, and caught by the Indians, in a Ware. 1820 *Niles' Reg.* XVIII. 362/2 They take them [*i.e.*, fish] with wares—they take them with dip net.
attrib. 1661 *Suffolk Deeds* III. 491 A percell of Land lying at Hinghome vpon ye waer necke. 1709 LAWSON *Carolina* 151 Water-Witch, or Ware-Coots, are a Fowl with Down and no Feathers.

*** Ware.**[2] *collect.* (in sing. and pl.) Articles of merchandise or manufactures.

1653 *Boston Rec.* X. 3 There may be a true Inventory taken . . . of all my wares, marchandize, ready money, plate [etc.]. 1677 *Ib.* VII. 111 All ware made of pewter or siluer whether brought to the Countrie or made here & exposed to sale [shall] be of ye. just alloy. 1773 *Mass. Province Acts* V. 248 No person . . . shall sell . . . any goods, chattels, wares, merchandizes or effects. 1838 HAWTHORNE *Notebooks* (1932) 31 He would send on quantities of his wares ahead to different stations. 1905 FREEMAN *Debtor* 419 He pictured himself . . . striving to dispose of his small and worthless wares for money enough to keep the machinery going.

b. *collect.* (in sing.) Articles made of baked clay. {1827-} Also attrib.

1733 *Maryland Hist. Mag.* XX. 61 Ware Tea Cups and Saucers. 1741 W. STEPHENS *Proc. Georgia* II. 199 He had lately drawn his Kiln of Ware, which was baking a second Time. 1881 *Harper's Mag.* Feb. 363/1 At least half of the ware has changed to a dull white and seems ready for the kiln.

+**War eagle.** The golden eagle (q.v., sense 1), the feathers of which were used by Plains Indians in their war bonnets. Also transf. — 1821 NUTTALL *Travels Arkansa* 88 The large feathers of the war-eagle . . . are sometimes distributed throughout the nation, as sacred presents. 1833 CATLIN *Indians* I. 68 A war-eagle. This noble bird is the one which the Indians in these regions, value so highly for their tail feathers. 1876 INGRAM *Centennial Exp.* 686 One of the chief attractions in Agricultural Hall . . . was the famous 'Old Abe,' the veteran War Eagle of Wisconsin. 1912 NICHOLSON *Hoosier Chron.* 328 The chairman of the state central committee was endeavoring to present as the temporary chairman of the convention a patriot known as the 'War Eagle of the Wabash.'

*** Warehouse.**

***1.** A building, or a part of a building, used for storing merchandise.

1639 *Dedham Rec.* 59 A parcell of ground & tymber for our towne to build a warehouse. 1699 *Boston Rec.* 50 Libertie is granted to Joseph Cocke to set vp a warehouse ouer the slip. 1715 *Boston News-Letter* 16 May 2/2 Sundry other European Goods, to be Sold by Messieurs Hedman and Lewis, at their Warehouse at the lower end of Kings-Street Boston. 1789 *Ky. Petitions* 132 They experience many Inconveniences on getting their Tobacco to the Different Warehouses Established by Law. 1835 HOFFMAN *Winter in West* I. 276 There are now five churches and two school-houses, and numerous brick stores and warehouses. 1884 WELLS *Practical Economics* 189n., 7,561,171 gallons were withdrawn from warehouse under the form of alcohol. 1905 *Richmond Wkly. Times-Dispatch* 4 Jan. 1 Fire broke out this morning in the tobacco district of the town, destroying two warehouses.

2. With descriptive terms.

See also *bonded warehouse* (under BONDED *ppl. a.* 2), *tobacco warehouse* (under TOBACCO 10).

1805 *Columbian Centinel* 31 July Extra 1/2 (Ernst), Patent medicine warehouse. 1827 Cotton warehouses [see COTTON 4 e]. 1835 *Stimpson's Boston Directory* Advt. 18 Furniture and Feather Warehouse. 1845 *Xenia Torch-Light* 31 July 2/1 The fire crossed Exchange street, riddling the

dry goods warehouses in its course. 1870 KEIM *Sheridan's Troopers* 254 Goods . . . had been tossed from a tarpaulin warehouse. 1872 Grain warehouse [see GRAIN *n.* 3 c].

3. Attrib. and comb. with *cellar, crowd, hire*, etc.

1641 *Mass. Bay Rec.* I. 341 They . . . are appointed to settell the rates of wharfige, portridge, & warehouse huire. 1704 *Providence Rec.* IV. 56 A warehouse lot of 40 foote square, bounded at Each Corner with stones. 1715 *Boston News-Letter* 21 Feb. 2/2 The following Goods were stolen out of the Ware-House Seller of Mr. James Smith in Fish-Market Boston viz 13 Cheshire Cheeses [etc.]. 1771 FRANKLIN *Autobiog.* 292, I was warehouseman, and everything, and, in short, quite a factotum. 1846 POLK *Diary* (1929) 141 He enumerated the great questions which had been settled, . . . and the establishment of the Warehouse system. 1851 *Polly Peablossom* 29 The singular failures of warehouse steelyards to make cotton-bales weigh as much in Augusta as at home. 1861 *Chicago Tribune* 15 April 1 Scale Beams, Warehouse Trucks, Baggage Barrows. 1902 NORRIS *Pit* ix, I've fixed the warehouse crowd. 1911 *Okla. Session Laws* 3 Legisl. 156 Such warehouse manager shall retain all moneys received for the sale of such alcohol.

Warehouse receipt. A certificate, usually negotiable, issued by a warehouseman, containing a description of property stored in a warehouse. Also attrib. — 1887 *Nation* 2 June 459/1 This state of things will continue after . . . the listing of silver warehouse receipts begins. 1890 WEEDEN *Econ. & Soc. Hist. New Eng.* I. 323 It could not have been mere loaning on warehouse receipts of property. 1913 *Cycl. Amer. Govt.* III. 590/2 The sales act has been adopted in eleven, and the warehouse receipts act in thirty, of our states and territories.

Wareroom. A room for the storage or display of merchandise. {1811-} Also with descriptive term. (See also CABINET WAREROOM, FURNITURE WAREROOM.) — 1833 *Knickerb.* I. 157 The ware-rooms of Phyfe's and McKinnan's are lumbered up with unsaleable cradles. 1853 *Harper's Mag.* March 558/1 The fairy-like sleighs . . . vanished from the carriage ware-rooms. 1887 *Courier-Journal* 16 Jan. 9 Removed. W. H. McKnight & Co., Carpet Warerooms. 1899 *Boston Transcript* 3 June 12/7 The Pianola may be seen any day at the warerooms.

+**War feast.** A feast held by the Indians in celebration of a victory. Also transf. — 1809 A. HENRY *Travels* 105 [It] had been the custom, among all the Indian nations, . . . to make a war-feast, from among the slain. 1811 *Niles' Reg.* I. 269/1 There were . . . many good men out of Congres[s] . . . whose appetites were prepared for a *war feast*. 1837 IRVING *Bonneville* I. 142, I joined no longer in the council, the hunt, or the war-feast. 1899 CUSHMAN *Hist. Indians* 254 Then followed war-feasts, scalp-dances, accompanied with war-songs, and shouts of victory.

+**War fever.** Enthusiasm for prosecution of a war. {1908} — 1812 *Steele P.* II. 668 The late report of the Secty. of the Treasy. will probably cool the war fever in some [people]. 1845 GREEN *Texian Exped.* 24 The President [of the Texan Republic] had succeeded in lulling the popular war-fever. 1884 *Century Mag.* Nov. 107 It was the news that the Sixth Massachusetts regiment had been mobbed by roughs on their passage through Baltimore which gave me the war fever.

+**Warfield.** Dried or jerked beef that is broiled. — 1840 KENNEDY *Quodlibet* 104 Take a plate on your knee, and fork up one of them warfields—and take care of your gown, they're dripping with butter.

War governor.

1. (Meaning uncertain.)

1775 ADAIR *Indians* 144 One [white man] . . . was deputed by the whimsical war-governor of Georgia, to awe the traders into an obedience of his despotic power.

+**2.** A governor of a state during the Civil War, or, in the South, during Reconstruction.

1884 BLAINE *20 Years of Congress* I. 305 The governors of the free States . . . became popularly known as the 'War Governors,' and they exercised a beneficent and decisive influenc upon the fortunes of the Union. 1894 *Harper's Mag.* June 138/1 Andrew's great fame as a War Governor was, of course, yet to come. 1900 *Miss. Hist. Soc. Pub.* III. 73 [General Charles Clark and his successor John P. Pettus] will be remembered as 'the war Governors of Mississippi.' 1925 BRYAN *Memoirs* 72 Richard Yates, son of Illinois' 'war governor,' . . . was the city attorney.

War ground. +An area in which Indians carry on hostilities. — 1845 FRÉMONT *Exped.* 115 Pawnees and other half-civilized tribes . . . for whom the intermediate country is a war ground. 1847 PARKMAN in *Knickerb.* XXX. 24 We came suddenly upon the great Pawnee trail, leading from their villages on the Platte, to their war and hunting-grounds to the southward. 1852 STANSBURY *Gt. Salt Lake* 229 Our rout : would lay [*sic*] directly through the war-ground of several powerful Indian tribes.

+**War hatchet.** Among the Indians, a hatchet or tomahawk used in carrying on war, or as a ceremonial symbol of a state of war. Freq. in phrases.

Cf. HATCHET *n.* 2.

1760 CROGHAN *Journal* (1904) 116 You [chiefs and warriors may] . . . bury the War Hatchet in the Bottomless Pitt. 1776 *N.H. Hist. Soc. Coll.* IX. 94 They have been . . . solicited by our most cruel unnatural Enemies to take up the War Hatchet against us. 1800 HAWKINS *Sk. Creek Country* 72 He lifts the war hatchet against the nation which has injured them. 1823 DODDRIDGE *Logan* II. ii, Must they be covered with the war hatchet? 1841 COOPER *Deerslayer* xxx, Our great fathers across the Salt Lake have sent each other the war-hatchet. 1876 BANCROFT *Hist. U.S.* V. 430 The young Cherokee warriors . . . [showed] a war-hatchet received about six years before. **1907** ANDREWS *Recoll.* 122 Full dress required his war-hatchet and weapons.

+War hawk.

1. One who is eager for war; a person urging entry into war. A term of reproach. **a.** One favoring war with France at the time of the X Y Z correspondence and the diplomatic crisis of 1798.

In general, applied to Federalists by Republicans.
1798 JEFFERSON *Writings* X. 33 At present, the war hawks talk of septembrizing, deportation, and the examples for quelling sedition set by the French executive. **1798** *Aurora* (Phila.) 10 Nov. (Th.), The warhawks will be now more than ever distracted.

b. One favoring the declaration of war upon England and the prosecution of the War of 1812.

In general, applied to Republicans by Federalists.
1812 *Columbian Centinel* 19 Feb. 4/1 Our War-Hawks when pot valiant grown, Could they the British King dethrone, Would sacrifice a man a day. **1814** *Ib.* 9 March 2/2 The War-Hawks and Vultures at Washington:— . . . may they be expelled from the capitol. **1815** CUTLER in *Life & Corr.* II. 332 Our war-hawks . . . affect to speak of it as a glorious war.

c. One favoring an aggressive policy in forcing England to recognize 54°40′ as the boundary of Oregon.

1846 *Congress. Globe* 18 April 687/1 The gentleman regarded 54°40′ men as 'war-hawks' and 'war-dogs!' **1846** L. BAKER *Lett. to J. Q. Adams on Oregon Question* 7 (Th. S.), With the war-hawks, the catchword is honor, but the meaning is fight.

2. A bird of war. Also transf.

1829 IRVING *Conquest of Granada* (1850) 350 These fierce warriors were nestled, like so many war-hawks, about their lofty cliff. **1865** PARKMAN *Pioneers of France* 308 The Indian tribes, war-hawks of the wilderness, . . . infested with their scalping parties the streams and pathways of the forest.

3. Attrib. in sense 1 b with *government, party, ruler*.

1814 *Columbian Centinel* 28 Sept. 1/2 The War, from the want of Capacity of the War-Hawk Government, has assumed a different aspect. *Ib.,* The people . . . will defend their possessions when invaded, . . . notwithstanding the imbecility and cowardice of the War-Hawk rulers. **1815** *Conn. Courant* 7 Feb. 3/1 Peaceable citizens have been stripped by the war-hawk party long since.

War horse.

1. A horse used in battle; a charger. {1653-}

1851 MELVILLE *Moby Dick* 128 [Thou] didst pick up Andrew Jackson, . . . [and] didst hurl him upon a war-horse. **1867** EDWARDS *Shelby* 149 Then there came, too, the presentation of a magnificent war-horse to Colonel Shelby. **1898** PAGE *Red Rock* 93 So he hitched his war-horses, Hotspur and Kate, to ploughs.

2. A veteran of military campaigns; an aggressive and 'regular' politician. Also used familiarly and contemptuously. *colloq.* {1902}

1837 BIRD *Nick* I. 68 Ar'nt thee the Pennsylvanny war-horse, the screamer of the meeting-house? **1867** RICHARDSON *Beyond Miss.* 151 That old war horse . . . threw off the black shaggy bearskin overcoat which he invariably wore. **1871** DE VERE 530 General Lee was *Mas Bob,* Johnston *Old Joe,* and Longstreet the *War-Horse.* **1885** *Wkly. New Mexican Rev.* 15 Jan. 4/4 There poured into the city by every train yesterday democratic 'war hosses' from the four corners of New Mexico. **1896** WHITE *Real Issue* 177 Colonel William Hucks, of Hucksville, the war-horse of Center Township, was in town last night.

+War kettle. A kettle used in war ceremonies by the Indians. {1764-} Also fig. — **1754** *World* (London) 12 Dec. 615 At a meeting of Sachems it was determined *to take up the hatchet,* and *make the war-kettle boil.* **1791** J. LONG *Voyages* 146 [They] brought him to the war-kettle to make his death-feast: which consisted of dog, tyger-cat, and bear's grease [etc.].

*Warm, *v.*

+1. *To warm over,* to heat again cooked food that has become cold; also, fig., to revive or reinvigorate. Also *ppl. a.*

1879 HOLMES *J. L. Motley* 162 [They] took up the old exceptions, [and] warmed them over into grievances. **1887** *Nation* 2 June 465/3 They will be spared the future bitterness of finding . . . themselves treated to insult and warmed-over excuses. **1916** BOWER *Phantom Herd* 246 He had a midnight supper of warmed-over coffee and cold bean sandwiches.

2. *To warm up,* to loosen up one's muscles, to get into condition for immediate play. Also transf. {1846-, to become more interested or energetic} Also *vbl. n.*

1883 *Chicago Inter-Ocean* 27 June 5 The players came on the diamond and began their practice play. This is called 'warming up.' **1887** *Courier-Journal* 24 Jan. 2/4 At first the stakes were small, but as the players warmed up the limit was raised. **1912** MATHEWSON *Pitching* 199 As I started to warm up, the ball refused to break.

Warm-air furnace. A furnace which gives out heat by causing the circulation of heated air. — **1886** J. A. PORTER *New Stand. Guide Washington* 208 Chas. G. Ball & Son, . . . Warm-Air Furnaces.

+War-making power. 1. The right of Congress, under the provisions of the Constitution (II. viii.), to declare war and to make provision for

the carrying on of war. **2.** The right of the federal government, as opposed to the government of an individual state or territory, to declare and carry on war. — **(1) 1833** *Niles' Reg.* XLIV. 148/1 Very few persons questioned the right of congress to lay an embargo, under the war-making power. **1859** BUCHANAN in *Pres. Mess. & P.* V. 569 The grant of this authority . . . would be a transfer of the war-making, or, strictly speaking, the war-declaring, power to the Executive. **(2) 1848** POLK *Ib.* IV. 598 The General Government, possessing exclusively the war-making power, had the right to take military possession of this disputed territory.

Warm blood. Unmixed thoroughbred blood; pure descent. — **1868** *Iowa State Agric. Soc. Rep. 1867* 120 With the exception of the one [stallion], there is not a drop of 'warm blood' in them. **1883** *Harper's Mag.* Oct. 724/2 The descendants of these [thoroughbred horses] constituted a stock of 'warm blood.'

+War measure. A law passed, an action taken, or a procedure adopted because of the needs and requirements of war. — **1808** W. EATON in *Life* (1813) 414 The Embargo was contemplated as a war measure. **1864** Cox *8 Yrs. in Congress* 35 Feeling the necessity of apologizing for the bill, . . . the gentleman terms it a war measure. **1884** BLAINE *20 Years of Congress* I. 354 [A number of Democrats accepted] the full responsibility of co-operating with the Republicans in war measures. **1918** *New International. Yrbk.* 716/1 The chief war measure of the government introduced in Congress was a bill 'to increase temporarily the military establishment of the United States.'

+War medicine. *To make* (a) *war medicine,* of an Indian, to engage in a ceremony calculated to secure supernatural assistance in war; transf., to become belligerent and aggressive. Also in allusive context. — **1805** [see MEDICINE 2 d]. **1893** *Chicago Tribune* 28 April 4/1 Gov. Altgeld . . . proceeded to administer a dose of war medicine he had been making for some time. **1897** LEWIS *Wolfville* 104 Word comes to Cherokee . . . that he's makin' war-medicine an' is growin' more hostile. **1906** *N.Y. Ev. Post* 8 May 1 Senator Dolliver was outside the breastworks, making war-medicine and refusing to be pacified.

*Warming pan. 1. A long-handled, covered pan for holding live coals, formerly used for warming beds. **2.** *transf.* A watch. {a1700} — **(1) 1636** *Essex Probate Rec.* I. 5 Inventory. . . . A broken warmeige pan. **1701** *Boston Rec.* 9 Ordered that no person or persons, do presume hereafter to carry fire from any House . . . unto any other House . . . but in a warming pan or other safe vessell. **1841** *Knickerb.* XVII. 235 [Mr. Dux was] engaged, for several hours, in an attempt to improve upon a new-fashioned warming-pan. **1884** 'MARK TWAIN' *H. Finn* xxxvii, He had a noble brass warming-pan. **(2) 1833** NEAL *Down-Easters* I. 127 The old quaker [was] trying to give boot for the bull-eyed warming-pan with a pewter face. **1884** [see WATCH PAPER].

+Warmouth. A fresh-water fish (*Chaenobryttus gulosus*) of the eastern states. Also attrib. with defining term. — **1883** *Nat. Museum Bul.* No. 27, 461 War-mouth; Red-eyed Bream; War-mouth Perch; Yawmouth. Eastern United States from Virginia to Florida. **1884** GOODE, etc. *Fisheries* I. 405 The Black Warmouth . . . abounds in the tributaries of the Upper Mississippi. **1903** T. H. BEAN *Fishes N.Y.* 470 The body of the warmouth is heavy and deep.

+Warm slaw. [?Formed by analogy with the erron. COLD SLAW (q.v. under COLESLAW).] (See quotation.) — **1796** F. BAILY *Tour* 136 A dish of stewed pork was served up, accompanied with some hot pickled cabbage, called in this part of the country 'warm slaw.'

Warm spring. A spring containing or producing warm water. Also pl. as proper name. — **1748** WASHINGTON *Diaries* I. 6 We this day call'd to see y. Fam'd Warm Springs. **1776** in *Amer. Sp.* XV. 407/2 A town at Warm Springs. **1837** SHERWOOD *Gaz. Georgia* (ed. 3) 203 The largest warm spring flows out of a spur of the Pine mountain. **1885** *Wkly. New Mexican Rev.* 16 April 4/3 The city of Socorro has been restrained . . . from using or interfering with the ojo caliente or warm spring there.

Warm-up. 1. The act of making one's self warm. **+2.** The power of generating enthusiasm. *colloq.* — **(1) 1878** STOWE *Poganuc People* 156 A knot of the talkers were gathered around the stove, having a final talk and warm-up. **(2) 1883** 'MARK TWAIN' *Life on Miss.* iii, The song didn't seem to have much warm-up to it.

+Warmus. (See WAMUS.)

War news. *pl.* Information concerning the progress of a war. — **1862** *Congregationalist* 31 Jan. (Chipman), Surely, the irreliability of our war news must be demoralizing all our channels of information. **1866** CARPENTER *At White House* 154 All war news of importance, of course, reached him [Lincoln] previous to its publication. **1891** in B. S. Heath *Labor & Finance Revol.* p. xvi, Mr. Heath . . . never failed to spend a portion of each evening writing up 'war news.'

*Warning. 1. (See quotation.) {*dial.,* 'the verbal invitation to attend a funeral'} **+2.** (See quot. 1851.) **+3.** A drink. — **(1) 1807** JANSON *Stranger in Amer.* 422 What they call 'warnings,' is the day before, or early in the morning, given of the funeral. This is a notice or warning of the event in writing, which is regularly carried from house to house, and shewn or read to some of the family. **(2) 1836** *Harvardiana* III. 98 Sadly I feel I should have been saved by numerous warnings. **1850** *Yale Lit. Mag.* XV. 210 No more shall 'warnings' in their hearing ring. **1851** HALL *College Words* 309 When it is ascertained that a student is not living in accordance with the laws of the institution, he is usually informed of the fact by a *warning,* as it is called, from one of the faculty, which consists merely of friendly caution and advice. **(3) 1908** LORIMER *J. Spurlock* 245 The Major looked out at the suburbs of Baltimore over his before-luncheon 'warning.'

+**War of 1812.** The war between the United States and Great Britain, 1812–15. — **1833** T. DWIGHT *Hist. Hartford Convention* 233 Such is a brief history of the origin and causes of the war of 1812. **1868** B. J. LOSSING *Pictorial Field-Bk. of War of 1812*, p. i, An account is given of . . . the origin and growth of political parties in the United States, and their relations to the War of 1812. **1900** *Congress. Rec.* 15 Feb. 1844/2 Let the blood of the heroes of the Revolution, of the war of 1812, and of the Spanish war incite in all Americans the true spirit of the founders.

War office. a. A government office or department in charge of military affairs {1721–}: (see also quot. 1801). +**b.** The United States War Department. Now *rare*. — **1776** *Jrnls. Cont. Congress* IV. 85 Resolved, That a committee of 7 be appointed to consider the propriety of establishing a war office. **1781** *Va. State P.* I. 586 All the Books belonging to the War Office being lost with the Council Books. **1801** *Steele P.* I. 219 My war office, or War accounts, for Rations, and house rent, and fire wood, I send on to the Secretary of War. **1808** *Ann. 10th Congress* 1 Sess. 2081, I was referred from the War Office to the Treasury Office.

War of independence. +**1.** *cap.* =REVOLUTIONARY WAR. **2.** The struggle of the Spanish possessions in North America for independence from the mother country. — (1) **1832** DUNLAP *Hist. Amer. Theatre* 45 The rocky foundation protruded, until the earth of the hill . . . was brought down, since the war of independence, to cover [the ramparts]. [**1883** FREEMAN *Some Impressions U.S.* 21 Still the War of Independence must be, on the American side, a formidable historic barrier in the way of perfect brotherhood.] **1914** *Cycl. Amer. Govt.* II. 390/2 *Man of the Revolution*, an effectionate nickname bestowed by the American people upon Samuel Adams . . . because of the leading part which he played in bringing about the War of Independence. (2) **1848** *Santa Fe Repub.* 3 May 1/2 It was not until the mother country, herself, became temporarily subjected to a foreign power, that the war of Independence was successfully commenced in her possessions on this continent.

+**War of Secession.** =CIVIL WAR b. — **1868** *N.Y. Herald* 31 July 4/5 M. Chevnier . . . [attempted] a parallel between the War of Independence and the War of Secession. **1907** *Harper's Mag.* Feb. 380 The War of Secession . . . [caused] a large number of Southern officers to leave the service.

+**War of (the) Rebellion.** =CIVIL WAR b. (Cf. REBELLION b.) — **1873** *Newton Kansan* 6 March 2/2 The Committee did not underrate the great services of the soldiers and sailors of the war of the rebellion in preserving our free-institutions. **1885** *Wkly. New Mexican Rev.* 5 March 3/4 Then . . . came on the war of rebellion before private enterprise in the way of mining could be taken up. **1900** *Congress. Rec.* 8 Jan. 679/1, I will accept the Senator's amendment; I will say war of the rebellion, if my words give any offense. **1913** LONDON *Valley of Moon* 430 It was at Sonoma that Clara's father had mustered in for the War of the Rebellion.

*****Warp. 1.** A towline. **2.** In growing trees and bushes, an inclination caused by the action of wind. {1679–, a twist or bending} — (1) **1675** *East-Hampton Rec.* I. 382 [The Indians] Doe ingage themselves . . . to preserve the boates Irons & warpes. **1759** *Essex Inst. Coll.* II. 286/1 Capt. Derby went on board a craft which . . . had cut our warp. **1851** SPRINGER *Forest Life* 104 Loads are eased down hill sides . . . by a strong 'warp,' taking a 'bite' round a tree, and hitching to one yoke of the oxen. (2) **1895** *Century Mag.* Sept. 677/2 When the wind beats up the peak, which it seldom does, as may be seen by the warp of the pines and tamaracks.

+**War paint.** {1859–}
1. Paint applied to themselves by Indians as a sign of entrance into war.
1826 COOPER *Mohicans* xxiii, The young Huron was in his war paint. **1845** *Knickerb.* XXV. 317 Wassatogo then . . . put on his war-paint. **1878** *Rep. Indian Affairs* p. xii, A Bannock Indian under the influence of whiskey and war-paint started out from the agency. **1890** HOWELLS *Boy's Town* 32 At most places under the banks there was clay of different colors, which they used for war-paint in their Indian fights. **1908** MULFORD *Orphan* 40 Show me the feather-dusters in war paint.
2. *fig.* **a.** A state of preparation for fighting. **b.** A fearful or frightening appearance masking the true character.
(a) 1869 'MARK TWAIN' *Sk., New & Old* 50 All the blackguards in the country arrive in their war-paint, and proceed to scare me to death with their tomahawks. **(b) 1883** CABLE *Dr. Sevier* 15 So his actions were right, he rather liked them to bear a hideous aspect: that was his war-paint.
3. *transf.* Rouge or other artificial coloring applied by women to their faces. *colloq.* and *facetious.* {1859–}
1869 HARTE *Luck of Roaring Camp* 84 The stranger . . . [brightened] through the color which Red Gulch knew facetiously as her 'war paint.' **1887** I. R. *Lady's Ranche Life Mont.* 19 They were got up, as he said, 'quite regardless' in feathers and war-paint—literally the latter.

War party.
+**1.** A number of Indian warriors joined as volunteers in the carrying on of war; the expedition of such an organization. Also *transf.*
1792 PUTNAM *Memoirs* 288 There is now a pack horse path the whole distance which has been much used by Indian war parties. **1808** PIKE *Sources Miss.* 123 The Little Osage had marched a war party against the Kans. **1835** HOFFMAN *Winter in West* II. 72 The appearance of some of these tribes, when on a war-party, must be singularly martial and picturesque. **1848** Crow war-party [see CROW 3]. **1858** BANCROFT *Hist. U.S.*

VII. 165 The backwoodsmen . . . were forming war parties along the frontier. **1868** WATERS *Life among Mormons* 35 A war party may be known by the absence of squaws, and of lodges, and by all the men being mounted. *a*1918 G. STUART *On Frontier* I. 183 War parties of Bannocks have the mountains on fire in all directions.
2. A political party favoring participation in war. {1835–}
1798 JEFFERSON *Writings* X. 31 Parker has completely gone over to the war party.

+**Warpath.**
I. 1. The route or way followed by Indians on a warlike expedition; a path regularly used by Indians going to war. Sometimes with specific reference to the Warriors' Path (q.v.).
1755 L. EVANS *Anal. Map Colonies* 29 Canoes may come up to the Crossing of the War Path. **1774** in Peyton *Adv. Grandfather* (1867) 132 We struck off in the direction of the head waters of the Kenewha, travelling the war path which has been immemorially used by the Indians. **1821** NUTTALL *Travels Arkansa* 104 These extensive and convenient routes . . . were their war and hunting-paths. **1852** WATSON *Nights in Block-House* 148 They travelled all that night on the war-path leading towards Wheeling.
2. Among the Indians, the state of war; war as an institution. Hence *to abandon, resume the warpath.*
1808 BARKER *Indian Princess* II. iii, I bring my father to the bloody war-path. **1827** COOPER *Prairie* viii, Their discretion was still too doubtful to permit them to be trusted on the war-path. **1844** S. M. FULLER *Summer on Lakes* 209 Even for the war path, . . . the brave prepares by a solemn fast. **1881** *Chicago Times* 16 April, The old man was greatly rejoiced to learn that the soldiers had not yet resumed the war-path. **1881** *Rep. Indian Affairs* 127 The war-path will thus be abandoned, and the white and red man be at peace.
3. An Indian war expedition.
1832 FERRALL *Ramble* 303 Some warrior, returning from the 'war path' or the chase, may have gazed with pleasure on the hills of his fathers. **1840** COOPER *Pathfinder* I. 69 A degree of glory . . . [had] fallen to . . . a brave on his first war-path. **1899** CUSHMAN *Hist. Indians* 254 On the return of a successful war-path, the village at once became a scene of festivity. **1916** EASTMAN *From Deep Woods* 32, I sent you on your first war-path.
transf. **1902** ALDRICH *Sea Turn* 286 'The idea of burning green wood on a war-path!' growled the scout.
4. (See quotation.)
1907 *Springfield W. Repub.* 14 March 1 The freak thoroughfare, which was called 'the midway' at Chicago and 'the pike' at St. Louis, will be called at Jamestown 'the warpath.'
II. In phrases in sense **2. 5. On (or upon) the warpath,** in a state of war.
1840 COOPER *Pathfinder* I. 68 We have been a whole moon on the war-path, and have found but one scalp. **1847** RUXTON *Adv. Rocky Mts.* (1848) 237 When on the war-path, more than ordinary care is taken to adorn the body. **1868** *Congress. Globe* 28 May 2638/3 The Indian will make a treaty in the fall, and in the spring he is again 'upon the war-path.' **1897** *Kissimmee* (Fla.) *Valley* 10 March 1/1 The outfit is said . . . to include almost everything that an eminent savage would require on the warpath.
b. *transf.* Used of persons not of Indian blood or of animals. {1888–}
1871 DE VERE 36 [The word] war-path . . . has led to the use of the phrase, he is out on the war-path, for a man who is about to make a deliberate attack on an adversary or a measure. **1884** W. SHEPHERD *Prairie Exper.* 39 The cows seldom interfere to protect their progeny; when you do find one on the war-path, it makes the ring lively. **1914** 'BOWER' *Flying U Ranch* 118 He's figurin' on gettin' us all out on the war-path, runnin' around in circles, so's't he can give us the laugh.
c. *To go* (*out*) *on* (*or upon*) *the warpath,* to engage in war; to begin aggressive hostilities.
1826 COOPER *Mohicans* xxviii, His nation would not go on the war-path, because they did not think it well. **1858** BANCROFT *Hist. U.S.* VII. 166 With chosen companions, he went out upon the war path, and added scalp to scalp. **1884** MATTHEWS & BUNNER *In Partnership* 28 Experienced Indian fighters say the signs of a speedy going on the war-path are not to be mistaken. **1925** TILGHMAN *Dugout* 22 For the grass was now good pasturage and it was time to go on the warpath.

*****Warper. 1.** One who winds or prepares yarn for the warp of a web. {1611–} **2.** A machine performing a similar function. — (1) **1845** *Lowell Offering* V. 281 We refer to dressers, warpers, drawers-in, harness-knitters, cloth-room girls, etc. (2) **1847** *Knickerb.* XXX. 517 A few [girls] tend the 'warpers,' the 'spoolers,' and the 'speeders.'

Warping anchor. An anchor used as a fixed point in warping a vessel. — **1817** *Ann. 14th Congress* 2 Sess. 1268 If warping anchors, with buoys, be laid down in the channel, . . . ships can, with any wind, be warped into the Roads.

War pipe. {1808} +A pipe smoked in an Indian war ceremonial. — **1775** ADAIR *Indians* 7 The beaus used to fasten the like [sc. pieces of tinkling metal] to their war pipes, with the addition of a piece of an enemy's scalp. **1827** in McKenney *Memoirs* I. 110 Across his breast . . . was his war-pipe, at least three feet long. **1899** CUSHMAN *Hist. Indians* 492 Some celebrated . . . old warrior, with the war-pipe in his hand, . . . delivered a speech.

+War pole. a. =WAR POST. **b.** *To strike the war pole,* to go on the warpath. — **1775** ADAIR *Indians* 162 And after they return home, hang it [their ark] on the leader's red-painted war pole. *Ib.* 187 The war-pole is a small peeled tree painted red, the top and boughs cut off short: it is fixt in the ground opposite to his [a war leader's] door, and all his implements of war are hung on the short boughs of it. **1818** EASTBURN & SANDS *Yamoyden* 148 Round and round the war pole whirling, Furious when the dancers grow. **1833** FLINT *D. Boone* 147 The *waiter,* or servant of the leader, . . . placed a couple of blocks of wood near the war-pole, opposite the door of a circular cabin. **1847** in Howe *Hist. Coll. Ohio* 422 Some time in September, 250 warriors *struck the war pole,* and took up their line of march.

+War post. A post, frequently painted red, put up by Indians for use in public ceremonies connected with war.
1779 *Mass. H. S. Proc.* 2 Ser. II. 463 [We] found a war post which the Indians had put up with marks cut in the same in token of their Scalps. **1788** W. BIGGS *Narr. Captivity* 18 They sung and danced around the war-post for half an hour. **1799** J. SMITH *Acct. Captivity* 12 He struck a war post with his tomahawk. **1835** J. HALL *Sk. of West* I. 202 Striking his tomahawk into the war-post, in the middle of the council-house, [he] said [etc.]. **1836** *Knickerb.* VII. 172 It would have gratified him little to have proclaimed at the war-post that he had shot an unsuspecting foe from an ambush. **1899** CUSHMAN *Hist. Indians* 493 The 'war-post,' painted red, was set up.

War power. {1766} Any one of various extraordinary powers assumed in time of war by the national government or the president. — **1863** KETTELL *Hist. Rebellion* II. 635 It was therefore asserted that . . . the government could exercise unlimited authority under the 'war-power' of the Constitution. **1870** *Nation* 3 March 129/1 We wonder whether this [inflation] was to be done under the 'war power.' **1904** *Springfield W. Republican* 12 Aug. 2 The ease with which the executive can exercise war powers without the express sanction of Congress.

＊Warrant, n.
＊1. A written order authorizing the performance of some act, as the payment of money.
See also TREASURY WARRANT b.
1633 *Plymouth Laws* 33 It is thought meet . . . to make payment to such [persons killing wolves] upon the Gov[erno]rs warrant as before. **1670** *Providence Rec.* III. 150 He had already receiued a warrant from the Gouounor requiring him to giue notice [etc.]. **1777** *Jrnls. Cont. Congress* VII. 350 Every warrant of a general officer . . . shall specify the particular service or account for which the same shall be drawn. **1879** *Ill. Rev. Statutes* 1171 Warrants payable on demand, shall hereafter be drawn and issued upon the treasurer of this state or of any county, township, city, school district or other municipal corporation. **1900** *Congress. Rec.* 23 Jan. 1064/1 Warrants on the State treasury went begging on Carondelet street at 20 cents on the dollar.

＊b. An order empowering an official to carry out a decision, make arrests, etc., with reference to the administration of justice.
See also BENCH WARRANT *n.*, DISTRESS WARRANT.
1639 *R.I. Col. Rec.* I. 68 If any shall refuse to make their personal appearance, . . . warrants shall be granted for the destraining for the due satisfaction of the endamaged. **1745** *Ga. Col. Rec.* VI. 145 A Warrant was immediately granted to apprehend him. **1857** *Harper's Mag.* Aug. 402/1 The Mayor, who affirms that he was not informed that the Coroner had a warrant for him, was . . . arrested. **1924** R. CUMMINS *Sky-high Corral* 36 You a sheriff? And where's your warrant?

+2. =LAND WARRANT 1. Also attrib.
See also MILITARY LAND WARRANT, TREASURY WARRANT a.
1636 *Md. Hist. Mag.* III. 158 A warrant to Capt. Henry ffleete for the 4000 Acres of Land due to him. **1783** in *Travels Amer. Col.* 669 The 1000 acre warrant survey . . . nearly joined Spangliss line. **1792** IMLAY *Western Territory* 13 After this period (i.e. 1781), a land office was opened by the state, granting warrants for any quantity of unlocated land. **1812** MARSHALL *Kentucky* 113 The warrant, in every instance, was an order to the surveyor, to lay off the quantity of land expressed, for the party.

+3. A formal notice of the calling of a town meeting, with a statement of the business to be considered.
1644 *Portsmouth Rec.* 32 It is ordered . . . that the businesse of such meetinge dayes shalbe specified in the warant of warninge to the metinge. **1664** *R.I. Col. Rec.* II. 52 The Leftenant, in each towne, is to give warrant to call the people together. **1720** *Boston Rec.* 147 The Town will proceed to the choyce of a Comittee to Consider ab[ou]t promoting of a Spinning School . . . as is exprest in the warr[an]t for the calling of this meeting. **1775** *Vt. Hist. Soc. Coll.* I. 11 There has been several warrants or notifications sent up the country for a general meeting. **1875** HOLLAND *Sevenoaks* 23 He read this article of the warrant, posted in the public places. **1914** *Cycl. Amer. Govt.* III. 542/2 A warrant . . . is posted in a public place, or mailed to the voters before the meeting; and no business can be transacted which is not mentioned in the warrant.

4. In the army and the navy, a certificate of appointment, inferior to a commission, issued to certain officers. {1786-} Also attrib.

1815 *Niles' Reg.* IX. 17/2 The table of the secretary of war was now crowded with applications for *cadet's warrants.* **1846** *Xenia Torch-Light* 2 April 1/5, I procured a Midshipman's warrant, and went to sea. **1864** 'PENNIMAN' *Tanner-Boy* 62 A warrant is a document, without the distinctive seals of a commission attached to it, given to officers below the rank of captain or lieutenant. **1880** LAMPHERE *U.S. Govt.* 146/1 The Adjutant-General's office . . . [keeps the] non-commissioned officers' warrant roll.

＊Warrant, v. **+** *tr.* To issue a warrant against (a person). — **1818** *Niles' Reg.* XIII. 406/1 You would be warranted or sued one hundred times every day.

+Warranted land. Land held by virtue of a land warrant. — **1774** *Penna. Gazette* 14 Dec. Suppl. 2/3 To be sold . . . Four tracts of warranted land . . . about 25 miles from Pittsburgh.

Warrantee, *n.* and *v.* (See WARRANTY *n.* and *v.*)

+Warrant machinist. In the United States Navy, a warrant officer serving as assistant to the engineer officer. — **1899** *U.S. Navy Dept. Ann. Rep.* 19 Section 14 . . . authorized the appointment of 100 warrant machinists. **1902** *Monthly Rev.* Aug. 93 Admiral Melville, in his report dealing with the warrant machinists of the U.S. Navy, says [etc.].

Warrant officer.
1. A naval officer appointed by a warrant. {1693-}
1717 *Mass. H. R. Jrnl.* I. 188 That there be allowed and paid out of the Publick Treasury . . . a Share and Half to each Warrant Officer, and a Single Share to each Foremast-Man, or Mariner. **1794** *Ann. 3d Congress* 1426 There shall be employed, in each of the said ships, the following warrant officers [etc.]. **1849** *Whig Almanac 1850* 27/1 H. Greeley proposed to add to section 1 . . . 'That no further appointments of warrant officers be made until Congress shall expressly direct a resumption of such appointments.' **1858** *S. Lit. Messenger* XXVI. 84/1 Masters' Mates constituted a grade of 'warrant officers.' **1899** *Congress. Rec.* 3 March 2873/2 Warrant Officers of the Navy. To be chief boatswain. . . . To be chief gunners. . . . To be chief carpenters.

2. 'An officer charged with the duty of serving a judicial warrant' (*Stand.*). {1901}
+Warrant trying. *local.* (See quot. 1859.) — **1829** *Va. Literary Museum* 185 His compliance was used as a justification for his attending a quarter race, a shooting match, a warrant trying, or a deer hunt. **1841** *S. Lit. Messenger* VII. 644/2 Not a 'warrant trying' can be held. **1859** BARTLETT 502 *Warrant-Trying,* the magistrates' monthly courts at the cross-roads. Virginia. **1877** BAGBY *Old Va. Gentleman* 11 Of church-going on Sunday, when the girls kept the carriage waiting; of warrant-tryings, vendues, election and general muster days.

＊Warranty, n. Also **warrantee.**
＊1. A covenant, stated or implied in a conveyance of real estate, by which the grantor gives the grantee assurance of the security of the title; a warranty deed.
1653 *Suffolk Deeds* II. 74 The said Dwelling howse . . . [is sold] to him the said Barnabass . . . wth Warranties against all person or persons whatsoeuer. **1743** *Md. Hist. Mag.* XX. 314, I make no other Warrantee than from me and mine and with that you will have as good a Title as the Law can give. **1845** COOPER *Chainbearer* vii, The old fellow . . . first asked for our deeds, and we showed them to him; as good and lawful warrantees as were ever printed and filled up by a 'squire.

＊2. A promise, on the part of a vendor, to answer for defects or omissions in the goods sold.
1874 WANAMAKER in Appel *Biog. Wanamaker* 385 A warrantee that will be honored as quickly as a good draft of the government. **1881** *Reinbeck (Iowa) Times* 26 May 4/7, 32 years of continuous and successful business . . . to 'back up' the broad warranty given on all our goods.

+Warranty, *v. tr.* To convey (land) with a covenant of warranty. — **1742** *Md. Hist. Mag.* XX. 264 Being obliged to Warrantee the Land called Hampton Court to Edward Flannigan [etc.].

+Warranty deed. A deed in which there is a covenant of warranty. Also *fig.* — **1779** E. PARKMAN *Diary* 106 His son in law had beguiled him to give a Warrantee Deed of his Place. **1831** PECK *Guide* 320 Purchasers for taxes . . . give general warrantee deeds for one dollar per acre. **1866** RICHARDSON *Secret Service* 188 Think of giving a man a warranty-deed for his own body and soul.

+War record. The facts known or recorded concerning the part played by an individual or a group in a war; a record of success in war. — **1890** CUSTER *Following Guidon* 2 They longed individually and as a regiment for a war 'record.' **1891** 'CRADDOCK' in *Harper's Mag.* Feb. 368/1 He had been a brave soldier, although the flavor of bushwacking clung to his war record. **1904** TARBELL *Hist. Standard Oil Co.* I. 31 The soldier . . . was welcomed into oil companies, stock being given him for the value of his war record.

＊Warrior. (See also BLACK WARRIOR.)
+1. An Indian fighting man; an Indian regarded as a soldier or fighter.
See also HEAD WARRIOR.
1739 W. STEPHENS *Proc. Georgia* I. 456 They were but few (under thirty) —but were pickt Men, all Warriors. **1755** *N. Carolina Col. Rec.* V. 635 Major Lewis is return'd from the Cherokee Country, and brought in only 7 Warriors and 3 Women. **1837** *Diplom. Corr. Texas* I. (1908) 237 He says that the Caddoes do not count more than from 130 to 150 warriors.

1881 *Rep. Indian Affairs* p. viii, The spirits had notified him that the dead warriors could not return to the country until the whites had left it.

+**b.** With preceding tribal name.

1775 ADAIR *Indians* 2 A large body of the English Indian traders . . . were escorted by a body of Creek and Choktah warriors. **1847** RUXTON *Adv. Rocky Mts.* (1848) 238 [Moccasin] attracted the attention of the Arapahô warriors. **1865** PIKE *Scout & Ranger* (1932) 41 The victim had probably ventured too far, while following the avocation of a Comanche warrior. **1907** ANDREWS *Recoll.* 127 Two Dacotah warriors were traveling on the shore.

+**c.** *transf.* A member of Tammany Hall.

1812 *Salem Gazette* 5 June 3/3 The Warriors of the Democratic Tribe will hold a powow at Agawam on Tuesday next.

2. Attrib. with *council, priest, statesman.*

1833 FLINT *D. Boone* 157 He attended a warrior-council. **1841** FOOTE *Texas* I. 93 The warrior-priest yet has under his command more than a hundred thousand Creoles. *Ib.* 152 A warrior statesman [Aaron Burr] . . . had been . . . maturing a scheme for revolutionizing all South America.

+**Warriors' Path.** A well-defined Indian warpath between the Ohio country (Shawnee and Wyandot) and western North Carolina (Catawba and Cherokee). Now hist. — **1770** WASHINGTON *Diaries* I. 425 At the Mouth of this C[ree]k . . . is the Warriors Path to the Cherokee Country. **1910** HODGE, etc. *Amer. Indians* II. 801/1 The great highway leading from Cumberland gap to the mouth of the Scioto was known as the Warriors' Path.

War road. +One of certain roads or ways used by Indians on the warpath. *Obs.* — **1782** in V. W. Howard *Heroes* (1932) 144 On the Southward side below where the War road crosses the said fork. **1822** J. FOWLER *Journal* 97, I now discover the men are all feerful of meeting With the Indeans as We are near the War Road.

+**Warsaw.** [See quotation.] The black grouper, *Garrupa nigrita.* — **1884** GOODE, etc. *Fisheries* I. 411 The Black Grouper . . . is at Pensacola known by the name 'Warsaw,' evidently a corruption of the Spanish name 'Guasa.'

*∗**Warship.** A ship built or equipped for use in war. — **1825** JOHN NEAL *Bro. Jonathan* III. 35 The great war-ship swung at her moorings. **1864** CUMMING *Hospital Life* 146/2 We were attacked by a fleet of war ships. **1896** *N.Y. Sun* 24 Aug. 1/1 The twelve vessels will constitute the first fleet of steel war ships ever gathered hereabouts.

War shout. A war cry or war whoop. {1866} Also fig. — **1830** COOPER *Water Witch* III. v, I am . . . fitter for the zephyr than the gale —the jest, than the war-shout. **1845** FRÉMONT *Exped.* 263 Giving the war shout, they instantly charged into camp. **1847** COYNER *Lost Trappers* 174 They raised a dreadful war-shout, and came bounding down the hill.

War signal. +Among the Indians, any one of various means for conveying a message concerning war. — **1775** ADAIR *Indians* 386 If they make a plain discovery, either of fresh tracks or of the enemy, they immediately pass the war-signal to each other. **1808** BARKER *Indian Princess* II. iii, Tell our chiefs to assemble; and show them the war-signal.

War song.

+**1.** Among the Indians, a song expressing or arousing warlike zeal; a song sung as an accompaniment to a war dance. {1818–, a song of defiance}

1755 *Va. State P.* I. 251 They sung the War Song, and four Indians went off in Two Canoes. **1789** MACLAY *Deb. Senate* 109 He had warmed himself with his own discourse, as the Indians do with their war song. **1823** JAMES *Exped.* I. 178 We were notified of their proximity by hearing their war-song. **1847** PARKMAN in *Knickerb.* XXX. 490 They circled round the area at full gallop, each warrior singing his war-song as he rode. *a*1918 G. STUART *On Frontier* I. 175 They had ten loose horses and halted on the hill and sang me a war song.

2. A song expressing popular sentiment during a war.

1897 BRODHEAD *Bound in Shallows* 115 That book of war-songs I sent for has come.

War steamer. A vessel of war operating by steam power. {1847} — **1840** *Niles' Nat. Reg.* 15 Aug. 384/3 Two war steamers . . . are in process of building in New York, for the Spanish government. **1847** POLK in *Pres. Mess. & P.* IV. 561 In addition to the four war steamers authorized by this act, the Secretary of the Navy has . . . entered into contracts for the construction of five steamers to be employed in the transportation of the United States mail. **1881–5** McCLELLAN *Own Story* 536 There was a war-steamer anchored off the White House, with steam up, ready to take off the President, cabinet, etc., at a moment's notice.

War talk. {1831} +Among the Indians, a speech proposing war, or a discussion concerning war. Also transf. — **1800** HAWKINS *Sk. Creek Country* 72 More than one half the nation have been for war at the same time; or taken, as they express it, the war talk. **1833** *Sketches D. Crockett* 185 His public harangues, or his war talks, as electioneering speeches are called in the west. **1850** *Western Journal* IV. 235 In the morning we learned from a Mexican captive that a war-talk had been held.

+**Warted squash.** A variety (*Cucurbita verrucosa*) of winter squash having a warted rind. {warted gourd, 1681} — **1847** DARLINGTON *Weeds & Plants* 143 Wårted Squash. Long-necked Squash. . . . Apt to produce worthless Hybrids among Pumpkins, when growing near them.

+**War trail.** A warpath. — **1840** COOPER *Pathfinder* III. iv, Warrior eat, drink, sleep, all time, when don't fight and go on war-trail. **1852** WATSON *Nights in Block-House* 89 The course pursued by Hewitt . . .

was in the direction of a favourite and well-known Indian war-trail, from Sandusky to Muskingum. **1870** KEIM *Sheridan's Troopers* 180 They follow what is familiar to the frontiersman as the Grand Comanche War-trail, crossing the Pecos and the Rio Grande. **1893** WISTER in *Harper's Mag.* Dec. 54/2 About young bucks goin' on the war-trail?

*∗**Warty,** *a.* **1.** Characterized by wartlike growths. {1693–} Used in the specific names of animals and plants. {c1711–} **2.** *Warty-flowered panic grass,* (see quotation). — **(1) 1842** *Nat. Hist. N.Y., Zoology* IV. 326 The Warty Balloon-fish. *Diodon verrucosus.* . . . This small fish . . . may prove to be the young of some species hitherto undescribed. **1843** *Ib.* VI. 20 This species . . . is sometimes distinguished as the *Warty Hermit Crab.* **1868** GRAY *Field Botany* 160 C[ucurbita] verrucosa, Warty, Long-neck, and Crook-neck Squash, Vegetable Marrow, &c. **(2) 1843** TORREY *Flora N.Y.* II. 428 *Panicum verrucosum.* . . . Warty-flowered Panic-grass. . . . Sandy swamps, Long Island.

+**War whoop,** *n.* Also war hoop, etc. {1798–}

1. A yell given by an Indian or by Indians as a signal for attack, or in order to terrify victims of attack.

The meaning of the term as used in the first quotation is uncertain.

[**1725** in *Travels Amer. Col.* 143 About Seven of the Clock in the Evening came in here the Warr hoop with the peice of a Scalp.] **1739** [see sense 2 a]. **1775** ADAIR *Indians* 159 The leader . . . goes three times round his dark winter-house, . . . sounding the war-whoop, singing the war-song. **1806** *Balance* V. 217/3 The war-whoop no longer resounded on the continent. **1827** COOPER *Prairie* xxiv, When the Pawnee war whoop is in their ears, the whole nation howls. **1847** PARKMAN in *Knickerb.* XXX. 490 Suddenly the wild yell of the war-hoop came pealing from the hills. **1900** *Congress. Rec.* 6 Feb. 1564/2 A war whose zone of conflict was . . . made hideous by the warwhoops of painted savages.

2. In various phrases. **a.** *To set up the* (or *a*) *war whoop,* to give a war cry or cries; to go on the warpath. Also transf.

1739 W. STEPHENS *Proc. Georgia* 474 In marching our Indians set up the war whoop. **1775** *S.C. Hist. Soc. Coll.* II. 33 If they are so foolish as to set up the war-whoop, . . . we can send a great many [warriors] into their country. **1823** THACHER *Military Jrnl.* 101 A party of Indians arriving and setting up the war whoop, . . . the Americans were induced to give way and retreat. **1876** 'MARK TWAIN' *Tom Sawyer* xvi, Then they set up a war-whoop of applause, and said it was 'splendid!'

b. *To give the* (or *a*) *war whoop,* =prec. sense.

1757 J. CARVER in *Arminian Mag.* XVII. (1794) 35 By this time the war-hoop was given, and the Indians began to murder those that were nearest to them. **1804** *Steele P.* I. 441 A disposition to conciliate prevails except with a few who are ready to give the war hoop. **1836** IRVING *Astoria* I. 184 One of them suddenly leaped up and gave a war-whoop. **1916** EASTMAN *From Deep Woods* 53, I was followed on the streets by gangs of little white savages, giving imitation war whoops.

c. *To raise a* (or *the*) *war whoop,* to utter a war cry; transf., to raise an outcry; to clamor for war. {1807, in transf. or fig. sense}

1834 CARRUTHERS *Kentuckian* I. 65, I jumped up and raised a war-whoop. **1836** EDWARD *Hist. Texas* 233 The Texian Representatives . . . raised the war-whoop. . . . To arms! To arms! **1851** MELVILLE *Moby Dick* 318 'Woo-hoo! Wa-hee!' screamed the Gay-Header in reply, raising some old war-whoop to the skies.

d. *In the name of the war whoop,* an exclamation emphasizing the speaker's astonishment. *colloq.*

1837 *S. Lit. Messenger* III. 663 In the name of the warwhoop, only to think, board $200 per day at Buffaloe!

+**War-whoop,** *v. intr.* To utter a war cry or a sound resembling a war cry. Also *ppl. a.* — **1837** *S. Lit. Messenger* III. 237 The Creeks warwhooped—the Cherokees were silent. **1883** 'MARK TWAIN' *Life on Miss.* 11, A tribe of war-whooping savages swarmed out to meet and murder them. *Ib.* lx, The lover goes war-whooping home.

+**Warwickite.** [f. *Warwick*, N.Y.] A titanate and borate of iron and magnesium, occurring in dark crystals. {1850} — **1838** C. U. SHEPARD in *Amer. Jrnl. Science* XXXIV. 314 A new species, which I designate Warwickite, from its original locality. **1857** DANA *Mineralogy* 212 *Warwickite* . . . occurs in prismatic crystals, of a brownish to an iron-gray color.

War widow. 1. The widow of a man killed in war. **2.** A woman whose husband is absent in war service. — **(1) 1866** *Rep. Indian Affairs* 164 These last came from Laramie during the winter, and claim to be war-widows. **(2) 1877** BARTLETT 261 During the rush to California, 1850 to 1860, . . . the new-found treasures of that country separated . . . many husbands from their wives. During the late war such were termed war-widows.

War woman. +**1.** Among the Indians, a priestess or female councilor. +**2.** *spec.* Nancy Hart, a Revolutionary heroine of Georgia, known for courage and resourcefulness in fighting Tories. — **(1) 1765** TIMBERLAKE *Memoirs* 71 Old warriors likewise, or war-women . . . have the title of Beloved. [**1786** FERRIAR in *Mem. Lit. & Philos. Soc. Manch.* (1790) III. 28 In every Indian village, the war-woman also is a kind of oracle; by dreams and presages, she directs the hunters to their prey, and the warriors to the enemy.] **(2) 1857** *Ladies' Repository* XVII. 81/1 The stream, called from her, 'War-Woman's Creek,' empties into it. *Ib.* 83/1 The 'war-woman's' skill in strategy and courage in action now appeared.

⁎ Wash, n.

┼1. The underground den of a beaver or bear.

1809 A. HENRY *Travels* 130 Their washes . . . are to be discovered, by striking the ice along the bank, and where the holes are, a hollow sound is returned. **1877** COUES *Fur-bearing Animals* II. 52 They [wolverines] bring forth in burrows under ground, probably old bear washes.

┼2. The erosion of topsoil and upper layers of earth by rain or running water; a place where such erosion has occurred.

1835 INGRAHAM *South-West* II. 88 Bermuda grass is used with great success to check the progress of a *wash.* **1857** *Ill. Agric. Soc. Trans.* III. 412 Land lying in such a position as to protect it from wash . . . may be kept in constant cultivation. **1913** BARNES *Western Grazing Grounds* 332 Traps were set in every trail and wash wherever the wolves had left a footprint.

┼3. (See quots. 1885 and 1891.) In full *wash sale.*

1848 W. ARMSTRONG *Stocks* 19 These wash sales are of course void between parties. **1859** *Watertown* (Wis.) *Democrat* 30 June, A Wash is a pretended sale, by special agreement between the seller and the buyer, for the purpose of getting a quotation reported. **1885** *Harper's Mag.* Nov. 842/2 A 'wash' . . . is an arrangement between brokers whereby one fictitiously buys what the other fictitiously sells of a certain stock, to keep up or advance the price, and thus to lay a foundation for real sales. **1891** *Cent.* 6830/3 *Wash,* a fictitious kind of sale, . . . in which a broker who has received orders from one person to buy and from another person to sell a particular . . . quantity of some particular stock or commodity simply transfers the stock or commodity from one principal to the other and pockets the difference.

┼4. *W.* The dry bed of an intermittent stream. (Cf. DRY WASH.)

1894 *Rev. of Revs.* Nov. 508/2 The centre of it [Pachango Valley] is occupied with the broad sandy 'wash' characteristic of Southern California streams. **1898** A. M. DAVIDSON *Calif. Plants* 112 In sandy washes . . . the prickly poppy will send out great white flowers. **1902** F. H. NEWELL *Irrigation in U.S.* 237 The flow of rainfall gradually disappears in the gravel and boulder channels or washes which extend out across the valley.

⁎ Wash, v.

⁎1. a. *tr.* To subject (auriferous earth or ore) to the action of water in order to obtain the metallic particles.

1847 *Santa Fe Repub.* 24 Sept. 1/3 The mineral [gold] is procured in different ways, but much the larger portion by washing the dirt. **1873** COZZENS *Marvellous Country* 202 The dirt to be washed had to be carried down to the river. **1889** MUNROE *Golden Days* 175 [They] moved along the shore, washing a little earth here and there.

┼b. *To wash gold,* to obtain gold by washing auriferous sand, earth, etc.

1863 *Rio Abajo Press* 5 May 2/1, I left him well and hearty at Real de San Francisco, day before yesterday washing gold. **1891** *Century Mag.* Feb. 533 The method of washing gold was then so simple . . . that they learned it quickly. **1907** WHITE *Arizona Nights* 164, I camped a while, washing gold, getting friendly with the Yumas.

c. *absol.* =senses a or b. {1604}

1848 *30th Congress 2 Sess.* H. R. Ex. Doc. No. 1, 57 About two hundred men are at work in the full glare of the sun washing for gold. **1850** N. KINGSLEY *Diary* 156 They washed this forenoon and got over two ounces amalgam. **1876** *Chicago Inter-Ocean* 4 June, Five hundred men are washing on rapid creek, thirty miles from Deadwood.

┼2. *Stock exchange. tr.* To enhance or endeavor to enhance the value of (stock) by fictitious sales. Also in phrases *to wash the market, to wash sales.* Cf. WASH *n.* 3 and WASHING 4.

1870 M. H. SMITH *20 Years Wall St.* 74 *Washing the Market. . . .* Two parties make an agreement to buy and sell from each other. The transaction is bogus. **1873** *Newton Kansan* 1 Jan. 1/6 Several brokers . . . are employed to 'wash' the stagnant stock. **1903** S. S. PRATT *Work of Wall St.* 146 The syndicate may be washing sales by matched orders through curb brokers in order to market watered stock.

Wash-, stem of WASH *v.* Used in combinations. In British use less frequent than *washing.*

┼1. In the names of garments and fabrics that are washable.

1888 *Boston Jrnl.* 23 June 6/3 [In] rural retreats . . . she can . . . wear wash-gowns, and live out of doors all day long. **1902** BANKS *Newspaper Girl* 168 He wore neckties of wash-ribbon. **1905** *N.Y. Ev. Post* 19 May 12 Their May Sale of Girls' Summer Wash Frocks.

2. In miscellaneous combinations.

Wash bluing, laundry bluing; *w. book,* a memorandum book used to list laundry; *w. earth,* alluvial earth; *w.-foot Baptist,* a Primitive Baptist (*colloq.*); *w. line,* a line upon which clothes are hung; *w. place,* a home where a washwoman goes to do the laundry; *w. pond,* a pond where washing is done; *w. stuff,* earth from which gold may be washed; *w.-trough,* a trough used for washing the face and hands.

1889 in J. F. Daly *Life A. Daly* 476, I wrote up the bill with a bottle of wash-blueing. **1840** MATHEWS *Politicians Prof.,* A manager looks upon

a manuscript American play, with, I imagine, about the same favor as he would peruse the wash-book of one of his supernumeraries. **1873** BEADLE *Undevel. West* 514 The soil is the richest kind of 'wash earth,' composed of the detritus of the volcanic hills. **1889** DELAND *Florida Days* 135 The Wash-foot Baptists worship in a single room. **1890** WIGGIN *Timothy's Quest* 48 There's lots of baby-clothes hanging on the wash-lines. **1875** STOWE *We & Neighbors* 177 Poll has gone to my wash-place to-day. **1741** *N.H. Probate Rec.* III. 66, I give . . . my Son Jonathan The farm he lives on near the wash pond. **1891** *Cent.* 6832/2 *Wash-stuff,* in *gold-mining,* same as *wash-dirt.* **1902** WISTER *Virginian* 16 It was not much of a toilet that I made in the first wash-trough of my experience.

Wash barrel. A barrel used, or similar to those used, in the process of washing clothes. — **1846** *Knickerb.* XXVII. 511 The 'doctor' . . . relieves his culinary labors by pounding away at some shirts and other 'duds' that are smoking in the wash-barrel. **1854** *Harper's Mag.* IX. 676/1 'How many mackerel did you get today?' 'About twenty wash-barrels, mostly large.'

Wash-basin. A basin in which to wash the hands and face. {1812–1855} 'Now chiefly *U.S.*' (*O.E.D.*).

1806 *Austin P.* I. (1924) 102, 3/12 doc. Wash basons, $6.50. **1829** B. HALL *Travels in N.A.* III. 263 There was but one wash-basin, as they called it, in the house. **1890** CUSTER *Following Guidon* 73 We had . . . a rude bunk for a bed, a stool, with a tin wash-basin. **1919** HOUGH *Sagebrusher* 27 They had used their single wash basin for their dish pan as well. *transf.* and *attrib.* **1860** HOLMES *Professor* 104 A new nursery, sir, with Lake Superior, and Huron, and all the rest of 'em for wash-basins! **1902** MACGOWAN *Last Word* 255 Miss Bucks . . . had just arrived in a hat of the wash-basin variety.

Washbear. 'The racoon or washing bear' (*Cent.*).

┼Wash bench. A bench upon which washing is done. — **1861** *Chicago Tribune* 15 April 1 We have sold the right to manufacture and sell . . . Cram's Patent Folding Furniture, comprising Ironing Tables, Wash Benches [etc.]. **1878** COOKE *Happy Dodd* 85 Then they all sat down on the wash-bench. **1891** RYAN *Pagan* 145 His landlady had noticed light curly rings showing about his temples . . . after his ablutions at the public bath—the wash bench.

┼Wash bill. A bill for washing; a laundry bill. — **1848** E. Bryant *California* App. 478, I have just seen . . . a wash bill, made out and paid, at the rate of eight dollars per dozen. **1873** HARTE *Episode Fiddletown* 26 His wash-bill [was] made out on the unwritten side of one of these squares. **1901** C. MORRIS *Life on Stage* 44 The three of us . . . set to work trying to solve the riddle how a girl was to pay . . . her wash-bill, and all the expenses of the theatre . . . all out of $5 a week.

Washboard. {1742-} ┼A board having a ribbed or fluted surface upon which clothes are rubbed when being washed. — **1845** J. W. NORRIS *Chicago Directory* 95 Manufacturer of the Improved Zinc Washboards. **1868** *Mich. Agric. Rep.* VII. 348 Saffel and Baldwin, Tiffin, O., [exhibited] half-dozen grooved wash-boards. **1902** BANKS *Newspaper Girl* 163 Clothes washed by her own hands on an American washboard in a big wooden tub.

┼Wash boiler. A large metal container in which white clothes are boiled. — **1853** FOWLER *Home for All* 119 A wash-boiler is stationed in the adjoining room. **1876** *Wide Awake* III. 43/2 Granny . . . [renewed] her attack upon the wash-boiler and its contents. **1913** STRATTON-PORTER *Laddie* vii, Sarah Hood cooked other things, and made a wash-boiler of coffee.

⁎ Washbowl. ┼A large, white, earthenware bowl for washing the face and hands. Freq. in phrase *washbowl and pitcher.*

1816 U. BROWN *Journal* I. 369 His wash-Bowl [is] the Knot of a tree. **1856** M. J. HOLMES *L. Rivers* 17 Now-a-days we allers has a wash-bowl and pitcher. **1883** 'MARK TWAIN' *Life on Miss.* xxxviii, Sometimes there was even a wash-bowl and pitcher. **1911** FERBER *Dawn O'Hara* 155, I still had enough to fill the wash-bowl. *transf.* a**1861** WINTHROP *J. Brent* 209 Men hatted with slouched hats, wash-bowls, and stove-pipes.

┼b. A utensil in which gold is washed.

1848 *Essex Inst. Coll.* XII. 106, I came from Salem City, With my washbowl on my knee.

Wash day. The day upon which the laundry work is done. {1864-} — **1846** *S. Lit. Messenger* XII. 508/1 Thursday is wash-day. **1882** *Century Mag.* March 659/2 The people of some countries believe that unless cats are well treated by the laundresses, they bring rain on wash-day. a**1918** G. STUART *On Frontier* I. 215 Most of us have selected some other day than Sunday for wash day.

Wash dish. {1825-} ┼=WASH-BASIN. — **1805** *Austin P.* I. (1924) 140, 1 Wash dish. **1839** KIRKLAND *New Home* 22 You'm lookin' for a wash-dish, a'n't ye! **1891** WILKINS *New Eng. Nun* 271, I've got my tin wash-dish there on the bench.

⁎ Washed, a. 1. Of land surfaces: Eroded by rains. ┼**2.** *Washed sale,* =WASH *n.* 3. — (1) **1787** WASHINGTON *Diaries* III. 259 From 56 sqr. yds. laid on a poor Washed Knowl, . . . 3 Pecks [of Irish potatoes]. **1835** LONGSTREET *Ga. Scenes* 187 In a washed field to our right, Music opened. (2) **1886** *Harper's Mag.* July 205/1 Washed or fictitious sales, or false reports of sales are also penal offences. **1900** NELSON *A B C Wall St.* 70 It will also be readily seen that the opportunity for washed sales is a very open one.

*Washer. ||1. =WASH n. 2. +2. =GOLD-WASHER 1. — (1) 1846 *Spirit of Times* (N.Y.) 18 April 89/3 Washers . . . can be [prevented] . . . by '*circular cultivation*,' which must sooner or later be adopted in all undulating lands. (2) 1850 TYSON *Diary in Calif.* 9 You will soon become accustomed to the mode of proceeding, either with a shovel, pickax, pan, or washer. 1885 *Wkly. New Mexican Rev.* 28 June 4/4 This washer of the 'Porter' pattern, does not operate well on anything but very dry dust or dry, fine tailings. 1901 WHITE *Westerners* 210 You has to have yore stamp mill and washer for all the group of claims.

Washerman. A man whose occupation is washing clothes. {1715-} Used chiefly of Chinese laundrymen. — 1845 JUDD *Margaret* 72 Nimrod became cook, washerman, porter. 1878 BEADLE *Western Wilds* 400 Chinamen . . . are porters, washer-men, railroad laborers, cigar makers. 1890 *Stock Grower & Farmer* 3 May 7/4 The treatment of these ignorant washermen consists partly of mutterings and incantat'ons.

Washerwoman. 1. A woman who washes clothes; a laundress. {1632-} +2. *Washerwoman's gig*, (see quotation). — (1) 1777 *Jrnls. Cont. Congress* VII. 163 The pay of the . . . Washerwomen, Servants &c [shall] be regulated by the Physicians and Surgeons General. 1816 WEEMS *Letters* III. 156 What can I ever make to defray carriages, taverns, . . . washerwomen, shoe blacks[?] 1900 *Congress. Rec.* 19 Jan. 1004/1, I traced a case in this city to find a pension attorney . . . and I found him . . . to be an Irish washerwoman. (2) 1890 *Ib.* 16 Aug. 8713/2 The 'washerwoman's gig'—4-11-14—[is] the chance that these three, or any other three numbers, will, in any order, be the first three numbers out of the thirteen taken from the wheel.

Washery. {1898-} +(See quot. 1909.) — 1895 *Columbus Dispatch* 6 May 7/6 The destruction of the washery and machinery was complete. 1897 *Ib.* 17 Sept. 1/3 Over 100 men reported for work at the Monarch washery. 1902 *Boston Globe* 20 May 9/1 Their onslaught was directed against the Grassy island washery of the Delaware & Hudson company. 1909 *Cent. Suppl.* 1432/3 *Washery*, . . . a place where coal is sorted and sized by the use of flowing water, and by the same process is concentrated and freed from dirt and incombustible gangue.

+Wash gold. Gold that occurs in alluvial deposits, as contrasted with that found in veins or lodes. — 1873 ARNY *Items regarding N. Mex.* 84 In Pinos Altos the main lead from which most of the wash-gold came has not been discovered yet. 1901 GRINNELL *Gold Hunting in Alaska* 87 The gold on the beach is not 'wash' gold.

+Wash goods. *pl.* Goods or fabrics that are washable. — 1878 *Decorum* 271 [This dress] may be of . . . wash-goods. 1887 *Courier-Jrnl.* 20 Feb. 1/6 We are selling great quantities of wash goods, such as French and Domestic Satteens, Fine Ginghams, White Goods. 1893 *Chicago Tribune* 23 April 44/3 Wash Goods. National bunting, for decorating.

Wash gravel. a. Alluvial deposits of gravel. b. Gravel or earth from which gold may be washed. — (a) 1873 BEADLE *Undevel. West* 494 Wash gravel and marine shells are heaped in fantastic piles by the wind. (b) 1891 *Cent.* 6831/2 *Wash-gravel*. Same as *wash-dirt*.

*Washhouse.

*1. A house, usually an outbuilding, in which washing is done.

1669 *Boston Rec.* 45 A parcell of Land . . . is bounded . . . from the S. West corner of James Whetcome wash house on a Line 100 foott. 1723 *Amer. Wkly. Mercury* 4 July 3/2 There is to be Exposed to sale by way of a Lottery, a new Brick House . . . with a good . . . Wash House. 1795 *Columbian Centinel* 21 Jan. 4/3 To be sold, A House . . . almost new, with Wash-House. 1828 *Yankee* April 125/1 What if the girl was 'flustrated' on coming into the room from the wash-house? 1863 CUMMING *Hospital Life* 69/1 The wash-house is a little ways from the rest of the hospital. 1885 *Rep. Indian Affairs* 99 The same parties also erected . . . a frame wash-house complete. 1923 WATTS *L. Nichols* 13 He preferred sleeping . . . stretched on the floor of the wash-house.

+2. A laundry. Used of Chinese laundries. *colloq.*

1872 McCLELLAN *Golden State* 427 Chinese wash-houses strike the eye at every corner. 1877 McCABE *Hist. Great Riots* 422 A portion of the crowd wrecked a Chinese wash-house in the neighborhood.

*Washing.

1. Washing away; erosion. {1726-}

1785 WASHINGTON *Diaries* II. 396 Track paths . . . may endanger the Banks if the Wood is stripped from them, which is their present security against washing. 1835 INGRAHAM *South-West* II. 87 [A ravine] has been formed by 'washing.' 1843 N. BOONE *Journal* 216 Near our camp, the hills had from the washing assumed various fantastic shapes.

*2. The act or process of subjecting earth to the action of water for the purpose of obtaining gold.

1825 *Amer. Jrnl. Science* IX. 11 Washings on a more limited scale are conducted here [in N. Carolina]. 1851 *Alta Californian* 17 July, The early adventurers in the gold-diggings required simply an Indian basket or a wooden bowl for their 'washings.' 1883 W. G. RITCH *Illust. N. Mex.* 75 Washing is still carried on upon a small scale by persons without capital, Mexicans principally.

3. A place where gold is obtained by washing ore or soil. {1865-}

1848 in Bryant *California* App. 458 Twenty-five miles above the lower washing, . . . the hills rise to about a thousand feet. 1889 J. D. WHITNEY *United States* 310 The earliest washings were along the rivers.

+4. *Stock exchange.* (See quotations and cf. WASH v. 2.)

1870 MEDBERY *Men Wall St.* 138 Washing, is where one broker arranges with another to buy a certain stock when he offers it for sale. The bargain is fictitious. 1894 S. LEAVITT *Our Money Wars* 287 In 1887 . . . by the process known as 'Washing,'—that is, by hiring one set of brokers to buy and another set of brokers to sell,—the price of shares was forced to fifteen times their value.

5. Attrib. (passing into adj.) and comb. with *bench, compound, fluid,* etc.

See also WASHING MACHINE, POWDER, TUB.

1775 *Essex Inst. Coll.* XIII. 187, 1 Washing Bench. 1843 *Nat. Hist. N.Y., Geology* I. 361 They were erecting shaking washing tables. 1844 KENDALL *Narr. Santa Fé Exped.* II. 400 The eyes of . . . a group of washing-girls, were drawn toward us. 1857 *Lawrence* (Kan.) *Republican* 28 May 4 This last is 'washing fluid,' which is valuable for cleaning casks. 1863 RANDALL *Pract. Shepherd* 165 The apprehension of contagious diseases, too, from using the same washing yards . . . [is] perfectly well founded. 1870 STEPHENS *Married in Haste* 86 This is washing-night, and I haven't quite got through. 1874 RAYMOND *6th Rep. Mines* 326 When there was snow on the mountain, they . . . managed to keep their washing holes supplied. 1876 — *8th Rep. Mines* 103 The washing-flume is 1¼ miles long, . . . paved with blocks. 1882 *4th Congress 1 Sess.* H. R. Ex. Doc. No. 216, 642 The dump for the gravel outside of the mine and the washing plant is variously arranged. 1884 *Harper's Mag.* LXIX. *Advt.*, Washing compounds and soap . . . are highly chemicaled.

Washing machine. 1. A machine for washing clothes. {1799-} +2. =GOLD-WASHER 1. — (1) 1818 *Niles' Reg.* XIV. 328/1, I have obtained an exclusive right from the president of the United States, for an improvement on the washing machine. 1847 *Rep. Comm. Patents* 1846 217 What we claim as our invention . . . is connecting the pounder or rubber of a washing machine with the hand lever. 1897 *McClure's Mag.* Nov. 64/2, I ain't even got a washin'-machine! (2) 1849 WIERZBICKI *California* 40 A washing machine is used when there are two or more working in partnership.

+Washing powder. A powder, usually saponaceous, used in washing. — 1869 FULLER *Flower Gatherers* 182 The old Proff . . . calls salt 'Chloride of Sodium' and sets me thinking of washing powders. 1896 *Internat. Typogr. Union Proc.* 55/1, 1 box B.S. washing powder, $6.

Washington. [George *Washington*, first president of the United States (1732–99).]

+1. A variety of plum. *Obs.* Also attrib.

1846 BROWNE *Trees Amer.* 246 *Washington* or *Bolmar Plum-tree.* This variety may be known by its roundish, yellow fruit. 1856 *Mich. Agric. Soc. Trans.* VII. 715 A gentleman noted for his noble Washingtons and imperial Gages. 1863 *Horticulturist* XVIII. 262 Of Plums, the following will probably be best for your purpose: Coe's Golden Drop, . . . Green Gage, McLaughlin, Washington.

+2. In special combinations.

Washington canvasback, =REDHEAD 1; *W. cedar*, (see quotation); *W. gun*, ?a type of cannon; *W. lily*, a large cultivated lily (*Lilium washingtonianum*) common on the west coast of the United States; *W. lottery wheel*, a lottery wheel operated at Washington, D.C.; *W. Monument*, a marble obelisk in Washington, D.C., erected as a national memorial to George Washington; *W. penny*, (see quotation); *W. pie*, a layer cake with a cream or jam filling; *W. press*, a type of hand-operated printing press; *W. territory*, the region organized as a territory in 1853 and admitted into the Union as a state in 1889.

1890 *Cent.* 5020/3 [An American variety of the redhead] is called more fully *red-headed duck*, . . . also *grayback, Washington canvasback*, and *American pochard.* 1889 *Ib.* 875/3 Washington cedar is the big-tree of California, *Sequoia gigantea.* 1874 B. F. TAYLOR *World on Wheels* 72 The cylinder is trained like a Washington gun, at an angle of about thirty-three and a third degrees. 1915 ARMSTRONG & THORNBER *Western Wild Flowers* 36 The flowers are even more deliciously fragrant than the Washington Lily. 1799 *Aurora* (Phila.) 31 Jan. (Th.), The gulls and goose-traps . . . come from the shop in which the Washington Lottery wheels remain undrawn. 1886 J. A. PORTER *New Stand. Guide of Washington* 51 Washington Monument. . . . The height of the obelisk from the foundation is 555 feet. 1888 *Amer. Notes & Q.* I. 238 The so-called 'Washington pennies,' which existed previous to this date [1793], were not issued by the Government and were models or medals. 1905 LINCOLN *Partners* 4 'Turnovers' [were] arranged cob-house fashion under a glass cover, with a dingy 'Washington' pie under another cover. 1896 SHINN *Story of Mine* 248 It contained an old-style Washington press, cases, desks, and editor's table. 1881 *Ore. State Jrnl.* 15 Jan. 4/1 The delegate from Washington Territory . . . succeeded in having two of his bills [passed].

+Washington eagle. The bald eagle in its immature stage. — 1839 PEABODY *Mass. Birds* 263 The Washington Eagle, *Falco Washingtonianus*, . . . sometimes wanders into New England. 1870 *Amer. Naturalist* IV. 525 The opinion long since advanced by some writers that the 'Washington Eagle' is but a very large immature Bald Eagle, is hence gaining ground. 1917 *Birds of Amer.* II. 80 Bald Eagle. . . . Black Eagle; Gray Eagle; Washington Eagle. The last three names refer to the immature Bald Eagle.

+Washington elm. A large elm in Cambridge, Mass., under which Washington took command of the Continental army on July 3, 1775. — 1846 BROWNE *Trees Amer.* 510 The Washington Elm. In the city of Cambridge, in Massachusetts, there stands, in the vicinity of Harvard University, a beautiful elm, named after General Washington. 1872

HOLMES *Poet* 23 You know the 'Washington elm,' or if you do not, you had better rekindle your patriotism by reading the inscription.

+Washingtonian, *n.*

1. A believer in the political principles of George Washington; a Federalist. *Obs.*

1806 FESSENDEN *Democracy Unveiled* I. 142 The measures by the imps are made A handle, plausible no doubt, To turn the Washingtonians out. **1814** *Niles' Reg.* VI. 2/1 Is it believed, then, that those persons are 'federalists' or 'Washingtonians'?

2. A member of the Washington Temperance Society. *Obs.*

1842 *Spirit of Times* (Phila.) 15 July (Th.), At a soiree recently given some young ladies urged a dashing and spirited young fellow to join the Washingtonians. **1845** *Lowell Offering* V. 69 The Washingtonians found the poor inebriate, and persuaded him to sign the pledge. **1854** SIMMS *Southward Ho!* 218 Because thou art a Washingtonian, shall there be no wine?

3. One who lives in Washington, D.C.

1852 EASTMAN *Aunt Phillis's Cabin* 234 The beautiful prospect, to which Washingtonians are so much accustomed that they are too apt not to notice it. **1881** *Century Mag.* Nov. 88/1 He met with Washingtonians who knew the family and gave him news of them. **1893** *Harper's Mag.* April 677/2 There are no simple picnics now . . . held at the hospitable country house of some Washingtonian with rural tastes.

+Washingtonian, *a.* **1.** Of or pertaining to the Washington Temperance Society. *Obs.* **2.** Emanating from, or resembling qualities of, George Washington. *Obs.* — (1) **1842** *Knickerb.* XX. 298 The festival was conducted on the Washingtonian principle. **1845** S. M. FULLER *Woman in 19th Century* 36 Presidents of Washingtonian societies [are] no less away from home than presidents of conventions. **1845** *Lowell Offering* V. 84 A brighter and more benignant day has dawned upon the homes of New England, ushered in by the Washingtonian star. — (2) **1876** *Wide Awake* III. 137/2 The little fishing band was now sadly broken and lessened by one of the Washingtonian demands upon Brother Jonathan. **1889** *Advance* 28 Feb., The cultivation of Washingtonian patriotism and Washingtonian citizenship was not ever more timely than now.

+Washingtonianism. 1. The principles of the Washington Temperance Society. *Obs.* **2.** Zeal for perpetuating the memory of George Washington. *Obs.* — (1) **1845** *Lowell Offering* V. 58 The first course consisted of beautiful thoughts, sublime resolutions and noble purposes, served in vessels bearing the inscription of *Washingtonianism.* **1859** *Harper's Mag.* Jan. 278/1 When Washingtonianism swept over the Western country he joined the army of its converts. (2) **1852** *Ib.* July 266/2 We suffer a kind of intermittent Washingtonianism, which now and then shows a very fever of drawings, and of small subscriptions.

+Washington's birthday. The day, Feb. 22, upon which George Washington was born, celebrated as a bank or school holiday. — **1841** *Picayune* 21 Feb. 2/2 Washington's Birth Day. To-morrow will be the anniversary of the birth day of George Washington—a day hallowed in the remembrance of Americans. **1881** *Cimarron News* 17 Feb. 3/2 Washington's birthday will be observed by a grand ball. **1907** *St. Nicholas* July 862/2 It was on Washington's Birthday in Central Park . . . that I had my first glimpse of this beautiful bird.

+Washington thorn. (See quot. 1891.) — **1846** BROWNE *Trees* 280 [The] Washington Thorn . . . was first cultivated . . . in the District of Columbia. **1858** WARDER *Hedges & Evergreens* 30 Then I planted the Washington thorn and buckthorn. **1891** *Cent.* 6300/2 *Washington thorn, Crataegus cordata,* found in Virginia, and thence southward and westward. It was formerly widely planted for hedges, being disseminated from near Washington City.

∗Washing tub. A tub used in washing. — **1766** in Chalkley *Scotch-Irish Settlement Va.* I. 127, 1 washing tub, 1 cooler, 1 tin saucepan. **1812** *Niles' Reg.* III. 59/1 It will not much amaze us . . . if these people go out to fight the enemy in *washing tubs.* **1863** 'G. HAMILTON' *Gala-Days* 73 Women stood at their washing-tubs.

+Wash kettle. A large open pot or cauldron in which water is heated for washing purposes. — **1787** *Kentucky Gazette* 24 Nov. 2/3 Samuel Blair, Has for sale, . . . a Quantity of excellent . . . copper and brass wash kettles. **1836** CROCKETT *Exploits* 91 He was possessed of considerable address, and had brass enough in his face to make a wash-kettle. **1884** 'CRADDOCK' *Tenn. Mts.* 7 The pine-knots flamed and glistered under the great wash-kettle. **1924** RAINE *Land of Saddle-Bags* 10 At the edge of the branch just outside the picket fence is the big iron wash kettle and the 'battling' bench for the family laundry.

+Wash kitchen. A kitchen or room in which clothes are washed. {1909-} — **1836** GILMAN *Recoll.* (1838) 206 Preparations were made for the wedding, which she chose to have performed in the wash-kitchen instead of our parlour. **1847** in Stowe *Key* 97/1 Dr. Peter Porcher.—Was called in by the coroner's jury to examine Maria's body; found it in the wash-kitchen. **1853** FOWLER *Home for All* 90 A wash-kitchen for the rough work of the family is much needed in every house.

+Washlady. A washerwoman. Also *washer lady.* — **1882** SWEET & KNOX *Texas Siftings* 196 A 'culled wash lady' told her that the 'white woman what lived here wanted to hire a cook.' **1901** GREENOUGH & KITTREDGE *Words & Their Ways* 322 It is the courtesy of democracy . . . that brings about the results which amuse us in 'saleslady' or 'washerlady' or the 'gentleman' who sweeps the crossing. **1904** *Brooklyn Standard Union* 29 May 4 'Blanchisseuses,' what some folks here call 'washladies.'

Wash leather. Very soft, washable leather such as that made from the skin of the chamois. {1662-} Also attrib. and transf. — **1634** WINTHROP in R. C. Winthrop *Life J. Winthrop* II. 126 [Bring] the best Irish stockings and wash leather stockings. **1692** SEWALL *Letter-Book* I. 133 A pair (of) Wash-Leather Dear-skin Gloves. **1711** *Springfield Rec.* II. 41 Four pair of washleather Gloves at 3 s the Pair. **1825** *Columbian Centinel* 5 Jan. 4/5 S. H. Parker . . . has just received . . . a fresh supply of Wash Leather, suitable for Waistcoats and Drawers, Toweling [etc.]. **1861** WINTHROP *C. Dreeme* 31 You can breakfast on . . . wash-leather cakes.

+Washman. =WASHERMAN. *local.* — **1879** *Harper's Mag.* Nov. 894/2 We saw in turn the smoke of a smelting works, a China 'washman's' shanty, a derrick [etc.].

+Washoe. [Indian tribal name.] Illustrated in attrib. uses only. Designating things found in, or characteristic of, Nevada or of the Washoe district of that state: (see quot. 1877). — **1877** W. WRIGHT *Big Bonanza* 114 A queer genius thus described the donkey, called by everybody in that region, 'The Washoe Canary.' **1880** *Cimarron News & Press* 13 May 3/2 Washoe Picks, . . . Hammers and Gold pans at Carey's. **1896** SHINN *Story of Mine* 110 Not merchants these . . . but a brave, honest outdoor race whose huge Washoe wagons were the forerunners of the railroads.

+Washoe process. (See quot. 1909.) — **1890** *Cent.* 4253/3. **1909** WEBSTER 2307/1 *Washoe process,* . . . the process of treating silver ores by grinding in pans or tubs with the addition of mercury, and sometimes of chemicals such as blue vitriol and salt.

+Washoe zephyr. A strong west wind that blows in Nevada in the fall and spring. — **1872** 'MARK TWAIN' *Roughing It* 160 The 'Washoe Zephyr' . . . is a peculiarly Scriptural wind, in that no man knoweth 'whence it cometh.' **1877** W. WRIGHT *Big Bonanza* 106 The early settlers at Virginia made the acquaintance of the 'Washoe Zephyr' during this first winter.

Washout. {1876-}

+1. The washing away by heavy rains of a part of a road or railway.

1873 *Newton Kansan* 29 May 3/2 Owing to a wash out on the Cottonwood last Sunday night, we had no train from the east until Tuesday afternoon. **1884** *Boston Jrnl.* 22 April, The biggest washout that has ever been known on the Lake Champlain division of the Delaware and Hudson Railroad occurred last night. **1911** LINCOLN *Cap. Warren's Wards* 5 If we get to Provincetown without a wash-out we'll be lucky.

+2. A gully, gulch, or ravine resulting from erosion.

1877 CAMPION *On Frontier* 20 It was . . . seamed with deep narrow gullies, 'wash-outs' of rain storms. **1886** *Outing* VIII. 135/1, [I] slid down into a little washout that opened into a small ravine. **1900** DRANNAN *Plains & Mts.* 76 Right down there by . . . that wash-out, is where I intend to make my last fight. **1923** J. H. COOK *On Old Frontier* 70, I discovered that this band of horses was in the habit of drinking from a little pool located in the washout of an old creek bed.

+Wash pan. A pan used for washing out gold; a wash-basin. — **1857** BORTHWICK *3 Years in Calif.* 124 A 'prospector' goes with a pick and shovel, and a wash-pan. **1884** 'MARK TWAIN' *H. Finn* xxxvii, [We] scratched around and found an old tin washpan. **1919** HOUGH *Sagebrusher* ix, It's only the wash pan.

+Wash pitcher. A pitcher or ewer for the toilet. — **1852** STOWE *Uncle Tom* i, Eliza had upset the wash-pitcher. **1902** BELL *Hope Loring* 93 Lord . . . emptied half a dozen bottles of beer into his wash-pitcher. **1920** HOWELLS *Vacation of Kelwyns* 6 She had . . . often undergone the hardship of making Kelwyn hurry out untimely in the morning to fill the wash-pitcher.

+Washrag. A rag or cloth used in making one's toilet or in scrubbing — **1890** E. L. BYNNER *Begum's Daughter* iv, She employed the interval while her guests were at their luncheon in plying the wash-rag and comb. **1908** CALHOUN *Miss Minerva* 22 Aunt Cindy gave him [a scrubbing] with a hard washrag. **1923** WYATT *Invis. Gods* 21 The scrubwoman . . . was wringing the dripping screw of her tightly twisted washrag over her pail.

+Washroom.

1. A room in which things, usually clothes, are washed.

1806 *Mass. H. S. Coll.* 1 Ser. X. 77 They have usually two good rooms in front, bed-rooms, kitchen, wash-room, and other convenient apartments in the rear. **1853** FOWLER *Home for All* 168 By the side of this work-kitchen or wash-room and ice-room near the pantry is an excellent place for a milk-room. **1869** E. PUTNAM *Receipt Bk.* 319 For the wash-room, have a place for tubs. **1878** *Vermont Bd. Agric. Rep.* 79 At the end from the road were the press and wash rooms.

2. A lavatory.

1854 *Harper's Mag.* IX. 851/1 A gentleman in the wash-room said to the Captain of the boat, 'Can't you give me a clean towel, Captain?' **1890** LANGFORD *Vigilante Days* (1912) 438 Barnhardt fled to the washroom. **1908** S. E. WHITE *Riverman* 101 After freshening up in the marbled and boarded washroom, he hunted up Newmark.

+Wash sink. A sink or washbowl at which one washes. — **1857** *Lawrence (Kan.) Republican* 2 July 4 'Here are all the conveniences for washing,' said the landlord, stepping to a mahogany wash sink and raising the lid. **1878** 'MARK TWAIN' & WARNER *Gilded Age* 270 It was a small room, with a stove in the middle . . . and a wash-sink in one corner.

Washstand. 1. A tablelike piece of furniture accommodating the basin, pitcher, towel, etc., used by one in washing the hands and face. {1839-} **+2.** (See quotation.) — (1) **1830** *Collegian* 25 A chest, surmounted by a wash-stand, in the third [room]. **1851** MITCHELL *Dream*

Life 192 You can . . . take a peep into the broken bit of looking-glass over the wash-stand. **1890** CUSTER *Following Guidon* 253 The wash-stands were similarly constructed. **1922** PARRISH *Case & Girl* 229 The metal wash-stand gave him an inspiration; its upper strip was thin. **(2) 1909** WEBSTER 2307/1 *Wash stand*, . . . in stables, a place in the floor prepared so that carriages may be washed there and the water run off.

Wash still. (See quot. 1909.) — **1816** *Ann. 14th Congress* 2 Sess. 1204 A wash still is used of one hundred and twenty gallons. **1909** *Cent. Suppl.* 1277/1 *Wash still*, a still for the distillation of the original fermented liquor, as distinguished from one used to redistil the condensed product from the former.

Wash-up. {1869-} +The act of washing oneself. — **1887** HARTE *Millionaire & Devil's Ford* 176 You boys can go there for a general wash-up. **1917** MATHEWSON *Sec. Base Sloan* 64 [They] dropped from the car and went back to the station for a wash-up.

* **Washwoman.** A woman who takes in washing; a washerwoman. ('Now *U.S.' O.E.D.*) — **1774** FITHIAN *Journal* I. 270, I gave to our Wash-Woman some old Linen. **1835** INGRAHAM *South-West* II. 262 An old negro wash-woman standing by. **1877** HALE *G. T. T.* 74 You may paint my portrait, or that dear old black wash-woman's.

Wastebasket. A waste-paper basket. {1850-} 'Now chiefly *U.S.*' (*O.E.D.*). — **1860** HOLMES *Professor* 228 We fling a nameless scribbler's impertinences into our waste-baskets. **1880** CABLE *Grandissimes* 214 It was a paper Sylvestre had picked out of a waste-basket. **1923** VANCE *Baroque* 38 Half a dozen essays had been consigned serially to the waste-basket.

* **Waste land.** Uncultivated or uninhabited land, freq., in colonial times, reserved for woodland or for other common purposes. — **1640** *Hartford Land Distrib.* 20 One parcell . . . abuttinge vpon the Great River on the west . . . & on the wast land on the East. **1654** *Conn. Rec.* I. 262 This Courte giues Mr. Will: Goodwin libberty to make vse of . . . Timber from the waste land belonginge to the Country. **1708** *Boston Rec.* 46 There has been dispute . . . relateing to the Wast Lands at Brantree. **1789** MORSE *Amer. Geog.* 249 Connecticut has no waste lands. **1866** *Rep. Indian Affairs* 285 There should be set apart a tract large enough to give a square mile to every four persons, as there is much waste land in this nation.

+**Wasteway.** A channel or outlet for surplus water. — **1882** THAYER *From Log-Cabin* 184 There was a waste-way just ahead. **1884** *Harper's Mag.* Sept. 621/2 Above these . . . is a wasteway . . . over which the surplus water can pour should the supply exceed the capacity of the dam.

Wasty, *a.* {1904-} +**1.** Wasteful. *Obs.* +**2.** 'Resembling cotton-waste' (*Cent.*). — **(1) 1823** COOPER *Pioneers* xxx, I won't have his wasty ways brought into my hut. **1839** TOWNSEND *Narrative* 238 We have now abandoned the 'wasty ways' which so disgraced us when game was abundant. **(2) 1886** *U.S. Consular Rep.* XVIII. 470 The wool becomes impoverished on account of the heat and dust, and is very tender, with a dry, wasty top.

Watap. Also **watape, wattap,** etc. [Can. Fr. from Amer. Indian.] (See quot. 1910.) — [**1789** A. MACKENZIE *Voyage from Montreal* (1801) 37*n.*, Watape is the name given to the divided roots of the spruce-fir.] **1806** LEWIS in *L. & Clark Exped.* (1905) IV. 84 We were visited by eight Cla[t]sops and Chinnooks from whom we purchased . . . two hats made of waytape and white cedar bark. *c***1836** CATLIN *Indians* II. 138 [The bark canoes of the Chippeways] are . . . sewed together, with roots of the tamarack, which they call *wat-tap*, [so] that they are water-tight. **1846** MCKENNEY *Memoirs* I. 102 The skin of the snake was . . . fastened by a root of the red cedar, called wattap, to a lock of the captor's hair. **1910** HODGE, etc. *Amer. Indians* II. 921/1 *Watap*, roots of the pine, spruce, tamarack, etc., used to sew birch-bark for canoes and other purposes.

* **Watch,** *n.*

1. In Colonial America, a body of watchmen who patrolled the streets of a town at night.

1633 *Plymouth Laws* 33 The Govr. and Councell of Assistants [shall] hire a watch & charge it upon the whole colony. **1662** *Boston Rec.* 8 The Towne hath beene many times betrusted with a watche consistinge of youths. **1714** SEWALL *Diary* II. 424 My son preaches the first Sermon after the New Watch being set up. **1787** *Baltimore Rec.* 60 This Board will meet on the first Monday in April to Settle with [the] Watch and then discharge them. **1808** *Amer. Law Journal* I. 73 Parker being one of the city watch, she used to hear him rap with his stick at the door to awaken his family.

***2.** A small instrument for showing the time, of a size convenient for being carried in a pocket.

1644 *Conn. Rec.* I. 471, I doe further giue to my sonne Samuell . . . my watch. **1677** in Earle *Sabbath* 77 [E. Needham, who died in 1677, left a] Striking clock, a watch, and a Larum that dus not Strike. **1735** HEMPSTEAD *Diary* 296, I got my watch rectified & a new Christial. **1771** FRANKLIN *Autobiog.* 260, I was better dress'd than ever while in his service, having a genteel new suit from head to foot, a watch [etc.]. **1815** *N. Amer. Rev.* I. 334 There is hardly any man, young or old, rich or poor, who does not own a watch of some kind. **1891** WELCH *Recoll. 1830-40* 180 The watch was carried in the fob of the trousers from which a heavy 'fob chain' depended. **1907** *St. Nicholas* June 721/2 He took from his pocket the heavy silver watch.

3. *attrib.* and *comb.* **a.** In sense 1 and also in the more general sense of the state of being awake or on the watch.

1645 *New Haven Col. Rec.* 204 This watchm[aste]r is to be appojnted yearly. **1711** *N.C. Col. Rec.* I. 783 [Our powder] will be as proper for their use, in their Signals, Watch guns and Salutes. **1835** AUDUBON *Ornith. Biog.* III. 55 The watch-note of the male [wood duck] . . . resembles *hoe-ĕĕk*. **1844** LEE & FROST *Oregon* 247 Here a watch-night had been held at the close of the year, and a happy state of religious feeling prevailed. **1852** *Knickerb.* XXXIX. 403 He will pay it off by riding the watch-officers. **1863** A. D. WHITNEY *F. Gartney* xxviii, The night-watchman . . . had left . . . but a few minutes, going his silent round . . . , and recording his faithfulness by the half-hour pin upon the watch-clock. **1866** GREGG *Life in Army* 222 As Methodists . . . we kept up the time-honored custom of watch-meeting, on the last evening of the year. **1866** W. REID *After War* 341, I run back to the watch-tank and waited. **1881** *Harper's Mag.* Oct. 690/2 If this watch ground be a runway in the woods or on some narrow stream, then the hunter must have a short and quick aim. **1887** GOODE, etc. *Fisheries* V. II. 229 The divisions of the crew are known as the starboard and larboard watches, commanded respectively by the first and second mates or the second and third mates, who are known as 'watch-headers.'

b. In sense 2 with *back, bracelet, charm*, etc.

1773 *Penna. Gazette* 16 June Suppl. 2/2 Clock and watch main-springs, watch-glasses, watch fusee chains, . . . clock and watch hands [etc.]. **1790** *Penna. Packet* 7 May 3/3 Imported and to be Sold by John Wood, Clock and Watch Maker, . . . watch magnifying glasses, . . . watch keys and steel chains, watch seals, . . . all kinds of clock and watch files. **1818** FLINT *Lett. from Amer.* 62 [There are in Pittsburgh] 5 Silversmiths and Watch Repairers. **1828** *Yankee* May 147/3 There have been four watch-drawings in this place within two months. **1867** *Atlantic Mo.* Feb. 202/2 I used to gild his watch-backs for him. **1890** *Ann Arbor Record* 13 March, A drawing of the first watch club organized in the City, was held at Watts' jewelry store, . . . and George Krauth became the possessor of a $30 watch which cost him but $1. **1896** *Godey's Mag.* April 449/1 The watch bracelet, with its setting of substantial leather, is a convenient adjunct to the cycler. **1898** CANFIELD *Maid of Frontier* 15 [How's] the little baby I gave the watch-charm to?

* **Watch,** *v.* +*To watch out*, to be on one's guard; to take care. — **1845** HOOPER *Simon Suggs' Adv.* 115 He determined therefore to 'watch out.' **1890** *Harper's Mag.* Sept. 557/2, I told Hiram to watch out. **1903** *N.Y. Sun* 16 Nov. 4 We advise the golfers to watch out, or else they may find themselves locked up.

Watch bill. A bill or halberd for the use of a watchman. {1665-} — **1661** *Essex Probate Rec.* I. 341 A sword & ammunition & a watchbill & a chopping knife. **1701** *Boston Rec.* 7 The Rounds [shall] walk with watch bills.

Watch boat. A boat used for patrol duty. {1789-} — **1778** *N.H. Hist. Soc. Coll.* IX. 368 Watch Boats being ordered constantly to Patrol near the Shore to prevent a Supprise. **1891** *Scribner's Mag.* X. 471 Extra watch-boats are employed if necessary.

Watch box. A small building used to shelter a man or men on watch; a sentry box. {1699-} — **1704** *N.H. Hist. Soc. Coll.* III. 54 Mr. Andrew Gardner, minister of Lancaster, coming down from the watch-box in the night, in a darkish colored gown, was mistaken for an Indian. **1748** J. NORTON *Redeemed Captive* 8 The Serj. . . . sent two Men up into the Watch-Box. **1835** in *S. Lit. Messenger* IV. 90/2 [There are] thousands of watch boxes for people to break their heads at every corner. **1878** PINKERTON *Strikers* 317 Three of the incendiaries then went to the watch-box at the end of the bridge.

Watch-burner. One who steals watches. *slang. Obs.* — **1849** *Cincinnati Commercial* 12 Dec. 1/6 Robberies. . . . A grown up St. Giles, formerly a young watch burner, . . . was caught at the cabin under suspicious circumstances.

+**Watch care.** Watchful care. {1908} Also *after watch care*, the care given someone *after* a certain event. — **1845** *Indiana Mag. Hist.* XXIII. 152 Very much, also, depends on the kind of preachers and leaders, who have the after watch-care of the persons that are brought into the church. **1866** GREGG *Life in Army* 67, I have often experienced the watch-care of one who is nigh at hand to help and save. **1896** *Peterson Mag.* March 253/1 The years of watch care which she had given to the child left in her charge.

Watch chain. A chain attached to a watch and usually secured at one end to a buttonhole. {1739-} Also attrib. — **1759** *Newport Mercury* 26 June 4/3 Imported . . . and to be sold by Jacob Richardson, . . . Gun-hammers, Gun-Locks, Watch Chains and Seals. **1773** *Penna. Gazette* 16 June Suppl. 2/2 Silver and steel watch chains. **1840** MATHEWS *Politicians* I. ii, I shall have another seal put to the bunch at the end of my watch-chain. **1876** WARNER *Gold of Chickaree* 189 Will you fasten this to your watch chain—to please me? **1907** ANDREWS *Recoll.* 169 A number of the prisoners . . . [made] out of peach stones, watch chain ornaments.

Watch coat. A warm overcoat of the type used by seamen or soldiers on watch. {1719-} Also attrib. — **1705** *Boston News-Letter* 10 Dec. 4/2 David Thomas Souldier, a Welsh-man, . . . hath on a new white Cape cloth Watch Coat. **1758** *Memoirs of Last War* 14 The Men employed in the Fishery . . . [have] each a Blanket, Watch Coat, Rug, Pea-Jacket. **1804** CLARK in *Lewis & C. Exped.* VI. (1905) 278 Necessary stores [include] . . . 1 Watch Coat, 2 pr ox hide Shoes. *c***1820** in *Knickerb.* XXIX. 470 Then generous from his watchcoat poke A jug of cider-brandy took. **1851** MELVILLE *Moby-Dick* 172 In cold weather you may carry your house aloft with you, in the shape of a watch-coat.

Watchcry. A slogan. {1882-} — **1837** *S. Lit. Messenger* III. 74/2 This indeed has now become the watch-cry of party. **1850** in A. C. Cole *Whig Party in So.* (1913) 169 'Tell the plotters to assemble elsewhere!' became the watch-cry.

+Watch crystal. A piece of glass used to protect the face of a watch. — **1873** BEADLE *Undevel. West* 542 The post trader at Defiance had a quart or so of these, which looked to be like those used as watch crystals. **1883** *Century Mag.* Sept. 732/2 Some of the shallow ones [glass jars] are like six-quart milk-pans, and the sizes of the others lessen to the minimum of a watch crystal.

Watchdog.

1. A dog kept chiefly to guard a house. {1610-}

1854 M. J. HOLMES *Tempest & Sunshine* 242 Fanny, who was accustomed to the savage watch-dogs of Kentucky, sprang back in terror. **1906** PRINGLE *Rice Planter* 404, I have been quite alone in the house and yard without MacDuff, my stanch little watch-dog.

+2. *Watchdog of the treasury,* or variant: A person, usually a member of Congress, who consistently tries to check the expenditure of public money.

1853 *Congress. Globe* 3 March 1141/1 If I were to select the man in this House who was the most faithful watchdog over the Treasury of the United States. I would select the gentleman from Alabama. **1869** *Ib.* 22 Jan. 532/1, I admire the ambition which seems to inspire him to be the 'watchdog of the Treasury.' **1872** *Chicago Tribune* 20 Nov. 1/6 In Congress he was the watch-dog of the Treasury. **1884** *Boston Jrnl.* 20 Sept., Cleveland . . . gave a promise of his ability to become the watch-dog of the United States Treasury. **1897** *Congress. Rec.* 8 July 2517/1 He became generally known as 'the watchdog of the Treasury.' **1913** LA FOLLETTE *Autobiog.* 52 Holman was always objecting—the watch-dog of the treasury.

*Watcher. 1. One who keeps watch by a sick person or a corpse. **+2.** One who watches at the polls on election day to assure honesty in the voting, or to make sure that nothing improper is done to the prejudice of the party which he represents. — **(1) 1716** SEWALL *Diary* III. 91 The Watcher, Mrs. Welsteed, and the Nurse had much adoe to turn her. **1726** *N.H. Probate Rec.* II. 285 My will is that . . . each of the watchers have one pr. of glov s. **1860** HOLMES *Professor* 342 Ask him if he don't want any watchers. I don't mind setting up any more 'n' a cat-owl. **(2) 1911** *Okla. Session Laws* 3 Legisl. 82 The challenger, pool book holder and watcher shall perform duties as provided by law, governing any general election.

Watch face. A watch dial. — **1794** *Mass. Spy* 1 May 4/2 Ready for Sale . . . Beautiful enamelled Clock and Watch Faces. **1893** *Scribner's Mag.* June 725/1 He felt for his matches and struck one to look at his watch-face.

+Watch fob. A short chain, ribbon, or other ornamental appendage to a watch. — **1864** *Hist. North-Western Soldiers' Fair* 124 [Donations include] 1 watch fob. **1882** *Century Mag.* April 884/2 The typical Southerner . . . wore a broad-brimmed Panama hat and a great watch-fob. **1901** HEGAN *Mrs. Wiggs* 80 Here's yer grandpa's watch-fob.

Watch guard. A watch chain or similar device for securing a watch. {1834-} — **1838** HAWTHORNE *Notebooks* (1932) 29 He has . . . a gold watch guard, with a seal appended. **1884** 'MARK TWAIN' *H. Finn* xliii, Tom's most well now, and got his bullet around his neck on a watch-guard for a watch.

*Watch-house.

*1. A house or building serving as the headquarters of a town watch. Now hist.

In Colonial times this was often a meetinghouse or a small structure attached to a meetinghouse.

1639 *Watertown Rec.* I. 1. 6 Ordered yt the Meetinghouse is appointed for a watchhouse to the vse of the Towne. **1640** *New Haven Col. Rec.* 34 The Ma[ste]r is to take care that one man alwayes stand sentinell in a sentinell posture without the watch house. **1678** *Springfield Rec.* II. 138 It was voted & agreed that the watch house to ye New meeting house should be, or serve instead of a schoole house. **1723** *Boston Rec.* 175 There [shall] be forth with five watch houses at the Least in the Most Sutable places of the Town. **1891** EARLE *Sabbath* 5 The meeting-house was at first a watch-house, from which to keep vigilant lookout for any possible approach of hostile or sneaking Indians.

attrib. **1799** BENTLEY *Diary* II. 316 Visited the watch house point upon which was buried the first person from the Hospital built on the point near it opposite to Beverly.

2. A house used by municipal night watchmen or police for the temporary custody of persons under arrest. {1716-1845}

1705 *Boston News-Letter* 3 Sept. 2/2 Search all Houses that are suspected to Entertain such Servants or Slaves contrary to Law, and finding any such . . . restrain them in the Common Prison, Watch House, or Constables House till morning. *a*1821 BIDDLE *Autobiog.* 8 They were taking us to their watch-house when we . . . made our escape. **1857** HAMMOND *Northern Scenes* 119, [I] came near being taken to the watch-house for smashing a window in the opposite block.

+3. In various special senses: (see quotations).

1775 ROMANS *Nat. Hist. Florida* App. p. lxxii, You will see . . . a watch-house (nick-named a fort). **1836** in *Jrnl. Southern History* I. 353 The Tavern at which I staid during the night is called a Watch House. It is immediately on the bank of the River, and keeps, as I had been told, a look out for Boats for Passengers. **1881** INGERSOLL *Oyster Industry* 249 *Watch House.*—A shanty built on the shore, or near the planted oyster beds, from which they may be guarded.

Watch key. A key used for winding a watch. {1723-} — **1773** *Penna. Gazette* 16 June Suppl. 2/2 Steel and brass watch keys. **1838** COOPER *Homeward B.* xxx, The mate, [was] diligently thumbing his watch-key. **1865** *Atlantic Mo.* April 458/1 Still Reuben looked . . . at the guard-chain . . . with a glittering watch-key upon it.

Watchmaker. One whose trade is the making of watches. {1630-} — **1708** *Boston News-Letter* 5 April 2/2 Isaac Webb Watch-maker and Clock-maker . . . is now Removed over-against the West-End of the said Town-House. **1808** *Centinel* 23 Nov. (Th.), One of the Embargoroons came into a Yankee watch maker's shop. **1892** *York County Hist. Rev.* 54 Alfred Cartwright, Watchmaker and Jeweler, Opposite Baptist Church, Main St.

*Watchman.

*1. One of a body of men employed to patrol the streets of a town at night. *Obsolescent.*

1636 *Watertown Rec.* I. 1. 3 Ordered . . . every man that is Souldier or watchman to come at his appointed time. **1723** *Boston Selectmen* 113 The Watch men are directed to walke Silently and Slowly, now and then to Stand Still and Listen. **1771** *Phila. Ordinances* (1812) 39 Watchmen . . . are also hereby empowered . . . to apprehend all night-walkers. **1839** BRIGGS *H. Franco* II. 168 An ivory-handled bowie-knife was found by my side by the watchman who picked me up. **1865** *Atlantic Mo.* June 678/2 She was found by the watchman on his midnight beat.

2. One employed to guard private property, esp. at night. {1600}

1704 *Boston News-Letter* 8 May 2/1 The Watchman on the Top of his House, not knowing who it was, call'd out, Stand. **1845** *Lowell Offering* V. 109n., The print-yard watchman's bell—that often rings. **1877** *Harper's Mag.* March 605/1, I secured the position of watchman at our store every other Sunday night. **1890** *Congress. Rec.* 4 Aug. 8123/2 On this list there are firemen, watchmen, elevator men.

+Watchout. *On the watchout,* on the lookout. — **1884** 'MARK TWAIN' *H. Finn* iv, I never tried to do anything, but just poked along low-spirited and on the watch-out. [**1887** *Nation* 27 Oct. 331/3 *Branch,* to designate a brook, is common in Ohio; so is *cavort,* . . . *trot-line* and *watchout.*] **1902** HARBEN *A. Daniel* 16 Peter Mosely is a man on the watch-out fer rail soft snaps.

Watch paper. A round piece of paper or other material fitted into the lid of a watch and decorated with a picture or design, or inscribed with words. {1777-} — **1858** HOLMES *Autocrat* 245 The watch-paper had been pink once, and had a faint tinge still. **1872** *Atlantic Mo.* Feb. 179 She had given him a watch-paper, cut and painted with her own lovely hands. **1884** *Harper's Mag.* July 249/1 A 'watch paper'—that is to say, the portrait of some fair one made of the shape and size to wear inside the lid of the 'warming-pans' of the period.

Watch pocket. A pocket placed in a garment for holding a watch; also, a pocket or pouch for safeguarding a watch, esp. at night. {1837-} Also attrib. — **1852** *Harper's Mag.* March 576/2 Every waistcoat has a little watch-pocket. **1861** *Vanity Fair* 19 Jan. 26/1 Her light brown curls were straying over his vest, on the watch-pocket side. **1864** *Hist. North-Western Soldiers' Fair* 74 [Donations include] 1 watch pocket, 4 lamp mats. **1890** HOWELLS *Boy's Town* 8 The deer . . . put one of the forelegs in at the watch-pocket.

Watch ribbon, Watch riband. A ribbon used in the same way as a watch chain. {1834-} — **1829** SANDS *Writings* II. 140 She transformed every straggling male customer who wanted to cheapen a pair of white gloves, or a watch-ribband, into a Romeo. **1850** S. WARNER *Wide, Wide World* xxv, At the end of a showy watch-ribbon hung some showy seals. **1861** *Vanity Fair* 26 Jan. 45/1 Whither could Fashion have wandered for the stupendous watch-ribands growing so much in favor of late?

Watch room. A room for the use of watchmen. — **1850** *Annual Sci. Discovery* 73 On the top of the structure [a lighthouse] is the watch-room, and lantern, or light-room. **1883** 'MARK TWAIN' *Life on Miss.* xxxi, From the ring a wire led to the ceiling, and thence to a bell in the watch-room.

Watch seal. One of the seals formerly worn as attachments to a watch chain. {1798-} — **1774** FITHIAN *Journal I.* 160 Bought a watch-seal. **1783** *Lowell Offering* IV. 83 'How d'ye do, Fanny?' asked a great fat man, with huge watch seals. **1872** EGGLESTON *End of World* 65 A man . . . a-weightin' hisself down with pewter watch-seals, gold-washed.

Watch string. A string or cord, usually of silk, used as a watch guard. {1789} — **1754** *S.C. Gazette* 27 June 2/2 Just imported, . . . silk watch strings, none-so-pretties, star and scarlet gartering. **1771** A. G. WINSLOW *Diary* 5, I intend to send Nancy Mackky . . . the fag end of Harry's watch string.

+Watch stuffer. One who induces an ignorant or gullible person to pay him a high price for a cheap or worthless watch. *slang.* — **1840** in *Amer. Speech* XVI. 231 A notorious watch stuffer . . . undertook yesterday to cheat and defraud Mr. Joseph Thompson . . . by palming off upon him a worthless brass watch as a gold one. **1859** A. VAN BUREN *Sojourn in South* 17, I noticed on the doors and walls of the Central depot, Chicago, this placard: 'Beware of pick-pockets and watch-stuffers!'

+Watch stuffing. The practice of selling cheap or worthless watches at high prices to ignorant purchasers. *slang.* — **1840** in *Amer. Speech* XVI. 231 More Watch Stuffing.—One would suppose so many cases of this description had been published that [etc.]. **1851** HALL *Manhattaner* 182 Gambling on the western waters, like watch-stuffing in goodly Manhattan, has come to be understood. **1860** *Atlantic Mo.* Dec. 671 Dog-smudging, ring-dropping, watch-stuffing . . . are all terms which have more or less outgrown the bounds of their Alsatia of Thieves' Latin and are known of men.

*__Watchtower.__ A tower at which watch was kept against attack, and which often could be used for signaling the approach of danger. Also fig. — 1766 STORK *Acct. E. Florida* 35 At the north end of this island is a watch-tower, or look-out, built of white stone. 1836 *S. Lit. Messenger* II. 764 We must ever be on the watch-tower ready to give the alarm. 1881 *Ore. State Jrnl.* 1 Jan. 6/4 No danger-signal gleamed from the watch-tower upon the bridge.

*__Water, n.__

I. 1. Fictitious capital created by watering stock. {1894–}

1883 *Nation* 8 Nov. 384/2 It is the dread of 'water' which is now keeping the foreign investor out of Wall Street. 1903 E. JOHNSON *Railway Transportation* 82 In general, non-dividend stocks stand for water instead of real investment.

*__2.__ *To take water*, +to recede, retreat, or back down from a position or undertaking. *colloq.*

1853 BALDWIN *Flush Times* 275 'If it please your honor, I believe *I will take water*' (a common expression, signifying that the person using it would take a nonsuit). 1880 N. BROOKS *Fairport Nine* 73 Jo immediately presented arms, having gained his point, which was to make the captain 'take water,' as the boys would say. 1891 C. ROBERTS *Adrift Amer.* 200 The fellow, who was really a coward, though nearly twice as big as myself, took water at once.

3. *To go in the water*, +to be baptized as a religious convert. *colloq.*

1863 E. W. Pearson *Lett. Port Royal* 145 Katrine is 'going in the water.'

II. *attrib.* and *comb.* *__4.__ Designating vessels for containing or ladling water.

1708 *Boston News-Letter* 15 March 2/2 Stollen on Monday the first Currant out of a Gentlemans House in Boston, . . . three water pouches or buckets. 1865 *Nation* I. 13 Our company got orders to fill their water-canteens. 1881 *Rep. Indian Affairs* 406 Dippers, water, 1-quart, retinned, long handles, riveted. 1893 *Scribner's Mag.* June 713/1 Soup is cooked in great water-boilers. 1905 PHILLIPS *Social Secretary* 103 She seemed to be hanging to his words like a thirsty bird to a water-pan. 1907 ANDREWS *Recoll.* 168 Our plates and water-cups were of tin.

*__5.__ Designating areas covered by water.

1711 in *Amer. Speech* 409/2 Begining at a marked Stooping white Oak. . . . Standing in a water Slash by ye road side. 1855 MAURY *Phys. Geog. Sea* 185 Now suppose the water-basins which hold the lakes to be over a thousand fathoms . . . deep. 1857 HAMMOND *Northern Scenes* 146 The season for moose hunting along the water pastures, was nearly over.

6. Designating persons and things connected in some way with city or other governmental control of the water supply.

1834 *New York Laws* 451 The governor shall nominate . . . five persons, to be known as the water commissioners for the city of New-York, . . . to examine and consider all matters relative to supplying the city of New-York with . . . pure and wholesome water. 1843 'CARLTON' *New Purchase* I. 200 With a calabash at the end of a proper pole Aunt Nancy could dip as from an artificial reservoir!—and all without a water tax! 1847 *Ass. Aldermen N.Y. Proc.* 31 Resolution removing Jesse Brush from the office of Water Purveyor. 1849 *Act to Amend Charter of City of N.Y.* 11 There shall be a bureau in this department for the collection of the revenues derived from the sale of the water, and the chief officer thereof, shall be called the 'Water Register.' 1853 *Inaugural Addresses Boston Mayors* II. 22 A subject which possesses . . . interest to every water taker and tax payer in the City . . . [is] wastefulness in the use of water. 1896 SHINN *Story of Mine* 81 Water claims and mill sites were taken up almost as soon as work had fairly begun on the Comstock. 1898 ATHERTON *Californians* 63 Teddy groans and tells me that his water bill is four hundred dollars a month.

*__7.__ In the specific names of plants that grow in the water or in marshy places.

Only a selection of examples is given. See also the separate entries below.

1850 *New Eng. Farmer* II. 109 The Water Andromeda is a low evergreen shrub, found in this vicinity, on the borders of Cedar Pond. 1818 DARBY *Emigrant's Guide* 80 The most important vegetable productions [include]: . . . *Gleditsia monosperma*, Water honey locust. 1897 *Kissimmee* (Fla.) *Valley* 3 March 2/3 The water hyacinth were not killed by the cold, as reported, and are just as much of an obstruction as ever. 1818 *Mass. H. S. Coll.* 2 Ser. VIII. 170 In August the eye is gratified with . . . the inflated, pale and water lobelias. 1853 SIMMS *Sword & Distaff* (1854) 93 The other is . . . somewhere among them water-myrtle and willow bushes. 1806 CLARK in *Lewis & C. Exped.* V. (1905) 110, I observe here . . . water penerial (pennyroyal), elder, coalts foot [etc.]. 1818 DARBY *Emigrant's Guide* 33 [Among] the most common timber trees found in the basin of the Mobile [is] . . . *Pinus taeda*, Loblolly, or water pine. 1785 MARSHALL *Amer. Grove* 122 *Quercus rubra ramosissima*, Water Red Oak, . . grows most naturally by creek sides, or in low wet places. 1672 JOSSELYN *New Eng. Rarities* 42 Water Plantane, here called Water-suckleaves. c1730 CATESBY *Carolina* I. 60 The Water-Tupelo . . . has a large trunk, especially near the ground, and grows very tall.

*__8.__ In the specific names of animals that live in or about the water.

Only a selection of examples is given. See also the separate entries below.

1884 GOODE, etc. *Fisheries* I. 199 The Spotted Sand Flounder, *Lophopsetta maculata*, . . . [is] variously known along the coast as Water Flounder, Window-pane, and Daylight. 1842 *Nat. Hist. N.Y., Zoology* I. 38 The Water Mink, is much larger [than the mountain mink], and of a chestnut red. 1781–2 JEFFERSON *Notes Va.* (1788) 77 Water pelican of the Missisipi, whose pouch holds a peck. 1859 BARTLETT 502 *Water-Dogs*, . . . sometimes called Water-puppies and Ground-puppies. 1864 WEBSTER 1497/2 *Water-rabbit*, . . . an American rabbit (*Lepus aquaticus*), found in Mississippi and Louisiana, and having the peculiarity of swimming and diving. 1832 WILLIAMSON *Maine* I. 159 The *Roach* . . . has been called the 'water-sheep['] for its simplicity. 1867 *Amer. Naturalist* I. 328 This species connects the Water-boatman with the Water-skaters, or Gerris, a familiar insect. 1889 *Harper's Mag.* Sept. 573/2 The clams, the water-skippers, were his nearest friends. 1881 *Amer. Naturalist* XV. 483, I send you by express a number of 'water-weevils' preserved in alcohol.

9. In special combinations.

Water Baptist, =BAPTIST 1; *w. campaign*, ?a fishing party; *w. cloud*, a rain cloud; *w. connection*, a section of a transportation route which must be traveled by water; *w. dumpling*, =DOUGHBOY 1; *w.-finder*, one who locates or endeavors to locate underground streams or water sources; *w.-finding fork*, a forked bough or twig used by a water-finder; *w. freight*, a means of transportation by water; *w. lick*, a moist or wet salt lick; *w. mirage*, a mirage or deceptive appearance of water; *w. paint*, a wash made by mixing powdered pigment in water, kalsomine; *w. prairie*, (see quotation); *w.-reading*, the art of detecting the characteristics of a stretch of water from its surface appearances; *w. sawmill*, a sawmill driven by water power; *w. scrape*, a hard journey over desert country; *w. set*, a water pitcher and accompanying glasses; *w. slip*, a narrow stretch of water; *w. soldier* {c1759}, a marine; *w. thief*, (see quotation).

1723 *Amer. Wkly. Mercury* 12 Feb. 4/2 All serious Persons, whether . . . Water-Baptists, or People called Quakers, . . . may advise with the said Person at his Lodgings. 1751 *Boston Ev. Post* 23 Sept., A number of gentlemen were out upon a Water-Campaign a few Days ago. 1869 J. R. BROWNE *Adv. Apache Country* 429 The only other instance known to me of the bursting of a water-cloud with such disastrous consequences occurred about four years ago. 1851 CIST *Cincinnati* 312 Then comes the Baltimore road, . . . to connect with this city, in almost a direct line, and without any water connection. 1843 *Amer. Pioneer* II. 153, I got a dough-boy or water-dumpling, and proceeded. 1883 *Harper's Mag.* Oct. 708/2 By trade he is a well-digger, but to this commonplace occupation he has added the more unusual profession of water-finder. *Ib.*, I spent . . . many hours sauntering about with the water-finding fork in my hands. 1892 *Vt. Agric. Rep.* XII. 121 Cheap water freights . . . may be obtained on the lake to the north. 1780 in *Travels Amer. Col.* 652 The Buffalo lick in No 2 is a water lick at the foot of a hill. 1848 ROBINSON *Santa Fe Exped.* 17 Water-mirage appears, but no water; and last and worst the dreaded Sirocco or hot wind blows. 1884 'MARK TWAIN' *H. Finn* xvii, sometimes they wash them [*sc.*, bricks] over with red water-paint. 1871 DE VERE 125 Those vast inland plains, known farther North as *salt* and *water* prairies, . . . [are] covered with a thick incrustation or nitrous efflorescence, known as *tesquite*, so as to give them the appearance of a large motionless lake. 1875 'MARK TWAIN' *Old Times* iii. 51 Mr. Bixby seemed to think me far enough advanced to bear a lesson on water-reading. 1831 PECK *Guide* 318 Vandalia contains . . . one water saw mill, one ox mill, one horse mill, and two schools. 1844 GREGG *Commerce of Prairies* I. 70 The whole party was busy in preparing for the 'water scrape,' as those droughty drives are very appropriately called by prairie travellers. 1904 *Century Mag.* Feb. 540/2 The many patches of color were subdued—a red table-cloth, a water-set of blue glass and a vase of paper roses. 1796 in *Amer. Speech* XV. 409/2 To four Chesnuts in the head of a deep Wallow by a water slip. 1861 F. Moore *Rebellion Rec.* I. III. 43 Three companies from Louisiana arrived today, also a hundred water soldiers (marines) from New Orleans. 1884 *Nat. Museum Bul.* No. 27, 778 Bung-bucket or water-thief. . . . Used instead of a pump for drawing drinking-water from the bung-hole of a cask.

*__Water, v.__

+**1.** *tr.* To pack (a jury). *Obs.*

1792 BELKNAP *Hist. New Hampshire* III. 256 The practice of watering the jury was familiarly known to those persons who had business in the Law.

+**2.** To supply (an engine) with water. Also with *up*.

1870 in De Vere 359, I question if it be wise in running a railroad to water anything but the engine. 1898 HAMBLEN *Gen. Manager's Story* 234 The onlookers [jeered] at the awkward attempts of the new men, to get the few remaining dead engines watered and fired-up. 1901 MERWIN & WEBSTER *Calumet 'K'* 203 One hot day after watering up the engine him and the conductor went off to get a drink.

3. To increase the nominal capital of an enterprise by issuing additional shares of (stock) without investing more money in the business. {1883–}

1870 MEDBERY *Men Wall St.* 138 Watering a stock, is the hydraulic artifice employed by modern managers to double the quantity of a stock without improving its quality. 1881 *Nation* XXXII. 434 He does not 'mean to be understood as saying' that a corporation can 'water' its stock. **1889** 'MARK TWAIN' *Conn. Yankee* 335, I do not approve of watering stock, but . . . you can water a gift as much as you want to.

+4. To put (logs) into the water for transport.
1877 *Lumberman's Gazette* 24 May, There have been 257,000,000 feet of logs watered on the various branches of the Muskegon.

***Water adder.** +Any one of various American snakes, esp. *Natrix sipedon*, which live in or frequent fresh water. (Cf. WATER MOCCASIN, WATER SNAKE.) — **1784** CUTLER in *Life & Corr.* I. 98 In [the] river we saw a very large snake swimming, which we supposed was either a black snake or a water adder. **1839** STORER *Mass. Reptiles* 228 The water adder . . . is frequently killed at Cambridge, four feet and more in length. **1899** *Animal & Plant Lore* 86 The water-adder . . . carries a poisonous sting in its tail.

+**Water arum.** =CALLA I. — **1817–8** EATON *Botany* (1822) 214 Water arum . . . grows in wet places. *a***1862** THOREAU *Maine Woods* 310 The characteristic flowers in *swamps* were: *Rubus triflorus* (dwarf raspberry), *Calla palustris* (water-arum) [etc.]. **1919** STURTEVANT *Notes on Edible Plants* 125 Water Arum. Water Dragon. . . . The rootstocks of this plant yield eatable starch.

+**Water ash.** **a.** Any one of several American ashes. **b.** =BOX ELDER I. — **1709** LAWSON *Carolina* 93 The Water-Ash is brittle. *a*1797 in Imlay *Western Territory* (ed. 3) 144 The sugar maple-trees are generally found mixed with the beech, hemlock, white and water ash. **1819** E. DANA *Geogr. Sk.* 171 The soil is . . . thickly covered with timber; such as various species of oak and water ash. **1892** APGAR *Trees Northern U.S.* 124 *Fraxinus platycarpa*, Water-Ash, . . . [is] a medium-sized tree in deep river-swamps, Virginia and south. **1897** SUDWORTH *Arborescent Flora* 291 Boxelder. . . . [Also called] Water Ash (Dakotas).

Water avens. =CURE-ALL I. {1777–} — **1784** [see CURE-ALL I]. **1814** BIGELOW *Florula Bostoniensis* 125 *Geum rivale*. Water avens. . . . A fine plant conspicuous in meadows for its high, nodding, dark coloured flowers. **1832** WILLIAMSON *Maine* I. 124 *Heal-all, Cure-all* or *Water-avens*, is of two varieties; one has circular, the other oval leaves. The former is used to check inflammations and eruptions of the skin. **1847** [see AVENS].

+**Water back.** (See quot. 1876.) — **1864** STOWE *House & Home P.* 294 The kitchen-range with its water-back I humbly salute. **1876** KNIGHT 2735/1 *Water-back*, a permanent reservoir at the back of a stove or range, to utilize the heat of the fire in keeping a supply of hot water.

Water bailiff.** In port towns, an officer charged with various duties such as keeping water fronts and sometimes streets freed from debris, enforcing fishing regulations, etc. *Obs.* — **1636** *Boston Rec.* II. 11 John Sampford and William Hudson shalbe Water baylies to see that noe annoying things eyther by fish, Wood or stone . . . be left or layd about the sea shore. **1649** *Ib.* 98 Edward Belcher is chossen watter Bayley to see that noe stones nor timber doe lye on the flats or shoor to the Dammage of boats or vessals. **1701** *Phila. Ordinances* (1812) 6 The sheriff of the said city . . . shall be the water-bailiff. *a1821** BIDDLE *Autobiog.* 30 The owner of the black who had run away intended to send the water bailiff after me.

Water bar. +A ridge or low barrier slanting across a hill or mountain road to deflect water flowing down it. — **1850** *N.H. Hist. Soc. Coll.* VI. 220 In passing a water bar, he was thrown from his carriage and killed. **1874** *Vermont Bd. Agric. Rep.* II. 657 It is a common custom in many places to construct what are called 'water-bars' on hill-roads. **1880** A. D. WHITNEY *Odd or Even* 102 The only break and safety were the water-bars, humping up across the way at frequent intervals.

Water barrel. A barrel serving as a container for water: (see also quot 1876). — **1849** *31st Congress 1 Sess.* Sen. Doc. No. 64, 205 After filling our water barrels, and giving our animals all they would drink, I made a start this evening at two o'clock. **1864** STOWE *House & Home P.* 103 Her aesthetic soul was at first greatly tried with the water-barrel which stood under the eaves-spout. **1876** KNIGHT 2375/2 *Water-barrel*, . . . a large wrought-iron barrel with a self-acting valve in the bottom, used in drawing water where there are no pumps. **1907** *St. Nicholas* July 771/1 Two tents by a driven well, . . . and a row of dusty water barrels comprised the new stage station.

+**Water battery.** *Milit.* A battery nearly on a level with the water of an adjacent river, lake, etc. — **1817** *Ann. 14th Congress* 2 Sess 983 There may be a water battery on Craney Island. **1862** in F. Moore *Rebellion Rec.* V. II. 189 The rebels also showed a water-battery from the beach at the ferry-landing. **1893** *Harper's Mag.* April 761/2 [Fort San Marco's] water-battery, where once stood the Spanish cannon, looks out to sea.

+**Water beech.** **a.** =PLANE TREE. **b.** =AMERICAN HORNBEAM. — **1756** KALM *Resa* II. 198 Af de härvarande Ängelska kallades den dels *Button-wood*, dels ock mäst *Water-Beech*. **1814** PURSH *Flora Amer.* II. 635 *Platanus occidentalis* . . . is known by the name of Button-wood, Water Beech, Sycamore and Plane Tree. **1865** BURROUGHS in *Atlantic Mo.* May 521/2 The chief feature [of the ground] . . . is a dense growth in the centre, consisting of Dog-wood, Water-Beech [etc.]. **1894** COULTER *Bot. W. Texas* III. 413 *Carpinus caroliniana*. (American hornbeam. Blue or water-beech.)

+**Water birch.** Any one of various American birches as the red birch (q.v.). Also attrib. — **1859** *S. Lit. Messenger* XXVIII. 143/1 Yisterday, I . . . had two lines out for cat, hitched to water-birch limbs. **1883** ZEIGLER & GROSSCUP *Alleghanies* 120 Lichens . . . decorate the trunk of the two-hundred-year-old water birch. **1897** SUDWORTH *Arborescent Flora* 141 *Betula nigra*, River Birch. . . . Water Birch (W. Va., Kans.).

Water biscuit. **1.** A biscuit made with water. {1854} +**2.** A cake-like mass of calcareous matter. — **(1)** *c*1790 COXE *View U.S.* 62 The produce, manufactures, and exports of Pennsylvania are very many and various, viz. . . . bran, shorts, ship-bread, white water biscuit [etc.]. **(2)** **1900** J. M. CLARKE (*title*), The Water Biscuit of Square Island, N.Y.

+**Water bitternut (hickory).** =WATER HICKORY. — **1810** MICHAUX *Arbres* I. 20 J[uglans] aquatica, *Water bitter nut*, nom donné par moi. **1832** BROWNE *Sylva* 172 Water Bitternut Hickory . . . is confined to the Southern States, and is confounded with the pignut hickory, though different from it in many respects. **1860** CURTIS *Woody Plants N.C.* 44 Water Bitter-nut Hickory. . . . The timber is rather inferior. **1897** SUDWORTH *Arborescent Flora* 112 Water Bitternut (S.C., Tenn.).

Water-bound, *a.* {1646–} **a.** Bounded on one or more sides by water. +**b.** Confined or detained by high water. — **(a)** **1781** in Sparks *Corr. Revol.* III. 410 The fleet might be well furnished with vegetables from the water-bound counties. **(b)** **1862** *N.Y. Tribune* 30 April 1/3 While water-bound, it [a foraging party] was attacked by guerrillas. **1865** PIKE *Scout & Ranger* (1932) 10 The prospect of being water-bound in the mountains for two or three days without provisions . . . was not very inviting. **1903** A. ADAMS *Log of Cowboy* 103 The Brazos had been unfordable for over a week, five herds being waterbound.

Water bucket.** A bucket for water, esp. one for the drinking water of a household. — **1640** *Md. Archives* IV. 91, 1. water-buckett. **1783** in Sherwood *Gaz. Georgia* (1860) 172 Let your water-bucket stand so high, that your children shall not dabble in it. **1867** 'E. KIRKE' *On Border* 264 With a water-bucket on his arm, he walked slowly along the mountain-side. *a1918** G. STUART *On Frontier* II. 136 Ice one-half inch thick froze in our water bucket.

Water bug. **a.** Any one of various hemipterous insects of aquatic habits. {1750–} +**b.** (See quot. 1891.) — **1778** CARVER *Travels* 493 The Water Bug is of a brown colour, about the size of a pea. **1854** THOREAU *Walden* 203 You can even detect a water-bug (*Gyrinus*) ceaselessly progressing over the smooth surface a quarter of a mile off. **1878** *N. Amer. Rev.* CXXVII. 485 Friendship [exists between] . . . the peacock and the pigeon, the water-bug and the leech. **1891** *Cent.* 6840/2 *Water-bug*, . . . the croton bug or German cockroach, *Blatta* (*Phyllodromia*) *germanica:* so called from its preference for water-pipes and moist places in houses.

+**Water call.** *Milit.* A signal summoning soldiers to assemble to get water or to water their horses. — **1781** E. DENNY *Mil. Jrnl.* 35 About eight or nine o'clock, as we found water, a short halt was made, the water-call beat. **1861** *Army Regulations* 39 *Water-calls* at the hours directed by the commanding officer. **1868** *Harper's Mag.* Feb. 303/2 When the men mounted at the 'water-call,' some were seen to mount from the right-hand side, Indian fashion.

+**Water chinquapin.** The wankapin or American lotus, *Nelumbo lutea.* — **1836** LINCOLN *Botany* App. 119 Water chinquepin, sacred bean, Indian lotus. . . . Flowers larger than those of any other plant in North America, except one species of magnolia. **1843** TORREY *Flora N.Y.* I. 38 Great Yellow Water-lily. Water Chinquepin. . . . Big Sodus Bay, Lake Ontario. **1850** S. F. COOPER *Rural Hours* 275 One of the noblest plants of our country belongs to this tribe of the water-lilies: . . . [the] water-chinquapin, as it is sometimes called.

+**Water-cooler.** A receptacle in which drinking water is kept cool. Also attrib. — **1869** *Boyd's Business Directory* 51 L. H. Mace & Co's Refrigerator, Meat Safe and Water Cooler Manufactory. **1887** *Courier-Journal* 21 June 3/6 By S. T. Moore & Co. . . . Water cooler; Water-hose and Reel. **1902** WHITE *Blazed Trail* 20 The interested spectators of the little drama included two men near the water-cooler.

Water cracker. {1799–} +**1.** A cracker made of flour, fat, salt, and water. +**2.** (See quotation.) — **(1)** **1825** *Mo. Intelligencer* 4 June 3/4 Ward and Parker Have Just Received For Sale at their Grocery and Liquor Store Molasses, Water Crackers [etc.]. **1845** *Xenia Torch-Light* 31 July 3/7 The subscriber has just opened a Grocery and Provision Store consisting of . . . Water Crackers, Mackerel [etc.]. **1877** *Harper's Mag.* Feb. 448/1 Aunt Helen threw her a bit of water-cracker. **(2)** **1887** *Scientific Amer.* LVI. 181/1, I have taken a water cracker, as they [Prince Rupert drops] are called in the factory, several feet long, and broken it four or five times.

***Water crow.** *S.* +=WATER TURKEY. — **1838** AUDUBON *Ornith. Biog.* IV. 138 At the mouths of the [Miss.] river it bears the name of 'Water Crow.' **1891** *Cent.* 6841/2 *Water crow*, . . . the darter, snake-bird, or water-turkey, *Plotus anhinga*. (Southern U.S.)

Water ditch. A ditch for water {1735–}, +esp. one for supplying water for mining or irrigation purposes. — **1654** *Boston Rec.* 34 [The lot] lyeth with in fence layd out, . . . one end at a water ditch. **1866** *Rep. Indian Affairs* 93 They have . . . constructed a water-ditch several miles in length, bringing in the waters of Tule river, for irrigation purposes. **1890** LANGFORD *Vigilante Days* (1912) 338 They, in company with five others, had purchased a water ditch in Boise Basin. **1902** WISTER *Virginian* 458 The scars of new-scraped water-ditches began to appear.

***Water dog.** +**1.** =HELLBENDER I. +**2.** ?A variety of dogfish. — **(1)** **1859** BARTLETT 502 *Water-Dogs*, the Western name for various species of salamanders, or lizard-shaped animals, with smooth, shiny, naked skins; sometimes called Water-puppies and Ground-puppies. **1882** *Amer. Naturalist* XVI. 140 The Menopona [*sic*] here called 'alligator' and 'water-dog,' is an exceedingly voracious animal. **(2)** **1892** A. E. LEE *Hist. Columbus, Ohio* I. 299 Suckers, catfish, gars and waterdogs were also taken [in the Scioto R.].

Watered stock. Stock in a business organization that has been increased without the addition of actual capital. Also attrib. — **1873** *Newton Kansan* 10 April 2/2 The only curse railroads can be to a country arises from the 'watered stock' process. **1887** *Courier-Journal* 29 Jan. 4/1

Watered stock sells for less than par. **1908** LORIMER *J. Spurlock* 119 An era of dilution—watered honah; watered stocks; watered whiskey.

+**Water elm.** Any one of various American trees of the family Ulmaceae. — **1884** SARGENT *Rep. Forests* 123 *Ulmus Americana*. . . . White Elm. American Elm. Water Elm. **1897** SUDWORTH *Arborescent Flora* 182 *Ulmus alata*, Wing Elm. . . . Water Elm (Ala.). *Ib.* 183 *Planera aquatica*, Planertree. . . . Water Elm (Fla.). **1903** 'O. HENRY' in *McClure's Mag.* Dec. 144/1 [I] noticed a rabbit-hawk sitting on a dead limb in a water-elm.

Water engine. An engine for pumping water to extinguish a fire. {1677–} Also attrib. — **1683** *Boston Rec.* 162 One man out of each Compa[ny] of the traines bands should take the care . . . of the water Engine. **1732** *Ib.* 41 The Petition of the Water Enginemen . . . [shall] be Granted. **1780** *Heath P.* III. 28 The fire might be extinguished if we had a water engine. **1889** BRAYLEY *Boston Fire Dept.* 7 The first mention of a water-engine is made in the records of March 1, 1653–4.

***Waterfall.** +A mass or bunch of hair, usually artificial, worn by women at the back of the head. {1875–} Also attrib. — **1864** STOWE *House & Home P.* 165 The one I wore yesterday was my waterfall-hat, with the green feather. **1889** CUSTER *Tenting on Plains* 384 Custom made it necessary to disfigure ourselves with the awkward water-fall, and no matter how luxuriant the hair. **1901** FITCH *Captain Jinks* 43 A spotted net over her 'waterfall.'

+**Water feather.** The featherfoil, *Hottonia inflata*. — **1818** NUTTALL *N. Amer. Plants* I. 120. **1840** DEWEY *Mass. Flowering Plants* 154 *Hottonia inflata*. Water-feather. . . . Near Boston and New Bedford. **1901** MOHR *Plant Life Ala.* 49 They are kept afloat . . . by the rosettes of their floating leaves, as in sundew (*Drosera intermedia*), water feather (*Hottonia inflata*) [etc.].

Water fence. 'Chiefly *U.S.*' (*O.E.D. Suppl.*). **a.** A ditch serving as a barrier or boundary. {1707–} **b.** A fence built out into a stream or other water so that animals cannot pass around its end; a fence built over a stream. — **1651** *Southampton Rec.* I. 79 Mr Iohn Gosmer [shall] have . . . authority to hier men or teams for the accomplishing of the water fence of the little plaine. **1673** *Ib.* 202 The Indians are to maintain a man at the said water fence as a gin keeper from time to time. **1738** HEMPSTEAD *Diary* 338 Ad[a]m & Josh helpt Jno. Harris make Water fence at Greens Harbour. **1791** *Huntington Rec.* III. 160 He petitions the Trustees to Grant him toleration to Run a water fence from the South part of his Land Down to the Channel. **1880** *Scribner's Mo.* Feb. 509/2 Of all fences, none is so simple as the water fence, only a pole spanning the stream.

+**Water flaxseed.** (See quot. 1891.) — **1817–8** EATON *Botany* (1822) 333 Water flaxseed. . . . The roots rarely reach the ground; but merely extend downwards a few inches into the water. **1839** in *Mich. Agric. Soc. Trans.* VII. 411. **1891** *Cent.* 6842/1 *Water-flaxseed*, . . . the larger duckweed, *Lemna polyrhiza:* so called from the shape and minute size of the fronds.

Water football. A game resembling football played in the water. — **1891** *Triangle* I. 83 Water Foot Ball [heading] . . . as played at our summer school differs somewhat from water polo, as it was played in deep water, where the players were obliged to keep swimming.

+**Water front.** Land, usually in a town, that fronts or abuts on a body of water. Also attrib. — **1856** EMERSON *Eng. Traits* 47 A people so skilful and sufficient in economizing water-front by docks, warehouses, and lighters. **1882** MCCABE *New York* 402 The men live on the steamer, and patrol the water front of the city in row boats. **1910** J. HART *Vigilante Girl* 28 Where he made his biggest clean-up was in buying some mud-flats out in the bay and then forcing a new water-front bill through the legislature.

+**Water gap.** A gap in a range of mountains through which a stream flows. (Cf. GAP 2.) — **1818** F. HALL *Travels* 164 There is a similar aperture some miles N.E. called the Water Gap. **1835** MARTIN *Descr. Virginia* 31 [The Blue Mountain chain] continues its original direction to the Delaware Water Gap. **1872** *Newton Kansan* 29 Aug. 4/1 At the Delaware water-gap is a widow. **1923** in *Amer. Speech* XV. 409/1 Some [of these rivers] break through the Blue Ridge from the Valley, making water-gaps in that formidable mountain barrier.

Water gristmill. A gristmill driven by water power. — **1723** *Amer. Wkly. Mercury* 19 Sept. 2/2 To be Sold . . . , the Farm, late of Thomas Stevenson, . . . with a Water Grist-Mill upon it. **1790** *Ky. Petitions* 145 [They] are destitute of Every advantage resulting from water Grist mills. **1831** PECK *Guide* 318 Vandalia contains . . . one water grist mill, one water saw mill [etc.].

Water guard. {1646–} +(See quot. 1866.) *Obs.* — **1823** THACHER *Military Jrnl.* 103, I did not think it possible you could escape the vigilance of the water guards. **1866** LOSSING *Hudson* 351 The 'water-guard' was an aquatic corps, in the pay of the revolutionary government.

+**Water haul.** In fishing, a haul of the net which takes no fish; fruitless effort of any kind. — **1871** *Congress. Globe* 17 Feb. 1356/1 It occurred to me, at all events, the gentleman from California had made what fishermen call a 'water haul.' **1882** *Critic* (Washington) 23 Feb. (Th.), Ostensibly I went to testify as an expert in the Star-route cases, but I did not testify. You know that was another water-haul. **1898** R. M. JOHNSON *P. Amerson's Will* 221, I 'tended to that business dilicate as I knowed how; but no use: a waterhaul, out an' out.

***Water hen.** Any one of various aquatic birds likened to a hen, +esp. the American coot (q.v.). — **1737** BRICKELL *N. Carolina* 200 The Blue-Peters, or Water-Hens, are very plenty. **1778** CARVER *Travels* 466. **1857** *Porter's Spirit of Times* 3 Jan. 290/2 The *Spirit*, still, will treat . . . of sora, and of water-hens. **1917** *Birds of Amer.* I. 212 Florida Gallinule. *Gallinula galeata*. . . . [Also called] Red-billed Mud Hen; Water Hen.

+**Water hickory.** The bitter pecan (*Carya aquatica*) of the southern states. — **1818** DARBY *Emigrant's Guide* 80 The most important vegetable productions [include]: . . . *Juglans amara*, Bitter nut hickory, *Juglans aquatica*, Water hickory [etc.]. **1884** SARGENT *Rep. Forests* 136. **1901** MOHR *Plant Life Ala.* 46 Water hickory (*Hicoria aquatica*) . . . and green ash (*Fraxinus lanceolata*) are frequent inhabitants of the forest-clad swamps.

Water hole. *W.* A hole or depression in the ground in which water collects. {1679–} — **1843** MARRYAT *M. Violet* xxii, At sun-down we came upon a water-hole, and encamped for the night. **1869** J. R. BROWNE *Adv. Apache Country* 279 In several places near the water-holes the deer tracks were so thick that they reminded me of a sheep corral. **1893** REMINGTON in *Harper's Mag.* Dec. 79/2 At intervals men are sent to bring back a steer from the water-holes. **1923** J. H. COOK *On Old Frontier* 30 The Indians knew . . . where water-holes along dry creeks were located.

***Watering,** *a.* Attrib. with *privilege, season, station.* — **1848** *Santa Fe Repub.* 31 May 2/4 His pastures and grazing grounds are large, and supplied with good watering privileges. **1854** BROMWELL *Locomotive Sk.* 89 Even the little watering-stations . . . rise far superior, in the spirit of the design, to any other on the route. **1857** DAVIS *El Gringo* 199 The land-owners and overseers watch the *acequias* during the watering season with great care.

Watering bucket. A bucket used in watering horses, etc. — **1845** *Indiana Mag. Hist.* XXIII. 212 He then wrote . . . to tell all to come with their wagons, and grain, and hay, and feed troughs and watering buckets. **1876** KNIGHT 2739/2 *Watering-bucket*. In the United States service the regulation bucket is made of sole leather, fastened with copper-rivets and having a copper rim.

***Watering place.** A place on a road where teams may be watered. — **1839** PLUMBE *Sk. Iowa* 46 Its streams are few, and consequently 'tis far between 'watering places.' **1844** GREGG *Commerce of Prairies* II. 56 Upon leaving one watering place, we never knew where we would find the next. **1851** *Polly Peablossom* 179 The sudden stopping of the coach at a watering-place aroused W. from his sleep. **1864** *Harper's Mag.* Oct. 568/2 The old stage-houses of the Overland Mail Company still stand by the watering-places.

Water jug. A jug for water. — **1779** *York Co., Va., Rec.: Wills* XXII. 28 April, 2 water jugs 30/. **1855** M. THOMPSON *Doesticks* 63 In the morning I found . . . my watch in the water-jug. **1873** *Amer. Naturalist* VII. 95 Two water-jugs, which are similar in shape to the decanters formerly furnished the guests of a hotel, . . . were taken from an ancient cemetery in Perry County, Missouri.

Water keg. A keg or small barrel for water. — **1839** *Knickerb.* XIII. 382 Line-tubs, water-kegs, and wafe-poles, were thrown hurriedly into the boats. **1870** KEIM *Sheridan's Troopers* 95 The supply brought in the water-kegs, greatly to our inconvenience was soon consumed. *a***1918** G. STUART *On Frontier* I. 47 We dug up enough to put into water-kegs and enjoyed the luxury of ice-water all that hot day.

***Water lily.** Any one of various aquatic plants, esp. of the genus *Nymphaea*, having showy flowers. Also attrib. — **1672** JOSSELYN *New Eng. Rarities* 44 Water Lilly, with yellow Flowers, the Indians Eat the Roots. **1737** BRICKELL *N. Carolina* 22 Oris, Water-lillies, Peony, Male and Female, Solomons-Seal, Agarick. **1818** *Mass. H. S. Coll.* 2 Ser. VIII. 171 Among the plants in the neighbouring towns, that are too interesting to be omitted, are rosemary-leaved andromeda, the white nymphea or fragrant water lily [etc.]. **1880** CABLE *Grandissimes* 237 Yonder where the sunbeams wedge themselves in, [there are] constellations of water-lilies. **1912** WOODROW *Sally Salt* 110 Get some water-lily buds!

Water line. {*a*1625–} +A river or rivers regarded as a means of transportation. Also attrib. — **1852** in *Amer. Speech* XV. 382/2 The stimulating effect of a water line transportation . . . will be soon and sensibly felt. **1873** *Harper's Mag.* Feb. 471 The Governor of Virginia . . . [spoke of] the proposed national water line and transalleghany route between Eastern and Western Virginia. **1881–5** MCCLELLAN *Own Story* 343 The water line of transportation would have insured the prompt and safe arrival of the 1st corps.

+**Water locust.** A species of honey locust (*Gleditsia aquatica*) found in moist regions in the South. — **1810** MICHAUX *Arbres* I. 36 G[leditschia] monosperma. . . . *Water Locust*, . . . nom secondaire. **1832** BROWNE *Sylva* 161 The Water Locust is first seen in the Atlantic States in the lower part of South Carolina. **1897** SUDWORTH *Arborescent Flora* 254.

+**Water lot. 1.** A lot or plot of ground which fronts on a body of water. **2.** (See quot. 1891.) — **(1) 1722** *Amer. Wkly. Mercury* 2 Aug. 2/2 A Water-Lot containing 40 Feet 9 Inches, on King-Street, and about 250 Feet back from said Street into the River Delaware. **1799** *Wilmington* (N.C.) *Gazette* 12 Dec., A water Lot with a Wharf and Warehouse thereon. **1804** *Phila. Ordinances* (1812) 273 An ordinance authorising the mayor to borrow ten thousand dollars for the purpose of purchasing a water lot on the north side of Chesnut-street. **1868** 'MARK TWAIN' *Sk., New & Old* 150 A memorial praying that the city's right to the water-lots upon the city front might be established by law of Congress. **(2) 1891** *Cent.* 6844/2 *Water-lot*, . . . a lot of ground which is under water; specifically, one of a regular system of city lots which are partly or wholly covered by the water of a bay, lake, or river, and may be filled in and converted into made ground for the erection of buildings, docks, etc.

+**Water maple.** Any one of various American maples, as the red maple and the silver maple. — **1802** ELLICOTT *Journal* 284 Water maple, (*acer negundo,*) . . . is met with as high as the Wabash. **1822** Woods *English Prairie* 49 The red or water-maple most resembles the sycamore of England. **1897** Sudworth *Arborescent Flora* 282 *Acer spicatum.* Mountain Maple. . . . [Also called] Water Maple (Ky.). *Ib.* 287 *Acer saccharinum.* Silver Maple. . . . [Also called] Water Maple (Pa., W. Va.). **1912** Cobb *Back Home* 137 [The] walk . . . [was] shaded well all the way by water maples.

Watermelon.

1. The large oblong or round fruit of the plant *Citrullus vulgaris;* the plant producing this fruit. {1615-}

*c*1629 *Mass. H. S. Coll.* 1 Ser. I. 124 Wee abound with such things . . . as musk-millions, water-millions, Indian pompions [etc.]. **1698** Thomas *Pensilvania* 18 There are . . . Water-Mellons, Muskmellons, . . . and Sarsaparilla. **1741** W. Stephens *Proc. Georgia* II. 149, [I] found all the Land that I had designed for Cultivation this year well fitted with . . . divers Sorts of Gourds, such as Pumpions, Water and Musk Melons. **1791** Bartram *Travels* 303 [We had] a feast of Water mellons and Oranges, the Indians having brought a canoe load of them to the trading-house. **1840** *Niles' Nat. Reg.* 29 Aug. 416/3 A Watermellon, sent by Charles Waters, esq. . . . weighed 50 lbs. **1918** Sandburg *Cornhuskers* 35 Why do I always think of niggers and buck-and-wing dancing whenever I see watermelon?

2. Attrib. and comb. with *cutting, day, party,* etc.

1748 Eliot *Field-Husb.* i. 10 Water Melon Seed . . . produces Melons which grow to a great Size. **1883** Riley *Old Swimmin'-Hole* 23 Old wortermelon time is a-comin' round again. **1888** Rittenhouse *Maud* 412 At eight Mr Blauvelt called to take me to the impromptu 'water-melon party.' **1890** *Stock Grower & Farmer* 9 Aug. 3/3 Mr. W. E. Anderson . . . sends a hearty invitation to be present at the novel celebration [at Rocky Ford, Colo.]. . . of 'watermelon day.' **1894** *McClure's Mag.* IV. 83/2 Why, we've got corn' beef . . . an' watermelon perserves. **1896** *Godey's Mag.* Feb. 220/2 The Georgia Watermelon Spoon is the newest departure in souvenir spoons. **1912** Cobb *Back Home* 50 The veterans adjourned back behind Floral Hall for a watermelon cutting.

+**Watermelon patch.** A small piece of ground planted in watermelons. — **1809** Irving *Knickerb.* 328 The Gardeniers of Hudson . . . [were] distinguished by many triumphant feats, such as robbing watermelonpatches. **1832** Ferrall *Ramble* 298, [I] slipped out . . . into the watermelon patch. **1888** 'Craddock' *Despot* 99 Thar's old Jer'miah Miles jes' drawed a pistol ter skeer some o' them bad boys out in his watermillion patch.

* **Water mill.** A grinding mill the machinery of which is driven by water. — **1634** Wood *New Eng. Prospect* 41 Water-milne called *Stony-river;* upon which is built a water-milne. **1696** *Narragansett Hist. Reg.* III. 280 Suffering a certain water-mill . . . to fall and go to decay . . . [is] a wrong and abuse to the Town. **1829** Weems *B. Franklin* 171 He would take the model of a double-geared water mill, turning two pairs of stones, . . . and set it in motion. **1883** Howe *Country Town* (1926) 26 Jo was often sent to a water-mill in the woods with a grist.

+**Water moccasin. a.** A pit viper (*Agkistrodon piscivorus*), found in or near water in the southern states. **b.** Any one of various harmless water snakes confused with this. — **1821** Nuttall *Travels Arkansa* 154 The other [snake] frequents waters, and is called the water-mockasin, and poisonous black-snake. **1835** Audubon *Ornith. Biog.* III. 90 The Congo snake and water-moccasin glide before you as they seek to elude your sight. **1882** C. C. Hopley *Snakes* 495 A 'water moccasin' . . . had been seen . . . unwelcomely close to a southern residence. **1891** *Cent.* 6845/1 *Water-moccasin.* . . . A name applied with little discrimination in the United States to several species of aquatic snakes; properly, the venomous . . . *Ancistrodon piscivorus*, with which the harmless *Tropidonotus* (or *Nerodia*) *sipedon* is sometimes confounded.

Water oak. +Any one of various American oaks often found near water, esp. *Quercus nigra* of the southeastern states. — **1709** Lawson *Carolina* 93 Willow-Oak is a sort of Water-Oak. **1797** Priest *Travels* 12 Water and barren oak are small and bushy and only used for firing. **1834** Peck *Gaz. Illinois* 23 Of oaks there are several species, as . . . swamp or water oak, white oak, red oak. **1897** Sudworth *Arborescent Flora* 172 ff. [5 species listed]. **1901** Mohr *Plant Life Ala.* 61 Water oak . . . ascends to the upper valley of Talladega Creek in Clay County.

+**Water oats. a.** =Indian rice. (Cf. Water rice, Wild rice 1.) **b.** (See quot. 1895.) — **1817-8** Eaton *Botany* (1822) 519 *Zizania clavulosa*, water-oats, wild-rice. **1843** Torrey *Flora N.Y.* II. 416 Water Oats. . . . Swamps, and borders of rivulets and lakes. **1895** *Dept. Agric. Yrbk. 1894* 430 A conspicuous grass of our southern shores, and belonging to the class of sand binders, is *water oats*, or beach grass. **1901** Mohr *Plant Life Ala.* 362 Water Oats. . . . Valuable for its highly nutritious seeds.

Water ouzel. {1622-} +=American dipper. — **1849** Audubon *Western Jrnl.* 118, I saw today the first water-ousel I ever saw alive in America. **1875** *Amer. Naturalist* IX. 76 The stream . . . was also the home of the water ouzel. **1917** *Birds of Amer.* III. 173 The Water Ouzel cares nothing for the cold.

Water poplar. A species of poplar. {1707 (Mortimer *Art. Husb.* 360)} — **1761** Kalm *Resa* III. 178 *Water-poplar*, växte här ymnigast af alla trän, trefs oförlikneligen väl på stränderna, och steg up til samma högd, som våra största Aspar. **1817-8** Eaton *Botany* (1822) 404 *Populus angulata*, balm-of-gilead, water poplar, cotton wood. **1821** *Mass. H. S. Coll.* 2 Ser. IX. 154 Plants, which are indigenous in the township of Middlebury, [Vt., include:] . . . Water poplar.

Water power.

1. Power derived from falling or moving water; a place where the utilization of such water is practicable. {1836-, in Canada}

1827 Drake & Mansfield *Cincinnati* 100 The extent of water-power, which the Miami Canal, when completed, will afford upon the city plain. **1854** Simms *Southward Ho!* 173 We have abundance of water-power, all over the South. **1874** *Vermont Bd. Agric. Rep.* II. 740 About 1854 or 1855 the company . . . leased a water power and mill of A. W. Hyde & Co. **1900** *Congress. Rec.* 8 Jan. 665/2, I should like to have . . . some official . . . tabulate . . . statistics in regard to the water power of the country.

2. Attrib. with *arrastra, course, grist mill,* etc.

1857 Braman *Texas* 38 Three large stores . . . and an excellent water-power grist-mill . . . indicate thrift and prosperity. **1872** Raymond *4th Rep. Mines* 332 The Treasury Mining Company has a 15-stamp water-power mill. **1877** W. Wright *Big Bonanza* 69 [They] were also beginning to work ores in mills and water-power arastras on the Carson River. **1883** *Century Mag.* Sept. 692/2 We observe that the foreground of the western division is profusely channeled with navigable waters and water-power courses. **1901** Merwin & Webster *Calumet 'K'* 20 We've been putting in a big rope drive on a water-power plant over at Stillwater. **1910** Pinchot *Fight for Conservation* 27 We are met at every turn by the indignant denial of the water-power interests.

+**Water privilege.** The right to make use of the water of, or the power generated by, a stream or other body of water; the place where such water or water power is available.

1749 *N.H. Probate Rec.* III. 755 We set off to Deborah Shackford, . . . the Water Privilege belonging to said Estate. **1815** Humphrey *Yankey* 53 She must be as big as the nation, and have a wonderful water privilege into the bargain. **1833** A. Fergusson *Notes Tour U.S.* 267 They have here, what is called in America, a valuable *water privilege* or *fall*, and have erected flour and saw-mills to a large extent. **1849** Thoreau *Week* 230 Some of the finest water privileges in the country still unimproved on the former stream. **1892** *Vt. Agric. Rep.* XII. 128 Good water privileges may be found on the Missisquoi river in the seventy-five miles of its devious course through the County.

transf. **1883** Peck *Bad Boy* 50 He was helping her put on her rubber waterprivilege to go home in the rain the night of the sociable.

***Water rat.** +a. =Muskrat 1 a. **b.** A wharf rat. — **1737** Brickell *N. Carolina* 129 There are four sorts of Rats in this Province, viz. the Musk, the Marsh, the Water, and the House-Rat. **1781-2** Jefferson *Notes Va.* (1788) 55 There remains then the buffalo, red deer, . . . and water rat. **1830** Cooper *Water Witch* I. 129 Your coasters are in and out, like water-rats on a wharf, at any hour of the twenty-four. **1873** Phelps *Trotty's Wedding* ix, It is an island, this rock . . . and there are wild roses on it, and a water-rat.

+**Water rattlesnake. 1.** ? =Water moccasin a. **2.** The diamond-back rattlesnake, *Crotalus adamanteus.* — (1) **1736** Catesby *Carolina* II. 43 *Vipera aquatica*, The Water Viper, . . . in Carolina commonly goes by the Name of the Water Rattle-Snake. (2) **1810** Lambert *Travels thro' U.S.* III. 60 The shores abounded with a species of *water rattle-snake*, whose bite was also of a deadly nature. **1861** *New Amer. Cycl.* XIII. 773 The diamond or water rattlesnake . . . is dark brown or dusky above, with a series of large rhomboidal spots continuous from head to tail.

+**Water rice.** =Indian rice: (see also quot. 1901). — **1878** Killibrew *Tenn. Grasses* 237 Water or Indian Rice . . . grows in swamps, and on borders of rivulets and lakes. **1901** Mohr *Plant Life Ala.* 49 Fresh-water plants which root in a water-soaked soil . . . include *Zizania, Zizianopsis* (water rice).

+**Water right.** W. The right to use the water in a particular region or place; a certificate attesting such a right; also, a stream or other source of water. {1907-} — **1813** *Ann. 13th Congress* 1 Sess. 50 Feeder, (nearly completed,) reservoirs, lock at the feeder, purchase of water-rights and land . . . [$]230,000. **1876** Raymond *8th Rep. Mines* 89 The Milton Company also owns a main ditch . . . and other water-rights. **1896** Shinn *Story of Mine* 41 His claims to the spring had some colour . . . , though no water-right was ever recorded. **1914** 'Bower' *Flying U Ranch* 69 He's got a water right on Flying U creek.

+**Water rot,** *n.* (See quotation.) — **1791** Bartram *Travels* 208 The traders and Indians call this disease [of horses and cattle] the water-rot or scald, and say it is occasioned by the warm waters of the savanna, . . . when these creatures wade deep to feed on the water-grass.

Water-rot, *v. tr.* To soak (hemp, etc.) in water; to water-ret. Also *vbl. n.* and *ppl. a.* {1794-} 'Chiefly U.S.' (O.E.D. Suppl.). — **1705** *Boston News-Letter* 30 July 2/2 For Hemp Water rotted, bright and clear, per Ton, containing 20 Gross Hundreds, Six Pounds. **1759** *Newport Mercury* 8 May 1/2 Some prefer Water-rotting [for flax]. **1843** *Amer. Pioneer* II. 450 The manner of making ropes of linn bark, was to cut the bark in strips . . . and water-rot it. **1883** Allen *New Farm Book* 252 The best plan for water rotting of hemp is in vats under cover, the water in which is kept at an equable temperature.

Water shield. {1846-} +An American aquatic plant (*Brasenia schreberi*) having large shieldlike leaves. Also with specifying term. — **1817-8** Eaton *Botany* (1822) 310 *Hydropeltis purpurea*, water shield. The leaves float on the surface of the water. **1839** in *Mich. Agric. Soc. Trans.* VII. 409. **1901** Mohr *Plant Life Ala.* 503 *Brasenia purpurea.* . . . Purple Water Shield.

Water snake. Any one of various snakes that frequent the water. {1601-} — **1676** GLOVER *Va.* in *Phil. Trans.* XI. 631 There are very many *Water-Snakes*, that keep the Springs and Rivers. **1778** CARVER *Travels* 167 Wreaths of water-snakes [lay] basking in the sun. **1822** WOODS *English Prairie* (1904) 290 The black, water, and garter-snakes, are all said to be harmless. **1890** HOWELLS *Boy's Town* 31 They believed that these deep holes were infested by water-snakes, though they never saw any.

+**Water star grass.** An American water plant (*Heteranthera dubia*) having star-shaped blossoms. — **1843** TORREY *Flora N.Y.* II. 313 *Heteranthera graminea.* Water Star-grass. . . . Flowing waters: frequent. **1898** CREEVEY *Flowers of Field* 128 Water Star-grass . . . has stamens all alike, with grass-like leaves which lie under water.

***Water starwort.** Any one of various plants of the genus *Callitriche.* Also attrib. — **1857** GRAY *Botany* 384 *Callitrichaceae.* (Water-Star-worts.) Aquatic small annuals. **1869** *Amer. Naturalist* III. 212 The common water-cress . . . will do well with water starwort. **1901** MOHR *Plant Life Ala.* 598 *Callitrichaceae.* Water Starwort Family. . . . North America, 11 [species].

+**Water station.** (See first quotation.) — **1840** TANNER *Descr. Canals & Rail Roads* 263 *Water stations*, places where locomotives obtain their supplies of water. **1865** *39th Congress 2 Sess.* H. R. Rep. No. 34, 1026 Water-stations out of order, having been dry for two years. **1898** NICHOLAS *Idyl of Wabash* 56 If I can reach the water-station I can warn the engineer.

+**Water street.** A street that leads to or extends along a water front. Usually as a proper name. Also attrib. — **1642** *Cambridge Prop. Rec.* 73 Comon ground adioyninge to waterstreet East the Cricke south. **1789** *Boston Directory* 180 Cambell Patrick, smith and farrier, Water-street. **1868** BEECHER *Sermons* (1869) I. 31 The Water street movement in New-York, to-day, is another such movement. **1902** WHITE *Blazed Trail* 183 Any old logger . . . will tell you of the 'Pen,' the 'White Row,' the 'Water Streets' of Alpena, Port Huron, Ludington.

Water tank. {1834-}
1. A large reservoir erected beside a railroad track for supplying locomotives with water. Also attrib.
1862 MOORE *Rebellion Rec.* V. II. 148 They got on a car, and ran up the road to cut a water-tank, and were ambushed. **1877** ROE *Army Lett.* 164 The dogs ran back almost a mile to the water tank. **1887** HARRIS *Free Joe* 165 The station consisted of a water-tank and a little pigeon-house where tickets were sold. **1890** H. Palmer *Stories of Base Ball Field* 65 'The Gladiator' would get out at every little water-tank town and introduce himself. **1907** LONDON *Road* 125, I proceeded to the water-tank.

2. A large or small container for water to be used for drinking and other purposes.
1873 COZZENS *Marvellous Country* 464 All the towns or villages have large water-tanks, or reservoirs, constructed upon the rock. **1886** H. D. BROWN *Two College Girls* 52, I'll go to the water-tank for some water. **1890** *Stock Grower & Farmer* 5 April 4/4 This warm weather brings out the cattle from the hills, and . . . at the water tank is a constant charging crowd. **1894** *Outing* June 172 Four or five rough-looking men . . . were clustered about the water-tank.

+**Water target.** =WATER SHIELD. — **1814** BIGELOW *Florula Bostoniensis* 135 *Hydropeltis purpurea.* Water target. . . . An aquatic plant . . . [growing in] stagnant waters. **1833** EATON *Botany* (ed. 6) 180. **1854** THOREAU *Walden* 194 A closer scrutiny . . . [detects] only a few small heart-leaves, . . . and perhaps a water-target or two.

+**Water terrapin.** An edible turtle of the family Testudinidae, esp. of the genus *Malaclemys*, found in fresh or brackish water; one of various water tortoises. (Cf. TERRAPIN 1 a.) — **1709** LAWSON *Carolina* 133 Water Terebins are small; containing about as much Meat as a Pullet, and are extraordinary Food. **1805** LEWIS in *L. & Clark Exped.* II. (1904) 186 See a number of water tarripens. **1856** *Porter's Spirit of Times* 20 Sept. 43/2 Fishermen in our waters are often annoyed by the water-terrapin.

Water thrush. {1668-} +Any one of various American warblers of the genus *Seiurus*, usually found near streams. Also with specifying terms. — **1811** WILSON *Ornithology* III. 66 [The] Water Thrush, *Turdus Aquaticus*, . . . is remarkable for its partiality to . . . shores, ponds, and streams of water. **1839** AUDUBON *Ornith. Biog.* V. 287, I cannot after all distinguish between the Louisiana Water Thrush and the Common Water Thrush. **1865** BURROUGHS in *Atlantic Mo.* May 521/2 In a remote clearing . . . by a stumpy, shallow pond, I am sure to find the Water-Thrush. **1917** *Birds of Amer.* III. 154 Water-Thrush. . . . Other Names.—New York Warbler; Small-billed Water-Thrush; Northern Water-Thrush.

+**Water-toter.** *S.* One who supplies a group of workers with water. *colloq.* — **1852** *Fla. Plantation Rec.* 549, 83 Negroes on Chemoonie and 43 Names goes into the Field, including the Driver and two water toters. **1860** OLMSTED *Back Country* 48 Each gang [of cotton pickers] was attended by a 'water-toter.'

Water tower. {1887-} +A piece of fire-fighting equipment consisting essentially of an adjustable pipe or frame by means of which water may be delivered at a greater height than would otherwise be possible. — **1894** B. MATTHEWS in *Harper's Mag.* Jan. 227/1 The water-tower . . . was speedily erected and in service. **1905** *N.Y. Times* 30 Jan. 6 It is a terrible task to pull a ponderous engine or water tower on wheels. **1911** A. B. REEVE *Poisoned Pen* 61 Four engines, two hook-and-ladders, a water-tower, the battalion chief and a deputy are hurrying to that fire.

+**Water turkey.** =DARTER 1. — **1836** HOLLEY *Texas* 100 Kingfishers and water-turkies . . . are found in great abundance. **1883** 'MARK

TWAIN' *Life on Miss.* App. A, A water-turkey now and again rises and flies ahead into the long avenue of silence. **1917** *Birds of Amer.* I. 94 The Water-Turkey is no more a 'Turkey' than the Nighthawk is a 'Hawk.'

+**Water viper.** =WATER MOCCASIN. — *c*1735 CATESBY *Carolina* II. 43 *Vipera Aquatica.* The Water Viper. . . . One of these Serpents I surprized swimming a Shore with a large Cat-Fish. **1789** MORSE *Amer. Geog.* 61 Of the Snakes which infest the United States, are the following, viz. The Rattle Snake . . . , Water Viper, Black Viper [etc.]. **1810** LAMBERT *Travels thro' U.S.* III. 60 There were a great number of *water vipers* reclining upon the branches. **1891** *Cent.* 6763/1 In the United States the name [viper] is commonly but erroneously applied to various spotted snakes, . . . as the water-*viper, Ancistrodon piscivorus*, the water-moccasin, poisonous.

Water wagtail. {1611-} +One of various American water thrushes. — **1781-2** JEFFERSON *Notes Va.* (1788) 77 Besides these, we have The Royston Crow, . . . Water Wagtail [etc.]. **1882** *Century Mag.* Jan. 361/2 New England [birds include]: . . . Water wagtail, Hermit thrush [etc.]. **1917** *Birds of Amer.* III. 153 The Louisiana Water-Thrush . . . bobs its tail as it proceeds, a peculiarity from which it derives its popular name of Water Wagtail.

***Water wave.** +A wave or undulation made in the hair when wet. — **1882** *Harper's Mag.* Nov. 877/2 She is pasting down her wetted hair into a semblance of the 'water-waves' of fashionable society. **1923** WYATT *Invis. Gods* 7 His grandmother . . . [was] bending over him her water waves and pearl powder.

***Water wheel.** A wheel utilizing the power of falling or flowing water. — **1688** *Essex Inst. Coll.* XXXV. 214 John Hale & John Emery . . . [are] to make . . . [a] water wheele. **1780** *N.J. Archives* 2 Ser. IV. 374 There are . . . three boulting mills, two of which go by a water-wheel. **1815-6** *Niles' Reg.* IX. Suppl. 182/2 The *re-acting water wheel* . . . is likely to supercede any other now in use. **1885** *Santa Fé Wkly. New Mexican* 20 Aug. 1/3 New comers [should] . . . build under-shot water wheels at the river bank, that would carry the water up twenty feet at a lift. **1903** A. ADAMS *Log of Cowboy* 286 The herd . . . continued going round and round like a water wheel.

+**Water white oak.** =OVERCUP OAK. — **1801** MICHAUX *Histoire des Chênes* 5 Chêne blanc aquatique. Chêne lyré. *Water white oak.* **1813** MUHLENBERG *Cat. Plants* 87 Swamp post oak, water white oak. *Quercus lyrata.* **1832** BROWNE *Sylva* 272 This interesting species . . . is called Swamp Post Oak, Over-Cup Oak and Water White Oak.

***Water willow.** Any one of various willowlike trees or shrubs, +esp. a species of *Dianthera.* Also with specifying term. — **1829** EATON *Botany* (ed. 5) 265 *Justicia pedunculosa*, water willow. **1857** GRAY *Botany* 297 *Dianthera*, Water-Willow. . . . Perennial herbs, growing in water. **1897** *Outing* March 536/1 Mallards, however, prefer . . . the roots of a species of water-willow. **1901** MOHR *Plant Life Ala.* 735 *Dianthera ovata.* . . . Low Water Willow.

Water witch. {1680-}
+1. Any one of various water birds especially quick in diving, as the horned grebe and the pied-billed grebe.
1789 MORSE *Amer. Geog.* 60 American Birds [include] . . . Water-wagtail, Water-hen, Water-witch. **1835** AUDUBON *Ornith. Biog.* III. 359 'Water-witches,' as they call you, I clearly see your bills, although you have withdrawn all of you save those parts. **1883** THAXTER *Poems for Children* 8 The swift and slender water-witch, Whose neck like silver shines. **1917** *Birds of Amer.* I. 5 Horned Grebes are commonly known as 'Hell-divers' or 'Water-Witches.'

+2. (See quot. 1859.) Also attrib.
1817 S. BROWN *Western Gazetteer* 96 This discovery [of a lead mine] was made by a water-witch. **1859** BARTLETT 502 *Water-Witch*, . . . a person who pretends to have the power of discovering subterranean springs by means of the divining rod. **1883** *Harper's Mag.* Oct. 708/2 Nor do his employers make any secret of their preference for a workman with a water-witch reputation. **1890** L. C. D'OYLE *Notches* 153 Injun heap water-witch. Show white man where to dig.

***Waterwork(s).**
*1. A structure erected on a stream or other body of water in order to utilize water or water power; a water mill.
1623 *Plymouth Col. Rec.* I. 8 Stephen Deane, desiring to set up a water worke, to beat corne upon the brooke adjoyning to the towne of Plymouth, . . . was referred to the Govr & Councell. **1668** *Springfield Rec.* II. 90 Thomas Miller shall & will make & mayteyne the water worke fence. **1746** *Duxbury Rec.* 170 The said stream may be forever used . . . to improve the water coming from her by any sort of Mill or water works. **1779** *N.J. Archives* 2 Ser. III. 684 A petition was presented . . . praying a law to authorise them to build a dam and water-works across said creek. **1825** *Austin P.* II. (1924) 1166 You must fit him with a league of land . . . with a stream on which, all kinds of water works, may be erected.

2. A plant or the machinery, buildings, etc., used to obtain water for distribution to a town or city. {1621-}
1810 CUMING *Western Tour* 12 This water steam engine, otherwise called the waterworks, is a work of great magnitude. It . . . is capable of raising about 4,500,000 gallons of water in 24 hours. **1834** R. BAIRD *Valley Miss.* 210 The Water Works, by which the city is supplied with water from the Cumberland, is a noble monument of the liberality and enterprise of the citizens. **1881** *Harper's Mag.* April 711/1 The beautiful tower of the water-works remains about the only really ornamental public edifice.

1925 (title), Water Works Practice, a Manual Issued by the American Water Works Association.

+**Wauregan,** a. local. [Amer. Indian.] Good, fine, showy. Obs. or Obsolescent. — [**1643** WILLIAMS Key (1866) 64 Wunêgin Well, or good.] a**1809** in Kendall Travels I. 307 For courage bold, for things waureegan, He was the glory of Moheagan. **1877** BARTLETT 741 Wauregan. . . . The word is still local in and about Norwich, Conn. **1910** HODGE, etc. Amer. Indians 923/2.

* **Wave.**

1. A natural or artificial undulation of the hair; hair, or a section of hair, having such undulation.

1866 A. D. WHITNEY L. Goldthwaite iv, Freedom's northern wind will take all the wave out of your hair. **1884** NYE Baled Hay 15 She blushed clear up under her 'wave.'

2. (See quot. 1909.)

1887 Nation 14 July 32/1 Pessimistic financiers are predicting a panicky wave as being likely . . . to follow the failure of . . . real-estate speculators to 'corner' the possible building sites. **1909** N.Y. Ev. Post 6 July (Th.), What other practical nations call movements, we characteristically call 'waves.' The fight against graft in municipal politics was a 'wave.'

3. attrib. Designating the action of waves, or things produced by such action, or things similar in appearance to waves.

1843 N. BOONE Journal 191 In the sandstone were noticed wave-lines. **1856** OLMSTED Slave States 397 For an hour or two we got above the sandy zone, and into the . . . 'wave' region of the State. The surface here was extremely undulating. **1880** DANA Manual Geol. 910 Index, Wave-action on coral reefs.

* **Waved,** a. In the specific names of plants and trees. {1668-} Also waved-leaved. {1822-} — **1813** MUHLENBERG Cat. Plants 84 Alnus undulata, Waved alder. **1817-8** EATON Botany (1822) 234 Cheiranthus fenestralis, waved-wall-flower. **1836** LINCOLN Botany App. 74 [Amaryllis] undulata, (waved lily, Sept.). The flowers numerous on each stalk. **1843** TORREY Flora N.Y. II. 121 Asclepias obtusifolia. Waved-leaved Milkweed. . . . Sandy woods and fields. Long Island.

+**Wavey.** [Canadian Fr. from Algonquin.] A North American goose of the genus Chen; a snow goose. — [**1795** S. HEARNE Journey North. Ocean 329 Wavey (or white goose). Ib. 442 Horned wavey. . . . Common Wavey, or Snow Goose.] **1884** COUES Key to Birds (ed. 2) 686 Chen rossi . . . Horned Wavey. Least Snow Goose. **1917** Birds of Amer. I. 155 Snow Goose. . . . Wavey; Common Wavey; Little Wavey. . . . Streaked on head and neck very faintly with darker [plumage]; more or less waved on back with same.

* **Waving,** a. Of land: Undulating. — **1796** HAWKINS Letters 29, [I] arrive . . . over waving lands 4 miles to the house of Mr. Grierson. **1800** [see RIVER FLAT 1]. **1817** BROWN Western Gazetteer 12 Sixty miles above the confluence of Coosa and Tallapoose, there is a high waving country.

+**Wavy oak.** (See quotation.) — **1885** HAVARD Flora W. & S. Texas 505 Quercus undulata, (Wavy Oak). Very common, scrubby Oak in foothills west of Devil's River.

+**Wavy-striped flea beetle.** (See quotations.) — **1868** Amer. Naturalist II. 514 The Wavy-striped Flea-Beetle. This beautiful little beetle, also called 'Striped Turnip-fly' . . . at the West, is well known and abundant. **1884** Rep. Comm. Agric. 301 The Wavy-Striped Flea-Beetle. . . . The wing-covers have each a broad, wavy, longitudinal band of a pale yellow color.

+**Wawa.** Also **way-way.** [Cree wehweh 'goose.'] =WAVEY. — **1768** Phil. Trans. LX. 126 There are various sorts of the geese, as the grey-goose, the way-way, the brant, the dunter. **1855** LONGFELLOW Hiawatha 28 When the Wawa has departed, When the wild-goose has gone southward.

* **Wax,** n.

* **1.** Beeswax or any of various substances resembling this derived from plants or from petroleum.

1649 WILLIAMS Letters (1874) 169, I want wax to seal. **1717** N.C. Col. Rec. II. 272, I beg some honest man may be employed to buy . . . some paper and wax [for me]. **1846** THORPE Myst. Backwoods 150 The hunter . . . prepares a candle, which he makes out of the wax taken from the comb of wild bees. **1888** in Tarbell Hist. Standard Oil Co. I. 155 We even got it down to making wax, and using the very last residuum in the boilers.

b. spec. A substance derived from the berries of the wild myrtle.

1696-8 Mass. H. S. Coll. 1 Ser. V. 127 There is great store of the myrtle-berries, which being boiled up to a wax, make as good candles as the best wax candles whatsoever. **1785** MARSHALL Amer. Grove 94 Candleberry Myrtle [has] . . . roundish berries, affording a kind of green wax which is sometimes used in making candles. **1806** in Ann. 9th Congress 2 Sess. 1128 The wax was no longer green, but had changed its colour to a grayish-white. **1880** CABLE Grandissimes 34, I am sending an aged lady there to gather the wax of the wild myrtle.

+**2.** local. (See quot. 1879.)

1845 JUDD Margaret II. 185 The 'Wax' is freely distributed to be cooled on lumps of snow. **1879** WEBSTER Suppl. 1585/1 Wax, . . . thick sirup made by boiling down the sap of the sugar-maple tree, and cooled by exposure to the air.

3. Son of wax, a shoemaker. A term derived from the use of wax in preparing thread for shoe-making.

1871 DE VERE 313 Sons of wax, is neither an uncommon nor an uncomplimentary name for them [boot- and shoemakers].

4. attrib. In the specific names of plants and birds.

1850 Conn. Public Acts 5 It shall not be lawful . . . for any person to shoot . . . [the] spider bird or wax bird. **1829** EATON Botany (ed. 5) 193 Cuphea viscosissima, wax-bush. **1856** STOWE Dred I. 53 That heliotrope, and these jessamines . . . and that wax camelia. **1817-8** EATON Botany (1822) 175 Anthoceros levis, wax liverwort. . . . On the earth in damp shaded situations. **1847** DARLINGTON Weeds & Plants 63 P[ortulaca] grandiflora, P. Gillesii and others . . . are now common in gardens; they are known in some places as 'Wax Pinks.' **1817-8** EATON Botany (1822) 257 Cuphea viscosissima, waxweed.

Wax, v. +tr. To excel, overcome, get the better of, or circumvent. colloq. — a**1861** WINTHROP J. Brent 22, I'll hev some of ther strychnine what'll wax Burbon County's much 's our inyans ken wax them low-lived smellers what they grow to old Pike. **1880** Cimarron News & Press 3 June 1/5 He waxed Shaffer once in Peoria, and then he tackled Slosson once, and Slosson didn't get the game. a**1889** W. D. O'CONNOR Three Tales 298 You've waxed the rebels, George!

Waxberry. {1835-} Any of various shrubs or bushes bearing waxy berries, esp. the snowberry and the candleberry. — **1848** BRYANT California xxiii. 236 A shrub, which growing in our gardens is called the wax-berry, I saw in several places to-day. **1872** POWERS Afoot & Alone 146 The wax-berry rips long scratches in his ankles. **1894** Amer. Folk-Lore VII. 90 Symphoricarpus racemosus, waxberry, N.Y. **1897** SUDWORTH Arborescent Flora 117 Myrica cerifera. Wax Myrtle. . . . [Also called] Waxberry (R.I., Pa., S.C.).

Wax doll. A doll with head, bust, and sometimes limbs made of wax. {1828-} — **1843** Lowell Offering III. 45 She is sure you have brought her a great wax doll. **1881** Ore. State Jrnl. 1 Jan. 7 Holiday Goods! Wax Dolls for 25¢.

Wax(ed) end. Waxed thread used by shoemakers. {1825-} — **1843** 'CARLTON' New Purchase II. 178 Wax-ends stuck in awl-holes! **1887** GEORGE 40 Yrs. on Rail 19 At odd times I did work on shoes, 'closing' them, as we used to call the process of sewing the parts together with waxed ends.

Wax figure. A figure, usually of some eminent or notorious person, made of wax. {1825-} — **1835** Knickerb. V. 275 Derfeuil, the proprietor of the museum, . . . set him repairing. and then making, wax-figures. **1862** BROWNE A. Ward: His Book 85, I shall show the vorst [i.e., vast] superiority of wax figgers and snakes over theatre plays, in a interlectooal pint of view.

Wax flower. An artificial flower made of wax. {1843-} Also attrib. — **1854** Penna. Agric. Rep. 176 There was but one specimen of wax flowers exhibited. **1869** Boyd's Business Directory 18 Artist and Wax Flower Materials. **1891** WILKINS New Eng. Nun 217 In one corner was a rude bracket holding a bouquet of wax flowers. **1905** LINCOLN Partners 29 There were . . . some wax flowers under a glass on the shelf, and a vase of dried 'feather grass' on a bracket in the corner.

Wax light. A wax candle. {a1700-} — **1648** Md. Archives IV. 388 To Tho: Mathewes for Mithridate & wax-lights [etc.]. **1879** Harper's Mag. June 68/1 One can imagine . . . the guests assembling in the ball-room, brilliant with wax-lights, the floor polished until it reflects a duplicate image of the bright scene above its surface.

Wax-myrtle. The bayberry or candleberry, Myrica cerifera; also, a shrub of other species of Myrica. Also with specifying term. {1813} — **1806** in Ann. 9th Congress 2 Sess. 1130 The cedar, and wax myrtle . . . attach themselves particularly to the calcareous region. **1842** BUCKINGHAM E. & W. States I. 161 The berries of the wax-myrtle, when boiled, yield a fine green wax. **1863** MITCHELL My Farm 56 The old flimsy pasture with its blotches of . . . wax myrtles. **1882** Harper's Mag. June 66 The wax-myrtle . . . takes us back to the early settlers, who . . . used these berries to make . . . an agreeable-smelling soap. **1897** SUDWORTH Arborescent Flora 117 Myrica californica. California Wax Myrtle. . . . [Also called] California Myrtle (Cal.). Wax Myrtle (Cal.). **1901** [see WAX TREE].

Wax plant. {1801-} The Indian pipe. — **1859** BARTLETT 503 Wax-Plant (Monotropa uniflora), a perfectly white, fleshy plant, looking as if made of wax. **1879** WEBSTER Suppl. 1585/1 Wax-plant, a white, fleshy plant . . . , growing parasitically on the roots of beech and pine trees, in shady moist places.

Wax tree. {c1792-} A scentless wax myrtle. — **1791** BARTRAM Travels 405 This very beautiful evergreen shrub, . . . the French inhabitants call the wax tree. **1843** DE SMET Lett. & Sk. 113 On the plains we find . . . now and then the willow, the alder, the wax tree. **1901** MOHR Plant Life Ala. 15 On one of these excursions he [Bartram] discovered the wax myrtle, a small tree called by the French the wax tree, which possessed none of the fragrance of the common wax or candleberry tree (Myrica cerifera).

Waxwing. Any passerine bird of the genus Bombycilla. (Cf. BOHEMIAN, CEDAR WAXWING.) {1817-} — **1828** BONAPARTE Ornithology III. 9 The waxwings, . . . when fruits are scarce, . . . seize upon insects. **1858** BAIRD Birds Pacific R.R. 317 Wax-wing [or] Bohemian Chatterer . . . [is] seen in the United States only in severe winters, except along the great lakes. **1870** Amer. Naturalist III. 34 The Shrikes, however, resemble these birds more than the Waxwings or the Vireos, with which Baird associates them.

Waxwork.

1. Modelling in wax; the articles made by such modelling. {1697-}

1731 in Odell *Annals N.Y. Stage* I. 13 [Martha Gazley] Makes and Teacheth . . . Artificial Fruit and Flowers, and other Wax-Work. *c*1750 in Singleton *Social N.Y.* 319 The fire-engines played into the house, but . . . most of the waxwork was destroyed. **1871** *Scribner's Mo.* II. 262 Perhaps the young ladies will make wax-work.

2. *pl.* An exhibition of articles made of wax. {sing., 1796-; pl., 1831-} Also *wax work show.*

1791 *Holyoke Diaries* 125 Evng at Wax Works. **1867** DALY *Under Gaslight* IV. 35 Bermudas says he's seen 'em in Barnum's wax-work show. **1883** *Harper's Mag.* July 257 [They] became lessees of a sort of wax works which they called 'the Infernal Regions.'

3. *Like waxwork,* in perfect order and condition.

1849 KINGSLEY *Diary* 14 Went on board the brig of war at night, found everything like waxwork. **1854** CUMMINS *Lamplighter* 34 Her rooms were like wax-work.

+4. Climbing bittersweet, *Celastrus scandens.*

1841 *Knickerb.* XVII. 334 The golden-berried wax-work weaves its wreath. **1860** CURTIS *Woody Plants N.C.* 119 Wax-work. Bittersweet.... This is to me the rarest plant in the State.

* Way, *n.*

*1. A road, path, or passage.

Cf. RIGHT OF WAY 1.

1627 *Plymouth Laws* 30 It was agreed . . . that the old path ways be still allowed and that every man be allowed a conveanient way to the water. **1687** *R.I. Col. Rec.* III. 235 Surveyors of Highways . . . [are] to take care for the repairing the ways in their respective townships. **1708** *Boston Rec.* 49 The way below the Late Deacon Eliots Barn leading from Orange Street Eastward by the Sea Side [is] *Beech Street.* **1790** *Phila. Ordinances* (1812) 123 If any driver . . . shall drive . . . on the side of the way on his left hand, . . . [he] shall forfeit . . . the sum of one dollar. **1880** CABLE *Grandissimes* 376 This way (corridor, the Creoles always called it) opened into a sunny court.

2. Phrases. **+a.** *No two ways about it* (or *that*), no conceivable doubt or difference of opinion about it (or that). *colloq.*

1818 FEARON *Sketches* 320 You and I have got to dovetail, and no two ways about it. **1858** *Texas Almanac 1859* 130 [The Indian's] memory is the rock of ages, there is no 'two ways' about it. **1885** CRAWFORD *Amer. Politician* 113 The old lady . . . 'expected there were no two ways about it.'

+b. *All the way from . . . to . . . ,* within a range between . . . and . . . ; limited by . . . and . . . .

1878 BEADLE *Western Wilds* 493 The value of the booty taken has been estimated all the way from $150,000 to $300,000. **1882** *Ib.* 579 The population is estimated all the way from fifteen to forty thousand: take your choice.

c. *(In) the worst way,* (see WORST *a.* 2).

3. *attrib.* Designating offices, equipment, fares, etc., pertaining to travel between intermediate points on a transportation line.

See also WAY FREIGHT, WAY PASSENGER, etc.

1837 *Jamestown* (N.Y.) *Jrnl.* 26 July 2/2 The agents do not perform any of the duties of postmasters, other than separating the packets for each of the way offices. **1847** WEBSTER 1253/3 *Way-Baggage,* the baggage or luggage of a way-passenger of a railroad, &c. **1874** PINKERTON *Expressman & Detective* 11 The safe was intended for way packages. **1879** BURDETTE *Hawkeyes* 240, I looked out of the way-car window. **1883** 'MARK TWAIN' *Life on Miss.* lii. She got out of the cars at a way place. **1883** SWEET & KNOX *Through Texas* III. 42 About the time you get to know them, they begin to get off at way-landings.

4. In special combinations.

Way line, a light rope used for hauling a heavier one; *w. log,* a log used in launching a boat; *w. pocket,* a pouch in which the waybill of a stagecoach is carried; *w. strip,* a piece of wood used in building ways for launching a boat.

1905 LINCOLN *Partners* 174 The smaller end of the 'way line,' a stout rope tapering from one inch to three inches in thickness, was spliced to the 'drag line.' **1716** HEMPSTEAD *Diary* 57, I was all day Getting Waylogs & Launching Timber. **1890** LANGFORD *Vigilante Days* (1912) 528, I handed the big man the way-pocket containing the way-bill. **1805** LEWIS in *L. & Clark Exped.* II. (1904) 201 We have therefore only the way strips now to obtain in order to complete the wood work.

* 'Way, Way, *adv.* (See also AWAY *adv.*)

'*Obs. exc. Sc., north.,* and *U.S.*' (O.E.D.).

*1. Used in various verb phrases.

1840 DANA *Two Years* 49 Go 'way! You think, 'cause you been to college you know better than anybody. **1888** CUSTER *Tenting on Plains* 614 [He destroyed the picture], thus taking way the sting of ridicule, which constant sight of the caricature might produce. **1908** *Collier's Mag.* 17 Oct. 13/2 Mr. Bryan has, during the past twelve years, eaten or otherwise made way with over 1,700 meals at railroad lunch-counters.

2. With prepositions in sense: At a considerable distance; far. {1891}

1849 W. S. MAYO *Kaloolah* 44 It was way towards Tupper's Lake. **1873** *Congress. Globe* 29 Jan. 948/1 Utah is way in advance of the age in one respect; . . . female suffrage has been adopted there. **1889** *Harper's Mag.* April 828/2 The gentleman whom we are about to nominate is a man 'way beyond suspicion. **1922** Z. GREY *To Last Man* 3 Dad's growin' old. . . . He must be 'way over sixty.

+3. With adverbs in sense: At or by a considerable distance; thoroughly.

1888 *Congress. Rec.* 3 Oct. 9122/1 He is way below, he is only 50 . . . in mathematics. **1898** NICHOLS *Idyl of Wabash* 79 These yellow things [violets] are way ahead of time. **1905** PHILLIPS *Social Secretary* 97, I'm 'way behind on sleep. **1908** WHITE *Riverman* 83 You got to feeling like the thing was never going to end, and . . . you got sick of it way through.

+b. With *back:* Far off; long ago. {1918} Freq. in phrase *from way back.* Also used attrib. or, in jocular use, as a noun.

1855 *Merry's Museum* XXIX. 58, I live 'way back in the woods.' **1884** *Boston Globe* Oct., His unkempt hair, gawky appearance, and homespun suit . . . all bespoke the citizen from wayback. **1885** *Santa Fé Wkly. New Mexican* 10 Sept. 1/2 A writer in giving a description of the plains of Kansas in the 'way back' time, speaks of it as a 'wilderness of grasses.' **1887** *New York Ev. Post* 4 Oct., The way-back delegates, those from the farms and the small villages. **1890** CUSTER *Following Guidon* 261 We were, in Western terms, 'waybacks from wayback.' **1905** *Springfield W. Repub.* 6 Oct. 10 Mrs. Thayer is American from way back. **1923** COOK *On Old Frontier* 227 This occurred 'way back,' when the Indians had no horses.

+c. With *down:* Far down; far below.

1851 WORTLEY *Travels in U.S.* 138 Less elaborately finished craft . . . are bound for . . . the trading and wealthy cities of far off Alabama and Louisiana, 'way down south.' **1866** LOWELL *Biglow P.* II. xi. 235 Nor these ain't matters thet with pol'tics swings, But goes 'way down amongst the roots o' things. **1913** LONDON *Valley of Moon* 332 Here I am, which proves that 'way down inside I must want the country.

+d. With *off:* At a considerable distance; far removed; very wrong.

1853 G. C. HILL *Dovecote* 29, I found her 'way off in them woods yonder! **1892** *Harper's Mag.* Feb. 438/2 The papers are generally 'way off in some things. **1903** R. HALL *Pine Grove House* 15 Way off here we can hear the noise.

+e. With *out:* Far away from a point regarded as central.

1868 G. A. CUSTER in *Following Guidon* 53 They had braved the perils . . . in order to bring us, 'way out here, news from our loved ones. **1882** *Congress. Rec.* 9 March 1758/1 Instead of that they go way out to Peoria, Illinois. **1908** 'YESLAH' *Tenderfoot S. Calif.* 139 Catalina is an island out at sea—way out.

+f. With *over:* Far over; as far as (a point named or implied).

1850 GARRARD *Wah-To-Yah* xvii. 200 Calyforny! way over yonder! **1896** JEWETT *Pointed Firs* 88 She's rode 'way over from Nahum Brayton's place. **1904** *N.Y. Times* 5 April 2 A thick, pungent smoke which soon became so great a cloud as to cause a stench way over to Broadway.

+g. With *up:* Far up; very high.

1850 S. WARNER *Wide, Wide World* xii, Do you live 'way up there? **1876** HABBERTON *Jericho Road* 20 The river is way up. **1904** 'O. HENRY' *Roads of Destiny* 299, I want to be manager of something way up—like a railroad or a diamond trust.

Waybill, *n.* **a.** A list showing the names of the passengers transported in a public vehicle or identifying the goods sent by a common carrier: (see also quot. 1839). {1791-}

+b. A document or label identifying and supplying information concerning a shipment of goods by freight or express. Also with defining terms.

1821 *Mass. Spy* 23 May (Th.), Packages of the larger kind . . . were always entered on the way-bill. **1839** *Diplom. Corr. Texas* I. (1908) 392 With every mail passing from the United States into Texas will be sent a way bill showing the exact amount of unpaid U.S. postage. **1848** BARTLETT 377 *Way-Bill,* a list of the passengers in a stage-coach, railroad car, steamboat, or other public conveyance. **1872** in Tarbell *Hist. Standard Oil Co.* I. 286 The party hereto of the second part . . . [agrees] to make manifests or way-bills of all petroleum or its products, transported over any portion of the railroads. **1883** RITTENHOUSE *Maud* 225, I found out what way-bills and manifests are. **1887** GUNTER *Mr. Barnes* 145 The old and dilapidated little dirty trunk covered with numerous way-bills. **1903** E. JOHNSON *Railway Transportation* 165 The goods shipped [by express] are accompanied by a way-bill similar to a freight way-bill, stating the weight and value of each package, the consignor and consignee, destination, and charges, prepaid or unpaid.

+Waybill, *v. tr.* To make a waybill for (goods). — **1877** W. H. BURROUGHS *Taxation* 140 Freight being way-billed through. **1890** *Railways Amer.* 412 [He] must count, seal, superscribe, and way-bill money packages and handle oyster-kegs and barrels of beer at a moment's notice.

+Wayfarer's tree. =next. — **1858** THOREAU *Maine Woods* 88 The mountain-ash was now very handsome, as also the wayfarer's tree or hobble-bush. **1860** CURTIS *Woody Plants N.C.* 91 The branches spread upon the ground, and . . . form well secured loops for tripping the feet of inexperienced wayfarers; a habit which has been revenged . . . in the names imposed upon it of *American Wayfarer's Tree* and the *Devil's Shoestrings.*

*Wayfaring tree. +The hobblebush, *Viburnum alnifolium.* Also with specifying term. — **1785** MARSHALL *Amer. Grove* 159 *Viburnum.* Pliant Meally, or Way-faring-Tree. **1857** GRAY *Botany* 168 V[*iburnum*] *lantanoides.* (Hobble-bush. American Wayfaring-tree.) **1899** GOING *Flowers* 57 The tender foliage of the 'wayfaring-tree' or 'hobble-bush' has had no protection save a coating of scurf.

+Way freight.
1. Goods destined for, or picked up at, an intermediate stopping place or way station; a consignment of these goods.
1833 *Niles' Reg.* XLIV. 260/2 The hatch . . . was open to get out a lot of way-freight. **1869** *Rep. Comm. Patents 1868* I. 774/2 The car has a plurality of metallic chambers for the respective reception of 'way' and 'through' freight. **1874** COLLINS *Kentucky* I. 195 [The legislature] authorizes Ky. Central Railroad to charge for way-freights not over 25 per cent. over through-freight rates. **1875** 'MARK TWAIN' *Old Times* vii. 131 No way-freights and no way-passengers were allowed.

2. A freight train making stops for way freight. Also attrib. and fig.
1879 BURDETTE *Hawkeyes* 64 It was a way freight going south. **1887** DALY *Railroad of Love* 15 If you are loaded with millions, you may court on way-freight time. **1898** HAMBLEN *Gen. Manager's Story* 37 It was the way freight that had crossed over to load some freight. **1903** E. JOHNSON *Railway Transportation* 135 Frequently the 'milk' trains and way-freight trains have passenger-coaches attached.

+Way letter. A letter accepted by a post rider or postman en route between two post offices. {1893} — **1773** FINLAY *Journal* 38 Way letters he makes his own perquisite. **1792** *Ann. 2d Congress* 62 The deputy postmasters . . . [shall] answer to him, for all by or way letters, and shall specify the same . . . in the post bill. **1836** in *P.O. Laws* (1843) I. 29 The Postmaster General shall submit . . . specific estimates of the sums of money expected to be required [for] . . . 'Ship, steam-boat, and way letters' [etc.]. **1880** LAMPHERE *U.S. Govt.* 98/1 The accounts of the postal service must be kept in such manner as to exhibit separately the amount of . . . expenditure made for . . . way letters.

+Way mail. Mail picked up at or destined for a way station. — **1818** *Amer. Monthly Mag.* II. 315 The way-mail . . . is so arranged as not to detain the coach more than three minutes at each post-office on the road. **1845** *S. Lit. Messenger* XI. 376/1 The passengers . . . will generally see . . . a mulatto, who has something to do with the transfer of the way mail.

Way-off, *a.* Far-off. — **1870** A. D. WHITNEY *We Girls* xiv, [They] had come from their way-off, beautiful Wisconsin home.

+Way passenger. A passenger boarding or leaving a coach, etc., at a way station, or a point en route. Also transf.
1786 *Mass. Spy* 5 Jan., Way passengers will be accommodated when the stages are not full. **1819** *Niles' Reg.* XV. 384/2 Way-passengers down, the same as up. **1824** *Mass. Spy* 28 July (Th.), Way Passenger. . . . A sturgeon leaped in and took passage [on the schooner]. **1850** *Rep. Comm. Patents 1849* 410 It has another convenience of giving notice to way passengers of the approach to their destinations. **1867** HOLMES *Guardian Angel* 65 The gentlemanly conductor . . . was always taking up and setting down way-passengers. **1879** BAGBY *Old Va. Gentleman* 236 The way-passengers . . . were dumped upon mattresses, placed on the dining-tables.

+Way point. A stopping place on a route or during a journey. — **1880** *Harper's Mag.* Dec. 53 The Ohio is plied by a line of Cincinnati and Pittsburgh packets, and by smaller craft earning a precarious existence between 'way' points. **1897** *Outing* March 555/2 Blue herons posed at way-points with all the dignity of sentinels. **1902** WISTER *Virginian* 276 The letter . . . [had] taken the stage-coach at a way-point.

*Ways and means. Committee on ways and means or ways and means committee, = COMMITTEE 2 d. — **1774** *Boston Rec.* 181 The Comittee [*sic*] on Ways & Means Reported verbally, that they had been considering the best Methods to Employ the Poor. **1867** *Ore. State Jrnl.* 5 Jan. 2/2 The Ways and Means Committee decided to postpone an action on Mr. Boutwell's bill. **1919** *Lit. Digest* 22 March 21/2 Mr. Fordney, of Michigan, . . . will probably be . . . Chairman of the Ways and Means Committee.

+Way station. A station intermediate between stations of major importance in a transportation system; a local station.
1849 *Mass. R.R. Rep.* 21 Whole number of way stations, nineteen. **1854** *Harper's Mag.* VIII. 566/2 The boats touched at most of the prominent towns on the river, to land such passengers as might desire to disembark at 'way-stations.' **1878** BEADLE *Western Wilds* 48 North Platte . . . [is] now a way station, with hotel and saloon attachment. **1882** McCABE *New York* 187 The throngs who wait at the way stations rush on board only to find standing room. **1906** *Springfield W. Repub.* 29 March 5 A through train with no stops for way stations.
fig. and transf. **1892** *Congress. Rec.* 23 March 2462/2 'Will the gentleman allow me to ask him a question?' . . . 'The gentleman will excuse me. On a fast schedule I can not stop at way stations.' **1912** F. J. HASKIN *Amer. Government* 210 Cities which are to-day mere way stations on the international routes of trade will grow into rich world centers.

attrib. **1885** JACKSON *Zeph* vii, It had been but five minutes,—only an insignificant way-station stop. **1908** *Atlantic Mo.* Nov. 683 Even if one neglects the way-station island of Curaçao, the extremes begin before foot is set on Venezuelan soil.

+Way traffic. Local traffic. — **1869** *Harper's Mag.* July 294/2 The 'way traffic' upon the line will for many years be inconsiderable. **1883** 'MARK TWAIN' *Life on Miss.* xxii, Freight and passenger way traffic remains to the streamers.

+Way train. A train stopping at local or way stations. — **1873** 'MARK TWAIN' & WARNER *Gilded Age* 269 Next morning . . . he descended, sleepy and sore, from a way-train. **1899** MUIRHEAD *Baedeker's U.S.* p. xxi, A slow train is called an *Accommodation* or *Way Train.* **1920** LEWIS *Main Street* 22 The hordes of the way-train were not altogether new to Carol.

+Way-up, *a.* Of superior quality or rank; excellent. *colloq.* (See 'WAY *adv.* 3 g.) — **1889** FARMER 553/2 *Way-up spread,* a good feast; something superlative in the matter of eating and drinking. **1898** POST *10 Years Cowboy* 239 Joe Anderson will fiddle for us, and we can have a way-up time. **1901** H. ROBERTSON *Inlander* 72, I didn't think her one of those way-up girls that would suit a way-up fellow like Rod.

Way warden. An official made responsible for the condition of roads and ways. Now hist. {1776–} — **1647** in Currier *Hist. Newbury, Mass.* 48. **1649** *Plymouth Col. Rec.* II. 137 Wee present the way wardens or surveyors of Taunton for neglecting to mend the hyewayes. **1673** *Jamaica Rec.* I. 31 Thomas Smith and John Skidmore shall be Way Wardings . . . to call . . . Men . . . for repayreing and cleareing the hyghe Wayes. **1691** *Providence Rec.* VIII. 178 Chosen for way wardens Sam: whipple & Joseph Hearnden.

*Weak, *a.*
1. In the specific names of plants.
1813 MUHLENBURG *Cat. Plants* 96 *Acacia miamensis,* Weak acacia. **1878** KILLEBREW *Tenn. Grasses* 229 *Poa Debilis,* Weak Meadow Grass. . . . A soft eatable, but too scattered growing grass. **1843** TORREY *Flora N.Y.* II. 352 *Scirpus debilis.* . . . Weak-stalked Clubrush. . . . Borders of lakes and rivulets, particularly in sandy soils. **1817–8** EATON *Botany* (1822) 514 *Viola debilis,* weak stem violet. Flowers small.

2. In special combinations.
Weak gas, (see quotation); *w.-kneed,* lacking in resolution and force; *w.-lunged,* with impaired lung; *w. spot,* the place of least strength, hence the person of least strength or dependability in a group; *w. ticket,* in politics, a ticket making little appeal.
1889 HOWELLS *Hazard of Fortunes* II. 118 They call it weak-gas when they tap it two or three hundred feet down. **1870** *N.Y. Times* 7 Sept. (De Vere), General Butler is setting a good example to his weak-kneed brethren. **1892** *Courier-Journal* 2 Oct. 9/6 Disease . . . gradually left me in the condition known as 'weak-lunged.' **1868** CHADWICK *Base Ball* 28 The batsmen on the other side, of course, regarding him as the weak spot in the nine. **1874** *Chicago Times* 11 June 5/4 A weak ticket was expected, inasmuch as the convention proposed to elevate the office men who were not known to the politicians.

*Weaken, *v.* +*intr.* To give way; to let go; to take a less firm stand in the face of opposition. *colloq.* {1809} — **1876** 'MARK TWAIN' *Tom Sawyer* xxvii, Don't you ever weaken, Huck, and I won't. **1882** HARTE *Flip* 31 The old man weakened. **1890** LANGFORD *Vigilante Days* (1912) 100 If I were to leave it would be reported that I had 'weakened' and fled from Patterson.

+Weakfish. [Du. *week visch* 'soft fish.'] An edible marine fish of the genus *Cynoscion* and allied genera of the family Otolithidae.
1796 MORSE *Univ. Geog.* I. 222 Bony Fish [found in the U.S. include the] . . . Minow, Week fish, King fish. **1814** MITCHILL *Fishes N.Y.* 396 The weak fish is so much the companion of the basse, that I once gave him the specific name of *comes.* **1835** AUDUBON *Ornith. Biog.* III. 606 An elderly man . . . asked if I had ever seen the 'Weak fish' along the coast without the [fish hawk]. **1855** BAIRD in *Smithsonian Rep. 1854* 339 The silver-side . . . makes an excellent bait for blue fish, [and] weak fish. **1875** *Fur, Fin & Feather* 122 You are always welcome to a seat in his boat, if disposed for . . . spot-fish, weak fish or blue fish. **1903** *N.Y. Ev. Post* 21 Nov., The soft fish without strong and flabby flesh—such as the bluefish and weakfish—spoil quickest.

+Weakfishing. Fishing for weakfish. — **1888** GOODE *Amer. Fishes* 125 Much the same rig . . . is used in weakfishing. **1904** *Brooklyn Eagle* 30 May 3 The reports of good weak fishing to be had in Jamaica Bay brought out scores of anglers.

*Weak-handed, *a.* Short-handed; lacking sufficient numbers. {1836} Also as *adv.* — **1775** *Essex Inst. Coll.* XIII. 156 The affair . . . of the Inhabitants removal has given us great trouble and we are but weak handed. **1784** WASHINGTON *Diaries* II. 325 In an infant settlement where the people are poor and weak handed. **1898** N. E. JONES *Squirrel Hunters of Ohio* 14 Much of the labor necessary to open up a new country of this character could not be performed 'weak-handed.'

+Weak sister. A person who cannot be depended upon; one who is likely to give way under pressure. *colloq.* — **1861** *N.Y. Tribune* 26 Dec. 4/3 There are White Unionists there, but they are weak sisters—overawed, terrorized, silenced. **1883** *Gringo & Greaser* 1 Sept. 2/2 John Sylvester, . . . a very 'weak sister,' was so scared in the Estancia fight that he ran all the way home.

Weaponless Christian. (See quotation.) — **1796** MORSE *Univ. Geog.* I. 283 [Mennonists] call themselves the Harmless Christians, Revengeless Christians, and Weaponless Christians.

∗ Wear, *v.*

1. *intr.* To get along; to succeed.

1831 ROYALL *Southern Tour* II. 136 The sons of this noble state [N.Y.] wear much better in the south than the Yankees.

2. In phrases. **a.** *To wear out,* to exhaust the fertility of (land); of land, to become exhausted. {'to wear out of heart,' 1607}

1632 *Plymouth Laws* 31 The said acres are for the most part worne out. **1748** ELIOT *Field-Husb.* i. 11 The Third sort of Land I would speak of is our old Land which we have worn out. **1758** *Newport Mercury* 19 Dec. 2/2 With a right Cultivation and Management, our Lands will not wear out. **1800** TATHAM *Agric. & Commerce* 49 This is *worn out* (as it is called) by the culture of maize and tobacco. **1834** J. HALL *Sk. of West* (1835) I. 195 The pioneers placed little value upon their lands, in consequence of an apprehension that the soil would soon 'wear out.'

+b. *To wear a collar,* (see COLLAR 2 b).

c. *To wear (up)on,* to deplete or exhaust; to injure; to prey upon.

1864 NORTON *Army Lett.* 245, I did not suppose these things were serious enough to wear upon your health. **1876** HABBERTON *Jericho Road* 12 I reckon it wore on him so bad that it killed him. **1891** WILKINS *New Eng. Nun* 109, I should think it would kill you, an' you don't look as if it wore on you a bit.

∗ Wear(e). Variant of WEIR(E).

∗ Wearing. *attrib.* Designating clothing or articles of dress.

1639 *Conn. Rec.* I. 444 A Inuentory of the goods and Cattle of John Brundish [includes:] . . . his weareing apparrell. **1645** *Suffolk Deeds* I. 60 I pray wife make sale of . . . all your weareing clothes. **1647** *Conn. Probate Rec.* I. 10, 1 weareing Coate. **1692** *Ib.* 456, I give to my son John the best pair of my wearing shoes. *Ib.* 492, I also give to my daughter . . . my wearing linen. **1850** LEWIS *La. Swamp Doctor* 51 The piece of wearin' truck wot's next the skin made a monstrous pretty flag as the old hoss . . . streakt it up the road.

∗ Weasel.

∗ 1. Any one of several small animals of the genus *Mustela.*

1612 SMITH, etc. *Virginia* I. 14 Martins, Powlecats, weessels and Minkes we know they haue, because we haue seen many of their skinnes. **1709** LAWSON *Carolina* 125 The Dormouse is the same as in England; and so is the weasel, which is very scarce. **1819** SCHOOLCRAFT *Mo. Lead Mines* 36 The following is a list of such animals as are still to be met with: . . . weasel, mink, go[p]har, otter. **1907** *St. Nicholas* Sept. 1021/2 Unfortunately there was a weasel in that hole.

b. With specifying words designating varieties of weasels or animals allied to weasels or similar to them.

1805 LEWIS in *L. & Clark Exped.* II. (1904) 379 The ermin[e] whic[h] is known to the traiders of the N.W. by the name of the white weasel is the genuine ermine. **1825** HARLAN *Fauna Amer.* 65 *Mustela canadensis.* . . . The fisher, . . . from the western states. Fisher weasel or martin of others. **1842** *Nat. Hist. N.Y., Zoology* I. 35 The Brown Weasel. *Mustela fusca.* . . . A new species. **1917** *Mammals of Amer.* 118 Arctic Weasel. . . . Related Species. . . . Bonaparte's Weasel. . . . Richardson's Weasel. . . . Mountain Weasel [etc.].

2. In allusions and comparisons.

1816 WEEMS *Letters* III. 166 Yr. Bible carts had been here as thick as weasels in a hen yard selling Bibles at nearly half price. **1830** COOPER *Water Witch* I. 11 Here have I been seven years trying to fatten the nags, and they still look . . . like weasels. **1842** 'UNCLE SAM' *Peculiarities* II. 10, I can suck melancholy out of hot corn and hominy, as a weazel sucks eggs. **1846** *Xenia Torch-Light* 2 July 4/1 They are as wide awake as weasels. **1856** DERBY *Phoenixiana* 111 Oh! no, my public, an ancient weasel may not be detected in the act of slumber, in that manner.

+3. *cap.* An inhabitant of South Carolina. A nickname.

1845 *Cincinnati Misc.* I. 240 The inhabitants of . . . S. Carolina [are called] Weasels. **1872** *Harper's Mag.* Jan. 318/1. **1888** WHITMAN *Nov. Boughs* 70 Those from . . . South Carolina, [were call'd] Weasels.

+4. = WEASEL SKIN.

1869 *Ore. State Jrnl.* 2 Jan. 1/6 Young man your weasel draw, or else prepare to die. **1890** LANGFORD *Vigilante Days* (1912) 46 Draw your weasel now.

5. *attrib.* and *comb.* **a.** In sense 1 with *cage, hunting.* **b.** *Weasel words,* intentionally ambiguous words.

(a) **1780** *Narragansett Hist. Reg.* I. 101 Made a weasel cage. **1884** ROE *Nature's Story* 308 Weasel-hunting has some drawbacks. (b) **1904** *Booklovers Mag.* Jan. 7 Should there be a recurrence to the old custom of noncommittal platforms, filled with 'weasel words,' the identity of the Democratic nominee will still be a matter of great interest.

∗ Weasel skin. **+A** purse. — **1887** TOURGEE *Button's Inn* 154 You're welcome to all you get out of that 'weasel-skin.' **1898** WESTCOTT *D. Harum* xvii, We'll see whose weasel-skin's the longest. **1903** A. ADAMS *Log of Cowboy* 356 Every rascal of us got his weasel skin out.

Weaser. *L.I.* (See quotations.) Also *weaser sheldrake.* — **1844** GIRAUD *Birds of L.I.* 340 The difference in plumage of the adult male, from the young male and female, is so strongly marked, that our gunners consider it a distinct species, calling the former 'Weaser,' or large 'Swamp-Shell-Drake.' **1888** TRUMBULL *Names of Birds* 65 [*Merganser americanus* is called] on Long Island at Moriches, Weaser Sheldrake; at Bellport and Seaford (Hempstead), Weaser. **1891** *Cent.* 6861/3.

∗ Weather.[1] = WETHER. — **1640** *Conn. Probate Rec.* I. 23, 3 Ewes, one Ewe kydd, 2 weathers. **1804** J. ROBERTS *Penna. Farmer* 25 The turnips were sufficient for fattening the weathers. **1866** *Oregon State Jrnl.* 24 Nov. 3/1 The two year old weathers of this breed are said to dress 200 lbs. net.

∗ Weather.[2]

1. In phrases. **+a.** *Under the weather,* indisposed; slightly ill. {1882-}

1836 DUNLAP *Mem. Water Drinker* (1837) I. 80 He seems a little under the weather, somehow; and yet he's not sick. **1850** *Knickerb.* XXXVI. 362/1 He complained of being under the weather. **1860** HOLLAND *Miss Gilbert's Career* 277 The old man is under the weather. **1887** *Lisbon (Dakota) Star* 22 May 4 Captain . . . Smith, who has been somewhat under the weather for a few days past, is again able to be around.

b. *To the weather,* uncovered.

1897 F. C. MOORE *How to Build a Home* 26 The slate should be laid with not more than seven inches 'to the weather.' *Ib.* 27 Shingles . . . [should not be] laid with a greater number of inches to the weather . . . than called for by the specifications.

2. Attrib. and comb. with *book, history, house,* etc.

Freq. used with reference to forecasting the weather.

1860 HOLMES *Professor* 247 The man and the woman in the toy called a 'weather-house' [are] both on the same wooden arm suspended on a pivot. **1871** *Scribner's Mo.* I. 402 The creation of the government Signal Service for obtaining weather-telegrams . . . [will] mark a new era in American commerce. **1872** *Atlantic Mo.* Feb. 184 His weather-book . . . is a wonder of neatness and minuteness,—fifty-nine days' weather history on one small page. **1876** INGRAM *Centennial Exp.* 119 The principal part of this exhibit was a signal station, or weather-observer's station. **1881** STODDARD *E. Hardery* 189 The climatic lines on the weather maps bend northwesterly after they cross the Alleghanies. **1883** SWEET & KNOX *Through Texas* 268 The weather-sharp is an alleged prophet, who tries to make people believe he is more intimate with the climate than anybody else. **1884** *N.Y. Herald* 27 Oct. 5/2 Midnight Weather Report. . . . Generally fair weather, followed by increasing cloudiness and local rains. **1895** *Advance* 1 Aug. 153/1 We had on suits of picturesque weather-wear and unconcealable shabbiness. **1902** LORIMER *Lett. Merchant* 203 The weather man usually guesses wrong. **1903** EARLE *Two Cent. Costume Amer.* II. 617 Another name for a safeguard was a weather-skirt.

∗ Weatherboard. A clapboard. — **1684** I. MATHER *Providences* (1856) v. 101 A burnt brick, and a piece of weather-board, were thrown in at the window. **1768** *Va. House of Burgesses* 162 [Soldiers] ripped off the Weather boards of the dwelling House and Stable. **1816** U. BROWN *Journal* I. 268 Weather boards [are] tumbling off very fast. **1891** *Century Mag.* April 846 The sides were of weather-boards ten to twelve inches wide.

+Weather Bureau. A governmental agency, since 1891 a bureau of the Department of Agriculture, which collects reports of weather conditions and issues predictions. Also in fig. context. — **1879** WEBSTER *Suppl.* 1585/1 *Weather-bureau,* a term applied to that bureau of the War Department of the government, which collects and compares meteorological observations, and publishes, by telegraph, reports and predictions concerning the weather. **1894** WARNER *Golden House* xiii, He didn't know anything more about the weather than the Weather Bureau knows. **1905** N. DAVIS *Northerner* 176 The weather vouchsafed to the valley of the Tennessee by the deities of the Weather Bureau was ideal.

Weather cloth. *Naut.* Canvas or tarpaulin used to protect boats and their equipment, and to shelter crew and passengers from rough weather. — **1856** KANE *Arctic Explor.* I. 315 A sort of weather-cloth . . . would certainly make her more comfortable in heavy weather. **1897** *Outing* XXIX. 547/1 A coil of rope for head-rest, a discarded sail for weather cloth.

∗ Weathercock. A weather vane, orig. in the form of a cock. Also in fig. context. — **1652** WILLIAMS *Hireling Ministry* (1847) 171 The Weather-Cock, according as the powerful wind of a prevailing Sword and Authority, shall blow from the various points and quarters of it. **1789** MORSE *Amer. Geog.* 258 The gable end is commonly of brick with . . . an iron horse for a weather cock, on the top. **1846** *Xenia Torch-Light* 30 July 1/6, I watched the weather-cock as close as I ever watched my anvil.

Weather-earing. A line used to fasten a sail to the yard or gaff on the windward side of a vessel; the fastening of such a line. — **1827** COOPER *Red Rover* III. 86 The fellow . . . thinks his equal is not to be found at a weather-earing. **1840** DANA *Two Years* 31 We began to haul out the reef-tackle, and have the weather earing passed before there was a man upon the yard. **1865** A. A. WHITNEY *Gayworthys* 253 The best sailor on board had the weather-earing on our yard.

‖**Weatherist.** A weather prophet. — **1869** *Northern Vindicator* (Estherville, Ia.) 26 Oct., We prophecy before the weather changes and we loose [*sic*] our reputation as a 'weatherist.'

‖**Weatherologist.** = prec. — **1870** *Northern Vindicator* (Estherville, Ia.) 19 Feb., The wisest weatherologists cannot tell what a day may bring forth.

+**Weather strip**, *n.* A strip of metal or wood so placed at the edge of a window or door casing as to be useful in keeping out cold air: (see also quot. 1869). — **1847** *Rep. Comm. Patents 1846* 94 One patent has been granted for improvements in fences, and another for a weather strip for doors. **1869** *Boyd's Business Directory* 304 Averill's Weather Strip consists of a beaded or corrugated strip, nailed or screwed to the door by its upper edge. **1875** *Chicago Tribune* 6 Nov. 1/3 Weather Strips! Have on hand, or will furnish to order, any kind desired, at lowest prices. **1908** A. WARNER *Seeing England with Uncle John* 9 Lee wanted to put weather-strips on the baby's windows [in England] and nobody even knew what weather-strips were.

+**Weather-strip**, *v. tr.* (See quot. 1891.) Also *ppl. a.* — **1891** *Cent.* 6863/3 *Weather-strip*, . . . to apply weather-strips to; fit or secure with weather-strips. **1908** STEVENS *Liberators* 8 The wind that shook the windows, weather-stripped as they were, crept into the room.

Weather vane. A device placed in some high position and so moving with the wind as to indicate the wind's direction. {1721-} — **1876** INGRAM *Centennial Exp.* 124 The weather-vane in turning revolves the rod to which it is attached. **1911** LINCOLN *Cap. Warren's Wards* 359, I tell her she'd sand-soap the weather vane if she could climb up to it.

Weather-wiser. {1667-1787} One who is skilled in interpreting weather signs. — **1816** *Niles' Reg.* X. 272/1 The *weatherwisers* may account for the fact [of the rain], if they can. **1883** *Homiletic Mo.* Aug. 622 Anybody can understand talk about the weather; and . . . all men are, in some sense, weather-wisers.

* **Weaver.**

* **1.** One whose trade is the weaving of cloth.

1644 *Essex Probate Rec.* I. 37, I giue Thomas my Son my Loomes . . . with there appurtenances concerning his trade of a weaver. **1729** *Amer. Wkly. Mercury* 22 May, There is just arrived from Scotland, a parcel of choice *Scotch Servants;* Taylors, Weavers, Shoemakers and ploughmen. **1892** *York County Hist. Rev.* 30 This is a two-story building . . . equipped with hand looms, and where six competent weavers are regularly employed.

+**2.** (See quotation.)

1920 *Nat. Museum Proc.* LVIII. 385 In parts of the Southern States the large dancing crane-flies pass by the name of 'weavers.'

* **3.** Used in possessive in combinations.

1673 *Essex Inst. Coll.* L. 27 In the shop [are] a weavers loome with Gears harnesses. **1815** *Niles' Reg.* IX. 36/1 Plane stocks, weaver's reeds, and the different productions of the lathe. **1847** *Rep. Comm. Patents 1846* 273 What I claim as new . . . [is] the forming of a true fisherman's or weaver's knot in netting woven in a loom. **1850** *Ib. 1849* 183 Improvement in Weavers' Temples.

+**Weave room.** A room in a factory in which cloth is woven. Also attrib. — **1845** *Lowell Offering* V. 281 The weave-room overseer who has sent out the most cloth . . . is entitled to a premium. **1850** JUDD *R. Edney* 94 There is a difference between the weave-room and the warping-room. **1899** JEWETT *Queen's Twin* 92 She'll . . . be kaping her plants in the weave-room windows this winter with the rest of the girls.

+**Weave shop.** =prec. — **1847** *Knickerb.* XXX. 517 Most of the girls work in the 'weave-shop.'

+**Webb.** An Indian woman or wife. *Obs.* — **1634** WOOD *New Eng. Prospect* (1865) 114 Web, a wife. **1672** JOSSELYN *New Eng. Rarities* 62 A Fisher-man, having burnt his Knee Pan, was healed again by an Indian Webb, or Wife. **1676** I. MATHER *K. Philip's War* (1862) 141 A party of English came in a Warlike posture upon some of their *Webbs* (as they call them) *i.e. Women* as they were gathering corn.

Web-fingered, *a.* {1781-} In the specific names of fishes. — **1814** MITCHILL *Fishes N.Y.* 431 Web-fingered Gurnard. *Trigla palmipes.* With bright yellow fringes on the fingers. **1842** *Nat. Hist. N.Y., Zoology* IV. 46 Web-Fingered Grunter. . . . This is a very rare species. **1873** T. GILL *Cat. Fishes E. Coast N.A.* 21 *Prionotus carolinus.* . . . Web-fingered sea-robin; Carolina robin.

Webfoot. {1765-}

+**1.** *cap.* A resident of Oregon. A nickname.

1864 *Ore. State Jrnl.* 6 Aug. 1/3 The thunder bellowed through those immense canyons in a way that would scare any Web-foot out of his boots. **1882** W. NASH *Two Years in Oregon* 164 Our neighbors in California call us 'Web-feet.' **1904** STEEDMAN *Bucking the Sagebrush* 88 The term 'Web-foot' was given to the settlers west of the Cascades range of mountains.

+**b.** *Old Webfoot,* Oregon.

c**1873** DE VERE *MS. Notes* 661 *Oregon*=Land of Red Apples. Affectionately=Old Webfoot on acc[oun]t of incessant rains which prevail.

+**c.** Attrib. in sense: Oregon or Oregonian.

1864 *Ore. State Jrnl.* 12 March 3/1 Today the rain is coming down in real web-foot style. **1874** GLISAN *Jrnl. Army Life* 497 Those persons . . . cannot be contented in the 'webfoot' country as the Willamette Valley is derisively called, because of its frequent rains in winter. **1882** W. NASH *Two Years in Oregon* 164 The State is called 'The Web-foot State.'

+**2.** An infantryman. *colloq.*

Cf. *Uncle Sam's web feet* (under UNCLE SAM 3) and *Uncle Samuel's web feet* (under UNCLE SAMUEL).

1884 CABLE *Dr. Sevier* 421 Compliments . . . flew back and forth from the 'web-foots' to the 'critter company,' and from the 'critter company' to the 'web-foots.'

+**Web press.** A printing press supplied with paper from a roll. Also *web perfecting press,* such a press with attachments for cutting, folding, etc. — **1876** KNIGHT 2751/2 The *web-press* is a late improvement. *Ib.,* In the Hoe web perfecting-press . . . the paper is printed from a roll containing a length of over four miles and a half. **1888** *Nation* 12 July p. iii/1 The New York Weekly Post . . . is printed . . . with new web presses.

+**Web saw.** A frame saw. — **1876** KNIGHT 2752/1 *Web-saw,* a saw strained between points or holders; a frame-saw. **1889** *Century Mag.* Jan. 418/2 The web-saw, the glue-pot, the plane, and the hammer are the principal tools used.

+**Webster.**[1] [Noah *Webster,* Amer. lexicographer (1758-1843).] Used in the possessive with reference to a spelling book prepared by Noah Webster or to a dictionary bearing his name. Also in nominative as the putative author of one of the late amplifications of his dictionary. — **1823** COOPER *Pioneers* vi, Elnathan, then about fifteen, was . . . furnished with a 'New Testament,' and a 'Webster's Spelling Book.' **1863** *Rio Abajo Press* 18 Aug. 3/1 Webster's Unabridged . . . spells the word Alburquerque and Albuquerque. **1900** *Congress. Rec.* 25 Jan. 1177/2 Some of the meanings or definitions of the word 'disorderly,' as given by Webster in his dictionary are [etc.].

+**Webster.**[2] [Daniel *Webster,* Amer. statesman (1782-1852).] Used attrib. with *ticket, Whig.* — **1835-7** HALIBURTON *Clockmaker* 1 Ser. iv. 25 I love the Quakers, I hope they'll go the Webster ticket yet. **1884** BLAINE *20 Years of Congress* I. 164 [The] conservative side [of the assemblage was typified] by the choice of an old Webster Whig.

+**Websterian**, *a.*[1] [From WEBSTER.[2]] **1.** Profound, impressive, solemn, prodigious. **2.** Of a type worn by Daniel Webster. — (1) **1856** *S. Lit. Messenger* XXII. 243/1 He felt within him in embryo Websterian thoughts. **1867** LOCKE *Swingin' Round* 62 When the idea flashed over my Websterian intelleck, I shouted Halleology! **1894** ALDRICH *Two Bites* 73 Among others came the Hon. Jedd Deane, with his most pronounced Websterian air. (2) **1883** *Century Mag.* Nov. 139/2 He was dressed in an ill-cut black Websterian coat.

+**Websterian**, *a.*[2] [From WEBSTER.[1]] Of or pertaining to Noah Webster or to one of the dictionaries based on his. — **1874** B. F. TAYLOR *World on Wheels* 28 Websterian 'probabilities' says that is not the derivation of 'scale' at all.

+**Webworm.** One of various larvae which spin large webs. Also attrib. (See also FALL WEBWORM.) — **1797** *Mass. H. S. Coll.* 1 Ser. V. 281 Having been in the habit of frequently visiting my trees, in order to destroy the canker and web-worms [etc.]. **1802** *Ib.* VIII. 190 The web worm, [is] a small taper worm, of a gray colour, about a half of an inch in length. **1876** *Field & Forest* I. 77 In the *Clisiocampas,* (the web-worms of the apple tree and wild cherry,) . . . the silk glands are well developed at an early age. **1885** *Rep. Indian Affairs* 84 Many of the Indians have gardens, but the 'web-worm' which came in June destroyed nearly all the growing vegetables. **1890** *Cent.* 3765/2 Common millers in the United States are *Spilosoma virginica,* a moth whose larva is one of the woolly-bear caterpillars, and *Hyphantria cunea,* the web-worm moth.

* **Wedding.** Illustrated in attrib. uses only.

See also the separate entries which follow.

1712 SEWALL *Diary* II. 367 Met with my Wedding Gloves and Bride-cake from Govr. Saltonstall. **1787** TYLER *Contrast* I. i, Mrs. Catgut was making a new cap for Miss Bloomsbury, which . . . it is very probable is designed for a wedding cap. **1801** WEEMS *Letters* II. 161, I send you ten dollars the amount of three wedding fees. **1831** POE *Poems* (1859) 74 Hear the mellow wedding bells, Golden bells! **1859** STOWE *Minister's Wooing* xii, Mrs. Scudder was not a little pleased to have in her possession a card of invitation to a splendid wedding-party. **1871** *Baltimore American* 19 Jan. (De Vere), [The newly-married couple] set out on a two years' wedding tour to Europe. **1875** STOWE *We & Our Neighbors* 476 Your wedding gift to me was something I meant to keep to myself.

Wedding cake. A large, elaborately decorated cake, cut and distributed at a wedding reception or feast. {1648-} — **1771** A. G. WINSLOW *Diary* 1, I had a bit of the wedding cake. **1845** *Lowell Offering* V. 4 Heaping plates of wedding-cake now make their appearance. **1884** RITTENHOUSE *Maud* 335 We slept with wedding-cake under our pillows. **1905** N. DAVIS *Northerner* 39, I'll make Milly Ann send you a piece of my wedding-cake.

Wedding card. A wedding announcement or invitation. — **1857** *Atlantic Mo.* Nov. 72/1 Not long after, I received a certain wedding-card. **1884** 'CRADDOCK' *Where Battle Was Fought* 216 A couple of wedding cards fell upon the floor from one of the open envelopes in his hand. **1894** B. MATTHEWS in *Harper's Mag.* April 681/2 [He] took from the bureau behind him an envelope containing the wedding-cards.

Wedding dress. A bride's wedding gown. {1863-} — **1825** WOODWORTH *Forest Rose* II. iv, Don't be cross, and here's something to buy you a wedding-dress. **1848** *Knickerb.* XXXI. 37 She has watched the silkworm . . . wrap itself up and die, without a thought of . . . wedding-dresses. **1875** STOWE *We & Our Neighbors* 406 The conversation here branched off into an animated discussion of some points in Angie's wedding-dress. **1907** *St. Nicholas* Aug. 895/1 The one with the white ribbon unlocks the trunk with your grandmother's wedding-dress.

+**Wedding fix(ings).** A bride's wedding outfit. *colloq.* — **1840** *Kentucky Rifle* 31 Oct., Sal was makin up her weddin fixins. **1896** WILKINS *Madelon* 212 D'ye want any money to buy your wedding-fixings with? **1903** — in *Harper's Mag.* Dec. 28 There was poor Flora wantin' some cotton cloth for her weddin' fix.

+**Wedding journey.** A trip taken by a married couple immediately after the wedding. — **1871** HOWELLS *(title),* Their Wedding Journey. **1878** *Decorum* 196 The newly-married couple start off on their wedding journey. **1894** *Outing* XXIV. 325/1 The wedding journey was short. **1907** LILLIBRIDGE *Trail* 96 Is it to be a wedding journey?

+Wedding journeyer. One who goes on a wedding trip. — **1871** HOWELLS *Wedding Journey* 57 Imagine the infinite comfort of our wedding-journeyers, transported . . . to the shelter and the quiet of that absurdly palatial steamboat.

Wedding present. A present sent to a bride and groom. {1898-} — **1863** 'M. HARLAND' *Husks* 132 We have always intended to give you just exactly what we would have done one of them, as a wedding-present. **1883** HOWELLS *Woman's Reason* x, I had been doing them for a wedding present. **1902** NORRIS *Pit* 416 Isabel sent us a wedding present—a lovely medicine chest full of homœopathic medicines.

Wedding trip. =WEDDING JOURNEY. — **1870** STEPHENS *Married in Haste* 382 To-day we are to start on our wedding-trip. **1888** *Milnor (Dak.) Teller* 18 May 6/5 Wait until the wedding-trip is over— . . . the wedding finery put away. **1900** MUNN *Uncle Terry* 354 Somebody will be taking a wedding-trip to the Land of the Midnight Sun in the near future.

Wedding visit. A visit paid to a newly-married couple or to a girl about to be married. ?*Obs.* — **1761** *Holyoke Diaries* 55 At Mrs. Cotnam's to make the Wedding visit. a**1809** in Morse *Life O. W. Holmes* I. 16 Mamma must pay the wedding visit.

* Wedge. (See also ENTERING WEDGE.)

* 1. A tool thicker at one end than at the other, used for splitting objects, raising heavy weights, etc.

Maul and wedges, (see MAUL *n.* 2).

1640 *Conn. Rec.* I. 448, 3 axes, 2 wedges. **1731** J. SECCOMBE *Father Abbey's Will* ii, An Iron Wedge and Beetle. **1848** COOPER *Oak Openings* I. 53 There were axes, and wedges, and a beetle in the canoe.

2. A strip of land narrower at one end than at the other. Also as place name. {1678, 1867-}

1700 *Md. Hist. Mag.* XX. 294 The Wedge, 65 acr[es] Sur[veyed] the 24 of Novemb[e]r 1673. **1707** *Providence Rec.* IV. 78 A considerable wedge of land neare unto ye said Abbotts. **1885** *Outing* VII. 59/1 Over the two longest sides of the wedge, dwarfed, upcurling spruces hang.

+3. *To knock out the wedges,* (see quot. 1871.)

1848 LOWELL *Biglow P.* 1 Ser. vii. 90, You'd ough' to leave a feller free, An' not go knockin' out the wedges, To ketch his fingers in the tree. **1871** DE VERE 320 To *knock out the wedges* . . . is used to express a painful embarrassment in which a man is left by his friends, after having been led into it by their urgency.

4. In combination with adjectives in *-ed.*

1785 MARSHALL *Amer. Grove* 88 *Mespilus cuneiformis.* Wedge leaved Mespilus. . . : The leaves are smooth, wedge, or inverse egg-shaped, and pointed. **1872** COUES *Key to Birds* 316 Genus *Rhodostethia.* . . . Wedge-tailed, or Ross' Rosy Gull.

Wedge tent. A tent the ends of which are shaped like a wedge or inverted V. — **1862** NORTON *Army Lett.* 49 We used to sleep on the ground or on pine boughs when we had the small or wedge tents. **1865** G. SABRE *Prisoner of War* 93 The prisoners' hospitals were composed of a limited number of very small 'wedge' tents. **1887** BILLINGS *Hardtack* 48 The A or Wedge tents are yet quite common. . . . It is *now* a canvas tent stretched over a horizontal bar. **1891** *Fur, Fin & Feather* March 169 The other two slept in a little wedge tent close to hand.

* Weed.[1]

* 1. A plant which grows wild, or is intrusive in cultivated ground, and is not valued either for its usefulness or its beauty.

1654 JOHNSON *Wonder-w. Prov.* 32 The great mingle mangle of Religion among you hath caused the Churches of Christ to increase so little with you, standing at a stay like Corne among Weeds. **1738** *Md. Hist. Mag.* XVIII. 21 He had been bitten by a rattlesnake in the weeds. **1823** JAMES *Exped.* I. 194 The weeds . . . are cut down and removed. **1901** MOHR *Plant Life Ala.* 339 Chicken Corn . . . [is] a pernicious weed in many parts of the Southern States.

+b. (See quotation.)

1900 BRUNCKEN *N. Amer. Forests* 68 An area is denuded of its merchantable timber and henceforth lies as an idle waste, stocked at best with scrub and inferior species of trees—weeds, as the forester calls them.

2. Tobacco or a cigar. Usually 'the weed.' {1606-}

See also VIRGINIA WEED.

1664 *Md. Council Proc.* 505 The London Merchants . . . Left that Unhappie Weede to Virginia and Maryland. **1827** COOPER *Red Rover* II. 262 He had freshened his ideas by an ample addition to the morsel of weed which he had kept all along thrust into one of his cheeks. **1858** VIELÉ *Following Drum* 65 We visited a cigar manufactory, and saw 'the weed' in every variety of form. **1889** *Century Mag.* Jan. 410/1 Cope lighted one of the weeds to keep Exall company. **1912** MATHEWSON *Pitching* 231 How about these ball-players who masticate the weed?

3. Attrib. and comb. in sense 1 and 1 b.

1841 W. KENNEDY *Texas* I. 155 The settlers highly estimate the productive power of the weed prairies. **1850** *Rep. Comm. Patents 1849* 297, I likewise claim the combination of the adjustive weed cutter and leveler F. **1863** MITCHELL *My Farm* 289 The scattered stones and debris . . . are feeding weed-crops in idle corners. **1905** *Forestry Bureau Bul.* No. 61, 26 *Weed tree,* a tree of a species which has little or no value.

* Weed.[2] Mourning apparel worn to indicate bereavement; also, **a** band of black material worn on the hat or around a sleeve for the same purpose. — **1748** *N.H. Probate Rec.* III. 537, I give and Bequeath to my Brother. . . . A paer of Gloves and a Morning Weed. **1764** *Essex Inst. Coll.* XLIX. 286 [We] will make use of no other mourning, than a weed in the hat, or a crape round the arm. **1856** STOWE *Dred* I. 150 Tiff stood by the side of the grave, . . . a deep weed of black upon his arm. **1873** ALDRICH *Marjorie Daw* 229 His hat had a weed on it, which struck me as being strange.

Weeding hoe. A hoe used for weeding. — **1638** *Md. Council Proc.* 76, I have seised . . . 6 weeding hoes. **1703** *N.C. Col. Rec.* I. 579 Grey did formerly adjust . . . two weeding hoes, one hilling hoe [etc.]. **1868** *Mich. Agric. Rep.* VII. 286 The cut . . . represents a weeding-hoe. **1907** *Dialect Notes* III. 238 *Weeding-hoe,* common hoe; garden hoe.

Weekly. A publication which appears once a week. {1846-} — **1833** *Knickerb. Mag.* I. 185 We have articles on Political Economy in the monthlys, the weeklys, and the dailys. **1870** *Scribner's Mo.* I. 124 Here is a news-stand . . . a pictorial array of . . . illustrated weeklies. **1892** *Courier-Journal* 4 Oct. 2/1 The Kentucky Baptist [is] a newsy weekly published at Ludlow. **1907** *St. Nicholas* June 679/2 In 1865 the young writer [*sc.* Thomas Bailey Aldrich] came to Boston to take charge of a weekly called *Every Saturday.*

* Weep. +*To weep a little weep,* to have a spell of crying. — **1869** ALCOTT *Little Women* I. 62 Being . . . a very human little girl, she often 'wept a little weep,' as Jo said. **1871** *Scribner's Mo.* II. 292 So, womanlike, I began to 'weep a little weep.' **1880** *Harper's Mag.* May 911/1 When the last pair of little feet had pattered down the steps I sat down by my desk and 'wept a little weep.'

* Weeper. A piece of crape depending from a hat, worn in token of mourning. {1832-} Also transf. — **1845** *Knickerb.* XXVI. 585 The long black crape 'weeper,' which it was the custom at that time to wear depending from the hat behind. **1857** TAYLOR *Northern Travel* 169 The firs were hung with weepers of black-green moss. **1879** B. F. TAYLOR *Summer-Savory* 54 The crape 'weeper' used to . . . sway in a slow and pensive way from side to side. **1895** WIGGIN *Village Watch-Tower* 156 Si, in his best suit, a broad weed and weepers, drove Cyse Higgins's black colt.

* Weeping, *a.* In the specific names of trees the branches and foliage of which droop. {1791-} (See also WEEPING WILLOW.) — **1858** WARDER *Hedges & Evergreens* 262 *Thuja pendula,* or Weeping Arbor Vitae, has filiform, drooping branches. **1879** *Scribner's Mo.* Nov. 44/2 How can we do justice to this specimen of a weeping beech! **1858** WARDER *Hedges & Evergreens* 264 *Cupressus pendula,* or Weeping Cypress, has a large, expanded head, with very pendulous branchlets. **1879** *Scribner's Mo.* Nov. 43/1 The weeping larch . . . brings us back once more to familiar forms—familiar and yet how strange!

Weeping willow. A species of willow (*Salix babylonica*) imported and cultivated for ornament. {1731-}

1779 FRENEAU *Poems* (1786) 104 There cedars dark, the osier, and the pine, Shorn tamerisks, and weeping willows grew. **1805** PARKINSON *Tour* 375, I saw some weeping-willows at Mount-Vernon growing by the sides of the lawn before the hall-door. **1830** WATSON *Philadelphia* 719 The first weeping willows were introduced into the city by Governor John Penn for his garden. **1873** ALDRICH *Marjorie Daw* ii, [It] has an obsequious retinue of fringed elms and oaks and weeping willows. **1893** *Harper's Mag.* Feb. 374/2 Weeping-willows lent a familiar aspect to the [cemetery] scene.

+Weequashing. [From Algonquian *wigwas,* 'birch-bark (canoe).'] The spearing of eels or other fish from a canoe by torchlight. — **1792** *Mass. H. S. Coll.* 1 Ser. I. 231 The Indians, when they go in a canoe with a torch, to catch eels in the night, call it Weequash, or anglicised, *weequashing.* **1888** GOODE *Amer. Fishes* 436 Vast quantities are taken in the sluiceways of dams, and by spearing by torchlight or 'weequashing.'

* Weevil. Also †**weavel,** etc. Any beetle of the group *Rhyncophora,* esp. the larva of beetles of this group which are destructive to grain, fruit, etc.; also, any other larva destructive to crops.

1624 SMITH *Gen. Hist. Va.* v. 197 It chanced a pretty secret to be discouered to preserue their corne from the fly, or weauell. **1676** *Conn. Rec.* II. 486 Their corn suffered much damage by the weavills. **1751** WASHINGTON *Diaries* I. 20 Bre[ad] which was almost Eaten up by Weavel and Maggots. **1814** J. TAYLOR *Arator* 153 As to the weavil they are certainly avoided by getting it [wheat] out early. **1858** *Mich. Agric. Soc. Trans.* IX. 252 In this extract we find the popular name 'weevil' used in speaking of the wheat-fly or midge. **1877** *Vermont Bd. Agric. Rep.* IV. 107 Our farmers have sustained [great loss] from the wheat midge—or 'weevil,' as it is frequently but most improperly called. **1895** *Dept. Agric. Yrbk. 1894* 279 The granary weevil is the 'curculio' and 'weevil' of early writings.

attrib. and *comb.* **1846** *Cultivator* ns. III. 210 The wheat was all weevil-eaten, and being unfit for bread, was sold to a distillery. **1864** *Ohio Agric. Rep.* XVIII. 149 The wheat is what is called the 'weevil proof.'

Weigh-, stem of *weigh* v. Comb. with *boss, house, lock, room.* — **1671** *Doc. Col. Hist. N.Y.* XII. 489 They shall soe Ship . . . upon the Weigh House at the Bridge. **1833** *Niles' Reg.* XLIV. 177/2 There was weighed at the Albany weighlock . . . 882 lbs. merchandise, exclusive of 19 empty boats. **1880** LAMPHERE *U.S. Govt.* 69/2, 1 assistant in weigh-room [receives] per diem $3.85. **1917** SINCLAIR *King Coal* 44 Scarcely an evening passed that some man did not break loose, shaking his fist at the sky, or at the weigh-boss.

*Weigher.

*1. A public officer who weighs or supervises the weighing of commodities; in later use, esp. at a customhouse.

1711 *Boston Rec.* 88 Voted. That Mesues Francis Thrasher, John Bennet . . . be ye Weighers of Hay for ye ensuing year. **1792** BENTLEY *Diary* I. 336 Ropes, Samuel, Cooper, Culler, Weigher & Gauger. **1822** *Ann. 17th Congress* 1 Sess. 134 These clerks were sometimes . . . weighers, who performed the duties of clerks for nothing. **1871** *Harper's Mag.* June 21/2 The 'weigher' may have neglected some article enumerated. **1891** O'BEIRNE *Leaders Ind. Territory* 113/2 At the present time he is Weigher for the Nation, as well as National Timber Contractor.

*2. A person employed by a business house to weigh goods.

1835 in Hoffman *Winter in West* II. 117n., When the hogs are received, they are first weighed by the weigher. **1901** MERWIN & WEBSTER *Calumet 'K'* 325 The wind . . . came whistling through the cracks in the cupola walls with a sting in it that set the weighers to shivering.

Weighership. The office of public weigher. — **1885** *American* XI. 68 After all, Mr. Sterling seems likely to miss the Brooklyn weighership.

*Weighing. *attrib.* Designating apparatus for weighing grain or places where it is weighed. — **1880** *Harper's Mag.* Oct. 726/1 Somebody pulls a lever, and, presto! away has gone that grain up into a weighing bin. **1901** MERWIN & WEBSTER *Calumet 'K'* 278 A water boy found him upon the weighing floor. *Ib.* 321 [The grain] came tumbling down again . . . into the great weighing hoppers.

Weighmaster. An official in charge of a public scales; a person, esp. at a mine, in charge of the weighing of a product. {1617-} — **1665** in *N.Y. State Lib. Hist. Bul.* No. 2 May (1899) 171 You are further required, to adjust Accompts with Jonas Bartleson the Weigh Master. **1808** *Ann. 10th Congress* 2 Sess. 490 David Williams . . . and a Mr. Kemper, weighmaster, . . . were present. **1877** WRIGHT *Big Bonanza* 226 Said the weigh-master, . . . 'A team of ten horses . . . hauled a load of ore which weighed over 73,000 pounds.'

*Weight, n. 1. A gymnasium appliance consisting of a piece of metal attached to a cord which runs over a pulley. **2.** That part of a track meet which consists of weight-throwing. — (1) **1887** *Century Mag.* XXXIV. 179/2 There were rings, weights, bars, clubs and dumb-bells. (2) **1895** *Outing* Sept. 461/2 The weight, of course, will go to Yale.

Weight, v. {1647-} **+To weight on,** to hold in place by means of weights. — **1881** PIERSON *In the Brush* 51 [The 'shakes'] were not nailed on, but 'weighted on'—kept in their places by small timbers laid across each row of 'shakes' over the entire roof.

+Weight pole. (See quot. 1882.) — **1791** in Jillson *Dark & Bl. Ground* 109 The weight poles . . . weigh down the clapboards upon which they lie. **1822** WOODS *English Prairie* 168 Some poles are laid along the building to keep the boards on . . . ; weight-poles as they are called. **1882** THAYER *From Log-Cabin* 31 The roof was covered with slabs, held in place by long weight-poles. **1908** HANDSAKER *Pioneer Life* 91 The roof was made of 'shakes' or clapboards, and in place of nails was secured by 'weight poles.'

*Weir(e). Also **wear(e).** (See also WARE.¹)

*1. An enclosure of stakes or brushwood placed in a river for the purpose of catching fish; also, a wicker basket or trap used for the same purpose.

1612 SMITH, etc. *Virginia* I. 24 They haue many artificiall weares in which they get abundance of fish. **1670** *Plymouth Rec.* 114 The hedge . . . shall stand untill such time as none appeeres to take ffish . . . before the said hedge or weire. **1738** BYRD *Dividing Line* (1901) 233 They are great enemies to weirs set up in the rivers to catch fish. **1851** *S. Lit. Messenger* XVII. 224/1 The Angler's lodge was . . . hung around with nets and wears. **1911** *Rep. Fisheries 1908* 311/2 [The horseshoe crab] is caught by hand and in pounds and weirs.

2. Attrib. with *dam, net, pocket,* etc.

1857 *Ohio Acts* LIV. 184 It shall be unlawful . . . to catch fish . . . by means of any . . . weir-pound. **1869** *Michigan Gen. Statutes* I. (1882) 573 It shall not be lawful for any person or persons to place a weir dam, fish weir, or weir net, across any race, drain, stream, or inland river of this state. **1896** JEWETT *Pointed Firs* (1910) 54 When 't is a poor catch in the weir pocket they just fly a little signal down by the shore. **1914** W. D. STEELE *Storm* 39 The man . . . had built a chicken-pen . . . , using a strange net of wire in place of the condemned weir-twine that ordinary folks used.

+Wejack, Wejag. [Amer. Indian. Cf. Cree *wuchak*.] **1.** =FISHER 2. **2.** ?A woodchuck. — (1) **1795** S. HEARNE *Journey N. Ocean* 377 The Wejack and Skunk are never found in the Northern Indian country. **1829** J. RICHARDSON, etc. *Fauna Bor.-Amer.* I. 52 *Mustela Canadensis.* The Pekan, or Fisher. . . . Wejack, or Fisher [of the] Fur Traders. (2) c1849 PAIGE *Dow's Sermons* I. 178 The poor man . . . feels as safe as a wejag in his winter's burrow.

*Well, n.

*1. A hole sunk in the earth to a water-bearing stratum.

1630 HIGGINSON *New-England* 12 Neere Salem . . . we may digge Wels and find Water where we list. **1751** in *Amer. Speech* XV. 410 The common Hall of this Borough will meet on Saturday next to receive Proposals of the Workmen to make four public Wells. **1843** N. BOONE *Journal* 201 Capt. Boone . . . discovered a well in the sand made by some Indians. **1907** *St. Nicholas* July 771/1 Two tents by a driven well, . . . and a row

of dusty water barrels comprised the new stage station set down in the heart of the Nevada desert.

+2. A rivulet flowing from a spring; a creek. *Obs.*

1649 *Md. Hist. Mag.* VIII. 51 A Well by Patowmeck River called St. Raphaell's Well vntill it fall into a Branch of St. Raphaells Creek. **1681** *N.H. Probate Rec.* I. 47 Tenn acres of land joyneing to the Lands I now possess beginneng from the Creek or Well.

+3. An oil well.

1865 *Atlantic Mo.* April 393/2 The Phillips Well . . . now pumps about three hundred and thirty [barrels per day], and is considered a first-class well. **1880** *Harper's Mag.* Dec. 50 Through miles of underground pipes giant pumps force crude petroleum from the wells. **1919** *Kay County Okla.* 45 They saw a well flowing 125 barrels of oil per day.

+4. *local.* A lake.

1877 HODGE *Arizona* 238 A number of curious and interesting lakes, or, as some of them are called, 'wells,' of pure fresh water.

5. Attrib. and comb. with *digging, drill,* etc.

1849 G. G. FOSTER *N.Y. in Slices* 8 An interminable line of crooked well-posts . . . meets your gaze. **1858** *Ill. Agric Soc. Trans.* III. 362 The men are now born . . . who will live to see . . . well digging . . . done by steam. **1865** A. D. WHITNEY *Gayworthys* 383 Tears, wrung up through the strong life of the man, along this well-shaft that had sounded down, suddenly, to the sweet springs of his boyhood, ran from his eyes. **1876** KNIGHT 2759/1 *Well-rig* is the term applied to the whole *plant* for well-boring, consisting of the *derrick,* its engine [etc.]. *Ib.* 2759/2 *Well-drill,* a tool for boring wells. **1883** *Century Mag.* July 332/2 One ‡certificate] he gives to the well manager who has signed with him. **1884** *Gringo & Greaser* 1 Feb. 1/1 We are connected with the only practical Tube Well-Drivers in the West. **1890** *Stock Grower & Farmer* 22 Feb. 1/1 Rust's well drilling machinery, Steam and Horse Power, for Deep and Shallow Wells.

*Well, a. In attrib. use: In good health; sound. {1628-1672} Also transf. (See also WELL MAN.) — c1835 CATLIN *Indians* II. 80 Of those who are alive, there are not well ones enough to take care of the sick. **1845** KIRKLAND *Western Clearings* 74 This third day had been 'well day' to most of the invalids. **1868** *Iowa State Agric. Soc. Rep.* 1867 97 Whatever disease they may have had is communicated to the well hogs. **1874** HOWELLS *Chance Acquaintance* (1882) 97 Calling Kitty's attention to his ingenuity by a pressure of her well foot. **1897** *Boston Jrnl.* 5 Jan. 4/5 'How sweet!' she exclaimed, with a glad light glowing in her well eye [one devoid of dust].

*Well, adv. Employed to introduce a remark, often as a stop-gap till the speaker decides what to say.

The following quotations show that British and American writers have noted the frequency of American use of this word. Any examples which could be quoted would not differ from British ones.

1840 A. M. MAXWELL *Run through U.S.* I. 16 *Well* is a great and never-to-be-neglected American word. **1841** BUCKINGHAM *America* I. 237 In answering a question when distinctly understood, as for instance, 'Where are you going today?' . . . the party answering usually begin[s], by saying, 'Well,' and, after a short pause, gives you the answer required. **1866** LOWELL *Biglow P.* 2 Ser. p. 1, A friend . . . told me that he once heard five 'wells' . . . precede the answer to an inquiry. **1885** *Amer. Soc. Psych. Research Proc.* I. 312 (*Cent.*), The 'wells' and 'ahs,' 'don't-you-know's' and other stop-gap interjections. **1891** COOKE *Huckleberries* 304 What would all New England speech be without 'well'?

+Well auger. An auger used in digging wells. Also attrib. — **1879** *Cimarron News & Press* 20 Nov. 1/3, $25 to $50 per day can actually be made with the Great Western Well Auger. **1890** *Stock Grower & Farmer* 22 Feb. 1/1 Empire Well auger company.

Well-borer. One who makes a business of boring wells. {1786-} — **1864** *Harper's Mag.* Dec. 60/2 In preparation for the expected influx of speculators and new well-borers. **1884** *Lisbon* (Dak.) *Star* 10 Oct., Experienced well-borers have leased 3,000 acres of land on the Monongahela river. **1895** GRAHAM *Stories of Foot-Hills* 234 Jarvis is my name, Colonel Bob Jarvis, well-borer.

*Well-born, a. The *well-born* {1841}, +the Federalists. A derisive nickname alluding to John Adams' use of the term in quot. 1787. — [1787 J. ADAMS *Defence of Constitution* I. p. x, The rich, the well-born, and the able, acquire an influence among the people.] **1788** *Amer. Museum* June (1792) 527 Under such a government, men of education, abilities, and property, commonly called *the well born,* will be the most likely to get into places of power and trust. **1883** McMASTER *People U.S.* I. 469 In most of the squibs and pasquinades that filled the papers the Federalists were reviled under the name of 'the well-born.'

Well-broke, a. {1731-1796} Of domestic animals: Effectively trained for service. (Cf. BROKE *ppl. a.* 2.) — **1825** *Austin P.* II. (1924) 1026, I wish you to Procure Me two yok of well Broke oxen. **1850** *Rep. Comm. Patents 1849: Agric.* 161 Good well-broke teams are worth per yoke from $35 to $60. **1871** *Rep. Indian Affairs* (1872) 422, I turned over to him . . . two good, well-broke work-oxen.

+Well curb. Also **well kerb.** The stone or cement border around the top of a well. {1886} — **1837** HAWTHORNE *Twice-told Tales* (1879) I. 155 [You] have passed by the taverns and stopped at the running brooks and well-curbs. **1845** *Knickerb.* XXV. 448, [I] hastened out to the great stone by the well-kerb to perform my matinal ablutions. **1872** EGGLESTON *End of World* 62 Jonas Harrison was leaning against the well-curb. **1903** WIGGIN *Rebecca* 135 Her eyes . . . fell to the well-curb.

Well-digger. One who makes a business of digging wells. {1693-} — **1789** *Boston Directory* 204 White William, well-digger. **1807** J. R.

SHAW *Life* (1930) 174 My name being established in the country as a well-digger, I was accordingly sent for. **1839** in *Mich. Agric. Soc. Trans.* VII. 372 Well-diggers assert that such a seam of gravel, at depth of twenty feet, is very general. **1883** *Harper's Mag.* Oct. 708/2 By trade he is a well-digger.

* **Well enough.** To let well enough alone, not to interfere with the present situation; to be satisfied with conditions as they are {to let well alone, 1740–} — **1842** FELT *Annals of Salem* I. 340 It would . . . be better to cry out when all was not well and let well enough alone. **1904** *N.Y. Ev. Post* 23 June 1 Secretary Johnson . . . induced the chairman to let well enough alone.

Well fixed, a. {1718–} +Well-to-do; well supplied with property. *colloq.* — **1822** *Murphey Papers* I. 263 His brother is well fixed. **1912** N. M. WOODROW *Sally Salt* 228, I'm well to do, Hilda, well fixed in the world. **1925** TILGHMAN *Dugout* 70 You'll be well fixed.

Wellington boot. A style of boot named after Arthur, first duke of Wellington, 1769–1852. {1839–} — [**1817** BIRKBECK *Notes Journey Amer.* (1818) 93 Nine out of ten, native Americans, are tall and longlimbed . . . ; in pantaloons and Wellington boots.] **1820** WEEMS *Letters* III. 280 The young Gentlemen will soon get out of conceit of their Wellington boots and fine jackets. **1845** *Xenia Torch-Light* 23 Oct. 3/5 His stock consists of . . . Napoleon and Wellington boots. **1886** EBBUTT *Emigrant Life* 60 My father took off one of his long Wellington boots for a weapon.

Well man. A man in good health. {1628–1759}
1699 *N.H. Hist. Soc. Coll.* I. 134 No less than four well men . . . were engaged in taking care of every one that was sick. **1840** DANA *Two Years* 86 A well man at sea has little sympathy with one who is sea-sick. **1860** HOLMES *Professor* 359 Those . . . so endowed look upon a well man and see a shroud. **1897** 'MARK TWAIN' *Following Equator* 31, I was a well man; so I gave thanks and took to those delicacies again. **1912** CROLY *M. A. Hanna* 447 Mr. Hanna had not been for years a thoroughly well man.

+**Well pole.** =WELL SWEEP. {1893} Also fig. — **1775** *Mass. H. S. Coll.* 1 Ser. I. 260 Seeing the well-pole drawing down, took aim at the place where he [an Indian] thought the man must stand. **1826** LONGFELLOW in S. Longfellow *H. W. Longfellow* I. 86 No green trees and orchards by the roadside; no slab-fences; no well-poles. **1845** *Knickerb.* XXV. 448 The old pear-tree by the well-pole . . . was all green and youthful. **1867** HARRIS *Sut Lovingood* 87 Du yu see these yere well-poles what I uses fur laigs?

+**Wells-Fargo.** A firearm issued to its guards by the well-known express company. — **1898** *Scribner's Mag.* XXIII. 86/2 Into the face the messenger fired one barrel of his Wells-Fargo.

+**Well sweep.** A long pole, pivoted to the top of a high post, by means of which water is raised in a bucket attached to the end of the pole. — **1841** WEBSTER II. 947/2. **1851** A. CARY *Clovernook* 73 She attached the towel to the end of the well-sweep, where it waved as a signal for Peter to come to supper. **1874** B. F. TAYLOR *World on Wheels* 217 The well-sweep . . . goes up forty times a day and comes down with a bang. **1903** K. M. ABBOTT *Old Paths New Eng.* 281 Children jumped for the long arm of the well-sweep.

* **Welsh, a.** Also **Welch.**
1. Of persons: Native to Wales, or of Welsh ancestry.
1708 *Boston News-Letter* 6 Dec. 4/2 We daily expect another Vessel from Millford with more Welsh Passengers. **1740** *Georgia Col. Rec.* IV. 673 The honourable Trustees would please to import . . . a Number of English or Welch Servants. **1855** A. JONES *Cymry of '76* 16 Francis Hopkinson was descended from a Welsh family, and was a member of the Continental Congress. **1913** LONDON *Valley of Moon* 214 The little Welsh baker had closed up shop and gone away.

2. In the specific names of plants and animals.
1843 TORREY *Flora N.Y.* II. 61 *Pycnanthemum incanum.* Common Mountain Mint. Welsh Mint. **1844** *Nat. Hist. N.Y., Zoology* II. 343 The Grey Duck, or Gadwall, *Anas strepera.* . . . In New-Jersey, it is called the Welsh or German Duck.

* **Welsh cotton.** A woolen cloth with a nap. *Obs.* {–1580} — **1725** *Md. Hist. Mag.* XVIII. 215, [I] desire . . . you to send by some Ship . . . 100 yards welsh Cotton. **1770** *Ib.* 69, 500 yards of Welsh Cotton the Best.

Welsher. =WELSHMAN 1. — **1827** COOPER *Prairie* xviii, There was a story of a nation of Welshers, that lived here-away in the prairies.

Welsh Indian. A member of a supposed tribe of Indians which spoke Welsh. (See Hodge, etc. *Amer. Indians* II. 931 f.) — **1804** JEFFERSON in *Lewis & Clark Exped.* VII. (1905) 292 Mr. Evans, a Welshman, was employed by the spanish government . . . to go in search of the Welsh Indians said to be up the Missouri. **1805** ORDWAY in *Journals of Lewis & O.* 282 We think that they [the Flatheads] are the welch Indians.

* **Welshman. 1.** A native of Wales settled in America; a descendant of such a settler. +**2.** *local.* A name given to various fishes, esp. to the large-mouthed black bass. — (1) [**1705** *Boston News-Letter* 10 Dec. 4/2 Lately Deserted Her Majesties Service . . . Thomas Souldier, a Welshman.] **1855** M. THOMPSON *Doesticks* 285, I had a powerful rival in the person of a six foot Welshman, . . . with a fist like a pile-driver. (2) **1709** LAWSON *Carolina* 159 The brown Pearch, which some call Welch-men, are the largest sort of Pearches that we have. **1884** *Century Mag.* April 908/1 A black bass . . . becomes . . . a 'welshman' in North Carolina. **1896** JORDAN & EVERMANN *Check-List Fishes* 338 *Holocentrus ascensionis.* Matejuelo; Squirrel-fish; Welshman. . . . Florida to St. Helena.

* **Welsh plain.** A kind of flannel made in Wales. *Obs.* {–1725} — **1732** *S.C. Gazette* 136/2 Lately imported, and to be sold, . . . welsh plains and kendal cottons. **1816** J. E. WHITE *Lett. on England* I. 179 Shrewsbury is the principal mart for the flannels that are made in Wales, . . . generally known in the United States by the name of Welsh plains.

Welsh rabbit. Also **Welsh rarebit.** A dish consisting essentially of melted cheese, butter, milk or other liquid, and various condiments. {1725–} — **1843** *Knickerb.* XXI. 588 If you wish to secure a few fragments of tremendous dreams, devour a Welch rare-bit. **1846** CORCORAN *Pickings* 130 His round, ruddy face told of roast beef, plum pudding, brown stout, and Welch-rabbits. **1877** *Harper's Mag.* March 577/2 Phenice brought in the Welsh rare-bit (good before bed, but a little indigestible). **1912** [see CARD PARTY].

Welting cord. Cord used in making welts in garments. {1887} — **1869** *Boyd's Business Directory* 694 J. Edwards, . . . manufacturer of 'Edwards' Core Wound, Cable Laid Welting Cord. **1893** HOLLEY *Samantha at World's Fair* 464, I should have been tempted to have bent a pin, and take some weltin' cord out of my pocket and go to fishin' for it.

* **Wench.** +A female Negro slave, servant, or girl. (See also NEGRO WENCH.) Now rare.
1717 *N.C. Col. Rec.* II. 310 A Wench for the House I want sore. **1760** WASHINGTON *Diaries* I. 118 Belinda, a Wench of mine, in Frederick. **1807** JANSON *Stranger in Amer.* 309 Female slaves, in this part of the world are uniformly called wenches. **1872** POWERS *Afoot & Alone* 30 The lazy swinging wenches, with buckets of water on their turbaned heads. **1909** *Dialect Notes* III. 393 Buck, . . . now applied almost exclusively to male negroes as the opposite of *wench.*
attrib. and *transf.* **1806** LEWIS in *L. & Clark Exped.* IV. (1905) 187, I think the most disgusting sight I have ever beheld is these dirty naked wenches [Indian squaws]. **1880** E. JAMES *Negro Minstrel's Guide* 10 The legs of wench dancers . . . are often padded.

+**Wenham (Lake) ice.** Ice from a lake in the township of Wenham, Mass. — **1846** *Niles' Nat. Reg.* 2 May 144/1 The barque Hannah Sprague . . . has been chartered to carry a cargo of Wenham Lake ice from Boston to London. **1860** HOLMES *Professor* 103 'The Model of all the Virtues' had a pair of searching eyes as clear as Wenham ice. **1885** HOWELLS *Silas Lapham* 178 They were so many blocks of Wenham ice for purity and rectangularity.

+**Werowance.** Also **weroance,** etc. [Amer. Indian.] In colonial times, an Indian chief. Now hist.
1588 HAKLUYT *Voyages* III. 255 There be sundry Kings, whom they call Werowances, and Countreys of great fertility. **1607** in Smith *Works* (1910) p. xlii, We found here a Wiroans (for so they call their kynges) who satt upon a matt of Reedes, with his people about him. **1650** *Md. Archives* I. 330 Provided that no one Copyhold Exceed above fifty Acres unless it be to the Werrowance or chief head of every of the said Six Nations. *c*1680 *Mass. H. S. Coll.* 2 Ser. I. 28 They sent out 6 of their Woerowances (chief men) to commence a treaty. **1705** BEVERLEY *Virginia* III. 57 A *Werowance* is a Military Officer, who of course takes upon him the command of all Parties. **1804** [see ROANOKE]. **1899** *Atlantic Mo.* June 725/2, I drove my boat in between the sloop of the commander of Shirley Hundred and the canoe of the Nansemond werowance.

Wesleyan, n. A member of the Methodist Church {1791–}, +esp. a member of the Wesleyan Methodist Connection of America. — **1849** CHAMBERLAIN *Ind. Gazetteer* 271 The Episcopal Methodists have five churches, the Wesleyans one. **1856** SIMMS *Charlemont* 184 These little acts of courtesy . . . were yet strangely at variance with the straightlaced practices of the thoroughgoing Wesleyan.

Wesleyan, a. Of or pertaining to John Wesley (1703–91) or to his doctrines. {1771–} — **1840** *Niles' Nat. Reg.* 10 Oct. 96 Wesleyan society. The following is an abstract of the returns made to the late conference. **1856** CARTWRIGHT *Autobiog.* 79 What would Methodism have been in the Wesleyan connection to-day? **1867** DIXON *New America* II. 307 The Wesleyan body . . . parted into two great sects—a Methodist Episcopal Church North, and a Methodist Episcopal Church South. **1882** 'M. HARLAND' *Eve's Daughters* 342 The Wesleyan sister . . . [was] in conscience bound to draw the line of demarcation between church and world somewhere.

Wesleyan Methodist. A member of the Wesleyan or Methodist church; a member of the Wesleyan Methodist Connection of America. {1839–} — **1796** MORSE *Univ. Geog.* I. 280 In 1788, the number of *Wesleian* Methodists in the United States, stood thus: Georgia, 2011 [etc.]. **1842** *Niles' Nat. Reg.* 7 May 160/3 The Wesleyan Methodists. . . . The number of members . . . in the United States in 1840, [is stated to be] 844,816. **1879** *Minutes Mich. Conf. of Wesleyan Methodist Connection of Amer.* 3 Conference convened in the Wesleyan Methodist church, at Brighton, Michigan.

* **West, n.** +At any particular time, that part of the present United States west of the more settled regions; now, roughly, that part of the United States west of the Mississippi River, esp. the Rocky Mountain region.
Where the *West* begins depends to a large extent upon the location of the user of the term. (See also FAR WEST, GREAT WEST, MIDDLE WEST, OUT WEST *n.* and *adv.*)
1818 BRYANT *Poetical Works* (1925) 26 The hunter of the West must go In depths of woods to seek the deer. **1820** *Niles' Reg.* XVIII. 386/1 Are all the people of the 'west'—of the many highly important states beyond the mountains, to be thus traduced by wholesale? **1835** *Jamestown* (N.Y.)

Jrnl. 14 Jan. 4/6 Theo. Butler respectfully informs the inhabitants of Chautauqua County that he is now receiving at his book store the largest assortment of books . . . ever offered in the West. **1845** [see EL DORADO]. **1870** *Scribner's Mo.* I. 143 The commercial intercourse of New England with the West has been greatly obstructed by [the Appalachian chain]. **1900** *Congress. Rec.* 16 Jan. 857/2 The people of the West have cattle, grain, and minerals. **1905** *Boston Ev. Traveler* 27 Jan. 11/2 'Rustler,' for example, as the term is used in the West.

* **West**, *adv.* +Toward the western part of the United States.

1836 DUNLAP *Mem. Water Drinker* (1837) I. 52 A Connecticut settler . . . was very glad to sell his buildings and go west. **1856** E. H. HALL *Ho! for the West!* (1858) 4 If bound still further west he has at Chicago a choice of several roads. **1874** B. F. TAYLOR *World on Wheels* 242 Pretty soon he took all that he had and went West. **1884** ROE *Nature's Story* 380 My fear was that you and Miss Hargrove both would send me West as a precious good riddance. **1900** *Congress. Rec.* 29 Jan. 1258/1 The President went West; . . . he was applauded everywhere on his way in Iowa, Illinois, and other Western States.

+**b.** *Go West, young man,* or variants: Settle in the West as the place of greatest opportunity.

Commonly ascribed to Horace Greeley.

1851 J. L. B. SOULE in *Terre Haute Express,* Go West, young man! Go West! **1879** W. SAUNDERS *Through Light Continent* 35 'Go West, young man,' was Horace Greeley's advice, and West I went accordingly. **1883** *Gringo & Greaser* 1 Sept. 1/2 Come West, young man, come West and see the sights.

‖**c.** In the West.

1889 HOWELLS *Annie Kilburn* xi, One of 'em married West, and her husband left her.

+**West-bound**, *a.* Of railroad trains or traffic: Going westward. Also *absol.* — **1881** *Chicago Times* 12 March, The west-bound express was laid up all night at Kearney. **1888** *Economist* 27 Oct. 3/2 The westbound freight does not make quite so good a showing but is on the increase. **1898** *McClure's Mag.* X. 390, I was ordered to couple in ahead of a west-bound passenger train. **1909** WASON *Happy Hawkins* 222 The west-bound had to take a sidin' and wait twenty minutes for the east-bound.

* **West country.** +=WEST *n.* Used attrib. *Obs.* — **1829** FLINT *G. Mason* 10 These consisted of the substantial materials of a west country-man's diet, corn, bacon, and sweet potatoes. **1839** C. A. MURRAY *Travels* II. 122, I heard this day a west-country phrase that was perfectly new to me.

Western, *n.* {1708-} +**1.** =WESTERNER. +**2.** An animal bred and raised in the West for meat. — (1) **1835** H. C. TODD *Notes* 8 Buckskin is the nickname for Southerns and Westerns. **1888** BRYCE *Amer. Commw.* II. III. lxv. 480 He [Jackson] was a raw rude Western, a man of the people. (2) **1890** *Stock Grower & Farmer* 26 April 7/3 The fed Westerns are about out of the way, while fat native sheep we are not now receiving any considerable number.

* **Western,** *a.* +Referring to the American 'West.'

1. Of geographical areas, etc.: Situated in the western part of the United States or constituting that part of the country that is in the West.

The areas so designated varied as the United States grew westward. The term formerly sometimes denoted territories outside the nation.

1785 WASHINGTON *Writings* X. 494 Instance your late ordinance respecting the disposal of the western lands. **1808** *Ann. 10th Congress* 1 Sess. 249 It appears that a Western empire, with *Cincinnati* for its capital, had been fully disclosed. **1814** *Niles' Reg.* VI. 393/2 There is not in the universe anything to compare with *western America* for the bounties that nature has bestowed upon it. **1834** A. PIKE *Sketches* 50 A part of the western desert is common ranging ground for both nations. **1836** *S. Lit. Messenger* II. 111 We begin to distinguish by his idiom and his pronunciation, the New Englander, the Southron, and the native of the great Western Valley. **1836** *Diplom. Corr. Texas* I. (1908) 95, I wrote him so soon as I determined to join the Tennessee Volunteers called to the Western borders. **1837** *S. Lit. Messenger* III. 663 Such are the steamboats of the western lakes. **1900** *Congress. Rec.* 16 Jan. 875/2 Go out to-day on the western coast, and after you pass the line of Colorado what do you strike? **1907** *St. Nicholas* May 599/1 Dick, [was] accustomed . . . to the intense cold of the western mountains and prairies.

2. Of persons or groups: Living in or coming from the western states.

1803 *Ann. 7th Congress* 2 Sess. 238 Our western brethren . . . look to us for decisive and effectual measures. **1833** J. HALL *Harpe's Head* 87 Two of the youngest of the company . . . were engaged in a *tussle*, an exercise common among our western youth. **1841** *S. Lit. Messenger* VII. 725/2 There would be rendered available to the country in war, the services of eight or ten thousand Western watermen. **1848** BURTON *Waggeries* 28 The old gentleman, too, brought home every single southern or western merchant that entered the store. **1850** *Knickerb.* XXXV. 371 Western preachers generally do not preach to men and women, but to ladies and gentlemen. **1865** [see EASTERN *a.* 2]. **1873** BEADLE *Undevel. West* 42 The inhabitants I found to be of the genus Western Yankee, willing to take a stranger in and *do* him. **1895** G. KING *New Orleans* 230 The short rifle of the English service proved also no match for the long bore of the Western hunters.

3. Of various commodities: Produced in the western states.

1827 COOPER *Prairie* xxxi, I will engage to get the brats acclimated to a fever-and-ague bottom in a week, and not a word shall be uttered harder to pronounce than the bark of a cherry-tree, with perhaps a drop or two of western comfort. **1841** *S. Lit. Messenger* VII. 774/2 The meat served out to them consists generally of bacon cured on the farms, to which . . . is added Western bacon. **1846** CORCORAN *Pickings* 57 Western turkeys were never known to thrive when they came south. **1851** *Polly Peablossom* 144 He determined to invest . . . in a barrel of Western whiskey. **1880** *Cimarron News & Press* 26 Aug. 2/3 In this fact may be seen one reason for the strength and steadiness of the Chicago market for the Texas and western beeves. **1894** *Vt. Agric. Rep.* XIV. 94 They did not dare let a customer take a Western horse to keep a while on trial.

4. Of aspects of society and culture: Characteristic of or prevailing in the western states.

1834 A. PIKE *Sketches* 34 [The Indians], to use a western phrase, 'barked up the wrong tree,' when they got hold of Tom Smith. **1835** HOFFMAN *Winter in West* I. 240 In western phraseology, 'The way in which folks'll stare, squire, will be a *caution*.' **1848** COOPER *Oak Openings* II. 223 At Detroit commenced our surprise at the rapid progress of western civilization. **1854** HAWTHORNE *Eng. Note-Books* I. 51, I judge him to be a very able man, with the Western sociability and free-fellowship. **1883** SHIELDS *S. S. Prentiss* 31 The captain had housed his all in an ark, called in our Western language a flat-boat. **1893** *Nation* 13 July 32/3 She is altogether the . . . cyclonish, Western type—a good-tempered girl with no end of go.

5. Of settlements, roads, etc.: Built or located in the West.

1853 McCONNEL *Western Char.* 137 Many a time, in the western highways, have I met with a sturdy 'mover.' **1873** *Newton Kansan* 3 April 3/4 Among Wichita's many hopes which are characteristic of every western town, she hopes for a large cattle trade. **1882** McCABE *New York* 274 Intruders on 'claims' are as summarily dealt with as they are in a western mining camp. **1883** *Century Mag.* Sept. 796/2 In railway circles, all roads east of Buffalo, Pittsburg, Wheeling, Bristol (Tennessee), etc., are distinctively known as Eastern roads, and the lines west of these points are spent upon a Western farm. **1900** *Congress. Rec.* 10 Jan. 749/2 His early life was spent upon a Western farm.

6. In specific names.

Only a selection of examples is given.

a. Of trees and plants.

1813 MUHLENBERG *Cat. Plants* 96 *Fraxinus sericea,* Western black ash. **1884** SARGENT *Rep. Forests* 115 *Catalpa speciosa.* . . . Western Catalpa. Valley of the Vermilion river, Illinois [etc.]. **1897** SUDWORTH *Arborescent Flora* 149 Goldenleaf Chinquapin. . . . Common names [include] Chinquapin (Cal., Oreg.), . . . Western Chinquapin. **1870** *Amer. Naturalist* IV. 582 Prominent among these are . . . sunflowers of several species . . . ; the western iron weed (*Vernonia fasciculata*). **1869** *Ib.* III. 412 Western Larch (*Larix occidentalis*). I found this fine Larch first near Bitterroot valley. **1915** ARMSTRONG & THORNBER *Western Wild Flowers* 436 Western Penny-royal, Mustang Mint. . . . An attractive plant, pretty in color and form. **1905** *Bureau of Forestry Bul.* No. 66, 33 The rock pine, western red cedar, Bebb willow [etc.] . . . have, without doubt, come down from the Rocky Mountains. **1897** SUDWORTH *Arborescent Flora* 286 Large-tooth Maple. . . . Common names. Western Sugar Maple, Hard Maple, . . . Large-toothed Maple. **1869** *Amer. Naturalist* III. 410 Western White Pine (*Pinus monticola*). I found scattered trees of this beautiful species on the highest parts of the Rocky Mountains.

b. Of birds and insects.

1917 *Birds of Amer.* II. 201 Black Phoebe. *Sayornis nigricans.* . . . Western Black Pewee. **1869** *Amer. Naturalist* III. 185 Other birds observed [near Cajon Pass, Calif.] were a flock of Pigeons . . . and the Western Bluebird. **1828** BONAPARTE *Synopsis* 394 The Western Duck . . . inhabits the western coast of North America. **1869** *Amer. Naturalist* III. 183 The Western Flicker (*Colaptes Mexicanus*) was the only one of its tribe observed in this nearly woodless plain. **1839** AUDUBON *Ornith. Biog.* V. 320 [The] Western Gull . . . is especially remarkable for the great depth and comparative shortness of its bill. **1876** *Field & Forest* II. 72 Mr. Bethune treats . . . the subject of the Western Locust, (*Caloptenus spretus*), devoting several pages to the means of reducing their ravages. **1893** ROOSEVELT *Wilderness Hunter* 64, I spoke above of the sweet singing of the western meadow lark. **1878** *Nat. Museum Proc.* I. 395 [The] Western Robin . . . visits the valleys only in winter, when it is sometimes abundant. **1868** *Amer. Naturalist* II. 161 Western Snow-bird (*Junco Oregonus*). A specimen [was] shot at Fort Whipple, Arizona. **1874** COUES *Birds N.W.* 248 The Western Wood Pewee is exceedingly abundant in Arizona.

7. In special combinations.

Western-born, born in the West; *w. end*, a person's posterior; *w. fire*, a generous fire like that found in western homes; *w. invitation*, such an invitation as westerners commonly make; *w. mail*, mail from the West; *w. swing*, a dance regarded as of Western origin; *w. tour*, a tour through the West; *w. trade*, sale to Western customers.

1859 *Ladies' Repository* XIX. 1/2 The Bishop was western-born, and he owes, doubtless, much of his endurance to his frontier boyhood. **1836** *Knickerb.* VII. 43 My earliest sufferings arose from certain applications on the part of my mother to 'my western end' for not keeping out of the gutter. **1819** E. EVANS *Pedestrious Tour* 128, I spent many a pleasant evening . . . seated by a huge western fire. **1890** RYAN *Told in Hills* 38 Say, Clara, that sounds like an invitation to drink, doesn't it?—a western invitation. **1703** *Mass. H. S. Coll.* 3 Ser. VII. 61 Letters from Piscataqua come in the Western mail. **1847** in H. Howe *Hist. Coll. Ohio* 121 [They] danced the scamper-down, double-shuffle, western-swing and half-moon, forty-six years ago in the log cabin of Major Carter. **1900** *Congress. Rec.* 16 Jan. 856/1 The President . . . stated repeatedly in his Western tour that he was an instrument of Providence. **1885** *Century Mag.* Jan. 402 [His] knowledge of art was limited to a commercial appreciation of the value of gilt decorations on red leather boot-tops designed for the Western trade.

Western country. + = WEST COUNTRY.

In very common use, 1785–1850.

1781 *Va. State P.* II. 298 My last Trip to the Western Country was attended with more hardships than this probably would be. **1788** *Ky. Convention Jrnl.* MS. B 13 Resolved, That . . . the president be requested to present him the thanks of the Convention for the regard which he therein manifested for the Interest of the Western Country. **1820** FLINT *Lett. from Amer.* 218 The greater part of the lands of the western country are cleared by deadening the timber. **1845** SOL. SMITH *Theatr. Apprent.* 91 Our intention was to make our way to the western country. **1880** *Cimarron News & Press* 23 Dec. 1/4 The sentiment . . . will find a warm echo in the hearts of many in this Western country. **1894** WISTER in *Harper's Mag.* May 909/2 When you kids have travelled this Western country awhile you'll keep your cards locked.

+**Western daisy.** (See quot. 1891.) — **1891** *Cent.* 6881/2 *Western daisy*, a plant, *Bellis integrifolia*, found from Kentucky southwestward, the only species of the true daisy genus native in the United States. **1901** MOHR *Plant Life Ala.* 778.

+**Westerner.** {1905–} One who lives in the West. — [**1837** MARTINEAU *Society* III. 21 'We are apt to think,' said a westerner to me, 'that however great and good another person may be, we are just as great and good.'] **1849** AUDUBON *Western Jrnl.* 186 The tall, raw-boned Westerner [was] bearded and moustached. **1864** E. W. Pearson *Lett. Port Royal* 259 My guests . . . [included] Judge Cooley, . . . a Westerner and also very pleasant. **1886** [see DROPPER 4]. **1905** *Springfield W. Repub.* 11 Aug. 1 The reciprocity conference at Chicago is called by westerners.

+**Western farmer.** One who farms in the West. — **1812** *Niles' Reg.* III. 53/1 The unnatural trade which we carry on with Philadelphia and Baltimore . . . affords not the least encouragement to the western farmer. **1909** PARKER *G. Cleveland* 134 The relation of the tariff to the Western farmer.

+**Western fever.** The desire to migrate westwards. Now hist. — **1835** A. PARKER *Trip to Texas* 20 The 'western fever' rages here [in New York] as violent as on the sterile hills of New-Hampshire. **1857** *Ladies' Repository* XVII. 100/1 Some relative . . . once went that way with the 'Western fever' and returned without it.

+**Western frontier.** That part of the United States which, on the west, bordered upon unoccupied territory. Now hist. (See also FRONTIER.) — **1721** *Mass. H. Rep. Jrnl.* III. 104, 50 more good Effective men [shall] be employed as Scouts for securing the Western Frontiers. **1778** *Jrnls. Cont. Congress* X. 66 A petition from sundry inhabitants of the western frontiers was read. **c1834** CATLIN *Indians* II. 15 Fort Leavenworth . . . is the extreme outpost on the Western Frontier, and built, like several others, in the heart of the Indian country. **1839** HOFFMAN *Wild Scenes* 30, [I] expected of course to see one of those roystering, 'cavorting,' rifle-shirted blades that I have seen upon our western frontier. **1883** SWEET & KNOX *Through Texas* 504 The past history of the western frontier is nothing more nor less than the history of one unending Indian war.

+**Western Indian.** An Indian located in the West. — **1713** *N.C. Col. Rec.* II. 26 The Tuscaroras have surprised and rob'ed our Traders going to the Western Indians. **1827** COOPER *Prairie* v, He glanced . . . after the flying cattle, with the longings of a Western Indian.

+**Westernism.** {1892–} An expression of speech supposed to be peculiar to the West. — **1838** *Knickerb.* XI. 447, I now recollect but few specimens of Jack's *westernisms*. **1852** EASTMAN *Aunt Phillis's Cabin* 174 [The cat] proceeded immediately to the hearth where the provender was deposited, and to use an inelegant Westernism, 'walked into it.' **1886** *Harper's Mag.* Oct. 773 'It hasn't—ah—panned out.' He involuntarily made a droll face as he uttered the Westernism.

‖**Westernite.** =WESTERNER. — **1886** *West Chester* (Penna.) *Republican*, The westernites are ahead of us.

Westernize, *v.* {1842–} +*tr.* To make Western in character and manner. — **1837** PECK *New Guide* 107 Emigrants from Europe . . . are fast losing their national manners and feelings, and to use a provincial term, will soon become 'westernized.' **1853** *La Crosse Democrat* 28 June 2/5 A man who has been perfectly westernized, naturally thinks and acts on a much greater scale than he did before he passed through this process. **1882** *Advance* 22 June, After a month's residence [in Lawrence, Kan.], I have come to feel that it was a New England town *westernized*.

Western life. +The manners and customs of life in the West. — **1850** GARRARD *Wah-To-Yah* ii. 37 We crowded together, listening with much interest to tales of western life. **1883** *Harper's Mag.* Jan. 283/1 The great festivals of Western life are camp-meetings, barbecues, and log-rollings.

Western man. +A Westerner; a man typical of the old West. — **1834** BRACKENRIDGE *Recollections* 175 A western man . . . informed me that there was but *one* lawyer in the town. **1845** SIMMS *Wigwam & Cabin* 1 Ser. 85 When did you ever find a western man unwilling for a horse-barter? **1885** *Harper's Mag.* March 642/1 The 'Western man' is fast dying out: the railways, rather than the saloons, have killed him.

Western paper. +A newspaper published in the West. — **1806** *Balance* V. 366 The following curious suggestions . . . are extracted from the file of western papers. **1902** BANKS *Newspaper Girl* 8, I would be bidden by the proprietor of the bustling Western paper to think up things for newspaper stories.

Western people. +The residents of the West. — **1806** *Balance* V. 366/1 A letter from a gentleman of Frankfort . . . declares the western people to be indissolubly attached to the union. **1850** J. GALLAHER *Western Sketch-Book* 34 The language employed at that time, by the plain western people, in describing the results of these meetings, was, that so many 'fell.' **1884** *Gringo & Greaser* 1 Jan. 1/2 Western people . . . have always taken these precautions, except those who wear no socks at all. **1895** G. KING *New Orleans* 154 The Western people saw themselves deprived of an outlet without which they could not exist.

+**Western plain. a.** The prairie country. *rare.* **b.** A western prairie. Usu. pl. — **1836** J. HALL *Statistics of West* 46 The western plain is the centre of our empire. **1851** GLISAN *Jrnl. Army Life* 54 This would be a real saving at frontier stations like ours—within easy range of the . . . wild animals of the western plains. **1870** *Rep. Comm. Agric. 1869* 95 A large development of meat products would naturally be looked for from the western plains. **1877** *Harper's Mag.* March 519/1 The buffalo [is found] on our broad Western plains.

+**Western prairie.** =PRAIRIE 1 *note d* and *e*. — **1806** *Ann. 9th Congress* 2 Sess. 1134 Very different are the western prairies, which expression signifies only a country without timber. **1837** *S. Lit. Messenger* III. 736 I here saw for the first time a western prairie. **1847** LONGFELLOW *Poetical Works* (1893) 83/2 Far in the western prairies or forests that skirt the Nebraska, . . . the wild horses affrighted sweep by. **1873** *Newton Kansan* 1 May 3/2 The law for encouraging the growth of timber upon western prairies is published upon the fourth page of this paper. **1879** *Scribner's Mo.* Dec. 239/2 The mellow Western prairie is at first a wild, untamed thing.

+**Western Reserve.** A part of the present state of Ohio (see quot. 1837) to which Connecticut had a legal claim and the ownership of the land in which she reserved when ceding her claim to the federal government. (Cf. FIRE LAND 1.)

1800 *Stat. at Large* II. 56 All that territory commonly called the Western Reserve of Connecticut . . . was excepted by said state of Connecticut out of the cession by the said state heretofore made to the United States. **1824** *New Eng. Farmer* II. 341 A settlement in the northern part of Ohio, called the 'western reserve,' has justly obtained much celebrity. **1837** W. JENKINS *Ohio Gaz.* 470 *Western Reserve*, oftentimes called New Connecticut, is situated in the northeast quarter of the state, between lake Erie on the north, Pennsylvania east, the parallel of the 41st degree of north latitude south, and Sandusky and Seneca counties on the west. **1872** *Vermont Bd. Agric. Rep.* I. 520 The 'Western Reserve' will not be long in spreading to the lake. **1889** P. BUTLER *Recollections* 11 The Western Reserve was settled mainly by New Englanders, who were intelligent and God-fearing men. **1913** LONDON *Valley of Moon* 22 And my mother was born in Ohio, or where Ohio is now. She used to call it the Great Western Reserve.

attrib. **1831** C. B. STORRS (*title*), An Address Delivered at the Western Reserve College, Hudson, Ohio, February 9, 1831, at His Inauguration. **1847** HOWE *Hist. Coll. Ohio* 255 There were 24000 acres of choice land scattered about the county of the Connecticut Western Reserve school land. **1892** *Western Reserve Hist. Soc. Tracts* III. 125 The present Western Reserve Historical society was first suggested by C. C. Baldwin . . . early in the year 1866.

+**Western settler.** A settler in the West. Now hist. — **1784** WASHINGTON *Diaries* II. 326 The Western Settlers—from my own observation—stand as it were on a pivot. **1835** HOFFMAN *Winter in West* I. 223 The oldest western settlers of this country are by . . . [no] means so familiar with books as the emigrants from the east. **1845** KIRKLAND *Western Clearings* 4 The years 1835 and 1836 will long be remembered by the Western Settler. **1913** BARNES *Western Grazing Grounds* 87 One peculiar class of western settler was the nester.

Western shore. +That part of Maryland and Virginia on the western side of Chesapeake Bay. (Cf. EASTERN SHORE.) — **1624** SMITH *Gen. Hist. Va.* IV. 143 Cleane contrary they on the Westerne shore, the younger bears the charge, and the elder the dignitie. **c1680** *Mass. H.S. Coll.* 2 Ser. I. 47 The Governour . . . ships himselfe for the western shore, being assisted with 5 ships and 10 sloops. **1746** E. KIMBER *Itinerant Observer* 51 The Inhabitants on the *Western Shore* are supply'd with prodigious Quantities of Beef, Pork and Grain.

+**Western state.** A state in the western part of the United States.

1794 T. COOPER *America* 8 These parts . . . furnish yearly a very considerable number of emigrants to the middle and western states. **1812** *Ann. 12th Congress* 1 Sess. II. 1227 At the time of the Indian or Western war, a peculiar organization had been made of the militia of the Western States. **1831** [see CUMBERLAND]. **1853** STOWE *Key* 218/1 Ministers both from New England and the Western States, did take a stronger and more decided ground. **1875** [see MIDDLE STATES b]. **1902** E. C. MEYER *Nominating Systems* 41 [Primary laws] vary from the most rudimentary beginnings, found mainly in the Western States, to more complicated and detailed systems, such as those of Massachusetts and Wisconsin.

+**Western territory.** Land in the West; spec., land northwest of the Ohio River and east of the Mississippi River together with an area south of the Ohio which was ceded to the national government by various states; also, a portion of this. *Obs.* — **1789** *Ann. 1st Congress* 63 In conformity to the law re-establishing the Western Territory, I nominate Arthur St. Clair, Governor. **1790** *Steele P.* I. 57 The Cession of Western territory offered by this State to the United States I am taught to believe is accepted. **1794** *U.S. Register 1795* 17, 220,000,000 of acres, lying west of the northern and middle states, and northwest of the river Ohio, . . . together with an extensive territory south of the Ohio, . . . forms what is usually denominated the Western Territory. **1806** *Balance* V. 292/2 General Bowles then at Montreal, was fixed upon . . . to carry his schemes into execution in Kentucky and the western territory. **1855** *S. Lit. Messenger* XXI. 669/1 The tide of emigration now set steadily towards the Western Territories.

+**Western warbling vireo.** (See quot. 1917.) — **1878** *Nat. Museum Proc.* I. 409. **1917** *Birds of Amer.* III. 105/2 In western North America there is a smaller and darker form of this bird, known as the Western, or Swainson's, Warbling Vireo (*Vireosylva gilva swainsoni*).

Western waters. *pl.* +The rivers and lakes of the West. — **1777** in *Amer. Speech* XV. 410/1 All persons who . . . had bona fide settled themselves . . . upon any waste and ungranted lands on the said Western Waters . . . shall be allowed for every family so settled four hundred acres of land. **1789** *Ann. 1st Congress* 154 A communication will be established with the river Ohio and the western waters. **1803** *Ann. 7th Congress* 2 Sess. 236 One-third of that population will probably be on the Western waters. **1827** COOPER *Prairie* vii, What will the Yankee Choppers say, when they have cut their path from the eastern to the western waters[?]

+**Western wilds.** *pl.* The West regarded as more or less a wilderness. — **1786** HUMPHREYS, etc. *Anarchiad* (1861) 20 O'er Western wilds, the tawny bands allied, Insult the States. **1803** *Ann. 7th Congress* 2 Sess. 193 Add to this the danger and the devastation from the troops of that country, aided by innumerable hosts of savages from the western wilds. **1841** BUCKINGHAM *America* I. 298 Daniel Boone, the celebrated American backwoodsman, [was] one of the early pioneers . . . in the western wilds. **1862** STRONG *Cadet Life W. Point* 19 Away in the depths of western wilds, . . . fell another gallant form. **1878** BEADLE (*title*), Western Wilds, and the Men Who Redeem Them.

Western World. America. — **1654** JOHNSON *Wonder-w. Prov.* 15 Let us tell of the marvelous doings of Christ preparing for his peoples arrivall in the Western World. **1671** *Plymouth Laws* 285 Gods providence having disposed us in this Corner of this Western world, so far from our Native Prince and People. **1744** FRANKLIN *Works* (1905) I. p. v, I shall add . . . my hearty Wish, that this first Translation of a *Classic* in this *Western World*, may be followed with many others. **1809** BARLOW *Columbiad* 21, I sing the Mariner who first unfurl'd An eastern banner o'er the western world. **1833** COKE *Subaltern's Furlough* xiii, [Boston] is the Athens of the western world.

+**West Florida.** A province formed after the treaty of Paris, 1763, comprising the lands west of the Chattahoochie and Apalachicola rivers and south of 31° N. lat. (later 32°81'). — **1789** MORSE *Amer. Geog.* 477 The principal town in West Florida is Pensacola.

+**West Florid(i)an.** A resident of West Florida. — **1775** ADAIR *Indians* 140 The West-Floridans, in order to keep their women subject to the law of adultery, bring some venison or buffalo's flesh to the house of their nominal wives, at the end of every winter's hunt. **1883** *Century Mag.* June 311/2 'Jools,' said the West-Floridian, laying his great hand tenderly upon the Creole's shoulder, 'do you think you have any shore hopes of heaven?'

* **West India.**

1. West India rum.

[**1789** *Ann. 1st Congress* 136 Mr. Ames stated the difference in the price of country rum and West India.] **1837** *Harvardiana* III. 238, I was obliged to down with a throat-rattler of West India.

2. *attrib.* Designating products of the West Indies.

[**1650** WILLIAMS *Virginia Richly Valued* 48 The West-Indie Potatoe . . . is a food excellently delicious and strongly nourishing.] **1770** in Summers *Ann. S.W. Va.* 64 For West India Rum they may demand ten shillings per gallon. **1790** *Columbian Centinel* 15 Sept. 4/2 West-India Fish received in barter for the Salt. **1832** CHILD *Frugal Housewife* 30 West India molasses is a gentle cathartic, while sugar-baker's molasses is slightly astringent. **1880** *Vt. Agric. Rep.* VI. 222 Our forefathers resorted to it (the cornstalk) as a means to furnish a substitute for West India sugar.

+**West India goods.** *pl.* Goods imported from the West Indies. — **1789** *Fayetteville* (N.C.) *Gaz.* 28 Aug., The subscriber has just received a good supply of West-India Goods. **1840** DANA *Two Years* 142 This was a small mud building, of only one room, in which were liquors, dry and West India goods [etc.]. **1860** HOLMES *E. Venner* vii, He used to deal in West India goods, such as coffee, sugar, and molasses, not to speak of rum. **1877** ALDRICH *Queen of Sheba* 12 Even the weather-beaten sign of 'J. Tibbets & Son, West India Goods & Groceries,' . . . emitted an elusive spicy odor.

* **West Indian.** A native of the West Indies of European descent. {1661-} — **1787** WASHINGTON *Diaries* III. 257 On my Return home I found a Mr. Dunlap (a West Indian), Mr. Cary, . . . and Mr. Porter here. **1873** HARTE *Fiddletown* 97 Here sat that young West Indian . . . Alexander Hamilton.

+**West Point.** [*West Point*, N.Y.]

1. The United States Military Academy, located at West Point. Also transf.

1856 GLISAN *Jrnl. Army Life* 359 We have not met since he was a cadet at West Point. **1868** *N.Y. Herald* 18 July 8/2 The following officers have been ordered to report for duty at West Point. **1892** M. A. JACKSON *Gen. Jackson* 53 This school . . . is called the 'West Point of the South.' **1894** ALLEN *Kentucky Cardinal* xvi, Joe is distinguishing himself at West Point.

2. Attrib. with *graduate, officer, phrase.*

1841 *Picayune* 3 Sept. 1/6 [The expedition] numbered about 450 men, . . . under the command of Hugh McLeod, a West Point graduate. **1874** ALDRICH *P. Palfrey* xv, I am one of the few West Point officers born in the South who have stuck to the old flag. **1887** CUSTER *Tenting on Plains* 286, I have known the General to 'bone up,' as his West Point phrase expressed it, on the smallest details of some question at issue.

+**West Pointer.** A cadet at the military academy at West Point, N.Y.; a graduate of the academy. Also attrib. — **1863** 'M. HARLAND' *Husks* 195 She promenaded past them leaning on the arm of a young West Pointer. **1878** *N. Amer. Rev.* CXXVI. 85 A detached brigade of Confederates [were] under the command of General Evans, of South Carolina, a West-Pointer enjoying the *sobriquet* of 'Shanks.' **1884** RITTENHOUSE *Maud* 282 [He] led me about in true West Pointer style, by my finger tips. **1903** HART *Actual Govt.* 469 All the greatest commanders in the Civil War were West Pointers.

* **West side.** That part of a city located in or towards the west. Also attrib. Hence *West sider.* — **1858** *Harper's Mag.* July 283/2 As our friend entered the door a well-known 'West side' operator made his bid. **1872** *Chicago Tribune* 19 Nov., The West Side places have fallen off. **1890** LANGFORD *Vigilante Days* (1912) 406 Thurmond came from the 'west side,' with a reputation for being a friend of the roughs. **1903** *Harper's Mo.* July 213 The abysmal craving of New Yorkers—West Side or East Side—is for friends. **1903** *N.Y. Ev. Post* 14 Nov. 4 The persistence with which the West Siders have followed up this question of the Broadway trees.

+**West Virginian.** One who lives or was born in West Virginia. — **1881-5** McCLELLAN *Own Story* 149 The executive never disowned my proclamation to the West Virginians. **1885** HOWELLS *Silas Lapham* 512 The young West Virginian . . . had come on to arrange the purchase of the Works.

Westward, *n.* {1652-} =WEST *n.* *Obs.* — **1778** *Jrnls. Cont. Congress* X. 9 Colonel Samuel Washington . . . declined the office of commissioner to the westward. **1815** [see EASTWARD (2)].

Westward, *a.* Western. *rare.* {1872-} — **1778** *Va. State P.* I. 315 The Northward and Westward Indians were bad people.

Wet, *n.* +A person who is opposed to prohibiting the legal sale of alcoholic liquors. — **1888** *Battle Creek Wkly. Jrnl.* 29 Feb., This is the first victory for the 'wets.' **1895** *Voice* 19 Sept. 2/1 There is great despondency among the 'wets.' **1896, 1907** [see DRY *n.* 2].

* **Wet,** *a.*

+**1.** Of places: Permitting the sale and consumption of alcoholic liquors.

1888 *Battle Creek Jrnl.* 3 July, A seemingly senseless rumor is afloat to the effect that since the county has gone 'dry' the Michigan Central dining car headquarters will be transferred to a 'wet' point. **1888** BRYCE *Amer. Commw.* II. III. liv. 350n., Some States, *e.g.* Georgia, have adopted a local option system, under which each county decides whether it will be 'wet' or 'dry.' **1890** *Congress. Rec.* 12 March 2172/1 Every spring election there is a contest as to whether the town is to be 'wet' or 'dry.' **1909** *N.Y. Ev. Post* 18 March (Th.), Nearly half the country is already openly against the saloon, and so are thousands of voters in the 'wet' regions.

+**b.** Of votes: In favor of permitting the sale of liquor.

1888 *Battle Creek Wkly. Jrnl.* 29 Feb., Ann Arbor gave a 'wet' majority of 473. **1896** *Chicago Record* 11 Feb. 6/5 The Ohio Anti-Saloon league . . . had a county system which provided that where the 'dry' vote exceeded the 'wet' vote . . . the whole county would go dry.

+**c.** *To vote* (or *go*) *wet,* to vote in favor of permitting or legalising the sale of alcoholic liquor.

1888 *American* (F.), In Missouri . . . forty-nine counties have voted wet, and thirty-three dry. Thirteen of the twenty towns went dry, and seven wet.

2. In combination with adjectives in -*ed.* {1660-}

1834 *Atlantic Mo.* XXVI. 485 Pine timber for ships is *docked*, or *wet-seasoned*; i.e. put under water 2 years, then sunned so as merely to dry the outside. **1876** RAYMOND *8th Rep. Mines* 419 The cost of drying the wet-crushed ore is to be avoided. **1885** *Harper's Mag.* Jan. 274/1 Hides brought to the tannery in this condition are known as 'wet salted.'

3. In special combinations.

Wet Grave, New Orleans; *wet mine,* a mine in danger of being flooded; *wet swamp,* a swamp, perhaps one that is wetter than most.

1833 J. E. ALEXANDER *Transatlantic Sk.* II. 30 New Orleans is called the 'Wet Grave,' because, in digging 'the narrow house,' water rises within eighteen inches of the surface. **1896** SHINN *Story of Mine* 99 Ophir, Justice, Uncle Sam, and Yellow Jacket won undesired pre-eminence as 'wet mines.' **1654** *Hartford Land Distrib.* 112 One parcell of land . . . abutting . . . upon a wett swamp ioyning to the neck of land on the west.

*Wet, v. 1. *tr.* To celebrate (receipt of a commission, promotion, etc.) by drinking {a1687–}: (see also quot. 1856). Also with *down.* 2. *To wet (someone's) jacket,* (see quotation). 3. *To wet the colors,* to furnish liquor to a ship's crew. — (1) 1746 HEMPSTEAD *Diary* 468 Danll Starr Wet his Commission. Treated both Companys at his house wth Cakes & Drink. 1856 HALL *College Words* (ed. 2) 476 *Wet,* to christen a new garment by treating one's friends when one first appears in it. 1894 'MARK TWAIN' *Those Twins* v, Lots of new friends carried Pudd'nhead Wilson off tavernward to feast him and 'wet down' his great and victorious entry into the legal arena. (2) 1856 CARTWRIGHT *Autobiog.* 149 He took a great deal of pleasure in . . . making them members of his church . . . by 'wetting their jackets,' that is, immersing them. (3) 1884 *Nat. Museum Bul.* No. 27, 717 The bridegroom is generally supposed to 'wet the colors' by furnishing his shipmates with a liberal supply of whatever beverages they may prefer.

*Wet day. +A rainy day; a time of misfortune and need. — 1867 CRAWFORD *Mosby* 83 Even the poor negro . . . had his little cabin searched and robbed of what little money he had laid aside for a '*wet day.*' 1908 'O. HENRY' *Strictly Business* 15 There are mighty few actors . . . who couldn't fix themselves for the wet days to come if they'd save their money.

+Wet diggings. *pl. Mining.* (See quot. 1889.) — 1884 *Encycl. Brit.* (ed. 9) *Amer. Suppl.* I. 197/2 In California the mountain-torrents flow through *gulches,* the *wet-diggings* of the gold-regions. 1889 MUNROE *Golden Days* 111 The wet or placer diggings were those in, or in the vicinity of, flowing streams.

+Wet-down. A wetting. — 1891 *Boston Jrnl.* 6 May 4/6 The bursting of a water-pipe caused a heavy wet-down at Miss Nellie H. Bonney's millinery establishment.

Wet goods. *pl.* 1. Liquids, spec., alcoholic liquors. {1882–} Also attrib. 2. ?Goods damaged by water. — (1) 1779 *Remembrancer* VIII. 277 Philadelphia, May 5. Saturday last arrived here from Cadiz, a polacre, with a large and general assortment of dry and wet goods. 1787 *Md. Gazette* 1 June 4/2 He is supplied as usual, with every Article in the Wet Goods Line, at the lowest Market prices. 1875 *Chicago Tribune* 13 Dec. 5/4 Another Day's Developments in the Mashing of the Great Complot in Wet Goods. 1917 McCUTCHEON *Green Fancy* 73 Two or three men visitors have come down from the place to sample our stock of wet goods. (2) 1858 *S. Lit. Messenger* XXVII. 31/2 It haunts places where what are called 'wet goods' are disposed of, and is there being constantly cheated.

+Wet groceries. =WET GOODS 1. — 1866 W. REID *After War* 136 Coarse dry goods were plenty, and so were what, I believe, are technically called 'wet groceries.' 1894 *Congress. Rec.* 6 April 3527/1, I do not know whether they were 'dry' groceries or 'wet' groceries that were sold there.

+Wet hawk. (See quotation.) — 1781–2 JEFFERSON *Notes Va.* (1788) 77 Besides these, we have . . . [the] Wet hawk, which feeds flying. 1808 ASHE *Travels* 162.

Wet hen. +(As) *mad as a wet hen,* or variant: Extremely angry. — 1881 STODDARD *E. Hardery* 28 He's as mad as a wet hen. 1881 *Harper's Mag.* April 729/2 He wuz as mad as forty thousan' wet hens. 1890 MUNN *Uncle Terry* 68 He came in yesterday, mad as a wet hen, and wanted his money back.

*Wether. A male sheep, esp. a castrated ram. Also attrib. — 1637 *Essex Inst. Coll.* IX. 42 Agreed to allowe a goatherd for keeping a whole year . . . one shilling an ew Lamb . . . & 6d a y[ea]r a wether lamb. 1650 *Essex Probate Rec.* I. 124 Fouer wether sheepe . . . ewe sheepe. 1768 WASHINGTON *Diaries* I. 301 Put up my Beeves and Weathers to Fatten. 1846 *Knickerb.* XXVII. 17 A faultless haunch of wether mutton . . . lies glowing and blushing at the sound of the praises that are bestowed upon it. 1890 *Stock Grower & Farmer* 5 April 5/1 Troy Bros. of Raton, have 3,000 wethers sold as feeders, at $2.50 per head.

Wether goat. A castrated goat. {1671–} — 1653 *East-Hampton Rec.* I. 46 The s[ai]d Lion Gardiner was fformerly possessed of . . . 4 weather goots worth 4£.

+Wet key. A Florida key consisting of a group of trees the roots of which are under water. — 1834 AUDUBON *Ornith. Biog.* II. 356 Groups of such trees [*i.e.,* trees whose roots are constantly immersed] occur of considerable extent, and are called 'Wet Keys.'

Wet land. Land which remains too wet or is covered by water part of the year. — 1804 J. ROBERTS *Penna. Farmer* 19 The first and principal improvement of wet land is draining. 1847 HOWE *Hist. Coll. Ohio* 98 'Wet land,' . . . by judicious cultivation, . . . rapidly improves in fertility. 1849 *New Eng. Farmer* I. 235 A large portion of the land in Indiana . . . is technically called 'flat woods,' 'wet lands,' 'black slashes,' &c.

Wet nurse. A woman employed to suckle and nurse a baby. {1620–} — 1714 *Boston News-Letter* 22 Nov. 2/2 A Certain Person wants a wet Nurse into the House, to Suckle a Child. 1871 *Scribner's Mo.* II. 481 At nine o'clock the wet nurse brought the baby in. 1882 'M. HARLAND' *Eve's Daughters* 33 A wet-nurse who is an honest woman, clean in body and in life, is beyond price.

+Wet prairie. A prairie on which water stands at least part of the year: (see also quot. 1897). — 1819 HULME *Journal* 280 Some of those [prairies] we passed over are called *wet prairies,* but, they are dry at this time of the year. 1849 CHAMBERLAIN *Ind. Gazetteer* 152 The wet prairies form the sources of the creeks. 1897 HOUGH *Story of Cowboy* 15 Sometimes such tanks run far into the open country back of the 'wet prairie' as the sea marsh is generally called.

+Wet store. A store that sells wet goods. — 1788 *Maryland Jrnl.* 25 July (Th.), [Notice] to those who would wish for the best stand for a Dry or Wet Store.

+Wet (weather) spring. A spring that runs in wet weather. — 1844 in *Filson Club Quarterly* IX. 232 There was . . . a wet spring, at times, there. 1901 HARBEN *Westerfelt* 87 Good gracious, it's runnin' like a wet-weather spring.

Weymouth pine. The white pine (*Pinus strobus*), a native of North America. {1766–} — 1799 WELD *Travels* 161 Smooth bark or Weymouth pines . . . seem almost peculiar to this part of the country. 1847 DARLINGTON *Weeds & Plants* 336 White Pine. Weymouth Pine. . . . This is also a most valuable tree. 1897 SUDWORTH *Arborescent Flora* 13.

Whack, n. {1737–}

+1. A chance or turn. Freq. in phrase *first whack. colloq.*
1884 *Century Mag.* Nov. 60 Lucky whack it was for me that I got here to-day, and in time to save the mine! 1890 *Stock Grower & Farmer* 17 May 3/1 We have first whack at the water and intend to take out all we need. 1904 W. H. SMITH *Promoters* 40 We can get the first whack at all of them too.

b. Time. *colloq.*
1886 *Century Mag.* Jan. 427/1 They fetches a feller every whack.

+2. *That's* (or *it's*) *a whack,* it's a deal or a bargain. *colloq.*
1876 'MARK TWAIN' *Tom Sawyer* vi. 70 'I'll stay if you will.' 'Good—that's a whack.' 1883 HAY *Bread-Winners* 149 Say the word, and it's a whack. 1902 McFAUL *Ike Glidden* 146, 'I'll guarantee to get him to take you to Grand Menan with him.' 'It's a whack,' said Jim.

+3. *To have* (or *take*) *a whack at,* to deliver a blow at; to have a chance at; to make a try at. *colloq.*
1891 *Boston Jrnl.* 22 June 2/2 There are thousands . . . who . . . are anxious to have a whack, at the polls, at the party that deceived them. 1900 *Congress. Rec.* 5 Feb. 1522/1 Senator Carter of Montana took a whack at this business not long ago. 1901 FLYNT *World of Graft* 159 The criminal lawyer also has his 'whack,' and a strenuous one it is, at the thief's pile.

+4. *Out of whack,* out of order. *colloq.*[2]
1899 ADE *Doc' Horne* 79 My stomach seems to be out of whack. 1903 — *People You Know* 70 If the Plumbing wasn't out of Whack, the Furnace required too much Coal.

Whack, v. {1719–} +1. *tr.* To drive (mules or oxen). Cf. MULE-WHACKER. 2. To cut (a way) through. 3. To defeat. — (1) 1873 BEADLE *Undevel. West* 691 One ought to be a 'Pioneer'—one of those who whacked mules or oxen across the Plains in the olden time. (2) a1890 CABLE in Webster (1890) 1642/2 Rodsmen were whacking their way through willow brakes. (3) 1897 *Outing* Aug. 466/2 His sisters had 'whacked' the champions scores of times.

Whacker. {1823–} +A driver of a team. (Cf. BULLWHACKER 1, MULE-WHACKER.) — 1827 C. BRYANT *Letter* 1 Jan. (MS.), If our doors were closed, the country whackers who bring in cotton, corn and other produce for sale, would never find the way in. 1880 *Harper's Mag.* April 679/1 A noisy train of long-horned, thin-bodied oxen comes round the corner . . . , the whacker's long whip cracking like pistol-shots.

Whackets. A noisy game of some kind. — 1782 S. E. BALDWIN *Simeon Baldwin* 100 The others exercised themselves with the most disagreeable of Games, *Whackets,* which they made so ridiculously noisy that it was disgusting.

‖Whack stamp. ?The stamp of unreliability. — 1887 *Courier-Journal* 23 Jan. 12/1 The consideration for which the princeling says that Washburn did this perilous work was $4 per letter. This feature puts the 'whack' stamp on the whole story.

+Whafler. A speckled woodpecker. *Obs.* — 1807 *Mass. H. S. Coll.* 2 Ser. III. 54 The birds, which frequent this and the adjacent islands, are the crow, . . . the wood-pecker, two species, the red-headed, and the speckled or whafler.

+Whahoo. 1. =WAHOO.[1] 2. (See quotations.) — (1) 1829 EATON *Botany* (ed. 5) 428 *Ulmus alata,* whahoo. 1875 *Field & Forest* I. 35 The winged Elm, or Whahoo, stands in the Botanic garden. 1897 SUDWORTH *Arborescent Flora* 182. (2) *Ib.* 197 *Magnolia fraseri,* Fraser Umbrella. . . . Whahoo. *Ib.* 267 *Ptelea trifoliata.* . . . Hoptree. Wafer Ash. Whahoo.

*Whale, n.

*1. Any large marine mammal of the order Cetacea.
1616 SMITH *New England* 29 [There were] Whales, Grampus, Porkpisces [etc.]. 1650 *East-Hampton Rec.* I. 8 If any whales be cast up within our bounds . . . every householder shall do his part of ye worke about cutting of them out. 1707 *Boston News-Letter* 10 March 2/1 Last Week a Whale about 40 foot long was struck a few miles to the Eastward of this City. 1773 in Singleton *Social N.Y.* 352 A considerable large whale was seen . . . in the East River of this City. 1806 CLARK in *Lewis & C. Exped.* III. (1905) 244 The Whale was already pillaged of every Valuable part by the Kilamox Inds. 1846 *Niles' Nat. Reg.* 28 March 64/3, 36 young whales were discovered in York river, Virginia, driven ashore by the late heavy gale. 1891 CHASE & CLOW *Industry* II. 129 While the body of the whale floats alongside the ship, men pass long ropes around the carcass.

+b. *A whale of a,* an intensive. *colloq.* {1930}
1913 *19th Cent.* Sept. 621 [They] had what the Americans call 'a whale of a good time.'

+2. *Old whale,* a sailor.
1861 *New Haven Palladium* 27 Dec. (Chipman), We 'Old Whales' or, as we are sometimes termed, 'Sardines,' are not supposed by some 'land crabs' to have much of a taste for the feathery tribe 'done up brown.'

3. Attrib. and comb. with *cry, design, grease*, etc.

1673 *Southampton Rec.* II. 246 Wee ingage ourselves to him to bee at his service to goe to sea for him the whale season upon the whale design. **1674** *East-Hampton Rec.* I. 367 All Whale scrapps that are at the several mens tryeinge places shalbee all buiried in the ground. **1713** *Boston News-Letter* 5 Oct. 2/2 The best sort of Greenland Whale Warps, to be Sold. **1769** *R.I. Commerce* I. 275 Have now sent 12 whale Irons . . . per Anthony's boy. **1793** *Huntington Rec.* III. 172 The two whale Houses on the Beach stood between Goose Island & Thatch Island. **1817** *Niles' Reg.* XIII. 36/2 Being in the South seas, he fell in with a Nantucket whale-ship. **1840** DANA *Two Years* 42 He had been forty years in the whale-trade. **1844** LEE & FROST *Oregon* 301 Our cook . . . made his feast upon bread and whale grease, of which they had had a great abundance during the past winter. **1850** CHEEVER *Whale & Captors* 45 The captain was killed by a single stroke of a whale-spade. **1851** MELVILLE *Moby-Dick* 269 Town-ho, . . . the ancient whale-cry upon first sighting a whale from the mast-head.

Whale, *v.*

1. *tr.* To beat or flog. Also *to whale it into.* {1790–1801} 'Now *U.S. colloq.*' (O.E.D.).

1831 *Maysville* (Ky.) *Eagle* 12 July, I'll just *whale* it *into* that Van Buren. **1848** LOWELL *Biglow P.* 1 Ser. 53 Their masters can cuss 'em, an' kick 'em, an' wale 'em. **1869** *Overland Mo.* III. 128 Some boasted that one Southerner could 'whale' ten Yankees. **1904** *Albany Wkly. Times* 26 May 4 When the lad comes home with his bruises and torn shirt, don't whale him until you find out all about it.

2. *To whale away,* +*fig.*, to talk continuously and violently.

1846 WHITCHER *Bedott P.* vi. 67 You remember that one that come round a spell ago, a whalin' away about human rights. *c*1847 *Ib.* x. 104 The elder . . . whaled away through his nose. **1890** BARRÈRE & LELAND (1897) II. 394/1.

+**b.** *To whale it at,* to pitch into (something or someone) energetically; to whale away at. *colloq.*

1873 'MARK TWAIN' & WARNER *Gilded Age* 47 Spread her wide open! Whale it at her! **1886** *Harper's Mag.* July 322/1 In tones of wrath . . . he whaled it at his opponent throughout the fifteen minutes allotted to him.

Whaleback. {1886} +A steamer whose main decks, being rounded over, look somewhat like the back of a whale. — **1891** *Pall Mall Gaz.* 10 June 2/2 The Americans claim that, in Captain Macdougall's steel 'whalebacks,' they possess the universal ship of the future. **1898** *Kansas City Star* 19 Dec. 4/1 At Detroit yesterday the powerful tugs . . . released from the ice a large fleet of whalebacks.

+**Whaleboat.** A long narrow rowboat sharp at both ends, used orig. in whaling and later for many purposes, esp. as a lifeboat on a steamer. {1871}

1682 *Conn. Rec.* III. 318 How cam you up into these parts? In a whale boat. **1712** *Boston News-Letter* 8 Dec. 2/2 Six Men going off the Gurnet Beach in a Whale-Boat . . . after a Whale, by reason of the Boisterousness of the sea, . . . they were all Drowned. **1782** CRÈVECŒUR *Letters* 154 It may appear strange to you, that so slender a vessel as an *American whale-boat* . . . should dare to pursue and to attack [whales]. **1807** *Mass. H. S. Coll.* 2 Ser. III. 31 A whaleboat . . . is built by five or six workmen in three days, and costs fifty dollars. **1886** *Outing* VIII. 45/2, I've been into a whaleboat, fast to a whale, and him a runnin' some fifteen or twenty mile a hour.

* **Whalebone.**

1. The horny substance derived from the upper jaws of baleen whales; freq. used to stiffen articles of dress. {1601–}

1640 *Mass. H. S. Coll.* 4 Ser. VI. 67 Tell goodman Nickerson I intreat him to send me a pound of whalebone by the first he can. **1775** *Amer. Husbandry* I. 59 Exports of this province since the peace [include] . . . Whale-bone, 28 tons. **1800** BOWNE *Life* 32 There is too much appearance of whalebone and buckram to please the depraved taste of the present age. **1850** CHEEVER *Whale & Captors* 28 Whalebone [in 1848], two million three thousand six hundred pounds, worth $508,762. **1904** *Glasgow Deliverance* 287 She's got to w'ar whalebones in her clothes when I'm aroun'.

2. A walking stick; a riding whip. {1842–, a whip}

1835 HOFFMAN *Winter in West* II. 252 There [you would see] . . . a gang of dandy-looking blackees, each with an enormous cudgel, in lieu of the gold-headed whale-bone which is elsewhere so much in vogue. **1868** WOODRUFF *Trotting Horse* 57 The right kind of touch is worth more in an emergency than all the whipcord and whalebone in the world.

3. Attrib. and comb. with *bonnet, busk, cutter*, etc.

1745 in Watson *Philadelphia* 179 Children's stays, jumps and bodice, whalebone and iron busks. **1789** *Boston Directory* 196 Pulsifer Thomas, whale-bone-cutter. **1830** WATSON *Philadelphia* 176 The 'mush-mellon' bonnet, used before the Revolution, had numerous whale-bone stiffeners in the crown. *Ib.*, The latest bonnet was the 'whale-bone bonnet,' having only the bones in the front as stiffeners. **1851** MELVILLE *Moby-Dick* 513 Fifty of these whale-bone whales are harpooned for one cachalot.

Whalebone cane. =WHALEBONE 2. — **1837** *S. Lit. Messenger* III. 3, I was startled by the apparition of a dandy . . . flourishing a little whalebone cane. **1867** RICHARDSON *Beyond Miss.* 51 A lithe, young man, armed only with a whalebone cane.

Whale fishery. The business or occupation of fishing for whales. {1704–}

1723 *New-Eng. Courant* 27 May 2/2 One — Ames of Scituate, employ'd in the Whale-fishery at Sea, was lately drowned. *a*1772 WOOLMAN *Journal* 171 They depend principally on the whale fishery. **1814** *Ann. 13th Congress* 1 Sess. 1118 [Nantucket and New Bedford] are the only towns . . . which could prosecute the whale fishery, to any considerable extent, without the aid and support of Government. **1850** CHEEVER *Whale & Captors* 28 The number of vessels in the American whale fishery the present year, 1849, . . . is estimated at six hundred and ten. **1891** *Century Mag.* April 928 The interests . . . of our whale fisheries . . . demand that you should exert the greatest vigilance.

* **Whale fishing.** =prec. Also attrib. — **1622** 'MOURT' *Relation* 4 Our master and his mate . . . preferred it before Greenland Whale-fishing. **1777** *N.J. Archives* 2 Ser. I. 437 The situation is very healthy and convenient either for hunting or fishing, even whale fishing. **1849** *Whig Almanac 1850* 17/1 An oceanic-canal . . . would get the U.S. China trade, the U.S. whale-fishing vessels, and many others.

Whale killer. One who kills whales. {1613} — **1690** *Plymouth Laws* 231 S[ai]d Whale killers . . . [shall] repair to some prudent person whome the Court shall appoint and there give in the wounds of s[ai]d Whale. **1817** *N. Amer. Rev.* V. 319 Maushop . . . preserved their lives by converting them into whale killers.

Whale louse. A small crustacean parasitic on whales. {1774} — **1737** BRICKELL *N. Carolina* 245 The Whale-Louse. Their Head is like that of a Louse, with four Horns. **1843** *Nat. Hist. N.Y., Zoology* VI. 40 This species, which is known under the name of Whale Louse, is usually found attached to the bodies of whales along our coast. **1869** *Amer. Naturalist* III. 244 The Whale-louse (*Cyamus*) . . . has a short and broad body, with stout legs and claws.

Whaleman.

+**1.** A man engaged in whaling. {1898}

1665 *East-Hampton Rec.* I. 230 The whaleman might strike a whale, and bringe her ashore at the said place. **1675** *Ib.* 375 An action entered by Thomas Dyament Senior in the behalfe of the Companie of Whalemen belongeinge to Mr. James. **1724** *New-Eng. Courant* 14 Dec. 1/2 Our Whalemen and Fishermen . . . demand extravagant Prices for their Wares. **1791** *Mass. H. S. Coll.* III. 154 The seamen are the most expert whalemen in the world. **1839** *Knickerb.* XIII. 381 His compliance . . . should not be construed into an admission, that Nantucket whalemen were the best boatmen in the world. **1888** [see DEVILFISH 2].

2. A ship engaged in whaling. {1860}

1767 CUTLER in *Life & Corr.* I. 19 Whalemen fitted out for the Straits of Belle Isle, and Davis Straits. **1854** BARTLETT *Personal Narr.* I. 504 Passed a whaleman, the ship Carlton. **1868** G. G. CHANNING *Recoll. Newport* 138 The Mount Hope changed hands, and was turned into a whaleman.

* **Whale oil.** Oil derived from whale blubber. Also attrib. — **1686** [see FISH OIL]. **1765** ROGERS *Acct. N. Amer.* 187 [The Northern Indians] feed chiefly on whale-oil and blubber. **1850** *Rep. Comm. Patents 1849: Agric.* 272, 3 gallons strong lye, 1 pint whale-oil soap. **1882** *Century Mag.* March 761/1 [On the mantel-piece] were arrayed the irons and the whale-oil lamps to which they still clung.

Whaler.

1. A man engaged in whaling. {1684–}

1775 ROMANS *Nat. Hist. Florida* p. lxxix, The North, or Grand Bahama bank, is little frequented but by whalers and turtlers. **1823** COOPER *Pilot* II. 41 Trust an old whaler, Captain Barnstable, . . . who has been used to these craft all his life. **1885** *Century Mag.* Jan. 423 There were Maine lumbermen, New Bedford Whalers [etc.]. **1900** *Congress. Rec.* 4 Jan. 643/1 The joint resolution . . . recognizing the . . . heroic services of . . . the overland expedition to Point Barrow, Arctic Ocean, for the relief of whalers.

2. A ship engaged in whaling. {1806–}

1830 N. AMES *Mariner's Sk.* 274 A lady on each arm answers precisely the same purpose as the 'ice pieces' on the bows of a Greenland whaler, they keep off shocks. **1848** BURTON *Waggeries* 9, I started on my first voyage in the Confidence whaler, Capting Coffing. **1883** HOWELLS *Woman's Reason* xxi, It is unnecessary even to record the details of his transfer . . . from the whaler which took him off.

b. =WHALEBOAT.

1835 AUDUBON *Ornith. Biog.* III. 186 Quickly was the whaler hauled on board.

+**3.** A huge person or animal. *colloq.*

1833 S. SMITH *Life J. Downing* 179 He's a whaler of a feller, as big as any two men in Downingville. **1845** HOOPER *Daddy Biggs' Scrape* (1928) 140 Boys, he's a whaler! **1891** COOKE *Huckleberries* 248 A whaler! my eye!

Whalery. {1878–} Whaling; an establishment for the use of whalers. — **1683** PENN *Acct. Prov. Penna.* 9 The Whalery [is conveniently posted] for a sound and fruitful Bank. **1685** — *Further Acct. Penna.* 8 We justly hope a considerable profit by a Whalery.

Whaling, *n.*[1]

1. The business or action of whale fishing. {1821–, attrib.; 1895}

1688 *Huntington Rec.* II. 9 If the said Willam have a good voyage In Whaling ye are before if not then to pay the for said sume. **1716** *Mass. H. Rep. Jrnl.* I. 138 Peter Thatcher Esq; and Mr. Benjamin Hawes, are

... Appointed to go to the said Island [Nantucket], and enquire into ... their Whaling. **1839** *Knickerb.* XIII. 378 Whaling was the most dignified and manly of all sublunary pursuits. **1902** *N.Y. Tribune* Wkly. Rev. 26 April 8/2, I'll be —— if I ever go a-whaling again!

2. *attrib.* **a.** Designating trade, employment, etc., in whaling.

1722 *New-Eng. Courant* 18 June 2/2 Huffey of Nantucket ... went out from thence on the Whaling Account. **1723** *Ib.* 25 March 2/2 The going off to Sea on the Whaling Employment in the Summer-Season, has prov'd ... advantageous. **1780** *N.J. Archives* 2 Ser. IV. 656 Wanted, Two experienced Harponiers in the whaling business. **1860** *Harper's Mag.* June 8/1 New Bedford is the chief seat of the whaling interest.

b. Designating ships and implements used in whaling.

1850 CHEEVER *Whale & Captors* 24 The first proper whaling harpoon used in America was wrought there [in Nantucket] or on Cape Cod. **1851** MELVILLE *Moby Dick* 466 The whaling-pike is similar to a frigate's boarding-weapon of the same name. **1866** *Ore. State Jrnl.* 1 Dec. 3/1 The steam whaling bark Pioneer arrived at New London. **1884** *Nat. Museum Bul.* No. 27, 302 Whaling-gun. Brand gun No. 2; muzzle-loading, skeleton iron stock. New Bedford, Massachusetts. *Ib.* 352 Whaleman's 'Bell.' ... Gift of Captain Henry Clay. Obtained from the whaling schooner Golden Eagle. **1891** *Century Mag.* Jan. 402/1 The whaling fleets and the hide drogers ... half a century ago wintered on the coast [of Calif.].

c. Designating persons, places, and times associated with whaling.

1839 *Knickerb.* XIII. 392 You are ever upon the whaling-ground of the American seaman. **1849** COOPER *Sea Lions* i, As a whaling town, Sag Harbor is the third or fourth port in the country. *Ib.*, New York can, and has often fitted whalers for sea, having sought officers in the regular whaling ports. **1851** MELVILLE *Moby Dick* 42 The wife of a whaling captain had provided the chapel with a handsome pair of red worsted man-ropes. **1856** *Porter's Spirit of Times* 8 Nov. 163/1 The Crescent City Whaling Company succeeded in killing two more whales. **1874** C. M. SCAMMON *Marine Mammals* 247 At the point where the enormous carcass was stripped of its fat, arose the 'whaling station,' where try-pots were set in rude furnaces ... and capacious vats were made of planks, to receive the blubber. **1885** *Rep. Indian Affairs* 188 After the whaling and sealing season is over they go to the hop-fields. **1896** JEWETT *Pointed Firs* 101 That was the time for folks to travel, 'way back in the old whalin' days!

+Whaling, *n.²* A beating or flogging. *colloq.* — **1847** *N.Y. Tribune* Aug. (B.), For which 'arrogant' demeanor we are bound to give her a whaling. **1859** *La Crosse Daily Union* 13 Nov. 2/1 The father of the girl gave him an awful whaling. **1860** GREELEY *Overland Journey* 52 The oxen ... are often treated very cruelly, not merely in respect to the beating and whaling ..., but with regard to food and drink. **1918** FREEMAN *Edgewater People* 298 Got a whalin' ef I didn't.

Whaling, *a.* +Immense, huge. *colloq.* — **1854** M. J. HOLMES *Tempest & Sunshine* 203 Tell Aunt Judy to get us up a whalin dinner. **1873** BEADLE *Undevel. West* 433 Splendid prospect for fruit—peaches sure of whalin' crop.

Whaling vessel. A ship used in whaling. — **1767** CUTLER in *Life & Corr.* I. 19 Our whaling vessels sailed for the Western Islands. **1894** WILKINS in *Harper's Mag.* March 499/1 The son, Ichabod, had gone to sea in a whaling-vessel.

Whaling voyage. A voyage undertaken for the purpose of whaling. {1823-} — **1807** *Mass. H. S. Coll.* 2 Ser. III. 29 The whaling voyages to the coast of Brazil last about ten months. **1840** *Niles' Nat. Reg.* 22 Aug. 400/3 Whaling voyage. The ship Hector arrived at New Bedford ... with a cargo of twenty-seven hundred barrels of oil. **1893** *Harper's Mag.* Jan. 314/1 There seemed to be good reasons why women would not ... make the crew for a three years' whaling voyage.

＊Whang, *n.¹* A thong made of deerskin or a deer sinew. Also attrib. — **1824** DODDRIDGE *Notes* 114 [Moccasins] were sewed together and patched with deer skin thongs, or whangs as they were commonly called. **1846** MONETTE *Miss. Valley* II. 4 The sinews of the deer ... were known by the general term of 'whangs.' **1913** BARNES *Western Grazing Grounds* 118 Reins ... were twenty-four-strand and plaited from the finest grade of whang leather.

Whang, *n.²* Variant of *twang*. — **1875** 'MARK TWAIN' *Old Times* iv. 68 An agonized voice, with the backwoods 'whang' to it, would wail out.

Whang, *n.³* +Formerly, in Maine and some other parts of New England, a house-cleaning party; a gathering of neighbors to aid one of their number in cleaning house' (*Cent.*).

Whang, *v.* {1684-} *To whang up,* to tie up with whangs. — **1859** G. A. JACKSON *Diary* 521, [I] stopped at noon two hours and whanged up my moccasins; nearly barefooted.

+Whangdoodle. 1. A fabulous animal of ludicrous but undefined characteristics. **2.** *Attrib.* and *transf.* or allusive, sometimes in sense: Loud, noisy. — **(1)** **1861** *N.Y. Times* 30 Nov. 4/4 The lion roared, but the whang-doodle did *not* mourn. **1894** CLARK *On Cloud Mt.* 21 Be ye goin' to teeter aroun' there till Jedgment Day, like a Whangdoodle on one leg? **(2)** **1859** *Harper's Mag.* March 568/1, I send you an anecdote of a whang-doodle hard-shell preacher. **1890** *Boston Jrnl.* 23 July, The rougher element among the boys ... formed the 'Whang Doodle' Club for the purpose of settling him.

+Whangdoodler. One intent on doing mischief. — **1890** *Boston Jrnl.* 23 July, Whang Doodlers. A Band of Youths Organized to Assault a Judge.

＊Whap, *v.* (See WHOP *v.*)

‖Whapperknocker. (See quotation.) — **1781** PETERS *Hist. Conn.* (1829) 189 The whapperknocker is somewhat bigger than a weazel, and of a beautiful brown-red color.

＊Wharf.
The following quotations illustrate the occasional American use of the plural *wharf(e)s.* The plural in common American usage, *wharves,* is represented in the *O.E.D.* by a single British example of 1442.

1649 *New Haven Col. Rec.* I. 457 The comittee formerly chosen to consider aboute makeing of wharfes ... were desired to issue [a report]. **1673** *Boston Rec.* 83 Libertie of egresse & regresse of vessells & lyeinge att theire wharfes for loadinge & unloadinge. **1711** [see WHARFINGER]. **1841** COOPER *Deerslayer* i, There is still standing ... within musket-shot of the wharfs of Albany, a residence of a younger branch of the Van Rensselaers.

1. A structure built along a shore so that vessels can take on and unload passengers and cargo.

1644 *Conn. Rec.* I. 267 The house neare adioyning to ye wharfe. **1701** [see COMMON COUNCIL]. **1774** JEFFERSON *Writings* (1859) I. 133 Two wharves are to be opened again when his Majesty shall think proper. **1800** *Mass. H. S. Coll.* 1 Ser. VI. 229 There are wharves constructed of piers on each side of the draw. **1827** *Western Mo. Rev.* I. 148 A brigade of British soldiers was encamped on the common, less than a mile from the wharf. **1862** NORTON *Army Lett.* 66 Two or three wharves have been built. **1909** RICE *Mr. Opp* 132 [He] cleared the rapidly widening space between the boat and the shore, and dropped upon the wharf.

2. Attrib. and comb. with *builder, ground, hand,* etc.

1654 *Suffolk Deeds* II. 77 Thomas Joy and Joane his wife ... have sold ye dam wharfe head & streame whereon the said mills doe stand. **1659** *Charlestown Land Rec.* 72 One dwelling House with a yard, ... Bounded south by the wharfway. **1704** *Providence Rec.* XI. 89 Betweene the ... Towne Wharfe place & the north side of the said Thomas Olney his said lott. **1749** *N.H. Probate Rec.* III. 757 The wharf and wharf ground and all Privileges and Appurtenances belonging to the Same. **1776** *Jrnls. Cont. Congress* VI. 901 The committee appointed to contract with, and send an active wharf builder, and proper assistants to General Washington. **1842** *Knickerb.* XX. 339 [He] could find no wharf-owners whose characters were immaculate. **1868** *Ore. State Jrnl.* 8 June 1/3 The company has secured fifteen acres of land with ample wharf privileges. **1882** *Harper's Mag.* Sept. 588/1 Trucks were leaning, with crooked handles, just as they had been dropped by the wharf hands. **1907** *St. Nicholas* Sept. 1039/2 Wharf Pile Bored by a Teredo.

＊Wharfage. *collect.* Wharfs; wharf accommodations. {1807-} — **1705** *Dedham Rec.* V. 342 His Meadow at the new Bridge over Charls River is much demnefied ... by the whorfage and other Stopage in the River. **1887** *Courier-Journal* 4 May 8/2 The Steamer Hibernia Brings Suit Against the City For Defective Wharfage.

+Wharf boat. A boat used instead of a wharf at a place on a river where the height of the water is too variable to permit use of a wharf. Also attrib.

1847 FIELD *Drama in Pokerville* 53 White, Waters, and Johnson, were stuck together, fenced in at one end ... by deaf Miss Smith of the wharfboat family. **1863** F. MOORE *Rebellion Rec.* V. 1. 22 A rebel gunboat ... dropped alongside the wharf-boat and destroyed all the cotton and molasses to be found. **1875** 'MARK TWAIN' *Old Times* vi. 116 At every good-sized town from one end of the river to the other, there was a 'wharf-boat' to land at, instead of a wharf or a pier. **1884** *Harper's Mag.* Sept. 503/2 [The] landing consisted ... of an immense wharf-boat ... moored at the shore. **1911** SAUNDERS *Col. Todhunter* 39 A mighty cheer rose from the crowd assembled on the Nineveh wharf-boat.

＊Wharfinger. The keeper of a wharf. — **1687** *Boston Rec.* X. 80 James Barnes, whaffenger, became surety ... for Arthur Powell. **1711** *Ib.* VIII. 79 No Wharfinger ... Shall Suffer any Sort of Fire-wood to be carted ... off their Wharfes. **1794** *Mass. H. S. Coll.* 1 Ser. III. 248 A number of proprietors ... appoint a wharfinger to collect the dockage and wharfage, and superintend all matters relative to the wharf. **1890** LANGFORD *Vigilante Days* (1912) 338 Rousing a wharfinger, they were informed that all navigation was suspended until the waters should abate. **1905** LINCOLN *Partners* 107 The trunk itself was stored in the wharfinger's office until its owner should call for it some time in the future.

Wharfing ground, land. Ground used for a wharf and for the storage of goods landed at a wharf. — **1653** *Suffolk Deeds* III. 468 Wharfeing Land Lying before his house from ye Streete or high way to the Seaward to the Low water marke. **1847** LANMAN *Summer in Wilderness* 13, I saw this wharfing ground ... crowded with merchandise of every possible variety.

Wharfmaster. =WHARFINGER. {a1618} — **1837** PECK *New Guide* 325 The following, from the register of a wharf-master, will exhibit the commerce for 1835. **1873** [see PORT WARDEN].

+Wharf rat.
1. The house rat.

1823 COOPER *Pilot* II. 13 To burrow like a rabbit, or jump from hole to hole, like a wharf-rat! **1851** *S. Lit. Messenger* XVII. 145/1 He was aware of an enormous wharf rat, jumping from step to step. **1917** *Mammals of Amer.* 222 House Rat. Epimys norvegicus. ... Barn Rat, Wharf Rat. ... The common Rat to be seen about cities.

2. A vagrant or petty criminal who haunts wharves; any person frequently found on or near wharves. *colloq.*

1837 NEAL *Charcoal Sk.* (1838) 98 Gauley, Ben, if he isn't a wharf-rat! **1863** HAWTHORNE *Our Old Home* 193, I saw the seafaring people . . . lolling on long-boats, . . . as sailors and old wharf-rats are accustomed to do. **1880** *Harper's Mag.* Jan. 306/1 Sam Patch was a waif, a 'wharf rat.' **1903** HARTE *Writings* XIX. 12 The fateful wharf [was] still deserted except by an occasional 'wharf-rat,'—as the longshore vagrant or petty thief was called.

∗Whatcheer. [The English words of greeting used by Indians upon the arrival of Roger Williams at the site of Providence, R.I.] +In allusive use in Rhode Island, esp. in place names. — **1662** *Providence Rec.* III. 14 The East end of that parcel of ground called What Cheere. **1832** DURFEE *Whatcheer* 159 Their shouts embodied sought the joyous sky With open arms, and greeting of Whatcheere. **1859** BARTLETT 506 There is in Providence a 'Whatcheer Bank,' a 'Whatcheer Church,' 'Whatcheer hotels' [etc.].

What is it. +A curiosity. Orig. a term for a puzzling exhibit in a show. — *a*1882 *Phila. Times* (Th.S.), The two negro girls, who figure as 'what-is-its,' are paid $200 a week. **1892** *Congress. Rec.* App. 6 June 568/2 In this strange combination, this congressional 'what is it,' half horse, half alligator, . . . it is safe to predict that the miller will get all the corn, and the farmer all the chaff. **1920** SANDBURG *Smoke & Steel* 53 Hound dogs with bronze paws looking to a long horizon with a shivering silver angel, a creeping mystic what-is-it.

∗Whatnot. A stand or set of shelves for the display of knick-knacks or curiosities. {1808-} — **1848** BARTLETT 380. **1863** HAWTHORNE *Our Old Home* 104 Such delicate trifles . . . we put upon a drawing-room table . . . or a what-not. **1873** 'MARK TWAIN' & WARNER *Gilded Age* 197 An absence of any 'what-nots' in the corners with rows of cheerful shells, and Hindu gods, and Chinese idols, and nests of useless boxes of lacquered wood. **1885** *Century Mag.* XXX. 582/1 Pleasant writing-desks, what-nots, and book-stands, are finding their way into the newly built houses. **1902** [see SAW FISH].

+**What say,** *interrog.* or *interj.* What do (or did) you say or think? What? — **1825** NEAL *Bro. Jonathan* I. 357 'Was he hurt, uncle Harwood?' 'What-say?' **1836** GILMAN *Recoll.* (1838) 39 The common southern expression is eh? or what say? pronounced almost like one word. **1855** SIMMS *Forayers* 52 What 'say, boys—won't a back-and-rush of the nags do it? **1891** WILKINS *New Eng. Nun* 31 Well, what say!

∗Wheat.

∗1. A well-known grain manufactured into flour and other cereal preparations; the cultivated grasslike plant (*Triticum vulgare*) producing this.

See also FALL WHEAT, RED WHEAT, etc.

1607 in Smith *Works* (1910) p. xlii, They had gotten . . . wheate, beanes and mulberyes. **1678** ANDROS in R. N. Toppan *Randolph* II. 303 The Comodityes of the Country to ye westward, are wheate, . . . timber, lumber & horses. **1703** *N.H. Probate Rec.* I. 503, I give unto my wife . . . yearly . . . one bushel of Wheat. **1786** WASHINGTON *Diaries* III. 12, I began to hand weed the drilled Wheat from the Cape behind the Stables. **1805** PARKINSON *Tour* 665 The Colonel . . . did not even raise wheat for his own use. **1890** *Stock Grower & Farmer* 24 May 3/4 Wheat does well [in N. Mex.] and the quality is superior. **1897** *Farmer's Bul.* No. 895, 5 In the northern section of the Great Plains . . . the earliest sown wheat does not go beyond the rosette stage in the fall.

b. This grain used in colonial times as a medium of payment.

1647 *Suffolk Deeds* I. 69 Twenty fyve pounds, to be payd ten pounds in present in wheat. **1682** *Braintree Rec.* 22 To be payd . . . in current pay at . . . prises following wheat 4s.: Rye 3s.: barley mailte 3s. **1731** *Md. Hist. Mag.* XIX. 293 They may be Enabled to discharge such Taxes with Wheat Hemp or Flax at Stated prices.

+**2.** In colloq. phrases.

a. *Good as wheat,* very good; quite satisfactory. **b.** *Wheat and Indian,* (see quotation). **c.** *It is (all) wheat,* (see quot. 1865).

(a) 1851 *Polly Peablossom* 150 'Spose we make it up!' 'Good as wheat,' sez he. **1876** 'MARK TWAIN' *Tom Sawyer* xxviii. 215 Agreed, and good as wheat. **(b) 1859** BARTLETT 506 *Wheat and Indian,* a mixture of wheat flour and the meal of Indian corn. **(c) 1865** S. BOWLES *Across Continent* 129 Porter . . . mutters that he supposes 'it is all wheat,' this being Utah idiom for all right. **1882** WAITE *Adv. Far West* 260 Anything that is all right with Rockwell, is 'on the square.' It is 'wheat.'

3. *attrib.* and *comb.* **a.** With *bin, cake, clay,* etc.

1688 CLAYTON *Va.* in *Phil. Trans.* XVII. 987 They might preserve their weakest Cattle, by these Methods, and the help of the Wheat-patch. **1827** DRAKE & MANSFIELD *Cincinnati* 66 From the following establishments . . . no returns have been received: . . . 1 Wheat Fan Factory. **1846** EMMONS *Agric. N.Y.* I. 293 Above it a soil is not uncommon, which is called locally a wheat sand, in contradistinction to a wheat clay. **1847** HOWE *Hist. Coll. Ohio* 116 This town is at present a great wheat depot on the canal. **1848** *Rep. Comm. Patents 1847* 97 The wheat climate to commence with May and end with August. **1853** B. F. TAYLOR *Jan. & June* 158 Perhaps it was a great, square, two-story device, with the architecture of a wheat-bin. **1865** A. D. WHITNEY *Gayworthys* 218 There are wheat-cakes and maple syrup for your breakfast. **1867** CRAWFORD *Mosby* 186 [They] had nothing to drink . . . but new wheat whiskey and apple brandy just from the still. **1870** *Rep. Comm. Agric. 1869* 5 The wheat farm-

er, with a full garner, is not joyous over his market returns. **1902** HARBEN *A. Daniel* 114 He jest rolled me about in his hands like a piece o' wheat dough.

b. Designating trade in or speculative activities involving wheat.

1849 CHAMBERLAIN *Ind. Gazetteer* 281 [Lafayette] is now reckoned the fourth city in the State . . . and as to the wheat and flour business, the first. **1887** *Courier-Journal* 4 May 4/1 It is given out that all the contract wheat in Chicago is now cliqued, which implies the successive sacrifice of outside speculators every month until August by the process of wheat-banking. **1892** *Nation* 14 Sept. 214/2 Bitter controversy [is] going on at Chicago over the 'July wheat deal.' **1893** M. HOWE *Honor* 264 In his calculations he omitted . . . the number of children robbed of their birthrights, that the great wheat corner might be responsible for. **1908** 'O. HENRY' *Strictly Business* 252 After I had taken some $9,000,000 out of the soap business I made the rest in corn and wheat futures.

c. In the specific names of insects, birds, etc., esp. those that are injurious to wheat.

1883 *Amer. Naturalist* XVII. 1073 The wheat-bulb worm . . . generally affects the base of the terminal joint. **1891** *Cent.* 6888/3 *Wheat-cutworm,* the larva of an American noctuid moth, *Laphygma frugiperda.* **1888** TRUMBULL *Names of Birds* 21 While shooting in Benton Co., Oregon, in 1885, he found this species [the American widgeon] in enormous flocks on the wheat-fields, and . . . it was there called the wheat-duck. **1845** J. J. BROWN *Amer. Angler's Guide* (1850) 170 It takes the various names of weak-fish, wheat-fish, and squeteauge [sic]. . . . The second name has its origin from the fact of its having made its appearance always at harvest time. **1890** *Cent.* 3422/3 *L*[*eucania*] *albilinea* is the adult of the wheat-head army-worm. **1748** ELIOT *Field-Husb.* III. 53 We find the other Wheat is subject to be destroyed in the Fall by Wheat-lice. **1854** EMMONS *Agric. N.Y.* V. 263 (*index*), Wheatstalk insect, 179. *Ib.,* Wheatworms, 243.

d. In special combinations.

Wheat coffee, parched wheat used as coffee; *w. doings, w. fixings,* bread, cakes, dumplings, etc., made of wheaten flour; *w. king,* a man who has become wealthy through dealings in wheat; *w. seeder,* a seeder for sowing wheat; *w. yard,* an inclosure in which wheat is threshed.

1840 DANA *Two Years* 203 Finding wheat-coffee and dry bread rather poor living, we clubbed together, and I went up to the town. **1846** *Knickerb.* XXVIII. 314 John has got all my wheat-doin's away from me! **1853** *Harper's Mag.* July 279/2 A relative in Galveston, . . . knowing the rarity of wheat fixins in his visitor's location, presented him with a genuine wheat biscuit, to be given to each of his children on his return. **1888** *Troy Daily Times* 7 Feb. (F.), They heard of Cattle Kings and Wheat Kings, and Iron Kings. **1879** *Scribner's Mo.* Nov. 133/2 You will see plows, harrows, wheat-seeders, corn-planters. **1788** WASHINGTON *Diaries* III. 397 The other hands, except the Carter, who was drawing rails to the Wheat yard, were Hoeing Corn.

+**Wheat belt.** A region where wheat is the prevailing crop. — **1863** *Harper's Mag.* Oct. 718/1 The enterprising town of A—, in Northern Ohio, is the wheat-market for a considerable section of the wheat-belt of that State. **1882** *Uncle Rufus & Ma* 40 We had at last struck the chief object of our trip—the great wheat-belt of Dakota. **1903** HART *Actual Govt.* 116 Illinois is divided into a wheat belt, a corn belt, and the city of Chicago.

Wheat bird. A bird that feeds on wheat {1898-, *dial.*}, +as the horned lark. — **1747** CATESBY in *Phil. Trans.* XLIV. 444 They arrive [in Va.] annually at the time that Wheat . . . is at a certain Degree of Maturity. . . . They have attain'd the Name of Wheat-Birds. **1858** *Texas Almanac 1859* 67 The wheat-bird and rust also injured the crop to some extent in places. **1917** *Birds of Amer.* II. 212 Horned Lark. *Otocoris alpestris alpestris.* . . . [Also called] Prairie Bird; Road Trotter; Wheat Bird.

∗Wheat bread. Bread made of wheat flour as distinguished from corn bread. Also *attrib.* — **1774** HUTCHINSON *Diary & Lett.* I. 171 They live upon coarse bread made of rye and corn mixed, and by long use they learn to prefer this to flour or wheat bread. **1847** DRAKE *Pioneer Life Ky.* 22 Their hearts yearned for . . . neat and abounding wheat-bread trays. **1880** 'MARK TWAIN' *Tramp Abroad* 574, I have selected . . . hot wheat-bread, Southern style.

+**Wheat country.** A section or region in which considerable wheat is or may be raised. — **1776** *N.J. Archives* 2 Ser. I. 133 To be Sold, . . . a very good Grist-Mill, . . . in a very good wheat country. **1848** *Rep. Comm. Patents 1847* 101 The states of New York, Pennsylvania, Maryland, and Virginia, . . . together with the north-western and western states reaching down to Tennessee, are properly the wheat country of the union. **1890** *Stock Grower & Farmer* 29 March 5/3 The panhandle country . . . is a fine wheat country.

Wheat fly. Any one of various flies injurious to wheat. {1844-} — **1790** [see FLY WEEVIL]. **1846** EMMONS *Agric. N.Y.* I. 324 The wheat fly has committed more extensive ravages in this than in the western part of the State. **1858** *Mich. Agric. Soc. Trans.* IX. 245 The Wheat-Midge (*Cecidomyia tritici,*) or wheat-fly, as it is commonly called, is nearly allied to the Hessian fly.

Wheat grass. Any one of various grasses of the genus *Agropyron.* {1668-} — **1817-8** EATON *Botany* (1822) 494 *Triticum repens,* wheat-grass, couch-grass, quack-grass. **1871** *Harper's Mag.* July 187/2 Among the more important of these plants the wheat-grass stands pre-eminent. **1894** *Amer. Folk-Lore* VII. 103 *Agropyrum glaucum,* . . . wheat-grass, Central Neb.

+Wheat insect. =HESSIAN FLY. *Obs.* — **1792** *N.Y. State Soc. Arts* I. 57 The wheat insect, or Hessian fly, as it is commonly called, put an end to this kind of husbandry. **1838** *Mass. Agric. Survey 1st Rep.* 98 Late sowing of wheat . . . has carried the season of flowering beyond the time of the wheat insect.

Wheat market. The center for dealings in wheat; the demand for wheat; the supply of wheat available at a particular time. — **1863** [see WHEAT BELT]. **1868** *N.Y. Herald* 1 July 9/3 The wheat market was dull. **1898** *Kansas City Star* 21 Dec. 8/1 The wheat market in Chicago was inclined to drag at the outset. **1904** HARBEN *Georgians* 60, I once tried to get some men together to corner the wheat market.

Wheat midge. A small fly, *Thecodiplosis mossellana*, or the Hessian fly. {1843-} — **1850** *Rep. Comm. Patents 1849: Agric.* 110 Some years ago, before the weevil or wheat-midge made its appearance, these northern towns produced large crops of winter wheat. **1868** *Rep. Comm. Agric. 1867* 238 The wheat midge, fruit blight, potato rot, black knot and hop louse were unknown. **1877** *Vermont Bd. Agric. Rep.* IV. 107 Our farmers have sustained [great loss] from the wheat midge—or 'weevil,' as it is frequently but most improperly called.

+Wheat pit. The part of an exchange devoted to trading in wheat. — **1884** in *Harper's Mag.* LXXIII. 217 In the Wheat Pit at Chicago in a single year was buried most of the future prosperity of this republic than the sum of all the traffic which flows through that great city in a decade. **1902** [see CORN PIT].

+Wheat-separator. (See quot. 1883.) — **1859** *Rep. Comm. Patents 1858* I. 500 Improvement in Wheat Separators. **1883** KNIGHT *Suppl.* 946/1 *Wheat separator.* The separation of mustard, cockle, and grass seed from the wheat is effected by passing the mixed grains over inclined plates perforated with holes.

* Wheel, *n.*

I. *1. A circular frame or disk used as a support for the weight of a moving object, serving as a device for enabling it to move.

See also CART WHEEL 1, CAR WHEEL, DRIVING WHEEL 1, 2.

1643 *Plymouth Rec.* 17 Rates . . . for a paire of wheels £01 10.s. **1775** *N.H. Probate Rec.* I. 759, I Give and bequeth . . . half my plow's chain's Sled's carts wheels, and all other appurtinance's thereto belonging, . . . to my Son Samuel. **1850** GLISAN *Jrnl. Army Life* 32 The only damage done to the stage was the breaking of several spokes of one of the wheels. **1893** *Harper's Mag.* Feb. 353/1 He suggested that each one of these men should give some part of a carriage—one the wheels, one the body, one the furnishings, etc.

*2. Any one of various mechanical devices.

See also BULL WHEEL, DRIVING WHEEL 3, etc.

* a. = SPINNING WHEEL.

1644 *Essex Probate Rec.* I. 39 One wheele to spin with, 4s. **1783** in Parkman *Diary* 299 One large Wheel 2/8, two foot Wheels 6/–. **1834** CROCKETT *Narr. Life* 68 My wife had a good wheel and knowed exactly how to use it. **1869** WHITTIER *Poetical Works* (1894) 101/2 The wheel with flaxen tangle, as it dropped from her sick hand!

* b. A mill or water wheel.

See also WATER WHEEL.

1656 *Suffolk Deeds* II. 271, [I] doe graunt Bargaine & sell vnto him the said Thomas Savage one ffurnace Bellowes, wheeles, floudgates Damme pond [etc.]. **1837** *Knickerb.* IX. 253, I reached a little mill-dam, and floating idly into the floom of a cloth-dressing establishment, became entangled under the wheel. **1900** MUNN *Uncle Terry* 364 He held her up that she might see the wheel go around and laugh and crow at its splashing.

3. A wheel used as a gambling device; = LOTTERY WHEEL. {1698-}

See also WHEEL OF FORTUNE.

1750 *N.J. Archives* 1 Ser. XII. 640 The Ticketts will be putting into the wheels on Wednesday. **1813** *Columbian Centinel* 4 Sept. 1/2 The wheels have gained the handsome sum of 10290 Dollars! **1840** *Picayune* 1 Aug. 2/5 Every day the judges of our courts . . . [were] assisting in putting lottery tickets in the wheel! **1890** *Congress. Rec.* 16 Aug. 8713/2 In the event that two of the numbers on your ticket correspond to any two of the thirteen numbers drawn from the wheel, a prize of $2.45 is paid.

+4. A dollar; = CART WHEEL 2. *colloq.*

1807 TUFTS *Autobiog. of a Criminal* (1930) 293 Quid, a guinea. Wheel, a dollar. **1825** NEAL *Bro. Jonathan* I. 160, I shows him a double handful o' the royal goold; the ginooine yeller stuff—wheels. **1906** *Harper's Mag.* Feb. 34 He brought out a silver dollar, called a 'wheel' in the language of the camp.

+5. *cap.* Any one of various political organizations of farmers. More fully, *Agricultural Wheel.*

The model was furnished by a society formed in 1882 in Arkansas, later growing into a national organization ultimately consolidated with the Farmers' Alliance and Co-operative Union of America.

1882 in W. S. Morgan *Hist. of Wheel* 62 [Our organization] was named the Wheel. . . . Every editor who is opposed to our principles raises a pitiful little wail, O Wheel, keep out of politics. **1886** in *Appletons' Ann. Cycl. 1886* 42/1 We have formed the National Agricultural Wheel of the United States of America, for the purpose of organizing and directing the powers of the industrial masses, but not as a political party. **1891** MOR-GAN *Hist. of Wheel* 81 A committee was appointed to assist the colored Wheelers to organize a State Wheel [in Tenn.].

+6. A bicycle or tricycle; cycling as a sport or recreation. *colloq.* {1888-}

1882 *Wheelman* I. 13, 'I love my wheel,' he said, 'as the yachtsman loves his boat.' **1895** CHAMBLISS *Diary* 314 Let the vulgar 'new woman' mount her 'wheel' and make pilgrimages. **1914** ELIOT in James *C. W. Eliot* 249 This morning we had to walk instead of riding our wheels.

+b. A ride on a bicycle.

1880 *Scribner's Mo.* Feb. 483/1 A few possessors of the birotate chariot . . . enjoyed a 'wheel around the Hub.' **1893** *Outing* XXII. 140/2 It would have been a lovely wheel had we chosen to explore it on bicycles.

+7. *Ferris wheel,* a large vertical wheel slowly rotated by power on a fixed axle, carrying passengers in cars or seats suspended from the rim.

Invented by G. W. G. Ferris and first displayed at the World's Columbian Exposition (1893); subsequently a common feature of places for public recreation and amusement.

1893 *Scientific Amer.* 9 Sept. 169/1 The World's Columbian Exposition —A view from the Ferris wheel. **1909** *Cent. Suppl.* 1443/2 *Ferris wheel*, a device intended to amuse the people at an exhibition, fair, or summer resort.

8. *To grease one's wheels* {1857-}, to take a drink of liquor.

1844 *S. Lit. Messenger* X. 489/2 Hoisting him upon their shoulders, [they] bore him off to 'grease his wheels.'

+9. *To throw sand in the wheels,* (see SAND 3 b).

II. *attrib.* and *comb.* **10.** In senses 1 and 2 with *carriage, chair, chamber,* etc.

See also WHEELBARROW, WHEEL(ED) CULTIVATOR, etc.

1756 *Lett. to Washington* II. 7 It appears to us the most imprudent step, to leave the only road fit for wheel-carriages, in the power of the enemy. **1840** *Boston Transcript* 19 June 3/1 Fall back top, elliptic springs, wheel guards. **1845** KIRKLAND *Western Clearings* 141 His familiar edged him along on his wheel-chair. **1851** HALL *Manhattaner* 175 Audacious dashing under the very wheel-paddles, were scores of little boats filled with pedlary. **1858** C. FLINT *Milch Cows* 193 In weeding, a little wheel-hoe is invaluable. **1879** *Scribner's Mo.* July 345/1 A gloomy echoing and gurgling sounded from the dark wheel-chamber, where the water was rushing under the wheel. **1880** *Cimarron News & Press* 23 Dec. 3/1 Wheel and Lead harness, collars, Lines . . . at Porter's. **1883** *Harper's Mag.* Aug. 327/2 The wheel foundry, in which 200 car wheels are cast every day. **1888** *Ib.* March 566/1 Shovels, carts, and wheelbarrows are of a past age; the big wheel-scraper does the business. **1896** *Vt. Agric. Rep.* XV. 101 The tools best suited to orchard use are the plough, wheel or disc harrow, and cultivator.

b. Designating animals occupying the position in a team directly in front of the wheels of the vehicle.

See also WHEEL HORSE 1.

1869 *Overland Mo.* III. 127 The Texan driver . . . has his 'wheel-steers,' his 'swing-steers,' and his 'lead-steers.' **1888** CODY *Wild West* 548 The wheel-horses—or rather the wheel-mules—were good on the hold-back. **1903** ADAMS *Log of Cowboy* 6 One of the wheel oxen . . . could be ridden.

+11. In sense 6 with *assembler, road,* etc.

1882 *Wheelman* I. 115 This is a great country, and its railroads are better than its wheel-roads. **1885** *Century Mag.* Oct. 913/2 To think of Riverside Park simply as a relief from the thronged wheelways of Central Park is to form a most inadequate and incomplete conception of that work. **1897** *Outing* XXX. 277/2 One manufacturer [supplies] . . . dropforgings, . . . another tires, . . . and so on all through the arts of the wheel-assemblers. **1903** R. HALL *Pine Grove House* 259 Surely that was Winifred Stowe in her new wheel suit.

12. In special combinations.

Wheel base, a measure of length in a vehicle, taken from the points of contact of front and rear wheels with the track or surface; *w. boat,* (see quotation); *w. moth,* (see quotation); *w. stock* {1835, *dial.*}, the wooden materials for making wheels.

1886 *Franklin Inst. Jrnl.* March 201 The distance between the supporting wheels is four feet, which thus forms the rigid wheel-base of the truck. **1828** WEBSTER, *Wheel-boat,* a boat with wheels, to be used either on water or upon inclined planes or railways. **1854** EMMONS *Agric. N.Y.* V. 271 (*index*), *Trochilium,* or Wheelmoth. **1884** SARGENT *Rep. Forests* 515 Manufacturers of cooperage and wheel stock . . . suffer from the exhaustion and deterioration of material.

* Wheel, *v.* (See also WHEELING.)

1. *intr.* To ride on a bicycle; to move on roller skates. {1721-, to travel in a wheeled vehicle}

1884 *Century Mag.* Sept. 643/2 One young girl . . . was attended by a youth on a bicycle, who wheeled attentively by her side. **1893** *Harper's Mag.* Jan. 204/2 You'll put on roller-skates yourself, and go wheeling off first this, then that way. **1897** *N.Y. Journal* 5 Sept. 41/5 Wheel east on Eastern Parkway.

2. *To wheel into line* {1859-}, fig., to move into a position of agreement with the majority or with the conventional point of view; to fall into step.

1856 *Democratic Conv. Proc.* 67 Quickly all the other States changed their votes, wheeled into line. **1860** ABBOTT *South & North* 309 When the question comes to a popular vote, . . . these four States will wheel into line on the side of liberty. **1900** *Congress. Rec.* 20 Feb. 1968/2 Under the lash and spur of party policy and expediency they have wheeled into line and now stand ready.

* **Wheelbarrow.**

* **1.** An open container mounted on a wheel or wheels and furnished with handles by which it may be pushed.

1634 WOOD *New Eng. Prospect* 42 Shoales of Basse have driven up shoales of Macrill from one end of the sandie beech to the other, which the inhabitants have gathered up in wheelbarrowes. **1771** [see PAPER *n.* 1]. **1842** [see HOT CORN]. **1872** *Atlantic Mo.* April 395 Having wheelbarrows with one wheel and others with two wheels, he was bound to ascertain, with the certainty of arithmetic, which the was more advantageous.

attrib. **1825** NEAL *Bro. Jonathan* III. 313 A prodigious black woman appeared—rolling away, with a wheel-barrow load of clothes. **1843** 'CARLTON' *New Purchase* I. 5 The porter, . . . as some compensation for his blunder and its consequences, . . . refused the usual fee of the wheelbarrow service.

b. A wheelbarrow kiss (see under sense 2).

1847 LANMAN *Summer in Wilderness* 190 The forfeits are redeemed by making 'wheelbarrows,' 'measuring tape and cutting it off,' and by 'bowing to the wittiest, kneeling to the prettiest, and kissing the one we love best.'

2. In special combinations.

Wheelbarrow bet, a bet involving, as a penalty, the giving of a wheelbarrow ride to the winner; *w. boat,* (see quotation); *w.-fashion,* (see quotation); *w. government,* a government pushed or goaded into action by the people; *w. kiss,* a kiss delivered wheelbarrow-fashion.

1869 *Ore. State Jrnl.* 2 Jan. 1/4 Two Germans of Louisville, Ky., were arrested by the Police for attempting to fulfill the conditions of a wheelbarrow bet on the Presidential election. **1877** BARTLETT 748 *Wheelbarrow-Boat,* a steamboat with a stern-wheel, used on some of the Western rivers, as well as in Canada and Oregon. **1828** *Yankee* April 106/2 They were . . . ordered to kiss each other 'wheelbarrow fashion.' You would then see a . . . young man, and a . . . girl meet on the floor; close their right and left hands, on both sides; and with a whirl . . . turn through their arms, bring the back part of their shoulders in contact—each with the head resting upon the other's right shoulder, their mouths meeting. **1885** CRAFTS *Sabbath for Man* 288 The political code now in vogue . . . leads to a wheelbarrow government, carried on . . . by the people pushing them [the legislators] from behind. **1828** *Yankee* Sept. 288/1 As for their delightful good old fashioned wheel-barrow kisses, I think, they are all of a piece with red-ear kisses, trundle-beds and bundling.

Wheelbarrow man. {1712} +A convict engaged in labor on the roads. *Obs.* — **1788** *Mass. Spy* 26 Nov. 2/1 It is said the perpetrators were of that class called wheelbarrow men. **1790** *Ann. 2d Congress* 1462 Those [executions] which have taken place have been generally of emigrant convicts, or fugitive wheel-barrow men.

+ **Wheel bug.** A large insect (*Arilus cristatus*) with a wheellike crest. — [**1815** KIRBY & SPENCE *Introd. Entomology* I. 110 *Reduvius serratus,* F., commonly known in the West Indies by the name of the *wheel-bug.*] **1869** *Rep. Comm. Agric.* 1868 316 The *Reduvius,* or wheel-bug, is found in gardens, feeding voraciously upon caterpillars. **1904** KELLOGG *Amer. Insects* 204 Another fairly well-known member of this family is the wheel-bug, *Prionidus cristatus,* especially common in the South.

+ **Wheel(ed) cultivator.** A cultivator provided with a wheel or wheels. — **1850** *Rep. Comm. Patents 1849* 156, I do not claim in this application the invention of a wheeled cultivator. **1868** *Mich. Agric. Rep.* VII. 345 Fords & Howe, Oneonta, N.Y., [exhibited] 1 two-horse wheel cultivator, or horse-hoe. **1891** *Cent.* 6891/1.

* **Wheeler.**

* **1.** A wheelwright or wheel-maker.

1654 JOHNSON *Wonder-w. Prov.* 209 Wheelers, Glovers, Fellmungers, and Furriers, are orderly turn'd to their trades.

2. In a team, an animal harnessed next to the wheel of the vehicle; a wheel horse. {1813–}

See also NIGH WHEELER, OFF WHEELER.

1852 BRISTED *Upper Ten Th.* 223 In the next quarter the wheeler instead of the leader was alongside the other team. **1887** TOURGEE *Button's Inn* 91 The team consisted of two iron-gray wheelers . . . and a span of bay leaders. **1913** LONDON *Valley of Moon* 351, I threw the back into the wheelers an' slammed on the brake an' stopped on the very precise spot.

+ **3.** A member, or potential member, or a candidate on the ticket of the Agricultural Wheel: (see WHEEL *n.* 5).

1890 *Congress. Rec.* 30 June 6802/2 [He] never left the Democratic party until he began his race for Congress, and even then he claimed to be a Democratic 'Wheeler.' **1891** [see WHEEL *n.* 5].

+ **Wheelerite.** (See quotation.) — **1874** *Amer. Jrnl. Science* 3 Ser. VII. 571 Wheelerite, a new Fossil Resin. . . . I have taken the liberty of naming this new mineral after Lieutenant George M. Wheeler, Corps of Engineers, U.S. Army.

+ **Wheeler pan.** *Metallurgy.* A container invented by Zenas Wheeler for the grinding and amalgamating of ores. — **1869** BROWNE *Adv. Apache Country* 396 The Real del Monte contains . . . thirty-six Wheeler pans, and other machinery in proportion.

Wheel horse.

1. In a team, a horse attached immediately in front of the wheels. {1708–}

1760 WASHINGTON *Diaries* I. 136 With much difficulty made my Chariot wheel horses plow. **1848** *Knickerb.* XVIII. 499 To this [stagecoach] were yoked two tolerably good wheel-horses. **1897** *Outing* XXX. 107/2, I alone had pointed the leader and held up the near wheel-horse.

+ **2.** *transf.* A strong person, esp. one carrying a heavy burden or responsibility; someone that can be expected to furnish loyal support, esp. to a political organization.

1845 HOOPER *Taking Census* 179, I'm jist a hunderd and forty seving pound *neat* weight, and I'm a wheel-horse! **1862** Moore *Rebellion Rec.* V. II. 551 Acting Major-Gen. Foster, the wheel-horse of the Burnside expedition, is chief officer in command. **1867** *Wkly. New Mexican* 24 Aug. 2/2 Carleton . . . worked like a beaver for Perea, and so did Perfecto Armijo, the Perea wheel horse in that county then. **1904** *N.Y. Times* 24 June 5 If any other of the old wheel horses of the party had been selected for Chairman.

attrib. **1906** LYNDE *Quickening* 213 His first care was to assure the 'wheel-horse' member of the municipal purchasing board that he was ready to talk business.

Wheelhouse. {1813–} +A structure enclosing the steering wheel of a vessel; a pilot house: (see also quot. 1860). — **1835** [see PILOT *n.* 1]. **1850** LEWIS *La. Swamp Doctor* 106, I descended from the upper deck, being partly hidden by the wheel-house. **1860** WORCESTER 1662/2 *Wheel-House,* a structure or box over a wheel in a steam-vessel; paddle-box. **1877** PHELPS *Story of Avis* 398 The cross couple on the after-deck, whose little boy he was now leading away to the wheel-house. **1922** PARRISH *Case & Girl* 216 He noted . . . a bridge forward of the wheel-house, together with a decidedly commodious cabin aft.

* **Wheeling. 1.** Transportation or travel by means of a wheeled vehicle. {1805} **2.** Travel by bicycle; bicycling as a recreation or sport. {1882} Also attrib. — **(1) 1846** FARNHAM *Prairie Land* 361 Thar's a right smart of snow, and it's about half melted now. That makes wheelin heavy. **1877** BARTLETT 748 At the North-west, wheeling is synonymous with *hauling.* **1883** *Harper's Mag.* Oct. 727/2 Wheeling is now everywhere easy. **(2) 1896** *Voice* 24 Sept. 7 [It is] eminently 'rational' to go a-wheeling in your shoes and stockings unhindered and unhampered by the one-time indispensable leg-covering. **1897** *Boston Jrnl.* 22 Jan. 3/4 (*caption*), Wheeling Whispers. Several of the bicycle stores are being newly painted. **1897** *Outing* July 346/1 Good wheeling was enjoyed back to Auburndale.

Wheel iron. An iron appliance attached to an axletree of a carriage or wagon to resist the action of the pull of the horses. *Obs.* {1829–} Also attrib. — **1788** *Ky. Gazette* 31 May 2/2 Turners tools & wheel-irons. **1815** *Niles' Reg.* VIII. 141/2 [In Pittsburgh there is] 1 wheel iron manufactory. **1845** *Xenia Torch-Light* 4 Dec. 1/1, I will sell at public sale . . . Saddle Irons, Buckles, Wheel Irons.

Wheelman. {1884}

+ **1.** A steersman or helmsman.

1865 *Ore. State Jrnl.* 12 Aug. 2/5 The wheelman says that large fragments of the bottom and a part of the rudder were afterwards seen alongside the wreck.

2. A male cyclist; a man who rides a bicycle or tricycle, esp. for pleasure or sport. {1884}

1880 *Century Mag.* Feb. 496/1 In the parlors the costumes of the wheelmen seemed not so much out of place. **1891** *Outing* May 137 The meet of the Keystone wheelmen in 1890. **1902** WILSON *Spenders* 467 When he came to a 'wheelman's rest,' he ate many sandwiches and drank much milk. **1910** FRANCK *Vagabond Journey* 16 The thoroughfare was thronged with vehicles, riders, and, above all, with wheelmen.

Wheel of fortune. {1760-2–} A wheel used as a device for the determining of chance {1763–}; a gambling game played with such a wheel (Cf. WHEEL *n.* 3.) — **1822** [see FARO TABLE]. **1865** PIKE *Scout & Ranger* (1932) 141 They might have hesitated before demanding a resort to the wheel of fortune. **1888** GRIGSBY *Smoked Yank* (1891) 106 Faro, poker, wheel of fortune, tricks and games of every variety were played and carried on openly and publicly. **1905** BELASCO *Girl of Golden West* (1925) I. 58 The proprietor of a wheel-of-fortune, which is set up in the dance-hall.

Wheel pit. {1828–, *dial.*} A hole or deep receptacle affording space for the turning of a wheel. — **1844** A. LAWRENCE *Diary & Corr.* 188, I can see the men, the machines, the wheel-pit, and the speed-gauge. **1860** HOLLAND *Miss Gilbert* 67 The room was full of the noise of heavy gearing, and the constant plash of water in the near wheel-pit.

+ **Wheelsman.** The pilot of a ship; =WHEELMAN 1. — **1885** *Harper's Mag.* March 643/1 She is everybody's pet, from the rather dandy wheelsman . . . down to the grizzled, grimy deck hands. **1887** *Courier-Journal* 4 May 4/6 A young farmer, seeing the peril of the wheelsman, plunged into the waves.

* **Wheelwright.** One whose business is the construction and repair of wheels and wheeled vehicles. Hence *wheelwrighting.*

1638 *Dedham Rec.* 47 Timothy Dwite . . . [is] to haue halfe an acre for situacion of his house next ye hether end of yt grownd w[hi]ch the wheel-write had. **1703** *N.C. Col. Rec.* I. 577 He Ingaging & promising before the

Courte to doe his endeavour to learne the boy the trade of a wheel-wright. **1770** [see CARIOLE 1]. **1835** JACKSON in *Pres. Mess. & P.* III. 172 Wheelwrights, millwrights, etc., are supported among them. **1867** CRAWFORD *Mosby* 119 The buildings of the town consist of one blacksmith-shop with residence attached thereto, and a wheel-wright's shop. **1883** *Rep. Indian Affairs* 253 Carpentry, harness-making, wheelwrighting.

* **Whelk.** Also **whilk.** Any one of various marine snails. (See also WILK.) — **1702** MATHER *Magnalia* (1852) I. 351 Whilks and crabs were their best food. **1868** *Amer. Naturalist* II. 247 Our attention is attracted by the unusual movements of a large shell, commonly called the whelk. **1884** *Nat. Museum Bul.* No. 27, 246 *Purpura lapillus*, . . . Drill or Whélk. Long Island Sound to Arctic Ocean. **1911** *Rep. Fisheries* 1908 313/2 The sea snail (*Littorina*) and whelk (*Fulga*) . . . are used for bait and sometimes for food on the north Atlantic coast.

* **Whelp.** +A native or inhabitant of Tennessee. — **1872** *Harper's Mag.* Jan. 318/1 Below will be found a careful compilation of the various nicknames given to the States and people of this republic . . . Tennessee, Whelps.

* **Where,** adv. *Where* . . . *at*, (see AT *prep.* 5.)

* **Wherry.** A light boat; a shallop or a light passenger boat for short trips. Also attrib. — **1624** SMITH *Gen. Hist. Va.* 6, I intended with two Wherries and fortie persons . . . to try this [river] presently. **1705** *Boston News-Letter* 2 April 2/1, 3 persons were drowned by the oversetting of a Wherry coming from Burlington hither. **1835** [see PUNT[1]]. **1876** TRIPP *Student-Life* 157 Scores of friendly students thronge the boat-houses and the wherry-raft.

+ **Whetsaw.** [See quot. 1778.] (See quotations.) — **1778** CARVER *Travels* 475 The Whetsaw . . . makes a noise like the filing of a saw; from which it receives its name. **1815** *Mass. H. S. Coll.* 2 Ser. IV. 273 The birds noticed thereabout are, the crow, . . . whetsaw (a bird of the cuckoo kind, always heard, but seldom seen in the groves,) grous.

* **Whetstone.** A stone suitable for sharpening edge tools; +*Arkansas whetstone,* Arkansas stone (q.v. under ARKANSAS *n.* and *a.* 7).

1643 WILLIAMS *Key* (1860) 177 *Cauómpsk,* a Whetstone. **1751** J. BARTRAM *Observations* 30 A steep hill side, full of excellent flat whet-stones of all sizes. **1843** [see RUBSTONE]. **1878** *Harper's Mag.* Jan. 204 In commerce, under the name of the Arkansas whetstone or Ouachita oil-stone, [novaculite rock] has almost eclipsed its Turkish rival. **1923** J. H. COOK *On Old Frontier* 150 After using my whetstone a few moments I picked up one of the forelegs of the big bull.

Whew, v. {1684-} *New Eng.* +*intr.* To bustle. — **1873** A. D. WHITNEY *Other Girls* 112 Nothing ever got ahead of her; she whewed round; when she was 'whewing' she neither wanted Bell to hinder nor help. **1878** COOKE *Happy Dodd* 151 Don't whew into everything as though there wan't no more days in the week. **1894** *Outing* XXIX. 103/1 She just whewed around after supper an' got her glasses an' silver washed an' her tables set.

Whey cure. A treatment consisting of the administration of whey. — **1792** *Md. Hist. Mag.* XII. 311 The subscriber . . . performs The Botanical (Herb) Whey Cures, Prepared by him.

* **Which,** pron. +(See quotations.) *colloq.* — **1835** A. PARKER *Trip to Texas* 88, Ask a question, and if they do not understand you, they reply '*which*?' **1859** BARTLETT 507 *Which?* An absurd word used by some persons instead of *What?* in asking for a repetition of what has been said.

Which way. (See EVERY *a.*)

+ **Whiffet.**[1] [Var. of *whippet.*]

1. A small dog. Also *whiffet dog.*

1801 *Olio* (Phila.) 41 (Th.), Who heeds the Whiffit's bark, when tempests howl? **1827** *Hallowell* (Me.) *Gaz.* 20 June 3/4 They report them to have . . . 1129 lap dogs, turnspits, whiffets and unknown. **1848** *Ladies' Repository* VIII. 315 The best protection to a house, with a family in it, that can be named—that is, a little, barking, noisy, cowardly, whiffet dog. **1879** BURROUGHS *Locusts & Wild Honey* 30 The king-bird will worry the hawk as a whiffet dog will worry a bear.

2. An insignificant man; a whippersnapper. *colloq.*

1839 *Congress. Globe* App. 17 Jan. 105/3 There was not a Whig whiffet in the country but could ask [etc.]. **1876** WHITMAN *Spec. Days* 89 How it [a tree] rebukes . . . this gusty-temper'd little whiffet, man, that runs indoors at a mite of rain or snow. **1883** L. A. LAMBERT *Notes on Ingersoll* 200 We hold ourselves responsible to him, and to all the glib little whiffets of his shallow school.

+ **Whiffet.**[2] (See quot. 1864.) — **1864** WEBSTER 1508/2 *Whiffet,* . . . a little whiff or puff; a whiff. **1910** J. HART *Vigilante Girl* 14 At last, of the heavy fog-bank there remained nothing but whiffets and rings and wreaths of mist.

+ **Whiffletree.** =WHIPPLETREE. — *a*1841 HAWES *Sporting Scenes* II. 69 Our whiffle-tree became detached from the vehicle, and fell upon the horse's heels. **1863** A. D. WHITNEY *F. Gartney* xviii, She managed . . . to slip out the fastening of the trace, on one side, where it held to the whiffletree. **1884** *Lisbon* (Dak.) *Star* 18 July, While they were driving along one of the whiffletrees suddenly broke. **1920** SANDBURG *Smoke & Steel* 255 The rings in the whiffletree count their secrets.

+ **Whiffling.** Vacillation, evasion. *colloq.* — **1841** COOPER *Deerslayer* i, I would carry the gal off to the Mohawk by force, make her marry me in spite of her whiffling. **1906** *Springfield W. Repub.* 18 Oct. 3 This outcome of a week of doubt and whiffling will be viewed with mixed emotions.

Whig. {1645-}

+**1.** A colonist who opposed the measures of the royal governors in the American colonies, esp. one of the revolting colonists during the Revolutionary War. Now hist.

1711 *N.C. Col. Rec.* I. 768 Sr Nathaniel Johnson being put out by the whigs [etc.]. **1768** (*title*), A Collection of Tracts from the late News Papers, &c. Containing particularly The American Whig, A Whip for the American Whig [etc.]. **1772** A. G. WINSLOW *Diary* 59 Coln brought in the talk of Whigs & Tories & taught me the difference between them. **1774** J. ADAMS *Familiar Lett.* 7 Dr. Gardiner . . . brings us news of a battle at the town meeting, between Whigs and Tories. **1884** A. JOHNSTON *Hist. Amer. Politics* 6 As soon as independence was announced, in 1776, to be the final object of the contest, the names Whig and Tory lost, in America, whatever of British significance they had ever possessed.

+**2.** One politically opposed to Andrew Jackson; a member of the Whig party. Now hist.

1834 *Niles' Reg.* 12 April 101/2 In New York and Connecticut the term 'whigs' is now used by the opponents of the administration when speaking of themselves. **1850** *Harper's Mag.* Dec. 123/1 Twenty-one members of Congress were elected, of whom 8 were Whigs, and 13 Democrats. **1884** BLAINE *20 Years of Congress* I. 104 For the first few weeks of the canvass the Whigs had strong hope of success. **1922** McCORMAC *Biog. Polk* 141 As its appearance in the *Union* was always accompanied by news of Democratic victory, the Whigs expressed their contempt by calling it [a spread-eagle woodcut] 'Harris's buzzard.'

3. attrib. and comb. **a.** In sense 1 with *boy, committee, inhabitant,* etc.

1776 TRUMBULL *M'Fingal* 70, I see afar the sack of cities, The gallows strung with Whig-committees. **1811** MEASE *Philadelphia* 201 A party of the society of Friends, who . . . [thought] it lawful to take up arms in defence of American liberty, . . . separated from the main body of Friends. . . . This society is styled 'Whig, or Free Quakers.' **1835** SIMMS *Partisan* (1854) 381 In one night ten, twenty, thirty, or more [tories], would collect together, and . . . rush with fire and sword upon their whig neighbors. **1844** *Lexington Observer* 2 Oct. 1/4 May the same success attend you now, that rewarded the . . . army of whig patriots. **1854** SIMMS *Southward Ho!* 299 The British conquerors . . . regarded [with perfect recklessness] . . . the interests, the rights, or the affections of the whig inhabitants of South Carolina. **1857** *Ladies' Repository* XVII. 83/1 [The Tories] went in an opposite direction to that of my Whig boy. **1922** *Friends Hist. Soc. Jrnl.* XIX. 12 While in New York he [Samuel Shoemaker] exerted himself for the relief of the Whig prisoners.

b. In sense 2 with *authority, candidate, convention,* etc.

1834 C. A. DAVIS *Lett. J. Downing* 316 Masonry and Anti-Masonry was pretty much all one, and goin to vote the entire Whig Ticket all over the country. **1838** *N.Y. Advertiser & Exp.* 11 April 3/1 Let the only *Deposite* be made at the *Ballot Box,* and the only paper in circulation be *Whig votes.* **1838** Whig authorities [see HEARSE 2]. **1840** *Niles' Nat. Reg.* 2 May 136/1 The young men's national whig convention . . . is to meet on Monday. **1844** *Lexington Observer* 5 Oct. 3/4 Great Whig Mass Meeting at Cumberland Gap. **1845** *Xenia Torch-Light* 31 July 2/4 The choice of a Whig candidate for this district was to be decided in Convention. **1848** *Niles' Nat. Reg.* LXXIV. 38/2 The Whig platform . . . is the broad platform of the Constitution. **1855** in Hambleton *H. A. Wise* 152 The majority of Whig Know-Nothings who affected the Winchester nominations were too keen for the spoils.

Whiggery. {1682-} +The principles or doctrines of the American Whig party. — **1835** C. P. BRADLEY *I. Hill* 163 Wherever there still lives a man, who was a prominent member of the old federal party, that man is an adherent of modern Whiggery. **1848** *N.Y. Herald* June 21 (B.), There is a chance . . . of General Taylor being vigorously opposed by some men of undoubted Whiggery. **1876** *N. Amer. Rev.* CXXIII. 213 Whiggery meant sound views on the tariff, good, quiet management of the elections, a deference for Southern opinion, . . . and a worship of Mr. Webster.

Whig party. {1683-} +The political party made up originally of those opposed to the principles and practices of Andrew Jackson and his followers. Now hist. — **1834** HONE *Diary* I. 101 This was the day of the great fete at Castle Garden to celebrate the triumph gained by the Whig Party in the late charter election in this city. **1856** *Democratic Conv. Proc.* 69 In many a tough contest, the old Whig party . . . have encountered the Democracy.

Whilk. (See WHELK.)

* **Whip,** *n.*

***1.** A slender, flexible twig or sprout; a growth or collection of these. {1585}

1853 B. F. TAYLOR *Jan. & June* 16 Some body planted a cherry stone, four or five years ago, and forgot it; but the 'whip' of a tree went right on. **1881** INGERSOLL *Oyster Industry* 250 *Whips,* slender branches used to mark the bounds of oyster-beds. (Connecticut.) **1908** WHITE *Riverman* 135 What, in the early year, had been merely a whip of brush, now had become a screen.

2. In specific names.

1891 *Cent.* 6902/3 *Whip-grass,* an American species of nut-grass, *Scleria triglomerata.* **1817-8** EATON *Botany* (1822) 348 *Malva virgata,* whip-stalk mallows. **1842** *Nat. Hist. N.Y., Zoology* IV. 373 The Whip Sting-ray. *Pastinaca hastata.* . . . When captured, this individual whipped its tail about with great activity in all directions. **1889** *Cent.* 2596/1 *Grampus,* ... the whip-tailed scorpion, *Thelyphonus giganteus.* ... (Florida, U.S.)

* **Whip,** *v.*

* **1.** *tr.* To chastise (a person) with or as with a whip, as a prescribed punishment for an offense.

1630 *Mass. Bay Rec.* I. 82 Bartholmewe Hill is adiudged to be whipt for stealeing a loafe of breade from John Hoskins. **1650** *Plymouth Laws* 92 Whosoever shall prophane the Lords day ... shall ... be whipte. **1705** *Boston News-Letter* 8 Oct. 2/2 A certain person ... brought some Tarr to be Sold, some whereof was mingl'd with dirt; for which he was Sentenced to be severely Whipt. **1826** FLINT *Recoll.* 348 He has been arrested and whipped. **1890** LANGFORD *Vigilante Days* (1912) 288 A man ... had been whipped for larceny at Nevada.

* **2.** To beat, vanquish, defeat. ('Now *U.S. colloq.' O.E.D.*)

1805 PARKINSON *Tour* 265 They have once *whipped* the British; and they will do it again (the term *whipping* arises from their whipping the negroes). **1898** PAGE *Red Rock* 230 You're always talkin' about havin' whipped us.

b. To surpass.

1835 HOFFMAN *Winter in West* II. 119 Old Kaintuck ... whips all 'Out-West' in prettiness.

+**3.** To reduce or bring (moss or hemp) into a desired condition by, or as by, threshing or beating with a whip.

1841 W. KENNEDY *Texas* I. 101 Let it [Spanish moss] remain in cold water to rot, like flax or hemp, after which it is dried, whipped, and put into the tick. **1850** *Rep. Comm. Patents 1849: Agric.* 331 It is an easy matter for one hand to clean 500 to 600 pounds [of hemp] per day, on the hand-brake; either by scutching or by whipping and shaking.

+**4.** To thresh *out* (rice) by beating.

1903 PRINGLE *Rice Planter* 44 The hands now are whipping out the seed rice, which is a tedious business.

+**5.** In colloquial phrases. **a.** *To whip the devil round a stump,* (see DEVIL *n.* 5).

+**b.** *To whip one's weight in wild cats,* or variants: To fight with uncommon ferocity and effectiveness.

1829 *Mass. Spy* 11 Feb. (Th.), Every man who could 'whip his weight in wildcats' burned with desire of reaping renown by an encounter with Francisco. **1846** *Spirit of Times* (N.Y.) 16 May 133/2 Courage enough to whip an acre of wild cats. **1852** WATSON *Nights in Block-House* 20 Not as long as I can whip my weight in catamounts or bar, I'll never gin in.

* **Whipper.** +A device for whipping or beating the dirt, trash, etc., from seed cotton. *Obs.* Also *attrib.* — **1861** *Fla. Plantation Rec.* 61 Your overseers are using the whippers. **1863** E. W. Pearson *Lett. Port Royal* 234 It was a busy scene—a whipper on each arbor with a child atop to fill the machine, which is used to lash the dirt out of the cotton before ginning. **1882** *Century Mag.* Jan. 477/1 A comparatively new machine ... consists of a suction fan, a 'whipper-wheel,' or light paddle, for stirring up the cotton.

* **Whipping.** A beating with a whip. Also *attrib.*

1638 *Mass. H. S. Coll.* 4 Ser. VI. 245 He hath suffred for his much vncleanenes 2 severall whippings. **1699** E. WARD *Trip to New-Eng.* 13 Whipping is a Punishment so Practicable in this Country, upon every slight Offence, ... that all the Inhabitants of that Place [New Haven], above the Age of Fourteen, had been Whip'd for some Misdemeanour or other (except two) the Minister and the Justice. **1769** *New-London Gazette* 2 June 1/3 There was very severe whippings the day before yesterday [in Boston]. *a*1853 in Stowe *Key* 35/1 He may have a private whipping-board on his own premises, and brutalise himself there. **1862** 'E. KIRKE' *Among Pines* 151 This was the whipping-rack, and hanging to it were several stout whips with short hickory handles, and long triple lashes.

+**Whipping house.** A house to which slaves were sent to be punished. *Obs.* — **1852** STOWE *Uncle Tom* xxix, It was the universal custom to send women and young girls to whipping houses. **1865** *Atlantic Mo.* April 510/2 Without thought of nine o'clock, pass, patrol, or whipping-house, [he was] rushing on the road ... to Tallahassee.

Whipping post. A post set up in a public place to which offenders were tied to be whipped. {1600-} — **1636** *Plymouth Laws* 41 In every Constablerick there [shall] be ... a whipping post. **1705** *Va. State P.* I. 94 The sd. negro ... [is] to receive thirty-one lashes ... att the Comon Whiping post. **1885** *Rep. Indian Affairs* 204 Every time he [an Indian] whipped ... his wife, he certainly would have to hug and take a sweat at the whipping-post.

Whippletree. The doubletree of a wagon; a singletree. {1733-} Also *attrib.* — **1819** *Plough Boy* I. 62 The tongue and whipple-tree of a waggon was shivered to pieces. **1854** *Mich. Agric. Soc. Trans. 1853* V. 77, 1 whippletree hook.

+**Whippoorwill.** [Echoic.] A nocturnal bird (*Antrostomus vociferus*) noted for its insistent call.

1709 LAWSON *Carolina* 146 Whippoo-Will, so nam'd, because it makes those Words exactly. **1789** MORSE *Amer. Geog.* 60 The whip-poor-will is remarkable for the plaintive melody of its notes. **1805** LEWIS in *L. & Clark Exped.* II. (1904) 200 We have not the whip-poor-will either. **1884** 'MARK TWAIN' *H. Finn* i, I heard an owl, away off, who-whooing about somebody that was dead, and a whippowill and a dog crying about somebody that was going to die. **1920** HOWELLS *Vacation of Kelwyns* 42 Kel-

wyn sat with his family on the door-step, and listened to ... the whippoorwills that whirred through the cool, damp air.

+**Whippoorwill('s) shoe. a.** =PITCHER PLANT. **b.** Any one of various American plants of the genus *Cypripedium.* — **1832** [see FORE-FATHERS'-PITCHER]. **1869** FULLER *Flower Gatherers* 182 Didn't I just tell you it is a 'Whippoor-Will's Shoe?' **1894** *Amer. Folk-Lore* VII. 100 *Cypripedium,* sp., whip-poor-will shoe, (Indians) N.Y.

* **Whipsaw,** *n.* A frame saw having a narrow blade. — **1633** [see FRAME SAW]. **1718** HEMPSTEAD *Diary* 75 Ye goods were ... 3 whip saws ... & two Cases of bottles. **1871** *Harper's Mag.* Dec. 54/1 [He was] not yet able to use the whip-saw, broad-axe and frow. **1903** N. H. BANKS *Round Anvil Rock* 19 The rich dark wood of its walls and floor—all rudely smoothed with the broadaxe and the whip-saw.

+**Whipsaw,** *v. tr.* To cut or get out (timber, plank, etc.) with a whipsaw; also *fig.,* to get the better of. — **1867** *Harper's Mag.* Oct. 572/2 Built on the lake in the winter of 1866, all her timbers were whip-sawed. **1884** *Hartford* (Conn.) *Post* Sept., Had Braddock been half as prudent as he was brave, he could ... have whipsawed the French and Indians in that campaign. **1891** *Century Mag.* Jan. 286 The great redwoods that were hewn in the Sonoma forests were 'whip-sawed' by hand for the plank required. **1900** ADE *More Fables* 174 The Astute Reader knows what happens in a Family when Mother and the Only Child put their Heads together to whipsaw the Producer. *a*1918 G. STUART *On Frontier* I. 203 We have succeeded in getting one thousand feet of lumber, at ten cents per foot, whipsawed for sluice boxes.

+**Whipsawing. a.** Using a whipsaw to procure lumber. **b.** *fig.* (See quots. 1885 and 1903.) — (a) **1847** *Santa Fe Repub.* 23 Oct. 2/2 The great cost of procuring lumber by whip-sawing. (b) **1885** *Mag. Amer. Hist.* May 496/1 *Whip-sawing,* the acceptance of fees or bribes from two opposing persons or parties. **1903** *N.Y. Sun* 8 Nov. 10 These speculators have subjected themselves to the process known in Wall Street as whip-sawing; that is, they have bought when the market was strong and sold when the market was weak, and found each time that they bought at the top and sold at the bottom.

+**Whipsawyer.** One who uses a whipsaw. — **1881** *Lumber World* March, Some of the first saw mills built in England ... were destroyed ... on the ground that it would ruin the occupation of the whip sawyers.

Whip snake. Any one of various slender snakes somewhat resembling a whip {1774-}, +esp. the coachwhip snake. — **1835** LATROBE *Rambler in N.A.* II. 46 The whip-snake ... would take hold of a tuft of grass with its mouth as you approached, and scutch you with its tail, till you removed yourself out of the way! **1883** *Harper's Mag.* Oct. 708/1 My venomous acquaintances [included] ... black-snake, whip-snake, coral-snake [etc.]. **1898** E. D. COPE *Crocodilians N. Amer.* (1900) 789 The species of this genus [*Zamenis*] are elongate in form and active in movement, so that the popular names of 'whip-snake' and 'racer' are appropriate.

Whip thong. The thong or lash of a whip. — **1827** *Hallowell* (Me.) *Gaz.* 20 June 4/5 They have also received a large supply of ... whips and whipthongs. **1897** *Outing* XXX. 252/2 If your whip thong gets caught in the harness drop your hand and push the stick forward, and the thong will, invariably, release itself.

* **Whirl.** +**a.** A trial or test; *to try a whirl,* to give a try to. *colloq.* +**b.** A spinning bait used in fishing. — (a) **1887** *Outing* X. 112/1 Bill will want to give Old Prince a whirl. **1900** DRANNAN *Plains & Mts.* 417 Shall we try them a whirl or not? **1916** 'BOWER' *Phantom Herd* 267 Seems like I've had beans before, this week, but I'll try them another whirl. (b) **1888** GOODE *Amer. Fishes* 71 People who live near the lake, ... using two lines with spoon-baits or 'whirl,' ... frequently take two hundred or more Crappies in a day.

+**Whirling exercise.** A fit of whirling or spinning around as the result of religious excitement. *Obs.* — **1834** *Biblical Repertory* VI. 345 One young woman had what I would call the *whirling exercise.* **1871** DE VERE 235 *Whirling Exercises* were still more grotesque affections, in which, during a sermon, persons spun round like a top for upward of an hour, without experiencing any fatigue.

Whisk broom. A small broom used for brushing off clothes. {1857-} Also *comb.* — **1861** NEWELL *Orpheus C. Kerr* I. 207 There being no fan she used a small whisk-broom. **1882** RITTENHOUSE *Maud* 49, I got for Christmas ... [a] satin whisk-broom-holder with broom. **1911** *Springfield W. Repub.* 5 Jan. 1 The health department of New York is against the brushing off of passengers by porters on arriving trains.... The whisk broom must go.

Whisky, Whiskey.

1. A spirituous liquor distilled from grain and containing a high percentage of alcohol. {1715-}

1748 WEISER *Journal* 23 Found a dead Man on the Road who had killed himself by Drinking too much Whisky. **1792** *Ann. 2d Congress* 1111 [Notes of discharge] were frequently sold for five dollars, or one gallon of whiskey. **1803** J. DAVIS *Travels* 336 He spoke full an hour for the repeal of the tax on domestic distilled liquors; that is, whiskey, and peach, and apple brandy. **1880** *Cimarron News & Press* 4 Nov. 3/1 The law against selling whiskey on that [election] day is one of the best on the statute book. **1912** WASON *Friar Tuck* iii, What most of us called a town was nothin' but a log shack with a barrel of cheap whiskey and a mailbag wanderin' once a month.

2. *attrib.* and *comb.* **a.** Designating spirituous liquors or drinks of which whisky forms a prominent part.

1786 in Summers *Hist. S.W. Va.* 416 He drank a share of a quart bowl of whiskey grog. **1865** PIKE *Scout & Ranger* (1932) 13 'Whiskey-cocktail,' 'gin-sling,' 'stone-wall,' and the names of a host of others arose in my mind. **1870** STEPHENS *Married in Haste* 339, I can get him a splendid whisky smash.

b. Designating receptacles for whisky.

1806 *Balance* V. 187/2 A number of toasts were washed down by 'the waters of the Great Spring' (probably meaning a whiskey-cask). **1807** J. R. SHAW *Life* (1930) 56 The inhabitants . . . were very generous in rolling out their whiskey-barrels to make us drunk. **1837** BIRD *Nick* II. 26 [The old warrior's finger] was pointed at the two or three little whiskey-kegs. **1843** 'CARLTON' *New Purchase* II. 242 He abstained, that day at least, from his whiskey bottle. **1855** *Knickerb.* XLVI. 502 The farmer . . . setting the whiskey-jug under a tree near at hand, departs for his neighbor's harvest-field. **1880** R. H. DAVIS *Silhouettes* 48 Slung about the man's waist was a whiskey flask and a horn.

c. Designating those who make, use, or otherwise have to do with whisky.

1817 *N. Amer. Rev.* IV. 185 An active, overreaching, bustling race, whisky-makers and drinkers, store-keepers, millers and traders. **1844** *Knickerb.* XXIII. 502 We know a whiskey-distiller who refused his daughter to a portrait-painter. **1873** *Newton Kansan* 19 June 3/5 That's the way with these whiskey guzzlers. **1886** *Rep. Ind. Affairs* 157 There are the intruding cowmen, farming intruders, coal and timber thieves . . . and whisky-peddlers. **1887** *Voice* 11 Aug., The whiskey men of this city [Louisville] put up piles of money . . . to defeat Prohibition in Texas.

d. Designating places where whisky is made or sold.

1835 BIRD *Hawks* II. 6 You would have some of the wherewithall smuggled up to this identical old woman's whiskey-house! **1867** RICHARDSON *Beyond Miss.* 81 The Border Ruffian capital . . . was composed of few dwelling-houses, many land-offices, and multitudinous whiskey saloons. **1869** A. K. MCCLURE *Rocky Mts.* 55 Forty 'whisky-mills,' or small groceries, where whisky, tobacco, and portable eatables are sold. **1883** *Harper's Mag.* July 261, I visited one of the largest whiskey distilleries. **1901** WHITE *Westerners* 2 Here and there a straight Indian, stalking solemnly towards some one of the numerous 'whiskey joints.'

e. In the specific names of plants.

1897 SUDWORTH *Arborescent Flora* 245 *Prunus serotina.* . . . Common Names. . . . Whisky Cherry (Minn.). **1871** DE VERE 399 The Whiskey-root . . . is a cactus, growing on the sandy hills along the Rio Grande. . . . [The Indians] dig up the root, slice it, chew the pieces, and swallow the juice, which has a powerful intoxicating effect.

f. In special combinations.

Whisky Baptist, (see quotation); *w. bloat,* a disreputable whisky drinker (*slang*); *w. cramp,* a cramp brought on by whisky drinking; *W. Democrat,* a Democrat who participated in the whisky insurrection in Pennsylvania; *w. license,* a license for making or selling whisky; *w. poker,* (see quotation); *w. pool,* a combination of whisky distillers or dealers; *W. Rebellion,* =WHISKY INSURRECTION; *w. tax,* a government tax on whisky; *w. trust,* a combination of those engaged or involved in the manufacture of whisky; *w. vote,* a vote favoring the whisky interests.

1871 EGGLESTON *Hoosier Schoolm.* xii. 102 The 'Hardshell Baptists' or, as they are otherwise called, the 'Whiskey Baptists' . . . , exist in all the old Western and South-western States. **1862** *N.Y. Tribune* 28 March 4/5 Private pilferers—the whisky-bloats—the bullies in ward elections . . . were out in full force. **1883** BEADLE *Western Wilds* 608 [He] died suddenly, in 1875, of whisky cramp. **1863** *Rio Abajo Press* 4 Aug. 2/2 If the editor of the Gazette intends to insinuate that Jefferson countenanced the Whiskey Democrats in their rebellion against the laws of the United States [etc.]. **1873** *Newton Kansan* 10 April 3/2 The whiskey licence . . . has since become the subject of considerable argument. **1864** DICK *Amer. Hoyle* (1866) 182 Whiskey Poker. . . . Each player contributes one chip to make a pool, and the same rules govern as at 'draw,' except that the strongest hand you can get is a straight flush. **1884** *Boston Herald* 23 May, The Whiskey Pool Weakening. **1863** *Congress. Globe* 31 Jan. 662/2 We now look [with amazement] upon those who, in the last century, maligned the great Washington for his efforts to suppress the whisky rebellion of Pennsylvania. **1812** *Niles' Reg.* II. 7/1 Mr. Gallatin recommended a whiskey tax. **1890** *Stock Grower & Farmer* 8 Feb. 6/3 The Whiskey trust . . . will resolve itself into an every-day corporation. **1873** *Newton Kansan* 14 Nov. 2/3 [Money] can buy whiskey saloons and perhaps a few whiskey votes.

+**Whisky boy.** One of the insurrectionists in the Whisky Insurrection. *Obs.* — **1799** FRENEAU *Letters* (1943) 27 If Washington had drawn and quartered thirty or forty of the whisky boys, we would not have had this rumpus. **1842** *S. Lit. Messenger* VIII. 10/1 Mr. Brackenridge led the whiskey boys . . . by the Monongahela road. **1850** FOOTE *Sk. Virginia* 560 The insubordinate, commonly called the Whiskey Boys, were many of them members of Presbyterian congregations.

+**Whisky fraud.** *Hist.* Evasion by distillers (c1865–75), often with the assistance of conniving politicians and officials, of the internal revenue duties on whisky. *Obs.* Also attrib. — **1875** *Chicago Tribune* 19 Nov. 4/1 Yesterday was a black-letter day in the annals of the St. Louis whisky-fraud exposures. **1894** FORD *P. Stirling* 91 What do yez say to the whisky frauds, an' black Friday, an' credit mobilier? **1900** *Congress. Rec.* 17 Jan. 913/2 One of the most discreditable things that has happened . . . since the Belknap scandal and the whisky frauds.

+**Whisky Insurrection.** (See quot. 1914.) Also attrib. and allusive. — [**1806** *Balance* V. 227/2 Mention is made of 'French outcasts and foreign renegadoes'—of 'whiskey insurrections,' etc.] **1824** *Mass. Spy* 28 July (Th.), In the whole county, we doubt whether there are an hundred

individuals who are tinctured with the duelling or whiskey-insurrection mania. **1914** *Cycl. Amer. Govt.* III. 687/1 An outbreak in western Pennsylvania in 1794 against the enforcement of a federal excise law on domestic spirits is commonly called the Whiskey Insurrection.

+**Whisky jack.** [Amer. Indian. Cf. Cree *wiskatjân.*] The Canada jay, *Perisoreus canadensis.* Also *whisky john.* — **1839** AUDUBON *Ornith. Biog.* V. 208 The description of the habits of the Canada Jay or 'Whiskey-Jack' . . . may here be referred to. **1870** *Amer. Naturalist* IV. 596 The Canada jay, known all over the northern country by the less euphonious name of 'whiskey jack,' had already laid and almost hatched its eggs. **1917** *Birds of Amer.* II. 225 Whiskey Jack; Camp Robber; Whiskey John . . . 'Whiskey Jack' always looks and acts fuddled, especially when he is planning to steal something.

+**Whisky pole.** A pole set up by participants in the Whisky Insurrection. *Obs.* — **1794** *Mass. Spy* 19 Nov. 3/1 The whiskey poles are all cut down [at Pittsburgh]. **1808** *Ib.* 21 Dec. (Th.), Albert Gallatin . . . kindled the flame of insurrection around a whiskey pole.

+**Whisky ring.** A combination for fraudulently furthering the whisky interests, esp. a group of distillers and revenue officers who, during Grant's administration, conspired to defraud the government of part of the tax on distilled spirits. *Obs.* Also *whisky ringer.* — **1868** *Congress. Globe* 9 July 3865/2 It is the 'money ring' which controls on that side, which has been charging that the 'whisky ring' controls on the other. **1868** *Ore. State Jrnl.* 25 July 2/1 The office holders and whisky ringers, are making up the expenses of the impeachment trial. **1875** *Chicago Tribune* 15 Nov. 4/3 For years the Whisky Ring was protected at Washington. **1886** DORSEY *Midshipman Bob* 232 A few months later some twenty or thirty fellows were involved in a 'whiskey-ring.'

Whisky-seller. One who sells whisky. — c**1834** CATLIN *Indians* II. 24 The small-pox, was accidentally introduced amongst them [Pawnee Indians] by the Fur Traders, and whiskey sellers. **1910** [see POKER[2] 2].

+**Whisky skin.** A drink containing whisky. *slang.* — **1856** *Yale Lit. Mag.* XXI. 146 (Th.), Nine whiskey skins, and our spirits rushed together. **1861** [see BRANDY SOUR]. **1891** SALA in *Times* (London) 22 Feb. 2/3 The scheme of [the London American club] . . . seemed to comprise unlimited cocktails, whiskey skins, corpse revivers [etc.].

+**Whisky sour.** (See quot. 1891.) — **1891** *Cent.* 6906/1 *Whisky sour,* a beverage consisting chiefly of whisky and water, acidulated with lemon-juice. **1904** LOVETT *R. Gresham* 186 Bring a couple o' whiskey sours there, barkeep.

+**Whisky straight.** (See STRAIGHT *a.* 1 c.)

+**Whisky trader.** One who sells whisky, esp. in trade with the Indians. — **1822** MORSE *Rep. Indian Affairs* I. 48 The business done in the factory at Chicago . . . does not average two hundred dollars a year, in consequence of the whiskey traders at that place. **1846** MCKENNEY *Memoirs* I. 90 The whiskey trader . . . sought only to rob them of their blankets and calicoes. **1871** [see WOLFER]. a**1918** G. STUART *On Frontier* I. 186, I wish those whiskey traders would go on to the Blackfoot country.

+**Whisky traffic.** Trade in whisky. — **1846** MCKENNEY *Memoirs* I. 25, I had . . . urged the passage of laws for the protection of the system from the inroads made upon it by the whiskey traffic of traders. **1866** *Rep. Indian Affairs* 86 The whiskey traffic, with all its demoralizing influences, will flourish. **1885** *Ib.* 5 The whiskey traffic continues.

* **Whistle,** *n.*

***1.** A wind or air instrument which produces a more or less shrill note when blown.

1644 *Essex Probate Rec.* I. 32 One silu[er] whissell & a Corall, 2s. 6d. **1761** [see FORGING]. a**1861** [see OUTDOORS *n.* 2]. **1907** LONDON *Road* 72 The whistle sounded.

attrib. **1883** 'MARK TWAIN' *Life on Miss.* xxiv, 'This one,' indicating the whistle-lever, 'is to call the captain.' **1901** MERWIN & WEBSTER *Calumet 'K'* 319 At last the engineer walked over and pulled the whistle cord.

+**b.** *To pay too dear for one's whistle,* or variant: To pay much more for a thing than it is worth; *to pay for one's whistle,* to pay the piper.

1779 FRANKLIN *Writings* VII. 416 Poor man, said I, you pay too much for your whistle. **1837** *S. Lit. Messenger* III. 176 That, rejoined he, would be paying too dear for the whistle. **1878** *Harper's Mag.* Jan. 199 When respectable people like the Mayor of the city of Hot Springs and his friends got drunk, they should pay for their whistle.

2. The cry *of* a moose or elk. {1839–, of other animals}

1890 LANGFORD *Vigilante Days* (1912) 512 Several times he mistook the whistle of an elk, and howl of the wolf, for the Indian.

* **Whistle,** *v.* **1.** *intr.* Of moose: To utter a short, loud whistle or roar. +**2.** *To whistle down* (or *off*), to signal (orders) by means of a locomotive whistle. — (1) **1839** HOFFMAN *Wild Scenes* 59 They were bent upon having a shot at the game, which dashed to and fro, snorting and whistling. **1891** *Scribner's Mag.* X. 447 A little later, about September 7th, the bulls begin to challenge each other, in hunting parlance, whistling. (2) **1869** HARTE *Poems* (1871) 37 Said the Engine from the East, . . . 'S'pose you whistle down your brakes.' **1891** C. ROBERTS *Adrift Amer.* 172 The engineer whistled the brakes off.

* **Whistler.**

1. Any one of various birds whose wings in flight make a peculiar whistling noise {1782–}, +esp. the golden-eye duck. Also with specifying term.

1709 LAWSON *Carolina* 149 Whistlers. These are called Whistlers, from the whistling Noise they make, as they fly. **1832** WILLIAMSON *Maine* I.

142 A Whistler is about as large as a Dipper. **1874** LONG *Wild-Fowl* 281 Local names [of the buffle-headed duck are:] butter-box, butter-ball, and little whistler. **1882** [see COOT 1]. **1917** *Birds of Amer.* I. 119 European Widgeon. *Mareca penelope.* . . . Widgeon; Whistler. *Ib.* I. 225 Woodcock. *Philohela minor.* . . . Whistler.

+2. = HOARY MARMOT.

1820 HARMON *Jrnl.* 427 A small animal, found only on the Rocky Mountain, denominated by the Natives, Quis-qui-su, or whistlers, from the noise which they frequently make. **1917** *Mammals of Amer.* 202 The Hoary Marmot is also called the Whistler, from its call—a shrill whistle used not only as a danger signal but as a means of communication at all times.

Whistlewood. {1825-} +(See quot. 1891.) — **1891** *Cent.* 6908/1 *Whistle-wood,* the striped maple, *Acer Pennsylvanicum,* thus named because used by boys to make whistles. . . . The name is also given to the basswood, *Tilia Americana.* **1897** SUDWORTH *Arborescent Flora* 283.

* **Whistling,** *n.* +The characteristic cry made by the male moose. Also attrib. — **1882** BAILLIE-GROHMAN *Camps in Rockies* 123 It was 'whistling time,' as the rutting season is called. **1886** *Outing* IX. 51/2 [The elk] moved away up the hill, uttering a whistling as they went. **1893** ROOSEVELT *Wilderness Hunter* 164 During the rut the bulls are very noisy; and their notes of amorous challenge are called 'whistling' by the frontiersman.

* **Whistling,** *a.* In the names of various American birds and animals. — **1806** CLARK in *Lewis & C. Exped.* V. (1905) 59 Labiech also brought a whisteling squirrel which he had killed on it's hole in the high plains. **1844** *Nat. Hist. N.Y., Zoology* II. 83 The Whistling Warbler. *Vermivora swainsoni.* . . . This is a southern species, and apparently rare. **1892** TORREY *Footpath-Way* 93, I heard a white-throated sparrow singing outside. . . . A sweet and home-felt strain is this of 'Whistling Jack.' **1917** *Mammals of Amer.* 201 Hoary Marmot. *Marmota caligata.* . . . [Also called] Whistling Marmot. **1917** *Birds of Amer.* I. 225 Woodcock. *Philohela minor.* . . . Whistling Snipe; Wood Snipe.

Whistling (field) plover. {1668} The black-bellied plover (*Squatarola squatarola*) or the golden plover. — **1682** [see CRANE 1]. **1709** LAWSON *Carolina* 140 The gray or whistling Plover, are very scarce amongst us. **1813** WILSON *Ornithology* VII. 41 Black-bellied Plover . . . is known in some parts of the country by the name of the large whistling Field Plover. **1844** *Nat. Hist. N.Y., Zoology* II. 214. **1917** *Birds of Amer.* I. 256, 257.

Whistling swan. {1785-} +The common American swan, *Cygnus columbianus.* — **1806** LEWIS in *L. & Clark Exped.* III. (1905) 307 The large, and small or whistling swan . . . still remain with us. **1828** BONAPARTE *Synopsis* 379 The Whistling Swan . . . [is] very numerous in winter in Chesapeake Bay. **1872** COUES *Key to Birds* 281 Whistling Swan. Tail (normally) of 20 feathers. A yellow spot on bill. **1917** *Birds of Amer.* I. 164.

* **White,** *n.*

1. A member of the white race. {1671-} **a.** As distinguished from Negroes.

1715 *Boston News-Letter* 15 Aug. 2/2 They are still daily Battling with the Indian Enemy, wherein they have lost a great many Whites & Blacks. **1788** BELKNAP *P.* II. 2 Have their children an equal right to education in the town schools with those of whites? **1837** *S. Lit. Messenger* III. 645 The true reason for the hostility of the whites to the blacks in the free states, is that given in the text. **1865** [see BLACK *n.* 1]. **1900** *Congress. Rec.* 8 Jan. 674/2 In a mixed community of whites and negroes the negro representative selected under this unnatural and purely arbitrary rule represents, in fact, the non-voters of both races.

b. As distinguished from Indians.

1741 *S.C. Hist. Soc. Coll.* IV. 13 He undertook an Expedition against it [St. Augustine] with five hundred whites and a few Indians. **1786** *Amer. Acad. Mem.* II. 1. 152 The Indians . . . had recourse to the whites . . . for a supply of bread corn. **1826** COOPER *Mohicans* Introd., The Whites have assisted greatly in rendering the traditions of the Aborigines more obscure by their own manner of corrupting names. **1890** *Stock Grower & Farmer* 15 Feb. 6/2 Neither Governor Prince nor the commander at Fort Marcy have received any information of serious trouble between the Navajo Indians and the Whites in northwestern New Mexico. **1905** COLE *Early Oregon* 60 We kept so close to the savages . . . that any general firing must have been nearly as fatal to the Indians as to the whites.

2. A variety of potato.

1837 *Mass. Agric. Survey 1st Rep.* 33 The kinds raised are the August whites, a very early variety; the English whites, a round potato.

* **White,** *a.*

I. 1. Of or pertaining to persons of the white race. **a.** As contrasted with Indians. {1604-}

1784 FILSON *Kentucke* 82 The White Flesh, the Americans, French, Spaniards, Dutch and English, this day smoke out the peace-pipe. **1835** SIMMS *Yemassee* I. 95 Does the white chief come to the great council of the Yemassee as a fur trader? **1849** *31st Congress 1 Sess.* Sen. Doc. No. 64, 188 Their Great Father, the President, having such a multitude of white children in the . . . East that there was not room sufficient for all of them. **1906** *Indian Laws & Tr.* III. 252 The roll of the Osage tribe of Indians [includes] . . . children of members of the tribe who have, or have had, white husbands. **1916** EASTMAN *From Deep Woods* 17 The white teacher will first teach you the signs by which you can make out the words on their books.

b. As contrasted with Negroes. {1777-}

1797 *Ann. 5th Congress* 336 Some observations were made as to the proportioning of men to each State, which it seems was made according to the number of white inhabitants and three-fifths of the blacks. **1845** F. DOUGLASS *Narrative* 32, I could not approach her as I was accustomed to approach other white ladies. **1853** POYAS *Peep into Past* 123 His dear old Mistress used to ride . . . to Charles Town . . . [to] attend the white meeting. **1868** *N.Y. Herald* 4 July 1868 5/2 The registered white vote has been very greatly increased. **1904** PRINGLE *Rice Planter* 127, I think the time has come when I really must try and 'get white help.'

+2. Honest, fair, decent. *colloq.* Also adv. in phrase *to treat white.* (Cf. WHITE MAN 4.)

1865 'MARK TWAIN' *Sk., New & Old* 74 The parson . . . was one among the whitest men I ever see. **1878** BEADLE *Western Wilds* 473, 'I'm white on this thing,' replied La Bonté. **1888** DORSEY *Midshipman Bob* 169 He's as clean and white a little man as ever stepped. **1896** ADE *Artie* 110 Jim's a good fellow and he's been white with me. **1903** DELAND *Dr. Lavendar's People* 88 'It's treating me white,' Algernon said.

3. American. *colloq.[2]* or *local.*

1902 WISTER *Virginian* 158 Us folks have been white for a hundred years.

II. In specific names. 4. Of various American fishes having white or silvery skins.

1709 LAWSON *Carolina* 157 The white Guard-Fish is shaped almost like a Pike, but slenderer. **1794** *Amer. Acad. Mem.* II. 11. 46 The first [fish] . . . was brought me by a boy who called it a white eel. **1820** White Chub [see SHINER 2]. **1842** *Nat. Hist. N.Y., Zoology* IV. 13 The White Lake Bass . . . is a very common fish in Lake Erie, and is known at Buffalo under the name White Bass. **1911** *Rep. Fisheries 1908* 311 Different species [of hake] are known as 'old English hake,' 'squirrel hake,' 'white hake,' [etc.].

5. Of various American birds having white plumage.

1844 *Nat. Hist. N.Y., Zoology* II. 333 The Eider Duck . . . is known on Long Island under the names of . . . White Coot, Big Sea Duck, and Shoal Duck. **1872** *Amer. Naturalist* VI. 400 The avocet, and the blacknecked stilt . . . are called 'white snipes!' **1917** *Birds of Amer.* II. 23 White-tailed Ptarmigan. . . . [Also called] White Quail.

6. Of various American animals having white fur.

1805 LEWIS in *Ann. 9th Congress* 2 Sess. 1049 They could furnish . . . the skins of a large species of white hare, a very delicate fur. **1840** EMMONS *Mass. Quadrupeds* 45 There is no occasion for mistaking this species for its cogenor, commonly called the White Weasel.

7. Of various American plants and trees having white bark, flowers, wood, etc.

1709 LAWSON *Carolina* 91 White, Scaly-bark Oak; This is used . . . in building Sloops and Ships. **1785** MARSHALL *Amer. Grove* 19 *Betula papyrifera.* White Paper Birch. This is a variety . . . having a very white smooth bark. **1814** BIGELOW *Florula Bostoniensis* 195 *Solidago bicolor.* White Golden rod. . . . Dry woods, Cambridge. **1833** White bush [see PEPPER BUSH 1]. **1895** *Dept. Agric. Yrbk. 1894* 211 [In] the true agricultural part of our country, . . . white potatoes, barley, and oats attain their highest perfection. **1920** HOWELLS *Vacation of Kelwyns* 60 Parthenope . . . had filled a tall jug with columbines, clover-heads, and pink and white laurel.

III. 8. In special combinations.

White aborigine, (see quotation and cf. WHITE INDIAN 1); *w. basis,* the white population thought of as serving as a basis for representation in a legislative assembly; *W. Brotherhood, W. Camelias,* in some of the southern states after the Civil War, organizations of white men seeking to regain white political supremacy; *w. Charlie, w. check* or *counter,* (see quotations); *w. dog,* (see quotation and cf. RED DOG 2); *w. dog feast,* a new year feast or ceremony among the Iroquois involving the sacrifice of dogs; *w. population,* white settlers.

1846 SAGE *Scenes Rocky Mts.* xxiv, The Munchies are a nation of *white aborigines,* actually existing in a valley among the Sierra de los Mimbros Chain. **1830** *Va. Lit. Museum* 509/1 Supposing . . . that there would be a few slave holding counties in the west, there was no danger that the 'white basis,' would carry power into unfriendly hands. **1870** W. W. HOLDEN *Proclamations Govr. N.C.* 31 There is a widespread and secret organization in this State, partly political and partly social in its objects . . . known . . . as 'The White Brotherhood.' **1877** BEARD *K.K.K. Sketches* 137 The K.K.K. . . . underwent a very positive metempsychosis, and became, thereafter, the White League, or White Camelias. **1842** *Congress. Globe* App. 28 Dec. 74/2 There seems to me as much prospect of the ultra Whigs—'the white Charlies'—coalescing with the Democrats, as there is of Tyler and his friends. **1864** DICK *Amer. Hoyle* (1866) 186 *White Check, or Counter.*—An ivory or bone token representing a certain coin as may be agreed upon, usually a decimal part of a dollar. **1875** *Chicago Tribune* 24 Aug. 6/1 'White Dog' was a State issue to pay for canal repairs. **1907** HODGE, etc. *Amer. Indians* I. 460/2 New fire was made in . . . the White-dog feast of the Iroquois. **1824** DODDRIDGE *Notes* 71 The honey bees . . . always kept a little in advance of the white population.

+White alder. The sweet-pepper bush. — **1857** GRAY *Botany* 254 *Clethra,* White Alder. Sweet Pepperbush. **1860** CURTIS *Woody Plants N.C.* 100 The leaves are a little like those of the common *Alder,* but are smaller and narrower. **1899** A. BROWN *Tiverton Tales* 320 The white alder crept farther and farther from its bounds.

White apple. +The prairie potato, *Psoralea esculenta*. — **1805** LEWIS in *L. & Clark Exped.* II. (1904) 10 The white apple . . . is confined to the highlands principally. **1846** SAGE *Scenes Rocky Mts.* xii, The *pomme blanc*, or white apple, is a native of the prairies and mountains.

+**White ash.**[1]

1. An American ash (*Fraxinus americana*) having leaves with whitish or pale green undersides. Also attrib.

1684 *Duxbury Rec.* 42 [The line runs] unto a white ash tree marked by the brook side. **1782** in W. W. Howard *Bryan Sta. Heroes* (1932) 144 S36 W200 poles to white ash and two small beeches. **1820** FLINT *Lett. from Amer.* 229 White and blue ash trees are easily split, pliant, and readily smoothed. **1859** HILLHOUSE tr. Michaux *Sylva* III. 49 The White Ash is one of the most interesting among the American species for the qualities of its wood. **1901** MOHR *Plant Life Ala.* 81 White ash . . . is apparently not rare in the cedar brakes of central and southeastern Tennessee.

b. The wood of this tree.

1683 *N.H. Hist. Soc. Coll.* VIII. 146 [They] did feloniously . . . use about one cord of white ash. *a*1797 [see BASSWOOD 1]. *a*1817 DWIGHT *Travels* I. 41 The *White Ash* . . . is excellent timber for a multitude of purposes; particularly for utensils on the farm and in the house.

2. An oar. {1906} Also collective.

1851 MELVILLE *Moby-Dick* 394 This clumsy lubber was trying to free his white-ash. **1866** 'MARK TWAIN' *Harper's Mag.* Dec. 105 Each boat took to the 'white-ash'—that is, to the oars.

White ash.[2] [ASH *n.*[2]] A variety of coal. Also attrib. — **1857** *Harper's Mag.* Sept. 460/2 The veins of the first, second, and third axes are of the white-ash variety. **1881** RAYMOND *Mining Gloss.*

Whiteback. {*a*1825-} +The canvasback duck. — **1813** [see SHELDRAKE]. **1917** *Birds of Amer.* I. 133 Canvas-back. *Marila valisineria.* . . . [Also called] White-back.

White-backed (three-toed) woodpecker. One of several regional American varieties of three-toed woodpeckers, esp. *Picoides americanus dorsalis.* — **1891** *Cent.* 691/10 *White-backed woodpecker*, a three-toed woodpecker of North America, *Picoides dorsalis* of Baird, having a long white stripe down the middle of the black back. **1917** *Birds of America* II. 149.

+**White bass.** One of several American fishes, esp. a fish of the Great Lakes and midwestern rivers, *Lepibema chrysops*. — **1813** *Niles' Reg.* IV. 317/1 Among those, not known in the Eastern states, is the *White Bass*, a fish resembling the herring but considerably larger. **1849** *31st Congress 1 Sess.* Sen. Doc. No. 64, 203 We caught a white bass that I have never seen anywhere before. **1884** GOODE, etc. *Fisheries* I. 429 The White Bass is a beautiful, clean-looking fish. **1911** *Rep. Fisheries 1908* 317 The name is sometimes applied to the white bass (*Roccus chrysops*) of the Great Lakes region.

+**White basswood.** A basswood (*Tilia heterophylla*) found in the Alleghany region. — **1884** SARGENT *Rep. Forests* 28 White Bass Wood. . . . Most common . . . along the western slopes of the southern Alleghany mountains. **1892** APGAR *Trees Northern U.S.* 73. **1897** SUDWORTH *Arborescent Flora* 302.

+**White bay.** The sweet bay, an American Magnolia, *M. virginiana*. Also attrib. — **1810** MICHAUX *Arbres* I. 33 *White Bay*, nom tombé en desuétude, autrefois dans le *New Jersey*. **1832** BROWNE *Sylva* 209 In the Southern States it [the magnolia] is generally called White Bay or Sweet Bay. **1847** WOOD *Botany* 150. **1901** MOHR *Plant Life Ala.* 505 White Bay. . . . The bark is used medicinally under the name of 'white bay bark.'

White bear. {1613-} +The grizzly bear. — **1791** J. LONG *Voyages* 95 The large white bear commonly called the grizly bear, is a very dangerous animal. **1852** REYNOLDS *Hist. Illinois* 172 He was destroyed there [in the Rocky Mts.] by a white bear.

White-bearded wheat. A variety of wheat having white awns. — **1788** WASHINGTON *Diaries* IV. 417 Also sowing . . . one bushel of the White bearded Wheat sent me by Beale Boardly. **1850** *Rep. Comm. Patents 1849: Agric.* 132 The white-bearded wheat, a valuable kind less liable to total failure than almost any other.

White beech. {1852, *dial.*} +The common American beech. — **1810** MICHAUX *Arbres* I. 27 Fagus sylvestris, *White beech*, . . . dans les Etats les plus septentrionaux et le District de Maine. **1832** BROWNE *Sylva* 153 On the banks of the Ohio the white beech attains the height of more than 100 feet. **1851** SPRINGER *Forest Life* 30 The distinctions of '*white*' and '*red*' Beech in common use among the people describes [*sic*] but one species. **1894** *Amer. Folk-Lore* VII. 99.

White bellied, *a.* {1611-} In the specific names of birds, animals, etc. {1774-}

1812 WILSON *Ornithology* V. 44 The White-Bellied Swallow . . . often takes possession of an apartment in the boxes appropriated to the Purple Martin. **1814** MITCHILL *Fishes N.Y.* 441 White-bellied Killifish. *Esox pisculentus.* **1858** BAIRD *Birds Pacific R.R.* 374 *Sitta Carolinensis.* White-bellied Nuthatch. . . . Eastern North America to the high central plains. **1869** *Amer. Naturalist* III. 186 The White-bellied Auk (*Brachyramphus hypoleucus*) . . . [has] not been found farther north. *Ib.* 474 The resident species not found westward of this valley [Colorado R. in Calif.] were the Ladder Woodpecker (*Picus scalaris*), the White-bellied Wren (*Thriothorus leucogaster*) [etc.]. **1917** *Mammals of Amer.* 172 White-bellied Fox Squirrel.—*Sciurus niger neglectus.* . . . Central Virginia and West Virginia to Pennsylvania. **1917** *Birds of Amer.* I. 93 Water-Turkey. *Anhinga*

anhinga. . . . [Also called] White-bellied darter (young). *Ib.* 214 Coot. *Fulica americana.* . . . [Also called] White-bellied Mud Hen.

White belly. +**a.** =SHARP-TAILED GROUSE. +**b.** =AMERICAN WIDGEON. — **1891** *Cent.* 6910/2. **1917** *Birds of America* I. 120, II. 27.

+**White bent grass.** =REDTOP 2. — **1868** GRAY *Field Botany* 543 *Agrostis alba*, White Bent-Grass. . . . Moist meadows and fields. **1901** MOHR *Plant Life Ala.* 370 White Bent Grass. . . . Extensively naturalized from Canada to the Mexican Gulf.

+**Whitebill. 1.** The coot. **2.** The slate-colored junco. — (1) **1844** *Nat. Hist. N.Y., Zoology* II. 273 The American Coot . . . [or] Whitebill . . . frequents low marshy spots near the coast. **1917** *Birds of Amer.* I. 214. (2) *Ib.* III. 45 Slate-colored junco. . . . [Also called] White Bill.

+**White-bill(ed) woodpecker.** =IVORY-BILLED WOODPECKER. Also with descriptive term. — *c*1728 CATESBY *Carolina* I. 16 The largest white-bill Woodpecker. Weighs twenty ounces. *Ib.* opp. p. 16 Largest White Bill'd Woodpecker. [1782 LATHAM *Gen. Syn. Birds* I. II. 553 Whitebilled W[oodpecker]. . . . This bird inhabits Carolina, Virginia, New Spain.]

White birch. {1830- (Loudon *Hortus Brit.*)} +The North American paper birch (*Betula papyrifera*) or the gray birch (*B. populifolia*).

1814 [see OLD-FIELD BIRCH]. **1841** COOPER *Deerslayer* ii, Yonder is a white birch with a broken top. **1864** NICHOLS *Amer. Life* I. 16 The great white birch (of whose bark the Indians made canoes). **1890** HOWELLS *Shadow of Dream* III. ii, I saw . . . the slim white birches on the lawn. **1905** WIGGIN *Rose* 11 A well-dressed white birch [was] growing on an irreproachable lawn.

attrib. **1868** *Amer. Naturalist* II. 178 After haunting . . . the white-birch swamps, it [the warbler] moves southward. **1871** STOWE *Sam Lawson* 195 She got her a little bit o' land, right alongside o' Old Black Hoss John's white-birch wood-lot. **1905** WIGGIN *Rose* 75 You're just like a white birch sapling.

Whitebird. {1875-} +=SNOW BUNTING. — **1844** *Nat. Hist. N.Y., Zoology* II. 178 The White Snow-Bird . . . is called White-bird [in some parts of the U.S.]. **1917** *Birds of Amer.* III. 19.

+**White brant.** The snow goose, *Chen hyperboreus*. — **1805** LEWIS in *L. & Clark Exped.* I. (1904) 370 Saw a great number of white brant. **1872** *Amer. Naturalist* VI. 400 The snow goose or 'white-brant' began to arrive in considerable numbers about October 1st. **1917** *Birds of Amer.* I. 155.

+**White-breasted (chicken) hawk.** The red-tailed hawk. — **1828** BONAPARTE *Synopsis* 32 [The] White-breasted Hawk, *Falco borealis*, . . . inhabits throughout North America. **1917** *Birds of Amer.* II. 71 Red-tailed Hawk. *Buteo borealis borealis.* . . . [Also called] White-breasted Chicken Hawk.

+**White-breasted nuthatch.** An American nuthatch (*Sitta carolinensis*) having bluish-gray and black upper parts and a white breast. — **1808** WILSON *Ornithology* I. 41 The White-breasted Nuthatch is common almost everywhere in the woods of North America. **1839** AUDUBON *Ornith. Biog.* V. 473. **1850** S. F. COOPER *Rural Hours* 33 A white-breasted nut-hatch among the trees on the lawn. **1912** *Dept. Agric. Yrbk. 1911* 242 A single species [of nuthatch is] on the list of enemies of the apple worm, namely, . . . the white-breasted nuthatch.

+**White buffalo.** The Rocky Mt. goat or sheep. *Obs.* — [**1801** A. MACKENZIE *Voyages* (1802) I. 202 Our conductor informed us that great numbers of bears, and small white buffaloes, frequent those mountains.] **1806** LEWIS in *L. & Clark Exped.* V. (1905) 165 The indians inform us that there is . . . an abundance of the mountain sheep or what they call white buffaloe. **1888** *Outing* May 130 The 'white buffaloes' alluded to by Mackenzie could not have been mountain sheep, as this species is dark brown.

White cap. {1668-} +A member of a voluntary group formed ostensibly for regulating public morals; also, pl., the group so formed. — **1888** *Battle Creek Jrnl.* 12 Dec., The White Caps left notices at several other saloons Saturday night. **1899** TARKINGTON *Gentleman from Ind.* iv, Usually White-Caps are a vigilance committee going after rascalities the law doesn't reach. **1903** *N.Y. Times* 14 Oct. 1 The whitecaps went to the negro's home and demanded that he open the door as they intended to whip him.

+**White cat(fish). a.** A catfish (*Haustor catus*) found chiefly in the eastern and southern states. **b.** The channel cat, *Ictalurus punctatus*. — **1836** [see BLUE CATFISH]. **1843** MARRYAT *M. Violet* xliv, The rivers and streams . . . abound with . . . the salmon and white-cat fish, the soft-shelled tortoise [etc.]. **1884** *Nat. Museum Bul.* No. 27, 491 *Ictalurus punctatus.* . . . White Cat. . . . This is a valuable food-fish. **1896** JORDAN & EVERMANN *Check-List Fishes* 232.

+**White cedar.** One of various North American coniferous trees, esp. one of the genus *Chamaecyparis;* also, the wood of such a tree.

1675 JOSSELYN *Two Voyages* 27 We had the sight of an Indian-Pinnace sailing by us made of Birch-bark, sewed together with the roots of spruce and white Cedar. **1709** LAWSON *Carolina* 89 Ever-Greens are here plentifully found, . . . white Cedar, the Pitch Pine, the yellow Pine [etc.]. **1796** WANSEY *Excursion U.S.* 107 The white Cedar is a native of this state [*sc.* Delaware], and is a very handsome tree. **1814** BIGELOW *Florula Bostoniensis* 236 The White Cedar grows naturally in wet situations. **1879** [see BOATBUILDING]. **1901** MOHR *Plant Life Ala.* 325.

Whitechapel needle. A needle, perhaps made in Whitechapel, London. *Obs.* {1828, in allusive use} — **1774** *Penna. Gazette* 10 Aug. Suppl. 2/2 Whitechapel and Glovers needles. **1776** *N.J. Archives* 2 Ser. I. 13 For Sale . . . : Whitechapel needles, knives and forks [etc.].

* **White clay.** Clay of a white or whitish appearance. Also attrib. — **1805** in *Ann. 9th Congress* 2 Sess. 1077 The land on which they now live is prairie, of a white clay soil, very flat. **1823** JAMES *Exped.* I. 144 Several [Indians] were painted with white clay, which had the appearance of being grooved in many places. **1846** SAGE *Scenes Rocky Mts.* xviii, The white clay is much used by the Indians in cleaning skins and robes.

* **White clover.** Dutch clover, *Trifolium repens.* Also attrib. — **1749** FRANKLIN *Writings* II. 384 The Grass which comes in first after Ditching is Spear-grass and white clover. **1771** [see ENGLISH GRASS]. **1806** CLARK in *Lewis & C. Exped.* V. (1904) 245, I observed . . . the white clover common in the Western parts of the U. States. **1889** [see DUTCH CLOVER]. **1901** MOHR *Plant Life Ala.* 561.

* **White corn.** +Indian corn the grains or kernels of which are white. — **1789** WASHINGTON *Diaries* IV. 4 Finished gathering . . . White Corn of the kind had in 1787 from Colo. Richard Henry Lee. **1888** [see HOMINY 1].

+**White crane.** The whooping crane, *Grus americana.* — **1846** THORPE *Myst. Backwoods* 156 The angler resumes his sport, and the flocks of white crane settle down in the shallows. **1872** COUES *Key to Birds* 271 White or Whooping Crane. . . . Adult plumage pure white. **1917** *Birds of Amer.* I. 198.

White-crowned, *a.* In the names of various birds having white crests. — **1811** WILSON *Ornithology* IV. 49 [The] White-crowned Bunting: *Emberiza leucophrys* . . . is one of the rarest of its tribe in the United States. **1844** GIRAUD *Birds of L.I.* 123 *Fringilla Leucophrys.* . . . White-Crowned Finch. . . . In the Western States it is more abundant. **1884** *Nat. Museum Bul.* No. 27, 144 *Nyctherodius violaceus.* White-crowned Night Heron. . . . Southern States, breeding north to the Carolinas and Southern Illinois and Indiana.

+**White-crowned sparrow.** A crown sparrow (*Zonotrichia leucophrys*) found throughout the greater part of the United States. — **1839** PEABODY *Mass. Birds* 321 The White-crowned Sparrow . . . is one of the finest of this family of birds. **1894** TORREY *Fla. Sketch-Book* 235, I discovered . . . perched at the top of the oak, tossing back his head and warbling—a white-crowned sparrow. **1917** *Birds of Amer.* III. 35.

+**White curlew.** The white ibis (*Guara alba*) of the southern states. — **1731** CATESBY *Carolina* I. 82 The White Curlew . . . frequent[s] the low watery lands. **1789** MORSE *Amer. Geog.* 59. **1917** *Birds of Amer.* I. 177/1 The old birds . . . are usually referred to as 'Spanish Curlews' or 'White Curlews.'

+**White cypress.** =BALD CYPRESS. — **1810** [see BALD CYPRESS]. **1832** BROWNE *Sylva* 143 The names of Black and White Cypress, in the Carolinas and Georgia, are founded only on the quality and color of the wood. **1897** SUDWORTH *Arborescent Flora* 59.

+**White egret.** A large American egret (*Casmerodius albus egretta*) formerly abundant in the Gulf States. Also *great white egret.* (Cf. *little white egret* under LITTLE *a.* 1) — **1835** AUDUBON *Ornith. Biog.* III. 137 [The Louisiana Heron] is at all seasons a social bird, moving about in company with the Blue Heron or the White Egret. **1872** COUES *Key to Birds* 267 Great White Egret. White Heron. No obviously lengthened feathers on the head at any time. **1917** *Birds of Amer.* I. 186.

+**White elm.** The American elm or the cork elm. — **1770** FORSTER tr. Kalm *Travels* I. 67 *Ulmus Americana,* the white elm. **1818** FLINT *Lett. from Amer.* 97. **1860** *Ill. Agric. Soc. Trans.* IV. 451 The White Elm . . . is not good timber—is hard to split. **1901** MOHR *Plant Life Ala.* 474 White Elm. . . . Frequently planted for shade.

White eye. {1848-} +New England rum. — **1827** *Western Mo. Rev.* I. 320 They found by experience that it [whisky] made them . . . more frisky than 'white eye.' **1845** JUDD *Margaret* I. 31 She will bring home some of . . . the real white-eye. **1875** BURNHAM *Three Years* p. viii.

+**White-eyed flycatcher.** =next. — **1810** WILSON *Ornithology* II. 166 [The] White-Eyed Flycatcher . . . has been observed in the neighborhood of Savannah, so late as the middle of November. **1865** *Atlantic Mo.* May 520/1 One of the most marvellous little songsters . . . is the White-Eyed Flycatcher.

+**White-eyed vireo.** A vireo (*Vireo griseus*) found chiefly in the eastern United States. — **1831** AUDUBON *Ornith. Biog.* I. 328 The White-eyed Flycatcher, or Vireo, *Vireo Noveboracensis.* **1871** BURROUGHS *Wake-Robin* (1886) 28 Still keeping among the unrecognized, the white-eyed vireo, or fly-catcher, deserves particular mention. **1917** [see KEY WEST].

White face. {1860-} +**1.** =BALD-FACE 1. *Obs.* +**2.** *White-face clay,* =WHITE CLAY. *Obs.* +**3.** =WHITE EYE. *Obs.* +**4.** *White-face act,* an act on the stage not done in black face. — **(1) 1709** LAWSON *Carolina* 151 The bald, or white Faces are a good Fowl. **(2) 1819** *Plough Boy* I. 190 My garden is what we call *white face clay,* though not quite the hardest kind. **(3) 1855** BARNUM *Life* 79 It is the meanest kind of New-England rum . . .—real white-face. **(4) 1895** *N.Y. Dramatic News* 9 Nov 14/4 Lew Dockstader, in his new white-face act, . . . will be seen at Keith's, November 18.

* **White-faced,** *a.* In special combinations.

White-faced clay, =WHITE CLAY; *white-faced glossy ibis,* an ibis (*Plegadis guarauna*) found chiefly in Florida; *white-faced hornet,* the bald-faced hornet, *Vespa maculata; white-faced New England,* =WHITE EYE. *Obs.*

1880 *Vt. Agric. Rep.* VI. 29 'White-faced' clay, not even discolored by the slightest amount of vegetable mould, is found everywhere. **1884** *Nat. Museum Bul.* No. 27, 145 White-faced Glossy Ibis. . . . Tropical and subtropical America. **1891** *Cent.* 6739/1 V[espa] *maculata* of North America is the so-called *white-faced hornet.* **1848** *Knickerb.* XXXII. 276 In a certain town in New-Hampshire, a certain inhabitant thereof required for his comfortable enjoyment at least a pint of 'white-faced New-England,' daily.

White father. +A white man regarded by the Indians as a friend and protector. *Obs.* — **1835** [see FATHER 2]. **1894** WISTER in *Harper's Mag.* Sept. 516/2 The White Father has sent me.

+**White fir.** One of various firs of the western states, esp. *Abies concolor.* — **1884** SARGENT *Rep. Forests* 9 The bottoms of the streams are lined with . . . an open growth of the white fir. **1897** SUDWORTH *Arborescent Flora* 53 ff.

* **Whitefish. a.** Any one of various fishes of the family Coregonidae, +esp. an American lake fish, *Coregonus clupeiformis.* **b.** *local.* One of various other fishes, as the menhaden.

1709 LAWSON *Carolina* 160 The white Fish . . . are found a great way up in the Freshes of the Rivers. **1791** J. LONG *Voyages* 43 At this place there is abundance of fine fish, particularly pickerill, trout, and white fish. **1815** *Lit. & Phil. Soc. N.Y. Trans.* I. 495 At the head of the western fishes, may be placed the *white fish,* which is universally admitted to be the most delicious. **1840** *S. Lit. Messenger* VI. 604/1 The white fish are caught with the seine, and abound in all the lakes surrounding Michigan. *a***1882** WEED *Autobiog.* 206 The whitefish, now in such general use and so highly appreciated, . . . was then seldom seen. **1896** JORDAN & EVERMANN *Check-List Fishes* 283 *Brevoortia tyrannus.* Menhaden; Mossbunker; Bony-fish; Whitefish. *Ib.* 462 *Caulolatilus princeps.* Blanquillo; Whitefish. **1911** *Rep. Fisheries 1908* 317/2 The California species [of tile-fish] . . . is also known as the 'whitefish.'

White flint. 1. Flint stone of a white or whitish color. **2.** A variety of flint or hard wheat the kernels of which are whitish in color. In full *white flint wheat.* +**3.** A variety of flint corn the kernels of which are white. In full *white flint corn.* — **(1) 1809** KENDALL *Travels* I. 243 The rock which bears the inscription is an isolated mass of stone, composed . . . of *white flint.* **(2) 1849** *New Eng. Farmer* I. 291 We have in our office a fine specimen of the White Flint wheat. **1849** EMMONS *Agric. N.Y.* II. 138 White Flint . . . is an esteemed variety, and is supposed to be of Spanish origin. **(3) 1855** *Amer. Inst. N.Y. Trans.* 589 A valuable variety of corn was obtained from New Mexico, bearing the name of 'white flint.' **1868** *Mich. Agric. Rep.* VII. 349 Wm. Hall, Greenfield, [exhibited a] variety [of] white flint corn.

+**White-footed (prairie) mouse.** Any one of various mice of the genus *Peromyscus.* — **1857** *Rep. Comm. Patents 1856: Agric.* 86 One of their greatest enemies in this vicinity is the Northern shrike, . . . the food of which consists almost wholly of arvicolae and a few white-footed prairie mice. **1869** *Amer. Naturalist* III. 120 When the axe-man struck the tree, a Whitefooted Mouse . . . rushed from the nest. **1876** [see DEER MOUSE]. **1917** *Mammals of Amer.* 239/1 The White-footed Mouse is by far the most beautiful species of the family to which it belongs.

White-fronted goose. {w.-f. wild goose, 1768} +=LAUGHING GOOSE. — **1823** James *Exped.* I. 266. **1874** LONG *Wild-Fowl* 241 The white-fronted goose . . . [is] the 'Brant' amongst Western sportsmen. **1917** *Birds of Amer.* I. 158/1 The White-fronted Goose . . . is now regarded as a mere straggler on the entire Atlantic coast.

+**White-fronted owl.** =KIRTLAND'S OWL. — **1872** *Amer. Naturalist* VI. 283. **1873** *Ib.* VII. 427 The 'white-fronted owl' (*Nyctale albifrons* Cass.) is now conceded by most if not all American ornithologists to be the young of the saw-whet. **1917** *Birds of Amer.* II. 107.

+**White goat.** =MOUNTAIN GOAT. — **1884** *Century Mag.* Dec. 193 The *Aplocerus montanus,* known to the frontiersman and to the fur-trader of the extreme North-west as the white goat of the Rocky Mountains. **1888** ROOSEVELT in *Century Mag.* June 206/2 White goats have been known to hunters ever since Lewis and Clarke crossed the continent.

+**White grub.** A grub or larva which is white, esp. that of the June bug. — *a***1817** DWIGHT *Travels* I. 77 The white-grub has . . . very extensively injured meadows and pastures. **1871** [see MAY BEETLE].

* **Whitehead.** +*Like a whitehead,* vigorously, hard, immediately. — **1830** *Mass. Spy* 28 July (Th.), Clear out like a whitehead. **1882** [see CIRCUS DAY]. **1917** MCCUTCHEON *Green Fancy* 129 It doesn't seem reasonable that they'd run like whiteheads with guns in.

* **White-headed,** *a.* +In the names of various American birds that have heads wholly or partially covered with white feathers. — **1805** CLARK in *Lewis & C. Exped.* III. (1905) 74 Blue jay, Small white headed hawk, Some Crows & ravins. **1835** AUDUBON *Ornith. Biog.* III. 174 The males [of the white ibis] evince their displeasure by uttering sounds which greatly resemble those of the White-headed Pigeon. **1858** BAIRD *Birds Pacific R.R.* 96 *Picus albolarvatus.* White-headed Woodpecker. . . . Cascade mountains of Oregon and southward into California. **1917** *Birds of Amer.* II. 226 In the West, in the Rocky Mountain region, . . . is the White-headed or Rocky Mountain Jay.

+**White-headed eagle.** =BALD EAGLE. — **1811** WILSON *Ornithology* IV. 89 White-headed, or bald eagle. . . . This distinguished bird . . . is the most beautiful of his tribe in this part of the world. **1871** [see FISH HAWK]. **1917** *Birds of Amer.* II. 80.

+**Whiteheart hickory.** =MOCKERNUT HICKORY. — **1810** MICHAUX *Arbres* I. 20 J[uglans] tomentosa. . . . *White heart hickery,* . . . usité dans ces deux Etats [N.Y. & N.J.]. **1884** SARGENT *Rep. Forests* 134 White-heart Hickory. . . . Generally on rich upland hillsides. **1897** SUDWORTH *Arborescent Flora* 114.

* **White hellebore.** Any one of various herbs of the genus *Veratrum,* +as American hellebore, also, their roots or rhizomes. — **1687** SEWALL *Diary* I. 179 Mr. Cook scrapes white Hellebore which he snuffs up. **1737**

[see Sarsaparilla 1]. **1820** *U.S. Pharmacopœia* 117 Decoction of White Hellebore. **1857** Gray *Botany* 476 V[eratrum] *viride.* (American White Hellebore. Indian Poke.) . . . Swamps and low grounds.

White heron. a. =White egret. **b.** *Little white heron,* =Snowy heron. — c1730 Catesby *Carolina* I. 77 *Ardea alba minor Carolinensis.* The little white Heron. . . . They feed on Fish, Frogs, &c., and frequent Rivers, Ponds and Marshes. **1804** Lewis in *L. & Clark Exped.* VI. (1905) 123 This day one of our Hunters brought me a *white Heron.* **1882** Godfrey *Nantucket* 243 Among these [rarer species are] . . . white heron, green heron, oriole [etc.]. **1917** *Birds of Amer.* I. 186, 188.

White House. +The residence in Washington, D.C., occupied by the Presidents of the United States while in office.

1811 F. J. Jackson in H. Adams *New-Eng. Federalism* (1877) 385 [Foster] goes . . . to act as a sort of political conductor to attract the lightning that may issue from the clouds round the Capitol and the White House at Washington. **1828** [see President's house]. **1867** *Harper's Mag.* Nov. 811/2, I called at the White House early one morning. **1884** *Century Mag.* April 803/1 There is no building quite as satisfying to my eye as the White House. **1913** La Follette *Autobiog.* 448, [I] called at the White House to pay my respects.

transf. and *attrib.* **1878** *Ill. Dept. Agric. Trans.* XIV. 146 Tecumseh had his thousands of braves encamped above and below Vincennes, Indiana, where Gen. Harrison occupied the 'White House' of this great Northwest. **1881** *Harper's Mag.* Feb. 369 Soup, fish, fruit, coffee, and tea dishes, for the new White House set.

+**White ibis.** =Spanish curlew. — **1813** Wilson *Ornithology* VIII. 43 [The] White Ibis . . . [is] pretty numerous on the borders of lake Ponchartrain. **1872** Coues *Key to Birds* 264. **1917** *Birds of Amer.* I. 175 The White Ibis is in no sense a Curlew, but its long, rounded, curved bill has doubtless suggested this name to many interested but unscientific observers.

+**White Indian. 1.** An Indian belonging to certain plains tribes of relatively light color or to other tribes, as the Zuñi and Menominee, where albinos are not infrequent. Also as name of a tribe. **2.** A white man living among the Indians. — (1) **1765** Rogers *Acct. N. America* 191 This fruitful country [upper Missouri] is at present inhabited by a nation of Indians, called by the others the White Indians, on account of their complexion, they being much the fairest Indians on the continent. **1800** D. R. D'Eres *Memoirs* 50 This nation was called the White Indian. **1873** Beadle *Undevel. West* 588 The prosaic fact is, these 'White Indians' are nothing but Indians, pure and simple. (2) **1837** *S. Lit. Messenger* III. 256 To his amazement, the proposal is rejected, and the savage rage of the 'white Indian' is awakened by the insult.

＊**White lead.** A heavy powder consisting chiefly of lead carbonate and used generally in paint-making. Also *attrib.* — **1724** Jones *Virginia* 32 Here . . . they build . . . most commonly with Timber . . . painted with white Lead and Oil. **1771** *Copley-Pelham Lett.* 173, I have been obliged to bye a hundred lb. of White lead. **1819** White-lead factory [see Nail-cutting machine]. **1899** [see Paint shop]. **1908** White-lead drummer [see Fur 3].

+**White league.** An organization formed to maintain white supremacy; esp. (*caps.*), those formed in Louisiana in 1874 to combat Negro political dominance. — **1874** in Fleming *Hist. Reconstruction* II. 144 White Leagues are forming to put down the negroes and carpetbaggers. **1875** *Congress. Globe* 13 Jan. 415/2 With a view to the late election in Louisiana, white men associated themselves together in armed bodies called 'White Leagues.' **1879** [see Night rider 1].

+**White Leaguer.** A member of the White League. *Obs.* — **1874** in Fleming *Hist. Reconstruction* II. 145, I told him . . . the Democrats or white-leaguers would not hurt the negroes if they could help it.

+**White lettuce.** Any one of various species of *Prenanthes.* — **1817-8** Eaton *Botany* (1822) 409 *Prenanthes alba,* white lettuce. . . . About two or three feet high. **1857** Gray *Botany* 238. **1861** Wood *Botany* 472.

+**White lime (tree).** Any one of various lime trees the leaves of which are white or whitish underneath. — **1810** Michaux *Arbres* I. 40 *Tilia alba,* White lime. **1832** Browne *Sylva* 305 The height of the white lime tree rarely exceeds 40 feet.

＊**White Line.** +A secret political organization formed about 1875 in some of the southern states to assist in securing white supremacy. *Obs.* Also *attrib.* — **1875** *Chicago Tribune* 6 Nov. 3/6 These figures teach the docility and gentleness of the colored race, all white line documents and lies to the contrary notwithstanding. **1877** *Congress. Rec.* 4 Aug. 5183/2 In their party pow-wow . . . , [Mr. Lamar and his friends] declared by formal resolution against the white-line policy. **1880** 'E. Kirke' *Garfield* 54 The horrors of the Ku-klux and the White-Lines should not run riot at the polls.

+**White Liner.** A member of the White Line organization. *Obs.* — **1875** *Chicago Tribune* 2 Nov. 4/7 The white-liners of Mississippi . . . expect to carry the election to-day. *Ib.* 6 Nov. 8/7 The White-Liners having carried Mississippi, it remains to be seen what they will do.

+**White locust.** *local.* The common American locust, *Robinia pseudoacacia,* or a variety of this having white heartwood. — **1832** [see Red locust]. **1846** Browne *Trees Amer.* 207 *White locust,* with a white heart, . . . is considered as the least valuable [of the locusts]. **1893** *Amer. Folk-Lore* VI. 140.

White man.

1. A man belonging to the white race. Also in generic sense. {1695-} +**a.** As distinguished from an Indian.

1725 in *Travels Amer. Col.* 105 Who was it that told You anything abt. White Men coming among You? **1822** Morse *Rep. Indian Affairs* II. 169 There are . . . fourteen or fifteen grist, and two saw mills owned by whitemen, who are married into native families. **1870** *Republican Rev.* 25 June 2/3 [The Zuñis] brag on never having killed a white man. **1923** J. H. Cook *On Old Frontier* 229 It was then or never that the white man could be stayed from doing as he pleased in the valuable hunting grounds.

+**b.** As distinguished from a Negro.

1789 Morse *Amer. Geog.* 430 All free whitemen of 21 years of age . . . are qualified to elect representatives. **1819** *Plough Boy* I. 14 In Georgia the poll tax on a free male of colour, is about 18 times as great as on a white man. **1874** J. S. Pike *Prostrate State* 12 [In] the House of Representatives [of S.C.] . . . sit one hundred and twenty-four members. Of these, twenty-three are white men. **1910** B. F. Riley *White Man's Burden* 37 The responsibility . . . rests not on the Negro, but on the white man.

+**c.** As distinguished from a Spaniard or a Mexican.

1857 Chandless *Visit Salt Lake* 316 The term 'a white man,' as distinctive from a Spaniard, shows how much more likely it is that the latter race should remain abject and die out. **1863** *Rio Abajo Press* 21 April 2/2 One of the 'delegates' elected by a 'county convention' composed of ten 'white men' and three 'cristianos.' **1905** 'O. Henry' *Roads of Destiny* 135 I got into a little gun frolic down in Laredo and plugged a white man.

+**2.** A Southerner as distinguished from a Yankee or Northerner.

1835 Hoffman *Winter in West* II. 204 Is he a Yankee or a white man? **1887** J. C. Harris in *Century Mag.* Aug. 545/2 Yonder's the Yankees on one side, and here's the blamed niggers on t'other, and betwixt and betweenst 'em a white man's got mighty little chance.

‖**3.** The language spoken by white people.

1878 Beadle *Western Wilds* 28, I'd never heard of any language but white-man and Injin.

+**4.** A man of honorable, dependable character. *colloq.* (Cf. White *a.* 2.)

1883 Howells *Woman's Reason* xx, You've behaved to me like a white man from the start. **1889** Munroe *Golden Days* 26, I've froze onto a white man.

5. Used in possessive to designate things suitable for, owned by, or characteristic of white people.

1845 *Big Bear Ark.* 37 To give him a white man's chance, I proposed alternatives to him. **1865** *Atlantic Mo.* April 405/2 After spending the night at a 'white man's' hotel in Buffalo, the next morning found her standing . . . before one of the world's great wonders. **1871** *Rep. Indian Affairs* (1872) 470 [He] openly avowed his determination to follow the 'white man's road.' **1899** Quinn *Penna. Stories* 17 It was 'white man's weather' the next day, and the town was alive.

+**White man's country. 1.** A country of superior excellences. **2.** A country governed by those of its citizens who are white. — (1) **1871** Hay *Pike Co. Ballads* 21 This is a white man's country. **1881** Hayes *New Colorado* 22 When you git out there on the range in Coloraydo, you'll say it's a white man's country. (2) **1900** *Congress. Rec.* 1 Feb. 1404/2 This is a white man's country . . . and the white people intend to rule it now and forever.

+**White man's fly.** In Indian speech: A bee. *Obs.* — **1796** Latrobe *Journal* 19 Wild bees . . . are called by the Indians the white man's fly. **1845** *S. Lit. Messenger* XI. 9/2 The bee, whose busy hum is so sure a herald of civilization, that it is known among the Indians as the 'white man's fly.'

+**White man's foot.** =Plantain.[1] *Obs.* — **1840** Dewey *Mass. Flowering Plants* 114. **1849** Longfellow in S. Longfellow H. W. Longfellow II. 158 Agassiz . . . pointed out by the roadside a weed called by the Indians 'the white man's foot,' because it advances into the wilderness with the white settlers. **1860** Holmes *Professor* 296 The broad, flat leaves of the plantain,—'the white man's foot,' as the Indians called it.

+**White man's party.** A political faction or group in the South particularly zealous for the maintenance of white supremacy. *Obs.* — [**1860** Greeley *Overland Journey* 37 They must be as harsh, and cruel, and tyrannical, toward the unfortunate blacks as possible, in order to prove themselves 'the white man's party.'] **1874** in Fleming *Hist. Reconstruction* II. 146 His action paralyzes the White Man's Party in New Orleans.

+**White maple.** Any one of several maples, as the red maple or silver maple, the bark of which is pale or whitish in appearance. — **1806** Lewis in *L. & Clark Exped.* V. (1905) 137 A small speceis of white maple are beginning to put fourth their leaves. **1832** Williamson *Maine* I. 108 The *white* Maple . . . has two varieties, one is smooth and straightgrained; the other has apparent curls and bird's eyes. **1872** McClellan *Golden State* 163 In the large variety in the State are the . . . dogwood, cherry, white maple. **1897** Sudworth *Arborescent Flora* 283, 287, 290.

White marl. (See quot. 1791.) {1756- (*Compl. Body Husb.* 43)} — **1791** Bartram *Travels* 32 The upper soil of these swamps is a . . . stiff mud, . . . on a foundation or stratum of calcareous fossil, which the inhabitants call white marle. **1883** *Century Mag.* Sept. 719/1 A mountain streamlet . . . bears along submerged or dissolved in it, . . . cloudings of earthy substance, ocherous, milky from white marl.

+**White miller (fly). 1.** Any one of various clothes moths, or an American tiger moth, *Diacrisia virginica.* **2.** An artificial fly used by anglers. — (1) **1854** Emmons *Agric. N.Y.* V. 229 White Miller. . . . Abdomen marked with three rows of black dots. **1859** *S. Lit. Messenger* XXIX. 416/1 Sober, white miller-flies proceeded here and there in an orderly, quiet way. **1899** *Animal & Plant Lore* 41 A white 'miller' coming into the house is a sign of bad news. New England. **(2) 1897** *Outing* XXX. 294/1 Useful trout-flies for the month [June] include: the hackles, white miller, alder [etc.].

White mulberry. The white fruit of a variety of mulberry (*Morus alba*), or the tree producing this fruit; formerly grown to supply food for silkworms. {1731– (P. Miller *Gard. Dict.* s.v. *Morus*)} Also attrib. — **1610** *Estate of Va.* 55 There are innumerable white Mulberry trees. **1737** WESLEY *Journal* I. 402 The white mulberry is not good to eat. **1804** J. ROBERTS *Penna. Farmer* 189 The leaves of both the black and white mulberry are used in raising silkworms. **1884** *Century Mag.* Jan. 432/1 In 1623, . . . law was invoked to compel the planting of white mulberries and the raising of silk.

White mullet. {1802–} **+a.** One of several suckers found in coastal streams of the south Atlantic states. **+b.** A marine mullet (*Querimana curema*) of silvery appearance, found along the Atlantic and Pacific coasts. — **1839** KEMBLE *Residence in Ga.* 53 Had I been the ingenious man who wrote a poem upon fish, the white mullet of the Altamaha should have been at least my heroine's cousin. **1842** *Nat. Hist. N.Y., Zoology* IV. 146 The White Mullet is in high repute among epicures. **1883** [see LIZA]. **1911** *Rep. Fisheries 1908* 312 Many suckers of the genus *Moxostoma* are called 'mullet,' 'white mullet,' 'sucking mullet,' etc.

+White-necked raven. (See quot. 1891.) — **1887** RIDGWAY *Manual N.A. Birds* 362. **1891** *Cent.* 6911/3 The *white-necked* raven, *Corvus cryptoleucus*, a small raven found in western parts of the United States, having the concealed bases of the feathers of the neck fleecy-white. **1917** *Birds of America* II. 228.

+White Negro. A Negro of an exceptionally light, often albinal, complexion. — **1775** J. WARREN in *Warren-Adams Lett.* I. 77 The [New] York troops . . . will amount to 9,000 at least, . . . including the black and white negroes engaged in their service in Boston. **1824** DODDRIDGE *Notes* 52 Mulattoes . . . are denominated white negroes. **1850** LEWIS *La. Swamp Doctor* 76 He was one of that peculiar class called Albinoes, or white negroes.

+White nigger. [f. prec.] A white person who does hard manual labor; a drudge. *Obs.* — **1837** FEATHERSTONHAUGH *Canoe Voyage* II. 195 That class . . . have the audacity to call those who contracted to their own class in the north, *white Niggers*. **1871** EGGLESTON *Hoosier Schoolm.* 52 'Ole Miss Meanses' white nigger,' as some of them called her, in allusion to her slavish life.

+White oak.

1. Any one of various species of American oak of which *Quercus alba* of the eastern half of the United States is typical; a tree of one of these species or the wood.

[**1637** MORTON *New Canaan* 62 Oakes are there of two sorts, white and redd.] **1644** *Essex Probate Rec.* I. 35, 2200 pipe stavs of whitt oake. **1698** *Boston Rec.* 233 [The way is] to run below a great white oake on the back side of said Tuttle's house. **1724** in *Amer. Speech* XV. 296 To a small white oak Standing on the Side of a large pocosin or Great Swamp calld the Marsh run. **1791** DENNY *Journal* 158 Upland thin, covered chiefly with white oak. **1860** CURTIS *Woody Plants N.C.* 31 White Oak . . . is probably of more general use . . . than any other of our Oaks. **1901** MOHR *Plant Life Ala.* 99 The rich black soil . . . prevails covered either with the white oaks and hickories, or with cedar hammocks.

2. *attrib.* and *comb.* **a.** Designating trees or shrubs of white oak, or parts of these.

1648 *Providence Rec.* XV. 21 The South-east corner is bounded with a gully and a white Oake tree. **1658** *Ib.* I. 42 On the South East Cornner a white oake Stumpe. **1672** JOSSELYN *New Eng. Rarities* 48 Out of the white Oak Acorns, . . . The Natives draw an Oyl. **1749** HEMPSTEAD *Diary* 538, I was . . . splitting a hard white oak Log. **1783** *Amer. Acad. Mem.* II. 1. 50, I boiled, for want of nutgalls, some shavings of white oak bark. **1822** J. FOWLER *Journal* 143 On the hill sides are some small white oak brush from one to fifteen feet high.

b. Designating things made of white oak or white oak lumber.

1663 *Plymouth Rec.* 66 Lot . . . bounded . . . with two white oake stakes. **1674** *Md. Archives* II. 405 The second story all to be made of good white Oke quartered Planck. **1682** *N.H. Hist. Soc. Coll.* VIII. 75 White-oak pipe-staves [shall be] three pounds per thousand. **1727** SEWALL *Letter-Book* II. 137 Ten Rods above Mr. Banister's Land, . . . a White Oak Post is set down by me. **1771** *N.H. Gazette* 30 Aug. (Ernst), This to inform such persons as are desirous of contracting for . . . white oak knees, or standards, white oak pipe [etc.] . . . to apply to me. **1830** S. SMITH *Life J. Downing* 76, I told the man I'd give him four good white oak ax handles. **1841** *S. Lit. Messenger* VII. 19/1 A white-oak merchantman . . . usually runs ten or twelve years. **1892** *York County Hist. Rev.* 89 J. M. Grim, Man'f'r of White Oak Baskets and Cigars.

c. Designating areas upon which white oak is the prevailing growth.

See also WHITE-OAK LAND, SWAMP.

1770 WASHINGTON *Diaries* I. 433 Some tolerable good white oak Ground, level, and meadowey. **1784** White Oak Ridges [see GLADY *a.*]. **1840** *S. Lit. Messenger* VI. 605/1 A great portion of Michigan is covered

by *white-oak openings*. **1891** RYAN *Fagan* 179 A big drove of hogs on a white-oak flat, when the acorns are a good crop.

+White-oak cheese. 'Tough, hard cheese made from skimmed milk' (B. '77). *Obs.* — **1853** *Harper's Mag.* VII. 850/1 [He saw] a stout arm reach up and take down from the shelf a heavy 'white-oak' cheese. **1889** *Ib.* LXXIX. 694/2 They had . . . the greatest app'tite for old-fashioned, hum-made, white-oak cheese.

+White-oak land. Land upon which white oak is the prevailing growth. — **1751** [see PINEY *a.*]. **1816** U. BROWN *Journal* I. 358 Thin White Oak Land Tollerably well timbered easily worn out. **1882** *Econ. Geol. Illinois* II. 21 These white oak lands are reckoned among the most fertile lands in the county.

+White-oak swamp. A low, swampy region heavily timbered with white oak. — **1720** in *Amer. Speech* XV. 290/2 Lying and being on the North side of the white Oake Swamp. **1788** *N.C. State Gazette* (Newbern) 27 March, 3000 acres; part of which is white-oak swamp of the best quality. **1862** *Va. State P.* XI. 217 You would . . . prevent a move to intercept me from the direction of the white oak swamp.

White owl. a. =BARN-OWL. {1770–} **b.** *Great white owl*, the snowy owl, *Nyctea nyctea.* — (a) **1812** [see BARN-OWL]. a**1841** W. HAYES *Sporting Scenes* I. 85 He and one of the boys brought in fifty-four brant, . . . a cormorant, and a white owl. **1917** *Birds of Amer.* II. 98. (b) **1817** [see WHITE PELICAN]. **1874** COUES *Birds* N.W. 309 *Nyctea Scandiaca*, . . . Great White or Snowy Owl. . . . It is not exclusively nocturnal. **1917** *Birds of Amer.* II. 115.

+White pelican. A large American pelican, *Pelecanus erythrorhynchos.* — **1817** S. BROWN *Western Gazetteer* 146 Those of the feathered tribe which may be considered as local, consist of the white pelican, . . . sandhill crane, great white owl [etc.]. **1894** TORREY *Fla. Sketch-Book* 66, I saw . . . a couple of white pelicans, the only ones I found in Florida. **1917** *Birds of Amer.* I. 102 The largest colonies of White Pelicans in the United States are found on Malheur Lake, Klamath Lake, and Clear Lake reservations.

White people. Members of the white race as distinguished from Indians or Negroes. — **1751** *Va. State P.* I. 245 Mr. Andrew Muntour . . . is the proper person to be our Interpreter, having a good Character, both amongst White people and Indians. **1853** RAMSEY *Tennessee* 112 The Indians were appeased by this instance of condescension in the white-people. **1875** *Chicago Tribune* 6 Nov. 5/6, I never before saw such determination to carry an election, the whole body of the white people being moved by a common impulse.

+White perch. Any one of various American fishes as the silver perch, calico bass, crappie, etc. Also attrib.

1775 BURNABY *Travels* 15 These waters are stored with incredible quantities of fish, such as sheeps-heads, rock-fish, drums, white pearch. **1814** MITCHILL *Fishes N.Y.* 420 White Perch. (*Bodianus pallidus*.) . . . Colour whitish, with a dark hue according to the angle of reflected light. **1869** *Rep. Comm. Agric. 1868* 331 On the 13th of May, I had also obtained a quantity of white-perch spawn. **1882** JORDAN & GILBERT *Fishes N. Amer.* 567 *H[aploidonotus] grunniens.* . . . White Perch; Croaker. . . . Great Lakes to Texas. **1897** *N.Y. Forest, Fish, & Game Comm. 2d Rep.* 241 *Morone americana*, . . . White Perch, . . . is abundant in fresh-water lakes of Central Park, New York, and Prospect Park, Brooklyn. **1911** *Rep. Fisheries 1908* 313 'White perch' [is applied] to a surf-fish (*Phanerodon furcatus*) on the California coast.

+White pine.

1. A species of pine (*Pinus strobus*) found in the East and Middle West; also, one of several other species of pine, as the sugar pine and the lodgepole pine.

1709 [see PITCH PINE 1]. **1792** BELKNAP *Hist. New Hampshire* III. 102 The White Pine . . . is undoubtedly the prince of the American forest. **1815** DRAKE *Cincinnati* 83 The white pine . . . is said to be occasionally seen on the waters of the Muskingum. **1860** CURTIS *Woody Plants N.C.* 25 White Pine. . . . The wood . . . is applied to a far greater variety of economical uses than that of any other Pine. **1897** SUDWORTH *Arborescent Flora* 4 ff. [7 species so called]. **1905** *Forestry Bureau Bul.* No. 63, 6 The seed of the white pine is borne in a cone.

2. A tree belonging to one of these species; also, the wood of these trees.

1682 *Providence Rec.* XIV. 113 A great white pine . . . is ye norwesterne corner bound. **1723** *Doc. Hist. N.Y. State* I. 720 But suppose the People could be restrained from cutting any White Pines. a**1797** [see BASSWOOD 1]. **1883** *Harper's Mag.* Jan. 209/1 The bedstead and bureaus . . . are made of varnished white pine. **1906** [see PITCH PINE 1].

3. *attrib.* and *comb.* **a.** Designating things made of white pine.

1742 *Boston Rec.* 300 The Committee . . . Are of Opinion . . . [that] there be Erected a Breast Work of Square White Pine Timber. **1771** *N.H. Gazette* 30 Aug. (Ernst), This to inform such persons as are desirous of contracting for white pine masts, yards and bowsprits, . . . to apply to me. **1833** *Niles' Reg.* XLIV. 395/1 The flooring was white pine plank, laid on oaken sleepers. **1834** in *Atlantic Mo.* XXVI. 742 Stood half an hour to see a man cutting shingles out of white-pine blocks, with a circular saw. **1844** *Knickerb.* May 444 The clean white-pine buckets, . . . into which the sap drips from the spiles, are made expressly for this use. **1872** 'MARK TWAIN' *Roughing It* 162, [I] took up quarters with the untitled plebeians in one of the fourteen white-pine cot-bedsteads.

b. Designating areas where white pine is the prevailing growth.

1789 MORSE *Amer. Geog.* 197 The tract . . . is white pine land. *a*1817 DWIGHT *Travels* II. 160 The white-pine plains are of stiff loam.

c. Designating insects that damage the white pine.

1868 *Rep. Comm. Agric. 1867* 73 The white pine worm, *Lophyrus abbottii*, . . . lives principally on white pine. **1905** *Forestry Bureau Bul.* No. 63, 14 The white pine weevil (*Pissodes strobi*) is a reddish-brown snout beetle.

∗**White poplar. a.** =SILVER POPLAR. +**b.** The aspen (*Populus tremuloides*) or a variety of this. +**c.** =TULIP TREE. — **1774** [see HOLLY 1]. **1814** PURSH *Flora Amer.* II. 383 *Liriodendron obtusiloba.* . . . Generally known by the name of Tulip-tree, or White and Yellow Poplar. **1837** PECK *Gaz. Illinois* 235 Besides other timber, here is yellow and white poplar. **1897** SUDWORTH *Arborescent Flora* 128 f., 136, 194 [4 species so called].

White rabbit. +Any one of various American hares, as the snow-shoe rabbit, that have white fur in winter. — **1789** MORSE *Amer. Geog.* 198 In this country are . . . brown squirrils, white rabbits, bears [etc.]. **1805** SIBLEY in *Ann. 9th Congress* 2 Sess. 1082 Wild hogs are likewise plenty in their country, and white rabbits, or hares. **1842** *Nat. Hist. N.Y., Zoology* I. 95 The Northern Hare . . . is often called the White Rabbit.

White race. The Caucasian, as contrasted, usually, with the black, race. — **1855** *Chicago Times* 2 March 2/1 Emancipation would degrade the slave and deteriorate the white race. **1900** *Congress. Rec.* 15 Feb. 1843/1 The negro . . . has been forced prematurely into political contests with the superior white race.

+**White Republican.** A white man, as distinguished from a Negro, who is a member of the Republican party. — **1863** HOPLEY *Life in South* I. 5 'Black and white republicans,' 'new and old line whigs,' 'fire-eaters' and 'democrats,' were given up in despair. **1893** *Congress. Rec.* 2 Oct. 2044/1 The affection of Damon and Pythias . . . is not a circumstance to the love of the white Republican for the negro while the ballots are going in. **1903** *Forum* Oct. 177 Many white Republicans are already leaving that party because they do not desire to affiliate themselves with the negro.

White ribbon. A ribbon or piece of ribbon of a white color +worn by those campaigning for prohibition of the sale of alcoholic liquors. — **1893** HOLLEY *Samantha at World's Fair* 275 Denmark has a display of seven little wimmen a-wearin' the white ribbon. **1899** *Scribner's Mag.* XXV. 104 If the wearers of the white ribbon were to make inquiries of the dealers in glass-ware, they would find that no fewer married couples . . . buy wine glasses as a necessary table article.

∗**White root.** +**a.** =BUTTERFLY WEED. +**b.** =NONDO. — **1791** BARTRAM *Travels* 47*n.*, [The carminative *Angelica lucida* is] called Nondo in Virginia: by the Creek and Cherokee traders, White Root. **1822** WOODS *English Prairie* 230 In moist places, there is a small shrub, named white-root, which must be grubbed up before it can be ploughed. **1894** *Amer. Folk-Lore* VII. 94 *Asclepias tuberosa*, white root, Mass.

White rot. One of various wood rots chiefly caused by fungi of the genus *Fomes*. — **1834** AUDUBON *Ornith. Biog.* II. 237 They cut at both its extremities [*sc.* of a fallen tree], and sound the whole of its bark, to enable them to judge if the tree has been attacked by the white rot.

+**White rule.** *S.* Rule or government exercised by white people as contrasted with Negroes. Also *white-ruled* a. — **1868** *N.Y. Herald* 4 July 4/3 The Texan delegates observe these instructions in their intercourse with representatives from the white-ruled States. **1876** [see DIVIDE *v.* 2]. **1884** *Century Mag.* April 863/2 There is a strong sentiment which would crystallize into perpetuity the present condition of absolute white rule and negro subjection in political affairs.

White rumped, *a.* Of birds: Having the rump covered with white feathers. {1782–} — **1839** AUDUBON *Ornith. Biog.* V. 336 White-Rumped Cormorant. *Phalacrocorax Leuconotus.* **1858** BAIRD *Birds Pacific R.R.* 113 *Melanerpes erythrocephalus.* . . . Red-headed woodpecker. . . . White-rumped woodpecker. **1874** COUES *Birds N.W.* 487 *Tringa fuscicollis.* Bonaparte's Sandpiper; White-rumped Sandpiper. **1881** *Amer. Naturalist* XV. 210 One of the earliest birds to nest in the vicinity of Los Angeles, was the white-rumped Shrike (*Collyrio excubitoroides*). **1917** *Birds of Amer.* II. 164 Marsh Hawk, *Circus hudsonius*. . . . White-rumped Hawk.

+**White sage (brush).** *W.* One of various western American shrubs having whitish leaves, as the sagebush (*Artemisia mexicana*). — **1870** BEADLE *Utah* 457 Tracts, entirely barren a score of years ago, . . . present a scant growth of grease-wood, which is succeeded in time by whitesage brush. **1877** W. WRIGHT *Big Bonanza* 278 In Nevada this white sage is the principal food of vast herds of cattle. **1884** W. SHEPHERD *Prairie Exper.* 253 The plains, besides grass, bear the white sage, which is very nutritious. **1898** A. M. DAVIDSON *Calif. Plants* 148 The white sage has a curiously folded lower lip that seems designed to bar out all but the strongest bees.

+**White salmon. a.** The silver salmon, *Oncorhynchus milktschitsch.* **b.** One of various other fishes, as the large-mouthed black bass, of a white or silvery appearance. — **1612** SMITH, etc. *Virginia* I. 15 Of fish we were best acquainted with . . . mullets, white Salmonds, Trowts, Soles [etc.]. **1809** CUMING *Western Tour* 20 The Susquehannah . . . abounds with rock-fish, . . . cat-fish and white salmon. **1856** *Porter's Spirit of Times* 25 Oct. 129/2 One or the other of these fish [the pike-perch and the growler] . . . is also, it is presumed, the *white salmon*, which Capt. John Smith describes. **1911** *Rep. Fisheries 1908* 315 The silver salmon, or white salmon . . . , is found in all rivers from the Sacramento River to Bering Strait.

+**White settlement. a.** A settlement or community of white people. **b.** Settlement or occupancy by white settlers.

(a) 1822 [see CORN-PLANTING]. **1850** GLISAN *Jrnl. Army Life* 18 Many small bands of Indians, removed to this part of our territory a few years ago, to give room for the great expansion of white settlements. **1901** DUNCAN & SCOTT *Allen & Woodson Co., Kansas* 9 The first white settlements in the county were made in the spring and summer of 1855. **(b) 1878** [see ENTERING WEDGE]. **1899** CUSHMAN *Hist. Indians* 145 Howls are heard . . . even this day, 'Open up to white settlement!'

White skin. =PALEFACE 1. *Obs.* {1874–} Also attrib. — **1772** in *Travels Amer. Col.* 525 There was a talk from the Quapas with a White Skin. **1823** DODDRIDGE *Logan* II. ii, Were I angry at Logan I would say that he . . . has been too fond of the white skins. **1840** COOPER *Pathfinder* I. 34 Though these torments belong only to the red-skin natur', . . . white-skin natur' may be, and often has been, agonized by them.

∗**Whitesmith.** A tinsmith. *Obs.* — **1720** *Amer. Wkly. Mercury* 20 Oct. 3/2 Edward Hunt of this City, White-Smith, was indicted for Counterfeiting the Spanish Silver Coin current here. **1788** *Mass. Spy* 12 June 3/1 Federal procession, and order of march . . . 9th whitesmiths. **1820** [see FIRE ENGINE b].

+**White snakeroot. a.** =WILD GINGER. **b.** An American plant (*Eupatorium urticaefolium*), having small white flowers. — **1817–8** EATON *Botany* (1822) 184 *Asarum canadense*, white snakeroot, wild ginger. . . . Root aromatic and stimulant. **1871** *Ill. Agric. Soc. Trans.* VIII. 7 Mr. William Jerry . . . claims to have discovered the cause of Milk-sickness in the plant *Eupatorium ageratoides* (or white Snake-root).

White spruce. {1830– (Loudon *Hortus Brit.* 388)} +Any one of various American spruces, esp. *Picea glauca*. Also attrib. — **1803** LAMBERT *Descr. Genus Pinus* 39 *Pinus alba*. White Spruce Fir. . . . In Canada, Nova Scotia, and the northern parts of New England, it grows in perfection. **1810** MICHAUX *Arbres* I. 18 Abies alba . . . *White or Single Spruce*, . . . dénomination également en usage dans les Etats du Nord, le District de Maine et la Nouvelle Ecosse. **1860** CURTIS *Woody Plants N.C.* 27 White spruce (*A. alba*). This has about the same range in the United States as the *Black Spruce*, but does not extend quite so far to the northward. **1897** SUDWORTH *Arborescent Flora* 34 ff. [4 species so called].

+**White squaw.** A white woman. — **1837** IRVING *Bonneville* II. 174 They . . . were especially eloquent about the white squaws. **1871, 1899** [see PAPOOSE *n.* 2].

White tail. {1611–} +=WHITE-TAILED DEER. Also attrib. — **1872** [see MULE DEER]. **1891** *Fur, Fin & Feather* 176 The white-tails have become scarce and difficult to kill. **1907** WHITE *Arizona Nights* 68 We succeeded in killing a nice, fat white-tail buck.

White-tailed, *a.* {1642–} Of birds and fishes: Having a white tail or one marked with white. (See also next.) — **1818** [see REMORA]. **1828** BONAPARTE *Ornithology* II. 18 [The] White-Tailed Hawk, *Falco Dispar*, . . . we recently discovered to be an inhabitant of North America. **1839** AUDUBON *Ornith. Biog.* V. 200 [The] White-tailed Grous, *Tetrao Leucurus*, . . . is an inhabitant of the Rocky Mountains. **1858** BAIRD *Birds Pacific R.R.* 636 White-tailed Ptarmigan. . . . Northern America to the west. **1872** COUES *Key to Birds* 211 White-tailed Kite. . . . Head, tail and under parts white. **1891** *Cent.* 6912/2 *White-tailed buzzard, Buteo albocaudatus,* a fine large hawk of Texas and southward, having the tail and its coverts white with broad black subterminal zone. *Ib., White-tailed longspur,* the black-shouldered or chestnut-collared longspur, *Centrophanes ornatus*.

+**White tailed deer.** The Virginia deer and allied species or varieties. Also with specifying term. — **1849** *31st Congress 1 Sess.* Sen. Doc. No. 64, 204 [Along the Pecos] we saw for the first time since leaving the Rio Grande the white-tailed or common deer of the States! **1897** HOUGH *Story of Cowboy* 227 In certain parts of the country, too, the white-tailed deer offers sport to the ranch pack. **1917** *Mammals of Amer.* 8 Texas White-tailed Deer.—*Odocoileus texanus.*

∗**White thorn.** Any one of various species of hawthorn, +esp. the American scarlet haw, *Crataegus coccinea*. — **1634** WOOD *New Eng. Prospect* 18 The white thorne affords hawes as bigge as an English Cherrie. **1785** WASHINGTON *Diaries* II. 335 There are great abundance of the White Thorn (now full of the red Berries in clusters). **1817** S. BROWN *Western Gazetteer* 82 These lands produce black walnut, . . . cotton wood, white thorn. **1897** SUDWORTH *Arborescent Flora* 230 *Cratægus tomentosa.* Black Haw. . . . [Also called] White Thorn.

Whitethroat. {1676–} +=next. — *a*1862 THOREAU *Maine Woods* 198 We heard the white throats along the shore. **1892** TORREY *Foot-Path Way* 52 Found to my delight a white-throat. **1904** [see OLIVE 3 b].

+**White-throated sparrow.** A brown sparrow (*Zonotrichia albicollis*) of eastern North America, having a conspicuous white square on the throat. — **1811** WILSON *Ornithology* III. 51 [The] White-Throated Sparrow . . . [winters] in most of the states south of New England. *a*1862 THOREAU *Maine Woods* 198 The note of the white-throated sparrow . . . was the first heard in the morning. **1903** S. E. WHITE *Forest* 90 The white-throated sparrow sings nine different variations of the same song.

White top boot. A boot having a white top or upper. *Obs.* — **1815** in Kittredge *Old Farmer* (1904) 220 To strut in white top boots, . . . drink brandy, and smoke segars, are not the most essential qualifications for a schoolmaster. **1847** J. S. HALL *Book of Feet* 141 The Hessian or Austrian boot . . . was soon afterward introduced into the United States, as was the white-top boot.

+**White top (grass).** +Any one of various pasture grasses, as fowl meadow grass and redtop. — **1819** WARDEN *Statistical Acct. U.S.* II. 8 The grasses are: White clover, white top and red top. **1840** BUEL *Farm-*

er's Companion 228 The white-top or foul meadow is said, by Muhlenburgh, to be a variety of the *A. vulgaris.* **1877** *Vermont Bd. Agric. Rep.* IV. 169 White-top Grass, (*Danthonia spicata,*) makes unwholesome hay.

White-topped, *a.* {1805-} Of wagons: Having a cover of white canvas. — **1849** PARKMAN in *Knickerb.* XXXIII. 10 The plain was covered with the long files of their white topped wagons. **1916** EASTMAN *From Deep Woods* 79 Every road leading to the agency was filled with white-topped lumber wagons.

+**White trash.** **a.** = POOR WHITE TRASH. Also attrib. **b.** An individual belonging to this class. — **1855** M. THOMPSON *Doesticks* 314 The appointments generally at this place might be considered very tasteful by the 'white trash.' **1868** *Putnam's Mag.* I. 705/2, 'I ketched him . . . ,' returned the venerable 'white trash,' indignantly. **1883** *Harper's Mag.* Feb. 423/1 North Carolina was the paradise of the 'white trash.' **1902** BANKS *Newspaper Girl* 149, I see I bein' yor perfessed cook wid a w'ite trash kitchen-maid underneaf me!

White trout. One of various fishes, usually ones having a pale or silvery skin, as the bastard weakfish. {c1640-} — **1737** BRICKELL *N. Carolina* 158 The Salt-Water Trouts, commonly called the White Trouts, . . . have blackish and not Red Spots. **1879** *Scribner's Mo.* Nov. 17/1 Hunters [in Michigan] . . . began to talk of a white-meated fish with all the game qualities of the trout. . . . It was known to them as the 'white trout.' **1897** *N.Y. Forest, Fish, & Game Comm. 2d Rep.* 185 The silvery sides of the fish in summer gave rise to that [name] of 'white trout.' **1911** *Rep. Fisheries 1908* 315 Sea trout.—A name given . . . to the white trout (*Cynoscion nothus*) along the southern coast.

+**White walnut.** **a.** = BUTTERNUT 1. **b.** = SHAGBARK 2. Also attrib.
1743 CLAYTON *Flora Virginica* 190 Juglans alba, . . . White Walnuts. **1785** MARSHALL *Amer. Grove* 67 Butter-nut, or White Walnut. . . . The bark and shells of the nuts dye a good brown colour, scarcely ever fading. **1805** in Young *Jessamine Co., Ky.* 69 The timber is white ash, hickory, . . . white and black walnut. **1857-8** [see BLACK WALNUT 1]. **1897** SUDWORTH *Arborescent Flora* 113 Hicoria ovata, Shagbark (Hickory). . . . [Also called] White Walnut (N.J.).

Whitewash, *n.* {1689-} +A defeat in a game, as baseball, in which the losing side fails to score. *colloq.* Also attrib. — **1875** *Chicago Tribune* 6 July 5/1 The Chicagos barely escaped a complete whitewash, being blanked in eight straight innings. **1884** *Boston Jrnl.* 13 Sept., The Bostons Give the Lawrence Team a Whitewash bath.

*Whitewash, v. +tr. In baseball, to prevent (an opposing team) from scoring in an inning or in a game. — **1868** CHADWICK *Base Ball* 46 A nine is said to be 'whitewashed' when they are put out in an inning without being able to score a single run. **1875** *Chicago Tribune* 10 Aug. 5/4 The St. Louis Club for the first time in their history, were whitewashed this afternoon by the underrated Philadelphias. **1884** *Boston Jrnl.* 2 Oct., Buffalo Whitewashes Providence.

Whitewash brush. A brush used in applying whitewash to a surface. — **1814** *Austin P.* I. (1924) 240, 1 White Wash Brush. **1886** *Boston Jrnl.* 10 July 2/3 A Buffalo street car recently carried . . . a darky with a whitewash brush. **1899** [see next].

Whitewasher. One whose occupation is whitewashing. {1752-} — **1733** *S.C. Gazette* 24 Feb., He's a Bricklayer, Plaisterer and White-washer. **1852** STOWE *Uncle Tom* xlv, G. D——. Three fourths black; whitewasher; from Kentucky; nine years free. **1899** CHESNUTT *Wife of His Youth* 249 He bought a whitewash brush, . . . and began work as a whitewasher.

+**Whiteweed.** Any one of various wild plants having a white flower, esp. the oxeye daisy. Also attrib. — **1803** *Mass. H. S. Coll.* IX. 200 On the upland and meadows grow . . . white weed, red top, clover, and herds grass. **1838** *Mass. Agric. Survey 2d Rep.* 68 The principal weeds that infest the fields . . . are the ox-eyed daisy or white weed . . . and the charlock. **1880** *Harper's Mag.* Sept. 500/2 White-weed [grew] knee-deep along all the straggling paths. **1907** WIGGIN *New Chron. Rebecca* i, [She] began to twine the whiteweed blossoms into a rope.

White wing. {1854-} +1. (See quot. 1891.) Also with specifying terms. +2. A street sweeper. — (1) **1891** *Cent.* 6912/3 *Whitewing,* . . . the white-winged or velvet scoter, sea-coot, or surf-duck. **1917** *Birds of America* I. 150 Black White-wing; . . . May White-wing; . . . Eastern White-wing. (2) **1898** *Kansas City Star* 21 Dec. 4/1 Alderman Herman Gerhart would have the white wings paid every Saturday night. **1904** *N.Y. Tribune* 3 April, Constantinople existed long centuries before Manhattan Island had streets, and yet the only 'white wings' have been the hungry pariah dogs.

*White-winged, a. In the names of birds having wings wholly or partly white. {1728-} — **1835** AUDUBON *Ornith. Biog.* III. 553 The White-Winged Silvery Gull, *Larus Leucopterus.* **1844** *Nat. Hist. N.Y., Zoology* II. 337 The White-winged Coot . . . is much prized for the quantity and quality of its down. **1872** COUES *Key to Birds* 294 Velvet Scoter. White-winged Surf-duck. **1884** *Nat. Museum. Bul* No. 27, 172 *Hydrochelidon leucoptera.* . . . White-winged Black Tern. **1891** *Cent.* 6913/1 *White-winged snowbird,* a variety of the common black snowbird, *Junco hiemalis aikeni,* with white wingbars, found in the mountains of Colorado. **1917** *Birds of Amer.* II. 181 Bobolink. . . . White-winged Blackbird. . . . United with various species of Blackbirds, it pillages the [rice] fields.

+**White-winged crossbill.** A crossbill (*Loxia leucoptera*) of eastern North America. — **1811** WILSON *Ornithology* IV. 48 The White-winged Crossbill is five inches and a quarter long. **1844** *Nat. Hist. N.Y., Zoology* II. 183. **1892** TORREY *Foot-Path Way* 27 Up flew two . . . white-winged crossbills!

+**White-wing(ed) dove.** A pigeon (*Melopelia asiatica*) of the southern states. — **1852** Stansbury *Gt. Salt Lake* 326 Columba Leucoptera. White-winged Dove. **1884** COUES *Key to Birds* 569 *Melopelia leucoptera.* White-wing Dove. **1917** *Birds of Amer.* II. 50 The White-winged Dove [is] perhaps the best known bird of the torrid cactus deserts and mesquite valleys of the southwest.

+**White wolf.** (See quot. 1891.) — **1807** GASS *Journal* 37 Here we found a white wolf dead. **1833** CATLIN *Indians* I. 257 The white wolves . . . follow the herds of buffaloes . . . from one season to another. **1847** PARKMAN in *Knickerb.* XXX. 23 These are the large white and gray wolves, whose deep and awful howl we heard at intervals. **1891** *Cent.* 6959/3 *White wolf,* a whitish variety of the common wolf of North America.

White woman. A woman who is white as distinguished from an Indian or Negro woman. — **1751** GIST *Journals* 41 We left Muskingum, and went W 5 M, to the White Woman's Creek, on which is a small Town; this White Woman was taken away from New England, when she was not above ten Years old, by the French Indians. **1900** *Congress. Rec.* 5 Feb. 1507/2 Manley slandered white women in a scurrilous negro newspaper having a local circulation.

Whitewood. {1683-} +One of various American trees having white or light-colored wood, as the tulip tree or the basswood. Also *whitewood tree.*
1663 *Plymouth Rec.* 66 Lott . . . bounded with . . . a great white wood tree. **1762** CLAYTON *Flora Virginica* 83. **1823** in Schoolcraft *Travels Mississippi Valley* 375 The country . . . is supplied with every variety of excellent timber, consisting chiefly of maple, . . . walnut, white wood, bass wood, &c. **1843** [see SADDLETREE]. **1860** CURTIS *Woody Plants N.C.* 78 These are handsome trees . . . known in the Northern States by the names of *Lime Tree* and *White Wood,* but more generally by that of *Bass Wood.* **1897** SUDWORTH *Arborescent Flora* 135, 198, 271, 273, 301 [5 species listed].

+**b.** The wood of a whitewood tree. Also attrib.
1855 HOLBROOK *Among Mail Bags* 432 'White wood' is considered the best material for the entire [letter] case. **1868** [see BEECH WOOD 2]. **1897** MOORE *How to Build a Home* 90 'White wood' holds nails well and paints and stains well.

*Whiting. +Any of several American fishes, esp. the hake and any species of *Menticirrhus.*
1790 [see DRUM *n.* 3]. **1839** STORER *Mass. Fishes* 132 The Hake . . . is generally known by the fishermen of Massachusetts as the 'Whiting.' **1842** [see KINGFISH 2]. **1888** [see PORKFISH]. **1911** *Rep. Fisheries 1908* 311 Kingfish (*Menticirrhus saxatilis*). . . . It is called . . . 'whiting' in the South.

*Whitlow grass. An early flowering plant (*Draba verna*) formerly thought to be a cure for whitlow. — **1791** MUHLENBERG *Index Florae* 173. **1843** TORREY *Flora N.Y.* I. 63 Common Whitlow-grass. . . . Fields and hillsides. **1891** COULTER *Bot. W. Texas* I. 18.

Whitney. A kind of cloth made at Witney, England. {Witney, 1716-; 1760-} Also attrib. — **1727** *Boston News-Letter* 29 June 2/2 To be Sold by Mr. Thomas Perkins. . . . Wadings, Whitney-Shaggs [etc.]. **1732** *S.C. Gazette* 28/2 Runaway from his Master . . . a white Servant, named Caleb Lowle, . . . having on a red Whitney Coat. **1776** *Essex Inst. Coll.* XLIX. 99 Sold at Mr. Flagg's store . . . grey, crimson and scarlet whitney.

*Whittle, v. tr. and absol. To cut thin shavings from (a stick or shingle) with a knife.
1825 NEAL *Bro. Jonathan* I. 144 One of the boys . . . [was] whittling in the corner. **1836** *S. Lit. Messenger* II. 434 We have seen advocates whittling during a defence, and judges whittling on the bench. **1864** *Wkly. New Mexican* 17 June 1/3 General Grant . . . deliberately whittled a rail until the guns were placed in position. **1884** HOWELLS *Silas Lapham* 69 Having found a pine stick of perfect grain, he abandoned himself to the pleasure of whittling it.

Whittler. One who whittles, esp. as a pastime. — **1839** MARRYAT *Diary Amer.* 1 Ser. I. 236 In some courts they put sticks before noted whittlers to save the furniture. **1853** *La Crosse Democrat* 15 Nov. 2/4 When a man refuses to pay a debt among the Mormons, they send 3 officers, called whittlers, who take their station in front of the debtor's house, each with a jack knife and a bundle of sticks, and whittle away . . . until the delinquent knocks under. **1879** B. F. TAYLOR *Summer-Savory* 138 It is here that in rainy days and winter nights the whittlers, smokers, spitters and talkers gather in. **1907** *St. Nicholas* Sept. 998/1 Ned Saunders, for so our whittler was named, was a city boy.

Whittling. The activity of cutting shavings from a stick. {1614} Also attrib. — **1836** *S. Lit. Messenger* II. 434 Whether the practice of 'whittling' during conversation, has any connection with ease of utterance, is a question too abstruse for my present cursory investigation. **1846** COOPER *Redskins* vii, The precaution of the landlord was far from being unnecessary, and appeared to be taken in good part by all to whom he offered 'whittling-pieces,' some six or eight in the whole. **1886** POORE *Reminisc.* I. 368 The sergeant at arms supplied Sam Houston, U.S. Senator from Texas, with sticks of soft pine wood. . . . There is a picture here of his whittling away, with the huge shavings lying about him.

Whiz(z), *n.* {1620-} **1.** A turmoil. **2.** A celebration. +**3.** *It's a whiz,* or variant: It's an agreement or bargain. *slang.* — (1) **1825** NEAL *Bro. Jonathan* III. 279, I could not—my blood was all in a whizz. (2) **1892** *Harper's Mag.* March 650/1 The prevailing American desire to indulge in what is widely known as an electoral whiz, accompanied by high stepping and a feeling of great wealth. **1905** 'O. HENRY' *Trimmed Lamp* 244 He's going on a whiz to-night. **(3) 1869** 'MARK TWAIN' *Innocents* 426 Each of the seven lifted up his voice and said, It is a whiz. **1888** *N.Y. Times* 30 Dec., I assured him that it was a whizz, rightly interpreting that strange word to mean, a go, or agreed to.

* **Whiz(z)**, *v. tr.* To send with a whiz; to hurry. {1880-} — **1836** IRVING *Astoria* II. 140 He was on the point of whizzing a bullet into the target so tauntingly displayed. **1868** A. D. WHITNEY *P. Strong* 26 They are whizzed to death with work. **1889** *Voice* 17 Jan., The Viceroy Li Hung Chang . . . was whizzed over the line at the rate of 35 or 40 miles an hour.

Whoa haw. A cry of command to a draft animal. Also attrib. — **1848** BRYANT *California* iii. 32 The crack of the ox-goad, the 'whoa-haws' in a loud voice, . . . altogether create a most Babel-like and exciting confusion. **1876** CROFUTT *Trans-continental Tourist* 42 It would never do to omit a description of this famous stream, up the banks of which so many emigrants toiled in the 'whoa haw' times.

* **Whole**, *a.*

See also *Committee of the whole* (under COMMITTEE 2 c), WHOLE HOG, etc.

***1.** Entire. Used, freq. with an effect of exaggeration, before various words of general meaning, usually collective nouns.

The whole biling, the whole boodle, etc., (see BILING *vbl. n.,* BOODLE 2, etc.).

1796 A. BARTON *Disappointment* II, ii, Troth! an here's the hole-tote of us. **1827** SHERWOOD *Gaz. Georgia* 139 *Whole heap,* for many, several, much, large congregation. **1843** STEPHENS *High Life N.Y.* I. 38 With that he flung a hull grist of papers among the crowd. **1904** *San Francisco Chron.* 24 July 22 The American farmer may not be 'the whole thing,' but he is so important a part of the industrial machine that he cannot suffer a serious injury without affecting all the running gear. **1922** SANDBURG *Slabs Sunburnt West* 8 It is easy to come here a stranger and show the whole works, write a book, fix it all up.

+**2.** *To go (for) the whole,* to go the whole way; to accept to the fullest extent.

1821 *Mass. Spy* 10 Jan. (Th.), Going for the whole. **1824** *Niles' Reg.* 20 March 36/2 This is what some people call 'going the whole.' **1836** *Jeffersonian* (Albany) 9 June 136 (Th.), I go the whole, sir. Intemperance is one of the greatest evils of our land. **1910** J. W. TOMPKINS *Mothers & Fathers* 79 We went the whole—I mean, we gave the baby the full Suzanna McMoogle.

+**b.** *To go the whole animal, creature,* etc.

To go the whole figure, (see FIGURE *n.* b); *to go (the) whole hog,* (see WHOLE HOG 1).

1833 *Sketches D. Crockett* 40 But didn't I go the whole animal? **1834** CARRUTHERS *Kentuckian* I. 188, I'm flabbergasted! if that ain't what I call goin the whole cretur. **1840** *Valentine Vox* xlii (Th.), Then of course you mean to go the whole quadruped. **1848** BURTON *Waggeries* 22 We go the hull shoat with them.

3. *Whole-wheat bread,* bread of flour made from the entire wheat kernel, +from which a portion of the bran may have been removed.

1903 *Harper's Bazar* Oct. 981 Two [sandwiches] of whole-wheat bread with peanut butter.

Whole-hearted, *a.* {1855-} +Of a person: Earnest, good-hearted, kind. — **1840** CHANNING *Let. to Miss Aikin* 18 July, What a whole-hearted man! as we Yankees say. **1873** 'MARK TWAIN' 323 He will help us, I suppose? Balloon is a whole-hearted fellow. **1890** JEWETT *Strangers* 58 You're real whole-hearted, Mis' Trimble.

Whole hog.

1. *To go (the) whole hog,* to involve one's self to the fullest extent; to go the limit. *slang.* {1830, in Canada; 1839-} Freq. in political use.

1829 D. WEBSTER *Private Corr.* (1857) I. 467 He [Andrew Jackson] will either go with the party, as they say in New York, or go the whole hog, as it is phrased elsewhere. **1835** H. C. TODD *Notes* 46 In Virginia originated *Go the whole hog,* a political phrase marking the democrat from a federalist. **1844** *Prophet* (N.Y.) 14 Sept. (Th.), We go 'whole hog' for Jeffersonian democracy. **1858** *Harper's Mag.* Jan. 278/2 Nobody but a Clay man would have [stolen half a pig]; . . . a Jackson man . . . would have gone the whole hog! **1870** *N.Y. Ledger* July (De Vere), He might just as well go the whole hog and run for Congress, instead of . . . trying to be sent to the Legislature.

2. In figurative or allusive use as a symbol of entireness, completeness, acceptability, etc. *slang.*

1832 CLAY *Speeches* (1860) II. 114 The senator modestly claimed only an old smoked, rejected joint; but the stomach of his excellency yearned after the whole hog! **1854** BENTON *30 Years' View* I. 470/1 The coin itself was burlesqued, in mock imitations of brass or copper, with grotesque figures, . . . the 'whole hog' and the 'better currency' . . . being the favorite devices. **1883** in Fleming *Hist. Reconstruction* II. 434 Some of them . . . proved better men than the Republicans, but still we don't put the whole hog on them.

3. Attrib., chiefly in political usage, in sense: Thoroughgoing. {whole-hogg defender, 1853}

See also WHOLE-HOG (JACKSON) MAN.

1833 *Congress. Deb.* 11 Feb. 1676 The gentleman from Kentucky . . . was designated by many as 'a whole hog' nullifier. **1836** *Raleigh* (N.C.) *Standard* 3 Nov. 2/1 (Th. S.), Mr. Hendricks [of Indiana] has lately declared himself 'a whole hog Van Buren man.' **1840** KENNEDY *Quodlibet* 51 [They were] thorough-bred, whole-hog democrats. **1846** *Xenia Torch-Light* 22 Jan. 2/1 Mr. Gallagher introduced some 'whole-hog' Oregon resolutions. **1912** *Congress. Rec.* 1 Jan. 4/2 Whole-hog standpatters are about as scarce as whole-hog progressives.

+**Whole-hog (Jackson) man.** A thoroughgoing supporter of Andrew Jackson or his political principles. Now hist. — **1832** BIDDLE *Senator Grundy's Polit. Conduct Reviewed* 22 (Th. S.), [Mr. Felix Grundy says, 'I claim to be a whole-hog Jackson man, because I voted for that fellow Biddle.' **1838** HONE *Diary* I. 308 Three other thorough whole-hog men . . . have no . . . notion of political honesty. **1847** FORD *Hist. Illinois* 105 Politicians in those days of the Jackson party were divided into whole hog men, and nominal Jackson men. **1855** I. C. PRAY *Mem. J. G. Bennett* 141 James Gordon Bennett . . . is a thorough-going, 'whole-hog' Jackson man.

Wholesale, *v.* **1.** *tr.* To sell at wholesale or in quantity; to sell at the wholesale price. Also transf. **2.** *intr.* **a.** Of a merchant: To engage in selling at wholesale. **b.** Of a commodity: To be sold in large quantities, or at a wholesale price. — **(1) 1800** WEEMS *Letters* II. 152 For this I w[oul]d instantly wholesale my books & quit the business forever. **1859** *Harper's Mag.* Feb. 426/2 Considering the way the rascal came by the goods, I don't think the Court can afford to wholesale them to him. **(2) 1881** *Ore. State Jrnl.* 1 Jan. 7 We are prepared to Wholesale and Retail Cheaper than any place in this city. **1885** *Harper's Mag.* Jan. 289/1 American ladies' shoes, wholesaling at $1.50 per pair.

Wholesale, *adv.* In large quantity or at a wholesale price; at or by wholesale. {1866-} — **1759** *Newport Mercury* 5 June 4/1 To be Sold, Wholesale, . . . Bearskins, Beaver Coating [etc.]. **1883** GOODE *Fisheries Industries U.S.* 47 'Count' Clams, the largest size, . . . sell for $3 per barrel, wholesale. **1908** GALE *Friendship Village* 4 Mis' Jeweller Sprague . . . had had only six bread and butter knives, her that could get wholesale too.

+**Whole-souled,** *a.* Hearty; generous; noble-minded. {1893} — **1834** CARRUTHERS *Kentuckian* I. 190 [The New Yorkers] are a whole-souled people, and I like 'em. **1888** *Manhattan Athletic Club Chronicle* (F.), If this whole-souled gentleman should ever visit New York City, he will be extended a right royal welcome by the Manhattan Athletic Club. **1908** *N.Y. Ev. Post* 22 Oct. (Th.), One of the things Mr. Taft does best is to smile upon people in a genuinely friendly, whole-souled, frank spirit, and make them like him.

Whoop, *n.* A loud cry, shout, or yell {1600-}; +a war whoop. Used chiefly of Indians.

See also DEATH WHOOP, INDIAN WHOOP.

1675 in I. Mather *K. Philip's War* (1862) 246 They signified their sense of approach by their whoops. **1753** GIST *Journals* 85 We grew uneasy, and then he said two whoops might be heard to his cabin. **1829** COOPER *Wish-ton-Wish* iv, I never knew an Indian raise his whoop when a scout had fallen into the hands of the enemy. **1905** BELASCO *Girl of Golden West* (1925) I. 57 The cheerful glow of kerosene lamps, the rattle of poker chips, and an occasional 'whoop,' show that life in the Polka is in full swing.

+**b.** In allusive use, with reference to the enthusiasm or triumph manifested by a whoop.

1889 'MARK TWAIN' *Conn. Yankee* 110 This . . . report lacked whoop and crash and lurid description. **1911** HARRISON *Queed* 318 If you'll only let her stand two years, take my word for it, she'll go through with a whoop.

* **Whoop,** *v.*

1. *tr.* and *intr.* Of Indians: To yell or shout; to utter with a cry or yell.

See also HOOP *v.* 1.

1754 *Mass. H. S. Coll.* 3 Ser. V. 25 [The Indians] take what rum they think proper, whooping and yelping as if they gloried in their depredations. **1775** ADAIR *Indians* 144 They fall on eager and merciless, whooping their revengeful noise, and thrashing their captive. **1865** PARKMAN *Pioneers of France* 44 An Indian chief . . . ran to meet them, whooping and clamoring welcome.

+**2.** *To whoop up. slang* or *colloq.²* **a.** To promote or praise unrestrainedly; to ballyhoo. **b.** To arouse enthusiasm in (people); to excite. **c.** To raise.

See also HOOP *v.* 2.

1885 *South Fla. Sentinel* (Orlando) 5 Aug. 3/3 Whoop up Florida to those Yankees. **1889** FARMER 78/1 The boys have whooped up the State to boom for Smith. **1894** HARTE *Protegee of Jack Hamlin's* 159 He's one of them McHulishes whose name in them old history times was enough to whoop up the boys and make 'em paint the town red. **1897** *Congress. Rec.* 6 July 2358/1 No amount of mere 'whooping up,' by press or otherwise, can make the mills appear to run and society to seem prosperous. **1904** *N.Y. Sun* 8 Sept. 10 The bail was reduced to $10,000, but was whooped up to $15,000 when Larry was rearrested.

+3. *To whoop things* (*it* or *them*) *up.* **a.** To indulge in noisy revelry; to make things lively.

1884 *Harper's Mag.* Aug. 472/2 He whoops it up with the plain people. **1887** T. STEVENS *Around World on Bicycle* I. 11 In the language of the gold fields, [they] 'turned themselves loose,' 'made things hum,' and 'whooped 'em up' around the bar-room of their village. **1903** *N.Y. Sun* 18 Nov. 4 Three boys broke into the Garden and began to whoop things up.

b. To act to stir up enthusiasm.

1888 *Century Mag.* May 156 His rival is a prominent politician, with an abundance of party workers to 'whoop it up' for him. **1891** HARTE *First Family Tasajara* 4 What did we whoop up things here last spring to elect Kennedy to the legislation [*sic*] for? **1906** *N.Y. Ev. Post* 29 Oct. 1 The Hearst contingent, spurred by the Hearst papers, will 'whoop it up' with increasing fervor.

+Whoopee, *interj.* and *n.* [f. WHOOP *n.*] **1.** *interj.* An exclamation of strong emotion. (See also HOOPEE *interj.*) **2.** *n.* An instance of exclaiming of *whoopee.* — (1) **1862** *Harper's Mag.* July 282/1 He yelled at the top of his voice, 'Whoopee! Whiskey only twenty-five cents a gallon!' **1874** G. C. EGGLESTON *Rebel's Recoll.* 56 You may reconstruct the men, . . . but how are you going to reconstruct the women? *Whoop-ee!* **1888** GRIGSBY *Smoked Yank* (1891) 61 Whoopee! How the old man did rave! **1906** 'O. HENRY' *Heart of West* 82 You eat chili-concarne-con-huevos and then holler 'Whoopee!' (2) **1880** 'MARK TWAIN' *Tramp Abroad* 80 Then I propped myself against M. Gambetta's back, and raised a rousing '*Whoop-ee!* **1895** *Outing* XXVI. 428/2 John's 'whoopee' had caused a little ebon . . . to set open the gates.

Whooper. {1660-} +A sand-hill crane. — **1886** *Leslie's Mo.* Oct. 503/1 The scattered fields of sod corn . . . are beset . . . with huge droves of long-legged 'whoopers.'

+Whoop hymn. 'A weird melody chanted by the colored fishermen of the Potomac river while hauling the seine: more fully called *fishing-shore whoop-hymn*' (*Cent.*).

+Whooping crane. The large white crane (*Grus americana*), or a related species. So called because of the loud, raucous cry. (See also HOOPING CRANE.) — **1791** W. BARTRAM *Travels* 433 They were geese, brant, gannet, and the great and beautiful whooping crane (*grus alber*). **1839** TOWNSEND *Narrative* 201 We saw here the whooping crane, and white pelican, numerous. **1879** BISHOP *4 Months in Sneak-box* 108 Whooping-cranes . . . and Sand-hill cranes . . . , in little flocks, dotted the grassy prairies. **1917** *Birds of Amer.* I. 200/2 The Whooping Crane is doomed to extinction.

+Whooping owl. A hoot owl. — **1781** S. PETERS *Hist. Conn.* (1829) 197 The tree-frogs, whipperwills, and whooping-owls, serenade the inhabitants every night with music. **1837** [see HORNED OWL].

‖**Whoop-jamboree,** *a.* High-flown. *slang.* — **1873** 'MARK TWAIN' & WARNER *Gilded Age* 21 He's come back to the Forks with jist a hell's-mint o' whoop-jamboree notions.

‖**Whoop-jamboreehoo.** A noisy demonstration or outcry. *slang.* — **1884** 'MARK TWAIN' *H. Finn* xxix, Don't do anything but just the way I am telling you; if you do, they will suspicion something and raise whoop-jamboreehoo. **1894** — in *St. Nicholas* March 399 Me and Jim went all to pieces with joy, and began to shout whoopjamboreehoo.

Whoosh, *v.* and *interj.* (See quotations.) {woosh, 1823, *dial.*; 1830-, *dial.*, in allied senses} — **1848** J. MITCHELL *Nantucketisms* 41 *Whoosh*, to whoosh is to back a horse. *a*1870 CHIPMAN *Notes on Bartlett* 511 *Whoosh.* . . . Often used in backing oxen.

* Whop, Whap, *v.* +*intr.* To move the body suddenly and violently. — **1824** *Mo. Intelligencer* 29 May 1/3, I wonder they don't break to splinters Things, they whop round so like thrashers. **1891** *Cent.* 6917/1 *Whop, whap,* . . . to plump suddenly down, as on the ground; flop; turn suddenly: as, she whopped down on the floor; the fish whopped over. (U.S.)

+Whore fair. (See quotation.) — **1699** E. WARD *Trip New-Eng.* 11 Their Lecture-Days [in New Eng.] are call'd by some amongst them, *Whore Fair*, from the Levity and Wanton Frollicks of the Young People.

* Whort(le). Short for WHORTLEBERRY. Also attrib. — **1764** HUTCHINSON *Hist. Mass.* I. 485 Travellers are wont to refresh themselves with . . . rasberries, cherries and whorts. **1791** MUHLENBERG *Index Florae* 168. **1852** ARTHUR & CARPENTER *Hist. Kentucky* 108 Downing slipped aside and hid himself in a thick cluster of whortle-bushes.

* Whortleberry. (See also HURTLEBERRY.)

1. +**a.** The fruit of any one of various species of *Gaylussacia*, or the plant bearing such fruit. *** b.** The fruit of any one of various other plants, esp. those of the genus *Vaccinium*, or the plant bearing such fruit.

1702 C. MATHER *Magnalia* (1853) II. 357 Sometimes we liv'd on wortle berries, sometimes on a kind of wild cherry. **1812** STODDARD *Sk. Louisiana* 168 The country to the north of lake Pontchartraine furnishes plenty of whortleberries. **1836** EDWARDS *Hist. Texas* 66 The names of the trees . . . [and] shrubs. . . [include] the Prickly Ash, the Shin-wood, the Spoon-wood, . . . the Whortleberry. *c*1891 O'BEIRNE in Dale & Rader *Okla. Hist.* (1930) 637 Bear hunting in these mountains is at its best when the huckleberry (or whortleberry) is ripening.

2. With specifying term.

See also BLACK WHORTLEBERRY, BLUE WHORTLEBERRY.

1784 *Amer. Acad. Mem.* I. 438 The Choke Whortleberry . . . is unpalatable. **1785** MARSHALL *Amer. Grove* 158 Privet-leaved Whortleberry. **1817-8** EATON *Botany* (1822) 505 Black-blue whortleberry. . . . Very

branching. **1836** LINCOLN *Botany* App. 147 High whortleberry. . . . Berries large, black, sub-acid.

3. Attrib. with *bush, cup, excursion,* etc.

1770 FORSTER tr. Kalm *Travels* I. 66 *Vaccinium* . . . , a species of whortleberry shrub. **1784** BELKNAP *Jrnl. Tour to White Mts.* (1876) 20 Pitch pine, mixed with white oak and whortleberry bushes. **1825** NEAL *Bro. Jonathan* II. 340, I wouldn't allow one of them to make up . . . a whortle-berry pudding. **1832** CHILD *Frugal Housewife* 67 Whortleberry Pie. Whortleberries make a very good common pie. **1836** *Knickerb.* VIII. 287 On they [the cattle] go, . . . now here, and anon far over the whortleberry plain. **1841** *Lowell Offering* I. 17 We younkers were on a whortleberry excursion. **1850** S. F. COOPER *Rural Hours* 73 The whortleberry-cups are hanging thickly on their low branches. **1860** *Harper's Mag.* Nov. 789/1 My brothers came one morning for me to . . . make one of a whortleberry party to the mountain. **1868** *Amer. Naturalist* II. 133, I was in Condersport [*sic*], Pa., in whortle-berry time.

Whortleberrying. The seeking or gathering of whortleberries. — **1815** *Holyoke Diaries* 176 Went Whortleberrying.

*Why, *interj.* +*Why, certainly,* (see quot. 1889). — **1889** FARMER 558/2 *Why, Certainly!*—An Eastern phrase—one of the more delicate American catch-phrases, signifying either acquiescence, or employed as a variant of 'Well, really!' **1903** R. HALL *Pine Grove House* 93 Harold gave the American assent, 'Why certainly.'

+Whyo. [O why-oh-why-oh, a signal cry.] A ruffian or holdup man. — **1889** FARMER 195 These nicknames are, like other fashions, continually changing, the *dead-rabbits* of the last decade being now called Whyos. **1901** RIIS *Making of American* 240, I knew them—the Why-ōs, the worst cutthroats in the city. *Ib.* 279 Headquarters of the Whyo Gang.

Wickerwork.

1. Work made with intertwined wickers; a structure made in this way. {1719-}

1758 *Lett. to Washington* II. 365 [This camp] is slightly fortified with a parapet of wicker work, extreamly neat, rammed full of earth **1847** EMORY *Military Reconn.* 85 Each abode consists of a dome-shaped wicker-work, . . . thatched with straw or cornstalks. *a*1861 WINTHROP *Canoe & Saddle* 35 [He] is stopped by a shield of wicker-work.

2. Attrib. with *cage, case,* etc.

1858 VIELÉ *Following Drum* 184 [The carriage-house] was full of wicker-work cages of strange and beautiful birds. *a*1861 WINTHROP *Canoe & Saddle* 204 This fashionable martyr was being papoosed in a tight-swathing wicker-work case. **1877** *Harper's Mag.* April 678/2 A wicker-work fence, inwoven with cedar, formed the boundary of what resembled the eyrie of a mountain eagle. **1884** *Rep. Comm. Agric.* 170 The wicker-work sofas and chairs of native workmanship are exceedingly comfortable looking articles. **1898** HARPER *S. B. Anthony* I. 267 The sure panacea for such ills . . . is a wicker-work cradle and a dimple-cheeked baby.

* Wicket.

+1. Cricket or a game based on cricket.

1726 SEWALL *Diary* III. 372 Sam. Hirst . . . went into the Common to play at Wicket. **1841** *Picayune* 25 May 2/2 Who has not played 'barn ball' in his boyhood, . . . and 'wicket' in his manhood? **1871** [see ROUND BALL]. **1904** *Hartford Courant* 19 Aug. 13 The ancient and honorable game of wicket . . . is practically cricket in an abridged form.

2. A hurdle.

1846 J. G. SAXE *Progress* (1847) 12 Each great science, to the student's pace, Stands like the wicket in a hurdle race.

+3. One of the hoops used in croquet.

1866 A. D. WHITNEY *L. Goldthwaite* vi, Leslie came in and found her at her window that overlooked the wickets. **1887** STOCKTON *Hundredth Man* viii, She went through her wickets as rapidly as possible, and ended in becoming a rover.

4. (See quotation.)

1891 *Amer. Folk-Lore* IV. 230 Kick the Wicket. . . . The boy who is 'it' places the wicket, which is sometimes made of wood, and sometimes of a piece of old rubber hose, against the tree or post chosen as home, and then stations himself . . . ready to catch it when it is kicked by the other players.

+Wickiup. [Algonquian.] **1.** A brush hut or mat-covered house used by Indians in the West. **2.** *transf.* A shanty used by a white man. (See also WAKIUP.) — (1) **1857** *Jrnl. of Discourses* V. 80 (Th.), We asked which was the way to Jacob's 'Wicky-up.' **1885** *Century Mag.* April 842 Many still adhere to the 'wicky-up'—a shapeless hut made from a combination of brush and mats woven from reeds. **1897** *Scribner's Mag.* XXII. 569/1 In the shade of the wickiup . . . sat Wet Dog. (2) **1876** *Sun* (N.Y.) 10 May 2/6 Come up and see me at my wickiup in Montana. **1897** LEWIS *Wolfville* 28 This Wilkins lives in a wickeyup out on the aige of the town.

+Wickup. 1. =WICOPY 1. Also attrib. **2.** =WICOPY 2. — (1) **1704** *Providence Rec.* V. 244 Two trees growing out of one Roote Called Wickupp trees. **1897** SUDWORTH *Arborescent Flora* 302 *Tilia americana.* Basswood. . . . [Also called] Wickup (Mass.). (2) **1891** *Amer. Folk-Lore* IV. 148 *Epilobium angustifolium* we only knew by the name our grandmother taught us, *Wickup*.

Wicky. {1681-} +Sheep laurel (*Kalmia angustifolia*) or hairy laurel (*K. hirsuta*). — **1860** CURTIS *Woody Plants N.C.* 99 Wicky . . . is a poisonous plant, especially to sheep, and in some places is called *Sheep Laurel*. **1901** MOHR *Plant Life Ala.* 654 Wicky. . . . Low sandy pine barrens.

+**Wicopy.** Also **wickopick, wickoby,** etc. [Algonquian; cf. Cree *wikupiy* 'inner bark.']

1. The leatherwood or the basswood.

1778 CARVER *Travels* 499 The Wickopick or Suckwick appears to be a species of the white wood. 1846 BROWNE *Trees Amer.* 422 The marsh dirca or leather-wood, (*Dirca palustris*,) sometimes also called *wickoby*, is a native from Maine and Canada to Georgia. 1870 *Amer. Naturalist* IV. 217 Leather-wood . . . , also called Wicopy, with pale yellowish flowers is a curious shrub. 1894 ROBINSON *Danvis Folks* 27 Sam saw a sprawling moose-wood or wicopy close at hand.

2. One or other species of willow herb; fireweed.

1844 S. M. FULLER *Summer on Lakes* 33 The flame-like flower I was taught afterward by an Indian girl to call the Wickopee.

Wide-awake.

1. A soft felt hat with a wide brim. {1837–}

1853 LOWELL in *Putnam's Mag.* Nov. 462/2 'This is a Maine dew,' said a shaggy woodman cheerily, as he shook the water out of his wide-awake. 1873 'MARK TWAIN' & WARNER *Gilded Age* 154 'Well,' said the vice-president . . . pulling his wideawake down over his forehead.

+**2.** In the political campaign of 1860 and later, a supporter of Abraham Lincoln; freq., in pl., an organization of supporters of Lincoln.

1860 E. COWELL *Diary* 203 Mr. Lincoln arrived on Tuesday last and was serenaded by a Band of Wideawakes. 1887 [see RAIL-SPLITTER 2]. 1917 B. MATTHEWS *These Many Years* 47 The torchlight procession of Lincoln's supporters, the glittering parade of the 'wide-awakes,' as they were called.

3. One who is wide-awake intellectually.

1890 C. MARTYN *W. Phillips* 122 There was then a circle of wide-awakes meeting at irregular intervals.

+**4.** The sooty tern. Also attrib.

1917 *Birds of Amer.* I. 68 Sooty Tern, *Sterna fuscata*. . . . [Also called] Egg Bird; Wide-awake. *Ib.* 71 They never rest or swim on the water and, apparently, get so little sleep that they are called the 'Wide-awake Terns.'

+**Wide-awake club.** The Wide-awakes (sense 2). — 1867 *Atlantic Mo.* June 662/1 The Wide-Awake Club . . . issued, in due time, in sixty-six regiments of loyal Missouri volunteers. 1870 *Congress. Globe* 23 June 4770/1, I remember the Wide Awake Club that I belonged to, and the Wide Awake cape that I wore.

Wide-awake hat. = WIDE-AWAKE 1. {1841–} — 1855 *Chicago Times* 17 May 1/7 Some friend sent us, the other day, a 'wide-awake' hat. 1884 'CRADDOCK' *Where Battle Was Fought* 62 His old wide-awake hat was pushed back.

* **Widgeon.** A wild duck of the genus *Mareca*, esp. *M. americana*. (Cf. AMERICAN WIDGEON.) — 1610 *Estate of Va.* 30 The riuers . . . are couered with flocks of Wild-foule: as . . . teal, wigeons, hearons, bitters. 1794 *Mass. H. S. Coll.* I Ser. III. 199 Sea fowl are plenty on the shores and in the bay; particularly the gannet, . . . widgeon, and peep. 1835 AUDUBON *Ornith. Biog.* III. 15 The whole surface of open water is covered with Mallards, Widgeons, . . . and Green-winged Teals. 1907 LILLIBRIDGE *Trail* 276 They were still there: . . . greyish speckled widgeon.

* **Widow.**

1. *Card-playing.* (See quotations.)

1864 DICK *Amer. Hoyle* (1866) 182 Five cards are dealt to each player, one at a time, and an extra hand is dealt on the table, which is called the 'widow.' 1887 KELLER *Draw Poker* 12 *Widow*, or *Kitty*—A percentage taken out of the pool to defray the expenses of the game or the cost of refreshments. 1898 DICK *Amer. Hoyle* (ed. 17) 228 [In] the game of cinch . . . after the draw, the card or cards remaining undealt must be placed, face down, on the table. This is called the 'widow.'

2. Used in the possessive. **a.** In miscellaneous combinations.

1907 *St. Nicholas* July 799/1 Her lovely, sad face under her widow's bonnet almost broke my heart. 1760 *Newport Mercury* 1 Jan. 3/2 Just Imported . . . and to be Sold by Andrew Heatly, . . . Widows Crape. 1653 *Boston Rec.* X. 3 The thirds of all my lands & housing . . . I give unto my . . . wife . . . according to the last law of our Generall Court made concerning widowes doueries. 1891 *Atlantic Mo.* June 814/1 In New Orleans, the colored people have started a widows' home. 1844 RUPP *Relig. Denominations* 418 In the larger communities, similar houses afford the same advantages to such widows as desire to live retired, and are called Widows' Houses. 1849 LONGFELLOW *Kavanagh* 38 She had on her forehead what is sometimes called a 'widow's peak,'—that is to say, her hair grew down to a point in the middle. 1900 *Congress. Rec.* 19 Jan. 991/2 Why this delay in granting widows' pensions under the old law? 1844 *Knickerb.* XXIII. 214 The lone woman . . . retired to the 'widow's pew,' a pew set apart, in country churches, for the gratuitous accommodation of those in that unhappy condition. 1754 *N.H. Probate Rec.* III. 493 Eleven acres of ye Said Eighty six acres of Land & ye Two thirds of ye house & barn are Inlocked by ye widows thirds. 1912 *Commoner* XII. 11 Mrs. Force . . . has ordered widow's weeds of white.

+**b.** In specific names.

1819 *Western Rev.* I. 371 Black dotted Perch. . . . The vulgar names of this fish are black perch, widow's perch, dotted bass, [etc.]. 1890 *Cent.* 5463/1 S[edum] *pulchellum* of the southern United States is sometimes cultivated under the name of *widow's cross*.

+**Wienerwurst.** [Ger.] Sausage stuffed in long, slender links. Also *wiener* and (colloq.) *wienie*. — 1899 [see FRANKFURTER]. 1904 H. R. MARTIN *Tillie* 34, I'm havin' fried smashed potatoes and wieners. 1920 LEWIS *Main Street* 287 Try some of the new wienies we got in. 1923 WATTS L. *Nichols* 27 [They made] occasional purchases of bananas, candy, wienerwürst, or like eatables.

Wig.

1. A covering of hair for the head, contrived usually with human hair and worn either for fashion or to conceal baldness. {1675–}

1711 *Boston News-Letter* 25 June 2/2 Deserted from Her Majesties Ship the Saphir, . . . Thomas Barrington, a short well set Man, of a brown Complexion, wearing a Wigg. 1858 COOPER *Water Witch* I. 258 Alderman Van Beverout . . . adjusted his wig, like one fully conscious of the value of appearances in this world. 1869 *Boyd's Business Directory* 34 Wigs so natural as to defy detection.

2. A mature, male seal. {1832}

1830 AMES *Mariner's Sk.* 145 These old wigs are more than twice as large as the female seal, and might be mistaken for another species. 1869 *Overland Mo.* III. 391 Full-aged males, [are] called 'wigs.'

3. Attrib. in sense 1 with *block, caul, ribbon, spring.*

1733 Wigg Caul [see LACED *a*]. 1759 *Newport Mercury* 26 June 4/3 Imported . . . and to be sold by Jacob Richardson, . . . Vices and Wig Springs. 1770 *Md. Hist. Mag.* III. 146 We will not hereafter . . . import or cause to be imported . . . Ribbons and Millenery of all Kinds, except Wig-ribbon. 1842 *Knickerb.* XIX. 116 'To judge by Mr. Stripe's expression . . . ' 'Expression! Did you ever hear of the expression of a wig-block?'

Wiggle.

1. (See quotation.)

1831 BUTTRICK *Travels* 78 The water was very bad. . . . After straining it would still exhibit live insects, which they call wiggles.

2. An irregularity of line; a quick movement.

1861 *N.Y. Tribune* 30 May 6/4 You will doubtless observe a certain wiggle in my handwriting. 1869 ALCOTT *Little Women* II. 355 Rob's footstool had a wiggle in its uneven legs. 1898 HAMBLEN *Gen. Manager's Story* 128 With a derisive wiggle of her drawhead she [a train] glided away.

3. A wriggling, twisting movement, esp. of a person's body {1808–, *Sc.* (weegle) and *dial.*}; *the wiggles*, a habit or a fit of making continuous quick movements.

1894 *Educator* (Phila.) Feb. 279 Every fleeting expression of their faces or wiggle of their bodies, [is] to be turned to advantage in teaching conversational language. 1908 'YESLAH' *Tenderfoot S. Calif.* 73 A kid in front of me . . . had the 'wiggles.'

Wiggler. {weegler, 1808 *Sc.*} Something that wiggles, esp. an insect on the surface of water or a worm. — 1859 BARTLETT 498 *Waggletail*, the larva of the mosquito, etc.; also called a wiggler. 1870 EGGLESTON *Queer Stories* 58 Catching wigglers . . . [is] not easy. 1895 *Outing* XXVI. 375/2 I baited with wigglers and cast astern.

Wiggletail. {1888} +The larva of a mosquito or other insect. — 1855 *Chicago Times* 9 Aug. 4/6 The mosquito proceeds from the animalculæ commonly termed the wiggle-tail. a1859 in Bartlett 512 The full development of any number of 'wiggle-tails' to the mosquito stage can be witnessed. a1918 G. STUART *On Frontier* I. 25 The water in the run . . . was so full of . . . 'wiggletails,' that we could neither drink nor use it until it was strained through a cotton cloth.

Wigmaker. One whose business is the making of wigs. {1755–} — 1714 *Boston News-Letter* 13 Sept. 2/2 One Irish Man Servant, who is a good Barber and Wiggmaker. 1775 E. Singleton *Social N.Y.* 247 Henry Wilmot, in Hanover Square, sells . . . prepared hairs of all sorts and wig-makers trimmings. 1885 EGGLESTON in *Century Mag.* April 888/2 The wig-maker's tortures fell upon the natural hair: it was curled, frizzled, and powdered.

* **Wigwag,** *n.* +A signal flag. *colloq.* Also transf. and attrib. — 1886 *Scientific Amer.* LIV. 16/2 In the army wig-wag system, a flag moved to the right and left during the day. 1888 DORSEY *Midshipman Bob* 42 The blood went a hummin' up inter his face, till it looked like a wig-wag. 1910 J. HART *Vigilante Girl* 15 The arrival of the steamer was being telegraphed by its wooden wigwags throughout the city.

Wigwag, *v.* **1.** *tr.* To send (a signal) by waving flags; to move (a lantern or the arms of a semaphore) in a particular way for the purpose of signalling. Also *vbl. n.* **2.** *intr.* To signal by waving flags. — (1) 1892 *Lippincott's Mag.* Dec. 764, I requested Lieutenant Marix to 'wigwag a signal' to Captain Whiting. 1893 *Columbus Dispatch* 27 April, From the flagship of each nation there was the wig-wagging or the swinging of semphamore [sic] arms. 1903 ADAMS *Log of Cowboy* 313 Some one in the lead wigwagged his lantern. (2) 1899 R. H. DAVIS in *Harper's Mag.* May 941 [He] stood on the crest of the hill to 'wigwag' to the war-ships. 1918 in *Liberty* 11 Aug. (1928) 8/1 We were still under quarantine on board, . . . wigwagging to the sailors on shore for definite information as to whether champagne was really ninety-five cents a quart.

Wigwag, *adv.* With a wiggling movement. — 1846 *Congress. Globe* 16 Jan. 208/1 High, dry, in the cornfield stood, Gun-boat, No. 1, Wigwag went her tail, Pop, went her gun.

Wigwagger. One who signals by moving flags rapidly. — 1898 *Scribner's Mag.* July 4/1 Wig-waggers beat the air from the bridges.

+Wigwam. [Algonquian; cf. Ojibway *wigiwam* 'a dwelling.'] {1743-}

1. An Indian house or tent, constructed of poles and covered with skins, mats, bark, or other material; a tepee.

Though *wigwam* is derived from an Eastern family of Indian languages, and may not have been used by Indians in the West, writers have called Indian habitations in all parts of the country *wigwams*.
1628 *Mass. H. S. Coll.* 3 Ser. VIII. 177 When any dies, they [Sagamores] say Tanto carries them to his *wigwam*, that is his house. **1674** JOSSELYN *Two Voyages* 126 Their houses which they call *Wigwams*, are . . . of a round form for the most part, sometimes square. **1724** KIDDER *Exped. Lovewell* (1865) 17 [We] came upon a Wigwam that the Indians had lately gone from. **1779** *N.H. Hist. Soc. Coll.* VI. 321 Their wigwams were all destroyed by themselves about a year ago, when they left the place. **1833** [see CROW 3]. **1872** POWERS *Afoot & Alone* 215 Each wigwam . . . is composed of a wickerwork frame, thatched with straw and covered with a layer of common earth a foot thick. **1903** WHITE *Forest* 206 His dwelling is the wigwam, and his habitation the wide reaches of the wilderness.

b. *transf.* An Indian family.
1845 DE SMET *Oregon Missions* 169 The Cree nation is considered very powerful, and numbers more than six hundred wigwams.

2. A hut used by white people.
*a***1649** WINTHROP *Hist.* I. 53 Finch of Watertown, had his wigwam burnt and all his goods. **1773** FINLAY *Journal* 5 We made a *wigwam* or hut of branches open in front. *c***1800** PLUMMER *Life & Adv.* 174, I was buying rags for paper, and conveying them to a barn near my wigwam. **1840** *Knickerb.* XVI. 161 They [the hunters] lived widely apart, in log-huts and wigwams, almost with the simplicity of Indians. **1869** [see BRUSHWOOD 1].

3. One of several buildings erected successively to serve as headquarters for the Tammany Society in New York; hence, the society itself.
1787 in Kilroe *St. Tammany* 120 The members of St. Tammany's Society in the City of New York are requested to meet at their wigwam. . . . By order of the Sachem. **1806** *Balance* V. 187/2 A gang of Indians, or white men, pretending to be Indians, late held a council . . . at a 'great wigwam' somewhere about New York. **1868** *N.Y. Herald* 3 July 4/1 Prominent . . . is the new wigwam of the Tammany Society, Columbian Order, in East Fourteenth street. **1895** *N.Y. Tribune* 26 Jan. 2/5 All connected with the Wigwam have been looking forward to this meeting. **1905** *N.Y. Ev. Post* 13 Oct. 1 The first mass meeting to ratify the Tammany ticket will be held at the wigwam next Thursday.

b. One of various other buildings used by political groups, esp. a large temporary structure erected to house a national political convention.
1885 *Mag. Amer. Hist.* May 496/2 The Tammany Society of Philadelphia called its place of meeting a wigwam as early as 1789. *Ib.*, As early as 1859-60 huge buildings of rough boards were erected for political purposes in large towns. . . . These, too, are known as wigwams. **1892** *Times* (London) 22 June 5/3 The wooden roof of the great wigwam in which the delegates [to the Democratic convention in Chicago] met was completed yesterday. **1896** *Chicago Record* 12 Feb. 6/3 Kerens . . . is against a wigwam [for a convention]. He says it is impossible to keep the heat out of a temporary building, constructed of thin boards. **1900** RHODES *Hist. U.S.* II. 456 Wigwam . . . is still applied in Western cities by Republicans to buildings used for party purposes.

4. A shelter on a boat or raft.
1851 MELVILLE *Moby-Dick* 77, I could not well overlook a strange sort of tent, or rather wigwam, pitched a little behind the main-mast. **1883** 'MARK TWAIN' *Life on Miss.* iii, Three or four wigwams [were] scattered about the raft's vast level space for storm-quarters.

5. A form of moccasin.
1887 *Milwaukee Sentinel* 12 Aug. 7/1 Philbrook's Waterproof Wigwams . . . will outwear three pair of the common kind and hold their shape.

6. Attrib. and comb. in sense 1 with *floor, pole,* etc.
1835 WHITTIER *Poetical Works* (1894) 497/2 Ruth will sit in the Sachem's door And braid the mats for his wigwam floor. **1843** 'CARLTON' *New Purchase* I. 75 The town itself stood on the site of their own wigwam village. **1847** LANMAN *Summer in Wilderness* 107 When the island was searched no tracks or wigwam-poles could be seen. **1901** WHITE *Claim Jumpers* 136 [He] built over the whole a wigwam-shaped pyramid of heavier twigs.

*Wild, *n.*

*1. An unsettled, uncultivated, or uncivilized region. Often pl. {now mostly *rhet.* or *poet.*}
1785 *Va. State P.* IV. 4 Our situation is such, inhabiting valleys intermixed with and environed by vast wilds of barren and inaccessible mountains [etc.]. **1817** *Essex Inst. Coll.* VIII. 288 Packed off about 3 o'clock, over the turnpike for the untried wilds of the West. **1861** NEWELL *Orpheus C. Kerr* I. 101 It seems but three seconds ago that all this beautiful scene was a savage wild. **1913** LONDON *Valley of Moon* 474 We've come out from two weeks in the real wilds of Curry County.

+2. *To play the wild* (*with*), to upset or confound; to behave recklessly or without restraint.

1856 J. B. JONES *Wild West Scenes* 1 Ser. 10 Love can play the 'wild' with any young man. **1869** TOURGEE *Toinette* (1881) 56 This abolition business at the North is playing the wild with our people's notions. **1911** SAUNDERS *Col. Todhunter* 143, I been playin' the wild in St. Louis.

*Wild, *a.*

*1. Of an area, region, or place: Uncultivated; uninhabited or sparsely settled; not supplied with the institutions of civilized society.
See also WILD LAND, WILD WEST.
1688 *Providence Rec.* XVII. 119 The Estate of Joseph Jenckes juin[io]r . . . [includes] about 30 acors of willd pastewer. **1748** WASHINGTON *Jrnl. Journey over Mts.* 50 We camped this Night in ye Woods near a Wild Meadow where was a Large Stack of Hay. **1775** FITHIAN *Journal* II. 148 [Mr. Elliott] welcomed me first to this 'wild country,' as he saw fit to term it. **1848** *Whig Almanac 1849* 46/1 If the poor man with a large family could but get rid of the $100 tax on his 80 acre wild lot. **1857** BENTON *Exam. Dred Scott Case* 40 They gave codes of law . . . over the wild territory, still in the hands of the Indians. **1902** HULBERT *Forest Neighbors* 171 He happened to alight one day on a certain wild pond down in Mississippi.

*2. Designating certain animals existing in the wild state.
See also WILD BEEF, WILDCAT *n.* 1.
1789 MORSE *Amer. Geog.* 381 English fallow-deer, and the American wild deer are seen through the thickets. **1807** GASS *Journal* 197, I saw the skin of a wild sheep, which had fine beautiful wool on it. **1809** A. HENRY *Travels* 276 Our supper was made on the tongues of the wild ox, or buffalo, boiled in my kettle. **1848** *S. Lit. Messenger* XIV. 169/2 A wild gobler with splendid plumage was strutting in a circle about a clump of dogwoods. **1881** INGERSOLL *Oyster Industry* 250 *Wild Oyster.*—One of natural growth; uncultivated or transplanted. (Massachusetts.) **1885** *Santa Fé Wkly. New Mexican* 27 Aug. 4/2 Mounted cowboy and wild steer in speed ring. **1891** *Cent.* 6924/2 *Wild dove,* in the United States, the common Carolina dove, or mourning-dove, *Zenaidura carolinensis*. **1894** *Scribner's Mag.* May 603/1 Lucky indeed will be the guest who shall be invited to partake of . . . stewed 'jabalin,' or wild boar.

3. *Baseball.* **a.** Of a pitched or thrown ball: Aimed wide of the mark; random. {*a*1810, in general sense} **b.** Of a pitcher or of his delivery: Inaccurate in aim.
See also WILD THROW.
1885 CHADWICK *Art of Pitching* 70 The errors charged to him on 'called' or wild pitched balls. **1886** — *Art of Batting* 21 The pitcher's delivery is rather wild. **1890** CAMP in *St. Nicholas* Aug. 831/1 The catcher . . . must begin by a resolution . . . to consider no ball beyond his reach, no matter how wild. **1891** *Harper's Wkly.* XXXV. 291/2 Spalding, last year's pitcher, . . . was speedy, but wild.

+4. *Wild and woolly West,* the untamed and lawless western country. Also *wild and lawless West.*
1886 *Boston Herald* 16 July, One of the most annoying things to be met with in the wild and woolly West is an 'alkali sink.' **1890** *Congress. Rec.* 20 June 6304/1, I had supposed . . . that these denunciations of culture and of scientific investigation were confined to the wild and lawless West. **1896** *Ib.* 1 May 4693/2 The one-sided, jug-handled proposition . . . which I thank God does not come from the 'wild and woolly West.' **1925** TILGHMAN *Dugout* 81 The bad men of the wild and woolly days.

+b. *Wild and woolly,* crude or unrefined; unpolished; suggestive of the lawless frontier.
1901 *Forum* Jan. 591 Any 'wild and woolly' Western college, whose whole life is poverty stricken, but vigorous and ambitious. **1902** WISTER *Virginian* 162, I'm wild, and woolly, and full of fleas.

*5. In the names of plants, fruits, and trees.
Only a very few examples are given here. Others may be found under various plant names and in botanical books. (See also WILD APPLE, WILD BARLEY, etc.)
1875 *Amer. Naturalist* IX. 17 A very common bushy shrub . . . is known [in Utah] under the appropriate name of '*wild almond*.' **1874** LONG *Wild-Fowl* 209 On the Chesapeake they are said to be particularly fond of the roots of the wild celery. **1778** CARVER *Travels* 520 Roses red and white, Wild Hollyhocks, Wild Pinks. **1795** WINTERBOTHAM *Hist. View* III. 398 The following have been employed for medical purposes: . . . Wild hyssop, . . . Common avens, or herb bennet. **1852** MARCY *Explor. Red River* (1854) 70 We also found the wild passion-flower, (*Passiflora incarnata*). **1709** LAWSON *Carolina* 77 Samphire in the Marshes excellent, so is the Dock or Wild-Rhubarb. **1800** TATHAM *Agric. & Commerce* 136 There is a species of wild plant, which, among the people of the country, is vulgarly called wild hemp, sometimes wild silk. **1791** W. BARTRAM *Travels* 137 It is exceedingly curious to behold the Wild Squash climbing over the lofty limbs of the trees. **1854** THOREAU *Walden* 139 Wild sumachs and blackberry vines [are] breaking through into your cellar. **1847** EMORY *Military Reconn.* 11 On the uplands the grass is luxuriant, and occasionally is found the wild tea, (*amorpha canescens*). **1848** BRYANT *California* iv. 54 The wild tulip . . . and several flowers of the campanella or bell-shaped classification, have ornamented the prairie to-day. **1877** *Rep. Comm. Agric.* 1876 69 *Liatris odoratissima* . . . is locally known [in Florida] as wild vanilla, but it has no relation whatever to the vanilla-plant that produces the fragrant pods of that name. **1682** ASH *Carolina* 7 The Wild Wallnut or Hiquery-Tree, gives the Indians, by boyling its Kernel, a wholesome Oyl. **1850** Wild wheat [see WILD BARLEY].

6. In special combinations.

Wild gardener, one who makes a garden in which wild plants are arranged in a natural setting; *w. hedge,* a natural, hedgelike growth of wild shrubbery; *w. tribe,* (see quotation).

1882 *Century Mag.* May 153/2 Does not our wild-gardener know . . . our matchless fringed gentian, looking regal amid the coarse September weeds? **1858** THOREAU *Maine Woods* 158 The farmer sometimes talks of 'brushing up,' . . . as if the wild hedges . . . were *dirt.* **1844** GREGG *Commerce of Prairies* I. 282 All the Indians of New Mexico not denominated Pueblos—not professing the Christian religion—are ranked as *wild tribes,* although these include some who have made great advances in arts, manufactures and agriculture.

Wild apple. Any species of apple growing wild. Also attrib. — **1799** J. SMITH *Acct. Captivity* 17 There is a large quantity of wild apple. **1804** CLARK in *Lewis & C. Exped.* I. (1904) 58 Vast quantities of wild apples. **1849** PARKMAN in *Knickerb.* XXXIII. 112 The young wild apple trees . . . were now hung thickly with ruddy fruit. **1869** *Amer. Naturalist* II. 567 Very singular and curious clusters of excrescences occur on the leaves . . . of the wild apple tree of the West. **1897** SUDWORTH *Arborescent Flora* 209 f. [2 species listed].

Wild barley. A species of barley growing wild, as *Hordeum nodosum,* a troublesome weed. — **1850** SAWYER *Way Sketches* 66 We saw in many parts of the valley wild wheat, oats and barley growing luxuriantly. **1894** COULTER *Bot W. Texas* III. 549 *Hordeum nodosum.* (Wild barley.)

+**Wild bean.** Any one of various wild plants of the pea family. Also with specifying adjective. — **1778** CARVER *Travels* 515 Herbs [include:] . . . Noble Liverwort, Bloodwort, Wild Beans [etc.]. **1821** *Mass. H. S. Coll.* 2 Ser. IX. 150 Plants, which are indigenous in the township of Middlebury, [Vt., include:] . . . *Glycine apios,* Slender wild bean. **1859** BARTLETT 512 Wild Bean. (*Phaseolus diversifolius.*) A plant common in the alluvial bottoms of the West, the Wild Potato of the Sioux Indians, much used as food. **1868** GRAY *Field Botany* 108 Ground-nut, Wild Bean, . . . *Apios tuberosa.* Wild on low grounds. **1891** *Amer. Folk-Lore* IV. 148 Several vines of the same genus [*Polygonum*] we knew only as *Wild Bean.*

+**Wild beef.** An American bison or its meat. — **1709** LAWSON *Carolina* 115 The Beasts of Carolina are the Buffalo, or wild Beef. Bear. Panther [etc.]. **1827** COOPER *Prairie* xxvi, It abounded in neither venison nor the wild beef of the prairies.

Wild berry. Any one of various small fruits growing wild, or the plant bearing such a fruit. {1855–} Also attrib. {a1850–} — **1819** CHINQUAPIN 2]. **1838** FLAGG *Far West* II. 15 A deep dingle, choked up with stunted trees and tangled underbrush of hazels, sumach, and wildberry. **1876** *Fur, Fin & Feather* Sept. 142 The short wildberry crop in the mountains . . . drove them [*sc.* bears] into the valleys for food.

+**Wild Bill.** [Of obscure origin.] (See quotation.) — **1886** *Harper's Mag.* June 61/1 'A wild Bill' [in the usage of Ky. mountaineers] is a bed made by boring auger-holes into a log, driving sticks into these, and overlaying them with hickory bark and sedge-grass—a favorite couch.

Wildbore. A woolen cloth used for women's clothes. {1798–} Now hist. — **1784** in Earle *Costume Colonial Times* 257 Marone Ribb'd Wildbores. **1788** *Mass. Spy* 23 Oct. 3/4 Wildbore Camblets, Crapes, Poplins [etc.]. **1812** *Niles' Reg.* II. 9/1 Much of it [*i.e.,* wool] . . . may be wrought into . . . wildbores.

+**Wild buckwheat.** Any one of various wild plants resembling the buckwheat, as *Eriogonum fasciculatum* of California or the heath aster, *Aster ericoides.* — **1878** JACKSON *Travel at Home* 186 There are solid knitted and knotted banks of vines on either hand,—woodbine, groundnut vine, wild or 'false' buckwheat [etc.]. **1898** A. M. DAVIDSON *Calif. Plants* 191 One of the Eriogonums, or wild buckwheats, is shrubby enough to be classed as chaparral. **1909** WEBSTER 2335/1 W[ild] buckwheat, . . . the heath aster. *Local, U.S.*

Wild cabbage. A plant in some way resembling the common cabbage, +as *Caulanthus crassicaulis* of California. — **1806** in *Ann. 9th Congress* 2 Sess. 1142 Wild carrot, wild onion, ginger, wild cabbage, and bastard indigo [grow in the vicinity of the Washita R.]. **1878** ROTHROCK *Geog. Survey Botany* 41 *Caulanthus crassicaulis,* . . . Wild Cabbage.—Sometimes used as food.

Wild camomile. 1. Any plant of the genus *Matricaria.* {1830– (Loudon *Hortus Brit.* 354)} Also with specifying term. **2.** The field camomile, *Anthemis arvensis.* — **(1) 1829** EATON *Botany* (ed. 5) *Matricaria chamomilla,* wild chamomile. **1901** MOHR *Plant Life Ala.* 813 *Matricaria inodora maritima.* . . . Seaside Wild Camomile. **(2) 1845** LINCOLN *Botany* App. 74/1 *Anthemis . . . arvensis,* (wild chamomile).

+**Wild canary.** *local.* **1.** (See quotations.) **2.** The yellow warbler, *Dendroica aestiva.* — **(1) 1891** *Cent.* 6924/2 *Wild canary,* the American goldfinch, *Spinus* or *Chrysomitris tristis.* **1917** *Birds of Amer.* III. 14/1 The male is such a bright yellow bird with black wings and tail that he readily becomes known as the Wild Canary in any community where he is commonly seen. **(2) 1893** *Stand.* 274/1. **1917** *Birds of Amer.* III. 126 Yellow Warbler. *Dendroica æstiva æstiva.* . . . [Also called] Wild Canary (incorrect).

Wild caper. 1. The caper spurge (*Tithymalus lathyrus*), or a related species. +**2.** =PIN CHERRY. — **(1) 1817–8** EATON *Botany* (1822) 279 *Euphorbia peplus,* wild caper. **1889** *Cent.* 803/1 *Wild caper,* the caper-spurge, *Euphorbia Lathyris,* whose immature capsules are used as a substitute for real capers. **(2) 1900** WEBSTER *Suppl.* 34/3 *Wild caper,* . . . a wild plum (*Prunus Pennsylvanica*) of the Eastern United States.

✳**Wild carrot.** +**1.** ?A poisonous herb of the carrot family. ✳**2.** The carrot plant (*Daucus carota*) in its wild form, widely distributed as a weed; also, the root of this. — **(1) 1790** [see FEVERROOT]. **(2) 1802** DRAYTON

S. Carolina 65 Wild carrot, or bird's nest. (*Daucus.*) **1846** *Knickerb.* XXVII. 55 It is very likely he would be eating an onion or a wild carrot. **1879** WHITMAN *Spec. Days* 138 Wherever I go over fields, through lanes, in by-places, blooms the white-flowering wild-carrot. **1899** GOING *Flowers* 349 There are places west of the Mississippi where wild-carrot . . . is cosseted and extolled under the appropriate alias of 'lace-flower.'

✳**Wildcat,** *n.*

I. ✳**1.** Any one of various wild animals of the cat family, +as the bobcat or a related American species.

To whip one's weight in wildcats, (see WHIP *v.* 5 b).

[**1612** SMITH, etc. *Virginia* I. 14 There is also a beast they call Vetchunquoyes in the forme of a wilde Cat.] **1634, 1699** [see OUNCE[1]]. **1709** LAWSON *Carolina* 118 Wild Cat. This Cat is quite different from those in Europe; being more nimble and fierce, and larger. **1743** CATESBY *Carolina* App. p. xxv, *Catus Americanus.* The Wild Cat. This beast is about three times the size of a common cat. **1804** CLARK in *Lewis & C. Exped.* I. (1904) 236, I line my Gloves and have a Cap made of the Skin of the *Louservia* (Lynx) (or wild Cat of the North). **1859** BARTLETT 512 *Wild-Cat.* A panther . . . is familiarly called there [in Mich.] a Wild-cat. **1913** BARNES *Western Grazing Grounds* 330 The wild cat and lynx, commonly known as 'bob cats,' cause sheepmen much loss.

✳**2.** Applied to persons. +**a.** One favoring entrance of the United States into the War of 1812. *colloq.* Now hist. +**b.** A member of a pro-slavery faction in Maine. *colloq.*

1812 *Columbian Centinel* 6 June 2/5 Some of the *Wildcats* of Congress have gone home, unable to incur the awful responsibility of unnecessary *War.* **1853** *Whig Almanac 1854* 40/1 Election Returns. . . . Maine. . . . Legislature. . . . House—Whigs, 65; Democrats, 58; Wildcats, 18.

3. *colloq.* +**a.** =WILDCAT BANK.

Said to have been so called because a representation of a panther or 'wildcat' appeared on the notes of a bank in Michigan.

1838 BENTON *30 Years' View* II. 92 Those called wild cats—The progeny of a general banking law in Michigan. **1863** *Congress. Globe* 15 Jan. 342/3 Governor Matteson, for several years, was king of the so-called 'wild cats'; he owned stock-banks in all directions. **1896** *Nation* 3 Dec. 417/2 The question now coming up is whether this feature of our banking system can be amended without giving the field to wildcats.

+**b.** A mine of doubtful value or one serving as the basis of fraudulent transactions.

1864 'MARK TWAIN' *Sketches* 149 Strategy is driven to the utmost limit by the friends of some pet wildcat or other, to effect sales of it to disinterested parties. **1875** *Scribner's Mo.* July 272/1 Two years ago the Consolidated Virginia mine was denounced on the street as a 'wild cat.' **1896** SHINN *Story of Mine* 70 These 'wild-cats' . . . were bought and sold with increasing energy for months.

+**c.** A successful oil well located in a region not previously known to have oil.

1903 TARBELL in *McClure's Mag.* Feb. 399/1 New territory had been opened up by unexpected wildcats.

+**4.** Used as a collective term, or quasi-adjectivally, with reference to unsound money or financially precarious undertakings. *colloq.*

1838 *N.Y. Advertiser & Exp.* 10 March 2/4 'Wild Cat' will buy provisions of no kind. **1853** *La Crosse Democrat* 26 July 3/2 More than half his money was Wild Cat and counterfeit. **1864** J. R. BROWNE in *Harper's Mag.* Oct. 554/2 Even at that early date there were speculators in 'wild cat.' c1868 'MARK TWAIN' *Sk., New & Old* 150 They would do with it just as they would with one of your silver-mines out there—they would try to make all the world believe it was 'wildcat.' **1889** — *Conn. Yankee* 532 It was wildcat, and everybody knew it. **1894** HARTE *Protégée of Jack Hamlin's* 142 Who'd have thought of your . . . ever doing anything but speculate in wild-cat or play at draw poker.

+**b.** (See quotation.) *colloq.*

1871 DE VERE 297 For many years afterward all irresponsible banks . . . were designated as Wild-Cat Banks, and their notes often very curtly and severely as wild cats.

+**5.** (See second quotation.) In full *wildcat train. colloq.*

1885 *Good Words* July 452/1 Every now and then the newspapers allude to 'wild-cat' trains. *Ib.,* The 'wild-cat' is the slowest of all trains. It is only used for freight, and reaches its destination when it can, running whenever the line is clear.

II. attrib. 6. In sense 1, esp. with reference to the fur of wildcats.

See also WILDCAT('S) SKIN.

1839 PLUMBE *Sk. Iowa* 59, I might find some of the law-makers of Wisconsin arrayed in wild cat caps and hunting shirts. **1852** BRISTED *Upper Ten Th.* 16 This one [sleigh] . . . has no back-robe at all, the black bear being placed in front, instead of the ordinary wildcat or wolf lap-skin. **1868** *Mich. Agric. Rep.* VII. 416 One striking feature of the exhibition [was] . . . a collection of . . . wild-cat robes, gloves, caps [etc.]. **1901** WHITE *Westerners* 283 He let out a wild-cat yell.

+**7.** Designating pieces of wildcat money. *colloq.*

See also WILDCAT BILL, CURRENCY, MONEY.

1839 in Sol. Smith *Autobiog.* 144, I would not t x your kindness by accepting of Illinois or wild-cat paper bills. **1853** *Daily Morning Herald*

(St. Louis) 5 Feb. (Th.), [We hope gold will] take the place of 'Wild-cat' shinplasters. *Ib.* 18 Feb. (Th.), All the 'individual issues,' 'wild-cat rags,' 'red dogs,' 'plank road,' 'Illinois river,' and all other fraudulent and swindling shinplaster notes should be driven from the city. 1855 M. THOMPSON *Doesticks* 38 You are called upon to . . . pay half a dollar to a man . . . who gives you wild-cat paper . . . in exchange for your Yankee gold. 1881 *Congress. Rec.* App. 18 Jan. 35/1 Anyone at all familiar with the old days of . . . 'wild-cat,' and 'shin-plaster' notes, will fully concede the incomparable superiority of the present system. 1888 Wild-cat bank-notes [see SHINPLASTER 1 b].

+8. Designating irresponsible or untrustworthy persons, especially those promoting or otherwise engaged in hazardous speculations or fraudulent enterprises. *colloq.*

Cf. WILDCATTER 3.

a1859 *Cincinnati Enquirer* (B.), Our banks are always willing to offer loans and facilities to speculators and wild-cat business men to operate with. 1888 *Puck* (F.), This was a wild cat broker. 1909 *N.Y. Ev. Post* 22 Feb. (Th.), The wild-cat mining promoter . . . flourished successfully in the old days of boom mining camps.

+9. Designating organizations, persons, etc., concerned with wildcat banks or irresponsible banking procedures. *colloq.*

1842 *Congress. Globe* App. 13 Jan. 65/3 It is the old, worn out . . . slang upon which every red dog, wild cat, owl creek, coon box, and Cairo, swindling shop which has disgraced our country, obtained their charters. 1853 BREWERTON *With Kit Carson* (1930) 179 There was a vague rumor in regard to certain 'wild-cat' banking operations. 1867 *Galaxy* III. 632 When [the Yankee mind stoops] . . . to criminal pursuits, it is more likely to manifest itself in the way of . . . wild-cat banking institutions. 1870 *Ib.* App. 26 March 224/2 [Ten years ago] the moneyed East knew not the richer West, save as the home of wild-cats, wild-cat financiers, and wild-cat banks. 1875 *Chicago Tribune* 27 Nov. 8/7 The wild-cat inflation organ. which believes only in irredeemable, fluctuating, depreciated scrip for money. 1881 *N.Y. Sun* 16 Nov. (Th.), Walsh next turned up in Washington as a wildcat banker. 1882 *Congress. Rec.* App. 16 May 303/1 The worst system we have ever had was the wild-cat State banking system. 1887 *Harper's Mag.* April 666 The bank officials of 'wildcat' times . . . issued their notes so long as they could find strength to affix their signatures.

+10. Designating properties or business enterprises irregularly, unsoundly, or dishonestly administered, sold, or financed. *colloq.*

See also WILDCAT MINE.

1871 DALY *Divorce* 53, I invested in some wild-cat stock. 1884 *Harper's Mag.* March 505/1 A conservatism and solidity in St. Louis business methods . . . have kept it out of wild-cat speculations. 1885 HOWELLS *Silas Lapham* 420 That scoundrel began to load me up with those wild-cat securities of his. 1890 *Stock Grower & Farmer* 18 Jan. 4/4 The promoters of one or two wild cat irrigation schemes in this territory have secured laudatory notices . . . by the use of liberal quantities of 'soap.' 1892 *Vt. Agric. Rep.* XII. 151 Millions of her 'surplus' have been dumped into all sorts of wild cat enterprises outside the State. 1902 HARBEN *A. Daniel* 286 That visionary gang . . . will spend all I leave you in their wild-cat investments.

+11. In special combinations. *colloq.*

Wildcat claim, a worthless mining claim represented to investors as valuable; *w. literature,* extravagant stories of wild adventure; *w. state,* a western state regarded as having been admitted to statehood for political reasons before it was ready; *w. still,* a still operated without a license; *w. well,* =WILDCAT n. 3 c; *w. whisky,* moonshine.

1872 'MARK TWAIN' *Roughing It* 311 One plan of acquiring sudden wealth was to 'salt' a wildcat claim and sell out while the excitement was up. 1875 *— Old Times* i. 21 He was . . . an untravelled native of the wilds of Illinois, who had absorbed wildcat literature and appropriated its marvels. 1872 *Chicago Tribune* 27 Dec. 4/7 Wild-cat States in the West have been created for the seeming purpose of giving two ambitious politicians seats in the Senate. 1883 'S. BONNER' *Dialect Tales* 143 You're up the Cumberland spyin' for wild-cat stills. 1883 *Century Mag.* July 331/2 When he begins to put down a wild-cat well, he usually leases all the land in the vicinity. 1881 T. HUGHES *Rugby, Tenn.* 64 They are sadly weak when wild-cat whisky—or 'moonshine,' as the favourite illicit beverage of the mountains is called—crosses their path.

+Wildcat, *v.* (See WILDCATTING.)

+**Wildcat bank.** A bank issuing notes in excess of its ability to redeem them; one of various western banks organized under lax state legislation in the period preceding the establishment (1863–64) of the national banking system. *colloq.* Now hist. — 1838 *N.Y. Advertiser & Exp.* 14 Feb. 1/2 These institutions have very properly received the *soubriquet,* of 'wild cat banks.' 1849 W. BROWN *America* 36 The reign of Andrew Jackson . . . was particularly famed for the great increase of . . . Wild Cat Banks. 1852 GOUGE *Fiscal Hist. Texas* 236 Other 'wild-cat banks' will have their branches in Texas. 1873 'MARK TWAIN' & WARNER *Gilded Age* 86 They want me to go in with them . . . and buy up a hundred and thirteen wildcat banks.

+**Wildcat bill.** A note issued by a bank lacking the ability to redeem it; a note of a wildcat bank. *colloq.* — 1838 *Jeffersonian* (Albany) 15 Sept. 244/1 We shall have . . . *Lumbermen's bills,* and *Wild-cat Bills,* that nobody knows who the father or the maker is. 1869 *Atlantic Mo.* July

85/2, I might have had imposed upon me some of the 'wild-cat' bills then afloat. 1894 'MARK TWAIN' *P. Wilson* viii, He held out the wild-cat bill.

+**Wildcat currency.** A medium of exchange consisting of notes issued without security, as the notes of wildcat banks. *colloq.* — 1858 *Baltimore Sun* 8 July (B.), We are overrun with a wild-cat currency from all God's creation. 1882 J. QUINCY *Figures of Past* 196 At Ashford, in Connecticut, . . . the bother of the wild-cat currency, as it was afterward called, was forced upon our attention. 1898 *Mo. So. Dakotan* I. 15 Those were the days of 'wild cat' currency when a man might be rich at sunrise, and a pauper at sunset.

+**Wildcat engine.** =WILD ENGINE. *colloq.* — 1888 *Mo. Republican* 23 Feb. (F.), The Montreal night express was thrown from the track . . . by a wild cat engine that had been turned loose at the Mechanicville yards by an evil-disposed person. 1891 ELLIS *Check 2134* 88 There was just one chance in a hundred of a wildcat engine approaching.

+**Wildcat mine.** A worthless mine represented to investors as a valuable one; a mine made to appear more valuable than it is. *colloq.* — 1872 'MARK TWAIN' *Roughing It* 307 Not a wildcat mine . . . yielded a ton of rock worth crushing. 1880 INGHAM *Digging Gold* 447 A Very Common Swindle is from what are called 'Wild-Cat Mines.'

+**Wildcat money.** Money in the form of worthless or depreciated bank notes. *colloq.* Now hist. — 1838 *N.Y. Advertiser & Exp.* 14 Feb. 1/2 Our almost entire circulation is now in 'wild cat money.' 1842 KIRKLAND *Forest Life* I. 91 We took our pay in wild-cat money; that turned to waste paper before we got it off our hands. 1891 'THANET' *Otto the Knight* 106 Billy . . . got ninety-five cents on the dollar. Pretty good for wild-cat money, hey? 1892 *Courier-Journal* 1 Oct. 3/2 This is the kind of money . . . which is to be superceded [*sic*] by the . . . wild-cat money.

Wildcat('s) skin. The skin of a wildcat. {1863, in Africa} — 1624 SMITH *Gen. Hist.* Va. 1. 17 [We] exchanged with them Kniues . . . for some . . . wilde Catte skinnes. 1720 D. NEAL *Hist. New-Eng.* I. 88 The Chief of them was distinguish'd by a wild Cat's-Skin on his Arm. 1841 [see PILLOW 1]. 1858 VIELÉ *Following Drum* 164 There is a wilderness . . . with the finest wild-cat skins.

+**Wildcatter.** *colloq.* **1.** (See quot. 1883.) **2.** An operator of an unlicensed still. **3.** A promoter of a wildcat mine. — **(1)** 1883 *Century Mag.* July 327/2 The 'wild-catters,' as the prospectors are called who take the risks of sinking wells in unknown territory. 1904 *Scientific Amer.* 18 June 474 Large oil producers do not prospect; they leave that dangerous business to the professional 'wildcatter.' **(2)** 1892 *Columbus Dispatch* 11 March, One of the moonshiners . . . was shot in the affray. . . . Three more of the wild catters . . . are seriously hurt. **(3)** 1909 *N.Y. Ev. Post* (s.w. ed.) 22 Feb. 6 The wildcatter would have few victims if the intended victim had the common-sense foresight to appeal to the mining engineer.

+**Wildcatting.** *colloq.*
1. (See quotations.) Also *wildcat* v.
1883 *Century Mag.* July 331/1 'Wild-catting' is the name applied to the venturesome business of drilling wells on territory not known to contain oil. 1897 *Boston News Bureau* 22 June, 'Wildcatting' . . . consists in leasing lands and sinking wells with the expectation of making a lucky strike. 1903 *Dialect Notes* II. 345 *Wild-cat,* . . . to prospect in territory not known to be good.

+**2.** The issuing of unsecured or worthless currency; the promotion and sale of valueless securities or property.
1890 *Stock Grower & Farmer* 4 Jan. 3/2 We want no wild-catting in irrigating enterprises such as we had in the cattle business a few years ago. 1893 *Nation* LVI. 76/3 Wild-catting . . . was rife before the war. 1923 'BOWER' *Parowan Bonanza* 132 He's a fine, straight fellow and everybody knows he wouldn't stand for any wildcatting.

Wild cattle. Ordinary cattle that have run wild; bovine animals of wild breeds {1771– (Pennant *Tour Scot.* 273)}; bison. (Cf. WILD COW 2.) — 1653 *Md. Council Proc.* 295 Mr. Willm Ettonhead and others . . . [desire] Some Course might be taken for the getting up and killing the wild Cattell. 1738 BYRD *Dividing Line* (1901) 122 We saw many Buffalo-Tracks. . . . These wild Cattle hardly ever range alone. 1863 MASSETT *Drifting About* 132, I was requested to sell 'several hundred head of wild cattle' in 'bands' of forty each. 1889 FARMER 560/1 A strange breed of wild cattle is found in the high hills skirting the Umpqua valley, Oregon. 1923 J. H. COOK *On Old Frontier* 25 It is a difficult thing to make a large majority of even present day cattlemen . . . understand what the words 'Wild Cattle' really meant in Southern Texas.

Wild cherry. The fruit of any one of various species of cherry growing wild, +as the chokecherry (*Padus virginiana*) and the black cherry (*P. serotina*); the tree producing such fruit. {1731– (Miller *Gard. Dict.*)} Also with specifying adj.

See also WILD RED CHERRY.

1666 *S.C. Hist. Coll.* II. 12 There are many sorts of fruit Trees, as Vines, Medlars, Peach, Wild Cherries. 1784 W. WALTON *Narr. Captivity B. Gilbert* 81 They were under the Necessity of eating wild Cherries. 1837 WILLIAMS *Florida* 114 Of Cherries we have only the black wild cherry. 1882 LATHROP *Echo of Passion* ii, [He] selected a straight wild cherry, which he attacked vigorously. 1901 MOHR *Plant Life Ala.* 61 Wild cherry (*Prunus serotina*) is only found here and there in the richest spots.

attrib. 1843 TALBOT *Journals* 34, I had just shot a ring-dove in a wild cherry grove. 1852 STANSBURY *Gt. Salt Lake* 59 We crossed the dry beds of several small streams, skirted, in some instances, with willows, box-elder, wild-cherry bushes. 1899 JEWETT *Queen's Twin* 81 She had a sprig of wild-cherry blossom in her dress.

+**Wild-cherry bark.** (See quots. 1836 and 1901.) — **1829** FLINT *G. Mason* 98 He gave an infusion of Dog Wood, Wild Cherry, and Yellow Poplar bark. **1836** WOOD & BACHE *Dispensatory* 525 *Prunus Virginiana.* U.S. Wild-cherry Bark. . . . The inner bark is the part employed in medicine. **1901** MOHR *Plant Life Ala.* 552 The inner bark [of the black cherry, *Padus serotina*] is the 'wild cherry bark,' '*Prunus virginiana*,' of the United States Pharmacopœia.

Wild cherry tree. Any one of various trees producing wild cherries. {1812– (Withering *Brit. Plants* III. 557)} — **1705** BEVERLEY *Virginia* II. 26 The Bark of the Sassafras-Tree and wild Cherry-Tree have been experimented to partake very much of the Virtue of the *Cortex Peruviana.* **1843** FRÉMONT *Explor. Rocky Mts.* 71 We now made a kind of tea from the roots of the wild cherry tree. **1907** *St. Nicholas* Aug. 895/2 There's a wild cherry tree on the bank.

Wild cinnamon. {1858, in Jamaica} A white-barked tree (*Canella winterana*) with an aromatic inner bark used as a spice. — **1837** WILLIAMS *Florida* 98 Wild Cinnamon.—Called by the inhabitants, Naked Wood. **1884** SARGENT *Rep. Forests* 24 *Canella alba.* . . . White Wood. Cinnamon Bark. Wild Cinnamon. Semi-tropical Florida. On the southern keys.

Wild clover. {*dial.*} Any one of various plants of the family Fabaceae growing wild. — **1775** CRESSWELL *Journal* 76 Wild Clover . . . in such plenty it might be mown and would turn out a good crop. **1833** FLINT *D. Boone* 113 Pawpaw, cane, and wild clover, marked exuberant fertility. **1846** SAGE *Scenes Rocky Mts.* xxiii, The wild clover of these valleys is much like the common red, and, in some places, is afforded in great abundance. **1886** Z. F. SMITH *Kentucky* 2 Amid the undulating pastures of wild clover, bluegrass, and cane, game most abounded.

Wild coffee. {1884, in Jamaica}

+**1.** = FEVERROOT c.
1833 EATON *Botany* (ed. 6) 372 *Triosteum perfoliatum,* fever root, horse-ginseng, wild coffee. . . . Berries purple or yellow. **1898** CREEVEY *Flowers of Field* 364 Feverwort. Horse-gentian. Wild Coffee. . . . Canada and New England to Minnesota and southward.

+**2.** (See quotations.) Also attrib.
1890 *Congress. Rec.* 12 June 5991/1 In California . . . this wild silk-worm feeds upon . . . the cascara sagrada, or wild coffee. **1893** *Amer. Folk-Lore* VI. 139 *Rhamnus Californica,* wild coffee; bearberry. S. Barbara Co., Cal. **1897** SUDWORTH *Arborescent Flora* 299 *Rhamnus purshiana.* Bearberry. . . . [Also called] Wild Coffee-bush (Cal.). . . . Wild Coffee (Cal.).

Wild columbine. +A native, wild, red-flowering species of *Aquilegia* (*A. canadensis*), called also *honeysuckle*. — **1814** BIGELOW *Florula Bostoniensis* 133 Wild columbine. . . . This early flower is more delicate in its habits and colours than the common garden species. **1855** *Harvard Mag.* I. 234 The Wild Columbine . . . is a well-known and very showy flower. **1898** CREEVEY *Flowers of Field* 277 Wild Columbine. . . . Insects find sweet honey at the end of the tiny horns.

Wild cotton. Any one of various plants resembling or suggesting in appearance the cotton plant. {1808, *Sc.*} — **1854** H. H. RILEY *Puddleford* 216 The 'paper-wasp' was gathering wild cotton and flax . . . for his palace. **1894** *Amer. Folk-Lore* VII. 94 *Asclepias cornuti,* . . . wild cotton, West Va.

Wild cow. 1. A domestic cow aroused to a state of fury. **2.** An undomesticated bovine animal; a bison. (Cf. WILD CATTLE.) — **(1) 1732** HEMPSTEAD *Diary* 245, 3. more [teeth] are lose & hath been Ever Since the wild Cow hitt them with her head. **(2) 1765** [see BEAVER 1]. **1809** FRENEAU *Poems* I. 257 On A Man Killed by a Buffaloe (or wild Cow).

* **Wild cucumber.** Any one of various wild plants {1535, of the fruit; 1630}, +as the wild balsam apple, *Echinocystis lobata.*
1784 *Amer. Acad. Mem.* I. 488 *Elaterium.* . . . Wild Cucumber. The stems, leaves and blossoms like those of the cucumber. **1805** LEWIS in *L. & Clark Exped.* II. (1904) 230 The lambsquarter, wild coucumber, sand rush and narrow dock are also common here. **1837** LINCOLN *Botany* 186/2 Wild cucumber. [*Momordica echinata* or *balsamina*]. **1850** S. F. COOPER *Rural Hours* 107 The wild cucumber, a very troublesome plant, . . . is clearly settled as belonging to this continent. **1892** *Amer. Folk-Lore* V. 91 *Anemone nemorosa,* wild cucumber, N.H. *Ib.* 96 *Echinocystis lobata,* wild cucumber, N.B., and U.S. generally. **1898** *Mo. So. Dakotan* I. 87 The trees along the river banks were heavily draped by . . . the trailing wild cucumbers. **1909** *Cent. Suppl.* 323/2 *Wild cucumber,* . . . in California, the big-root or man-root *Micrampelis fabacea,* and doubtless other species.

Wild currant. The fruit of any one of various species of the genus *Ribes,* or the plant bearing such fruit. — **1833** CATLIN *Indians* I. 72 Clusters of plum trees . . . and wild currants, loaded down with their fruit. **1873** ARNY *Items regarding N. Mex.* 27 The natural productions of the prairies, mesas, valleys . . . [include] wild currant, china berries, wild grapes. **1898** A. M. DAVIDSON *Calif. Plants* 68 Some are in flower, the wild currants and gooseberries, for instance.

* **Wild duck.** Any undomesticated duck, as the mallard. Also comb. — **1743** CATESBY *Carolina* App. p. xxxvii, The Black Duck is considerably bigger than the common Wild Duck. **1796** [see KINGFISHER]. **1819** LATROBE *Journal* 163 Along the levee [were sold] . . . innumerable wild ducks. **1873** *Harper's Mag.* March 639/1 Gentlemen also are to be found frequenting these places later in the season for the purpose of wild-duck shooting. **1917** *Birds of Amer.* I. 113 Wild Ducks fall naturally into the two groups known as River or Pond Ducks and Sea or Bay or Diving Ducks.

+**Wild engine.** 'A locomotive running over a railway without regard to schedule time. . . . A locomotive which by some accident or derangement has escaped from the control of its driver' (*Cent.*). *colloq.*

* **Wilderness.**

* **1.** An area of uncleared, uncultivated, unsettled, or sparsely settled land.
1638 *R.I. Col. Rec.* I. 34 Parcells of land in this barbarous wilderness. **1791** [see INDIAN *attrib.* and *adj.* 4 d]. **1851** SPRINGER *Forest Life* 83 These roads . . . ramify the wilderness to all the principal 'clumps' and 'groves of pine.'

+**b.** In the Atlantic colonies, used to distinguish unsettled areas from settled areas.
1666 *Conn. Hist. Soc. Coll.* VI. 54 Each of the Said parties are to haue thair parte in that Land which abuteth on the wilderness. **1770** *N.H. Hist. Soc.* IX. 56 A great number of Towns are now settling at once by Persons who have removed into the Wilderness.

+**2.** Used to designate specific areas in the United States. **a.** An unsettled mountainous region along the eastern border of Kentucky. **b.** The difficult terrain along the Mississippi River near Vicksburg, Mississippi. **c.** A forested region of Virginia south of the Rapidan River, famous as a scene of hostilities in the Civil War. **d.** A remote mountainous area in West Virginia near the Maryland boundary.
(a) 1792 IMLAY *Western Territory* 9 These mountains . . . ramify into a country 200 miles over from east to west, called the wilderness. **1829** *Va. Lit. Museum* 85 This elevated tract, . . . from its dreariness and want of improvement, or population, was called 'the wilderness.' **(b) 1864** 'PENNIMAN' *Tanner-Boy* 282 He laid Grand Gulf to plunge into the 'Wilderness' of Mississippi. **(c) 1865** *Atlantic Mo.* June 744/1 An article . . . gives an outline of the operations of the Army of the Potomac . . . through the tangled thickets of the Wilderness. **(d) 1880** *Harper's Mag.* July 171/1 The Wilderness comprises seven hundred square miles of virgin forest.

3. *attrib.* **a.** In sense 1 with *barrier, condition,* etc.
1659 *R.I. Col. Rec.* I. 415 Wee dare not interrupt your high affayres with the particulars of our wilderness conditions. **1675** *Conn. Rec.* II. 259 Seek the Lord by solemne fasting and prayer, that he would bless his wilderness people. **1701** *Hartford Land Distrib.* 488 Sayd Lott is bounded . . . with wilderness undivided Land on the East. **1716** *Mass. H. Rep. Jrnl.* I. 144 [The inhabitants of Framingham petition] That a Tract of Wilderness Land . . . may be Granted or Sold to them. **1809** *Ann. 10th Congress* 2 Sess. 1093 The wide extent of wilderness country, which separates the population. **1854** BENTON *30 Years' View* I. 15/1 The new boundaries . . . establish a wilderness barrier between Missouri and New Mexico.

+**b.** In special combinations.
Wilderness cure, a method of treating illness by life in the open air; *W. Road,* the historic route from Virginia into Kentucky by way of the Cumberland Gap.
1860 *Harper's Mag.* Aug. 342/2 [From the Virginia frontier] they struck into the forest, that stretched, unbroken, to the banks of the Kentucky River . . . following what was called the 'Wilderness Road.' **1881** *Ib.* May 868/1 The Reporter pitched his tent and began the trial of the wilderness cure.

Wild fig. Any one of various uncultivated species of *Ficus,* +as, in Florida, the golden fig, *F. aurea.* — **1709** LAWSON *Carolina* 105 The wild Fig grows in Virginia. **1775** *Amer. Husbandry* I. 381 The wild fig . . . grows only on the mountains or their neighbourhood. **1884** SARGENT *Rep. Forests* 127 Wild Fig. . . . Semi-tropical Florida. **1897** SUDWORTH *Arborescent Flora* 191 [2 species listed].

* **Wildfire.** An inflammable material used in warfare. — *a*1649 WINTHROP *Hist.* I. 28 Our captain shot a ball of wild-fire fastened to an arrow out of a cross-bow. **1675** *N.H. Hist. Soc. Coll.* II. 14 They also used several stratagems to fire us, namely, by wild fire in cotton and linen rags with brimstone in them. **1721** *New-Eng. Courant* 20 Nov. 2/2 The Granado passing thro' the Window had . . . such a Turn given to it, that in falling on the Floor, the fired Wildfire in the Fuse, was violently shaken out. **1764** HUTCHINSON *Hist. Mass.* II. 275 The fuze was fortunately beat off by the passing of the shell through the window, and the wild fire spent itself upon the floor. **1839** *Knickerb.* XIII. 445 The man who stood sentinel . . . cried out, 'Wild fire, by ——!'

* **Wild flax.** An uncultivated plant resembling the true flax,' as the toadflax (*Linaria vulgaris*) or the gold-of-pleasure (*Camelina sativa*). — **1792** IMLAY *Western Territory* 209 Wild flax, *Linum Virginianum.* **1848** ROBINSON *Santa Fé Exped.* 18 We found . . . wild flax four feet high. **1873** ARNY *Items regarding N. Mex.* 27 The natural productions of the prairies, mesas, valleys . . . [are] wild flax, wild oats [etc.]. **1894** *Amer. Folk-Lore* VII. 96 *Linaria vulgaris,* wild flax, devil's flax, . . . West Va.

Wild-fowl shooting. The shooting of wild fowl. Also *wild-fowling.* {1859} — **1851** *S. Lit. Messenger* XVII. 45/1 Wild-fowl-shooting . . . is peculiar to the tide water region. **1874** LONG *Wild-Fowl* 13 Wild-fowling as an art is but very little understood by the great majority of sportsmen. **1898** *Outing* April 54/1 For me wild-fowl shooting stands pre-eminent.

* **Wild garlic.** Any one of various species of *Allium.* — **1787** WASHINGTON *Diaries* III. 183 The others . . . had been culled from the wild garlick. **1843** [see FIELD GARLIC]. **1894** COULTER *Bot. W. Texas* III. 433 Wild Garlic. . . . Extending, westward to central Texas.

Wild ginger. Any one of various wild plants of the birthwort family, +esp. *Asarum canadense,* which has a ginger-flavored rootstock. — **1804** LEWIS in *L. & Clark Exped.* VI. (1904) 154 Wild ginger grows in rich bottom Land. **1847** WOOD *Botany* 465 Wild Ginger . . . has been considered useful in whooping-cough. **1860** CURTIS *Woody Plants N.C.* 120 Wild Ginger. . . . In some parts of the United States, it has gotten the name of *Dutchman's Pipe.* **1901** MOHR *Plant Life Ala.* 481.

* **Wild goat.** A goatlike animal found wild; a prong-horned antelope. — **1804** LEWIS in *L. & Clark Exped.* VI. (1904) 129 This day Capt Clark killed a male wild goat. **1820** *Amer. Antiq. Soc. Coll.* I. 72 We found above the half of a fat wild goat which the wolves had strangled.

* **Wild goose.**

1. Any undomesticated goose, +esp. the Canada goose; also, the flesh of this bird cooked and served as food.

1622 'MOURT' *Relation* 25 Wee saw great flockes of wild Geese and Duckes. **1724** JONES *Virginia* 12 They count their Time by Days, or by the Return of the Moon, and *Cohonks,* a sort of wild Geese. **1767** J. ADAMS *Diary* Works II. 206 [Tufts determined] to bring my wife and child over, to dine upon wild goose, and cranberry sauce. **1821** NUTTALL *Travels Arkansa* 75 This morning I accompanied the doctor to shoot wild geese. **1845** *Big Bear Ark.* 134, I'd seen . . . more swan, wild goose, and duck, than you ever will see. **1905** N. DAVIS *Northerner* 146 A flight of wild geese passed overhead.

2. In special combinations.

Wild-goose plum, (see quot. 1890); *wild-goose rye,* a variety of rye said to have been grown from seed found in the crop of a wild goose.

1884 *Lisbon* (Dak.) *Star* 15 Aug., 'Wild Goose Rye' in time will no doubt become one of the greatest of Dakota products. **1890** *Cent.* 4566/1 *Wild-goose plum,* an improved variety of the Chickasaw, said to have been raised from a stone found in the crop of a wild goose.

Wild gooseberry. The fruit of any one of various plants of the genus *Grossularia* growing wild, esp. the pasture gooseberry (*G. cynosbati*), or a shrub similar to these; the plant bearing the fruit. Also with specifying term.

a**1686** in Alvord & Bidgood *Trans-Allegheny Region* 190 As we march'd we met with some wild gooseberries and exceeding large haws. **1785** MARSHALL *Amer. Grove* 133 *Ribes cynosbati.* Prickly fruited Wild Goose-berry. **1805** PARKINSON *Tour* 112 There were wild gooseberries in abundance in the woods. **1889** *Cent.* 2576/2 The wild gooseberries of North America include several species, the fruit of which is rarely eaten. **1898** A. M. DAVIDSON *Calif. Plants* 70 Some early wild gooseberries have long, bright red flowers that serve honey to humming bird guests. **1901** MOHR *Plant Life Ala.* 67 In rocky but somewhat rich soil on these ridges . . . [grows] *V[accinium] melanocarpum,* the so-called wild gooseberry, remarkable for its large fruit.

* **Wild grape.** The fruit of any one of various species of grapevine found growing wild; the plant bearing the fruit.

1763 *S.C. Hist. Coll.* II. 468 Wild grapes grow on this land. **1849** CHAMBERLAIN *Ind. Gazetteer* 17 Wild grapes . . . and strawberries of excellent qualities grow spontaneously. **1882** RITTENHOUSE *Maud* 132 We drove to the woods, had a jolly time and returned at 6 p.m. laden with wild-grapes and scarlet berries. **1907** [see PAWPAW 1].

Wild grass. Green herbage growing wild. — **1748** [see CRAMBERRY]. **1872** *Vermont Bd. Agric. Rep.* I. 288 Under the popular name of 'Wild Grass,' they [species of sedge] are much cut for hay.

+**Wild hay.** Hay made from wild grass. — **1835** HOFFMAN *Winter in West* I. 163 Settlers . . . , for the sake of the wild hay, locate themselves near the great marshes. **1881** *Rep. Indian Affairs* 33 The bottom lands furnish an abundant supply of nutritious wild hay. **1884** VASEY *Agric. Grasses* 61 *Muhlenbergia glomerata.* (Spiked Muhlenbergia.) . . . In the Eastern States it is utilized as one of the native products of wet meadows in the making of what is called wild hay.

* **Wild hemp.** Any one of various plants valued for their fiber; + = INDIAN HEMP. — **1641** *Mass. Bay Rec.* I. 322 There is a kind of wild hempe groweing plentifully all over the countrey. **1765** CROGHAN *Journal* 23 The ground is exceedingly rich, and partly overgrown with wild hemp. **1806** in *Ann. 9th Congress* 2 Sess. 1142.

Wild hog. A domestic swine unmarked or running at large; any wild animal of the family Suidae {1835}; +a peccary (q.v.).

1650 *Md. Council Proc.* 255 Divers Licences . . . haue beene heretofore granted . . . for the killing of Wild Hoggs. **1782** CRÈVECŒUR *Letters* 237 I found them out by following the track of some wild hogs. **1805** in *Ann. 9th Congress* 2 Sess. 1082 Wild hogs are likewise plenty in their country. **1831** PATTIE *Personal Narr.* 67 In these bottoms are great numbers of wild hogs. **1872** McCLELLAN *Golden State* 204 Wild hogs and goats abound in the mountains. **1916** THOBURN *Stand. Hist. Oklahoma* I. 47 The Mexican wild hog (peccary) was reported to be quite common in the valley of the Red River.

+**b.** Used as an opprobrious term: (see quotation).

1884 *Congress. Rec.* 4 June 4821/1 A distinguished railroad king, who talks about this House as 'wild hogs' in letters which are of record—I refer to Mr. Huntington.

+**Wild-hog sense.** Common sense; sufficient awareness to protect one's own comfort and well-being. *colloq.* — **1868** *Congress. Globe* App. 18 March 286/2 This common perception is called by the 'old settlers' 'wild-hog sense.' **1903** 'O. HENRY' *Roads of Destiny* 374 Be intelligent, now, and use at least wild-hog sense.

Wild honeysuckle. Any one of various wild plants, esp. species of *Lonicera* and *Azalea,* with fragrant flowers. {1731– (Miller *Gard. Dict.* s.v. *Caprifolium*)}

1761 KALM *Resa* III. 109 Af Ängelsmännerna heta de wild Honeysuckle, emedan de äro på långt håll mycket like Periclymenum eller Caprifolium. **1786** FRENEAU *Misc. Works* 152 [Poem entitled] The Wild Honey Suckle. **1832** S. J. HALE *Flora* 73 Honeysuckle, wild. . . . *Azalea procumbens.* . . . This species, so much esteemed for the beauty and fragrance of its flower, exists chiefly in North America. **1850** S. F. COOPER *Rural Hours* 134 They gather violets, and then again, the azalea, or 'wild honeysuckle,' as they call it. **1898** CREEVEY *Flowers of Field* 454 Sweet Wild Honeysuckle. *L. grata.* . . . Often cultivated, but found growing wild in rocky woodlands in New England, New Jersey, and southward.

Wild hop. Any one of various plants {1877, *dial.*}: **a.** A vine of the genus *Humulus.* **b.** (See quot. 1891.) {*dial.*} +**c.** The virgin's-bower, *Clematis virginiana.* — **1781–2** JEFFERSON *Notes Va.* (1788) 36 Wild hop. *Humulus lupulus.* **1795** [see GINGER 1]. **1819** E. DANA *Geogr. Sk.* 85 Divers species may be collected from the forests, which are useful in medicine and the arts; such as . . . Indian turnip, wild hops. **1891** *Cent.* 6924/3 Wild hop, the common bryony, *Bryonia dioica.* **1892** *Amer. Folk-Lore* V. 91 *Clematis Virginiana,* traveller's joy; wild hops, N.H.

* **Wild horse.** A horse living in a wild state; a mustang. — **1808** C. SCHULTZ *Travels* II. 144 Wild horses are likewise sometimes seen on the west side of the river. **1831** PECK *Guide* 164 *Wild horses* are found ranging the prairies. **1873** ARNY *Items regarding N. Mex.* 63 The wild horses of our plains occasionally excite the warm admiration of critical observers. **1923** J. H. COOK *On Old Frontier* 64 In a few places so-called 'wild horses' may be found; but they are not the original breed of mustang.

Wild hyacinth. {1812– (Withering *Brit. Plants* II. 422)} +**1.** The camass, *Camassia esculenta.* +**2.** The squirrel corn, *Dicentra canadensis.* — (1) **1847** [see EASTERN *a.* 7]. **1894** COULTER *Bot. W. Texas* III. 435. **1909** C. H. STERNBERG *Life of Fossil Hunter* 223 The Indians were roasting camus, the bulb of the wild hyacinth. (2) **1893** *Amer. Folk-Lore* VI. 137 *Dicentra Canadensis,* wild hyacinth. N.Y.

+**Wild Indian.** An Indian regarded as primitive, savage, or roving rather than settled; *spec.,* in the Southwest, an Indian not a Pueblo.

1840 *Texas Sentinel* (Austin) 22 Jan. 4/2 The wild Indians committed the depredations. **1851** *N. Mex. H. Rep. Jrnl.* 86 There are other persons who are opposed to all amicable relations with the wild Indians. **1866** *Rep. Indian Affairs* 78 The 'wild' Indian never thinks of owning any particular spot of ground. **1873** ARNY *Items regarding N. Mex.* 64 The wild Indians of New Mexico number . . . Navajos, 8,500 Apaches, 4,502 Utes, 1,347. **1913** LONDON *Valley of Moon* 295 He cut a swath through the Johnny Rebs . . . yellin' like a wild Indian.

attrib. **1854** BENTON *30 Years' View* I. 15/1 Shelter the wild Indian depredators upon the lives and property of all who undertook to pass from one to the other.

Wild indigo. +**a.** Any one of various American plants of the genus *Baptisia,* esp. *B. tinctoria,* used in dyeing. {1866} +**b.** Any one of various plants of the genus *Amorpha;* false indigo, from which a coarse indigo is said to have been made in early Carolina. **c.** (See quot. 1901.)

1778 CARVER *Travels* 519 Wild Indigo is an herb of the same species as that from whence Indigo is made in the southern colonies. **1819** *Western Rev.* I. 92 *Baptisia cerulea,* Blue wild Indigo. **1860** Darlington *Weeds & Plants* 108 The Wild Indigo . . . is conspicuous when in flower, especially in sandy woods and fields. **1877** BAGBY *Old Va. Gentleman* 3 Everybody is obliged to have wild indigo to keep flies off his horse's head in summer. **1889** *Cent.* 180/2 The false indigo, *A[morpha] fruticosa,* is occasionally cultivated for ornament. . . . Also called *bastard* or *wild indigo.* **1901** MOHR *Plant Life Ala.* 565 *Indigofera caroliniana.* . . . Wild Indigo. . . . Coast of North Carolina to Florida, west to western Louisiana.

* **Wilding.** ‖A wild animal. — **1897** *Advance* 23 Sept. 409/3 Not a specimen of these wildings [*sc.* deer, turkey, and otter] can be seen now.

+**Wild ipecac. a.** The ipecac spurge (*Tithymalopsis ipecacuanhae*), having a root used as an emetic and a purgative. **b.** = FEVERROOT c. — (a) **1815** DRAKE *Cincinnati* 87 Emetics. . . . *Euphorbia ipecacuanha*—wild ipecac, the root. **1843** TORREY *Flora N.Y.* II. 177 Wild Ipecac . . . is emetic, and is sometimes used as a substitute for the Ipecacuanha of the shops. **1857** GRAY *Botany* 387. (b) **1832** WILLIAMSON *Maine* I. 129 Also, we may mention *Fever-root,* which is perennial, and called *wild Ipecac.*

Wild ivy. Any one of various (usually creeping or climbing) plants growing wild. — **1775** BURNABY *Travels* 37 It was a delightful valley, . . . covered with . . . wild ivy, in full flower. **1802** DRAYTON *S. Carolina* 69 Calico flower, wild ivy, or laurel . . . kills sheep and other animals which eat its leaves. **1832** KENNEDY *Swallow Barn* I. 129 Some prim old maidish poplar . . . was furbelowed with wild ivy.

Wild jalap. +**1.** (See quotation.) **2.** = MAN-OF-THE-EARTH 1. {1884} — (1) **1863** PORCHER *Resources of Southern Fields* 21 *Podophyllum peltatum.* Wild jalap; May-apple; wild lemon; duck-weed. Diffused in rich swamp lands. (2) **1891** *Cent.* 6924/3.

Wild land. +Land either uncultivated or uncultivable; unsettled or unoccupied land; forest. — **1813** J. ADAMS *Works* X. 26 We had so much wild land, . . . that many years must pass before we should be ambitious of power upon the ocean. **1848** *S. Lit. Messenger* XIV. 312/2

[Carabas] had made a great blind purchase of wild lands, on a speculative credit. **1885** *Wkly. New Mexican Rev.* 22 Jan. 3/5 Trouble Brewing in Colfax County—opposed to Fencing Wild Lands. **1905** VALENTINE *H. Sandwith* 418 The coal mining company would make you a good offer for the wild land you own.

* **Wild lettuce. a.** Any one of various species of *Lactuca* growing wild, +esp. *L. canadensis.* **b.** Any one of various other plants, as various species of white lettuce (*Prenanthes*) {1760} +and a species of *Claytonia* sometimes used as a pot herb. Also with specifying term.

1784 [see PEPPERGRASS]. **1784** *Amer. Acad. Mem.* I. 475 *Prenanthes....* Ivyleaf. Ivy-leafed Wild Lettuce. **1847** WOOD *Botany* 359 *L*[*actuca*] *elongata.* Wild Lettuce.... A common, rank plant, growing in hedges, thickets, &c., where the soil is rich and damp. **1893** *Amer. Folk-Lore* VI. 138 *Claytonia perfoliata,* wild lettuce. S. Barbara Co., Cal. **1901** MOHR *Plant Life Ala.* 754.

+**Wild lily of the valley. 1.** The yellow clintonia (*Clintonia borealis*), or a related species. **2.** The shinleaf, *Pyrola elliptica.* **3.** =BEAD RUBY. — (1) **1829** EATON *Botany* (ed. 5) 184 *Convallaria borealis,* wild lily of the valley, dragoness-plant. **1909** WEBSTER 2385/2 W[*ild*] *lily of the valley,* ... the liliaceous plant *Clintonia umbellata.* (2) **1894** *Amer. Folk-Lore* VII. 93 *Pyrola elliptica,* wild lily-of-the-valley, Concord, Mass. (3) **1909** WEBSTER 2335/2 W[*ild*] *lily of the valley,* ... the bead-ruby (*Unifolium canadense*).

Wild lime. {1866–, in India, etc.} +**a.** =HOG PLUM 1. +**b.** = LAUREL CHERRY. +**c.** The Ogeechee lime, *Nyssa ogeche.* Also *wild limetree.* +**d.** The ironwood, *Zanthoxylum fagara.* — **1767** in Darlington *Mem. Bartram & Marshall* 292 The Wild Lime is a singular plant. **1791** W. BARTRAM *Travels* 94 These shelly ridges have a vegetable surface of loose black mould ... which naturally produces ... Tallow-nut or Wild Lime. **1813** MUHLENBERG *Cat. Plants* 48 *Prunus Caroliniana,* ... Wild lime. **1832** BROWNE *Sylva* 221 In Georgia this tree is known by the name of Sour Tupelo and Wild Lime. **1884** SARGENT *Rep. Forests* 31 *Xanthoxylum Pterota....* Wild Lime. **1897** SUDWORTH *Arborescent Flora* 266 *Xanthoxylum fagara....* Wild Lime. *Ib.* 311 *Nyssa ogeche.* Sour Tupelo.... Wild Limetree.

* **Wild oat.** Any one of various plants growing wild. Usually pl.

+**a.** The wild rice, *Zizania aquatica.* ***b.** Any one of various wild species of *Avena,* esp. *A. fatua.* +**c.** The poverty grass or oat grass, *Danthonia spicata.* +**d.** The bellwort, *Uvularia sessifolia.* **e.** The tall oat grass, *Arrhenatherum elatius.* +**f.** The Indian grass or wood grass, *Sorghastrum nutans.*

1705 [see BREAD 1 c]. **1775** CRESSWELL *Journal* 76 Wild Oats and Wild Rye in such plenty it might be mown and would turn out a good crop. **1781-2** JEFFERSON *Notes Va.* (1788) 36 Wild oat. *Zizania aquatica.* **1817-8** EATON *Botany* (1822) 262 *Danthonia spicata,* wild oats.... Leaves undulate, short. **1840** DEWEY *Mass. Flowering Plants* 237 Wild Oat. A small grass of no considerable importance. **1847** WEBSTER 1265/1 *Wild Oats,* ... a tall, oat-like kind of soft grass; the *Holcus avenaceus.* **1847** WOOD *Botany* 554 *Uvularia sessifolia.* Bellwort. Wild Oats. **1874** LONG *Wild-Fowl,* The entire surface [of a 300-acre pond] is covered with the dense growth of the wild oats or rice. **1884** VASEY *Agric. Grasses* 75 *Avena fatua.* (Wild oats) This species is very common in California. **1889** *Ib.* 36 *Chrysopogon nutans* (*Sorghum nutans*) (Wild Oats).... It grows rather sparsely and forms a thin bed of grass.

attrib. **1857** *Harper's Mag.* Nov. 817 [He] built a cabin of cedar logs in the 'wild oats country.' **1890** HARTE *Waif of Plains* 154 He was forced to defer his first self-prepared breakfast until he had reached ... a less dangerous place than the wild-oat field to build his first camp fire.

Wild oat grass. {1812– (Withering *Br. Plants* II. 201)} +**1.** Any one of various American species of *Danthonia.* Also with specifying terms. **2. a.** (See quotation.) +**b.** The Indian grass, *Sorghastrum nutans.* +**c.** The feather bunch grass, *Stipa viridula.* — (1) **1843** TORREY *Flora N.Y.* II. 454 *Danthonia spicata.* Wild Oat-grass.... Dry open woods and in fields. **1901** MOHR *Plant Life Ala.* 373 *Danthonia compressa....* Mountain Wild Oat Grass.... *Danthonia glabra....* Smooth Wild Oat Grass. ... *Danthonia sericea....* Silky Wild Oat Grass. (2. a) **1909** *Cent. Suppl.* 882/1 *Wild oat-grass,* ... the wild oat, *Avena fatua.* (b) *Ib., Wild oat-grass,* ... the Indian grass, *Sorghastrum avenaceum.* (c) *Ib., Wild oat-grass,* ... same as *feather bunch-grass.*

* **Wild olive.** Any one of various plants resembling the cultivated olive or bearing a similar fruit.

+**a.** The tupelo gum of the genus *Nyssa.* (See OLIVE TREE c.) +**b.** = SILVER BELL. Also *wild olive tree.* +**c.** =MASTIC. +**d.** The devilwood or American olive, *Osmanthus americanus.*

1806 in *Ann. 9th Congress* 2 Sess. 1142 The silk plant, wild endive, wild olive [grow in the vicinity of the Washita R.]. **1813** MUHLENBERG *Cat. Plants* 96 *Nyssa tomentosa,* ... Wild olive. **1831** AUDUBON *Ornith. Biog.* I. 122 The Wild Olive ... is small, brittle and useless. **1846** BROWNE *Trees Amer.* p. xi/2 Olive, Wild, 366. *Ib.* 366 *Halesia tetraptera,* The Common Snowdrop-Tree.... Wild Olive-tree, Britain and Anglo-America. **1897** SUDWORTH *Arborescent Flora* 317 *Sideroxylon mastichodendron.* Mastic.... Wild Olive (Fla.). *Ib.* 332 *Osmanthus americanus....* Devilwood. ... Wild Olive (Fla.). **1919** [see SILVER BELL].

+**Wild onion.** A plant of any one of various wild species of *Allium,* as the nodding onion, *A. cernuum.*

1654 JOHNSON *Wonder-w. Prov.* 54 With Fish, wild Onions and other Herbs were sweetly satisfied until other provisions came in. **1709** [see CIVE]. **1797** HAWKINS *Letters* 112 The old fields ... [are] covered with wild onion. **1805** ORDWAY in *Journal of Lewis & O.* 194 Found wild Inions. **1843** TORREY *Flora N.Y.* II. 309. **1915** ARMSTRONG & THORNBER *Western Wild Flowers* 14 Wild Onions are easily recognized by their characteristic taste and odor.

Wild orange. An orange tree growing wild, or any one of various other plants, as the laurel cherry, the angelica tree, the Osage orange, and the prickly ash (sense 1 c). {1866–, in W. Indies}

1802 DRAYTON *S. Carolina* 8 Small rising grounds sometimes present themselves; on which grow ... wild orange, ... and dwarf palmetto. **1810** MICHAUX *Arbres* I. 36 *Cerasus caroliniana, Wild orange,* ... seul nom donné à cet arbre dans la partie maritime des Etats méridionaux. **1858** WARDER *Hedges & Evergreens* 44 Our beautiful Wild Orange (*Cerasus caroliniana*) ... is much planted about Southern residences, for hedges. **1891** *Cent.* 6382/2 *Toothache-tree,* ... [the] *Aralia spinosa,* or angelica-tree, sometimes called *wild orange.* **1894** *Amer. Folk-Lore* VII. 98 *Maclura aurantiaca,* wild orange, N.J. **1897** SUDWORTH *Arborescent Flora* 265 *Xanthoxylum clava-herculis.* Prickly Ash. ... Wild Orange.

attrib. **1832** BROWNE *Sylva* 136 Wild Orange Tree. *Cerasus Caroliniana.* **1843** *Knickerb.* XXI. 225 The oaks seem[ed] like sheeted ghosts as we rode rapidly on ... [until] we came to the gate of the wild-orange hedge which enclosed the plantation.

* **Wild parsnip.** The common parsnip (*Pastinaca sativa*) in its wild form; also, any one of various other wild plants of the carrot family. — **1778** [see BLACK HELLEBORE]. **1790** [see FEVERROOT]. **1821** [see GRASS 1 b]. **1847** DARLINGTON *Weeds & Plants* 149 Cow-bane. Wild Parsnip. ... This is reputed to be an active poison, particularly to horned cattle. **1913** BARNES *Western Grazing Grounds* 267 Water Hemlock ... sometimes is called cowbane or wild parsnip.

Wild pea. Any one of various wild plants of the pea family. — **1778** CARVER *Travels* 515 Herbs [include:] ... Scabious, Mullen, Wild Pease. **1808** PIKE *Sources Miss.* 104 Their craws were filled with acorns and the wild pea. **1844** LEE & FROST *Oregon* 85 On the ridge next the ocean, ... the wild pea abounds. **1892** *Amer. Folk-Lore* V. 94 *Lupinus perennis,* wild pea. Worcester Co., Mass. **1893** *Ib.* VI. 140 *Crotalaria sagittalis,* wild pea. Ia.

+**Wild peach.** S. =LAUREL CHERRY. Also attrib. — **1831** HOLLEY *Texas* (1833) 50 The leaves resemble those of the peach tree. Hence it is called by the colonists, wild peach. **1836** — *Texas* 88 Among the underwood are found ... the wild peach tree—an evergreen bearing a white blossom. **1857** BRAMAN *Texas* 40 Its surface is covered with ... cane and wild-peach brakes. **1901** [see LAUREL CHERRY].

Wild pear (tree). {1812– (Withering *Br. Plants* III. 560)} +**1.** New Eng. The shadbush, *Amelanchier canadensis.* +**2.** (See quotation.) — (1) **1810** MICHAUX *Arbres* I. 32 *Mespilus arborea, June berry.... Wild pear* ..., dans le district de Maine. **1832** BROWNE *Sylva* 216 In the northern section of the Union, it is called *Wild Pear Tree* and *Sugar Plum.* (2) **1897** SUDWORTH *Arborescent Flora* 310 *Nyssa sylvatica.* Black Gum. ... [Also called] Wild Peartree (Tenn.).

+**Wild pea vine.** A wild vine, as the hog peanut, resembling the cultivated plant bearing the pea. — **1786** WASHINGTON *Diaries* III. 123 Some of the Wild Pea vine ... had been pulled. **1834** BRACKENRIDGE *Recollections* 34 We gathered the wild pea vine, and made ourselves soft beds under the shade of the trees. **1851** *S. Lit. Messenger* XVII. 565/1 We will ... let the horses eat the luxuriant wild pea-vine until the wagons come up.

Wild pigeon. {1719–} +Any native American, undomesticated pigeon, esp. the now extinct passenger pigeon. — **1738** BYRD *Dividing Line* (1901) 156 A Prodigious Flight of Wild Pigeons ... flew high over our Heads to the Southward. **1805** CLARK in *Lewis & C. Exped.* II. (1904) 226 A fiew wild pigions about our camp. **1842** *Niles' Nat. Reg.* 9 July 304/3, 3000 live wild pigeons, will arrive at 5 o'clock this afternoon ... by the freight train from Albany. **1880** *Cimarron News & Press* 23 Dec. 1/5 There are ... three species [of pigeons found here], the band-tailed pigeon, the wild pigeon—a plump bird found in large flocks, ... and the Carolina dove.

Wild pine. Any one of various pines growing wild. Also attrib. {1811} — **1848** THOREAU *Maine Woods* 71 Perchance where *our* wild pines stand ... husbandmen planted grain. **1881** *Rep. Indian Affairs* 131 Wild pine nuts and seeds they gather in the fall. **1894** *Harper's Mag.* Aug. 338/2 The wild pine region is far more interesting and attractive than those bits of forest with modern improvements.

Wild pink. a. Any one of various pinks growing wild, as the Deptford pink, *Dianthus armeria.* {1753–} +**b.** Any one of various American species of *Silene,* esp. *S. pennsylvanica.* +**c.** (See quot. 1894.)

1778 CARVER *Travels* 520 Wild Hollyhock, Wild Pinks, Golden Rod. **1814** BIGELOW *Florula Bostoniensis* 108 Wild pink.... This small species of pink has a leafy pubescent stem, ending in erect branches. *Ib.* 110 *Silene Pennsylvanica.* Catchfly.... Sometimes called *wild pink,* from its similarity in habit to some of that genus. **1836** EDWARD *Hist. Texas* 42 [He] recognizes ... [the] *wild-pinks.* **1893** *Amer. Folk-Lore* VI. 138 *Silene laciniata,* wild pink. S. Barbara Co., Cal. **1894** *Ib.* VII. 100 *Arethusa bulbosa,* wild pink, Atlantic City, N.J.

Wild plum. {1880, in S. Africa} The fruit of any one of various wild species of *Prunus*, +esp. the red plum (*P. americana*); also, the tree bearing such fruit. {wild plum tree, 1812– (Withering *Br. Plants* III. 558)}

1709 LAWSON *Carolina* 105 The wild Plums of America are of several sorts. **1786** [see CHEROKEE 6 a]. **1802** ELLICOTT *Journal* 286 The following will be met with in various parts of the country. Sassafras. . . . Locust, . . . wild plum, (*prunus chickasaw*) tulip tree [etc.]. **1838** FLAGG *Far West* II. 177 Endless thickets of the wild plum . . . were to be seen stretching for miles along the plain. **1851** BARRY *Fruit Garden* 120 The Canada or Wild Plum . . . abounds in Ohio, Michigan, and other western States. **1884** SARGENT *Rep. Forests* 65. **1897** SUDWORTH *Arborescent Flora* 236 ff. [5 species listed]. **1925** TILGHMAN *Dugout* 56 Fan being gone after some wild plums down the creek.

attrib. **1737** BRICKELL *N. Carolina* 77 The Wild Plum Tree, whereof there are two sorts, if not more, one is much sooner ripe than the other. **1888** *Insect Life* I. 89 The egg-laying habits of the Wild-Plum Weevil . . . have been described. *a*1918 G. STUART *On Frontier* II. 117 There are many wild plum thickets along the streams.

Wild potato. {in Jamaica} Any one of various wild plants.

+**a.** The man-of-the-earth. +**b.** The potato bean or groundnut, *Apios tuberosa.* +**c.** =HORSE NETTLE. +**d.** The spring beauty, *Claytonia virginica.*

1772 ROMANS in P. L. Phillips *Notes B. Romans* (1924) 124 The Savages are not so well provided with Bread as the Spaniards. . . . But both . . . [use] a Species of Convolvulus known by the Name of Wild Potatoe. **1778** CARVER *Travels* 511 Wild Potatoes, Liquorice, Snake Root, [etc.]. **1803–4** LEWIS in *L. & Clark Exped.* VI. (1905) 138 The common wild pittatoe also forms another article of food in savage life. **1819** *Amer. Farmer* I. 109 This is probably the *glycine apios,* or wild potato, which is nearly as good as the common. **1847** [see MAN-OF-THE-EARTH 1]. **1864** [see HORSE NETTLE]. **1892** *Amer. Folk-Lore* V. 93 *Claytonia Virginica,* wild potatoes. Union Co., Pa.

+**Wild potato vine. 1.** =MAN-OF-THE-EARTH 1. **2.** =MANROOT. — (1) **1833** [see MAN-OF-THE-EARTH 1]. **1898** CREEVEY *Flowers of Field* 459 Wild Potato-vine. . . . The root is tuberous, very large. (2) **1871** [see MAN-OF-THE-EARTH 2].

+**Wild red cherry. 1.** =PIN CHERRY. **2.** (See quotation.) — (1) **1847** WOOD *Botany* 240 C[*erasus*] *Pennsylvanica*. . . . Wild Red Cherry. . . . This tree is of rapid growth, and quickly succeeds a forest-clearing if neglected. **1919** STURTEVANT *Notes on Edible Plants* 462 Wild Red Cherry. . . . The fruit is sour and unpleasant. (2) **1897** SUDWORTH *Arborescent Flora* 237 *Prunus angustifolia.* Chickasaw Plum. . . . Wild Red Cherry (La.).

+**Wild rice.**

1. A tall aquatic plant (*Zizania aquatica*), the seeds of which were much used as food by the Indians.

1778 CARVER *Travels* 522 Wild Rice . . . grows in the greatest plenty throughout the interior parts of North America. **1819** E. DANA *Geogr. Sk.* 266 Lac du Bœuf . . . extends 12 miles, and is covered with *folles avoines,* or wild rice. **1846** MCKENNEY *Memoirs* I. 104 Savannas of wild rice grew out of it in all directions. **1897** *Outing* XXX. 544/1 The duck finds snails, wild rice, etc.

2. =RICE CUT-GRASS.

1847 DARLINGTON *Weeds & Plants* 369 False or wild Rice . . . is in the Northern States considered not only worthless, but rather a nuisance.

3. Attrib. and comb. with *eater, lake, tract.*

1824 KEATING *Narrative* (1825) I. 177 The Menomone, or wild rice eaters . . . [appear] to be fast decreasing in numbers. **1856** *Porter's Spirit of Times* 13 Dec. 242/1 The Canada goose and Hutchins' goose . . . rest at night . . . in reedy marshes and wild-rice lakes. **1874** COUES *Birds N.W.* 179 [Bobolinks throng] in countless hordes the wild-rice tracts and the grain fields.

Wild rose. Any one of various roses growing wild {1781–}, +as the swamp rose. Also attrib. — **1784** *Amer. Acad. Mem.* I. 451 Wild Rose. . . . This species is generally preferred for conserves. **1796** [see EGLANTINE]. **1850** COOPER *Rural Hours* 122 The wild roses are in flower. We have them of three varieties: the early rose . . . ; the low rose . . . ; and the tall many-flowered swamp rose. **1880** *Harper's Mag.* Aug. 333/1 The buttonwood-trees . . . must, with the undergrowth of blackberry vines and wild-rose bushes, have hidden me from sight. **1896** JEWETT *Pointed Firs* 30 A late golden robin . . . was singing close by in a thicket of wild roses.

Wild rosemary. {1611–} **1.** The moorwort, *Andromeda polifolia.* {1760} +**2.** (See quotation.) — (1) **1833** EATON *Botany* (ed. 6) 17 *Andromeda polifolia,* wild rosemary. **1891** *Cent.* 5231/3. (2) **1894** *Amer. Folk-Lore* VII. 96 *Conradina canescens,* . . . wild rosemary, Fla.

∗**Wild rye.** Any one of various grasses of the genus *Elymus,* or a similar plant. — **1751** GIST *Journals* 43 The wild Rye appeared very green and flourishing. **1794** T. COOPER *America* 32 A species of rush-grass, commonly called wild rye, from the similarity of its stalk to the rye so called among us. **1822** DEWEES *Lett. from Texas* 27 The wild rye . . . grows very plentifully here in the bottoms. **1884** VASEY *Agric. Grasses* 110 Wild rye, Lyme Grass, Terrell Grass. . . . In some localities this is common in low meadows, and is cut . . . for hay.

∗**Wild sage.**

1. A species of *Salvia,* +esp. meadow sage, *S. lyrata.*

The identity of the plant referred to in the first quotation is not certain.

1804 LEWIS in *L. & Clark Exped.* VI. (1905) 148 From it's resemblence in taste smell &c to the common Sage I have called it the wild Sage. **1817–8** EATON *Botany* (1822) 445. **1836** LINCOLN *Botany* App. 136.

+**2.** Any one of various species of *Artemisia;* sagebrush.

1807 GASS *Journal* 127 A kind of wild sage, . . . as high as a man's head . . . grows in these bottoms. **1847** RUXTON *Adv. Rocky Mts.* (1848) 208 Wild sage . . . is the characteristic plant in all the elevated plains of the Rocky Mountains. *a*1918 G. STUART *On Frontier* I. 20 Now I see fields of alfalfa and moving grain where were once the bunch grass and wild sage.

attrib. **1849** PARKMAN *Oregon Trail* 146 The restless young Indians . . . [often started] an antelope from the thick growth of wild-sage bushes.

Wild service (berry). Any one of various wild plants of the apple family {1741–}, +esp. the shadberry, *Amelanchier canadensis.* Also attrib. — **1785** MARSHALL *Amer. Grove* 90 *Mespilus nivea.* Early ripe, Esculent fruited Medlar, or wild Service. **1813** MUHLENBERG *Cat. Plants* 49 *Pyrus botryapium,* June berries, wild service, snowy pear. **1846** BROWNE *Trees Amer.* 325 *Pyrus aucuparia.* . . . Mountain Ash. Wild Service-tree, Anglo-America. **1847** WOOD *Botany* 245 A[*melanchier*] *Canadensis.* . . . Shad Berry. June Berry. Wild Service Berry.

+**Wild snakeroot. 1.** The black cohosh, *Cimicifuga racemosa.* **2.** The ground ivy, *Glecoma hederacea.* — (1) **1743** CLAYTON *Flora Virginica* 58 *Actæa racemis longissimis.* . . . Black or Wild-Snake-root. (2) **1892** *Amer. Folk-Lore* V. 102 *Nepeta Glechoma,* wild snake-root. Cambridge, Mass.

Wild strawberry. The fruit of any one of several uncultivated species of *Fragaria* {1620}, +esp. the Virginia strawberry (*F. virginiana*); also, the plant bearing this fruit. — **1814** BIGELOW *Florula Bostoniensis* 123 The common wild strawberry is a very delicious fruit. **1843** TORREY *Flora N.Y.* I. 212. **1852** *Knickerb.* XXXIX. 295 Uncle Theodore . . . sought to break his early morning's fast by partaking of some delicious wild straw-berries. **1891** WELCH *Recoll.* 1830–40 119 This basket was the receptacle . . . for bringing to market wild strawberries.

+**Wild throw.** Baseball. (See quot. 1868.) — **1866** *N.Y. Herald* 28 Aug. 8/2 The latter . . . [was] helped by . . . a wild throw by Osborne to Brentnall. **1868** CHADWICK *Base Ball* 46 A ball thrown beyond the reach of a fielder or base player . . . is counted as a wild throw. **1892** *Courier-Journal* 4 Oct. 5/1 A wild throw by Bierbauer, Merritt's sacrifice and a single by Clausen scored two runs.

+**Wild tobacco. 1.** The Indian tobacco, *Lobelia inflata.* **2.** Any one of various uncultivated plants of the genus *Nicotiana.* **3.** The toadflax, *Linaria vulgaris.* — (1) **1817–8** EATON *Botany* (1822) 340. **1832** WILLIAMSON *Maine* I. 125 The Lobelia, wild, or Indian tobacco, . . . is a powerful emetic and has given relief in asthmatic complaints. (2) **1885** HAVARD *Flora W. & S. Texas* 513 *Nicotiana repanda* . . . and *N. trigonophylla.* . . . Wild Tobacco . . . [does] not seem of much account for smoking. **1894** *Amer. Folk-Lore* VII. 95 *Nicotiana Bigelovii,* wild tobacco, Santa Barbara Co., Cal. (3) *Ib.* 96 *Linaria vulgaris,* . . . wild tobacco, Indian hemp, impudent lawyer, West Va.

+**Wild tomato.** Any one of various plants resembling or suggestive of the common cultivated tomato. — **1873** BEADLE *Undevel. West* 708 After strawberries and wild tomatoes came in the whole family usually took to the prairie on Sunday and 'browsed.' **1894** *Scribner's Mag.* May 603/1 'Cabrito,' or goat meat, [is] made into a stew with frijoles and the wild tomato. **1894** *Amer. Folk-Lore* VII. 95 *Physalis grandiflora,* . . . wild tomato, No. Minn.

+**Wild train.** (See quot. 1877 and cf. WILDCAT *n.* 5.) *colloq.* — **1877** BARTLETT 760 *Wild Train,* a railroad train not on the time-tables of the road, and therefore irregular, and 'not entitled to the track,' as the railroad phrase is, as against a regular train. **1888** *Chicago Inter-Ocean* 7 March 1/3 The dispatcher at Marshalltown was at fault, forgetting a wild train that was running north from Marshalltown.

Wild turkey. A large American bird (*Meleagris gallopavo*) formerly found wild over a large area of the United States; the flesh of this bird cooked as food. {1830–}

1612 SMITH, etc. *Virginia* I. 15 Wilde Turkies are as bigge as our tame. **1670** *S.C. Hist. Soc. Coll.* V. 168 Wilde turke . . . is not soe pleasant to eate of as ye tame, but very fleshy & farr bigger. **1709** LAWSON *Carolina* 149 The wild Turkeys I should have spoken of, when I treated of the Land-Fowl. **1779** *New Eng. Hist. & Gen. Reg.* XVI. 29 Went out this day gunning, saw deer and wild Turkey. **1822** WOODS *English Prairie* 122 I passed fourteen or fifteen wild turkeys, in a field. **1833** FLINT *D. Boone* 115 Venison and wild turkey, sweet potatoes and pies, smoked on their table. **1917** *Birds of Amer.* II. 31/1 Wild Turkeys are polygamists.

comb. **1846** THORPE *Myst. Backwoods* 61 The wild turkey-hunter is a being of solitude. *Ib.* 64 We, then, here have the best specimen of wild turkey-hunting.

∗**Wild turnip. a.** The turnip or the rutabaga growing wild. +**b.** The jack-in-the-pulpit, *Arisaema triphyllum.* — **1835** *S. Lit. Messenger* I. 394 Eight of our women who were gathering wild turnip in the prairies, had been captured and carried away by the Flat-heads. **1837** LINCOLN *Botany* 78 *Arum* . . . *triphyllum,* (Indian turnip, wild turnip, wakerobin). **1838** [see MUSTARD 1]. **1869** FULLER *Flower Gatherers* 73 Botanists call this plant *Arisaema triphyllum,* but common country people are content with the name of 'Wild Turnip.' **1898** A. M. DAVIDSON *Calif. Plants* 200 Some weeds are only cultivated plants relapsed into a natural condition; the wild turnip, which we call mustard, . . . for instance.

+**Wild West.** The western area of the United States, regarded as the scene of lawlessness and primitive ways of life. Also attrib. — **1851** [see METROPOLITAN *a*.]. **1857** *Quinland* II. 193, I now see how this wild West will regenerate the expiring East. **1887** *Courier-Journal* 18 Feb. 1/1 Their gang played before the members of the 'Wild West' organization of cowboys and Indians.

+**Wild western,** *a.* Of or pertaining to the wild West. — **1872** *Chicago Ev. Jrnl.* 3 July, The spirit of the wild Western piece is the same as that . . . of the Bret Harte and John Hay school of verse. **1901** WHITE *Claim Jumpers* 27 In the afternoon the young man took a vacation and hunted Wild Western adventures.

+**Wild West show.** A circus specializing in cowboy and Indian feats. — **1887** *Courier-Journal* 18 Feb. 5/4 Nate Salisbury, one of the proprietors of the Wild West show, was playing at the queer audience. **1888** W. F. CODY *Story of Wild West* 694 In the spring of 1883 (May 17th) I opened the Wild West Show at the fair grounds in Omaha. **1894** *Harper's Mag.* 475/1 The smart and flippant Parisian writers were sincerely disappointed because the exhibition at Chicago was not an exaggerated Wild West Show. **1923** *Outlook* 26 Sept. 136/1 The line of descent of the Stampede leads through the Wild West Show.

Wild yam(-root). {1756–, in W. Indies} +A twining vine (*Dioscorea paniculata*) growing wild in North America; the root of this, used medicinally. — **1843** TORREY *Flora N.Y.* II. 293 *Dioscorea villosa.* Wild Yam-root. . . . Thickets, borders of woods, etc. **1875** *Amer. Naturalist* IX. 392 Some of these [vines], as the wild yam, moonseed, . . . and other allied forms . . . , fill many a thicket with masses of tangled cords. **1901** MOHR *Plant Life Ala.* 449 *Dioscorea villosa.* . . . Wild Yam. . . . The root, under the name of 'wild yam root,' is used nonofficially in medicine.

***Wilk.** Variant of WHELK. — **1616** SMITH *New England* 29 [There are found] Pearch, Eels, Crabs, Lobsters, Muskles, Wilkes, Oysters, and diuerse others, &c. **1709** [see PERIWINKLE[1]]. **1794** *N.Y. State Soc. Arts* I. 134 The remaining two acres I manured with . . . the shells of clams, oysters, wilks and scollops.

+**Willet.** [Imitative of a bird cry.] The semipalmated snipe. — [**1709** LAWSON *Carolina* 147 Will Willet is so called from his Cry, which he very exactly calls Will Willet, as he flies.] **1791** BARTRAM *Travels* 70 [We] procured plenty of sea fowl, such as curlews, willets, snipes, sand birds, and others. **1813** WILSON *Ornithology* VII. 27 The willet is peculiar to America. **1855** [see DUSKY DUCK]. **1917** *Birds of Amer.* I. 247 The Willet . . . is another of our rapidly 'vanishing shore birds.'

William.** +A confederate bill for $100. — **1869** *Overland Mo.* III. 128 $100 bills were there called 'Williams,' and $50 bills 'Blue Williams.' *a1889** in Farmer 560/2 A Texan once told me . . . that he had 100,000 dollars in Williams laid up against that day . . . when he could exchange it, dollar with dollar, for greenbacks.

+**Williamsite.** [L. W. *Williams*, Amer. mineralogist.]. An American variety of serpentine. — **1848** *Amer. Jrnl. Science* 2 Ser. VI. 249 New Minerals. . . . Williamsite. . . . This mineral was sent to me by L. White Williams, . . . of West Chester, Chester Co., Penn.

+**Williamson's woodpecker.** A western woodpecker (*Sphyrapicus thyroideus*), the female of which was, for a time, regarded as a separate species and named the brown-headed woodpecker. — **1858** BAIRD *Birds Pacific R.R.* 105 Williamson's Woodpecker . . . has as yet only been found in the Rocky mountains, about latitude 40°, and westward. **1874** COUES *Birds N.W.* 289 Williamson's Woodpecker in Colorado . . . arrives in the neighborhood of Idaho Springs in the early or middle part of April. **1917** *Birds of Amer.* II. 152 Williamson's Woodpecker . . . has no red feathers on the top of his head.

+**Willies.** *pl. The willies*, a feeling of nervous discomfort; 'the creeps.' *colloq.*[2] — **1900** BONNER *Hard Pan* 99 It just gives me the willies to think of your being down on your luck. **1913** LONDON *Valley of Moon* 105 Bert gives me the willies the way he's always lookin' for trouble.

***Willow.**

***1.** A tree or bush of the genus *Salix;* the genus itself.

1674 *Cal. State P., Amer. & W.I.* VII. 581 Maine is . . . well furnished with . . . hills, and fruitful valleys, where grow . . . willow, buttonwood, poplar [etc.]. **1778** CARVER *Travels* 505 There are several species of the willow, the most remarkable of which is a small sort that grows on the banks of the Mississippi. **1832** BROWNE *Sylva* 301 The most common of the American willows . . . is . . . called Black Willow or simply Willow. *a***1918** G. STUART *On Frontier* I. 153 The creek in the center of the valley, [was] bordered by a heavy growth of willows.

***2.** The wood or osiers of such a tree.

1805 ORDWAY in *Jrnls. Lewis & O.* 272 [We] made a fish drag of willows and caught 520 fine pan fish. **1849** WIERZBICKI *California* 69 The saddle-tree is made of light wood—willow principally. **1869** BRACE *New West* 138 Around her were conical baskets of willow or osier. **1881** *Rep. Indian Affairs* 131 [They] live in camps made of limbs of trees or else willows placed in the form of a somewhat irregular horse-shoe, or in Southeastern Nevada in huts of adobe.

3. With specifying terms denoting particular species or varieties of willow.

1804 LEWIS in *L. & Clark Exped.* VI. (1905) 146 The wide leaf willow . . . grows in similar situations to that discribed with rispect to the narrow leaf willow. **1805** CLARK *Ib.* II. (1904) 168 A fine spring . . . near which place 4 cotton willow trees grew. **1817–8** EATON *Botany* (1822) 444 *Salix nigra*, brittle-point willow, black-willow. **1843** TORREY *Flora N.Y.* II. 212 *Salix rigida.* Rigid Heart-leaved Willow. . . . Wet places along rivers. **1845** LINCOLN *Botany* App. 161/1 *Salix discolor*, (bog willow). **1847** DARLINGTON *Weeds & Plants* 328 *S[alix] viminalis.* . . . Osier. Basket Willow. A large shrub or small bushy tree. **1869** *Rep. Comm. Agric. 1868* 202 Weeping and drooping trees.—Babylonian willow (*Salix Babylonica.*)—[It is] of rapid growth. *Ib.*, Kilmarnock willow (*Salix caprea*) . . . [is] one of the most distinct of the hardy weeping plants. **1891** *Cent.* 6929/1 *Sandbar willow, Salix longifolia*, a small tree often forming dense clumps of great beauty on river sandbars and banks.

4. *attrib.* and *comb.* **a.** Designating things made of parts of willow trees.

1663 *Plymouth Rec.* 67 On the north side and west end it is bounded with a willow stake by a smale Rocke stone. **1793** *Mass. Spy* 19 Sept. 4/3 John Nazro . . . will sell . . . Chip and willow Hats. **1848** BRYANT *California* xii. 167 Willow-baskets . . . contained service-berries. **1852** *S. Lit. Messenger* XVIII. 364/1 His hut was the depository wherein had lain at different times, thousands of birch-bark, willow-skin or parchment letters. **1882** 'M. HARLAND' *Eve's Daughters* 109 A half-teaspoonful of powdered willow-charcoal is a harmless and in most cases an effectual corrective. **1883** *Century Mag.* Oct. 897/1 He sat in a large willow chair very much at his ease. **1887** *Courier-Journal* 6 Feb. 3/6 For Sale . . . willow rockers and settees. **1899** *Boston Traveller* 25 July, No one seems to know how the name of 'Willow Stateroom' first came to this piece of furniture.

b. Designating places characterized by a growth of willows.

1804 CLARK in *Lewis & C. Exped.* I. (1904) 47 Behind a Small Willow Island in the bend is a Prarie. **1804** LEWIS *Ib.* VI. (1905) 146 These willow bars form a pleasant beacon to the navigator at that season when the banks of the river are tumbling in. **1807** GASS *Journal* 23 We . . . landed on a willow bank. *Ib.* 51 We passed a willow bottom. *Ib.* 274 A cotton tree island . . . rears itself predominant over the surrounding willow marsh. **1827** COOPER *Prairie* iv, If the travellers who lie near the willow brake are not awoke out of their sleep by a visit from these miscreants. **1869** J. R. BROWNE *Adv. Apache Country* 146 He flung himself into a willow thicket and there made battle. **1880** CABLE *Grandissimes* 347 Out to westward rose conspicuously the old house and willow-copse of Jean-Poquelin.

c. In the specific names of insects and birds.

1854 EMMONS *Agric. N.Y.* V. 207 The antiope or willow butterfly survives the winter. **1888** RITTENHOUSE *Maud* 411 Dr Bower . . . brushed a willow-fly from my belt. **1917** *Birds of Amer.* III. 15 On the Pacific coast the differences are . . . great enough to make a separate variety called the Willow Goldfinch (*Astragalinus tristis salicamans*). **1872** COUES *Key to Birds* 235 *Lagopus albus.* Willow Ptarmigan. **1917** *Birds of Amer.* III. 229 The Willow Thrush (*Hylocichla fuscescens salicicola*) is a form of the Veery which is a little duller in coloration. **1839** PEABODY *Mass. Birds* 312 The Willow Wren, *Sylvia trochilus*, . . . is named from its attachment to the willow.

Willow brush. A mass of willow branches. — **1867** *Ore. State Jrnl.* 5 Jan. 1/2 This structure . . . consisted of three lines of piles substantially driven, carefully filled in with willow brush.

Willow bush. A willow shrub. {1876} — **1723** *Providence Rec.* XVI. 223 The afore Said Line . . . Begining at a willow bush or tree marked. **1805** LEWIS in *L. & Clark Exped* II. (1904) 234 Early this morning we passed about 40 little booths formed of willow bushes to shelter them from the sun. **1902** WHITE *Blazed Trail* 102 It was a little painted frame house, . . . with a willow bush at one corner.

+**Willow grouse.** The willow ptarmigan. (Cf. PTARMIGAN 1.) — **1825** RICHARDSON in Wilson & Bonaparte *Amer. Ornith.* IV. 327 The willow grouse inhabits the fur countries from the fiftieth to the seventieth parallels of latitude, . . . breeding in the valleys of the Rocky Mountains. **1872** [see PTARMIGAN 1]. **1902** WISTER *Virginian* 142 He had showed her where a covey of young willow-grouse were hiding as their horses passed.

***Willow-herb.** A plant of the genus *Epilobium* or *Chamaenerion*, esp. the fireweed, *E.* or *C. angustifolium.*

1784 *Amer. Acad. Mem.* I. 438. **1850** S. F. COOPER *Rural Hours* 154 The showy willow-herb, with its pyramid of lilac flowers [is opening]. **1882** *Harper's Mag.* May 861 Those 'pink spikes of the willow-herb,' also called fire-weed. **1915** ARMSTRONG & THORNBER *Western Wild Flowers* 316 Willow Herb. *Epilobium Franciscanum.* . . . A perennial, not especially pretty, with a stout, reddish stem.

b. With specifying terms denoting various species of these and other genera.

1784 *Amer. Acad. Mem.* I. 415 *Lysimachia.* . . . Yellow Willowherb. . . . In woodland. June. **1814** BIGELOW *Florula Bostoniensis* 90 *Epilobium coloratum.* Coloured Willow herb. . . . Meadows and swamps. **1843** TORREY *Flora N.Y.* I. 231 *Epilobium angustifolium.* Rose-bay Willow-herb. *Ib.* 233 *Epilobium palustre.* Narrow-leaved Willow-herb.

***Willow-leaf.** *attrib.* +In the specific names of plants and trees: Bearing leaves similar to those of a willow. — **1817–8** EATON *Botany* (1822) 467 *Solidago stricta*, willow-leaf golden-rod. **1844** GREGG *Commerce of Prairies* I. 159 Willow-leaf or bitter cottonwood . . . has been reckoned by some a species of cinchona. **1897** SUDWORTH *Arborescent Flora* 216 *Cratægus crus-galli salicifolia*, . . . Willowleaf Cockspur. *Ib.* 246 *Prunus salicifolia*, Willowleaf Cherry.

Willow-leaved, *a.* =prec. {1731–} — **1785** MARSHALL *Amer. Grove* 124 *Quercus Phellos latifolia.* Broad Willow-leaved Oak. **1796** B. HAWKINS *Letters* 51 The growth pine, not large, with blackjack and willow leaved hickory. **1814** BIGELOW *Florula Bostoniensis* 198 *Aster salicifolius.* Willow leaved Aster. . . . A very tall, slender species.

+**Willow oak.** An oak of the eastern states, *Quercus phellos*, or the laurel oak, *Q. laurifolia.*

1709 LAWSON *Carolina* 93 Willow-Oak is a sort of Water-Oak. 1775 *Amer. Husbandry* I. 377 *Willow oak*, so called from the near resemblance of the leaf to that of a willow. 1832 BROWNE *Sylva* 279 The willow oak, in favorable situations, attains the height of 50 or 60 feet. 1897 SUDWORTH *Arborescent Flora* 175, 177. 1901 MOHR *Plant Life Ala.* 87 The willow oak . . . is most abundant in wet, undrained flats of an impervious soil.

b. With adjectives denoting particular varieties or a related species of this oak.

See also UPLAND WILLOW OAK.

c1729 CATESBY *Carolina* I. 22 The Highland Willow Oak . . . grows on dry poor land. 1817 S. BROWN *Western Gazetteer* 24 [There are] three [species] of willow oak, upland, swamp, and *shingle*, so called from its being an excellent material for shingles. 1837 WILLIAMS *Florida* 76 Oak, high willow. *Quercus cinera*—on barren hills. 1894 COULTER *Bot. W. Texas* III. 417 *Quercus cinerea*. (High-ground willow-oak.)

+**Willow swamp.** A swamp in which willows grow. {1901, in Siberia} Also attrib. — 1644 *R.I. Col. Rec.* I. 83 No more landes shall be layed out . . . from the brooke to the great swamp; that is to say, the willow swamp footpath. 1883 *Century Mag.* Oct. 922/1 Occasionally in the spring . . . they [snipe] may be found in alder or willow swamps near their usual haunts.

*Willow tree. =WILLOW 1. — 1658 *Charlestown Land Rec.* 81 [The land] is boundid . . . ffrom the sayd stump to a mapell stump, and so by a willow tree. 1785 MARSHALL *Amer. Grove* 139. 1868 HAWTHORNE *Note-Books* II. 70 A large and beautiful willow tree . . . sweeps against the overhanging eaves. 1914 STEELE *Storm* 304, [I] ran on, grazing a wall and veering into a willow-tree.

+**Willowware. 1.** Articles made from willow osiers. **2.** Crockery decorated with a well-known willow pattern. Also attrib. — (1) 1851 CIST *Cincinnati* 172 Baskets, Cradles, Wagons, and other willow-ware. 1869 J. R. BROWNE *Adv. Apache Country* 276 They [the Papago Indians] . . . are expert in the manufacture of pottery and willow ware. 1892 *York County Hist. Rev.* 43 The premises are conveniently arranged . . . with two warehouses, one for the storage of crockeryware wood and willow-ware. (2) c1885 R. COLLYER in J. H. Holmes *Life & Lett.* (1917) I. 24 A great rack for the pewter dishes and willow ware. 1893 *Post Harvard Stories* 109 It was like the bridge in a blue willow-ware plate. 1904 GLASGOW *Deliverance* 58 The china consisted of some odd, broken pieces of old willow-ware.

Willow whistle. A whistle made from the bark of a willow wand. — 1843 STEPHENS *High Life N.Y.* II. 203, I was sartin that the old fox would peel me, as he would peel bark for a willow whistle. 1853 *Knickerb.* XLII. 171 The bobolinkums . . . utter many a wise and witty criticism on willow-whistles and musical instruments in general. 1883 [see MELODEON[1]].

+**Wilmot Proviso.** (See quot. 1885.) Also attrib. and transf. (See also PROVISO b.)

1847 in *Amer. Hist. Ass. Rep.* II. 1138 If the Wilmot proviso . . . should receive the sanction of Congress, it will strongly tend to favor the views which we entertain. 1848 *Congress. Globe* 18 May 781/2 The Baltimore Convention . . . would consist of Wilmot-proviso men and anti-Wilmot-proviso men. 1851 in Stowe *Key* 188/1 It is useless to talk about strict construction, State rights, or Wilmot provisos. 1857 BENTON *Exam. Dred Scott Case* 117 Some [voted] because they deemed it the best kind of a Wilmot proviso. 1863 KETTELL *Hist. Rebellion* II. 643 The 'Wilmot Proviso' act . . . had been settled in the compromises of 1850. 1885 *Mag. Amer. Hist.* May 496/2 *Wilmot Proviso.*—A measure introduced into Congress by David Wilmot, of Pennsylvania, in 1846, absolutely excluding slavery from the new territories then about to be acquired from Mexico.

+**Wilson.** [Alexander *Wilson*, Amer. ornithologist (1766–1813).] Used in the possessive in the names of various birds. (See also WILSON'S PETREL, PHALAROPE, etc.). — 1839 PEABODY *Mass. Birds* 368 Wilson's Sandpiper . . . is found, in its season, on all the shores and in all the markets of the Union. 1869 *Amer. Naturalist* II. 597 Wilson's Owl (*Otus Wilsonianus*). . . . It seems to be generally distributed across the continent. 1891 *Cent.* 6930/3 Wilson's bluebird, the common eastern bluebird of the United States, *Sialia sialis*. *Ib.*, Wilson's stint. 1892 Wilson's black-cap warbler [see BLACK-CAP 1]. 1902 WHITE *Blazed Trail* 296 Wilson's warblers, pine creepers, black-throats [etc.] . . . passed silently or noisily, each according to his kind. 1917 *Birds of Amer.* I. 60 Common Tern. . . . Sea Swallow; Wilson's Tern.

+**Wilson's petrel.** The common stormy petrel, *Oceanites oceanicus.* — 1844 *Nat. Hist. N.Y., Zoology* II. 290 Wilson's Petrel, *Thalassidroma Wilsoni*, . . . or *Mother Carey's Chicken*, occurs commonly along our coast from Mexico to high northern latitudes. 1884 *Nat. Museum Bul.* No. 27, 175. 1917 *Birds of Amer.* I. 85/1 Leach's Petrel and Wilson's Petrel are supplementary each of the other.

+**Wilson's phalarope.** A rather large phalarope (*Steganopus tricolor*), found in the West. — 1828 BONAPARTE *Synopsis* 342. 1874 COUES *Birds N.W.* 468 Wilson's Phalarope is of very general distribution . . . from the Mississippi Valley westward. 1917 *Birds of Amer.* I. 221 To find Wilson's Phalarope one has to journey to the northwest interior.

+**Wilson's plover.** A ring plover (*Pagolla wilsonia*) found in the southern states. — 1828 BONAPARTE *Synopsis* 299 Wilson's Plover . . . inhabits the sea shores of the southern and middle states during summer. 1844 *Nat. Hist. N.Y., Zoology* II. 211. 1917 *Birds of Amer.* I. 266 Wilson's Plover looks like a bleached and faded copy of the Semipalmated.

+**Wilson('s) snipe.** A common snipe of the United States, *Capella delicata.* — 1857 *Rep. Comm. Patents: Agric. 1856* 159 The summer range of Wilson's snipe . . . extends northward far beyond the limits of the United States. 1883 Wilson snipe [see FEEDING GROUND 2]. 1917 *Birds of Amer.* I. 229 The food of Wilson's Snipe is known to include crane-flies ('leather-jackets'), locusts, grasshoppers [etc.].

+**Wilson('s) thrush.** =VEERY. — 1839 PEABODY *Mass. Birds* 306 Wilson's Thrush . . . is described by Nuttall as a common bird, resembling the wood thrush in its voice and song. 1858 BAIRD *Birds Pacific R.R.* 214. 1876 WHITMAN *Spec. Days* 84, I could make out the bobolink, tanager, Wilson's thrush. 1882 GODFREY *Nantucket* 241/1 Wilson Thrush (*Turdus fuscescens*). 1917 *Birds of Amer.* III. 228 Alexander Wilson, in whose honor the bird is often called 'Wilson's Thrush,' . . . [never] heard the unique and beautiful song of this bird.

Wilt, *v.*
Of dial. origin. Chiefly U.S. in early nineteenth century.

1. *intr.* Of plants: To become limp; to droop. Also quasi-passive: To be wilted. {1691–}

1750 *Mass. H. S. Coll.* VII. 240 The Indian corn rolled up and wilted. 1810 CUTLER in *Life & Corr.* II. 343 One flower . . . continued to open until 11 o'clock at night, when it began to close; in the morning quite wilted. 1817 *Mass. Spy* 5 March (Th.), You perceived that [the rod] was dry and tough; it was wilted in the ashes of the great conflagration. 1866 LOWELL *Biglow P.* 2 Ser. p. xl, We express the first stage of withering in a green plant suddenly cut down by the verb *to wilt*. 1904 GLASGOW *Deliverance* 166 The first ripe stalk . . . hung, slowly wilting, on the earth.
fig. 1899 QUINN *Penna. Stories* 48 [His] loud shirt was wilting under the influence of his great exertions.

+**b.** *transf.* Of persons: To lose confidence or vigor; to become limp. Freq. with *down*.
1787 A. ADAMS *Familiar Lett.* 333 Mrs. Cranch . . . is wilted just enough to last to perpetuity. 1847 ROBB *Squatter Life* 99, I wilted down, and gin up right straight. 1866 LOWELL *Biglow P.* 2 Ser. p. xli, The imaginative phrase 'he wilted right down,' like 'he caved right in,' is a true Americanism. 1885 WILKINS in *Harper's Mag.* March 595/1 He begun to look kind of ashamed, an' wilted right down. 1912 *N.Y. Ev. Post* 15 July 1/1 (Th. S.), The English runners entirely wilted and were unable to approach their ordinary records.

2. *tr.* To make limp; to cause to lose vigor or confidence.
1809 T. DWIGHT *Theology* (1819) IV. 165 Despots . . . have wilted the human race into sloth and imbecility. 1878 *Scribner's Mo.* XVI. 55/2 No breeze stirs it; no sun wilts it. 1888 DELAND *John Ward* 233 The full blaze of sunshine . . . was wilting the dish of violets.

Wilted, *a.* Limp, exhausted. {1830–} — 1809 IRVING *Knickerb.* III. vii, The rest of the house . . . is decorated with fanciful festoons of wilted peaches and dried apples. 1833 *Knickerb.* II. 152 In the forests, their [locusts'] course is marked by the wilted and sallow leaves of the young and tender branches. 1860 HAWTHORNE *Works* (1883) VI. 493 The combatants . . . now pelted one another with mock sugar-plums and wilted flowers. 1908 'YESLAH' *Tenderfoot S. Calif.* 39 After you've carted a wilted bunch [of poppies] around for a few hours, you aint much stuck on 'em.

Wilton. {1904} A kind of cloth made in Wilton, England. Also attrib. — 1773 *Penna. Gazette* 21 April 1/1 Fine broadcloths, cassimers, saggathies, and Wiltons. 1777 *N.J. Archives* 2 Ser. I. 420 A fellow who calls himself William Glan . . . had on when he went away a yellowish wilton coat.

Wilton carpet. A kind of carpet manufactured in Wilton, Eng.; carpeting of a similar type. {1889–} — 1774 *Penna. Gazette* 10 Aug. Suppl. 2/2 Wilton and Scotch carpets. 1789 in *Century Mag.* XXXVII. 852/2 The floors [are] covered with the richest kind of Turkey and Wilton carpets. 1876 KNIGHT 2776/2 *Wilton-carpet*, a carpet made like Brussels, excepting that the wire is flattened instead of being round.

*Wimble. A gimlet, auger, or other tool for boring. Also attrib. — 1640 *Conn. Rec.* I. 448 An Inventory of the goods and Cattell of James Olmestead [includes]: . . . 4 brueing vessells, . . . wymbles. 1641 *Essex Probate Rec.* I. 14, 2 wimble trees. 1673 *Essex Inst. Coll.* L. 27 Wimble stocks wimble bitts 2 saddles & bridles.

*Win, *v.*
To win in a walk, (see WALK *n.* 6 b).

+**1.** *To win beef*, to shoot so well at a shooting match as to secure beef as a prize; *to win hands down*, to win decisively or impressively; *to win by a nose*, fig., to win by a narrow margin.
1835 LONGSTREET *Ga. Scenes* 217 He called his rifle the Soap-stick, and . . . he was very confident of winning beef with her. 1896 *Internat. Typogr. Union Proc.* 24/2 A cut down of about 25 per cent., . . . was successfully resisted by me winning 'hands down.' 1907 *St. Nicholas* Sept. 997 Won by a nose! Score 10 to 9.

*2. *To win out*, +to be victorious or successful. *colloq.*
1896 *Voice* 9 April 4/5 McKinley will lead on the first ballot, but 'who will win out' is a different question. 1902 McFAUL *Ike Glidden* 170 Quite a party of our people are here hoping to see your horse win out. 1923 HERRICK *Lilla* 72 'Old Lil' had won out!

Winchester. + =next. [1871 *Standard* 1 Feb., The arms . . . being the Remington and the Chassepot, with some few Winchesters.] 1883 M. H. FOOTE *Led-Horse Claim* 160 They dassent try it on with less than fifty Winchesters. **1898** CANFIELD *Maid of Frontier* 121 Under their knees they felt the Winchesters in the long scabbards. **1925** [see REPEATING a.].

+**Winchester rifle.** [Oliver F. *Winchester*, Amer. manufacturer (1810–80).] A breech-loading rifle, usually of a lever-loading, tubular magazine type, manufactured by the Winchester Arms Co. Also *Winchester repeating rifle.* — **1877** in Fleming *Hist. Reconstruction* II. 79 There was issued . . . a large number of Winchester rifles. **1885** *Outing* VII. 18/1 From the dead Chiricahuas had been taken four nickel-plated, breech-loading Winchester repeating rifles. **1899** in *Congress. Rec.* 25 Jan. (1900) 1169/2 The city had ordered several thousand Winchester rifles. **1906** C. D. WRIGHT *Battles of Labor* 131 The Pinkertons were armed with Winchester rifles.

* **Wind.**

+**1.** In colloq. phrases. **a.** *To throw up in(to) the wind,* to bring into an unsettled state. **b.** *To slip one's wind,* to die.

(a) **1809** *Steele P.* II. 612 Sectry Smith has quarrelled with Jackson, and thrown the whole business 'again up in the wind.' **1810** *Ib.* 640 [He] proceeded from a disposition to . . . throw the whole business *up into the wind* again. (b) **1883** *Gringo & Greaser* 1 Sept. 2/2 He had entirely slipped his wind—for want of which he was buried the 11th ult. **1884** *Ib.* 1 Jan. 1/1 The old darky-fraud, who dubbed herself Sojourner Truth, has slipped her wind.

+**2.** In special combinations.

Wind pox, chicken pox; *w. pump,* (see quotation); *w. reef,* a ripple on the water caused by the wind but apparently produced by a reef; *w. sucker,* a horse afflicted with crib-biting, a crib-biter; *w. work,* talk, discussion, planning, etc., that precedes active work on an undertaking.

1868 *N.Y. Herald* 1 July 5/6 The children were all well, with the exception that they had the wind pox and were weakly. **1876** KNIGHT 2783/2 *Wind-pump,* a pump driven by a wind-wheel. **1876** 'MARK TWAIN' *Old Times* iii. 56 It wasn't a bluff reef. . . . It wasn't anything but a wind reef. **1850** *New Eng. Farmer* II. 55 How to cure a 'Wind Sucker.' **1873** BEADLE *Undevel. West* 130 The wind-work is all done, and grading will commence about September first.

Windbreak. Any one of various obstacles or barriers, as a row of trees, a hill, etc., that breaks the force of the wind or gives protection from it. {1894–} 'Chiefly *U.S.*' (*O.E.D.*). — **1861** *Ill. Agric. Soc. Trans.* IV. 449 These trees, which are valuable as shade and as wind-breaks, should be planted. **1883** W. G. RITCH *Illust. N. Mex.* 116 No expense need be incurred for shelter during the winter, . . . the timber, hills, and valleys furnishing natural wind-breaks. **1891** *Century Mag.* March 653 He would . . . erect a small 'wind-break' of brush and fat stones, such as the Indians make. **1924** CROY *R.F.D. No. 3* 48 He could see . . . the 'wind-break' on the northwest.

+**Windbreaker.** Something which breaks the force of the wind; a windbreak. — **1873** BEADLE *Undevel. West* 730 If there is any windbreaker northwest, between there and Alaska, I had no evidence of it. **1893** *Dialect Notes* I. 334 *Wind breaker:* a screen or the like used to break the force of the wind. [N.J.]

* **Windfall.** A heap of blown-down trees; a tract upon which the trees have been leveled by a wind. {1830, in Canada} — **1838** *Knickerb.* XII. 491 The 'wind-fall' had been set on fire, leaving nothing but the long blackened bodies of the pines. **1877** W. WRIGHT *Big Bonanza* 329 This region somewhat resembles the track of a tornado in a timbered country —what is called a 'windfall.' **1894** *Outing* XXIV. 416/2 You may catch a passing glimpse of a black body clambering frantically through a windfall. **1924** R. CUMMINS *Sky-high Corral* 78 He wallowed through the windfall and climbed out of the gulch.

Windfish. +**1.** (See quotation.) +**2.** The fallfish, *Leucosomus corporalis.* — (1) **1842** *Nat. Hist. N.Y., Zoology* IV. 192 The Variegated Bream. *Abramis versicolor.* . . . The name of Wind-fish is derived from one of its habits. Whenever a light flaw of wind ruffles the water, thousands of these fish may be seen darting to the surface, and as suddenly disappearing. (2) **1891** *Cent.* 6935/2 *Windfish,* the fall-fish, or silver chub, . . . the largest cyprinoid of eastern North America. **1896** JORDAN & EVERMANN *Check-List Fishes* 246 Wind-fish; Corporal. Abundant from St. Lawrence River to the James, east of the Alleghanies.

* **Windflower.** One of various species of *Anemone.* — **1817–8** EATON *Botany* (1822) 174 *Anemone virginiana,* wind flower. **1835** BIRD *Hawks* I. 62 There is such an array of azaleas below, with blood-roots and wind-flowers, and dog-wood, as has half-turned my brain. **1882** *Century Mag.* Sept. 778/1 Flowers grew in abundance among the snow-banks— . . . yellow violets, wind-flowers and half a dozen other species. **1914** 'BOWER' *Flying U Ranch* 189, I sure do like them wind-flowers scattered all over the ground.

+**Windgap.** (See quot. 1889.) — **1779** *N.H. Hist. Soc. Coll.* VI. 314 This morning the troops . . . pass the Windgap, so called, for its being the only pass for a number of miles through a long chain of mountains. *a*1813 WILSON *Foresters* 85 This pass in the Blue mountain is usually called the Wind Gap. **1889** J. D. WHITNEY *United States* 223 Gaps . . . in which the depression in the ridge is not sufficiently deep to give passage to a watercourse are known as 'wind-gaps.'

* **Winding blade.** +A step in dancing. *Obs.* — *a*1846 *Quarter Race Ky.* 179 He even introduced a new step, which would be as difficult to describe as to perform. He called it the *windin blades.* **1848** JUDSON *Mysteries N.Y.* I. 91 Every step in the hornpipe, fling, reel, &c., was brought in; . . . and, then, to close up, the richest step of all . . . , the winding-blade.

* **Windmill.** A mill the machinery of which is driven by the wind.

1634 WOOD *New Eng. Prospect* 78 These Indians . . . doe much extoll and wonder at the English for their strange Inventions, especially for a Wind-mill. **1724** JONES *Virginia* 53 As for grinding Corn, &c. they have good Mills . . . ; besides Hand-Mills, Wind-Mills [etc.]. **1803** *Mass. H. S. Coll.* 1 Ser. IX. 202 Windmills may be seen on almost every eminence in this part of the country. **1892** *York County Hist. Rev.* 112 He has a fine windmill and water pipes conveniently arranged in the house. **1906** J. S. GARLAND *New Eng. Town Law* R.I. 119 The town council of any town may remove all such windmills within their towns as are located . . . contrary to the provisions of this chapter.

attrib. **1684** *Portsmouth Rec.* 222 Two acres of Land on the windmill hill. **1831** *Louisville Pub. Adv.* 1 Sept., Bark Mills, Wind Mill Irons, . . . for Sale. **1891** C. ROBERTS *Adrift Amer.* 149 He had bought the exclusive right to sell and set up a kind of patent windmill-pump in Texas.

* **Window.**

***1.** An opening for air and light in a wall or side of a building.

1622 'MOURT' *Relation* 142 Bring Paper, and Linced oyle for your Windowes. **1652** *Suffolk Deeds* I. 194 The sajd John Capen shall have libertje to make windowes for light on that side next to me. **1786** [see FISHING SEASON]. **1852** MITCHELL *Dream Life* 166 Honey-suckle . . . grew over the window. **1892** M. A. JACKSON *Gen. Jackson* 196 On either side of the fireplace is a window. **1922** TARKINGTON *Gentle Julia* 151 The open windows of the dining-room revealed an evening of fragrant clarity.

+**b.** An opening in a canebrake.

1855 *Harper's Mag.* Oct. 604/1 After crossing one or two lagoons, the hunters came to a 'window,' and among the matted limbs of trees and cane the dogs halted.

2. Attrib. with *arch, bolt, cap,* etc.

*c*1645 *Harvard Rec.* I. 10 It[em] for window-hookes, 4[d]. **1713** *Va. State P.* I. 175 Rubbing, Cutting, & Setting ye Window Arches. **1815** *Niles' Reg.* IX. 94/2 Straw knives and window bolts. **1857** VAUX *Villas* 280, I am not aware of any existing example in the United States of a window-hood constructed of stone. **1866** *Harper's Mag.* Oct. 635/1 It had been a stanch fire-proof dwelling-house in its day, with marble cornice and carved window-caps. **1886** *Harper's Mag.* July 196/1, 3500-pound barred window-guards intercept the sunlight. **1887** WILKINS *Humble Romance* 250 Unpainted walls with white windowfacings.

3. In special combinations.

Window balcony, a balcony before a window; *w. display,* a display of merchandise in a shop window; *w. garden,* flowers growing in pots or boxes on a window sill or ledge; *w. hanger,* an advertising bill or poster suitable for displaying in a window; *w.-maker,* one who makes windows; *w. mirror,* (see quotation); *w. privilege,* the privilege of displaying an advertising poster in a shop window; *w. weight,* a weight serving as a counterpoise for a window.

1883 *Century Mag.* Nov. 41/2 Much lattice-work also will be observed . . . at the angle formed by a window-balcony with some lofty court-wall. **1898** CAHAN *Imported Bridegroom* 228 Straying forlornly by inexorable window displays, men and women would pause here and there. **1883** CABLE *Dr. Sevier* 81 The asylumed widows of 'St. Anna's' could glance down . . . over their poor little window-gardens. **1895** *N.Y. Dramatic News* 19 Oct. 3/4 After the window hangers and Sunday 'ads' were all out, the play was omitted. **1820** FLINT *Lett. from Amer.* 213 [There are:] a window maker; . . . and one fanning mill maker. **1883** KNIGHT *Suppl.* 948/2 *Window Mirror,* a mirror mounted outside the window, . . . to reflect the passing objects in the street. **1895** *N.Y. Dramatic News* 26 Oct. 5/3 What with 'window privileges,' 'press applications,' . . . it is about time a firm stand was taken. **1776** E. DRINKER *Journal* (1889) 41 Two or three men called to look at our window weights—found them to be of Iron.

+**Window casing.** A window frame or case. — **1853** B. F. TAYLOR *Jan. & June* 205 Here are So-and-so's initials on the window-casings. **1888** *Harper's Mag.* Dec. 32/1, I was knocking on the window-casing to make you hear. **1906** GUNTER *Prince in Garret* ix, The gaunt Ambigue slips an agile leg over the window casing, and climbs into his own apartment.

Window glass. Glass for use in a window. {1634–} — **1714** *Boston News-Letter* 15 March 2/2 To be Sold by Publick Vendue or Outcry . . . Looking Glass, and Window Glass. **1815** *Niles' Reg.* IX. 35/2 A manufactory of green window glass and hollow ware, is about to go into operation. **1885** EGGLESTON in *Century Mag.* April 874/1 Window-glass was not then [in colonial times] in general use . . . , and oiled paper for a long time let a dusky light into the obscure rooms of many settlers' houses.

Windowpane. {1819–} +An exceptionally thin, translucent flounder, *Lophopsetta maculata.* — **1873** T. GILL *Cat. Fishes E. Coast N. Amer.* 17 *Lophopsetta maculata.* . . . Spotted turbot; window-pane (New Jersey). **1884** GOODE, etc. *Fisheries* I. 199 The Spotted Sand Flounder, . . . variously known along the coast as Water Flounder, Window-pane, and Daylight.

Window sash. **1.** The light frame in which the panes of glass of a window are set. {1806–} +**2.** *W.* A cattle brand. — (1) **1763** in H. M. Brooks *Gleanings* IV. 35 Russell has a number of Window Sashes . . . to Sell. **1835** *Jamestown* (N.Y.) *Jrnl.* 13 May 2/4 Amongst our very numerous arrivals, . . . are two large covered flat boats, . . . one entirely laden with patent window sash. **1890** *Rep. Secy. Agric. 1899* 131 The ordinary way of glazing window-sashes is to set in the glass, fasten it with triangular bits of tin [etc.]. (2) **1903** ADAMS *Log of Cowboy* 92 [We] cut out three head in the blotched brand called the 'Window Sash.'

Window screen. {1850-} +A screen, consisting usually of mesh wire mounted on a light frame, placed in a window frame to bar out flies, mosquitoes, etc., when the window is open. — **1892** *Vt. Agric. Rep.* XII. 135 [There are] mills manufacturing . . . furniture and window screens. **1907** *St. Nicholas* May 614/1 We tried to buy wire netting—the sort we use for window screens at home.

Window shade. {1810-} +=SHADE *n.* 5. Also attrib. — **1851** CIST *Cincinnati* 261 [There are] window shade factories. **1869** *Boyd's Business Directory* 601 Till & Senn, manufacturers of Window Shades. **1894** 'MARK TWAIN' *P. Wilson* vii, Wilson was able to see the girl very well, the window-shades . . . being up. **1906** FREEMAN *Light of Soul* 402 Directly Martha was in her own room she pulled down her window-shades.

Window shutter. A shutter or blind used to darken or secure a window. {1683-} Cf. SHUTTER 1. — **1747** *Georgia Col. Rec.* VI. 189 The Boards for . . . Window Shutters . . . were bespoke of Mr. Bolzius some Months past. **1806** PIKE *Sources Miss.* I. App. 38 The doors and window-shutters are musket-proof. **1860** HOLMES *Professor* 203, I see the light through cracks in his window-shutters. **1900** DIX *Deacon Bradbury* 2 The window-shutters, green or sometimes blue, were uniformly 'drawn to' or 'bowed.'

Windowy, *a.* {1631-} +Having many or large windows. — **1863** 'G. HAMILTON' *Gala-Days* 353 The homes of the students . . . [were] formal, stiff, windowy, bricky. **1888** *Harper's Mag.* June 130/2 Several large, ugly, windowy wooden bulks grew up for shoe shops.

***Windrow.** +=WINDFALL. — **1829** COOPER *Wish-ton-Wish* ii, Here and there [was] a wind-row, along which trees had been uprooted by the furious blasts which sometimes sweep off acres of our trees in a minute. **1840** — *Pathfinder* I. 13 The particular wind-row of which we are writing, lay on the brow of a gentle acclivity. **1891** SWASEY *Early Days Calif.* 15 In some portions of the West these tornado tracks are termed 'windrows.'

Windscreen. {1903-} +=WINDBREAK. — **1858** WARDER *Hedges & Evergreens* 240 The common Cedar is . . . much used . . . where a quick, permanent, and effective wind-screen is wanted. **1887** *Century Mag.* March 740/2 That department . . . was nearly surrounded by a windscreen of hemlock boughs and odd pieces of canvas.

+**Wind slash.** =WINDFALL. — **1886** *N.Y. Times* 13 April (*Cent.*), All persons having occasion to . . . start a fire in any old chopping, wind-slash, bush or berry lot, . . . shall give five days' notice. **1905** *Forestry Bureau Bul.* No. 61, 53 Windfall, an area upon which the trees have been thrown by wind. . . . Syn.: blow down, wind slash.

Windsor chair. {1724} A wooden chair, usually with arms, having a stick back, turned ranging legs, and a flat or saddle seat. {1740-} Also *Windsor chair-maker.* — **1778** *Jrnl. Cont. Congress* XI. 719 There is due to William Widdifield, for 6 windsor chairs for the use of the treasury office, 42 dollars. **1789** *Boston Directory* 174 Adams Joseph, cabinet and Windsor chair-maker. **1800** *Aurora* (Phila.) 30 Aug. (Th.), Bureaus, Dukes, sophas, windsor chairs, &c. [at auction]. **1848** 'UNCLE SAM' *Peculiarities* II. 272, I gave a 'loafer' three cents for liberty to sit down on a 'Windsor chair.'

+**Wind-splitter.** Something so sharp that it splits the wind. *jocular.* Also *wind-splitting* a. — **1890** ALLEN in *Harper's Mag.* Dec. 58/2 A tall thinnish man, with . . . a white wind-splitting face. **1893** M. A. OWEN *Voodoo Tales* 28, I seed dem ole win'-splittehs (wind-splitter)—(the name in the vernacular of a species of long, lean hog that ranges half-wild). [**1900** *Daily Express* (London) 13 July 6/6 The 'wind-splitting train' was tested over the line between Baltimore and Washington recently. *Ib.*, The wind-splitter . . . keeps up a wonderful pace, but glides along as if on glass.]

*Wind storm. A storm characterized by exceptionally high wind with little or no rain. — **1835** REED & MATHESON *Visit* I. 32 While at Washington, I first witnessed the windstorm, which is common in this country. **1874** GLISAN *Jrnl. Army Life* 501 The northwest has fewer and less destructive windstorms. **1918** *Nation* 7 Feb. 164/1 It is necessary for him [the farmer] to carry insurance against possible loss from tornado or wind storm.

+**Windy City.** Chicago, Illinois. A nickname. — **1887** *Courier-Journal* 31 Jan. 5/1 A Gauzy Story of an Alleged Anarchist Dynamite Plot from the Windy City. **1890** *Congress. Rec.* 21 April 3598/1 We hear descriptions of a 'Windy City' on the west coast of a lake which all know to be flat and low, with an atmosphere filled with smoke and soot. **1908** McGAFFEY *Show-Girl* 58 Chicago is sure rightly named when they call it the Windy City.

*Wine.

*1. The fermented juice of grapes or other fruits used as a beverage.
1624 *Va. House of Burgesses* 29 He had some small provisions of bread and wine. **1714** [see BISCUIT I]. **1806** *Austin P.* I. (1924) 104, 10 h[ea]ds red Wine if cheap. **1866** *Rep. Indian Affairs* 132 This race of Indians . . . manufacture considerable wine from the native grape. **1907** *St. Nicholas* July 799/2 He sent for wine and made her drink it.

b. As the subject of legal enactments or regulations.
1633 *Plymouth Laws* 35 None [shall] be suffered to retale wine or strong water. **1691** [see LIQUOR *n.* 1]. **1721** *Mass. H. Repr. Jrnl.* III. 22 A Bill, Intituled, An Act, For Granting unto His Majesty, an Excise upon Wines. **1891** *Reg. Concerning Withdrawal of Wine Spirits for Fortification of Pure Sweet Wines* (Office Internal Revenue) 6 Stamps and seals [shall be affixed] to the packages containing such wines as may be prescribed by the Commissioner of Internal Revenue.

2. In special combinations.

Wine crop, a crop or yield of grapes; *w. julep,* a spirituous drink of which wine forms the principal part; *w. plant,* (see quotation); *w. room,* a shop where wine is sold; *w. sangaree,* =SANGAREE *n.; w. supper,* a social supper at which wine is drunk; *w. tap,* a device used for drawing wine from a cask.
1885 *Santa Fé Wkly. New Mexican* 9 July 2/4 Frank Huning, of Albuquerque, has ordered 100 gross of wine bottles for this season's wine crop. **1847** FIELD *Drama in Pokerville* 31 Let us drive on to the hotel, . . . and find Mrs. Oscar Dust taking a wine julep, as, in summer, she always did. **1887** *Harper's Mag.* Jan. 303/1 There is . . . rhubarb, sold in some instances under the name of 'wine-plant.' **1887** *Courier-Journal* 9 May 1/8 The two men were in Fleisch's wine room, sampling some Prohibition bitters. **1832** WATSON *Hist. Tales N.Y.* 123 At funerals, the Dutch gave *hot* wine in winter; and in summer they gave wine-sangaree. **1859** *Harper's Mag.* Sept. 503/2 The course of wine-suppers and billiards into which her husband is enticed. **1651** *Essex Probate Rec.* I. 144, 1 wine tap . . . 1 saltseller.

Wine biscuit. A small, light biscuit served with wine. *Obs.* — **1832** *Louisville Pub. Adv.* 10 March 1/2 J. Wolf . . . keeps constantly on hand an extensive assortment of . . . Water Crackers, Wine Biscuit, &c. **1835** HOFFMAN *Winter in West* II. 90 On a broad rock [reposed] . . . a tray of wine-biscuits and a fragrant Ohio cheese.

+**Winebrennerians.** [Named from the founder, Rev. John Winebrenner (1797-1860).] *pl.* (See quot. 1884.) — **1867** DIXON *New America* II. 309 No sect escaped this rage for separation . . . [neither] River Brethren, nor Winebrennarians. **1884** Schaff *Religious Encycl.* III. 2538 Winebrennerians, the popular designation of a Baptist denomination officially called 'The Church of God.'

+**Wine card.** A list of wines available in a hotel, restaurant, etc. — **1851** M. REID *Scalp Hunters* ii, Whenever I took up a wine-card or a pencil, these articles were snatched out of my fingers. **1852** *Harper's Mag.* V. 267/1 Summer visitors to the favorite watering places are not unapt to call for a wine-card.

Wine cooper. A cooper who makes barrels, casks, etc., for wine. {1635-} — **1643** *Mass. H. S. Coll.* 4 Ser. VI. 180 There is one Samuell Crum, a wine cooper, lately come from sea. **1678** *Boston Rec.* 125 Peter Choke wine Coop[er] reported to be of vitious conversation. **1704** *Boston News-Letter* 31 July 2/1 Several Persons . . . are now in Prison, . . . [including] Daniel Amos Wine-Cooper. **1774** J. ANDREWS *Lett.* 334 Met Abra Hunt, wine cooper . . . with his wife. **1848** *Rep. Comm. Patents 1847* 465 It induced me . . . to send to Champaigne in France, for a skilful wine cooper.

*Wine grape. +Any one of various grapes used in making wine. Also attrib. — **1775** ADAIR *Indians* 228 Hemp, and wine-grapes grow there [340 miles n.w. of Charleston] to admiration. **1856** *Rep. Comm. Patents 1855: Agric.* 305 The 'Catawba' . . . is the 'Wine' grape. **1869** *Rep. Comm. Agric. 1868* 212 What varieties are in highest repute as wine grapes? **1913** LONDON *Valley of Moon* 509 This is a wine-grape valley.

Wine jelly. Jelly made with wine. — **1865** A. D. WHITNEY *Gayworthys* 336 She would like some wine-jelly made. **1876** *Wide Awake* III. 309/2 She had fed him with beef-tea and mutton-broth, and gruel, and wine-jelly. **1893** *Post Harvard Stories* 30 There is a can of wine-jelly.

+**Winery.** An establishment for making wine. {1912} — **1882** *Harper's Mag.* Dec. 55/1 The road to the large substantial buildings of the winery was bordered by a deep orchard of oranges. **1891** *Boston Jrnl.* 30 April 2/3 The wine-grape growers . . . complain that there is no profit in their business, . . . because of the combination of the great wineries. **1913** LONDON *Valley of Moon* 433 There were dams and lakes, . . . a stone winery, stone barns.

+**Winesap.** A variety of medium-sized, roundish, deep red winter apple; a tree bearing such apples. — **1817** W. COXE *Fruit Trees* 153 Winesap. This is one of our best cider fruits. **1868** *Mich. Agric. Rep.* VII. 430 Apples [recommended] . . . as promising well . . . : King, Wine-sap [etc.]. **1895** 'CRADDOCK' *Mystery Witch-Face Mt.* 111 The red-freighted boughs of an old winesap bent above the girl's head. **1913** [see RAMBO].

*Wine tree. *local.* +=MOUNTAIN ASH. — **1860** CURTIS *Woody Plants N.C.* 70 Mountain Ash . . . is called *Wine Tree* (from a kind of liquor said to be made from it). **1897** SUDWORTH *Arborescent Flora* 211 *Pyrus americana . . .*, Mountain Ash. . . . [Also called] Wine Tree (N.C.).

*Wing. *attrib.*

1. In the specific names of plants.
1817-8 EATON *Botany* (1822) 428 *Rhus copallina*, wing-rib sumach, mountain sumach. . . . Berries red. **1894** *Amer. Folk-Lore* VII. 90 *Actinomeris squarrosa*, wing-stem, stickweed, West Va. **1843** TORREY *Flora N.Y.* II. 36 *Mimulus alatus*, Wing-stemmed Monkey-flower. . . . Wet meadows.

2. In special combinations.
Wing shot, one who shoots birds on the wing; *w. sweep,* a plow the share of which has winglike lateral extensions for increasing the width of furrow cut.
1875 *Fur, Fin & Feather* 118 Bogardus, Champion Wing-Shot of America, uses Orange Lightning [powder] for Trap-Shooting. **1854** *Fla. Plantation Rec.* 553/1, 5 Wing Sweapes.

Wing and wing, *adv.* With sails boomed out on each side similar to wings. {1893-} Also *transf.* — **1781** *Md. Hist. Mag.* V. 129 We were now wing and wing, that is right before the wind. **1827** COOPER *Red Rover* I. 84 That yonder bit of a schooner would make more way, going wing-and-wing, than jammed up on a wind. **1886** *Outing* IX. 76/1 This [North Sea Harbor] we made with fresh breeze and heavy sea, *Outing* running wing and wing, with reef in dandy. [**1894** H. D. LLOYD *Wealth against Commonwealth* 182 The panic of 1857 caught him with sails wing-a-wing, conducting all at once, and prosperously, grist-mills, oil-mills, grain distilleries [etc.].]

+**Wing dam,** *n.* A dam or barrier built out into a stream to deflect or deepen the current. Also attrib. and fig. — **1809** FESSENDEN *Pills Poetical* 36 His rhetorick was directed towards . . . wingdam bills. **1836** J. HALL *Statistics of West* 45 Wing-dams [thrown] from each side of the river . . . confine the current within narrow bounds. **1883** 'MARK TWAIN' *Life on Miss.* xxviii, They are building wing-dams here and there to deflect the current. **1905** *Forestry Bureau Bul.* No. 61, 43.

+**Wing-dam,** *v. tr.* To provide (a mining claim or river) with a wing dam. — **1857** BORTHWICK *3 Years in Calif.* 265 A company of fifteen or twenty white men would have wing-dammed this claim. **1872** MCCLELLAN *Golden State* 257 Gold-seekers . . . [are] wing-damming the rivers. **1882** *47th Congress 1 Sess.* H. R. Ex. Doc. No. 216, 20 Other attempts to flume or wing-dam the river have been only partially successful.

+**Winged elm.** The cork elm, *Ulmus alata.* — **1857** GRAY *Botany* 396 Winged Elm. Whahoo. . . . Wood fine-grained. valuable. **1875** *Field & Forest* I. 35 The winged Elm, or Whahoo, stands in the Botanic garden. **1894** COULTER *Bot. W. Texas* III. 406. **1901** MOHR *Plant Life Ala.* 89 Box elder, winged elm, willow, . . . shade the rocky banks of the swift mountain stream.

+**Winkle hawk.** (See quotation.) — **1848** BARTLETT 386 Winkle-Hawk. (Dutch *winkel-haak.*) A rent in the shape of the letter L, frequently made in cloth.

+**Winnebago.** [Amer. Indian.] An Indian of a Siouan tribe first encountered by Europeans in Wisconsin, on Green Bay; also, pl., the tribe of such an Indian.

[**1640** *Jesuit Rel. & Allied Doc.* XVIII. 230 Ces peuples se nomment Ouinipigou, pource qu'ils viennent des bords d'vne mer dont nouns n'auons point de cognoissance.] **1812** *Niles' Reg.* II. 6/2 Two young Winibiegoes . . . went near some of the American sentinels, and were shot at. **1839** SCHOOLCRAFT *Algic Researches* I. 13 The Winnebagoes are clearly of the Abanic stock. **1888** [see PONCA].

attrib. **1835** HOFFMAN *Winter in West* I. 257 The Winnebago chief . . . [had] just left the establishment. **1854** *La Crosse Democrat* 18 April 1/5 Dr. Andros has received an appointment . . . as physician to the Winnebago Indians.

b. The language of this tribe.
1860 *Harper's Mag.* Sept. 568/2 As he could not speak Winnebago, the first thing to be done was to find an interpreter.

* **Winter.** *attrib.* passing into *adj.*

+**1.** Designating places occupied by, or involved in trading operations with, Indians in winter.
1677 HUBBARD *Narrative* II. 58 He was put to paddle . . . to an Island called Mount Desart, where his Peteroon used to keep his Winter Station. **1775** ADAIR *Indians* 322 A hunting camp of the Chikkasah went out to the extent of their winter-limits. **1799** J. SMITH *Acct. Captivity* 18 Here they made their wintercabbin. **1815** *Niles' Reg.* IX. 216/2 The Potawattamies . . . are daily passing for the purpose of making their winter hunt. **1835** HOFFMAN *Winter in West* I. 189 Several winter lodges of the Pottawattamies . . . were plainly perceptible over the plain. **1870** KEIM *Sheridan's Troopers* 103 [Instructions were] to proceed . . . towards the Washita river, the supposed winter seat of the hostile tribe. **1877** *Rep. Indian Affairs* 15 The winter camp of this chief was about two hundred miles north.

2. Designating or relating to clothing and bedding used in winter.
1759 *Essex Inst. Coll.* III. 104 Cold weather . . . will make us . . . put on our Winter Clothing. **1774** FITHIAN *Journal* I. 179 This afternoon is so cool that I should be glad of a winter suit. **1866** A. D. WHITNEY *L. Goldthwaite* xiv, The third trunk . . . had been 'full of old winter-dresses to be made over. **1878** Winter comfortable [see COMFORTABLE 2]. **1910** TOMPKINS *Mothers & Fathers* 102 Wait till you've worn your winter flannels there in August.

3. In the specific names: **a.** Of birds in some way associated with the winter season.
1884 COUES *Key to Birds* 379 S[pizella] monticola. . . . Tree Sparrow. Winter Chip-bird. Abundant in the U.S. in winter. **1848** Winter duck [see PIGEONTAIL]. **1811** Winter falcon [see FALCON 2]. **1839** Winter goose [see FLIGHT GOOSE]. **1891** *Cent.* 6943/3 *Winter redbird,* the cardinal grosbeak, which winters in the United States.

b. Of varieties of apples.
1874 *Rep. Comm. Agric. 1873* 210 Winter Horse . . . [is a variety] of the Southern States. **1817** COXE *Fruit Trees* 122 Wine Apple. . . . It is called . . . in some places in New-Jersey, the fine Winter, and large Winter Red. **1910** Winter russet [see COOKIE]. **1850** *Rep. Comm. Patents 1849: Agric.* 281 Baldwin, Roxbury russet, and Danvers winter-sweet comprise the chief varieties.

c. Of other fruits, vegetables, etc., that keep well or grow in winter.
1855 *Amer. Inst. N.Y. Trans. 1854* 430 Rarely does any but the winter bell [a pear] . . . hang upon its branches. **1775** *Amer. Husbandry* I. 137 The sort [cultivated] is the great white winter cabbage. **1775** ADAIR *Indians* 358 Grape-vines . . . on the hills of the Mississippi . . . produce winter-canes. **1846** SAGE *Scenes Rocky Mts.* xxvii, A small ground-vine of evergreen, with a leaf assimilating the winter-clover in shape, and is

found only in mountainous regions. **1832** CHILD *Frugal Housewife* 28 Winter evergreen is considered good for all humors. **1913** BARNES *Western Grazing Grounds* 57 The forage is greatly augmented by . . . sweet sage or 'winter fat' (*Eurotia lanata*). **1709** LAWSON *Carolina* 102 The other Winter Fox-Grapes, are much of the same Bigness. **1800** HAWKINS *Sk. Creek Country* 44 They call this the winter reed, as it clusters like the cane. **1784** W. WALTON *Narr. Captivity B. Gilbert* 69 [Mouldy corn was] their only Food, excepting a few Winter Turneps. **1787** WASHINGTON *Diaries* III. 255 Began to sow at the No. Wt. Corner of this enclosure under furrow the Winter Vetches. **1785** MARSHALL *Amer. Grove* 157 *Vaccinium arboreum.* Winter, or Tree Whortle-Berry.

4. In special combinations.
Winter beaver, beaver fur taken in winter; *w. count,* a pictographic record made by Indians, often on a hide, of the chief events of a year; *w. crop,* a crop, as oats, wheat, etc., sown in late autumn; *w. fever,* a fever prevalent in winter; *w. meat,* meat for use in winter; *w. operation,* logging operations conducted in the winter; *w. privilege,* (see quotation); *w. school,* a school held during the winter; *w. sickness, w. succotash,* (see quotations); *w. yard,* =MOOSE-YARD.
1684 *Va. State P.* I. 18 Statement of Nicholas Spencer . . . in regard to . . . 'the sum of 128 pounds best winter beaver, Killed in Season.' **1901** *Smithsonian Rep. 1900* 67 The calendars, or winter-counts . . . play so large, yet so obscure a role in Indian life. **1754** *Va. State P.* I. 249 He was obliged to . . . Leave his winter Crop in the Ground. **1874** GLISAN *Jrnl. Army Life* 444 They would be prostrated by various forms of malarious fever—such as . . . winter-fever. **1919** *Maine My State* 21 When the winter weather set in, we usually made a regular hunt to get the winter meat. **1895** [see KENNEBUNKER]. a**1870** CHIPMAN *Notes on Bartlett* 514 *Winter-Privileges,* separate meetings from those in the central parochial church, allowed to be held by the people in out-districts. **1903** WIGGIN *Rebecca* 173 The winter school, from which the younger children of the place stayed away during the cold weather. **1847** DEWEES *Lett. from Texas* 303 The winter sickness . . . generally commences with a bad cold and terminates in pneumonia. **1850** *New Eng. Farmer* II. 66 Winter Saccatash.—This is made of dried shelled beans, and hard corn. **1893** ROOSEVELT *Wilderness Hunter* 215 The winter-yard is usually made . . . on high ground, away from the swamps.

Winter apple. Any one of various apples that ripen in late autumn and keep well in winter. {**1744**- (Ellis *Mod. Husb.* I. ii. 138)} — **1702** *Essex Inst. Coll.* VIII. 202 I was gathering winter Apples. **1714** *Ib.* XXXVI. 326 Gathered 40 bushels winter apples. **1856** *Rep. Comm. Patents: Agric. 1855* 292 Good winter apples usually sell here [Mich.] from $1 to $1.50 a barrel. **1902** C. L. PIDGIN *Stephen Holton* 279 Father expects me to barrel up those winter apples.

Winterberry. (See quot. 1891 and cf. VIRGINIA WINTERBERRY.) {**1759**-} — **1784** *Amer. Acad. Mem.* I. 430 Winterberry. . . . Berries red and generally remain on the shrub through the winter. **1843** TORREY *Flora N.Y.* II. 3 Common Winter-berry. . . . A decoction of it [the bark] is used for washing ill-conditioned ulcers. **1891** *Cent.* 6943/3 *Winterberry,* . . . a name of several shrubs of the genus *Ilex,* belonging to the section (once genus) *Prinos,* growing in eastern North America.

Winter butter. Butter made in winter. {**1675**-} — **1794** *Mass. H. S. Coll.* 1 Ser. III. 197 Winter butter, . . . cheese, and beans, . . . are procured from the markets at Boston. **1873** *Vermont Bd. Agric. Rep.* III. 186 This butter is not what is usually called 'winter butter.' **1879** *Harper's Mag.* July 217 Winter butter . . . will cost you a cent less.

+**Winter dairy.** A dairy operated in winter. — a**1858** in C. Flint *Milch Cows* 233 The process for the winter dairy is similar to that of the summer. **1888** *Vt. Agric. Rep.* X. 24 [Mr. Allen] thinks winter dairies pay the best. **1894** *Ib.* XIV. 37, I would not know how to manage a winter-dairy without a winter silo.

Winter egg. 1. A thick-shelled egg of various invertebrates that survives the winter and hatches in spring. Also attrib. **2.** An egg laid in winter. — (1) **1881** *Amer. Naturalist* XV. 484 We cannot apply to it [the egg of vastatrix], the term 'winter egg.' **1884** *Rep. Comm. Agric.* 406 The insect may be carried on the roots of the vines during the winter . . . in the 'winter-egg' state. (2) **1894** *Vt. Agric. Rep.* XIV. 165 If you want to be sure of winter eggs, you should prepare for it this winter.

+**Winter flounder.** A small, edible American flounder, *Pseudopleuronectes americanus.* — **1814** MITCHILL *Fishes N.Y.* 387 [The] New-York Flatfish . . . is called the winter flounder. **1855** [see NEW YORK 2 b]. **1911** *Rep. Fisheries 1908* 310/1.

Winter grain. Autumn-sown grain that ripens in the spring or summer. {**1697**-} — **1659** *Conn. Rec.* I. 345 Winter graine is sowed on the land. **1791** WASHINGTON *Diaries* IV. 150 The Winter grain . . . appeared promising and abundant. **1804** J. ROBERTS *Penna. Farmer* 50 Some sow it [timothy grass] with winter grain. **1872** TICE *Over Plains* 48 The winter grains have . . . succeeded most admirably.

+**Winter grape.** The chicken grape, *Vitis cordifolia.* — **1771** WASHINGTON *Diaries* II. 43 Began to Plant Cuttings of the Winter Grape. **1814** BRACKENRIDGE *Views La.* 60 Formerly a wretched sort of wine was made of the *winter grape.* **1862** *Rep. Comm. Patents 1861: Agric.* 484 The Winter grape is frequently a high climber.

Winter grass. A specific variety of grass that grows in winter or any winter-growing grass. — **1795** WINTERBOTHAM *Hist. View* II. 68 The uppermost vegetation is a species of grass, called winter grass. **1797** HAWKINS *Letters* 107 We saw some fine grass in bloom, the small winter grass common on the hills in bloom. **1850** *Rep. Comm. Patents 1849: Agric.* 157 The 'winter-grass' of this region [Washington, Miss.], the nearly universal *Poa annua,* . . . [reaches] a height of from four to eight inches.

*Wintergreen. a. =SHINLEAF. **+b.** Any one of various American evergreen shrubs of the genus *Gaultheria*, esp. *G. procumbens.* **c.** =PIPSISSEWA. **d.** *fig.* Freshness or vigor in old age.

1672 [see PYROLA]. **1778** CARVER *Travels* 509 Winter Green. This is an ever-green of the species of the myrtle. **1850** HAWTHORNE *Scarlet Letter* 18 This Inspector . . . was . . . one of the most wonderful specimens of winter-green that you would be likely to discover in a life-time's search. **1876** T. HILL *True Order of Studies* 81 Our American plant Gaultheria is called in some sections Wintergreen. **1884** MILLSPAUGH *Amer. Med. Plants* 104 *Chimaphila umbellata.* . . . Common names pipsissewa, winter green [etc.]. **1891** *Cent.* 6944/2.

+Wintergreen berry. The edible, scarlet berry of *Gaultheria procumbens.* — **1810** M. DWIGHT *Journey to Ohio* 46 We found winter green berrys in abundance. *a*1861 WINTHROP *Open Air* 113 At this dam the reddest, spiciest . . . wintergreen-berries . . . are to be found. **1881** McLEAN *Cape Cod Folks* 243 Life was mainly supported on winter-green-berries, or box berries.

+Winter hawk. =RED-SHOULDERED HAWK. — **1831** AUDUBON *Ornith. Biog.* I. 364 The Winter Hawk is not a constant resident in the United States. **1884** COUES *Key to Birds* 545. **1917** *Birds of Amer.* II. 74.

*Winter house. +A house or structure serving as the abode of Indians in the winter. *Obs.* — **1756** in *Century Mag.* XXIII. 505/1 We must be at the Expenses of building Winter-Houses for them if more should come. **1775** [see WAR WHOOP *n.* 1]. **1833** FLINT *D. Boone* 158 All [the Indians] . . . then adjourned to their 'winter house.'

*Wintering. *attrib.* +Designating places occupied in the winter by Indians. — **1804–5** CLARK in *Lewis & C. Exped.* VI. (1905) 61 [From Fort Mandan] to Menatarras Wintering Village. **1807** GASS *Journal* 51 At the mouth of this river is a wintering camp of the Rickarees of 60 lodges. **1817** BRADBURY *Travels* 51, I set out . . . at sunrise, for the wintering house.

+Wintering ground. The ground or place where an individual or party spends the winter. — **1808** PIKE *Sources Miss.* 33 This day's march made me think seriously of our wintering-ground. **1837** IRVING *Bonneville* I. 96 There was no good wintering ground in the neighborhood. **1852** REYNOLDS *Hist. Illinois* 190 Mr. Hay got out into the wintering ground, and erected his quarters for winter.

+Wintering post. A post or station at which a military force spends the winter. — **1823** in *S. Dak. Hist. Coll.* I. 192 Part of the men . . . deserted from their wintering post at the Big Horn. **1831** R. COX *Adv. Columbia R.* 106 Messrs. Farnham and Pillet returned from their wintering posts. *c*1836 CATLIN *Indians* II. 149 [Camp Des Moines] is the wintering post of Colonel Kearney.

+Winterkill, *n.* Plant death caused by the cold of winter. — **1850** *Rep. Comm. Patents 1849: Agric.* 199 Wheat . . . is now subject to rust, blast, and winter-kill. *Ib.* 204 The fly, rust, and winter-kill have materially injured the wheat crop.

+Winterkill, *v.*

1. *tr.* To kill (plants) by exposure to the cold of winter.

1817 S. BROWN *Western Gazetteer* 49 That wheat . . . never gets winter-killed. **1864** *Ohio Agric. Rep.* XVIII. p. xxxvii, Farmers complain . . . of the crops having been 'winter killed.' **1880** *Scribner's Mo.* April 807/1 In regions where they [blackberry bushes] are badly winter-killed I would keep them under three feet, so that the snow might be a protection. **1918** *Nation* 7 Feb. 129/2 Though the farmers sowed a million acres more winter wheat than ever before, . . . much has been winter-killed.

2. *intr.* Of plants or crops: To die from exposure to the cold of winter.

1846 EMMONS *Agric. N.Y.* I. 281 The grain very rarely winter-kills. **1871** *Ill. Agric. Soc. Trans.* VIII. 174 The Lawton . . . [is] apt to winter-kill. **1882** *Maine Agric. Rep.* XXVI. 338 The Mann apple . . . winter-kills badly with me.

+Winterkilling. The killing of crops, etc., by the cold of winter. — **1853** *Mich. Agric. Soc. Trans.* IV. 159 [Draining] prevents . . . 'winter-killing.' **1869** *Rep. Comm. Agric. 1868* 248 The Osage quicks will be more likely to escape winter-killing. **1876** *Ill. Dept. Agric. Trans.* XIII. 308 The young growth [of wheat] was less luxuriant, . . . and winter-killing became more common.

+Winter range. An area that affords grazing for cattle in winter. — **1874** [see FIRE GUARD *v.*]. **1890** *Stock Grower & Farmer* 18 Jan. 5/3 Al Doyle . . . has just come in from the winter range. **1895** [see BREAK *n.*[1] 1 b].

Winter resort. A place to which people go for health and pleasure during the winter. — **1875** C. NORDHOFF *Communistic Soc. U.S.* 65 [Economy] during many years was a favorite winter as well as summer resort for Pittsburghers. **1893** *Harper's Mag.* Feb. 365/1 [New Orleans] is the best of all the American winter resorts. **1913** LONDON *Valley of Moon* 496, I saw from the car windows . . . hotels, springs, summer resorts, winter resorts.

Winter rye. Rye sown in the autumn and harvested in the following spring or summer. {1756– (*Compl. Body Husb.* 382/2)} — **1764** *N.H. Hist. Soc. Coll.* IX. 161, [I] reaped winter rye. **1798** I. ALLEN *Hist. Vermont* 273 Winter wheat and winter rye are sown in September and October. **1832** *N.H. Hist. Soc. Coll.* III. 72 Winter rye succeeds very well. **1893** HOLLEY *Samantha at World's Fair* 558, I could explain . . . all about my winter rye.

+Winter snipe. The dunlin or the purple sandpiper. — **1844** *Nat. Hist. N.Y., Zoology* II. 240 In the autumn, . . . its plumage is so changed that it obtains another name, and is then called Winter Snipe. **1917** *Birds of Amer.* I. 232, 237.

Winter wheat. A variety of wheat suitable for sowing in the autumn and harvesting the following spring or summer; wheat of this variety. {1825– (Loudon *Encycl. Agric.* 747)} Also attrib.

1671 *New Castle Court Rec.* 81 The Pl[ain]t[iff] demands . . . foure thousand one hundred & twenty gilders . . . payable in . . . winter wheat. **1721** *Boston Rec.* 154 They Promote . . . the raising of Good winter wheat. **1800** [see FALL WHEAT]. **1876** *Ill. Dept. Agric. Trans.* XIII. 287 Randolph, Monroe, St. Clair, Madison, etc., [counties of Illinois] lead in winter wheat. **1887** *Courier-Journal* 19 Feb. 7/4 The news from the winter-wheat belt was rather bearish. **1925** TILGHMAN *Dugout* 81 It was found that winter wheat would grow there.

+Winter wren. A small American wren, *Nannus hiemalis hiemalis.* — **1808** WILSON *Ornithology* I. 139 [The] Winter Wren . . . frequents the projecting banks of creeks. **1839** PEABODY *Mass. Birds* 316 The Winter Wren . . . is found in Maine in summer. **1892** TORREY *Foot-Path Way* 102 The ear . . . [catches] now and then the distant tinkle of a winter wren's tune. **1904** WHITE *Silent Places* 84 Instantly a winter-wren . . . went into ecstatic ravings.

+Winter yellowlegs. The greater yellowlegs, *Totanus melanoleucus.* — **1844** *Nat. Hist. N.Y., Zoology* II. 250 The Varied Tatler . . . is the Big Yellow-leg, or Winter Yellow-leg of our sportsmen. **1917** *Birds of Amer.* I. 244/1 There is a widespread idea that these birds appear later in the autumn than the Lesser Yellow-legs, so that they are much called 'Winter Yellow-legs.'

*Wipe, *v.*

1. To wipe out, (see quot. 1870).

1870 M. H. SMITH *20 Years Wall St.* 69 When a margin is closed and the stock sold by the broker, the operator is said to be 'wiped out.' **1902** WILSON *Spenders* 410 Uncle Peter, we're wiped out.

2. To wipe up the floor with (one), or variants: To beat (someone) decisively; to get the better of (someone). *colloq.*[2] {1905–}

1887 *Courier-Journal* 4 Jan. 2/6 Two Brothers Wipe up the Floor With a Missouri Newspaper Man. **1888** *Detroit Free Press* Aug., He'd wipe up the ground with him; he'd walk all over him. **1890** *Congress. Rec.* 2 June 550/1 Dr. J. V. Harris . . . in a short but vigorous speech completely wiped the ground up with the Colonel.

*Wiper.

1. A piece of cloth or tow used for wiping the bore of a gun.

1803 [see GUN *n.* 6 a]. **1846** SAGE *Scenes Rocky Mts.* 11, Upon the strap attached to it [a powder-horn], are affixed this bullet mould, . . . wiper [etc.].

2. A blackboard eraser.

1858 *Ill. Agric. Soc. Trans.* III. 581 On the top of the wainscot should be a trough . . . to hold chalk and wipers.

3. *Railroading.* A worker in a roundhouse whose chief function is to clean locomotives.

1883 FULTON *Sam Hobart* 31 Some [engines] are in the hands of the wipers. **1898** HAMBLEN *Gen. Manager's Story* 80 The wipers are everybody's helpers. **1901** NORRIS *Octopus* 18 They cut my pay down just as off-hand as they do the pay of any dirty little wiper in the yard.

Wiping rod. A rod equipped with a piece of cloth or tow and used for cleaning the bore of a gun. — **1805** LEWIS in *L. & Clark Exped.* II. (1904) 197 S(h)arbono lost his gun, shot pouch, horn, tomahawk, and my wiping rod. **1876** KNIGHT 1961/1 *Rod*, a straight, slender piece of wood or metal, as the ramrod, wiping-rod [etc.].

Wiping stick. =prec. {1848–} — **1817** BRADBURY *Travels* 167 They often take from them the furs they have collected, and beat them severely with their *wiping sticks.* **1837** WETMORE *Gaz. Missouri* 325 We made a few . . . new wiping-sticks. **1862** *Harper's Mag.* Sept. 450/2 Having fastened this ghastly mark [*sc.* a skull] upon the end of a wiping stick, they . . . commenced trying their rifles at one of the eyes.

*Wire.

*1. Metal drawn out into a slender thread.

1744 FRANKLIN *Acct. Fire-Places* 33 A little Grate of Wire will keep them [*sc.* mice] out. **1805** in *Ann. 9th Congress* 2 Sess. 966 During the American Revolution, he engaged in making Wire. **1885** *South Fla. Sentinel* (Orlando) 8 April 2/2 J. M. Bryan, M. C. Osborn and W. D. Moore have received 6 tons of wire with which to fence in a large portion of their 2000 A. ranch.

b. *Under wire,* fenced. (Cf. DITCH *n.* 2 c, FENCE *n.* 1 b.) **1919** HOUGH *Sagebrusher* 6 She's all under wire.

2. *Horse racing.* An imaginary line marking the finish.

1887 *Courier-Journal* 5 May 1/1 Eva K., Little Munch . . . were first under the wire. **1902** McFAUL *Ike Glidden* 200 They were but a few lengths from the wire. *Ib.* 202 The conquering colt swept under the wire. **1920** SANDBURG *Smoke & Steel* 138 He flashed his heels to other ponies . . . and hardly ever came under the wire behind the other runners.

+3. *To pull (the) wires*, or variants: To manipulate or control as one does puppets attached to wires; to exert influence. Usually in political context. {to pull *at* wires, 1834}

1813 *Ann. 12th Congress* 2 Sess. 562 When those who pulled the wires saw fit, they passed away. **1826** *Mass. Spy* 12 April (Th.), Mr. McDuffie said he was perfectly aware who was the skulking manager who moved the wires. **1855** I. C. PRAY *Mem. J. G. Bennett* 137 Mr. Bennett was active . . . in moving the wires in behalf of Mr. Van Buren's nomination. **1872** MORRELL *Flowers & Fruits* 20 Sam. Houston was then in Texas among the Cherokee Indians, pulling the wires. **1894** [see CAUCUS *v.*]. **1913** LA FOLLETTE *Autobiog.* 46 There was no influence they did not use; no wires they did not pull.

+b. *To lay wires for*, to make preparations for.

1908 *N.Y. Ev. Post* (s.w. ed) 12 Nov. 1 Woodruff began to lay wires for the coming Senatorial vacancy.

4. *attrib.* and *comb.* **a.** Designating objects made of, or with, wire.

1654 *Essex Probate Rec.* I. 184, 1 wire Candle stick. **1785** WASHINGTON *Diaries* II. 447 Wire riddles—course, 4. **1816** *Portfolio* June 521 The wire bridge near Philadelphia . . . is supported by six wires each 3-8ths of an inch in diameter. **1839** BRIGGS *H. Franco* I. 19 The gentleman who sat behind me said . . . wire cushions . . . attracted the electric fluid in a thunder storm. **1850** *Western Jrnl.* III. 339 Comparative Expense . . . of strong rough plank and strong rough wire fencing. **1859** L. WILMER *Press Gang* 377 The wire-telegraph . . . is as much an 'institution' as journalism. **1868** *Mich. Agric. Rep.* VII. 356 E. T. Barnum, Detroit, [had a] general display of wire goods. **1881** BUEL *Border Bandits* 55 The young man started off . . . , carrying the treasure box by a wire handle. **1885** *Harper's Mag.* Sept. 567/2 Mary Leithe . . . passed slowly through the wire-net doors. **1894** WISTER in *Harper's Mag.* May 913/2 Cutler knocked at the wire door.

b. Designating establishments which make wire, and craftsmen who work with wire.

1777 in *S. Lit. Messenger* XXVII. 253/1 Wire mills are in great forwardness. **1796** *Boston Directory* 295 Witherle, Joshua, wire manufacturer. **1812** MELISH *Travels* II. 55 The following [is an] enumeration of the professions exercised in Pittsburg . . . Wire-drawers, wire-workers [etc.]. **1812** *Niles' Reg.* III. 9/2 On Wednesday . . . the corner stone of the card and wire factory . . . was laid. **1813** *Ib.* IV. 294/2 Many *wire* manufactories are established or establishing. **1837** W. JENKINS *Ohio Gazetteer* 318, 1 wire weaver.

c. Designating products or things which have stiffness produced by wire or like that of wire.

1820 *Columbian Centinel* 5 Jan. 4/2 C. J. Adams . . . has just received . . . Wire Cottons. **1881** HAYES *New Colorado* 108 A gentleman in a wire hat . . . accosted him.

d. Designating tools used for work with wire.

1876 KNIGHT 2797/2 *Wire-stretcher*, a tool for straining lightly telegraph or fence wires. **1887** *Courier-Journal* 20 Feb. 3/2 Printing-Office. . . . Card Cutter, Wire Stitcher [etc.]. **1914** 'BOWER' *Flying U Ranch* 168 Want me to go back and get the wire nippers?

e. Designating metals found in a form resembling wire.

1878 BEADLE *Western Wilds* 483 Wire silver . . . [looks like a] mass of tangled hair turned to pure silver. **1880** *Cimarron News & Press* 9 Sept. 2/3 The rock is . . . full of wire gold.

f. In special combinations.

Wire binder, a binder which puts wire around sheaves of grain; *w. ferry*, a ferry which uses a wire cable; *w. house*, a brokerage house which has private telegraph wires connecting it with exchanges and perhaps with branches; *w. jerker*, (see quotation) *humorous*.

1902 *Scientific Amer.* Suppl. 20 Dec. 22546/3 It would cost more to harvest grain with a wire binder. *a***1918** G. STUART *On Frontier* II. 102 Went down ten miles to Huntley and crossed the river on a wire ferry. **1904** *N.Y. Ev. Post* 18 June, The so-called 'wire house' . . . is a product of the boom times. **1875** *Chicago Tribune* 22 Aug. 16/1 A slim-looking, smooth faced individual . . . informed him that he was the wire-jerker [in a telegraph office].

Wire cloth. Netting or screening made of wire. {1798-} Also attrib. — **1850** *Rep. Comm. Patents 1849* 238, I also claim the employment of the gravitation hammers or beaters V, for . . . detaching the flour from the meshes of the wire cloth. **1875** KNIGHT 848/2 A cylindrical wire-cloth sieve in the paper-making machine . . . allows the finely ground stuff to pass. **1881** *Amer. Naturalist* XV. 196 Two specimens of Anolis that I have kept for months in a wire-cloth cage, have shown some interesting habits.

Wire communication. 1. A line of wire. **2.** Communication by telegraph.. — (1) **1751** FRANKLIN *Exper. on Electricity* 90 Had there been a good wire communication from the spindle heads to the sea, that could have conducted more freely than tarred ropes. (2) **1862** *N.Y. Tribune* 10 June 8/2 For a week past we have had no wire communication further East than Green Spring Run, 15 miles beyond Cumberland.

Wire-cutter. 1. An instrument for cutting wire. {1905} **2.** A person who cuts wire fences. — (1) **1876** KNIGHT 2790/1 *Wire-cutter*, a nippers for cutting off wire. **1904** [see PLIERS]. (2) **1888** [see FENCE-CUTTER].

Wire edge. A turned-over edge produced on a cutting tool by faulty grinding. {1846-} In fig. uses.

*c***1804** BRACKENRIDGE *Mod. Chivalry* 214 In the course of mixing with good company, the wire edge of art would wear off, and an ease of demeanor be attained. **1834** CARRUTHERS *Kentuckians* I. 220 They may set people's teeth on a wire edge. **1838** COOPER *Home as Found* 352 [It was] as much in rule for the legal tyro to take off the wire-edge of his wit in a Fourth of July oration, as it was formerly for a mousquetaire to prove his spirit in a duel. **1866** 'MARK TWAIN' *Lett. Sandwich Isl.* 28 The tamarinds . . . sharpened my teeth up like a razor, and put a 'wire edge' on them that I think likely will wear off when the enamel does. **1883** SWEET & KNOX *Through Texas* 422, I wonder . . . if the landlord has hired him to take the wire edge off our appetites. **1903** A. ADAMS *Log of Cowboy* 203 Most of the boys had worn off the wire edge for gambling.

Wire fence.

1. A fence or fencing made of wire. {1832-} Hence *wire-fenced* a.

1850 *Western Jrnl.* III. 339 Comparative cost of wire and plank fences. **1873** BEADLE *Undevel. West* 40 Wire fences were the only kind in use in this vicinity. **1880** *Cimarron News & Press* 22 Jan. 2/1 A wire fenced enclosure . . . [keeps] the cattle within fixed boundaries. **1898** CANFIELD *Maid of Frontier* 142 His wire fence measured 130 miles.

2. Attrib. with *man, plan, staple*.

1880 *Cimarron News & Press* 22 Jan. 2/1 The wire fence plan will ultimately become the most popular. **1882** *Rep. Indian Affairs* 444 Wire fence staples, steel, galvanized. **1907** MULFORD *Bar-20* 107, I'll have time to 'tend to th' wire-fence men, too.

Wire grass. {1824-}

+1. A European meadow grass, *Poa compressa*.

1751 [see BLUE GRASS 1]. **1790** DEANE *New-Eng. Farmer* 115 Wire grass is of a bluish colour. **1843** TORREY *Flora N.Y.* II. 457 Wire-grass . . . is much esteemed for pasturage. **1878** KILLEBREW *Tennessee Grasses* 163 Wire Grass . . . is very hardy.

+2. One or other of several coarse, useless grasses, esp. *Aristida stricta*.

1775 ROMANS *Nat. Hist. Florida* 16 The most natural grass on this soil is of a very harsh nature, and . . . is known by the name of wire grass. **1797** [see SAW PALMETTO]. **1878** *Rep. Indian Affairs* 157 The land is . . . full of alkali, with flats of wire-grass. **1883** SMITH *Geol. Survey Ala.* 540 Coarse tufts of wire-grass form the undergrowth almost universally. **1901** MOHR *Plant Life Ala.* 113 Wire-grass, is extremely abundant in the coast region of South Carolina.

+3. a. A cultivated grass, *Eleusine indica*.

1840 DEWEY *Mass. Flowering Plants* 245 *Eleusine*. . . . Wire Grass. . . . From Eleusis, a name of Ceres, the goddess of grasses. **1843** TORREY *Flora N.Y.* II. 447 Wire-grass. . . . Cultivated grounds, and about houses. **1857** GRAY *Botany* 554. **1894** *Amer. Folk-Lore* VII. 104.

+b. (See quotation.)

1885 HAVARD *Flora W. & S. Texas* 529 The most common grass on bottoms and low prairies is *Hilaria mutica*, sometimes called Wire-Grass.

+4. a. The soil that bears wire grass. **b.** A territory abounding in wire grass.

1869 *Overland Mo.* III. 130 [In] Texas . . . there is . . . the 'hummock,' (yielding principally small honey-locusts) and the 'wire-grass.' **1905** *Montgomery Wkly. Adv.* 17 Feb. 3 The main run of land throughout the Wiregrass is clayey and sandy.

+5. Attrib. in sense 2 with *country, county*, etc.

1847 *Knickerb.* XXIX. 202 Let him go . . . into the 'wire-grass' region. **1858** *S. Lit. Messenger* XXVI. 230/1, We were teaching an 'academ[y'] down in the wire grass country of South Georgia. **1859** *Harper's Mag.* Dec. 134/1 A regular wire-grass piny woodsman. **1885** *Century Mag.* April 849/1 Miss Priscilla Mattox . . . had come up from one of the wire-grass counties.

Wire netting. Netting or screening made of wire. {1854-} Also attrib. — **1801** *Ann. 7th Congress* 2 Sess. 1292 The books shall be . . . set up in portable cases . . . with wire-netting doors and locks. **1897** HOWELLS *Open-eyed Conspiracy* i, We go and look at the deer . . . behind their wire netting. **1907** *St. Nicholas* May 614/2 We tried to buy wire netting . . . for window screens.

+Wirepuller. One who 'pulls wires,' esp. one who uses underhand methods of political manipulation. {1859-} — **1833** in *Commons*, etc. *Doc. Hist.* VIII. 340 Wirepullers . . . for the furtherance of . . . party interest. **1869** J. H. BROWNE *Great Metropolis* 646 As a wire-puller, caucus-controller, and manager of men, he is said to eclipse his astutest predecessors. **1889** EGGLESTON in *Century Mag.* March 791/2 He is surely wrong in supposing that the choice of a Senate . . . can generally be fixed by wire-pullers in advance.

+Wirepulling. Intrigue; underhand manipulation; freq. in political affairs. {1876-} — **1847** *Congress. Globe* 26 Jan. 262/3 Neither by demonstrations here, nor by figuring and wire-pulling at home, am I engaged to the support of this bill. **1871** BAGG *At Yale* 203 Hence the amount of political intrigue, and wire-pulling, and log-rolling, expended. **1884** *Century Mag.* Nov. 110 Many [officers] . . . won their positions by political wire-pulling at Washington. **1911** HARRISON *Queed* 220 Through much subtle wire-pulling, he got himself put on the toast list.

+Wire-tapper. One who taps, or pretends to tap, a telegraph or telephone wire for the purpose of getting prior information as to the results of races, thus being able, or pretending to be able, to bet on a sure thing.

— **1894** *Columbus Dispatch* 5 Jan., An attempt to tap the wires and 'work' the bookmakers and pool rooms . . . has been foiled. . . . The wire tappers escaped. **1910** [see BUNCO STEERER].

+Wire taste. A tape with fine wire woven into it, used in millinery work. — **1820** *Columbian Centinel* 1 April 4/3 Wire Taste for Millinery . . . will be sold . . . at reduced prices.

+Wire weed. (See quot. 1894.) — **1884** 'CRADDOCK' *Where Battle Was Fought* 75 [She] gazed far away at the billowy sweep of the wire-weeds. **1894** *Amer. Folk-Lore* VII. 91 *Aster diffusus*, . . . Gray, white devil, wireweed, devil weed. . . . West Va.

+Wirework, *v. tr.* To manipulate by wirepulling. — **1843** J. Q. ADAMS *Diary* 547 Mr. James Monroe was recalled by President Washington through Thomas Pickering, wireworked by Alexander Hamilton.

Wireworker.

1. A craftsman who works in wire. {1670-}

1808 *Ann. 10th Congress* 2 Sess. 90 The jeweller, and the wire-worker, have made distinguished progress. **1812** MELISH *Travels* II. 55 The professions exercised in Pittsburg . . . [include] wire-drawers, wire-workers.

+2. A wirepuller; a party worker.

1835 *Jamestown Jrnl.* 10 June 1/3 The wire workers lacked sense. **1844** *Shawnee Chief* (Shawneetown, Ill.) 3 Aug. 2/2 His independent course has displeased some of the wire workers. **1870** *Republican Rev.* 26 March 2/1 For some reason best known to the wireworkers of the Fusionists, the base of operations has been changed to Santa Fé. **1883** WILDER *Sister Ridnour* 130 The politician grasps the hand of his wire-worker and tool.

Wireworm. One of various larvae, similar to a wire in appearance, and destructive, esp. to corn and other grain. {1709-} — **1838** *Mass. Zool. Survey Rep.* 62 The wire-worm of America . . . belongs to the class *Myriapoda*. **1848** *Rep. Comm. Patents 1847* 113 The grain became a prey to . . . the wire worm. **1854** EMMONS *Agric. N.Y.* V. 86 *Elateridae* . . . are known in New-York and New-England by the name of wireworms, from their form and hardness. **1865** *Atlantic Mo.* June 657/2 The wire-worms . . . she divides for her chicks. **1924** CROY *R.F.D. No. 3* 182 There were so many . . . wire worms . . . in the corn.

Wiry grass. + =WIRE GRASS 2. In attrib. use. — **1887** *Courier-Journal* 12 Jan. 2/6 The wiry-grass region is infested by a band which has stolen millions of acres of the finest timber lands in the State.

+Wishbone. The V-shaped bone in front of the breast bone in a fowl. Also *wishing-bone*. Also transf. — **1853** B. F. TAYLOR *Jan. & June* 92 [We] grasped the 'wish-bone' and wished. **1860** in *Amer. Jrnl. Education* XIII. 130 A boy . . . had brought into the school the breastbone of a chicken, (commonly called the *wishing-bone*). **1884** COUES *Key to Birds* 147 The Clavicles . . . are the pair of bones which when united together form the object well known as the . . . 'wish-bone.' **1888** 'CRADDOCK' *Broomsedge Cove* 17 Bowles air ez lucky ez a wishbone. **1905** 'O. HENRY' *Trimmed Lamp* 51 Ragged he was, with a split shirt front open to the wishbone.

+Wishtonwish. [Amer. Ind.] **1.** The prairie dog. **2.** The whippoorwill or a similar bird. — **(1) 1808** [see PRAIRIE SQUIRREL 1]. **1819** WARDEN *Statistical Acct. U.S.* I. 226 This animal . . . is called by the Indians *Wishtonwish* from its cry; and by white hunters and traders, Prairie dog, or squirrel. **(2) 1826** COOPER *Last of Mohicans* xxii, ''Tis a pleasing bird, . . . and has a soft and melancholy note.' . . . 'He speaks of the wish-ton-wish,' said the scout. **1829** — *Wish-ton-Wish* xvii, The Whip-poor-Will; a name that the most unlettered traveller in those regions would be likely to know was vulgarly given to the Wish-Ton-Wish, or the American night-hawk. **1838** FLAGG *Far West* II. 109 Here [near Kaskaskia R., Ill.] is found the jay; . . . the thrush; the wishton-wish; the plaintive whippoorwill.

Wisp broom. A whisk broom. — **1848** *Knickerb.* XXXII. 80 It looked like a barber's wisp-broom. **1867** COZZENS *Sayings* 71 Spruce trees not bigger than a wisp broom grow in some patches.

Wistaria. [Caspar *Wistar*, Amer. anatomist (1761-1818).] A plant of the genus *Wistaria*, native to North America, Japan, and China. {1842-} Also attrib. (Cf. AMERICAN WISTARIA.) — **1847** DARLINGTON *Weeds & Plants* 101 Wistaria. . . . Virginia, South and West. **1857** GRAY *Botany* 96 Wistaria. . . . Large and showy lilac-purple flowers. **1875** *Amer. Naturalist* IX. 392 Chief of all our native vines, is the Wistaria, found native in southern Illinois. **1888** HARRIS *Free Joe* 199 A wistaria vine running helter-skelter across the roof of the little cabin. **1905** N. DAVIS *Northerner* 320 She sat in the wistaria arbor.

+Wistar party. [See prec.] In Philadelphia, a social gathering of men for the discussion of current subjects. — **1829** B. HALL *Travels in N.A.* II. 340, I shall never forget these agreeable and instructive Wistar parties at Philadelphia. **1839** GRUND *Aristocracy in Amer.* II. 157 His dislike of the Wistar parties,—a sort of half literary, half fashionable, weekly convention of gentlemen, at which a tolerable supper is added to a great deal of indifferent conversation. **1889** LOWELL *Letters* II. 363 Philadelphia was very dinnery, of course, with lunches and Wister parties thrown in.

∗Witch, *n.*

∗1. A woman supposed to have dealings with the devil or evil spirits.

1648 *Mass. H. S. Coll.* 4 Ser. VI. 68 The witche is condemned, and to be hanged to-morrow. **1693** C. MATHER *Wonders Invis. World* (1862) 214 A Further Account of the Tryals of the New-England Witches. **1767** HUTCHINSON *Hist. Mass.* II. 35 Your daughter said she was at the witches meeting.

b. Applied to an Indian man or woman.

1649 ELIOT *Glorious Progress* 9 Old Papassaconnaway . . . hath been a great Witch in all mens esteem . . . and a very politick wise man. **1825** NEAL *Bro. Jonathan* II. 11 [He] struck into a path which led . . . up to the cabin door, of the old Mohawk witch.

c. Phrases. *The witch is in it,* it is bewitched; *as nervous as a witch,* very restless.

1885 HOWELLS *Silas Lapham* 325 [She] said aloud to herself, 'Well, the witch is in it.' **1911** F. M. CRAWFORD *Uncanny Tales* 132 She's been as nervous as a witch all day.

2. Attrib. with *cake, hanger, pie,* etc.

1693 I. MATHER *Further Acct. Tryals* (1862) 287, I hear that of late there was a *Witch-cake* made with the Urine of bewitched Creatures, as one Ingredient. **1693** C. MATHER *Wonders Invis. World* (1862) 15 The Dæmons might Impose the Shapes of Innocent Persons . . . , (which may perhaps prove no small part of the Witch-Plot in the issue). **1828** ROYALL *Black Book* II. 65 He was one of those right old witch-hangers. **1852** STOWE *Uncle Tom* xxxv, 'It's a witch thing, mas'r!' 'A what?' 'Something that niggers gets from witches.' **1884** 'MARK TWAIN' *H. Finn* xxxvi, You make them a witch pie.

∗Witch, *v.* +*intr.* To engage in mischief *with*. Also transf. — **1862** STOWE in *Independent* 6 March 1/1, I'd forgive him his share of this summer's mischief . . . , for I witched with him. **1875** HOLLAND *Sevenoaks* 441 The summer moon witches with the mist.

+Witch alder. Any shrub of the genus *Fothergilla.* — **1817-8** EATON *Botany* (1822) 282 *Fothergilla alnifolia,* witch alder. **1836** LINCOLN *Botany* App. 98. **1895** *Stand.* 2073/2.

Witch ball. (See quotation.) {1866-} — **1878** BEADLE *Western Wilds* 483, I have seen specimens [of wire silver] that looked like a 'witchball,' or mass of tangled hair turned to pure silver.

∗Witchcraft. The practices of witches, esp., in later use, with respect to Indians. — **1636** *Plymouth Laws* 43 Solemn Compaction or conversing with the divell by way of witchcraft conjuracion or the like. **1692** SEWALL *Letter-Book* I. 132 Are perplexed per witchcrafts; six persons have already been condemned and executed at Salem. **1764** HUTCHINSON *Hist. Mass.* II. 52 The old colony law . . . makes witchcraft a capital offence. **1822** MORSE *Rep. Indian Affairs* II. 18 The Wyandots still retain their faith in witchcraft. **1881** *Rep. Indian Affairs* 3, I instructed them . . . to prohibit absolutely the execution of the death penalty for witchcraft.

Witch elm. {1626-} + Any of several American trees, esp. the wing elm. Also attrib. — **1685** *Providence Rec.* XIV. 151 The Norwesterne Cornner being bounded with a witch Elme tree haveing some stones layd about it. **1840** HOFFMAN *Greyslaer* I. 144 A clump of witch-elms growing in the centre cast their drooping branches nearly to the middle of the stream. **1897** SUDWORTH *Arborescent Flora* 182 *Ulmus alata,* Wing Elm. . . . [Also called] Witch Elm (W.Va.).

+Witch grass. =TWITCH GRASS. — **1790** S. DEANE *New-Eng. Farmer* 230/2 Witch-Grass . . . [is] a most obstinate and troublesome weed. **1833** see PUS(S)LEY]. **1894** *Outing* XXIV. 166/1 Their pathway lay . . . through reaches of white, dry sand, coaxed into a settled abiding place by a reluctant growth of witch-grass.

∗Witch-hazel.

+1. An American shrub, *Hamamelis virginiana;* also, the bark of this or an extract made from it.

1671 *S.C. Hist. Soc. Coll.* V. 333 Here is some holly, elder, & witch hazell. **1778** CARVER *Travels* 508 The Witch Hazle grows very bushy, about ten feet high. **1784** *Amer. Acad. Mem.* I. 412 Witch-Hazel. . . . The Indians considered this tree as a valuable article in their materia medica. **1832** WILLIAMSON *Maine* I. 116 The *Witch Hazel* . . . is used by the natives as a remedy for inflammations. **1850** *Knickerb.* XXXVI. 388 Get out in the woods and scrape enough witch-hazel to make you some more ink. **1891** *Cent.* 6951/3 Witch-hazel is now much in vogue as a cure for bruises and sprains, as also for various internal difficulties. **1919** HOUGH *Sagebrusher* 70 Can't you put some witch hazel on your knee?

+2. Attrib., esp. with reference to the use of parts of the shrub in locating water, gold, or oil.

1847 DARLINGTON *Weeds & Plants* 144 Hamamelaceæ. (Witch-hazel Family.) Shrubs or trees with alternate, simple leaves. **1848** PARKMAN in *Knickerb.* XXXI. 400, I would like to have one of those fellows . . . go about with his witch-hazel rod . . . [to locate] a gold mine. **1873** 'MARK TWAIN' & WARNER *Gilded Age* 272 A witch-hazel professor . . . could walk over the land with his wand and tell him infallibly whether it contained coal. **1875** *Scribner's Mo.* Nov. 130/1 Some few women have that witch-hazel power which enables them to find out the human nature in their cook or washerwoman. **1886** [see FORK n. 7]. **1892** TORREY *Foot-Path Way* 61 Such witch hazel blossoms as can be gathered in December are . . . nothing but belated specimens. **1894** ROBINSON *Danvis Folks* 179 I should admire tu know if he ever tried the myraculous paower of a witch hazel crotch. . . . I c'n find veins of water with 'em. **1904** TARBELL *Hist. Standard Oil Co.* I. 24 In January there had suddenly been struck on Pithole Creek . . . a well, located with a witch-hazel twig.

+Witch hopple. =HOBBLEBUSH. — **1840** HOFFMAN *Greyslaer* II. 44 Tangled thickets of moss wood and wytch-hopple, gave now the springy footing the tired hunter loves. **1894** *Outing* XXIV. 186/2 We had to . . . take the walking as it came, hills and valleys, marshes and witchhopple. **1895** REMINGTON *Pony Tracks* 143 The miserable 'witchhoppel' leads its lusty plebeian life. **1906** *N.Y. Ev. Post* 10 Nov. Sat. Suppl. 1 The undergrowth consists chiefly of witchhopple and moosewood.

∗Withdraw. Withdrawal. *Obs.* {1444} — **1693** C. MATHER *Wonders Invis. World* (1862) 126 One of these Witnesses was over-perswaded by some Persons, to be out of the way upon G. B.'s Tryal; but he came afterwards with Sorrow for his withdraw. **1720** SEWALL *Diary* III. 276 Went not to Mm. Winthrop's. This is the 2d Withdraw. **1770** T. HUTCHINSON *Diary & Lett.* I. 28, I determined therefore to give an order for the withdraw of the garrison.

Withdrawal card. A card made out when one withdraws from a union. — **1874** *Internat. Typogr. Union Proc.* 15 A member taking a Withdrawal Card severs his connection with the Union, and vacates any office he may hold in the Union. **1895** *Ib.* 35/1, [I] settled by having these proprietors take out withdrawal cards.

∗Withe, *n.* A twig, esp. one of hickory, used for securing something in place, for making chair bottoms, and, by Indians, for making handles of stone hammers. Also fig.
See also HICKORY WITHE.
1637 *Dedham Rec.* 28 Poles [are] to be bownd to ye Rayles with poles & withes. **1785** in Darlington *Mem. Bartram & Marshall* 544 By twisting a withe of Hickory round the stone, they make a helve, and so cut and bruised the bark round the trees. **1852** MARCY *Expl. Red River* (1854) 98 They also make use of a war-club, made by bending a withe around a hard stone. **1867** EDWARDS *Shelby* 13 The habits, and traditions, and prejudices, and withes of system which bound the slaveholders of Missouri, would drop from about them like burned flax.
comb. and *attrib.* **1845** *Knickerb.* XXV. 444 The chairs around the room were . . . withe-bottomed. **1864** *Maine Agric. Soc. Returns 1863* 66 Sawed slats . . . would be cheaper than the withe hurdles.

∗Withe, *v. tr.* To bind (a person) with withes; to catch (a deer) with a noose of withes. {c1630–1732} Also *vbl. n.* — **1835–7** HALIBURTON *Clockmaker* 1 Ser. xvi. 142 If their fences . . . aint [good], they ought to stake 'em [*sc.* cattle] up, and with them well. **1839** HOFFMAN *Wild Scenes* I. xix, What, . . . you are not a-going to withe the deer? *Ib.* 114 I always said that withing is a good way. **1841** COOPER *Deerslayer* xxviii, The body of Deerslayer was withed in bark sufficiently to create a lively sense of helplessness. **1858** D. K. BENNETT *Chronology N.C.* 25 The Indians . . . withed him to a sapling.

+Withe rod. An American shrub, *Viburnum nudum.* {1866} — **1847** WOOD *Botany* 302 Withe Rod. . . . A shrub or small tree, 10–15 f[eet] high. *a*1862 THOREAU *Maine Woods* 310 The prevailing shrubs and small trees along the shore were: . . . cranberry-tree and withe-rod. **1875** EMERSON *Trees Mass.* II. 411 The Naked Viburnum. Withe Rod. *V. nudum.* . . . A slender, erect shrub, . . . found growing in swamps and wet woods.

+Witness stand. In a court room, the place, usually a somewhat elevated stand beside the judge's bench, occupied by a witness when giving his testimony. — **1885** [see OFFICER 1 b]. **1894** 'MARK TWAIN' *P. Wilson* xx, He would not call him to the witness-stand. **1905** N. DAVIS *Northerner* 132 He had sweated his nefarious dealings from him on the witness-stand.

+Witness (tree). *Surveying.* (See quot. 1845.) — **1845** KIRKLAND *Western Clearings* 3 The corners [are] especially distinguished by stakes whose place is pointed out by trees called Witness-trees. **1898** POST *10 Years Cowboy* 169 They could have marked three trees . . . ; in which case the corner would be found somewhere in the circle made by the three 'witnesses.'

∗Wizard.

∗1. A man who practices witchcraft.
1680 *N.H. Hist. Soc. Coll.* VIII. 47 Rachel Fuller told us of several persons that she reckoned for witches and wizzards in this town. **1698** in Burr *Witchcraft Cases* (1914) 74 To give Punishment to the Witch or Wizard (that might be the wicked Procurer or Contriver of this Stone Affliction). **1845** SIMMS *Wigwam & Cabin* 2 Ser. 110 The negroes all around . . . look upon his powers as a wizard, with a degree of dread.

2. A professional prestidigitator.
1895 *N.Y. Dramatic News* 14 Dec. 6/1 The wonderful record established at the California theatre by Herrmann the Great . . . has finally been broken . . . [by] the wonderful wizard [himself].

Wizened up, *a.* Wizened, shrivelled. *colloq.* — **1881** JEWETT *Country By-Ways* 38 Stephen seemed to be all wizened up since cold weather come. **1902** LORIMER *Lett. Merchant* 122 Chauncey was . . . wizened up like a late pippin.

+Wizzle, *v. intr.* (See quotation.) — *a*1870 CHIPMAN *Notes on Bartlett* 515 To Wizzle, to shrink up; to wrinkle; to be shrunk, to be wrinkled. New England.

+Wizzled up, *a.* =WIZENED UP. *colloq.* — **1843** STEPHENS *High Life N.Y.* I. 219 She had on a cap all bowed off with pink ribbons, that looked queer enough round her leetle wizzled up face. **1853** *Knickerb.* XLIII. 539 No one followed up the meetings more constantly than a little old woman with a wizzled-up face.

∗Woad. A plant (*Isatis tinctoria*) formerly grown for the blue coloring matter obtained from the leaves. (See also *dyer's woad* (under DYER'S d.).) — **1815** *Niles' Reg.* VIII. 56/1 Woad and madder, essential dyes in our manufactures, are already successfully cultivated. **1847** WOOD *Botany* 164 The Woad is . . . occasionally cultivated for the sake of its leaves.

∗Woadwaxen. The woodwaxen or dyer's-broom (*Genista tinctoria*), yielding a yellow dye. — **1847** WOOD *Botany* 234 Wood-waxen. . . . A naturalized species, found occasionally in dry, hilly grounds. **1886** *Harper's Mag.* Dec. 102/1 The woad-waxen . . . [is] the identical 'whin' of the English downs, now sparingly naturalized in some sections of New England.

Wobble, *v.* (See WABBLE *v.*)

+Wokas, Wocus. [Klamath *wókas.*] The seeds of a yellow water lily of the West (*Nuphar polysepalum*), dried and roasted by the Indians for food. — **1881** *Rep. Indian Affairs* 144 This lake . . . produces in abundance a small seed known by the name of 'wocus.' **1900** DRANNAN *Plains & Mts.* 482 Jack came to my camp one day and said: . . . 'Wocus nearly all gone.' **1902** *Nat. Museum Rep.* 728 The Indians harvest their crop of wokas, or waterlily seed.

∗Wolf.

∗1. A wild animal of the genus *Canis*, +as the American gray wolf.
1602 [see OTTER 1]. **1633** *Plymouth Laws* 33, 2d was allowed p[er] head to any, that should kill a wolfe. **1750** WALKER *Journal* 58 We found the Wolf's Den and caught 4 of the young ones. **1790** S. DEANE *New-Eng. Farmer* 327/1 New-England . . . has been much infested with wolves. **1873** ARNY *Items regarding N. Mex.* 30 Wolves . . . are found in all parts of the grant [on the Red River]. **1913** [see MOUNTAIN LION].

b. With specifying or defining terms.
See also *barking wolf* (under BARKING *ppl. a.*), BLACK WOLF, etc.
1804–6 CLARK in *Lewis & C. Exped.* VI. (1904) 122 The Small burrowing wolf of the prairie is found as low as the Mahars. **1838** S. PARKER *Tour Rocky Mts.* 189 There are five different species of wolves; the common gray wolf, the black, blue, white, and the small prairie wolf. **1890** *Cent.* 4479/2 *Pied wolf*, a pied variety of *Canis occidentalis*, the common American wolf.

2. The skin of a wolf.
1805 CLARK in *Lewis & C. Exped.* II. (1904) 377, I have also observed some robes among them of beaver, moonox, and small wolves. **1876** *Smithsonian Misc. Coll.* XIII. vi. 69 Furs. . . . Wolf, (*Canis lupus*)—linings, rugs, and robes. White wolf. Black wolf. . . . Red wolf.

3. Wrath, desire to fight.
*a*1846 *Quarter Race Ky.* 89 [A licking] wakened my wolf wide awake, so I begin to look about for a man I *could* lick and *no mistake!*

4. *attrib.* and *comb.* **a.** With *bait, baiter,* etc.
See also WOLF HOOK, WOLF HUNT, etc.
1636 *Mass. H. S. Coll.* 2 Ser. VIII. 229, 6 wolf bullets with adders tongues. **1640** *Conn. Hist. Soc. Coll.* XIV. 258 One p[ar]sell Lying Neere the Wolffe Pound. **1646** *Portsmouth Rec.* 33 The wolfe Catcher shall be payed out of the tresuery. **1661** *Oyster Bay Rec.* I. 3 Every Townesman shall bring in all ther dews for wolf killing. **1835** HOFFMAN *Winter in West* I. 181 Wolf, bear, and badger-baiting have each their active followers. **1845** SIMMS *Wigwam & Cabin* 1 Ser. 121 He had put to shame the best wolf-takers of the tribe. **1846** SAGE *Scenes Rocky Mts.* xii, Numerous wolf tracks . . . appeared on all sides. **1868** *Iowa State Agric. Soc. Rep. 1867* 130, [I] used the carcass [of a cow] for 'wolf bait.' **1891** *Fur, Fin & Feather* 187 From buffalo hunters to wolf-baiters is but a step. **1891** EARLE *Sabbath* 11 In 1664, if the wolf-killer wished to obtain the reward, he was ordered to bring the wolf's head.

b. In the specific names of plants, animals, etc. Also in possessive.
See also WOLF DOG, WOLF FISH.
1884 GOODE, etc. *Fisheries* I. 250 This species [*Anarrichthys ocellatus* is commonly known as the 'Eel,' or 'Wolf-eel,' the latter name probably having been given by some one familiar with the Atlantic Wolf-fish. **1786** WASHINGTON *Writings* (1835) IX. 164, I would write to you for the wolfhound, if to be had conveniently. **1895** *Dept. Agric. Yrbk.* **1894** 286 The wolf moth or little grain moth . . . is not particularly destructive in America. **1796** HAWKINS *Letters* 46 There is a plant in bloom called by the whites wolfs tongue.

5. In special combinations.
Wolf castle, an area enclosed by dense and nearly impenetrable shrubbery; *w. chase*, a wolf hunt; *w. dance*, an Indian dance in which the participants imitate the actions of wolves; *w. meat*, flesh to be eaten by wolves; *w. pup*, a wolf whelp; *w. tail*, a disease of cattle.
1853 SIMMS *Sword & Distaff* (1854) 81 The place in which the latter found himself was a sort of wolf-castle. **1835** HOFFMAN *Winter in West* I. 207 Arrangements were accordingly made by the several gentlemen present for that most exciting of sports, a wolf-chase on horseback. **1908** *Sunset Mag.* April 566/1 [He went] among the Shoshone tepees to an unexpected entertainment—a wolf-dance. **1850** GARRARD *Wah-To-Yah* ix. 119 Thar be heap of wolf-meat afore long—sartain! **1827** COOPER *Prairie* v, Old Esther . . . has no more fear of a red-skin than of a suckling cub or of a wolf-pup. **1879** *Diseases of Swine* 195 Cattle are afflicted with wolf-tail and hollow-horn.

Wolfberry. (See quot. 1891.) — [**1834** G. DON *Gen. System Gardening* III. 451.] **1847** WOOD *Botany* 300. **1891** *Cent.* 6959/3 *Wolfberry*, a shrub, *Symphoricarpos occidentalis*, of northern North America, in the United States ranging from Michigan and Illinois to the Rocky Mountains.

Wolf dog. a. A dog used to hunt wolves or to keep them away, or suitable for such purposes. {1652–} Also in fig. context. **b.** A dog representing or supposed to represent a cross between the domestic dog and the wolf. {1736–} — **1637** *Mass. Bay Rec.* I. 198 John Sweete, being presented by the grandiury for shooting a woolfe dog . . . , was fined 5l. **1825** NEAL *Bro. Jonathan* I. 188 A tall, shaggy, wolf dog . . . followed after the boy. **1860** HOLMES *Professor* ii. 45 There is never a collar on the American wolf-dog such as you often see on the English mastiff. **1890**

WEBSTER 1661/1 *Wolf dog*, a dog bred between a dog and a wolf, as the Eskimo dog.

Wolfe hat. [?James *Wolfe*, Eng. general (1727-59).] A kind of cocked hat. — **1889** *Century Mag.* April 861/1 [Washington in his portrait] wears the cocked hat usually called the Wolfe hat.

+**Wolfer.** A wolf-hunter. — **1871** *Rep. Indian Affairs* (1872) 410 A regular stampede took place out of that section of the country of 'wolfers' and whiskey traders. **1913** BARNES *Western Grazing Grounds* 332 One of the most experienced 'wolfers' . . . was called from some distance to try his hand.

* **Wolf fish. 1.** Any one of various fishes of the family Anarhichadidae; +also, a similar fish of the Pacific coast. Also attrib. +2. (See quotations.) — (1) **1792** BENTLEY *Diary* I. 381 We succeeded in taking . . . the wolf fish. **1832** WILLIAMSON *Maine* I. 151 The body of the Wolf-fish is round and slender, the head large and blunt. **1884** GOODE, etc. *Fisheries* I. 248 The Wolf-fish family is represented on our Atlantic coast by three species. **1909** *Cent. Suppl.* 47/1 *Anarrhichthys*, . . . a genus of wolf-fishes of the family *Anarrhichadidæ.* . . . *A. ocellatus* is found on the coast of California. (2) **1882** *Nat. Museum Proc.* V. 661 It is said to be not an uncommon thing for the 'wolf-fish,' as this *Alepidosaurus* is styled, to throw itself on the beach at Iliulink. **1896** JORDAN & EVERMANN *Check-List Fishes* 305 *Alepisaurus æsculapius.* . . . Sabatka; Wolf-fish. Coast of Alaska to California.

+**Wolf hook.** A device for catching wolves. Now hist. — **1636** *Mass. H. S. Coll.* 2 Ser. VIII. 229 An account of certain ammunition. . . . 200 wolfhooks, 20 wolfhooks to hang. **1891** A. M. EARLE *Sabbath* 12 The wary wolf was not easily destroyed either by musket or wolf-hook.

+**Wolf hunt.** A hunting of wolves. — **1835** HOFFMAN *Winter in West* II. 18, I was on a wolf-hunt by moonlight several hours before dawn. **1853** 'P. PAXTON' *Yankee in Texas* 92 The wolf-hunt was declared the order of the day. **1886** *Century Mag.* Nov. 25/2 Men came together for . . . wolf-hunts, where a tall pole was erected in the midst of a prairie or clearing, and a great circle of hunters, . . . with shouts and yells, drove all the game in the woods together at the pole for slaughter.

+**Wolfing.** The hunting of wolves. Also attrib. — **1848** RUXTON *Life Far West* i, Some of 'em got their flints fixed this side of Pawnee Fork, and a heap of mule-meat went wolfing. [**1875** BUCKLAND *Log-Book* 109 When the wolfing season has commenced on the prairies, the hunter impregnates the carcase of a buffalo . . . with strychnine and places it in a likely position.] **1897** HOUGH *Story of Cowboy* 12 These dogs are used in the constant wolfing operations. *a*1918 G. STUART *On Frontier* II. 172 Wolfing became quite an important industry in Montana.

* **Wolfish,** *a.*
1. Wolflike, savage.
1775 ADAIR *Indians* 259 To keep the [Indian] wolf from our own doors, by engaging him with his wolfish neighbours. **1848** BURTON *Waggeries* 16 He felt sorter wolfish, and lookin' at the strannger darned savagerous. **1854** J. S. C. ABBOTT *Napoleon* (1855) II. 242 Swarms of Cossacks, on fleet and wolfish horses.

+**2.** Ravenously hungry; eager; insatiable. *colloq.*
1806 WEBSTER 352/2 *Wolfish* or *Wolvish*, like a wolf, ravenous. *a*1848 PORTER *Tales of Southwest* 121 (B.), They'd been fightin' the barrel of whiskey mightily comin' up, and were perfectly wolfish arter mar of the dog. **1895** REMINGTON *Pony Tracks* 125 By 12 M. we acquire a wolfish yearning for the 'flesh-pots.'

+**Wolf pen.** An enclosure made with logs for trapping wolves; a cage or enclosure for the exhibition of wolves. Also transf. — **1647** *Watertown Rec.* I. 1. 12 The Towne gaue: to John Witherll: there Right in the palisado that inclosed the woulfe pen. **1667** *East-Hampton Rec.* I. 269 Mr James shall have the fence belonging to the wolfe pen. **1835** A. PARKER *Trip to Texas* 52 A man on Fox river . . . made a wolf pen over a cow that got accidentally killed, and caught twelve wolves in one week! **1866** C. H. SMITH *Bill Arp* 129 They marched me to the wolf pen and there I stayed till the fuss was over. **1876** INGRAM *Centennial Exp.* 106 The places of interest are . . . the Aviary, the Fox Pens, the Wolf-Pens.

+**Wolf pit.** A hollow prepared as a trap for wolves. — **1658** *Norwalk Hist. Rec.* 47 [They] have undertaken to make and provide a good and sufficient wolfe-pitt. **1678** *New Castle Court Rec.* 177 Itt was . . . Resolved and ordered by the Court . . . [that there] bee made and erected fitting woolfe pitts or houses. **1694** *Conn. H. S. Coll.* XIV. 296 From thence to the Top of the Hill by the wolfe pits. **1835** AUDUBON *Ornith. Biog.* III. 339 Mine host . . . asked if I should like to pay a visit to the wolf-pits.

+**Wolf scalp.** The skin of a wolf's head, exhibited as evidence of the killer's claim to a bounty. Also comb. — **1800** in Rothert *Muhlenberg Co.* 116 Sharp Garness Brought before me . . . four Groan Wolf Sculps and proved them as the Law directs. **1847** ROBB *Squatter Life* 70 Among the wolf-scalp hunters of the western border of Missouri, . . . *Hoss* Allen is all *powerful* popular. **1891** *Fur, Fin & Feather* 187 One dollar each [is paid] for wolf scalp and fifty cents for coyotes.

* **Wolfskin.** The skin of a wolf, used as clothing or for similar purposes; a garment or blanket made of this. Also attrib.
1612 SMITH, etc. *Virginia* I. 9 His arrowes . . . hee wore in a woolues skinne at his backe for his quiuer. **1649** [see RAC(C)OON *n.* 3 b]. **1805** LEWIS in *Ann. 9th Congress* 2 Sess. 1055 Buffalo robes and wolf skins [are supplied by the Yankton Indians]. **1835** HOFFMAN *Winter in West* I. 244 A hard-featured borderer, with long sandy hair flowing from under a cap of wolf-skin. **1858** VIELÉ *Following Drum* 203 Several squaws accompanied them, dressed in wolf-skins. **1864** TAYLOR *H. Thurston* 78 With

a wolf-skin robe on his knees, Woodbury sat in luxurious warmth. **1880** *Harper's Mag.* Aug. 368/1 An old hunter sat smoking on a roll of wolf-skins. **1898** N. E. JONES *Squirrel Hunters of Ohio* 9 A wolf-skin 'hunting shirt' made the weather right at all times with the hunter.

+**Wolf('s) robe.** (See quot. 1891.) — **1873** PHELPS *Trotty's Wedding* xix, Deb drew the great gray wolf's-robe over her face and head. **1891** *Cent.* 6960/1 *Wolfrobe*, . . . the skin or pelt of a wolf made into a robe for use in carriages, etc.

Wolf trap. {1780} A place so arranged as to attract and imprison wolves; a device for catching a wolf. {1883} Also attrib. and transf. — **1642** *Plymouth Laws* 70 All the Townes . . . shall make woolfe Trapps. **1687** *Manchester Town Rec.* 32 The sd tree . . . [stands] on the east of woolf trap brook. **1824** DODDRIDGE *Notes* 63 The wolf trap . . . fastened on his foot with its merciless jaws. **1874** B. F. TAYLOR *World on Wheels* 163 The ambulance that was used in the late war . . . , with wolf-trap springs . . . , is, for a merciful device, certainly the most cruel. **1886** *Century Mag.* Nov. 30/1 A preacher in Sangamon County . . . had set a wolf-trap in view of his pulpit.

+**Wolfy,** *a.* Wolflike; suggestive of the presence of wolves or the appearance of wolves. — **1837** NEAL *Charcoal Sk.* (1838) 35 Dabbs was decidedly out of sorts—perhaps bony, as well as wolfy. **1838** DRAKE *Tales Queen City* 36 It looks rather wolfy in these parts. **1839** PLUMBE *Sk. Iowa* 59, I might find some of the law-makers of Wisconsin . . . rather 'wolfy about the head and shoulders.'

* **Wolverine, Wolverene.**
+**1.** A North American mammal (*Gulo luscus*) closely related to the glutton of Europe.
1736 GYLES *Mem. Captivity* 25 The Wolverin is a very fierce and mischievous Creature, about the bigness of a middling Dog. **1796** MORSE *Univ. Geog.* I. 196 The Wolverene . . . seems to be a grade between the bear and the woodchuck. **1832** [see CARCAJOU 1]. **1850** [see BLACK CAT 1]. **1868** *Amer. Naturalist* II. 215 The Wolverine follows the Beaver and preys upon them. **1904** WHITE *Silent Places* 3 Unfamiliar names of beasts . . . , the wolverine, the musk-ox, parka, . . . —these and others sang like arrows cleaving the atmosphere of commoner words.

+**2.** *cap.* A native or resident of Michigan, the Wolverine State. A nickname.
1835 HOFFMAN *Winter in West* I. 179 [His] white capot, Indian moccasins, and red sash, proclaimed . . . the genuine *wolverine*, or naturalized Michiganian. **1839** *Cadiz* (Ohio) *Sentinel* 20 Nov. (Th.), The Wolvereens close side by side. **1904** *Grand Rapids Ev. Press* 23 June 3 Wolverines At Fair. Many Michigan Persons Enjoy the St. Louis Show.

3. *attrib.* and *comb.* **a.** In sense 1 with *skin.* +**b.** In sense 2 with *audacity, thing, wildcat.*
1779 *Essex Inst. Coll.* XLIX. 112 Sold . . . 21 wolverene skins, at £1. **1843** 'CARLTON' *New Purchase* II. 239 Like all hoosiery and woolverine things, they are regardless of dignities. **1847** *Congress. Globe* 5 Feb. 332/2 Set up a great Government bank— . . . a full-grown undeniable Wolverine wild-cat. **1852** *Mich. Agric. Soc. Trans.* III. 332 We have . . . about 10,000 things which Wolverine audacity have denominated swine.

+**Wolverine State.** The state of Michigan. A nickname. — **1846** *Knickerb.* XXVIII. 360 In the Wolverine state, on one occasion, Judge M—. . . was alone upon the bench. **1875** [see LAKE STATE 2]. **1904** *N.Y. Ev. Post* 6 Aug., The Wolverine State has its shield supported by a stag and an elk.

* **Woman.**
The following quotations, all by British writers, give evidence of the reluctance of Americans to use *woman* in polite speech.
1832 KEMBLE *Journal* I. 311 The ladies here have an extreme aversion to being called *women.* . . . Their idea is, that that term designates only the lower or less refined classes of female humankind. **1837** MARTINEAU *Society* III. 83 The view was strange, after being told . . . that I was about to see a very fine woman, to meet in such cases almost the only plain women I saw in the country. . . . This is almost the only connexion in which the word woman is used. **1842** BUCKINGHAM *Slave States* II. 29 A female negro is called 'a wench,' or a 'woman'; and it is this, perhaps, which makes the term 'woman' so offensive to American ears, when applied to white females, who must all be called 'ladies.' **1887** I. R. *Lady's Ranche Life Mont.* 72 If he . . . remarks, 'What a nice woman Mrs. So-and-so is,' they always reply, 'Yes, she's a very nice *lady*,' with a great stress on the *lady.*

1. *To make a woman of* (someone), to force (someone) to occupy a position of subjection or to do woman's work.
1742 *Penna. Col. Rec.* IV. 579 We conquer'd You, we made Women of you. **1836** IRVING *Astoria* I. 221 Where was his squaw, that he should be obliged to make a woman of himself?

2. *attrib.* and *comb.* in sing. and pl. ***a.** Designating women of specified occupations.
1642 *Md. Archives* IV. 189 John Skinner . . . bargained to deliver unto the said Leonard Calvert, fourteene negro men-slaves, & three women slaves. **1715** Woman Servant [see COUNTRY WORK]. **1878** *Harper's Mag.* March 602/2 The established physicians . . . never believed in 'women doctors.' **1883** *Nation* XXXVI. Index 1/3 Woman lawyer in contempt of court. **1887** *Ib.* XLIV. 362/3 Prohibition amendments are said to have been carried by the efforts of women-workers at the polls. **1902** Women students [see CALICO *n.* 3 b].

b. In special combinations.

Woman movement, the movement to give women more opportunities and greater freedom in society, industry, and government; *w. question*, the question of woman's place in business and politics; *w. scrape*, a petty quarrel or offense concerning a woman or women; *women stairs*, the steps leading to the gallery seats for women in a meeting house; *woman-whipper*, one who whips women.

1883 *Harper's Mag.* Aug. 468/2 Whether the great progress of the 'woman movement' . . . is due to the agitation of 'woman's rights,' or proceeds in spite of it. **1871** [see sense 3 c]. **1855** *Chicago Times* 3 March 3/1 A 'woman scrape' of a comico-tragico laughable and supremely ridiculous character 'came off' at the City Hotel. **1717** *Narragansett Hist. Reg.* III. 279 The Pew that was built . . . in a corner as we go up the Women Stairs. **1849** F. DOUGLASS *Narrative* 119 They have men-stealers for ministers, women-whippers for missionaries.

3. In combinations in the possessive, in sing. or pl. **a.** Designating places or parts of places reserved for women or in some way associated with them.

1703 *Topsfield Rec.* 130 Mr. Tillton should have 7 or 8 of the pla[n]ck of ye wimens seats . . . for his charge of taking down the Pulpit. **1725** *New-Eng. Courant* 8 Feb. 1/2 Those who have the Unhappiness of sitting near the Stairs that lead up into the Women's Gallery's, can hardly hear the Minister's first Prayer for . . . the Screiks of English Pattoons. **1853** G. C. HILL *Dovecote* 68 This room was professedly 'the woman's room.' **1894** *Harper's Mag.* July 322/2 In the Woman's Building at the fair . . . we encountered a boy with tear-stained . . . face.

b. Designating various organizations of women.

See also WOMAN'S AID SOCIETY.

1866 MOORE *Women of War* 573 A company of women . . . organized themselves into . . . the 'Woman's Central Relief Association of New York.' **1878** (*title*), Massachusetts Woman's Christian Temperance Union Cuisine. **1880** *Harper's Mag.* Dec. 102/1 In the summer of 1872 the Woman's Education Association of Boston petitioned Harvard College to offer examinations similar to those which the English universities held. **1893** HOLLEY *Samantha at World's Fair* 518 What solid comfort I took through the hull caboodle of 'em—Peace Societies, Temperance, . . . Woman's protective union [etc.]. **1909** *Nat. Conservation Congress Proc.* 61 The Women's Clubs are working for forestry.

c. In special combinations.

Woman's department, in a newspaper or periodical, a special section devoted to women's interests; *w. doctor*, a person attending a woman in the capacity of a physician; *w. exchange*, a public establishment for the display and sale of handwork, baked goods, and other products of the home industry of women; *w. reformatory*, an institution for reforming delinquent women; *w. righter*, a person favoring, or working in behalf of, woman's rights {1885-}; *w. wear*, cloth used for women's dresses.

1875 C. F. WINGATE *Views & Interviews* 146, [I] asked the editor to make a 'women's department,' and give me charge of it. **1882** 'M. HARLAND' *Eve's Daughters* 25 The old women and 'women's doctors' of our foremothers' times physicked the mother. **1893** *Harper's Mag.* Feb. 456 It's a Woman's Exchange. **1912** NICHOLSON *Hoosier Chron.* 53 You're coming to the State House to talk about the Woman's Reformatory. **1871** EGGLESTON in *Scribner's Mo.* I. 380 We were discussing the woman question. I am a 'woman's righter.' **1823** COOPER *Pioneer* xi, [One woman wore] a shawl . . . over an awkwardly-fitting gown, of rough, brown 'woman's-wear.'

+Woman's aid society. Also **women's aid society.** **1.** =LADIES' AID (SOCIETY) 1. **2.** =LADIES' AID (SOCIETY) 2. — (1) **1865** *Atlantic Mo.* June 676/2 Their names appeared . . . as liberal contributors . . . to women's-aid societies, to the sick and wounded soldiers. (2) **1879** BURDETTE *Hawkeyes* 56 The woman's aid society . . . had been unable to fulfill their pledge to pay for the pew cushions.

Woman school. A school kept by a woman. *Obs.* — **1769** *Essex Inst. Coll.* XXI. 238 Voted to carry two Papers one for a man Scool and one for a woman Scool. **1798** MANNING *Key of Liberty* 36 Every Town to be obliged to keep . . . twelve weeks of a woman school in the summer. **1838** *U.S. Mag.* I. 404 He went to a 'woman school' each summer.

Woman's-rightism. The doctrine of woman's rights. — **1855** in Hambleton *H. A. Wise* 303 That section of country [is] fruitful in isms, in abolitionism, . . . women's-rightism and every other ism imaginable.

Woman's rights. Also **women's rights.** *pl.*

1. The rights of women in society {1840-}; spec., legal and political status equal to that of men; woman suffrage.

1842 KIRKLAND *Forest Life* II. 183, [I am] no champion of 'woman's rights' in a technical sense. **1852** *Harper's Mag.* V. 833/1 The annual gathering of the advocates of Women's Rights took place at Syracuse in the middle of September. **1870** 'F. FERN' *Ginger-Snaps* 148 [She] couldn't tell a snuffbox from a patent reaper, and has a bank-book and dividends: . . . and Woman's Rights has done it. **1882** LATHROP *Echo of Passion* xvii, I have been talking woman's rights this afternoon.

2. Attrib. with *convention, man, meeting*, etc.

1850 (*title*), Women's Rights Convention. **1853** J. R. DIX *Transatlantic Tracings* 275, I should like . . . to present the reader with a sketch of the proceedings of a Woman's Rights Meeting. **1855** *Knickerb.* XLVI. 376 Aunt Tabitha Strong would have made a capital 'woman's-rights' man. **1855** *Chicago W. Times* 18 Oct. 1/2 He had been charged . . . with being . . . a woman's rights man. **1868** *N.Y. Herald* 16 July 4/3 Framingham, in Massachusetts, . . . has long been a favorite resort of the long haired

philosophers of the free love, woman's rights, negro worshipping school. **1882** PECK *Sunshine* 11 The *Sun* is a woman's rights paper.

‖**Woman's-rightsy**, *a.* Of or pertaining to woman's rights. — **1863** 'G. HAMILTON' *Gala-Days* 270, I do not design now to open anew any vulgar, worn-out, woman's rightsy question.

Woman suffrage. Also **women's suffrage.** {1867-} In attrib. use with *amendment, association*, etc. — **1868** *N.Y. Herald* 1 July 6/5 The Central Committee of the Women's Suffrage Association of America . . . have prepared a women's rights platform for the coming National Democratic Convention. **1872** *Newton Kansan* 21 Nov. 2/3 The Chase County *Leader* takes up the Woman Suffrage question. **1882** *Nation* 16 Nov. 411/3 The returns from Nebraska are at last decisive as to the fate of the woman-suffrage amendment at the late election in that State. **1898** *Mo. So. Dakotan* I. 60 It was not until after the beginning of the concerted action of the woman suffrage movement that a finger was lifted towards the betterment of woman's condition in this professed free land.

Woman suffragist. Also **woman's suffragist.** One working to secure woman suffrage, or favoring this cause. — **1882** [see ELECTIONEERING *n.* b]. **1883** RITTENHOUSE *Maud* 259 You'll be a . . . woman's suffragist before you know it. **1887** *Harper's Mag.* May 989/1 The woman suffragists . . . proceed almost always by resolutions and lobbying. **1900** *New Eng. Hist. & Gen. Reg.* LIV. p. cxxxi, She has been especially active in prosecuting the cause of the woman suffragists.

✱**Womble-cropped,** *a.* (See WAMBLE-CROPPED *a.*)

✱**Wonder.** *New Eng.* +A variety of sweet fried cake; a cruller. — **1845** *Knickerb.* XXV. 447, I gave my good aunt ocular assurance that her . . . 'wonders' were as acceptable as they used to be. **1848** DRAKE *Pioneer Life Ky.* 97 They were . . . 'wonders,' . . . being known to you under the name of crullers. **1859** STOWE *Minister's Wooing* iv, A plate of crullers or wonders, as a sort of sweet fried cake was commonly called.

+**Wonderation.** Wondering, amazement. Also used as a mild oath. — **1824** [see JIGAMAREE]. **1857** *Knickerb.* XLIX. 35, I passed the time in wonderation.

+**Wongen.** Variant of WANGUN. — **1853** LOWELL *Fireside Travels* 128 We . . . took possession of a deserted *wongen*, in which to cook and eat our dinner.

✱**Wonted,** *a.* Accustomed *to* (something); absol., familiar with a place or thing, at home. {1610-1692} 'Now *U.S.*' (O.E.D.). — **1847** EMERSON *Representation Men* 192 The accumulated dramatic materials to which the people were already wonted. **1861** R. T. COOKE in *Atlantic Mo.* Aug. 147/2 We kinder fed him up for a few days back, till he got sorter wonted. **1871** LOWELL *My Study Windows* 14 [The crows] grew so wonted as . . . to tolerate my near approach. **1893** *Harper's Mag.* May 855/1 He gradually became wonted to his new position. **1901** JEWETT in *McClure's Mag.* June 171 Jakey's the only one that's got wonted.

✱**Wood,** *n.*

I. ✱**1.** A forest or portion of forest; land overgrown by trees, shrubs, etc. Usually pl.

The plural *woods* is sometimes construed as a singular, as in quot. 1907.

1608 SMITH *Virginia* 11 In coasting the shore, divers out of the woods would meet with us with corn and trade. **1683** *Conn. Probate Rec.* 344 My Farme of Land lying in the Woods. **1710** *Providence Rec.* XVII. 271 Having a very considerable Knowledge of the Woods. **1817** S. BROWN *Western Gazetteer* 47 These natural meadows . . . are separated by strips of woods. **1890** HOWELLS *Boy's Town* 51 The boys had gone into the vast woods . . . for pawpaws. **1907** NORRIS *Veil* 3 Suddenly [a narrow road] pitched down a long hill through a thick woods of venerable trees.

b. With contextual allusion to the former practice of burning the woods annually to increase the growth of grass, etc., for cattle going at large.

1642 *New Haven Col. Rec.* I. 70 The woods and meadowes Shall be burned the tenth of March every yeare. **1683** *Derby Rec.* 134 To Burn ye woods for fed of Cattil . . . [3] men Shal Be paid by ye town. **1704** *R.I. Col. Rec.* III. 573 No person or persons whatsoever shall . . . set any fire or fires in order to burn the woods.

✱**2.** Felled timber or firewood.

1636 *Watertown Rec.* I. 1. 3 Whosoever shall take any wood of the 40 Acres of ground . . . shall pay for every Cart load. **1734** *Harvard Rec.* I. 151 Every Scholar Graduate & Undergraduate shall find his proportions of furniture, wood and Candles, during the whole time of his having a Study assigned to him. **1837** *S. Lit. Messenger* III. 684 Notwithstanding several stoppages for wood and water . . . we reached Utica in little more than five hours. **1903** [see CHIP *n.* 4].

+**3.** *pl.* A rural, as contrasted with an urban, region; the 'backwoods.'

1845 COOPER *Chainbearer* xviii, What has an attorney to do with me and mine, out here in the woods? **1889** 'MARK TWAIN' *Conn. Yankee* 309 You have lived in the woods, and lost much by it. **1916** EASTMAN *From Deep Woods* 152, I should have long ago gone back to the woods.

II. In phrases.

To saw wood, (see SAW *v.* 3).

4. *To take in wood*, to take wood for fuel aboard a steamboat. *Obs.* Also *fig.*

1823 JAMES *Exped.* I. 31 We left Shawneetown . . . and stopped three miles below, to take in wood. **1839** MARRYAT *Diary* 1 Ser. II. 36 In the West, where steam-navigation is so abundant, when they ask you to drink they say, 'Stranger, will you take in wood?'

+5. *To take to the woods*, fig., to depart without ceremony; to abstain from voting.

1903 *Nation* 24 Sept. 237 Conservative Gold Democrats . . . are preparing to take to the woods on election day. **1906** *Springfield W. Repub.* 18 Jan. 9 A large proportion of them [*sc.* congressmen], however, 'took to the woods' and did not vote at all.

6. *To knock wood*, to tap or strike on something made of wood, as a supposed way of avoiding bad luck. {to touch wood, 1908}

1905 S. HALE *Letters* 406, I feel as if I must knock wood all the time to keep the charm up.

III. *attrib.* and *comb.* 7. Designating areas of woods.

See also WOODLAND, WOOD LAWN, WOOD LOT.

1698 *N.H. Probate Rec.* I. 438 My wood fields lying on the Creek behind my house. **1824** DODDRIDGE *Notes* 105 The wood range was eaten out. **1856** *Mich. Agric. Soc. Trans.* VIII. 754 His wood patch was nicely cleaned up and saved for future use.

8. Designating vessels, vehicles, etc., designed for, or engaged in, transporting wood.

1704 *Boston News-Letter* 7 Aug. 2/2 Next day they took a Wood Boat & two Slaves. **1780** *Md. Hist. Mag.* IX. 243 We have taken but few of the wood waggons which Supply the town. **1785** *Ib.* XX. 42 He hath gone up and down frequently in . . . wood-flats. **1828** in Quincy *Hist. Harvard* II. 561 The sloop *Harvard*, which was . . . employed as a wood-coaster. **1856** HALE *If, Yes, & Perhaps* 147 The sledge . . . is in general contour not unlike a Yankee wood-sled. **1863** CUMMING *Hospital Life* 59/2 We came up to town on a wood-car. **1872** Wood train [see GRAVEL TRAIN]. **1883** *Century Mag.* Sept. 651/2 A wood-packet runs regularly from Cotuit to Nantucket.

9. In specific names: **a.** Of plants growing in the woods.

See also WOOD ASTER, WOOD HAIR GRASS, etc.

1833 EATON *Botany* (ed. 6) 155 *Geranium dissectum*, wood geranium. **1844** WHITTIER *Poetical Works* (1894) 390/2 When wood-grapes were purpling. **1785** WASHINGTON *Diaries* II. 375 The Wood honey suckle . . . is an agreeable looking flower. **1897** SUDWORTH *Arborescent Flora* 315 *Kalmia latifolia*. Mountain Laurel. . . . [Also called] Wood Laurel (Pa.). **1878** KILLEBREW *Tenn. Grasses* 94 Wood Meadow Grass, *Poa nemoralis*, . . . has not been utilized as a meadow grass in Tennessee. **1784** *Amer. Acad. Mem.* I. 442 *Jussiæa*. . . . Wood Plantain. Rattle-Snake Plantain. . . . It is said to cure the bite of a rattle-snake.

b. Of birds, animals, etc., found in the woods, or of insects boring in wood.

See also WOOD BUFFALO, WOODCOCK, etc.

1891 *Cent.* 6964/2 *Wood-ant*, . . . a white ant, or termite, as *Termes flavipes*, which lives in the wood of old buildings. *Ib.* 6966/2 *Wood-engraver*, . . . any one of several bark-beetles of the genus *Xyleborus* and allied genera; specifically, *X. cælatus*. This works in the cambium layer of pine-trees in the United States in such a way that, on removing the loosened bark, the surface of the wood is seen furrowed in a regular and artistic manner. **1840** EMMONS *Mass. Quadrupeds* 31 *Vulpes Virginianus* . . . is termed by furriers the Wood-gray Fox. **1854** *Agric. N.Y.* V. 242 *Eurydas grata*. Woodnymph. . . . This beautiful moth is rare here. **1884** COUES *Key to Birds* (ed. 2) 653 American Wood Stork or Wood 'Ibis.' **1917** *Birds of Amer.* II. 32 Wild Turkey. *Meleagris gallopavo silvestris*. . . . [Also called] Wood Turkey. **1844** *Knickerb.* XXIII. 72 A wood-turtle [is] fast asleep, near the stump of a tree.

10. In special combinations. **a.** In the singular.

Wood-and-water station, a place where a railway train stops for wood and water; *w. bee*, (see quotation); *w. contractor*, one who is under contract to supply wood; *W. Crees*, the Cree Indians living in the forest, as distinguished from those on the plains; *w. cry*, (see quotation); *w. interest*, a wooded area from which a designated person may get wood; *w. mill*, a sawmill; *w. mold*, mold consisting of decayed wood; *w.-passer*, a fireman; *w. rank*, a pile of wood; *w. rift*, a rift of wood; *w. strap*, a strap used in carrying burdens of wood; *w.-surveyor*, a surveyor or measurer of wood; *w. tag*, (see quotation); *w. tree*, a tree that is to be used as firewood; *w. work*, (see quotation).

1873 'MARK TWAIN' & WARNER *Gilded Age* 270 Ilium . . . [had been] made a wood-and-water station of the new railroad. **1857** *Quinland* I. 91 The whole neighbourhood would assemble . . . to prepare for each other the wood necessary to keep such a fire going during the winter as we have described at the beginning of this narrative; hence a 'wood bee.' **1881** *Rep. Indian Affairs* 39 The axes of the Indian, the wood-chopper, and military wood-contractor have cleared nearly all. **1885** *Boston Jrnl.* 23 June 1/8 The Wood Crees have gone back to get a cache of provisions. **1852** WATSON *Nights in Block-House* 340, I was struck with the greatest terror at hearing the wood-cry, as it is called, which the savages I had left were making, upon missing their charge. **1663** *Charlestown Land Rec.* 84 Graunted unto Peeter Tufts . . . to Cutt . . . Twentie small trees, . . . from of[f] our wood interest on Maulden Common. **1768** J. LEES *Journal* 15 [He] has a Wood and flour Mill erected, and also set up a manufactury of Potash. **1869** *Rep. Comm. Agric. 1868* 424 A small portion of the field was manured with a compost of night-soil and wood-mold. **1876** RAYMOND *8th Rep. Mines* 330 Wages of one wood-passer, . . . [$]1 33. **1884** 'MARK TWAIN' *H. Finn* xviii, Then up gets one of the boys, draws a steady bead over the wood-rank, and drops one of them out of his saddle. **1846** W. G. STEWART *Altowan* I. 196 The last tributary . . . burst its

banks . . . and brought down whole herds of buffalo, and deposited them on islands and wood-rifts. **1915** G. M. WHITE *Rose o' Paradise* 154 The girl came in sight, with her wood-strap on her shoulders. **1845** *Knickerb.* XXVI. 466, I was a wood-surveyor, Sir. **1891** *Amer. Folk-Lore* IV. 222 Wood Tag. In this game, the one who is 'it' tries to tag any player who is not touching wood, objects of wood being regarded as a 'home' or 'hunk.' **1636** *Essex Inst. Coll.* IV. 94/2 Every p[er]son that shall fell any tymber or wood trees within the lib[er]tyes of Salem . . . shall pay a fyne or penaltye of five shillings. **1637** *Mass. H. S. Coll.* 4 Ser. VII. 122 Their worke wilbe to deale in wood-worke, as stubbing of trees, cleareing of grounds, &c.

b. In the plural.

Woods Chippewas, the Chippewa Indians dwelling in the forest, as distinguished from those on the plains; *w. gate*, a gate in the woods or giving access to the woods; *w. litter*, vegetable mold from the woods; *w. lot*, =WOODLOT; *w. partner*, a member of a logging firm whose duties are chiefly in the woods; *w. pasturage*, pasturage afforded by an area of woods; *w. pound*, a pound or enclosure in the woods; *w. prairie*, (see quotation); *w. walker*, one accustomed to walking in the woods; *w. woman*, a woman accustomed to life in the woods.

1849 *31st Congress 1 Sess.* H. R. Ex. Doc. No. 5, II. 1030 'The Chippewas are small in person' (this remark . . . does not apply exactly to the woods Chippewas west of the Mississippi). **1845** F. DOUGLASS *Narrative* 59, I stopped my oxen to open the woods gate. **1869** *Rep. Comm. Agric. 1868* 391 Any land . . . may be improved by the addition of vegetable matter, such as woods litter. **1895** 'CRADDOCK' *Mystery Witch-Face Mt.* 196 The chase leads . . . past 'woods-lots.' **1902** WHITE *Blazed Trail* 5 Mr. Daly, the 'woods partner' of the combination, would flit away to the scenes of new and perhaps more extensive operations. **1787** *Va. State P.* IV. 233 A large area of woods-pasturage [was] destroyed by the Horses. **1722** *Providence Rec.* XIII. 58 Ensign James Whipple is Chosen Pound Keeper for the woods Pound. **1883** SMITH *Geol. Survey Ala.* 474 The post-oak Prairie soil [is] . . . sometimes also distinguished as 'woods prairies.' **1902** WHITE *Blazed Trail* 131 They were . . . plodding along with the knee-bent persistency of the woods-walker. **1840** THOMPSON *Green Mt. Boys* II. 55 The woodswoman, if the term be admissible, [was] wary as she was fearless.

∗ **Wood,** *v.* With *up*.

+1. *intr.* or *absol.* To get or bring in a supply of wood. Also *transf.*

1840 *Picayune* 22 Oct. 2/4 A Van Buren paper in New York calls on the party in the Tenth Ward to 'wood up,' and says 'register your brothers, uncles, aunts,' &c. **1843** *N.Y. Semi-Weekly Express* 4 Jan. 3/2 Another editor invites his Subscribers to 'wood up' while the sleighing lasted.

+2. *intr.* Of a steamboat or a locomotive: To take on wood as fuel.

1848 *Commercial* (Wilmington, N.C.) 29 Aug. 1/6 (Th. S.), A steamer stopped at the landing to wood up. **1858** W. P. SMITH *Railway Celebrations* II. 47 This requires . . . a special stoppage of the passenger train . . . in order to 'wood up.' **1870** LOGAN *Before Footlights* 200 [At] the occasional stoppages to 'wood up,' . . . all was bustle and commotion. **1891** C. ROBERTS *Adrift Amer.* 220 We went on down the river . . . stopping . . . occasionally to 'wood up,' as taking in fuel was termed.

+b. *transf.* Of a person: To take a drink of liquor.

1840 *Picayune* 31 Oct. 2/3 He 'wooded up' as he came along. **1846** *Spirit of Times* (N.Y.) 25 April 100/3 If he had been [a teetotaler], he never would have stopped three times between Dracut and Tewksbury, to 'wood up.' *a*1855 J. F. KELLY *Humors* 175 Jake Hinkle . . . made a straight bend for Sanders' 'Grocery,' and began to 'wood up.'

+3. *tr.* To supply (a stove) with wood as fuel.

1850 JUDD *R. Edney* 52 Richard . . . very quietly went to wooding up the stove.

+ **Wood aster.** Any one of various asters . . . that grow in the woods.

— **1833** EATON *Botany* (ed. 6) 37 *Aster ledifolius*, wood aster. . . . About a foot high. **1883** THAXTER *Poems for Children* 73 Where hides the wood-aster?

∗ **Woodbine.** Also **woodbind.**

∗ **1.** Any one of various climbing plants, as the honeysuckle, hedge bindwood, Virginia creeper, etc. Also attrib.

1709 [see JESSAMINE 1]. **1737** BRICKELL *N. Carolina* 57 The Spontaneous Shrubs of this Country . . . [include] four sorts of Honey-suckle Tree, or Woodbine. **1785** WASHINGTON *Diaries* II. 373 The Woodbine (or Honey Suckle) which I cut and set out, appears to be about half alive. **1803** J. DAVIS *Travels* 88 Of flowers, the jessamine and woodbine grow wild. **1881** RITTENHOUSE *Maud* 16, [I] fixed the wood-bine vines and bright blossoms. **1903** *Critic* XLIII. 305 The woodbine reaches its blazing lines.

2. *To go where the woodbine twineth*, to come to naught; to depart for regions unknown. *colloq.*

1870 *N.Y. Tribune* 24 Jan. 1/4 'What became of the $50,000,000 gold carried for Mrs. Grant [etc.]'? [Jim Fisk:] 'Oh! that has gone with all the rest. Where the woodbine twineth!' **1870** *Congress. Globe* 29 April 3096/1 My bill went 'where the woodbine twineth.' **1879** *Daily State Jrnl.* (Lincoln, Neb.) 12 March 4/2 The two lads . . . found guilty of burglary, have 'gone where the woodbine twineth.' **1897** *Congress. Rec.* 18 Jan. 907/1 The bill . . . goes 'where the woodbine twineth.'

Wood box. A box in which firewood or stove wood is kept. — **1850** JUDD *R. Edney* 135 The Old Man . . . [adjusted the fire] to the necessities of the room, and the state of the wood-box. **1891** 'THANET' *Otto the Knight* 72 After he had filled our wood-boxes he always carried a load to Aunt Callie. **1916** PORTER *David* 103 [There were] woodboxes to be filled.

+**Wood buffalo.** The wood bison, *Bison bison athabascae.* — **1871** *Amer. Naturalist* V. 250 The wood buffalo . . . was never found in herds, but singly. **1884** [see MOUNTAIN BUFFALO 2].

+**Wood butcher.** (See quotations.) *slang.* — **1888** M. STEWART *From Nile to Nile* 75 Every jackleg carpenter, or, to use the wild western nomenclature, 'wood butcher,' . . . had been set to work. **1902** WHITE *Blazed Trail* 202 The blacksmith is also a good wood-butcher (carpenter). **1917** J. A. MOSS *Officers' Manual* 485 *Wood-butcher*—company artificer.

+**Wood camp.** A camp of woodcutters. — **1866** *Wkly. New Mexican* 22 Feb. 1/4 At a wood camp . . . six soldiers were stationed cutting wood. **1887** *Outing* X. 5/1 A path . . . led us to . . . the site of a Mexican wood-camp. *c*1908 CANTON *Frontier Trails* 220, I found my three men in a wood camp.

Woodchopper. One who chops wood, usually as a vocation; a lumberer. — **1779** *Mass. H. S. Coll.* 2 Ser. II. 458 The Centry discov[er]ed a man creeping towards the wood choppers. **1819** DEWEES *Lett. from Texas* 9 Most of them were pale-faced, sickly looking people, apparently fishermen and wood-choppers. **1881** *Rep. Indian Affairs* 39 The axes of the Indian, the wood-chopper, and military wood-contractor have nearly cleared all. **1907** *St. Nicholas* June 747/1 The size of the trees cut down . . . would do credit to our skilful wood-choppers.

Woodchopping. 1. The chopping of wood. {1897-} Also attrib. +**2.** =CHOPPING BEE. — (1) **1855** *Knickerb.* XLVI. 225 These versatile shoremen . . . turn from farming and trading to wrecking, wood-chopping [etc.]. **1879** HOWELLS *Lady of Aroostook* 250 It suggests a wood-chopping period. (2) **1872** EGGLESTON *End of World* 51, I never went to a wood-chopping.

+**Woodchuck.** [Modification of Amer. Indian name.]
1. =GROUND HOG 1.
1674 *Cal. State P., Amer. & W.I.* VII. 581 The natural inhabitants of the woods, hills, and swamps, are . . . rabbits, hares, and woodchucks. **1778** CARVER *Travels* 454 The Wood-chuck is a ground animal of the fur kind. **1832** WILLIAMSON *Maine* I. 140 The Woodchuck is about 14 inches in length. **1879** [see HAND TRUNK]. **1919** *Maine My State* 249 A woodchuck . . . had dug a hole for his winter home.
b. In phrases of comparison.
1835 BIRD *Hawks* I. 170 Here's a dose for the dog will make him sleep like a wood-chuck at Christmas. **1860** HOLMES *Professor* 104 He will come all right by-and-by, sir—as sound as a wood-chuck. **1907** G. M. WHITE *Boniface to Burglar* 131 Here they are, like woodchucks in their holes.
c. *The land of woodchucks,* a country area.
1851 ROSS *In New York* 46 But what could a 'greenhorn,' right from the land of woodchucks do?
2. Attrib. and comb. with *hole, hunt, skin, society.*
1817 *Mass. Spy* 18 June (Th.), Woodchuck Hunt. Woodchucks have appeared in great numbers. **1845** JUDD *Margaret* I. 17 Vigorously plied he his whip of wood-chuck skin on a walnut stock. **1873** PHELPS *Trotty's Wedding* xx, The Chairman of the Woodchuck Society coughed. **1893** HOLLEY *Samantha at World's Fair* 410 That is a woodchuck hole—the woodchuck wuz took in it.

* **Woodcock.**
1. +**a.** =AMERICAN WOODCOCK. +**b.** Either of two species of woodpecker, the ivory-billed woodpecker or the pileated woodpecker.
See also BLACK WOODCOCK, IVORY-BILL WOODCOCK.
1666 ALSOP *Maryland* (1869) 41 The Turkey, the Woodcock, . . . the Pigeon, and others. **1709** LAWSON *Carolina* 139 The Woodcocks live and breed here. **1824** J. DODDRIDGE *Notes* 69 The different kinds of woodpeckers still remain . . . , with the exception of the largest genus . . . , the wood-cock which is now very scarce. **1885** M. THOMPSON *By Ways & Bird Notes* 24, I allus called 'em air birds woodcocks. **1917** *Birds of Amer.* II. 138, 154.
2. Attrib. with *brake, ground, supper.*
1835 HOFFMAN *Winter in West* I. 17 [There was] no woodcock-ground within five miles of the court-house. **1844** *Knickerb.* XXIV. 192 Pleasant was . . . our friend the captain's woodcock supper. **1891** *Cent.* 6965/2 The woodcock . . . is found in bogs and . . . alder-brakes (sometimes called *woodcock-brakes* in consequence).

+**Wood-corder.** =CORDER 1. — **1681** [see OVERSEER 2 g]. **1781** *Baltimore Rec.* 43 The Commiss[ion]ers . . . appointed him Wood-corder. **1850** [see DOG-KILLER 1].

+**Woodcutter.** {1821-} =WOODCHOPPER.
1761 NILES *Indian Wars* II. 417 A party of men were appointed to cover some bateaux and wood-cutters. **1800** in *Harper's Mag.* VI. 7 No woodcutters or carters [are] to be had at any rate. **1817** PAULDING *Lett. from South* I. 154 We came suddenly upon a brace of wood-cutters. **1905** [see CHARCOAL BURNER].

+**Wood-cutting.** {1722-} The cutting of firewood; cutting down trees; timbering. {1893-} Also attrib. — **1683** *Harvard Rec.* I. 75 The Cook [shall] be allowed . . . what he shall expend annually for Wood-cutting. **1784** ELLICOTT in Mathews *Life A. Ellicott* 23 We finished the Wood

Cutting of the 5° West Longitude. **1884** *Century Mag.* 594/1 At the wood-cutting camps more than half the entire average population died within the two years. **1905** WIGGIN *Rose* 171 Logging was to begin that day; then harvesting; then wood-cutting.

+**Wood duck.** {1847, in Australia} **a.** The summer duck, *Aix sponsa.* **b.** =HOODED MERGANSER. — **1777** J. ADAMS in *Familiar Lett.* 272 Mr. Arnold's collection of . . . mooses, wood-ducks, . . . have all been thought of. **1815** *Lit. & Phil. Soc. N.Y. Trans.* I. 63 [The] wood duck, and prairie hen, have in many instances, been tamed. **1894** *Outing* May 150/2 Once I roused a pair of wood-duck . . . from the roots of a hemlock. **1917** *Birds of Amer.* I. 112 Hooded Merganser. . . . [Also called] Wood Duck. *Ib.* 130/1 The Wood Duck is one of the most richly and beautifully colored birds of the United States.

* **Wooden,** *a.*
* **1.** Made of wood.
1641 *Conn. Rec.* I. 443, 1 payle & a wooden platter. **1648** *Ib.* 490 Wooden dishes. *a*1656 BRADFORD *Hist.* 320 Meatheglin, drawne out in wooden flackets. **1676** Wooden bowls [see EARTHEN *a.*]. **1817** FORDHAM *Narr. Travels* 79 [Flat boats] are stuck together with wooden pins. **1835** *Knickerb.* V. 275 He was sent . . . to collect his wooden-clock debts. **1847** HOWE *Hist. Coll. Ohio* 126 Chagrin Falls contains . . . 1 wooden bowl and three woolen factories. **1868** *Putnam's Mag.* Oct. 415/2 A little 'fancy store' in a modest wooden house nestled between two pretentious 'marble-fronts.'
+**2.** Wooded or forested. Freq. *wooden country.*
1816 U. BROWN *Journal* 1. 358 To Smith field a Wooden Town in a Wooden Country & a wooden bred set of Tavern-keepers. **1843** 'CARLTON' *New Purchase* I. 62 Our wooden country's mighty rough. **1891** RYAN *Pagan* 130 Many people from the 'wooden' country tramped over the mountain.
3. In special combinations.
Wooden chimney, =STICK-AND-CLAY CHIMNEY; *w. railway,* a railway made entirely of wood; *w. saddle,* a harness saddle made of wood; *w. slate,* (see quotation); *w. tent,* =LOG TENT.
1836 J. HALL *Statistics of West* 104 Great wooden chimnies . . . occupy nearly the whole gable end of a house. **1837** PECK *New Guide* 181 Coal . . . [is] brought to the works on wooden rail-ways. **1863** A. D. WHITNEY *F. Gartney* xi, Higher up . . . was the 'wooden saddle' fabricated for the back of the placid, slow-moving ox. **1832** WATSON *Hist. Tales N.Y.* 32 The Dutch Reformed Church . . . [was] a Stone Structure, with split oaken shingles then called 'wooden slate.' **1758** *Essex Inst. Coll.* XII. 145 Lay dry in my new wooden tent.

+**Wooden Indian.** A wooden image of an Indian in a standing posture, formerly used as a sign before a cigar store; a silent, dull, or phlegmatic person. — **1895** *N.Y. Dramatic News* 5 Oct. 5/2 Hoey would draw tears from a wooden Indian. **1901** CHURCHILL *Crisis* 279 [He would] sit against the wall as silent as a wooden Indian. **1907** *St. Nicholas* May 607/1, I've been hibernating over at Hammond for two whole days with a dozen wooden Indians who would n't even say 'Good Morning' to me until I shouted it!

+**Wooden island.** (See quot. 1808.) *Obs.* — **1808** ASHE *Travels* 366 *Wooden Islands,* are places, where . . . large quantities of drift-wood, have, through time, been arrested and matted together in different parts of the [Mississippi] river. **1846** LEVINGE *Echoes from Backwoods* II. 20 The Mississippi is obstructed by *planters, sawyers,* and *wooden islands,* which are frequently the cause of injury.

+**Wooden nutmeg.**
1. An imitation nutmeg made of wood, facetiously ascribed to the inventive genius of sharp Yankee traders of New England, particularly Connecticut; fig., a device of any sort for deception or trickery.
1830 *Mass. Spy* 28 July (Th.), Yankee boasters—may they be . . . primed with wooden nutmegs. **1835** HOFFMAN *Winter in West* I. 90 The effects of the Yankee were generally limited to . . . some knick-knack in the way of a machine for . . . manufacturing wooden nutmegs for family use. **1871** DE VERE 620 In the press and Congress wooden nutmegs have to answer for forged telegrams, political tricks, and falsified election-returns. **1897** *Congress. Rec.* 7 Jan. 574/1 [In] the New England States, . . . the boys serve apprenticeship in making wooden nutmegs.
2. A New Englander, esp. one from Connecticut. A nickname.
1839 *Jamestown (N.Y.) Jrnl.* 24 July 1 Do you mean to insinuate, you Yankee pedler—you infernal wooden nutmeg, that I have cheated? **1888** WHITMAN *Nov.* 406 Those from . . . Connecticut . . . [were call'd] Wooden Nutmegs.
b. *The land of wooden nutmegs,* New England or Connecticut.
1826 *Mass. Spy* 6 Sept. (Th.), The land of 'wooden nutmegs' and horn gun-flints. **1868** *N.Y. Herald* 2 July 4/1 From the land of wooden nutmegs, and humbugs, generally, they have winged their way.
3. Attrib. with *chap, man, memory,* etc., in facetious allusion to the alleged vending of wooden nutmegs by Yankee peddlers from New England.
1824 *Microscope* (Albany, N.Y.) 27 March 4/1 (Th.), All the heroes of wooden nutmegs, horn gun-flint, and bass-wood button memory. **1827** *Western Mo. Rev.* I. 85 The tin wagon, . . . *wooden nutmeg,* and *wooden clock* missionaries find . . . harvest beginning to fall short. **1841** FOOTE

Texas II. 391 The tricks . . . of the *moral wooden-nutmeg trade*. **1852** *S. Lit. Messenger* XVIII. 675/2 It was doing business on the wooden-nutmeg . . . principle. **1861** NEWELL *Orpheus C. Kerr* I. 191 The moment those wooden-nutmeg chaps got their breath, they went to work. **1899** TARKINGTON *Gentleman from Ind.* xvi, I believe him to be the original wooden-nutmeg man.

+**Wooden-Nutmeg State.** The state of Connecticut. A nickname. — *a***1855** J. F. KELLY *Humors* 38 John Bulkley . . . [was] one of the best edicated men of his day in the wooden nutmeg State. **1867** *Ore. State Jrnl.* 18 May 2/2 They only carried the 'wooden nutmeg state' by a few hundred. **1907** [see NUTMEG 2].

+**Wooden (over)coat.** A coffin. *slang.* — **1859** MATSELL *Vocabulum* 96 *Wooden coat,* a coffin **1871** J. H. BROWNE *Sights & Sensations* 21 Anything, from an infant's robe to a wooden overcoat, as they used to call it in the army, can be supplied at the Compton.

Wooden spoon. {1803-}

1. A spoon made of wood.

1797 HAWKINS *Letters* 252, I will give . . . an earth pot, pan and large wooden spoon. **1916** EASTMAN *From Deep Woods* 149 You will find us still Indians, eating with wooden spoons out of the bowls of wood.

+**2.** *Yale.* A spoon made of wood, presented to a student in a ceremony, usually one constituting a burlesque upon the junior exhibition; also, the ceremony, or the recipient of the award: (see note). {1803-, at Cambridge Univ.} Also attrib. and in allusive context.

Sometimes traced from an early custom of presenting a wooden spoon to the greatest glutton in a class. In the early years, a doubtful distinction conferred upon the man taking the lowest of the junior appointments; subsequently bestowed, without regard to scholarship, as an indication of great popularity.

1849 [see BOOTLICK *n.* 1]. **1849** *Gallinipper* Dec., The 'Wooden Spoon' exhibition passed off without any such hubbub. **1851** HALL *College Words* 311 *Wooden Spoon* . . . this title is conferred on the student who takes the last appointment at Commencement. **1867** COZZENS *Sayings* 86 There is old Geoffrey Chaucer (commonly known among the wooden spoons of Boston as Daniel Chaucer). **1871** BAGG *At Yale* 405 The 'Presentation of the Wooden Spoon' by the junior class . . . had come to be *the* exhibition of the whole college year. *Ib.* 419 The great problem . . . was, How to procure good seats at the Wooden Spoon?

Woodenware. Articles, usually household utensils, as bowls, dishes, etc., turned from solid blocks of wood. {1727-} — 164[7] *Conn. Rec.* I. 477 A parcell of wooden ware. **1711** *Essex Inst. Coll.* IV. 187/1 All my wooden ware. **1843** *Niles' Nat. Reg.* 176/1 The New York packet ships are carrying out large quantities of wooden ware to London. **1892** *York County Hist. Rev.* 50 On the first floor is carried an extensive and varied line of . . . wooden ware.

Wood frog. {1698-} +The common American frog, *Rana sylvatica*. — **1839** STORER *Mass. Reptiles* 239 The Wood Frog . . . is very difficult to be taken on account of its agility in leaping. **1857** *Rep. Comm. Patents 1856: Agric.* 114 In its [the broad-winged buzzard's] stomach have been found wood-frogs. **1901** *Chambers's Encycl.* V. 13/1 Widely distributed in the United States . . . [is] the Wood-frog.

Wood grouse. {1776-} +(See quots. 1917). — **1862** WINTHROP *J. Brent* 245 The brace of wood grouse he had shot that morning . . . had never made journey in a crowded box. **1917** *Birds of Amer.* II. 14 Hudsonian Spruce Partridge. *Canachites canadensis canadensis.* . . . [Also called] Wood Grouse; Wood Partridge. *Ib.* 16 Franklin's Grouse. *Canachites franklini.* . . . [Also called] Wood Grouse; Tyee Grouse.

+**Wood hair grass.** A tough grass, *Deschampsia flexuosa*. — **1870** *Rep. Comm. Agric.* 1869 89 Wood hair grass . . . [is] of no agricultural value. **1878** KILLEBREW *Tenn. Grasses* 197 Wood Hair Grass . . . is readily eaten by cattle and sheep.

+**Wood-hauler.** One who hauls wood. — **1897** *Outing* Feb. 438/2 Jean walked down by an old wood-hauler's road. *a***1918** G. STUART *On Frontier* II. 166 It was decided to pay . . the wood hauler out of the roundup funds.

+**Wood hog.** (See quot. 1805.) *Obs.* — **1805** PARKINSON *Tour* 290 The real American hog is what is termed the wood-hog; they are long in the leg; narrow on the back, short in the body, [etc.]. **1840** *Cultivator* VII. 81 The next fall, *mast* was plenty, and 'wood hogs' were fat.

+**Woodhorse. 1.** =SAWHORSE 1. **2.** (See quotation.) — (1) **1845** F. DOUGLASS *Narrative* 116 Mr. Johnson kindly let me have his wood horse and saw. **1879** STOCKTON *Rudder Grange* xiii, They knocked over the wood-horse. (2) **1891** *Cent.* 5943/1 *Stick-bug,* . . . any orthopterous insect of the family *Phasmidæ:* particularly applied to *Diapheromera femorata,* . . . also called *wood-horse*.

Woodhouse. A house, shed, etc., in which wood is stored. Also attrib. — **1655** *Suffolk Deeds* III. 210 Dwelling howse in Boston . . . with one smale shead or wood house. **1795** *Columbian Centinel* 21 Jan. 4/3 To be sold, A House . . . almost new, with Wash-House, Wood-House. **1887** ALDEN *Little Fishers* iv, Maybe you would like to sleep in the woodhouse chamber. **1893** HALE *New Eng. Boyhood* 43 Behind it was a little yard, with a wood-house. **1920** HOWELLS *Vacation of Kelwyns* 97, I'll git my lantern here in the woodhouse.

Wood ibis. The Colorado turkey (*Mycteria americana*), of temperate and tropical America. — **1785** LATHAM *Gen. Synopsis Birds* V. 104 Wood Ibis. . . . Found in Carolina. **1813** WILSON *Ornithology* VIII. 39 The

Wood Ibis inhabits the lower parts of Louisiana, Carolina, and Georgia; is very common in Florida. **1874** [see BAY IBIS]. **1917** *Birds of Amer.* I. 179/2 Thirty-seven Wood Ibises had taken possession of this pool.

Wooding. Attrib. with *place, station.* — **1831** AUDUBON *Ornith. Biog.* I. 343, On a steam-boat's reaching what we call a *wooding-place,* the *strangers* were very apt to pay a quarter of a dollar for two or three heads of this Woodpecker. **1863** RUSSELL *Diary North & South* I. 269 The scenery and the scenes were just the same as yesterday's—high banks, cotton-slides, wooding stations.

Woodland.

1. Land covered with trees; a wooded region.

1638 *Charlestown Land Rec.* 2 [List of possessions] ffive acres of wood land, . . scituate in mistick feilde, . . situate upon the high way betwixt that and the meadow. **1726** *Boston News-Letter* 16 June 2/2 Several Lotts of very good Wood Land in Brookfield, To be Sold. **1876** *Ill. Dept. Agric. Trans.* XIII. 288 The prairies and woodland into which the State is divided. **1903** Fox *Little Shepherd* viii, The lesser men of to-day . . . resemble those giants of old as the woodlands of the Bluegrass to-day resemble the primeval forests from which they sprang.

2. *attrib.* **a.** With *ground.* **b.** In the names of plants.

(a) **1624** SMITH *Gen. Hist. Va.* IV. 111 Hee hath laid out . . . many miles of Champian and Woodland ground. (b) **1901** MOHR *Plant Life Ala.* 706 *Stachys cordata.* . . . Woodland Woundwort. . . . Flowers red; June. **1915** ARMSTRONG & THORNBER *Western Wild Flowers* 198 Woodland Star, *Lithophragma heterophylla,* . . . is sometimes called Star of Bethlehem.

+**Woodland caribou.** The American reindeer, *Rangifer caribou.* — **1859** BARTLETT 69 There are two species [of American reindeer], the Barren Ground, and the Woodland, Caribou. **1917** *Mammals of Amer.* 27/2 The Woodland Caribou is a forest rover.

+**Wood lawn.** A portion of level land overgrown with trees. Also attrib. — **1815** DRAKE *Cincinnati* 43 On the western side, it is principally woodlawn. **1871** *Ill. Agric. Soc. Trans.* VIII. 80 Mr. Sodowsky's farm is located in one of the finest woodlawn blue-grass regions of the State.

+**Wood lot.** A piece of land upon which wood for fuel, etc., grows. Also attrib.

1658 *Suffolk Deeds* III. 174, I heeretofore purchased . . . all the rights to any wood Lott. **1698** *Conn. Probate Rec.* 578, I give him ½ of my 2 Woodlotts. **1706** *Manchester Rec.* I. 115 It is Voted and agreed to lay out 50 or 60 Acors of land at the west end of our common for a wood lot. **1818** FEARON *Sketches* 72 The farm contains about 150 acres, 15 of which are a fine wood lot. **1886** *Century Mag.* April 863/1, I can't bear any of your cheap wood-lot stuff. **1920** HOWELLS *Vacation of Kelwyns* 104 He had found pasturage for him in a wood-lot.

Wood louse. {1611-}

1. =BED-BUG 1. *Obs.*

1675 [see CHINCH].

2. Any one of various small invertebrate terrestrial animals found in or near wood, as a pill bug or a mite {1611-}; locally, a white ant or termite.

1743 CATESBY *Carolina* App. p. xxxvii, [Insects] I observed in Carolina [include] . . . The Wood-louse. **1819** D. B. WARDEN *Acc. U.S.* I. 496 Musquitoes and wood-lice [note, *Acarus Americanus*] are most troublesome in thickly wooded vallies. *Ib.* II. 525 The wood louse, or Chigo, or Bete Rouge (*Acarus sanguinis*) . . . is also very troublesome. **1860** HOLMES *Professor* v. 132 A few score years ago, sick people were made to swallow . . . the expressed juice of wood-lice. **1891** *Cent.* 6967/1 *Wood-louse,* . . . a termite, or white ant, as *Termes flavipes*.

3. Any one of various marine mollusks. Also attrib.

1860 *Smithsonian Rep.* 1859 207 Eleven species of *Chitonidæ* or Wood-louse shells. *a***1884** [see RATTLESNAKE'S TAIL 2]. **1911** *Rep. Fisheries* 1908 315/2 Sea snails (*Gasteropoda*) . . . are found on all our coasts, and are known as . . . 'wood-lice,' 'lobster tails,' 'sea-bugs,' etc.

Woodman. =WOODSMAN. — **1758** *Lett. to Washington* II. 314 My Son Matt . . . will have none but what is Select Gunners and good woodmen. **1804** C. B. BROWN tr. Volney *View* 213, I shall be disposed to attribute these fires . . . to the negligence of woodmen or travellers. **1857** [see DEER PATH]. **1899** CUSHMAN *Hist. Indians* 507 No sound of the woodman's ax . . . broke the profound silence of the vast forests. **1905** [see LUMBERJACK].

+**Wood meeting.** 'The name given by the Mormons to a Camp-meeting' (B. '59).

Wood mouse. Any one of various mice that live in the woods {1601-}, +esp., in the United States, a white-footed mouse. — **1840** HOFFMAN *Greyslaer* I. 59 Here, now, is dried venison . . . , if the woodmice haven't got it. **1876** MILLER *First Fam'lies* 120 They heard the little brown wood-mice nibble and nibble at the bits of bacon rind. **1902** HULBERT *Forest Neighbors* 104 She was in the habit of occasionally bringing [home] . . . a wood-mouse.

+**Wood nettle.** An American herb (*Laportea canadensis*) found in fertile woods. — **1857** GRAY *Botany* 398. **1882** *Harper's Mag.* Nov. 847/2 A nodding leaf upon the wood-nettle arrested my attention. **1901** MOHR *Plant Life Ala.* 477.

Wood owl. An owl living in woods {1809-}, +as the barred owl. — [**1871** BRYANT tr. Homer *Odyssey* 103 [In the] boughs Birds of broad wing, wood-owls and falcons, built Their nests.] **1884** COUES *Key to Birds* (ed. 2) 508 *Strix.* . . . Brown Owls. Wood Owls. . . . A large genus of 'earless' owls. **1917** *Birds of Amer.* II. 103.

Wood path. A path through woods. — **1829** WILLIS *Fugitive Poetry* 23, [I] take Woodpath, or stream, or sunny mountain side. **1841** HAWTHORNE *Notebooks* (1932) 81 A little while ago, mushrooms or toad-stools were very numerous, along the wood-paths, and road sides, especially after rain. **1920** HOWELLS *Vacation of Kelwyns* 142 The young man . . . struck into a wood-path from the road.

* **Woodpecker.** Any one of various widely distributed birds of the family Picidae, having bills suited for drilling bark and tree trunks for insect food.

1709 LAWSON *Carolina* 142 Of Wood-Peckers, we have four sorts. **1778** CARVER *Travels* 471 The Woodpecker . . . is a very beautiful bird. **1806** *Balance* V. 265/1 A wood-pecker lighting on the roof of his house . . . called 'George! George!' **1891** WILKINS *New Eng. Nun* 162 A woodpecker flew into the tree and began tapping at the trunk. **1906** *N.Y. Ev. Post* 22 May 9 This big woodpecker spends half of his time on the ground.

b. With specifying words.

See also AUDUBON'S WOODPECKER, DOWNY WOODPECKER, etc.
*c*1728 Larger red-crested Wood-pecker [see RED-CRESTED *a*.]. **1815** in Shaw *Gen. Zool.* IX. I. 173 Canada spotted Woodpecker. **1839** AUDUBON *Ornith. Biog.* V. 186 Phillips's Woodpecker. *Picus Phillipsii.* **1869** *Amer. Naturalist* II. 598 Arctic Woodpecker. (*Picoides arcticus*). **1878** Californian Woodpecker [see CALIFORNIAN *a.* 2]. **1891** *Cent.* 7017/1 *Yellow-winged woodpecker,* the yellow-shafted flicker, or golden-winged woodpecker. **1898** M. R. AUDUBON *Audubon & Jrnls.* II. 51 [They] returned with several birds, among which was a female Red-patched Woodpecker.

+ **Wood pelican.** = WOOD IBIS. — *c*1731 CATESBY *Carolina* I. 81 *Pelicanus Americanus.* The Wood Pelican. *Ib., Pelicanus Sylvaticus.* The Wood Pelican. **1791** W. BARTRAM *Travels* 293 *Tantalus loculator;* the wood pelican. **1918** *Cambridge Hist. Amer. Lit.* I. 197 We see the solitary, dejected 'wood-pelican,' alone on the topmost limb of a dead cypress.

+ **Wood pewee.** An American tyrant flycatcher (*Myiochanes virens*); with specifying adjective, a related species. Also *wood pewee flycatcher.* — **1810** WILSON *Ornithology* II. 81 Wood Pewee Flycatcher. *Muscicapa rapax.* I have given the name Wood Pewee to this species. **1839** PEABODY *Mass. Birds* 295 The Wood Pewee . . . arrives in Massachusetts in the middle of May. **1874** Western Wood Pewee [see WESTERN *a.* 6 b]. **1917** *Birds of Amer.* II. 205 The animal food of the Wood Pewee is made up of insects.

* **Woodpile.** A pile of wood, esp. firewood. {−1699} For *nigger in the woodpile,* see NIGGER *n.* 12. — **1701** *Boston Rec.* 10 Whosoever Shall Kindle or make any fire open or abroad, within two rodds of any wooden house, warehouse, wood pile or any other combustable matter . . . Shall forfit . . . ten Shillings. **1834** AUDUBON *Ornith. Biog.* II. 81 In winter it frequently visits the wood-pile of the farmer, close to his house. **1917** H. T. COMSTOCK *The Man* 168 But fo' she started forth Marg spilled every jug onto the wood pile.

+ **Wood pussy.** (See quotations.) *local.* — **1899** *Animal & Plant Lore* 61 Wood pussy, skunk, *Mephitica mephitica,* Craigville, Mass. **1917** *Mammals of Amer.* 132/1 The Skunk . . . is known in different localities by special names, such as 'wood-pussy,' 'essence-peddler,' and 'pole-cat.'

+ **Wood ranger.** A member of a military force operating in the woods or forest; a scout or woodsman. — **1734** *Georgia Col. Rec.* III. 414 [The French] have Five hundred Men in Pay, constantly employed as Wood-Rangers, to keep their neighboring Indians in Subjection. **1757** E. BURKE *Acct. Settlements Amer.* II. 270 A company of wood rangers . . . scour the country near our settlements. **1896** *Harper's Mag.* April 712/1 The white wood-rangers were as ruthless as their red foes.

+ **Wood rat.** Any one of various native American rats of the genus *Neotoma,* found in the woods. — **1766** J. BARTRAM *Journal* 30 We found a great nest of a wood-rat. **1826** GODMAN *Amer. Nat. Hist.* II. 69 The Wood-Rat . . . is to be found throughout this country in certain situations. **1876** [see KANGAROO MOUSE 1]. **1912** *Univ. Calif. Public. in Zool.* X. 127 Two specimens [of cony] were trapped in . . . rat-traps . . . set for wood rats.

+ **Wood road.** An unimproved road through a wooded region or forest. — **1821** COOPER *Spy* vii, Finding a wood-road, . . . [he] turned down its direction. **1884** W. SHEPHERD *Prairie Exper.* 96 The latter is a wood-road for hauling lumber. a**1918** G. STUART *On Frontier* II. 101 We wandered around on an old wood road.

+ **Wood robin.** = WOOD THRUSH. — **1808** [see GROUND ROBIN 2]. **1844** *Nat. Hist. N.Y., Zoology* II. 71 The Wood Thrush . . . has various popular names, such as Wood Robin, Ground Robin. **1890** *Harper's Mag.* Dec. 148/1 His voice was like a wood-robin.

* **Wood sage.** +The American germander, *Teucrium canadense.* — **1784** [see GERMANDER]. **1843** TORREY *Flora N.Y.* II. 82 Woodsage . . . [is found in] low and rather shady grounds. **1898** CREEVEY *Flowers of Field* 162 Wood Sage . . . [grows] along Greenwood Lake, New Jersey.

+ **Wood saw.** A saw, as a bucksaw, used for sawing wood. — **1816** AUSTIN P. I. (1924) 264, 1 Wood Saw. **1845** in *Tall Tales of S.W.* (1930) 26, I would sooner have my leg taken off with a wood-saw. **1876** KNIGHT 2035/2 Wood-saw.

+ **Wood sawyer.** One whose occupation is sawing wood. — **1815** N. *Amer. Rev.* II. 143 Mr. John Wood, killed in the street by Patrick Hart, a wood-sawyer. **1868** G. G. CHANNING *Recoll. Newport* 254 By swinging my arms backwards and forwards, after the fashion of wood-sawyers, . . . I got into a glow. **1891** WILKINS *New Eng. Nun* 43 Matilda's antecedents had come of wood-sawyers and garden-laborers.

Woodshed. A shed in which wood for fuel is kept {1844−}; also, contextually, such a place as the scene of the administration of parental

discipline. — **1868** HAWTHORNE *Note-Books* II. 9 We have been employed partly in an augean labor of clearing out a wood-shed. **1907** *St. Nicholas* July 826/2 He could save himself and most of his companions from unpleasant reckonings in various and sundry woodsheds.

Woodsman. A man, as a hunter, scout, or woodcutter, accustomed to life in the woods. {1699−} 'Chiefly *U.S.*' (O.E.D.). — **1733** BYRD *Journey to Eden* (1901) 299 One of our Woodsmen alarm'd us with the news that he had follow'd the Track of a great Body of Indians. **1792** *Ann. 2d Congress* 347 Those rangers . . . were expert woodsmen, perfectly inured to the Indian mode of warfare. **1816** U. BROWN *Journal* II. 358 We would get a Woods Man on our way thence. **1867** DIXON *New America* II. 289 One of the most popular Presidents since Washington died, was a log-clearer, a woodsman. **1910** TOMPKINS *Mothers & Fathers* 219 For once in his woodsman's life, [he was careless] of where he was.

+ **Wood sparrow.** = FIELD SPARROW. — **1858** *Atlantic Mo.* Dec. 864/2 While listening to the notes of the Wood-Sparrow, we are continually saluted by the . . . song of the Chewink, or Ground Robin. **1865** BURROUGHS in *Atlantic Mo.* May 521/1 You [are directed] where to look for the Hooded Warbler, the Wood-Sparrow, or the Chewink. **1917** *Birds of Amer.* III. 43.

+ **Wood spell.** (See quotations.) *Obs.* Also attrib. — **1864** WEBSTER 1269/2 *Spell,* a gratuitous helping forward of another's work; as, a wood-spell. (U.S.) **1869** STOWE *Oldtown Folks* 478 The minister's 'wood-spell' . . . was a certain day set apart in the winter, . . . when every parishioner brought the minister a sled-load of wood. *Ib.,* Tina, Harry, and I had been busy . . . in helping Esther create the wood-spell cake. **1880** S. PERLEY *Hist. Boxford, Mass.* 177 The 'wood-spell' was recognized as one of the few holiday seasons of our ancestors.

+ **Wood stove.** A stove adapted for burning wood. — **1847** *Rep. Comm. Patents* 1846 304 The common wood stove and cylindrical coal stove [are combined]. **1878** COOKE *Happy Dodd* 98 The dining-room was darker, and a wood-stove replaced the fire. **1898** WESTCOTT *D. Harum* xxiii, His appliance for warmth consisted of a small wood stove.

+ **Woods violet.** (See WOOD VIOLET.)

+ **Woodsy,** *a.* Of or pertaining to the woods; sylvan. — [1860 in Brewster *Life J. D. Whitney* 179 Your gallery would be rather monotonously 'lake and wood'sy.] **1883** 'MARK TWAIN' *Life on Miss.* xxx, Ship Island region was as woodsy and tenantless as ever. **1903** *Munsey's Mag.* May 190 From out a woodsy side road, . . . a big automobile . . . glided.

+ **Wood terrapin.** The wood tortoise, *Clemmys insculpta.* — **1774** FITHIAN *Journal* I. 198 Tom the Coachman came in with a wood Tarripin. **1842** *Nat. Hist. N.Y., Zoology* III. 14 The Wood Terrapin . . . is a harmless species.

Wood thrush. {1817−} +The swamp robin, *Hylocichla mustelina.* — **1791** W. BARTRAM *Travels* 181 The shrill tuneful songs of the wood-thrush. **1808** WILSON *Ornithology* I. 31 The Wood Thrush . . . is also fond of a particular species of lichen. **1875** BURROUGHS *Winter Sunshine* 161 The wood-thrush now and then comes out of the grove near by. **1917** *Birds of Amer.* III. 227/2 The Wood Thrush is a decidedly useful species.

Wood tick. 1. Any one of various ticks, as *Dermacentor electus,* found in the woods. {1668−} +2. A deathwatch or some other insect that makes a ticking sound. — (1) **1745** E. KIMBER *Itinerant Observer* 13 There are Abundance of other Torments in these Climates, as Cock-Roaches, Wood-Ticks, &c. **1819** WARDEN *Statistical Acct. U.S.* II. 180 The wood tick . . . resembles a bug, and lives upon trees and rushes. **1890** *Stock Grower & Farmer* 31 May 4/1 According to a Colorado paper, a wood-tick in that state is making life miserable. (2) **1891** *Harper's Mag.* Oct. 815/1 The wood-tick was held to be a death-watch. *Ib.* 825/2 There was a long silence broken only by the wood-ticks.

Wood violet. {hairy wood violet, *c*1710; 1829−} Any one of various violets growing in the woods, esp. the bird's-foot violet. Also *woods violet.* — **1817–8** EATON *Botany* (1822) 314 *Viola canadensis,* woods violet, . . . in damp woods. **1869** FULLER *Flower Gatherers* 13 They were not wood-violets. **1905** VALENTINE *H. Sandwith* 225 She was, apparently, studying a bunch of wood violets she had picked.

+ **Wood wagtail.** = OVENBIRD. — **1869** BURROUGHS *Wake-Robin* (1886) 198 The well-known golden-crowned thrush (*Seiurus aurocapillus*) or wood-wagtail. **1875** — *Winter Sunshine* 205 We have . . . the wood-wagtail, whose air song is of a similar character to . . . the skylark's. **1917** *Bird of Amer.* III. 152/1 The Oven-bird is known as the Wood Wagtail.

Wood warbler. {1817−} +Any one of various American warblers. — **1883** *Century Mag.* Sept. 727/2 [Striking color] is easily observable . . . in the . . . quill-feathers of the wood warbler. **1891** [see CAPE MAY 2].

Woodware. = WOODENWARE. {1859−, in Australia} — **1760** WASHINGTON *Diaries* I. 134 Bought . . . wood ware and Bees Wax. **1872** McCLELLAN *Golden State* 357 Wood-ware, rolling stock . . . and wine form no inconsiderable feature of the prosperity of the State.

Wood wren. {1792−} +(See quot. 1891.) — **1839** AUDUBON *Ornith. Biog.* V. 469. **1844** *Nat. Hist. N.Y., Zoology* II. 54 The Wood Wren . . . has probably been confounded with the House Wren, and has thus been overlooked. **1891** *Cent.* 6970/3 *Wood-wren,* . . . a supposed species of true wren, described by Audubon in 1834 as *Troglodytes americanus,* but not different from the common house-wren of the United States. **1917** *Birds of Amer.* III. 192 House Wren . . . Wood Wren. . . . Hollow limbs or trunks of fruit trees are also often utilized [for nesting].

* **Wood yard.**

*1. A place where wood, esp. firewood, is chopped, sawed, or stored.

1634 in *Amer. Speech* XV. 294 A piece of land known by the name of the woodyard. **1766** FRANKLIN *Writings* IV. 409 As you have a WoodYard, perhaps they may not be necessary. **1825** LONGFELLOW in *S. Longfellow H. W. Longfellow* I. 62 There is no wood to be had from the College wood-yard. **1884** [see FEED YARD].

+2. *spec.* A place on the bank of a river where firewood for steamboats is kept for sale.

1837 FEATHERSTONHAUGH *Canoe Voyage* II. 125 We moored at a wood-yard on the left bank to repair it. **1853** *Harper's Mag.* March 433/2 We are at the wood-yard of South Manitou. **1883** [see HEAD *v.* 2].

+Woohoo. [Amer. Sp. *guebucú*.] A sailfish of the genus *Istiophorus.* —
1884 GOODE, etc. *Fisheries* I. 337 The 'Sail-fish,' *Histiophorus americanus*, is called by sailors in the south the 'Boohoo' or 'Woohoo.'

* Wool, *n.*

* 1. The fine hair comprising the fleece of a sheep.

1645 *Suffolk Deeds* I. 66 [He was to pay] in Bever corne cattle wines or wooll. **1776** HUTCHINSON *Diary & Lett.* II. 68 The American Colonies have not wool enough of their own. **1863** *Rio Abajo Press* 17 Feb. 2/1 About one million pounds of wool were last year taken from this Terri-tory to Kansas City.

2. In phrases.
See also DYED-IN-THE-WOOL *a.*

+a. *To pull the wool over* (some one's) *eyes*, or variants: To deceive (some one).

1839 *Jamestown* (N.Y.) *Jrnl.* 24 April 1/6 That lawyer . . . has been trying to spread wool over your eyes. **1842** *Spirit of Times* (Phila.) 29 Sept. (Th.), Look sharp, or they'll pull wool over your eyes. **1875** HOL-LAND *Sevenoaks* 259 She 'pulled the wool' over the eyes of his wife. **1894** WILKINS *Pembroke* 185 'Tain't very hard to pull the wool over Caleb Thayer's eyes.

+b. *All wool* (*a yard long*) *and a yard wide*, genuine.

1885 HOWELLS *Silas Lapham* 237 Mother held up her head as if she were all wool and a yard wide. **1913** LONDON *Valley of Moon* 60 You're a live one, all wool, a yard long and a yard wide.

3. *attrib.* and *comb.* **a.** Designating activities and things having to do with the production of wool and with wool in the crude state.

1811 *Niles' Reg.* I. 101/2 No spoliation will injure our home wool mar-ket. **1830** *Collegian* 41 A dull sound, resembling that made by the rolling of a well-packed wool-bag down stairs. **1845** *29th Congress 1 Sess.* H. R. Doc. No. 6, 445 Fattening pork . . . is not generally considered as profit-able as wool-growing or dairying. **1850** *Rep. Comm. Patents 1849: Agric.* 181, I think that wool depots are of great advantage. **1862** *Ib.* **1861:** *Agric.* 131 The wool clip of New England commands a ready cash market in Boston. **1872** *Atlantic Mo.* April 422 [He] was directed to come and begin work as a porter at the wool-warehouse. **1876** Wool-pack [see JUTE 1]. **1884** *Century Mag.* Feb. 518/2 The wool-bench was set up, and the reel full of twine was made ready in its place. **1890** *Stock Grower & Farmer* 3 May 6/1 In two weeks the town will be full of wool wagons. **1902** CAS-PER *Wyoming Derrick* (Casper) 2 Oct., To identify the sheep a wool brand is used.

b. Designating persons connected with wool as laborers or merchants.

1825 *Columbian Centinel* 29 Jan. 1/1 Wanted, three Wool Staplers. **1835** PAULDING *J. Bull & Bro. Jon.* (new ed.) 187 [He was] a great hand at raising sheep, which he called being a wool-grower. **1850** *Rep. Comm. Patents 1849: Agric.* 254 The common practice is for farmers to sell their clip . . . to the . . . wool dealers in the large cities. **1863** RANDALL *Pract. Shepherd* 173 The fleece having been deposited on the folding table, . . . the wool-tyer first spreads it out. **1876** *Wide Awake* III. 30/1 The wool buyers are to be here this afternoon.

c. Designating products made of wool.

1833 Wool homespun [see HOMESPUN]. **1848** *Rep. Comm. Patents 1847* 213 In Appendix, No. 14, will be found a paper . . . recommending wool mattresses. *Ib.* 510 Wool flannel, and all substances made of wool, keep our bodies warm. **1896** *Godey's Mag.* Feb. 212/2 The severity of wool suits is relieved by velvet collars.

d. In special combina tions.

Wool-pulling, pulling the wool over other people's eyes, used attrib.; *wool-sower*, (see quotation); *w. sponge*, an American commercial sponge of soft fiber, as *Hippospongia canaliculata gossypina*.

1847 ROBB *Squatter Life* 16 In short I'm up to the whole 'wool pulling' system. **1891** *Cent.* 6972/3 *Wool-sower*, a woolly many-celled cynipid gall occurring on white-oak twigs in the United States, and made by the gall-fly *Andricus seminator*. **1877** HYATT *Revision of N. A. Poriferæ* 16 The grades [of American sponges] are Glove Sponge . . . , Wool Sponge . . . , and Yellow and Hard Head.

Wool, *v.* {1660-} **+** *tr.* To pull the wool or hair off (a person or animal); to beat or punish; *to wool lightning out of* (someone), to whip (someone) thoroughly. *slang.*

1832 PAULDING *Westward Ho!* I. 122, I'll wool lightning out of you. **1845** HOOPER *Simon Sugg's Adv.* 63 Now, I'll wool you. **1853** BALDWIN *Flush Times Ala.* 41 He wooled him, then skinned him. **1884** *Congress. Rec.* 5 May 3796/1 If ever there was a man who wooled the British lion, he was the man. **1895** REMINGTON *Pony Tracks* 265 The pups again flew into him [the bear] and 'wooled him,' as the cowboys put it.

Woolang. (See WOOLYNEAG.)

* Wool card. A device used for carding wool.

1651 *Mayflower Descendant* X. 39, I give her . . . two spining Wheeles a paire of wool cardes. **1768** ROWE *Diary* 154 We will not for one year send for any European Commodities excepting . . . Wool Cards. **1893** M. A. OWEN *Voodoo Tales* 11 Not one of them ever went to bed at night with-out hanging up a . . . pair of wool-cards at the bed's head.

b. Attrib. and comb. with *factory, maker, manufacturer.*

1789 *Boston Directory* 197 Richards, Giles & Co., wool and cotton card manufacturers. **1811** *Niles' Reg.* I. 101/2 The trade of dressing skins should be diffused . . . in the morocco style, and for book binders, glovers, wool card-makers and others. *a*1817 DWIGHT *Travels* IV. 486, 4 Wool Card factories . . . [are worth] $78,998.

Wool-carding. *attrib.* passing into *adj.* Designating mills or similar establishments employed in the carding of wool. — **1827** DRAKE & MANSFIELD *Cincinnati* 65 Two Woolcarding and Fulling Mills. **1835** J. MARTIN *Descr. Virginia* 134 The county contains . . . 5 wool-carding estab-lishments. **1847** L. COLLINS *Kentucky* 228 Carrollton . . . contains . . . one wool carding factory.

Wool-carding machine. A machine that cards wool. — **1806** *Bal-ance* V. 288/2, I was, lately, much pleased with seeing a wool-carding machine in operation. **1896** HARRIS *Sister Jane* 207 [He] invested in a wool-carding machine.

Wool-comber. One engaged in combing wool. {1702-} — **1617** *Mayflower Descendant* X. 193 Robert Cushman, woolcomber, from Can-terbury in England. **1725** *New-Eng. Courant* 19 April 2/2 John Head, . . . Wooll-Comber.

Wool-dyed, *a.* {1844} *fig.* **+** =DYED-IN-THE-WOOL *a.* — **1832** *Niles' Reg.* XLIII. 65/2 Messrs. Randolph and Ritchie . . . are chiefs of the 'wool-dyed democrats' of the present day. **1904** *Charlotte* (N.C.) *Ob-server* 19 June 2 Higginson is one of the old abolition gang, is wool-dyed and blind.

* Woolen, Woollen. Cloth made of wool. — **1705** *Boston News-Letter* 16 April 2/1 Foreign Ships may not bring in or Import any European . . . Woolens. **1778** *Jrnl. Cont. Congress* X. 23 A recommendation [shall] be sent to the clergy . . . to solicit charitable donations of woollens. **1822** *Ann. 17th Congress 1 Sess.* I. 282, $75,000 for the purchase of woollens for the army for the year 1823. **1843** *Whig Almanac 1844* 26/2 One is forci-bly struck with . . . the high prices paid for blankets, and other articles of woolen. **1898** WESTCOTT *D. Harum* i, I smelt woolen stronger'n ever.

+Woolenet. A thin woolen cloth. Also attrib. — **1820** *Columbian Centinel* 1/2 Just received . . . a few pieces of Woolinetts. **1825** MOTLEY *Correspondence* I. 3, I wish you would send me up some nankeen pantaloons, as my woolenet ones are so tight that they are uncomfortable.

Woolery. The wool-growing interest. — **1890** *Columbus Dispatch* 2 Sept., David Harpster . . . the head of the Ohio woolery is here.

+Wool grass. Any of various grasses or grasslike plants. — **1854** THOREAU *Walden* 331, I am particularly attracted by the arching and sheaf-like top of the wool-grass. **1857** GRAY *Botany* 501 *S[cirpus] Erio-phorum.* (Wool-Grass.) **1899** GOING *Flowers* 191 One of the stateliest of native sedges is the so-miscalled 'wool-grass.'

Woolgrowing, *a.* Producing wool. — **1847** HOWE *Hist. Coll. Ohio* 105 [Columbiana Co.] is the greatest wool-growing county in Ohio. **1872** *Newton Kansan* 5 Sept. 4/1 The wool-growing states . . . are showing a considerable increase in the number of sheep. **1900** *Congress. Rec.* 31 Jan. 1369/2 Our woolgrowing and manufacturing interests are also aroused.

Wool hat. 1. A hat made of wool felt. {1856} **+2.** One who wears a wool hat; a yokel or rustic. *colloq.* — (1) *c*1792 COXE *Views U.S.* 314 Wool hats, of Winchester make, are in much repute. **1839** BRIGGS *H. Franco* I. 158 On his head he wore a low crowned drab wool hat. **1867** RICHARDSON *Beyond Miss.* 24 A backwoods Missouri boy in white wool hat . . . throws the dice. **1898** YOUNG *Jessamine Co., Ky.* 163 They made wool hats. (2) **1880** *Harper's Mag.* Dec. 159/1 An old 'wool-hat' came along with a cart drawn by a single ox.

+Woolhead. 1. A Negro. *slang.* 2. An addle-pate. *slang.* 3. *local.* The bufflehead duck. — (1) **1828** COOPER *Red Rover* I. 218 Yonder is a slaver, off the fort, if you like a cargo of wool-heads for your money. (2) **1887** DALY *Railroad of Love* 64 Oh, you poor, dear wool-head! (3) **1888** TRUMBULL *Names of Birds* 83.

* Woollen. (See WOOLEN.)

Woolly, *n.* {1865-} **+1.** A windstorm: (see quotation). **+2.** *W.* A sheep. — (1) **1897** *Outing* XXX. 263/1 'We're going to have a "woolly,"' sure. . . . ' These winds, sudden and strong, beat the water into wool-white foam; hence their name. (2) **1914** 'BOWER' *Flying U Ranch* 101 Who owns these woollies?

* Woolly, *a.*

+1. Of the West or a westerner: Rude, untutored.

See also *wild and woolly West* and *wild and woolly* (under WILD *a.* 4 and 4 b).

1891 RYAN *Told in Hills* 191 Let us 'move our freight,' 'hit the breeze,' or any other term of the woolly West that means action. **1904** *N.Y. Ev. Post* 22 June 7 A young woman who ropes steers with as much ease and expedition as the 'wooliest' cowboy. **1910** MCCUTCHEON *Rose in Ring* 334 If it wasn't for you, Davy, I'd cut it in a minute and dig for the wooly West.

* 2. In the specific names of plants and trees. **a.** As sim-ple modifier.

1813 MUHLENBERG *Cat. Plants* 24 *Bumelia lanuginosa*, Woolly Iron-wood. *Ib.* 96 *Diospyros Caroliniana*, Woolly persimon. **1817-8** EATON *Botany* (1822) 465 *Solidago nemoralis*, woolly golden-rod. . . . Of a grey aspect. **1840** Dewey *Mass. Flowering Plants* 81 *Lechea thymifolia*, Woolly Pin Weed, . . . [is] found in the eastern part of our State. *Ib.* 242 *Holcus lanatus*, Woolly Soft Grass, . . . [is] little desired by animals. **1843** Torrey *Flora N.Y.* II. 503 *Osmunda cinnamomea*, Woolly Flowering-fern, . . . occurs near New-York, and has also been found near Cambridge, in Washington county. **1897** Sudworth *Arborescent Flora* 115 *Hicoria glabra villosa*. . . . Woolly Pignut (Hickory). **1915** Armstrong & Thornber *Western Wild Flowers* 454 Romero, Woolly Blue-curls, . . . grows on dry plains and low hills in the Northwest.

b. In combination with adjectives in *-ed.* {1822–}
1846 Browne *Trees Amer.* 52 *Gordonia lasianthus*, The Woolly-flowered Gordonia. **1885** Havard *Flora W. & S. Texas* 528 Woolly-jointed Grama (*Bouteloua eriopoda*); . . . forming dense and excellent pastures. **1892** Apgar *Trees Northern U.S.* 118 *Bumelia lanuginosa*, (Woolly-Leaved Buckthorn), . . . [grows in] the woods of southern Illinois and southward. **1894** Coulter *Bot. W. Texas* III. 532 *Bouteloua eriopoda*. (Woolly-stemmed grama.) . . . Dry gravelly plains, Western Texas to Arizona.

3. In the specific names of insects or larvae. {1805–}
1868 *Mich. Agric. Rep.* VII. 170 The wooly lice . . . suck much of the vitality from the beautiful beeches of our forests. **1909** Webster 2349/1 *Woolly worm*. . . . The larva of any sawfly that covers itself with a white woolly secretion, as the larva of *Selandria caryæ*, which feeds upon the hickory and butternut.

Woollyhead. {1767–} *slang.* +**1.** A Negro. +**2.** *Polit.* A person opposed to slavery; an abolitionist. — (1) **1827** Cooper *Prairie* xv, Some people think woolly-heads are miserable, working on hot plantations under a broiling sun. **1856** Stowe *Dred* II. 23, I'm all eaten up with woolly-heads, like locusts. (2) **1853** *Knickerb.* XLII. 653 'Woolly-Heads' were 'about.' **1864** Sala in *Daily Telegraph* 20 Sept., I get it quite as hot from the Woollyheads as from the Copperheads. **1888** M. Lane in *America* 8 Nov. 16 *Woolly-Heads*, the name given to the opposing party in 1850 by the Silver-Grays.

+**Woollypate.** =Woollyhead 1. — **1868** *N.Y. Herald* 1 Aug. 8/3 This representative of his Satanic majesty . . . created . . . a consternation among the little wooly pates.

+**Woolly sheep.** A variety of Rocky Mountain sheep. — **1837** Irving *Bonneville* I. 47 The mountain sheep . . . is often confounded with another animal, the 'woolly sheep' found more to the northward

+**Wool-picking.** (See quot. 1817.) In full *wool-picking frolic*. — **1817** Birkbeck *Notes Journey Amer.* (1818) 58 The wife was at a neighbour's on a 'wool-picking frolic,' which is a merry meeting of gossips at each other's houses, to pick the year's wool and prepare it for carding. **1872** *Harper's Mag.* June 33/1 Zed had a wool-pickin', . . . and all the gals and fellers was there. **1882** *Ib.* May 918/2 It wuz at a wool-pickin'.

Woolsey. =Linsey-woolsey. {1737} — **1881** Pierson *In the Brush* 50 [She] approached . . . with a dress of woolsey woven in her own loom. **1881** Buel *Border Outlaws* 61 The curb [of a bridle] was of homespun woolsey.

+**Woolyneag, Woolang.** [Abnaki *wulanikw* 'handsome squirrel.'] (See quot. 1910.) Also attrib. — **1722** in Temple & Sheldon *Hist. Northfield, Mass.* 160 To 3 fox skins and 1/2 a woolang skin, £0 13 6. **1832** [see Black cat 1]. **1875** Temple & Sheldon *Hist. Northfield, Mass.* 162 *Woolang* or woolaneaque, was the name for the fisher, which is the largest of the mink family. **1910** Hodge, etc. *Amer. Indians* II. 974/2 *Woolyneag*, a name in the northern parts of New England for the fisher or pekan. . . . The name . . . is evidently a misapplication.

+**Woozy,** *a.* **1.** Befuddled or intoxicated. *colloq.²* {1917} Also fig. **2.** Fuzzy. — (1) **1897** Lewis *Wolfville* 66 When Jim says all this it seems like I'm in a daze an' sorter woozy. **1908** 'O. Henry' *Roads of Destiny* 64 A man spends his on highballs, and a woman gets woozy on clothes. (2) **1903** *N.Y. Sun* 29 Nov. 27 He has a whole lot of woozy hair.

+**Wopse,** *v. New Eng. tr.* To wrap *up*. — **1875** Holland *Sevenoaks* 60 We'll wopse 'im up in some blankits. **1897** Robinson *Uncle Lisha* 45 There's a poor leetle muskrat . . . all wopsed up in a mess o' weeds.

Worcestershire (sauce). A sharp sauce, orig. made in Worcester, England, used esp. as a relish with meat. {Worcester sauce, 1863; 1889–} — **1846** *Knickerb.* XXVII. 18 He sent Jim to the pocket of the chaise for a bottle of Worcestershire Sauce. **1869** Lowell *My Study Windows* 25 Making missionaries go down better with the Fejee-Islanders by balancing the hymn-book . . . with a bottle of Worcestershire.

***Word.** *S.* +In special senses: (see quotations). — **1836** *Quarter Race Ky.* (1846) 19 Crump . . . had won the word—that is, he was to ask 'are you ready?' and if answered 'yes!' it was to be a race. **1881** *Harper's Mag.* Aug. 395/1 [Whoever was] overcome and prostrate, cried 'Enough!' Such conduct was understood merely as an admission, technically termed 'word,' that the defeated yielded for the present only.

Word-firing. In a pistol-shooting match, the firing of the pistols at the call of a word or words from the referee. — **1856** *Porter's Spirit of Times* 22 Nov. 192/3 By the ordinary rule of word-firing, for instance, between the words 'one' and 'three,' it would be impossible for such skilful shots as Mr. Travis and Mr. Snydam to miss.

***Work,** *n.*
***1.** *pl.* A place where work, esp. manufacturing, is carried on, including buildings, housing, machinery, etc.
See also Bottling works, Gas works, etc.
1649 *Perfect Descr. Virginia* 5 Skilfull Iron-men for the Works sent out of England. **1764** [see Distilling]. **1875** *Chicago Tribune* 11 Sept. 4/1 The North Chicago Rolling-Mill Company, a gigantic corporation with gigantic works on the North Branch of the Chicago River. **1911** Rolt-

Wheeler *Boy with Census* 90 His father before him was a barrel-sighter and his son has just entered the works.

2. *attrib.* ***a.** Designating persons who work or have to do with work.
*a***1649** Winthrop *Hist.* I. 166 Here arrived a small Norsey bark . . . with one Gardiner, an expert engineer or work base, and provisions. **1851** Cist *Cincinnati* 244 The manufacture of tobacco conduces to the health of the work hands. **1865** *Atlantic Mo.* March 322/1 They call us workwomen! **1894** *Missionary Herald* Oct. 426/2 The interest among our workboys continues.

***b.** Designating animals that perform work.
1763 Washington *Diaries* I. 184, 7 Work Steers. **1866** *Rep. Indian Affairs* 143 The Indians . . . must be provided with work-cattle. **1871** *Ib.* (1872) 320 The work-animals belonging to this agency . . . are entirely worn out. **1877** *Ib.* 22 Unprecedented storms and heavy roads had . . . broken down our light Indian work-stock. **1885** *Ib.* 41 The desire to obtain work-teams . . . has been great. **1894** 'Mark Twain' *P. Wilson* xviii, On'y de work-mules to ride [on].

***c.** Designating articles used in work.
1781–2 Jefferson *Notes Va.* (1788) 175 Let us never wish to see our citizens occupied at a work-bench, or twirling a distaff. **1823** Cooper *Pioneers* xii, There was a trifling air of better life in a tea-table and work-stand. **1842** Kirkland *Forest Life* II. 216 As she spoke she took from her 'work-pocket' a guard-chain. **1871** *Harper's Mag.* Aug. 381 Her work-apron was twisted half round her body. **1923** *Dialect Notes* V. 235 A work shirt made of crossbarred cotton cloth, which is called *hickory shirtin'*.

d. In special combinations.
*Work day, +the part of a day required for work {working day, 1875–}; *w. train*, a railway train used in maintaining the road bed.
1884 *Lisbon* (Dak.) *Star* 10 Oct., The work-train is again engaged in hauling gravel. **1898** *Kansas City Star* 18 Dec. 2/1 High wages and the added leisure of the short workday will be an inspiration.

***Work,** *v.*
1. *tr.* To operate on or in; to exploit in some way; to rob or swindle. {1851–, in related senses}
1882 McCabe *New York* 520 Even vessels lying at anchor in the harbor, are busily worked by [thieves]. **1887** *Courier-Journal* 20 Jan. 2/6 Lee Ayres was . . . locked up in the city prison for working the Berry National Bank. **1892** Howells *Quality of Mercy* 251 They were a pair of confidence-men trying to work him. **1903** Shuman *Pract. Journalism* 38 Brown was almost able to tell when he was being worked.

2. *To work off.* {1655–} **a.** To get rid of (slow-moving merchandise) by selling it.
1813 Weems *Letters* III. 92 The Maps . . . may be work[e]d off and in time to give you bank interest on your money. **1884** Nye *Baled Hay* 59 We can't work off wheezy parlor organs.

+**b.** To use up.
1837 Martineau *Society* II. 53 It was found the best economy to *work off* the stock of negroes once in seven years. **1894** *Vt. Agric. Rep.* XIV. 93 When the present supply [of horses] is worked off they will be high again.

+**c.** *To work one's self off as* (someone), to impersonate (someone) for some fraudulent purpose.
1897 'Thanet' *Missionary Sheriff* 7 The lightning-rods ain't in it with this last scheme—working hisself off as a Methodist parson.

***3.** *To work out.* **a.** To serve as a hired helper.
1842 *Letter* 31 Jan. (MS.), Chloe works out. **1858** Weed *Autobiog.* 18 I had 'worked out,' and earned leather . . . enough for a pair of shoes.

b. (See first quotation.)
1905 *Harper's Wkly.* 28 Jan. 136/1 The ship had returned to Liverpool, where the whole crew was 'worked out,' as the process of getting rid of men in foreign ports is termed. *Ib.*, The officers had quit after working out the crew.

***4.** *To work up*, +to move, as a result of one's own effort, into a position of greater importance or to a higher salary.
1850 Mitchell *Lorgnette* I. 77 They say she wants to 'work up.' **1902** Lorimer *Lett. Merchant* 109 He was . . . drawing ten thousand a year, which was more than he could have worked up to in the leather business in a century.

***Worker.**
***1.** A craftsman; one who works.
1719 *Manchester Rec.* 147 Ye Commetty Shall . . . agree with a arte-feshal workmen to oversee ye works. **1891** O'Beirne *Leaders Ind. Territory* 180/2 He is . . . a painstaking worker. **1920** *3d Nat. Country Life Conf Proc.* 51 The cigar-box workers have done the same thing.

2. A draft horse. {1617}
1788 Washington *Diaries* III. 403 The Horses were . . . 8 Workers. **1894** *Vt. Agric. Rep.* XIV. 99 There are three kinds of horses that we can breed—trotters, drivers, workers.

+**3.** One who works for a political party; a minor member of a political machine.
1873 'Mark Twain' & Warner *Gilded Age* 399 In Washington he was . . . a 'worker' in politics. **1886** [see Heeler]. **1905** *McClure's Mag.* XXIV. 338 'Workers' are paid 'to get out the vote.'

+**Workey.** (See Worky.)

+**Workeyism.** [f. WORKY.] A social or political theory emphasizing the rights of labor. — **1835** *New Eng. Mag.* VIII. 143 They who get up the cry of workeyism, as if, forsooth, every man in New England did not work.

* **Workhouse.**

***1.** A house in which work is performed; a workshop.
1647 *Essex Probate Rec.* I. 91 One dwelling house, one barne and worke house with foure Akers of land. **1714** *Boston News-Letter* 8 Feb. 2/2 A Convenient work-House, fit to make Candles and Sope . . . to be Let. **1882** *Rep. Indian Affairs* 4 Their work-houses are all underground.

2. A public institution in which paupers are lodged and put to work. {1652-}
1653 *Boston Rec.* X. 26 My thoughts . . . have beene about . . . the setting up of a Bridewell or Workehouse for Prisonrs Malefactors & some sort of poore people. **1712** *Ib.* VIII. 96 Not only Such persons as thro' Age or other Infirmities are rendered uncapable of Labour, but others who are Capable but not willing to worke may be entertained at the Almes House or worke House and properly imployed, provided . . . that they be kept in Seperate Apartmts. from those poor honest people who are Sent there Only as Objects of Charrity. **1755** *Bristol* (Va.) *Vestry Bk.* 160 They will Join with this parish towards Building a workhouse, to keep the poor of the three parishes in. **1883** *Harper's Mag.* June 138/1 As if the charity of the land had not provided workhouses, homes, and asylums by hundreds.

b. (See quotation.)
1871 DE VERE 568 In Boston . . . a *workhouse* has been established for weak girls, . . . [who] learn ostensibly how to cultivate flowers, but in reality to accustom them gradually to such hard work as will restore them to health.

+**3.** A house of correction for minor offenders: (see also first quot. 1772).
1653 [see sense 2 above]. **1740** *S.C. Gazette* 14 June, Brought to the Work-House in Charlestown, a Negro Fellow, . . . taken up on Savannah River. **1772** HABERSHAM *Letters* 178 The Work House . . . for confining and punishing fugitive and Criminal Slaves, is also in the same Condition with the Goal. **1772** A. G. WINSLOW *Diary* 36 [She] soon got into the workhouse for new misdemeanours. **1846** CORCORAN *Pickings* 10 Thirty days in the new workhouse may have more virtue. **1907** *Springfield W. Repub.* 18 July 1 Twenty-three leading business men of the city have been . . . sentenced to six months in the workhouse.

4. Attrib. with *fence, yard.*
1741 *Boston Rec.* 281 Another line Eastward bevelling with the Work house fence. **1784** *Independent Gazetteer* 17 July (Ernst), The American Aerostatic balloon will rise from the New Work-house yard, with a person in it.

* **Working.** *attrib.*

***1.** Designating places suited for performing work.
1648 *Conn. Rec.* I. 491 In the working shopp . . . [are] axes, handsaw, beetle rings [etc.]. **1870** STEPHENS *Married in Haste* 157 She withdrew into the working-chamber. **1900** *Congress. Rec.* 8 Jan. 688/1 That reference library . . . will become not a mere reference library, but a working library, with rooms which can be utilized as reading and writing rooms. **1901** MERWIN & WEBSTER *Calumet 'K'* 127 In the working story . . . is the machinery for unloading cars and for lifting the grain.

2. Designating articles of attire worn when a person is working. {1769-}
1771 FRANKLIN *Autobiog.* 254, I was in my working dress. **1865** *Atlantic Mo.* Jan. 94/1 [We] were promoted to . . . the patching of his working clothes. **1866** W. REID *After the War* 116 He must have working suits and Sunday suits. **1900** DIX *Deacon Bradbury* 91 He seized his straw working-hat.

3. In special combinations.
Working frolic, =BEE² 1; *w. harness,* harness for use by a horse pulling a heavy wagon; *w. plan,* a plan or sketch used as the basis for laying out an area or building a structure; *w. table,* a table used for work; *w. train,* a train used in the construction or repair of railroad tracks.
1852 REYNOLDS *Hist. Illinois* 167 The neighbors . . . organized themselves into a kind of working frolic. **1842** KIRKLAND *Forest Life* I. 18 The old lumber-wagon, with a pair of plough-horses, equipped in working-harness, to withstand the *corduroy* and swamp-holes, received me and my luggage. **1880** 'MARK TWAIN' *Tramp Abroad* 370 The ghastly desolation of the place was as tremendously complete as if Doré had furnished the working-plans for it. **1879** A. D. WHITNEY *Just How* 306 Have all the things ready . . . upon your working-table. **1872** HUNTINGTON *Road-Master's Asst.* 57 It is better to stop working or irregular trains, than to allow them to run over track before it is really prepared for them.

+**Working card.** A card permitting a man to work in a union shop. (Cf. *Travel(l)ing card,* under TRAVEL(L)ING *n.* 2, and UNION CARD.) Also attrib. — **1874** *Internat. Typogr. Union Proc.* 34 Subordinate Unions are recommended to fearlessly enforce the 'working-card' system. **1896** *Ib.* 35/2 It was agreed to issue him a working card.

‖**Workinger.** =next. — **1866** *Ore. State Jrnl.* 1 Dec. 2/3 How much contempt he always entertained for that class of beings whose very instinct seemed to condemn it to be a 'workinger.'

Workingman. A man belonging to the laboring class. {1816-}

1638 *Essex Inst. Coll.* IX. 67 Euery working man [to mend the highway] vpon the 7th day of this moneth. **1729** FRANKLIN *Writings* II. 138 Working-Men and their Families are thereby induced to be more . . . extravagant. **1877** [see COMMUNISM 1]. **1906** PRINGLE *Rice Planter* 336 When a working-man loses a good wife he is indeed bereft.

b. In possessive combinations in plural, used in names of organizations of workingmen.
1844 *Lexington Observer* 2 Oct. 3/1 The Working Men's Clay Club of this city will hold an adjourned meeting. *a*1870 CHIPMAN *Notes on Bartlett* 517 In 1832, the 'Working Men's Party' was in active operation in the U.S. **1888** *Amer. Almanac* 249, 726 [votes were cast in Ore.] for the Workingmen's Candidate [for president].

* **Workman.** A man working on a job as a mechanic, artisan, etc.; one skilled in some branch of the manual arts. — **1639** *Conn. Rec.* I. 42 The workemen are much taken vp and imployed in making a bridge and meeting house. **1771** FRANKLIN *Autobiog.* 238 [I was] able to do little jobs myself in my house when a workman could not readily be got. **1850** *Harper's Mag.* Nov. 722/1 Workmen were . . . laying out the grounds. **1903** BELL *Dowager Countess* 42 Workmen were in half of the rooms.

* **Workshop.** A room or building in which work, usually of a manual or industrial nature, is carried on. Also comb. — **1725** *Boston Selectmen* 135 In answer to the Petition of Wm. Bond of Boston House wright for Liberty to Build of Timber a Shede for a work-shop. **1760** WASHINGTON *Diaries* I. 148 Sowd 17½ Drills of Trefoil Seed . . . , numbering from the side next the Stable (or Work Shop). **1854** [see ENGINE HOUSE 2]. **1911** PERSONS, etc. *Mass. Labor Laws* 242 When there is a vacancy in the force of building inspectors, one of the factory and workshop inspectors is transferred.

+**Worky.** Also **workey.** A worker, esp. a factory worker or operative; in pl., an organization of workpeople. Now rare. Also transf. (Cf. WORKEYISM.)
1830 *Niles' Reg.* XXXVIII. 231/2 The regencies and the juntas, the squads of contemptible politicians, . . . &c. . . . call the 'workies' many hard names. **1833** T. HAMILTON *Men & Manners* I. 299 The operative class have already formed themselves into a society, under the name of 'The Workies.' **1839** *Knickerb.* XIV. 138 [The woodpecker] is a practical body—a regular 'worky.' **1849** WILLIS *Rural Letters* 194 You would either remain stationary, a mere 'workey,' or your genius would discover . . . where, in the well-searched bowels of literature, lay an unworked vein of ore. *Ib.* 236 The clerks and workies have passed down an hour before the nine o'clock tide. **1894** *Sunday Reform Leaflet* (Columbus, O.) Sept. 5 Take away this rest-day, and you . . . turn us into a nation of mere 'workies.'

* **World.**

1. *attrib.* passing into *adj.* **a.** Of a scope embracing the entire world; universal. {1839-}
See also WORLD SERIES.
1870 MEDBERY *Men Wall St.* 114 Every step toward the development of New York as a world-mart must be an advancement of themselves. **1900** *Congress. Rec.* 29 Jan. 1259/1 We have become a 'world power.' **1909** *World To-Day* Sept. 981/2 All that is required to make Chicago verily the world-market is the same push and energy directed to foreign trade.

b. *World-outside,* the world not included in a given religious community.
1920 HOWELLS *Vacation of Kelwyns* 139 There was an unusual attendance from the world-outside, especially of summer-folks from Ellison.

2. Used in possessive sense similar to that of 1 a.
See also WORLD'S FAIR.
1867 *Ore. State Jrnl.* 9 Feb. 1/2 The French Emperor . . . [made enormous preparations] for the approaching 'World's Congress.' **1877** E. C. BRUCE *The Century: Its Fruits* 60 [Philadelphia had become] comparable to Vienna as a site for a World's Exposition. **1885** *Wkly. New Mexican Rev.* 29 Jan. 3/3 The World's Exhibition had 20,000 visitors on Saturday. **1893** *Outing* XXII. 154/2 He has . . . held the world's record in the pole vault for distance.

+**World-beater.** A champion; a prize-winner. *colloq.*² — **1893** *Outing* XXII. 103/1 The master of Palo Alto believed that the filly would prove to be a world-beater. **1912** MATHEWSON *Pitching* 25 'Rube' Marquard came to the Giants . . . heralded as a world-beater.

+**World series, World's (championship) series.** *Baseball.* A succession of post-season games played between the champion teams of two professional leagues. Also attrib. — **1888** *Spalding's Base Ball Guide* 47 In 1887 the world's championship series had become an established supplementary series of contests. **1913** *Collier's* 4 Oct. 5/1 In this next impending world-series carnival between Giants and Athletics we have had the hunch [etc.]. **1918** *Everybody's Mag.* Aug. 105 World's Series Opened.

+**World's fair.** An international exposition, containing exhibits from various countries.
The first two examples refer to the International Exposition held in London in 1851.
1850 *New Eng. Farmer* II. 413 The State Board of Agriculture are making up a collection of samples of Indian corn for the World's Fair. **1851** GREELEY *Glances at Europe* 29 'The World's Fair,' as we Americans have been accustomed to call it, has now been open five days. **1876** INGRAM *Centennial Exp.* 18 The story of the grandest World's Fair that has ever been held. **1884** *N. Mex. Terr. Rep.* 17 Present the opportunities for future development, with special reference to . . . the World's Fair at New Or-

leans next winter. **1890** *Stock Grower & Farmer* 25 Jan. 6/3 On last Saturday the senate committee on the world's fair of 1892 concluded its hearing of arguments in behalf of New York and Chicago. **1915** *Outlook* 14 April 895 The Spectator at the World's Fair. . . . He returns to San Francisco [after] nine years.

b. Attrib. with *bond, commission, main building.*

1893 *Chicago Tribune* 21 April 4/3 The bonded debt of Chicago, including the World's Fair bonds, is but eighteen and a half millions. **1899** *Dept. Agric. Yrbk.* 5 In 1892 the first soil map . . . was issued by the World's Fair Commission of Maryland. **1909** 'O. HENRY' *Options* 279, I rang the door-bell of that World's Fair main building.

World's people. People not members of the specific religious group in the mind of the speaker or writer. A term used by Friends and some others. — **1824** 'SINGLETON' *Lett. South & West* 19 If a quaker love a lady out of the society, he must ask liberty, and pardon for the sin of loving one of the world's people. **1824** BLANE *Excursion U.S.* 452 These children . . . are constantly impressed with the charitable belief that the 'world's people' (thus they designate all who are not Shakers) will inevitably go to everlasting punishment. **1848** *Wilmington* (N.C.) *Commercial* 8 Aug. 1/6 (Th. S.), My conscience [said the Rogerite, from Conn.] will not permit me to marry her in the forms of the world's people. **1862** WINTHROP *J. Brent* 116 We of the Latter Day Church think much of such associations; more so, I suppose, than you world's people.

+World's series. (See WORLD SERIES.)

* Worm.

I. *1. An earthworm or angleworm (qq.v.), or any one of various creatures, frequently of a destructive nature, regarded as similar to it.

1705 BEVERLEY *Virginia* II. 6 The Damage occasion'd by these Worms, may be . . . avoided. **1759** ELIOT *Field-Husb.* vi. 144 These Worms [*sc.* silkworms] will feed freely on Lettice, and the Leaves of other Plants. **1832** WILLIAMSON *Maine* I. 168 We have among us, in summer, a variety of native worms, . . . the Earthworm, the Brandling, the Angleworm. **1880** CABLE *Grandissimes* 240 One night the worm came upon the indigo.

+2. The outline of a worm fence, as indicated by the placing of the bottom rails; the bottom rail of a worm fence, or the length of rail between the vertical supports, excluding the laps.

1760 WASHINGTON *Diaries* I. 128 Laid in part the Worm of a fence round my Peach Orchard. **1800** TATHAM *Tobacco* 10 The worm (as it is called) being thus laid, the same process is repeated until the fence rises to the height of nine or ten rails. **1838** ELLSWORTH *Valley of Wabash* 50 The eighth rail . . . rests on crotches eight feet long, crossing at each corner of the 'worm.' **1855** *Mich. Agric. Soc. Trans.* VI. 177 The fence is laid with seven feet worm, and one foot lap at each end. **1891** RYAN *Pagan* 59 [He] would stop his work of laying the 'worm' for the new fence.

II. *attrib.* and *comb.* **3.** Designating diseases or conditions, or remedies prepared for diseases or conditions, attributed to the presence of worms in the body. {1702-}

1773 *Penna. Gazette* Suppl. 23 June 2/3 His never failing worm cake, which destroys that vermin so pernicious to children. *Ib.* 30 June 3/3 A new invented Worm-Syrup. **1775** ROMANS *Nat. Hist. Florida* 254 The Worm fever . . . is common through all America. **1848** DUNGLISON *Med. Lexicon* 418/1 *Helminthiasis.* . . . It is, also, called . . . Worm disease. **1850** PEREIRA *Elem. Mat. Med.* (ed. 3) II. 1478 A preparation kept in the shops of the United States . . . under the name of *worm tea,* consists of spigelia root, senna, manna, and savine, mixed together. **1853** *La Crosse Democrat* 17 May 3/4 Like a child in a worm fit. **1887** *Courier-Journal* 5 Feb. 8/1 Wintersmith's Worm Candy the best.

+4. With reference to worm fences.

See also WORM FASHION.

1846 *Xenia Torch-Light* 23 July 4/1, I found a single log cabin, surrounded by a low fence of rails, wormlaid. **1862** *Ill. Agric. Soc. Trans.* V. 209 Fourteen miles of fence . . . laid in the worm form with stakes and riders. **1880** *Fergus' Hist. Ser.* No. 14, 107 The fences were made of rails, . . . laid up, in what was called the 'worm' or 'Virginia' style.

5. In specific names. {1666-}

See also WORM-EATER, WORM-EATING WARBLER, etc.

1884 GOODE, etc. *Fisheries* I. 201 Fish which live near the shore . . . [include] 'Worm Cod,' 'Clam Cod,' 'Black Snappers.' [**1860** *Smithsonian Rep. 1859* 206 The Ivory Worm-shell (*V[ermetus] eburneus*) . . . is perhaps the most beautiful species.] **1819** *Western Rev.* I. 92 *Chenopodium anthelmenthicum,* Worm weed.

6. In special combinations.

Worm gum, an albuminous substance found in raw silk; *W. People,* a division of the Piegan, a tribe related to the Blackfoot tribe of Indians; *w. punch,* (see quotation).

1869 *Rep. Comm. Agric. 1868* 289 It loses eighteen to twenty-five per cent. of the weight in dyeing by the boiling off of the worm gum. **1892** GRINNELL *Blackfoot Lodge Tales* 225 Gentes of the Pi-kun-i [include] . . . Worm People. **1891** *Cent.* 6981/1 *Worm-punch,* . . . a small, rather slender punch, used by coopers for clearing out worm-holes in staves or heads of casks, for the purpose of stopping the holes with wooden plugs to prevent leaking.

+Worm-eater. A bird that feeds on worms, as the worm-eating warbler. Also with specifying term. — **1760** G. EDWARDS *Gleanings Nat.*

Hist. II. 200 The Worm-eater's bill is pretty sharp-pointed. **1831** SWAINSON & RICHARDSON *Fauna Bor.-Amer.* II. 221 *Sylvicola (Vermivora) peregrina.* . . . Tennessee Worm-eater. **1868** *Amer. Naturalist* II. 174 The Blue-winged Yellow Warbler . . . is one of that subdivision of the warbler family called the 'Worm-eaters.' **1917** *Birds of Amer.* III. 116/1 The Worm-eater is a quiet bird that spends most of his time on the ground or within a few feet of it.

+Worm-eating warbler. A bird of the genus *Helmitherus,* esp. the common worm-eater (*H. vermivorus*) of the eastern states. — **1811** WILSON *Ornithology* III. 74 [The] Worm-Eating Warbler . . . is remarkably fond of spiders. **1872** COUES *Key to Birds* 93 Worm-eating Warbler. . . . Eastern United States; . . . rather common. **1917** *Birds of Amer.* III. 116/1 The Worm-eating Warbler is distinctly a ground Warbler.

Wormer. {1602-} +A screw attached to the end of a rod, used for withdrawing the charge from a gun. — **1702** *Essex Inst. Coll.* XLII. 162 A gunne mallet, two formers, . . . a wormer, & scourer for small arms. **1891** *Cent.* 6980/3.

Worm fashion. +The manner of construction characteristic of a worm fence. Also as *adv.* — **1819** FAUX *Memorable Days* 320 All the wood to be cut down and burnt, save what is wanted for fencing the land with rails in the worm fashion. **1840** HOFFMAN *Greyslaer* I. 83 Two fields, separated by a high rail-fence, laid 'worm-fashion.' **1880** 'MARK TWAIN' *Tramp Abroad* 245 Lucerne is a charming place . . . with here and there a bit of ancient embattled wall bending itself over the ridges, worm-fashion.

+Worm fence. Also **worm rail fence.**

1. A fence built with rails laid so that the ends cross each other at angles; a zigzag rail fence.

See also VIRGINIA WORM FENCE and SNAKE FENCE.

1652 *East-Hampton Rec.* I. 22 The worme fence on the litel plaine. **1741** *Ga. Hist. Soc. Coll.* II. 107 They made an attempt to enclose the whole with a worm fence of six feet high. **1818** FORDHAM *Narr. Travels* 163 The worm rail fences running in straight-lines . . . have little of beauty. **1836** CROCKETT *Exploits* 31 My poetry looked as zigzag as a worm fence. **1872** *Amer. Naturalist* VI. 199 One of the largest axes we have seen . . . was found supporting a section of worm-fence. **1913** [see REDWOOD 4 c].

b. Hence *worm-fencing* n., *worm-fenced* a.

1789 *Amer. Philos. Soc.* III. p. ix, Worm-fencing and similar expedients of infant cultivation, should never be seen. **1904** T. E. WATSON *Bethany* 8 [It] was striving, unsuccessfully, to look at ease among . . . negro cabins, and worm-fenced cotton fields.

2. Attrib. with *bucking, enclosure, fashion.*

1836 SIMMS *Mellichampe* xx, A little cornfield, with its worm-fence enclosure, lay on one hand, and, on the other, the woods were open and free from undergrowth. **1867** HARRIS *Sut Lovingood* 41 The road wer sprinkled worm fence fashun. **1897** LEWIS *Wolfville* 193 That Remorse pony . . . gives way to sech a fit of real old worm-fence buckin' as lands Slim Jim on his sombrero.

* Worm grass. Any one of various species of the genus *Spigelia* {1756-, in W. Indies}, +esp. the pinkroot (*S. marilandica*), used as a vermifuge. — **1786** ABERCROMBIE *Gardeners Daily Assist.* I. 66 *Spigelia marilandica,* or Mariland worm grass, or Carolina India pink. **1831** AUDUBON *Ornith. Biog.* I. 361 The Indian Pink-root or Worm-grass . . . grows in rich soil by the margins of woods. **1857** GRAY *Botany* 174. **1898** CREEVEY *Flowers of Field* 377 Pinkroot. Worm-grass. . . . New Jersey southward and westward.

+Worm rail fence. (See WORM FENCE.)

* Wormseed. The fruit or seed, or the plant as a whole, of any one of various species of plants, +esp. *Chenopodium ambrosioides* (also called *American wormseed*), used, or formerly used, as a vermifuge. {1831} Also attrib.

1653 *Mass. H. S. Coll.* 4 Ser. VII. 466 Wee gave him wormeseed. **1709** [see RUE]. **1756** KALM *Resa* II. 291 Chenopodium anthelminticum eller *Wormseed.* **1791** MUHLENBERG *Index Florae* 174 *Erysimum,* Worm-seed. **1830** LINDLEY *Nat. Syst. Bot.* 167 The essential oil of *Chenopodium anthelminticum,* known in North America under the name of Worm-seed Oil, is powerfully anthelmintic. **1857** Wormseed mustard [see MUSTARD 1 b]. **1891** *Cent.* 6981/1 *Wormseed,* . . . the fruit of the American herb *Chenopodium ambrosioides,* especially var. *anthelminticum,* which is often reckoned a distinct species. . . . Distinguished as *American wormseed.* **1901** MOHR *Plant Life Ala.* 488 *Chenopodium anthelminticum.* . . . Wormseed. . . . The seeds, 'American wormseed,' Chenopodium United States Pharmacopœia, are used medicinally.

Worm snake. 1. Any one of various harmless snakes {1885, in Australia}, +as the ground snake, *Carphophis amoena.* +**2.** A snakeworm (q.v. under SNAKE *n.* 11). — (1) **1885** J. S. KINGSLEY, etc. *Stand. Nat. Hist.* III. 362 The snake *Carphophis* is very generally distributed; in the United States, the species *amœna,* . . . as the thunder, ground, or worm-snake, is most familiar. (2) **1891** *Cent.* 6981/1.

* Wormwood.

*1. Any one of various plants of the genus *Artemisia,* or a preparation made from one of these plants; +sagebrush.

1672 JOSSELYN *New Eng. Rarities* 46 We made our Beer of Molosses, Water, Bran, chips of Sassafras Root, and a little Wormwood. **1709** LAWSON *Carolina* 44/1 Our pot herbs and others of use [are] . . . Tansey, Wormwood [etc.]. **1774** *Holyoke Diaries* 82 Nurse ointed it with Parsley, wormwood & Camomel. **1818** [see BITTERS 1]. **1837** IRVING *Bonneville*

I. 57 The valleys were . . . scantily clothed with a stunted species of wormwood. 1870 [see RAGWEED].

b. With specifying terms.

Roman wormwood, see ROMAN *a.* 1, quot. 1784.

1847 WOOD *Botany* 349 A[rtemisia] *Canadensis.* Sea Wormwood. . . . Shores of the great lakes. **1857** GRAY *Botany* 227 A[rtemisia] *Canadensis.* (Canada Wormwood.) . . . Shore of all the Great Lakes, and northward. *Ib., A. caudata.* (Slender Wormwood.) . . . Sandy soil, coast of New Hampshire to New Jersey; and in Illinois. **1909** *Cent. Suppl.* 1163/3 A[rtemisia] *filifolia* . . . , of the dry plains of western North America, . . . [is] called *silvery wormwood.*

2. attrib. a. With bush, tea.

1851 *Harper's Mag.* Sept. 482/2, I came opposite to a small clump of wormwood bushes. **1868** G. G. CHANNING *Recoll. Newport* 125 Wormwood tea, [was used] as an emetic.

+b. Wormwood sage, (see quotation).

1909 *Cent.* 1163/3 *Wormwood sage,* either of two narrow-leaved species of *Artemisia, A. filifolia* and *A. frigida,* of the dry plains of western North America, having a sage-like aspect.

*Wormy, a. +Of fish: Infested with lice. — **1884** *Springfield* (Mass.) *Wheelmen's Gaz.* Nov. 110/3 The stream was fairly alive with trout but the large ones were wormy.

Worn-out, a. Of land or a piece of land: Exhausted, wasted. {1852} — **1748** ELIOT *Field-Husb.* i. 12 Another Way to help Worn-out Land is to sow it with Clover Seed. **1796** DABNEY *Address to Farmers* 23 A young and flourishing orchard, has rendered many an old and worn-out farm saleable. **1844** in Commons, etc. *Doc. Hist.* I. 170 It will be rich inheritance for your children, instead of an old worn out place. **1880** *Vt. Agric. Rep.* VI. 28 Let us . . . determine . . . the nature of the change which has come over the soil of these so called worn-out pastures.

Worriment. A state of worry, or an act or instance of worrying or causing worry; something causing or representing worry. *colloq.* {1887–, *dial.*} 'Chiefly *U.S.*' (O.E.D.). — **1832** S. SMITH *Life Downing* 161, I've had a good many head-flaws and worriments in my life time. **1866** W. BAKER *Inside* 9 It was a special weapon in her arsenal in the worriment of her husband. **1886** MACCHETTA *Copper Queen* I. 165 Ready with vinegar, hartshorn, and the usual worriments towards resuscitation. **1904** *N.Y. Times* 20 May 1 The cause of the suicide was worriment resulting from business troubles.

*Worry, v.

+1. tr. (See quot. 1828.)

1828 WEBSTER, *Worry,* . . . to fatigue; to harass with labor; a popular sense of the word. **1875** HOLLAND *Sevenoaks* 66 For three steady hours he went on, the horse no more worried than if he had been standing in the stable.

2. *To worry along,* to make progress in spite of obstacles or difficulties; +also, *colloq.,* to manage somehow to keep going.

1758 *Essex Inst. Coll.* XII. 141 Worried along 13 miles to day. **1871** 'MARK TWAIN' *Sk., New & Old* 296 You seem to have pretty much all the tunes there are, and you worry along first rate. **1885** HOWELLS *Silas Lapham* 214, I think I can manage to worry along.

3. *To worry down,* to swallow with difficulty or effort. Also *fig.*

1870 HALE *Ten Times One* 61 She 'worried down' the tea, and ate a slice of toast. **1883** 'MARK TWAIN' *Life on Miss.* iii, I can swaller a thirteenth of the yarn, if you can worry down the rest.

4. *To worry through* {1876–}, to arrive at an objective by labor and effort, as against obstacles {1901}; also, *colloq.,* to keep going during a period of difficulty. {1899}

1764 *N.H. Hist. Soc. Coll.* IX. 171 The snow so drifted . . . 'twas with difficulty we worried through. **1869** HARTE *Luck of Roaring Camp* 52 Jim and I managed to worry through.

Worsely, adv. {*dial.*} (See quotation.) — c**1870** CHIPMAN *Notes on Bartlett* 517 *Worsely,* humorously used for 'in a worse way,' &c. Colloquial.

*Worst, a.

1. *(The) worst kind,* +the severest, most extreme, or most drastic kind; as adverbial phrase, to an extreme, as much as possible. Also *worse kind. colloq.*

1839 MARRYAT *Diary in Amer.* 1 Ser. II. 227 He loves Sal, the worst kind. **1859** BARTLETT 517 *Worst Kind.* Used in such phrases as, 'I gave him the worst kind of a licking.' **1892** *Harper's Mag.* Feb. 437/2, I want something to read the worst kind. **1893** POST *Harvard Stories* 140 Then he begged worse kind just to let him look out of a window where he could see you. **1904** *N.Y. Tribune* 26 June, 'So you want to go to Cuba, do you?' asked Colonel Roosevelt. 'I do, worst kind.'

2. *(In) the worst way,* +as much as possible. *colloq.*

c**1870** CHIPMAN *Notes on Bartlett* 517 'It was wanted in the worst way.' Said July 18, 1860, with reference to a shower which, after a drought, fell the night before. **1902** CLAPIN 422 *Worst way.* In parts of Pennsylvania, used for very strongly, as in the following: 'He wants to see you the worst way.' **1908** 'YESLAH' *Tenderfoot S. Calif.* 32 Jones . . . needed that diamond scarf-pin the worst way.

*Worsted.

*1. A yarn, or a fabric made from a yarn, made from long-staple wool combed with the fibers parallel; also, a soft woolen yarn for knitting or embroidery, or a mixed yarn similar to this.

1691 SEWALL *Letter-Book* I. 117 Send Fring for the Fustian Bed the Worsted is for. **1747** HEMPSTEAD *Diary* 493, I went to Capt David Crockers and carried home worsted to make me a pr of Stockings. **1831** [see SMOKING 2]. **1875** STOWE *We & Neighbors* 157 There sat Angelique, . . . her lap full of worsteds. **1903** *Boston Transcript* 2 Sept. 12/2 The use of combed and carded cotton yarns . . . as a substitute for worsted . . . has grown apace.

*2. attrib. passing into *adj.* **a.** Designating garments or other goods made of worsted.

1666 SANFORD *Letter Book* 14, I would desiere . . . Sume wosted and Iresh Stockings. **1676** *N.H. Probate Rec.* I. 173 To Abigail Gilman [she bequeathes] . . . one feather pillow and wistead rug. **1691** SEWALL *Letter-Book* I. 116 Send 4 p[iece]s of worsted Damask stuffs. **1744** *Md. Hist. Mag.* XXI. 246, 1 Dozn. double Worsted Caps. **1863** TAYLOR *H. Thurston* 57 A worsted apron was tied over her drab gown. **1870** 'F. FERN' *Ginger-Snaps* 54 Worsted cats and dogs come next in the shape of mats, chair-covers, etc. **1891** *Cent.* 7010/2 *Worsted yarn,* yarn made from long-haired or combed wool, and consisting either entirely of wool, or of wool combined with mohair and alpaca, or of wool and cotton, or of wool and silk. **1891** WILKINS *New Eng. Nun* 217 Upon the walls hung various little worsted and cardboard decorations. **1908** [see FASCINATOR].

b. With reference to the manufacture or the use of worsted.

1714 HEMPSTEAD *Diary* 41, I bought a pr Woosted Combs for 30s. **1779** E. PARKMAN *Diary* 143 Mrs. P. has rid unto ye South of ye Town to procure Worsted Combings. **1843** *Knickerb.* XXI. 409 The friend looks up from her worsted work in horror. **1876** KNIGHT 2819 *Worsted machinery,* machinery for the manufacture of combing or long-stapled wool.

Worsted-comber. One whose business is to comb worsted. {1702} — **1684** *Boston Rec.* X. 75 John Woodmansey became surety to the town for Charles Scott by trade a worsted comer. **1708** SEWALL *Diary* II. 241 Bouroughs, a worsted-comber, was at Mr. Colman's Meeting. **1796** *Boston Directory* 231 Burge, Joseph, worsted comber, Newbury street.

*Wort. An infusion of malt or some other grain, as in beer-making. — **1712** *Essex Inst. Coll.* X. 1. 94 He made her [the cow] some flip of the wort. **1779** E. PARKMAN *Diary* 108 Went to see Sam Dalrymple, whose Leggs were lately scalled with hot wort. **1875** KNIGHT 2820/2 When fermented, the wort becomes beer; or wash for distillation.

*Worth, a. +a. *For all it is worth,* or variants: With an effort to secure the utmost return. +b. *For all (one) is worth,* with every effort of which (one) is capable. {1897}

For use in comparisons, as *not . . . worth a cent,* see the nouns.

1874 'MARK TWAIN' *Sk:, New & Old* 310 We shall fly our comet for all it is worth. **1880** TOURGEE *Bricks* 451 A man who comes here must pitch in and count for all he's worth. **1883** *N.Y. Mercury* (Ware *Passing English*), Scalchi, to use a side-walk phrase, played Siebel for all the character was worth. **1889** GUNTER *That Frenchman* 298 [The steamer] is driving, for everything she is worth, down the waters of the Finnish Gulf. **1897** 'THANET' *Missionary Sheriff* 19 Paisley played his cough and his hollow cheeks for all they were worth.

Worth-while. The quality of being worth while. *rare.* {1899} — **1867** A. D. WHITNEY *L. Goldthwaite* ii, How did the world seem to such a person, and where was the *worth-while* of it?

*Would, v. Used in place of *had,* in *would better, would best.* — **1898** [see BOODLER 2]. **1898** *Dial* XXV. 294/1 In this part of the English-speaking world [the Middle West] . . . a form of expression that is becoming wide-spread, at least in colloquial, newspaper, and schoolmaster English, . . . [is] the use of 'would better' for the idiomatic 'had better.' **1903** W. G. BROWN *Foe of Compromise* 174 We would best begin.

*Woundwort. A plant of the genus *Stachys,* regarded as useful in the healing of wounds. — **1791** MUHLENBERG *Index Florae* 172 *Stachys,* Wound-wort. **1814** [see HEDGE NETTLE]. **1892** COULTER *Bot. W. Texas* II. 343.

*Wrangler. +=HORSE WRANGLER. (See also *freight-wrangler* under FREIGHT *n.* 8.) — **1896** G. W. DICE *Counterfeiting Exposed* 23 [The] 'wrangler' had been killed by a bullet from a needle gun. **1905** A. ADAMS *Outlet* 93 The remuda and team were taken in charge by the wrangler and cook.

*Wrapper.

1. A loose-fitting outer garment, esp. a robe or gown for wear indoors. {1734–}

'In later use chiefly *U.S.*' (O.E.D.).

1764 HABERSHAM *Letters* 17 What are called Short Gowns or wrappers with petticoats are best for women. **1860** HOLLAND *Miss Gilbert* 108 Arthur took his accustomed seat at the head of the table, with Leonard at his right hand, robed in a very comely morning wrapper. **1893** SANBORN *S. Calif.* 5, I believe in taking along a loose wrapper to wear in the cars. **1914** JAMES *Ivory Tower* 1 The large loose ponderous girl . . . lived, as they said about her, in wrappers and tea-gowns.

+2. In various special applications.
a. A form of legging or boot. **b.** A cigar. **c.** (See quotation.) **d.** (See quot. 1901.) In full *wrapper chain.*

(a) **1808** PIKE *Sources Miss.* III. App. 36 The lower class of men are generally dressed in . . . a kind of leather boot or wrapper. (b) **1834** HAWTHORNE *Twice-told Tales* (1879) I. 118 Our friend . . . [expended] a whole bunch of Spanish wrappers among at least twenty horrified audiences. (c) *c*1870 CHIPMAN *Notes on Bartlett* 517 *Wrapper*, . . . an undershirt. (d) **1901** WHITE in *Munsey's Mag.* (Eng. ed.) XXV. 391/2 Two men cautiously unhook the 'wrappers'—chains whose function it is to bind on the load. **1905** *Forestry Bureau Bul.* No. 61, 30 *Binding chain*, a chain used to bind together a load of logs. . . . Syn.: wrapper chain. (N[orthern] F[orest].)

*✱**Wrapping.** In special combinations.
Wrapping boot, =WRAPPER 2 a; *w. cord*, cord or string used to tie up packages; *w. machine, w. silk*, (see quotations).
1808 PIKE *Sources Miss.* III. App. 41 Their dress is . . . the wrapping boot with the jack boot. **1865** *Harper's Mag.* April 665/2 You can spin some cotton . . . , then double and twist it . . . , and sell it to some merchant for wrapping-cord. **1915** *Scientific Amer.* 30 Jan. 106/1 Wrapping machines . . . are adapted to wrap, seal, and label automatically newspapers or similar articles. **1891** *Cent.* 5630/1 *Wrapping-silk*, a fine strong floss employed in the manufacture of artificial flies.

Wrapping paper. Strong, coarse paper for wrapping up parcels, etc. {1842–} — **1768** [see PACKAGE]. *c*1790 COXE *View U.S.* 62 The produce, manufactures, and exports of Pennsylvania . . . [include] wrapping, blotting, sheathing and hanging paper. **1813** *Niles' Reg.* V. 190/1 Sheathing and wrapping paper. **1893** [see MANIL(L)A]. **1909** RICE *Mr. Opp* 83 Mr. Opp . . . gazed for inspiration at the brown wrapping-paper.

*✱**Wrath.** +*Like all wrath*, in an excessive or violent manner. *colloq*.—
1832 PAULDING *Westward Ho!* II. 182 He held back like all wrath, and wouldn't take any thing. **1850** *Commercial* (Wilmington, N.C.) May 30 2/3 (Th.S.), [The barber] began to tub my head like *all wrath*. **1857** *S. Lit. Messenger* XXV. 305/2 He will whale you like all wrath.

+**Wrathily,** *adv.* Wrathfully. — **1847** WEBSTER 1275/1 *Wrathily*, very angrily. **1879** CABLE *Old Creole Days* 206 The negro begged; the master wrathily insisted.

+**Wrathy,** *a.* Of persons: Full of wrath, angry. {1859–} Also transf. and in fig. expressions. *colloq*.² — **1828** COOPER *Red Rover* I. 221 You are wrathy, friend, without reason. **1843** STEPHENS *High Life N.Y.* I. 223 She looked wrathy enough to spit fire. **1872** TALMAGE *Sermons* 100 The wrathiest tempest that ever blackened the sky. **1900** DIX *Deacon Bradbury* 217 A huge, wrathy figure made two strides.

Wrecker.
1. One who secures salvage from wrecked vessels; a salvager. {1804–, in W. Indies, etc.} Also transf.
1802 ELLICOTT *Journal* 246 [The island] is much frequented by the turtlers, and wreckers. **1870** *Amer. Naturalist* III. 228 Wherever a storm has thrown upon the shore an unusual accumulation of garbage, we find these sagacious wreckers [crows] on the alert. **1883** *American* VI. 37 Lawyers and agents . . . might be described with fairness as 'wreckers' and . . . generally manage to absorb the assets. **1891** *Harper's Mag.* Sept. 592/1 The old 'wreckers' about Key West know every one of them. **1905** LINCOLN *Partners* 150 Brad, how'd you like to be a wrecker?

+**2.** One appointed to recover as much as possible of the assets of insolvent firms.
1846 LYELL *Second Visit* II. 39 'A wrecker' . . . [had] the unenviable task . . . of seeking out and recovering bad debts.

+**3.** (See quot. 1904.)
1904 *Booklovers Mag.* May 663 This special train . . . dubbed the 'Wrecker' . . . is a relief train, ready to respond to any call for aid in case of accident.

+**Wreck heap.** An obstruction or drift of stumps, logs, etc., in a river. *Obs.* — **1826** FLINT *Recoll.* 92 These wreck-heaps are immense piles of trees. **1868** *Putnam's Mag.* May 506/1 The bars, the 'tow-heads,' the wreck-heaps, . . . phenomena of the Mississippi.

Wrecking. {1804–} +In special combinations.
Wrecking car, a railroad car used in clearing the tracks after wrecks; *w. crane*, a railroad crane used in clearing up wrecks; *w. crew*, a crew of wreckers or salvagers, in transf. use; *w. gang, w. outfit*, a group of workers who clear up train wrecks.
1862 *Ashcroft's Railway Directory* 76 No. of . . . Wrecking Cars [on the Central Railroad of New Jersey], 1. **1874** KNIGHT 644/1 Fairbairn's travelling crane . . . is adapted for a wrecking-crane for railroad use. **1878** HARTE *Drift from Two Shores* 27 A wrecking crew of curlew hastily manned the uprooted tree that tossed wearily beyond the bar. **1901** MERWIN & WEBSTER *Calumet 'K'* 8 Bannon . . . was chief of the wrecking gang on a division of the Grand Trunk. **1898** *Engineering Mag.* XVI. 68 The wrecking outfit should be immediately available.

Wrecking company. A company that salvages wrecked or stranded ships {1891–}, +or one that tears down and removes buildings, etc., preparatory for new construction work. — **1895** *Dept. Agric. Yrbk.* 1894 30 The nearest Weather Bureau observer . . . telegraphed a wrecking company at Norfolk. **1898** *Kansas City Star* 20 Dec. 9/1 The board of construction has had under consideration several propositions from engineers and wrecking companies. **1905** LINCOLN *Partners* 297 The train brought representatives of three large wrecking companies to Orham.

+**Wrecking train.** A relief train for service at the scene of a wreck. — **1887** *Courier-Journal* 17 Jan. 1/7 Wrecking trains have arrived. **1891** [see BOILER 1]. **1909** *N.Y. Times* 26 June, A wrecking train with physicians from Livingston Manor was soon on the spot.

+**Wreck master.** A person appointed to take charge of wrecks or wreckage. {*a*1868, in W. Indies} — **1799** *Md. Laws* lxxxii, The governor . . . [shall] appoint one discreet and sensible person . . . to act in the office of a wreck-master. *a*1841 HAWES *Sporting Scenes* I. 205 If . . . the wreck-master did come to look for the wreck, it couldn't be expected that [etc.]. **1904** *Booklovers Mag.* May 665 When the wreck-master and his gang reach the scene this is the first question that arises: Is there anyone, living or dead, under the debris?

*✱**Wren.**
1. Any one of various small birds of the family Troglodytidae, or any one of various other birds resembling these.
1709 LAWSON *Carolina* 144 The Wren is the same as in Europe. **1805** LEWIS in *L. & Clark Exped.* II. (1904) 130, I observed among them the . . . wren and several other birds. **1882** *Vt. Agric. Rep.* VII. 67 The blue bird, cat bird, wren and ground sparrows are acknowledged to be beneficial.

b. Preceded by specifying terms.
See also BEWICK'S WREN, CACTUS WREN, etc.
1806 LEWIS in *L. & Clark Exped.* (1905) III. 309 The little brown ren . . and the beatiful Buzzard of the columbia still continue with us. **1808** Golden-Crested Wren [see GOLDEN-CRESTED *a*.]. **1827** WILLIAMS *West Florida* 30 Green Wren. *M[uscicapa] cantatrix*. **1917** *Birds of Amer.* III. 194 Winter Wren. *Nannus hiemalis hiemalis*. . . . Other Names.—Wood Wren; Mouse Wren; Spruce Wren; Short-tailed Wren.

+**2.** *attrib.* In the specific names of other birds.
1872 COUES *Key to Birds* 79 *Chamœidæ.* Wren-tits . . . much like a titmouse in general appearance, . . . with the general habits of wrens. **1891** *Cent.* 6989/2 *Wren-babbler*, a babbler of small size or otherwise resembling a wren.

*✱**Wrestle,** *v.* Also *dial.* **wrastle.** +**1.** *tr.* To eat or devour (food). *slang. Obs.* +**2.** *W.* To throw or hold down (a calf) for branding. — (1) **1871** HAY *Pike Co. Ballads* 24 He'll wrastle his hash to-night in hell. **1881** HAYES *New Colorado* 92 A prominent gentleman from Dakota . . . wrastles his hash at the Occidental. **1897** LEWIS *Wolfville* 82 The O. K. House, where them Britons has been wrastlin' their chuck. (2) **1888** ROOSEVELT in *Century Mag.* April 861/2 A fire is built, the irons heated, and a dozen men dismount to, as it is called, 'wrestle' the calves. **1893** *Wilderness Hunter* 26 The other men dismounted to 'wrestle' and brand them.

+**Wring-jaw.** (See quot. 1800.) *slang. Obs.* — **1800** BOUCHER *Glossary* p. l, *Wring-jaw*; hard cider. **1845** COOPER *Chainbearer* iii, His weakness in favor of 'wring-jaw' . . . [was] a well-established failing.

*✱**Wrist.** +**1.** A pin or projection from the side of a wheel, crank, etc., to which a connecting rod is attached. +**2.** The grip of a gunstock. — (1) **1864** WEBSTER 1529/3 *Wrist*, . . . a stud or pin. **1876** KNIGHT 1720/1 *Pitman-box*, the stirrup and brasses which embrace the wrist of the driving-wheel. **1883** — *Suppl.* 229/2 A wrist on a crank wheel. (2) **1874** LONG *Wild-Fowl* 27 The stock should be of English or German walnut, with a strong, thick wrist.

+**Wrister.** A knitted covering for the wrist. — **1879** WEBSTER *Suppl.* 1585/3 *Wrister*, a covering for the wrist. **1896** *Chautauquan* Oct. 83/1 The old lady wore gray yarn wristers.

*✱**Writ.** *Law.*
✱1. A written order lawfully issued by a court, government official, etc., commanding the performance or nonperformance, by the person to whom it is directed, of a specified act.
1648 *Mass. H. S. Coll.* 4 Ser. VI. 322 The Court grants him a writt of enquiry, upon a non suit. **1731** *Boston Rec.* 23 Voted. . . . The Committe to whome that afair was betrusted, be Desired to bring forward Such Writt of Reveiw. **1856** *Huntington Rec.* III. 431 Resolved that J. Lawrence Smith be authorized to serve a writ of ejectment and dispossess Samuel P. Hartt.

2. *Writ of error*, a writ issued in an effort to secure the reversal of a judgment on the ground of error. {1663–}
1698 SEWALL *Diary* I. 484 The Judgm't of the Court in the Writt of Error was not declar'd till Septr. 15. **1789** *Phila. Ordinances* (1812) 70 When any writ of error shall be granted upon any judgment [etc.]. **1822** *Ann. 17th Congress* 1 Sess. 145 A writ of error was immediately taken to the supreme court of the State. **1905** *Indian Laws & Tr.* III. 158 Cases taken by appeal or writ of error from the circuit courts of the United States to the circuit court of appeals.

+**Write-up.** A somewhat extended newspaper account of a person, place, etc., often of a laudatory nature. — **1885** *Wkly. New Mexican Rev.* 19 Feb. 4/1, I have prepared quite an extensive 'write-up' of the resources of this country. **1892** *Church Union* Aug. 15 A writer in the New York *World* recently undertook to eulogize the character of Mr. Stevenson. . . . We quote the following paragraphs from his write-up. **1911** in R. T. Bye *Capital Punishment in U.S.* 36 [The condemned man] said upon the scaffold that if he did not get a 'good write-up' from the newspapers he would haunt them to-night.

Writing desk. A writing table, esp. one fitted with compartments for holding writing materials {1611–}; a portable case used for a similar purpose. {1862–} — **1715** *Boston News-Letter* 2 May 2/2 Tables, Beaufetts, Writing Desks, . . . Sold by William Randle. **1807** IRVING, etc. *Salmagundi* 11, [He] packed up . . . his old-fashioned writing-desk. **1856** SIMMS *Charlemont* 227 He carefully locked them up in his portable writing-desk. **1920** HOWELLS *Vacation of Kelwyns* 159 They went on the business of selecting the stuff for a writing-desk.

∗Writing master. A teacher of penmanship. — **1686** *Boston Rec.* 191 They [shall] raise a schoole-house . . . [and] maineteine an able readinge and Writinge Master. **1721** SEWALL *Letter-Book* II. 135 Ames Angier is now Writingmaster. **1836** [see GRAMMAR MASTER]. **1883** *Harper's Mag.* Sept. 643/1 Excepting the people who write like the writing-master, . . . the handwriting is sprawling, flourishy, unformed.

Writing room. {1825-} +**a.** A room in which instruction in writing is given. **b.** A room in a hotel where writing facilities are at the disposal of the guests. — **1810** *Columbian Centine l*3 Nov. 1/2 Exercises in Writing. . . . Females can be attended to in the afternoon at the Writing Room in classes. **1922** *Hotel Mo.* XXX. 57/2 Around the lobby is the writing room, the ladies' lounge [etc.].

∗Writing school. A school in which writing is taught. Also attrib. — **1686** *Boston Rec.* 184 A Motion of the Inhabitants of Muddy River for a writinge Schoole for their Children was read. **1719** *Boston Selectmen* 51 Mr. John Briggs [is] to be Master at ye New Writing School House at ye North. **1792** *Mass. H. S. Coll.* 1 Ser. I. 115 On the lower floor are two apartments; one intended for a grammar school, and the other for a writing school. **1829** in Commons, etc. *Doc. Hist.* I. 234 Attended Writing School & got home at night. **1873** *Winfield* (Kan.) *Courier* 25 Jan. 3/1 The writing school in the new school house, under the supervision of J. M. Read, is doing well.

Wrought iron. Iron capable of being wrought or welded; malleable iron. {1703-} Also attrib. — **1678** *New Castle Court Rec.* 350, 117 lb of wrought Iorn. **1788** in *Rep. Comm. Patents 1849* 534 The greatest part must consist of copper or brass, . . . together with curious wrought iron. **1847** *Ib. 1846* 77 One patent has been granted within the year . . . for improvements in the machinery for welding wrought iron or steel cannon. **1883** Wrought-iron frame [see ELECTRIC LIGHT b]. **1909** 'O. HENRY' *Options* 164 A negro man wearing a white jacket came through the iron gate, with its immense granite posts and wrought-iron lamp-holders.

Wrymouth. {1652-} +A large blenny (*Cryptacanthodes maculatus*). of the north Atlantic coast of the United States, or any one of various fishes related to this. Also with specifying term. — **1839** STORER *Mass. Fishes* 28 *Cryptacanthodes maculatus.* The spotted Wry-mouth. **1890** *Science* April 212/1 The cod-fish, the cunner, the sea-raven, the rock-eel and the wry-mouth, which inhabit these brilliant groves are all colored to match their surroundings.

+**Wyandot(te).** [Fr. *Ouendat*, rendering a native name.]

1. An Indian of a once powerful Iroquoian tribe at one time included in the Huron confederacy; also, pl., the tribe of such an Indian.

The name has been used loosely and with varying meaning.

[**1640** *Relations des Jésuites* (1858) 35/2 Depuis le sault S. Louis montant tousiours sur ce grand fleuue, on trouue . . . les Ouendat [etc.].] **1749** *Doc. Col. Hist. N.Y.* VI. 531 The Twitchwees & Wayandotts . . . for two or three years past have dealt largely with our Traders. **1804** *Md. Hist. Mag.* IV. 6 The Indian chief, Tarhie, a Wyandote, . . . [was] hunting bears. **1824** DODDRIDGE *Notes* 301 A party of seven Wyandots, made an incursion into a settlement. **1896** *Harper's Mag.* April 709/1 The victors were a party of Wyandots and Ottawas.

2. A variety of Indian corn. *Obs.*

1856 *Rep. Comm. Patents 1855: Agric.* 173 The 'Wyandotte' is certainly the most prolific corn I have ever grown.

3. (See quot. 1910.)

1884 *Bazaar* 12 Sept. 866/1 Wyandottes. Wanted a few early pullets, pure bred. **1894** *Vt. Agric. Rep.* XIV. 173 Select . . . for broilers, Plymouth Rocks or Wyandottes. **1910** HODGE, etc. *Amer. Indians* II. 977/2 *Wyandotte*, an American breed of fowls, earlier known as Sebright Cochins, said to have sprung from the mating of a Sebright bantam cock and a Cochin hen.

4. Attrib. with *Indian, nation, pony,* etc.

1789 *Ann. 1st Congress* 72 The Governor of the Western Territory . . . entered into [a treaty] . . . with the sachems and warriors of the Wyandot, Delaware, Ottawa [etc.] . . . nations. **1795** *Amer. Philos. Soc.* IV. 123 This Dipus, as I am informed by a Wyandot-Indian, is common at Sandusky. **1799** J. SMITH *Acct. Captivity* 44 The warriors were preparing to go to war, in the Wiandot, Pottowatomy, and Ottawa towns. **1835** HOFFMAN *Winter in West* I. 127, I have seen nothing of the natives yet except a couple of Wyandott squaws. **1842** TYLER in *Pres. Mess. & P.* IV. 157 I transmit herewith to the Senate a treaty recently concluded with the Wyandott tribe of Indians. **1847** PARKMAN in *Knickerb.* XXX. 126 His sturdy Wyandot pony stood quietly behind him.

+**Wyandotte Constitution.** *Hist.* The constitution drafted for the state of Kansas in 1859 by a convention in Wyandotte, now Kansas City. (Cf. *Lecompton Constitution,* under LECOMPTON 1.) — **1877** JOHNSON *Anderson Co., Kansas* 128 On the first Tuesday of July, 1859, the delegates elected assembled at Wyandotte to frame the constitution, afterwards known as the Wyandotte constitution.

X

∗X. The twenty-fourth letter of the alphabet.

+**1.** *Hist.* Used, in conjunction with 'Y' and 'Z,' to indicate one of certain French emissaries engaged in negotiations with three envoys sent to Paris by the United States government in 1797. Also attrib.

1797 *Amer. State P.: For. Relations* II. 158 M. X. . . . said his communication was not immediately with M. Talleyrand but through another gentleman in whom M. Talleyrand had great confidence. This proved to be M. Y. **1798** *Ib.* 157 The names designated by the letters W. X. Y. Z. in the following copies of letters. **1841** TRUMBULL *Autobiog.* 222, [I] visited the American X, Y, Z negotiators, Pinckney, Marshall, and Gerry.

+**2.** A ten-dollar bill.

1837 *Knickerb.* IX. 96 My wallet . . . distended with V's and X's to its utmost capacity. **1859** J. B. JONES *Southern Scenes* 155, I've just borrowed an X. **1893** POST *Harvard Stories* 295 Perhaps you had better lend me an X now.

3. Something shaped like the letter 'X.'

[**1874** B. F. TAYLOR *World on Wheels* 51 Your Railway Hog . . . takes two seats, turns them *vis-a-vis,* and makes a letter X of himself, so as to keep them all.] *Ib.,* A meek-faced man, as thin and pale as an ivory paper-cutter, . . . made an X of *himself.*

Xebeck. A small three-masted vessel. {1756-, in the Mediterranean} — **1777** *N.J. Archives* 2 Ser. I. 496 The xebecks Repulse and Champion, . . . with the two floating batteries and three fire-ships, were accordingly set on fire and destroyed.

XX. +A twenty-dollar bill. — **1883** CRAWFORD *Dr. Claudius* 346 The Custom-House officials . . . know the green side of a XX, and are seldom troubled with gloomy forebodings.

Xylograph. A wood engraving. {1878-} — **1864** WEBSTER 1531/3 *Xylograph,* an engraving on wood, or the impression from such an engraving. **1865** *Atlantic Mo.* Jan. 56/1 [Cruikshank's] wondrous wood-cuts —xylographs, if you wish a more pretentious word—will be long remembered.

Y

* **Y.** The twenty-fifth letter of the alphabet.

+**1.** *Hist.* Used to indicate a person: (see X 1).

+**2.** *Railroad.* **a.** = SWITCHBACK. **b.** (See quot. 1864.)

1858 W. P. SMITH *Railway Celebrations* 42 Mr. Engineer Latrobe's original triumph in crossing great elevations with locomotive and cars, by means of a series of steep inclines, called Y's. **1864** WEBSTER 1532/1 *Y*, . . . a portion of track consisting of two converging tracks connected by a cross-track. **1873** BEADLE *Undevel. West* 209 They will have a Y put in with the right branch terminating at their town. **1879** BURDETTE *Hawk-eyes* 205, I know every switch, side-track and Y in the State of Iowa.

+**3.** Abbrev. for *Yale* or for *Y.M.C.A.* Also attrib.

1892 *Outing* March 455/1 The old 'Y' rule . . . required a man to win a point either in the Yale or Harvard games, or at the Intercollegiate meeting, before he could wear the university 'Y.' **1894** *Harper's Mag.* July 184/1 As the Yale crew have not arrived, no large blue flag with a white 'Y' in the centre graces the top of the staff. **1923** HERRICK *Lilla* 234, I see that they are recruiting men for the Y.M.C.A. I should think you would make a splendid Y secretary.

* **Yacht.** A small, light, sailing or motor vessel used chiefly for pleasure cruising, racing, etc.

1688 SEWALL *Diary* I. 225 The Duke of Albemarl's Yott arrives. **1766** [see PLEASURE BOAT]. **1830** WATSON *Philadelphia* App. 18 The Dutch *yachts* (then so called) were from one to two weeks in a voyage to Hudson and Albany. **1897** *Outing* XXX. 191/1 The display of yachts and smaller craft was excellent. **1922** [see MACHINE 2 b].

Yacht club. A club or organized group of yacht-owners interested in promoting yachting. {1837–} Also attrib. — **1868** *N.Y. Herald* 4 July 5/2 The House Committee of the New York Yacht Club announces . . . that the new club house is open. **1894** *Outing* Sept. 458/1 The yacht-club reception was the topic of the day. **1902** ALDRICH *Sea Turn* 63 Mr. Brandon wandered over to the Eastern Yacht Club.

Yachting. {1836–} *attrib.* Designating clothing or articles of clothing worn when yachting.

1879 HOWELLS *Lady of Aroostook* 110 [She] found her yachting-dress perfectly adapted to tramping over the South Bradfield hills. **1880** *Harper's Mag.* Aug. 399/1 A blue flannel yachting shirt . . . [and] a coat of substantial stuff, are almost indispensable for a two weeks' cruise. **1890** DAVIS *Gallegher* 235 This is the first time I ever appeared . . . [in] a blue serge yachting suit. **1891** *Scribner's Mag.* X. 198 He returned to his study of the effects of her dark hair under a yachting cap. **1897** *Outing* XXX. 561/1 Golf and bicycle uniforms . . . cannot compare with the really smart yachting rigs of the incomparable American girls. **1898** ATHERTON *Californians* 183 Magdaléna sat amidst iridescent billows of ball-gowns, dinner-gowns, . . . yachting-frocks, summer-frocks.

Yager. {1804–} +A rifle of a type now obsolete. In full *Yager rifle.*

1840 C. HOFFMAN *Greyslaer* I. 18 He instantly brought his yager to his shoulder. **1865** PIKE *Scout & Ranger* (1932) 30 We had discharged a portion of our yagers and pistols. **1890** LANGFORD *Vigilante Days* (1912) 410 My armory consisted of one rifle, fifteen United States yagers [etc.]. *a*1918 G. STUART *On Frontier* I. 178 Nine Pipes, a Flathead, came to get a nipple put on his Yager rifle.

+**Yalensian.** A student or graduate of Yale. — **1852** BRISTED *5 Years in Eng. Univ.* II. 153 The necessary expenses of a Cantab will . . . be brought very nearly on a par with those of a Yalensian. **1860** E. C. PORTER *Songs of Yale* p. v, A locality well known to Yalensians as 'Tutor's Lane.' **1912** NICHOLSON *Hoosier Chron.* 219 Dan, finding several Yalensians in the company, . . . made them all acquainted with Sylvia and her friends.

+**Yaller gal.** = YELLOW GIRL. *slang.* — **1847** ROBB *Squatter Life* 135 He was puttin' up a picaninny 'yaller gal,' about five years old. **1869** TOURGEE *Toinette* (1881) 136 The place was first deeded from old man Tommy Gray to Arthur Lovett, as trustee for a yaller gal, Belle. **1899** CHESNUTT *Conjure Woman* 116 He lef' a wife behin' 'im,—a monst'us good-lookin' yaller gal, name' Sally.

* **Yam. a.** The edible root of any one of various species of the genus *Dioscorea*, or one of these plants; a root or plant related to or resembling these. (See also WILD YAM(-ROOT).)

+**b.** *S.* A variety of sweet potato. Also attrib.

1676 GLOVER *Va.* in *Phil. Trans.* XI. 629 Their Gardens have . . . Carrets, Potatoes, and Yams. **1748** CATESBY *Carolina* II. p. xix, The Yam. . . . Carolina is the farthest North I have known them to grow, and there more for curiosity than advantage. **1844** *Lexington Observer* 9 Oct. 3/6 Our friend R. C. Boggs, has left upon our table a potatoe of the yam

species. **1905** N. DAVIS *Northerner* 155 The possum . . . reposed in a nest of golden yams dripping with butter.

+**Yamassee.** Also **Yammasee, Yemassee.** [Amer. Indian.] An Indian of a tribe of Muskhogean stock formerly occupying the coast region in South Carolina and Georgia; also, pl., the tribe. Also attrib.

1699 J. DICKINSON *God's Protecting Providence* 84 The Carolina-Indians, called the Yammasees, . . . [were] Trading for Deer-Skins. **1741** *S.C. Hist. Soc. Coll.* IV. 14 The Yemassee Indians, . . . had lived in amity with the Government at St. Augustine. **1744** MOORE *Voy. Georgia* 107 The Indians . . . rowed . . . by taking a short and long stroke alternately, which they called the Yamassee stroke. **1835** SIMMS (*title*), The Yemassee.

+**Yamp.** Also **yampa(h).** [Shoshonean Indian.] The edible potato-like tuber of a western herb (*Atenia gairdneri*), or a related species (*A. kelloggii*). Also attrib. — **1845** FRÉMONT *Exped.* 158 This morning we breakfasted on *yampah.* **1847** Yampa root [see PIGNUT 3]. **1896** *Garden & Forest* IX. 303 *Yamp*, or *Yampah.* . . . The root . . . is highly esteemed by these and other Indians as an article of food.

Yank.[1] {1818–} +A sudden jerk, pull, or tug. Also *fig.* — **1885** *Milnor* (Dak.) *Free Press* 28 March 1/5 The other shoe pulled hard, and . . . Mr. Crane gave it a sudden yank. **1888** GUNTER *Mr. Potter* viii, Her brother giving her a masculine yank [from the gondola], and jumping her upon the steps. **1906** *N.Y. Globe* 20 Aug. 6 A fantastic proposition from Germany . . . takes one back with an unpleasant yank into the middle ages.

+**Yank.**[2] Short for YANKEE *n.* — **1778** *Conquerors* 14 I'll drive the Yanks from north to south again. **1862** *Phila. Inquirer* The 'Yank' has got up a superior article, which it is very difficult to detect. **1890** [see CONFED *n.* and *a.* 1]. **1918** SANDBURG *Cornhuskers* 50 Out of . . . coal towns in Colorado Sprang a vengeance of Slav miners, Italians, Scots, Cornishmen, Yanks.

Yankee, *n.* [Of unknown origin: see note.]

The fullest and most competent discussion of *Yankee* is that by O. G. T. Sonneck, *Report on 'The Star Spangled Banner'* . . . *and 'Yankee Doodle'* (1909) 79 ff. Mr. Sonneck analyzes the many theories that have been advanced to account for the origin of this word. The earliest to appear in print (in the *Penna. Ev. Post* of May 25, 1775, and reprinted in the *N.Y. Gazetteer* of June 1, 1775) attributed it to an Indian tribe, the *Yankoos* or 'invincible ones.' Unfortunately, no such tribe is known. Other Indian derivations, from a Cherokee word, *eankke*, or from Indian corruption of the word *English* to *Yengeese* to *Yankees*, lack supporting evidence.

One Jonathan Hastings who lived in Cambridge, Mass., circa 1713 has also been alleged to be the inventor of the word which he used to mean 'excellent.' (See 1788 W. Gordon *Hist. Independence U.S.A.* (1789) I. 325.) Though such a person existed, it is improbable that his use of the word had any bearing on its subsequent currency as a nickname.

The theory that the term is from Du. *Janke,* dim. of *Jan,* 'John,' given as a nickname by the Dutch of New York to the English of Connecticut, is probably untenable; but the use of the word in names or as a name, sometimes with Dutch associations, is shown in the following examples: [**1683** *Cal. State P., Amer. & W.I.* XI. 457 [The pirates] sailed from Bonaco . . . ; chief commanders, Vanhorn, Laurens, and Yankey Duch. *Ib.*, [They] put eight hundred man into Yankey's and another ship.] **1725** *Notes & Q.* 5 Ser. X. 467 Item one negroe man named Yankee to be sold. **1788** W. GORDON *Hist. Independence U.S.A.* I. 325 The students . . . gave him [Jonathan Hastings] the name of Yankee Jon.

+**1.** A nickname applied originally to New Englanders.

In the first group of examples New Englanders are clearly meant. In the second group they seem to be referred to by implication.

(1) **1765** *Oppression,* From meanness first this Portsmouth Yankey rose. **1784** SMYTH *Tour* II. 366 The New Englanders are disliked by the inhabitants of all the other provinces, by whom they are called *Yankeys.* **1824** HODGSON *Letters from N.A.* II. 34 In America, the term Yankee is applied to the natives of New England only, and is generally used with an air of pleasantry. **1883** SWEET & KNOX *Through Texas* 18, I can lick daylight out'n the biggest Yankee ever grew in New England. **1916** EASTMAN *From Deep Woods* 66, I found Yankees of the uneducated class very Indian-like in their views and habits.

(2) **1802** D. G. COWARD *Let.* (Pettigrew P.), Men who have stood high, and held positions with honor in the County, now are Yankees at heart. **1828** A. LAWRENCE *Diary & Corr.* 83, I wish to see you, as long as you live, a well-bred, upright *Yankee.* **1840** [see PIGEON 4]. **1870** NOWLAND *Indianapolis* 123 At the time Mr. F. first came to Indianapolis there was a strong prejudice existing among the people against the Yankees (as all Eastern people were called). **1903** [see CLAM *n.* 1].

2. A native or inhabitant of the United States; an American.

The first quotations indicate that this more inclusive application was first given to the name by British writers and speakers.

(1) c1784 NELSON in A. Duncan *Life Nelson* 321, I . . . am determined not to suffer the Yankies to come where the ship is. a1800 TWINING *Visit* 385 Their wit was particularly directed against a 'Yankee.' We apply this designation . . . to the inhabitants of all parts of the United States. 1833 COKE *Subaltern's Furlough* xi, In England we are apt to designate all Americans as Yankees, whether they are born under the burning sun of Louisiana, or frozen up five months in the year on the shores of the Lake of the Woods.

(2) 1815 HUMPHREYS *Yankey* 14 The word Yankey . . . has sometimes been applied to Americans of the United States in general. 1832 PAULDING *Westward Ho!* II. 135 He [a Frenchman living in Mo.] did not like the Yankees, by which term he designated the Americans in general. 1874 *Congress. Rec.* App. 7 May 257/2 When I say a Yankee, I mean an American. 1893 *Harper's Mag.* April 786/1 [The descendants of the Spanish in California] have caught the spirit of the times; they too are 'Yankees.'

+3. Used, esp. by Southerners during the Civil War, of Federal soldiers.

1861 NORTON *Army Lett.* 27 The soil may be sacred, but we sacrilegious Yankees can't help observing that it is awfully deficient in manure. 1865 RICHARDSON *Secret Service* 354 Look out Rebs! The Yankees are coming! 1895 CHAMBLISS *Diary* 305 The malignant epithets, 'Yankee' and 'Rebel,' . . . were invented by fanatics and foreigners to aggravate our interstate quarrel. 1907 ANDREWS *Recoll.* 172 Some negro boys peered into the car windows to look at us Yankees.

+b. An inhabitant of the northern states.

1865 RICHARDSON *Secret Service* 90 [The] newspapers have persuaded the masses that the Yankees (a phrase which they no longer apply distinctively to New Englanders, but to every person born in the North) . . are arrant cowards. 1872 POWERS *Afoot & Alone* 23 One of those gigantic negroes . . . had never seen a Yankee before.

+4. Whisky sweetened with molasses. *colloq. Obs.*

1804 FESSENDEN *Orig. Poems* (1806) 78 Call on me, when you come this way, And take a dram of *Yankee.* 1843 [see NUMBER-ONE *n.*].

5. The English used by Yankees; American English.

[1824 J. GILCHRIST *Etymologic Interpreter* 8 The naked savages of Indiana already speak a corrupt English (or Yankee).] 1828 *Yankee* I. 197/3 Why not say, as people do say that either speak or write either English or Yankee—such a one. 1850 S. WARNER *Wide, Wide World* xxxix, I am sorry that is Yankee, for I suppose one must speak English. 1866 LOWELL *Biglow P.* 2 Ser. p. xix, I should be half inclined to name the Yankee a *lingo* rather than a dialect.

+6. In phrases. **a.** *To catch a Yankee,* to catch a tartar. **b.** *To play Yankee,* to behave in the manner of a Yankee, as by replying to a question by asking one.

(a) 1811 *Niles' Reg.* I. 71/2 The irritation in England on account of the attack of the *Little Belt* on our Frigate the *President,* in which the former 'caught a yankee,' still continues. (b) 1896 *Congress. Rec.* 30 March 3366/1 Now I will play Yankee with my friend.

Yankee. *attrib.* passing into *adj.*

+1. Of or pertaining to Yankees; American.

See also YANKEE CLOCK, YANKEE GRIT, etc.

1776 TRUMBULL *M'Fingal* 15 The true war-dance of Yankey-reels, And manual exercise of heels. 1806 *Balance* V. 67/1 We will, in our Yankee way, ask another question. 1814 *Niles' Reg.* VI. 180/2 What southern port is there that a 'yankee' vessel does not enter? 1836 DUNLAP *Mem. Water Drinker* (1837) I. 13 The Yankee journals are as flat as the whole surface of society in this country. 1849 W. BROWN *America* 68 The following struck me as original, and one which would bear transplanting into our own country, viz., the Yankee Pile Driver. 1855 *Mich. Agric. Soc. Trans.* VI. 144 This farm as a whole, exhibits a rare instance of Yankee go-a-headativeness. 1867 RICHARDSON *Beyond Miss.* 50 Lawrence was distinctively a Yankee town. 1880 *Harper's Mag.* Sept. 645/1 Talk of Yankee 'cuteness! 1900 *Congress. Rec.* 1 Feb. 1406/2, I would like to ask the gentleman Yankee fashion another question.

+2. Of a person: Of Yankee birth or residence. Applied especially to persons from New England or the northern states.

1784 Yankee bundler [see BUNDLER]. 1803 LEWIS in *Jrnls. of L. & Ordway* 43 Continued our rout and took up the N.W. Shore near a yankey farmer from whom I perchased some corn. 1822 DEWEES *Lett. from Texas* 26 Our little yankee preacher seemed to enjoy himself very well during the trip. a1841 HAWES *Sporting Scenes* II. 44, I think Yankee schoolmasters ought to be taken up as vagrants. 1857 M. J. HOLMES *Meadow-Brook* xxxviii, The new 'Yankee engineer' was a daring, reckless fellow. 1873 MILLER *Amongst Modocs* 37 A sort of Yankee sailor was this boatman. 1901 Yankee colonist [see COLONIST 1 c].

+b. Esp. used in the South with reference to the northern soldiers during the Civil War and to school-teachers from the northern and New England states.

1865 BOUDRYE *Fifth N.Y. Cavalry* 35 The valley [was] cleared of the Yankee army. 1866 W. REID *After the War* 282 A couple of Yankee

school-mistresses were . . . the teachers of the boys and girls of Mr. Davis' slaves. 1867 GOSS *Soldier's Story* 46 Yankee prisoners . . . became engaged in the transactions of cheating and stealing from their more miserable companions. 1871 *Congress. Globe* 5 April 205/3 A Yankee school-marm was stoned and murdered by her own pupils. 1871 EGGLESTON *Hoosier Schoolm.* 39 Squire Hawkins was a poor Yankee schoolmaster. 1880 Yankee 'nigger teacher' [see NIGGER *n.* 9].

+3. Used of, or with reference to, the Yankee dialect or speech.

See also YANKEE DIALECT.

1803 *Balance* 15 Nov. 363 It would (to use a Yankee phrase) puzzle a dozen Philadelphia lawyers to unriddle the conduct of the democrats. 1847 WHITTIER *Writings* V. 391 Small, squeaking voices spoke in a sort of Yankee-Irish dialect. 1858 *Harper's Mag.* Aug. 428/1 Dr. Chapman made the acquaintance of a country doctor—a clever man in the Yankee sense of the word. 1866 MOORE *Women of War* 174 Your speech savors of the Yankee twang. 1880 *Harper's Mag.* Sept. 613/1 The familiar twang given to the Yankee speech of words like *now* and *cow* . . . was extended beyond the limits of perversion.

+4. Used in combination with participles and other adjectives.

1787 TYLER *Contrast* III. i, I'm a true born Yankee American son of liberty. 1799 *Aurora* (Phila.) 30 Sept. (Th.), Faith, 'twill be Yankee-like, and plagued funny. 1800 *Ib.* 15 Oct. (Th.), The Yankee built squab boat skipper is obstinate. 1835–7 HALIBURTON *Clockmaker* 1 Ser. xvii. 145, I heard him ax the groom who that are Yankee lookin' feller was. 1839 KEMBLE *Residence in Ga.* 117 All these infamous articles are Yankee made. 1866 A. D. WHITNEY *L. Goldthwaite* x, Over all looked forth a face . . . that had undoubtedly always been, what it now was, emphatically Yankee-smart.

+5. In special combinations.

Yankee beverage, Y. cart, (see quotations); *Y.-Catcher,* a member of a company of Confederate soldiers organized in Virginia; *Y. evening,* = EVENING 1; *Y. farming, Y. jacket,* (see quotations); *Y.-lover,* in the South, a term of opprobrium for a person regarded as sympathetic to northerners and northern ideals; *Y. music,* florid contrapuntal choral music popular in New England churches in the late eighteenth century; *Y. nigger,* a term of contempt among southerners for a northern white man; *Y. nutmeg,* = WOODEN NUTMEG 1; *Y. shilling, Y. sled,* (see quotations); *Y. wood sled,* a heavy sled for hauling wood; *Y. yoke,* during the Civil War, the rule of the federal government, or of those favoring the Union cause.

1830 PICKERING *Inquiries Emigrant* 26 Vinegar and water, sweetened with molasses, is much drank in this hot weather, and called switchel, or 'Yankee beverage.' 1834 CARRUTHERS *Kentuckian* I. 26 He drove what we call a Yankee cart, half wagon and half carriage. 1861 Moore *Rebellion Rec.* I. III. 71 The Yankee-Catchers will report and be ready to enter service in a few days. 1828 ROYALL *Black Book* II. 323, I arrived at Thomastown in the evening—not the *Yankee* evening—I mean about sundown. 1902 G. C. EGGLESTON *D. South* 318 He had shipped and sold the large surplus crops of apples and sweet potatoes—a thing wholly unprecedented in that part of Virginia, where no product of the soil except tobacco and wheat were ever turned to money account. He was laughed at for what his neighbors characterized as 'Yankee farming.' 1816 'SCENE PAINTER' *Emigrant's Guide* 52 He commanded some of the crew to furnish the d—d English rascal with a *good Yankee Jacket,* which in plain English is a quantity of tar besmeared over the naked body, upon which an abundance of feathers is immediately strewed. 1879 TOURGEE *Fool's Errand* 130 My children are insulted every now and then as 'nigger-worshipers,' and . . . 'Yankee-lovers.' 1822 *Mass. Spy* 1 May (Th.), A few years since, most of the choirs in New-England were running mad after what was termed Yankee musick. 1839 HOFFMAN *Wild Scenes* II. 66 You and Humphrey take the Yankee nigger by his shoulders. 1874 B. F. TAYLOR *World on Wheels* 75 That's the way betting comes. It is not a mere invention, like a Yankee nutmeg. 1891 WELCH *Recoll. 1830–40* 168 The common silver coin known as Pistareen . . . was worth sixteen and two-thirds cents and halves of it, eight and one-third cents, a Yankee shilling, or sixpence. 1876 KNIGHT 2204/1 The *Yankee* sled has wide runners which elevate the benches sufficiently. 1856 HALE *If, Yes, & Perhaps* 141 They would be gone three months and more, . . . dragging a sled very like a Yankee wood-sled . . . , over ice and snow. 1862 CUMMING *Hospital Life* 42/2 General Bragg has every hope that the Kentuckians will be glad to roll themselves of the hated Yankee yoke.

+Yankee, *v. tr.* To defraud, cheat, outsmart. *slang. Obs.* {1837} — 1801 in Cist *Cincinnati* (1841) 177, I generally yankees them once a month, and they stand that like lambs. 1838 DRAKE *Tales Queen City* 88 The partisans of Captain Leatherwood . . . had placed themselves around the polls, to prevent the friends of their favorite candidate, from being *yankeed* out of the opportunity of voting. 1859 [see JEW *v.* 1].

+Yankee clock. A clock of American manufacture, esp. one of a kind made in New England and formerly sold by Yankee peddlers. — 1839 [see NOTION 3]. 1851 CIST *Cincinnati* 313 A Yankee clock is now produced for sixty cents that formerly cost three dollars. 1867 'E. KIRKE' *On Border* 57 [On] a broad mantle of unpainted oak . . . a Yankee clock is ticking.

+Yankee dialect. The dialect or variety of English used by Yankees, esp. those of New England. — 1832 DUNLAP *Hist. Amer. Theatre* 71 'The Contrast' . . . [has] a degree of humour and knowledge of what is termed Yankee dialect. 1840 *Knickerb.* XV. 43 My guide . . . [was] a man of few words, and those few of the purest Yankee dialect. 1881 *Harper's Mag.*

Jan. 258/2 Mr. Lowell wrote a letter to the Boston *Courier*, . . . inclosing a poem in the Yankee dialect.

+Yankeedom. The realm of the Yankees; the United States, esp. New England; Americans in general. {1851–} — **1843** *Yale Lit. Mag.* VIII. 308 All Yankeedom might be searched through and through, and no lovelier spot be found, than Bodkinville. **1847** ROBB *Squatter Life* 176 The old fashion defies the ingenuity of Yank*eedom* to improve on it. **1865** *Public Opinion* (London) 28 Jan. 93 He meant merely to perpetrate one of those grim jokes in which Yankeedom so much delights. **1894** ALDRICH *Two Bites* 193, I have come to Yankeedom to make my fortune. **1902** HARBEN *A. Daniel* 110, I met a feller from up in Yankeedom that said 'darn,' an' another from out West that said 'dang.'

+Yankee-Doodle. [Of unknown origin: see note.]

Sonneck (see YANKEE *n.*, note), upon careful investigation, eliminated or cast grave doubts upon the validity of every theory as to the origin of the term, including the one attributing the song to Dr. Richard Shuckburgh.

1. The title of a well-known American song and air. Also transf.

1767 in Sonneck *Report* (1909) 110 Air IV, Yankee Doodle. **1775** *Penna. Ev. Post* 22 July 317/2 General Gage's troops are much dispirited . . . and are heartily disposed to leave off dancing any more to the tune of Yankey Doodle. **1812** *Niles' Reg.* II. 367/2 Our brave citizens giving three hearty cheers, and greeting his majesty's faithful subjects with the well remembered tune of *Yankee Doodle.* **1863** HOPLEY *Life in South* I. 172 The tune of 'Yankee Doodle' was hissed, and forbidden at the Mobile Theatre. **1900** *Congress. Rec.* 16 Feb. 1874/2 There we find the boys in blue and the boys in gray . . . marching to the blended strains of Yankee Doodle and Dixie.

b. *To give Yankee-Doodle,* to give Hail Columbia (q.v. under HAIL COLUMBIA 2). *slang.*

1866 MOORE *Women of War* 102 Sheridan gave the rebs 'Hail Columbia' and 'Yankee Doodle' combined, . . . and I do not think their army will trouble us again this winter.

2. A Yankee; collect., the Yankees. {a1807–1814} *Obs.*

1770 *R.I. Commerce* I. 330 The many favours allready conferred on Poor Old yankey dodle. **1846** *Knickerb.* XXVII. 50 Vagabonds for Texas, but Yankee-Doodles for Vermont. **1847** ROBB *Squatter Life* 147 He'd cuss de Yankee doodels, and grit his teeth most owdaciously. **1869** *Harper's Mag.* Sept. 619/1 Here's Yankee Doodle's been and come And beat your crackest yatches.

b. Attrib. with *business, college, invitation.*

1825 NEAL *Bro. Jonathan* II. 319 One of your yankee doodle invitations, that—happy to see you another time. **1846** *Knickerb.* XXVII. 50 The writer of this was educated at a Yankee-Doodle College at New Haven. **1894** *Scribner's Mag.* May 605/2 There is little of the Yankee-Doodle business about [the music].

+Yankee-Doodledom. The home or realm of the Yankee-Doodles, esp. New England or the northern states. *Obs.* — **1845** HONE *Diary* II. 248 The ladies of this family (natives though they be of Yankee-doodle-dom) seem to possess, in a high degree, the power of capturing the aristocracy of England. **1846** *Knickerb.* XXVII. 57 [In Vermont] are the quintessence of subtile character and strong-hold of Yankee-Doodledom. **1861** in Bartlett (1877) 769 Abe Lincoln, and all his Northern scum, Shall own our independence of *Yankee Doodledom.*

+Yankee grit. Unflinching, persevering courage and determination such as a Yankee is supposed to possess. — **1865** BOUDRYE *Fifth N.Y. Cavalry* 178 With trusty carbines and Yankee grit, our boys scattered the enemy before them. **1884** B. MATTHEWS in *Harper's Mag.* May 906/1 His mother left him her full share of Yankee grit. **1894** *Vt. Agric. Rep.* XIV. 125 That Yankee grit . . . will see us through this blight of one of our greatest industries.

+Yankeeish, *a.* Resembling a Yankee, or suggestive of Yankee manners and customs. — **1830** *Collegian* 117 Comparisons are generally 'odorous,' particularly Yankeeish, and decidedly condemned by Captain Basil Hall. **1848** *Ladies' Repository* VIII. 8 That Yankeeish aspect of equality and comfortable competence . . . is found equaled nowhere out of New England. **1852** *Knickerb.* XXXIX. 152 The inhabitants of that part of the world, [near Cape Cod] being somewhat Yankeeish, called it 'Eating Hall.'

+Yankeeism. {1820–}

1. A trait, whim, peculiarity, etc., characteristic of Yankees. {1836–}

1792 *New-York Mag.* III. 244 Yankeyism [title of an anecdote showing New England character]. **1850** *Knickerb.* XXXVI. 175/1 When an earnest man, who wants to do good, *adopts* . . . a certain method or style, no matter if it be Yankyism, or Carlylism, . . . it answers his porpoise tolerabul well. **1868** *Putnam's Mag.* I. 34/1 He glanced at the superscription and express seals (in that little act cropped out the hopeless 'Yankeeism' of the pork-merchant's character).

2. A word or expression characteristic of Yankee speech; an Americanism. {1820–}

1806 FESSENDEN *Democracy Unveiled* II. 177 *Twistical* is a *Yankeyism.* **1855** BRISTED in *Cambridge Ess.* 58 'Yankeeisms' in this century have taken the place occupied by *bulls* and other Hibernicisms in the last. **1892** *Nation* LIV. 287/1 In scientific philology, *Yankeeism* and *Americanism* are, respectively, species and genus.

+Yankeeland. The land of the Yankees, esp. New England. Also *Yankeelander.*

1788 FRENEAU *Misc. Works* 69 In Yanky land there stands a town Where learning may be purchas'd low. **1813** PAULDING *J. Bull & Bro. Jon.* (ed. 2) 93 The Southlanders came at last to consider all the Yankeylanders downright cheats. **1855** BRISTED in *Cambridge Ess.* 66 To begin with the New England States, those six lying east of the Hudson, and constituting the veritable 'Yankeeland.' **1867** *Atlantic Mo.* May 539/2 The Wilcox and Gibbs [sewing] machine, [is] the only one . . . which was not invented by a Yankee, or in Yankee land. **1908** 'O. HENRY' *Options* 93, I can't conceive that even ten years in Yankeeland could change a boy of mine.

attrib. **1836** *S. Lit. Messenger* II. 192 The clever young writer . . . was cut dead in his Yankee-land habiliments.

+Yankee nation. New England; the northern states. (See also *universal Yankee nation,* under UNIVERSAL *a.*[1]) — **1859** *Ladies' Repository* XIX. 507/1 In other portions of the 'Yankee nation' [than Boston], ingenuity is tasked chiefly to advance material gains. **1870** O. LOGAN *Before Footlights* 236 The rebel prisoners . . . [were] rather sarcastic when referring to the Yankee nation.

+Yankee notion. A small article of merchandise of the kind sold by Yankee peddlers, as a bowl or pan. Usually pl. Also attrib.

The first quotation refers to ideas.

[c1815 PAULDING *Amer. Comedies* (1847) 51, I suppose these are what they call Yankee notions.] **1825** NEAL *Bro. Jonathan* II. 298 We found him stowed away among the [articles] . . . which we had got in exchange for a load of Yankee notions. **1843** 'UNCLE SAM' *Peculiarities* I. 167 At this guessing party there war a Yankee notion-seller trying to clear himself of a clock by swearing it were the last. **1848** IRVING *Knickerb.* (rev. ed.) IV. vi, An immense store of oysters and clams, . . . and Yankee 'notions' formed the *spolia opima.* **1872** *Newton Kansan* 22 Aug. 5/5 For a nice bottle of perfumery or Yankee notions, go to G. D. Munger's. **1903** WIGGIN *Rebecca* 245 The Perkins' attic was still a treasure-house of ginghams, cottons, and 'Yankee notions.' **1904** *Hartford Courant* 29 Oct. 25 The 'Yankee Notion' state, as it [Conn.] has often been called, earned its title in the early part of the 19th century, when there was a great impetus given to the manufacture of almost all sorts of useful implements for the farm and for the household.

+Yankee peddler. A peddler from New England whose stock in trade consists of Yankee notions. — **1834** SIMMS *Guy Rivers* I. 64 The regulators have made out to catch a certain Yankee pedler. **1853** [see NOTION 1]. **1870** *Scribner's Mo.* I. 122 [He] won much reputation as a genuine 'Yankee peddler.'

+Yankee rum. =NEW ENGLAND RUM. — **1777** CRESSWELL *Journal* 263 They [the people of New England] import large quantities of Molasses from the West Indies, which they distill and sell to Africa and the other Colonies, which goes by the name of Yankee Rum or Stink-e-buss. **1807** JANSON *Stranger in Amer.* 28 At Boston they distil large quantities of that detestable spirit, there called New England, but in the Southern States, Yankee rum. **1842** 'UNCLE SAM' *Peculiarities* I. 43 On the outside . . . is printed the following thirsty announcement:— . . . Jamaica Spirits, Yankee Rum [etc.].

+Yankee State. The state of Ohio. A nickname. — **1826** FLINT *Recoll.* 45 This is properly designated 'the Yankee state.' **1884** *Harper's Mag.* June 125/1 Ohio was called 'the Yankee State.'

+Yankee trick. A trick, fraud, or deception thought to be typical of a Yankee. — **1776** TRUMBULL *M'Fingal* 62 Was there a Yanky trick you knew, They did not play as well as you? **1813** *Niles' Reg.* V. 175/2 It won't do to play yankee tricks with *yankees.* **1867** GOSS *Soldier's Story* 45 The rebels prided themselves on the performance of what they termed a 'Yankee trick.'

+Yankee wagon. A light wagon, as a dearborn, used chiefly for pleasure. *Obs.* — **1818** PALMER *Travels U.S.* 188 Their pleasure waggons, called Yankee waggons, are in miniature on four wheels, neatly painted, and drawn by one horse. **1847** *Santa Fe Repub.* 17 Sept. 2/4 For Sale, A strong and well finished Yankee Wagon and Harness.

+Yankton. [Amer. Indian.] An Indian belonging to one of the seven divisions of the Sioux, or a related division sometimes confounded with it; also, pl., the division. Also attrib. — **1708** in Neill *Hist. Minnesota* 164. **1805** [see INDIAN attrib. and adj. 9]. **1827** in McKenney *Memoirs* I. 109 He was clothed in a yankton dress—new and beautiful. **1894** EGGLESTON in *Harper's Mag.* Feb. 469/1 The Yanktons . . . seem to have been scouring the Coteau in hope of slaughtering some Cree or Assiniboin hunting party. **1910** HODGE, etc. *Amer. Indians* II. 991/1 The so-called 'Yankton Sioux' under the Ft. Peck agency, Mont., are in reality chiefly Yanktonai.

+Yapon. (See YAUPON.)

* Yard, *n.*

*1. An area of ground enclosed by, enclosing, or situated adjacent to or near, a building or buildings, as a garden adjoining a house {now *dial.*}, or, chiefly U.S., the part of a town lot surrounding a house.

See also BACK YARD, BARN-YARD, etc.

1638 *Charlestown Land Rec.* 9 One dwelling house, with a yard and garden. **1741** *N.H. Probate Rec.* III. 83, I Give to my wife Huldah the House that we now Live in & the Garden or yard before the door. **1815** BENTLEY *Diary* IV. 349 Several late instances of paving yards. **1835** INGRAHAM

South-West II. 88 Striped grass, cultivated in yards at the north. **1840** *Picayune* 12 Aug. 2/3 Prentiss . . . is to address a meeting of the citizens, . . . in the Park (*Yard*, not Theatre), on Monday evening. **1894** [see FLAGSTONE 1]. **1924** CROY *R.F.D. No. 3* 62 Josie came up the path of the hard-baked yard.

b. = PRISON YARD {1777-}; +*liberty of the yard*, (see quot. 1828).

[**1660** *Plymouth Rec.* 127 An adition [to the house of correction] shalbee erected . . . ; with a yard afore it.] **1777** *N.H. Comm. Safety Rec.* 97 Ordered Simeon Ladd, Gaol keeper, to give Jno Powell the Liberty of the yard. **1809** [see FIVES]. **1828** WEBSTER s.v. *Yard, Liberty of the yard*, is a liberty granted to persons imprisoned for debt, of walking in the yard, or within any other limits prescribed by law. **1844** 'UNCLE SAM' *Peculiarities* II. 47 You are aware that I send my help into the yard every day for *my* share of the firing.

+c. = COLLEGE YARD.

[**1665** in Hutchinson *Coll. Papers Mass.-Bay* 421 At Cambridg they have a wooden collidg and, in the yard, a brick pile of two bayes for the Indians.] **1841** *Harvard Faculty Orders & Regul.* 6 Collecting in groups round the doors of the College buildings or in the yard [shall be considered a violation of decorum]. **1871** BAGG *At Yale* 27 Besides the fourteen buildings already described, the only others within the yard . . . were the two wooden dwelling-houses. **1902** [see GOLD COAST 4].

*2. A pen or similar enclosure for animals.

See also CATTLE YARD, CHICKEN YARD, etc.

1637 *Dedham Rec.* 28 In ye greate Iland under ye Rocke shall a yard be paled in for Swyne. **1643** WILLIAMS *Key* (1866) 118 If man provide eke for his Birds, In Yard, in Coops, in Cage. **1772** *Huntington Rec.* II. 515 All People that have sheep on the Commons should attend to search & Drive the same into Yard. **1884** ROE *Nature's Story* 59 It does not often happen in the country that fowls are restricted to a narrow yard or run.

+b. An enclosure for animals which are to be shipped or slaughtered for meat. Often pl.

See also STOCKYARD.

1865 *Atlantic Mo.* Jan. 83/2 The average weekly expenditure by butchers at the New York yards during the year 1863 was $328,865. **1868** [see FIRE PLUG]. **1879** *Cimarron News & Press* 27 Nov. 3/2 The company will at once build suitable yards at Dorsey station.

*3. A piece of ground, with or without buildings, set apart for some specific purpose or business: (see also quot. 1891).

See also ARTILLERY YARD, BRICKYARD, etc.

1798 in Hawkins *Letters* 495 Mr. Cornell did not chuse for him to work in his yard [of a smithy]. **1851** *Polly Peablossom* 121 Mr. T. incidentally mentioned the bursting of a steamboat at his yard. **1891** W. K. BROOKS *Oyster* 131 Around each claire is built a levee or dirt wall called a yard. . . . This yard retains the water filling the basin. **1905** *Forestry Bureau Bul.* No. 61, 41 *Landing*, . . . a place to which logs are hauled or skidded preparatory to transportation by water or rail. . . . [Also called] log dump, rollway, yard.

b. On a railroad, an area of track, switches, buildings, etc., near a station or terminus. {1903} Also *railroad yard*. Often pl.

See also FREIGHT YARD.

1877 McCABE *Hist. Great Riots* 32 The Federal troops took possession of the railroad yards and property at Martinsburg. **1883** FULTON *Sam Hobart* 40 The skill acquired in the yard . . . enabled him to move out of the depot quickly and stop at the stations without a jar. **1924** J. TULLY *Beggars of Life* 56, I hears 'em talkin' in the yards.

4. In a forest, a place where moose or deer herd, esp. in winter. {1829-, in Canada}

See also DEER YARD, MOOSE-YARD.

1834 AUDUBON *Ornith. Biog.* II. 431 A moose . . . had been driven from its haunt or yard by Indians. **1839** HOFFMAN *Wild Scenes* 59 A yard with three moose in it . . . was discovered. **1893** ROOSEVELT *Wilderness Hunter* 223 A 'yard' is . . . the spot which a moose has chosen for its winter home. **1902** WHITE *Blazed Trail* 323 The deer, herded together, tramped 'yards' where the feed was good.

5. *attrib.* **a.** In senses 1 and 2 with *bar, door, fence*, etc.

1809 A. HENRY *Travels* 79 Behind the yard-door of my own house . . . there was a low fence. **1831** PECK *Guide* 160 It then requires an annual dressing of stable or yard manure. **1835** BIRD *Hawks* II. 166 An axe and a few crowbars . . . might soon make way through the yard-gate. **1849** LANMAN *Lett. Alleghany Mts.* 145 He even went so far . . . as to consume for fire wood . . . the top most rail of his yard-fence. **1868** *Iowa State Agric. Soc. Rep.* 1867 187 Along the yard-walks, against the side of the house, stable or shed, . . . they plant the vine. **1868** A. D. WHITNEY *P. Strong* 10 Everybody's little yard-room opens into all out-doors. **1869** — *Hitherto* xi, The lowing of cattle at their yard-bars. **1879** *Diseases of Swine* 214, Yard hogs—*i.e.*, that are fed on dish-water and kitchen slops— seldom or never take the cholera. **1885** *Century Mag.* June 294/1, I saw an officer leaning over the yard-paling.

b. In sense 3 b with *boss, conductor, crew*, etc.

1877 McCABE *Hist. Great Riots* 77 Two yard crews . . . refused [to take out the train], and were discharged. **1887** *Courier-Journal* May 9/3 The yard officer came around and told him he would have to leave the yards.

1891 C. ROBERTS *Adrift Amer.* 93 The brakesman was standing by to couple the cars that the yard engine was backing down on to the rest of the train. *Ib.* 144, I went at once to the yard-boss asking him for a job. **1898** *Engineering Mag.* XVI. 67 With the ordinary yard-handling of, say, an army corps, . . . trains *en route* . . . must be held back. **1909** *Cent. Suppl.* 1458/3 *Yard-locomotive*, . . . a locomotive specially designed to operate in the station- or terminal-yards of a railway for making up and distributing trains.

Yard, *v.* [f. YARD *n.*] See also YARDING.

'Colonial' and *U.S.*' (*O.E.D.*).

1. *tr.* To enclose (cattle or other animals) in a yard or pen. {1855-}

1758 *Essex Inst. Coll.* XII. 140 The Dutch here have a nasty practice of yarding their cows in ye Street before their doors. **1863** RANDALL *Pract. Shepherd* 141 In the northern regions . . . sheep are yarded and fed only on dry feed in winter. **1874** *Vermont Bd. Agric. Rep.* II. 195 One and perhaps the great cause of the impoverishment of our cow pastures is that we yard our cows nights.

+2. To pile or store *up* (wood) in a yard or on a landing.

1878 *Lumberman's Gaz.* 12 Jan. 35/3 The logs . . . have been yarded or piled up in the woods during the fall. [**1903** *Windsor Mag.* Sept. 405/2 [Beavers] commence to build their houses and yard-up wood for the winter in September.]

3. *intr.* **a.** Of a moose or deer: To occupy a yard. (See YARD *n.* 4). Also with *up.*

1852 H. W. HERBERT *Field Sports* (ed. 4) II. 199 Here it [*sc.* the moose] still breeds, and yards in winter. **1878** *Scribner's Mo.* Feb. 453/1 The bull moose never yards with the females and young. **1894** *Century Mag.* Jan. 354/2 [Moose] do not . . . yard up until the deep snow comes.

b. Of domestic live stock: To occupy a yard or pen.

1861 *Ill. Agric. Soc. Trans.* IV. 399 [Cattle and swine] yarding together when the latter are not with pig.

Yardage. The use of a yard or enclosure, or the charge made for this. Also attrib. — **1868** *Ill. Agric. Soc. Trans.* VI. 322 Net cash receipts for yardage, and profit on feed, 1866. **1889** *Public Opinion* 16 Feb., The furnace-master paying the company yardage at the rate of 25 cents per ton. **1903** ADAMS *Log of Cowboy* 201, I'll not ship any more cattle to your town, . . . until you adjust your yardage charges.

Yard grass. Any one of various grasses growing in yards {1848, in Barbados}, +esp. the crab grass, *Eleusine indica.* — **1822** WOODS *English Prairie* 199 Yard-grass comes on land that has been much trodden; it is something like cock's-foot-grass. **1847** DARLINGTON *Weeds & Plants* 378 Yard Grass. . . . Cattle and hogs are fond of it. **1850** [see QUITCH GRASS]. **1901** MOHR *Plant Life Ala.* 135 Far the largest part of the cultivated fields, however, is left to a luxuriant growth of weedy grasses, chiefly . . . yard grasses.

Yarding. 1. The action, in various senses, of YARD *v.* {1865-} Also attrib. +**2.** (See quotation.) +**3.** (See quotation.) — (1) **1699** *Huntington Rec.* II. 246 Ye said thomas Ketcham Doth Reserve yarding Roome forever for to fodder his cattle in ye winter time. **1887** *Harper's Mag.* Feb. 458/1 By the end of November the bulls [*i.e.*, moose] forsake the cows, and move for high land. . . . They locate on north-west faces of the highest mountains the country affords. This is 'yarding.' (2) **1840** BUEL *Farmer's Companion* 315 Summer yarding, stuff carted into the yard, and trodden by the cattle, for manure. (3) **1887** H. HALL, etc. *Tribune Book of Sports* 432 'Pot-hunters' have other methods of shooting the Adirondack deer, such as 'yarding' . . . , [in which] the deer are traced to their winter herding grounds and are then shot down.

+Yard limit. (See quot. 1891.) Also attrib. — **1891** *Cent.* 7010/1 *Yard-limit*, . . . on a railway, the extreme end of the yard-space occupied by sidings and switches: usually indicated by a sign beside the track. **1898** *McClure's Mag.* X. 306 [The] switch to the outward or down-hill track . . . came under the 'yard-limit' rule. **1917** MATHEWSON *Sec. Base Sloan* 13 Beyond the bridge a 'Yard Limit' sign met them.

*Yardman. {1819-, *dial.*} A man working in a railroad yard. {1889 (*Electrical Rev.* XXV. 432/1)} Also *yardsman.* {1888} — **1877** BARTLETT 769 *Yardsman*, a man employed in the yard of a railroad station. **1878** PINKERTON *Strikers* 221 Up to this time the movement had been almost entirely controlled by such brakemen and yardmen as had been inveigled into the Trainmen's Union.

+Yardmaster. On a railroad, an official in charge of a yard. — **1872** *Newton Kansan* 10 Oct. 3/3 W. W. Fagan . . . was busy . . . introducing the new officials, . . . Geo. McCutcheon, yard-master [etc.]. **1877** McCABE *Hist. Great Riots* 346 The yard-master of the Erie division has seemed to be very slow. **1895** *Chicago Strike of 1894* 101, [I] have been a switchman, brakesman, yard master, and freight conductor.

Yardsman. (See YARDMAN.)

+Yardstick.

1. A rule or similar device one yard in length, used in measuring. {1883, in special sense}

1816 PICKERING 206 *Yard-wand* . . . is still sometimes used, by *old* people, for what we now call a *yard-stick.* **1843** *Knickerb.* XXII. 111 The shop-keeper was there with his yard-stick. **1872** 'MARK TWAIN' *Roughing It* 32 He lays his long ears down on his back, straightens himself out like a yardstick. **1907** *St. Nicholas* June 735 She's sure that the yardsticks buy shoes for their feet.

b. *fig.* A standard or measure.

1844 EMERSON *Miscellanies* 352 The railroad . . . has great value as a sort of yard-stick, and surveyor's line. **1878** *N. Amer. Rev.* CXXVI. 507 Senator Thurman was content to measure the Bland Bill with the yard-stick of the constitutional lawyer.

c. In quasi-adverbial use.

1884 'MARK TWAIN' *H. Finn* xl, She was just in a sweat about every little thing that wasn't yard-stick straight.

2. In various figurative expressions.

1848 MITCHELL *Nantucketisms* 42 'He looks as if he had swallowed a yard stick.' Stiff, reserved. **1870** 'F. FERN' *Ginger-Snaps* 72, I know of a merchant, helplessly fastened to the yardstick, who should be an editor. **1887** TOURGEE *Button's Inn* 133 Now you're talking by the yardstick. . . . If you only had nerve to practise what you preach!

* Yarn.

* 1. Spun fiber, as for use in weaving; a strand made of loosely twisted threads, as for knitting. Also with defining terms.

See also COTTON YARN.

1644 *Conn. Rec.* I. 104 By reson of the badnes and rottennes of much yarne . . . many weauers are discouridged. **1686** *Narragansett Hist. Reg.* III. 104 Woolen yarn & cotton wool. **1751** MACSPARRAN *Diary* 64, I wrote a Letter at her Request to Mrs. Wilkinson to go with Stocking yarn. **1768** *Boston Gazette* 9 May (Ernst), The young Women of the Pres-byterian Congregation . . . generously gave Mrs. Parsons the spinning of two Hundred and seventy Skeins of good Yarn. **1800** [see BARN-FLOOR]. **1845** JUDD *Margaret* I. 29 She's as bad as a hang-bird that steals my yarn on the grass. **1893** *Harper's Mag.* April 805/1 Her ball of yarn had fallen to the floor. **1919** HOUGH *Sagebrusher* 23 She still had in her hands the long knitting needles, [and] the ball of yellowish yarn.

b. *Paper yarn*, (see quotation).

1909 *Cent. Suppl.* 1458/3 *Paper yarn*, yarn made from cellulose fiber con-verted into flat strips and spun or twisted.

2. *attrib.* *** a.** Designating articles of clothing made of yarn.

1705 *Boston News-Letter* 10 Dec. 4/2 He has on . . . black breeches, gray yarn Stockings, a black hat almost new. **1775** *Essex Inst. Coll.* XLIII. 95 [He] had a dark coloured Yarn Cap on. **1857** STROTHER *Vir-ginia* 130 Crayon's supply of yarn socks were distributed round to serve as overshoes. **1898** E. C. HALL *Aunt Jane* 19 She had on her old black poke-bonnet and some black yarn mitts.

b. *Yarn basket*, a basket for yarn.

1878 STOWE *Poganuc People* 112 He had been known to upset all Miss Cushing's nicely arranged yarn-baskets.

Yarn-spinner. {1813–} *** 1.** *Polit.* ?One who engages in manipu-lations in order to introduce illegal votes. *slang.* **2.** A teller of yarns or stories. *colloq.* — (1) **1840** *Richmond Enquirer* Nov. (Th.), The profuse use of gold, corruption of the franchise by pipe layers and yarn spinners, . . . have conspired to elect W. H. Harrison. (2) **1865** A. D. WHITNEY *Gayworthys* 252 'Oh, I'm no yarn-spinner,' said the young Captain, eva-sively. **1883** *Harper's Mag.* Jan. 323/2 The story was 'improved' by the marine yarn-spinners of that port. **1911** ROLT-WHEELER *Boy with Census* 185 If Meacham had been as good a farmer as a yarn-spinner there would have been no question as to his success.

* Yarrow. =MILFOIL. Also attrib. — **1622** 'MOURT' *Relation* 62 We found here in Winter, . . . Sorrell, Yarow, Caruell [etc.]. **1709** [see MUL-LEIN]. **1784** *Amer. Acad. Mem.* I. 483 Yarrow. Blossoms white. **1836** EDWARD *Hist. Texas* 42 [A] few examples [of the herb varieties] are the water-cresses, and the yarrow-root. **1878** WHITMAN *Spec. Days* 123 These perennial blossoms and friendly weeds [include] . . . yarrow, coreopsis, wild pea.

+ Yarrup. =FLICKER. — **1865** [see FLICKER]. **1893** *Scribner's Mag.* June 773/2 The flicker has a long array of names, many of them, like flicker, clape, wake-up, yarrup, etc., . . . derived from his notes. **1917** *Birds of Amer.* II. 164/2 Another person has heard the bird calling its *Yarrup-yarrup* while flying about . . . in quest of food; hence the com-mon name of Yarrup.

Yaup, *n.* and *v.* (See YAWP *n.* and YAWP *v.*)

+ Yaupon. Also *yop(p)on, yapon,* etc. [Catawba *yo-pún* 'a little bush.']

1. A holly (*Ilex vomitoria*) of the southern states; a plant related to this.

1709 LAWSON *Carolina* 90 This *Yaupon*, call'd by the South-Carolina Indians, *Cassena*, is a Bush, that grows chiefly on the Sand Banks and Islands. **1775** [see CASSINE 1 (b).]. **1836** HOLLEY *Texas* 88 Among these the Yawpan or tea tree deserves a special notice. **1860** DARLINGTON *Weeds & Plants* 217 One of our own southern species, *I. Cassine,* known as Yau-pon, furnished the black drink of the North Carolina Indians. **1897** SUD-WORTH *Arborescent Flora* 278 *Ilex cassine.* Dahoon. . . . [Also called] Yau-pon (Fla.). *Ib.* 279 *Ilex vomitoria.* Yaupon. . . . [Also called] Yopon (N.C., Ga., Ala., Miss., Tex.). Yaupon (N.C., S.C., Fla., Miss., La.).

attrib. **1837** WILLIAMS *Florida* 29 Scrub oaks and yapon bushes, tangled with vines, form impenetrable thickets. **1901** MOHR *Plant Life Ala.* 45 The following species form . . . thickets more or less free from larger trees: . . . *Ilex vomitoria* (yaupon holly).

2. =YAUPON TEA.

1709 LAWSON *Carolina* 221 As for Purging and Emeticks . . . they never apply themselves to, unless in drinking vast Quantities of their *Yaupon* or Tea. **1790** FRENEAU *Poems* (1809) II. 205 We left this dreary place, Nor staid to drink their dear Yoppon.

+ Yaupon tea. A beverage prepared from the leaves of the yaupon. — **1737** BRICKELL *N. Carolina* 319 They drink great quantities of *Yaupan Tea.* **1895** *Advance* 19 Dec. 909/1 The very sight of that horrid yupon and sassafras tea makes me fairly sick.

Yaw-haw, *v. intr.* To laugh loudly. — **1835–7** HALIBURTON *Clock-maker* 1 Ser. xix. 169, I had to pucker up my mouth . . . to keep from yawhawin in her face. **1836** *Knickerb.* VII. 21 'T would be too bad . . . [to be] laughed at . . . by every yaw-hawing land-loafer.

Yawl, *n.*

1. A ship's small boat; any one of various kinds of sailing boats. {1670–}

1732 *S.C. Gazette* 8 April, They came up with him & demanded his Yawl out. **1742** *Essex Inst. Coll.* XLV. 338 The Long Boat yawl & booms [were] driving from side to side of the ship. **1824** DEWEES *Lett. from Texas* 50 An old gentleman . . . in company with two Mexicans, had coasted round in a yawl, to the mouth of the Colorado. **1845** *Cincinnati Misc.* I. 125/1 The yawl . . . was sent out ahead with a coil of rope. **1881** *Ore. State Jrnl.* 1 Jan. 2/4 The seas swept your decks and carried off your yawl at the davits. **1897** *Outing* XXX. 113/1 The *Wanderer* was a sixteen-foot yawl.

2. Attrib. with *boat, duty, skiff.*

1800 *Columbian Centinel* 1 Jan. 3/3 Picked up a Yawl Boat. **1865** *At-lantic Mo.* May 546/1 He lay on the wet floor of a yawl skiff. **1876** 'MARK TWAIN' *Tom Sawyer* xv, He crept down the bank . . . and climbed into the skiff that did 'yawl' duty at the boat's stern.

Yawl, *v. tr.* To convey in a yawl. — **1884** 'MARK TWAIN' *H. Finn* xxiv, When we got to the village they yawled us ashore.

Yawp, Yaup, *n.* {1824–} **+** Useless talk; unjustified criticism. Often contemptuous. *colloq.²* — **1835** INGRAHAM *South-West* I. 29 Hold your yaup, you youngster you. **1864** TROWBRIDGE *Cudjo's Cave* 18 You better shet your yaup, and be a bringin' that ar kittle. **1884** *Gringo & Greaser* 1 Jan. 1/1 The old darky-fraud . . . found plenty of fools to listen to her apish harangues and to swallow her silly yawp. **1904** *Buffalo Com-mercial* 25 Aug. 6 The insincere and ridiculous yawp about the fierce belligerency of Theodore Roosevelt will be laid away.

* Yawp, *v. intr.* To talk loudly or blatantly; to shout abuse *at. colloq.²* Also as *ppl. a.* and *vbl. n.* — **1872** S. HALE *Letters* 90 Perhaps it is just as well, however, not to yawp much about our going *alone.* **1884** NYE *Baled Hay* 56 Their relatives . . . lifted up their yawp and yawped at them. **1887** *Courier-Journal* 21 June 4/1 The yawping scribblers of the Bloody Shirt . . . are the basest, the meanest, the most cowardly traitors and bullies who ever lived. **1899** M. ROBERTSON *Where Angels Fear* (1921) 96 It's just this same yawping at one another in the forecastles that makes it easy for the buckoes aft to hunt you.

+ Yawpan. (See YAUPON.)

+ Yazoo. *attrib.* [Of unknown origin.] Used with reference to the sale (1795) by Georgia, under a contract later rescind-ed as fraudulent, of lands near the Yazoo River, and to the subsequent legal claims of the purchasers against the United States government.

1796 *Aurora* (Phila.) 5 Dec. (Th.), The Yazoo men (as they are called in this place [Savannah, Ga.]) were making every exertion to prevent General Jackson from being elected a representative. **1805** *Ann. 8th Con-gress* 2 Sess. 1148 The Legislature of Georgia . . . made the fraudulent and villanous contract with the Yazoo speculators of 1795. *Ib.* 1156, I shall now proceed to a brief investigation of the legality of the Yazoo claims. *Ib.,* Now, if the sale to the Yazoo companies was just and valid, . . . any subsequent purchase by Congress must be invalid. *Ib.* 1169 He inferred that the Yazoo act of 1795 was as justifiable as any grant ever made by that State. *Ib.* 1171, I hope he will not, lest the red dragon should devour him, as well as his brethren, the Yazoo claimants. **1806** *Balance* V. 37/3 Only seven or eight of Randolph's Yazoo friends clung to him. **1808** *Ann. 10th Congress* 1 Sess. 1279 To grant the Yazoo country to speculators? **1850** BUCKINGHAM *Newspaper Lit.* II. 203 A three-act comedy, called 'The Georgia Spec, or Land in the Moon,' . . . censured the wickedness of the speculators in what was called the Yazoo purchase.

* Yea.

1. An affirmative vote. {1657–1781}

1774 [see NAY]. **1811** *Niles' Reg.* I. 205/2 The question was decided as follows: Yeas.—Messrs. Anderson, Archer [etc.]. **1886** LOGAN *Great Con-spiracy* 394 The vote on its passage in the Senate was 29 yeas to 14 nays.

2. *Yeas and nays,* used with reference to the longest and most elaborate method of taking a vote in American parlia-mentary procedure: (see quot. 1903). Also attrib. in sing.

1790 STEELE *P.* I. 65, I have opposed this bill in every stage of its passage and tomorrow will have the yeas and nays on the last reading. **1854** BENTON *30 Years' View* I. 204/2 Mr. Webster called for the vote, and to be taken by yeas and nays. **1900** *Congress. Rec.* 11 Jan. 782/2, I trust the Senator will not demand a yea-and-nay vote at this hour in the afternoon. **1903** HART *Actual Govt.* 252 More formal is vote by yeas and nays, in which the clerk calls the roll and each member as his name is called answers 'aye' or 'no.' The importance of the yeas and nays is that they are recorded in the journals.

*Year. *Year in (and) year out,* year after year. {1881} — **1830** *Mass. Spy* 28 July (Th.), I've been at school year in and year out. **1868** ALCOTT *Little Women* I. 203 You see other girls having splendid times, while you grind, grind, year in and year out. **1910** *N.Y. Ev. Post* 7 March (Th.), Year in, year out, these tasters of literature appraise the motley flux.

Yearling tick. One of the stages in the development of a tick. — **1863** [see STAR 3 b]. **1869** *Amer. Naturalist* III. 51 When ready for a new meal or a new transformation (now called 'yearling ticks'), they again ascend bushes.

*Yeast. Attrib. and comb. with *bottle, brewing, cart,* etc.
1851 *Harper's Mag.* July 283/2 A lady . . . was awakened in the night by the bursting of a yeast bottle. **1852** EASTMAN *Aunt Phillis's Cabin* 47 The cork that is lifting itself from the jug standing on it, belongs to the yeast department. **1854** *Penna. Agric. Rep.* 141 It too frequently happens that a watchful care of the yeast pot is neglected. **1864** STOWE *House & Home P.* 234 The daughters of New England have abandoned the old respectable mode of yeast-brewing and bread-raising. **1869** — *Oldtown Folks* 270 She dared to peep into her yeast-jug at the very moment of projection. **1880** *Harper's Mag.* Dec. 85/1 'Gosh!' said old Israel Tucker, jogging along in his yeast cart. **1898** HARPER *S. B. Anthony* I. 160 In those days . . . the process of yeast-making was long and difficult.

Yeast bread. Bread raised with yeast. — **1864** STOWE *House & Home P.* 226 There was really nothing to eat! . . . Sour yeast-bread,— . . . strong butter! **1883** *Rep. Indian Affairs* 115 Most of the young women of this tribe have learned . . . to make sweet yeast bread, from hop yeast. **1898** NICHOLAS *Idyl of Wabash* 6 They don't know how to make yeast bread.

*Yell, *n.*

+1. =INDIAN WHOOP.
1796 S. HASTINGS *Captivity of Mrs. Johnson* 21 They then, with a true savage yell, gave the war whoop. **1812** MARSHALL *Kentucky* 51 The effect . . . was augmented tenfold by the yell, and the war whoop. **1840** *Knickerb.* XVI. 45 They were startled by the well known yell of the Indians. **1870** KEIM *Sheridan's Troopers* 52 With yells, and violent gestures, on came the surging savage hord[e]s.

+2. A cheer, rhythmical and having a fixed order of syllables, shouted in chorus by college students. Also transf.
1890 *St. Nicholas* Aug. 837/2 The young men . . . are giving the mountain calls or 'yells,' cries adopted [for the different resort hotels] according to the well-known college custom. **1903** *N.Y. Ev. Post* 30 Sept. 2 The students sang the college song and gave the 'varsity yell from the steps of the library.

+3. (See quotation.) More fully *cattle yell.*
1914 'BOWER' *Flying U Ranch* 219 He fired again and again, and gave the range-old cattle-yell; the yell which had sent many a tired herd over many a weary mile.

+4. *Southern yell,* =REBEL YELL.
1864 POLLARD *So. Hist. of War: 3d Year* 89 Our men . . . gave a Southern yell in response to the Yankee cheer.

*Yell, *v.* Of an Indian: To utter a characteristic cry or whoop. Also *vbl. n.* — **1736** GYLES *Mem. Captivity* 2 The Yelling of the Indians . . . terrified me. **1823** JAMES *Exped.* I. 127 The Indians collected around the fire in the centre of the lodge, yelling incessantly. **1856** GLISAN *Jrnl. Army Life* 302 Some Indians . . . commenced whooping and yelling. **1885** *Rep. Indian Affairs* 79 The frightened and desperate animals . . . [are] pursued by from one to a dozen savages, yelling, whooping, and firing their guns.

*Yellow, *n.* Also *colloq.*[2] **yeller.**

+1. *pl.* =PEACH YELLOWS.
1846 LOWELL *Biglow P.* 1 Ser. i. 9 Like a peach thet's got the yellers. **1851** BARRY *Fruit Garden* 363 The Yellows in the Peach . . . exhibits itself in a yellow, sickly foliage, feeble shoots, and small fruits prematurely ripened. [**1862** *Rep. Comm. Patents 1861: Agric.* 543 Diseases called 'yellow,' and cracking of the bark, destroy the [peach and cherry] trees.] **1886** *Harper's Mag.* June 48/2, I can almost taste the yellows in much of the fruit bought in market.

+2. *fig.* Cowardice. *slang.*
1896 ADE *Artie* 57 This is how I found the streak o' yellow in him. **1914** 'BOWER' *Flying U Ranch* 146 Honest to grandma, I was just b'ginnin' to think this bunch was gitting all streaked up with yeller.

3. *pl.* Publications depending for effect upon the exploitation of sensational aspects of the news. *colloq.*
[**1898** *Daily News* (London) 27 July 5/7 This deliberate attempt to stir up animosities . . . is worthy of 'the yellows' at their worst.] **1903** *N.Y. Times Sat. Rev.* 7 Nov. 796 A pretty Southern widow who did newspaper work for the yellows.

*4. Something of a yellow color. **+a.** Gold. **+b.** A yellow poker chip.
(a) 1901 RYAN *Montana* 227 She would watch some strange miner dig and wash the soil in his search for the precious 'yellow.' **(b) 1908** LORIMER *J. Spurlock* 184 Each time I would find . . . that his stack of yellows had a new bay-window or cupola on it.

*Yellow, *a.* Also *colloq.*[2] **yeller, yallow, yaller.**

I. 1. Of a person: Having a light brown or yellowish skin {1834-}; +of mulatto or quadroon blood.
See also YELLOW BOY 2, GIRL, WOMAN.
1814 *Niles' Reg.* VII. 284/2 The owner, a yellow man, not liking to lose his all without a struggle, made for a small creek. **1834** CARRUTHERS *Kentuckian* I. 22 It used to make me laugh to see the yallow raskals sculpin their kin. **1850** M. REID *Rifle Rangers* I. 146 Yellow fellows [Mexicans]. **1867** LOCKE *Swingin' Round* 287 The per cent. uv yeller niggers in this State attests how faithful Kentucky hez bin. **1898** DUNBAR *Folks from Dixie* 38 He's one o' dese little yaller men, an' you know dey kin be powahful contra'y.

b. Used, often with *peril,* with reference to Chinese or Oriental influence {1892-}, +esp. with reference to immigration to the United States.
1876 W. M. FISHER *Californians* 62 Even as far east as Massachusetts the advancing yellow wave is creating a 'bore' in the mouth of some of the largest white rivers of trade. *Ib.,* Men laughed a long time at the *ifs* advanced regarding 'the negro question.' . . . The yellow comedy has now the boards as a kind of after-piece. **1904** *Forum* Jan. 460 The far-seeing statesmen of Europe . . . have dreaded the approach . . . of a coming 'Yellow Peril.' **1914** *Cycl. Amer. Govt.* I. 262/1 The 'Yellow Peril' Period (1871–1898).

+2. Used of sensational books and magazines issued in inexpensive form, as in yellow covers.
See also YELLOW COVER 2.
1855 'CARLTON' *New Purchase* (ed. 2) 3 Although published near the noon of the Yellow Literature Day, the First Edition of the Work was all immediately sold.

+3. *Yellow behind the gills,* having fever and ague. *colloq.*
1878 BEADLE *Western Wilds* 26 He was, in local phrase, 'yaller behind the gills.'

II. In fig. and transferred senses. **+4.** Mean-spirited; cowardly; of poor quality; false. *slang.*
1856 in Barnum *Struggles* 400 Though you thought our minds were green, We never thought your heart was yellow. **1896** ADE *Artie* 8 It was a yellow show, and I'm waitin' for forty-five cents change. **1901** NORRIS *Octopus* 123 This business we talked over to-night—I'm out of it. It's yellow. **1922** PARRISH *Case & Girl* 335 The whole outfit is yellow.

+5. *Baseball.* Of a game, a play, or a player: Of poor quality, as if because of fear or nervousness. *colloq.*
1890 *N.Y. Press* 6 July (E. J. Nichols). **1907** *McClure's Mag.* April 684/1 Outside of a few what Billy designated 'yellow' plays . . . [the game] was a good one.

+6. Of newspapers or journals, singly or collectively: Characterized by sensationalism.
Said to have been suggested by the experimental use of yellow color printing in 1895 in a cartoon ('The Yellow Kid') in the *New York World.* (See also YELLOW JOURNAL.)
[**1898** *Daily News* (London) 2 March 7/2 The yellow Press is for a war with Spain, at all costs.] **1904** *Brooklyn Eagle* 31 May 4 The yellowness of yellow papers consists in their falsehoods, their sensations, their brag, their vulgarity. **1907** FIELD *Six-Cylinder Courtship* 58 Rooker was city editor of the yellowest morning newspaper published in New York!

+b. Of a writer or publisher: Connected in some way with yellow journals; unscrupulously sensational in method.
1902 PHILLIPS *Woman Ventures* 248 Gammell was a sensationalist— 'the yellowest yet.' [**1906** *Times* (London, wkly. ed.) 9 Nov. 714 The President of the United States sent his Secretary of State to New York to throw the whole weight of Mr. Roosevelt's . . . authority and influence against the 'yellow' candidate [sc. Hearst].] **1909** *N.Y. Ev. Post* (s.-w ed.) 15 Feb. 4 Our morals are . . . under the management . . . of yellow editors.

III. In specific names.
Only a selection of examples is given.

7. Of plants.
See also YELLOW ASH, YELLOW BIRCH, etc.
1738 W. STEPHENS *Proc. Georgia* I. 200, I planted almost wholly with that yellow Corn. **1784** *Amer. Acad. Mem.* I. 473 *Trifolium.* . . . The indigenous species [include] . . . The Red Honeysuckle. The Yellow Clover. **1812** STODDARD *Sk. Louisiana* 161 No other wood than white and yellow cypress, was sawed. a**1817** DWIGHT *Travels* I. 81 Even the proper maize of New-England, commonly styled the *yellow flint corn,* . . . [yields] but an indifferent harvest. **1817-8** EATON *Botany* (1822) 486 *Thlaspi campestre,* yellow-seed, false-flax, . . . was probably introduced with flax-seed. **1824** IRVING *Tales of Traveller* I. 251 He had been watching a lark . . . rising from a bed of daisies and yellow-cups. **1847** DARLINGTON *Weeds & Plants* 197 C[irsium] horridulum. . . . Yellow Thistle. . . . A rugged and repulsive plant, which is very common on the seashore. **1891** *Cent.* 7015/2 *Yellow cypress,* a tree, Chamæcyparis Nutkaensis, of northwestern North America, . . . is somewhat used in boat- and ship-building. . . . Also *Sitka cypress, yellow cedar.* **1891** *Amer. Folk-Lore* IV. 147 The only Buttercup we then knew . . . we called *Yellow Daisy.* **1892** *Ib.* V. 104 *Erythronium Americanum,* yellow bells.

b. In combination with adjectives in *-ed*.

See also YELLOW-BARK(ED) OAK, YELLOW-EYED GRASS, YELLOW-FRUITED *a*.

1738 W. STEPHENS *Proc. Georgia* I. 200 The Failure of a Crop . . . was principally owing to that yellow skin'd Corn. **1806** SHECUT *Flora Carolinæensis* I. 106 *Æ[sculus] Flava*, Yellow flowered Horse Chesnut, . . . a native of the western parts of Pennsylvania, and Virginia. **1817–8** EATON *Botany* (1822) 334 *Leptanthus gramineus*, yellow-eyed water grass.

8. Of birds.

See also YELLOWBACK 1, YELLOWBELLY 2, etc.

1709 LAWSON *Carolina* 146 These Yellow-Wings are a very small Bird, of a Linnet's Colour, but Wings as yellow as Gold. **1748** CATESBY *Carolina* II. p. xxxvi, Land-Birds which breed and abide in Carolina in the Summer, and retire in Winter [include] . . . the yellow Titmouse, the purple Martin. **1838** J. HALL *Statistics of West* 124 The yellow plover frequents the prairies in the spring. **1868** *Amer. Naturalist* II. 494 The farmers of Kansas are under great obligations to the little yellow-heads. **1917** *Birds of Amer.* III. 162 Yellow-breasted Chat. *Icteria virens virens*. . . . [Also called] Yellow Mockingbird.

b. In combination with adjectives in *-ed*.

See also *yellow-backed warbler* (under YELLOW-BACKED *a*. 1), YELLOW-BELLIED *a*., etc.

[**1758** G. EDWARDS *Gleanings Nat. Hist.* I. 49/1 The Yellow-faced Parakeet . . . has a long and pointed tail.] **1839** PEABODY *Mass. Birds* 324 The Yellow Shouldered Sparrow, *Fringilla Canadensis*, arrives from the north at the approach of winter. **1887** RIDGWAY *Manuel N.A. Birds* 7 Western Arctic America and northeastern Asia. . . . *U[rinator] adamsii*. . . . Yellow-billed Loon.

9. Of fishes and other animals.

See also YELLOWBACK 3, YELLOW BASS, etc.

1778 CARVER *Travels* 479 The Rattle Snake. There appears to be two species of this reptile; one of which is commonly termed the Black, and the other the Yellow. **1782** CRÈVECŒUR *Letters* 43 The yellow wasps, which build under ground, in our meadows, are much more to be dreaded. **1814** MITCHILL *Fishes N.Y.* 382 Yellow scorpaena, *Scorpaena flava*, . . . resembles the bullheads by his large mouth. **1815** DRAKE *Cincinnati* 141 Yellow-cat and sword-fish are most esteemed. **1835** SIMMS *Yemassee* I. 191 [The young chief can] rise to strike him in the heel like the yellow-belly moccasin. **1836** KIRTLAND in *Ohio Geol. Survey* 169 *Noturus flavus*, . . . Yellow-back-tail. **1838** *S. Lit. Messenger* IV. 25/1 The yellow flies and moschetoes swarmed in myriads. **1856** *Rep. Comm. Patents 1855: Agric.* 83 The Yellow Caterpillar. . . . Found on the cotton-plant in September and October. **1856** *Porter's Spirit of Times* 20 Sept. 40/3 The Pike-perch, *Lucioperca Americana*, . . . [is known as] the Yellow Pike. **1877** Yellow sponge [see WOOL *n*. 3 d]. **1884** GOODE, etc. *Fisheries* I. 362 About Buzzard's Bay and in the vicinity the largest [of the squeteagues], are known as 'Yellow-fins.' *Ib.* 421 At Cleveland and Dover, Ohio, this species [the wall-eyed pike] is known as 'Yellow Pickerel.' **1909** STRATTON-PORTER *Girl of Limberlost* 188 On the day she added these big Yellow Emperors she would get a check for three hundred dollars.

b. In combination with adjectives in *-ed*.

See also *yellow-backed rockfish* (under YELLOW-BACKED *a*. 4), YELLOW-BELLIED *a*., YELLOW-TAILED *a*.

1842 *Nat. Hist. N.Y., Zoology* IV. 85 The Yellow-finned Red-mouth, *Hemulon chrysopteron*, . . . [is] highly prized as food. **1842** *Ib.* I. 90 The Yellow-cheeked Meadow-Mouse, *Arvicola Xanthognathus*, . . . burrows in banks. **1868** *Amer. Naturalist* II. 533 Yellow-footed Marmot (*Arctomys flaviventer?*). **1882** *Nat. Museum Bul.* No. 16, 576 *U[mbrina] roncador*. . . . Yellow-finned Roncador. **1891** *Cent.* 7016/3 The yellow-necked caterpillar, the larva of a common North American bombycid moth, *Datana ministra*, which feeds in communities on the foliage of apple, hickory, and walnut in the United States.

IV. +10. In miscellaneous special combinations and phrases.

Yellow Day, (see quotation); *y. dip*, crude turpentine allowed to remain all winter in the box on the tree; *y. dust*, =GOLD DUST; *y. iron*, (see quotation); *Yellowknife*, an Indian of a Canadian tribe formerly noted for manufacturing and selling large numbers of copper knives; *y. pepper*, spiteful or sharp-tongued comment; *y. slip*, (see quotation); *y. streak*, a cowardly or treacherous strain in a person's character; *y. tobacco*, a high grade of tobacco; *y. water*, a disease of horses.

1881 *Harper's Mag.* Dec. 944/1 [On] the 'yellow day' of 1881 in America . . . the sun rose clear, but within an hour the moist air . . . seemed to thicken into a heavy screen of mist, that . . . was of a strange yellow hue. **1859** G. W. PERRY *Turpentine Farming* 123 'Yellow dip' . . . makes more spirits than any other turpentine. **1905** BEACH *Pardners* 25 When the river broke we cleaned up one hundred and eighty-seven dollars' worth of lovely, yellow dust. **1875** *Chicago Tribune* 21 Aug. 5/5 The Indians cannot be made to believe that all the prospect-holes in Custer Gulch have not yielded a large amount of yellow iron, as they call the gold. [**1870** DALL *Alaska* 429 *The Âh-tenâ* . . . have been called . . . *Yellow Knife*, or Nehâunee, by the English.] **1850** *Knickerb.* XXXVI. 73 The feeling that she seasons too liberally with her 'yellow pepper,' prevails with those who know her and her ways. **1900** NELSON *A B C Wall St.* 154 The news slips of the New York News Bureau are known as the 'yellow slips.' **1911** FERBER *Dawn O'Hara* 96, I'll swear there is no yellow streak. **1850** *Rep. Comm. Patents 1849: Agric.* 322 There ought, if the quality of the crop will permit, to be four sorts of tobacco, 'Yellow,' 'Bright,' 'Dull,' and 'Second.' **1796** HAWKINS *Letters* 46 The distemper which has for 3 or 4 years past destroyed the horses in the Southern States, . . . called there the yellow water, was introduced into this country from St. Antoine, and Appaluca.

***Yellow**, *v. tr.* To produce a yellow color in (tobacco). Also *vbl. n.* used attrib. — **1863** *Ill. Agric. Soc. Trans.* V. 667 If the weather is wet, it is best to . . . let the yellowing process take place in the house. *Ib.* 668 To make a really fancy article, the tobacco must be thoroughly yellowed before, and cured entirely by fire.

+**Yellow ash. 1.** (See quotations.) **2.** The yellowwood, *Cladrastis lutea*. — (**1**) **1778** CARVER *Travels* 497 The yellow ash . . . is only found near the head branches of the Mississippi. **1832** WILLIAMSON *Maine* I. 106 Of this species [the black ash], the *red* and *yellow* are only varieties. (**2**) **1884** SARGENT *Rep. Forests* 57 Yellow Wood. Yellow Ash . . . yielding a clear yellow dye.

Yellowback. {1796–} +**1.** *Blue yellowback*, the blue yellow-backed warbler, *Compsothlypis americana*. +**2.** A legal-tender note with the back printed in a yellowish color. *colloq.* +**3.** A fresh-water mussel of the Mississippi Valley and the southeastern states. — (**1**) **1892** TORREY *Foot-Path Way* 83, I wondered why this particular little grove . . . should be the favorite resort of . . . blue yellow-backs. **1917** *Birds of Amer.* III. 123/1 The Parula Warbler has been called the Blue Yellowback. (**2**) **1902** WILSON *Spenders* 150 She was dead in love with the nice long yellow-backs that I've piled up. (**3**) **1909** WEBSTER 1209/1.

Yellow-backed, *a.* {1874} **1.** *Yellow-backed warbler*, the Parula warbler, *Compsothlypis americana*. ‖**2.** *Yellow-backed pamphleteering*, the writing or publication of pamphlets issued in yellow covers. **3.** *Yellow-backed fiddle*, a cheap violin with its back finished in a light color. +**4.** *Yellow-backed rockfish*, a food fish of the Pacific coast, *Pteropodus maliger*. — (**1**) **1783** LATHAM *Gen. Synopsis Birds* IV. 440 Yellow-backed Warbler. (**2**) **1846** POE *Works* (1902) XV. 112 [Fashion has condemned] her more modern rivals . . . to the eternal insignificance of the yellow-backed pamphleteering. (**3**) **1877** W. WRIGHT *Big Bonanza* 29 The orchestra—a 'yaller-backed fiddle'—struck up. (**4**) **1884** GOODE, etc. *Fisheries* I. 264 Yellow-backed Rock-fish. . . . It ranges from Monterey to Puget Sound.

+**Yellow-bark(ed) oak.** =QUERCITRON OAK. — **1847** DARLINGTON *Weeds & Plants* 315 *Q[uercus] tinctoria*, . . . Yellow-barked Oak, . . . is exported in large quantities to Europe, where it is employed in dyeing yellow. **1884** SARGENT *Rep. Forests* 149 Yellow-bark Oak . . . is occasionally used medicinally in the form of decoctions. **1892** APGAR *Trees Northern U.S.* 156 *Quercus coccinea*. . . . Var. *tinctoria*. (Quercitron. Yellow-barked or Black Oak.) . . . Bark . . . with the inner color orange.

+**Yellow bass. 1.** The small-mouthed black bass, *Micropterus dolomieu*. **2.** A yellow fresh-water fish (*Chrysoperca interrupta*) found in the lower Mississippi. — (**1**) **1820** RAFINESQUE in *Western Rev.* II. 50 Pale River-Bass. *Lepomis pallida*. . . . Vulgar name Yellow Bass, common Bass, &c. (**2**) **1884** GOODE, etc. *Fisheries* I. 431 The Yellow Bass . . . is found throughout the lower course of the Mississippi.

+**Yellow bear. 1.** =GRIZZLY BEAR. **2.** The yellow larva of the Virginia tiger moth, *Diacrisia virginica*. — (**1**) **1805** WHITEHOUSE in *Lewis & Clark Exped.* VII. (1905) 93 Towards evening the hunters killed a yallow bear in a bottom of cotton wood. (**2**) **1867** *Amer. Naturalist* I. 162 Many [insects] winter in the caterpillar or larva state, such as the larvæ of several Noctuidæ and the 'yellow-bear.'

Yellow-bellied, *a.* {1709} In the specific names of birds, fishes, and other animals. {1783}

1814 MITCHILL *Fishes N.Y.* 440 Yellow-bellied Killifish. *Esox pisciculus*. . . . Frequents the salt tide waters. **1827** WILLIAMS *W. Florida* 30 Black-head fly catcher. . . . Yellow-bellied do. *M[uscicapa] cristata*. **1842** *Nat. Hist. N.Y., Zoology* III. 45 The Yellow-bellied Snake, *Tropidonotus leberis*, . . . is said to affect water and moist places. *Ib.* 73 The Yellow-bellied Salamander, *Salamandra symmetrica*, . . . is extensively distributed throughout the Union. *Ib.* IV. 192 The Variegated Bream, *Abramis versicolor*, . . . is also called the yellow-bellied Perch. **1884** GOODE, etc. *Fisheries* I. 155 *Pseudemys scabra*, a species which occurs in the Carolinas, Georgia, and Northern Florida, . . . is known popularly as the 'Yellow-bellied Terrapin.'

+**Yellow-bellied woodpecker.** A sapsucker (*Sphyrapicus varius*) of the eastern states. — *c***1729** CATESBY *Carolina* I. 21 *Picus Varius Minor, Ventre Luteo*. The Yellow belly'd Wood-pecker. **1825** BONAPARTE *Ornithology* I. 75 [The] Young Yellow-Bellied Woodpecker, *Picus Varius*, . . . is introduced on account of its anomalous plumage. **1839** PEABODY *Mass. Birds* 336 The Yellow Bellied Woodpecker . . . keeps itself within the shade of the forest. **1892** TORREY *Foot-Path Way* 190 The first yellow-bellied woodpecker of the season was hammering in a tree over my head.

Yellowbelly. {1796–} +**1.** *S.W.* A Mexican. A contemptuous term. +**2.** The yellow-bellied flycatcher, *Empidonax flaviventris*. **3.** The name of various fishes {1890–, in New Zealand, etc.}: +(see quotations). — (**1**) **1850** M. REID *Rifle Rangers* 12n., Yellow bellies—a name given by Western hunters and soldiers of the U.S.A. to the Mexicans. (**2**) **1892** TORREY *Foot-Path Way* 9 In his notes, the yellow-belly may be said to take after both the least flycatcher and the wood pewee. (**3**) **1896** JORDAN & EVERMANN *Check-List Fishes* 247 *Ptychocheilus oregonensis*. . . . Yellow-belly; Sacramento Pike. Rivers of Oregon and Washington. *Ib.* 355 *Lepomis auritus*. . . . Yellowbelly; Redbreast Bream. Maine to Louisiana.

+**Yellow-billed magpie.** (See MAGPIE 2 b.)

+**Yellow birch.** A North American tree (*Betula lutea*) having a yellow or gray bark; the wood of this tree. Also attrib. — **1787** *Amer. Acad. Mem.* II. I. 158 Black and Yellow Birch. . . . The bark of the latter is used by the Indians for making canoes. *c*1840 NEAL *Beedle's Sleigh Ride* 15 Nothing was heard but a cricket under the hearth, keeping tune with a sappy yellow birch forestick. **1848** THOREAU *Maine Woods* 17 These camps were about twenty feet long by fifteen wide, built of logs,—hemlock, cedar, spruce, or yellow birch. *Ib.* 18 They are very proper forest houses, ... made of living green logs, hanging with ... the curls and fringes of the yellow-birch bark. **1899** JEWETT *Queen's Twin* 208 There's Aunt Cynthy's lane right ahead, there by the great yellow birch.

Yellowbird. {*a*1705–}

+1. a. = GOLDFINCH 1. **b.** = SUMMER YELLOWBIRD.

1775 BURNABY *Travels* 17 In the woods [of Va.] there are ... the bluebird, the yellow-bird. **1808** WILSON *Ornithology* I. 20 Yellow-Bird, or Goldfinch. *Fringilla Tristis.* This bird is ... of a rich lemon yellow. **1887** WILKINS *Humble Romance* 81 She often paused between her stitches to gaze absorbedly at a yellow-bird. **1891** *Cent.* 7016/1 *Yellowbird*, ... the summer warbler.

+2. A gold coin. *slang.*

1853 SIMMS *Sword & Distaff* 469 Think over the different draws, or holes, whar' you hides away your yallow-birds.

Yellow-blossom. *pl.* = ST.-JOHN'S-WORT. — **1753** HEMPSTEAD *Diary* 611 Wee pulld up the yellow Blossoms (alias Johnsworth) in the upper end & back Side the Lot.

Yellow boy.

1. A gold coin. *slang.* {1662–} Also attrib.

1809 WEEMS *Marion* (1833) 173 But at parting, [he] launches out for me a fist full of yellow boys! **1841** *Congress. Globe* 7 July 129/3 They would calmly discuss the principles of the measure— ... laying aside their Jackson notions of yellow-boy currency. **1883** 'MARK TWAIN' *Life on Miss.* XXXVI, She's all there—a round ten thousand dollars in yellow-boys.

+2. A mulatto boy or man. Sometimes with allusion to sense 1.

1833 NEAL *Down-Easters* I. 65 Thats what they call gettin' the yeller-boys, I spose. **1836** CROCKETT *Exploits* 110 [She] left the poor politician destitute of every thing except a fine 'yellow boy,' [mulatto child] but of widely different description from those which Benton put in circulation. **1861** LOWELL *Biglow P.* 2 Ser. i. 29 Though yaller boys is thick anough, eagles hez kind o' flown.

Yellow-breasted, *a.* {1776–, in Ceylon} In the specific names of birds. — *c*1730 CATESBY *Carolina* I. 50 The yellow breasted Chat.... They frequent the Banks of great rivers. **1828** BONAPARTE *Synopsis* 335 The Yellow-breasted Rail, *Rallus noveboracensis*, ... inhabits throughout North America. **1831** AUDUBON *Ornith. Biog.* I. 121 The Yellow-breasted Warbler, or Maryland Yellow-throat. **1865** *Atlantic Mo.* May 521/1 [I] find ... the Redstart, the Yellow-Throat, the Yellow-Breasted Flycatcher [etc.].

+Yellow cotton. Cotton having fiber of a yellowish tinge. Also attrib. — **1829** B. HALL *Travels in N.A.* III. 220 The different kinds of cotton are, 'first quality white,' 'second quality white,' and 'yellow.' **1865** E. W. Pearson *Lett. Port Royal* 300 Celia wanted her 'yellow-cotton-money' 'by himself.'

Yellow cover. **+1.** (See quotation.) *slang.* **2.** A book cover of a yellowish hue, commonly used for sensational books; hence, literature of a cheap, sensational order. *colloq.* Also attrib. — **(1)** **1859** BARTLETT 520 *Yellow Cover*, ... a notice of dismissal from government employment. So called from its being usually enclosed in a yellow envelope. **(2)** **1862** BROWNE *A. Ward: His Book* 197 My tower threw the southern Conthieveracy ... was thrilling enuff for yeller covers. **1864** LELAND *Art of Conversation* 234 *Yellow cover.* Applied to cheap and vulgar literature; so called first in 1840, from the twenty-five cent editions of Paul de Kock's novels, and similar works. **1866** *Chicago Tribune* 13 Feb. 13 The remainder of the outside was filled with yellow-cover literature, clipped from the New York *Police Gazette, Sunday Mercury,* and sheets of that description.

Yellow-covered, *a.* Of a literary production: Having a yellow cover or +depending for effect upon sensation or cheap thrills. *colloq.* — **1858** *Harper's Mag.* Sept. 564/1 The greater number were lounging in easy postures about the cabin, ... deeply immersed in the 'yellow-covered literature' so plentiful on our Western waters. **1860** GREELEY *Overland Journey* 235 Even quack medicines ... and yellow-covered novels are sold at double the prices borne on their labels or covers.

+Yellow-crowned (night) heron. A heron (*Nyctanassa violacea*) of the southern states, the crest of which has a pale tawny tinge. — **1813** WILSON *Ornithology* VIII. 26 [The] Yellow-crowned Heron ... inhabits the lower parts of South Carolina, Georgia, and Louisiana. **1844** *Nat. Hist. N.Y., Zoology* II. 228 The Yellow-Crowned Night Heron ... is no where very abundant. **1917** *Birds of Amer.* I. 195/1 [The] Yellow-crowned Night Heron ... is quite as diurnal in its habits as any of the more common Herons.

+Yellow-crowned warbler. 1. The chestnut-sided warbler, *Dendroica pensylvanica.* **2.** The myrtle bird, *Dendroica coronata.* — **(1)** **1817** SHAW *Gen. Zool.* X. 623 Yellow-crowned Warbler. (*Sylvia icterocephala.*) ... This inhabits the continent of North America, appearing in ... Pennsylvania in April. **1917** *Birds of Amer.* III. 133. **(2)** **1839** PEABODY *Mass. Birds* 307 The Yellow-crowned Warbler ... is quite common here for two or three weeks in May. **1868** *Amer. Naturalist* II. 171 The Yellow-crowned Warbler ... [arrives] from the fifteenth to the twentieth of April. **1917** *Birds of Amer.* III. 128.

Yellow dock. The curled dock (*Rumex crispus*), or a related species; also, a preparation made from this. — **1676** GLOVER *Va.* in *Phil. Trans.* XI. 629 There grow wild in the Woods, Plantane of all sorts, Yellow-Dock, Bur-Dock, Solomons-seal. **1839** in *Mich. Agric. Soc. Trans.* VII. 418. **1853** *La Crosse Democrat* 7 June 2/4 Dr. Gyott's Yellow Dock and Sarsaparilla. **1872** [see RHEUMATISM WEED 1].

Yellow dog. {*c*1770}

+1. A cur or mongrel. *colloq.*

1833 J. S. JONES *Green Mt. Boy* II. iv, That yaller dog has broke his chain, and bit a nigger! **1865** BROWNE *A. Ward; His Travels* 49 Columbus was a four-horse team fillibuster, and a large yaller dog under the waggin. **1909** 'O. HENRY' *Options* 299, I'll buy ... a shotgun and a yellow dog.

+b. Used as a symbol of worthlessness or insignificance.

1895 HARTE *Clarence* III. iii, In Illinois we wouldn't hang a yellow dog on that evidence. **1907** WHITE *Arizona Nights* 344 You wouldn't do that to a yellow dog.

+c. In fig. and transferred use. *slang.*

1903 *Everybody's Mag.* Oct. 562 If there are five magazines in the [cut-rate] combination, two of them are good. The rest are 'yellow dogs.' **1908** LORIMER *J. Spurlock* 60 That's going altogether too far—to force me to brand myself a sneak like that yellow dog Rawden!

+2. attrib. **a.** With reference to notes issued by wildcat banks. (Cf. RED DOG 2.) **b.** With reference to agreements or political commitments regarded as discreditable, esp. those aimed at injury to organized labor.

(a) **1875** *Chicago Tribune* 26 Aug. 4/1 The grand mass-meeting in Detroit in favor of cheap imitation money of the 'blue-pup' and 'yellow dog' variety proved to be a wretched failure. **(b)** **1902** *United Mine Workers' Jrnl.* 3 July 1/1 (*headlines*), Below is an Exact Copy of the Housing Lease, Better Known as the 'Yellow Dog' Lease, Which is Creating Such a Stir Among the Miners on Loup Creek. **1903** *Outlook* 15 Aug. 931/2 In preference to a Tammany 'yellow dog' ticket his organization [*sc.* the German-American Reform Union] would support the fusion candidate. **1920** *Motorman & Conductor* Oct. 34/1 Yellow dog contracts ... provide that the miner shall not join a union while in the employ of the company.

+Yellow-eyed grass. Any one of various plants of the genus *Xyris.* Also attrib. — **1814** BIGELOW *Florula Bostoniensis* 13 Yellow eyed grass. ... Small yellow florets. **1857** GRAY *Botany* 487 Xyridaceæ. (Yellow-eyed Grass Fam[ily]) Rush-like herbs. **1899** GOING *Flowers* 187 The seeds of both water-rushes and yellow-eyed-grass are small and light.

+Yellow fever.

1. An infectious tropical or semitropical fever characterized by jaundice, hemorrhages, etc. {1758–, in W. Indies}

1740 W. STEPHENS *Proc. Georgia* II. 17 From Charles-Town we hear of a dangerous Distemper raging there, which they call the Yellow Fever, from the Corpse immediately so changing, after Death. **1800** *Columbian Centinel* 2 July 4/1 The Pestilence known by the name of the *Yellow Fever*, has excited the attention of the learned in Medicine. **1823** *New Eng. Farmer* II. 24 The following circumstance is a remarkable instance of the non-contagion of the Yellow Fever. **1898** *Boston Jrnl.* 31 July 10/2 (Ernst), Our so-called immunes are persons who have had yellow fever. **1904** 'O. HENRY' *Roads of Destiny* 353 He'd ... treat anything from yellow fever to a personal friend.

b. (See quotation.)

1835 INGRAHAM *South-West* II. 282 One half [of the cotton] in the rows, and sometimes whole acres together, die with the 'rust,' 'sore skin,' or 'yellow fever.'

2. Attrib. with *captain, epidemic, fly,* etc.

1833 J. E. ALEXANDER *Transatlantic Sk.* II. 16 The only chance I had was a yellow-fever captain, ... who ventures down the river from Cincinnati, or St. Louis, in the fall, to see if he can pick up a few stray passengers. **1860** ABBOTT *South & North* 113 The yellow-fever epidemic is a very serious drawback to the idea of a residence in Mobile. **1880** *Psyche* III. 111/1 At Norfolk in 1855, a fly appeared in swarms, which the people ... called the yellow fever fly. **1881** *Harper's Mag.* Jan. 204/2 The last entertainment [was] ... a concert, in aid of the yellow-fever sufferers. *a*1882 in McCabe *New York* 99 Dix [Island] ... is used for the reception of cholera and yellow fever patients.

Yellow fir. {1667–} W. **+a.** The Douglas fir, *Pseudotsuga taxifolia.* **+b.** The white fir, *Abies grandis.* — **1882** *Garden* 30 Sept. 301/3 The principal tree in these forests [near Puget Sound] is the yellow Fir.] **1884** SARGENT *Rep. Forests* 209 Two varieties [of the Douglas fir], red and yellow fir, are distinguished by lumbermen, dependent probably upon the age of the tree. **1894** COULTER *Bot. W. Texas* III. 555 In the Guadalupe Mountains and northwestward.... 'Yellow Fir.' **1897** SUDWORTH *Arborescent Flora* 54 *Abies grandis.* Great Silver Fir. ... [Also called] Yellow Fir (Mont., Idaho).

Yellowfish. **+1.** The niggerfish, *Cephalopholis fulvus.* **+2.** The Atka fish, *Pleurogrammus monopterygius.* — **(1)** *c*1733 CATESBY *Carolina* II. 10 The Yellow Fish. ... This had small thin scales of a reddish yellow colour. **(2)** **1884** *Nat. Museum Bul.* No. 27, 392 The 'Atka fish,' 'Atka Mackerel,' or 'Yellow fish' (*Pleurogrammus monopterygius*), ... is extremely plentiful off Atka and the Shumagin islands and elsewhere in Alaska.

Yellow flower. + = HALF HORSE (AND) HALF ALLIGATOR 1. Also transf. in attrib. use. In full *yellow flower of the forest.* — **1833** COKE *Subaltern's Furlough* I. 35 The effect of his performance in the West . . . incensed the 'half-horse, half-aligator boys,' 'the yellow flowers of the forest,' as they call themselves. **1836** (*title*), Crockett's Yaller Flower Almanac for '36. **1844** 'UNCLE SAM' *Peculiarities* I. 169, I'm a yeller flower in the forest, I am.

Yellow-flowering, *a.* In the specific names of plants. {1832} — **1785** MARSHALL *Amer. Grove* 81 *Lonicera Diervilla,* Yellow flowering Diervilla, . . . grows most natural upon mountains. **1806** LEWIS in *L. & Clark Exped.* V. (1905) 138, I observed . . . the yelow flowering pea in blume. **1833** EATON *Botany* (ed. 6) 393 *Xyris caroliniana,* yellow-eyed grass, yellow-flowering-rush.

Yellow-fruited, *a.* In the specific names of plants. — **1785** MARSHALL *Amer. Grove* 29 American Yellow-Fruited Nettle-Tree. . . . The juice of the fruit is said to be astringent. **1813** MUHLENBERG *Cat. Plants* 48 *Crataegus flava,* Yellow-fruited hawthorn.

+**Yellow girl.** A mulatto woman or girl; a light-skinned woman of Negro blood. *colloq.* or *slang.* (See also YALLER GAL.) — *a*1866 in Hullah *Song-Book* 350, I lov'd a dark-eyed yellow girl, And thought that she lov'd me. **1888** [see BRIGHT *a.* 3 b].

*** Yellow-hammer.** *local.* +The flicker or golden-winged woodpecker (*Colaptes auratus*), or a related bird. — **1832** WILLIAMSON *Maine* I. 150 The *Yellow-hammer* is also a Woodpecker. **1857** [see HIGH-HOLDER]. **1874** BAIRD, etc. *N. Amer. Birds* II. 581 This bird [*sc. Colaptes Mexicanus*], in some parts of California, is known as the Yellow-Hammer. **1896** JEWETT *Pointed Firs* 143, I could hear . . . the clink of a yellow-hammer over in the woods.

Yellow-headed, *a.* In the specific names of birds. {1743-} — **1823** JAMES *Exped.* I. 265 *Oriolus (Zanthornus) icterocephalus*—Yellow-headed oriole. **1878** *Nat. Museum Proc.* I. 405 *Dendrœca occidentalis.*—Yellow-headed Gray Warbler. **1891** *Cent.* 7016/2 The yellow-headed tit or titmouse, the gold tit, *Auriparus flaviceps.* **1917** *Birds of Amer.* III. 216 Verdin. *Auriparus flaviceps flaviceps.* . . . [Also called] Gold-Tit; Yellow-headed Bush-Tit.

+**Yellow-headed blackbird.** A large blackbird (*Xanthocephalus xanthocephalus*) common in western North America. — **1846** *30th Congress 1 Sess.* H. R. Ex. Doc. No. 41, 436 [We saw] large flocks of the yellow headed black bird, or troopial. **1872** *Vermont Bd. Agric. Rep.* I. 332 Large flocks of the Yellow-headed Black Bird passed through the region and entirely destroyed the insects. **1895** *Dept. Agric. Yrbk. 1894* 237 The yellow-headed blackbird did considerable damage by pulling the corn just as it came through the ground.

+**Yellow-headed troopial.** = prec. — **1825** BONAPARTE *Ornithology* I. 29 The Yellow-headed Troopials assemble in dense flocks. **1839** TOWNSEND *Narrative* 142 Here we saw a number of beautiful yellow-headed troopials. **1858** *New Amer. Cycl.* III. 283/1 The yellow-headed troopials of North America.

Yellow honeysuckle. +*a.* The trumpet honeysuckle (*Lonicera flava*), of the southern states, or a related plant. +*b.* = FLAME AZALEA. — **1836** LINCOLN *Botany* App. 113 *Lonicera . . . flava,* (yellow honeysuckle,) . . . flowers bright yellow. **1850** S. F. COOPER *Rural Hours* 70 The yellow honeysuckle grows in the Catskill Mountains. **1860** CURTIS *Woody Plants N.C.* 98 Yellow Honeysuckle . . . is found only at a considerable elevation on our mountains.

Yellow jacket. {1898-, in Australia}

+**1.** Any one of various American wasps having yellow markings. Also transf.

1796 LATROBE *Journal* 106 The yellow jacket . . . appears to be on the wing very like the common wasp. **1828** ROYALL *Black Book* II. 376 Black coats as thick as yellow-jackets; preaching here sixteen times a week. **1866** C. H. SMITH *Bill Arp* 127, I rolled some twenty feet . . . and cotch up agin an old pine stump that was full of yaller jakets. **1877** W. WRIGHT *Big Bonanza* 63 The claim was called the Yellow Jacket because of the fact of the locators finding a nest of yellow-jackets in the surface rock. **1920** HOWELLS *Vacation of Kelwyns* 104 A swarm of yellow-jackets had stung him.

attrib. **1817** PAULDING *Lett. from South* I. 228 Oliver's horse being stung by a yellow-jacket hornet.

transf. **1823** DODDRIDGE *Logan* I. i, Why so large an encampment of Indians? . . . Why do these Yellow-jackets come so near us?

+**2.** A fish of the genus *Oligoplites;* a leather jacket.

1883 *Nat. Museum Bul.* No. 27, 440 *Oligoplites occidentalis.* . . . Yellow Jacket; Yellow Tail.

*** Yellow jasmin(e), jessamine.** A plant having sweet-scented yellow flowers, +esp. the American Carolina jessamine, *Gelsemium sempervirens.* Also attrib. — **1709** LAWSON *Carolina* 89 The yellow Jessamin is wild in our Woods. **1775** BURNABY *Travels* 12 They are likewise adorned and beautified with . . . magnolias, yellow jasamines [etc.]. **1802** [see SEA ISLAND 1]. **1894** TORREY *Fla. Sketch-Book* 105 Here and there in the undergrowth were yellow jessamine vines.

+**Yellow journal.** A newspaper or similar publication depending upon sensational reporting as a method of attracting readers. Also attrib. — **1900** *Congress. Rec.* 5 Feb. 1511/2 We have been branded in the yellow journals, . . . as 'traitors' and 'copperheads.' **1903** *Forum* July 87 Even the yellow journal critics . . . are capable of keen, synthetic analysis. **1908** SINCLAIR *Metropolis* 105 As for the 'yellow' journals, they would have discussions of the costumes by 'experts.'

+**Yellow journalism.** The use of sensational reporting and conspicuous display as means of attracting readers to a newspaper or journal. — **1898** BANKS in *19th Cent.* Aug. 328 All American journalism is not 'yellow,' though all strictly 'up-to-date' yellow journalism is American! **1924** E. P. MITCHELL *Memoirs of Editor* 126 The phrase 'yellow journalism' . . . [was] put into circulation by my dear friend the late Ervin Wardman.

+**Yellow lady's-slipper.** Any one of various orchids of the genus *Cypripedium* having yellow flowers, as the species *C. parviflorum.* Also with defining adjectives. — **1738** CATESBY *Carolina* II. 73 The Yellow Lady's Slipper. . . . These grow on the sandy banks of rivers in Carolina, Virginia, and Pensylvania. **1817-8** EATON *Botany* (1822) 261. **1869** *Amer. Naturalist* III. 8 Raising their heads above the foliage of that miniature grove of wild mandrakes are a few specimens of the Yellow Ladies' Slipper. **1890** *Cent.* 3329/2 In America the most conspicuous wild lady's-slippers are the larger yellow, *C. pubescens;* the smaller yellow, *C. parviflorum* [etc.].

Yellowleg. {1830-3, *dial.*}

+**1.** Either one of two American shore birds having long yellow legs, the lesser yellowlegs (*Totanus flavipes*) or the greater yellowlegs (*Totanus melanoleucus*). Usu. pl. Also with specifying terms.

[**1772** FORSTER in *Phil. Trans.* LXII. 410 *Scolopax, Totanus.* Spotted Woodcock. . . . This bird is called a yellow leg at Albany fort.] **1844** *Nat. Hist. N.Y., Zoology* II. 248 The Yellow-Legs . . . [eats] insects, worms, and small aquatic animals. **1862** *N.H. Laws* 2609 [If any person shall] take, kill or destroy any of the birds called yellow-legs, or sandpipers; . . . he shall forfeit for every [one] . . . , the sum of one dollar. **1870** [see YELLOW-LEGGED *a.*]. **1882** GODFREY *Nantucket* 241/2, I have met with the . . . Yellow-Leg (*Gambetta flavipes*). **1884** *Nat. Museum Bul.* No. 27, 151 Greater Yellow-legs; Tell-tale. . . . Breeding in colder portions of North America. **1894** TORREY *Fla. Sketch-Book* 181 About the edges of the water were . . . at least half a dozen of the smaller yellowlegs. **1895** *Outing* XXVI. 70/2 The winter yellowlegs were less numerous.

+**b.** *local.* Bastard yellowlegs, = LONG-LEGGED SANDPIPER.

1909 WEBSTER 190/3 *B*[*astard*] *yellowlegs,* the stilt sandpiper. *Mass. & Long Island.* **1917** *Birds of Amer.* I. 231/1 The similarity of the two species is acknowledged by the popular name, 'Bastard Yellow-legs,' which the sportsmen of Long Island have given to the Stilt Sandpiper.

2. (See quotation.)

1848 *S. Lit. Messenger* XIV. 531/1 Acres of frogs— . . . from the innocent little yellow legs, . . . to the lethargic and aldermanic patriarch of the Glades.

+**3.** A Confederate soldier.

1869 *Harper's Mag.* April 716/1 If you will be kind enough to bring out one of those 'yellow legs' (Confederates) in the guard house, and let me shoot him, I can *die in peace!*

+**4.** A mounted representative of government authority, as a cavalryman or a forest ranger. *slang.* Also attrib.

1895 REMINGTON *Pony Tracks* 174 'We can catch him before he pulls out in the morning, I think,' said the yellow-leg. *c*1917 in *Dialect Notes* V. 59 The detachment of Yellow Legs imported at the behest of the Commercial Club. **1917** J. A. MOSS *Officers' Manual* 485 *Yellow-leg,* cavalryman. **1924** R. CUMMINS *Sky-high Corral* 25 Set yeller-leg kids in here to tell us how to raise cows.

Yellow-legged, *a.* {1752} +In the specific names of American birds. — **1781-2** Yellow-legged snipe [see SNIPE 2]. **1805** LEWIS in *L. & Clark Exped.* VI. (1905) 133 [*Symphemia semi-palmata*] is about the size of the yellow leged plover. **1870** *Amer. Naturalist* IV. 547 Yellow-legged Sandpiper (*Gambetta flavipes*). . . . 'Yellow-legs' have been found breeding in Mercer county, New Jersey. **1889** *Cent.* 2576/1 *Yellow-legged goose,* the American white-fronted goose. (San Diego, California, U.S.).

+**Yellow-legger. 1.** (See quotation.) **2.** *local.* (See quotation.) — (1) **1891** *Cent.* 7016/3 *Yellow-legger,* . . . the yellowlegs. (2) *Ib., Yellow-legger,* . . . a fisherman from Eastham. (Provincetown, Massachusetts.)

*** Yellow lily.** +*a.* The Canada lily, *Lilium canadense.* Also *wild yellow lily.* +*b.* A trout lily. Also attrib. — **1784** *Amer. Acad. Mem.* I. 433 Yellow Lily. Blossoms Yellow, with black spots. **1806** [see LILY 2]. **1843** TORREY *Flora N.Y.* II. 305 *Lilium Canadense.* Wild Yellow Lily. . . . Moist meadows. **1858** THOREAU *Maine Woods* 98 There were a few yellow-lily-pads still left. **1894** *Amer. Folk-Lore* VII. 102 *Erythronium Americanum,* yellow lily, Ferrisburgh, Vt.

+**Yellow locust. 1.** The common American locust, *Robinia pseudoacacia.* **2.** (See quotation.) — (1) **1810** MICHAUX *Arbres* I. 38 Locust. . . . *Yellow Locust* (Acacia jaune), . . . [nom donné] a cet arbre sur les bords de la rivière Susquehannah. **1884** SARGENT *Rep. Forests* 55 Yellow Locust. . . . Widely and generally naturalized throughout the United States. (2) **1897** SUDWORTH *Arborescent Flora* 257 *Cladrastis lutea.* . . . Yellow-wood. . . . [Also called] Yellow Locust (Ky., Tenn.).

+**Yellow mackerel.** Either one of two cavallas, the jurel or hardtail (*Paratractus crysos*) or the related species (*Caranx hippos*). — **1814** MITCHILL *Fishes N.Y.* 424 Yellow Mackerel. . . . A marine fish, taken in the bay of New-York. **1855** BAIRD in *Smithsonian Rep. 1854* 336 Yellow Mackerel. . . . Only one specimen of this fish was seen during my stay. **1883** *Nat. Museum Bul.* No. 27, 439 *Caranx hippos.* . . . Yellow Mackerel. . . . Atlantic coast of the United States north to Cape Cod. **1911** *Rep. Fisheries 1908* 311 Jurel. . . . [Known] about New York and on the coast of New Jersey as the 'yellow mackerel.'

+**Yellow oak.** Any one of various American oaks, as the black or quercitron oak (*Quercus velutina*) or the chinquapin oak. — **1686** *Topsfield Rec.* 59 A heape of rocks [is] near to a . . . yealow oack at the southwesterly corner [of the parsonage land]. **1778** CARVER *Travels* 495 There are several sorts of oaks in these parts; the black, the white, the red, the yellow, the grey. **1810** MICHAUX *Arbres* I. 23 Q[uercus] p[in]us acuminata. . . . *Yellow oak* (Chêne jaune), nom donné . . . dans le comté de Lancaster en Pensylvanie. **1813** MUHLENBERG *Cat. Plants* 87 *Quercus castanea*, Yellow oak. **1897** SUDWORTH *Arborescent Flora* 156 *Quercus acuminata*. . . . Chinquapin Oak. . . . [Also called] Yellow Oak. *Ib.* 168 *Quercus velutina*. Yellow Oak. . . . [Also called] Quercitron Oak.

+**Yellow perch.** Any one of various American fresh-water fishes, esp. the common perch (*Perca flavescens*) and the small-mouth black bass (*Micropterus dolomieu*): (see also quot. 1903). — **1805** PARKINGTON *Tour* 311 The Baltimore market consists of rock; perch, white and yellow [etc.]. **1814** MITCHILL *Fishes N.Y.* 421 Yellow Perch. *Bodianus flavescens*. . . . A beautiful fresh-water fish, of a foot or more in length. **1820** RAFINESQUE in *Western Rev.* II. 51 Streaked-cheeks River-Bass. *Lepomis trifasciata*. . . . Vulgar names Yellow bass, Gold bass, Yellow perch [etc.]. **1855** LONGFELLOW *Hiawatha* 67 [He] saw the yellow perch, the Sakwa, Like a sunbeam in the water. **1903** T. H. BEAN *Fishes N.Y.* 529 In Great Egg Harbor bay individuals [of *Morone americana*, the white perch] taken from salt water are sometimes called yellow perch or peerch.

+**Yellow pine.**

1. One of various American pines.

a. =GEORGIA PINE. **b.** The shortleaf pine, *Pinus echinata*. **c.** The bull pine, *P. ponderosa*. **d.** The Arizona pine, *P. arizonica*. **e.** =JEFFREY PINE. **f.** The common white pine. **g.** A Rocky Mountain species, *P. ponderosa scopulorum*. **h.** =LOBLOLLY PINE. **i.** The pitch pine, *P. rigida*.

1709 LAWSON *Carolina* 89 Ever-Greens are here plentifully found, of a very quick Growth, and pleasant Shade; . . . the yellow Pine, the white Pine [etc.]. **1781–2** JEFFERSON *Notes Va.* (1788) 39 Yellow pine. *Pinus Virginica*. **1791** [see LONG-LEAVED (PITCH) PINE]. **1810** MICHAUX *Arbres* I. 16 Pinus mitis. . . . *Yellow pine* (Pin jaune), dénomination générale dans tous les Etats du milieu. **1854** WHIPPLE etc. *Explor. Ry. Route* I. 79 It is a species of yellow pine, called by the botanist *Pinus brachyptera*. **1878** WHEELER *Geog. Survey Rep.* VI. 260 *Pinus Arizonica* . . . [is found] on the Santa Rita Mountains, in Southern Arizona. . . . 'There called yellow pine.' **1884** SARGENT *Rep. Forests* 578 The eastern slopes of the Sierra Nevada are covered with a heavy forest, in which yellow pines (*Pinus ponderosa* and *P. Jeffreyi*) are the prevailing and most important trees. **1897** SUDWORTH *Arborescent Flora* 20 *Pinus ponderosa scopulorum*. Rock Pine. . . . [Also called] Yellow Pine (Mont., Nebr.). *Ib.* 26 *Pinus tæda*. Loblolly Pine. . . . [Also called] Yellow Pine (north Ala., N.C.). **1908** BRITTON & SHAFER *N. Amer. Trees* 31 Pitch pine . . . is known [as] . . . Yellow pine.

2. With defining terms.

1834 A. PIKE *Sketches* 37, I observed that it was only one particular kind of pine which they used, viz. the rough yellow pine. **1849** *31st Congress 1 Sess.* Sen. Doc. No. 64, 97 The *sylva*, to-day, has been the large yellow pine and the piñon. **1892** APGAR *Trees Northern U.S.* 174 *Pinus ponderosa*. (Western Yellow or Heavy-wooded Pine.) . . . A large Pacific coast species. **1897** SUDWORTH *Arborescent Flora* 20 *Pinus ponderosa scopulorum*. Rock Pine. . . . [Also called] Rocky Mountain Yellow Pine (lit.).

3. The wood of a yellow pine, or a yellow pine considered with reference to its value as wood. Also with defining term.

See also *long-leaf yellow pine* (under LONG-LEAF PINE 2).

1812 STODDARD *Sk. Louisiana* 123 They produce vast quantities of yellow and pitch pine. **1832** WILLIAMSON *Maine* I. 110 The yellow Pine . . . is used for flooring and for planking vessels. **1880** *Cimarron News & Press* 18 March 2/3 More than one million feet of yellow pine and seven or eight hundred thousand feet of oak will be called for. **1891** *Cent.* 4496/3 *Yellow pine*, . . . a commercial name of the common white pine.

4. Attrib. with *beam, blaze, lumber*, etc.

1796 *Ann. 4th Congress* 2 Sess. 2789 No. of feet of yellow pine plank, . . . 35,679. **1799** *Wilmington* (N.C.) *Gazette* 19 April, About 30 tons of good yellow pine timber. a**1817** DWIGHT *Travels* II. 57 Whateley . . . consists also of three divisions: an interval, a yellow-pine plain, and a collection of hills. **1850** GARRARD *Wah-To-Yah* xix. 216 His eyes were fast fixed on an imaginary object in the yellow-pine blaze. **1858** WARDER *Hedges & Evergreens* 246 This tree furnishes the yellow-pine lumber much used in civil and naval architecture. **1872** 'MARK TWAIN' *Roughing It* 171 It was yellow-pine timber-land. **1897** F. C. MOORE *How to Build a Home* 21, I think yellow-pine beams well worth the difference in cost.

Yellow plum. {1707– (Mortimer *Art Husbandry* 547)} +The common wild plum (*Prunus americana*), or a variety of this. Also *large yellow sweet plum, wild yellow plum*. — **1785** MARSHALL *Amer. Grove* 111 Large Yellow Sweet Plumb. This generally rises to the height of twelve or fifteen feet. **1813** MUHLENBERG *Cat. Plants* 48 *Prunus nigra* (*Americana*), Yellow plumb. **1885** HAVARD *Flora W. & S. Texas* 512 *Prunus Americana*, var. *mollis*. Wild Yellow Plum. . . . Yellow fruit, smaller and less palatable than that of the species in the Northern States.

Yellow poll. +The yellow warbler, *Dendroica aestiva*. Also *yellow-poll warbler*. — [**1783** LATHAM *Gen. Synopsis Birds* IV. 515 Yellow-Poll. . . . This species is found in America. **1785** PENNANT *Arctic Zool.* II. 402 Yellow-poll Warbler. . . . Inhabits Canada.] **1831** AUDUBON *Ornith. Biog.*

I. 476 The Yellow-Poll Warbler . . . is heard in spring. **1867** 'LACKLAND' *Homespun* I. 72 Perhaps a bustling little yellow-poll answers in the copse. **1917** *Birds of Amer.* III. 126.

+**Yellow pond lily.** Any plant of the genus *Nuphar*. Also with defining adjective. — **1821** *Mass. H. S. Coll.* 2 Ser. IX. 152 *Nuphar advena*, Yellow pond lily. . . . [*Nuphar*] *kalmiana*, . . . Little yellow pond lily. **1878** *Rep. Indian Affairs* 115 [The] seed of the yellow pond-lily, the camas and other roots, are both nutritious and palatable. **1890** *Cent.* 4616/1 The yellow pond-lily of Oregon, etc., is *N[ymphæa] polysepala*. **1898** HARPER *S. B. Anthony* I. 50 Here and there [is] a large patch of yellow pond lilies.

+**Yellow poplar.** Any one of various soft-wood trees or the wood yielded by them, esp. the tulip tree, *Liriodendron tulipifera*.

1774 in Peyton *Adv. Grandfather* (1867) 127 The forest of Kentucky consists of yellow and white poplar, walnut, red bud, hiccory. **1810** MICHAUX *Arbres* I. 37 Yellow or White Poplar, en égard a la couleur du bois. **1821** NUTTALL *Travels Arkansa* 58 On the river lands . . . [are] enormous cotton-wood trees . . . commonly called yellow poplar. **1832** BROWNE *Sylva Amer.* 204 The mechanics who employ it [the tulip tree] distinguish it by the names of White Poplar and Yellow Poplar. **1897** SUDWORTH *Arborescent Flora* 198.

attrib. **1829** FLINT *G. Mason* 98 He gave an infusion of Dog Wood, Wild Cherry, and Yellow Poplar bark. **1834** PECK *Gaz. Illinois* 210 Yellow poplar boards and plank are brought across the lake from the St. Joseph's river.

+**Yellow redpoll.** A subspecies (*Dendroica palmarum hypochrysea*) of the palm warbler, or the palm warbler itself. Also *yellow redpoll*, or *red-polled, warbler*. — [**1764** G. EDWARDS *Gleanings Nat. Hist.* III. 295 The Yellow Red-pole . . . hath its upper mandible dusky.] **1811** WILSON *Ornithology* IV. 19 [The] Yellow-Red-poll Warbler: *Sylvia petechia* . . . [frequents] low swampy thickets. **1858** BAIRD *Birds Pacific R.R.* 288 Yellow Red Poll. . . . In one specimen there is scarcely any yellow about the head and neck. **1868** *Amer. Naturalist* II. 171 Soon after the pine-warbler has arrived, . . . the Yellow Red-polled Warbler . . . makes his appearance. **1917** *Birds of Amer.* III. 149.

Yellow rocket. {1812–} **1.** (See quotation.) **2.** The winter rocket or winter cress, *Barbarea vulgaris*. {1812– (Withering *Brit. Plants* III. 723)} — (1) **1817–8** EATON *Botany* (1822) 304 *Hesperis tristis*, yellow rocket. (2) **1890** *Rep. Secy. Agric. 1889* 383 Yellow rocket . . . may be identified readily by the comparatively many times shorter beak of the capsule.

+**Yellowroot.** One of various American plants having yellow roots.

a. A shrub, *Zantorrhiza apiifolia*. Also with defining term. **b.** = GOLDENSEAL. **c.** =GOLDTHREAD.

1785 Shrub Yellow Root [see SHRUB[1]]. [**1796** NEMNICH *Allg. Lexicon Naturgeschichte* III. 944 Yellow root, *Hydrastis canadensis*.] **1804** LEWIS in *L. & Clark Exped.* VI. (1905) 143 This plant is known in Kentucky and many other parts of this western country by the name of the yellow root. **1815** DRAKE *Cincinnati* 88 Yellow root [is used in dyeing]. **1839** [see GOLDENSEAL]. **1892** *Amer. Folk-Lore* V. 91 *Coptis trifolia*, yellowroot. N.H.

+**Yellowrump.** The myrtle bird (*Dendroica coronata*), having a yellow patch on the rump; with qualifying term, a related species. Also *yellowrump warbler*. — c**1730** CATESBY *Carolina* I. 58 The Yellow-rump . . . is a creeper. [**1785** PENNANT *Arctic Zool.* II. 400 Yellow-rump Warbler.] **1810** WILSON *Ornithology* II. 138 [The] Yellow-Rump Warbler . . . frequents the cedar trees, devouring the berries with great avidity. **1891** *Cent.* 7017/1 Western yellowrump, Audubon's warbler, *Dendræca auduboni*. **1892** TORREY *Foot-Path Way* 96 This yellow-rump, or myrtle bird, is one of the thrifty members of his great family.

+**Yellow-rumped warbler.** =prec.; also, with qualifying terms, a warbler related to the yellowrump. — [**1783** LATHAM *Gen. Synopsis Birds* II. 481 Yellow-rumped w[arbler]. . . . Throat, breast, and rump, fine yellow. . . . Inhabits Pensylvania.] **1884** [see CREEPER 2]. **1917** *Birds of Amer.* III. 130 Because of its resemblance to the Myrtle Warbler . . . Audubon's Warbler is often called the Western Yellow-rumped Warbler. *Ib.* 131 Magnolia Warbler. *Dendroica magnolia*. . . . [Also called] Blue-headed Yellow-rumped Warbler.

+**Yellowshank.** =YELLOWLEG 1. Freq. pl. Also attrib. and with specifying adjectives. — [**1785** PENNANT *Arctic Zool.* II. 468 Yellow-shanks Sn[ipe]. With a.slender black bill.] **1835** AUDUBON *Ornith. Biog.* III. 573 The Yellowshank is much more abundant in the interior . . . than along our Atlantic coast. **1839** PEABODY *Mass. Birds* 369 The Yellow Shanks . . . often gives an alarm to others that are less on their guard. **1844** *Nat. Hist. N.Y., Zoology* II. 248 This small species . . . is described under the name of Yellowshank Tatler. **1874** COUES *Birds N.W.* 496 *Totanus Melanoleucus*. . . . Greater Telltale; Greater Yellowshanks; Tattler. *Ib.* 497 *Totanus Flavipes*. . . . Lesser Telltale; Lesser Yellowshanks. *Ib.* 498 The Yellowshank . . . nests only in high latitudes.

Yellowskin. A person having a yellowish skin {1904}, as a Mexican. — **1850** GARRARD *Wah-To-Yah* i. 8 Every man [was] armed, equipped and ready . . . for a fight with the 'yellow skins.' **1851** M. REID *Rifle Rangers* (1853) 89, I was in hopes we'd have a brush with the yellowskins.

+**Yellowstone trout.** A cutthroat trout (*Salmo lewisi*) found in the headwaters of the Yellowstone River and in Yellowstone Lake. — **1884**

Nat. Museum Bul. No. 27, 426 *Salmo purpuratus.* . . . Yellowstone Trout; Rocky Mountain Brook Trout.

Yellowtail. {1608–}

1. Any one of various fishes having a yellow or yellowish tail. {1709–}

+**a.** The mademoiselle, *Bairdiella chrysura.* **b.** The spot, *Leiostomus xanthurus.* +**c.** The menhaden, *Brevoortia tyrannus.* +**d.** = YELLOW JACKET 2. +**e.** A rockfish of California, *Sebastodes flavidus.* +**f.** An amber fish of California, *Seriola dorsalis.* Also with specifying term. +**g.** = RUNNER 4 b. +**h.** The sailor's choice, *Lagodon rhomboides.* **i.** The yellow-tailed snapper, *Ocyurus chrysurus.* +**j.** The mayfish, *Fundulus majalis.*

1775 [see JEWFISH]. [**1796** NEMNICH *Allg. Lexicon Naturgeschichte* III. 944 Yellow tail. . . . *Perca punctata.*] **1838** *Encycl. Metropolitana* XXIV. (1845) 370/2 S[ciæna] *Xanthurus;* . . . Yellow-tailed Smooth-mouth. . . . Found on the Carolina coast, where it is called the Yellow-tail. **1878** [see FATBACK]. **1882** *Nat. Museum Bul.* No. 16, 570 *Sciæna punctata,* Silver Perch; Yellow-tail. **1883** *Ib.* No. 27, 440 *Oligoplites occidentalis.* . . . Yellow Jacket; Yellow Tail. **1884** GOODE, etc. *Fisheries* I. 266 At Monterey it [*sc.* the yellowtail rockfish] is always known by the appropriate name of 'Yellow-tail,' the caudal fin being always distinctly yellow. *Ib.* 331 The California Yellow-tail . . . , according to Jordan, . . . is known under the names 'Yellow-tail,' 'White Salmon,' and 'Cavasina.' *Ib.* 332 *Elagatis pinnulatus* . . . , [known] at Pensacola as 'Yellow-tail' or 'Shoemaker,' is, according to Stearns, 'abundant on the western and southern coasts of Florida.' *Ib.* 393 The 'Sailor's Choice' . . . [is known] in the Indian River region as the 'Sailor's Choice,' 'Scup,' and 'Yellow-tail.' **1896** JORDAN & EVERMANN *Check-List Fishes* 382 *Ocyurus chrysurus.* . . . Yellow-tail; Rabirubia. West Indies, southern Florida to Brazil. **1897** *Outing* XXX. 259/1 The doctor and myself . . . had taken nearly one thousand and eighty pounds of fish, especially yellowtail. **1903** T. H. BEAN *Fishes N.Y.* 309 The striped killifish, also known as the . . . mayfish, yellow-tail, and New York gudgeon, is the largest member of its family known on our eastern coast.

2. Used attrib. in specific names.

1785 PENNANT *Arctic Zool.* II. 406 Yellow-tail Warbler. With an ash-colored crown. . . . Taken . . . off Hispaniola, at sea. **1884** GOODE, etc. *Fisheries* I. 266 Yellow-tail Rock-fish, (*Sebastichthys flavidus*). . . . About Monterey and San Francisco it is very abundant. *Ib.* 569 In North Carolina . . . the names 'Yellow-tail Shad' are occasionally heard.

Yellow-tailed, *a.* +In specific names of American birds and fishes. — [**1758** G. EDWARDS *Gleanings Nat. Hist.* I. 101 The Yellow-tailed Flycatcher. **1823** LATHAM *Gen. Hist. Birds* VI. 232 Yellow-tailed Warbler.] **1884** GOODE, etc. *Fisheries* I. 379 *Umbrina roncador* . . . is generally known as the 'Yellow-tailed' or 'Yellow-finned Roncador.'

+**Yellowthroat.**

1. Any one of various warblers of the genus *Geothlypis.* Also with defining terms.

See also MARYLAND YELLOWTHROAT.

1844 *Nat. Hist. N.Y., Zoology* II. 80 The Yellow-Throat. *Trichas Marilandica.* **1865** *Atlantic. Mo.* May 521/1, [I find] the Yellow-Throat, the Yellow-Breasted Flycatcher [etc.]. **1887** RIDGWAY *Manual N.A. Birds* 523 Western United States, east to Mississippi Valley. . . . G[eothlypis] *trichas occidentalis.* Western Yellow-throat. **1917** *Birds of Amer.* III. 161/2 The Pacific Yellow-throat (*Geothlypis trichas arizela*) . . . [breeds] from southern British Columbia to southern California. *Ib.,* The Salt Marsh Yellow-throat (*Geothlypis trichas sinuosa*) is limited to the salt marshes about San Francisco Bay.

2. The yellow-throated warbler, or a variety of this. Also with defining terms.

1873 in Coues *Birds N.W.* 67 The Yellow-throat prefers the trees along the banks of streams. **1917** *Birds of Amer.* III. 139/1 The clear song of this Dominican Yellow-throat . . . is very distinctive. *Ib.* 140/2 The Sycamore Warbler of the south-central States . . . is well named the Sycamore Yellow-throat.

+**3.** = YELLOW-THROATED VIREO.

1904 F. S. MATHEWS *Field Book of Wild Birds* 158 The Yellow-throat has a violin quality to his voice.

Yellow-throated, *a.* {1859} +In the specific names of American birds. — *c*1730 Yellow-throated Creeper [see CREEPER 2]. **1808** WILSON *Ornithology* I. 117 [The] Yellow-Throated Flycatcher, *Muscicapa Sylvicola,* . . . is found chiefly in the woods, hunting among the high branches. **1844** *Nat. Hist. N.Y., Zoology* II. 120 The Yellow-Throated Greenlet, *Vireo flavifrons,* . . . winters in Texas and Mexico.

+**Yellow-throated vireo.** A greenlet (*Vireo flavifrons*) in which the throat and breast are of a canary-yellow color. — **1839** AUDUBON *Ornith. Biog.* V. 428 Yellow-Throated Vireo. *Vireo Flavifrons.* **1878** COUES *Birds Colo. Valley* 489 Most of the Greenlets, including . . . , the Yellow-throated, and the Warbling Vireos, inhabit high open woods. **1917** *Birds of Amer.* III. 105.

+**Yellow-throated warbler.** A wood warbler (*Dendroica dominica*) of the southern states. Also *yellowthroat warbler, yellow-throated gray warbler.* — **1810** WILSON *Ornithology* II. 64 [The] Yellow-Throat Warbler, *Sylvia Flavicollis,* . . . pass[es] the summer in Virginia, and in the southern parts of Maryland. **1828** BONAPARTE *Synopsis* 80 The Yellow-throated Warbler . . . inhabits the northern parts of the United States. **1874** COUES *Birds N.W.* 66 One of the most remarkable nests I ever saw, was

built by a Yellow-throated Warbler at Wilmington, North Carolina. **1891** *Cent.* 6820/3 *Yellow-throated warbler.* . . . Also *yellow-throated gray warbler.* **1917** *Birds of Amer.* III. 139/1 The Yellow-throated and Sycamore Warblers are geographical variations of the same species of Warbler.

Yellowtop. {1892–4–, *dial.*} +**1.** A species of grass: (see quotations). **2.** (See quotation.) — (1) **1846** WORCESTER 833/1 *Yellow-Top,* a species of grass; called also *white-top. Farm. Ency.* **1909** *Cent. Suppl.* 1460/1 *Yellow-top,* . . . a reed-grass, *Calamagrostis hyperborea Americana,* common in low meadows and on shady river-banks throughout the northwestern United States. (2) **1891** *Cent.* 7017/1 *Yellow-top,* . . . a variety of turnip: so called from the color of the skin on the upper part of the bulb.

*✳**Yellow violet.** Any one of various yellow-flowered violets, +as the downy species (*Viola pubescens*) of the eastern states.

[**1657** COLES *Adam in Eden* 175 Yellow Violets of Virginia.] **1784** *Amer. Acad. Mem.* I. 485 Yellow Violet. It is said the Indians applied the bruised leaves to boils and painful swellings. **1814** BRYANT *Poetical Works* (1903) 23 The yellow violet's modest bell Peeps from the last year's leaves below. **1832** HALE *Flora* 185 Yellow Violet, *Viola, nuttalli.* . . . The only species of Viola found on the plains of Missouri, from the confluence of the river Platte to Fort Mandan. **1895** WIGGIN *Village Watch-Tower* 135 He could tell where to look for the rare fringed gentian, the yellow violet, the Indian pipe.

b. With descriptive or specifying adjectives.

1857 GRAY *Botany* 44 Downy Yellow Violet. . . . Woods; common. **1901** MOHR *Plant Life Ala.* 628 *Viola scabriuscula.* . . . Smoothish Yellow Violet. . . . Pennsylvania, Kentucky, and Tennessee.

Yellow warbler. +A small bird of a bright yellow color (*Dendroica aestiva*); also, with defining terms, any one of various other yellow or yellowish birds of the family Compsothlypidae.

See also *Blue-eyed yellow warbler* (under BLUE-EYED *a.* 1).

1783 LATHAM *Gen. Synopsis Birds* II. 482 Spotted Yellow Warbler, *Le Figuier brun de Canada.* **1810–** Blue-Winged Yellow Warbler [see BLUE-WINGED *a.*]. **1845** JUDD *Margaret* I. 160 The leafless Butternut, whereon . . . the yellow warbler made its nest, sprawls its naked arms. **1858** BAIRD *Birds Pacific R.R.* 282 *Dendroica Aestiva.* . . . Yellow Warbler. . . . United States from Atlantic to Pacific. **1871** BURROUGHS *Wake-Robin* (1886) 184 The yellow warbler . . . is conspicuous [among the permanent summer residents near Washington, D.C.]. **1917** *Birds of Amer.* III. 127/2 Regional varieties of the Yellow Warbler are: the Sonora Yellow Warbler (*Dendroica æstiva sonorana*), found in the southwestern part of North America . . . ; the Alaska Yellow Warbler (*Dendroica æstiva rubiginosa*) . . . ; and the California, or Brewster's, Yellow Warbler (*Dendroica æstiva brewsteri*).

Yellowweed. {1760–} +**a.** Any one of various crowfoots or buttercups of the genus *Ranunculus.* +**b.** *local.* Any one of various species of goldenrod. +**c.** A yellow-flowered herb of the genus *Helenium;* a sneezeweed.

1790 [see CROWFOOT I b]. **1847** WOOD *Botany* 142 R[anunculus] *acris,* . . . Yellow Weed, . . . is the most common species from Penn. to Hudson's Bay. **1863** MITCHELL *My Farm* 123 In some fields, stunted, draggled cedar bushes, and masses of yellow-weed. **1891** *Cent.* 7017/1 *Yellow-weed,* . . . a common name of coarse species of goldenrod. **1900** WEBSTER *Suppl.* 237/2 *Yellowweed,* . . . a common composite annual weed (*Helenium tenuifolium*) growing abundantly in waste places throughout the Southern United States.

attrib. **1874** *Vermont Bd. Agric. Rep.* II. 777 The beetles are often common upon yellow-weed blossoms.

Yellow willow. The golden osier (*Salix vitellina*) {1742– (Ellis *Timber-Tree* II. 186)}, having yellow twigs used in basket-making, or a related or similar plant. Also attrib.

1785 WASHINGTON *Diaries* II. 346 Planted the remainder of the . . . yellow Willow in the Shrubberies. **1807** *Gales's N.C. Almanack* 35 A friend to agricultural improvements is desirous that some of our farmers would make the experiment in manufacturing sugar from the sap of the Yellow Willow. **1813** MUHLENBERG *Cat. Plants* 91 *Salix vitellina,* Yellow willow. **1847** HOWE *Hist. Coll. Ohio* 521 The Indians were quietly smoking their pipes filled with a mixture of tobacco, sumach leaves and kinnickinnick, or yellow willow bark. **1897** SUDWORTH *Arborescent Flora* 124 *Salix cordata lutea.* . . . Yellow Willow.

Yellow-winged, *a.* In the specific names of birds and insects. {1764} — **1811** Yellow-Winged Sparrow [see SPARROW 2]. **1839** AUDUBON *Ornith. Biog.* V. 497 Yellow-Winged Bunting. *Fringilla Passerina.* **1841** T. W. HARRIS *Rep. Insects Mass.* 143 *Locusta sulphurea.* Yellow-winged locust. . . . It is a rare species in this vicinity. **1891** *Cent.* 7017/1 Blue yellow-winged warbler, *Helminthophaga chrysoptera.*

+**Yellow woman. 1.** A woman of mixed blood, as a mulatto or quadroon, having a yellowish complexion. **2.** A Chinese woman. — (1) **1831** PECK *Guide* 72 Much has been said about certain connections that are winked at with the yellow women of [New Orleans]. (2) **1873** BEADLE *Undevel. West* 302 We plunge into the dark alleys lined by little cubby-holes alive with yellow women.

Yellowwood. Any one of various trees having yellow wood, or the wood of such a tree. {1666-}
+**a.** =OSAGE ORANGE 1. +**b.** =GOPHER WOOD. +**c.** =SWEETLEAF. +**d.** The boxwood of Florida, *Schaefferia frutescens.* +**e.** The shrub yellowroot, *Zanthorrhiza apiifolia.* +**f.** The American smoke tree, *Cotinus cotinoides.* +**g.** =BUCKTHORN 1.
1806 in *Ann. 9th Congress* 2 Sess. 1138 At this place Mr. Dunbar obtained one or two slips of the 'bois d'arc,' (bow wood, or yellow wood). **1810** MICHAUX *Arbres* I. 39 Virgilia lutea. . . . *Yellow wood* (Bois jaune), nom donné à cet arbre dans l'Etat de Tennessée. **1821** *Amer. Jrnl. Science* III. 44 On the Arkansas and on Red River, we have a great quantity of yellow wood. **1860** CURTIS *Woody Plants N.C.* 65 Yellow Wood. (*Symplocos tinctoria.*) . . . The leaves . . . afford, by decoction, a beautiful yellow color. **1884** SARGENT *Rep. Forests* 39 *Schaefferia frutescens.* . . . Yellow Wood. Box Wood. Semi-tropical Florida, southern keys from Metacombe Key eastward. **1891** *Cent.* 5386/3 A small tree of southern Florida and the neighboring islands, produces a valuable wood which from its color and hardness is known by the names of *yellow-wood* and *boxwood.* *Ib.* 7017/2 *Yellow-wood,* . . . the shrub-yellowroot, *Xanthorrhiza apiifolia.* **1897** SUDWORTH *Arborescent Flora* 274 *Cotinus cotinoides.* . . . American Smoke-tree. . . . [Also called] Yellowwood (Ala.). *Ib.* 298 *Rhamnus caroliniana.* . . . Indian Cherry. . . . [Also called] Yellow-wood (Ala., Fla., La.). *Ib.* 299 *Rhamnus purshiana.* Bearberry. . . . [Also called] Yellow-wood (Oreg.).

*** Yelp,** *n.* +The short, repetitious, staccato note of the turkey hen, or a call imitative of this. — **1846** [see CRITTER 2]. **1885** *Outing* VII. 65/1 The yelp, or call, was answered by a gobbler.

*** Yelp,** *v.* +*tr.* To call *up* (a wild turkey) by imitating the yelp or call of a turkey hen. — **1894** *Harper's Mag.* Nov. 885/2 The hunter hastily improvises a 'blind' of pine boughs, and 'yelps them up' if he can.

+**Yengeese.** *pl.* [Said to be a corruption by American Indians of *English.*] Used by Indians of the New England settlers, and, later, of white people in general. Also, in sing., *Yengee. Obs.*
Sometimes regarded as the source of *Yankee.* See YANKEE *n.* note.
1818 HECKEWELDER *Acct. Ind. Nations* 133 What a number of people are coming along! . . . Not one *long knife.* All *Yengees!* **1841** COOPER *Deerslayer* x, I no Mingo—good Delaware—Yengeese friend. [**1865** W. BOYD *Swartzen* 4 Yengee sled or roomy traineau.] **1867** DIXON *New America* I. 68 The Yengee has taught the Indian to drink whisky.

*** Yeoman.** Also †yeaman. The owner of a small farm; a countryman. Now *rare.*
1654 *Suffolk Deeds* II. 35 Edward Deuotion of Muddy Ryuer within the presinckts of boston aforesayd yeaman. **1705** *Charlestown Land Rec.* 171 Robert Wyer, Inholder, and Eleizer Bateman, Yeoman, . . . Lett unto the said John Wesson, one Certain Tract or parcel of Land. **1836** DUNLAP *Mem. Water Drinker* (1837) I. 55 Nor could the yeomen's daughters tolerate her manners or caprices. **1872** *Atlantic Mo.* Jan. 16 The yeomen of Virginia . . . were sometimes sorely put to it when a sum of money was to be raised. **1900** *Congress. Rec.* 3 Feb. 1477/2 On every side . . . are scattered the towns . . . of the sturdy and industrious yeomen of Berks [Co., Pa.].

+**b.** *Yeoman of the gun room,* formerly, in the United States Navy, a petty officer having charge of the gun room on a warship. *Obs.*
1794 *Ann. 3d Congress* 1426 The following petty officers . . . shall be appointed by the captains of the ships . . . : two gunner's mates, one yeoman of the gun room [etc.]. **1796** *Ann. 4th Congress* 2 Sess. 2787 Pay of the officers, seamen, and marines [per month]: . . . 2 Yeomen of the Gun Rooms, [$]13.

+**Yep,** *adv.* Yes. *colloq.* — **1891** *Harper's Mag.* Nov. 970/1 He gently and peacefully murmured, 'Yep.' **1914** STEELE *Storm* 45 'Tobacco?' asked one of the whisperers. 'Yep,' another answered.

+**Yerba buena.** [Sp., 'good herb.'] **1.** *cap.* A name formerly given to San Francisco: (see also second quot. 1872). **2.** (See quot. 1915.) Also attrib. — (1) **1843** MARRYAT *M. Violet* xvi, This settlement [on San Francisco Bay] . . . is called *Yerba buena* (the good grass), from the beautiful meadows of wild clover which extend around it for hundreds of miles. **1872** McCLELLAN *Golden State* 144 Their unmarked graves occupy their uncertain tenure in the shifting sands of *Yerba Buena! Ib.* 196 Directly in the line between San Francisco and Oakland, midway in the bay, is *Yerba Buena,* or *Goat island.* **1875** *Scribner's Mo.* July 266/2 Its [San Francisco's] very name—'Yerba Buena'—was strange to American ears. (2) **1882** HARTE *Flip* 15 He seized a few of the young, tender green leaves of the yerba buena vine . . . and ate them. **1915** ARMSTRONG & THORNBER *Western Wild Flowers* 436 Yerba Buena, Tea-vine. *Micromeria Chamissonis.* . . . It was used medicinally by California Indians, so it was called 'good herb' by the Mission Fathers, and is still used as a tea by Spanish-Californians.

+**Yerba mansa.** [Sp., 'mild herb.'] (See quot. 1891.) — **1891** *Cent.* 7018/3 *Yerba mansa,* a Californian herb, *Anemopsis Californica,* of the *Piperaceae.* **1898** A. M. DAVIDSON *Calif. Plants* 174 Many people think the yerba mansa useful as a medicine.

+**Yerba santa.** *W.* [Sp., 'holy herb.'] Any one of several shrubs of the genus *Eriodictyon.* (Cf. BEAR-WEED.) — **1894** *Amer. Folk-Lore* VII. 94 *Eriodictyon glutinosum,* palo santo, yerba santa, Cal. **1910** J. HART *Vigilante Girl* 344 The keener odor of the yerba santa reached her nostrils.

Yerb tea. (See HERB TEA.)

+**Yes sir-ee,** *adv.* An emphatic form of *yes.* (Cf. NO SIR-EE *adv.*) — **1852** *Knickerb.* XXXIX. 474 'Do you know you were not [knocked down]?' 'Yes, Sir-ee!' **1853** BUNN *Old Eng. & New Eng.* p. iii, The more accepted mode of answering, nowadays, when an American means there should be no mistake, is, 'Yes, Sir-ee.' **1898** HARRIS *Tales of Home Folks* 225 Cassy Tatum! Yes, siree! The very gal!

*** Yew.**
*** 1.** Any one of various trees and shrubs of the genus *Taxus* or a similar or related genus. Also *yew tree.*
+**a.** The native species of the eastern United States, the ground hemlock, *Taxus canadensis.* **b.** The English yew (*T. baccata*), cultivated in the United States. +**c.** The Pacific or short-leaved yew (*T. brevifolia*) of the western states. +**d.** Locally, any one of various plants resembling either the English or the American species.
1785 MARSHALL *Amer. Grove* 150 *Taxus.* The Yew-Tree. **1815** DRAKE *Cincinnati* 83 [The] yew, mountain maple, . . . and witch hazle I have only found at the falls of the Little Miami. **1844** DE SMET *Oregon Missions* 82 In no part of this region have I met with a more luxuriant growth of pine, fir, elm, oak, buttonball, and yew-trees. **1873** *Amer. Naturalist* VII. 628 A Yew Flowering in Winter. **1884** SARGENT *Rep. Forests* 186 *Taxus Floridana.* . . . Yew. . . . Rare and very local. **1897** SUDWORTH *Arborescent Flora* 76 *Cupressus guadalupensis.* . . . Arizona Cypress. . . . [Also called] Yew (Ariz.). *Ib.* 102 *Tumion californicum.* . . . California Torreya. . . . [Also called] Yew (Idaho).

2. With specifying or qualifying terms.
See also AMERICAN YEW.
1785 MARSHALL *Amer. Grove* 151 *Taxus canadensis.* Canadian Yew-Tree. . . . A beautiful evergreen shrub, capable of being formed into any shape. **1847** WOOD *Botany* 518 *T[axus] Canadensis.* Dwarf Yew. Ground Hemlock. **1863** European Yew [see EUROPEAN *a.* 1]. **1897** SUDWORTH *Arborescent Flora* 102 f.

Yiddish. A mixed language of German origin spoken by European and American Jews {1886-} — **1899** *Boston Globe* 3 Dec. 33/1 Yiddish is . . . 70 percent German, 20 percent Hebrew and 10 percent Slavic. **1920** SANDBURG *Smoke & Steel* 30 The front rooms hither and yon and signs in Yiddish.

*** Yield,** *v. tr.* To relinquish (the right to speak on the floor of a legislative assembly); to relinquish (a part or a given amount of one's speaking time). Also *absol.* — **1846** *Congress. Globe* 18 April 687/2 Mr. Jefferson Davis took the floor; but yielded it for a moment to Mr. Daniel. **1864** *Ib.* 5 March 934/2, I ask the gentleman from Vermont to yield to me for about five minutes. **1908** STEVENS *Liberators* 224 No member should yield his time to any other member.

Y.M.C.A. Abbrev. for YOUNG MEN'S CHRISTIAN ASSOCIATION. {1881-} Also attrib. — **1880** CABLE *Grandissimes* 17 There were no 'Howards' or 'Y.M.C.A.'s' in those days. **1883** FULTON *Sam Hobart* 131 Edwin D. Ingersoll, Railroad Secretary of the Y.M.C.A., . . . traversed the field of his labors years after he went higher. **1893** POST *Harvard Stories* 5 Hardly anyone knows him except . . . some of his Y.M.C.A. pals. **1896** *Columbus Dispatch* 3 Oct. 2/5 The first pentathlon contest . . . will take place in the Y.M.C.A. gymnasium. **1917** MATHEWSON *Second Base Sloan* 135 Pattern preferred his room at the Y.M.C.A.

+**Yo-hah, Yohay, Yo-ho.** [Imitative.] Among the Indians, an interjection expressive of pleasure or approval. — **1751** GIST *Journals* 49 We send You these four Strings of Wampum, to which they gave the usual Yo Ho. **1751** J. BARTRAM *Observations* 22 They gave us the *Yohay,* a particular *Indian* expression of approbation. **1791** J. LONG *Voyages* 56 These gifts were received with a full yo-hah, or demonstration of joy.

*** Yoke. a.** A device for joining two draft animals, as oxen. **b.** A collar or frame placed on a pig or other animal running loose, in order to limit freedom of action. — **1636** [see RING *n.* 2]. **1682** *Jamaica* (L.I.) *Rec.* I. 223 Hogs . . . [shall be] yoked with a yoke a foot and halfe long. **1746** *N.H. Probate Rec.* III. 420, I also Give to my sd. Wife all my . . . Farming Tackling . . . Excepting . . . ye Yoke in which ye aboves[ai]d Steers have Commonly Wrought. **1850** BROWNE *Poultry Yard* 215 It is usual to prevent them [*sc.* geese] getting through the gaps in fences, by hanging a stick or 'yoke' across their breasts.

+**Yokeag(e).** Also **yokeke(a)g.** ['A corruption of Pequot-Mohegan *yok'hig,* an abbreviation of *yok'higan* '(what is) made soft' (Hodge).] =ROKEAG(E). — **1697** SEWALL *Letter-Book* I. 188, I pray your acceptance of a little Boston Yokeheag. **1701** — *Diary* II. 27 Eat Yokeheg in Milk. **1848** [see ROKEAG(E).]. **1910** HODGE, etc. *Amer. Indians* II. 999/1 *Yokeag* . . . is still prepared by the Pequot-Mohegan of the Indian reservation on Thames r., Conn., and is sometimes sold by them to their white neighbors, who eat it with milk and sometimes with ice cream.

+**Yonkapin.** Also **yoncopin, yonkypin.** Variants of WANKAPIN. Also attrib. — **1872** *Amer. Naturalist* VI. 726 Very curious peltate leaves, looking somewhat like miniatures of the great lotus or 'yonkapins.' **1891** *Cent.* 6816/1 *Wankapin.* . . . Also *yoncopin.* **1920** COOPER *Under Big Top* 73 Hard, black affairs, such as we knew in kidhood days as 'yonkypin nuts.'

*** Yonker, Younker.** [Du. *jonker.*] A man of property and position in society; a proprietor of lands; a patroon. *Obs.* {-c1645} +Also *Yonkers* (orig. possessive), as a place name.
1666 *N.Y. Council Minutes* I. 234 Mary [Oneale] . . . laid clayme to a certaine parcell of Land . . . Commonly called ye Younckers Land . . . [and] brought seuerall Indians before ye Governor to acknowledg the

purchase of ye said Lands by Vander Dunck commonly called ye Younker. **1668** *Ib.* 23 The Def[endan]t . . . hath purchased Land near adjoyning that was the Youncker Van der Duncks. **1734** *N.-Y. Wkly. Jrnl.* 12 Aug. 4/1 From the Country Seat of Fred. Philipse, Esq; in Westchester County, commonly called the Yonkers, we hear that [etc.]. **1754** *Doc. Col. Hist. N.Y.* VI. 839 Even if the real line of Jersey is to run from the Forks of Delaware . . . to the Station on Hudson's River opposite to the lower Yonkers. [**1870** *Putnam's Mag.* Sept. 243/1 Before the Revolution, Mr. Phillipse . . . was always spoken of by his tenantry as 'the Yonker'—*the* gentleman—*par excellence.*]

+Yop(p)on. (See YAUPON.)

+York. [Short for NEW YORK.]

1. New York City or New York State. *colloq.*[2]

1840 in *Amer. Speech* XVI. 231/1 'A stuffer' . . . persuaded Robert that he could not live here in York, without a watch. **1855** BARNUM *Life* 22 He had been to 'York.' **1871** DE VERE 653 The 'Associated Press' . . . at once adopted certain well-known abbreviations: . . . New York and New Orleans appeared [in telegraph and cable messages] simply as *York* and *Orleans.* **1901** 'FLYNT' *World of Graft* 91 York has always been my hangout.

2. *ellipt.* = NEW YORK CURRENCY. Used adverbially. *Obs.*

1845 COOPER *Chainbearer* xxviii, The lot's worth forty pounds York.

3. *attrib.* **a.** Designating units or systems of exchange acceptable in, or belonging to, New York.

See also YORK SHILLING.

1688 *N.J. Archives* 1 Ser. II. 31, I have secured yo[u]r money & have got it payed in this day being 26 lib . . 2d York money. **1758** *Lett. to Washington* II. 279 The York Bill you Inclosed will over pay the postage of your Letter. **1765** ROGERS *Journals* 161 My own sley was taken with 1196 l. York currency in cash.

b. Designating persons or things associated in some way with New York.

1705 *Boston News-Letter* 12 March 2/2 A French Privateer . . . supposed the York man to be a Merchant man. **1789** MACLAY *Deb. Senate* 148 The York Senators and representatives were in the committee-room. **1843** STEPHENS *High Life N.Y.* II. 240 For a York gal, she has a snakish turn for business. **1894** FORD *P. Stirling* 73 His mother . . . had always known her Peter was a hero, and needed no 'York papers' to teach her the fact.

*Yorker.

+1. A person born in, living in, or coming from, New York City or New York State; a New Yorker.

1758 *Essex Inst. Coll.* XVIII. 102 A party of Rangers, Regulars and Yorkers were in ye Front. **1776** A. ADAMS *Familiar Lett.* 229 A regiment of Yorkers refused to quit the city. **1784** *Mass. Centinel* 30 June 3/2 Animosities [are] subsisting between the Yorkers and the Green Mountain Boys. **1836** HILDRETH *Campaigns Rocky Mts.* 15 They are all 'Yorkers,' that is, from the western portion of our state. **1901** FLYNT *World of Graft* 91, I'm a Yorker really.

+2. = YORK SHILLING.

1909 *Dialect Notes* III. 418 *Yorker,* twelve and a half cents.

+Yorkino. (See quotation.) — **1836** EDWARD *Hist. Texas* 125 The Creole party is divided into several factions. First, the *Aristocratic.* . . . They are also called *Yorkinos* and *Anglicans* because under English influence, and leaning towards European connections.

+York River. [Estuary in Virginia.] An oyster of an American variety. — **1839** *S. Lit. Messenger* V. 837/1 A Steak—a dozen of 'York River,' done with a pinch of salt, but no butter, in their own liquor, over a slow fire—and the repast crowned with a bunch of Grapes. **1844** *Knickerb.* XXIII. 500 Here we are with . . . our York-rivers.

+York shilling. {1883, in Canada} A New York shilling (q.v.), valued ordinarily at 12½ cents. Also *attrib.* (Cf. ELEVENPENNY BIT.) — **1824** *Mass. Spy* 8 Sept. (Th.), This remark quickly brought a York shilling out of my pocket for toll. **1855** 'CARLTON' *New Purchase* (ed. 2) 4 The Mass-men resolving to devour only a Penneth of Book at a time, or at most a York-Shilling worth. **1898** HARPER *S. B. Anthony* I. 123 At the evening session a 'York shilling' admittance fee was charged. **1900** DIX *Deacon Bradbury* 241, I would n't give a York shilling for it. **1909** *Dialect Notes* III. 418 *York shilling,* same as *Yorker.*

*Yorkshire. 1. A breed of swine. {attrib., 1770-} **2.** *attrib.* Designating cloths or goods coming from, or associated in some way with, Yorkshire. {1612-} — **(1)** **1895** *Bur. Animal Industry Circ.* No. 4, 3 A few instances of disease among my 'improved breeds,' Poland, Chester Whites, Durocs, and Yorkshires. **(2)** **1732** [see KERSEY 1]. **1784** *Mass. Centinel* 26 June 3/3 For Sale, a Variety of Goods, by wholesale, amongst which are, . . . Yorkshire Planes, Shalloons, [etc.].

+York State. New York State. Also *attrib.* — **1823** *Daily Nat. Intelligencer* 1 May 1/4. **1828** J. HALL *Lett. from West* 170 On arriving at an inn . . . in New England [I answered] the tedious inquiries whether I was a *southerner,* or a *York-state* man. **1855** BARNUM *Life* 111 Several eccentric individuals from 'York State' were in the habit of visiting Bethel. **1904** WALLER *Wood-Carver* 103, I can . . . keep him answering questions as to how he did things when he was a boy over in York State.

+York wagon. a. A substantial wagon of a kind built in York, Pennsylvania, for carrying goods. **b.** A carriage of a certain type: (see quot. 1841). — **1824** *Mass. Yeoman* 11 Feb. (Th.), In an instant he cap-

sized a York-waggon, threw out the riders, and threw down the horse. **1838** 'UNCLE SAM' in *Bentley's Misc.* IV. 134 Purchasing a 'York waggon,' or shandy, to convey myself and goods, I bade adieu to the 'city of brotherly love.' **1841** PARK *Pantology* 480 The York waggon has a single seat, without a top; but . . . four wheels. **1843** 'UNCLE SAM' *Peculiarities* I. 155 In the county of Columbia . . . stands a country 'tavern and hotel,' much frequented by travellers in stage-coaches, gigs, sulkies, 'York wagons. **1856** *Porter's Spirit of Times* 4 Oct. 67/1 They didn't have no York waggins and the likes at that time [1835].

+Yosemite. [See note.] The name given to a valley, a series of falls, and a public park in California. Used *attrib.*

'Powers states that the name Yosemite is a distorted form of the Miwok *uzumaiti,* 'grizzly bear,' a term never used by the Indians to designate the valley itself or any part of it' (Hodge).

1868 *Calif. Geol. Survey* (*title*), The Yosemite Book: A Description of the Yosemite Valley. **1881** *Ore. State Jrnl.* 1 Jan. 5/5 Our enterprising druggist . . . [has] secured the agency for Slaven's Famous Yosemite Cologne. **1915** ARMSTRONG & THORNBER *Western Wild Flowers* 192 Yosemite Stonecrop. *Sedum Yosemitense.* . . . On moss-covered rocks, moistened by the glistening spray blowing from the Yosemite waterfalls, we find these beautiful plants.

+Yosemitic, *a.* [f. prec.] Associated in some way with the Yosemite Valley. *rare.* — **1894** MUIR *Mountains of Calif.* 276, [I have found] countless waterfalls . . . in the Sierra, . . . among the icy peaks, or warm foot-hills, or in the profound yosemitic cañons of the middle region.

+You-all(s), *pron.* You. Used in addressing a number of persons, and also in addressing two persons or an individual: (see note). *colloq.* Chiefly *S.*

'It is commonly believed in the North that Southerners use *you-all* in the singular, but this is true, if it is ever true at all, of only the most ignorant of them. The word may be addressed to individuals, but only when they are thought of as representatives of a group. . . . The literature of the subject is extensive and full of bitterness' (1936 Mencken *Amer. Language* (ed. 4) 449n.). Of the examples below, quot. 1901, a literary treatment of a western scene, is the only clear instance of the use of the singular.

1869 *Overland Mo.* III. 131 During the war we all heard enough of 'we-uns' and 'you-uns,' but 'you-alls' was to me something fresh. **1896** HARRIS *Sister Jane* 51, I don't want to worry you-all. **1901** WHITE *Westerners* 8 Reckon you-all fills the bill. **1911** SAUNDERS *Col. Todhunter* 165 Angelica's been confidin' in you and Mrs. Todhunter, and you-all have sided with her.

+b. Used as an indefinite pronoun.

1897 LEWIS *Wolfville* 54 When you-all stampedes a bunch of ponies that a-way they don't hold together like cattle. *Ib.* 179 You-alls can't run no brand on melodies.

*Young, *a.*

+1. *Young America.* **a.** *Polit.* A name or slogan used with reference to a wave of expansionist sentiment beginning in the 1840's and culminating in a movement within the Democratic party characterized by desire to spread American ideals and institutions and to extend American influence. **b.** A single representative, or, collect., the entire body of American youth; the characteristics attributed to young Americans. *colloq.* Also *fig.*

1845 E. DE LEON (*title*), Position and Duties of 'Young America,' an Address Delivered before the Two Literary Societies of the South Carolina College. **1850** *Knickerb.* XXXVI. 288, I heard 'Young America' shout, . . . 'Pa, you go back now!' **1852** in *Amer. Hist. Rev.* XXXII. 45 The grand ideas which are the most potent in the election are . . . the ideas for which the term *Young America* is the symbol. **1853** *S. Lit. Messenger* XIX. 70/1 It was the old fogy against young America. a1861 WINTHROP *J. Brent* 22 It [a wine] is romantic old Spain, with ardent young America interfused. **1873** *Newton Kansan* 10 July 3/4 Young America's [*sic*], like small armies in battle, assisted in the grand jubilee. **1918** LINCOLN *Shavings* 234 He seemed to typify young america setting cheerfully forth to face—anything.

attrib. and *comb.* **1852** *Harper's Mag.* Dec. 128/1 There is . . . the absurd yet dangerous spirit of 'Young-America-ism.' **1855** M. THOMPSON *Doesticks* 325 The waxen boy in a scratch wig and full suit of Young America clothes. **1886** *Outing* April 94/2 One of the most flourishing base-ball clubs in the country is the Young America Base-Ball Club of Philadelphia.

+2. In the specific names of animals and plants.

1814 MITCHILL *Fishes N.Y.* 405 Grunts. *Labrus grunniens.* . . . This fish is called, by the fishermen, *young sheep's head,* and young drum, from its resemblance to those creatures. **1825** *Amer. Jrnl. Science* XI. 278 *Menopoma Alleghaniensis.* . . . Hell-bender. . . . Young Alligator. **1892** *Amer. Folk-Lore* V. 100 *Gaultheria procumbens,* young plantlets; . . . young chinks; . . . young ivories.

+3. In special combinations.

Young Democracy, the radical faction of the Democratic party in New York State in the period following the nomination of Polk (see BARNBURNER); *Y. Napoleon,* Gen. George B. McClellan (1826-85); *Y. Republic,* Texas; *Y. Scratcher,* in the Republican party in New York State, a member of a faction expressing its disapproval of party leadership by scratching certain candidates' names from the ticket (now hist.).

1851 J. F. W. JOHNSTON *Notes N. Amer.* I. 218 [Radical Democrats] are stigmatised as *Barnburners*, but call themselves the '*Young Democracy*,' or the '*Progressive Young Democracy.*' **1871** DE VERE 250 General McClellan was *Little Mac* or *Young Napoleon.* **1852** *Knickerb.* XL. 387 While on a visit to Texas, I was induced, by the favorable accounts I had received from the 'West,' to reconnoitre that portion of the 'Young Republic.' **1879** *Nation* 9 Oct. 233/3 These young Scratchers will not be stopped from scratching by hearing that the venerable editor of the *Tribune* . . . thinks it foolishness.

+Young American, *n.* and *a.* **1.** *n.* A representative or symbol of the idealism characteristic of the Young America movement. **2.** *adj.* Progressive, enterprising. — **(1) 1844** R. W. EMERSON (*title*), The Young American. **1870** — *Soc. & Solitude* 135 They are so many Young Americans announcing a better era,—more bread. **(2) 1856** *Merry's Museum* XXXI. 79 If ever a city had any reason to be called 'Young American' in its character, that city is St. Paul.

‖**Youngerly**, *a.* [*younger* and *-ly.* Cf. *elderly.*] Belonging to the younger group; not yet middle-aged. *colloq.* — **1868** *Church Union* 11 Jan. (*Cent.*), The life-blood of Christendom flows in the veins of her youngerly men.

Younger set. The coterie of young people regarded as the leaders in society; the smart set among young people. — **1900** NORRIS *Blix* 29 They two . . . had been in a measure identified with what was known as the Younger Set. **1917** [see PACK PEDDLER].

+Young Hickory. *Polit.* Any one of various men in public life. A nickname given with allusion to Andrew Jackson as 'Old Hickory' (q.v.).

The use of this nickname for Martin Van Buren, reported by Charles Ledyard Norton in *Mag. Amer. Hist.* XIII. 496/2 and also given by Farmer, Clapin, and *Cycl. Amer. Govt.*, has no supporting citations.

1. James Knox Polk (1795-1849), eleventh president of the United States (1845-49).

1844 *Congress. Globe* App. 3 June 598/2 In consequence of the intimate personal relations between them [*sc.* Jackson and Polk], as well as the perfect concurrence in their political opinions, and principles, and action, he [*sc.* Polk] has been called the 'Young Hickory.' **1846** *Ib.* 24 Dec. 225/1 When 'Young Hickory' went to the White House, the spirit of 'Old Hickory' did not go with him, but the spirit of Kinderhook—no, of Lindenwold, did. **1864** NICHOLS *Amer. Life* I. 255 The President—the veritable Young Hickory, sixty years old, I think, . . . received me with dignified politeness.

2. David Bennett Hill (1843-1910), governor of New York (1885-91).

1892 MCKEE *U.S.* 'Snap Shots' 248.

Young idea. A child, or, collect., children. *colloq.* (Perhaps with allusion to Thomson's line: To teach the young Idea how to shoot.) {1728} — **1840** HONE *Diary* II. 17 When I was a lad, the 'young idea' [was] first beginning to put on its percussion-caps. **1866** *Ore. State Jrnl.* 24 Nov. 3/1 It is impossible to keep a supply of schoolmarms on hand to teach the young ideas.

Young man. +Among the Indians, a male who is, by reason of youth, not yet entitled ordinarily to play an important part in formal deliberations of representatives of the social group; a young warrior. — **1822** Morse *Rep. Indian Affairs* II. 143 We address our Chiefs and Council by the terms, Brothers, Chiefs, and Warriors, and lately, Young Men. **1848** COOPER *Oak Openings* II. 84 Even the 'young men,' unless chiefs, were to be merely distant spectators.

Young men's. The possessive pl. of *young man* in the names of organizations composed of young men or formed to help young men. {1858-} — **1835** S. *Lit. Messenger* I. 273 In all the cities, and many of the larger and middling towns . . . there are . . . Young Men's Societies. **1865** *Atlantic Mo.* March 362/2 A lecture before the Young Men's Associations . . . is any characteristic utterance of any man who speaks in their employment. **1883** *Century Mag.* May 76/1 We thought of a Young Men's Club, like that at New Albion.

Young Men's Christian Association. An international organization, founded in England in 1844, working for the welfare of young men, as by educational work, organized recreation, and the provision of suit-able living quarters. Also attrib. (Cf. Y.M.C.A.) — **1851** in L. L. Doggett *History of Y.M.C.A.* I. 116 The name of this society shall be the 'Boston Young Men's Christian Association,' and its object the improvement of the spiritual and mental condition of young men. **1872** MCCLELLAN *Golden State* 399 There are about five thousand five hundred volumes in the Young Men's Christian Association library. **1882** MCCABE *New York* 313 The Young Men's Christian Association Building stands opposite the Academy of Design. *Ib.* 314 The building is the property of the New York branch of the Young Men's Christian Association. **1900** *Congress. Rec.* 19 Feb. 1919/2 This section, if allowed to apply to the Territory of Hawaii, would interfere with . . . the Young Men's Christian Association ownership of property.

Young Women's Christian Association. An organization working, by methods similar to those of the Young Men's Christian Association (q.v.), to promote the welfare of young women. — **1867** in *Boston Y.W.C.A. Rep.* 1868 2 Pauline A. Durant, Ann Maria Sawyer, Hannah A. Bowen, Clara S. Wells, their associates and successors, are hereby made a Corporation by name of the 'Boston Young Women's Christian Association.' **1915** E. PACKARD *Study of Living Conditions* 9 'Investigate before, not afterwards,' was the principle which made the Young Women's Christian Association decide to investigate the living conditions of girls in New York City.

+Younker. (See YONKER.)

+You-uns, *pron. pl.* S. You. *dial.* {you yins 1885, *Sc.*} Also in sing. sense. — **1810** M. DWIGHT *Journey to Ohio* 37 Youns is a word I have heard used several times, but what it means I don't know. **1871** HAY *Pike Co. Ballads* 25 But I'll tell the yarn to youans. **1880** *Harper's Mag.* Sept. 534/2 You-uns had better keep close, single file. **1885** 'CRADDOCK' *Prophet* 7, I hev no call ter spen' words . . . with a free-spoken man like you-uns. **1923** *Dialect Notes* V. 214 Has you-uns ever met up afore?

* **Yucca.**

1. A plant belonging to an American genus of liliaceous plants having a woody stem, stiff, pointed leaves, and a cluster of large white flowers. {1664-}

1774 in Peyton *Adv. Grandfather* (1867) 68 We made the first day in the scorching sun twenty-six miles through a sandy desert, covered with cactus, endemis, yuccas [etc.]. **1823** JAMES *Exped.* II. 192 The first range of primitive rocks . . . [is] destitute of vegetation, except a few prickly pears and yuccas. **1895** G. KING *New Orleans* 260 The great moat, alive with fish, with on its farther bank a thick hedge of yucca, or Spanish dagger. **1910** J. HART *Vigilante Girl* 350 Interminable files of the tall yucca marched like silent soldiers toward the horizon.

2. Attrib. and comb. with *cactus, borer, fibre*, etc.

1845 FRÉMONT *Exped.* 256 Yucca trees . . . suited well with the dry and desert region we were approaching. *Ib.* 257 We . . . emerged from the *yucca* forest at the foot of an *outlier* of the Sierra before us. **1851** M. REID *Scalp Hunters* xviii, She was standing under one of the yuca palm trees that grew up from the azotea. **1870** *Amer. Naturalist* IV. 581 Other remarkable forms are . . . the yucca-leaved rattlesnake master, or button snakeroot (*Cryngium yuccæfolium*). **1873** *Ib.* VII. 475 The yucca is incapable of self-fertilization, and . . . the yucca moth [*Pronuba yuccasella*] . . . effects it. **1885** *Wkly. New Mexican Rev.* 8 Jan. 3/6 A mammoth English syndicate . . . will engage in raising yucca plant on a large scale. **1887** *Century Mag.* May 44/2 This Yucca palm is commonly known as the Spanish bayonet and oftentimes as the soap-weed. **1891** *Cent.* 7026/2 *Yucca-borer.* 1. A large North American castnioid moth, *Megathymus yuccæ*, whose larva bores into the roots of plants of the genus *Yucca*. 2. A Californian weevil, *Yuccaborus frontalis.* **1893** LUMMIS *Land of Poco Tiempo* 36 In 1540 the Pueblo dressed in . . . tunics of yucca fibre. **1897** SUDWORTH *Arborescent Flora* 106 *Yucca arborescens*, . . . Joshua Yucca. . . . [Also called] Yucca cactus (Cal.).

+Yucker. =FLICKER. Also *yawker bird.* — **1808** WILSON *Ornithology* I. 53 [The Gold-winged woodpecker] has numerous provincial appellations . . . , such as . . . 'Yucker,' 'Piut,' 'Flicker.' **1844** [see HIGH-HOLE]. **1917** *Birds of Amer.* II. 163 Flicker. . . . [Also called] Yawker Bird; Walk-up.

+Yukon stove. (See quot. 1898.) — **1898** W. B. HASKELL *2 Yrs. in Klondike* 75 The 'Yukon stove' . . . is a small sheet iron box with an oven at the back and a telescope pipe. **1908** CANTON *Frontier Trails* 156, I took his advice and bought a Yukon stove, which is a flat sheet-iron stove and very light.

Z

∗Z. The twenty-sixth letter of the alphabet. *Hist.* +Used to indicate a person: (see X 1). — **1797** *Amer. State P.: For. Relations* II. 162 On the 22d of October, M. Z. a French gentleman of respectable character informed Mr. Gerry, that [etc.]. **1798, 1841** [see X 1].

Zambo. A person of mixed Negro and Indian blood. *Obs.* {1819-, of S. Amer., etc.} — **1836** EDWARD *Hist. Texas* 120 Their offspring [those of Indians and Negroes], called Washinangoes or *Zambos*, are very hardy and clever. **1850** COLTON *Deck & Port* 279 Zambos are generally employed as household servants.

+**Zanjero.** *S.W.* [Sp.] (See quot. 1877.) — **1877** BARTLETT 771 *Zanjero*, . . . one whose duty it is to take charge of ditches, when used for purposes of irrigation. **1882** *Harper's Mag.* Dec. 49/1 A Zangiero . . . is the official overseer of the water and irrigation system.

+**Zapato.** *S.W.* [Sp.] A shoe or boot. — **1849** T. T. JOHNSON *Sights Gold Region* 70 He was dressed with loose gay linen pants, yellow leather, or buckskin zapatos, or shoes. **1887** *Scribner's Mag.* II. 510/1 The true cow-boy . . . will hop and roll about until he has worn out his *zapatos*. **1907** WHITE *Arizona Nights* 168 He had on . . . the rawhide home-made zapatos the Mexicans wore then instead of boots.

+**Zarape.** (See SARAPE.)

+**Zebra caterpillar.** The striped larva of an American moth, *Ceramica picta.* — **1891** *Cent.* 7030/3 *Zebra-caterpillar.* . . . It feeds on clover, peas, beans, cabbages [etc.]. **1925** HERRICK *Man. Injurious Insects* 253 The Zebra Caterpillar . . . occurs occasionally in sufficient numbers to cause injury to garden crops.

+**Zebra swallowtail.** A large swallow-tailed butterfly (*Iphiclides marcellus*) found in the East. — **1891** *Cent.* 7031/1. **1904** KELLOGG *Amer. Insects* 448 One of the best-known butterflies of the east is the zebra swallowtail.

+**Zenaida dove.** A tropical American pigeon, *Zenaida zenaida.* — **1828** BONAPARTE *Ornithology* III. 23 [The] Zenaida Dove, *Columba Zenaida*, . . . inhabits the Florida keys. **1839** AUDUBON *Ornith. Biog.* V. 558 Zenaida Dove, *Columba Zenaida*, . . . is raised with ease in aviaries. **1895** [see QUAIL 3 b].

∗**Zephyr.** +=WASHOE ZEPHYR. — **1877** W. WRIGHT *Big Bonanza* 253 The 'zephyr' is one of the peculiar institutions of Washoe.

+**Zequia.** (See SEQUIA.)

Zigzag. {1712-} +**1.** =ZIGZAG RAIL FENCE. *Obs.* **2.** (See quotation.) — (1) **1832** TROLLOPE *Domestic Manners* I. 144 And what does a broken zig-zag signify? **1843** 'UNCLE SAM' *Peculiarities* I. 169, I ran like lightning, and getting over a zig-zag, . . . tore my trowsers. **1867** *Atlantic Mo.* Jan. 103/1 Git together enough to make about ten rods o' zigzag, two rails high. (2) **1876** KNIGHT 2829/1 Zigzag, a winding chute on the face of a dam to enable fish to ascend.

+**Zigzag rail fence.** =WORM FENCE 1. — **1898** CANFIELD *Maid of Frontier* 102 The zigzag rail fences looked as straight as a rule.

Zinc. A well-known bluish white metal, used widely in alloys such as brass, nickel, silver, etc., and as a roofing material. {1651-} Also attrib. — **1789** MORSE *Amer. Geog.* 227 Zink or spelter, a semi-metal, and several other fossils and metals have been found in Connecticut. **1819** *Plough Boy* I. 148 In New-York Zinc has lately been tried as a covering for houses. **1867** RICHARDSON *Beyond Miss.* 91 A stout squaw . . . wore zinc ear-rings as large as silver dollars. **1888** *Harper's Mag.* June 48/1 Along the line of Spring River, lead, . . . galena, and zinc, as blende or black-jack and amber-jack, are abundant. **1922** Zinc mine [see LEAD MINE].

+**Zinkite.** (See quot. 1891.) Also attrib. — **1854** DANA *Mineralogy* (ed. 4) II. 100 Zincite Group. **1891** *Cent.* 7035/2 Zinkite, . . . a native

oxid of zinc, found at Franklin Furnace and Stirling Hill, . . . in Sussex county, New Jersey.

Zinnia. Any one of various plants of the tropical American genus *Zinnia*, esp. the common garden plant, *Z. elegans.* {1767-} — **1832** HALE *Flora* 194 Zinnia, *Zinnia multiflora*. . . . Found on the banks of the Mississippi. **1887** WILKINS *Humble Romance* 399 Beyond the dahlias on either side were zinnias and candytuft and marigolds. **1914** E. STEWART *Lett. of Woman Homesteader* 252, I have zinnias, marigolds, hollyhocks, and many other dear old flowers that my mother loved.

+**Zip,** *v. intr.* To go rapidly or with a zip. Also *zipping* n. *colloq.* — **1852** *Knickerb.* XL. 182 How we did 'z-i-p!' **1881** BATTEN *Reminisc. U.S. Navy* 72, I heard the zipping of bullets in the air close to my head. **1914** 'BOWER' *Flying U Ranch* 152 The bullet zipped close over the head of Big Medicine. **1917** McCUTCHEON *Green Fancy* 94 In a few weeks I shall be on my feet again, zipping along on the crest of the wave.

+**Zombi.** [App. from African dialect. Cf. Kongo *zumbi* 'fetish.'] (See quot. 1871.) — **1871** DE VERE 138 Zombi, a phantom or a ghost, not unfrequently heard in the Southern States in nurseries and among the servants, . . . is a Creole corruption of the Spanish *sombra.* **1880** CABLE *Grandissimes* 234 Bras-Coupé hears the voice of zombis.

Zouave. {1830-} +In the Civil War, a member of any one of various volunteer regiments in the Union army adopting features of the dress and the drill of the French Zouaves. Also attrib. (See also FIRE ZOUAVE.) — **1861** E. COWELL *Diary* 311 Colonel William Wilson's Battalion of Zouaves was completed yesterday. **1861** in W. Lawrence *A. A. Lawrence* 168, I am chosen quartermaster of our zouave regiment. **1862** NORTON *Army Lett.* 77 That Zouave cap . . . is dark blue, and, of course, it has no front, that's Zouave style. **1870** O. LOGAN *Before Footlights* 194 A battalion of ferocious Zouaves bayonetting nothing with undiminished ardor during the somewhat protracted space of four years.

+**Zou-Zou.** (See ZU-ZU.)

+**Zuñi.** Also **Suni.** [Sp., from native term of unknown meaning.] An Indian of a tribe residing in a pueblo of the same name in western New Mexico; also, pl., the tribe. Also attrib.

1834 [see MOQUI]. **1863** *Rio Abajo Press* 1 Dec. 2/3 The Zuñi Indians had a war-dance here day before yesterday. **1870** *Republican Rev.* 25 June 2/3 The Zuni village, the first settlement on this road in New Mexico. **1873** [see MOQUI]. **1897** *Outing* XXIX. 345/2 The Zuñis were then a mighty people. **1910** HODGE, etc. *Amer. Indians* II. 1017/2 Fray Martin de Arvide . . . was killed by 5 Zuñi.

b. The language of these Indians.

1883 *Century Mag.* Dec. 201 [From this] amalgamation of Spanish and Zuñi, . . . I inferred that he regarded . . . Zuñi food prepared in Zuñi fashion as worthy of emphatic recommendation.

+**Zuñian.** A Zuñi Indian. — **1848** ROBINSON *Santa Fe Exped.* (1932) 53 The Zunians are a tribe somewhat similar in their habits to the Lagoonies. **1855** WHIPPLE, etc. *Explor. Ry. Route* III. 40 The Zuñians that escaped built the town . . . upon a high mesa.

+**Zu-Zu.** Also **Zou-Zou.** (See quot. 1909.) — **1863** *Harper's Mag.* March 569/2 A Zou-zou . . . found himself arrested by the guard. *c*1870 CHIPMAN *Notes on Bartlett* 521 Zouzou, pet name for a Zouave. **1884** *Century Mag.* Oct. 814/2 You shall have your rations, Zou Zous, to-night. **1909** WEBSTER 2373 Zu-Zu, . . . a familiar nickname for the Zouaves in the Union Army.

BIBLIOGRAPHY

THE PURPOSE of the present bibliography is twofold. It is designed, first, to serve as a record of the bulk of the reading done for the Dictionary, an indication of the documentary evidence for the edited material in the finished book. Second, by expanding into completeness the short-title references used in citations—frequently varied slightly in the text to meet the requirements of space—it will enable the user readily to trace individual quotations to their sources. In accordance with these general aims, books and other sources only occasionally quoted in the Dictionary, and cited in such form that they are readily identifiable, have been omitted from the list.

With respect to fullness of treatment the entries fall into two groups, which in a general way correspond to the two objectives indicated above. The first class, comprising those entires for which the information is limited to author, short title, (sometimes) place of publication, and date, includes two general groups: (1) books of general currency, frequently read from various editions for the Dictionary and cited in it by chapter or by some other reference form appropriate to any edition; and (2) periodicals and other publications for which the title, with the addition of place of publication, is sufficient identification. The second class consists of those sources which, because of obscurity, appearance in a multiplicity of editions, or some other peculiarity, require further identification. Entries in this second group, accordingly, have been supplied with concise but bibliographically adequate descriptions.

NOTES

(1) For works appearing in a number of editions, the effort has been to enter all editions actually used for the Dictionary, although, because of the chronological and geographical distribution of the reading done for the project, and the use made of material read for the *Oxford English Dictionary*, it has not always been easy to be certain of these. In general, notes following imprint ("1st ed. 1885"; "Also: 3d ed. Bost., 1897"; etc.) indicate editions actually read or quoted; purely historical notes ("First publ. 1883"; etc.), however, have been occasionally added in order to explain, without implying actual use of the version cited, apparent discrepancies between dates of actual publication and those assigned to quoted materials.

(2) Exact reprints of texts, as well as originals, have been cited for works read in both versions, even though reprinted texts have been frequently quoted by page numbers of the originals.

(3) The sign of equality (=) indicates that the editions referred to are equivalent in paging.

(4) Boldface dates (and the substitute form "v.d." for "various dates," given to diaries, collections of letters, volumes of short stories, etc.) represent the dates actually assigned in the Dictionary to quoted matter; publication dates, if different from these, have been left in lightface type.

(5) Serials and similar publications, and works issued in more volumes than one, in order to facilitate ready identification, are usually cited as complete files or sets, with inclusive dates; in exceptional circumstances, however, the specific volumes used are individually identified.

BIBLIOGRAPHY

A

ABBOTT, J. S. C. *Christopher Carson.* N.Y., 1875 [cop. **1873**]
South and North. N.Y., **1860**
ABDY, E. S. *Journal of a Residence and Tour in the United States of North America, from April 1833, to October, 1834.* Lond., **1835**
ABERCROMBIE, JOHN. *The Gardener's Daily Assistant in the Modern Practice of English Gardening.* Lond. [**1786**]
ACADEMY OF NATURAL SCIENCES OF PHILADELPHIA *Journal.* Phila., **1817–1918**
ADAIR, JAMES. *The History of the American Indians.* Lond., **1775**
ADAMS, A. See ADAMS, J., and ADAMS, A.
ADAMS, ANDY. *The Log of a Cowboy.* Bost., **1903**. Also: Lond. [n.d.]. (Page references altered to fit Bost. ed.)
ADAMS, JOHN. *Works.* Bost., 1850–6. **v.d.** Includes his: *Diary*
ADAMS, JOHN, and ADAMS, ABIGAIL. *Familiar Letters . . . during the Revolution.* Ed. C.F. Adams. N.Y., 1876. **v.d.**
ADAMS, JOHN QUINCY. *The Diary of John Quincy Adams, 1794–1845.* Ed. Allan Nevins. N.Y., 1929. =1928. **v.d.**
The Duplicate Letters, the Fisheries and the Mississippi. Wash., 1822. **v.d.**
Memoirs. Ed. C.F. Adams. Phila., 1874–7. **v.d.**
ADAMS, S. H. *The Clarion.* Bost., **1914**
ADAMS, W. See CAULKINS
ADAMS, WILLIAM TAYLOR. *Field and Forest; or, The Fortunes of a Farmer.* Bost., 1874. =**1870**
In Doors and Out. [New ed.] Bost., 1876. =1875. First publ. **1854**
ADE, GEORGE. *Artie.* Chic., **1896**
Doc' Horne. Chic., **1899**
Fables in Slang. Lond., 1902. =**1899**
Forty Modern Fables. N.Y., **1901**
In Babel. N.Y., 1906. =**1903**
More Fables. Chic., **1900**
People You Know. N.Y. [**1903**]
Pink Marsh. N.Y. [cop. **1897**]
Advance. Chic., **1867–1917**
The Affecting History of Dreadful Distresses of Frederick Manheim's Family. To Which Are Added, An Encounter between a White Man and Two Savages. . . . [N.p.] Printed for Chapman Whitcomb [1792–3]. **1792**
'AGRICOLA.' *A Series of Essays on Agriculture & Rural Affairs.* Raleigh [N.C.] **1819**
Agricultural Museum. Ed. David Wiley. Georgetown [D.C.] **1810–12**
Ainsworth's Magazine. Lond., **1843–54**. Vols. I–IV include miscellaneous contributions by 'Uncle Sam' (q.v.). **v.d.**
ALABAMA. GEOLOGICAL SURVEY. *Report for the Years 1881 and 1882.* By E. A. Smith. Montgomery, Ala., **1883**
Albany, Annals of. See MUNSELL
ALBANY INSTITUTE. *Transactions.* Albany, 1830–92. **v.d.**
ALCOTT, A. B. *The Journals of Bronson Alcott.* Ed. Odell Shepard. Bost., 1938. **v.d.**
ALCOTT, LOUISA M. *Jo's Boys.* Bost., 1899 = [**1886**]. Also: Bost., 1903. Lond., 1914
Little Women. Bost., **1869**. 2 vols. Vol. I first publ. **1868**
ALDEN, ISABELLA (MCDONALD). *Little Fishers and Their Nets.* **1887**
ALDEN, J. B. *Living Topics Cyclopedia.* Vol. I. N.Y., **1896**
ALDRICH, T. B. *Marjorie Daw, and Other People.* Bost., **1873**
Prudence Palfrey. **1874**
The Queen of Sheba. Bost., **1877**
A Sea Turn, and Other Matters. Bost., **1902**
The Stillwater Tragedy. **1880**
The Story of a Bad Boy. Bost., 1877, 1911. =1870. Also: Bost., 1923. First publ. **1869**
Two Bites at a Cherry, with Other Tales. Bost., **1894**
'ALEXANDER.' See HECTOR
ALLARDICE, R. B. *Agricultural Tour in the United States and Upper Canada.* Edinb., **1842**

ALLEN, A. V. G. *Life and Letters of Phillips Brooks.* N.Y., 1901. **v.d.**
ALLEN, I. *Hist. Vermont.* See VERMONT HISTORICAL SOCIETY
ALLEN, JAMES L. *The Blue-Grass Region of Kentucky, and Other Kentucky Articles.* N.Y., **1892**
The Choir Invisible. N.Y., **1897**
A Kentucky Cardinal. **1894**
ALLEN, JOEL A. *The American Bisons, Living and Extinct.* Cambridge, **1876**. Also as: *History of the American Bison, Bison Americanus.* (In U.S. GEOLOGICAL AND GEOGRAPHICAL SURVEY OF THE TERRITORIES. *Annual Report.* No. 9, 1875. Wash., 1877. Pp. 443–587)
ALLEN, R. L. *The New American Farm Book.* New ed. Rev. and enl. by L. F. Allen. N.Y., **1883**
ALLYN, JOHN. *A Sermon, Delivered at Plimouth, December 22, 1801.* Bost., 1802. **1801**
ALSOP, GEORGE. *A Character of the Province of Maryland.* New ed. By J. G. Shea. N.Y., 1869. (Reprinted: Balt., 1880.) Also publ.: Cleveland, 1902. First publ. **1666**
Alta California. San Francisco, **1849–91**
'ALTON.' See BAILEY, E. A.
ALVORD, C. W., and BIDGOOD, LEE. *The First Explorations of the Trans-Allegheny Region by the Virginians, 1650–1674.* Cleveland, 1912. **v.d.**
America: A Journal for Americans. Chic., **1888–91**. Includes: M. LANE. *American Political Catch-Words, Names, and Phrases.* 13 Sept.—8 Nov. **1888**
American. Phila., **1880–1900**
AMERICAN ACADEMY OF ARTS AND SCIENCES. *Memoirs.* 1780–1821. Bost. [etc.] 1785–[1821]. New ser., 1826–current. Cambridge, 1833–current. **v.d.**
Proceedings. 1846–current. Bost., 1848–current. **v.d.**
AMERICAN ACADEMY OF POLITICAL AND SOCIAL SCIENCE. *Annals.* Phila., **1890–current**
American Almanac and Repository of Useful Knowledge. Bost., **1830–61**
American Almanac and Treasury of Facts. Ed. A. R. Spofford. N.Y., **1878–89**
American Annual Cyclopædia. See *Appletons' Annual Cyclopædia*
AMERICAN ANTIQUARIAN SOCIETY. *Transactions and Collections.* Worcester, 1820–1911. **v.d.** Vols. I–VII as: *Archæologia Americana.* Vol. IV includes: JOSSELYN. *New Eng. Rarities* (q.v.). **1672**. Vol. VII contains: LECHFORD. *Note-Book.* **v.d.** Vol. III includes: J. HULL. *Diaries.* **v.d.** (Cited also as: *Diary Occurr.*)
American Archives. [Comp.] Peter Force. [Wash., 1837–53.] **v.d.**
American Baptist Magazine and Missionary Intelligencer. Bost., **1817–24**
The American Cyclopædia. See *The New American Cyclopædia*
American Encyclopædia of Printing. See RINGWALT
American Farmer. Balt.; Wash., **1819–97**
American Folk-Lore. See *Journal of American Folk-Lore*
AMERICAN FOLK-LORE SOCIETY. *Memoirs.* Bost.; N.Y., **1894–current**. Vol. VII includes: *Animal and Plant Lore.* Ed. F. D. Bergen. **1899**
AMERICAN HISTORICAL ASSOCIATION. *Annual Report.* 1884–. N.Y.; Wash., 1885–. 1907, Vol. II, 1908, Vol. II, Parts I–II: *Diplomatic Correspondence of the Republic of Texas.* Parts I–III. 1908–11. **v.d.** 1919, Vol. II, Parts I–II, 1922, Vol. II: M. AUSTIN. *The Austin Papers.* Ed. E. C. Barker. **v.d.**
American Historical Review. N.Y.; Lancaster, Pa., **1895–current**. Vol. VI includes: J. HARROWER. *Diary.* **v.d.**
The American Home Cook Book. Detroit, **1878**
American Husbandry. Lond., **1775**
American Ind. Society. See *A Documentary History of American Industrial Society*
AMERICAN INSTITUTE OF THE CITY OF NEW YORK. *Transactions . . . for the Year 1854.* Albany, **1855**
American Journal of Science (and Arts). New Haven, **1818–current**. (Also as: *Silliman's Journal of Science*)
American Law Journal. Phila., **1808–17**

American Magazine, or a Monthly View of the Political State of the British Colonies. Phila., **1741**
American Mineralogical Journal. N.Y., **1814**
American Monthly Magazine and Critical Review. N.Y., **1817–19**
American Museum, or, Universal Magazine. Phila., 1787–92. **v.d.**
American Natural History. See GODMAN
American Naturalist. Salem, Mass., etc., **1867–current**. (Also as: *A Year in Natural History*)
American Notes and Queries. Phila., **1888–92**
AMERICAN PHILOLOGICAL ASSOCIATION. *Transactions and Proceedings.* 1869–current. Hartford [etc.] 1871–current. **v.d.** Vols. XIV and XVII include: C. F. SMITH. *On Southernisms.* 1883, **1886**
AMERICAN PHILOSOPHICAL SOCIETY. *Proceedings.* 1744–current. Phila., 1840–current *Transactions.* 1769–1804. Phila., 1771–1809. New ser., 1818–current. Phila., 1818–current. (Cited as: *Amer. Philos. Soc.*) **v.d.** Vol. III (old ser.) includes: H. MUHLENBERG. *Index Floræ Lancastriensis.* **1791**
American Pioneer. Chillicothe, Ohio; Cinc., **1842–3**
American Poems, Selected and Original. [Ed. E. H. Smith.] Litchfield [Conn., **1793**]
American Review of History and Politics. Phila., **1811–2**
American Review of Reviews. See *Review of Reviews.* N.Y.
American Speech. Balt.; N.Y., **1925–current**. Vol. IX includes: A. W. READ. *Nantucketisms of 1848* [printing a list comp. in 1848 by James Mitchell]. **1848**
American State Papers. See U.S. CONGRESS
American Traveller. Bost., **1825–42**
American Weekly Mercury. Phila., **1719–46**
AMES, NATHAN. *Childe Harvard.* Bost., **1848**
AMES, NATHANIEL. *A Mariner's Sketches.* Providence, **1830**
AMHERST, MASS. *Records of the Town . . . from 1735 to 1788.* Ed. J. F. Jameson. Amherst, 1884. **v.d.**
AMPHLETT, WILLIAM. *The Emigrant's Directory to the Western States of North America.* Lond., **1819**
Analectic Magazine. Phila., **1813–19**; n.s. **1820**
Anarchiad. See HUMPHREYS, D., et al.
ANBUREY, THOMAS. *Travels through the Interior Parts of America.* Lond., **1789**
ANDREAS, A. T. *History of the State of Kansas.* Chic., **1883**
ANDREWS, C. C. *Recollections.* Cleveland, 1928. **1907**
ANDREWS, JOHN. *Letters . . . , 1772–1776.* Ed. Winthrop Sargent. Cambridge, 1866. **v.d.** See also MASSACHUSETTS HISTORICAL SOCIETY. *Proceedings*
Andros Tracts. See PRINCE SOCIETY
Animal and Plant Lore. See AMERICAN FOLK-LORE SOCIETY
Animals of America: 'Mammals of America.' [Ed.] H. E. Anthony. Garden City, N.Y. [**1937**]. First publ. under title: *Mammals of America.* N.Y. [cop. **1917**]
Annals of Albany. See MUNSELL
Annals of Congress. See U.S. CONGRESS. *The Debates and Proceedings*
Annals of Southwest Virginia. See SUMMERS
Annual Cyclopædia. See *Appletons' Annual Cyclopædia*
Annual of Scientific Discovery. Bost., **1850–71**
Annual Register. 1758–. Lond., **1761–**
Anthony's Photogr. Bul. See *International Annual*
APGAR, A. C. *Trees of the Northern United States.* N.Y. [cop. **1892**]
APPEL, J. H. *The Business Biography of John Wanamaker.* N.Y., 1930. **v.d.**
Appletons' Annual Cyclopædia. 1861–1902. N.Y., 1862–1903. **v.d.** Also as: *(American) Annual Cyclopædia*
Archæologia Americana. See AMERICAN ANTIQUARIAN SOCIETY. *Transactions*
Archives of Maryland. Balt., 1883–current. **v.d.** Vol. III: *Proceedings of the Council,* [Vol. I.] 1636–1667. **v.d.**
Arkansaw Doctor, The Life and Adventures of. See BYRN

ARMSTRONG, MARGARET N., and THORNBER, J. J. *Field Book of Western Wild Flowers.* N.Y., 1915
ARMSTRONG, WILLIAM. *Stocks and Stock-Jobbing in Wall Street.* N.Y., 1848
Army Orders. See LOUDOUN and LYMAN
Army Regulations. See U.S. WAR DEPT. *Revised Regulations*
ARNY, W. F. M. *Interesting Items regarding New Mexico.* Santa Fe, 1873
'ARP.' See SMITH, C. H.
'ARR.' See ROLLINS
ARTHUR, T. S., and CARPENTER, W. H. *The History of Kentucky, from Its Earliest Settlement to the Present Time.* Phila., 1852
ASBURY, FRANCIS. *Journal.* N.Y., 1821. **v.d.**
ASH, THOMAS. *Carolina.* Lond., 1682
ASHE, THOMAS. *Travels in America Performed in 1806.* Lond.: Phillips, 1808. 3 vols. Also publ.: Newburyport [Mass.]: Re-printed for W. Sawyer & Co., 1808. 366 pp.
ASPINWALL. See BOSTON. REGISTRY DEPT.
The Association . . . of the Delegates. See 'JINGLE'
ATHERTON, GERTRUDE F. (HORN). *The Californians.* Lond., 1898
Perch of the Devil. [London, 1924.] =1914
ATKINSON, ELEANOR (STACKHOUSE). *Johnny Appleseed.* N.Y., 1915
Atlantic Monthly. Bost., 1857–current. Vols. XXVI–XXVII include: MINOR. *Diary.* 1834. Vols. XL–XLI include: CLEMENS. *Some Rambling Notes of an Idle Excursion* (see also his: *Punch, Brothers, Punch!*) **v.d.**
AUDUBON, JOHN JAMES. *Ornithological Biography.* Phila.; Bost.; Edinb., 1831–39
AUDUBON, JOHN WOODHOUSE. *Audubon's Western Journal: 1849–50.* Cleveland, 1906. **v.d.**
AUGUSTA CO., VA. *Chronicles of the Scotch-Irish Settlement in Virginia: Extracted from the Original Court Records. . . .* By Lyman Chalkley. Rosslyn, Va. [cop. 1912–3]. **v.d.**
AULD, JOSEPH. *Picturesque Burlington.* Burlington, Vt., 1893
Aurora. Phila., 1790–1835
Austin Papers. See AMERICAN HISTORICAL ASSOCIATION
AVERY, E. K., defendant. *A Full Report of the Trial. . . .* By B. F. Hallett. Bost., 1833

B

BACHE, ANNA. *The Fire-Screen, or Domestic Sketches.* Phila., 1841
BACHELLOR, IRVING. *Eben Holden.* Bost. [cop. 1900]
BACON, MATTHEW. *A New Abridgment of the Law.* Ed. Sir Henry Gwyllim [*et al.*], with notes by John Bouvier. Phila., 1852
BAEDEKER, KARL, firm. *The United States.* [By J. F. Muirhead.] 2d rev. ed. Leipsic, 1899
BAGBY, G. W. *The Old Virginia Gentleman, and Other Sketches.* Ed. T. N. Page. N.Y., 1911. =1910. **v.d.**
BAGG, L. H. *Four Years at Yale.* New Haven, 1871
BAILEY, E. A. *Among the Law-Makers.* N.Y., 1900. =1886
BAILEY, J. M. *Folks in Danbury; or, Mr. Miggs and His Neighbours.* Lond. [1877]
Life in Danbury. Bost., 1873
BAILLIE-GROHMAN, W. A. *Camps in the Rockies.* Lond., 1882
BAILY, FRANCIS. *Journal of a Tour in Unsettled Parts of North America in 1796 & 1797.* Lond., 1856. **v.d.**
BAIRD, ROBERT. *Impressions and Experiences of the West Indies and North America in 1849.* Phila., 1850
View of the Valley of the Mississippi. Phila., 1832. 2d ed. Phila., 1834
BAIRD, S. *Birds Pacific R.R.* See U.S. WAR DEPT. *Reports*
BAKER, B. A. *A Glance at New York.* N.Y. [n.d.]. First perf. 1848
BAKER, L. C. *History of the United States Secret Service.* Phila., 1867
BAKER, W. M. *The New Timothy.* N.Y., 1870
Balance (and Columbian Repository). Hudson, N.Y., 1801–8
BALDWIN, J. G. *The Flush Times of Alabama and Mississippi.* N.Y., 1853. N.Y., 1855. =1853
BALDWIN, S. E. *Life and Letters of Simeon Baldwin.* New Haven [1919]. **v.d.**
BALTIMORE, MD. *First Records of Baltimore Town and Jones' Town, 1729–1797.* Balt., 1905. **v.d.**
Baltimore Sun. See *Sun*
BANCROFT, GEORGE. *History of the United States.* Bost., 1852–74 [cop. 1834–74]. Rev. ed. Bost., 1876
BANKS, ELIZABETH L. *The Autobiography of a Newspaper Girl.* Lond., 1902. 328 pp. Also publ.: N.Y., 1902. 317 pp.
Baptist Mag. See *American Baptist Magazine*
BARKER. See MOSES. *Representative Plays.* Vol. I
BARLOW, JOEL. *The Columbiad.* Phila., 1807

BARNES, H. F. *Charles Fenno Hoffman.* N.Y., 1930. Includes letters and poems by Hoffman. **v.d.**
BARNES, T. W. See WEED. *Life*
BARNES, W. C. *Western Grazing Grounds and Forest Ranges.* Chic., 1913
BARNET, H. L. *A Dictionary with Legal Notes, for Commercial Use throughout the United States of America.* 3d ed. Chic., 1882. First publ. 1880
BARNETT, EVELYN S. (SNEAD). *The Dragnet.* N.Y., 1909
BARNUM, FRANCES C. (BAYLOR). *On Both Sides.* Phila., 1885
BARNUM, P. T. *The Life of P. T. Barnum.* N.Y., 1855
Struggles and Triumphs. N.Y., 1871. Buffalo 1872. Pp. 25–780 = 1st ed. 1869. **v.d.**
BARRÈRE, ALBERT, and LELAND, C. G., eds. *A Dictionary of Slang, Jargon & Cant.* [Edinb.] 1889–90. [2d ed.] Lond., 1897
BARRY, PATRICK. *The Fruit Garden.* N.Y., 1851
BARTLETT, J. R. *Dictionary of Americanisms.* N.Y., 1849. =1848. 3d ed. Bost., 1860. =2d ed., 1859. 4th ed. Bost., 1896. =1877
Personal Narrative of Explorations . . . Connected with the United States and Mexican Boundary Commission. N.Y., 1854. Also publ.: Lond., 1854
'BARTON, ANDREW.' *The Disappointment; or, The Force of Credulity.* 2d ed. Phila., 1796
BARTON, W. E. *A Hero in Homespun.* Bost., 1897
Sim Galloway's Daughter-in-Law. Bost., 1897
The Truth about the Trouble at Roundstone. Bost., 1897
BARTRAM, JOHN. *Journal.* See STORK
Observations on the Inhabitants, Climate, Soil, [etc.] . . . from Pensilvania to . . . Lake Ontario. Lond., 1751
BARTRAM, WILLIAM. *Travels through North and South Carolina* [etc.]. Lond., 1792. Also: Dublin, 1793. (Page references taken from ed.: Phila., 1791.) Also: [Ed. Mark Van Doren.] [N.Y.] 1928.
BASSETT, J. S. *The Southern Plantation Overseer as Revealed in His Letters.* Northampton, Mass., 1925. **v.d.**
BATEMAN. See MOSES. *Representative Plays.* Vol. II
BATES, C. A., ed. *The Clothing Book.* N.Y., 1898
The Battle of Brooklyn. Brooklyn, 1873. First publ. 1776
BAXTER, RICHARD, and ELIOT, JOHN. *Some Unpublished Correspondence.* Ed. F. J. Powicke. Manchester [Eng.] 1931. **v.d.**
BAY STATE TRANSPORTATION LEAGUE. *A Bill to Incorporate the Boston and Chicago Railway Trust Company.* Bost., 1874
BAYLOR. See BARNUM, F. C.
BEACH, R. E. *The Barrier.* N.Y., 1908
BEADLE, J. H. *Life in Utah.* Phila. [cop. 1870]
The Undeveloped West. Phila. [1873]
Western Wilds, and the Men Who Redeem Them. Detroit [n.d.]. 1883. First publ. 1878
BEADLE & CO. *The Dime Base-Ball Player.* N.Y. [cop. 1860–81]
BEARD, J. M. *K.K.K. Sketches.* Phila., 1877
BEAUDRY, L. N. *Historic Records of the Fifth New York Cavalry, First Ira Harris Guard.* Albany, 1874. =1865
The Beauties of Brother Bull-us, by His Loving Sister Bull-a. N.Y., 1812
BECKWOURTH, J. P. *Life and Adventures.* Ed. T. D. Bonner. N.Y., 1931. First publ. 1856
BEECHER, H. W. *Life Thoughts.* [1st Ser. By E. D. Proctor.] N.Y., 1860. =1858. 2d Ser. as his: *Notes from Plymouth Pulpit* (q.v.)
Norwood. N.Y., 1868
Notes from Plymouth Pulpit. By Augusta Moore. N.Y., 1859
Sermons . . . in Plymouth Church, Brooklyn, New York. 1st Ser. Lond., 1869. (Page references from ed.: N.Y., 1869.) **v.d.**
BELASCO. See MOSES. *Representative American Dramas*
Belcher Papers. See MASSACHUSETTS HISTORICAL SOCIETY. *Collections*
BELKNAP, JEREMY. *The History of New-Hampshire.* Bost., 1784–92
Belknap, Life of. See MARCOU
Belknap Papers. See MASSACHUSETTS HISTORICAL SOCIETY. *Collections*
BELL, ANDREW. *Men & Things in America.* 2d ed. Southampton [Eng.] 1862. First publ. 1838
BELL, LILIAN L. *Carolina Lee.* Bost., 1906
Hope Loring. Bost., 1908
A Little Sister to the Wilderness. Chic., 1895
BELL, MARGARET V. (DWIGHT). *A Journey to Ohio in 1810.* Ed. Max Farrand. New Haven, 1920. =1912. Written 1810
BELLAMY, EDWARD. *Looking Backward.* Bost., 1888
BENEFIELD, BARRY. *The Chicken-Wagon Family.* N.Y. [cop. 1925]
BENNETT, D. K. *Chronology of North Carolina, . . . from the Year 1584 to the Present Time.* N.Y., 1858
BENNETT, EMERSON. *Mike Fink.* Rev. ed. Cinc. [1852]

BENTLEY, WILLIAM. *Diary.* Salem, Mass., 1905–14. **v.d.**
Bentley's Miscellany. Lond., 1837–68. Vols. IV, VI–VII (Amer. ed., N.Y., Vols. II, IV–V) include: 'UNCLE SAM.' *Uncle Sam's Peculiarities* (q.v.). **v.d.**
BENTON, T. H. *Historical and Legal Examination of That Part of the Decision of the Supreme Court . . . in the Dred Scott Case. . . .* N.Y., 1860. = 1857. **v.d.**
Thirty Years View. N.Y., 1854–6. **v.d.**
BENWELL, J. *An Englishman's Travels in America.* Lond. [?1853]
BERNARD, JOHN. *Retrospections of America, 1797–1811.* Ed. Mrs. Bayle Bernard. N.Y., 1887. 1827
BESSEY, C. E. *Botany for High Schools and Colleges.* N.Y., 1880
BEVERLEY, ROBERT. *The History and Present State of Virginia.* Lond., 1705. 2d ed. Lond., 1722
Biblical Repertory and Theological Review. Phila., 1830–6
Bibliography of the Negro American. See DU BOIS
BIDDLE, CHARLES. *Autobiography.* Phila., 1883. a1821
BIDDLE, N. See LEWIS, M., and CLARK, W. *History*
BIDWELL, BARNABAS. *The Mercenary Match.* New Haven [?1784]. First perf. ?1785
Big Bear Ark. See PORTER, W. T.
BIGELOW, JACOB. *American Medical Botany.* Bost., 1817–20
Florula Bostoniensis. Bost., 1814
BIGGS, WILLIAM. *Narrative of the Captivity of William Biggs among the Kickapoo Indians in Illinois in 1788.* [N.Y.] 1922. 1st ed. 1825
BILLINGS, JOHN D. *Hardtack and Coffee.* Bost., 1888. =1887
'BILLINGS, J.' See SHAW, H. W.
Biography of Isaac Hill. See BRADLEY
Biography of N. Hale. See JOHNSTON, H. P.
BIRD, I. L. See BISHOP, I. L.
BIRD, R. M. *The Hawks of Hawk-Hollow.* Phila., 1835
Nick of the Woods. Phila., 1837
Robin Day. Lond., 1840. First publ. 1839
Birds of America. Ed.-in-Chief, T. G. Pearson. Garden City, N.Y., 1936. =1917
BIRKBECK, MORRIS. *Letters from Illinois.* Phila., 1818
Notes on a Journey in America. 2d ed. Lond., 1818. First publ. 1817
BIRKET, JAMES. *Some Cursory Remarks Made . . . in His Voyage to North America 1750–1751.* New Haven, 1916. **v.d.**
BISHOP, ISABELLA L. (BIRD). *A Lady's Life in the Rocky Mountains.* Lond., 1879. N.Y., 1879–80. First publ. 1878
BISHOP, N. L. *Four Months in a Sneak-Box.* Bost., 1879
BISHOP, R. H. *An Outline of the History of the Church in the State of Kentucky.* Lexington [Ky.] 1824
Black Cat. Bost. [etc.] 1895–1920
BLAINE, J. G. *Twenty Years of Congress.* Norwich, Conn., 1884–6
BLAIR. See PRINCETON UNIVERSITY. *An Account of the College*
BLAKE, MORTIMER. *A Centurial History of the Mendon Association of Congregational Ministers.* Bost., 1853
BLAND, THEODORICK, JR. *The Bland Papers.* Ed. Charles Campbell. Petersburg [Va.] 1840–3. **v.d.**
BLANE, W. N. *An Excursion through the United States and Canada during the Years 1822–23.* Lond., 1824
BLEECKER, ANN E. (SCHUYLER). *The History of Maria Kittle.* Hartford, 1797. Written 1779
BLOME, RICHARD. *The Present State of His Majesties Isles and Territories in America.* London, 1687
BLOODGOOD, S. D. *An Englishman's Sketch-Book.* N.Y., 1828
BOK, E. W. *The Americanization of Edward Bok.* N.Y. 1921. =1920
BONAPARTE, C. L. *American Ornithology.* Phila., 1825–33. (Vols. IV–V) **v.d.**
Synopsis. See NEW YORK ACADEMY OF SCIENCES
BOND, J. W. *Minnesota and Its Resources.* N.Y., 1854. Pp. 9–361 = 1st ed., 1853
'BONNER, S.' See MACDOWELL
BONNER, T. See BECKWOURTH
BOONE. See PELZER
BORTHWICK, J. D. *Three Years in California.* Edinb., 1857
BOSTON. CITY COUNCIL. *Documents of the City of Boston.* Bost. **v.d.**
BOSTON. REGISTRY DEPT. *Records Relating to the Early History of Boston.* Bost., 1876–. (Vols. I–XXVIII have title: *Report of the Record Commissioners*.) Individual vols. of series cited by specific titles as follows:
ASPINWALL, WILLIAM. *Notarial Records from 1644 to 1651.* n.d. (Vol. XXXII)
Boston Selectmen. Records of Boston Selectmen. 1701–15 (Vol XI); 1716–36 (Vol. XIII);

1736–42 (Vol. XV). *Selectmen's Minutes.* 1742/3–53 (Vol. XVII); 1754–63 (Vol. XIX); 1764–8 (Vol. XX); 1769–75 (Vol. XXIII); 1776–86 (Vol. XXV); 1787–98 (Vol. XXVII); 1799–1810 (Vol. XXXIII); 1811–18 (Vol. XXXVIII); 1818–22 (Vol. XXXIX)

Boston (Town) Records. 1634–61 (Vol. II); 1660–1701 (Vol. VII); 1700–28 (Vol. VIII); 1729–42 (Vol. XII); 1742–57 (Vol. XIV); 1758–69 (Vol. XVI); 1770–7 (Vol. XVIII); 1778–83 (Vol. XXVI); 1784–96 (Vol. XXXI); 1796–1813 (Vol.XXXV); 1814–22 (Vol. XXXVII)

Charlestown Land Rec. v.d. (Vol. III)

Dorchester Records. v.d. (Vol. IV)

Miscellaneous Papers (Vol. X). Includes: 'The Last Will and Testament of Me, Robert Keayne.' **1653.** Boston Directory (q.v.). **1789, 1796**

Roxbury Land and Church Records. v.d. (Vol. VI)

BOSTON COURIER. *The Eighty-second Anniversary of American Independence.* Bost., **1858**

Boston Directory. Bost., **1789**–current. Also as: *Stimpson's Boston Directory.* See also BOSTON. REGISTRY DEPT. *Records. Miscellaneous Papers*

Boston Documents. See BOSTON. CITY COUNCIL

Boston Gazette. **1800–15**

Boston Gazette (and Country Journal). **1719–98**

Boston News-Letter. **1704–76.** Also under title: *Massachusetts Gazette*

Boston Orations (1785). See *Orations*

Boston Records. See BOSTON. REGISTRY DEPT.

Boston Selectmen. See BOSTON. REGISTRY DEPT.

BOSTONIAN SOCIETY. *Proceedings.* Bost. [1882]–current

BOSTWICK, A. E. *The American Public Library.* N.Y., **1910**

BOUCHER, JONATHAN. *Boucher's Glossary of Archaic and Provincial Words.* Ed. Joseph Hunter and Joseph Stevenson. Lond., 1832–3. **v.d.**

BOUDRYE. See BEAUDRY

BOURKE, J. G. (See also *Scribner's Magazine.*) *Journals.* MS., West Point Military Academy. **v.d.**

'BOWER.' See SINCLAIR, B.

BOWLES, SAMUEL. *Our New West.* Hartford, Conn., **1869**

BOWNAS, SAMUEL. *An Account of the Life . . . of Samuel Bownas.* Lond., **1756**

BOWNE, ELIZA (SOUTHGATE). *A Girl's Life Eighty Years Ago.* N.Y., 1887. **v.d.**

Boyd's Business Directory of over One Hundred Cities and Villages in New York State. 1869–70. Albany, **1869**

BOYLAN. See [North Carolina Almanacs]

BRACE, C. L. *The Dangerous Classes of New York.* N.Y., 1872. **v.d.**

The New West. N.Y., **1869**

BRACKENRIDGE, HENRY M. *Recollections of Persons and Places in the West.* Phila.. [1834]

Views of Louisiana; together with a Journal of a Voyage up the Missouri River, in 1811. Pittsb., **1814**

BRACKENRIDGE, HUGH H. *Bunkers-Hill.* See MOSES. *Representative Plays.* Vol. I

Modern Chivalry, or the Adventures of Captain Farrago and Teague O'Regan. Phila., 1846. Also: N.Y..1926. N.Y. [cop. 1937]. **v.d.**

BRACKETT, G. E. *Farm Talk.* Bost., **1868**

BRADBURY, JOHN. *Travels in the Interior of America.* Lond., **1817**

BRADFORD, JOHN. *Historical Notes on Kentucky.* San Fran., 1932 **1826**

BRADFORD, WILLIAM. *Bradford's History 'Of Plimoth Plantation.' From the Original Manuscript.* Bost., 1899. =1898. 555 pp. Also publ. as: *History of Plymouth Plantation 1620–1647.* Bost..1912. 2 vols. a1656

BRADLEY, C. P. *Biography of Isaac Hill, of New-Hampshire.* Concord, N.H., **1835**

BRADMAN, ARTHUR. *A Narrative of the Extraordinary Sufferings of Robert Forbes.* Phila., 1794. First publ. **1791**

BRADSTREET, ANNE (DUDLEY). *The Poems of Mrs. Anne Bradstreet.* [N.Y.] 1897. **v.d.**

BRADY, C. T. *The Bishop.* N.Y., **1903**

BRAINERD, DAVID. *Diary* [and *Journal*]. Lond., 1902. **v.d.**

Braintree, Mass. Records of the Town . . . 1640 to 1793. Ed. S. A. Bates. Randolph, Mass., 1886. **v.d.**

BRAMAN, D. E. E. *Braman's Information about Texas.* Phila., **1857**

BRAYLEY, A. W. *A Complete History of the Boston Fire Department.* Bost., 1889. **v.d.**

BRECK, SAMUEL. *Recollections . . . , with Passages from His Notebooks (1761–1862).* Ed. H. E. Scudder. Phila., 1877. **v.d.**

BRERETON, JOHN. *A Briefe and True Relation of the Discouerie of the North Part of Virginia.* N.Y., 1903. =1602

BREVARD, JOSEPH. *Diary,* 1791. MS., Univ. of N.C. **1791**

Brevard Papers. MS., North Carolina Historical Commission, Raleigh, N.C. **v.d.**

BREWER, W. H. *Rocky Mountain Letters, 1869.* [Ed. E. B. Rogers.] Denver, 1930. **1869**

BREWERTON, G. D. *Overland with Kit Carson.* [Ed.] Stallo Vinton. N.Y., 1930. First publ. **1853**

BREWSTER, E. T. *Life and Letters of Josiah Dwight Whitney.* Bost., 1909. **v.d.**

BRICKELL, JOHN. *The Natural History of North-Carolina.* Dublin, **1737.** [Raleigh [N.C.]: Reprinted by Authority of the Trustees of the Public Libraries, 1911.]

BRIGGS, C. F. *The Adventures of Harry Franco.* N.Y., **1839**

The Trippings of Tom Pepper. N.Y., **1847–50**

BRISTED, C. A. *Eng. Lang. in Amer.* See *Cambridge Essays*

Five Years in an English University. 2d ed. N.Y., **1852**

The Upper Ten Thousand. 2d ed. rev. N.Y., **1852**

BRISTED, JOHN. *The Resources of the United States of America.* N.Y., **1818**

BRISTOL PARISH, VA. *Vestry Book and Register . . . 1720–1789.* Transcribed and published by C. G. Chamberlayne. Richmond, 1898. **v.d.**

Broadside Verse. See WINSLOW, O. E.

BROCKENBROUGH. See MARTIN, J.

BROCKETT, L. P.,ed. *Our Country's Progress.* Balt., 1885. First publ. as: *Our Country's Wealth and Influence.* Hartford, **1882**

BRODHEAD, EVA W. (McGLASSON). *Bound in Shallows.* N.Y., **1897**

BROMWELL, WILLIAM. *Locomotive Sketches, with Pen and Pencil.* Phila., **1854**

BROOKHAVEN, N.Y. *Records . . . Up to 1800.* Patchogue, N.Y., 1880. **v.d.**

BROOKS, C. T. *A Poem Pronounced before the Phi Beta Kappa Society, at Cambridge.* Bost., **1845**

BROOKS, H. M. *The Olden Time Series: Gleanings Chiefly from Old Newspapers of Boston and Salem, Massachusetts.* Bost., 1886. 6 vols. **v.d.** No. 2. *The Days of the Spinning-Wheel in New England.* No. 4. *Quaint and Curious Advertisements*

BROOKS, NOAH. *The Boys of Fairport.* N.Y., 1924. =1898. First publ., in part, as: *The Fairport Nine.* N.Y., **1880**

BROTHERS, THOMAS. *The United States of North America as They Are.* Lond., 1840. **v.d.**

BROWN, ALICE. *Meadow-Grass.* Bost., **1895**

Old Crow. N.Y., **1922**

Tiverton Tales. Bost. [cop.1899]

BROWN, C. B. *Arthur Mervyn.* Phila., 1887. First publ. **1799–1800**

Wieland. **1798**

tr. See VOLNEY

BROWN, HELEN D. *Two College Girls.* Bost., **1886**

BROWN, JAMES. *The Letter Book of James Brown of Providence.* Providence, 1929. **v.d.**

BROWN, S. R. *The Western Gazetteer; or, Emigrant's Directory.* Auburn, N.Y., **1817**

BROWN, THOMAS. *A Plain Narrative of the Uncommon Sufferings . . . of Thomas Brown.* Bost., **1760**

BROWN, U. See MARYLAND HISTORICAL MAGAZINE

BROWN, WILLIAM, of Leeds. *America: A Four Years' Residence in the United States and Canada.* Leeds, **1849**

BROWNE, C. F. *Artemus Ward: His Book.* N.Y., 1864. =1862

Artemus Ward: His Travels. N.Y., **1865**

BROWNE, D. J. *The American Poultry Yard.* N.Y., 1855. =1850

The Sylva Americana. Bost., **1832**

The Trees of America. N.Y., **1846**

BROWNE, J. See BROWN, J.

BROWNE, JOHN R. *Adventures in the Apache Country.* N.Y., **1869**

BROWNE, JUNIUS H. *The Great Metropolis; a Mirror of New York.* Hartford, **1869**

BROWNE, MARTHA (GRIFFITH). *Autobiography of a Female Slave.* N.Y., **1857**

BRUCE, P. A. *Economic History of Virginia in the Seventeenth Century.* N.Y., **1896**

BRUCE'S NEW YORK TYPE-FOUNDRY. *An Abridged Specimen of Printing Types.* N.Y., **1869**

BRUNCKEN, ERNEST. *North American Forests and Forestry.* N.Y., **1900**

BRYAN, W. J. *Memoirs . . . by Himself and His Wife, Mary Baird Bryan.* Phila. [cop. 1925]. **v.d.**

BRYANT, EDWIN. *What I Saw in California.* N.Y., 1848. Also publ. as: *Rocky Mountain Adventures.* N.Y. [?1885]

BRYANT, W. C. *Poetical Works.* Roslyn Ed. N.Y., 1925. =1903. **v.d.** (Some poems cited by individual titles and line numbers)

BRYCE, JAMES BRYCE, Viscount. *The American Commonwealth.* Lond., **1888.** 3 vols.

Buckeye Cookery. See WILCOX

Buckeye Informer. ?Delphos, Ohio, **1906–15**

BUCKINGHAM, JAMES S. *America, Historical, Statistic, and Descriptive.* Lond. [1841]. 3 vols. Also: N.Y., **1841.** 2 vols.

The Eastern and Western States of America. Lond. [1842]

The Slave States of America. Lond. [1842]

BUCKINGHAM, JOHN, *i.e.,* THOMAS. See KNIGHT, S.

BUCKINGHAM, JOSEPH T. *Specimens of Newspaper Literature: With Personal Memoirs, Anecdotes, and Reminiscences.* Bost., 1850. **v.d.**

BUCKINGHAM, THOMAS. See KNIGHT, S.

Buckskin Mose. See PERRIE

BUDD, THOMAS. *Good Order Established in Pennsylvania and New Jersey.* Reprinted from the original ed. of 1685. Cleveland, 1902. **1685**

BUEL, JAMES W. *The Border Outlaws.* St. Louis, 1881. Includes, with sep. paging, his: *The Border Bandits . . . Jesse and Frank James*

BUEL, JESSE. *The Farmer's Companion.* Bost. [1840]. **1839**

'BUFFALO BILL.' See CODY, W. F.

BULKELEY. See CONNECTICUT HISTORICAL SOCIETY

BULLOCK, WILLIAM. *Sketch of a Journey through the Western States of North America.* Lond., **1827**

BUNN, ALFRED. *Old England and New England.* Lond., **1853**

BUNNER, H. C. *Zadoc Pine, and Other Stories.* N.Y., **1891**

BURDETTE, R. J. *Hawk-Eyes.* N.Y., **1880**

The Rise and Fall of the Mustache and Other 'Hawkeyetems.' Burlington, Iowa, **1877**

BUREAU OF AMER. ETHNOL. See U.S. BUREAU OF AMERICAN ETHNOLOGY

BUREAU OF FORESTRY. See U.S. FOREST SERVICE

BURGESS, GELETT. *Find the Woman.* Indianapolis [cop. 1911]

BURK, J. D. *The History of Virginia, from the First Settlement to the Present Day.* Petersburg, Va. **1804–16**

BURKE, EMILY P. *Reminiscences of Georgia.* [Oberlin, Ohio] **1850**

BURKE, T. A., ed. *Polly Peablossom's Wedding; and Other Tales.* Phila. [cop. 1851]

BURNABY, ANDREW. *Travels through the Middle Settlements in North-America.* 2d ed. Lond., **1775**

BURNETT, P. H. *Recollections and Opinions of an Old Pioneer.* N.Y., **1880**

BURNHAM, CLARA L. (ROOT). *Jewel; a Chapter in Her Life.* N.Y. [1903]

BURNHAM, G. P. *Three Years with Counterfeiters.* Bost. [1875]

BURR, G. L., ed. *Narratives of the Witchcraft Cases, 1648–1706.* N.Y., 1914. Includes: R. CHAMBERLAIN. *Lithobolia.* 1698

BURRITT, ELIHU. *A Walk from London to Land's End and Back.* Lond., **1865**

BURROUGHS, JOHN. *Birds and Poets; with Other Papers.* Bost., 1893. =1877

Fresh Fields. Bost., 1885 [1884]

Pepacton. Bost. [cop. 1909]. First publ. **1881**

Wake-Robin. [2d ed.] Bost., 1886. First publ. **1871**

Winter Sunshine. Edinb., 1883. **1875**

BURROUGHS, W. H. *A Treatise on the Law of Taxation.* N.Y., **1877**

BURTON, W. E. *Waggeries and Vagaries.* Phila., **1848**

BUSHNELL, HORACE. *Forgiveness and Law.* N.Y., **1874**

Work and Play. N.Y., 1864. **v.d.**

A Business Advertiser and General Directory of the City of Chicago for the Year 1845–6. By J. W. Norris. Chic., **1845**

BUTLER, FRANCES A. (KEMBLE). See KEMBLE

BUTLER, PARDEE. *Personal Recollections of Pardee Butler.* Cinc., **1889**

BUTTRICK. See THWAITES

BYNNER, E. L. *Agnes Surriage.* Bost. [cop. 1886]

BYRD, WILLIAM. *Writings.* Ed. J. S. Bassett. N.Y., 1901. Includes: *History of the Dividing Line.* **1738.** *A Journey to the Land of Eden.* **1733.** *A Progress to the Mines.* **1732**

BYRN, M. L. *The Life and Adventures of an Arkansaw Doctor.* Phila., **1851**

C

CABLE, G. W. *Bonaventure.* Lond., **1888**

John March, Southerner. **1894**

Dr. Sevier. N.Y., 1889. =1885. First publ. 1883–4. **v.d.**

The Grandissimes. N.Y., 1922. =1880

Caddo (Okla.) *Herald.* **1895**–current

CAHAN, ABRAHAM. *The Imported Bridegroom, and Other Stories of the New York Ghetto.* Bost., **1898**

Calendar of State Papers. See GREAT BRITAIN. PUBLIC RECORD OFFICE

Calendar of Va. State Papers. See VIRGINIA

CALHOUN, FRANCES (BOYD). *Miss Minerva and William Green Hill.* Chic., **1909**

CALHOUN, J. C. *Works.* [Ed. R. K. Crallé.] N.Y., 1851–6. (Reprinted with various dates.) **v.d.**

California Chronicle. See *Daily California Chronicle*

Calif. Claims. In: 30th Congress, 1 Sess. Senate Rep. No. 75. 23 Feb. 1848. **v.d.**

Cambridge Essays, Contributed by Members of the University. 1855. Lond. [?1855]. Includes: BRISTED. *Eng. Lang. in Amer.* **1855**

CAMBRIDGE, MASS. *The Records of the Town of Cambridge (formerly Newtowne) Massachusetts. 1630–1703.* Cambridge, 1901. **v.d.**

PROPRIETORS. *The Register Book of the Lands and Houses . . . , with the Records of the Proprietors of the Common Lands.* Cambridge, 1896. **v.d.**

CAMP, W. C. *Walter Camp's Book of College Sports.* N.Y., 1893. **v.d.**

CAMPBELL, DAISY R. *The Proving of Virginia.* **1915**

CAMPION, J. S. *On the Frontier.* Lond., 1878. First publ. **1877**

CANFIELD, C. D., ed. *The Diary of a Forty-Niner* [Alfred T. Jackson]. Bost., 1920. First publ.: N.Y., 1906. **v.d.**

CANFIELD, H. S. *A Maid of the Frontier.* Chic. [cop. **1898**]

CANTON, F. M. *Frontier Trails.* Bost., 1930. Written **c1908**

Cape-Fear Recorder. Wilmington, N.C., **1816–current**

CARLETON, H. G. *Lectures before the Thompson Street Poker Club.* N.Y. [cop. **1889**]

The Thompson Street Poker Club. Lond. [1889]. First publ., in part, 1884. **v.d.**

CARLETON, WILL. *Farm Ballads.* N.Y. [cop. 1882]. First publ. **1873**

Farm Legends. N.Y. [cop. **1875**]

Farm Festivals. N.Y., **1881**

CARLISLE, G. W. F. H., 7th Earl of. *Travels in America. The Poetry of Pope. Two Lectures Delivered . . . December 5th and 6th, 1850.* N.Y., 1851. **1850**

'CARLTON.' See HALL, B. R.

Carolina, The Fundamental Constitutions of. See *Old South Leaflets*

CARPENTER, F. B. *Six Months at the White House with Abraham Lincoln.* N.Y., **1866**

CARROLL, B. R., ed. *Historical Collections of South Carolina.* N.Y., 1836. **v.d.** Vol. II includes: J. GLEN. *Descr. S. Carolina* (q.v.). **1761**

CARROLL, EDWARD, JR. *Principles and Practice of Finance.* N.Y. 1902. **=1895**

Carroll Papers. See *Maryland Historical Magazine*

CARRUTHERS. See CARUTHERS

CARSON, CHRISTOPHER. *Kit Carson's Own Story of His Life, as Dictated to Col. and Mrs. D. C. Peters about 1856–57, and Never Before Published.* Ed. B. C. Grant. Taos, N.M., 1926. **c1857**

CARTWRIGHT, PETER. *Autobiography.* Ed. W. P. Strickland. **N.Y.**, 1857 [cop. **1856**]

CARUTHERS, W. A. *The Kentuckian in New York.* N.Y., **1834**

CARVER, JONATHAN. *A Detail of the Massacre of the English, by the French Indians, at Fort William Henry, in America, in 1757.* (Extract from: *Arminian Magazine* (Lond.), XVII (Jan., 1794), 33–38)

Travels through the Interior Parts of North-America. Lond., **1778**

CARWARDINE, W. H. *The Pullman Strike.* 4th ed. Chic., **1894**

CARY, ALICE. *Ballads, Lyrics, and Hymns.* N.Y., **1866**

Clovernook, or, Recollections of Our Neighborhood in the West. N.Y., 1852 [cop. **1851**]

Married, not Mated. N.Y., **1856**

Pictures of Country Life. N.Y., 1876. **=1859**

The Casquet of Literature. See GIBBON

CASSIN, JOHN. *Illustrations of the Birds of California, Texas, Oregon, British and Russian America. Intended to Contain . . . a General Synopsis of North American Ornithology.* Phila., **1856.** (Cited as: *N. Amer. Birds*)

CASWALL, HENRY. *America, and the American Church.* Lond., **1839**

Catawba Journal. Charlotte, N.C., **1824–7**

CATESBY, MARK. *The Natural History of Carolina, Florida and the Bahama Islands.* Lond., 1731–43. Appendix, 1748. [New ed.] by George Edwards. Lond., 1754. **v.d.**

CATHERWOOD, MARY (HARTWELL). *Mackinac and Lake Stories.* N.Y., **1899**

CATLIN, GEORGE. *Illustrations of the Manners, Customs, and Condition of the North American Indians.* 8th ed. Lond., 1851. Also as: *Letters and Notes on the Manners, Customs, and Condition of the North American Indians.* 3d ed. N.Y., 1844. **=1841. v.d.**

CAULKINS, FRANCES M. *Memoir of the Rev. William Adams of Dedham, Mass. and of the Rev. Eliphalet Adams of New London, Conn.* Cambridge, 1849. **v.d.** See also MASSACHUSETTS HISTORICAL SOCIETY. *Collections*

Causes Reduct. Tonnage. See U.S. CONGRESS. HOUSE. COMMITTEE ON CAUSES OF REDUCTION OF AMERICAN TONNAGE

The Centennial Exposition. See INGRAM

Centennial West Point. See U.S. MILITARY ACADEMY

Central Watchtower and Farmer's Journal. Harrodsburg, Ky., **1827–30**

The Century Dictionary: An Encyclopedic Lexicon of the English Language. Prepared under the superintendence of W. D. Whitney. N.Y. [1889–91]. 24 pts. **v.d.** Suppl. **1909.** 2 vols.

Century Magazine. Vols. XXIII–CXX. N.Y., **1881–1930.** (For Vols. I–XXII see *Scribner's Monthly.*) Includes: CLEMENS. *Pudd'nhead Wilson.* (XLVII–XLVIII.) **v.d.** EGGLESTON. *Faith Doctor.* (XLI–XLII.) **1891.** EGGLESTON. *Graysons.* (XXXV–XXXVI.) **v.d.** HOWELLS. *Woman's Reason.* (XXV–XXVI.) **1883.** STOCKTON. *Dusantes.* (XXXV.) **v.d.** STOCKTON. *Hundredth Man.* (XXXIII–XXXIV.) **v.d.** STOCKTON. *Mrs. Lecks.* (XXXII.) **1886**

CHADWICK, HENRY. *The Art of Batting and Base Running.* N.Y. [cop. **1886**]

The Art of Pitching and Fielding. Chic. [cop. **1885**]

The Base Ball Player's Book of Reference. N.Y., **1867**

The Dime Base-Ball Player. See BEADLE & Co.

The Game of Base Ball. How to Learn It, How to Play It, and How to Teach It. N.Y. [cop. **1868**]

CHALKLEY, L. See AUGUSTA CO., VA.

CHALKLEY, THOMAS. *A Journal or, Historical Account of the Life, Travels and Christian Experiences, of . . . Thomas Chalkley.* 2d ed. Lond., 1751. **v.d.**

CHAMBERLAIN, E. *The Indiana Gazetteer.* 3d ed. Indianapolis, **1849**

CHAMBERLAIN, R. See BURR

Chambers's Journal. Edinb.; London, **1832–current**

CHAMBLISS, W. H. *Chambliss Diary; or, Society as It Really Is.* N.Y., **1895**

CHANDLESS, WILLIAM. *A Visit to Salt Lake.* Lond., **1857**

CHANNING, G. G. *Early Recollections of Newport, R.I.* Newport, **1868**

CHANNING, W. E. *Complete Works.* Lond., 1884. Also publ. as: *Works.* Bost., 1886. **v.d.**

CHAPMAN, A. W. *Flora of the Southern United States.* N.Y., **1860**

Charlestown Land Rec. See BOSTON. REGISTRY DEPT.

Charlotte (N.C.) *Observer.* **1886–current**

CHASE, ANNIE, and CLOW, E. *Stories of Industry.* Bost. [cop. **1891**]

CHASE, C. M. *The Editor's Run in New Mexico and Colorado, Embracing Twenty-eight Letters.* [Montpelier, Vt., 1882.] **1881**

CHASE, FREDERICK. *A History of Dartmouth College and the Town of Hanover, New Hampshire.* Cambridge, 1891–1913. **v.d.**

CHEEVER, H. T. *The Whale and His Captors.* N.Y., **1850**

CHENEY, MARY A. (BUSHNELL), ed. *Life and Letters of Horace Bushnell.* N.Y., 1880. **v.d.**

CHESNUT, MARY B. (MILLER). *A Diary from Dixie.* Ed. I. D. Martin and M. L. Avary. N.Y., 1905. Also: Lond., 1905. **v.d.**

CHESNUTT, C. W. *The Conjure Woman.* Bost., **1900**

CHETWOOD, W. R. *The Voyages, Dangerous Adventures and Imminent Escapes of Captain Richard Falconer.* Lond., **1720**

CHICAGO ASSOCIATION OF COMMERCE. *A Guide to the City of Chicago.* [Chic., cop. **1909**]

Chicago Chronicle. **1895–1907**

Chicago Evening Journal. **1861–71**

Chicago Inter-Ocean. See *Inter-Ocean*

Chicago Record. **1881–1901**

Chicago Strike of 1894. See U.S. STRIKE COMMISSION, 1894

Chicago Times. [Daily.] **1854–95.** [Weekly.] **1854–93.** (Note: 1855 citations are from a mixed vol. Citations of 29 March or later date are from weekly ed.; those of earlier date are from daily ed.)

Chicago Tribune. **1847–current**

CHICKEN. See MERENESS

CHILD, LYDIA M. (FRANCIS). *The American Frugal Housewife.* Bost., **1832**

Fact and Fiction. N.Y., **1846**

Letters from New York. 3d ed. N.Y., 1846. =1845. **v.d.**

A Romance of the Republic. Bost., **1867**

CHIPMAN, REV. RICHARD MANNING, 1815–93. Manuscript notes in a copy of 2d ed. (1859) of Bartlett's *Dict. Americanisms.* Lent through the courtesy of the owner, Professor Richard H. Shryock, Duke Univ. **c1870**

CHOPIN, KATE (O'FLAHERTY). *Bayou Folk.* Bost., **1894**

Christian Banner. Fredericksburg, Va. **1848–62**

CHRISTISON, J. S. *Crime and Criminals.* Chic., **1897**

CHRISTY, G. N. *George Christy's Ethiopian Joke Book, No. 3.* Phila., **1860**

Chronicles of Oklahoma. Oklahoma City, **1921–current**

Chunkey's Fight with the Panthers. See PORTER, W. T. *The Big Bear of Arkansas*

CHURCH, BENJAMIN. *Entertaining Passages Relating to Philip's War.* Bost., **1716.** Also reprinted in 2 vols.: I. *The History of King Philip's War.* [Ed.] H. M. Dexter. Bost., 1865. II. *The History of the Eastern Expeditions . . . against the Indians and French.* [Ed.] H. M. Dexter. Bost., 1867

CHURCHILL, WINSTON. *The Crisis.* N.Y., **1901**

Cimarron (N.M.) *News and Press.* See *News and Press*

Cincinnati Misc. See CIST

CIST, CHARLES. *Cincinnati in 1841.* Cinc., **1841**

comp. *The Cincinnati Miscellany, or, Antiquities of the West.* Cinc., 1845–6. Chiefly from Vol. I. **v.d.**

Sketches and Statistics of Cincinnati in 1851. Cinc., **1851**

Civil Engineer and Architect's Journal. Lond., **1837–68**

CLAIBORNE, J. F. H. *Life and Correspondence of John A. Quitman.* N.Y., 1860. **v.d.**

Life and Times of Gen. Sam. Dale. N.Y., **1860**

CLAP, THOMAS. *The Annals or History of Yale-College, in New-Haven.* New-Haven, 1766. **v.d.**

CLAPIN, SYLVA. *A New Dictionary of Americanisms.* N.Y. [**1902**]

CLAPPE, LOUISE A. K. (SMITH). *The Shirley Letters from California Mines in 1851–52.* San Fran., 1922. **v.d.**

CLARK, F. T. *On Cloud Mountain.* N.Y., **1894**

'CLAVERS.' See KIRKLAND, C. M.

CLAY, HENRY. *Life and Speeches.* Phila., 1860. **v.d.**

Speeches. [Comp.] Richard Chambers. Cinc., 1842. **v.d.**

CLAY-CLOPTON, VIRGINIA. *A Belle of the Fifties.* Ed. Ada Sterling. N.Y., 1904. **v.d.**

CLAYTON. [*Accounts of Virginia.*] See ROYAL SOCIETY OF LONDON

Flora Virginica. See GRONOVIUS

CLEMENS, S. L. *Writings.* Definitive Ed. [N.Y., 1922–5.] **v.d.**

The Adventures of Huckleberry Finn. Lond., **1884.** N.Y., 1885. Lond., 1886

The Adventures of Thomas Jefferson Snodgrass. Chic., 1928. **v.d.**

The Adventures of Tom Sawyer. Hartford, **1876**

The American Claimant. N.Y., **1892**

The Celebrated Jumping Frog of Calaveras County, and Other Sketches. N.Y., 1867. **v.d.**

A Connecticut Yankee in King Arthur's Court. N.Y., **1889**

The Curious Republic of Gondour, and Other Whimsical Sketches. N.Y., 1919. **v.d.**

Following the Equator. Hartford, **1897**

The Gilded Age. See CLEMENS and WARNER

The Innocents Abroad. Hartford, **1869**

Jumping Frog. See his: *The Celebrated Jumping Frog;* also his: *Mark Twain's Sketches, New and Old*

Mark Twain's Letters. N.Y., 1917. **v.d.**

Letters from the Sandwich Islands, Written for the Sacramento Union. Stanford Univ., Calif., 1938. First publ. **1866**

Life on the Mississippi. N.Y. [cop. 1911]. First publ. **1883.** Chaps. iv–xvii as: *Old Times on the Mississippi.* **1875.** (Page references from 1st ed.: Toronto, 1876)

The £1,000,000 Bank-Note and Other New Stories. N.Y., **1893**

The Mysterious Stranger. N.Y. [1916]. **1898**

Old Times on the Mississippi. Toronto, 1876. First publ. **1875.** See also his: *Life on the Mississippi*

Pudd'nhead Wilson. See *Century Magazine*

Punch, Brothers, Punch! and Other Sketches. N.Y. [cop. 1878]. **v.d.** Includes: *Random Notes* [= *Some Rambling Notes,* q.v.] *of an Idle Excursion.* **v.d.** *Speech on the Weather.* **1877**

Roughing It. Hartford, **1872.** Chaps. xlvi–lxxix issued also as: *The Innocents at Home.* Lond., **1872**

Screamers. Lond. [?1871]. 166 pp. **v.d.**

Mark Twain's Sketches, New and Old. Hartford, 1875. Also: *Sketches, New and Old.* N.Y. [cop. 1903.] (*Writings,* Author's National Ed., Vol. XIX.) **v.d.** Includes: *The 'Jumping Frog'* (q.v.). **1865**

Sketches of the Sixties. 1926. See HARTE and CLEMENS

Some Rambling Notes of an Idle Excursion. See *Atlantic Monthly;* also his: *Punch, Brothers, Punch!*

Those Extraordinary Twins. **1894**

A Tramp Abroad. Hartford, **1880**

CLEMENS, S. L., and WARNER, C. D. *The Gilded Age.* Hartford, **1873**

CLOVER, S. T. *Paul Travers' Adventures.* Chic., **1897**

COALE. See SUMMERS. *Annals of Southwest Virginia*

COBB, I. S. *Back Home.* N.Y. [cop. **1912**]

COBBETT, WILLIAM. *A Treatise on Cobbett's Corn.* Lond., **1828**

A Year's Residence in the United States of America. Lond., **1818–9**

CODY, LOUISA (FREDERICI), and COOPER, C. R. *Memories of Buffalo Bill.* N.Y., **1919**

CODY, W. F. *Story of the Wild West and Camp-Fire Chats.* Phila. [**1888**]

COFFIN, JOSHUA. *A Sketch of the History of Newbury, Newburyport, and West Newbury, from 1635 to 1845.* Bost., 1845. **v.d.**

COHEN, A. J. *Wanted: A Cook.* Indianapolis [cop. **1904**]

COKE, E. T. *A Subaltern's Furlough.* **1833**
COLE, A. C. *The Whig Party in the South.* Wash., 1913. **v.d.**
COLE, G. E. *Early Oregon.* [Spokane, cop. **1905**]
Collegian. Cambridge, **1830**
COLLINS, LEWIS. *Historical Sketches of Kentucky.* Maysville, Ky., **1847**
Collins' Historical Sketches of Kentucky. History of Kentucky. Rev. by R. H. Collins. Covington, Ky., **1874**
COLLINS, R. H. See COLLINS, L.
COLLINS, S. H. *The Emigrant's Guide to and Description of the United States of America.* 4th ed. Hull [Eng., **1830**]
COLLYER, R. H. *Lights and Shadows of American Life.* Bost. [?**1844**]
COLMAN. See MASSACHUSETTS. AGRICULTURAL SURVEY
[*Colonial Records of Pennsylvania.* 1683–1790.] Phila., 1852; Harrisburg, 1851–3. Binder's title: *Pennsylvania Colonial Records.* **v.d.**
The Colonial Records of the State of Georgia. [Ed.] A. D. Candler. Atlanta, 1904–. **v.d.** Vol. IV (with suppl.) includes: W. STEPHENS. *Journal of the Proceedings in Georgia.* . . . . **v.d.**
COLONIAL SOCIETY OF MASSACHUSETTS. *Publications.* Vols. XV–XVI, XXXI: *Harvard Rec.* **v.d.** Vols. XXII–XXIII: *Plymouth Church Rec.* **v.d.**
COLTON, J. H., pub. *The State of Indiana Delineated.* N.Y., **1838**
COLTON, WALTER. *Deck and Port.* N.Y., **1850**
Three Years in California. N.Y., **1850**
Columbian Centinel. Boston. **1784–1840.** Also under title: *Massachusetts Centinel*
Columbian Magazine. See *Universal Asylum*
Columbus (Ohio) *Dispatch.* [Weekly.] **1874–?1900**
Columbus (Ohio) *Evening Dispatch.* **1871**–current
COMBE, GEORGE. *Notes on the United States of America, during a Phrenological Visit in 1838–9–40.* Phila., **1841**
COMER. See RHODE ISLAND HISTORICAL SOCIETY. *Collections*
Commerce of Rhode Island. See MASSACHUSETTS HISTORICAL SOCIETY. *Collections*
Commercial Advertiser. N.Y., **1797–1904**
COMMISSIONER OF INTERNAL REVENUE. *Decisions.* See U.S. TREASURY DEPT. *Treasury Decisions under the Customs . . . Laws*
Common Sense Cook Book. N.Y., **1867**
Commoner. Lincoln, Neb., **1901–23**
COMMONS. See *A Documentary History*
COMSTOCK, HARRIET T. (SMITH). *The Man Thou Gavest.* Garden City, N.Y., **1917**
CONDICT, ADELAIDE (BURNET). *Philip Eckert's Struggles and Triumphs.* N.Y., 1869 [**1868**]
CONGREGATIONAL CHURCHES IN MASSACHUSETTS. CAMBRIDGE SYNOD, 1648. *The Original Constitution, Order and Faith of the New-England Churches.* Bost., 1812. Includes: *A Platform of Church Discipline.* 1648. *Propositions* . . . *Answered by the Synod of 1662.* 1662. *A Confession of Faith Adopted* . . . *1680.* **1680**
A Platform of Church-Discipline. Bost., 1772. **1648.** See, under this heading, *The Original Constitution;* see also WISE
Congregational Confession of Faith. See CONGREGATIONAL CHURCHES IN MASSACHUSETTS. CAMBRIDGE SYNOD, 1648. *The Original Constitution.* See also WISE
Congressional Debates. See U.S. CONGRESS. *Register of Debates in Congress*
Congressional Globe. See U.S. CONGRESS
Congressional Record. See U.S. CONGRESS
CONNECTICUT (COLONY). *Public Records.* Hartford, 1850–90. **v.d.**
Connecticut Courant. Hartford, **1764–1914**
CONNECTICUT HISTORICAL SOCIETY. *Collections.* Hartford, 1860–1932. **v.d.** Contents include: G. BULKELEY. *Will & Doom.* 1692 (III); S. DEANE. *Correspondence.* **v.d.** (II); *Deane Papers.* **v.d.** (XXIII); *Distribution of Lands in Hartford.* **v.d.** (XIV); *Hartford Town Votes.* **v.d.** (VI); *Records of the Particular Court of Connecticut.* **v.d.** (XXII); *Talcott Papers.* **v.d.** (IV); *Wyllys Papers.* **v.d.** (XXI)
Connecticut Particular Court Rec. See CONNECTICUT HISTORICAL SOCIETY. *Collections*
Conn. Probate Rec. See MANWARING
Consular Rep. See U.S. BUREAU OF FOREIGN COMMERCE
CONTINENTAL CONGRESS. See U.S. CONTINENTAL CONGRESS
COOK, EBENEZER. *The Sot-Weed Factor: or, A Voyage to Maryland.* Lond., **1708.** [N.Y.: Reprinted, 1865]
COOK, JAMES H. *Fifty Years on the Old Frontier.* New Haven, **1923**
COOK, JOHN R. *The Border and the Buffalo.* Topeka, Kan., **1907**
COOKE, E. V. *Baseballogy.* Chic., **1912**
COOKE, J. E. *Beatrice Hallam.* N.Y., **1892.** First publ. as Vol. I of his: *The Virginia Comedians.* N.Y., **1854**

Ellie: or, the Human Comedy. Richmond, **1855**
Surry of Eagle's Nest. N.Y., **1866**
COOKE, ROSE (TERRY). *The Deacon's Week.* Bost. [n.d.]. **1885**
Happy Dodd. Bost., **1878**
Huckleberries Gathered from New England Hills. Bost., 1896. =1891. **v.d.**
Somebody's Neighbors. Bost., 1881. **v.d.**
Steadfast: the Story of a Saint and a Sinner. Bost., **1889**
COOPER, C. R. *Under the Big Top.* Bost., 1923. =**1920**
COOPER, J. F. *The Chainbearer.* **1845**
The Deerslayer. **1841**
Gleanings. See his: *Recollections in Europe*
Home as Found. **1838**
Homeward Bound. **1838**
The Last of the Mohicans. **1826**
Lionel Lincoln. **1825**
The Monikins. **1835**
Notions of the Americans. Lond., **1828**
The Oak Openings. N.Y., **1848**
The Pathfinder. Phila., **1840**
The Pilot. N.Y., **1823**
The Pioneers. **1823**
The Prairie. **1827**
Recollections of Europe. Lond., **1837.** Also publ. under title: *Gleanings in Europe.* Ed. R. E. Spiller. Vol. I. *France.* N.Y., 1928
The Red Rover. Lond., **1827.** Also publ.: N.Y., 1881
The Redskins. **1846**
The Sea Lions. **1849**
The Spy. **1821**
The Water Witch. Lond., **1830.** Also publ.: Lond., 1834
The Wept of Wish-ton-Wish. **1829**
Wing-and-Wing. **1842**
COOPER, SUSAN F. *Rural Hours.* N.Y., **1850**
COOPER, THOMAS. *Some Information respecting America.* Lond., **1794**
COPLEY, J. S., and PELHAM, HENRY. *Letters & Papers* . . . , *1739–1776.* [Bost.] 1914. **v.d.**
CORCORAN, D. *Pickings from the Portfolio of the Reporter of the New Orleans 'Picayune.'* Phila. [**1846**]
Cosmopolitan. N.Y., **1886–1925**
COTTOM. See [North Carolina Almanacs]
COUES, ELLIOTT. *Birds of the Northwest.* Wash., **1874**
Key to North American Birds. Salem [Mass.] 1872. 2d ed. Bost., 1884. 3d ed. Bost., **1887** ed. See FOWLER, JACOB; LEWIS and CLARK, *History;* and PIKE, Z. M.
COULTER, JOHN. *Adventures in the Pacific.* Dublin, **1845**
COULTER, JOHN MERLE. *Botany of Western Texas.* Wash., **1891–4**
COUPEE. See [North Carolina Almanacs]
Courier-Journal. Louisville, Ky. **1868**–current
COURTENAY, FLORENCE. *Physical Beauty, How to Develop and Preserve It.* N.Y. [cop. **1922**]
COWELL, EMILIE M. (EBSWORTH). *The Cowells in America, Being the Diary of Mrs. Sam Cowell.* Lond., 1934. **v.d.**
COWELL, JOSEPH. *Thirty Years Passed among the Players in England and America.* N.Y., **1844**
COWLES, JULIA. *Diaries* . . . *1797–1803.* Ed. L. H. Moseley. New Haven, **1931.** **v.d.**
COX, ROSS. *Adventures on the Columbia River.* N.Y., 1832. 1st ed. Lond., **1831**
COX, SAMUEL S. *A Buckeye Abroad.* Columbus, 1860. =**1852**
Eight Years in Congress, from 1857 to 1865. N.Y., 1865. **v.d.**
COX, SANDFORD C. *Recollections of the Early Settlement of the Wabash Valley.* Lafayette [Ind.] **1860**
COXE, DANIEL. *A Description of the English Province of Carolana.* Lond., **1722**
COXE, TENCH. *A View of the United States of America.* Phila., **1794.** Also publ.: Dublin, 1795
COXE, W. *A View of the Cultivation of Fruit Trees.* Phila., **1817**
COYNER, D. H. *The Lost Trappers.* Cinc., 1859. =**1847**
COZZENS, F. S. *Prismatics.* N.Y., **1853**
The Sayings of Dr. Bushwhacker and Other Learned Men. N.Y., **1867**
Sparrowgrass Papers. N.Y., 1860. =**1856**
COZZENS, S. W. *The Marvellous Country, or, Three Years in Arizona and New Mexico.* Bost. [cop. 1876]. First publ.: Bost., **1873**
'CRADDOCK.' See MURFREE
CRANE, STEPHEN. *George's Mother.* N.Y., **1896**
Maggie: A Girl of the Streets. N.Y., 1896. First publ. **1892**
The Third Violet. N.Y., **1897**
CRAWFORD, F. M. *An American Politician.* Bost., **1885**
CRAWFORD, J. M. *Mosby and His Men.* N.Y., **1867**
CRAWFORD, M. See *Sources of the History of Oregon*
CRESSWELL, NICHOLAS. *Journal* . . . , *1774–1777.* N.Y., 1924. **v.d.**
CRÈVECŒUR, M. G. ST. J. DE. *Letters from an American Farmer.* Lond., 1783. =**1782**

CRIM, MATT. *Elizabeth: Christian Scientist.* N.Y., **1893**
Crisis. Columbus, Ohio, **1861–71**
CRISSEY, FORREST. *Tattlings of a Retired Politician.* Chic., **1904**
CROCKETT, DAVID. *An Account of Col. Crockett's Tour to the North and Down East, in the Year of the Lord One Thousand Eight Hundred and Thirty-four.* Phila., **1835**
Col. Crockett's Exploits and Adventures in Texas. Phila., **1836**
A Narrative of the Life of David Crockett. Phila., **1834.** Also publ. as: *Autobiography.* N.Y., 1923
Sketches. See *Sketches*
[*Crockett Almanacs, 1835–52.*] Published in various places and under varying titles: *Davy Crockett's Almanac; Crockett's Yaller Flower Almanac;* etc.
CROFUTT, G. A. *Trans-continental Tourist.* N.Y., **1876**
CROGHAN, GEORGE. *Journal.* [Burlington, N.J., 1875.] (Reprinted from *Monthly American Journal of Geology and Natural Science,* I. (Dec., 1831), 257–72.) **1765.** See also THWAITES
CROY, HOMER. *R.F.D. No. 3.* N.Y., **1924**
Cultivator. Albany, **1834–65**
CUMING, FORTESCUE. *Sketches of a Tour to the Western Country.* Pittsb., 1810. **v.d.**
CUMINGS, SAMUEL. *The Western Pilot.* Cinc., **1829.** Also publ.: Cinc., 1832. Cinc., 1843
CUMMING, KATE. *A Journal of Hospital Life.* Louisville [cop. 1866]. **v.d.**
CUMMINGS, H. S., comp. *Dartmouth College. Sketches of the Class of 1862.* Wash., 1909. **v.d.**
CUMMINS, MARIA S. *The Lamplighter.* Bost., 1890. =**1854**
CUMMINS, RALPH. *Sky-high Corral.* Lond. [cop. **1924**]
CURTIS, GEORGE W. *Horses, Cattle, Sheep and Swine.* 2d ed. N.Y., **1893**
CURTIS, GEORGE WILLIAM. *Prue and I.* N.Y., 1892. First publ. **1856**
CURTIS, M. *Woody Plants N.C.* See HALE, P. M.
CUSHING, M. H. *The Story of Our Post Office.* Bost., **1893**
CUSHMAN, H. B. *History of the Choctaw, Chickasaw and Natchez Indians.* Greenville, Tex., **1899**
CUSTER, ELIZABETH (BACON). *'Boots and Saddles'; or, Life in Dakota with General Custer.* N.Y., **1885**
Following the Guidon. N.Y., **1890**
Tenting on the Plains. N.Y., 1889. =**1887**
CUTLER, JERVIS. *A Topographical Description of the State of Ohio.* Bost., **1812**
CUTLER, W. P., and CUTLER, J. P. *Life, Journals, and Correspondence of Rev. Manasseh Cutler, LL.D.* Cinc., 1888. **v.d.**
Cyclopædia of Biblical Lit. See McCLINTOCK, J., and STRONG, J.
The Cyclopaedia of Temperance and Prohibition. N.Y., **1891**
Cyclopedia of American Government. Ed. A. C. McLaughlin and A. B. Hart. N.Y., **1914**

D

DABNEY, JOHN, comp. *An Address to Farmers.* Salem [Mass.] **1796**
Daily California Chronicle. San Fran., **1853–8**
Daily Chronicle. Lond., **1869–1930**
Daily Inter-Ocean. See *Inter-Ocean.*
Daily Picayune. New Orleans, **1836–1914**
DAKOTA MISSION CONF. See METHODIST EPISCOPAL CHURCH. MISSION CONFERENCES. DAKOTA
'DALE, A.' See COHEN
DALE, E. E., and RADER, J. L. *Readings in Oklahoma History.* Evanston, Ill. [cop. 1930]. **v.d.**
DALRYMPLE, LUCINDA L. *Journal of a Young Lady of Virginia.* 1782. [Ed. E. V. Mason.] Balt., 1871. **1782**
DALTON, WILLIAM. *Travels in the United States of America, and Part of Upper Canada.* Appleby [Eng.] **1821**
DALY, AUGUSTIN. *After Business Hours.* N.Y.: Priv. pr. **1886**
The Big Bonanza. N.Y.: Priv. pr. 1884. First perf. **1875**
Divorce. N.Y.: Priv. pr. 1884. First perf. **1871**
The Great Unknown. N.Y.: Priv. pr. 1890. First perf. **1889**
A Legend of 'Norwood'; or, Village Life in New England. N.Y.: Priv. pr. **1867**
Little Miss Million. [N.Y.] Priv. pr. 1893. First perf. **1892**
The Lottery of Love. [N.Y.] Priv. pr. 1889. First perf. **1888**
Love in Harness. [N.Y.] Priv. pr. 1887. First perf. **1886**
Nancy and Company. N.Y.: Priv. pr. **1886**
Our English Friend. N.Y.: Priv. pr. 1884. First perf. **1882**

Pique. N.Y.: Priv. pr. 1884. First perf. **1875**
The Railroad of Love. [N.Y.] Priv. pr. [1887]
A Test Case; or, Grass versus Granite. N.Y.: Priv. pr. 1893. First perf. **1892**
Under the Gaslight. N.Y.: Author's ed. **1867**
Daly, J. F. *The Life of Augustin Daly*. N.Y., 1917. **v.d.**
Daly, W. H. *Alaska and Its Resources*. Bost., **1897**
Dana, C. W. *The Great West*. Bost., **1857**. =his: *The Garden of the World*. 1856
Dana, Charles A. *Recollections of the Civil War*. N.Y., 1902 [cop. 1898]. **1897**
Dana, Edmund. *Geographical Sketches on the Western Country*. Cinc., **1819**
Dana, J. D. *Geology*. Phila., **1849**
Manual of Geology. Phila., 1863 [cop. **1862**]
Manual of Mineralogy. New ed., rev. and enl. Lond., 1872. New ed. first publ.: New Haven, **1857**. (Other editions cited occasionally)
Dana, R. H. *The Seaman's Manual. Containing a Treatise on Practical Seamanship*. Lond., **1841**
Two Years before the Mast. N.Y., 1862. =**1840**. Also publ.: Chic.: Conkey [n.d.]. New ed. Bost., 1884. =**1869**
Darby, William. *The Emigrant's Guide to the Western and Southern Territories, with a Map of the United States*. N.Y., **1818**
A Geographical Description of the State of Louisiana. Phila., **1816**
Darlington, William. *American Weeds and Useful Plants*. Rev. by George Thurber. N.Y., **1860**. =1859. 1st ed. as: *Agricultural Botany*. Phila., **1847**
Memorials of John Bartram and Humphry Marshall. Phila., 1849. **v.d.**
Darrow, C. S. *Farmington*. Chic., **1904**
Dartmouth. Hanover [N.H.] **1839–44**
Darusmont, Frances (Wright). *Views of Society and Manners in America*. N.Y., 1821. **v.d.**
Davidson, Alice M. *California Plants in Their Homes*. Los Angeles, **1898**
Davidson, Robert. *History of the Presbyterian Church in the State of Kentucky*. N.Y., **1847**
Davies, Ebenezer. *American Scenes and Christian Slavery*. Lond., **1849**
Davis, A. McF., ed. *Tracts Relating to the Currency of the Massachusetts Bay, 1682–1720*. Bost., 1902. **v.d.**
Davis, Charles Augustus. *Letters of J. Downing*. N.Y., **1834**
Davis, Charles Belmont. *The Borderland of Society*. Chic., **1898**
Davis, Charles Henry. *Polaris Exp.* See U.S. Navy Dept. *Narrative*
Davis, John. *Travels of Four Years and a Half in the United States of America*. Lond., **1803**. Also publ.: N.Y., 1909
Davis, Norah. *The Northerner*. N.Y., **1905**
Davis, Parke H. *Football, the American Intercollegiate Game*. N.Y., 1911. **v.d.**
Davis, Peter S. *The Young Parson*. Phila., **1863**
Davis, Rebecca B. (Harding). *Silhouettes of American Life*. N.Y., 1892. **v.d.**
Davis, Richard H. *Gallegher and Other Stories*. N.Y., 1913. **v.d.**
Davis, W. W. H. *El Gringo*. N.Y., **1857**
Day, H. F. *King Spruce*. N.Y., **1908**
Deane, Samuel. *Diary; Journal*. See Smith, T.
The New-England Farmer. Worcester: Thomas, **1790**. 2d ed. **1797**
Deane, S. *Correspondence. Deane Papers*. See Connecticut Historical Society
Deane Papers. See Connecticut Historical Society
Dearborn, Benjamin. *The Columbian Grammar*. Bost., **1795**
Debates in Congress. See U.S. Congress
Debates in Mass. Convention. See Massachusetts. Convention
Decorum: A Practical Treatise on Etiquette and Dress, of the Best American Society. N.Y., 1880. **1878**
Dedham, Mass. *Early Records*. Dedham, 1886–99. **v.d.** Vol. III: 1636–59. Vol. IV: 1659–73. Vol. V: 1672–1706
Deland, Margaret. *Florida Days*. Bost., **1889**
John Ward, Preacher. Bost., **1888**
Old Chester Tales. N Y. [cop. **1898**]
Delaney, Matilda J. (Sager). *A Survivor's Recollections of the Whitman Massacre*. Spokane [cop. **1920**]
Delaware County (N.Y.) *Deeds*. Cited in *Dialect Notes*, II, 132
Deming, Philander. *Adirondack Stories*. Bost., **1880**
Democratic Party. *Official Proceedings of the National Democratic Convention, Held in Cincinnati, June 2–6, 1856*. Cinc., **1856**
Democratic Review. See *United States Magazine*
Denison, C. W. *The Tanner-Boy and How He Became Lieutenant-General*. Bost., **1864**
Denny, Ebenezer. *Military Journal*. Phila., 1859. **v.d.** See also Pennsylvania, Historical Society of
Denton, Daniel. *A Brief Description of New-York*. Lond., **1670**. Facsimile: N.Y., 1937. Also: Ed. John Pennington. [Phila.] 1845. Cleveland, 1902
Department of Agriculture. See U.S. Dept. of Agriculture
Derby, G. H. *Phoenixiana; or, Sketches and Burlesques*. 12th ed. N.Y., 1859. =**1856**
Derby, Conn. *Town Records*. Derby, 1901. **v.d.**
D'Eres. See Rouso d'Eres
Derville, Leslie. *The Other Side of the Story*. N.Y. [**1904**]
A Description of Kentucky. See Toulmin
A Description of South Carolina. See Glen
Description of Virginia, A Perfect. See Force. *Tracts*. Vol. II, No. 8
De Smet. See Smet
Devens, R. M. *The Pictorial Book of Anecdotes and Incidents of the War of the Rebellion*. Hartford, **1866**
De Vere, M. S. *Americanisms; the English of the New World*. N.Y., 1872 [cop. **1871**]. Copy at Univ. of Virginia includes author's marginal notes of *c*1873. See also *Encyclopædia Britannica*
Dewees, Mary (Coburn). *Journal of a Trip from Philadelphia to Lexington in Kentucky*. MS., Univ. Chicago Lib. **1788**
Dewees, W. B. *Letters from an Early Settler of Texas*. Comp. Cara Cordelle. Louisville, 1852. **v.d.**
Dewey. See Massachusetts. Zoological and Botanical Survey. *Reports on the Herbaceous Plants*
De Witt's Base-Ball Guide for 1878. Ed. Henry Chadwick. N.Y., cop. **1878**
Dialect Notes. Bost.; Norwood, Mass.; New Haven, **1890–1939**. Contents include: Vol. V: J. L. B. Taylor. *Snake County Talk*. **1923**. Vol. VI: R. H. Thornton. *An American Glossary* (q.v.). Vol. III (supplement). Ed. Louise Hanley. **v.d.** G. E. Ellis. *Let. to Bartlett*. **1848**. *Memo of R. I. Words*. **1848**
Diary of Daly Débutante. See Ranous
Dick, W. B. *The American Hoyle*. 3d ed. N.Y. [?1866; cop. **1864**]. 13th ed. N.Y., **1880**
Dickens, Charles. *American Notes for General Circulation*. N.Y., Harper, **1842**. Also: Lond., **1842**. 2 vols.
Dickenson. See Dickinson, J.
Dickinson, Emily. *Complete Poems*. Bost., 1924. *a***1886**
Further Poems. Ed. M. D. Bianchi and A. L. Hampson. Bost., 1929. *a***1886**
Dickinson, Jonathan. *Gods Protecting Providence Man's Surest Help and Defence*. Phila., **1699**
Dickson, A. J. *Covered Wagon Days: A Journey across the Plains in the Sixties*. Ed. A. J. Dickson. Cleveland, 1929. **v.d.**
Diplomatic Corr. Tex. See American Historical Association
Diseases of Swine. See U.S. Dept. of Agriculture. *Special Report*
Dix, E. A. *Deacon Bradbury*. N.Y., **1900**
Dix, John. *Transatlantic Tracings; or, Sketches of Persons and Scenes in America*. Lond., **1853**
Dixon, James. *Personal Narrative of a Tour through a Part of the United States and Canada*. N.Y., **1849**
Dixon, W. H. *New America*. 6th ed. Lond., **1867**
A Documentary History of American Industrial Society. Ed. J. R. Commons, *et al*. Cleveland, 1910–1. **v.d.**
The Documentary History of the State of New-York. By E. B. O'Callaghan. Albany, 1849–51. **v.d.** Vol. II includes: C. Williamson. *Descr. Genesee*. **1798**
Documents & Recs. Relative to the Province of New-Hampshire. See New Hampshire. [*Provincial and State Papers*]
Documents Relating to the Colonial, Revolutionary and Post-Revolutionary History of the State of New Jersey. (*Archives of the State of New Jersey*. 1st Ser.) Newark, 1880–. **v.d.**
Documents Relating to the Revolutionary History of the State of New Jersey. (*Archives of the State of New Jersey*. 2d Ser.) Trenton, 1901–17. **v.d.**
Documents Relative to the Colonial History of the State of New-York. Albany, 1853–87. **v.d.**
Doddridge, Joseph. *Logan*. . . . [With] *The Dialogue of the Backwoodsman and the Dandy*. Cinc., 1868. **1823**, **1821**
Notes, on the Settlement and Indian Wars, of the Western Parts of Virginia & Pennsylvania. Wellsburgh, Va., **1824**
Dodge, John. *An Entertaining Narrative of the Cruel and Barbarous Treatment and Extreme Sufferings of Mr. John Dodge during His Captivity*. 2d ed. Danvers [Mass.] **1780**
Dodge, Mary A. *Country Living and Country Thinking*. Bost., 1865. =**1862**
Gala-Days. Bost., 1865. =**1863**
A New Atmosphere. Bost., **1865**
Skirmishes and Sketches. Bost., 1866. =**1865**
Twelve Miles from a Lemon. N.Y., **1874**
'Doesticks.' See Thomson, M. N.
Dorchester Antiquarian and Historical Society. *Collections*. No 3. 2d ed. Bost., 1874. Includes: R. Mather. *Journal*. **1635**. I. Mather. *Life R. Mather*. **1670**
Dorchester Rec. See Boston. Registry Dept.
Dorsey, Ella L. *Midshipman Bob*. N.Y., **1888**
Douglass, Frederick. *Narrative of the Life of Frederick Douglass*. Bost., 1849. =**1845**
Douglass, William. *A Summary . . . of the First Planting, Progressive Improvements, and Present State of the British Settlements in North America*. Bost., 1749–[52]. Also publ. 1755 and 1760 **v.d.**
'Dow, Jr.' See Paige
Dow, G. F., ed. *The Holyoke Diaries, 1709–1856*. Salem, Mass., 1911. **v.d.**
Dow, Lorenzo. *History of Cosmopolite; or, The Four Volumes of Lorenzo's Journal*. N Y., 1814. 3d ed. Wheeling, Va., 1848. **v.d.**
'Downing, Maj. Jack.' (See also Smith, Seba; Davis, C. A.) *The Life of Andrew Jackson*. Phila., **1834**
D'Oyle, L. C. *Notches on the Rough Edge of Life*. [Lond., 1890.] **v.d.**
Drake, Benjamin. *Tales and Sketches, from the Queen City*. Cinc., **1838**
Drake, Benjamin, and Mansfield, E. D. *Cincinnati in 1826*. Cinc., **1827**
Drake, Daniel. *Natural and Statistical View, or Picture of Cincinnati and the Miami Country*. Cinc., **1815**
Pioneer Life in Kentucky. Ed. C. D. Drake. Cinc., 1870. **v.d.**
Drake, S. G. *Tragedies of the Wilderness*. Bost., **1841**
Dramatic Comps. Copyrighted. See U.S. Copyright Office
Drannan, W. F. *Thirty-one Years on the Plains and in the Mountains*. Chic. [cop. **1900**]
Draper, J. W. *History of the American Civil War*. N.Y. [cop. **1867–70**]
Drayton, John. *Letters Written during a Tour through the Northern and Eastern States of America*. Charleston, **1794**
A View of South-Carolina, as Respects Her Natural and Civil Concerns. Charleston, **1802**
Dreiser, Theodore. *The Financier*. N.Y. [**1912**]
Drinker, Elizabeth (Sandwith). *Extracts from the Journal*. . . . Ed. H. D. Biddle. Phila., 1889. **v.d.**
Duane, William, ed. *Letters to Benjamin Franklin*. N.Y., 1859. **v.d.**
Du Bois, W. E. B. *A Select Bibliography of the Negro American*. Atlanta, 1905. **v.d.**
Dumont, Frank. *Lew Benedict's Congress Broke Loose Songster*. N.Y., **1869**
Dunbar, P. L. *Folks from Dixie*. N.Y., **1898**
Duncan, J. M. *Travels through Part of the United States and Canada*. Glasgow, **1823**
Duncan, L. W., and Scott, C. F. *History of Allen and Woodson Counties, Kansas*. Iola, Kan., **1901**
Duncan, Mary (Grey) L. *America as I Found It*. N.Y., **1852**
Dunglison, Robley. *A New Dictionary of Medical Science and Literature*. Bost., **1833**. Subsequent eds. (2d, **1839**; 7th, **1848**; 8th, **1851**; 11th, **1854**) publ. at Phila. under title: *Medical Lexicon*
Dunlap, James. *A Book of Forms*. 4th ed. Phila., **1857**
Dunlap, William. *André*. See Moses. *Representative Plays*. Vol. I
Darby's Return. N.Y., **1789**
The Father; or, American Shandyism. N.Y., 1887. First publ. **1789**
A History of the American Theatre. N.Y., **1832**
The Memoirs of a Water Drinker. N.Y., 1837. First publ. as: *Thirty Years Ago: or, The Memoirs of a Water Drinker*. N.Y., **1836**
Dunmore, J. M., Earl of. *Correspondence*. Colonial Office Papers, Class 5, No. 1353 (formerly America & W. Indies, No. 213). MS., Great Britain, Public Record Office. **v.d.**
Du Puy, W. A. *Uncle Sam, Detective*. N.Y. [**1916**]
Durfee, Job. *Whatcheer, or, Roger Williams in Banishment*. Providence, **1832**
Durivage, F. A., and Burnham, G. P. *Stray Subjects, Arrested and Bound Over*. Phila. [n.d.] = **1848**
Durrett. See Filson Club.
Dutton, C. J. *The Shadow on the Glass*. N.Y., **1923**
Duxbury, Mass. *Copy of the Old Records of the Town*. . . . *From 1642 to 1770*. Plymouth, 1893. **v.d.**
Dwight, M. V. See Bell, M. V.
Dwight, Timothy. *Remarks on the Review of Inchiquin's Letters, Published in the Quarterly Review*. Bost., **1815**
Travels; in New-England and New-York. New Haven, 1821–2. *a***1817**

E

EARLE, ALICE (MORSE). *Colonial Days in Old New York.* N.Y., 1896. **v.d.**
Curious Punishments of Bygone Days. N.Y., 1907. =1896. **v.d.**
The Sabbath in Puritan New England. N.Y., 1891. **v.d.**
Early Conn. Probate Rec. See MANWARING
EAST HAMPTON, N.Y. *Records of the Town.* Sag Harbor, 1887-1905. **v.d.**
EASTBURN, J. W., and SANDS, R. C. *Yamoyden, a Tale of the Wars of King Philip.* N.Y., 1820. See also SANDS
EASTBURN, ROBERT. *A Faithful Narrative of the Many Dangers and Sufferings . . . of Robert Eastburn during His Late Captivity among the Indians.* Phila., 1758
EASTMAN, C. A. *From the Deep Woods to Civilization.* Bost., 1929. =1916
EASTMAN, MARY (HENDERSON). *Aunt Phillis's Cabin.* Phila., 1852
EASTON, JOHN. *A Narrative of the Causes Which Led to Philip's Indian War of 1675 and 1676. . . . With Other Documents.* [Ed.] F. B. Hough. Albany, 1858. **1675**
EATON, AMOS. *Manual of Botany for the Northern and Middle States of America.* 3d ed. Albany, 1822. 1817-8. 5th ed., 1829. 6th ed., 1833. 7th ed., **1836**
EBBUTT, P. G. *Emigrant Life in Kansas.* Lond., **1886**
Economical Geology of Illinois. See ILLINOIS. GEOLOGICAL SURVEY
Economist. Chic., **1888**-current
EDWARD, D. B. *History of Texas.* Cinc., **1836**
EDWARDS, GEORGE. *A Natural History of Uncommon Birds, and of Some Rare and Undescribed Animals.* Lond. [1743]-51
EDWARDS, J. N. *Shelby and His Men.* Cinc., **1867**
EGGLESTON, EDWARD. *The Book of Queer Stories, and Stories Told on a Cellar Door.* N.Y., 1871. First publ. 1870
The Circuit Rider. N.Y., **1874**
Duffels. N.Y., **1893**
The End of the World. Chic. [cop. 1900]. =1872
The Graysons. See *Century Magazine*
The Hoosier School-Boy. N.Y., 1899. =**1883**
The Hoosier Schoolmaster. N.Y. [cop. 1871]
Mr. Blake's Walking-Stick. Chic., 1872. =**1870**
The Mystery of Metropolisville. N.Y. [cop. 1873]
EGGLESTON, G. C. *Dorothy South.* N.Y. [cop. 1902]
The First of the Hoosiers. Phila. [1903]
A Rebel's Recollections. N.Y., **1874**
The Wreck of the Red Bird. N.Y., **1882**
The Eighty-second Anniversary of American Independence. See BOSTON COURIER
ELIOT, JARED. *A Continuation of the Essay upon Field-Husbandry.* New-London [Conn.] 1751
Essays upon Field-Husbandry. Bost., 1760. **v.d.**
ELIOT, JOHN. *A Brief Narrative of the Progress of the Gospel among the Indians of New England.* [Ed.] W. T. R. Marvin. Bost., 1868. 1670. See also *Old South Leaflets*
Day-Breaking. See MASSACHUSETTS HISTORICAL SOCIETY. *Collections.* See also *Old South Leaflets*
The Glorious Progress of the Gospel. See WINSLOW, E.
ELIOT, S. A. *A Sketch of the History of Harvard College.* Bost., 1848
ELLET, ELIZABETH F. (LUMMIS). *The Pioneer Women of the West.* Phila., 1873. =**1852**
ELLICOTT, ANDREW (See also MATHEWS, C. V.). *Journal.* Phila., 1814. =1803. **v.d.**
ELLIOT, JONATHAN, ed. *The Debates . . . on the Adoption of the Federal Constitution.* Wash., 1827-45. **v.d.**
ELLIOT, MAUD (HOWE). *Honor.* St. Paul [cop. 1893]
ELLIOTT, F. R. *Elliott's Fruit Book.* N.Y., 1854. New ed. as: *The Western Fruit Book.* N.Y. [cop. 1859]
ELLIS, E. S. *Check 2134.* N.Y. [cop. 1891]
ELLIS, G. E. *Letter to J. R. Bartlett.* MS. (Bartlett Papers). John Carter Brown Lib., Providence, R.I. 1848. See also *Dialect Notes*
ELLIS, J. B. *Lahoma.* Indianapolis [cop. 1913]
ELLSWORTH, H. W. *Valley of the Upper Wabash, Indiana.* N.Y., 1838
'ELMWOOD.' See GREENE, A.
ELWYN, A. L. *Glossary of Supposed Americanisms.* Phila., 1859
EMERSON, ALICE B. *Ruth Fielding at Snow Camp.* N.Y., 1913
EMERSON, C. N., ed. *The Internal Revenue Guide.* Springfield, Mass., 1866. **v.d.**
EMERSON, G. See MASSACHUSETTS. ZOOLOGICAL AND BOTANICAL SURVEY. *Report*
EMERSON, R. W. *Complete Works.* [Ed.] E. W. Emerson. [Centenary Ed. Bost., 1903-4.] v.d. Vol. IX: *Poems* (q.v.). **v.d.** Also: *Works.* Lond., 1888-90. 3 vols. (Bohn's Standard Lib.) **v.d.**

The Conduct of Life. Bost., **1860**
Essays. [1st Ser.] Bost., 1841. 2d Ser. Bost., 1854. **v.d.**
Letters and Social Aims. Bost., 1876 [1875]. 314 pp. Also: New and rev. ed. 1876 (and in subsequent reprints). 285 pp.
Miscellanies. Bost., 1892. =1883. (*Complete Works,* Riverside Ed., Vol. XI.) **v.d.**
Miscellanies: Embracing Nature, Addresses, and Lectures. Bost., 1856. 383 pp. Also: New and rev. ed. Bost., 1876 (and in subsequent reprints). 315 pp. **v.d.**
Poems. Bost., 1857. =1847. Also: Concord Ed. Bost., 1904. See also his: *Complete Works*
Representative Men. Bost., **1850**
Society and Solitude. Bost., 1870. 300 pp. Also: Bost., 1876 (and in subsequent reprints). 269 pp. **v.d.**
EMMONS. *Agric. N.Y.* See NEW YORK (STATE). NATURAL HISTORY SURVEY. *Natural History of New York.* [Div. 5]
Mass. Quadrupeds. See MASSACHUSETTS. ZOOLOGICAL AND BOTANICAL SURVEY. *Reports on the Herbaceous Plants*
EMORY. *Notes Mil. Reconnoissance.* See U.S. ENGINEER DEPT.
Report on U.S. & Mex. Boundary Survey. See U.S. DEPT. OF THE INTERIOR
Emporia (Kan.) *Gazette.* 1890-current
Emporium of Arts and Sciences. Phila., 1812-4
Encyclopædia Americana. Ed. Francis Lieber. Phila., 1829-33
Encyclopædia Americana, 1884-9. See *Encyclopædia Britannica*
The Encyclopædia Britannica. 9th ed. [American] Supplement. Also issued as: *Encyclopædia Americana.* N.Y., 1884 [cop. 1883]-9. Vol. I includes: DE VERE. *Americanisms*
Encyclopedia Americana. Ed. F. C. Beach, *et al.* N.Y. [cop. 1903-4]. Also: N.Y., 1918-20. **v.d.**
Engineer. Lond., 1856-current
An Englishman's Sketch-Book. See BLOODGOOD
ESSEX CO., MASS. PROBATE COURT. *The Probate Records.* Salem, 1916-20. **v.d.**
ESSEX INSTITUTE. *Historical Collections.* Salem, 1859- (Note: Some quots. from Vol. XLV erroneously cited as from Vol. XLII; some from Vol. X, Part III, erroneously cited as from Vol. XIII)
Material in individual vols. is cited under specific titles as below:
A. FULLER. *Journal.* 1758. (Vol. XLVI)
D. GIDDINGS. *Journal.* v.d. (Vol. XLVIII)
Gloucester Records. v.d. (Vols. XXI-XXII)
S. HOLTEN. *Journal.* v.d. (Vols. LV-LVI)
C. REA. *Journal* (q.v.). 1758. (Vol. XVIII)
J. STEVENS. *Journal.* v.d. (Vol. XLVIII)
L. WOOD. *Journal.* v.d. (Vols. XIX-XXI)
Estate of Virginia, A True Declaration of the. See FORCE. *Tracts.* Vol. III, No. 1
EVANS, A. J. See WILSON, A. J.
EVANS, E. See THWAITES
EVANS, LEWIS. *An Analysis of a General Map of the Middle British Colonies in America; and of the Country of the Confederate Indians.* Phila., 1755
Evanston (Ill.) *Press.* 1889-1916
Evening Standard. Lond., 1827-current
Examiner. Lond., 1808-81

F

FALCONER. See CHETWOOD
FANNING, DAVID. *Narrative . . . as Written by Himself.* N.Y., 1865. 1790
FARMER, J. S., ed. *Americanisms—Old and New.* Lond., 1889
FARMER, J. S., and HENLEY, W. E. *Slang and Its Analogues Past and Present.* Lond., 1890-1904
Farmers' Bul. See U.S. DEPT. OF AGRICULTURE
FARMERS' MUSEUM, Walpole, N.H. *The Spirit of the Farmers' Museum, and Lay Preacher's Gazette. Being a Judicious Selection.* Walpole, 1801. 6 pp.
FARNHAM, ELIZA W. (BURHANS). *Life in Prairie Land.* N.Y., 1846
FARNHAM, T. J. *Life and Adventures in California.* N.Y., 1846
Travels. See THWAITES
Father Abbey's Will. See SECCOMB(E)
FAUX, WILLIAM. *Memorable Days in America.* Lond., 1823
FEARON, H. B. *Sketches of America.* Lond., 1818
FEATHERSTONHAUGH, G. W. *A Canoe Voyage up the Minnay Sotor.* Lond., 1847
Excursion through the Slave States, from Washington on the Potomac to the frontier of Mexico. N.Y., 1844
The Federalist. 1788
FELT, J. B. *The Customs of New England.* Bost., 1853

FELTON, MRS. *Life in America.* Hull [Eng.]. 1838
FERBER, EDNA. *Dawn O'Hara.* N.Y. [1911]
FERGUSON, C. D. *The Experiences of a Forty-Niner during Thirty-four Years Residence in California and Australia.* Cleveland, 1888
FERGUSSON, ADAM. *Practical Notes Made during a Tour in Canada, and a Portion of the United States.* Edinb., 1833
'FERN.' See PARTON
FERNOW. See *Documents Relative to the Colonial History of the State of New-York*
FERRALL. See O'FERRALL
FESSENDEN, T. G. *Democracy Unveiled; or, Tyranny Stripped of the Garb of Patriotism.* 3d ed. N.Y., 1806
The Ladies Monitor. Bellows Falls, Vt., 1818
Original Poems. Phila., 1806. **v.d.**
FIDLER, ISAAC. *Observations on Professions, Literature, Manners, and Emigration, in the United States and Canada.* N.Y., 1833
FIELD, E. S. *The Sapphire Bracelet.* N.Y. [cop. 1910]
A Six-Cylinder Courtship. N.Y. [1907]
FIELD, H. M. *Bright Skies and Dark Shadows.* N.Y., 1890
FIELD, J. M. *The Drama in Pokerville.* Phila. [?1847]
Field and Forest. Wash., 1875-8
FILSON, JOHN. *The Discovery, Settlement and Present State of Kentucke.* Wilmington [Del.] 1784
FILSON CLUB. *Filson Club Publications.* Louisville, 1884-. No. 3: PERRIN. *Ky. Pioneer Press.* 1888. v.d. No. 7: *Ky. Centenary Celebr.* 1892. No. 8: R. T. DURRETT. *The Centenary of Louisville.* v.d. No. 9: T. SPEED. *Polit. Club, Danville, Ky.* 1894. v.d. No. 13: J. S. JOHNSTON. *First Explorations of Kentucky.* 1898. Includes: T. WALKER. *Journal of an Exploration of Kentucky.* 1750. C. GIST. *Journal of a Tour through Ohio and Kentucky.* 1751. No. 16: RAUCK. *Boonesborough.* 1901. v.d. No. 27: ROBERTSON. *Ky. Petitions.* 1914. v.d. No. 31: LITTELL. *Polit. Trans. Ky.* 1806. NICHOLAS. *Let. to Friend.* 1798. WILKINSON. *Memorial.* 1787
FINCH, JOHN. *Travels in the United States of America and Canada.* Lond., 1833
FINLAY, HUGH. *Journal.* Brooklyn, 1867. **v.d.**
FINLAY, J. B. *Autobiography.* Cinc., 1855. First publ. 1854
FINN, H. J., ed. *American Comic Annual.* Bost., 1831
FINN, H. J., *et al.* See *Whimwhams*
First Planters of New-England. See *Massachusetts, or the First Planters of New-England*
FISHER, W. M. *The Californians.* Lond., 1876
Fisheries Exhibition Cat. See LONDON. INTERNATIONAL FISHERIES EXHIBITION, 1883
FISK, J. L. *Expedition . . . to the Rocky Mountains.* [Wash., 1864.] 1863
FISKE, STEPHEN. *Holiday Stories.* Lond., 1900. First publ. 1891
FITCH, ASA. *Report on the Noxious, Beneficial and Other Insects of the State of New York.* Albany, 1865
FITCH, CLYDE. *Captain Jinks of the Horse Marines.* N.Y., 1902. First perf. 1901
The City. See MOSES. *Representative American Dramas*
Plays. Ed. M. J. Moses and Virginia Gerson. Bost., 1915. Vol. II includes: *Captain Jinks of the Horse Marines.* 1901
FITCH, T. See MERENESS
FITHIAN, P. V. *Philip Fithian Vickers, Journal and Letters, 1767-1774.* Ed. J. R. Williams [*et al.*]. Princeton, 1900-34. v.d. Vol. I, pp. 1-43, also cited as: *Princetoniana*
FITZGERALD, HUGH. *Sam Steele's Adventures on Land and Sea.* Chic. [cop. 1906]
FLAGG, E. See THWAITES
FLAGG, W. J. See *Harper's Magazine*
FLANDRAU, C. M. *Harvard Episodes.* Bost., 1897
FLEMING, WALTER L., ed. *Documentary History of Reconstruction.* Cleveland, 1906-7. **v.d.**
FLEMING, W. See MERENESS
FLINT, C. L. *Milch Cows and Dairy Farming.* N.Y., 1858
FLINT, JAMES. *Letters from America.* Edinb., 1822. v.d. See also THWAITES
FLINT, TIMOTHY. *Biographical Memoir of Daniel Boone, the First Settler of Kentucky.* Cinc., 1833
Francis Berrian; or, The Mexican Patriot. Bost., 1826
George Mason, the Young Backwoodsman. Bost., 1829
The Life and Adventures of Arthur Clenning. Phila., 1828
Recollections of the Last Ten Years, Passed in Occasional Residences and Journeyings in the Valley of the Mississippi. Bost., 1826
Florida Plantation Records. See JONES, G. N.
FLOWER, R. See THWAITES
'FLYNT.' See WILLARD
FOBES. See *Magazine of History*
FOLSOM, GEORGE. *History of Saco and Biddeford.* Saco [Me.] 1830. **v.d.**

Foote, H. S. *Texas and the Texans.* Phila., **1841**
Foote, Mary (Hallock). *The Led-Horse Claim.* Bost. [cop. **1883**]
Foote, W. H. *Sketches of Virginia, Historical and Biographical.* Phila., **1850**
Force, Peter, comp. *American Archives.* See *American Archives*
comp. *Tracts and Other Papers Relating . . . to . . . the Colonies.* Wash., 1836–46. Contents include: Vol. I, No. 12. F. Higginson. *New Englands Plantation* (q.v.). **1630.** Vol. II, No. 1. J. Smith. *A Description of New England* (q.v.). **1616.** No. 5. T. Morton. *New English Canaan* (q.v.). **1632** [*i.e.*,] **1637.** No. 8. *A Perfect Description of Virginia.* **1649.** Vol. III, No. 1. *A True Declaration of the Estate of . . . Virginia.* **1610.** Vol. IV, No. 1. R. Hakluyt, tr. *Virginia Richly Valued* (q.v. under *Relaçam verdadeira*). **1609**
Ford, Emily E. (Fowler). *Notes on the Life of Noah Webster.* N.Y., 1912. **v.d.**
Ford, P. L. *The Honorable Peter Stirling.* N.Y., 1899. =**1894**
Tattle-Tales of Cupid. N.Y., **1898**
Ford, Thomas. *A History of Illinois, from . . . 1818 to 1847.* Chic., 1859. =1854. a**1850**
Fordham, E. P. *Personal Narrative of Travels.* Ed. F. A. Ogg. Cleveland, 1906. **v.d.**
Foreign Missionary Chronicle. Pittsb.; N.Y., **1833–41**
Forestry Bureau. See U.S. Forest Service
Forster. See Kalm
Fort, Charles. *The Outcast Manufacturers.* N.Y., **1909**
Foster, G. G. *New York in Slices.* N.Y., **1849**
Foster, Hannah (Webster). *The Coquette; or, The History of Eliza Wharton.* Bost., **1797**
Fowler, Jacob. *Journal.* Ed. Elliott Coues. N.Y., 1898. **v.d.**
Fowler, John. *Journal of a Tour in the State of New York, in the Year 1830.* Lond., **1831**
Fowler, O. S. *A Home for All; or, the Gravel Wall and Octagon Mode of Building.* N.Y. [cop. **1853**]
Fox, John, Jr. *The Kentuckians.* N.Y., **1898**
The Little Shepherd of Kingdom Come. **1903**
Foxhall. See Toxhall
Francis, Francis, Jr. *Saddle and Mocassin* [*sic*]. Lond., **1887**
Frank Leslie's Popular Monthly. N.Y., **1876**–current
Franklin, Benjamin. *Writings.* Ed. A. H. Smyth. N.Y., 1905–7. **v.d.** Vol. I includes: *Autobiography.* **v.d.** Vol. II includes: *Dogood Papers.* **1722.** *Journal.* **1726.** *A Modest Enquiry into the Nature . . . of a Paper Currency.* **1729.** Selections from *Pennsylvania Gazette.* **1732.** *Plain Truth* (q.v.). **1747.** *Proposals Relating to the Education of the Youth in Pennsylvania.* **1749**
Complete Works. Comp. and ed. John Bigelow. N.Y., 1887–8. **v.d.**
An Account of the New Invented Pennsylvania Fire-Places. Phila., **1744**
Experiments and Observations on Electricity. Lond., **1751.** [4th ed.] 1769. **v.d.**
The Medical Side of Benjamin Franklin. See Pepper
Plain Truth. [Phila.] **1747.** See also his: *Writings.* Vol. II
Poor Richard, 1733. Phila. [**1732**]. Also subsequent issues
Poor Richard Improved: Being an Almanack and Ephemeris . . . for the Bissextile Year, 1748. Phila. [**1747**]
Proposals Relating to the Education. . . . See his: *Writings*
Frazer, Lilly Grove, Lady, *et al. Dancing.* Lond., **1895**
Frederic, Harold. *The Damnation of Theron Ware.* Chic., 1900. =**1896**
The Deserter, and Other Stories. Bost. [cop. **1898**]
The Lawton Girl. N.Y., 1899. =**1890**
Seth's Brother's Wife. N.Y., **1887**
Free Press. Halifax, N.C.; Tarboro, N.C., **1824**–current. Title varies
Freeburg, V. O. *The Art of Photoplay Making.* N.Y., **1918**
Freeman, E. A. See *Longman's Magazine*
Freeman, Mary E. (Wilkins). *By the Light of the Soul.* N.Y., **1906**
The Copy-Cat, & Other Stories. N.Y., 1914. **v.d.**
The Debtor. N.Y., **1905**
Edgewater People. N.Y. [cop. **1918**]
Giles Corey, Yeoman. N.Y., **1893**
A Humble Romance and Other Stories. N.Y. [cop. **1887,** 1915]
In Colonial Times. Bost., **1899**
Jane Field. N.Y., 1893. First publ. **1892**
Jerome, A Poor Man. N.Y., **1897**
Madelon. N.Y., **1896**
A New England Nun and Other Stories. N.Y. [cop. **1891**]
Pembroke. N.Y., **1894**
The Portion of Labor. N.Y., **1901**
The Pot of Gold, and Other Stories. Bost. [cop. **1892**]
The Shoulders of Atlas. N.Y., **1908**
Six Trees. N.Y., **1903**
The Winning Lady, and Others. N.Y., 1909. **v.d.**
Young Lucretia, and Other Stories. N.Y., **1892**
Freeman, Mary E. (Wilkins), and Kingsley, Florence M. *An Alabaster Box.* N.Y., **1917**
Freemason's Magazine and General Miscellany. Phila., **1811–2**
Frémont, J. C. *Report of the Exploring Expedition to the Rocky Mountains in the Year 1842, and to Oregon and North California in the Years 1843–'44.* Wash., 1845. Cited as: *Explor. Rocky Mts.* **1843.** *Exped.* **1845**
French, Alice. *The Missionary Sheriff.* N.Y., **1897**
Otto the Knight, and Other Trans-Mississippi Stories. Bost., **1891**
Stories of a Western Town. N.Y., 1897. =**1893**
French, Allen. *The Barrier.* N.Y., **1904**
Freneau, P. M. *Miscellaneous Works.* Phila., **1788**
Poems Written and Published during the Revolutionary War. Phila., 1809. **v.d.**
Poems Written between the Years 1768 & 1794. New ed. Monmouth [N.J.] **1795**
Poems. . . . Written Chiefly during the Late War. Phila., **1786**
Friis. See North Carolina. Historical Commission
Frothingham, Richard. *The History of Charlestown, Massachusetts.* Charlestown, 1845–9. **v.d.**
Fuller, A. See Essex Institute
Fuller, Jane G. *Uncle John's Flower-Gatherers.* N.Y., **1869**
Fuller, Sarah M. See Ossoli
Fulton, J. D. *Sam Hobart, the Locomotive Engineer.* N.Y. [**1883**]
The Fundamental Constitutions of Carolina. See *Old South Leaflets*
Fur, Fin, and Feather, a Bi-monthly Periodical . . . , Being a Compilation of the Game Laws. [March–April, 1891.] N.Y., cop. 1880. **v.d.**
Fur, Fin, and Feather: A Compilation of the Game Laws. . . . [2d ed., rev.] N.Y. [cop. 1870]. 1872. **v.d.**
Fur, Fin, and Feather: A Compilation of the Game Laws. [March–May, 1873.] N.Y. [cop. 1870]. **v.d.**
Fur, Fin, and Feather: A Compilation of the Game Laws. [3d ed., 1875.] N.Y., cop. 1870. **v.d.**
Fur, Fin, and Feather: A Quarterly Periodical . . . , Being a Compilation of the Game Laws. [Sept., 1876.] N.Y., cop. 1876. **v.d.**

G

Gale, Zona. *Friendship Village.* N.Y., 1910. = **1908**
Gales. See [North Carolina Almanacs]
Gallaher, James. *The Western Sketch-Book.* Bost., **1850**
Gallatin, James. *A Great Peace Maker: The Diary of James Gallatin.* N.Y., 1914. **v.d.**
Gallinipper. New Haven, **1846–58.** Published irregularly
Ganilh, Anthony. *Mexico versus Texas, A Descriptive Novel.* Phila., **1838**
Garden and Forest. N.Y., **1888–97**
Garland, Hamlin. *The Eagle's Heart.* N.Y., **1900**
Main-travelled Roads. Border ed. N.Y. [1922]. **v.d.**
Garland, Hugh A. *The Life of John Randolph of Roanoke.* N.Y., 1851. =1850. **v.d.**
Garrard, L. H. *Wah-To-Yah and the Taos Trail.* Ed. W. S. Campbell. Oklahoma City, 1927. First publ. **1850**
Garrison, W. P., and Garrison, F. J. *William Lloyd Garrison, 1805–1879: The Story of His Life Told by His Children.* N.Y., 1885–9. **v.d.**
Gass, Patrick. *A Journal of the Voyages and Travels of a Corps of Discovery, under the Command of Capt. Lewis and Capt. Clarke.* Pittsb., **1807.** 3d ed. Phila., 1811. Also publ. as: *Lewis and Clarke's Journal . . . as Related by Patrick Gass.* New ed. Dayton [Ohio] 1847
Gay, Bunker. *Narrative of the Captivity of Mrs. Jemima Howe . . . 1755.* [Rutland, Vt., 1818.] (Extract from: C. Bingham, comp. *The American Preceptor.*) **1755**
Gazette of the United States. N.Y., **1789–90.** Phila., **1790–1804**
General Orders of 1757. See Loudoun and Lyman
George, C. B. *Forty Years on the Rail.* Chic., **1887**
George, Henry. *Progress and Poverty.* Lond., 1881. =**1879**
Georgia Colonial Records. See *Colonial Records of the State of Georgia*
Georgia Historical Society. *Collections.* Savannah, 1840–1916. **v.d.** Contents include: Vol. I. F. Moore. *A Voyage to Georgia.* **1744.** Vol. II. W. Stephens. *A State of the Province of Georgia.* **1740.** Vol. III, Part I. B. Hawkins. *A Sketch of the Creek Country.* **1800.** Vol. IV, Part I. C. C. Jones, Jr. *The Dead Towns of Georgia.* **1878.** Vol. IV, Part II. E. Kimber. *Itinerant Observer.* **v.d.** Vol. VI, Part I. J. Habersham. *Letters.* **v.d.** Vol. IX. B. Hawkins. *Letters.* **v.d.**
Gerrard. See Garrard
Gerry, Margarita (Spalding). *The Masks of Love.* N.Y., **1914**
Gesner, Abraham. *A Practical Treatise on Coal, Petroleum, and Other Distilled Oils.* N.Y., **1861.** 2d ed. [Ed.] G. W. Gesner. N.Y., 1865. a**1864**
Gibbon, Charles, ed. *The Casquet of Literature: Being a Selection . . . from the Works of the Most Admired Authors.* Lond., 1873–4. **v.d.**
Giddings. See Essex Institute
Gilbert, B. See Walton
Gilbert, G. K. See U.S. Geographical and Geological Survey
Gilman, Caroline (Howard). *Recollections of a Southern Matron.* N.Y., 1838. First publ. **1836**
Gilman, Chandler R. *Life on the Lakes.* N.Y., **1836**
Gilmore, J. R. *Among the Pines.* N.Y., **1862.** Also publ. as: *Life in Dixie's Land.* Lond., 1863 [**1862**]
My Southern Friends. N.Y., **1863**
On the Border. Bost., **1867**
Girard. See Simpson, S.
Gist, Christopher. *Christopher Gist's Journals.* Pittsb., 1893. **v.d.** See also Filson Club. *Filson Club Publications.* No. 13
Given, J. L. *Making a Newspaper.* N.Y., **1907**
A Glance at New York. See Baker, B. A.
Glasgow, Ellen A. G. *The Deliverance.* N.Y., **1904**
The Descendant. N.Y., 1905. =**1897**
Glen, James. *A Description of South Carolina.* Lond., **1761.** See also Carroll, B. R.
Glisan, Rodney. *Journal of Army Life.* San Fran., 1874. **v.d.**
Gloucester Rec. See Essex Institute
Glover. See Royal Society of London
Godfrey, E. K. *The Island of Nantucket.* Bost., **1882**
Godfrey, T. See Moses. *Representative Plays.* Vol. I
Godley, J. R. *Letters from America.* Lond., **1844**
Godman, J. D. *American Natural History.* Phila., **1826–8**
Gods Protecting Providence. See Dickinson, J.
Going, Maud. *Field, Forest, and Wayside Flowers.* N.Y. [**1899**]
Goode, G. B. *American Fishes.* N.Y., **1888**
A Review of the Fishery Industries of the United States. See London. International Fisheries Exhibition, 1883
Goode, G. B., *et al. The Fisheries and Fishery Industries of the United States.* Wash., 1884–7. **v.d.** Sect I: *Natural History of Aquatic Animals.* **v.d.** Sect. V: *History and Methods of the Fisheries.* **v. l.**
Goodlander, C. W. *Memories and Recollections . . . of the Early Days of Fort Scott.* Fort Scott, Kan., **1900**
Goodrich, S. G. *Recollections of a Lifetime.* N.Y., **1856**
The Travels, Voyages, and Adventures of Gilbert Go-Ahead, in Foreign Parts. N.Y., 1859. = **1856**
Goodwin, H. K., defendant. *The Official Report of the Trial. . . .* By J. M. W. Yerrington. Bost., **1887**
Gookin. See Massachusetts Historical Society. *Collections*
Gordon, Clarence. *Boarding-School Days.* N.Y., **1873**
Gordon, H. See Mereness
Gordon, William. *The History of the Rise, Progress, and Establishment of the Independence of the United States of America.* N.Y., 1789. First publ. **1788**
Gordon, William St. Clair. *Recollections of the Old Quarter.* Lynchburg, Va., **1902**
Gorges. See Prince Society
Goss, W. L. *The Soldier's Story of His Captivity.* Bost., **1867.** Also publ. 1871
Gouge, W. M. *The Fiscal History of Texas.* Phila., **1852**
Grace, Henry. *The History of the Life and Sufferings of Henry Grace.* Reading [Eng.] **1764**
Graham, J. A. *A Descriptive Sketch of the Present State of Vermont.* Lond., **1797**
Graham, Margaret (Collier). *Stories of the Foot-Hills.* Bost., **1895**
Graham's American Monthly Magazine of Literature, Art, and Fashion. Phila., **1826–58**
Grant, Anne (MacVicar). *Memoirs of an American Lady.* Lond., **1808**
Grant, Robert. *An Average Man.* Bost., **1884**
Unleavened Bread. N.Y., **1900**
Gray, Asa. *Field, Forest, and Garden Botany.* N.Y. [cop. **1868**]
First Lessons in Botany and Vegetable Physiology. N.Y., 1866. =**1857**

Manual of the Botany of the Northern United States. Rev. ed. N.Y., 1860. =1857. Also: 4th rev. ed. N.Y., 1866. =1863. 5th ed. N.Y., 1874. =1867
GRAY, J. C., and ROPES, J. C. *War Letters, 1862–1865.* Bost., 1927. **v.d.**
GREAT BRITAIN. PUBLIC RECORD OFFICE. *Calendar of State Papers, Colonial Series. America and West Indies.* 1574/1660–. Ed. W. N. Sainsbury [*et al.*]. Lond., 1860–current. **v.d.** Cited by vol. nos. as assigned to entire *Colonial Ser.* in a single chronological sequence. Vol. III of *Amer. & W.I.* ser. (1669/74) cited as *Colonial Ser.*, Vol. VII; Vol. VI of *Amer. & W.I.* ser. (1681/5) cited as *Colonial Ser.*, Vol. XI
The Great Kalamazoo Hunt. See PORTER, W. T. *The Big Bear of Arkansas*
GREELEY, HORACE. *An Overland Journey, from New York to San Francisco, in the Summer of 1859.* N.Y., 1860
GREEN, B. W. *Word-Book of Virginia Folk-Speech.* Richmond, 1899
GREEN, S. B. *Forestry in Minnesota.* Delano [Minn.] 1898
GREEN, T. J. *Journal of the Texian Expedition against Mier.* N.Y., 1845
GREENE, ASA. *The Life and Adventures of Dr. Dodimus Duckworth.* N.Y., 1833
A Yankee among the Nullifiers. N.Y., 1833
GREENE, SARAH P. (McLEAN). *Cape Cod Folks.* Bost., 1881
GREER, HENRY. *A Dictionary of Electricity.* N.Y., 1883
GREER-PETRIE, CORDIA. *Angeline at the Seelbach.* Louisville, 1923. =1921
GREGG, JOHN C. *Life in the Army, in the Departments of Virginia, and the Gulf.* Phila., 1866
GREGG, JOSIAH. *Commerce of the Prairies.* N.Y., 1844
GRIFFITH. See BROWNE, M.
GRIGSBY, MELVIN. *The Smoked Yank.* 3d ed. Chic., 1899 [cop. 1888]. =1891
Gringo and Greaser. Manzano, N.M., 1883–4
GRINNELL, JOSEPH. *Gold Hunting in Alaska.* Elgin, Ill. [cop. 1901]
GRISWOLD, R. W. *Passages from the Correspondence and Other Papers of Rufus W. Griswold.* Ed. W. M. Griswold. Cambridge, 1898. **v.d.**
The Republican Court; or, American Society in the Days of Washington. N.Y., 1856. =1855. **v.d.**
GRONOVIUS, J. F. *Flora Virginica, Exhibens Plantas Quas V. C. Johannes Clayton in Virginia Observavit atque Collegit.* Lugduni Batavorum, 1743. First publ. 1739–43. Also publ. 1762
GROSVENOR, W. M. *Does Protection Protect?* N.Y., 1871
GROTON, MASS. *Early Records. . . . 1662–1707.* Ed. S. A. Green. Groton, 1880. **v.d.**
GROVE. See FRAZER
GRUND, F. J. *Aristocracy in America.* Lond., 1839
A Guide to City of Chicago. See CHICAGO ASSOCIATION OF COMMERCE
GUNN, T. B. *The Physiology of New York Boarding-Houses.* N.Y., 1857
GUNTER, A. C. *Miss Dividends.* Lond., 1892
Miss Nobody of Nowhere. 1890
GWINNETT. See JENKINS, C. F.
GYLES, JOHN. *Memoirs of Odd Adventures, Strange Deliverances, &c. in the Captivity of John Gyles.* Bost., 1736

H

HABBERTON, JOHN. *The Jericho Road.* Chic., 1877 [cop. 1876]
HABERSHAM. See GEORGIA HISTORICAL SOCIETY. *Collections.* Vol. VI, Part I
HAKLUYT. See *Relaçam verdadeira;* also, FORCE. *Tracts.* Vol. IV, No. 1
HALE, E. E. *G. T. T.; or, The Wonderful Adventures of a Pullman.* Bost., 1877
If, Yes, and Perhaps. Bost., 1868. **v.d.**
The Ingham Papers. Bost., 1869. **v.d.**
Kanzas and Nebraska. Bost., 1854
Margaret Percival in America. Bost., 1850
A New England Boyhood. Bost. [1893]
A New England Boyhood, and Other Bits of Autobiography. Bost., 1905 [pref. 1899]. =1900. **v.d.** (*Works,* Library Ed., Vol. VI)
Philip Nolan's Friends. See *Scribner's Monthly*
Sybaris and Other Homes. Bost., 1869
Ten Times One Is Ten. Bost., 1871 [cop. 1870]
HALE, N. See JOHNSTON, H. P.
HALE, P. M., comp. *The Woods and Timbers of North Carolina.* Raleigh, 1883. Pt. 1, pp. 9–196 are from CURTIS. *Woody Plants N.C.* 1860. (Page references taken from ed. 1860 of Curtis)
HALE, R. L. *The Log of a Forty-Niner.* [Ed.] C. H. Russ. Bost., 1923. c1900
HALE, SARAH J. (BUELL). *Flora's Interpreter.* 14th ed. Bost. [cop. 1833]. (Page references and textual alterations from ed.: Bost., 1832)

HALE, SUSAN. *Letters.* Ed. C. P. Atkinson. Bost., 1919. **v.d.**
HALIBURTON, T. C. *The Attaché.* See his: *Sam Slick in England*
The Clockmaker. [1st Ser.] Lond., 1838. 329 pp. First publ.: Halifax, 1836. 1835–7. 2d Ser. Lond., 1838. 354 pp. 3d Ser. cited from 1852 Lond. ed. containing all three series: 160, 193, 179 pp. 3d Ser. first publ.: Lond., 1840
Nature and Human Nature. Lond., 1859. 344 pp. 1st ed. Lond., 1855. 2 vols.
Sam Slick in England; or, The Attaché. Lond., 1858. 395 pp. 1st ed. as: *The Attaché; or, Sam Slick in England.* [1st Ser.] Lond., 1843. 2 vols. 2d Ser. Lond., 1844. 2 vols.
ed. *Traits of American Humour.* By native authors. . . . Lond., 1852. 3 vols.
HALL, A. O. *The Manhattaner in New Orleans.* N.Y., 1851
HALL, BASIL. *Travels in North America, in the Years 1827 and 1828.* Edinb., 1829
HALL, BAYNARD R. *The New Purchase.* Indiana Centennial Ed., ed. J. A. Woodburn. Princeton, 1916. (Page references from 1st ed. N.Y., 1843. 2 vols.) 2d ed. New Albany, Ind. [cop. 1855]
HALL, BENJAMIN H. *A Collection of College Words and Customs.* Cambridge, 1851. [2d ed.] Rev. and enl. Cambridge, 1856
HALL, C. C., ed. *Narratives of Early Maryland, 1633–1684.* N.Y., 1910. Contains: A. WHITE. *Brief Rel. Maryland.* 1634. L. STRONG. *Babylon's Fall.* 1655
HALL, EDWIN. *The Ancient Historical Records of Norwalk, Conn.* Norwalk, 1847. **v.d.**
'HALL, E. C.' See OBENCHAIN
HALL, FRANCIS. *Travels in Canada and the United States, in 1816 and 1817.* Bost., 1818
HALL, FRANK. *History of the State of Colorado.* Chic., 1889–95. Vol. II includes: G. A. JACKSON. *Diary* (q.v.).
HALL, JAMES. *The Harpe's Head; a Legend of Kentucky.* Phila., 1833
Legends of the West. 2d ed. Phila., 1833. First publ. 1832
Letters from the West. Lond., 1828
Notes on the Western States. Phila., 1838. Includes his: *Statistics of the West* (q.v.)
Sketches of History, Life, and Manners in the West. Phila., 1835. Vol. I first publ.: Cinc., 1834. **v.d.**
Statistics of the West. Cinc., 1836. See also his: *Notes on the Western States*
HALL, T. W. *Tales.* N.Y. [1899]
HALLOCK, CHARLES. *The Sportsman's Gazetteer and General Guide.* Rev., enl. N.Y., 1883. Includes his: *Sportsman's Glossary.* 1878
Hallowell (Me.) *Gazette.* 1814–27
Hall's Wilmington Gazette. See *Wilmington Gazette*
HALSEY, MINA D. *A Tenderfoot in Southern California.* N.Y., 1908.
HAMBLEN, H. E. *The General Manager's Story.* N.Y., 1898
HAMBLETON, J. P. *A Biographical Sketch of Henry A. Wise.* Richmond, 1856. **v.d.**
HAMILTON, ALEXANDER, 1712–56. *Hamilton's Itinerarium.* Ed. A. B. Hart. St. Louis, Mo., 1907. 1744
HAMILTON, ALEXANDER, 1757–1804. *Works.* Ed. H. C. Lodge. N.Y., 1885–6. **v.d.** Citations from other sources include publication dates
'HAMILTON, G.' See DODGE, M. A.
HAMILTON, S. M., ed. *Letters to Washington, and Accompanying Papers.* Bost., 1898–1902. **v.d.**
HAMILTON, THOMAS. *Men and Manners in America.* Lond., 1833
HAMMETT, S. A. *A Stray Yankee in Texas.* N.Y., 1853
The Wonderful Adventures of Captain Priest. N.Y., 1855
HAMMOND, J. D. *The History of Political Parties in the State of New-York.* Albany, 1842
HAMMOND, S. H. *Hunting Adventures in the Northern Wilds.* Phila. [1863]. =1856. First publ. as: *Hills, Lakes, and Forest Streams.* 1854
Wild Northern Scenes. N.Y., 1857
HANDSAKER, SAMUEL. *Pioneer Life.* Eugene, Ore., 1908. **v.d.**
HAPGOOD, HUTCHINS. *An Anarchist Woman.* N.Y., 1909
The Autobiography of a Thief. N.Y., 1903
The Hapless Orphan; or, Innocent Victim of Revenge. Bost., 1793
HARBEN, W. N. *Abner Daniel.* N.Y., 1902
The Georgians. N.Y., 1904
Westerfelt. N.Y., 1901
HARIOT. See HARRIOT
'HARLAND.' See TERHUNE
HARMON, D. W. *A Journal of Voyages and Travels in the Interior of North America.* N.Y., 1903. First publ.: Andover, 1820

HARPER, I. D. *The Life and Work of Susan B. Anthony.* Indianapolis, 1898–1908. **v.d.**
Harper's Magazine. N.Y., 1850–current. Vols. XLIV–XLV include: FLAGG. *Good Investment.* **v.d.**
HARRIGAN, EDWARD. *The Mulligans.* N.Y., 1901
HARRIOT, THOMAS. *A Briefe and True Report of the New Found Land of Virginia.* Lond., 1588. (Cited from facsimile reproduction. Ann Arbor, 1931)
HARRIS, CORRA M. (WHITE). *Eve's Second Husband.* Phila. [cop. 1911]
HARRIS, G. W. *Sut Lovingood: Yarns Spun by a 'National Born Durn'd Fool.'* N.Y. [cop. 1867]. **v.d.**
HARRIS, J. C. *Mingo and Other Sketches in Black and White.* Bost., 1884. **v.d.**
On the Plantation; a Story of a Georgia Boy's Adventures during the War. N.Y., 1892
On the Wing of Occasions. N.Y., 1900
Sister Jane, Her Friends and Acquaintances. Bost. [cop. 1896]
Tales of the Home Folks. Bost., 1898
HARRIS, MIRIAM (COLES). *The Tents of Wickedness.* N.Y., 1907
HARRIS, THADDEUS MASON. *The Journal of a Tour into the Territory Northwest of the Alleghany Mountains. . . . With a Geographical and Historical Account of the State of Ohio.* Bost., 1805
HARRIS, THADDEUS WILLIAM. *A Treatise on Some of the Insects of New England Which Are Injurious to Vegetation.* Cambridge, 1842. 2d ed. Bost., 1852. New ed. as: *A Treatise on Some of the Insects Injurious to Vegetation.* 1862
HARRIS, W. T. *Remarks Made during a Tour through the United States of America.* Lond., 1821. **v.d.**
Harrisburgh (Pa.) *Journal, and the Weekly Advertiser.* 1789
HARRISON, H. S. *Queed.* Bost., 1911
HARRISON, W. H. *Messages and Letters.* See *Indiana Historical Collections*
HARROWER. See *American Historical Review*
HART, JEROME. *A Vigilante Girl.* Chic., 1910
HARTE, BRET. *Writings.* Standard Library Ed. [Bost., cop. 1896–1914]. **v.d.** Vol. III: *The Story of a Mine, and Other Tales.* 1896. Vols. XIII–XIV: *Gabriel Conroy* (q.v.), *Bohemian Papers, Stories of and for the Young.* **v.d.**
The Argonauts of North Liberty. Bost., 1888
Barker's Luck, and Other Stories. Bost., 1896
The Bell-Ringer of Angel's, etc. Leipzig, 1894
Clarence. Bost., 1895
Colonel Starbottle's Client, and Some Other People. Bost., 1892
Condensed Novels. And Other Papers. N.Y., 1867
The Crusade of the Excelsior. Bost., 1887
Drift from Two Shores. Bost., 1879. =1878
East and West Poems. Bost., 1871
A First Family of Tasajara. Bost., 1892. First publ. 1891
Flip and Found at Blazing Star. Bost., 1882
Gabriel Conroy. Hartford, Conn., 1876. See also *Scribner's Monthly* and his: *Writings,* Vols. XIII–XIV. **v.d.**
The Heritage of Dedlow Marsh, and Other Tales. Bost., 1890. =1889
In the Carquinez Woods. Bost., 1884. First publ.: Lond., 1883
The Luck of Roaring Camp, and Other Sketches. Bost., 1871. **v.d.**
Maruja. Bost., 1885
A Millionaire of Rough-and-Ready and Devil's Ford. Bost., 1887
Mr. Jack Hamlin's Mediation, and Other Stories. Bost., 1899
Mrs. Skaggs's Husbands, and Other Sketches. Bost., 1873
On the Frontier. Bost., 1884
Poems. Bost., 1871
Poetical Works. Bost., 1883
Poetical Works. Household Ed. Bost. [cop. 1912]. **v.d.**
A Protégée of Jack Hamlin's, and Other Stories. Bost., 1894
A Sappho of Green Springs, and Other Stories. Bost., 1891
Snow-bound at Eagle's. Bost., 1886
Stories in Light and Shadow. Bost., 1898
Story of Mine. See his: *Writings*
Susy, a Story of the Plains. Bost., 1893
Tales of the Argonauts, and Other Sketches. Bost., 1875. **v.d.**
Three Partners; or, The Big Strike on Heavy Tree Hill. Bost., 1897
Two Men of Sandy Bar. Bost., 1876
Under the Redwoods. Bost., 1901
A Waif of the Plains. Bost., 1890
HARTE, BRET, and CLEMENS, S. L. *Sketches of the Sixties.* San Fran., 1926. **v.d.**
Hartford Land Distrib. See CONNECTICUT HISTORICAL SOCIETY
Hartford Town Votes. See CONNECTICUT HISTORICAL SOCIETY
Harvard Magazine. Cambridge, 1854–61
Harvard Mem. Biog. See HIGGINSON, T. W.

Harvard Rec. See Colonial Society of Massachusetts
Harvard Register. Cambridge, **1827–8**
Harvard University. [Laws, etc.] **v.d.** 1. *The Laws of Harvard College.* Bost., 1790. Also: Bost., 1798; Cambridge, 1807, 1814, 1816, 1820. 2. *The Constitution of the University at Cambridge.* Cambridge, 1812. 3. *Statutes and Laws of the University in Cambridge, Massachusetts.* Cambridge, 1825. Also: Cambridge, 1826, 1828. 4. *Laws of Harvard University, Relative to Undergraduates.* Cambridge, 1841. Also: Cambridge, 1845. Includes: *Orders and Regulations of the Faculty*
Harvardiana. Cambridge, **1834–38**
Haskins, C. W. *The Argonauts of California.* N.Y., **1890**
Hastings, Susannah (Willard) Johnson. *A Narrative of the Captivity of Mrs. Johnson.* Walpole, Newhampshire, **1796**
Havard. See U.S. National Museum. *Proceedings*
Hawes, W. P. *Sporting Scenes and Sundry Sketches.* N.Y., 1842. *a***1841**
Hawkins, Abigail D. *Hannah: The Odd Fellows Orphan.* Indianapolis, **1879**
Hawkins, B. *Letters.* See Georgia Historical Society. *Collections.* Vol. IX
Sk. Creek Country. See Georgia Historical Society. *Collections.* Vol. III, Part I
Hawks, F. L. *The Adventures of Daniel Boone, the Kentucky Rifleman.* N.Y., 1844 [cop. **1843**]
Hawley, Zerah. *A Journal of a Tour through Connecticut* [etc.]. New Haven, 1822. **v.d.**
Haws. See Tomlinson
Hawthorne, Julian. *Fortune's Fool.* Lond., **1883**
Nathaniel Hawthorne and His Wife: A Biography. Bost., 1885. =1884. **v.d.**
Hawthorne, Nathaniel. *Works.* Standard Library Ed. Bost., 1891. =1883–9. Vol. XIII: *Dr. Grimshawe's Secret.* *a***1864**
American Notebooks. Ed. Randall Stewart. New Haven, 1932. **v.d.**
The House of the Seven Gables. Bost., **1851.** Also publ. 1897
Mosses from an Old Manse. N.Y., **1846**
Our Old Home. Bost., **1863**
Passages from the American Note-Books. [Ed. Sophia Hawthorne.] Bost., **1868.** 2 vols.
Passages from the English Note-Books. [Ed. Sophia Hawthorne.] Bost., 1870. 2 vols. Also publ.: Lond., 1870. 2 vols. **v.d.**
Passages from the French and Italian Note-Books of Nathaniel Hawthorne. Bost., 1872. 2 vols. Also publ.: Lond., 1871. 2 vols. **v.d.**
The Scarlet Letter. Bost., **1850**
Twice-told Tales. 13th ed. Bost. [1879]. Also publ.: Rev. ed. Bost., 1851. **v.d.**
Hay, John. *The Bread-Winners: A Social Study.* N.Y. [cop. **1883**]
Pike County Ballads and Other Pieces. Bost., **1871**
Hayden, H. C. *Poems.* Bost., 1888. =**1887**
'Haywarde.' See Cozzens, F. S.
Hazard, Caroline. *Thomas Hazard Son of Robt., Call'd College Tom.* Bost., 1893. **v.d.**
Hazard, Ebenezer. *Historical Collections; Consisting of State Papers and Other Authentic Documents.* Phila., 1792–4. **v.d.**
Heath, B. S. *Labor and Finance Revolution.* Chic., **1891.** =1880
Heath Papers. See Massachusetts Historical Society. *Collections*
Hector, Annie (French). *Going West; or, Homes for the Homeless.* Indianapolis, **1881**
Hedley, F. Y. *Marching through Georgia.* Chic., 1890 [cop. **1884**]
Hegan. See Rice
Helper, H. R. *The Land of Gold.* Balt., **1855**
Hempstead, Joshua. *Diary . . . from September, 1711, to November, 1758.* New London, Conn., 1901. **v.d.**
Hempstead, N.Y. *Records of the Towns of North and South Hempstead, Long Island, N.Y.* Ed. B. J. Hicks. Jamaica, N.Y., 1896–1904. **v.d.**
Henderson, G. C. *Keys to Crookdom.* N.Y., **1924**
Henderson, Mary N. (Foote). *Practical Cooking and Dinner Giving.* N.Y., 1883 [cop. **1876**]
Henderson, T. See [North Carolina Almanacs]
Hennepin, Louis. *A New Discovery of a Vast Country in America.* Lond., **1698.** [Part I] 12 p.l., 299 pp. [Part II] 16 p.l., 178 [i.e., 182], [2], 303–55 pp.
Henry, Alexander. *Travels and Adventures in Canada and the Indian Territories between the Years 1760 and 1776.* N.Y., **1809.** New ed., ed. James Bain. Toronto, 1901
Henry, J. J. *An Accurate and Interesting Account . . . of That Band of Heroes, Who Traversed the Wilderness in the Campaign against Quebec in 1775.* Lancaster [Pa.] 1812. *a***1811**
'Henry, O.' See Porter, W. S.
Henry, W. S. *Campaign Sketches of the War with Mexico.* N.Y., **1847**
Herald of Freedom. Edenton, N.C., **1799.** See also *Kansas Herald of Freedom*
Heriot. See Harriot
Herrick, Robert. *Homely Lilla.* N.Y. [cop. **1923**]
Higginson, Ella (Rhoads). *From the Land of the Snow-Pearls: Tales from Puget Sound.* N.Y., 1897. Chiefly a republ. of her: *The Flower That Grew in the Sand, and Other Stories.* **1896**
Higginson, Francis. *New-Englands Plantation.* [1st ed.] Lond., **1630.** See also Force. *Tracts.* Vol. I, No. 12. Also: 3d ed. **1630**
Higginson, T. W., ed. *Harvard Memorial Biographies.* Cambridge, **1866**
Oldport Days. Bost., **1873**
Hildeburn, C. S. R. *A Century of Printing. The Issues of the Press in Pennsylvania, 1685–1784.* Phila., 1885–6. **v.d.**
Hildreth, James. *Dragoon Campaigns to the Rocky Mountains.* N.Y., **1836**
Hill, G. C. *Homespun; or, Five and Twenty Years Ago.* N.Y., **1867**
Hill, Isaac, Biogr. See Bradley
Hillhouse. See Michaux, F. A.
Hillsborough Recorder. Hillsboro, N.C., **1820–79; 1895–6**
Hines, Gustavus. *Wild Life in Oregon.* N.Y. [n.d.]. =his: *A Voyage round the World.* Buffalo, 1850. **v.d.**
Hirst, H. B. *The Coming of the Mammoth, . . . and Other Poems.* Bost., **1845**
Historical & Scientific Sk. Mich. See Michigan, Historical Society of
Historical Collections of Ohio. See Howe, H.
Historical Collections of South Carolina. See Carroll, B. R.
An Historical Digest of the Provincial Press. Comp. L. H. Weeks and E. M. Bacon. Bost., 1911. **v.d.**
An Historical Review and Directory of North America. Cork, **1801**
Historical Review of the Industrial and Commercial Growth of York County. [?York, Pa., **1892**]
The History of Charlestown, Massachusetts. See Frothingham
History of Congress. Phila., **1834**
History of Northampton, Mass. See Trumbull, J. R.
History of Pelham, Mass. See Parmenter
History of Saco. See Folsom
History of the North-western Soldiers' Fair. Chic., **1864**
Hitchcock, David. *A Poetical Dictionary; or, Popular Terms Illustrated in Rhyme.* Lenox [Mass.] **1808**
Hitchcock, E. A. *A Traveler in Indian Territory: The Journal of Ethan Allen Hitchcock.* Ed. Grant Foreman. Cedar Rapids, Iowa, 1930. **v.d.**
Hobart, G. V. *John Henry.* N.Y. [**1901**]
Hodge, A. See [North Carolina Almanacs]
Hodge, F. W., *et al. Handbook of American Indians North of Mexico.* Wash., **1907–10**
Hodge, H. C. *Arizona as It Is; or, The Coming Country.* N.Y., **1877**
Hodgkinson,? *Letters on Emigration.* By a Gentleman, Lately Returned from America. Lond., **1794**
Hodgson, Adam. *Letters from North America Written during a Tour.* Lond., **1824**
Hoffman, C. F. *Greyslaer: A Romance of the Mohawk.* N.Y., **1840**
[Letters and Poems.] See Barnes, H. F.
Wild Scenes in the Forest and Prairie, N.Y., 1843. Also publ. as: *Wild Scenes in the Forest.* Lond. [?1839]. **1838**
A Winter in the West. N.Y., **1835.** Also publ. as: *A Winter in the Far West.* Lond., **1835**
Holbrook, James. *Ten Years among the Mail Bags.* Phila., **1855**
Holbrook, John E. *North American Herpetology.* Enl. ed. Phila., **1842**
Holder, C. F. *Marvels of Animal Life.* N.Y., **1885**
Holditch, Robert. *The Emigrant's Guide o the United States of America.* Lond., **1818**
Holland, J. G. *Arthur Bonnicastle.* **1873**
The Bay-Path. N.Y., **1857**
Letters to the Joneses. N.Y., 1864. =**1863**
Miss Gilbert's Career. N.Y., 1866.= **1860**
Sevenoaks, a Story of To-day. N.Y., 1901. =**1875**
Titcomb's Letters to Young People, Single and Married. N.Y., **1858**
Holley, Marietta. *My Opinions and Betsey Bobbet's.* Hartford, 1901. =**1873**
Samantha at the World's Fair. N.Y., **1893**
Holley, Mary (Austin). *Texas. Observations . . . 1831.* Balt., 1833. **1831.** Also, greatly enl.: *Texas.* Lexington, Ky., **1836**
Holmes, Abiel. *The Life of Ezra Stiles.* Bost., **1798**
Holmes, Isaac. *An Account of the United States of America, Derived from Actual Observation.* Lond. [**1823**]
Holmes, Mary J. (Hawes). *Aikenside.* See her: *Madeline*
Cousin Maude. N.Y., **1860**
The Homestead on the Hillside, and Other Tales. **1856.** I. *The Homestead on the Hillside.* II. *Rice Corner.* III. *The Gilberts; or, Rice Corner Number Two.* IV. *The Thanksgiving Party and Its Consequences.* V. *The Old Red House among the Mountains.* VI. *Glen's Creek.* VII. *The Gableroofed House at Snowdon*
'Lena Rivers. N.Y., 1870. =**1856**
Madeline. N.Y., **1881.** Also publ., altered, as: *Aikenside.* N.Y. [n.d.] *c***1900**
Meadow-Brook. **1857**
Tempest and Sunshine. N.Y., 1860. =**1854**
Holmes, O. W. *The Autocrat of the Breakfast-Table.* Bost., **1858**
Elsie Venner. **1860**
The Guardian Angel. Bost., **1867**
Humorous Poems. Bost., 1865. **v.d.**
Life and Lett. See Morse, J. T.
A Mortal Antipathy. **1885**
Over the Teacups. Bost., **1891**
Poems. New and enl. ed. Bost., **1855.** =1849. Frequently reprinted
The Poet at the Breakfast-Table. Bost., **1872**
Complete Poetical Works. Cambridge Ed. Bost. [cop. 1908]. =1895. **v.d.**
The Professor at the Breakfast-Table. Bost., 1880. =**1860.** Also publ.: Lond.: Scott [n.d.]. (Page refs. altered to fit ed. 1860.) [Handy Volume Ed.] Bost., 1902
Wit and Humour: Poems. Lond.: Hotten [n.d.] =1867. **v.d.**
Holten. See Essex Institute
Holyoke Diaries. See Dow, G. F.
Home Cook Book. See *American Home Cook Book*
Home Missionary. N.Y., **1829–1909**
Hone, Philip. *Diary . . . , 1828–1851.* Ed Bayard Tuckerman. N.Y., 1889. **v.d.**
Hooker, Thomas. *Works.* Lond., **1637–45**
Hooker, Sir W. J. *Flora Boreali-Americana.* Lond. [**1829**]**–40**
Hooper, E. J. *Address, Delivered before the Literary Society of Pittsborough.* Hillsborough [N.C.] **1835**
Hooper, J. J. *Simon Suggs' Adventures.* Phila. [n.d.] =**1845.** Includes: *Taking the Census. Daddy Biggs' Scrape.* Bound with: *The Widow Rugby's Husband* (q.v.). Also publ., without *The Widow Rugby's Husband:* Americus, Ga., 1928
The Widow Rugby's Husband. Phila. [n.d.] = **1851.** Bound with: *Simon Suggs' Adventures* (q.v.)
Hopkins, Esek. *Correspondence.* Ed. A. S. Beck. Providence, 1933. **v.d.**
Hopley, Catherine C. *Life in the South; from the Commencement of the War.* Lond., **1863**
Hoppe, A. *Englisch-Deutsches Supplement-Lexicon.* Berlin, **1871**
Hornblow, Arthur. *The Profligate.* N.Y. [cop. **1908**]
Horticulturist and Journal of Rural Art and Rural Taste. Albany, **1846–75**
Horry. See Weems. *The Life of Gen. Francis Marion*
Hough, Emerson. *The Sagebrusher.* N.Y., **1919**
The Story of the Cowboy. N.Y., **1897**
Hough, F. B. *Papers Relating to Pemaquid.* Albany, 1856. **v.d.**
Houstoun, Matilda C. (Jesse) F. *Texas and the Gulf of Mexico.* Phila., 1845. First publ.: Lond., **1844**
Howard, B. W. See Teuffel
Howard, H. R., comp. *The History of Virgil A. Stewart.* N.Y., **1836**
Howard, Virginia W. *Bryan Station Heroes and Heroines.* [Lexington, Ky., cop. 1932.] **v.d.**
Howe, E. W. *A Moonlight Boy.* Bost., **1886**
The Mystery of the Locks. Bost., **1885**
The Story of a Country Town. N.Y., 1926. =1884. First publ. **1883**
Howe, Henry. *Historical Collections of Ohio.* Cinc., 1847. **v.d.**
Howe, J. See *Magazine of History*
Howe, M. See Elliott, M.
Howells, W. D. *A Boy's Town.* N.Y., **1890**
A Chance Acquaintance. Bost., **1873.** Also publ.: Edinb., 1882
The Coast of Bohemia. N.Y., **1893**
A Hazard of New Fortunes. N.Y. [cop. **1889**]
An Imperative Duty. **1891**
The Lady of the Aroostook. Bost., **1879.** Also publ. 1882
Literary Friends and Acquaintances. N.Y., **1902.** First publ. 1900
The Minister's Charge. Bost. [cop. **1886**]
A Modern Instance. **1882**
An Open-eyed Conspiracy. **1897**
Out of the Question. **1877**
The Quality of Mercy. N.Y., **1892**
The Rise of Silas Lapham. Bost., 1885. First publ. **1884–85**
The Shadow of a Dream. **1890**
Their Wedding Journey. Bost., 1874 [cop. **1871**]
The Undiscovered Country. Bost., **1880**
The Vacation of the Kelwyns. N.Y. [cop. **1920**]
A Woman's Reason. See *Century Magazine*
Howison, John. *Sketches of Upper Canada . . . and Some Recollections of the United States of America.* Edinb., **1821.** 2d ed. 1822

HOWITT, EMANUEL. *Selections from Letters Written during a Tour through the United States.* Nottingham **[1820]**

HOWLAND, S. A. *Steamboat Disasters and Railroad Accidents in the United States.* Worcester, 1846. =1840. **v.d.**

HOYLE, EDMOND. *Hoyle's Games. . . . With American Additions.* Phila., 1882. [advt. **1857]**

HOYT, C. See MOSES. *Representative American Dramas*

HOYT, W. H. See NORTH CAROLINA. HISTORICAL COMMISSION. *Publications.* (2)

HUBBARD, WILLIAM. *General Hist. of New Eng.* See MASSACHUSETTS HISTORICAL SOCIETY. *Collections*

A Narrative of the Troubles with the Indians in New-England. Bost., **1677.** Also publ. as: *The Present State of New-England.* Lond., **1677.** Reprinted, in British version, as: *The History of the Indian Wars in New England.* [Ed.] S. G. Drake. Roxbury, Mass., 1865

HUDSON, FREDERIC. *Journalism in the United States.* N.Y., **1873**

HUGHES, J. T. *Doniphan's Expedition.* Cinc., 1848. =**1847.** Also publ.: [Ed.] W. E. Connelley. Topeka, Kan., 1907. Includes his: *Diary.* **v.d.**

HULBERT, W. D. *Forest Neighbors.* N.Y., 1903. First publ. **1902**

HULL. See AMERICAN ANTIQUARIAN SOCIETY

HULME. See THWAITES

HUMBOLDT, ALEXANDER, and BONPLAND, A. J. A. *Personal Narrative of Travels to the Equinoctial Regions of America.* Tr. Thomasina Ross. Lond., **1852**

HUMPHREYS, DAVID. *A Poem on Industry.* Phila., **1794**

The Yankee in England. [n.p., **1815]**

HUMPHREYS, DAVID, *et al. The Anarchiad: A New England Poem.* Ed. L. G. Riggs. New Haven, 1861. **1786–7**

HUNTER, J. M., comp. and ed. *The Trail Drivers of Texas.* [San Antonio, cop. **1920]–3**

HUNTINGTON, W. S. *The Road-Master's Assistant and Section-Master's Guide.* N.Y., **1872**

HUNTINGTON, N.Y. *Huntington Town Records.* [Ed.] C. R. Street. [Huntington] 1887–9. **v.d.**

HUNTLEY, H. V. *California: Its Gold and Its Inhabitants.* Lond., 1856. **v.d.**

HUTCHINS, THOMAS. *A Topographical Description of Virginia, Pennsylvania, Maryland, and North Carolina.* Lond., **1778.** Also: Bost., 1787

HUTCHINSON, THOMAS. *A Collection of Original Papers Relative to the History of the Colony of Massachusetts-Bay.* Bost., 1769. **v.d.**

Diary and Letters. Comp. P. O. Hutchinson. Lond., 1883–6. **v.d.**

The History of the Colony of Massachusets-Bay. Bost., **1764–1828.** Vols. I–II publ. also as: *The History of Massachusetts.* 3d ed. Salem [etc.] 1795. (Both eds. cited as: *Hist. Mass.*)

HUTTON. See MOSES. *Representative Plays.* Vol. II

HYDE, G. M. *Newspaper Reporting and Correspondence.* N.Y., **1912**

I

ILLINOIS. DEPT. OF AGRICULTURE. *Transactions.* 1853–1918. Springfield, 1855–[1921]. **v.d.** Vols. I–VIII as: *Transactions of the Illinois State Agricultural Society*

GEOLOGICAL SURVEY. *Economical Geology of Illinois.* By A. H. Worthen. Springfield [1882]

LAWS, STATUTES, ETC. *Revised Statutes, 1883.* Chic., 1883. **v.d.**

Illinois Central (Employes') Magazine. Chic., **1909**–current

Illinois Monthly Magazine. Vandalia; Cinc., **1830–2**

ILLINOIS STATE AGRICULTURAL SOCIETY. See ILLINOIS. DEPT. OF AGRICULTURE

IMLAY, GILBERT. *A Topographical Description of the Western Territory of North America.* Lond., **1792.** Also: 3d ed. Lond., 1797. **v.d.**

Independent Chronicle. Bost., **1776–1840**

Index to Patents. See U.S. PATENT OFFICE. *Subject-Matter Index of Patents*

INDIANA. GENERAL ASSEMBLY. *Documents . . . at the Thirty-third Session* [1848–9]. Indianapolis, 1849. **v.d.**

GENERAL ASSEMBLY. HOUSE OF REPRESENTATIVES. *Journal . . . at the Twenty-third Session* [1838–9]. Indianapolis, 1839. **v.d.**

GENERAL ASSEMBLY. SENATE. *Journal . . . during the Twentieth Session* [1835–6]. Indianapolis, 1835 [1836]. **v.d.**

GENERAL ASSEMBLY. SENATE. *Journal . . . during the Twenty-ninth Session* [1844–5]. Indianapolis, 1844 [1845]. **v.d.**

Indiana Gazetteer. 1833: see SCOTT. 1849: see CHAMBERLAIN, E.

Indiana Historical Collections. Indianapolis, **1916**–current. Vols. VII, IX contain: W. H. HARRISON. *Messages and Letters.* Ed. Logan Esarey. **v.d.**

INDIANA HISTORICAL SOCIETY. *Publications.* Indianapolis, **1895**–current

Indiana (Quarterly) Magazine of History. Indianapolis; Bloomington, **1905**–current

INGERSOLL, ERNEST. *The Oyster-Industry.* Wash., **1881**

INGHAM, G. T. *Digging Gold among the Rockies.* Phila. **[1880]**

INGRAHAM, J. H. *Burton; or, The Sieges.* N.Y., **1838**

The South-West. N.Y., **1835**

INGRAM, J. S. *The Centennial Exposition.* Phila. [cop. **1876]**

Inter-Ocean. Chicago, **1872–1914**

INTERNAL REVENUE, COMMISSIONER OF. *Decisions.* See U.S. TREASURY DEPT. *Treasury Decisions under the Customs . . . Laws*

Internal Revenue Guide. See EMERSON, C. N.

International Annual of Anthony's Photographic Bulletin and American Process Yearbook. N.Y., **1888–1902**

INTERNATIONAL TYPOGRAPHICAL UNION OF NORTH AMERICA. *Report of Proceedings.* Indianapolis, etc., **1874**–current

IOWA STATE AGRICULTURAL SOCIETY. [Annual] *Report . . . for the Year 1867.* Des Moines, **1868.** Includes: *Iowa State Hort. Soc. Rep. 1867*

IPSWICH, MASS. *The Ancient Records of the Town of Ipswich, Vol. 1.—From 1634 to 1650.* Ed. G. A. Schofield. Ipswich, 1899 [1900]. Unpaged. **v.d.**

IRVING, P. M. *The Life and Letters of Washington Irving.* N.Y., 1864–9 [cop. 1862–3]. 4 vols. ([*Works*], Vols. XX–XXIII.) **v.d.**

IRVING, WASHINGTON. *Astoria.* Phila., 1841. 2 vols. =**1836.** Also publ.: Lond., 1836. 3 vols. Author's rev. ed. Lond., 1850. 340 pp. N.Y. [cop. 1868]. 698 pp. (*Works*, Hudson Ed., Vol. III)

Bonneville. See his: *The Rocky Mountains*

Bracebridge Hall. [2d ed.] N.Y., **1822.** Also publ.: Lond., 1824

Chronicles of Wolfert's Roost and Other Papers. Author's Ed. Edinb., 1855. Also publ. as: *Wolfert's Roost, and Other Papers.* N.Y., 1855. **v.d.**

Diedrich Knickerbocker's A History of New York. Ed. Stanley Williams and Tremaine McDowell. N.Y.: Harcourt, Brace [cop. 1927]. **1809.** Also publ., rev., as: *Knickerbocker's History of New York.* Knickerbocker Ed. N.Y.: Putnam [1897]. 2 vols. **1848**

Life. See IRVING, P. M.

The Rocky Mountains. Phila., 1843. **1837.** 2 vols. Also publ. as: *Adventures of Captain Bonneville.* Lond., **1837.** 3 vols. (Amer. ed. cited usually as: *Bonneville*)

The Sketch Book of Geoffrey Crayon. [2d ed.] N.Y., **1819–20.** 7 parts. (No. 7 appears to be from ed. 1.) Also publ.: Lond., 1820. 2 vols.

Tales of a Traveller. Lond., **1824**

A Tour on the Prairies. Phila., **1835**

IRVING, WASHINGTON, *et al. Salmagundi.* N.Y., 1814. Also: [Ed.] E. A. Duyckinck. N.Y. [cop. 1860]. Knickerbocker Ed. N.Y. [1897]. (Occasional citations from other eds. usually include chapter nos.) **v.d.**

IRWIN, W. H. *The Red Button.* N.Y. [cop. **1912]**

IVES, J. M. *New England Book of Fruit.* Salem, **1847**

J

JACKSON, A. T. See CANFIELD, C. D.

JACKSON, G. A. *Diary.* MS., State Historical Soc. of Colo., Denver. **v.d.** See also HALL, FRANK

JACKSON, HELEN M. (FISKE) H. *Between Whiles.* Bost., **1887**

Bits of Travel at Home. Bost., **1878**

Zeph. Bost., **1885**

JACKSON, MARY A. (MORRISON). *Life and Letters of General Thomas J. Jackson (Stonewall Jackson).* N.Y., **1892.** [2d ed.] under title: *Memoirs of Stonewall Jackson.* Louisville [1895]

JACOBS, HARRIET (BRENT). *Incidents in the Life of a Slave Girl.* Ed. L. M. Child. Bost., **1861**

JAMAICA, N.Y. *Records of the Town of Jamaica, Long Island, New York.* Ed. J. C. Frost. Brooklyn, 1914. **v.d.**

JAMES, ED. *The Amateur Negro Minstrel's Guide.* N.Y., **1880**

JAMES, EDWIN, comp. *Account of an Expedition from Pittsburgh to the Rocky Mountains. . . . Comp. from the Notes of Major Long, Mr. T. Say, and Other Gentlemen of the Party.* Lond., **1823.** 3 vols. Reprinted: see THWAITES. Also publ.: Phila., 1823. 2 vols.

JAMES, HENRY. *The Bostonians.* Lond., **1886**

The Ivory Tower. N.Y., 1917. Written **1914**

The Portrait of a Lady. Bost. [cop. **1881]**

Roderick Hudson. Bost., 1876. First publ. **1875**

The Sacred Fount. N.Y., **1901**

JAMES, T. H. *Rambles in the United States and Canada during the Year 1845.* Lond., **1846**

Jamestown (N.Y.) *Journal.* **1826–1904**

JANSON, C. W. *The Stranger in America.* Lond., **1807**

JAY, JOHN. *Correspondence and Public Papers.* Ed. H. P. Johnston. N.Y., 1890–3. **v.d.**

JAY, WILLIAM. *The Life of John Jay.* N.Y., 1833. **v.d.**

JEFFERDS, C. M., defendant. *Trial . . . for Murder.* By C. E. Wilbour. N.Y., **1862**

JEFFERSON, JOSEPH. *Autobiography.* N.Y. **[1890]**

JEFFERSON, THOMAS. *Writings.* **v.d.** (a) Definitive Ed. [Ed.] A. A. Lipscomb and A. E. Bergh. Wash., 1905. =1903–4. 20 vols. (Usually cited without publication date.) (b) Ed. P. L. Ford. N.Y., 1892–9. 10 vols. (In early parts of Dict., cited without publication date.) (c) Ed. H. A. Washington. N.Y., 1853–4. (Also reprinted with various dates and imprints.) 9 vols. Vol. I includes his: *Autobiography.* **v.d.**

Memoir, Correspondence, and Miscellanies. Ed. T. J. Randolph. Charlottesville [Va.] 1829. **v.d.**

Notes on the State of Virginia. Phila., 1788. Also publ.: Lond., 1787. **1781–2**

Jefferson Papers. See MASSACHUSETTS HISTORICAL SOCIETY. *Collections*

JENKINS, C. F. *Button Gwinnett.* Garden City, N.Y., 1926. Includes: GWINNETT. *Letters.* **v.d.**

JENKINS, WARREN. *The Ohio Gazetteer, and Traveler's Guide.* Columbus **[1837]**

JENNESS, J. S., ed. *Transcripts of Original Documents in the English Archives Relating to the Early History of the State of New Hampshire.* N.Y., 1876. **v.d.**

JEWETT, SARAH O. *Betty Leicester.* N.Y., 1890 [cop. **1889]**

Country By-Ways. Bost., **1881**

A Country Doctor. Bost., **1884**

The Country of the Pointed Firs. Bost., **1896.** Also: Bost. [cop. 1910]

Deephaven. Bost., **1877**

King of Folly Island, and Other People. Bost., **1888**

Life of Nancy. Bost., **1895**

Marsh Island. Bost., **1885**

The Mate of the Daylight and Friends Ashore. Bost., **1883**

Old Friends and New. Bost., **1879**

Play Days. Bost., **1878**

The Queen's Twin, and Other Stories. Bost., **1899.** Also: Lond. [cop. **1899]**

Strangers and Wayfarers. Bost., **1890**

The Tory Lover. Bost., **1901**

A White Heron. Bost., **1886**

JILLSON, W. R. *Tales of the Dark and Bloody Ground.* Louisville, 1930. **v.d.**

'JINGLE, BOB.' *The Association, &c. of the Delegates of the Colonies.* [?N.Y.] **1774**

JOHNSON, C. B. *Letters from the British Settlement in Pennsylvania.* Phila., **1819**

JOHNSON, EDWARD. *Wonder-working Providence of Sions Saviour in New England.* [Ed.] W. F. Poole. Andover [Mass.] 1867. (A reprint, page for page, of his: *A History of New-England.* Lond., **1654.**) Also publ. as: *Johnson's Wonder-working Providence, 1628–1651.* Ed. J. F. Jameson. N.Y., 1910

JOHNSON, EMORY R. *American Railway Transportation.* N.Y., 1907. =**1903**

JOHNSON, SUSANNAH (WILLARD). See HASTINGS

JOHNSON, T. T. *Sights in the Gold Region and Scenes by the Way.* N.Y., **1849**

JOHNSON, W. A. *The History of Anderson County, Kansas.* Garnett, Kan., **1877**

JOHNSTON, H. P. *Nathan Hale, 1776: Biography and Memorials.* N.Y., 1901. **v.d.**

JOHNSTON, J. F. W. *Notes on North America, Agricultural, Economical, and Social.* Bost., **1851**

Jonathan's Visit. See *Poor Will's Almanack*

JONES, C. C., JR. *Dead Towns of Ga.* See GEORGIA HISTORICAL SOCIETY. *Collections.* Vol. IV, Part I

JONES, G. N., b. 1811. *Florida Plantation Records.* Ed. U. B. Phillips and J. D. Glunt. St. Louis, 1927. **v.d.**

JONES, HUGH. *The Present State of Virginia.* Lond., **1724**

JONES, JOHN B. *Adventures of Col. Gracchus Vanderbomb, of Sloughcreek, in Pursuit of the Presidency.* Phila., **1852**

Wild Southern Scenes. Phila. [cop. **1859]**

Wild Western Scenes. [1st Ser.] New Stereotype Ed. Phila., 1865. =**1856.** First publ.: N.Y., **1841**

JONES, JOSEPH. *Letters of Joseph Jones, of Virginia. 1777–1787.* Wash., 1889. **v.d.**

JONES, JOSEPH STEVENS. *The Green Mountain Boy.* Bost. [18–?]. First perf. **1833**

The People's Lawyer. See MOSES. *Representative Plays.* Vol. II

JONES, N. E. *The Squirrel Hunters of Ohio; or, Glimpses of Pioneer Life.* Cinc., **1898.** First publ. 1897

JOSSELYN, JOHN. *An Account of Two Voyages to New-England.* Lond., **1674.** See also MASSACHUSETTS HISTORICAL SOCIETY. *Collections.* 3d Ser. Vol. III

New Englands Rarities Discovered. Lond., **1672.**
See also AMERICAN ANTIQUARIAN SOCIETY
Journal of American Folk-Lore. Bost.; N.Y.; Lancaster, Pa., **1888**–current
Journal of an Excursion to the United States and Canada in the Year 1834. Edinb., **1835**
Journal of Discourses. Liverpool, **1854–85**
Journal of Science. See *American Journal of Science*
Journals of the Continental Congress. See U.S. CONTINENTAL CONGRESS
Journals of the Massachusetts House of Representatives. See MASSACHUSETTS (COLONY). GENERAL COURT
JUDD, SYLVESTER. *Margaret.* Bost., **1845.** [Rev. ed.] Bost., **1882.** First publ. **1851**
Richard Edney and the Governor's Family. Bost., **1850**
JUDSON, E. Z. C. *The Mysteries and Miseries of New York.* N.Y., **1848**

K

KALM, PEHR. *Pehr Kalms Resa till Norra Amerika.* [Ed.] Fredrik Elfving and Georg Schauman. Helsingfors, 1904–15. (Page references from orig. ed., as reprinted: Stockholm, 1753–61.) Also: Tr. J. R. Forster. Lond., **1770–1.** 2d ed. **1772**
KANE, E. K. *Arctic Explorations: The Second Grinnell Expedition in search of Sir John Franklin.* Phila., **1856**
The U.S. Grinnell Expedition in Search of Sir John Franklin. N.Y., **1853**
Kansas City Star. **1880**–current
Kansas Herald of Freedom. Lawrence, **1854–60**
KANSAS STATE HISTORICAL SOCIETY. *Collections.* [1875]–1928. Topeka, 1881–1928. [1875]–1908 as: *Transactions.* **v.d.**
KEATE, J. H. *The Destruction of Mephisto's Greatest Web.* Salt Lake City, **1914**
KEATING, W. H. *Narrative of an Expedition to the Source of St. Peter's River . . . under the Command of Stephen H. Long.* Lond., 1825. First publ.: Phila., **1824**
KEAYNE. *Will.* See BOSTON. REGISTRY DEPT. *Records. Miscellaneous Papers.* Also quoted in *Mass. H. S. Coll.* 5th Ser. V. 16*n*.
KEIM, D. R. *Sheridan's Troopers on the Border.* Phila., 1885. =**1870**
Keith, Capt. Thomas. See *Struggles of Capt. Thomas Keith*
KELLER, J. W. *The Game of Draw Poker.* N.Y., **1887**
KELLOGG, R. H. *Life and Death in Rebel Prisons.* Hartford, **1865**
KELLOGG, V. L. *Common Injurious Insects of Kansas.* [Lawrence, Kan.] **1892**
KELLY, J. F. *The Humors of Falconbridge.* Phila. [cop. **1856**]
KELLY, WILLIAM. *A Stroll through the Diggings of California.* Lond., 1852. First publ. as: *An Excursion to California.* Lond., **1851**
KEMBLE, FRANCES A. *Journal.* [Aug. 1, 1832, to July 17, 1833.] Lond., 1835. **v.d.**
Journal of a Residence on a Georgian Plantation in 1838–1839. N.Y., 1863. **1839**
KENDALL, E. A. *Travels through the Northern Parts of the United States.* N.Y., **1809**
KENDALL, G. W. *Narrative of the Texan Santa Fé Expedition.* N.Y., **1844**
KENNEDY, ARCHIBALD. *The Importance of Gaining and Preserving the Friendship of the Indians to the British Interest Considered.* Lond., **1752.** First publ.: N.Y., 1751
KENNEDY, J. P. *Horse Shoe Robinson.* Phila., **1835**
Memoirs of the Life of William Wirt. Phila., 1860. =1850. First publ. **1849**
Quodlibet: Containing Some Annals Thereof. Phila., **1840**
Rob of the Bowl. Phila., **1838**
Swallow Barn. Phila., **1832**
KENNEDY, P. P. *The Blackwater Chronicle.* N.Y., **1853**
KENNEDY, WILLIAM. *Texas: The Rise, Progress, and Prospects of the Republic of Texas.* Lond., **1841**
Kentucky Centenary Celebration. See FILSON CLUB. *Filson Club Publications.* No. 7
Kentucky Gazette. Lexington, **1787–1848**
Kentucky Petitions. See FILSON CLUB. *Filson Club Publications.* No. 27
Kentucky Rifle. Danville, **1840–?**
KERSEY. See PHILLIPS, E.
KETTELL, T. P. *History of the Great Rebellion.* Worcester, 1862–3. **v.d.**
KIDDER, FREDERIC. *The Expeditions of Capt. John Lovewell, and His Encounters with the Indians.* Bost., 1865. **v.d.**
KILBOURN, JOHN. *The Ohio Gazetteer.* 8th ed. Columbus, **1826.** Also: 10th ed. **1831.** 11th ed. **1833**
KILLEBREW, J. B. *The Grasses of Tennessee.* Nashville, 1878. **v.d.**

KIMBER. See GEORGIA HISTORICAL SOCIETY. *Collections.* Vol. IV, Part II
KING, CHARLES. *Fort Frayne.* Lond. [n.d.]. First publ.: N.Y. [**1895**]
Sunset Pass; or, Running the Gauntlet through Apache Land. N.Y. [cop. **1890**]
A Trooper Galahad. Phila., **1899**
KING, CLARENCE. *Mountaineering in the Sierra Nevada.* Bost., **1872**
Rep. Precious Metals. See U.S. BUREAU OF THE MINT
KING, GRACE E. *New Orleans; the Place and the People.* N.Y., 1904. =**1895**
KING, RUFUS. *Life and Correspondence.* Ed. C. R. King. N.Y., **1894–1900. v.d.**
KINGSBURY, SUSAN M., ed. *Labor Laws and Their Enforcement, with Special Reference to Massachusetts.* By C. E. Persons [*et al.*]. N.Y., **1911. v.d.**
KINGSLEY, J. S., et al. *The Standard Natural History.* Bost., **1884–5.** Also publ. as: *The Riverside Natural History.* Bost. [cop. **1888**]
KINGSLEY, NELSON. *Diary.* Ed. F. J. Teggart. Berkeley, 1914. **v.d.**
Kiote. Lincoln, Neb., **1898–1901; 1911**
KIP. See *Sources of the History of Oregon*
KIRK, ELLEN W. (OLNEY). *Queen Money.* Bost., **1888**
'KIRKE.' See GILMORE
KIRKLAND, CAROLINE M. (STANSBURY). *Forest Life.* N.Y., **1842**
A New Home—Who'll Follow? 2d ed. N.Y., 1840. First publ. **1839**
Western Clearings. N.Y., 1845. **v.d.**
KIRKLAND, F.' See DEVENS
KIRKLAND, JOSEPH. *The McVeys (An Episode).* Bost., **1888**
Zury: The Meanest Man in Spring County. Bost., **1887**
Kissimmee Valley (Gazette). Kissimmee, Fla., **1894**–current
Kit Carson's Own Story of His Life. See CARSON
KITTREDGE, G. L. *The Old Farmer and His Almanack.* Bost., 1904. **v.d.**
Knickerbocker. N.Y., **1833–65.** Vols. XXIX–XXXIII include: PARKMAN. *Oregon Trail.* **1847–9**
KNIGHT, E. H. [Vols. I–II:] *The Practical Dictionary of Mechanics.* Lond. [n.d.]. [Vol. III:] *Knight's American Mechanical Dictionary.* N.Y., 1876. Set first publ. as: *Knight's American Mechanical Dictionary.* N.Y., **1874–6.** Suppl. publ. as: *Knight's New Mechanical Dictionary.* Bost. [pref. **1883**]
KNIGHT, H. C. *Letters from the South and West.* Bost., 1824. **v.d.**
KNIGHT, SARAH (KEMBLE). *The Journals of Madam Knight, and Rev. Mr. Buckingham.* N.Y., 1825. Includes: S. KNIGHT. *The Private Journal Kept . . . on a Journey from Boston to New-York.* 1704. T. BUCKINGHAM. *The Private Journals Kept by Rev. John [i.e., Thos.] Buckingham of the Expedition against Canada [including] A Diary of the Naval Expedition against Port Royal, in the Year 1710 [and] A Diary of the Land Expedition against Crown Point, in the Year 1711.* **1710, 1711**
Knowledge. Lond., **1881–1917**
Ku Klux Klan Rep. See U.S. CONGRESS. JOINT SELECT COMMITTEE

L

'LACKLAND.' See HILL, G. C.
La Crosse (Wis.) Democrat. [Daily.] 1859–72. (Also as: *La Crosse Daily Union.*) [Weekly.] **1852–72**
Ladies' Repository. Cinc.; N.Y., **1841–76**
Lady's Magazine and Repository of Entertaining Knowledge. Phila., **1792–3**
LAFOLLETTE, R. M. *Autobiography.* Madison [Wis.] **1913**
LAMBERT, A. B. *A Description of the Genus* Pinus. Lond., **1803**
LAMBERT, JOHN. *Travels through Lower Canada, and the United States of North America.* Lond., 1810. 2d ed. as: *Travels through Canada,* etc. Lond., **1813**
LAMPHERE, G. N. *The United States Government: Its Organization and Practical Workings.* Phila., **1880**
LANCASTER, MASS. *Early Records. . . . 1643–1725.* Ed. H. S. Nourse. Lancaster, 1884. **v.d.**
Land We Love. Charlotte, N.C., **1866–9**
LANE. See *America: A Journal for Americans*
LANGFORD, N. P. *Vigilante Days and Ways.* Chic., 1912. First publ. **1890**
LANMAN, CHARLES. *Letters from the Alleghany Mountains.* N.Y., **1849**
A Summer in the Wilderness. N.Y., **1847**
LATHROP, G. P. *Echo of Passion.* **1882**
LATROBE, B. H. *Journal.* N.Y., 1905. **v.d.**

LATROBE, C. J. *The Rambler in Mexico.* N.Y., **1836**
The Rambler in North America. Lond., **1835**
LAWRENCE, AMOS. *Extracts from the Diary and Correspondence of the Late Amos Lawrence.* Ed. W. R. Lawrence. Bost., 1855. **v.d.**
LAWRENCE, WILLIAM. *Life of Amos A. Lawrence, with Extracts from His Diary and Correspondence.* Bost., 1889. =1888. **v.d.**
LAWRENCE AND LEMAY. See [*North Carolina Almanacs*]
Lawrence (Kan.) Republican. **1857–69**
LAWSON, HENRY. *Over the Sliprails.* Sydney [Australia] **1900**
LAWSON, JOHN. *A New Voyage to Carolina.* Lond., **1709**
LEACOCK. See MOSES. *Representative Plays.* Vol. I
LEAVITT, SAMUEL. *Our Money Wars.* 2d ed. Bost., 1896. =1st ed. **1894**
LECHFORD. *Note-Book.* See AMERICAN ANTIQUARIAN SOCIETY
Plain Dealing. See MASSACHUSETTS HISTORICAL SOCIETY. *Collections*
LEDERER, J. See TALBOT, W.
LEE, DANIEL, and FROST, J. H. *Ten Years in Oregon.* N.Y., **1844**
LEE, J. P. *Golf in America.* N.Y., **1895**
LEGGETT, WILLIAM. *Tales and Sketches.* N.Y., **1829**
LEGISLATIVE COUNCIL OF NEW YORK. See NEW YORK (COLONY). COUNCIL
LELAND, C. G. *Memoirs.* Lond., **1893.** 2 vols. Also publ.: N.Y., 1893. 439 pp.
LEONARD, MARY F. *The Story of the Big Front Door.* N.Y. [cop. **1898**]
LEONARD, ZENAS. *Leonard's Narrative; Adventures of Zenas Leonard, Fur Trader and Trapper.* Cleveland, 1904. First publ. as: *Narrative of the Adventures of Zenas Leonard.* Clearfield [Penna.] **1839**
LESLIE, ELIZA. *Seventy-five Receipts for Pastry, Cakes, and Sweetmeats.* Bost., **1828**
Leslie's Mo. See *Frank Leslie's Popular Monthly*
L'ESTRANGE, R. See *Relaçam verdadeira*
Letters from Ala. See ROYALL
Letters to Benjamin Franklin. See DUANE
Letters to Washington. See HAMILTON, S. M.
LETTS, J. M. *California Illustrated.* N.Y., **1852**
LEVETT. See MASSACHUSETTS HISTORICAL SOCIETY. *Collections*
LEVINGE, R. G. A. *Echoes from the Backwoods; or, Sketches of Transatlantic Life.* Lond., **1846**
LEWIS, A. H. *The Boss, and How He Came to Rule New York.* N.Y., **1903**
Wolfville. N.Y. [cop. **1897**]
LEWIS, C. B. *Brother Gardner's Lime-Kiln Club.* Chic., **1882**
LEWIS, E. J. *The American Sportsman.* Phila., 1863. =3d ed., 1857 [cop. 1856]. Enl. from his: *Hints to Sportsmen.* Phila., **1851**
LEWIS, H. C. *Odd Leaves from the Life of a Louisiana 'Swamp Doctor.'* Phila. [1850]. (See also his: *The Swamp Doctor's Adventures*)
The Swamp Doctor's Adventures in the South-West. Phila. [cop. 1858]. Includes, separately paged: H. C. LEWIS. *Odd Leaves from the Life of a Louisiana 'Swamp Doctor'* (q.v.) **1850.** J. S. ROBB. *Streaks of Squatter Life.* 1847
LEWIS, MERIWETHER, and CLARK, WILLIAM. *History of the Expedition . . . to the Sources of the Missouri.* [Written by Nicholas Biddle. Ed.] Paul Allen. Phila., 1814. Also: Reprinted, ed. Elliott Coues. N.Y., 1893. **v.d.**
Original Journals of the Lewis and Clark Expedition, 1804–1806. Ed. R. G. Thwaites. N.Y., 1904–5. **v.d.** (Cited as: LEWIS & CLARK *Exped.*)
LEWIS, MERIWETHER, and ORDWAY, JOHN. *Journals . . . Kept on the Expedition of Western Explorations, 1803–1806.* Ed. M. M. Quaife. Madison, Wis., 1916. **v.d.**
LEWIS, SINCLAIR. *Main Street.* N.Y., **1920**
LEWIS, W. M. *The People's Practical Poultry Book.* N.Y. [cop. **1871**]
Lexington (Ky.) Observer & Reporter. [Semi-weekly.] 1832–73. Also publ. daily, weekly, and triweekly under varying titles
Library of Universal Knowledge. N.Y., 1881 [cop. **1880**]
Life among Mormons. See WATERS
Life in the West: Back-Wood Leaves and Prairie Flowers. Lond., **1842**
Life on Lakes. See GILMAN, C. R.
LILLIBRIDGE, W. O. *Where the Trail Divides.* N.Y., **1907**
LINCOLN, A. See PHELPS, A. L.
LINCOLN, J. C. *Cap'n Warren's Wards.* N.Y., **1911**
Mr. Pratt. N.Y., 1920. First publ. 1906
Partners of the Tide. N.Y., **1905**
Shavings. N.Y. [cop. **1918**]
LINCOLN, LEVI. *A Farmer's Letters to the People.* Phila., **1802**
LINDLEY, JOHN, and MOORE, THOMAS, eds. *The Treasury of Botany.* Lond., **1866**
LIPPINCOTT'S *Magazine.* Phila., **1868–1916**
LITERARY AND PHILOSOPHICAL SOCIETY OF NEW-YORK. *Transactions.* N.Y., 1815–[25]. Vol. I includes: MITCHILL. *Fishes N.Y.* **1814**

Literary Magazine and American Register. Phila., 1803–7
Literary Record. See *Trübner's American . . . Literary Record*
LITTELL. See FILSON CLUB. *Filson Club Publications.* No. 31
'LITTLE.' See MACAULAY
LIVERMORE. See NEW HAMPSHIRE HISTORICAL SOCIETY
Living Topics Cycl. See ALDEN, J. B.
LOCKE, D. R. *The Struggles . . . of Petroleum V. Nasby.* Bost., 1872
'Swingin round the Cirkle.' Bost., 1867
LOCKE, J. *Fundamental Constitutions.* See *Old South Leaflets*
The Log Cabin & Hard Cider Melodies. Bost., 1840
Log of Chasseur. See *Maryland Historical Magazine*
LOGAN, JAMES. *Notes of a Journey through Canada, the United States of America, and the West Indies.* Edinb., 1838
LOGAN, JOHN A. *The Great Conspiracy.* N.Y., 1886. v.d.
LOGAN, OLIVE. *Before the Footlights.* Phila., 1870
LONDON, JACK. *The Road.* N.Y., 1916. =1907
The Valley of the Moon. N.Y., 1913
LONDON. INTERNATIONAL FISHERIES EXHIBITION, 1883. *The Fisheries Exhibition Literature.* Lond., 1883–84. Includes: Vol. XII. *Official Catalogue.* 1883. Vol. XIII, Pt. II [No. 1]. G. B. GOODE. *A Review of the Fishery Industries of the United States and the Work of the U.S. Fish Commission.* 1883
LONG, JOHN. *Voyages and Travels of an Indian Interpreter and Trader.* Lond., 1791
LONG, JOSEPH W. *American Wild-Fowl Shooting.* N.Y., 1874
LONG, S. H. *Exped.* See JAMES, EDWIN; also KEATING
LONGFELLOW, H. W. *The Courtship of Miles Standish, and Other Poems.* Bost., 1858
Evangeline. Bost., 1848. =1847
Hyperion. N.Y., 1839
Kavanagh. Bost., 1849
Life. See LONGFELLOW, S.
Complete Poetical Works. [Cambridge Ed., ed. H. E. Scudder.] Bost. [cop. 1893]. v.d.
The Song of Hiawatha. Bost., 1855
Tales of a Wayside Inn. Bost., 1863
LONGFELLOW, SAMUEL, ed. *Life of Henry Wadsworth Longfellow, with Extracts from His Journals and Correspondence.* Bost., 1896. =1891. v.d.
Longman's Magazine. Lond., 1883–1905. Vol. I includes: E. A. FREEMAN. *Some Points in American Speech and Customs.* 1882–3
LONGSTREET, A. B. *Georgia Scenes, Characters, Incidents, &c., in the First Half Century of the Republic.* Augusta, Ga., 1835. 2d ed. N.Y., 1843. =1840. New ed. N.Y., 1897
LORAIN, JOHN. *Nature and Reason Harmonized in the Practice of Husbandry.* Phila., 1825
LORIMER, G. H. *Jack Spurlock—Prodigal.* 1908
Letters from a Self-made Merchant to His Son. Bost., 1902
LOSSING, B. J. *Harpers' Popular Cyclopaedia of United States History from the Aboriginal Period to 1876.* N.Y., 1882. =1881. v.d.
The Hudson, from the Wilderness to the Sea. N.Y. [1866]
LOUDOUN, J. C., 4th Earl of, and LYMAN, PHINEAS. *General Orders of 1757.* N.Y., 1899. 1757
Louisville Courier-Journal. See *Courier-Journal*
The Louisville Directory for the Year 1832. Louisville, 1832
Louisville Public Advertiser. Louisville, 1830–42
LOVETT, R. M. *Richard Gresham.* N.Y., 1904
LOW. See MOSES. *Representative Plays.* Vol. I
LOWELL, J. R. *Writings.* Riverside Ed. Bost., 1890. v.d. Vols. I–VI sometimes cited as: *Prose Works.* Vol. VI also cited as: *Literary and Political Addresses.* v.d. Includes: *Place of the Independent in Politics* (publ. also as his: *The Independent in Politics* (q.v.). 1888
Among My Books. Bost., 1870
The Biglow Papers. [1st Series.] Bost., 1876. = 1848. v.d. 2d Series. Bost., 1867 [cop. 1866]. v.d.
Democracy, and Other Addresses. Bost., 1887 [1886]. v.d. Includes his: [*On*] *Democracy* (q.v.). 1884
Fireside Travels. Bost., 1864. Also publ.: Lond., 1864. Includes: *A Moosehead Journal.* 1853
The Independent in Politics. N.Y., 1888. See also his: *Literary and Political Addresses* (under *Writings*)
Letters. Ed. C. E. Norton. N.Y., 1894. v.d.
Literary and Political Addresses. See his: *Writings*
A Moosehead Journal. See his: *Fireside Travels*; also *Putnam's (Monthly) Magazine*
My Study Windows. Bost., 1871. Also publ.: Lond., 1871. v.d.
On Democracy. Birmingham [Eng., 1884]. See also his: *Democracy, and Other Addresses*
Poetical Works. Complete Ed. Bost., 1882 [cop. 1876]. v.d.

Complete Poetical Works. Cambridge Ed. Bost. [cop. 1924]. =1896. v.d.
Prose Works. See his: *Writings*
Lowell Offering. Lowell, Mass., 1840–5
Loyal Verses. See STANSBURY, J., and ODELL, J.
LUDLOW, J. M. F. *A Sketch of the History of the United States.* Cambridge [Eng.] 1862
Lumberman's Gazette. Bay City, Mich., 1871–86
LUMMIS, C. F. *The Land of Poco Tiempo.* N.Y., 1897. =1893
LUMSDEN, JAMES. *American Memoranda, . . . during a Short Tour in the Summer of 1843.* Glasgow, 1844. 1843
LUNENBURG, MASS. *Early Records of the Town . . . 1719–1764.* Comp. W. A. Davis. Fitchburg, 1896. v.d.
PROPRIETORS. The Proprietors' Records . . . 1729–1833. Comp. W. A. Davis. Fitchburg, 1897. v.d.
LYCEUM OF NATURAL HISTORY OF NEW YORK. See NEW YORK ACADEMY OF SCIENCES
LYELL, SIR CHARLES. *A Second Visit to the United States of North America.* N.Y., 1849. Also publ.: Lond., 1849. v.d.
Travels in North America. Lond., 1845. v.d.
LYLE, REV. JOHN, 1769–1925. *Diary, 1801–3.* Typewritten copy (74 ll.), Univ. of Chicago Lib., of MS. (140 ll.). v.d.
LYNDE, BENJAMIN. *The Diaries of Benjamin Lynde and of Benjamin Lynde, Jr.* Bost.: Priv. pr. 1880. v.d.
LYNDE, FRANCIS. *The Grafters.* Indianapolis, 1904
The Quickening. Indianapolis, 1906
LYON. See TOMLINSON

M

McALLISTER, WARD. *Society as I Have Found It.* N.Y. [cop. 1890]
MACAULAY, FANNIE (CALDWELL). *The Lady of the Decoration.* N.Y., 1906
McCABE, J. D. *The History of the Great Riots.* Phila. [1877]
New York by Sunlight and Gaslight. Phila. [pref. 1882]. v.d.
McCLELLAN, G. B. *McClellan's Own Story.* N.Y., 1887 [1886]. v.d.
McCLELLAN, R. G. *The Golden State.* Phila., 1874. First publ. 1872
McCLELLAND, MARGARET G. *St. John's Wooing.* N.Y., 1895
M'CLINTOCK, CAPT. *John Beedle's Sleigh Ride, Courtship, and Marriage.* Attributed to Capt. M'Clintock. N.Y., 1841. c1840
McCLINTOCK, JOHN, and STRONG, JAMES. *Cyclopædia of Biblical, Theological, and Ecclesiastical Literature.* N.Y., 1873–91. =1867–87
McCLUNG, J. A. *Sketches of Western Adventure.* Maysville, Ky., 1832
McCLURE, A. K. *Three Thousand Miles through the Rocky Mountains.* Phila., 1869
McCLURE, DAVID. *Diary.* N.Y., 1899. v.d.
McClure's Magazine. N.Y., 1893–1926
McCONNEL, J. L. *Western Characters.* N.Y., 1853
McCORMAC, E. I. *James K. Polk, a Political Biography.* Berkeley, Calif., 1922
McCOY, J. G. *Historic Sketches of the Cattle Trade of the West and Southwest.* Kansas City, Mo., 1874
McCUTCHEON, G. B. *Graustark.* N.Y., 1903. = 1901
Green Fancy. N.Y., 1917
The Rose in the Ring. N.Y., 1910
McDONOGH, JOHN. *Some Interesting Papers.* Ed. J. T. Edwards. McDonogh, Md., 1898. v.d.
MacDOWELL, KATHERINE S. (BONNER). *Dialect Tales.* N.Y., 1883
McELROY, W. H., and McBRIDE, ALEXANDER, eds. *Life Sketches of Executive Officers and Members of the Legislature of the State of New York for 1873.* Albany, 1873
McFAUL, A. D. *Ike Glidden in Maine.* Bost. [cop. 1903]. 1902
McGAFFEY, KENNETH. *The Sorrows of a Show Girl.* Chic., 1908
MacGOWAN, ALICE. *The Last Word.* Bost., 1903 [1902]
MacGREGOR, JOHN. *British America.* Edinb., 1832
'McHUGH.' See HOBART
MACKAY, ALEXANDER. *The Western World; or, Travels in the United States in 1846–47.* Phila., 1849
MACKAYE, H. S. *The Panchronicon.* N.Y., 1904
McKENNEY, T. L. *Memoirs Official and Personal, with Sketches of Travel.* N.Y., 1846
Sketches of a Tour to the Lakes. Balt., 1827
MACKENZIE, W. L. *The Life and Times of Martin Van Buren.* Bost., 1846. v.d.
McLAUGHLIN AND HART. See *Cyclopedia of American Government*
MACLAY, WILLIAM. *Sketches of Debate in the First Senate of the United States, in 1789–90–91.* Ed. G. W. Harris. Harrisburg [cop. 1880]. v.d.
McLEAN. See GREENE, S. P.

MacLEOD, X. D. *Biography of Hon. Fernando Wood.* N.Y., 1856. v.d.
McMURTRIE, HENRY. *Sketches of Louisville and Its Environs.* Louisville, 1819
McNEMAR, RICHARD. *The Kentucky Revival.* Cinc., 1807
MACRAE, DAVID. *The Americans at Home.* Edinb., 1870
M'ROBERT, PATRICK. *A Tour through Part of the Northern Provinces of America.* 1776
MacSPARRAN, JAMES. *A Letter Book and Abstract of Out Services, Written during the Years 1743–1751.* Ed. Daniel Goodwin. Bost., 1899. v.d. (Cited as: *Diary*)
MACTAGGART, JOHN. *Three Years in Canada.* Lond., 1829
MADISON, JAMES. *Writings.* Ed. Gaillard Hunt. N.Y., 1900–10. v.d.
Magazine of American History, with Notes and Queries. N.Y., 1877–93. Vols. XII–XIII include the first form of: C. L. NORTON. *Polit. Americanisms.* 1884–5
Magazine of History, with Notes and Queries. Extra Numbers. Tarrytown, N.Y. [etc.], 1907–35. v.d. No. 126 (Vol. XXXII, No. 2): F. P. WIERZBICKI. *California as It Is.* 1849. No. 130 (Vol. XXXIII, No. 2): S. FOBES. *Journal of a Member of Arnold's Expedition.* c1835. No. 132 (Vol. XXXIII, No. 4): J. HOWE. *Journal.* v.d.
Magnolia Place Journal. MS., Univ. of North Carolina. v.d.
MAGOFFIN, SUSAN (SHELBY). *Down the Santa Fé Trail and into Mexico.* Ed. S. M. Drumm. New Haven, 1926. v.d.
MAILLARD, A. S. *An Account of the Customs and Manners of the Micmakis and Maricheets Savage Nations.* Lond., 1758
MAINE. BOARD OF AGRICULTURE. *Agriculture of Maine. Annual Report of the Secretary of the Board of Agriculture,* [2d Series] 1856–1901. Augusta, 1857–1901. Some vols. include also: *Abstract of Returns from the Agricultural Societies of Maine.* v.d.
Maine Doc. Hist. See MAINE HISTORICAL SOCIETY. *Documentary History*
MAINE HISTORICAL SOCIETY. *Collections.* Portland, 1831–1906. v.d.
Documentary History of the State of Maine. Portland, 1869–1916. v.d.
Maine, My State. See MAINE WRITERS RESEARCH CLUB
Maine Wills. See SARGENT, W. M.
MAINE WRITERS RESEARCH CLUB. *Maine, My State.* [Lewiston, Me., cop. 1919]
Major Jack Downing. (Northern Humour.) Author's Unabridged Ed. Lond. [?1867]. v.d.
MAJORS, ALEXANDER. *Seventy Years on the Frontier.* Chic., 1893
Mammals of America. See *Animals of America*
MANCHESTER, MASS. *Town Records.* Salem, Mass., 1889–91. v.d.
MANHEIM, FREDERICK. See *The Affecting History*
MANNING, WILLIAM. *The Key of Libberty . . . ; Written in the Year 1798.* [Ed.] S. E. Morison. Billerica, Mass., 1922. 1798
MANSFIELD, E. D. *The Life of General Winfield Scott.* N.Y., 1846
MANWARING, C. W., comp. *A Digest of the Early Connecticut Probate Records.* Hartford, 1904–6. v.d. Vol. I: 1635–1700
MARCHMONT, A. W. *When I Was Czar.* N.Y. [1903]
MARCOU, JANE (BELKNAP). *Life of Jeremy Belknap.* N.Y., 1847. v.d.
MARCY, R. B. *Exploration of the Red River of Louisiana in the Year 1852.* Wash., 1854. 1852
The Prairie Traveler. N.Y., 1859
Report. See U.S. CONGRESS. 31ST CONGRESS, 1 SESS. SENATE
MARRYAT, FRANK S. *Mountains and Molehills.* N.Y., 1855
MARRYAT, FREDERICK. *A Diary in America.* Lond., 1839. 3 vols. Also publ.: Phila., 1839. 2 vols. *Travels and Adventures of Monsieur Violet in California, Sonora, and Western Texas.* 1843
MARSHALL, HUMPHREY. *The History of Kentucky.* Frankfort [Ky.] 1812. [2d ed.] Frankfort [Ky.] 1824
MARSHALL, HUMPHRY. *Arbustrum Americanum: The American Grove.* Phila., 1785
'MARTIN, E.' See McCABE
MARTIN, GEORGE (MADDEN). *Emmy Lou.* N.Y. [1902]
MARTIN, HELEN (REIMENSNYDER). *Tillie, a Mennonite Maid.* N.Y., 1904
MARTIN, JOSEPH, ed. *A Comprehensive Description of Virginia, and the District of Columbia. . . . To Which Is Added a History of Virginia, from Its First Settlement to the Year 1754. . . .* By W. H. Brockenbrough. Richmond [n.d.] = his: *A New and Comprehensive Gazetteer of Virginia.* Charlottesville [Va.] 1835
MARTINEAU, HARRIET. *Harriet Martineau's Autobiography.* [Ed.] M. W. Chapman. Lond., 1877. Written 1855
Retrospect of Western Travel. Lond., 1838
Society in America. Lond., 1837

Maryland (Colony). Council. *Proceedings.* See *Archives of Maryland*
Maryland, Archives of. See *Archives of Maryland*
Maryland Gazette. Annapolis, **1727–34**
Maryland Gazette. Annapolis, **1745–1839**
Maryland Gazette. Balt., **1778–9, 1783–91.** Issue of 1 June 1787
Maryland Historical Magazine. Balt., **1906–current.** Vol. I includes: *Log of Chasseur.* **v.d.** Vols. X–XI include: U. Brown. *Journal.* **v.d.** Vols. X–XVI include: *Carroll Papers.* **v.d.**
Maryland Journal. Balt., **1773–97**
Mason, Capt. John. See Prince Society
Mason, R. B. [*Report on Gold-Mining in California,* 17 Aug. 1848.] In: 30th Congress, 2 Sess. House. Ex. Doc. No. 1. Pp. 56–64. (Also widely distributed in other publications.) **1848**
Massachusetts (Colony). *Records of the Governor and Company of the Massachusetts Bay in New England.* Ed. N. B. Shurtleff. Bost., 1853–4. **v.d.** Vol. I includes: *Mass. Charter.* **1629**
Court of Assistants. *Records . . . 1630–1692.* [Ed.] John Noble and J. F. Cronin. Bost., 1901–28. **v.d.**
General Court. House of Representatives. *Journals.* 1715–. [Bost.] 1919–. **v.d.**
Governor, 1741–1757 (William Shirley). *A Letter from William Shirley . . . : With a Journal of the Siege of Louisbourg.* Bost.: Draper, 1746. **1745**
Laws, Statutes, etc. *The Acts and Resolves, Public and Private, of the Province of the Massachusetts Bay.* 1692–1780. Bost., 1869–1922. 21 vols. (Running title: *Province Laws.*) **v.d.**
Laws, Statutes, etc. *The Charters and General Laws of the Colony and Province of Massachusetts Bay.* Bost., 1814. **v.d.**
Massachusetts. Agricultural Survey. *First Report.* By Henry Colman. Bost., **1838.** *Second Report.* Bost., **1839**
Board of Agriculture. *Annual Report.* 1853–1917. Bost., 1854–1918. **v.d.**
Convention, 1788. *Debates and Proceedings in the Convention . . . Held in the Year 1788.* Ed. B. K. Peirce and Charles Hale. Bost., 1856. **1788**
Laws, Statutes, etc. *Acts and Resolves.* (Binder's title.) 1780–1806. Bost., 1890–8. 13 vols. **v.d.**
Laws, Statutes, etc. *Acts and Resolves.* 1839–current. Bost., 1842–current. **v.d.**
Laws, Statutes, etc. *Laws.* 1805–38. Bost., 1806–38. 11 vols. 8vo. (Vols. IV (new series)–XIV of: (*Acts and*) *Laws,* 1780–1838.) **v.d.**
Laws, Statutes, etc. *Resolves.* 1806–38. Bost., 1806–38. 9 vols. 8vo. (Vols. XII–XX of: *Resolves,* 1776–1838.) **v.d.**
Zoological and Botanical Survey. *A Report on the Trees and Shrubs Growing Naturally in the Forests of Massachusetts.* By G. B. Emerson. Bost., **1846**
Zoological and Botanical Survey. *Reports of the Commissioners on the Zoological Survey.* Bost., **1838**
Zoological and Botanical Survey. *Reports on the Fishes* [by Storer], *Reptiles* [by Storer] *and Birds* [by Peabody] *of Massachusetts.* Bost., **1839**
Zoological and Botanical Survey. *Reports on the Herbaceous Plants* [by Dewey] *and on the Quadrupeds* [by Emmons] *of Massachusetts.* Cambridge, **1840**
Massachusetts. See *Massachusetts, or the First Planters of New-England*
Massachusetts Bay Acts. See Massachusetts (Colony). Laws, Statutes, etc.
Massachusetts Bay Currency Tracts. See Davis, A. McF.
Massachusetts Bay Rec. See Massachusetts (Colony). *Records*
Massachusetts (Body of) Liberties. See Massachusetts Historical Society. *Collections.* See also Whitmore, W. H.
Massachusetts Centinel. See *Columbian Centinel*
Massachusetts Charter. 1629. See Massachusetts (Colony). *Records*
Massachusetts Charters and Laws. See Massachusetts (Colony). Laws, Statutes, etc.
Massachusetts, Colonial Society of. See Colonial Society of Massachusetts
Massachusetts Debates & Proc. See Massachusetts. Convention, 1788
Massachusetts Gazette. 1763–8, 1769–76. See *Boston News-Letter*
[Semi-weekly.] Bost., **1768–9**
Massachusetts Historical Society. *Collections.* [Cambridge, etc.] **1792–current.** Also reprinted with various dates. Material in individual vols. is cited under specific titles as follows:
Belcher Papers. **v.d.** (6th Ser., Vols. VI–VII)
Belknap Papers. **v.d.** (5th Ser., Vols. II–III; 6th Ser., Vol. IV)
Bowdoin & Temple Papers. (6th Ser., Vol. IX)
Caulkins. *Mem. of W. Adams & E. Adams.* **v.d.** (4th Ser., Vol. I)
Commerce of Rhode Island. **v.d.** (7th Ser., Vols. IX–X)
Eliot. *Day-Breaking* (q.v.). **1647.** (3d Ser., Vol. IV)
Good News from New-England. **1648.** (4th Ser., Vol. I)
Gookin. *Indians.* **1674.** (1st Ser., Vol. I)
Heath Papers. **v.d.** (5th Ser., Vol. IV; 7th Ser., Vols. IV–V)
Higginson. *New-England.* **1630.** (1st Ser., Vol. I)
W. Hubbard. *A General History of New England.* *a*1704. (2d Ser., Vols. V–VI)
Jefferson Papers. **v.d.** (7th Ser., Vol. I)
Josselyn. *Two Voyages* (q.v.). 1675. **=1674.** (3d Ser., Vol. III)
Lechford. *Plain Dealing.* **1642.** (3d Ser., Vol. III)
Levett. *Voyage to New England.* **1628.** (3d Ser., Vol. VIII)
Massachusetts (Body of) Liberties (q.v.). **1641.** (3d Ser., Vol. VIII)
C. Mather. *Diary.* **v.d.** (7th Ser., Vols. VII–VIII)
New England's First Fruits. Part II. **1643.** (1st Ser., Vol. I)
Niles. *Indian Wars.* **v.d.** (3d Ser., Vol. VI; 4th Ser., Vol. V)
Sewall. *Diary.* **v.d.** (5th Ser., Vols. V–VII)
Sewall. *Letter-book.* **v.d.** (6th Ser., Vols. I–II)
Shepard. *Clear Sun-Shine.* **1648.** (3d Ser., Vol. IV)
J. Smith. *Adv. Planters* (q.v.). **1631.** (3d Ser., Vol. III.) Also cited as his: *Pathway*
Underhill. *Newes from America.* **1638.** (3d Ser., Vol. VI)
Warren-Adams Letters. **v.d.** (Vols. LXXII–LXXXIII)
E. Winslow, ed. *The Glorious Progress of the Gospel* (q.v.). **1649.** (3d Ser., Vol. IV)
Winthrop Papers. **v.d.** (In 6 parts: 4th Ser., Vols. VI–VII; 5th Ser., Vols. I, VIII; 6th Ser., Vols. III, V.) Part I also cited without part no. Part IV (5th Ser., Vol. VIII) also cited as: J. Winthrop. *Letters*
Massachusetts Historical Society. *Proceedings.* Bost., **1791–current.** 1st Ser., Vol. VII, includes: S. Sewall. *The Selling of Joseph.* **1700.** 1st Ser., Vol. VIII, includes: J. Andrews. *Letters* (q.v.). **v.d.**
Massachusetts House of Representatives. See Massachusetts (Colony). General Court. House of Representatives.
Massachusetts Liberties. See *Massachusetts (Body of) Liberties*
Massachusetts; or, The First Planters of New-England. Bost., 1696. **v.d.**
Massachusetts Province Acts, Laws. See Massachusetts (Colony). Laws, Statutes, etc. *The Acts and Resolves*
Massachusetts Spy. Bost.; Worcester, **1770–1904**
Massett, S. C. *'Drifting About.'* N.Y., **1863**
Mather, Cotton. *Diary.* See Massachusetts Historical Society. *Collections*
Magnalia Christi Americana. [Ed.] Thomas Robbins. Hartford, 1853. Also publ. 1855. First publ. **1702**
A Memorial. See 'Philopolites'
The Wonders of the Invisible World. Lond., 1862. First publ. **1693.** Vol. includes also: I. Mather. *A Further Account of the Tryals of the New-England Witches. . . . To Which Is Added, Cases of Conscience.* **1693**
Mather, Increase. *Cases of Conscience.* See Mather, C. *The Wonders of the Invisible World*
An Essay for the Recording of Illustrious Providences. Bost., **1684.** Also publ. as: *Remarkable Providences Illustrative of the Earlier Days of American Colonisation.* Lond., 1890. =1856. ("Library of Old Authors")
A Further Account of the Tryals of the New-England Witches. See C. Mather. *The Wonders of the Invisible World*
The History of King Philip's War. [Ed.] S. G. Drake. Bost., 1862. First publ. **1676**
Life R. Mather. See Dorchester Antiquarian and Historical Society
Remarkable Providences. See his: *An Essay*
Mather, Richard. *Journal.* See Dorchester Antiquarian and Historical Society
Mathews, Anne (Jackson). *Memoirs of Charles Mathews, Comedian.* Lond., 1839. **v.d.**
Mathews, Catharine V. *Andrew Ellicott, His Life and Letters.* N.Y. [cop. 1908]. **v.d.**
Mathews, Cornelius. *Various Writings.* N.Y., 1863 [*i.e.,* 1843]. **v.d.** Includes: *The Politicians.* **1840**
Moneypenny; or, The Heart of New York. N.Y., **1850**
The Motley Book. 3d ed. N.Y., 1840. **=1838**
Mathews, Frances A. *Billy Duane.* N.Y., **1905**
Mathews, Lyman. *Lectures on Eloquence and Style.* Andover [Mass.] **1836**
Mathews, William. *Getting on in the World.* Chic., **1873**
Mathewson, Christopher. *Pitching in a Pinch.* N.Y., **1912**
Second Base Sloan. N.Y. [cop. **1917**]
Matsell, G. M. *Vocabulum, or, The Rogue's Lexicon.* N.Y., **1859**
Matthews, Brander. *A Confident To-Morrow.* N.Y., **1900**
These Many Years. N.Y., **1917**
Matthews, Brander, and Bunner, H. C. *In Partnership.* Edinb., 1885. First publ. **1884**
Maude, John. *Visit to the Falls of Niagara in 1800.* Lond., 1826. **1800**
Maverick, Augustus. *Henry J. Raymond and the New York Press.* Hartford, **1870**
Maxwell, A. M. *A Run through the United States, during the Autumn of 1840.* Lond., **1841**
May, John. *Journal and Letters . . . 1788 and '89* Cinc., 1873. **v.d.**
Mayflower Descendant. Bost., **1899–current**
Mayo, Robert. *Political Sketches of Eight Years in Washington.* Balt., 1839. **v.d.**
Maysville (Ky.) *Eagle.* [Weekly.] **1814–?87**
Mease, James. *The Picture of Philadelphia.* Phila., **1811**
Medbery, J. K. *Men and Mysteries of Wall Street.* Bost., 1871. **=1870**
Meine, F. J., ed. *Tall Tales of the Southwest.* N.Y., 1930. **v.d.**
Meline, J. F. *Two Thousand Miles on Horseback.* N.Y., **1867**
Melish, John. *Travels in the United States of America.* Phila., **1812**
Mellen, Grenville. *Our Chronicle of '26.* Bost., **1827**
Melville, Herman. *Moby-Dick; or, The Whale.* N.Y., **1851.** Also: N.Y. [1926]. ("Modern Library")
Typee: A Peep at Polynesian Life. Lond., **1846.** Also: Ed. S. A. Leonard. N.Y. [cop. 1920]
Memoirs of the American Academy. See American Academy of Arts and Sciences. *Memoirs*
Memoirs of the Principal Transactions of the Last War between the English and French in North America. [Attrib. to Wm. Shirley.] 3d ed. Bost., **1758**
Mereness, N. D., ed. *Travels in the American Colonies.* N.Y., 1916. **v.d.** Includes materials by G. Chicken, T. Fitch, W. Fleming, H. Gordon, P. Stevens, and D. Taitt
Merwin, Samuel, and Webster, H. K. *Calumet 'K.'* N.Y., 1905. **=1901**
Messages and Papers of the Presidents. See U.S. President
Methodist Episcopal Church. Mission Conferences. Dakota. *Minutes of the Third [–Fifth] Annual Session.* Sioux City, Iowa [etc.], **1882[–4]**
Meyer, E. C. *Nominating Systems.* Madison, Wis., **1902**
Michaux, André. *Histoire des chênes de l'Amérique.* Paris, **1801.** (4 unnumbered pages of text cited as pp. 5–8)
Michaux, F. A. *Histoire des arbres forestiers de l'Amérique septentrionale.* Paris, **1810–3**
The North American Sylva. [Tr. A. L. Hillhouse.] Notes by J. J. Smith. Phila., **1857–9**
Michigan. Laws, Statutes, etc. *The General Statutes of the State.* Chic., 1882–3. **v.d.**
State Board of Agriculture. *Annual Report of the Secretary.* Lansing, 1862–current. **v.d.**
Michigan Agricultural Society. See Michigan State Agricultural Society
Michigan Agriculture Rep. See Michigan. State Board of Agriculture
Michigan, Historical Society of. *Historical and Scientific Sketches of Michigan.* Detroit, **1834**
Michigan State Agricultural Society. *Transactions.* 1849–59. Lansing, 1850–61. **v.d.**
Micmakis and Maricheets. See Maillard
Miles, William, of Carlisle, Pa. *Journal of the Sufferings and Hardships of Captain Parker H. French's Overland Expedition to California.* [N.Y., 1916.] =1851. **1850**
The Military Journals of Two Private Soldiers. See Tomlinson
Miller, Joaquin. *First Fam'lies of the Sierras.* Chic., **1876**
Life amongst the Modocs: Unwritten History. Lond., **1873.** Also under title: *Unwritten History. Life amongst the Modocs.* Hartford 1874
Miller, John. *A Description of the Province and City of New York.* Lond., 1843. **c1695**
Miller, Philip. *The Gardeners Dictionary.* Lond., **1731.** Abridged ed., **1735.** 2d ed., **1741.** Frequently reissued
Miller, William, botanist. *A Dictionary of English Names of Plants.* Lond., **1884**
Mills, S. J., and Smith, Daniel. *Report of a Missionary Tour.* Andover, **1815**
Miner. See Richardson, C. F., and Richardson, E. M.
Mineralogical Journal. See *American Mineralogical Journal*
Minor. *Diary.* See *Atlantic Monthly*
Minturn, William. *Travels West.* Lond., **1877**

Mirror (of Literature, Amusement, and Instruction). Lond., **1822–49**
Missionary Herald. Bost., **1805–current**
Missouri Intelligencer. Columbia, **1819–35**
MITCHELL, D. G. *Works.* [Edgewood Ed.] N.Y., 1907. **v.d.** Vol. IX contains: *Seven Stories with Basement and Attic*
Dream Life. N.Y., 1852. =**1851**
Fudge Doings. N.Y., **1855**
The Lorgnette. N.Y., **1850.** Vol. I
My Farm of Edgewood. N.Y., **1863**
Reveries of a Bachelor. N.Y., **1850.** Also publ.: N.Y., 1897
Seven Stories. See his: *Works*
MITCHELL, JAMES. *Nantucketisms.* See *American Speech*
MITCHELL, JOHN. *Reminiscences of Scenes and Characters in College: by a Graduate of Yale.* New Haven, **1847**
MITCHELL, JOHN A. *Dr. Thorne's Idea.* N.Y., **1910**
MITCHELL, S. W. *Roland Blake.* N.Y., 1895. = **1886**
MITCHILL. *Fishes N.Y.* See LITERARY AND PHILOSOPHICAL SOCIETY OF NEW-YORK
MOE, A. K. *A History of Harvard.* Cambridge, **1896**
MOHR, C. T. *Plant Life of Alabama.* Wash., **1901**
MONETTE, J. W. *History of the Discovery and Settlement of the Valley of the Mississippi.* N.Y., **1846**
Monthly South Dakotan. See *South Dakotan*
Monthly Weather Rev. See U.S. WEATHER BUREAU
MOORE, F. *Voy. Georgia.* See GEORGIA HISTORICAL SOCIETY. *Collections.* Vol. I
MOORE, FRANCIS C. *How to Build a Home.* N.Y., **1897**
MOORE, FRANK, ed. *Rebel Rhymes and Rhapsodies.* N.Y., 1864. **v.d.**
ed. *The Rebellion Record.* See *The Rebellion Record*
ed. *Songs and Ballads of the American Revolution.* N.Y., 1856. **v.d.**
Women of the War. Hartford, **1866**
MOORE, M. H. *Sketches of the Pioneers of Methodism in North Carolina and Virginia.* Nashville, **1884**
MORDECAI, SAMUEL. *Virginia, Especially Richmond, in By-gone Days.* Richmond, **1860**
MORLEY, MARGARET W. *The Carolina Mountains.* Bost., **1913**
Morning Star. Lond., **1856–69**
MORRELL, Z. N. *Flowers and Fruits from the Wilderness.* Bost., 1873. =**1872**
MORRIS, CLARA. *Life on the Stage.* N.Y., **1901**
Stage Confidences; Talks about Players and Play Acting. Bost. **[1902]**
MORRIS, G. See SPARKS
MORSE, JEDIDIAH, comp. *The American Gazetteer.* Bost., **1797.** 2d ed. **1798**
The American Geography. Elizabeth Town [N.J.] **1789.** New ed. Lond., **1794**
The American Universal Geography. 3d ed. Bost., **1796**
A Report to the Secretary of War . . . on Indian Affairs. New Haven, 1822. **v.d.**
MORSE, JEDIDIAH, and MORSE, R. C., comps. *The Traveller's Guide: or, Pocket Gazetteer of the United States.* New Haven, **1823.** 2d ed., **1826**
MORSE, JOHN T. *Life and Letters of Oliver Wendell Holmes.* Bost., 1896. **v.d.**
MORTON, NATHANIEL. *New-Englands Memoriall.* Cambridge, **1669.** 6th ed. Bost., 1855
MORTON, THOMAS. *New English Canaan.* 1632 [*i.e.,* 1637]: see FORCE. *Tracts.* Vol. II, No. 5. 1637: see PRINCE SOCIETY
MOSES, M. J., ed. *Representative American Dramas.* Bost., 1925. **v.d.** Contents include: BELASCO. *The Girl of the Golden West.* **1905.** FITCH. *The City.* **1909.** HOYT. *A Texas Steer.* **1894.** THOMAS. *The Witching Hour.* **1907**
Representative Plays by American Dramatists. N.Y., 1918–[25]. **v.d.** Vol. I contains: BARKER. *The Indian Princess.* **1808.** BRACKENRIDGE. *The Battle of Bunkers-Hill.* **1776.** DUNLAP. *André.* **1798.** GODFREY. *The Prince of Parthia.* **1765.** LEACOCK. *The Fall of British Tyranny.* **1776.** LOW. *The Politician Out-witted.* **1789.** NOAH. *She Would Be a Soldier* (q.v.). **1819.** ROGERS. *Ponteach* (q.v.). **1766.** TYLER. *The Contrast* (q.v.). **1787.** WARREN. *The Group.* **1775.** Vol. II includes: BATEMAN. *Self.* **1856.** HUTTON. *Fashionable Follies.* **1815.** J. S. JONES. *The People's Lawyer.* **1839.** MOWATT [*i.e.,* RITCHIE]. *Fashion.* **1850**
MOTLEY, J. L. *Correspondence.* Ed. G. W. Curtis. N.Y., 1889. **v.d.**
Mourt's Relation or Journal of the Plantation at Plymouth. [Ed.] H. M. Dexter. Bost., 1865. First publ. **1622**
MOWATT. See MOSES. *Representative Plays.* Vol. II
MUHLENBERG, HENRY. *Catalogus Plantarum Americæ Septentrionalis.* Lancaster [Pa.] **1813**
Index Florae. See AMERICAN PHILOSOPHICAL SOCIETY. *Transactions*
MUIRHEAD. See BAEDEKER
MULFORD, C. E. *Bar-20.* N.Y., **1907**
The Bar-20 Three. Lond., **1921.** Also publ.: Chic., 1921
Rustlers' Valley. **1924**
MUMFORD, LEWIS. *Sticks and Stones.* N.Y. [cop. **1924**]
Munitions of War. See NORTON, C. B., and VALENTINE, W. J.
MUNN, C. C. *Uncle Terry.* N.Y., **1900**
MUNROE, KIRK. *Dorymates.* N.Y. [cop. **1889**]
The Golden Days of '49 N.Y. **[1889]**
MUNSELL, JOEL. *The Annals of Albany.* Albany, 1850–9. **v.d.**
Munsey's Magazine. N.Y., **1889–1929.** (Eng. ed., sometimes quoted for Vol. XXV, varies)
MURFREE, MARY N. *The Despot of Broomsedge Cove.* Bost., 1889 [cop. **1888**]
In the Tennessee Mountains. Bost., **1884**
The Mystery of Witch-Face Mountain. Bost., **1895**
The Prophet of the Great Smoky Mountains. Bost., **1885**
The Story of Keedon Bluffs. Bost., 1891 [cop. **1887**]
Where the Battle Was Fought. Bost., 1885. =**1884**
Murphey Papers. See NORTH CAROLINA. HISTORICAL COMMISSION
MURRAY, AMELIA M. *Letters from the United States, Cuba, and Canada.* Lond., 1856. **v.d.**
MURRAY, SIR C. A. *Travels in North America.* N.Y., **1839.** 3d ed. Lond., 1854
MURRAY, W. H. H. *Adventures in the Wilderness.* Bost., **1869**
MYERS, A. O. *Bosses and Boodle in Ohio Politics.* Cinc., **1895**
MYERS, GUSTAVUS. *The History of Tammany Hall.* N.Y., 1901. **v.d.**

N

N. Hawthorne & Wife. See HAWTHORNE, J.
NADAL, E. S. *Impressions of London Social Life.* N.Y., **1875**
NARRAGANSETT CLUB. *Publications.* Providence, 1866–74. **v.d.** Vol. I includes: R. WILLIAMS. *A Key into the Language of America* (q.v.). Ed. J. H. Trumbull. **1643.** Vol. VI contains: R. WILLIAMS. *Letters.* Ed. J. R. Bartlett. **v.d.**
Narragansett Historical Register. Providence, **1882–91**
Narrative of Privations and Sufferings of . . . Prisoners of War. See UNITED STATES SANITARY COMMISSION
Narratives Career De Soto. See *Relaçam verdadeira*
Narratives of Early Maryland. See HALL, C. C.
'NASBY.' See LOCKE, D. R.
NASON, DANIEL. *A Journal of a Tour from Boston to Savannah.* Cambridge, **1849**
Nation. N.Y., **1865–current**
NATIONAL CONSERVATION CONGRESS. *Proceedings.* Wash. [1910]. **1909**
NATIONAL COUNTRY LIFE CONFERENCE. *Rural Organization: Proceedings of the Third National Country Life Conference, Springfield, Mass., 1920.* Wash., 1921. **1920**
National Intelligencer. [Tri-weekly; semi-weekly.] Wash., **1800–69.** Issue of 1 May 1823 includes: *Provincial Dictionary*
NATIONAL MUSEUM. See U.S. NATIONAL MUSEUM
NATIONAL PARK SERVICE. See U.S. NATIONAL PARK SERVICE
National Republican. Wash., **1860–88**
Natural History of New York. See NEW YORK (STATE). NATURAL HISTORY SURVEY
A Naval Encyclopædia. Phila., **1881**
Naval War Records. See U.S. NAVY DEPT. *Official Records*
NEAL, DANIEL. *The History of New-England.* Lond., **1720**
NEAL, JOHN. *Brother Jonathan.* Edinb., **1825**
The Down-Easters. N.Y., **1833**
John Beedle's Sleigh Ride. See M'CLINTOCK, CAPT.
Rachel Dyer. Portland [Me.] **1828**
NEAL, JOSEPH C. *Charcoal Sketches.* Phila., 1838. First publ. **1837**
Peter Ploddy, and Other Oddities. Phila., **1844**
NEILL, E. D. *Virginia Carolorum . . . 1625–1685.* Albany, 1886. **v.d.**
NELSON, S. A. *The A B C of Wall Street.* N.Y. **[1900]**
The New American Cyclopædia. Ed. George Ripley and C. A. Dana. N.Y., 1869–72. =1858 [1857]–63. Revised as: *The American Cyclopædia.* With suppl. N.Y., **1883–4.** First publ. without suppl.: **1873–6**
NEW CASTLE, DEL. COURT. *Records . . . , 1676–1681.* Lancaster, Pa., 1904. **v.d.**
New-England Courant. Bost., **1721–6**
New England Farmer. Bost., **1848–64, 1867–71**
New England Farmer. (Fessenden) Bost., **1822–46. 1865–1913**
New England Historical and Genealogical Register. Bost., 1847–current. **v.d.**
New-England Magazine. Bost., **1831–5**
New England Magazine: An Illustrated Monthly. Bost., **1884–8.** New ser. Bost., **1889–1917**
New-England Weekly Journal. Bost., **1727–41**
New England's First Fruits. Lond., **1643.** See MASSACHUSETTS HISTORICAL SOCIETY. *Collections.* See also *Old South Leaflets*
NEW HAMPSHIRE. [*Provincial and State Papers.* Ed. Nathaniel Bouton, *et al.*] Concord [etc.] 1867–current. **v.d.** Vols. I–VII have title: *Provincial Papers. Documents and Records Relating to the Province of New-Hampshire.* Vols. XXXI–: *The Probate Records of the Province of New Hampshire*
COMMITTEE OF SAFETY. See NEW HAMPSHIRE HISTORICAL SOCIETY
FORESTRY AND RECREATION COMMISSION. *Report.* Concord, **1885–1919**
New Hampshire, Documents and Records. See NEW HAMPSHIRE. [*Provincial and State Papers*]
NEW HAMPSHIRE HISTORICAL SOCIETY. *Collections.* Concord, 1824–current. **v.d.** Vol. I includes: PENHALLOW. *The History of the Wars of New England with the Eastern Indians.* **1726.** Vol. VI includes: D. LIVERMORE. *A Journal of the March of General Poor's Brigade.* **1779.** Vol. VII includes: *Records of the New Hampshire Committee of Safety.* **v.d.** Vol. IX includes: T. WALKER. *Diaries.* **v.d.**
New Hampshire Orig. Docs. See JENNESS
New Hampshire Probate Records. See NEW HAMPSHIRE. [*Provincial and State Papers*]
New Hampshire State Papers. See NEW HAMPSHIRE. [*Provincial and State Papers*]
NEW HAVEN (COLONY). *Records of the Colony and Plantation . . . , from 1638 to 1649.* Ed. C. J. Hoadly. Hartford, 1857. **v.d.**
Records of the Colony or Jurisdiction . . . , from May, 1653, to the Union. Ed. C. J. Hoadly. Hartford, 1858. **v.d.**
NEW HAVEN COLONY HISTORICAL SOCIETY, New Haven. *Ancient Town Records.* Vols. I–II: *New Haven Town Records,* 1649–1684. New Haven, 1917–19. **v.d.**
New-Jersey Almanac, for . . . 1823. [By] David Young. Elizabeth-Town [?1822]. Includes: *Yankee Phrases.* **1822**
New Jersey Archives. 1st Series: see *Documents Relating to the Colonial, Revolutionary and Post-Revolutionary History of the State of New Jersey.* 2d Series: see *Documents Relating to the Revolutionary History of the State of New Jersey*
New Jersey Journal. Chatham, **1779–83**
New Mexican. Santa Fe. 1849: see *Santa Fe New Mexican.* 1863–8: see *Weekly New Mexican*
New Mexican Review. Santa Fe, **1862–1918.** (Also as: *Weekly New Mexican Review; New Mexican Review and Live Stock Journal; Santa Fé Weekly New Mexican and Live Stock Journal*)
NEW MEXICO (TERRITORY). *Official Reports . . . for the Years 1882 and 1883.* Santa Fe, 1884. **v.d.**
New Mexico Press. Albuquerque, **1864–7.** (Preceded by: *Rio Abajo Weekly Press*)
NEW PLYMOUTH COLONY. *Records.* Ed. N. B. Shurtleff [and David Pulsifer]. Bost., 1855–61. **v.d.**
LAWS, STATUTES, etc. *The Compact with the Charter and Laws of the Colony of New Plymouth.* Bost., 1836. **v.d.**
(New) Voice. N.Y.; Chic., **1884–1906.** Also as: *New York Voice*
A New Voyage to Georgia. 2d ed. Lond., 1737. = **1735**
NEW YORK (COLONY). COUNCIL. *Journal of the Legislative Council of the Colony of New-York.* Albany, 1861. **v.d.**
NEW YORK (STATE). FOREST, FISH, AND GAME COMMISSION. *Annual Report [1895]–1909.* Albany, **1896–1910**
NATURAL HISTORY SURVEY. *Natural History of New York.* Albany, 1842–94. [Div. 1] *Zoology of New-York.* By J. E. DeKay. Albany, **1842–4.** [Div. 2.] *A Flora of the State of New-York.* By John Torrey. Albany, **1843.** [Div. 4.] *Geology of New-York.* By W. W. Mather [*et al.*]. Albany, **1842–3.** [Div. 5.] *Agriculture of New-York.* By Ebenezer Emmons. Albany, **1846–54**
NEW YORK ACADEMY OF SCIENCES. *Annals of the Lyceum of Natural History of New York. . . . Sept. 1823–June 1877.* N.Y., 1824–76. Vol. II includes: C. L. BONAPARTE. *The Genera of North American Birds, and a Synopsis of the Species.* **1828**
New York Advertiser and Express. See *New York Semi-Weekly Express*
New York Colonial Documents. See *Documents Relative to the Colonial History of the State of New-York*
New York Commercial Advertiser. See *Commercial Advertiser*
New York Dramatic News. N.Y., **1894–6**
New York Evening Post. **1802–1919**
New York Herald. **1835–1924**
NEW YORK HISTORICAL SOCIETY. *Collections. John Watts de Peyster Publication Fund Ser.* N.Y., 1868–current. **v.d.** Vols. XXV–XLI include:

NEW YORK (COUNTY). SURROGATE'S COURT. *Abstracts of Wills on File.* 1665–1800. **v.d.**
New York Library Bulletin, Hist. See NEW YORK. STATE LIBRARY
NEW YORK. PUBLIC LIBRARY. *Bulletin.* 1897–current
New York Semi-weekly Express. 1836–79. Also as: *New York Advertiser and Express*
New York State Agric. Trans. See SOCIETY FOR THE PROMOTION OF USEFUL ARTS
New York State Col. Hist. See *Documents Relative to the Colonial History of the State of New-York*
New York State Doc. Hist. See *The Documentary History of the State of New-York*
NEW YORK. STATE LIBRARY. *History Bulletin.* Albany, 1898–1919
New York State Soc. Arts. See SOCIETY FOR THE PROMOTION OF USEFUL ARTS
New York Tribune. 1841–1924
New York Voice. See *(New) Voice*
New York Wills. See NEW YORK HISTORICAL SOCIETY
Newbury Rec. See COFFIN
NEWELL, CHESTER. *History of the Revolution in Texas.* N.Y., **1838**
NEWELL, R. H. *The Orpheus C. Kerr Papers.* 1st Ser. N.Y., 1863. =1862. **v.d.**
Newport (R.I.) *Mercury.* 1758–current
News and Press. Cimarron, N.M. 1870–1910
Newton (Kan.) *Kansan.* 1872–99
NICHOLAS, ANNA. *An Idyl of the Wabash, and Other Stories.* Indianapolis, **1899**
NICHOLS, E. J. *An Historical Dictionary of Baseball Terminology.* [State College, Pa., 1939.] Microfilm copy of typewritten thesis
NICHOLS, J. L. *The Business Guide; or, Safe Methods of Business.* 28th ed. Naperville, Ill., **1891**
NICHOLS, T. L. *Forty Years of American Life.* Lond., **1864**
NICHOLSON, MEREDITH. *A Hoosier Chronicle.* Lond., **1912**
The Hoosiers. N.Y., **1900**
NICKLIN, P. H. *Letters Descriptive of the Virginia Springs.* Phila., **1835**
A Pleasant Peregrination through the Prettiest Parts of Pennsylvania. Phila., **1836**
NILES. See MASSACHUSETTS HISTORICAL SOCIETY. *Collections*
Niles' Weekly Register. Phila., 1811–49. Also as: *Niles' National Register*
NOAH, M. M. *Gleanings from a Gathered Harvest.* N.Y., **1845**
She Would Be a Soldier. N.Y., **1819**. See also MOSES. *Representative Plays.* Vol. I
NORRIS, FRANK. *Blix.* N.Y., 1900. =1899
Frank Norris of 'the Wave': Stories and Sketches from the San Francisco Weekly, 1893 to 1897. San Francisco, 1931. **v.d.**
McTeague. N.Y., 1904. =1899
The Octopus. N.Y., **1901**
The Pit. N.Y., 1922. =1903 [cop. 1902]
The Third Circle. N.Y., **1909**. **v.d.**
Vandover and the Brute. Garden City, N.Y., 1914. c1895
NORRIS, J. W. *Chicago Directory.* See *A Business Advertiser and General Directory*
NORRIS, MARY H. *The Veil.* Bost., **1907**
North American Miscellany and Dollar Magazine. Bost.; N.Y., **1851–2**
North American Review. Bost.; N.Y., 1815–1939
NORTH CAROLINA (COLONY). *Colonial Records.* Ed. W. L. Saunders. Raleigh, 1886–90. **v.d.**
NORTH CAROLINA. HISTORICAL COMMISSION. *Publications.* Raleigh, 1907–current. **v.d.** (1) ADELAIDE L. FRIES, ed. *Records of the Moravians in North Carolina* ([Vols. XII ff.]), including: J. J. FRIIS. *Diary.* 1754 ([Vol. XV]); C. G. REUTER. *Wachau.* 1764 (Vol. XVI]). (2) A. D. MURPHEY. *Papers.* Ed. W. H. Hoyt. **v.d.** ([Vols. IV–V.]) (3) J. STEELE. *Papers.* Ed. H. M. Wagstaff. **v.d.** ([Vols. XIII–XIV])
[*North Carolina Almanacs.*] (Dates of issue; places of publ.) *Boylan's North-Carolina Almanack.* 1811. Raleigh. *Cottom's New Virginia & North Carolina Almanack.* 1820. Richmond, Va. *Coupee's North-Carolina Almanac.* 1809. Salisbury. *Gales's North-Carolina Almanack.* 1807, 1814–6, 1821–2. Raleigh. *Henderson's Almanack.* 1813–4, 1816, 1820, 1823. Raleigh. *Hodge & Boylan's North-Carolina Almanack.* 1801. Halifax. *Hodge's North Carolina Almanack.* 1796. Halifax. *Lawrence & Lemay's North-Carolina Almanack.* 1828. Raleigh. (Read at Univ. of N.C. Lib.). **v.d.**
NORTHALL, W. K. *Before and Behind the Curtain.* N.Y., 1851. **v.d.**
ed. *Life and Recollections of Yankee Hill.* N.Y., 1850. **v.d.**
Northern Vindicator. Estherville, Iowa, 1868–1902
NORTON, CHARLES BENJAMIN, and VALENTINE, W. J. *Report to the Government of the United States on the Munitions of War.* N.Y., 1868
NORTON, CHARLES LEDYARD. *Political Americanisms. A Glossary of Terms and Phrases.* Lond., 1890. See also *Magazine of American History*

NORTON, JOHN. *The Redeemed Captive.* Bost., **1748**
NORTON, O. W. *Army Letters, 1861–1865.* [Chic., 1903]. **v.d.**
Norwalk Hist. Rec. See HALL, E.
Notes and Queries. Lond., 1849–current
NOTT, H. J. *Novellettes of a Traveller.* N.Y., **1834**
NOWLAND, J. H. B. *Early Reminiscences of Indianapolis.* Indianapolis, **1870**
NUTTALL, THOMAS. *The Genera of North American Plants.* Phila., **1818**
A Journal of Travels into the Arkansa Territory, during the Year 1819. Phila., **1821**. See also THWAITES
NUTTING, WALLACE. *Massachusetts Beautiful.* Framingham [cop. 1923]
NYE, E. W. *Baled Hay.* N.Y. [cop. **1884**]

O

O'BEIRNE, H. F., comp. *Leaders and Leading Men of the Indian Territory.* Chic., **1891**
OBENCHAIN, ELIZA C. (CALVERT). *Aunt Jane of Kentucky.* Bost., 1907. **v.d.**
O'BRYAN, WILLIAM. *A Narrative of Travels in the United States of America.* Lond., **1836**
Observer & Rep. See *Lexington* (Ky.) *Observer*
O'CONNOR, W. D. *Three Tales.* Bost., 1892. a1889
ODELL, G. C. D. *Annals of the New York Stage.* N.Y., 1927–current. **v.d.**
O'FERRALL, S. A. *A Ramble through Six Thousand Miles through the United States of America.* Lond., **1832**
Official Congress. Directory. See U.S. CONGRESS
OHIO. BOARD OF AGRICULTURE. *Eighteenth Annual Report . . . , for the Year 1863.* Columbus, **1864**
OKLAHOMA. GOVERNOR. *Report . . . to the Secretary of the Interior.* Wash., **1897**
LAWS, STATUTES, etc. *Session Laws of 1910–1911* [3d legislature]. Guthrie, **1911**. **v.d.**
Oklahoma Chronicles. See *Chronicles of Oklahoma*
Old South Leaflets. [General Series.] Bost. [1896–current.] Contents include: Vol. I, No. 21. J. ELIOT. *Brief Narrative* (q.v.). **1670**. Vol. III, No. 51. *New England's First Fruits* (q.v.). **1643**. Vol. VI, No. 143. J. ELIOT. *The Day-breaking of the Gospel* (q.v.). **1647**. Vol. VII, No. 172. *The Fundamental Constitutions of Carolina.* **1669**
OLMSTED, F. L. *A Journey in the Back Country.* Lond., **1860**
A Journey in the Seaboard Slave States. N.Y., 1861. =1856
Onward. N.Y., 1869–70. Cover-title: *Mayne Reid's Magazine: Onward*
Orations Delivered at the Request of the Inhabitants of . . . Boston, to Commemorate the Evening of the Fifth of March, 1770. Bost. [1785]. **v.d.**
Oregon State Journal. Eugene, 1864–1909
O'REILLY, HARRINGTON. *Fifty Years on the Trail: A True Story of Western Life.* Lond., **1889**
OSSOLI, SARAH M. (FULLER), MARCHESA D'. *Summer on the Lakes, in 1843.* Bost., **1844**.
OSTRANDER, ISABEL E. *How Many Cards?* N.Y., **1920**
Our Country's Progress. See BROCKETT.
OUSELEY, W. G. *Remarks on the Statistics and Political Institutions of the United States.* Phila., **1832**
Outing. Albany, 1882–1923
Overland Monthly. San Fran., 1868–1875; 1883–1935
OWEN, MARGARET B. *The Secret of Typewriting Speed.* Chic., 1918. =1917.
OWEN, MARY A. *Voodoo Tales, as Told among the Negroes of the Southwest.* N.Y., 1893. Also publ. as: *Old Rabbit, the Voodoo, and Other Sorcerers.* Lond., 1893
OWENS, FRANCES E. (JOHNSTON). *Mrs. Owens' Cook Book.* Chic., 1882. Rev. ed., 1888. =1884
Oyster Bay, N.Y. Oyster Bay Town Records. Vol. I: 1653–90. N.Y., 1916. **v.d.**

P

Pacific R.R. Rep. See U.S. WAR DEPT. *Reports*
PAGE, T. N. *Red Rock.* N.Y., **1898**
PAIGE, E. G. *Dow's Patent Sermons. First Series.* Phila. [cop. 1857]. c1849
PAINE, R. D. *Comrades of the Rolling Ocean.* Bost., 1923 [cop. 1921, 1923]
Pall Mall Gazette. Lond., 1865–current
PALMER, G. H. *The Life of Alice Freeman Palmer.* Bost., **1908**
PALMER, H. C. *Stories of the Base Ball Field.* Chic., **1890**
PALMER, J. See THWAITES
PALMER, JOHN. *Journal of Travels in the United States of North America, and in Lower Canada.* Lond., 1818
'PANSY.' See ALDEN, I.

PANTHER, ABRAHAM. *A Very Surprising Narrative, of a Young Woman Discovered in a Rocky-Cave; after Having Been Taken by the Savage Indians . . . in the Year 1777.* Jaffrey, N.H. [n.d.]. **1777**
Papers Relating to Pemaquid. See HOUGH, F. B.
PARK, ROSWELL. *Pantology; or, A Systematic Survey of Human Knowledge.* Phila., **1841**
PARKER, A. A. *A Trip to the West and Texas.* Concord, **1835**
PARKER, F. W. *Talks on Pedagogics.* N.Y. [1894]
PARKER, G. F. *Recollections of Grover Cleveland.* N.Y., 1911. =1909
PARKER, SAMUEL. *Journal of an Exploring Tour beyond the Rocky Mountains.* Ithaca, N.Y., **1838**
PARKINSON, JOHN. *Paradisi in Sole Paradisus Terrestris. Faithfully Reprinted from the Edition of 1629.* Lond., 1904. **1629**
Theatrum Botanicum: The Theater of Plants. Lond., **1640**
PARKINSON, RICHARD. *A Tour in America in 1798, 1799, and 1800.* Lond., **1805**
PARKMAN, EBENEZER. *Diary.* Ed. H. M. Forbes. [Westborough, Mass.] 1899. **v.d.**
PARKMAN, FRANCIS. *The California and Oregon Trail.* N.Y., 1849. **v.d.** See also *Knickerbocker*
PARMENTER, C. O. *History of Pelham, Mass., from 1738 to 1898.* Amherst, Mass., 1898. **v.d.**
PARRISH, RANDALL. *The Case and the Girl.* N.Y., **1922**
PARTON, SARA P. (WILLIS). *Ginger-Snaps.* N.Y., **1870**
Patents. See U.S. PATENT OFFICE
PATTIE, J. O. *Personal Narrative.* Ed. Timothy Flint. Cinc., **1831**. See also THWAITES
PAULDING, J. K. *The Backwoodsman.* Phila., **1818**
The Beauties of Brother Bull-us. See *The Beauties of Brother Bull-us*
The Book of Saint Nicholas. N.Y., **1836**
A Book of Vagaries. N.Y., **1868**
Chronicles of the City of Gotham. N.Y., **1830**
The Diverting History of John Bull and Brother Jonathan. 2d ed. N.Y., **1835**. First publ.: N.Y., **1812**. Republ.: Lond., 1814
John Bull in America. N.Y., **1825**
The Lay of the Scottish Fiddle. 1st Amer. from 4th ed. Lond., 1814. First publ. 1813
Letters from the South. N.Y., **1817**
Westward Ho! N.Y., **1832**
PAULDING, J. K., and PAULDING, W. I. *American Comedies.* Phila., 1847. Includes: *The Bucktails* [by J. K. Paulding], c1815; and *The Noble Exile, Madmen All,* and *Antipathies* [all by W. I. Paulding], c1845
'PAXTON.' See HAMMETT
PEABODY. *Mass. Birds.* See MASSACHUSETTS. ZOOLOGICAL AND BOTANICAL SURVEY. *Reports on the Fishes*
PEARS, SARAH. *Narrative.* MS., Newberry Lib., Chic., c1785
PEARSON, ELIZABETH W., ed. *Letters from Port Royal Written at the Time of the Civil War.* Bost., 1906. **v.d.**
PECK, G. W. *Peck's Bad Boy and His Pa.* Chic., **1883**
Peck's Sunshine. Chic., 1883. =1882
PECK, J. M. *A Gazetteer of Illinois.* Jacksonville [Ill.] 1834. 2d ed. Phila., **1837**
A Guide for Emigrants. Bost., **1831**
A New Guide for Emigrants to the West. 2d ed. Bost., **1837**
PEIRCE, AUGUSTUS. *The Rebelliad.* Bost., 1842. **1819**
PEIRCE, BENJAMIN. *A History of Harvard University, from Its Foundation . . . to the Period of the American Revolution.* Cambridge, 1833. **v.d.**
Pelham, Hist. See PARMENTER
PELZER, LOUIS. *Marches of the Dragoons in the Mississippi Valley.* Iowa City, 1917. Includes: N. BOONE. *Journal.* 1843
Pemaquid, Papers rel. to. See HOUGH, F. B.
'PENCIL.' *White Sulphur Papers; or, Life at the Springs of Western Virginia.* N.Y., **1839**
PENHALLOW. See NEW HAMPSHIRE HISTORICAL SOCIETY
PENN, WILLIAM. *Select Works.* 3d ed. Lond., 1782. **v.d.**
Penn-Logan Corr. See PENNSYLVANIA, HISTORICAL SOCIETY OF
'PENNIMAN.' See DENISON
Pennsylvania Agricultural Report. See PENNSYLVANIA STATE AGRICULTURAL SOCIETY
Pennsylvania Archives. Phila., 1852–6; Harrisburg, 1874–1935
Pennsylvania Chronicle. Phila., 1767–74.
Pennsylvania Colonial Records. See [*Colonial Records of Pennsylvania*]
Pennsylvania Evening Herald. Phila., 1785–8
Pennsylvania Evening Post. Phila., 1775–84
Pennsylvania Gazette. Phila., 1728–1815
PENNSYLVANIA, HISTORICAL SOCIETY OF. *Memoirs.* Phila., 1827–95. **v.d.** Vol. VII includes: E. DENNY. *Military Journal* (q.v.). **v.d.** Vols. IX–X include: *Penn-Logan Correspondence.* **v.d.**

Pennsylvania Journal. Phila., **1742–93**
Pennsylvania Magazine of History and Biography. Phila., **1877–current**
Pennsylvania Packet. Phila., **1771–90**
PENNSYLVANIA STATE AGRICULTURAL SOCIETY. *First Annual Report of the Transactions.* Harrisburg, **1854**
The Penny Cyclopædia of the Society for the Diffusion of Useful Knowledge. Lond., **1833–43**
PEPPER, WILLIAM. *The Medical Side of Benjamin Franklin.* Phila., 1911. **v.d.**
PERCY, ADRIAN. *Twice Outlawed. A Personal History of Ed and Lon Maxwell, alias the Williams Brothers.* Chic. [?1882]
A Perfect Description of Virginia. See FORCE. *Tracts.* Vol. II, No. 8
PERRIE, G. W. *Buckskin Mose.* Ed. C. G. Rosenberg. N.Y., 1890 [cop. 1889]. **=1873**
PERRIN. See FILSON CLUB. *Filson Club Publications.* No. 3
PERRY, G. W. *A Treatise on Turpentine Farming.* Newbern, N.C., **1859**
PERRY, NORAH. *A Flock of Girls and Their Friends.* Bost., 1888 [cop. 1887]
PERRY, W. S., ed. *Historical Collections Relating to the American Colonial Church.* [Hartford] 1870–8. **v.d.**
PERSONS. See KINGSBURY
Peter Gott. See REYNOLDS, JOSEPH
PETERS, D. C. *The Life and Adventures of Kit Carson.* N.Y., **1858**
PETERS, SAMUEL. *A General History of Connecticut.* Lond., **1781**. Also: New-Haven, 1829. N.Y., 1877
Peterson('s) Magazine. N.Y.; Phila., **1840–98**
Pettigrew Papers. Letters and documents (MS.) in lib. of Univ. of North Carolina
PEYTON, J. L. *The Adventures of My Grandfather.* Lond., **1867**
The Pharmacopœia of the United States of America. Bost., **1820**
PHELPS, ALMIRA (HART) L. *Familiar Lectures on Botany.* 5th ed. Hartford, 1837. **=1836.** New ed. N.Y., **1845**
PHELPS, E. S. See WARD, E. S.
Phil. Trans. See ROYAL SOCIETY OF LONDON
PHILADELPHIA. ORDINANCES, etc. *Ordinances of the Corporation of the City of Philadelphia.* Phila., 1812. **v.d.**
PHILADELPHIA, ACADEMY OF NATURAL SCIENCES OF. See ACADEMY OF NATURAL SCIENCES OF PHILADELPHIA
Philadelphia Spirit of the Times. See *Spirit of the Times.* Phila.
PHILIPS, MELVILLE, ed. *The Making of a Newspaper.* N.Y., **1893**
PHILLIPS, D. G. *The Social Secretary.* N.Y., **1905**
A Woman Ventures. N.Y. [cop. 1902]
PHILLIPS, EDWARD. *The New World of English Words: or, A General Dictionary.* Lond., **1658.** 4th ed. as: *The New World of Words.* 1678. 6th ed. [Ed.] J[ohn] K[ersey]. **1706**
PHILLIPS, HENRY. *Historical Sketches of the Paper Currency of the American Colonies, Prior to the Adoption of the Federal Constitution.* Roxbury, Mass., **1865–6**
PHILLIPS, P. L. *Notes on the Life and Works of Bernard Romans.* Deland, Fla., 1924. **v.d.**
PHILLIPS, WENDELL. *Speeches, Lectures, and Letters.* Bost., 1863. **v.d.**
'PHILOPOLITES' [?Cotton Mather]. *A Memorial of the Present Deplorable State of New-England.* [Lond.] **1707**
Philosophical Society. See AMERICAN PHILOSOPHICAL SOCIETY
Philosophical Transactions. See ROYAL SOCIETY OF LONDON
Picayune. See *Daily Picayune*
PICKERING, JOHN. *A Vocabulary, or Collection of Words and Phrases . . . Supposed to be Peculiar to the United States of America. . . .* Boston, 1816. First publ., in substance, in: AMERICAN ACADEMY OF ARTS AND SCIENCES. *Memoirs.* Vol. III, Pt. 1. **1815**
PICKERING, JOSEPH. *Inquiries of an Emigrant.* New ed. Lond., 1831. 3d ed., 1832. First publ. as: *Emigration, or No Emigration.* Lond., 1830. **v.d.**
PIDGIN, C. F. *Blennerhassett.* N.Y. [cop. 1901]
Stephen Holton. Bost., **1902**
Zachariah, the Congressman. Chic., **1880**
PIERSON, H. W. *In the Brush.* N.Y., **1881**
PIKE, ALBERT. *Prose Sketches and Poems.* Bost., **1834**
PIKE, JAMES. *Scout and Ranger.* Princeton, 1932. First publ. **1865**
PIKE, Z. M. *An Account of Expeditions to the Sources of the Mississippi.* Phila., 1810. **v.d.** Publ. also as: *The Expeditions of Zebulon Montgomery Pike, to Headwaters of the Mississippi River.* Ed. Elliott Coues. N.Y., **1895**
PINCHOT, GIFFORD. *The Fight for Conservation.* N.Y., **1910**
PINE, G. W. *Beyond the West.* 2d ed. Utica, N.Y., 1871. First publ. **1870**

PINKERTON, ALLAN. *The Expressman and the Detective.* Chic., 1875. **=1874**
Strikers, Communists, Tramps and Detectives. N.Y., 1884. **=1878**
PITTENGER, WILLIAM. *Daring and Suffering: A History of the Great Railroad Adventure.* Phila., 1864. **=1863.** Also publ. as: *The Great Locomotive Chase.* Phila., 1901
PITTMAN, HANNAH (DAVIESS). *The Belle of the Blue Grass Country.* Bost., 1906
PITTMAN, PHILIP. *The Present State of the European Settlements on the Mississippi.* Lond., 1770
Plantation Missionary. Oberlin, Ohio, 1890–1918
A Platform of Church-Discipline. See CONGREGATIONAL CHURCHES IN MASSACHUSETTS
PLAYFAIR, HUGO. *The Hugo Playfair Papers; or, Brother Jonathan, the Smartest Nation in All Creation.* Lond., 1841
Plough Boy, and Journal of the Board of Agriculture. Albany, 1819–23
PLUMBE, JOHN. *Sketches of Iowa and Wisconsin.* St. Louis, 1839
PLUMMER, JONATHAN. *Sketches of the History of the Life and Adventures of Jonathan Plummer.* [?Bost., c1800]
Plymouth Church Rec. See COLONIAL SOCIETY OF MASSACHUSETTS
Plymouth Col. Rec. See NEW PLYMOUTH COLONY
Plymouth Laws. See NEW PLYMOUTH COLONY
PLYMOUTH, MASS. *Records of the Town.* Plymouth, 1889–1903. **v.d.**
The Pocumtuc Housewife. [Deerfield, Mass., 1906.] First publ. **1805**
POE, E. A. *Complete Works.* Ed. J. A. Harrison. [Virginia Ed.] N.Y. [1902]. Also: Ed. E. C. Stedman and G. E. Woodberry. N.Y., 1914. **=1894–5. v.d.**
Poker. See WELSH
POLK, J. K. *Diary.* Ed. M. M. Quaife. Chic., 1910. 4 vols. **v.d.**
Polk: The Diary of a President, 1845–1849. Ed. Allan Nevins. Lond., 1929. **v.d.**
POLLARD, E. A. *Southern History of the War.* N.Y., 1866. 2 vols. in 1
Southern History of the War. The First Year of the War. N.Y., 1863. First publ. 1862
Southern History of the War. The Third Year of the War. N.Y., 1865. **=1864**
Polly Peablossom. See BURKE, T. A.
POOL, MARIA L. *In Buncombe County.* Chic., 1896
Poor Will's Almanack. 1839. Phila. [?1838]. Includes: *Jonathan's Visit.* 1838
POORE, B. P. *Perley's Reminiscences of Sixty Years in the National Metropolis.* Phila. [1886]
POPE, JOHN. *A Tour through the Southern and Western Territories of the United States of North-America.* Richmond, 1792
POPKIN, J. S. *Memorial.* Ed. Cornelius Felton. Cambridge, 1852. **v.d.**
Popular Science Monthly. N.Y., 1872–current
Port Folio. Phila., 1801–27
PORTER, D. D. *Incidents and Anecdotes of the Civil War.* N.Y., 1886. **=1885**
PORTER, EDWARD C., ed. *The Songs of Yale.* New Haven, 1860
PORTER, ELEANOR (HODGMAN). *Just David.* N.Y., 1916
PORTER, GENE (STRATTON). *Freckles.* N.Y., 1904
The Girl of the Limberlost. N.Y., 1909
PORTER, HORACE. *West Point Life: An Anonymous Communication.* [N.Y., ?1859]
PORTER, J. A. *New Standard Guide of the City of Washington.* Wash., 1886
PORTER, WILLIAM SYDNEY. *Cabbages and Kings.* Lond., 1916. First publ.: N.Y., 1904. **v.d.**
The Four Million. Lond., 1916. (Page references from ed.: N.Y., 1915. **=1913.**) First publ.: N.Y., 1906. **v.d.**
Heart of the West. N.Y., 1927. **=1913.** First publ. 1907. **v.d.**
Options. N.Y. [1909]. Lond., 1916. (Page references altered.) Also publ.: N.Y., 1915. **=1913. v.d.**
Roads of Destiny. N.Y., 1909. Also publ.: N.Y., 1915. **=1913. v.d.**
Rolling Stones. N.Y., 1915, 1920. **=1912.** Lond. [n.d.]. (Page references from ed. 1912.) **v.d.**
Strictly Business. Lond. [n.d.]. First publ.: N.Y., 1910. **v.d.**
The Trimmed Lamp. N.Y., 1915. **=1907. v.d.**
PORTER, WILLIAM TROTTER, ed. *The Big Bear of Arkansas, and Other Sketches.* Phila. [Pref., 1845.] **v.d.** Includes: *The Great Kalamazoo Hunt. Chunkey's Fight with the Panthers* ed. *A Quarter Race in Kentucky and Other Sketches.* Phila. [cop. 1846, 1854]. First publ. 1846. **v.d.**
Porter's Spirit of the Times. N.Y., 1856–1860
PORTSMOUTH, R.I. *Early Records.* [Ed. A. Perry and C. S. Brigham.] Providence, 1901. **v.d.**
PORY, JOHN. *John Pory's Lost Description of Plymouth Colony.* Bost., 1918. 1622, c1622
POST, C. C. *Ten Years a Cowboy.* Chic., 1898. **=1896**
POST, C. F. See THWAITES
POST, W. K. *Harvard Stories.* N.Y., 1893

Post Express. Rochester, N.Y., 1859–1923
POTE, WILLIAM. *The Journal of Captain William Pote, Jr. during His Captivity in the French and Indian War.* N.Y., 1896. **v.d.**
POWER, TYRONE. *Impressions of America.* Lond., 1836
POWERS, STEPHEN. *Afoot and Alone.* Hartford, 1872
POYAS, ELIZABETH A. *A Peep into the Past.* Charleston, 1853
Practical Housekeeping. See WILCOX
PRAY, I. C. *Memoirs of James Gordon Bennett and His Times.* N.Y., 1855
PRENTICE, ARCHIBALD. *A Tour in the United States.* Manchester [Eng.] 1853. **1848**
PRESCOTT, G. B. *History, Theory, and Practice of the Electric Telegraph.* Bost., 1860. **v.d.**
The Speaking Telephone, Talking Phonograph, and Other Novelties. N.Y., 1878. Enlarged as: *The Speaking Telephone, Electric Light, and Other Recent Electrical Inventions.* N.Y., 1879
The Present State of the Country and Inhabitants . . . of Louisiana. Lond., 1744
President, Message to Congress, 1849. See U.S. CONGRESS. 31ST CONGRESS, 1 SESS. HOUSE
Presidents, Messages and Papers of the. See U.S. PRESIDENT
PRICE, THOMAS D., Welsh Hills, near Newark, Ohio. Excerpts from diaries, 1850 to 1898. MS. **v.d.**
PRIEST, WILLIAM. *Travels in the United States of America.* Lond., 1802. Written 1797
PRINCE SOCIETY. *Publications.* Bost., 1865–current. **v.d.** Vol. I.: W. WOOD. *New Eng. Prospect.* (q.v.). **1634.** Vols. V–VII: *The Andros Tracts.* **v.d.** Vol. XIV: T. MORTON. *New English Canaan* (q.v.). **1637.** Vol. XVII: J. W. DEAN, ed. *Capt. John Mason.* **v.d.** Vol. XIX: SIR F. GORGES. *A Briefe Narration . . . Especially, Showing the Beginning . . . of New England.* Running title: *A Description of New-England.* a1647
PRINCETON UNIVERSITY. *An Account of the College of New-Jersey.* Woodbridge, N.J., 1764
The Princeton Book. Bost., 1879. **v.d.**
PRINGLE, ELIZABETH W. (ALLSTON). *A Woman Rice Planter.* N.Y., 1913. **v.d.**
PRITTS, JOSEPH. *Mirror of Olden Time Border Life.* 2d ed. Abingdon, Va., 1849. Includes: A. S. WITHERS. *Chron. Border Warfare* (q.v.). 1831
PROVIDENCE, R.I. RECORD COMMISSIONERS. *Early Records.* Providence, 1892–1909. **v.d.**
Provincial Press Mass. See *An Historical Digest*
Publishers' Weekly. N.Y., 1872–current
PURCHAS, SAMUEL. *Pvrchas His Pilgrimage.* Lond., 1613
PURSH, FREDERICK. *Flora Americæ Septentrionalis.* Lond., 1814
PUSEY, W. A. *The Wilderness Road to Kentucky, Its Location and Features.* N.Y. [cop. 1921]. **v.d.**
PUTNAM, ELIZABETH H. L. *Mrs. Putnam's Receipt Book.* New and enl. ed. N.Y., 1869. **=1867**
PUTNAM, RUFUS. *Memoirs.* Bost., 1903. **v.d.**
Putnam's (Monthly) Magazine. N.Y., 1853–7; 1868–70. Vol. II includes: LOWELL. *Moosehead Jrnl.* 1853

Q

Quarter Race Ky. See PORTER, W. T.
QUICK, HERBERT. *Double Trouble.* Indianapolis [1906]
Yellowstone Nights. Indianapolis [cop. 1911]
QUINCY, JOSIAH. *The History of Harvard University.* Cambridge, 1840. **v.d.**
Quinland; or, Varieties in American Life. Lond., 1857
QUINN, A. H. *Pennsylvania Stories.* Phila., 1899
QUITMAN. See CLAIBORNE

R

R., I. *A Lady's Ranche Life in Montana.* Lond., 1887
RAE, W. F. *Westward by Rail.* N.Y., 1871. =Lond., 1870
'RAIMOND.' See ROBINS
RAINE, J. W. *The Land of Saddle-Bags.* Richmond, 1924
RAINE, W. M. *Brand Blotters.* N.Y. [cop. 1912]
Bucky O'Connor, a Tale of the Unfenced Border. N.Y. [cop. 1910]
Raleigh (N.C.) Register. [Weekly.] 1799–?
RAMSEY, J. G. M. *The Annals of Tennessee to the End of the Eighteenth Century.* Charleston, 1853. **v.d.**
RANDALL, H. S. *The Practical Shepherd.* Rochester, N.Y., 1864. **=1863**
Randolph, John, Life of. See GARLAND, H. A.
RANKIN, D. S. *Kate Chopin and Her Creole Stories.* Phila., 1932. **v.d.**

RANOUS, DORA K. (THOMPSON). *Diary of a Daly Débutante.* N.Y., 1910. **v.d.**
'RATTLEHEAD.' See BYRN, M. L.
RAUCK. See FILSON CLUB. *Filson Club Publications.* No. 16
RAWLINSON. See ROWLANDSON
RAYMOND, R. W. *A Glossary of Mining and Metallurgical Terms.* Easton, Pa., **1881**
Mines & Mining; Rep. Mines. See U.S. TREASURY DEPT. *Statistics*
Silver and Gold: An Account of the Mining and Metallurgical Industry of the United States. N.Y., **1873**
RAYNOLDS. See U.S. ENGINEER DEPT. *Report*
REA, CALEB. *Journal. . . . Written during the Expedition against Ticonderoga in 1758.* Ed. F. M. Ray. Salem, Mass., 1881. **1758.** See also ESSEX INSTITUTE
READ, O. P. *The Jucklins.* Chic. [cop. **1896**]
The Rebellion Record: A Diary of American Events. Ed. Frank Moore. N.Y., 1862–71. **v.d.**
Records of the Governor and Company of the Massachusetts Bay in New England. See MASSACHUSETTS (COLONY)
Records of the Moravians. See NORTH CAROLINA. HISTORICAL COMMISSION
REDFORD, A. H. *The History of Methodism in Kentucky.* Nashville, **1868–70**
REED, ANDREW, and MATHESON, JAMES. *A Narrative of the Visit to the American Churches, by the Deputation from the Congregational Union of England and Wales.* N.Y., **1835**
REED, W. B. *Life and Correspondence of Joseph Reed.* Phila., 1847. **v.d.**
REID, MAYNE. *The Scalp Hunters.* **1851**
REID, WHITELAW. *After the War.* Cinc., **1866**
Reinbeck (Iowa) *Times.* **1879–84?**
Relaçam verdadeira. 1557. Various translations: (1) RICHARD HAKLUYT. *Virginia Richly Valued.* Lond., **1609.** See also FORCE. *Tracts.* Vol. IV, No. 1. (2) [Anon.] *A Relation of the Invasion and Conquest of Florida . . . under the Command of Fernando de Soto.* Lond., **1686.** [Licenser: R. L'Estrange.] (3) BUCKINGHAM SMITH. *Narratives of the Career of Hernando de Soto in the Conquest of Florida.* N.Y., **1866**
A Relation of Maryland, Reprinted from the London Edition of 1635. Ed. F. L. Hawks. N.Y., 1865. **1635**
A Relation of the Invasion and Conquest of Florida. See *Relaçam verdadeira*
A Relation of the Successefull Beginnings of the Lord Baltemore's Plantation in Mary-Land. . . . 1634. [Albany, 1865.] **1634**
Relations des Jésuites. Québec, 1858. **v.d.**
Remarks on the Trial of J. P. Zenger, Printer of the New York Weekly Journal. Lond., **1738**
REMINGTON, FREDERICK. *Pony Tracks.* N.Y., **1895**
Report of the Commissioner of Agriculture. See U.S. DEPT. OF AGRICULTURE. *Report of the Secretary*
Report of the Commissioner of Education. See U.S. OFFICE OF EDUCATION
Report of the Commissioner of Fisheries. See U.S. BUREAU OF FISHERIES
Report of the Commissioner of Indian Affairs. See U.S. OFFICE OF INDIAN AFFAIRS
Report of the Commissioner of Patents. See U.S. PATENT OFFICE. *Annual Report*
Report of the Geological Survey. See U.S. GEOLOGICAL SURVEY
Report of the Joint Committee on Reconstruction. See U.S. CONGRESS. JOINT COMMITTEE
Report of the Secretary of Agriculture. See U.S. DEPT. OF AGRICULTURE
Report of the Secretary of the Navy. See U.S. NAVY DEPT. *Annual Report*
Report of the Secretary of the Treasury. See U.S. TREASURY DEPT. *Annual Report*
[Report on] *Fisheries of the United States, 1908.* See U.S. BUREAU OF THE CENSUS
Report on Prec. Metals. See U.S. BUREAU OF THE MINT
Report . . . on the Munitions of War. See NORTON, C. B., and VALENTINE, W. J.
Reports of Explor. R.R. Route. See U.S. WAR DEPT. *Reports*
Republic. Wash., **1849–53**
Republic: A Monthly Magazine. Wash., **1873–7**
Republican Review. Albuquerque, N.M., **1870–3**
REUTER. See NORTH CAROLINA. HISTORICAL COMMISSION
Review of Reviews. Lond., **1890–1936**
Review of Reviews. N.Y., **1890–1937.** (Also as: *American Review of Reviews*)
Revolutionary Diplom. Corr. See U.S. DEPT. OF STATE
REYNOLDS, JOHN. *The Pioneer History of Illinois.* Belleville, Ill., **1852**
REYNOLDS, JOSEPH. *Peter Gott, the Cape Ann Fisherman.* Bost., **1856**
RHODE ISLAND (COLONY). *Records.* Ed. J. R. Bartlett. Providence, 1856–65 **v.d.**
COURT OF TRIALS. *Rhode Island Court Records.* Providence, 1920–2. **v.d.**
Rhode Island Commerce. See *Commerce of Rhode Island*, under MASSACHUSETTS HISTORICAL SOCIETY. *Collections*
RHODE ISLAND HISTORICAL SOCIETY. *Collections.* Providence, 1827–1941. **v.d.** Vol. I: R. WILLIAMS. *Key* (q.v.). **1643.** Vol. VIII: J. COMER. *Diary.* Ed. C. E. Barrows and J. W. Willmarth. **v.d.**
Publications. 1893–1901. Providence, 1893–1900. **v.d.** Vol. VIII includes: R. WILLIAMS. *Ten Letters.* **v.d.**
Rhode Island Words. MS. (Bartlett Papers), John Carter Brown Lib., Providence, R.I. **1848.** See also *Dialect Notes*
RICE, ALICE C. (HEGAN). *Mr. Opp.* N.Y., **1909**
Mrs. Wiggs of the Cabbage Patch. N.Y., 1913. = **1901**
Sandy. N.Y., **1905**
RICH, O. O. *A Synopsis of the Genera of American Plants.* Georgetown, D.C., **1814**
RICHARDS, LAURA E. (HOWE). *Mrs. Tree.* Bost. [cop. **1902**]
RICHARDSON, A. D. *Beyond the Mississippi.* Hartford [cop. **1867**]
The Secret Service, the Field, the Dungeon, and the Escape. Hartford, 1866. =**1865**
RICHARDSON, C. F., and RICHARDSON, ELIZABETH M. (THOMAS). *Charles Miner, a Pennsylvania Pioneer.* Wilkes-Barre, Pa., 1916. **v.d.**
RICHARDSON, SIR JOHN, *et al. Fauna Boreali-Americana.* Lond., **1829–37.** Vol. II: SWAINSON AND RICHARDSON. *Birds.* **1831**
RIDEOUT, H. M. *The Key of the Fields, and Boldero.* N.Y., **1918**
RIIS, J. A. *The Making of an American.* N.Y., 1902. =**1901**
RILEY, H. H. *Puddleford, and Its People.* N.Y., **1854**
RILEY, J. W. *Eccentric Mr. Clark.* N.Y., **1913**
'The Old Swimmin'-Hole,' and 'Leven More Poems. Indianapolis, **1883**
Pipes o' Pan at Zekesbury. Indianapolis, **1889**
RINGWALT, J. L., ed. *American Encyclopædia of Printing.* Phila., **1871**
Rio Abajo Weekly Press. Albuquerque, N.M., **1863–4.** (Continued as: *New Mexico Press*)
RITCH, W. G. *Illustrated New Mexico.* 4th ed. Santa Fé **1883**
RITCHIE. See MOSES. *Representative Plays.* Vol. II
RITTENHOUSE, ISABELLA M. *Maud.* Ed. R. L. Strout. N.Y., 1939. **v.d.**
Riverside Nat. Hist. See KINGSLEY, J. S.
ROBB, J. S. *Streaks of Squatter Life.* See LEWIS, H. C. *The Swamp Doctor's Adventures*
ROBERTS, CECIL. *Adrift in America.* Lond., **1891**
ROBERTS, JOB. *The Pennsylvania Farmer.* Phila. **1804**
ROBERTS, WILLIAM. *An Account of the First Discovery and Natural History of Florida.* Lond., **1763**
ROBERTSON, HARRISON. *The Inlander.* N.Y., **1901**
Red Blood and Blue. N.Y., **1900**
ROBERTSON, MORGAN. *Land Ho!* N.Y., **1905**
'Where Angels Fear to Tread' and Other Tales of the Sea. N.Y., 1921. =**1899**
ROBINS, ELIZABETH. *The Magnetic North.* N.Y. [cop. **1904**]. 417 pp. Also: [Tauchnitz Ed.] Leipzig, **1904.** 2 vols.
ROBINSON, H. P. *Men Born Equal.* N.Y., **1895**
ROBINSON, J. S. *Sketches of the Great West. A Journal of the Santa-Fe Expedition.* Portsmouth [N.H.] **1848.** Also: [Ed.] C. L. Cannon. Princeton, 1932
ROBINSON, R. E. *Danvis Folks.* Bost., 1899. = **1894**
Uncle Lisha's Outing. Bost., 1898. =**1897**
ROBINSON, SARA T. D. (LAWRENCE). *Kansas: Its Interior and Exterior Life.* Bost., **1856**
ROBLEY, T. F. *History of Bourbon County, Kansas.* Fort Scott, Kan., **1894**
Rochester (N.Y.) *Post Express.* See *Post Express*
ROE, E. P. *Barriers Burned Away.* N.Y., **1872**
Nature's Serial Story. N.Y., 1885 [**1884**]. Also publ.: N.Y., 1902. (*Works*, Vol. I.)
ROE, FRANCES M. A. (MACK). *Army Letters from an Officer's Wife, 1871–1888.* N.Y., 1909. **v.d.**
ROGERS, J. See STONE, B. W.
ROGERS, ROBERT. *A Concise Account of North America.* Lond., **1765**
Journals of Major Robert Rogers. Lond., **1765**
Ponteach. Lond., **1766.** See also MOSES. *Representative Plays.* Vol. I
ROLLINS, ELLEN C. (HOBBS). *New England Bygones.* New ed. Phila., 1883. First publ. **1880**
ROLT-WHEELER, F. W. *The Boy with the U.S. Census.* Bost. [**1911**]
ROMANS, BERNARD. *A Concise Natural History of East and West Florida.* N.Y., 1776. =**1775**
ROOSEVELT, EDITH K. (CAROW), and ROOSEVELT, KERMIT, comps. *American Backlogs: The Story of Gertrude Tyler and Her Family 1660–1860.* N.Y., 1928. **v.d.**
ROOSEVELT, THEODORE. *The Wilderness Hunter.* N.Y., 1909. =**1893**
ROOT, N. W. T., and LOMBARD, J. K., comps. *Songs of Yale.* New Haven, **1853**
ROSIER, JAMES. *Rosier's Relation of Waymouth's Voyage to the Coast of Maine, 1605.* By H. S. Burrage. Portland, Me., 1887. **1605**
ROSS, J. H. *What I Saw in New-York.* Auburn, N.Y., **1851**
ROSS, T. See HUMBOLDT and BONPLAND
ROTHERT, O. A. *A History of Muhlenberg County.* Louisville, 1913. **v.d.**
ROUSO D'ERES, C. D. *Memoirs.* Exeter [N.H.] **1800**
ROWE, JOHN. *Letters and Diary of John Rowe, Boston Merchant, 1759–1762, 1764–1779.* Ed. A. R. Cunningham. Bost., 1903. **v.d.**
ROWLANDSON, MARY (WHITE). *The Soveraignty & Goodness of God . . . ; being a Narrative of the Captivity and Restauration of Mrs. Mary Rowlandson.* Cambridge, **1682**
ROWLEY, MASS. *Early Records. . . . 1639–1672.* Rowley, 1894. **v.d.**
Roxbury Land Rec. See BOSTON. REGISTRY DEPT.
Royal Gazette. [Semi-weekly.] Charleston, S.C., **1781–2**
ROYAL SOCIETY OF LONDON. *Philosophical Transactions.* Lond., 1665–current. **v.d.** Vol. XI includes: T. GLOVER. *Account of Virginia.* **1676.** Vols. XVII–XVIII, XLI include: CLAYTON. [*Accounts of Virginia*]. **v.d.**
ROYALL, ANNE (NEWPORT). *The Black Book.* Wash., **1828–9**
Letters from Alabama on Various Subjects. Wash., 1830. **v.d.**
Mrs. Royall's Pennsylvania; or, Travels Continued in the United States. Wash., **1829**
Mrs. Royall's Southern Tour; or, Second Series of the Black Book. Wash., **1830–1**
RUPP, I. D. *An Original History of the Religious Denominations at Present Existing in the United States.* Phila., **1844**
Rural Organization. See NATIONAL COUNTRY LIFE CONFERENCE
RUSSELL, OSBORNE. *Journal of a Trapper.* [Ed. L. A. York. 2d ed. Boise, Idaho] cop. 1921. **v.d.**
RUXTON, G. F. A. *Adventures in Mexico and the Rocky Mountains.* N.Y., 1848. First publ.: Lond., **1847.** Republ. in part as his: *Wild Life in the Rocky Mountains* (q.v.)
Life in the Far West. N.Y., 1849. Also publ. as: *In the Old West.* Ed. Horace Kephart. N.Y., 1924. =1915. First publ. **1848**
Wild Life in the Rocky Mountains. Ed. Horace Kephart. N.Y., 1924. =1916. (Chaps. xx–xxxvi, pp. 182–308, of his: *Adventures in Mexico* (q.v.). **1847**)
RYAN, MARAH E. (MARTIN). *A Pagan of the Alleghanies.* Chic. [cop. **1891**]
That Girl Montana. Chic. [cop. **1901**]
Told in the Hills. Chic. [cop. **1891**]

S

S. Lit. Messenger. See *Southern Literary Messenger*
SABINE, LORENZO. *Principal Fisheries of the American Seas.* 32d Congress, 2 Sess. House. Ex. Doc., No. 23. **1852**
SABRE, G. E. *Nineteen Months a Prisoner of War.* N.Y., **1865**
SAGE, R. B. *Rocky Mountain Life.* Bost., 1859. First publ. as: *Scenes in the Rocky Mountains.* Phila., **1846**
The St. Clair Papers. See SMITH, WILLIAM HENRY
'ST. JOHN.' See CRÈVECŒUR
St. Nicholas. N.Y., **1873–1940**
SALA, G. A. H. *America Revisited.* Lond., **1882.** Also publ. 1883, 1885
SALEM, MASS. *Town Records.* Salem, 1868–current. **v.d.**
Salem (Mass.) *Gazette.* **1781**
Salem (Mass.) *Gazette.* **1790–1908**
SALMONS, C. H., comp. *The Burlington Strike: Its Motives and Methods.* Aurora, Ill., **1889**
SALTUS, E. E. *The Paliser Case.* N.Y., **1919**
SANBORN, KATHERINE A. *A Truthful Woman in Southern California.* N.Y., 1900. =**1893**
SANDBURG, CARL. *Chicago Poems.* N.Y., **1916**
Cornhuskers. N.Y., **1918**
Slabs of the Sunburnt West. N.Y. [cop. **1922**]
Smoke and Steel. N.Y., **1920**
SANDS, R. C. *Writings . . . in Prose and Verse.* N.Y., 1834. **v.d.** Vol. I includes: EASTBURN and SANDS. *Yamoyden.* **1820.** See also EASTBURN, J. W., and SANDS, R. C.
SANFORD, PELEG. *Letter Book . . . 1666–1668.* Transcribed by H. W. Preston. Providence, 1928. **v.d.**
Sanitary Commission. See UNITED STATES SANITARY COMMISSION
Santa Fe Gazette. See *Santa Fe (Weekly) Gazette*
Santa Fe (N.M.) *New Mexican.* **1848**–current
Santa Fe (N.M.) *Republican.* **1847–?**
Santa Fe (N.M.) (*Weekly*) *Gazette.* **1851–69**
Santa Fé Weekly New Mexican and Live Stock Journal. See *New Mexican Review*

Sargent, C. S. *Report on the Forests of North America.* Wash., **1884**
Sargent, William M. *Maine Wills. 1640–1760.* Portland, 1887. **v.d.**
Sargent, Winthrop, 1753–1820. *Diary . . . during the Campaign of MDCCXCI.* Wormsloe [Ga.] 1851. **1791**
Sargent, Winthrop, 1825–70, ed. *The History of an Expedition against Fort Du Quesne, in 1755; under Major-General Edward Braddock.* Phila., **1855**
Saturday Review of Politics, Literature, Science and Art. Lond., **1855–1938**
Saunders, R. D. *Colonel Todhunter of Missouri.* N.Y. [cop. **1911**]
Savage, R. H. *The Midnight Passenger.* Lond., 1901 [**1900**]
Sawyer, Lorenzo. *Way Sketches.* Ed. Edward Eberstadt. N.Y., 1926. **1850**
Saxe, J. G. *Progress: A Satirical Poem.* N.Y., **1846**
'Scene Painter.' *The Emigrant's Guide.* Lond. **1816**
Schaff, Philip, ed. *A Religious Encyclopædia.* Edinb., 1883 [cop. **1882**]–**4**
Schaw, Janet. *Journal of a Lady of Quality.* Ed. E. W. Andrews and C. M. Andrews. New Haven, 1922. =1921. **v.d.**
Schoolcraft, H. R. *The American Indians.* New rev. ed. Rochester [N.Y.] **1851.** First publ. (in part) **1848**
Journal of a Tour into the Interior of Missouri and Arkansaw. Lond., 1821. **v.d.**
A View of the Lead Mines of Missouri. N.Y., **1819**
Schultz, Christian. *Travels on an Inland Voyage.* N.Y., 1810. **v.d.**
Scott, John, of Centreville, Ind. *The Indiana Gazetteer, or Topographical Dictionary.* 2d ed. Indianapolis, **1833**
Scottow, Joshua. See *Massachusetts, or the First Planters of New England*
Scribner's Magazine. N.Y., **1887–1939.** Vol. XV includes: J. G. Bourke. *The American Congo.* **1894**
Scribner's Monthly. N.Y., **1870–81.** Vols. XI–XII include: B. Harte. *Gabriel Conroy* (q.v.). **v.d.** Vols. XI–XIII include: E. E. Hale. *Philip Nolan's Friends.* **v.d.**
Scudder, H. E. *The Dwellers in Five-Sisters Court.* N.Y., **1876**
Sealsfield, Charles. *The Americans as They Are.* Lond., **1828**
Seccomb(e), John. *Father Abbey's Will.* **1731.** See also Winslow, O. E.
Secretary of Agriculture. See U.S. Dept. of Agriculture. *Report of the Secretary*
Sedgwick, Catherine M. *Tales and Sketches.* Phila., **1835.** 2d Series. N.Y., **1844**
Seitz, D. C. *Training for the Newspaper Trade.* Phila. [cop. **1916**]
Select Circulating Library. Phila., **1832–42.** (Also under title: *Waldie's Select Circulating Library*)
Sewall. *Diary; Letter-Book.* See Massachusetts Historical Society. *Collections*
The Selling of Joseph. See Massachusetts Historical Society. *Proceedings*
Seward, William. *Journal of a Voyage from Savannah to Philadelphia, and from Philadelphia to England.* Lond., **1740**
Shaw, H. W. *Josh Billings' Farmer's Allminax.* 1870–9. N.Y., 1870 [1869]–78. **v.d.**
Shaw, J. R. *A Narrative of the Life & Travels of John Robert Shaw, the Well-Digger. . . . Written by Himself.* [Louisville, 1930.] First publ. **1807**
Shecut, J. L. E. W. *Flora Carolinæensis.* Charleston, **1806**
Sheldon, George. *A History of Deerfield, Massachusetts.* Deerfield, 1895–6. **v.d.**
Sheldon, H. S., ed. *Documentary History of Suffield* [Conn.] . . . *1660–1749.* Springfield, Mass., 1879–88. **v.d.**
Shelton, Jane D. *The Salt-Box House: Eighteenth Century Life in a New England Hill Town.* N.Y., 1929. =1900. **v.d.**
Shepard, Thomas. *The Clear Sunshine of the Gospel Breaking Forth upon the Indians in New-England.* N.Y., 1865. First publ.: Lond., **1648.** See also Massachusetts Historical Society. *Collections*
Shepherd, William. *Prairie Experiences in Handling Cattle and Sheep.* Lond., **1884**
Sherburne, Andrew. *Memoirs.* 2d ed. Providence, **1831.** First publ. **1828**
Sheridan, P. H. *Personal Memoirs.* N.Y., **1888**
Sherman, W. T., and Sherman, John. *The Sherman Letters: Correspondence between General and Senator Sherman from 1837 to 1891.* Ed. R. S. Thorndike. N.Y., 1894. **v.d.**
Sherwood, Adiel. *Gazetteer of the State of Georgia.* Charleston, **1827.** 2d ed. Phila., **1829.** 3d ed. Wash., **1837**
Shields, J. D. *The Life and Times of Seargent Smith Prentiss.* Phila., **1883**
Shillaber, B. P. *Life and Sayings of Mrs. Partington.* N.Y., **1854**
Shinn, C. H. *The Story of the Mine.* N.Y., **1897**
Shirley. See Massachusetts (Colony). Governor; also *Memoirs of the Principal Transactions*
Shirreff, Patrick. *A Tour through North America.* Edinb., **1835**
Shuman, E. L. *Steps into Journalism.* Evanston, Ill., **1894**
Siddons, Leonora. *The Female Warrior.* Balt., 1844 [cop. **1843**]
Silliman, Benjamin. *Manual on the Cultivation of the Sugar Cane.* Wash., **1833**
Silliman's Journal. See *American Journal of Science*
Simmonds, P. L. *A Dictionary of Trade Products* [etc.]. Lond., **1858.** New ed. Lond. [**1867**]
Simmonds, W. See Smith, John. *Works*
Simms, W. G. *Border Beagles.* Phila., **1840.** 2 vols. New and rev. ed. N.Y., 1855. 495 pp.
Cabin and Wigwam. See his: *Wigwam and Cabin*
Charlemont; or, The Pride of the Village. N.Y., 1882. =**1856**
The Forayers; or, The Raid of the Dog-Days. Chic. [n.d.]. =**1855**
Guy Rivers. N.Y., **1834**
The Kinsmen. Phila., **1841.** Also publ. as: *The Scout.* New and rev. ed. Chic. [n.d.]. =**1854**
Mellichampe. **1836**
The Partisan. N.Y., **1835.** 2 vols. New and rev. ed. Chic. [n.d.]. =1854. 531 pp.
The Scout. See his: *The Kinsmen*
Southward Ho! N.Y., **1854**
The Sword and the Distaff. See his: *Woodcraft*
The Wigwam and the Cabin. N.Y., **1845.** 2 vols. (1st and 2d Ser.) in 1. Also publ. 1882 as: [*Works*, Vol. XVI]
Woodcraft; or, Hawks about the Desert. New and rev. ed. N.Y., 1854. 1st ed. as: *The Sword and the Distaff.* **1853**
The Yemassee. N.Y., **1835**
Simonin, L. L. *Le Grand-Ouest des États-Unis.* Paris, **1869**
Simpson, J. H. See U.S. Congress. 31st Congress, 1 Sess. Senate
Simpson, Stephen. *Biography of Stephen Girard, with His Will Affixed.* Phila., 1832. **v.d.**
Sinclair, Bertha (Muzzey). *Flying U Ranch.* N.Y. [cop. **1914**]
The Parowan Bonanza. Bost., **1923**
The Phantom Herd. Bost., **1916**
Sinclair, Sir John, Bart. *Correspondence.* Lond., 1831. **v.d.**
Sinclair, Upton. *King Coal.* N.Y., **1917**
The Metropolis. N.Y., **1908**
'Singleton, A.' See Knight, H. C.
Singleton, Esther. *Social New York under the Georges, 1714–1776.* N.Y., 1902. **v.d.**
Sketches and Eccentricities of Col. David Crockett, of West Tennessee. Louisville [n.d.]. =**1833**
'Slick, J.' See Stephens, A. S.
'Slick, S.' See Haliburton
Slocomb, William. *The American Calculator.* Phila., **1831**
Smedes, Susan (Dabney). *Memorials of a Southern Planter.* 3d ed. Balt., 1888. =**1887**
Smet, P. J. de. *Oregon Missions and Travels over the Rocky Mountains in 1845.* N.Y., 1847. **v.d.**
Smith, B. See *Relaçam verdadeira*
Smith, C. H. *Bill Arp, So Called. A Side Show of the Southern Side of the War.* N.Y., **1866**
Smith, Edward. *Account of a Journey through North-eastern Texas.* Lond., **1849**
Smith, Eliakin [*et al.*]. *Account Books.* In Judd MSS., Forbes Lib., Northampton, Mass. **v.d.**
Smith, Elihu H. See *American Poems*
Smith, Eugene A. See Alabama. Geological Survey
Smith, F. H. *Caleb West, Master Diver.* Bost., **1898**
Smith, James. *An Account of the Remarkable Occurrences in the Life and Travels of Col. James Smith . . . during His Captivity with the Indians.* Lexington [Ky.] **1799.** Also publ.: Cinc., 1870
Smith, John. *Works.* Ed. Edward Arber. Birmingham [Eng.] 1884. New ed. by A. G. Bradley as: *Travels and Works.* Edinb., 1910. **v.d.** Includes: *A True Relation of . . . Occurrences and Accidents . . . in Virginia* (also cited as: *Newes from Virginia*). **1608.** *A Map of Virginia. With a Description of the Countrey* [Part II: W. Simmonds. *The Proceedings of the English Colonie in Virginia*]. **1612.** *A Description of New England.* **1616.** *The Generall Historie of Virginia* (q.v.). **1624.** *Advertisements for the Unexperienced Planters of New-England, or Anywhere. Or, The Path-Way to Experience to Erect a Plantation* (q.v.). **1631**
Advertisements for the Unexperienced Planters of New-England, or Anywhere. Or, The Path-Way to Experience to Erect a Plantation. Lond., **1631.** See also Massachusetts Historical Society. *Collections.* See also his: *Works*
A Description of New England. See his: *Works.* See also Force. *Tracts.* Vol. II, No. 1
The Generall Historie of Virginia, New-England, and the Summer Isles. Lond., **1624.** See also his: *Works*
Newes from Virginia. See his: *Works*
The Path-Way to Experience. See his: *Advertisements*
Smith, J. J. See Michaux, F. A.
Smith, M. H. *Sunshine and Shadow in New York.* Hartford, **1868**
Twenty Years among the Bulls and Bears of Wall Street. N.Y., 1871. =**1870**
Smith, Samuel S. *An Essay on the Causes of the Variety of Complexion and Figure in the Human Species.* Edinb., 1788. First publ.: Phila., **1787**
Smith, Seba. *Jack Downing's Letters.* Phila. [cop. **1845**]. Also under title: *May-Day in New-York.* N.Y., **1845**
The Life and Writings of Major Jack Downing. 2d ed. Bost., 1834. =1st ed. 1833. **v.d.**
(Supposed author.) *The Life of Andrew Jackson.* See 'Downing'
Major Downing. 1830, 1831, 1832, 1833, or 1834: see his: *The Select Letters.* 1830–3: see Davis, C.
(Supposed author.) *Major Jack Downing.* (*Northern Humour.*) See *Major Jack Downing*
May-Day in New-York. See his: *Jack Downing's Letters*
My Thirty Years Out of the Senate. N.Y., 1859. **v.d.**
The Select Letters of Major Jack Downing. Phila., 1834. (Pirated.) **v.d.**
'Way Down East. N.Y., 1856. =**1854**
Smith, Solomon F. *Autobiog.* See his: *Theatrical Management*
The Theatrical Apprenticeship and Anecdotical Recollections of Sol. Smith. Phila., **1846**
Theatrical Management in the West and South for Thirty Years. Interspersed with Anecdotical Sketches Autobiographically Given by Sol. Smith. N.Y., **1868**
Smith, Thomas. *Journals of the Rev. Thomas Smith, and the Rev. Samuel Deane.* [Ed.] William Willis. [2d ed.] Portland [Me.] 1849. **v.d.**
Smith, William Hawley. *The Promoters.* Chic. [**1904**]
Smith, William Henry. *The St. Clair Papers.* Cinc., 1882. **v.d.**
Smith, William Prescott. *The Book of the Great Railway Celebrations of 1857.* N.Y., **1858**
Smith, Z. F. *The History of Kentucky.* Louisville, 1886. Also: Centennial Ed. Louisville, 1892. **v.d.**
Smithsonian Institution. *Annual Report of the Board of Regents.* [1846]–current. Wash., **1847**–current. (Part II, 1884–current, issued as: U.S. National Museum. *Report*)
Smithtown, N.Y. *Records.* [Huntington, N.Y., 1898.] **v.d.**
Smithwick, Noah. *The Evolution of a State; or, Recollections of Old Texas Days.* Comp. N. S. Donaldson. Austin, Tex. [**1900**]
Smyth, J. F. D. *A Tour in the United States of America.* Lond., **1784**
Snake County Talk. See *Dialect Notes*
Society for the Promotion of Useful Arts. *Transactions.* Albany, **1792–1919.** Vol. I publ. as: *Transactions of the Society . . . for the Promotion of Agriculture, Arts, and Manufactures*
Songs of Yale. 1853: see Root and Lombard. 1860: see Porter, E. C.
Soulé, Frank, *et al. The Annals of San Francisco.* N.Y., **1855**
Sources of the History of Oregon. [Ed. F. G. Young.] Eugene, Ore., 1897–9. Part I: M. Crawford. *Journal.* **1842.** Part II: L. Kip. *Indian Council Walla Walla.* **1855.** Parts III–VI: N. Wyeth. *Correspondence and Journals.* **v.d.**
South-Atlantic. Wilmington, N.C., **1877–?82**
South Atlantic Quarterly. Durham, N.C., **1902**–current
South Carolina Historical and Genealogical Magazine. Charleston, **1900**–current
South Carolina, Historical Collections of. See Carroll, B. R.
South Carolina Historical Society. *Collections.* Charleston, 1857–[9]. **v.d.**
South Dakota Historical Collections. Pierre, **1902**–current
South Dakotan. Mitchell, **1898–1904.** (Also as: *Monthly South Dakotan*)
South Florida Sentinel. Orlando, Fla., **1885–?1918**
Southampton, N.Y. *Records of the Town.* Sag Harbor, N.Y., 1874–1915. **v.d.**
Southern Literary Messenger. Richmond, Va., **1834–64**
Southold, N.Y. *Southold Town Records.* [Ed.] J. W. Case. [N.Y.] 1882–4. **v.d.**
Spalding's (Official) Base Ball Guide. N.Y., **1878–1914**
Sparks, Jared. *The Life of Gouverneur Morris, with Selections from His Correspondence and Miscellaneous Papers.* Bost., 1832. **v.d.**
Speed. See Filson Club. *Filson Club Publications.* No. 9
The Spirit of the Farmers' Museum. See Farmers' Museum

Spirit of the Times. N.Y. See *Spirit of the Times: A Chronicle;* see also *Porter's Spirit of the Times*

Spirit of the Times. Phila., **1838–?51**

Spirit of the Times: A Chronicle of the Turf. N.Y., **1831–61**

Springer, J. S. *Forest Life and Forest Trees*. N.Y., **1851**

Springfield, Mass. *The First Century of the History of Springfield: The Official Records from 1636 to 1736*. Springfield, 1898–9. **v.d.**

Springfield (Mass.) *(Daily) Republican*. **1844**–current

Springfield (Mass.) *(Weekly) Republican*. **1824**–current

Stacey, May Humphreys. *Uncle Sam's Camels: The Journal of May Humphreys Stacey*. Ed. L. B. Lesley. Cambridge, 1929. **v.d.**

Standard Guide of Washington. See Porter, J. A.

Standard Nat. Hist. See Kingsley, J. S.

Stansbury, H. See U.S. Engineer Dept. *Exploration*

Stansbury, Joseph, and Odell, Jonathan. *Loyal Verses*. Ed. Winthrop Sargent. Albany, 1860. **v.d.**

Stapleton, Patience. *The Major's Christmas, and Other Stories*. Denver, **1886**

State of the British and French Colonies in North America, with Respect to Number of People [etc.]. Lond., **1755**

A State of the Province of Georgia. See Georgia Historical Society. *Collections*. Vol. II

State Papers and Publick Documents of the United States. 2d[–3d] ed. Bost., 1817–9. **v.d.** See also U.S. Congress. *American State Papers*

Statutes at Large. See U.S. Laws, Statutes, etc.

Steamboat Disasters. See Howland

Steedman, C. J. *Bucking the Sagebrush*. N.Y., **1904**

Steele, Eliza R. *A Summer Journey in the West*. N.Y., **1841**

Steele, W. D. *Storm*. N.Y., **1914**

Steele Papers. See North Carolina. Historical Commission

Stephens, Alexander H. *Recollections . . . : His Diary . . . at Fort Wilson, Boston Harbour, 1865*. Ed. M. L. Avary. N.Y., 1910. **1865**

Stephens, Ann S. (Winterbotham). *High Life in New York*. By Jonathan Slick. Lond., 1844. First publ. **1843**

Married in Haste. N.Y. [cop. 1890]. =**1870**

Stephens, W. *Proc. Georgia*. See *The Colonial Records of the State of Georgia*

State of Province of Georgia. See Georgia Historical Society. *Collections*. Vol. II

Stevens, I. N. *The Liberators*. N.Y., **1908**

Stevens, J. See Essex Institute

Stevens, P. See Mereness

Stevenson. See U.S. Geographical Surveys

Stewart, C. D. *Partners of Providence*. Bost., **1907**

Stewart, Elinore (Pruitt). *Letters of a Woman Homesteader*. Bost., **1914**

Stewart, Sir W. G. D. 7th Bart. *Altowan; or, Incidents of Life and Adventure in the Rocky Mountains*. Ed. J. W. Webb. N.Y., **1846**

Stiles, Ezra. *Extracts from the Itineraries and Other Miscellanies of Ezra Stiles*. Ed. F. B. Dexter. New Haven, 1916. **v.d.**

Literary Diary. Ed. F. B. Dexter. N.Y., 1901. **v.d.**

Stillman, W. J. *The Autobiography of a Journalist*. Bost., **1901**

Stimpson's Boston Directory. See *Boston Directory*

Stock Grower and Farmer. Las Vegas, N.M., **1890**

Stockton, F. R. *Afield and Afloat*. N.Y., **1900**

The Casting Away of Mrs. Lecks and Mrs. Aleshine. N.Y. [cop. **1886**]. See also *Century Magazine*

The Dusantes. N.Y. [cop. **1888**]. See also *Century Magazine*

The Hundredth Man. See *Century Magazine*

Rudder Grange. N.Y., 1907. =**1879**

Stoddard, Amos. *Sketches, Historical and Descriptive, of Louisiana*. Phila., **1812**

Stoddard, W. O. *Esau Hardery*. N.Y., **1881**

Stone, B. W. *The Biography of Eld. Barton Warren Stone, Written by Himself*. [Ed.] John Rogers. Cinc., 1847. **v.d.**

Stone, E. M. *The Life and Recollections of John Howland*. Providence, **1857**

Storer. See Massachusetts. Zoological and Botanical Survey. *Reports on the Fishes*

Stork, William. *An Account of East-Florida*. Lond. **[1766]**. Includes: J. Bartram. *Journal*. **v.d.**

Stowe, Harriet E. (Beecher). *Betty's Bright Idea. Also, Deacon Pitkin's Farm, and the First Christmas of New England*. N.Y., 1876. **v.d.**

Dred: A Tale of the Great Dismal Swamp. Bost., **1856**. Lond., **1856**

The First Christmas. See her: *Betty's Bright Idea*

House and Home Papers. Bost., 1865. First publ. **1864**

A Key to Uncle Tom's Cabin. Bost., **1853**. Lond., **1853**

The Mayflower. N.Y., 1844. =**1843**

The Minister's Wooing. **1859**

Oldtown Folks. Bost., **1869**

The Pearl of Orr's Island. Lond., **1861–2**

Pink and White Tyranny. Bost., **1871**

Poganuc People. N.Y. [cop. **1878**]

Sam Lawson's Oldtown Fireside Stories. Bost. [cop. **1871**]

Uncle Tom's Cabin. **1852**

We and Our Neighbors. N.Y. [cop. **1875**]

Strachey, William. *The Historie of Travaile into Virginia Britannia*. Ed. R. H. Major. Lond., 1849. Written *c***1618**

Stratton-Porter. See Porter, G.

Stray Subjects. See Durivage and Burnham

Strickland, William. *Observations on the Agriculture of the United States of America*. Lond., **1801**

Strickland, W. P. See Cartwright

Strong, G. C. *Cadet Life at West Point*. Bost., **1862**

Strong, L. See Hall, C. C.

Strother, D. H. *The Blackwater Chronicle*. See Kennedy, P. P.

Virginia Illustrated. N.Y., **1857**

Struggles of Capt. Thomas Keith in America. Lond. **[?1808]**

Stuart, Granville. *Forty Years on the Frontier*. Ed. P. C. Phillips. Cleveland, 1925. *a***1918**

Stuart, James. *Three Years in North America*. Edinb., **1833**

Stuart, Ruth (McEnery). *In Simpkinsville*. N.Y., **1897**

The River's Children. N.Y., **1904**

Stuart-Wortley, Emmeline C. E. (Manners). *Travels in the United States*. N.Y., **1851**

Sturge, Joseph. *A Visit to the United States in 1841*. Lond., **1842**

Sturtevant, E. L. *Notes on Edible Plants*. Albany, **1919**

Sudworth, G. B. *Nomenclature of the Arborescent Flora of the United States*. Wash., **1897**

Suffield Doc. Hist. See Sheldon, H. S.

Suffolk Co., Mass. *Suffolk Deeds*. Bost., 1880–1906. **v.d.**

Sullivan, T. R. *The Heart of Us*. Bost., **1912**

Summers, L. P. *Annals of Southwest Virginia, 1769–1800*. Abingdon, Va., 1929. **v.d.** Includes: C. Coale. *W. Waters*. **1878**

History of Southwest Virginia, 1746–1786, Washington County, 1777–1870. Richmond, 1903. **v.d.**

Sumner, Charles. *The Scholar, the Jurist, the Artist, the Philanthropist*. Bost., **1846**

Sun. Balt., **1837**–current

Sutcliff, Robert. *Travels in Some Parts of North America*. 2d ed. York [Eng.] 1815. First publ. **1811**

Swainson. See Richardson, J.

Swasey, W. F. *The Early Days and Men of California*. Oakland [Calif., **1891**]

Sweet, A. E., and Knox, J. A. *On a Mexican Mustang through Texas*. Lond., 1884. =1st ed. Hartford, **1883**

Sketches from 'Texas Siftings.' N.Y., **1882**

T

Taber, E. M. *Stowe Notes, Letters and Verses*. Bost., 1913. **1890–3**

Taitt. See Mereness

Talbot, Theodore. *Journals . . . , 1843 and 1849–52*. Ed. C. H. Carey. Portland, Ore., 1913. **v.d.**

Talbot, Sir William, tr. *The Discoveries of John Lederer, in Three Several Marches from Virginia*. Rochester, N.Y., 1902. First publ.: Lond., **1672**

Talcott Papers. See Connecticut Historical Society

Tall Tales. See Meine

Talmage, T. D. *Abominations of Modern Society*. N.Y., **1872**

Sermons . . . Delivered in the Brooklyn Tabernacle. Lond., **1872**

Tarbell, Ida M. *The History of the Standard Oil Company*. N.Y., 1904. **v.d.**

Tarkington, Booth. *The Gentleman from Indiana*. **1899**

Tatham, William. *Communications concerning the Agriculture and Commerce of the United States of America: Being an Auxiliary to a Report Made by W. Strickland . . . to the Board of Agriculture*. Lond., **1800**

An Historical and Practical Essay on the Culture and Commerce of Tobacco. Lond., **1800**

Taylor, Bayard. *Eldorado*. Lond., **1850**. Also publ.: N.Y., 1862

Hannah Thurston: A Story of American Life. N.Y., 1864. =**1863**

Taylor, Benjamin F. *Between the Gates*. Chic., **1878**

January and June. N.Y., 1854. Also: N.Y., 1871. =**1853**

Summer-Savory, Gleaned from Rural Nooks in Pleasant Weather. Chic., **1879**

The World on Wheels. Chic., **1874**

Taylor, J. L. B. *Snake County Talk*. See *Dialect Notes*

Taylor, John. *Arator*. 2d ed. Georgetown, D.C., **1814**. 4th–6th eds. Petersburg [Va.] **1818**

Taylor, W. M. *David, King of Israel*. **1874**

Temple, J. H., and Sheldon, George. *A History of the Town of Northfield, Massachusetts, for 150 Years*. Albany, 1875. **v.d.**

Terhune, Mary V. (Hawes). *Common Sense in the Household*. N.Y., **1884**. =1881

The Empty Heart; or, Husks. 'For Better, for Worse.' N.Y., 1871. Contains: *Husks*. **1863**. *For Better, for Worse*. **1870**

Eve's Daughters. N.Y., **1882**

Teuffel, Blanche W. (Howard) von. *One Summer*. **1875**

Texas (Republic). *Diplomatic Correspondence*. See American Historical Association

Texas Almanac and State Industrial Guide. 1857–current. Galveston, 1856–current. **v.d.**

'Texian.' See Ganilh

Thacher, James. *A Military Journal . . . from 1775 to 1783*. Bost., 1823. **v.d**

'Thanet.' See French, Alice

Thaxter, A. W. *A Poem Delivered before the Iadma of Harvard College*. Cambridge, **1850**

Thaxter, Celia (Laighton). *Among the Isles of Shoals*. Bost., 1885. =**1873**

Poems for Children. Bost., 1884 [cop. **1883**]

Thayer, W. M. *From Log Cabin to the White House*. Norwich, Conn., **1882**

Thoburn, J. B. *A Standard History of Oklahoma*. Chic., 1916. 5 vols. **v.d.**

Thomas, Augustus. *Arizona*. Chic. [cop. **1899**]

The Witching Hour. See Moses. *Representative American Dramas*

Thomas, F. W. *John Randolph, of Roanoke*. Phila., **1853**

Thomas, Gabriel. *An Historical and Geographical Account of the Province and Country of Pensilvania; and of West-New-Jersey in America*. Lond., **1698**. Reprinted, page for page: [N.Y., 1848]. (Part II., sep. paged, as: *An Historical Description of the Province and Country of West-New-Jersey in America*.) Also publ. as: *An Account of Pennsylvania and West New Jersey*. Cleveland, 1903

Thomas, I. See Deane, Samuel. *The New-England Farmer*

Thompson, D. P. *The Adventures of Timothy Peacock*. Middlebury [Vt.] **1835**

The Green Mountain Boys. Rev. ed. Bost., 1848. 2 vols. in 1. 11–170, 171–364 pp. Also: N.Y. [n.d.]. 360 pp. First publ. 1839. **1840**

Locke Amsden. Bost., **1848**. =1847

Thompson, Maurice. *Byways and Bird Notes*. N.Y., **1885**

Thompson, M. N. See Thomson

Thompson, W. T. *Chronicles of Pineville*. Phila., 1849. =**1845**

Major Jones's Courtship. Rev. and enl. N.Y., 1872. First publ., in part, 1843. **v.d.**

Major Jones's Courtship and Travels. Phila. [1857]. Includes, separately paged: *Major Jones's Courtship*. First publ., in part, 1843. **v.d.** *Major Jones's Sketches of Travel*. =**1848**

Thompson, Zadock. *History of Vermont, Natural, Civil and Statistical*. Burlington [Vt.] **1842**

Thompson Street Poker Club. See Carleton, H. G.

Thomson, M. N. *Doesticks' Letters: And What He Says*. Phila. [cop. **1855**]. Also as: *Doesticks: What He Says*. N.Y., **1855**

Plu-ri-bus-tah. N.Y., **1856**

Thoreau, H. D. *Writings*. Riverside Ed. Bost., 1894 [1893]. **v.d.** Vol. I: *A Week on the Concord and Merrimack Rivers* (q.v.). **1849**. Vol. III: *The Maine Woods* (q.v.) **v.d.** Also: Walden Ed. Bost., 1906. **v.d.** Vols. VII–XX: *Journal*. Vols. I–XIV. Ed. Bradford Torrey. **v.d.**

Autumn. . . . Ed. by H. G. O. Blake. Bost.; N.Y., **1892**

Cape Cod. Bost., 1865. **v.d.**

Excursions. Bost., 1863. *a***1862**

Journal. See his: *Writings*, Walden Ed.

The Maine Woods. Bost., 1864. Also publ. 1891. **v.d.** See also his: *Writings*, Riverside Ed.

Walden. Bost., **1854**

A Week on the Concord and Merrimack Rivers. Bost., 1862. =**1849**. Also: New and rev ed. Bost., 1879. =1868 [cop. 1867]. See also his: *Writings*, Riverside Ed.

A Yankee in Canada, with Anti-Slavery and Reform Papers. Bost., 1866. *a***1862**

Thornton, R. H. *An American Glossary*. Phila., 1912. 2 vols. **v.d.** For Vol. III (supplement) see *Dialect Notes*

Thorpe, T. B. *The Mysteries of the Backwoods*. Phila., **1846** [1845]

Thwaites, R. G., ed. *Early Western Travels, 1748–1846*. Cleveland, 1904–7. **v.d.** 32 vols. Includes: M. Birkbeck. *Extract of a Letter*. **1821** (Vol. X). T. Buttrick. *Voyages, Travels, and Discoveries*. **1831** (Vol. VIII). G. Croghan. *Journal* (q.v.). **1765** (Vol. I). E. Evans. *Pedestrious Tour*. **1819** (Vol. VIII). T. J. Farn-

HAM. *Travels in the Great Western Prairies.* **1841** (Vols. XXVIII–XXIX). E. FLAGG. *The Far West.* **1838** (Vols. XXVI–XXVII). J. FLINT. *Letters from America* (q.v.). **v.d** (Vol. IX). R. FLOWER. *Letters.* **v.d.** (Vol. X). T. HULME. *Journal.* **v.d.** (Vol. X.) E. JAMES, comp. *Account of an Expedition* (q.v.). **1823** (Vols. XIV–XVII). T. NUTTALL. *Travels into the Arkansas Territory* (q.v.). **1821** (Vol. XIII). J. PALMER. *Journal of Travels over the Rocky Mountains.* **1847** (Vol. XXX). J. O. PATTIE. *Personal Narrative* (q.v.). **1831** (Vol. XVIII). C. F. POST. *Journal.* **v.d.** (Vol. I). J. K. TOWNSEND. *Narrative.* **1839** (Vol. XXI). C. WEISER. *Journal.* **1748** (Vol. I). J. WOODS. *Two Years' Residence . . . on the English Prairie* (q.v.). **1822** (Vol X). J. B. WYETH. *Oregon.* **1833** (Vol. XXI)

TICE, J. H. *Over the Plains.* St. Louis, Mo., **1872**

TICKNOR, GEORGE. *Life, Letters and Journals.* Bost., 1876. **v.d.**

TILGHMAN, Z. A. *The Dugout.* Oklahoma City, **1925**

TIMBERLAKE, HENRY. *The Memoirs of Lieut. Henry Timberlake.* Lond., **1765**

TODD, H. C. *Notes upon Canada and the United States of America.* Toronto, **1835**

TODD, JOHN. *The Student's Manual.* 3d ed. Northampton, **1835**

Tom Pepper. See BRIGGS

TOMES, ROBERT. *The Bazar Book of Decorum.* N.Y. [cop. **1870**]

TOMLINSON, ABRAHAM, comp. *The Military Journals of Two Private Soldiers, 1758–1775.* Poughkeepsie [N.Y.] 1855. **v.d.**

TOMPKINS, JULIET W. *Mothers and Fathers.* N.Y., **1910**

TOMPSON, BENJAMIN. *Benjamin Tompson, 1642–1714. . . . His Poems Collected with an Introduction by Howard Judson Hall.* Bost., 1924. **v.d.** Includes: *New-Englands Crisis.* **1676**

TOPSFIELD, MASS. *Town Records.* 1659–1778. Topsfield, 1917–20. **v.d.**

TORREY, BRADFORD. *A Florida Sketch-Book.* Bost., **1894**

The Foot-Path Way. Bost., 1893. **=1892**

TORREY, JOHN. *Flora N.Y.* See NEW YORK (STATE). NATURAL HISTORY SURVEY

TOULMIN, HARRY. *A Description of Kentucky, in North America.* Lond., **1792**

TOURGEE, A. W. *Bricks without Straw.* N.Y. [cop. **1880**]

Button's Inn. Bost., **1887**

A Fool's Errand. New, enl. ed. N.Y. [cop. **1880**]. 1st ed. **1879.** Part II: *The Invisible Empire.* **1880**

A Royal Gentleman. . . . And 'Zouri's Christmas. N.Y. [cop. **1881**]. *A Royal Gentleman* first publ. 1874 as: *Toinette.* Written 1868–9. **1869**

Toinette; 'Zouri's Christmas. See his: *A Royal Gentleman*

Town and Country Magazine. Lond., **1769–96**

TOWNSEND, G. A. *The Mormon Trials at Salt Lake City.* N.Y., **1871**

TOWNSEND, J. K. See THWAITES

TOXHALL. *Inventories of Toxhall's Estate, Bertie Co., N.C.* MS., N.C. Historical Commission, Raleigh. **c1728**

Tragedies of the Wilderness. See DRAKE, S. G.

Travels Amer. Col. See MERENESS

The Travels of Capts. Lewis and Clarke. Lond., **1809**

TRENT, WILLIAM. *Journal . . . A.D. 1752.* Ed. A. T. Goodman. Cinc., 1871. **1752**

Triangle. Pub. by Physical Department of Y.M.C.A. Training School, Springfield, Mass. Springfield, **1891–2**

Tribune Almanac. 1838–1914. N.Y., 1838–1913. Also as: *Whig Almanac.* Issues 1838–54 read in photolithographic reprod. under title: *The Tribune Almanac for the Years 1838 to 1868, Inclusive.* N.Y., 1868. Vol. I. **v.d.**

TRIPP, G. H. *Student-Life at Harvard.* Bost., **1876**

TROBRIAND, P. R. D. DE K., Comte de. *Vie militaire dans le Dakota . . . (1867–1869).* Paris, 1926. **v.d.**

TROLLOPE, ANTHONY. *North America.* Lond., **1862**

TROLLOPE, FRANCES (MILTON). *Domestic Manners of the Americans.* Lond., **1832**

TROWBRIDGE, J. T. *Cudjo's Cave.* Bost., **1864**

Trübner's American and Oriental Literary Record. Lond., **1865–90**

TRUMBULL, GURDON. *Names and Portraits of Birds Which Interest Gunners.* N.Y., **1888**

TRUMBULL, JAMES R. *History of Northampton, Massachusetts, from Its Settlement in 1654.* Northampton, 1898–1902. **v.d.**

TRUMBULL, JOHN. *Autobiography, Reminiscences and Letters.* N.Y., 1841. **v.d.**

M'Fingal. Bost., 1785. Also: Ed. B. J. Lossing. N.Y., 1881. **v.d.**

The Progress of Dulness. Exeter [N.H.] 1794. **v.d.**

TUCKERMAN. See HONE

TUDOR, WILLIAM. *Letters on the Eastern States.* N.Y., **1820**

The Life of James Otis, of Massachusetts. Bost., 1823. **v.d.**

'TWAIN.' See CLEMENS

TWINING, THOMAS. *Travels in America 100 Years Ago.* N.Y., 1894. **a1800**

Travels in India a Hundred Years Ago, with a Visit to the United States. Ed. W. H. G. Twining. Lond., 1893. **a1800**

TYLER, L. G. *The Letters and Times of the Tylers.* Richmond, 1884–96. **v.d.**

TYLER, ROYALL. *The Contrast.* Ed. T. J. McKee. N.Y., 1887. First publ.: Phila., 1790. First perf.: **1787.** See also MOSES. *Representative Plays.* Vol. I

The Yankey in London. N.Y., **1809**

TYLER, W. S. *History of Amherst College during Its First Half Century. 1821–1871.* Springfield, Mass., **1873.** Rev. ed. [1821–91]. **1895**

Typographical Journal. Indianapolis, **1889**–current

TYSON, J. L. *Diary of a Physician in California.* N.Y., **1850**

U

'Uncle Rufus' and 'Ma,' the Story of a Summer Jaunt. [?Chic.] **1882**

'UNCLE SAM.' *Uncle Sam's Peculiarities.* Lond. [**1844**]. (See also *Bentley's Miscellany.*) Based partly on material from *Ainsworth's Magazine* (q.v.)

UNDERHILL, E. F., and THOMSON, MORTIMER *The History and Records of the Elephant Club.* N.Y., **1857**

UNDERHILL, J. See MASSACHUSETTS HISTORICAL SOCIETY. *Collections*

U.S. BUREAU OF AMERICAN ETHNOLOGY. *Annual Report.* 1879/80–current. Wash., 1881–current. **v.d.**

U.S. BUREAU OF FISHERIES. *Report of the Commissioner.* 1871/2–current. Wash., 1873–current. **v.d.**

U.S. BUREAU OF FOREIGN COMMERCE. *Consular Reports. Commerce, Manufactures, etc.* Wash., **1880–1903**

U.S. BUREAU OF THE CENSUS. *Fisheries of the United States, 1908.* Wash., **1911**

U.S. BUREAU OF THE MINT. *Report of the Director of the Mint upon the Statistics of the Production of the Precious Metals* [1881]. Wash., **1882.** (Also publ. as: 47th Congress, 1 Sess. House. Ex. Doc. No. 216. Erroneously cited as: C. KING. *Rep. Precious Metals*)

U.S. COMMISSIONER OF EDUCATION. See U.S. OFFICE OF EDUCATION

U.S. CONGRESS. *American State Papers.* Wash., 1832–61. **v.d.**

The Congressional Globe. 1833–73. Wash., 1834–73. **v.d.**

Congressional Record. Wash., 1873–current. **v.d.**

The Debates and Proceedings in the Congress of the United States. 1789–1824. Wash., 1834–56. **v.d.** (Cited as: *Annals . . . Congress*)

Official Congressional Directory. Wash., **1809**–current

Register of Debates in Congress. 1824–37. Wash., 1825–37. **v.d.**

JOINT COMMITTEE ON RECONSTRUCTION. *Report.* Wash., **1866**

JOINT SELECT COMMITTEE ON THE CONDITION OF AFFAIRS IN THE LATE INSURRECTIONARY STATES. *Report.* Wash., 1872. **v.d.**

HOUSE. COMMITTEE ON CAUSES OF REDUCTION OF AMERICAN TONNAGE. *Causes of the Reduction of American Tonnage and the Decline of Navigation Interests.* Wash., **1870**

31ST CONGRESS, 1 SESS. HOUSE. *Ex. Doc.* No. 5. *Message from the President of the United States to the Two Houses of Congress.* **1849.** Part I: 850 pp. Part II: 1–370, 937–1215 pp. Part III: 371–935 pp.

31ST CONGRESS, 1 SESS. SENATE. *Ex. Doc.* No. 64. 24 Jan. 1850. Includes: J. H. SIMPSON. *Journal of a Military Reconnaissance from Santa Fe, New Mexico, to the Navajo Country.* **1849.** R. B. MARCY. *Report of Route from Fort Smith to Santa Fe.* **1849**

U.S. CONTINENTAL CONGRESS. *Journals . . . , 1774–1789.* Wash., 1904–37. **v.d.** (Cited without publication dates)

Journals of the American Congress: from 1774 to 1778. Wash., 1823. **v.d.**

U.S. COPYRIGHT OFFICE. *Dramatic Compositions Copyrighted . . . 1870 to 1916.* Wash., 1918. **v.d.**

U.S. DEPT. OF AGRICULTURE. *Annual Reports.* 1894–current. Wash., 1895–current. **v.d.**

Farmers' Bulletins. Wash., **1889**–current

Report of the Secretary of Agriculture. 1849–93. Wash., 1850–94. **v.d.** 1849–61 as: *Rep. Comm. Patents: Agric.* 1862–88 as: *Rep. Comm. Agric.*

Special Report, No. 12. Investigation of Diseases of Swine and Infectious and Contagious Diseases Incident to Other Classes of Animals. Wash., **1879**

Yearbook. 1894–current. Wash., 1895–current. **v.d.**

U.S. DEPT. OF STATE. *Revolutionary Diplomatic Correspondence of the United States.* Ed. Francis Wharton. Wash., 1889. **v.d.**

U.S. DEPT. OF THE INTERIOR. *Report on the United States and Mexican Boundary Survey.* By W. H. Emory [*et al.*]. Wash., 1857–9. (34th Congress, 1 Sess. House. Ex. Doc. No. 135.) **v.d.**

U.S. ENGINEER DEPT. *Exploration and Survey of the Valley of the Great Salt Lake of Utah.* By Howard Stansbury. Wash., 1853. First publ.: Phila., **1852**

Notes of a Military Reconnoissance. By W. H. Emory. Wash., 1848. **v.d.**

Report on the Exploration of the Yellowstone River. By W. F. Raynolds. Wash., **1868**

U.S. FOREST SERVICE. *Bulletin.* Wash., **1887–1913**

U.S. GEOGRAPHICAL AND GEOLOGICAL SURVEY OF THE ROCKY MOUNTAIN REGION. *Report on the Geology of the Henry Mountains.* By G. K. Gilbert. Wash., **1877**

U.S. GEOGRAPHICAL SURVEYS WEST OF THE 100TH MERIDIAN. *Report upon United States Geographical Surveys West of the One Hundredth Meridian, in Charge of First Lieut. Geo. M. Wheeler.* Wash., **1875–89.** Vol. III includes: J. J. STEVENSON. *Geology of a Portion of Colorado.* **1875**

U.S. GEOLOGICAL SURVEY. *Annual Report.* 1879/80–current. Wash., 1880–current. **v.d.**

U.S. LAWS, STATUTES, ETC. *Indian affairs. Laws and treaties.* Comp. C. J. Kappler. Wash., 1903–. **v.d.**

The Statutes at Large of the United States of America. Bost.; Wash., 1845–current. **v.d.**

U.S. MILITARY ACADEMY, WEST POINT. *The Centennial of the United States Military Academy.* Wash., 1904. **v.d.**

U.S. NATIONAL MUSEUM. *Bulletin.* Wash., **1875**–current

Proceedings. 1878–current. Wash., 1879–current. **v.d.** Vol. VIII includes: HAVARD. *Report on the Flora of Western and Southern Texas.* **1885**

Report. 1884–current. Wash., 1885–current. (Publ. also as Part II of: SMITHSONIAN INSTITUTION. *Annual Report* (q.v.). **v.d.**

U.S. NATIONAL PARK SERVICE. *Annual Report of the Director.* 1916–7–current. Wash., **1917**–current

U.S. NAVY DEPT. *Annual Report of the Secretary of the Navy.* 1862–current. Wash., 1863–current. **v.d.**

Narrative of the North Polar Expedition . . . U.S. Ship Polaris. Ed. C. H. Davis. Wash., **1876**

Official Records of the Union and Confederate Navies in the War of the Rebellion. Wash., 1894–1922. **v.d.**

U.S. OFFICE OF EDUCATION. *Annual Report of the Commissioner.* 1867/8–1931/2. Wash., 1868–1932. **v.d.**

U.S. OFFICE OF INDIAN AFFAIRS. *Annual Report of the Commissioner.* Wash., 1849–current. **v.d.**

U.S. PATENT OFFICE. *Annual Report of the Commissioner of Patents.* 1837–current. Wash., 1838–current. **v.d.** (For agricultural portions of reports see U.S. DEPT. OF AGRICULTURE. *Report*)

Official Gazette. Wash., **1872**–current

Subject-Matter Index of Patents from 1790 to 1873. Wash., **1874**

U.S. Pharmacopœia. See *Pharmacopœia*

U.S. POST-OFFICE DEPT. *Laws and Regulations for the Government of the Post Office Department.* Wash., **1843**

The Postal Laws and Regulations of the United States of America. Wash., **1887**

U.S. PRESIDENT. *A Compilation of the Messages and Papers of the Presidents, 1789–1897.* Publ. J. D. Richardson. Wash., 1896–99. **v.d.**

U.S. STRIKE COMMISSION, 1894. *Report on the Chicago Strike of June-July, 1894.* Wash., **1895**

U.S. TREASURY DEPT. *Annual Report of the Secretary of the Treasury.* 1790–current. Wash., 1828–current. **v.d.**

Statistics of Mines and Mining in the States and Territories West of the Rocky Mountains; Being the [1st–8th] *Annual Report of Rossiter W. Raymond.* Wash., 1869–77. **v.d.** 3d rep. publ. also as: RAYMOND. *Mines, Mills, and Furnaces of the Pacific States and Territories.* N.Y., **1871**

Treasury Decisions. 1868–1897. Wash., 1869–1898. **v.d.**

Treasury Decisions under the Customs, Internal Revenue, Industrial Alcohol, Narcotic and Other Laws. [Weekly.] Wash., **1898**–current

U.S. WAR DEPT. *Reports of Explorations and Surveys, to Ascertain the Most Practicable and Economical Route from the Mississippi River to the Pacific Ocean.* Wash., 1855–60. **v.d.** Contents include: Vol. III. A. W. WHIPPLE [*et al.*]. *Explor. Ry. Route* [including] *Indian Tribes.* **v.d.** Vol. IX. S. F. BAIRD. *Birds Pacific R.R.* **1858**

Revised Regulations for the Army of the United States, 1861. Phila. [**1861**]

U.S. WEATHER BUREAU. *Monthly Weather Review.* Wash., **1872**–current

United States Magazine and Democratic Review. Wash.; N.Y., **1837–59**

UNITED STATES SANITARY COMMISSION. *Narrative of Privations and Sufferings of United States Officers and Soldiers While Prisoners of War in the Hands of the Rebel Authorities.* Phila., **1864**
The Sanitary Commission of the United States Army. N.Y., **1864**
Universal Asylum and Columbian Magazine. Phila., **1786–92.** (Title, Sept., 1786–Feb., 1790: *Columbian Magazine, or Monthly Miscellany*)

V

VALENTINE, E. U. *Hecla Sandwith.* Indianapolis **[1905]**
VAN BUREN, A. D. *Jottings of a Year's Sojourn in the South.* Battle Creek, **1859**
VANCE, L. J. *Baroque.* N.Y. [cop. **1923**]
Cynthia-of-the-Minute. N.Y., **1911**
VAN DYKE, HENRY. *Fisherman's Luck and Some Other Uncertain Things.* N.Y., 1900. **=1899**
Vanity Fair. N.Y., **1859–63**
VASEY, GEORGE. *The Agricultural Grasses of the United States.* Wash., 1884. New ed. Wash., **1889**
VAUX, CALVERT. *Villas and Cottages.* N.Y., **1857.** [2d ed.] N.Y., **1864**
VERMONT. *Vermont State Papers.* Comp. William Slade. Middlebury, 1823. **v.d.**
BOARD OF AGRICULTURE. *Annual Report.* 1871/2–1907/8. Montpelier, 1872–1908. **v.d** Vol. VI–XXVIII as: *Vt. Agric. Rep.* 1880–1908. Vol. IV includes, with separate paging: *Vt. Dairymen's Ass. Rep.* Vol. VIII. **1877**
VERMONT DAIRYMEN'S ASSOCIATION. See VERMONT. BOARD OF AGRICULTURE
VERMONT HISTORICAL SOCIETY. *Collections.* Montpelier, 1870–1. **v.d.** Vol. I includes: I. ALLEN. *The Natural and Political History of the State of Vermont.* **1798**
Vermont State Papers. See VERMONT
Victims of Gaming. Bost., **1838**
VICTOR, O. J. *The History, Civil, Political and Military, of the Southern Rebellion.* N.Y. [1861–8]. **v.d.**
VIELÉ, TERESA (GRIFFIN). *'Following the Drum': A Glimpse of Frontier Life.* N.Y., **1858**
A View of the New York State Prison in the City of New-York. N.Y., **1815**
VIRGINIA (COLONY). GENERAL ASSEMBLY. HOUSE OF BURGESSES. *Journals.... 1619–1658/59.* Ed. H. R. McIlwaine. Richmond, 1915. **v.d.**
VIRGINIA. *Calendar of Virginia State Papers and Other Manuscripts ... Preserved in the Capitol at Richmond.* Richmond, 1875–93. **v.d.**
LAWS, STATUTES, etc. *The Statutes at Large; Being a Collection of All the Laws of Virginia from ... 1619.* [Ed.] W. W. Hening. Richmond, etc., 1819–23. **v.d.**
Virginia Carolorum. See NEILL
Virginia Literary Museum and Journal of Belles Lettres. Charlottesville, **1829–30**
Virginia Magazine of History and Biography. Richmond, 1893–current. **v.d.**
A Visit to Texas: Being the Journal of a Traveller through Those Parts Most Interesting to American Settlers. N.Y., **1834**
Voice. See *(New) Voice*
VOLNEY, C. F. C., Comte de. *A View of the Soil and Climate of the United States of America.* Tr. C. B. Brown. Phila., **1804.** Also publ. as: *View of the Climate and Soil of the United States of America.* Tr. [anon.] Lond., **1804**
Voodoo Tales. See OWEN, M. A.

W

W., J. See WINSHIP
WADSWORTH, DANIEL. *Diary.* [Ed. G. L. Walker.] Hartford, Conn., 1894. **v.d.**
WAITE, CATHERINE (VAN VALKENBURG). *Adventures in the Far West; and Life among the Mormons.* Chic., **1882**
WALCOTT, E. A. *The Open Door.* N.Y., **1910**
Waldie's Select Circulating Library. See *Select Circulating Library*
WALKER, THOMAS. *Journal of an Exploration of Kentucky.* See FILSON CLUB. *Filson Club Publications.* No. 13
WALKER, T. See NEW HAMPSHIRE HISTORICAL SOCIETY
WALLACE, LEWIS. *Ben-Hur, A Tale of the Christ.* N.Y. [cop. **1880**]. 560 pp. Also: Garfield Ed. N.Y., 1893 [cop. 1891]. 2 vols.
WALLER, MARY E. *The Wood-Carver of 'Lympus.* Bost., **1904**
WALSH, W. S. *Handy-Book of Literary Curiosities.* Phila. [cop. **1892**]
WALTON, WILLIAM. *A Narrative of the Captivity and Sufferings of Benjamin Gilbert and His Family.* Phila., **1784**
WANSEY, HENRY. *The Journal of an Excursion to the United States of North America, in the Summer of 1794.* Salisbury [Eng.] **1796**
WARBURTON, G. D. *Hochelaga; or, England in the New World.* N.Y., **1846**
'WARD, A.' See BROWNE, C. F.
WARD, EDWARD. *A Trip to New-England.* Lond., **1699.** See also WINSHIP
WARD, ELIZABETH S. (PHELPS). *Old Maids, and Burglars in Paradise.* Bost. [1887]. Includes: *An Old Maid's Paradise.* 1885. First publ.: Lond., **1879.** *Burglars in Paradise.* **1886**
A Singular Life. Bost. [cop. **1894**]
The Story of Avis. Bost., **1877**
Trotty's Wedding Tour, and Story-Book. Bost. [cop. 1901]. **=1873**
WARDEN, D. B. *A Chorographical and Statistical Description of the District of Columbia.* Paris, **1816**
A Statistical, Political, and Historical Account of the United States of North America. Edinb., **1819**
WARDER, J. A. *American Pomology.* N.Y. [cop. **1867**]
Hedges and Evergreens. N.Y., **1858**
WARE, J. R. *Passing English of the Victorian Era.* Lond. **[1909]**
WARFIELD, WILLIAM. *The Theory and Practice of Cattle-Breeding.* Chic., **1889**
WARNER, C. D. *The Golden House.* **1894**
On Horseback, a Tour in Virginia, North Carolina and Tennessee. Bost., 1896. **=1888**
My Summer in a Garden. **1870**
WARNER, SUSAN B. *The Wide, Wide World.* **1850**
WARNER, SUSAN B., and WARNER, ANNA B. *The Gold of Chickaree.* N.Y., **1876**
WARREN, M. See MOSES. *Representative Plays.* Vol. I
Warren-Adams Lett. See MASSACHUSETTS HISTORICAL SOCIETY. *Collections*
WARWICK, R.I. *Early Records.* Ed. [H. M. Chapin]. Providence, 1926. **v.d.**
WASHINGTON, GEORGE. *Writings.* Ed. W. C. Ford. N.Y., 1889–93. **v.d.**
Diaries ... 1748–1799. Ed. J. C. Fitzpatrick. Bost., 1925. **v.d.**
Washington [George], *Letters to.* See HAMILTON, S. M.
WASON, R. A. *Friar Tuck.* **1912**
Happy Hawkins. Bost. [cop. **1909**]
WATERBURY, CONN. PROPRIETORS. *Proprietors' Records of the Town ... 1677–1761.* Ed. K. A. Prichard. [Waterbury] 1911. **v.d.**
WATERS, W. E. *Life among the Mormons.* N.Y., **1868**
WATERTOWN, MASS. *Watertown Records.* Vol. I. Watertown, 1894. (Quots. chiefly from Part I.) **v.d.**
WATSON, ELKANAH. *Men and Times of the Revolution.* Ed. W. C. Watson. 2d ed. N.Y., 1861. =1856. **v.d.**
WATSON, H. C. *Camp-Fires of the Revolution.* N.Y., 1874. **=1850**
Nights in a Block-House. Phila., **1852**
WATSON, J. F. *Annals of Philadelphia.* Phila., **1830.** Also publ. 1870
Historic Tales of Olden Time: Concerning the Early Settlement and Advancement of New-York City and State. N.Y., **1832**
Historic Tales of Olden Time, concerning the Early Settlement and Progress of Philadelphia and Pennsylvania. Phila., **1833**
WATSON, T. E. *Bethany: A Story of the Old South.* Thomson, Ga., 1920. **=1904**
WATTERSON, HENRY, ed. *Oddities in Southern Life and Character.* Bost., 1883. **v.d.**
WATTS, MARY (STANBERY). *Luther Nichols.* N.Y., **1923**
Nathan Burke. N.Y., **1910**
WAYLEN, EDWARD. *Ecclesiastical Reminiscences of the U.S.* N.Y., **1846**
WEBB, JAMES JOSIAH. *Memoirs.* Typewritten copy (Historical Soc. of New Mexico, Santa Fe) of orig. MS. Printed as: *Adventures in the Santa Fe Trade, 1844–1847.* Ed. R. P. Bieber. Glendale, Calif., 1931. **1888**
WEBB, J. W. See STEWART, W. G. D.
WEBB, W. S. See LOUDOUN and LYMAN
WEBSTER, DANIEL. *Works.* Bost., 1851. **v.d.**
Private Correspondence. Ed. Fletcher Webster. Bost., 1857. **v.d.**
WEBSTER, NOAH. *An American Dictionary of the English Language....* N.Y., **1828.** 2 vols. Rev. eds.: New Haven, **1841.** Springfield, Mass., 1856. **1847.** Springfield, Mass., 1884. **1864.** With Suppl. **1879**
A Compendious Dictionary of the English Language. [New Haven] **1806**
Dissertations on the English Language. Bost., **1789**
Webster's International Dictionary of the English Language. Springfield, Mass., 1900. **1890.** Suppl. **1900**
A Letter to the Honorable John Pickering on the Subject of His Vocabulary. Bost., **1817**
Webster's New International Dictionary of the English Language. Springfield, Mass., 1928. First publ. **1909**
WEED, THURLOW. *Letters from Europe and America.* Albany, 1866. **v.d.**
Life of Thurlow Weed. [Bost., 1883–4.] Vol. I: *Autobiography.* Ed. H. A. Weed. Vol. II: *Memoir.* By T. W. Barnes. **v.d.**
A Week in Wall Street. N.Y., **1841**
Weekly Mercury. See *American Weekly Mercury*
(Weekly) New Mexican. Santa Fe, **1863–83**
Weekly New Mexican Review. See *New Mexican Review*
WEEMS, M. L. *Letters.* See his: *Mason Locke Weems, His Works and Ways*
The Life of Benjamin Franklin. Phila. [cop. **1829**]
The Life of Gen. Francis Marion. By Peter Horry and M. L. Weems. Phila., 1833. First publ. **1809**
The Life of George Washington. 10th ed. Phila., **1810.** Enl. ed.: Phila., **1840**
Mason Locke Weems, His Works and Ways. N.Y., 1929. Vols. II–III: *Letters.* **v.d.**
WEISER. See THWAITES
WELBY, ADLARD. *A Visit to North America and the English Settlements in Illinois.* Lond., **1821**
WELCH, S. M. *Home History. Recollections of Buffalo during the Decade from 1830 to 1840.* Buffalo, **1891**
WELD, ISAAC. *Travels through the States of North America.* Lond., **1799**
WELLS, D. A. *Our Burden and Our Strength.* Troy, N.Y., **1864**
Practical Economics. N.Y., 1885. **v.d.**
WELLS, D. A., and DAVIS, S. H. *Sketches of Williams College.* Williamstown, Mass., **1847**
WELLS, H. P. *The American Salmon Fisherman.* N.Y., **1886**
WELSH, CHARLES. *Poker: How to Play It.* Lond., **1882**
WESLEY, JOHN. *Journal ... From October 14th, 1735, to October 24th, 1790.* With Introd. Essay by Thomas Jackson. Lond., 1903. Also: *Journal.* Ed. Nehemiah Curnock. Lond. [1909–16]. **v.d.**
West Point Life. See PORTER, H.
WESTCOTT, E. N. *David Harum.* **1898**
Western Carolinian. Salisbury, N.C., **1820–44**
Western Gleaner, or Repository for Arts, Sciences and Literature. Pittsb., **1813–4**
Western Journal (and Civilian). St. Louis, **1848–56**
Western Monthly Review. Cinc., **1827–30**
Western Review and Miscellaneous Magazine. Lexington, Ky., **1819–21**
WESTON, RICHARD. *A Visit to the United States and Canada in 1833.* Edinb., **1836**
WETMORE, ALPHONSO, comp. *Gazetteer of the State of Missouri.* St. Louis, **1837**
WHEELEYS BAPTIST CHURCH, BUSHYFORK TOWNSHIP, PERSON COUNTY, N.C. *Minutes,* 1791–1898. MS., Univ. of N.C. Lib. **v.d.**
Wheelman. Bost., **1882–3**
Whig Almanac. See *Tribune Almanac*
WHILLDIN, M., comp. *A Description of Western Texas.* Galveston, **1876**
Whimwhams. By [H. J. Finn, *et al.*] Bost., **1828**
WHIPPLE. *Explor. Ry. Route; Indian Tribes.* See U.S. WAR DEPT. *Reports.*
WHITCHER, FRANCES M. (BERRY). *The Widow Bedott Papers.* N.Y., 1856. **v.d.**
WHITE, A. See HALL, C. C.
WHITE, CHARLES. *Oh Hush! or, The Virginny Cupids.* N.Y. **[1856]**
The Policy Players. N.Y. [cop. 1874]. First perf. **1847**
WHITE, GEORGE M. *From Boniface to Bank Burglar.* N.Y., **1907.** =1905
WHITE, GRACE M. *Rose o' Paradise.* N.Y. **[1915]**
WHITE, S. E. *Arizona Nights.* Garden City, N.Y., 1916. **=1907**
Blazed Trail. N.Y. [cop. **1902**]
Blazed Trail Stories. Garden City, N.Y., 1916. **v.d.**
The Claim Jumpers. Garden City, N.Y., 1916. **=1901**
Conjuror's House. N.Y. [cop. **1903**]
The Forest. N.Y., 1907. **=1903**
The Riverman. Garden City, N.Y., 1916. **=1908**
The Silent Places. Garden City, N.Y., 1916. **= 1904**
The Westerners. N.Y. [cop. **1901**]
WHITE, W. A. *The Real Issue.* Chic., 1897. **=1896**
WHITLOCK, BRAND. *The 13th District.* Indianapolis [cop. **1902**]
WHITMAN, WALT. *Complete Prose Works.* Phila., 1892. **v.d.**
Democratic Vistas. Wash., **1871.** Also in his: *Complete Prose Works*
November Boughs. Phila., **1888**
Specimen Days & Collect. Phila., 1882–3. **v.d.**
Walt Whitman's Diary in Canada. Ed. W. S. Kennedy. Bost., 1904. **v.d.**
WHITMORE, W. H. *A Bibliographical Sketch of the Laws of the Massachusetts Colony from 1630 to 1686.* Includes: *Mass. Body of Liberties* (q.v.). **1641**
WHITNEY, ADELINE D. (TRAIN). *Faith Gartney's Girlhood.* **1863**
The Gayworthys. Bost., **1865**

Just How; a Key to Cook-Books. Bost., **1879**
The Other Girls. **1873**
Patience Strong's Outings. Bost., 1869. [cop. **1868**]
Real Folks. Bost., 1872. =**1871**
Sights and Insights. Bost., **1876**
A Summer in Leslie Goldthwaite's Life. Bost. [cop. 1894]. =1893. Also: N.Y.: Hurst [n.d.]. First publ. **1866**
We Girls. **1870**
WHITNEY, J. D. *Life and Letters.* See BREWSTER
WHITTIER, J. G. *Writings.* [Riverside Ed. Bost., 1892.] **v.d.** Vols. I–IV: *Poetical Works.* Vols. V–VII: *Prose Works,* Vols. I–III
Complete Poetical Works. Bost., 1882. Cambridge Ed. Bost. [1894]. **v.d.**
Wide Awake. Bost., **1875–93.** Vol. III, July–Dec., **1876**
WIERZBICKI. See *Magazine of History*
WIGGIN, KATE D. (SMITH). *Rebecca of Sunnybrook Farm.* Bost., **1903**
Rose o' the River. Bost., **1905**
Timothy's Quest. Bost., 1892. =**1890**
The Village Watch-Tower. Bost., **1895**
WILCOX, ESTELLE WOODS. *Buckeye Cookery.* Rev. and enl. Minneapolis, 1885 [cop. 1880]. 536 pp. Enl. as: *Practical Housekeeping.* Minneapolis, 1883 [cop. 1881]. 688 pp.
WILDER, CHARLOTTE F. (FELT). *Sister Ridnour's Sacrifice.* Cinc., **1883**
WILDER, G. *Diary.* 1850–63. MS. **v.d.**
WILEY, C. H. *Life in the South.* Phila. [1852]
WILKINS, M. E. See FREEMAN, M. E.
WILKINSON. See FILSON CLUB. *Filson Club Publications.* No. 31
WILLARD, J. F. *Notes of an Itinerant Policeman.* Bost., **1900**
Tramping with Tramps. N.Y., 1900. =**1899**
The World of Graft. N.Y., **1901**
WILLIAMS, H. L. *Love and Lockjaw.* N.Y., **1895**
WILLIAMS, JESSE L. *Princeton Stories.* N.Y., **1895**
WILLIAMS, JOHN. *The Redeemed Captive, Returning to Zion. A Faithful History of Remarkable Occurrences in the Captivity . . . of Mr. John Williams.* Bost., 1758. **1707**
WILLIAMS, JOHN LEE. *The Territory of Florida.* N.Y., **1837**
A View of West Florida. Phila., **1827**
WILLIAMS, ROGER. *Roger Williams's 'Christenings Make Not Christians' 1845. . . . Ed. by H. M. Dexter. Followed by . . . Letters Written by Roger Williams.* Providence, 1881. **v.d.**
Key. 1827: see RHODE ISLAND HISTORICAL SOCIETY. *Collections.* 1866: see NARRAGANSETT CLUB
Letters. 1874. See NARRAGANSETT CLUB
Ten Letters. 1900. See RHODE ISLAND HISTORICAL SOCIETY. *Publications*
Unpublished Letters. See his: *Roger Williams's 'Christenings Make Not Christians'*
WILLIAMS, SAMUEL. *The Natural and Civil History of Vermont.* Walpole, Newhampshire, 1794. 2d ed. Burlington, Vt., **1809**
WILLIAMSON, CHARLES. *Descr. Genesee.* See *The Documentary History of the State of New-York*
WILLIAMSON, W. D. *The History of the State of Maine.* Hollowell [Me.] **1832**
WILLIS, N. P. *The Convalescent.* N.Y., 1859. **v.d.**
Rural Letters. N.Y., **1849**
WILLS, H. O. *Twice Born.* Cinc., **1890**
WILMER, L. A. *Our Press Gang.* Phila., **1859**
Wilmington (N.C.) *Gazette.* **1797–1816.** (1797–8 as: *Hall's Wilmington Gazette*)
WILSON, ALEXANDER. *American Ornithology.* Phila., 1808–14. **v.d.**
The Foresters: A Poem, Descriptive of a Pedestrian Journey to the Falls of Niagara, in the Autumn of 1804. West Chester, Pa., 1839. First publ. 1818. a**1813**
WILSON, ALEXANDER, and BONAPARTE, C. L. *American Ornithology.* Ed. Robert Jameson. Edinb., 1831. Also publ.: Lond., 1832. **v.d.** See also BONAPARTE
WILSON, AUGUSTA J. (EVANS). *Vashti.* **1867**
WILSON, C. H. *The Wanderer in America.* 4th ed. Thirsk [Eng.] **1823**
WILSON, H. L. *Ma Pettengill.* **1919**
Somewhere in Red Gap. Lond., 1920. =**1916**
The Spenders. N.Y. [1902]

WILSON, J. F. *The Land Claimers.* Bost., **1911**
WILSON, ROBERT. *The Travels of That Well-known Pedestrian, Robert Wilson.* Lond., **1807**
WINANS, W. H. *Reminiscences and Experiences in the Life of an Editor.* Newark, N.J., **1875**
WINCHELL, ALEXANDER. *Walks and Talks in the Geological Field.* N.Y., **1886**
WINCHESTER, C. W. *The Victories of Wesley Castle.* Buffalo, 1901. =**1900**
WINES, E. C. *Two Years and a Half in the American Navy.* Phila., **1832**
Winfield (Kan.) *Courier.* **1873–1919**
WINGATE, C. F. *Views and Interviews on Journalism.* N.Y., **1875**
WINSHIP, G. P., ed. *Boston in 1682 and 1699: A Trip to New-England, by Edward Ward, and A Letter from New England, by J. W.* Providence, 1905. **v.d.**
WINSLOW, ANNA. *Diary of Anna Green Winslow, a Boston School Girl of 1771.* Ed. A. M. Earle. Bost., 1894. **v.d.**
WINSLOW, B. D. *Class Poem, Delivered . . . at the Valedictory Exercises of the Class of 1835.* Cambridge, **1835**
WINSLOW, EDWARD, ed. *The Glorious Progress of the Gospel, amongst the Indians in New England. Manifested by Three Letters, under the Hand of . . . Mr. John Eliot* [etc.]. Lond., 1649. See also MASSACHUSETTS HISTORICAL SOCIETY. *Collections*
Good Newes from New-England. Lond., **1624**
WINSLOW, OLA E., comp. *American Broadside Verse from Imprints of the 17th & 18th Centuries.* New Haven, 1930. **v.d.** Includes: J. SECCOMB(E) *Father Abbey's Will* (q.v.). **1731**
WINTERBOTHAM, WILLIAM. *An Historical, Geographical, Commercial, and Philosophical View of the American United States.* Lond., **1807**
WINTHROP, JOHN, 1588–1649. *Hist.* See his: *Winthrop's Journal*
Winthrop's Journal: 'History of New England.' . . . Ed. J. K. Hosmer. N.Y., 1908. a**1649**
Letters. See WINTHROP, R. C.
WINTHROP, JOHN, 1606–76. *Letters.* See *Winthrop Papers*
WINTHROP, R. C. *Life and Letters of John Winthrop.* Bost., 1869. =1864–7. **v.d.**
WINTHROP, THEODORE. *The Canoe and the Saddle.* Bost., 1863. a**1861**
Cecil Dreeme. Bost., **1861**
John Brent. Bost., 1862. a**1861**
Life in the Open Air, and Other Papers. Bost., 1863. a**1861**
Winthrop Papers. See MASSACHUSETTS HISTORICAL SOCIETY. *Collections*
WISE, JOHN. *A Vindication of the Government of the New-England Churches.* Bost., 1772. Includes: *A Platform of Church-Discipline.* 1648. *A Confession of Faith . . . of the Churches Assembled at Boston in New England, May 12, 1680.* **1680**
WISTER, OWEN. *Lin McLean.* N.Y., 1898 [1897]. **v.d.**
Red Men and White. N.Y. [cop. 1895]
The Virginian. N.Y., **1902**
Witchcraft Cases. See BURR
WITHERS, A. S. *Chronicles of Border Warfare.* Ed. R. G. Thwaites. Cinc., 1895. First publ.: Clarksburg, Va., **1831.** See also PRITTS
WITHERSPOON, JOHN. *The Druid* [Papers]. Nos. 5–7. Publ. orig. in: *Pennsylvania Journal and The Weekly Advertiser* (Phila.), 9, 16, 23, 30 May, **1781.** Reprinted in: M. M. MATHEWS, ed. *The Beginnings of American English.* Chic. [1931], pp. 14–30
Lectures on Moral Philosophy, and Eloquence. Phila., 1810. **v.d.**
WOLLEY, CHARLES. *A Two Years Journal in New York: and Part of Its Territories in America.* Lond., 1701. Also: Ed. E. B. O'Callaghan. N.Y., 1860. [Ed.] E. G. Bourne. Cleveland, **1902**
WOOD, ALPHONSO. *A Class-Book of Botany.* 10th ed. Claremont, N.H., 1850 [pref. 1847]. Also: N.Y., 1864. **1861**
WOOD, F. See MACLEOD
WOOD, J. G. *Homes without Hands.* N.Y., 1866. First publ.: Lond., **1865**
WOOD, L. See ESSEX INSTITUTE

WOOD, SAMUEL. *Letters from the United States.* [Lond., **1838**]
WOOD, WILLIAM. *New Englands Prospect.* Lond., **1634.** See also PRINCE SOCIETY
WOOD, WILLIAM BURKE. *Personal Recollections of the Stage.* Phila., **1855**
WOODROW, NANCY M. (WADDEL). *Sally Salt.* Indianapolis [cop. **1912**]
WOODRUFF, H. W. *The Trotting Horse of America.* N.Y., **1868**
WOODS, D. B. *Sixteen Months at the Gold Diggings.* Lond., **1851**
WOODS, JOHN. *Two Years' Residence in the Settlement on the English Prairie, in the Illinois Country.* Lond., **1822.** See also THWAITES
WOODWORTH, SAMUEL. *The Forest Rose; or, American Farmers.* N.Y., **1825**
WOOLMAN, JOHN. *Journal.* Bost., 1882. =1871. a**1772**
WOOLSEY, T. D. *An Historical Discourse Pronounced before the Graduates of Yale College.* New Haven, 1850. **v.d.**
WORCESTER, J. E. *A Dictionary of the English Language.* New ed., with suppl. Phila., 1887. First publ. 1860. Suppl. first publ. **1881**
A Universal Critical and Pronouncing Dictionary of the English Language. Lond., 1848. =**1846**
WORTHEN. See ILLINOIS. GEOLOGICAL SURVEY
Worthington's Illustrated Monthly Magazine. Hartford, Conn., **1893–?4**
WORTLEY. See STUART-WORTLEY
WRIGHT, F. See DARUSMONT
WRIGHT, WILLIAM. *History of the Big Bonanza.* Hartford, **1877**
WYATT, EDITH F. *The Invisible Gods.* N.Y., **1923**
WYETH, J. B. See THWAITES
WYETH, N. See *Sources of the History of Oregon*
Wyllys Papers. See CONNECTICUT HISTORICAL SOCIETY
WYSE, FRANCIS. *America, Its Realities and Resources.* Lond., **1846**

X

Xenia (Ohio) *Torch-Light.* **1838–88**

Y

Yale Banger. New Haven, **1845–50, 1852.** Publ. by Sigma Theta
Yale Battery. New Haven, **1850.** Publ. by Delta Kappa
Yale Literary Magazine. New Haven, **1836**–current
YALE UNIVERSITY. *The Laws of Yale-College.* New Haven, **1774.** (Also MS. laws of earlier date)
Yankee. Portland, Me., **1828–9**
Yankee Phrases. See *New-Jersey Almanac*
The Yankee Traveller: or, The Adventures of Hector Wigler. Concord, **1817**
Year in Natural History. See *American Naturalist*
'YESLAH.' See HALSEY
YORK CO., ME. REGISTER OF DEEDS. *York Deeds.* 1642–1737. Portland, 1887–1910. **v.d.**
York Co. [Pa.] *Hist. Rev.* See *Historical Review*
YORK CO., VA. *Records.* MS. **v.d.**
YOUMANS, E. L. *The Hand-Book of Household Science.* N.Y., 1881 [cop. **1857**]
YOUNG, B. H. *A History of Jessamine County, Kentucky, from Its Earliest Settlement to 1898.* Louisville, 1898. **v.d.**
The Young Parson. See DAVIS, P. S.

Z

ZEIGLER, WILBUR G., and GROSSCUP, BEN S. *The Heart of the Alleghanies.* Raleigh, N.C. [cop. **1883**]